THE AUTHORITY SINCE 1868

THE WORLD ALMANAC

AND BOOK OF FACTS

1988

WORLD ALMANAC
AN IMPRINT OF PHAROS BOOKS • A SCRIPPS HOWARD COMPANY
NEW YORK

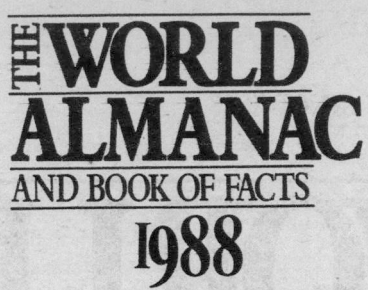

THE WORLD ALMANAC
AND BOOK OF FACTS
1988

Editor: Mark S. Hoffman
Associate Editor: June Foley **Senior Assistant Editor:** Thomas McGuire
Chronology & Special Features: Donald Young **Index:** Deborah G. Felder
Administrative Assistant: Angella Cummings

Cover design: Lawrence Ratzkin

Pharos Books
Senior Vice President & Publisher: David Hendin
Vice President & Associate Publisher: Phyllis Henrici
Editor-in-Chief: Hana Umlauf Lane **Sales Manager:** Kevin McDonough
Editorial Assistant: Jo-Anne Mercado Volkers **Production Manager:** Marie Mulcahy

---

The editors acknowledge with thanks the many letters of helpful comment and criticism from readers of THE WORLD ALMANAC, and invite further suggestions and observations. Because of the volume of mail directed to the editorial offices, it is not possible to reply to each letter writer. However, every communication is read by the editors and all comments and suggestions receive careful attention. Inquiries regarding contents should be sent to: The World Almanac, 200 Park Avenue, New York, NY 10166.

THE WORLD ALMANAC is published annually in November.

THE WORLD ALMANAC does not decide wagers.

The first edition of THE WORLD ALMANAC, a 120-page volume with 12 pages of advertising, was published by the New York World in 1868, 120 years ago. Annual publication was suspended in 1876. Joseph Pulitzer, publisher of the New York World, revived THE WORLD ALMANAC in 1886 with the goal of making it a "compendium of universal knowledge." It has been published annually since then. In 1931, it was acquired by the Scripps Howard Newspapers; until 1951, it bore the imprint of the New York World-Telegram and thereafter, until 1967, that of the New York World-Telegram and Sun. It is now published in paper and clothbound editions by Pharos Books, a Scripps Howard company.

THE WORLD ALMANAC & BOOK OF FACTS 1988

Library of Congress Catalog Card Number 4-3781
International Standard Serial Number (ISSN) 0084-1382
Pharos Books (softcover) ISBN 0-88687-334-7
Pharos Books (hardcover) ISBN 0-88687-335-5
Ballantine Books (softcover) ISBN 0-345-34891-5
Ballantine Books (hardcover) ISBN 0-345-34890-7
Microform Edition since 1868: University Microfilms Intl.
Printed in the United States of America
The Ballantine softcover and hardcover editions distributed in the United States by Ballantine Books, a division of Random House, Inc.

WORLD ALMANAC
An Imprint of Pharos Books
A Scripps Howard Company
200 Park Avenue, New York, NY 10166

1988 HIGHLIGHTS

GENERAL INDEX

—G—

—J—

—O—

— T —

— U —

Bork's Nomination to Supreme Court is Rejected

After one of the most bitter battles ever waged over a Supreme Court nominee, the Senate, **Oct. 23**, rejected the nomination of Judge Robert H. Bork. The vote was 58 against confirmation and 42 in favor, the biggest margin by which the Senate has ever rejected a Supreme Court nomination. Judge Bork was the 27th Supreme Court nominee to be rejected in U.S. history, and the first since, 1970, when Pres. Nixon's nomination of G. Harrold Carswell was rejected. Pres. Reagan responded to the resounding defeat of his nominee by saying: "I am saddened and disappointed that the Senate has bowed today to a campaign of political pressure." He added that his next nominee for the court "will share Judge Bork's belief in judicial restraint—that a judge is bound by the Constitution to interpret laws, not make them." Senate Judiciary Chairman Joseph Biden Jr. (D-Del.) said there was "no possibility" a new nominee could be investigated and confirmed by Thanksgiving, when Congress tentatively was scheduled to adjourn for the year.

Reagan/Gorbachev Summit Plans Stalled

Top-level negotiations between the U.S. and the Soviet Union unexpectedly broke off, **Oct. 23**, after Mikhail Gorbachev refused to set a date for a summit meeting with Pres. Reagan. The Soviet leader insisted that differences over the development of space-based defense weapons must be resolved first. The apparent deadlock over Pres. Reagan's Strategic Defense Initiative ("Star Wars") seemed to be similar to that which ended the last meeting between the leaders one year ago in Reykjavik, Iceland. Gorbachev told Sec. of State George Shultz that while most of the remaining obstacles to a treaty abolishing medium and shorter-range nuclear missiles had been resolved, and that progress had been made toward reducing longer-range weapons, it was not enough to justify the promised meeting tentatively scheduled for late 1987.

Addenda, Late News, Changes

AIDS (pp. 35-36)

A new study of homosexual men in Finland found that some who became infected with the AIDS virus through sexual intercourse did not form antibodies for more than a year, far longer than most experts had expected. This could mean that some people may have been declared free of the virus prematurely.

A handbook, "AIDS and the Education of Our Children: A Guide for Parents and Teachers," was issued by the U.S. Dept. of Education. It stressed "appropriate moral and social conduct" and encouraged sexual abstinence or monogamy.

The chairman, the vice chairman, and the only medical staff officer of the President's AIDS commission resigned on Oct. 7, 1987. James D. Watkins, a retired admiral who had been Chief of Naval Operations, was named the new chairman. He appointed Polly L. Gault as the commission's new executive director.

Area Codes (pp. 547-547)

The following places in California have had their area codes changed from 714 to 619: Apple Valley, Bonita, Calexico, Cardiff-by-the-Sea, Casa De Oro-Mt. Helix, Castle Park-Otay, Coachella, Lakeside, Leucadia, Ramona, Solana Beach, and Spring Valley.

Awards

Books and Allied Arts (p. 349)

Ingersoll Prizes, by Ingersoll Foundation, to authors of abiding importance whose works affirm the moral principles of Western civilization, $15,000 each: Eliot Award for creative writing: Octavio Paz; Weaver Award for scholarly letters: Josef Pieper.

Journalism (p. 349)

Livingston Awards, for young journalists, $5,000: international reporting: Barbara Fischkin, *New York Newsday;* national reporting: Mark Zieman, *Kansas City Star:* local reporting: Benjamin L. Weiser, *Washington Post.*

Broadcasting and Theater (p. 350)

Emmy Awards, by Academy of Television Arts and Sciences, for nighttime programs, 1986-87: Dramatic series: *L.A. Law,* NBC; actress, drama: Sharon Gless, *Cagney & Lacey;* actor, drama: Bruce Willis, *Moonlighting,* ABC; supporting actress: Bonnie Bartlett, *St. Elsewhere,* NBC; supporting actor: John Hillerman, *Magnum, P.I.,* CBS. Comedy series: *Golden Girls,* NBC; actress: Rue McClanahan, *Golden Girls;* actor: Michael J. Fox, *Family Ties,* NBC; supporting actress: Jackee Harry, *227,* NBC; supporting actor: John Larroquette, *Night Court,* NBC; series guest actress: Alfre Woodard, *L.A. Law;* actor: John Cleese, *Cheers,* NBC; series direction: Gregory Hoblit, *L.A. Law.* Variety, music or comedy program: *The 1987 Tony Awards,* CBS; mini-series: *Year in the Life,* NBC; animated special: *Cathy,* CBS; actress, special: Gena Rowlands, *The Betty Ford Story,* ABC; actor, special: James Woods, *Promise,* NBC; supporting actress: Piper Laurie, *Promise;* actor: Dabney Coleman, *Sworn to Silence,* ABC.

Miscellaneous (p. 350)

American Comedy Awards: female performer of the year: Bette Midler; male performer of the year: Woody Allen; female movie comic, Bette Midler, "Ruthless People"; male movie comic: Woody Allen, "Hannah and Her Sisters"; female TV comic: Betty White, "Golden Girls"; male TV comic: Johnny Carson, "Tonight Show"; newcomer: Woody Harrelson, "Cheers"; female stand-up comic: Lily Tomlin; male stand-up comic: Robin Williams; lifetime creative achievement: Norman Lear; lifetime achievement trophies: Bette Midler, Lucille Ball, Carol Burnett, Mary Tyler Moore, Lily Tomlin, Sid Caesar, Steve Allen, Woody Allen, Mel Brooks, Jonathan Winters.

Dance Magazine Awards: Merrill Ashley, New York City Ballet; Trisha Brown, choreographer; Liz Thompson, director, Jacobs Pillow Dance Festival; David White, director, Dance Theater Workshop; Doris Hering, director, National Assn. for Regional Ballet.

Golden Globe Awards, by Hollywood Foreign Press Assn.: dramatic movie: "Platoon"; director, dramatic movie: Oliver Stone, "Platoon"; actress, dramatic movie: Marlee Matlin, "Children of a Lesser God"; actor, dramatic movie: Bob Hoskins, "Mona Lisa"; comedy or musical movie: Woody Allen, "Hannah and Her Sisters"; actress, comedy or musical movie: Sissy Spacek, "Crimes of the Heart"; actor, comedy or musical movie: Paul Hogan, "Crocodile Dundee"; DeMille Award, for career achievement: Anthony Quinn.

Grawemeyer Award, by Univ. of Louisville, for achievement by a composer, $150,000: Harrison Birtwistle, "The Mask of Orpheus."

House and Garden Design Awards, for residential design, $25,000 each: architecture: Frank Gehry; interior design and decoration: Patrick Naggar.

Kennedy Center Awards, for lifetime achievement in the performing arts, gold medallions: Lucille Ball, Ray Charles, Yehudi Menuhin, Antony Tudor, Jessica Tandy, Hume Cronyn.

Lasker Medical Research Awards: Susumu Tonegawa, M.I.T.; Philip Leder, Harvard Medical School; Leroy Hood, Calif. Inst. of Technology; Mogens Schou, Aarhus Univ. Psychiatric Inst., Denmark.

National Medal of Arts, for creators and philanthropists: Romare Bearden, painter; J.W. Fisher, opera patron; Ella Fitzgerald, singer; Armand Hammer, art patron; Sydney and Frances Lewis, art patrons; Howard Nemerov, writer and scholar: Alwin Nikolais, choreographer; Isamu Noguchi, sculptor; William Schuman, composer; Robert Penn Warren, poet and novelist.

National Society of Film Critics Awards: best film: "Blue Velvet"; actor: Bob Hoskins, "Mona Lisa"; actress: Chloe Webb, "Sid and Nancy"; supporting actor: Dennis Hopper, "Blue Velvet"; supporting actress: Dianne Wiest, "Hannah and Her Sisters"; screeenplay: Hanif Kureishi, "My Beautiful Laundrette"; cinematography: "Blue Velvet"; documentary "Marlene."

New York Film Critics Awards: best film: "Hannah and Her Sisters"; director: Woody Allen; actor: Bob Hoskins, "Mona Lisa"; actress: Sissy Spacek, "Crimes of the Heart"; supporting actor: Daniel Day Lewis, "A Room With a View"; supporting actress: Dianne Wiest, "Hannah and Her Sisters"; screenplay: Hanif Kureishi, "My Beautiful Laundrette"; cinematography: "A Room With a View"; foreign language film: "The Decline of the American Empire."

Nobel Prizes (p. 341-343)

Nobel Prize in Physiology or Medicine: Susumu Tonegawa, a Japanese scientist working at M.I.T., won the Nobel Prize in medicine, for his discoveries of how the body can suddenly marshal its immunological defenses against millions of different disease agents it has never previously encountered. He was the first Japanese scientist to win the Nobel Prize in Physiology or Medicine. The prize amounts to $340,000 this year.

Nobel Prize in Chemistry: The award went to Donald J. Cram, an American professor at the Univ. of California at Los Angeles; Charles J. Pederson, an American research chemist with E.I. du Pont de Nemours & Co. until his retirement in 1969; and Jean-Marie Lehn, a French professor at Louis Pasteur Univ. in Strasbourg and the College de France in Paris. The three men were pioneers in wide-ranging research, including the creation of artificial molecules.

Nobel Prize in Physics: K. Alex Muller, a Swiss I.B.M. fellow, and J. Georg Bednorz, a German working at I.B.M.'s Zurich Research Lab, shared the prize for their pioneering work in superconductivity.

Nobel Peace Prize: The award went to President Oscar Arias Sanchez of Costa Rica, the main architect of the regional peace plan signed by five Central American countries in August, 1987, and scheduled to take full effect on Nov. 7, 1987.

Nobel Memorial Prize in Economics: Robert M. Solow, an American professor at M.I.T., won the prize for seminal contributions to the theory of economic growth, including a mathematical model illustrating that long-term growth depends on technological progress as well as increases in capital and labor.

Nobel Prize in Literature: Joseph Brodsky, born in the U.S.S.R. and now living in New York, was awarded the prize for his poetry and essays. The Academy honored him for "an all-embracing authorship, imbued with clarity of thought and poetic intensity."

Miss America (p. 353)

Miss Michigan, Kaye Lani Rae Rafko, was named Miss America for 1988.

Business Directory (pp. 783, 784, 786)

David W. Johnson was name chairman, president, and chief executive officer of Gerber Products Co.

Joseph E. Antonini was named chief exeutive officer of K mart.

William F. Schmied was named chief executive officer of Singer Co.

Chronology (pp. 57, 60, 63)

"Subway Vigilante" Found Not Guilty — On Oct. 20, Goetz was sentenced to six months in jail for carrying an unlicensed concealed pistol. He was also sentenced to five years' probation and ordered to undergo psychiatric counseling.

Child Survives Crash Fatal to 155 — According to evidence presented to the National Transportation Safety Board, **Oct. 16,** the pilot was not warned that the plane's wing flaps were improperly positioned because an alarm system was not working. The revised death toll is 156.

U.S. Involvement in Persian Gulf Continues — U.S. naval forces struck back at Iran, **Oct. 19,** for attacks on American-registered vessels and other Persian Gulf shipping by shelling and destroying two connected offshore platforms that American officials said were a base for Iranian gunboats. A third platform was boarded, and commandoes destroyed radar and communications equipment. No American casualties were reported.

Congress (p. 280)

The U.S. representative of the First District of Texas is Jim Chapman, a Democrat from Sulphur Springs, not Sam B. Hall Jr. Congressman Chapman, the incumbent, ran unopposed in 1986.

Constitution of the U.S. (p. 435)

Proposed amendment relating to congressional pay: Montana, Connecticut, and Wisconsin ratified in 1987.

1986 Immigration Law (p. 747)

The Reagan administration liberalized the rules for illegal aliens seeking amnesty under the new immigration law. It was expected that some 100,000 would benefit from the change. The new regulation affects persons who were residing illegally in the U.S., left the country, then fraudulently used documents obtained at overseas consulates to re-enter the U.S. to resume their illegal residence.

Mayors (p. 285)

Richard Arrington Jr. was reelected mayor of Birmingham, Ala. in Oct.

Metropolitan Areas (p. 537)

As of July 1, 1986, the Dallas-Fort Worth metropolitan area moved up from ninth to eighth place, passing Houston which slipped to number nine. The estimated population of Dallas-Fort Worth is 3,655,300.

Mountains (pp. 514-515)

Height of Mount Everest: In Oct. 1987, it was reported that scientists had used a combination of four navigation satellites to make measurements showing Mt. Everest to be 800 feet higher than K-2.

Nations (pp. 659, 660)

Burkina Faso: Pres. Thomas Sankara was overthrown and executed by a military coup.

Burundi: President Jean-Baptiste Bagaza was overthrown by a military coup.

Population (p. 532)

According to a Census Bureau report released in Sept. 1987, the Hispanic population of the U.S. has increased 30 percent since 1980. This increase is five times the rate of the rest of the population. The Hispanic population is now estimated to be 18.8 million, up 4.3 million from 1980.

According to a Census Bureau report released in Oct. 1987, the median age of Americans reached 31.7 years in 1986.

Poverty (p. 542)

The proportion of Americans living in poverty in 1986 was 13.6 percent. The national poverty rate was higher in 1986 than in any year from 1969 through 1980, but was at its lowest level since Pres. Reagan took office.

Reagan Administration (pp. 262, 263, 264, 265, 328)

C. William Verity was confirmed as Secretary of Commerce.

James H. Burley was nominated for Secretary of Transportation. Elizabeth Dole resigned in Sept. 1987.

William S. Sessions was confirmed as director of the Federal Bureau of Investigation.

William E. Brock resigned as U.S. Secretary of Labor, effective Nov. 1.

Scientific Achievements and Discoveries (p. 154)

Collaborative Research Inc. announced Oct. 7, 1987, that it had completed the first full map of the 23 pairs of human chromosomes.

Sports (p. 895)

Li Huirong leaped 46 feet, 3/4 in. to set a new women's world record in the triple jump.

States and Territories (p. 629)

Palau: The people of Palau voted, Aug. 21, in favor of a compact of self-government in association with the U.S., ending the Pacific island group's status as the world's last United Nations trust territory. The compact gave Palau independence, with Washington retaining control of the island group's defense.

Zip Codes (p. 548)

The correct zip code for Vernon, Connecticut is 06066.

Frantic Trading Shakes Wall Street

Wall Street suffered its worst day in history, **Oct. 19,** as the Dow Jones Industrial Average plummeted a record 508 points. The 22.6 percent one-day decline was the largest since World War I, and was far greater than the 12.82 percent drop on Oct. 28, 1929, that along with the following day's 11.7 percent decline preceded the Great Depression.

The Dow had hit a record high of 2,722.42 on Aug. 25. The 200 points it had fallen since that time was called a correction by most market analysts, many of whom had predicted that the Dow would reach 3,000 by the end of 1987 and challenge the 3,500 mark in 1988.

The debacle began on Friday, **Oct. 16,** when the DJIA fell a record 108.35 points on record volume of 338.5 million shares. The 508-point decline the following Monday saw a previously unheard of 604.3 million shares change hands, almost double the record set during the previous trading session

When trading ended, the Dow was down almost 1,000 points, or 36 percent, from its Aug. 25 high. Wilshire Associates, which tracks over 5,000 stocks, reported that the rout took $500 billion in equity value from the nation's stock portfolios.

The crash sent market anaylsts searching for an explanation. Many blamed the federal budget deficit, rising interest rates, and the falling dollar.

The following day, **Oct. 20,** the DJIA rose a record 102.27 points on another record-volume 608.1 million shares. In the days that followed, the market was volatile and erratic: **Oct. 21** saw a record surge of 186.84 points to be followed by a 77.42 drop the next day.

European, Japanese, and Canadian stock markets were also dramatically effected.

Heroes of Young America: The Eighth Annual Poll

Tom Cruise, the young star of such popular films as *Risky Business, Top Gun,* and *The Color of Money,* was named the "Top Hero" of Young America in our eighth annual polling of high school students. Students in grades 8 through 12 were asked to select those individuals in public life they admired most. The schools chosen to participate represented a geographic cross-section of the United States. In addition to choosing a top hero, the teenagers were asked to make selections in 8 other categories.

The Top Hero

Born in 1962, Tom Cruise is the youngest personality to be named top hero. Within a year of its release, Mr. Cruise's smash hit, *Top Gun,* became one of the top 20 all-time box office hits. Finishing in second place was last year's winner, the ubiquitous Bill Cosby. The third place winner was the number one sports hero, Michael Jordan of the NBA's Chicago Bulls. Jordan was followed, in order of ranking, by: Eddie Murphy (winner in 1985); Kirk Cameron; Bruce Willis; Michael J. Fox; Mel Gibson; Arnold Schwarzenegger; and Clint Eastwood. In an interesting development, the write-in choice "Mother" (as in "my mother") received enough votes to tie Michael J. Fox for seventh place, and was the only female receiving enough votes to place among the top 15 finishers.

Previous winners of the top hero honor were: Burt Reynolds (1980 and 1981); Alan Alda (1982); and Michael Jackson (1984).

What Makes a Hero?

This year, for the first time, the students were also asked to indicate which qualities they considered most important in making their selection for "Top Hero." Of the 22 qualities on the ballot, "**intelligent**" received the most votes, followed by honest, funny, brave, responsible, good looking, cool, sexy, daring, and compassionate, while "articulate" received the least votes. Among the many write-in choices were: awesome, talented, athletic, strong, and "just like I am."

Top Sports Hero

Michael Jordan, the basketball star of the Chicago Bulls, was named the top sports hero by an almost 2 to 1 margin over second place finisher Magic Johnson of the world champion Los Angeles Lakers. Jordan, the NBA's leading scorer for the 1986-87 season, was last year's runner-up to another Chicago-based athlete, William "Refrigerator" Perry, who finished fourth in this year's balloting. Michael Jordan's popularity was equal among males and females. In addition to his outstanding and sometimes amazing performances on the basketball court, Jordan's many commercial endorsement and his engaging personality have made him a popular figure for all teenagers, as demonstrated by his third place finish in the top hero category.

Larry Bird, of the Boston Celtics, finished third in the balloting, thus marking the first time that basketball players had finished first, second, and third, in this category. Other top vote-getters were: Sugar Ray Leonard; Walter Payton; Kareem Abdul-Jabbar; Julius Erving; Debi Thomas; and Chris Evert.

Top Hero

Tom Cruise, movie actor

Movie Performers/Non-comedy

Tom Cruise, actor
Whoopi Goldberg, actress, comedienne

Television Performers/Non-comedy

Bruce Willis, actor, "Moonlighting"
Cybill Shepherd, actress, "Moonlighting"

Comedy

Bill Cosby, actor, comedian
Lisa Bonet, actress "The Cosby Show"

Music and Dance

Janet Jackson, pop singer
Phil Collins, rock singer

News and Sports Media

Tom Brokaw, anchorman, "NBC Evening News"
Barbara Walters, TV journalist, ABC News

Artists and Writers

Stephen King, author, *Pet Sematary, Christine.*
Judy Blume, author, *Tiger Eyes, Deenie*

Politicians and Newsmakers

Dr. Ruth Westheimer, sex advisor
Neil Armstrong, former astronaut

Top Sports Hero

Michael Jordan, basketball player, Chicago Bulls

America's Concerns

Source: The Conference Board, 1987

What problems concern us most:

1. Drug Abuse
2. Cost of medical care
3. Federal budget deficit
4. Unemployment
5. Crime
6. Loss of manufacturing jobs
7. Alcoholism
8. Plight of farmers
9. AIDS
10. Poverty

People over 55 are most concerned about the cost of medical care, while those earning more than $50,000 per year say the budget deficit is America's biggest economic or social problem.

National Spelling Bee Champions

The Scripps Howard National Spelling Bee, conducted by Scripps Howard Newspapers and other leading newspapers since 1939, was instituted by the Louisville (Ky.) Courier-Journal in 1925. Children under 16 years of age and not beyond the eighth grade are eligible to compete for cash prizes at the finals, which are held annually in Washington, D.C.

In the 1987 spelldown, the runner-up missed "dyscalculia" (impairment of mathematical ability due to organic condition of the brain). The winner spelled it correctly, and also the final word, "staphylococci" (a genus of bacterium). **The 1987 winners are:**

1. Stephanie Petit, 13, Bethel Park, PA (The Pittsburgh Press, PA). 2. Rachel E. Nussbaum, 13, Ithaca, NY (Herald-Journal/Herald American, Syracuse, NY). 3. Lynn Cabral, 13, El Paso, TX (El Paso Herald-Post, TX).

120th ANNIVERSARY EDITION

The World Almanac

and Book of Facts for 1988

The Top 10 News Stories

Just one day before the 1986 congressional elections, a Beirut magazine reported that the U.S. had sent spare parts and ammunition to Iran. After much investigation, including that of the U.S. congress, it was revealed that additional sales of arms had been made to Iran, and that profits from the sales had been diverted to fund the contra rebels fighting in Nicaragua. The Iran-Contra affair became the most serious crisis of the Reagan Administration.

Oil tankers in the Persian Gulf became the targets of Iranian and Iraqi missiles and warplanes as the U.S. and other nations became embroiled in the bitter war between Iran and Iraq. The U.S. retaliated with limited military strikes against selected Iranian targets.

How AIDS is and is not spread became just one of the many medical and social issues surrounding the deadly disease in 1987.

Nominated by Pres. Reagan to fill the vacancy on the Supreme Court left by the resignation of Justice Powell, Robert Bork was rejected by the Senate.

Marked by a record 508-point decline of the Dow Jones Industrial Average, Wall Street suffered its worst day in history.

Led by Mikhail Gorbachev's policy of openness or "glasnost," the Soviet Union entered a new era of proposed social and economic reforms.

Already tarnished by the scandals that ended the aspirations of Gary Hart and Joseph Biden, the 1988 presidential race began to take shape with a plethora of Republican and Democratic candidates.

Unthinkable before recent medical advances, surrogate parenting became an issue of national debate as a result of the custody battle for "Baby M" between Mary Beth Whitehead and William and Elizabeth Stern.

Raising hopes that the U.S. and the U.S.S.R. would sign a treaty in the near future, the two nations reached tentative agreement on a worldwide ban on medium-range nuclear missiles.

A scandal involving the sexual activities of Jim Bakker, one of the best-known TV evangelists, forced Bakker to leave his ministry and left his PTL organization in disarray.

AIDS

By B.D. Colen

By late 1987, almost 50,000 cases of Acquired Immune Deficiency Syndrome had been reported to the federal Centers for Disease Control (CDC) in Atlanta, Ga. Almost half the people represented by that stark number were dead of the disease known by layman and scientist alike as AIDS.

While researchers were in general agreement by then that the prospects for the development of a safe vaccine against AIDS were dim indeed—a least a decade off, if that soon—there was some encouragement in the statistics being compiled by the CDC since the epidemic's first recognition in June 1981. To begin with, a quick glance at the numbers made it quite evident that, at least at that point, the disease was still confined to the same so-called risk groups in which it had first appeared six years earlier: sexually active homosexual and bisexual men; intravenous drug abusers and their sexual partners and offspring; hemophiliacs and their sex partners and offspring; and those who received AIDS-infected blood transfusions and their sex partners and offspring.

Although there was ever-increasing talk of AIDS spreading among heterosexuals, there was no evidence of that spread by the end of 1987. Indeed, the number of heterosexual AIDS cases was increasing, but there were still less than 1,000 cases in the so-called "no identified risk" category, which means those patients who either do not belong to a risk group or who deny having had sex with a risk group member.

Additionally, there has probably been more useful information compiled and confirmed about AIDS, in a shorter period of time, than has been similarly gathered on any other disease in history. When one considers how little was known when the disease was first recognized in 1981—otherwise healthy gay men were, for some inexplicable reason, developing rare cancers and infections usually seen only in those whose immune systems had been intentionally suppressed following organ transplantation—one realizes that what is astounding is how much we know about AIDS, rather than how much we do not know.

Among the things we know are the following:

• **What causes AIDS:** AIDS is caused by a retrovirus, called HIV—for Human Immune deficiency Virus—first isolated in 1983 by Dr. Robert Gallo at the National Cancer Institute, in Bethesda , Md., and Dr. Luc Montagnier at the Institute Pasteur, in Paris. The virus's primary target of opportunity in the body appears to be the T-Lymphocytes, the white blood cells, that constitute the body's first line of defense against infection. As the immune system is weakened, the AIDS carrier may become an AIDS patient, falling victim to any number of infections that might not even cause any disease in an individual with a healthy immune system. This period from infection to disease may take as little as six months, or longer than seven years.

• **How AIDS is spread:** The best way to describe the spread of AIDS is to say that it is an infection of inoculation. The virus usually must be injected into the blood stream for an individual to become infected. Thus, we see AIDS in intravenous drug abusers who share needles. An infected individual will pass a needle, containing a residue of virus-carrying blood, to another drug abuser, and when that individual uses the needle, the AIDS virus is injected into his or her blood stream along with the narcotics in the syringe. Or, an infected individual has intimate sexual relations with an uninfected person and in an exchange of body fluids, the virus is passed. Those most at risk in this manner are the receptive partners in anal sex, when virus carrying semen is ejaculated into the rectum, and the virus can then make its way through the permeable anal tissue into the blood stream. AIDS may also be contracted through oral sex, and vaginal intercourse, although the risks are lower. Prior to the development of a test for the antibodies produced by exposure to the HIV virus, AIDS was also being spread in transfused blood and blood products. However, the screening of the blood supply has greatly reduced that risk; it is infinitely riskier to refuse a needed transfusion than to accept donated blood.

• **How to prevent AIDS:** Sexual abstinence is virtually 100 percent effective in protecting against HIV infection. By the same token, sex with an HIV-free individual is 100 percent safe. Thus, health officials are urging those who are not abstinent to attempt to limit their sex lives to the confines of a mutually monogamous relationship. Outside of monogamy and abstinence, the use of condoms and a spermicide offer a great deal of protection against the HIV virus, but are not 100 percent effective.

(continued)

• **How AIDS is NOT spread:** Researchers knew by at least 1983, and have only had their findings repeatedly confirmed since, that AIDS is **NOT** spread by casual contact of *any* kind. Here are some of the ways you can *not* get AIDS: From a swimming pool; from casually kissing an AIDS patient; from sharing a room, or bed, with an AIDS patient; from working with an AIDS patient or carrier; from going to school with an AIDS carrier; or from sharing a sandwich with an AIDS patient or carrier. In short, if you do not share needles, or have sex with someone who is AIDS infected, you cannot get AIDS from that person.

The Future

Considered in the perspective of the history of medicine and disease, it is amazing that we already know this much about a disease that was unknown to us just six years ago; however, there are some areas in which progress in AIDS research has been agonizingly slow. Because the AIDS virus is extremely complex, and because it mutates at a faster rate than influenza virus—heretofore one of the most rapidly mutating viruses—developing a vaccine to prevent the spread of AIDS is proving to be far more difficult than anyone thought it would be.

Despite grandiose promises several years ago by top health officials, responsible researchers now predict an effective AIDS vaccine is at least a decade away, if we ever see one at all. In the late summer of 1987, both Nobel Laureate biologist David Baltimore and U.S. Surgeon General C. Everett Koop said, in unrelated talks, that they were quite pessimistic about prospects for the early development of a vaccine. Baltimore, who chaired the National Academy of Science's Institute of Medicine Committee on a National Strategy for AIDS, said he was even less hopeful about vaccine development this fall than he was a year ago. And Koop said that what virologists are telling him makes him wonder if there will ever be a vaccine.

Things are a bit brighter on the treatment scene, but, here too, progress has been painfully slow. As of late fall 1987, there was only one partially effective treatment for AIDS, the new drug, azidothymidine (AZT). This drug appears to both extend life, and improve its quality, for *some* AIDS patients. On the other hand, there are a large number of patients it cannot help, and it has serious side effects in many patients.

Where did all this leave us at the end of 1987? Confronting an uncertain future. While public opinion poll after public opinion poll has shown that the public knows a great deal about AIDS, and probably more people have heard of the disease and know at least a little about it than know who the Vice President is, people are still unnecessarily fearful and are willing to drastically curtail the rights of those with AIDS. The formation this past summer of a Presidential Commission to recommend national AIDS policy proved about as controversial as everything else connected to the disease, with virtually everyone outside the White House criticizing the makeup of the commission and its chances of producing a worthwhile report.

In the meantime, the report of the prestigious Institute of Medicine, *Confronting AIDS*, which predicts that by 1991, in the U.S. alone, there will have been a total of more than 270,000 cases of AIDS, and 179,000 deaths. And in parts of Central Africa, the committee reported, there may already be as many as 10 million AIDS-infected individuals.

But at the same time, as 1987 came to an end, at least one renowned epidemiologist was willing to make a positive prediction. According to Dr. Alexander Langmuir, the retired founder of the CDC's Epidemic Intelligence Service, the AIDS epidemic will peak in late 1988 and will then begin to fade, until, by the turn of the century, the disease will be at a very low, endemic, level in the current high-risk groups. According to Langmuir, there is no chance of the disease exploding into the general population. But even if he is correct, Langmuir warns that everyone must exercise care if they want to be sure of avoiding what is now the most frightening disease to a majority of Americans.

B.D. Colen, 1984 Pulitzer Prize-winning science editor and writer for *New York Newsday*, is the author of *The Essential Guide To A Living Will*, Pharos Books, 1987.

Iran-Contra Affair

By Jack Anderson and Dale Van Atta

What became known as the "Iran-Contra Affair" throughout the world centered on two concurrent secret initiatives undertaken by President Reagan and top aides: 1) to attempt a back-channel strategic opening to pro-Western "moderate" elements in the radical Iranian regime of the Ayatollah Ruhollah Khomeini as well as secure the release of the American hostages; and 2) to supervise and fund military re-supply efforts to the rebels collectively known as the "contras" battling the Marxist Sandinista regime in Nicaragua.

These two secret Reagan Administration policies, running throughout 1985 and 1986, proved to be a political bombshell after becoming public. In relatively rapid succession, the affair came under the scrutiny of the Senate Select Committee on Intelligence, a presidentially-appointed panel, the FBI and an independent counsel, and an unusual joint committee of specially-selected Senate and House members. In the wake of the scandal, the President's Chief of Staff, Donald Regan; his national security adviser, Adm. John Poindexter; a top National Security Council aide, Lt. Col. Oliver North; and other officials resigned. In short, the Iran-contra affair became the worst crisis of the Reagan Administration.

Beginnings

If a single date marked the beginning of the Iran-contra affair, it was March 16, 1984, when William Buckley, Central Intelligence Agency station chief in Beirut, Lebanon, was kidnapped and held hostage by pro-Iranian Shiite extremists known as Hezbollah. There were many efforts to win his release, and these efforts increased after top officials of the administration secretly learned he was being tortured to extract his extensive, classified knowledge of CIA anti-terrorist operations and agents. Buckley's chief, CIA director William Casey, vowed to do whatever was necessary to secure his release.

There was little Casey could actually do. America had suffered repeated humiliations from Khomeini and his followers since he had unseated the Shah of Iran in a Feb. 1979 coup. On Nov. 4, 1979, Iranians seized 66 hostages at the U.S. Embassy in Teheran. Fifty-two were held for 444 days, and were finally released on the day President Reagan was inaugurated, Jan. 20, 1981. The new President declared: "Let terrorists be aware than when the rules of international behavior are violated, our policy will be one of swift and effective retribution."

The President had been unable to implement the policy, other than instituting an American embargo on arms to Iran that was fitfully adhered to by allied countries. Until 1985, U.S. intelligence had established an Iranian planning and/or operational role in four anti-American terrorist incidents resulting in 262 American deaths. (These included the suicide car-bombing of the American embassy in Beirut, Apr. 1983, 17 American dead; suicide truck bombing of Marine barracks in Beirut, Oct. 1983, 241 dead; bombing of the American Embassy annex in Beirut, Sept. 1984, two dead; and the hijacking of Kuwait Air Lines Flight 221 ending in Teheran, Dec. 1984, two dead.) Not only did Pres. Reagan fail to retaliate, he was also unable to secure the release of an increasing number of hostages held by the pro-Iranian Hezbollah.

By late 1984, a formal reappraisal of the U.S. policy toward Iran was underway. But it was not until May and June 1985 that trading arms for a new strategic opening with Iran—and for hostages—coalesced in official administration circles. The events included: 1) a five-page memorandum the CIA produced in May which suggested that if the U.S. allowed allies to sell Iran arms, Western influence in Iran might increase; 2) a May trip to Israel by a National Security Council consultant, Michael A. Ledeen, who reported that high Israeli government officials believed such an arms-engineered opening with Iran was possible, and encouraged it, and 3) a draft National Security Decision Directive circulated in June proposing a new opening to Iran which might involve arms sales; and 4) secret Iranian help in obtaining the release in Beruit of American passengers from a TWA flight hijacked in June out of Athens.

Finally, there was an intriguing plan Col. North backed to rescue seven other American hostages, including Buckley. It involved Drug Enforcement Administration agents, Texas billionaire H. Ross Perot, and a ransom of $1 million per hostage. In a June 7, 1985 memo from North to then-national security adviser Robert (Bud) McFarlane, North foreshadowed the future when he reported that "travel arrangements and operational costs are currently being financed from funds normally available to the Nicaraguan resistance." At this early date, Col. North was already directing unusual NSC covert activities using unorthodox funding practices.

It was the Israelis who picked up the ball at this point. David Kimche, director general of the Israeli Foreign Ministry, met with McFarlane in July in Washington and urged him to give Israel the green light on opening-enhancing arms shipments. As the two continued to huddle, McFarlane briefed Reagan who finally sanctioned August and September Israeli shipments of 508 anti-tank TOW missiles to Iran, knowing that it could result in release of American hostages as well as open a back-channel dialogue with "moderate" Iranians. Since the President and other Reagan administration officials had identified Iran as the primary culprit in anti-American terrorist acts, this meant a clandestine reversal of the administration's public refusal to deal with terrorists. On Sept. 14, 1985, the Rev. Benjamin F. Weir, a Presbyterian minister, was released after having been held 16 months.

In mid-November 1985, the Israelis proceeded with another arms shipment—18 Hawk anti-aircraft missiles. But Portuguese officials refused to allow the planeload to land in transit, and McFarlane called his staffer, Col. North, to help. At the time, McFarlane was in Geneva, Switzerland, for the superpower summit between Pres. Reagan and Mikhail Gorbachev. North solved the problem after first turning to the CIA for help, and then enlisting the aide of a retired Air Force officer, Maj. Gen. Richard V. Secord. North's note to Secord said his "discrete (sic) assistance is again requested in support of our national interests." The two had already been working closely together for 16 months, funding and directing the "secret" war in Nicaragua through a network of private American donors, foreign potentates, and on-the-scene soldiers of fortune.

Throughout his administration, Pres. Reagan tried to fund the contras, who were largely a creation of the CIA. But Congress, which was reluctant to conduct a *not-so-secret* war against the Nicaraguan government, had an on-again off-again affair with the contras. Under Congressional pressure, Pres. Reagan, on Dec. 21, 1982, signed a defense appropriations bill containing the first restrictive amendment proposed by Rep. Edward P. Boland (D-Mass.). It prohibited the CIA and the Pentagon from providing military equipment, training, or advice to any group "for the purpose of overthrowing the government of Nicaragua." On Dec. 8, 1983, another defense appropriations bill mandated that "not more than" $24 million could be spent by U.S. agencies for the contras. Congressional outrage in April 1984 over the clandestine CIA mining of Nicaraguan harbors led to the most restrictive Boland Amendment of all which said no federal funds from the Pentagon, CIA or any other agency "involved in intelligence activities" could be used for the contras between Oct. 1, 1984 and Dec. 3, 1985.

Anticipating this, Col. North contacted the retired Gen. Secord in July 1984 and asked him to aid the contras. Gen. Secord arranged the first of four arms shipments to the contras in Nov. 1984, a small shipload of munitions from the Far East. Both he and North were heartened in their aggressive contra aid effort by foreign contributions such as Saudi Arabian officials—and by a Presidential speech in March 1985 when Reagan publicly hailed the contras as "the moral equivalent of our Founding Fathers." About the same time, Secord arranged a 90,000-pound planeload shipment of grenades and ammunition from Europe. Another shipload occurred in May 1985, but by Aug. 1985, Congress expressed concern about North's involvement with the contras. The inquiry was parried, barely slowing North and Secord down. So it had become inevitable that North would turn to Secord for private help in the Iranian initiative in Nov. 1985, in addition to the contra resupply efforts.

Linking the Two Efforts

The two different covert Reagan Administration efforts became intertwined in Jan. 1986. McFarlane had resigned as national security adviser the previous Dec. 4, and Adm. Poindexter, his deputy, was promoted to the top position. The same day began another period—until Oct. 17, 1986—when a Congressional bill again stated no funds from the CIA, Pentagon or other "entity involved in intelligence activities" could be used for the contras.

Poindexter decided it would be covert action as usual. He relied on North for both the Iranian initiative and the contra resupply efforts. North relied on Secord. And both relied on an Iranian intermediary used by the Israelis, Manucher Ghorbanifar, who was considered unreliable by the CIA and a liar by their polygraph experts. It was during a London hotel meeting in Jan. 1986, when Ghorbanifar met with North in the bathroom, that the Ghorbanifar-originated idea for diverting profits from the Iran arms sales to the contras first came up, according to North's subsequent testimony (Actually, Secord had already placed an excess $800,000 from the Nov. 1985 Hawk missile shipment in the "contra account" of his company, Lake Resources.)

On Jan. 17, 1986, the President secretly signed a one-page "finding" which authorized the Iran initiative. It had been under discussion since early December, and been through several drafts. The final version stated the U.S. government would "establish contact with moderate elements within and outside the Government of Iran by providing these elements with arms, equipment and related material." Three purposes were stated in the finding; "(1) establishing a more moderate government in Iran, (2) obtaining from them significant intelligence (on Iranian) intentions with respect to its neighbors and with respect to terrorist acts, and (3) furthering the release of the American hostages held in Beruit and preventing additional terrorist acts by these groups."

The first direct U.S. shipment of arms—1,000 TOW missiles—was delivered on Feb. 22. Col. North ordered Secord to make the $2.6 million in profits, and all subsequent surpluses, available to the contras. North wrote the so-called "Diversion Memo," the most famous of the scandal, between Apr. 4 and 7 to Adm. Poindexter. In a five-page memo, North stated that of the "residual funds" from the Iranian arms transactions, "$12 million will be used to purchase critically needed supplies for the Nicaraguan Democratic Resistance Forces." In the end, less than $4 million of the more than $30 million from the arms sales was actually diverted to the contras. (The contra resupply effort continued throughout the summer, peaking in Sept. 1986).

The last three of four direct U.S. shipments of arms to Iran occurred on May 25 (a pallet of Hawk missile spare parts); Aug. 3 (another pallet of Hawk missile spare parts); and Oct. 30-31 (500 TOW missiles). McFarlane, North and others actually flew on the May spare parts flight to Iran and underwent days of frustrating talks with the so-called Iranian "moderates." McFarlane broke off the discussions, and flew back to the U.S. on May 28 in disgust. But the Rev. Lawrence Martin Jenco, a Roman Catholic priest, was released on July 26. On Sept. 9, another American, Frank Herbert Reed, was taken hostage and yet another, Joseph James Cicippio, was kidnapped Sept. 12. A third American, Edward Austin Tracy, was taken hostage on Oct. 21. On Nov. 2, David Jacobsen was released. After little over a year of the Iranian arms-for-hostages deal, three hostages were released and three more were taken.

Reaction

The administration's secret initiatives began unraveling publicly on Apr. 28, 1986. The first five stories on the Iranian arms-for-hostage deal was published by nationally-syndicated columnists Jack Anderson and Dale Van Atta. Van Atta had first learned of the deal in Dec. 1985, but was asked to hold it by administration officials who charged hostages might be killed if the initiative was publicized. In a one-on-one interview with Van Atta on Feb. 24, Pres. Rea-

(continued)

gan personally asked the columnists to continue suppressing the story. But the Reagan-ordered bombing raid on Libya convinced the columnist to reveal some of the story. In a June 29 column, they stated flatly: "We can reveal that the secret negotiations (with Iran) over arms supply and release of American hostages have involved members of the National Security Council and a former official of the CIA." North fretted over the publicity, though no other news organizations ran similar accounts since they were unable to confirm the stories. He complained in one secret memo the following Sept. 17 that one person "could well be the source of the Jack Anderson (/Van Atta) stuff we have seen periodically." Col. North's contra resupply program received irreparable public exposure after Oct. 5, when the Nicaraguans shot down a C-123K cargo plane and captured an American, Eugene Hasenfus.

The final nail in the coffin for the covert initiatives came with the Nov. 3 publication of *Al Shiraa*, a Beirut weekly magazine, whose story disclosed the U.S. had sent spare parts and ammunition to Iran after a secret visit by McFarlane. The following day, Hashemi Rafsanjani, speaker of the Iranian parliament, confirmed that McFarlane and four other Americans had come on such a mission to Iran. The story quickly snowballed until Pres. Reagan was forced to defend his "secret diplomatic initiative to Iran" in a Nov. 13 nationally-televised speech. The speech was full of inaccuracies, including the assertion that the shipments involved only "small amounts of defensive weapons and spare parts." He concluded: "We did not—repeat—we did not trade weapons or anything else for hostages."

The affair became a full-fledged scandal on Nov. 25 with an announcement by Attorney General Edwin Meese that the "Diversion Memo" had been discovered, and a criminal investigation of the principals was beginning. On the same day, Pres. Reagan announced Poindexter's resignation and North's dismissal. After the announcement, North's secretary, Fawn Hall, sneaked key documents out of their office to North in her boots and under the back of her clothing. She later testified that even earlier, on the evening of Nov. 21, she and North had altered critical documents relating to the initiatives, and shredded a foot and a half high pile of documents over the course of half an hour.

The Senate Select Committee on Intelligence was the first out with an official investgative report, a 65-page document released Jan. 29, 1987, which concluded that the President's Iranian arms initiative was fueled by a desire to free the hostages and establish a covert dialogue with "moderate" Iranians, and resulted also from pressures by the Israelis, as well as private citizens and foreign arms dealers out to make money or gain influence with the Reagan Administration.

The next report came from a Presidentially-appointed three-member "Special Review Board," chaired by former Sen. John Tower. (The other two members were former Secretary of State and Sen. Edmund Muskie and former national security adviser Brent Scowcroft). Their report, issued on Feb. 26, 1987, contained a remarkable collection of private computer-sent notes between McFarlane, North, Poindexter and Secord. It also reported on the only interrogations of the President concerning his own role in the affair. The President was quoted as saying he had no knowledge of the diversion of Iranian arms profits to the contras. Finally, the Tower Commission report was sharply critical of Reagan's management style which had allowed aides to run amok implementing the President's policies. Reagan quickly acted on the report's recommendations, but confessed in a nationally-televised speech on March 4: "I told the American people I did not trade arms for hostages. My heart and my best intentions still tell me that's true. But the facts and the evidence tell me it is not . . . What began as a strategic opening to Iran deteriorated in its implementation into trading arms for hostages."

The third report, from the specially-impanelled committees of the House and Senate, was due on Oct. 30, 1987 (after *World Almanac* press time). The 11-member (six Democrats; five Republicans) U.S. Senate Select Committee on Secret Military Assistance to Iran and the Nicaraguan Opposition was chaired by Sen. Daniel Inouye (D-Hawaii). The 15-member (nine Democrats; six Republicans) U.S. House Select Committee to Investigate Covert Arms Transactions with Iran was chaired by Rep. Lee H. Hamilton (D-Ind.). The committees met jointly for 40 days of public hearings from May 5 to Aug. 3. More than 1,000 administration documents were entered into the record. Pres. Reagan waived "executive privilege" not only for all of his aides and their documents, but also for himself. He provided relevant notes from his personal diary.

In all, the committees heard from 28 public witnesses. Gen. Secord and McFarlane were heard from first, followed by a series of minor witnesses. Fawn Hall, North's secretary, provided temporary "sex appeal" for the mostly-male scandal—but also managed to raise serious questions about the attitude at the White House that lead to the North "shredding party." She said that sometimes they found it necessary "to go above the written law." Toward the end, Secretary of State George Shultz offered riverting testimony on the internal "battle(s) royal" of the administration. He also left on the record eloquent soliloquies on the flaws in Reagan policies, the tragedy of conducting the nation's business as North and Poindexter had done, and the need to consult with Congress and otherwise follow the guiding principles of the Constitution.

The popular highlight of the nationally-televised hearings was the early July appearance of "Ollie" North—the gung-ho Marine in full be-medaled uniform, attractive and an all-American can-do type of guy. In the days preceding his testimony, witnesses had impugned North's personal integrity at the same time they praised his patriotism, misguided or not. His days on the stand were charged with emotion and eloquence as he defended potentially illegal action, and made no apologies for lying to Congress and deceiving the American public. As for the diversion, he though it was "a neat idea," and still did. Substantively, he added detail to the record and a new view of the late CIA director William Casey as a Svengali in the affair, frequently closeting himself with North and spurring him on to create a self-sustaining off-the-shelf covert action capability with the help of entities like Secord's "enterprise."

North was hailed as a new American hero, and reduced interrogating Congressmen to utterance of speeches about their own patriotism and/or the folly of North's causes and course of action. One effective, polite voice of rebuttal was Sen. George J. Mitchell's (D-Maine), who told North: "It is possible for an American to disagree with you on aid to the contras and still love the country as much as you do." Others later charged that North and friends had operated a "junta," a government-within-a-government which, if its operations were not denounced, threatened the foundations of American democracy.

The historically significant highlight of the hearings was the testimony of the dry, pipe-smoking Adm. Poindexter. Poindexter revealed that, because he thought it might be embarrassing to the President as the scandal unfolded, he had destroyed a Dec. 4, 1985, finding signed by Pres. Reagan. The purported document authorized the Hawk missile sales retroactively and portrayed them as nothing more than an arms-for-hostages swap. On July 15, 1987, Poindexter answered the most critical question of the hearings: What did the President know about the possibly illegal diversion of Iran arms sales profits and when? "I made a very deliberate decision not to ask the President so that I could insulate hime from the decision and provide some future deniability for the President if it ever leaked out," Poindexter testified. "The buck stops here with me." As in other highly-charged national American investigations in the past—such as the Watergate hearings—this lone witness's testimony was not automatically considered the final word on the President's knowledge. Indeed, Poindexter was generally believed to be the least credible witness, frequently professing his inability to recall past events when given a series of tough questions.

Pres. Reagan once again addressed the nation Aug. 12, at the close of the public hearings. He was clearly buoyed by Poindexter's confirmation that the President had not been told about the diversion, But he was almost sanguine on the Iran initiative itself: "Our original initiative rapidly got all tangled up in the sale of arms, and the sale of arms got tangled up with the hostages," he said. "I let my preoccupation with the hostages intrude into areas where it didn't belong . . . I was stubborn in my pursuit of a policy that went astray."

Meanwhile, independent counsel Lawrence E. Walsh,

named by a special federal court Dec. 19, 1986, continued a separate criminal investigation with the aid of a grand jury, the Justice Department and the FBI. Indictments were expected before the end of 1987. (*See Chronology for additional details.*)

Jack Anderson won the Pulitzer for national reporting in 1972. "Washington Merry-Go-Round," the nationally syndicated column, written and reported by Mr. Anderson and Dale Van Atta, is distributed by United Feature Syndicate.

U.S. Education in 1987

Four years after the start of an educational reform movement in the U.S., some changes had been effected in the schools, but their significance was unclear.

In 1983, American education was characterized by a "rising tide of mediocrity" that undermined U.S. competitiveness in the world economy, according to the report "A Nation at Risk," by the National Commission on Excellence in Education. The commission's recommendations included requiring all high school students to study English, math, science, social studies, computer science, and foreign languages; paying, promoting, and granting tenure to teachers based on merit, not seniority; considering a longer year for high schools; and adopting higher admissions standards for colleges. In that election year, Pres. Reagan made education a major political issue, calling for a return to "the basics," and endorsing merit pay for teachers. Governors and legislatures in all 50 states took such steps as increasing teachers' salaries, instituting merit pay plans, and requiring more basic academic courses for a high school diploma, all of which required pumping billions of dollars into the schools.

In 1987, the *New York Times* reported on many new programs and new approaches, but concluded: "There is not yet proof that students are learning better. Moreover, as the first rush of political enthusiasm has worn off, some of the new measures have begun to erode in several states under pressure from unhappy teachers and tight state budgets."

According to the *Times*, since 1980, all but five states raised the minimum requirements for high school graduation; 42 raised mathematics requirements; 34, science requirements; 38 created some form of merit pay for good teachers or passed incentives for local districts to do so; 24, most in the South, passed comprehensive educational packages. Overall, state support for public schools grew by 26 percent beyond inflation since 1980.

Mixed Results

Still, results remained unclear or mixed. South Carolina passed one of the nation's broadest reforms in 1984, and since then, standardized test scores for primary and secondary school students increased dramatically and average Scholastic Aptitude Tests scores rose more than in any other state—by 36% since 1982. Meanwhile, in Louisiana, almost half of the students who began high school failed to graduate. And from Florida came reports that educational "reforms" contributed to an increase in the dropout rate—to 40%.

The idea of merit pay—more money for superior teachers—proved controversial. New Jersey gave up its plan to award $5,000 stipends to "master teachers" after only one district chose to participate. The major complaint: the evaluation was an inadequate measure of good teaching. Many experts contended that the school reform movement was hindered by an emphasis on politics over learning.

An annual U.S. Education Dept. survey released early in 1987 found "some gain, a little slippage" among U.S. public schools in 1986. "We have basically held steady," said Education Secretary William J. Bennett. In 1985, when the S.A.T. scores had increased substantially for the first time in two decades, some politicians had attributed the gains to the changes in the schools. "Bravo!" Bennett had said. "We begin to see here the impact of the reform movement on the past several years." Over the next two years, the College Board and the American College Testing Program reported that S.A.T. and A.C.T. scores were virtually unchanged. President of the College Board, Donald M. Stewart, said, "It makes me wonder about the real impact of the national reform movement. I'm not sure that improved learning is taking place." Others claim that it would take more time for the effects of the changes in schools to be demonstrated in standardized tests.

Japanese Schools Praised

Americans could find no solace in the results of four studies released in 1987 that compared U.S. education with that in other countries. A U.S. Education Dept. study of Japanese education praised Japan as a "learning society of formidable dimensions." Education Secretary Bennett said these schools had been "demonstrably successful in providing . . . a powerfully competitive economy," and listed a dozen pluses, including orderly classrooms and hallways, memorization, high expectation for students, and the teaching of a clear-cut morality. The study also found that the Japanese school week was five and a half days, the school year 210 days—30 more than in the U.S.; curricula were well-defined; parents were extensively involved; and teachers' pay, status, and responsibility were greater than in the U.S. Further, the study found that Japanese elementary and high school students spent "about one-third more time during a typical class period engaged in learning" than U.S. students did; Japanese teachers could generally count on peer pressure to make sure students were well-behaved and ready to work; discipline and deference to authority were instilled through character-building practices, such as a daily cleanup of classrooms and hallways, and private, fee-charging tutorial services gave students extra help after school, with almost half of Japanese ninth-graders attending.

Three reports on the poor showing by U.S. students in international test of mathematic skills were issued by the Mathematical Sciences Research Board. One found U.S. students mediocre at all math skills except straightforward computation, compared with students from 20 other countries, and blamed the "diffuse" U.S. math curricula, with their emphasis on "repetition and review." A report of American children compared with Chinese and Japanese children arrived at the same findings. A third study, of American, Taiwanese, and Japanese students noted that Taiwanese and Japanese mothers were more likely to think that effort brought success and, therefore, worked with their children in mastering their lessons. In contast, U.S. mothers tended to leave education to the schools and to assume that children needed innate ability in math to do well.

Positive News

However, there was some positive news about education in 1987. Black high school students were found to be making steady gains on the Scholastic Aptitude Tests and American College Tests. The College Board reported that from 1977 to 1987, the average scores of black students on the SATs rose by 21 points on the verbal section, to 351, and by 20 points on the mathematics section, to 377, on a scale of 200 to 800. American College Testing reported that the average composite scores of blacks on its tests increased from 13.0 in 1986 to 13.4 in 1987, on a scale of one to 36, continuing a trend that began in 1976 when the average was 11.9.

Also, the number of college freshman interested in teaching careers increased in 1986, for the fourth consecutive year, according to an annual poll by the American Council on Education and the Univ. of Calif. at Los Angeles. Seven percent of male and female college and university students said they were interested in becoming elementary or secondary teachers, compared with 6.2 in 1985, and an all-time low of 4.7 in 1982.

U.S. education was found to be worthwhile in at least one sense. A Bureau of the Census study issued in Sept. 1987 measured the average income of adults, based on how much schooling they received. The study found that only about one in five Americans had a college degree, but this 20 percent were those who earned the most money. At the head of the list were professionals, such as lawyers, doctors, and dentists, who took home an average of $3,178 a month, more than five times the pay of those who hadn't completed high school. Following professionals were those who received doctorates, averaging $3,265 a month; those with a master's degree, $2,288; holders of a bachelor's degree, $1,841; an associate's degree, $1,346; those who received vocational training, $1,219; those who attended college but left without a degree, $1,169; high school graduates, $1,045; and high school dropouts, $693.

June Foley

CHRONOLOGY OF THE YEAR'S EVENTS

Reported Month by Month in 3 Categories: National, International, and General — Nov. 1, 1986 to Oct. 16, 1987

NOVEMBER

National

Voters Hand Senate to Democrats — The big prize in the midterm Congressional election, **Nov. 4,** was control of the U.S. Senate. The Republicans had held a majority for 6 years, ever since Ronald Reagan was first elected president. But the Democrats came out of the 1986 voting with a 55-45 majority, a net gain of 8 seats. Thus, for the first time, Reagan would face opposing majorities in both houses. The president campaigned vigorously for GOP Senate candidates, but with little success. The Democrats easily retained their majority in the U.S. House, adding on 5 seats for a division of 258 to 177 over the Republicans. The Senate sweep was particularly satisfactory for the Democrats because they picked up 4 seats in the South, their longtime base that the Republicans had been eroding in recent elections. The big southern winner was Florida Gov. Bob Graham, who unseated the incumbent Sen. Paula Hawkins in an especially bitter contest. Sen. Alan Cranston (D, Cal.) turned back a strong challenge from Rep. Ed Zschau. The narrow losses by the Republicans in the House was some consolation, but the slight shift was expected to be costly on issues in which the House had been closely divided, such as the fight over aid to antigovernment contras opposing the leftist Sandinista regime in Nicaragua. The gubernatorial contests were a success story for Republicans. The Democratic majority in the state houses fell from 34-16 before the election to 26-24, with such large prizes as Florida and Texas moving to the Republican column.

Leaders Chosen for 100th Congress — Both parties chose their leaders for the 100th Congress, which would convene in January 1987. Robert Byrd (W. Va.) was renamed Democratic leader in the Senate, **Nov. 20,** and thus would become majority leader when the Democrats took control of the upper house in January. Byrd had been majority leader from 1977 to 1981 and minority leader thereafter, when the Republicans held a majority. J. Bennett Johnston (La.) had made an effort to replace Byrd, but had given up when it became apparent that he did not have enough support. Sen. Alan Cranston was chosen by his colleagues to continue as Democratic whip. In their caucus, **Nov. 20,** the Republicans renamed as their leader Robert Dole (Kan.), who in January would make the change from majority leader to minority leader. Republicans renamed Alan Simpson (Wyo.) as party whip.

Stock Trader Must Pay $100 Million — The most scandal-ridden year in Wall Street history was marked by another milestone—the agreement by a wealthy stock trader to pay $100 million in a fine and to return illicit profits. The Securities and Exchange Commission had alleged that Ivan Boesky had traded stock on the basis of inside information (facts not available to the general public) about corporate takeovers. The government announced, **Nov. 14,** that Boesky had agreed to plead guilty to an unspecified criminal count. He was barred for life from trading in securities. The investigation of Boesky had grown out of a similar inquiry into illegal trading by Dennis Levine, an investment banker who had pleaded guilty in June. The SEC said that Boesky had agreed to pay Levine 5 percent of the profits made on stocks bought on Levine's advice. The fine, by far the largest ever for insider trading, consisted of a $50 million fine and $50 million in returned profits. On **Dec. 22,** 2 ex-employees of Lazard Freres & Co. who had been implicated by Levine pleaded guilty to felonies, one for giving information on corporate takeovers to Levine and the second for filing false tax returns.

G.M. Cutback Jolts Economy — General Motors Corp. announced, **Nov. 6,** that it would close 11 plants employing about 29,000 people—about 5 percent of its U.S. work force. The move, described as part of G.M.'s program to replace obsolete facilities with modern, efficient plants, would be a setback for the economy of Michigan, in particular. Otherwise, the U.S. economy appeared to be holding steady. The unemployment rate remained at 6.9 percent in October, the Labor Department reported, **Nov. 7.** Prices paid by producers for consumer goods edged upward 0.3 percent in October, the Department reported, **Nov. 14.** Inflation continued in check, with the consumer price index advancing only 0.2 percent in October, the Department said, **Nov. 25.**

Reagan Vetoes Clean Water Bill — Defying the unanimous sentiment of both houses of Congress, Pres. Ronald Reagan, **Nov. 6,** vetoed legislation that would have spent $18 billion for sewage treatment facilities. He said that the bill, aimed at strengthening the Clean Water Act, would have cost three times the amount of money that he had advocated. The so-called pocket veto—Reagan simply declined to sign the bill within 10 days after receiving it while Congress was not in session—was opposed by Reagan's appointee Lee Thomas, administrator of the Environmental Protection Agency. Congressional supporters vowed to reintroduce the bill in the new Congress in January.

International

Aquino Ousts Foe in Cabinet — A long-festering crisis within the government of Pres. Corazon Aquino of the Philippines came to a head with the removal of Defense Minister Juan Ponce Enrile. Enrile's support for Aquino had been a key factor in her rise to power earlier in the year, but he had since been identified with dissidents in the military who opposed her efforts to negotiate with Communist insurgents. Despite reports early in November that Enrile might lead a coup, Aquino went on with a state visit to Japan, **Nov. 10-13.** The armed forces chief of staff, Gen. Fidel Ramos, a supporter of Aquino, kept troops on alert around the capital during her absence. On **Nov. 22,** Ramos took similar action to prevent a coup, ordering tanks to surround Aquino's residence. On **Nov. 23,** Aquino asked her entire cabinet to resign. She replaced Enrile with Rafael Ileto, the deputy defense minister and a retired general. She also called on the Communists to accept a cease-fire within a week or negotiations would be cut off. A cease-fire agreement was in fact reached, **Nov. 26,** to take effect Dec. 10 for 60 days. The cessation of fighting would be the first since the New People's Army was founded in 1969.

U.S. Violates Arms Treaty Limits — On **Nov. 28,** by deploying a B-52 bomber capable of carrying cruise missiles, the United States violated the limits of the unratified Strategic Arms Limitation Treaty (SALT II) that had been signed by the United States and the Soviet Union in 1979. Despite the failure by the U.S. Senate to accept the treaty and charges that the Soviet Union was already ignoring its provisions, Pres. Ronald Reagan had previously stayed within its bounds. The treaty limited each signatory to 1,320 strategic delivery systems, but the bomber's flight between Air Force bases near Fort Worth and San Antonio, Tex. put the United States above that level. During a state visit to India, **Nov. 28,** Soviet leader Mikhail Gorbachev called the violation a "major mistake" and said it showed a lack of U.S. interest in arms control. Congress had added a nonbinding resolution to the 1987 defense authorization bill calling on the administration to continue to observe SALT II limits.

American Convicted in Nicaragua — Eugene Hasenfus, a U.S. citizen captured by government forces in Nicaragua in October after his plane, which was carrying arms to government opponents, was shot down, was convicted by a government tribunal, **Nov. 15.** Hasenfus, who had admitted participating in an operation to aid the contras, was sentenced to 30 years in prison for having violated Nicaragua's security law. Three other men had been killed when the plane was downed. During his trial, Hasenfus said he had made at least 10 flights into Nicaragua to drop weapons for the contras. In his testimony, he denied working for the U.S. Central Intelligence Agency and said he did not know who was running the operation.

General

Organized Crime Leaders Convicted — Eight men, identified by prosecutors as top leaders of organized crime, were convicted, **Nov. 20,** in New York City, mostly for racketeering, conspiracy, and extortion. U.S. Attorney Rudolph Giuliani said, "The verdict reached today has resulted in dismantling the ruling council of La Cosa Nostra." Three defendants convicted as bosses of crime families were Anthony (Fat Tony) Salerno, Anthony (Tony Ducks) Corallo, and Carmine (Junior) Persico. Prosecutors said that the organizations they and the others ran were engaged in illegal gambling, narcotics trafficking, and labor racketeering. During the 10-week trial prosecutors developed a case utilizing surveillance photographs and taped conversations as well as scores of witnesses. One defendant, Anthony (Bruno) Indelicato, was convicted of participating in the 1979 slayings of Carmine Galante, a rival crime figure, and 2 of his associates. On **Jan. 13**, seven of the defendants received 100-year prison terms. Indelicato was sentenced to 40 years in prison.

Global Fight Against AIDS Begun — The World Health Organization, a United Nations body, **Nov. 20**, launched a worldwide fight against acquired immune deficiency syndrome (AIDS). Dr. Halfdan Mahler, head of the WHO, called the disease "a health disaster of pandemic proportions" and added that he could not imagine "a worse health problem in this century." He estimated that by 1990 cases of AIDS could total 3.5 million and that 100 million persons might be infected with the virus while remaining free of its symptoms. Mahler criticized some countries for not making a sufficient effort to combat the disease and acknowledged that he had previously underestimated the AIDS threat. He said his organization hoped to be raising $1.5 billion a year by 1990. Strategies of the WHO offensive would include education campaigns, a global information-gathering system, a network to share information among scientists worldwide, utilizing skills of professionals outside the public-health field, and the education of health workers on how AIDS spreads.

Disasters — An Iranian military transport plane crashed into a mountain in eastern Iran, killing all 103 persons aboard, most of them soldiers, the Iranian press agency said, **Nov. 3**. . . . Up to 200 persons drowned, **Nov. 11**, when an overcrowded ferry sank in rough seas near Montrouis, Haiti.

DECEMBER

National

Record Year Ends on Wall Street — The stock market again dominated economic news in December as the busiest and one of the most profitable years in Wall Street history came to an end. The Dow Jones industrial average posted another all-time high on **Dec. 2**, closing at 1955.57. Otherwise, economic signs were mixed. The Commerce Department reported, **Dec. 2**, that the index of leading economic indicators had risen 0.6 percent in October. The unemployment rate held at 6.9 percent in November for the third straight month, the Labor Department reported, **Dec. 5**. The department said, **Dec. 12**, that the index of prices paid by consumers for finished goods had risen 0.2 percent in November. The Commerce Department reported, **Dec. 16**, that, using the broadest measure of trade with other countries, the U.S. balance of payments had posted a record deficit of $36.28 billion in the third quarter of 1986. The consumer price index rose 0.3 percent in November, the Labor Department reported, **Dec. 19**. The excitement on Wall Street was measured, **Dec. 19**, in the record volume of more than 244 million shares traded on the New York Stock Exchange. The Commerce Department said, **Dec. 30**, that the index of leading economic indicators had risen 1.2 percent in November. The department reported, **Dec. 31**, that the U.S. deficit on merchandise trade rose sharply to a record $19.2 billion in November. **Dec. 31** was a down day on Wall Street, with the Dow Jones average declining to 1895.95, but the advance for the year totaled 349.14 points, representing a gain of 22.6 percent.

U.S. Employees' Smoking Curbed — The U.S. General Services Administration directed, **Dec. 5**, that nonsmoking federal government employees must be assured of a "reasonably smoke-free environment" at their jobs. The new rules would cover some 2.3 million workers, and followed similar actions by the U.S. armed services. Many scientific reports had linked lung cancer in nonsmokers with exposure to the cigarette smoke from others. The new regulations, effective Feb. 8, 1987, required that office areas be divided into smoking and nonsmoking areas. In general, large areas used by many employees, such as auditoriums, conference rooms, classrooms, and libraries, would be nonsmoking areas. Smoking would be permitted where it could be "configured so as to limit the involuntary exposure of nonsmokers to secondhand smoke to a minimum." In releasing his annual report on smoking and health, **Dec. 16**, Surgeon General C. Everett Koop asserted, "The right of a smoker to smoke stops at the point where his or her smoking increases the disease risk in those occupying the same environment."

Wright to Become Speaker of House — Rep. Jim Wright (D, Tex.) was assured, **Dec. 8**, of becoming the next Speaker of the U.S. House of Representatives. For more than a year, Wright had openly campaigned for Speaker, the office being vacated by the retiring Thomas P. (Tip) O'Neill (D, Mass.). Wright's election went without challenge in the Democratic caucus. Rep. Thomas Foley (Wash.) was elected majority leader by his Democratic colleagues, and Rep. Tony Coelho (Cal.) was elected majority whip. Wright quickly made news by suggesting that the tax-rate cuts embodied in the 1986 tax law be delayed as a means of reducing the federal budget deficit. The Republican House members, also meeting, **Dec. 8**, again chose Robert Michel (Ill.) as their leader and Rep. Trent Lott (Miss.) as minority whip.

U.S. Shuts Down Nuclear Reactor — The U.S. Department of Energy announced, **Dec. 12**, that a nuclear reactor that was an important source of plutonium for nuclear weapons would be shut down for 6 months while safety improvements were made. The reactor, a part of the department's Hanford nuclear complex near Richland, Wash., resembled in design the Soviet Union's reactors at Chernobyl, one of which released a lethal cloud of radiation in 1986 after its core melted down. Like the Chernobyl reactors, the N reactor at Hanford lacked a containment dome that would keep radioactive steam from escaping into the atmosphere if an accident occurred. The N reactor, which had opened in 1963 with a projected lifespan of 20 years, had been in the news because of frequent reports of safety violations. The Energy Department said renovations would cost $50 million.

International

5 in Argentina Convicted for Abuses — A former police chief and 4 other men were convicted by an Argentine court on **Dec. 2**, for human-rights abuses during the period of military rule in the 1970s. Retired Gen. Ramón Camps, who as provincial police chief of Buenos Aires had been responsible for the torture of newspaper editor Jacobo Timmerman, was found guilty of torturing 73 persons. The other defendants were also convicted of torture, a practice commonly used by authorities against those believed to be leftist opponents of the military regime, which had subsequently been replaced by a civilian government. Pres. Raúl Alfonsín said, **Dec. 5**, that in an effort to achieve national reconciliation he would ask Congress to set a deadline for filing similar charges against military officers. Congress adopted a law setting a 60-day limit for the filing of charges, and Alfonsín signed it into law, **Dec. 26**. The Argentine Supreme Court, **Dec. 30**, upheld an earlier conviction of 5 former members of the ruling junta for the torture and killing of political prisoners.

U.S. Aids Hondurans Against Nicaragua — Nicaraguan and Honduran forces clashed near their common border, and, for the second time in 1986, U.S. helicopters transported Honduran soldiers to the vicinity of the fighting. On **Dec. 4**, Nicaraguan soldiers overran a Honduran border post in pursuit of Nicaraguan contras who opposed the leftist Sandinista regime in Nicaragua and who had established a base inside Honduras. Nicaraguan civilian refugees who had crossed into Honduras were caught up in the subsequent fighting in the Las Vegas area of Honduras. Although Nicaragua denied its forces were inside Honduras, reports said they had pushed to within a half mile of the contra base camp. On **Dec. 6** and **7**, using U.S.-made A-37 planes, the Hondurans bombed Sandinista troops. On **Dec. 7** and **8**, unarmed U.S. helicopters flown by Americans carried Honduran soldiers to an airfield near the conflict. An American citizen, Sam Hall, was arrested by Nicaraguan authorities, **Dec. 12**, at a military air base on suspicion of espionage.

Hall, a brother of U.S. Rep. Tony Hall (D, Ohio), had reportedly served as a mercenary in several countries. Eugene Hasenfus, an American convicted in November of supplying arms to the contras, was pardoned, **Dec. 17,** by the Nicaragua National Assembly in response to a request by Pres. Daniel Ortega. Hasenfus immediately returned to the United States in the company of Sen. Christopher Dodd (D, Conn.). The Nicaraguan foreign ministry freed Hall, **Jan. 27,** declaring that his instability and occasional incoherence exempted him from criminal responsibility.

Chinese Students Demand Democracy — Protests by Chinese students calling for more democracy spread throughout the country in December. The mass demonstrations appeared to come in response to encouragement by China's leaders that intellectuals be more outspoken. Students demonstrated peacefully in Hefei, **Dec. 5** and **9,** and began an illegal poster campaign, **Dec 12,** that was also reported in other cities. Up to 35,000 students took to the streets of Shanghai, **Dec. 20,** and on **Dec. 21** as many as 50,000 were reported to have gathered in People's Square. The New China News Agency reported, **Dec. 21,** that the government had accused the students of "illegal actions" that "will affect social stability and unity." On **Dec. 22,** Shanghai police banned any further unauthorized demonstrations in the city. Meanwhile, mass protests were reported in several other cities, but they seemed, in general, to be disorganized and unfocused on precise objectives.

OPEC to Cut Oil Production — The Organization of Petroleum Exporting Countries agreed to cut production and set a fixed price for oil. Meeting in Geneva, **Dec 11-20,** ministers representing the members of the cartel agreed that, effective Jan. 1, 1987, they would reduce their combined oil output by about one million barrels per day; the current level was about 16.6 million barrels per day. Every OPEC member except Iran and Iraq would reduce production by about 5 percent. Iran's actual production was running far below its former and new (slightly reduced) quotas because of the disruption of its facilities caused by the war with Iraq. Iraq rejected its new quota, which was set at about 9 percent below its current production. The price for oil would be pegged at about $18 a barrel, effective Feb. 1, 1987, reflecting a shift from the price-war policy of Sheik Ahmed Yamani, the recently ousted oil minister of Saudi Arabia.

Forced Exile Ends for Sakharovs — Andrei Sakharov, the dissident Russian physicist, and his wife, Yelena Bonner, were freed from internal exile in the Soviet Union in December. Sakharov reported that Soviet leader Mikhail Gorbachev had informed him by phone, **Dec. 16,** that he and his wife would be free to leave the city of Gorky, to which he had been exiled in 1980 for supporting human rights causes. Bonner, who had been convicted of anti-Soviet activities in 1984, was pardoned. The Soviet Union made the formal announcement, **Dec. 19,** and said Sakharov would be allowed to return to work at the Soviet Academy of Sciences. On their return to Moscow, **Dec. 23,** the couple was greeted by some 200 supporters and journalists. As outspoken as ever, Sakharov denounced the war in Afghanistan and the treatment of Soviet dissidents.

60 Killed in Skyjacking — About 60 persons were reported to have been killed, **Dec. 25,** when a hijacked Iraqi airliner crashed in Saudi Arabia. Saudi authorities did not acknowledge officially that a hijacking had taken place. Survivors of the incident—variously reported as 30 to 44 in number—said that the hijackers had exploded 2 grenades and exchaged gunfire with guards while the plane was in the air, and that most of the casualties had occurred when the plane attempted a emergency landing near Arar in northwest Saudi Arabia.

General

Billionaire Perot Ousted by G.M. — The General Motors Corporation, **Dec. 1,** expelled billionaire H. Ross Perot from its board of directors after Perot continued to criticize G.M. Chairman Roger Smith. Perot had been the automobile giant's largest stockholder since 1984, when it had purchased Electronic Data Systems Corp., the computer services company Perot had founded. Perot had frequently criticized the G.M. leadership, which he had found to be isolated from its work force and prospective customers. He especially deplored large perquisites available to the company's executives.

Plane Circles Earth Without Refueling — Aviation history was made when the U.S. aircraft *Voyager* circled the earth nonstop without taking on additional fuel. The experimental craft, whose main wings were to the rear and whose small wings—designed to provide lift and to prevent stalling—were near the nose, took off from Edwards Air Force Base near Los Angeles on **Dec. 14.** The pilots were Richard Rutan and Jeana Yeager. The plane, carrying 1,200 gallons of gasoline, declined in weight from 9,750 pounds to 1,858 pounds during the flight. Storms encountered during the flight forced the pilots to change the flight plan 5 times. Some 7½ hours before landing, the plane plunged from 8,500 feet to 5,000 feet when the rear engine stalled. The pilots switched to the front engine to avert disaster. The plane landed at Edwards, **Dec. 23,** after being in the air 9 days, 3 minutes, and 44 seconds. It had covered 25,012 miles for an average speed of 115.8 miles per hour. The miles flown and the length of time in the air were both records for endurance.

Merger of Banks Among Biggest Ever — Chemical New York Corp. announced, **Dec. 15,** that it had agreed to buy Texas Commerce Bancshares, Inc. The purchase price, about $1.1 billion, made this one of the largest banking mergers ever. As a result, Chemical would rise from 7th to 5th in size among U.S. banking concerns. A recent Texas law had allowed mergers between Texas banks and between Texas and out-of-state banks. The recent slump in the oil-based Texas economy had adversely affected Texas Commerce's profits.

96 Die in San Juan Hotel Fire — A fire of suspicious origin engulfed the Dupont Plaza Hotel in San Juan, Puerto Rico on **Dec. 31,** and claimed 96 lives, making it one of the worst hotel fires in U.S. history. More than 140 persons were injured. The fire began in mid-afternoon in the ballroom and continued for 6 hours. The 22-story, 423-room hotel was packed with holiday visitors, many of whom were gambling in the hotel casino when the fire broke out. Many persons were rescued by helicopters from the rooftop and balconies. An investigation into the cause of the fire began immediately.

Disasters — The crash of a Soviet airliner, **Dec. 12,** while on its approach to a landing in East Berlin resulted in the deaths of 69 of the 81 persons aboard.

JANUARY

National

100th Congress Convenes — The 100th U.S. Congress, whose 2-year term would carry the nation to the end of its second century under the 1787 Constitution, convened in January. Rep. Jim Wright (D, Tex.), the Speaker-elect of the House, said, **Jan. 2,** that the U.S. trade deficit was the most important economic problem facing the nation, and he called for the enactment of a trade bill aimed at reducing the deficit. Sen. Robert Byrd (D, W. Va.), the new Senate majority leader, said, **Jan. 4,** that the voters wanted checks and balances between the branches of government, and would "get them" from the Democratic-controlled Congress. Congress formally convened, **Jan. 6.** Two contests for important positions developed. On **Jan. 6,** Republicans on the Senate Foreign Relations Committee voted 7-0 to keep Sen. Richard Lugar (Ind.) as the ranking minority member; Lugar had been committee chairman when the Republicans had controlled the Senate. House Democrats voted 130-124, **Jan. 7,** to unseat Rep. Les Aspin (Wis.) as chairman of the Armed Services Committee. Both of these votes were reversed. Sen. Jesse Helms (R, N.C.) challenged Lugar's designation, and on **Jan. 20,** the full Republican caucus, voting by secret ballot, picked Helms over Lugar, 24-17, to be ranking Republican on the Foreign Relations Committee. Helms's victory supported the seniority system; he had more seniority in the Senate than Lugar. Helms's strong anticommunist views may also have been a factor. Seniority also figured in Aspin's case. He had been chosen to head the Armed Services Committee in 1985 over more senior members who were regarded as less able than he. But lingering resentment over his challenge to seniority, plus disapproval among some Democratic liberals of his support for some administration policies, had resulted in the **Jan. 7** vote against Aspin. On **Jan. 22,** however, no other single candidate could marshal enough votes against Aspin, who was restored to the chairmanship; he prevailed on the third ballot, 133-116, against his last remaining challenger, Rep. Marvin Leath (Tex.).

Reagan Has Prostate Surgery — Pres. Ronald Reagan entered Bethesda (Md.) Navy Medical Center, **Jan. 4,** for long-scheduled surgery and tests. An examination revealed no recurrence of intestinal cancer (he had been operated on in 1985), but 4 small polyps were removed. On **Jan. 5,** the president underwent "routine" surgery for an enlarged prostate gland. The doctors found no evidence that his cancer had recurred or spread. Reagan, saying "I feel great," returned to the White House, **Jan. 8,** for a recovery period that was expected to last 6 weeks.

Reagan Submits Trillion-Dollar Budget — Pres. Ronald Reagan produced the nation's first trillion-dollar budget in January. His federal budget for fiscal 1988, submitted to Congress, **Jan. 5,** called for outlays of $1,024.3 billion and revenues of $916.6 billion, for a projected deficit of $107.8 billion. Spending for 1987 was projected at slightly above one trillion dollars, but the budget Reagan actually submitted for 1987 had been just below that figure. The deficit projected for 1988 met the requirements of the Gramm-Rudman balanced budget act, which had mandated a deficit for 1988 of no more than $108 billion. Although Reagan claimed that the budget contained no new taxes, it included various fees and levies for the use of government properties and services. Reagan proposed to eliminate or scale back a number of domestic programs. His request for a 3 percent real growth in defense spending was the smallest of his presidency. The Treasury Department said, **Jan. 13,** that over the next 5 years the new federal tax code would bring in $15.7 billion less than the code it replaced. The Congressional Budget Office estimated, **Jan. 20,** that Reagan's proposed budget would create a deficit $27 billion to $32 billion greater than the government had claimed. The Treasury reported, **Jan. 27,** that the deficit for the first quarter of fiscal 1987 (October through December 1986) was $64.34 billion, down 14 percent from a year earlier.

Unemployment at 6-Year Low — The nation's jobless rate was reported in January to be at its lowest point since 1980. The *Wall Street Journal* reported, **Jan. 8,** that a record total of 11.4 million cars were sold in the United States in 1986. U.S.-produced cars accounted for 71.8 percent of the total, down from 74.4 percent in 1985, establishing that imports remained a growing threat to American industry. General Motors made 55.2 percent of the domestic sales, Ford 25.2 percent, and Chrysler 14.3 percent. Toyota led foreign-car manufacturers with 633,806 sales. The Labor Department, **Jan. 9,** reported that the unemployment rate for December was 6.6 percent, down 0.2 percent from November and at the lowest level since March 1980. The Labor Department said, **Jan. 9,** that for all of 1986 the prices paid by producers for finished goods had declined 2.5 percent, the sharpest fall since 1949 and the first since 1963. In international currency markets, the dollar continued to decline against other major currencies; on **Jan. 14,** it was valued at 152.77 Japanese yen, a post-World War II low for the dollar. The Federal Reserve Board said, **Jan. 16,** that in 1986 the output of the nation's factories, mines, and utilities had risen 0.9 percent. The Labor Department said, **Jan. 21,** that consumer prices had advanced just 1.1 percent in all of 1986, the lowest annual rise since the 0.7 percent of 1961. Energy costs had brought the rate down, falling 19.7 percent in 1986; gasoline prices had dropped 30.7 percent. The Commerce Department reported, **Jan. 22,** that the gross national product had risen at an annual rate of 1.7 percent during the last quarter of 1986, with the result that the rate of increase for the entire year stood at only 2.5 percent, the smallest advance in 4 years. The department said, **Jan. 23,** that personal income, adjusted for inflation, had risen 3 percent in 1986. The Labor Department said, **Jan. 27,** that wage and salary increases had advanced 3.5 percent in 1986, a decline from the 4.4 percent increase for 1985. Although the U.S. deficit on merchandise trade had been a comparatively modest $10.6 billion in December, the Commerce Department said, **Jan. 30,** that the total deficit for the year stood at nearly $170 billion, easily a record.

Dow Jones Stock Average Tops 2000 — The U.S. stock market continued to rise at a phenomenal pace in Janaury, with records broken in rapid succession. In the first week of the year the Dow Jones industrial average climbed more than 100 points and on **Jan. 8,** closed at 2002.25, its first finish above 2000. The average had closed above 1000 for the first time in 1972. A record 253.1 million shares changed hands on the New York Stock Exchange, **Jan. 15;** the DJIA closed, **Jan. 20,** at 2104.47, having advanced for 13 consecutive trading days, another record. After slipping for one day, the average soared 51.60 points, **Jan. 22,** a one-day record. On **Jan. 23,** on record volume of 302.4 million shares, the market gyrated wildly, rising 64 more points by mid-day before plunging 114 points in barely an hour. The market finally closed down 44.15 that day, but quickly resumed its advance, posting another new high of 2163.39 on **Jan. 28.** The cumulative advance for the month of more than 250 points was unprecedented.

10,000 March in Georgia Town — In a scene reminiscent of the demonstrations of the 1960s, civil rights supporters took to the streets of a Georgia town in January. The target of the protest march was Cumming, in Forsyth County. The county had been all-white since 1912. Cumming's population was about 2,000, the county's 38,000. A small march by blacks and whites, **Jan. 17**—to show that "it would be OK for black people to come visit"—was disrupted by members of the Ku Klux Klan and their supporters. On **Jan. 24,** some 10,000 persons came to Cumming, about 25 miles northeast of Atlanta. Mrs. Coretta Scott King, Mayor Andrew Young of Atlanta, the Rev. Jesse Jackson, and Sen. Sam Nunn (D, Ga.) were among the leaders. Again, the marchers encountered protestors, but they were protected by 1,700 Georgia National Guardsmen and 500 Georgia state troopers.

Speakes Leaves White House Post — Larry Speakes, principal spokesman for Pres. Ronald Reagan since Press Secretary James Brady was seriously wounded in 1981 during the attempt on the president's life, left the White House in January to take a position with Merrill Lynch, the brokerage firm. Marlin Fitzwater succeeded Speakes, **Jan. 31.** Two other presidential aides, Political Director Mitchell Daniels and Communications Director Patrick Buchanan, announced their resignations within a few days, both effective March 1. Buchanan had sought to project a militant conservative point of view from the president.

International

Chinese Community Party Leader Quits — In the culmination of an apparent power struggle, Hu Yaobang resigned as general secretary of the Chinese Communist Party's Central Committee. Continuing public display of political opposition by students was considered to be one factor reflecting the tense situation in China. Students rallied in Beijing, **Jan. 1,** endorsing Chinese supreme leader Deng Xiaoping and declaring their support for democracy and for his modernization program. Deng, however, issued a directive, **Jan. 1,** ordering the suppression of any further protests. Beijing University students, **Jan. 5,** burned copies of the *People's Daily.* An editorial in the *People's Daily,* **Jan. 6,** blamed unnamed party officials for failing to halt the spread of Western ideas—asserting that some officials had "turned a blind eye" to attempts by some to introduce capitalism. In a communiqué issued, **Jan. 16,** after a meeting of the party's ruling politburo, it was announced that Hu, 71, had stepped down and had been succeeded as acting secretary by Premier Zhao Ziyang. The communiqué said Hu had been accused of "mistakes on major issues of political principle." Hu, once considered the likely successor to Deng, delivered a self-criticism at the meeting of the Politburo. He had supported political and economic reforms advocated by Deng. Perhaps paradoxically, the **Jan. 16** communiqué endorsed Deng's reforms and approaches to the West.

Afghan Leader Declares Cease-Fire — Najibullah, leader of the Soviet-supported regime in Afghanistan, announced, **Jan. 1,** that government forces would observe a cease-fire against Muslim rebels, effective **Jan. 15.** The Soviet news agency Tass reported that the truce was part of a national reconciliation program and that the Afghan government would be willing to form a coalition including opposition figures. The organization of 7 rebel groups, based in Pakistan, rejected the offer. The rebels proposed, **Jan. 6,** direct talks with the Soviet Union aimed at total withdrawal of Soviet forces from Afghanistan. On **Jan. 15,** as the truce went into effect, Najibullah declared an amnesty for army deserters and a release of many prisoners.

Libyans Pushed Back in Chad — The conflict in Chad took a new turn, **Jan. 2,** when the forces of Chad's Pres. Hissen Habré attacked and captured the oasis town of Fada. During the advance, the Chadians reportedly killed several hundred Libyan soldiers. The thrust carried the Chadians north of the 16th parallel, which had separated Chad into a northern sector controlled by Libya and a southern sector controlled by the government of Chad, which was supported by France. Libyan jets, **Jan. 4,** bombed 4 towns south of the 16th parallel. On **Jan. 7,** French fighter-bombers struck Libyan radar installations in northern Chad. In turn, Libyan planes bombed a government post.

"Glasnost" Is Key to New Soviet Era — By January, strong signals pointed to a new era in the Soviet Union under the leadership of General Secretary Mikhail Gorbachev. Since coming to power in 1985, he had concentrated on rejuvenating the stagnant and inefficient Soviet economy, and he had clearly embraced a strategy summed up by the word "glasnost"—meaning openness. Newspapers were now publishing unfavorable economic news, such as the failure to meet agricultural-production goals. Data showing an infant-mortality rate twice that in the United States were made known. News relating to earthquakes, airplane crashes, shipwrecks, and hijacking was also being reported. In the new climate, the government encouraged frank discussions of alcoholism, drug abuse, and prostitution, the kinds of activities once described as endemic to the West. Indeed, Pravda reported, **Jan. 6,** that there were 46,000 registered drug addicts in the Soviet Union and that 4,000 pushers had been arrested. Gorbachev's strategy took other forms. Prominent officials were ousted from their jobs on charges ranging from alcoholism, corruption, negligence, and falsifying records. In Uzbekistan, some 2,600 officials were fired or otherwise punished. Gorbachev's shakeup of the leadership in Kazakhstan in December sparked street riots that were reported in the press. In an astonishing development, Viktor Chebrikov, head of state security, admitted, **Jan. 8,** that a number of KGB officials had been involved in the arrest of a Soviet journalist on a false charge. The release from exile in December of the Soviet dissident physicist Andrei Sakharov and his wife was seen as part of a relaxation of internal controls. Some shackles on the arts were coming off. A private art market flourished in Moscow. Rock music was encouraged. Books, films, and plays dealt with themes once frowned on. One film, *Repentence,* stunned audiences with its indictment of crimes during the Stalin era. It remained to be seen whether the new openness would undermine the cardinal Soviet principles of collectivization and rigid central planning or threaten the authority of the Communist Party. But Gorbachev pressed on. Addressing the Communist Party Central Committee, **Jan. 27,** he called for major political reforms and criticized economic failures during the rule (1964-1982) of Leonid Brezhnev. The Committee, **Jan. 28,** gave a general but not altogether specific endorsement to Gorbachev's proposals. These had included allowing more than one candidate to seek a party office, changing the way in which members of the ruling Politburo and Secretariat were chosen, bringing more women and young people into the party, and permitting citizens to take grievances against party officials to the courts. Dinmukhamed Kunayev, ousted leader of the Kazakhstan party, announced his retirement—probably forced—from the Politburo, **Jan. 28.**

Shultz Meets South African Rebel Leader — U.S. Secretary of State George Shultz met for the first time with a leader of the African National Congress, the principal group seeking to overthrow the white regime in South Africa. Earlier, on **Jan. 8,** the State Department had asserted that the ANC was "deeply beholden" to the South African Communist Party and to the Soviet Union for military weapons and training. After meeting with Shultz, **Jan. 28,** ANC leader Oliver Tambo said they had agreed on the need to abolish the apartheid system and on ways to accomplish that. The State Department said Shultz had voiced concern about Soviet influence on ANC and on ANC's use of violent means. During his visit to the United States, Tambo admitted that the ACN was allied with the South African Communist Party and had gotten arms from the Soviet Union, but denied that the Communists controlled the ANC.

Iran Opens New Attack in Iraq — Iran, **Jan. 9,** launched a massive assault on Iraqi positions near the city of Basra. Most ground fighting occurred east of Basra in the Fish Lake region. Iranian artillery pounded the city. Iraq, in turn, bombed a number of Iranian cities, including Teheran and the holy city of Qom. Iran fired long-range missiles into Baghdad. Iranian ground forces reportedly made some headway, but at a cost, according to U.S. estimates, of up to 50,000 casualties. The same estimates put Iraqi casualties as high as 20,000. The *New York Times,* **Jan. 12,** quoted intelligence sources as asserting that the Reagan administration had intentionally provided false information to both Iran and Iraq in recent years in order to prevent either side from winning the war.

Ecuador President Seized by Soldiers — Pres. León Febres Cordero and about 30 members of his military staff were seized, **Jan. 16,** by air force troops and held for 12 hours until the president met his captors' demands and agreed to the release of an imprisoned air force general. During a military review at a base near Guyaquil, the air force troops opened fire on Febres Cordero's party, killing 2 bodyguards and wounding 7 other persons. The president and the others, including the defense minister and the air force chief of staff, were seized. The captors were all enlisted men except for a major and a captain. The president eventually agreed to free Gen. Frank Vargas Pazzos, who had been jailed in Quito for an attempted rebellion in 1986. Febres Cordero was freed after Vargas came to the base. The president later said he had been beaten by his captors. He promised not to punish them, but the government said, **Jan. 21,** it would investigate the incident.

More Men Kidnapped in Lebanon — Terry Waite, representative of the Archbishop of Canterbury, who had been seeking the release of Western hostages, was the most prominent person to disappear. Waite was last seen in Beirut, **Jan. 20.** Gunmen abducted 3 American teachers and an Indian professor from the campus of Beirut University College, **Jan. 24.** Three more men, one from Saudi Arabia, were seized in Beirut, **Jan. 26.** The U.S. State Department, **Jan. 28,** barred U.S. citizens from traveling to Lebanon and gave the approximately 1,500 Americans in Lebanon 30 days to leave. On **Jan. 29,** the previously unknown group claiming to have seized the 4 teachers threatened to kill them if the United States attacked Lebanon.

Marcos Coup Foiled in Philippines — An attempt by the deposed and exiled Ferdinand Marcos to regain power in the Philippines was thwarted in January. In another incident, troops fired on leftist demonstrators in Manila, **Jan. 22,** killing 18 and wounding 96, the first such assault on civilians during the presidency of Corazon Aquino. Since his ouster as president in February 1986, Marcos and his wife Imelda had lived in Hawaii. Speculation had grown that Marcos would seek to overthrow the government. On **Jan. 24,** Mrs. Marcos went shopping and spent $2,000 on military gear, including combat boots. On **Jan. 27,** some 500 rebel soldiers attacked at least 6 sites in and near Manila and gained control of a broadcasting complex. They were unable to take over any military installations. The U.S. State Department determined, **Jan. 28,** that a jetliner that had arrived in Honolulu had been chartered by Marcos and was to fly him back to the Philippines. Marcos told reporters, **Jan. 29,** that the State Department had warned him he would be prevented from going to the Philippines. The rebels subsequently gave up their insurrection. Gen. Fidel Ramos, chief of staff of the armed forces, ordered the arrest, on **Jan. 30,** of 4 officers linked to the attempted coup.

Kohl Retains Power in Germany — Chancellor Helmet Kohl kept his job as a result of the **Jan. 25** general election in West Germany, but his Christian Democratic Union and its conservative Bavarian sister party lost ground. The 2 parties polled 44.3 percent of the vote, the lowest level of the postwar era, but retained a reduced majority in the Bundestag. Kohl had campaigned on the basis of respectable if not spectacular economic growth and declining inflation; however, unemployment stood at 8.7 percent on election day.

General

Maryland Rail Crash Kills 16 — An Amtrak passenger train carrying about 600 persons collided with 3 linked Conrail locomotives near Chase, Md., **Jan. 4,** killing 16 persons and injuring about 175. The northbound passenger train struck the Conrail engines from behind. An ensuing investigation found that both trains had been speeding, that the Conrail engineer had passed a junction stop signal and gone through a closed switch and then onto the same tracks as the passenger train, and that traces of marijuana were in the systems of the Conrail engineer and brakeman. On **May 4,** the Conrail engineer, Ricky Gates, was indicted on 16 counts of manslaughter.

3 Hotel Workers Charged in Fire — Three employees of the Dupont Plaza Hotel in San Juan were charged in connection with the fire that swept the hotel on New Year's Eve and killed 96 persons. Investigators focused on a possible link between the fire and negotiations between the management and the International Brotherhood of Teamsters, which represented more than half the employees. The talks had been acrimonious, and three small fires had occurred in the 2 weeks before the fatal fire. Anonymous warnings and threats had been reported. The labor dispute involved management's desire to replace 60 union workers with nonunion workers. Just before the fatal fire, the Teamsters members had met in the hotel ballroom and voted unanimously to reject a contract offer from management. On **Jan. 13,** Héctor Escudero Aponte, a maintenance worker, was arraigned on 96 counts of murder. The Federal Bureau of Investigation said he had confessed to starting the fire, which he had intended only as a small fire. Two more men were charged in the case, **Jan. 14,** and **Jan. 29.** On **Apr. 24,** Escudero and the two other men pleaded guilty to setting the fire. Escudero also pleaded guilty to the murder of a U.S. Secret Service agent who had been at the hotel investigating a counterfeiting case. On **June 22,** the 3 defendants were sentenced to terms ranging from 75 to 99 years in prison.

Condom Ads OK'd to Fight AIDS — Ads for condoms were becoming prominent in the U.S. media in January. The acceptance of the ads reflected growing concern about the need for Americans to practice "safe sex" to prevent the spread of acquired immune deficiency syndrome (AIDS). The fatal condition had heretofore affected mostly male homosexuals and intravenous drug users in the United States, but there was evidence it was spreading among heterosexuals. Condom ads were already appearing widely in some European nations. KRON in San Francisco became, **Jan. 16,** the first major-market television station in the United States to accept commercials for condoms. By month's end, stations in 2 other cities had followed suit, as had *Newsweek.* The *New York Times* said, **Jan. 23,** that it would run a condom ad March 1. American public opinion appeared to be sharply divided on the advertising of condoms, with one point of view being that sharply reduced sexual activity was the moral and ultimately safer approach. AIDS, by now, was claiming a growing toll of prominent persons, including the pianist and entertainer Liberace, who died, **Feb. 4.** Surgeon Gen. C. Everett Koop, **Feb. 10,** endorsed the advertising of condoms on television.

Disasters — A Brazilian jetliner crashed 12 miles east of Abidjan, capital of the Ivory Coast, **Jan. 3,** killing 50 of the 51 persons aboard. . . . All 54 persons aboard an Ethiopian air force plane died, **Jan. 13,** when it crashed shortly after takeoff from Asmara, in Eritrea province. . . . At least 50 persons died, **Jan. 16,** when a boat carrying passengers to a Roman Catholic festival sank near Abugan Island in the central Philippines.

FEBRUARY

National

Consumer Price Index Jumps — A sharp increase in consumer prices was the most riveting economic news in February. The Commerce Department reported, **Feb. 3,** that the index of leading economic indicators had risen 2.1 percent in December. The Labor Department announced, **Feb. 6,** that the unemployment rate held steady at 6.6 percent in January, continuing at a 6-year low. The department said, **Feb. 13,** that the prices charged by producers for finished goods rose 0.6 percent in January. The Federal Reserve Board announced, **Feb. 13,** that industrial production rose 0.4 percent in January. The stock market boom continued, with the Dow Jones industrial average rising a record 54.14 points, **Feb. 18,** and then hitting another all-time high, 2244.09, on **Feb. 19.** Two statistics released, **Feb. 27,** could cause concern on Wall Street. Inflation had been held in firm check for several years, but the Labor Department said that consumer prices had risen 0.7 percent in January. The Commerce Department announced more bad news on merchandise trade, a deficit of $14.78 billion in January.

Clean Water Bill Passed Over Veto — A $20 billion bill aimed at cleaning up the nation's water supply became law over Pres. Ronald Reagan's veto. Most of the money would be spent for sewer construction. Polluted estuaries and runoff from polluted rainwater would be targeted, as would water poisoned by toxic dumps. Reagan had killed the bill by pocket veto in November, and had vetoed an identical bill, **Jan. 30,** calling it a "budget-buster." Congress easily overrode the veto, the House by 401-26 on **Feb. 3,** and the Senate by 86-14 on **Feb. 4.**

Reagan OKs "Catastrophic" Coverage — Pres. Ronald Reagan, **Feb. 12,** said he would submit legislation to expand the Medicare system to help cover costs of catastrophic illness. Medicare was the federal insurance program for persons 65 or older. Under the new plan, monthly premiums would be increased, the beneficiaries would receive an unlimited number of days of hospital care after paying an initial deductible, and out-of-pocket expenses would not exceed $2,000 a year. Under present law, only 60 days of hospital care were covered after an initial deductible, and out-of-pocket expenses were unlimited. Long-term nursing-home care would not be covered.

Cuomo Won't Seek Presidency — In a surprise announcement, Gov. Mario Cuomo of New York said that he would not seek the Democratic presidential nomination in 1988. Most polls showed that Cuomo, who had been reelected in 1986 in a landslide, was running second to former Sen. Gary Hart (Col.) among Democratic voters as their choice to head the ticket. Cuomo had frequently made speeches across the country, and the general expectation was that he would run. But on **Feb. 19,** at the end of a radio call-in show, Cuomo said he would not be a candidate, and that the decision was the best for his state and for his family. On **Feb. 21,** Sen. Sam Nunn (Ga.), regarded as the leading authority in his party on national defense, said that he would not seek the Democratic nomination for the time being, but would keep his options "completely open." Rep. Richard Gephardt (Mo.) became the first official Democratic entry in the presidential sweepstakes, **Feb. 23,** when he opened his campaign in St. Louis. Gephardt had made his reputation in the House as a defender of U.S. industry against the threat of foreign imports, and he restated his concerns in his announcement.

International

Ethiopians OK Communist Constitution — Ethiopian voters, **Feb. 1,** gave their overwhelming approval to a new constitution that established a civilian Communist government. The country's leader, Lt. Col. Mengistu Haile Mariam, said, **Feb. 22,** that 96 percent of the eligible voters had turned out, and that 81 percent of those voting had favored the constitution. The country would now be called the People's Republic of Ethiopia. The Worker's Party, of which there were about 50,000 members, would be the "vanguard" in the one-party state. Later in 1987, party-approved candidates would seek election to the parliament, which in turn would choose a president.

Moslem Factions Clash in Beirut — Moslems fought each other in Beirut as the violence there took a new turn. Three Americans and an Indian kidnapped in January became the center of international tension. Israeli Prime Minister Yitzhak Shamir, **Feb. 2,** rejected a demand by their captors, the Islamic Jihad for the Liberation of Palestine, that Israel free 400 Arab prisoners in exchange for the 4. Another group, the Revolutionary Justice Organization, threatened to kill its captives, who included 2 Americans. The Islamic Jihad let its **Feb. 9** deadline pass without killing its hostages. Moslem militias, who had been allied against the Christians, fought each other, beginning **Feb. 15**, for control of West Beirut, the Moslem sector of the city. Syria, which supported the feuding Shiite Amal militiamen as well as the Druse-led faction, stepped in and imposed a truce, **Feb. 19**. Lebanese Premier Rashid Karami and Shiite and Druse leaders asked Syria, **Feb. 20**, to intervene militarily. Pres. Amin Gemayel of Lebanon warned, **Feb. 21**, against Syrian intervention, but the Syrian forces entered West Beirut, **Feb. 22**. By then, some 300 persons had been killed and 1,300 wounded. In taking control of neighborhood militia offices, **Feb. 24**, the Syrians encountered resistance, and, in one battle, they killed 23 Shiites.

Filipinos Approve New Constitution — Philippine voters handed Pres. Corazon Aquino a big victory, approving a draft constitution on which she had staked her leadership. The public campaign had unfolded against the threat of military insurrection. Aquino's supporters repeatedly proclaimed, "Vote yes for democracy, yes for stability, yes for Cory." A leading opponent of the constitution, former Defense Minister Juan Ponce Enrile, had predicted that rejection of the constitution would bring about her resignation. The constitution, prepared by an Aquino-appointed commission, provided for a bicameral national legislature, a president with defined limits on his or her power, and a judiciary to be appointed free from political influence. In the voting, **Feb. 2**, 76 percent of the ballots cast favored the constitution. The result provided firm political footing for Aquino, who had abrogated the previous constitution after succeeding the deposed Ferdinand Marcos in 1986. Negotiators for communist insurgents said, **Feb. 7**, that they would no longer participate in peace talks or extend a 60-day cease-fire after its expiration, **Feb. 8**.

Calero Quits Contra Unity Group — The United Nicaraguan Opposition, the civilian umbrella organization nominally in control of the forces opposed to the Nicaraguan government, was shaken by new quarrels. The UNO was created with U.S. support as a veneer of civilian control and to provide a means of channeling U.S. aid to the contras. Its directorate consisted of Arturo José Cruz, Alfonso Robelo Callejas, and Adolfo Calero Portocarrero. Calero also headed the Nicaraguan Democratic Force (FDN), the largest contra army, which had resisted reforms agreed to by the 3 directors that would have increased civilian control over the FDN. This prompted Cruz to confirm, **Feb. 6**, that he was resigning as a director of UNO. Aside from being lukewarm on civilian control, Calero favored the overthrow of the Nicaraguan government, while Cruz and Robelo were willing to negotiate a settlement with the Sandinista regime. Calero announced, **Feb. 16**, that he, too, would resign from the UNO. Cruz said, **Feb. 17**, that he would go through with his resignation unless the FDN agreed to take orders from the directors, and, on that day, Col. Enrique Bermudez, the FDN military commander, said he would do so. Cruz, **Feb. 19**, then dropped his threat to resign.

140 Soviet Dissidents Freed — In another apparent move to improve its human-rights image, the Soviet Union, **Feb. 10**, pardoned and freed 140 dissidents who had been held in prisons and labor camps. They had been convicted of "anti-Soviet agitation and propaganda." The announcement by the foreign ministry appeared to cover the largest number of dissidents freed at one time in more than 3 decades. White House spokesman Marlin Fitzwater said, **Feb. 10**, the United States welcomed the announcement and hoped that more prisoners would be released soon.

Brazil Stops Paying on Debt —Brazil, the developing world's largest debtor nation, stunned the financial world, **Feb. 20**, when Pres. José Sarney announced that payment of interest on debts to foreign commercial banks would be suspended. The action, taken unilaterally, was aimed at protecting Brazil's hard currency reserves, which had fallen from $11 billion to $4 billion in a year. In a televised address, Sarney said he hoped that forthcoming negotiations with creditors would yield a "definitive and lasting solution" to Brazil's debt problems. Brazil's action involved some $67 billion. U.S. Secretary of the Treasury James Baker said that Brazil's action was no cause for panic.

Soviets End A-Test Moratorium — The Soviet Union ended, **Feb. 26**, its 18-month unilateral moratorium on nuclear tests. The moratorium had been accompanied by frequent appeals that the United States follow suit, which the Reagan administration had rebuffed. Maj. Gen. Geli Batenin, speaking for the Soviet defense ministry, said that the underground test had been conducted 1,700 miles southeast of Moscow and that it had an explosive yield of under 20 kilotons. He deplored the 2 U.S. nuclear tests in 1987 and said the Soviet Union would resume its moratorium as soon as the United States announced a halt of its own tests.

Terrorist Gets Life Term in Killings — A Lebanese convicted of planning the 1982 murders in Paris of a U.S. military attaché and an Israeli diplomat and complicity in the 1984 attack on the U.S. consul general in Strasbourg was sentenced to life in prison, **Feb. 28**. The sentence against Georges Abdallah was handed down in Paris by a special panel of 7 magistrates despite a request by the prosecutor that he be given no more than 10 years in prison. It was expected that the harsh sentence would make it more difficult for the French government to negotiate with terrorists to win freedom for hostages or secure other concessions. Terrorists demanding Abdallah's release had killed 11 persons in Paris in September 1986 in a series of bombings.

Hopes Rise for Europe Missile Accord — Prospects for the removal of medium-range nuclear missiles from Europe brightened in February. Soviet leader Mikhail Gorbachev called, **Feb. 28**, for the superpowers to reach an agreement separately from any other arms-control issue. This appeared to be a reversal of his position at Reykjavik, Iceland, in October, when he told Pres. Ronald Reagan that any such agreement must be linked to a curb on development of the U.S. strategic defense initiative ("Star Wars"). The "linkage" problem aside, Reagan and Gorbachev had reportedly agreed in principle in Iceland to remove their medium-range missiles from Europe over a 5-year period. In response to Gorbachev's appeal, the White House announced it was ready to "move very rapidly to an agreement."

General

U.S. Infant Death Rate High — Figures showed that the United States had one of the highest infant mortality rates among industrialized nations. The Children's Defense Fund, a nonprofit advocacy organization, said, in a report issued **Feb. 2**, that the United States, with 10.8 deaths for every 1,000 live births, stood at the bottom of the list in 1984 with Belgium and East and West Germany. Finland, Iceland, and Japan, with 6 deaths per 1,000 live births, had the lowest death rates. Among the 50 states, South Carolina had the highest rate, South Dakota the lowest. The death rate for black babies was double the rate for whites. Marian Wright Edelman, president of the CDF, charged that cuts in federal programs had left many poor families with no access to adequate prenatal and postnatal care.

Another Wall Street Figure Pleads Guilty — The Wall Street scandal continued when an investment banker pleaded guilty to insider trading. Three prominent brokers were arrested, **Feb. 12**. Two were, or had been, affiliated with Kidder, Peabody & Co., and the 3rd was associated with Goldman, Sachs & Co.—2 of the profession's most respected firms. Martin Siegel, formerly a mergers and acquisitions specialist at Kidder, who had implicated the others, pleaded guilty, **Feb. 13**. Siegel, in turn, had been fingered by Ivan Boesky, a confessed inside trader who had paid $100 million in punishment in 1986 and who was cooperating with the ongoing investigation. Dennis Levine, whose confession to securities fraud in 1986 had helped unravel the scandal, was sentenced, **Feb. 20**, to 2 years in prison. Boyd Jeffries, another associate of Boesky, agreed, **Mar. 19**, to plead guilty to 2 securities law violations. Boesky pleaded guilty, **Apr. 23**, to one count of conspiracy to make false statements to the federal government. As part of his $100 million settlement with the SEC in 1986, Boesky had agreed to plead guilty to one felony charge at a later date.

Supernova Appears in Southern Sky — An exploding star, known as a supernova, was identified in the sky over the southern hemisphere, **Feb. 24**, by Ian Shelton, an astronomer at a University of Toronto observatory in Chile. Estimated to be 163,000 light years distant, it still became the closest supernova since 1604. Although only moderately bright to earthbound observers, it was estimated that the object had the brilliance of a billion suns, and that it was expanding at the rate of 9,300 miles per second. The star appeared in the Greater Magellanic Cloud, one of several small galaxies that are regarded as satellites of the Milky Way, in which our sun is situated. It was later determined that the supernova had a companion object, one tenth the brightness of the supernova and apparently related to it in some way.

SMU Football Season Canceled — The National Collegiate Athletic Association, **Feb. 25**, canceled Southern Methodist University's 1987 football season as partial punishment for violation of NCAA rules. The governing body of collegiate sports found that SMU officials had given illegal payments to football players at a time when the school was already on probation for other rules violations. The school had been penalized 6 other times since 1958. In the latest incident, the NCAA said 13 football players had received $61,000 from officials in the athletic department. The money apparently came from a wealthy booster. SMU was also limited to 7 games for the 1988 season, instead of the usual 11. (SMU later canceled its entire 1988 season.) Appearances on television and in post-season bowl games were barred until 1990. Gov. Bill Clements of Texas revealed, **Mar. 3**, that he and others of the school's board of governors had allowed payments to continue in 1985 even after they had been uncovered by the NCAA because "commitments had been made" to the players. Clements had been chairman of the SMU board before being elected governor in 1986.

MARCH

National

Trade Deficit Continues to Rise — The index of leading economic indicators fell 1 percent in January, the Commerce Department announced, **Mar. 3**. The Labor Department said, **Mar. 6**, that the nation's unemployment rate had held steady at 6.6 percent in February for the 3d straight month. The Commerce Department said, **Mar. 18**, that corporate profits had risen 6.1 percent in the 4th quarter of 1986. The Labor Department reported, **Mar. 13**, that prices charged by producers for finished goods had risen 0.1 percent in February. The U.S. balance of payments on current account—the broadest measure of trade with other nations—showed a deficit of $36.84 billion in the 4th quarter of 1986 and $140.57 billion for the entire year, both records. The surge on Wall Street continued, with the Dow Jones industrial average posting another all-time high of 2372.59 on **Mar. 26**. Consumer prices rose 0.4 percent in February, the Labor Department said, **Mar. 27**. The Commerce Department said, **Mar. 31**, that the index of leading economic indicators had risen 0.7 percent in February. Two leading banks, Citibank and Chase Manhattan, surprised financial experts, **Mar. 31**, by raising their prime lending rate, their base rate for corporate loans, from 7.5 percent to 7.75 percent—the first increases by major banks since 1984.

Babbitt, Dukakis, Haig in '88 Race — Three more aspirants entered the contest for the presidency in March. Former Gov. Bruce Babbitt of Arizona announced his candidacy for the Democratic nomination, **Mar. 10**. Little known nationally, Babbitt took some bold positions at odds with the Democratic mainstream. He said federal benefits, including Social Security, should be taxable for a couple earning more than $32,000 a year, with the revenues to fund catastrophic illness coverage for the elderly. He said he opposed unilateral retaliation for trade imbalances. Gov. Michael Dukakis of Massachusetts said, **Mar. 17**, he would enter the Democratic race. Regarded as center-to-liberal in political philosophy, Dukakis had presided over a strong economic recovery in Massachusetts, which had one of the lowest unemployment rates in the nation. The governor stressed that voters should consider a candidate's competence and personal character in choosing a president. Saying he was "throwing my helmet into the ring," Alexander Haig announced, **Mar. 24**, that he was seeking the Republican nomination. Haig had capped his military career as commander of the North Atlantic Treaty Organization, and he had then served as White House chief of staff during the last embattled days of the Nixon presidency and as secretary of state under Ronald Reagan in 1981-82. Haig urged more presidential vetoes to curb federal spending and continued support for the contras fighting the Nicaraguan regime. He said he would not renounce first use of nuclear weapons.

Deaver, Ex-Reagan Aide, Indicted — Michael K. Deaver, a longtime friend of Ronald and Nancy Reagan and a key White House aide during the president's first term, was indicted in March on 5 counts of perjury. The indictment was secured by an independent counsel, Whitney North Seymour, Jr. A legal challenge by Deaver to Seymour's authority was rejected, **Mar. 18**, by U.S. Chief Justice William Rehnquist. Deaver's lawyers had questioned the constitutionality of the 1978 law under which Seymour had been appointed, contending that its provision that a federal court appoint the counsel infringed on the executive's authority to conduct prosecutions. Rehnquist said the appeal was premature, and that Deaver had not been charged with any crimes. However, within hours of Rehnquist's ruling, the indictment was returned. Seymour, who had been empowered to investigate possible illegal lobbying activities by Deaver after he left the White House, said Deaver had lied to a federal grand jury and to Congress when asked about those activities.

Reagan Imposes Duties on Japanese Products — Pres. Ronald Reagan said, **Mar. 27**, that the United States would impose duties that would double the import prices of many electronic products imported from Japan. His action came in response to what the United States said was Japan's failure to abide by a 1986 agreement forbidding Japanese companies from selling semiconductor chips in the United States for less than a "fair market value" (as determined by the United States). The tariffs could affect imports of television sets, and stereo and computer equipment. The decline of the U.S. dollar against the Japanese yen—a contributor to the trade deficit—continued, with the dollar hitting a post-World War II low against the yen on **Mar. 31**.

International

Israel Acts in U.S. Spy Case —The Israeli government, under criticism from the United States for its possible involvement in the Jonathan Pollard spy case, set up an inquiry into the affair in March. A federal grand jury in Washington, D.C., **Mar. 3**, indicted an Israeli air force officer, Aviem Sella, and said he and 3 other Israelis had conspired with Pollard to get secret military data from the United States. Sella could not be arrested unless he came to the United States voluntarily. The United States, **Mar. 3**, officially protested Sella's new assignment as commander of Israel's 2d-largest air force base. Pollard, who had been convicted in 1986 of spying for Israel, was sentenced, **Mar. 4**, to life in prison. His wife was sentenced to 5 years in prison as an accessory. Israel's trade minister, Ariel Sharon, said, **Mar. 9**, that the Pollard espionage operation was necessary because the United States had not given Israel all the intelligence data that it needed. In an attempt to blunt suspicion that the spy plot had the official approval of the government, the Israeli cabinet announced the inquiry, **Mar. 11**. Sella, **Mar. 29**, resigned as commander of the air force base.

U.S. Soviet Missile Plans Submitted — The 2 superpowers formally submitted their proposals on removing medium-range nuclear weapons from Europe. The Soviet proposal, presented at the bilateral talks in Geneva, **Mar. 2**, had been unveiled publicly in February. The U.S. plan, put on the table at Geneva, **Mar. 4**, included the understanding reached at the 1986 Reykjavik summit that each side could keep 100 intermediate nuclear force warheads away from Europe. U.S. negotiators, **Mar. 12**, offered a 6-point package of verification measures related to its proposal for the removal of the missiles from Europe. The package, if approved, would include on-site inspections, the uncoding of data transmissions from missile tests to permit electronic monitoring of the tests, and an agreement on the disposition of missiles once they were removed from Europe.

Congess Debates Contra Aid Again — A sharply divided U.S. Congress again grappled with the issue of financial aid to the Nicaraguan contras in March. Following through on an earlier threat, Arturo Cruz resigned, **Mar. 9**, as a director of the United Nicaraguan Opposition, saying he did not see that the contras had the will to make reforms he wanted, including establishment of greater civilian control over the anti-government movement. The U.S. House voted 230-196, **Mar. 11,** to suspend aid to the contras until Pres. Ronald Reagan accounted for funds approved by Congress and received from other sources. A portion of millions of dollars in gifts from private citizens, profits from the sale of arms to Iran, and donations from foreign governments appeared to be unaccounted for. The vote put in some jeopardy $40 million of $100 million approved for the contras in 1986 but not yet paid out. The Senate, **Mar. 18,** voted 52-48 against a similar resolution to block the payment.

Haitians Approve New Constitution — Haitian voters, in a nearly unanimous vote, approved a new constitution. The Constituent Assembly had approved the document, **Mar. 10,** and the national vote was held on **Mar. 29.** The referendum came more than a year after the ouster of the dictator Jean-Claude Duvalier. The new constitution created a power-sharing arrangement among a president as head of state, a premier as head of government, and a legislature to which the premier would be responsible.

Libyans Suffer Costly Rout in Chad — Libya's occupation of northern Chad appeared to be nearing a bloody end in March. The recent deterioration in Libya's military position began to approach a climax, **Mar. 19** and **21,** when Chadian government forces ambushed 2 Libyan columns south of Wadi Doum, site of a Libyan air base. Some 800 Libyans were reported killed in the ambushes, and Wadi Doum itself fell to the Chadians, **Mar. 22,** as the Libyans reportedly suffered 1,269 more deaths. Soviet-built weapons were captured or destroyed. The forces of Pres. Hissen Habre were armed with French and U.S. antiaircraft and antitank missiles and received logistical aid from the French. French sources reported, **Mar. 25,** that the Libyans were withdrawing from Faya-Largeau, their last major stronghold in Chad, after destroying fuel and ammunition depots, and on **Mar. 27,** Chad said its army had taken the town without a fight.

Aquino Vows Military Action — Pres. Corazon Aquino abandoned her conciliatory approaches toward her politcal opponents. She told graduating military cadets, **Mar. 22,** that attempts to reach compromise settlements with Communist rebels and right-wing plotters had not succeeded. She asserted, "The answer to the terrorism of the left and the right is not social and economic reform but police and military action." She deplored the "bloody and insolent rejections" of her overtures by her opponents. Peace talks with the Communists had broken off in February.

Marine Embassy Guards Face Charges — A serious breach in security at the U.S. Embassy in Moscow became apparent in March. On **Jan. 10,** the Marine Corps had announced the arrest in December of an Embassy guard, Sgt. Clayton Lonetree, and on **Mar. 24,** the Corps said that another guard, Cpl. Arnold Bracy, had been arrested. By late March, Lonetree faced 24 charges, including espionage and failure to report suspected espionage. Military prosecutors said, **Mar. 27,** that the two had been enticed by Soviet women into working for the KGB and that they had provided Soviet agents with access to sensitive areas of the Embassy, including the room where secret messages were coded and decoded. Defense Secretary Caspar Weinberger said, **Mar. 28,** that the United States had suffered a "very great loss" from the incident. It was announced, **Mar. 30,** that the entire 28-Marine guard contingent would be replaced with other Marines. Formal charges were filed against Bracy, **Mar. 31.**

Salvadoran Rebels Score Bloody Victory — Leftists seeking to overthrow the government of El Salvador killed at least 69 soldiers—the official count—in a raid on a major military base. An American military adviser also died in the raid. Earlier, when a Salvadoran military helicopter crashed, **Mar. 26,** a U.S. Central Intelligence Agency officer was killed. In the **Mar. 31** raid on the military headquarters at El Paraiso, 36 miles north of the capital, the soldiers were killed in a surprise night strike that included mortar and rocket fire. An American adviser, Staff Sgt. Gregory Fronius, was among the victims. All the Salvadorans killed were enlisted men; officers reportedly fled to an underground bunker. Some 60 defenders were reported to be wounded, but unofficial accounts put the number of dead and wounded even higher. Only 8 guerrillas were reported killed in the assault.

Thatcher Visits Soviet Union — British Prime Minister Margaret Thatcher traveled to the Soviet Union and conferred with Soviet leader Mikhail Gorbachev for 11 hours. She was the first British prime minister to visit the Soviet Union in 12 years. Thatcher, who arrived, **Mar. 28,** was guest of honor at a banquet, **Mar. 30,** and took the opportunity to call on the Soviets to withdraw from Afghanistan and to make more progress on human rights. She made public a plan to break the U.S.-USSR deadlock over the U.S. Strategic Defense Initiative that, in effect, supported Pres. Ronald Reagan's broad interpretation of the 1972 antiballistic missile treaty, which, in turn, would facilitate SDI research. Gorbachev rejected Thatcher's ABM proposal as "unrealistic" and suggested that the debate over human rights be broadened to include millions of unemployed and homeless people in the West. After visiting the republic of Georgia, Thatcher returned to London, **Apr. 1.**

1,500 Sudanese Civilians Massacred — The civil strife in Sudan reached a peak of tragedy on **March 26** and **27,** when about 1,500 civilians of the Dinka tribe were massacred, apparently by local police and militiamen. The Dinkas were the backbone of the rebel movement, which consisted of animists and Christian blacks living in the southern part of Sudan. The government was controlled by Moslems. The massacre of the Dinkas appeared to be in retaliation for a rebel raid in which 70 militiamen were killed. The victims, among some 6,000 Dinkas who had fled to the vicinity of the town of El Daein in Darfur province to escape the fighting elsewhere, were attacked with machine guns and herded into a train and police station and burned alive.

General

Reputed Crime Leader Acquitted — Federal prosecutors fighting organized crime suffered a setback when an alleged kingpin in the Mafia was found not guilty of criminal charges. Earlier, on **Mar. 2,** the government had won another victory when 17 men were convicted in New York City in the 17-month "Pizza Connection" trial. They were found to be part of a ring that had distributed heroin and cocaine through a network of pizza parlors in the Midwest and Northeast. Gaetano Badalamenti, former head of the Sicilian Mafia, was among those convicted. But on **Mar. 13,** a jury in New York City found reputed Mafia boss John Gotti and 6 of his alleged lieutenants not guilty of charges that included murder, kidnapping, and loansharking. The government contended that the men had operated a criminal enterprise over an 18-year period.

Chrysler to Buy American Motors — The Chrysler Corp. agreed, **Mar. 9,** to buy American Motors Corp., by far the smallest of the 4 U.S. auto manufacturers. Chrysler would buy 46% of AMC from Renault, the French company, and get the rest directly from AMC. The cost of the deal was estimated at $1.5 billion. Approval would be required by the AMC and Renault boards, AMC shareholders, and the U.S., Canadian, and French governments. AMC had made its mark in the 1950s and 1960s with its compact Rambler cars that appealed to economy-minded drivers. But foreign imports had taken much of the compact market, and in 1986 AMC had less than 1 percent of the overall U.S. market. AMC's 4-wheel drive jeep was its most popular vehicle.

Vatican Opposes Birth Technologies — The Vatican, **Mar. 10,** took a strong stand against artificial fertilization and generation of human life outside the body. In announcing the Roman Catholic Church's position on the new birth technologies, the Congregation for the Doctrine of the Faith said it could approve only those medical or scientific techniques that would assist married couples who engaged in "normal" intercourse. The document asked governments to forbid surrogate motherhood and experiments on living embryos, and asserted that "The one conceived must be the fruit of his parents' love." The document opposed test-tube fertilization as well as artificial insemination of an unmarried woman—or of a widow even if her husband had donated the sperm.

Surrogate Mother Denied Custody — A surrogate-mother contract was tested in court for the first time in 1987, and the custody decision handed down favored the biological father and his wife over the surrogate. In 1985, Mary Beth Whitehead of Brick, N.J., had signed a contract with William Stern to bear his child for a payment of $10,000. Stern's wife, Elizabeth, had been fearful of becoming pregnant after contracting a mild case of multiple sclerosis. Nationwide, some 500 babies had been born under similar agreements. Shortly after giving birth to a girl in March 1986, Whitehead declined the $10,000 and took the infant to Florida, where it was subsequently seized at the home of Whitehead's mother. The Sterns were then awarded temporary custody of "Baby M," as she was called. A subsequent custody trial was held in Bergen County (N.J.) Superior Court with Judge Harvey Sorkow presiding. The trial ended **Mar. 12.** In his ruling, announced **Mar. 31,** Sorkow held that the contract was "constitutionally protected" and awarded custody to William Stern. The judge also said the Sterns were better able to care for the child. He signed documents allowing Stern's wife to adopt the baby, which they called Melissa. He terminated all parental rights for Whitehead. On **Apr. 10,** the New Jersey Supreme Court granted Whitehead the right to visit the child for 2 hours a week pending outcome of her appeal in the case.

TV Evangelist Quits in Sex Scandal — Jim Bakker, an Assemblies of God minister who was one of the best-known television evangelists in the United States, resigned his ministry after admitting having sex with a young admirer in 1980. Bakker had run the PTL Club in Fort Mill, S.C.—the initials stood for Praise the Lord and People that Love—and he and his wife, Tammy Faye, were hosts of a daily television program carried by hundreds of stations through the PTL network. The PTL also operated a Christian theme park in South Carolina. Bakker revealed to the Charlotte (N.C.) *Observer,* **Mar. 19,** that "treacherous former friends" had betrayed him into a sexual encounter in a Clearwater (Fla.) hotel with Jessica Hahn, then 21. Bakker said he then "succumbed" to paying blackmail to Hahn to protect his family and ministry. Bakker called in Jerry Falwell, another leading Christian preacher on TV, to take over his ministry. Still another TV evangelist, Oral Roberts, made news, **Mar. 22,** by entering the prayer tower at Oral Roberts University and saying he would remain there until he raised $8 million for medical scholarships. He had said God would "call him home" if the money wasn't collected. The Bakker plot thickened when his lawyer, Roy Grutman, said, **Mar. 24,** that yet another TV preacher, Jimmy Swaggart, had plotted a hostile takeover of PTL. Swaggart denied it. Another evangelist, Marvin Gorman, sued Swaggart for $90 million, saying Swaggart had spread sexual rumors about him. Hahn said, **Mar. 24,** that she had received only "a few dollars" of the money allegedly extorted from Bakker. Roberts said, **Apr. 1,** that the $8 million had been raised and that God had spared him.

Drug to Fight AIDS Approved — The U.S. government, **Mar. 20,** approved for the first time the use of a drug in the fight against acquired immune deficiency syndrome (AIDS). Both the government and the Burroughs Wellcome Company, manufacturer of the drug, emphasized that it was not a cure for the deadly condition. However, the drug, azidothymidine, or AZT, had proved successful in clinical tests in inhibiting the ability of the AIDS virus to duplicate inside body cells. Drawbacks to the drug, which would be marketed under the brand name Retrovir, included its high cost and its potentially severe side effects. Ending a long international dispute, Pres. Ronald Reagan and French Premier Jacques Chirac announced at the White House, **Mar. 31,** that researchers from the United States and France would share credit for discovery of the AIDS virus. Patent rights to a blood test that emerged from the discovery would also be shared.

Van Gogh Canvas Sets Auction Record — "Sunflowers," a painting by Vincent Van Gogh, which he created in 1889 not long before committing suicide, was auctioned, **Mar. 30,** for the equivalent of $39.9 million, easily the highest amount ever paid for a work of art at auction. The painting, a part of the Beatty collection, had been exhibited for some time in Great Britain's National Gallery. It was auctioned in just 4 minutes and 20 seconds at Christie's in London, with the prize going to an anonymous telephone bidder.

Disasters — Earthquakes that hit the northeastern jungle of Ecuador, **Mar. 5** and **6,** killed 300 persons and left 4,000 missing and perhaps 20,000 homeless. . . . A British ferry, the *Herald of Free Enterprise,* traveling from Zeebrugge, Belgium, to Dover, capsized in the English Channel, **Mar. 6,** and the death toll was put at 188; about 350 persons were rescued.

APRIL

National

Reagan Overridden on Highway Veto — An $87.5 billion highway and mass transit bill became law when the U.S. Senate overrode a veto by Pres. Ronald Reagan. The bill, originally passed by both houses in March, was controversial. Providing millions of dollars to every state for highway repair, it was far more expensive than what Reagan would accept. Furthermore, it contained a provision that would allow states to raise the speed limit on rural interstate highways from 55 miles per hour to 65 mph. Many states, especially those in the West where long isolated stretches of highway are common, had long argued for the increase. But opponents said that a breach in the national 55 mph limit would result in greater consumption of gasoline and in an increase in traffic deaths. In his **Mar. 27** veto, Reagan denounced the bill's "pork barrel politics." The House, **Mar. 31,** overrode the veto by a 350-73 margin. The Senate voting was close. On **Apr. 1,** the Senate initially cast a 66-34 vote to override, one vote short of the required two-thirds margin. Parliamentary maneuvering led to a second vote, **Apr. 2.** Reagan went to Capitol Hill, met with Republican senators, and pleaded for the 13 Republicans who had voted against him the first time to switch their votes. But none did so, and the Senate overrode the veto, 67-33, when the one Democrat to support Reagan on the first vote, Terry Sanford (N.C.), switched positions.

Unemployment Trend Still Down — The U.S. unemployment rate edged downward to 6.5 percent in March, a 7-year low, the Labor Department reported, **Apr. 3.** Some economists said the decline was mostly due to the fact that discouraged job-seekers were leaving the labor force. On Wall Street, the Dow Jones industrial average registered a record one-day advance, **Apr. 3,** of 69.89 points and closed at a record high of 2390.34. The average posted another new high, **Apr. 6,** closing at 2405.54. The Labor Department said, **Apr. 10,** that prices paid by producers for finished goods rose 0.4 percent in March. The U.S. deficit on merchandise trade continued to rise, to $15.06 billion in February, the Commerce Department reported, **Apr. 14.** The department said, **Apr. 23,** that the U.S. gross national product grew at an annual rate of 4.3 percent in the first quarter. The Labor Department said, **Apr. 24,** that consumer prices had risen 0.4 percent in March. The sharp run-up on Wall Street was primarily responsible for the advance in the index of leading economic indicators of 0.4 percent in March, as reported by the Commerce Department, **Apr. 29.**

Kemp, Hart Seek Presidency — The crowded field for the 1988 presidential election grew again in April. Rep. Jack Kemp (R, N.Y.) announced his candidacy for the Republican nomination, **Apr. 6.** A former professional football player, Kemp had become a leading spokesman on the national scene for lower taxes and greater economic opportunity for all. He regarded himself as a true defender of conservative political ideology and had sometimes even criticized the Reagan White House for compromising conservative principles. He said he would make his campaign a referendum on early development of the Strategic Defense Initiative ("Star Wars"). Gary Hart, a former senator from Colorado who had made a strong bid for the Democratic nomination in 1984, announced, **Apr. 13,** that he would try again. Standing on a boulder at Red Rocks Park near Denver, he asserted that during the Reagan presidency, "We've let personal greed replace a sense of social justice and equity and the national good." Hart, who had always emphasized the importance of ideas and issues, was leading the polls among Democratic voters for the 1988 nomination.

Mayor of Chicago Reelected — Mayor Harold Washington of Chicago, a Democrat, was reelected to a second 4-year term on **Apr. 7.** He received 54 percent of the vote to 42 percent for his principal challenger, Edward Vrdolyak, a

Democrat who ran as the Solidarity Party candidate. The Republican candidate, Donald Haider, received 4 percent. Washington received 97 percent of the black vote and 15 percent of the white vote. Jane Byrne, whom Washington had defeated in the Democratic primary in February, had endorsed him. Washington supporters won a majority on the city council. During Washington's first term, Vrdolyak supporters had held a majority and had defeated the mayor on many important issues.

House OKs Trillion-Dollar Budget — The U.S. House of Representatives approved a trillion-dollar budget that would increase taxes and put a cap on defense spending. In its first vote on **Apr. 9**, the House rejected, 394-27, the budget Pres. Reagan had submitted in January. In forcing that vote, the Democratic leadership sought to embarrass the Republicans, most of whom voted against Reagan's budget. The House then approved, 230-192, a budget essentially the same as that reported by the House Budget Committee. No Republicans voted for it, and 19 Democrats voted against it. The budget bill allowed increases in a few domestic programs and froze the rest at previous levels. The increase approved for defense would be less than the rate of inflation. The bill called for $18 billion in unspecified tax increases and would result in a deficit of $132.5 billion, based on assumptions by the Congressional Budget Office.

International

Pope Visits Latin America — Political realities intruded on religious events when Pope John Paul II visited Latin America. The pope's first stop was Montevideo, Uruguay, **Mar. 31**, after which he proceeded to Santiago, Chile, **Apr. 1**, where Pres. Augusto Pinochet welcomed him. The pope met, **Apr. 3**, with 19 opposition leaders, ranging in political views from far left to far right, who pledged to use peaceful means to seek a restoration of democracy. The pope also met, **Apr. 3**, with Carmen Gloria Quintana, 19, who reportedly was doused with gasoline and set afire by Chilean security officers in 1986; a companion died in the incident. On the evening of **Apr. 3**, the pope conducted an outdoor mass for one million persons in Santiago that was marred by violence when youths opposing the government set bonfires and stoned police. The police struck back with water cannons and tear gas. The pope continued the service, but admonished the crowd, "We will not tire of repeating everywhere that violence is not Christian." Proceeding to Argentina, Pope John Paul II received a warm welcome in Buenos Aires, **Apr. 6**. Mindful of abuses committed by the Argentine military in the recent past, he told a gathering of political leaders that it was their "inescapable duty" to show the way in respecting human rights. Half a million people attended a Palm Sunday mass conducted by the pope in Buenos Aires, **Apr. 12**.

Mulroney, Reagan Hold 3d Summit — Canadian Prime Minister Brian Mulroney and Pres. Ronald Reagan held their third summit conference in Ottawa on **Apr. 5** and **6**. As in the recent past, acid rain and free trade were the principal bones of contention. Mulroney wanted a bilateral agreement to eliminate half of acid rain emissions by 1994, and he reportedly pressed the president to come up with a timetable for the reduction of U.S. air pollutants that caused acid rain to fall on both countries. Addressing Parliament, **Apr. 6**, Reagan mentioned no timetable but said he and Mulroney had agreed to consider a bilateral accord on acid rain. He also said his administration was committed to "good-faith negotiations" to achieve free trade between the countries. Political opponents in both countries dismissed Reagan's statements as only vague promises.

Reagan Fears New Embassy Bugged — In the wake of the security breach at the U.S. Embassy in Moscow, Pres. Ronald Reagan, **Apr. 7**, ordered an investigation of security at the future U.S. embassy compound now being built. Some $100 million had already been spent on the new compound, which was being constructed by Soviet workers under U.S. supervision. Following the arrest of 2 U.S. Marines on espionage charges, the concern grew that Soviet intelligence might have been able to plant bugs in the new complex. Reagan said he might even order it to be torn down. On **Apr. 8**, a third Marine was charged with failure to disclose sexual contact with at least one Soviet woman and a fourth was arrested on suspicion of espionage. A Soviet spokesman, **Apr. 8**, said the United States had invented the spy episode, and on **Apr. 9**, at a press conference in Moscow, Soviet officials displayed bugging devices they said had been planted at Soviet missions in the United States by U.S. intelligence.

Gorbachev Visit Excites Czechs — Soviet leader Mikhail Gorbachev visited Czechoslovakia and received a warm welcome from citizens who appeared to approve the economic, social, and cultural reforms that he was promoting in the USSR. However, the Czech leadership, headed by 76-year-old Pres. Gustav Husak, had reportedly been cool to the proposed reforms, and the leaders displayed stiff formality toward Gorbachev during his visit. On the evening of **Apr. 9**, their first night in Prague, Gorbachev and his wife Raisa strolled through the streets and drew cheers and applause from thousands of people in an apparently spontaneous display of affection. Addressing the Czechoslovak-Soviet Friendship Society in Prague, **Apr. 10**, Gorbachev acknowledged that some East-bloc countries were reluctant to follow the new path of reform, but he said he was not asking anyone "to copy us" and that other Socialist countries were solving their problems in their own ways. A letter to Gorbachev from Czech reformers, made public **Apr. 10**, asserted that Gorbachev had revived hopes for "socialist democracy" in Czechoslovakia. Visiting Bratislava, **Apr. 11**, before returning to Moscow, Gorbachev was mobbed by thousands of persons.

South African Strike Turns Violent — A strike by black South African railway workers, which had begun in March after an employee was dismissed on a petty issue, became violent in April. The state-owned South African Transport Services refused to recognize the black union as legitimate and threatened to dismiss the strikers. The union denied responsibility for a series of firebomb attacks on commuter trains that began **Apr. 13**. Within a week, 60 trains were destroyed or damaged. On **Apr. 22**, as the deadline expired for the 16,000 black workers to return to work or lose their jobs, thousands of other blacks stayed away from their jobs in a show of sympathy with the strikers. Police entered the headquarters of the Congress of South African Trade Unions and arrested hundreds of union members. In Johannesburg, blacks protesting the dismissals clashed with police, and at least 6 blacks were killed.

Soviets Offer New Euromissile Plan — Soviet leader Mikhail Gorbachev surprised visiting U.S. Secretary of State George Shultz, **Apr. 14**, by making a new proposal on European missiles. As described by the Soviet news agency Tass, Gorbachev "expressed the readiness to record in an agreement on medium-range missiles the Soviet Union's obligation to eliminate its shorter-range missiles within a relatively short and clearly defined time period." Tass also said that Gorbachev, in a major concession, agreed that research on the U.S. Strategic Defense Initiative could include "work on the ground—in institutes, at proving grounds, at plants." As new evidence of the Soviet trend toward openness, Shultz was interviewed, virtually uncensored, for 30 minutes on Soviet television, **Apr. 15**. In Geneva, **Apr. 27**, the Soviet raised a new demand—that there could be no agreement on shorter-range missiles in Europe unless 72 Pershing IA missiles based in West Germany were removed. The short-range Pershings could carry either nuclear or conventional warheads.

Army Revolt Flares in Argentina — An army major accused of human-rights abuses refused to appear before a civilian court in Argentina, **Apr. 15**, and fled to an army base in Córdoba. Ernesto Barreiro had been accused of interrogating prisoners at a detention camp during the "dirty war" against leftists in the 1970s. Many of the prisoners had been tortured and murdered. Pres. Raúl Alfonsín had accepted legislation setting a February 1987 cutoff for filing further charges against military personnel for such abuses. Barreiro's case had been brought before the court prior to the deadline. Refusing to appear in court, he was protected by the Córdoba base commander and other officers, who, on **Apr. 15**, issued demands for an amnesty for all crimes committed during the "dirty war." Alfonsín refused to negotiate and 100,000 persons demonstrated in support of him in Buenos Aires, **Apr. 16**. The revolt spread, **Apr. 17**, as 50 to 350 rebels occupied an army school at Campo de Mayo. This group continued to hold out after Barreiro fled th

Córdoba base and the officers there surrendered, **Apr. 17.** Alfonsín went to the Campo de Mayo, **Apr. 19,** and persuaded the remaining holdouts to surrender. The president, **Apr. 20,** accepted the resignation of the army chief of staff, reportedly because the rebellion had not been ended quickly.

Reagan, Nakasone Meet on Trade Crisis — Premier Yasuhiro Nakasone of Japan arrived in Washington, D.C., **Apr. 29,** as tensions related to trade seemed to be reaching a peak. He and Pres. Ronald Reagan met, **Apr. 30,** and **May 1,** and Nakasone appealed to Reagan to lift the tariffs announced by the United States in March and formally imposed, **Apr. 17.** Seeking to respond to U.S. anger prompted by the soaring trade deficit with Japan, Nakasone said that work on a major Japanese airport would be opened to foreign bids. He also reaffirmed a promise to buy more U.S. superconductors, promised to step up loans to the third world, and said he would push a spending package aimed at stimulating Japan's economy. Nakasone said he would support lower interest rates by the Bank of Japan as another step to help reduce Japan's trade surplus. The U.S. House, **Apr. 30,** passed a bill requiring the president to retaliate against countries that did not open their markets to U.S. products. Japan announced, **May 1,** that its trade surplus stood at a record $101.4 billion during fiscal 1986. The United States accounted for about half of that total.

Hundreds Die in Sri Lanka Attacks — Hundreds of persons were killed in Sri Lanka in a series of violent incidents known or assumed to have been perpetrated by Tamil separatists. About 127 were killed and 60 were wounded, **Apr. 17,** when rebels stopped 3 buses and 3 other vehicles along a jungle highway, identified which travelers were members of Sri Lanka's Sinhalese majority, and attacked them with machine guns and grenades. Another attack, **Apr. 20,** not far from where the first one took place, resulted in 15 deaths. A bomb blast in Colombo, the capital, **Apr. 21,** killed 105 and wounded 200.

U.S. Sends Accused Nazi to Soviet Union — For the first time, the United States deported an accused war criminal to the Soviet Union against his will. Karl Linnas, 67, had come to the United States in 1951, describing himself as a displaced person. He settled on Long Island, New York, and became a U.S. citizen in 1959. Linnas was sentenced to death in absentia by the Soviet Union in 1962 for having headed an Estonian concentration camp where 12,000 persons were killed. Deportation proceedings were begun against Linnas and the legal fight came to a conclusion, **Apr. 20,** when the U.S. Supreme Court denied his request for a delay in deportation. The U.S. Department of Justice supported the deportation, asserting that evidence was overwhelming that he had committed war crimes. Pat Buchanan, the former White House communications director, was among those who opposed the deportation, arguing that the evidence—much of it from the Soviet bloc—was suspect and that it was innappropriate for the United States to surrender anyone to Soviet justice. Within hours after the Supreme Court decision, Linnas, still protesting vehemently, was put on a plane for the Soviet Union. While awaiting the outcome of an appeal for a pardon, Linnas died, **July 2,** in Leningrad after undergoing 2 operations.

Arafat Tightens Grip on PLO — Leaders of the Palestine Liberation Organization met in Algiers and the result was a surprising show of unity under the leadership of oft-embattled PLO Chariman Yasir Arafat. The Palestine National Council, regarded by the PLO as its parliament in exile, convened, **Apr. 20.** Some extremists, including the faction headed by the terrorist Abu Nidal, had either left Algiers during preliminary meetings or boycotted the gathering altogether. Nonetheless, Arafat appeared at the podium on the opening day with George Habash and Nayef Hawatmeh, two factional leaders of Marxist groups who had often opposed Arafat. During the week-long meeting, Pres. Hafez al-Assad of Syria traveled to Moscow, **Apr. 23-25,** where he reportedly was urged to go easy in his own long feud with Arafat. In addition to Syria, Libya emerged as a mediator among PLO factions. On **Apr. 26,** at the end of the PNC conference, compromises on divisive issues were announced and Arafat appeared to have firmed up his powers as chairman. Egypt, responding to a PNC resolution criticizing the Camp David accord between Egypt and Israel, said, **Apr. 27,** it would close most PLO offices in Egypt.

U.S. Bars Waldheim — In the first such action every taken against the head of a friendly country, the U.S. Justice Department barred Austrian Pres. Kurt Waldheim from entering the United States. The department announced its decision, **Apr. 27,** after a year's investigation. It found a "prima facie case" that during World War II Waldheim had taken part in Nazi war crimes, including the execution of civilians and the mass deportation of civilians to concentration camps and death camps. Waldheim's wartime activities while serving in the German army had become public knowledge in 1986 during his successful campaign for the Austrian presidency. He had formerly served as secretary-general of the United Nations.

American Killed in Nicaragua — Benjamin Linder, 27, of Portland, Ore., was killed in Nicaragua, **Apr. 28,** during an attack on his work crew by contra guerrillas. A mechanical engineer, Linder was working on a rural hydroelectric project near the border with Honduras. He was believed to be the first U.S. volunteer working for the Sandinista government to be killed. Two Nicaraguans were also killed in the contra attack.

Biggest Wheat Sale Announced — The United States announced, **Apr. 30,** that the Soviet Union had agreed to buy 4 million metric tons of subsidized wheat—the largest sale ever of subsidized wheat to one country. The deal fell within the framework of a 5-year commitment by the Soviet Union for the purchase of wheat. Commodities analysts estimated the value of the sale at about $375 million.

General

Reagan Backs AIDS Education — Pres. Ronald Reagan, speaking to the College of Physicians of Philadelphia, **Apr. 1,** declared that acquired immune deficiency syndrome was "public health enemy No. 1" and said that the federal government would spend $766 million and $1 billion to fight it in fiscal years 1987 and 1988. He endorsed education about AIDS in the schools, and said that emphasis should be on the importance of sexual abstinence in young people and fidelity in marriage. Surgeon Gen. C. Everett Koop favored greater emphasis on explicit instruction in schools on how to use condoms to reduce the risk of transmitting the AIDS virus. Responding to a question, Reagan said, "I don't quarrel with that," but he added that not enough attention had been given to the teaching of what was right and wrong in sexual matters.

Texaco Files for Bankruptcy — Texaco Inc., unable to resolve its costly legal dispute with Pennzoil Co., became, on **Apr. 12,** the largest U.S. company ever to file for bankruptcy. Texaco had been ordered by a Texas court to pay Pennzoil $8.53 billion for having wrongfully interfered with a merger agreement between Pennzoil and Getty Oil Co. Additionally, Texaco had been required to post a $12 billion bond while it appealed the original judgment. By filing under Chapter 11 of the U.S. bankruptcy code, Texaco could avoid posting the bond. Negotiations between Texaco and Pennzoil on a settlement continued.

New Animal Forms to Be Patented — The U.S. Commerce Department announced, **Apr. 16,** that inventors would be permitted to patent new forms of animal life through such techniques as gene splicing and genetic engineering. The policy forbade the patenting of new genetic characteristcs in humans. Recent advances in reproductive technologies had as their objective such practical creations as cows that would give more milk or pigs that would contain less fat. A Supreme Court decision in 1980 had allowed for the patenting of new organisms. A coalition of animal welfare and public policy groups was immediately formed to oppose the new policy. Dr. Michael Fox, a veterinarian and scientific director of the Humane Society, warned that "the entire creative process . . . is going to be redirected or controlled to satisfy purely human ends." He added, "We are not only playing God, we are assuming dominion over God."

Bakker's Return to TV Ministry Barred — The Rev. Jerry Falwell, the new chairman of the PTL board of directors, said that the board had formally ended the ministry of the Rev. Jim Bakker. Bakker had stepped down from the ministry in March after admitting a liaison with a young woman in 1980. During April, more charges of sexual misconduct were made against Bakker, who denied them. It was also reported that Bakker and his wife Tammy Faye had received remunerations from PTL totaling $4.8 million since 1984. Falwell, whom Bakker had asked to take over PTL, said, **Apr. 27**, that Bakker had implied to him that "there'll be a holy war" if he were not permitted to resume his ministry. Falwell said, **Apr. 28**, that the PTL board had cut off all income to the Bakkers; obtained the resignation of the Rev. Richard Dortch, PTL's president and a longtime associate of Bakker's; and stopped payments from a $265,000 fund established for Jessica Hahn, the church secretary with whom Bakker had had sex in 1980. Falwell said that PTL was $50 million in debt. The Assemblies of God, **May 6**, dismissed Bakker and Dortch as ministers. Bakker was cited for his "sexual encounter" with Hahn and for "his alleged misconduct involving bisexual activity." Dortch was dismissed for concealing "the immoral conduct of a fellow minister" and for his apparent role in a "coverup," a reference to the fact that he had negotiated a financial settlement with Hahn.

MAY

National

Scandal Ends Hart's '88 Campaign — Gary Hart abruptly dropped out of the contest for the 1988 Democratic presidential nomination after a newspaper reported that a young woman had spent the night with him in his Washington, D.C., town house. A former senator from Colorado, Hart had made a strong bid for the nomination in 1984. He had declared his candidacy for 1988 in April, and was ahead in public-opinion polls both for the nomination and in matchups with potential Republican nominees. Hart had been plagued by rumors of "womanizing" for years, and he and his wife, Lee, had been separated twice. Annoyed by the speculation, Hart was quoted in the *New York Times*, **May 3**, as saying, "If anybody wants to put a tail on me, go ahead. They'd be very bored." That same day, a Sunday, the *Miami Herald* reported that Hart had spent much of the weekend with a young woman at his house. Lee Hart was in Colorado at the time. The author of the article, Jim McGee, said he and other reporters had staked out the house after receiving an anonymous tip. But the reporters' observations had not been uninterrupted, and not all doors to the house had been watched, so the story was not airtight. Emerging from the house late Saturday to confront reporters outside his house, Hart said that his guest was "a friend of a friend of mine" and "an acquaintance." The story stirred considerable debate not only about Hart, but also about journalistic ethics. Many deplored not only the appropriateness of the pursuit of a candidate's private life, but also the way in which the reporters had done their job. On **May 4**, Hart's guest was identified as Donna Earle Rice, 29, a Miami model. It also became known that Hart, Rice, and another man and woman had sailed from Florida to Bimini Island in the Bahamas aboard a yacht named *Monkey Business*. Addressing the American Newspaper Publishers Association in New York City, **May 5**, Hart said, "At no time did we, the woman involved and I, spend an evening, a night, together." While campaigning in New Hampshire, **May 6**, Hart was asked by a reporter if he had ever committed adultery, and replied, "I do not have to answer that question." Saying she believed her husband's assertions, Lee Hart flew to New Hampshire, **May 6**. On **May 7**, the Harts cancelled scheduled campaign appearances and returned to Colorado. Meeting the press, **May 8**, Hart bowed out of his presidential campaign in the face of polls showing a precipitous drop in his support. He said, "I refuse to submit my family and friends and innocent people and myself to further rumors and gossip. It's simply an intolerable situation." Hart asserted that the system for selecting national leaders "reduces the press of this nation to hunters and presidential candidates to being hunted." Hart's withdrawal came as the *Washington Post* was planning a story about Hart's relationship with another woman.

Senate Gives Reagan Option on Tax Hike — The Senate joined the House in confronting Pres. Ronald Reagan with a budget bill not to his liking. The bill approved by the Senate, **May 7**, would avoid an effective reduction in defense spending for the 1988 fiscal year only if Reagan agreed to sign a separate bill approving $18.3 billion in tax increases. If he did not do so, defense spending would be frozen at the 1987 level, with no allowance for inflation. The House bill, approved in April, also provided for an $18 billion tax increase, but neither the Senate nor the House had specified where the new money was to come from. Reagan had repeatedly refused to consider any tax increase. Focusing on the defense authorization portion of the budget, the House, **May 20**, approved, 239-177, $289 billion for the Pentagon for the 1988 fiscal year—a figure that no more than matched the 1987 authorization. The House attached several arms-control provisions to the bill, which required that the United States adhere to a narrow interpretation of the 1972 antiballistic missile treaty, banned funding for any weapons that exceeded limits in the 1979 Strategic Arms Limitation Treaty, required that the United States limit underground atomic tests to one kiloton if the Soviets did the same, and banned funding for any use of U.S. combat troops in Nicaragua unless American lives were in danger.

Jobless Rate Falls Again — The Labor Department reported, **May 8**, that the nation's unemployment rate had declined to 6.2 percent in April from 6.5 percent in March, continuing a long-term trend. The percentage of unemployed was the lowest of any time during the Reagan presidency. The U.S. deficit on merchandise trade stood at $13.63 billion in March, somewhat smaller than in February, the Commerce Department reported, **May 14**. The Labor Department said, **May 15**, that the prices paid by producers for finished goods rose 0.7 percent in April, a harbinger of an increase in the rate of inflation. Major banks raised their prime lending rate to 8.25 percent from 8 percent, **May 15**, their third increase in less than 2 months. The Commerce Department said, **May 22**, that after-tax profits of U.S. corporations fell 5.5 percent during the first quarter of 1987. The consumer price index rose 0.4 percent in April, holding steady for the third consecutive month, the Labor Department said, **May 22**. The index of leading economic indicators fell 0.6 percent in April, the Commerce Department reported, **May 29**.

Meese Asks Criminal Probe of Himself — Attorney Gen. Edwin Meese 3d asked that an independent counsel investigate his ties to the scandal-ridden Wedtech Corporation. Wedtech, a Bronx, New York, defense contractor, was also the target of several state and federal investigations. Four former Wedtech officials had already pleaded guilty in federal court in New York City to falsely claiming $5 million from the Pentagon, taking money illegally from the company, conspiring to bribe public officials, and paying off members of Congress and the Reagan administration. Subsequently, several politicans were indicted on charges involving Wedtech. Since **Feb. 2**, an independent counsel (formerly known as a special prosecutor), James McKay, had been investigating the involvement in Wedtech of Lyn Nofziger, a former aide and adviser to Pres. Ronald Reagan. It was reported that E. Robert Wallach, a friend of Meese, and W. Franklyn Chinn, a San Francisco financial consultant, were also targets of the investigation. Meese admitted, **Apr. 6**, that, while he was the counselor to Reagan in 1982, he had received memos from Wallach about Wedtech's efforts to get a no-bid Army contract as part of the government's minority-business program, and that he had acted to see that the company got "a fair hearing." Wedtech later received a $30 million contract to build generator engines. In 1985, Meese had given $60,000 to Chinn, who had just become a consultant for Wedtech, for investment in a "limited blind trust." Meese said later he did not know whether Chinn put the money in Wedtech stock. On **May 11**, Meese asked that McKay broaden his investigation to include an inquiry into Meese's relationship with Wedtech, and later that day the independent counsel agreed to do so.

Sen. Simon Joins Presidential Race — Sen. Paul Simon of Illinois, styling himself as a traditional New Deal Democrat, declared, **May 19**, that he would seek his party's nomination for president in 1988. Simon, at 58, was the oldest candidate pursuing the nomination. If elected, he would be the only 20th century president, aside from Harry Truman, who had not graduated from college. A former newspaper publisher and the author of 11 books, Simon had served years in the U.S. House before election to the Senate in 1984. He was a leading supporter of jobs programs, civil rights, and arms control.

Ex-Labor Secretary Acquitted — Raymond Donovan, who served as secretary of labor under Pres. Ronald Reagan from 1981 to 1985, was acquitted, **May 25,** of larceny and fraud charges. Donovan and 7 other men were found not guilty of all charges after an 8-month trial in the borough of the Bronx in New York City. Five of the men were present or former officials of the Schiavone Construction Co., of which Donovan was a co-owner. The defendants had been charged with a scheme to defraud the New York City Transit Authority of $7.4 million. The company had been awarded a contract to construct a subway tunnel. Judge John Collins had instructed the jury that the prosecution had to prove that the company never intended to make "good faith" efforts to allocate 10 percent of the work to minority businesses.

International

Korean Unrest Leads to Shake-Up — Rising political tensions in South Korea brought about major changes in the cabinet. On **May 1,** the new Party for Reunification and Democracy named Kim Young Sam as its leader. He and another opposition leader, Kim Dae Jung, had formed the new party after the breakup in the opposition New Korea Democratic Party. On **May 23,** protests erupted in Seoul, the capital, over the death (in January) of a student while undergoing interrogation by police. The riots appeared to be an immediate cause of a shake-up in the government, **May 26.** Those losing their jobs included Prime Minister Lho Shin Yong, the deputy prime minister, the national police chief, the home affairs minister, and the minister of justice. By **May 5,** police officers had been arrested in connection with the student's death.

U.S. Offers Strategic Weapons Treaty — The Geneva talks on strategic weapons reopened, **May 5,** and on **May 8,** the United States presented to the Soviet Union a draft treaty on reducing strategic (long-range) offensive weapons. The U.S. plan would have each side reduce its strategic arsenal by 50 percent over 7 years, and leave each with 1,600 delivery vehicles (missiles and bombers) and 6,000 nuclear warheads. Soviet leader Mikhail Gorbachev said, **May 19,** that the Soviet Union would remove its SS-20 medium-range missiles targeted on Asia if the United States agreed to eliminate its nuclear weapons in Japan, South Korea, and the Philippines, and also withdraw its aircraft carriers beyond certain lines in the Pacific Ocean.

S. African Government Stays in Power — Parliamentary elections, on **May 6,** gave the governing party in South Africa a slightly increased majority. The voting was seen as a show of popular support for Pres. Pieter Botha's apartheid policies. The far-right Conservative Party also increased its strength and displaced the Progressive Federal Party as the second-largest party. The PFP had backed the type of sweeping politcal reforms that its supporters argued were needed to achieve racial peace. Blacks were not permitted to vote. Members of Asian and mixed-race minorities would elect their members of parliament at a later time. Botha said, **May 7,** "The outside world must now have a clear picture that they cannot dictate to South Africa."

Nicaraguan Contras Pick New Leaders — The Nicaraguan contras, plagued for years by feuds among their political and military leaders, came up with a new leadership team in May. Representatives of various factions, seemingly united only by their desire to overthrow the leftist Sandinista regime in Nicaragua, met in Miami, **May 6,** and on **May 13,** they named 6 members of a new 7-member directorate. Two of the 3 members of the previous leadership group, Adolfo Calero and Alfonso Robelo, representing the Conservative and Social Democractic parties, were part of the new structure, which was to be called the Nicaraguan Resistance.

8 IRA Bombers Killed by British — The outlawed Irish Republican Army suffered a costly setback, **May 8,** when 8 of their members, including 3 senior leaders, were killed by British security forces after they bombed a police station in Loughgall, County Armagh, Northern Ireland. Three IRA men carried the bombs in the shovel of a hijacked bulldozer. After detonating the bombs, the 3 joined 5 other men in a van, where all were attacked by the British, who were lying in wait. All of the IRA men, plus a bystander, were killed.

Candidates Backed by Aquino Win — Filipino voters elected a national legislature, **May 11,** and candidates supported by Pres. Corazon Aquino swept to victory. The voting, following the approval of a new constitution in February, consolidated Aquino's position as the democratic leader of the nation. The nation, as a whole, voted for the members of the Senate, with the 24 top vote-getters being chosen for that chamber. The 200 members of the House of Representatives were chosen in individual districts. Aquino did not actually form a political party, but her endorsed candidates were generally referred to as the Laban, the name of the party founded by her late husband Begnino in 1978. Candidates endorsed by Aquino included both conservatives and reformers.

Soviets Launch Biggest Rocket Ever — The Soviet Union, **May 16,** successfully tested the world's most powerful rocket, one able to lift 5 times as much weight as its next-largest launch vehicle. The Soviet news agency Tass reported that the total weight of the rocket and its dummy payload was 2,000 tons. The rocket was capable of putting a 100-ton space shuttle into orbit. The "Energia" had 8 liquid hydrogen engines.

Romania Cool to Gorbachev — Soviet leader Mikhail Gorbachev visited Romania, **May 25-27,** and appeared to find little support for his package of social and economic reforms. Romania's leader, Nicolas Ceausecu, a critic of Gorbachev's program, met Gorbachev and his wife at the airport in Bucharest and the leaders drove past crowds far more restrained than the ones that had welcomed Gorbachev to Czechoslovakia in April. Gorbachev, addressing 5,000 Communist Party officials in Bucharest, **May 26,** drew no applause when he referred to complaints from Hungary about mistreatment of ethnic Hungarians in Romania, or when he criticized nepotism without mentioning the Romanian regime, which practiced it. Likewise, his explanation of his reform program brought no applause. Gorbachev attended a summit of Warsaw Pact leaders in East Berlin, **May 28-29.** The meetings took place behind closed doors, and the East German press gave only limited coverage to Gorbachev.

German Pilot, 19, Lands in Red Square — Mathias Rust, a 19-year-old resident of Hamburg, West Germany, embarrassed Soviet officials, **May 29,** when he flew his single engine Cessna from Helsinki across 400 miles of Soviet air space and landed in Red Square, just a few yards from the Kremlin wall. Leaving his plane, Rust visited with onlookers before being seized and imprisoned. The daring flight raised serious questions about Soviet air defenses. The Politburo, **May 30,** abruptly dismissed Defense Minister Marshal Sergei Sokolov as well as the commander in chief of air defense, Marshal Aleksandr Koldunov. Gen. Dimitri Yazov was named the new defense minister.

General

Reagan Calls for More Tests for AIDS — Pres. Ronald Reagan called for a step-up in testing of individuals for exposure to the virus that caused acquired immune deficiency syndrome. Earlier, fear of the fatal condition took on a new dimension when the Centers for Disease Control announced, **May 19,** that 3 health-care workers had been infected with the virus after their skin was splashed by the blood of infected hospital patients. The 3 workers had skin abrasions through which the virus could have reached their bloodstream. Reagan, addressing the American Foundation for AIDS research, **May 31,** in Washington, D.C., urged mandatory testing for federal, state, and local prisoners as well as for new immigrants. The president also endorsed "routine" testing for marriage license applicants and for anyone seeking treatment for drug abuse or sexually transmitted diseases.

Fatal "Twilight Zone" Case Settled — Director John Landis and 4 others were found not guilty of criminal charges in the deaths in 1982 of actor Vic Morrow and 2 children during the filming of a scene for the motion picture *Twilight Zone.* The trial was the first to arise from an accident on the set of a Hollywood film. The accident occurred when a special-effects explosive caused the crash of a helicopter that struck Morrow and the 2 children, ages 6 and 7, who were on the ground. Landis, producer Steven Spielberg, and Warner Brothers subsequently faced civil suits. Landis and 4 others were also charged with involuntary manslaughter. James Camomile, a technician who had been granted immunity from prosecution in return for his testimony, admitted during the trial that he set off the explosives before the helicopter was a safe distance from Morrow and the children. The jury acquitted all of the defendants on May 29.

Disasters — All 183 passengers and crew were killed, **May 9,** when a Polish jetliner crashed on the outskirts of Warsaw soon after beginning its flight to New York ... More than 90 persons were feared dead, **May 8,** after a ferry and a tugboat collided in the Yangtze River near Nantong ... A fire in northern China's province of Heilungkiang burned from **May 6** to **June 2,** devastating 2.47 million acres, killing 191, and leaving 51,000 homeless.

---

37 U.S. Sailors Killed by Iraqi Missile in Persian Gulf; U.S. Responds and Protects Kuwaiti Oil Tankers

A missile from an Iraqi warplane killed 37 sailors on a U.S. frigate in the Persian Gulf. In the complex diplomatic and military maneuvering that followed, which was tied to the Iran-Iraq war and superpower rivalry in the region, the United States took the dangerous step of escorting Kuwaiti oil tankers in the gulf and reflagging them with the U.S. flag.

The *U.S.S. Stark,* a guided missile frigate and one of 7 ships in the U.S. Middle East Force in the gulf, was in international waters about 85 miles northeast of Bahrain on the night of **May 17.** An Iraqi Mirage F-1 jet flew south along the coast of Saudi Arabia, turned east, and fired at least one missile toward the *Stark* from a distance of about 10 miles. The *Stark* had twice radioed the jet and warned it off. The missile was in flight for about 90 seconds before it struck the ship's bridge and exploded in the sleeping quarters of the crew. Most of the victims were killed in their bunks. The surviving crew put out the fire and the ship was towed to port in Bahrain.

Pres. Saddam Hussein of Iraq said, **May 19,** that Iraq was responsible, and that the "unintentional accident" would not affect relations between the 2 countries. Both Iraq and Iran had frequently attacked ships in the gulf, usually oil tankers, but the *Stark* was 40 miles south of any previous Iraqi night attack. Pres. Ronald Reagan, **May 19,** said Iran "was the real villain" because it had refused to negotiate an end to the war.

The tragedy refocused attention on a plan for the United States to protect Kuwaiti oil tankers in the gulf. The Reagan administration said, **May 19,** that it had reached "general agreement" with Kuwait to fly the U.S. flag over 11 of its tankers, which would also be escorted by U.S. Navy ships and protected from attack by Iran. Kuwait, which supported Iraq in the war, had asked for U.S. protection, but it had also arranged to lease 3 Soviet tankers that could be protected by Soviet warships.

The *Stark's* commander, Capt. Glenn Brindel, said, **May 20,** that the Iraqi attack had caught the ship by surprise because Iraqi planes had been regarded as friendly. He said that the ship's electronic equipment had failed to detect the launching of the missile. A sailor on lookout sighted the incoming missile and gave warning, but the frigate's main defense, its Phalanx gatling gun, was in its manual rather than automatic mode and was unable to respond in time.

The U.S. Senate, **May 21,** voted 91-5 to require the administration to report to Congress on the situation in the gulf before reflagging the Kuwaiti tankers. Those concerned about the reflagging and escort plan were struck by 2 major ironies. First, the U.S. defensive action against Iran had been hastened by the attack by Iraq. Second, the United States, unlike Western Europe and Japan, imported only a small part of its oil from the gulf. No other national showed any initial interest in helping to protect the Kuwaiti tankers.

Following the Senate's lead, the House, **June 2,** voted to require the administration to explain how it would protect U.S. warships and the Kuwaiti tankers flying the American flag.

National Security Adviser Frank Carlucci said, **June 6,** that he did not believe China's denials that it was selling Silkworm antiship missiles to Iran. White House Chief of Staff Howard Baker said, **June 7,** that the United States might retaliate if the Silkworms were deployed.

After it became apparent that Congress would veto the sale of 1,600 Maverick air-to-ground missiles to Saudi Arabia, Reagan announced, **June 11,** he was temporarily abandoning the plan. The United States was seeking Saudi cooperation in protecting the reflagged tankers.

The House Armed Services Committee found, in a report released **June 14,** that negligence on the part of the Stark's officers had been a major factor in the May 17 disaster. The report said that the Iraqi jet had not been warned in time, that weapons had not been brought into action in time, and that an audio alarm designed to warn the ship of incoming missiles had been turned off because it had given false alarms.

The Navy said, **June 19,** that Brindel and 2 other officers on the Stark were being relieved of duty because of "lack of confidence in their performance."

After a month's lull, Iraq, **June 20,** resumed the gulf shipping war with an attack on a tanker carrying Iranian oil, and followed with more attacks. Iran reentered the fray **June 27,** attacking 2 tankers.

The first 2 Kuwaiti tankers raised their U.S. flags, **July 21.** Escorted by 3 U.S. Navy warships, they passed through the Strait of Hormuz into the Persian Gulf, **July 22.** On **July 24,** when the convoy was about 120 miles from Kuwait, the tanker *Bridgeton,* at 400,000 tons one of the world's biggest ships, struck a mine. It took on water, but no one was injured, and the convoy continued to Kuwait. A White House spokesman said it was not clear who planted the mine, although Iran was thought to be responsible.

The Navy said, **July 27,** it would not court-martial the captain and chief weapons officer of the *Stark,* but the 2 officers received reprimands and were allowed to leave the Navy.

The U.S. Coast Guard gave permission, **July 28,** for the *Bridgeton* to take on two-thirds of the oil cargo that was its normal capacity. The Pentagon, **July 29,** ordered 8 minesweeping helicopters to be flown to the Gulf. Otherwise, the United States had virtually no modern minesweeping equipment. France, **July 29,** ordered an aircraft carrier and other ships into the Gulf to protect French interests. Four U.S. sailors were lost, **July 30,** in the crash of a helicopter preparing to land on the *USS LaSalle,* the Navy's command ship in the Gulf. U.S. diplomats asked 5 European governments to help with minesweeping of the Gulf. Great Britain declined to do so, **July 31.**

Iran staged so-called Martyrdom maneuvers in the Gulf, **Aug. 4–7,** that reportedly involved training by volunteers to ram U.S. warships with speedboats carrying explosives. After leaving the Persian Gulf and entering the Gulf of Oman, **Aug. 10,** the Texaco *Caribbean,* an American-operated (but Panamanian-registered) supertanker struck a mine and spilled 10,000 barrels of oil. Previously, no mines had been reported outside the Persian Gulf. On **Aug. 8,** a Navy Tomcat fighter fired 2 missiles at an Iranian jet perceived to be hostile, but both missed. The U.S. Navy, **Aug. 8–11,** escorted 3 more reflagged Kuwaiti tankers into the Persian Gulf and to Kuwait. Britain and France changed their minds, **Aug. 11,** and ordered their own minesweepers into the Persian Gulf region.

On **Aug. 15,** the supply ship *Anita,* flying the flag of the United Arab Emirates, hit a mine in the Gulf of Oman, blew up, and sank with one crewman dead and 5 missing. An explosion at the Arabian-American Oil Co. gas plant on the Persian Gulf coast of Saudi Arabia killed up to 22 persons. The U.S. Navy escorted 4 more Kuwaiti tankers into the Gulf, **Aug. 19.**

The mine-damaged *Bridgeton* was among 4 loaded tankers escorted out of the Gulf, beginning **Aug. 22.** On **Aug. 24,** the *USS Kidd,* an escorting destroyer, fired machine guns in front of 2 small wooden boats that had approached the convoy. They turned away. Iraq, **Aug. 29,** attacked Iranian tankers and offshore oil installations by air. Iran responded, beginning **Aug. 31,** by attacking Arab tankers and freighters with speedboats.

JUNE

National

Volcker to Resign as "Fed" Chairman — Pres. Ronald Reagan announced, June 2, that Paul Volcker, who had served 8 years as chairman of the Federal Reserve Board, would retire at the end of his second term, **Aug. 6.** In retrospect, Volcker's leadership was regarded as a great success, although his policy of holding interest rates high between 1979 and 1982 to suppress inflation had been unpopular. Inflation, which was running at 13.3 percent when Volcker became chairman, eventually declined to 1.1 percent. In 1982, when recession became a bigger worry than inflation, Volcker let interest rates fall slowly. A period of steady economic growth evolved from the recession. Reagan named Alan Greenspan, chairman of the Council of Economic Advisers under Pres. Gerald Ford, to succeed Volcker.

Congressman Indicted in Wedtech Case — The scandal involving the Wedtech Corporation broadened with the indictment of Rep. Mario Biaggi (D, N.Y.). A federal grand jury, **June 3,** charged Biaggi and 6 other men with various crimes involving the company, which the indictment described as a "racketeering enterprise." Biaggi was accused of perjury and extortion. Attorney Gen. Edwin Meese 3d, who had previously acknowledged having intervened in behalf of Wedtech while an aide to Pres. Ronald Reagan, was criticized by the director of the Office of Government Ethics. The director, David Martin, asserted in a letter made public, **June 30,** that Meese did not comply with federal ethics regulations when he invested $60,000 in 1985 with W. Franklyn Chinn, then an adviser to Wedtech. Martin said Meese had failed to get the approval of the ethics office for the investment.

Continuing Economic Growth Foreseen — Statistics released in June suggested that the prolonged period of growth in the U.S. economy would continue. The Labor Department said, **June 5,** that the unemployment rate had held steady at 6.2 percent in May, the lowest level of the Reagan presidency. The department said, **June 12,** that prices charged by producers for finished goods had risen 0.3 percent in May. The Commerce Department reported, **June 12,** that the U.S. deficit on merchandise trade had fallen slightly to $13.3 billion in April. The consumer price index, closely watched for any evidence of a return to high inflation, edged upward only 0.3 percent in May, the Labor Department reported, **June 23.** The Dow Jones industrial average continued to post new highs on Wall Street and closed, **June 25,** at 2431.03. The Commerce Department, **June 30,** corrected a previous estimate, saying that the index of leading economic indicators had risen 0.2 percent, not declined 0.6 percent, in April. Furthermore, the department said, the index had risen 0.7 percent in May.

2 More Democrats in '88 Field — Two Democratic senators entered the race for their party's 1988 presidential nomination. Sen. Joseph Biden (Del.) declared his intentions, **June 9,** in a speech in Wilmington, Del. Biden, a spirited orator who had become chairman of the Senate Judiciary Committee in 1987, asserted that a climate of selfishness in public and private life had emerged in recent years, and said, "We must rekindle the fire of idealism in our society." Sen. Albert Gore, Jr. (Tenn.) entered the contest, **June 29,** in a speech in his hometown of Carthage, Tenn. Gore, the son of a senator, had served 8 years in the U.S. House before being elected to the Senate in 1984. The candidate's wife, Mary, or Tipper, was an active critic of sexual and violent themes in the recording industry to which children were exposed. Gore, who was only 39 and who would become the youngest president if elected in 1988, described himself as the candidate of the New South.

General Dynamics Charges Dropped — Fraud charges against General Dynamics and 4 current or former executives were dismissed, **June 19,** in a federal district court in Los Angeles. The U.S. Attorney had informed the court that the counts in the indictment were not supported by sufficient evidence. The indictments asserted that the government had suffered a loss of $3.2 million because cost overruns incurred in production of the Sergeant York antiaircraft weapons had been charged to other federal projects. James M. Beggs, who resigned as director of the National Aeronautics and Space Administration when he was indicted in the case, was among those absolved.

Congress Approves $1 Trillion Budget for 1988 — The House, **June 20,** and the Senate, **June 24,** gave final approval to a budget resolution for the 1988 fiscal year that continued to promise an eventual showdown with the White House. The vote in both houses was essentially along party lines, and the resolution reflected Democratic priorities in rejecting Pres. Ronald Reagan's call for increased defense spending. The Pentagon would get $289 billion, no more than in 1987, but the total would be increased to $7 billion if Reagan agreed to unspecified tax increases of $19 billion. The resolution provided for expenditures of $1,055.5 billion and revenues of $921.6 billion, for a deficit of $133.9 billion. The president could not veto the resolution, but appropriations bills adopted in accord with its provisions would be subject to veto.

Powell Retires From Supreme Court — Justice Lewis F. Powell, Jr. announced, **June 26,** his retirement from the U.S. Supreme Court. Powell, who was 79, said he was leaving because of his age and concern "that I could handicap the court in the event of reoccurrences of serious health problems." Pres. Richard Nixon had named Powell to the Court in 1971. In a court that was sharply divided on many issues, Powell usually took a moderate stance and often cast the deciding vote in 5-4 decisions.

International

Panama's Leader Accused of Crimes — Published charges against the de facto leader of Panama, Gen. Manuel Antonio Noriega, set off widespread public demonstrations in June. The accusations came from Col. Roberto Diaz Herrera, who had been forced out as chief of the general staff, **June 1.** In articles published in the newspaper *La Prensa,* **June 7-9,** Diaz charged that Noriega had rigged the 1984 election that had given the presidency to Nicolas Ardito Barletta and that he had then brought about the ouster of Ardito Barletta in 1985. In more serious charges, Diaz said that Noriega had planned the death of Panama's strongman, Gen. Omar Torrijos Herrera, in a plane accident in 1981 and that he was implicated in the murder in 1985 of Dr. Hugh Spadafora, a critic of the military regime. U.S. government agencies had already gathered data linking Noriega to Spadafora's death and to drug smuggling. The Roman Catholic Church called, **June 9,** for an investigation of the charges. Public demonstrations against the regime began to spread, and on **June 11,** the government suspended many civil and political rights. The U.S. Senate voted 84-2, **June 26,** for a resolution calling for free elections in Panama. Pres. Eric Arturo Delvalle, **June 27,** denounced U.S. interference in his country's affairs, and on **June 30,** 5,000 demonstrators, including government officials, attacked the U.S. Embassy, some pelting it with rocks and bottles.

Bomb Kills Lebanese Premier — Lebanese Premier Rashid Karami was killed, **June 1,** when a bomb exploded in his helicopter during a flight to Beirut from his hometown of Tripoli. It was believed that the bomb had been placed either in his briefcase or under his seat. The interior minister and several others were injured. The copilot made an emergency landing. Karami, who had served as premier 10 times since 1955, had submitted his resignation, **May 4,** amid the continuing chaos in Lebanon, but Pres. Amin Gemayel had not yet formally accepted it.

Noncommunist Leaders Attend 13th Summit — Venice was the site for the 13th summit conference of the leaders of the 7 major noncommunist industrial nations. Pres. and Mrs. Ronald Reagan arrived in Venice, **June 3,** and on **June 6,** the president met with Pope John Paul II in Rome. Reagan announced, **June 8,** that the United States would lift tariffs on some Japanese television sets because of Japanese efforts to redress the serious U.S.-Japanese trade imbalance. The **June 8-10** summit conference was relatively uneventful. It included declarations of support for efforts to resolve the international trade problems and preserve "the principle of freedom of navigation" in the Persian Gulf. At a press conference in Venice, **June 11,** Reagan caused brief alarm in financial markets when he said it was "within reason that there could still be some lowering of the value [of the dollar] in relation to other currencies." In a speech in West Berlin,

June 12, Reagan challenged Soviet leader Mikhail Gorbachev to tear down the Berlin wall.

Partial Rebuilding of Embassy Recommended — Former Defense Secretary James Schlesinger, after completing a 10-day investigation, said at a news conference, **June 8,** that the chancery building of the new U.S. Embassy in Moscow was loaded with Soviet listening devices. He said U.S. officials were naive for allowing concrete sections to be prefabricated away from the site of the construction. Schlesinger had been named to head a State Department investigation team after U.S. Marine guards at the old Embassy were arrested for espionage. The Marine Corps, **June 12,** dismissed charges against one of the guards, Cpl. Arnold Bracy, for lack of evidence. In his formal report, **June 26,** Schlesinger recommended that the top 3 floors of the chancery, still under construction, be demolished and rebuilt. He said this would cost $35 million.

Pope Visits Poland 3d Time — Pope John Paul II visited his native Poland for the third time as leader of the Roman Catholic Church. He conferred, **June 8,** with Polish leader Gen. Wojciech Jaruzelski. On **June 9,** a million persons attended the pope's mass in Lublin. At Tarnow, **June 10,** he supported the right of farmers to resist the government's attempts to collectivize their land. In addresses, **June 11,** he gave unmistakable endorsement to the outlawed Solidarity labor movement, and granted an audience in Gdansk to Lech Walesa, founder of Solidarity. A number of persons were injured in Gdansk, **June 12,** when a melee broke out between police and demonstrators who had attended the pope's mass. The pope concluded his visit, **June 14,** by conducting an outdoor mass in Warsaw.

Antigovernment Riots Sweep Korea — Public demands for political reform in South Korea became more widespread and violent in June, but by month's end it appeared that an accommodation might be in sight. On **June 10,** the ruling Democratic Justice Party chose Roh Tae Woo, the party's chief and a friend of Pres. Chun Doo Hwan, to be its candidate for president in the December 1987 election. The country's indirect voting system appeared to assure Roh's election. He backed Chun's decision not to consider any alternative electoral procedure until after the 1988 Olympic Games were held in Seoul. The response to Roh's choice was renewed street demonstrations, again led by students but now apparently supported by other elements of the population. The riots continued day after day, with the government's defense in the hands of the nation's police, who frequently used tear gas; the regime feared that the use of Army troops might cost the nation the right to host the Olympics. On **June 18,** tens of thousands of students, supported by many middle-class citizens, effectively gained control of downtown Seoul for several hours. The Reagan administration, **June 18,** called on the South Korean government to permit a renewal of debate over changing the constitution. Chun met for the first time, **June 24,** with opposition leader Kim Young Sam after agreeing on 2 conditions: to free several hundred protestors seized during the riots; and to free Kim Dae Jung, another opposition leader, from house arrest. Chun offered to Kim Young Sam a renewal of constitutional debate, which Chun had muzzled, but Kim insisted, **June 25,** on a guarantee that the next election would not be held under the current constitution. He urged that the issue of changing the constitution be put to a national referendum. On returning, **June 26,** from meetings with Chun and Kim Dae Jung, U.S. Assistant Secretary of State Gaston Sigur, Jr., said that the government was showing a little flexibility. He had warned the regime against a military crackdown. After a march in 30 cities of some 100,000 persons, **June 26,** the demonstrations began to die down. Roh surprised both sides, **June 29,** by saying that he accepted most opposition demands. He supported a constitutional amendment to provide a direct presidential election, amnesty and restoration of civil rights for Kim Dae Jung, release of most political detainees, "bold social reforms," and a crackdown on crime and corruption.

Thatcher Wins 3d Term in Britain — For the first time since the 1820s, a British prime minister was elected to a third consecutive term. Margaret Thatcher and her Conservative Party, which had first come to power in 1979, swept to victory, **June 11,** in parliamentary elections. The Tories ran on a record of having reduced taxes, inflation, and labor strife. Thatcher's party won 375 seats in Parliament, a slight decline from 392 in the old Parliament. Labour won 229 seats and the centrist Alliance of the Liberal and Social Democratic parties won 22 seats. In the popular vote, the results were closer: Tories 42 percent, Labour 33 percent, and the Alliance 23 percent.

Ex-African Leader Sentenced to Death — Jean-Bedel Bokassa, former president and then self-proclaimed emperor of the Central African Republic, was found guilty and sentenced to die, **June 12,** for his involvement in at least 20 murders. Bokassa, who was overthrown in 1979, had fled to France and had been sentenced to death in absentia. Returning to the Central African Republic in 1986, in an attempt to clear his name, he was arrested and retried. The court found that he had ordered real or imagined opponents put to death in prison. Bokassa was also convicted of ordering the arrest of 100 children who had objected to wearing uniforms produced in a factory owned by Bokassa's wife. Many of the children were subsequently killed in prison.

U.S. TV Reporter Seized in Beirut — Charles Glass, a correspondent for the ABC network, who was on leave of absence to write a book on the Middle East, was kidnapped in Beirut, **June 17.** The son of the Lebanese defense minister and his driver were also seized, but freed, **June 24.** Glass had covered the TWA hostage crisis in Beirut in June 1985. A heretofore unknown group, the Organization for the Defense of Free People, claimed responsibility for the kidnapping, **July 1.** In a videotape released by the group, **July 7,** Glass was shown claiming he was a spy for the CIA, but his appearance and pattern of speech suggested that the statement had been forced from him.

Gorbachev's Reforms Take Shape — The overhaul of the Soviet system under the forceful leadership of Mikhail Gorbachev began to take shape in June. Multi-candidate elections became a reality, **June 21,** when contests were permitted for 76 of 52,000 Communist Party soviets (local councils) around the nation. Gorbachev had endorsed the idea of contested elections in January. However, those contesting the elections had all been approved by the party. Addressing the Party's Central Committee, **June 25,** Gorbachev called for a "radical reorganization of economic management" by the end of the 1980s. Naming some names, he rebuked officials who he said were working to sabotage restructuring. Gorbachev endorsed competition for state-owned enterprises, reduced central control over pricing and distribution of goods, and more decision-making by local party organizations. The Committee, **June 26,** endorsed the guidelines proposed by Gorbachev and also elevated 3 of his allies to full membership in the ruling Politburo. The nation's parliament, the Supreme Soviet, passed a law, **June 30,** that embodied Gorbachev's economic reforms.

Pope Meets With Waldheim — Despite criticism from Jewish leaders, Pope John Paul II held an audience in Rome, **June 25,** with Austrian Pres. Kurt Waldheim. After their private talks, the pope publicly praised Waldheim for his work at the United Nations as secretary general. The pope said nothing publicly about accounts that Waldheim had been involved in human rights abuses while serving in the German army in World War II, but the church said it was "surprised and grieved" by Jewish opposition to the meeting.

General

3d World Chaos Seen as AIDS Spreads — The Third International Conference on AIDS (acquired immune deficiency syndrome) drew 6,300 scientists and health professionals to Washington, D.C., **June 1-5.** Dr. Jonathan Mann, an official of the World Health Organization, warned that the anticipated rise in AIDS cases could bring political and economic upheaval to Third World countries, especially those in Africa, where, in some cities, 10 percent or more of pregnant women were infected with the AIDS virus. He said that 5 million to 10 million people worldwide were infected and that active cases might reach 1 million by 1991. Expanding on a policy announced in May by Pres. Ronald Reagan, Attorney Gen. Edwin Meese 3d said, **June 8,** that federal prisoners, would-be immigrants, and illegal aliens applying for legal status would be tested for exposure to the virus. Prospective immigrants testing positive would be barred from entry into the United States. Illegal aliens testing positive would be denied permanent legal status. Feder probation officers would be notified of prisoners testing positive, and released prisoners might thereafter be barred from obtaining some kinds of jobs.

"Subway Vigilante" Found Not Guilty — Bernhard Goetz, the New York City subway rider who had shot 4 black youths on a train in 1984 after they had approached him, was found not guilty of attempted murder and assault by a State Supreme Court jury, **June 16.** He was convicted only of carrying a loaded, concealed weapon. The prosecution played a taped confession in which Goetz said, "I wanted to kill those guys," but the defense attacked it as the unreliable statements of a "traumatized, sick, psychologically upset individual." One of the wounded victims, Troy Canty, testified that he did not intend to rob Goetz but was just panhandling when he asked him for $5. Another wounded youth, Darrell Cabey, remained partially paralyzed and brain damaged. Though the issue of a racial motive in the shootings was not addressed in the trial, it was widely discussed outside the courtroom. Some black political leaders criticized the verdict, but many black citizens approved of it.

Japan Blames Boeing for 520 Deaths — In their final report on the worst single-plane disaster in history, Japanese investigators said, **June 19,** that faulty repairs by Boeing Company employees were responsible for the crash in 1985 in Japan that killed 520 persons. The report said that the repair crew had placed a single line of rivets, rather than a double line as required, in a rear bulkhead when repairing a broken tail section. In flight, the bulkhead, which separated the pressurized and unpressurized sections of the cabin, ruptured. This destroyed the jet's vertical tail fin and its 4 hydraulic control systems, causing the plane to careen for more than 30 minutes before hitting the side of a mountain. The report cited Japan Air Lines and the Japanese Ministry of Transport for not detecting cracks in the bulkhead during routine inspections. Boeing, **June 19,** said it accepted the report's findings.

Disasters — A Philippine Airlines plane crashed into a mountain in northern Luzon, **June 26,** killing all 50 aboard.

JULY

National

Reagan Nominates Bork for Supreme Court — Pres. Ronald Reagan announced, **July 1,** that Judge Robert Bork of the U.S. Court of Appeals for the District of Columbia was his choice to fill the vacancy on the U.S. Supreme Court created by the retirement of Justice Lewis F. Powell, Jr. Reagan had named Bork to the Appeals Court in 1982. Bork had taught law at Yale and was U.S. Solicitor General from 1973 to 1977. He gained national attention in 1973 when Pres. Richard Nixon sought to dismiss Watergate special prosecutor Archibald Cox. Bork's two superiors in the Justice Department refused to obey the order and resigned. Bork then dismissed Cox. In nominating Bork, Reagan called him a "prominent and intellectually powerful advocate of judicial restraint." Judiciary Committee Chairman Joseph Biden (D, Del.) predicted, **July 1,** that the Senate confirmation fight would be contentious. Sen. Edward Kennedy (D, Mass.) attacked Bork, **July 1,** as an extremist, and Sen. Robert Packwood (R, Ore.) said, **July 3,** he would filibuster the nomination unless Bork agreed to abide by Roe v. Wade, the 1973 Court decision that established a constitutional right to abortion. Bork had criticized the landmark ruling. Organizations opposing Bork included the National Education Association, **July 5,** and the National Organization for Women and the National Association for the Advancement of Colored People, **July 6.** Conservative groups, equally active, hailed the nomination as the chance to obtain a Court majority against abortion and on such issues as affirmative action (which they opposed) and prayer in the public schools (which they supported).

LaRouche Indicted for Conspiracy — Lyndon H. LaRouche, Jr., a perennial presidential candidate who was generally regarded as an extremist, was charged in an indictment unsealed on **July 2** with conspiring to thwart an investigation of a $1 million credit-card fraud. Five organizations and 13 individuals associated with LaRouche were indicted in 1986. The alleged fraud involved unauthorized charges to credit cards of persons who had used the cards to purchase LaRouche publications. The new indictment charged that LaRouche and some of his associates had sought to obstruct a grand jury investigation by destroying records, by attacking the U.S. attorney investigating the case, and by slipping 3 of the original defendants out of the country.

Unemployment Falls Again — The Labor Department said, **July 2,** that the steady decline in unemployment continued in June, to 6 percent from 6.2 percent in May. The figure was at its lowest since December 1979. The department reported, **July 10,** that the prices charged by producers for finished goods rose 0.2 percent in June. The Commerce Department said, **July 15,** that the U.S. deficit on merchandise trade grew to $14.4 billion in May. The department reported, **July 24,** that the gross national product grew at an annual rate of 2.6 percent in the second quarter. It said, **July 30,** that the index of leading economic indicators rose 0.8 in June. The bull market continued on Wall Street, with the Dow Jones industrial average closing at an all-time high of 2572.07 on **July 31.**

Ex-Aide to Reagan Indicted — More indictments were handed down in the Wedtech scandal, and a former longtime adviser to Pres. Ronald Reagan, Lyn Nofziger, was included. Earlier, on **July 6,** Attorney Gen. Edwin Meese 3d released detailed information on his partnership with W. Franklyn Chinn, a former Wedtech official, whom he had given $60,000 to invest. The money had not been invested in Wedtech stock, but Chinn made about $35,000 in profits on 1-day stock trades. The indictment of Nofziger, unsealed **July 17,** evolved from an investigation by independent counsel James McKay. Nofziger was indicted on 6 counts of violating the federal ethics law prohibiting high public officials from lobbying their former agencies for a year after leaving the government. The indictments cited Meese as one of the officials he had lobbied. A single charge was filed against Mark Bragg, Nofziger's business partner. Nofziger, **July 17,** denied "any deliberate violation" of the law.

Commerce Secretary Killed at Rodeo — Sec. of Commerce Malcolm Baldrige was killed, **July 25,** when the horse he was riding reared and fell on top of him. Baldrige was practicing for an event at the fairgrounds in Walnut Creek, Calif. A veteran horseman, the 64-year-old Baldrige had participated in many rodeos. He had served in Pres. Ronald Reagan's cabinet since 1981, supporting free trade while urging Reagan to act against unfair international trade practices. Reagan, **Aug. 10,** nominated C. William Verity, Jr., a retired chairman of Armco Inc., a steelmaking company, and a supporter of increased trade with the Soviet Union, to succeed Baldrige.

International

U.S.-Panama Ties Strained — Relations between the United States and Panama grew tense in July. On **July 1,** the United States charged that a rock-throwing attack on the U.S. Embassy the previous day took place with the "unmistakable involvement" of the government of Panama. Business leaders seeking the ouster of strongman Gen. Manuel Antonio Noriega called a general strike for **July 3–5.** The government had charged that the opponents of the regime were wealthy whites who had the backing of the United States. On **July 7,** Pres. Eric Arturo Delvalle banned mass demonstrations, and hundreds of antigovernment demonstrators were arrested, **July 10,** when they sought to defy the ban. Within days, dozens of the marchers were sentenced to prison. It was reported in late July that the United States had suspended economic and military aid to Panama. The government shut down 3 newspapers, **July 26.** They were charged with inciting rebellion and rioting. On **July 27,** riot troops arrested Roberto Díaz Herrera, a retired colonel who had accused Noriega of serious crimes. Forty-five others were arrested during a gunfight between his bodyguards and soldiers. A general strike, **July 27** and **July 28,** paralyzed major cities.

South Korea to Get Direct Election — Pres. Chun Doo Hwan of South Korea announced, **July 1,** that the next president would be chosen by direct popular vote and that he would step down on **Feb. 25, 1988.** By endorsing the June 29 reform plan of his political ally and party leader, Roh Tae Woo, who was also the party's candidate for president, Chun appeared to have ended the political unrest that had swept the country for months. Chun bowed to what he acknowledged was the public's "ardent desire" for direct democracy in place of the indirect system that virtually assured continued rule by his party. Opposition leaders hailed Chun's announcement. On **July 4**, 5 policemen were sentenced to 5 to 15 years in prison for the death in January of a student. Hundreds of thousands of people took to the streets, **July 9**, to honor another student who had been injured fatally during a street demonstration. The government, **July 9**, restored political rights to 2,335 former political prisoners, including opposition leader Kim Dae Jung.

Barbie Convicted of War Crimes — Klaus Barbie was convicted, **July 4**, of crimes against humanity in a court in Lyons, France, where, during World War II, he had been chief of the Nazi Gestapo. Previously sentenced to death in absentia, Barbie this time was convicted on new charges of deportations of 842 people that resulted in 370 deaths. In an especially abhorrent incident, he was convicted of deporting 44 children and 7 adults from a children's home to the Auschwitz death camp, where all but one died. Barbie had lived in Bolivia for 32 years until he was brought back to France in 1983. The death penalty was no longer legal in France, and Barbie was sentenced to life in prison.

72 Killed in India in Bus Attacks — Attacks by Sikh separatists on busses in India brought death to 72 persons on **July 6** and **7**. The attacks, following a now-familiar pattern, resulted in the deaths of one gunman and 71 Hindus. More than 50 persons were wounded.

Marcos Boasts of Vast Fortune — Ferdinand Marcos, the ousted president of the Philippines, claimed, in a conversation with 2 Americans that was made public in July, that he had a "secret cache" of $14 billion in gold hidden in the Philippines and $500 million in Swiss bank accounts. The Reagan administration, on learning of Marcos's boast and of his stated plan, on a tape recorded without his knowledge, to try to overthrow the Philippines government, told Marcos that he could not leave the Hawaiian island of Oahu without the permission of the Philippines government. The Americans, Richard Hirschfeld and Robert Chastain, told a House Foreign Affairs subcommittee, **July 9**, that they had signed a contract with the Philippines government to take a share of any funds reclaimed from Marcos as a result of information that they had gathered. On the tape, which had been made May 21, Marcos claimed a 10,000-man force would welcome him back to the Philippines. He spoke of kidnapping Pres. Corazon Aquino. Marcos said, **July 12**, that he would act against the government only to prevent a communist takeover.

France Breaks Relations With Iran — France broke off diplomatic relations with Iran in July. On **June 30**, French police surrounded the Iranian embassy in Paris, where they believed that an Iranian wanted for questioning in the bombings in Paris in 1986 had taken refuge. Iran, in turn, blockaded the French embassy in Teheran, and on **July 12**, Iran accused French authorities of assaulting an Iranian diplomat in Geneva. On **July 16**, Iran threatened to end relations if the diplomat's attackers were not punished and if the guard on the embassy was not lifted. France broke relations, **July 17**. For the past year, France had been seeking Iran's help in obtaining freedom for French hostages kidnapped in Lebanon.

386 Reported Slain in Mozambique — The official news agency of Mozambique said, **July 21**, that antigovernment rebels had killed 386 civilians—some of them hospital patients—and wounded 76 in and near the town of Homoine, **July 18**. A spokesman for the Renamo guerrilla movement said that government troops dressed as rebels had massacred the victims. The government was supported by Soviet bloc and black African countries, the rebels allegedly by South African and other unknown sources.

USSR Offers New Arms Concession — In an interview published **July 22**, Soviet leader Mikhail Gorbachev said the Soviet Union could accept worldwide elimination of intermediate nuclear forces. He offered to drop his insistence on basing INF warheads in Soviet Asia. As part of their tentative agreement to remove their longer-range INF systems from Europe, the superpowers had contemplated retaining 100 warheads on their own soil. In his new concession, formally presented at the Geneva arms-control talks, **July 23**, Gorbachev offered to forgo the basing of warheads anywhere in its territory if the United States would do the same. In a draft treaty on curtailing weapons in space, presented at Geneva, **July 29**, the Soviet Union insisted that the United States abide by the 1972 anti-ballistic missile treaty for 10 years. On **July 31**, 2 months after the United States had done the same, the Soviet Union presented a draft treaty on reducing long-range nuclear weapons. As before, Moscow linked such an agreement to curbs on the U.S. Strategic Defense Initiative.

Sri Lanka, India Sign Pact on Tamils — Pres. J.R. Jayewardene of Sri Lanka and Prime Minister Rajiv Gandhi of India signed an agreement, **July 29**, that sought to end the armed rebellion by the Tamil minority against Sri Lanka's government. The terms included a cease-fire and amnesty for the rebels and political prisoners. A de facto Tamil homeland would be formed by the creation of a single semi-autonomous government in 2 provinces where most of the Tamils lived. The accord also permitted deployment of an Indian peacekeeping force, and, in fact, 3,000 Indian troops were deployed in the Jaffna Peninsula, **July 30**. The agreement provoked opposition from both Tamils and Sri Lanka's Sinhalese majority, and some 40 persons were killed during violent demonstrations.

Hundreds Die in Violence at Mecca — Iranian pilgrims battled Saudi police, **July 31**, near the Grand Mosque in the holy city of Mecca, and hundreds were killed or injured. Though political protests were banned in Mecca during the annual pilgrimage, thousands of Iranians reportedly shouted denunciations of the United States, the Soviet Union, and Israel, and raised portraits of the Iranian leader Ayatollah Ruhollah Khomeini. The demonstration turned violent, and many, including women, children, and pilgrims from other countries, were trampled to death. The incident portended a new crisis between Iran and Saudi Arabia.

200 Haitians Die in Massacre — More than 200 people were killed and 100 wounded, **July 23**, in the farming town of Jean-Rabel, Haiti in a clash between wealthy landowners and a land-reform group. The basic facts were established by an investigatory commission that made its report public Aug. 20. The report said the reformers attacked first, killing 10 people. Hundreds of the reformers were then killed or wounded when attacked by supporters of the landowners with machetes and clubs.

72 Die in Karachi Explosion — Two car-bomb explosions in a crowded section of Karachi, Pakistan, **July 14**, killed at least 72 persons and injured some 300. President Muhammad Zia ul-Haq attributed the bombings to Pakistan's support of the Afghanistan resistance, but domestic opponents of the president's regime could have been responsible.

General

18 Suffocate in Boxcar — A locked railroad boxcar became a tomb for 18 young Mexicans in early July. The men, all but 2 of them reportedly illegal aliens, entered the boxcar on the afternoon of **July 1**. The aliens had agreed to pay $400 each to a smuggler who slipped illegal aliens across the border. The other 2 men were reportedly accomplices of the smuggler. The smuggler locked the men—19 in all, one of whom would survive—in the car, which proved to be airtight. Tools he had given the men could not be used to open a hole. The victims were found dead by border patrol agents on the morning of **July 2**, in Sierra Blanca, Tex., 90 miles southeast of El Paso. The survivor recounted the horror of the fatal entrapment.

Reagan Names AIDS Commission — Pres. Ronald Reagan, **July 23**, announced the names of the 13 members of the commission that would advise him on acquired immune deficiency syndrome (AIDS). In keeping with controversies that surrounded all aspects of the fatal condition, the makeup of the commission had been hotly debated. After gay rights groups complained that no homosexuals would be on the commission, Reagan added Dr. Frank Lilly, a geneticist and former board member of the Gay Men's Health Crisis. The commission was also criticized because some of its members had little familiarity with the disease.

Disasters —More than 300 persons were believed to have died, **July 5**, when a barge crossing the Luapula River between Zaire and Zambia hit a sandbar, overturned, and sank. . . . A Miami-bound cargo plane carrying 10 people and 18 prize jumping horses crashed just after takeoff from Mexico City, **July 30**, killing one passenger and 53 persons on the ground, and all of the horses.

AUGUST

National

FCC Drops Fairness Doctrine — The fairness doctrine, which had required radio and television broadcasters to offer balanced coverage of controversial issues, was abolished, **Aug. 4**, by the Federal Communications Commission. Consumer advocate Ralph Nader saw the decision as a setback for those who wanted to espouse minority views, but the broadcasters argued that the doctrine had tended to discourage them from presenting controversial issues at all. Congress's attempt earlier in the year to write the fairness doctrine into law had fallen before a presidential veto.

Economic Data Remain Encouraging — Statistics released in August continued to reflect a healthy economic environment. The unemployment rate continued to edge downward, to 5.9 percent in July, the Labor Department said, **Aug. 7.** The Department said, **Aug. 14** that the prices charged by producers for finished goods edged upward only 0.2 percent in July. The trade deficit, however, rose in June to $15.71 billion, the Commerce Department reported, **Aug. 16.** The Department said, **Aug. 21**, that the consumer price index rose by 0.2 percent in July. It reported, **Aug. 21,** that after-tax profits of U.S. corporations rose a strong 4.2 percent in the second quarter of 1987. The phenomenal boom on Wall Street carried the Dow Jones industrial average to an all-time high of 2722.42 on **Aug. 25.**

Reagan's Helicopter Nearly Hit — In a year in which near misses among aircraft had become a growing concern, Pres. Ronald Reagan had a brush with tragedy, **Aug. 13.** As his helicopter approached his ranch in Santa Barbara, Calif., where he was to begin a vacation, a small private plane flew within 200 feet of it. The helicopter took evasive action, and security guards in a second copter pursued the plane, which landed at Orange County Airport. The pilot, Army Pvt. Ralph Myers, was questioned and then held when it was learned that he was absent without leave from a base in Washington state.

Courts Overturn Textbook Rulings — On **Aug. 24**, in Cincinnati, a 3-judge panel reversed a Federal District Court ruling that public schools in Hawkins County, Tenn., could excuse children from classes because textbooks offended their parents' relgious beliefs. The lower court had held that the parents could take their children elsewhere and be reimbursed for the costs of private lessons. The appeals panel unanimously found no proof "that any plaintiff student was ever called upon to say or do anything that required the student to affirm or deny a religious belief. . . ." On **Aug. 26,** in Atlanta, Ga., a 3-judge panel unanimously reversed a district court ruling banning 44 textbooks from Alabama public schools because they promoted the "religion" of "secular humanism." The district judge, W. Brevard Hand, had held that the textbooks violated the constitutional ban on government establishment of religion. The panel found no evidence that the "omission of certain facts regarding religion from these textbooks of itself constituted an advancement of secular humanism" or hostility to other religions. The ruling held that a constitutional mandate requiring neutrality on religion had been stretched incorrectly "into an affirmative obligation to speak about religion."

International

Iran Denounces Saudis for 402 Deaths — Saudi Arabia, **Aug. 1**, put the death toll in the previous day's violence near the Grand Mosque in Mecca at 402, including 275 Iranians, 85 Saudis, and 42 pilgrims from other countries. The Saudis blamed Iran for the riot, and said that police had not fired any shots. On **Aug. 1,** a mob in Teheran sacked the Saudi and Kuwaiti embassies. Arab nations rallied to the support of the Saudis. Ayatollah Ruhollah Khomeini, the Iranian leader, charged, **Aug. 3**, that the United States was to blame, called the Saudi ruling family "vile and ungodly," and said it was unworthy of the responsibility of guarding the Islamic shrines. King Fahd responded, **Aug. 5**, saying the government would "never relent in the defense of our homeland and sacred shrines."

Nicaraguan Peace Plans Offered — Pres. Ronald Reagan and the presidents of 5 Central American countries both came up with plans that sought to bring peace to the region —and especially to Nicaragua. Reagan, with bipartisan collaboration from House Speaker Jim Wright (D, Tex.), announced his plan, **Aug. 4.** It called for an immediate cease-fire between Nicaragua's Sandinista government and contras who were fighting against it. The United States would suspend military aid to the contras and Nicaragua would stop accepting similar aid from the Soviet Union and Cuba. Foreign combat troops would be withdrawn from the region, and Nicaragua would grant democratic reforms and provide amnesty to the rebels. At that point, the U.S. economic embargo would be lifted, and the United States and regional governments would conduct talks. If Nicaragua failed to implement the changes by Sept. 30, the United States would be free to resume aid to the contras. Contra leaders, after meeting with Reagan, **Aug. 5**, said they could accept the plan. The presidents of Nicaragua, El Salvador, Honduras, Costa Rica, and Guatamala signed their own preliminary peace agreement in Guatamala City, **Aug. 7.** It incorporated the main points of a proposal set forth in February by Pres. Oscar Arias Sánchez of Costa Rica. It provided for a 90-day time frame for implementing its provisions. The plan called for a dialogue between governments and unarmed internal opposition groups in each country, cease fires where guerrillas were operating, a cessation of states of emergency, and an end to regional or outside aid to antigovernment forces. Although the agreement would end U.S. aid to the contras and prevent them from using their bases in Costa Rica and Honduras, Reagan gave cautious support for the plan, **Aug. 8.** Defense Secretary Caspar Weinberger, however, faulted the plan, **Aug. 11,** saying that influence over the Nicaraguan government's actions would be curtailed if the contras' effectiveness was reduced. Pres. Daniel Ortega met with Cuban Pres. Fidel Castro in Havana, **Aug. 12,** and on **Aug. 13** Cuba endorsed the plan. Philip Habib, Reagan's special envoy to Central America, resigned, **Aug. 14,** apparently unhappy at having had no major role in developing U.S. initiatives in the region. Contra leaders, meeting with Pres. José Napoleón Duarte of El Salvador, **Aug. 21,** accepted the presidents' plan but demanded direct negotiation with the Sandinista government, a guarantee of safety for contras accepting amnesty, and the right to continue to receive arms until the cease-fire was secured.

Chad Regains Territory — After Libyans attacked Chadian positions, the Chadians counterattacked, and on **Aug. 8,** drove the Libyans out of the Aozou Strip, the northernmost section of Chad, which Libya had occupied in 1973 on the basis of an unratified 1935 treaty. The area was believed to be rich in uranium and phosphates. Libya still controlled a large air base on the border between the 2 countries.

South African Miners' Strike Fails — More than 250,000 black South African miners went on strike in August, but ultimately returned to work without the wage increase they had demanded. The walkout, **Aug. 9,** by the gold miners and coal miners had potentially serious consequences for South Africa, which derived 80 percent of its foreign earnings from mining. The union asked for a 30 percent pay increase, but the mine owners refused to agree to increases beyond their offer of 15 percent to 23 percent. White employees of the mines earned much more than the blacks. Twenty thousand striking miners were dismissed, **Aug. 27.** Clashes during the strike resulted in 11 miners dead, 300 wounded, and 400 arrested. The strike ended, **Aug. 30,** with the union accepting the mine owners' wage offer.

American "Escapes" Beirut Captors — American journalist Charles Glass, who had been kidnapped in Beirut, **June 16,** escaped, **Aug. 18,** in circumstances that were not entirely clear. He said he had slipped out of his chains and locked his sleeping guards inside the apartment in which he had been held. He made contact with Syrians who drove him to Damascus, where he was turned over to U.S. officials. It was considered possible that his escape had been permitted because Syria—angered by the kidnapping—had threatened to move militarily into the Shiite districts of Beirut unless he was freed. The ABC newsman said he had been kept blindfolded and that the "confession" that had been videotaped had been made at gunpoint.

New Korean Constitution Drafted — The political process continued to move forward in South Korea with the drafting of a new constitution. Earlier, the new reformist trend was seen when the nation's largest industrial company, Hyundai Group, yielded to government pressure, **Aug. 19,** and agreed to recognize a new union. Such an intervention by the government was without precedent. The 70,000 Hyundai employees went back to work, **Aug. 20,** but labor strife remained widespread. It was reported that up to 500 other industrial disputes remained unresolved as workers stepped up demands for a greater share of the prosperity that the nation was experiencing. The low wage rates had been a major factor in the success Korean exports had found in many countries. After a month of negotiations between the ruling party and its principal opposition, the draft of a new constitution was completed, **Aug. 31.** The president, who would serve for 5 years, would be chosen in a direct popular election. He could not dissolve the National Assembly and could declare martial law only with difficulty. The military would be kept neutral in politics, and some new legal rights, including habeas corpus, would be recognized.

Marine Convicted in Embassy Case —Sgt. Clayton Lonetree was convicted of espionage, **Aug. 21,** as a result of activities he had engaged in while serving as a Marine guard at the U.S. embassies in Moscow and Vienna. He had been court-martialed on 13 charges that included unauthorized contacts with foreign nationals, conspiring with Soviet intelligence agents, disclosing the identities of U.S. intelligence agents, and giving blueprints of the embassies to Soviet agents. Convicted on all counts, Lonetree was sentenced to 30 years in prison, **Aug. 24,** and given a dishonorable discharge.

Missile Treaty Prospects Improve — West German Chancellor Helmut Kohl offered, **Aug. 26,** to dismantle 72 Pershing missiles in order to clear a roadblock to a superpower treaty on intermediate nuclear forces. West Germany controlled the missiles, but the United States controlled their nuclear warheads. The Soviet Union wanted the missiles eliminated as part of an overall treaty on INF forces.

Filipino Troops Revolt Again — In August, for at least the fifth time since she became president in 1986, Corazon Aquino of the Philippines put down an uprising, but this one, by mutinous army troops, was the most serious yet. The revolt was led by officers linked to a reform movement in the military that had helped topple former Pres. Ferdinand Marcos. They struck in the early hours of **Aug. 28,** but were repulsed about 300 yards from the presidential palace in Manila. The president's son was wounded and 3 of his bodyguards were killed. Other rebels seized Cebu City, the islands' second-largest city, and Camp Aguinaldo military base. Col. Gregorio Honasan, leader of the revolt, said he was not attempting a military coup, but was acting because the government had lost its "political will" and because Aquino had established a personality cult. By **Aug. 29,** Camp Aguinaldo had been retaken and the rebels gave up their control of Cebu City. Honasan disappeared.

General

Child Survives Crash Fatal to 155 — At least 155 persons died as the result of a crash **Aug. 16,** of a Northwest Airlines jet that had just taken off from Detroit Metropolitan Airport in Romulus, Mich. Miraculously, a 4-year-old girl, Cecilia Cichan, of Tempe, Ariz., survived. Her father, mother, and brother all died. The death toll was the second-highest ever for a U.S. plane crash. The number of persons aboard the plane was uncertain. Two persons were killed on the ground. The cause of the disaster was not immediately determined.

Humans to Test AIDS Vaccine — U.S. health officials and MicroGeneSys Inc. announced, **Aug. 18,** that the first test on humans of an experimental vaccine for AIDS would begin in October. The company, based in West Haven, Conn., developed the vaccine, which had already been tested on animals. In the human tests, 81 volunteers would be recruited in the Washington, D.C., area for the tests, which would be conducted at a National Institutes of Health unit at Bethesda, Md. Public anxiety concerning AIDS was underscored by an incident in Arcadia, Fla. Three young brothers, all hemophiliacs who had received blood transfusions, had been exposed to the AIDS virus but showed no symptoms of AIDS. They had been barred from school in 1986, but a federal judge had ordered their admittance for the fall 1987 term. On their return to school, **Aug. 24,** many local citizens withdrew their children from classes. On **Aug. 28,** a fire of unknown origin destroyed the family's home, and on **Aug. 29,** the boys' mother, Louise Ray, said that they would move elsewhere.

Hospital Orderly Admits Killing 24 — A 35-year-old hospital orderly pleaded guilty in Hamilton County Court, **Aug. 18,** to killing 24 people, 21 of them at Daniel Drake Memorial Hospital in Cincinnati in 1986 and 1987. The orderly, Donald Harvey of Middletown, Ohio, reportedly confessed to 30 other killings since the 1970s. He said he had poisoned most of his victims. An investigation got under way when an autopsy showed that a patient had died of a lethal dose of cyanide. Harvey was sentenced to 3 consecutive life terms.

Gunman Kills 16 in England — A young man armed with a semiautomatic rifle, a carbine, and 3 hand guns rampaged through the small town of Hungerford, England, **Aug. 19,** killing or fatally wounding 16 persons. Fourteen more were wounded. The dead included the mother of the gunman, Michael Ryan, a 25-year-old laborer and gun collector. Ryan took refuge in a school, and after a standoff with police he apparently shot and killed himself.

Disasters — Up to 100 persons may have died when a bus crashed into a canal in Uttar Pradesh in India, **Aug. 7.** . . . At least 50 miners were killed near Welkom, South Africa, **Aug. 31,** when an explosion in a gold mine caused an elevator to fall more than 4,000 feet down a shaft. . . . A Thai Airways jet plunged into the Andaman Sea, **Aug. 31,** killing all 83 aboard.

SEPTEMBER

National

Economic Indicators Continue to Rise — Twice in September the Commerce Department reported additional increases in the index of leading economic indicators. The department said, **Sept. 1,** that the index had risen 0.5 percent in July. The unemployment rate held at 5.9 percent in August, the Labor Department reported, **Sept. 4.** The Federal Reserve Board, **Sept. 4,** raised its discount rate—the rate charged on loans to financial institutions—to 6 percent from 5.5 percent. The U.S. trade deficit rose to a record $16.5 billion in July, the Commerce Department reported, **Sept. 11.** After having backed off from its August all-time high, the Dow Jones industrial average rebounded, **Sept. 22,** with a record one-day gain of 75.23 points, closing at 2568.05. The Labor Department reported, **Sept. 23,** that consumer prices had jumped 0.5 percent in August. The Commerce Department said, **Sept. 30,** that the index of leading economic indicators had risen 0.6 percent in August.

Court Nominee Defends Views — Judge Robert Bork, Pres. Ronald Reagan's choice for a seat on the U.S. Supreme Court, gave a spirited defense of his views in testimony before the Senate Judiciary Committee, which would vote on whether to recommend his appointment to the full Senate. The Standing Committee on Federal Judiciary of the American Bar Association approved the nomination, **Sept. 8.** But its vote, 10 to 4, that Bork was "well-qualified" may have set back the nomination. A 15th panelist said only that he was "not opposed" to Bork. The panel usually had given unanimous approval to Federal Court nominees. Bork appeared before the Senate committee, **Sept. 15-19.** He said he was "neither liberal nor conservative," but said he based his judgement on the "original intent" of the framers of the Constitution. When senators cited outspoken positions that he had taken—including criticisms of Supreme Court decisions—in his writings before joining the U.S. Court of Appeals in 1982, Bork said he had modified some views and that in other instances he would accept the principle that established precedents should not, as a rule, be overturned. Bork asserted that there was no constitutional protection of privacy and that he therefore continued to disagree with Court decisions protecting the private conduct of married couples and the right of a woman to an abortion that was based on that presumed right. He said that political speech was the core of the 1st Amendment protection of free speech, but that some other forms of speech—not including pornography—were also protected, though perhaps less clearly. He contended that although the equal protection clause of the 14th Amendment protected "any person," the authors had intended to apply it only to racial and ethnic minorities and that, therefore, the protection of women under the amendment fell into a gray area. The committee hearings continued through **Sept. 30**, with many prominent figures testifying both for and against the nomination. Members of the Senate found themselves under unprecedented public pressure from constituents, who vociferously argued Bork's alleged virtues and shortcomings.

Pope Hears Critics on U.S. Tour — Pope John Paul II visited the United States for the second time as leader of the Roman Catholic Church—he had also come in 1979—and he heard from a number of U.S. Catholics who disagreed with Church teachings. Pres. Ronald Reagan greeted the Pope in Miami, **Sept. 10.** At a meeting with priests, Father Frank McNulty, who had been chosen as their representative, politely asked the Pope to address the issues of priestly celibacy and the restricted role of women in the Church. Meeting with Jewish leaders in Miami, **Sept. 11**, John Paul defended Israel as a homeland for the Jewish people, but also supported the formation of a Palestinian homeland. A storm forced the Pope to curtail a mass before 250,000 people in Miami, **Sept. 11.** In Columbia. S.C., **Sept. 11**, in the heart of the Protestant Bible Belt, the Pope attended an ecumenical prayer service. At a youth rally in the New Orleans Superdome, **Sept. 12**, he watched a "Mini Mardi Gras" featuring bands and floats. Meeting with black Catholic leaders, he spoke out against "economic deprivation" experienced by American blacks. Some 300,000 attended his Sunday mass in San Antonio, **Sept. 13.** In Phoenix, **Sept. 14**, he called on Catholic health-care workers to reject abortion, euthanasia, and the new reproductive technologies. Also in Phoenix, he asked American Indians to forget past abuses by the Church and to concentrate on the Church's current efforts in behalf of Indian rights. Addressing leaders of the entertainment world in Los Angeles, **Sept. 15**, the Pope deplored the depiction of sex and violence in the mass media. In a meeting with Catholic bishops, **Sept. 16**, he heard their spokesmen contend that U.S. Catholics could experience deep faith even while questioning Church teachings. John Paul replied that sacraments could be denied those who ignored Church teachings on divorce, birth control, and similar issues. Confronting another touchy issue among U.S. Catholics, he declared that "women are not called to the priesthood." In San Francisco, **Sept. 27**, 2,000 persons demonstrated in protest against the Pope's strictures on homosexual behavior. In an address, the Pope emphasized the love of God for all people and His forgiveness of sin. Sixty-two victims of acquired immune deficiency syndrome were among those who received the Pontiff's blessing. In Detroit, **Sept. 18**, Donna Hanson, representing 52 million lay Catholics, appealed to John Paul to give lay people a greater voice in the Church, and the Pope responded by warning against confusing the roles of priests and laity. Concluding his U.S. tour, **Sept. 19**, the Pope visited the heavily Polish city of Hamtramck, Mich., and then, in an address in Detroit, declared that the "ultimate test" of America's greatness was "to respect every human person, especially . . . those as yet unborn"—a reference to abortion. The Pope flew to Canada and conducted a mass, **Sept. 20**, for 4,000 Indians at Fort Simpson, Northwest Territories. He then returned to the Vatican.

Plagiarism Ends Biden's '88 Race — Sen. Joseph Biden (Del.) bowed out of the race for the 1988 Democratic presidential nomination after it became known that he had borrowed passages from speeches by other public figures without attributing them and that he had exaggerated his academic credentials. In a story datelined, **Sept. 11**, the *New York Times* compared a summation Biden had given at a debate in Iowa with excerpts from a speech by Neil Kinnock, leader of Britain's Labour Party. The words of a long passage were nearly identical, with Biden applying details of Kinnock's life and ancestry to himself and his own family. Subsequently, the press cited similarities between Biden speeches and those by Robert Kennedy and Hubert Humphrey. After it was reported that he had been disciplined by Syracuse University for plagiarism, Biden said, **Sept. 17**, that he had been failed in the course but had passed after repeating it. He said he had almost always credited Kinnock when quoting him. After an additional revelation that he had described himself in a talk in New Hampshire as a better student than he actually was, Biden withdrew as a candidate, **Sept. 23.** The story then took a bizarre turn. Gov. Michael Dukakis (Mass)., regarded as one of the foremost contenders for the nomination, denied reports, **Sept. 28**, that his staff had leaked the documentation unfavorable to Biden. Then, on **Sept. 30**, Dukakis announced that his campaign manager, John Sasso, had resigned after admitting that he had provided videotapes of Biden's speeches to reporters. Another aide, Paul Tully, resigned after admitting that he had told *Time* magazine, untruthfully, that the Dukakis campaign had not spread information about Biden.

Robertson Gains in Early '88 Tests — The contest for the 1988 Republican presidential nomination began to move into the range of serious politicking in September. In a widely publicized straw poll at an Ames, Iowa party gathering, **Sept. 12**, the Rev. Pat Robertson easily defeated his better known rivals. Sen. Robert Dole (Kan.) was second and Vice Pres. George Bush ran third. None of the 3 had formally announced his candidacy. Transportation Secretary Elizabeth Dole announced, **Sept. 14**, that she would step down from her Cabinet post, effective **Oct. 1**, to join her husband's presidential campaign. Robertson, who had not been taken seriously as a likely nominee, also seemed strong in Michigan, where his forces joined with those of Rep. Jack Kemp (N.Y.), **Sept. 15**, to prevent some 1,200 Bush supporters from participating in the state's delegate-selection process. On the Democratic side, Rep. Patricia Schroeder (Col.) announced, **Sept. 28**, that she would not seek the presidential nomination. She had been campaigning nationally, but had raised less than half of the $2 million she had said that she needed for the campaign. She said she had not been able to figure out how to run and continue to serve her constituents.

UAW and Ford OK Contract — The United Automobile Workers and the Ford Motor Company reached a tentative new 3-year contract settlement in September. As negotiations neared their conclusion, a **Sept. 14** strike deadline passed without a walkout. The tenative settlement of **Sept. 17** guaranteed that Ford's 104,000 workers would not be laid off unless the industry as a whole went into a decline. Ford agreed to close no plants during the term of the contract. The workers would get a 3 percent increase in their base wage in the first year and would be given 3 percent lump-sum payments in the next 2 years.

U.S. Observes Constitution Bicentennial — The 200th anniversary of the signing of the U.S. Constitution was observed, **Sept. 17.** At the principal celebration, in Philadelphia, Pres. Ronald Reagan stood near Independence Hall and asserted, "In a very real sense, it was then—in 1787—that the revolution truly began." He said it was a revolution "to free man from tyranny of every sort and secure his freedom the only way possible in this world; through the checks and balances and institutions of limited, democratic government." Former Chief Justice Warren Burger, chairman of the Bicentennial Commission, struck a replica of the Liberty Bell. Floats and marching bands containing citizens from all 50 states paraded past Independence Hall.

International

Aquino Shakes Up Cabinet — In the wake of the short-lived but serious military revolt of late August, Philippines Pres. Corazon Aquino revamped her government in September. Commenting on the cause of the revolt, **Sept. 1**, Army Chief of Staff Fidel Ramos said that the factionalism was a serious problem in the armed forces and that army pay must be increased sharply. He also called for a review of the government's fight against Communist and Moslem rebels. The Aquino government said, **Sept. 2**, it would back the pay raise. The government said, **Sept. 2**, that 12 government troops, 19 insurgents, and 22 civilians had been killed in the August fighting. Of the 1,350 soldiers who had joined the revolt, 1,033 were in custody. On **Sept. 9**, more than 2 dozen Cabinet members and other officials offered to resign to permit Aquino to restructure the government. Vice-Pres. Salvador Laurel, **Sept. 16**, confirmed his resignation from his second post, foreign minister, saying he had fundamental differences with Aquino on the Communist insurgency. Aquino also replaced her finance minister. On **Sept. 17,** she removed her closest adviser, Joker Arroyo, and another assistant. Both had been regarded as leftists by the military.

Persian Gulf Fighting Continues — The U.N. Security Council, in an attempt to settle the Iran/Iraq war, **Sept. 4,** approved a peace mission to the Middle East by Secretary Gen. Javier Pérez de Cuéllar. An Iranian surface-to-surface missle struck the coast of Kuwait, **Sept. 4,** and Kuwait, **Sept. 5,** expelled 5 Iranian diplomats. Iraq said, **Sept. 9,** it had revenged the attack on Kuwait by bombing 13 cities, oil facilities, and other sites in Iran. Pérez de Cuéllar met separately with Iranian and Iraqi leaders between **Sept. 11** and **15,** but with no announced evidence of success. Within hours after his departure, the combatants resumed attacks on each other. A U.S. helicopter gunship fired on and hit an Iranian ship laying mines in the Gulf, **Sept. 21.** Three Iranian sailors were killed and 26 taken prisoner. The captives were returned to Iranian control, **Sept. 26.**

German Pilot Gets Soviet Prison Term — The teen-age pilot who flew a small plane from Helsinki to a dramatic landing in Red Square in Moscow in May was sentenced to 4 years in a Soviet labor camp. Mathias Rust, 19, of West Germany asserted on the opening day of his trial, **Sept. 2,** that he had come on a peace mission and had hoped to meet with Soviet leaders. The prosecution emphasized the danger to aircraft and to people on the ground that Rust had presented. Rust pleaded guilty to violating the Soviet border and international flight rules, and he was found guilty of "hooliganism." He was sentenced, **Sept. 4.**

Superpowers Close to Missile Treaty — The United States and the Soviet Union reached tentative agreement on a worldwide ban on medium-range nuclear missiles. Earlier, on **Sept. 5,** 3 members of the U.S. House visited a Soviet radar facility and later challenged the Reagan administration's claim that it was part of a system to guard against nuclear attacks. The 1972 antiballistic missile treaty had banned most such defenses. The Congressmen were allowed to take photographs and videotapes. Progress on the superpower arms talks emerged from meetings, **Sept. 15-17,** in Washington, D.C. between U.S. Secretary of State George Shultz and Soviet Foreign Minister Eduard Shevardnadze and their staffs. They signed an agreement, **Sept. 15,** to create "risk-reduction centers" to help avoid an accidental nuclear war. In the move toward the treaty on intermediate nuclear forces (INF), the U.S. agreed, **Sept 15,** that it would begin removing its missiles from Europe as soon as the treaty became effective. The Soviet Union agreed, **Sept. 17,** that West Germany's 72 Pershing missiles would not be included in the treaty, and, in return, Shultz reportedly said that the nuclear warheads for the missiles, which the United States controlled, would be dismantled. Soviet leader Mikhail Gorbachev said, **Sept. 17,** an INF treaty could be concluded by the end of the year and would pave the way for a treaty on long-range weapons in 1988. Pres. Ronald Reagan announced, **Sept. 18,** that the 2 sides had reached a tentative agreement for worldwide elimination of INF weapons. He said the 2 countries would next seek to reduce strategic (long-range) weapons by 50 percent. Reagan said arrangements would soon be made for a summit meeting with Gorbachev in the United States.

East German Leader Visits West Germany — Erich Honecker, who had presided over the construction of the Berlin Wall in 1961, came to West Germany in September—an unprecedented visit for an East German leader. At a banquet, **Sept. 7,** West German Chancellor Helmut Kohl said that reunification of the 2 Germanys would be in accord with the wishes of the German people, but Honecker replied by stressing the "realities" of the existence of 2 soverign German states. A communiqué issued, **Sept. 8,** outlined agreements in the fields of science, the environment, and nuclear safety. Honecker met with West German industrialists, **Sept. 9,** and on **Sept. 10,** he visited his birthplace at Wiebelskirchen, in Saarland, for the first time since the 2 German states were created in 1949.

Increased Aid for Contras Sought — Secretary of State George Shultz said, **Sept. 10,** that the administration would ask Congress for $270 million in military and nonlethal aid for the Nicaraguan contras for an 18-month period, from Sept. 30 through the rest of the Reagan presidency. By the end of September, the Sandinista regime in Nicaragua had taken several steps in response to the peace plan approved in August by 5 Central American countries. A National Reconciliation Commission was formed with Cardinal Miguel Obando y Bravo, a critic of the Sandinistas, as its head. An opposition newspaper, *La Presna,* was permitted to reopen, and the government lifted a 21-month ban on Radio Católica, another opposition voice. Pres. Daniel Ortega said his government was ready to do what was necessary to achieve a cease-fire with the contras.

General

Anti-Cholesterol Drug Approved — The U.S. Food and Drug Administration, **Sept. 1,** approved a new drug to lower the levels of cholesterol in the blood. High blood cholesterol was regarded as the most important factor related to atherosclerosis and coronary heart disease. Some 20 million Americans had risky levels of cholesterol. The drug, lovastatin, would be sold by its developer, Merck & Company, under the trade name Mevacor. Medical experts warned that the drug, which could cost users $3,000 a year, was not a substitute for proper diet and exercise, but should be used only when diet and exercise failed to lower cholesterol levels.

Siamese Twins Are Separated — Seven-month-old Siamese twin brothers were separated, **Sept. 5** and **6,** in a 22-hour surgical marathon that involved a 70-person medical team at Johns Hopkins Hospital in Baltimore. The boys, Patrick and Benjamin Binder, who were born in West Germany, were attached at the back of the head. They shared a broad area of skull and brain tissue. For one hour during the unprecedented surgical procedure, their blood supplies were drained, their hearts were stopped, and their brain function was reduced. At this time, neurosurgeons were able to cut through the vein they shared that drains much of the brain. The severed vessel was then reconstructed in each twin and circulation was restarted. After the operation, the twins were reported to be in critical but stable condition.

Treaty to Protect Ozone Signed — A treaty designed to preserve the ozone layer in the atmosphere was approved, **Sept. 16,** by representatives of 24 countries in Montreal. The signatories agreed to freeze world production of the most commonly used chlorofluorocarbons—chemicals used in refrigerators, solvents, and aerosol propellants—which were regarded as responsible for the destruction of the ozone. The treaty also provided for a 50 percent reduction of world output of the chemicals by 1999. Production of another group of compounds, halons, would be frozen in 1992. The treaty would become effective when ratified by 11 countries representing at least two-thirds of all consumption of chlorofluorocarbons.

Disasters — The government of Bangladesh reported, **Sept. 2,** that floods beginning in early August had left 24 million—one-fifth of the population—homeless or without food. At least 670 people had died. . . . Colombian officials said, **Sept. 28,** that an avalanche of mud killed at least 175 persons at Medellin.

OCTOBER

National

Court Nominee's Chances Fade — During early October it became apparent that Judge Robert Bork, who had bee nominated by Pres. Ronald Reagan to a seat on the U.S Supreme Court, would not be confirmed by the U.S. Senate Almost every day brought new declarations of oppositio from individual senators. Conservative and moderate south-ern Democrats disappointed the White House by heedin the opposition to Bork by their black constituents—whos votes in most cases had been decisive in sending the senator to Washington. Sen. Arlen Specter (R, Pa.), a previously un-committed member of the Judiciary Committee, came ou against Bork, **Oct. 1.** Reagan lobbied individual senator and on **Oct. 3,** in his weekly radio address, he urged Bor supporters to flood Capitol Hill with appeals for him. H warned that Bork foes, in the intensity of their oppositio were trying to politicize the court system. Democrats ob-jected that Reagan himself had politicized the Court in 198 when he campaigned for GOP senatorial candidates con-tending that a Republican Senate would approve his conse vative nominees. Sen. Alan Cranston (D, Cal.), the Democratic whip, said, **Oct. 5**, that a majority of 53 senators were firmly aligned against Bork. The Judiciary Committee, **Oct. 6**, voted 9-5 to recommend to the full Senate that the nomination be rejected. Sen. Howell Heflin (D, Ala.), the last uncommitted member, said he was voting against Bork because of his concern that Bork might be an extremist. Bork said, **Oct. 9**, that he would not ask that his nomination be withdrawn. He said if he withdrew the "campaign of distortions" against him "would be seen as a success, and it would be mounted against future nominees." Reagan, angered by the impending defeat of the nomination, vowed, **Oct. 13**, to send up another nominee who would upset the Democrats "just as much" as Bork had. Responding to further criticisms from the president, Sen. Terry Sanford (D, N.C.) said, **Oct. 14**, that opponents of Bork were tired of having their integrity impugned, their sincerity questioned, and their intelligence insulted. The majority report of the Judiciary Committee, issued **Oct. 15**, asserted that Bork was unfit for the Court because he was insensitive to individual rights and liberties.

Stock Market Prices Plunge — The Dow Jones industrial average, the most widely followed barometer of stock market activity, suffered its three biggest one-day point losses ever during the first half of October. A decline of 91.55 in the average on **Oct. 6** was attributed to concern over rising interest rates. On **Oct. 7**, major banks raised their prime lending rates from 8.75 percent to 9.25 percent, the fifth increase of the year. The Commerce Department reported, **Oct. 14**, that the U.S. trade deficit had shrunk to $15.7 billion in August, but it had been widely expected that the deficit would be much smaller. As a result, stock prices fell again, with the Dow Jones average declining by 95.46 points. On **Oct. 16**, the Dow tumbled 108.36 points, the first time the Dow had lost 100 points in a single session. In terms of percentages, the declines of October 1987 were still substantially smaller that the disastrous declines of October 1929. By **Oct. 16**, the Dow Jones average had slipped some 450 points below its all-time August highs.

Robertson, Jackson, Bush in '88 Field — Three more aspirants officially declared for president in early October. Shortly after resigning his Christian ministry, Pat Robertson announced his candidacy for the Republican nomination in New York City, **Oct. 1**. He stood in front of a brownstone in a predominantly black area where, he said, 27 years earlier God had called him to minister to the poor. The Rev. Jesse Jackson formally launched his second campaign in Raleigh, N.C., **Oct. 10**. He called Raleigh the heart of "the new South," an apparent target of his campaign. Polls showed Jackson with the support of about 20 percent of Democratic voters, more than any other contender. Vice Pres. George Bush officially began his second try for the Republican nomination—he had lost to Ronald Reagan in 1980—in a speech in Houston, **Oct. 12**. Not since 1836 had an incumbent vice president been elected directly to the presidency. A loyal supporter of Pres. Reagan, Bush was expected to distance himself somewhat from the president as the campaign unfolded in order to broaden his appeal.

International

Tibetans Protest Chinese Rule — Protests by Tibetans against Chinese control of Tibet turned violent in October. The initial demonstration, **Sept. 27**, calling for Tibetan independence had led to the arrest of at least 27 Buddhist monks. A crowd of Tibetans stoned and burned a police station in Lhasa, **Oct. 1**, and 9 persons were reported to have died. The official paper of China's Communist party, **Oct. 3**, blamed the trouble on the Dalai Lama, Tibetan Buddhism's highest religious figure, and his "clique." Chinese police, **Oct. 5**, occupied part of Jokhang Cathedral, center of Buddhist religious life in Tibet. The U.S. Senate, **Oct. 6**, condemned China for its crackdown. The Dalai Lama urged his followers, **Oct. 7**, to continue their protests against Chinese rule but to do so peacefully. Meanwhile, the Chinese continued to arrest more Tibetans.

U.S. Involvement in Persian Gulf Continues — U.S. helicopter gunships sank 3 Iranian patrol boats in the Persian Gulf, **Oct. 8**. At least one had fired on a patrolling helicopter. At least 2 Iranians were killed. The American-owned tanker *Sungari*, flying the Liberian flag, was struck by an Iranian missile, **Oct. 15**, in Kuwaiti waters. In a more serious incident, the Kuwaiti tanker *Sea Isle City*, flying the American flag, was struck by a missile, **Oct. 16**, and 18 were injured. (Editor's note: at press-time, U.S. military reprisal was reported to be under consideration.)

Reagan Pressures Nicaragua — Pres. Ronald Reagan stepped up his pressure on the Sandinista government of Nicaragua. By **Oct. 3**, the White House had developed a list of demands that went beyond the terms of the Central American peace agreement announced in August. To avert an administration request for more military aid to the contras, Nicaragua would have to conduct a free election before the one scheduled in 1990, free 2,300 political prisoners, negotiate a cease-fire with the contras, allow them to run for office, and expel Soviet and Cuban military advisers. Addressing the Organization of American States in Washington, **Oct. 7**, Reagan said he would fight for renewed aid for the contras until "full democracy is established." Addressing the U.N. General Assembly, **Oct. 8**, Pres. Daniel Ortega of Nicaragua called on the U.S. government to enter direct talks with his government. On **Oct. 13**, Pres. Oscar Arias of Costa Rica, the instigator of the peace plan approved by 5 Central American countries in August, was awarded the Nobel Peace Prize.

U.S., Canada OK Trade Pact — After 16 months of negotiations, representatives of the United States and Canada agreed, **Oct. 3**, to a historic trade pact that would eliminate tariffs and other barriers to trade by the year 2000. Tariffs would be eliminated in 3 stages, some immediately, some in 5 years, and the rest in 10 years. Most trade between the 2 countries already entered duty-free. Under the agreement, arbitration panels would handle unresolved disputes. The agreement was subject to the approval of the U.S. Congress and the Canadian Parliament.

Soviets to Pay U.N. Debts — The Soviet Union announced, **Oct. 15**, that it was paying all its debts to the United Nations, including $197 million owed for peacekeeping operations. These bills dated from 1973. The USSR had just paid $28 million to bring it up to date on its regular contributions. The United States, having refused to pay for activities it did not approve, owed a total of $414.2 million to the United Nations.

General

Quake Hits Southern California — A moderately severe earthquake, measuring 6.1 on the Richter Scale, struck southern California, **Oct. 1**, causing 6 deaths, more than 100 injuries, and $59 million in damages. At least 15 aftershocks were felt within a few hours, and more occurred in subsequent days. Many residents chose to live outdoors. The city of Whittier was hardest hit. The quake leveled buildings and started fires. It was the worst to hit the area since 1971. A truly immense quake was being forecast for California within the next 50 years.

Falwell Quits PTL Ministry — The Rev. Jerry Falwell resigned as chairman of the PTL television ministry. A Federal bankruptcy court, **Oct. 7**, rejected a reorganization plan submitted by Falwell and ordered creditors of PTL to submit their own plan. The ministry was more than $50 million in debt. Falwell and the entire board then resigned, **Oct. 8**.

Pro Football Strike — A strike by pro football players ended in October without achieving its objectives. The National Football League Players Association ended its 24-day strike, **Oct. 15**. Negotiation committees had reached agreement on 8 minor issues but not on free agency, the players' biggest demand, which would permit them to move from one club to another when contracts expired. During the strike, the club owners brought in nonunion players who performed erratically before small crowds and reduced television audiences. The strike was weakened when players defected and began to return to their teams. The union filed an antitrust lawsuit against the league.

Disasters — South African officials, **Oct. 3**, put the death toll at 174, with 86 missing, in floods that had struck in Natal Province. The floodwaters caused an estimated $500 million in damage . . . From 50 to 100 persons drowned or were killed by sharks, **Oct. 6**, when a boat carrying them from the Dominican Republic to Puerto Rico capsized and sank.

(See *Addenda* for late-breaking news.)

Summary of Iran-Contra Affair: Nov. 1986-Aug. 1987

The scandal first came to light, **Nov. 3, 1986,** in a report in *Al Shiraa,* a pro-Syrian magazine in Beirut, which quoted Iranian sources as saying that former U.S. National Security Adviser Robert McFarlane had come in secret to Teheran to discuss a cessation of Iranian support for terrorists in return for the delivery of spare parts for weapons. Hojatolislam Hashemi Rafsanjani, speaker of the Iranian parliament, confirmed, **Nov. 4,** that McFarlane and 4 other Americans had arrived illegally in Iran and had been detained and then expelled after making the proposal reported by *Al Shiraa.* News reports in the United States in early November linked the release of U.S. hostage David Jacobsen in Beirut and the freeing of 2 other U.S. hostages during the past year to an agreement by the United States to transfer military spare parts to Iran by way of Israel. The Reagan administration had stated publicly that it would not negotiate with terrorists, and the 1979 Arms Export Control Act had embargoed arms sales to Iran.

Meeting with congressional leaders, **Nov. 12,** Reagan acknowledged authorizing the arms shipment; members of Congress said later they had had no previous notice of the arms deals with Iran, although the law required the president to notify Congress of covert operations and of arms shipments to Iran. In a televised speech, **Nov. 13,** Reagan said the United States had sent "defensive weapons and spare parts" to Iran—but not enough to fill one planeload. He said he had sought to improve relations with Iran, to end the Iran-Iraq war, to eliminate terrorism by Iran, and to "effect the safe return of all hostages"—though he insisted that the arms sales were not part of an actual deal to free the hostages. He said McFarlane had gone to Iran with the equipment in the spring of 1986. Press reports said that in January 1986 Reagan had signed an executive order reversing the key legal barrier imposed by the 1979 law—but, to confuse matters further, shipments to Iran had begun 4 months before that, in September 1985. On **Nov. 14,** the Arab League, a supporter of Iraq in its war with Iran, denounced what it called a "flagrant violation" of America's declared neutrality in the war.

At a **Nov. 19** news conference, Reagan acknowledged that the arms deal was controversial and that some top advisers had opposed it. He said the responsibility for the decision and the operation "is mine, and mine alone." The president said the United States had sold 1,000 TOW antitank missiles and spare parts for Hawk antiaircraft missile batteries, but added that no more arms would be sent to Iran. He denied that the United States had condoned the shipment of arms to Iran by any other countries, contradicting a previous statement by Donald Regan that Israel had shipped arms. After the press conference, the White House issued a statement acknowledging "a third country [was] involved in our secret project with Iran."

Appearing briefly before reporters, **Nov. 25,** Reagan said, "I was not fully informed on the nature of one of the activities undertaken in connection with this initiative." He announced that John Poindexter, his adviser for national security affairs, had resigned, and that Lt. Col. Oliver North, a member of the National Security Council staff, had been relieved of his duties. He said he would appoint a review board to study the role and procedures of the NSC staff. Attorney Gen. Edwin Meese 3d followed the president's statements by announcing that profits from the arms deal had been transferred to antigovernment forces, known as contras, who, with the support of the Reagan administration, were fighting to overthrow the leftist Sandanista government in Nicaragua. Based on his own inquiries undertaken at Reagan's request, Meese reconstructed this sequence of events:

Between January and September, the Central Intelligence Agency at the behest of the NSC sent $12 million in weapons to Israel. Representatives of Israel sold the arms to Iran for $10 million to $30 million more than their cost. The Israelis returned $12 million to the CIA, which reimbursed the Pentagon. Someone, operating with North's knowledge, then put the rest of the money into Swiss bank accounts controlled by the contras. Meese said that North was the only government official who knew precisely about these events, but that Poindexter knew something was going on and that McFarlane—who by then was out of government—had learned of the diversion of funds in the spring.

North, according to subsequent press reports, had been involved in other foreign policy activities, including the civil war in Nicaragua, the invasion of Grenada in 1983, and the airborne capture of the hijackers of the *Achille Lauro* cruise ship in 1985.

Adolfo Calero, a leader of the contras, denied, **Nov. 25,** that his group had received any of the money. The Israeli government acknowledged, **Nov. 26,** its involvement in the secret shipment of arms to Iran but denied any role in providing funds for the contras. Donald Regan, seeking to emphasize his lack of knowledge of the widening affair, asked reporters, **Nov. 26,** "Does a bank president know whether a bank teller is fiddling around with the books? No."

Pres. Reagan, **Nov. 26,** named a 3-member review board to investigate the NSC. Members were John Tower, a former senator from Texas, chairman; Brent Scowcroft, a former NSC adviser for Pres. Gerald Ford; and Edmund Muskie, a former senator and secretary of state. Administration officials said, **Nov. 27,** that on the previous weekend North had destroyed documents from the NSC files. The Senate Intelligence Committee announced, **Nov. 28,** that it had begun to investigate the affair. In an inteview with *Time* magazine made public **Nov. 30,** Reagan called North a national hero and blamed the press for playing up the Iran-contra revelations.

The Senate committee investigation opened behind closed doors, **Dec. 1,** with testimony by McFarlane. North (**Dec. 1**) and Poindexter (**Dec. 3**) declined to testify, invoking their right against self-incrimination provided by the 5th Amendment to the U.S. Constitution. Reagan, **Dec. 2,** named Frank Carlucci, former deputy director of the CIA, as his new national security adviser. The president also called for the appointment of an independent counsel, formerly known as a special prosecutor, to investigate the Iran-contra affair. Vice Pres. George Bush said, **Dec. 3,** that "clearly mistakes were made" by the administration, but said he knew nothing of the diversion of funds to the contras or the paying of ransom for the hostages.

Shultz told the House Foreign Affairs Committee, **Dec. 8,** that he was, "to put it mildly, shocked" to learn that the White House, without informing him, had approached directly the U.S. ambassador to Lebanon, John Kelly, to enlist his help in arranging the arms deal. Shultz said that Assistant Secretary of State Elliott Abrams had persuaded the Sultan of Brunei to give money to the contras through a Swiss bank account. McFarlane told the committee, **Dec. 8,** that Reagan had approved Israeli shipments to Iran as early as August 1985. Poindexter and North declined, **Dec. 9,** to answer the committee's questions. CIA Director William Casey told a closed session of the committee, **Dec. 10** and **11,** that CIA officials had erred seriously in allowing North to use the agency's resources for the arms shipments. Casey said Reagan had told him not to tell Congress about the shipment of arms to Iran.

A Saudi Arabian billionaire, Adnan Khashoggi, said in a **Dec. 10** interview that he had arranged the financing for the purchase of U.S. arms by Iran, but that the Saudi government was not involved. An Iranian arms dealer, Manucher Ghorbanifar, said, **Dec. 11,** that he had gone to Lebanon to arrange the release of U.S. hostages in exchange for U.S. arms sales to Iran. The 2 men denied that they had made any money for their efforts. It was later reported that Ghorbanifar had flunked a CIA polygraph test that sought to determine if he could be trusted.

Sen. Joseph Biden (D, Del.), **Dec. 12,** called for an investigation of whether the Justice Department had tried to interfere with an FBI investigation into the Iran-contra affair. The department inspector subsequently opened an inquiry into why the department had asked the FBI in October to delay an investigation. Attorney Gen. Meese had claimed that he knew nothing of the affair until late November. A chronology of events issued by Bush's office, **Dec. 15,** suggested that the administration knew more than it had acknowledged about the supplying of the contras by private U.S. citizens.

The Credit Suisse bank, **Dec. 15,** froze 2 accounts reportedly used by North, retired USAF Gen. Richard Secord and Iranian-born U.S. businessman Albert Hakim to funnel arms-sales profits to the contras. Reagan, **Dec. 16,** proposed that Poindexter and North be granted limited immunity from prosecution to compel their testimony about the affair.

Contradicting McFarlane's testimony, Donald Regan told the Senate committee, **Dec. 16,** that in 1985 the president had disapproved the selling of arms through Israel. Regan said that neither he nor the president had known of the diversion of funds from the sales to the contras. Casey, scheduled to testify, **Dec. 16,** fell ill, and on **Dec. 18,** a tumor—later found to be cancerous—was removed from his brain.

A panel of 3 federal judges, **Dec. 19,** named Lawrence Walsh, a former prosecutor, judge, and deputy U.S. attorney general, as the independent counsel. The panel asked Walsh to investigate support for the contras by anyone in or out of government since 1984, as well as the sales to Iran. On **Dec. 23,** Gen. Secord refused to answer questions by the House Intelligence Committee.

The White House, **Jan. 9, 1987,** released the text of Reagan's Jan. 17, 1986 intelligence finding, depicting the arms sale as part of an effort to promote a more moderate Iranian government. A cover memo written by North said that the sale might be the only hope for freeing the hostages, and said Israel had initiated the plan to send arms to Iran.

Shultz told the House Foreign Affairs Committee, **Jan. 21,** that U.S. and Iranian officials had met as late as December 1986, at which time the Iranians proposed further arms sales and asked for U.S. pressure on Kuwait to free 17 Shiite terrorists in exchange for U.S. hostages. At that point, Shultz directed that the talks be terminated.

The Defense Department said, **Jan. 23,** that antitank missiles delivered to Iran were underpriced by $2.6 million when sold by the department to the CIA. This kept the price below the $14 million figure that would have required that Congress be told of the sale.

The White House confirmed, **Jan. 26,** that Donald Regan, although he had attended several meetings to discuss the arms sales, told Shultz in the spring of 1986 that rumors of such sales "couldn't be true."

In his State of the Union speech, **Jan. 27,** Reagan said he had "one major regret"—that he had not succeeded in his attempt to improve relations with moderates in Iran and free all the hostages. In Teheran, **Jan. 28,** Rafsanjani produced a Bible that Reagan had signed and that North had presented to Iranian officials in October 1986.

The White House announced, **Feb. 2,** that Casey had resigned as director of central intelligence, and that Reagan had nominated Robert Gates, deputy director of the CIA, to succeed him. McFarlane was hospitalized, **Feb. 9,** after taking an overdose of a tranquilizer in an apparent suicide attempt. He soon recovered.

The Tower Commission report, released **Feb. 27,** proved to be a powerful, if unofficial, indictment of the way in which the administration had handled the Iran-contra affair. The 300-page document depicted the president as confused and uninformed, and said that his relaxed "personal management style" had prevented him from controlling or even determining what was being done by his subordinates. The commission put "primary responsibility for the chaos" that descended on the White House on Chief of Staff Regan, who, it said, had given Reagan bad advice and had failed to grasp the serious legal and political problems presented by the Iran initiative. The report said McFarlane did not fully inform Cabinet members about the Iran initiative and that Poindexter had "actively misled" them. Casey was reproached for failing to control the NSC activities and for not telling Reagan what it was up to. The report noted that Shultz and Weinberger, while opposing the Iran initiative, had "actively distanced themselves from the march of events." The report acknowledged that its account of the scandal was "necessarily incomplete," because Poindexter, North, and Secord had refused to testify and because other witnesses and many documents were unavailable.

The report said the Iran initiative had evolved from 2 desires by Pres. Reagan: to free the hostages and to improve ties with Iran in order to check Soviet influence, but it concluded that the arms shipments soon evolved into a simple arms-for-hostages swap. A key question was: When had Reagan approved the shipment by Israel of U.S. arms to Iran? The president had first told the commission that he approved the shipment in August 1985, corroborating the account by McFarlane. In a second interview, Reagan had told the commission that, after discussing the matter with Donald Regan, he recalled that he had approved the shipment only after he had discovered that it had occurred. Reagan had then written to the commission saying that he did not remember when he had approved the shipment. The sequence of events was further obscured, the report said in an appendix, when, according to McFarlane, a chronology of events prepared for Reagan in advance of his Nov. 19 press conference was rewritten several times in an attempt "to blur and leave ambiguous the President's role."

The commission said in its report that it was unable to determine much about the diversion of profits from the arms sales to the contras. It did say that North had directed a private network supplying the contras, calling that another "case study" in the misuse of the NSC. The report rebuked Poindexter for letting North operate "largely outside the orbit of the U.S. government." The report did not challenge the president's claim that he knew nothing of the diversion until 1986.

The report said North had a secret airstrip built for the contras in neighboring Costa Rica in 1985. It said that after Costa Rican Pres. Oscar Arias Sanchez threatened to expose the airstrip, North called Arias and threatened that the U.S. would cut off foreign aid to Costa Rica if he did so.

Donald Regan resigned as White House chief of staff, **Feb. 27,** and Reagan named former Senate Majority Leader Howard Baker (R, Tenn.) to succeed him. Regan's departure had been widely expected after he had feuded with First Lady Nancy Reagan and after widespread criticism of his failure to head off the Iran fiasco. Baker, who had been considering a campaign for the Republican presidential nomination, was generally welcomed as someone who could repair the administration's frayed relations with Congress.

Gates withdrew, **Mar. 2,** as the nominee to head the CIA. He had reportedly had major input into testimony on the Iran-contra affair prepared for Casey in November 1986 that was inaccurate. Some senators were also concerned about Gates's ability to keep the CIA independent of White House pressures. On **Mar. 3,** Reagan nominated FBI Director William Webster as the new CIA director.

Reagan, **Mar. 4,** denounced reports that his wife had played a key role in government decisions or in the dismissal of Donald Regan. Later, on **Mar. 4,** in an address to the nation, Reagan retreated somewhat from his denial that he had sought to trade arms for hostages, asserting "My heart and my best intentions still tell me that is true, but the facts and the evidence tell me it is not." He said that what had begun "as a strategic opening to Iran deteriorated in its implementation into trading arms for hostages." Reagan said he had told the Tower commission that he had known nothing of the diversion of money to the contras. Shultz and Weinberger, **Mar. 5,** rejected the commission assertion that they had sought to distance themselves from the sale of arms to Iran. Weinberger said he and Shultz had argued against the sale to the president many times.

In records made public, **Mar. 5,** Calero revealed that the contras had received $32 million in anonymous contributions during the 2 years when direct U.S. military support had been banned. On **Mar. 6,** he said $200,000 had come to the contras from a Swiss bank account controlled by North, the first confirmation that Iran arms-sale funds had gone to the contras.

House and Senate committees investigating the affair voted, **Mar. 18,** to hold joint hearings, merge their staffs, and share evidence. During a press conference, **Mar. 19,** in response to a question on the Iran arms sale, Reagan said, "I would not go down that road again."

The public hearings by the 26-member Senate and House committees investigating the Iran-contra affair began in May. Gen. Secord, testifying without immunity, appeared before the committee, **May 5-8.** He said that North had recruited him in 1984 to organize delivery by air of weapons for the contras, that McFarlane had asked him in 1985 to play a role in the Iranian arms delivery, and that North first mentioned diverting Iranian money to the contras to him in December 1985. Secord said Iran deposited $30 million in payment for the arms in a Swiss bank account controlled by his partner Albert Hakim in the name of Lake Resources, Inc. Of this, $12.3 million went to the U.S. government to pay for the weapons, $3 million was spent on transporting them, $3.5 million was diverted to the contras, and $1 million went to other projects. Of the remainder, according to Secord, $6.53 million in the Swiss account was for the "benefit" of Hakim, there was an additional $1.36 million in the Lake account, and $2 million could not be accounted for. Secord said he and North decided on what to charge the Iranians, with the desire to aid the contras being one factor. Secord testified that he had taken no money aside from a salary of $6,000 a month from Stanford Technology Trading Group Inc., the company he and Hakim owned jointly. But he admitted that $520,000, which he called a loan, had been transferred to Stanford from a Swiss financial institution controlled by an associate of Hakim.

Secord said North had used some of the Iranian profits to pay employees of the U.S. Drug Enforcement Administration assigned to rescue U.S. hostages in Lebanon. According to Secord, the DEA was not willing to pay the expenses of the agents. Secord said North had told him that on several occasions he had told Reagan about the diversion of money to the contras.

Former CIA Director Casey, whose role in the mystery had appeared to grow larger as the investigation unfolded, died, **May 6**, of pneumonia, 5 months after undergoing brain surgery.

Richard Miller, already named by Carl Channell a fundraiser for conservative causes, as a coconspirator, pleaded guilty, **May 6**, to conspiracy. A former campaign worker for Reagan, Miller had founded a public relations firm used to funnel money from Channell's organization to the Lake Resources account in Switzerland. From there, it was used to arm the contras.

McFarlane, testifying, **May 11-14**, said that Pres. Reagan, reacting to a congressional ban on support for the contras, had repeatedly made clear in public and private that he would not break faith with the contras. He said Reagan had not directly solicited money for the contras from King Fahd, who had doubled his donation from $1 million to $2 million a month after meeting with Reagan in 1985. McFarlane said he had repeatedly briefed Reagan on what his staff was doing to aid the contras. He repeated a previous statement that he had learned about the diversion of the Iranian funds to the contras from North in May 1986.

McFarlane recounted how an Israeli official, David Kimche, had called him in September 1985 and asked him to choose a hostage to be released in exchange for the arms Israel was selling to Iran. McFarlane said he chose William Buckley, the former CIA station chief in Beirut who, as it turned out, had already died under torture. Instead, the Rev. Benjamin Weir was released at that time.

The question of the inaccurate chronology prepared by McFarlane, North, and Poindexter in November 1986 brought an indignant outburst from McFarlane. He insisted that in preparing the chronology he had recalled that Israel had shipped oil-drilling equipment, not Hawk missiles, to Iran in 1985. He said he later accepted Meese's assertion that Hawks had been shipped.

One mystery was solved, **May 12**, when congressional investigators said that $10 million donated to the contras by the Sultan of Brunei and subsequently unaccounted for had in fact been deposited in the Swiss account of a wealthy businessman because North had given the wrong bank account number to Abrams, who had solicited the contribution. A Swiss judge froze the account into which the businessman had transferred the money.

Reversing earlier statement that he did not know the details of aid to the contras, Reagan said, **May 15**, that he had been briefed on contra aid regularly because it was "my idea to begin with." He asserted "As a matter of fact, I was very definitely involved in the decisions about support to the freedom fighters."

Maj. Gen. John Singlaub (ret.), testifying before the committees, **May 20** and **21**, said Abrams had told him he would assure the governments of Taiwan and South Korea that Singlaub had the authority to solicit aid for the contras from them.

Hakim, Secord's business partner, testifying, **June 3** and **4**, acknowledged that he had been motivated by the prospect of profits when he agreed to open the "second channel" to Iran after the arms dealer Ghorbanifar proved unreliable. Hakim described his affection for North and his family and said that, although he knew gifts to government officials were illegal, he had set up a $200,000 account as a "death benefit" for North. He said he had also provided $2 million for North in his will in the event of the deaths of both Secord and himself.

Bretton Sciaroni, counsel to the President's Intelligence Oversight Board, testified, **June 8**. He had written the legal opinion cited by Reagan and others that the Boland amendment banning covert aid to the contras did not apply to the National Security Council. Sciaroni, who had failed his first 4 bar exams and who had taken his White House job before he knew that he had passed the fifth, said his legal opinion was based on talks with North and a NSC lawyer and on a brief review of documents he was told were relevant.

The appearance before the committees, **June 8** and **9**, by Fawn Hall, a part-time model who had been North's secretary, gave a lift to the television ratings for the hearings. Testifying under a grant of limited immunity from prosecution, she said that on Nov. 21, 1986, on North's instructions, she had altered 4 memos dealing with aid to the contras, sent by North to McFarlane in 1985, to make them seem innocuous. She recounted the massive shredding of documents on the last days before North was dismissed from his White House job. She smuggled other documents out of the building by concealing them in her clothing. Hall defended her actions by saying, "Sometimes you have to go above written law."

Glen Robinette, a private security consultant, testified, **June 23**, that he had installed a $13,900 security system at North's home and that North had subsequently written 2 fake letters to conceal the fact that Secord had paid for the system.

Testifying, **June 25**, Assistant Attorney Gen. Charles Cooper described a meeting on Nov. 20, 1986, at which North insisted that Casey tell the Senate and House Intelligence Committees that U.S. officials had believed that Israel had shipped oil-drilling equipment, not missiles, to Iran. Cooper said that Casey and Poindexter went along with this tactic. In a deposition by Abraham Sofaer, legal adviser to the State Department, Sofaer said he had insisted that this false explanation be deleted from the prepared statement that Casey was to give. This was done, though Casey returned to the cover story during the course of questioning by members of the committees. Sofaer said other evidence made him conclude that the administration was trying to cover up the diversion of Iranian money to the contras.

North testified **July 7–10, 13**, and **14**. He said he had come to tell the truth, "the good, the bad, and the ugly." According to North, who was appearing with a grant of limited immunity, the idea of diverting arms-sales profits to the contras had come from Ghorbanifar, and North had thought it "a neat idea." Poindexter and Casey, who was said to be "very enthusiastic," approved of the plan. Casey, in fact, emerged in North's testimony as the driving force behind the diversion and in other efforts in behalf of the contras and in the attempt to keep Congress in the dark. North said he wrote 5 memos recommending the diversion, all of them addressed to Poindexter and all bearing a space for the president's initialed approval. North said he had destroyed 4 of the memos, and the fifth was found by Assistant Attorney Gen. William Bradford Reynolds. North said he had never "personally discussed" the diversion with Reagan, but "assumed that the President was aware of what I was doing and had, through my superiors, approved it."

Revealing a new dimension to the covert White House activities, North said Casey envisioned using profits from the arms sales to fund an ongoing covert network that would flourish independently of congressional appropriations and oversight. North said that some of the projected activities would be conducted with intelligence services from other friendly countries.

North said he was willing to accept the role designed for him by the administration, to be the scapegoat protecting his superiors, including Reagan, but he said he was no longer willing to take all the blame once a criminal investigation got underway. He admitted deceiving Congress on several occasions, because members of Congress, he said, often leaked classified documents. He said McFarlane had told him to include false statements in a chronology that he prepared in November 1986. North said he began destroying documents in October 1986, at Casey's recommendation, after a contra supply plane was shot down in Nicaragua. An assertion that he continued to shred, on Nov. 22, 1986, even in the presence of investigating officials from the Justice Department left members incredulous.

North's bedrock defense of his conduct as a member of the NSC staff for 5 years was that he had believed that all his activities had been authorized by his superiors.

As for the security system installed at his home with profits from the arms sales, North said he had been threatened by the terrorist Abu Nidal and that the government had not been willing to provide protection. He said that his backdated letters indicating he would pay for the security system constituted "probably the grossest misjudgment that I have made in my life."

Poindexter was questioned, **July 15-21,** about the "finding" prepared in November 1985 that authorized the sale to Iran as an arms-for-hostages trade. Though several witnesses had testified as to the existence of the finding, Pres. Reagan said he could not recall signing it and no copy had been found. Poindexter said he had seen Reagan sign the finding, but he (Poindexter) had destroyed it in November 1986 because it was "politically embarrassing."

Poindexter claimed he never saw the 5 memos North said he had written suggesting that Poindexter get Reagan's approval for the diversion of money to the contras. As for the 4 that supposedly disappeared into North's shredder, Poindexter said, "I frankly don't think those existed." He said he had made the decision to allow the diversion. "I felt I had the authority to do it. I thought it was a good idea. I was convinced that the President would, in the end, think it was a good idea. But I did not want him to be associated with the idea." He added, "The buck stops with me." More explicitly, Poindexter said his purpose was to "provide some future deniability for the President if it ever leaked out."

Sen. Sam Nunn (D, Ga.) asked Poindexter about a lunch he had with Casey, Nov. 22, 1986, but Poindexter remembered virtually nothing about it. Nunn observed, "This was an enormously important meeting. . . . And yet, you seem to not recall anything about it except that you had sandwiches." Nunn read a Navy fitness report citing Poindexter's "photographic memory."

An angry Shultz, testifying, **July 23** and **24,** depicted intrigue and duplicity in the White House that added up to "guerrilla warfare." He said he had waged a "battle royal" against the Iran deal, and that Casey, McFarlane, and Poindexter had lied to him and deceived the president in order to perpetuate the Iran initiative and protect themselves. He said U.S. negotiators "got taken to the cleaners" by the Iranians.

Shultz identified Reagan as a strong advocate for the arms sales. Shultz said he warned Reagan, in advance of his disastrous press conference of Nov. 19, 1986, that he was receiving inaccurate information, and he said Reagan responded, "You're telling me things that I don't know, that are news to me." He told the president after the conference that he had made many "wrong or misleading" statements. Shultz said that the CIA tailored its intelligence reports to fit administration policy. Shultz said he had not known in advance of NSC solicitation of money for the contras from foreign countries, aside from the $10 million obtained from Brunei.

Edwin Meese, testifying, **July 28** and **29,** defended his November 1986 investigation of the scandal. He said he had no reason to suppose North would attempt to shred documents and therefore had taken no action to secure his files. Meese acknowledged he had not asked Poindexter whether he had authorized the diversion to the contras, whether he had told Reagan, or who else outside the government might know about it.

Former Chief of Staff Donald Regan testified, **July 30** and **31,** that he had had nothing to do with preparing the false chronology. He said Pres. Reagan had been told all the details about the November 1985 shipment of Hawk missiles by Israel to Iran. Regan recalled a Nov. 10, 1986, White House meeting at which the president defended the arms deal on the ground that Iran was the weaker of the Gulf War combatants and that the weapons would help even up the war; at the time, Iran was generally regarded as having the upper hand over Iraq, but Regan said no one corrected the president. Regan attributed his ouster from the White House to Nancy Reagan, who, he said, told him she wanted everyone who had "let Ronnie down" to leave.

In testimony, **July 31** and **Aug. 3,** Weinberger said he repeatedly tried to stop the arms sales on the ground that there was no moderate element in Iran with whom the United States could negotiate. He said Poindexter and others had kept the sales going by preventing Pres. Reagan from hearing opposing views. Weinberger said that the Army had undercharged the CIA for 4,000 TOW missiles not in order to provide greater profit margins on the sales, but because of "a series of unfortunate but totally innocent errors."

With the conclusion of public hearings, **Aug. 3,** the committee proceeded to interview several witnesses in executive session. Beyond that, they faced the task, in writing their final report, of reconciling the many discrepancies in the testimony that they had heard.

Pres. Reagan said, **Aug. 1,** "I haven't heard a single word that indicated in any of the testimony that laws were broken." In an address, **Aug. 12,** he acknowledged being "stubborn in pursuit of a policy that went astray" but said again he had not known of the diversion of funds. He declared, "The buck does not stop with Adm. Poindexter, as he stated in his testimony. It stops with me. I am the one who is ultimately accountable to the American people." In his response, Sen. George Mitchell (D, Me.) said, "The mistakes were not only in the execution of policies, the major mistakes were in the policies themselves. And the policies were the President's."

How a Bill Becomes a Law

1. A Senator or Representative introduces a bill by sending it to the clerk of the House, who assigns it a number and title. This procedure is termed the *first reading.* The clerk then refers the bill to the appropriate Senate or House committee.
2. If the committee opposes the bill, they immediately *table,* or kill it. Otherwise, the committee holds hearings to listen to opinions and facts offered by members and other interested people. The committee then debates the bill and possibly offers amendments. A vote is taken, and if favorable, the bill is sent back to the clerk of the House.
3. The clerk reads the bill to the House. This is termed the *second reading.* Members may then debate the bill and suggest amendments.
4. *The third reading* is simply by title, and the bill is put to a voice or roll call vote.
5. The bill then goes to the other house, where it may be defeated, or passed with or without amendments. If defeated, the bill dies. If passed with amendments, a joint Congressional committee works out the differences and arrives at a compromise.
6. After its final passage by both houses, the bill is sent to the President. If he signs it, the bill becomes a law. However, he may *veto* the bill by refusing to sign it and sending it back to the house where it originated, with his reasons for the veto.
7. The President's objections are then read and debated, and a roll-call vote taken. If the bill receives less than a two-thirds vote, it is defeated. If it receives at least two-thirds, it is sent to the other house. If that house also passes it by at least two-thirds, the President's veto is *overridden,* and the bill becomes a law.
8. If the President wishes neither to sign nor to veto the bill, he may retain it for 10 days—not including Sunday—after which it automatically becomes a law even without his signature. However, if Congress has adjourned within those 10 days, the bill is automatically killed; this indirect rejection is termed a *pocket veto.*

Major Decisions of the U.S. Supreme Court, 1986-87

(For further information, see *Supreme Court, Chronology*, and *Addenda*)

The 1986-87 Supreme Court term, from October to July, was the first with William J. Rehnquist as chief justice. In the year's decisions, Rehnquist and the court's newest justice, Antonin Scalia, often disagreed with the rest of the court. Frequently, the decisive role in determining which faction would prevail was played by Justice Lewis F. Powell, Jr., who announced his retirement at the end of the term. Of the 189 five to four decisions made over the past 6 years, Powell voted with the majority in 134, or 71%. Although only 25% of those decisions when Powell was part of the majority were on the "liberal" side of the issue, some of the 25% were landmark rulings, including those on abortion and affirmative action.

The court opened its new term, Oct. 5, with only 8 members. It declined to review nearly 1,000 appeals, and agreed to hear 21 cases, including: whether a newspaper had a constitutional right to defy a court order barring publication of certain facts, instead of appealing the order; a challenge to the constitutionality of a 1984 New York City law that prohibited clubs deemed not "distinctly private" from excluding women as members; and whether the Fifth Amendment privilege against self-incrimination barred prosecutors and courts from requiring suspects to help them obtain the suspects' foreign bank records by signing consent forms. Also on its first day, the court left standing: a regulation permitting state-chartered banks that were not members of the Federal Reserve System to underwrite corporate securities; a decision barring publication of author J.D. Salinger's biography unless brief quotations from Salinger's private letters were deleted; and rulings that multibillion-dollar lawsuits against Union Carbide Corp. over the 1984 Bophal chemical plant disaster that killed more than 2,000 people, should be tried in India, not the U.S.

Summaries of notable actions follow. The Court:

Ruled, 5-3, that Arizona could not deny state aid to a private family-planning organization because it provided abortions and abortion counseling. (Nov. 3)

Ruled, 8-1, that employers should make a "reasonable" attempt to accommodate an employee's religion. (Nov. 17)

Ruled, 6-2, to control the efforts of companies to challenge mergers by competitors on antitrust grounds. (Dec. 9)

Ruled, 5-4, that the Constitution did not prohibit independent voters from participating in a political party's primary election if the party permitted this activity. (Dec. 10)

Ruled, 5-4, to strike down as unconstitutional, a federal regulation banning direct political expenditures by non-profit, issue-oriented corporations. (Dec. 15)

Ruled, 6-3, to uphold a California law requiring employers to give women disability leave for pregnancy and childbirth and to guarantee them reinstatement to their jobs. (Jan. 13)

Ruled, 8-0, to uphold the establishment of discount brokerage services by national banks across state lines. (Jan. 14)

Ruled, 6-3, to uphold using evidence obtained improperly by police through an honest mistake. (Feb. 24)

Ruled, 5-4, to uphold an affirmative action program in Alabama that called for promotions of equal numbers of black and white state troopers. (Feb. 25)

Ruled, 8-1, that states may not refuse unemployment benefits to employees fired for refusing to work on the Sabbath. (Feb. 25)

Ruled, 7-2, that a 1973 law prohibiting discrimination against the handicapped in federally-aided programs protected those suffering from contagious diseases, but said the ruling would not apply to someone who posed "a significant risk of communicating an infectious disease to others in the workplace." (Mar. 3)

Ruled, 6-3, that aliens asking for political asylum need not prove a "clear probability" that they would be killed, tortured or otherwise persecuted for their beliefs if returned to their homeland. The Court said asylum could be granted if persecution was "a reasonable possiblity." (Mar. 9)

Ruled, 5-4, to uphold the use of evidence obtained by police under a law found to be unconstitutional, providing the police reasonably believed the law to be constitutional. (Mar. 9)

Declined to hear, thus let stand, an affirmative action plan for the promotion of blacks in the Cincinnati fire department. (Mar. 23)

Ruled, 6-3, to uphold a voluntary affirmative action plan for public employees to correct sex discrimination. In its first ruling on affirmative action for women, the Court said an employer may act voluntarily to correct a "manifest imbalance" in the work force through an affirmative action plan, providing the rights of other workers were not "unnecessarily trammeled." (Mar. 25)

Ruled, 7-2, to strike down a Utah law restricting cable TV's broadcasting of nudity and sex acts that the state considered "indecent," although they were not legally obscene. (Apr. 6)

Ruled, 9-0, to take away a lower federal court protection for Texaco, Inc. against having to post a $12 billion appeals bond in its court fight with Pennzoil Co. (Apr. 6)

Ruled, 5-4, to uphold the state regulation of corporate takeovers. (Apr. 21)

Ruled, 5-4, that defendants who played a major role in a crime resulting in murder could be sentenced to death if they showed a "reckless indifference" to life. (Apr. 21)

Ruled, 5-4, to reject a general racial challenge to the death penalty, as insufficient proof that the defendant in the specific case had been the victim of discrimination. (Apr. 22)

Ruled, unanimously, that states may require private, all-male public service clubs to admit women as members. The Court specified in a footnote that the justices were expressing no opinion about the First Amendment rights of members "in the many clubs and other entities with selective memberships that are found throughout the country." (May 4)

Ruled, 6-3, to specify that one of its three standing tests for obscene material should be based on a national standard—one upon which reasonable people would agree—rather than on local community values." (May 4)

Ruled, unanimously, in two cases, that a 121-year-old civil rights law barring racial discrimination could be applied to prohibit any form of discrimination that Congress deemed racial when the law was passed. (May 18)

Ruled, 5-4, to extend a prohibition against suing the government for negligence involving personnel to include cases where the negligence originated with a civilian employee. (May 18)

Ruled, 6-3, to uphold "preventive detention" before trial if a federal court determined that the suspect was a danger to the public. (May 18)

Ruled, 8-1, to affirm a state court's ruling ordering a disabled veteran to pay child support from veteran's disability benefits, his sole means of support. (May 18)

Ruled, 6-3, that local governments could be liable for damages if their zoning or other regulations deprived landowners of the use of their land, even temporarily. (June 9)

Rule, 5-4, to affirm the use of arbitration to resolve securities-fraud claims, if the agreement between the investor and broker called for arbitration. (June 8)

Ruled, 5-4 against the use of "victim impact statements" at sentencing hearings of a capital case. (June 8)

Ruled, 7-2, to uphold the Federal Extradition Act of 1793, requiring state courts to honor the legal requests of another state to extradite those sought for alleged criminal activity in their state. (June 9)

Ruled, unanimously, to strike down a Los Angeles airport regulation that barred any "First Amendment activities." (June 15)

Ruled, 7-2, to strike down a Louisiana law requiring public schools teaching evolution to teach "creation science" as well. The Court ruled that the 1981 state law violated the separation of church and state required by the First Amendment "because it seeks to employ the symbolic and financial support of government to achieve a religious purpose." (June 19)

Ruled, 7-2, to restrict the use of the mail-fraud law to protection of property rights. (June 24)

Ruled, unanimously, to affirm an exemption for religious groups from the federal law prohibiting discrimination in employment based on religion. However, four of the justices specified that their agreement was restricted to cases involving nonprofit activities of churches. (June 24)

Ruled, 7-2, to affirm Congress's authority to require states to raise the drinking age to 21 or lose federal highway aid. (June 24)

Ruled, 5-4, to uphold the First Amendment right of a public employee to slur the U.S. president privately without punishment. (June 24)

Ruled, 5-4, to disallow damage suits by military personnel against the superior officers or the government, even for violations of constitutional rights. The Court also approved court-martialing of military personnel, even for crimes occurring off base and unrelated to their service. (June 25)

Ruled, 6-3, that law enforcement officers were immune from liability when they conducted an illegal, warrantless search, if they reasonably believed that the search was legal. (June 25)

Major Actions of the 100th Congress, 1987

(For further information, see *Congress, Chronology*, and *Addenda*)

The 100th Congress convened on Jan. 6, 1987. For the first time in the Reagan presidency, Democrats controlled both houses, having regained control of the Senate, 55-45, in the Nov. 1986 elections, and having a 258-177 margin in the House.

Among the problems remaining from the 99th Congress: (1) The Iran-contra arms scandal, which was scheduled to be investigated by both houses; (2) The budget deficit, which had risen to more than $160 billion, although the 1985 Gramm-Rudman balanced-budget law had mandated its reduction to $108 billion in fiscal 1988; (3) Foreign trade—To make U.S. industry more competitive, a trade bill would be the 100th Congress's "highest priority," Speaker-elect Jim Wright (D., Tex.) said on Jan. 2; (4) The environment—the House again passed an extension of the Clean Water Act, which had been vetoed by Pres. Reagan following the previous session; (5) Transportation—Bills included a major highway measure deadlocked in the last Congress over a 555-mile-an-hour national speed limit; (6) Banking and securities—Efforts to shore up the Federal Savings and Loan Insurance Corp.; possible changes in the regulation of the banking system; and possible action to control corporate takeovers; (7) Taxes—a package of technical corrections that would repair errors in the tax reform law of 1986.

Major actions during the first three-quarters of the session included the following:

Legislation Passed by Congress and Signed or Vetoed by Pres. Reagan

Clean Water Act. Despite Pres. Reagan's veto, Congress enacted the Clean Water Act on Feb. 4. The bill authorized $18 billion through 1994 for revolving loan funds and sewer construction grants; $2 billion for cleaning up estuaries and toxic "hot spots" and dealing with polluted runoff in rainwater from urban streets and farms. Pres. Reagan had vetoed an identical measure after Congress adjourned in 1986. The same bill was introduced at the start of the 100th Congress, and was passed 93-6 by the Senate on Jan. 21, and 406-8 by the House on Jan. 8. The vote to override was cast by the House on Feb. 3, 401-26; and by the Senate on Feb. 4, 86-14.

Emergency Aid for the Homeless. Pres. Reagan signed a bill, on Feb. 12, providing the homeless with emergency aid. The House, by voice vote on Feb. 4, had okayed the Senate's version of a bill to earmark $50 million in federal disaster relief funds for aid to the homeless. The bill had passed the House on Jan. 27, 296-79, and the Senate—with several amendments—on Jan. 29, 77-6. To avoid increasing the federal deficit, the $50 million would be transferred within the Federal Emergency Management Agency from its program for disaster relief to its food and shelter program.

Appliance Energy Conservation. Pres. Reagan signed the National Appliance Energy Conservation Act of 1987 on Mar. 17, requiring the Energy Dept. to establish energy efficiency standards for household electrical appliances. The Senate had passed the bill, 89-6, on Feb. 17, and the House had agreed by voice vote on Mar. 3. The bill was almost identical to one pocket-vetoed by Pres. Reagan at the end of the 1986 congressional session.

Highway and Mass Transit. Over Pres. Reagan's veto, Congress passed, on Apr. 2, a $87.5 billion highway and mass transit bill. The bill provided millions of dollars to each state. It also permitted the states to raise the speed limit on rural interstate highways to 65 miles per hour. The bill had been adopted by the House, 407-17, on Mar. 18, and by the Senate, 79-17, on Mar. 20. A separate vote by the House, on Mar. 18, on the speed limit was 217-206 in favor of 65 miles per hour.

National Debt Increase. Pres. Reagan signed a bill on May 15 that temporarily increased the national debt by about $20 million, to $2.32 trillion. This enabled the government to continue borrowing through July 17. Without the increase, the debt limit would have reverted that midnight to $2.111 trillion. Since actual federal debt already exceeded that figure, all federal borrowing would have had to stop.

Statue of Liberty. Pres. Reagan signed a bill on June 19 that prohibited entrance fees at the Statue of Liberty. The Senate had passed the bill on Apr. 7, the House on June 7.

G.I. Bill. Pres. Reagan signed legislation on June 1 to make permanent a new G.I. Bill program set up on a 3-year basis in 1984. The program provided veterans of 3 years of duty and an honorable discharge with $300 per month in education benefits, to a maximum of $10,800. The House approved on Mar. 17, the Senate on May 8. Both houses endorsed the final version on May 13.

Emergency Aid for the Homeless. A bill authorizing more than $1 billion in emergency aid to the country's homeless over the next 2 years was approved by Congress on June 30 and signed by Pres. Reagan on July 22. The measure was approved in final form by the Senate on June 27, 65-8, and by the House on June 30, 301-115. The legislation authorized $443 million in aid to the homeless in fiscal 1987 and $616 million in fiscal 1988, to begin Oct. 1. An Interagency Council on the Homeless would be created to coordinate federal programs for the homeless and to determine the scope of the problem in America.

Other Legislation Passed—Final Action

Underground Nuclear Test. The House of Representatives passed a resolution on Feb. 4 that urged Pres. Reagan to cancel the first underground nuclear test of the year. Press accounts had maintained that the detonation was scheduled for Feb. 5, so the congressional Democrats scheduled a Feb. 4 vote on the resolution. However, the detonation actually occurred at a Nevada site about 86 miles northwest of Las Vegas on Feb. 3. The resolution was passed after the fact.

Peace Plan for Central America. The Senate, in a 77-1 non-binding vote on Mar. 12, endorsed a peace plan for Central America proposed in Jan. by Oscar Arias Sanchez, Costa Rica's president. The plan required El Salvador and Guatemala, as well as Nicaragua, to offer an amnesty and cease-fire to rebels fighting the governments of these countries.

Retaliatory Duties Against Japan. The Senate unanimously passed a resolution on Mar. 20, asking Pres. Reagan to impose duties on a wide range of Japanese electronics as retaliation against Japan's persistent trade surplus and Tokyo's alleged failure to live up to a 1986 agreement barring Japanese companies from selling semiconductor chips to the U.S. for less than a fair market value.

(continued)

Legislation Passed—Preliminary Action

Suspension of Aid to Contras. The House voted on Mar. 11, 230-196, to suspend further aid to the Nicaraguan contras until Pres. Reagan accounted for funds the contras had so far received from the U.S. and elsewhere. The resolution gave the president 180 days to come up with an accounting.

Comprehensive Banking Bill. The Senate approved, 79-11 on Mar. 27, a comprehensive banking bill that would put a one-year moratorium on banks offering new securities, insurance, or real estate services. The bill would also enable the insolvent Federal Savings and Loan Insurance Corp. to borrow as much as $7.5 billion over 2 years in the bond market. Other provisions would limit the establishment of new limited-service banks; give new options to the Federal Deposit Insurance Corp. to close failing banks; and limit the time financial institutions could hold a depositor's check before clearing it.

Catastrophic Medical Costs. The House passed a bill, 302-127 on July 22, to expand the Medicare program to protect disabled and elderly people against "catastrophic medical costs." The 5-year, $33 billion program would be funded totally through higher premiums paid by Medicare beneficiaries. However, only the 40% of these beneficiaries with enough income to file tax returns would pay the increased premiums.

100 Years Ago

Benjamin Harrison, a 55-year-old Indiana Republican, was elected the 23rd U.S. President. President Cleveland actually got a 100,000-vote plurality in the popular vote, but Harrison received 233 electoral votes to Cleveland's 168. Harrison's grandfather, William Henry Harrison, had been the 9th U.S. President; his great-grandfather, Benjamin Harrison, a signer of the Declaration of Independence; and several successive generations of Benjamins Harrisons, distinguished civic leaders.

At least 500 people died in the "Blizzard of 1888," which swept the Northeast, March 12 to 14, leaving New York City without transportation, communication, or food supplies, and causing damages estimated at $25 million.

After more than 40 years of off-again, on-again construction, the Washington Monument opened to the public in Washington, D.C. Standing 555 feet high, the unadorned white marble shaft was the world's tallest masonry structure. It had the same proportions as the ancient Egyptian obelisks.

Congress enacted a U.S. Department of Labor, but it would not have Cabinet status until 1903.

Chicago's Tacoma Building showed the first basic advance in building construction since the Medieval Gothic arch and flying buttress: its steel skeleton employed load-bearing metal throughout its structure. This construction method for tall buildings would revolutionize Chicago's skyline.

Anti-Chinese riots broke out in Seattle. The laborers had been imported to help build the railroads that were pushing westward, and some white workmen feared that the newcomers would depress wages.

International

The Convention of Constantinople guaranteed passage through the Suez Canal to ships of all nations in both peace and war. The guarantee would be honored until 1956-1957, when Egypt would deny the use of the canal to Israeli ships and ships bearing Israeli goods; and then after the Israeli-Arab War, from 1967 to 1975, Egypt would close the canal to all ships.

Brazil's Negro slaves were freed, May 13, under terms of a law put through under Pedro II, ruling since 1840. The 1871 Rio Branco law had freed the children of slaves, an 1885 law had freed slaves over 60, and the new law completed emancipation.

"Jack the Ripper" stalked London, spreading panic, from August to November. Striking at night, the killer slit the throats of at least six East End prostitutes, then disemboweled them. Scotland Yard failed to solve the murders.

Science & Inventions

A new law of chemistry—that if one of the factors in any chemical equilibrium changes, the system readjusts to minimize the change—was formulated by French chemist Henri Louis Le Chatelier.

An alternating-current (ac) electric motor was developed by Croatian-American inventor Nikola Tesla. It would largely supplant direct-current (dc) motors. Tesla's induction, synchronous, and split-phase motors would make possible the production and distribution of alternating current. This would make the universal transmission and distribution of electricity practicable. By the turn of the century, Tesla's name would be as famous worldwide as Edison's.

The first successful electric trolley cars went into service in Richmond, Va., on 12 miles of track laid by engineer-inventor Frank Sprague.

The first patent for a pneumatic bicycle tire was given to Scottish veterinary surgeon John Boyd Dunlop at Belfast, Ireland.

The first ball-point pen patent was issued to J.J. Loud, who designed a coarse marker for rough surfaces. However, the patent would expire before the design could be developed.

The Kodak camera revolutionized photography. Introduced by George Eastman with the slogan, "You press the button, we do the rest," the Kodak made it possible for an amateur to take satisfactory snapshots. The $25 camera, which was small and light, came loaded with a roll of stripping paper long enough for 100 exposures. When the film was exposed, the entire camera was sent to Rochester, N.Y. There the exposed strip was developed and printed, a new strip inserted for $10, and the camera returned to its owner with the finished prints.

Business

The Parker Pen Company was established at Janesville, Wis., by George Safford Parker. It would become the world's largest producer of fountain pens.

A new shorthand system was introduced in Liverpool by John Robert Gregg, an Irish-born inventor. The Gregg system featured symbols that utilized the natural motion of the hand. Gregg would move to the U.S. in 1893, and after a few years his system would spread rapidly here, largely supplanting the Pitman system. Eventually the Gregg system would be adapted into 20 languages.

Arts & Entertainment

The National Geographic Society was founded by Alexander Graham Bell's father-in-law, Gardiner Greene Hubbard. Chartered as a nonprofit scientific and educational organization, the Society promoted research and exploration in geography as well as publishing the monthly magazine, *National Geographic.*

Looking Backward, 2000-1887, a utopian novel by socialist Edward Bellamy, pictured a peaceful, happy U.S. in the year 2000, with industry nationalized and wealth fairly distributed. The book sold 1 million copies.

The poem "Casey at the Bat" was published in the San Francisco Examiner. Author Ernest Lawrence Taylor was paid $5.

Oscar Wilde published "The Happy Prince," a children's story written for his two small sons.

Gilbert and Sullivan's operetta, "The Yeoman of the Guard," opened at London's Savoy Theatre.

Gustav Mahler became musical director of the Budapest Opera.

Auguste Rodin sculpted "The Thinker."

Paul Gaughin painted "The Vision of the Sermon" (Jacob and the Angel), his friend Vincent Van Gogh painted "Sunflowers," and Henri Toulouse-Lautrec painted "Place Clichy."

Milestones

Born in 1888 were French singer Maurice Chevalier; New Zealand-born British author Katherine Mansfield; British adventurer T.E. Lawrence, who would be known as "Lawrence of Arabia;" Anglo-American poet T.S. Eliot; American dramatist Eugene O'Neill; American popular composer Irving Berlin; and Native American Jim Thorpe, one of the greatest all-around athletes in history.

TAXES

Federal Income Tax

Source: Internal Revenue Service

Prepared by the Internal Revenue Service, this section provides an overview of the many changes that will be in effect, for the first time, as a result of the 1986 Tax Reform Act. To simplify the extensive changes made by the new law, the IRS has provided a summary for 14 major categories that includes information on the old law, the changes as a result of the new law, examples, and comments.

Tax Rates

Old Law: There were as many as fifteen taxable income brackets, and the rates began above a zero bracket amount (ZBA).

New Law:

1987—For 1987 there will be five tax rates, ranging from 11 to 38.5%.

1988—Beginning in 1988 there will be two tax rates.

Married Filing Joint Returns and Surviving Spouses

Tax Rate	Bracket
15%	$0 to $29,750
28%	Over $29,750

Married Filing Separately

Tax Rate	Bracket
15%	$0 to $14,875
28%	Over $14,875

Heads of Households

Tax Rate	Bracket
15%	$0 to $23,900
28%	Over $23,900

Single Persons

Tax Rate	Bracket
15%	$0 to $17,850
28%	Over $17,850

Beginning in 1988, upper income married taxpayers filing jointly lose the benefit of the 15 percent tax-rate. A five percent net adjustment to their taxable income will begin at $71,900.

Heads of households' taxable income of between $61,560 and $89,560 will be subject to the five percent adjustment, as will single individuals' taxable income between $43,150 and $89,560. The rate adjustment for married taxpayers filing separately will apply when their taxable income is between $39,950 and $113,300.

1989—Beginning in 1989, the taxable income amounts at which the 28 percent rate starts will be adjusted for inflation.

Comments: The last change in the tax rates came with the Economic Recovery Act of 1981, which lowered the top rate from 70 to 50 percent starting in 1982. That law also provided for adjusting the rates for inflation starting with 1985 returns.

Standard Deductions

Old Law: Under previous law, most taxpayers had the benefit of a zero bracket amount, which was built into the tax rates and schedules.

Zero Bracket Amounts for 1986

Single	$2,480
Head of household	$2,480
Married filing jointly	$3,670
Married filing separately	$1,835

New Law: The new Act replaces the zero bracket amount with a standard deduction consisting of a basic standard deduction and an additional standard deduction. The standard deduction is a flat amount subtracted from adjusted gross income (AGI) for taxpayers who do not itemize deductions. The amount of the standard deduction depends on the taxpayer's filing status, age and blindness.

Taxpayers whose itemized deductions, such as medical expenses, charitable contributions, mortgage interest, state and local taxes, etc., total more than their standard deduction amount do not use the standard deduction. Instead, they subtract their itemized deductions from their AGI to arrive at their taxable income.

Basic Standard Deduction Amouts

For 1987	
Joint returns & surviving spouses	$3,760
Heads of households	$2,540
Single taxpayers	$2,540
Married filing separately	$1,880
For 1988	
Joint returns & surviving spouses	$5,000
Heads of households	$4,400
Single taxpayers	$3,000
Married filing separately	$2,500

Individuals claimed as dependents on other returns may claim the larger of $500 *or* the amount of their earned income up to the amount of the standard deduction to which the taxpayer would be allowed. Earned income includes income from wages, tips, services or self-employed business activity.

Examples: A dependent parent, age 60, had unearned income (interest and dividends) of $900 during 1987. He had no earned income. His standard deduction would be $500.

In 1987, a dependent child had $10,000 unearned income and $100 earned income, he claimed a $500 standard deduction. He is limited to this amount because he is a dependent and because his earned income is less than $500. He would, therefore, have $9,500 in taxable income.

For 1987, a dependent child with $4,000 earned income and $600 unearned income would claim a $2,540 standard deduction because her earned income was greater than the standard deduction. She would have taxable income of $1,460.

Comments: Most taxpayers do not itemize deductions. For example, in 1985 the IRS received 100 million individual income tax returns and only 38 percent claimed itemized deductions. Of course taxpayers who file the long Form 1040 are more likely to be itemizers and 59 percent of the 61 million Forms 1040 filed for 1985 claimed itemized deductions. But the facts show that the majority of taxpayers do not claim itemized deductions.

A person who can be claimed as a dependent by another taxpayer may use up to $500 of the standard deduction to offset unearned income.

Additional Standard Deductions

Old Law: Taxpayers could claim an additional exemption for old age or for blindness. There was no additional standard deduction.

New Law: Beginning in 1987, elderly and blind taxpayers will claim additional standard deductions instead of the extra personal exemptions. Taxpayers who are over age 65 at the end of 1987 qualify for the additional standard deduction for the elderly. Those taxpayers who claim the additional standard deduction for blindness must still attach a doctor's statement to their return.

Additional Standard Deduction Amounts for 1987 and 1988

Joint return, elderly *or* blind (per person)	$600
Joint return, ederly *and* blind (per person)	$1,200
Single, elderly *or* blind	$750
Single, elderly *and* blind	$1,500

The additional standard deductions are effective Jan. 1, 1987. Persons eligible for the additional standard deductions may also use the 1988 basic standard deductions beginning Jan. 1, 1987.

Examples: In 1987, a sixty-five year old woman would claim $3,750 for her standard deduction. Because she qualifies for the additional standard deduction, she would use the 1988 amounts.

1988 standard deduction for single person	$3,000
Additional standard deduction for age	750
	$3,750

On a joint return for 1987, a seventy year old man and a fifty-eight year old blind woman would be entitled to a standard deduction totaling $6,200.

1988 standard deduction for joint returns	$5,000
Additional deduction for husband's age	600
Additional deduction for wife's blindness	600
	$6,200

Exemptions

Old Law: Taxpayers claimed personal exemptions of $1,080 for themselves and an equal amount for their spouses and other dependents in 1986.

Additional exemptions of $1,080 were allowed for aged (over 65) and blind taxpayers for 1986.

New Law: The personal exemption amount rises over three years:

1987	$1,900
1988	$1,950
1989	$2,000

After 1989, the personal exemption amount will be changed for inflation each year.

Beginning in 1988, the personal exemption will be phased out for high income taxpayers by increasing their taxable income by five percent when taxable income reaches $149,250 (married filing joint return). Extra personal exemptions for age and blindness end with tax year 1986; beginning in 1987, additional standard deduction amounts will replace these exemptions. There is no change to the regulations governing exemptions for dependents living in Canada or Mexico.

Comments: For tax year 1985, Americans claimed almost 213 million exemptions on their tax returns, an average of 2.2 exemptions per return.

Capital Gains and Losses

Old Law: A capital gain is the amount of gain arising from the sale of property such as stocks and bonds held for appreciation, as opposed to a business inventory held for resale to customers. Taxpayers who sold property held for more than six months were said to have long-term capital gain; if the property was sold before six months, the gain was called short-term.

Taxpayers can deduct 60 percent of their net capital gain in 1986. The effect was that they paid tax on only 40 percent of their profit.

New Law: Tax reform repeals the capital gains deduction, effective Jan. 1, 1987. The maximum tax rate on individual long-term capital gains will not exceed 28 percent, a rise of eight percent over the prior maximum rate of 20 percent.

The new provisions do not change the character of gains as ordinary vs. capital or as long-term or short-term capital gains. Capital loss treatment will be unchanged; i.e. netted against capital gains and limited to $3,000 of the excess claimed in a given year. In 1987, capital loss can offset other income on a dollar for dollar basis and not the two for one under current law.

Comments: If the sale results in a loss and if the property was held more than six months, the taxpayer may deduct only half the net loss (that is, the excess of long-term losses over long-term gains).

In 1985, 10 million Schedule E's (capital Gains and Losses) were filed with individual income tax returns.

Adjustments to Income

Of the seven statutory adjustments to income allowable in 1985, tax reform affects four of them in various degrees. Each of these is discussed in the text that follows.

Individual Retirement Arrangements (IRAs)

Effective date: Tax years beginning Jan. 1, 1987

Old Law: All taxpayers with earned income could deduct contributions to IRAs up to $2,000 a year on their earned income, whichever is less. Taxpayers who had no earned income could claim a "spousal" IRA if their spouse had earned income. In the latter case, the total contributions for the IRAs could not be more than $2,250 a year.

New Law: The old law applies to 1986, so taxpayers may still claim deductions for 1986 contributions made until April 15, 1987.

All taxpayers with earned income may still make contributions to their IRAs after tax year 1986; however, there may be limits to the amount they can deduct. Income from IRAs will remain tax-free until the taxpayer withdraws it.

For tax year 1987, married taxpayers whose adjusted gross income is less than $40,000 on their joint return may take an IRA deduction whether or not they are active participants in a qualified retirement plan. Single taxpayers in qualified retirement plans may deduct IRAs if their adjusted gross income is below $25,000. The IRA deduction phases out over the next $10,000 of AGI. Married couples filing jointly with AGI over $50,000 or single filers with AGI over $35,000 may not deduct any contributions to IRAs. For married taxpayers filing separately, the IRA is totally phased out for either spouse with AGI of $10,000.

Examples: For every $1,000 over the AGI limit, the allowable IRA deduction is lowered by $200; ($5 AGI = $1 deduction); the computed limit is rounded to the next lowest $10. Thus, a single taxpayer with AGI of $26,785 would have an allowable IRA deduction of $1,650:

Taxpayer's AGI	$26,785
Less unconditional limit	25,000
	$1,785
	÷ 5 = $357, rounded to $350
Therefore:	
Maximum IRA contribution	$2,000
Less limit	−350
Total deductible IRA contribution	$1,650

Spousal IRAs are also reduced if over the AGI limit.

For IRAs, adjusted gross income does not include deductible IRAs, but does include taxable Social Security benefits and passive loss limitations.

Taxpayers who don't have a qualified retirement plan at work may take an IRA deduction up to the lesser of $2,000 or the amount of their earned income regardless of their AGI. However, if one spouse is a qualified plan member, neither spouse may have a deductible IRA.

Taxpayers are considered to belong to their employers' qualified plans if they are eligible, even if they choose not to participate.

Taxpayers may treat deductible IRAs as non-deductible; doing so might help taxpayers whose deductions other than IRAs are more than their taxable income.

Taxpayers who take or continue a loan to make an IRA contribution, may not deduct the interest on that loan.

Comments: In 1984, 15 million returns, just under 16 percent of all returns, claimed IRA deductions totaling $36 million. Preliminary figures for 1985 returns show little increase in this figure.

NOTE—A qualified retirement plan means: (1) a qualified pension, profit-sharing or stock bonus plan; (2) a qualified annuity plan (sec.403(a)); (3) a simplified employee pension plan (sec.408(k)); (4) a plan established for its employees by the federal, state or other political subdivision or by any agency of these entities; (5) a plan described in section 501(c)(18); or (6) a tax-sheltered annuity (sec.403(b)).

Two-Earner Deduction

Effective date: Jan. 1, 1987

Old Law: Under the Economic Recovery Tax Act of 1981, married couples who both worked were allowed a deduction of the lesser of 10 percent of the earnings of the lower paid spouse or $3,000. The purpose of this deduction was to counteract the so-called marriage penalty, which sometimes caused married couples to pay more tax on a joint return than they would have paid as single taxpayers.

New Law: The two-earner deduction is repealed because the tax rates are lower and the personal exemption and standard deduction amounts are higher. The increased personal exemption amounts and standard deductions and the decreased tax rates will relieve the loss of this deduction.

Comments: In 1985, 44 million returns were filed by married couples filing jointly and more than one half of all joint returns claimed the two-earner deduction.

Employee Business Expense

Effective date: Jan. 1, 1987

Old Law: Employees may claim some job-related expenses, such as meals and lodging during overnight travel, and the cost of entertaining clients, as adjustments to income. Even taxpayers who do not itemize can claim these expenses before 1987.

New Law: All employee business expenses except reimbursed expenses will be allowed only as itemized miscellaneous deductions, subject to a floor of 2 percent of the adjusted gross income. Only 80 percent of the cost of meals and entertaining customers is deductible starting in 1987. These expenses are then subject to the two percent floor on miscellaneous deductions.

Comments: In 1985, 6 million returns showed employee business expenses under adjustments to income.

Moving Expenses

Effective date: Jan. 1, 1987

Old Law: Taxpayers who changed jobs usually could deduct moving expenses, including the cost of moving household goods, travel to the new home, househunting trips, and other related expenses. To qualify, the move must be job-related and it must meet several other requirements. The expenses for moving household goods and traveling to a new home had some limits. All other deductible moving expenses, such as househunting trips or temporary quarters, are subject to a $3,000 ceiling. Before 1987, taxpayers who qualified would claim these expenses even if they did not itemize deductions.

New Law: Employees or self-employed persons will now claim moving expenses as miscellaneous itemized deductions, subject to the earlier requirements and dollar limits.

Comments: Almost 1.4 million taxpayers claimed the moving expense adjustment in 1985.

Itemized Deductions

Effective date: Jan. 1, 1987

Old Law: Taxpayers who had certain expenses which added up to more than the zero bracket amount for their filing status could take deductions for the following:

—Medical expenses adding up to more than five percent of adjusted gross income;

—State and local income taxes, real estate taxes, personal property and sales taxes;

—Interest paid on debts, including home mortgage, credit cards and charge accounts, and other loans;

—Charitable contributions;

—Casualty and theft losses exceeding 10 percent of adjusted gross income;

—Miscellaneous deductions including union dues, tax preparation fees and some business expenses like uniform maintenance.

New Law: Taxpayers may take deductions subject to the following changes:

—Medical expenses are deductible above 7.5 percent of adjusted gross income;

—State and local sales taxes are no longer deductible after Jan. 1, 1987;

—Interest deduction has changed as follows:

Nonbusiness interest expense deductions will phase out over four years:

Tax Year	Amount of Personal Interest Deductible
1987	65%
1988	40%
1989	20%
1990	10%
1991	0

—Only mortgage interest on the taxpayer's first and second homes will remain fully deductible;

—Taxpayers who signed mortgages after August 16, 1986, can deduct only the interest on a mortgage amount no larger than the "cost basis" of the home, plus the cost of improvements. The Act makes some exceptions for home equity loans to meet some medical or educational expenses. For purposes of interest deductions, "cost basis" does not include considerations for "rollovers" or involuntary conversions. "Cost basis" usually means the purchase price, unless it is above fair market value;

—Ministers with tax-free parsonage allowances and military personnel with tax-free housing allowances may deduct mortgage interest and property taxes on their residences, effective retroactively.

Charitable contribution deductions no longer are allowed to those who do not itemize deductions. Itemizers may deduct contributions as under earlier rules.

Casualty and theft losses also remain deductible under the old rules.

Miscellaneous deductions now include most employee business expenses, including moving, travel and entertainment expenses. Except for moving expenses, which are deductible in full, the taxpayer must subtract two percent of adjusted gross income from total miscellaneous expenses to figure the deductible amount. The taxpayer can take only 80 percent off the cost of business related meals and entertainment.

Comments: In 1985, 38 percent of all tax returns and 59 percent of all Forms 1040 filed included itemized deductions. This figure represents 38 million returns with total itemized deductions of $277 billion. In 1984, 34 million returns claimed interest deductions totalling $155 billion.

In 1985, 26 percent of non-itemizers claimed charitable contributions on 25 million returns. In 1984, non-itemizers' charitable contributions totalled $1 billion. Itemizers claimed $10 billion for charitable contributions in 1985.

In 1984, employee business expense adjustments to income were $19 billion.

Earned Income Credit

Effective date: Jan. 1, 1987

Old Law: Low income taxpayers with one or more dependent children were eligible for a refundable credit of 11 percent of the first $5,000 of earned income to a maximum credit of $550. Beginning at earned income of $6,500, the credit was reduced, with no credit allowable for those with earned income above $11,000.

New Law: Eligible taxpayers will now be able to claim a top credit of up to $800. More important, the IRS plans to

(continued)

publish a table providing the credit for taxpayers thereby eliminating the need for detailed computation.

Comments: The earned income credit began in 1975 with a top credit of $400 for taxpayers earning $4,000 or less. In 1985, 6 million taxpayers claimed the earned income credit and more than one half of those had adjusted gross income above $5,000, but less than $10,000. It is important for all low income taxpayers to consider this because they may be eligible for the credit even if they do not need to file a return for other reasons.

Income Averaging

Effective date: Jan. 1, 1987

Old Law: Eligible taxpayers could elect to apply a lower tax rate to the taxable year's income that was more than 40 percent higher than the average of their three prior years' taxable income. This election favored taxpayers whose income increased greatly from one year to the next.

New Law: Income averaging is no longer allowed, beginning in 1987.

Comments: Over 3 million taxpayers used income averaging in 1985.

Unemployment Compensation

Effective date: Jan. 1, 1987

Old Law: Taxpayers had to pay tax on part of their unemployment benefits if these benefits plus adjusted gross income totaled more than $12,000 if single, or $18,000 if married filing jointly.

New Law: All unemployment benefits are subject to tax.

Comments: In 1985, taxpayers reported taxable unemployment benefits on more than 7 million tax returns.

Dividend Exclusion for Individuals

Old Law: The first $100 of single taxpayers' qualifying dividends from stocks and similar investments and the first $200 of married taxpayers' qualifying dividends were not subject to tax.

New Law: The exclusion ends for dividends received after 1986.

Comments: In 1985, almost 18 million tax returns reported dividend income.

Taxing Income of Children

Effective date: Jan. 1, 1987

Old Law: Income from assets transferred to minor children was taxed to them at their lower rate. For example, a married couple at the 50 percent bracket could open a savings account for their dependent child, whose asset is taxed at only 11 percent. If the child earned $3,000 of interest, the tax would be $211, based on taxable income of $1,920 ($3,000 − $1,080, the exemption amount for 1986). The parents would have paid $1,500 on the same income.

New Law: Individuals who may be claimed as dependents by other taxpayers may not claim their own exemptions on their return. Further, children under age 14 with at least one living parent may use up to $500 of their standard deduction against unearned income. If the child's unearned income is more than $1,000, that income will be taxed at the child's rate or the parent's rate, whichever is higher.

Comments: The effect of this change is to charge a higher tax rate on children's unearned income by taxing it at the parent's rate when that rate is higher. However, because only the amount of unearned income over $1,000 is subject to this treatment, the child does get the benefit of a lower rate on that amount.

In the above example, assuming the same $3,000 income, the child's taxable income would be $2,500, allowing for the $500 standard deduction. Assuming that the parent's rate is 28 percent, the child's tax rate would be $530 (.11 × $1,000 + .28 × $1,500). At the parent's rate, the $3,000 income would be taxed at a straight 28 percent, or $840. Although the tax is still lower on the child's return, the difference is only $310, compared to $1,289 under the old law.

Social Security Numbers Required for Dependents

Effective date: Returns due on or after Jan. 1, 1988

Old Law: Taxpayers were required to enter on their tax returns Social Security numbers only for themselves and their spouses. They were not required to provide numbers for their claimed dependents.

New Law: Taxpayers must report the Social Security number for each person five years or older claimed as a dependent.

W-4's and the New Withholding

Effective date: Oct. 1, 1987

Old Law: Employees claim withholding allowances on Form W-4, which determines how much will be withheld from their wages for federal tax. Employees may claim allowances for personal exemptions, tax credits and estimated itemized deductions. The form remains in effect until the employee changes or revokes it.

New Law: Because IRS will publish new withholding tables to reflect the major changes in exemption amounts, standard deductions and tax rates, all employees must have filed a revised Form W-4 before Oct. 1, 1987. If the employee does not file a new W-4 by this date, the employer must withhold taxes from wages as if single employees were claiming only one allowance or married employees were claiming only two allowances.

Comments: Although the new requirement did not go into effect until Oct. 1, 1987, employees should have reviewed their withholding tax status around Jan. 1, 1987. The new Act makes dramatic changes to exemptions, the standard deduction and several types of income and deductions. These changes could result in too much or too little tax withheld if the employee waited until Oct. 1, 1987, to take action.

Who Must File

Whether U.S. citizens or residents must file tax returns depends on their gross income, their filing status, their age, and whether they are blind. The filing requirements for tax years beginning after 1986 have changed. Generally, the Tax Reform Act raised the amount of income a person can have before he or she is required to file a return. This means fewer taxpayers will have to file returns.

Generally, U.S. citizens or residents will have to file tax returns if their gross income for the year is at least as much as the amount shown for their situation in the table below.

Filing Status	1987 Gross Income	1988 Gross Income
Single		
Under 65 and not blind	$4,440	$4,950
Under 65 and blind	4,900	4,950
65 or older	5,650	5,700
Married Filing Joint Return		

(continued)

Both spouses under 65 and neither blind	$7,560	$8,900
Both spouses under 65 and one or both spouses blind	8,800	8,900
One spouse 65 or older	9,400	9,500
Both spouses 65 or older	10,000	10,100
Married Filing Separate Return		
All—whether 65 or older or blind	1,900	1,950
Head of Household		
Under 65 and not blind	4,440	6,350
Under 65 and blind	6,300	6,350
65 or older	7,050	7,100
Qualifying Widow(er)		
Under 65 and not blind	5,660	6,950
Under 65 and blind	6,900	6,950
65 or older	7,500	7,550

Example: John and Mary Smith intend to file a joint return for 1987. John's income is all from wages. Mary receives no income subject to tax. Neither John nor Mary is blind. John is 67 years old but Mary will not be 65 until 1990. In 1987 their combined gross income subject to tax will be $9,800. They will have to file a return for 1987 because their gross income will be at least $9,400.

If Mary would be 65 by the end of 1987, they would not have to file a 1987 tax return because their gross income would be less than $10,000.

When To File

You should file as soon as you can after January 1, but not later than April 15, 1988.

If you file late, you may have to pay penalties and interest.

If you know that you cannot file by the due date, you should ask for an extension using Form 4868, Application for Automatic Extension of Time To File U.S. Individual Income Tax Return.

If you are living or traveling outside the United States and Puerto Rico on April 15, you can get an automatic 2-month extension of time to file. Just attach a statement to your return explaining the details.

Which Form To File

You may be able to use Form 1040EZ if:

- You were single and do not claim any dependents.
- You were not 65 or over or blind.
- You had only wages, salaries, and tips, and not more than $400 of interest income.
- Your taxable income is less than $50,000.
- You do not itemize deductions or claim any adjustments to income or tax credits.

You may be able to use Form 1040A if:

- You had income only from wages, salaries, tips, unemployment compensation, interest, or dividends.
- Your taxable income is less than $50,000.
- You do not itemize deductions.

You can also use Form 1040A to claim the deduction for certain contributions to an Individual Retirement Arrangement (IRA) and the credit for child and dependent care expenses.

Since Forms 1040A and 1040EZ are easier to complete than Form 1040, you should use one of them unless using Form 1040 lets you pay less tax. However, even if you meet the above tests, you must file Form 1040 if any of the following situations applies to you.

You must use Form 1040 if:

- Your taxable income is $50,000 or more.
- You itemize deductions.
- You are a qualifying widow(er) with a dependent child.
- You received, as a nominee, interest or dividends that actually belong to another person.
- You received or paid accrued interest on securities transferred between interest payment dates.
- You received any nontaxable dividends or capital gain distributions.
- You are required to fill in Part III of Schedule B for foreign accounts and foreign trusts.
- You had any of the kinds of income shown on Form 1040, lines 11 through 18, 20b, and 21, such as taxable social security or railroad retirement benefits.
- You take any of the adjustments to income shown on Form 1040, lines 23, 25 through 28, or any write-in amount included on line 29.
- You claim any of the credits on Form 1040, lines 41, 44, 45, or any write-in amount included on lines 42 or 46.
- You owe any of the taxes on Form 1040, lines 38, 48 through 52, or any write-in amount included on line 53 (other than advance EIC payments).
- You claim any of the payments on Form 1040, lines 55, 59, 60, or any write-in amount included on lines 60 or 61.
- You file any of these forms:

Form 1040-ES, Estimated Tax for Individuals, for 1987 (or if you want to apply any part of your 1987 overpayment to estimated tax for 1988).

Form 2210, Underpayment of Estimated Tax by Individuals.

Form 2555, Foreign Earned Income.

Form 4563, Exclusion of Income From Sources in American Samoa.

Form 8271, Investor Reporting of Tax Shelter Registration Number.

1987 Tax Rates

Married Filing Jointly or Qualifying Widow(er)

Tax Rate	Bracket
11%	$0-$3,000
15%	$3,001-$28,000
28%	$28,001-$45,000
35%	$45,001-$90,000
38.5%	Over $90,000

Married Filing Separately

Tax Rate	Bracket
11%	$0-$1,500
15%	$1,501-$14,000
28%	$14,001-$22,500
35%	$22,501-$45,000
38.5%	Over $45,000

Single

Tax Rate	Bracket
11%	$0-$1,800
15%	$1,801-$16,800
28%	$16,801-$27,000
35%	$27,001-$54,000
38.5%	Over $54,000

Head of Household

Tax Rate	Bracket
11%	$0-$2,500
15%	$2,501-$23,000
28%	$23,001-$38,000
35%	$38,501-$80,000
38.5%	Over $80,000

Federal Individual Income Tax—Effective (Average) and Marginal Tax Rates for Selected Income Groups: 1954 to 1985

Source: U.S. Dept. of the Treasury.

Refers to income after exclusions. Effective rate represents tax liability divided by stated income. The marginal tax rate is the percentage of the first additional dollar of income which would be paid in income tax. Computations assume the low income allowance, standard deduction, zero bracket amount, or itemized deductions equal to 10 percent of adjusted gross income, whichever is greatest. Excludes self-employment tax.

Adjusted Gross Income Current Dollars	Tax Liability				Effective Rate (percent)				Marginal Tax Rate (percent)			
	1954-1963	1970[1]	1979-1980[2]	1985	1954-1963	1970[1]	1979-1980[2]	1985	1954-1963	1970[1]	1979-1980[2]	1985
Single person, no dependents:												
$5,000	818	683	250	177	16.4	13.7	5.0	3.5	22	19.5	16	12
$10,000	2,096	1,726	1,177	888	21.0	17.3	11.8	8.9	34	25.6	21	16
$20,000	5,900	4,405	3,837	2,845	29.5	22.0	19.2	14.3	50	34.8	34	26
$25,000	8,324	6,091	5,484	4,125	33.3	24.4	21.9	16.5	56	39.0	39	26
$35,000	13,778	10,028	9,194	6,916	39.4	28.1	26.3	19.8	62	46.1	44	34
$50,000	22,788	17,235	16,032	12,067	45.6	34.5	32.1	24.1	72	61.5	55	42
$75,000	39,702	31,560	29,487	22,195	52.9	42.1	39.3	29.6	78	65.5	63	48
Married couple, 2 dependents:[3]												
$5,000	420	290	−500[4]	−550[4]	8.4	5.8	−10.0[4]	−11.0[4]	20	15.0	—	—
$10,000	1,372	1,112	374	132[4]	13.7	11.2	3.7	−1.3[4]	22	19.5	16	24.2[4]
$20,000	3,800	3,213	2,265	1,682	19.0	16.1	11.3	8.4	30	25.6	24	16
$25,000	5,318	4,490	3,497	2,566	21.3	18.0	14.0	10.3	38	28.7	28	18
$35,000	9,037	7,677	6,571	4,916	25.8	21.9	18.8	14.0	47	40.0	37	25
$50,000	15,976	13,674	12,118	9,086	32.0	27.3	24.2	18.2	56	49.2	43	33
$75,000	29,635	25,594	23,404	17.649	39.5	34.1	32.1	23.5	65	56.4	54	42

State Individual Income Taxes: Rates, Exemptions

Source: Tax Foundation, Inc. Data as of August 1, 1987
Footnotes at end of table.

State	Taxable income	Percentage rates	Taxable income	Percentage rates	Personal exemp.[1] Single	Married family head	Each dependent
Alabama[2,4]	First $1,000	2	Over $6,000	5	$1,500	$3,000	$300
	1,001-6,000	4					
Arizona[2,3,4]	First 1,155	2	3,465.01-4,620	5 Less $69	1,996	3,992	1,198
	1,155.01-2,310	3 Less $12	4,620.01-5,775	6 Less $115			
	2,310.01-3,465	4 Less $35	5,775.01-6,930	7 Less $173			
			Over 6,930.01	8 less $243			
Arkansas	First 2,999	1	9,000-14,999	4.5	20 (tax credit)	40	20
	3,000-5,999	2.5	15,000-24,999	6			
	6,000-8,999	3.5	25,000 and over	7			
California[2,3,5,6]	First 3,420	0	31,421-36,660	6	(tax credit) 43	86	14
	3,421-10,420	1	36,661-41,860	7			
	10,421-15,620	2	41,861-47,120	8			
	15,621-20,840	3	47,121-52,360	9			
	20,841-26,160	4	52,361-57,580	10			
	26,161-31,420	5	Over 57,580	11			
Colorado[7]	5% of modified federal taxable income, with special rate tables for nonitemizers.						
Connecticut	7% tax on adjusted capital gains; tax on dividends earned if federal adjusted gross income is greater than or equal to $54,000; tax ranges from 1% on $54,000 through 12% on $100,000 and over.				100	200	
Delaware[9]	First 2,000	0	20,001-25,000	6.6	1,250	2,500	1,250
	2,001-5,000	3.2	25,001-30,000	7.0			
	5,001-10,000	5.0	30,001-40,000	7.6			
	10,001-20,000	6.0	Over 40,000	7.7			
Dist. of Col.[9]	First 2,000	0	10,001-20,000	8	1,025	2,050	1,025
	2,001-10,000	6	Over 20,000	9.5			
Georgia[2]	First 1,000	1	5,001-7,000	4	1,500	3,000	1,500
	1,001-3,000	2	7,001-10,000	5			
	3,001-5,000	3	Over 10,000	6			

State	Taxable Income	Percentage rates	Taxable income	Percentage rates	Personal exemp.[1] Single	Married family head	Each Dependent
Hawaii[9]	First $2,400	2.25	$10,401-20,400	8.25	$1,040	$2,080	$1,040
	2,401-4,400	4.25	20,401-28,400	9.25			
	4,401-6,400	6.25	28,401-40,400	9.75			
	6,401-10,400	7.25	Over 40,400	10.00			
Idaho[5]	First 999	2	4,000-4,999	6.5	Federal exemptions.		
	1,000-1,999	4	5,000-7,499	7.5			
	2,000-2,999	4.5	7,500-19,999	7.8			
	3,000-3,999	5.5	Over 20,000	8.2			
Illinois	Total net income		2.5		1,000	2,000	1,000
Indiana	Adjusted gross	3.4			1,000	2,000	1,000
Iowa[4,7]	First 1,023	0.5	3,070-4,092	3.5	20*	40*	15*
	1,024-2,046	1.25	4,093-7,161	5	*Tax credit		
	2,047-3,069	2.75	7,162-9,207	6	On up to 13% over $76,725		
Kansas[4]	First 2,000	2	5,001-7,000	5	1,000	2,000	1,000
	2,001-3,000	3.5	7,001-10,000	6.5	20,001-25,000	8.5	
	3,001-5,000	4	10,001-20,000	7.5	Over 25,000	9.0	
Kentucky[4]	First 3,000	2	4,001-5,000	4	20*	40*	20*
	3,001-4,000	3	5,001-8,000	5	*Tax credit		
			Over 8,000	6			
Louisiana[4,5]	First 10,000	2	Over 50,000	6	4,500	9,000	1,000
	10,001-50,000	4					
Maine[2,3,7]	First 4,400	1	17,301-21,500	7	1,000	2,000	1,000
	4,401-8,600	2	21,501-32,400	8			
	8,601-12,900	3	32,401-50,000	9.2			
	12,901-17,300	6	Over 50,000	10			
Maryland	First 1,000	2	2,001-3,000	4	1,000	2,000	1,000
	1,001-2,000	3	Over 3,000	5			
Massachusetts	Earned and business income:	5*			2,200	4,400	700
	Interest, divs., net capital gains:	10*	No tax on income below $12,000 for husband and wife or $8,000 for single individual. Rates shown apply above these amounts. Exemptions apply to earned income only.				
Michigan	All taxable income	4.6			1,500	3,000	1,500
Minnesota[2,3,7,9]	1-19,000	6	Over 19,000	8	Federal exemptions.		
Mississippi	First 5,000	3	Next 5,000	4	6,000	9,500	1,500
			Over 10,000	5			
Missouri[4]	First 1,000	1.5	5,001- 6,000	4	1,200	2,400	400
	1,001-2,000	2	6,001- 7,000	4.5			
	2,001-3,000	2.5	7,001- 8,000	5			
	3,001-4,000	3	8,001-9,000	5.5			
	4,001-5,000	3.5	Over 9,000	6			
Montana[3,4]	First 1,300	2	10,601-13,200	7	1,060	2,120	1,060
	1,301-2,600	3	13,201-18,500	8	Surtax equal to 10% of Montana personal income tax liability from 1987 through 1989.		
	2,601-5,300	4	18,501-26,500	9			
	5,301-7,900	5	26,501-46,400	10			
	7,901-10,600	6	Over 46,400	11			
Nebraska[2]	First 3,000	2.0	28,001-45,000	5.0	1,100	2,200	1,100
	3,001-28,000	3.2	Over 45,000	5.9			
New Hampshire	Interest and dividends (with some exceptions).	5			$1,200 each income is exempt.		

State	Taxable Income	Percentage rates	Taxable income	Percentage rates	Personal exemp.[1] Single	Married family head	Each Dependent
New Jersey	First $20,000	2			$1,000	$2,000	$1,000
	Next 30,000	2.5					
	Over 50,000	3.5					
A taxpayer or married filing jointly with gross income of $3,000 ($1,500 if filing separately) or less is not taxable.							
New Mexico[2,5]	First 8,000	2.4	36,001-48,000	6.9	Federal exemptions.		
	8,001-16,000	3.8	48,001-64,000	7.7			
	16,001-24,000	4.8	Over 64,000	8.5			
	24,001-36,000	5.9					
New York[2,9]	First 6,000	3	18,801-24,800	7	0	0	0
	6,001-10,200	4	24,801-34,000	8	In 1987 and 1988, a tax is imposed on certain unearned income: 3% in 1987; 2% in 1988.		
	10,201-14,600	5	Over 34,000	8.375			
	14,601-18,000	6					
North Carolina.	First 2,000	3	6,001-10,000	6	1,100	2,200*	800
	2,001-4,000	4	Over 10,000	7	*An additional exemption of $1,100 is allowed the spouse having the lower income; is joint returns are not permitted.		
	4,001-6,000	5					
North Dakota[4]*	First 3,000	2.67	25,001-35,000	9.33	Federal exemptions. Surtax imposed for 1987 only equal to 10% of taxpayers income tax liability.		
	3,001-5,000	4	35,001-50,000	10.67			
	5,001-8,000	5.33	Over 50,000	12			
	8,000-15,000	6.67					
	15,001-25,000	8	*Optional tax is 14% of federal income tax liability.				
Ohio	First 5,000	0.751	20,001-40,000	4.506	650	1,300	650
	5,001-10,000	1.502	40,001-80,000	5.257	Additional exemption equal to $350 times the number of exemptions or a credit equal to $20 times the number.		
	10,001-15,000	3.004	80,001-100,000	6.008			
	15,001-20,000	3.755	Over 100,000	6.9			
Oklahoma[2,4,6]	First 2,000	0.5	10,001-12,500	4	1,000	2,000	1,000
	2,001-5,000	1	12,501-15,000	5			
	5,001-7,500	2	Over 15,000	6			
	7,501-10,000	3					
Oregon[2,3,4]	First 2,000	5	Over 5,000	9	85*	170*	85*
	2,001-5,000	7					
Pennsylvania	2.1% of specified classes of taxable income, including earned income.						
Rhode Island	22.96% of modified federal income tax liability.						
South Carolina[2]	First 4,000	3	8,001-10,000	6	Federal exemptions. Credit for married persons filing jointly is .7% of the lesser of $30,000 or the qualified earned income of the spouse with the lower income.		
	4,001-6,000	4	Over 10,000	7			
	6,001-8,000	5					
Tennessee	Interest and dividends	6			No tax on the first $1,250 for each individual return; or $2,500 or combined income for persons filing jointly; or from persons 65 or older with certain income levels.		
Utah[2]	First 1,500	2.75	4,501-6,000	5.75	75% of federal exemptions.		
	1,501-3,000	3.75	6,001-7,500	6.75			
	3,001-4,500	4.75	Over 7,500	7.75			
Vermont[9]	2.5% of modified federal income tax liability; not to exceeed Vermont tax liability computed on the basis of the IRC in effect January 1, 1987.						

State	Taxable Income		Percentage rates	Taxable income	Per-centage rates	Personal exemp.[1] Single	Married family head	Each Dependent
Virginia[9]	First	$3,000	2	$5,001-15,000	5	$800	$1,600	$800
		3,001-5,000	3	Over 15,000	5.75			
West Virginia[2]	First	10,000	3	40,001-60,000	6	2,000	4,000	2,000
		10,001-25,000	4	Over 60,000	6.5			
		25,001-40,000	4.5					
Wisconsin[2]	First	10,000	5	20,001-40,000	7.5	20*	40*	20*
		10,001-20,000	6.6	Over 40,00	7.9	*Tax credit		

(1) Does not include exemptions or credits for age or blindness, to offset sales or property taxes paid, or for any special purpose. (2) Rates shown are for married persons filing jointly in Alabama, California, Georgia, Hawaii, Maine, Minnesota, Nebraska, New Mexico, New York, Oklahoma, South Carolina, Utah, West Virginia, and Wisconsin; separate rate schedules apply for single taxpayers and in some cases to heads of households. Rates shown for Arizona and Oregon are for single taxpayers; in the case of joint returns, the tax is twice the tax that would be due if taxable income of husband and wife were cut in half. (3) Rates and/or exemptions are subject to annual adjustment for inflation. Data here are for 1986 tax year. Iowa data is for 1987 tax year; in Minnesota indexing begins in 1991. (4) All or part of federal income tax liability is deductible in computing state income tax. (5) Community property state in which, in general, half of community income is taxed to each spouse. (6) Different rate schedules apply for taxpayers who choose to deduct Federal income tax in Oklahoma. (7) Alternative minimum tax imposed. (8) Additional tax imposed on sum of tax preference items. (9) Rates are for taxable years beginning after December 31, 1987, and for Hawaii, New York, and Virginia, ending before 1989.

State Estate Tax Rates and Exemptions

Source: Compiled by Tax Foundation from Commerce Clearing House data

As of August 1987. *See p. 79 for state inheritance tax rates and exemptions.*

State (a)	Rates (on net estate after exemptions) (b)	Maximum rate applies above	Exemption
Alabama	Maximum Federal credit (c, d)	$10,040,000	$60,000
Alaska	Maximum Federal credit (c, d)	10,040,000	60,000
Arizona	Maximum Federal credit (c, d)	10,040,000	60,000
Arkansas	Maximum Federal credit (c, d)	10,040,000	60,000 (e)
California	Maximum Federal credit (c, d)	10,040,000	60,000
Colorado	Maximum Federal credit (c, d)	10,040,000	60,000
District of Columbia	Maximum Federal credit (c, d)	10,040,000	60,000
Florida	Maximum Federal credit (c, d)	10,040,000	60,000
Georgia	Maximum Federal credit (c, d)	10,040,000	60,000
Hawaii	Maximum Federal credit (c, d)	10,040,000	60,000
Illinois	Maximum Federal credit (c, d)	10,040,000	60,000
Maine	Maximum Federal credit (c, d)	10,040,000	60,000
Massachusetts	5% on first 50,000 to 16% (g)	4,000,000	1,500 (e, f)
Minnesota	Maximum Federal credit (c, d)	10,040,000	60,000
Mississippi	1% on first 60,000 to 16% (g)	10,000,000	175,625 (e)
Missouri	Maximum Federal credit (c, d)	10,040,000	60,000
Nevada	Maximum Federal credit (c, d)	10,040,000	60,000
New Mexico	Maximum Federal credit (c, d)	10,040,000	60,000
New York	2% on first 50,000 to 21% (g, h)	10,100,000	(e,i)
North Dakota	Maximum Federal credit (c, d)	10,040,000	60,000 (e)
Ohio	2% on first 40,000 to 7% (g)	500,000	500 (j, k)
Oklahoma	.5% on first 10,000 to 15% (g)	10,000,000	(l, m)
Oregon	Maximum Federal credit (c, d)	10,040,000	60,000 (e)
Rhode Island	2% on first 25,000 to 9% (c, g, o)	1,000,000	25,000 (e, n)
South Carolina	6% on first 40,000 to 8% (d, g)	100,000	120,000 (e, p)
Utah	Maximum Federal credit (c, d)	10,040,000	60,000 (e)
Vermont	Maximum Federal credit (c, d)	10,040,000	60,000 (e)
Virginia	Maximum Federal credit (c, d)	10,040,000	60,000
Washington	Maximum Federal credit (c, d)	10,040,000	60,000
West Virginia	Maximum Federal credit (c, d)	10,040,000	60,000
Wyoming	Maximum Federal credit (c, d)	10,040,000	60,000

(a) Excludes states shown in table on page 79 which levy an estate tax, in addition to their inheritance taxes, to assure full absorption of the federal credit. (b) The rates generally are in addition to graduated absolute amounts. (c) Maximum federal credit allowed under the 1954 code for state estate taxes paid is expressed as a percentage of the taxable estate (after $60,000 exemption) in excess of $40,000, plus a graduated absolute amount. In Rhode Island on net estates above $250,000. (d) A tax on nonresident estates is imposed on the proportionate share of the net estate which the property located in the state bears to the entire estate wherever situated. (e) Transfers to religious, charitable, educational, and municipal corporations generally are fully exempt. Limited in Mississippi to those located in United States or its possessions. (f) Credit. Applies to net estates above $200,000. Otherwise, exemption is equal to Massachusetts net estate. (g) An additional estate tax is imposed to assure full absorption of the federal credit. In New York, this applies only to residents. In Rhode Island on net estates above $250,000. (h) On net estate before exemption. Federal marital deduction allowed. (i) The credit is variable, ranging from the full amount of tax if estate tax is $2,750 or less to $500 if estate tax is $5,000 or more. (j) Marital deduction is equal to the lesser of the modified federal marital deduction; or to half of the difference between the value of the gross estate and deductions or $500,000, whichever is greater. (k) Credit is $500 or the amount of the tax if it is lesser than $500. (l) An estate valued at $100 or less is exempt. (m) Exemption is a total aggregate of $175,000 for father, mother, child and named relatives. Property passed to surviving spouse is excluded. (n) Marital deduction is $175,000. (o) From 1986 through 1990 tax is levied at a declining percentage of the tax that would otherwise be payable; 60% for decedents dying in 1988, 40% in 1989. (p) Exemption is increased to $140,000 June 30, 1988 to July 1, 1989. Federal marital deduction allowed.

State Inheritance Tax Rates and Exemptions

Source: Compiled by Tax Foundation from Commerce Clearing House data.
August 1, 1987

State (a)	Rates (b) (percent) Spouse, child, or parent	Brother or sister	Other than relative	Max. rate applies above ($1,000)	Exemptions (c) ($1,000) Spouse	Child or parent	Brother or sister	Other than relative
Connecticut (d)	3-8	4-10	8-14	1,000	300	50	6	1
Delaware	1-6	5-10	10-16	200	70	10	3	1
Idaho	2-15	4-20	8-30	500	All	30(e)	10	10
Indiana	1-10	7-15	10-20	1,500	All	10(5)(e)	0.5	0.1
Iowa	1-8	5-10	10-15	150	180	15(e)	None	None
Kansas	1-5	3-12.5	10-15	500	All	30	5	None
Kentucky	2-10	4-16	6-16	500	All	5	1	0.5
Louisiana	2-3	5-7	5-10	20	25(f)	25	1	0.5
Maryland (g)	1	10	10	(h)	.15(i)	.15(i)	0.15(i)	0.15(i)
Michigan	2-10 (j)	2-10 (j)	12-17 (j)	750	65(k)	10(e)	10	None
Montana	2-8	4-16	8-32	100	All	7(e)	1.0	None
Nebraska	1	1	6-18	60	All	10	10	0.5
New Hampshire	(l)	15	15	(h)	(l)	(l)	None	None
New Jersey	6-16 (m)	11-16	15-16	3,200	All	250(n)	0.5(o)	0.5(o)
North Carolina	1-12	4-16	8-17	3,000	All	20.15 (p)	None	None
Pennsylvania	6	15	15	(h)	None(q)	None(q)	None	None
South Dakota	3-15	4-20	6-30	100	All	30(r)	0.5	0.1
Tennessee	5.5-9.5	5.5-9.5	5.15-13	440	600(s)	600	600	250 (t)
Wisconsin	2.5-10	5-20	10-20	100	All	50	1	0.5

(a) In addition to an inheritance tax, all states listed also levy an estate tax, generally to assure full absorption of the federal credit.

(b) Rates generally apply to excess above graduated absolute amounts.

(c) Generally, transfers to governments or to solely charitable, educational, scientific, religious, literary, public, and other similar organizations in the U.S. are wholly exempt. Some states grant additional exemptions either for insurance, homestead, joint deposits, support allowance, disinherited minor children, orphaned, incompetent or blind children, and for previously or later taxed transfers. In many states, exemptions are deducted from the first bracket only. Adopted children generally receive the same consideration as natural children.

(d) On estates an additional inheritance tax equal to 30% of the basic tax is imposed. A second additional tax equal to 10% of the basic tax and the first additional tax is imposed, except on the farmland passing to a descendant.

(e) Exemption for child (in thousands); $50 in Iowa; and $30 in S.D. Exemption for minor child is (in thousands): $50 in Idaho; $10 in Indiana ($5 per parent and child over 21); $20 in Ky. In Mich. a widow receives $5,000 for every minor child to whom no property is transferred in addition to the normal exemption for a spouse; in Montana, all property is exempt.

(f) Community property state in which, in general, either all community property to the surviving spouse is exempt, or only one-half of the community property is taxable on the death of either spouse.

(g) Where property of a decedent subject to administration in Md. is $10,000 or less, no inheritance taxes are due.

(h) Rate applies to entire share.

(i) All real property and the first $100,000 of non-real property transferred to a spouse is exempt. For other beneficiaries, no exemption if share exceeds amount stated.

(j) There is no tax on the share of any beneficiary if the value of the share is less than $100.

(k) Spouse entitled to another $10,000 exemption.

(l) Spouses, children, parents, and adopted children in the decedent's line of succession are entirely exempt.

(m) July 1, 1987 through June 30, 1988; thereafter no tax.

(n) Exemption July 1, 1987 through June 30, 1988; thereafter entirely exempt.

(o) No exemption if share exceeds amount stated. For brothers and sisters, $25,000 exemption effective July 1, 1988.

(p) Credit in effect 1988; $26,150 in 1989 and thereafter.

(q) However, the $2,000 family exemption is specifically allowed as a deduction.

(r) The rates range from 3.75-7.5% for a child and from 3-15% for parents. Parent exemption is $3,000.

(s) There is a marital deduction equal to 50% of the value of the taxable transfer.

(t) $250,000 in 1988; $350,000 in 1989.

Residential Property Tax Rates in Selected Cities: 1985

Source: Government of the District of Columbia, Department of Finance and Revenue

City	Effective tax rate per $100 Rank	Rate	Assessment level (percent)	Nominal rate per $100	City	Effective tax rate per $100 Rank	Rate	Assessment level (percent)	Nominal rate per $100
Newark, NJ	1	5.46	45.8	11.93	Houston	24	1.68	100.0	1.68
Wilmington, DE	2	4.26	92.0	4.63	Boston	25	1.64	100.0	1.64
Bridgeport	3	4.21	63.8	6.60	Chicago	26	1.63	16.0	10.16
Detroit	4	4.16	50.0	8.32	Jackson, MS	27	1.61	15.0	10.75
Indianapolis	5	3.32	33.3	9.96	Boise City	28	1.50	98.7	1.52
Milwaukee	6	3.22	99.3	3.24	Fargo	29	1.47	4.5	32.58
Providence	7	3.21	44.3	7.25	New York City	30	1.37	15.0	9.10
Des Moines	8	2.73	72.5	3.76	Louisville	31	1.30	92.0	1.41
Baltimore	9	2.70	43.5	6.21	New Orleans	32	1.30	92.0	1.41
Philadelphia	10	2.62	35.0	7.48	Billings	33	1.26	3.7	34.09
Portland, OR	11	2.57	100.0	2.57	Charlotte	34	1.16	90.5	1.28
Manchester	12	2.38	30.0	7.93	Norfolk	35	1.15	92.0	1.25
Minneapolis	13	2.27	20.8	10.89	Columbia	36	1.15	4.0	28.65
Cleveland	14	2.08	35.0	5.94	Washington, DC	37	1.14	93.7	1.22
Sioux Falls	15	2.05	29.8	6.89	Phoenix	38	1.09	10.0	10.89
Portland, ME	16	2.03	75.0	2.71	Charleston, WV	39	1.07	62.0	1.73
Omaha	17	2.01	72.4	2.77	Salt Lake City	40	1.04	11.9	8.75
Jacksonville	18	1.93	98.9	1.95	St Louis	41	1.04	19.0	5.48
Albuquerque	19	1.82	33.3	5.48	Seattle	42	.99	93.8	1.06
Memphis	20	1.75	25.0	7.01	Wichita	43	.99	7.8	12.68
Atlanta	21	1.75	37.0	4.73	Anchorage	44	.94	100.0	.94
Burlington	22	1.71	23.0	7.44	Little Rock	45	.92	20.0	4.61
Oklahoma City	23	1.71	13.5	12.64	Las Vegas	46	.85	35.0	2.44

Federal Estate and Gift Tax

Source: Tax Foundation, Inc.

Estate Tax

As a result of the Economic Recovery Tax Act of 1981, the lifetime unified credit against combined estate and gift taxes increased in steps from $47,000 in 1981 to $62,800 in 1982, $79,300 in 1983, $96,300 in 1984, $121,800 in 1985, $155,800 in 1986, and $192,800 in 1987 and thereafter. Thus, cumulative transfers exempt from estate and gift taxes increased from $175,625 in 1981, to $225,000 in 1982, $275,000 in 1983, $325,000 in 1984, $400,000 in 1985, $500,000 in 1986, and $600,000 in 1987 and thereafter. The maximum estate and gift tax rate, which was 70 percent in 1981, has been reduced gradually to 50 percent in 1988 and thereafter. The schedule for 1988 is shown below.

Estate taxes are computed by applying the unified rate schedule, shown below, to the total estate minus allowable deductions, such as funeral expenses, administrative expenses, debts and charitable contributions, plus taxable gifts made after 1976. Gift taxes paid are subtracted from tax due, and credit also may be taken for state death taxes. The amount of the state tax credit is determined by the schedule shown in the table below or the actual state taxes paid, whichever is less. No state tax credit is available to an adjusted taxable estate (i.e., taxable estate minus $60,000) smaller than $40,000. Transfers to a surviving spouse are generally tax exempt.

The law provides for real property passed on to family members for use in a closely held business, such as farming, to be valued in basis of such use, rather than fair market value on basis of highest and best use. In no case may this special valuation reduce the gross estate by more than $600,000 in 1981, $700,000 in 1982, and $750,000 in 1983 and thereafter.

The generation-skipping transfer tax effective since April 30, 1976 was expanded by the Tax Reform Act of 1986. Under prior law, terminations or distributions from trusts were subject to taxes substantially equivalent to those that would have been imposed had the property been transferred outright to each successive generation. The tax now also applies to "direct skips" which are generation-skipping transfers, such as gifts or transfers of property to a trust, occuring after October 22, 1986 with some exceptions. The tax rate is 55% in 1987 and 50% thereafter. Each grantor is allowed a lifetime exemption of $1 million, as well as, prior to 1990, up to $2 million for "direct skips" to each grandchild.

A return must be filed for the estate of every U.S. citizen or resident whose gross estate exceeds $600,000 in 1987 and thereafter ($60,000 for the estate of a nonresident not a citizen). The return is due nine months after death unless an extension is granted.

Gift Tax

Any citizen or resident alien whose gifts to any one person exceed $10,000 within a calender year will be liable for payment of a gift tax, at rates determined under the unified estate and gift tax schedule. Gift tax returns are filed on an annual basis and ordinarily are due by April 15 of the following year.

Gifts made by a husband and wife to a third party may be considered as having been made one-half by each, provided both spouses consent to such division.

Unified Rate Schedule for Estate and Gift Tax for 1988[1]

If the amount with respect to which the tentative tax to be computed is:	The tentative tax is:		
Not over $10,000	18 percent of such amount.		
Over $10,000 but not over $20,000	$1,800, plus 20%	of the excess over	$10,000.
Over $20,000 but not over $40,000	$3,800, plus 22%	of the excess over	$20,000.
Over $40,000 but not over $60,000	$8,200, plus 24%	of the excess over	$40,000.
Over $60,000 but not over $80,000	$13,000, plus 26%	of the excess over	$60,000.
Over $80,000 but not over $100,000	$18,200, plus 28%	of the excess over	$80,000.
Over $100,000 but not over $150,000	$23,800, plus 30%	of the excess over	$100,000.
Over $150,000 but not over $250,000	$38,800, plus 32%	of the excess over	$150,000.
Over $250,000 but not over $500,000	$70,800, plus 34%	of the excess over	$250,000.
Over $500,000 but not over $750,000	$155,800, plus 37%	of the excess over	$500,000.
Over $750,000 but not over $1,000,000	$248,300, plus 39%	of the excess over	$750,000.
Over $1,000,000 but not over $1,250,000	$345,800, plus 41%	of the excess over	$1,000,000.
Over $1,250,000 but not over $1,500,000	$448,300, plus 43%	of the excess over	$1,250,000.
Over $1,500,000 but not over $2,000,000	$555,800, plus 45%	of the excess over	$1,500,000.
Over $2,000,000 but not over $2,500,000	$780,800, plus 49%	of the excess over	$2,000,000.
Over $2,500,000 but not over $3,000,000	$1,025,800, plus 50%	of the excess over	$2,500,000.

State Death Tax Credit for Estate Tax

Adjusted taxable estate from	to	Credit = +	%	Of excess over
$ 0	$ 40,000	0	0	$ 0
40,000	90,000	0	.8	40,000
90,000	140,000	400	1.6	90,000
140,000	240,000	1,200	2.4	140,000
240,000	440,000	3,600	3.2	240,000
440,000	640,000	10,000	4	440,000
640,000	840,000	18,000	4.8	640,000
840,000	1,040,000	27,600	5.6	840,000
1,040,000	1,540,000	38,800	6.4	1,040,000
1,540,000	2,040,000	70,800	7.2	1,540,000
2,040,000	2,540,000	106,800	8	2,040,000
2,540,000	3,040,000	146,800	8.8	2,540,000
3,040,000	3,540,000	190,800	9.6	3,040,000
3,540,000	4,040,000	238,800	10.4	3,540,000
4,040,000	5,040,000	290,800	11.2	4,040,000
5,040,000	6,040,000	402,800	12	5,040,000
6,040,000	7,040,000	522,800	12.8	6,040,000
7,040,000	8,040,000	650,800	13.6	7,040,000
8,040,000	9,040,000	786,800	14.4	8,040,000
9,040,000	10,040,000	930,800	15.2	9,040,000
10,040,000		1,000,000	16	10,040,000

(1) The unified credit for estates of decedents dying during 1987 and thereafter is $192,800.

EMPLOYMENT

U.S. Labor Force, Employment and Unemployment

Source: Bureau of Labor Statistics, U.S. Labor Department

(numbers in thousands; monthly data are seasonally adjusted)

Employment status	Annual averages 1984	1985	1986	1987 Jan.	Feb.	March	April	May	June
Civilian labor force	113,544	115,561	111,303	119,034	119,349	119,212	119,335	119,993	119,517
Employed	105,005	107,150	109,597	111,011	111,382	111,368	111,835	112,447	112,257
Agriculture	3,321	3,179	3,163	3,145	3,236	3,284	3,290	3,335	3,178
Nonagricultural industries	101,685	103,971	106,434	197,866	108,146	108,084	108,545	109,112	119,079
Unemployed	8,539	8,312	8,237	8,023	7,967	7,854	7,500	7,546	7,260
Unemployment rates (unemployment in each group as a percent of the groups' civilian labor force)									
Total, 16 years and over	7.5	7.2	7.0	0.7	6.7	6.6	6.3	6.3	6.1
Men, 20 years and over	6.6	6.1	6.1	6.0	5.9	5.8	5.6	5.5	5.5
Women, 20 years and over	6.8	6.7	6.2	5.9	5.8	5.8	5.5	5.4	5.2
Both sexes, 16 to 19 years	18.9	18.8	18.3	17.7	18.0	18.1	17.4	17.7	15.9
White, total	6.5	5.7	6.0	5.9	5.7	5.6	5.4	5.3	5.2
Men, 20 years and over	5.7	5.3	5.3	5.3	5.2	5.1	4.8	4.7	5.4
Women, 20 years and over	5.8	5.6	5.4	5.1	4.9	4.8	4.6	4.5	5.4
Both sexes, 16 to 19 years	16.0	16.9	15.6	13.8	14.3	13.9	13.1	13.1	15.9
Black, total	15.9	14.5	14.5	14.3	14.3	13.9	13.0	13.8	12.7
Men, 20 years and over	14.3	13.1	12.9	12.2	12.0	11.5	10.9	12.5	11.5
Women, 20 years and over	13.5	13.0	12.4	12.8	12.9	13.0	11.5	16.1	11.1
Both sexes, 16 to 19 years	42.7	42.2	39.3	39.5	38.9	37.6	38.0	39.0	33.3
Married men, spouse present	4.6	4.3	4.4	4.2	4.2	4.1	4.1	3.9	4.0
Married women, spouse present	5.7	5.6	5.2	4.8	4.8	4.5	4.4	4.1	4.0
Women who maintain families	10.3	10.5	9.9	9.8	9.5	9.7	9.3	9.6	9.7
Full-time workers	9.5	7.2	NA	6.4	6.3	6.2	5.9	5.9	5.7
Part-time workers	9.3	9.3	NA	9.0	8.7	9.2	8.6	8.7	6.9
Nonagricultural w/s workers	7.4	7.2	7.0	6.7	6.6	6.5	6.2	6.3	6.2
Construction	14.3	13.1	13.5	13.2	11.6	12.5	11.9	12.1	11.6
Manufacturing	7.5	7.7	13.1	6.8	6.8	6.9	6.2	6.4	5.6
Durable goods	7.2	7.6	7.1	6.8	6.8	6.7	6.2	6.3	5.3
Wholesale & retail trade	8.0	7.6	5.1	6.9	7.3	6.2	6.6	6.0	5.9
Finance & service industries	6.6	6.2	7.6	7.5	7.2	7.3	7.0	6.9	7.2
Agricultural w/s workers	13.5	13.2	12.2	11.6	11.2	10.7	9.0	8.7	8.8

Employed Persons by Major Occupational Groups and Sex

1986 Averages Occupational group	Thousands of persons Both sexes	Males	Females	Percent distribution Both sexes	Males	Females
Total employed	109,597	60,892	48,706	100.0	100.0	100.0
Managerial and professional specialty	26,554	15,029	11,525	24.2	24.7	23.7
Executive, administration and managerial	12,642	7,990	4,653	11.5	13.1	9.6
Professional specialty	13,911	7,039	6,872	12.7	11.6	14.1
Technical, sales and administrative support	34,354	12,130	22,223	31.3	19.9	45.6
Technicians and related support	3,364	1,783	1,581	3.1	2.9	3.2
Sales occupations	13,245	6,862	6,383	12.1	11.3	13.1
Administrative support, including clerical	17,745	3,485	14,260	16.2	5.7	29.3
Service occupations	14,680	5,775	8,905	13.4	9.5	18.3
Private household	981	39	942	.9	.1	1.9
Protective service	1,787	1,566	221	1.6	2.6	.5
Service, except private household and protective	11,913	4,170	7,542	10.9	6.8	15.9
Precision production, craft, and repair	13,405	12,256	1,150	12.2	20.1	2.4
Mechanics and repairers	4,374	4,222	151	—	—	—
Construction trades	4,924	4,826	99	—	—	—
Other precision production, craft, and repair	4,108	3,208	900	—	—	—
Operators, fabricators, and laborers	17,160	12,805	4,355	15.7	21.0	8.9
Machine operators, assemblers, and inspectors	7,911	4,485	3,187	7.2	7.8	6.5
Transportation and material moving occupations	4,564	4,158	406	4.2	6.8	.8
Handlers, equipment cleaners, helpers, and laborers	4,685	3,923	762	4.3	6.4	1.6
Farming, forestry, and fishing	3,444	2,896	548	3.1	4.8	1.1

Employment and Unemployment in the U.S.

Civilian labor force, persons 16 years of age and over (in thousands)

Year*	Employed	Unemployed	Unemployment Rate	Year*	Employed	Unemployed	Unemployment Rate
1940[1]	47,520	8,120	14.6%	1978	96,048	6,202	6.1
1950	58,918	3,288	5.0	1980	99,303	7,637	7.1
1960	65,778	3,852	5.5	1981	100,397	8,273	7.6
1965	71,088	3,366	4.5	1982	99,526	10,678	9.7
1970	78,678	4,093	4.9	1983	100,834	10,717	9.6
1975	85,846	7,929	8.5	1984	105,005	8,539	7.5
1976	88,752	7,406	7.7	1985	107,150	8,312	7.2
1977	92,017	6,991	7.1	1986[2]	109,597	8,237	7.0

[1]Persons 14 years of age and over; (2) Not strictly comparable with prior years.
***Early unemployment rates:** 1915, 9.7; 1916, 4.8; 1917, 4.8; 1918, 1.4; 1919, 2.3; 1920, 4.0; 1921, 11.9; 1922, 7.6; 1923, 3.2; 1924, 5 1925, 4.0; 1926, 1.9; 1927, 4.1; 1928, 4.4; 1929, 3.2; 1930, 8.7; 1931, 15.9; 1932, 23.6; 1933, 24.9; 1934, 21.7; 1935, 20.1; 1936, 16.9; 193 14.3; 1938, 19.0; 1939, 17.2.

Employment by Broad Occupational Group and Selected Occupations, 1986 and Projected to 2000

Source: Bureau of Labor Statistics

Occupation	1986	Projected 2000 alternatives: Low	Moderate	High	Change, 1986-2000 moderate alternative: Number change	Percent change	Annual rate of change
Total employment	**111,623**	**126,432**	**133,030**	**137,533**	**21,407**	**19.2**	**1.3**
Executive, administrative, and managerial workers	10,583	12,900	13,616	14,105	3,033	28.7	1.8
Education administrators	288	316	325	336	37	12.9	0.9
Financial managers	638	747	792	824	154	24.1	1.6
General managers and top executives	2,383	2,820	2,965	3,052	582	24.4	1.6
Marketing, advertising, and public relations managers	323	402	427	444	105	32.5	2.0
Accountants and auditors	945	1,251	1,322	1,371	376	39.8	2.4
Personnel, training, and labor relations specialists	230	264	278	288	49	21.2	1.4
Professional workers	13,538	16,438	17,192	17,793	3,654	27.0	1.7
Electrical and electronics engineers	401	544	592	616	192	47.8	2.8
Computer systems analysts	331	544	582	607	251	75.6	4.1
Lawyers	527	676	718	748	191	36.3	2.2
Teachers, preschool	176	233	240	248	64	36.3	2.2
Teachers, kindergarten and elementary	1,527	1,778	1,826	1,883	299	19.6	1.3
Teachers, secondary school	1,128	1,246	1,280	1,320	152	13.4	0.9
College and university faculty	754	703	722	745	-32	-4.2	-0.3
Dentists	151	184	196	203	45	29.6	1.9
Physicians and surgeons	491	645	679	700	188	38.2	2.3
Registered nurses	1,406	1,951	2,018	2,077	612	43.6	2.6
Technicians and related support workers	3,726	4,884	5,151	5,325	1,424	38.2	2.3
Licensed practical nurses	631	835	869	891	238	37.7	2.3
Drafters	348	331	354	366	5	1.6	0.1
Computer programmers	479	758	813	850	335	69.9	3.9
Sales workers	12,606	15,522	16,334	16,760	3,728	29.6	1.0
Cashiers	2,165	2,616	2,740	2,798	575	26.5	1.7
Sales agents, real estate	313	422	451	468	138	43.9	2.6
Salespersons, retail	3,579	4,563	4,780	4,871	1,201	33.5	2.1
Administrative support workers, including clerical	19,851	21,028	22,109	22,885	2,258	11.4	0.8
Switchboard operators	279	313	330	343	51	18.3	1.2
Computer operators, except peripheral equipment operators	263	364	387	403	124	47.2	2.8
Bookkeeping, accounting, and auditing clerks	2,116	2,085	2,208	2,291	92	4.3	0.3
Payroll and timekeeping clerks	204	171	180	186	-25	-12.0	-0.9
General office clerks	2,361	2,688	2,824	2,916	462	19.6	1.3
Receptionists and information clerks	682	913	964	997	282	41.4	2.5
Secretaries	3,234	3,470	3,658	[illegible]	424	13.1	0.9
Typists and word processors	1,002	[illegible]	[illegible]	[illegible]	-140	-13.9	-1.1
Private household workers	981	883	955	970	-26	-2.6	-0.2
Service workers, except private household workers	16,555	21,051	21,962	22,562	5,407	32.7	2.0
Janitors and cleaners, including maids/housekeepers	2,676	3,144	3,280	3,382	604	22.6	1.5
Waiters and waitresses	1,702	2,360	2,454	2,503	752	44.2	2.6
Nursing aides, orderlies, and attendants	1,224	1,584	1,658	1,691	433	35.4	2.2
Hairdressers, hairstylists, and cosmetologists	562	627	662	683	99	17.7	1.2
Police patrol officers	349	400	409	422	61	17.4	1.2
Guards	794	1,104	1,177	1,241	383	48.3	2.9
Precision production, craft, and repair workers	13,923	14,722	15,590	16,225	1,666	12.0	0.8
Carpenters	1,010	1,134	1,192	1,252	182	18.1	1.2
Electricians	556	617	644	676	89	15.9	1.1
Painters and paperhangers, construction and maintenance	412	475	502	526	90	21.9	1.4
Plumbers, pipefitters, and steamfitters	402	452	471	493	69	17.2	1.1
Aircraft mechanics and engine specialists	107	122	129	130	22	20.1	1.3
Automotive mechanics	748	758	808	830	60	8.0	0.6
Machinists	378	345	373	385	-5	-1.5	-0.1
Operators, fabricators, and laborers	16,300	15,774	16,724	17,411	424	2.6	0.2
Sewing machine operators, garment	633	526	541	567	-92	-14.5	-1.1
Electrical and electronics assembers	249	105	116	119	-134	-53.7	-5.3
Welders and cutters	287	284	307	320	19	6.7	0.5
Bus drivers	478	541	555	572	77	16.2	1.1
Truck drivers	2,463	2,821	2,968	3,050	505	20.5	1.3
Industrial truck and tractor operators	426	265	283	296	-143	-33.6	-2.9
Farming, forestry, and fishing workers	3,556	3,229	3,393	3,497	-163	-4.6	-0.3
Gardeners and groundskeepers, except farming	767	964	1,005	1,033	238	31.1	2.0
Farm workers	940	705	750	779	-190	-20.3	-1.6
Farm operators and managers	1,336	1,001	1,051	1,078	-285	-21.3	-1.7

Note: Data do not add to totals due to rounding.

State Per Capita Income in 1986

Source: Bureau of Economic Analysis, U.S. Dept. of Commerce

U.S. total	$14,641
Connecticut	19,600
D.C.	19,397
New Jersey	18,626
Alaska	17,796
Massachusetts	17,722
New York	17,111
California	16,904
Maryland	16,684
New Hampshire	15,911
Illinois	15,586
Nevada	15,437
Virginia	15,408
Colorado	15,234
Delaware	15,010
Washington	15,009
Minnesota	14,994
Hawaii	14,886
Michigan	$14,775
Kansas	14,650
Florida	14,646
Rhode Island	14,579
Pennsylvania	14,249
Ohio	13,933
Wisconsin	13,909
Missouri	13,789
Nebraska	13,742
Texas	13,478
Arizona	13,474
Georgia	13,446
Iowa	13,348
Vermont	13,348
Oregon	13,328
Indiana	13,136
Maine	12,790
Wyoming	12,781
North Dakota	$12,472
North Carolina	12,438
Oklahoma	12,283
Tennessee	12,002
South Dakota	11,814
Montana	11,803
New Mexico	11,422
Alabama	11,336
South Carolina	11,299
Kentucky	11,238
Idaho	11,223
Louisiana	11,193
Arkansas	11,073
Utah	10,981
West Virginia	10,576
Mississippi	9,716

Mothers in the Work Force

Source: Bureau of Labor Statistics

Age of children and family type	1977 Total children	1977 Mother in the labor force Number	1977 Mother in the labor force Percent of total	1982 Total children	1982 Mother in the labor force Number	1982 Mother in the labor force Percent of total	1987 Total children	1987 Mother in the labor force Number	1987 Mother in the labor force Percent of total
Total children under 18 years old	60,584	28,892	47.7	58,312	32,008	54.9	58,438	35,170	60.2
6 to 17 years	43,467	22,462	51.7	39,820	23,534	59.1	38,637	24,657	63.8
Under 6 years	17,117	6,431	37.6	18,492	8,473	45.8	19,801	10,513	53.1
1 year or younger	5,532	1,721	31.1	6,340	2,640	41.6	6,470	3,248	50.2
2 years	2,741	1,052	38.4	3,138	1,472	46.9	3,264	1,750	53.6
3 years	2,750	1,056	38.4	3,051	1,476	48.4	3,285	1,760	53.6
4 years	2,917	1,235	42.3	3,011	1,461	48.5	3,388	1,846	54.5
5 years	3,178	1,366	43.0	2,953	1,424	48.2	3,394	1,908	56.2
In married-couple families	50,279	23,341	46.4	46,293	25,130	54.3	45,464	27,870	61.3
6 to 17 years	35,499	17,930	50.5	30,908	30,908	58.7	29,355	19,113	65.1
Under 6 years	14,780	5,411	36.6	15,385	7,000	45.5	16,109	8,756	54.4
1 year or younger	4,949	1,542	31.2	5,483	2,312	42.2	5,448	2,836	52.1
2 years	2,386	898	37.6	2,602	1,225	47.1	2,661	1,478	55.5
3 years	2,356	878	37.3	2,513	1,203	47.9	2,682	1,444	53.8
4 years	2,439	995	40.8	2,390	1,133	47.4	2,706	1,503	55.5
5 years	2,650	1,098	41.4	2,397	1,127	47.0	2,612	1,495	57.2
In families maintained by women	9,499	5,551	58.4	10,968	6,878	62.7	11,492	7,301	63.5
6 to 17 years	7,266	4,532	62.4	8,093	5,405	66.8	8,180	5,543	67.8
Under 6 years	2,233	1,020	45.7	2,876	1,473	51.2	3,312	1,757	53.0
1 year or younger	553	179	32.4	777	328	42.2	902	412	45.7
2 years	333	154	46.2	495	247	49.9	533	272	51.0
3 years	380	178	46.8	491	273	55.6	551	316	57.4
4 years	457	240	52.5	587	328	55.9	609	343	56.3
5 years	509	268	52.7	526	297	56.5	718	413	57.5
In families maintained by men	807	—	—	1,050	—	—	1,483	—	—

Blacks in Management and the Professions

Source: Bureau of Labor Statistics
Percentage of jobs filled by blacks in 1986.

Managerial and professional specialty	**6.0%**
Officials and administrators, public administration	8.4
Financial managers	3.0
Personnel and labor relation managers	5.5
Purchasing managers	4.1
Managers: marketing, advertising and public relations	2.5
Administrators: education and related fields	8.9
Managers: medicine and health	8.1
Managers: properties and real estate	5.2
Accountants and auditors	5.6
Underwriters and other financial officers	6.0
Personnel, training and labor relations specialists	11.9
Buyers, wholesale and retail trade (except farm products)	3.2
Construction inspectors	4.5
Professional specialties	**6.7%**
Architects	3.2
Engineers	3.7
Mathematical and computer scientists	7.2
Natural scientists	2.5
Physicians and dentists	3.3
Nurses	6.7
Pharmacists	4.0
Dieticians	17.7
Therapists	7.8
Teachers: college and university	4.0
Other teachers	9.5
Conselors: educational and vocational	12.9
Librarians, archivists and curators	7.4
Social scientists and urban planners	5.5
Social, recreation and religious workers	12.5
Lawyers and judges	3.0
Writers, artists, entertainers and athletes	5.2

Civilian Employment of the Federal Government

Source: Workforce Analysis and Statistics Division, U.S. Office of Personnel Management as of May 1987
(Payroll in thousands of dollars)

	All Areas		United States		Wash., D.C. MSA		Overseas	
	Employ-ment	Payroll	Employ-ment	Payroll	Employ-ment	Payroll	Employ-ment	Payroll
Total, all agencies[1]	**3,095,712**	**6,833,984**	**2,947,089**	**6,402,891**	**349,509**	**932,788**	**148,623**	**431,093**
Legislative branch	**37,880**	**94,048**	**37,819**	**93,832**	**35,508**	**87,776**	**61**	**216**
Congress	19,446	46,222	19,446	46,222	19,446	46,222	—	—
Senate	7,352	17,347	7,352	17,347	7,352	17,347	—	—
House of Representatives	12,078	28,835	12,078	28,835	12,078	28,835	—	—
Comm. on Security and Coop. in Europe	16	40	16	40	16	40	—	—
Architect of the Capitol	2,132	4,373	2,132	4,373	2,132	4,373	—	—
Botanic Garden	55	128	55	128	55	128	—	—
Congressional Budget Office	213	965	213	965	213	965	—	—
Copyright Royalty Tribunal	7	28	7	28	7	28	—	—
General Accounting Office	5,388	15,691	5,335	15,515	3,506	10,374	53	176
Government Printing Office	5,152	13,506	5,152	13,506	4,675	12,603	—	—
Library of Congress	4,920	11,337	4,912	11,297	4,912	11,297	8	40
Office of Technology Assessment	202	652	202	652	202	652	—	—
Physician Payment Rev Comm	7	27	7	27	7	27	—	—
Prospective Payment Assessment Committee	25	76	25	76	25	76	—	—
Tax Court	333	1,043	333	1,043	328	1,031	—	—
Judicial branch	**19,629**	**47,563**	**19,396**	**46,984**	**1,749**	**4,903**	**233**	**579**
Supreme Court	345	1,101	345	1,101	345	1,101	—	—
United States Courts	19,284	46,462	19,051	45,883	1,404	3,802	233	579
Executive branch	**3,038,203**	**6,692,373**	**2,889,874**	**6,262,075**	**312,252**	**840,109**	**148,329**	**430,298**
Executive Office of the President	1,497	4,665	1,489	4,635	1,489	4,635	8	30
White House Office	365	1,087	365	1,087	365	1,087	—	—
Office of the Vice President	23	64	23	64	23	64	—	—
Office of Management and Budget	529	1,778	529	1,778	529	1,778	—	—
Office of Administration	192	431	192	431	192	431	—	—
Council of Economic Advisors	33	113	33	113	33	113	—	—
Council on Environmental Quality	11	45	11	45	11	45	—	—
Office of Policy Development	31	104	31	104	31	104	—	—
Executive Residence	88	296	88	296	88	296	—	—
National Security Council	59	190	59	190	59	190	—	—
Office of Science and Tech.	9	25	9	25	9	25	—	—
Office of US Trade Representatives	147	507	139	477	139	477	8	30
WH Conf. Drug Free America	10	25	10	25	10	25	—	—
Executive departments	**1,095,654**	**4,093,654**	**1,670,335**	**3,709,716**	**229,082**	**618,196**	**125,319**	**383,938**
State	26,571	61,234	8,462	25,246	7,321	22,688	17,109	35,988
Treasury	151,106	[illegible]	150,000	295,920	19,218	51,202	1,046	3,054
Defense, Total	1,083,855	2,456,189	981,861	2,125,293	88,378	228,645	101,994	330,896
Department of the Army	395,268	918,809	348,630	670,860	28,984	64,918	46,638	247,940
Department of the Navy	340,926	777,750	315,273	747,966	37,808	105,939	25,653	29,784
Department of the Air Force	255,520	537,161	230,272	514,770	6,575	14,092	16,248	22,391
Defense Logistics Agency	52,276	115,237	51,855	114,240	3,026	6,042	421	997
Other Defense Activities	39,865	107,232	26,831	77,457	11,985	37,054	13,034	29,775
Justice	68,484	170,380	67,334	167,074	18,221	46,175	1,150	3,306
Interior	75,306	172,381	74,953	171,479	9,090	26,318	353	902
Agriculture	112,639	220,035	111,184	217,813	12,020	31,111	1,455	2,222
Commerce	34,460	82,322	33,678	78,766	18,066	48,522	782	3,556
Labor	17,757	49,778	17,718	49,662	6,124	18,940	39	116
Health and Human Services	129,947	284,053	129,208	282,391	29,200	75,332	739	1,662
Housing and Urb. Develop.	12,775	31,439	12,633	31,096	3,212	9,567	142	343
Transportation	62,046	205,461	61,542	203,597	9,168	31,274	504	1,864
Energy	16,669	47,487	16,664	47,461	5,803	18,439	5	26
Education	4,719	13,913	4,718	13,910	3,261	9,983	1	3
Independent agencies[1]	**1,241,052**	**2,594,054**	**1,218,050**	**2,547,724**	**81,681**	**217,278**	**23,002**	**46,330**
Environmental Protection Agency	14,696	36,613	14,682	36,570	4,914	13,933	14	43
Equal Employment Oppor. Comm.	3,112	8,177	3,112	8,177	773	1,893	—	—
Fed. Deposit Insurance Corp.	9,141	20,480	9,033	20,234	1,141	3,225	108	246
Federal Emergency Mgt. Agency	2,552	6,844	2,545	6,827	1,230	3,510	7	17
General Services Admin.	21,981	49,303	21,875	49,062	8,179	20,472	106	241
National Aeronautics and Space Admin.	22,580	73,819	22,573	73,789	4,821	16,096	7	30
National Archives & Records Adm.	3,085	4,251	3,085	4,251	1,051	2,213	—	—
Nuclear Regulatory Comm.	3,476	12,439	3,476	12,439	2,266	8,351	—	—
Office of Personnel Mgmt.	6,140	11,008	6,110	10,976	2,445	5,713	30	32
Panama Canal Commission	8,488	14,656	18	39	6	18	8,470	14,617
Small Business Admin.	4,900	11,737	4,806	11,529	1,395	2,429	94	208
Smithsonian Summary	4,989	9,651	4,877	9,446	4,640	8,856	112	205
Tennessee Valley Authority	32,258	85,896	32,258	85,896	16	65	—	—
US Information Agency	8,879	21,685	4,348	13,227	4,061	12,093	4,531	8,458
US International Development Cooperative Agency	4,779	14,471	2,265	7,008	2,251	6,937	2,514	7,463
U.S. Postal Service	816,989	1,653,095	813,601	1,644,942	20,447	47,157	3,388	8,153
Veterans Administration	249,029	494,014	246,311	488,940	6,415	18,839	2,718	5,074

(1) Included in total are independent agencies with fewer than 2,500 employees.

Women in Professional Occupations, 1983 and 1986

Source: Bureau of Labor Statistics

As of February, 1987, women held the majority of professional jobs in the U.S. While men's traditional dominance of some professions, such as medicine, law, and engineering, continued, women made sufficient advances in even those fields over the previous few years to gain the overall majority in the nearly 50 professional occupations surveyed by the Bureau of Labor Statistics.

Occupational category	1983		1986	
	Number of women (in thousands)	As percent of total employed in occupation	Number of women (in thousands)	As percent of total employed in occupation
Professional specialty workers, total	6,169	48.1	6,872	49.4
Engineers, surveyors, and architects	104	6.1	119	6.2
Mathematical and computer scientists	137	29.6	228	36.2
Natural scientists	73	20.5	86	22.5
Health diagnosing occupations	98	13.3	109	15.0
Health assessment and treating occupations	1,629	85.8	1,728	85.3
Teachers, college and university	220	36.3	230	36.0
Teachers, except college and university	2,386	70.9	2,613	73.4
Counselors, educational and vocational	98	53.1	93	53.1
Librarians, archivists, and curators	180	84.4	176	82.9
Social scientists and urban planners	122	46.8	143	46.0
Social, recreation, and religious workers	358	43.1	427	46.9
Lawyers and judges	103	15.8	118	18.1
Writers, artists, entertainers, and athletes	660	42.7	801	45.0

Employees in Non-Agricultural Establishments

Source: Bureau of Labor Statistics, U.S. Department of Labor (thousands)

Annual Average by Industry Division

Year	Total	Mining	Construction	Manufacturing	Trans. and public utilities	Whole., retail trade	Finance, insur., real estate	Services	Government
1955	50,641	792	2,839	16,882	4,141	10,535	2,298	6,240	6,914
1960	54,189	712	2,926	16,796	4,004	11,391	2,629	7,378	8,353
1965	60,765	632	3,232	18,062	4,036	12,716	2,977	9,036	10,074
1970	70,880	623	3,588	19,367	4,515	15,040	3,645	11,548	12,554
1975	76,945	752	3,525	18,323	4,542	17,060	4,165	13,892	14,686
1980	90,406	1,027	4,346	20,285	5,146	20,310	5,160	17,890	16,241
1982	89,566	1,128	3,905	18,781	5,082	20,457	5,341	19,036	15,837
1983	90,200	952	3,948	18,434	4,954	20,881	5,468	19,694	15,870
1984	94,406	966	4,383	19,378	5,159	22,100	5,689	20,797	16,032
1985 (Revised)	97,519	927	4,673	19,260	5,238	23,073	5,955	23,073	15,394
1986	99,610	763	4,904	18,994	5,244	23,580	6,297	23,099	16,710

Employment and Training Services and Unemployment Insurance

Source: Employment and Training Administration, U.S. Department of Labor

Employment Service

The Federal-State Employment Service consists of the United States Employment Service and affiliated state employment services which make up the nation's public employment service system. During program year 1984, the public employment service made 5.1 million placements—4.7 million in nonagricultural and .4 million in agricultural industries. Overall, 3.5 million different individuals were placed in employment.

The employment service refers employable applicants to job openings that use their highest skills and helps the unemployed obtain services or training to make them employable. It also provides special attention to handicapped workers, migrants and seasonal farmworkers, workers who lose their jobs because of foreign trade competition, and other worker groups. Veterans receive priority services including referral to jobs and training. During program year 1984, almost 799,000 veterans were placed in jobs.

Job Training

The Job Training Partnership Act (JTPA) of 1984 went into full effect on October 1, 1983, replacing the Comprehensive Employment and Training Act (CETA), with training programs focusing almost entirely on the private sector.

State governors will receive bloc grants from the Labor Department. The funds will be distributed to Service Delivery Areas—areas of 200,000 population or more where local elected officials will work with Private Industry Councils to plan and conduct training projects in local areas.

Key differences in the new act are that at least 70 cents of each training dollar must be used for direct training costs, as compared to CETA's 18 cents. (CETA wound up nine years of existence at a total cost of $58 billion with 27 million enrollees and a 15 percent placement rate for training participants.)

JTPA has provisions for the retraining and job placement of dislocated workers—persons with long attachment to the labor force who have lost their jobs through plant closings and technological change, with little chance of returning to their old jobs. In program year 1985, approximately $1.9 billion was provided for block grants to serve about 1.1 million participants. In addition, states were provided $222 million to serve over 250,000 dislocated workers.

(continued)

For the first time in the history of such programs, specific performance standards have been established and each Service Delivery Area and each state will have to match its performance to the minimum standards initially set by the Employment and Training Administration.

All in all, approximately 1 million unemployed workers are expected to be trained or assisted in obtaining employment through JTPA.

Other sections of JTPA include the Job Corps, which will enroll approximately 100,000 youth between the ages of 16 through 21 in 107 centers throughout the country for job and educational training; the summer jobs for youth program which will provide temporary summer work for nine weeks to approximately 785,000 youths; the migrant and seasonal farmworker program, which will provide job, social, and educational services to thousands of agricultural workers; and the Indian and Native American program which is expected to spend about $62 million on job and training programs, mostly on reservations.

Other National Training Programs

The Work Incentive (WIN) program for employable recipients of Aid to Families of Dependent Children has been placing approximately 350,000 persons, mostly women, in private sector jobs.

Trade Ajustment Assistance for Workers

The Trade Adjustment Assistance (TAA) is available to workers who lose their jobs or whose hours of work and wages are reduced as a result of increased imports. TAA includes a variety of benefits and reemployment services to help unemployed workers prepare for and obtain suitable employment. Workers may be eligible for training, job search, relocation and other reemployment services. Additionally, weekly trade readjustment allowances (TRA) may be payable to eligible workers following their exhaustion of unemployment insurance benefits. In fiscal year 1986, about 39,500 workers received $115.5 million in TRA payments; about 12,000 workers entered training; about 1,650 workers conducted in job search visits; and about 2,900 workers relocated in order to obtain long term jobs.

The TAA program is administered by the Employment and Training Administration of the U.S. Department of Labor. States serve as agents to the Labor Department in administering the benefit provisions of the Trade Act of 1974.

Unemployment Insurance

Unlike old-age and survivors insurance, entirely a federal program, the unemployment insurance program is a Federal-State system that provides insured wage earners with partial replacement of wages lost during involuntary unemployment. The program protects most workers. During calendar year 1985, an estimated 93 million workers in commerce, industry, agriculture, and government, including the armed forces, were covered under the Federal-State system. In addition, an estimated 350,000 railroad workers were insured against unemployment by the Railroad Retirement Board.

Each state, as well as the District of Columbia, Puerto Rico, and the Virgin Islands, has its own law and operates its own program. The amount and duration of the weekly benefits are determined by state laws, based on prior wages and length of employment. States are required to extend the duration of benefits when unemployment rises to and remains above specified state levels; costs of extended benefits are shared by the state and federal governments.

Under the Federal Unemployment Tax Act, as amended in 1985, the tax rate is 6.2% on the first $7,000 paid to each employee of employers with one or more employees in 20 weeks of the year or a quarterly payroll of $1,500. A credit of up to 5.4% is allowed for taxes paid under state unemployment insurance laws that meet certain criteria, leaving the federal share at 0.8% of taxable wages.

Social Security Requirement

The Social Security Act requires, as a condition of such grants, prompt payment of due benefits. The Federal Unemployment Tax Act provides safeguards for workers' right to benefits if they refuse jobs that fail to meet certain labor standards. Through the Unemployment Insurance Service of the Employment and Training Administration, the Secretary of Labor determines whether states qualify for grants and for tax offset credit for employers.

Benefits are financed solely by employer contributions, except in Alaska, Alabama, Pennsylvania, New Jersey, and West Virginia, where employees also contribute. Benefits are paid through the states' public employment offices, at which unemployed workers must register for work and to which they must report regularly for referral to a possible job during the time when they are drawing weekly benefit payments. During the 1986 calendar year, $15.9 billion in benefits was paid under state unemployment insurance programs to 8.3 million beneficiaries. They received an average weekly payment of $135.68 for total unemployment for an average of 14.6 weeks.

Selected Unemployment Insurance Data by State

Calendar year 1986, state programs only.

	Insured claimants[1] (1,000)	Beneficiaries[2] (1,000)	Exhaustions[3] (1,000)	Initial claims[4] (1,000)	Benefits paid[5] (1,000)	Avg. weekly benefit for total unemployment	Employers subject to state law (1,000)
Alabama	202	175	42	426	$186,813	$99.97	75
Alaska	59	56	30	98	139,697	158.59	15
Arizona	111	74	20	193	108,451	113.33	72
Arkansas	124	96	22	249	128,199	119.35	48
California	1,455	1,114	409	2,947	2,093,444	118.38	674
Colorado	147	102	33	204	218,248	157.33	87
Connecticut	108	111	18	211	181,257	155.45	86
Delaware	24	21	6	40	43,926	145.33	15
District of Columbia	28	22	11	39	66,487	163.74	20
Florida	241	182	70	385	298,259	124.48	276
Georgia	277	220	55	436	226,871	110.35	128
Hawaii	35	27	7	62	52,951	146.13	24
Idaho	50	47	18	119	78,607	131.98	24
Illinois	460	364	144	772	906,653	141.10	231
Indiana	198	151	45	391	190,448	100.84	98
Iowa	107	85	27	179	168,408	140.06	61
Kansas	95	83	28	179	168,447	150.76	59
Kentucky	160	120	33	279	184,057	106.59	67
Louisiana	263	217	125	459	570,078	149.98	85
Maine	51	36	15	123	59,481	123.38	29
Maryland	133	110	28	237	215,046	138.15	97
Massachusetts	148	203	55	422	457,554	156.31	139
Michigan	312	406	107	933	754,662	154.92	183
Minnesota	156	[illegible]	[illegible]	[illegible]	[illegible]	[illegible]	94
Mississippi	117	93	27	267	112,464	94.43	46
Missouri	212	172	47	473	223,840	108.39	119

(continued)

	Insured claimants[1] (1,000)	Beneficiaries[2] (1,000)	Exhaustions[3] (1,000)	Initial claims[4] (1,000)	Benefits paid[5] (1,000)	Avg. weekly benefit for total unemployment	Employers subject to state law (1,000)
Montana	37	31	13	73	53,312	128.84	24
Nebraska	51	43	15	80	61,916	110.85	40
Nevada	69	41	11	86	73,880	134.13	23
New Hampshire	29	23	1	43	16,022	116.89	31
New Jersey	297	268	107	497	656,966	157.31	186
New Mexico	49	42	15	90	85,966	121.81	33
New York	589	541	190	1,138	1,210,305	135.54	423
North Carolina	324	224	48	723	241,719	119.14	123
North Dakota	23	22	10	47	50,928	149.39	18
Ohio	383	340	99	798	139,828	148.94	194
Oklahoma	126	112	44	217	233,737	145.84	69
Oregon	141	130	33	335	250,201	139.55	69
Pennsylvania	566	487	129	1,282	1,106,247	155.07	219
Puerto Rico	93	72	39	263	102,821	71.63	46
Rhode Island	59	45	12	108	73,131	131.33	26
South Carolina	143	102	31	381	111,399	100.66	63
South Dakota	12	11	2	29	13,675	107.89	18
Tennessee	208	166	45	493	176,506	92.37	86
Texas	710	528	205	1,038	1,231,954	161.94	313
Utah	61	49	16	102	99,178	156.35	32
Vermont	23	18	3	35	28,636	122.12	17
Virgin Islands	3	2	1	4	3,993	109.99	3
Virginia	156	124	25	306	135,943	127.95	111
Washington	219	177	49	502	378,551	142.08	106
West Virginia	74	72	20	107	148,548	144.35	34
Wisconsin	217	201	61	457	370,572	141.35	97
Wyoming	30	24	8	55	62,768	165.85	16
Total	**9,965**	**8,322**	**2,703**	**19,670**	**$15,899,442**	**$135.72**	**5,265**

(1) Claimants whose base-period earnings or whose employment, covered by the unemployment insurance program, was sufficient to make them eligible for unemployment insurance benefits as provided by state law. (2) First payments. (3) Final payments. Claimants who exhaust their benefit rights in one benefit year may be entitled to further benefits in the following benefit year. (4) Excludes intrastate transitional claims. (5) Adjusted for voided benefit checks and transfers under interstate combined wage plan.

Extent of Unemployment by Race, Hispanic Origin, and Sex, 1985-86

Source: Bureau of Labor Statistics
(numbers in thousands)

Extent of unemployment, race, and Hispanic origin	Total		Men		Women	
	1985	1986	1985	1986	1985	1986
White						
Total who worked or looked for work	109,060	110,725	59,924	60,628	49,136	50,098
Percent with unemployment	15.6	15.0	16.2	15.9	14.9	13.9
Total with unemployment	17,054	16,623	9,718	9,648	7,336	6,974
Did not work but looked for work	1,626	1,531	660	661	966	870
Worked during the year	15,428	15,091	9,059	8,987	6,369	6,104
Median weeks of unemployment for all workers	12.0	12.4	13.0	13.4	10.4	10.7
Percent who worked during the year[1]	100.0	100.0	100.0	100.0	100.0	100.0
Year-round workers[2] with 1 or 2 weeks of unemployment	5.2	5.5	5.7	6.5	4.4	4.0
Part-year workers[3] with unemployment	94.8	94.5	94.3	93.5	95.6	96.0
1 to 4 weeks	21.4	20.1	17.4	16.0	27.2	26.1
5 to 14 weeks	33.7	33.3	34.1	33.4	33.0	33.2
15 weeks or more	39.7	41.1	42.8	44.2	35.4	36.6
With 2 spells or more of unemployment	31.6	31.6	35.6	33.9	25.9	28.1
Black						
Total who worked or looked for work	13,297	13,601	6,504	6,596	6,793	7,004
Percent with unemployment	25.0	25.1	25.9	25.3	24.1	24.8
Total with unemployment	3,321	3,409	1,685	1,671	1,636	1,738
Did not work but looked for work	730	744	292	276	438	468
Worked during the year	2,591	2,665	1,393	1,394	1,199	1,270
Median weeks of unemployment for all workers	16.8	15.7	17.2	16.2	16.2	15.3
Percent who worked during the year[1]	100.0	100.0	100.0	100.0	100.0	100.0
Year-round workers[2] with 1 or 2 weeks of unemployment	3.0	3.8	3.0	3.1	2.9	4.6
Part-year workers[3] with unemployment	97.0	96.2	97.0	96.9	97.1	95.4
1 to 4 weeks	13.7	13.7	12.0	13.5	15.6	13.8
5 to 14 weeks	30.0	31.3	30.6	31.5	29.3	31.1
15 weeks or more	53.4	51.2	54.4	51.9	52.2	50.5
With 2 spells or more of unemployment	35.6	36.4	38.1	40.1	32.7	32.4
Hispanic Origin						
Total who worked or looked for work	8,252	8,789	4,891	5,199	3,361	3,590
Percent with unemployment	22.6	22.3	24.4	23.6	19.9	20.5
Total with unemployment	1,865	1,962	1,194	1,226	670	735
Did not work but looked for work	229	205	97	83	132	122
Worked during the year	1,636	1,757	1,097	1,144	539	613
Median weeks of unemployment for all workers	14.5	14.7	15.2	16.4	13.1	12.7
Percent who worked during the year[1]	100.0	100.0	100.0	100.0	100.0	100.0
Year-round workers[2] with 1 or 2 weeks of unemployment	3.6	4.3	3.6	4.0	3.8	4.9
Part-year workers[3] with unemployment	96.4	95.7	96.4	96.0	96.2	95.1
1 to 4 weeks	16.5	15.6	13.6	13.7	22.3	19.2
5 to 14 weeks	31.9	31.1	32.4	29.3	30.8	34.2
15 weeks or more	48.0	49.0	50.4	53.0	43.2	41.6
With 2 spells or more of unemployment	33.9	32.7	37.9	35.0	25.6	28.4

(1) Time worked includes paid vacation and sick leave. (2) Worked 50 or 51 weeks. (3) Worked less than 50 weeks.

Average Annual Pay, by State, 1985-1986

Source: Bureau of Labor Statistics

State	1986	% Change from 1985	Rank
Ala.	$17,638	+3.6	37
Alaska	28,442	−0.9	1
Ariz.	18,870	+4.6	22
Ark.	16,162	+3.9	46
Calif.	21,995	+5.0	7
Colo.	20,275	+3.6	10
Conn.	22,516	+6.1	5
Del.	19,639	+2.6	15
D.C.	27,137	+3.7	2
Fla.	17,679	+4.2	35
Ga.	18,746	+4.6	23
Hawaii	18,101	+4.4	31
Idaho	16,602	+1.5	42
Ill.	21,452	+4.1	8
Ind.	19,024	+2.8	18
Iowa	16,598	+3.1	44
Kan.	17,934	+3.5	32
Ky.	17,357	+2.5	38
La.	18,290	+0.4	29
Maine	16,326	+5.8	45
Md.	20,121	NA	11
Mass.	20,925	+6.6	9
Mich.	22,720	+3.8	4
Minn.	19,630	+4.3	16
Miss.	15,420	+3.1	50
Mo.	18,915	+3.1	21
Mont.	$16,085	+1.0	48
Neb.	16,106	+3.1	47
Nev.	18,739	+3.1	24
N.H.	18,303	+6.4	28
N.J.	22,309	+5.8	6
N.M.	17,301	+1.8	39
N.Y.	23,200	+5.9	3
N.C.	17,001	+4.8	40
N.D.	15,778	+1.2	49
Ohio	19,902	+2.4	13
Okla.	18,345	+0.8	26
Ore.	18,322	+2.7	27
Pa.	19,404	+4.0	17
R.I.	17,733	+5.2	34
S.C.	16,600	+4.1	43
S.D.	14,477	+3.5	51
Tenn.	17,661	+4.0	36
Texas	19,934	+1.6	12
Utah	17,863	+1.6	33
Vt.	16,857	+5.2	41
Va.	18,972	+3.9	19
Wash.	19,645	+3.6	14
W.Va.	18,405	+2.2	25
Wis.	18,202	+3.5	30
Wyo.	18,969	+0.1	20
Avg.	**19,966**	+4.0	

Average Weekly Earnings of Production Workers[1]

Source: Bureau of Labor Statistics, U.S. Labor Department

Year, month	Manufacturing workers Gross average weekly earnings Current dollars	Manufacturing workers Gross average weekly earnings 1977 dollars	Private nonagricultural workers Gross average weekly earnings Current dollars	Private nonagricultural workers Gross average weekly earnings 1977 dollars
1975	190.79	214.85	163.53	184.16
1980	288.62	212.08	235.10	172.74
1984	374.03	220.67	292.86	172.78
1985	385.97	219.93	299.09	170.42
1986	396.01	222.23	304.85	171.07
1987 Jan.	401.47	222.30	306.16	169.52
Feb.	401.47	221.44	307.74	169.74
Mar.	402.87	221.24	308.63	169.48
Apr.	398.75	217.78	308.29	168.28
May	403.68	210.75	310.70	169.17
June	406.07p	220.09p	312.20p	169.21p
July	401.13p	—	311.85p	—

(1) Data relate to production workers in mining and manufacturing; to construction workers in contract construction, and to nonsupervisory workers in transportation and public utilities; wholesale and retail trade; finance, insurance, and real estate; and services. (p)—preliminary.

Federal Minimum Hourly Wage Rates Since 1950

Source: U.S. Department of Labor.

(Employee estimates as of September 1984, except as indicated. The Fair Labor Standards Act of 1938 and subsequent amendments provide for minimum wage coverage applicable to specified nonsupervisory employment categories. Exempt from coverage are executives and administrators or professionals).

Effective date	Minimum Rates for Nonfarm Workers: Laws prior to 1966[1]	Percent, avg earnings[2]	1966 and later[3]	Minimum rates for farm workers[4]
Jan. 25, 1950	$.75	54	(X)	(X)
Mar. 1, 1956	1.00	52	(X)	(X)
Sept. 3, 1961	1.15	50	(X)	(X)
Sept. 3, 1963	1.25	51	(X)	(X)
Feb. 1, 1967	1.40	50	$1.00	$1.00
Feb. 1, 1968	1.60	54	1.15	1.15
Feb. 1, 1969	(5)	(5)	1.30	1.30
Feb. 1, 1970	(5)	(5)	1.45	(5)
Feb. 1, 1971	(5)	(5)	1.60	(5)
May 1, 1974	2.00	46	1.90	1.60
Jan. 1, 1975	2.10	45	2.00	1.80
Jan. 1, 1976	2.30	46	2.20	2.00
Jan. 1, 1977	(5)	(5)	2.30	2.20
Jan. 1, 1978	2.65	44	2.65	2.65
Jan. 1, 1979	2.90	45	2.90	2.90
Jan. 1, 1980	3.10	45	3.10	3.10
Jan. 1, 1981	3.35	43	3.35	3.35
Sept. 1, 1985	(5)	(5)	(5)	(5)
*				

(X) Not applicable. (1) Applies to workers covered prior to 1961 Amendments and, after Sept. 1965, to workers covered by 1961 Amendments. Rates set by 1961 Amendments were: Sept. 1961, $1.00; Sept. 1964, $1.15; and Sept. 1965, $1.25. (2) Percent of gross average hourly earnings of production workers in manufacturing. (3) Applies to workers newly covered by Amendments of 1966, 1974, and 1977, and Title IX of Education Amendments of 1972. (4) Included in coverage as of 1966, 1974, and 1977 Amendments. (5) No change in rate.

*On Mar. 25, 1987, Sen. Edward M. Kennedy (D, Mass.) introduced the Minimum Wage Restoration Act, which would increase the minimum wage rates from $3.35 to $4.65 an hour over the next 3 years—50¢ in 1988, 40¢ in 1989, 40¢ in 1990. The legislation also mandated subsequent increases based on an index of 50% of the average private, nonsupervisory, and nonagricultural hourly wage rate. On March 26, 1987, Rep. Augustus Hawkins (D., Cal.) introduced a similar bill in the House.

Employed Wage and Salary Workers Paid at Minimum Hourly Wage Rate, 1986

Source: U.S. Department of Labor

	# Hourly Workers (in thousands)	# Hourly Workers at $3.35 (in thousands)	% of All Workers Paid Hourly	% of All Workers at $3.35
Total, 16 yrs, and over	**57,529**	**3,461**	**8.8**	**6.0**
16-24	15,649	2,146	19.2	13.7
16-19 yrs.	5,727	1,361	32.3	23.8
25 yrs. and over	41,880	1,314	4.9	3.1
Men, 16 yrs. and over	29,666	1,336	5.9	4.5
Women, 16 yrs. and over	27,863	2,125	7.6	4.3
Men who maintain families	938	20	3.1	2.1
Women who maintain families	3,457	213	9.7	6.2
White	48,713	2,765	8.6	5.7
Men	25,186	1,044	5.5	4.1
Women	23,527	1,722	11.9	7.3
Black	7,216	612	10.3	8.5
Men	3,666	254	8.2	6.9
Women	3,550	358	12.4	10.1
Full-time workers	42,808	1,174	4.1	2.7
Part-time workers	14,721	2,287	22.6	15.5
Private industry	**50,391**	**3,461**	**8.8**	**6.0**
Agriculture	832	92	17.7	11.1
Mining	459	1	.2	.2
Construction	3,881	42	1.6	1.1
Manufacturing	13,688	346	2.9	2.5
Transportation & public utilities	3,154	32	1.4	1.0
Wholesale trade	1,748	61	3.8	3.5
Retail trade	12,233	1,729	21.6	14.1
Finance, insurance, & real estate	2,036	53	3.0	2.6
Services	12,358	768	10.0	6.2
Private households	604	64	47.7	10.6
Business & repair	2,668	144	6.3	5.4
Personal	1,374	141	16.4	10.3
Entertainment & recreation	569	85	19.3	14.9
Government	**7,138**	**337**	**5.7**	**4.7**
Federal	1,972	31	2.0	1.6
State	1,580	132	9.8	8.4
Local	3,586	175	5.9	4.9

Work Stoppages (Strikes) in the U.S.

(involving 1,000 workers or more)

Source: Bureau of Labor Statistics, U.S. Department of Labor

Year	Number stoppages[1]	Workers involved[1] (thousands)	Man days idle[1] (thousands)
1952	470	2,746	48,820
1955	363	2,055	21,180
1958	332	1,587	17,900
1960	222	896	13,260
1961	195	1,031	10,140
1962	211	793	11,760
1963	181	512	10,020
1964	246	1,183	16,220
1965	268	999	15,140
1966	321	1,300	16,000
1967	381	2,192	31,320
1968	392	1,855	35,567
1969	412	1,576	29,397
1970	381	2,468	52,761
1971	298	2,516	35,538
1972	250	975	16,764
1973	317	1,400	16,260
1974	424	1,796	31,809
1975	235	965	17,563
1976	231	1,519	23,962
1977	298	1,212	21,258
1978	219	1,006	23,774
1979	235	1,021	20,409
1980	187	795	20,844
1981	145	729	16,908
1982	96	656	9,061
1983	81	909	17,461
1984	62	376	8,499
1985	54	324	7,079
1986	69	533	11,861

(1) The number of stoppages and workers relate to stoppages that began in the year. Days of idleness include all stoppages in effect. Workers are counted more than once if they were involved in more than one stoppage during the year.

Injuries and Illnesses in Industry

(in thousands)

Source: Bureau of Labor Statistics, U.S. Labor Dept.

Industry division	Total cases[1, 2]		Lost workday cases		Nonfatal cases without lost workdays		Lost workdays	
	1985	1984	1985	1984	1985	1984	1985	1984
Injuries and Illnesses[3]	**5,507.2**	**5,419.7**	**2,537.0**	**2,501.2**	**2,965.9**	**2,913.4**	**45,189.0**	**42,983.8**
Agriculture, forestry, and fishing[3]	91.7	93.6	46.1	47.4	45.4	46.0	736.4	709.6
Mining[4]	78.0	94.1	44.3	52.0	33.3	41.7	1,342.4	1,560.7
Construction	613.3	582.0	275.0	258.8	337.1	322.4	5,196.0	4,794.9
Manufacturing	1,937.6	1,988.6	857.1	873.6	1,079.6	1,114.1	14,973.7	14,644.1
Durable goods	1,226.8	1,261.3	531.2	543.0	694.9	717.8	9,261.0	9,071.9
Nondurable goods	710.8	727.3	325.9	330.7	384.6	396.3	5,712.7	5,572.2
Transportation and public utilities	422.7	427.9	246.2	251.6	175.7	175.4	5,268.7	5,131.5
Wholesale and retail trade	1,356.7	1,314.5	592.9	579.1	763.2	734.4	9,261.4	8,925.9
Wholesale trade	386.5	379.8	189.7	181.1	196.4	198.1	3,224.9	2,910.3
Retail trade	970.2	934.7	403.2	398.0	566.8	536.3	6,036.5	6,015.6
Finance, insurance, and real estate	103.6	98.6	47.0	45.1	56.5	53.3	818.2	691.[illegible]
Services	903.8	820.5	428.3	393.9	475.1	426.0	7,592.1	6,525.[illegible]
Injuries[3]	**5,381.7**	**5,294.8**	**2,484.7**	**2,449.7**	**2,893.1**	**2,841.1**	**44,050.3**	**41,921.[illegible]**
Illnesses[3]	**125.6**	**124.8**	**52.3**	**51.8**	**72.8**	**72.3**	**1,138.6**	**1,061.[illegible]**

(1) To maintain comparability with the rest of the series, a statistical method was used for generating the estimates to represent the small nonfarm employers in low-risk industries who were not surveyed for 1983 and 1984. The estimating procedure involved averaging the data reported by small employers for the 1980, 1981, and 1982 surveys. (2) Includes fatalities. (3) Excludes farms with fewer than 11 employees. (4) Excludes independent mining contractors. NOTE: Components may not add to the totals because of rounding.

Labor Union Directory

Source: Bureau of Labor Statistics; World Almanac Questionnaire

(*) Independent union; all others affiliated with AFL-CIO.

American Federation of Labor & Congress of Industrial Organizations (AFL-CIO), 815 16th St. NW, Washington, DC 20006; 13.1 mln. members.

Actors and Artistes of America, Associated (AAAA), 165 W. 46th St., New York, NY 10036; founded 1919; Frederick O'-Neal, Pres. (since 1970); no individual members, 9 National Performing Arts Unions are affiliates; approx. 220,000 combined membership.

Actors' Equity Association, 165 W. 46th St., New York, NY 10036; founded 1913; Colleen Dewhurst, Pres.; 37,500 active members.

Air Line Pilots Association, 1625 Massachusetts Ave. NW, Washington, DC 20036. Henry A. Duffy, Pres.; 34,000 members.

Aluminum Brick & Glass Workers International Union (ABGWIU), 3362 Hollenberg Drive, Bridgeton, MO 63044; founded 1953; Ernie Labaff, Pres. (since 1985); 55,000 members, 415 locals.

Automobile, Aerospace & Agricultural Implement Workers of America, International Union, United (UAW), 8000 E. Jefferson Ave., Detroit, MI 48214; founded 1935; Owen Bieber, Pres. (since 1983); 1,150,000 members, 1,320 locals.

Bakery, Confectionery & Tobacco Workers International Union (BC&T), 10401 Connecticut Ave., Kensington, MD 20895; founded 1886; John DeConcini, Pres. (since 1978); 145,000 members, 190 locals.

Boilermakers, Iron Shipbuilders, Blacksmiths, Forgers and Helpers, International Brotherhood of (IBBISB/BF&H), 570 New Brotherhood Bldg., 8th and State Ave., Kansas City, KS 66101; founded 1880; Charles W. Jones, Pres. (since 1983) 115,000 members, 600 locals.

Bricklayers and Allied Craftsmen, International Union of, 815 15th St. NW, Washington, DC 20005; John T. Joyce, Pres.; 110,000 members, 540 locals.

Carpenters and Joiners of America, United Brotherhood of, 101 Constitution Ave. NW, Washington, DC 20001; founded 1881; Patrick J. Campbell, Gen. Pres.; 650,000 members, 1,800 locals.

Chemical Workers Union, International (ICWU), 1655 West Market St., Akron, OH 44313; founded 1944; Frank D. Martino, Pres. (since 1975); 70,000 members, 400 locals.

Clothing and Textile Workers Union, Amalgamated (ACTWU), 15 Union Square, New York, NY 10003; founded 1976; union founded 1914; Murray H. Finley, Pres. (since 1976); 280,564 members, 1,490 locals.

Communications Workers of America, (AFL-CIO, CLC) 1925 K St. NW, Washington, DC 20006; Morton Bahr, Pres.; 700,000 members, 1,200 locals.

Distillery, Wine & Allied Workers International Union (DWU), 66 Grand Ave., Englewood, NJ 07631; founded 1940; George J. Orlando, Pres. (since 1984); 25,000 members, 67 locals.

***Education Association, National,** 1201 16th St. NW, Washington, DC 20036; Mary H. Futrell, Pres.; 1,700,000 members, 12,000 affiliates.

Electrical Workers, International Brotherhood of (IBEW), 1125 15th St., NW, Washington, DC 20005; founded 1891; J.J. Barry, Int'l Pres. (since 1986); 1,000,000 members, 1,400 locals.

Electronic, Electrical, Salaried, Machine and Furniture Workers, International Union of (IUE), 1126 16th St. NW, Washington, DC 20036; founded 1949; William H. Bywater, Pres. (since 1982); 200,000 members, 550 locals.

Farm Workers of America, United (UFW), La Paz, Keene, CA 93531; founded 1962; Cesar E. Chavez, Pres. (since 1962); 100,000 members.

***Federal Employees, National Federation of (NFFE),** 1016 16th St. NW, Washington, DC 20036; founded 1917; James M. Peirce Jr., Pres. (since 1976); 52,000+ members, 487 locals.

Fire Fighters, International Association of, 1750 New York Ave. NW, Washington, DC 20006; John A. Gannon, Pres.; 172,401 members, 1,943 locals.

Firemen and Oilers, International Brotherhood of, 122 C. St. NW, Washington, DC 20006; George J. Francisco, Pres.; 32,000 members.

Food and Commercial Workers International Union, United, (UFCW) 1775 K St., NW, Washington, DC 20006; founded 1979 following merger; William H. Wynn, Int'l Pres. (since 1977); 1.3 million members, 600 locals.

Garment Workers of America, United (UGWA), 4207 Lebanon Rd., Hermitage, TN 37076; founded 1891; Earl W. Carroll, Gen. Pres. (since 1987); 25,000 members, 125 locals.

Glass, Pottery, Plastics & Allied Workers Intl. Union (GPPAW), 608 E. Baltimore Pike, P.O. Box 607, Media, PA 19063; founded 1842; James E. Hatfield, Int'l Pres. (since 1977); 80,000 members, 289 locals.

Government Employees, American Federation of (AFGE), 80 F St., NW, Washington, DC 20001; founded 1932; Kenneth T. Blaylock, Natl. Pres. (since 1976); 225,000 members, 1,300 locals.

Grain Millers, American Federation of (AFGM), 4949 Olson Memorial Hwy., Minneapolis, MN 55422; founded 1948; Robert W. Willis, Gen. Pres.; 35,000 members, 210 locals.

Graphic Communications International Union (GCIU), 1900 L St., NW, Washington, DC 20036; founded 1983; James J. Norton, Pres. (since 1985); 191,291 members, 602 locals.

Hotel Employees and Restaurant Employees International Union, 1219-28th St., NW, Washington, DC 20007; Edward T. Hanley, Gen. Pres.; 330,000 members, 190 locals.

Industrial Workers of America, International Union, Allied (AIW), 3520 W. Oklahoma Ave., Milwaukee, WI 53215; founded 1935; Dominick D'Ambrosio, Intl. Pres. (since 1975); 70,000 members, 370 locals.

Iron Workers, International Association of Bridge Structural and Ornamental, 1750 New York Ave. NW, Washington, DC 20006; Juel D. Drake, Pres.; 153,015 members, 305 locals.

Laborers' International Union of North America (LIUNA), 905 16th St. NW, Washington, DC 20006; founded 1903; Angelo Fosco, Gen. Pres. (since 1976); 430,000 members, 800 locals.

Ladies Garment Workers Union, International (ILGWU), 1710 Broadway, New York, NY 10019; founded 1900; Jay Mazur, Pres. (since 1986); 200,000 members, 340 locals.

Leather Goods, Plastic and Novelty Workers' Union, International, 265 W. 14th St., New York, NY 10011; Domenic DiPaolo, Gen. Pres.; 25,000 members, 85 locals.

Letter Carriers, National Association of (NALC), 100 Indiana Ave. NW, Washington, DC 20001; founded 1889; Vincent R. Sombrotto, Pres. (since 1978); 290,000 members, 3,940 locals.

***Locomotive Engineers, Brotherhood of (BLE),** 1365 Ontario St., Cleveland, OH 44114; founded 1863; R.E. Delaney, Pres. (since 1986); 55,483 members, 674 divisions.

Longshoremen's Association, International, 17 Battery Pl., New York, NY 10004; Thomas W. Gleason, Pres.; 76,579 members, 367 locals.

***Longshoremen's & Warehousemen's Union, International (ILWU),** 1188 Franklin St., San Francisco, CA 94109; founded 1937; James R. Herman, Pres. (since 1977); 55,000 members, 81 locals.

Machinists and Aerospace Workers, International Association of (IAM), 1300 Connecticut Ave. NW, Washington, DC 20036; founded 1888; William W. Winpisinger, Int'l Pres.; 800,000 members, 1,610 locals.

Maintenance of Way Employes, Brotherhood of (BMWE), 12050 Woodward Ave., Detroit, MI 48203; founded 1887; Geoffrey N. Zeh, Pres. (since 1986); 75,000 members, 910 locals.

Marine & Shipbuilding Workers of America, Industrial Union of (IUMSWA), 5101 River Rd., #110, Bethesda, MD 20816; founded 1934; Arthur E. Batson Jr., Pres. (since 1982); 15,000 members, 32 locals.

Maritime Union of America, National, 346 W. 17th St., New York NY 10001; Shannon Wall, Pres.; 35,000 members.

***Mine Workers of America, United (UMWA),** 900 15th St. NW, Washington, DC 20005; founded 1890; Richard Trumka, Int'l Pres. (since 1982); 225,000 members, 900 locals.

Molders' and Allied Workers' Union, International (IM & AWU), 1225 E. McMillan St., Cincinnati, OH 45206; founded 1859; Bernard Butsavage, Pres. (since 1983); 40,000 members, 191 locals.

Musicians of the United States and Canada, American Federation of (AF of M), 1501 Broadway, Suite 600, New York, NY 10036; founded 1896; Victor W. Fuentealba, Pres. (since 1978); 206,000 members, 480 locals.

Newspaper Guild, The (TNG), 1125 15th St. NW, Washington, DC 20005; founded 1933; Charles A. Perlik Jr., Pres. (since 1969); 34,000 members, 80 locals.

Novelty & Production Workers, Intl. Union of Allied, 147-149 E. 26th St., New York, NY 10010; Julius Isaacson, Pres. 30,000 members, 18 locals.

***Nurses Association, American,** 2420 Pershing Rd., Kansas

City, MO 64108; Margretta M. Styles, Pres.; 53 constituent state assns.

Office and Professional Employees International Union (OPEIU), 265 W. 14th St., New York, NY 10011; founded 1945 (AFL Charter); John Kelly, Int'l Pres. (since 1979); 135,00 members, 300 locals.

Oil, Chemical and Atomic Workers International Union (OCAW), PO Box 2812, Denver, CO 80201; Joseph M. Misbrener Pres. (since 1983); 115,000 members, 443 locals.

Operating Engineers, International Union of (IUOE), 1125 17th St. NW, Washington, DC 20036; founded 1896; Larry Dugan, Jr., Gen. Pres. (since 1985); 375,000 members, 200 locals.

Painters and Allied Trades, International Brotherhood of (IBPAT), 1750 New York Ave. NW, Washington, DC 20006; founded 1887; William A. Duval, Gen. Pres. (since 1984); 161,516 members, 667 locals.

Paperworkers International Union, United (UPIU), 3340 Perimeter Hill Dr., Nashville, TN 37202; founded 1884; Wayne E. Glenn, Pres. (since 1978); 245,000 members, 1,150 locals.

***Plant Guard Workers of America, International Union, United (UPGWA),** 25510 Kelly Rd., Roseville, MI 48066; founded 1948; Henry E. Applen, Pres.; 28,000 members, 176 locals.

Plasterers' and Cement Mason's International Association of the United States & Canada; Operative, 1125 17th St. NW, Washington, DC 20036; Robert J. Holton, Pres.; Vincent J. Panepinto, Secy.-Treas.; 65,000 members, 365 locals.

Plumbing and Pipe Fitting Industry of the United States and Canada, United Association of Journeymen and Apprentices of the, 901 Massachusetts Ave. NW, Washington, DC 20001; Marvin J. Boede, Pres.; 350,000 members.

***Police, Fraternal Order of,** 2100 Gardiner Lane, Louisville, KY 40205; Richard A. Boyd, Natl. Pres. and Charles R. Orms, Natl. Secy.; 173,071 members, 1,742 affiliates.

***Postal Supervisors, National Association of,** 490 L'Enfant Plaza SW, Suite 3200, Washington, DC 20024-2120; Rubin Handelman, Pres.; 41,000 members, 460 locals.

Postal Workers Union, American (APWU), 1300 L St. NW, Washington, DC 20005; founded 1971; Moe Biller, Pres. (since 1980); 330,000 members, 2,500 locals.

Railway, Airline and Steamship Clerks, Freight Handlers, Express and Station Employees; Brotherhood of (BRAC), 3 Research Place, Rockville, MD 20850; Richard I. Kilroy, Int'l Pres. (since (1981); 160,000 members, 750 locals.

Railway Carmen of the United States and Canada, Brotherhood (BRC of US&C), 4929 Main St., Kansas City, MO 64112; founded 1888; C.E. Wheeler, Gen. Pres. (since 1983); 72,054 members, 520 locals.

Retail, Wholesale and Department Store Union, 30 E. 29th St., New York, NY 10016; Lenore Miller, Pres.; 250,000 members, 315 locals.

Roofers, Waterproofers & Allied Workers, United Union of, 1125 17th St. NW, Washington, DC 20036; Earl J. Kruse, Pres.; 27,000 members, 138 locals.

Rubber, Cork, Linoleum and Plastic Workers of America, United (URW), 87 South High St., Akron, OH 44308; founded 1935; Milan Stone; Int'l Pres. (since 1981); 116,000 members, 443 locals.

***Rural Letter Carriers' Association, National,** Suite 100, 1448 Duke St., Alexandria, VA 22314; founded 1903; Olin F. Armentrout, Pres. (since 1986); 70,000 members; state organizations, 47.

Seafarers International Union of North America (SIUNA), 5201 Auth Way, Camp Springs, MD 20746; founded 1938; Frank Drozak, Pres.; 90,000 members.

Service Employees International Union (SEIU), 1313 L St. NW, Washington, DC 20005; founded 1921; John J. Sweeney, Pres. (since 1980); 850,000 members, 300 locals.

Sheet Metal Workers' International Association (SMWIA), 1750 New York Ave. NW, Washington, DC 20006; founded 1888; Edward J. Carlough, Gen. Pres. (since 1970); 150,000 members, 282 locals.

State, County and Municipal Employees, American Federation of, 1625 L St. NW, Washington, DC 20036; Gerald McEntee, Pres.; 1,000,000 members, 2,991 locals.

Steelworkers of America, United (USWA), 5 Gateway Center, Pittsburgh, PA 15222; founded 1936; Lynn Williams, Int'l Pres. (since 1984); 832,748 members, 4,125 locals.

Teachers, American Federation of (AFT), 555 New Jersey Ave. NW, Washington, DC 20001; founded 1916; Albert Shanker, Pres. (since 1974); 640,000 members, 2,200 locals.

***Teamsters, Chauffeurs, Warehousemen and Helpers of America, International Brotherhood of (IBT),** 25 Louisiana Ave. NW, Washington, DC 20001; founded 1903; Jackie Presser, Gen. Pres.; 2,000,000 members, 694 locals.

Television and Radio Artists, American Federation of, 1350 Ave. of the Americas, New York, NY; founded 1937; Frank Maxwell, Pres.; 67,000 members, 38 locals.

Textile Workers of America, United (UTWA), 2 Echelon Plaza, Laurel Rd., P.O. Box 749, Vorhees, NJ 08043-0749; founded 1901; Vernon Mustard, Intl. Pres. (since 1986); 26,000 members, 180 locals.

Theatrical Stage Employees and Moving Picture Operators of the United States and Canada, International Alliance of, 1515 Broadway, New York, NY 10036; Alfred W. Di Tolla, Pres.; 61,471 members, 750 locals.

Transit Union, Amalgamated (ATU), 5025 Wisconsin Ave. NW, Washington, DC 20016; founded 1892; John W. Rowland, Intl. Pres. (since 1981); 160,000 members, 295 locals.

Transport Workers Union of America, 80 West End Ave., New York, NY 10023; founded 1934; John E. Lawe; Int'l Pres. (since 1985); 91,000 members, 74 locals.

***Transportation Union, United (UTU),** 14600 Detroit Ave., Cleveland, OH 44107; founded 1969; Fred A. Hardin, Pres. (since 1979); 120,000 members; 862 locals.

***Treasury Employees Union, National (NTEU),** 1730 K St. NW, Suite 1101, Washington, DC 20006; founded 1938; Robert M. Tobias, Natl. Pres. (since 1983); 120,000 represented, 250 chapters.

***University Professors, American Association of (AAUP),** 1012-14th St., Washington, DC 20005; founded 1915; Julius G. Gelman, Pres.; 53,000 members, 1,300 locals.

Upholsterers' International Union of North America (UIU), 25 N. 4th St., Philadelphia, PA 19106; founded 1882; John Serembus, Pres.; 31,827 members, 133 locals.

Utility Workers Union of America (UWUA), 815 16th St. NW Washington, DC 20006; founded 1945; James Joy Jr., Natl Pres. (since 1980); 60,000 members, 220 locals.

Woodworkers of America, International (IWA), 1622 N. Lombard St., Portland, OR 97217; founded 1937; Keith Johnson Intl. Pres. (since 1973); 100,000 members, 200 locals.

Percent of Workers in Unions

Source: U.S. Bureau of Labor Statistics

	Percent union members[1] 1984	1985
Total	**18.8**	**18.0**
16-24 years	7.9	7.3
25-34 years	18.2	16.7
35-44 years	23.9	22.7
45-54 years	25.5	25.1
55-64 years	25.0	24.8
65 years and over	9.8	8.7
Men, total	**23.0**	**22.1**
Women, total	**13.8**	**13.2**
Occupation		
Managerial and professional specialty	15.8	15.2
Technical sales, and administrative support	11.2	10.8
Service occupations	15.1	14.4

	Percent unior members[1] 1984	198
Precision, production, craft, and repair	30.1	28.
Operators, fabricators, and laborers	33.1	31.
Farming, forestry, and fishing	5.5	5.
Industry		
Agricultural wage and salary workers	2.6	2.
Private nonagricultural wage and salary workers	15.5	14.
Mining	17.7	17.
Construction	23.5	22
Manufacturing	26.0	24
Transportation and public utilities	38.7	37
Wholesale and retail trade, total	7.9	7
Finance, insurance, and real estate	2.7	2
Services	7.3	6
Government	35.8	35

1. Members of labor union or employee association.

ECONOMICS

U.S. Budget Receipts and Outlays—1983-1986

Source: U.S. Treasury Department, Bureau of Govt. Financial Operations
(Fiscal years end Sept. 30)
(millions of dollars)

Classification	Fiscal 1983	Fiscal 1984	Fiscal 1985[1]	Fiscal 1986
Net Receipts				
Individual income taxes	$288,938	$295,955	$334,560	$348,959
Corporation income taxes	37,022	56,893	61,331	63,143
Social insurance taxes and contributions:				
Federal old-age and survivors insurance	128,972	152,444	169,882	182,518
Federal disability insurance	18,348	15,907	16,348	17,711
Federal hospital insurance	35,641	40,262	44,871	51,335
Railroad retirement fund	2,805	3,321	2,213	2,103
Total employment taxes and contributions	**185,766**	**212,184**	**234,646**	**255,062**
Other insurance and retirement:				
Unemployment	18,799	25,138	25,758	24,098
Federal employees retirement	4,351	4,494	4,672	4,645
Civil service retirement and disability	78	86	87	96
Total social insurance taxes and contributions	**208,994**	**241,902**	**265,163**	**283,901**
Excise taxes	35,300	37,361	35,992	32,919
Estate and gift taxes	6,053	6,010	6,422	6,958
Customs duties	8,655	11,370	12,079	13,323
Deposits of earnings-Federal Reserve Banks	14,492	15,684	17,059	18,374
All other miscellaneous receipts	1,109	1,281	1,451	1,514
Net Budget Receipts	**$600,562**	**$666,457**	**$734,057**	**$769,091**
Net Outlays				
Legislative Branch	$1,448	$1,579	$1,610	1,665
The Judiciary	787	866	966	1,069
Executive Office of the President:				
The White House Office	21	16	24	23
Office of Management and Budget	35	37	41	37
Total Executive Office	**94**	**95**	**111**	**107**
Funds appropriated to the President:				
Disaster relief	202	243	192	333
International security assistance	3,677	5,034	9,295	10,371
Multinational assistance	1,460	1,699	1,763	1,838
Agency for International Development	...	1,083	1,208	1,220
International Development Assistance	2,352	2,819	3,008	3,121
Total funds appropriated to the President	**5,427**	**8,481**	**12,050**	**11,377**
Agriculture Department:				
Food stamp program	11,839	11,561	11,701	11,619
Farmer's Home Admin.	4,303	6,066	11,093	8,001
Total Agriculture Department	**46,391**	**37,160**	**55,523**	**58,666**
Commerce Department	1,929	1,863	2,140	2,084
Defense Department:				
Military personnel	45,523	47,655	67,842	71,511
Operation and maintenance	64,915	67,369	72,348	75,259
Procurement	53,624	61,879	70,381	76,517
Research, development, test, evaluation	20,554	23,117	27,103	32,283
Military construction	3,524	3,706	4,260	5,067
Total Defense Department (military)	**207,045**	**240,382**	**245,371**	**265,636**
Defense Department (civil)	—	—	18,842	20,480
Education Department	14,567	15,511	16,682	17,673
Energy Department	8,356	8,289	10,586	11,025
Health and Human Services Department:				
Food and Drug Administration	364	390	418	417
National Institutes of Health	3,750	4,157	4,670	5,115
Public Health Service	7,856	8,184	8,866	9,493
Health Care Financing Adm.	—	—	113,359	119,318
Human Development Services	5,344	5,896	6,056	5,998
Total Health and Human Services Dept.	**276,453**	**292,313**	**132,103**	**143,251**
Social Security	—	—	183,434	190,684
Housing and Urban Development Department	15,315	16,520	28,720	14,193
Interior Department	4,569	4,961	4,826	4,791
Justice Department:				
Federal Bureau of Investigation	824	916	1,072	1,183
Total Justice Department	**2,849**	**3,165**	**3,586**	**3,768**
Labor Department:				
Unemployment Trust Fund	32,655	26,089	23,826	21,819
Total Labor Department	**38,194**	**24,522**	**23,893**	**24,141**
State Department	2,267	2,403	2,645	2,864
Transportation Department	20,616	23,956	25,022	27,365
Treasury Department:				
Internal Revenue Service	6,391	6,095	6,746	7,188
Interest on the public debt	128,813	153,838	178,945	187,117
Total Treasury Department	**116,248**	**141,105**	**164,987**	**176,180**
Environmental Protection Agency	4,299	4,057	4,511	4,868
General Services Administration	145	192	−214	286
National Aeronautics and Space Administration	6,664	7,048	7,251	7,403
Office of Personnel Management	21,278	22,590	23,727	23,955
Small Business Administration	479	255	680	490

(continued)

Classification	Fiscal 1983	Fiscal 1984	Fiscal 1985	Fiscal 1986
Net Outlays				
Veterans Administration	24,816	25,593	26,333	26,536
Independent agencies:				
Action	126	133	129	154
Board for International Broadcasting	91	105	97	127
Consumer Product Safety Commission	33	34	35	35
Corporation for Public Broadcasting	137	138	151	160
District of Columbia	427	486	548	530
Equal Employment Opportunity Commission	152	152	158	159
Export-Import Bank of the United States	578	1,068	−384	−1,167
Federal Communications Commission	82	87	94	92
Federal Deposit Insurance Corporation	−613	−248	−1,942	262
Federal Emergency Management Agency	506	596	469	658
Federal Home Loan Bank Board	−453	−561	414	1,060
Federal Trade Commission	65	66	65	62
Intragovernmental Agencies	55	39	278	218
Appalachian Regional Commission	264	212	204	159
Interstate Commerce Commission	65	56	50	45
Legal Services Corporation	234	271	300	305
National Archives & Record Adm.	—	—	100	96
Merit Systems Protection Board	24	26	23	23
National Foundation on the Arts and Humanities	269	302	317	320
National Labor Relations Board	123	130	134	132
National Science Foundation	1,055	1,198	1,313	1,550
National Transportation Safety Board	NA	21	22	22
Nuclear Regulatory Commission	515	462	468	421
Postal Service	789	879	1,210	716
Railroad Retirement Board	3,963	3,606	4,129	3,980
Securities and Exchange Commission	90	92	103	104
Smithsonian Institution	194	211	226	224
Tennessee Valley Authority	820	351	1,010	905
U.S. Information Agency	508	574	694	780
U.S. Railway Association	4	2	25	2
Other Independent agencies	327	339	373	354
Total independent agencies	**10,350**	**10,946**	**9,580**	**11,422**
Undistributed offsetting receipts	−35,565	−52,351	−58,973	−62,118
Net Budget Outlays	**795,916**	**841,800**	**945,987**	**989,789**
Less net receipts	600,562	666,457	734,057	769,091
Deficit	**−$195,354**	**−$175,342**	**−211,931**	**−220,698**
Off budget items	−12,357	−9,996	—	—

(1) In accordance with the Balanced Budget and Emergency Deficit Control Act of 1985, all former off-budget entities are now presented on-budget. The Federal Financing Bank activities are now shown as separate accounts under the agencies that use the FFB to finance their programs. In addition, 2 Social Security trust funds (Federal old-age survivors insurance and Federal disability insurance trust funds) have been moved off-budget.

U.S. Net Receipts and Outlays

Source: U.S. Treasury Department; annual statements for year ending June 30[3] (thousands of dollars)

Yearly average	Receipts	Outlays	Yearly average	Receipts	Outlays	Yearly average	Receipts	Outlays
1789-1800[1]	5,717	5,776	1871-1875	336,830	287,460	1916-1920[6]	3,483,652	8,065,333
1801-1810[2]	13,056	9,086	1876-1880	288,124	255,598	1921-1925	4,306,673	3,578,989
1811-1820[2]	21,032	23,943	1881-1885	366,961	257,691	1926-1930	4,069,138	3,182,807
1821-1830[2]	21,928	16,162	1886-1890	375,448	279,134	1931-1935[4]	2,770,973	5,214,874
1831-1840[2]	30,461	24,495	1891-1895	352,891	363,599	1936-1940[4]	4,960,614	10,192,367
1841-1850[2]	28,545	34,097	1896-1900	434,877	457,451	1941-1945[4]	25,951,137	66,037,928
1851-1860	60,237	60,163	1901-1905	559,481	535,559	1946-1950[5,7]	39,047,243	42,334,534
1861-1865	160,907	683,785	1906-1910	628,507	639,178			
1866-1870	447,301	377,642	1911-1915	710,227	720,252			

Fiscal Year	Receipts	Outlays	Fiscal year	Receipts	Outlays	Fiscal year	Receipts	Outlays
1955	60,389,744	64,569,973	1973	232,191,842	246,603,359	1980	520,056,012	579,602,970
1960	77,763,460	76,539,413	1974	264,847,484	268,342,952	1981	602,612,295	660,544,033
1964	89,458,664	97,684,375	1975	281,037,466	324,641,586	1982	617,766,000	728,424,000
1965	93,071,797	96,506,904	1976	300,005,077	365,610,129	1983	600,562,000	795,916,000
1968[9]	153,675,705	172,803,186	1976 Trans[3]	81,772,766	94,472,996	1984	666,457,000	841,800,000
1970	193,843,791	194,968,258	1977[3]	356,861,331	401,896,376	1985[10]	734,057,000	945,987,000
1971	188,332,129	210,652,667	1978	401,997,000	450,758,000	1986	769,091,000	989,789,000
1972[8]	215,262,639	238,285,907	1979	465,954,656	493,607,095			

(1) Average for period March 4, 1789, to Dec. 31, 1800. (2) Years ended Dec. 31, 1801 to 1842; average for 1841-1850 is for the period Jan. 1, 1841, to June 30, 1850. (3) Effective fiscal year 1977, fiscal year is reckoned Oct. 1-Sept. 30; transition quarter covers July 1, 1976-Sept. 30, 1976. (4) Expenditures for years 1932 through 1946 have been revised to include Government corps. (wholly owned) etc. (net). (5) Effective January 3, 1949, amounts refunded by the Government, principally for the overpayment of taxes, are being reported as deductions from total receipts rather than as expenditures. Also, effective July 1, 1948, payments to the Treasury, principally by wholly owned Government corporations for retirement of capital stock and for disposition of earnings, are excluded in reporting both budget receipts and expenditures. Neither of these changes affects the size of the budget surplus or deficit. Beginning 1931 figures in each case have been adjusted accordingly for comparative purposes. (6) Figures for 1918 through 1946 are revised to exclude statutory debt retirement (sinking fund, etc.). (7) Excludes $3 billion transferred to Foreign Economics Corporation Trust Fund, and includes $3 billion representing expenditures made from the FEC Trust Fund. (8) Effective fiscal year 1972 loan repayments and loan disbursements will be netted against expenditures and known as outlays. (9) From 1968, figures include trust funds (e.g. Social Security). (10) Since 1985, off-budget items are incl.; some social security trust funds moved off-budget.

National Income by Industry

Source: Bureau of Economic Analysis, U.S. Commerce Department
(billions of dollars)

	1960	1965	1970	1975	1980	1985	1986
National income without capital consumption adjustment	**428.6**	**583.6**	**835.1**	**1,315.0**	**2,263.9**	**3,198.3**	**3,394.5**
Domestic industries	**425.1**	**577.8**	**827.8**	**1,297.4**	**2,216.3**	**3,158.5**	**3,360.7**
Private industries	371.6	500.8	695.4	1,088.3	1,894.5	2,689.9	2,864.7
Agriculture, forestry, fisheries	17.8	21.0	25.9	46.5	61.4	76.6	82.9
Mining	5.6	6.1	8.4	21.2	43.8	44.2	40.2
Construction	22.5	32.3	47.4	69.9	126.6	167.6	181.8
Manufacturing	125.3	171.6	215.6	317.5	532.1	672.0	684.4
Durable goods	73.4	105.6	127.7	185.0	313.7	402.7	410.7
Nondurable goods	52.0	66.1	87.9	132.5	218.4	269.3	273.7
Transportation, public utilities	35.8	47.0	64.4	101.1	177.3	256.4	269.5
Transportation	18.5	23.7	31.5	48.0	85.8	109.2	113.8
Communication	8.2	11.5	17.6	26.8	48.1	67.8	70.9
Electric, gas, and sanitary services	9.1	11.7	15.2	26.2	43.4	79.4	84.7
Wholesale trade	25.0	32.5	47.5	83.0	143.3	202.5	210.1
Retail trade	41.3	55.1	79.9	123.1	189.4	282.8	301.3
Finance, insurance, and real estate	51.3	67.4	96.4	143.9	279.5	411.1	465.6
Services	46.9	67.9	109.8	182.1	341.0	576.7	629.0
Government, government enterprises	**53.5**	**76.9**	**132.4**	**209.1**	**321.8**	**468.6**	**496.1**
Rest of the world	**3.5**	**5.8**	**7.3**	**17.5**	**47.6**	**39.8**	**33.7**

National Income by Type of Income

Source: Bureau of Economic Analysis, U.S. Commerce Department
(billions of dollars)

	1960	1965	1970	1975	1980	1985	1986
National income	**424.9**	**585.2**	**832.6**	**1,289.1**	**2,203.5**	**3,229.9**	**3,422.0**
Compensation of employees	**296.7**	**399.8**	**618.3**	**948.7**	**1,638.2**	**2,370.8**	**2,504.9**
Wages and salaries	272.8	363.7	551.5	814.7	1,372.0	1,974.7	2,089.1
Government	49.2	69.9	117.1	176.1	260.1	372.1	394.8
Other	223.7	293.8	434.3	638.6	1,111.8	1,602.6	1,604.3
Supplements to wages, salary	23.8	36.1	66.8	134.0	266.3	396.1	415.8
Employer contrib. for social ins.	12.6	18.3	34.3	68.0	127.9	203.8	214.7
Other labor income	11.2	17.8	32.5	65.9	138.4	192.3	201.1
Proprietors' income	**52.1**	**65.1**	**80.2**	**125.4**	**180.7**	**257.3**	**289.8**
Farm	11.6	13.0	14.7	25.4	20.5	29.7	37.2
Nonfarm	40.5	52.1	65.4	100.0	160.1	227.6	252.6
Rental income of persons	**15.3**	**18.1**	**18.2**	**13.5**	**6.6**	**9.0**	**16.7**
Corp. prof., with inv. adjust.	**49.8**	**76.2**	**69.5**	**123.9**	**194.0**	**277.6**	**284.4**
Corp. profits before tax	49.9	77.4	76.0	134.8	237.1	224.8	231.9
Corp. profits tax liability	22.7	30.9	34.4	50.9	84.8	96.7	105.0
Corp. profits after tax	27.2	46.5	41.7	83.9	152.3	128.1	126.8
Dividends	12.9	19.1	22.5	29.6	54.7	81.3	86.8
Undistributed profits	14.3	27.4	19.2	54.3	97.6	46.8	40.0
Inventory valuation adj.	-.2	-1.2	-6.6	-11.0	-43.1	.7	6.5
Net interest	**11.3**	[illegible]	**41.2**	[illegible]	**200.9**	**315.3**	**326.1**

Gross National Product, Net National Product, National Income, and Personal Income

Source: Bureau of Economic Analysis, U.S. Commerce Department
(billions of dollars)

	1960	1970	1975	1980	1985	1986
Gross national product	**515.3**	**1,015.5**	**1,598.4**	**2,732.0**	**4,010.3**	**4,235.0**
Less: Capital consumption allowances	46.4	88.8	161.8	303.8	437.6	456.7
Equals: Net national product	**468.9**	**926.6**	**1,436.6**	**2,428.1**	**3,572.7**	**3,778.4**
Less: Indirect business tax and nontax liability	45.3	94.0	140.0	213.3	333.2	347.7
Business transfer payments	2.0	4.1	7.4	12.1	21.6	22.3
Statistical discrepancy	−2.8	−1.1	2.5	4.9	−5.6	−4.9
Plus: Subsidies less current surplus of government enterprises	.4	2.9	2.4	5.7	6.3	8.7
Equals: National income	**424.9**	**832.6**	**1,289.1**	**2,203.5**	**3,229.9**	**3,422.0**
Less: Corporate profits with inventory valuation and capital consumption adjustment	49.5	74.7	117.6	177.2	277.6	284.4
Net interest	11.3	41.2	83.8	200.9	315.3	326.1
Contributions for social insurance	21.9	62.2	118.5	216.5	352.7	374.3
Wage accruals less disbursement	.0	.0	.1	.0	−.2	0
Plus: Government transfer payment to persons	27.5	81.8	185.7	312.6	468.2	496.0
Personal interest income	24.9	69.3	122.5	271.9	476.5	497.6
Personal dividend income	12.9	22.2	28.7	52.9	76.3	81.2
Business transfer payments	2.0	4.1	7.4	12.1	21.6	22.3
Equals: Personal income	**409.4**	**831.8**	**1,313.4**	**2,258.5**	**3,327.0**	**3,534.3**

Third World Debt

Outstanding external debt of Third World nations totaled over $1 trillion at the end of 1986, according to a survey by the World Bank. The following are the leading debtor nations at the beginning of 1987.

Country	Dollars	Country	Dollars	Country	Dollars
Brazil	107.8 billion	Venezuela	34.1 billion	Peru	14.7 billion
Mexico	102.0 billion	Philippines	28.1 billion	Colombia	14.7 billion
Argentina	53.0 billion	Nigeria	22.1 billion	Ecuador	9.1 billion
Indonesia	43.9 billion	Chile	21.2 billion		

Public Debt of the U.S.

Source: U.S. Treasury Department, Financial Management Service, Bureau of the Census

Fiscal year	Debt (billions)	Per. cap. (dollars)	Interest paid (billions)	Pct. of federal outlays	Fiscal year	Debt (billions)	Per. cap. (dollars)	Interest paid (billions)	Pct. of federal outlays
1870	$2.4	$61.06	—	—	1972	426.4	2,037	21.8	9.4
1880	2.0	41.60	—	—	1973	457.3	2,164	24.2	9.8
1890	1.1	17.80	—	—	1974	474.2	2,223	29.3	10.9
1900	1.2	16.60	—	—	1975	533.2	2,475	32.7	9.8
1910	1.1	12.41	—	—	1976	620.4	2,852	37.1	10.0
1920	24.2	228	—	—	1977	698.8	3,170	41.9	10.2
1930	16.1	131	—	—	1978	771.5	3,463	48.7	10.6
1940	43.0	325	1.0	10.5	1979	826.5	3,669	59.8	11.9
1945	258.7	1,849	3.8	4.1	1980	907.7	3,985	74.9	12.7
1950	256.1	1,688	5.7	13.4	1981	997.9	4,338	95.6	14.1
1955	272.8	1,651	6.4	9.4	1982	1,142.0	4,913	117.4	15.7
1960	284.1	1,572	9.2	10.0	1983	1,377.2	5,870	128.8	15.9
1965	313.8	1,613	11.3	9.6	1984	1,572.3	6,640	153.8	18.1
1970	370.1	1,814	19.3	9.9	1985	1,823.1	7,598	178.9	18.9
1971	397.3	1,921	21.0	10.0	1986	2,034.0	8,546	187.1	24.3

Note: Through 1976 the fiscal year ended June 30. From 1977 on, fiscal year ends Sept. 30.

Foreign Direct Investment in the U.S.

Source: Bureau of Economic Analysis; U.S. Commerce Department

(billions of dollars)

Country	1970	1975	1980	1983	1984	1985	1986
Total	**13.2**	**27.6**	**83.0**	**137.0**	**164.5**	**184.6**	**209.3**
Canada	3.1	5.3	12.1	11.4	15.2	17.1	18.3
Europe	9.5	18.5	37.4	92.9	108.2	121.4	141.6
Netherlands	2.1	5.3	19.1	29.1	33.7	37.0	42.8
Switzerland	1.5	2.1	5.0	7.4	8.1	10.5	12.1
United Kingdom	4.1	6.3	14.1	32.1	38.3	43.5	51.3
W. Germany	0.680	1.4	7.5	10.8	12.3	14.8	17.3
Other Europe	1.0	3.3	8.7	13.2	15.6	14.3	17.3
Japan	0.229	0.591	4.7	11.3	16.0	19.3	23.4
Other areas	0.370	3.1	11.4	21.3	25.0	26.2	

U.S. Direct Investment Abroad in Selected Countries

Source: Bureau of Economic Analysis, U.S. Commerce Department

(millions of dollars)

	1985	1986
All countries	**229,748**	**259,890**
Africa	4,496	4,263
Egypt	2,423	2,027
Libya	1,922	1,798
Nigeria	44	588
Asia and Pacific	15,330	16,023
Hong Kong	3,296	3,580
India	386	450
Indonesia	4,434	4,305
Malaysia	1,141	1,074
Philippines	1,011	1,117
Singapore	1,884	2,291
South Korea	743	792
Taiwan	747	860
Thailand	1,054	1,048
Other	635	505
Australia	8,427	8,384
Canada	47,106	50,178
Europe	105,371	123,183
European Communities	81,337	96,226
Belgium	5,333	6,302
Denmark	1,304	1,317
France	7,870	9,471
Germany, West	16,743	20,344
Greece	209	194
Ireland	3,608	4,250
Italy	5,711	6,987
Luxembourg	471	495
Netherlands	7,286	11,874
United Kingdom	32,801	34,990
Other Europe	24,034	26,958
Austria	493	420
Finland	258	294
Norway	3,216	3,798
Portugal	236	283
Spain	2,510	3,111
Sweden	942	1,043
Switzerland	15,765	17,458
Turkey	226	224
Japan	9,246	11,333
South America	18,028	18,402
Argentina	2,713	2,986
Brazil	8,889	9,135
Chile	85	193
Colombia	2,142	2,049
Ecuador	361	536
Peru	1,652	1,118
Venezuela	1,588	1,843
Other	597	542
Central America	9,630	9,685
Mexico	5,070	4,826
Panama	4,004	4,352
Middle East	4,811	5,353
Israel	784	710
Saudi Arabia	2,468	2,480
United Arab Emirates	904	982

U.S. International Transactions

Source: Bureau of Economic Analysis, U.S. Commerce Department
(millions of dollars)

	1960	1965	1970	1975	1980	1984	1985	1986
Exports of goods and services[1]	**28,861**	**41,087**	**65,674**	**155,729**	**342,485**	**360,778**	**359,458**	**372,807**
Merchandise, adjusted, excluding military[2]	19,650	26,461	42,469	107,088	224,269	219,900	215,635	224,361
Transfers under U.S. military agency sales contracts	335	830	1,501	4,049	8,274	9,954	8,670	8,903
Travel	919	1,380	2,331	4,697	10,588	11,353	11,675	12,913
Passenger fares	175	271	544	1,039	2,591	3,028	3,040	3,562
Other transportation	1,607	2,175	3,125	5,840	11,618	13,809	14,066	15,190
Royalties and license fees from affiliated foreigners[3]	590	1,199	1,758	3,543	5,780	3,921	4,224	4,715
Royalties and license fees from unaffiliated foreigners	247	335	573	757	1,305	1,724	1,942	2,147
Other private services from affiliated foreigners	—	—	—	—	—	2,483	2,516	3,084
Other private services from unaffiliated foreigners	570	714	1,294	2,920	5,158	7,985	8,215	9,122
U.S. Government miscellaneous services	153	285	332	446	398	711	876	602
Receipts of income on U.S. assets abroad:								
Direct investment	3,621	5,506	8,169	16,595	37,146	21,217	32,665	36,697
Other private receipts	646	1,421	2,671	7,644	32,798	59,464	50,131	45,191
U.S. Government receipts	349	510	907	1,112	2,562	5,229	5,603	6,321
Transfers of goods and services under U.S. military grant programs, net	**1,695**	**1,636**	**2,713**	**2,207**	**756**	**153**	**46**	**101**
Imports of goods and services	**-23,670**	**-32,708**	**-59,901**	**-132,745**	**-333,020**	**-455,612**	**-460,550**	**-498,501**
Merchandise, adjusted, excluding military[2]	-14,758	-21,510	-39,866	-98,185	-249,749	-332,422	-338,083	-368,700
Direct defense expenditures	-3,087	-2,952	-4,855	-4,795	-10,511	-11,896	-12,009	-12,565
Travel	-1,750	-2,438	-3,980	-6,417	-10,397	-15,449	-16,482	-17,627
Passenger fares	-513	-717	-1,215	-2,263	-3,607	-6,502	-7,313	-6,842
Other transportation	-1,402	-1,951	-2,843	-5,708	-11,790	-14,843	-15,852	-17,099
Royalties and license fees to affiliated foreigners[3]	-35	-68	-111	-287	-428	-597	-467	-616
Royalties and license fees to unaffiliated foreigners	-40	-67	-114	-186	-297	-359	-425	-461
Other private services to affiliated foreigners	—	—	—	—	—	478	696	1,324
Other private services to unaffiliated foreigners	-593	-461	-827	-1,551	-2,909	-5,074	-5,983	-6,853
U.S. Government miscellaneous services	-254	-457	-576	-789	-1,214	-1,531	-1,733	-1,696
Payments of income on foreign assets in the U.S.								
Direct investment	-394	-657	-875	-2,234	-8,635	-9,229	-6,079	-5,846
Other private payments	-511	-942	-3,617	-5,788	-20,893	-38,421	-35,516	-38,912
U.S. Government payments	-332	-489	-1,024	-4,542	-12,592	-19,769	-21,306	-22,607
U.S. military grants of goods and services, net	**-1,695**	**-1,636**	**-2,713**	**-2,207**	**-756**	**-153**	**-46**	**-101**
Unilateral transfers (excl. military grants of goods and services), net	**-2,367**	**-2,948**	**-3,443**	**-4,868**	**-7,593**	**-12,178**	**-15,301**	**-15,658**
U.S. Government grants (excluding military grants of goods and services)	-1,672	-1,808	-1,736	-2,894	-4,731	-8,541	-11,222	-11,773
U.S. Government pensions and other transfers	-273	-463	-611	-1,068	-1,818	-2,193	-2,171	-2,231
Private remittances and other transfers	-423	-677	-1,096	-906	-1,044	-1,444	-1,908	-1,654
U.S. assets abroad, net (increase/capital outflow (-))	**-4,099**	**-5,716**	**-9,337**	**-39,703**	**-86,118**	**-22,291**	**-31,399**	**-95,982**
U.S. official reserve assets, net	2,145	1,225	2,481	-849	-8,155	-3,131	-3,858	-312
U.S. Government assets, other than official reserve assets, net	-1,100	-1,605	-1,589	-3,474	-5,162	-5,476	-2,831	-1,920
U.S. private assets, net	-5,144	-5,336	-10,229	-35,380	-72,802	-13,685	-24,711	-94,374
Foreign assets in U.S., net (increase/capital inflow (+))	2,294	742	6,359	15,670	58,112	102,467	129,872	213,386
Statistical discrepancy (sum of above items with sign reversed)	-1,019	-157	-219	5,917	24,982	26,837	17,920	23,947
Memoranda:								
Balance on merchandise trade	**4,892**	**4,951**	**2,603**	**8,903**	**-25,480**	**-112,522**	**-122,148**	**-144,339**
Balance on goods and services	5,191	8,378	5,773	22,984	9,466	-94,835	-101,093	-125,694
Balance on goods , services, and remittances	4,496	7,238	4,067	21,011	6,604	-98,472	-105,171	-129,579
Balance on current account	2,824	5,431	2,331	18,116	1,873	-107,013	-116,393	-141,352

(1) Excludes transfers of goods and services under U.S. military grant programs. (2) Excludes exports of goods under U.S. military agency sales contracts identified in Census export documents, excludes imports of goods under direct defense expenditures identified in Census import documents, and reflects various other adjustments. (3) Redefined in 1982.

Dow Jones Industrial Average Since 1954

High		Year	Low		High		Year	Low	
Dec. 31	404.39	1954	Jan. 11	279.87	Apr. 28	950.82	1971	Nov. 23	797.97
Dec. 30	488.40	1955	Jan. 17	388.20	Dec. 11	1036.27	1972	Jan. 26	889.15
Apr. 6	521.05	1956	Jan. 23	462.35	Jan. 11	1051.70	1973	Dec. 5	788.31
July 12	520.77	1957	Oct. 22	419.79	Mar. 13	891.66	1974	Dec. 6	577.60
Dec. 31	583.65	1958	Feb. 25	436.89	July 15	881.81	1975	Jan. 2	632.04
Dec. 31	679.36	1959	Feb. 9	574.46	Sept. 21	1014.79	1976	Jan. 2	858.71
Jan. 5	685.47	1960	Oct. 25	566.05	Jan. 3	999.75	1977	Nov. 2	800.85
Dec. 13	734.91	1961	Jan. 3	610.25	Sept. 8	907.74	1978	Feb. 28	742.12
Jan. 3	726.01	1962	June 26	535.76	Oct. 5	897.61	1979	Nov. 7	796.67
Dec. 18	767.21	1963	Jan. 2	646.79	Nov. 20	1000.17	1980	Apr. 21	759.13
Nov. 18	891.71	1964	Jan. 2	766.08	Apr. 27	1024.05	1981	Sept. 25	824.01
Dec. 31	969.26	1965	June 28	840.59	Dec. 27	1070.55	1982	Aug. 12	776.92
Feb. 9	995.15	1966	Oct. 7	744.32	Nov. 29	1287.20	1983	Jan. 3	1027.04
Sept. 25	943.08	1967	Jan. 3	786.41	Jan. 6	1286.64	1984	July 24	1086.57
Dec. 3	985.21	1968	Mar. 21	825.13	Dec. 16	1553.10	1985	Jan. 4	1184.96
May 14	968.85	1969	Dec. 17	769.93	Dec. 2	1955.57	1986	Jan. 22	1502.29
Dec. 29	842.00	1970	May 6	631.16	Aug. 25	2722.42	1987*	Jan. 2	1927.31

*As of 9/15/87

Components of Dow Jones Industrial Average

Allied-Signal
Aluminum Co. of Amer.
American Express
AT&T
Bethlehem Steel
Boeing
Chevron
Coca-Cola
DuPont
Eastman Kodak
Exxon
General Electric
General Motors
Goodyear
IBM
International Paper
McDonald's
Merck
Minn. Mining & Manuf.
Navistar
Philip Morris
Primerica
Procter & Gamble
Sears Roebuck
Texaco
Union Carbide
United Technologies
USX Corp.
Westinghouse
Woolworth

Components of Dow Jones Transportation Average

Allegis
AMR Corp.
American President
Burlington Northern
CSX
Canadian Pacific
Carolina Freight
Consolidated Freightways
Consolidated Rail
Delta Air Lines
Federal Express
NWA
Norfolk Southern
Pan Am
Piedmont Aviation
Ryder System
Santa Fe Southern Pacific
TWA
Union Pacific
USAir Group

Components of Dow Jones Utility Average

American Electric Power
Centerior Energy
Columbia Gas System
Commonwealth Edison
Consolidated Edison
Consolidated Natural Gas
Detroit Edison
Houston Industries
Niagara Mohawk Power
Pacific Gas & Electric
Panhandle Eastern
Peoples Energy
Philadelphia Electric
Public Service Enterprises
Southern California Edison

Stocks Exchanges

N.Y. Stock Exchange Transactions

Year	Yearly volumes Stock shares	Yearly volumes Bonds par values	Year	Yearly volumes Stock shares	Yearly volumes Bonds par values
1900	138,981,000	$579,293,000	1960	766,693,818	$1,346,419,750
1905	260,569,000	1,026,254,000	1970	2,937,359,448	4,494,864,600
1910	163,705,000	634,863,000	1975	4,693,427,000	5,178,300,000
1915	172,497,000	961,700,000	1980	11,352,294,000	5,190,304,000
1920	227,636,000	3,868,422,000	1981	11,853,740,659	5,733,071,000
1925	459,717,623	3,427,042,210	1982	16,458,036,768	7,155,443,000
1929	1,124,800,410	2,996,398,000	1983	21,589,576,997	7,572,315,000
1930	810,632,546	2,720,301,800	1984	23,071,031,447	6,982,291,000
1935	381,635,752	3,339,458,000	1985	27,510,706,353	9,046,453,000
1940	207,599,749	1,669,438,000	1986	35,680,016,341	10,475,399,000
1950	524,799,621	1,112,425,170			

American Stock Exchange Transactions

Year	Yearly volume Stock shares	Yearly volume Bonds[1] princ. amts.	Year	Yearly volume Stock shares	Yearly volume Bonds[1] princ. amts.	Year	Yearly volume Stock shares	Yearly volume Bonds[1] princ. amts.
1929	476,140,375	$513,551,000	1960	286,039,982	$32,670,000	1983	2,081,270,000	$395,190,000
1930	222,270,065	863,541,000	1970	843,116,260	641,270,000	1984	1,545,010,000	371,990,000
1940	42,928,337	303,902,000	1980	1,626,072,625	355,723,000	1985	2,100,860,000	645,182,000
1945	143,309,392	167,333,000	1981	1,343,400,220	301,226,000	1986	2,978,540,000	810,264,000
1950	107,792,340	47,549,000	1982	1,485,831,536	325,240,000			

(1) Corporate

Most Active Stocks in 1986

New York Exchange

Stock	Volume (millions of shares)
A.T.&T.	528.7
USX	435.1
I.B.M.	407.6
Mobil	262.7
Exxon	241.3
Eastman Kodak	240.4
Phillips Petroleum	227.6
Goodyear	225.4
General Motors	221.4
Navistar	217.2
Sears	210.1
Texaco	206.5
American Express	201.5
Commonwealth Edison	198.0
BankAmerica	197.9

American Exchange

Stock	Volume (millions of shares)
Wickes Companies	270.2
BAT Industries	120.2
Wang Labs B	108.1
Lorimar-Telepictures	59.0
Texas Air	57.3
AM International	47.7
Echo Bay Mines	43.5
Horn & Hardart	41.1
First Australia Prime	41.1
Amdahl	39.8
Hasbro	36.5
Home Group	35.5
TIE/Communications	32.1
Husky Oil Limited	28.6
Home Shopping Network	27.5

NASDAQ

Stock	Volume (millions of shares)
MCI	447.1
Glaxo Holding	276.7
Jaguar	254.1
Apple Computer	238.0
Intel	192.5
Seagate	176.7
Henley Group	130.0
Convergent Tech	121.9
Integraph Corp.	121.4
THT Lyd	117.3
U.S. Health Care	113.6
Tandon Corp.	113.2
HBO	112.4
DSC Communications	106.1
Tandem Computers	104.1

Wall Street Celebrates Fifth Year of Bull Market

On Aug. 12, 1987, the Dow Jones industrial average closed at 2,669.32, up over 243 percent since the great bull market of the 1980s began on Aug. 12, 1982 when the DJIA closed at 776.92. The following is the record of how the 30 stocks currently in the DJIA fared during that period.

Stock	Price 8/12/87	Percent Change From 8/12/82
F.W. Woolworth	57.00	577.00
Merck	198.375	512.74
Westinghouse Electric	70.75	433.96
Boeing	53.00	354.31
Philip Morris	102.625	346.86
American Express	38.875	334.99
Coca-Cola	50.25	334.94
McDonald's	59.00	333.64
Du Pont	128.25	319.59
General Electric	63.50	303.17
Exxon	99.00	295.50
Primerica	48.25	269.36
Dow Jones industrial average	**2,669.32**	**243.58**
Goodyear	74.50	239.20
Sears Roebuck	58.375	223.45
Minnesota Mining & Mfg.	79.50	205.03
International Paper	53.625	193.84
United Technologies	57.875	191.48
IBM	170.375	173.49
Alum. Co. of America	61.75	168.48
AT&T	34.625	160.81
Chevron	60.125	140.00
Procter & Gamble	99.375	136.96
USX	38.625	134.09
Allied-Signal	47.125	128.04
General Motors	90.00	125.39
Navistar	8.125	116.67
Eastman Kodak	98.75	106.46
Union Carbide	28.50	102.39
Texaco	44.75	70.48
Bethlehem Steel	17.75	18.33

Top Volume Days on the New York Stock Exchange

(As of Sept. 9, 1987)

Date	NYSE volume (millions)	Dow change	Dow close
1/23/87	302.39	−44.15	2101.52
8/11/87	278.13	+44.64	2680.48
4/14/87	266.54	−34.09	2252.98
2/5/87	256.66	+10.26	2201.49
1/15/87	253.12	+35.72	2070.73
12/19/86	244.68	+16.03	1928.85
9/8/87	242.80	−16.26	2545.12
9/12/86	240.49	−34.17	1758.72
9/11/86	237.57	−86.61	1792.89
8/3/84	236.57	+36.00	1202.08

Stock Ownership—Characteristics of Shareowners

Source: N.Y. Stock Exchange
(in thousands)

	1970	1980	1983	1985
Total[1]	**30,850**	**30,200**	**42,360**	**47,040**
Male	15,689	15,666	20,864	23,699
Female	15,161	14,534	21,496	23,341
Age:				
Under 21 years	2,221	2,308	2,749	2,260
21-34 years	4,500	6,407	10,552	11,093
35-44 years	5,801	5,925	8,346	10,982
45-54 years	7,556	5,456	6,586	7,899
55-64 years	6,084	5,144	6,850	8,217
65 years and over	4,330	4,589	7,277	6,589
Education:				
High school:				
3 years or less	3,566	1,746	2,356	2,513
4 years	8,697	5,737	8,788	7,869
College:				
1-3 years	5,867	9,353	13,529	13,937
4 years or more	9,999	10,613	14,375	19,854
Minors[2]	2,221	2,308	2,749	2,260
Income[3]				
Under $5,000	2,389 }	1,742	1,460	2,151
$5,000-$9,999	5,779 }			
$10,000-$14,999	8,346	3,180	2,596	1,193
$15,000-$24,999	7,670	6,930	8,579	7,116
$25,000-$49,999		11,623	17,168	21,369
$50,000 and over	4,114	3,982	7,918	11,321
Residence by MSA size:				
Under 100,000	175	204	262	307
100,000-249,999	2,245	1,883	3,060	3,448
250,000-499,999	2,686	2,921	3,962	4,293
500,000-999,999	3,712	4,345	6,555	6,950
1,000,000 and over	14,881	15,447	21,730	24,751
Nonmetropolitan areas	6,913	5,400	6,791	7,291

(1) Represents all publicly owned issues of common and preferred stock, incl. stock mutual funds. Data based on national probability samples; (2) Those whose stock holdings are registered in accordance with the Gifts to Minors Statutes; (3) Adults only.

Financial Data on Selected Companies

(For additional information on the companies see pages 781-787.)

Company	Ticket Symbol	1986 Gross Revenues	Earnings per share 1984	1985	1986	Price[1]	PE[1] Ratio	Dividend[1] Yield %
Abbott Laboratories	ABL	$3.8 bln.	$1.67	$1.94	$2.32	$63	25	1.6
Albertson's Inc.	ABS	5.3 bln.	2.42	2.57	3.00	62⅝	19	1.5
American Express	AXP	14.6 bln.	1.40	1.78	2.78	38	22	2.0
American Home Products	AHP	4.9 bln.	4.26	4.70	5.18	89⅞	16	3.7
Anheuser-Busch	BUD	7.6 bln.	1.24	1.42	1.69	37⅞	20	1.6
Bausch & Lomb	BOL	698 mln.	1.98	2.23	2.47	45¾	18	1.9
Bell & Howell	BHW	853 mln.	3.04	3.06	3.10	71½	29	0.9
Boeing	BA	16.3 bln.	5.39	3.75	4.28	51⅜	14	2.7
Borden	BN	5.0 bln.	2.38	2.50	3.00	59¼	18	2.2
Bristol-Myers	BMY	4.8 bln.	1.73	1.93	2.07	50⅞	22	2.8
Campbell Soup	CPB	4.3 bln.	2.97	3.06	3.45	66⅝	17	2.2
Chrysler	C	22.5 bln.	5.22	6.25	6.31	44⅜	8	2.3
Clorox	CLX	1.0 bln.	1.55	1.64	1.80	32⅛	17	2.7
Coleman	CLN	501 mln.	2.37	1.46	2.48	39	16	3.1
Colgate-Palmolive	CL	4.9 bln.	0.64	2.13	2.52	48¾	18	2.8
Deere	DE	3.5 bln.	1.55	0.45	d3.88	37	—	0.7
Digital Equipment	DEC	7.5 bln.	2.87	3.71	4.81	191	22	—
Echlin	ECH	901 mln.	1.06	1.10	1.11	18	17	3.1
Fort Howard Paper	FHP	1.5 bln.	2.11	2.47	2.18	59½	27	1.8
Gannett	GCI	2.8 bln.	1.40	1.58	1.71	54¼	29	1.7
General Electric	GE	35.2 bln.	2.51	2.56	2.73	67½	21	2.1
Grumman	GQ	3.5 bln.	3.62	2.65	2.32	27⅜	13	3.7
Hasbro	HAS	1.3 bln.	1.29	1.78	1.71	23½	21	0.4
Hershey Foods	HSY	2.1 bln.	1.16	1.28	1.42	31⅛	20	2.0
Hewlett-Packard	HWP	7.1 bln.	2.59	1.91	2.02	65⅝	29	0.4
IBM	IBM	51.2 bln.	10.77	10.67	7.81	162	22	2.7
Jostens	JOS	581 mln.	.84	.88	.96	22½	18	2.1
Kellogg	K	3.3 bln.	1.68	2.28	2.58	64½	22	2.1
Kimberly-Clark	KMB	4.3 bln.	2.39	2.92	2.94	58½	19	2.5
Knight-Ridder	KRI	1.9 bln.	2.15	2.19	2.41	57¾	23	1.7
Limited, The	LTD	3.1 bln.	0.51	0.80	1.21	40½	30	0.6
Lockheed	LK	10.2 bln.	5.28	6.10	6.18	55⅜	9	2.5
Maytag	MYG	1.7 bln.	1.50	1.65	1.70	56¼	16	3.2
McDonald's	MCD	4.2 bln.	1.95	2.22	2.49	57⅛	22	0.9
McGraw-Hill	MHP	1.5 bln.	2.86	2.92	3.04	79¾	27	2.1
Melville	MES	5.2 bln.	3.60	4.07	4.40	75¼	16	2.3
Merck	MRK	4.1 bln.	3.09	3.79	4.85	212	37	1.5
Motorola	MOT	5.8 bln.	3.27	0.61	1.53	66½	37	1.0
NYNEX	NYN	11.3 bln.	5.05	5.42	6.01	73⅝	12	5.2
Ohio Matress	OMT	297 mln.	0.89	0.53	0.72	20⅛	25	2.0
Olsten	OLS	313 mln.	0.49	0.60	0.75	26¾	31	0.7
Parker Hannifen	PH	1.7 bln.	1.79	2.04	1.98	43½	23	1.8
Penney (J.C.)	JCP	14.7 bln.	2.91	2.66	3.53	58¾	16	2.5
Petrie Stores	PST	1.1 bln.	1.30	1.81	1.58	36⅜	23	1.9
Pfizer	PFE	4.4 bln.	3.08	3.44	3.90	70½	17	2.6
Pitney Bowes	PBI	1.9 bln.	1.76	1.83	2.10	47⅝	21	1.6
Polaroid	PRD	1.6 bln.	0.42	0.60	1.67	36	19	1.7
Procter & Gamble	PG	1.4 bln.	2.07	2.34	2.27	99⅞	53	27
Quaker Oats	OAT	3.6 bln.	1.68	1.88	2.18	53¾	17	1.9
Ramada	RAM	687 mln.	0.24	0.46	0.27	7⅞	27	—
Raytheon	RTN	7.3 bln.	4.02	4.60	5.10	81¾	15	2.2
Reebok	RBK	919 mln.	0.16	0.91	2.55	20	14	—
Rite Aid	RAD	1.7 bln.	1.69	1.65	1.89	41¼	21	1.6
Rockwell International	ROK	12.2 bln.	1.63	2.00	2.06	26½	12	2.5
Royal Dutch Petroleum	RD	38.8 bln.	11.14	9.13	8.65	129⅞	13	4.7
Rubbermaid	RBD	795 mln.	0.70	0.79	0.96	34⅜	33	1.0
Ryder System	RDR	3.7 bln.	1.65	1.73	2.09	37⅜	16	1.4
Sara Lee	SLE	7.9 bln.	1.63	1.81	2.02	44½	19	2.2
Schering-Plough	SGP	2.3 bln.	1.75	1.89	2.17	53⅞	22	1.9
Scott Paper	SPP	3.4 bln.	3.83	4.52	4.96	84¾	16	1.6
Sears, Roebuck	S	44.2 bln.	4.01	3.53	3.62	53¼	13	3.8
Smithkline Beckman	SKB	3.7 bln.	3.10	3.28	3.39	59	15	2.8
Snap-on Tools	SNA	670 mln.	1.47	1.46	1.59	42⅜	24	1.8
Sterling Drug	STY	1.9 bln.	2.39	2.56	2.91	63⅛	20	2.4
Stop & Shop	SHP	3.8 bln.	2.30	1.10	1.60	34⅜	19	1.9
Supermarkets General	SGL	5.5 bln.	1.48	1.78	1.65	37⅞	34	0.7
Tandy	TAN	3.0 bln.	2.75	2.11	2.22	48⅜	18	1.0
Tootsie Roll	TR	111.4 mln.	0.99	1.24	1.45	32¼	22	0.7
Toys "R" Us	TOY	2.4 bln.	0.87	0.93	1.17	39¼	32	—
Union Camp	UCC	2.0 bln.	2.48	1.30	1.77	44	19	2.6
Unocal	UCL	8.5 bln.	4.03	2.36	1.51	37	22	2.7
USAir Group	U	1.8 bln.	4.92	4.05	3.34	49¼	10	0.2
VF Corp	VFC	1.5 bln.	1.96	2.25	2.05	42¼	19	1.7
Wal-Mart	WMT	11.9 bln.	0.96	1.16	1.59	39¼	42	0.3
Walgreen	WAL	3.6 bln.	1.39	1.53	1.67	42½	28	1.3
Westinghouse Electric	WX	10.7 bln.	3.04	3.52	4.42	70	15	2.5
Whirlpool	WHR	4.0 bln.	2.59	2.49	2.70	39	15	2.8
Woolworth	Z	6.5 bln.	2.23	2.75	3.25	51⅝	15	2.6

(1) As of Sept. 15, 1987. d = deficit.

Leading Stock Mutual Funds

Source: Lipper Analytical Services Inc.

Ten Years
12/31/76 To 12/31/86

	Percent
Fidelity Magellan Fund	1577.50
Twentieth Century Select	943.18
Amer Capital Pace	843.26
20th Century Growth	817.40
Quasar Associates*	816.07
Lindner Fund*	797.27
International Investors	797.10
Lehman Capital Fund	789.07
Weingarten Equity	783.82
Evergreen Fund	782.14
Loomis-Sayles Capital*	741.41
Nicholas Fund	682.14
Amev Growth Fund	659.42
Lindner Dividend*	652.77
Phoenix Stock	647.05
Merrill Lynch Pacific	640.51
NEL Growth Fund	636.29
Value Line Lvge. Growth	624.89
Fidelity Destiny I	613.79
Franklin Gold Fund	611.09
US Gold Shares	598.41
Over-The-Counter Sec.	591.47
Growth Fund of America	590.08
IDS Growth Fund	584.88
New York Venture	584.81

Five Years
12/31/81 To 12/31/86

	Percent
Fidelity Magellan Fund	270.75
Merrill Lynch Pacific	257.66
Vanguard Qual. Dvd 1*	257.20
Vanguard World-Intl. Gro	256.82
Loomis-Sayles Capital*	256.41
Pru-Bache Utility	245.86
Fidelity Sel. Financial	228.77
BBK International	227.14
Putnam Intl. Equities	221.40
Fidelity Sel. Health	219.11
Phoenix Growth	218.04
Strong Total Return	211.21
Eaton Vance Total Return	208.31
Lindner Dividend*	206.89
Fairmont Fund	205.81
Fidelity Destiny I	203.06
T Rowe Price Intl. Fund	201.54
United Income	200.74
Evergreen Total Return	200.48
Phoenix Stock	200.42
Washington Mutual Inv.	198.57
Strong Investment	198.26
Quest for Value Fund	197.56
NEL Growth Fund	197.35
United Contl. Income	196.44

1986
12/31/85 To 12/31/86

	Percent
New England Zenith Cap Growth	95.21
Merrill Lynch Pacific	78.05
Nomura Pacific Basin	74.48
Newport Far East	73.26
Financial Port-Pacific	72.49
GT Pacific Growth Fund	70.04
Fidelity Overseas	69.25
BBK International	61.97
T Rowe Price Intl. Fund	61.29
GT Japan Growth	60.62
Fidelity Destiny II	60.45
Strong Opportunity	59.90
Vanguard World-Intl. Growth	56.71
FT International	55.70
USAA Gold	55.60
Benham Target 2010	54.42
IDS International	53.95
GT International Growth	53.83
Transatlantic Fund	52.62
Intl. Fund for Institutions	50.72
Scudder International	50.70
Trustees Commingled Intl.	50.59
Vanguard Special-Gold	49.88
Fundtrust International	49.65
Keystone International	49.06

*Fund closed to new accounts.

NASDAQ Sets Record Volume

NASDAQ, The National Association of Securities Dealers Automated Quotations, reported turnover volume of 26.6 billion shares in 1986. This was an increase of 38.2% over 1985. The number of companies with shares traded in this market was 4,417 in 1987, making NASDAQ the third-largest market in the world, after the New York and Tokyo exchanges.

Federal Reserve System

The Federal Reserve System is the central bank for the United States. The system was established on December 23, 1913, originally to give the country an elastic currency, to provide facilities for discounting commercial paper, and to improve the supervision of banking. Since then, the System's responsibilities have been broadened. Over the years, stability and growth of the economy, a high level of employment, stability in the purchasing power of the dollar, and reasonable balance in transactions with foreign countries have come to be recognized as primary objectives of governmental economic policy.

The Federal Reserve System consists of the Board of Governors, the 12 District Reserve Banks and their branch offices, and the Federal Open Market Committee. Several advisory councils help the Board meet its varied responsibilities.

The hub of the System is the seven member Board of Governors in Washington. The members of the Board are appointed by the President and confirmed by the Senate, to serve 14-year terms. The President also appoints the Chairman and Vice-Chairman of the Board from among the board members for 4-year terms that may be renewed. Currently, the board members are: Alan Greenspan, Chairman; Manuel H. Johnson, Vice Chairman; Edward W. Kelley, Jr.; Martha R. Seger; Wayne D. Angell; H. Robert Heller.

The Board is the policy-making body. In addition to its policy making responsibilities, it supervises the budget and operations of the Reserve Banks, approves the appointments of their presidents and appoints 3 of each District Bank's directors, including the chairman and vice chairman of each Reserve Bank's board.

The 12 Reserve Banks and their branch offices serve as the decentralized portion of the System, carrying out day-to-day operations such as circulating currency and coin, providing fiscal agency functions and payments mechanism services. The District Banks are located in Boston, New York, Philadelphia, Cleveland, Richmond, Atlanta, Chicago, St. Louis, Minneapolis, Kansas City, Dallas and San Francisco.

The System's principal function is monetary policy, which it controls using three tools: reserve requirements, the discount rate and open market operations. Uniform reserve requirements, set by the Board, are applied to the transaction accounts and nonpersonal time deposits of all depository institutions. Responsibility for setting the discount rate (the interest rate at which depository institutions can borrow money from the Reserve Banks) is shared by the Board of Governors and the Reserve Banks. Changes in the discount rate are recommended by the individual Boards of Directors of the Reserve Banks and are subject to approval by the Board of Governors. The most important tool of monetary policy is open market operations (the purchase and sale of government securities). Responsibility for influencing the cost and availability of money and credit through the purchase and sale of government securities lies with the Federal Open Market Committee (FOMC). This committee is composed of the 7 members of the Board of Governors, the president of the Federal Reserve Bank of New York, and 4 other Federal Reserve Bank presidents, who serve one-year terms on a rotating basis. The committee bases its decisions on current economic and financial developments and outlook, setting yearly growth objectives for key measures of money supply and credit. The decisions of the committee are carried out by the Domestic Trading Desk of the Federal Reserve Bank of New York.

The Federal Reserve Act prescribes a Federal Advisory Council, consisting of one member from each Federal Reserve District, elected annually by the Board of Directors of each of the 12 Federal Reserve Banks. They meet with the Federal Reserve Board at least four times a year to discuss business and financial conditions and to make advisory recommendations.

The Consumer Advisory Council is a statutory body, including both consumer and creditor representatives, which advises the Board of Governors on its implementation of consumer regulations and other consumer-related matters. Following the passage of the Monetary Control Act of 1980, the Board of Governors established the Thrift Institutions Advisory Council to provide information and views on the special needs and problems of thrift institutions. The group is comprised of representatives of mutual savings banks, savings and loan associations, and credit unions.

Largest U.S. Commercial Banks

Source: American Banker; based on deposits Dec. 31, 1986.
(thousands)

Rank	Deposits	Rank	Deposits
Citibank NA, New York	$102,933,000	Union Bank, Los Angeles	$8,122,922
Bank of America NT&SA, San Francisco	76,084,000	Seattle-First National Bank	7,753,514
Chase Manhattan Bank NA, New York	60,899,893	First Union National Bank, Charlotte	7,597,348
Manufacturers Hanover Trust Co., New York	46,117,000	Pittsburgh National Bank	7,421,031
Morgan Guaranty Trust Co., New York	44,935,863	Bank of New England NA, Boston	7,337,376
Chemical Bank, New York	39,163,000	Fidelity Bank NA, Malvern, PA	7,242,812
Security Pacific National Bank, Los Angeles	34,574,626	Connecticut Bank & Trust Co. NA, Hartford	7,215,016
Bankers Trust Co., New York	34,162,759	First Fidelity Bank NA, Newark	7,209,772
Wells Fargo Bank NA, San Francisco	33,286,916	Citizens & Southern National Bank, Atlanta	7,198,992
First National Bank, Chicago	24,909,690	Connecticut National Bank, Hartford	7,045,299
Continental Illinois Nat'l Bank & Trust Co., Chicago	18,695,628	City Federal Savings Bank, Elizabeth, N.J.	6,998,588
Great Western Bank, Beverly Hills, Cal.	18,130,530	Crossland Savings FSB, New York	6,876,465
First Interstate Bank of California, Los Angeles	18,115,591	Boston Safe Deposit & Trust Co.	6,830,142
Marine Midland Bank NA, Buffalo	17,034,413	NCNB National Bank of Florida, Tampa	6,746,423
First National Bank, Boston	16,689,981	Anchor Savings Bank FSB, Northport, N.Y.	6,468,025
Mellon Bank NA, Pittsburgh	15,049,613	Dime Savings Bank of N.Y. FSB	6,464,274
Bank of New York	14,970,194	Philadelphia National Bank	6,442,770
American Express Bank LTD, New York	13,406,000	Rainier National Bank, Seattle	6,316,803
Meritor Savings Bank, Philadelphia	12,676,100	United Virginia Bank, Richmond	6,111,774
Irving Trust Co., New York	12,662,578	Harris Trust & Savings Bank, Chicago	6,096,175
Republic National Bank, New York	11,139,069	AmeriTrust Co. NA, Cleveland	6,081,623
First Nationwide Bank, San Francisco	11,079,351	Comerica Bank-Detroit	5,911,414
Goldome FSB, Buffalo, N.Y.	11,016,213	First National Bank, Minneapolis	5,826,850
NCNB National Bank of North Carolina, Charlotte	9,847,559	Florida National Bank, Jacksonville	5,795,374
National Bank of Detroit	9,714,319	Maryland National Bank, Baltimore	5,789,068
Southeast Bank NA, Miami	9,461,003	First Interstate Bank of Arizona NA, Phoenix	5,702,441
Valley National Bank, Phoenix	9,216,623	United States National Bank, Portland	5,638,056
Great American First Savings Bank, San Diego	8,877,414	Texas Commerce Bank NA, Houston	5,607,112
Republic Bank Dallas NA	8,623,009	MBank Dallas NA	5,465,242
National Westminster Bank USA, New York	8,784,311	Huntington National Bank, Columbus, Oh.	5,414,927
Wachovia Bank & Trust Co. NA, Winston-Salem	8,608,159	Meridian Bank, Reading, PA	5,359,657
Sovran Bank NA, Richmond	8,352,879	First Union Bank of Florida, Jacksonville	5,346,832
		California First Bank, San Francisco	5,268,106
		State Street Bank & Trust Co., Boston	5,254,894
		Manufacturers National Bank, Detroit	5,237,695
		Bank of Tokyo Trust Co., New York	5,168,657

Largest Banks Outside the U.S.

Source: American Banker; based on deposits Dec. 31, 1986, or nearest fiscal year-end.
(thousands of U.S. dollars)

Bank, country	Deposits	Bank, country	Deposits
Dai-Ichi Kangyo Bank Ltd., Tokyo, Japan	$186,029,628	Dresdner Bank, Frankfurt, W. Germany	95,656,271
Fuji Bank, Ltd., Tokyo, Japan	166,547,333	Taiyo Kobe Bank, Ltd., Kobe, Japan	91,240,394
Sumitomo Bank Ltd., Osaka, Japan	164,507,271	Daiwa Bank, Ltd., Osaka, Japan	88,296,103
Mitsubishi Bank Ltd., Tokyo, Japan	158,671,131	Bank of Tokyo, Ltd., Japan	86,863,648
Sanwa Bank Ltd., Osaka, Japan	151,871,893	Yasuda Trust & Banking Co. Ltd., Tokyo, Japan	85,901,361
Norinchukin Bank, Tokyo, Japan	144,233,722	Union Bank of Switzerland, Zurich, Switzerland	81,743,463
Industrial Bank of Japan, Ltd., Tokyo, Japan	137,424,332	Hongkong and Shanghai Banking Corp., Hong Kong	77,975,856
Credit Agricole Mutuel, Paris, France	133,396,066	Swiss Bank Corp., Basle, Switzerland	74,603,109
Banque Nationale de Paris, France	121,830,138	Commerzbank, Frankfurt, W. Germany	72,143,790
Deutsche Bank, Frankfurt, W. Germany	121,574,053	Toyo Trust & Banking Co. Ltd., Tokyo, Japan	71,515,662
Credit Lyonnais, Paris, France	115,235,251	Westdeutsche Landesbank Girozentrale, Duesseldorf, W. Germany	71,512,709
Tokai Bank Ltd., Nagoya, Japan	113,260,733	Nippon Credit Bank, Ltd., Tokyo, Japan	68,801,207
Mitsubishi Trust & Banking Corp., Tokyo, Japan	110,529,232	Bayerische Vereinsbank, Munich, W. Germany	68,383,919
Sumitomo Trust & Banking Co., Ltd., Osaka, Japan	110,136,767	Midland Bank Plc, London, U.K.	68,293,524
National Westminster Bank Plc, London, U.K.	107,831,802	Banca Nazionale del Lavoro, Rome, Italy	64,609,892
Mitsui Bank Ltd., Tokyo, Japan	104,352,303	Shoko Chukin Bank, Tokyo, Japan	64,259,656
Societe Generale, Paris, France	99,084,964	Lloyds Bank Plc, London, U.K.	63,171,732
Mitsui Trust & Banking Co., Ltd., Tokyo, Japan	98,919,395	Royal Bank of Canada, Montreal, Canada	60,645,504
Long-Term Credit Bank of Japan Ltd., Tokyo, Japan	98,645,684	Bayerische Hypotheken-und Wechsel-Bank, Munich, W. Germany	59,504,546
Barclays Plc, London, U.K.	96,793,866		

Bank Failures

Source: Federal Deposit Insurance Corp

Year	Closed	Year	Closed	Year	Closed	Year	Closed
1934	61	1958	9	1967	4	1978	7
1935	32	1959	3	1969	9	1979	10
1936	72	1960	2	1970	8	1980	10
1937	84	1961	9	1971	6	1981	10
1938	81	1963	2	1972	3	1982	42
1939	72	1964	8	1973	6	1983	48
1940	48	1965	9	1975	14	1984	79
1955	5	1966	8	1976	17	1985	120
						1986	138

All Banks in U.S.—Number, Deposits

Source: Federal Reserve System

Comprises all national banks in the United States and all state commercial banks, trust companies, mutual stock savings banks, private and industrial banks, and special types of institutions that are treated as banks by the federal bank supervisory agencies. Data as of June 30 prior to 1975.

Year	Number of banks						Total deposits (millions of dollars)					
		F.R.S. members			Nonmembers			F.R.S. members			Nonmembers	
	Total all banks	Total	Nat'l	State	Mutual savings	Other	Total all banks	Total	Nat'l	State	Mutual savings	Other
1925 . .	**26,479**	9,538	8,066	1,472	621	18,320	**51,641**	32,457	19,912	12,546	7,089	12,095
1930 . .	**23,855**	8,315	7,247	1,068	604	14,936	**59,828**	38,069	23,235	14,834	9,117	12,642
1935 . .	**16,047**	6,410	5,425	985	569	9,068	**51,149**	34,938	22,477	12,461	9,830	6,381
1940 . .	**14,955**	6,398	5,164	1,234	551	8,008	**70,770**	51,729	33,014	18,715	10,631	8,410
1945 . .	**14,542**	6,840	5,015	1,825	539	7,163	**151,033**	118,378	76,534	41,844	14,413	18,242
1950 . .	**14,674**	6,885	4,971	1,914	527	7,262	**163,770**	122,707	82,430	40,277	19,927	21,137
1955 . .	**14,309**	6,611	4,744	1,867	525	7,173	**208,850**	154,670	98,636	56,034	27,310	26,870
1960 . .	**14,006**	6,217	4,542	1,675	513	7,276	**249,163**	179,519	116,178	63,341	35,316	34,328
1965 . .	**14,295**	6,235	4,803	1,432	504	7,556	**362,611**	259,743	171,528	88,215	50,980	51,889
1970 . .	**14,167**	5,805	4,638	1,167	496	7,866	**502,542**	346,289	254,322	91,967	69,285	86,968
1975 . .	**15,108**	5,787	4,741	1,046	475	8,846	**896,879**	590,999	447,590	143,409	110,569	195,311
1980 . .	**15,145**	5,422	4,425	997	460	9,263	**1,333,399**	843,030	651,848	191,182	150,000	340,369
1983 . .	**14,922**	5,821	4,756	1,065	366	8,735	**1,686,035**	1,083,149	864,495	218,654	161,543	441,343
1984 . .	**14,739**	5,973	4,905	1,068	267	8,498	**1,759,000**	1,170,013	945,033	224,980	121,559	467,433
1985 . .	**14,713**	6,044	4,964	1,080	344	8,325	**1,973,816**	1,285,562	1,033,631	251,931	137,535	500,179
1986 . .	**14,494**	5,978	4,870	1,108	357	8,159	**2,104,284**	1,406,949	1,126,093	280,956	148,245	549,090

Federal Deposit Insurance Corporation (FDIC)

The primary purpose of the Federal Deposit Insurance Corporation (FDIC) is to insure deposits in all banks approved for insurance coverage benefits under the Federal Deposit Insurance Act. The major functions of the FDIC are to pay off depositors of insured banks closed without adequate provision having been made to pay depositors' claims, to act as receiver for all national banks placed in receivership and for state banks placed in receivership when appointed receiver by state authorities, and to prevent the continuance or development of unsafe and unsound banking practices. The FDIC's entire income consists of assessments on insured banks and income from investments; it receives no appropriations from Congress. It may borrow from the U.S. Treasury not to exceed $3 billion outstanding, but has made no such borrowings since it was organized in 1933. The FDIC surplus (Deposit Insurance Fund) as of July 1, 1987 was $18.4 billion.

Gold Reserves of Central Banks and Governments

Source: IMF, *International Financial Statistics*
(Million fine troy ounces)

Year end	All countries[1]	United States	Canada	Japan	Belgium	France	West Germany	Italy	Netherlands	Switzerland	United Kingdom
1970	1,057.89	316.34	22.59	15.22	42.01	100.91	113.70	82.48	51.06	78.03	38.52
1971	1,028.44	291.60	22.69	19.42	44.12	100.66	116.47	82.40	54.53	83.11	22.18
1972	1,019.68	275.97	21.95	21.10	43.08	100.69	117.36	82.37	54.17	83.11	21.08
1973	1,022.24	275.97	21.95	21.11	42.17	100.91	117.61	82.48	54.33	83.20	21.01
1974	1,020.24	275.97	21.95	21.11	42.17	100.93	117.61	82.48	54.33	83.20	21.03
1975	1,018.71	274.71	21.95	21.11	42.17	100.93	117.61	82.48	54.33	83.20	21.03
1976	1,014.23	274.68	21.62	21.11	42.17	101.02	117.61	82.48	54.33	83.28	21.03
1977	1,029.19	277.55	22.01	21.62	42.45	101.67	118.30	82.91	54.63	83.28	22.23
1978	1,036.82	276.41	22.13	23.97	42.59	101.99	118.64	83.12	54.78	83.28	22.83
1979	944.44	264.60	22.18	24.23	34.21	81.92	95.25	66.71	43.97	83.28	18.25
1980	952.99	264.32	20.98	24.23	34.18	81.85	95.18	66.67	43.94	83.28	18.84
1981	953.26	264.11	20.46	24.23	34.18	81.85	95.18	66.67	43.94	83.28	19.03
1982	948.69	264.03	20.26	24.23	34.18	81.85	95.18	66.67	43.94	83.28	19.01
1983	945.27	263.39	20.17	24.23	34.18	81.85	95.18	66.67	43.94	83.28	19.01
1984	946.09	262.79	20.14	24.23	34.18	81.85	95.18	66.67	43.94	83.28	19.03
1985	949.00	262.65	20.11	24.33	34.18	81.85	95.18	66.67	43.94	83.28	19.03
1986	948.80	262.04	19.72	24.23	34.18	81.85	95.18	66.67	43.94	83.28	19.01

(1) Covers IMF members with reported gold holdings. For countries not listed above, see *International Financial Statistics*, a monthly publication of the International Monetary Fund.

U.S. and World Silver Production

Source: Bureau of Mines, U.S. Interior Department

(troy ounces)

Largest production of silver in the United States in 1915—74,961,075 troy ounces.

Year	United States	World	Year	United States	World	Year	United States	World
1930 . .	50,748,127	248,708,426	1960 . .	36,000,000	241,300,000	1983 . .	43,431,000	386,533,000
1935 . .	45,924,454	220,704,231	1965 . .	39,806,033	257,415,000	1984 . .	44,592,000	412,069,000
1940 . .	69,585,734	275,387,000	1970 . .	45,006,000	310,891,000	1985p . .	39,433,000	421,041,000
1945 . .	29,063,255	162,000,000	1975 . .	34,938,000	303,112,000	1986e . .	34,220,000	419,781,000
1950 . .	43,308,739	203,300,000	1980 . .	32,329,000	339,382,000			
1955 . .	36,469,610	224,000,000	1982 . .	40,248,000	371,159,000			

(p) preliminary. (e) estimate.

World Gold Production

(Troy Ounces)

Year	world prod.	Africa: South Africa	Africa: Ghana	Africa: Zaire	North and South America: United States	North and South America: Canada	North and South America: Mexico	North and South America: Colombia	Australia	Other: China	Other: Philippines	Other: USSR
1972	44,843,374	29,245,273	724,051	140,724	1,449,943	2,078,567	146,061	188,137	754,866	—	606,730	—
1974	40,124,290	24,388,203	614,007	130,603	1,126,886	1,698,392	134,454	265,195	512,611	—	537,615	—
1975	38,476,371	22,937,820	523,889	103,217	1,052,252	1,653,611	144,710	308,864	526,821	—	502,577	—
1976	39,024,485	22,936,018	532,473	91,093	1,048,037	1,691,806	162,811	300,307	502,741	—	501,210	—
1977	38,906,145	22,501,886	480,884	80,418	1,100,347	1,733,609	212,709	257,070	624,270	—	558,554	—
1978	38,983,019	22,648,558	402,034	76,077	998,832	1,735,077	202,003	246,446	647,579	—	586,531	—
1979	38,768,978	22,617,179	362,000	69,992	964,390	1,644,265	190,364	269,369	596,910	—	535,166	—
1980	39,197,315	21,669,468	353,000	39,963	969,782	1,627,477	195,991	510,439	547,591	—	753,452	8,425,000
1982	43,082,814	21,355,111	331,000	62,233	1,465,686	2,081,230	214,349	472,674	866,815	1,800,000	834,439	8,550,000
1983	44,995,806	21,847,310	276,000	192,930	2,002,526	2,363,411	198,177	438,579	983,522	1,850,000	816,536	8,600,000
1984	46,475,191	21,860,933	287,000	117,115	2,084,615	2,682,786	270,998	799,889	1,295,963	1,900,000	827,149	8,650,000
1985p	48,673,292	21,565,230	299,363	63,022	2,427,232	2,815,118	265,693	1,142,830	1,881,491	1,950,000	1,062,997	8,700,000
1986e	50,937,043	20,513,665	290,000	60,000	3,733,190	3,364,700	280,000	1,400,000	2,479,000	2,100,000	1,295,000	8,850,000

(e) estimated (p) preliminary

U.S. Industrial Corporations with Largest Sales in 1986

Source: FORTUNE Magazine

Company (1985 rank)	Sales (billions)	Income (or loss) (millions)	Company (1985 rank)	Sales (billions)	Income (or loss) (millions)
General Motors (1)	$102.81	$2,945	Eastman Kodak (33)	$11.55	$374
Exxon (2)	69.89	5,360	Dow Chemical (28)	11.11	732
Ford (4)	62.72	3,285	Westinghouse Electric (32)	10.73	671
IBM (5)	51.25	4,789	Goodyear Tire & Rubber (35)	10.33	124
Mobil (3)	44.87	1,407	Lockheed (36)	10.27	408
General Electric (10)	35.21	2,492	Phillips Petroleum (17)	9.79	228
AT&T (8)	34.09	139	Xerox (40)	9.38	465
Texaco (6)	31.61	725	Sun (20)	9.38	385
Du Pont (9)	27.15	1,538	PepsiCo (41)	9.29	458
Chevron (7)	24.35	715	Standard Oil (24)	9.22	(345)
Chrysler (13)	22.51	1,403	General Dynamics (42)	9.21	(53)
Philip Morris (27)	20.68	1,478	Kraft (34)	8.74	413
Amoco (11)	18.28	747	Coca-Cola (44)	8.67	934
RJR Nabisco (23)	17.00	1,604	3M (47)	8.60	779
Shell Oil (14)	16.83	883	Sara Lee (45)	7.94	223
Boeing (21)	16.34	665	ITT (25)	7.90	494
United Technologies (16)	15.67	72	Union Carbide (39)	7.83	496
Procter & Gamble (22)	15.44	709	Anheuser-Busch (51)	7.68	518
Occidental Petroleum (19)	15.34	151	Digital Equipment (55)	7.59	617
Atlantic Richfield (12)	14.59	615	Unocal (31)	7.48	176
Tenneco (18)	14.56	(39)	Unisys (72)	7.43	(43)
USX (15)	14.00	(1,833)	Caterpillar (52)	7.32	(76)
McDonnell Douglas (29)	12.66	277	Raytheon (60)	7.31	393
Rockwell International (30)	12.30	611	LTV (43)	7.27	(3,252)
Allied-Signal (37)	11.79	605	Georgia-Pacific (54)	7.22	296

Largest Corporate Mergers or Acquisitions in U.S.

(as of mid-1987)

Company	Acquirer	Dollars	Year	Company	Acquirer	Dollars	Year
Gulf Oil	Chevron	13.3 bln.	1984	Texasgulf	Elf Aquitaine	4.2 bln.	1981
Getty Oil	Texaco	10.1 bln.	1984	Cities Service	Occidental Petroleum	4.0 bln.	1982
Standard Oil	British Petroleum	7.5 bln.*	1987	Midcon	Occidental Petroleum	3.8 bln.	1986
Conoco	DuPont	7.4 bln.	1981	American Hospital	Baxter Travenol	3.8 bln.	1986
Marathon Oil	U.S. Steel	6.5 bln.	1981	Owens-Illinois	Kohlberg Kravis Roberts	3.6 bln.	1987
Beatrice	Kohlberg Kravis Roberts	6.2 bln.	1986	Belridge Oil	Shell Oil	3.6 bln.	1979
RCA	General Electric	6.2 bln.	1986	ABC Broadcasting	Capital Cities Comm.	3.5 bln.	1985
Superior Oil	Mobil Oil	5.7 bln.	1984	Viacom	National Amusements	3.4 bln.	1987
Newmont Mining	T. Boone Pickens	5.6 bln.	(1)	Texas Oil and Gas	USX Corp.	3.0 bln.	1985
General Foods	Philip Morris	5.6 bln.	1986	Esmark	Beatrice Foods	2.7 bln.	1984
Southern Pacific	Santa Fe Railroad	5.2 bln.	1983	G.D. Searle	Monsanto	2.7 bln.	1986
Southland	J.T. Acquisition	5.1 bln.	1987	Continental Group	Kiewit-Murdock	2.7 bln.	1984
Hughes Aircraft	General Motors	5.0 bln.	1985	St. Joe Minerals	Fluor	2.6 bln.	1981
Nabisco	R.J. Reynolds	4.9 bln.	1985	Electronic Data Systems	General Motors	2.6 bln.	1984
Signal Cos.	Allied Corp.	4.9 bln.	1986	Associated Dry Goods	May Dept. Stores	2.5 bln.	1986
Sperry	Burroughs	4.8 bln.	1986				
Connecticut General	INA	4.3 bln.	1981				

*For the 45% of Standard Oil that British Petroleum did not already own. (1) Still pending, Sept. 1987.

In the first half of 1987, 927 mergers and acquisitions were announced, a sharp drop from the 1,527 merger announcements in the year-earlier period. The value of the deals, however, rose to $91.3 billion, compared with $77.1 billion a year earlier, a rise of 18 percent.

U.S. Currency and Coin

Source: U.S. Treasury Department; Financial Management Service (June 30, 1986)

Amounts Outstanding and in Circulation

	Amounts outstanding	Less amounts held by: United States Treasury	Less amounts held by: Federal Reserve Banks[1]	Amounts in circulation
Currency				
Federal Reserve Notes[1]	$215,964,649,114	$4,231,880	$32,928,966,653	$183,031,450,581
United States Notes	322,539,016	30,043,339	9	292,495,668
Currency No Longer Issued	270,821,617	190,859	26,076	270,604,682
Total	$216,558,009,747	$34,466,078	$32,928,992,738	$183,594,550,931
Coin[2]				
Dollars[3]	$2,024,703,898	$352,481,112	$122,028,662	$1,550,194,124
Fractional Coin	14,712,135,000	186,643,062	361,061,104	14,164,430,834
Total	16,736,838,898	539,124,174	483,089,766	15,714,624,958
Total currency and coin	$233,294,848,645	$573,590,252	$33,442,082,504	$199,309,175,889

Currency in Circulation by Denominations

Denomination	Total currency in circulation	Federal Reserve Notes[1]	U.S. Notes	Currency no longer issued
1 Dollar	$3,701,589,632	$3,548,726,209	$143,481	$152,719,942
2 Dollars	718,748,002	585,802,142	132,932,862	12,998
5 Dollars	5,055,175,325	4,904,699,020	112,278,505	38,197,800
10 Dollars	11,523,770,350	11,498,820,850	5,950	24,943,550
20 Dollars	54,780,940,120	54,760,723,260	3,380	20,213,480
50 Dollars	23,837,026,100	23,825,387,700	—	11,638,400
100 Dollars	83,641,102,800	83,571,637,900	47,131,400	22,333,500
500 Dollars	153,212,000	153,021,500	—	190,500
1,000 Dollars	177,701,000	177,492,000	—	209,000
5,000 Dollars	1,805,000	1,760,000	—	45,000
10,000 Dollars	3,480,000	3,380,000	—	100,000
Fractional parts	487	—	—	487
Partial notes[4]	115	—	90	25
Total currency	$183,594,550,931	$183,031,450,581	$292,495,668	$270,604,682

Comparative Totals of Money in Circulation — Selected Dates

Date	Amounts (in millions)	Per capita[5]	Date	Amounts (in millions)	Per capita[5]	Date	Amounts (in millions)	Per capita[5]
June 30, 1986	$199,309.2	$825.35	June 30, 1965	$39,719.8	$204.14	June 30, 1930	$4,522.0	$36.74
June 30, 1985	185,890.7	778.58	June 30, 1960	32,064.6	177.47	June 30, 1925	4,815.2	41.56
June 30, 1984	175,059.6	739.64	June 30, 1955	30,229.3	182.90	June 30, 1920	5,467.6	51.36
June 30, 1983	162,027.1	691.74	June 30, 1950	27,156.3	179.03	June 30, 1915	3,319.6	33.01
June 30, 1980	127,097.2	558.28	June 30, 1945	26,746.4	191.14	June 30, 1910	3,148.7	34.07
June 30, 1975	81,196.4	380.08	June 30, 1940	7,847.5	59.40			
June 30, 1970	54,351.0	265.39	June 30, 1935	5,567.1	43.75			

(1) Issued on and after July 1, 1929. (2) Excludes coin sold to collectors at premium prices. (3) Includes $481,781,898 in standard silver dollars. (4) Represents value of certain partial denominations not presented for redemption. (5) Based on Bureau of the Census estimates of population.

The requirement for a gold reserve against U.S. notes was repealed by Public Law 90-269 approved Mar. 18, 1968. Silver certificates issued on and after July 1, 1929 became redeemable from the general fund on June 24, 1968. The amount of security after those dates has been reduced accordingly.

U.S. Money in Circulation, by Denominations

Outside Treasury and Federal Reserve Banks. (millions of dollars)

Source: U.S. Treasury Department, Financial Management Service

Fiscal year	Total in circulation	Coin and small denomination: Coin	$1	$2	$5	$10	$20	$50	$100	Large denomination currency: $500	$1,000	$5,000	$10,000
1950	27,741	1,554	1,113	64	2,049	5,998	8,529	2,422	5,043	368	588	4	12
1960	32,869	2,427	1,533	88	2,246	6,691	10,536	2,815	5,954	249	316	3	10
1970	57,093	6,281	2,310	136	3,161	9,170	18,581	4,896	12,084	215	252	3	4
1975	86,547	8,959	2,809	135	3,841	10,777	28,344	8,157	23,139	175	204	2	4
1980	137,244	12,419	3,499	677	4,635	11,924	40,739	13,731	49,264	163	189	2	3
1985	170,739	15,150	3,571	707	4,939	11,363	51,586	21,715	76,516	154	179	2	3

Seigniorage on Coin and Silver Bullion

Source: U.S. Treasury Department, Financial Management Service

Seigniorage is the profit from coining money; it is the difference between the monetary value of coins and their cost, including the manufacturing expense.

Fiscal year	Total	Fiscal year	Total
Jan. 1, 1935-June 30, 1965, cumulative	$2,525,927,763.84	1982	390,407,804.91
1968	383,141,339.00[1]	1983	477,479,387.58
1970	274,217,884.01	1984	498,371,724.09
1972	580,586,683.00	1985	515,906,969.31
1974	320,706,638.49	1986	392,445,674.57
1975	660,898,070.69	Cumulative Jan. 1, 1935-Sept. 30, 1986	12,798,894,096.69
1980	$662,814,791.48		

(1) Revised to include seigniorage on clad coins.

United States Mint

Source: United States Mint, U.S. Treasury Department

The United States Mint was created by Act of April 2, 1792, which established the U.S. national coinage system. Initially, operations were conducted at Philadelphia, then the nation's capital. Supervision of the Mint was a function of the secretary of state, but in 1799, it became an independent agency reporting directly to the president. The Mint was made a statutory bureau of the Treasury Department in 1873, with a director appointed by the president to oversee its operations from headquarters offices in the Treasury Department in Washington, D.C.

The Mint manufactures all U.S. coins and distributes them through the Federal Reserve banks and branches. The Mint also maintains physical custody of the treasury's monetary stocks of gold and silver, moving, storing and releasing from custody as authorized. There are 6 field facilities. Mints are located in Philadelphia and Denver; the San Francisco Assay Office and San Francisco Old Mint perform coinage operations and numismatic functions; two depositories, one at Fort Knox, Ky., for the storage of gold, and the other at West Point, N.Y., where gold and silver are stored and coinage is produced by congressional authorization. A museum is maintained at the San Francisco Old Mint.

The traditional 90% silver coinage was phased out and cupronickel clad coinage introduced when the Coinage Act of 1965 removed all silver from the dime and quarter and reduced the silver content of the half dollar to 40%. In 1970, legislative action removed the remaining silver from the half dollar and in providing for the resumption of dollar coinage, directed that both denominations produced for circulation also be cupronickel clad metal. Changes in the design, weight and size of the standard silver dollar were approved by Congress in 1978, and beginning in 1979, a smaller cupronickel dollar coin bearing the likeness of Susan B. Anthony and the Apollo II moon landing was released.

A change in the composition of the cent was effected in 1982, when the current copper-plated zinc cent was introduced to replace the traditional 95% copper cent.

The Mint manufactures and sells bronze medals of a national character, produces numismatic coins and coin sets, and as scheduling permits, manufactures coinage for foreign governments. Special government-sponsored numismatic coinage includes congressionally authorized 90% silver half dollars produced in 1982 to mark the 250th anniversary of George Washington's birth, and 90% gold $10 coins dated 1984 and two 90% silver dollars dated 1983 and 1984, respectively, commemorating the 1984 Olympic games, and a 90% gold $5 coin, a 90% silver dollar coin and a cupronickel half dollar for the Statue of Liberty Centennial in 1986. The Mint issued a 1987 dated 90% gold $5 coin and a 1987 dated 90% silver dollar coin honoring the 200th Anniversary of the U.S. Constitution. Congress has also directed the U.S. Mint to commence the production and sale of legal tender gold and silver bullion coins designated as "American Eagle Bullion Coins" by the mint. The coins in the series contain .9167 fine gold, and have a face value of $50 (1 oz.), $25 (½ oz.), $10 (¼ oz.), and $5 (1/10 oz.). The American Eagle silver bullion coin has a face value of $1 and contains 1 troy ounce of .999 fine silver. Information concerning these and other Mint coin programs and coin availability, may be secured from the United States Mint, 10001 Aerospace Road, Lanham, MD 20706.

Domestic Coinage Executed During Calendar Year 1986

Denomination	Philadelphia	Denver	West Point	Total value	Total pieces
Dollars—non-silver	—0—	—0—	—0—	—0—	—0—
Subsidiary					
Half dollars	$ 6,553,816.50	$ 7,683,072.50	$0.00	$ 14,236,889.00	28,473,778
Quarter dollars	137,799,833.25	126,074,665.00	0.00	263,874,498.25	1,055,497,993
Dimes	68,264,969.30	47,332,697.40	0.00	115,597,666.70	1,155,976,667
Total subsidiary	**212,618,619.05**	**181,090,434.90**	**0.00**	**393,709,053.95**	**2,239,918,438**
Minor					
Five-cent pieces	$26,844,174.65	$18,090,957.00	0.00	$ 44,935,131.65	898,702,633
One-cent pieces[1]	44,909,954.93	44,428,666.98	$4,000.00	89,342,621.91	8,934,262,191
Total minor,	**$71,754,129.58**	**$62,519,623.98**	**$4,000.00**	**$134,277,753.56**	**9,832,964,824**
Total domestic coinage	**$284,372,748.63**	**$243,610,058.88**	**$4,000.00**	**$527,986,807.51**	**12,072,913,262**

Portraits on U.S. Treasury Bills, Bonds, Notes and Savings Bonds

Denomination	Savings bonds	Treas. bills	Treas. bonds	Treas. notes
25	Washington			
50	F.D. Roosevelt		Jefferson	
75	Truman			
100	Eisenhower		Jackson	
200	Kennedy			
500	Wilson		Washington	
1,000	T. Roosevelt	H. McCulloch	Lincoln	Lincoln
5,000	McKinley	J.G. Carlisle	Monroe	Monroe
10,000	Cleveland	J. Sherman	Cleveland	Cleveland
50,000		C. Glass		
100,000		A Gallatin	Grant	Grant
1,000,000		O. Wolcott	T. Roosevelt	T. Roosevelt
100,000,000				Madison
500,000,000				McKinley

Large Denominations of U.S. Currency Discontinued

The largest denomination of United States currency now being issued is the $100 bill. Issuance of currency in denominations larger than $100 was discontinued in 1969.

As large denomination bills reach the Federal Reserve Bank they are removed from circulation.

Because some of the discontinued currency is expected to be in the hands of holders for many years, the description of the various denominations below is continued:

Amt.	Portrait	Embellishment on back	Amt.	Portrait	Embellishment on back
$ 1	Washington	Great Seal of U.S.	$ 100	Franklin	Independence Hall
2	Jefferson	Signers of Declaration	500	McKinley	Ornate denominational marking
5	Lincoln	Lincoln Memorial	1,000	Cleveland	Ornate denominational marking
10	Hamilton	U.S. Treasury	5,000	Madison	Ornate denominational marking
20	Jackson	White House	10,000	Chase	Ornate denominational marking
50	Grant	U.S. Capitol	100,000	Wilson	Ornate denominational marking

*For use only in transactions between Federal Reserve System and Treasury Department.

State Finances

Revenues, Expenditures, Debts, Taxes, U.S. Aid

For fiscal 1985 ending June 30, 1983, except: Alabama and Michigan, Sept. 30; New York, Mar. 31; Texas, Aug. 31. Taxes are State income and sales (or gross receipts) taxes, and vehicle, etc., fees.

Sources: Census Bureau, U.S. Teasury Dept.

	Revenue (thousands)	Expenditures (thousands)	Debt (thousands)	Per cap. Debt	Per cap. taxes	Per cap. U.S. aid
Alabama	$6,618,332	$6,082,189	$3,239,853	$806	$731	$428
Alaska	5,917,595	4,949,743	5,692,101	10,925	3,620	1,228
Arizona	5,330,494	4,598,782	683,889	215	924	352
Arkansas	3,342,458	3,018,212	824,708	350	740	430
California	57,894,216	51,839,954	16,056,548	609	1,098	402
Colorado	5,300,834	4,817,165	1,520,473	471	708	361
Connecticut	6,299,535	5,428,688	6,389,163	2,013	1,112	434
Delaware	1,684,264	1,335,206	1,831,524	2,945	1,316	511
Florida	13,768,320	12,853,957	5,014,494	441	733	275
Georgia	8,759,703	7,618,371	2,157,591	361	757	397
Hawaii	2,676,984	2,538,693	2,709,596	2,571	1,293	413
Idaho	1,610,156	1,440,021	629,247	626	730	443
Illinois	17,573,049	16,490,504	9,787,199	848	800	406
Indiana	7,916,853	7,084,020	1,730,339	315	789	332
Iowa	4,097,391	4,029,705	1,325,543	400	000	404
Kansas	3,713,641	3,247,655	318,865	130	782	349
Kentucky	6,178,424	5,447,024	3,633,273	975	809	473
Louisiana	8,156,067	7,580,812	8,094,673	1,806	860	398
Maine	2,136,786	1,947,767	1,224,601	1,052	864	567
Maryland	8,193,494	7,364,722	5,091,055	1,159	984	412
Massachusetts	11,485,335	11,028,037	10,100,950	1,735	1,137	488
Michigan	17,719,929	15,633,890	5,903,899	650	1,006	436
Minnesota	9,378,366	8,121,012	3,502,627	835	1,247	473
Mississippi	3,922,729	3,561,410	1,006,930	385	693	455
Missouri	6,682,144	5,816,977	3,319,406	660	667	385
Montana	1,738,331	1,557,424	744,503	901	776	707
Nebraska	2,143,559	2,136,580	1,028,066	640	648	421
Nevada	1,909,081	1,642,917	1,108,496	1,184	1,005	414
New Hampshire	1,382,376	1,194,676	1,979,239	1,983	435	421
New Jersey	15,904,710	14,080,179	13,364,830	1,767	1,021	389
New Mexico	3,625,018	3,040,879	1,277,455	881	993	615
New York	46,762,391	40,106,103	32,355,192	1,819	1,164	624
North Carolina	9,878,777	8,492,053	2,156,628	345	831	341
North Dakota	1,651,233	1,541,117	585,866	855	1,011	660
Ohio	21,242,350	17,568,417	8,204,063	764	805	387
Oklahoma	5,672,035	5,077,154	3,581,385	1,085	903	374
Oregon	6,337,286	4,811,712	6,606,048	2,458	738	539
Pennsylvania	20,336,975	18,067,350	7,269,221	615	857	419
Rhode Island	2,128,519	2,009,683	2,814,124	2,907	890	592
South Carolina	5,825,035	5,253,955	3,402,857	1,017	816	395
South Dakota	1,081,777	1,004,515	1,086,446	1,535	502	678
Tennessee	6,142,245	5,439,026	1,913,389	402	630	430
Texas	21,360,783	19,074,421	5,192,530	317	706	273
Utah	3,133,347	2,818,208	1,333,302	811	805	462
Vermont	1,109,092	1,033,824	900,616	1,683	857	629
Virginia	8,916,267	7,800,178	3,316,926	581	783	318
Washington	9,780,504	9,011,557	3,029,948	687	1,040	414
West Virginia	3,665,280	3,343,268	1,628,348	841	955	467
Wisconsin	9,786,843	8,665,304	4,473,094	937	1,071	442
Wyoming	1,945,554	1,497,392	756,811	1,487	1,584	989
United States	**$439,416,467**	**$390,742,488**	**$211,916,930**	**$890**	**$907**	**$100,828**

Business Starts in the U.S.

Source: Dun & Bradstreet Corp.

There was a 0.7 percent increase in business starts in the United States in 1986 over the previous year. Business starts were uneven throughout the country—from a 20.6 percent increase in New England to a decline of 13.9 percent in the oil-dominated region of Arkansas, Oklahoma, Louisiana, and Texas.

State	Business starts 1985	Business starts 1986	Change
Alabama	3,221	3,236	+0.5%
Alaska	1,018	705	−30.7%
Arizona	4,736	4,283	−9.6%
Arkansas	1,965	1,903	−2.9%
California	28,937	29,851	+3.2%
Colorado	5,265	5,292	+0.5%
Connecticut	3,223	3,822	+18.6%
District of Columbia	880	848	−3.6%
Delaware	648	631	−2.6%
Florida	18,491	17,709	−4.2%
Georgia	6,790	7,303	+7.6%
Hawaii	1,019	1,065	+4.5%
Idaho	1,071	1,017	−5.0%
Illinois	11,958	10,504	−12.2%
Indiana	3,968	4,023	+1.4%

(continued)

State	Business starts 1985	1986	Change
Iowa	1,864	1,618	−13.2%
Kansas	2,515	2,191	−12.9%
Kentucky	2,934	3,269	−11.4%
Louisiana	4,402	4,141	−5.9%
Maine	814	1,011	+24.2%
Massachusetts	5,222	6,239	+19.5%
Maryland	4,766	5,132	+7.7%
Michigan	8,144	8,495	+4.3%
Minnesota	3,521	3,535	+0.4%
Mississippi	1,600	1,877	+17.3%
Missouri	4,424	4,316	−2.4%
Montana	920	812	−11.7%
North Carolina	5,278	5,225	−1.0%
North Dakota	453	448	−1.1%
New Hampshire	1,074	1,415	+31.8%
New Jersey	8,596	10,341	+20.3%
New Mexico	1,454	1,407	−3.2%
New York	19,190	21,609	+12.6%
Nebraska	1,237	1,161	−6.1%
Nevada	1,204	1,092	−9.3%
Ohio	8,262	8,869	+7.3%
Oklahoma	3,475	2,954	−15.0%
Oregon	2,767	2,975	+7.5%
Pennsylvania	9,136	9,809	+7.4%
Rhode Island	765	834	+9.0%
South Carolina	2,801	2,864	+2.2%
South Dakota	474	464	−2.7%
Tennessee	4,502	4,312	−4.2%
Texas	26,073	21,913	−16.0%
Utah	1,796	1,731	−3.6%
Virginia	5,783	6,030	+4.3%
Vermont	511	685	+34.1%
West Virginia	1,200	1,418	+18.2%
Washington	5,311	5,238	−1.4%
Wisconsin	3,591	3,448	−4.0%
Wyoming	521	525	+0.8%

Federal Aid to State and Local Governments

Source: U.S. Office of Management and Budget
(million of dollars)

Type of aid, function, and major program	1970	1975	1980	1984	1985	1986[1]
Grant-in-aid shared revenue	**24,065**	**49,791**	**91,451**	**97,577**	**105,897**	**108,802**
National defense	37	74	93	95	157	150
Natural resources & environment	411	2,437	5,363	3,779	4,069	3,918
Energy	25	43	499	534	529	528
Agriculture	604	404	569	1,832	2,420	1,922
Transportation[2]	4,599	5,864	13,087	15,013	17,055	18,178
Airports	83	292	590	694	789	776
Highways	4,395	4,702	9,209	10,522	12,841	13,854
Railroads	—	(z)	54	34	35	35
Urban mass transit	105	689	3,129	3,483	2,797	2,673
Commerce & housing credit	4	2	3	2	2	2
Community & regional development[2]	1,780	2,842	6,486	5,157	5,221	5,245
Urban renewal	1,054	1,374	214	24	28	35
Education, employment, training, social services[2]	6,393	12,133	21,862	16,669	17,817	18,108
Health[2]	3,849	8,810	15,758	21,837	24,451	26,530
Alcohol, drug abuse, & mental health	146	590	679	501	501	461
Medicaid[4]	2,727	6,840	13,957	20,061	22,655	24,686
Income security[2]	5,819	9,352	18,495	25,678	27,153	27,530
Assistance payment program	4,142	5,121	6,888	8,311	8,592	9,041
Food stamps, administration	559	136	413	732	886	939
Child nutrition & special milk programs	379	1,565	3,388	3,361	3,480	3,669
Housing assistance	436	1,326	3,435	5,750	6,407	6,156
Veterans benefits & services	18	33	90	66	91	96
Administration of justice	42	725	529	69	95	145
General government	49	101	138	171	182	187
General purpose fiscal assistance	430	6,971	8,478	6,677	6,656	6,264

(1) Estimate. (2) Includes items not shown separately. z = not applicable.

Prime Military Contract Awards by State

Source: U.S. Defense Dept.

(millions of dollars)

State	Contract[1] Awards 1984	1985
Alabama	$1,132	$1,418
Alaska	437	550
Arizona	1,764	2,006
Arkansas	692	810
California	28,520	29,115
Colorado	1,153	1,563
Connecticut	5,459	5,543
Delaware	226	261
Dist. of Col.	815	1,104
Florida	4,034	5,271
Georgia	3,123	3,520
Hawaii	537	626
Idaho	51	50
Illinois	1,476	1,693
Indiana	2,522	3,177
Iowa	405	590
Kansas	2,362	2,139
Kentucky	448	506
Louisiana	1,855	2,175
Maine	532	957
Maryland	4,013	4,608
Massachusetts	7,029	7,714
Michigan	2,510	2,789
Minnesota	1,826	2,298
Mississippi	2,190	1,310
Missouri	6,520	7,613
Montana	83	102
Nebraska	167	193
Nevada	129	128
New Hampshire	663	678
New Jersey	3,278	3,862
New Mexico	552	492
New York	9,515	10,033
North Carolina	863	1,029
North Dakota	201	207
Ohio	2,804	4,648
Oklahoma	535	602
Oregon	230	256
Pennsylvania	3,253	4,149
Rhode Island	396	431
South Carolina	478	490
South Dakota	47	78
Tennessee	796	793
Texas	8,750	10,562
Utah	880	789
Vermont	170	163
Virginia	4,605	6,167
Washington	2,884	3,559
West Virginia	72	90
Wisconsin	959	1,065
Wyoming	74	125
Total	**124,015**	**140,096**

(1) Military awards for supplies, services, and construction. Net value of contracts of over $25,000 for work in each state. Figures reflect impact of prime contracting on state distribution of defense work. Often the state in which a prime contractor is located is not the state in which the subcontracting work is done.

Index of Leading Economic Indicators

Source: Bureau of Economic Analysis, U.S. Dept. of Commerce

The index of leading economic indicators, which is issued to project the economy's performance six months or a year ahead, rose .52 percent in July 1987. Analysts said that the increase suggests that the economy is likely to continue to grow, but at a lackluster pace.

The index is made up of twelve measurements of economic activity that tend to change direction long before the overall economy does. The volatility of the index, caused in part by the fact that many of the statistics covered do not reach the Commerce Department until weeks after the initial report, usually results in at least one revision after the initial reporting.

Two companion indexes—those of coincident and lagging indicators—rose in July by 0.5 percent and fell 0.5 percent, respectively. The coincident index reflects current economic conditions. Its components are: employees on nonagricultural payrolls; personal income less transfer payments; industrial production; and manufacturing and trade sales. The lagging index consists of items that tend to lag behind the business cycle.

Leading Indicators: Component Analysis

Components	Contribution to change June to July 1987
Average workweek of production workers in manufacturing	0.00
Average weekly claims for state unemployment insurance[1]	0.00
New orders for consumer goods and materials, 1982 dollars	−0.25
Vendor performance (companies receiving slower deliveries from suppliers)	+0.27
Index of net business formation	NA
Contracts and orders for plant and equipment, 1962 dollars	+0.01
Building permits issued	−0.08
Change in inventories on hand and on order, 1982 dollars	NA
Change in sensitive materials prices	+0.21
Index of stock prices	−0.24
Money supply: M-2, 1982 dollars	−0.01
Change in credit (business and consumer borrowing)	NA
Leading indicators index, percent change	**+0.52**

(1) Series is inverted in computing index; that is, a decrease in the series is considered upward movement. (NA) Not available.

Consumer Price Index

The Consumer Price Index (CPI) is a measure of the average change in prices over time in a fixed market basket of goods and services. From Jan. 1978, the Bureau of Labor Statistics began publishing CPI's for two population groups: (1) a CPI for All Urban Consumers (CPI-U) which covers about 80% of the total population; and (2) a CPI for Urban Wage Earners and Clerical Workers (CPI-W) which covers 32% of the total population. The CPI-U includes, in addition to wage earners and clerical workers, groups such as professional, managerial, and technical workers, the self-employed, short-term workers, the unemployed, retirees and others not in the labor force.

The CPI is based on prices of food, clothing, shelter, and fuels, transportation fares, charges for doctors' and dentists' services, drugs, and the other goods and services bought for day-to-day living. The index measures price changes from a designated reference date—1967—which equals 100.0. An increase of 203%, for example, is shown as 303.0. This change can also be expressed in dollars as follows: The price of a base period "market basket" of goods and services in the CPI has risen from $10 in 1967 to $30.30.

Which Index For You?

Which index should you use to calculate the impact of inflation on your life? If your income is near the poverty level, or if you are retired on a moderate income, you should probably use the CPI-U. Otherwise, even if you are moderately rich, the CPI-W will probably be the best indicator for you.

The CPI (W and U) emerges each month as single numbers. At the end of the year an average is computed from the monthly figures. (Averaging does away with fluctuations caused by special situations that have nothing to do with inflation.)

For example, the average CPI at the end of 1986 was 331.1. This means that the value of goods and services, which was set at 100% in 1967, cost 231.1% more in 1986.

Changes in prices and how they affect you can be calculated by comparing the CPI of one period against another. The 1986 CPI reading of 331.1 can be compared to the 1985 reading of 322.2. Dividing by 322.2, the excess over 1 is the percentage increase for the year 1986; in this case, 1.1%, the lowest increase in the index since 1961.

Did your income increase by enough to keep up with this inflation? To make the comparison, dig out your old W-2 or income tax return forms, or find your old paycheck stubs. Both gross and takehome pay comparisons will be of interest to you, but take care to compare equals. Overtime pay should not be counted. Also, watch out for changes in deductions such as those for tax exemptions, credit union payments and payroll bonds. These have nothing to do with inflation and should be added back to your take home pay.

Measuring Your Paycheck

A. To compare year-to-year earnings in percent form, divide your 1986 earnings by those of 1985 and express the result as a percentage. For example, if you earned the gross wages of the average U.S. worker, your paychecks in 1985 showed about $299.09 per week as compared with $304.85 per week in 1986, an increase of 1.1%. Since prices rose by 1.1% during 1986, the average worker gained 0.8% in real gross income that year. You can do the same kind of calculation on your total 1985 and 1986 earnings by using your total annual income figures in place of weekly earnings figures.

Average Consumer Price Indexes

Source: Bureau of Labor Statistics, U.S. Labor Department

The Consumer Price Index (CPI-U) measures the average change in prices of goods and services purchased by urban wage earners and clerical workers. (1967 = 100). NA = Not available.

	1980		1981		1982		1983		1984		1985		1986	
	Index	%+	Index	%+	Index	%+	Index	%+	Index	%+	Index	%+	Index	%+
All items	247.0	13.5	273.3	10.2	288.6	6.0	298.4	3.2	311.1	4.3	322.2	3.6	331.1	1.1
Food, drink	248.7	8.7	267.8	7.7	278.5	4.0	284.7	2.2	295.1	3.7	302.0	2.3	317.0	3.7
Housing	263.2	12.3	293.2	11.4	314.7	7.3	322.0	2.3	336.5	4.5	349.9	4.0	362.1	1.8
Apparel, upkeep	177.4	6.6	186.6	5.2	190.9	2.3	195.6	2.5	200.2	2.4	206.0	2.9	210.9	0.9
Transportation	250.5	17.7	281.3	12.3	293.1	4.2	300.0	2.4	311.7	3.9	319.9	2.6	308.4	-5.9
Medical care	267.2	11.3	295.1	10.4	326.9	10.8	355.1	8.6	379.5	6.9	403.1	6.2	446.8	7.7
Entertainment	203.7	8.5	219.0	7.5	232.4	6.1	242.4	4.3	255.1	5.2	265.0	3.9	277.4	3.4
Other	213.6	8,8	233.3	9.2	257.0	10.2	286.3	11.4	307.7	7.5	326.6	6.1	355.2	5.6

Consumer Price Indexes, 1987

Source: Bureau of Labor Statistics, U.S. Labor Department

(seasonally adjusted indexes)

(1967=100)	Mar. CPI-U	Mar. CPI-W	Apr. CPI-U	Apr. CPI-W	May CPI-U	May CPI-W
Food, beverages	320.6	320.3	321.5	321.1	323.9	323.1
Housing	267.2	359.6	368.2	360.4	368.2	361.0
Apparel, upkeep	215.4	213.6	218.6	216.9	219.1	217.6
Transportation	311.8	312.0	313.4	314.0	314.4	315.1
Medical care	453.7	451.0	456.5	453.9	459.1	456.9
Entertainment	279.7	274.3	281.3	275.9	282.1	277.1
Other goods, services	362.2	356.8	363.9	358.4	366.0	360.2
Services	412.6	407.3	414.1	408.7	415.3	409.8
Rent, for home[1, 2]	124.1	112.5	124.8	113.0	125.1	113.4
Household, less rent[1, 2]	111.5	102.5	111.4	102.4	112.3	103.2
Medical care	490.1	487.2	493.7	491.1	496.5	494.1
Other services	345.2	339.5	347.2	341.6	349.0	343.3
All items less food	335.9	329.7	337.5	331.3	338.4	332.3
Commodities	289.3	288.4	290.8	290.0	291.9	291.3
Commodities less food	268.3	267.6	270.1	269.6	270.8	270.5
Nondurables[1]	296.8	296.9	299.1	299.2	300.0	300.1
Energy	365.2	363.0	366.2	364.3	366.8	364.8
All items less energy	336.7	330.4	338.2	331.7	339.3	333.0

(1) Not seasonally adjusted. (2) Indexes on a Dec. 1984 = 100 base.

Consumer Price Indexes for Selected Items and Groups

Source: Bureau of Labor Statistics, U.S. Labor Dept.

(1967 = 100 except as noted. Annual averages of monthly figures; seasonally adjusted)

	1970	1975	1980	1982	1983	1984	1985	1986 Dec.
All items	**116.3**	**161.2**	**246.8**	**289.1**	**298.4**	**311.1**	**322.2**	**331.1**
Food and beverages	**114.7**	**172.1**	**248.0**	**278.2**	**284.4**	**295.1**	**302.0**	**316.8**
Food	114.9	175.4	254.6	285.7	291.7	302.9	309.8	324.8
Food at home	113.7	175.8	251.5	279.2	282.2	292.6	296.8	308.7
Cereals, bakery prods.[1]	108.9	184.8	246.4	283.4	292.5	305.3	317.0	328.0
Meats, poultry, fish, eggs	117.3	176.4	242.2	262.1	261.0	266.6	263.4	386.6
Dairy prods.[1]	111.8	156.6	227.4	247.0	250.0	253.2	258.0	360.9
Fruits, vegetables	113.4	171.0	246.7	291.4	292.2	317.4	325.7	323.4
Sugar, sweets[1]	115.1	246.2	341.3	367.5	374.4	389.1	398.8	411.2
Fats, oils[1]	105.8	198.6	241.2	259.6	263.1	288.0	294.4	285.5
Nonalcoholic beverages	117.4	178.9	395.8	424.2	432.2	443.0	451.7	470.3
Other prepared foods	109.4	163.0	231.1	268.1	276.5	284.9	294.2	306.6
Food away from home	119.9	174.3	267.0	306.5	319.9	333.4	346.6	370.5
Alcoholic beverages	112.3	142.1	186.3	208.5	216.5	222.1	229.5	243.9
Housing	**118.2**	**164.5**	**263.3**	**314.7**	**323.1**	**336.5**	**349.9**	**354.8**
Shelter	123.6	169.7	281.7	337.0	344.8	361.7	382.0	398.1
Rent	110.1	137.3	191.6	224.0	236.9	249.3	264.6	285.1
Maintenance, repairs[1]	124.0	187.6	285.7	334.1	346.3	359.2	368.9	274.6
Fuel, other utilities	107.6	167.8	278.6	350.8	370.3	387.3	393.6	371.1
Electricity	106.2	167.0	253.4	320.3	330.6	351.8	364.1	351.2
Household furnishings & operation	111.5	151.0	205.4	233.2	238.5	242.5	247.2	248.5
House furnishings	109.3	137.4	174.2	193.8	197.5	199.1	200.1	199.7
Apparel & upkeep	**116.1**	**142.3**	**178.4**	**191.8**	**196.5**	**200.2**	**206.0**	**209.6**
Apparel commodities	116.5	141.2	171.1	181.0	184.5	187.0	191.6	194.5
Apparel commodities[2]	116.3	140.6	167.8	177.0	180.8	183.2	188.1	190.9
Men's & boys'	117.1	142.2	168.4	183.9	188.9	192.4	197.9	202.1
Women's & girls'	116.0	138.1	155.1	159.1	161.9	163.6	169.5	173.1
Footwear	117.7	144.2	190.3	205.5	206.9	209.5	212.1	214.9
Transportation	**112.7**	**150.6**	**249.7**	**291.5**	**298.4**	**311.7**	**319.9**	**304.2**
Private	111.1	149.8	249.2	287.5	293.9	306.6	314.2	297.5
Automobiles, new	107.6	127.6	179.3	197.5	202.6	208.5	215.2	231.4
Automobiles, used	104.3	146.4	208.1	296.4	329.7	375.7	379.7	356.6
Gasoline	105.6	170.8	369.1	389.3	376.3	370.2	373.3	262.5
Auto insurance rates[1]	126.7	145.9	247.4	275.7	302.7	326.3	359.5	423.9
Public[1]	128.5	158.6	251.6	346.0	362.6	385.2	402.8	425.8
Airline fares[1]	118.5	159.0	284.8	395.0	417.8	443.0	470.9	503.7
Medical care	**120.6**	**168.6**	**265.9**	**328.7**	**357.3**	**379.5**	**403.1**	**443.9**
Prescription drugs	101.2	109.3	154.8	192.7	213.8	234.3	256.5	289.6
Physicians' services	121.4	169.4	269.3	327.1	352.3	376.8	398.8	446.4
Dental services[1]	119.4	161.9	240.2	283.6	302.7	327.3	347.9	372.3
Hospital room	145.4	236.1	418.9	556.7	619.7	670.9	710.5	763.0
Entertainment	**116.7**	**152.2**	**205.3**	**235.8**	**246.0**	**255.1**	**265.0**	**272.3**
Newspapers[1]	119.4	174.5	238.2	283.5	302.4	314.3	328.0	346.7
Entertainment services[1]	121.0	152.4	201.6	231.8	245.3	258.3	271.8	292.0
Other goods & services	**116.8**	**153.9**	**214.5**	**259.9**	**288.3**	**307.7**	**326.6**	**349.5**
Tobacco products[1]	121.2	153.9	202.6	243.5	291.0	310.0	328.5	357.2
Personal care[1]	113.2	150.7	213.1	248.3	261.1	271.4	281.9	291.3
Toilet goods,[1, 3]	110.4	150.0	206.1	246.1	260.6	269.6	278.5	290.3
Personal care services[1]	116.0	151.4	219.9	251.2	262.5	274.1	286.0	292.7
Personal, educational expenses	118.2	162.4	236.2	301.0	333.3	365.7	397.1	450.0

(1) Not seasonally adjusted, (2) Except footwear (3) Incl. personal care appliances.

Consumer Price Index by Region and Selected Cities

Source: Bureau of Labor Statistics, U.S. Labor Department

Area (1967 = 100)	CPI-U Indexes Mar. 1987	CPI-U Indexes Apr. 1987	CPI-U Indexes May 1987	CPI-U Percent change to May 1987 from— May 1986	CPI-W Indexes Mar. 1987	CPI-W Indexes Apr. 1987	CPI-W Indexes May 1987	CPI-W Percent change to May 1987 from— May 1986
U.S. city average	335.9	337.7	338.7	3.8	330.5	332.3	333.4	3.7
Northeast urban	**179.9**	**181.0**	**181.7**	—	**177.0**	**178.2**	**178.9**	—
More than 1,200,000	177.5	178.8	179.5	—	173.0	174.4	175.2	—
500,000 to 1,200,000	180.7	182.3	182.8	—	177.7	179.3	179.7	—
50,000 to 500,000	188.8	188.9	189.0	—	193.1	193.1	193.5	—
North Central urban	**179.5**	**180.4**	**180.8**	—	**175.3**	**176.2**	**176.7**	—
More than 1,200,000	183.2	184.0	184.5	—	177.3	178.3	178.8	—
360,000 to 1,200,000	177.8	179.5	179.5	—	173.1	174.6	174.8	—
50,000 to 360,000	175.3	176.1	176.9	—	171.5	172.2	173.0	—
Less than 50,000	174.0	174.6	174.9	—	175.1	175.7	176.2	—
South urban	**180.2**	**180.9**	**181.4**	—	**179.0**	**179.7**	**180.3**	—
More than 1,200,000	180.4	181.5	182.0	—	179.6	180.7	181.4	—
450,000 to 1,200,000	182.3	183.0	183.2	—	178.1	178.7	179.1	—
50,000 to 450,000	178.8	179.2	179.8	—	179.3	179.8	180.4	—
Less than 50,000	177.8	178.0	178.9	—	178.4	178.6	179.5	—
West urban	**182.7**	**183.8**	**184.4**	—	**180.1**	**181.1**	**181.7**	—
More than 1,250,000	186.1	187.2	188.1	—	181.0	182.1	182.9	—
330,000 to 1,250,000	181.4	182.7	183.2	—	181.5	182.8	183.5	—
50,000 to 330,000	175.2	175.8	175.2	—	173.3	173.8	173.2	—
Selected areas								
Chicago, Ill.–NW Ind	335.5	337.1	338.4	4.4	320.1	321.6	322.7	4.2
L.A.–Long Beach, Anaheim, Cal.	341.4	342.8	345.1	4.8	333.4	334.8	337.1	4.5
New York, N.Y.–NE N.J.	334.7	337.0	339.0	5.7	325.7	328.2	330.2	5.7
Philadelphia, Pa.–N.J.	329.4	333.8	336.2	5.4	330.4	334.9	337.5	5.2
San Francisco–Oakland, Cal.	349.6	353.0	353.5	—	343.4	346.9	347.0	—
Baltimore, Md.	335.9	—	340.1	3.3	333.2	—	337.4	3.2
Boston, Mass.	336.8	—	335.1	3.0	334.7	—	332.9	4.0
Cleveland, Oh.	356.8	—	357.5	—	333.3	—	334.2	—
Miami, Fla.	178.4	—	179.1	3.5	178.6	—	179.2	3.3
St. Louis, Mo.–Ill.	328.8	—	330.5	3.7	324.3	—	326.3	3.9
Washington, D.C.–Md.—Va.	338.0	—	340.5	3.3	340.1	—	343.2	3.9
Dallas–Fort Worth, Tex.	—	351.8	—	—	—	344.4	—	—
Detroit, Mich.	—	330.5	—	—	—	319.9	—	—
Houston, Tex.	—	341.1	—	—	—	338.5	—	—
Pittsburgh, Pa.	—	338.2	—	—	—	316.6	—	—

Percent Change in Consumer Prices in Selected Countries

Source: Organization for Economic Cooperation and Development

Country	1970-1975, avg.	1975-1980, avg.	1980-1985, avg.
United States	6.7	8.9	5.5
Australia	10.2	10.6	8.3
Austria	7.3	5.3	4.9
Belgium	8.4	6.4	7.0
Canada	7.3	8.7	7.4
Denmark	9.3	10.4	7.9
Finland	11.7	10.7	8.6
France	8.8	10.5	9.6
Germany, W.	6.1	4.1	3.9
Greece	12.3	16.3	20.7
Ireland	13.3	14.1	12.3
Italy	11.3	16.3	13.7
Japan	11.5	6.5	2.7
Luxembourg	7.2	6.1	6.9
New Zealand	10.2	14.8	12.0
Netherlands	8.6	6.0	4.2
Norway	8.4	8.4	9.0
Portugal[1]	15.4	21.8	23.2
Spain	12.1	18.6	12.2
Sweden	8.0	10.5	9.0
Switzerland	7.7	2.3	4.3
Turkey[1]	18.6	50.1	37.8
United Kingdom	13.0	14.4	7.2

(1) Excludes rent.

Distribution of Total Personal Income

(in billions)

Source: Bureau of Economic Analysis; U.S. Commerce Department

Year	Personal income	Personal taxes	Disposable Personal income	Personal outlays	Personal Savings: Amount	Personal Savings: As a pct. of disposable income
1960	$ 402.3	$ 50.4	$ 352.0	$ 332.3	$ 19.7	5.6%
1965	540.7	64.9	475.8	442.1	33.7	7.1
1970	811.1	115.8	695.3	639.5	55.8	8.0
1972	951.4	141.0	810.3	757.7	52.6	6.5
1973	1,065.2	150.7	914.5	835.5	79.0	8.6
1974	1,168.6	170.2	998.3	913.2	85.1	8.5
1975	1,265.0	168.9	1,096.1	1,001.8	94.3	8.6
1976	1,391.2	196.8	1,194.4	1,111.9	82.5	6.9
1977	1,540.4	226.4	1,314.0	1,236.0	78.0	5.9

(continued)

Year	Personal income	Personal taxes	Disposable Personal income	Personal outlays	Personal Savings: Amount	Personal Savings: As a pct. of disposable income
1978	$1,732.7	$258.7	$1,474.0	$1,384.6	$89.4	6.1%
1979	1,951.2	301.0	1,650.2	1,553.5	96.7	5.9
1980	2,165.3	336.5	1,828.9	1,718.7	110.2	6.0
1981	2.429.5	387.7	2,041.7	1,904.3	137.4	6.7
1982	2,584.6	404.1	2,180.5	2,044.5	136.0	6.2
1983	2,838.6	410.5	2,428.1	2,297.4	130.6	5.4
1984	3,108.7	44.2	2,668.6	2,504.5	164.1	6.1
1985	3,327.0	485.9	2,841.1	2,714.1	127.1	4.5
1986	3,534.3	512.2	3,022.1	2,891.5	130.6	4.3

Producer Price Indexes

Source: Bureau of Labor Statistics, U.S. Labor Department

Producer Price Indexes measure average changes in prices received in primary markets of the U.S. by producers of commodities in all stages of processing.

Commodity group (1967 = 100)	Annual Avg. 1985	Annual Avg. 1986	1986 Jan.	1986 June	1987 Jan.	1987 June
All commodities	**308.7**	**299.8**	**308.9**	**298.9**	**300.9**	**308.5**
Farm products processed foods and feeds	**250.5**	**252.0**	**251.5**	**249.5**	**251.6**	**263.0**
Farm products	220.5	224.7	227.4	221.4	220.8	239.1
Processed foods and feeds	260.4	265.1	263.3	263.4	266.8	274.8
Industrial commodities	**323.8**	**312.1**	**323.8**	**311.6**	**313.5**	**320.2**
Textile products and apparel	210.4	211.1	210.7	211.1	212.0	214.3
Hides, skins, leathers, and related products	286.1	296.7	293.7	299.0	301.9	316.2
Fuels and related products and power	633.6	483.5	620.3	483.5	461.6	494.0
Chemicals and allied products	303.2	299.7	305.1	298.0	301.1	313.0
Rubber and plastic products	245.9	246.1	246.9	246.4	245.0	247.0
Lumber and wood products	303.6	305.3	298.9	306.4	307.9	317.0
Pulp, paper, and allied products	327.2	335.3	330.6	334.0	345.0	349.7
Metals and metal products	314.9	311.3	311.0	311.0	312.8	319.0
Machinery and equipment	298.9	303.3	301.1	303.0	306.1	306.7
Furniture and household durables	221.6	223.9	222.7	223.6	225.5	227.0
Nonmetallic mineral products	347.8	352.0	252.5	252.8	350.0	352.3
Transportation equipment (Dec. 1968 = 100)	269.5	276.2	273.3	275.5	282.3	281.6
Miscellaneous products	302.3	308.5	307.3	306.6	312.6	314.5

Indexes of Manufacturing, Industrial Countries

Source: Bureau of Labor Statistics, U.S. Labor Department (1977=100)

Output per hour

Country	1960	1965	1970	1975	1980	1983	1984	1985	1986
United States	62.2	76.6	80.8	92.9	101.4	112.0	116.6	121.7	126.0
Canada	50.7	65.0	75.6	88.6	98.2	106.9	110.2	112.7	112.1
Japan	23.2	35.0	64.8	87.7	122.7	142.3	152.2	163.7	168.2
Belgium	32.8	40.6	59.9	85.9	119.7	144.7	149.8	153.3	NA
Denmark	37.2	48.4	65.5	94.6	112.3	120.2	118.9	117.2	116.6
France	36.4	49.2	69.6	88.5	112.0	128.8	133.8	138.3	140.9
West Germany	40.3	54.0	71.2	90.1	108.6	119.1	123.5	128.9	131.4
Italy	36.5	52.9	72.7	91.1	116.9	126.6	134.7	136.8	138.4
Netherlands	32.4	42.1	64.3	86.2	113.9	127.5	141.2	145.6	NA
Norway	54.6	64.4	81.7	96.8	106.7	117.2	123.9	125.2	122.1
Sweden	42.3	58.5	80.7	100.2	112.7	125.5	131.0	134.5	136.4
United Kingdom	55.5	65.7	79.7	95.2	101.7	123.0	129.5	134.2	138.2

Unit Labor Costs in U.S. dollars

Country	1960	1965	1970	1975	1980	1983	1984	1985	1986
United States	58.7	55.8	71.0	91.7	130.6	145.0	144.2	145.1	144.3
Canada	59.4	50.4	64.5	93.1	121.5	143.1	139.9	135.2	137.9
Japan	28.5	35.4	39.1	86.7	116.8	111.5	107.2	104.3	148.7
Belgium	30.2	38.6	42.0	89.7	133.7	77.4	71.7	72.3	NA
Denmark	29.5	36.2	44.4	89.6	129.0	95.1	89.9	94.0	128.9
France	41.7	48.4	46.8	99.5	154.1	113.7	103.8	103.9	138.0
West Germany	25.9	32.6	42.9	88.7	147.9	113.3	102.7	99.6	139.2
Italy	32.5	41.2	50.6	104.3	141.4	126.8	114.7	114.8	151.4
Netherlands	25.1	35.2	41.2	92.8	134.2	97.1	81.8	80.7	NA
Norway	21.7	26.9	34.5	81.4	129.3	107.9	99.1	101.3	129.8
Sweden	30.1	35.4	41.1	83.2	125.3	80.4	78.2	80.6	102.5
United Kingdom	44.2	51.0	54.2	103.7	220.5	160.8	144.3	144.8	171.9

NOTE: The data relate to all employed persons (wage & salary, the self-employed, and unpaid family workers) in the U.S. and Canada, and all employees (wage & salary earners) in the other countries.

Personal Consumption Expenditures in the U.S.

Source: Bureau of Economic Analysis, U.S. Commerce Department

(billions of dollars)

	1981	1982	1983	1984	1985	1986
Personal consumption expenditures	**1,915.1**	**2,050.7**	**2,234.5**	**2,430.5**	**2,629.4**	**2,799.8**
Food & Tobacco	**399.2**	**423.5**	**450.1**	**479.0**	**504.8**	**532.0**
Food purchased for off-premise consumption	262.6	278.4	290.4	305.8	320.6	333.3
Purchased meals and beverages	106.7	112.9	123.5	134.1	143.2	155.2
Tobacco products	22.7	24.7	28.2	30.5	32.0	34.2
Clothing, accessories, jewelry	**148.2**	**153.3**	**167.2**	**181.8**	**194.9**	**209.1**
Shoes	18.8	18.9	20.2	21.6	23.2	24.6
Clothing and accessories less shoes	100.9	105.4	114.7	125.0	133.9	142.7
Jewelry and watches	16.7	16.7	18.0	19.9	20.8	23.5
Personal care	**29.3**	**30.6**	**34.1**	**36.4**	**38.9**	**41.4**
Toilet articles, preparations	17.9	18.8	20.3	21.9	23.0	24.2
Barbershops, beauty parlors, baths, health clubs	11.4	11.7	13.8	14.5	15.8	17.2
Housing	**295.6**	**321.1**	**344.1**	**371.3**	**402.4**	**436.9**
Owner-occupied nonfarm dwellings space rent	200.7	218.1	233.9	252.3	272.7	296.0
Tenant-occupied nonfarm dwellings rent	71.1	77.9	84.7	92.2	103.0	114.5
Rental value of farm dwellings	12.6	12.9	12.1	12.2	10.9	9.9
Household operation	**255.2**	**272.4**	**294.1**	**316.9**	**331.9**	**343.0**
Furniture, incl. bedding	22.1	21.6	23.8	26.5	28.1	30.6
Kitchen, other household applicances	17.5	17.7	19.6	21.6	23.5	24.7
China, glassware, tableware, utensils	10.0	10.4	11.2	12.2	12.8	13.4
Other durable house furnishings	21.1	21.5	24.4	27.1	28.3	30.3
Semidurable house furnishings	10.8	11.4	12.3	13.3	13.9	14.8
Cleaning, household supplies, paper products	21.6	22.6	23.6	25.1	26.2	27.3
Household utilities	93.4	103.2	110.8	117.5	122.9	121.1
Telephone, telegraph	31.2	35.6	37.9	39.8	40.1	42.1
Medical care	**219.3**	**245.4**	**288.7**	**298.4**	**326.8**	**257.8**
Drug preparations, sundries	20.8	22.1	24.4	26.3	27.9	29.7
Physicians	49.0	54.4	61.1	67.1	73.3	80.2
Dentists	16.1	17.4	18.5	19.8	21.3	22.5
Privately controlled hospitals and sanitariums	96.8	110.3	119.6	130.6	140.0	152.1
Health insurance	13.2	15.1	16.0	19.0	21.7	23.9
Personal business	**103.5**	**116.3**	**136.7**	**145.8**	**174.0**	**195.1**
Brokerage charges, investment counseling	7.6	8.4	11.8	11.6	14.8	19.2
Bank service charges, trust services, safe deposit box rental	6.6	8.1	9.0	10.2	11.7	13.0
Legal services	16.6	18.8	21.7	24.6	28.2	31.3
Funeral, burial expenses	4.6	4.9	5.2	5.6	6.2	6.4
Transportation	**261.5**	**267.6**	**295.4**	**329.5**	**358.8**	**365.3**
User-operated transportation	238.0	243.7	270.5	301.6	329.7	335.8
New autos	50.7	53.3	66.2	77.6	86.9	101.5
Used autos	17.8	19.6	21.6	30.2	34.5	33.8
Accessories & other parts	19.1	20.2	21.9	23.3	25.0	25.0
Repair, greasing, washing, parking, storage, rental	34.8	35.4	38.4	42.8	48.3	51.8
Gasoline and oil	92.7	89.1	90.2	90.0	92.6	75.3
Tolls	1.1	1.2	1.2	1.3	1.3	1.4
Insurance premiums less claims paid	8.9	9.1	10.3	10.0	9.9	12.4
Purchased local transportation	6.2	6.4	6.5	6.9	7.1	7.6
Transit systems	2.7	3.0	3.1	3.4	3.5	3.8
Taxicab	3.2	3.0	2.9	3.0	3.1	3.3
Railway (commutation)	.4	.4	.4	.5	.5	.5
Purchased intercity transportation	17.3	17.6	18.4	21.0	22.0	21.9
Railway (excl. commutation)	.4	.4	.5	.6	.6	.7
Bus	1.3	1.3	1.2	1.2	1.2	1.1
Airline	14.5	14.7	15.3	17.5	18.3	18.1
Recreation	**128.6**	**138.3**	**152.1**	**168.3**	**183.8**	**198.0**
Books, maps	6.2	6.6	7.2	7.8	8.2	8.7
Magazines, newspapers, sheet music	11.0	11.4	12.0	12.7	12.9	13.7
Nondurable toys and sport supplies	16.0	16.8	18.0	19.7	20.9	21.8
Wheel goods, durable toys, sports equipment, boats, pleasure aircraft	18.7	19.3	20.4	24.8	25.9	27.0
Radio and TV receivers, records, musical instruments	22.0	24.5	28.2	31.5	36.1	40.8
Flowers, seeds, potted plants	4.4	4.5	4.8	5.2	5.7	6.5
Admissions to specified spectator amusements	6.9	7.8	8.6	9.5	9.6	10.3
Motion picture theaters	2.9	3.3	3.6	3.9	3.7	3.9
Legitimate theater, opera	2.0	2.1	2.4	2.7	3.0	3.4
Spectator sports	2.0	2.3	2.6	2.9	2.9	3.1
Clubs, fraternal organizations	3.4	3.8	4.2	4.5	5.1	5.4
Commerical amusements	11.7	12.5	13.6	14.1	14.9	15.6
Private education, research	**30.6**	**32.6**	**35.8**	**39.1**	**43.1**	**46.9**
Higher education	11.3	12.1	13.2	14.4	16.0	16.7
Elementary and secondary schools	10.3	10.8	11.8	12.6	13.6	14.8
Religious and welfare activities	**41.0**	**44.4**	**47.8**	**52.6**	**56.8**	**62.4**
Foreign travel and other, net	**3.0**	**5.1**	**8.5**	**11.3**	**13.2**	**11.9**

Economic and Financial Glossary

The following are some of the terms currently being used in business and finance.

Acquisition: The purchase of one company by another.

Balanced Budget: The federal government budget is balanced when receipts are equal to current expenditure.

Balance of payments: The difference between all payments made to foreign countries and all payments coming in from abroad over a set period of time. A *favorable* balance exists when more payments are coming in than going out and an *unfavorable* balance exists when the reverse is true. Payments include gold, the cost of merchandise and services, interest and dividend payments, money spent by travelers, and repayment of principal on loans.

Balance of trade (trade gap): The difference between exports and imports, both in actual funds and credit. A nation's balance of trade is *favorable* when exports exceed imports and *unfavorable* when the reverse is true.

Bear Market: A market in which prices are falling.

Bearer Bond: A bond issued in bearer form rather than being registered in the owner's name. Ownership is determined by possession.

Bond: A written promise or IOU by the issuer to repay a fixed amount of borrowed money on a specified date and to pay a set annual rate of interest in the meantime, usually at semi-annual intervals. Bonds are generally considered safe because the borrower (whether a company or the government) usually must make interest payments before the money is spent on anything else.

Bull Market: A market in which prices are on the rise.

Commercial Paper: An extremely short-term corporate IOU, generally due in 270 days or less. Available in face amounts of $100,000, $250,000, $500,000, $1,000,000 and combinations thereof.

Convertible Bond: A corporate bond (see below) which may be converted into a stated number of shares of common stock. Its price tends to fluctuate along with fluctuations in the price of the stock as well as with changes in interest rates.

Corporate Bond: Evidence of debt by a corporation. The bond normally has a stated life and pays a fixed rate of interest. Considered safer than the common or preferred stock of the same company.

Cost of living: The cost of maintaining a particular standard of living measured in terms of purchased goods and services. The rise in the cost of living is the same as the rate of inflation.

Cost-of-living benefits: Benefits that go to those persons whose money receipts increase automatically as prices rise.

Credit crunch (liquidity crisis): The period when cash for lending to business and consumers is in short supply.

Debenture: An unsecured long-term debt obligation backed only by the general credit of the issuing corporation.

Deficit spending: The practice whereby a government goes into debt to finance some of its expenditures.

Depression: A long period of economic decline when prices are low, unemployment is high, and there are many business failures.

Devaluation: The official lowering of a nation's currency, decreasing its value in relation to foreign currencies.

Discount Rate: The rate of interest set by the Federal Reserve that member banks are charged when borrowing money through the Federal Reserve System.

Disposable income: Income after taxes which is available to persons for spending and saving.

Dividend: Payment by a corporation to its shareholders. It may be in the form of cash, stock shares, or other property.

Economic Growth: The steady process of increasing productive capacity of the economy, and hence of increasing national income.

Federal Deposit Insurance Corporation (FDIC): A government-sponsored corporation that insures accounts in national banks and other qualified institutions.

Federal Reserve System: The entire banking system of the U.S., incorporating 12 Federal Reserve banks (one in each of 12 Federal Reserve districts), and 24 Federal Reserve branch banks, all national banks and state-chartered commercial banks and trust companies that have been admitted to its membership. The system greatly influences the nation's monetary and credit policies.

Full employment: The economy is said to be at full employment when only fractional unemployment exists. That is, everyone who wishes to work at the going wage-rate for his type of labor is employed. Since it takes time to switch from one job to another, there will be at any given time a small amount of unemployment.

Dow-Jones Industrial Average: A measure of stock market prices, based on 30 leading companies on the New York Stock Exchange.

Golden Parachute: Provisions in the employment contracts of executives guaranteeing substantial severance benefits if they lose their jobs or authority in a corporate takeover.

Government Bond: An IOU of the U.S. Treasury, considered the safest security in the investment world. They are divided into two categories, those that are not marketable and those that are. *Savings Bonds* cannot be bought and sold once the original purchase is made. These include the familiar Series EE bonds. You buy them at 50 percent of their face value and when they mature, 5 years later, they will pay you back 100 percent of face value if you cash them in. Another type, Series H, are not discounted, but issued in amounts of $500, $1,000, $5,000, and $10,000 and pay their interest in semiannual checks. They pay 8 percent the first year of their 10-year life, 5.8 percent for the next 4 years, and 6 percent for the last 5 years. Marketable bonds fall into 3 categories. *Treasury Bills* are short-term U.S. obligations, maturing in 3, 6, or 12 months. They are sold at a discount of the face value, and the minimum denomination is $10,000. *Treasury Notes* mature in up to 10 years. Denominations range from $500, $1,000 to $5,000, $10,000 and up. *Treasury Bonds* mature in 10 to 30 years. The minimum investment is $1,000.

Greenmail: A company buys back its own shares from a suitor for more than the going market price to avoid a hostile takeover.

Gross National Product (GNP): The market value of all goods and services that have been bought for final use during a year. The GNP is generally considered to be the most comprehensive measure of a nation's economic activity. The *Real* GNP is the GNP adjusted for inflation.

Individual Retirement Account (IRA): A self-funded retirement plan that allows employed individuals to contribute a maximum yearly sum toward their retirement. Interest earned in the account is tax deferred.

Inflation: An increase in the average level of prices; double-digit inflation occurs when the percent increase rises above 9.9.

Insider Information: Important facts about the condition or plans of a corporation that have not been released to the general public.

Junk Bonds: Debt securities that sell at relatively low prices, because of the low credit rating of their issuers. They pay significantly higher yields than top-grade bonds to reflect their added risk. In the 1980s, they have been used to finance hostile takeovers.

Key leading indicators: A series of a dozen indicators from different segments of the economy used by the Commerce Department to foretell what will happen in the economy in the near future.

Leveraged Buy-Out: An acquisition of a public company by a small group, often including the company's management, which takes the company private. Much of the purchase price is borrowed with the debt repaid from company profits or by selling company assets.

Liquid Assets: Assets that include cash or those items that are easily converted into cash.

Margin Account: A brokerage account that allows a person to trade securities on credit.

Money supply: The currency held by the public plus checking accounts in commercial banks and savings institutions.

Mortgage-Backed Securities: Created when a bank, builder or government agency gathers together a group of mortgages and then sells bonds to other institutions and the public. The investors receive their proportionate share of the interest payments on the loans as well as the principal payments. Usually, these mortgages are guaranteed by the government, making them a fairly safe investment despite the fact that their market value does fluctuate.

Municipal Bond: Issued by governmental units such as states, cities, local taxing authorities and other agencies. Interest is exempt from U.S. — and sometimes state and local — income tax. *Municipal Bond Unit Investment Trusts* allow you to invest with as little as $1,000 in a portfolio of many different municipal bonds chosen by professionals. The income is exempt from federal income taxes.

Mutual Fund: A portfolio, or selection, of professionally bought and managed stocks in which you pool your money along with thousands of other people. A share price is based on net asset value, or the value of all the investments owned by the funds, less any debt, and divided by the total number of shares. The major advantage is less risk — it is spread out over many stocks and, if one or two do badly, the remainder may shield you from the losses. *Bond Funds* are mutual funds that deal in the bond market exclusively. *Money Market Mutual Funds* buy in the so-called "Money Market" — institutions that need to borrow large sums of money for short terms. Usually the individual investor cannot afford the denominations required in the "Money Market" (i.e. treasury bills, commercial paper, certificates of deposit), but through a money market mutual fund he can take advantage of these instruments when interest rates are high. These funds offer special checking account advantages. The minimum investment is generally $1,000.

National debt: The debt of the national government as distinguished from the debts of the political subdivisions of the nation and private business and individuals.

National debt ceiling: Limit set by Congress beyond which the national debt cannot rise. This limit is periodically raised by congressional vote.

Option: A contractual agreement between a buyer and a seller to buy or sell shares of a security. A **Call** option contract gives the right to purchase shares of a specific stock at a stated price within a given period of time. A **Put** option contract gives the buyer the right to sell shares of a specific stock at a stated price within a given period of time.

Per capita income: The nation's total income divided by the number of people in the nation.

Prime interest rate: The rate charged by banks on short-term loans to large commercial customers with the highest credit rating.

Producer price index: A statistical measure of the change in the price of wholesale goods. It is reported for 3 different stages of the production chain: crude, intermediate, and finished goods.

Public debt: The total of the nation's debts owed by state, local, and national government. This is considered a good measure of how much of the nation's spending is financed by borrowing rather than taxation.

Recession: A mild decrease in economic activity marked by a decline in real GNP, employment, and trade, usually lasting 6 months to a year, and marked by widespread decline in many sectors of the economy. Not as severe as a depression.

Seasonal adjustment: Statistical changes made to compensate for regular fluctuations in data that are so great they tend to distort the statistics and make comparisons meaningless. For instance, seasonal adjustments are made in midwinter for a slowdown in housing construction and for the rise in farm income in the fall after the summer crops are harvested.

Stagnation: A period of economic slowdown in which there is little growth in GNP, capital investment, and real income.

Stock: *Common Stocks* are shares of ownership in a corporation; they are the most direct way to participate in the fortunes of a company. There can be wide swings in the prices of this kind of stock. *Preferred Stock* is a type of stock on which a fixed dividend must be paid before holders of common stock are issued their share of the issuing corporation's earnings. Prices are higher and yields lower than comparable bonds and are, consequently, not the best investment for individuals. However, they are attractive to corporate investors because 85 percent of preferred dividends are tax exempt to corporations. *Convertible Preferred Stock* can be converted into the common stock of the company that issued the preferred. This stock has the advantage of producing a higher yield than common stock and it also has appreciation potential. *Over-the-Counter Stock* is not traded on the major or regional exchanges, but rather through dealers from whom you buy directly. These stocks tend to belong to smaller companies. Prices of OTC stocks are based on the dealer's supply and demand. *Blue Chip* stocks are so called because they have been leading stocks for a long time. They usually do not show dramatic growth, but often yield good dividends over time. *Growth* stocks are stocks whose earnings have grown over several years.

Supply-side economics: The school of economic thinking which stresses the importance of the costs of production as a means of revitalizing the economy. Advocates policies that raise capital and labor output by increasing the incentives to produce.

Takeover: The passing of control of one company by another company or group by sale or merger. A friendly takeover occurs when the acquired company's management is agreeable to the merger; when management is opposed to the merger it is an unfriendly takeover. Takeover arbitrage is the purchase and/or selling of the securities of companies involved in takeover situations in order to realize a profit.

Tax incidence: The point at which the tax burden ultimately rests. For example, the imposition of a specific tax on a commodity may cause firms to increase the price by the amount of the tax. If consumers do not reduce their purchases of that commodity, then the entire burden of the tax will have shifted onto them.

Tender Offer: A public offer to buy a company's stock; usually priced at a premium above the market.

Unit Investment Trust: A portfolio of many different corporate bonds, preferred stocks, government-backed securities or utility common stocks in which you can invest with as little as $1,000. Professional managers choose the securities, arrange for safe-keeping and collect the income. You receive your pro rata share of income every month.

Zero Coupon Bond: A corporate or government bond that is issued at a deep discount from the maturity value and pays no interest during the life of the bond. It is redeemable at face value.

World Wheat, Rice and Corn Production, 1985

Source: UN Food and Agriculture Organization

(thousands of metric tons)

Country	Wheat	Rice	Corn
World, total	**510,029**	**465,970**	**490,155**
Afghanistan	2,850[1]	480[2]	800[2]
Argentina	8,500[2]	400	12,600
Australia	16,550	864	311
Austria	1,563	NA	1,727
Bangladesh	1,464	21,900[2]	1[1]
Belgium[2]	1,204[3]	NA	90[2,3]
Brazil	4,247	9,019	22,017
Bulgaria	3,500[1]	75[1]	2,600[1]
Burma	206	15,400[2]	403
Canada	23,900	NA	7,393
Chile	1,165	157	772
China	85,286[1]	171,479[1]	62,250[1]
Columbia	79	1,764	882
Cuba	NA	524	97[1]
Czechoslovakia	6,023	NA	1,114
Denmark	1,996	NA	NA
Ecuador	19[2]	300[1]	250[1]
Egypt	1,874[2]	2,312[2]	3,982[2]
Ethiopia	700[1]	NA	1,400[1]
Finland	472	NA	NA
France	29,030	61	11,839
German Dem. Rep.	3,806[2]	NA	2[1]
Germany, Fed. Rep.	9,866	NA	1,204
Greece	1,792	106	1,800
Hungary	6,573	36	6,798
India	44,229	91,500[2]	7,000[1]
Indonesia	NA	38,660[2]	5,300[2]
Iran	6,000[1]	1,100	50[2]
Iraq	650[1]	105[1]	32[1]
Ireland	500[2]	NA	NA
Israel	110[2]	NA	26[1]
Italy	8,516	1,064	6,352
Japan	874	14,578	NA
Kampuchea	NA	1,900[1]	78[1]
Korea, Dem. Peo. Rep.[1]	680[1]	5,600[1]	2,680[1]
Korea, Republic of	11[2]	7,855[2]	132
Laos	NA	1,400[1]	45[1]
Madagascar	NA	2,178[2]	140[2]
Malaysia	NA	1,895[2]	24[2]
Mexico	5,228	988	15,013
Nepal	534	2,800	770[1]
Netherlands	851	NA	2[1]
New Zealand	382	NA	220
Pakistan	11,600[2]	4,500[2]	1,030[1]
Panama	NA	199[2]	70[2]
Peru	90	973	708
Philippines	NA	8,300[2]	3,542[2]
Poland	6,461	NA	69
Portugal	385	147	570
Romania	6,800[1]	85[1]	13,800[1]
South Africa	1,600[2]	3[1]	7,550
Soviet Union	83,000[1]	2,600[1]	15,000[1]
Spain	5,326	459	3,331
Sri Lanka	NA	2,634[2]	38[1]
Sweden	1,378	NA	NA
Switzerland	547	NA	157
Syria	1,714[2]	NA	63
Thailand	NA	19,521	4,686
Turkey	17,032	265	1,900
United Kingdom	11,700	NA	1[1]
United States	65,992	6,171	225,180
Uruguay	440[2]	423	108
Venezuela	1[2]	472[2]	900[2]
Vietnam	NA	15,600[1]	500[2]
Yugoslavia	4,859	36	9,891

(1) FAO estimate; (2) Unofficial figure; (3) Includes Luxembourg; NA = Not available.

Wheat, Rice and Corn—Exports and Imports of 10 Leading Countries

Source: Economic Research Service, U.S. Agriculture Department

(thousands of metric tons.)

Leading Exporters	Exports[1] 1980	1985	1986[p]
Wheat			
United States	41,204	24,902	27,624
Canada	16,262	17,682	21,000
France	13,423	16,969	15,675
Australia	9,577	15,962	15,000
Argentina	3,845	4,300	4,450
Hungary	700	1,900	1,100
United Kingdom	1,100	2,600	5,800
Italy	1,620	2,534	2,470
Germany, Fed Rep.	1,502	2,817	2,100
Greece	887	742	310
Rice			
Thailand	3,049	4,338	3,700
United States	3,028	1,885	2,576
China, People's Rep.	590	950	900
Pakistan	1,163	1,297	1,100
Italy	475	667	600
Burma	674	636	600
Australia	468	390	375
Korea, DPR	200	250	250
Uruguay	184	260	220
Argentina	95	150	150
Corn			
United States	61,163	31,528	38,102
Argentina	9,098	7,367	5,000
China, People's Rep	125	6,400	4,000
France	2,380	4,877	5,900
Thailand	2,142	3,674	2,800
Belgium/Luxembourg	1,742	759	850
Yugoslavia	300	1,430	1,800
Romania	770	200	750
Canada	1,056	653	150
Italy	19	315	380

Leading Importers	Imports[1] 1980	1985	1986[p]
Wheat			
Soviet Union	16,000	15,700	17,000
China, People's Rep	13,789	6,600	7,500
Egypt	5,423	6,236	6,332
Japan	5,840	5,532	5,500
Brazil	3,910	2,000	2,400
Italy	3,028	5,040	5,400
Iran	1,896	2,200	2,700
Korea, Rep. of	2,095	3,032	3,800
Iraq	1,366	1,700	2,600
Algeria	2,294	2,800	3,500
Rice			
Brazil	0	1,300	50
Bangladesh	84	39	300
Iran	583	450	850
Saudi Arabia	356	500	500
Iraq	350	500	600
Nigeria	394	360	320
Malaysia	167	480	325
Philippines	0	353	0
Vietnam	30	500	450
Indonesia	2,040	34	21
Corn			
Soviet Union	11,800	10,400	8,500
Japan	13,989	14,553	15,500
Taiwan	2,703	3,071	3,400
Spain	4,251	2,238	1,200
Korea, Rep of	2,355	3,625	3,600
Netherlands	2,638	2,183	2,075
Belgium/Luxembourg	2,927	1,859	1,806
Egypt	984	1,881	2,035
Mexico	3,833	1,736	3,400
Italy	2,666	1,118	950

(1) Marketing years; (p) Preliminary

Agricultural Products — U.S. and World Production and Exports

Source: Foreign Agricultural Service, U.S. Agriculture Department

1985/86 Commodity	Unit	Production U.S.	Production World	Production % U.S.	Exports[1] U.S.	Exports[1] World	Exports[1] % U.S.
Wheat	MMT	66.0	502.4	13.1	24.9	95.8	26.0
Oats	MMT	7.5	47.1	15.9	0.03	1.4	2.1
Corn	MMT	225.2	480.3	46.9	31.1	62.3	49.9
Barley	MMT	12.8	177.6	7.2	0.5	17.0	2.9
Rice (milled basis)	MMT	4.4	316.3	1.4	1.8	11.8	15.3
Sorghum	MMT	28.3	72.4	39.1	4.4	9.0	48.9
Soybeans	MMT	57.1	96.2	59.4	20.7	26.5	78.1
Tobacco, unmfd.	MMT	0.69	6.8	10.1	0.25	1.4	17.9
Edible, Veg. Oils	MMT	6.4	47.7	13.4	1.2	15.5	7.7
Cotton (lint)	MB[2]	13.4	78.1	17.2	2.0	19.3	10.4

(1) Standard Trade Years Wheat: July-June (85/86); Oats: Oct.-Sept. (85/86); Corn: Oct.-Sept. (85/86); Barley: Oct.-Sept. (85/86); Rice: Aug.-July (85/86); Sorghum: Oct.-Sept. (85/86); Soybeans: Sept.-Aug. (85/86); Tobacco: Jan.-Dec. (85); Edible Veg. Oils: Jan.-Dec. (85); Cotton: Aug.-July (85/86). (2) Million Bales.

Grain, Hay, Potato, Cotton, Soybean, Tobacco Production

Source: Economic Research Service, U.S. Agriculture Department

1986 State	Barley 1,000 bushels	Corn, grain 1,000 bushels	Cotton lint 1,000 bales[1]	All Hay 1,000 tons	Oats 1,000 bushels	Potatos 1,000 cwt.	Soybeans 1,000 bushels	Tobacco 1,000 pounds	All Wheat 1,000 bushels
Alabama	—	15,390	330	1,120	1,200	1,668	14,490	—	5,720
Alaska	—	—	—	—	—	—	—	—	—
Arizona	2,900	2,640	825	1,262	—	1,298	—	—	8,688
Arkansas	—	8,480	605	1,945	2,211	—	69,300	—	31,980
California	23,600	38,000	2,250	8,628	3,150	18,457	—	—	51,525
Colorado	21,000	99,400	—	3,642	2,200	20,296	—	—	96,430
Connecticut[2]	—	—	—	209	—	225	—	3,124	—
Delaware	3,050	14,027	—	50	—	1,311	6,000	—	1,530
Florida	—	9,920	34	676	—	8,543	3,220	13,303	3,100
Georgia	—	42,340	200	901	1,365	—	15,300	67,815	15,400
Hawaii	—	—	—	—	—	—	—	—	—
Idaho	72,150	7,800	—	4,720	2,070	87,320	—	—	81,750
Illinois	—	1,404,000	—	3,664	13,800	783	366,000	—	36,080
Indiana	—	695,400	—	2,236	6,390	990	161,500	12,600	30,100
Iowa	—	1,626,750	—	8,000	37,800	332	363,125	—	1,680
Kansas	10,440	181,560	1	6,390	10,800	—	59,840	—	336,600
Kentucky	527	139,040	—	3,500	252	—	37,440	331,055	8,910
Louisiana	—	44,660	680	781	—	35	38,220	—	7,350
Maine[2]	—	—	—	448	2,600	21,000	—	—	—
Maryland	4,820	42,340	—	508	825	272	10,820	24,300	6,815
Massachusetts[2]	—	—	—	325	—	667	—	702	—
Michigan	3,245	257,250	—	5,743	17,010	11,190	30,400	—	30,600
Minnesota	55,000	707,600	—	9,675	43,350	15,293	170,400	—	103,666
Mississippi	—	13,500	1,200	1,160	—	—	44,100	—	6,200
Missouri	—	280,720	197	6,028	5,000	—	177,550	4,884	18,810
Montana	85,020	1,495	—	4,320	4,140	2,233	—	—	138,520
Nebraska	5,535	896,000	—	7,258	21,240	2,399	95,550	—	76,000
Nevada	2,970	—	—	1,376	—	2,800	—	—	1,720
New Hampshire[2]	—	—	—	198	—	—	—	—	—
New Jersey	1,240	11,128	—	297	216	1,944	3,393	—	1,290
New Mexico	1,040	8,250	82	1,319	—	2,745	—	—	10,120
New York	—	64,350	—	5,280	12,350	7,780	—	—	7,595
North Carolina	1,620	93,840	110	573	2,200	2,264	38,400	444,380	14,260
North Dakota	175,950	49,290	—	5,425	38,500	21,600	16,685	—	289,820
Ohio	—	476,160	—	4,307	12,160	2,377	150,470	15,080	48,300
Oklahoma	1,260	5,220	240	4,295	4,400	—	4,800	—	150,800
Oregon	20,805	4,800	—	3,134	7,600	23,172	—	—	58,405
Pennsylvania	3,900	127,720	—	5,124	16,740	5,160	5,600	21,830	9,680
Rhode Island[2]	—	21,160	—	23	—	416	—	—	—
South Carolina	588	—	87	328	1,008	—	14,960	75,480	7,500
South Dakota	35,910	233,700	—	9,330	46,200	2,340	41,230	—	108,660
Tennessee	—	56,980	400	2,092	—	234	37,500	92,734	10,725
Texas	1,750	148,960	2,542	7,460	8,400	3,591	4,370	—	120,000
Utah	11,552	2,250	—	2,135	864	1,760	—	—	9,750
Vermont[2]	—	21,600	—	938	—	20	—	—	—
Virginia	3,960	—	2	1,464	460	1,112	14,750	73,649	6,970
Washington	45,000	20,400	—	2,874	2,145	60,180	—	—	116,850
West Virginia	—	6,300	—	801	500	20,125	—	2,848	396
Wisconsin	4,845	365,800	—	10,775	52,700	—	11,520	14,480	8,040
Wyoming	10,720	5,814	—	2,445	2,700	536	—	—	8,445
Total U.S.	**610,497**	**8,252,834**	**9,785**	**155,271**	**384,546**	**354,468**	**2,007,033**	**1,198,264**	**2,086,780**

(1) Equiv. to 480 lbs. (2) All harvested corn acreage is for silage.

Production of Chief U.S. Crops

Source: National Agricultural Statistics Service: U.S. Agriculture Department

Year	Corn for grain 1,000 bushels	Oats 1,000 bushels	Barley 1,000 bushels	Sorghums for grain 1,000 bushels	All wheat 1,000 bushels	Rye 1,000 bushels	Flax-seed 1,000 bushels	Cotton lint 1,000 bales	Cotton seed 1,000 tons
1970 . .	4,152,243	915,236	416,091	683,179	1,351,558	36,840	29,416	10,192	4,068
1975 . .	5,828,961	638,960	379,162	754,354	2,126,927	15,924	15,553	8,302	3,218
1980 . .	6,639,396	458,792	361,135	579,343	2,380,934	15,958	7,728	11,122	4,470
1981 . .	8,118,650	509,529	473,512	875,835	2,785,357	18,187	7,289	15,646	6,397
1982 . .	8,235,101	592,630	515,935	835,083	2,764,967	19,533	10,278	11,963	4,744
1983 . .	4,174,678	476,961	508,925	487,521	2,419,824	27,116	6,903	7,771	3,076
1984 . .	7,674,020	473,661	599,204	866,241	2,594,777	32,463	7,022	12,982	5,149
1985 . .	8,876,706	520,800	591,383	1,120,271	2,425,105	20,537	8,293	13,432	5,279
1986 . .	8,252,834	384,546	510,497	941,634	2,086,780	19,498	11,538	9,785	3,857

Year	Tobacco 1,000 lbs.	All hay 1,000 tons	Beans dry edible 1,000 cwt.	Peas dry edible 1,000 cwt.	Peanuts 1,000 lbs.	Soy-beans 1,000 bushels	Pota-toes 1,000 cwt.	Sweet pota-toes 1,000 cwt.
1970	1,906,453	126,969	17,399	3,315	2,983,121	1,127,100	325,716	13,164
1975	2,182,304	132,397	17,442	2,731	3,846,722	1,548,344	321,978	12,891
1980	1,786,225	130,740	26,729	3,285	2,302,762	1,797,543	303,905	10,953
1981	2,063,589	142,520	32,751	2,290	3,981,850	1,989,110	340,623	12,799
1982	1,994,494	149,241	25,563	—	3,440,255	2,190,297	355,131	14,833
1983	1,428,969	140,764	15,520	—	3,295,530	1,635,772	333,911	12,083
1984	1,727,962	150,648	21,070	—	4,405,745	1,860,863	362,612	12,986
1985	1,511,638	148,601	22,175	—	4,122,787	2,098,531	407,109	14,853
1986	1,165,927	155,271	22,898	3,196	3,700,745	2,007,033	354,468	12,754

Year	Five seed crops* 1,000 lbs.	Sugar-cane 1,000 tons	Sugar beets 1,000 tons	(1)Pecans million lbs.	Al-monds million lbs.	(1)Wal-nuts 1,000 tons	(1)Fil-berts 1,000 tons	Oranges** 1,000 boxes	Grape-fruit** 1,000 boxes
1970	251,934	23,996	26,378	77.6	124.0	111.8	9.3	185,770	53,910
1975	161,609	28,344	29,704	246.8	186.0	199.3	12.1	237,810	61,610
1980	131,070	26,963	23,502	183.5	322.0	197.0	15.4	273,630	73,200
1981	159,195	27,408	27,538	339.1	408.0	225.0	14.7	244,580	67,860
1982	—	29,770	20,894	218.6	347.0	234.0	18.8	176,690	70,550
1983	—	28,161	20,992	270.0	242.0	199.0	8.2	225,180	60,600
1984	—	27,340	22,134	232.4	590.0	213.0	13.4	169,510	53,610
1985	—	28,213	22,529	244.4	465.0	219.0	24.6	158,750	55,860
1986	—	30,311	25,224	225.3	250.0	180.0	15.5	176,410	57,770

*Fine seed crops include alfalfa, red clover, lespedeza, and timothy. **Crop year ending in year cited. (1) In shells.

Harvested Acreage of Principal U.S. Crops

Source: National Agricultural Statistics Service: U.S. Agriculture Department (thousands of acres)

State	1984	1985	1986
Alabama	3,656	3,321	2,535
Arizona	895	809	681
Arkansas	8,507	7,778	7,344
California	5,764	5,609	5,091
Colorado	6,686	6,846	6,166
Connecticut	150	151	140
Delaware	539	554	536
Florida	1,332	1,344	1,222
Georgia	5,652	5,071	3,843
Hawaii	95	89	90
Idaho	4,835	4,738	4,730
Illinois	23,496	23,111	22,050
Indiana	12,513	12,362	11,661
Iowa	24,724	25,030	24,096
Kansas	21,355	21,615	20,694
Kentucky	5,674	5,484	5,187
Louisiana	4,895	4,632	4,370
Maine	384	403	383
Maryland	1,622	1,639	1,582
Massachusetts	169	164	166
Michigan	7,730	7,685	7,010
Minnesota	20,761	20,426	19,246
Mississippi	6,291	5,604	4,878
Missouri	14,514	14,247	13,252
Montana	9,183	7,613	9,415
Nebraska	18,584	18,509	17,473
Nevada	596	565	583
New Hampshire	112	113	112
New Jersey	472	466	437
New Mexico	1,310	1,381	1,179
New York	4,038	4,048	3,810
North Carolina	5,404	5,418	4,657
North Dakota	20,975	20,495	20,571
Ohio	10,608	10,845	10,257
Oklahoma	8,677	8,978	8,573
Oregon	2,721	2,739	2,711
Pennsylvania	4,546	4,569	4,426
Rhode Island	17	17	15
South Carolina	2,912	2,778	2,179
South Dakota	16,270	15,246	15,966
Tennessee	5,406	5,136	4,670
Texas	20,036	21,094	17,750
Utah	1,109	1,129	1,132
Vermont	537	540	530
Virginia	3,116	3,002	2,810
Washington	4,769	5,052	4,713
West Virginia	769	732	683
Wisconsin	9,424	9,221	9,013
Wyoming	1,904	1,669	1,962
***Total U.S.**	**335,732**	**330,063**	**312,578**

* States may not add to U.S. due to rounding. (1) Crop acreages included: corn, sorghum, oats, barley, wheat, rice, rye, soybeans, flax-seed, peanuts, sunflower, cotton, all hay, dry edible beans, potatoes, sweet-potatoes, tobacco, sugar-cane and sugar-beets; harvested acreages for winter wheat, rye, all hay, tobacco, and sugar-cane are used in computing planted acreage.

Farms—Number and Acreage, by States

Source: Natl. Agricultural Statistics Service: U.S. Agriculture Department

State	Farms (1,000) 1985	Acreage (Mil) 1985	Acreage per farm 1985	Farms (1,000) 1985	Acreage (Mil) 1985	Acreage per farm 1985
US	2,275	1,008	443	2,212	1,002	453
Ala.	54	12	222	51	11	216
Alas.	1	2	2,000	1	1	1,000
Ariz.	9	38	4,222	9	37	4,111
Ark.	53	16	302	50	16	320
Calif.	79	33	418	79	33	418
Colo.	27	34	1,259	27	34	1,259
Conn.	4	(z)	—	4	(z)	—
Del.	4	1	250	3	1	125
Fla.	39	13	333	39	13	333
Ga.	50	14	280	49	13	265
Haw.	5	2	400	4	2	500
Idaho	25	15	600	24	14	583
Ill.	90	29	322	86	29	337
Ind.	80	16	200	77	16	208
Iowa	111	34	306	109	34	312
Kans.	72	48	666	70	48	686
Ky.	100	15	150	99	15	152
La.	36	10	278	36	10	278
Maine	8	2	250	8	2	250
Md.	18	3	167	17	3	176
Mass.	6	1	167	6	1	167
Mich.	62	11	177	60	11	183
Minn.	96	30	313	93	30	323
Miss.	48	14	292	46	14	304
Mo.	115	31	270	115	31	270
Mont.	24	61	2,542	24	61	2,542
Nebr.	59	47	797	57	47	825
Nev.	3	9	3,000	2	9	4,500
N.H.	3	.5	167	3	.5	167
N.J.	9	1	111	8	1	125
N. Mex.	14	45	3,214	14	45	3,214
N.Y.	44	9	205	42	9	214
N.C.	76	11	145	73	11	151
N. Dak.	34	41	1,206	33	41	1,242
Ohio	89	16	180	88	16	182
Okla.	71	33	465	71	33	465
Oreg.	37	18	486	37	18	486
Pa.	58	9	155	57	9	158
R.I.	1	(z)	—	1	(z)	—
S.C.	28	5	179	27	5	185
S. Dak.	37	45	1,216	36	45	1,250
Tenn.	98	13	133	96	13	135
Tex.	177	134	757	162	133	821
Utah	14	11	786	14	11	786
Vt.	7	2	286	7	2	286
Va.	54	10	185	50	10	200
Wash.	38	16	1,421	38	16	421
W. Va.	21	4	190	21	4	190
Wis.	83	18	217	82	18	220
Wyo.	9	35	3,889	9	35	3,889

(z) Less than 500 farms or 500,000 acres.

Livestock on Farms in the U.S.

Source: Natl. Agricultural Statistics, Service: U.S. Agriculture Department (thousands)

Year (On Jan. 1)	All cattle	Milk cows	All sheep	Hogs[3]
1890	60,014	15,000	44,518	48,130
1900	59,739	16,544	48,105	51,055
1910	58,993	19,450	50,239	48,072
1920	70,400	21,455	40,743	60,159
1925	63,373	22,575	38,543	55,770
1930	61,003	23,032	51,565	55,705
1935	68,846	26,082	51,808	39,066
1940	68,309	24,940	52,107	61,165
1945	85,573	27,770	46,520	59,373
1950	77,963	23,853	29,826	58,937
1955	96,592	23,462	31,582	50,474
1960	96,236	19,527	33,170	59,026
1965	109,000	[2]15,380	25,127	50,792
1970	112,369	12,091	20,423	57,046
1975	132,028	11,220	14,515	54,693
1980	111,242	10,758	12,699	67,318
1981	114,351	10,849	12,947	64,462
1982	115,444	10,986	12,997	58,698
1983	115,001	11,047	12,140	54,534
1985	109,749	10,805	10,443	54,073
1986	105,468	11,177	9,983	52,313
1987[1]	102,031	10,547	10,328	50,960

(1) Total estimated value on farms as of Jan. 1, 1987, was as follows (avg. value per head in parentheses): cattle and calves $41,491,630,000 ($407); sheep and lambs $781,800,000 ($75.70); hogs and pigs $4,669,498,000 ($91.60). (2) New series, milk cows and heifers that have calved, beginning 1965. (3) As of Dec. 1 of preceding year.

U.S. Meat and Lard Production and Consumption

Source: Economic Research Service, U.S. Agriculture Department (million lbs.)

Year	Beef Production	Beef Consumption	Veal Production	Veal Consumption	Lamb and mutton Production	Lamb and mutton Consumption	Pork (exclud. lard) Production	Pork (exclud. lard) Consumption	All meats Production	All meats Consumption	Lard Production	Lard Consumption[1]
1940	7,175	7,257	981	981	876	873	10,044	9,701	19,076	18,812	2,288	1,901
1950	9,534	9,529	1,230	1,206	597	596	10,714	10,390	22,075	21,721	2,631	1,891
1960	14,753	15,147	1,109	1,093	768	852	13,905	13,838	30,535	30,930	2,562	1,358
1970	21,685	22,926	588	581	551	657	14,699	14,661	37,523	38,825	1,913	939
1980	21,664	23,321	400	412	318	350	16,615	16,562	38,979	40,645	1,207	540
1985	23,728	25,345	515	525	359	383	14,807	15,651	39,444	41,943	927	401
1986	24,387	25,824	526	545	335	371	14,063	14,918	39,014	41,659	876	264

(1) Direct use. Excludes lard used in indirect food use such as table spreads and shortenings.

Selected Indexes of Farm Inputs: 1960 to 1985

Source: Economic Research Service, U.S. Agriculture Department

(1977 = 100. Inputs based on physical quantities of resources used in production.)

Input	1960	1965	1970	1975	1978	1980	1981	1982	1983	1984	1985p
Total	**99**	**97**	**96**	**97**	**102**	**103**	**102**	**100**	**97**	**96**	**94**
Farm labor	177	144	112	106	96	96	96	93	97	92	85
Farm real estate[2]	103	103	105	97	100	103	103	103	101	99	97
Mechanical power and machinery	83	80	85	96	104	101	98	94	90	88	83
Agricultural chemicals[3]	32	49	75	83	107	123	129	118	105	121	123
Feed, seed, and livestock purchases[4]	77	86	96	93	108	114	108	106	108	104	110
Taxes and interest	95	101	102	100	99	100	99	99	99	95	96

(p) Preliminary. (2) Includes service buildings, improvements. (3) Includes fertilizer, lime, and pesticides. (4) Nonfarm portion.

Average Prices Received by U.S. Farmers

Source: Natl. Agricultural Statistics Service, U.S. Agriculture Department

The figures represent dollars per 100 lbs. for hogs, beef cattle, veal calves, sheep, lamb, and milk (wholesale), dollars per head for milk cows; cents per lb. for milk fat (in cream), chickens, broilers, turkeys, and wool; cents for eggs per dozen.

Weighted calendar year prices for livestock and livestock products other than wool. 1943 through 1963, wool prices are weighted on marketing year basis. The marketing year has been changed (1964) from a calendar year to a Dec.-Nov. basis for hogs, chickens, broilers and eggs.

Year	Hogs	Cattle (beef)	Calves (veal)	Sheep	Lambs	Cows (milk)	All milk	Chickens- (excl. broilers)	Broilers	Turkeys	Eggs	Wool
1930	8.84	7.71	9.68	4.74	7.76	74	2.21	...	...	20.2	23.7	19.5
1940	5.39	7.56	8.83	3.95	8.10	61	1.82	13.0	17.3	15.2	18.0	28.4
1950	18.00	23.30	26.30	11.60	25.10	198	3.89	22.2	27.4	32.8	36.3	62.1
1960	15.30	20.40	22.90	5.61	17.90	223	4.21	12.2	16.9	25.4	36.1	42.0
1970	22.70	27.10	34.50	7.51	26.40	332	5.71	9.1	13.6	22.6	39.1	35.4
1975	46.10	32.20	27.20	11.30	42.10	412	8.75	9.9	26.3	34.8	54.5	44.8
1979	41.80	66.10	88.80	26.30	66.70	1,040	12.00	14.4	25.9	41.3	58.3	86.3
1980	38.00	62.40	76.80	21.30	63.60	1,190	13.05	11.0	27.7	41.3	56.3	88.1
1983	46.80	55.50	61.70	15.70	53.90	1,030	13.58	12.7	28.6	38.0	61.1	61.3
1984	47.10	57.30	59.90	16.40	60.10	895	13.46	15.9	33.7	48.9	72.3	79.5
1985	44.00	53.70	62.10	23.90	67.70	860	12.75	14.8	30.1	49.1	57.1	63.3
1986	49.30	52.60	61.10	25.60	69.00	820	12.50	12.5	34.5	47.1	61.6	66.8

The figures represent cents per lb. for cotton, apples, and peanuts; dollars per bushel for oats, wheat, corn, barley, and soybeans; dollars per 100 lbs. for rice, sorghum, and potatoes; dollars per ton for cottonseed and baled hay.

Weighted crop year prices. Crop years are as follows: apples, June-May; wheat, oats, barley, hay and potatoes, July-June; cotton, rice, peanuts and cottonseed, August-July; soybeans, September-August; and corn and sorghum grain, October-September.

	Corn	Wheat	Upland cotton[1]	Oats	Barley	Rice	Soybeans	Sorghum	Peanuts	Cottonseed	Hay	Potatoes	Apples
1930	.598	.663	9.46	0.311	.420	1.74	1.34	1.02	5.01	22.00	11.00	1.47	...
1940	.618	.674	9.83	0.298	.393	1.80	.892	.873	3.72	21.70	9.78	.850	...
1950	1.52	2.00	39.90	0.788	1.19	5.09	2.47	1.88	10.9	86.60	21.10	1.50	...
1960	13.00	1.74	30.08	0.599	.840	4.55	2.13	1.49	10.0	42.50	21.70	2.00	2.72
1970	1.33	1.33	21.86	0.623	.973	5.17	2.85	2.04	12.8	56.40	26.10	2.21	6.52
1975	2.54	3.55	51.10	1.45	2.42	8.35	4.92	4.21	19.6	97.00	52.10	4.48	8.80
1979	2.52	3.78	62.3	1.36	2.29	10.50	6.28	4.18	20.6	121.00	59.50	3.43	15.40
1980	3.11	3.91	74.4	1.79	2.86	12.80	7.57	5.25	25.1	129.00	71.00	6.55	12.1
1983	3.21	3.51	66.0	1.62	2.47	8.57	7.83	4.89	34.7	166.00	75.80	5.82	14.9
1984	2.63	3.39	57.5	1.67	2.29	8.04	5.84	4.15	27.9	99.50	72.70	5.69	15.5
1985	2.23	3.08	56.1	1.23	1.98	6.53	5.05	3.45	34.4	66.00	67.60	3.92	17.3
1986	1.45	2.41	51.5	1.18	1.59	3.80	4.67	2.39	28.7	78.50	59.60	4.94	19.2

(1) Beginning 1964, 480 lb. net weight bales.

Grain Storage Capacity at Principal Grain Centers in U.S.

Source: Chicago Board of Trade Market Information Department, July 1987

(bushels)

Cities	Capacity	Cities	Capacity
Atlantic Coast	37,100,000	Texas High Plains	95,100,000
Great Lakes		Enid	79,000,000
Toledo	46,500,000	Gulf Points	
Buffalo	14,300,000	South Mississippi	45,400,000
Chicago	54,500,000	North Texas Gulf	30,000,000
Milwaukee	9,100,000	South Texas Gulf	14,800,000
Duluth	74,100,000	Plains	
River Points		Wichita	47,900,000
Minneapolis	102,200,000	Topeka	54,900,000
Peoria	5,900,000	Salina	56,000,000
St. Louis	17,700,000	Hutchinson	42,000,000
Sioux City	7,800,000	Hastings-Grand Island	29,600,000
Omaha-Council Bluffs	32,500,000	Lincoln	33,700,000
Atchison	26,500,000	Pacific N.W.	
St. Joseph	19,600,000	Puget Sound (incl. Portland)	37,100,000
Kansas City, Mo.	75,100,000	California ports	11,000,000
Southwest			
Fort Worth	70,700,000		

Atlantic Coast — Albany, N.Y., Philadelphia, Pa., Baltimore, Md., Norfolk, Va. **Gulf Points** — New Orleans, Baton Rouge, Ama. Belle Chase, La., Mobile, Ala. **North Texas Gulf** — Houston, Galveston, Beaumont, Port Arthur, Texas. **South Texas Gulf** — Corpus Christi, Brownsville, Texas. **Pacific N.W.** — Seattle, Tacoma, Wash., Portland, Oreg., Columbia River **Calif. Ports** — San Francisco, Stockton, Sacramento, Los Angeles. **Texas High Plains** — Amarillo, Lubbock, Hereford, Plainview, Texas.

Consumption of Major Food Commodities per Person

Source: Economic Research Service: U.S. Agriculture Department

Commodity[1]	1984	1985	1986
Meats	144.7	144.4	141.7
Beef	78.5	79.1	79.8
Veal	1.8	1.8	1.9
Lamb and mutton	1.5	1.4	1.4
Pork	61.8	62.0	58.6
Fish (edible weight)	13.7	14.4	14.7
Poultry products:			
Eggs	33.0	32.0	32.0
Chicken (ready-to-cook)	55.7	58.0	59.1
Turkey (ready-to-cook)	11.4	12.1	13.4
Dairy products:			
Cheese	21.6	22.6	23.2
Condensed and evaporated milk	7.5	7.5	8.4
Fluid milk and cream (product weight)	243	245	245
Ice cream (product weight)	18.0	18.0	18.3
Fats and Oils—Total fat content	58.7	64.1	64.2
Butter (actual weight)	4.8	4.8	4.6
Margarine (actual weight)	10.4	10.8	11.4
Lard	3.7	3.7	3.5
Shortening	21.3	22.9	22.1
Other edible fats and oils	21.5	25.0	25.8
Fruits:			
Fresh	87.5	86.5	91.7
Citrus	23.0	22.6	25.1
Noncitrus	64.5	63.9	66.6
Processed:			
Canned fruit	8.9	8.4	8.8
Juice	18.6	19.8	19.9
Frozen	3.0	3.3	3.5
Chilled citrus juices	3.6	3.2	3.7
Dried	2.8	2.9	2.8
Vegetables:			
Fresh[2]	78.5	78.5	79.4
Canned (excluding potatoes and sweet potatoes)	47.1	43.1	NA
Frozen (excluding potatoes)	8.6	8.7	NA
Potatoes[3]	113.5	120.3	NA
Sweet potatoes[3]	5.1	5.6	NA
Grains:			
Wheat flour[4]	118	123	130
Rice	8.5	9.3	12.3
Other:			
Coffee	7.5	7.4	NA
Tea	0.7	0.7	NA
Cocoa	3.5	3.6	NA
Peanuts (shelled)	5.9	6.0	NA
Dry edible beans	6.1	NA	NA
Sugar (refined)	67.5	63.4	61.0

(1) Quantity in pounds, retail weight unless otherwise shown. Data on calendar year basis except for dried fruits, fresh citrus fruits, peanuts, and rice which are on a crop-year basis, and eggs which are on a marketing year basis. Data are as of August 1987. (2) Commercial production for sale as fresh produce. (3) Including fresh equivalent of processed. (4) White, whole wheat, and semolina flour including use in bakery products. NA = Not available.

U.S. Egg Production

Source: Economic Research Service. U.S. Agriculture Department (millions of eggs)

State	1983	1984	1985	1986
Ala.	2,813	2,783	2,794	2,723
Alas.	15.6	13.6	11.7	12.8
Ariz.	102	105	99	121
Ark.	3,768	3,560	3,655	3,731
Cal.	8,173	8,325	8,052	7,850
Col.	619	637	568	575
Conn.	1,073	1,199	1,173	1,281
Del.	142	140	126	135
Fla.	2,965	2,912	2,692	2,683
Ga.	4,671	4,474	4,080	4,010
Ha.	197.3	209.7	220.5	227
Ida.	240	258	239	230
Ill.	1,004	876	732	663
Ind.	4,624	4,997	5,538	5,561
Ia.	1,827	1,769	1,600	1,441
Kan.	481	466	472	463
Ky.	457	434	431	420
La.	417	396	348	336
Me.	1,402	1,355	1,237	1,239
Md.	836	840	813	890
Mass.	265	268	257	316
Mich.	1,484	1,519	1,693	1,644
Minn.	2,508	2,443	2,267	2,312
Miss.	1,285	1,253	1,251	1,274
Mo.	1,352	1,357	1,351	1,397
Mont.	193	198	202	201
Neb.	792	773	844	829
Nev.	1.8	0.0	0.0	0.0
N.H.	142	125	121	95
N.J.	240	234	474	501
N.M.	287	282	273	280
N.Y.	1,741	1,710	1,710	1,523
N.C.	3,152	3,246	3,294	3,400
N.D.	119	120	118	61
Oh.	2,980	3,445	3,592	3,868
Okla.	841	879	868	809
Ore.	630	678	649	659
Pa.	4,716	4,282	4,774	4,692
R.I.	62	74	80	58
S.C.	1,594	1,617	1,573	1,615
S.D.	374	378	391	395
Tenn.	822	744	756	663
Tex.	3,089	3,181	3,131	3,355
Ut.	456	436	418	457
Vt.	69	65	67	67
Va.	839	843	850	914
Wash.	1,232	1,306	1,355	1,205
W.Vir.	136	132	121	109
Wis.	906	884	836	830
Wyo.	8.7	7.2	6.8	4.5
Total	**68,169**	**68,230**	**68,407**	**68,515**

Note: The egg and chicken production year runs from Dec. 1 of the previous year through Nov. 30. (1) Included are eggs destroyed because of possible PCB contamination.

Farm-Real Estate Debt Outstanding by Lender Groups

Source: Economic Research Service, U.S. Agriculture Department

		Amounts held by principal lender groups				
Dec. 31	Total farm-real estate debt[1] $1,000	Federal land banks[1] $1,000	Farmers Home Administration[2] $1,000	Life insurance companies[3] $1,000	All commercial banks $1,000	Other[4] $1,000
1955	9,012,016	1,480,204	412,670	2,271,784	1,275,429	3,571,929
1960	12,820,304	2,539,044	722,870	2,974,609	1,591,762	4,992,019
1965	21,186,886	4,240,227	1,497,313	4,801,677	2,607,404	8,040,265
1970	30,346,083	7,145,363	2,440,043	5,610,300	3,772,377	11,378,000
1975	49,682,502	16,029,468	3,368,747	6,726,000	6,296,286	17,262,000
1980	96,030,619	36,196,103	8,163,259	12,927,800	8,563,457	30,180,000
1981	105,888,323	43,825,202	8,876,976	13,073,900	8,342,245	31,770,000
1982	110,062,585	47,699,376	9,169,863	12,801,546	8,391,800	32,000,000
1983	112,715,359	48,811,040	9,549,619	12,717,600	9,317,100	32,320,000
1984	111,705,915	49,102,581	10,073,202	12,443,999	10,186,133	29,900,000
1985	105,414,291	44,596,302	10,426,969	11,806,100	11,384,920	27,200,000
1986	97,338,597	39,286,000	10,348,597	10,998,000	12,706,000	24,000,000

(1) Includes data for joint stock land banks and Federal Farm Mortgage Corporations. (2) Includes loans made directly by FmHA for farm ownership, soil and water loans to individuals, Indian tribe land acquisition, grazing associations, and irrigation drainage and soil conservation associations. Also includes loans for rural housing on farm tracts and labor housing. (3) American Council of Life Insurance. (4) Estimated by ERS, USDA.

Government Payments by Programs and State

Source: Economic Research Service, U.S. Agriculture Department

(thousands)

1986 State	Conservation	Feed Grain	Wheat	Cotton	Wool Act	Rice	Miscellaneous	Total
Alabama	$3,945	$6,545	$8,831	$42,828	$9	$612	$17,003	$79,773
Alaska	193	222	1	0	12	0	363	791
Arizona	1,385	2,606	4,290	65,949	2,096	0	7,239	88,565
Arkansas	2,666	11,246	48,231	59,796	56	177,964	13,758	313,717
California	3,961	17,324	43,441	119,601	9,476	82,272	111,785	387,860
Colorado	4,877	63,813	109,432	0	6,057	0	50,453	234,632
Connecticut	237	583	0	0	44	0	3,049	3,913
Delaware	180	5,916	468	0	3	0	404	6,971
Florida	2,551	3,875	1,744	2,802	19	395	14,734	26,120
Georgia	3,776	30,625	33,003	26,981	28	0	21,694	116,107
Hawaii	412	0	0	0	6	0	6,363	6,781
Idaho	2,502	31,942	145,555	0	3,873	0	39,357	223,229
Illinois	4,569	747,916	60,480	0	831	0	68,723	882,519
Indiana	2,492	357,242	29,004	0	485	0	22,052	411,275
Iowa	4,196	1,026,192	1,768	1	2,317	0	126,708	1,161,182
Kansas	4,377	216,997	609,439	8	1,300	0	38,647	870,768
Kentucky	3,580	57,099	11,937	76,015	140	0	16,348	165,119
Louisiana	2,456	3,658	4,792	1,368	49	65,960	5,560	83,843
Maine	1,847	1,161	4	0	124	0	3,667	6,803
Maryland	839	21,371	1,842	0	121	0	8,028	32,201
Massachusetts	387	360	0	0	61	0	4,935	5,743
Michigan	2,533	151,624	24,579	0	657	0	41,517	220,910
Minnesota	3,352	452,814	196,169	1	1,458	0	148,559	802,353
Mississippi	3,950	5,150	13,129	128,932	24	28,815	12,553	192,553
Missouri	4,778	159,560	63,785	29	602	12,617	34,495	275,866
Montana	3,121	45,080	269,830	21,625	7,396	0	19,023	366,075
Nebraska	4,876	596,020	138,571	9,351	1,198	0	117,747	867,763
Nevada	922	474	1,227	0	801	0	28	3,452
New Hampshire	380	164	0	0	46	0	2,274	2,864
New Jersey	296	4,410	769	0	45	0	975	6,495
New Mexico	2,099	14,982	22,326	236	5,438	0	17,347	62,428
New York	2,693	40,100	6,094	0	389	0	27,414	76,690
North Carolina	3,338	50,357	9,996	10,076	57	0	16,455	90,279
North Dakota	3,424	115,067	511,090	0	1,743	0	68,856	700,180
Ohio	2,511	205,692	43,782	0	1,388	0	15,599	268,972
Oklahoma	4,626	12,930	328,592	28,174	578	87	18,037	393,024
Oregon	2,277	6,176	94,281	0	3,234	0	21,679	127,647
Pennsylvania	2,581	27,440	1,985	0	579	0	11,989	44,574
Rhode Island	40	9	0	0	18	0	401	468
South Carolina	2,435	17,347	13,738	14,132	2	0	6,791	54,445
South Dakota	2,508	178,676	157,316	147	6,695	0	37,513	382,855
Tennessee	3,450	23,279	16,188	34,112	52	40	21,310	98,431
Texas	14,145	181,233	225,158	400,133	33,956	54,007	69,752	978,384
Utah	2,741	4,996	11,716	0	5,957	0	10,563	35,973
Vermont	1,719	621	4	0	106	0	9,899	12,349
Virginia	2,329	23,767	7,046	95	879	0	8,453	42,569
Washington	3,289	23,701	212,432	0	627	0	58,671	298,720
West Virginia	3,612	2,580	97	0	531	0	1,548	8,368
Wisconsin	2,853	203,115	3,868	0	584	0	56,004	266,424
Wyoming	1,683	3,981	11,691	0	9,775	0	2,198	29,328
Total	**$139,989**	**$5,158,038**	**$3,499,721**	**$1,042,392**	**$111,922**	**$422,769**	**$1,438,520**	**$11,813,351**

(1) Includes both cash payments and payment-in-kind (PIK). (2) Includes amount paid under agriculture and conservation programs (Agriculture Conservation, Emergency Conservation, and Great Plains Program). (3) The programs included are: Rural Clean Water, Clean Lakes, Conservation Reserve, Animal Waste Management, Forest Incentive, Water Bank, Dairy Indemnity, Dairy Termination, Emergency Feed, Extended Warehouse Storage, Extended Storage, PIK Storage, and Milk Diversion.

Federal Food Program Costs[1]

Source: Management Information Division, Food and Nutrition Service, USDA (millions of dollars)

Fiscal year	Food stamps benefits[7]	Food distribution[4]				Child nutrition (Cash payments)					Total food costs
		WIC[3]	Needy persons[5]	Schools	Institutions	School lunch	School breakfast	Child care	Summer food	Special milk	
1978	5,165	312	68	543	28	1,808	181	150	100	135	8,490
1979	6,478	429	96	745	54	1,984	231	189	109	134	10,449
1980	8,686	584	125	905	71	2,282	288	239	118	145	13,443
1981	10,630	708	158	895	78	2,381	332	335	110	101	15,728
1982	9,532[2]	756	351[6]	766	111	2,185	317	310	93	20	14,447
1983	11,155[2]	902	1,208[6]	840	158	2,406	351	351	98	18	17,487
1984	10,703[2]	1,386	1,335[6]	830	199	2,506	369	364	106	17	16,480
1985	10,743	1,487	1,041	829	171	2,579	379	410	113	16	19,810

(1) Cost data are direct federal benefits to recipients; they exclude federal administrative payments and applicable State and local contributions. (2) Excludes Puerto Rico Nutrition Assistance Program. (3) Special Supplemental Food Program for Women, Infants and Children. (4) Includes cost of commodity entitlements, cash-in-lieu of commodities and bonus foods. (5) Includes Food Distribution Program on Indian Reservations, Needy Family Program in Trust Territory, Commodity Supplemental Food Program and Nutrition Program for the Elderly. (6) Includes Temporary Emergency Food Assistance Program. (7) Average benefits per participant per month: 1970—$10.55; 1975—$21.41; 1981—$39.49; 1982—$39.05; 1983—$42.98; 1984—$42.76.

Farm Income—Cash Receipts from Livestock Marketing

Source: Economic Research Service, U.S. Department of Agriculture

(thousands)

State	1980	1981	1982	1983	1984	1985
Alabama	$1,174,522	$1,252,258	$1,215,464	$1,267,461	1,388,335	1,301,247
Alaska	4,116	5,088	6,393	7,325	6,969	8,033
Arizona	783,266	729,583	707,114	744,902	753,056	701,622
Arkansas	1,477,283	1,621,147	1,540,938	1,494,656	1,885,353	1,825,284
California	4,088,614	4,218,829	4,392,892	4,212,875	4,528,777	4,165,410
Colorado	2,211,592	2,009,458	2,014,019	2,000,471	2,204,710	2,019,129
Connecticut	171,407	188,215	198,727	202,503	220,387	205,521
Delaware	236,699	268,166	288,268	315,957	383,358	352,327
Florida	978,525	1,026,286	1,018,326	1,078,395	1,090,603	1,015,307
Georgia	1,534,433	1,752,763	1,677,790	1,716,316	1,848,315	1,727,111
Hawaii	81,225	88,138	78,408	86,487	87,015	82,821
Idaho	855,277	965,891	841,696	885,633	900,988	862,271
Illinois	2,323,680	2,219,766	2,368,522	2,294,568	2,172,888	2,063,183
Indiana	1,664,833	1,710,208	1,758,458	1,849,815	1,801,292	1,727,602
Iowa	5,311,538	5,678,816	5,906,599	5,140,272	5,014,616	4,811,147
Kansas	3,376,625	3,366,481	3,289,518	3,182,353	3,614,089	3,263,760
Kentucky	1,345,084	1,352,584	1,281,395	1,475,139	1,414,944	1,351,905
Louisiana	471,938	452,321	508,497	499,991	479,901	491,476
Maine	298,786	286,190	258,440	282,817	283,933	250,343
Maryland	622,037	693,694	707,425	719,191	810,066	769,723
Massachusetts	126,887	134,888	132,634	137,261	130,993	124,396
Michigan	1,123,606	1,112,551	1,176,317	1,266,835	1,297,626	1,231,315
Minnesota	3,289,825	3,392,072	3,546,839	3,337,287	3,359,873	3,370,127
Mississippi	892,590	863,542	939,578	926,782	1,046,290	1,010,043
Missouri	2,174,935	2,303,698	2,071,683	2,262,784	2,166,168	1,930,078
Montana	746,877	629,224	654,022	657,285	716,563	802,004
Nebraska	4,016,003	3,795,910	4,336,468	4,217,716	4,524,309	4,112,810
Nevada	158,216	132,985	166,093	153,020	172,372	143,924
New Hampshire	71,136	71,969	76,695	77,720	77,019	70,722
New Jersey	123,405	104,040	132,138	136,783	134,746	144,454
New Mexico	912,822	585,201	632,123	634,384	656,588	717,640
New York	1,776,547	1,873,165	1,854,532	1,918,213	1,921,201	1,844,989
North Carolina	1,447,138	1,604,212	1,620,572	1,679,102	1,940,667	1,934,315
North Dakota	773,398	592,259	606,259	647,590	693,387	686,066
Ohio	1,372,093	1,431,931	1,529,863	1,524,056	1,625,641	1,510,952
Oklahoma	2,150,514	1,829,923	2,090,515	1,689,453	1,775,807	1,725,716
Oregon	536,260	613,567	658,655	566,757	630,281	621,877
Pennsylvania	1,943,365	2,147,899	2,162,347	2,222,559	2,242,027	2,183,827
Rhode Island	14,094	15,274	14,232	12,412	13,925	13,408
South Carolina	409,810	396,147	394,654	409,230	427,241	414,973
South Dakota	1,841,837	1,881,871	1,639,297	1,649,350	1,804,348	1,903,097
Tennessee	904,440	852,482	898,177	906,468	1,053,683	999,973
Texas	5,196,423	5,448,215	5,421,060	5,521,428	5,900,842	5,440,501
Utah	387,033	407,076	[illegible]	400,227	449,099	408,363
Vermont	353,667	362,133	380,227	402,039	371,856	351,864
Virginia	957,192	907,548	988,591	892,026	1,121,157	1,004,456
Washington	835,263	957,838	973,743	921,936	1,031,471	932,300
West Virginia	172,746	163,186	170,169	170,111	182,654	191,606
Wisconsin	3,751,494	4,182,816	4,107,380	4,140,416	4,075,081	4,099,748
Wyoming	519,426	460,231	416,917	481,802	471,991	478,750
Total U.S.	**$67,990,522**	**$69,150,543**	**$70,248,825**	**$69,453,159**	**$72,904,501**	**$69,400,516**

Value of Farmland, By State

Source: Economic Research Service, U.S. Agriculture Department

State	Per acre 1987 value	1-year change
New Jersey	$5,321	36%
Rhode Island	4,217	9%
Connecticut	4,056	9%
Massachusetts	2,999	9%
Maryland	1,831	−3%
New Hampshire	1,794	9%
Delaware	1,775	1%
Pennsylvania	1,725	19%
Florida	1,464	2%
Alaska	1,437	−24%
California	1,366	−13%
Vermont	1,286	9%
Virginia	1,111	−3%
North Carolina	1,096	−3%
Maine	1,082	9%
Illinois	1,040	−9%
Tennessee	1,012	2%
Ohio	$942	−7%
New York	931	13%
Indiana	931	−12%
Georgia	846	3%
Michigan	833	−11%
South Carolina	794	−9%
Kentucky	791	−9%
Iowa	748	−11%
Louisiana	734	−27%
Alabama	731	−4%
Washington	723	−11%
Mississippi	654	−13%
Arkansas	634	−10%
Wisconsin	626	−12%
Idaho	567	−12%
Missouri	552	−9%
West Virginia	527	−2%
Minnesota	$493	−19%
Texas	482	−11%
Oregon	479	−8%
Utah	454	−5%
Oklahoma	428	−11%
Colorado	364	2%
Kansas	340	−12%
Nebraska	335	−8%
North Dakota	282	−11%
Arizona	242	5%
Nevada	211	6%
South Dakota	178	−17%
Montana	167	−18%
Wyoming	151	−2%
New Mexico	122	−9%
Continental U.S. Average	**$548**	**−8%**

ENERGY

World Nuclear Power

(Source: *Nuclear News*, Aug. 1986)

Country	Plants Operating[1] (number)	Plants Operating[1] (megawatts)	Plants Under Construction (number)	Plants Under Construction (megawatts)	Total Commitment (number)	Total Commitment (megawatts)
United States	92	78,618	28	30,849	120	109,467
France	44	38,948	18	22,210	62	61,158
Soviet Union	44	27,338	29	28,950	73	56,288
Japan	33	23,639	11	8,768	44	32,407
West Germany	16	16,114	7	6,877	23	22,991
Canada	17	11,145	5	4,361	22	15,506
United Kingdom	38	11,748	4	2,720	42	14,468
Sweden	12	9,435	—	—	12	9,435
Spain	8	5,682	2	1,979	10	7,661
South Korea	5	3,580	4	3,686	9	7,266
Czechoslovakia	6	2,380	7	3,230	13	5,610
Belgium	7	5,450	—	—	7	5,450
Taiwan	6	4,884	—	—	6	4,884
East Germany	5	1,702	5	2,532	10	4,234
Bulgaria	4	1,760	2	1,906	6	3,666
Italy	3	1,285	3	2,004	6	3,289
Switzerland	5	2,930	—	—	5	2,930
Finland	4	2,310	—	—	4	2,310
South Africa	2	1,840	—	—	2	1,840
India	6	1,244	2	440	8	1,684
Romania	—	—	3	1,680	3	1,680
Hungary	2	820	2	820	4	1,640
Argentina	2	935	1	692	3	1,627
Mexico	—	—	2	1,308	2	1,308
Poland	—	—	2	880	2	880
Cuba	—	—	2	880	2	880
Other	5	1,883	1	300	6	2,183
World	**366**	**255,670**	**140**	**127,072**	**506**	**382,742**

(1) Includes several plants in long-term shutdowns that may not be restarted due to safety concerns.

U.S. Nuclear Power Plant Operations

Source: Energy Information Administration, Monthly Energy Review, Feb. 1987

	Operable Reactors Number	Nuclear-Based Electricity Generation Million Net Kilowatthours	Nuclear Portion of Domestic Electricity Generation Percent		Operable Reactors Number	Nuclear-Based Electricity Generation Million Net Kilowatthours	Nuclear Portion of Domestic Electricity Generation Percent
1973	39	83,479	4.5	1981	74	272,674	11.9
1974	48	113,976	6.1	1982	77	282,773	12.6
1975	54	172,505	9.0	1983	80	293,677	12.7
1976	61	191,104	9.4	1984	86	327,634	13.6
1977	65	250,883	11.8	1985	95	383,691	15.5
1978	70	276,403	12.5	1986	100	414,038	16.6
1979	68	255,155	11.4	1987 January	102	39,975	17.9
1980	70	251,116	11.0	1987 February	102	36,598	18.9

Status of U.S. Nuclear Reactor Units

Source: Energy Information Administration, Monthly Energy Review, Feb. 1987

	Licensed for Operation		Construction Permits					Total Design Capacity Million Net Kilowatts
	Operable	In Startup	Granted	Pending	On Order	Announced	Total	
	Number of Reactor Units							
1973	39	3	51	58	48	20	219	212
1974	48	5	58	80	28	16	235	234
1975	54	2	69	73	19	19	236	236
1976	61	0	72	66	16	19	234	236
1977	65	1	80	52	13	9	220	220
1978	70	0	90	32	9	4	205	204
1979	68	0	91	21	3	0	183	179
1980	70	2	82	12	3	0	169	163
1981	74	0	75	11	3	0	163	157
1982	77	2	60	3	2	0	144	135
1983	80	3	53	0	2	0	138	129
1984	86	6	38	0	2	0	132	123
1985	95	3	30	0	2	0	130	121
1986	100	7	19	0	2	0	128	119
1987 January	102	6	18	0	2	0	128	119
1987 February	102	6	18	0	2	0	128	119

U.S. Total Energy Production by Source, 1952-1986

Source: Energy Information Administration, Annual Energy Review, 1986 (quadrillion Btu, except as noted)

Year	Coal	Natural Gas[1]	Crude Oil[2]	Natural Gas Plant Liquids	Hydroelectric Power[3]	Nuclear Electric Power[4]	Geothermal[4]	Total	Percent Change[5]
1952	12.73	7.96	13.28	1.00	1.47	0	0	36.45	−2.1
1953	12.28	8.34	13.67	1.06	1.41	0	0	36.77	0.9
1954	10.54	8.68	13.43	1.11	1.36	0	0	35.13	−4.5
1955	12.37	9.34	14.41	1.24	1.36	0	0	38.73	10.2
1956	13.31	10.00	15.18	1.28	1.43	0	0	41.21	6.4
1957	13.06	10.61	15.18	1.29	1.52	0	0	41.65	1.1
1958	10.78	10.94	14.20	1.29	1.59	(6)	0	38.81	−6.8
1959	10.78	11.95	14.93	1.38	1.55	(6)	0	40.60	4.6
1960	10.82	12.66	14.93	1.46	1.61	0.01	0	41.49	2.2
1961	10.45	13.10	15.21	1.55	1.66	0.02	(6)	41.99	1.2
1962	10.90	13.72	15.52	1.59	1.82	0.03	(6)	43.58	3.8
1963	11.85	14.51	15.97	1.71	1.77	0.04	(6)	45.85	5.2
1964	12.52	15.30	16.16	1.80	1.89	0.04	(6)	47.72	4.1
1965	13.06	15.78	16.52	1.88	2.06	0.04	(6)	49.34	3.4
1966	13.47	17.01	17.56	2.00	2.06	0.06	(6)	52.17	5.7
1967	13.83	17.94	18.65	2.18	2.35	0.09	0.01	55.04	5.5
1968	13.61	19.07	19.31	2.32	2.35	0.14	0.01	56.81	3.2
1969	13.86	20.45	19.56	2.42	2.65	0.15	0.01	59.10	4.0
1970	14.61	21.67	20.40	2.51	2.63	0.24	0.01	62.07	5.0
1971	13.19	22.28	20.03	2.54	2.82	0.41	0.01	61.29	−1.3
1972	14.09	22.21	20.04	2.60	2.86	0.58	0.03	62.42	1.8
1973	13.99	22.19	19.49	2.57	2.86	0.91	0.04	62.06	−0.6
1974	14.07	21.21	18.57	2.47	3.18	1.27	0.05	60.84	−2.0
1975	14.99	19.64	17.73	2.37	3.15	1.90	0.07	59.86	−1.6
1976	15.65	19.48	17.26	2.33	2.98	2.11	0.08	59.89	0.1
1977	15.76	19.57	17.45	2.33	2.33	2.70	0.08	60.22	0.5
1978	14.91	19.49	18.43	2.25	2.94	3.02	0.06	61.10	1.5
1979	17.54	20.08	18.10	2.29	2.93	2.78	0.08	63.80	4.4
1980	18.60	19.91	18.25	2.25	2.90	2.74	0.11	64.76	1.5
1981	18.38	19.70	18.15	2.31	2.76	3.01	0.12	64.42	−0.5
1982	18.64	18.25	18.31	2.19	3.26	3.13	0.10	63.89	−0.8
1983	17.25	16.53	18.39	2.18	3.50	3.20	0.13	61.19	−4.2
1984	19.72	17.93	18.85	2.27	3.31	3.55	0.16	65.81	7.6
1985	19.33	16.92	18.99	2.24	2.94	4.15	0.20	64.78	−1.6
1986p	19.48	16.49	18.35	2.17	3.04	4.48	0.22	64.25	−0.8

(1) Dry natural gas; (2) Includes lease condensate; (3) Electric utility and industrial generation of hydroelectric power; (4) Generated by electric utilities; (5) Percent change from previous year calculated from data prior to rounding; (6) Less than 0.005 quadrillion Btu; (p) = preliminary.

U.S. Total Energy Consumption by Source, 1952-1986

Source: Energy Information Administration, Annual Energy Review, 1986 (quadrillion Btu, except as noted)

Year	Coal	Natural Gas	Petroleum[1]	Hydroelectric Power[2]	Nuclear Electric Power[3]	Geothermal[3]	Total	Percent Change[4]
1952	11.31	7.55	14.96	1.50	0	0	35.30	−0.5
1953	11.37	7.91	15.56	1.44	0	0	[illegible]	[illegible]
1954	9.71	8.33	15.84	1.39	0	0	35.27	−2.8
1955	11.17	9.00	17.25	1.41	0	0	38.82	10.1
1956	11.35	9.61	17.94	1.49	0	0	40.38	4.0
1957	10.82	10.19	17.93	1.56	0	0	40.48	0.3
1958	9.53	10.66	18.53	1.63	(5)	0	40.35	−0.3
1959	9.52	11.72	19.32	1.59	(5)	0	42.14	4.4
1960	9.84	12.39	19.92	1.66	0.01	(5)	43.80	3.9
1961	9.62	12.93	20.22	1.68	0.02	(5)	44.46	1.5
1962	9.91	13.73	21.05	1.82	0.03	(5)	46.53	4.7
1963	10.41	14.40	21.70	1.77	0.04	(5)	48.32	3.9
1964	10.96	15.29	22.30	1.91	0.04	(5)	50.50	4.5
1965	11.58	15.77	23.25	2.06	0.04	(5)	52.68	4.3
1966	12.14	17.00	24.40	2.07	0.06	(5)	55.66	5.6
1967	11.91	17.94	25.28	2.34	0.09	0.01	57.57	3.4
1968	12.33	19.21	26.98	2.34	0.14	0.01	61.00	6.0
1969	12.38	20.68	28.34	2.66	0.15	0.01	64.19	5.2
1970	12.26	21.79	29.52	2.65	0.24	0.01	66.43	3.5
1971	11.60	22.47	30.56	2.86	0.41	0.01	67.89	2.2
1972	12.08	22.70	32.95	2.94	0.58	0.03	71.26	5.0
1973	12.97	22.51	34.84	3.01	0.91	0.04	74.28	4.2
1974	12.66	21.73	33.45	3.31	1.27	0.05	72.54	−2.3
1975	12.66	19.95	32.73	3.22	1.90	0.07	70.55	−2.8
1976	13.58	20.35	35.17	3.07	2.11	0.08	74.36	5.4
1977	13.92	19.93	37.12	2.51	2.70	0.08	76.29	2.6
1978	13.77	20.00	37.97	3.14	3.02	0.06	78.09	2.4
1979	15.04	20.67	37.12	3.14	2.78	0.08	78.90	1.0
1980	15.42	20.39	34.20	3.12	2.74	0.11	75.96	−3.7
1981	15.91	19.93	31.93	3.11	3.01	0.12	73.99	−2.6
1982	15.32	18.51	30.23	3.56	3.13	0.10	70.84	−4.3
1983	15.90	17.36	30.05	3.87	3.20	0.13	70.50	−0.5
1984	17.07	18.51	31.05	3.72	3.55	0.16	74.06	5.1
1985	17.48	17.85	30.92	3.36	4.15	0.20	73.96	−0.1
1986p	17.32	16.53	31.89	3.50	4.48	0.22	73.93	−0.1

(1) Petroleum products supplied including natural gas plant liquids and crude oil burned as fuel; (2) Electric utility and industrial generation of hydroelectric power and net electricity imports; (3) Generated by electric utilities; (4) Percent change from previous year calculated from data prior to rounding; (5) Less than 0.005 quadrillion Btu; (p) = preliminary.

World Production of Crude Oil,[1] 1960-1986

Source: Energy Information Administration, Annual Energy Review, 1986 (millions of barrels per day)

Year	Total[2] OPEC	Canada	China	Mexico	United Kingdom	United States	U.S.S.R.	Other Non-OPEC	Total World
1960	8.70	0.52	0.10	0.27	(4)	7.04	2.91	1.42	20.96
1961	9.36	0.61	0.11	0.29	(4)	7.18	3.28	1.60	22.43
1962	10.51	0.67	0.12	0.31	(4)	7.33	3.67	1.71	24.32
1963	11.51	0.71	0.13	0.32	(4)	7.54	4.07	1.85	26.13
1964	12.98	0.75	0.18	0.32	(4)	7.61	4.60	1.92	28.36
1965	14.34	0.81	0.23	0.32	(4)	7.80	4.79	2.01	30.30
1966	15.77	0.88	0.29	0.33	(4)	8.30	5.23	2.13	32.93
1967	16.85	0.96	0.28	0.37	(4)	8.81	5.68	2.42	35.37
1968	18.79	1.19	0.30	0.39	(4)	9.10	6.08	2.79	38.64
1969	20.91	1.13	0.48	0.46	(4)	9.24	6.48	2.99	41.69
1970	23.41	1.26	0.60	0.49	(4)	9.64	6.97	2.92	45.29
1971	25.33	1.35	0.78	0.49	(4)	9.46	7.44	2.99	47.84
1972	27.09	1.53	0.90	0.51	(4)	9.44	7.88	2.91	50.26
1973	30.99	1.80	1.09	0.47	(4)	9.21	8.33	3.69	55.57
1974	30.73	1.68	1.32	0.57	(4)	8.77	8.86	3.84	55.77
1975	27.16	1.44	1.49	0.71	0.01	8.38	9.47	4.12	52.76
1976	30.74	1.30	1.67	0.83	0.25	8.13	9.99	4.30	57.19
1977	31.30	1.32	1.87	0.98	0.77	8.25	10.49	4.55	59.52
1978	29.81	1.31	2.08	1.21	1.08	8.71	10.95	4.72	59.87
1979	30.93	1.50	2.12	1.46	1.57	8.55	11.19	5.04	62.35
1980	26.89	1.44	2.11	1.94	1.62	8.60	11.46	5.17	59.23
1981	22.65	1.29	2.01	2.31	1.81	8.57	11.55	5.36	55.55
1982	18.87	1.27	2.05	2.75	2.07	8.65	11.62	5.64	52.90
1983	17.58	1.36	2.12	2.69	2.29	8.69	11.68	6.24	52.65
1984	17.48	1.44	2.30	2.78	2.48	8.88	11.58	6.90	53.83
1985	16.07	1.47	2.48	2.74	2.53	8.97	11.25	7.46	52.95
1986p	18.37	1.48	2.52	2.42	2.55	8.67	11.65	7.82	55.47

(1) Includes lease condensate, excludes natural gas plant liquids; (2) Current membership of the Organization of the Petroleum Exporting Countries includes Algeria, Ecuador, Gabon, Indonesia, Iran, Iraq, Kuwait, Libya, Nigeria, Qatar, Saudi Arabia, United Arab Emirates, and Venezuela.

U.S. Coal Production and Consumption, 1949-1986

Source: Energy Information Administration, Annual Energy Review, 1986 (Million Short tons)

	Production					Consumption				
Year	Bituminous Coal	Sub-bituminous Coal	Lignite	Anthracite	Total	Electric Utilities	Coke Plants	Trans-portation	Residential & Com-mercial	Total
1949	437.9	(1)	(1)	42.7	480.6	84.0	91.4	70.2	116.5	483.2
1950	516.3	(1)	(1)	44.1	560.4	91.9	104.0	63.0	114.6	494.1
1951	533.7	(1)	(1)	42.7	576.3	105.8	113.7	56.2	101.5	505.9
1952	466.8	(1)	(1)	40.6	507.4	107.1	97.8	39.8	92.3	454.1
1953	457.3	(1)	(1)	30.9	488.2	115.9	113.1	29.6	79.2	454.8
1954	391.7	(1)	(1)	29.1	420.8	118.4	85.6	18.6	69.1	389.9
1955	464.6	(1)	(1)	26.2	490.8	143.8	107.7	17.0	68.4	447.0
1956	500.9	(1)	(1)	28.9	529.8	158.3	106.3	13.8	64.2	456.9
1957	492.7	(1)	(1)	25.3	518.0	160.8	108.4	9.8	49.0	434.5
1958	410.4	(1)	(1)	21.2	431.6	155.7	76.8	4.7	47.9	385.7
1959	412.0	(1)	(1)	20.6	432.7	168.4	79.6	3.6	40.8	385.1
1960	415.5	(1)	(1)	18.8	434.3	176.7	81.4	3.0	40.9	398.1
1961	403.0	(1)	(1)	17.4	420.4	182.2	74.2	0.8	37.3	390.4
1962	422.1	(1)	(1)	16.9	439.0	193.3	74.7	0.7	36.5	402.3
1963	458.9	(1)	(1)	18.3	477.2	211.3	78.1	0.7	31.5	423.5
1964	487.0	(1)	(1)	17.2	504.2	225.4	89.2	0.7	27.2	445.7
1965	512.1	(1)	(1)	14.9	527.0	244.8	95.3	0.7	25.7	472.0
1966	533.9	(1)	(1)	12.9	546.8	266.5	96.4	0.6	25.6	497.7
1967	552.6	(1)	(1)	12.3	564.9	274.2	92.8	0.5	22.1	491.4
1968	545.2	(1)	(1)	11.5	556.7	297.8	91.3	0.4	20.0	509.8
1969	547.2	8.3	5.0	10.5	571.0	310.6	93.4	0.3	18.9	516.4
1970	578.5	16.4	8.0	9.7	612.7	320.2	96.5	0.3	16.1	523.2
1971	521.3	22.2	8.7	8.7	560.9	327.3	83.2	0.2	15.2	501.6
1972	556.8	27.5	11.0	7.1	602.5	351.8	87.7	0.2	11.7	524.3
1973	543.5	33.9	14.3	6.8	598.6	389.2	94.1	0.1	11.1	562.6
1974	545.7	42.2	15.5	6.6	610.0	391.8	90.2	0.1	11.4	558.4
1975	577.5	51.1	19.8	6.2	654.6	406.0	83.6	(2)	9.4	562.6
1976	588.4	64.8	25.5	6.2	684.9	448.4	84.7	(2)	8.9	603.8
1977	581.0	82.1	28.2	5.9	697.2	477.1	77.7	(2)	9.0	625.3
1978	534.0	96.8	34.4	5.0	670.2	481.2	71.4	(2)	9.5	625.2
1979	612.3	121.5	42.5	4.8	781.1	527.1	77.4	(2)	8.4	680.5
1980	628.8	147.7	47.2	6.1	829.7	569.3	66.7	(2)	6.5	702.7
1981	608.0	159.7	50.7	5.4	823.8	596.8	61.0	(2)	7.4	732.6
1982	620.2	160.9	52.4	4.6	838.1	593.7	40.9	(2)	8.2	706.9
1983	568.6	151.0	58.3	4.1	782.1	625.2	37.0	(2)	8.4	736.7
1984	649.5	179.2	63.1	4.2	895.9	664.4	44.0	(2)	9.1	791.3
1985	613.9	192.7	72.4	4.7	883.6	693.8	41.1	(2)	7.8	818.0
1986p	626.2	184.6	73.6	3.8	888.2	685.1	37.1	(2)	7.9	806.2

(1) Included in bituminous; (2) Less than 0.05 million short tons; (p) = preliminary.

U.S. Household Energy[1] Consumption by Census Region, 1978-82 and 1984[2]

Source: Energy Information Administration, Annual Energy Review, 1986 (Quadrillion Btu, except as noted)

Census Region	1978	1979	1980	1981	1982	1984
Northeast						
Natural Gas	1.14	1.05	0.92	1.06	0.99	0.93
Electricity[3]	0.39	0.39	0.39	0.42	0.38	0.41
Distillate Fuel Oil and Kerosene	1.32	1.03	1.09	0.96	0.79	0.93
Liquefied Petroleum Gases	0.03	0.03	0.03	0.03	0.02	0.03
Total	2.89	2.50	2.43	2.47	2.18	2.29
Consumption per household (million Btu)	166	145	138	138	122	125
North Central						
Natural Gas	2.53	2.48	2.02	2.24	1.76	1.99
Electricity[3]	0.60	0.59	0.60	0.57	0.57	0.55
Distillate Fuel Oil and Kerosene	0.46	0.31	0.16	0.17	0.15	0.13
Liquefied Petroleum Gases	0.12	0.10	0.15	0.13	0.11	0.13
Total	3.70	3.48	2.92	3.12	2.60	2.80
Consumption per household (million Btu)	180	168	139	147	122	129
South						
Natural Gas	0.96	0.91	1.11	1.16	1.13	1.15
Electricity[3]	1.00	0.97	1.06	1.03	1.05	1.06
Distillate Fuel Oil and Kerosene	0.32	0.28	0.27	0.16	0.17	0.16
Liquefied Petroleum Gases	0.15	0.14	0.15	0.12	0.12	0.12
Total	2.43	2.30	2.59	2.46	2.46	2.50
Consumption per household (million Btu)	99	92	96	89	88	85
West						
Natural Gas	0.95	0.88	0.89	0.93	0.89	0.91
Electricity[3]	0.48	0.47	0.41	0.46	0.42	0.47
Distillate Fuel Oil and Kerosene	0.09	0.09	0.04	0.03	0.03	0.04
Liquefield Petroleum Gases	0.03	0.04	0.04	0.04	0.04	0.03
Total	1.54	1.47	1.38	1.47	1.38	1.45
Consumption per household (million Btu)	110	100	86	90	84	85
United States						
Natural Gas	5.58	5.31	4.94	5.39	4.77	4.98
Electricity[3]	2.47	2.42	2.46	2.48	2.42	2.48
Distillate Fuel Oil and Kerosene	2.19	1.71	1.55	1.33	1.14	1.26
Liquefied Petroleum Gases	0.33	0.31	0.36	0.31	0.29	0.31
Total	10.56	9.74	9.32	9.51	8.62	9.04
Consumption per household (million Btu)	138	126	114	114	103	105

(1) Major energy items only, as shown; (2) Data for April of year shown through March of following year; (3) Includes electricity generated for distribution from wood, waste, geothermal, wind, photovoltaic, and solar thermal energy. Note: No data available for 1983.

Net Electricity Generation at Electric Utilities by Energy Source

Source: Energy Information Administration, Monthly Energy Review, Feb. 1987 (Million kilowatthours)

	Coal	Petroleum	Natural Gas	Nuclear Electric Power	Hydro-electric Power	Other[1]	Total
1973	847,651	314,343	340,858	83,479	272,083	2,294	1,860,710
1974	828,400	000,931	320,065	113,976	301,032	2,703	1,867,140
1975	852,786	289,095	299,778	172,505	300,047	3,437	1,917,649
1976	944,391	319,999	[illegible]	191,101	[illegible]	[illegible]	[illegible]
1977	985,219	358,179	305,505	250,883	220,475	4,063	2,124,323
1978	975,742	365,060	305,391	276,403	280,419	3,315	2,206,331
1979	1,075,037	303,525	329,485	255,155	279,783	4,387	2,247,372
1980	1,161,562	245,994	346,240	251,116	276,021	5,506	2,286,439
1981	1,203,203	206,421	345,777	272,674	260,684	6,054	2,294,812
1982	1,192,004	146,797	305,260	282,773	309,213	5,164	2,241,211
1983	1,259,424	144,499	274,098	293,677	332,130	6,456	2,310,285
1984	1,341,681	119,808	297,394	327,634	321,150	8,638	2,416,304
1985	1,402,128	100,202	291,946	383,691	281,149	10,724	2,469,841
1986	1,385,831	136,585	248,508	414,038	290,844	11,503	2,487,310
1987 January	126,624	11,924	17,788	39,975	25,409	1,017	222,736
1987 February	109,641	10,504	15,120	36,598	21,216	940	194,019
2-month total	236,265	22,427	32,908	76,573	46,624	1,957	416,755

(1) Electricity produced from geothermal, wood, waste, wind, photovoltaic, and solar thermal energy sources connected to electric utility distribution systems.

U.S. Passenger Car Efficiency, 1960-1985

Source: Energy Information Administration, Annual Energy Review, 1986

	Average[1] Annual Mileage		Fuel Consumption		Fuel Rate	
Year	Thousand Miles per Car	Index 1973 = 100.0	Gallons per Car	Index 1973 = 100.0	Miles Gallon	Index 1973 = 100.0
1960	9.45	94.6	661	86.6	14.3	109.2
1965	9.39	94.0	667	87.4	14.1	107.6
1970	9.98	99.9	735	96.3	13.6	103.8
1975	9.63	96.4	712	93.3	13.5	103.1
1976	9.76	97.7	711	93.2	13.7	104.6
1978	10.05	100.6	715	93.7	14.1	107.6
1979	9.48	94.9	664	87.0	14.3	109.2
1980	9.14	91.5	603	79.0	15.2	116.0
1981	9.00	90.1	579	75.9	15.5	118.3
1982	9.53	95.4	587	76.9	16.3	124.4
1983	9.65	96.6	578	75.8	16.7	127.5
1984	9.79	98.0	553	72.5	17.7	135.1
1985p	9.83	98.4	549	72.0	17.9	136.6

(1) Arithmetic mean (p) =preliminary

U.S. Net Imports of Energy by Source, 1952-86

Source: Energy Information Administration, Annual Energy Review, 1986 (quadrillion Btu)

	Net Imports[1]						Net Imports[1]				
Year	Coal	Petroleum[2]	Natural Gas (Dry)	Other[3]	Total	Year	Coal	Petroleum[2]	Natural Gas (Dry)	Other[3]	Total
1952	−1.40	1.20	−0.02	0.02	−0.20	1970	−1.93	6.92	0.77	−0.04	5.72
1953	−0.97	1.44	−0.02	0.02	0.47	1971	−1.54	8.07	0.88	(4)	7.41
1954	−0.91	1.58	−0.02	0.02	0.67	1972	−1.53	9.83	0.97	0.05	9.32
1955	−1.46	1.98	−0.02	0.04	0.54	1973	−1.42	12.98	0.98	0.14	12.68
1956	−1.98	2.26	−0.03	0.04	0.30	1974	−1.57	12.66	0.91	0.19	12.19
1957	−2.16	2.26	(4)	0.02	0.12	1975	−1.74	12.51	0.90	0.08	11.75
1958	−1.41	3.14	0.10	0.03	1.86	1976	−1.57	15.20	0.92	0.09	14.65
1959	−1.04	3.46	0.12	0.03	2.57	1977	−1.40	18.24	0.98	0.20	18.02
1960	−1.02	3.57	0.15	0.04	2.74	1978	−1.00	17.06	0.94	0.33	17.32
1961	−0.98	3.82	0.22	0.02	3.08	1979	−1.70	16.93	1.24	0.27	16.75
1962	−1.08	4.20	0.40	(4)	3.53	1980	−2.39	13.50	0.96	0.18	12.25
1963	−1.35	4.21	0.40	−0.01	3.25	1981	−2.92	11.38	0.86	0.33	9.65
1964	−1.33	4.53	0.44	0.01	3.65	1982	−2.77	9.05	0.90	0.28	7.46
1965	−1.37	5.01	0.44	−0.02	4.06	1983	−2.01	9.08	0.89	0.35	8.31
1966	−1.35	5.21	0.47	−0.01	4.32	1984	−2.12	9.89	0.79	0.39	8.95
1967	−1.35	4.91	0.50	−0.02	4.04	1985	−2.39	8.95	0.89	0.41	7.87
1968	−1.37	5.73	0.58	−0.02	4.90	1986p	−2.19	11.11	0.70	0.44	10.06
1969	−1.53	6.42	0.70	−0.02	5.56						

(1) Net imports = imports minus exports; (2) Includes imports to Strategic Petroleum Reserve, from 1977; (3) Coal Coke and small amounts of electricity transmitted across U.S. borders with Canada and Mexico; (4) Less than 0.005 quadrillion Btu; (p) = preliminary.

Net Imports of Crude Oil and Petroleum Products by Country of Origin, 1960-1986

Source: Energy Information Administration, Annual Energy Review, 1986 (thousand barrels per day, except as shown)

	Organization of Petroleum Exporting Countries (OPEC)								U.S. Dependence on OPEC	
Year	Total OPEC[1]	Arab Members of OPEC[2]	Canada	Mexico	United Kingdom	Virgin Is. and Puerto Rico	Total Net Imports	Total Net Imports Percent of Consumption[3]	Percent of Net Imports[4]	Percent of Consumption[5]
1960	1,311	292	86	−2	−12	34	1,613	16.5	81.3	13.4
1961	1,283	284	167	27	−10	42	1,743	17.5	73.6	12.9
1962	1,210	241	229	35	−6	40	1,913	18.4	63.3	11.6
1963	1,282	258	243	29	−7	43	1,915	17.8	67.0	11.9
1964	1,359	293	272	23	−9	45	2,057	18.7	66.1	12.3
1965	1,475	324	297	21	−11	45	2,281	19.8	64.7	12.8
1966	1,470	291	352	6	−6	58	2,375	19.7	61.9	12.2
1967	1,258	177	400	13	−51	89	2,230	17.8	56.4	10.0
1968	1,302	272	468	15	13	143	2,609	19.5	49.9	9.7
1969	1,336	276	564	10	7	186	2,933	20.8	45.5	9.4
1970	1,343	196	736	9	−1	270	3,161	21.5	42.5	9.1
1971	1,671	327	831	−14	1	365	3,701	24.3	45.2	11.0
1972	2,061	529	1,082	−20	−1	428	4,519	27.6	45.6	12.6
1973	2,991	914	1,294	−28	(6)	426	6,025	34.8	49.6	17.3
1974	3,277	752	1,038	−27	1	475	5,892	35.4	55.6	19.7
1975	3,599	1,382	824	29	7	484	5,846	35.8	61.6	22.0
1976	5,063	2,423	571	53	24	488	7,090	40.6	71.4	29.0
1977	6,190	3,184	446	155	117	560	8,565	46.5	72.3	33.6
1978	5,747	2,962	359	291	173	436	8,002	42.5	71.8	30.5
1979	5,633	3,054	438	418	196	353	7,985	43.1	70.5	30.4
1980	4,293	2,549	347	506	169	256	6,365	37.3	67.4	25.2
1981	3,315	1,844	358	497	370	169	5,401	33.6	61.4	20.6
1982	2,136	852	397	632	442	154	4,298	28.1	49.7	14.0
1983	1,843	630	471	802	374	178	4,312	28.3	42.7	12.1
1984	2,037	817	547	714	388	184	4,715	30.0	43.2	13.0
1985	1,821	470	696	755	295	114	4,286	27.3	42.5	11.6
1986p	2,760	1,148	708	638	342	154	5,289	32.8	52.2	17.1

(1) Includes Nigeria, Saudi Arabia, Venezuela, Ecuador, Gabon, Indonesia, Iran, Iraq, Kuwait, Libya, Qatar, and United Arab Emirates; (2) Includes Algeria, Iraq, Kuwait, Libya, Qatar, Saudi Arabia, and United Arab Emirates; (3) Calculated by dividing total net petroleum imports by total U.S. petroleum products supplied; (4) Calculated by dividing net petroleum imports from OPEC countries by total net petroleum imports; (5) Calculated by dividing net petroleum imports from OPEC countries by total U.S. petroleum product supplied; (6) Less than 500 barrels per day; (p) = preliminary.

World's Largest Capacity Hydro Plants

Rank order	Name	Country	Rated capacity now (MW)	Rated capacity planned (MW)	Rank order	Name	Country	Rated capacity now (MW)	Rated capacity planned (MW)
1	Lower Tunguska*	USSR		20,000	5	Tucurui	Brazil	3,960	8,000
2	Itaipu	Brazil/Paraguay	4,900	12,600	6	Sayano Shushensk*	USSR	6,400	6,400
3	Grand Coulee	USA	6,494	10,830					
4	Guri (Raúl Leoni-final stage)	Venezuela		10,300					

(continued)

Rank order	Name	Country	Rated capacity now (MW)	Rated capacity planned (MW)
7=	Corpus Posadas	Argentina/ Paraguay		6,000
7=	Krasnoyarsk	USSR	6,000	6,000
9	La Grande 2	Canada	2,000	5,328
10	Churchill Falls	Canada	5,225	5,225
11	Tarbela	Pakistan	1,750	4,678
12=	Bratsk	USSR	4,500	4,500
12=	Ust-Ilim	USSR	3,675	4,500
14	Yacyreta-Apipe*	Argentina/ Paraguay	2,760	4,140
15	Cabora Bassa	Mozambique	2,000	4,000
16=	Rogun*	USSR		3,600
16=	Oak Creek	USA	3,600	3,600
18	Paulo Afonso I	Brazil	1,524	3,409
19	Pati*	Argentina		3,300
20=	Ilha Solteira	Brazil	3,200	3,200
20=	Brumley Gap	USA	3,200	3,200
22	Chapetón*	Argentina		3,000
23	Gezhouba	China	2,715	2,715
24	John Day	USA	2,160	2,700
25	São Simão	Brazil	2,680	2,680

*Planned or under construction.

Major Dams of the World

Source: T.W. Mermel, *Intl. Water Power & Dam Construction, Handbook '87.*

World's Highest Dams

Rank order	Name	Country	Height above lowest formation (m)
1	Rogun*	USSR	335
2	Nurek	USSR	300
3	Grand Dixence	Switzerland	285
4	Inguri	USSR	272
5	Boruca*	Costa Rica	267
6	Vaiont	Italy	262
7=	Chicoasén	Mexico	261
7=	Tehri*	India	261
9	Kishau*	India	253
10	Sayano-Shushensk*	USSR	245
11	Guavio*	Colombia	243
12	Mica	Canada	242
13=	Mauvoisin	Switzerland	237
13=	Chivor	Colombia	237
15	Chirkei	USSR	233
16	Oroville	USA	230
17=	Bhakra	India	226
17=	El Cajón*	Honduras	226
19	Hoover	USA	221
20=	Contra	Switzerland	220
20=	Dabaklamm	Austria	220
20=	Mratinje	Yugoslavia	220
20=	Seti*	Nepal	220
24	Dworshak	USA	219
25	Glen Canyon	USA	216

*Planned or under construction.

World's Largest Volume Dams

Rank order	Name	Country	Dam volume $m^3 \times 10^3$
1	Syncrude Tailings*	Canada	540,000
2	Chapetón*	Argentina	296,200
3	Pati	Argentina	238,180
4	New Cornelia Tailings	USA	209,500
5	Tarbela	Pakistan	105,570
6	Fort Peck	USA	96,050
7	Lower Usuma	Nigeria	93,000
8	Cipasang	Indonesia	90,000
9	Atatürk*	Turkey	85,000
10	Guri	Venezuela	77,971
11	Rogun*	USSR	75,500
12	Oahe	USA	70,339
13	Gardiner	Canada	65,440
14	Mangla	Pakistan	65,379
15	Tucurui	Brazil	64,300
16	Afsluitdijk	Netherlands	63,430
17	Yacyretá-Apipe*	Paraguay/Argentina	61,200
18	Oroville	USA	59,635
19	San Luis	USA	59,559
20	Nurek	USSR	58,000
21	Garrison	USA	50,845
22	Cochiti	USA	50,230
23	Oosterschelde	Netherlands	50,000
24	Tabqua (Thawra)	Syria	46,000
25	Aswan (High)	Egypt	44,300

*Planned or under construction.

World's Largest Capacity Reservoirs

Rank order	Name	Country	Reservoir capacity $m^3 \times 10^6$
1	Owen Falls**	Uganda	2,700,000
2	Bratsk	USSR	169,270
3	Aswan (High)	Egypt	168,900
4	Kariba	Zimbabwe	160,368
5	Akosombo	Ghana	148,000
6	Daniel Johnson	Canada	141,852
7	Guri (Raúl Leoni-final stage)	Venezuela	138,000
8	Krasnoyarsk	USSR	73,300
9	Bennett W.A.C. (Portage Mt.)	Canada	70,309
10	Zeya	USSR	68,400
11	Cabora Bassa	Mozambique	63,000
12	La Grande 2	Canada	61,715
13	Chapetón*	Argentina	60,600
14	La Grande 3	Canada	60,020
15	Ust Ilim	USSR	59,300
16	Volga-V.I. Lenin (Kuibyshev)	USSR	58,000
17	São Felix	Brazil	55,200
18	Caniapiscau (KA-3, KA-4 & KA-5)	Canada	53,800
19	Bukhtarma	USSR	49,800
20	Atatürk*	Turkey	48,700
21	Bakun*	Malaysia	43,800
22	Cerros Colorados	Argentina	48,000
23	Irkutsk	USSR	46,000
24	Lower Tunguska	USSR	45,000
25	Tucurui	Brazil	43,000

*Planned or under construction.
** The major part of this reservoir is the natural capacity of a lake.

U.S. Energy Expenditures Per Capita, by State, 1983

Source: Energy Information Administration

Division and State	Dollars	Rank
U.S.	**1,728**	(x)
New England	**1,604**	(x)
Maine	1,874	15
New Hampshire	1,473	46
Vermont	1,467	47
Massachusetts	1,566	40
Rhode Island	1,418	49
Connecticut	1,694	26
Middle Atlantic	**1,580**	(x)
New York	1,416	50
New Jersey	1,965	8
Pennsylvania	1,582	37
East North Central	**1,758**	(x)
Ohio	1,900	12
Indiana	1,734	21
Illinois	1,986	7
Michigan	1,542	42
Wisconsin	1,643	30
West North Central	**1,814**	(x)
Minnesota	1,711	22
Iowa	1,962	9
Missouri	1,705	23
North Dakota	2,056	5
South Dakota	1,816	18
Nebraska	1,857	16
Kansas	1,940	10
South Atlantic	**1,603**	(x)
Delaware	1,878	13
Maryland	1,606	34
District of Columbia	1,771	(x)
Virginia	1,610	33
West Virginia	1,686	29
North Carolina	1,573	38
South Carolina	1,639	31
Georgia	1,512	43
Florida	1,701	(x)
East South Central	**1,732**	(x)
Kentucky	1,694	26
Tennessee	1,749	20
Alabama	1,827	17
Mississippi	1,613	32
West South Central	**2,418**	(x)
Arkansas	1,780	19
Louisiana	2,896	3
Oklahoma	1,875	14
Texas	2,492	4
Mountain	**1,682**	(x)
Montana	1,699	25
Idaho	1,556	41
Wyoming	3,031	2
Colorado	1,584	35
New Mexico	1,693	28
Arizona	1,584	35
Utah	1,496	44
Nevada	2,017	6
Pacific	**1,486**	(x)
Washington	1,493	45
Oregon	1,572	39
California	1,426	48
Alaska	3,082	1
Hawaii	1,940	10

(1) Includes sources not shown separately. (2) Based on estimated resident population as of July 1. (3) Includes net imports of coal coke not shown separately by State.

Major U.S. Public and Private Dams and Reservoirs

Source: Corps of Engineers, U.S. Army, mid-1987
Heights over 400 feet.

Height—Difference in elevation in feet, between lowest point in foundation and top of dam, exclusive of parapet or other projections. **Length**—Overall length of barrier in feet, main dam and its integral features as located between natural abutments. **Volume**—Total volume in cubic yards of all material in main dam and its appurtenant works. **Year**—Date structure was originally completed for use. (UC) Under construction subject to revision. **River**—Mainstream. **Purpose**—I-Irrigation; C-Flood Control; H-Hydroelectric; N-Navigation; S-Water Supply; R-Recreation; D-Debris Control; O-Other. **Parentheses** after name indicate type of dam as follows: (RE)-Earth; (PG)-Gravity; (ER)-Rockfill; (CB)-Buttress; (VA)-Arch; (MV)-Multi-arch; (OT)-Other.

Name of dam	State	River	Ht.	Lgth.	Vol. (1,000)	Purpose	Year
Oroville (RE)	Cal.	Feather River	756	6800	78000	RCSH	1968
Hoover (VA)	Nev.	Colorado River	726	1242	4400	IHCO	1936
Dworshak (PG)	Ida.	North Fork of Clearwater	717	3287	6450	HCR	1973
Glen Canyon (VA)	Ariz.	Colorado River	710	1560	4901	HCSR	1966
New Bullards Bar (VA)	Cal.	North Yuba River	635	2200	2600	SH	1970
New Melones (ER)	Cal.	Stanislaus River	625	1560	16000	IHCR	1979
Swift (RE)	Wash.	North Fork Lewis River	610	2100	15400	HRC	1958
Mossyrock (VA)	Wash.	Cowlitz River	606	1648	1270	HCR	1968
Shasta (PG)	Cal.	Sacramento River	602	3460	8711	ISHN	1945
Don Pedro (RE)	Cal.	Tuolumne River	568	1800	16000	H	1971
Hungry Horse (VA)	Mon.	South Fork of Flathead River	564	2115	3086	IHCN	1953
Grand Coulee (PG)	Wash.	Columbia River	550	4173	10585	IHCN	1942
Ross (VA)	Wash.	Skagit River	540	1300	919	HR	1949
Trinity (RE)	Cal.	Trinity River	537	2450	29410	IHCR	1962
Yellowtail (VA)	Mon.	Bighorn River	525	1480	1546	ICHR	1966
Cougar (ER)	Ore.	South Fork McKenzie River	519	1600	13000	HCIR	1964
Flaming Gorge (VA)	Ut.	Green River	502	1285	987	HCSR	1964
Fontana (PG)	N.C.	Little Tennessee River	480	2365	3576	H	1944
New Exchequer (ER)	Cal.	Merced River	479	1240	5169	H	1926
Little Blue Run (RE)	Penn.	Little Blue Run	400	2100	13000	—	1977
Morrow Point (VA)	Col.	Gunnison River	468	741	365	HCR	1968
Carters (ER)	Ga.	Coosawattee River	464	1950	15000	CHR	1974
Detroit (PG)	Ore.	North Santiam River	463	1580	1500	HCRI	1953
Anderson Ranch (RE)	Ida.	South Fork Boise River	456	1350	9653	IHCR	1950
Union Valley (RE)	Cal.	Silver Creek	453	1800	10000	S	1963
Round Butte (RE)	Ore.	Deschutes River	440	1450	9600	HR	1964
Pine Flat Lake (PG)	Cal.	Kings River	440	1840	2400	CIRH	1954
Jocassee (ER)	S.C.	Keowee River	435	1800	11600	H	1973
O'Shaughnessy (PG)	Cal.	Moccasin Creek	430	900	663	HS	1923
Mud Mountain (ER)	Wash.	White River	425	700	2300	C	1948
Libby (PG)	Mon.	Kootenai River	422	2890	3760	HCR	1973
Pacoima (VA)	Cal.	Pacoima Creek	420	640	226	C	1929
Owyhee (VA)	Ore.	Owyhee River	417	833	538	ICR	1932
Lower Hell Hole (ER)	Cal.	Rubicon River	410	1550	8315	SH	1966
Castaic (RE)	Cal.	Castaic Creek	410	5200	44000	IRS	1973
Mammoth Pool (RE)	Cal.	San Joaquin River	406	820	5355	HS	1960
San Gabriel No. 1 (ER)	Cal.	San Gabriel River	405	1520	10600	CS	1939
Navajo (RE)	N.M.	San Juan River	402	3648	26840	IR	1963
No name (RE)	S.C.	Jocassee River	400	1000		H	1972
Pyramid (ER)	Cal.	Piru Creek	400	1080	6952	IRSH	1973
Bath County Upper (ER,RE)	Va.	Little Bush Creek	470	2398	23544	H	1984

MANUFACTURES AND MINERALS

General Statistics for Major Industry Groups

Source: Bureau of the Census

The data in the following table are based upon information from the 1985 Annual Survey of Manufacturers.

Industry Number	All employees (1,000)	All employees Payroll (millions)	Production workers Number (1,000)	Production workers Hours (millions)	Production workers Wages (millions)	Value added by mfr. (millions)
Food and kindred products	1,422.5	28,077.3	993.6	1,941.2	17,427.7	104,146.0
Tobacco products	49.2	1,369.4	36.9	67.8	940.9	11,893.7
Textile mill products	658.4	9,967.1	565.3	1,101.4	7,609.2	20,693.3
Apparel, other textile prods.	1,059.2	12,470.6	904.0	1,580.7	9,003.4	27,728.4
Lumber and wood products	612.9	10,407.4	514.2	996.4	7,835.8	21,065.5
Furniture and fixtures	472.3	7,754.6	380.0	726.8	5,345.5	16,478.8
Paper and allied products	604.1	15,350.8	462.1	943.7	10,783.4	40,387.2
Printing and publishing	1,359.8	28,169.2	742.1	1,384.4	13,554.4	73,054.3
Chemicals, allied products	826.2	23,344.9	476.0	951.2	11,662.0	95,257.5
Petroleum and coal products	127.5	4,131.8	83.5	177.6	2,533.9	17,111.6
Rubber, misc. plastics prod.	742.5	14,722.9	578.4	1,137.7	9,794.2	35,708.3
Leather, leather products	146.7	1,863.2	124.8	225.1	1,342.3	4,107.5
Stone, clay, glass products	519.5	11,476.1	403.8	813.0	8,196.2	28,841.8
Primary metal industries	742.0	19,853.8	571.0	1,134.5	14,277.4	38,081.9
Fabricated metal products	1,472.8	33,150.0	1,103.5	2,200.1	21,976.8	69,161.5
Machinery, except electric	1,991.1	50,904.6	1,236.6	2,434.7	26,510.5	110,224.1
Electric, electronic equip.	2,007.1	48,504.0	1,233.1	2,373.6	23,658.8	109,861.5
Transportation equipment	1,757.0	54,591.8	1,179.6	2,406.6	33,171.4	120,953.1
Instruments, related prods.	604.3	14,666.4	348.0	676.4	6,692.6	40,278.3
Misc. manufacturing indus.	328.0	5,725.7	234.6	452.5	3,415.3	14,031.6
Auxiliaries[2]	1,288.1	46,484.6	—	—	—	—
All industries, total	**18,791.2**	**442,986.2**	**12,171.1**	**23,725.4**	**235,731.7**	**999,065.8**

*Not including government owned and operated establishments.

Manufacturing Production Worker Statistics

Source: Bureau of Labor Statistics, U.S. Labor Department (p — preliminary)

Year	All employees	Production workers	Constant Dollars[1]	Avg. weekly earnings	Avg. hourly earnings	Avg. hrs. per wk.
1955	16,882,000	13,288,000	—	$75.30	$1.85	40.7
1960	16,796,000	12,586,000	183.5	89.72	2.26	39.7
1965	18,062,000	13,434,000	206.4	107.53	2.61	41.2
1970	19,367,000	14,044,000	208.0	133.33	3.35	39.8
1975	18,323,000	13,043,000	214.9	190.79	4.83	39.5
1979	21,040,000	15,068,000	224.6	269.34	6.70	40.2
1980	20,285,000	14,214,000	212.0	288.62	7.27	39.7
1985	19,260,000	13,092,000	220.15	386.37	9.54	40.5
1986	18,994,000	12,895,000	222.23	396.01	9.73	40.7
1987 Jan.	18,956,000	12,884,000	222.30	401.47	9.84	40.9
Feb.	18,980,000	12,910,000	221.44	401.47	9.84	41.1
Mar.	18,995,000	12,925,000	221.24	402.87	9.85	40.9
Apr.	19,011,000	12,941,000	217.66	398.75	9.87	40.6
May[p]	19,016,000	12,955,000	NA	403.27	9.86	41.0

(1) Earnings in current dollars divided by the Consumer Price Index on a 1977 basis.

Retail Store Sales

Source: Bureau of the Census, U.S. Department of Commerce
(millions of dollars)

Kind of business	1985	1986
Retail trade, total	**1,379,621**	**1,454,411**
Durable goods, total	**517,981**	**568,057**
Automotive dealers	311,859	335,822
Motor vehicle, other miscellaneous automotive dealers	285,479	309,248
Auto and home supply stores	26,380	26,574
Furniture, home furnishings, equipment stores	69,584	78,487
Furniture, home furnishings stores	37,451	41,830
Household appliance, radio, and TV stores	27,403	31,147
Building materials, hardware, garden supply, and mobile home dealers	75,556	88,093
Building materials and supply stores	55,695	65,572
Hardware stores	10,397	10,706
Nondurable goods stores, total	**861,640**	**886,354**
Apparel and accessory stores	74,321	80,775

Kind of business	1985	1986
Men's, boys' clothing, furnishings stores	8,826	9,567
Women's clothing, specialty stores, furriers	30,901	33,899
Shoe stores	14,010	14,927
Food stores	283,987	296,040
Grocery stores	267,004	278,483
General merchandise group stores	149,952	155,262
Department stores	135,528	142,503
Variety stores	8,854	8,449
Eating and drinking places	133,457	144,966
Restaurants, lunchrooms, cafe	73,209	77,986
Drinking places	10,534	11,581
Gasoline service stations	101,266	86,618
Drug stores	46,191	49,316
Liquor stores	19,491	19,792

Total retail stores sales (millions of dollars) — (1955) 183,851; (1958) 200,353; (1959) 215,413; (1960) 219,529; (1961) 218,992; (1962) 235,563; (1963) 246,666; (1964) 261,870; (1965) 284,128; (1966) 303,956; (1967) 292,956; (1968) 324,358; (1969) 346,717; (1970) 368,403; (1971) 406,234; (1972) 449,069; (1973) 509,538; (1974) 540,988; (1975) 588,146; (1976) 657,375; (1977) 725,212; (1978) 806,773; (1979) 899,116; (1980) 959,561; (1981) 1,041,327; (1982) 1,072,100; (1983) 1,174,298; (1984) 1,289,373.

Sales and Profits of Manufacturing Corporations by Industry Group

Source: Bureau of the Census—Economic Surveys Division

(millions of dollars)

Industry group	Sales			Income after taxes		
	1Q 1986	4Q 1986	1Q 1987	1Q 1986	4Q 1986	1Q 1987
All manufacturing corporations	543,986	564,457	553,233	19,386	18,706	23,959
Nondurable manufacturing corporations	273,254	274,486	273,150	11,605	12,276	13,890
Food and kindred products, incl. tobacco	74,301	80,475	77,880	2,686	4,153	2,879
Textile mill products	11,529	11,265	11,211	339	498	379
Paper and allied products	17,521	19,948	19,941	583	957	996
Printing and publishing	25,057	29,327	27,471	1,519	2,121	1,273
Chemicals and allied products	51,249	49,849	51,605	3,134	2,139	4,251
Industrial chemicals and synthetics	20,325	19,788	20,713	1,343	549	1,477
Drugs	9,312	9,552	10,088	1,179	1,600	1,476
Petroleum and coal products	65,806	52,703	54,562	2,720	1,539	2,821
Rubber and miscellaneous plastics products	14,437	15,533	14,732	351	295	821
Other nondurable manufacturing corporations	13,355	15,385	15,747	273	574	470
Durable manufacturing corporations	270,732	289,971	280,083	7,781	6,431	10,068
Stone, clay, and glass products	11,242	14,051	12,288	187	614	660
Primary metal industries	21,221	21,032	21,465	−189	−290	630
Iron and steel	11,651	11,647	11,951	−343	−470	352
Nonferrous metals	9,570	9,385	9,514	155	180	278
Fabricated metal products	27,773	29,539	29,747	835	617	513
Machinery, except electrical	48,072	52,031	48,993	1,352	1,404	751
Electrical and electronic equipment	47,128	49,764	47,295	1,746	1,967	1,982
Transportation equipment	79,233	83,981	82,867	3,545	1,770	3,920
Motor vehicles and equipment	49,776	49,870	51,935	2,464	1,759	2,903
Aircraft, guided missiles, and parts	25,802	30,159	27,309	1,047	−75	1,034
Instruments and related products	14,960	16,358	15,535	−116	−472	980
Other durable manufacturing corporations	21,103	23,216	21,891	422	821	631
All mining corporations*	**9,557**	**7,904**	**7,870**	**−1,070**	**−1,121**	**−338**
All retail trade corporations*	**110,569**	**140,833**	**NA**	**1,588**	**5,064**	**NA**
All wholesale trade corporations*	**142,498**	**141,418**	**139,927**	**1,033**	**1,827**	**1,683**

*With assets over $25 million.

Annual Percent Change in Productivity and Related Data, 1975-1986

Source: Bureau of Labor Statistics, U.S. Labor Department

Item	1975	1976	1977	1978	1979	1980	1981	1982	1983	1984	1985	1986
Business sector:												
Output per hour of all persons	2.0	2.8	1.7	0.8	−1.2	−0.3	1.4	−0.4	2.7	2.5	1.8	1.9
Real compensation per hour	0.5	2.9	1.3	0.8	−1.4	−2.7	−1.0	1.6	1.0	−0.2	1.1	2.0
Unit labor cost	7.6	5.9	6.0	7.6	11.1	10.9	7.7	8.3	1.4	1.5	2.8	2.0
Unit nonlabor payments	15.5	5.8	7.1	6.7	5.4	5.6	13.4	1.5	7.2	6.9	2.4	2.2
Implicit price deflator	10.3	5.9	6.4	7.3	9.0	9.0	9.6	5.9	3.3	3.3	2.7	2.1
Nonfarm business section:												
Output per hour of all persons	1.8	2.6	1.6	0.8	−1.6	−0.4	1.0	−0.6	3.3	2.1	1.2	1.6
Real compensation per hour	0.5	2.5	1.2	0.9	−1.6	−2.7	−0.9	1.5	1.1	−0.3	0.8	1.9
Unit labor cost	7.8	5.7	6.1	7.7	11.2	11.0	8.3	8.4	1.0	1.8	3.2	2.2
Unit nonlabor payments	17.1	7.4	7.5	5.6	4.6	7.3	12.6	2.2	8.7	5.5	3.2	2.4
Implicit price deflator	10.8	6.3	6.6	7.0	8.9	9.7	9.7	6.3	3.5	3.0	3.2	2.3
Manufacturing:												
Output per hour of all persons	2.5	4.6	3.0	1.5	−0.1	0.0	2.2	2.2	5.8	5.5	5.1	3.7
Real compensation per hour	2.4	2.3	2.0	0.5	−1.4	−1.7	−0.7	2.2	−0.1	−0.8	1.6	1.3
Unit labor cost	9.1	3.5	5.4	6.6	9.7	11.7	7.3	6.2	−2.5	−1.9	0.2	−0.4
Unit nonlabor payments	29.2	6.9	6.9	1.9	−2.9	−1.1	14.3	1.9	12.7	7.9	−2.8	2.4
Implicit price deflator	14.1	4.4	5.9	5.2	6.2	8.4	8.9	5.1	1.1	0.7	−0.7	0.4

U.S. Reliance on Foreign Supplies of Minerals

Source: Bureau of Mines, U.S. Interior Department

Mineral	Percent imported in 1986	Major sources (1982-85)	Major uses
Columbium	100%	Brazil, Canada, Thailand, Nigeria	Steelmaking and aerospace alloys
Graphite	100	Mexico, China, Brazil, Madagascar	Metallurgical processes
Manganese	100	South Africa, France, Brazil, Gabon	Steelmaking
Mica (sheet)	100	India, Belgium, France, Japan	Electronic and electrical equipment
Strontium	100	Mexico, Spain	Television picture tubes, pyrotechnics
Platinum group	98	South Africa, Britain, USSR	Catalytic converters for autos, electrical and electronic equipment
Bauxite and alumina	97	Australia, Guinea, Jamaica, Suriname	Aluminum production
Cobalt	92	Zaire, Zambia, Canada, Norway	Aeorspace alloys
Diamonds (industrial)	92	South Africa, Britain, Ireland, Belgium	Machinery for grinding and cutting
Tantalum	91	Thailand, Brazil, Australia, Malaysia	Electronic components
Fluorspar	88	Mexico, South Africa, China, Italy	Raw material for metallurgical and chemical industries
Chromium	82	South Africa, Zimbabwe, Turkey, Yugoslavia	Stainless steel
Nickel	78	Canada, Australia, Norway, Botswana	Stainless steel and other alloys
Potash	78	Canada, Israel, East Germany, USSR	Fertilizer
Tin	77	Thailand, Brazil, Indonesia, Bolivia	Cans, electrical construction
Zinc	74	Canada, Mexico, Peru, Australia	Construction and transportation materials
Cadmium	69	Canada, Australia, Mexico, West Germany	Plating and coating of metals
Silver	69	Canada, Mexico, Britain, Peru	Photography, electrical and electronic components
Barite	66	China, Morocco, India, Chile	Oil drilling fluids

U.S. Pig Iron and Steel Output

Source: American Iron and Steel Institute (net tons)

Year	Total pig iron	Raw steel	Year	Total pig iron	Raw steel
1940	46,071,666	66,982,686	1975	101,208,000	116,642,000
1945	53,223,169	79,701,648	1980	68,721,000	111,835,000
1950	64,586,907	96,836,075	1981	73,570,000	120,828,000
1955	76,857,417	117,036,085	1982	43,309,000	74,577,000
1960	66,480,648	99,281,601	1984	51,904,000	92,528,000
1965	88,184,901	131,461,601	1985	50,446,000	88,259,000
1970	91,435,000	131,514,000	1986	43,952,000	81,606,000

Steel figures include only that portion of the capacity and production of steel for castings used by foundries which were operated by companies producing steel ingots.

U.S. Copper, Lead, and Zinc Production

Source: Bureau of Mines, U.S. Interior Department

Year	Copper		Lead		Zinc		Year	Copper		Lead		Zinc	
	Quantity (metric tons	Value ($1,000)	Quantity (metric tons)	Value ($1,000)	Quantity (metric tons)	Value ($1,000)		Quantity (metric tons)	Value ($1,000)	Quantity (metric tons)	Value ($1,000)	Quantity (metric tons	Value ($1,000)
1950	827	379,122	390,839	113,078	565,516	167,000	1982	1,147	1,840,856	512,516	288,579	303,160	257,116
1960	1,037	733,706	223,774	57,722	395,013	112,365	1983	1,038	1,751,476	449,295	214,745	275,294	251,204
1965	1,226	957,028	273,196	93,959	554,429	178,284	1984	1,103	1,625,116	322,677	181,745	252,768	270,833
1970	1,560	1,984,484	518,698	178,609	484,560	163,650	1985	1,106	1,632,483	413,955	174,008	226,545	201,607
1975	1,282	1,814,763	563,783	267,230	425,792	366,097	1986	1,147	1,670,665	339,793	165,150	202,983	170,049
1980	1,181	2,666,931	550,366	515,189	317,103	261,671							

Cotton, Wool, Silk, and Man-Made Fibers Production

Source: Economics, Statistics, and Cooperatives Service, U.S. Agriculture Department

Cotton and wool from reports of the Agriculture Department; silk, rayon, and non-cellulosic man-made fibers from Textile Organon, a publication of the Textile Economics Bureau, Inc.

Year	Cotton[1]		Wool[2]		Silk	Man-made fibers[3]			
						Cellulosic		Non-cellulosic[4]	
	U.S.	World	U.S.	World	World	U.S.	World	U.S.[4]	World[6]
	(million bales)[5]		(million pounds)		(mil. lbs.)	(million pounds)		(million pounds)	
1940	12.6	31.2	434.0	4,180	130	471.2	2,485.3	4.6	4.6
1950	10.0	30.6	249.3	4,000	42	1,259.4	3,552.8	145.9	177.4
1960	14.2	46.2	298.9	5,615	68	1,028.5	5,749.1	854.2	1,779.1
1965	14.9	55.0	224.8	5,731	72	1,527.0	7,359.4	2,062.4	4,928.9
1970	10.2	50.0	170.0	6,107	90	1,373.2	7,573.9	4,053.5	10,361.7
1975	8.3	54.0	125.5	5,911	104	749.0	6,523.2	6,432.2	17,344.6
1980	11.1	[illegible]	106.6	[illegible]	[illegible]	[illegible]	[illegible]	[illegible]	[illegible]
1981	15.6	70.8	110.9	6,367	126	770.1	7,063.8	9,047.0	23,869.2
1983	7.8	67.9	102.9	6,466	121	630.3	6,661.0	8,705.6	24,414.9
1984	13.0	85.8	92.9	6,539	121	620.1	6,784.2	8,865.7	26,216.6

(1) Year beginning Aug. 1. (2) Grease basis. (3) Includes filament yarn and staple and tow fiber. (4) Includes textile glass fiber. (5) 480-pound net weight bales, U.S. beginning 1960 and world beginning 1965. (6) 1966 to date, excludes Olefin.

Clean Water Act Funds by State

In 1987, Congress voted to spend $20 billion dollars to reduce water pollution in the United States. The Clean Water Act allocated construction grants and funds through 1994. The annual allotments of federal funds from fiscal year 1988 to fiscal year 1990 are shown below. Allocations from 1991-1994 will be determined at a later date.

State	Millions of Dollars	State	Millions of Dollars	State	Millions of Dollars
Alabama	27.1	Kentucky	30.9	North Dakota	11.9
Alaska	14.5	Louisiana	26.7	Ohio	136.6
Arizona	16.4	Maine	18.8	Oklahoma	19.6
Arkansas	15.9	Maryland	58.7	Oregon	27.4
California	173.6	Massachusetts	82.4	Pennsylvania	96.1
Colorado	19.4	Michigan	104.4	Rhode Island	16.3
Connecticut	29.7	Minnesota	44.6	South Carolina	24.9
Delaware	11.9	Mississippi	21.9	South Dakota	11.9
Dist. of Col.	11.9	Missouri	67.3	Tennessee	35.3
Florida	81.9	Montana	11.9	Texas	110.9
Georgia	41.0	Nebraska	12.4	Utah	12.8
Hawaii	18.8	Nevada	11.9	Vermont	11.9
Idaho	11.9	New Hampshire	24.3	Virginia	49.7
Illinois	109.8	New Jersey	99.2	Washington	42.2
Indiana	58.5	New Mexico	11.9	West Virginia	37.8
Iowa	32.9	NewYork	267.9	Wisconsin	65.6
Kansas	21.9	North Carolina	43.8	Wyoming	11.9

U.S. Nonfuel Mineral Production

Source: Bureau of Mines, U.S. Interior Department

Production as measured by mine shipments, sales, or marketable production (including consumption by producers)

		1984		1985	
Metals		Quantity	Value (thousands)	Quantity	Value (thousands)
Antimony ore and concentrate	short tons, antimony content	557	W	W	W
Bauxite	thousand metric tons, dried equivalent	856	$15,643	[p]565	[p]$9,000
Copper (recoverable content of ores, etc.)	metric tons	1,091,284	1,608,422	[p]1,050,000	[p]1,500,000
Gold (recoverable content of ores, etc.)	troy ounces	[r]2,084,615	751,833	2,475,436	786,345
Iron ore, usable (excluding byproduct iron sinter) thousand long tons, gross weight		W	W	W	W
Iron oxide pigments, crude	short tons	53,017	2,819	46,585	2,826
Lead (recoverable content of ores, etc.)	metric tons	[r]322,677	181,745	413,955	174,008
Manganiferous ore (5% to 35% Mn)	short tons, gross weight	88,423	860	19,882	W
Mercury	76-pound flasks	19,048	W	16,530	W
Molybdenum (content of concentrate)	thousand pounds	102,405	326,780	111,936	347,812
Nickel (content of ore and concentrate)	short tons	14,540	W	6,127	W
Silver (recoverable content of ores, etc.)	thousand troy ounces	44,440	361,773	[p]43,000	[p]267,000
Titanium concentrate:					
Ilmenite	short tons, gross weight	W	W	W	W
Tungsten ore and concentrate	metric tons, contained W	1,173	13,409	983	9,143
Vanadium (recoverable in ore and concentrate)	short tons	1,617	24,551	W	W
Zinc (recoverable content of ores, etc.)	metric tons	252,768	270,833	[p]225,000	[p]200,000
Combined value of beryllium concentrates, magnesium chloride for magnesium metal, rare-earth metal concentrate, tin, titanium concentrates (rutile), zircon concentrate, and values indicated by symbol W		XX	2,427,624	XX	2,291,386
Total metals		**XX**	**5,986,000**	**XX**	**5,588,000**
Nonmetals (except fuels)					
Abrasive stones[2]	short tons	1,290	602	1,157	515
Asbestos	metric tons	57,422	24,238	57,457	20,485
Barite	thousand short tons	775	25,445	739	21,501
Boron minerals	do	1,367	456,687	NA	NA
Bromine	thousand pounds	385,000	95,000	320,000	80,000
Calcium chloride	short tons	[e]838,000	[e]93,000	W	W
Cement:					
Masonry	thousand short tons	3,281	219,877	[p]3,400	231,000
Portland	do	74,376	3,810,446	[p]76,000	3,970,000
Clays	do	44,236	1,037,233	[p]45,630	1,000,000
Diatomite	do	627	120,926	635	127,030
Feldspar	short tons	710,000	23,500	700,000	22,800
Fluorspar	do	72,000	W	66,000	W
Garnet (abrasive)	do	29,647	[e]2,487	36,727	2,212
Gem stones(e)		NA	7,450	NA	7,425
Gypsum	thousand short tons	14,319	113,671	14,726	114,229
Helium (Grade A) Crude	million cubic feet	[r]1,642	[r]61,575	1,865	69,938
Lime	thousand short tons	15,922	811,183	15,713	812,249
Magnesium compounds	short tons	W	W	W	W
Mica:					
Scrap	thousand short tons	161	7,139	138	6,330
Peat	do	814	19,907	882	21,892
Perlite	short tons	498,000	16,638	507,000	17,160
Phosphate rock	thousand metric tons	49,197	1,182,244	50,835	1,203,265
Potassium salts	thousand metric tons, $K^{2}O$ equivalent	1,639	241,800	1,266	178,400
Pumice	thousand short tons	502	4,929	508	4,553
Pyrites	thousand metric tons	W	W	W	W
Salt	thousand short tons	39,225	675,099	[p]39,700	[p]690,000
Sand and gravel (construction)	do	773,900	2,244,000	[p]801,000	2,434,500
Sand and gravel (industrial)	do	29,380	377,200	29,900	389,100
Sodium sulfate (natural)	do	435	40,125	389	35,860
Stone[4] (crushed)	do	[e]956,000	[e]3,755,600	[p]1,005,000	[p]4,167,000
Stone[4] (dimension)	do	[e]1,157	[3]154,949	[p]1,299	[p]169,785
Sulfur, Frasch process	thousand metric tons	5,001	546,106	4,678	573,570
Talc and pyrophyllite	thousand short tons	1,170	24,745	1,269	29,188
Tripoli	short tons	124,482	699	W	W
Vermiculite	thousand short tons	315	31,500	314	32,000
Combined value of aplite, asphalt (native), emery, graphite, helium (crude), iodine, kyanite, lithium minerals, magnesite, marl (greensand), olivine, sodium carbonate (natural), staurolite, wollastonite, and values indicated by symbol W		XX	937,900	XX	1,096,796
Total nonmetals		**XX**	**[r]17,164,000**	**XX**	**17,530,000**
Grand total		**XX**	**25,150,000**	**XX**	**23,120,000**

(e) Estimate. (p) Preliminary. (r) Revised. (W) Withheld to avoid disclosing company proprietary data; included in "Combined value" figures. (XX) Not applicable. (NA) Not available.
(1) Production as measured by mine shipments, sales, or marketable production (including consumption by producers).
(2) Grindstones, pulpstones, sharpening stones, excludes mill liners & grinding pebbles.
(3) Excludes output in New Mexico, withheld to avoid disclosing company proprietary data.
(4) Excludes abrasive stone, bituminous limestone and sandstone; all included elsewhere in table.

Minerals

Source: Bureau of Mines, U.S. Interior Department, 1986

Aluminum: the 2d most abundant metal element in the Earth's crust after silicon. Bauxite is the main source of aluminum; convert to aluminum equivalent by multiplying by 0.211. Guinea and Australia have 46 percent of the world's reserves. It is used in the U.S. in packaging 30%, transportation 22% and building 22%.

Chromium: some 99 percent of the world's chromite is found in South Africa and Zimbabwe. The chemical and metallurgical industries use about 85% of the chromite consumed in the U.S.

Cobalt: used in jet engine parts, cutting tools, electronic devices, and pigments for paints and allied products. Principal cobalt producing countries include Zaire, Zambia, and the USSR. The U.S. uses about one-third of total world consumption. Although resources are relatively large, the U.S. has produced no cobalt since 1971; cobalt resources are low grade and production from these deposits is not economically feasible.

Columbium: used mostly as an alloying element in steels and superalloys. Brazil and Canada are the world's leading producers. There is no significant U.S. columbium mining industry.

Copper: main uses of copper in the U.S. are in building construction 41%, electrical and electronic products 23%, industrial machinery and equipment 14%, transportation 12%. The leading producer is Chile, followed by the U.S., USSR, Canada, Zambia, and Zaire. Principal mining states are Arizona, New Mexico, and Utah.

Gold: used in the U.S. in jewelry and arts 48%, industrial (mainly electronic) 35%, dental 16%. South Africa has about half of the world's resources; significant quantities are also present in the U.S., Canada, USSR, and Brazil. Gold mining in the U.S. takes place in nearly all of the western states and Alaska.

Iron ore: the source of primary iron for the world's iron and steel industries. Major iron ore producers include the USSR, Brazil, Australia, and China.

Lead: the U.S. is the world's largest producer and consumer of lead metal. Transportation accounted for the major end use in the U.S. with 71% used in batteries, gasoline additives, and other applications. Other uses include emergency power supply batteries, construction sheeting, sporting ammunition and TV tubes. Other major mine producers include the USSR, Australia, and Canada.

Manganese: essential to iron and steel production. The U.S., Japan, and Western Europe are all nearly deficient in economically minable manganese. South Africa and the USSR have nearly 80% of the world's reserves.

Nickel: vital to the iron and steel industry and played a key role in the development of the chemical and aerospace industries. Leading producers include the USSR, Canada, Japan and Australia.

Platinum-Group Metals: the platinum group comprises 6 closely related metals: platinum, palladium, rhodium, ruthenium, iridium, and osmium. They commonly occur together in nature and are among the scarcest of the metallic elements. They are consumed in the U.S. by the following industries: automotive 46%, electrical and electronic 18%, and dental and medical 15%. The USSR and South Africa have over 90% of the world's reserves.

Silver: used in the following U.S. industries: photography 46%; electrical and electronic products 26%; sterlingware, electroplated ware, and jewelry 10%. Silver is mined in more than 54 countries. Idaho produces over 30% of the U.S. silver.

Tantalum: a refractory metal with unique electrical, chemical, and physical properties which is mostly used in the U.S in electrical machinery and transportation industries. Thailand, Australia, and Brazil are the leading producers. There is no significant U.S. tantalum mining industry.

Titanium: a metal which is mostly used in jet engines, airframes, and space and missile applications. It is produced in the USSR, Japan, and the western and central U.S.

Vanadium: used as an alloying element in steel. The USSR and South Africa are the world's largest producers.

Zinc: used as protective coating on steel, as diecastings, as an alloying metal with copper to make brass, and as chemical compounds in rubber and paints. It is mined in over 50 countries with Canada the leading producer, followed by the USSR, Australia, Peru and Spain. In the U.S., mine production comes mostly from Tennessee, Missouri, and New York.

World Mineral Reserve Base

Source: Bureau of Mines, U.S. Interior Department

Mineral	Reserve Base[1]	Mineral	Reserve Base[1]
Aluminum	23,000 mln. metric tons[2]	Nickel	111,000 thousand short tons
Chromium	7,500 mln. short tons	Platinum—Group Metals	2,100 mln. troy oz.
Cobalt	18,400 mln. lbs.	Silver	10,800 mln. troy oz.
Columbium	11,000 mln. lbs.	Tantalum	90 mln. lbs.
Copper	566 mln. metric tons	Titanium	NA
Gold	1,490 mln. troy oz.	Vanadium	18,300 thousand short tons
Iron	206,000 mln. long tons[3]	Zinc	290 mln. metric tons
Lead	142 mln. metric tons		
Manganese	4,000,000 thousand short tons		

(1) Includes demonstrated resources that are currently economic (reserves), marginally economic (marginal reserves), and some of those that are currently subeconomic. (2) Bauxite. (3) Crude ore.

U.S. Nonfuel Mineral Production—Leading States

Source: Bureau of Mines, U.S. Interior Department

1986 State	Value (thousands)	Principal minerals
California	$2,300,000	Cement, boron minerals, sand and gravel (construction), stone (crushed).
Texas	1,900,000	Cement, stone (crushed), sand and gravel (construction), lime, salt.
Arizona	1,600,000	Copper, gold, silver, molybdenum.
Florida	1,500,000	Stone (crushed), cement, phosphate rock.
Michigan	1,400,000	Cement, sand & gravel, salt.
Minnesota	1,200,000	Iron ore, sand and gravel (construction), stone (crushed), sand and gravel (industrial).
Georgia	1,100,000	Clays, stone (crushed).
Pennsylvania	833,000	Cement, stone (crushed), lime, sand and gravel (construction).
Missouri	764,500	Cement, lead, zinc.
New York	647,000	Stone (crushed), salt, cement.
New Mexico	608,400	Sand & gravel, potassium salts.

TRADE AND TRANSPORTATION

U.S. Foreign Trade with Leading Countries

Source: Office of Industry and Trade Information, U.S. Commerce Department

(millions of dollars)

Exports from the U.S. to the following areas and countries and imports into the U.S. from those areas and countries:	Exports			Imports		
	1980	1985	1986	1980	1985	1986
Total	**220,705**	**213,146**	**217,304**	**240,834**	**345,276**	**387,081**
Western Hemisphere	**74,114**	**78,271**	**76,411**	**78,489**	**115,916**	**110,201**
Canada	35,395	47,251	45,333	41,455	69,006	68,253
20 Latin American Republics	36,030	27,850	27,969	29,851	43,448	39,541
Central American Common Market	1,951	1,622	1,768	1,849	1,722	2,061
Dominican Republic	795	742	921	786	982	1,085
Panama	699	675	712	330	410	366
Bahamas	396	786	761	1,382	626	442
Jamaica	305	404	457	383	273	299
Netherlands Antilles	448	427	398	2,564	808	471
Trinidad and Tobago	680	504	532	2,378	1,358	793
Western Europe	**71,372**	**56,763**	**61,642**	**47,849**	**79,756**	**89,825**
OECD countries (excludes depend. and Yugo.)	66,654	56,084	61,003	45,952	79,165	89,130
European Economic Community	53,679	48,994	53,154	35,958	64,761	75,736
Belgium and Luxembourg	6,661	4,918	5,399	1,914	3,387	4,006
Denmark	863	706	758	725	1,665	1,757
France	7,485	6,096	6,216	5,247	9,482	10,129
Germany, Federal Republic of	10,960	9,050	10,561	11,681	20,239	25,124
Ireland	836	1,342	1,434	411	901	1,003
Italy	5,511	4,625	4,838	4,313	9,674	10,607
Netherlands	8,669	7,269	7,848	1,910	4,081	4,066
United Kingdom	12,694	11,273	11,418	9,755	14,937	15,396
Austria	448	441	464	388	834	864
Finland	505	438	381	439	895	908
Iceland	79	38	80	200	248	238
Norway	843	666	937	2,632	1,164	1,079
Portugal	911	695	638	256	546	552
Sweden	1,767	1,925	1,871	1,617	4,124	4,420
Switzerland	3,781	2,288	2,977	2,787	3,476	5,253
Greece	922	498	430	292	395	395
Spain	3,179	2,524	2,615	1,209	2,515	2,702
Turkey	540	1,295	1,160	175	602	633
Yugoslavia	756	595	528	446	542	646
Eastern Europe	**3,860**	**3,215**	**1,900**	**1,433**	**1,936**	**2,001**
USSR	1,513	2,423	1,248	453	409	558
Asia	**60,168**	**60,745**	**64,532**	**78,848**	**131,885**	**153,869**
Near East	**11,900**	**9,709**	**8,415**	**17,280**	**6,267**	**7,890**
Iran	23	74	34	339	725	569
Iraq	724	427	528	352	474	440
Israel	2,045	2,580	2,239	943	2,123	2,418
Jordan	407	377	332	3	14	10
Kuwait	886	551	657	472	184	267
Lebanon	303	141	106	33	19	30
Saudi Arabia	5,769	4,474	3,449	12,509	1,907	3,612
Syria	239	106	59	26	3	8
Japan	**20,790**	**22,631**	**26,882**	**30,701**	**68,783**	**81,911**
East and South Asia	**27,478**	**24,530**	**26,099**	**30,867**	**52,969**	**59,296**
Bangladesh	292	219	165	85	196	230
China, People's Republic of	3,755	3,856	3,106	1,054	3,862	4,771
China (Taiwan)	4,337	4,700	5,524	6,850	16,396	19,791
Hong Kong	2,686	2,786	3,030	4,736	8,396	12,729
India	1,689	1,642	1,536	1,098	2,295	2,283
Indonesia	1,545	795	946	5,183	4,569	3,112
Korea, Republic of	4,685	5,956	6,355	4,147	10,013	12,729
Malaysia	1,337	1,539	1,730	2,577	2,300	2,421
Pakistan	642	1,042	830	128	274	325
Philippines	1,999	1,379	1,363	1,730	2,145	1,972
Singapore	3,033	3,476	3,380	1,920	4,260	4,725
Thailand	1,263	1,113	936	816	1,326	1,746
Oceania	**4,876**	**6,399**	**6,659**	**3,392**	**3,819**	**3,717**
Australia	4,093	5,441	5,551	2,509	2,837	2,632
New Zealand and Samoa	599	729	883	703	883	984
Africa	**9,060**	**7,388**	**5,978**	**32,251**	**11,964**	**10,348**
Algeria	542	430	553	6,577	2,333	1,831
Botswana	...	16	20	...	29	2
Egypt	1,874	2,323	1,982	458	79	112
Gabon	48	91	25	278	502	
Ghana	127	54	84	206	90	191
Ivory Coast	185	70	60	288	525	425
Kenya	141	97	70	54	92	141
Liberia	113	73	65	128	83	82
Libya	509	311	46	7,124	44	2
Morocco	344	279	487	35	39	43
Nigeria	1,150	676	409	10,905	3,002	2,530
South Africa, Rep. of	2,464	1,205	1,159	3,321	2,071	2,365
Sudan	143	243	90	17	9	22
Tunisia	174	256	163	60	13	11
Zaire	155	105	105	361	401	221

U.S. Exports and Imports of Leading Commodities

Source: Office of Industry and Trade Information, U.S. Commerce Department (millions of dollars)

Commodity	Exports 1980	Exports 1985	Exports 1986	Imports 1980	Imports 1985	Imports 1986
Food and live animals	**27,744**	**19,268**	**17,303**	**15,763**	**18,649**	**20,803**
Cattle, except for breeding	...	...	...	228	301	422
Meat and preparations	1,293	1,153	1,424	2,346	2,237	2,367
Dairy products and eggs	255	388	407	318	406	415
Fish	915	1,016	1,297	2,612	3,985	4,691
Grains and preparations	18,079	11,050	7,368	...	...	...
Wheat, including flour	6,586	3,959	3,217	...	...	...
Rice	1,285	665	621	...	...	...
Grains and Animal feed	2,878	1,890	2,622	331	699	737
Vegetables and Fruit	...	2,435	2,657	1,188	3,978	4,200
Sugar	...	...	...	1,988	936	670
Coffee, crude	...	...	...	3,872	3,130	4,293
Cocoa or cacao beans	...	...	...	395	564	418
Tea	...	...	...	131	166	133
Beverages and tobacco	**2,663**	**2,958**	**2,902**	**2,772**	**3,727**	**3,866**
Alcoholic beverages	...	...	...	2,220	2,966	3,066
Tobacco, unmanufactured	2,390	1,521	1,210	422	535	591
Crude materials, inedible, except fuels	**23,791**	**16,936**	**17,324**	**10,496**	**10,391**	**10,432**
Hides and skins	694	1,088	1,314	88	73	65
Oilseeds, oil nuts, oil kernels	5,883	3,906	4,334	...	98	65
Synthetic rubber and rubber latex	695	584	649	...	...	...
Lumber and rough wood	2,675	2,037	2,240	2,134	3,087	3,140
Wood pulp and pulpwood	2,454	1,955	2,318	1,725	1,551	1,547
Textile fibers and wastes	2,864	1,633	...	242	16	358
Ores and metal scrap	4,518	2,692	2,802	3,696	2,331	2,148
Mineral fuels and related materials	**7,982**	**9,971**	**8,115**	**9,058**	**53,917**	**37,310**
Coal	4,523	8,952	7,867	...	...	...
Petroleum and products	2,833	4,707	3,640	73,771	49,607	34,140
Natural gas	...	...	...	5,155	4,136	2,994
Animal and vegetable oils and fats	**1,946**	**1,434**	**1,015**	**533**	**672**	**516**
Chemicals	**20,740**	**21,759**	**22,766**	**8,583**	**14,533**	**15,001**
Medicines and pharmaceuticals	1,932	2,708	3,090	508	1,084	1,240
Fertilizers, manufactured	2,265	2,160	1,935	1,104	967	865
Plastic materials and resins	3,884	3,777	4,301	...	...	...
Machinery and transport equip.	**84,629**	**94,278**	**95,290**	**60,546**	**137,264**	**161,562**
Machinery	55,790	59,488	60,397	31,904	75,299	87,549
Aircraft engines and parts	1,915	3,316	3,729			
Auto engines and parts	1,688	2,494	2,269	...	...	4,495
Agricultural machinery	3,104	1,601	1,421	682	1,431	1,584
Tractors and parts	1,809	775	...	...	1,156	972
Office machines and computers	8,709	14,928	15,456	2,929	11,562	14,669
Transport equipment	28,839	34,790	34,893	28,642	61,965	74,013
Road motor vehicles and parts	14,590	17,579	18,575	24,134	45,476	54,661
Aircraft and parts except engines	12,816	14,373	15,106	1,885	3,578	4,494
Other manufactured goods	**42,714**	**39,347**	**16,629**	**55,900**	**94,982**	**103,559**
Tires and tubes	511	343	315	1,143	1,923	1,986
Wood and manufactures, exc. furniture	2,675	...	...	632	820	901
Paper and manufactures	2,831	2,329	2,602	3,587	3,977	6,360
Glassware and pottery	...	...	...	1,224	2,195	2,492
Diamonds, excl. industrial	...	...	...	2,252	3,006	3,459
Nonmetallic mineral manuf.	2,209	1,820	1,886	...	...	...
Metal manufactures	4,205	3,253	3,008	...	6,560	7,129
Pig iron and ferroalloys	3,123	...	...	...	...	...
Iron and steel-mill products	2,998	1,157	1,081	6,686	4,237	8,168
Nonferrous base metals	2,964	1,534	...	7,623	2,445	7,699
Textiles, other than clothing	3,632	627	573	2,493	4,897	9,221
Clothing	1,203	6,505	899	6,427	14,949	17,288
Footwear	...	...	...	2,808	5,695	6,473
Furniture	521	560	534	...	...	...
Professional, scientific, controlling instruments	6,763	7,815	6,733	...	3,211	3,888
Printed matter	1,097	1,279	1,342	613	1,116	1,376
Clocks and watches	133	84	83	1,097	1,367	1,536
Toys, games, sporting goods	1,012	579	628	1,914	4,074	4,728
Artworks and antiques	...	...	...	2,672	2,188	2,092
Other transactions	**8,496**	**10,971**	**11,011**	**7,183**	**11,141**	**14,914**
Total	**220,705**	**213,446**	**206,376**	**240,834**	**345,276**	**369,961**

Value of U.S. Exports, Imports, and Merchandise Balance

Source: Office of Trade and Investment Analysis, U.S. Dept. of Commerce

(millions of dollars)

	Principal Census trade totals					Other Census totals		
Year	U.S. exports and reexports excluding military grant-aid	U.S. general imports f.a.s. transaction values[1]	U.S. merchandise balance f.a.s.[1]	U.S. general imports c.i.f.	U.S. balance exports f.a.s. imports c.i.f.	Military grant-aid shipments	Exports of domestic merchandise	Re-exports
1950	9,997	8,954	1,043	—	—	282	10,146	133
1955	14,298	11,566	2,732	—	—	1,256	15,426	128
1960	19,659	15,073	4,586	—	—	949	20,408	201
1965	26,742	21,520	5,222	—	—	779	27,178	343
1970	42,681	40,356	2,325	42,833	−152	565	42,612	634
1975	107,652	98,503	9,149	105,935	1,716	461	106,622	1,490
1980	220,626	244,871	−24,245	256,984	−36,358	156	216,668	4,115
1983	200,486	258,048[2]	−57,562	269,878	−69,392	52	195,969	4,568
1984	217,865	325,726	−107,861	341,177	−123,312	23	212,057	5,831
1985	213,133	345,276	−132,143	361,626	−148,493	13	206,925	6,221
1986	217,292	369,961	−152,669	387,082	−169,790	12	206,376	10,928

Note: Export values include both commercially-financed shipments and shipments under government-financed programs such as AID and PL-480. (1) Prior to 1974, imports are customs values, i.e. generally at prices in principal foreign markets. (2) In 1981 import value changes back to customs value.

U.S. Foreign Trade, by Economic Classes

(millions of dollars)

Economic class	1965	1970	1975	1980	1984	1985	1986
Exports, total	**29,128**	**45,114**	**106,622**	**216,672**	**212,057**	**206,925**	**206,376**
Excluding military grant-aid	—	—	**106,161**	**216,515**	**212,034**	**206,912**	**206,364**
Crude foods	2,587	2,748	11,804	9,695	8,330	7,938	9,120
Manufactured foods	1,590	1,921	4,221	13,197	12,810	9,947	9,303
Crude materials	2,887	4,492	10,883	18,776	16,985	13,319	10,729
Agricultural	1,942	2,524	5,747	—	—	—	—
Semimanufactures	4,114	6,866	12,815	37,312	40,627	38,006	36,335
Finished manufactures	16,008	26,563	66,379	126,518	133,305	137,717	140,889
Excluding military grant-aid	—	—	65,918	126,362	133,282	137,704	140,877
Imports, total[1]	**22,293**	**40,748**	**99,305**	**245,262**	**325,726**	**345,276**	**369,961**
Crude foods	2,008	2,579	3,642	7,737	8,809	9,351	11,125
Manufactured foods	1,877	3,519	5,953	10,385	12,289	12,562	13,058
Crude materials	3,709	4,126	23,570	76,380	49,264	44,404	41,395
Agricultural	864	797	1,280	2,336	2,782	2,593	2,601
Semimanufactures	4,964	7,263	17,326	34,072	48,233	44,043	41,395
Finished manufactures	8,871	22,464	46,411	112,620	207,130	234,914	268,096

(1) Customs values are shown for imports.

Total Exports and Exports Financed by Foreign Aid

(millions of dollars)

	1965	1970	1975	1980	1982	1984	1985	1986
Exports, total	**27,530**	**43,224**	**107,592**	**220,783**	**212,275**	**217,888**	**213,146**	**217,304**
Agricultural commodities	6,306	7,349	22,097	41,757	37,011	38,231	29,619	26,679
Nonagricultural commodities	20,445	35,310	85,094	178,948	175,264	179,657	183,527	190,686
Manufactured goods (domestic)	17,439	29,343	70,950	143,971	139,738	143,148	145,384	148,690
Military grant—aid	779	565	461	156	82	23	13	12
Export financed under P.L.-480	1,323	1,021	1,181	1,094	956	995	1,083	804
Sales for foreign currency	899	276	—	—	—	—	—	—
Donations, including disaster relief	253	255	257	329	228	177	270	108
Long-term dollar credit sales	152	490	924	765	727	814	813	530
AID expend. for U.S. goods for export	—	—	665	673	567	646	838	378

Value of Principal Agricultural Exports

(millions of dollars)

Commodity	Avg. 1961-65	Avg. 1966-70	1965	1970	1975	1980	1984	1985	1986
Wheat and wheat products	1,268	1,197	1,214	1,144	5,292	6,660	6,740	3,898	3,280
Feed grains	841	1,082	1,162	1,099	5,492	9,759	8,110	6,023	3,098
Rice	178	311	244	314	858	1,288	845	665	621
Fodders and feeds	179	386	278	496	987	1,126	1,183	1,013	1,382
Oilseeds and products	774	1,182	1,029	1,642	NA	9,393	8,369	5,794	6,464
Cotton, raw	639	408	495	377	991	2,864	2,441	1,633	773

Top U.S. Industrial Exporters

Source: *Fortune* magazine

U.S. industrial corporations ranked by sales to foreign countries (in billions)

1986 rank	Company	Sales	1985 rank
1.	General Motors	$8.37	1
2.	Boeing	7.33	3
3.	Ford Motor	7.24	2
4.	General Electric	4.35	4
5.	IBM	$3.06	5
6.	du Pont	2.96	8
7.	Chrysler	2.81	6
8.	McDonnell Douglas	2.80	7
9.	United Technologies	$2.13	9
10.	Eastman Kodak	2.04	11

Merchant Fleets of the World

Source: Maritime Administration, U.S. Commerce Department

Oceangoing steam and motor ships of 1,000 gross tons and over as of July 1, 1986, excludes ships operating exclusively on the Great Lakes and inland waterways and special types such as channel ships, icebreakers, cable ships, etc., and merchant ships owned by any military force. Tonnage is in thousands. Gross tonnage is a volume measurement; each cargo gross ton represents 100 cubic ft. of enclosed space. Deadweight tonnage is the carrying capacity of a ship in long tons (2,240 lbs.).

	Total			Type of Vessel Freighters			Bulk Carriers			Tankers		
	Number	Gross Tons	Dwt. Tons	Number	Gross Tons	Dwt. Tons	Number	Cross Tons	Dwt. Tons	Number	Gross Tons	Dwt. Tons
All Countries	25,555	395,056	656,323	13,937	97,284	126,542	5,787	135,366	235,833	5,456	158,508	292,345
United States[1]	737	16,034	24,339	417	6,383	7,353	25	693	1,152	258	8,444	15,535
Privately Owned[3]	477	13,490	21,196	209	4,494	4,889	25	693	1,152	235	8,164	15,081
Government Owned	260	2,544	3,143	208	1,889	2,464	—	—	—	23	280	454
Reserve Fleet	228	2,201	2,754	186	1,654	2,177	—	—	—	20	250	408
Other[2]	32	343	389	22	235	287	—	—	—	3	30	46
Algeria	63	1,090	1,496	36	199	286	4	57	93	22	830	1,114
Argentina	187	2,275	3,439	99	787	1,072	20	523	879	67	961	1,485
Australia	76	1,877	2,984	26	275	325	31	936	1,518	19	666	1,141
Belgium	82	2,210	3,653	31	369	447	33	1,379	2,506	17	450	685
Brazil	345	6,036	9,953	169	1,166	1,549	90	2,752	4,677	83	2,113	3,723
British Columbia	450	9,825	16,078	196	1,404	1,768	204	6,480	11,065	48	1,927	3,241
*Bulgaria	117	1,274	1,878	51	307	372	45	610	947	17	337	538
*China (People's Rep.)	1,025	10,278	15,624	692	4,985	7,024	180	3,567	5,954	139	1,584	2,558
China (Taiwan)	214	4,552	7,025	127	1,545	1,845	68	2,369	4,040	18	636	1,140
Cyprus	716	8,900	15,322	451	2,174	3,324	168	3,152	5,320	91	3,530	6,657
Denmark	255	4,390	6,794	159	1,652	1,816	13	333	589	79	2,392	4,382
Finland	120	1,480	2,305	58	364	482	27	278	384	32	795	1,431
France	268	7,615	13,057	138	1,531	1,840	38	1,356	2,351	86	4,691	8,850
*German Dem. Rep.	161	1,299	1,715	133	874	1,104	21	337	529	4	50	75
Germany (Fed. Rep. Of)	528	4,931	6,865	414	3,068	3,789	23	646	1,037	88	1,159	2,010
Greece	1,835	32,092	57,130	733	5,448	8,112	760	15,145	26,943	309	11,290	21,978
India	358	6,434	10,597	108	1,629	2,357	116	2,955	5,093	57	1,816	3,122
Indonesia	330	1,449	2,148	229	776	1,134	12	139	207	80	469	772
Iran	108	2,276	3,873	42	428	592	46	896	1,506	20	952	1,775
Iraq	35	858	1,518	16	108	154	—	—	—	18	743	1,363
Italy	569	7,855	13,000	230	1,223	1,580	102	3,115	5,406	227	3,368	5,969
Japan	1,604	37,366	60,287	633	6,302	6,280	497	14,780	25,535	468	16,239	28,456
Korea (Republic Of)	487	6,575	11,154	240	1,257	1,778	176	4,210	7,264	71	1,108	2,112
Kuwait	74	2,343	3,485	42	725	953	—	—	—	32	1,618	2,532
Liberia	1,852	62,126	119,080	386	3,517	4,818	764	21,391	40,072	694	37,082	74,137
Malaysia	183	1,652	2,390	125	578	801	23	476	825	33	594	760
Malta	191	2,175	3,514	122	725	1,028	58	967	1,602	9	464	878
Mexico	78	1,223	1,879	21	147	195	12	309	511	45	767	1,173
Nassau Bahamas	129	5,063	9,051	40	270	360	20	565	1,004	58	4,061	7,649
Netherlands	464	4,361	6,867	363	1,858	2,491	28	657	1,107	69	1,738	3,250
Norway	424	12,572	21,116	130	1,147	1,431	90	3,584	6,212	182	7,483	13,406
Panama	3,620	42,101	69,710	2,068	12,964	18,123	952	18,225	31,683	565	10,447	19,685
Philippines	300	4,802	8,152	193	979	1,374	153	3,327	5,724	40	532	1,023
Poland	285	3,054	4,385	104	1,320	1,370	90	1,442	2,277	9	000	529
Portugal	73	1,278	2,272	44	240	314	8	181	298	19	844	1,653
*Romania	268	3,012	4,606	194	1,024	1,312	64	1,511	2,446	9	470	846
Saudi Arabia	164	3,013	5,148	78	736	1,027	18	449	756	65	1,816	3,356
Singapore	480	6,652	11,200	298	2,343	3,292	83	2,213	3,985	97	2,086	3,915
Spain	489	5,191	9,613	308	966	1,483	79	1,349	2,396	101	2,873	5,733
Sweden	206	2,591	3,764	116	1,156	1,321	20	375	593	68	1,048	1,848
Turkey	322	3,541	6,139	203	669	1,023	58	1,222	2,072	55	1,617	3,032
*U.S.S.R.	2,514	18,717	24,858	1,793	9,841	11,967	221	3,356	5,222	448	5,042	7,546
United Kingdom	541	12,744	20,256	206	2,576	2,853	96	2,807	4,924	227	7,034	12,407
Yugoslavia	263	2,680	4,139	186	1,311	1,859	63	1,139	1,922	10	213	351

(*) Source material limited. (1) Excludes 205 non—merchant type and/or Navy—owned vessels currently in the Natl. Defense Reserve Fleet.

Commerce at Principal U.S. Ports

Source: Corps of Engineers, Department of the Army (short tons per year, 1985)

	Total	Foreign
New York, N.Y.	152,053,796	48,986,868
New Orleans, La.	146,677,720	53,562,964
Valdez Hrbr., Alas.	99,624,406	40,296
Houston, Tex.	90,669,169	41,283,935
Baton Rouge, La.	70,715,564	20,305,302
Norfolk Hrbr., Va.	47,180,824	36,649,092
Tampa Harbor, Fla.	46,904,727	20,617,953
Long Beach, Calif.	43,977,333	20,841,557
Corpus Christi Ship Chnl., Tex.	42,682,399	21,961,188
Mobile, Ala.	37,749,120	17,853,467
Baltimore Hrbr., Md.	36,425,293	25,626,170
Los Angeles, Calif.	36,373,907	16,958,870
Texas City, Tex.	33,440,917	14,597,911
Philadelphia, Pa.	32,690,108	21,497,651
Duluth-Supr., Minn.	28,816,841	5,097,613
Pittsburgh, Pa.	28,551,728	0
Marcus Hook, Pa.	27,417,581	15,560,089
Beaumont, Tex.	26,842,008	10,770,776
St. Louis, Metro.	26,620,294	0
Lake Charles, La.	25,944,452	13,446,342
Chicago, Ill.	22,574,041	4,044,992
Portland, Ore.	21,844,843	10,886,995
Pascagoula, Miss.	20,006,414	10,778,621
Huntington, W. Va.	19,643,608	0
Newport News, Va.	19,168,548	17,527,222
Toledo Hrbr., Oh.	18,400,468	1,734,500
Boston, Mass.	17,268,816	7,608,705
Richmond, Calif.	17,177,609	3,953,488
Seattle, Wash.	16,230,013	8,603,491
Cincinnati, Oh.	16,215,227	0
Paulsboro, N.J.	16,101,261	10,011,062
Tacoma Hrbr., Wash.	15,794,532	9,780,543
Port Arthur, Tex.	15,754,931	9,163,594
Detroit, Mich.	15,612,344	1,850,635
Cleveland, Oh.	13,767,174	1,163,267
Indiana, Ind.	13,549,278	649,719
Freeport, Tex.	12,918,289	6,002,897
Port Everglades, Fla.	11,648,543	3,005,153

Commerce on U.S. Inland Waterways

Source: Corps of Engineers, Department of the Army 1985

Mississippi River System and Gulf Intracoastal Waterway

Waterway	Tons
Mississippi River, Minneapolis to the Gulf	383,964,109
Mississippi River, Minneapolis to St. Louis	72,039,185
Mississippi River, St. Louis to Cairo	92,667,520
Mississippi River, Cairo to Baton Rouge	149,874,491
Mississippi River, Baton Rouge to New Orleans	256,962,743
Mississippi River, New Orleans to Gulf	223,879,690
Gulf Intracoastal Waterway	102,463,665
Mississippi River System	527,808,570

Ton-Mileage of Freight Carried on Inland Waterways

System	Ton-miles
Atlantic Coast waterways	24,810,851
Gulf Coast waterways	36,502,065
Pacific Coast waterways	19,908,394
Mississippi River System, including Ohio River and tributaries	224,697,416
Great Lakes system, U.S. commerce only	75,774,612
Total:	**381,693,338**

Important Waterways and Canals

The St. Lawrence & Great Lakes Waterway, the largest inland navigation system on the continent, extends from the Atlantic Ocean to Duluth at the western end of Lake Superior, a distance of 2,342 miles. With the deepening of channels and locks to 27 ft., ocean carriers are able to penetrate to ports in the Canadian interior and the American midwest.

The major canals are those of the St. Lawrence Great Lakes waterway — the 3 new canals of the St. Lawrence Seaway, with their 7 locks, providing navigation for vessels of 26-foot draught from Montreal to Lake Ontario; the Welland Ship Canal by-passing the Niagara River between Lake Ontario and Lake Erie with its 8 locks, and the Sault Ste. Marie Canal and lock between Lake Huron and Lake Superior. These 16 locks overcome a drop of 580 ft. from the head of the lakes to Montreal. From Montreal to Lake Ontario the former bottleneck of narrow, shallow canals and of slow passage through 22 locks has been overcome, giving faster and safer movement for larger vessels. The new locks and linking channels now accommodate all but the largest ocean-going vessels and the upper St. Lawrence and Great Lakes are open to 80% of the world's saltwater fleet.

Subsidiary Canadian canals or branches include the St. Peters Canal between Bras d'Or Lakes and the Atlantic Ocean in Nova Scotia; the St. Ours and Chambly Canals on the Richelieu River, Quebec; the Ste. Anne and Carillon Canals on the Ottawa River; the Rideau Canal between the Ottawa River and Lake Ontario, the Trent and Murrary Canals between Lake Ontario and Georgian Bay in Ontario and the St. Andrew's Canal on the Red River. The commercial value of these canals is not great but they are maintained to control water levels and permit the passage of small vessels and pleasure craft. The Canso Canal, completed 1957, permits shipping to pass through the causeway connecting Cape Breton Island with the Nova Scotia mainland.

The Welland Canal overcomes the 326-ft. drop of Niagara Falls and the rapids of the Niagara River. It has 8 locks, each 859 ft. long, 80 ft. wide and 30 ft. deep. Regulations permit ships of 730-ft. length and 75-ft. beam to transit.

Shortest Navigable Distances Between Ports

Source: Distances Between Ports. Defense Mapping Agency Hydrographic/Topographic Center

Distances shown are in nautical miles (1,852 meters or about 6,076.115 feet). To get statute miles, multiply by 1.15.

TO / FROM	New York	Montreal	Colon[1]
Algiers, Algeria	3,618	3,592	4,737
Amsterdam, Netherlands	3,411	3,318	4,829
Baltimore, Md.	410	1,820	1,904
Barcelona, Spain	3,721	3,695	4,840
Boston, Mass.	378	1,309	2,136
Buenos Aires, Argentina	5,845	6,440	5,344
Cape Town, S. Africa[2]	6,789	7,115	6,425
Cherbourg, France	3,127	3,034	4,545
Cobh, Ireland	2,878	2,780	4,320
Copenhagen, Denmark	3,934	3,841	5,352
Dakar, Senegal	3,336	3,562	3,689
Galveston, Tex.	1,862	3,224	1,485
Gibraltar[3]	3,210	3,184	4,329
Glasgow, Scotland	3,324	3,231	4,742
Halifax, N.S.	593	958	2,298
Hamburg, W. Germany	3,636	3,543	5,054
Hamilton, Bermuda	697	1,621	1,644
Havana, Cuba	1,167	2,528	990
Helsinki, Finland	4,484	4,391	5,902
Istanbul, Turkey	5,006	4,980	6,125
Kingston, Jamaica	1,472	2,690	555
Lagos, Nigeria	4,870	5,130	5,033
Lisbon, Portugal	2,980	2,941	4,155
Marseille, France	3,896	3,870	5,015
Montreal, Quebec	1,516		3,190
Naples, Italy	4,185	4,159	5,304
Nassau, Bahamas	961	2,274	1,165
New Orleans, La.	1,707	3,069	1,403
New York, N.Y.		1,516	1,972
Norfolk, Va.	287	1,697	1,781
Oslo, Norway	3,888	3,795	5,306
Piraeus, Greece	4,687	4,661	5,806
Port Said, Egypt	5,119	5,093	6,238
Rio de Janeiro, Brazil	4,743	5,342	4,246
St. John's, Nfld.	1,097	1,038	2,697
San Juan, Puerto Rico	1,399	2,445	992
Southampton, England	3,156	3,063	4,514

TO / FROM	San. Fran.	Vancouver	Panama[1]
Acapulco, Mexico	1,834	2,612	1,426
Anchorage, Alas.	1,892	1,347	5,127
Bombay, India	9,791	9,513	9,248
Calcutta, India	9,006	8,728	10,929
Colon, Panama[1]	3,290	4,065	44
Jakarta, Indonesia	7,657	7,413	10,570
Haiphong, Vietnam	6,657	6,358	9,806
Hong Kong	6,044	5,756	9,196
Honolulu, Hawaii	2,095	2,419	4,688
Los Angeles, Cal.	369	1,162	2,912
Manila, Philippines	6,223	5,946	9,355
Melbourne, Australia	6,966	7,342	7,916
Pusan, S. Korea	4,922	4,623	8,074
Ho Chi Min City, Vietnam	6,890	6,606	9,822
San Francisco, Cal.		812	3,246
Seattle, Wash.	796	126	4,005
Shanghai, China	5,398	5,110	8,571
Singapore	7,356	7,078	10,495
Suva, Fiji	4,760	5,183	6,312
Valparaiso, Chile	5,146	5,915	2,615
Vancouver, B.C.	812		4,021
Vladivostok, USSR	4,554	4,262	7,738
Yokohama, Japan	4,547	4,260	7,687

TO / FROM	Port Said	Cape Town[2]	Singapore
Bombay, India	3,046	4,599	2,435
Calcutta, India	4,691	5,489	1,650
Dar es Salaam, Tanzania	3,129	2,369	4,041
Jakarta, Indonesia	5,276	5,184	527
Hong Kong	6,474	7,071	1,460
Kuwait	3,306	5,169	3,845
Manila, Philippines	6,355	6,952	1,341
Melbourne, Australia	7,837	6,104	3,842
Ho Chi Min City, Vietnam	5,660	6,263	646
Singapore	5,014	5,611	
Yokohama, Japan	7,906	8,503	2,892

(1) Colon on the Atlantic is 44 nautical miles from Panama (port) on the Pacific. (2) Cape Town is 35 nautical miles northwest of the Cape of Good Hope. (3) Gibraltar (port) is 24 nautical miles east of the Strait of Gibraltar.

Notable Ocean Passages by Ships

Compiled by N.R.P. Bonsor

Sailing Vessels

Date	Ship		From	To	Nautical miles	Time D. H. M	Speed (knots)
1846	Yorkshire		Liverpool	New York	3150	16. 0. 0	8.46†
1853	Northern Light		San Francisco	Boston	—	76. 6. 0	—
1854	James Baines		Boston Light	Light Rock	—	12. 6. 0	—
1854	Flying Cloud		New York	San Francisco	15091	89. 0. 0	7.07†
1868-9	Thermopylae		Liverpool	Melbourne	—	63.18.15	—
—	Red Jacket		New York	Liverpool	3150	13. 1.25	10.05†
—	Starr King		50 S. Lat	Golden Gate	—	36. 0. 0	—
—	Golden Fleece		Equator	San Francisco	—	12.12. 0	—
1905	Atlantic		Sandy Hook	England	3013	12. 4. 0	10.32
	Atlantic Crossing by Passenger Steamships						
1819 (5/22 - 6/20)	Savannah (a)	US	Savannah	Liverpool	—	29. 4. 0	—
1838 (5/7 - 5/22)	Great Western	Br	New York	Avonmouth	3218	14.15.59	9.14
1840 (8/4 - 8/14)	Britannia (b)	Br	Halifax	Liverpool	2610	9.21.44	10.98†
1854 (6/28 - 7/7)	Baltic	US	Liverpool	New York	3037	9.16.52	13.04
1856 (8/6 - 8/15)	Persia	Br	Sandy Hook	Liverpool	3046	8.23.19	14.15†
1876 (12/16-12/24)	Britannic	Br	Sandy Hook	Queenstown	2882	7.12.41	15.94
1895 (5/18 - 5/24)	Lucania	Br	Sandy Hook	Queenstown	2897	5.11.40	22.00
1898 (3/30 - 4/5)	Kaiser Wilhelm der Grosse	Ger	Needles	Sandy Hook	3120	5.20. 0	22.29
1901 (7/10 - 7/17)	Deutschland	Ger	Sandy Hook	Eddystone	3082	5.11. 5	23.51
1907 (10/6 - 10/10)	Lusitania	Br	Queenstown	Sandy Hook	2780	4.19.52	23.99
1924 (8/20 - 8/25)	Mauretania	Br	Ambrose	Cherbourg	3198	5. 1.49	26.25
1929 (7/17 - 7/22)	Bremen*	Ger	Cherbourg	Ambrose	3164	4.17.42	27.83
1933 (6/27 - 7/2)	Europa	Ger	Cherbourg	Ambrose	3149	4.16.48	27.92
1933 (8/11 - 8/16)	Rex	It	Gibraltar	Ambrose	3181	4.13.58	28.92
1935 (5/30 - 6/3)	Normandie*	Fr	Bishop Rock	Ambrose	2971	4. 3. 2	29.98
1938 (8/10 - 8/14)	Queen Mary	Br	Ambrose	Bishop Rock	2938	3.20.42	31.69
1952 (7/11 - 7/15)	United States	US	Bishop Rock	Ambrose	2906	3.12.12	34.51
1952 (7/3 - 7/7)	United States* (e)	US	Ambrose	Bishop Rock	2942	3.10.40	35.59
	Other Ocean Passages						
1928 (June)	USS Lexington		San Pedro	Honolulu	2226	3. 0.36	30.66
1944 (Jul-Sep)	St. Roch (c) (Can)		Halifax	Vancouver	7295	86. 0. 0	—
1945 (7/16-7/19)	USS Indianapolis (d)		San Francisco	Oahu, Hawaii	2091	3. 2.20	28.07
1945 (11/26)	USS Lake Champlain		Gibraltar	Newport News	3360	4. 8.51	32.04
1950 (Jul-Aug)	USS Boxer		Japan	San Francisco	5000	7.18.36	26.80†
1951 (6/1-6/9)	USS Philippine Sea		Yokohama	Alameda	5000	7.13. 0	27.62†
1958 (2/25-3/4)	USS Skate (f)		Nantucket	Portland, Eng	3161	8.11. 0	15.57
1958 (3/22-3/29)	USS Skate (f)		Lizard, Eng	Nantucket	—	7. 5. 0	—
1958 (7/23-8/7)	USS Nautilus (g)		Pearl Harbor	Iceland (via N. Pole)	—	15. 0. 0	—
1960 (2/16-5/10)	USS Triton (h)		New London	Rehoboth, Del	41500	84. 0. 0	20.59†
1960 (8/15-8/20)	USS Seadragon (i)		Baffin Bay	NW Passage, Pac	850	6. 0. 0	—
1962 (10/30-11/11)	African Comet* (U.S.)		New York	Cape Town	[illegible]	12.10.22	22.00
1973 (8/20)	Sea-Land Exchange (k) (U.S.)		Bishop Rock	Ambrose	2912	3.11.24	34.92
1973 (8/24)	Sea-Land Trade (U.S.)		Kobe	Race Rock, BC	4126	5. 6. 0	32.75

† The time taken and/or distance covered is approximate and so, therefore, is the average speed.

* Maiden voyage. (a) The Savannah, a fully rigged sailing vessel with steam auxiliary (over 300 tons, 98.5 ft. long, beam 25.8 ft., depth 12.9 ft.) was launched in the East River in 1818. It was the first ship to use steam in crossing any ocean. It was supplied with engines and detachable iron paddle wheels. On its famous voyage it used steam 105 hours. (b) First Cunard liner. (c) First ship to complete NW Passage in one season. (d) Carried Hiroshima atomic bomb in World War II. (e) Set world speed record; average speed eastbound on maiden voyage 35.59 knots (about 41 m.p.h.). (f) First atomic submarine to cross Atlantic both ways submerged. (g) World's first atomic submarine also first to make undersea voyage under polar ice cap, 1,830 mi. from Point Barrow, Alaska, to Atlantic Ocean, Aug. 1-4, 1958, reaching North Pole Aug. 3. Second undersea transit of the North Pole made by submarine USS Skate Aug. 11, 1958, during trip from New London, Conn., and return. (h) World's largest submarine. Nuclear-powered Triton was submerged during nearly all its voyage around the globe. It duplicated the route of Ferdinand Magellan's circuit (1519-1522) 30,708 mi., starting from St. Paul Rocks off the NE coast of Brazil, Feb. 24-Apr. 25, 1960, then sailed to Cadiz, Spain, before returning home. (i) First underwater transit of Northwest Passage. (k) Fastest freighter crossing of Atlantic.

Fastest Scheduled Passenger Train Runs in U.S. and Canada

Source: Donald M. Steffee, figures are based on 1987 timetables

Railroad	Train	From	To	Dis. miles	Time min.	Speed mph.
Amtrak	Five Metroliners	Baltimore[1]	Wilmington	68.4	42	97.8
Amtrak	Metroliner 101	Metro Park	Princeton Junction	23.9	15	95.6
Amtrak	Five Metroliners	Wilmington	Baltimore	68.4	43	95.4
Amtrak	Thirteen Metroliners	Baltimore[1]	Wilmington	68.4	44	93.3
Amtrak	Five Metroliners	Baltimore[1]	Wilmington	68.4	45	91.2
Amtrak	Metroliner 122	Trenton	Newark	48.1	32	90.2
Amtrak	Four Metroliners	Philadelphia	Metro Park	66.4	45	88.5
Amtrak	Four trains	Rensselear	Hudson	28.4	19	88.4
Amtrak	Metroliner 112	Philadelphia	Newark	80.5	55	87.8
Via Rail Canada	Capital	Kingston	Belleville	44.6	31	86.3
Amtrak	Four Metroliners	Philadelphia	Newark	80.5	56	86.2
Amtrak	Three Metroliners	Wilmington	Baltimore	68.4	48	85.5
Amtrak	Four Metroliners	Philadelphia	Newark	80.5	57	84.7
Via Rail Canada	York	Guildwood	Kingston	145.1	104	83.7
Amtrak	Three trains	Wilmington	Baltimore	68.4	49	83.7
Amtrak	Three Metroliners	Newark	Philadelphia	80.5	58	83.2
Via Rail Canada	Renaissance	Dorval	Kingston	165.8	120	82.9
Via Rail Canada	Three trains	Guildwood	Kingston	145.1	105	82.9

Railroad	Train	From	To	Dis. miles	Time min.	Speed mph.
Amtrak	Benjamin Franklin	N. Philadelphia	Newark	76.0	55	82.9
Amtrak	Metroliner 100	New Carrollton	BWI Airport Sta.	20.7	15	82.8
Amtrak	Broadway Limited	Trenton	Newark	48.1	35	82.4
Via Rail Canada	La Salle	Dorval	Brockville	115.3	84	82.3
Via Rail Canada	Two trains	Cornwall	Kingston	108.1	79	82.1
Amtrak	Six Metroliners	Newark	Philadelphia	80.5	59	81.9
Vai Rail Canada	La Salle	Belleville	Kingston	50.5	37	81.9
Via Rail Canada	Capital	Guildwood	Belleville	100.5	74	81.5
Amtrak	Four trains	Metro Park[1]	Trenton	33.9	25	81.3
Amtrak	Three Metroliners	Metro Park	Philadelphia	66.4	49	81.3
Via Rail Canada	Capital	Belleville	Kingston	44.6	33	81.1
Amtrak	Metroliner 121	Newark	Philadelphia	80.5	60	80.5
Amtrak	Five trains	Wilmington[1]	Baltimore	68.4	51	80.5
Amtrak	Two trains	Trenton	Newark	48.1	36	80.2

Fastest Scheduled Passenger Train Runs in Foreign Countries

France	TGV trains (2 runs)	Paris	Macon	225.7	100	135.4
Japan	Yamabiko trains (6 runs)	Moricka	Sendai	106.3	50	127.6
Great Britain	High Speed Train	Swindon	Didcot	24.2	14	103.6
West Germany	Riemenschneider	Celle	Uelzen	32.5	20	97.5
Spain	Talgo 115	Manzonares	Alcazar	30.4	20	91.2
Soviet Union	High Speed Train[2]	Leningrad[1]	Moscow[3]	403.6	279	86.8
Sweden	City Express (2 runs)	Hallsberg[1]	Skvode	70.8	49	86.7
Italy	Inter City 523	Florence	Rome	165.5	115	86.3
Australia	Riverina XPT	Culcairn	Wagga Wagga	47.0	35	80.6

(1) Runs listed in both directions. (2) Once weekly: Thursday from Leningrad, Fri. from Moscow. (3) Probable operating stop at Bologuye; times unavailable

Passenger Car Production, U.S. Plants

Source: Motor Vehicle Manufacturers Association; mid-Year 1987

	1985	1986	1987 5 Mos.
Renault Alliance	73,422	46,095	15,331
Renault Encore	36,497	3,408	—
Total American Motors Corp.	**109,919**	**49,503**	**15,331**
Horizon	142,611	171,882	32,997
Reliant	162,690	151,695	51,984
Sundance	—	36,856	46,137
Caravelle (K)	1,776	1,008	51,984
Caravelle (E)	44,785	41,292	24,300
Caravelle (M)	2,446	2,068	135
Gran Fury	15,179	17,818	1,717
Total Plymouth	**369,487**	**422,619**	**157,270**
Laser	52,209	25,327	—
LeBaron	96,339	83,163	37,104
LeBaron GTS	95,187	68,699	18,539
Fifth Avenue	106,116	122,442	17,036
New Yorker (E)	64,342	64,964	37,657
Total Chrysler-Plymouth	**783,680**	**791,210**	**315,584**
Omni	136,823	163,416	28,363
Shadow	—	35,107	45,515
Daytona	47,746	33,063	24,044
Aries	135,186	126,311	49,450
Dodge 600 (K)	28,664	20,451	—
Dodge 600 (E)	38,171	43,612	21,544
Lancer	65,097	47,817	11,843
Diplomat	30,701	35,593	2,639
Total Dodge	**482,388**	**506,370**	**183,398**
Total Chrysler Corp.	**1,266,068**	**1,297,580**	**498,982**
Ford	7,122	—	—
Thunderbird	170,513	131,289	72,184
LTD	184,431	—	—
Taurus	12,250	335,689	192,410
Tempo	188,124	198,824	85,564
Escort	344,548	378,341	162,158
EXP	3,863	—	—
Mustang	187,776	177,728	95,824
Total Ford	**1,098,627**	**1,221,871**	**608,140**
Grand Marquis	4,733	—	—
Cougar	129,788	101,788	70,252
Marquis	84,862	—	—
Sable	5,810	127,343	61,016
Topaz	54,060	57,560	27,367
Lynx	75,098	60,297	19,754
Capri	20,095	12,344	—
Lincoln	119,787	137,280	60,534
Mark	18,031	26,126	12,099
Continental	25,259	19,626	8,077
Total Lincoln—Mercury	**537,523**	**542,364**	**259,189**
Total Ford Motor Co.	**1,636,150**	**1,764,235**	**867,329**
Nova*	64,601	191,475	64,748
Chevette	152,769	102,537	46,024

*Produced by NUMMI (50% owned by General Motors Corp.)

	1985	1986	1987 5 Mos.
Cavalier	492,004	395,151	160,566
Citation	28,697	—	—
Camaro	214,429	172,584	46,918
Beretta—Corsica	0	17,200	120,515
Celebrity	264,097	257,283	162,954
Monte Carlo	138,532	110,048	32,970
Chevrolet	289,821	223,842	94,409
Corvette	46,304	28,410	13,110
Total Chevrolet	**1,691,254**	**1,499,230**	**696,190**
Acadian	17,716	19,490	—
1000	24,895	16,814	8,658
Sunbird	142,947	130,167	—
Fiero	109,569	69,735	16,038
Firebird	114,290	105,110	35,527
Grand Am	143,259	231,318	113,094
6000	58,952	132,385	37,708
Bonneville/Parisienne	90,989	89,718	66,381
Total Pontiac	**702,617**	**794,737**	**319,848**
Firenza	62,152	38,212	7,839
Calais	149,829	120,629	53,412
Ciera	356,798	236,613	78,732
Supreme	235,496	107,036	32,133
Delta 88	192,400	291,346	96,939
Oldsmobile 98	143,277	114,558	33,247
Toronado	29,030	18,779	8,034
Total Oldsmobile	**1,168,982**	**927,173**	**310,336**
Skyhawk	105,617	82,429	14,740
Skylark	40,953	—	—
Somerset and Skylark	125,593	112,773	31,956
Century	299,104	230,137	83,044
Regal	137,018	60,897	20,103
LeSabre	106,612	172,061	58,561
Electra	138,682	91,559	45,284
Riviera	47,882	26,110	7,492
Total Buick	**1,001,461**	**775,966**	**261,180**
Cimarron	26,703	23,241	6,839
Cadillac C	214,083	171,562	74,946
Cadillac D	—	76,514	33,331
Eldorado	53,301	25,246	8,394
Seville	28,678	22,474	10,772
Allante	—	—	1,728
Total Cadillac	**322,765**	**319,037**	**136,010**
Total General Motors	**4,887,079**	**4,316,143**	**1,723,564**
Accord	145,337	213,811	97,104
Civic	—	24,348	45,535
Total Honda of America	**145,337**	**238,159**	**142,639**
Toyota	—	**13,649**	**17,026**
Volkswagen of America	**96,458**	**84,397**	**32,687**
Total Passenger Cars	**8,184,821**	**7,828,783**	**3,358,249**

Selected Motor Vehicle Statistics

Source: Federal Highway Adm.; National Transportation Safety Board

State, 1986	Driver's age Jan. 1, 1987 (1) Regular	(2) Juvenile	Licensed drivers[3] (1000)	Registered autos, buses & trucks[3] (1000)	State gas tax gal. cents (Dec. 31, 1986)	Motorfuel consumption[3] Highway 1,000 gallons	Non-Highway 1,000 gallons	Safety belt use law[4, 5] (July 23, 1987)
Alabama	16	—	2,484	3,461,000	13	2,326,000	70,000	No
Alaska	16	—	302	348,000	8	289,000	52,000	No
Arizona	16	—	2,394	2,353,000	16	1,866,000	42,000	No
Arkansas	16	—	1,767	1,435,000	13.5	1,422,000	71,000	No
California	16/18	14	17,822	19,703,000	9	13,181,000	347,000	S
Colorado	18	16	2,307	2,769,000	18	1,790,000	46,000	S
Connecticut	16/18	—	2,335	2,537,000	17	1,571,000	30,000	P
Delaware	16/18	—	454	485,000	13	350,000	11,000	No
Dist. of Col.	18	16	394	345,000	15.5	180,000	4,000	S
Florida	16	—	8,008	10,349,000	9.7	6,110,000	264,000	S
Georgia	16	—	3,957	4,686,000	7.5	3,935,000	106,000	No
Hawaii	15	—	604	672,000	11	352,000	16,000	P
Idaho	16	14	706	862,000	14.5	517,000	35,000	S
Illinois	16/18	—	7,026	7,785,000	13	5,414,000	127,000	P
Indiana	16/18	—	3,616	4,090,000	14	3,080,000	81,000	S
Iowa	16/18	—	1,878	2,764,000	16	1,512,000	96,000	P
Kansas	16	14	1,652	2,171,000	11	1,417,000	66,000	S
Kentucky	16	—	2,273	2,641,000	15	2,127,000	70,000	No
Louisiana	15/17	15	2,789	3,054,000	16	2,307,000	105,000	S
Maine	15/17	15	817	861,000	14	681,000	30,000	No
Maryland	16/18	16	2,954	3,359,000	13.5	2,330,000	24,000	S
Massachusetts	17/18	16½	3,824	3,737,000	11	2,636,000	64,000	No
Michigan	16/18	14	6,307	7,187,000	15	4,582,000	147,000	S
Minnesota	16/18	15	2,502	3,548,000	17	2,105,000	144,000	P
Mississippi	15	—	1,834	1,810,000	9	1,479,000	58,000	No
Missouri	16	—	3,424	2,593,000	10	3,050,000	90,000	S
Montana	15/16	13	588	628,000	17	510,000	37,000	S
Nebraska	16	14	1,089	1,262,000	16.7	901,000	74,000	No
Nevada	16	14	714	696,000	13	600,000	16,000	S
New Hampshire	16/18	16	754	1,019,000	14	533,000	11,000	No
New Jersey	17	16	5,904	4,926,000	8	3,968,000	91,000	S
New Mexico	15/16	—	1,005	1,155,000	11	934,000	27,000	P
New York	17/18	16	9,967	9,373,000	8	6,960,000	202,000	P
North Carolina	16/18	—	4,196	4,536,000	15.5	3,688,000	109,000	P
North Dakota	16	14	448	649,000	13	426,000	51,000	No
Ohio	16/18	14	7,329	8,331,000	12	5,641,000	111,000	S
Oklahoma	16	—	2,279	2,915,000	10	2,062,000	80,000	S
Oregon	16	14	1,940	[illegible]	11	1,500,000	10,000	P
Pennsylvania	17/18	16	7,631	7,340,000	12	4,949,000	96,000	No
Rhode Island	16/18	—	626	615,000	15	413,000	14,0000	No
South Carolina	16	15	2,166	2,276,000	13	1,947,000	75,000	No
South Dakota	16	14	405	677,000	13	465,000	39,000	No
Tennessee	16	14	3,071	3,914,000	17	3,037,000	69,000	S
Texas	16/18	15	10,755	12,612,000	10	10,393,000	421,000	P
Utah	16/18	—	989	1,105,000	14	895,000	23,000	S
Vermont	18	16	394	418,000	13	200,000	10,000	No
Virginia	16/18	—	3,861	4,463,000	11	3,253,000	76,000	S
Washington	16/18	—	3,014	3,767,000	18	2,168,000	81,000	S
West Virginia	16/18	16	1,308	1,239,000	10.5	907,000	28,000	No
Wisconsin	16/18	14	3,259	32,811,000	17.5	2,321,000	99,000	No
Wyoming	16	14	312	507,000	8	425,000	30,000	No
Total			**158,594**	**176,532,000**		**125,797,000**	**4,115,000**	

(1) Unrestricted operation of private passenger car. When 2 ages are shown, license is issued at lower age upon completion of approved driver education course. (2) Juvenile license issued with consent of parent or guardian. (3) Estimated, 1986. (4) P = an officer may stop a vehicle for a violation (primary); S = an officer may only issue a seat belt citation when the vehicle is stopped for another moving violation (secondary); (5) Seat belt laws were credited with holding the 1986 traffic fatality rate at its 1985 level, the lowest since the statistic was first recorded in 1940.

Automobile Factory Sales

Source: Motor Vehicle Manufacturers Association

Year	Passenger cars Number	Motor trucks, buses Number	Total Number	Year	Passenger cars Number	Motor trucks, buses Number	Total Number
1900	4,192	—	4,190	1970	6,546,817	1,692,440	8,239,257
1910	181,000	6,000	187,000	1981	6,255,340	1,700,908	7,956,248
1920	1,905,560	321,789	2,227,349	1982	5,049,184	1,906,455	6,955,639
1930	2,787,456	575,364	3,362,820	1983	6,739,223	2,413,897	9,153,120
1940	3,717,385	754,901	4,472,286	1984	7,621,176	3,075,325	10,696,501
1950	6,665,863	1,337,193	8,003,056	1985	8,002,259	3,356,905	11,359,164
1960	6,665,863	1,194,475	7,869,271	1986	7,516,189	3,392,885	10,909,074

After July 1, 1964 all tactical vehicles are excluded. Federal excise taxes are excluded in all years.

Federal Outlays for Transportation, 1970-1986

Source: U.S. Office of Management and Budget

Function	1970	1975	1980	1981	1982	1983	1984	1985	1986, est.
Total outlays	**7,008**	**10,918**	**21,329**	**23,379**	**20,625**	**21,334**	**23,669**	**25,838**	**27,106**
Percent of total outlays	3.6	3.3	3.6	3.4	2.8	2.6	2.8	2.7	2.8
Average annual percent change	7.4	9.3	21.7	9.6	−11.8	3.4	10.9	9.2	4.9
Ground transportation	4,678	7,027	15,274	17,074	14,321	14,265	16,158	17,606	18,615
Air transportation	1,408	2,387	3,723	3,814	3,526	4,000	4,415	4,895	4,954
Water transportation	895	1,430	2,229	2,381	2,687	2,969	3,010	3,201	3,397
Other transportation	26	74	104	110	90	99	85	137	140

Personal Consumption Expenditures for Transportation, 1960-1985

Source: U.S. Bureau of Economic Analysis. *Survey of Current Business*

[In billions of dollars, except percent. Represents market value of purchases of goods and services by individuals and nonprofit institutions]

Type of product or service	1960	1965	1970	1975	1977	1980	1982	1983	1984	1985
Total expenditures	**42.4**	**58.4**	**80.6**	**129.4**	**179.3**	**236.6**	**267.3**	**291.9**	**319.5**	**349.8**
Percent of total personal consumption	**13.1**	**13.6**	**13.0**	**13.3**	**14.9**	**14.2**	**13.5**	**13.5**	**13.6**	**13.5**
User-operated transportation	39.1	54.5	74.3	119.7	167.0	218.5	246.7	269.9	295.7	320.3
New autos	14.0	21.4	21.9	29.3	44.3	46.3	52.8	65.2	75.9	87.2
Net purchases of used autos	2.6	3.9	5.3	8.9	13.2	15.5	20.8	23.0	26.4	28.1
Other motor vehicles	.6	1.3	2.9	7.1	13.9	10.1	14.0	18.2	23.0	29.8
Tires, tubes, accessories, other parts	2.5	3.4	6.1	10.5	13.5	18.9	21.2	22.8	24.6	24.1
Repair, greasing, washing, parking[1]	5.1	6.9	11.2	18.8	25.1	32.3	37.0	38.8	42.4	47.8
Gasoline and oil	12.0	14.7	22.4	40.4	48.1	84.8	90.4	90.0	91.4	91.9
Bridge, tunnel, ferry, road tolls	.3	.5	.7	.8	.9	1.0	1.1	1.1	1.3	1.4
Insurance premiums less claims paid	2.0	2.4	3.8	3.9	8.1	9.7	9.5	10.6	10.9	10.0

(1) Includes rental and storage.

Volume and Characteristics of Travel

Source: U.S. Federal Highway Administration Survey for 1983; covers only day trips regardless of trip length.

Characteristic	Household			Person		Percent Distribution			
						Household		Persons	
	Numbers of trips (mil.)	(bil.)	Average trip length (miles)	Number of trips (mil.)	(bil.)	Number of trips	Vehicle-miles	Number of trips	Person-miles
Total	**126,874**	**1,002,139**	**7.9**	**224,385**	**1,946,662**	**100.0**	**100.0**	**100.0**	**100.0**
Purpose:									
Trip to work	35,375	302,185	8.5	45,826	391,544	27.9	30.3	20.4	20.2
Work-related business	3,696	42,223	11.4	15,283	115,605	2.9	4.2	2.4	5.9
Shopping	25,363	133,823	5.2	40,655	219,112	20.0	13.3	18.1	11.2
Other family or personal business	23,245	155,131	6.7	36,158	256,929	18.3	15.5	16.1	13.2
School/church	7,444	40,990	5.5	26,486	129,953	5.9	4.1	11.8	6.7
Visit friends or relatives	12,543	135,801	10.8	24,743	283,520	9.9	13.6	11.0	14.6
Other social or recreational	15,416	133,417	8.7	35,457	302,145	12.2	13.3	15.8	15.5
Vacation	187	21,317	114.0	630	155,551	.1	2.1	.3	8.0
Other	3,605	37,252	7.2	9,147	92,303	2.8	3.6	4.1	4.7
Means of transportation:									
Automobile	95,497	742,301	9.8	139,387	1,181,626	75.3	74.2	62.1	60.8
Station wagon	10,920	81,471	7.5	16,194	139,253	8.6	8.1	7.2	7.2
Passenger van	2,803	21,401	7.6	4,746	51,269	2.2	2.1	2.1	2.6
Pickup truck[1]	13,851	122,504	8.8	18,372	176,926	10.9	12.2	8.2	9.1
Other	3,803[2]	34,462[2]	9.0	45,686[3]	397,588[3]	3.0[2]	3.4[2]	20.4[3]	20.4[3]

(1) Excludes pickup with camper and other trucks. (2) Includes other vans, pickups with campers, other trucks, motorized campers, motorcycles, motorized bicycles and other privately owned vehicles not listed elsewhere. (3) Includes other vans, motorized campers, motorcycles, trains, streetcars, elevated rail, airplane, commercial taxis, buses, school buses, bicycles, walking and other forms of transportation not included elsewhere.

Public Transportation Usage

Source: U.S. Bureau of the Census

(percentage of workers 16 years and older in each region or SMSA.)

	1970	1980		1970	1980		1970	1980
United States	**9.0**	**6.4**	Los Angeles	5.6	7.0	Minneapolis	8.5	8.7
			San Francisco	15.5	16.4	Cleveland	13.4	10.6
Northeast	**19.1**	**14.2**	Anaheim	0.4	2.1	**South**	**5.0**	**3.3**
New York	52.5	45.1	San Diego	4.3	3.3	Washington, D.C.	16.3	15.5
Philadelpha	20.7	14.0	Denver	4.4	6.1	Dallas	5.1	3.4
Boston	19.7	15.6	**North Central**	**6.7**	**4.9**	Houston	5.4	3.0
Nassau-Suffolk, N.Y.	15.5	12.5	Chicago	23.3	18.0	Baltimore	13.8	10.3
Pittsburgh	14.6	11.5	Detroit	7.9	3.7	Atlanta	8.4	7.6
West	**4.6**	**5.0**	St. Louis	8.0	5.7			

Air Distances Between Selected World Cities in Statute Miles

Point-to-point measurements are usually from City Hall

	Bangkok	Berlin	Cairo	Cape Town	Caracas	Chicago	Hong Kong	Honolulu	Lima	London
Bangkok	...	5,352	4,523	6,300	10,555	8,570	1,077	6,609	12,244	5,944
Berlin	5,352	...	1,797	5,961	5,238	4,414	5,443	7,320	6,896	583
Cairo	4,523	1,797	...	4,480	6,342	6,141	5,066	8,848	7,726	2,185
Cape Town	6,300	5,961	4,480	...	6,366	8,491	7,376	11,535	6,072	5,989
Caracas	10,555	5,238	6,342	6,366	...	2,495	10,165	6,021	1,707	4,655
Chicago	8,570	4,414	6,141	8,491	2,495	...	7,797	4,256	3,775	3,958
Hong Kong	1,077	5,443	5,066	7,376	10,165	7,797	...	5,556	11,418	5,990
Honolulu	6,609	7,320	8,848	11,535	6,021	4,256	5,556	...	5,947	7,240
London	5,944	583	2,185	5,989	4,655	3,958	5,990	7,240	6,316	...
Los Angeles	7,637	5,782	7,520	9,969	3,632	1,745	7,240	2,557	4,171	5,439
Madrid	6,337	1,165	2,087	5,308	4,346	4,189	6,558	7,872	5,907	785
Melbourne	4,568	9,918	8,675	6,425	9,717	9,673	4,595	5,505	8,059	10,500
Mexico City	9,793	6,056	7,700	8,519	2,234	1,690	8,788	3,789	2,639	5,558
Montreal	8,338	3,740	5,427	7,922	2,438	745	7,736	4,918	3,970	3,254
Moscow	4,389	1,006	1,803	6,279	6,177	4,987	4,437	7,047	7,862	1,564
New York	8,669	3,979	5,619	7,803	2,120	714	8,060	4,969	3,639	3,469
Paris	5,877	548	1,998	5,786	4,732	4,143	5,990	7,449	6,370	214
Peking	2,046	4,584	4,698	8,044	8,950	6,604	1,217	5,077	10,349	5,074
Rio de Janeiro	9,994	6,209	6,143	3,781	2,804	5,282	11,009	8,288	2,342	5,750
Rome	5,494	737	1,326	5,231	5,195	4,824	5,774	8,040	6,750	895
San Francisco	7,931	5,672	7,466	10,248	3,902	1,859	6,905	2,398	4,518	5,367
Singapore	883	6,164	5,137	6,008	11,402	9,372	1,605	6,726	11,689	6,747
Stockholm	5,089	528	2,096	6,423	5,471	4,331	5,063	6,875	7,166	942
Tokyo	2,865	5,557	5,958	9,154	8,808	6,314	1,791	3,859	9,631	5,959
Warsaw	5,033	322	1,619	5,935	5,559	4,679	5,147	7,366	7,215	905
Washington, D.C.	8,807	4,181	5,822	7,895	2,047	596	8,155	4,838	3,509	3,674

	Los Angeles	Madrid	Melbourne	Mexico City	Montreal	Moscow	New Delhi	New York	Paris	Peking
Bangkok	7,637	6,337	4,568	9,793	8,338	4,389	1,813	8,669	5,877	2,046
Berlin	5,782	1,165	9,918	6,056	3,740	1,006	3,598	3,979	548	4,584
Cairo	7,520	2,087	8,675	7,700	5,427	1,803	2,758	5,619	1,998	4,698
Cape Town	9,969	5,308	6,425	8,519	7,922	6,279	5,769	7,803	5,786	8,044
Caracas	3,632	4,346	9,717	2,234	2,438	6,177	8,833	2,120	4,732	8,950
Chicago	1,745	4,189	9,673	1,690	745	4,987	7,486	714	4,143	6,604
Hong Kong	7,240	6,558	4,595	8,788	7,736	4,437	2,339	8,060	5,990	1,217
Honolulu	2,557	7,872	5,505	3,789	4,918	7,047	7,412	4,969	7,449	5,077
London	5,439	785	10,500	5,558	3,254	1,564	4,181	3,469	214	5,074
Los Angeles	...	5,848	7,931	1,542	2,427	6,068	7,011	2,451	5,601	6,250
Madrid	5,848	...	10,758	5,643	3,448	2,147	4,530	3,593	655	5,745
Melbourne	7,931	10,758	...	8,426	10,395	8,950	6,329	10,359	10,430	5,643
Mexico City	1,542	5,643	8,426	...	2,317	6,676	9,120	2,090	5,725	7,753
Montreal	2,427	3,448	10,395	2,317	...	4,401	7,012	331	3,432	6,519
Moscow	6,068	2,147	8,950	6,676	4,401	...	2,698	4,683	1,554	3,607
New York	2,451	3,593	10,359	2,090	331	4,683	7,318	...	3,636	6,844
Paris	5,601	655	10,430	5,725	3,432	1,554	4,102	3,636	...	5,120
Peking	6,250	5,745	5,643	7,753	6,519	3,607	2,353	6,844	5,120	...
Rio de Janeiro	6,330	5,045	8,226	4,764	5,078	7,170	8,753	4,801	5,684	10,768
Rome	6,326	851	9,929	6,377	4,104	1,483	3,684	4,293	690	5,063
San Francisco	347	5,803	7,856	1,887	2,543	5,885	7,691	2,572	5,577	5,918
Singapore	8,767	7,080	3,759	10,327	9,203	5,228	2,571	9,534	6,673	2,771
Stockholm	5,454	1,653	9,630	6,012	3,714	716	3,414	3,986	1,003	4,133
Tokyo	5,470	6,706	5,062	7,035	6,471	4,660	3,638	6,757	6,053	1,307
Warsaw	5,922	1,427	9,598	6,337	4,022	721	3,277	4,270	852	4,325
Washington, D.C.	2,300	3,792	10,180	1,885	489	4,876	7,500	205	3,840	6,942

	Rio de Janiero	Rome	San Francisco	Singapore	Stockholm	Teheran	Tokyo	Vienna	Warsaw	Wash., D.C.
Bangkok	9,994	5,494	7,931	883	5,089	3,391	2,865	5,252	5,033	8,807
Berlin	6,209	737	5,672	6,164	528	2,185	5,557	326	322	4,181
Cairo	6,143	1,326	7,466	5,137	2,096	1,234	5,958	1,481	1,619	5,822
Cape Town	3,781	5,231	10,248	6,008	6,423	5,241	9,154	5,656	5,935	7,895
Caracas	2,804	5,195	3,902	11,402	5,471	7,320	8,808	5,372	5,559	2,047
Chicago	5,282	4,824	1,859	9,372	4,331	6,502	6,314	4,698	4,679	596
Hong Kong	11,009	5,774	6,905	1,605	5,063	3,843	1,791	5,431	5,147	8,155
Honolulu	8,288	8,040	2,398	6,726	6,875	8,070	3,859	7,632	7,366	4,838
London	5,750	895	5,367	6,747	942	2,743	5,959	771	905	3,674
Los Angeles	6,330	6,326	347	8,767	5,454	7,682	5,470	6,108	5,922	2,300
Madrid	5,045	851	5,803	7,080	1,653	2,978	6,706	1,128	1,427	3,792
Melbourne	8,226	9,929	7,856	3,759	9,630	7,826	5,062	9,790	9,598	10,180
Mexico City	4,764	6,377	1,887	10,327	6,012	8,184	7,035	6,320	6,337	1,885
Montreal	5,078	4,104	2,543	9,203	3,714	5,880	6,471	4,009	4,022	489
Moscow	7,170	1,483	5,885	5,228	716	1,532	4,660	1,043	721	4,876
New York	4,801	4,293	2,572	9,534	3,986	6,141	6,757	4,234	4,270	205
Paris	5,684	690	5,577	6,673	1,003	2,625	6,053	645	852	3,840
Peking	10,768	5,063	5,918	2,771	4,133	3,490	1,307	4,648	4,325	6,942
Rio de Janeiro	...	5,707	6,613	9,785	6,683	7,374	11,532	6,127	6,455	4,779
Rome	5,707	...	6,259	6,229	1,245	2,127	6,142	477	820	4,497
San Francisco	6,613	6,259	...	8,448	5,399	7,362	5,150	5,994	5,854	2,441
Singapore	9,785	6,229	8,448	...	5,936	4,103	3,300	6,035	5,843	9,662
Stockholm	6,683	1,245	5,399	5,936	...	2,173	5,053	780	494	4,183
Tokyo	11,532	6,142	5,150	3,300	5,053	4,775	...	5,689	5,347	6,791
Warsaw	6,455	820	5,854	5,843	494	1,879	5,689	347	...	4,472
Washington, D.C.	4,779	4,497	2,441	9,662	4,183	6,341	6,791	4,438	4,472	...

AEROSPACE

Memorable Manned Space Flights

Sources: National Aeronautics and Space Administration and The World Almanac.

Crew, date	Mission name	Orbits[1]	Duration	Remarks
Yuri A. Gagarin (4/12/61)	Vostok 1	1	1h 48m	First manned orbital flight.
Alan B. Shepard Jr. (5/5/61)	Mercury-Redstone 3	(2)	15m 22s	First American in space.
Virgil I. Grissom (7/21/61)	Mercury-Redstone 4	(2)	15m 37s	Spacecraft sank. Grissom rescued.
Gherman S. Titov (8/6-7/61)	Vostok 2	16	25h 18m	First space flight of more than 24 hrs.
John H. Glenn Jr. (2/20/62)	Mercury-Atlas 6	3	4h 55m 23s	First American in orbit.
M. Scott Carpenter (5/24/62)	Mercury-Atlas 7	3	4h 56m 05s	Manual retrofire error caused 250 mi. landing overshoot.
Andrian G. Nikolayev (8/11-15/62)	Vostok 3	64	94h 22m	Vostok 3 and 4 made first group flight.
Pavel R. Popovich (8/12-15/62)	Vostok 4	48	70h 57m	On first orbit it came within 3 miles of Vostok 3.
Walter M. Schirra Jr. (10/3/62)	Mercury-Atlas 8	6	9h 13m 11s	Closest splashdown to target to date (4.5 mi.).
L. Gordon Cooper (5/15-16/63)	Mercury-Atlas 9	22	34h 19m 49s	First U.S. evaluation of effects on man of one day in space.
Valery F. Bykovsky (6/14-6/19/63)	Vostok 5	81	119h 06m	Vostok 5 and 6 made 2d group flight.
Valentina V. Tereshkova (6/16-19/63)	Vostok 6	48	70h 50m	First woman in space.
Vladimir M. Komarov, Konstantin P. Feoktistov, Boris B. Yegorov (10/12/64)	Voskhod 1	16	24h 17m	First 3-man orbital flight: first without space suits.
Pavel I. Belyayev, Aleksei A. Leonov (3/18/65)	Voskhod 2	17	26h 02m	Leonov made first "space walk" (10 min.)
Virgil I. Grissom, John W. Young (3/23/65)	Gemini-Titan 3	3	4h 53m 00s	First manned spacecraft to change its orbital path.
James A. McDivitt, Edward H. White 2d, (6/3-7/65)	Gemini-Titan 4	62	97h 56m 11s	White was first American to "walk in space" (20 min.).
L. Gordon Cooper Jr., Charles Conrad Jr. (8/21-29/65)	Gemini-Titan 5	120	190h 55m 14s	First use of fuel cells for electric power; evaluated guidance and navigation system.
Frank Borman, James A. Lovell Jr. (12/4-18/65)	Gemini-Titan 7	206	330h 35m 31s	Longest duration Gemini flight
Walter M. Schirra Jr., Thomas P. Stafford (12/15-16/65)	Gemini-Titan 6-A	16	25h 51m 24s	Completed world's first space rendezvous with Gemini 7.
Neil A. Armstrong, David R. Scott (3/16-17/66)	Gemini-Titan 8	6.5	10h 41m 26s	First docking of one space vehicle with another; mission aborted, control malfunction.
John W. Young, Michael Collins (7/18-21/66)	Gemini-Titan 10	43	70h 46m 39s	First use of Agena target vehicle's propulsion systems.
Charles Conrad Jr., Richard F. Gordon Jr. (9/12-15/66)	Gemini-Titan 11	44	71h 17m 08s	Docked, made 2 revolutions of earth tethered; set Gemini altitude record (739.2 mi.).
James A. Lovell Jr., Edwin E. Aldrin Jr. (11/11-15/66)	Gemini-Titan 12	59	94h 34m 31s	Final Gemini mission; record 5½ hrs. of extravehicular activity.
Vladimir M. Komarov (4/23/67)	Soyuz 1	17	26h 40m	Crashed after re-entry killing Komarov.
Walter M. Schirra Jr., Donn F. Eisele, R. Walter Cunningham (10/11-22/68)	Apollo-Saturn 7	163	260h 09m 03s	First manned flight of Apollo spacecraft command-service module only.
Georgi T. Beregovoi (10/26-30/68)	Soyuz 3	64	94h 51m	Made rendezvous with unmanned Soyuz 2.
Frank Borman, James A. Lovell Jr., William A. Anders (12/21-27/68)	Apollo-Saturn 8	10[3]	147h 00m 42s	First flight to moon (command-service module only); views of lunar surface televised to earth.
Vladimir A. Shatalov (1/14-17/69)	Soyuz 4	45	71h 14m	Docked with Soyuz 5.
Boris V. Volyanov, Aleksei S. Yeliseyev, Yevgeny V. Khrunov (1/15-18/69)	Soyuz 5	46	72h 46m	Docked with Soyuz 4; Yeliseyev and Khrunov transferred to Soyuz 4.
James A. McDivitt, David R. Scott, Russell L. Schweickart (3/3-13/69)	Apollo-Saturn 9	151	241h 00m 54s	First manned flight of lunar module.

Crew, date	Mission name	Orbits[1]	Duration	Remarks
Thomas P. Stafford, Eugene A. Cernan, John W. Young (5/18-26/69)	Apollo-Saturn 10	31[4]	192h 03m 23s	First lunar module orbit of moon.
Neil A. Armstrong, Edwin E. Aldrin Jr., Michael Collins (7/16-24/69)	Apollo-Saturn 11	30[3]	195h 18m 35s	First lunar landing made by Armstrong and Aldrin; collected 48.5 lbs. of soil, rock samples; lunar stay time 21 h, 36m, 21 s.
Georgi S. Shonin, Valery N. Kubasov (10/11-16/69)	Soyuz 6	79	118h 42m	First welding of metals in space.
Anatoly V. Filipchenko, Vladislav N. Volkov, Viktor V. Gorbatko (10/12-17/69)	Soyuz 7	79	118h 41m	Space lab construction tests made; Soyuz 6, 7 and 8 — first time 3 spacecraft 7 crew orbited earth at once.
Charles Conrad Jr., Richard F. Gordon, Alan L. Bean (11/14-24/69)	Apollo-Saturn 12	45[3]	244h 36m 25s	Conrad and Bean made 2d moon landing; collected 74.7 lbs. of samples, lunar stay time 31 h, 31 m.
James A. Lovell Jr., Fred W. Haise Jr., John L. Swigart Jr. (4/11-17/70)	Apollo-Saturn 13	...	142h 54m 41s	Aborted after service module oxygen tank ruptured; crew returned safely using lunar module oxygen and power.
Alan B. Shepard Jr., Stuart A. Roosa, Edgar D. Mitchell (1/31-2/9/71)	Apollo-Saturn 14	34[3]	216h 01m 57s	Shepard and Mitchell made 3d moon landing, collected 96 lbs. of lunar samples; lunar stay 33 h, 31 m
Georgi T. Dobrovolsky, Vladislav N. Volkov, Viktor I. Patsayev (6/6-30/71)	Soyuz 11	360	569h 40m	Docked with Salyut space station; and orbited in Salyut for 23 days; crew died during re-entry from loss of pressurization.
David R. Scott, Alfred M. Worden, James B. Irwin (7/26-8/7/71)	Apollo-Saturn 15	74[3]	295h 11m 53s	Scott and Irwin made 4th moon landing; first lunar rover use; first deep space walk; 170 lbs. of samples; 66 h, 55 m, stay.
Charles M. Duke Jr., Thomas K. Mattingly, John W. Young (4/16-27/72)	Apollo-Saturn 16	64[3]	265h 51m 05s	Young and Duke made 5th moon landing; collected 213 lbs. of lunar samples; lunar stay line 71 h, 2 m.
Eugene A. Cernan, Ronald E. Evans, Harrison H. Schmitt (12/7-19/72)	Apollo-Saturn 17	75[3]	301h 51m 59s	Cernan and Schmitt made 6th manned lunar landing; collected 243 lbs. of samples; record lunar stay of 75 h.
Charles Conrad Jr., Joseph P. Kerwin, Paul J. Weitz (5/25-6/22/73)	Skylab 2	...	672h 49m 49s	First American manned orbiting space station; made long-flights tests, crew repaired damage caused during boost.
Alan L. Bean, Jack R. Lousma, Owen K. Garriott (7/28-9/25/73)	Skylab 3	...	1,427h 09m 04s	Crew systems and operational tests, exceeded pre-mission plans for scientific activities; space walk total 13h, 44 m.
Gerald P. Carr, Edward G. Gibson, William Pogue (11/16/73-2/8/74)	Skylab 4	...	2,017h 16m 30s	Final Skylab mission; record space walk of 7 h, 1 m., record space walks total for a mission 22 h, 21 m.
Alexi Leonov, Valeri Kubason (7/15-7/21/75)	Soyuz 19	96	143h 31m	
Vance Brand, Thomas P. Stafford, Donald K. Slayton (7/15-7/24/75)	Apollo 18	136	217h 30m	U.S.-USSR joint flight. Crews linked-up in space, conducted experiments, shared meals, and held a joint news conference.
Leonid Kizim, Vladmir Solovyov, Oleg Atkov (2/8-10/2/84)	Salyut 7	...	237 days	Set space endurance record.

(1) The U.S. measures orbital flights in revolutions while the Soviets use "orbits." (2) Suborbital. (3) Moon orbits in command module. (4) Moon orbits.

Fire aboard spacecraft Apollo I on the ground at Cape Kennedy, Fla. killed Virgil I. Grissom, Edward H. White and Roger B. Chaffee on Jan. 27, 1967. They were the only U.S. astronauts killed in space tests.

U.S. Space Shuttles

Name, date	Crew
Columbia (4/12-14/81)	Robert L. Crippen, John W. Young.
Columbia (11/12-14/81)	Joe Engle, Richard Truly.
Columbia (3/22-30/82)	Jack Lousma, C. Gordon Fullerton.
Columbia (6-27/7-4/82)	Thomas Mattingly 2d, Henry Hartsfield Jr.
Columbia (11/11-16/82)	Vance Brand, Robert Overmyer, William Lenoir, Joseph Allen.

Name, date	Crew
Challenger (4/4-9/83)	Paul Weitz, Karol Bobko, Story Musgrave, Donald Peterson.
Challenger (6/18-24/83)	Robert L. Crippen, Norman Thagard, John Fabian, Frederick Hauck, Sally K. Ride (1st U.S. woman in space).
Challenger (8/30-9/5/83)	Richard Truly, Daniel Brandenstein, William Thornton,

U.S. Space Shuttles

Name, date	Crew
	Guion Bluford (1st U.S. black in space), Dale Gardner.
Columbia (11/28-12/8/83)	John Young, Brewster Shaw Jr., Robert Parker, Owen Garriott, Byron Lichtenberg, Ulf Merbold.
Challenger (2/3-11/84)	Vance Brand, Robert Gibson, Ronald McNair, Bruce McCandless, Robert Stewart.
Challenger (4/6-13/84)	Robert L. Crippen, Francis R. Scobee, George D. Nelson, Terry J. Hart, James D. Van Hoften.
Discovery (8/30-9/5/84)	Henry W. Hartsfield Jr., Michael L. Coats, Steven A. Hawley, Judith A. Resnik, Richard M. Mullane, Charles D. Walker.
Challenger (10/5-13/84)	Robert L. Crippen, Jon A. McBride, Kathryn D. Sullivan, Sally K. Ride, Marc Garneau (first Canadian), David C. Leestma, Paul D. Scully-Power.
Discovery (11/8-16/84)	Frederick H. Hauck, David M. Walker, Dr. Anna L. Fisher, Joseph P. Allen, Dale A. Gardner.
Discovery (1/24-27/85)	Thomas K. Mattingly, Loren J. Shriver, James F. Buchli, Ellison S. Onizuka, Gary E. Payton.
Discovery (4/12-19/85)	Karol J. Bobko, Donald E. Williams, Sen. Jake Garn, Charles D. Walker, Jeffrey A. Hoffman, S. David Griggs, M. Rhea Seddon.
Challenger (4/29-5/6/85)	Robert F. Overmyer, Frederick D. Gregory, Don L. Lind, Taylor G. Wang, Lodewijk van den Berg, Norman Thagard, William Thornton.
Discovery (6/17-6/24/85)	John O. Creighton, Shannon W. Lucid, Steven R. Nagel, Daniel C. Brandenstein, John W. Fabian, Prince Sultan Salman al-Saud (first Arab), Patrick Baudry.
Challenger (7/29-8/6/85)	Roy D. Bridges Jr., Anthony W. England, Karl G. Henize, F. Story Musgrave, C. Gordon Fullerton, Loren W. Acton, John-David F. Bartoe.
Discovery (8/27-9/3/85)	John M. Lounge, James D. van Hoften, William F. Fisher, Joe H. Engle, Richard O. Covey.
Atlantis (10/4-10/7/85)	Karol J. Bobko, Ronald J. Grabe, David C. Hilmers, William A. Pailes, Robert C. Stewart.
Challenger (10/30-11/6/85)	Henry W. Hartsfield Jr., Steven R. Nagel, Bonnie J. Dunbar, James F. Buchli, Guion S. Bluford Jr., Ernst Messerschmid, Reinhard Furrer, Wubbo J. Ockels.
Atlantis (11/26-12/3/85)	Brewster H. Shaw Jr., Bryan D. O'Connor, Charles Walker, Rodolfo Neri (first Mexican), Jerry L. Ross, Sherwood C. Spring, Mary L. Cleave.
Columbia (1/12-1/18/86)	Robert L. Gibson, Charles F. Bolden Jr., George D. Nelson, Bill Nelson (first congressman), Franklin R. Chang-Diaz, Steven A. Hawley, Robert J. Cenker.
Challenger (1/28/86-exploded after takeoff)	Francis R. Scobee, Michael J. Smith, Robert E. McNair, Ellison S. Onizuka, Judith A. Resnik, Gregory B. Jarvis, Sharon Christa McAuliffe (*See Chronology*).

Notable U.S. Unmanned and Planetary Missions

Spacecraft	Launch date (GMT)	Mission	Remarks
Mariner 2	Aug. 27, 1962	Venus	Passed within 22,000 miles from Venus 12/14/62; contact lost 1/3/63 at 54 million miles
Ranger 7	July 28, 1964	Moon	Yielded over 4,000 photos
Mariner 4	Nov. 28, 1964	Mars	Passed behind Mars 7/14/65; took 22 photos from 6,000 miles
Ranger 8	Feb. 17, 1965	Moon	Yielded over 7,000 photos
Surveyor 3	Apr. 17, 1967	Moon	Scooped and tested lunar soil
Mariner 5	June 14, 1967	Venus	In solar orbit; closest Venus fly-by 10/19/67
Mariner 6	Feb. 25, 1969	Mars	Came within 2,000 miles of Mars 7/31/69; sent back data, photos
Mariner 7	Mar. 27, 1969	Mars	Came within 2,000 miles of Mars 8/5/69
Mariner 9	May 30, 1971	Mars	First craft to orbit Mars 11/13/71; sent back over 7,000 photos
Pioneer 10	Mar. 3, 1972	Jupiter	Passed Jupiter 12/3/73; exited the solar system 6/14/83
Mariner 10	Nov. 3, 1973	Venus, Mercury	Passed Venus 2/5/74; arrived Mercury 3/29/74. First time gravity of one planet (Venus) used to whip spacecraft toward another (Mercury)
Viking 1	Aug. 20, 1975	Mars	Landed on Mars 7/20/76; did scientific research, sent photos; functioned 6 1/2 years
Viking 2	Sept. 9, 1975	Mars	Landed on Mars 9/3/76; functioned 3 1/2 years
Voyager 1	Sept. 5, 1977	Jupiter, Saturn	Encountered Jupiter 3/5/79; Saturn 11/13/80
Voyager 2	Sept. 20, 1977	Jupiter, Saturn, Uranus	Encountered Jupiter 7/9/79; Saturn 8/26/81; Uranus 1/8 and 1/27/86
Pioneer 12	May 20, 1978	Venus	Entered Venus orbit 12/4/78
Pioneer 13	Aug. 8, 1978	Venus	Encountered Venus 12/9/78

Successful Space Launches: 1957 to 1985

(Criterion of success is attainment of Earth orbit or Earth escape)

Year	Total[1]	USSR	United States	Japan	European Space Agency	India	China
Total	**2,642**	**1,733**	**844**	**27**	**9**	**3**	**14**
1957-1959	21	6	15	—	—	—	—
1960-1964	268	76	192	—	—	—	—
1965-1969	586	302	279	—	—	—	—
1970-1974	555	405	139	5	—	—	2
1975-1979	607	461	126	10	1	—	6
1980	105	89	13	2	—	1	—
1981	123	98	18	3	2	1	1
1982	121	101	18	1	—	—	1
1983	127	98	22	3	2	1	1
1984	129	97	22	3	4	—	3
1985	121	98	17	2	3	—	1

(1) Incl. launches in countries not shown.

NASA Outlays for Research and Development

Source: U.S. Office of Management and Budget

(millions of dollars)

			Performance				Facilities			
Year	Total outlays	Percent change	Total	Space flight	Space science applications	Air transport and other	Total	Space flight	Space science applications	Air transport and other
1966	$5,933	16.5[1]	$5,361	$3,819	$1,120	$422	$572	$391	$63	$118
1967	5,426	−8.5	5,137	3,477	1,160	500	289	172	47	70
1968	4,726	−12.9	4,599	3,028	1,061	510	127	69	29	29
1969	4,252	−10.0	4,187	2,754	893	540	65	27	21	17
1970	3,753	−11.7	3,699	2,195	963	541	54	14	21	19
1971	3,382	−9.9	3,338	1,877	926	535	44	8	6	30
1972	3,423	1.2	3,373	1,727	1,111	535	50	13	7	30
1973	3,316	−3.1	3,271	1,532	1,220	519	45	5	11	29
1974	3,256	−1.8	3,181	1,448	1,156	577	75	25	12	38
1975	3,266	.3	3,181	1,500	1,076	606	85	35	9	42
1976	3,670	12.4	3,549	1,934	969	646	121	66	11	43
1977	3,945	7.5	3,840	2,195	1,002	643	105	56	4	45
1978	3,984	1.0	3,860	2,204	964	692	124	56	8	60
1979	4,187	5.0	4,054	2,175	1,144	735	133	41	9	83
1980	4,850	15.8	4,710	2,556	1,341	813	140	38	5	97
1981	5,241	11.8	5,274	3,026	1,380	868	147	26	4	117
1982	6,035	11.3	5,926	3,526	1,454	946	109	17	3	89
1983	6,664	10.4	6,556	4,027	1,486	1,043	108	26	—	82
1984	7,048	5.8	6,856	4,037	1,667	1,152	192	44	20	128
1985 est.	7,321	3.9	7,073	3,893	1,868	1,312	248	75	22	151

(1) Change from 1965.

National Aviation Hall of Fame

The National Aviation Hall of Fame at Dayton, Oh., is dedicated to honoring the outstanding pioneers of air and space.

Allen, William M.
Andrews, Frank M.
Armstrong, Neil A.
Arnold, Henry H. "Hap"
Atwood, John Leland
Balchen, Bernt
Baldwin, Thomas S.
Beachey, Lincoln
Beech, Olive A.
Beech, Walter H.
Bell, Alexander Graham
Bell, Lawrence D.
Boeing, William E.
Bong, Richard I.
Borman, Frank
Boyd, Albert
Brown, George "Scratchley"
Byrd, Richard E.
Cessna, Clyde V.
Chamberlin, Clarence D.
Chanute, Octave
Chennault, Claire L.
Cochran (Odlum), Jacqueline
Collins, Michael
Conrad Jr., Charles
Crossfield, A. Scott
Cunningham, Alfred A.
Curtiss, Glenn H.
deSeversky, Alexander P.
Doolittle, James H.
Douglas, Donald W.
Draper, Charles S.
Eaker, Ira C.
Earhart, (Putnam), Amelia
Eielson, C. Benjamin
Ellyson, Theodore G.
Ely, Eugene B.
Fairchild, Sherman M.
Fleet, Reuben H.
Fokker, Anthony H.G.
Ford, Henry
Foss, Joseph
Foulois, Benjamin D.
Gabreski, Francis S.
Glenn Jr., John H.
Goddard, George W.
Goddard, Robert H.
Godfrey, Arthur
Goldwater, Barry M.
Grissom, Virgil I.
Gross, Robert E.
Grumman, Leroy R.
Guggenheim, Harry F.
Haughton, Daniel J.
Hegenberger, Albert F.
Heinemann, Edward H.
Hughes, Howard R.
Ingalls, David S.
Johnson, Clarence L.
Kenney, George C.
Kettering, Charles F.
Kindelberger, James H.
Knabenshue, A. Roy
Lahm, Frank P.
Langley, Samuel P.
Lear, William P. Sr.
LeMay, Curtis E.
LeVier, Anthony W.
Lindbergh, Anne M.
Lindbergh, Charles A.
Link, Edwin A.
Lockheed, Allan H.
Loening, Grover
Luke Jr., Frank
Macready, John A.
Martin, Glenn L.
McDonnell, James S.
Mitchell, William "Billy"
Montgomery, John J.
Moss, Sanford A.
Neumann, Gerhard
Northrop, John K.
Patterson, William A.
Piper Sr., William T.
Post, Wiley H.
Read, Albert C.
Reeve, Robert C.
Rentschler, Frederick B.
Richardson, Holden C.
Rickenbacker, Edward V.
Rodgers, Calbraith P.
Rogers, Will
Ryan, T. Claude
Schirra, Walter M.
Schriever, Bernard A.
Selfridge, Thomas E.
Shepard Jr., Alan B.
Sikorsky, Igor I.
Six, Robert F.
Smith, C.R.
Spaatz, Carl A.
Sperry Sr., Elmer A.
Sperry Sr., Lawrence B.
Stapp, John P.
Taylor, Charles E.
Towers, John H.
Trippe, Juan T.
Turner, Roscoe
Twining, Nathan F.
von Braun, Wernher
von Karman, Theodore
Wade, Leigh
Walden, Henry W.
Wilson, Thornton A.
Wright, Orville
Wright, Wilbur
Yeager, Charles E.

Notable Around the World and Intercontinental Trips

	From/To	Miles	Time	Date
Nellie Bly	New York/New York		72d 06h 11m	1889
George Francis Train	New York/New York		67d 12h 03m	1890
Charles Fitzmorris	Chicago/Chicago		60d 13h 29m	1901
J. W. Willis Sayre	Seattle/Seattle		54d 09h 42m	1903
J. Alcock-A.W. Brown (1)	Newfoundland/Ireland	1,960	16h 12m	June 14-15, 1919
Two U.S. Army airplanes	Seattle/Seattle	26,103	35d 01h 11m	1924
Richard E. Byrd (2)	Spitsbergen/N. Pole	1,545	15h 30m	May 9, 1926
Amundsen-Ellsworth-Nobile Expedition	Spitsbergen/Teller, Alaska		80h	May 11-14,1926
E.S. Evans and L. Wells (N. Y.World) (3)	New York/New York	18,400	28d 14h 36m 05s	June 16-July 14, 1926
Charles Lindbergh (4)	New York/Paris	3,610	33h 29m 30s	May 20-21, 1927
Amelia Earhart, W. Stultz, L. Gordon	Newfoundland/Wales		20h 40m	June 17-18, 1928
Graf Zepppelin	Friedrichshafen, Ger./Lakehurst, N.J.	6,630	4d 15h 46m	Oct. 11-15, 1928
Graf Zeppelin	Friedrichshafen, Ger./Lakehurst, N.J.	21,700	20d 04h	Aug. 14-Sept. 4, 1929
Wiley Post and Harold Gatty (Monoplane Winnie Mae)	New York/New York	15,474	8d 15h 51m	July 1, 1931
C. Pangborn-H. Herndon Jr. (5)	Tokyo/Wenatchee, Wash.	4,458	41h 34m	Oct. 3-5, 1931
Amelia Earhart (6)	Newfoundland/Ireland	2,026	14h 56m	May 20-21, 1932
Wiley Post (Monoplane Winnie Mae) (7)	New York/New York	15,596	115h 36m 30s	July 15-22, 1933
Hindenburg Zeppelin	Lakehurst, N.J./Frankfort, Ger.		42h 53m	Aug. 9-11, 1936
H. R. Ekins (Scripps-Howard Newspapers in race) (Zeppelin Hindenburg to Germany air planes from Frankfurt)	Lakehurst, N.J./Lakehurst, N.J.	25,654	18d 11h 14m 33s	Sept, 30-Oct. 19, 1936
Howard Hughes and 4 assistants	New York/New York	14,824	3d 19h 08m 10s	July 10-13, 1938
Douglas Corrigan	New York/Dublin		28h 13m	July 17-18, 1938
Mrs. Clara Adams (Pan American Clipper)	Port Washington, N.Y./Newark, N.J.		16d 19h 04m	June 28-July 15, 1939
Globester, U.S. Air Transport Command	Wash., D.C./Wash., D.C.	23,279	149h 44m	Oct. 4, 1945
Capt. William P. Odom (A-26 Reynolds Bombshell)	New York/New York	20,000	78h 55m 12s	Apr. 12-16, 1947
America, Pan American 4-engine Lockheed Constellation (8)	New York/New York	22,219	101h 32m	June 17-30, 1947
Col. Edward Eagan	New York/New York	20,559	147h 15m	Dec. 13, 1948
USAF B-50 Lucky Lady II (Capt. James Gallagher) (9)	Ft. Worth, Tex./Ft. Worth, Tex.	23,452	94h 01m	Feb. 26-Mar. 2, 1949
Col. D. Schilling, USAF (10)	England/Limestone, Me.	3,300	10h 01m	Sept. 22, 1950
C.F. Blair Jr.	Norway/Alaska	3,300	10h 29m	May 29, 1951
Two U.S. S-55	Massachusetts/Scotland	3,410	42h 30m	July 15-31, 1952
Canberra Bomber (11)	N. Ireland/Newfoundland	2,073	04h 34m	Aug. 26, 1952
	Newfoundland/N. Ireland	2,073	03h 25m	Aug. 26, 1952
Three USAF B-52 Stratofortresses (12)	Merced, Cal./Cal.	24,325	45h 19m	Jan. 15-18, 1957
Max Conrad	Chicago/Rome	5,000	34h 03m	Mar. 5-6, 1959
USSR TU-114 (13)	Moscow/New York	5,092	11h 06m	June 28, 1959
Boeing 707-320	New York/Moscow	c.5090	08h 54m	July 23, 1959
Peter Gluckmann (solo)	San Francisco/San Francisco	22,800	29d	Aug. 22-Sept. 20, 1959
Sue Snyder	Chicago/Chicago	21,219	62h 59m	June 22-24, 1960
Max Conrad (solo)	Miami/Miami	25,946	8d 18h 35m 57s	Feb. 28-Mar. 8, 1961
Sam Miller & Louis Fodor	New York/New York		46h 28m	Aug. 3-4, 1963
Robert & Joan Wallick	Manila/Manila	23,129	05d 06h 17m 10s	June 2-7, 1966
Arthur Godfrey, Richard Merrill Fred Austin, Karl Keller	New York/New York	23,333	86h 9m 01s	June 4-7, 1966
Trevor K. Brougham	Darwin, Australia/Darwin	24,800	5d 05h 57m	Aug. 5-10, 1972
Walter H. Mullikin, Albert Frink, Lyman Watt, Frank Cassaniti, Edward Shields	New York/New York	23,137	1d 22h 50s	May 1-3,1976
David Kunst (15)	Waseca, Minn./Waseca, Minn.	14,500	4yrs 3mos 16d	June 10, 1970-Oct. 5, 1974
Arnold Palmer	Denver/Denver	22,985	57h 25m 42s	May 17-19, 1976
Boeing 747 (14)	San Francisco/San Francisco	26,382	54h 7m 12s	Oct. 28-31, 1977
Concorde	London/Wash., D.C.	1,023 mph	03h 34m 48s	May 29, 1976
Concorde	Paris/New York	1,037.50 mph	03h 30m 11s	Aug. 22, 1978
Richard Rutan & Jeana Yeager (16)	Edwards AFB, Cal.	25,012	09d 03m 44s	Dec. 14-23, 1986

(1) Non-stop transtlantic flight. (2) Polar flight. (3) Mileage by train and auto, 4,110; by plane, 6,300; by steamship, 8,000. (4) Solo transatlantic flight in the Ryan monoplane the "Spirit of St. Louis". (5) Non-stop Pacific flight. (6) Woman's transoceanic solo flight. (7) First to fly solo around northern circumference of the world, also first to fly twice around the world. (8) Inception of regular commercial global air service. (9) First non-stop round-the-world flight, refueled 4 times in flight. (10) Non-stop jet transatlantic flight. (11) Transatlantic round trip on same day. (12) First non-stop global flight by jet planes; refueled in flight by KC-97 aerial tankers; average speed approx. 525 mph. (13) Non-stop between Moscow and New York. (14) Speed record around the world over both the earth's poles. (15) First to circle the earth on foot. (16) Circled the earth nonstop without refueling.

International Aeronautical Records

Source: The National Aeronautic Association, 1763 R St. NW, Washington, DC 20009, representative in the United States of the Federation Aeronautique Internationale, certifying agency for world aviation and space records. The International Aeronautical Federation was formed in 1905 by representatives from Belgium, France, Germany, Great Britain, Spain, Italy, Switzerland, and the United States, with headquarters in Paris. Regulations for the control of official records were signed Oct. 14, 1905. World records are defined as maximum performance, regardless of class or type of aircraft used. Records to Aug., 1987.

World Absolute Records—Maximum Performance in Any Class

Speed over a straight course — 3,529.56 kph. (2,193.16 mph) — Capt. Elden W. Joersz, USAF, Lockheed SR-71; Beale AFB, Cal., July 28, 1976.

Speed over a closed circuit — 3,367.221 kph. (2,092.294 mph) — Maj. Adolphus H. Bledsoe Jr., USAF, Lockheed SR-71; Beale AFB, Cal., July 27, 1976.

Distance in a straight line — 20,168.78 kms (12,532.28 mi.) — Maj. Clyde P. Evely, USAF, Boeing B52-H; Kadena, Okinawa to Madrid, Spain, Jan. 11, 1962.

Distance over a closed circuit — 18,658.15 kms (11,593.68 mi.) — Richard Rutan & Jeana Yeager, U.S., Voyager, Vandenberg AFB to Mojave Airport, Cal., July 10-15, 1986.

Altitude — 37,650 meters (123,523.58 feet) — Alexander Fedotov, USSR, E-266M; Podmoskovnoye, USSR, Aug. 31, 1977.

Altitude in horizontal flight — 25,929.031 meters (85,068.997 ft.) — Capt. Robert C. Helt, USAF, Lockheed SR-71; Beale AFB, Cal., July 28, 1976.

Class K Spacecraft

Duration — 236 days, 22 hrs., 49 min., 4 sec. — Leonid Kizim, Vladimir Solovyov, Oleg Atkov, USSR, Soyuz T-10, Salyut 7, Soyuz T-11; Feb. 8-Oct. 2, 1984.

Altitude — 377,668.9 kms (234,672.5 mi.) — Frank Borman, James A. Lovell Jr., William Anders, Apollo 8; Dec. 21-27, 1968.

Greatest mass lifted — 127,980 kgs. (282,197 lbs.) — Frank Borman, James A. Lovell Jr., William Anders, Apollo 8; Dec. 21-27, 1968.

Distance — 140,800,200 kms. (87,436,800 mi.) — Anatoly Beresovoy & Valentin Lebedev, USSR, Salyut 7, Soyuz T5, Soyuz T7; May 13-Dec. 10, 1982.

World "Class" Records

All other records, international in scope, are termed World "Class" records and are divided into classes: airships, free balloons, airplanes, seaplanes, amphibians, gliders, and rotorplanes. Airplanes (Class C) are sub-divided into four groups: Group I — piston engine aircraft, Group II — turboprop aircraft, Group III — jet aircraft, Group IV — rocket powered aircraft. A partial listing of world records follows:

Airplanes (Class C-I, Group I—piston engine)

Distance, closed circuit — 18,658.16 kms (11,593.18 mi.) — Richard Rutan & Jeana Yeager, U.S., Voyager; Vandenberg AFB to Mojave Airport, Cal., July 10-15, 1986.

Distance, straight line — 18,081.99 kms. (11,235.6 miles) — Cmdr. Thomas D. Davies, USN; Cmdr. Eugene P. Rankin, USN; Cmdr. Walter S. Reid, USN, and Lt. Cmdr. Ray A. Tabeling, USN; Lockheed P2V-1; from Pearce Field, Perth, Australia to Columbus, Oh., Sept. 29-Oct. 1, 1946.

Speed over 3-kilometer measured course — 803.138 kph. (499.04 mph) — Steve Hinton; P-51D; Tonopah, Nev., Aug. 14, 1979.

Speed for 100 kilometers (62.137 miles) without payload — 755.668 kph. (469.549 mph.) — Jacqueline Cochran, U.S.; North American P-51; Coachella Valley, Cal., Dec. 10, 1947.

Speed for 1,000 kilometers (621.369 miles) without payload — 693.78 kph. (431.09 mph.) — Jacqueline Cochran, U.S.; North American P 51; Santa Rosa Summit, Cal. Flagstaff, Ariz. course, May 24, 1948.

Speed for 5,000 kilometers (3,106.849 miles) without payload — 544.59 kph. (338.39 mph.) — Capt. James Bauer, USAF, Boeing B-29; Dayton, Oh., June 28, 1946.

Speed around the world — 327.73 kph (203.64 mph) — D.N. Dalton, Australia; Beechcraft Duke; Brisbane, Aust., July 20-25, 1975. Time: 5 days, 2 hours, 19 min., 57 sec.

Light Airplanes—(Class C-1.d)

Distance in a straight line — 12,341.20 kms. (7,668.48 miles) — Max Conrad, U.S.; Piper Comanche; Casablanca, Morocco to Los Angeles, June 2-4, 1959.

Speed for 100 kilometers — (62,137 miles) in a closed circuit — 519.480 kph. (322.780 mph.) — Ms. R. M. Sharpe, Great Britain; Vickers Supermarine Spitfire 5-B; Wolverhampton, June 17, 1950.

Helicopters (Class E-1)

Distance in a straight line — 3,561.55 kms. (2,213.04 miles) — Robert G. Ferry, U.S.; Hughes YOH-6A helicopter; Culver City, Cal., to Ormond Beach, Fla., Apr. 6-7, 1966.

Speed over 3-km. course — 348.971 kph. (216.839 mph.) — Byron Graham, U.S.; Sikorsky S-67 helicopter; Windsor Locks, Conn., Dec. 14, 1970.

Speed around the world —56.97 kph. (35.40 mph) — H. Ross Perot Jr.; Bell 206 L-11 Long Ranger N39112; Dallas, Tex.–Dallas, Tex.; Sept. 1-30, 1982; 29 days, 3 hrs., 8 min., 13 sec.

Gliders (Class D-I—single place)

Distance, straight line — 1,460.8 kms. (907.7 miles) — Hans Werner Grosse, West Germany; ASK12 sailplane; Luebeck to Biarritz, Apr. 25, 1972.

Distance to a goal & return — 1,646.68 kms. (1,023.25 miles) — Thomas Knauff, U.S. Nimbus III; Williamsport, Pa., Apr. 25, 1983.

Airplanes (Class C-I, Group II—Turboprop)

Distance in a straight line — 14,052.95 kms. (8,732.09 miles) — Lt. Col. Edgar L. Allison Jr., USAF, Lockheed HC-130 Hercules aircraft; Taiwan to Scott AFB, Ill.; Feb. 20, 1972.

Altitude — 15,549 meters (51,014 ft.) — Donald R. Wilson, U.S.; LTV L450F aircraft; Greenville, Tex., Mar. 27, 1972.

Speed for 1,000 kilometers (621.369 miles) without payload — 871.38 kph. (541.449 mph.) — Ivan Soukhomline, USSR; TU-114 aircraft; Sternberg, USSR; Mar. 24, 1960.

Speed for 5,000 kilometers (3,106.849 miles) without payload — 877.212 kph. (545.072 mph.) — Ivan Soukhomline, USSR; TU-114 aircraft, Sternberg, USSR; Apr. 9, 1960.

(continued)

Airplanes (Class C-1, Group III—Jet-powered)

Distance in a straight line — 20,168.78 kms. (12,532.28 mi.) — Maj. Clyde P. Evely, USAF, Boeing B-52-H, Kadena, Okinawa to Madrid, Spain, Jan. 10-11, 1962.
Distance in a closed circuit — 18,245.05 kms. (11,336.92 miles) — Capt. William Stevenson, USAF, Boeing B-52-H, Seymour-Johnson, N.C., June 6-7, 1962.
Altitude — 36,650 meters (123,523.58 ft.) — Alexander Fedotov, USSR; E-226M airplane; Podmoskovnoye, USSR, Aug. 31, 1977.
Speed for 100 kilometers in a closed circuit — 2,605 kph. (1,618.7 mph.) — Alexander Fedotov, USSR; E-266 airplane, Apr. 8, 1973.
Speed for 500 kilometers in a closed circuit — 2,981.5 kph. (1,852.61 mph.) — Mikhail Komarov, USSR; E-266 airplane, Oct. 5, 1967.
Speed for 1,000 kilometers in a closed circuit — 3,367.221 kph (2,092.294 mph) — Maj. Adolphus H. Bledsoe Jr., USAF; Lockheed SR-71; Beale AFB, Cal., July 27, 1976.
Speed for 2,000 kilometers without payload — 2,012,257 kph. (1,250.42 mph.) — S. Agapov, USSR; Podmoscovnde, USSR; July 20, 1983.
Speed around the world — 825.32 kph. (512.853 mph) — Brooke Knapp, U.S., Gulfstream III; Washington, D.C., Feb. 13-15, 1984.

Balloons-Class A

Altitude — 34,668 meters (113,739.9 feet) — Cmdr. Malcolm D. Ross, USNR; Lee Lewis Memorial Winzen Research Balloon; Gulf of Mexico, May 4, 1961.
Distance —8,382.4 kms. (5,208.67 mi.) — Ben Abruzzo; Raven Experimental; Nagashima, Japan to Covello, Cal., Nov. 9-12, 1981.

Duration —137 hr., 5 min., 50 sec. — Ben Abruzzo and Maxie Anderson; Double Eagle II; Presque Isle, Maine to Miserey, France (3,107.61 mi.); Aug. 12-17, 1978.

FAI Course Records

Los Angeles to New York — 1,954.79 kph (1,214.65 mph) — Capt. Robert G. Sowers, USAF; Convair B-58 Hustler; elapsed time: 2 hrs. 58.71 sec., Mar. 5, 1962.
New York to Los Angeles — 1,741 kph (1,081.80 mph) — Capt. Robert G. Sowers, USAF; Convair B-58 Hustler; elapsed time: 2 hrs. 15 min. 50.08 sec., Mar. 5, 1962.
New York to Paris — 1,753.068 kph (1,089.36 mph) — Maj. W. R. Payne, U.S.; Convair B-58 Hustler; elapsed time: 3 hrs 19 min. 44 sec., May 26, 1961.
London to New York — 945.423 kph (587.457 mph) — Maj. Burl Davenport, USAF; Boeing KC-135; elapsed time: 5 hrs. 53 min. 12.77 sec.; June 27, 1958.
Baltimore to Moscow, USSR — 906.64 kph (563.36 mph) — Col. James B. Swindal, USAF; Boeing VC-137 (707); elapsed time: 8 hrs. 33 min. 45.4 sec., May 19, 1963.
New York to London — 2,908.026 kph (1,806.964 mph) — Maj. James V. Sullivan, USAF; Lockheed SR-71; elapsed time 1 hr. 54 min. 56.4 sec., Sept. 1, 1974.
London to Los Angeles — 2,310.353 kph (1,435.587 mph) — Capt. Harold B. Adams, USAF; Lockheed SR-71; elapsed time: 3 hrs. 47 min. 39 sec., Sept. 13, 1974.

The Busiest U.S. Airports in 1986

Source: Air Transport Association of America (Passengers arriving & departing)

Chicago O'Hare	54,770,673	Boston	21,862,718
Atlanta	45,191,480	St. Louis	20,352,383
Los Angeles	41,417,867	Honolulu	18,235,154
Dallas/Ft. Worth	39,945,326	Detroit	17,604,583
Denver	34,685,944	Minneapolis/St. Paul	17,073,605
Newark	29,433,046	Pittsburgh	15,989,507
San Francisco	27,813,595	Washington, D.C. (DCA)	14,307,980
New York (JFK)	27,223,733	Houston	13,996,015
New York (LGA)	22,188,817	Phoenix	13,274,015
Miami	21,947,368	Philadelphia	12,780,306

U.S. Scheduled Airline Traffic

Source: Air Transport Association of America (thousands)

	1984	1985	1986
Passenger traffic			
Revenue passengers enplaned	344,683	382,022	418,493
Revenue passenger miles	305,115,855	336,403,021	366,283,158
Available seat miles	515,323,339	547,788,432	606,847,601
Revenue passenger load factor(%)	—	61.4	60.4
Cargo traffic (ton miles)	8,185,366	7,689,003	9,017,136
Freight and express	6,566,571	6,030,543	7,335,942
U.S. Mail	1,583,531	1,625,500	1,624,312
Foreign Mail	35,264	32,960	56,882
Overall traffic and service			
Total revenue ton miles—charter service	2,580,969	2,825,521	3,181,516
Total revenue ton miles—all services	41,277,948	44,154,779	48,827,582
Total available ton miles—all services	76,298,288	80,565,182	90,124,424

U.S. Airline Safety

Source: National Transportation Safety Board

	Departures (millions)	Fatal accidents	Fatalities	Fatal accidents per 100,000 departures		Departures (millions)	Fatal accidents	Fatalities	Fatal accidents per 100,000 departures
1976	4.8	2	38	0.041	1982	5.0	3	233	0.060
1977	4.9	3	78	0.061	1983	5.0	4	15	0.080
1978	5.0	5	160	0.100	1984	5.4	1	4	0.019
1979	5.4	4	351	0.074	1985	5.7	4	197	0.070
1980	5.3	0	0	0.000	1986p	6.4	1	1	0.016
1981	5.2	4	4	0.077					

(p) = preliminary. For 1987, see *Disasters, 1986-7* in Index.

SCIENCE AND TECHNOLOGY

Scientific Achievements and Discoveries: 1987

As of September 1, 1987

Origins of Life on Earth

An **asteroid,** believed to have hit the earth 2.3 million years ago, was found to be 10 times larger than had been estimated, and its impact to have created an explosion 172 times larger than the biggest hydrogen bomb ever detonated. Frank Kyte, a geochemist at the Univ. of California, Los Angeles, one of the scientists studying seafloor sediment samples collected in the 1960s, said that the blast might have helped create the **Ice Age.** This period, when the earth started getting colder, began about 3.5 million years ago, and sheets of ice covered parts of the continents from about 1.5 million years ago to about 10,000 years ago, in the Pleistocene Ice Age. Geochemists speculated that the asteroid might have stimulated the cooling by throwing up debris that blocked sunlight.

A new **fossil discovery** in Tanzania suggested that the species believed to be the earliest tool user and a direct ancestor of modern humans was apparently much smaller and more apelike than had been thought. This discovery, along with other recent findings, led some scientists to speculate that an abrupt transition in early **human evolution** had occurred about 1.6 million years ago. Other scientists cautioned that the known fossil remains were still too few and far between to justify definitive statements on the course of human evolution. Early Homo Sapiens evolved about 400,000 years ago, and truly modern humans emerged about 35,000 years ago. The discovery was made by a team led by Donald C. Johanson, of the Inst. of Human Origins in Berkeley, Calif.

Dr. Solomon H. Katz, an anthropologist at the Univ. of Pennsylvania, reported that the accidental discovery by **prehistoric humans** that wild wheat and barley soaked in water to make gruel, did not spoil if left out in the open air, was directly related to the decision to settle down and cultivate and reap crops. Natural yeast converted the gruel to a dark, **bubbling brew** that made whoever drank it feel good. In addition, the brew made people robust, and at the time, it was second only to animal protein as a nutritional source. This combination of mood-altering and nutritional properties would have been incentive enough to cause neolithic hunter-gatherers in the Near East to begin cultivating the grains. Dr. Katz said that "almost invariably, individuals and societies appear to invest enormous amounts of effort and even risk" in the pursuit of mind-altering foods and beverages. According to the *New York Times*, the world's oldest recipe written on Sumerian tablets, was for beer. Another tablet contained a hymn to the beer goddess, Ninkasi.

Astronomical Findings

An **exploding star (supernova)** appeared over the Southern Hemisphere in Feb. 1987, producing a shower of subnuclear particles across the earth, and gave scientists important new evidence concerning the ultimate fate of the universe. The exploding star, believed to be 163,000 light years from earth, was the closest and brightest such deluge known to have occurred since 1604. The cosmic blast had occurred 50,000 years ago, but the light it generated was only now reaching earth. John N. Bahcall of the Inst. for Advanced Study at Princeton Univ. and Sheldon L. Glashow of Harvard Univ. reported that the **neutrinos** (subnuclear particles lacking an electric charge and extremely difficult to detect) had a lower mass than some theories predicted. This, in turn, meant that the combined mass of all neutrinos was insufficient to halt the **expansion of the universe** and cause it to **collapse.** The new findings did not prove that a collapse would not occur, but they indicated that some other undiscovered mass in the universe would have to be present for that to happen. The alternative to such a final collapse was a universe that expanded forever.

Astronomers believed they had witnessed the **birth of a giant galaxy** for the first time, finding evidence that perhaps a billion suns had ignited within a huge gas cloud 71 billion trillion miles from earth. The object, a proto-galaxy, was too far away for scientists to be certain what it was, but, according to Hyron Spinrad of the Univ. of California at Berkeley, it was believed to be "the first evidence for a massive galaxy seen during its formation stages long ago and far away." The observations were made with a radio telescope in New Mexico and with optical telescopes at Lick Observatory and at Kitt Peak National Observatory in Arizona. The object was 12 billion light years from earth. A light year is the distance light travels in one year, so the birth of the galaxy occurred 12 billion years ago.

George Djorgovski of the Harvard/Smithsonian Center for Astrophysics, George Meylan of the European Southern Observatory, Richard Perley of the Natl. Radio Astronomy Observatory, and Patrick McCarthy of the Univ. of California, Berkeley, discovered what appeared to be the first **binary quasar** (quasi-stellar object), a pair of extremely massive, violently energetic objects far away in space. This discovery would allow astronomers to calculate the minimum size, or mass, of a quasar for the first time. It was estimated that each of the two quasars contained enough mass for 100 billion suns. The pair of objects were about 12 billion light years away from the earth in a constellation known as Crater. Quasars are the most distant, fastest-moving, oldest objects known in the universe.

The Jet Propulsion Laboratory in Pasadena, Calif. reported a significant atmosphere on Pluto. The finding enhanced the stature of the smallest and most distant planet from the sun whose small size and odd orbit had led some astronomers to call it an asteroid. New measurements showed that the diameter of Pluto was 1,370 miles and that of its moon, Charon, 800 miles. The diameter of Ceres, the largest known asteroid, was 590 miles.

Medicine

Under the direction of Dr. Ignacio Madrazo Navarro, of La Raza Medical Center in Mexico City, a radical new surgical procedure was developed (and utilized in 19 patients as of July 21, 1987) to treat severe cases of **Parkinson's disease.** The procedure was marked by the **implantation of the patient's adrenal tissue into the brain.** Parkinson's disease is a progressive neurological disorder characterized by loss of muscle control, often accompanied by tremors, slurred speech, extreme fatigue, and the inability to perform ordinary tasks. Implantation of the adrenal tissue appeared to cause the production in the brain of dopamine, the substance whose deficiency was believed responsible for the disease's symptoms. The adrenal gland normally produced a related chemical. Doctors have suggested that tissue implants in the brain could have applications in treating other disorders affecting the central nervous system, possibly including Huntington's disease, Alzheimer's disease, epilepsy, strokes, spinal injuries, and schizophrenia.

A clinical trial of an **experimental drug,** THA (tetrahydroaminocrydine), that had shown some promise of reducing memory loss in victims of **Alzheimer's disease,** but whose value had been questioned by many experts, was announced in Aug. 1987 by federal health officials. Dr. Kenneth L. Davis of Mount Sinai Medical Center in New York City, who would direct the the new clinical trial, predicted that the drug would help slow the loss of some patients' mental capacities. Approximately 2.5 million Americans suffer from Alzheimer's disease, a progressive mental deterioration for which there is no cure and no treatment for those with major symptoms. The study would take two years to complete. Dr. Davis and others at Mount Sinai School of Medicine reported, in May 1987, that the risk of developing Alzheimer's was four to five times as great among close relatives of patients as in the general population. A **hereditary basis** has been difficult to detect in a disease such as Alzheimer's because it tends to occur so late in life that many potential victims die before symptoms appeared.

A protein called **tissue factor,** the master molecule governing the formation of **blood clots,** was isolated and cloned,

(*continued*)

which scientists believed would lead to new methods to treat heart attacks, strokes, and possibly cancer. Tissue factor initiates the formation of both blood clots that are beneficial, such as those that heal cuts, and blood clots that are harmful, such as those that block coronary arteries and cause strokes. Scientists hoped to develop techniques using tissue factor to test theories about why some people were predisposed to heart disease. Others hoped to develop a new class of antithrombotic drugs to prevent blood clots.

New studies of people who came close to death provided insights into the **nature of death** and showed it might be less painful, less frightening, and more peaceful than generally thought. These suppositions were based on the **near-death experiences** of people who came close to death or were revived from a state of clinical death, usually after a painful accident or illness. According to Kenneth Ring of the Univ. of Connecticut, people underwent "a brief but powerful thrust into a higher state of consciousness." Near-death experiences varied in length and intensity, but followed similar patterns. People who underwent them reported feeling abrupt separation from their bodies and looking down upon themselves. Their pain dissolved, and they were overwhelmed by an inexpressible peace and contentment. Many said they entered a tunnel of darkness and moved towards a brilliant white light that emitted warmth and love, that they were flooded with knowledge beyond their ordinary capabilities, and that they discerned the pattern or **meaning of life.** A Gallup poll reported that 8 million people had near-death episodes and found that no relationship existed between the experience and a person's religious or cultural background. Studies have also shown that children had these experiences.

Genetic Engineering

A panel of the National Academy of Sciences, a private organization chartered by Congress, concluded that there was no evidence that organisms developed by the techniques of genetic engineering presented any "unique" **ecological hazard.** Genetic engineering involves the deliberate rearrangement, removal or addition of specific pieces of DNA, the active substance of genes, which determines the **hereditary characteristics** of all living things. On the risks of releasing organisms altered in this manner, the panel stated that they were "the same in kind as those associated with the introduction into the environment of unmodified organisms and organisms modified by other genetic techniques." Their report said that although "the mechanisms of heredity were unknown to early breeders, their procedures for selective breeding were a form of genetic engineering." The academy's report was drafted by experts representing a cross-section of scientific fields and was chaired by Dr. Arthur Kelman of the Univ. of Wisconsin in Madison.

On Apr. 24, 1987, **genetically altered bacteria** were released outdoors for the first time. In this historic experiment, the bacteria, designed to prevent frost damage on crops, were sprayed on 2,300 strawberry plants in Brentwood, Calif.

Collaborative Research, a company in Bedford, Mass., a leader in developing **genetic tests,** was believed to be two years away from completing a map of the 23 pairs of human chromosomes. This would let scientists pinpoint all the genes associated with human illness, from obscure metabolic disorders to leading killers such as arteriosclerosis (hardening of the arteries). Michael McGinnin, director of the U.S. Office of Disease Prevention and Health Promotion, predicted (according to a report in *U.S. News & World Report*) that most people would be getting genetic profiles by the year 2000. The ability to anticipate the risk or potential of individuals to acquire a particular disease or disorder would be greatly enhanced by such genetic testing. The reliability and accuracy of many of these tests had not yet been established, nor were there guidelines for use of such personal data.

Superconductors

The discovery of a new class of superconductors—materials capable of carrying electric current without the resistance that normally wastes energy in the form of heat—led scientists to anticipate a multitude of practical applications. **Superconducting transmission lines** would mean recapturing the energy now lost with ordinary wires. Before transmission lines would become feasible on a large scale, many technical problems, such as their capacity for carrying current, would have to be solved. Replacing the nation's electrical transmission system would take many years and would be very costly. Superconducting lines could safely carry far more current for much greater distances than conventional underground cables. This would allow utilities to locate nuclear power plants or fields of solar cells far from populated areas.

Passing current through any conductor creates a magnetic field. This magnetic field is basic to the operation of electric motors, television picture tubes, and much of modern technology. A large enough coil of superconducting material could store a huge current in the form of a magnetic field. If **superconducting magnets** were put on the bottom of a train, and pulled along a track of ordinary metal, the magnetism would cause the train to levitate, rising into the air and floating on the magnetic fields. **Magnetic levitation** had been studied in the past by such groups as the General Motors Corp., and the research was now being revived. Because they were not subject to friction, **levitating trains** could travel at 300 miles per hour, smoothly and quietly. Other possible applications included storage of current without losing power, smaller computers that would work faster, nuclear fusion, and beam weapons.

It was reported, Aug. 29, 1987, that the U.S. Patent and Trademark Office would accelerate the processing of patent applications involving superconductivity.

Patents

In the 1986 fiscal year, which ended Sept. 30, 76,993 patents were issued by the U.S. Patent Office. This total exceeded the 1985 figure by 1,691. Patent applications reached a record total of 131,403.

U.S. residents were granted 38,124 patents, about 54 percent of the total, while non-U.S. residents from 100 nations received nearly 33,000 patents. Japanese citizens were awarded two of every five foreign patents for a total of 13,857 in 1986, by far the largest number of any other nation. In 1966, by comparison, 16 percent of the patents issued went to non-U.S. citizens.

In 1986, there were 1,121 patents that became ineffective because their owners failed to pay the required maintenance fees. The charges apply to utility patents, which have a normal life of 17 years, but not to design or plant patents. The fees, which start at $225, are due three and a half years after patent issuance. A total of 17,209 patents were renewed in 1986 after the payment of fees totaling more than $3.8 million.

Since it started counting, in 1836, the U.S. Patent Office has issued 4,658,440 patents (through Apr. 14, 1987).

Patent Piracy

In May 1987, the Senate Judiciary Committee's Subcommittee on Patents, Copyrights and Trademarks unanimously approved a bill to allow American companies, for the first time, to seek Federal court relief against foreign pirating of their patented manufacturing processes. The pirating is estimated to cost American industry billions of dollars annually. The bill seeks to give U.S. manufacturers greater legal protection for processes that were patented in the U.S., but have been copied by foreign concerns to make products for sale in the U.S. A similar measure has passed the House of Representatives.

Congress passed legislation in 1984 that made trademark counterfeiting a criminal offense, cracking down on foreign competitors that copied names and trademarks used to identify popular products such as designer clothing, jewelry, and luggage.

Patents for Animals

A bill that would temporarily prevent the U.S. Patent and

Trademark Office from issuing patents for animals produced by artificial genetic manipulations was introduced in Aug. 1987 in the House of Representatives. The measure came nearly four months after the Patent Office announced its intention to consider applications to patent higher forms of animal life that have been altered by new biological technologies, including genetic engineering. If enacted by Congress, the bill would prohibit the Patent Office from issuing any animal patent for at least two years. None have been issued to date (Sept. 1987), but 15 applications have been filed.

In its Apr. 1987 announcement, the Patent and Trademark Office said it would consider genetically engineered animals to be "products of human ingenuity," and therefore patentable. According to some industrialists, the decision to patent animals will have a significant impact on hundreds of thousands of jobs, and the U.S.'s ability to compete in global agricultural markets. It is said that the issue involves tens of billions of dollars in future trade and agriculture.

In reaction to the announcement by the Patent Office, religious leaders, ethicists, national farm organizations, and animal welfare groups protested, and asserted that the policy raised potential problems that Congress needed to consider.

In the 197-year history of the American patent system, legislation has never been proposed to block a policy that the Patent and Trademark Office has already put into effect.

Inventions of 1987

Some of the more "interesting" inventions issued patents during 1987 were: **survival structures** and campsites to provide safety for city populations in case of a nuclear war; an **antiterrorist patrol vehicle**, nicknamed the Viking, that has a conventional appearance, but carries a machine gun that can be fired through a roof hatch; an apparatus, called the **Bubble-Thing**, to make soap bubbles, eight feet in diameter, (the shape may resemble a whale or a tractor tire); a method of producing cumulus **rain clouds**; an apparatus that can ride and guide a **horse by remote control**; an electronic **anti-snoring device**, which operates with an audio signal that irritates the sleeper and causes the snoring to stop; a **bathing suit** made with fabric that changes color with the body temperature of the wearer; a system to **identify individuals by the iris**, the colored portion of the eye, by storing an image of the iris; a **yarn caddy**, called the Happy Hooker, to prevent tangling of yarn while knitting or crocheting; an electronic device that **dissuades dogs from barking** by directing a spray of material to the nose and eyes; and a method of **making chocolate** products that will not stick to wrappers or fingers even at high temperatures.

Personal Computers

In the past few years, sales of home computers have fallen short of earlier expectations as the industry continues to be faced with an oversupply of products and overcrowding of companies into the market. Foreign competition is also seen as a major factor in the industry's setback.

The home computer industry (a small but significant component of the whole computer industry) has also seen a marked decrease in demand. Sales of personal computers, which almost doubled year after year for several years, are expected to grow no more than 10–20 percent in 1987.

There is a growing realization among home computer companies that they have not necessarily been satisfying their customers. Many people use their computers for only one task, rather than the multiple tasks that computer makers had envisioned and promised the public. A more fundamental problem now facing the home computer industry, is convincing the consumer of the *need* for a home computer. After the wave of growth in the late 1970's and early 1980's, the novelty of owning a home computer has worn out, and consumers are now questioning the computer's value and usefulness. The cost effectiveness of a "home" computer (not a personal computer used in the home) has not been convincingly demonstrated, as many consumers still find it more efficient to maintain hand-written grocery lists, recipes, check books, etc.

Computers in Education

The number of personal computers for instructional use in public elementary and secondary schools has risen dramatically, from 250,000 to 1 million between 1983 and 1985 (according to a Johns Hopkins Univ. study), and is expected to double in each of the next five years, according to the National Center for Education Statistics. Despite the presence of computers in more than half the nation's schools, organizations such as the National Education Assn. claim that relatively few students actually receive any computer instruction. The equipment is primarily used for administrative purposes, or for the classes of a few isolated instructors, generally those who teach computer skills. The general failure to utilize the available computer technology seems to be the result of inadequate planning and funding, the lack of curriculum development and suitable educational software, and poor teacher training. To date, there is no national policy on integrating computers into American public education, and little cooperation or agreement on methodology among educators, government officials, and the private sector.

Some educators and social activists have voiced their concern about a widening gap in computer literacy between more affluent suburban school districts and poorer urban ones. Some have stated that federal cutbacks in aid to education have added to this discrepancy. It is argued that wealthier school districts will find the means to purchase the necessary equipment, while less affluent school districts will not, therefore perpetuating the economic status quo.

The rapid development and commercialization of the computer has caused educators, sociologists, and psychologists to become concerned with the possible adverse impact on some children. Questions being investigated about the social and emotional effects of computerization in the home and schools are strikingly similar to those raised in response to the influence of television. Studies, just beginning to be undertaken, will examine the influence of computers on child development, as well as on the quality of family life.

Computers in the Work Force

Source: U.S. Department of Labor

Occupational Group	Percent of workers with desk-top PC's* 1985	1990
Technical	55.9%	76.2%
Managerial	36.5%	64.4%
Professional	39.2%	63.7%
Armed forces	20.3%	40.0%
Clerical	25.0%	38.5%
Sales	16.6%	32.7%
Services, including firefighters, police, food preparation	11.9%	25.2%
Skilled crafts, including carpenters, plumbers	5.7%	16.8%
Farm	4.3%	7.6%
Operators of manufacturing and transportation machines	1.6%	4.7%
Laborers	0.4%	1.6%

*Estimated.

Computer Language

The following is a glossary of key words or terms that consumers should learn if they are considering buying their own personal computer.

Access: the ability to get information or use a computer or program.

Acoustic coupler: a device that allows other electronic devices to communicate by making, and also listening to sounds made over an ordinary telephone. See **Modem.**

Address: designates the location of an item of information stored in the computer's memory.

ASCII: acronym for American Standard Code for Information Interchange. A 7-bit code used to represent alphanumeric characters.

Assembly language: a machine oriented language in which mnemonics are used to represent each machine-language instruction. Each CPU has its own specific assembly language.

Backup file: a copy of a current file used if the current file is destroyed.

BASIC: a popular computer language that is used by many small and personal computer systems. It means—Beginner's All-purpose Symbolic Instruction Code.

Baud rate: serial-data transmission speed. Originally a telegraph term, expressed in terms of the number of events that take place in one second. One baud is equal to one bit per second.

Binary: refers to the base-2 number system in which the only allowable digits are 0 and 1.

Bit: short for binary digit, the smallest unit of information stored in a computer. It always has the binary value of "O" or "1."

Bubble memory: a relatively new type of computer memory, it uses tiny magnetic "pockets" or "bubbles" to store data.

Buffer: a place to put information before further processing.

Bug: a mistake that occurs in a program within a computer or in the unit's electrical system. When a mistake is found and corrected, it's called debugging.

Bundling: the practice of selling the hardware and software as a single package.

Byte: an 8-bit sequence of binary digits. Each byte corresponds to 1 character of data, representing a single letter, number, or symbol. Bytes are the most common unit for measuring computer and disk storage capacity.

Cathode Ray Tube Terminal: a device used as a computer terminal which contains a television-like screen for displaying data. Most CRT terminals also have a typewriter-like keyboard.

COBOL: Common Business Oriented Language; one of the most widely used business programming languages.

Compiler: a program that translates a high-level language, such as BASIC, into machine language.

CPU: the Central Processing Unit within the computer that executes the instructions that the user gives the system.

Chip: a term for the integrated circuit and its package which contains coded signals.

Cursor: the symbol on the computer monitor that marks the place where the operator is working.

Database: a large amount of data stored in a well organized format. A database management system is a program that allows access to the information.

Dedicated: designed for a single use.

Density: the amount of data that can be stored on one sector of one track of a disk.

Disk: a revolving plate on which information and programs are stored. See also **Floppy disk.**

Disk Drive: a peripheral machine that stores information on disks.

Documentation: user or operator instructions that come with some hardware and software that tells how to use the material.

DOS: "Disk Operating System," a collection of programs designed to facilitate the use of a disk drive and floppy disk.

Dump: a printout of the contents of any file.

Error Message: a statement by the computer indicating that the user has done something incorrectly.

File: a logical group of pieces of information labelled by a specific name; considered a single unit by the computer. It is used commonly on microcomputers and word processors.

Floppy disk: a small inexpensive disk used to record and store information. It must be used in conjunction with a disk drive.

Format: the arrangement by which information is stored.

Hardware: the physical apparatus or "nuts and bolts" that make up a computer. It includes silicon chips, transformers, boards and wires, etc. Also used to describe various pieces of equipment including the CPU, printer, modem, CRT (cathode ray tube), etc.

Hexadecimal: refers to the base-16 number system. Machine language programs are often written in hexadecimal notation.

Interface: the hardware or software necessary to connect one device or system to another.

K: abbreviation for Kilo-byte used to denote 1,024 units of stored matter.

Language: any set of compiled, unified, or related commands or instructions that are acceptable to a computer.

Load: the actual operation of putting information and data into the computer or memory.

Menu: programs, functions or other choices displayed on the monitor for user selection.

Memory: the internal storage of information.

Microcomputer: a small, complete computer system. Most personal computers now in use are microcomputers.

Minicomputer: an intermediate computer system sized between the very small microcomputer and the large computer.

Modem: short for modulating-demodulating. An acoustic or non-acoustic coupler, used either with a telephone or on a direct-line, for transmitting information from one computer to another.

Noise: random disturbances that degrade or disrupt data communications.

Printer: a computer output device that, when attached to a computer, will produce printed copy on paper.

Program: coded instructions telling a computer how to perform a specific function.

RAM: abbreviation for random-access-memory. A type of microchip, its patterns can be changed by the user and the information it generates stored on tape, disk, or in printed form.

Random access: the ability to retrieve records in a file without reading any previous records.

ROM: abbreviation for read-only-memory. A type of microchip that is different from RAM in that it cannot be altered by the user.

Software: the programs, or sets of instructions, procedural rules, and, in some cases, documentation that make the computer function.

Terminal: a work station away from the main computer that allows several people to have access to a single, main computer.

User friendly: hardware or software designed to help people become familiar with their computer. Usually includes simple and easy to follow instructions.

Window: portion of a video display screen devoted to displaying specific categories of information.

Word Processor: a text–editing program or system that allows electronic writing and correcting of articles, books, etc.

Inventions and Discoveries

Invention	Date	Inventor	Nation.
Adding machine	1642	Pascal	French
Adding machine	1885	Burroughs	U.S.
Addressograph	1892	Rotheim	Norwegian
Aerosol spray	1926	Goodhue	U.S.
Air brake	1868	Westinghouse	U.S.
Air conditioning	1911	Carrier	U.S.
Air pump	1654	Guericke	German
Airplane, automatic pilot	1912	Sperry	U.S.
Airplane, experimental	1896	Langley	U.S.
Airplane jet engine	1939	Ohain	German
Airplane with motor	1903	Wright bros.	U.S.
Airplane, hydro	1911	Curtiss	U.S.
Airship	1852	Giffard	French
Airship, rigid dirigible	1900	Zeppelin	German
Arc welder	1919	Thomson	U.S.
Autogyro	1920	de la Cierva	Spanish
Automobile, differential gear	1885	Benz	German
Automobile, electric	1892	Morrison	U.S.
Automobile, exp'mtl	1864	Marcus	Austrian
Automobile, gasoline	1889	Daimler	German
Automobile, gasoline	1892	Duryea	U.S.
Automobile magneto	1897	Bosch	German
Automobile muffler	...	Maxim, H.P.	U.S.
Automobile self-starter	1911	Kettering	U.S.
Babbitt metal	1839	Babbitt	U.S.
Bakelite	1907	Baekeland	Belg., U.S.
Balloon	1783	Montgolfier	French
Barometer	1643	Torricelli	Italian
Bicycle, modern	1885	Starley	English
Bifocal lens	1780	Franklin	U.S.
Block signals, railway	1867	Hall	U.S.
Bomb, depth	1916	Tait	U.S.
Bottle machine	1895	Owens	U.S.
Braille printing	1829	Braille	French
Burner, gas	1855	Bunsen	German
Calculating machine	1833	Babbage	English
Camera—see also Photography			
Camera, Kodak	1888	Eastman, Walker	U.S.
Camera, Polaroid Land	1948	Land	U.S.
Car coupler	1873	Janney	U.S.
Carburetor, gasoline	1893	Maybach	German
Card time recorder	1894	Cooper	U.S.
Carding machine	1797	Whittemore	U.S.
Carpet sweeper	1876	Bissell	U.S.
Cash register	1879	Ritty	U.S.
Cathode ray tube	1878	Crookes	English
Cellophane	1900	Brandenberger	Swiss
Celluloid	1870	Hyatt	U.S.
Cement, Portland	1824	Aspdin	English
Chronometer	1761	Harrison	English
Circuit breaker	1925	Hilliard	U.S.
Clock, pendulum	1657	Huygens	Dutch
Coaxial cable system	1929	Affel, Espensched	U.S.
Coke oven	1893	Hoffman	Austrian
Compressed air rock drill	1871	Ingersoll	U.S.
Comptometer	1887	Felt	U.S.
Computer, automatic sequence	1944	Aiken et al.	U.S.
Condenser microphone (telephone)	1916	Wente	U.S.
Corn, hybrid	1917	Jones	U.S.
Cotton gin	1793	Whitney	U.S.
Cream separator	1878	DeLaval	Swedish
Cultivator, disc	1878	Mallon	U.S.
Cystoscope	1878	Nitze	German
Diesel engine	1895	Diesel	German
Dynamite	1866	Nobel	Swedish
Dynamo, continuous current	1871	Gramme	Belgian
Dynamo, hydrogen cooled	1915	Schuler	U.S.
Electric battery	1800	Volta	Italian
Electric fan	1882	Wheeler	U.S.
Electrocardiograph	1903	Einthoven	Dutch
Electroencephalograph	1929	Berger	German
Electromagnet	1824	Sturgeon	English
Electron spectrometer	1944	Deutsch, Elliott, Evans	U.S.
Electron tube multigrid	1913	Langmuir	U.S.
Electroplating	1805	Brugnatelli	Italian
Electrostatic generator	1929	Van de Graaff	U.S.
Elevator brake	1852	Otis	U.S.
Elevator, push button	1922	Larson	U.S.
Engine, coal-gas 4-cycle	1876	Otto	German
Engine, compression ignition	1883	Daimler	German
Engine, electric ignition	1883	Benz	German
Engine, gas, compound	1926	Eickemeyer	U.S.
Engine, gasoline	1872	Brayton, Geo.	U.S.
Engine, gasoline	1889	Daimler	German
Engine, steam, piston	1705	Newcomen	English
Engine, steam, piston	1769	Watt	Scottish
Engraving, half-tone	1852	Talbot	U.S.
Filament, tungsten	1913	Coolidge	U.S.
Flanged rail	1831	Stevens	U.S.
Flatiron, electric	1882	Seely	U.S.
Furnace (for steel)	1858	Siemens	German
Galvanometer	1820	Sweigger	German
Gas discharge tube	1922	Hull	U.S.
Gas lighting	1792	Murdoch	Scottish
Gas mantle	1885	Welsbach	Austrian
Gasoline (lead ethyl)	1922	Midgley	U.S.
Gasoline, cracked	1913	Burton	U.S.
Gasoline, high octane	1930	Ipatieff	Russian
Geiger counter	1913	Geiger	German
Glass, laminated safety	1909	Benedictus	French
Glider	1853	Cayley	English
Gun, breechloader	1811	Thornton	U.S.
Gun, Browning	1897	Browning	U.S.
Gun, magazine	1875	Hotchkiss	U.S.
Gun, silencer	1908	Maxim, H.P.	U.S.
Guncotton	1847	Schoenbein	German
Gyrocompass	1911	Sperry	U.S.
Gyroscope	1852	Foucault	French
Harvester-thresher	1818	Lane	U.S.
Helicopter	1939	Sikorsky	U.S.
Hydrometer	1768	Baume	French
Ice-making machine	1851	Gorrie	U.S.
Iron lung	1928	Drinker, Slaw	U.S.
Kaleidoscope	1817	Brewster	Scottish
Kinetoscope	1889	Edison	U.S.
Lacquer, nitrocellulose	1921	Flaherty	U.S.
Lamp, arc	1847	Staite	English
Lamp, incandescent	1879	Edison	U.S.
Lamp, incand., frosted	1924	Pipkin	U.S.
Lamp, incand., gas	1913	Langmuir	U.S.
Lamp, Klieg	1911	Kliegl, A.&J.	U.S.
Lamp, mercury vapor	1912	Hewitt	U.S.
Lamp, miner's safety	1816	Davy	English
Lamp, neon	1909	Claude	French
Lathe, turret	1845	Fitch	U.S.
Launderette	1934	Cantrell	U.S.
Lens, achromatic	1758	Dollond	English
Lens, fused bifocal	1908	Borsch	U.S.
Leydenjar (condenser)	1745	von Kleist	German
Lightning rod	1752	Franklin	U.S.
Linoleum	1860	Walton	English
Linotype	1884	Mergenthaler	U.S.
Lock, cylinder	1851	Yale	U.S.
Locomotive, electric	1851	Vail	U.S.
Locomotive, exp'mtl	1802	Trevithick	English
Locomotive, exp'mtl	1812	Fenton et al.	English
Locomotive, exp'mtl	1813	Hedley	English
Locomotive, exp'mtl	1814	Stephenson	English
Locomotive practical	1829	Stephenson	English
Locomotive, 1st U.S.	1830	Cooper, P.	U.S.
Loom, power	1785	Cartwright	English
Loudspeaker, dynamic	1924	Rice, Kellogg	U.S.
Machine gun	1861	Gatling	U.S.
Machine gun, improved	1872	Hotchkiss	U.S.
Machine gun (Maxim)	1883	Maxim, H.S.	U.S., Eng.
Magnet, electro	1828	Henry	U.S.
Mantle, gas	1885	Welsbach	Austrian
Mason jar	1858	Mason, J.	U.S.
Match, friction	1827	John Walker	English
Mercerized textiles	1843	Mercer, J.	English

Invention	Date	Inventor	Nation.
Meter, induction	1888	Shallenberg	U.S.
Metronome	1816	Malezel	German
Micrometer	1636	Gascoigne	English
Microphone	1877	Berliner	U.S.
Microscope, compound	1590	Janssen	Dutch
Microscope, electronic	1931	Knoll, Ruska	German
Microscope, field ion	1951	Mueller	Germany
Monitor, warship	1861	Ericsson	U.S.
Monotype	1887	Lanston	U.S.
Motor, AC	1892	Tesla	U.S.
Motor, DC	1837	Davenport	U.S.
Motor, induction	1887	Tesla	U.S.
Motorcycle	1885	Daimler	German
Movie machine	1894	Jenkins	U.S.
Movie, panoramic	1952	Waller	U.S.
Movie, talking	1927	Warner Bros.	U.S.
Mower, lawn	1831	Budding, Ferrabee	English
Mowing machine	1822	Bailey	U.S.
Neoprene	1930	Carothers	U.S.
Nylon synthetic	1930	Carothers	U.S.
Nylon	1937	Du Pont lab	U.S.
Oil cracking furnace	1891	Gavrilov	Russian
Oil filled power cable	1921	Emanueli	Italian
Oleomargarine	1869	Mege-Mouries	French
Ophthalmoscope	1851	Helmholtz	German
Paper machine	1809	Dickinson	U.S.
Parachute	1785	Blanchard	French
Pen, ballpoint	1888	Loud	U.S.
Pen, fountain	1884	Waterman	U.S.
Pen, steel	1780	Harrison	English
Pendulum	1583	Galileo	Italian
Percussion cap	1807	Forsythe	Scottish
Phonograph	1877	Edison	U.S.
Photo, color	1892	Ives	U.S.
Photo film, celluloid	1893	Reichenbach	U.S.
Photo film, transparent	1884	Eastman, Goodwin	U.S.
Photoelectric cell	1895	Elster	German
Photographic paper	1835	Talbot	U.S.
Photography	1835	Talbot	English
Photography	1835	Daguerre	French
Photography	1816	Niepce	French
Photophone	1880	Bell	U.S.-Scot.
Phototelegraphy	1925	Bell Labs	U.S.
Piano	1709	Cristofori	Italian
Piano, player	1863	Fourneaux	French
Pin, safety	1849	Hunt	U.S.
Pistol (revolver)	1836	Colt	U.S.
Plow, cast iron	1785	Ransome	English
Plow, disc	1896	Hardy	U.S.
Pneumatic hammer	1890	King	U.S.
Powder, smokeless	1884	Vieille	French
Printing press, rotary	1845	Hoe	U.S.
Printing press, web	1865	Bullock	U.S.
Propeller, screw	1804	Stevens	U.S.
Propeller, screw	1837	Ericsson	Swedish
Punch card accounting	1889	Hollerith	U.S.
Radar	1940	Watson-Watt	Scottish
Radio amplifier	1906	De Forest	U.S.
Radio beacon	1928	Donovan	U.S.
Radio crystal oscillator	1918	Nicolson	U.S.
Radio receiver, cascade tuning	1913	Alexanderson,	U.S.
Radio receiver, heterodyne	1913	Fessenden	U.S.
Radio transmitter triode modulation	1914	Alexanderson	U.S.
Radio tube-diode	1905	Fleming	English
Radio tube oscillator	1915	De Forest	U.S.
Radio tube triode	1906	De Forest	U.S.
Radio, signals	1895	Marconi	Italian
Radio, magnetic detector	1902	Marconi	Italian
Radio FM 2-path	1933	Armstrong	U.S.
Rayon	1883	Swan	English
Razor, electric	1928	Schick	U.S.
Razor, safety	1895	Gillette	U.S.
Reaper	1834	McCormick	U.S.
Record, cylinder	1887	Bell, Tainter	U.S.
Record, disc	1887	Berliner	U.S.
Record, long playing	1947	Goldmark	U.S.
Record, wax cylinder	1888	Edison	U.S.
Refrigerants, low-boiling fluorine compound	1930	Midgely and co-workers	U.S.

Invention	Date	Inventor	Nation.
Refrigerator car	1868	David	U.S.
Resin, synthetic	1931	Hill	English
Rifle, repeating	1860	Spencer	U.S.
Rocket engine	1926	Goddard	U.S.
Rubber, vulcanized	1839	Goodyear	U.S.
Saw, band	1808	Newberry	English
Saw, circular	1777	Miller	English
Searchlight, arc	1915	Sperry	U.S.
Sewing machine	1846	Howe	U.S.
Shoe-sewing machine	1860	McKay	U.S.
Shrapnel shell	1784	Shrapnel	English
Shuttle, flying	1733	Kay	English
Sleeping-car	1865	Pullman	U.S.
Slide rule	1620	Oughtred	English
Soap, hardwater	1928	Bertsch	German
Spectroscope	1859	Kirchoff, Bunsen	German
Spectroscope (mass)	1918	Dempster	U.S.
Spinning jenny	1767	Hargreaves	English
Spinning mule	1779	Crompton	English
Steamboat, exp'mtl	1778	Jouffroy	French
Steamboat, exp'mtl	1785	Fitch	U.S.
Steamboat, exp'mtl	1787	Rumsey	U.S.
Steamboat, exp'mtl	1788	Miller	Scottish
Steamboat, exp'mtl	1803	Fulton	U.S.
Steamboat, exp'mtl	1804	Stevens	U.S.
Steamboat, practical	1802	Symington	Scottish
Steamboat, practical	1807	Fulton	U.S.
Steam car	1770	Cugnot	French
Steam turbine	1884	Parsons	English
Steel (converter)	1856	Bessemer	English
Steel alloy	1891	Harvey	U.S.
Steel alloy, high-speed	1901	Taylor, White	U.S.
Steel, electric	1900	Heroult	French
Steel, manganese	1884	Hadfield	English
Steel, stainless	1916	Brearley	English
Stereoscope	1838	Wheatstone	English
Stethoscope	1819	Laennec	French
Stethoscope, binaural	1840	Cammann	U.S.
Stock ticker	1870	Edison	U.S.
Storage battery, rechargeable	1859	Plante	French
Stove, electric	1896	Hadaway	U.S.
Submarine	1891	Holland	U.S.
Submarine, even keel	1894	Lake	U.S.
Submarine, torpedo	1776	Bushnell	U.S.
Tank, military	1914	Swinton	English
Tape recorder, magnetic	1899	Poulsen	Danish
Telegraph, magnetic	1837	Morse	U.S.
Telegraph, quadruplex	1864	Edison	U.S.
Telegraph, railroad	1887	Woods	U.S.
Telegraph, wireless high frequency	1895	Marconi	Italian
Telephone	1876	Bell	U.S.-Scot.
Telephone amplifier	1912	De Forest	U.S.
Telephone, automatic	1891	Stowger	U.S.
Telephone, radio	1900	Poulsen, Fessenden	Danish
Telephone, radio	1906	De Forest	U.S.
Telephone, radio, l. d	1915	AT&T	U.S.
Telephone, recording	1898	Poulsen	Danish
Telephone, wireless	1899	Collins	U.S.
Telescope	1608	Lippershey	Neth.
Telescope	1609	Galileo	Italian
Telescope, astronomical	1611	Kepler	German
Teletype	1928	Morkrum, Kleinschmidt	U.S.
Television, iconoscope	1923	Zworykin	U.S.
Television, electronic	1927	Farnsworth	U.S.
Television, (mech. scanner)	1923	Baird	Scottish
Thermometer	1593	Galileo	Italian
Thermometer	1730	Reaumur	French
Thermometer, mercury	1714	Fahrenheit	German
Time recorder	1890	Bundy	U.S.
Time, self-regulator	1918	Bryce	U.S.
Tire, double-tube	1845	Thomson	Scottish
Tire, pneumatic	1888	Dunlop	Scottish
Toaster, automatic	1918	Strite	U.S.
Tool, pneumatic	1865	Law	English
Torpedo, marine	1804	Fulton	U.S.
Tractor, crawler	1904	Holt	U.S.
Transformer A.C.	1885	Stanley	U.S.
Transistor	1947	Shockley, Brattain, Bardeen	U.S.

Invention	Date	Inventor	Nation.
Trolley car, electric	1884-87	Van DePoele, Sprague	U.S.
Tungsten, ductile	1912	Coolidge	U.S.
Turbine, gas	1849	Bourdin	French
Turbine, hydraulic	1849	Francis	U.S.
Turbine, steam	1884	Parsons	English
Type, movable	1447	Gutenberg	German
Typewriter	1867	Sholes, Soule, Glidden	U.S.
Vacuum cleaner, electric	1907	Spangler	U.S.
Washer, electric	1901	Fisher	U.S.
Welding, atomic hydrogen	1924	Langmuir, Palmer	U.S.
Welding, electric	1877	Thomson	U.S.
Wind tunnel	1912	Eiffel	French
Wire, barbed	1874	Glidden	U.S.
Wire, barbed	1875	Haisn	U.S.
Wrench, double-acting	1913	Owen	U.S.
X-ray tube	1913	Coolidge	U.S.
Zipper	1891	Judson	U.S.

Discoveries and Innovations: Chemistry, Physics, Biology, Medicine

	Date	Discoverer	Nation.
Acetylene gas	1892	Wilson	U.S.
ACTH	1949	Armour & Co.	U.S.
Adrenalin	1901	Takamine	Japanese
Aluminum, electrolytic process	1886	Hall	U.S.
Aluminum, isolated	1825	Oersted	Danish
Analine dye	1856	Perkin	English
Anesthesia, ether	1842	Long	U.S.
Anesthesia, local	1885	Koller	Austrian
Anesthesia, spinal	1898	Bier	German
Anti-rabies	1885	Pasteur	French
Antiseptic surgery	1867	Lister	English
Antitoxin, diphtheria	1891	Von Behring	German
Argyrol	1901	Barnes	U.S.
Arsphenamine	1910	Ehrlich	German
Aspirin	1889	Dresser	German
Atabrine	...	Mietzsch, et al.	German
Atomic numbers	1913	Moseley	English
Atomic theory	1803	Dalton	English
Atomic time clock	1947	Libby	U.S.
Atom-smashing theory	1919	Rutherford	English
Aureomycin	1948	Duggar	U.S.
Bacitracin	1945	Johnson, et al.	U.S.
Bacteria (described)	1676	Leeuwenhoek	Dutch
Barbital	1903	Fischer	German
Bleaching powder	1798	Tennant	English
Blood, circulation	1628	Harvey	English
Bordeaux mixture	1885	Millardet	French
Bromine from sea	1924	Edgar Kramer	U.S.
Calcium carbide	1888	Wilson	U.S.
Calculus	1670	Newton	English
Camphor synthetic	1896	Haller	French
Canning (food)	1804	Appert	French
Carbomycin	1952	Tanner	U.S.
Carbon oxides	1925	Fisher	German
Chlorine	1774	Scheele	Swedish
Chloroform	1831	Guthrie, S.	U.S.
Chloromycetin	1947	Burkholder	U.S.
Classification of plants and animals	1735	Linnaeus	Swedish
Cocaine	1860	Niermann	German
Combustion explained	1777	Lavoisier	French
Conditioned reflex	1914	Pavlov	Russian
Conteben	1950	Belmisch, Mietzsch, Domagk	German
Cortisone	1936	Kendall	U.S.
Cortisone, synthesis	1946	Sarett	U.S.
Cosmic rays	1910	Gockel	Swiss
Cyanimide	1905	Frank, Caro	German
Cyclotron	1930	Lawrence	U.S.
DDT (not applied as insecticide until 1939)	1874	Zeidler	German
Deuterium	1932	Urey, Brickwedde, Murphy	U.S.
DNA (structure)	1951	Crick	English
		Watson	U.S.
		Wilkins	English
Electric resistance (law)	1827	Ohm	German
Electric waves	1888	Hertz	German
Electrolysis	1852	Faraday	English
Electromagnetism	1819	Oersted	Danish
Electron	1897	Thomson, J.	English
Electron diffraction	1936	Thomson, G.	English
		Davisson	U.S.
Electroshock treatment	1938	Cerletti, Bini	Italian
Erythromycin	1952	McGuire	U.S.
Evolution, natural selection	1858	Darwin	English
Falling bodies, law	1590	Galileo	Italian
Gases, law of combining volumes	1808	Gay-Lussac	French
Geometry, analytic	1619	Descartes	French
Gold (cyanide process for extraction)	1887	MacArthur, Forest	British
Gravitation, law	1687	Newton	English
Holograph	1948	Gabor	British
Human heart transplant	1967	Barnard	S. African
Indigo, synthesis of	1880	Baeyer	German
Induction, electric	1830	Henry	U.S.
Insulin	1922	Banting, Best, Macleod	Canadian, Scottish
Intelligence testing	1905	Binet, Simon	French
Isinazid	1952	Hoffman-La-Roche	U.S.
		Domagk	German
Isotopes, theory	1912	Soddy	English
Laser (light amplification by stimulated emission of radiation)	1958	Townes, Schawlow	U.S.
Light, velocity	1675	Roemer	Danish
Light, wave theory	1690	Huygens	Dutch
Lithography	1796	Senefelder	Bohemian
Lobotomy	1935	Egas Moniz	Portuguese
LSD-25	1943	Hoffman	Swiss
Mendelian laws	1866	Mendel	Austrian
Mercator projection (map)	1568	Mercator (Kremer)	Flemish
Methanol	1925	Patard	French
Milk condensation	1853	Bordon	U.S.
Molecular hypothesis	1811	Avogadro	Italian
Motion, laws of	1687	Newton	English
Neomycin	1949	Waksman, Lechevalier	U.S.
Neutron	1932	Chadwick	English
Nitric acid	1648	Glauber	German
Nitric oxide	1772	Priestley	English
Nitroglycerin	1846	Sobrero	Italian
Oil cracking process	1891	Dewar	U.S.
Oxygen	1774	Priestley	English
Ozone	1840	Schonbein	German
Paper, sulfite process	1867	Tilghman	U.S.
Paper, wood pulp, sulfate process	1884	Dahl	German
Penicillin	1929	Fleming	Scottish
practical use	1941	Florey, Chain	English
Periodic law and table of elements	1869	Mendeleyev	Russian
Planetary motion, laws	1609	Kepler	German
Plutonium fission	1940	Kennedy, Wahl, Seaborg, Segre	U.S.
Polymixin	1947	Ainsworth	English
Positron	1932	Anderson	U.S.
Proton	1919	Rutherford	N. Zealand
Psychoanalysis	1900	Freud	Austrian
Quantum theory	1900	Planck	German
Quasars	1963	Matthews, Sandage	U.S.

	Date	Discoverer	Nation.
Quinine synthetic	1918	Rabe	German
Radioactivity	1896	Becquerel	French
Radium	1898	Curie, Pierre	French
		Curie, Marie	Pol.-Fr.
Relativity theory	1905	Einstein	German
Reserpine	1949	Jal Vaikl	Indian
Salvarsan (606)	1910	Ehrlich	German
Schick test	1913	Schick	U.S.
Silicon	1823	Berzelius	Swedish
Streptomycin	1945	Waksman	U.S.
Sulfadiazine	1940	Roblin	U.S.
Sulfanilamide	1934	Domagk	German
Sulfanilamide theory	1908	Gelmo	German
Sulfapyridine	1938	Ewins, Phelps	English
Sulfathiazole	...	Fosbinder, Walter	U.S.
Sulfuric acid	1831	Phillips	English
Sulfuric acid, lead	1746	Roebuck	English
Terramycin	1950	Finlay, et al.	U.S.
Tuberculin	1890	Koch	German

	Date	Discoverer	Nation.
Uranium fission (theory)	1939	Hahn, Meitner, Strassmann	German
		Bohr	Danish
		Fermi	Italian
		Einstein, Pegram, Wheeler	U.S.
Uranium fission, atomic reactor	1942	Fermi, Szilard	U.S.
Vaccine, measles	1954	Enders, Peebles	U.S.
Vaccine, polio	1953	Salk	U.S.
Vaccine, polio, oral	1955	Sabin	U.S.
Vaccine, rabies	1885	Pasteur	French
Vaccine, smallpox	1796	Jenner	English
Vaccine, typhus	1909	Nicolle	French
Van Allen belts, radiation	1958	Van Allen	U.S.
Vitamin A	1913	McCollum, Davis	U.S.
Vitamin B	1916	McCollum	U.S.
Vitamin C	1912	Holst, Froelich	Norwegian
Vitamin D	1922	McCollum	U.S.
Wassermann test	1906	Wassermann	German
Xerography	1938	Carlson	U.S.
X-ray	1895	Roentgen	German

Chemical Elements, Discoverers, Atomic Weights

Atomic weights, based on the exact number 12 as the assigned atomic mass of the principal isotope of carbon, carbon 12, are provided through the courtesy of the International Union of Pure and Applied Chemistry and Butterworth Scientific Publications.

For the radioactive elements, with the exception of uranium and thorium, the mass number of either the isotope of longest half-life (*) or the better known isotope (**) is given.

Chemical element	Symbol	Atomic number	Atomic weight	Year discov.	Discoverer
Actinium	Ac	89	227*	1899	Debierne
Aluminum	Al	13	26.9815	1825	Oersted
Americium	Am.	95	243*	1944	Seaborg, et al.
Antimony	Sb	51	121.75	1450	Valentine
Argon	Ar	18	39.948	1894	Rayleigh, Ramsay
Arsenic	As	33	74.9216	13th c.	Albertus Magnus
Astatine	At	85	210*	1940	Corson, et al.
Barium	Ba	56	137.34	1808	Davy
Berkelium	Bk	97	249**	1949	Thompson, Ghiorso, Seaborg
Beryllium	Be	4	9.0122	1798	Vauquelin
Bismuth	Bi	83	208.980	15th c.	Valentine
Boron	B	5	10.811a	1808	Gay-Lussac, Thenard
Bromine	Br	35	79.904b	1826	Balard
Cadmium	Cd	48	112.40	1817	Stromeyer
Calcium	Ca	20	40.08	1808	Davy
Californium	Cf	98	251*	1950	Thompson, et al.
Carbon	C	6	12.01115a	B.C.	
Cerium	Ce	58	140.12	1803	Klaproth
Cesium	Cs	55	132.905	1860	Bunsen, Kirchhoff
Chlorine	Cl	17	35.453b	1774	Scheele
Chromium	Cr	24	51.996b	1797	Vauquelin
Cobalt	Co	27	58.9332	1735	Brandt
Copper	Cu	29	63.546b	B.C.	
Curium	Cm	96	247*	1944	Seaborg, James, Ghiorso
Dysprosium	Dy	66	162.50	1886	Boisbaudran
Einsteinium	Es	99	254*	1952	Ghiorso, et al.
Erbium	Er	68	167.26	1843	Mosander
Europium	Eu	63	151.96	1901	Demarcay
Fermium	Fm	100	257*	1953	Ghiorso, et al.
Fluorine	F	9	18.9984	1771	Scheele
Francium	Fr	87	223*	1939	Perey
Gadolinium	Gd	64	157.25	1886	Marignac
Gallium	Ga	31	69.72	1875	Boisbaudran
Germanium	Ge	32	72.59	1886	Winkler
Gold	Au	79	196.967	B.C.	
Hafnium	Hf	72	178.49	1923	Coster, Hevesy
Hahnium	Ha	105	262*	1970	Ghiorso, et al.
Helium	He.	2	4.0026	1868	Janssen, Lockyer
Holmium	Ho	67	164.930	1878	Soret, Delafontaine
Hydrogen	H	1	1.00797a	1766	Cavendish
Indium	In.	49	114.82	1863	Reich, Richter
Iodine	I	53	126.9044	1811	Courtois
Iridium	Ir.	77	192.2	1804	Tennant
Iron	Fe	26	55.847b	B.C.	
Krypton	Kr	36	83.80	1898	Ramsay, Travers
Lanthanum	La	57	138.91	1839	Mosander
Lawrencium	Lr.	103	260*	1961	Ghiorso, T. Sikkeland, A.E. Larsh, and R.M. Latimer
Lead	Pb	82	207.19	B.C.	
Lithium	Li	3	6.939	1817	Arfvedson
Lutetium	Lu	71	174.97	1907	Welsbach, Urbain
Magnesium	Mg	12	24.312	1829	Bussy

Chemical element	Symbol	Atomic number	Atomic weight	Year discov.	Discoverer
Manganese	Mn	25	54.9380	1774	Gahn
Mendelevium	Md	101	258*	1955	Ghiorso, et al.
Mercury	Hg	80	200.59	B.C.	
Molybdenum	Mo	42	95.94	1782	Hjelm
Neodymium	Nd	60	144.24	1885	Welsbach
Neon	Ne	10	20.183	1898	Ramsay, Travers
Neptunium	Np	93	237*	1940	McMillan, Abelson
Nickel	Ni	28	58.71	1751	Cronstedt
Niobium[1]	Nb	41	92.906	1801	Hatchett
Nitrogen	N	7	14.0067	1772	Rutherford
Nobelium	No	102	258*	1958	Ghiorso, et al.
Osmium	Os	76	190.2	1804	Tennant
Oxygen	O	8	15.9994a	1774	Priestley, Scheele
Palladium	Pd	46	106.4	1803	Wollaston
Phosphorus	P	15	30.9738	1669	Brand
Platinum	Pt	78	195.09	1735	Ulloa
Plutonium	Pu	94	242**	1940	Seaborg, et al.
Polonium	Po	84	210**	1898	P. and M. Curie
Potassium	K	19	39.102	1807	Davy
Praseodymium	Pr	59	140.907	1885	Welsbach
Promethium	Pm	61	147**	1945	Glendenin, Marinsky, Coryell
Protactinium	Pa	91	231*	1917	Hahn, Meitner
Radium	Ra	88	226*	1898	P. & M. Curie, Bemont
Radon	Rn	86	222*	1900	Dorn
Rhenium	Re	75	186.2	1925	Noddack, Tacke, Berg
Rhodium	Rh	45	102.905	1803	Wollaston
Rubidium	Rb	37	85.47	1861	Bunsen, Kirchhoff
Ruthenium	Ru	44	101.07	1845	Klaus
Rutherfordium	Rf	104	261*	1969	Ghiorso, et al.
Samarium	Sm	62	150.35	1879	Boisbaudran
Scandium	Sc	21	44.956	1879	Nilson
Selenium	Se	34	78.96	1817	Berzelius
Silicon	Si	14	28.086a	1823	Berzelius
Silver	Ag	47	107.868b	B.C.	
Sodium	Na	11	22.9898	1807	Davy
Strontium	Sr	38	87.62	1790	Crawford
Sulfur	S	16	32.064a	B.C.	
Tantalum	Ta	73	180.948	1802	Ekeberg
Technetium	Tc	43	99**	1937	Perrier and Segre
Tellurium	Te	52	127.60	1782	Von Reichenstein
Terbium	Tb	65	158.924	1843	Mosander
Thallium	Tl	81	204.37	1861	Crookes
Thorium	Th	90	232.038	1828	Berzelius
Thulium	Tm	69	168.934	1879	Cleve
Tin	Sn	50	118.69	B.C.	
Titanium	Ti	22	47.90	1791	Gregor
Tungsten (Wolfram)	W	74	183.85	1783	d'Elhujar
Uranium	U	92	238.03	1789	Klaproth
Vanadium	V	23	50.942	1830	Sefstrom
Xenon	Xe	54	131.30	1898	Ramsay, Travers
Ytterbium	Yb	70	173.04	1878	Marignac
Yttrium	Y	39	88.905	1794	Gadolin
Zinc	Zn	30	65.37	B.C.	
Zirconium	Zr	40	91.22	1789	Klaproth

(1) Formerly Columbium. (a) Atomic weights so designated are known to be variable because of natural variations in isotopic composition. The observed ranges are: hydrogen±0.0001; boron±0.003; carbon±0.005; oxygen±0.0001; silicon±0.001; sulfur±0.003. (b) Atomic weights so designated are believed to have the following experimental uncertainties: chlorine±0.001; chromium±0.001; iron±0.003; bromine±0.001; silver±0.001; copper±0.001.

Compact Discs

Compact disc (CD) technology was developed by Sony and N.V. Philips of the Netherlands, and introduced in the U.S. in 1982. The sound is represented by millions of pitted and flat dots molded into three miles of grooves that spiral around each plastic disc.

The growth of CDs has been stimulated by lower prices for CD players, which are now available for as little as $100. In 1986, nearly 3 million CD players were sold in the U.S., and 4 million are expected to be sold in 1987. By the end of 1987, 7% of U.S. households are expected to have one CD player.

The same laser disc technology is being applied to greatly increase the memory storage capacity of the personal computer. Compact discs with read-only memory (CD ROMs), even as limited as they now are in their production and applications, offer the consumer potential access to approximately 200,000 pages of printed information storable on each 4.72-inch disc, with retrieval at speeds far surpassing present technology. One such disc product, made available in March 1987 by Microsoft Corp., includes a dictionary, a national zip code directory, a thesaurus, Barlett's *Familiar Quotations*, and *The World Almanac and Book of Facts*.

Video Cassette Recorders

Video cassette recorders (VCRs), a technology originated in the U.S. in 1961, but today dominated by Japan, continue to change the home entertainment habits of millions of Americans. According to a report by the Electronic Industries Association, sales of videocassette recorders increased 11% in 1986 over 1985, from 11.9 to 13.2 million. It is estimated that 40% of U.S. households now include a VCR.

There are more than 15,000 video stores, as well as retail stores offering tapes in the U.S. In addition to these retail outlets, the first vending machine to carry videocassettes was installed in 1986, with more planned for convenience stores, hotels, motels, all-night restaurants, and office-building cafeterias. At the same time, public libraries across the nation are now making videocassettes available for borrowing at no cost.

A January 1984 Supreme Court decision established that federal copyright laws were not violated by the taping of television broadcasts at home for later viewing. This practice, called "time shifting" in the industry, has been one of the strongest selling points for VCRs.

The 1986 Survey of U.S. VCR Owners, conducted by National Demographics & Lifestyles of Denver, found 36% rent movies one or twice a week, while 48% record television programs to be played back at another time.

WEIGHTS AND MEASURES

Source: National Bureau of Standards, U.S. Commerce Department

U.S. Moving, Inch by 25.4 mm, to Metric System

On July 2, 1971, following the report of a metric conversion study committee, Commerce Secy. Maurice H. Stans recommended a gradual U.S. changeover during a 10-year period at the end of which the U.S. would be predominantly, but not exclusively, on the metric system. The Metric Conversion Act of 1975, signed Dec. 23, 1975, declared a national policy of coordinating voluntary increasing use of the Metric System and established a U. S. Metric Board to coordinate the change over. That Board terminated its operations on Sept. 30, 1982 and transferred its functions to the Office of Metric Programs, U.S. Department of Commerce.

Currently conversion to metric for the most part is confined to the following industries: automotive, construction and farm equipment, computer, and bottling. In addition, with encouragement of the National Council of Teachers of Mathematics, our school systems are placing more emphasis on teaching the metric system.

The International System of Units

Two systems of weights and measures exist side by side in the United States today, with roughly equal but separate legislative sanction: the U.S. Customary System and the International (Metric) System. Throughout U.S. history, the Customary System (inherited from, but now different from, the British Imperial System) has been, as its name implies, customarily used; a plethora of federal and state legislation has given it, through implication, standing as our primary weights and measures system. However, the Metric System (incorporated in the scientists' new SI or Systeme International d'Unites) is the only system that has ever received specific legislative sanction by Congress. The "Law of 1866" reads:

> It shall be lawful throughout the United States of America to employ the weights and measures of the metric system; and no contract or dealing, or pleading in any court, shall be deemed invalid or liable to objection because the weights or measures expressed or referred to therein are weights or measures of the metric system.

Over the last 100 years, the Metric System has seen slow, steadily increasing use in the United States. In science and also in the pharmaceutical industry, the use of metrics has for many years been predominant; today, the manufacturing industry is steadily increasing its use of the metric system largely motivated by the automotive industry, which is now predominantly metric.

On Feb. 10, 1964, the National Bureau of Standards issued the following bulletin:

> Henceforth it shall be the policy of the National Bureau of Standards to use the units of the International System (SI), as adopted by the 11th General Conference on Weights and Measures (October 1960), except when the use of these units would obviously impair communication or reduce the usefulness of a report.

What had been the Metric System became the International System (SI), a more complete scientific system.

Seven units have been adopted to serve as the base for the International System as follows: **length**—meter; **mass**—kilogram; **time**—second; **electric current**—ampere; **thermodynamic temperature**—kelvin; **amount of substance**—mole; and **luminous intensity**—candela.

Prefixes

The following prefixes, in combination with the basic unit names, provide the multiples and submultiples in the International System. For example, the unit name "meter," with the prefix "kilo" added, produces "kilometer," meaning "1,000 meters."

Prefix	Symbol	Multiples	Equivalent	Prefix	Symbol	Submultiples	Equivalent
exa	E	10^{18}	quintillionfold	deci	d	10^{-1}	tenth part
peta	P	10^{15}	quadrillionfold	centi	c	10^{-2}	hundredth part
tera	T	10^{12}	trillionfold	milli	m	10^{-3}	thousandth part
giga	G	10^{9}	billionfold	micro	μ	10^{-6}	millionth part
mega	M	10^{6}	millionfold	nano	n	10^{-9}	billionth part
kilo	k	10^{3}	thousandfold	pico	p	10^{-12}	trillionth part
hecto	h	10^{2}	hundredfold	femto	f	10^{-15}	quadrillionth part
deka	da	10	tenfold	atto	a	10^{-18}	quintillionth part

Tables of Metric Weights and Measures

Linear Measure

10 millimeters (mm)	= 1 centimeter (cm)
10 centimeters	= 1 decimeter (dm) = 100 millimeters
10 decimeters	= 1 meter (m) = 1,000 millimeters
10 meters	= 1 dekameter (dam)
10 dekameters	= 1 hectometer (hm) = 100 meters
10 hectometers	= 1 kilometer (km) = 1,000 meters

Area Measure

100 square millimeters (mm^2)	= 1 square centimeter (cm^2)
10,000 square centimeters	= 1 square meter (m^2) = 1,000,000 square millimeters
100 square meters	= 1 are (a)
100 ares	= 1 hectare (ha) = 10,000 square meters
100 hectares	= 1 square kilometer (km^2) = 1,000,000 square meters

Fluid Volume Measure

10 milliliters (mL)	= 1 centiliter (cL)
10 centiliters	= 1 deciliter (dL) = 100 milliliters
10 deciliters	= 1 liter (L) = 1,000 milliliters
10 liters	= 1 dekaliter (daL)
10 dekaliters	= 1 hectoliter (hL) = 100 liters
10 hectoliters	= 1 kiloliter (kL) = 1,000 liters

Cubic Measure

1,000 cubic millimeters (mm^3)	= 1 cubic centimeter (cm^3)
1,000 cubic centimeters	= 1 cubic decimeter (dm^3) = 1,000,000 cubic millimeters
1,000 cubic decimeters	= 1 cubic meter (m^3) = 1 stere = 1,000,000 cubic centimeters = 1,000,000,000 cubic millimeters

Weight

10 milligrams (mg)	= 1 centigram (cg)
10 centigrams	= 1 decigram (dg) = 100 milligrams
10 decigrams	= 1 gram (g) = 1,000 milligrams
10 grams	= 1 dekagram (dag)
10 dekagrams	= 1 hectogram (hg) = 100 grams
10 hectograms	= 1 kilogram (kg) = 1,000 grams
1,000 kilograms	= 1 metric ton (t)

Table of U.S. Customary Weights and Measures

Linear Measure

12 inches (in)	= 1 foot (ft)
3 feet	= 1 yard (yd)
5 ½ yards	= 1 rod (rd), pole, or perch (16 ½ feet)
40 rods	= 1 furlong (fur) = 220 yards = 660 feet
8 furlongs	= 1 statute mile (mi) = 1,760 yards = 5,280 feet
3 miles	= 1 league = 5,280 yards = 15,840 feet
6076.11549 feet	= 1 International Nautical Mile

Liquid Measure

When necessary to distinguish the liquid pint or quart from the dry pint or quart, the word "liquid" or the abbreviation "liq" should be used in combination with the name or abbreviation of the liquid unit.

4 gills	= 1 pint (pt) = 28.875 cubic inches
2 pints	= 1 quart (qt) = 57.75 cubic inches
4 quarts	= 1 gallon (gal) = 231 cubic inches = 8 pints = 32 gills

Area Measure

Squares and cubes of units are sometimes abbreviated by using "superior" figures. For example, ft^2 means square foot, and ft^3 means cubic foot.

144 square inches	= 1 square foot (ft^2)
9 square feet	= 1 square yard (yd^2) = 1,296 square inches
$30\frac{1}{4}$ square yards	= 1 square rod (rd^2) = $272\frac{1}{4}$ square feet
160 square rods	= 1 acre = 4,840 square yards = 43,560 square feet
640 acres	= 1 square mile (mi^2)
1 mile square	= 1 section (of land)
6 miles square	= 1 township = 36 sections = 36 square miles

Cubic Measure

1 cubic foot (ft^3)	= 1,728 cubic inches (in^3)
27 cubic feet	= 1 cubic yard (yd^3)

Gunter's or Surveyors' Chain Measure

7.92 inches (in)	= 1 link
100 links	= 1 chain (ch) = 4 rods = 66 feet
80 chains	= 1 survey mile (mi) = 320 rods = 5,280 feet

Troy Weight

24 grains	= 1 pennyweight (dwt)
20 pennyweights	= 1 ounce troy (oz t) = 480 grains
12 ounces troy	= 1 pound troy (lb t) = 240 pennyweights = 5,760 grains

Dry Measure

When necessary to distinguish the dry pint or quart from the liquid pint or quart, the word "dry" should be used in combination with the name or abbreviation of the dry unit.

2 pints (pt)	= 1 quart (qt) = 67.2006 cubic inches
8 quarts	= 1 peck (pk) = 537.605 cubic inches = 16 pints
4 pecks	= 1 bushel (bu) = 2,150.42 cubic inches = 32 quarts

Avoirdupois Weight

When necessary to distinguish the avoirdupois ounce or pound from the troy ounce or pound, the word "avoirdupois" or the abbreviation "avdp" should be used in combination with the name or abbreviation of the avoirdupois unit.

(The "grain" is the same in avoirdupois and troy weight.)

$27\frac{11}{32}$ grains	= 1 dram (dr)
16 drams	= 1 ounce (oz) = $437\frac{1}{2}$ grains
16 ounces	= 1 pound (lb) = 256 drams = 7,000 grains
100 pounds	= 1 hundredweight (cwt)°
20 hundredweights	= 1 ton = 2,000 pounds°

In "gross" or "long" measure, the following values are recognized.

112 pounds	= 1 gross or long hundredweight°
20 gross or long hundredweights	= 1 gross or long ton = 2,240 pounds°

°When the terms "hundredweight" and "ton" are used unmodified, they are commonly understood to mean the 100-pound hundredweight and the 2,000-pound ton, respectively; these units may be designated "net" or "short" when necessary to distinguish them from the corresponding units in gross or long measure.

Tables of Equivalents

In this table it is necessary to distinguish between the "international" and the "survey" foot. The international foot, defined in 1959 as exactly equal to 0.3048 meter, is shorter than the old survey foot by exactly 2 parts in one million. The survey foot is still used in data expressed in feet in geodetic surveys within the U.S. In this table the survey foot is italicized.

When the name of a unit is enclosed in brackets thus, [1 hand], this indicates (1) that the unit is not in general current use in the United States, or (2) that the unit is believed to be based on "custom and usage" rather than on formal definition.

Equivalents involving decimals are, in most instances, rounded off to the third decimal place except where they are exact, in which cases these exact equivalents are so designated.

Lengths

1 angstrom (A)	0.1 nanometer (exactly) 0.000 1 micrometer (exactly) 0.000 000 1 millimeter (exactly) 0.000 000 004 inch
1 cable's length	120 fathoms (exactly) 720 *feet* (exactly) 219 meters
1 centimeter (cm)	0.3937 inch
1 chain (ch) (Gunter's or surveyors)	66 *feet* (exactly) 20.1168 meters
1 chain (engineers)	100 feet 30.48 meters (exactly)
1 decimeter (dm)	3.937 inches
1 degree (geographical)	364,566.929 feet 69.047 miles (avg.) 111.123 kilometers (avg.)
-of latitude	68.708 miles at equator 69.403 miles at poles
-of longitude	69.171 miles at equator
1 dekameter (dam)	32.808 feet
1 fathom	6 *feet* (exactly) 1.8288 meters (exactly)
1 foot (ft)	0.3048 meters (exactly)
1 furlong (fur)	10 chains (surveyors) (exactly) 660 *feet* (exactly) $\frac{1}{8}$ statute mile (exactly) 201.168 meters
[1 hand] (height measure for horses from ground to top of shoulders)	4 inches
1 inch (in)	2.54 centimeters (exactly)
1 kilometer (km)	0.621 mile 3,281.5 feet
1 league (land)	3 survey miles (exactly) 4.828 kilometers
1 link (Gunter's or surveyors)	7.92 inches (exactly) 0.201 meter
1 link engineers	1 foot 0.305 meter
1 meter (m)	39.37 inches 1.094 yards
1 micrometer (μm) [the Greek letter mu]	0.001 millimeter (exactly) 0.000 039 37 inch
1 mil	0.001 inch (exactly) 0.025 4 millimeter (exactly)
1 mile (mi) (statute or land)	5,280 *feet* (exactly) 1.609 kilometers
1 international nautical mile (nmi)	1.852 kilometers (exactly) 1.150779 survey miles 6,076.11549 feet
1 millimeter (mm)	0.039 37 inch
1 nanometer (nm)	0.001 micrometer (exactly) 0.000 000 039 37 inch
1 pica (typography)	12 points
1 point (typography)	0.013 837 inch (exactly) 0.351 millimeter
1 rod (rd), pole, or perch	$16\frac{1}{2}$ *feet* (exactly) 5.029 meters
1 yard (yd)	0.9144 meter (exactly)

Areas or Surfaces

1 acre	43,560 square *feet* (exactly) 4,840 square yards 0.405 hectare
1 are (a)	119.599 square yards 0.025 acre

(continued)

1 bolt (cloth measure):	
length	100 yards (on modern looms)
width	42 inches (usually, for cotton) 60 inches (usually, for wool)
1 hectare (ha)	2.471 acres
[1 square (building)]	100 square feet
1 square centimeter (cm^2)	0.155 square inch
1 square decimeter (dm^2)	15.500 square inches
1 square foot (ft^2)	929.030 square centimeters
1 square inch (in^2)	6.4516 square centimeters (exactly)
1 square kilometer (km^2)	247.104 acres 0.386 square mile
1 square meter (m^2)	1.196 square yards 10.764 square feet
1 square mile (mi^2)	258.999 hectares
1 square millimeter (mm^2)	0.002 square inch
1 square rod (rd^2) sq. pole, or sq. perch	25.293 square meters
1 square yard (yd^2)	0.836 square meter

Capacities or Volumes

1 barrel (bbl) liquid	31 to 42 gallons°

°There are a variety of "barrels," established by law or usage. For example: federal taxes on fermented liquors are based on a barrel of 31 gallons: many state laws fix the "barrel for liquids" as 31 $\frac{1}{2}$ gallons; one state fixes a 36-gallon barrel for cistern measurement; federal law recognizes a 40-gallon barrel for "proof spirits"; by custom, 42 gallons comprise a barrel of crude oil or petroleum products for statistical purposes, and this equivalent is recognized "for liquids" by 4 states.

1 barrel (bbl), standard, for fruits, vegetables, and other dry commodities except dry cranberries	7,056 cubic inches 105 dry quarts 3.281 bushels, struck measure
1 barrel (bbl), standard, cranberry	5,826 cubic inches $86\frac{45}{64}$ dry quarts 2.709 bushels, struck measure
1 board foot (lumber measure)	a foot-square board 1 inch thick
1 bushel (bu) (U.S.) (struck measure)	2,150.42 cubic inches (exactly) 35.239 liters
[1 bushel, heaped (U.S.)]	2,747.715 cubic inches 1.278 bushels, struck measure°

°Frequently recognized as $1\frac{1}{4}$ bushels, struck measure.

[1 bushel (bu) (British Imperial) (struck measure)]	1.032 U.S. bushels struck measure 2,219.36 cubic inches
1 cord (cd) firewood	128 cubic feet (exactly)
1 cubic centimeter (cm^3)	0.061 cubic inch
1 cubic decimeter (dm^3)	61.024 cubic inches
1 cubic inch (in^3)	0.554 fluid ounce 4.433 fluid drams 16.387 cubic centimeters
1 cubic foot (ft^3)	7.481 gallons 28.317 cubic decimeters
1 cubic meter (m^3)	1.308 cubic yards
1 cubic yard (yd^3)	0.765 cubic meter
1 cup, measuring	8 fluid ounces (exactly) $\frac{1}{2}$ liquid pint (exactly)
[1 dram, fluid (fl dr) (British)]	0.961 U.S. fluid dram 0.217 cubic inch 3.552 milliliters
1 dekaliter (daL)	2.642 gallons 1.135 pecks
1 gallon (gal) (U.S.)	231 cubic inches (exactly) 3.785 liters 0.833 British gallon 128 U.S. fluid ounces (exactly)
[1 gallon (gal) British Imperial]	277.42 cubic inches 1.201 U.S. gallons 4.546 liters 160 British fluid ounces (exactly)
1 gill (gi)	7.219 cubic inches 4 fluid ounces (exactly) 0.118 liter
1 hectoliter (hL)	26.418 gallons 2.838 bushels
1 liter (L) (1 cubic decimeter exactly)	1.057 liquid quarts 0.908 dry quart 61.025 cubic inches
1 milliliter (mL) (1 cu cm exactly)	0.271 fluid dram 16.231 minims 0.061 cubic inch
1 ounce, liquid (U.S.)	1.805 cubic inches 29.573 milliliters 1.041 British fluid ounces
[1 ounce, fluid (fl oz) (British)]	0.961 U.S. fluid ounce 1.734 cubic inches 28.412 milliliters
1 peck (pk)	8.810 liters
1 pint (pt), dry	33.600 cubic inches 0.551 liter
1 pint (pt), liquid	28.875 cubic inches (exactly) 0.473 liter
1 quart (qt) dry (U.S.)	67.201 cubic inches 1.101 liters 0.969 British quart
1 quart (qt) liquid (U.S.)	57.75 cubic in (exactly) 0.946 liter 0.833 British quart
[1 quart (qt) (British)]	69.354 cubic inches 1.032 U.S. dry quarts 1.201 U.S. liquid quarts
1 tablespoon	3 teaspoons°(exactly) 4 fluid drams $\frac{1}{2}$ fluid ounce (exactly)
1 teaspoon	$\frac{1}{3}$ tablespoon°(exactly) $1\frac{1}{3}$ fluid drams°

°The equivalent "1 teaspoon—$1\frac{1}{3}$ fluid drams" has been found by the bureau to correspond more closely with the actual capacities of "measuring" and silver teaspoons than the equivalent "1 teaspoon—1 fluid dram" which is given by many dictionaries.

Weights or Masses

1 assay ton°° (AT)	29.167 grams

°°Used in assaying. The assay ton bears the same relation to the milligram that a ton of 2,000 pounds avoirdupois bears to the ounce troy; hence the weight in milligrams of precious metal obtained from one assay ton of ore gives directly the number of troy ounces to the net ton.

1 bale (cotton measure)	500 pounds in U.S. 750 pounds in Egypt
1 carat (c)	200 milligrams (exactly) 3.086 grains
1 dram avoirdupois (dr avdp)	$27\frac{11}{32}$ (=27.344) grains 1.772 grams
gamma, see microgram	
1 grain	64.799 milligrams
1 gram	15.432 grains 0.035 ounce, avoirdupois
1 hundredweight, gross or long°°° (gross cwt)	112 pounds (exactly) 50.802 kilograms
1 hundredweight, net or short (cwt. or net cwt.)	100 pounds (exactly) 45.359 kilograms
1 kilogram (kg)	2.205 pounds
1 microgram (μg [The Greek letter mu in combination with the letter g])	0.000001 gram (exactly)
1 milligram (mg)	0.015 grain
1 ounce, avoirdupois (oz avdp)	437.5 grains (exactly) 0.911 troy ounce 28.350 grams
1 ounce, troy (oz t)	480 grains (exactly) 1.097 avoirdupois ounces 31.103 grams
1 pennyweight (dwt)	1.555 grams
1 pound, avoirdupois (lb avdp)	7,000 grains (exactly) 1.215 troy pounds 453.592 37 grams (exactly)
1 pound, troy (lb t)	5,760 grains (exactly) 0.823 avoirdupois pound 373.242 grams
1 ton, gross or long°°° (gross ton)	2,240 pounds (exactly) 1.12 net tons (exactly) 1.016 metric tons

°°°The gross or long ton and hundredweight are used commercially in the United States to only a limited extent, usually in restricted industrial fields. These units are the same as British "ton" and "hundredweight."

1 ton, metric (t)	2,204.623 pounds 0.984 gross ton 1.102 net tons
1 ton, net or short (sh ton)	2,000 pounds (exactly) 0.893 gross ton 0.907 metric ton

Tables of Interrelation of Units of Measurement

Units of length and area of the international and survey measures are included in the following tables. Units unique to the survey measure are italicized. See pg 163, Tables of Equivalents, 1st para.

1 international foot	= 0.999 998 survey foot (exactly)
1 survey foot	= 1200/3937 meter (exactly)
1 international foot	= 12 × 0.0254 meter (exactly)

Bold face type indicates exact values

Units of Length

Units	Inches	*Links*	Feet	Yards	*Rods*	*Chains*	Miles	cm	Meters
1 inch=	**1**	0.126 263	0.083 333	0.027 778	0.005 051	0.001 263	0.000 016	**2.54**	**0.025 4**
1 *link*=	**7.92**	**1**	**0.66**	**0.22**	**0.04**	**0.01**	**0.000 125**	20.117	0.201 168
1 foot=	**12**	1.515 152	**1**	0.333 333	0.060 606	0.015 152	0.000 189	**30.48**	**0.304 8**
1 yard=	**36**	4.545 45	**3**	**1**	0.181 818	0.045 455	0.000 568	**91.44**	**0.914 4**
1 *rod*=	**198**	**25**	**16.5**	**5.5**	**1**	**0.25**	**0.003 125**	502.92	5.029 2
1 *chain*=	**792**	**100**	**66**	**22**	**4**	**1**	**0.012 5**	2011.68	20.116 8
1 mile=	**63 360**	**8000**	**5280**	**1760**	**320**	**80**	**1**	**160 934.4**	**1609.344**
1 cm=	0.3937	0.049 710	0.032 808	0.010 936	0.001 988	0.000 497	0.000 006	**1**	**0.01**
1 meter=	39.37	4.970 960	3.280 840	1.093 613	0.198 838	0.049 710	0.000 621	**100**	**1**

Units of Area

Units	Sq. inches	*Sq. links*	Sq. feet	Sq. yards	*Sq. rods*	*Sq. chains*
1 sq. inch=	**1**	.015 942 3	0.006 944	0.000 771 605	0.000 025 5	0.000 001 594
1 sq. *link*=	62.726 4	**1**	**0.435 6**	**0.0484**	**0.0016**	**0.000 1**
1 sq. foot=	**144**	2.295 684	**1**	0.111 111 1	0.003 673 09	0.000 229 568
1 sq. yard=	**1296**	20.661 16	**9**	**1**	0.033 057 85	0.002 066 12
1 sq. *rod*=	**39 204**	**625**	**272.25**	**30.25**	**1**	**0.062 5**
1 sq. *chain*=	**627 264**	**10 000**	**4 356**	**484**	**16**	**1**
1 *acre*=	**6 272 640**	**100 000**	**43 560**	**4 840**	**160**	**10**
1 sq. mile=	**4 014 489 600**	**64 000 000**	**27 878 400**	**3 097 600**	**102 400**	**6400**
1 sq. cm=	0.155 000 3	0.002 471 05	0.001 076	0.000 119 599	0.000 003 954	0.000 000 247
1 sq. meter=	1550.003	24.710 44	10.763 91	1.195 990	0.039 536 70	0.002 471 044
1 *hectare*=	15 500 031	247 104	107 639.1	11 959.90	395.367 0	24.710 44

Units	*Acres*	Sq. miles	Sq. cm	Sq. meters	*Hectares*
1 sq. inch=	0.000 000 159 423	0.000 000 000 249 10	**6.451 6**	**0.000 645 16**	0.000 000 065
1 sq. *link*=	**0.000 01**	**0.000 000 015 625**	404.685 642 24	0.040 468 56	0.000 004 047
1 sq. foot=	0.000 022 956 84	0.000 000 035 870 06	929.034 1	0.092 903 41	0.000 009 290
1 sq. yard=	0.000 206 611 6	0.000 000 322 830 6	**8 361.273 6**	**0.836 127 36**	0.000 083 613
1 sq. *rod*=	**0.006 25**	**0.000 009 765 625**	252 929.5	25.292 95	0.002 529 295
1 sq. *chain*=	**0.1**	**0.000 156 25**	4 046 873	404.687 3	0.040 468 73
1 *acre*=	**1**	**0.001 562 5**	40 468 73	4 046.873	0.404 687 3
1 sq. mile=	**640**	**1**	25 899 881 103	2 589 988.11	258.998 811 034
1 sq. cm=	0.000 000 024 711	0.000 000 000 038 610	**1**	**0.000 1**	**0.000 000 01**
1 sq. meter=	0.000 247 104 4	0.000 000 386 102 2	**10 000**	**1**	**0.0001**
1 *hectare*=	2.471 044	0.003 861 006	**100 000 000**	**10 000**	**1**

Units of Mass Not Greater than Pounds and Kilograms

Units	Grains	Pennyweights	Avdp drams	Avdp ounces
1 grain=	**1**	0.041 666 67	0.036 571 43	0.002 285 71
1 pennyweight=	**24**	**1**	0.877 714 3	0.054 857 14
1 dram avdp=	**27.343 75**	1.139 323	**1**	**0.062 5**
1 ounce avdp=	**437.5**	18.229 17	**16**	**1**
1 ounce troy=	**480**	**20**	17.554 29	1.097 143
1 pound troy=	**5760**	**240**	210.651 4	13.165 71
1 pound avdp=	**7000**	291.666 7	**256**	**16**
1 milligram=	0.015 432	0.000 643 015	0.000 564 383	0.000 035 274
1 gram=	15.432 36	0.643 014 9	0.564 383 4	0.035 273 96
1 kilogram=	15 432.36	643.014 9	564.383 4	35.273 96

Units	Troy ounces	Troy pounds	Avdp pounds	Milligrams	Grams	Kilograms
1 grain=	0.002 083 33	0.000 173 611	0.000 142 857	**64.798 91**	**0.064 798 91**	0.000 064 799
1 pennyw't.=	**0.05**	0.004 166 667	0.003 428 571	**1555.173 84**	**1.555 173 84**	0.001 555 174
1 dram avdp=	0.056 966 15	0.004 747 179	0.003 906 25	1771.845 195	1.771 845 195	0.001 771 845
1 oz avdp=	0.911 458 3	0.075 954 86	**0.062 5**	**28 349.523 125**	**28.349 523 125**	0.028 349 52
1 oz troy=	**1**	0.083 333 333	0.068 571 43	**31 103.476 8**	**31.103 476 8**	0.031 103 48
1 lb troy=	**12**	**1**	0.822 857 1	**373 241.721 6**	**373.241 721 6**	0.373 241 722
1 lb avdp=	14.583 33	1.215 278	**1**	**453 592.37**	**453.592 37**	**0.453 592 37**
1 milligram=	0.000 032 151	0.000 002 679	0.000 002 205	**1**	**0.001**	**0.000 001**
1 gram=	0.032 150 75	0.002 679 229	0.002 204 623	**1000**	**1**	**0.001**
1 kilogram=	32.150 75	2.679 229	2.204 623	**1 000 000**	**1000**	**1**

Units of Mass Not Less than Avoirdupois Ounces

Units	Avdp oz	Avdp lb	Short cwt	Short tons	Long tons	Kilograms	Metric tons
1 oz av=	**1**	**0.0625**	**0.000 625**	**0.000 031 25**	0.000 027 902	0.028 349 523	0.000 028 350
1 lb av=	**16**	**1**	**0.01**	**0.000 5**	0.000 446 429	**0.453 592 37**	0.000 453 592
1 sh cwt=	**1 600**	**100**	**1**	**0.05**	0.044 642 86	**45.359 237**	**0.045 359 237**
1 sh ton=	**32 000**	**2000**	**20**	**1**	0.892 857 1	**907.184 74**	**0.907 184 74**
1 long ton=	**35 840**	**2240**	**22.4**	**1.12**	**1**	**1016.046 908 8**	1.016 046 909
1 kg=	35.273 96	2.204 623	0.022 046 23	0.001 102 311	0.000 984 207	**1**	**0.001**
1 metric ton=	35 273.96	2 204.623	22.046 23	1.102 311	0.984 206 5	**1000**	**1**

(continued)

Units of Volume

Units	Cubic inches	Cubic feet	Cubic yards	Cubic cm	Cubic dm	Cubic meters
1 cubic inch=	1	0.000 578 704	0.000 021 433	16.387 064	0.016 387	0.000 016 387
1 cubic foot=	1728	1	0.037 037 04	28 316.846 592	28.316 847	0.028 316 847
1 cubic yard=	46 656	27	1	764 554.857 984	764.554 858	0.764 554 858
1 cubic cm=	0.061 023 74	0.000 035 315	0.000 001 308	1	0.001	0.000 001
1 cubic dm=	61.023 74	0.035 314 67	0.001 307 951	1 000	1	0.001
1 cubic meter	61 023.74	35.314 67	1.307 951	1 000 000	1000	1

Units of Capacity (Liquid Measure)

Units	Minims	Fluid drams	Fluid ounces	Gills	Liquid pt
1 minim=	1	0.016 666 7	0.002 083 33	0.000 520 833	0.000 130 208
1 fluid dram=	60	1	0.125	0.031 25	0.007 812 5
1 fluid ounce=	480	8	1	0.25	0.062 5
1 gill=	1920	32	4	1	0.25
1 liquid pint=	7680	128	16	4	1
1 liquid quart=	15 360	256	32	8	2
1 gallon=	61 440	1024	128	32	8
1 cubic inch=	265.974	4.432 900	0.554 112 6	0.138 528 1	0.034 632 03
1 cubic foot=	459 603.1	7 660.052	957.506 5	239.376 6	59.844 16
1 milliliter=	16.230 73	0.270 512 18	0.033 814 02	0.008 453 506	.002 113 376
1 liter=	16 230.73	270.512 18	33.814 02	8.453 506	2.113 376

Units	Liquid quarts	Gallons	Cubic inches	Cubic feet	Liters
1 minim=	0.000 065 104 17	0.000 016 276 04	0.003 759 766	0.000 002 175 790	0.000 061 611 52
1 flu. dram=	0.003 906 25	0.000 976 562 5	0.225 585 9	0.000 130 547 4	0.003 696 691
1 fluid oz=	0.031 25	0.007 812 5	1.804 687 5	0.001 044 379	0.029 573 53
1 gill=	0.125	0.031 25	7.218 75	0.004 177 517	0.118 294 118
1 liquid pt=	0.5	0.125	28.875	0.016 710 07	0.473 176 473
1 liquid qt=	1	0.25	57.75	0.033 420 14	0.946 352 946
1 gallon=	4	1	231	0.133 680 6	3.785 411 784
1 cubic in.=	0.017 316 02	0.004 329 004	1	0.000 578 703 7	0.016 387 064
1 cubic foot=	29.922 08	7.480 519	1728	1	28.316 846 592
1 liter=	1.056 688	0.264 172 05	61.023 74	0.035 314 67	1

Units of Capacity (Dry Measure)

Units	Dry pints	Dry quarts	Pecks	Bushels	Cubic in.	Liters
1 dry pint=	1	0.5	0.062 5	0.015 625	33.600 312 5	0.550 610 47
1 dry quart=	2	1	0.125	0.031 25	67.200 625	1.101 220 9
1 peck=	16	8	1	0.25	537.605	8.809 767 5
1 bushel=	64	32	4	1	2150.42	35.239 07
1 cubic inch=	0.029 761 6	0.014 880 8	0.001 860 10	0.000 465 025	1	0.016 387 06
1 liter=	1.816 166	0.908 083	0.113 510 37	0.028 377 59	61.023 74	1

Miscellaneous Measures

Caliber—the diameter of a gun bore. In the U.S., caliber is traditionally expressed in hundredths of inches, eg. .22 or .30. In Britain, caliber is often expressed in thousandths of inches, eg. .270 or .465. Now, it is commonly expressed in millimeters, eg. the 7.62 mm. M14 rifle and the 5.56 mm. M16 rifle. Heavier weapons' caliber has long been expressed in millimeters, eg. the 81 mm. mortar, the 105 mm. howitzer (light), the 155 mm. howitzer (medium or heavy).

Naval guns' caliber refers to the barrel length as a multiple of the bore diameter. A 5-inch, 50-caliber naval gun has a 5-inch bore and a barrel length of 250 inches.

Carat, karat—a measure of the amount of alloy per 24 parts in gold. Thus 24-carat gold is pure; 18-carat gold is one-fourth alloy.

Decibel (dB)—a measure of the relative loudness or intensity of sound. A 20-decibel sound is 10 times louder than a 10-decibel sound; 30 decibels is 100 times louder; 40 decibels is 1,000 times louder, etc. One decibel is the smallest difference between sounds detectable by the human ear. A 140-decibel sound is painful.

10 decibels	– a light whisper
20	– quiet conversation
30	– normal conversation
40	– light traffic
50	– typewriter, loud conversation
60	– noisy office
70	– normal traffic, quiet train
80	– rock music, subway
90	– heavy traffic, thunder
100	– jet plane at takeoff

Em—a printer's measure designating the square width of any given type size. Thus, an em of 10-point type is 10 points. An en is half an em.

Gauge—a measure of shotgun bore diameter. Gauge numbers originally referred to the number of lead balls of the gun barrel diameter in a pound. Thus, a 16 gauge shotgun's bore was smaller than a 12-gauge shotgun's. Today, an international agreement assigns millimeter measures to each gauge, eg:

Gauge	Bore diameter in mm
6	23.34
10	19.67
12	18.52
14	17.60
16	16.81
20	15.90

Horsepower—the power needed to lift 550 pounds one foot in one second, or to lift 33,000 pounds one foot in one minute. Equivalent to 746 watts or 2,546.0756 Btu/h.

Quire—25 sheets of paper

Ream—500 sheets of paper

Electrical Units

The **watt** is the unit of power (electrical, mechanical, thermal, etc.). Electrical power is given by the product of the voltage and the current.

Energy is sold by the **joule**, but in common practice the billing of electrical energy is expressed in terms of the **kilowatt-hour**, which is 3,600,000 joules or 3.6 megajoules.

The **horsepower** is a non-metric unit sometimes used in mechanics. It is equal to 746 watts.

The **ohm** is the unit of electrical resistance and represents the physical property of a conductor which offers a resistance to the flow of electricity, permitting just 1 ampere to flow at 1 volt of pressure.

Compound Interest

Compounded Annually

Principal	Period	4%	5%	6%	7%	8%	9%	10%	12%	14%	16%
$100	1 day	0.011	0.014	0.016	0.019	0.022	0.025	0.027	0.033	0.038	0.044
	1 week	0.077	0.096	0.115	0.134	0.153	0.173	0.192	0.230	0.268	0.307
	6 mos.	2.00	2.50	3.00	3.50	4.00	4.50	5.00	6.00	7.00	8.00
	1 year	4.00	5.00	6.00	7.00	8.00	9.00	10.00	12.00	14.00	16.00
	2 years	8.16	10.25	12.36	14.49	16.64	18.81	21.00	25.44	29.96	34.56
	3 years	12.49	15.76	19.10	22.50	25.97	29.50	33.10	40.49	48.15	56.09
	4 years	16.99	21.55	26.25	31.08	36.05	41.16	46.41	57.35	68.90	81.06
	5 years	21.67	27.63	33.82	40.26	46.93	53.86	61.05	76.23	92.54	110.03
	6 years	26.53	34.01	41.85	50.07	58.69	67.71	77.16	97.38	119.50	143.64
	7 years	31.59	40.71	50.36	60.58	71.38	82.80	94.87	121.07	150.23	182.62
	8 years	36.86	47.75	59.38	71.82	85.09	99.26	114.36	147.60	185.26	227.84
	9 years	42.33	55.13	68.95	83.85	99.90	117.19	135.79	177.31	225.19	280.30
	10 years	48.02	62.89	79.08	96.72	115.89	136.74	159.37	210.58	270.72	341.14
	12 years	60.10	79.59	101.22	125.22	151.82	181.27	213.84	289.60	381.79	493.60
	15 years	80.09	107.89	139.66	175.90	217.22	264.25	317.72	447.36	613.79	826.55
	20 years	119.11	165.33	220.71	286.97	366.10	460.44	572.75	864.63	1,274.35	1,846.08

Ancient Measures

Biblical

Cubit	=	21.8 inches
Omer	=	0.45 peck 3.964 liters
Ephah	=	10 omers
Shekel	=	0.497 ounce 14.1 grams

Greek

Cubit	=	18.3 inches
Stadion	=	607.2 or 622 feet
Obolos	=	715.38 milligrams
Drachma	=	4.2923 grams
Mina	=	0.9463 pounds
Talent	=	60 mina

Roman

Cubit	=	17.5 inches
Stadium	=	202 yards
As, libra, pondus	=	325.971 grams, .71864 pounds

Weight of Water

1	cubic inch	.0360 pound
12	cubic inches	.433 pound
1	cubic foot	62.4 pounds
1	cubic foot	7.48052 U.S. gal
1.8	cubic feet	112.0 pounds
35.96	cubic feet	2240.0 pounds
1	imperial gallon	10.0 pounds
11.2	imperial gallons	112.0 pounds
224	imperial gallons	2240.0 pounds
1	U.S. gallon	8.33 pounds
13.45	U.S. gallons	112.0 pounds
269.0	U.S. gallons	2240.0 pounds

Density of Gases and Vapors

at 0°C and 760 mmHg

Source: National Bureau of Standards (kilograms per cubic meter)

Gas	Wgt.	Gas	Wgt.	Gas	Wgt.
Acetylene	1.171	Ethylene	1.260	Methyl fluoride	1.545
Air	1.293	Fluorine	1.696	Mono methylamine	1.38
Ammonia	.759	Helium	.178	Neon	.900
Argon	1.784	Hydrogen	.090	Nitric oxide	1.341
Arsene	3.48	Hydrogen bromide	3.50	Nitrogen	1.250
Butane-iso	2.60	Hydrogen chloride	1.639	Nitrosyl chloride	2.99
Butane-n	2.519	Hydrogen iodide	5.724	Nitrous oxide	1.997
Carbon dioxide	1.977	Hydrogen selenide	3.66	Oxygen	1.429
Carbon monoxide	1.250	Hydrogen sulfide	1.539	Phosphine	1.48
Carbon oxysulfide	2.72	Krypton	3.745	Propane	2.020
Chlorine	3.214	Methane	.717	Silicon tetrafluoride	4.67
Chlorine monoxide	3.89	Methyl chloride	2.25	Sulfur dioxide	2.927
Ethane	1.356	Methyl ether	2.091	Xenon	5.897

Temperature Conversion Table

The numbers in bold face type refer to the temperature either in degrees Celsius or Fahrenheit which are to be converted. If converting from degrees Fahrenheit to Celsius, the equivalent will be found in the column on the left, while if converting from degrees Celsius to Fahrenheit the answer will be found in the column on the right.

For temperatures not shown. To convert Fahrenheit to Celsius subtract 32 degrees and multiply by 5, divide by 9; to convert Celsius to Fahrenheit, multiply by 9, divide by 5 and add 32 degrees.

Celsius		Fahrenheit	Celsius		Fahrenheit	Celsius		Fahrenheit
−273.2	**−459.7**	....	−17.8	**0**	32	35.0	**95**	203
−184	**−300**	....	−12.2	**10**	50	36.7	**98**	208.4
−169	**−273**	−459.4	−6.67	**20**	68	37.8	**100**	212
−157	**−250**	−418	−1.11	**30**	86	43	**110**	230
−129	**−200**	−328	4.44	**40**	104	49	**120**	248
−101	**−150**	−238	10.0	**50**	122	54	**130**	266
−73.3	**−100**	−148	15.6	**60**	140	60	**140**	284
−45.6	**−50**	−58	21.1	**70**	158	66	**150**	302
−40.0	**−40**	−40	23.9	**75**	167	93	**200**	392
−34.4	**−30**	−22	26.7	**80**	176	121	**250**	482
−28.9	**−20**	−4	29.4	**85**	185	149	**300**	572
−23.3	**−10**	14	32.2	**90**	194			

Boiling and Freezing Points of Water

Water boils at 212°F at sea level. For every 550 feet above sea level, boiling point of water is lower by about 1°F. Methyl alcohol boils at 148°F. Average human oral temperature, 98.6°F. Water freezes at 32°F. Although "Centigrade" is still frequently used, the International Committee on Weights and Measures and the National Bureau of Standards have recommended since 1948 that this scale be called "Celsius."

Breaking the Sound Barrier; Speed of Sound

The prefix Mach is used to describe supersonic speed. It derives from Ernst Mach, a Czech-born German physicist, who contributed to the study of sound. When a plane moves at the speed of sound it is Mach 1. When twice the speed of sound it is Mach 2. When it is near but below the speed of sound its speed can be designated at less than Mach 1, for example, Mach .90. Mach is defined as "in jet propulsion, the ratio of the velocity of a rocket or a jet to the velocity of sound in the medium being considered."

When a plane passes the sound barrier—flying faster than sound travels—listeners in the area hear thunderclaps, but pilots do not hear them.

Sound is produced by vibrations of an object and is transmitted by alternate increase and decrease in pressures that radiate outward through a material media of molecules—somewhat like waves spreading out on a pond after a rock has been tossed into it.

The frequency of sound is determined by the number of times the vibrating waves undulate per second, and is measured in cycles per second. The slower the cycle of waves, the lower the frequency. As frequencies increase, the sound is higher in pitch.

Sound is audible to human beings only if the frequency falls within a certain range. The human ear is usually not sensitive to frequencies of less than 20 vibrations per second, or more than about 20,000 vibrations per second—although this range varies among individuals. Anything at a pitch higher than the human ear can hear is termed ultrasonic.

Intensity or loudness is the strength of the pressure of these radiating waves, and is measured in decibels. The human ear responds to intensity in a range from zero to 120 decibels. Any sound with pressure over 120 decibels is painful.

The speed of sound is generally placed at 1,088 feet per second at sea level at 32°F. It varies in other temperatures and in different media. Sound travels faster in water than in air, and even faster in iron and steel. If in air it travels a mile in 5 seconds, it does a mile under water in 1 second, and through iron in 1/3 of a second. It travels through ice cold vapor at approximately 4,708 feet per second, ice-cold water, 4,938; granite, 12,960; hardwood, 12,620; brick, 11,960; glass, 16,410 to 19,690; silver, 8,658; gold, 5,717.

Colors of the Spectrum

Color, an electromagnetic wave phenomenon, is a sensation produced through the excitation of the retina of the eye by rays of light. The colors of the spectrum may be produced by viewing a light beam refracted by passage through a prism, which breaks the light into its wave lenghts.

Customarily, the primary colors of the spectrum are thought of as those 6 monochromatic colors that occupy relatively large areas of the spectrum: red, orange, yellow, green, blue, and violet. However, Sir Isaac Newton named a 7th, indigo, situated between blue and violet on the spectrum. Aubert estimated (1865) the solar spectrum to contain approximately 1,000 distinguishable hues of which according to Rood (1881) 2 million tints and shades can be distinguished; Luckiesh stated (1915) that 55 distinctly different hues have been seen in a single spectrum.

Many physicists recognize only 3 primary colors: red, yellow, and blue (Mayer, 1775); red, green, and violet (Thomas Young, 1801); red, green, and blue (Clerk Maxwell, 1860).

The color sensation of black is due to complete lack of stimulation of the retina, that of white to complete stimulation. The infra-red and ultra-violet rays, below the red (long) end of the spectrum and above the violet (short) end respectively, are invisible to the naked eye. Heat is the principal effect of the infra-red rays and chemical action that of the ultra-violet rays.

Common Fractions Reduced to Decimals

8ths	16ths	32ds	64ths	
			1	.015625
		1	2	.03125
			3	.046875
	1	2	4	.0625
			5	.078125
		3	6	.09375
			7	.109375
1	2	4	8	.125
			9	.140625
		5	10	.15625
			11	.171875
	3	6	12	.1875
			13	.203125
		7	14	.21875
			15	.234375
2	4	8	16	.25
			17	.265625
		9	18	.28125
			19	.296875
	5	10	20	.3125
			21	.328125
		11	22	.34375

8ths	16ths	32ds	64ths	
			23	.359375
3	6	12	24	.375
			25	.390625
		13	26	.40625
			27	.421875
	7	14	28	.4375
			29	.453125
		15	30	.46875
			31	.484375
4	8	16	32	.5
			33	.515625
		17	34	.53125
			35	.546875
	9	18	36	.5625
			37	.578125
		19	38	.59375
			39	.609375
5	10	20	40	.625
			41	.640625
		21	42	.65625
			43	.671875
	11	22	44	.6875

8ths	16ths	32ds	64ths	
			45	.703125
		23	46	.71875
			47	.734375
6	12	24	48	.75
			49	.765625
		25	50	.78125
			51	.796875
	13	26	52	.8125
			53	.828125
		27	54	.84375
			55	.859375
7	14	28	56	.875
			57	.890625
		29	58	.90625
			59	.921875
	15	30	60	.9375
			61	.953125
		31	62	.96875
			63	.984375
8	16	32	64	1.

Spirits Measures

- Pony . . . . 0.5 jigger
- Shot . . . . 0.666 jigger; 1.0 ounce
- Jigger . . . . 1.5 shot
- Pint . . . . 16 shots; 0.625 fifth
- Fifth . . . . 25.6 shots; 1.6 pints; 0.8 quart; 0.75706 liter

- Quart . . . . 32 shots; 1.25 fifth
- Magnum . . . . 2 quarts; 2.49797 bottles (wine)

For champagne and brandy only:

- Jeroboam . . . . . 6.4 pints; 1.6 magnum; 0.8 gallon

For champagne only:

- Rehoboam . . . . 3 magnums
- Methuselah . . . . 4 magnums
- Salmanazar . . . . 6 magnums
- Balthazar . . . . . 8 magnums
- Nebuchadnezzar . 10 magnums

Wine bottle (standard):

- . . . . 0.800633 quart; 0.7576778 liter

Mathematical Formulas

To find the CIRCUMFERENCE of a:

Circle — Multiply the diameter by 3.14159265 (usually 3.1416).

To find the AREA of a:

Circle — Multiply the square of the diameter by .785398 (usually .7854).

Rectangle — Multiply the length of the base by the height.

Sphere (surface) — Multiply the square of the radius by 3.1416 and multiply by 4.

Square — Square the length of one side.

Trapezoid — Add the two parallel sides, multiply by the height and divide by 2.

Triangle — Multiply the base by the height and divide by 2.

To find the VOLUME of a:

Cone — Multiply the square of the radius of the base by 3.1416, multiply by the height, and divide by 3.

Cube — Cube the length of one edge.

Cylinder — Multiply the square of the radius of the base by 3.1416 and multiply by the height.

Pyramid — Multiply the area of the base by the height and divide by 3.

Rectangular Prism — Multiply the length by the width by the height.

Sphere — Multiply the cube of the radius by 3.1416, multiply by 4 and divide by 3.

Playing Cards and Dice Chances

Poker Hands

Hand	Number possible	Odds against
Royal flush	4	649,739 to 1
Other straight flush	36	72,192 to 1
Four of a kind	624	4,164 to 1
Full house	3,744	693 to 1
Flush	5,108	508 to 1
Straight	10,200	254 to 1
Three of a kind	54,912	46 to 1
Two pairs	123,552	20 to 1
One pair	1,098,240	4 to 3 (1.37 to 1)
Nothing	1,302,540	1 to 1
Total	**2,598,960**	

Dice
(probabilities on 2 dice)

Total	Odds against (Single toss)	Total	Odds against (Single toss)
2	35 to 1	8	31 to 5
3	17 to 1	9	8 to 1
4	11 to 1	10	11 to 1
5	8 to 1	11	17 to 1
6	31 to 5	12	35 to 1
7	5 to 1		

Dice
(Probabilities of consecutive winning plays)

No. consecutive wins	By 7, 11, or point	No. consecutive wins	By 7, 11 or point
1	244 in 495	6	1 in 70
2	6 in 25	7	1 in 141
3	3 in 25	8	1 in 287
4	1 in 17	9	1 in 582
5	1 in 34		

Pinochle Auction
(Odds against finding in "widow" of 3 cards)

Open places	Odds against	Open places	Odds against
1	5 to 1	4	3 to 2 for
2	2 to 1	5	2 to 1 for
3	Even		

Bridge

The odds—against suit distribution in a hand of 4-4-3-2 are about 4 to 1, against 5-4-2-2 about 8 to 1, against 6-4-2-1 about 20 to 1, against 7-4-1-1 about 254 to 1, against 8-4-1-0 about 2,211 to 1, and against 13-0-0-0 about 158,753,389,899 to 1.

Measures of Force and Pressure

Dyne = force necessary to accelerate a 1-gram mass 1 centimeter per second squared = 0.000072 poundal

Poundal = force necessary to accelerate a 1-pound mass 1 foot per second squared = 13,825.5 dynes = 0.138255 newtons

Newton = force needed to accelerate a 1-kilogram mass 1 meter per second squared

Pascal (pressure) = 1 newton per square meter = 0.020885 pound per square foot

Atmosphere (air pressure at sea level) = 2,116.102 pounds per square foot = 14.6952 pounds per square inch = 1.0332 kilograms per square centimeter = 101,323 newtons per square meter.

Large Numbers

U.S.	Number of zeros	French British, German
million	6	million
billion	9	milliard
trillion	12	billion
quadrillion	15	1,000 billion
quintillion	18	trillion
sextillion	21	1,000 trillion
septillion	24	quadrillion
octillion	27	1,000 quadrillion
nonillion	30	quintillion
decillion	33	1,000 quintillion

Roman Numerals

I	1	VI	6	XI	11	L	50	CD	400	$\overline{X}$	10,000
II	2	VII	7	XIX	19	LX	60	D	500	$\overline{L}$	50,000
III	3	VIII	8	XX	20	XC	90	CM	900	$\overline{C}$	100,000
IV	4	IX	9	XXX	30	C	100	M	1,000	$\overline{D}$	500,000
V	5	X	10	XL	40	CC	200	$\overline{V}$	5,000	$\overline{M}$	1,000,000

ENVIRONMENT

Environmental Quality Index

Source: Feb.-Mar. 1987 issue of NATIONAL WILDLIFE Magazine.

Wildlife: In 1986, there were signs that the federal government was finally committed to attacking the sources of toxic threats to wildlife. But this task was a daunting one. All over the country, poisons continued to kill numerous plants and animals—including many in wildlife refuges.

On the positive side, bald eagles increased from 500 nesting pairs in the early 1960s to more than 1,700 in 1986; and the Dept. of Interior announced a phase-out of the use of lead shot for waterfowl hunting by 1991. Also, for the first time, the EPA restricted the use of two pesticides solely on the basis of their harmful effects on wildlife.

Ducks began to recover from their disastrous 1985 decline, with the 10 most common U.S. species estimated to have increased 14 percent in 1986. However, this was still 12 percent below the previous 30-year average.

Habitat loss continued. More than half the nation's original 215 million acres of swamps, bogs, and marshes had disappeared by 1986, with the loss continuing at a pace of about 400,000 acres a year. Still, in 1986 the Army Corps of Engineers continued to issue permits for dozens of dredge-and-fill projects. And the Dept. of Agriculture proposed regulatory loopholes that would weaken the impact of "swampbuster" provisions in the 1985 Farm Act.

Other wildlife areas were under siege as well: all over the country the habitat was becoming tainted by increasing amounts of toxic chemicals, which were even damaging perhaps one in every five National Wildlife Refuges. Due to habitat loss, 1986 saw a dramatic decline in a number of fish populations. Finally, the outlook for beleaguered species became even bleaker when Congress failed to renew the Endangered Species Act.

Air: On the bright side, efforts to control acid rain got an important boost in 1986 when, for the first time, Pres. Reagan formally acknowledged that action was necessary. Studies showed that at least 75 percent of the lakes in New Hampshire and Rhode Island and at least 60 percent of those in Massachusetts and Maine would be seriously damaged if acid rainfall were to continue; and that 43 percent of the upper Midwest's lakes could become devoid of all life as a result of high acidity.

There was also concern about a spate of dangerous chemical air pollutants largely ignored by federal regulators. One study found that more than 62 million pounds of highly toxic chemicals were being released annually into the air. Although the Clean Air Act gave the federal government authority to control all airborne toxic chemicals, as of 1986, only six out of hundreds of substances had been regulated.

The EPA announced, further, that more than a third of 84 metro areas being monitored for another air pollutant, ozone, would fail to meet the law's 1987 deadline for reducing ozone pollution to a "safe" level. Nearly 80 million Americans were breathing unhealthful levels of ozone. And new research found that ozone could damage crops.

Perhaps most discouraging, Harvard scientist Lance Wallace reported the results of his five-year, seven-city EPA study: levels of toxic pollutants were as much as five times higher inside homes than outdoors. The culprits included paint, plastics, cigarettes, building material, and other consumer products.

Water: Major improvements came from a national cleanup campaign, but the water problems, far from being solved, were found to be even more pervasive and entrenched than ever suspected.

"Nonpoint" pollution, from diffuse sources, was increasingly found to be a problem, and was generally not regulated by the Clean Water Act. One study discovered that nearly one in every four miles of U.S. rivers and one in every five lakes were being spoiled or threatened by nonpoint pollutants cascading from farms, mines, and urban areas. In 1986 Congress passed an improved Clean Water Act that required some control of nonpoint pollution. However, Pres. Reagan vetoed the bill.

Enforcement of existing legislation proved another problem. The *Washington Post* found that, of 124 major industrial and sewage treatment plants discharging into Chesapeake Bay, every one dumped more than permits allowed, and penalties were rare—even when permit levels were exceeded by 2,000 percent.

A U.S.-Canadian study found that the 37 million people living around the Great Lakes generally had 20 percent higher levels of toxic chemicals in their bodies than did other North Americans. The purity of water in U.S. aquifers was also suspect: in California, it was found that one-fifth of the drinking water wells were contaminated at levels above legal safety limits; in Iowa, pesticides were found in at least half of the state and city wells. Further, the EPA estimated that more than one-third of the country's 800,000 underground storage tanks were leaking motor fuels and chemical solvents into groundwater.

Good news: Congress took a major step toward controlling groundwater pollution by revising the 12-year-old Safe Drinking Water Act. And Congress extended for five years, at a cost of $9 billion, the federal Superfund program, which was charged with cleaning up toxic dump sites.

Energy: The big story combined an oil glut, the collapse of OPEC, and a dramatic decline in oil prices. The oil industry was seriously hurt as prices fell and domestic drilling dropped, but conservationists knew less exploration and development meant less adverse impact on wildlife and fisheries. And fortunately, the cheap oil failed to increase U.S. energy consumption, raising hopes that conservation measures may have become part of American life.

Meanwhile, disputes over the use of federal lands reemerged. Based on a decades-old shale-mining claim, the Dept. of Interior agreed to give 82,000 acres of prime grazing and recreation land in Colorado to an oil consortium for a token $2.50 per acre. This set a precedent for 28 million additional acres of federal land under other mining claims.

Environmentalists also battled abusive mining practices, including the failure of the federal government and some states to enforce strip-mining regulations and collect fees from mine operators.

Other concerns included the "greenhouse effect"—a warming of the Earth caused by the burning of fossil fuels; and the accident at the Soviet nuclear plant at Chernobyl.

Although low oil prices and the phasing out of tax credits made many projects using wind, solar, or geothermal power uneconomical, renewable energy did make strides. By 1990, the California Energy Commission estimated, wind and hydro power would be the two cheapest energy sources in the state. Also, a Stanford Univ. solar cell set a new record for efficiency of conversion of sunlight into electricity. And the Alabama Power company dedicated a solar power plant, the first large-scale facility to use the thin-film technology powering solar calculators and watches.

Soil: The nation took an historic step forward in the fight against soil erosion as the Dept. of Agriculture began to implement key provisions of a new farm bill. The 1985 law authorized the government to create a "conservation reserve," by paying farmers for each acre of highly erodible land that they took out of crop production and replanted to soil-saving vegetation. By November, nearly 9,000,000 acres of land had been placed in reserve.

The new law also included a "sodbuster" provision, penalizing farmers who plowed and planted fragile grasslands without approved plans to control wind and water erosion. Further, by 1990 all farmers had to have soil-conservation plans for their entire farms or lose crop subsidies.

The program promised to benefit wildlife, as well. Land enrolled had to be kept in vegetation for at least 10 years, and could not be grazed or cut for hay. The resulting meadows and groves could restore crucial wildlife habitat.

Unfortunately, the soil conservation reserve proved less popular than had been hoped. The problem was cold cash:

despite an average payment of $45 per acre per year from the USDA for land placed in the reserve, farmers could get even more money in crop supports by continuing to cultivate their erodible land. Officials had hope for the future, however, since in 1990 farmers would lose the lucrative crop subsidies on their erodible land unless they complied with conservation plans that could require the construction of expensive terraces and waterways.

Forests: 1986 was a troubled year for the nation's "woodbaskets"—the rich forests of the Northwest and South. Forest-product companies, having depleted virtually all of the valuable virgin forests on Western private land, were fighting to harvest portions of the three million acres of this "old growth" remaining on public forests.

The industry increasingly looked to the South, where favorable climate and geography let foresters grow genetically refined "supertrees" that produced wood in record time. But the South's rise in forestry was clouded in 1986 by a report that trees there were growing more slowly than previously, and that air pollution could be a factor. Yellow pines showed as much as 30 percent less growth between 1972 and 1982 than in the previous decade, and 15 percent tree deaths compared to nine percent a decade earlier.

The South's future as a forestry center was also under question because the Forest Service reported that some 85 percent of cutover forestlands in the region were not being reforested.

The concern over the future of forest resources heated the battle over the 195 million acres of national forest land, as the U.S. Forest Service reached the halfway point in a planning process that would decide the fate of 155 national forests in 44 states and two territories.

Hazardous Waste Sites

Source: Environmental Protection Agency, Natl. Priorities List Fact Book, June 1986

State	Final Sites	Proposed Sites	Total Sites
Alabama	8	2	10
Alaska	0	0	0
Arizona	5	4	9
Arkansas	7	1	8
California	34	27	61
Colorado	12	3	15
Connecticut	6	1	7
Delaware	9	5	14
Florida	32	7	39
Georgia	3	2	5
Hawaii	0	6	6
Idaho	4	0	4
Illinois	14	11	25
Indiana	23	5	28
Iowa	6	7	13
Kansas	6	1	7
Kentucky	9	1	10
Louisiana	5	2	7
Maine	5	2	7
Maryland	6	2	8
Massachusetts	21	0	21
Michigan	56	10	66
Minnesota	36	2	38
Mississippi	2	0	2
Missouri	12	5	17
Montana	7	2	9
Nebraska	2	3	5
Nevada	0	0	0
New Hampshire	12	1	13
New Jersey	91	6	97
New Mexico	4	0	4
New York	57	8	65
North Carolina	6	2	8
North Dakota	1	0	1
Ohio	27	3	30
Oklahoma	4	1	5
Oregon	4	1	5
Pennsylvania	48	17	65
Rhode Island	8	0	8
South Carolina	10	2	12
South Dakota	1	0	1
Tennessee	7	1	8
Texas	21	5	26
Utah	3	7	10
Vermont	2	0	2
Virginia	7	6	13
Washington	19	9	28
West Virginia	5	1	6
Wisconsin	26	4	30
Wyoming	1	0	1
Guam	1	0	1
Puerto Rico	8	0	8
TOTAL	**703**	**185**	**888**

U.S. Municipal Solid Waste, 1960-1984

Source: U.S. Environmental Protection Agency

(millions of tons, unless otherwise indicated)

Item, material[1]	1960	1965	1970	1975	1977	1979	1980	1981	1982	1983	1984
Gross waste generated	82.3	98.3	118.3	122.7	133.3	140.7	139.1	140.9	137.8	144.1	148.1
Per person per day (lb.)	2.50	2.77	3.16	3.11	3.32	3.43	3.35	3.36	3.25	3.37	3.43
Materials recovered	5.9	6.2	8.0	9.1	11.6	13.0	13.4	13.2	12.9	13.9	15.1
Per person per day (lb.)	.18	.17	.21	.23	.29	.32	.32	.31	.30	.32	.35
Percent of gross discards recovered:											
Paper and paperboard	18.0	15.0	16.9	19.2	20.7	20.9	21.9	20.6	20.6	20.7	20.8
Glass	1.5	1.2	1.2	2.7	3.5	4.0	5.0	5.0	5.2	5.9	7.2
Ferrous metals	.5	1.0	1.2	1.9	2.4	3.1	3.2	3.1	2.8	2.7	2.8
Aluminum	(NA)	(NA)	1.6	12.4	13.1	13.0	19.6	28.4	30.9	29.3	29.4
Processed for energy recovery	(NA)	.2	.4	.7	1.4	2.3	2.7	2.3	3.5	5.0	6.5
Per person per day (lb.)	(NA)	.01	.01	.02	.03	.06	.06	.05	.08	.12	.15
Net waste disposed of	76.4	91.9	109.9	112.8	120.3	125.4	123.0	125.4	121.4	125.2	126.5
Per person per day (lb.)	2.32	2.59	2.94	2.86	2.99	3.05	2.96	2.99	2.86	2.92	2.93
Percent distribution of net discards[2]											
Paper and paperboard	32.1	35.0	33.1	30.4	33.1	34.4	33.6	34.5	33.2	35.3	37.1
Glass	8.4	9.2	11.3	11.6	11.4	11.3	11.3	11.3	11.0	10.4	.97
Metals	13.7	11.6	12.2	11.8	10.9	10.6	10.3	10.0	10.1	9.9	9.6
Plastics	.5	1.5	2.7	3.9	5.3	6.4	6.0	6.1	6.7	7.0	7.2
Rubber and leather	2.2	2.4	2.7	3.3	2.8	3.3	3.3	3.2	3.0	2.6	2.5
Textiles	2.6	2.4	2.0	2.2	2.0	2.3	2.3	2.4	2.4	2.3	2.1
Wood	3.9	3.8	3.6	3.8	3.9	2.6	3.9	3.5	4.0	4.0	3.8
Food wastes	14.6	13.1	11.5	11.8	10.6	9.6	9.2	8.9	8.8	8.5	8.1
Yard wastes	20.3	19.2	19.0	19.5	18.2	17.7	18.2	18.2	18.7	18.1	17.9
Other wastes	1.7	1.7	1.7	1.9	1.8	1.8	1.9	1.9	2.0	1.9	1.9

NA = Not Available. (1) Includes post-consumer residential and commercial solid wastes, the major portion of typical municipal collections; excludes mining, agriculture and industrial processing, demolition and construction wastes, sewage sludge, junked cars, and obsolete equipment wastes. (2) Net discards after materials recovery and before energy recovery.

Land Cover and Land Use, by State

Source: U.S. Dept. of Agriculture, Soil Conservation service, 1982

			Nonfederal							
						Rural land				
State	Total surface area[1]	Federal surface area	Total	Urban and builtup land	Rural trans-portation	Total[2]	Crop-land	Pas-ture land	Range-land	Forest land
U.S.	**1,937,726**	**404,063**	**1,495,436**	**46,416**	**26,914**	**1,412,011**	**420,994**	**132,356**	**405,914**	**393,197**
Alabama	33,091	904	31,553	906	639	29,697	4,510	3,817	—	20,633
Arizona	72,960	32,056	40,603	711	291	39,582	1,206	79	30,948	4,760
Arkansas	34,040	3,114	30,221	636	540	28,770	8,102	5,794	162	14,340
California	101,572	45,552	54,471	3,265	1,037	49,833	10,518	1,393	18,125	15,218
Colorado	66,618	23,611	42,696	672	609	41,271	10,603	1,260	24,223	4,030
Connecticut	3,212	9	3,109	603	55	2,401	245	114	—	1,828
Delaware	1,309	33	1,204	128	26	1,039	519	35	—	348
Florida	37,545	3,129	31,528	2,770	601	27,730	3,557	4,273	3,804	12,430
Georgia	37,702	2,068	35,078	1,632	504	32,536	6,568	2,977	—	21,884
Hawaii	4,141	342	3,771	126	23	3,610	333	974	—	1,474
Idaho	53,481	33,445	19,449	189	255	18,934	6,390	1,274	6,733	3,977
Illinois	36,061	493	35,137	1,846	870	32,076	24,727	3,157	—	3,429
Indiana	23,159	489	22,514	1,192	517	20,597	13,781	2,212	—	3,640
Iowa	36,016	172	35,644	623	1,061	33,709	26,441	4,536	—	1,756
Kansas	52,658	585	51,785	721	1,104	49,655	29,118	2,241	16,909	626
Kentucky	25,862	1,125	24,278	636	570	22,866	5,934	5,880	—	10,158
Louisiana	30,561	1,104	27,103	823	546	25,256	6,409	2,369	241	12,895
Maine	21,290	135	19,702	212	270	19,066	953	569	—	16,770
Maryland	6,695	158	6,114	763	114	5,173	1,794	534	—	2,425
Massachusetts	5,302	89	4,923	883	128	3,839	297	202	—	2,970
Michigan	37,457	3,087	33,368	1,966	873	30,265	9,443	2,911	—	15,360
Minnesota	54,017	3,373	47,457	904	1,154	45,036	23,024	3,590	199	13,956
Mississippi	30,521	1,618	28,558	582	539	27,063	7,415	3,975	—	15,243
Missouri	44,606	2,094	41,983	1,117	977	39,543	14,998	12,573	168	10,986
Montana	94,109	27,107	65,947	197	784	64,665	17,197	3,036	37,837	5,228
Nebraska	49,507	639	48,449	415	826	46,990	20,277	2,125	23,096	732
Nevada	70,759	60,189	10,159	199	152	9,788	860	304	7,908	357
New Hampshire	5,938	727	5,033	236	109	4,629	158	125	—	4,085
New Jersey	4,984	145	4,635	1,163	69	3,342	809	240	—	1,848
New Mexico	77,819	26,420	51,247	267	382	50,535	2,413	163	40,982	4,734
New York	31,429	237	30,084	1,811	594	27,386	5,912	3,872	—	16,517
North Carolina	33,708	2,116	29,111	1,622	727	26,481	6,695	1,980	—	16,729
North Dakota	45,250	1,879	42,434	198	1,036	41,021	27,039	1,272	10,948	438
Ohio	26,451	346	25,892	2,187	645	22,859	12,447	2,714	—	6,380
Oklahoma	44,772	1,192	42,783	851	789	40,795	11,568	7,138	15,060	6,539
Oregon	62,127	32,122	29,332	526	365	28,291	4,356	1,966	9,392	11,889
Pennsylvania	28,997	668	28,060	2,073	613	25,144	5,896	2,593	—	15,300
Rhode Island	776	4	672	140	14	508	27	36	—	406
South Carolina	19,912	1,150	18,173	839	475	16,681	3,579	1,208	—	11,026
South Dakota	49,354	2,824	45,762	231	833	44,506	16,947	2,703	22,784	562
Tennessee	26,972	1,343	24,980	1,000	588	23,189	51,592	5,356	—	11,529
Texas	17,075	2,998	164,765	4,388	2,234	157,431	33,320	17,043	95,353	9,324
Utah	54,336	35,819	16,703	274	152	16,247	2,039	490	8,489	3,235
Vermont	6,153	315	5,619	97	101	5,377	648	501	—	4,087
Virginia	26,091	2,347	23,063	1,219	329	21,292	3,397	3,392	—	13,625
Washington	43,609	12,474	30,092	990	492	28,462	7,793	1,345	5,637	12,690
West Virginia	15,508	1,104	14,330	312	205	13,722	1,093	1,869	—	10,423
Wisconsin	35,938	1,800	33,064	1,125	770	30,890	11,457	3,394	—	13,393
Wyoming	62,598	29,315	32,803	148	330	32,240	2,587	755	26,915	987

— Represents zero. (1) Includes 107.9 million acres of water areas and minor land cover and uses not shown separately; (2) Includes 59.55 million acres of minor land cover and uses not shown separately.

Pollution Abatement and Control Expenditures, 1975-1984

Source: U.S. Environmental Protection Agency

(in millions of dollars, except percent)

										1984p		
Type	1975	1977	1978	1979	1980	1981	1982	1983	Total[1]	Air	Water	Solid waste
Current Dollars												
Total	**30,177**	**37,566**	**42,706**	**48,736**	**53,538**	**57,470**	**57,680**	**61,357**	**68,539**	**30,853**	**25,927**	**12,260**
% government	28.9	26.8	28.1	26.8	25.3	22.1	21.8	20.8	20.9	3.6	32.3	32.4
Pollution abatement	28,420	35,256	40,109	45,892	50,491	54,343	54,500	58,061	65,205	29,337	25,199	12,010
Personal consumption	3,243	4,299	4,787	5,428	6,589	8,152	8,318	9,737	10,659	10,659	—	—
Business	17,602	22,360	24,922	29,088	32,283	35,545	35,610	37,619	42,271	18,130	17,433	8,271
Government	7,576	8,596	10,399	11,377	11,620	10,647	10,571	10,705	12,275	548	7,766	3,739
Federal	432	490	472	548	494	506	550	795	860	117	415	188
State & local	1,752	1,963	2,212	2,461	2,778	3,053	3,274	3,552	4,008	15	361	3,552
Govt. enterprise fixed capital	5,392	6,144	7,716	8,368	8,347	7,088	6,747	6,358	7,407	416	6,991	—
Regulation & monitoring	653	833	949	1,067	1,296	1,378	1,397	1,385	1,405	351	459	158
Research & development	1,104	1,478	1,647	1,777	1,751	1,749	1,783	1,911	1,930	1,166	269	92

P = preliminary; — Represents zero. (1) includes "other and unallocated" expenditures, such as for noise, radiation, and pesticide pollution, and business expenditures not assigned to media, which may be either positive or negative; therefore, data may not add.

Some Endangered Species in the World

Source: U.S. Fish and Wildlife Service, U.S. Interior Department; as of April 10, 1987

Common name	Scientific name	Historic range
Mammals		
Asian wild ass	Equus hemianus	Southwestern & Central Asia
Bobcat	Felis rufus escuinapae	Central Mexico
Cheetah	Acinonyx jubatus	Africa to India
Asian elephant	Elephas maximas	S. Central & E. Africa
Bactrian camel	Camelus bactrianus	Mongolia, China
Gorilla	Gorilla gorilla	Central & W. Africa
Leopard	Panthera pardus	Africa, Asia
Asiatic lion	Panthera leo persica	Turkey to India
Howler monkey	Alouatta pigra	Mexico to S. America
Giant panda	Ailuropoda melanoleuca	China
Black rhinoceros	Diceros bicornis	Sub-Saharan Africa
Tiger	Panthera tigris	Asia
Gray whale	Eschrichtius robustus	N. Pacific Ocean
Wild yak	Bos grunniens	China (Tibet), India
Mountain zebra	Equus zebra zebra	South Africa
Birds		
Hooded crane	Grus monacha	Japan, USSR
Indigo macaw	Anodorhynchus leari	Brazil
West African ostrich	Struthio camelus spatzi	Spanish Sahara
Golden parakeet	Aratinga guarouba	Brazil
Australian parrot	Geopsittacus occidentalis	Australia

Some Endangered Species in North America

Source: U.S. Fish and Wildlife Service, U.S. Interior Department; as of April 10, 1987

Common name	Scientific name	Range
Mammals		
Ozark big-eared bat	Plecotus townsendii ingens	U.S. (Mo., Okla., Ariz.)
Brown or grizzly bear	Ursus arctos horribilis	U.S. (48 conterminous states)
Eastern cougar	Felis concolor cougar	Eastern N.A.
Columbian white-tailed deer	Odocoileus virginianus leucurus	U.S. (Wash., Ore.)
San Joaquin kit fox	Vulpes macrotis mutica	U.S. (Cal.)
Fresno kangaroo	Dipodomys nitratoides exiles	U.S. (Cal.)
Ocelot	Felis pardalis	U.S. (Tex., Ariz.)
Southern sea otter	Enhydra lutris hereis	U.S. (Wash., Ore., Cal.)
Florida panther	Felis concolor coryi	U.S. (La., Ark. east to S.C., Fla.)
Utah prairie dog	Cynomys parvidens	U.S. (Ut.)
Morro Bay kangaroo rat	Dipodomys heermanni morroensis	U.S. (Cal.)
Carolina northern flying squirrel	Glaucomys sabrinus coloratus	U.S. (N.C., Tenn.)
Red wolf	Canis rufus	U.S. (Southeast to central Tex.)
Birds		
Masked bobwhite (quail)	Colinus virginianus ridgwayi	U.S. (Ariz.)
California condor	Gymnogyps californianus	U.S. (Ore., Cal.)
Whooping crane	Grus americana	U.S. (Rky. Mntns. east to Carolinas), Canada
Eskimo curlew	Numenius borealis	Alaska and N. Canada
Bald eagle	Haliaeetus leucocephalus	U.S. (most states), Canada
American peregrine falcon	Falco peregrinus anatum	Canada to Mexico
Hawaiian hawk	Buteo solitarius	U.S. (Hi.)
Attwater's greater prairie-chicken	Tympanuchus cupido attwateri	U.S. (Tex.)
Bachman's warbler (wood)	Vermivora bachmanii	U.S. (Southeast), Cuba
Kirtland's warbler (wood)	Dendroica kirtlandii	U.S., Canada, Bahama Is.
Ivory-billed woodpecker	Campephilus principalis	U.S. (Southcentral and Southeast), Cuba
Reptiles		
American alligator	Alligator mississippiensis	U.S. (Southeast)
American crocodile	Crocodylus acutus	U.S. (Fla.)
Atlantic salt marsh snake	Nerodia fasciatia taeniata	U.S. (Fla.)
Plymouth red-bellied turtle	Pseudemys rubiventris bangsi	U.S. (Mass.)
Fishes		
Yaqui catfish	Ictalupus pricei	U.S. (Ariz.)
Bonytail chub	Gila elegans	U.S. (Ariz., Cal., Col., Nev., Ut., Wyo.)
Gila trout	Salmo gilae	U.S. (Ariz., N.M.)

Young of Animals Have Special Names

The young of many animals, birds and fish have come to be called by special names. A young eel, for example, is an elver. Many young animals, of course, are often referred to simply as infants, babies, younglets, or younglings.

bunny: rabbit.
calf: cattle, elephant, antelope, rhino, hippo, whale, etc.
cheeper: grouse, partridge, quail.
chick, chicken: fowl.
cockerel: rooster.
codling, sprag: codfish.
colt: horse (male).
cub: lion, bear, shark, fox, etc.

(continued)

cygnet: swan.
duckling: duck.
eaglet: eagle.
elver: eel.
eyas: hawk, others.
fawn: deer.
filly: horse (female).
fingerling: fish generally.
flapper: wild fowl.
fledgling: birds generally.
foal: horse, zebra, others.
fry: fish generally.
gosling: goose.
heifer: cow.
joey: kangaroo, others.
kid: goat.
kit: fox, beaver, rabbit, cat.
kitten, kitty, catling: cats, other fur-bearers.
lamb, lambkin, cosset, hog: sheep.
leveret: hare.
nestling: birds generally.
owlet: owl.
parr, smolt, grilse: salmon.
piglet, shoat, farrow, suckling: pig.
polliwog, tadpole: frog.
poult: turkey.
pullet: hen.
pup: dog, seal, sea lion, fox.
puss, pussy: cat.
spike, blinker, tinker: mackerel.
squab: pigeon.
squeaker: pigeon, others.
whelp: dog, tiger, beasts of prey.
yearling: cattle, sheep, horse, etc.

Speeds of Animals

Source: Natural History magazine, March 1974.

Animal	Mph	Animal	Mph	Animal	Mph
Cheetah	70	Mongolian wild ass	40	Human	27.89
Pronghorn antelope	61	Greyhound	39.35	Elephant	25
Wildebeest	50	Whippet	35.50	Black mamba snake	20
Lion	50	Rabbit (domestic)	35	Six-lined race runner	18
Thomson's gazelle	50	Mule deer	35	Wild turkey	15
Quarterhorse	47.5	Jackal	35	Squirrel	12
Elk	45	Reindeer	32	Pig (domestic)	11
Cape hunting dog	45	Giraffe	32	Chicken	9
Coyote	43	White-tailed deer	30	Spider (Tegenaria atrica)	1.17
Gray fox	42	Wart hog	30	Giant tortoise	0.17
Hyena	40	Grizzly bear	30	Three-toed sloth	0.15
Zebra	40	Cat (domestic)	30	Garden snail	0.03

Most of these measurements are for maximum speeds over approximate quarter-mile distances. Exceptions are the lion and elephant, whose speeds were clocked in the act of charging; the whippet, which was timed over a 200-yard course; the cheetah over a 100-yard distance; man for a 15-yard segment of a 100-yard run (of 13.6 seconds); and the black mamba, six-lined race runner, spider, giant tortoise, three-toed sloth, and garden snail, which were measured over various small distances.

Gestation, Longevity, and Incubation of Animals

Longevity figures were supplied by Ronald T. Reuther. They refer to animals in captivity; the potential life span of animals is rarely attained in nature. Maximum longevity figures are from the Biology Data Book, 1972. Figures on gestation and incubation are averages based on estimates by leading authorities.

Animal	Gestation (day)	Average longevity (years)	Maximun longevity (yrs., mos.)
Ass	365	12	35-10
Baboon	187	20	35-7
Bear: Black	219	18	36-10
Grizzly	225	25	—
Polar	240	20	34-8
Beaver	122	5	20-6
Buffalo (American)	278	15	—
Bactrian camel	406	12	29-5
Cat (domestic)	63	12	28
Chimpanzee	231	20	44-6
Chipmunk	31	6	8
Cow	284	15	30
Deer (white-tailed)	201	8	17-6
Dog (domestic)	61	12	20
Elephant (African)	—	35	60
Elephant (Asian)	645	40	70
Elk	250	15	26-6
Fox (red)	52	7	14
Giraffe	425	10	33-7
Goat (domestic)	151	8	18
Gorilla	257	20	39-4
Guinea pig	68	4	7-6
Hippopotamus	238	25	—
Horse	330	20	46
Kangaroo	42	7	—
Leopard	98	12	19-4
Lion	100	15	25-1
Monkey (rhesus)	164	15	—
Moose	240	12	—
Mouse (meadow)	21	3	—
Mouse (dom. white)	19	3	3-6
Opossum (American)	14-17	1	—
Pig (domestic)	112	10	27
Puma	90	12	19
Rabbit (domestic)	31	5	13
Rhinoceros (black)	450	15	—
Rhinoceros (white)	—	20	—
Sea lion (California)	350	12	28
Sheep (domestic)	154	12	20
Squirrel (gray)	44	10	—
Tiger	105	16	26-3
Wolf (maned)	63	5	—
Zebra (Grant's)	365	15	—

Incubation time (days)

Chicken	21
Duck	30
Goose	30
Pigeon	18
Turkey	26

A Collection of Animal Collectives

The English language boasts an abundance of names to describe groups of things, particularly pairs or aggregations of animals. Some of these words have fallen into comparative disuse, but many of them are still in service, helping to enrich the vocabularies of those who like their language to be precise, who tire of hearing a group referred to as "a bunch of," or who enjoy the sound of words that aren't overworked.

band of gorillas
bed of clams, oysters
bevy of quail, swans
brace of ducks
brood of chicks
cast of hawks
cete of badgers
charm of goldfinches
chattering of choughs
cloud of gnats
clowder of cats
clutch of chicks
clutter of cats
colony of ants
congregation of plovers
covey of quail, partridge
crash of rhinoceri
cry of hounds
down of hares
drift of swine
drove of cattle, sheep
exaltation of larks
flight of birds
flock of sheep, geese
gaggle of geese
gam of whales
gang of elks
grist of bees
herd of elephants
horde of gnats
husk of hares
kindle or **kendle** of kittens
knot of toads
leap of leopards
leash of greyhounds, foxes
litter of pigs
mob of kangaroos
murder of crows
muster of peacocks
mute of hounds

nest of vipers
nest, nide of pheasants
pack of hounds, wolves
pair of horses
pod of whales, seals
pride of lions
school of fish
sedge or **siege** of cranes
shoal of fish, pilchards
skein of geese
skulk of foxes
sleuth of bears
sounder of boars, swine
span of mules
spring of teals
swarm of bees
team of ducks, horses
tribe or **trip** of goats
troop of kangaroos, monkeys
volery of birds
watch of nightingales
wing of plovers
yoke of oxen

Major Venomous Animals

Snakes

Coral snake - 2 to 4 ft. long, in Americas south of Canada; bite is nearly painless; very slow onset of paralysis, difficulty breathing; mortality high without antivenin.

Rattlesnake - 2 to 8 ft. long, throughout W. Hemisphere. Rapid onset of symptoms of severe pain, swelling; mortality low, but amputation of affected limb is sometimes necessary; antivenin. Probably higher mortality rate for Mojave rattler.

Cottonmouth water moccasin - up to 5 ft. long, wetlands of southern U.S. from Virginia to Texas. Rapid onset of symptoms of severe pain, swelling; mortality low, but tissue destruction can be extensive; antivenin.

Copperhead - less than 4 ft. long, from New England to Texas; pain and swelling; very seldom fatal; antivenin seldom needed.

Bushmaster - up to 12 ft. long, wet tropical forests of C. and S. America; few bites occur, but mortality rate is high.

Barba Amarilla or **Fer-de-lance** - up to 7 ft. long, from tropical Mexico to Brazil; severe tissue damage common; moderate mortality; antivenin.

Asian pit vipers - from 2 to 5 ft. long throughout Asia; reactions and mortality vary but most bites cause tissue damage and mortality is generally low.

Sharp-nosed pit viper or **One Hundred Pace Snake** - up to 5 ft. long, in southern Vietnam and Taiwan, China; the most toxic of Asian pit vipers; very rapid onset of swelling and tissue damage, internal bleeding; moderate mortality; antivenin.

Boomslang - under 6 ft. long, in African savannahs; rapid onset of nausea and dizziness, often followed by slight recovery and then sudden death from internal hemorrhaging; bites rare, mortality high; antivenin.

European vipers - from 1 to 3 ft. long; bleeding and tissue damage; mortality low; antivenins.

Puff adder - up to 5 ft. long, fat; south of the Sahara and throughout the Middle East; rapid large swelling, great pain, dizziness; moderate mortality often from internal bleeding; antivenin.

Gaboon viper - over 6 ft. long, fat; 2-inch fangs; south of the Sahara; massive tissue damage, internal bleeding; few recorded bites.

Saw-scaled or carpet viper - up to 2 ft. long, in dry areas from India to Africa; severe bleeding, fever; high mortality, causes more human fatalities than any other snake; antivenin.

Desert horned viper - in dry areas of Africa and western Asia; swelling and tissue damage; low mortality; antivenin.

Russell's viper or tic-palonga - over 5 ft. long, throughout Asia; internal bleeding; moderate mortality rate; bite reports common; antivenin.

Black mamba - up to 14 ft. long, fast-moving; S. and C. Africa; rapid onset of dizziness, difficulty breathing, erratic heart-beat; mortality high, nears 100% without antivenin.

Kraits - in S. Asia; rapid onset of sleepiness; numbness; up to 50% mortality even with antivenin treatment.

Common or Asian cobra - 4 to 8 ft. long, throughout S. Asia; considerable tissue damage, sometimes paralysis; mortality probably not more than 10%; antivenin.

King cobra - up to 16 ft. long, throughout S. Asia; rapid swelling, dizziness, loss of consciousness, difficulty breathing, erratic heart-beat; mortality varies sharply with amount of venom involved, most bites involve non-fatal amounts; antivenin.

Yellow or Cape cobra - 7 ft. long, in southern Africa; most toxic venom of any cobra; rapid onset of swelling, breathing and cardiac difficulties; mortality high without treatment; antivenin.

Ringhals, or spitting, cobra - 5 ft. and 7 ft. long; southern Africa; squirt venom through holes in front of fangs as a defense; venom is severely irritating and can cause blindness.

Australian brown snakes - very slow onset of symptoms of cardiac or respiratory distress; moderate mortality; antivenin.

Tiger snake - 2 to 6 ft. long, S. Australia; pain, numbness, mental disturbances with rapid onset of paralysis; may be the most deadly of all land snakes though antivenin is quite effective.

Death adder - less than 3 ft. long, Australia; rapid onset of faintness, cardiac and respiratory distress; at least 50% mortality without antivenin.

Taipan - up to 11 ft. long, in Australia and New Guinea; rapid paralysis with severe breathing difficulty; mortality nears 100% without antivenin.

Sea snakes - throughout Pacific, Indian oceans except NE Pacific; almost painless bite, variety of muscle pain, paralysis; mortality rate low, many bites are not envenomed; some antivenins.

Notes: Not all snake bites by venomous snakes are actually envenomed. Any animal bite, however, carries the danger of tetanus and anyone suffering a venomous snake bite should seek medical attention. Antivenins are not certain cures; they are only an aid in the treatment of bites. Mortality rates above are for envenomed bites; low mortality, up to 2% result in death; moderate, 2–5%; high, 5–15%. Even when the victim recovers fully, prolonged hospitalization and extensive medical procedures are usually required.

Lizards

Gila monster - up to 24 inches long with heavy body and tail, in high desert in southwest U.S. and N. Mexico; immediate severe pain followed by vomiting, thirst, difficulty swallowing, weakness approaching paralysis; no recent mortality.

Mexican beaded lizard - similar to Gila monster, Mexican westcoast; reaction and mortality rate similar to Gila monster.

Insects

Ants, bees, wasps, hornets, etc. Global distribution. Usual reaction is piercing pain in area of sting. Not directly fatal, except in cases of massive multiple stings. Many people suffer allergic reactions - swelling, rashes, partial paralysis –and a few may die within minutes from severe sensitivity to the venom (anaphylactic shock).

Spiders, scorpions

Black widow - small, round-bodied with hour-glass marking; the widow and its relatives are found around the world in tropical and temperate zones; sharp pain, weakness, clammy skin, muscular rigidity, breathing difficulty and, in small children, convulsions; low mortality; antivenin.

Recluse or fiddleback and brown spiders - small, oblong body; throughout U.S.; pain with later ulceration at place of bite; in severe cases fever, nausea, and stomach cramps; ulceration may last months; very low mortality.

Atrax **spiders** - several varieties, often large, in Australia; slow onset of breathing, circulation difficulties; low mortality.

Tarantulas - large, hairy spiders found around the world; American tarantulas, and probably all others, are **harmless,** though their bite may cause some pain and swelling.

Scorpions - crab-like body with stinger in tail, various sizes, many varieties throughout tropical and subtropical areas; various symptoms may include severe pain spreading from the wound, numbness, severe emotional agitation, cramps; severe reactions include vomiting, diarrhea, respiratory failure; low mortality, usually in children; antivenins.

Sea Life

Sea wasps - jellyfish, with tentacles up to 30 ft. long, in the S. Pacific; very rapid onset of circulatory problems; high mortality largely because of speed of toxic reaction; antivenin.

Portuguese man-of-war - jellyfish-like, with tentacles up to 70 ft. long, in most warm water areas; immediate severe pain; not fatal, though shock may cause death in a rare case.

Octopi - global distribution, usually in warm waters; all varieties produce venom but only a few can cause death; rapid onset of paralysis with breathing difficulty.

Stingrays - several varieties of differing sizes, found in tropical and temperate seas and some fresh water; severe pain, rapid onset of nausea, vomiting, breathing difficulties; wound area may ulcerate, gangrene may appear; seldom fatal.

Stonefish - brownish fish which lies motionless as a rock on bottom in shallow water; throughout S. Pacific and Indian oceans; extraordinary pain, rapid paralysis; low mortality.

Cone-shells - molluscs in small, beautiful shells in the S. Pacific and Indian oceans; shoot barbs into victims; paralysis; low mortality.

Major U.S. Public Zoological Parks

Source: World Almanac questionnaire, 1987; budget and attendance in millions. (*) park has not provided up-to-date data.

Zoo	Budget	Attendance	Acres	Species	Major attractions
Arizona-Sonora Desert Museum (Tucson)	$2.5	0.5	15	500	Earth Science Center, Sonora Desert Exhibit
Audubon (New Orleans)	6.0	1.0	58	371	Asian Domain, Louisiana Swamp, Australia Exhibit
Bronx (N.Y.C.)	20.0	2.4	265	674	Himalayan Highlands, African Plains, Jungle World, Wild Asia
Buffalo	2.6	0.4	23	234	Gorilla Habitat, Asian Rain Forest, giraffes
Chicago	16.0	1.9	200	500	7 Seas Panorama, Tropic World, Baboon Island
Cincinnati	5.3	1.2	67	723	Cat House, Insectarium, gorillas, Red Pandas
Cleveland	3.0	0.9	164	460	African Plains, Birds of Prey, rhino/cheetah
Dallas*	2.4	0.6	50	507	Okapi, bongo antelope, Grevy's zebra
Denver	3.8	0.9	73	368	Northern Shores, hooved animals, Feline House
Detroit	8.0	0.8	122	256	Reptiles, Bird House, Penguinarium
Houston*	2.6	2.0	55	649	Children's Zoo, Aquarium
Lincoln Park (Chicago)	5.5	4.0	35	450+	Free Zoo, Farm-in-the-Zoo, Bird Walks, Zoo-to-You
Los Angeles	4.0	1.5	113	500	Koalas, white tigers, elephant & camel rides
Louisville	2.5	0.4	73	245	African Panorama, polar bear, Siberian tiger
Memphis	2.4	0.5	36	399	Tropical Bird House, Aquarium, waterfowl
Miami Metrozoo	6.8	0.8	280	283	Wings of Asia, white Bengal tigers, gorilla family, Wildlife Show
Milwaukee	8.9	1.6	185	538	Dolphin Show, Dairy Complex/Farm, Great Apes
Minnesota	6.0	1.0	500	450	Beluga whale/dolphins, Bird Show, Monorail
National (Wash. D.C.)*	9.2	3.3	168	395	Lion/tiger complex, Beaver Valley, giant pandas
Oklahoma City	6.2	0.6	180+	750	Aquaticus Science Park, hoofstock collection
Philadelphia	10.2	1.3	42	457	African Plains, World of Primates, Treehouse
Phoenix*	2.6	0.7	125	275	Arabian oryx herd, Orangutans, Arizona exhibit
Rio Grande (Albuquerque)	2.8	0.5	60	246	Rain forest exhibit, reptile house
Riverbanks (Columbia, S.C.)	2.1	0.5	153	185	Eco-system Birdhouse/Rainstorm, penguins
St. Louis	6.6	2.5	83	660	Big Cat Country, Herpetarium, Primate House
San Antonio	4.8	1.1	49	700+	Children's Zoo, Monkey Island, elephant shows
San Diego	28.0	3.3	100	780	African kopje, Southeast Asian exhibit, Skyfari, koalas, golden monkeys
San Diego (Wild Animal Park)	16.0	1.3	1,800	225	Mixed-species enclosures; exotic species, monorail
San Francisco	8.8	1.2	65	270	Primate Discovery Center, Koala Crossing, Gorilla World, Penguin Island
Toledo	4.0	0.7	30	400	Hippoquarium, botanical gardens, Children's Zoo
Washington Pk (Portland)	18.9	0.9	64	125	Cascade Stream and Pond, Alaska Tundra, Penguinarium
Woodland Pk (Seattle)	3.4	0.8	90	350	African Savanna, gorillas, Asian Elephant Forest

Top 50 American Kennel Club Registrations

	Rank	1986	Rank	1985		Rank	1986	Rank	1985
Cocker Spaniels	1	98,330	1	96,396	Maltese	26	11,393	26	10,556
Poodles	2	85,500	2	87,250	Great Danes	27	9,145	27	9,698
Labrador Retrievers	3	77,371	3	74,271	Pugs	28	8,750	31	7,753
Golden Retrievers	4	59,057	5	56,131	West Highland White Terriers	29	8,635	30	8,048
German Shepherd Dogs	5	55,958	4	57,598	Dalmations	30	8,170	33	6,880
Chow Chows	6	43,026	8	39,167	Samoyeds	31	8,169	29	8,192
Beagles	7	39,849	7	40,803	Bulldogs	32	7,961	32	7,329
Miniature Schnauzers	8	38,961	9	38,134	German Shorthaired Pointers	33	7,840	28	8,351
Dachshunds	9	35,537	11	33,903	Keeshonden	34	6,732	34	6,640
Shetland Sheepdogs	10	35,064	10	34,350	Bichon Frises	35	6,538	40	5,447
Doberman Pinschers	11	33,442	6	41,532	Cairn Terriers	36	6,030	37	5,807
Yorkshire Terriers	12	32,485	12	31,034	Alaskan Malamutes	37	6,021	35	6,506
Shih Tzu	13	31,742	14	28,274	Scottish Terriers	38	5,974	38	5,750
Lhasa Apsos	14	29,556	13	28,823	Airedale Terriers	39	5,465	36	5,836
Rottweilers	15	28,257	16	22,886	Akitas	40	5,269	41	4,858
Pomeranians	16	25,056	15	22,962	Old English Sheepdogs	41	4,724	39	5,573
Siberian Huskies	17	19,988	18	20,144	Chesapeake Bay Retrievers	42	4,275	42	4,386
English Springer Spaniels	18	19,933	17	20,628	St. Bernards	43	3,798	45	3,732
Chihuahuas	19	19,310	21	18,518	Weimaraners	44	3,727	43	3,938
Collies	20	19,169	19	19,702	Miniature Pinschers	45	3,590	47	3,143
Pekingese	21	18,601	22	18,371	Norwegian Elkhounds	46	3,480	46	3,720
Basset Hounds	22	18,546	20	19,029	Irish Setters	47	3,179	44	3,804
Boxers	23	17,870	23	17,638	Pembroke Welsh Corgis	48	3,068	49	2,820
Brittanys	24	13,440	24	15,058	Wire Fox Terriers	49	2,796	52	2,376
Boston Terriers	25	12,814	25	12,381	Newfoundlands	50	2,781	51	2,578

Cat Breeds

There are 27 cat breeds recognized: abyssinian, american shorthair, balinese, birman, bombay, burmese, colorpoint shorthair, egyptian mau, exotic shorthair, havana brown, himalayan, japanese bobtail, korat, leopard cat, lilac foreign shorthair, maine coon cat, manx, ocicat, oriental shorthair, persian, rex, russian blue, scottish fold, siamese, sphynx, turkish angora, wirehair shorthair.

Mammals: Orders and Major Families

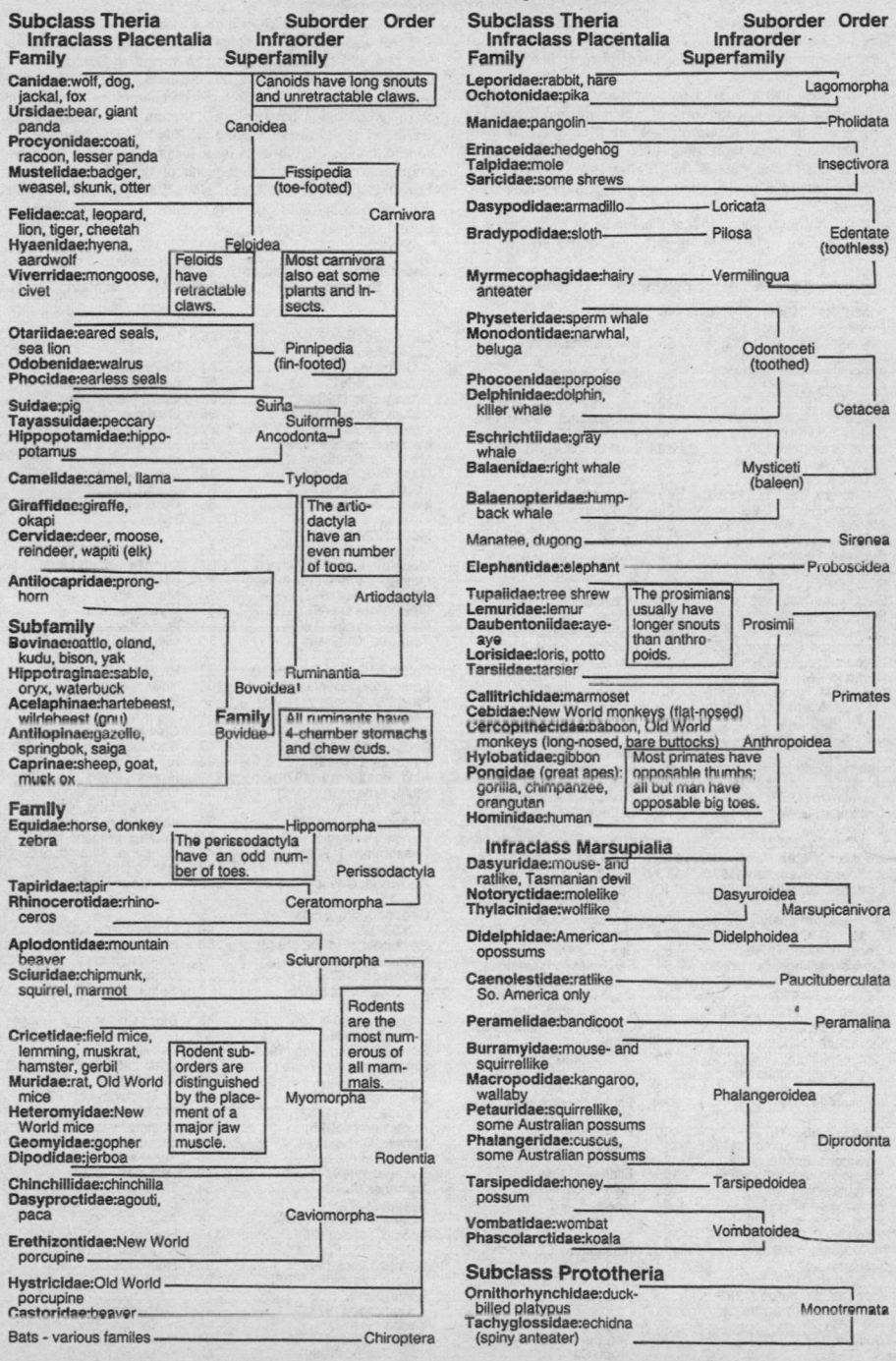

Subclass Theria

Infraclass Placentalia

Family	Superfamily	Suborder / Infraorder	Order
Canidae: wolf, dog, jackal, fox	Canoidea	Fissipedia (toe-footed)	Carnivora
Ursidae: bear, giant panda	Canoidea	Fissipedia (toe-footed)	Carnivora
Procyonidae: coati, racoon, lesser panda	Canoidea	Fissipedia (toe-footed)	Carnivora
Mustelidae: badger, weasel, skunk, otter	Canoidea	Fissipedia (toe-footed)	Carnivora
Felidae: cat, leopard, lion, tiger, cheetah	Feloidea	Fissipedia (toe-footed)	Carnivora
Hyaenidae: hyena, aardwolf	Feloidea	Fissipedia (toe-footed)	Carnivora
Viverridae: mongoose, civet	Feloidea	Fissipedia (toe-footed)	Carnivora
Otariidae: eared seals, sea lion		Pinnipedia (fin-footed)	Carnivora
Odobenidae: walrus		Pinnipedia (fin-footed)	Carnivora
Phocidae: earless seals		Pinnipedia (fin-footed)	Carnivora
Suidae: pig		Suina — Suiformes	Artiodactyla
Tayassuidae: peccary		Suina — Suiformes	Artiodactyla
Hippopotamidae: hippopotamus		Ancodonta — Suiformes	Artiodactyla
Camelidae: camel, llama		Tylopoda	Artiodactyla
Giraffidae: giraffe, okapi		Ruminantia	Artiodactyla
Cervidae: deer, moose, reindeer, wapiti (elk)		Ruminantia	Artiodactyla
Antilocapridae: pronghorn		Ruminantia	Artiodactyla
Subfamily (Family Bovidae)			
Bovinae: cattle, eland, kudu, bison, yak	Bovoidea[1]	Ruminantia	Artiodactyla
Hippotraginae: sable, oryx, waterbuck	Bovoidea[1]	Ruminantia	Artiodactyla
Acelaphinae: hartebeest, wildebeest (gnu)	Bovoidea[1]	Ruminantia	Artiodactyla
Antilopinae: gazelle, springbok, saiga	Bovoidea[1]	Ruminantia	Artiodactyla
Caprinae: sheep, goat, musk ox	Bovoidea[1]	Ruminantia	Artiodactyla
Family			
Equidae: horse, donkey zebra		Hippomorpha	Perissodactyla
Tapiridae: tapir		Ceratomorpha	Perissodactyla
Rhinocerotidae: rhinoceros		Ceratomorpha	Perissodactyla
Aplodontidae: mountain beaver		Sciuromorpha	Rodentia
Sciuridae: chipmunk, squirrel, marmot		Sciuromorpha	Rodentia
Cricetidae: field mice, lemming, muskrat, hamster, gerbil		Myomorpha	Rodentia
Muridae: rat, Old World mice		Myomorpha	Rodentia
Heteromyidae: New World mice		Myomorpha	Rodentia
Geomyidae: gopher		Myomorpha	Rodentia
Dipodidae: jerboa		Myomorpha	Rodentia
Chinchillidae: chinchilla		Caviomorpha	Rodentia
Dasyproctidae: agouti, paca		Caviomorpha	Rodentia
Erethizontidae: New World porcupine		Caviomorpha	Rodentia
Hystricidae: Old World porcupine			Rodentia
Castoridae: beaver			Rodentia
Bats - various familes			Chiroptera

Canoids have long snouts and unretractable claws.

Feloids have retractable claws.

Most carnivora also eat some plants and insects.

The artiodactyla have an even number of toes.

Family Bovidae

All ruminants have 4-chamber stomachs and chew cuds.

The perissodactyla have an odd number of toes.

Rodents are the most numerous of all mammals.

Rodent suborders are distinguished by the placement of a major jaw muscle.

Family	Superfamily	Suborder / Infraorder	Order
Leporidae: rabbit, hare			Lagomorpha
Ochotonidae: pika			Lagomorpha
Manidae: pangolin			Pholidata
Erinaceidae: hedgehog			Insectivora
Talpidae: mole			Insectivora
Saricidae: some shrews			Insectivora
Dasypodidae: armadillo		Loricata	Edentate (toothless)
Bradypodidae: sloth		Pilosa	Edentate (toothless)
Myrmecophagidae: hairy anteater		Vermilingua	Edentate (toothless)
Physeteridae: sperm whale		Odontoceti (toothed)	Cetacea
Monodontidae: narwhal, beluga		Odontoceti (toothed)	Cetacea
Phocoenidae: porpoise		Odontoceti (toothed)	Cetacea
Delphinidae: dolphin, killer whale		Odontoceti (toothed)	Cetacea
Eschrichtiidae: gray whale		Mysticeti (baleen)	Cetacea
Balaenidae: right whale		Mysticeti (baleen)	Cetacea
Balaenopteridae: hump-back whale		Mysticeti (baleen)	Cetacea
Manatee, dugong			Sirenea
Elephantidae: elephant			Proboscidea
Tupaiidae: tree shrew		Prosimii	Primates
Lemuridae: lemur		Prosimii	Primates
Daubentoniidae: aye-aye		Prosimii	Primates
Lorisidae: loris, potto		Prosimii	Primates
Tarsiidae: tarsier		Prosimii	Primates
Callitrichidae: marmoset		Anthropoidea	Primates
Cebidae: New World monkeys (flat-nosed)		Anthropoidea	Primates
Cercopithecidae: baboon, Old World monkeys (long-nosed, bare buttocks)		Anthropoidea	Primates
Hylobatidae: gibbon		Anthropoidea	Primates
Pongidae (great apes): gorilla, chimpanzee, orangutan		Anthropoidea	Primates
Hominidae: human		Anthropoidea	Primates

The prosimians usually have longer snouts than anthropoids.

Most primates have opposable thumbs; all but man have opposable big toes.

Infraclass Marsupialia

Family	Superfamily	Order
Dasyuridae: mouse- and ratlike, Tasmanian devil	Dasyuroidea	Marsupicanivora
Notoryctidae: molelike	Dasyuroidea	Marsupicanivora
Thylacinidae: wolflike	Dasyuroidea	Marsupicanivora
Didelphidae: American opossums	Didelphoidea	Marsupicanivora
Caenolestidae: ratlike So. America only		Paucituberculata
Peramelidae: bandicoot		Peramalina
Burramyidae: mouse- and squirrellike	Phalangeroidea	Diprodonta
Macropodidae: kangaroo, wallaby	Phalangeroidea	Diprodonta
Petauridae: squirrellike, some Australian possums	Phalangeroidea	Diprodonta
Phalangeridae: cuscus, some Australian possums	Phalangeroidea	Diprodonta
Tarsipedidae: honey possum	Tarsipedoidea	Diprodonta
Vombatidae: wombat	Vombatoidea	Diprodonta
Phascolarctidae: koala	Vombatoidea	Diprodonta

Subclass Prototheria

Family	Order
Ornithorhynchidae: duck-billed platypus	Monotremata
Tachyglossidae: echidna (spiny anteater)	Monotremata

Giant Trees of the U.S.

Source: The American Forestry Association, Washington, D.C.

There are approximately 748 different species of trees native to the continental U.S., including a few imports that have become naturalized to the extent of reproducing themselves in the wild state.

The oldest living trees in the world are reputed to be the bristlecone pines, the majority of which are found growing on the arid crags of California's White Mts. Some of them are estimated to be more than 4,600 years old. The largest known bristlecone pine is the "Patriarch," believed to be 1,500 years old. The oldest known redwoods are about 3,500 years old.

Recognition as the National Champion of each species is determined by total mass of each tree, based on this formula: the circumference in inches as measured at a point 4 1/2 feet above the ground plus the total height of the tree in feet plus 1/4 of the average crown spread in feet. Trees are compared on the basis of this formula. Trees within five points of each other are declared co-champions. The Giant Sequoia champion has the largest circumference, 83 ft. 2 in., Gallberry Holly the smallest, 5 in. Anyone can nominate the candidates for the National Register of Big Trees. For information, write to National Register of Big Trees, American Forestry Assn., 1319 18th St. NW, Wash., D.C. 20036. Or call toll-free at (800) 368-5748. Following is a small selection of the trees registered.

(Figure in parentheses is year of most recent measurement)

Species	Height (ft.)	Location
Acacia, Koa (1969)	140	Kau, Ha.
Ailanthus, Tree-of-Heaven (1972)	64	Long Island, N.Y.
Alder, European (1982)	70	Princeton, Ill.
Apple, Common (1984)	35	Santa Fe, N.M.
Ash, White (1983)	95	Palisades, N.Y.
Avocado (1982)	42	Hallandale, Fla.
Bayberry, Pacific (1972)	38	Siuslaw Natl. Forest, Ore.
Beech, American (1984)	130	Ashtabula Co., Oh.
Birch, Gray (1982)	59	East Windsor, Conn.
Birch, River (1983)	86	Anne Arundel Co., Md.
Birch, Yellow (1983)	76	Deer Isle, Me.
Blackbead, Catclaw (1976)	88	Sarasota, Fla.
Blackhaw, Rusty (1961)	25	nr. Washington, Ark.
Bladdernut, Amer. (1972)	36	nr. Utica, Mich.
Boxelder (1976)	110	Lenawee Co., Mich.
Buckeye, Painted (1984)	144	Union County, Ga.
Buckthorn, Cascara (1977)	35	Coos County, Ore.
Buckthorn, Cascara (1977)	37	Seaside, Ore.
Buckwheat-tree (1981)	44	Wash. County, Fla.
Buffaloberry, Silver (1975)	22	Malheur Co., Ore.
Bumelia, Gum (1977)	80	Robertson Co., Tex.
Buttonbush, Common (1977)	23	nr. High Springs, Fla.
Cajeput Tree (1983)	83	Davie, Fla.
Camphor-tree (1977)	72	Hardee Co., Fla.
Casuarina, Horsetail (1968)	89	Olowalo, Maui, Ha.
Catalpa, Northern (1984)	98	Lansing, Mich.
Cedar, Port-Orford (1972)	219	Siskiyou Natl. Forest, Ore.
Cercocarpus, Birchleaf (1972)	34	Central Point, Ore.
Cherry, Black (1984)	93	Allegan Co., Mich.
Chestnut, American (1979)	82	Oregon City, Ore.
Chinaberry (1967)	75	Koahe, So. Kuona, Ha.
Chinkapin, Giant (1979)	75	Cottage Grove, Ore.
Chokecherry, Common (1982)	67	Ada, Mich.
Coconut (1979)	92.5	Hilo, Ha.
Coffeetree, Kentucky (1976)	110	Van Buren Co., Mich.
Cottonwood, Black (1982)	148	Rainbow Falls St. Park, Wash.
Cypress, Monterey (1975)	97	Brookings, Ore.
Dahoon (1975)	72	Osceola For., Fla.
Desert-Willow (1976)	56	Gila Co., Ariz.
Devil's-walkingstick (1982)	51	San Felasco Hammock, Fla.
Devilwood (1972)	37	Mayo, Fla.
Dogwood, Pacific (1975)	50	nr. Clatskanie, Ore.
Douglas-fir, Coast (1975)	221	Olympic Natl. Park, Wash.
Doveplum (1965)	45	Miami, Fla.
Elm, American (1978)	125	Southampton Co., Va.
Eucalyptus, Longbeak (1983)	171	Kern Co., Cal.
Fir, Noble (1972)	278	Gifford Pinchot Natl. Forest, Wash.
Gumbo-limbo (1973)	50	Homestead, Fla.
Hackberry, Common (1972)	118	Allegany Co., Mich.
Hawthorn, Scarlet, (1980)	37	Clinton, N.Y.
Hemlock, Western (1978)	195	Tillamook, Ore.
Hercules-club (1961)	38	Little Rock, Ark.
Hickory, sand (1983)	94	Vineland, N.J.
Holly, American (1983)	50	St. Mary's City, Md.
Honeylocust, Thornless (1976)	130	Washtenaw Co., Mich.
Hophornbeam, Eastern (1976)	73	Grand Traverse Co., Mich.
Hoptree, Common (1982)	35	Ada, Mich.
Hornbeam, American (1982)	69	Milton, N.Y.
Joshua-tree (1967)	32	San Bernardino Natl. Forest, Cal.
Larch, Western (1980)	175	Libby, Mont.
Laurelcherry, Carolina (1972)	44	Dellwood, Fla.
Lebbek (1968)	65	Lahaina, Maui, Ha.
Lobolly-Bay (1983)	94	Ocala Natl. Forest, Fla.
Locust, Black (1974)	96	Dansville, N.Y.
Lysiloma, Bahama (1973)	79	Homestead, Fla.
Madrone, Pacific (1955)	79	Ettersburg, Cal.
Magnolia, Southern (1978)	86	Bladen Co., N.C.
Mangrove, Red (1975)	75	Everglades Natl. Pk., Fla.
Maple, Bigleaf (1977)	101	Jewell, Ore.
Mesquite, Velvet (1952)	55	Coronado Natl. Forest, Ariz.
Mountain-Ash, Showy (1982)	58	nr. Gould City, Mich.
Mountain-Laurel (1981)	28	Oconee County, S.C.
Mulberry, White (1982)	55	Leavenworth, Kan.
Oak, Scarlet (1978)	150	Maud, Ala.
Oak, White (1945)	107	Wye Mills, Md.
Osage-Orange (1969)	51	nr. Brookneal, Va.
Palmetto, Cabbage (1978)	90	Highlands Hammock State Pk., Fla.
Paloverde, Blue (1976)	53	Riverside Co., Cal.
Paulownia, Royal (1969)	105	Philadelphia, Pa.
Pawpaw, Common (1981)	56	Pickens County, S.C.
Peach (1978)	57	Sacramento, Cal.
Pear (1976)	57	Clawson, Mich.
Peppertree (1973)	47	San Juan Capistrano, Cal.
Pinckneya (1982)	32	nr. Orange Springs, Fla.
Pine, Ponderosa (1974)	223	Plumas, Cal.
Plum, American (1972)	35	Oakland Co., Mich.
Poison Sumac (1972)	20	Robin's Island, N.Y.
Pondcypress (1972)	135	nr. Newton, Ga.
Poplar, Balsam (1982)	98	South Egremont, Mass.
Possumhaw (1981)	42	Congaree Swamp, S.C.
Redbay (1972)	58	Randolph City, Ga.
Redwood, Coast (1972)	362	Humboldt Redwoods State Park, Cal.
Rhododendron, Rosebay (1981)	40	Oconee Co., S.C.
Royalpalm, Florida (1973)	80	Homestead, Fla.
Sassafras (1972)	100	Owensboro, Ky.
Seagrape (1972)	57	Miami, Fla.
Sequoia, Giant (1975)	275	Sequoia Natl. Pk., Cal.
Serviceberry, Downy (1984)	63	Barry Co., Mich.
Silktree (1971)	41	Gilmer, Tex.
Silverbell, Two-wing (1982)	66.5	Ashville, S.C.
Smoketree, American (1984)	35	West Lafayette, Ind.
Soapberry, Western (1984)	72	Coyle, Okla.
Sourwood (1972)	118	nr. Robbinsville, N.C.
Spruce, Blue (1982)	148	Rio Blanca Co., Col.
Sugarberry (1976)	78	Society Hills, S.C.
Sumac, Shining (1974)	55	Grenada Co., Miss.
Sweetleaf (1972)	55	Tallahassee, Fla.
Sycamore (1974)	129	Jeromesville, Oh.
Tamarisk (1981)	34	Columbus, N.M.
Tesota (1972)	32	nr. Quartzsite, Ariz.
Trifoliate-Orange (1984)	14	Aiken Co., SC
Tupelo, Black (1969)	117	Harrison Co., Tex.
(1971)	139	nr. Houston, Tex.
Walnut, Black (1975)	122	Humboldt Co., Cal.
Willow, Weeping (1982)	97	Asheville, N.C..
Winterberry, Common (1971)	40	Wildwood, Fla.
Yaupon (1972)	45	nr. Devers, Tex.
Yellow-Poplar (1972)	124	Bedford, Va.
Yew, Pacific (1969)	60	nr. Mineral, Wash.

METEOROLOGY

National Weather Service Watches and Warnings

Source: National Weather Service, NOAA, U.S. Commerce Department; *Glossary of Meteorology*, American Meteorological Society

National Weather Service forecasters issue a Tornado Watch for a specific area where tornadoes are most likely to occur during the valid time of the watch. A Watch alerts people to check for threatening weather, make plans for action, and listen for a Tornado Warning. A Tornado Warning means that a tornado has been sighted or indicated by radar, and that safety precautions should be taken at once. A Hurricane Watch means that an existing hurricane poses a threat to coastal and inland communities in the area specified by the Watch. A Hurricane Warning means hurricane force winds and/or dangerously high water and exceptionally high waves are expected in a specified coastal area within 24 hours.

Tornado—A violent rotating column of air in contact with the ground and pendant from a thundercloud, usually recognized as a funnel-shaped vortex accompanied by a loud roar. With rotating winds est. up to 300 mph., on a local scale, it is the most destructive storm. Tornado paths have varied in length from a few feet to nearly 300 miles (avg. 5 mi.); diameter from a few feet to over a mile (average 220 yards); average forward speed, 30 mph.

Cyclone—An atmospheric circulation of winds rotating counterclockwise in the northern hemisphere and clockwise in the southern hemisphere. Tornadoes, hurricanes, and the lows shown on weather maps are all examples of cyclones having various sizes and intensities. Cyclones are usually accompanied by precipitation or stormy weather.

Hurricane—A severe cyclone originating over tropical ocean waters and having winds 74 miles an hour or higher. (In the western Pacific, such storms are known as typhoons.) The area of strong winds takes the form of a circle or an oval, sometimes as much as 500 miles in diameter. In the lower latitudes hurricanes usually move toward the west or northwest at 10 to 15 mph. When the center approaches 25° to 30° North Latitude, direction of motion often changes to northeast, with increased forward speed.

Blizzard—A severe weather condition characterized by strong winds bearing a great amount of snow. The National Weather Service specifies a wind of 35 miles an hour or higher, and sufficient falling and/or blowing snow to reduce visibility to less than 1/4 of a mile for a duration of three hours or longer.

Severe Thunderstorm—A thunderstorm with winds of 58 mph. or greater and/or hail three-fourths of an inch or larger in diameter.

Flood—The condition that occurs when water overflows the natural or artificial confines of a stream or other body of water, or accumulates by drainage over low-lying areas.

National Weather Service Marine Warnings and Advisories

Small Craft Advisory: A Small Craft Advisory alerts mariners to sustained (exceeding two hours) weather and/or sea conditions either present or forecast, potentially hazardous to small boats. Hazardous conditions may include winds of 18 to 33 knots and/or dangerous wave or inlet conditions. It is the responsibility of the mariner, based on his experience and size or type of boat, to determine if the conditions are hazardous. When a mariner becomes aware of a Small Craft Advisory, he should immediately obtain the latest marine forecast to determine the reason for the Advisory.

Gale Warning indicates that winds within the range 34 to 47 knots are forecast for the area.

Tropical Storm Warning indicates that winds of 34 to 63 knots are forecast in a specified coastal area in 24 hours or less.

Storm Warning indicates that winds 48 knots and above, no matter how high the speed, are forecast for the area.

Hurricane Warning indicates that winds 64 knots and above are forecast for the area.

Special Marine Warning: A warning for potentially hazardous weather conditions, usually of short duration (2 hours or less) and producing wind speeds of 34 knots or more, not adequately covered by existing marine warnings.

Primary sources of dissemination are commercial radio, TV, U.S. Coast Guard Radio stations, and NOAA VHF-FM broadcasts. These broadcasts on 162.40 to 162.55 MHz can usually be received 20-40 miles from the transmitting antenna site, depending on terrain and quality of the receiver used. Where transmitting antennas are on high ground, the range is somewhat greater, reaching 60 miles or more.

Speed of Winds in the U.S.

Source: Natl. Climatic Data Center, NESDIS, NOAA, U.S. Department of Commerce

Miles per hour — average through 1986. High through 1986. Wind velocities in true values.

Station	Avg.	High	Station	Avg.	High	Station	Avg.	High
Albuquerque, N.M.	9.0	90	Honolulu, Ha.	11.5	67	New York, N.Y.(c)	9.4	70
Anchorage, Alas.	6.9	64	Jacksonville, Fla.	8.1	82	Omaha, Neb.	10.6	109
Atlanta, Ga.	9.1	60	Key West, Fla.	11.1	58	Pensacola, Fla.	8.3	53
Bismarck, N.D.	10.3	72	Knoxville, Tenn.	7.1	36	Philadelphia, Pa.	9.5	73
Boston, Mass.	12.4	61	Lexington, Ky.	9.4	46	Pittsburgh, Pa.	9.1	58
Buffalo, N.Y.	12.1	91	Little Rock, Ark.	7.9	65	Portland, Ore.	7.9	88
Cape Hatteras, N.C.	11.3	(b)110	Louisville, Ky.	8.3	61	Rochester, N.Y.	9.7	73
Chattanooga, Tenn.	6.1	37	Memphis, Tenn.	9.0	46	St. Louis, Mo.	9.7	60
Chicago, Ill.	10.2	58	Miami, Fla.	9.2	(a)74	Salt Lake City, Ut.	8.8	71
Cleveland, Oh.	10.7	74	Minneapolis, Minn.	10.6	92	San Diego, Cal.	6.9	56
Denver, Col.	8.8	56	Mobile, Ala.	9.0	(b)63	San Francisco, Cal.	8.7	47
Detroit, Mich.	10.2	46	Montgomery, Ala.	6.7	72	Savannah, Ga.	7.9	66
Fort Smith, Ark.	7.6	60	Mt. Washington, N.H.	35.1	231	Spokane, Wash.	8.8	59
Galveston, Tex.	11.0	(d)100	Nashville, Tenn.	8.0	41	Toledo, Oh.	9.4	72
Helena, Mont.	7.8	73	New Orleans, La.	8.2	(b)98	Washington, D.C.	9.3	78

(a) Highest velocity ever recorded in Miami area was 132 mph. at former station in Miami Beach in September, 1926.
(b) Previous location. (c) Data for Central Park, Battery Place data through 1960, avg. 14.5, high 113. (d) Recorded before anemometer blew away. Estimated high 120.

The Meaning of "One Inch of Rain"

An acre of ground contains 43,560 square feet. Consequently, a rainfall of 1 inch over 1 acre of ground would mean a total of 6,272,640 cubic inches of water. This is equivalent of 3,630 cubic feet.

As a cubic foot of pure water weights about 62.4 pounds, the exact amount varying with the density, it follows that the weight of a uniform coating of 1 inch of rain over 1 acre of surface would be 226,512 pounds, or about 113 short tons. The weight of 1 U.S. gallon of pure water is about 8.345 pounds. Consequently a rainfall of 1 inch over 1 acre of ground would mean 27,143 gallons of water.

Tides and Their Causes

Source: NOAA, National Ocean Service, U.S. Department of Commerce

The tides are a natural phenomenon involving the alternating rise and fall in the large fluid bodies of the earth caused by the combined gravitational attraction of the sun and moon. The combination of these two variable force influences produces the complex recurrent cycle of the tides. Tides may occur in both oceans and seas, to a limited extent in large lakes, the atmosphere, and, to a very minute degree, in the earth itself. The period between succeeding tides varies as the result of many factors and force influences.

The tide-generating force represents the difference between (1) the centrifugal force produced by the revolution of the earth around the common center-of-gravity of the earth-moon system and (2) the gravitational attraction of the moon acting upon the earth's overlying waters. Since, on the average, the moon is only 238,852 miles from the earth compared with the sun's much greater distance of 92,956,000 miles, this closer distance outranks the much smaller mass of the moon compared with that of the sun, and the moon's tide-raising force is, accordingly, 2⅕ times that of the sun.

The effect of the tide-generating forces of the moon and sun acting tangentially to the earth's surface (the so-called "tractive force") tends to cause a maximum accumulation of the waters of the oceans at two diametrically opposite positions on the surface of the earth and to withdraw compensating amounts of water from all points 90° removed from the positions of these tidal bulges. As the earth rotates beneath the maxima and minima of these tide-generating forces, a sequence of two high tides, separated by two low tides, ideally is produced each day.

Twice in each lunar month, when the sun, moon, and earth are directly aligned, with the moon between the earth and the sun (at new moon) or on the opposite side of the earth from the sun (at full moon), the sun and the moon exert their gravitational force in a mutual or additive fashion. Higher high tides and lower low tides are produced. These are called *spring* tides. At two positions 90° in between, the gravitational forces of the moon and sun — imposed at right angles—tend to counteract each other to the greatest extent, and the range between high and low tides is reduced. These are called *neap* tides. This semi-monthly variation between the spring and neap tides is called the *phase inequality.*

The inclination of the moon's orbit to the equator also produces a difference in the height of succeeding high tides and in the extent of depression of succeeding low tides which is known as the *diurnal inequality.* In extreme cases, this phenomenon can result in only one high tide and one low tide each day.

The actual range of tide in the waters of the open ocean may amount to only one or two feet. However, as this tide approaches shoal waters and its effects are augmented the tidal range may be greatly increased. In Nova Scotia along the narrow channel of the Bay of Fundy, the range of tides or difference between high and low waters, may reach 43 1/2 feet or more (under spring tide conditions) due to resonant amplification.

At New Orleans, the periodic rise and fall of the tide varies with the state of the Mississippi, being about 10 inches at low stage and zero at high. The Canadian Tide Tables for 1972 gave a maximum range of nearly 50 feet at Leaf Basin, Ungava Bay, Quebec.

In every case, actual high or low tide can vary considerably from the average, due to weather conditions such as strong winds, abrupt barometric pressure changes, or prolonged periods of extreme high or low pressure.

The Average Rise and Fall of Tides

Places	Ft.	In.	Places	Ft.	In.	Places	Ft.	In.
Baltimore, Md.	1	1	Mobile, Ala.	1	6[1]	San Diego, Cal.	5	9[1]
Boston, Mass.	9	6	New London, Conn.	2	7	Sandy Hook, N.J.	4	8
Charleston, S.C.	5	3	Newport, R.I.	3	6	San Francisco, Cal.	5	10[1]
Cristobal, Panama	1	1[1]	New York, N.Y.	4	7	Savannah, Ga.	7	5
Eastport, Me.	18	4	Old Pt. Comfort, Va.	2	6	Seattle, Wash.	11	4[1]
Galveston, Tex.	1	5[1]	Philadelphia, Pa.	6	2	Tampa, Fla.	2	10[1]
Halifax, N.S.	4	5	Portland, Me.	9	1	Vancouver, B.C.	10	6[1]
Key West, Fla.	1	10[1]	St. John's, Nfld.	2	7	Washington, D.C.	2	9

(1) Diurnal range.

Hurricane Names in 1988

U.S. government agencies responsible for weather and related communications have used girls' names to identify major tropical storms since 1953. A U.S. proposal that both male and female names be adopted for hurricanes, starting in 1979, was accepted by a committee of the World Meteorological Organization.

Names assigned to Atlantic hurricanes, 1988 — Alberto, Beryl, Chris, Debby, Ernesto, Florence, Gilbert, Helene, Isaac, Joan, Keith, Leslie, Michael, Nadine, Oscar, Patty, Rafael, Sandy, Tony, Valerie, William.

Names assigned to Eastern Pacific hurricanes, 1988 — Aletta, Bud, Carlotta, Daniel, Emilia, Fabio, Gilma, Hector, Iva, John, Kristy, Lane, Miriam, Norman, Olivia, Paul, Rosa, Sergio, Tara, Vicente, Willa.

Hurricane Hotlines

When tropical storms or hurricanes threaten, you will be able to get updates on the telephone from the National Oceanic and Atmospheric Administration. Recorded messages will identify areas under a hurricane watch or warning, the location of the storm, its forecast movement and wind speeds and tidal effects.

Two Hurricane Hotlines will be set up, one to be activated when hurricanes or tropical storms threaten the Eastern and Gulf Coast states, another for Hawaii. The number for the East Coast hot line is (900) 410-6622 (or NOAA). For Hawaii, the number is (900) 410-2263 (or CANE).

Callers will be billed 50 cents for the first minute and 35 cents for each additional minute. The average call is expected to cost about 85 cents.

Explanation of Normal Temperatures

Normal temperatures listed in the tables on pages 181 and 182 are based on records of the National Weather Service for the 30-year period from 1951-1980 inclusive. To obtain the average maximum or minimum temperature for any month, the daily temperatures are added; the total is then divided by the number of days in that month.

The normal maximum temperature for January, for example, is obtained by adding the average maximums for Jan., 1951, Jan., 1952, etc., through Jan., 1980. The total is then divided by 30. The normal minimum temperature is obtained in a similar manner by adding the average minimums for each January in the 30-year period and dividing by 30. The normal temperature for January is one half of the sum for the normal maximum and minimum temperatures for that month. The mean temperature for any one day is one-half the total of the maximum and minimum temperatures for that day.

Monthly Normal Temperature and Precipitation

Source: Natl. Climatic Data Center, NESDIS, NOAA, U.S. Department of Commerce

These normals are based on records for the 30-year period 1951 to 1980 inclusive. (See explanation on page 180.) For stations that did not have continuous records from the same instrument site for the entire 30 years, the means have been adjusted to the record at the present site.

Airport station; *city office stations. T, temperature in Fahrenheit; P, precipitation in inches; L, less than .05 inch.

Station	Jan.		Feb.		Mar.		Apr.		May		June		July		Aug.		Sept.		Oct.		Nov.		Dec.	
	T.	P.	T.	P.	T.	P.	T.	P.	T.	P.	T.	P.	T.	P.	T.	P.	T.	P.	T.	P.	T.	P.	T.	P.
Albany, N.Y.	21	2.4	23	2.3	34	3.0	47	2.9	58	3.3	67	3.3	71	3.0	69	3.3	61	3.2	51	2.9	39	3.0	26	3.0
Albuquerque, N.M.	35	0.4	39	0.4	46	0.5	55	0.4	64	0.5	75	0.5	79	1.3	76	1.5	69	0.9	57	0.9	44	0.4	36	0.5
Anchorage, Alas.	13	0.8	18	0.9	24	0.7	35	0.7	46	0.6	54	1.1	58	2.0	56	2.1	48	2.5	35	1.7	22	1.1	14	1.1
Asheville, N.C.	37	3.5	39	3.6	46	5.1	56	3.8	63	4.2	70	4.2	73	4.4	73	4.8	70	4.0	56	3.3	46	3.3	39	3.5
Atlanta, Ga.	42	4.9	45	4.4	53	5.9	62	4.4	69	4.0	76	3.4	79	4.7	78	3.4	73	3.2	62	2.5	52	3.4	45	4.2
Atlantic City, N.J.	34	3.3	35	3.2	42	3.7	51	3.1	60	2.9	68	2.9	74	3.9	74	4.5	68	2.7	58	2.8	48	3.5	38	3.5
Baltimore, Md.	33	3.0	35	3.0	43	3.7	54	3.4	63	3.4	72	3.8	77	3.9	76	4.6	69	3.5	57	3.1	46	3.1	37	3.4
Barrow, Alas.	-14	0.2	-20	0.2	-16	0.2	-2	0.2	19	0.2	33	0.4	39	0.9	38	1.0	31	0.6	14	0.6	-1	0.3	-13	0.2
Birmingham, Ala.	42	5.2	46	4.7	54	6.6	63	5.0	70	4.5	77	3.7	80	5.4	80	3.9	74	4.3	62	2.7	52	3.6	45	5.0
Bismarck, N.D.	7	0.5	15	0.5	26	0.7	43	1.5	55	2.2	64	3.0	70	2.0	69	1.7	57	1.4	46	0.8	29	0.5	15	0.5
Boise, Ida.	30	1.6	36	1.1	41	1.0	49	1.2	57	1.2	66	1.0	75	0.3	72	0.4	63	0.6	52	0.8	40	1.3	32	1.3
Boston, Mass.	30	4.0	31	3.7	38	4.1	49	3.7	59	3.5	68	2.9	74	2.7	72	3.7	65	3.4	55	3.4	45	4.2	34	4.9
Buffalo, N.Y.	24	3.0	25	2.4	33	3.0	45	3.0	56	2.9	68	2.7	71	3.0	69	4.2	62	3.4	52	2.9	40	3.6	29	3.4
Burlington, Vt.	17	1.9	18	1.7	29	2.2	43	2.8	55	3.0	65	3.6	70	3.4	67	3.9	59	3.2	48	2.8	37	2.8	23	2.4
Caribou, Me.	11	2.4	13	2.1	24	2.4	37	2.6	50	2.9	60	3.2	65	4.0	63	4.0	54	3.5	43	3.1	31	3.2	16	3.1
Charleston, S.C.	49	3.3	51	3.4	57	4.4	66	2.6	73	4.4	79	6.5	82	7.3	81	6.5	77	4.9	68	2.9	59	2.2	52	3.1
Chicago, Ill.	21	1.6	26	1.3	36	2.6	49	3.7	59	3.2	69	4.1	73	3.6	72	3.5	65	3.4	54	2.3	40	2.1	28	2.1
Cleveland, Oh.	26	2.5	27	2.2	37	3.0	48	3.3	58	3.3	68	3.5	72	3.4	70	3.4	64	2.9	53	2.5	42	2.8	31	2.8
Columbus, Oh.	27	2.8	30	2.2	40	3.2	51	3.4	61	3.8	70	4.0	74	4.0	72	3.7	66	2.8	54	1.9	42	2.6	32	2.6
Dallas-Ft. Worth, Tex.	44	1.7	49	1.9	56	2.4	66	3.6	74	4.3	82	2.6	86	2.0	86	1.8	79	3.3	68	2.5	56	1.8	48	1.7
Denver, Col.	30	0.5	34	0.7	38	1.2	47	1.8	57	2.5	67	1.6	73	1.9	71	1.5	63	1.2	52	1.0	39	0.8	33	0.6
Des Moines, Ia.	19	1.0	25	1.1	35	2.2	51	3.2	62	4.0	72	4.2	76	3.2	74	4.1	65	3.1	54	2.2	39	1.5	26	1.5
Detroit, Mich.	23	1.9	26	1.7	35	2.5	47	3.2	58	2.8	68	3.4	72	3.1	71	3.2	63	2.3	52	2.1	40	2.3	29	2.5
Dodge City, Kan.	30	0.5	35	0.5	42	1.5	54	1.8	64	3.3	75	3.0	80	3.1	78	2.5	69	1.9	58	1.3	43	0.8	34	0.5
Duluth, Minn.	6	1.2	12	0.9	23	1.8	38	2.2	50	3.2	59	4.0	65	4.0	63	4.1	54	3.3	44	2.2	28	1.7	14	1.3
Eureka, Cal.*	47	7.0	49	5.2	48	5.1	49	2.9	52	1.6	55	0.6	56	0.1	57	0.4	57	0.9	54	2.7	51	5.9	48	6.2
Fairbanks, Alas.	-13	0.5	-4	0.5	9	0.4	30	0.3	48	0.6	59	1.3	62	1.8	57	1.9	45	1.1	25	0.7	4	0.7	-10	0.7
Fresno, Cal.	46	2.0	51	1.9	54	1.6	60	1.2	68	0.3	75	0.1	81	L	79	L	74	0.2	65	0.4	53	1.2	45	1.6
Galveston, Tex.*	54	3.0	56	2.3	62	2.1	69	2.6	76	3.3	81	3.5	83	3.8	83	4.4	80	5.8	73	2.6	63	3.2	57	3.6
Grand Junction, Col.	26	0.6	34	0.5	42	0.8	52	0.7	62	0.8	72	0.4	79	0.5	76	0.9	67	0.7	55	0.9	40	0.6	28	0.6
Gr. Rapids, Mich.	22	1.9	24	1.5	33	2.5	46	3.6	58	3.0	67	3.9	71	3.0	70	3.5	62	3.1	51	2.9	39	2.9	27	2.6
Hartford, Conn.	25	3.5	28	3.2	37	4.2	49	4.0	59	3.4	69	3.4	73	3.1	71	4.0	63	3.9	52	3.5	42	4.1	29	4.2
Helena, Mon.	18	0.7	26	0.4	32	0.7	42	1.0	52	1.7	60	2.0	68	1.0	66	1.2	56	0.8	45	0.7	31	0.5	23	0.6
Honolulu, Ha.	73	3.8	73	2.7	74	3.5	76	1.5	78	1.2	79	0.5	80	0.5	81	0.6	81	0.6	80	1.9	77	3.2	74	3.4
Houston, Tex.	51	3.2	55	3.3	61	2.7	69	4.2	75	4.7	81	4.0	83	3.3	83	3.7	78	4.9	70	3.7	60	3.4	54	3.7
Huron, S.D.	11	0.4	18	0.8	29	1.2	46	2.0	57	2.7	68	3.3	74	2.3	72	2.0	61	1.4	49	1.4	32	0.7	19	0.5
Indianapolis, Ind.	26	2.7	30	2.5	40	3.6	52	3.7	63	3.7	72	4.0	75	4.3	73	3.5	67	2.7	55	2.5	42	3.0	32	3.0
Jackson, Miss.	46	5.0	49	4.9	56	5.9	65	5.9	73	4.8	79	2.9	82	4.4	81	3.7	76	3.6	65	2.6	55	4.2	49	5.4
Jacksonville, Fla.	53	3.1	55	3.5	61	3.7	68	3.3	74	4.9	79	5.4	81	6.5	81	7.2	78	7.3	70	3.4	61	1.9	55	2.6
Juneau, Alas.	22	3.7	28	3.7	31	3.3	39	2.9	46	3.4	53	3.0	56	4.1	55	5.0	49	6.4	42	7.7	33	5.2	27	4.7
Kansas City, Mo.	26	1.0	32	1.0	42	2.1	55	2.7	65	3.4	76	4.1	79	3.5	77	3.2	68	3.3	58	2.5	43	1.2	32	1.1
Knoxville, Tenn.	38	4.7	42	4.2	50	5.5	60	3.9	67	3.7	74	4.0	78	4.3	77	3.0	72	3.0	60	2.7	49	3.8	41	4.6
Lander, Wyo.	20	0.5	26	0.6	32	1.1	42	2.2	53	2.7	62	1.5	71	0.7	69	0.5	58	0.9	47	1.2	31	0.8	23	0.5
Lexington, Ky.	32	3.6	35	3.3	44	4.8	55	4.0	64	4.2	72	4.3	76	5.0	75	4.0	69	3.3	57	2.3	45	3.3	36	3.8
Little Rock, Ark.	40	3.9	44	3.8	52	4.7	62	5.4	71	5.3	79	3.7	82	3.6	81	3.1	74	4.3	63	2.8	51	4.4	43	4.2
Los Angeles, Cal.*	57	3.7	59	3.0	60	2.4	62	1.2	65	0.2	69	L	74	L	75	0.1	73	0.3	69	0.2	63	1.9	58	2.0
Louisville, Ky.	33	3.4	36	3.2	45	4.7	57	4.1	65	4.2	74	3.6	78	4.1	76	3.3	70	3.6	58	2.6	46	3.5	37	3.5
Marquette, Mich.*	12	2.0	14	1.9	23	2.8	37	3.6	50	4.0	60	3.9	65	3.2	63	3.3	54	3.0	44	3.3	30	3.0	18	2.1
Memphis, Tenn.	40	4.6	44	4.3	52	5.4	63	5.8	71	5.1	79	3.6	82	4.0	81	3.7	74	3.6	63	2.4	51	4.2	43	4.9
Miami, Fla.	67	2.1	68	2.1	72	1.9	75	3.1	79	6.5	81	9.2	83	6.0	83	7.0	82	8.1	78	7.1	73	2.7	69	1.9
Milwaukee, Wis.	19	1.6	23	1.3	32	2.6	45	3.4	55	2.6	65	3.6	71	3.5	69	3.1	62	2.9	51	2.3	37	2.0	25	2.0
Minneapolis, Minn.	11	0.8	18	0.9	29	1.7	46	2.1	59	3.2	68	4.1	73	3.5	71	3.6	61	2.5	50	1.9	33	1.3	19	0.9
Mobile, Ala.	51	4.6	54	4.9	60	6.5	68	5.4	75	5.5	81	5.1	82	7.7	82	6.8	78	6.6	69	2.6	59	3.7	53	5.4
Moline, Ill.	20	1.6	25	1.3	36	2.8	50	4.0	61	4.2	71	4.3	75	4.9	73	3.8	65	3.7	54	2.7	39	2.0	26	1.9
Nashville, Tenn.	37	4.5	40	4.0	49	5.6	60	4.8	68	4.6	76	3.7	79	3.8	78	3.4	72	3.7	60	2.6	49	3.5	41	4.6
Newark, N.J.	31	3.1	33	3.1	41	4.2	52	3.6	62	3.6	72	2.9	77	3.9	76	4.3	68	3.7	57	3.1	47	3.6	36	3.4
New Orleans, La.	52	5.0	55	5.2	61	4.7	69	4.5	75	5.1	80	4.6	82	6.7	82	6.0	79	5.9	69	2.7	60	4.1	55	5.3
New York, N.Y.*	32	3.2	33	3.1	41	4.2	53	3.8	62	3.8	71	3.2	77	3.8	75	4.0	68	3.7	58	3.4	47	4.1	36	3.8
Nome, Alas.	9	0.8	3	0.5	7	0.6	18	0.6	36	0.5	45	1.2	51	2.2	50	3.1	42	2.3	28	1.3	16	0.9	4	0.7
Norfolk, Va.	40	3.7	41	3.3	49	3.9	58	2.9	67	3.8	76	3.5	78	5.2	78	5.3	72	4.4	61	3.4	52	2.9	44	3.2
Okla. City, Okla.	36	1.0	41	1.3	49	2.1	60	2.9	68	5.5	77	3.9	82	3.0	81	2.4	73	3.4	62	2.7	49	1.5	40	1.2
Omaha, Neb.	19	0.8	25	0.9	35	1.9	50	2.9	62	4.3	71	4.1	76	3.6	74	4.1	64	2.5	54	2.1	38	1.3	26	0.8
Pago Pago, Amer. Samoa	81	13	81	13	81	11	81	11	80	11	80	8.6	79	6.5	79	7.1	79	6.7	80	11	80	11	81	14
Philadelphia, Pa.	31	3.2	33	2.8	42	3.9	53	3.5	63	3.2	72	3.9	77	3.9	75	4.1	68	3.4	57	2.8	46	3.3	36	3.5
Phoenix, Ariz.	52	0.7	56	0.6	61	0.8	68	0.3	77	0.1	87	0.2	92	0.7	90	1.0	85	0.6	73	0.6	61	0.5	53	0.8
Pittsburgh, Pa.	27	2.9	29	2.4	39	3.6	50	3.3	60	3.5	68	3.3	72	3.8	71	3.3	64	2.8	53	2.5	42	2.3	31	2.6
Portland, Me.	22	3.8	23	3.6	32	4.0	43	3.9	53	3.3	62	3.1	68	2.8	67	2.8	59	3.3	49	3.8	38	4.7	26	4.5
Portland, Ore.	39	6.2	43	3.9	46	3.6	50	2.3	57	2.1	63	1.5	68	0.5	67	1.1	63	1.6	54	3.1	46	5.2	41	6.4
Providence, R.I.	28	4.1	29	3.7	37	4.3	48	4.0	58	3.5	67	2.8	73	3.0	71	4.0	64	3.5	53	3.8	43	4.2	32	4.5
Raleigh, N.C.	40	3.6	42	3.4	49	3.7	59	2.9	67	3.7	74	3.7	78	4.4	77	4.4	71	3.3	60	2.7	50	2.9	42	3.1
Rapid City, S.D.	21	0.4	26	0.6	33	1.0	45	2.0	56	2.6	65	3.3	73	2.1	71	1.4	61	1.0	50	0.8	35	0.5	26	0.5
Reno, Nev.	32	1.2	37	1.0	41	0.7	46	0.5	55	0.7	62	0.3	70	0.3	67	0.3	60	0.3	50	0.3	40	0.6	33	1.2
Richmond, Va.	37	3.2	39	3.1	47	3.6	58	2.9	66	3.6	74	3.6	78	5.1	77	5.0	70	3.5	59	3.7	49	3.3	40	3.4
St. Louis, Mo.	29	1.7	34	2.1	43	3.3	56	3.6	66	3.5	75	3.7	79	3.6	77	2.6	70	2.7	58	2.3	45	2.5	34	2.2
Salt Lake City, Ut.	29	1.4	34	1.3	41	1.7	49	2.2	59	1.5	68	1.0	78	0.7	75	0.9	65	0.9	53	1.1	40	1.2	30	1.4
San Antonio, Tex.	50	1.6	54	1.9	62	1.3	70	2.7	76	3.7	82	3.0	85	1.9	84	2.7	79	3.8	70	2.9	60	2.3	53	1.4
San Diego, Cal.	57	2.1	58	1.4	59	1.6	61	0.8	63	0.2	66	0.1	70	L	72	0.1	71	0.2	68	0.3	62	1.1	57	1.4
San Francisco, Cal.	49	4.7	52	3.2	53	2.6	55	1.5	58	0.3	61	0.1	62	L	63	0.1	64	0.2	61	1.1	55	2.4	49	3.6
San Juan, P.R.	77	3.0	77	2.0	78	2.3	80	3.6	79	5.6	80	4.7	82	4.9	82	5.9	82	6.0	81	5.9	80	5.6	78	4.7
Sault Ste. Marie, Mich.*	13	2.2	14	1.7	24	2.0	38	2.4	50	2.9	58	3.3	64	3.0	63	3.5	55	3.9	45	2.9	33	3.2	20	2.6
Savannah, Ga.	49	3.1	52	3.2	58	3.8	66	3.2	73	4.6	79	5.7	81	7.4	81	6.7	77	5.2	67	2.3	58	1.9	51	2.8
Seattle, Wash.	39	6.0	43	4.2	44	3.6	49	2.4	55	1.6	60	1.4	65	0.7	64	1.3	60	2.0	52	3.4	45	5.6	41	6.3
Spokane, Wash.	26	2.5	32	1.6	38	1.4	46	1.1	54	1.4	62	1.2	70	0.5	68	0.7	60	0.7	48	1.1	35	2.1	29	2.5
Springfield, Mo.	32	1.6	36	2.1	45	3.4	56	4.0	65	4.3	73	4.7	78	3.6	77	2.8	70	4.2	58	3.2	45	2.9	36	2.6
Syracuse, N.Y.	23	2.6	24	2.7	33	3.1	46	3.3	57	3.2	66	3.6	71	3.8	69	3.8	62	3.3	51	3.1	41	3.5	28	3.2
Tampa, Fla.	60	2.2	61	3.0	66	3.5	72	1.8	77	3.4	81	5.3	82	7.4	82	7.6	81	6.2	74	2.3	67	1.9	61	2.1
Washington, D.C.	31	2.8	34	2.6	42	3.4	53	3.1	62	3.6	71	4.2	76	3.8	74	4.2	67	3.3	55	3.0	45	3.0	35	3.3
Wilmington, Del.	31	3.1	33	3.0	42	3.9	52	3.4	62	3.2	71	3.5	76	3.9	75	4.0	68	3.6	56	2.9	46	3.3	36	3.5

Normal Temperatures, Highs, Lows, Precipitation

Source: Natl. Climatic Data Center, NESDIS, NOAA, U.S. Commerce Department

These normals are based on records for the thirty-year period 1951-1980. (See explanation on page 180.) The extreme temperatures (through 1985) are listed for the stations shown and may not agree with the states records shown on page 184-185.

Airport stations; * designates city office stations. The minus (−) sign indicates temperatures below zero. Fahrenheit thermometer registration.

State	Station	Normal temperature — January		Normal temperature — July		Extreme temperature		Normal annual precipitation (inches)
		Max.	Min.	Max.	Min.	Highest	Lowest	
Alabama	Mobile	61	41	91	73	104	3	64.64
Alabama	Montgomery	57	36	92	72	105	0	49.16
Alaska	Juneau	27	16	64	47	90	−22	53.15
Arizona	Phoenix	65	39	105	80	118	17	7.11
Arkansas	Little Rock	50	30	93	71	109	−5	49.20
California	Los Angeles*	67	48	84	64	110	28	14.85
California	San Francisco	55	42	71	53	106	20	19.71
Colorado	Denver	43	16	88	59	104	−30	15.31
Connecticut	Hartford	34	17	85	62	102	−26	44.39
Delaware	Wilmington	39	23	86	66	102	−14	41.38
Dist. of Col.	Washington	43	28	88	70	103	−5	39.00
Florida	Jacksonville	65	42	91	72	105	7	52.76
Florida	Key West	72	66	89	80	95	41	39.42
Florida	Miami	75	59	89	76	98	30	57.55
Georgia	Atlanta	51	33	88	69	105	−8	48.61
Hawaii	Honolulu	80	65	87	73	94	53	23.47
Idaho	Boise	37	23	91	59	111	−23	11.71
Illinois	Chicago-Midway	29	14	83	63	102	−27	33.34
Indiana	Indianapolis	34	18	85	65	104	−22	39.12
Iowa	Des Moines	27	10	86	66	108	−24	30.83
Iowa	Dubuque	24	7	82	62	99	−28	38.59
Kansas	Wichita	40	19	93	70	113	−21	28.61
Kentucky	Louisville	41	24	88	68	105	−20	43.56
Louisiana	New Orleans	62	43	91	74	102	14	59.74
Maine	Portland	31	12	79	57	103	−39	43.52
Maryland	Baltimore	41	24	87	67	105	−7	41.84
Massachusetts	Boston	36	23	82	65	102	−12	43.84
Michigan	Detroit	31	16	83	61	102	−21	30.97
Michigan	Sault Ste. Marie*	21	5	75	52	98	−36	33.48
Minnesota	Minn.-St. Paul	20	2	83	63	104	−34	26.36
Mississippi	Jackson	57	35	93	68	106	2	52.82
Missouri	St. Louis	38	20	89	69	107	−18	33.91
Montana	Helena	28	8	84	52	105	−42	11.37
Nebraska	Omaha	30	10	89	67	114	−23	30.34
Nevada	Winnemucca	42	17	93	51	108	−34	7.87
New Hampshire	Concord	31	9	83	56	102	−37	36.53
New Jersey	Atlantic City	41	23	84	65	106	−11	41.93
New Mexico	Albuquerque	47	22	93	65	105	−17	8.12
New Mexico	Roswell	55	27	94	69	109	−9	9.70
New York	Albany	30	12	83	60	100	−28	35.74
New York	New York-La Guardia	37	26	84	69	107	−3	42.82
No. Carolina	Charlotte	50	31	88	69	104	−5	43.16
No. Carolina	Raleigh	50	29	88	67	105	−9	41.76
No. Dakota	Bismarck	18	−4	84	56	109	−44	15.36
Ohio	Cincinnati-Greater	37	20	86	65	102	−25	40.14
Ohio	Cleveland	33	19	82	61	103	−19	35.40
Oklahoma	Oklahoma City	47	25	94	71	110	−4	30.89
Oregon	Portland	44	34	80	56	107	−3	37.39
Pennsylvania	Harrisburg	37	22	86	65	107	−9	39.09
Pennsylvania	Philadelphia	39	24	86	67	104	−7	41.42
Rhode Island	Block Island	37	25	76	64	92	−4	41.91
So. Carolina	Charleston	59	37	89	72	103	6	51.59
So. Dakota	Huron	22	0	87	61	112	−39	18.66
So. Dakota	Rapid City	32	9	87	59	110	−27	16.27
Tennessee	Nashville	46	28	90	69	107	−17	48.49
Texas	Amarillo	49	22	91	66	108	−14	19.10
Texas	Galveston*	59	48	87	79	101	8	40.24
Texas	Houston	62	41	94	73	107	11	44.76
Utah	Salt Lake City	37	20	93	62	107	−30	15.31
Vermont	Burlington	25	8	81	59	101	−30	33.69
Virginia	Norfolk	48	32	90	70	104	−3	45.22
Washington	Seattle-Tacoma	44	34	75	54	99	0	38.60
Washington	Spokane	31	20	84	55	108	−25	16.71
West Virginia	Huntington	41	25	86	65	100	−16	40.74
Wisconsin	Madison	25	7	83	58	104	−37	30.84
Wisconsin	Milwaukee	26	11	80	61	101	−26	30.94
Wyoming	Cheyenne	37	15	83	55	100	−34	13.31
Puerto Rico	San Juan	83	70	88	76	98	60	53.99

Mean Annual Snowfall (inches) based on record through 1980: Boston, Mass. 42; Sault Ste. Marie, Mich., 113; Albany, N.Y. 65.2; Rochester, N.Y. 89.2; Burlington, Vt., 78.6; Cheyenne, Wyo., 53.3; Juneau, Alas. 105.8.

Wettest Spot: Mount Waialeale, Ha., on the island of Kauai, is the rainiest place in the world, according to the National Geographic Society, with an average annual rainfall of 460 inches.

Highest Temperature: A temperature of 136° F. observed at Azizia, Tripolitania in Northern Africa on Sept. 13, 1922, is generally accepted as the world's highest temperature recorded under standard conditions.

The record high in the United States was 134° in Death Valley, Cal., July 10, 1913.

Lowest Temperature: A record low temperature of −128.6° F. was recorded at the Soviet Antarctica station Vostok on July 21, 1983.

The record low in the United States was −80° at Prospect Creek, Alas., Jan. 23, 1971.

The lowest official temperature on the North American continent was recorded at 81 degrees below zero in February, 1947, at a lonely airport in the Yukon called Snag.

These are the meteorological champions—the official temperature extremes—but there are plenty of other claimants to thermometer fame. However, sun readings are unofficial records, since meteorological data to qualify officially must be taken on instruments in a sheltered and ventilated location.

Annual Climatological Data

Source: Natl. Climatic Data Center, NESDIS, NOAA, U.S. Department of Commerce

1985		Temperature °F				Precipitation[1]			Sleet or snow			Fastest Wind		No. of days			
Station	Elev. ft.	Highest	Date	Lowest	Date	Total (in.)	Greatest in 24 hrs.	Date	Total (in.)	Greatest in 24 hours.	Date	MPH	Date	Clear*	Cloudy*	Prec. .01 in. or more	Snow, sleet 1 in. or more
Albany, N.Y.	275	92	8/15	−7	12/26	29.95	1.73	9/26	50.7	6.5	3/4	36	1/15	62	190	138	15
Albuquerque, N.M.	5311	100	7/6	5	2/1	10.75	1.17	4/28	7.1	2.0	2/3	—	—	149	101	74	1
Anchorage, Alas.	114	76	6/30	−10	2/22	15.51	0.99	8/12	—	5.6	4/8	35	11/26	51	232	121	16
Asheville, N.C.	2140	93	6/5	−16	1/21	35.94	3.61	8/16	8.5	2.4	2/12	33	1/12	91	156	115	3
Atlanta, Ga.	1010	99	6/6	−8	1/21	49.80	3.93	10/1	1.9	1.5	2/11	36	2/11	114	151	119	0
Baltimore, Md.	148	99	8/14	−6	1/21	36.77	6.04	9/26	10.9	3.7	1/31	47	12/2	106	159	114	2
Barrow, Alas.	31	68	8/2	−42	2/25	3.80	0.48	7/3	22.5	1.6	9/21	37	11/9	58	182	95	4
Birmingham, Ala.	678	100	6/5	−6	1/21	50.67	5.47	7/27	0.3	0.3	2/12	—	—	—	—	113	0
Bismarck, N.D.	1647	100	7/7	−34	2/4	17.84	2.54	5/11	51.5	9.4	11/25	45	12/26	91	182	96	16
Boise, Ida.	2838	101	7/9	−12	2/4	11.14	0.78	7/30	41.6	6.0	11/28	40	3/26	116	145	82	15
Boston, Mass.	15	93	8/15	6	1/21	36.59	4.63	8/1	27.2	5.9	2/5	61	9/27	72	174	126	11
Buffalo, N.Y.	705	91	7/25	−10	1/21	46.00	2.33	11/4	168.2	16.9	1/19	56	4/6	43	221	185	41
Burlington, Vt.	332	89	8/14	−15	12/19	33.34	2.69	7/15	82.0	9.2	3/4	33	12/31	54	213	164	29
Charleston, S.C.	40	100	6/2	6	1/21	50.35	4.58	7/24	T	T	4/28	37	11/22	112	157	111	0
Charleston, W. Va.	939	96	8/13	−15	1/21	41.17	2.45	11/4	49.2	7.8	2/12	29	4/6	75	187	161	12
Chicago, Ill.	658	99	9/7	−27	1/20	40.07	2.80	11/1	38.8	7.5	1/1	37	3/4	79	190	135	16
Cincinnati, Oh.	869	92	9/9	−21	1/20	44.13	4.47	10/19	28.8	6.2	2/12	36	4/5	77	195	132	12
Cleveland, Oh.	777	92	7/8	−18	1/20	41.28	2.73	11/4	74.2	8.1	2/13	39	4/5	56	220	168	28
Columbus, Oh.	812	92	9/8	−19	1/20	38.67	3.56	7/14	43.8	6.3	2/12	37	1/1	62	204	150	18
Concord, N.H.	342	93	8/15	−19	2/4	30.89	2.07	9/5	55.5	10.4	3/4	34	2/27	75	172	113	17
Dallas, Tex.	551	106	9/1	7	2/2	30.70	2.39	6/5	5.1	2.4	2/1	58	8/2	130	138	69	4
Denver, Co.	5283	98	7/7	−15	1/31	16.31	1.57	7/18	67.5	8.7	9/28	41	4/3	113	125	95	20
Des Moines, Ia.	938	101	1/8	−20	1/20	28.50	2.19	8/21	45.3	10.9	12/1	54	3/4	127	155	110	15
Detroit, Mich.	633	91	9/7	−15	2/3	40.08	2.57	10/18	60.9	5.5	3/3	40	12/2	73	195	156	20
Dodge City, Kan.	2582	18	6/8	−7	1/12	22.48	1.84	10/8	26.5	6.4	1/9	41	6/10	124	141	82	6
Duluth, Minn.	1428	85	7/13	−13	1/19	31.83	2.69	9/2	110.0	15.0	9/2	57	3/4	73	183	151	27
Fairbanks, Alas.	436	83	6/3	−48	2/21	11.72	0.59	6/25	54.4	5.4	11/16	31	12/24	77	208	129	18
Fresno, Cal.	328	107	7/3	29	12/14	8.40	0.84	11/10	0.0	T	4/11	28	4/25	173	103	43	0
Galveston, Tex.	7	95	9/1	20	1/21	41.24	2.66	2/23	T	T	1/12	70	10/27	—	—	96	0
Grand Rapids, Mich.	784	92	7/13	−12	2/9	40.90	1.95	8/23	88.1	9.1	2/11	40	11/20	55	216	107	27
Hartford, Conn.	169	97	8/14	−3	2/4	36.88	2.73	8/11	27.2	4.4	2/5	43	9/27	79	189	123	9
Helena, Mont.	3828	101	7/9	−27	11/23	8.95	1.26	8/10	45.5	7.2	12/11	42	6/20	86	168	95	13
Honolulu, Ha.	7	93	9/16	54	2/1	17.38	4.43	10/19	0.0	0.0	—	30	5/23	79	99	87	0
Houston, Tex.	96	102	9/1	16	1/21	49.14	3.43	6/18	1.7	1.0	1/12	31	8/20	85	165	110	1
Huron, S.D.	1281	105	7/7	−30	12/18	24.95	2.82	3/3	80.5	18.3	3/3	50	5/12	108	152	92	20
Indianapolis, Ind.	792	91	7/14	−22	1/20	46.98	2.74	11/19	29.8	4.9	2/10	35	3/31	74	214	142	13
Jackson, Miss.	291	99	6/4	2	1/21	47.36	4.45	8/15	1.7	1.4	2/1	37	7/11	104	157	110	1
Jacksonville, Fla.	26	100	6/4	7	1/21	58.39	7.31	9/1	T	T	1/20	29	1/4	74	167	114	0
Kansas City, Mo.	1014	98	7/13	−14	1/20	52.72	4.35	10/9	27.9	7.6	1/9	37	3/26	113	160	130	10
Lander, Wyo.	5567	96	7/10	−22	1/31	10.69	1.26	12/8	100.9	22.7	11/12	50	5/26	131	121	67	24
Little Rock, Ark.	257	102	8/1	−2	1/20	49.02	5.08	4/22	11.3	6.3	2/1	—	—	—	—	105	5
Los Angeles, Cal.	97	97	7/1	39	12/12	9.32	2.36	11/24	0.0	0.0	—	—	—	154	86	30	0
Louisville, Ky.	477	96	7/14	−16	1/20	37.75	1.55	10/19	15.7	5.5	2/1	41	6/10	77	197	119	5
Marquette, Mich.	1415	86	7/13	−27	2/1	51.59	3.66	10/4	269.3	25.8	12/1	37	6/9	—	—	179	48
Memphis, Tenn.	258	97	6/4	−4	1/20	47.66	4.35	4/22	20.7	8.1	1/3	—	—	—	—	108	5
Miami, Fla.	7	98	6/4	30	1/22	56.26	3.25	8/9	0.0	0.0	—	38	11/19	106	104	127	0
Milford, Ut.	5028	101	6/6	11	2/5	11.21	1.40	9/19	62.6	20.4	3/27	47	9/17	156	102	71	14
Milwaukee, Wis.	[illegible]	[illegible]	[illegible]	[illegible]	[illegible]	[illegible]	[illegible]	[illegible]	[illegible]	[illegible]	1/1	[illegible]	[illegible]	77	170	[illegible]	[illegible]
Minneapolis, Minn.	834	102	6/8	−25	1/19	31.66	2.42	8/12	91.9	14.7	3/31	43	1/24	93	177	130	23
Mobile, Ala.	211	99	6/6	3	1/21	69.97	5.65	10/29	T	T	2/11	46	9/2	94	146	115	0
Moline, Ill.	582	97	9/7	−21	1/20	41.31	2.42	3/3	35.7	8.8	1/1	47	12/26	102	166	131	16
Nashville, Tenn.	590	98	7/14	−17	1/21	30.92	1.89	11/26	18.3	6.7	1/1	37	3/4	92	168	124	3
Newark, N.J.	7	97	8/15	−8	1/21	37.29	3.35	9/26	21.6	3.9	2/5	44	9/27	78	117	115	6
New Orleans, La.	4	94	6/5	14	1/21	66.98	4.91	10/27	0.4	0.4	1/20	35	10/28	77	169	119	0
New York, N.Y.	132	95	8/15	−2	1/21	38.82	3.54	9/6	19.5	5.7	2/5	28	12/14	—	—	122	5
Nome, Alas.	13	83	7/19	−28	2/20	21.24	1.50	10/5	52.0	3.6	5/6	44	5/18	101	195	143	15
Norfolk, Va.	24	97	9/3	−3	1/21	44.81	5.65	9/26	4.3	2.3	1/20	46	9/27	95	150	99	2
Oklahoma City, Okla.	1285	104	5/30	1	1/20	44.18	4.55	6/4	6.7	2.8	12/12	46	4/4	132	146	80	3
Omaha, Neb.	997	99	6/8	−18	1/20	21.21	2.07	7/18	23.5	6.0	3/30	—	—	—	—	80	11
Philadelphia, Pa.	5	93	8/14	−6	1/21	35.20	4.64	9/26	17.8	3.5	1/17	44	7/10	96	165	113	10
Phoenix, Ariz.	1110	115	8/24	28	2/1	7.92	0.98	11/11	0.1	0.1	12/11	32	7/15	203	71	38	0
Pittsburgh, Pa.	1137	92	8/13	−18	1/21	38.51	1.98	5/27	45.4	4.8	4/8	36	2/24	60	206	166	17
Portland, Me.	43	91	8/15	−9	2/4	34.01	3.01	11/5	49.1	9.9	3/4	51	9/27	84	171	124	20
Portland, Ore.	21	101	7/19	13	11/24	22.48	1.58	6/6	9.8	2.2	2/4	53	12/1	86	181	112	6
Providence, R.I.	51	93	8/15	2	1/21	40.42	3.43	8/30	24.8	7.6	2/5	52	9/27	85	178	130	9
Raleigh, N.C.	434	95	7/10	−9	1/21	38.17	3.09	11/20	4.1	2.4	1/28	31	3/12	111	152	101	2
Rapid City, S.D.	3162	104	7/7	−19	12/2	13.64	1.16	8/19	66.9	10.4	3/2	46	12/23	117	128	104	14
Reno, Nev.	4404	101	6/18	4	11/14	4.99	0.82	11/9	31.2	15.4	11/9	74	10/21	146	119	44	9
Richmond, Va.	164	100	8/14	−6	1/21	49.08	5.58	8/18	9.6	4.2	1/20	31	7/25	95	172	105	4
Rochester, N.Y.	547	91	8/13	−19	1/21	30.00	1.81	11/4	99.8	6.3	3/4	—	—	59	208	170	33
St. Louis, Mo.	535	97	7/14	−18	1/20	50.73	3.71	11/18	12.1	2.9	12/19	39	12/2	80	184	125	4
Salt Lake City, Ut.	4221	102	7/5	−9	2/1	16.97	1.34	5/9	74.7	10.7	12/7	39	7/26	118	155	92	22
San Antonio, Tex.	788	103	9/2	14	2/2	41.43	5.53	7/3	15.9	13.2	1/12	32	1/20	114	140	93	2
San Diego, Cal.	13	98	10/3	38	12/13	8.66	2.37	11/24	T	T	11/12	30	11/11	140	99	37	0
San Francisco, Cal.	8	99	7/1	33	12/12	12.57	2.23	2/7	0.0	0.0	—	46	11/29	150	96	50	0
Sault Ste Marie, Mich.	721	85	8/9	−26	2/2	39.37	1.64	9/2	174.3	12.4	12/1	42	10/24	61	222	190	52
Savannah, Ga.	46	104	6/2	3	1/21	38.64	3.62	6/7	0.0	0.0	—	40	11/22	99	150	118	0
Seattle, Wash.	400	93	7/19	10	11/23	25.13	2.08	6/6	24.9	7.8	11/21	33	3/20	66	205	123	6
Shreveport, La.	254	103	8/31	10	1/21	51.30	3.49	7/2	4.8	4.4	2/1	31	6/9	95	162	93	1
Sioux City, Ia.	1095	103	6/8	−18	12/18	23.37	2.01	9/12	33.8	10.3	3/30	48	1/14	98	157	109	11
Spokane, Wash.	2356	100	7/9	−21	11/23	11.21	0.74	11/3	61.4	8.1	11/8	42	4/23	97	189	99	25
Springfield, Mo.	1268	101	7/12	−13	1/20	56.50	4.53	11/17	25.9	4.6	1/19	34	1/18	100	177	128	9
Syracuse, N.Y.	410	91	8/15	−7	2/4	32.50	1.94	9/26	124.2	10.8	1/22	41	1/20	53	216	191	40
Tampa, Fla.	19	99	6/5	21	1/21	44.60	4.99	9/3	0.0	0.0	—	31	8/31	112	87	102	0
Washington, D.C.	10	98	8/15	−4	1/21	35.86	3.96	9/26	10.7	3.9	1/17	37	12/18	85	172	115	3
Wilmington, Del.	74	94	8/14	−14	1/21	33.73	3.75	9/26	16.7	3.9	1/25	38	9/27	100	168	113	7

*To get partly cloudy days deduct the total of clear and cloudy days from 365 (1 yr.). T—trace. (1) Date shown is the starting date of the storm (in some cases it lasted more than one day).

Record Temperatures by States Through 1986

Source: Natl. Climatic Data Center, NESDIS, NOAA, U.S. Commerce Department

State	Lowest °F	Highest	Latest date	Station	Approximate elevation in feet
Alabama	−27		Jan. 30, 1966	New Market	725
		112	Sept. 5, 1925	Centerville	345
Alaska	−80		Jan. 23, 1971	Prospect Creek Camp	1,100
		100	June 27, 1915	Fort Yukon	419
Arizona	−40		Jan. 7, 1971	Hawley Lake	8,180
		127	July 7, 1905 [1]	Parker	345
Arkansas	−29		Feb. 13, 1905	Pond	1,250
		120	Aug. 10, 1936	Ozark	396
California	−45		Jan. 20, 1937	Boca	5,532
		134	July 10, 1913	Greenland Ranch	−178
Colorado	−61		Feb. 1, 1985	Maybell	5,920
		118	July 11, 1888	Bennett	5,484
Connecticut	−32		Feb. 16, 1943	Falls Village	585
		105	July 22, 1926	Waterbury	409
Delaware	−17		Jan. 17, 1893	Millsboro	20
		110	July 21, 1930	Millsboro	20
Dist. of Col.	−15		Feb. 11, 1899	Washington	112
		106	July 20, 1930	Washington	112
Florida	−2		Feb. 13, 1899	Tallahassee	193
		109	June 29, 1931	Monticello	207
Georgia	−17		Jan. 27, 1940	CCC Camp F-16	1,000
		112	Jul. 24, 1952	Louisville	132
Hawaii	12		May 17, 1979	Mauna Kea	13,770
		100	Apr. 27, 193	Pahala	850
Idaho	−60		Jan. 16, 1943	Island Park Dam	6,285
		118	July 28, 1934	Orofino	1,027
Illinois	−35		Jan. 22, 1930	Mount Carroll	817
		117	July 14, 1954	E. St. Louis	410
Indiana	−35		Feb. 2, 1951	Greensburg	954
		116	July 14, 1936	Collegeville	672
Iowa	−47		Jan. 12, 1912	Washta	1,157
		118	July 20, 1934	Keokuk	614
Kansas	−40		Feb. 13, 1905	Lebanon	1,812
		121	July 24, 1936 [1]	Alton (near)	1,651
Kentucky	−34		Jan. 28, 1963	Cynthiana	719
		114	July 28, 1930	Greensburg	581
Louisiana	−16		Feb. 13, 1899	Minden	194
		114	Aug. 10, 1936	Plain Dealing	268
Maine	−48		Jan. 19, 1925	Van Buren	510
		105	July 10, 1911 [1]	North Bridgton	450
Maryland	−40		Jan. 13, 1912	Oakland	2,461
		109	July 10, 1936 [1]	Cumberland and Frederick	623-325
Massachusetts	−35		Jan. 12, 1981	Chester	640
		107	Aug. 2, 1975	Chester and New Bedford	120-640
Michigan	−51		Feb. 9, 1934	Vanderbilt	785
		112	July 13, 1936	Mio	963
Minnesota	−59		Feb. 16, 1903 [1]	Pokegama Dam	1,280
		114	July 6, 1936 [1]	Moorhead	904
Mississippi	−19		Jan. 30, 1966	Corinth	420
		115	July 29, 1930	Holly Springs	600
Missouri	−40		Feb. 13, 1905	Warsaw	700
		118	July 14, 1954 [1]	Warsaw and Union	687-560
Montana	−70		Jan. 20, 1954	Rogers Pass	5,470
		117	July 5, 1937	Medicine Lake	1,950
Nebraska	−47		Feb. 12, 1899	Camp Clarke	3,700
		118	July 24, 1936 [1]	Minden	2,169
Nevada	−50		Jan. 8, 1937	San Jacinto	5,200
		122	June 23, 1954 [1]	Overton	1,240
New Hampshire	−46		Jan. 28 1925	Pittsburgh	1,575
		106	July 4, 1911	Nashua	125
New Jersey	−34		Jan. 5, 1904	River Vale	70
		110	July 10, 1936	Runyon	18
New Mexico	−50		Feb. 1, 1951	Gavilan	7,350
		116	July 14, 1934 [1]	Orogrande	4,171
New York	−52		Feb. 18, 1979	Old Forge	1,720
		108	July 22, 1926	Troy	35
North Carolina	−34		Jan. 21, 1985	Mt. Mitchell	6,525
		110	Aug. 21, 1983	Fayetteville	213
North Dakota	−60		Feb. 15, 1936	Parshall	1,929
		121	July 6, 1936	Steele	1,857
Ohio	−39		Feb. 10, 1899	Milligan	800
		113	July 21, 1934 [1]	Gallipolis (near)	673
Oklahoma	−27		Jan. 18, 1930	Watts	958
		120	July 26, 1943 [1]	Tishmoningo	670
Oregon	−54		Feb. 10, 1933 [1]	Seneca	4,700
		119	Aug. 10, 1938	Pendleton	1,074
Pennsylvania	−42		Jan. 5, 1904	Smethport	1,469
		111	July 10, 1936 [1]	Phoenixville	100
Rhode Island	−23		Jan. 11, 1942	Kingston	100
		104	Aug. 2, 1975	Providence	51
South Carolina	−19		Jan. 21, 1985	Caesar's Head	3,100
		111	June 28, 1954 [1]	Camden	170
South Dakota	−58		Feb. 17, 1936	McIntosh	2,277
		120	July 5, 1936	Gannvalley	1,750

State	Lowest °F	Highest	Latest date	Station	Approximate elevation in feet
Tennessee	−32		Dec. 30, 1917	Mountain City	2,471
		113	*Aug. 9, 1930* [1]	*Perryville*	*377*
Texas	−23		Feb. 8, 1933	Seminole	3,275
		120	*Aug. 12, 1936*	*Seymour*	*1,291*
Utah	−69		Feb. 1, 1985	Peter's Sink	8,092
		117	*Jul. 5, 1985*	*Saint George*	*2,880*
Vermont	−50		Dec. 30, 1933	Bloomfield	915
		105	*July 4, 1911*	*Vernon*	*310*
Virginia	−30		Jan. 22, 1985	Mtn. Lake Bio. Stn.	3,870
		110	*July 15, 1954*	*Balcony Falls*	*725*
Washington	−48		Dec. 30, 1968	Mazama	2,120
	−48		Dec. 30, 1968	Winthrop	1,755
		118	*Aug. 5, 1961* [1]	*Ice Harbor Dam*	*475*
West Virginia	−37		Dec. 30, 1917	Lewisburg	2,200
		112	*July 10, 1936* [1]	*Martinsburg*	*435*
Wisconsin	−54		Jan. 24, 1922	Danbury	908
		114	*July 13, 1936*	*Wisconsin Dells*	*900*
Wyoming	−63		Feb. 9, 1933	Moran	6,770
		114	*July 12, 1900*	*Basin*	*3,500*

(1) Also on earlier dates at the same or other places.

International Temperature and Precipitation

Source: Environmental Data Service, U.S. Commerce Department

A standard period of 30 years has been used to obtain the average daily maximum and minimum temperatures and precipitation. The length of record of extreme maximum and minimum temperatures includes all available years of data for a given location and is usually for a longer period.

		Temperature F°						Average annual
		Average Daily				Extreme		precipitation
	Elev.	January		July				
Station	Ft.	Max.	Min.	Max.	Min.	Max.	Min.	(inches)
Addis Ababa, Ethiopia	8,038	75	43	69	50	94	32	48.7
Algiers, Algeria	194	59	49	83	70	107	32	30.0
Amsterdam, Netherlands	5	40	34	69	59	95	3	25.6
Athens, Greece	351	54	42	90	72	109	20	15.8
Auckland, New Zealand	23	73	60	56	46	90	33	49.1
Bangkok, Thailand	53	89	67	90	76	104	50	57.8
Beirut, Lebanon	111	62	51	87	73	107	30	35.1
Belgrade, Yugoslavia	453	37	27	84	61	107	−14	24.6
Berlin, Germany	187	35	26	74	55	96	−15	23.1
Bogota, Colombia	8,355	67	48	64	50	75	30	41.8
Bombay, India	27	88	62	88	75	110	46	71.2
Bucharest, Romania	269	33	20	86	61	105	−10	[illegible]
Budapest, Hungary	394	35	26	82	61	103	−10	24.2
Buenos Aires, Argentina	89	85	63	57	42	104	22	37.4
Cairo, Egypt	381	65	47	96	70	117	34	1.1
Capetown, South Africa	56	78	60	63	45	103	28	20.0
Caracas, Venezuela	3,418	75	56	78	61	91	45	32.9
Casablanca, Morocco	164	63	45	79	65	110	31	15.9
Copenhagen, Denmark	43	36	29	72	55	91	−3	23.3
Damascus, Syria	2,362	53	36	96	64	113	21	8.8
Dublin, Ireland	155	47	35	67	51	86	8	29.7
Geneva, Switzerland	1,329	39	29	77	58	101	−1	33.9
Havana, Cuba	80	79	65	89	75	104	43	48.2
Hong Kong	109	64	56	87	78	97	32	85.1
Istanbul, Turkey	59	45	36	81	65	100	17	31.5
Jerusalem, Israel	2,654	55	41	87	63	107	26	19.7
Lagos, Nigeria	10	88	74	83	74	104	60	72.3
La Paz, Bolivia	12,001	63	43	62	33	80	26	22.6
Lima, Peru	394	82	66	67	57	93	49	1.6
London, England	149	44	35	73	55	99	9	22.9
Madrid, Spain	2,188	47	33	87	62	102	14	16.5
Manila, Philippines	49	86	69	88	75	101	58	82.0
Mexico City, Mexico	7,340	66	42	74	54	92	24	23.0
Moscow, U.S.S.R.	505	21	9	76	55	96	−27	24.8
Nairobi, Kenya	5,971	77	54	69	51	87	41	37.7
Oslo, Norway	308	30	20	73	56	93	−21	26.9
Paris, France	164	42	32	76	55	105	1	22.3
Prague, Czechoslovakia	662	34	25	74	58	98	−16	19.3
Reykjavik, Iceland	92	36	28	58	48	74	4	33.9
Rome, Italy	377	54	39	88	64	104	20	29.5
San Salvador, El Salvador	2,238	90	60	89	65	105	45	70.0
Santiago, Chile	1,706	85	53	59	37	99	24	14.2
Sao Paolo, Brazil	2,628	77	63	66	53	100	32	57.3
Shanghai, China	16	47	32	91	75	104	10	45.0
Singapore	33	86	73	88	75	97	66	95.0
Stockholm, Sweden	146	31	23	70	55	97	−26	22.4
Sydney, Australia	62	78	65	60	46	114	35	46.5
Teheran, Iran	3,937	45	27	99	72	109	−5	9.7
Tokyo, Japan	19	47	29	83	70	101	17	61.6
Tripoli, Libya	72	61	47	85	71	114	33	15.1
Vienna, Austria	664	34	20	75	59	90	−14	25.6
Warsaw, Poland	294	30	21	75	56	98	−22	22.0

Record Maximum 24-Hour Precipitation by State

(through 1985)

Source: Natl. Climatic Data Center, NESDIS, NOAA, U.S. Department of Commerce

State	Precip. (inches)	Date	Station	Elevation (feet)
Ala. . .	20.33	4/13/55	Axis	36
Alas. . .	15.20	10/12/82	Angoon	15
Ariz. . .	11.40	9/4-5/70	Workman Creek	6,970
Ark. . .	14.06	12/3/82	Big Fork	1,100
Cal. . .	26.12	1/22-23/43	Hoegees Camp	2,760
Colo.. .	11.08	6/17/65	Holly	3,390
Conn. .	12.77	8/19/55	Burlington	460
Del. . .	8.50	7/13/75	Dover	30
Fla.. . .	38.70	9/5/50	Yankeetown	5
Ga.. . .	18.00	8/28/11	St. George	77
Ha.. . .	38.00	1/24-25/56	Kilauea Plantation	180
Id. . . .	7.17	11/23/09	Rattlesnake Creek	4,000
Ill. . . .	16.54	6/14-15/57	East St. Louis	410
Ind.. . .	10.50	8/6/05	Princeton	480
Ia. . . .	16.70	8/5-6/59	Decatur Co.	1,110
Kan. . .	12.59	5/31-6/1/41	Burlington	1,010
Ky.. . .	10.40	6/28/60	Dunmor	610
La.. . .	22.00	8/28-29/62	Hackberry	10
Me.. . .	8.05	9/11/54	Brunswick	70
Md.. . .	14.75	7/26-27/97	Jewell	152
Mass. .	18.15	8/18-19/55	Westfield	220
Mich.. .	9.78	8/31-9/1/14	Bloomingdale	750
Minn.. .	10.84	7/21-22/72	Fort Ripley	1,140
Miss.. .	15.68	7/9/68	Columbus	190
Mo.. . .	18.18	7/20/65	Edgarton	850
Mont. .	11.50	6/20/21	Circle	2,440
Neb. . .	13.15	7/8-9/50	York	1,610
Nev. . .	7.40	3/19/07	Lewer's Ranch	5,200
N.H. . .	10.38	2/10-11/70	Mount Washington	6,260
N.J. . .	14.81	8/19/39	Tuckerton	20
N.M. . .	11.28	5/18-19/55	Lake Maloya	7,400
N.Y. . .	11.17	10/9/03	NYC Central Park	130
N.C. . .	22.22	7/15-16/16	Altapass	2,600
N.D. . .	8.10	6/29/75	Litchville	1,470
Ohio . .	10.51	7/12/66	Sandusky	610
Okla.. .	15.50	9/3-4/40	Sapulpa	740
Ore. . .	10.17	12/21/15	Glenora	575
Pa.. . .	34.50*	7/17/42	Smethport	1,510
R.I.. . .	12.13	9/16-17/32	Westerly	40
S.C. . .	13.25	7/14-15/16	Effingham	110
S.D. . .	8.00	9/10/00	Elk Point	1,127
Tenn. .	11.00	3/28/02	McMinnville	900
Texas .	43.00*	7/25-26/79	Alvin	50
Utah . .	6.00*	9/5/70	Bug Point	6,600
Vt. . . .	8.77	11/3-4/27	Somerset	2,080
Va.. . .	27.00*	8/20/69	Nelson Co.	est. 500
Wash. .	12.00	1/21/35	Quinault R.S.	220
W.Va. .	19.00*	7/18/89	Rockport	700
Wis. . .	11.72	6/24/46	Mellen	1,150
Wyo.. .	6.06	8/1/85	Cheyenne	6,126

*Estimated

Wind Chill Table

Source: National Weather Service, NOAA, U.S. Commerce Department

Both temperature and wind cause heat loss from body surfaces. A combination of cold and wind makes a body feel colder than the actual temperature. The table shows, for example, that a temperature of 20 degrees Fahrenheit, plus a wind of 20 miles per hour, causes a body heat loss equal to that in minus 10 degrees with no wind. In other words, the wind makes 20 degrees feel like minus 10.

Top line of figures shows actual temperatures in degrees Fahrenheit. Column at left shows wind speeds.

MPH	35	30	25	20	15	10	5	0	−5	−10	−15	−20	−25	−30	−35	−40	−45
5	33	27	21	16	12	7	0	−5	−10	−15	−21	−26	−31	−36	−42	−47	−52
10	22	16	10	3	−3	−9	−15	−22	−27	−34	−40	−46	−52	−58	−64	−71	−77
15	16	9	2	−5	−11	−18	−25	−31	−38	−45	−51	−58	−65	−72	−78	−85	−92
20	12	4	−3	−10	−17	−24	−31	−39	−46	−53	−60	−67	−74	−81	−88	−95	−103
25	8	1	−7	−15	−22	−29	−36	−44	−51	−59	−66	−74	−81	−88	−96	−103	−110
30	6	−2	−10	−18	−25	−33	−41	−49	−56	−64	−71	−79	−86	−93	−101	−109	−116
35	4	−4	−12	−20	−27	−35	−43	−52	−58	−67	−74	−82	−89	−97	−105	−113	−120
40	3	−5	−13	−21	−29	−37	−45	−53	−60	−69	−76	−84	−92	−100	−107	−115	−123
45	2	−6	−14	−22	−30	−38	−46	−54	−62	−70	−78	−85	−93	−102	−109	−117	−125

(Wind speeds greater than 45 mph have little additional chilling effect.)

Heat Index

The index is a measure of the contribution that high humidity makes with abnormally high temperatures in reducing the body's ability to cool itself. For example, the index shows that for an actual air temperature of 100 degrees Fahrenheit and a relative humidity of 50 percent, the effect on the human body would be same as 120 degrees. Sunstroke and heat exhaustion are likely when the heat index reaches 105. This index is a measure of what hot weather "feels like" to the average person for various temperatures and relative humidities.

Relative Humidity	Air Temperature* 70	75	80	85	90	95	100	105	110	115	120
	Apparent Temperature*										
0%	64	69	73	78	83	87	91	95	99	103	107
10%	65	70	75	80	85	90	95	100	105	111	116
20%	66	72	77	82	87	93	99	105	112	120	130
30%	67	73	78	84	90	96	104	113	123	135	148
40%	68	74	79	86	93	101	110	123	137	151	
50%	69	75	81	88	96	107	120	135	150		
60%	70	76	82	90	100	114	132	149			
70%	70	77	85	93	106	124	144				
80%	71	78	86	97	113	136					
90%	71	79	88	102	122						
100%	72	80	91	108							

*Degrees Fahrenheit.

Average Relative Humidity (%)

Source: Natl. Climatic Data Center, NESDIS, NOAA, U.S. Department of Commerce

(M-morning; A-afternoon; through 1986)

	Jan.		Feb.		Mar.		Apr.		May		June		July		Aug.		Sept.		Oct.		Nov.		Dec.	
	M	A	M	A	M	A	M	A	M	A	M	A	M	A	M	A	M	A	M	A	M	A	M	A
Mobile, Ala.	80	60	81	55	84	55	87	52	87	54	87	54	89	60	90	61	88	59	86	53	85	57	83	61
Juneau, Alas.	79	75	82	74	83	68	81	63	79	63	80	65	84	70	88	74	91	76	88	78	84	79	83	81
Phoenix, Ariz.	67	32	61	27	58	24	43	16	35	13	32	12	45	20	51	23	51	23	52	23	59	28	68	34
Little Rock, Ark.	80	61	80	59	79	56	82	57	86	58	86	55	87	56	88	57	89	58	86	53	83	59	80	62
Los Angeles, Calif.	63	50	71	52	74	52	78	54	81	55	85	56	84	53	84	55	78	54	76	56	61	49	62	50
San Francisco, Calif.	81	63	83	63	81	61	82	61	89	68	89	72	92	74	93	73	87	66	81	60	82	63	80	63
Denver, Colo.	63	49	66	43	67	40	67	35	70	38	69	35	68	34	68	35	68	34	65	36	68	49	65	51
Hartford, Conn.	71	56	72	54	71	51	68	44	73	47	77	51	78	50	83	53	85	54	83	51	79	56	76	60
Wilmington, Del.	75	60	75	57	73	52	72	50	76	53	78	54	79	54	83	56	85	55	84	54	80	56	77	60
Dist. of Colo.	77	59	78	55	77	52	76	48	83	56	85	57	87	55	89	56	90	56	88	56	83	57	79	58
Jacksonville, Fla.	87	57	86	53	86	50	86	48	85	50	87	57	88	58	91	60	91	63	91	58	89	56	88	59
Miami, Fla.	84	59	83	57	82	56	79	54	81	60	85	66	85	63	86	65	88	67	86	64	85	62	83	60
Atlanta, Ga.	78	59	76	54	77	51	78	50	83	54	84	56	89	61	90	61	89	60	85	54	82	56	79	59
Columbus, Ga.	84	60	83	54	85	52	85	48	85	51	86	53	90	58	91	57	90	57	90	52	88	54	85	58
Honolulu, Ha.	82	62	78	59	73	58	70	56	67	54	67	53	68	52	69	53	68	52	69	55	75	59	79	61
Boise, Ida.	80	70	79	61	74	45	70	36	69	34	67	30	54	22	52	23	60	30	67	40	77	60	81	71
Chicago, Ill.	76	67	77	66	79	61	77	55	77	54	78	56	82	57	85	57	85	58	82	56	81	64	80	70
Indianapolis, Ind.	80	70	80	67	80	63	78	56	82	56	82	57	87	60	90	61	90	59	86	58	85	67	83	73
Des Moines, Ia.	75	67	78	66	78	61	78	56	77	55	79	56	81	57	84	58	84	59	79	56	79	64	79	70
Dubuque, Ia.	74	67	76	65	78	62	76	56	79	57	83	61	84	60	86	61	86	61	82	59	81	65	80	72
Wichita, Kan.	78	63	79	60	77	54	78	52	83	55	82	53	77	48	79	49	82	55	80	54	80	58	80	62
Louisville, Ky.	76	64	76	62	75	57	75	52	82	55	83	57	85	58	88	58	88	59	85	56	79	61	77	65
New Orleans, La.	84	66	83	63	84	60	87	60	89	60	89	62	91	66	91	66	89	65	87	59	86	61	86	66
Portland, Me.	76	61	76	59	75	58	73	55	75	58	79	61	80	59	83	59	86	60	84	59	83	63	79	62
Baltimore, Md.	71	57	71	55	71	50	71	48	76	52	79	52	80	53	83	55	84	55	82	54	77	55	74	57
Boston, Mass.	66	57	67	56	68	57	67	54	71	59	74	59	73	56	76	59	79	60	77	58	74	60	71	60
Detroit, Mich.	79	69	79	65	79	61	78	55	78	53	80	54	82	53	86	56	87	57	84	57	82	66	81	71
Minneapolis-St. Paul, Minn.	73	66	75	66	76	62	75	53	76	52	79	55	80	54	83	56	85	60	82	59	80	66	77	70
Jackson, Miss.	86	65	87	59	87	57	91	55	92	56	91	56	93	59	94	59	94	59	93	54	91	59	88	63
Kansas City, Mo.	74	63	76	64	78	61	78	57	84	59	85	59	83	56	86	59	85	60	81	58	79	63	78	66
St. Louis, Mo.	83	66	83	64	82	60	79	55	83	56	84	57	85	56	89	57	90	59	86	57	85	64	84	69
Helena, Mont.	70	62	71	55	71	46	69	38	70	37	71	37	66	29	66	30	72	37	73	42	74	58	72	65
Omaha, Neb.	77	66	79	64	78	58	77	53	79	54	82	55	83	56	86	59	86	60	82	57	81	63	80	68
Las Vegas, Nev.	55	31	50	26	44	22	35	15	31	13	24	10	29	15	35	17	34	17	38	19	40	27	50	33
Reno, Nev.	79	51	74	40	70	34	67	28	66	25	66	22	65	19	67	20	70	23	73	28	75	42	77	52
Concord, N.H.	74	58	76	56	76	53	74	45	77	48	83	53	84	51	88	53	90	55	87	53	84	60	80	63
Atlantic City, N.J.	77	58	79	56	77	54	76	51	78	55	81	57	83	56	86	57	87	58	87	56	84	58	78	59
Albuquerque, N.M.	71	40	65	32	56	24	49	18	48	18	46	17	60	27	66	30	62	31	62	30	66	36	71	43
Buffalo, N.Y.	79	73	80	71	80	66	76	58	75	56	77	57	78	55	83	58	84	60	82	61	81	70	81	74
New York-LaGuardia, N.Y.	65	57	65	55	66	53	66	50	70	53	72	54	72	53	76	55	76	56	73	55	71	58	68	60
Charlotte, N.C.	78	55	76	52	79	50	78	47	83	53	85	56	87	58	89	59	90	57	87	54	84	54	79	57
Bismarck, N.D.	73	67	77	68	80	63	79	52	78	48	84	53	83	47	83	46	82	50	79	52	80	64	78	70
Cleveland, Ohio	77	70	78	68	77	63	75	56	77	57	79	58	81	57	85	60	84	60	80	60	77	66	77	70
Oklahoma City, Okla.	77	59	78	57	75	52	77	52	83	57	83	56	79	48	79	49	82	54	79	52	79	56	78	58
Eugene, Ore.	92	80	92	73	91	64	90	57	91	54	90	49	87	38	88	40	89	43	94	63	93	78	92	84
Portland, Ore.	[illegible]	70	[illegible]	[illegible]	[illegible]	[illegible]	[illegible]	55	[illegible]	50	[illegible]	40	[illegible]	45	[illegible]	46	[illegible]	40	[illegible]	63	88	71	87	70
Philadelphia, Pa.	72	59	71	56	71	53	70	48	74	52	77	54	79	54	81	54	83	56	83	54	78	56	74	59
Pittsburgh, Pa.	75	65	74	62	74	57	72	50	75	52	78	52	82	53	85	56	85	56	81	54	78	62	76	67
Providence, R.I.	70	56	70	54	70	52	68	47	72	52	75	56	77	55	79	56	81	55	79	53	77	57	74	58
Charleston, S.C.	83	55	81	52	83	50	83	49	85	54	86	59	88	62	90	63	90	62	89	56	86	53	84	55
Huron, S.D.	73	67	78	69	83	66	83	56	84	54	87	57	86	52	89	53	87	54	82	56	82	64	78	69
Memphis, Tenn.	78	63	78	59	76	56	78	54	82	55	83	56	84	57	86	57	86	56	84	52	80	56	79	61
Nashville, Tenn.	79	63	79	59	78	53	80	51	86	56	87	55	90	57	91	59	90	59	87	55	82	60	80	63
Dallas-Ft. Worth, Tex.	79	60	79	59	79	57	82	58	87	60	85	55	80	48	80	50	85	56	82	55	81	57	79	59
Houston, Tex.	85	64	86	60	87	59	89	59	92	59	92	59	92	50	90	59	[illegible]	62	[illegible]	58	80	60	86	61
Salt Lake City, Ut.	78	69	77	59	71	47	67	39	65	33	60	26	52	21	55	23	62	29	69	41	74	58	78	71
Burlington, Vt.	70	63	73	63	74	59	73	53	75	51	78	56	79	53	83	57	86	62	81	61	78	67	75	69
Norfolk, Va.	74	59	74	57	73	53	73	50	77	55	79	56	82	59	84	61	83	61	83	60	79	56	75	58
Seattle-Tacoma, Wash.	80	74	80	67	82	61	83	57	82	54	81	53	81	49	83	51	86	58	86	67	83	74	82	77
Huntington, W.Va.	77	66	76	62	75	55	75	49	84	53	88	57	90	60	92	60	92	60	87	55	80	61	78	66
Milwaukee, Wis.	75	68	76	67	79	65	78	61	78	60	80	61	82	61	87	63	87	64	82	63	80	67	80	72
Cheyenne, Wyo.	57	50	60	47	64	46	67	41	70	43	70	41	69	38	68	37	66	38	60	41	60	49	58	52
San Juan, P.R.	81	64	79	62	77	60	75	62	78	65	78	66	78	66	79	66	79	67	80	66	81	67	81	66

Average Annual Snowfall

Source: Natl. Climatic Data Center, NESDIS, NOAA, U.S. Department of Commerce

(inches; through 1986)

The following are among the "snowiest" places in the U.S.:

Anchorage, Alas.	68.2	South Bend, Ind.	72.4	Mt. Washington, N.H.	248.9
Bettles, Alas.	77.8	Caribou, Me.	112.7	Albany, N.Y.	65.2
Cold Bay, Alas.	61.2	Portland, Me.	71.4	Binghamton, N.Y.	83.3
Fairbanks, Alas.	66.2	Blue Hill, Mass.	59.6	Buffalo, N.Y.	93.0
Homer, Alas.	59.3	Worcester, Mass.	69.6	Rochester, N.Y.	89.3
Juneau, Alas.	101.9	Alpena, Mich.	85.7	Syracuse, N.Y.	109.8
Kodiak, Alas.	77.9	Grand Rapids, Mich.	72.6	Youngstown, Ohio	55.7
McGrath, Alas.	90.1	Houghton Lake, Mich.	79.0	Sexton Summit, Ore.	98.4
Nome, Alas.	55.2	Marquette, Mich.	121.7	Erie, Pa.	83.7
St. Paul Is., Alas.	55.9	Muskegon, Mich.	97.8	Salt Lake City, Ut.	58.6
Talkeetna, Alas.	106.6	Sault St. Marie, Mich.	115.2	Burlington, Vt.	78.3
Valdez, Alas.	295.1	Duluth, Minn.	77.6	Stampede Pass, Wash.	432.5
Yakutat, Alas.	208.4	Intl. Falls, Minn.	61.1	Beckley, W.Va.	60.3
Flagstaff, Ariz.	96.2	Billings, Mont.	57.2	Elkins, W.Va.	72.3
Blue Canyon, Calif.	243.2	Great Falls, Mont.	58.8	Caspar, Wyo.	81.2
Mt. Shasta, Calif.	104.9	Kalispell, Mont.	65.5	Lander, Wyo.	105.2
Denver, Colo.	59.6	Concord, N.H.	64.2	Sheridan, Wyo.	70.7

ASTRONOMY AND CALENDAR

Edited by Dr. Kenneth L. Franklin, Astronomer Emeritus
American Museum-Hayden Planetarium

Celestial Events Highlights, 1988

(Greenwich Mean Time, or as indicated)

We can look for a good show from the planets this year. In the beginning, Jupiter gradually gives domination of our evening sky to Venus, the pair passing each other only 2° apart on March 6. The moon helps the beauty of the twilight by standing as a crescent between them a couple of evenings in February and March. Of course, the moon will almost always put on a show in the evening or morning twilight as it passes one of these bright planets each month. In the spring, Saturn joins Venus to entertain us, but rising in the east as Venus sets in the west. In early July, a few hours after midnight, scanning from the west to the east, we can find Saturn, Mars, Jupiter, and Venus, all quite bright. In September, Mars, having brightened almost a hundred-fold since January, is the star of the show as it reaches one of its very close approaches to earth, just 36.56 million miles this year. This is closer than 2 years ago, and this time it is very near the equator. This combination gives northern hemisphere observers a fine chance to observe the red planet's tantalizing features without too much blurring from looking through a long air path. While Mars is still brighter than it usually becomes at its oppositions, Jupiter outshines all but the goddess of beauty, Venus (who dominates the eastern morning sky), during November.

Of 32 lunar occultations this year, 6 are of planets. Antares and Spica have been in this list for a few years, but Regulus begins its series in June. Only the July, October, and late November Regulus events may be seen from some place in the U.S. Consider these listings, and mentions of close approaches among the planets, as opportunities to see the participating bodies quite close in the sky. In many cases, binoculars will enhance the view, or even be necessary for observation. Students of the following list may perceive that, while there is a distinct regularity to the occultations of stars, some will be missing. This is an indication that the event occurs too close to New Moon, i.e., the sun, for anything to be seen, even when it actually takes place.

January

Mercury is moving into the evening twilight all month, even at -0.9 magnitude a difficult object to see, standing nearly above the sun after sunset, at greatest elongation on the 26th, 19° east of the sun.

Venus is occulted by the crescent moon about 2 PM EST on the 21st; the event may be glimpsed through a telescope, and the two parties may be seen still close in the evening twilight.

Mars, looking like a hard-to-find reddish star of magnitude 1.5 rising after 3 AM local time, moves from Libra, through Scorpius, and into Ophiuchus, approaching Saturn during this month.

Jupiter, due south a little after sunset, is very bright (−2.4 magnitude) among the faint stars of Pisces.

Saturn, about 0.6 magnitude, is becoming easier to see in the eastern morning twilight, over the first weekend this month passing from Ophiuchus into Sagittarius, north of the scorpion's tail.

Moon occults Spica on the 12th, passes Mars and occults Antares on the 15th, passes Saturn, Uranus, and Neptune on the 17th, Mercury on the 20th, occults Venus on the 21st, and passes Jupiter on the 25th.

Jan. 3—The Quadrantid meteor shower is seriously impacted by the nearly full moon.

Jan. 4—Earth is at perihelion, 91.4 million miles from the sun.

Jan. 12—For southern hemisphere observers, the last quarter of moon occults Spica about 7 AM EST, but northern observers will find them very close together, nearly due south, in the dawn twilight.

Jan. 16—Before the moon rises about 5 AM, local time, it passes Antares, occulting it for observers on the other side of the earth.

Jan. 19—The sun enters Capricornus.

Jan. 21—The 2-day crescent moon will be above bright Venus in the western twilight this evening, a pleasant sight.

Jan. 26—Mercury is at greatest eastern elongation from the sun this evening, but is considerably below Venus in the evening twilight.

February

Mercury is stationary east of the sun on the 1st, passes between the earth and the sun at inferior conjunction on the 11th to become a morning object, and stationary again but west of the sun on the 23rd, lost to sight all month.

Venus is the very bright "evening star," below fainter Jupiter in the western evening twilight, with the moon between them on the evening of the 20th.

Mars, nearly as bright as a 1st magnitude star, moves rapidly eastward through Ophiuchus into Sagittarius by mid-month, speedily passing 0°.01 north of 6th magnitude Uranus on the 22nd and 1°.03 south of 0.6 magnitude Saturn on the 23rd, gradualy brightening as it goes.

Jupiter, still a dominant object in Pisces, is being approached from below by brilliant Venus in the evening twilight, with the crescent moon standing between them the evening of the 20th.

Saturn is easily seen in the morning sky as a star that "does not belong" in Sagittarius, passed by another interloper, Mars, on the 23rd.

Moon occults Spica on the 8th and Antares on the 12th, passes Mars, Saturn, and Uranus on the 13th, Neptune on the 14th, Venus on the 20th, and Jupiter on the 21st.

Feb. 1—Mercury stationary, beginning its retrograde motion.

Feb. 11—Mercury passes inferior conjunction with the sun.

Feb. 13—Saturn passes 1°.3 north of Uranus.

Feb. 16—Sun enters Aquarius.

Feb. 18—Pluto stationary, beginning its retrograde motion.

Feb. 20—Note the crescent moon between Venus, below, and Jupiter, above, in the western evening twilight.

Feb. 22—Mars passes 0°.01 north of Uranus.

Feb. 23—Mercury stationary, resuming its direct motion; Mars passes 1°.3 south of Saturn.

March

Mercury remains in the morning sky all month, being at greatest elongation, 27° west of the sun, the morning of the 8th, an interesting challenge for early risers.

Venus, clearly the beauty of the evening twilight, passes 2° north of Jupiter the evening of the 6th, but they make a handsome couple.

Mars, becoming perceptibly brighter, crosses nearly the whole of Sagittarius this month, passing 1°.4 south of 8th magnitude Neptune on the 7th.

Jupiter, now in Aries, is passed by Venus on the 6th, becoming the lower of the two "evening stars."

Saturn moves a little more than 1° eastward all month, firmly placed in Sagittarius.

Moon is partially eclipsed on the 3rd, occults Spica on the 7th and Antares on the 10th, passes Uranus, Saturn, and

Neptune on the 12th, Mars on the 13th, occults Mercury on the 16th, totally eclipses the sun on the 18th, passes Jupiter on the 20th, and Venus on the 21st.

Mar. 3.—Partial lunar eclipse.

Mar. 6—Venus passes 2° north of Jupiter.

Mar. 8—Mercury at greatest elongation, 27° west of the sun.

Mar. 11—Sun enters Pisces.

Mar. 18—Total solar eclipse.

Mar. 20—The vernal equinox occurs at 9:39 this morning, Greenwich time (4:39 AM EST), when the sun stands directly over the earth's equator in its northward journey; spring begins in the northern hemisphere, autumn in the southern; NOTE the thin crescent moon between low, bright Jupiter, and high, brighter Venus this evening.

April

Mercury is totally lost to view this month as it passes through superior conjunction, beyond the sun, on the 20th, technically becoming an evening object.

Venus is at greatest elongation on the 3rd, standing 46° east of the sun.

Mars outshines every star of Capricornus, entering this constellation during the first week of the month.

Jupiter bows out of our sky early this month as it plunges deeper into the evening twilight every night.

Saturn gradually brightens in Sagittarius as it begins its retrograde motion on the 11th.

Moon occults Spica on the 3rd, Antares on the 6th, passes Uranus and Saturn on the 8th, Neptune on the 9th, and Mars on the 10th, occults Venus on the 20th, and Spica again on the 30th.

Apr. 3—Venus is at greatest elongation, 46° east of the sun.

Apr. 4—Uranus is stationary, beginning its retrograde motion.

Apr. 11—Saturn and Neptune are stationary this date, each beginning its retrograde motion.

Apr. 18—Sun enters Aries.

Apr. 20—Mercury in superior conjunction.

Apr. 22—Lyrid meteor shower best after midnight, when the nearly first quarter moon will be out of the sky.

May

Mercury may be visible in the western evening twilight by mid-month as it is farthest east and north of the sun, perhaps the most favorable combination for our viewing this year; it appears as a star of minus 2nd magnitude, and is just 3° south of the thin crescent moon on the 17th.

Venus is at its brightest this month, truly dazzling in the evening twilight at magnitude minus 4.5, especially as the thin crescent moon passes very close on the 18th; a view through a telescope shows Venus to be crescent, also.

Mars at mid-month passes into Aquarius, now looking like a ruddy zero magnitude star.

Jupiter, in conjunction with the sun on the 2nd, becomes an object located in the morning sky, but is completely lost in the sun's glare, barely improving to merely difficult to observe by the end of the month.

Saturn, noticeably brighter than it was earlier in the year, outshines any star in Sagittarius.

Moon occults Antares on the 4th, passes Uranus and Saturn on the 5th, Neptune on the 6th, occults Mars on the 9th, passes Mercury on the 17th, and Venus on the 18th, occults Spica on the 27th, and Antares again on the 31st.

May 1—Pluto is at opposition to the sun in our midnight sky, appearing as nearly a 14th magnitude star in northeastern Virgo.

May 2—Jupiter is in conjunction with the sun.

May 4—The full moon 2 nights ago will seriously interfere with observation of the shower of meteors seeming to radiate from the vicinity of Eta Aquarii.

May 6—Venus is at greatest brilliancy in our evening sky.

May 8—As this day approaches its end to change to the 9th, around midnight, watchers in the east will see the last quarter moon and Mars get quite close, the moon passing just south of Mars; they will still be close even for western observers who wait for them to rise.

May 13—Sun enter Taurus.

May 17—This evening, the thin crescent moon will be above and to the right of Mercury, and Venus will be considerably higher than the moon in the sky.

May 18—This evening, the crescent moon will be above and to the right of brilliant Venus, a great tableau.

May 19—Mercury is at greatest elongation, 22° east of the sun.

May 22—Venus is stationary, beginning its retrograde motion.

June

Mercury is lost to view all month, beginning its retrograde motion on the 1st, and passing through inferior conjunction on the 13th, 4 hours after Venus does, to be a planet in our morning sky.

Venus is lost to view all month, passing through inferior conjunction on the 13th, 4 hours before Mercury does, to be a planet in our morning sky.

Mars remains in Aquarius all month, clearly outshining even Fomalhaut, the nearest bright star, far to its south, in Piscis Austrinus.

Jupiter, the brightest "star" in this month's morning sky, moves from Aries to Taurus in the middle of the month.

Saturn, in Sagittarius, is the night's guiding light as it is up all night, passing through opposition to the sun on the 20th.

Moon passes Uranus and Satun on the 1st, Neptune on the 2nd, Mars on the 6th, Jupiter on the 12th, occults Regulus on the 19th, Spica on the 24th, and Antares on the 27th, and for the second time this month passes Saturn, Uranus, and Neptune, on the 29th.

Jun. 1—Mercury is stationary, beginning its retrograde motion.

Jun. 13—Venus and Mercury each in inferior conjunction, becoming morning objects.

Jun. 20—Uranus and Saturn each in opposition, becoming evening objects; sun enters Gemini.

Jun. 21—The summer solstice occurs at 3:57 Greenwich time (10:57 PM June 20, EST); summer begins in the northern hemisphere, winter in the southern.

Jun. 24—Mercury is stationary, resuming its direct motion.

Jun. 27—Saturn passes 1°.3 north of Uranus.

Jun. 30—Neptune is at opposition, becoming an evening object.

July

Mercury, although reaching 21° west of the sun on the 6th, is lost in the morning twilight all month.

Venus, stationary on the 4th, rapidly becomes prominent in the dawn twilight, achieving it greatest brilliancy on the 19th.

Mars, brightening ever more, passes from Aquarius to Pisces on the 7th, and into Cetus, a non-zodiacal constellation, on the 25th.

Jupiter, the very bright object above Venus in the dawn sky, moves south of the Pleiades.

Saturn, a bright "star" in Sagittarius, has the evening sky all to itself.

Moon passes Mars on the 5th, Jupiter on the 9th, Venus on the 11th, Mercury on the 12th, occults Regulus on the 17th, Antares on the 25th, passes Saturn and Uranus on the 26th, and Neptune on the 27th.

Jul. 4—Venus is stationary on the western side of the sun, resuming its direct motion.

Jul. 6—Earth is at aphelion, its farthest from the sun this year, 94.4 million miles away; Mercury at greatest elongation, 21° west of the sun.

Jul. 19—Venus at greatest brilliancy, magnitude minus 4.5.

Jul. 20—Sun enters Cancer.

Jul. 25—Pluto is stationary in Virgo, resuming its direct (westward) motion.

August

Mercury moves from the morning to the evening sky as it passes through superior conjunction with the sun on the 3rd, but it will be almost impossible to see all month for northern hemisphere observers.

Venus is the dominant object in the eastern dawn sky, moving through Orion's club from Taurus into Gemini early this month, rising about 2 AM, local time in most of the US, standing 46° west of the sun on the 22nd, and resuming its eastward motion on the 30th.

Mars, brightening rapidly, begins its retrograde motion when it becomes stationary on the 26th, still south of Pisces in Cetus.

Jupiter is becoming brighter as it glides between the Pleiades and the Hyades in Taurus.

Saturn ends its retrograde motion on the 30th, when, in their mutual motions around the sun, the earth is moving directly away from Saturn; Saturn will continue to fade as our separation increases.

Moon passes Mars on the 2nd, Jupiter on the 6th, Venus on the 8th, occults Antares on the 21st, passes Saturn and Uranus on the 22nd, Neptune on the 23rd, suffers a partial eclipse on the 27th, and passes Mars again on the 30th.

Aug. 3—Mercury in superior conjunction, entering our evening sky.

Aug. 10—Sun enters Leo.

Aug. 11/12--The moon, being new, will be completely out of the way for observation of the Perseid meteor shower these nights; the meteors appear to streak away from a point in Perseus near Casseiopeia, high in the northeast, especially after midnight.

Aug. 22—Venus at greatest elongation, 46° west of the sun.

Aug. 27—Partial lunar eclipse.

Aug. 30—Saturn stationary, resuming its direct motion.

September

Mercury, while a poor prospect for observation from the northern hemisphere, is fine for watchers in the southern hemisphere, and almost always great in the tropics, reaching its greatest elongation this month on the 15th, stretching 27° from the sun into the evening sky.

Venus remains the brightest object in the pre-dawn sky, but brightening Jupiter appears to be drawing away from her with increasing speed.

Mars, nearly a week before opposition on the 28th, reaches its minimum separation from earth in many years on the 23rd, just 36.56 million miles apart, close enough to outshine Jupiter for a few days.

Jupiter stops its eastward motion, becoming stationary in Taurus as the earth seems to approach it directly; retrograde motion before opposition begins.

Saturn fades slightly as it begins to pick up eastward speed in Sagittarius.

Moon passes Jupiter on the 2nd, Venus on the 6th, occults Regulus on the 9th, eclipses the sun on the 11th, occults Mecury on the 13th, Antares on the 17th, passes Saturn, Uranus, and Neptune on the 19th, passes Mars on the 26th, and Jupiter again on the 30th.

Sept. 6—Uranus stationary, resuming its direct motion.

Sept. 11—Annular solar eclipse.

Sept. 15—Mercury at greatest elongation, 27° east of the sun.

Sept. 16—Sun enters Virgo.

Sept. 18—Neptune stationary, resuming its direct motion.

Sept. 21—Mercury passes 1°.3 south of Spica at 0400 GMT.

Sept. 22—Mars at closest approach to earth, 36.56 million miles away; autumnal equinox at 19:29 Greenwich time (2:29 PM EST); autumn begins in the northern hemisphere; spring in the southern.

Sept. 24—Jupiter stationary, beginning its retrograde motion.

Sept. 28—Mars at opposition; Mercury stationary, beginning its retrograde motion.

October

Mercury, now in retrograde motion, returns to come to about 1°.2 of Spica on the 5th, then passes from our evening into our morning wky when it moves through inferior conjunction on the 11th, ends its retrograde motion on the 19th when it is stationary, and is at its greatest elongation, 18° west of the sun, on the 26th, not a bad show for a planet that can't even be seen this month.

Venus, rising around 3 AM, local time, is the brightest planet in the eastern morning sky, clearly outshining Leo's brightest star, Regulus, which it passes only 0°.2 on the morning of the 4th, but Jupiter and Mars are vying for attention in the western AM sky.

Mars, as the month opens, has reteated from Cetus into Pisces where it is stationary at month's end to resume its westward motion, still dazzling but noticeably fainter than Jupiter.

Saturn is holding its own as the evening star, low in the southwest as twilight fades.

Moon occults Regulus on the 6th, Venus on the 7th, Antares on the 15th, passes Saturn and Uranus on the 16th, Neptune on the 17th, Mars on the 23rd, and Jupiter on the 27th.

Oct. 4—Venus passes 0°.2 from Regulus this morning, the pair visible along the east coast about the time they rise.

Oct. 7—Venus is occulted by the moon for observers in the longitudes of Europe, but another beautifully close combination of bright planet and crescent moon for the western hemisphere in the morning sky.

Oct. 11—Mercury in inferior conjunction.

Oct. 17—About 9 PM EST this evening, Saturn passes 1°.1 north of Uranus.

Oct. 18—Saturn passes 1°.1 north of Uranus.

Oct. 19—Mercury is stationary.

Oct. 21—Orionid meteor shower hampered by the neraly full moon.

Oct. 26—Mercury is at greatest elongation, 18° west of the sun.

Oct. 30—Mars is stationary, resuming its direct motion; sun enters Libra.

November

Mercury is lost in the evening twilight all month.

Venus, rising around 4 AM, local time, is nearly alone in the morning sky, but still the brightest planet anywhere.

Mars fades rapidly all month, managing to stay in Pisces.

Jupiter attains its greatest brilliancy, magnitude minus 2.9, at mid-month, still lying between the Pleiades and the Hyades, the two prominent star clusters in Taurus.

Saturn is still obvious in the southwestern twilight after sunset.

Moon occults Regulus on the 3rd, passes Venus on the 6th, occults Antares on the 11th, passes Uranus and Saturn on the 12th, Neptune on the 13th, Mars on the 19th, Jupiter on the 23rd, and occults Regulus again on the 30th.

Nov. 4—Pluto in conjunction with the sun.

Nov. 18—Leonid meteor shower best after moonset.

Nov. 22—Sun enters Scorpius.

Nov. 23—Jupiter at opposition.

Nov. 29—Sun enters Ophiuchus.

December

Mercury ends the year hidden by the glare of the sun.

Venus, rising around 5 in the morning, has begun its slide into the morning twilight, having given dawn and dusk nearly equal time this year.

Mars, fading fast but still bright, begins to move rapidly among the faint stars of eastern Pisces.

Jupiter is the only very bright planet left in our sky this month, still in its retrograde motion.

Saturn, having spent all year in our night sky, is now a difficult object in the southwest twilight at the beginning of the month, but is soon lost to the sun as it passes conjunction the day after Christmas.

Moon passes Venus on the 7th, Neptune on the 10th,

Mars on the 17th, Jupiter on the 20th, and occults Regulus on the 27th.

Dec. 1—Mercury in superior conjunction.

Dec. 14—Geminid meteor shower not hurt by the first quarter moon; watch for occasional fireballs.

Dec. 16—Sun enters Sagittarius.

Dec. 21—Winter solstice 15:28 GMT (20:28 AM EST); winter begins in the northern hemisphere, summer in the southern.

Dec. 22—Uranus in conjunction with the sun.

Dec. 26—Saturn in conjunction.

Dec. 31—Neptune in conjunction.

Planets and the Sun

The planets of the solar system, in order of their mean distance from the sun, are Mercury, Venus, Earth, Mars, Jupiter, Saturn, Uranus, Neptune and Pluto. Both Uranus and Neptune are visible through good field glasses, but Pluto is so distant and so small that only large telescopes or long exposure photographs can make it visible.

Since Mercury and Venus are nearer to the sun than is the earth, their motions about the sun are seen from the earth as wide swings first to one side of the sun and then to the other, although they are both passing continuously around the sun in orbits that are almost circular. When their passage takes them either between the earth and the sun, or beyond the sun as seen from the earth, they are invisible to us. Because of the laws which govern the motions of planets about the sun, both Mercury and Venus require much less time to pass between the earth and the sun than around the far side of the sun, so their periods of visibility and invisibility are unequal.

The planets that lie farther from the sun than does the earth may be seen for longer periods of time and are invisible only when they are so located in our sky that they rise and set about the same time as the sun when, of course, they are overwhelmed by the sun's great brilliance. None of the planets has any light of its own but each shines only by reflecting sunlight from its surface. Mercury and Venus, because they are between the earth and the sun, show phases very much as the moon does. The planets farther from the sun are always seen as full, although Mars does occasionally present a slightly gibbous phase — like the moon when not quite full.

The planets move rapidly among the stars because they are very much nearer to us. The stars are also in motion, some of them at tremendous speeds, but they are so far away that their motion does not change their apparent positions in the heavens sufficiently for anyone to perceive that change in a single lifetime. The very nearest star is about 7,000 times as far away as the most distant planet.

Planets of the Solar System

Mercury

Mercury, nearest planet to the sun, is the second smallest of the nine planets known to be orbiting the sun. Its diameter is 3,100 miles and its mean distance from the sun is 36,000,000 miles.

Mercury moves with great speed in its journey about the sun, averaging about 30 miles a second to complete its circuit in 88 of our days. Mercury rotates upon its axis over a period of nearly 59 days, thus exposing all of its surface periodically to the sun. It is believed that the surface passing before the sun may have a temperature of about 800° F., while the temperature on the side turned temporarily away from the sun does not fall as low as might be expected. This night temperature has been described by Russian astronomers as "room temperature" — possibly about 70°. This would contradict the former belief that Mercury did not possess an atmosphere, for some sort of atmosphere would be needed to retain the fierce solar radiation that strikes Mercury. A shallow but dense layer of carbon dioxide would produce the "greenhouse" effect, in which heat accumulated during exposure to the sun would not completely escape at night. The actual presence of a carbon dioxide atmosphere is in dispute. Other research, however, has indicated a nighttime temperature approaching −300°.

This uncertainty about conditions upon Mercury and its motion arise from its shorter angular distance from the sun as seen from the earth, for Mercury is always too much in line with the sun to be observed against a dark sky, but is always seen during either morning or evening twilight.

Mariner 10 made 3 passes by Mercury in 1974 and 1975. A large fraction of the surface was photographed from varying distances, revealing a degree of cratering similar to that of the moon. An atmosphere of hydrogen and helium may be made up of gases of the solar wind temporarily concentrated by the presence of Mercury. The discovery of a weak but permanent magnetic field was a surprise. It has been held that both a fluid core and rapid rotation were necessary for the generation of a planetary magnetic field. Mercury may demonstrate these conditions to be unnecessary, or the field may reveal something about the history of Mercury.

Venus

Venus, slightly smaller than the earth, moves about the sun at a mean distance of 67,000,000 miles in 225 of our days. Its synodical revolution — its return to the same relationship with the earth and the sun, which is a result of the combination of its own motion and that of the earth — is 584 days. Every 19 months, then, Venus will be nearer to the earth than any other planet of the solar system. The planet is covered with a dense, white, cloudy atmosphere that conceals whatever is below it. This same cloud reflects sunlight efficiently so that when Venus is favorably situated, it is the third brightest object in the sky, exceeded only by the sun and the moon.

Spectral analysis of sunlight reflected from Venus' cloud tops has shown features that can best be explained by identifying the material of the clouds as sulphuric acid (oil of vitriol). Infrared spectroscopy from a balloon-borne telescope nearly 20 miles above the earth's surface gave indications of a small amount of water vapor present in the same region of the atmosphere of Venus. In 1956, radio astronomers at the Naval Research Laboratories in Washington, D. C., found a temperature for Venus of about 600° F., in marked contrast to minus 125° F., previously found at the cloud tops. Subsequent radio work confirmed a high temperature and produced evidence for this temperature to be associated with the solid body of Venus. With this peculiarity in mind, space scientists devised experiments for the U.S. space probe Mariner 2 to perform when it flew by in 1962. Mariner 2 confirmed the high temperature and the fact that it pertained to the ground rather than to some special activity of the atmosphere. In addition, Mariner 2 was unable to detect any radiation belts similar to the earth's so-called Van Allen belts. Nor was it able to detect the existence of a magnetic field even as weak as 1/100,000 of that of the earth.

In 1967, a Russian space probe, Venera 4, and the American Mariner 5 arrived at Venus within a few hours of each other. Venera 4 was designed to allow an instrument package to land gently on the planet's surface via parachute. It ceased transmission of information in about 75 minutes when the temperature it read went above 500° F. After considerable controversy, it was agreed that it still had 20 miles to go to reach the surface. The U.S. probe, Mariner 5, went around the dark side of Venus at a distance of about 6,000 miles. Again, it detected no significant magnetic field but its radio signals passed to earth through Venus' atmosphere twice — once on the night side and once on the day side. The results are startling. Venus' atmosphere is nearly all carbon dioxide and must exert a pressure at the planet's surface of up to 100 times the earth's normal sea-level pressure of one atmosphere. Since the earth and Venus are about the same size, and were presumably formed at the same time by the same general process from the same mixture of chemical elements, one is faced with the question: which is the planet with the unusual history — earth or Venus?

Radar astronomers using powerful transmitters as well as sensitive receivers and computers have succeeded in determining the rotation period of Venus. It turns out to be 243 days clockwise — in other words, contrary to the spin of most of the other planets and to its own motion around the sun. If it were exactly 243.16 days, Venus would always present the same face toward the earth at every inferior conjunction. This rate and sense of rotation allows a "day" on Venus of 117.4 earth days. Any part of Venus will receive sunlight on its clouds for over 58 days and will be in darkness for 58 days. Recent radar observations have shown surface features below the clouds. Large craters, continent-sized highlands, and extensive, dry "ocean" basins have been identified.

Mariner 10 passed Venus before traveling on to Mercury in 1974. The carbon dioxide molecule found in such abundance in the atmosphere is rather opaque to certain ultraviolet wavelengths, enabling sensitive television cameras to take pictures of the Venusian cloud cover. Photos radioed to earth show a spiral pattern in the clouds from equator to the poles.

In December, 1978, two U. S. Pioneer probes arrived at Venus. One went into orbit about Venus, the other split into 5 separate probes targeted for widely-spaced entry points to sample different conditions. The instrumentation ensemble was selected on the basis of previous missions that had shown the range of conditions to be studied. The probes confirmed expected high surface temperatures and high winds aloft. Winds of about 200 miles per hour, there, may account for the transfer of heat into the night side in spite of the low rotation speed of the planet. Surface winds were light at the time, however. Atmosphere and cloud chemistries were examined in detail, providing much data for continued analysis. The probes detected 4 layers of clouds and more light on the surface than expected solely from sunlight. This light allowed Russian scientists to obtain at least two photos showing rocks on the surface. Sulphur seems to play a large role in the chemistry of Venus, and reactions involving sulphur may be responsible for the glow. To learn more about the weather and atmospheric circulation on Venus, the orbiter takes daily photos of the daylight side cloud cover. It confirms the cloud pattern and its circulation shown by Mariner 10. The ionosphere shows large variability. The orbiter's radar operates in 2 modes: one, for ground elevation variability, and the second for ground reflectivity in 2 dimensions, thus "imaging" the surface. Radar maps of the entire planet that show the features mentioned above have been produced.

Mars

Mars is the first planet beyond the earth, away from the sun. Mars' diameter is about 4,200 miles, although a determination of the radius and mass of Mars by the space-probe, Mariner 4, which flew by Mars on July 14, 1965 at a distance of less than 6,000 miles, indicated that these dimensions were slightly larger than had been previously estimated. While Mars' orbit is also nearly circular, it is somewhat more eccentric than the orbits of many of the other planets, and Mars is more than 30 million miles farther from the sun in some parts of its year than it is at others. Mars takes 687 of our days to make one circuit of the sun, traveling at about 15 miles a second. Mars rotates upon its axis in almost the same period of time that the earth does — 24 hours and 37 minutes. Mars' mean distance from the sun is 141 million miles, so that the temperature on Mars would be lower than that on the earth even if Mars' atmosphere were about the same as ours. The atmosphere is not, however, for Mariner 4 reported that atmospheric pressure on Mars is between 1% and 2% of the earth's atmospheric pressure. This thin atmosphere appears to be largely carbon dioxide. No evidence of free water was found.

There appears to be no magnetic field about Mars. This would eliminate the previous conception of a dangerous radiation belt around Mars. The same lack of a magnetic field would expose the surface of Mars to an influx of cosmic radiation about 100 times as intense as that on earth.

Deductions from years of telescopic observation indicate that 5/8ths of the surface of Mars is a desert of reddish rock, sand, and soil. The rest of Mars is covered by irregular patches that appear generally green in hues that change through the Martian year. These were formerly held to be some sort of primitive vegetation, but with the findings of Mariner 4 of a complete lack of water and oxygen, such growth does not appear possible. The nature of the green areas is now unknown. They may be regions covered with volcanic salts whose color changes with changing temperatures and atmospheric conditions, or they may be gray, rather than green. When large gray areas are placed beside large red areas, the gray areas will appear green to the eye.

Mars' axis of rotation is inclined from a vertical to the plane of its orbit about the sun by about 25° and therefore Mars has seasons as does the earth, except that the Martian seasons are longer because Mars' year is longer. White caps form about the winter pole of Mars, growing through the winter and shrinking in summer. These polar caps are now believed to be both water ice and carbon dioxide ice. It is the carbon dioxide that is seen to come and go with the seasons. The water ice is apparently in many layers with dust between them, indicating climatic cycles.

The canals of Mars have become more of a mystery than they were before the voyage of Mariner 4. Markings forming a network of fine lines crossing much of the surface of Mars have been seen there by men who have devoted much time to the study of the planet, but no canals have shown clearly enough in previous photographs to be universally accepted. A few of the 21 photographs sent back to earth by Mariner 4 covered areas crossed by canals. The pictures show faint, ill-defined, broad, dark markings, but no positive identification of the nature of the markings.

Mariners 6 & 7 in 1969 sent back many more photographs of higher quality than those of the pioneering Mariner 4. These pictures showed cratering similar to the earlier views, but in addition showed 2 other types of terrain. Some regions seemed featureless for many square miles, but others were chaotic, showing high relief without apparent organization into mountain chains or craters.

Mariner 9, the first artificial body to be placed in an orbit about Mars, has transmitted over 10,000 photographs covering 100% of the planet's surface. Preliminary study of these photos and other data shows that Mars resembles no other planet we know. Using terrestrial terms, however, scientists describe features that seem to be clearly of volcanic origin. One of these features is Nix Olympica, (now called Olympus Mons), apparently a shield volcano whose caldera is over 50 miles wide, and whose outer slopes are over 300 miles in diameter, and which stands about 90,000 feet above the surrounding plain. Some features may have been produced by cracking (faulting) of the surface and the sliding of one region over or past another. Many craters seem to have been produced by impacting bodies such as may have come from the nearby asteroid belt. Features near the south pole may have been produced by glaciers that are no longer present. Flowing water, non-existent on Mars at the present time, probably carved canyons, one 10 times longer and 3 times deeper than the Grand Canyon.

Although the Russians landed a probe on the Martian surface, it transmitted for only 20 seconds. In 1976, the U.S. landed 2 Viking spacecraft on the Martian surface. The landers had devices aboard to perform chemical analyses of the soil in search of evidence of life. The results have been inconclusive. The 2 Viking orbiters have returned the best pictures yet of Martian topographic features. Many features can be explained only if Mars once had large quantities of flowing water.

Mars' position in its orbit and its speed around that orbit in relation to the earth's position and speed bring Mars fairly close to the earth on occasions about two years apart and then move Mars and the earth too far apart for accurate observation and photography. Every 15-17 years, the close approaches are especially favorable to close observation.

Mars has 2 satellites, discovered in 1877 by Asaph Hall. The outer satellite, Deimos, revolves around Mars in about 31 hours. The inner satellite, Phobos, whips around Mars in a little more than 7 hours, making 3 trips around the planet each Martian day. Mariner and Viking photos show these bodies to be irregularly shaped and pitted with numerous craters. Phobos also shows a system of linear grooves, each about 1/3-mile across and roughly parallel. Phobos measures about 8 by 12 miles and Deimos about 5 by 7.5 miles in size.

Jupiter

Jupiter is the largest of the planets. Its equatorial diameter is 88,000 miles, 11 times the diameter of the earth. Its polar diameter is about 6,000 miles shorter. This is an equilibrium condition resulting from the liquidity of the planet and its extremely rapid rate of rotation: a Jupiter day is only 10 earth hours long. For a planet this size, this rotational speed is amazing, and it moves a point on Jupiter's equator at a speed of 22,000 miles an hour, as compared with 1,000 miles an hour for a point on the earth's equator. Jupiter is at an average distance of 480 million miles from the sun and takes almost 12 of our years to make one complete circuit of the sun.

The only directly observable chemical constituents of Jupiter's atmosphere are methane (CH_4) and ammonia (NH_3), but it is reasonable to assume the same mixture of elements available to make Jupiter as to make the sun. This would mean a large fraction of hydrogen and helium must be present also, as well as water (H_2O). The temperature at the tops of the clouds may be about minus 260° F. The clouds are probably ammonia ice crystals, becoming ammonia droplets lower down. There may be a space before water ice crystals show up as clouds; in turn, these become water droplets near the bottom of the entire cloud layer. The total atmosphere may be only a few hundred miles in depth, pulled down by the surface gravity (= 2.64 times earth's) to a relatively thin layer. Of course, the gases become denser with depth until they may turn into a slush or a slurry. Perhaps there is no surface — no real interface between the gaseous atmosphere and the body of Jupiter. Pioneers 10 and 11 provided evidence for considering Jupiter to be almost entirely liquid hydrogen. Long before a rocky core about the size of the earth is reached, hydrogen mixed with helium becomes a liquid metal at very high temperature and pressure. Jupiter's cloudy atmosphere is a fairly good reflector of sunlight and makes it appear far brighter than any of the stars.

Fourteen of Jupiter's 17 or more satellites have been found through earth-based observations. Four of the moons are large and bright, rivaling our own moon and the planet Mercury in diameter, and may be seen through a field glass. They move rapidly around Jupiter and their change of position from night to night is extremely interesting to watch. The other satellites are much smaller and in all but one instance much farther from Jupiter and cannot be seen except through powerful telescopes. The 4 outermost satellites are revolving around Jupiter clockwise as seen from the north, contrary to the motions of the great majority of the satellites in the solar system and to the direction of revolution of the planets around the sun. The reason for this retrograde motion is not known, but one theory is that Jupiter's tremendous gravitational power may have captured 4 of the minor planets or asteroids that move about the sun between Mars and Jupiter, and that these would necessarily revolve backward. At the great distance of these bodies from Jupiter — some 14 million miles — direct motion would result in decay of the orbits, while retrograde orbits would be stable. Jupiter's mass is more than twice the mass of all the other planets put together, and accounts for Jupiter's tremendous gravitational field and so, probably, for its numerous satellites and its dense atmosphere.

In December, 1973, Pioneer 10 passed about 80,000 miles from the equator of Jupiter and was whipped into a path taking it out of our solar system in about 50 years, and beyond the system of planets, on June 13, 1983. In December, 1974, Pioneer 11 passed within 30,000 miles of Jupiter, moving roughly from south to north, over the poles.

Photographs from both encounters were useful at the time but were far surpassed by those of Voyagers I and II. Thousands of high resolution multi-color pictures show rapid variations of features both large and small. The Great Red Spot exhibits internal counterclockwise rotation. Much turbulence is seen in adjacent material passing north or south of it. The satellites Amalthea, Io, Europa, Ganymede, and Callisto were photographed, some in great detail. Each is individual and unique, with no similarities to other known planets or satellites. Io has active volcanoes that probably have ejected material into a doughnut-shaped ring enveloping its orbit about Jupiter. This is not to be confused with the thin flat disk-like ring closer to Jupiter's surface. Now that such a ring has been seen by the Voyagers, older uncertain observations from Earth can be reinterpreted as early sightings of this structure.

Saturn

Saturn, last of the planets visible to the unaided eye, is almost twice as far from the sun as Jupiter, almost 900 million miles. It is second in size to Jupiter but its mass is much smaller. Saturn's specific gravity is less than that of water. Its diameter is about 71,000 miles at the equator; its rotational speed spins it completely around in a little more than 10 hours, and its atmosphere is much like that of Jupiter, except that its temperature at the top of its cloud layer is at least 100° lower. At about 300° F. below zero, the ammonia would be frozen out of Saturn's clouds. The theoretical construction of Saturn resembles that of Jupiter; it is either all gas, or it has a small dense center surrounded by a layer of liquid and a deep atmosphere.

Until Pioneer 11 passed Saturn in September 1979 only 10 satellites of Saturn were known. Since that time, the situation is quite confused. Added to data interpretations from the fly-by are earth-based observations using new techniques while the rings were edge-on and virtually invisible. It was hoped that the Voyager I and II fly-bys would help sort out the system. It is now believed that Saturn has at least 22 satellites, some sharing orbits. The Saturn satellite system is still confused.

Saturn's ring system begins about 7,000 miles above the visible disk of Saturn, lying above its equator and extending about 35,000 miles into space. The diameter of the ring system visible from Earth is about 170,000 miles; the rings are estimated to be no thicker than 10 miles. In 1973, radar observation showed the ring particles to be large chunks of material averaging a meter on a side.

Voyager I and II observations showed the rings to be considerably more complex than had been believed, so much so that interpretation will take much time. To the untrained eye, the Voyager photographs could be mistaken for pictures of a colorful phonograph record.

Uranus

Voyager II, after passing Saturn in August 1981, headed for a rendezvous with Uranus culminating in a fly-by January 24, 1986. This encounter answered many questions, and raised others.

Uranus, discovered by Sir William Herschel on Mar. 13, 1781, lies at a distance of 1.8 billion miles from the sun, taking 84 years to make its circuit around our star. Uranus has a diameter of about 32,000 miles and spins once in some 16.8 hours, according to fly-by data. One of the most fascinating features of Uranus is how far it is tipped over. Its north pole lies 98° from being directly up and down to its orbit plane. Thus, its seasons are extreme. When the sun rises at the north pole, it stays up for 42 years; then it sets and the north pole will be in darkness (and winter) for 42 years.

The satellite system of Uranus, consisting of at least 15 moons, (the 5 largest having been known before the fly-by) have orbits lying in the plane of the planet's equator. In that plane there is also a complex of rings, 9 of which were discovered in 1978. Invisible from Earth, the 9 original rings were found by observers watching Uranus pass before a star. As they waited, they saw their photoelectric equipment register several short eclipses of the star. Then the planet occulted the star as expected. After the star came out from behind Uranus, the star winked out several more times. Subsequent observations and analyses indicated the 9 narrow, nearly opaque rings circling Uranus. Evidence from the Voyager II fly-by has shown the ring particles to be predominantly a yard or so in diameter.

In addition to the 10 new, very small satellites, Voyager II returned detailed photos of the 5 large satellites. As in the case of other satellites newly observed in the Voyager program, these bodies proved to be entirely different from each other and any others. Miranda has grooved markings, reminiscent of Jupiter's Ganymede, but often arranged in a chevron pattern. Ariel shows rifts and channels. Umbriel is extremely dark, prompting some observers to regard its surface as among the oldest in the system. Titania has rifts and fractures, but not the evidence of flow found on Ariel. Oberon's main feature is its surface saturated with craters, unrelieved by other formations.

The structure of Uranus is subject to some debate. Basically, however, it may have a rocky core surrounded by a thick icy mantle on top of which is a crust of hydrogen and helium that gradually becomes an atmosphere. Perhaps continued analysis of the wealth of data returned by Voyager II will shed some light on this problem.

Neptune

Neptune, currently the most distant planet from the sun (until 1999), lies at an average distance of 2.8 billion miles. Having a diameter of about 31,000 miles and a rotation period of 18.2 hours, it is a virtual twin of Uranus. It is significantly more dense than Uranus, however, and this increases the debate over its internal structure. Neptune circles the sun in 164 years in a nearly circular orbit.

Neptune has 3 satellites, the third being found in 1981. The largest, Triton, is in a retrograde orbit suggesting that it was captured rather than being co-eval with Neptune. Triton is sufficiently large to raise significant tides on Neptune which will one day, say 100 million years from now, cause Triton to come close enough to Neptune for it to be torn apart. Nereid was found in 1949, and is in a long looping orbit suggesting it, too, was captured. The orbit of the third body is under analysis at this writing. Observations made in 1968 but not interpreted until 1982 suggest that Neptune, too, has a ring system.

As with the other giant planets, Neptune is emitting more energy than it receives from the sun. These excesses are thought to be cooling from internal heat sources and from the heat of the formation of the planets.

Little is known of Neptune beyond its distance, but Voyager II, if all continues to operate, will send us pictures and observations in 1989.

Pluto

Although Pluto on the average stays about 3.6 billion miles from the sun, its orbit is so eccentric that it is now approaching its minimum distance of 2.7 billion miles, less than the current distance of Neptune. Thus Pluto, until 1999, is temporarily planet number 8 from the sun. At its mean distance, Pluto takes 247.7 years to circumnavigate the sun. Until recently that was about all that was known of Pluto.

About a century ago, a hypothetical planet was believed to lie beyond Neptune and Uranus. Little more than a guess, a mass of one Earth was assigned to the mysterious body and mathematical searches were begun. Amid some controversy about the validity of the predictive process, Pluto was found nearly where it was predicted to be. It was found by Clyde Tombaugh at the Lowell Observatory in Flagstaff, Ariz., in 1930.

At the U.S. Naval Observatory, also in Flagstaff, on July 2, 1978, James Christy obtained a photograph of Pluto that was distinctly elongated. Repeated observations of this shape and its variation were convincing evidence of the discovery of a satellite of Pluto. Now named Charon, it may be 500 miles across, at a distance of over 10,000 miles, and taking 6.4 days to move around Pluto, the same length of time Pluto takes to rotate once. Gravitational laws allow these interactions to give us the mass of Pluto as 0.0017 of the Earth and a diameter of 1,500 miles. This makes the density about the same as that of water.

It is now clear that Pluto, the body found by Tombaugh, could not have influenced Neptune and Uranus to go astray. Theorists are again at work looking for a new planet X.

Greenwich Sidereal Time for 0^h GMT, 1988

(Add 12 hours to obtain Right Ascension of Mean Sun)

Date		h	m	Date		h	m	Date		h	m	Date		h	m
Jan.	1	06	39.5	Apr.	10	13	13.8	July	9	19	08.6	Oct.	7	01	03.4
	11	07	18.9		20	13	53.2		19	19	48.0		17	01	42.9
	21	07	58.4		30	14	32.6		29	20	27.4		27	02	22.3
	31	08	37.7	May	10	15	12.0	Aug.	8	21	06.9	Nov.	6	03	01.7
Feb.	10	09	17.6		20	15	51.5		18	21	46.3		16	03	41.1
	20	09	56.6		30	16	30.9		28	22	25.7		26	04	20.6
Mar.	1	10	36.1	June	9	17	10.3	Sept.	7	23	05.1	Dec.	6	05	00.0
	11	11	15.5		19	17	49.7		17	23	44.6		16	05	39.4
	21	11	54.9		29	18	29.2		27	00	24.0		26	06	18.8
	31	12	34.3												

Astronomical Signs and Symbols

☉	The Sun	⊕	The Earth	♅	Uranus	□	Quadrature
☾	The Moon	♂	Mars	♆	Neptune	☍	Opposition
☿	Mercury	♃	Jupiter	♇	Pluto	☊	Ascending Node
♀	Venus	♄	Saturn	☌	Conjunction	☋	Descending Node

Two heavenly bodies are in "conjunction" (☌) when they are due north and south of each other, either in Right Ascension (with respect to the north celestial pole) or in Celestial Longitude (with respect to the north ecliptic pole). If the bodies are seen near each other, they will rise and set at nearly the same time. They are in "opposition" (☍) when their Right Ascensions differ by exactly 12 hours, or their Celestial Longitudes differ by 180°. One of the two objects in opposition will rise while the other is setting. "Quadrature" (□) refers to the arrangement when the coordinates of two bodies differ by exactly 90°. These terms may refer to the relative positions of any two bodies as seen from the earth, but one of the bodies is so frequently the sun that mention of the sun is omitted; otherwise both bodies are named. The geocentric angular separation between sun and object is termed "elongation." Elongation is limited only for Mercury and Venus; the "greatest elongation" for each of these bodies is noted in the appropriate tables and is approximately the time for longest observation. When a planet is in its "ascending" (☊) or "descending" (☋) node, it is passing northward or southward, respectively, through the plane of the earth's orbit, across the celestial circle called the ecliptic. The term "perihelion" means nearest to the sun, and "aphelion," farthest from the sun. An "occultation" of a planet or star is an eclipse of it by some other body, usually the moon.

Planetary Configurations, 1988

Greenwich Mean Time (0 designates midnight; 12 designates noon; * = star; ☽ = moon)

Mo.	D. h. m.		
Jan.	4 00	-	⊕ at Perihelion (Earth)
	12 12	- ☌ ☽ *	Spica 0°.4 N, Occ'n
	15 16	- ☌ ☽ ♂	♂ 5° N (Mars)
	15 23	- ☌ ☽ *	Antares 0°.3 N, Occ'n

Mo.	D. h. m.		
	17 04	- ☌ ☽ ♄	♄ 6° N (Saturn)
	17 06	- ☌ ☽ ♆	♆ 5° N (Uranus)
	17 21	- ☌ ☽ ♆	♆ 6° N (Neptune)
	20 09	- ☌ ☽ ☿	☿ 2° N (Mercury)
	21 19	- ☌ ☽ ♀	♀ 0°.07 N, Occ'n (Venus)
	21 22	- ☌ ♂ *	♂ 5° N of Antares
	25 02	- ☌ ☽ ♃	♃ 4° S (Jupiter)
	26 17	-	☿ Gr Elong 19° E of ☉ (Sun)
Feb.	1 16	-	☿ stationary
	8 19	- ☌ ☽ *	Spica 0°.7 N Occ'n
	11 04	- ☌ ☿ ☉	Inferior
	12 08	- ☌ ☽ *	Antares 0°.5 N, Occ'n
	13 01	- ☌ ♄ ♅	♄ 1°.3 N
	13 09	- ☌ ☽ ♂	♂ 5° N
	13 19	- ☌ ☽ ♄	♄ 6° N
	13 19	- ☌ ☽ ♅	♅ 5° N
	14 09	- ☌ ☽ ♆	♆ 6° N
	18 23	-	♇ stationary (Pluto)
	20 17	- ☌ ☽ ♀	♀ 1°.9 S
	21 18	- ☌ ☽ ♃	♃ 4° S
	22 21	- ☌ ♂ ♅	♂ 0°.01 N
	23 04	-	☿ stationary
	23 13	- ☌ ♂ ♃	♂ 1°.3 S
Mar.	3 16	-	Partial Lunar Eclipse
	6 20	- ☌ ♀ ♄	♀ 2° N
	7 01	- ☌ ☽ *	Spica 0°.7 N, Occ'n
	7 22	- ☌ ☽ ♆	♂ 1°.4 S
	8 06	-	☿ Gr Elong 27° W of ☉
	10 15	- ☌ ☽ *	Antares 0°.6 N, Occ'n
	12 04	- ☌ ☽ ♅	♅ 5° N
	12 06	- ☌ ☽ ♄	♄ 6° N
	12 19	- ☌ ☽ ♆	♆ 6° N
	13 00	- ☌ ☽ ♂	♂ 5° N
	16 05	- ☌ ☽ ☿	☿ 0°.5 N, Occ'n
	18 02	-	Total Solar Eclipse
	20 09 39		Vernal Equinox; Spring begins, N Hemisphere
	20 14	- ☌ ☽ ♄	♄ 5° S
	21 12	- ☌ ☽ ♀	♀ 2° S
Apr.	3 07	- ☌ ☽ *	Spica 0°.7 N, Occ'n
	3 08	-	♀ Gr Elong 46° E of ☉
	4 19	-	♅ stationary
	6 20	- ☌ ☽ *	Antares 0°.5 N, Occ'n
	8 10	- ☌ ☽ ♅	♅ 5° N
	8 13	- ☌ ☽ ♄	♄ 6° N
	9 01	- ☌ ☽ ♆	♆ 6° N
	10 15	- ☌ ☽ ♂	♂ 3° N
	11 02	-	♄ stationary
	11 12	-	♆ stationary
	15 14	- ☌ ☽ *	♀ 10° N of Aldebaran
	20 00	- ☌ ☽ ♀	♀ 1°.0 S, Occ'n
	20 15	- ☌ ☿ ☉	superior
	30 14	- ☌ ☽ *	Spica 0°.7 N, Occ'n
May	1 09	- ☍ ♇ ☉	
	2 21	- ☌ ♄ ☉	
	4 02	- ☌ ☽ *	Antares 0°.4 N, Occ'n
	5 15	- ☌ ☽ ♅	♅ 5° N
	5 17	- ☌ ☽ ♄	♄ 6° N
	6 07	- ☌ ☽ ♆	♆ 6° N
	6 20	-	♀ Gr Brilliancy
	9 06	- ☌ ☽ ♂	♂ 0°.8 N, Occ'n
	11 06	- ☌ ☿ *	☿ 8° N of Aldebaran
	17 17	- ☌ ☽ ☿	☿ 3° S
	18 13	- ☌ ☽ ♀	♀ 1°.2 S
	19 02		☿ Gr Elong 22° E of ☉
	22 13	-	♀ stationary
	27 23	- ☌ ☽ *	Spica 0°.8 N, Occ'n
	31 10	- ☌ ☽ *	Antares 0°.4 N, Occ'n
June	1 01	-	☿ stationary
	1 21	- ☌ ☽ ♅	♅ 5° N
	1 22	- ☌ ☽ ♄	♄ 6° N
	2 12	- ☌ ☽ ♆	♆ 6° N
	6 20	- ☌ ☽ ♂	♂ 2° S
	12 03	- ☌ ☽ ♄	♄ 6° S
	13 00	- ☌ ♀ ☉	Inferior
	13 04	- ☌ ☿ ☉	Inferior
	19 18	- ☌ ☽ *	Regulus 1°.2 S, Occ'n
	20 04	- ☍ ♅ ☉	
	20 09	- ☍ ♄ ☉	
	21 03 57		Summer Solstice; Summer begins; N Hemisphere
	24 08	- ☌ ☽ *	Spica 1°.1 N, Occ'n
	24 23	-	☿ stationary
	27 02	- ☌ ♄ ♅	♄ 1°.3 N
	27 19	- ☌ ☽ *	Antares 0°.4 N, Occ'n
	29 04	- ☌ ☽ ♄	♄ 6° N
	29 04	- ☌ ☽ ♅	♅ 5° N
	29 20	- ☌ ☽ ♆	♆ 6° N
	30 10	- ☍ ♆ ☉	
July	4 08	-	♀ stationary
	5 07	- ☌ ☽ ♂	♂ 5° S
	6 00	-	⊕ at Aphelion
	6 16	-	☿ Gr Elong 21° W of ☉
	9 19	- ☌ ☽ ♄	♄ 6° S
	11 01	- ☌ ☽ ♀	♀ 10° S
	12 04	- ☌ ☽ ☿	☿ 7° S
	17 01	- ☌ ☽ *	Regulus 1°.0 S, Occ'n
	19 18	-	♀ Gr Brilliancy
	25 05	- ☌ ☽ *	Antares 0°.6 N, Occ'n
	25 18	-	♇ Stationary
	26 11	- ☌ ☽ ♄	♄ 6° N
	26 12	- ☌ ☽ ♅	♅ 5° N
	27 05	- ☌ ☽ ♆	♆ 6° N
Aug.	2 11	- ☌ ☽ ♂	♂ 8° S
	3 04	- ☌ ☿ ☉	Superior
	6 08	- ☌ ☽ ♄	♄ 6° S
	8 12	- ☌ ☽ ♀	♀ 9° S
	21 14	- ☌ ☽ *	Antares 0°.7 N, Occ'n
	22 12	-	♀ Gr Elong 46° W of ☉
	22 19	- ☌ ☽ ♄	♄ 6° N
	22 21	- ☌ ☽ ♅	♅ 5° N
	23 14	- ☌ ☽ ♆	♆ 6° N
	26 23	-	♂ stationary
	27 11	-	Partial Lunar Eclipse
	30 03	- ☌ ☽ ♂	♂ 9° S
	30 11	-	♄ stationary
Sept.	2 08	- ☌ ☽ *	Venus 9° S of Pollux
	2 20	- ☌ ☽ ♄	♄ 6° S
	5 10	-	♅ stationary
	6 23	- ☌ ☽ ♀	♀ 6° S
	9 13	- ☌ ☽ *	Regulus 1°.0 S, Occ'n
	11 05	-	Annular Solar Eclipse
	13 16	- ☌ ☽ ☿	☿ 0°.6 N, Occ'n
	15 22	-	☿ Gr Elong 27° E of ☉
	17 21	- ☌ ☽ *	Antares 0°.7 N, Occ'n
	18 17	-	♆ stationary
	19 03	- ☌ ☽ ♄	♄ 6° N
	19 05	- ☌ ☽ ♅	♅ 5° N
	19 22	- ☌ ☽ ♆	♆ 6° N
	21 04	- ☌ ☿ *	☿ 1°.3 S of Spica
	22 03	-	♂ closest approach to ⊕
	22 19 29		Autumnal Equinox; Fall begins; N Hemisphere
	24 16	-	♄ stationary
	26 04	- ☌ ☽ ♂	♂ 7° S
	28 04	- ☍ ♂ ☉	
	28 21	-	☿ stationary
	30 05	- ☌ ☽ ♄	♄ 6° S
Oct.	4 08	- ☌ ♀ *	♀ 0°.2 S of Regulus
	5 18	- ☌ ☿ *	☿ 1°.2 S of Spica
	6 20	- ☌ ☽ *	Regulus 1°.0 S, Occ'n
	7 03	- ☌ ☽ ♀	♀ 0°.6 S, Occ'n
	11 07	- ☌ ☿ ☉	Inferior
	15 02	- ☌ ☽ *	Antares 0°.6 N, Occ'n
	16 12	- ☌ ☽ ♄	♄ 6° N
	16 12	- ☌ ☽ ♅	♅ 5° N
	17 05	- ☌ ☽ ♆	♆ 6° N
	18 02	- ☌ ♄ ♅	♄ 1°.1 N
	19 16	-	☿ stationary
	23 04	- ☌ ☽ ♂	♂ 5° S
	26 21	-	☿ Gr Elong 18° W of ☉
	27 12	- ☌ ☽ ♄	♄ 6° S
	30 14	-	♂ stationary
Nov.	1 07	- ☌ ☿ *	☿ 4° N of Spica
	3 03	- ☌ ☽ *	Regulus 0°.8 S, Occ'n
	4 17	- ☌ ♇ ☉	
	6 15	- ☌ ☽ ♀	♀ 5° N
	11 08	- ☌ ☽ *	Antares 0°.5 S, Occ'n

Mo.	D. h. m.	
	12 19	- ☌ ☽ ♅ ♅ 5° N
	12 21	- ☌ ☽ ♄ ♄ 6° N
	13 11	- ☌ ☽ ♆ ♆ 5° N
	17 04	- ☌ ♀ * ♀ 4° N at Spica
	19 16	- ☌ ☽ ♂ ♂ 3° S
	23 03	- ☍ ♄ ☉
	23 17	- ☌ ☽ ♄ ♄ 6° S
	30 11	- ☌ ☽ * Regulus 0°.5 S, Occ'n
Dec.	1 09	- ☌ ☿ ☉ Superior
	7 06	- ☌ ☽ ♀ ♀ 7° N
	10 20	- ☌ ☽ ♆ ♆ 5° N
	17 16	- ☌ ☽ ♂ ♂ 3° S
	20 09	- ☌ ☿ ♆ ☿ 3° S
	20 20	- ☌ ☽ ♄ ♄ 6° S
	21 15 28	Winter Solstice; Winter begins; N Hemisphere
	22 20	- ☌ ♅ ☉
	24 18	- ☌ ♀ * ♀ 6° N of Antares
	26 12	- ☌ ♄ ☉
	27 20	- ☌ ☽ * Regulus 0°.2 S, Occ'n
	31 09	- ☌ ♆ ☉

Rising and Setting of Planets, 1988

Greenwich Mean Time (0 designates midnight)

		20° N. Latitude		30° N. Latitude		40° N. Latitude		50° N. Latitude		60° N. Latitude	
		Rise	Set	Rise	Set	Rise	Set	Rise	Set	Rise	Set
						Venus, 1988					
Jan.	10	8:52	20:06	9:06	19:52	9:23	19:35	9:46	19:12	10:23	18:35
	20	8:52	20:20	9:02	20:11	9:14	19:59	9:30	19:43	9:55	19:18
	30	8:50	20:33	8:55	20:28	9:02	20:21	9:10	20:13	9:24	19:59
Feb.	9	8:47	20:44	8:47	20:43	8:48	20:43	8:49	20:41	8:51	20:40
	19	8:42	20:55	8:38	20:58	8:33	21:03	8:27	21:09	8:18	21:19
	29	8:37	21:05	8:29	21:13	8:19	21:23	8:05	21:37	7:43	21:58
Mar.	10	8:32	21:15	8:20	21:27	8:04	21:42	7:43	22:04	7:09	22:38
	20	8:28	21:24	8:12	21:40	7:51	22:01	7:22	22:30	6:35	23:17
	30	8:25	21:32	8:04	21:52	7:39	22:18	7:03	22:53	6:01	23:56
Apr.	9	8:21	21:38	7:58	22:01	7:29	23:31	6:47	23:13	5:28	0:31
	19	8:17	21:41	7:52	22:06	7:20	22:38	6:32	23:25	4:59	0:59
	29	8:09	21:37	7:43	22:03	7:09	22:37	6:19	23:27	4:35	1:11
May	9	7:55	21:23	7:29	21:50	6:55	22:24	6:04	23:14	4:17	1:01
	19	7:30	20:56	7:05	21:22	6:32	21:55	5:43	22:44	4:03	0:24
	29	6:51	20:12	6:26	20:36	5:56	21:07	5:10	21:52	3:43	23:19
June	8	5:56	19:10	5:34	19:32	5:06	19:59	4:27	20:39	3:15	21:51
	18	4:56	18:00	4:36	18:19	4:12	18:43	3:39	19:17	2:41	20:15
	28	4:02	16:59	3:45	17:16	3:24	17:37	2:55	18:06	2:06	18:55
July	8	3:22	16:16	3:06	16:32	2:46	16:52	2:19	17:19	1:33	18:04
	18	2:55	15:49	2:39	16:05	2:19	16:25	1:51	16:52	1:06	17:38
	28	2:37	15:34	2:21	15:50	2:00	16:11	1:31	16:40	0:44	17:27
Aug.	7	2:28	15:26	2:11	15:44	1:49	16:05	1:19	16:35	0:28	17:26
	17	2:25	15:24	2:07	15:42	1:45	16:04	1:14	16:35	0:22	17:27
	27	2:26	15:25	2:08	15:43	1:47	16:05	1:16	16:35	0:24	17:27
Sept.	6	2:31	15:28	2:15	15:44	1:54	16:05	1:25	16:34	0:37	17:22
	16	2:39	15:30	2:24	15:45	2:05	16:04	1:40	16:30	0:57	17:12
	26	2:49	15:32	2:36	15:44	2:20	16:00	1:59	16:22	1:24	16:56
Oct.	6	2:59	15:32	2:49	15:42	2:37	15:54	2:21	16:10	1:55	16:36
	16	3:10	15:32	3:04	15:38	2:56	15:46	2:46	15:57	2:29	16:13
	26	3:22	15:31	3:19	15:34	3:16	15:37	3:11	15:41	3:04	15:48
Nov.	5	3:34	15:30	3:35	15:28	3:36	15:27	3:38	15:25	3:41	15:22
	15	3:46	15:29	3:51	15:24	3:58	15:17	4:06	15:09	4:19	14:56
	25	4:00	15:29	4:09	15:20	4:20	15:09	4:35	14:54	4:58	14:30
Dec.	5	4:14	15:31	4:27	15:18	4:43	15:03	5:04	14:41	5:39	14:06
	15	4:30	15:36	4:46	15:20	5:06	15:00	5:34	14:32	6:20	13:46
	25	4:47	15:44	5:06	15:25	5:29	15:01	6:02	14:28	6:59	13:31
						Mars, 1988					
Jan.	10	3:11	14:10	3:29	13:52	3:51	13:29	4:23	12:58	5:16	12:04
	20	3:02	13:56	3:21	13:37	3:45	13:13	4:20	12:38	5:19	11:39
	30	2:52	13:44	3:13	13:23	3:39	12:57	4:15	12:21	5:20	11:16
Feb.	9	2:43	13:32	3:04	13:10	3:31	12:44	4:10	12:05	5:18	10:57
	19	2:34	13:21	2:55	12:59	3:23	12:32	4:02	11:52	5:13	10:41
	29	2:24	13:11	2:46	12:49	3:13	12:21	3:53	11:41	5:04	10:30
Mar.	10	2:14	13:01	2:35	12:39	3:02	12:12	3:41	11:33	4:52	10:23
	20	2:02	12:52	2:23	12:31	2:50	12:04	3:28	11:26	4:35	10:19
	30	1:50	12:43	2:11	12:23	2:36	11:57	3:12	11:21	4:14	10:19
Apr.	9	1:38	12:34	1:57	12:15	2:20	11:51	2:54	11:18	3:51	10:20
	19	1:24	12:25	1:41	12:07	2:03	11:45	2:34	11:15	3:24	10:23
	29	1:09	12:15	1:25	11:59	1:45	11:39	2:13	11:12	2:58	10:26
May	9	0:53	12:05	1:08	11:51	1:25	11:33	1:50	11:09	2:29	10:29
	19	0:37	11:55	0:49	11:42	1:05	11:27	1:26	11:05	2:00	10:32
	29	0:19	11:43	0:30	11:32	0:43	11:19	1:01	11:01	1:29	10:33
June	8	0:01	11:31	0:09	11:22	0:20	11:11	0:35	10:56	0:58	10:33
	18	23:41	11:17	23:48	11:10	23:57	11:01	0:09	10:49	0:27	10:31
	28	23:20	11:02	23:25	10:56	23:32	10:49	23:41	10:40	23:55	10:26
July	8	22:58	10:44	23:02	10:40	23:07	10:36	23:13	10:29	23:23	10:19
	18	22:34	10:25	22:36	10:22	22:40	10:19	22:44	10:15	22:51	10:08
	28	22:08	10:02	22:09	10:01	22:11	9:59	22:14	9:56	22:18	9:52
Aug.	7	21:39	9:36	21:39	9:35	21:40	9:34	21:42	9:33	21:44	9:31
	17	21:06	9:05	21:06	9:04	21:07	9:04	21:07	9:04	21:08	9:03
	27	20:29	8:28	20:29	8:28	20:30	8:28	20:30	8:27	20:31	8:26
Sept.	6	19:47	7:46	19:48	7:45	19:49	7:44	19:50	7:43	19:51	7:42
	16	19:01	6:57	19:02	6:56	19:04	6:55	19:05	6:53	19:08	6:51
	26	18:12	6:06	18:13	6:04	18:16	6:02	18:18	5:59	18:23	5:55
Oct.	6	17:22	5:14	17:24	5:12	17:26	5:10	17:30	5:06	17:35	5:01
	16	16:33	4:26	16:36	4:23	16:38	4:21	16:42	4:17	16:48	4:11
	26	15:49	3:42	15:51	3:40	15:53	3:37	15:56	3:34	16:02	3:29

		20° N. Latitude		30° N. Latitude		40° N. Latitude		50° N. Latitude		60° N. Latitude	
		Rise	Set	Rise	Set	Rise	Set	Rise	Set	Rise	Set
Nov.	5	15:08	3:04	15:10	3:03	15:11	3:01	15:13	2:59	15:17	2:55
	15	14:32	2:31	14:32	2:31	14:33	2:30	14:33	2:30	14:34	2:29
	25	13:59	2:03	13:58	2:04	13:57	2:05	13:55	2:07	13:53	2:09
Dec.	5	13:29	1:38	13:27	1:40	13:24	1:43	13:20	1:48	13:13	1:54
	15	13:02	1:16	12:58	1:20	12:52	1:25	12:46	1:32	12:35	1:43
						Jupiter, 1988					
Jan.	10	11:54	0:14	11:48	0:20	11:40	0:28	11:30	0:38	11:15	0:53
	20	11:17	23:39	11:11	23:45	11:03	23:53	10:53	0:04	10:36	0:20
	30	10:42	23:05	10:35	23:12	10:27	23:20	10:15	23:32	9:58	23:49
Feb.	9	10:07	22:32	10:00	22:40	9:51	22:49	9:39	23:01	9:20	23:20
	19	9:33	22:00	9:25	22:08	9:16	22:18	9:02	22:31	8:42	22:52
	29	9:00	21:29	8:51	21:37	8:41	21:48	8:26	22:02	8:04	22:24
Mar.	10	8:27	20:58	8:18	21:07	8:06	21:19	7:51	21:34	7:27	21:58
	20	7:55	20:28	7:45	20:38	7:32	20:50	7:16	21:07	6:50	21:33
	30	7:23	19:59	7:12	20:09	6:59	20:22	6:41	20:40	6:13	21:08
Apr.	9	6:51	19:29	6:40	19:41	6:26	19:55	6:06	20:14	5:36	20:44
	19	6:19	19:00	6:07	19:12	5:52	19:27	5:32	19:47	5:00	20:20
	29	5:48	18:31	5:35	18:44	5:20	19:00	4:58	19:21	4:23	19:56
May	9	5:17	18:02	5:04	18:16	4:47	18:32	4:24	18:55	3:47	19:32
	19	4:46	17:33	4:32	17:48	4:14	18:05	3:50	18:29	3:11	19:08
	29	4:15	17:04	4:00	17:19	3:42	17:37	3:17	18:03	2:36	18:44
June	8	3:44	16:35	3:28	16:50	3:09	17:09	2:43	17:36	2:00	18:45
	18	3:12	16:06	2:56	16:21	2:37	16:41	2:09	17:08	1:24	17:53
	28	2:41	15:36	2:24	15:52	2:04	16:12	1:36	16:41	0:40	17:27
July	8	2:09	15:05	1:52	15:22	1:31	15:43	1:02	16:12	0:13	17:00
	18	1:36	14:34	1:19	14:51	0:58	15:13	0:28	15:43	23:38	16:33
	28	1:03	14:02	0:46	14:20	0:24	14:42	23:53	15:12	23:02	16:04
Aug.	7	0:30	13:30	0:12	13:47	23:49	14:10	23:18	14:41	22:26	15:33
	17	23:55	12:56	23:37	13:14	23:14	13:37	22:43	14:08	21:50	15:02
	27	23:20	12:21	23:02	12:39	22:39	13:02	22:07	13:34	21:13	14:28
Sept.	6	22:43	11:45	22:25	12:03	22:02	12:26	21:30	12:59	20:35	13:53
	16	22:06	11:08	21:47	11:26	21:24	11:49	20:52	12:21	19:57	13:16
	26	21:27	10:29	21:08	10:47	20:45	11:10	20:13	11:42	19:18	12:37
Oct.	6	20:46	9:48	20:28	10:07	20:05	10:30	19:33	11:02	18:38	11:56
	16	20:05	9:06	19:47	9:25	19:24	9:47	18:52	10:20	17:58	11:14
	26	19:22	8:23	19:04	8:41	18:42	9:04	18:10	9:36	17:16	10:29
Nov.	5	18:39	7:39	18:21	7:57	17:58	8:19	17:27	8:50	16:34	9:43
	15	17:54	6:54	17:37	7:11	17:15	7:33	16:44	8:04	15:52	8:56
	25	17:10	6:08	16:52	6:26	16:30	6:47	16:00	7:18	15:09	8:08
Dec.	5	16:25	5:23	16:08	5:40	15:46	6:01	15:17	6:31	14:27	7:21
	15	15:41	4:38	15:24	4:55	15:03	5:16	14:34	5:45	13:45	6:34
						Saturn, 1988					
Jan.	10	5:04	15:56	5:25	15:35	5:50	15:09	6:27	14:33	7:31	13:29
	20	4:30	15:21	4:50	15:00	5:16	14:35	5:52	13:58	6:56	12:54
	30	3:55	14:46	4:15	14:25	4:41	14:00	5:17	13:23	6:22	12:19
Feb.	9	3:19	14:10	3:40	13:50	4:06	13:24	4:42	12:48	5:46	11:43
	19	2:43	13:35	3:04	13:14	3:30	12:48	4:06	12:12	5:10	11:08
	29	2.07	12.58	2.28	12.38	2.53	12:12	3:30	11:36	4:34	10:32
Mar.	10	1:30	12:22	1:51	12:01	2:16	11:35	2:53	10:59	3:57	9:55
	20	0:53	11:44	1:13	11:24	1:39	10:58	2:15	10:21	3:19	9:17
	30	0:14	11:06	0:35	10:45	1:01	10:20	1:37	9:43	2:41	8:39
Apr.	9	23:36	10:27	23:56	10:06	0:22	9:41	0.58	9.04	2:02	8:00
	19	22:56	9:47	23:16	9:27	23:42	9:01	0:18	8:25	1:22	7:21
	29	22:16	9:07	22:36	8:47	23:02	8:21	23:38	7:44	0:42	6:41
May	9	21:35	8:26	21:55	8:06	22:21	7:40	22:57	7:03	0:01	6:00
	19	20:53	7:44	21:13	7:24	21:39	6:58	22:16	6:22	23:19	5:18
	29	20:11	7:02	20:31	6:42	20:57	6:16	21:34	5:40	22:38	4:36
June	8	19:29	6:20	19:49	6:00	20:15	5:34	20:51	4:57	21:55	3:53
	18	18:46	5:37	19:07	5:17	19:32	4:51	20:09	4:15	21:13	3:11
	28	18:04	4:55	18:24	4:34	18:50	4:09	19:26	3:32	20:30	2:28
July	8	17:21	4:12	17:41	3:52	18:07	3:26	18:44	2:50	19:48	1:45
	18	16:39	3:30	16:59	3:10	17:25	2:44	18:02	2:07	19:06	1:03
	28	15:57	2:48	16:18	2:28	16:43	2:02	17:20	1:25	18:24	0:21
Aug.	7	15:16	2:07	15:36	1:46	16:02	1:21	16:39	0:44	17:43	23:40
	17	14:35	1:26	14:56	1:06	15:21	0:40	15:58	0:03	17:03	22:59
	27	13:55	0:46	14:16	0:26	14:42	0:00	15:18	23:23	16:23	22:18
Sept.	6	13:16	0:07	13:36	23:46	14:02	23:20	14:39	22:43	15:44	21:39
	16	12:37	23:28	12:58	23:07	13:24	22:42	14:01	22:05	15:06	21:00
	26	11:59	22:50	12:20	22:29	12:46	22:03	13:23	21:26	14:28	20:21
Oct.	6	11:22	22:13	11:43	21:52	12:09	21:26	12:46	20:49	13:51	19:44
	16	10:46	21:36	11:06	21:15	11:33	20:49	12:10	20:12	13:15	19:07
	26	10:10	21:00	10:30	21:39	10:57	20:13	11:34	19:36	12:39	18:30
Nov.	5	9:34	20:24	9:55	20:03	10:21	19:37	10:58	19:00	12:04	17:54
	15	8:59	19:49	9:20	19:28	9:46	19:02	10:23	18:25	11:29	17:19
	25	8:24	19:14	8:45	18:53	9:11	18:27	9:48	17:50	10:54	16:44
Dec.	5	7:49	18:40	8:10	18:19	8:37	17:52	9:14	17:15	10:20	16:09
	15	7:15	18:05	7:36	17:44	8:02	17:18	8:39	16:41	9:45	15:35

Moonrise Tonight

The idea of estimating the time of moonrise tonight may have scared you off in the past because you assumed that it involved a difficult and mysterious series of calculations. The actual process is quite easy to do, however, especially with the little pocket calculators that seem ubiquitous today. The first major step involves finding three numbers for your city ob-

(continued)

tained from the latitude and longitude figures listed on pages 218 to 219. If your city is not here, find the information from a map, atlas or other source. These answers are permanent and never need to be determined for that city again. You can write these numbers down and use them every year you stay in that city. The second step involves taking the correct four figures from the tables of moonrise and moonset for the date you want. The third major step involves adjusting this answer to standard time.

Let us determine the time the gibbous moon rises July 4, in Rapid City, South Dakota.

First, we determine the 3 numbers for Rapid City:

I. Latitude: 44°04′52″ north; Longitude: 103°13′11″ west from p. 219.

A. Convert the Lat. and Long. to decimal numbers:

Lat.

52″ ÷ 60 = 0.′8667
4′ + 0.′8667 = 4.′8667
4.′867 ÷ 60 = 0.°0811
44° + 0.°081 = 44.°0811 for the Lat.

Long.

11″ ÷ 60 = 0.′1883
13′ + 0.′1883 = 13.′1883
13.′1883 ÷ 60 = 0.°2197
103° + 0.°2197 = 103.°2197 for the Long.

B. Fraction between 40° and 50° that Rapid City lies:

50° − 40° = 10°
44.°08 − 40° = 4.°08
4.°08 ÷ 10° = 4.°408

C. Fraction of world that Rapid City lies to the west of Greenwich, England:

103.°22 ÷ 360 = 0.287

D. Correction from Local to Standard time:
(Standard time meridian for Pacific Time is 105°.)

105 − 103.°22 = 1.°78 east, or earlier than at the standard meridian by 4 minutes for each degree, thus 4 × 1.78 = 7.°12, or, in round numbers 7 minutes early.

E. These 4 numbers, 1A, 1B, 1C, 1D, are constants for Rapid City and never have to be calculated again.

II. Find time of moonrise for Rapid City's latitude:

A. From the calendar page 212, find

	40°	50°
July 4	22:49	22:52
July 5	23:13	23:06

B. What we want lies 0.408 (Ans. IB) times the difference between the times for 40° and 50°, added to the time for 40° for each date. This is the prorated, or proportioned, time of the event at each latitude.

For the 4th: 22:49 − 22:52 = +3 minutes; +3 × 0.41 = + 1.23, or plus 1 minute
For the 5th: 23:13 − 23:06 = −7 minutes; −7 × 0.41 = −2.87, or minus 3 minutes
July 4 22:49 + 1 = 22:50
July 5 23:13 − 3 = 23:10

C. Now take the proportion of the time between these 2 dates that happened while the earth turned from Greenwich, England, to Rapid City, South Dakota:

23:10 − 22:50 = 20 minutes; 20 × 0.287 (Ans. 1C) = 5.74 minutes, or 6 minutes.
22:50 + 6 = 22:56, the local time that the moon rises.

D. Now correct for the fact that it rises 7 minutes earlier (Ans 1D) at Rapid City than at the standard meridian:

22:56 − 7 = 22:49, or 10:49 PM CST

At this date, however, they are on daylight time, so add 1 hour:

10:49 + 1 = 11:49 PM CDT.

Star Tables

These tables include stars of visual magnitude 2.5 and brighter. Co-ordinates are for mid-1988. Where no parallax figures are given, the trigonometric parallax figure is smaller than the margin for error and the distance given is obtained by indirect methods. Stars of variable magnitude designated by v.

To find the time when the star is on meridian, subtract R.A.M.S. of the sun table on page 194 from the star's right ascension, first adding 24h to the latter, if necessary. Mark this result P.M., if less than 12h; but if greater than 12, subtract 12h and mark the remainder A.M.

Star	Magnitude	Parallax ″	Light yrs.	Right ascen. h. m.	Declination ° ′
α Andromedae (Alpheratz)	2.06	0.02	90	0 07.8	+29 02
β Cassiopeiae	2.27v	0.07	45	0 08.6	+59 05
α Phoenicis	2.39	0.04	93	0 25.7	−42 22
α Cassiopeiae (Schedir)	2.23	0.01	150	0 39.8	+56 28
β Ceti	2.04	0.06	57	0 43.0	−18 03
γ Cassiopeiae	2.47v	0.03	96	0 56.0	+60 39
β Andromedae	2.06	0.04	76	1 09.1	+35 34
α Eridani (Achernar)	0.46	0.02	118	1 37.3	−57 18
γ Andromedae	2.26		260	2 03.2	+42 16
α Arietis	2.00	0.04	76	2 06.5	+23 24
o Ceti	2.00v	0.01	103	2 18.8	−3 02
α Ursae Min. (Pole Star)	2.02v		680	2 19.8	+89 13
β Persei (Algol)	2.12v	0.03	105	3 07.4	+40 55
α Persei	1.80	0.03	570	3 23.5	+49 49
α Tauri (Aldebaran)	0.85v	0.05	68	4 35.3	+16 29
β Orionis (Rigel)	0.12v		900	5 14.0	−8 13
α Aurigae (Capella)	0.08	0.07	45	5 15.8	+45 59
γ Orionis (Bellatrix)	1.64	0.03	470	5 24.5	+6 20
β Tauri (El Nath)	1.65	0.02	300	5 25.6	+28 36
δ Orionis	2.23v		1500	5 31.5	−0 18
ε Orionis	1.70		1600	5 35.6	−1 13
ζ Orionis	2.05	0.02	1600	5 40.2	−1 57
κ Orionis	2.06	0.01	2100	5 47.2	−9 40
α Orionis (Betelgeuse)	0.50v		520	5 54.5	+7 24
β Aurigae	1.90	0.04	88	5 58.7	+44 57
β Canis Majoris	1.98	0.01	750	6 22.2	−17 57
α Carinae (Canopus)	−0.72	0.02	98	6 23.7	−52 41
γ Geminorum	1.93	0.03	105	6 37.0	+16 25
α Canis Majoris (Sirius)	−1.46	0.38	8.7	6 44.6	−16 42
ε Canis Majoris	1.50		680	6 58.2	−28 57
δ Canis Majoris	1.86		2100	7 07.9	−26 22
η Canis Majoris	2.44		2700	7 23.6	−29 17
α Geminorum (Castor)	1.99	0.07	45	7 33.9	+31 55
α Canis Minoris (Procyon)	0.38	0.29	11.3	7 38.7	+5 15
β Geminorum (Pollux)	1.14	0.09	35	7 44.6	+28 03
ζ Puppis	2.25		2400	8 03.2	−39 58
γ Velorum	1.82		520	8 09.1	−47 18
ε Carinae	1.86		340	8 22.3	−59 28
δ Velorum	1.96	0.04	76	8 44.4	−54 40
λ Velorum	2.21	0.02	750	9 07.6	−43 23
β Carinae	1.68	0.04	86	9 13.1	−69 40
ι Carinae	2.25		750	9 16.8	−59 14
κ Velorum	2.50	0.01	470	9 21.8	−54 58
α Hydrae	1.98	0.02	94	9 27.0	−8 36
α Leonis (Regulus)	1.35	0.04	84	10 07.8	+12 01
γ Leonis	1.90	0.02	90	10 19.3	+19 54
β Ursae Majoris (Merak)	2.37	0.04	78	11 01.2	+56 27
α Ursae Majoris (Dubhe)	1.79	0.03	105	11 03.0	+61 49
β Leonis (Denebola)	2.14	0.08	43	11 48.5	+14 38
γ Ursae Majoris (Phecda)	2.44	0.02	90	11 53.2	+53 46
α Crucis	1.58		370	12 26.0	−63 02
γ Crucis	1.63		220	12 30.5	−57 03
γ Centauri	2.17		160	12 40.9	−48 54
β Crucis	1.25v		490	12 47.0	−59 38
ε Ursae Majoris (Alioth)	1.77v	0.01	68	12 53.5	+56 01
ζ Ursae Majoris (Mizar)	2.05	0.04	88	13 23.5	+54 59
α Virginis (Spica)	0.97v	0.02	220	13 24.6	−11 06
ε Centauri	2.30v		570	13 39.2	−53 24
η Ursae Majoris (Alkaid)	1.86		210	13 47.1	+49 22
β Centauri	0.61v	0.02	490	14 03.0	−60 19

Star	Magnitude	Parallax "	Light yrs.	Right ascen. h. m.	Declination ° ′
θ Centauri	2.06	0.06	55	14 06.0	−36 19
α Bootis (Arcturus)	−0.04	0.09	36	14 15.1	+19 15
η Centauri	2.31v		390	14 34.8	−42 06
α Centauri	−0.01	0.75	4.3	14 38.8	−60 47
α Lupi	2.30v		430	14 41.2	−47 20
ε Bootis	2.40	0.01	103	14 44.5	+27 07
β Ursae Minoris	2.08	0.03	105	14 50.7	+74 12
α Coronae Borealis	2.23v	0.04	76	15 34.2	+26 45
δ Scorpii	2.32		590	15 59.7	−22 35
α Scorpii (Antares)	0.96v	0.02	520	16 28.7	−26 24
α Trianguli Australis	1.92	0.02	82	16 47.4	−69 00
ε Scorpii	2.29	0.05	66	16 49.4	−34 16
η Ophiuchi	2.43	0.05	69	17 09.7	−15 43
λ Scorpii	1.63v		310	17 32.8	−37 06
α Ophiuchi	2.08	0.06	58	17 34.4	+12 34
θ Scorpii	1.87	0.02	650	17 36.5	−42 59
κ Scorpii	2.41v		470	17 41.7	−39 02
γ Draconis	2.23	0.02	108	17 56.3	+51 29
ε Sagittarii	1.85	0.02	124	18 23.4	−34 23
α Lyrae (Vega)	0.03	0.12	26.5	18 36.6	+38 46
σ Sagittarii	2.02		300	18 54.6	−26 19
α Aquilae (Altair)	0.77	0.20	16.5	19 50.2	+8 50
γ Cygni	2.20		750	20 21.8	+40 13
α Pavonis	1.94		310	20 24.7	−56 46
α Cygni (Deneb)	1.25		1600	20 41.0	+45 14
ε Cygni	2.46	0.04	74	20 45.7	+33 56
α Cephei	2.44	0.06	52	21 18.3	+62 32
ε Pegasi	2.39		780	21 43.6	+9 49
α Gruis	1.74	0.05	64	22 07.5	−47 01
β Gruis	2.11v		280	22 42.0	−46 57
α Piscis Austrinis (Fomalhaut)	1.16	0.14	22.6	22 57.0	−29 41
β Pegasi	2.42v	0.02	210	23 03.2	+28 01
α Pegasi	2.49	0.03	109	23 04.2	+15 09

Constellations

Culturally, constellations are imagined patterns among the stars that, in some cases, have been recognized through millenia of tradition. In the early days of astronomy, knowledge of the constellations was necessary in order to function as an astronomer. For today's astronomers, constellations are simply areas on the entire sky in which interesting objects await observation and interpretation.

Because western culture has prevailed in establishing modern science, equally viable and interesting constellations and celestial traditions of other cultures (of Asia or Africa, for example) are not well known outside of their regions of origin. Even the patterns with which we are most familiar today have undergone considerable change over the centuries, because the western heritage embraces teachings of cultures disparate in time as well as place.

Today, students of the sky the world over recognize 88 constellations that cover the entire celestial sphere. Many of these have their origins in ancient days; many are "modern," contrived out of unformed stars by astronomers a few centuries ago. Unformed stars were those usually too faint or inconveniently placed to be included in depicting the more prominent constellations. When astronomers began to travel to South Africa in the 16th and 17th centuries, they found a sky that itself was unformed, and showing numerous brilliant stars. Thus, we find constellations in the southern hemisphere like the "air pump," the "microscope," the "furnace," and other technological marvels of the time, as well as some arguably traditional forms, such as the "fly."

Many of the commonly recognized constellations had their origins in ancient Asia Minor—Syria, Babylon, etc. These were adopted by the Greeks and Romans who translated their names and stories into their own languages, some details being modified in the process. After the declines of these cultures, most such knowledge entered oral tradition, or remained hidden in monastic libraries. Beginning in the 8th century, the Moslem explosion spread through the Mediterranean world. Wherever possible, everything was translated into Arabic to be taught in the universities the Moslems established all over their new-found world.

In the 13th century, Alphonsus XX of Spain, an avid student of astronomy, succeeded in having Claudius Ptolemy's *Almagest*, as its Arabian title was known, translated into Latin. It thus became widely available to European scholars. In the process, the constellation names were translated, but the star names were retained in their Arabic forms. Transliterating Arabic into the Roman alphabet has never been an exact art, so many of the star names we use today only "seem" Arabic to all but scholars.

Names of stars often indicated what parts of the traditional figures they represented: Deneb, the tail of the swan; Betelgeuse, the armpit of the giant. Thus, the names were an indication of the position in the sky of a particular star, provided one recognized the traditional form of the mythic figure.

In English, usage of the Latin names for the constellations couples often inconceivable creatures, represented in unimaginable configurations, with names that often seem unintelligible. Avoiding traditional names, astronomers may designate the brighter stars in a constellation with Greek letters, usually in order of brightness. Thus, the "alpha star" is often the brightest star of that constellation. The "of" implies possession, so the genetive (possessive) form of the constellation name is used, as in Alpha Orionis, the first star of Orion (Betelgeuse). Astronomers usually use a 3 letter form for the constellation name, understanding it to be read as either the nominative or genitive case of the name.

Until the 1920's, astronomers used curved boundaries for the constellation areas. As these were rather arbitrary at best, the International Astronomical Union adopted boundaries that ran due north-south and east-west, filling the sky much as the contiguous states fill up the area of the "lower 48" United States.

Within these boundaries, and occasionally crossing them, popular "asterisms" are recognized: the Big Dipper is a small part of Ursa Major, the big bear; the Sickle is the traditional head and mane of Leo, the lion; one of the horntips of Taurus, the bull, properly belongs to Auriga, the charioteer; the northeast star of the Great Square of Pegasus is Alpha Andromedae.

It is unlikely that further change will occur in the realm of the celestial constellations.

Name	Genitive	Abbreviation	Meaning
Andromeda	Andromedae	And	Chained Maiden
Antlia	Antliae	Ant	Air Pump
Apus	Apodis	Aps	Bird of Paradise
Aquarius	Aquarii	Aqr	Water Bearer
Aquila	Aquilae	Aql	Eagle
Ara	Arae	Ara	Altar
Aries	Arietis	Ari	Ram
Auriga	Aurigae	Aur	Charioteer
Bootes	Bootis	Boo	Herdsmen
Caelum	Caeli	Cae	Chisel
Camelopardalis	Camelopardalis	Cam	Giraffe
Cancer	Cancri	Cnc	Crab
Canes Venatici	Canum Venaticorum	CVn	Hunting Dogs
Canis Major	Canis Majoris	CMa	Great Dog
Canis Minor	Canis Minoris	CMi	Little Dog
Capricornus	Capricorni	Cap	Sea-goat
Carina	Carinae	Car	Keel
Cassiopeia	Cassiopeiae	Cas	Queen
Centaurus	Centauri	Cen	Centaur
Cepheus	Cephei	Cep	King
Cetus	Ceti	Cet	Whale
Chamaeleon	Chamaeleontis	Cha	Chameleon
Circinus	Circini	Cir	Compasses (art)
Columba	Columbae	Col	Dove
Coma Berenices	Comae Berenices	Com	Berenice's Hair
Corona Australis	Coronae Australis	CrA	Southern Crown
Corona Borealis	Coronae Borealis	CrB	Northern Crown
Corvus	Corvi	Crv	Crow
Crater	Crateris	Crt	Cup
Crux	Crucis	Cru	Cross (southern)
Cygnus	Cygni	Cyg	Swan

(continued)

Name	Genitive	Abbreviation	Meaning
Delphinus	Delphini	Del	Dolphin
Dorado	Doradus	Dor	Goldfish
Draco	Draconis	Dra	Dragon
Equuleus	Equulei	Equ	Little Horse
Eridanus	Eridani	Eri	River
Fornax	Fornacis	For	Furnace
Gemini	Geminorum	Gem	Twins
Grus	Gruis	Gru	Crane (bird)
Hercules	Herculis	Her	Hercules
Horologium	Horologii	Hor	Clock
Hydra	Hydrae	Hya	Water Snake (female)
Hydrus	Hydri	Hyi	Water Snake (male)
Indus	Indi	Ind	Indian
Lacerta	Lacertae	Lac	Lizard
Leo	Leonis	Leo	Lion
Leo Minor	Leonis Minoris	LMi	Little Lion
Lepus	Leporis	Lep	Hare
Libra	Librae	Lib	Balance
Lupus	Lupi	Lup	Wolf
Lynx	Lyncis	Lyn	Lynx
Lyra	Lyrae	Lyr	Lyre
Mensa	Mensae	Men	Table Mountain
Microscopium	Microscopii	Mic	Microscope
Monoceros	Monocerotis	Mon	Unicorn
Musca	Muscae	Mus	Fly
Norma	Normae	Nor	Square (rule)
Octans	Octantis	Oct	Octant
Ophiuchus	Ophiuchi	Oph	Serpent Bearer
Orion	Orionis	Ori	Hunter
Pavo	Pavonis	Pav	Peacock
Pegasus	Pegasi	Peg	Flying Horse
Perseus	Persei	Per	Hero
Phoenix	Phoenicis	Phe	Phoenix
Pictor	Pictoris	Pic	Painter
Pisces	Piscium	Psc	Fishes
Piscis Austrinis	Piscis Austrini	PsA	Southern Fish
Puppis	Puppis	Pup	Stern (deck)
Pyxis	Pyxidis	Pyx	Compass (sea)
Reticulum	Reticuli	Ret	Reticle
Sagitta	Sagittae	Sge	Arrow
Sagittarius	Sagittarii	Sgr	Archer
Scorpius	Scorpii	Sco	Scorpion
Sculptor	Sculptoris	Scl	Sculptor
Scutum	Scuti	Sct	Shield
Serpens	Serpentis	Ser	Serpent
Sextans	Sextantis	Sex	Sextant
Taurus	Tauri	Tau	Bull
Telescopium	Telescopii	Tel	Telescope
Triangulum	Trianguli	Tri	Triangle
Tringulum Australe	Trianguli Australis	TrA	Southern Triangle
Tucana	Tucanae	Tuc	Toucan
Ursa Major	Ursae Majoris	UMa	Great Bear
Ursa Minor	Ursae Minoris	UMi	Little Bear
Vela	Velorum	Vel	Sail
Virgo	Virginis	Vir	Maiden
Volans	Volantis	Vol	Flying Fish
Vulpecula	Vulpeculae	Vul	Fox

Aurora Borealis and Aurora Australis

The Aurora Borealis, also called the Northern Lights, is a broad display of rather faint light in the northern skies at night. The Aurora Australis, a similar phenomenon, appears at the same time in southern skies. The aurora appears in a wide variety of forms. Sometimes it is seen as a quiet glow, almost foglike in character; sometimes as vertical streamers in which there may be considerable motion; sometimes as a series of luminous expanding arcs. There are many colors, with white, yellow, and red predominating.

The auroras are most vivid and most frequently seen at about 20 degrees from the magnetic poles, along the northern coast of the North American continent and the eastern part of the northern coast of Europe. They have been seen as far south as Key West and as far north as Australia and New Zealand, but rarely.

While the cause of the auroras is not known beyond question, there does seem to be a definite correlation between auroral displays and sun-spot activity. It is thought that atomic particles expelled from the sun by the forces that cause solar flares speed through space at velocities of 400 to 600 miles per second. These particles are entrapped by the earth's magnetic field, forming what are termed the Van Allen belts. The encounter of these clouds of the solar wind with the earth's magnetic field weakens the field so that previously trapped particles are allowed to impact the upper atmosphere. The collisions between solar and terrestrial atoms result in the glow in the upper atmosphere called the aurora. The glow may be vivid where the lines of magnetic force converge near the magnetic poles.

The auroral displays appear at heights ranging from 50 to about 600 miles and have given us a means of estimating the extent of the earth's atmosphere.

The auroras are often accompanied by magnetic storms whose forces, also guided by the lines of force of the earth's magnetic field, disrupt electrical communication.

Eclipses, 1988

(E.S.T.)

There are four eclipses, two of the sun and two of the moon.

1. Partial eclipse of the moon, March 3. The umbral phase lasts less than 14 minutes, and is visible in Asia, central and eastern Europe, northeast Africa, Wilkes Land of Antarctica, Australia, New Zealand, Alaska, Hawaii, the Arctic regions, the Indian Ocean and the west half of the Pacific Ocean.

Circumstances of the Eclipse

Moon enters penumbra	March	3	8:44 E.S.T.
Moon enters umbra		3	11:06
Middle of eclipse		3	11:13
Moon leaves umbra		3	11:20
Moon leaves penumbra		3	13:42

Magnitude of the eclipse, 0.003

2. Total eclipse of the sun, March 17. The partial phases of this eclipse are visible about dawn in most of India and south into the Indian Ocean, and about sunset in the Arctic regions north of eastern Siberia, all of Alaska, and parts of western Canada. The path of totality begins west of Sumatra, passes over Borneo, southern Philippines, across the Pacific south of the Aleutians, ending at sea. The maximum duration of totality is 3 minutes 51 seconds in the Pacific Ocean between Japan and New Guinea.

Circumstances of the Eclipse

Eclipse begins	March	17	18:24 E.S.T.
Central eclipse begins		17	19:24
Central eclipse at local noon		17	21:22
Central eclipse ends		17	22:32
Eclipse ends		17	23:32

3. Partial eclipse of the moon, August 27. The beginning of the umbral phase is visible on the east coast of Asia, most of Antarctica, Australia, New Zealand, the eastern half of South America, Central America, North America except east of Hudson's Bay, and the Pacific Ocean. The ending is visible in eastern Asia, most of Antarctica, Australia, New Zealand, northern Central America, central and western North America, and the Pacific Ocean.

Circumstances of the Eclipse

Moon enters penumbra	August	27	3:52 E.S.T.
Moon enters umbra		27	5:08
Middle of eclipse		27	6:04
Moon leaves umbra		27	7:02
Moon leaves penumbra		27	8:18

Magnitude of eclipse, 0.297

4. Annular eclipse of the sun, September 11-12. The partial phases of this eclipse are generally visible about dawn in eastern Africa and southern Arabian peninsula; during the

day in India, Southeast Asia, Indonesia, and most of Australia, the Indian Ocean, and parts of Antarctica; near sunset in New Zealand and parts of Antarctica. The path of central eclipse—annularity—begins on the equator at the eastern shore of Africa and runs solely over the Indian Ocean. Maximum duration of annularity is 6 minutes 52 seconds.

Circumstances of the Eclipse

Eclipse begins	September	11	20:46 E.S.T.
Central eclipse begins		11	21:59
Central eclipse at local noon		12	0:14
Central eclipse ends		12	1:28
Eclipse ends		12	2:41

The Planets and the Solar System

Planet	Mean daily motion "	Orbital velocity miles per sec.	Sidereal revolution days	Synodical revolution days	Dist. from sun in millions of mi. Max.	Min.	Dist. from Earth in millions of mi. Max.	Min.	Light at[1] perihelion	Light at[1] aphelion
Mercury . .	14732	29.75	88.0	115.9	43.4	28.6	136	50	10.58	4.59
Venus . . .	5768	21.76	224.7	583.9	67.7	66.8	161	25	1.94	1.89
Earth. . . .	3548	18.51	365.3	—	94.6	91.4	—	—	1.03	0.97
Mars	1886	14.99	687.0	779.9	155.0	128.5	248	35	0.524	0.360
Jupiter . . .	299	8.12	4332.1	398.9	507.0	460.6	600	368	0.0408	0.0336
Saturn . . .	120	5.99	10825.9	378.1	937.5	838.4	1031	745	0.01230	0.00984
Uranus. . .	42	4.23	30676.1	369.7	1859.7	1669.3	1953	1606	0.00300	0.00250
Neptune . .	21	3.38	59911.1	367.5	2821.7	2760.4	2915	2667	0.00114	0.00109
Pluto	14	2.95	90824.2	366.7	4551.4	2756.4	4644	2663	0.00114	0.00042

1. Light at perihelion and aphelion is solar illumination in units of mean illumination at Earth.

Planet	Mean longitude of:* ascending node °	'	"	perihelion °	'	"	Inclination* of orbit to ecliptic °	'	"	Mean* distance**	Eccentricity* of orbit	Mean longitude at the epoch* °	'	"
Mercury. . . .	48	11	46	77	16	48	7	00	17	0.387099	0.205629	211	23	37
Venus.	76	34	37	131	37	12	3	23	41	0.723327	0.006792	21	47	25
Earth	—	—	—	102	45	25	—	—	—	0.999999	0.016732	335	27	03
Mars	49	28	23	335	51	43	1	50	59	1.523652	0.093273	343	25	58
Jupiter	100	22	23	15	30	22	1	18	18	5.20316	0.048191	49	52	10
Saturn.	113	33	25	91	42	43	2	29	13	9.52355	0.054690	271	13	10
Uranus	73	58	52	169	15	36	0	46	21	19.1690	0.047313	264	35	32
Neptune . . .	131	40	48	43	57	36	1	46	13	30.0468	0.010382	280	07	11
Pluto	110	07	08	223	57	04	17	08	44	39.3395	0.246171	222	18	01

*Consistent for the standard Epoch: 1988 Aug. 27 Ephemeris Time **Astronomical units

Sun and planets	Semi-diameter at unit distance ' "	at mean least dist. ' "	in miles mean s.d.	Volume ⊕=1.	Mass. ⊕=1.	Density ⊕=1.	Sidereal period of rotation d.	h.	m.	s.	Gravity at surface ⊕=1.	Reflecting power Pct.	Probable temperature °F.
Sun	959.62	—	432560	1303730	332830	0.26	24	16	48		27.9	—	+ 10,000
Mercury . . .	3.37	5.5	1515	0.0559	0.0553	0.99	58	21	50		0.37	0.06	+ 620
Venus	8.34	30.1	3760	0.8541	0.8150	0.95	243	R			0.88	0.72	+ 900
Earth			3963	1.000	1.000	1.00		23	56	4.1	1.00	0.39	+ 72
Moon	2.40	932.4	1080	0.020	0.0123	0.62	27	7	43		0.17	0.07	− 10
Mars	4.69	8.95	2108.4	0.1506	0.1074	0.71		24	37	23	0.38	0.16	− 10
Jupiter	98.35	23.4	44362	1403	317.83	0.23		9	3	30	2.64	0.70	− 240
Saturn	80.80	0.7	37280	832	95.16	0.11		10	30		1.15	0.75	− 300
Uranus	35.4	1.9	15800	63	14.50	0.23		15	00	[illegible]	1.15	0.00	− 340
Neptune . . .	33.4	1.2	15100	55	17.20	0.31		18	26		1.12	0.82	− 370
Pluto*	1.9	0.05	930	0.01	0.0025	0.25	6	9	17		0.04	0.14	? ?

*Observers at the U.S. Naval Observatory have derived values similar to these after having discovered that Pluto has a satellite. It apparently revolves about Pluto in a period equal to Pluto's rotation period. (R) retrograde of Venus and Uranus.

Largest Telescopes Are in Northern Hemisphere

Most of the world's major astronomical installations are in the northern hemisphere, while many of astronomy's major problems are found in the southern sky. This imbalance has long been recognized and is being remedied.

In the northern hemisphere the largest reflector is the 236-inch mirror at the Special Astrophysical Observatory in the Caucasus in the Soviet Union. The largest reflectors in the U.S. include 3 in California: at Palomar Mtn., 200 inches; at Lick Observatory, Mt. Hamilton, 120 inches; and at Mt. Wilson Observatory, 100 inches. Also in the U.S. are a 158 inch reflector at Kitt Peak, Arizona, dedicated in June 1973, and a 107-inch telescope at the McDonald Observatory on Mt. Locke in Texas. A telescope at the Crimean Astrophysical Observatory in the Soviet Union has a 104-inch mirror.

Placed in service in 1975 were three large reflectors for the southern hemisphere. Associated Universities for Research in Astronomy (AURA), the operating organization of Kitt Peak National Observatory, dedicated the 158-inch reflector (twin of the telescope on Kitt Peak) at Cerro Tololo International Observatory, Chile; the European Southern Observatory has a 141-inch reflector at La Silla, Chile; and the Anglo-Australian telescope, 152 inches in diameter, is at Siding Spring Observatory in Australia.

Optical Telescopes

Optical astronomical telescopes are of two kinds, refracting and reflecting. In the first, light passes through a lens which brings the light rays into focus, where the image may be examined after being magnified by a second lens, the eye-piece, or directly photographed.

The reflector consists of a concave parabolic mirror, generally of Pyrex or now of a relatively heat insensitive material, cervit, coated with silver or aluminum, which reflects the light rays back toward the upper end of the telescope, where they are either magnified and observed by the eye-piece or, as in the case of the refractors, photographed. In most reflecting telescopes, the light is reflected again by a secondary mirror and comes to a focus after passing through a hole in the side of the telescope, where the eye-piece or camera is located, or after passing through a hole in the center of the primary mirror.

World's Largest Refractors

Location and diameter in inches

Yerkes Obs., Williams Bay, Wis.	40
Lick Obs., Mt. Hamilton, Cal.	36

(continued)

Astrophys. Obs., Potsdam, E. Germany	32
Paris Observatory, Meuden, France	32
Allegheny Obs., Pittsburgh, Pa.	30
Univ. of Paris, Nice, France	30
Royal Greenwich Obs., Herstmonceux, England	28
Union Obs., Johannesburg, South Africa	26.5
Universitats-Sternwarte, Vienna, Austria	26.5
Leander McCormick Obs., Univ. of Virginia, Charlottesville, Va.	26
Obs., Academy of Sciences, Pulkova, USSR	26
Astronomical Obs., Belgrade, Yugoslavia	26
Obs. Mitaka, Tokyo-to, Japan	26
US Naval Obs., Washington, D.C.	26
Mt. Stromlo Obs., Canberra, Australia	26

The Sun

The sun, the controlling body of our solar system, is a star whose dimensions cause it to be classified among stars as average in size, temperature, and brightness. Its proximity to the earth makes it appear to us as tremendously large and bright. A series of thermo-nuclear reactions involving the atoms of the elements of which it is composed produces the heat and light that make life possible on earth.

The sun has a diameter of 864,000 miles and is distant, on the average, 92,900,000 miles from the earth. It is 1.41 times as dense as water. The light of the sun reaches the earth in 499.012 seconds or slightly more than 8 minutes. The average solar surface temperature has been measured by several indirect methods which agree closely on a value of 6,000° Kelvin or about 10,000° F. The interior temperature of the sun is about 35,000,000 F.°.

When sunlight is analyzed with a spectroscope, it is found to consist of a continuous spectrum composed of all the colors of the rainbow in order, crossed by many dark lines. The "absorption lines" are produced by gaseous materials in the atmosphere of the sun. More than 60 of the natural terrestrial elements have been identified in the sun, all in gaseous form because of the intense heat of the sun.

Spheres and Corona

The radiating surface of the sun is called the **photosphere,** and just above it is the **chromosphere.** The chromosphere is visible to the naked eye only at times of total solar eclipses, appearing then to be a pinkish-violet layer with occasional great prominences projecting above its general level. With proper instruments the chromosphere can be seen or photographed whenever the sun is visible without waiting for a total eclipse. Above the chromosphere is the **corona,** also visible to the naked eye only at times of total eclipse. Instruments also permit the brighter portions of the corona to be studied whenever conditions are favorable. The pearly light of the corona surges millions of miles from the sun. Iron, nickel, and calcium are believed to be principal contributors to the composition of the corona, all in a state of extreme attenuation and high ionization that indicates temperatures on the order of a million degrees Fahrenheit.

Sunspots

There is an intimate connection between sunspots and the corona. At times of low sunspot activity, the fine streamers of the corona will be much longer above the sun's equator than over the polar regions of the sun, while during high sunspot activity, the corona extends fairly evenly outward from all regions of the sun, but to a much greater distance in space. Sunspots are dark, irregularly-shaped regions whose diameters may reach tens of thousands of miles. The average life of a sunspot group is from two to three weeks, but there have been groups that have lasted for more than a year, being carried repeatedly around as the sun rotated upon its axis. The record for the duration of a sunspot is 18 months. Sunspots reach a low point every 11.3 years, with a peak of activity occurring irregularly between two successive minima.

The sun is 400,000 times as bright as the full moon and gives the earth 6 million times as much light as do all the other stars put together. Actually, most of the stars that can be easily seen on any clear night are brighter than the sun.

The Zodiac

The sun's apparent yearly path among the stars is known as the **ecliptic.** The zone 16° wide, 8° on each side of the ecliptic, is known as the **zodiac.** Inside of this zone are the apparent paths of the sun, moon, earth, and major planets. Beginning at the point on the ecliptic which marks the position of the sun at the vernal equinox, and thence proceeding eastward, the zodiac is divided into twelve signs of 30° each, as shown herewith.

These signs are named from the twelve constellations of the zodiac with which the signs coincided in the time of the astronomer Hipparchus, about 2,000 years ago. Owing to the precession of the equinoxes, that is to say, to the retrograde motion of the equinoxes along the ecliptic, each sign in the zodiac has, in the course of 2,000 years, moved backward 30° into the constellation west of it; so that the sign Aries is now in the constellation Pisces, and so on. The vernal equinox will move from Pisces into Aquarius about the middle of the 26th century. The signs of the zodiac with their Latin and English names are as follows:

Spring	1.	♈ Aries.	The Ram.
	2.	♉ Taurus.	The Bull.
	3.	♊ Gemini.	The Twins.
Summer	4.	♋ Cancer.	The Crab.
	5.	♌ Leo.	The Lion.
	6.	♍ Virgo.	The Virgin.
Autumn	7.	♎ Libra.	The Balance.
	8.	♏ Scorpius.	The Scorpion.
	9.	♐ Sagittarius.	The Archer.
Winter	10.	♑ Capricorn.	The Goat.
	11.	♒ Aquarius.	The Water Bearer.
	12.	♓ Pisces.	The Fishes.

Moon's Perigee and Apogee, 1988

Perigee

Day	GMT	EST	Day	GMT	EST
Jan	19	21	July	30	08
Feb	17	10	Aug	27	17
Mar	16	20	Sept	25	04
Apr	13	23	Oct	23	12
May	10	22	Nov	20	10
June	5	00	Dec	16	04
July	2	06			

*Previous day

Apogee

Day	GMT	EST	Day	GMT	EST
Jan	7	6	July	18	00
Feb	3	10	Aug	14	12
Mar	1	12	Sept	10	15
Mar	29	00	Oct	07	20
Apr	25	19	Nov	4	11
May	23	14	Dec	2	06
June	20	08	Dec	30	04

Astronomical Constants; Speed of Light

The following were adopted in 1968, in accordance with the resolutions and recommendations of the International Astronomical Union (Hamburg 1964): Velocity of light, 299,792.5 kilometers per second, or about 186,282.3976 statute miles per second; solar parallax, 8″.794; constant of nutation, 9″.210; and constant of aberration, 20″.496.

The Moon

The moon completes a circuit around the earth in a period whose mean or average duration is 27 days 7 hours 43.2 minutes. This is the moon's sidereal period. Because of the motion of the moon in common with the earth around the sun, the mean duration of the lunar month — the period from one new moon to the next new moon — is 29 days 12 hours 44.05 minutes. This is the moon's synodical period.

The mean distance of the moon from the earth according to the American Ephemeris is 238,857 miles. Because the orbit of the moon about the earth is not circular but elliptical, however, the maximum distance from the earth that the moon may reach is 252,710 miles and the least distance is 221,463 miles. All distances are from the center of one object to the center of the other.

The moon's diameter is 2,160 miles. If we deduct the radius of the moon, 1,080 miles, and the radius of the earth, 3,963 miles from the minimum distance or perigee, given above, we shall have for the nearest approach of the bodies' surfaces 216,420 miles.

The moon rotates on its axis in a period of time exactly equal to its sidereal revolution about the earth — 27.321666 days. The moon's revolution about the earth is irregular because of its elliptical orbit. The moon's rotation, however, is regular and this, together with the irregular revolution, produces what is called "libration in longitude" which permits us to see first farther around the east side and then farther around the west side of the moon. The moon's variation north or south of the ecliptic permits us to see farther over first one pole and then the other of the moon and this is "libration in latitude." These two libration effects permit us to see a total of about 60% of the moon's surface over a period of time. The hidden side of the moon was photographed in 1959 by the Soviet space vehicle Lunik III. Since then many excellent pictures of nearly all of the moon's surface have been transmitted to earth by Lunar Orbiters launched by the U.S.

The tides are caused mainly by the moon, because of its proximity to the earth. The ratio of the tide-raising power of the moon to that of the sun is 11 to 5.

Harvest Moon and Hunter's Moon

The Harvest Moon, the full moon nearest the Autumnal Equinox, ushers in a period of several successive days when the moon rises soon after sunset. This phenomenon gives farmers in temperate latitudes extra hours of light in which to harvest their crops before frost and winter come. The 1988 Harvest Moon falls on Sept. 25 GMT. Harvest moon in the south temperate latitudes falls on Apr. 2.

The next full moon after Harvest Moon is called the Hunter's Moon, accompanied by a similar phenomenon but less marked; — Oct. 25, northern hemisphere; May 1, southern hemisphere.

The Earth: Size, Computation of Time, Seasons

Size and Dimensions

The earth is the fifth largest planet and the third from the sun. Its mass is 6 sextillion, 588 quintillion short tons. Using the parameters of an ellipsoid adopted by the International Astronomical Union in 1964 and recognized by the International Union of Geodesy and Geophysics in 1967, the length of the equator is 24,901.55 miles, the length of a meridian is 24,859.82 miles, the equatorial diameter is 7,926.41 miles, and the area of this reference ellipsoid is approximately 196,938,800 square miles.

The earth is considered a solid, rigid mass with a dense core of magnetic, probably metallic material. The outer part of the core is probably liquid. Around the core is a thick shell or mantle of heavy crystalline rock which in turn is covered by a thin crust forming the solid granite and basalt base of the continents and ocean basins. Over broad areas of the earth's surface the crust has a thin cover of sedimentary rock such as sandstone, shale, and limestone formed by weathering of the earth's surface and deposition of sands, clays, and plant and animal remains.

The temperature in the earth increases about 1°F. with every 100 to 200 feet in depth, in the upper 100 kilometers of the earth, and the temperature near the core is believed to be near the melting point of the core materials under the conditions at that depth. The heat of the earth is believed to be derived from radioactivity in the rocks, pressures developed within the earth, and original heat (if the earth in fact was formed at high temperatures).

Atmosphere of the Earth

The earth's atmosphere is a blanket composed of nitrogen, oxygen, and argon, in amounts of about 78, 21, and 1% by volume. Also present in minute quantities are carbon dioxide, hydrogen, neon, helium, krypton, and xenon.

Water vapor displaces other gases and varies from nearly zero to about 4% by volume. The height of the **ozone** layer varies from approximately 12 to 21 miles above the earth. Traces exist as low as 6 miles and as high as 35 miles. Traces of methane have been found.

The atmosphere rests on the earth's surface with the weight equivalent to a layer of water 34 ft. deep. For about 300,000 ft. upward the gases remain in the proportions stated. Gravity holds the gases to the earth. The weight of the air compresses it at the bottom, so that the greatest density is at the earth's surface. Pressure, as well as density, decreases as height increases because the weight pressing upon any layer is always less than that pressing upon the layers below.

The temperature of the air drops with increased height until the **tropopause** is reached. This may vary from 25,000 to 60,000 ft. The atmosphere below the tropopause is the **troposphere;** the atmosphere for about twenty miles above the tropopause is the **stratosphere,** where the temperature generally increases with height except at high latitudes in winter. A temperature maximum near the 30-mile level is called the **stratopause.** Above this boundary is the **mesosphere** where the temperature decreases with height to a minimum, the **mesopause,** at a height of 50 miles. Extending above the mesosphere to the outer fringes of the atmosphere is the **thermosphere,** a region where temperature increases with height to a value measured in thousands of degrees Fahrenheit. The lower portion of this region, extending from 50 to about 400 miles in altitude, is characterized by a high ion density, and is thus called the **ionosphere.** The outer region is called **exosphere;** this is the region where gas molecules traveling at high speed may escape into outer space, above 600 miles.

Latitude, Longitude

Position on the globe is measured by means of meridians and parallels. Meridians, which are imaginary lines drawn around the earth through the poles, determine **longitude.** The meridian running through Greenwich, England, is the **prime meridian of longitude,** and all others are either east or west. Parallels, which are imaginary circles parallel with the equator, determine **latitude.** The length of a degree of longitude varies as the cosine of the latitude. At the equator a degree is 69.171 statute miles; this is gradually reduced toward the poles. Value of a longitude degree at the poles is zero.

Latitude is reckoned by the number of degrees north or south of the equator, an imaginary circle on the earth's surface everywhere equidistant between the two poles. According to the IAU Ellipsoid of 1964, the length of a degree of latitude is 68.708 statute miles at the equator and varies slightly north and south because of the oblate form of the globe; at the poles it is 69.403 statute miles.

Computation of Time

The earth rotates on its axis and follows an elliptical orbit around the sun. The rotation makes the sun appear to move across the sky from East to West. It determines day and

(continued)

night and the complete rotation, in relation to the sun, is called the **apparent** or **true solar day.** This varies but an average determines the **mean solar day** of 24 hours.

The mean solar day is in universal use for civil purposes. It may be obtained from apparent solar time by correcting observations of the sun for the equation of time, but when high precision is required, the mean solar time is calculated from its relation to sidereal time. These relations are extremely complicated, but for most practical uses, they may be considered as follows:

Sidereal time is the measure of time defined by the diurnal motion of the vernal equinox, and is determined from observation of the meridian transits of stars. One complete rotation of the earth relative to the equinox is called the **sidereal day.** The **mean sidereal day** is 23 hours, 56 minutes, 4.091 seconds of mean solar time.

The **Calendar Year** begins at 12 o'clock midnight precisely local clock time, on the night of Dec. 31-Jan. 1. The day and the calendar month also begin at midnight by the clock. The interval required for the earth to make one absolute revolution around the sun is a **sidereal year;** it consisted of 365 days, 6 hours, 9 minutes, and 9.5 seconds of mean solar time (approximately 24 hours per day) in 1900, and is increasing at the rate of 0.0001-second annually.

The **Tropical Year,** on which the return of the seasons depends, is the interval between two consecutive returns of the sun to the vernal equinox. The tropical year consists of 365 days, 5 hours, 48 minutes, and 46 seconds in 1900. It is decreasing at the rate of 0.530 seconds per century.

In 1956 the unit of time interval was defined to be identical with the second of **Ephemeris Time,** 1/31,556,925.9747 of the tropical year for 1900 January Od 12th hour E.T. A physical definition of the second based on a quantum transition of cesium (atomic second) was adopted in 1964. The atomic second is equal to 9,192,631,770 cycles of the emitted radiation. In 1967 this atomic second was adopted as the unit of time interval for the Intern'l System of Units.

The Zones and Seasons

The five zones of the earth's surface are Torrid, lying between the Tropics of Cancer and Capricorn; North Temperate, between Cancer and the Arctic Circle; South Temperate, between Capricorn and the Antarctic Circle; The Frigid Zones, between the polar Circles and the Poles.

The inclination or tilt of the earth's axis with respect to the sun determines the seasons. These are commonly marked in the North Temperate Zone, where spring begins at the vernal equinox, summer at the summer solstice, autumn at the autumnal equinox and winter at the winter solstice.

In the South Temperate Zone, the seasons are reversed. Spring begins at the autumnal equinox, summer at the winter solstice, etc.

If the earth's axis were perpendicular to the plane of the earth's orbit around the sun there would be no change of seasons. Day and night would be of nearly constant length and there would be equable conditions of temperature. But the axis is tilted 23° 27′ away from a perpendicular to the orbit and only in March and September is the axis at right angles to the sun.

The points at which the sun crosses the equator are the equinoxes, when day and night are most nearly equal. The points at which the sun is at a maximum distance from the equator are the solstices. Days and nights are then most unequal.

In June the North Pole is tilted 23° 27′ toward the sun and the days in the northern hemisphere are longer than the nights, while the days in the southern hemisphere are shorter than the nights. In December the North Pole is tilted 23° 27′ away from the sun and the situation is reversed.

The Seasons in 1988

In 1988 the 4 seasons will begin as follows: add one hour to EST for Atlantic Time; subtract one hour for Central, two hours for Mountain, 3 hours for Pacific, 4 hours for Yukon, 5 hours for Alaska-Hawaii and six hours for Bering Time. Also shown in Greenwich Mean Time.

		Date	GMT	EST
Vernal Equinox	**Spring**	Mar. 20	09:39	04:39
Summer Solstice	**Summer**	June 21	03:57	22:57*
Autumnal Equinox	**Autumn**	Sept. 22	19:29	14:29
Winter Solstice	**Winter**	Dec. 21	15:28	10:28

*Previous Day

Poles of The Earth

The geographic (rotation) poles, or points where the earth's axis of rotation cuts the surface, are not absolutely fixed in the body of the earth. The pole of rotation describes an irregular curve about its mean position.

Two periods have been detected in this motion: (1) an annual period due to seasonal changes in barometric pressure, load of ice and snow on the surface and to other phenomena of seasonal character; (2) a period of about 14 months due to the shape and constitution of the earth.

In addition there are small but as yet unpredictable irregularities. The whole motion is so small that the actual pole at any time remains within a circle of 30 or 40 feet in radius centered at the mean position of the pole.

The pole of rotation for the time being is of course the pole having a latitude of 90° and an indeterminate longitude.

Magnetic Poles

The **north magnetic pole** of the earth is that region where the magnetic force is vertically downward and the **south magnetic pole** that region where the magnetic force is vertically upward. A compass placed at the magnetic poles experiences no directive force in azimuth.

There are slow changes in the distribution of the earth's magnetic field. These changes were at one time attributed in part to a periodic movement of the magnetic poles around the geographical poles, but later evidence refutes this theory and points, rather, to a slow migration of "disturbance" foci over the earth.

There appear shifts in position of the magnetic poles due to the changes in the earth's magnetic field. The center of the area designated as the north magnetic pole was estimated to be in about latitude 70.5° N and longitude 96° W in 1905; from recent nearby measurements and studies of the secular changes, the position in 1970 is estimated as latitude 76.2° N and longitude 101° W. Improved data rather than actual motion account for at least part of the change.

The position of the south magnetic pole in 1912 was near 71° S and longitude 150° E; the position in 1970 is estimated at latitude 66° S and longitude 139.1° E.

The direction of the horizontal components of the magnetic field at any point is known as magnetic north at that point, and the angle by which it deviates east or west of true north is known as the magnetic declination, or in the mariner's terminology, the **variation of the compass.**

A compass without error points in the direction of magnetic north. (In general this is *not* the direction of the magnetic north pole.) If one follows the direction indicated by the north end of the compass, he will travel along a rather irregular curve which eventually reaches the north magnetic pole (though not usually by a great-circle route). However, the action of the compass should not be thought of as due to any influence of the distant pole, but simply as an indication of the distribution of the earth's magnetism at the place of observation.

Rotation of The Earth

The speed of rotation of the earth about its axis has been found to be slightly variable. The variations may be classified as:

(A) **Secular.** Tidal friction acts as a brake on the rotation and causes a slow secular increase in the length of the day, about 1 millisecond per century.

(B) **Irregular.** The speed of rotation may increase for a number of years, about 5 to 10, and then start decreasing. The maximum difference from the mean in the length of the day during a century is about 5 milliseconds. The accumulated difference in time has amounted to approximately 44 seconds since 1900. The cause is probably motion in the interior of the earth.

(C) **Periodic.** Seasonal variations exist with periods of one year and six months. The cumulative effect is such that each year the earth is late about 30 milliseconds near June 1 and is ahead about 30 milliseconds near Oct. 1. The maximum seasonal variation in the length of the day is about 0.5 millisecond. It is believed that the principal cause of the annual variation is the seasonal change in the wind patterns of the Northern and Southern Hemispheres. The semiannual variation is due chiefly to tidal action of the sun, which distorts the shape of the earth slightly.

The secular and irregular variations were discovered by comparing time based on the rotation of the earth with time based on the orbital motion of the moon about the earth and of the planets about the sun. The periodic variation was determined largely with the aid of quartz-crystal clocks. The introduction of the cesium-beam atomic clock in 1955 made it possible to determine in greater detail than before the nature of the irregular and periodic variations.

Morning and Evening Stars 1988

(GMT)

	Morning	Evening
Jan.	Mars Saturn	Mercury Venus Jupiter
Feb.	Mercury (from 11) Mars Saturn	Mercury (to 11) Venus Jupiter
Mar.	Mercury Mars Saturn	Venus Jupiter
Apr.	Mercury (to 20) Mars Saturn	Mercury (from 20) Venus Jupiter
May	Mars Jupiter (from 2) Saturn	Mercury Venus Jupiter (to 2)
June	Mercury (from 13) Venus (from 13) Mars Jupiter Saturn (to 20)	Mercury (to 13) Venus (to 13) Saturn (from 20)
July	Mercury Venus Mars Jupiter	Saturn
Aug.	Mercury (to 3) Venus Mars Jupiter	Mercury (from 3) Saturn
Sept.	Venus Mars (to 28) Jupiter	Mercury Mars (from 28) Saturn
Oct.	Mercury (from 11) Venus Jupiter	Mercury (to 11) Mars Saturn
Nov.	Mercury Venus Jupiter (to 23)	Mars Jupiter (from 23) Saturn
Dec.	Mercury (to 1) Venus Saturn (from 26)	Mercury (from 1) Mars Jupiter Saturn (to 26)

Astronomical Twilight—Meridian of Greenwich

Date 1988	20°		30°		40°		50°		60°	
	Begin	End	Begin	End	Begin	End	Begin	End	Begin	End
	h m	h m	h m	h m	h m	h m	h m	h m	h m	h m
Jan. 1	5 16	6 50	5 30	6 35	5 45	6 21	6 00	6 07	6 10	5 40
11	5 19	6 56	5 33	6 43	5 46	6 30	6 00	6 17	6 15	6 01
21	5 21	7 01	5 32	6 51	5 43	6 40	5 55	6 30	6 06	6 18
Feb. 1	5 21	7 07	5 29	6 58	5 38	6 51	5 45	6 44	5 51	6 38
11	5 18	7 11	5 24	7 05	5 20	7 01	5 32	6 59	5 32	7 01
21	5 13	7 15	5 17	7 12	5 17	7 12	5 16	7 14	5 09	7 23
Mar. 1	5 08	7 18	5 08	7 19	5 06	7 21	4 59	7 29	4 44	7 45
11	5 00	7 21	4 58	7 24	4 50	7 32	4 38	7 46	4 12	8 12
21	4 52	7 24	4 45	7 32	4 33	7 44	4 14	8 04	3 37	8 43
Apr. 1	4 42	7 28	4 31	7 39	4 14	7 57	3 47	8 25	2 53	9 21
11	4 32	7 32	4 18	7 47	3 56	8 09	3 20	8 47	2 03	10 10
21	4 23	7 36	4 04	7 54	3 37	8 23	2 52	9 11	0 37	11 47
May 1	4 14	7 41	3 52	8 04	3 19	8 37	2 22	9 39		
11	4 08	7 46	3 41	8 13	3 03	8 53	1 49	10 09		
21	4 02	7 52	3 32	8 22	2 48	9 07	1 13	10 46		
June 1	3 58	7 58	3 26	8 30	2 36	9 20	0 21	11 52		
11	3 56	8 03	3 22	8 36	2 29	9 30				
21	3 57	8 06	3 22	8 40	2 28	9 35				
July 1	3 59	8 07	3 25	8 41	2 30	9 35				
11	4 03	8 06	3 30	8 39	2 40	9 30				
21	4 08	8 03	3 39	8 33	2 52	9 18	1 12	11 23		
Aug. 1	4 15	7 56	3 48	8 23	3 09	9 01	1 49	10 20		
11	4 20	7 50	3 56	8 13	3 22	8 46	2 21	9 46		
21	4 24	7 41	4 05	8 01	3 34	8 27	2 47	9 15		
Sept. 1	4 29	7 31	4 14	7 46	3 51	8 08	3 13	8 43	1 40	10 02
11	4 32	7 20	4 20	7 33	4 02	7 50	3 33	8 16	2 36	9 12
21	4 35	7 11	4 26	7 19	4 14	7 31	3 52	7 52	3 11	8 31
Oct. 1	4 38	7 02	4 33	7 05	4 25	7 13	4 10	7 28	3 41	7 54
11	4 40	6 53	4 40	6 53	4 35	6 58	4 26	7 05	4 07	7 23
21	4 43	6 47	4 45	6 44	4 45	6 43	4 41	6 46	4 32	6 55
Nov. 1	4 46	6 41	4 52	6 34	4 56	6 30	4 58	6 27	4 56	6 27
11	4 50	6 38	4 59	6 28	5 06	6 21	5 13	6 14	5 17	6 08
21	4 55	6 36	5 06	6 25	5 16	6 15	5 26	6 04	5 37	5 52
Dec. 1	5 00	6 37	5 13	6 24	5 25	6 11	5 38	5 58	5 53	5 42
11	5 06	6 40	5 20	6 26	5 34	6 12	5 48	5 57	6 06	5 38
21	5 11	6 45	5 25	6 30	5 39	6 16	5 55	6 00	6 15	5 40
31	5 15	6 50	5 30	6 35	5 44	6 21	6 00	6 06	6 18	5 48

1st Month — January, 1988 — 31 days

Greenwich Mean Time

NOTE: Light numbers indicate Sun. **Dark** numbers indicate **Moon.** *Degrees are North Latitude.*

CAUTION: Must be converted to local time. For instruction see page 197.

Day of month week year	Sun on Meridian **Moon phase** h m s	Sun's Declination ° ′	20° Rise Sun **Moon** h m	20° Set Sun **Moon** h m	30° Rise Sun **Moon** h m	30° Set Sun **Moon** h m	40° Rise Sun **Moon** h m	40° Set Sun **Moon** h m	50° Rise Sun **Moon** h m	50° Set Sun **Moon** h m	60° Rise Sun **Moon** h m	60° Set Sun **Moon** h m
1 Fr	12 03 02	−23 05	6 35	17 32	6 56	17 11	7 22	16 44	7 59	16 08	9 02	15 04
1			**15 19**	**4 19**	**14 52**	**4 45**	**14 18**	**5 17**	**13 29**	**6 06**	**11 50**	**7 43**
2 Sa	12 03 31	−23 00	6 36	17 32	6 56	17 11	7 22	16 45	7 59	16 09	9 02	15 06
2			**16 10**	**5 16**	**15 42**	**5 44**	**15 06**	**6 20**	**14 12**	**7 13**	**12 14**	**9 11**
3 Su	12 03 59	−22 55	6 36	17 33	6 56	17 12	7 22	16 46	7 59	16 10	9 02	15 07
3			**17 04**	**6 10**	**16 36**	**6 38**	**16 00**	**7 15**	**15 07**	**8 09**	**13 10**	**10 06**
4 Mo	12 04 27	−22 49	6 36	17 33	6 56	17 13	7 22	16 47	7 59	16 11	9 01	15 09
4	**01 40** ○		**17 59**	**7 00**	**17 33**	**7 27**	**17 00**	**8 01**	**16 12**	**8 51**	**14 34**	**10 30**
5 Tu	12 04 47	−22 43	6 37	17 34	6 57	17 13	7 22	16 48	7 58	16 12	9 00	15 10
5			**18 53**	**7 46**	**18 31**	**8 09**	**18 03**	**8 39**	**17 22**	**9 22**	**16 08**	**10 39**
6 We	12 04 54	−22 37	6 37	17 34	6 57	17 14	7 22	16 49	7 58	16 14	9 00	15 12
6			**19 46**	**8 26**	**19 28**	**8 46**	**19 06**	**9 10**	**18 34**	**9 44**	**17 40**	**10 41**
7 Th	12 05 21	−22 30	6 37	17 35	6 57	17 15	7 22	16 50	7 58	16 15	8 59	15 14
7			**20 37**	**9 03**	**20 24**	**9 18**	**20 07**	**9 36**	**19 45**	**10 02**	**19 08**	**10 42**
8 Fr	12 06 13	−22 22	6 37	17 36	6 57	17 16	7 22	16 51	7 58	16 16	8 58	15 16
8			**21 26**	**9 36**	**21 18**	**9 46**	**21 08**	**9 59**	**20 54**	**10 15**	**20 33**	**10 42**
9 Sa	12 06 39	−22 15	6 37	17 36	6 57	17 16	7 22	16 52	7 57	16 18	8 56	15 18
9			**22 14**	**10 07**	**22 11**	**10 13**	**22 08**	**10 19**	**22 03**	**10 27**	**21 56**	**10 40**
10 Su	12 07 04	−22 06	6 37	17 37	6 57	17 17	7 22	16 53	7 57	16 19	8 55	15 19
10			**23 02**	**10 38**	**23 05**	**10 38**	**23 08**	**10 38**	**23 12**	**10 39**	**23 18**	**10 39**
11 Mo	12 07 29	−21 57	6 37	17 38	6 57	17 18	7 22	16 54	7 56	16 20	8 54	15 21
11			**23 52**	**11 09**		**11 04**		**10 58**		**10 50**		**10 37**
12 Tu	12 07 53	−21 48	6 37	17 39	6 57	17 19	7 21	16 55	7 55	16 21	8 53	15 23
12	**07 04** ☾			**11 42**		**11 32**	**0 10**	**11 19**	**0 23**	**11 02**	**0 44**	**10 36**
13 We	12 08 16	−21 39	6 38	17 39	6 57	17 20	7 21	16 56	7 55	16 22	8 52	15 25
13			**0 45**	**12 18**	**0 58**	**12 03**	**1 15**	**11 44**	**1 38**	**11 17**	**2 15**	**10 36**
14 Th	12 08 39	−21 29	6 38	17 40	6 57	17 21	7 21	16 57	7 54	16 24	8 50	15 28
14			**1 41**	**13 00**	**2 00**	**12 39**	**2 23**	**12 13**	**2 57**	**11 37**	**3 54**	**10 36**
15 Fr	12 09 01	−21 18	6 38	17 41	6 57	17 22	7 20	16 58	7 53	16 25	8 49	15 30
15			**2 42**	**13 48**	**3 06**	**13 23**	**3 36**	**12 51**	**4 20**	**12 06**	**5 43**	**10 40**
16 Sa	12 09 23	−21 07	6 38	17 41	6 57	17 23	7 20	16 59	7 52	16 27	8 47	15 32
16			**3 47**	**14 45**	**4 14**	**14 17**	**4 50**	**13 41**	**5 42**	**12 47**	**7 35**	**10 53**
17 Su	12 09 44	−20 56	6 38	17 42	6 56	17 23	7 20	17 00	7 52	16 28	8 46	15 34
17			**4 54**	**15 50**	**5 22**	**15 21**	**6 00**	**14 44**	**6 55**	**13 49**	**9 03**	**11 41**
18 Mo	12 10 04	−20 45	6 38	17 42	6 56	17 24	7 19	17 02	7 51	16 30	8 44	15 37
18			**5 58**	**17 00**	**6 26**	**16 33**	**7 01**	**15 59**	**7 52**	**15 09**	**9 38**	**13 25**
19 Tu	12 10 23	−20 33	6 38	17 43	6 56	17 25	7 19	17 03	7 50	16 32	8 42	15 39
19	**05 26** ●		**6 57**	**18 11**	**7 20**	**17 49**	**7 50**	**17 22**	**8 33**	**16 42**	**9 48**	**15 30**
20 We	12 10 42	−20 20	6 38	17 44	6 56	17 26	7 18	17 04	5 49	16 34	8 40	15 42
20			**7 49**	**19 19**	**8 07**	**19 04**	**8 29**	**18 44**	**9 00**	**18 17**	**9 51**	**17 31**
21 Th	12 11 00	−20 07	6 38	17 44	6 55	17 27	7 18	17 05	7 48	16 35	8 38	15 44
21			**8 35**	**20 24**	**8 46**	**20 15**	**9 01**	**20 04**	**9 21**	**19 48**	**9 51**	**19 23**
22 Fr	12 11 18	−19 54	6 38	17 45	6 55	17 28	7 17	17 06	7 47	16 36	8 37	15 46
22			**9 16**	**21 25**	**9 21**	**21 23**	**9 28**	**21 20**	**9 37**	**21 15**	**9 51**	**21 09**
23 Sa	12 11 34	−19 41	6 38	17 46	6 55	17 29	7 16	17 07	7 46	16 38	8 35	15 49
23			**9 54**	**22 24**	**9 53**	**22 28**	**9 52**	**22 33**	**9 51**	**22 39**	**9 50**	**22 49**
24 Su	12 11 50	−19 27	6 38	17 46	6 54	17 30	7 16	17 08	7 45	16 40	8 33	15 52
24			**10 31**	**23 21**	**10 24**	**23 31**	**10 16**	**23 44**	**10 05**		**9 48**	
25 Mo	12 12 05	−19 12	6 37	17 47	6 54	17 30	7 15	17 10	7 44	16 41	8 31	15 54
25	**21 53** ☽		**11 08**		**10 56**	**10 56**	**10 40**		**10 20**	**0 01**	**9 48**	**0 28**
26 Tu	12 12 19	−18 58	6 37	17 47	6 54	17 31	7 14	17 11	7 42	16 42	8 29	15 56
26			**11 48**	**0 19**	**11 30**	**11 30**	**11 08**	**0 54**	**10 37**	**1 21**	**9 48**	**2 07**
27 We	12 12 33	−18 43	6 37	17 48	6 53	17 32	7 14	17 12	7 41	16 44	8 27	15 59
27			**12 30**	**1 16**	**12 07**	**12 07**	**11 39**	**2 03**	**11 00**	**2 41**	**9 50**	**3 48**
28 Th	12 12 45	−18 27	6 36	17 49	6 53	17 33	7 13	17 13	7 40	16 46	8 25	16 02
28			**13 16**	**2 14**	**12 50**	**12 50**	**12 17**	**3 11**	**11 29**	**3 57**	**9 56**	**5 28**
29 Fr	12 12 57	−18 12	6 36	17 49	6 52	17 34	7 12	17 14	7 39	16 48	8 22	16 04
29			**14 06**	**3 11**	**13 38**	**13 38**	**13 02**	**4 14**	**12 08**	**5 07**	**10 13**	**7 02**
30 Sa	12 13 08	−17 56	6 36	17 50	6 52	17 35	7 11	17 16	7 37	16 49	8 20	16 07
30			**14 59**	**4 06**	**14 31**	**14 31**	**13 54**	**5 11**	**13 00**	**6 06**	**10 57**	**8 08**
31 Su	12 13 18	−17 39	6 36	17 51	6 51	17 36	7 10	17 17	7 36	16 51	8 18	16 09
31			**15 53**	**4 57**	**15 27**	**15 27**	**14 52**	**6 00**	**14 02**	**6 51**	**12 16**	**8 38**

2nd Month **February, 1988** **29 Days**

Greenwich Mean Time

NOTE: Light numbers indicate Sun. **Dark** numbers indicate **Moon.** *Degrees are North Latitude.*

CAUTION: Must be converted to local time. For instruction see page 197.

Day of month week year	Sun on meridian **Moon phase**	Sun's Declination	20° Rise Sun **Moon**	20° Set Sun **Moon**	30° Rise Sun **Moon**	30° Set Sun **Moon**	40° Rise Sun **Moon**	40° Set Sun **Moon**	50° Rise Sun **Moon**	50° Set Sun **Moon**	60° Rise Sun **Moon**	60° Set Sun **Moon**
	h m s	° ′	h m	h m	h m	h m	h m	h m	h m	h m	h m	h m
1 Mo	12 13 27	−17 23	6 36	17 52	6 50	17 37	7 09	17 18	7 34	16 53	8 16	16 12
32			**16 40**	**5 44**	**16 24**	**6 08**	**15 54**	**6 40**	**15 11**	**7 25**	**13 49**	**8 49**
2 Tu	12 13 35	−17 06	6 36	17 52	6 50	17 38	7 08	17 20	7 33	16 54	8 14	16 14
33	**20 51** ○		**17 41**	**6 25**	**17 22**	**6 46**	**16 57**	**7 13**	**16 22**	**7 50**	**15 22**	**8 53**
3 We	12 13 43	−16 49	6 35	17 52	6 49	17 38	7 08	17 21	7 32	16 56	8 11	16 17
34			**18 32**	**7 03**	**18 18**	**7 20**	**17 59**	**7 40**	**17 34**	**8 08**	**16 52**	**8 54**
4 Th	12 13 50	−16 31	6 35	17 53	6 49	17 39	7 07	17 22	7 30	16 58	8 09	16 20
35			**19 22**	**7 37**	**19 12**	**7 49**	**19 00**	**8 03**	**18 44**	**8 23**	**18 18**	**8 53**
5 Fr	12 13 56	−16 13	6 34	17 53	6 48	17 40	7 06	17 23	7 28	17 00	8 06	16 23
36			**20 10**	**8 09**	**20 06**	**8 16**	**20 00**	**8 24**	**19 53**	**8 35**	**19 41**	**8 52**
6 Sa	12 14 01	−15 55	6 34	17 54	6 48	17 40	7 04	17 24	8 27	17 02	8 04	16 26
37			**20 58**	**8 40**	**20 59**	**8 41**	**21 00**	**8 44**	**21 01**	**8 46**	**21 04**	**8 51**
7 Su	12 14 05	−15 37	6 33	17 54	6 47	17 41	7 03	17 26	7 26	17 03	8 02	16 28
38			**21 47**	**9 10**	**21 53**	**9 07**	**22 01**	**9 03**	**22 11**	**8 57**	**22 27**	**8 49**
8 Mo	12 14 09	−15 18	6 33	17 55	6 46	17 42	7 02	17 27	7 24	17 05	7 59	16 31
39			**22 38**	**9 42**	**22 49**	**9 33**	**23 03**	**9 23**	**23 23**	**9 09**	**23 55**	**8 47**
9 Tu	12 14 11	−14 59	6 32	17 55	6 45	17 43	7 01	17 28	7 22	17 07	7 56	16 34
40			**23 31**	**10 16**	**23 48**	**10 02**		**9 45**		**9 22**		**8 46**
10 We	12 14 13	−14 40	6 32	17 56	6 44	17 44	7 00	17 29	7 20	17 08	7 54	16 36
41	**23 01** ☾			**10 54**		**10 35**	**0 09**	**10 12**	**0 39**	**9 40**	**1 29**	**8 46**
11 Th	12 14 15	−14 21	6 31	17 56	6 44	17 45	6 59	17 30	7 19	17 10	7 51	16 38
42			**0 29**	**11 38**	**0 50**	**11 15**	**1 18**	**10 45**	**1 58**	**10 03**	**3 11**	**8 47**
12 Fr	12 14 15	−14 01	6 31	17 57	6 43	17 46	6 58	17 31	7 17	17 12	7 48	16 41
43			**1 30**	**12 29**	**1 56**	**12 02**	**2 29**	**11 28**	**3 18**	**10 37**	**4 59**	**8 54**
13 Sa	12 14 15	−13 41	6 30	17 57	6 42	17 47	6 57	17 33	7 15	17 14	7 46	16 44
44			**2 34**	**13 28**	**3 02**	**12 59**	**3 39**	**12 22**	**4 34**	**11 26**	**6 42**	**9 18**
14 Su	12 14 14	−13 21	6 30	17 58	6 42	17 48	6 56	17 34	7 14	17 16	7 43	16 46
45			**3 37**	**14 34**	**4 06**	**14 06**	**4 43**	**13 30**	**5 38**	**12 36**	**7 40**	**10 35**
15 Mo	12 14 12	−13 01	6 29	17 58	6 41	17 48	6 54	17 35	7 12	17 17	7 40	16 49
46			**4 38**	**15 44**	**5 04**	**15 19**	**5 37**	**14 48**	**6 25**	**14 02**	**7 57**	**12 32**
16 Tu	12 14 10	−12 41	6 29	17 59	6 40	17 49	6 53	17 36	7 10	17 19	7 38	16 52
47			**5 33**	**16 53**	**5 54**	**16 34**	**6 21**	**16 10**	**6 58**	**15 36**	**8 02**	**14 36**
17 We	12 14 07	−12 20	6 28	17 59	6 39	17 50	6 52	17 37	7 08	17 21	7 35	16 54
48	**15 54** ●		**6 22**	**18 01**	**6 37**	**17 48**	**6 56**	**17 33**	**7 22**	**17 11**	**8 03**	**16 35**
18 Th	12 14 03	−11 59	6 28	18 00	6 38	17 50	6 50	17 38	7 06	17 22	7 32	16 57
49			**7 06**	**19 05**	**7 14**	**18 59**	**7 25**	**18 52**	**7 40**	**18 42**	**8 02**	**18 26**
19 Fr	12 13 58	−11 38	6 27	18 00	6 37	17 51	6 49	17 40	7 05	17 24	7 30	17 00
50			**7 46**	**20 07**	**7 48**	**20 08**	**7 51**	**20 09**	**7 55**	**20 10**	**8 01**	**20 13**
20 Sa	12 13 53	−11 17	6 27	18 01	6 36	17 52	6 48	17 41	7 03	17 26	7 27	17 02
51			**8 25**	**21 07**	**8 21**	**21 15**	**8 16**	**21 24**	**8 10**	**21 36**	**8 00**	**21 56**
21 Su	12 13 47	−10 55	6 26	18 01	6 35	17 53	6 46	17 42	7 01	17 28	7 24	17 04
52			**9 03**	**22 07**	**8 53**	**22 20**	**8 41**	**22 37**	**8 24**	**23 01**	**7 59**	**23 39**
22 Mo	12 13 40	−10 33	6 26	18 02	6 34	17 54	6 45	17 43	6 59	17 29	7 31	17 07
53			**9 43**	**23 07**	**9 27**	**23 26**	**9 08**	**23 50**	**8 41**		**7 58**	
23 Tu	12 13 33	−10 12	6 25	18 02	6 33	17 54	6 44	17 44	6 57	17 30	7 18	17 10
54			**10 26**		**10 05**		**9 39**		**9 02**	**0 24**	**7 59**	**1 23**
24 We	12 13 25	−09 50	6 24	18 03	6 32	17 55	6 42	17 45	6 55	17 32	7 15	17 12
55	**12 15** ☽		**11 12**	**0 06**	**10 47**	**0 30**	**10 15**	**1 00**	**9 29**	**1 44**	**8 03**	**3 08**
25 Th	12 13 16	−09 28	6 23	18 03	6 31	17 56	6 40	17 46	6 53	17 34	7 12	17 15
56			**12 01**	**1 05**	**11 33**	**1 32**	**10 58**	**2 07**	**10 05**	**2 58**	**8 15**	**4 48**
26 Fr	12 13 07	−09 05	6 22	18 04	6 30	17 56	6 39	17 48	6 51	17 36	7 10	17 18
57			**12 54**	**2 01**	**12 25**	**2 30**	**11 48**	**3 06**	**10 53**	**4 02**	**8 48**	**6 07**
27 Sa	12 12 57	−08 43	6 22	18 04	6 29	17 57	6 38	17 49	6 49	17 37	7 07	17 20
58			**13 48**	**2 54**	**13 20**	**3 22**	**12 45**	**3 58**	**11 52**	**4 51**	**9 58**	**6 47**
28 Su	12 12 47	−08 20	6 21	18 04	6 28	17 58	6 36	17 50	6 47	17 39	7 04	17 23
59			**14 43**	**3 42**	**14 18**	**4 08**	**13 46**	**4 41**	**13 00**	**5 28**	**11 29**	**7 01**
29 Mo	12 12 36	−07 58	6 20	18 05	6 27	17 59	6 34	17 51	6 45	17 41	7 01	17 26
60			**15 36**	**4 25**	**15 15**	**4 47**	**14 49**	**5 16**	**14 11**	**5 55**	**13 04**	**7 06**

3rd Month March, 1988 31 Days

Greenwich Mean Time

NOTE: Light numbers indicate Sun. **Dark** numbers indicate **Moon.** *Degrees are North Latitude.*

CAUTION: Must be converted to local time. For instruction see page 197.

Day of month week year	Sun on meridian **Moon phase** h m s	Sun's Declination ° ′	20° Rise Sun **Moon** h m	20° Set Sun **Moon** h m	30° Rise Sun **Moon** h m	30° Set Sun **Moon** h m	40° Rise Sun **Moon** h m	40° Set Sun **Moon** h m	50° Rise Sun **Moon** h m	50° Set Sun **Moon** h m	60° Rise Sun **Moon** h m	60° Set Sun **Moon** h m
1 Tu	12 12 25	−07 35	6 20	18 05	6 26	18 00	6 33	17 52	6 43	17 42	6 58	17 28
61			**16 28**	**5 04**	**16 12**	**5 22**	**15 51**	**5 44**	**15 23**	**6 15**	**14 35**	**7 07**
2 We	12 12 13	−07 12	6 19	18 06	6 25	18 00	6 32	17 53	6 41	17 44	6 55	17 30
62			**17 18**	**5 39**	**17 07**	**5 52**	**16 53**	**6 09**	**16 33**	**6 31**	**16 02**	**7 06**
3 Th	12 12 00	−06 49	6 18	18 06	6 24	18 01	6 30	17 54	6 39	17 46	6 52	17 33
63	**16 01 ○**		**18 07**	**6 11**	**18 01**	**6 20**	**17 53**	**6 30**	**17 43**	**6 44**	**17 27**	**7 05**
4 Fr	12 11 47	−06 26	6 17	18 06	6 23	18 01	6 28	17 55	6 37	17 48	6 49	17 36
64			**18 55**	**6 42**	**18 54**	**6 46**	**18 53**	**6 50**	**18 52**	**6 55**	**18 50**	**7 03**
5 Sa	12 11 34	−06 03	6 16	18 06	6 22	18 02	6 27	17 56	6 35	17 49	6 46	17 38
65			**19 44**	**7 13**	**19 48**	**7 11**	**19 54**	**7 09**	**20 02**	**7 06**	**20 13**	**7 02**
6 Su	12 11 20	−05 40	6 16	18 07	6 20	18 02	6 26	17 58	6 33	17 50	6 43	17 40
66			**20 34**	**7 44**	**20 44**	**7 37**	**20 56**	**7 29**	**21 13**	**7 17**	**21 40**	**7 00**
7 Mo	12 11 06	−05 17	6 15	18 07	6 19	18 03	6 24	17 59	6 31	17 52	6 40	17 43
67			**21 27**	**8 17**	**21 42**	**8 05**	**22 01**	**7 50**	**22 27**	**7 30**	**23 12**	**6 58**
8 Tu	12 10 51	−04 53	6 14	18 07	6 18	18 04	6 22	18 00	6 29	17 54	6 37	17 46
68			**22 22**	**8 54**	**22 42**	**8 37**	**23 08**	**8 15**	**23 45**	**7 46**		**6 58**
9 We	12 10 36	−04 30	6 14	18 08	6 17	18 04	6 21	18 01	6 26	17 56	6 34	17 48
69			**23 21**	**9 35**	**23 46**	**9 13**		**8 45**		**8 06**	**0 50**	**6 58**
10 Th	12 10 21	−04 06	6 13	18 08	6 16	18 05	6 20	18 02	6 24	17 57	6 31	17 50
70				**10 23**		**9 57**	**0 17**	**9 23**	**1 04**	**8 35**	**2 35**	**7 02**
11 Fr	12 10 06	−03 43	6 12	18 08	6 15	18 06	6 18	18 03	6 22	17 59	6 28	17 53
71	**10 56 ☾**		**0 22**	**11 17**	**0 50**	**10 48**	**1 26**	**10 12**	**2 20**	**9 17**	**4 20**	**7 16**
12 Sa	12 09 50	−03 19	6 11	18 09	6 14	18 06	6 16	18 04	6 20	18 00	6 25	17 56
72			**1 24**	**12 18**	**1 53**	**11 49**	**2 30**	**11 12**	**3 27**	**10 16**	**5 37**	**8 06**
13 Su	12 09 33	−02 56	6 10	18 09	6 12	18 07	6 14	18 05	6 18	18 02	6 22	17 58
73			**2 24**	**13 24**	**2 51**	**12 57**	**3 27**	**12 23**	**4 18**	**11 33**	**6 05**	**9 48**
14 Mo	12 09 17	−02 32	6 09	18 10	6 11	18 07	6 13	18 06	6 15	18 04	6 19	18 00
74			**3 19**	**14 31**	**3 43**	**14 09**	**4 13**	**13 41**	**4 56**	**13 01**	**6 13**	**11 47**
15 Tu	12 09 00	−02 08	6 08	18 10	6 10	18 08	6 11	18 07	6 13	18 05	6 16	18 03
75			**4 09**	**15 38**	**4 28**	**15 22**	**4 51**	**15 02**	**5 22**	**14 33**	**6 15**	**13 46**
16 We	12 08 43	−01 44	6 07	18 10	6 09	18 09	6 10	18 08	6 11	18 07	6 13	18 06
76			**4 55**	**16 43**	**5 07**	**16 33**	**5 22**	**16 21**	**5 42**	**16 05**	**6 14**	**15 39**
17 Th	12 08 26	−01 21	6 07	18 11	6 08	18 10	6 08	18 09	6 09	18 08	6 10	18 08
77			**5 36**	**17 46**	**5 42**	**17 43**	**5 49**	**17 39**	**5 59**	**17 35**	**6 13**	**17 27**
18 Fr	12 08 09	−00 57	6 06	18 11	6 06	18 10	6 07	17 10	6 07	18 10	6 07	18 10
78	**02 02 ●**		**6 16**	**18 47**	**6 15**	**18 51**	**6 14**	**18 56**	**6 14**	**19 02**	**6 12**	**19 13**
19 Sa	12 07 52	−00 33	6 05	18 11	6 05	18 11	6 05	18 11	6 05	18 12	6 04	18 13
79			**6 55**	**19 48**	**6 48**	**19 59**	**6 39**	**20 11**	**6 28**	**20 29**	**6 11**	**20 58**
20 Su	12 07 34	−00 10	6 04	18 11	6 04	18 11	6 03	18 12	6 03	18 14	6 01	18 15
80			**7 35**	**20 50**	**7 22**	**21 06**	**7 06**	**21 27**	**6 44**	**21 56**	**6 10**	**22 45**
21 Mo	12 07 16	+00 14	6 03	18 11	6 02	18 12	6 02	18 13	6 00	18 15	5 58	18 18
81			**8 17**	**21 51**	**7 59**	**22 13**	**7 35**	**22 41**	**7 03**	**23 21**	**6 10**	
22 Tu	12 06 58	+00 38	6 02	18 12	6 01	18 12	6 00	18 14	5 58	18 16	5 55	18 20
82			**9 03**	**22 52**	**8 40**	**23 18**	**8 10**	**23 52**	**7 28**		**6 13**	**0 33**
23 We	12 06 40	+01 02	6 01	18 12	6 00	18 13	5 58	18 15	5 56	18 18	5 52	18 22
83			**9 53**	**23 52**	**9 26**		**8 51**		**8 01**	**0 41**	**6 20**	**2 20**
24 Th	12 06 22	+01 25	6 00	18 12	5 59	18 14	5 56	18 16	5 54	18 20	5 49	18 24
84			**10 46**		**10 17**	**0 20**	**9 40**	**0 56**	**8 45**	**1 51**	**6 43**	**3 53**
25 Fr	12 06 04	+01 49	5 59	18 12	5 58	18 14	5 55	18 17	5 52	18 21	5 46	18 27
85	**04 41 ☽**		**11 40**	**0 47**	**11 12**	**1 16**	**10 36**	**1 52**	**9 42**	**2 47**	**7 40**	**4 49**
26 Sa	12 05 46	+02 12	5 59	18 13	5 56	18 15	5 54	18 18	5 49	18 22	5 43	18 30
86			**12 36**	**1 37**	**12 10**	**2 04**	**11 36**	**2 39**	**10 47**	**3 29**	**9 08**	**5 10**
27 Su	12 05 28	+02 36	5 58	18 13	5 55	18 16	5 52	18 19	5 47	18 24	5 40	18 32
87			**13 30**	**2 23**	**13 07**	**2 46**	**12 39**	**3 16**	**11 58**	**3 59**	**10 43**	**5 17**
28 Mo	12 05 10	+02 59	5 57	18 13	5 54	18 16	5 50	18 20	5 45	18 26	5 37	18 34
88			**14 22**	**3 03**	**14 04**	**3 23**	**13 42**	**3 47**	**13 10**	**4 21**	**12 16**	**5 19**
29 Tu	12 04 51	+03 23	5 56	18 14	5 52	18 17	5 49	18 21	5 43	18 28	5 34	18 37
89			**15 13**	**3 39**	**15 00**	**3 54**	**14 44**	**4 13**	**14 21**	**4 38**	**13 44**	**5 19**
30 We	12 04 33	+03 46	5 55	18 14	5 51	18 17	5 48	18 22	5 41	18 29	5 31	18 40
90			**16 02**	**4 12**	**15 54**	**4 23**	**15 44**	**4 35**	**15 31**	**4 52**	**15 10**	**5 18**
31 Th	12 04 15	+04 09	5 54	18 14	5 50	18 18	5 46	18 23	5 39	18 31	5 28	18 42
91			**16 51**	**4 44**	**16 48**	**4 49**	**16 45**	**4 55**	**16 40**	**5 04**	**16 33**	**5 16**

4th Month **April, 1988** **30 Days**

Greenwich Mean Time

NOTE: Light numbers indicate Sun. **Dark** numbers indicate **Moon.** *Degrees are North Latitude.*

CAUTION: Must be converted to local time. For instruction see page 197.

			20°		30°		40°		50°		60°	
Day of month week year	Sun on meridian **Moon phase** h m s	Sun's Declination ° ′	Rise Sun **Moon** h m	Set Sun **Moon** h m	Rise Sun **Moon** h m	Set Sun **Moon** h m	Rise Sun **Moon** h m	Set Sun **Moon** h m	Rise Sun **Moon** h m	Set Sun **Moon** h m	Rise Sun **Moon** h m	Set Sun **Moon** h m
1 Fr	12 03 57	+04 33	5 53	18 14	5 49	18 19	5 44	18 24	5 37	18 32	5 25	18 44
92			**17 40**	**5 15**	**17 42**	**5 15**	**17 45**	**5 15**	**17 50**	**5 15**	**17 57**	**5 15**
2 Sa	12 03 39	+04 56	5 52	18 14	5 48	18 20	5 42	18 25	5 34	18 34	5 22	18 47
93	**09 21 ○**		**18 30**	**5 46**	**18 38**	**5 41**	**18 48**	**5 34**	**19 01**	**5 26**	**19 23**	**5 13**
3 Su	12 03 21	+05 19	5 52	18 16	5 47	18 20	5 41	10 20	5 02	10 30	5 19	18 50
94			**19 22**	**6 19**	**19 35**	**6 08**	**19 52**	**5 56**	**20 16**	**5 38**	**20 54**	**5 12**
4 Mo	12 03 04	+05 42	5 51	18 15	5 46	18 21	5 39	18 27	5 30	18 37	5 16	18 52
95			**20 17**	**6 54**	**20 36**	**6 39**	**20 59**	**6 20**	**21 33**	**5 53**	**22 31**	**5 11**
5 Tu	12 02 46	+06 04	5 50	18 15	5 44	18 22	5 38	18 28	5 28	18 38	5 13	18 54
96			**21 15**	**7 35**	**21 39**	**7 14**	**22 09**	**6 48**	**22 52**	**6 12**		**5 11**
6 We	12 02 29	+06 27	5 50	18 16	5 43	18 22	5 36	18 29	5 26	18 40	5 10	18 56
97			**22 16**	**8 20**	**22 43**	**7 55**	**23 18**	**7 24**		**6 38**	**0 15**	**5 14**
7 Th	12 02 12	+06 50	5 49	18 16	5 42	18 23	5 34	18 30	5 23	18 42	5 07	18 59
98			**23 17**	**9 12**	**23 46**	**8 44**		**8 09**	**0 10**	**7 16**	**2 01**	**5 24**
8 Fr	12 01 55	+07 12	5 48	18 16	5 41	18 23	5 33	18 31	5 21	18 43	5 04	19 01
99				**10 11**		**9 42**	**0 23**	**9 05**	**1 19**	**8 09**	**3 29**	**5 59**
9 Sa	12 01 38	+07 35	5 47	18 16	5 40	18 24	5 32	18 32	5 19	18 44	5 01	19 04
100	**19 21 ☾**		**0 17**	**11 14**	**0 45**	**10 46**	**1 21**	**10 11**	**2 15**	**9 18**	**4 10**	**7 24**
10 Su	12 01 22	+07 57	5 46	18 17	5 38	18 24	5 30	18 34	5 17	18 46	4 58	19 06
101			**1 12**	**12 19**	**1 38**	**11 55**	**2 10**	**11 25**	**2 56**	**10 41**	**4 22**	**9 17**
11 Mo	12 01 06	+08 19	5 45	18 17	5 37	18 25	5 28	18 35	5 15	18 48	4 55	19 08
102			**2 03**	**13 24**	**2 23**	**13 05**	**2 49**	**12 42**	**3 25**	**12 09**	**4 26**	**11 12**
12 Tu	12 00 50	+00 41	5 44	18 17	5 36	18 25	5 27	18 36	5 13	18 49	4 52	19 11
103			**2 48**	**14 27**	**3 03**	**14 15**	**3 21**	**13 59**	**3 40**	**13 38**	**4 26**	**13 03**
13 We	12 00 35	+09 03	5 43	18 18	5 35	18 26	5 26	18 37	5 11	18 51	4 49	19 14
104			**3 29**	**15 28**	**3 38**	**15 22**	**3 49**	**15 15**	**4 03**	**15 05**	**4 26**	**14 49**
14 Th	12 00 20	+09 25	5 42	18 18	5 34	18 26	5 31	18 38	5 00	10 50	4 40	19 10
105			**4 09**	**16 25**	**4 11**	**16 29**	**4 14**	**16 30**	**4 18**	**16 31**	**4 25**	**16 33**
15 Fr	12 00 05	+09 46	5 42	18 19	5 33	18 27	5 22	18 39	5 07	18 54	4 43	19 18
106			**4 47**	**17 29**	**4 43**	**17 36**	**4 39**	**17 45**	**4 33**	**17 51**	**4 23**	**18 16**
16 Sa	11 50 51	+10 07	5 41	18 19	5 32	18 28	5 21	18 40	5 05	18 56	4 40	19 21
107	**12 00 ●**		**5 26**	**18 30**	**5 16**	**18 43**	**5 04**	**19 00**	**4 48**	**19 24**	**4 23**	**20 02**
17 Su	11 59 37	+10 29	5 40	18 19	5 31	18 28	5 20	18 41	5 03	18 58	4 37	19 24
108			**6 07**	**19 32**	**5 52**	**19 51**	**5 32**	**20 16**	**5 05**	**20 50**	**4 22**	**21 50**
18 Mo	11 59 23	+10 50	5 40	18 19	5 30	18 29	5 18	18 42	5 01	18 59	4 34	19 26
109			**6 52**	**20 35**	**6 31**	**20 59**	**6 05**	**21 30**	**5 27**	**22 14**	**4 24**	**23 40**
19 Tu	11 59 10	+11 11	5 39	18 20	5 29	18 29	5 16	18 43	4 59	19 00	4 31	19 28
110			**7 41**	**21 36**	**7 16**	**22 04**	**6 43**	**22 39**	**5 57**	**23 31**	**4 29**	
20 We	11 58 57	+11 31	5 38	18 20	5 28	18 30	5 15	18 44	4 57	19 02	4 28	19 31
111			**8 34**	**22 35**	**8 06**	**23 04**	**7 30**	**23 40**	**6 37**		**4 44**	**1 23**
21 Th	11 58 45	+11 52	5 37	18 20	5 27	18 31	5 14	18 45	4 55	19 04	4 25	19 34
112			**9 29**	**23 29**	**9 01**	**23 57**	**8 24**		**7 29**	**0 35**	**5 26**	**2 39**
22 Fr	11 58 33	+12 12	5 36	18 21	5 26	18 32	5 12	18 46	4 53	19 05	4 22	19 36
113			**10 25**		**9 59**		**9 24**	**0 32**	**8 33**	**1 24**	**6 45**	**3 13**
23 Sa	11 58 22	+12 32	5 36	18 21	5 25	18 32	5 10	18 47	4 51	19 06	4 20	19 38
114	**22 32 ☽**		**11 21**	**0 17**	**10 57**	**0 42**	**10 27**	**1 14**	**9 43**	**2 00**	**8 19**	**3 25**
24 Su	11 58 10	+12 52	5 35	18 21	5 24	18 33	5 09	18 48	5 49	19 08	4 17	19 41
115			**12 15**	**1 00**	**11 55**	**1 21**	**11 30**	**1 48**	**10 55**	**2 25**	**9 54**	**3 29**
25 Mo	11 58 00	+13 12	5 34	18 22	5 23	18 34	5 08	18 49	4 47	19 10	4 14	19 44
116			**13 06**	**1 37**	**12 51**	**1 54**	**12 32**	**2 15**	**12 06**	**2 44**	**11 24**	**3 30**
26 Tu	11 57 50	+13 31	5 34	18 22	5 22	18 34	5 06	18 50	4 46	19 11	4 12	19 46
117			**13 56**	**2 12**	**13 46**	**2 24**	**13 33**	**2 39**	**13 17**	**2 59**	**12 50**	**3 30**
27 We	11 57 40	+13 50	5 34	18 23	5 21	18 35	5 05	18 51	4 44	19 12	4 09	19 48
118			**14 44**	**2 44**	**14 40**	**2 51**	**14 34**	**2 59**	**14 26**	**3 11**	**14 14**	**3 29**
28 Th	11 57 31	+14 09	5 33	18 23	5 20	18 36	5 04	18 52	4 42	19 14	4 06	19 51
119			**15 33**	**3 15**	**15 33**	**3 17**	**15 34**	**3 19**	**15 35**	**3 22**	**15 37**	**3 27**
29 Fr	11 57 22	+14 28	5 32	18 23	5 19	18 36	5 03	18 53	4 40	19 16	4 03	19 54
120			**16 22**	**3 46**	**16 28**	**3 43**	**16 36**	**3 39**	**16 46**	**3 34**	**17 02**	**3 26**
30 Sa	11 57 14	+14 47	5 02	10 24	5 18	18 37	5 02	18 54	4 38	19 17	4 00	19 56
121			**17 14**	**4 18**	**17 25**	**4 10**	**17 40**	**3 59**	**17 59**	**3 46**	**18 31**	**3 24**

5th Month May, 1988 31 days

Greenwich Mean Time

NOTE: Light numbers indicate Sun. **Dark** numbers indicate **Moon.** *Degrees are North Latitude.*

CAUTION: Must be converted to local time. For instruction see page 197.

Day of month week year	Sun on meridian **Moon phase** h m s	Sun's Decli- nation ° ′	20° Rise Sun **Moon** h m	20° Set Sun **Moon** h m	30° Rise Sun **Moon** h m	30° Set Sun **Moon** h m	40° Rise Sun **Moon** h m	40° Set Sun **Moon** h m	50° Rise Sun **Moon** h m	50° Set Sun **Moon** h m	60° Rise Sun **Moon** h m	60° Set Sun **Moon** h m
1 Su	11 57 06	+15 05	5 31	18 24	5 17	18 38	5 00	18 55	4 36	19 18	3 58	19 58
122	**23 41** ○		**18 09**	**4 53**	**18 26**	**4 39**	**18 47**	**4 23**	**19 16**	**4 00**	**20 07**	**3 23**
2 Mo	11 56 59	+15 23	5 30	18 24	5 16	18 38	4 59	18 56	4 34	19 20	3 55	20 01
123			**19 07**	**5 32**	**19 29**	**5 13**	**19 56**	**4 50**	**20 36**	**4 17**	**21 49**	**3 23**
3 Tu	11 56 53	+15 41	5 30	18 24	5 15	18 39	4 58	18 57	4 32	19 22	3 52	20 04
124			**20 08**	**6 17**	**20 34**	**5 53**	**21 07**	**5 24**	**21 57**	**4 41**	**23 37**	**3 26**
4 We	11 56 46	+15 58	5 29	18 25	5 14	18 39	4 56	18 58	4 31	19 24	3 50	20 06
125			**21 11**	**7 08**	**21 39**	**6 41**	**22 15**	**6 06**	**23 10**	**5 15**		**3 33**
5 Th	11 56 41	+16 15	5 29	18 25	5 14	18 40	4 55	18 59	4 30	19 25	3 47	20 08
126			**22 12**	**8 05**	**22 40**	**7 36**	**23 17**	**6 59**		**6 04**	**1 15**	**3 59**
6 Fr	11 56 36	+16 32	5 28	18 25	5 13	18 41	4 54	19 00	4 28	19 27	3 44	20 11
127			**23 09**	**9 07**	**23 35**	**8 39**		**8 04**	**0 11**	**7 10**	**2 11**	**5 11**
7 Sa	11 56 32	+16 49	5 28	18 26	5 12	18 41	4 53	19 01	4 26	19 28	3 42	20 13
128				**10 12**		**9 47**	**0 08**	**9 16**	**0 56**	**8 29**	**2 30**	**6 58**
8 Su	11 56 28	+17 05	5 27	18 26	5 12	18 42	4 52	19 02	4 24	19 30	3 39	20 16
129			**0 00**	**11 16**	**0 22**	**10 57**	**0 49**	**10 31**	**1 28**	**9 55**	**2 35**	**8 51**
9 Mo	11 56 25	+17 22	5 27	18 26	5 11	18 42	4 51	19 03	4 23	19 31	3 36	20 18
130	**01 23** ☾		**0 46**	**12 19**	**1 03**	**12 05**	**1 23**	**11 47**	**1 51**	**11 22**	**2 37**	**10 41**
10 Tu	11 56 22	+17 37	5 26	18 27	5 10	18 43	4 50	19 04	4 21	19 32	3 34	20 20
131			**1 28**	**13 19**	**1 38**	**13 11**	**1 52**	**13 01**	**2 09**	**12 48**	**2 37**	**12 26**
11 We	11 56 20	+17 53	5 26	18 27	5 09	18 44	4 49	19 05	4 20	19 34	3 32	20 22
132			**2 06**	**14 18**	**2 11**	**14 16**	**2 17**	**14 14**	**2 24**	**14 11**	**2 36**	**14 07**
12 Th	11 56 19	+18 08	5 25	18 28	5 08	18 44	4 48	19 06	4 18	19 35	3 29	20 25
133			**2 44**	**15 16**	**2 42**	**15 21**	**2 41**	**15 27**	**2 38**	**15 34**	**2 35**	**15 46**
13 Fr	11 56 18	+18 23	5 25	18 28	5 08	18 45	4 47	19 07	4 16	19 36	3 26	20 28
134			**3 21**	**16 15**	**3 14**	**16 26**	**3 05**	**16 40**	**2 53**	**16 58**	**2 34**	**17 28**
14 Sa	11 56 18	+18 38	5 24	18 29	5 07	18 46	4 46	19 08	4 15	19 38	3 24	20 30
135			**4 01**	**17 16**	**3 47**	**17 33**	**3 31**	**17 54**	**3 09**	**18 23**	**2 34**	**19 12**
15 Su	11 56 18	+18 52	5 24	18 29	5 06	18 46	4 45	19 09	4 14	19 40	3 22	20 32
136	**22 11** ●		**4 43**	**18 18**	**4 24**	**18 40**	**4 01**	**19 07**	**3 29**	**19 48**	**2 35**	**21 00**
16 Mo	11 56 19	+19 06	5 24	18 30	5 06	18 47	4 44	19 10	4 12	19 41	3 20	20 34
137			**5 30**	**19 20**	**5 06**	**19 46**	**4 37**	**20 19**	**3 55**	**21 08**	**2 39**	**22 47**
17 Tu	11 56 21	+19 20	5 23	18 30	5 05	18 47	4 43	19 10	4 11	19 42	3 17	20 37
138			**6 21**	**20 21**	**5 54**	**20 49**	**5 20**	**21 25**	**4 30**	**22 19**	**2 49**	
18 We	11 56 23	+19 33	5 23	18 30	5 05	18 48	4 42	19 11	4 10	19 44	3 15	20 39
139			**7 16**	**21 17**	**6 48**	**21 45**	**6 11**	**22 21**	**5 17**	**23 15**	**3 18**	**0 18**
19 Th	11 56 26	+19 46	5 23	18 31	5 04	18 49	4 41	19 12	4 09	19 45	3 13	20 41
140			**8 13**	**22 09**	**7 45**	**22 35**	**7 10**	**23 08**	**6 17**	**23 56**	**4 23**	**1 10**
20 Fr	11 56 29	+19 59	5 22	18 31	5 04	18 49	4 40	19 13	4 08	19 46	3 11	20 44
141			**9 10**	**22 54**	**8 45**	**23 17**	**8 13**	**23 45**	**7 26**		**5 54**	**1 30**
21 Sa	11 56 32	+20 11	5 22	18 31	5 03	18 50	4 40	19 14	4 06	19 48	3 09	20 46
142			**10 05**	**23 34**	**9 44**	**23 53**	**9 17**		**8 38**	**0 26**	**7 29**	**1 38**
22 Su	11 56 37	+20 23	5 22	18 32	5 03	18 51	4 39	19 15	4 05	19 49	3 07	20 48
143			**10 58**		**10 41**		**10 20**	**0 15**	**9 51**	**0 47**	**9 01**	**1 40**
23 Mo	11 56 41	+20 35	5 22	18 32	5 02	18 51	4 38	19 16	4 04	19 50	3 05	20 50
144	**16 49** ☽		**11 48**	**0 10**	**11 36**	**0 24**	**11 22**	**0 41**	**11 01**	**1 04**	**10 29**	**1 40**
24 Tu	11 56 47	+20 46	5 21	18 32	5 02	18 52	4 38	19 16	4 03	19 52	3 03	20 52
145			**12 37**	**0 43**	**12 30**	**0 52**	**12 22**	**1 02**	**12 11**	**1 17**	**11 53**	**1 40**
25 We	11 56 52	+20 57	5 21	18 33	5 01	18 52	4 37	19 17	4 02	19 53	3 01	20 55
146			**13 25**	**1 14**	**13 23**	**1 18**	**13 22**	**1 22**	**13 19**	**1 29**	**13 15**	**1 38**
26 Th	11 56 58	+21 08	5 21	18 33	5 01	18 53	4 36	19 18	4 01	19 54	2 59	20 57
147			**14 14**	**1 44**	**14 17**	**1 43**	**14 22**	**1 42**	**14 29**	**1 40**	**14 39**	**1 37**
27 Fr	11 57 05	+21 18	5 21	18 34	5 01	18 53	4 36	19 19	4 00	19 55	2 57	20 59
148			**15 04**	**2 16**	**15 13**	**2 10**	**15 25**	**2 02**	**15 40**	**1 52**	**16 05**	**1 36**
28 Sa	11 57 12	+21 28	5 20	18 34	5 00	18 54	4 35	19 20	3 59	19 56	2 56	21 00
149			**15 57**	**2 50**	**16 12**	**2 38**	**16 30**	**2 24**	**16 56**	**2 05**	**17 38**	**1 35**
29 Su	11 57 20	+21 37	5 20	18 35	5 00	18 54	4 34	19 20	3 58	19 57	2 54	21 02
150			**16 54**	**3 27**	**17 14**	**3 10**	**17 39**	**2 49**	**18 15**	**2 21**	**19 18**	**1 35**
30 Mo	11 57 28	+21 46	5 20	18 35	5 00	18 55	4 34	19 21	3 57	19 58	2 52	21 04
151			**17 55**	**4 09**	**18 19**	**3 48**	**18 51**	**3 21**	**19 36**	**2 42**	**21 05**	**1 36**
31 Tu	11 57 36	+21 55	5 20	18 36	5 00	18 56	4 33	19 22	3 56	19 59	2 50	21 06
152	**10 53** ○		**18 58**	**4 59**	**19 26**	**4 33**	**20 01**	**4 00**	**20 54**	**3 13**	**22 50**	**1 42**

6th Month — June, 1988 — 30 days

Greenwich Mean Time

NOTE: Light numbers indicate Sun. **Dark** numbers indicate **Moon.** *Degrees are North Latitude.*

CAUTION: Must be converted to local time. For instruction see page 197.

Day of month / week / year	Sun on meridian / Moon phase (h m s)	Sun's Declination (° ′)	20° Rise Sun / Moon (h m)	20° Set Sun / Moon (h m)	30° Rise Sun / Moon (h m)	30° Set Sun / Moon (h m)	40° Rise Sun / Moon (h m)	40° Set Sun / Moon (h m)	50° Rise Sun / Moon (h m)	50° Set Sun / Moon (h m)	60° Rise Sun / Moon (h m)	60° Set Sun / Moon (h m)
1 We	11 57 45	+22 03	5 20	18 36	5 00	18 56	4 33	19 22	3 56	20 00	2 49	21 08
153			**20 01**	**5 55**	**20 30**	**5 27**	**21 07**	**4 50**	**22 02**	**3 56**		**2 00**
2 Th	11 57 54	+22 11	5 20	18 36	4 59	18 57	4 32	19 23	3 55	20 01	2 48	21 09
154			**21 02**	**6 57**	**21 29**	**6 29**	**22 03**	**5 52**	**22 53**	**4 58**	**0 05**	**2 55**
3 Fr	11 58 04	+22 19	5 20	18 37	4 59	18 58	4 32	19 24	3 54	20 02	2 46	21 11
155			**21 56**	**8 03**	**22 19**	**7 37**	**22 49**	**7 04**	**23 30**	**6 15**	**0 35**	**4 35**
4 Sa	11 58 14	+22 26	5 20	18 37	4 59	18 58	4 32	19 25	3 54	20 03	2 45	21 12
156			**22 45**	**9 09**	**23 03**	**8 48**	**23 25**	**8 20**	**23 56**	**7 41**	**0 44**	**6 31**
5 Su	11 58 24	+22 33	5 20	18 37	4 58	18 58	4 32	19 25	3 53	20 04	2 44	21 14
157			**23 28**	**10 13**	**23 40**	**9 57**	**23 55**	**9 37**		**9 10**	**0 47**	**8 23**
6 Mo	11 58 35	+22 39	5 20	18 38	4 58	18 59	4 31	10 26	3 52	20 05	2 42	21 16
158				**11 14**		**11 05**		**10 52**	**0 16**	**10 36**	**0 48**	**10 09**
7 Tu	11 58 46	+22 45	5 20	18 38	4 58	18 59	4 31	19 27	3 52	20 06	2 41	21 17
159	**06 21** ☾		**0 07**	**12 13**	**0 13**	**12 10**	**0 21**	**12 05**	**0 31**	**11 59**	**0 47**	**11 50**
8 We	11 58 57	+22 51	5 20	18 38	4 58	19 00	4 31	19 27	3 52	20 07	2 40	21 18
160			**0 44**	**13 11**	**0 44**	**13 13**	**0 45**	**13 17**	**0 45**	**13 21**	**0 46**	**13 28**
9 Th	11 59 08	+22 56	5 20	18 39	4 58	19 00	4 31	19 28	3 52	20 08	2 40	21 19
161			**1 21**	**14 08**	**1 15**	**14 17**	**1 08**	**14 28**	**0 59**	**14 43**	**0 46**	**15 07**
10 Fr	11 59 20	+23 01	5 20	18 39	4 58	19 01	4 31	19 28	3 51	20 08	2 39	21 21
162			**1 59**	**15 07**	**1 47**	**15 21**	**1 33**	**15 40**	**1 14**	**16 06**	**0 45**	**16 48**
11 Sa	11 59 32	+23 05	5 20	18 39	4 58	19 01	4 31	10 20	5 51	20 09	2 38	21 22
163			**2 39**	**16 06**	**2 22**	**16 27**	**2 01**	**16 52**	**1 32**	**17 28**	**0 46**	**18 32**
12 Su	11 59 45	+23 09	5 20	18 40	4 58	19 02	4 31	10 20	3 51	20 10	2 38	21 23
164			**3 23**	**17 08**	**3 02**	**17 32**	**2 34**	**18 03**	**1 55**	**18 49**	**0 48**	**20 18**
13 Mo	11 59 57	+23 13	5 20	18 40	4 58	19 02	4 30	19 30	3 50	20 10	2 37	21 24
165			**4 12**	**18 08**	**3 46**	**18 36**	**3 14**	**19 11**	**2 26**	**20 03**	**0 56**	**21 55**
14 Tu	12 00 10	+23 16	5 20	18 40	4 58	19 03	4 30	19 30	3 50	20 11	2 37	21 24
166	**09 14** ●		**5 05**	**19 08**	**4 37**	**19 35**	**4 02**	**20 11**	**3 09**	**21 05**	**1 16**	**23 03**
15 We	12 00 23	+23 19	5 20	18 41	4 58	19 03	4 30	19 31	3 50	20 11	2 36	21 25
167			**6 02**	**20 00**	**5 33**	**20 27**	**4 57**	**21 01**	**4 04**	**21 52**	**2 05**	**23 34**
16 Th	12 00 36	+23 21	5 20	18 41	4 58	19 03	4 30	19 31	3 50	20 12	2 36	21 26
168			**6 59**	**20 48**	**6 33**	**21 12**	**5 59**	**21 42**	**5 10**	**22 26**	**3 29**	**23 45**
17 Fr	12 00 49	+23 23	5 20	18 42	4 58	19 04	4 30	19 32	3 50	20 12	2 36	21 26
169			**7 55**	**21 30**	**7 32**	**21 50**	**7 03**	**22 15**	**6 22**	**22 50**	**5 05**	**23 49**
18 Sa	12 01 02	+23 25	5 21	18 42	4 59	19 04	4 31	19 32	3 50	20 12	2 35	21 27
170			**8 49**	**22 07**	**8 30**	**22 23**	**8 07**	**22 42**	**7 35**	**23 08**	**6 39**	**23 50**
19 Su	12 01 15	+23 26	5 21	18 42	4 59	19 04	4 31	19 32	3 50	20 13	2 35	21 27
171			**9 40**	**22 45**	**9 27**	**22 52**	**9 10**	**23 05**	**8 46**	**23 23**	**8 08**	**23 50**
20 Mo	12 01 28	+23 26	5 21	18 42	4 59	19 04	4 31	19 32	3 50	20 13	2 35	21 27
172			**10 29**	**23 13**	**10 21**	**23 19**	**10 10**	**23 26**	**9 56**	**23 35**	**9 33**	**23 49**
21 Tu	12 01 41	+23 27	5 21	18 42	4 59	19 04	4 32	19 32	3 50	20 13	2 35	21 28
173			**11 17**	**23 43**	**11 14**	**23 44**	**11 10**	**23 45**	**11 04**	**23 46**	**10 55**	**23 48**
22 We	12 01 54	+23 26	5 22	18 42	5 00	19 05	4 32	19 33	3 51	20 13	2 36	21 28
174	**10 23** ☽		**12 05**		**12 07**		**12 09**		**12 12**	**23 57**	**12 17**	**23 47**
23 Th	12 02 07	+23 26	5 22	18 42	5 00	19 05	4 32	19 33	3 51	20 13	2 36	21 28
175			**12 54**	**0 14**	**13 01**	**0 10**	**13 10**	**0 04**	**13 22**		**13 41**	**23 46**
24 Fr	12 02 20	+23 25	5 22	18 42	5 00	19 05	4 32	19 33	3 52	20 13	2 37	21 28
176			**13 45**	**0 46**	**13 58**	**0 37**	**14 13**	**0 25**	**14 35**	**0 10**	**15 09**	**23 45**
25 Sa	12 02 33	+23 24	5 23	18 42	5 00	19 05	4 32	19 33	3 52	20 13	2 38	21 28
177			**14 40**	**1 21**	**14 58**	**1 07**	**15 20**	**0 49**	**15 51**	**0 24**	**16 45**	**23 46**
26 Su	12 02 45	+23 22	5 23	18 43	5 01	19 05	4 33	19 33	3 52	20 13	2 38	21 27
178			**15 38**	**2 01**	**16 01**	**1 41**	**16 30**	**1 17**	**17 11**	**0 43**	**18 28**	**23 49**
27 Mo	12 02 58	+23 20	5 23	18 43	5 01	19 05	4 33	19 33	3 53	20 13	2 39	21 27
179			**16 41**	**2 47**	**17 07**	**2 22**	**17 41**	**1 52**	**18 31**	**1 08**	**20 16**	
28 Tu	12 03 10	+23 17	5 23	18 43	5 01	19 05	4 34	19 33	3 53	20 13	2 40	21 26
180			**17 45**	**3 40**	**18 13**	**3 12**	**18 50**	**2 37**	**19 45**	**1 46**	**21 49**	
29 We	12 03 22	+23 14	5 24	18 43	5 01	19 05	4 34	19 33	3 54	20 12	2 40	21 26
181	**19 46** ○		**18 48**	**4 40**	**19 16**	**4 12**	**16 51**	**3 35**	**20 45**	**2 40**	**22 37**	**0 35**
30 Th	12 03 34	+23 10	5 24	18 43	5 02	19 05	4 34	19 33	3 54	20 12	2 41	21 25
182			**19 46**	**5 47**	**20 11**	**5 19**	**20 42**	**4 44**	**21 28**	**3 52**	**22 52**	**2 01**

7th Month — July, 1988 — 31 Days

Greenwich Mean Time

NOTE: Light numbers indicate Sun. **Dark** numbers indicate **Moon.** *Degrees are North Latitude.*

CAUTION: Must be converted to local time. For instruction see page 197.

Day of month week year	Sun on meridian **Moon phase** h m s	Sun's Declination ° ′	20° Rise Sun **Moon** h m	20° Set Sun **Moon** h m	30° Rise Sun **Moon** h m	30° Set Sun **Moon** h m	40° Rise Sun **Moon** h m	40° Set Sun **Moon** h m	50° Rise Sun **Moon** h m	50° Set Sun **Moon** h m	60° Rise Sun **Moon** h m	60° Set Sun **Moon** h m
1 Fr	12 03 46	+23 07	5 24	18 43	5 02	19 05	4 35	19 33	3 55	20 12	2 42	21 21
183			**20 38**	**6 55**	**20 58**	**6 31**	**21 23**	**6 02**	**21 58**	**5 07**	**22 57**	**3 57**
2 Sa	12 03 57	+23 02	5 24	18 43	5 02	19 05	4 35	19 33	3 56	20 12	2 43	21 24
184			**21 25**	**8 02**	**21 39**	**7 44**	**21 56**	**7 21**	**22 20**	**6 41**	**22 58**	**5 55**
3 Su	12 04 08	+22 58	5 24	18 44	5 03	19 05	4 36	19 32	3 56	20 11	2 44	21 23
185			**22 06**	**9 06**	**22 14**	**8 54**	**22 24**	**8 40**	**22 38**	**8 14**	**22 58**	**7 47**
4 Mo	12 04 19	+22 53	5 25	18 44	5 03	19 05	4 36	19 32	3 57	20 11	2 46	21 22
186			**22 45**	**10 07**	**22 47**	**10 01**	**22 49**	**9 55**	**22 52**	**9 44**	**22 57**	**9 32**
5 Tu	12 04 30	+22 47	5 25	18 44	5 04	19 05	4 37	19 32	3 58	20 11	2 47	21 21
187			**23 22**	**11 06**	**23 18**	**11 07**	**23 13**	**11 08**	**23 06**	**11 10**	**22 57**	**11 12**
6 We	12 04 40	+22 42	5 25	18 44	5 04	19 05	4 37	19 32	3 59	20 10	2 48	21 20
188	**11 36** ☾		**23 59**	**12 03**	**23 49**	**12 11**	**23 37**	**12 20**	**23 21**	**12 35**	**22 56**	**12 51**
7 Th	12 04 50	+22 35	5 26	18 44	5 05	19 04	4 38	19 31	4 00	20 10	2 50	21 18
189				**13 02**		**13 15**		**13 31**	**23 38**	**14 00**	**22 56**	**14 31**
8 Fr	12 04 59	+22 29	5 26	18 43	5 05	19 04	4 38	19 31	4 00	20 09	2 52	21 17
190			**0 39**	**14 01**	**0 23**	**14 19**	**0 04**	**14 43**	**23 59**	**15 25**	**22 58**	**16 14**
9 Sa	12 05 08	+22 22	5 27	18 43	5 06	19 04	4 39	19 31	4 01	20 09	2 53	21 16
191			**1 21**	**15 00**	**1 01**	**15 24**	**0 35**	**15 54**		**16 49**	**23 03**	**17 58**
10 Su	12 05 17	+22 14	5 27	18 43	5 06	19 04	4 40	19 30	4 02	20 08	2 55	21 14
192			**2 08**	**16 00**	**1 43**	**16 27**	**1 12**	**17 02**	**0 27**	**18 07**	**23 17**	**19 39**
11 Mo	12 05 26	+22 07	5 28	18 43	5 07	19 03	4 40	19 30	4 03	20 07	2 56	21 13
193			**2 59**	**16 59**	**2 31**	**17 27**	**1 56**	**18 03**	**1 04**	**19 13**	**23 55**	**20 58**
12 Tu	12 05 33	+21 58	5 28	18 43	5 07	19 03	4 41	19 29	4 04	20 06	2 58	21 12
194			**3 54**	**17 53**	**3 25**	**18 21**	**2 49**	**18 56**	**1 55**	**20 03**		**21 38**
13 We	12 05 41	+21 50	5 28	18 43	5 08	19 03	4 42	19 29	4 05	20 05	3 00	21 10
195	**21 53** ●		**4 50**	**18 43**	**4 23**	**19 08**	**3 48**	**19 40**	**2 57**	**20 39**	**1 08**	**21 54**
14 Th	12 05 48	+21 41	5 28	18 43	5 08	19 03	4 43	19 28	4 06	20 04	3 02	21 08
196			**5 46**	**19 27**	**5 22**	**19 48**	**4 52**	**20 15**	**4 07**	**21 03**	**2 42**	**21 59**
15 Fr	12 05 54	+21 32	5 29	18 42	5 09	19 02	4 43	19 28	4 08	20 04	3 04	21 06
197			**6 41**	**20 06**	**6 21**	**20 23**	**5 56**	**20 44**	**5 20**	**21 21**	**4 17**	**22 01**
16 Sa	12 06 00	+21 22	5 29	18 42	5 09	19 02	4 44	19 27	4 09	20 03	3 06	21 05
198			**7 33**	**20 41**	**7 18**	**20 53**	**6 59**	**21 08**	**6 32**	**21 34**	**5 48**	**22 01**
17 Su	12 06 06	+21 12	5 30	18 42	5 10	19 02	4 45	19 27	4 10	20 02	3 08	21 03
199			**8 23**	**21 13**	**8 13**	**21 20**	**8 00**	**21 29**	**7 43**	**21 45**	**7 15**	**22 00**
18 Mo	12 06 11	+21 02	5 30	18 42	5 10	19 01	4 46	19 26	4 11	20 01	3 10	21 01
200			**9 12**	**21 43**	**9 07**	**21 46**	**9 00**	**21 49**	**8 52**	**21 54**	**8 38**	**21 59**
19 Tu	12 06 15	+20 51	5 30	18 42	5 11	19 01	4 47	19 26	4 12	20 00	3 12	20 59
201			**9 59**	**22 14**	**9 59**	**22 11**	**9 59**	**22 08**	**9 59**	**22 03**	**9 59**	**21 58**
20 We	12 06 19	+20 40	5 31	18 41	5 11	19 00	4 48	19 25	4 14	19 58	3 14	21 57
202			**10 47**	**22 45**	**10 52**	**22 37**	**10 59**	**22 28**	**11 07**	**22 12**	**11 21**	**21 56**
21 Th	12 06 22	+20 28	5 31	18 41	5 12	19 00	4 49	19 24	4 15	19 57	3 16	20 55
203			**11 36**	**23 18**	**11 47**	**23 05**	**12 00**	**22 50**	**12 18**	**22 23**	**12 46**	**21 55**
22 Fr	12 06 25	+20 17	5 31	18 41	5 13	18 59	4 50	19 23	4 16	19 56	3 18	20 53
204	**02 14** ☽		**12 28**	**23 54**	**12 44**	**23 37**	**13 04**	**23 15**	**13 31**	**22 37**	**14 17**	**21 55**
23 Sa	12 06 27	+20 05	5 32	18 40	5 13	18 59	4 50	19 22	4 18	19 54	3 20	20 51
205			**13 24**		**13 44**		**14 11**	**23 46**	**14 48**	**22 56**	**15 54**	**21 57**
24 Su	12 06 28	+19 52	5 32	18 40	5 14	18 58	4 51	19 21	4 19	19 53	3 23	20 49
206			**14 23**	**0 36**	**14 48**	**0 14**	**15 20**		**16 07**	**23 24**	**17 39**	**22 02**
25 Mo	12 06 29	+19 39	5 33	18 40	5 15	18 58	4 52	19 20	4 20	19 52	3 25	20 47
207			**15 26**	**1 25**	**15 54**	**0 59**	**16 30**	**0 26**	**17 23**		**19 22**	**22 22**
26 Tu	12 06 29	+19 26	5 33	18 39	5 15	18 57	4 53	19 19	4 21	19 51	3 27	20 44
208			**16 29**	**2 21**	**16 58**	**1 53**	**17 34**	**1 16**	**18 30**	**0 22**	**20 33**	**23 22**
27 We	12 06 29	+19 13	5 33	18 39	5 16	18 56	4 54	19 18	4 22	19 50	3 30	20 42
209			**17 30**	**3 25**	**17 56**	**2 57**	**18 30**	**2 20**	**19 20**	**1 25**	**20 59**	
28 Th	12 06 28	+18 59	5 34	18 38	5 16	18 56	4 55	19 18	4 24	19 48	3 32	20 40
210			**18 25**	**4 33**	**18 48**	**4 07**	**19 16**	**3 25**	**19 56**	**2 46**	**21 07**	**1 10**
29 Fr	12 06 27	+18 45	5 34	18 38	5 17	18 55	4 56	19 17	4 25	19 47	3 34	20 37
211	**03 25** ○		**19 15**	**5 42**	**19 32**	**5 21**	**19 53**	**4 55**	**20 22**	**4 18**	**21 09**	**3 11**
30 Sa	12 06 24	+18 31	5 34	18 37	5 18	18 54	4 57	19 16	4 26	19 46	3 36	20 34
212			**20 00**	**6 49**	**20 11**	**6 35**	**20 24**	**6 16**	**20 42**	**5 51**	**21 09**	**5 09**
31 Su	12 06 22	+18 16	5 35	18 37	5 18	18 54	4 58	19 15	4 28	19 44	3 38	20 32
213			**20 41**	**7 53**	**20 45**	**7 45**	**20 51**	**7 36**	**20 58**	**7 22**	**21 09**	**7 01**

8th Month **August, 1988** **31 Days**

Greenwich Mean Time

NOTE: Light numbers indicate Sun. **Dark** numbers indicate **Moon.** *Degrees are North Latitude.*

CAUTION: Must be converted to local time. For instruction see page 197.

Day of month week year	Sun on meridian **Moon phase** h m s	Sun's Declination °	20° Rise Sun **Moon** h m	20° Set Sun **Moon** h m	30° Rise Sun **Moon** h m	30° Set Sun **Moon** h m	40° Rise Sun **Moon** h m	40° Set Sun **Moon** h m	50° Rise Sun **Moon** h m	50° Set Sun **Moon** h m	60° Rise Sun **Moon** h m	60° Set Sun **Moon** h m
1 Mo	12 06 18	+18 01	5 36	18 36	5 19	18 53	4 58	19 14	4 30	19 42	3 41	20 30
214			**21 20**	**8 55**	**21 18**	**8 54**	**21 15**	**8 52**	**21 12**	**8 50**	**21 08**	**8 47**
2 Tu	12 06 14	+17 46	5 36	18 36	5 20	18 52	4 59	19 13	4 31	19 41	3 43	20 27
215			**21 58**	**9 55**	**21 50**	**10 00**	**21 40**	**10 07**	**21 27**	**10 16**	**21 07**	**10 29**
3 We	12 06 10	+17 30	5 36	18 36	5 20	18 51	5 00	19 12	4 32	19 39	3 46	20 24
216			**22 38**	**10 55**	**22 24**	**11 06**	**22 07**	**11 20**	**21 43**	**11 40**	**21 07**	**12 12**
4 Th	12 06 04	+17 15	5 37	18 35	5 21	18 50	5 01	19 10	4 34	19 38	3 48	20 22
217	**18 22** ☾		**23 20**	**11 55**	**23 00**	**12 12**	**22 36**	**12 34**	**22 03**	**13 04**	**21 08**	**13 56**
5 Fr	12 05 59	+16 58	5 37	18 35	5 21	18 50	5 02	19 09	4 36	19 36	3 50	20 17
218				**12 55**	**23 42**	**13 17**	**23 12**	**13 46**	**22 29**	**14 26**	**21 11**	**15 41**
6 Sa	12 05 52	+16 42	5 37	18 34	5 22	18 49	5 03	19 08	4 37	19 34	3 53	20 17
219			**0 06**	**13 55**		**14 21**	**23 54**	**14 55**	**23 03**	**15 44**	**21 21**	**17 25**
7 Su	12 05 45	+16 25	5 37	18 34	5 22	18 48	5 04	19 07	4 38	19 32	3 55	20 14
220			**0 55**	**14 54**	**0 28**	**15 22**		**15 58**	**23 49**	**16 53**	**21 49**	**18 53**
8 Mo	12 05 38	+16 09	5 38	18 33	5 23	18 48	5 05	19 06	4 39	19 30	3 58	20 12
221			**1 49**	**15 49**	**1 20**	**16 18**	**0 44**	**16 54**		**17 48**	**22 52**	**19 44**
9 Tu	12 05 30	+15 51	5 38	18 32	5 23	18 47	5 06	19 04	4 41	19 29	4 00	20 09
222			**2 44**	**16 40**	**2 17**	**17 06**	**1 41**	**17 40**	**0 48**	**18 28**		**20 04**
10 We	12 05 21	+15 34	5 38	18 32	5 24	18 46	5 07	19 03	4 42	19 27	4 02	20 06
223			**3 40**	**17 25**	**3 15**	**17 48**	**2 43**	**18 17**	**1 56**	**18 58**	**0 22**	**20 11**
11 Th	12 05 12	+15 16	5 38	18 31	5 25	18 45	5 08	19 02	4 44	19 25	4 04	20 03
224			**4 35**	**18 05**	**4 14**	**18 24**	**3 47**	**18 47**	**3 08**	**19 20**	**1 58**	**20 13**
12 Fr	12 05 02	+14 58	5 39	18 31	5 25	18 44	5 09	19 00	4 45	19 23	4 07	20 00
225	**12 31** ●		**5 28**	**18 41**	**5 11**	**18 55**	**4 50**	**19 13**	**4 20**	**19 36**	**3 30**	**20 13**
13 Sa	12 04 52	+14 40	5 39	18 30	5 26	18 43	5 10	18 59	4 46	19 22	4 10	19 58
226			**6 19**	**19 14**	**6 07**	**19 23**	**5 52**	**19 35**	**5 32**	**19 50**	**4 59**	**20 13**
14 Su	12 04 41	+14 22	5 40	18 29	5 27	18 42	5 11	18 58	4 48	19 20	4 12	19 55
227			**7 08**	**19 45**	**7 01**	**19 49**	**6 52**	**19 54**	**6 41**	**20 01**	**6 23**	**20 11**
15 Mo	12 04 30	+14 03	5 40	18 28	5 27	18 41	5 12	18 56	4 50	19 18	4 14	19 52
228			**7 55**	**20 15**	**7 51**	**20 11**	**7 53**	**20 13**	**7 40**	**20 10**	**7 44**	**20 10**
16 Tu	12 04 18	+13 44	5 40	18 28	5 28	18 40	5 12	18 55	4 51	19 16	4 17	19 49
229			**8 43**	**20 46**	**8 46**	**20 40**	**8 51**	**20 33**	**8 56**	**20 23**	**9 06**	**20 08**
17 We	12 04 05	+13 25	5 41	18 27	5 28	18 39	5 13	18 54	4 52	19 14	4 20	19 47
230			**9 31**	**21 18**	**9 40**	**21 07**	**9 51**	**20 53**	**10 05**	**20 35**	**10 29**	**20 07**
18 Th	12 03 52	+13 06	5 41	18 26	5 29	18 38	5 14	18 52	4 54	19 12	4 22	19 44
231			**10 21**	**21 52**	**10 35**	**21 36**	**10 52**	**21 17**	**11 17**	**20 50**	**11 56**	**20 06**
19 Fr	12 03 39	+12 47	5 41	18 25	5 29	18 37	5 15	18 51	4 55	19 10	4 24	19 41
232			**11 14**	**22 31**	**11 33**	**22 10**	**11 57**	**21 45**	**12 31**	**21 08**	**13 29**	**20 07**
20 Sa	12 03 25	+12 27	5 42	18 24	5 30	18 36	5 16	18 49	4 57	19 08	4 26	19 38
233	**15 51** ☽		**12 11**	**23 16**	**12 34**	**22 51**	**13 04**	**22 19**	**13 47**	**21 34**	**15 09**	**20 10**
21 Su	12 03 10	+12 07	5 42	18 24	5 30	18 35	5 17	18 48	4 58	19 06	4 29	19 36
234			**13 10**		**13 37**	**23 39**	**14 12**	**23 04**	**15 04**	**22 11**	**16 53**	**20 20**
22 Mo	12 02 55	+11 47	5 42	18 23	5 31	18 34	5 18	18 47	5 00	19 04	4 31	19 33
235			**14 12**	**0 07**	**14 40**		**15 17**		**16 13**	**23 04**	**18 21**	**20 56**
23 Tu	12 02 40	+11 27	5 42	18 22	5 32	18 33	5 19	18 46	5 02	19 02	4 34	19 30
236			**15 12**	**1 06**	**15 40**	**0 37**	**16 16**	**0 00**	**17 10**		**19 03**	**22 23**
24 We	12 02 24	+11 06	5 43	18 22	5 32	18 32	5 20	18 44	5 03	19 00	4 36	19 27
237			**16 09**	**2 10**	**16 34**	**1 43**	**17 06**	**1 08**	**17 52**	**0 15**	**19 16**	
25 Th	12 02 08	+10 46	5 43	18 21	5 33	18 30	5 21	18 42	5 04	18 58	4 38	19 24
238			**17 02**	**3 18**	**17 22**	**2 54**	**17 47**	**2 25**	**18 22**	**1 41**	**19 20**	**0 19**
26 Fr	12 01 51	+10 25	5 43	18 20	5 34	18 29	5 22	18 41	5 06	18 56	4 41	19 21
239			**17 49**	**4 26**	**18 03**	**4 08**	**18 20**	**3 46**	**18 44**	**3 14**	**19 21**	**2 20**
27 Sa	12 01 34	+10 04	5 43	18 19	5 34	18 28	5 23	18 39	5 08	18 54	4 43	19 18
240	**10 56** ○		**18 32**	**5 32**	**18 04**	**5 21**	**18 49**	**5 07**	**19 02**	**4 47**	**19 21**	**4 16**
28 Su	12 01 16	+09 43	5 44	18 18	5 35	18 27	5 24	18 38	5 09	18 52	4 45	19 15
241			**19 13**	**6 36**	**19 14**	**6 32**	**19 15**	**6 26**	**19 17**	**6 18**	**19 20**	**6 06**
29 Mo	12 00 58	+09 22	5 44	18 18	5 35	18 26	5 25	18 36	5 10	18 50	4 48	19 12
242			**19 53**	**7 39**	**19 47**	**7 41**	**19 41**	**7 44**	**19 32**	**7 48**	**19 19**	**7 54**
30 Tu	12 00 40	+09 00	5 44	18 17	5 36	18 25	5 26	18 34	5 12	18 48	4 50	19 09
243			**20 33**	**8 41**	**20 21**	**8 50**	**20 07**	**9 01**	**19 48**	**9 16**	**19 18**	**9 40**
31 We	12 00 22	+08 39	5 44	18 16	5 36	18 24	5 27	18 32	5 14	18 46	4 45	19 06
244			**21 15**	**9 43**	**20 58**	**9 58**	**20 36**	**10 17**	**20 07**	**10 43**	**19 19**	**11 27**

9th Month — September, 1988 — 30 Days

Greenwich Mean Time

NOTE: Light numbers indicate Sun. **Dark** numbers indicate **Moon.** *Degrees are North Latitude.*

CAUTION: Must be converted to local time. For instruction see page 197.

Day of month week year	Sun on meridian **Moon phase** h m s	Sun's Decli-nation °	20° Rise Sun **Moon** h m	20° Set Sun **Moon** h m	30° Rise Sun **Moon** h m	30° Set Sun **Moon** h m	40° Rise Sun **Moon** h m	40° Set Sun **Moon** h m	50° Rise Sun **Moon** h m	50° Set Sun **Moon** h m	60° Rise Sun **Moon** h m	60° Set Sun **Moon** h m
1 Th	12 00 03	+08 17	5 44	18 15	5 37	18 22	5 28	18 31	5 15	18 44	4 55	19 03
245			**22 01**	**10 45**	**21 39**	**11 06**	**21 10**	**11 32**	**20 31**	**12 09**	**19 21**	**13 16**
2 Fr	11 59 44	+07 55	5 45	18 14	5 38	18 21	5 29	18 30	5 16	18 41	4 58	19 00
246			**22 51**	**11 47**	**22 24**	**12 12**	**21 51**	**12 45**	**21 02**	**13 32**	**19 28**	**15 04**
3 Sa	11 59 24	+07 33	5 45	18 13	5 38	18 20	5 30	18 28	5 18	18 39	5 00	18 57
247	**03 50 ☾**		**23 44**	**12 48**	**23 15**	**13 16**	**22 39**	**13 52**	**21 45**	**14 45**	**19 48**	**16 42**
4 Su	11 59 05	+07 11	5 46	18 12	5 38	18 19	5 31	18 26	5 20	18 37	5 02	18 54
248				**13 45**		**14 14**	**23 35**	**14 50**	**22 40**	**15 45**	**20 39**	**17 47**
5 Mo	11 58 45	+06 49	5 46	18 12	5 39	18 18	5 32	18 25	5 21	18 35	5 04	18 51
249			**0 39**	**14 37**	**0 11**	**15 05**		**15 39**	**23 46**	**16 30**	**22 04**	**18 13**
6 Tu	11 58 25	+06 27	5 46	18 11	5 40	18 16	5 32	18 24	5 22	18 33	5 07	18 48
250			**1 36**	**15 24**	**1 09**	**15 48**	**0 36**	**16 19**		**17 03**	**23 40**	**18 23**
7 We	11 58 04	+06 04	5 46	18 11	5 40	18 15	5 33	18 22	5 24	18 31	5 09	18 45
251			**2 31**	**16 06**	**2 08**	**16 26**	**1 39**	**16 51**	**0 57**	**17 26**		**18 26**
8 Th	11 57 44	+05 42	5 47	18 09	5 41	18 14	5 34	18 20	5 26	18 29	5 12	18 42
252			**3 24**	**16 43**	**3 06**	**16 58**	**2 43**	**17 18**	**2 10**	**17 44**	**1 13**	**18 26**
9 Fr	11 57 37	+05 19	5 47	18 08	5 41	18 12	5 35	18 18	5 27	18 26	5 14	18 39
253			**4 15**	**17 16**	**4 02**	**17 27**	**3 45**	**17 40**	**3 21**	**17 58**	**2 43**	**18 26**
10 Sa	11 57 02	+04 56	5 47	18 07	5 42	18 11	5 36	18 17	5 28	18 24	5 16	18 36
254			**5 12**	**17 48**	**4 56**	**17 54**	**4 45**	**18 01**	**4 31**	**18 10**	**4 08**	**18 24**
11 Su	11 56 41	+04 34	5 47	18 06	5 42	18 10	5 37	18 15	5 30	18 22	5 19	18 33
255	**04 49 ●**		**5 55**	**18 18**	**5 49**	**18 19**	**5 45**	**18 20**	**5 39**	**18 21**	**5 30**	**18 23**
12 Mo	11 56 20	+04 11	5 47	18 05	5 43	18 09	5 38	18 14	5 32	18 20	5 21	18 30
256			**6 38**	**18 48**	**6 42**	**18 44**	**6 44**	**18 39**	**6 47**	**18 32**	**6 52**	**18 21**
13 Tu	11 55 59	+03 48	5 47	18 04	5 43	18 08	5 39	18 12	5 33	18 18	5 24	18 27
257			**7 22**	**19 20**	**7 35**	**19 10**	**7 44**	**18 59**	**7 56**	**18 44**	**8 14**	**18 20**
14 We	11 55 38	+03 25	5 47	18 04	5 44	18 06	5 40	18 10	5 34	18 15	5 26	18 24
258			**8 07**	**19 53**	**8 30**	**19 39**	**8 45**	**19 21**	**9 06**	**18 57**	**9 40**	**18 19**
15 Th	11 55 17	+03 02	5 47	18 03	5 45	18 05	5 41	18 09	5 36	18 13	5 28	18 21
259			**8 54**	**20 30**	**9 27**	**20 11**	**9 48**	**19 47**	**10 19**	**19 14**	**11 11**	**18 19**
16 Fr	11 54 55	+02 39	5 47	18 02	5 45	18 04	5 42	18 07	5 38	18 11	5 30	18 18
260			**9 45**	**21 12**	**10 26**	**20 49**	**10 54**	**20 19**	**11 34**	**19 37**	**12 47**	**18 21**
17 Sa	11 54 34	+02 15	5 48	18 01	5 46	18 02	5 43	18 06	5 39	18 08	5 32	18 15
261			**10 39**	**22 00**	**11 27**	**21 33**	**12 00**	**20 59**	**12 49**	**20 08**	**14 29**	**18 27**
18 Su	11 54 13	+01 52	5 48	18 00	5 46	18 01	5 44	18 04	5 40	18 06	5 35	18 12
262			**11 36**	**22 54**	**12 29**	**22 25**	**13 05**	**21 49**	**14 00**	**20 54**	**16 04**	**18 49**
19 Mo	11 53 51	+01 29	5 48	17 58	5 47	18 00	5 45	18 02	5 42	18 04	5 37	18 09
263	**03 18 ☽**		**12 35**	**23 54**	**13 28**	**23 26**	**14 05**	**22 50**	**15 00**	**21 55**	**17 03**	**19 53**
20 Tu	11 53 30	+01 06	5 48	17 57	5 47	17 59	5 46	18 00	5 44	18 02	5 40	18 06
264			**13 34**		**14 23**		**14 57**		**15 47**	**23 13**	**17 24**	**21 37**
21 We	11 53 09	+00 42	5 48	17 56	5 48	17 58	5 47	17 58	5 45	18 00	5 42	18 02
265			**14 30**	**0 59**	**15 12**	**0 33**	**15 40**	**0 01**	**16 20**		**17 31**	**23 33**
22 Th	11 52 48	+00 19	5 49	17 55	5 48	17 56	5 48	17 57	5 46	17 58	5 44	17 59
266			**15 22**	**2 04**	**15 55**	**1 44**	**16 16**	**1 18**	**16 45**	**0 40**	**17 33**	
23 Fr	11 52 26	−00 04	5 49	17 54	5 49	17 55	5 49	17 55	5 48	17 56	5 47	17 56
267			**16 12**	**2 10**	**16 33**	**2 55**	**16 46**	**2 37**	**17 04**	**2 11**	**17 33**	**1 28**
24 Sa	11 52 05	−00 28	5 49	17 54	5 49	17 54	5 50	17 54	5 50	17 54	5 49	17 53
268			**16 59**	**4 14**	**17 08**	**4 06**	**17 13**	**3 56**	**17 21**	**3 42**	**17 32**	**3 20**
25 Su	11 51 45	−00 51	5 49	17 53	5 50	17 52	5 50	17 52	5 51	17 52	5 52	17 50
269	**19 07 ○**		**17 45**	**5 17**	**17 41**	**5 16**	**17 39**	**5 14**	**17 36**	**5 12**	**17 31**	**5 08**
26 Mo	11 51 24	−01 46	5 50	17 52	5 50	17 51	5 51	17 50	5 52	17 49	5 54	17 47
270			**18 31**	**6 20**	**18 15**	**6 26**	**18 05**	**6 32**	**17 51**	**6 41**	**17 31**	**6 56**
27 Tu	11 51 03	−01 38	5 50	17 51	5 51	17 50	5 52	17 49	5 54	17 47	5 56	17 44
271			**19 19**	**7 23**	**18 52**	**7 35**	**18 34**	**7 50**	**18 09**	**8 11**	**17 31**	**8 44**
28 We	11 50 43	−02 01	5 50	17 50	5 51	17 49	5 53	17 47	5 55	17 45	5 58	17 41
272			**20 10**	**8 28**	**19 32**	**8 46**	**19 06**	**9 08**	**18 31**	**9 41**	**17 32**	**10 36**
29 Th	11 50 23	−02 25	5 50	17 49	5 52	17 48	5 54	17 46	5 57	17 42	6 01	17 38
273			**21 03**	**9 32**	**20 17**	**9 55**	**19 45**	**10 25**	**19 00**	**11 08**	**17 37**	**12 29**
30 Fr	11 50 03	−02 48	5 51	17 48	5 52	17 46	5 55	17 44	5 58	17 40	6 04	17 35
274			**21 59**	**10 36**	**21 07**	**11 03**	**20 32**	**11 37**	**19 40**	**12 29**	**17 51**	**14 16**

10th Month — October, 1988 — 31 Days

Greenwich Mean Time

NOTE: Light numbers indicate Sun. **Dark** numbers indicate **Moon.** *Degrees are North Latitude.*

CAUTION: Must be converted to local time. For instruction see page 197.

Day of month week year	Sun on meridian **Moon phase** h m s	Sun's Declination °	20° Rise Sun **Moon** h m	20° Set Sun **Moon** h m	30° Rise Sun **Moon** h m	30° Set Sun **Moon** h m	40° Rise Sun **Moon** h m	40° Set Sun **Moon** h m	50° Rise Sun **Moon** h m	50° Set Sun **Moon** h m	60° Rise Sun **Moon** h m	60° Set Sun **Moon** h m
1 Sa	11 49 43	−03 11	5 51	17 48	5 53	17 45	5 56	17 42	6 00	17 38	6 06	17 32
275			**22 31**	**11 36**	**22 03**	**12 05**	**21 26**	**12 41**	**20 31**	**13 36**	**18 29**	**15 38**
2 Su	11 49 23	−03 34	5 51	17 47	5 54	17 44	5 57	17 40	6 02	17 36	6 08	17 29
276	**16 58** ☾		**23 28**	**12 32**	**23 01**	**13 00**	**22 27**	**13 35**	**21 35**	**14 28**	**19 46**	**16 18**
3 Mo	11 49 05	−03 58	5 52	17 46	5 54	17 43	5 58	17 39	6 03	17 34	6 10	17 26
277				**13 21**		**13 47**	**23 30**	**14 19**	**22 46**	**15 05**	**21 20**	**16 32**
4 Tu	11 48 47	−04 21	5 52	17 45	5 55	17 42	5 59	17 38	6 04	17 31	6 10	17 23
278			**0 25**	**14 05**	**0 01**	**14 26**		**14 53**	**23 58**	**15 31**	**22 56**	**16 37**
5 We	11 48 29	−04 44	5 52	17 44	5 56	17 41	6 00	17 36	6 06	17 29	6 15	17 20
279			**1 19**	**14 43**	**0 59**	**15 00**	**0 34**	**15 22**		**15 51**		**16 38**
6 Th	11 48 11	−05 07	5 52	17 43	5 56	17 40	6 01	17 34	6 08	17 27	6 18	17 17
280			**2 11**	**15 18**	**1 56**	**15 30**	**1 37**	**15 45**	**1 10**	**16 06**	**0 26**	**16 38**
7 Fr	11 47 53	−05 30	5 53	17 42	5 57	17 38	6 02	17 32	6 10	17 25	6 20	17 14
281			**3 01**	**15 50**	**2 51**	**15 57**	**2 38**	**16 06**	**2 20**	**16 19**	**1 53**	**16 37**
8 Sa	11 47 36	−05 53	5 53	17 42	5 58	17 37	6 03	17 31	6 11	17 23	6 22	17 11
282			**3 49**	**16 21**	**3 44**	**16 23**	**3 38**	**16 26**	**3 29**	**16 30**	**3 16**	**16 36**
9 Su	11 47 20	−06 16	5 53	17 41	5 58	17 36	6 04	17 29	6 13	17 21	6 25	17 08
283			**4 37**	**16 51**	**4 37**	**16 48**	**4 37**	**16 45**	**4 37**	**16 41**	**4 37**	**16 34**
10 Mo	11 47 04	−06 39	5 53	17 40	5 59	17 35	6 05	17 28	6 14	17 19	6 28	17 05
284	**21 49** ●		**5 25**	**17 22**	**5 30**	**17 14**	**5 36**	**17 05**	**5 45**	**16 52**	**5 59**	**16 33**
11 Tu	11 46 48	−07 01	5 54	17 40	5 59	17 34	6 06	17 26	6 16	17 17	6 30	17 02
285			**6 14**	**17 55**	**6 24**	**17 42**	**6 37**	**17 27**	**6 55**	**17 05**	**7 24**	**16 32**
12 We	11 46 33	−07 24	5 54	17 39	6 00	17 32	6 07	17 24	6 18	17 15	6 32	16 59
286			**7 05**	**18 31**	**7 21**	**18 13**	**7 41**	**17 52**	**8 08**	**17 21**	**8 54**	**16 32**
13 Th	11 46 18	−07 46	5 54	17 38	6 01	17 31	6 08	17 23	6 19	17 13	6 35	16 56
287			**7 59**	**19 12**	**8 20**	**18 49**	**8 46**	**18 22**	**9 23**	**17 42**	**10 29**	**16 33**
14 Fr	11 46 04	−08 09	5 54	17 37	6 02	17 30	6 09	17 22	6 20	17 11	6 38	16 53
288			**8 56**	**19 57**	**9 21**	**19 32**	**9 52**	**18 59**	**10 39**	**18 11**	**12 09**	**16 39**
15 Sa	11 45 50	−08 31	5 55	17 36	6 02	17 29	6 10	17 20	6 22	17 09	6 40	16 50
289			**9 55**	**20 49**	**10 22**	**20 21**	**10 58**	**19 45**	**11 51**	**18 51**	**13 46**	**16 55**
16 Su	11 45 37	−08 53	5 55	17 36	6 03	17 28	6 12	17 18	6 24	17 07	6 42	16 48
290			**10 53**	**21 47**	**11 22**	**21 18**	**11 59**	**20 42**	**12 54**	**19 47**	**14 58**	**17 43**
17 Mo	11 45 25	−09 15	5 55	17 35	6 03	17 27	6 13	17 17	6 25	17 05	6 45	16 45
291			**11 50**	**22 48**	**12 17**	**22 22**	**12 52**	**21 48**	**13 44**	**20 58**	**15 29**	**19 14**
18 Tu	11 45 13	−09 37	5 55	17 34	6 04	17 26	6 14	17 16	6 27	17 03	6 48	16 42
292	**13 01** ☽		**12 42**	**23 51**	**13 06**	**23 29**	**13 37**	**23 00**	**14 20**	**22 19**	**15 39**	**21 03**
19 We	11 45 02	−09 59	5 56	17 34	6 04	17 25	6 15	17 14	6 28	17 01	6 50	16 39
293			**13 30**		**13 50**		**14 14**		**14 47**	**23 45**	**15 43**	**22 54**
20 Th	11 44 51	−10 20	5 56	17 33	6 05	17 24	6 16	17 13	6 30	16 59	6 52	16 36
294			**14 14**	**0 55**	**14 28**	**0 38**	**14 45**	**0 16**	**15 08**		**15 44**	
21 Fr	11 44 41	−10 42	5 57	17 32	6 06	17 23	6 17	17 12	6 32	16 57	6 55	16 33
295			**14 55**	**1 57**	**15 03**	**1 46**	**15 12**	**1 32**	**15 25**	**1 13**	**15 44**	**0 42**
22 Sa	11 44 31	−11 03	5 57	17 31	6 07	17 22	6 18	17 10	6 34	16 55	6 58	16 30
296			**15 35**	**2 58**	**15 36**	**2 54**	**15 38**	**2 48**	**15 40**	**2 40**	**15 43**	**2 28**
23 Su	11 44 23	−11 24	5 57	17 30	6 08	17 21	6 19	17 09	6 35	16 53	7 00	16 28
297			**16 14**	**4 00**	**16 09**	**4 02**	**16 03**	**4 04**	**15 55**	**4 07**	**15 43**	**4 12**
24 Mo	11 44 15	−11 45	5 58	17 30	6 08	17 20	6 20	17 08	6 36	16 51	7 02	16 25
298			**16 55**	**5 02**	**16 44**	**5 10**	**16 30**	**5 21**	**16 11**	**5 35**	**15 42**	**5 58**
25 Tu	11 44 07	−12 06	5 58	17 29	6 09	17 19	6 21	17 06	6 38	16 49	7 05	16 22
299	**04 35** ○		**17 39**	**6 05**	**17 22**	**6 20**	**17 01**	**6 39**	**16 31**	**7 05**	**15 43**	**7 48**
26 We	11 44 00	−12 27	5 58	17 28	6 10	17 18	6 22	17 05	6 40	16 47	7 08	16 20
300			**18 28**	**7 11**	**18 05**	**7 31**	**17 37**	**7 57**	**16 57**	**8 35**	**15 47**	**9 42**
27 Th	11 43 54	−12 47	5 59	17 28	6 10	17 17	6 24	17 04	6 42	16 42	7 10	16 17
301			**19 21**	**8 16**	**18 54**	**8 41**	**18 21**	**9 14**	**17 32**	**10 01**	**15 57**	**11 35**
28 Fr	11 43 49	−13 07	5 59	17 27	6 11	17 16	6 25	17 02	6 43	16 44	7 12	16 14
302			**20 18**	**9 20**	**19 50**	**9 48**	**19 13**	**10 24**	**18 19**	**11 17**	**16 23**	**13 13**
29 Sa	11 43 45	−13 27	6 00	17 27	6 12	17 15	6 26	17 01	6 45	16 42	7 15	16 12
303			**21 17**	**10 20**	**20 49**	**10 48**	**20 13**	**11 24**	**19 20**	**12 18**	**17 25**	**14 13**
30 Su	11 43 41	−13 47	6 00	17 26	6 13	17 14	6 27	17 00	6 47	16 40	7 18	16 09
304			**22 15**	**11 13**	**21 50**	**11 40**	**21 17**	**12 13**	**20 30**	**13 02**	**18 57**	**14 37**
31 Mo	11 43 38	−14 06	6 01	17 26	6 14	17 14	6 28	16 58	6 48	16 00	7 20	10 00
305			**23 11**	**12 00**	**22 50**	**12 23**	**22 23**	**12 52**	**21 44**	**13 33**	**20 34**	**14 45**

11th Month — November, 1988 — 30 Days

Greenwich Mean Time

NOTE: Light numbers indicate Sun. **Dark** numbers indicate **Moon.** *Degrees are North Latitude.*

CAUTION: Must be converted to local time. For instruction see page 197.

Day of month week year	Sun on meridian **Moon phase** h m s	Sun's Declination ° ′	20° Rise Sun **Moon** h m	20° Set Sun **Moon** h m	30° Rise Sun **Moon** h m	30° Set Sun **Moon** h m	40° Rise Sun **Moon** h m	40° Set Sun **Moon** h m	50° Rise Sun **Moon** h m	50° Set Sun **Moon** h m	60° Rise Sun **Moon** h m	60° Set Sun **Moon** h m
1 Tu	11 43 36	−14 26	6 02	17 26	6 14	17 13	6 29	16 57	6 50	16 37	7 22	16 04
306	**10 11 ☾**			**12 41**	**23 48**	**13 00**	**23 26**	**13 23**	**22 57**	**13 55**	**22 07**	**14 48**
2 We	11 43 35	−14 45	6 02	17 25	6 15	17 12	6 30	16 56	6 52	16 35	7 25	16 01
307			**0 04**	**13 17**		**13 31**		**13 49**		**14 12**	**23 35**	**14 49**
3 Th	11 43 35	−14 56	6 02	17 24	6 16	17 11	6 31	16 55	6 54	16 33	7 28	15 58
308			**0 55**	**13 50**	**0 43**	**14 00**	**0 28**	**14 11**	**0 08**	**14 26**		**14 49**
4 Fr	11 43 35	−15 22	6 03	17 24	6 16	17 10	6 32	16 54	6 55	16 32	7 30	15 56
309			**1 44**	**14 21**	**1 37**	**14 26**	**1 28**	**14 31**	**1 17**	**14 37**	**0 59**	**14 48**
5 Sa	11 43 36	−15 41	6 03	17 23	6 17	17 10	6 34	16 53	6 56	16 30	7 33	15 54
310			**2 31**	**14 52**	**2 30**	**14 51**	**2 28**	**14 50**	**2 25**	**14 49**	**2 20**	**14 47**
6 Su	11 43 38	−15 59	6 04	17 23	6 18	17 09	6 35	16 52	6 58	16 28	7 36	15 51
311			**3 19**	**15 23**	**3 23**	**15 17**	**3 27**	**15 10**	**3 33**	**15 00**	**3 42**	**14 45**
7 Mo	11 43 41	−16 17	6 04	17 23	6 19	17 08	6 36	16 51	7 00	16 26	7 38	15 48
312			**4 08**	**15 55**	**4 17**	**15 44**	**4 27**	**15 31**	**4 42**	**15 13**	**5 06**	**14 45**
8 Tu	11 43 45	−16 34	6 05	17 22	6 20	17 08	6 38	16 50	7 02	16 25	7 41	15 46
313			**4 59**	**16 30**	**5 13**	**16 14**	**5 30**	**15 55**	**5 54**	**15 28**	**6 34**	**14 44**
9 We	11 43 50	−16 52	6 05	17 22	6 20	17 07	6 39	16 49	7 03	16 24	7 44	15 44
314	**14 20 ●**		**5 53**	**17 10**	**6 12**	**16 49**	**6 35**	**16 23**	**7 09**	**15 47**	**8 07**	**14 46**
10 Th	11 43 55	−17 09	6 06	17 22	6 21	17 07	6 40	16 48	7 05	16 22	7 46	15 41
315			**6 49**	**17 55**	**7 13**	**17 30**	**7 42**	**16 59**	**8 26**	**16 14**	**9 47**	**14 50**
11 Fr	11 43 59	−17 25	6 06	17 21	6 22	17 06	6 41	16 47	7 06	16 21	7 48	15 39
316			**7 48**	**18 45**	**8 15**	**18 18**	**8 49**	**17 43**	**9 40**	**16 51**	**11 26**	**15 03**
12 Sa	11 44 09	−17 42	6 07	17 21	6 22	17 06	6 42	16 46	7 08	16 20	7 51	15 36
317			**8 48**	**19 42**	**9 16**	**19 14**	**9 53**	**18 37**	**10 47**	**17 43**	**12 49**	**15 41**
13 Su	11 44 17	−17 58	6 07	17 20	6 23	17 05	6 43	16 45	7 10	16 18	7 54	15 34
318			**9 45**	**20 43**	**10 13**	**20 16**	**10 49**	**19 41**	**11 41**	**18 49**	**13 31**	**17 00**
14 Mo	11 44 25	−18 14	6 08	17 20	6 24	17 04	6 44	16 44	7 11	16 17	7 56	15 32
319			**10 39**	**21 45**	**11 04**	**21 22**	**11 36**	**20 52**	**12 21**	**20 08**	**13 47**	**18 45**
15 Tu	11 44 35	−18 29	6 09	17 20	6 25	17 04	6 45	16 43	7 13	16 16	7 58	15 30
320			**11 28**	**22 47**	**11 49**	**22 29**	**12 14**	**22 05**	**12 51**	**21 32**	**13 52**	**20 34**
16 We	11 44 46	−18 44	6 09	17 20	6 26	17 04	6 46	16 42	7 14	16 14	8 01	15 28
321	**21 35 ☽**		**12 12**	**23 48**	**12 28**	**23 35**	**12 46**	**23 19**	**13 12**	**22 57**	**13 54**	**22 20**
17 Th	11 44 57	−18 59	6 10	17 20	6 27	17 03	6 48	16 42	7 16	16 13	8 04	15 26
322			**12 53**		**13 02**		**13 14**		**13 30**		**13 54**	
18 Fr	11 45 09	−19 14	6 11	17 20	6 28	17 03	6 49	16 41	7 18	16 12	8 06	15 24
323			**13 31**	**0 48**	**13 35**	**0 41**	**13 39**	**0 33**	**13 45**	**0 21**	**13 54**	**0 02**
19 Sa	11 45 22	−19 28	6 11	17 20	6 29	17 02	6 50	16 40	7 20	16 11	8 08	15 22
324			**14 09**	**1 47**	**14 07**	**1 46**	**14 04**	**1 46**	**14 00**	**1 44**	**13 54**	**1 43**
20 Su	11 45 36	−19 42	6 12	17 20	6 30	17 02	6 51	16 40	7 21	16 10	8 11	15 20
325			**14 48**	**2 46**	**14 39**	**2 52**	**14 29**	**2 59**	**14 15**	**3 09**	**13 53**	**3 24**
21 Mo	11 45 50	−19 55	6 13	17 19	6 30	17 01	6 52	16 40	7 22	16 09	8 14	15 18
326			**15 29**	**3 47**	**15 15**	**3 59**	**14 57**	**4 14**	**14 33**	**4 35**	**13 54**	**5 08**
22 Tu	11 46 06	−20 08	6 13	17 19	6 31	17 01	6 53	16 39	7 24	16 08	8 16	15 16
327			**16 15**	**4 50**	**15 55**	**5 08**	**15 30**	**5 31**	**14 55**	**6 03**	**13 57**	**6 57**
23 We	11 46 22	−20 21	6 14	17 19	6 32	17 01	6 54	16 38	7 26	16 07	8 18	15 14
328	**15 53 ○**		**17 06**	**5 55**	**16 41**	**6 18**	**16 10**	**6 48**	**15 25**	**7 30**	**14 03**	**8 50**
24 Th	11 46 39	−20 33	6 14	17 19	6 32	17 01	6 56	16 38	7 27	16 06	8 20	15 13
329			**18 01**	**7 00**	**17 34**	**7 27**	**16 59**	**8 01**	**16 07**	**8 52**	**14 21**	**10 37**
25 Fr	11 46 57	−20 45	6 15	17 19	6 33	17 00	6 57	16 37	7 28	16 05	8 23	15 12
330			**19 00**	**8 03**	**18 32**	**8 31**	**17 56**	**9 07**	**17 03**	**10 01**	**15 06**	**11 58**
26 Sa	11 47 15	−20 57	6 16	17 19	6 34	17 00	6 58	16 37	7 30	16 04	8 25	15 10
331			**20 00**	**9 00**	**19 34**	**9 27**	**19 00**	**10 02**	**18 10**	**10 53**	**17 28**	**12 37**
27 Su	11 47 34	−21 08	6 16	17 19	6 35	17 00	6 59	16 36	7 32	16 04	8 27	15 08
332			**20 59**	**9 51**	**20 36**	**10 15**	**20 06**	**10 46**	**19 24**	**11 30**	**18 06**	**12 51**
28 Mo	11 47 56	−21 18	6 17	17 19	6 36	17 00	7 00	16 36	7 33	16 03	8 29	15 07
333			**21 54**	**10 35**	**21 36**	**10 56**	**21 12**	**11 21**	**20 39**	**11 57**	**19 42**	**12 57**
29 Tu	11 48 15	−21 29	6 18	17 19	6 37	17 00	7 01	16 36	7 34	16 02	8 31	15 06
334			**22 47**	**11 14**	**22 33**	**11 30**	**22 16**	**11 49**	**21 52**	**12 16**	**21 13**	**12 59**
30 We	11 48 36	−21 39	6 18	17 19	6 38	17 00	7 02	16 36	7 36	16 02	8 33	15 04
335			**23 37**	**11 49**	**23 28**	**12 00**	**23 17**	**12 13**	**23 02**	**12 31**	**22 39**	**12 59**

12th Month **December, 1988** 31 days

Greenwich Mean Time

NOTE: Light numbers indicate Sun. **Dark** numbers indicate **Moon.** *Degrees are North Latitude.*

CAUTION: Must be converted to local time. For instruction see page 197.

Day of month week year	Sun on meridian **Moon phase** h m s	Sun's Declination ° ′	20° Rise Sun **Moon** h m	20° Set Sun **Moon** h m	30° Rise Sun **Moon** h m	30° Set Sun **Moon** h m	40° Rise Sun **Moon** h m	40° Set Sun **Moon** h m	50° Rise Sun **Moon** h m	50° Set Sun **Moon** h m	60° Rise Sun **Moon** h m	60° Set Sun **Moon** h m
1 Th	11 48 58	−21 48	6 19	17 19	6 39	17 00	7 03	16 36	7 37	16 02	8 35	15 03
336	**06 49 ☾**			**12 21**		**12 27**		**12 34**		**12 44**		**12 58**
2 Fr	11 49 21	−21 57	6 20	17 19	6 40	17 00	7 04	16 36	7 38	16 01	8 37	15 02
337			**0 25**	**12 51**	**0 21**	**12 52**	**0 17**	**12 53**	**0 11**	**12 55**	**0 01**	**12 57**
3 Sa	11 49 44	−22 06	6 20	17 20	6 40	17 00	7 05	16 35	7 40	16 01	8 39	15 00
338			**1 12**	**13 22**	**1 14**	**13 18**	**1 16**	**13 13**	**1 18**	**13 06**	**1 22**	**12 56**
4 Su	11 50 08	−22 14	6 21	17 20	6 41	17 00	7 06	16 35	7 41	16 00	8 41	14 59
339			**2 00**	**13 53**	**2 07**	**13 44**	**2 15**	**13 33**	**2 27**	**13 18**	**2 44**	**12 56**
5 Mo	11 50 33	−22 22	6 22	17 20	6 42	17 00	7 07	16 35	7 42	16 00	8 43	14 58
340			**2 50**	**14 27**	**3 02**	**14 13**	**3 17**	**13 56**	**3 37**	**13 32**	**4 10**	**12 55**
6 Tu	11 50 58	−22 30	6 22	17 20	6 42	17 00	7 07	16 35	7 43	15 59	8 44	14 58
341			**3 43**	**15 05**	**3 59**	**14 46**	**4 21**	**14 23**	**4 51**	**13 50**	**5 41**	**12 56**
7 We	11 51 23	−22 37	6 23	17 21	6 43	17 00	7 08	16 35	7 44	15 59	8 46	14 57
342			**4 38**	**15 48**	**5 00**	**15 25**	**5 27**	**14 56**	**6 07**	**14 14**	**7 18**	**13 00**
8 Th	11 51 50	−22 43	6 23	17 21	6 44	17 00	7 09	16 35	7 45	15 58	8 48	14 56
343			**5 37**	**16 37**	**6 03**	**16 11**	**6 35**	**15 37**	**7 23**	**14 47**	**9 00**	**13 09**
9 Fr	11 52 16	−22 49	6 24	17 21	6 44	17 00	7 10	16 35	7 46	15 58	8 49	14 56
344	**05 36 ●**		**6 38**	**17 33**	**7 05**	**17 05**	**7 41**	**16 28**	**8 35**	**15 34**	**10 32**	**13 37**
10 Sa	11 52 43	−22 55	6 24	17 22	6 45	17 00	7 11	16 35	7 47	15 58	8 51	14 55
345			**7 37**	**18 34**	**8 05**	**18 06**	**8 41**	**17 31**	**9 35**	**16 38**	**11 30**	**14 43**
11 Su	11 53 11	−23 00	6 25	17 22	6 46	17 01	7 12	16 35	7 48	15 58	8 52	14 54
346			**8 34**	**19 37**	**9 00**	**19 13**	**9 33**	**18 41**	**10 20**	**17 55**	**11 53**	**16 25**
12 Mo	11 53 39	−23 05	6 26	17 22	6 46	17 01	7 13	16 35	7 49	15 58	8 54	14 54
347			**9 25**	**20 41**	**9 47**	**20 21**	**10 15**	**19 56**	**10 53**	**19 19**	**12 01**	**18 15**
13 Tu	11 54 07	−23 09	6 26	17 23	6 47	17 01	7 14	16 35	7 50	15 58	8 55	14 54
348			**10 11**	**21 43**	**10 28**	**21 29**	**10 49**	**21 10**	**11 17**	**20 45**	**12 04**	**20 03**
14 We	11 54 35	−23 13	6 27	17 23	6 48	17 02	7 14	16 36	7 51	15 58	8 56	14 53
349			**10 53**	**22 43**	**11 04**	**22 35**	**11 18**	**22 24**	**11 36**	**22 09**	**12 05**	**21 46**
15 Th	11 55 04	−23 16	6 27	17 24	6 48	17 02	7 15	16 36	7 52	15 58	8 57	14 53
350			**11 32**	**23 41**	**11 37**	**23 39**	**11 43**	**23 36**	**11 52**	**23 32**	**12 05**	**23 26**
16 Fr	11 55 33	−23 19	6 28	17 24	6 49	17 02	7 16	16 36	7 53	15 59	8 58	14 53
351	**05 40 ☽**		**12 09**		**12 08**		**12 07**		**12 06**		**12 04**	
17 Sa	11 56 02	−23 21	6 28	17 25	6 50	17 02	7 16	16 36	7 54	15 59	8 59	14 53
352			**12 46**	**0 39**	**12 40**	**0 43**	**12 31**	**0 48**	**12 21**	**0 54**	**12 04**	**1 05**
18 Su	11 56 32	−23 23	6 29	17 25	6 50	17 03	7 17	16 37	7 54	16 00	9 00	14 54
353			**13 26**	**1 38**	**13 13**	**1 48**	**12 58**	**2 00**	**12 37**	**2 17**	**12 04**	**2 45**
19 Mo	11 57 01	−23 25	6 29	17 26	6 51	17 03	7 17	16 37	7 55	16 00	9 00	14 54
354			**14 08**	**2 38**	**13 50**	**2 54**	**13 28**	**3 14**	**12 57**	**3 42**	**12 06**	**4 29**
20 Tu	11 57 31	−23 26	6 30	17 26	6 51	17 04	7 18	16 38	7 56	16 00	9 01	14 54
355			**14 56**	**3 41**	**14 33**	**4 02**	**14 04**	**4 29**	**13 23**	**5 07**	**12 11**	**6 17**
21 We	11 58 01	−23 26	6 30	17 26	6 52	17 04	7 18	16 38	7 56	16 00	9 01	14 54
356			**15 48**	**4 44**	**15 22**	**5 10**	**14 48**	**5 42**	**13 59**	**6 30**	**12 22**	**8 04**
22 Th	11 58 31	−23 27	6 31	17 27	6 52	17 05	7 19	16 39	7 56	16 01	9 02	14 55
357			**16 45**	**5 47**	**16 17**	**6 15**	**15 41**	**6 50**	**14 48**	**7 43**	**12 53**	**9 38**
23 Fr	11 59 00	−23 26	6 31	17 27	6 53	17 05	7 19	16 39	7 57	16 01	9 02	14 55
358	**05 29 ○**		**17 45**	**6 46**	**17 17**	**7 14**	**16 42**	**7 50**	**15 50**	**8 42**	**14 00**	**10 33**
24 Sa	11 59 30	−23 25	6 32	17 28	6 53	17 06	7 20	16 40	7 57	16 02	9 03	14 56
359			**18 44**	**7 40**	**18 20**	**8 06**	**17 48**	**8 38**	**17 03**	**9 26**	**15 35**	**10 56**
25 Su	12 00 00	−23 24	6 32	17 28	6 54	17 07	7 20	16 40	7 57	16 03	9 03	14 57
360			**19 42**	**8 28**	**19 21**	**8 50**	**18 56**	**9 17**	**18 19**	**9 56**	**17 13**	**11 05**
26 Mo	12 00 29	−23 22	6 33	17 29	6 54	17 08	7 20	16 41	7 58	16 03	9 03	14 58
361			**20 36**	**9 09**	**20 21**	**9 27**	**20 01**	**9 48**	**19 34**	**10 19**	**18 48**	**11 08**
27 Tu	12 00 59	−23 20	6 33	17 29	6 55	17 08	7 21	16 41	7 58	16 04	9 04	14 59
362			**21 28**	**9 46**	**21 17**	**9 58**	**21 04**	**10 14**	**20 46**	**10 35**	**20 17**	**11 09**
28 We	12 01 28	−23 17	6 34	17 30	6 55	17 09	7 21	16 42	7 58	16 05	9 04	15 00
363			**22 17**	**10 19**	**22 11**	**10 27**	**22 04**	**10 36**	**21 55**	**10 49**	**21 41**	**11 09**
29 Th	12 01 58	−23 14	6 34	17 30	6 55	17 09	7 21	16 43	7 58	16 06	9 04	15 01
364			**23 04**	**10 50**	**23 04**	**10 53**	**23 04**	**10 56**	**23 03**	**11 01**	**23 02**	**11 08**
30 Fr	12 02 27	−23 10	6 34	17 31	6 56	17 10	7 21	16 44	7 58	16 07	9 03	15 02
365			**23 52**	**11 20**	**23 57**	**11 18**		**11 16**		**11 12**		**11 07**
31 Sa	12 02 56	−23 06	6 35	17 31	6 56	17 10	7 22	16 44	7 59	16 08	9 05	15 04
366	**04 57 ☾**			**11 51**		**11 44**	**0 03**	**11 35**	**0 11**	**11 24**	**0 23**	**11 06**

Latitude, Longitude, and Altitude of North American Cities

Source: National Oceanic and Atmospheric Administration, U.S. Commerce Department for geographic positions.
Source for Canadian cities: Geodetic Survey of Canada, Dept. of Energy, Mines, and Resources.
Altitudes U.S. Geological Survey and various sources. *Approx. altitude at downtown business area U.S.; in Canada at city hall except where (a) is at tower of major airport.

City	Lat. N °	'	"	Long. W °	'	"	Alt.* feet
Abilene, Tex.	32	27	05	99	43	51	1710
Akron, Oh.	41	05	00	81	30	44	874
Albany, N.Y.	42	39	01	73	45	01	20
Albuquerque, N.M.	35	05	01	106	39	05	4,945
Allentown, Pa.	40	36	11	75	28	06	255
Alert, N.W.T.	82	29	50	62	21	15	95
Altoona, Pa.	40	30	55	78	24	03	1,180
Amarillo, Tex.	35	12	27	101	50	04	3,685
Anchorage, Alas.	61	10	00	149	59	00	118
Ann Arbor, Mich.	42	16	59	83	44	52	880
Asheville, N.C.	35	35	42	82	33	26	1,985
Ashland, Ky.	38	28	36	82	38	23	536
Atlanta, Ga.	33	45	10	84	23	37	1,050
Atlantic City, N.J.	39	21	32	74	25	53	10
Augusta, Ga.	33	28	20	81	58	00	143
Augusta, Me.	44	18	53	69	46	29	45
Austin, Tex.	30	16	09	97	44	37	505
Bakersfield, Cal.	35	22	31	119	01	18	400
Baltimore, Md.	39	17	26	76	36	45	20
Bangor, Me.	44	48	13	68	46	18	20
Baton Rouge, La.	30	26	58	91	11	00	57
Battle Creek, Mich.	42	18	58	85	10	48	820
Bay City, Mich.	43	36	04	83	53	15	595
Beaumont, Tex.	30	05	20	94	06	09	20
Belleville, Ont.	44	09	42	77	23	11	257
Bellingham, Wash.	48	45	34	122	28	36	60
Berkeley, Cal.	37	52	10	122	16	17	40
Bethlehem, Pa.	40	37	16	75	22	34	235
Billings, Mon.	45	47	00	108	30	04	3,120
Biloxi, Miss.	30	23	48	88	53	00	20
Binghamton, N.Y.	42	06	03	75	54	47	865
Birmingham, Ala.	33	31	01	86	48	36	600
Bismarck, N.D.	46	48	23	100	47	17	1,674
Bloomington, Ill.	40	28	58	88	59	36	800
Boise, Ida.	43	37	07	116	11	58	2,704
Boston, Mass.	42	21	24	71	03	25	21
Bowling Green, Ky.	36	59	41	86	26	33	510
Brandon, Man.	49	51	00	99	57	00	1,265(a)
Brantford, Ont.	43	08	34	80	15	39	705(a)
Brattleboro, Vt.	42	51	06	72	33	48	300
Bridgeport, Conn.	41	10	49	73	11	22	10
Brockton, Mass.	42	05	02	71	01	25	130
Brownsville, Tex.	25	54	07	97	29	58	35
Buffalo, N.Y.	42	52	52	78	52	21	585
Burlington, Ont.	43	19	33	79	47	57	284
Burlington, Vt.	44	28	34	73	12	46	110
Butte, Mon.	46	01	06	112	32	11	5,765
Calgary, Alta.	51	02	46	114	03	24	3,427
Cambridge, Mass.	42	22	01	71	06	22	20
Camden, N.J.	39	56	41	75	07	14	30
Canton, Oh.	40	47	50	81	22	37	1,030
Carson City, Nev.	39	10	00	119	46	00	4,680
Cedar Rapids, Ia.	41	58	01	91	39	53	730
Central Islip, N.Y.	40	47	24	73	12	00	80
Champaign, Ill.	40	07	05	88	14	48	740
Charleston, S.C.	32	46	35	79	55	53	9
Charleston, W.Va.	38	21	01	81	37	52	601
Charlotte, N.C.	35	13	44	80	50	45	720
Charlottetown, P.E.I.	46	14	07	63	07	49	31
Chattanooga, Tenn.	35	02	41	85	18	32	675
Cheyenne, Wy.	41	08	09	104	49	07	6,100
Chicago, Ill.	41	52	28	87	38	22	595
Churchill, Man.	58	45	15	94	10	00	94(a)
Cincinnati, Oh.	39	06	07	84	30	35	550
Cleveland, Oh.	41	29	51	81	41	50	660
Colorado Springs	38	50	07	104	49	16	5,980
Columbia, Mo.	38	57	03	92	19	46	730
Columbia, S.C.	34	00	02	81	02	00	190
Columbus, Ga.	32	28	07	84	59	24	265
Columbus, Oh.	39	57	47	83	00	17	780
Concord, N.H.	43	12	22	71	32	25	290
Corpus Christi, Tex.	27	47	51	97	23	45	35
Dallas, Tex.	32	47	09	96	47	37	435
Dartmouth, N.S.	44	39	50	63	34	08	24
Davenport, Ia.	41	31	19	90	34	33	590
Dawson, Yukon	64	03	30	139	26	00	1,211(a)
Dayton, Oh.	39	45	32	84	11	43	574
Daytona Beach, Fla.	29	12	44	81	01	10	7
Decatur, Ill.	39	50	42	88	56	47	682
Denver, Col.	39	44	58	104	59	22	5,280
Des Moines, Ia.	41	35	14	93	37	00	805
Detroit, Mich.	42	19	48	83	02	57	585
Dodge City, Kan.	37	45	17	100	01	09	2,480
Dubuque, Ia.	42	29	55	90	40	08	620
Duluth, Minn.	46	46	56	92	06	24	610
Durham, N.C.	36	00	00	78	54	45	405
Eau Claire, Wis.	44	48	31	91	29	49	790
Edmonton, Alta.	53	32	43	113	29	21	2,186
El Paso, Tex.	31	45	36	106	29	11	3,695
Elizabeth, N.J.	40	39	43	74	12	59	21
Enid, Okla.	36	23	40	97	52	35	1,240
Erie, Pa.	42	07	15	80	04	57	685
Eugene, Ore.	44	03	16	123	05	30	422
Eureka, Cal.	40	48	08	124	09	46	45
Evansville, Ind.	37	58	20	87	34	21	385
Fairbanks, Alas.	64	48	00	147	51	00	448
Fall River, Mass.	41	42	06	71	09	18	40
Fargo, N.D.	46	52	30	96	47	18	900
Flagstaff, Ariz.	35	11	36	111	39	06	6,900
Flint, Mich.	43	00	50	83	41	33	750
Ft. Smith, Ark.	35	23	10	94	25	36	440
Fort Wayne, Ind.	41	04	21	85	08	26	790
Fort Worth, Tex.	32	44	55	97	19	44	670
Fredericton, N.B.	45	57	47	66	38	38	29
Fresno, Cal.	36	44	12	119	47	11	285
Gadsden, Ala.	34	00	57	86	00	41	555
Gainesville, Fla.	29	38	56	82	19	19	175
Gallup, N.M.	35	31	30	108	44	30	6,540
Galveston, Tex.	29	18	10	94	47	43	5
Gary, Ind.	41	36	12	87	20	19	590
Grand Junction, Col.	39	04	06	108	33	54	4,590
Grand Rapids, Mich.	42	58	03	85	40	13	610
Great Falls, Mon.	47	29	33	111	18	23	3,340
Green Bay, Wis.	44	30	48	88	00	50	590
Greensboro, N.C.	36	04	17	79	47	25	839
Greenville, S.C.	34	50	50	82	24	01	966
Guelph, Ont.	43	32	35	80	14	54	1,065
Gulfport, Miss.	30	22	04	89	05	36	20
Halifax, N.S.	44	38	54	63	34	30	60
Hamilton, Ont.	43	15	20	79	52	30	329
Hamilton, Oh.	39	23	59	84	33	47	600
Harrisburg, Pa.	40	15	43	76	52	59	365
Hartford, Conn.	41	46	12	72	40	49	40
Helena, Mon.	46	35	33	112	02	24	4,155
Hilo, Hawaii	19	43	30	155	05	24	40
Holyoke, Mass.	42	12	29	72	36	36	115
Honolulu, Ha.	21	18	22	157	51	35	21
Houston, Tex.	29	45	26	95	21	37	40
Hull, Que.	45	25	42	75	42	41	185
Huntington, W.Va.	38	25	12	82	26	33	565
Huntsville, Ala.	34	44	18	86	35	19	640
Indianapolis, Ind.	39	46	07	86	09	46	710
Iowa City, Ia.	41	39	37	91	31	53	685
Jackson, Mich.	42	14	43	84	24	22	940
Jackson, Miss.	32	17	56	90	11	06	298
Jacksonville, Fla.	30	19	44	81	39	42	20
Jersey City, N.J.	40	43	50	74	03	56	20
Johnstown, Pa.	40	19	35	78	55	03	1,185
Joplin, Mo.	37	05	26	94	30	00	990
Juneau, Alas.	58	18	12	134	24	30	50
Kalamazoo, Mich.	42	17	29	85	35	14	755
Kansas City, Kan.	39	07	04	94	38	24	750
Kansas City, Mo.	39	04	56	94	35	20	750
Kenosha, Wis.	42	35	43	87	50	11	610
Key West, Fla.	24	33	30	81	48	12	5
Kingston, Ont.	44	13	53	76	28	48	264
Kitchener, Ont.	43	26	58	80	29	12	1,100
Knoxville, Tenn.	35	57	39	83	55	07	890
Lafayette, Ind.	40	25	11	86	53	39	550
Lancaster, Pa.	40	02	25	76	18	29	355
Lansing, Mich.	42	44	01	84	33	15	830
Laredo, Tex.	27	30	22	99	30	30	440
La Salle, Que.	45	25	30	73	39	30	110
Las Vegas, Nev.	36	10	20	115	08	37	2,030
Laval, Que.	45	33	05	73	44	42	142
Lawrence, Mass.	42	42	16	71	10	08	65
Lethbridge, Alta.	49	41	38	112	49	58	2,985
Lexington, Ky.	38	02	50	84	29	46	955
Lihue, Ha.	21	58	48	159	22	30	210
Lima, Oh.	40	44	35	84	06	20	865
Lincoln, Neb.	40	48	59	96	42	15	1,150
Little Rock, Ark.	34	44	42	92	16	37	286
London, Ont.	42	59	17	81	14	03	822
Long Beach, Cal.	33	46	14	118	11	18	35
Lorain, Oh.	41	28	05	82	10	49	610
Los Angeles, Cal.	34	03	15	118	14	28	340
Louisville, Ky.	38	14	47	85	45	49	450
Lowell, Mass.	42	38	25	71	19	14	100
Lubbock, Tex.	33	35	05	101	50	33	3,195

City	Lat. N °	′	″	Long. W °	′	″	Alt.* Feet
Macon, Ga.	32	50	12	83	37	36	335
Madison, Wis.	43	04	23	89	22	55	860
Manchester, N.H.	42	59	28	71	27	41	175
Marshall, Tex.	32	33	00	94	23	00	410
Memphis, Tenn.	35	08	46	90	03	13	275
Meriden, Conn.	41	32	06	72	47	30	190
Mexico City, Mexico	19	25	45	99	07	00	7,347
Miami, Fla.	25	46	37	80	11	32	10
Milwaukee, Wis.	43	02	19	87	54	15	635
Minneapolis, Minn.	44	58	57	93	15	43	815
Minot, N.D.	48	14	09	101	17	38	1,550
Mississauga, Ont.	43	33	00	79	35	00	260(a)
Mobile, Ala.	30	41	36	88	02	33	5
Moline, Ill.	41	30	31	90	30	49	585
Moncton, N.B.	46	05	18	64	46	41	38
Montgomery, Ala.	32	22	33	86	18	31	160
Montpelier, Vt.	44	15	36	72	34	41	485
Montreal, Que.	45	30	33	73	33	14	90
Moose Jaw, Sask.	50	23	34	105	32	04	1,784
Muncie, Ind.	40	11	28	85	23	16	950
Nashville, Tenn.	36	09	33	86	46	55	450
Natchez, Miss.	31	33	48	91	23	30	210
Newark, N.J.	40	44	14	74	10	19	55
New Bedford, Mass.	41	38	13	70	55	41	15
New Britain, Conn.	41	40	08	72	46	59	200
New Haven, Conn.	41	18	25	72	55	30	40
New Orleans, La.	29	56	53	90	04	10	5
New York, N.Y.	40	45	06	73	59	39	55
Niagara Falls, N.Y.	43	05	34	79	03	26	570
Niagara Falls, Ont.	43	06	22	79	03	51	590
Nome, Alas.	64	30	00	165	25	00	25
Norfolk, Va.	36	51	10	76	17	21	10
North Bay, Ont.	46	18	35	79	27	45	670
Oakland, Cal.	37	48	03	122	15	54	25
Ogden, Ut.	41	13	31	111	58	21	4,295
Oklahoma City	35	28	26	97	31	04	1,195
Omaha, Neb.	41	15	42	95	56	14	1,040
Orlando, Fla.	28	32	42	81	22	38	70
Oshawa, Ont.	43	53	46	78	51	57	350
Ottawa, Ont.	45	26	24	75	41	42	185
Paducah, Ky.	37	05	13	88	35	56	345
Pasadena, Cal.	34	08	44	118	08	41	830
Paterson, N.J.	40	55	01	74	10	21	100
Pensacola, Fla.	30	24	51	87	12	56	15
Peoria, Ill.	40	41	42	89	35	33	470
Peterborough, Ont.	44	18	32	78	19	13	673
Philadelphia, Pa.	39	56	58	75	09	21	100
Phoenix, Ariz.	33	27	12	112	04	28	1,090
Pierre, S.D.	44	22	18	100	20	54	1,480
Pittsburgh, Pa.	40	26	19	80	00	00	745
Pittsfield, Mass.	42	26	53	73	15	14	1,015
Pocatello, Ida.	42	51	38	112	27	01	4,460
Port Arthur, Tex.	29	52	30	93	56	15	10
Portland, Me.	43	39	33	70	15	19	25
Portland, Ore.	45	31	06	122	40	35	77
Portsmouth, N.H.	43	04	30	70	45	24	[illegible]
Portsmouth, Va.	36	50	07	76	18	14	10
Prince Rupert, B.C.	54	19	00	130	19	00	125(a)
Providence, R.I.	41	49	32	71	24	41	80
Provo, Ut.	40	14	06	111	39	24	4,550
Pueblo, Col.	38	16	17	104	36	33	4,690
Quebec City, Que.	46	48	51	71	12	30	163
Racine, Wis.	42	43	49	87	47	12	630
Rapid City, S.D.	44	04	52	103	13	11	3,230
Raleigh, N.C.	35	46	38	78	38	21	365
Reading, Pa.	40	20	09	75	55	40	265
Regina, Sask.	50	26	55	104	36	50	1,894(a)
Reno, Nev.	39	31	27	119	48	40	4,490
Richmond, Va.	37	32	15	77	26	09	160
Roanoke, Va.	37	16	13	79	56	44	905
Rochester, Minn.	44	01	21	92	28	03	990
Rochester, N.Y.	43	09	41	77	36	21	515
Rockford, Ill.	42	16	07	89	05	48	715
Sacramento, Cal.	38	34	57	121	29	41	30
Saginaw, Mich.	43	25	52	83	56	05	595
St. Catharines, Ont.	43	09	33	79	14	50	362(a)
St. Cloud, Minn.	45	34	00	94	10	24	1,040
Saint John, N.B.	45	16	22	66	03	48	27
St. John's, Nfld.	47	33	42	52	42	48	200(a)
St. Joseph, Mo.	39	45	57	94	51	02	850
St. Louis, Mo.	38	37	45	90	12	22	455
St. Paul, Minn.	44	57	19	93	06	07	780
St. Petersburg, Fla.	27	46	18	82	38	19	20
Salem, Ore.	44	56	24	123	01	59	155

City	Lat. N °	′	″	Long. W °	′	″	Alt.* Feet
Salina, Kan.	38	50	36	97	36	46	1,229
Salt Lake City, Ut.	40	45	23	111	53	26	4,390
San Angelo, Tex.	31	27	39	100	26	03	1,845
San Antonio, Tex.	29	25	37	98	29	06	650
San Bernardino, Cal.	34	06	30	117	17	28	1,080
San Diego, Cal.	32	42	53	117	09	21	20
San Francisco, Cal.	37	46	39	122	24	40	65
San Jose, Cal.	37	20	16	121	53	24	90
San Juan, P.R.	18	27	00	66	04	15	35
Santa Barbara, Cal.	34	25	18	119	41	55	100
Santa Cruz, Cal.	36	58	18	122	01	18	20
Santa Fe, N.M.	35	41	11	105	56	10	6,950
Sarasota, Fla.	27	20	05	82	32	30	20
Saskatoon, Sask.	52	07	49	106	39	35	1,587
Sault Ste. Marie, Ont.	46	30	24	84	20	04	589
Savannah, Ga.	32	04	42	81	05	37	20
Schenectady, N.Y.	42	48	42	73	55	42	245
Scranton, Pa.	41	24	32	75	39	46	725
Seattle, Wash.	47	36	32	122	20	12	10
Sheboygan, Wis.	43	45	03	87	42	52	630
Sherbrooke, Que.	45	24	27	71	51	07	535(a)
Sheridan, Wy.	44	47	55	106	57	10	3,740
Shreveport, La.	32	30	46	93	44	58	204
Sioux City, Ia.	42	29	46	96	24	30	1,110
Sioux Falls, S.D.	43	32	35	96	43	35	1,395
Somerville, Mass.	42	23	15	71	06	07	13
South Bend, Ind.	41	40	33	86	15	01	710
Spartanburg, S.C.	34	57	03	81	56	06	875
Spokane, Wash.	47	39	32	117	25	33	1,890
Springfield, Ill.	09	47	50	09	00	51	610
Springfield, Mass.	42	06	21	72	35	32	85
Springfield, Mo.	37	13	03	93	17	32	1,300
Springfield, Oh.	39	55	38	83	48	29	980
Stamford, Conn.	41	03	09	73	32	24	35
Steubenville, Oh.	40	21	42	80	36	53	660
Stockton, Cal.	37	57	30	121	17	16	20
Sudbury, Ont.	46	29	24	80	59	24	850(a)
Superior, Wis.	46	43	14	92	06	07	630
Sydney, N.S.	46	08	15	60	11	48	15
Syracuse, N.Y.	43	03	04	76	09	14	400
Tacoma, Wash.	47	14	59	122	26	15	110
Tallahassee, Fla.	30	26	30	84	16	56	150
Tampa, Fla.	27	56	58	82	27	25	15
Terre Haute, Ind.	39	28	03	87	24	26	496
Texarkana, Tex.	33	25	48	94	02	30	324
Thunder Bay, Ont.	48	22	54	89	14	42	616
Toledo, Oh.	41	39	14	83	32	39	585
Topeka, Kan.	39	03	16	95	40	23	930
Toronto, Ont.	43	39	10	79	23	00	300
Trenton, N.J.	40	13	14	74	46	13	35
Trois-Rivieres, Que.	46	20	36	72	32	37	115(a)
Troy, N.Y.	42	43	45	73	40	58	35
Tucson, Ariz.	32	13	15	110	58	08	2,390
Tulsa, Okla.	36	09	12	95	59	34	804
Urbana, Ill.	40	06	42	88	12	06	725
Utica, N.Y.	43	06	12	75	13	33	415
Vancouver, B.C.	49	18	56	123	04	44	141
Victoria, B.C.	48	25	43	123	21	49	57
Waco, Tex.	31	33	12	97	08	00	405
Walla Walla, Wash.	46	04	08	118	20	24	936
Washington, D.C.	38	53	51	77	00	33	25
Waterbury, Conn.	41	33	13	73	02	31	260
Waterloo, Ia.	42	29	40	92	20	20	850
West Palm Beach, Fla.	26	42	36	80	03	07	15
Wheeling, W. Va.	40	04	03	80	43	20	650
Whitehorse, Yukon	60	43	17	135	03	03	2,305(a)
White Plains, N.Y.	41	02	00	73	45	48	220
Wichita, Kan.	37	41	30	97	20	16	1,290
Wichita Falls, Tex.	33	54	34	98	29	28	945
Wilkes-Barre, Pa.	41	14	32	75	53	17	640
Wilmington, Del.	39	44	46	75	32	51	135
Wilmington, N.C.	34	14	14	77	56	58	35
Windsor, Ont.	42	18	56	83	02	10	603
Winnipeg, Man.	49	53	56	97	08	23	762
Winston-Salem, N.C.	36	05	52	80	14	42	860
Worcester, Mass.	42	15	37	71	48	17	475
Yakima, Wash.	46	36	09	120	30	39	1,060
Yellowknife, N.W.T.	62	27	16	114	22	33	674(a)
Yonkers, N.Y.	40	55	55	73	53	54	10
York, Pa.	39	57	35	76	43	36	370
Youngstown, Oh.	41	05	57	80	39	02	840
Yuma, Ariz.	32	42	54	114	37	24	160
Zanesville, Oh.	39	56	18	82	00	30	720

World Cities

City	Lat.	Long.	Alt. Feet
London, UK (Greenwich)	51 30 00N	0 0 0	245
Paris, France	48 50 14N	2 20 14E	300
Berlin, Germany	52 32 00N	13 25 00E	110
Rome, Italy	41 53 00N	12 30 00E	95
Warsaw, Poland	52 15 00N	21 00 00E	360
Moscow, USSR	55 45 00N	37 42 00E	394
Athens, Greece	37 58 00N	23 44 00E	300
Jerusalem, Israel	31 47 00N	35 13 00E	2,500
Johannesburg, So. Afr.	26 10 00S	28 02 00E	5,740
New Delhi, India	28 38 00N	77 12 00E	770
Peking, China	39 54 00N	116 28 00E	600
Rio de Janeiro, Brazil	22 53 43S	43 13 22W	30
Tokyo, Japan	35 45 00N	139 45 00E	30
Sydney, Australia	33 52 00S	151 12 00E	25

Perpetual Calendar

The number shown for each year indicates which Gregorian calendar to use. For 1583-1802, or for Julian calendar, see page 222. For years 1803-1820, use numbers for 1983-2000, respectively.

1821....2	1847....6	1873....4	1899....1	1925....5	1951....2	1977....7	2003....4	2029....2	2055....6
1822....3	1848....14	1874....5	1900....2	1926....6	1952....10	1978....1	2004....12	2030....3	2056....14
1823....4	1849....2	1875....6	1901....3	1927....7	1953....5	1979....2	2005....7	2031....4	2057....2
1824....12	1850....3	1876....14	1902....4	1928....8	1954....6	1980....10	2006....1	2032....12	2058....3
1825....7	1851....4	1877....2	1903....5	1929....3	1955....7	1981....5	2007....2	2033....7	2059....4
1826....1	1852....12	1878....3	1904....13	1930....4	1956....8	1982....6	2008....10	2034....1	2060....12
1827....2	1853....7	1879....4	1905....1	1931....5	1957....3	1983....7	2009....5	2035....2	2061....7
1828....10	1854....1	1880....12	1906....2	1932....13	1958....4	1984....8	2010....6	2036....10	2062....1
1829....5	1855....2	1881....7	1907....3	1933....1	1959....5	1985....3	2011....7	2037....5	2063....2
1830....6	1856....10	1882....1	1908....11	1934....2	1960....13	1986....4	2012....8	2038....6	2064....10
1831....7	1857....5	1883....2	1909....6	1935....3	1961....1	1987....5	2013....3	2039....7	2065....5
1832....8	1858....6	1884....10	1910....7	1936....11	1962....2	1988....13	2014....4	2040....8	2066....6
1833....3	1859....7	1885....5	1911....1	1937....6	1963....3	1989....1	2015....5	2041....3	2067....7
1834....4	1860....8	1886....6	1912....9	1938....7	1964....11	1990....2	2016....13	2042....4	2068....8
1835....5	1861....3	1887....7	1913....4	1939....1	1965....6	1991....3	2017....1	2043....5	2069....3
1836....13	1862....4	1888....8	1914....5	1940....9	1966....7	1992....11	2018....2	2044....13	2070....4
1837....1	1863....5	1889....3	1915....6	1941....4	1967....1	1993....6	2019....3	2045....1	2071....5
1838....2	1864....13	1890....4	1916....14	1942....5	1968....9	1994....7	2020....11	2046....2	2072....13
1839....3	1865....1	1891....5	1917....2	1943....6	1969....4	1995....1	2021....6	2047....3	2073....1
1840....11	1866....2	1892....13	1918....3	1944....14	1970....5	1996....9	2022....7	2048....11	2074....2
1841....6	1867....3	1893....1	1919....4	1945....2	1971....6	1997....4	2023....1	2049....6	2075....3
1842....7	1868....11	1894....2	1920....12	1946....3	1972....14	1998....5	2024....9	2050....7	2076....11
1843....1	1869....6	1895....3	1921....7	1947....4	1973....2	1999....6	2025....4	2051....1	2077....6
1844....9	1870....7	1896....11	1922....1	1948....12	1974....3	2000....14	2026....5	2052....9	2078....7
1845....4	1871....1	1897....6	1923....2	1949....7	1975....4	2001....2	2027....6	2053....4	2079....1
1846....5	1872....9	1898....7	1924....10	1950....1	1976....12	2002....3	2028....14	2054....5	2080....9

1

1989

JANUARY

S	M	T	W	T	F	S
1	2	3	4	5	6	7
8	9	10	11	12	13	14
15	16	17	18	19	20	21
22	23	24	25	26	27	28
29	30	31				

FEBRUARY

S	M	T	W	T	F	S
			1	2	3	4
5	6	7	8	9	10	11
12	13	14	15	16	17	18
19	20	21	22	23	24	25
26	27	28				

MARCH

S	M	T	W	T	F	S
			1	2	3	4
5	6	7	8	9	10	11
12	13	14	15	16	17	18
19	20	21	22	23	24	25
26	27	28	29	30	31	

APRIL

S	M	T	W	T	F	S
						1
2	3	4	5	6	7	8
9	10	11	12	13	14	15
16	17	18	19	20	21	22
23	24	25	26	27	28	29
30						

MAY

S	M	T	W	T	F	S
	1	2	3	4	5	6
7	8	9	10	11	12	13
14	15	16	17	18	19	20
21	22	23	24	25	26	27
28	29	30	31			

JUNE

S	M	T	W	T	F	S
				1	2	3
4	5	6	7	8	9	10
11	12	13	14	15	16	17
18	19	20	21	22	23	24
25	26	27	28	29	30	

JULY

S	M	T	W	T	F	S
						1
2	3	4	5	6	7	8
9	10	11	12	13	14	15
16	17	18	19	20	21	22
23	24	25	26	27	28	29
30	31					

AUGUST

S	M	T	W	T	F	S
		1	2	3	4	5
6	7	8	9	10	11	12
13	14	15	16	17	18	19
20	21	22	23	24	25	26
27	28	29	30	31		

SEPTEMBER

S	M	T	W	T	F	S
					1	2
3	4	5	6	7	8	9
10	11	12	13	14	15	16
17	18	19	20	21	22	23
24	25	26	27	28	29	30

OCTOBER

S	M	T	W	T	F	S
1	2	3	4	5	6	7
8	9	10	11	12	13	14
15	16	17	18	19	20	21
22	23	24	25	26	27	28
29	30	31				

NOVEMBER

S	M	T	W	T	F	S
			1	2	3	4
5	6	7	8	9	10	11
12	13	14	15	16	17	18
19	20	21	22	23	24	25
26	27	28	29	30		

DECEMBER

S	M	T	W	T	F	S
					1	2
3	4	5	6	7	8	9
10	11	12	13	14	15	16
17	18	19	20	21	22	23
24	25	26	27	28	29	30
31						

2

JANUARY

S	M	T	W	T	F	S
	1	2	3	4	5	6
7	8	9	10	11	12	13
14	15	16	17	18	19	20
21	22	23	24	25	26	27
28	29	30	31			

FEBRUARY

S	M	T	W	T	F	S
				1	2	3
4	5	6	7	8	9	10
11	12	13	14	15	16	17
18	19	20	21	22	23	24
25	26	27	28			

MARCH

S	M	T	W	T	F	S
				1	2	3
4	5	6	7	8	9	10
11	12	13	14	15	16	17
18	19	20	21	22	23	24
25	26	27	28	29	30	31

APRIL

S	M	T	W	T	F	S
1	2	3	4	5	6	7
8	9	10	11	12	13	14
15	16	17	18	19	20	21
22	23	24	25	26	27	28
29	30					

MAY

S	M	T	W	T	F	S
		1	2	3	4	5
6	7	8	9	10	11	12
13	14	15	16	17	18	19
20	21	22	23	24	25	26
27	28	29	30	31		

JUNE

S	M	T	W	T	F	S
					1	2
3	4	5	6	7	8	9
10	11	12	13	14	15	16
17	18	19	20	21	22	23
24	25	26	27	28	29	30

JULY

S	M	T	W	T	F	S
1	2	3	4	5	6	7
8	9	10	11	12	13	14
15	16	17	18	19	20	21
22	23	24	25	26	27	28
29	30	31				

AUGUST

S	M	T	W	T	F	S
			1	2	3	4
5	6	7	8	9	10	11
12	13	14	15	16	17	18
19	20	21	22	23	24	25
26	27	28	29	30	31	

SEPTEMBER

S	M	T	W	T	F	S
						1
2	3	4	5	6	7	8
9	10	11	12	13	14	15
16	17	18	19	20	21	22
23	24	25	26	27	28	29
30						

OCTOBER

S	M	T	W	T	F	S
	1	2	3	4	5	6
7	8	9	10	11	12	13
14	15	16	17	18	19	20
21	22	23	24	25	26	27
28	29	30	31			

NOVEMBER

S	M	T	W	T	F	S
				1	2	3
4	5	6	7	8	9	10
11	12	13	14	15	16	17
18	19	20	21	22	23	24
25	26	27	28	29	30	

DECEMBER

S	M	T	W	T	F	S
						1
2	3	4	5	6	7	8
9	10	11	12	13	14	15
16	17	18	19	20	21	22
23	24	25	26	27	28	29
30	31					

3

JANUARY

S	M	T	W	T	F	S
		1	2	3	4	5
6	7	8	9	10	11	12
13	14	15	16	17	18	19
20	21	22	23	24	25	26
27	28	29	30	31		

FEBRUARY

S	M	T	W	T	F	S
					1	2
3	4	5	6	7	8	9
10	11	12	13	14	15	16
17	18	19	20	21	22	23
24	25	26	27	28		

MARCH

S	M	T	W	T	F	S
					1	2
3	4	5	6	7	8	9
10	11	12	13	14	15	16
17	18	19	20	21	22	23
24	25	26	27	28	29	30
31						

APRIL

S	M	T	W	T	F	S
	1	2	3	4	5	6
7	8	9	10	11	12	13
14	15	16	17	18	19	20
21	22	23	24	25	26	27
28	29	30				

MAY

S	M	T	W	T	F	S
			1	2	3	4
5	6	7	8	9	10	11
12	13	14	15	16	17	18
19	20	21	22	23	24	25
26	27	28	29	30	31	

JUNE

S	M	T	W	T	F	S
						1
2	3	4	5	6	7	8
9	10	11	12	13	14	15
16	17	18	19	20	21	22
23	24	25	26	27	28	29
30						

JULY

S	M	T	W	T	F	S
	1	2	3	4	5	6
7	8	9	10	11	12	13
14	15	16	17	18	19	20
21	22	23	24	25	26	27
28	29	30	31			

AUGUST

S	M	T	W	T	F	S
				1	2	3
4	5	6	7	8	9	10
11	12	13	14	15	16	17
18	19	20	21	22	23	24
25	26	27	28	29	30	31

SEPTEMBER

S	M	T	W	T	F	S
1	2	3	4	5	6	7
8	9	10	11	12	13	14
15	16	17	18	19	20	21
22	23	24	25	26	27	28
29	30					

OCTOBER

S	M	T	W	T	F	S
		1	2	3	4	5
6	7	8	9	10	11	12
13	14	15	16	17	18	19
20	21	22	23	24	25	26
27	28	29	30	31		

NOVEMBER

S	M	T	W	T	F	S
					1	2
3	4	5	6	7	8	9
10	11	12	13	14	15	16
17	18	19	20	21	22	23
24	25	26	27	28	29	30

DECEMBER

S	M	T	W	T	F	S
1	2	3	4	5	6	7
8	9	10	11	12	13	14
15	16	17	18	19	20	21
22	23	24	25	26	27	28
29	30	31				

4

JANUARY

S	M	T	W	T	F	S
			1	2	3	4
5	6	7	8	9	10	11
12	13	14	15	16	17	18
19	20	21	22	23	24	25
26	27	28	29	30	31	

FEBRUARY

S	M	T	W	T	F	S
						1
2	3	4	5	6	7	8
9	10	11	12	13	14	15
16	17	18	19	20	21	22
23	24	25	26	27	28	

MARCH

S	M	T	W	T	F	S
						1
2	3	4	5	6	7	8
9	10	11	12	13	14	15
16	17	18	19	20	21	22
23	24	25	26	27	28	29
30	31					

APRIL

S	M	T	W	T	F	S
		1	2	3	4	5
6	7	8	9	10	11	12
13	14	15	16	17	18	19
20	21	22	23	24	25	26
27	28	29	30			

MAY

S	M	T	W	T	F	S
				1	2	3
4	5	6	7	8	9	10
11	12	13	14	15	16	17
18	19	20	21	22	23	24
25	26	27	28	29	30	31

JUNE

S	M	T	W	T	F	S
1	2	3	4	5	6	7
8	9	10	11	12	13	14
15	16	17	18	19	20	21
22	23	24	25	26	27	28
29	30					

JULY

S	M	T	W	T	F	S
		1	2	3	4	5
6	7	8	9	10	11	12
13	14	15	16	17	18	19
20	21	22	23	24	25	26
27	28	29	30	31		

AUGUST

S	M	T	W	T	F	S
					1	2
3	4	5	6	7	8	9
10	11	12	13	14	15	16
17	18	19	20	21	22	23
24	25	26	27	28	29	30
31						

SEPTEMBER

S	M	T	W	T	F	S
	1	2	3	4	5	6
7	8	9	10	11	12	13
14	15	16	17	18	19	20
21	22	23	24	25	26	27
28	29	30				

OCTOBER

S	M	T	W	T	F	S
			1	2	3	4
5	6	7	8	9	10	11
12	13	14	15	16	17	18
19	20	21	22	23	24	25
26	27	28	29	30	31	

NOVEMBER

S	M	T	W	T	F	S
						1
2	3	4	5	6	7	8
9	10	11	12	13	14	15
16	17	18	19	20	21	22
23	24	25	26	27	28	29
30						

DECEMBER

S	M	T	W	T	F	S
	1	2	3	4	5	6
7	8	9	10	11	12	13
14	15	16	17	18	19	20
21	22	23	24	25	26	27
28	29	30	31			

5

1987

JANUARY

S	M	T	W	T	F	S
				1	2	3
4	5	6	7	8	9	10
11	12	13	14	15	16	17
18	19	20	21	22	23	24
25	26	27	28	29	30	31

FEBRUARY

S	M	T	W	T	F	S
1	2	3	4	5	6	7
8	9	10	11	12	13	14
15	16	17	18	19	20	21
22	23	24	25	26	27	28

MARCH

S	M	T	W	T	F	S
1	2	3	4	5	6	7
8	9	10	11	12	13	14
15	16	17	18	19	20	21
22	23	24	25	26	27	28
29	30	31				

APRIL

S	M	T	W	T	F	S
			1	2	3	4
5	6	7	8	9	10	11
12	13	14	15	16	17	18
19	20	21	22	23	24	25
26	27	28	29	30		

MAY

S	M	T	W	T	F	S
					1	2
3	4	5	6	7	8	9
10	11	12	13	14	15	16
17	18	19	20	21	22	23
24	25	26	27	28	29	30
31						

JUNE

S	M	T	W	T	F	S
	1	2	3	4	5	6
7	8	9	10	11	12	13
14	15	16	17	18	19	20
21	22	23	24	25	26	27
28	29	30				

JULY

S	M	T	W	T	F	S
			1	2	3	4
5	6	7	8	9	10	11
12	13	14	15	16	17	18
19	20	21	22	23	24	25
26	27	28	29	30	31	

AUGUST

S	M	T	W	T	F	S
						1
2	3	4	5	6	7	8
9	10	11	12	13	14	15
16	17	18	19	20	21	22
23	24	25	26	27	28	29
30	31					

SEPTEMBER

S	M	T	W	T	F	S
		1	2	3	4	5
6	7	8	9	10	11	12
13	14	15	16	17	18	19
20	21	22	23	24	25	26
27	28	29	30			

OCTOBER

S	M	T	W	T	F	S
				1	2	3
4	5	6	7	8	9	10
11	12	13	14	15	16	17
18	19	20	21	22	23	24
25	26	27	28	29	30	31

NOVEMBER

S	M	T	W	T	F	S
1	2	3	4	5	6	7
8	9	10	11	12	13	14
15	16	17	18	19	20	21
22	23	24	25	26	27	28
29	30					

DECEMBER

S	M	T	W	T	F	S
		1	2	3	4	5
6	7	8	9	10	11	12
13	14	15	16	17	18	19
20	21	22	23	24	25	26
27	28	29	30	31		

6

JANUARY

S	M	T	W	T	F	S
					1	2
3	4	5	6	7	8	9
10	11	12	13	14	15	16
17	18	19	20	21	22	23
24	25	26	27	28	29	30
31						

FEBRUARY

S	M	T	W	T	F	S
	1	2	3	4	5	6
7	8	9	10	11	12	13
14	15	16	17	18	19	20
21	22	23	24	25	26	27
28						

MARCH

S	M	T	W	T	F	S
	1	2	3	4	5	6
7	8	9	10	11	12	13
14	15	16	17	18	19	20
21	22	23	24	25	26	27
28	29	30	31			

APRIL

S	M	T	W	T	F	S
				1	2	3
4	5	6	7	8	9	10
11	12	13	14	15	16	17
18	19	20	21	22	23	24
25	26	27	28	29	30	

MAY

S	M	T	W	T	F	S
						1
2	3	4	5	6	7	8
9	10	11	12	13	14	15
16	17	18	19	20	21	22
23	24	25	26	27	28	29
30	31					

JUNE

S	M	T	W	T	F	S
		1	2	3	4	5
6	7	8	9	10	11	12
13	14	15	16	17	18	19
20	21	22	23	24	25	26
27	28	29	30			

JULY

S	M	T	W	T	F	S
				1	2	3
4	5	6	7	8	9	10
11	12	13	14	15	16	17
18	19	20	21	22	23	24
25	26	27	28	29	30	31

AUGUST

S	M	T	W	T	F	S
1	2	3	4	5	6	7
8	9	10	11	12	13	14
15	16	17	18	19	20	21
22	23	24	25	26	27	28
29	30	31				

SEPTEMBER

S	M	T	W	T	F	S
			1	2	3	4
5	6	7	8	9	10	11
12	13	14	15	16	17	18
19	20	21	22	23	24	25
26	27	28	29	30		

OCTOBER

S	M	T	W	T	F	S
					1	2
3	4	5	6	7	8	9
10	11	12	13	14	15	16
17	18	19	20	21	22	23
24	25	26	27	28	29	30
31						

NOVEMBER

S	M	T	W	T	F	S
	1	2	3	4	5	6
7	8	9	10	11	12	13
14	15	16	17	18	19	20
21	22	23	24	25	26	27
28	29	30				

DECEMBER

S	M	T	W	T	F	S
			1	2	3	4
5	6	7	8	9	10	11
12	13	14	15	16	17	18
19	20	21	22	23	24	25
26	27	28	29	30	31	

7

JANUARY

S	M	T	W	T	F	S
						1
2	3	4	5	6	7	8
9	10	11	12	13	14	15
16	17	18	19	20	21	22
23	24	25	26	27	28	29
30	31					

FEBRUARY

S	M	T	W	T	F	S
		1	2	3	4	5
6	7	8	9	10	11	12
13	14	15	16	17	18	19
20	21	22	23	24	25	26
27	28					

MARCH

S	M	T	W	T	F	S
		1	2	3	4	5
6	7	8	9	10	11	12
13	14	15	16	17	18	19
20	21	22	23	24	25	26
27	28	29	30	31		

APRIL

S	M	T	W	T	F	S
					1	2
3	4	5	6	7	8	9
10	11	12	13	14	15	16
17	18	19	20	21	22	23
24	25	26	27	28	29	30

MAY

S	M	T	W	T	F	S
1	2	3	4	5	6	7
8	9	10	11	12	13	14
15	16	17	18	19	20	21
22	23	24	25	26	27	28
29	30	31				

JUNE

S	M	T	W	T	F	S
			1	2	3	4
5	6	7	8	9	10	11
12	13	14	15	16	17	18
19	20	21	22	23	24	25
26	27	28	29	30		

JULY

S	M	T	W	T	F	S
					1	2
3	4	5	6	7	8	9
10	11	12	13	14	15	16
17	18	19	20	21	22	23
24	25	26	27	28	29	30
31						

AUGUST

S	M	T	W	T	F	S
	1	2	3	4	5	6
7	8	9	10	11	12	13
14	15	16	17	18	19	20
21	22	23	24	25	26	27
28	29	30	31			

SEPTEMBER

S	M	T	W	T	F	S
				1	2	3
4	5	6	7	8	9	10
11	12	13	14	15	16	17
18	19	20	21	22	23	24
25	26	27	28	29	30	

OCTOBER

S	M	T	W	T	F	S
						1
2	3	4	5	6	7	8
9	10	11	12	13	14	15
16	17	18	19	20	21	22
23	24	25	26	27	28	29
30	31					

NOVEMBER

S	M	T	W	T	F	S
		1	2	3	4	5
6	7	8	9	10	11	12
13	14	15	16	17	18	19
20	21	22	23	24	25	26
27	28	29	30			

DECEMBER

S	M	T	W	T	F	S
				1	2	3
4	5	6	7	8	9	10
11	12	13	14	15	16	17
18	19	20	21	22	23	24
25	26	27	28	29	30	31

8

JANUARY

S	M	T	W	T	F	S
1	2	3	4	5	6	7
8	9	10	11	12	13	14
15	16	17	18	19	20	21
22	23	24	25	26	27	28
29	30	31				

FEBRUARY

S	M	T	W	T	F	S
			1	2	3	4
5	6	7	8	9	10	11
12	13	14	15	16	17	18
19	20	21	22	23	24	25
26	27	28	29			

MARCH

S	M	T	W	T	F	S
				1	2	3
4	5	6	7	8	9	10
11	12	13	14	15	16	17
18	19	20	21	22	23	24
25	26	27	28	29	30	31

APRIL

S	M	T	W	T	F	S
1	2	3	4	5	6	7
8	9	10	11	12	13	14
15	16	17	18	19	20	21
22	23	24	25	26	27	28
29	30					

MAY

S	M	T	W	T	F	S
		1	2	3	4	5
6	7	8	9	10	11	12
13	14	15	16	17	18	19
20	21	22	23	24	25	26
27	28	29	30	31		

JUNE

S	M	T	W	T	F	S
					1	2
3	4	5	6	7	8	9
10	11	12	13	14	15	16
17	18	19	20	21	22	23
24	25	26	27	28	29	30

JULY

S	M	T	W	T	F	S
1	2	3	4	5	6	7
8	9	10	11	12	13	14
15	16	17	18	19	20	21
22	23	24	25	26	27	28
29	30	31				

AUGUST

S	M	T	W	T	F	S
			1	2	3	4
5	6	7	8	9	10	11
12	13	14	15	16	17	18
19	20	21	22	23	24	25
26	27	28	29	30	31	

SEPTEMBER

S	M	T	W	T	F	S
						1
2	3	4	5	6	7	8
9	10	11	12	13	14	15
16	17	18	19	20	21	22
23	24	25	26	27	28	29
30						

OCTOBER

S	M	T	W	T	F	S
	1	2	3	4	5	6
7	8	9	10	11	12	13
14	15	16	17	18	19	20
21	22	23	24	25	26	27
28	29	30	31			

NOVEMBER

S	M	T	W	T	F	S
				1	2	3
4	5	6	7	8	9	10
11	12	13	14	15	16	17
18	19	20	21	22	23	24
25	26	27	28	29	30	

DECEMBER

S	M	T	W	T	F	S
						1
2	3	4	5	6	7	8
9	10	11	12	13	14	15
16	17	18	19	20	21	22
23	24	25	26	27	28	29
30	31					

9

JANUARY

S	M	T	W	T	F	S
	1	2	3	4	5	6
7	8	9	10	11	12	13
14	15	16	17	18	19	20
21	22	23	24	25	26	27
28	29	30	31			

FEBRUARY

S	M	T	W	T	F	S
				1	2	3
4	5	6	7	8	9	10
11	12	13	14	15	16	17
18	19	20	21	22	23	24
25	26	27	28	29		

MARCH

S	M	T	W	T	F	S
					1	2
3	4	5	6	7	8	9
10	11	12	13	14	15	16
17	18	19	20	21	22	23
24	25	26	27	28	29	30
31						

APRIL

S	M	T	W	T	F	S
	1	2	3	4	5	6
7	8	9	10	11	12	13
14	15	16	17	18	19	20
21	22	23	24	25	26	27
28	29	30				

MAY

S	M	T	W	T	F	S
			1	2	3	4
5	6	7	8	9	10	11
12	13	14	15	16	17	18
19	20	21	22	23	24	25
26	27	28	29	30	31	

JUNE

S	M	T	W	T	F	S
						1
2	3	4	5	6	7	8
9	10	11	12	13	14	15
16	17	18	19	20	21	22
23	24	25	26	27	28	29
30						

JULY

S	M	T	W	T	F	S
	1	2	3	4	5	6
7	8	9	10	11	12	13
14	15	16	17	18	19	20
21	22	23	24	25	26	27
28	29	30	31			

AUGUST

S	M	T	W	T	F	S
				1	2	3
4	5	6	7	8	9	10
11	12	13	14	15	16	17
18	19	20	21	22	23	24
25	26	27	28	29	30	31

SEPTEMBER

S	M	T	W	T	F	S
1	2	3	4	5	6	7
8	9	10	11	12	13	14
15	16	17	18	19	20	21
22	23	24	25	26	27	28
29	30					

OCTOBER

S	M	T	W	T	F	S
		1	2	3	4	5
6	7	8	9	10	11	12
13	14	15	16	17	18	19
20	21	22	23	24	25	26
27	28	29	30	31		

NOVEMBER

S	M	T	W	T	F	S
					1	2
3	4	5	6	7	8	9
10	11	12	13	14	15	16
17	18	19	20	21	22	23
24	25	26	27	28	29	30

DECEMBER

S	M	T	W	T	F	S
1	2	3	4	5	6	7
8	9	10	11	12	13	14
15	16	17	18	19	20	21
22	23	24	25	26	27	28
29	30	31				

10

JANUARY

S	M	T	W	T	F	S
		1	2	3	4	5
6	7	8	9	10	11	12
13	14	15	16	17	18	19
20	21	22	23	24	25	26
27	28	29	30	31		

FEBRUARY

S	M	T	W	T	F	S
					1	2
3	4	5	6	7	8	9
10	11	12	13	14	15	16
17	18	19	20	21	22	23
24	25	26	27	28	29	

MARCH

S	M	T	W	T	F	S
						1
2	3	4	5	6	7	8
9	10	11	12	13	14	15
16	17	18	19	20	21	22
23	24	25	26	27	28	29
30	31					

APRIL

S	M	T	W	T	F	S
		1	2	3	4	5
6	7	8	9	10	11	12
13	14	15	16	17	18	19
20	21	22	23	24	25	26
27	28	29	30			

MAY

S	M	T	W	T	F	S
				1	2	3
4	5	6	7	8	9	10
11	12	13	14	15	16	17
18	19	20	21	22	23	24
25	26	27	28	29	30	31

JUNE

S	M	T	W	T	F	S
1	2	3	4	5	6	7
8	9	10	11	12	13	14
15	16	17	18	19	20	21
22	23	24	25	26	27	28
29	30					

JULY

S	M	T	W	T	F	S
		1	2	3	4	5
6	7	8	9	10	11	12
13	14	15	16	17	18	19
20	21	22	23	24	25	26
27	28	29	30	31		

AUGUST

S	M	T	W	T	F	S
					1	2
3	4	5	6	7	8	9
10	11	12	13	14	15	16
17	18	19	20	21	22	23
24	25	26	27	28	29	30
31						

SEPTEMBER

S	M	T	W	T	F	S
	1	2	3	4	5	6
7	8	9	10	11	12	13
14	15	16	17	18	19	20
21	22	23	24	25	26	27
28	29	30				

OCTOBER

S	M	T	W	T	F	S
			1	2	3	4
5	6	7	8	9	10	11
12	13	14	15	16	17	18
19	20	21	22	23	24	25
26	27	28	29	30	31	

NOVEMBER

S	M	T	W	T	F	S
						1
2	3	4	5	6	7	8
9	10	11	12	13	14	15
16	17	18	19	20	21	22
23	24	25	26	27	28	29
30						

DECEMBER

S	M	T	W	T	F	S
	1	2	3	4	5	6
7	8	9	10	11	12	13
14	15	16	17	18	19	20
21	22	23	24	25	26	27
28	29	30	31			

11

JANUARY

S	M	T	W	T	F	S
			1	2	3	4
5	6	7	8	9	10	11
12	13	14	15	16	17	18
19	20	21	22	23	24	25
26	27	28	29	30	31	

FEBRUARY

S	M	T	W	T	F	S
						1
2	3	4	5	6	7	8
9	10	11	12	13	14	15
16	17	18	19	20	21	22
23	24	25	26	27	28	29

MARCH

S	M	T	W	T	F	S
1	2	3	4	5	6	7
8	9	10	11	12	13	14
15	16	17	18	19	20	21
22	23	24	25	26	27	28
29	30	31				

APRIL

S	M	T	W	T	F	S
			1	2	3	4
5	6	7	8	9	10	11
12	13	14	15	16	17	18
19	20	21	22	23	24	25
26	27	28	29	30		

MAY

S	M	T	W	T	F	S
					1	2
3	4	5	6	7	8	9
10	11	12	13	14	15	16
17	18	19	20	21	22	23
24	25	26	27	28	29	30
31						

JUNE

S	M	T	W	T	F	S
	1	2	3	4	5	6
7	8	9	10	11	12	13
14	15	16	17	18	19	20
21	22	23	24	25	26	27
28	29	30				

JULY

S	M	T	W	T	F	S
			1	2	3	4
5	6	7	8	9	10	11
12	13	14	15	16	17	18
19	20	21	22	23	24	25
26	27	28	29	30	31	

AUGUST

S	M	T	W	T	F	S
						1
2	3	4	5	6	7	8
9	10	11	12	13	14	15
16	17	18	19	20	21	22
23	24	25	26	27	28	29
30	31					

SEPTEMBER

S	M	T	W	T	F	S
		1	2	3	4	5
6	7	8	9	10	11	12
13	14	15	16	17	18	19
20	21	22	23	24	25	26
27	28	29	30			

OCTOBER

S	M	T	W	T	F	S
				1	2	3
4	5	6	7	8	9	10
11	12	13	14	15	16	17
18	19	20	21	22	23	24
25	26	27	28	29	30	31

NOVEMBER

S	M	T	W	T	F	S
1	2	3	4	5	6	7
8	9	10	11	12	13	14
15	16	17	18	19	20	21
22	23	24	25	26	27	28
29	30					

DECEMBER

S	M	T	W	T	F	S
		1	2	3	4	5
6	7	8	9	10	11	12
13	14	15	16	17	18	19
20	21	22	23	24	25	26
27	28	29	30	31		

12

JANUARY

S	M	T	W	T	F	S
				1	2	3
4	5	6	7	8	9	10
11	12	13	14	15	16	17
18	19	20	21	22	23	24
25	26	27	28	29	30	31

FEBRUARY

S	M	T	W	T	F	S
1	2	3	4	5	6	7
8	9	10	11	12	13	14
15	16	17	18	19	20	21
22	23	24	25	26	27	28
29						

MARCH

S	M	T	W	T	F	S
	1	2	3	4	5	6
7	8	9	10	11	12	13
14	15	16	17	18	19	20
21	22	23	24	25	26	27
28	29	30	31			

APRIL

S	M	T	W	T	F	S
				1	2	3
4	5	6	7	8	9	10
11	12	13	14	15	16	17
18	19	20	21	22	23	24
25	26	27	28	29	30	

MAY

S	M	T	W	T	F	S
						1
2	3	4	5	6	7	8
9	10	11	12	13	14	15
16	17	18	19	20	21	22
23	24	25	26	27	28	29
30	31					

JUNE

S	M	T	W	T	F	S
		1	2	3	4	5
6	7	8	9	10	11	12
13	14	15	16	17	18	19
20	21	22	23	24	25	26
27	28	29	30			

JULY

S	M	T	W	T	F	S
				1	2	3
4	5	6	7	8	9	10
11	12	13	14	15	16	17
18	19	20	21	22	23	24
25	26	27	28	29	30	31

AUGUST

S	M	T	W	T	F	S
1	2	3	4	5	6	7
8	9	10	11	12	13	14
15	16	17	18	19	20	21
22	23	24	25	26	27	28
29	30	31				

SEPTEMBER

S	M	T	W	T	F	S
			1	2	3	4
5	6	7	8	9	10	11
12	13	14	15	16	17	18
19	20	21	22	23	24	25
26	27	28	29	30		

OCTOBER

S	M	T	W	T	F	S
					1	2
3	4	5	6	7	8	9
10	11	12	13	14	15	16
17	18	19	20	21	22	23
24	25	26	27	28	29	30
31						

NOVEMBER

S	M	T	W	T	F	S
	1	2	3	4	5	6
7	8	9	10	11	12	13
14	15	16	17	18	19	20
21	22	23	24	25	26	27
28	29	30				

DECEMBER

S	M	T	W	T	F	S
			1	2	3	4
5	6	7	8	9	10	11
12	13	14	15	16	17	18
19	20	21	22	23	24	25
26	27	28	29	30	31	

13

1988

JANUARY

S	M	T	W	T	F	S
					1	2
3	4	5	6	7	8	9
10	11	12	13	14	15	16
17	18	19	20	21	22	23
24	25	26	27	28	29	30
31						

FEBRUARY

S	M	T	W	T	F	S
	1	2	3	4	5	6
7	8	9	10	11	12	13
14	15	16	17	18	19	20
21	22	23	24	25	26	27
28	29					

MARCH

S	M	T	W	T	F	S
		1	2	3	4	5
6	7	8	9	10	11	12
13	14	15	16	17	18	19
20	21	22	23	24	25	26
27	28	29	30	31		

APRIL

S	M	T	W	T	F	S
					1	2
3	4	5	6	7	8	9
10	11	12	13	14	15	16
17	18	19	20	21	22	23
24	25	26	27	28	29	30

MAY

S	M	T	W	T	F	S
1	2	3	4	5	6	7
8	9	10	11	12	13	14
15	16	17	18	19	20	21
22	23	24	25	26	27	28
29	30	31				

JUNE

S	M	T	W	T	F	S
			1	2	3	4
5	6	7	8	9	10	11
12	13	14	15	16	17	18
19	20	21	22	23	24	25
26	27	28	29	30		

JULY

S	M	T	W	T	F	S
					1	2
3	4	5	6	7	8	9
10	11	12	13	14	15	16
17	18	19	20	21	22	23
24	25	26	27	28	29	30
31						

AUGUST

S	M	T	W	T	F	S
	1	2	3	4	5	6
7	8	9	10	11	12	13
14	15	16	17	18	19	20
21	22	23	24	25	26	27
28	29	30	31			

SEPTEMBER

S	M	T	W	T	F	S
				1	2	3
4	5	6	7	8	9	10
11	12	13	14	15	16	17
18	19	20	21	22	23	24
25	26	27	28	29	30	

OCTOBER

S	M	T	W	T	F	S
						1
2	3	4	5	6	7	8
9	10	11	12	13	14	15
16	17	18	19	20	21	22
23	24	25	26	27	28	29
30	31					

NOVEMBER

S	M	T	W	T	F	S
		1	2	3	4	5
6	7	8	9	10	11	12
13	14	15	16	17	18	19
20	21	22	23	24	25	26
27	28	29	30			

DECEMBER

S	M	T	W	T	F	S
				1	2	3
4	5	6	7	8	9	10
11	12	13	14	15	16	17
18	19	20	21	22	23	24
25	26	27	28	29	30	31

14

JANUARY

S	M	T	W	T	F	S
						1
2	3	4	5	6	7	8
9	10	11	12	13	14	15
16	17	18	19	20	21	22
23	24	25	26	27	28	29
30	31					

FEBRUARY

S	M	T	W	T	F	S
		1	2	3	4	5
6	7	8	9	10	11	12
13	14	15	16	17	18	19
20	21	22	23	24	25	26
27	28	29				

MARCH

S	M	T	W	T	F	S
			1	2	3	4
5	6	7	8	9	10	11
12	13	14	15	16	17	18
19	20	21	22	23	24	25
26	27	28	29	30	31	

APRIL

S	M	T	W	T	F	S
						1
2	3	4	5	6	7	8
9	10	11	12	13	14	15
16	17	18	19	20	21	22
23	24	25	26	27	28	29
30						

MAY

S	M	T	W	T	F	S
	1	2	3	4	5	6
7	8	9	10	11	12	13
14	15	16	17	18	19	20
21	22	23	24	25	26	27
28	29	30	31			

JUNE

S	M	T	W	T	F	S
				1	2	3
4	5	6	7	8	9	10
11	12	13	14	15	16	17
18	19	20	21	22	23	24
25	26	27	28	29	30	

JULY

S	M	T	W	T	F	S
						1
2	3	4	5	6	7	8
9	10	11	12	13	14	15
16	17	18	19	20	21	22
23	24	25	26	27	28	29
30	31					

AUGUST

S	M	T	W	T	F	S
		1	2	3	4	5
6	7	8	9	10	11	12
13	14	15	16	17	18	19
20	21	22	23	24	25	26
27	28	29	30	31		

SEPTEMBER

S	M	T	W	T	F	S
					1	2
3	4	5	6	7	8	9
10	11	12	13	14	15	16
17	18	19	20	21	22	23
24	25	26	27	28	29	30

OCTOBER

S	M	T	W	T	F	S
1	2	3	4	5	6	7
8	9	10	11	12	13	14
15	16	17	18	19	20	21
22	23	24	25	26	27	28
29	30	31				

NOVEMBER

S	M	T	W	T	F	S
			1	2	3	4
5	6	7	8	9	10	11
12	13	14	15	16	17	18
19	20	21	22	23	24	25
26	27	28	29	30		

DECEMBER

S	M	T	W	T	F	S
					1	2
3	4	5	6	7	8	9
10	11	12	13	14	15	16
17	18	19	20	21	22	23
24	25	26	27	28	29	30
31						

Julian and Gregorian Calendars; Leap Year

Calendars based on the movements of sun and moon have been used since ancient times, but none has been perfect. The Julian calendar, under which western nations measured time until 1582 A.D., was authorized by Julius Caesar in 46 B.C., the year 709 of Rome. His expert was a Greek, Sosigenes. The Julian calendar, on the assumption that the true year was 365 1/4 days long, gave every fourth year 366 days. The Venerable Bede, an Anglo-Saxon monk, announced in 730 A.D. that the 365 1/4-day Julian year was 11 min., 14 sec. too long, making a cumulative error of about a day every 128 years, but nothing was done about it for over 800 years.

By 1582 the accumulated error was estimated to have amounted to 10 days. In that year Pope Gregory XIII decreed that the day following Oct. 4, 1582, should be called Oct. 15, thus dropping 10 days.

However, with common years 365 days and a 366-day leap year every fourth year, the error in the length of the year would have recurred at the rate of a little more than 3 days every 400 years. So 3 of every 4 centesimal years (ending in 00) were made common years, not leap years. Thus 1600 was a leap year, 1700, 1800 and 1900 were not, but 2000 will be. Leap years are those divisible by 4 except centesimal years, which are common unless divisible by 400.

The Gregorian calendar was adopted at once by France, Italy, Spain, Portugal and Luxembourg. Within 2 years most German Catholic states, Belgium and parts of Switzerland and the Netherlands were brought under the new calendar, and Hungary followed in 1587. The rest of the Netherlands, along with Denmark and the German Protestant states made the change in 1699-1700 (German Protestants retained the old reckoning of Easter until 1776).

The British Government imposed the Gregorian calendar on all its possessions, including the American colonies, in 1752. The British decreed that the day following Sept. 2, 1752, should be called Sept. 14, a loss of 11 days. All dates preceding were marked O.S., for Old Style. In addition New Year's Day was moved to Jan. 1 from Mar. 25. (e.g., under the old reckoning, Mar. 24, 1700 had been followed by Mar. 25, 1701.) George Washington's birth date, which was Feb. 11, 1731, O.S., became Feb. 22, 1732, N.S. In 1753 Sweden too went Gregorian, retaining the old Easter rules until 1844.

In 1793 the French Revolutionary Government adopted a calendar of 12 months of 30 days each with 5 extra days in September of each common year and a 6th extra day every 4th year. Napoleon reinstated the Gregorian calendar in 1806.

The Gregorian system later spread to non-European regions, first in the European colonies, then in the independent countries, replacing traditional calendars at least for official purposes. Japan in 1873, Egypt in 1875, China in 1912 and Turkey in 1917 made the change, usually in conjunction with political upheavals. In China, the republican government began reckoning years from its 1911 founding — e.g., 1948 was designated the year 37. After 1949, the Communists adopted the Common, or Christian Era year count, even for the traditional lunar calendar.

In 1918 the revolutionary government in Russia decreed that the day after Jan. 31, 1918, Old Style, would become Feb. 14, 1918, New Style. Greece followed in 1923. (In Russia the Orthodox Church has retained the Julian calendar, as have various Middle Eastern Christian sects.) For the first time in history, all major cultures have one calendar.

To change from the Julian to the Gregorian calendar, add 10 days to dates Oct. 5, 1582, through Feb. 28, 1700; after that date add 11 days through Feb. 28, 1800; 12 days through Feb. 28, 1900; and 13 days through Feb. 28, 2100.

A century consists of 100 consecutive calendar years. The 1st century consisted of the years 1 through 100. The 20th century consists of the years 1901 through 2000 and will end Dec. 31, 2000. The 21st century will begin Jan. 1, 2001.

Julian Calendar

To find which of the 14 calendars printed on pages 220-221 applies to any year, starting Jan. 1, under the Julian system, find the century for the desired year in the three left-hand columns below; read across. Then find the year in the four top rows; read down. The number in the intersection is the calendar designation for that year.

Year (last two figures of desired year)

				01	02	03	04	05	06	07	08	09	10	11	12	13	14	15	16	17	18	19	20	21	22	23	24	25	26	27	28
				29	30	31	32	33	34	35	36	37	38	39	40	41	42	43	44	45	46	47	48	49	50	51	52	53	54	55	56
				57	58	59	60	61	62	63	64	65	66	67	68	69	70	71	72	73	74	75	76	77	78	79	80	81	82	83	84
Century			00	85	86	87	88	89	90	91	92	93	94	95	96	97	98	99													
0	700	1400	12	7	1	2	10	5	6	7	8	3	4	5	13	1	2	3	11	6	7	1	9	4	5	6	14	2	3	4	12
100	800	1500	11	6	7	1	9	4	5	6	14	2	3	4	12	7	1	2	10	5	6	7	8	3	4	5	13	1	2	3	11
200	900	1600	10	5	6	7	8	3	4	5	13	1	2	3	11	6	7	1	9	4	5	6	14	2	3	4	12	7	1	2	10
300	1000	1700	9	4	5	6	14	2	3	4	12	7	1	2	10	5	6	7	8	3	4	5	13	1	2	3	11	6	7	1	9
400	1100	1800	8	3	4	5	13	1	2	3	11	6	7	1	9	4	5	6	14	2	3	4	12	7	1	2	10	5	6	7	8
500	1200	1900	14	2	3	4	12	7	1	2	10	5	6	7	8	3	4	5	13	1	2	3	11	6	7	1	9	4	5	6	14
600	1300	2000	13	1	2	3	11	6	7	1	9	4	5	6	14	2	3	4	12	7	1	2	10	5	6	7	8	3	4	5	13

Gregorian Calendar

Pick desired year from table below or on page 220 (for years 1800 to 2059). The number shown with each year shows which calendar to use for that year, as shown on pages 220-221 (The Gregorian calendar was inaugurated Oct. 15, 1582. From that date to Dec. 31, 1582, use calendar 6.)

1583-1802

1583 . . 7	1603 . . 4	1623 . . 1	1643 . . 5	1663 . . 2	1683 . . 6	1703 . . 2	1723 . . 6	1743 . . 3	1763 . . 7	1783 . . 4
1584 . . 8	1604 . 12	1624 . . 9	1644 . 13	1664 . 10	1684 . 14	1704 . 10	1724 . 14	1744 . 11	1764 . . 8	1784 . 12
1585 . . 3	1605 . . 7	1625 . . 4	1645 . . 1	1665 . . 5	1685 . . 2	1705 . . 5	1725 . . 2	1745 . . 6	1765 . . 3	1785 . . 7
1586 . . 4	1606 . . 1	1626 . . 5	1646 . . 2	1666 . . 6	1686 . . 3	1706 . . 6	1726 . . 3	1746 . . 7	1766 . . 4	1786 . . 1
1587 . . 5	1607 . . 2	1627 . . 6	1647 . . 3	1667 . . 7	1687 . . 4	1707 . . 7	1727 . . 4	1747 . . 1	1767 . . 5	1787 . . 2
1588 . 13	1608 . 10	1628 . 14	1648 . 11	1668 . . 8	1688 . 12	1708 . . 8	1728 . 12	1748 . . 9	1768 . 13	1788 . 10
1589 . . 1	1609 . . 5	1629 . . 2	1649 . . 6	1669 . . 3	1689 . . 7	1709 . . 3	1729 . . 7	1749 . . 4	1769 . . 1	1789 . . 5
1590 . . 2	1610 . . 6	1630 . . 3	1650 . . 7	1670 . . 4	1690 . . 1	1710 . . 4	1730 . . 1	1750 . . 5	1770 . . 2	1790 . . 6
1591 . . 3	1611 . . 7	1631 . . 4	1651 . . 1	1671 . . 5	1691 . . 2	1711 . . 5	1731 . . 2	1751 . . 6	1771 . . 3	1791 . . 7
1592 . 11	1612 . . 8	1632 . 12	1652 . . 9	1672 . 13	1692 . 10	1712 . 13	1732 . 10	1752 . 14	1772 . 11	1792 . . 8
1593 . . 6	1613 . . 3	1633 . . 7	1653 . . 4	1673 . . 1	1693 . . 5	1713 . . 1	1733 . . 5	1753 . . 2	1773 . . 6	1793 . . 3
1594 . . 7	1614 . . 4	1634 . . 1	1654 . . 5	1674 . . 2	1694 . . 6	1714 . . 2	1734 . . 6	1754 . . 3	1774 . . 7	1794 . . 4
1595 . . 1	1615 . . 5	1635 . . 2	1655 . . 6	1675 . . 3	1695 . . 7	1715 . . 3	1735 . . 7	1755 . . 4	1775 . . 1	1795 . . 5
1596 . . 9	1616 . 13	1636 . 10	1656 . 14	1676 . 11	1696 . . 8	1716 . 11	1736 . . 8	1756 . 12	1776 . . 9	1796 . 13
1597 . . 4	1617 . . 1	1637 . . 5	1657 . . 2	1677 . . 6	1697 . . 3	1717 . . 6	1737 . . 3	1757 . . 7	1777 . . 4	1797 . . 1
1598 . . 5	1618 . . 2	1638 . . 6	1658 . . 3	1678 . . 7	1698 . . 4	1718 . . 7	1738 . . 4	1758 . . 1	1778 . . 5	1798 . . 2
1599 . . 6	1619 . . 3	1639 . . 7	1659 . . 4	1679 . . 1	1699 . . 5	1719 . . 1	1739 . . 5	1759 . . 2	1779 . . 6	1799 . . 3
1600 . 14	1620 . 11	1640 . . 8	1660 . 12	1680 . . 9	1700 . . 6	1720 . . 9	1740 . 13	1760 . 10	1780 . 14	1800 . . 4
1601 . . 2	1621 . . 6	1641 . . 3	1661 . . 7	1681 . . 4	1701 . . 7	1721 . . 4	1741 . . 1	1761 . . 5	1781 . . 2	1801 . . 5
1602 . . 3	1622 . . 7	1642 . . 4	1662 . . 1	1682 . . 5	1702 . . 1	1722 . . 5	1742 . . 2	1762 . . 6	1782 . . 3	1802 . . 6

The Julian Period

How many days have you lived? To determine this, you must multiply your age by 365, add the number of days since your last birthday until today, and account for all leap years. Chances are your answer would be wrong. Astronomers, however, find it convenient to express dates and long time intervals in days rather than in years, months and days. This is done by placing events within the Julian period.

The Julian period was devised in 1582 by Joseph Scaliger and named after his father Julius (not after the Julian calendar). Scaliger had Julian Day (JD) #1 begin at noon, Jan. 1, 4713 B. C., the most recent time that three major chronological cycles began on the same day — 1) the 28-year solar cycle, after which dates in the Julian calendar (e.g., Feb. 11) return to the same days of the week (e.g., Monday); 2) the 19-year lunar cycle, after which the phases of the moon return to the same dates of the year; and 3) the 15-year indiction cycle, used in ancient Rome to regulate taxes. It will take 7980 years to complete the period, the product of 28, 19, and 15.

Noon of Dec. 31, 1987, marks the beginning of JD 2,447,160; that many days will have passed since the start of the Julian period. The JD at noon of any date in 1988 may be found by adding to this figure the day of the year for that date, which is given in the left hand column in the chart below. Simple JD conversion tables are used by astronomers.

Days Between Two Dates

Table covers period of two ordinary years. Example—Days between Feb. 10, 1987 and Dec. 15, 1988; subtract 41 from 714; answer is 673 days. For leap year, such as 1988, one day must be added: final answer is 674.

Date	Jan.	Feb.	Mar.	April	May	June	July	Aug.	Sept.	Oct.	Nov.	Dec.
1	1	32	60	91	121	152	182	213	244	274	305	335
2	2	33	61	92	122	153	183	214	245	275	306	336
3	3	34	62	93	123	154	184	215	246	276	307	337
4	4	35	63	94	124	155	185	216	247	277	308	338
5	5	36	64	95	125	156	186	217	248	278	309	339
6	6	37	65	96	126	157	187	218	249	279	310	340
7	7	38	66	97	127	158	188	219	250	280	311	341
8	8	39	67	98	128	159	189	220	251	281	312	342
9	9	40	68	99	129	160	190	221	252	282	313	343
10	10	41	69	100	130	161	191	222	253	283	314	344
11	11	42	70	101	131	162	192	223	254	284	315	345
12	12	43	71	102	132	163	193	224	255	285	316	346
13	13	44	72	103	133	164	194	225	256	286	317	347
14	14	45	73	104	134	165	195	226	257	287	318	348
15	15	46	74	105	135	166	196	227	258	288	319	349
16	16	47	75	106	136	167	197	228	259	289	320	350
17	17	48	76	107	137	168	198	229	260	290	321	351
18	18	49	77	108	138	169	199	230	261	291	322	352
19	19	50	78	109	139	170	200	231	262	292	323	353
20	20	51	79	110	140	171	201	232	263	293	324	354
21	21	52	80	111	141	172	202	233	264	294	325	355
22	22	53	81	112	142	173	203	234	265	295	326	356
23	23	54	82	113	143	174	204	235	266	296	327	357
24	24	55	83	114	144	175	205	236	267	297	328	358
25	25	56	84	115	145	176	206	237	268	298	329	359
26	26	57	85	116	146	177	207	238	269	299	330	360
27	27	58	86	117	147	178	208	239	270	300	331	361
28	28	59	87	118	148	179	209	240	271	301	332	362
29	29	—	88	119	149	180	210	241	272	302	333	363
30	30	—	89	120	150	181	211	242	273	303	334	364
31	31	—	90	—	151	—	212	243	—	304	—	365

Date	Jan.	Feb.	Mar.	April	May	June	July	Aug.	Sept.	Oct.	Nov.	Dec.
1	366	397	425	456	486	517	547	578	609	639	670	700
2	367	398	426	457	487	518	548	579	610	640	671	701
3	368	399	427	458	488	519	549	580	611	641	672	702
4	369	400	428	459	489	520	550	581	612	642	673	703
5	370	401	429	460	490	521	551	582	613	643	674	704
6	371	402	430	461	491	522	552	583	614	644	675	705
7	372	403	431	462	492	523	553	584	615	645	676	706
8	373	404	432	463	493	524	554	585	616	646	677	707
9	374	405	433	464	494	525	555	586	617	647	678	708
10	375	406	434	465	495	526	556	587	618	648	679	709
11	376	407	435	466	496	527	557	588	619	649	680	710
12	377	408	436	467	497	528	558	589	620	650	681	711
13	378	409	437	468	498	529	559	590	621	651	682	712
14	379	410	438	469	499	530	560	591	622	652	683	713
15	380	411	439	470	500	531	561	592	623	653	684	714
16	381	412	440	471	501	532	562	593	624	654	685	715
17	382	413	441	472	502	533	563	594	625	655	686	716
18	383	414	442	473	503	534	564	595	626	656	687	717
19	384	415	443	474	504	535	565	596	627	657	688	718
20	385	416	444	475	505	536	566	597	628	658	689	719
21	386	417	445	476	506	537	567	598	629	659	690	720
22	387	418	446	477	507	538	568	599	630	660	691	721
23	388	419	447	478	508	539	569	600	631	661	692	722
24	389	420	448	479	509	540	570	601	632	662	693	723
25	390	421	449	480	510	541	571	602	633	663	694	724
26	391	422	450	481	511	542	572	603	634	664	695	725
27	392	423	451	482	512	543	573	604	635	665	696	726
28	393	424	452	483	513	544	574	605	636	666	697	727
29	394	—	453	484	514	545	575	606	637	667	698	728
30	395	—	454	485	515	546	576	607	638	668	699	729
31	396	—	455	—	516	—	577	608	—	669	—	730

Lunar Calendar, Chinese New Year, Vietnamese Tet

The ancient Chinese lunar calendar is divided into 12 months of either 29 or 30 days (compensating for the fact that the mean duration of the lunar month is 29 days, 12 hours, 44.05 minutes). The calendar is synchronized with the solar year by the addition of extra months at fixed intervals.

The Chinese calendar runs on a sexagenary cycle, i.e., 60 years. The cycles 1876-1935 and 1936-1995, with the years grouped under their twelve animal designations, are printed below. The Year 1988 (Lunar Year 4686) is found in the fifth column, under Dragon, and is known as a "Year of the Dragon." Readers can find the animal name for the year of their birth, marriage, etc., in the same chart. (Note: the first 3-7 weeks of each of the western years belong to the previous Chinese year and animal designation.)

Both the western (Gregorian) and traditional lunar calendars are used publicly in China, and two New Year's celebrations are held. On Taiwan, in overseas Chinese communities, and in Vietnam, the lunar calendar has been used only to set the dates for traditional festivals, with the Gregorian system in general use.

The four-day Chinese New Year, Hsin Nien, and the three-day Vietnamese New Year festival, Tet, begin at the first new moon after the sun enters Aquarius. The day may fall, therefore, between Jan. 21 and Feb. 19 of the Gregorian calendar. Feb. 17, 1988 marks the start of the new Chinese year. The date is fixed according to the date of the new moon in the Far East. Since this is west of the International Date Line the date may be one day later than that of the new moon in the United States.

Rat	Ox	Tiger	Hare (Rabbit)	Dragon	Snake	Horse	Sheep (Goat)	Monkey	Rooster	Dog	Pig
1876	1877	1878	1879	1880	1881	1882	1883	1884	1885	1886	1887
1888	1889	1890	1891	1892	1893	1894	1895	1896	1897	1898	1899
1900	1901	1902	1903	1904	1905	1906	1907	1908	1909	1910	1911
1912	1913	1914	1915	1916	1917	1918	1919	1920	1921	1922	1923
1924	1925	1926	1927	1928	1929	1930	1931	1932	1933	1934	1935
1936	1937	1938	1939	1940	1941	1942	1943	1944	1945	1946	1947
1948	1949	1950	1951	1952	1953	1954	1955	1956	1957	1958	1959
1960	1961	1962	1963	1964	1965	1966	1967	1968	1969	1970	1971
1972	1973	1974	1975	1976	1977	1978	1979	1980	1981	1982	1983
1984	1985	1986	1987	1988	1989	1990	1991	1992	1993	1994	1995

Chronological Eras, 1988

The year 1988 of the Christian Era comprises the latter part of the 212th and the beginning of the 213th year of the independence of the United States of America.

Era	Year	Begins in 1987		Era	Year	Begins in 1987	
Byzantine	7497	Sept.	14	Grecian (Seleucidae)	2300	Sept. or Oct.	14 / 14
Jewish	5749	Sept. (sunset)	11	Diocletian	1705	Sept.	11
Roman (Ab Urbe Condita)	2741	Jan.	14	Indian (Saka)	1909	Mar.	22
Nabonassar (Babylonian)	2737	Apr.	26	Mohammedan (Hegira)	1409	Aug.	13
Japanese	2648	Jan.	1				

Chronological Cycles, 1987

Dominical Letter	CB	Golden Number (Lunar Cycle)	XIII	Roman Indiction	11
Epact	31	Solar Cycle	9	Julian Period (year of)	6701

Standard Time Differences — North American Cities

At 12 o'clock noon, Eastern Standard Time, the standard time in N.A. cities is as follows:

Akron, Oh.	12.00	Noon	Frankfort, Ky.	12.00	Noon	Pierre, S.D.	11.00	A.M.
Albuquerque, N.M.	10.00	A.M.	Galveston, Tex.	11.00	A.M.	Pittsburgh, Pa.	12.00	Noon
Atlanta, Ga.	12.00	Noon	Grand Rapids, Mich.	12.00	Noon	Portland, Me.	12.00	Noon
Austin, Tex.	11.00	A.M.	Halifax, N.S.	1.00	P.M.	Portland, Ore.	9.00	A.M.
Baltimore, Md.	12.00	Noon	Hartford, Conn.	12.00	Noon	Providence, R.I.	12.00	Noon
Birmingham, Ala.	11.00	A.M.	Helena, Mon.	10.00	A.M.	*Regina, Sask.	11.00	A.M.
Bismarck, N.D.	11.00	A.M.	*Honolulu, Ha.	7.00	A.M.	Reno, Nev.	9.00	A.M.
Boise, Ida.	10.00	A.M.	Houston, Tex.	11.00	A.M.	Richmond, Va.	12.00	Noon
Boston, Mass.	12.00	Noon	*Indianapolis, Ind.	12.00	Noon	Rochester, N.Y.	12.00	Noon
Buffalo, N.Y.	12.00	Noon	Jacksonville, Fla.	12.00	Noon	Sacramento, Cal.	9.00	A.M.
Butte, Mon.	10.00	A.M.	Juneau, Alas.	8.00	A.M.	St. John's, Nfld.	1.30	P.M.
Calgary, Alta.	10.00	A.M.	Kansas City, Mo.	11.00	A.M.	St. Louis, Mo.	11.00	A.M.
Charleston, S.C.	12.00	Noon	Knoxville, Tenn.	12.00	Noon	St. Paul, Minn.	11.00	A.M.
Charleston, W.Va.	12.00	Noon	Lexington, Ky.	12.00	Noon	Salt Lake City, Ut.	10.00	A.M.
Charlotte, N.C.	12.00	Noon	Lincoln, Neb.	11.00	A.M.	San Antonio, Tex.	11.00	A.M.
Charlottetown, P.E.I.	1.00	P.M.	Little Rock, Ark.	11.00	A.M.	San Diego, Cal.	9.00	A.M.
Chattanooga, Tenn.	12.00	Noon	Los Angeles, Cal.	9.00	A.M.	San Francisco, Cal.	9.00	A.M.
Cheyenne, Wy.	10.00	A.M.	Louisville, Ky.	12.00	Noon	Santa Fe, N.M.	10.00	A.M.
Chicago, Ill.	11.00	A.M.	*Mexico City	11.00	A.M.	Savannah, Ga.	12.00	Noon
Cleveland, Oh.	12.00	Noon	Memphis, Tenn.	11.00	A.M.	Seattle, Wash.	9.00	A.M.
Colorado Spr., Col.	10.00	A.M.	Miami, Fla.	12.00	Noon	Shreveport, La.	11.00	A.M.
Columbus, Oh.	12.00	Noon	Milwaukee, Wis.	11.00	A.M.	Sioux Falls, S.D.	11.00	A.M.
Dallas, Tex.	11.00	A.M.	Minneapolis, Minn.	11.00	A.M.	Spokane, Wash.	9.00	A.M.
*Dawson, Yuk.	9.00	A.M.	Mobile, Ala.	11.00	A.M.	Tampa, Fla.	12.00	Noon
Dayton, Oh.	12.00	Noon	Montreal, Que.	12.00	Noon	Toledo, Oh.	12.00	Noon
Denver, Col.	10.00	A.M.	Nashville, Tenn.	11.00	A.M.	Topeka, Kan.	11.00	A.M.
Des Moines, Ia.	11.00	A.M.	New Haven, Conn.	12.00	Noon	Toronto, Ont.	12.00	Noon
Detroit, Mich.	12.00	Noon	New Orleans, La.	11.00	A.M.	*Tucson, Ariz.	10.00	A.M.
Duluth, Minn.	11.00	A.M.	New York, N.Y.	12.00	Noon	Tulsa, Okla.	11.00	A.M.
El Paso, Tex.	10.00	A.M.	Nome, Alas.	8.00	A.M.	Vancouver, B.C.	9.00	A.M.
Erie, Pa.	12.00	Noon	Norfolk, Va.	12.00	Noon	Washington, D.C.	12.00	Noon
Evansville, Ind.	11.00	A.M.	Okla. City, Okla.	11.00	A.M.	Wichita, Kan.	11.00	A.M.
Fairbanks, Alas.	8.00	A.M.	Omaha, Neb.	11.00	A.M.	Wilmington, Del.	12.00	Noon
Flint, Mich.	12.00	Noon	Peoria, Ill.	11.00	A.M.	Winnipeg, Man.	11.00	A.M.
*Fort Wayne, Ind.	12.00	Noon	Philadelphia, Pa.	12.00	Noon			
Fort Worth, Tex.	11.00	A.M.	*Phoenix, Ariz.	10.00	A.M.			

*Cities with an asterisk do not observe daylight saving time. During much of the year, it is necessary to add one hour to the cities which do observe daylight savings time to get the proper time relation.

Standard Time Differences—World Cities

The time indicated in the table is fixed by law and is called the legal time, or, more generally, Standard Time. Use of Daylight Saving Time varies widely. *Indicates morning of the following day. At 12:00 noon, Eastern Standard Time, the standard time (in 24-hour time) in foreign cities is as follows:

Addis Ababa	20 00	Caracas	13 00	Lima	12 00	Rome	18 00
Alexandria	19 00	Casablanca	17 00	Lisbon	18 00	Santiago (Chile)	13 00
Amsterdam	18 00	Copenhagen	18 00	Liverpool	17 00	Seoul	2 00*
Athens	19 00	Dacca	23 00	London	17 00	Shanghai	1 00*
Auckland	5 00*	Delhi	22 30	Madrid	19 00	Singapore	1 00*
Baghdad	20 00	Dublin	17 00	Manila	1 00*	Stockholm	18 00
Bangkok	0 00	Gdansk	18 00	Mecca	20 00	Sydney (Australia)	3 00*
Belfast	17 00	Geneva	18 00	Melbourne	3 00*	Tashkent	23 00
Berlin	18 00	Havana	12 00	Mexico City	11 00	Teheran	20 30
Bogota	12 00	Helsinki	19 00	Montevideo	14 00	Tel Aviv	19 00
Bombay	22 30	Ho Chi Minh City	1 00*	Moscow	20 00	Tokyo	2 00*
Bremen	18 00	Hong Kong	1 00*	Nagasaki	2 00*	Valparaiso	13 00
Brussels	18 00	Istanbul	19 00	Oslo	18 00	Vladivostok	3 00*
Bucharest	19 00	Jakarta	0 00	Paris	18 00	Vienna	18 00
Budapest	18 00	Jerusalem	19 00	Peking	1 00*	Warsaw	18 00
Buenos Aires	14 00	Johannesburg	19 00	Prague	18 00	Wellington (N.Z.)	5 00*
Cairo	19 00	Karachi	22 00	Rangoon	23 30	Yokohama	2 00*
Calcutta	22 30	Le Havre	18 00	Rio De Janeiro	14 00	Zurich	18 00
Cape Town	19 00	Leningrad	20 00				

Standard Time, Daylight Saving Time, and Others

Source: Defense Mapping Agency Hydrographic Center; Department of Transportation; National Bureau of Standards; U.S. Naval Observatory

Standard Time

Standard time is reckoned from Greenwich, England, recognized as the Prime Meridian of Longitude. The world is divided into 24 zones, each 15° of arc, or one hour in time apart. The Greenwich meridian (0°) extends through the center of the initial zone, and the zones to the east are numbered from 1 to 12 with the prefix "minus" indicating the number of hours to be subtracted to obtain Greenwich Time. Each zone extends 7½° on either side of its central meridian.

Westward zones are similarly numbered, but prefixed "plus" showing the number of hours that must be added to get Greenwich Time. While these zones apply generally to sea areas, it should be noted that the Standard Time maintained in many countries does not coincide with zone time. A graphical representation of the zones is shown on the Standard Time Zone Chart of the World published by the Defense Mapping Agency Hydrographic/Topographic Center, Washington, DC 20315-0030.

The United States and possessions are divided into eight Standard Time zones, as set forth by the Uniform Time Act of 1966, which also provides for the use of Daylight Saving Time therein. Each zone is approximately 15° of longitude in width. All places in each zone use, instead of their own local time, the time counted from the transit of the "mean sun" across the Standard Time meridian which passes near the middle of that zone.

These time zones are designated as Atlantic, Eastern, Central, Mountain, Pacific, Alaska, Aleutian-Hawaii, and Bering, and the time in these zones is basically reckoned from the 60th, 75th, 90th, 105th, 120th, 135th, 150th, 165th meridians west of Greenwich. The line wanders to conform to local geographical regions. The time in the various zones is earlier than Greenwich Time by 4, 5, 6, 7, 8, 9, 10, and 11 hours respectively.

24-Hour Time

24-hour time is widely used in scientific work throughout the world. In the United States it is used also in operations of the Armed Forces. In Europe it is used in preference to the 12-hour a.m. and p.m. system. With the 24-hour system the day begins at midnight and hours are numbered 0 through 23.

International Date Line

The Date Line is a zig-zag line that approximately coincides with the 180th meridian, and it is where each calendar day begins. The date must be advanced one day when crossing in a westerly direction and set back one day when crossing in an easterly direction.

The line is deflected eastward through the Bering Strait and westward of the Aleutians to prevent separating these areas by date. The line is again deflected eastward of the Tonga and New Zealand Islands in the South Pacific for the same reason.

Daylight Saving Time

Daylight Saving Time is achieved by advancing the clock one hour. Under the Uniform Time Act, which became effective in 1967, all states, the District of Columbia, and U.S. possessions were to observe Daylight Saving Time beginning at 2 a.m. on the last Sunday in April and ending at 2 a.m. on the last Sunday in October. Any state could, by law, exempt itself; a 1972 amendment to the act authorized states split by time zones to take that into consideration in exempting themselves. Arizona, Hawaii, Puerto Rico, the Virgin Islands, American Samoa, and part of Indiana are now exempt. Some local zone boundaries in Kansas, Texas, Florida, Michigan, and Alaska have been modified in the last several years by the Dept. of Transportation, which oversees the act. To conserve energy Congress put most of the nation on year-round Daylight Saving Time for two years effective Jan. 6, 1974 through Oct. 26, 1975; but a further bill, signed in October, 1974, restored Standard Time from the last Sunday in that month to the last Sunday in February, 1975. At the end of 1975, Congress failed to renew this temporary legislation and the nation returned to the older end-of April to end-of October DST system.

On July 8, 1986, Pres. Ronald Reagan signed legislation moving up the start of daylight saving time to the first Sunday in April. Daylight Saving Time, which used to start the last Sunday in April, will still end the last Sunday in October. The Transportation Dept. estimated that the earlier starting date will help save more than $28 million in traffic accident costs and prevent more than 1,500 injuries and 20 deaths. The new law, opposed by some farm state lawmakers, takes effect in 1987.

International

Adjusting clock time to be able to use the added daylight on summer evenings is common throughout the world.

Western Europe is on daylight saving time generally from the last Sunday in March to the last Sunday in September; however, the United Kingdom continues until the last Sunday in October.

The Soviet Union lies over 11 time zones, but maintains its standard time 1 hour fast of the zone designation. Additionally, it proclaims daylight saving time as does Europe.

China lies across 5 time zones, but has decreed that the entire country be placed on zone time minus 8 hours with daylight saving time from April 12 to September 12.

Many of the countries in the Southern Hemisphere maintain daylight saving time generally from October to March; however, most countries near the equator do not deviate from standard time.

Legal or Public Holidays, 1988

Technically there are no national holidays in the United States; each state has jurisdiction over its holidays, which are designated by legislative enactment or executive proclamation. In practice, however, most states observe the federal legal public holidays, even though the President and Congress can legally designate holidays only for the District of Columbia and for federal employees.

Federal legal public holidays are New Year's Day, Martin Luther King Day, Washington's Birthday, Memorial Day, Independence Day, Labor Day, Columbus Day, Veterans' Day, Thanksgiving, and Christmas.

Chief Legal or Public Holidays

When a holiday falls on a Sunday or a Saturday it is usually observed on the following Monday or preceding Friday. For some holidays, government and business closing practices vary. In most states, the office of the Secretary of State can provide details of holiday closings. In most states, the following will be legal or public holidays in 1987:

Jan. 1 (Friday) — New Year's Day.

Feb. 12 (Friday) — Lincoln's Birthday.

Feb. 15 (3d Mon. in Feb.) — Washington's Birthday, or Presidents' Day, or Washington-Lincoln Day:

May 30 (last Mon. in May) — Memorial Day, or Decoration Day.

July 4 (Monday) — Independence Day.

Sept. 5 (1st Mon. in Sept.) — Labor Day.

Oct. 10 (2d Mon. in Oct.) — Columbus Day, or Discoverers' Day, or Pioneers' Day.

Nov. 11 (Friday) — Veterans' Day.

Nov. 24 (4th Thurs. in Nov.) — Thanksgiving Day.

Dec. 25 (Sunday) — Christmas Day.

In some states, the following will be legal or public holidays in 1988:

Jan. 15 (Friday) — Martin Luther King Day. In some states, combined with Robert E. Lee Day and/or observed on Jan. 18, the 3rd Mon. in Jan.

Apr. 1 (Friday) — Good Friday. In some states, observed for half or part of day.

Nov. 8 (1st Tues. after the 1st Mon. in Nov.) — Election Day.

Some Days Usually Observed

Arbor Day. Tree-planting day. First observed April 10, 1872, in Nebraska. Now observed in most states, usually on the last Friday in Apr. (Apr. 24 in 1987).

Armed Forces Day (May 21 in 1988). Always third Saturday of May, by presidential proclamation. Replaces Army, Navy, and Air Force Days.

Bill of Rights Day, Dec. 15. By Act of Congress. Bill of Rights took effect Dec. 15, 1791.

Bird Day. Often observed with Arbor Day.

Child Health Day (Oct. 3 in 1988). Always first Monday in Oct., by presidential proclamation.

Citizenship Day, Sept. 17. President Truman, Feb. 29, 1952, signed bill designating Sept. 17 as annual Citizenship Day. It replaced I Am An American Day, formerly 3d Sunday in May, and Constitution Day, formerly Sept. 17.

Easter Sunday (Apr. 3 in 1988).

Easter Monday (Apr. 4 in 1988). A statutory day in Canada.

Elizabeth Cady Stanton Day, Nov. 12. Birthday of pioneer leader for equal rights for women.

Father's Day (June 19 in 1988). Always third Sunday in June.

Forefathers' Day, Dec. 21. Landing on Plymouth Rock, in 1620. Is celebrated with dinners by New England societies, especially "Down East."

Gen. Pulaski Memorial Day, Oct. 11. Native of Poland and Revolutionary War hero; died (Oct. 11, 1779) from wounds received at the siege of Savannah, Ga.

Georgia Day, Feb. 12. Observed in that state. Commemorates landing of first colonists in 1733.

Grandparents' Day (Sept. 11 in 1988). Always first Sunday after Labor Day. Legislated in 1979.

Groundhog Day, Feb. 2. A popular belief is that if the groundhog sees his shadow on this day, he returns to his burrow and winter continues 6 weeks longer.

Halloween, Oct. 31. The evening before All Saints or All-Hallows Day. Informally observed in the U.S. with masquerading and pumpkin decorating. Traditionally an occasion for children to play pranks.

Loyalty Day, May 1. By Act of Congress.

May Day. Name popularly given to May 1st. Celebrated as Labor Day in most of the world, and by some groups in the U.S. Observed in many schools as a Spring Festival.

Mother's Day (May 8 in 1988). Always second Sunday in that month. First celebrated in Philadelphia in 1908, Mother's Day has become an international holiday.

National Day of Prayer. By presidential proclamation each year on a day other than a Sunday.

National Freedom Day, Feb. 1. To commemorate the signing of the Thirteenth Amendment, abolishing slavery, Feb. 1, 1865. By presidential proclamation.

National Maritime Day, May 22. First proclaimed 1935 in commemoration of the departure of the SS Savannah, from Savannah, Georgia, on May 22, 1819, on the first successful transatlantic voyage under steam propulsion. By presidential proclamation.

Pan American Day, Apr. 14. In 1890 the First Intl. Conference of American States, meeting in Washington, was held on that date. A resolution was adopted which resulted in the creation of the organization known today as the Pan American Union. By presidential proclamation.

Primary Election Day. Observed usually only when presidential or general elections are held.

Reformation Day, Oct. 31. Observed by Protestant groups.

Sadie Hawkins Day (Nov. 12 in 1988). First Saturday after November 11.

St. Patrick's Day, Mar. 17. Observed by Irish societies, especially with parades.

St. Valentine's Day, Feb. 14. Festival of a martyr beheaded at Rome under Emperor Claudius. Association of this day with lovers has no connection with the saint and probably had its origin in an old belief that on this day birds begin to choose their mates.

Susan B. Anthony Day, Feb. 15. Birthday of a pioneer crusader for equal rights for women.

United Nations Day, Oct. 24. By presidential proclamation, to commemorate founding of United Nations.

Verrazano Day, Apr. 7. Observed by New York State, to commemorate the probable discovery of New York harbor by Giovanni da Verrazano in April, 1524.

Victoria Day (May 23 in 1988). Birthday of Queen Victoria, a statutory day in Canada, celebrated the first Monday before May 25.

World Poetry Day, Oct. 15.

Wright Brothers Day, Dec. 17. By presidential designation, to commemorate first successful flight by Orville and Wilbur Wright, Dec. 17, 1903.

Some Other Legal or Public Holidays

Source: Questionnaires to states

Jan. 18 — Confederate Heroes' Day or Robert E. Lee Day. In various southern states.

Jan. 30 — Franklin D. Roosevelt's Birthday. In Kentucky.

Mar. 2 — Texas Independence Day. In that state.

Mar. 12 — Thomas Jefferson's Birthday. In Alabama.

Mar. 16 — Mardi Gras Day (Tuesday before Ash Wednesday). In Alabama and Louisiana.

Mar. 21 — San Jacinto Day. In Texas.

Mar. 28 — Seward's Day. In Alaska.

Apr. 1 — Confederate Memorial Day. In Alabama; April 25 in Mississippi.

Apr. 18 — Patriots Day (3rd Mon. in April). In Maine and Massachusetts.

May 8 — Harry S. Truman's Birthday. In Missouri.

May 30 — Jefferson Davis Birthday. In Mississippi.

June 1 — Jefferson Davis's Birthday (Observed 1st Mon. in June). In Alabama; June 3 in Kentucky.

June 3 — Confederate Memorial Day. In Kentucky.

June 11 — King Kamehameha I Day. In Hawaii.

June 19 — Emancipation Day. In Texas.

July 16 — Bennington Battle Day. In Vermont.

July 25 — Pioneer Day. In Utah.

Aug. 1 — Colorado Day. In that state.

Aug. 8 — Victory Day. In Rhode Island.

Oct. 18 — Alaska Day. In that state.

Oct. 30 — Nevada Day. In that state.

Nov. 25 — Day after Thanksgiving. In some states.

Dec. 24 — Christmas Eve. In some states.

EDUCATION

Educational Attainment by Age, Race, and Sex

Source: U.S. Bureau of the Census unpublished data as of March, 1986 (Number of persons in thousands)

Race, age, and sex	Years of school completed					Percent			
	All persons	Less than high school, 4 years	High school, 4 years	College, 1 to 3 years	College, 4 years or more	Less than high school 4 years	High school, 4 years	College, 1 to 3 years	College, 4 years or more
March 1986									
All races									
18 to 24 years	27,112	5,696	12,128	7,337	1,951	21.0	44.7	27.1	7.2
25 years and over	146,606	37,050	56,338	24,729	28,489	25.3	38.4	16.9	19.4
25 to 34 years	42,053	5,543	17,311	9,104	10,094	13.2	41.2	21.6	24.0
35 to 44 years	32,508	4,931	12,630	6,655	8,292	15.2	38.9	20.5	25.5
45 to 54 years	22,662	5,348	9,521	3,455	4,337	23.6	42.0	15.2	19.1
55 to 64 years	22,061	7,364	8,743	2,786	3,170	33.4	39.6	12.6	14.4
65 years and over	27,322	13,863	8,133	2,729	2,597	50.7	29.8	10.0	9.5
Male, 25 years and over	69,503	17,296	24,260	11,856	16,091	24.9	34.9	17.1	23.2
Female, 25 years and over	77,102	19,754	32,078	12,874	12,399	25.6	41.6	16.7	16.1
White									
18 to 24 years	22,618	4,528	10,132	6,198	1,758	20.0	44.8	27.4	7.8
25 years and over	127,269	30,349	49,660	21,708	25,551	23.8	39.0	17.1	20.1
25 to 34 years	35,574	4,445	14,553	7,652	8,924	12.5	40.9	21.5	25.1
35 to 44 years	28,001	3,929	10,938	5,799	7,334	14.0	39.1	20.7	26.2
45 to 54 years	19,543	4,192	8,411	3,050	3,890	21.5	43.0	15.6	19.9
55 to 64 years	19,522	5,925	8,041	2,595	2,960	30.4	41.2	13.3	15.2
65 years and over	24,629	11,859	7,718	2,611	2,442	48.2	31.3	10.6	9.9
Male, 25 years and over	60,770	14,293	21,372	10,489	14,615	23.5	35.2	17.3	24.1
Female, 25 years and over	66,500	16,057	28,288	11,219	10,936	24.1	42.5	16.9	16.4
Black									
18 to 24 years	3,707	1,003	1,720	864	121	27.1	46.4	23.3	3.3
25 years and over	15,234	5,740	5,422	2,406	1,666	37.7	36.6	15.8	10.9
25 to 34 years	5,101	926	2,328	1,152	696	18.2	45.6	22.6	13.6
35 to 44 years	3,408	826	1,385	698	498	24.2	40.6	20.5	14.6
45 to 54 years	2,403	988	866	318	231	41.1	36.0	13.2	9.6
55 to 64 years	2,050	1,237	522	156	135	60.3	25.5	7.6	6.6
65 years and over	2,273	1,765	320	82	105	77.7	14.1	3.6	4.7
Male, 25 years and over	6,779	2,609	2,324	1,086	759	38.5	34.3	16.0	11.2
Female, 25 years and over	8,455	3,131	3,098	1,320	907	37.0	36.6	15.6	10.7
Spanish Origin[1]									
18 to 24 years	2,571	1,079	951	462	79	42.0	37.0	18.0	3.1
25 years and over	9,030	4,653	2,566	1,051	761	51.5	28.4	11.6	8.4
25 to 34 years	3,476	1,440	1,170	523	343	41.4	33.7	15.0	9.9
35 to 44 years	2,209	1,045	644	305	217	47.3	29.2	13.8	9.8
45 to 54 years	1,453	795	417	132	108	54.7	28.7	9.1	7.4
55 to 64 years	976	634	219	63	60	65.0	22.4	6.5	6.1
65 years and over	915	739	116	27	33	80.8	12.7	3.0	3.6
Male, 25 years and over	4,397	2,232	1,203	543	419	50.8	27.4	12.3	9.5
Female, 25 years and over	4,633	2,421	1,363	508	341	52.3	29.4	11.0	7.4

(1) Persons of Spanish origin may be of any race.

Historical Summary of Public Elementary and Secondary Schools

Source: Natl. Center for Education Statistics, U.S. Dept. of Education

Pupils and teachers (thousands)	1899-1900	1909-10	1919-20	1929-30	1939-40	1949-50	1959-60	1969-70	1979-80	1984-85
Total U.S. population	75,995	90,492	104,512	121,770	130,880	148,665	179,323	203,212	224,567	236,495
Population 5-17 years of age	21,573	24,009	27,556	31,417	30,150	30,168	43,881	52,490	48,040	44,942
Percent aged 5-17 years	28.4	26.5	26.4	25.8	23.0	20.3	24.5	25.8	21.4	19.0
Enrollment (thousands)										
Elementary and secondary	15,503	17,814	21,578	25,678	25,434	25,111	36,087	45,619	41,645	39,293
Percent pop. 5-17 enrolled	71.9	74.2	78.3	81.7	84.4	83.2	82.2	86.9	86.7	87.4
Percent in high schools	3.3	5.1	10.2	17.1	26.0	22.7	23.5	28.5	32.9	31.5
High school graduates	62	111	231	592	1,143	1,063	1,627	2,589	2,748	2,420
Average school term (in days)	144.3	157.5	161.9	172.7	175.0	177.9	178.0	178.9	178.5	...
Total instructional staff	...	...	678	880	912	962	1,464	2,253	2,441	...
Teachers, librarians: Men	127	110	93	140	195	195	402	691	782[4]	...
Women	296	413	565	703	681	719	985	1,440	1,518[4]	...
Percent men	29.9	21.1	14.1	16.6	22.2	21.3	29.0	33.4	34.0[4]	...
Revenue & expenditures (millions)										
Total revenue	$219	$433	$970	$2,088	$2,260	$5,437	$14,746	$40,267	$96,881	$137,351
Total expenditures	214	426	1,036	2,316	2,344	5,837	15,613	40,683	95,962	136,500[4]
Current elem. and secondary	179	356	861	1,843	1,941	4,687	12,329	34,218	86,984[1]	125,887[1]
Capital outlay	35	69	153	370	257	1,014	2,661	4,659	6,506	...
Interest on school debt	...	...	18	92	130	100	489	1,171	1,874	...
Other	...	...	3	9	13	35	132	636	598	...
Salaries and pupil cost				(Data in unadjusted dollars)						
Average annual teacher salary[2]	$325	$485	$871	$1,420	$1,441	$3,010	$5,174	$8,840	$16,715	$24,644
Expenditure per capita total pop.	2.83	4.71	9.91	19.03	17.91	39	87	200	424	577[4]
Current expenditure per pupil ADA[3]	16.67	27.85	53.32	86.70	88.09	209	375	816	2,272	3,449

(1) Because of a modification of the scope, "current expenditures for elementary and secondary schools" data for 1959-60 and later years are not entirely comparable with data for prior years. (2) Includes supervisors, principals, teachers and other non-supervisory instructional staff. (3) "ADA" means average daily attendance in elementary and secondary day schools. (4) Estimated.

Fall Enrollment and Teachers in Full-time Day Schools

Elementary and Secondary Day Schools, Fall 1985

Source: National Center for Education Statistics, U.S. Dept. of Education; National Education Assn.

	Local school districts (1983) Total	Total enrollment	Pupils per teacher	Classroom teachers	Teacher's average pay (1985-1986)	Instructional aides	Expenditure per pupil
United States	15,747	39,513,379	17.9	2,210,425	$25,257	305,591	$3,449
Alabama	128	730,460	20.2	36,138	22,934	3,510	2,325
Alaska	53	107,345	15.8	6,814	41,480	966	7,843
Arizona	221	548,252	19.6	27,935	24,680	3,950	2,724
Arkansas	367	433,410	17.5	24,767	19,538	2,606	2,353
California	1,030	4,255,554	23.1	184,151	29,750	45,435	3,256
Colorado	181	550,642	18.4	29,894	25,900	3,716	3,697
Connecticut	165	462,026	14.0	32,903	26,610	—	4,738
Delaware	19	92,901	16.2	5,745	24,625	619	4,184
District of Columbia	1	87,092	14.2	6,137	33,990	483	4,571
Florida	67	1,562,872	16.6	93,958	22,296	16,639	3,238
Georgia	187	1,079,594	18.8	57,374	22,080	8,902	2,657
Hawaii	1	164,169	22.6	7,276	5,845	1,006	3,465
Idaho	115	208,669	20.3	10,255	20,969	863	2,401
Illinois	1,009	1,826,478	17.8	102,657	27,190	9,967	3,538
Indiana	305	966,106	18.6	51,976	24,333	7,601	3,051
Iowa	439	485,332	15.3	31,770	21,690	3,129	3,439
Kansas	385	410,229	15.4	26,686	22,768	2,437	3,560
Kentucky	180	643,833	19.2	33,506	20,940	3,683	2,390
Louisiana	66	792,704	18.6	42,729	20,460	6,700	2,905
Maine	282	206,101	14.5	14,226	19,583	2,171	3,024
Maryland	24	671,560	17.5	38,433	27,186	4,846	4,102
Massachusetts	404	844,330	14.9	56,845	25,849	7,159	4,026
Michigan	574	1,689,828	20.6	82,193	30,168	11,488	3,848
Minnesota	437	705,140	17.1	41,314	26,970	5,648	3,674
Mississippi	154	471,195	18.1	26,102	18,443	7,279	2,357
Missouri	545	795,107	16.5	48,170	21,884	3,100	2,958
Montana	561	153,869	15.9	9,705	22,492	1,268	3,847
Nebraska	994	265,819	15.0	17,687	20,939	2,229	3,471
Nevada	17	154,948	20.0	7,751	25,620	—	2,829
New Hampshire	169	160,974	15.9	10,104	20,148	1,433	3,271
New Jersey	604	1,116,194	15.0	74,236	28,216	7,425	4,504
New Mexico	89	277,551	18.8	14,781	22,526	2,714	3,153
New York	720	2,621,378	15.8	165,573	30,200	20,974	5,492
North Carolina	142	1,086,165	18.8	57,638	22,476	16,437	2,625
North Dakota	321	118,570	16.2	7,299	20,816	904	3,210
Ohio	616	1,793,775	18.3	98,264	24,500	7,151	3,257
Oklahoma	615	592,327	16.6	35,752	21,419	4,088	2,850
Oregon	309	447,527	18.2	24,605	25,788	3,805	3,889
Pennsylvania	500	1,683,221	16.6	101,665	26,009	9,329	4,237
Rhode Island	40	133,442	15.1	8,844	29,470	803	4,285
South Carolina	92	606,643	17.5	34,645	21,428	5,439	2,591
South Dakota	195	124,291	14.9	8,340	18,095	1,734	2,892
Tennessee	143	813,753	20.3	40,023	21,800	4,738	2,363
Texas	1,075	3,131,705	17.4	180,118	24,419	26,068	3,043
Utah	40	403,395	23.6	17,126	22,341	2,739	2,220
Vermont	273	90,157	14.1	6,397	20,325	1,278	3,651
Virginia	138	968,104	16.9	57,339	23,382	7,780	3,155
Washington	299	749,706	20.7	36,202	26,015	4,371	3,723
West Virginia	55	357,923	15.7	22,733	20,625	2,780	3,244
Wisconsin	432	768,234	16.5	46,482	26,800	5,166	3,816
Wyoming	49	102,779	14.4	7,162	27,876	1,035	4,799

Programs for the Handicapped

Source: Office of Special Educ. and Rehabilitative Services, U.S. Dept. of Education

Number of children 3 to 21 years old served annually in educational programs for the handicapped and percent of total public school enrollment.

Type of Handicapped	1976-77	1978-79	1980-81	1981-82	1982-83	1983-84	1984-85
			Number Served, in Thousands				
All conditions	**3,692**	**3,889**	**4,142**	**4,198**	**4,255**	**4,324**	**4,355**
Learning disabled	796	1,130	1,462	1,622	1,741	1,803	1,836
Speech impaired	1,302	1,214	1,168	1,135	1,131	1,129	1,128
Mentally retarded	959	901	829	786	757	748	716
Seriously emotionally disturbed	283	300	346	339	352	361	373
Hard of hearing and deaf	87	85	79	75	73	74	71
Orthopedically handicapped	87	70	58	58	57	56	59
Visually handicapped	38	32	31	29	28	30	30
Deaf-blind	NA	2	3	2	2	2	2
			As Percent of Total Enrollment				
All conditions	**8.33**	**9.14**	**10.11**	**10.47**	**10.73**	**10.99**	**11.08**
Learning disabled	1.80	2.66	3.57	4.05	4.39	4.58	4.67
Speech impaired	2.94	2.85	2.85	2.83	2.85	2.87	2.87
Mentally retarded	2.16	2.12	2.02	1.96	1.91	1.90	1.82
Seriously emotionally disturbed	.64	.71	.85	.85	.89	.92	.95
Hard of hearing and deaf	.20	.20	.19	.19	.18	.19	.18
Orthopedically handicapped	.20	.16	.14	.14	.14	.14	.15
Visually handicapped	.09	.08	.08	.07	.07	.08	.08
Deaf-blind	—	.01	.01	.01	.01	.01	.01

Note: Counts are based on reports from the 50 States and District of Columbia only (i.e., figures from U.S. territories are not included). Percentages of total enrollment are based on the total annual enrollment of U.S. public schools, preprimary through 12th grade. Details may not add to totals because of rounding.

Enrollment in Private Elementary and Secondary Schools¹: Fall 1980

Source: National Center for Education Statistics, U.S. Dept. of Education

	Total	Not Church-related	Church-related: Total	Baptist	Catholic	Christian	Episcopal	Jewish	Lutheran	Seventh Day Adventist	Other
United States	**4,961,755**	**795,260**	**4,166,495**	**232,125**	**3,138,209**	**111,810**	**76,388**	**84,542**	**218,278**	**81,507**	**223,636**
Alabama	62,669	24,653	38,016	7,016	14,720	3,206	1,058	62	1,319	988	9,647
Alaska	3,800	568	3,232	830	1,029	731	—	—	64	161	417
Arizona	40,261	10,946	29,315	1,248	18,306	2,885	551	316	2,072	1,267	2,670
Arkansas	18,423	5,195	13,228	1,340	7,223	153	642	—	626	798	2,446
California	513,709	103,134	410,575	28,198	262,690	29,877	6,984	6,250	24,295	18,811	33,470
Colorado	35,250	7,257	27,993	2,244	17,120	1,087	193	550	2,783	1,459	2,557
Connecticut	88,404	21,005	67,339	250	61,760	372	1,873	885	814	381	1,064
Delaware	23,374	4,352	19,022	1,700	14,725	554	230	114	—	39	1,660
District of Columbia	21,203	4,636	16,567	152	12,214	210	2,184	—	—	499	1,308
Florida	204,988	50,084	154,904	31,704	74,268	7,580	9,072	3,791	9,337	3,688	15,464
Georgia	82,505	44,453	38,052	11,615	13,297	4,390	1,206	655	433	2,400	4,056
Hawaii	37,147	13,166	23,981	2,570	15,059	1,283	1,731	—	1,337	939	1,062
Idaho	5,839	377	5,462	65	2,189	524	—	—	620	1,200	864
Illinois	349,463	25,782	323,681	4,683	278,240	2,951	212	2,587	26,720	2,154	6,134
Indiana	100,234	7,433	92,801	8,629	63,237	2,887	455	359	9,226	1,229	6,779
Iowa	55,227	1,342	53,885	1,071	44,790	207	—	18	2,640	293	4,866
Kansas	33,889	3,514	30,375	320	25,610	1,021	183	167	1,759	408	907
Kentucky	69,728	11,033	58,695	3,977	50,226	1,737	82	132	179	735	1,627
Louisiana	158,921	30,176	128,745	4,451	112,099	649	4,642	110	1,994	1,284	3,516
Maine	17,540	8,002	9,538	867	6,733	591	—	33	—	291	1,023
Maryland	106,447	18,889	87,558	4,755	68,168	1,429	1,897	3,082	2,979	2,407	2,841
Massachusetts	138,333	28,405	109,928	316	104,720	386	901	1,582	—	1,088	935
Michigan	211,871	15,978	195,893	13,300	129,992	1,994	491	871	25,089	5,587	18,569
Minnesota	88,996	4,441	84,525	2,811	64,418	1,845	939	249	10,909	662	2,692
Mississippi	50,116	30,336	19,780	3,105	11,342	826	2,008	—	—	474	2,025
Missouri	126,319	8,857	117,462	2,666	95,194	1,104	300	312	11,399	1,335	5,152
Montana	7,668	925	6,743	201	4,684	16	—	—	535	528	779
Nebraska	38,574	1,367	37,207	245	30,169	261	315	25	4,944	955	293
Nevada	6,599	944	5,655	274	4,305	248	—	63	330	215	220
New Hampshire	20,721	5,886	14,835	838	11,239	555	852	—	—	71	1,280
New Jersey	229,878	23,463	206,415	1,701	189,876	1,764	408	6,427	1,341	1,059	3,839
New Mexico	18,027	5,173	12,854	786	9,217	740	20	80	224	523	1,264
New York	579,670	70,694	508,976	4,303	425,981	2,336	5,296	47,815	10,916	3,483	8,846
North Carolina	58,078	24,605	33,743	16,373	9,323	1,835	1,071	101	797	1,840	2,133
North Dakota	10,659	1,571	9,088	—	8,230	—	—	—	538	255	65
Ohio	268,357	14,294	254,063	6,336	227,888	6,318	117	2,064	5,569	1,700	4,071
Oklahoma	16,335	2,218	14,117	237	7,381	1,206	2,494	39	657	1,077	1,026
Oregon	27,828	4,059	23,769	775	14,357	2,014	551	118	744	3,968	1,242
Pennsylvania	402,058	39,978	362,080	6,880	314,367	8,175	2,361	2,684	1,676	1,446	24,491
Rhode Island	29,875	2,643	27,232	70	25,015	17	380	284	110	—	1,356
South Carolina	49,619	24,354	25,265	9,448	7,555	2,947	2,699	153	508	194	1,761
South Dakota	10,898	1,790	9,108	72	6,882	471	59	—	510	146	968
Tennesee	71,617	20,794	50,823	13,636	15,185	2,256	2,132	356	1,543	3,372	12,343
Texas	148,534	17,994	130,540	11,102	79,766	3,058	13,562	1,475	8,437	2,799	10,341
Utah	5,555	1,862	3,693	—	3,055	—	—	—	371	148	119
Vermont	7,555	3,264	4,291	69	4,082	35	46	—	—	59	—
Virginia	75,069	26,807	48,262	10,961	23,060	2,053	5,454	260	1,773	1,177	3,524
Washington	55,950	8,901	47,049	3,047	27,356	2,958	582	228	2,401	4,355	6,122
West Virginia	12,608	840	11,768	1,865	8,466	876	—	—	—	329	232
Wisconsin	162,361	6,060	156,301	2,485	110,014	1,192	155	245	37,551	1,089	3,570
Wyoming	3,036	760	2,276	538	1,387	—	—	—	209	142	—

(1) Includes enrollment in special education, vocational/technical, and alternative schools.

Federal Funds for Education, 1986

Source: U.S. Office of Management and Budget

Federal funds obligated for major programs administered by the Dept. of Education (thousands of dollars, est.).

Total	**19,495,346**
Elementary-secondary education	**4,657,475**
Grants for the disadvantaged	3,699,753
Special programs	715,687
Bilingual education	174,964
Indian education	67,071
School asst.—federally affected areas	**698,954**
Maintenance and operation	665,000
Construction	21,663
Disaster assistance	12,291
Education for the handicapped	**2,816,285**
State grant programs	1,215,550
Early childhood education	32,462
Special centers, projects, and research	96,100
Captioned films and media services	37,728
Personnel training	71,410
Handicapped rehab. service and res.	1,363,035
Vocational education and adult programs	**1,088,320**
Basic programs	922,181
Adult education, grants to States	119,448
Postsecondary student financial assistance	**8,819,650**
Educational opportunity grants	4,258,655
Work study	593,788
Direct student loans	224,486
Guaranteed student loans	3,707,471
Other student assistance programs	35,250
Direct aid to postsecondary institutions	**330,684**
Aid to minority and developing institutions	139,914
Special programs for the disadvantaged	176,370
Cooperative education	14,400
Higher education facilities	**258,640**
College housing loans	159,462
Other higher education programs	**52,010**
International education and foreign languages	32,050
Fund for improvement of postsecondary education	12,710
Public library services	**136,959**
Payments to special institutions	**263,740**
Departmental accounts	**372,629**
Educational research and improvement	59,978
Departmental management account	312,639

Scholastic Aptitude Test (SAT) Scores and Characteristics of College Bound Seniors: 1967 to 1986

Source: College Entrance Examination Board

(For school year ending in year shown)

Type of Test and Characteristic	Unit	1967	1970	1975	1977	1980	1981	1982	1983	1984	1985	1986
Test Scores[1]												
Verbal, total[1]	Point	466	460	434	429	424	424	426	425	426	431	431
Male	Point	463	459	437	431	428	430	431	430	433	437	437
Female	Point	468	461	431	427	420	418	421	420	420	425	426
Math, total[2]	Point	492	488	472	470	466	466	467	468	471	475	475
Male	Point	514	509	495	497	491	492	493	493	495	499	501
Female	Point	467	465	449	445	443	443	443	445	449	452	451
Participants												
Total	1,000	NA	NA	996	979	992	994	989	963	965	977	1,001
Male	Percent	NA	NA	49.9	48.9	48.2	48.0	48.1	48.2	48.2	48.3	48.1
White	Percent	NA	NA	86.0	83.9	82.1	81.9	81.7	81.1	80.3	80.0	NA
Black	Percent	NA	NA	7.9	8.8	9.1	9.0	8.9	8.8	9.1	8.9	NA
Obtaining scores[1] of—600 or above:												
Verbal	Percent	NA	NA	7.9	8.0	7.2	7.0	7.1	6.9	7.0	7.0	8.0
Math	Percent	NA	NA	15.6	16.1	15.1	14.4	15.3	15.9	17.0	17.0	17.0
Below 400:												
Verbal	Percent	NA	NA	37.8	39.1	41.8	41.6	40.2	41.1	40.0	40.0	38.0
Math	Percent	NA	NA	28.5	29.7	30.2	29.5	29.5	30.1	29.0	28.0	28.0

(NA) Not available. (1) Minimum score, 200; maximum score, 800. (2) 1967 and 1970 are estimates based on total number of persons taking SAT.

American College Testing (ACT) Program Scores and Characteristics of College-Bound Students: 1970 to 1986

Source: The American College Testing Program

Data for academic year ending in year shown. Test scores and characteristics of college-bound students based on a 10% sample.

Type of Test and Characteristic	Unit	1970	1975	1978	1980	1981	1982	1983	1984	1985[2]	1986
Test Scores[1]											
Composite	Point	19.9	18.6	18.5	18.5	18.5	18.4	18.3	18.5	18.6	18.8
Male	Point	20.3	19.5	19.3	19.3	19.3	19.2	19.1	19.3	19.4	19.6
Female	Point	19.4	17.8	17.8	17.9	17.8	17.8	17.6	17.9	17.9	18.1
English	Point	18.5	17.7	17.9	17.9	17.8	17.9	17.8	18.1	18.1	18.5
Male	Point	17.6	17.1	17.4	17.3	17.3	17.3	17.3	17.5	17.6	17.9
Female	Point	19.4	18.3	18.3	18.3	18.2	18.4	18.2	18.6	18.6	18.9
Math	Point	20.0	17.6	17.5	17.4	17.3	17.2	16.9	17.3	17.2	17.3
Male	Point	21.1	19.3	19.1	18.9	18.9	18.6	18.4	18.6	18.6	18.8
Female	Point	18.8	16.2	16.2	16.2	16.0	16.0	15.7	16.1	16.0	16.0
Social Studies	Point	19.7	17.4	17.1	17.2	17.2	17.3	17.1	17.3	17.4	17.6
Male	Point	20.3	18.7	18.0	18.2	18.3	18.1	18.0	18.1	18.3	18.6
Female	Point	19.0	16.4	16.4	16.4	16.4	16.6	16.4	16.5	16.6	16.9
Natural Science	Point	20.8	21.1	20.9	21.1	21.0	20.8	20.9	21.0	21.2	21.4
Male	Point	21.6	22.4	22.3	22.4	22.3	22.2	22.4	22.4	22.6	22.7
Female	Point	20.0	20.0	19.8	20.0	20.0	19.7	19.6	19.9	20.0	20.2
Participants											
Total	1,000	788	714	770	822	836	805	835	849	739	730
Male	Percent	52	46	45	45	45	45	46	46	46	46
White	Percent	(NA)	77	76	83	83	83	82	82	82	82
Black	Percent	4	7	7	8	8	8	9	9	8	8
Obtaining composite scores of—											
26 or above	Percent	14	14	13	13	13	13	13	13	14	14
15 or below	Pecent	21	33	34	33	33	34	35	33	32	31

(NA) Not available. (1) Minimum score, 1; maximum score, 36. (2) Begining in 1985, these data are now based on the performance of all ACT-tested students who graduated in the spring of a given school year and who took the ACT Assessment during junior or senior year of high school.

Current Languages Other Than English Spoken at Home: 1980

Source: U.S. Bureau of the Census

Current language spoken	Persons 5 to 17 years old: Total (1,000)	Persons 5 to 17 years old: Difficulty with English[1] (percent)	Persons 18 yrs. old and over: Total (1,000)	Persons 18 yrs. old and over: Difficulty with English[1] (percent)
Total persons	47,494	x	162,753	x
Speaking a language other than English	4,568	14.0	18,492	19.4
Spanish	2,952	15.4	8,164	27.6
Italian	147	5.4	1,471	14.0
French	223	6.8	1,328	7.2
German	192	6.2	1,395	4.7
Polish	41	5.7	780	10.6
Chinese	114	20.9	516	31.6
Greek	66	5.2	336	17.0
Philippine languages	63	8.9	411	9.4
Portuguese	68	10.3	284	31.6
Japanese	34	18.7	303	19.6
Korean	60	17.0	207	32.4
Vietnamese	64	36.0	130	38.7
All other	544	12.3	3,167	11.2

(x) Not applicable. (1) Persons reported as speaking English "not well" or "not at all."

Bachelor's Degrees Conferred, 1984-85

Source: National Center for Education Statistics, U.S. Dept. of Education

Major field of study	Degrees conferred	% change 1974-84	Major field of study	Degrees conferred	% change 1974-84
All Fields	**979,477**	**3**	Letters (English, Philosophy, etc.)	34,091	−39
			Liberal/general studies	19,191	93
Agric. & Natural Resources	18,107	19	Library Science	202	−78
Architecture & Envir. Design	9,325	17	Life sciences	38,445	−20
Area and Ethnic Studies	2,867	−23	Mathematics	15,146	−39
Bus. & Management	233,351	75	Military Sciences	299	−38
Communications	40,358	137	Multi/interdisciplinary studies	15,727	13
Communications technologies	1,725	87	Parks and recreation	4,593	28
Computer & Info. Sciences	38,878	576	Philosophy and religion	6,400	−32
Education	88,161	−50	Physical Sciences	6,039	40
Engineering	77,154	77	Protective services	23,732	12
Engineering technologies	18,951	151	Psychology	39,811	−23
Foreign Languages	9,954	+50	Public Affairs & Services	12,510	53
Health Sciences	64,513	55	Social Sciences	13,838	−14
Home Economics	15,555	6	Theology	91,461	−38
Law	1,157	157	Visual and Performing Arts	37,936	0

Private Schools by Level and Affiliation, 1983

Source: National Center for Education Statistics, U.S. Dept. of Education

Level and affiliation of school	Schools	Enrollment	Staff (in full-time equivalents)[1] Total	Teachers	Pupils per teacher
All private schools	**27,694**	**5,715,000**	**542,342**	**337,185**	**16.9**
Elementary schools	15,631	3,240,000	234,880	157,759	20.5
Catholic	7,897	2,260,000	137,909	94,519	23.9
Other religiously affiliated	5,109	630,000	56,838	37,968	16.6
Not religiously affiliated	2,624	351,000	40,132	25,272	13.9
Secondary schools	2,621	1,047,000	104,309	64,624	16.2
Catholic	1,490	848,000	68,897	45,563	18.2
Other religiously affiliated	669	106,000	17,569	4,391	11.3
Not religiously affiliated	462	43,000	17,843	8,670	10.7
Combined elementary and secondary schools	5,241	1,130,000	127,143	80,729	14.0
Catholic	191	70,000	7,145	4,219	16.6
Other religiously affiliated	3,185	556,000	57,054	36,529	15.2
Not religiously affiliated	1,865	504,000	62,944	39,781	12.6
Other schools[2]	4,201	297,000	76,010	34,072	8.7
Catholic	161	14,000	5,828	2,004	7.0
Other religiously affiliated	1,002	64,000	8,663	5,007	12.0
Not religiously affiliated	3,037	220,000	61,518	27,061	8.1

(1) Includes principals, assistant principals, teachers, guidance counselors, librarians and media specialists, teacher aides, and other professional and nonprofessional staff. (2) Includes special education schools, alternative schools, and vocational schools. Because of rounding, details may not add to totals.

High School Dropouts: 1970 to 1986

Source: U.S. Bureau of the Census

Age and Race	Number of dropouts (1,000) 1970	1975	1980	1985	1986	Percent of population 1970	1975	1980	1985	1986
Total dropouts[1]	**4,670**	**4,974**	**5,212**	**4,456**	**4,318**	**12.2**	**11.5**	**12.0**	**10.6**	**10.5**
16-17 years	617	715	709	505	455	8.0	8.6	8.8	7.0	6.1
18-21 years	2,138	2,557	2,578	2,095	1,961	16.4	16.3	15.8	14.1	13.6
22-24 years	1,770	1,553	1,798	1,724	1,726	18.7	14.5	15.2	14.1	14.3
White[1]	**3,577**	**3,861**	**4,169**	**3,583**	**3,497**	**10.8**	**10.5**	**11.3**	**10.3**	**10.3**
16-17 years	485	594	619	424	394	7.3	8.4	9.2	7.1	6.5
18-21 years	1,618	1,980	2,032	1,678	1,566	14.3	14.7	14.7	13.6	13.1
22-24 years	1,356	1,169	1,416	1,372	1,408	16.3	12.6	14.0	13.3	13.9
Black[1]	**1,047**	**1,024**	**934**	**748**	**707**	**22.2**	**18.5**	**16.0**	**12.6**	**12.0**
16-17 years	125	116	80	70	52	12.8	10.2	6.9	6.5	4.7
18-21 years	500	540	486	376	345	30.5	27.0	23.0	17.5	16.5
22-24 years	397	337	346	279	272	37.8	27.8	24.0	17.8	17.3

(1) Includes ages 14 and 15 and race groups not shown separately.

Esperanto

In 1887, Dr. L. L. Zamenhof, a linguist and physician, published a slim textbook on his "Internacia Lingvo" (International Language) under the pseudonym "Doktoro Esperanto." The term "Esperanto" became attached to the language itself as it gained adherents rapidly until the outbreak of World War I. Hardly recovered from the effects of the war, Esperanto was savaged by Nazism, Stalinism, Fascism, the Japanese militarists of the 1930's, and chauvinistic groups in many other countries. Not until the late 1950's did the number of speakers begin to show the steady increase which continues as Esperanto begins its second century.

Controlled experiments show that because of its logical structure, phonemic spelling, and regular grammar Esperanto can be learned to a given criterion of performance in from one-twentieth to one-fifth the time needed for the learning of a typical national language.

Inteligenta persono lernas la lingvon Esperanto rapide kaj facile. Esperanto estas la moderna, kultura lingvo por la tuta mondo.

Preprimary School Enrollment of Children 3 to 5 Years Old: 1970 to 1986

Source: U.S. Bureau of the Census

Civilian noninstitutional population. Includes public and non-public nursery school and kindergarten programs. Excludes 5 year olds enrolled in elementary school.

	Number of children (1,000)								Enrollment rate		
	1970	1975	1980	1981	1983	1984	1985	1986	1970	1985	1986
Population, 3–5 years old	10,877	10,183	9,284	9,644	10,252	10,612	10,733	10,866	—	—	—
Total Enrolled[1]	**4,075**	**4,954**	**4,878**	**4,936**	**5,385**	**5,480**	**5,865**	**5,971**	**37.5**	**54.6**	**54.9**
Nursery	1,093	1,745	1,982	2,055	2,347	2,335	2,477	2,545	10.0	23.1	23.4
Kindergarten	2,982	3,209	2,896	2,881	3,038	3,145	3,388	3,426	27.4	31.6	31.5
White	3,414	4,105	3,994	4,038	4,430	4,411	4,757	4,851	37.8	54.7	55.2
Black	585	731	725	725	758	845	919	892	34.9	55.8	54.1
Spanish origin[3]	NA	NA	370	399	406	380	496	593	NA	43.3	47.8
3 years old	454	683	857	891	1,005	1,004	1,035	1,041	13.0	28.8	28.9
4 years old	1,003	1,418	1,423	1,442	1,619	1,603	1,765	1,772	27.9	49.1	49.0
5 years old	2,617	2,852	2,598	2,604	2,762	2,872	3,065	3,157	69.2	86.5	86.7
Labor Force Status of Mother											
All races:[2] With mother in labor force[4]	1,345	2,168	2,480	2,515	2,853	2,969	3,306	3,403	38.8	58.1	58.9
3 and 4 years old	526	973	1,252	1,204	1,453	1,490	1,656	1,686	23.5	43.6	44.1
5 years old	818	1,195	1,229	1,311	1,399	1,479	1,649	1,717	66.6	87.2	88.0
Married, spouse present	1,131	1,733	1,976	1,999	2,296	2,366	2,729	2,715	39.5	58.8	59.1
Other marital status	214	435	504	517	556	603	577	688	36.0	55.1	58.1
Employed	1,246	1,948	2,256	2,264	2,578	2,702	2,999	3,159	39.3	59.1	59.8
Full-time	770	1,236	1,445	1,444	1,655	1,740	1,969	2,066	38.6	57.4	59.9
Mother not in labor force	2,694	2,704	2,266	2,254	2,378	2,311	2,372	2,361	37.0	50.4	50.0

(NA) Not available. (1) Includes children with mothers whose labor force status is unknown and children with no mother present in household, not shown separately. (2) Includes other races not shown separately. (3) Person of Spanish origin may be of any race. (4) Includes children with mothers who are unemployed, not shown separately.

Public Libraries

Source: World Almanac questionnaire (1985)

First figure in parentheses denotes number of branches-2d figure indicates number of bookmobiles. (*) indicates county library system; (†) indicates state library system; (C) Canadian dollars; (A) library has not provided up-to-date information.

City	No. bound volumes	Circulation	Cost of operation
Akron, Oh.* (18-2)	1,200,677	1,953,376	$ 4,991,407
Albuquerque, N.M. (8-2)(A)	NA	1,630,000	2,568,716
Atlanta, Ga.* (25-0)	1,600,000	2,183,274	9,452,587
Austin, Tex. (16-0)	887,002	2,124,421	6,499,624
Baton Rouge, La.* (10-0)	493,506	1,640,686	2,631,607
Boston, Mass. (25-2)(A)	4,916,277	1,454,414	11,500,000
Buffalo, N.Y.* (52-3)	3,425,918	6,228,129	12,343,977
Cincinnati, Oh.* (40-2)	3,413,334	6,592,469	16,020,795
Cleveland, Oh. (31-1)	2,483,283	4,102,968	17,800,000
Columbus, Oh.* (21-1)	1,353,261	4,320,000	11,500,000
Dallas, Tex. (18-0)	1,777,073	3,874,425	14,847,539
Dayton, Oh.* (19-1)	1,344,584	5,012,236	9,040,820
Denver, Col. (21-1)	1,177,785	2,570,396	11,398,400
Des Moines, Ia. (5-2)	548,244	1,218,816	2,437,592
Detroit, Mich. (25-4)	2,446,111	1,441,476	14,690,093
El Paso, Tex. (9-2)	1,060,000	1,200,000	3,500,000
Ft. Worth, Tex. (8-0)(A)	798,608	1,650,930	3,784,161
Honolulu, Ha. (47-7)	442,482	517,066	12,400,000
Indianapolis, Ind.* (22-2)	1,476,674	3,988,952	11,265,372
Jacksonville, Fla.* (11-1)(A)	1,013,497	2,026,528	3,808,000
Kansas City, Mo. (14-0)	1,346,364	875,040	5,091,058
Long Beach, Cal. (12-0)(A)	709,815	1,986,085	7,501,378
Los Angeles, Cal. (62-5)	5,107,313	10,538,792	22,928,548
Louisville, Ky.* (A-2)	1,410,381	3,031,941	6,400,000
Memphis, Tenn.* (22-2)	1,535,556	2,500,000	8,726,456
Miami, Fla.* (25-6)(A)	2,000,000	3,700,000	
Minneapolis, Minn. (14-0)	1,691,597	2,595,421	11,700,000
Mobile, Ala. (5-1)	371,657	766,420	2,433,475
Nashville, Tenn.* (15-2)	581,276	1,699,291	5,000,000
New Haven, Conn.(8-0)(A)	550,000	450,000	1,600,000
New Orleans, La. (11-0)(A)	802,934	1,176,304	3,735,693
New York (resrch)	7,271,592	780,171	3,737,693
N.Y.C. brches (82-2)(A)	3,450,969	8,107,362	
Brooklyn* (58-0)(A)	3,885,530	6,970,799	18,759,885
Queens* (59-0)(A)	4,260,930	6,877,351	25,434,000
Norfolk, Va. (11-1)	748,684	964,340	3,310,823
Okla. City, Okla.* (13-5)	600,000	2,350,000	7,376,199
Oakland, Calif. (17-3)	778,753	1,633,352	5,868,967
Omaha, Neb. (9-0)	561,028	1,690,478	3,652,008
Philadelphia, Pa. (51-0)	3,038,638	5,205,332	22,379,832
Phoenix, Ariz. (9-1)	1,332,400	4,137,000	8,794,000
Pittsburgh, Pa. (21-3)(A)	1,907,373	2,837,534	8,539,756
Portland, Ore.* (14-2)	1,178,703	3,237,547	5,526,054
Richmond, Va. (7-2)	696,966	961,000	2,771,504
Rochester, N.Y. (11-2)	959,207	1,457,210	
St. Louis, Mo. (13-2)	1,457,314	1,101,640	6,416,180
St. Paul, Minn. (11-1)	656,679	1,942,816	4,640,703
San Antonio, Tex.* (13-3)(A)	1,200,000	2,217,603	6,672,424
San Diego, Cal. (30-1)(A)	1,733,387	4,191,538	7,391,165
San Francisco, Cal. (26-1)(A)	1,749,129	2,470,091	9,146,080
San Jose, Cal. (17-1)(A)	1,250,000	2,800,000	5,800,000
Syracuse, N.Y.* (8-1)	509,386	1,189,319	5,655,999
Tucson, Ariz.* (15-2)	760,000	3,900,000	7,876,000
Tulsa, Okla. (20-1)	600,000	2,000,000	7,000,000
Wash. D.C. (26-1)	1,354,564	1,724,846	13,003,000
Wichita, Kan. (10-0)	854,046	1,224,426	2,853,098
Yonkers, N.Y. (3-1)	230,347	849,529	3,486,634

The Principal Languages of the World

Source: Sidney S. Culbert, Guthrie Hall NI-25 — University of Washington

Total number of speakers (native plus non-native) of languages spoken by at least one million persons (midyear 1987)

Language	Millions
Achinese (N Sumatra, Indonesia)	2
Afrikaans (So. Africa)	9
Akan (or Twi-Fante) Ghana	6
Albanian (Albania; Yugoslavia)	4
Amharic (Ethiopia)	13
Arabic	182
Armenian (USSR)	5
Assamese[1] (Assam, India; Bangladesh)	18
Aymara (Bolivia; Peru)	2
Azerbaijani (Iran; Azer. SSR, USSR)	11
Balinese (Indonesia)	3
Baluchi (Baluchistan, Pakistan)	3
Bashkir (Bashkir ASSR, USSR)	1
Batak (Indonesia) (see also Karo)	3
Baule (Ivory Coast)	1
Beja (Kassala, Sudan; Ethiopia)	1
Bemba (Zambia)	2
Bengali[1]	175
Berber[2]	
Beti (Cameroon; Gabon; Eq. Guinea)	2
Bhili (India)	3
Bikol (SE Luzon, Philippines)	3
Bulgarian (Bulgaria)	9
Burmese (Burma)	28
Buyi (S Guizhou, S China)	2

(continued)

Language	Millions
Byelorussian (Byelorussian SSR, USSR)	9
Cantonese (or Yue) (China; Hong Kong)	60
Catalan (NE Spain; S France; Andorra)	8
Cebuano (Bohol Sea area, Philippines)	11
Chagga (Kilimanjaro area, Tanzania)	1
Chiga (Ankole, Uganda)	1
Chinese[3]	
Chuvash (Chuvash ASSR, USSR)	2
Czech (Czechoslovakia)	12
Danish (Denmark)	5
Dogri (Jammu-Kashmir, C and E India)	1
Dong (Guizhou, Hunan, Guangxi, China)	2
Dutch-Flemish (Netherlands; Belgium)	21
Dyerma (SW Niger)	1
Edo (Bendel, S Nigeria)	1
English	426
Esperanto	1
Estonian (Estonian SSR, USSR)	1
Ewe (SE Ghana; S Togo)	3
Fang-Bulu (Dialects of Beti, q. v.)	
Farsi (Iranian form of Persian, q. v.)	
Finnish (Finland; Sweden)	5
Flemish (see Dutch-Flemish)	
Fon (SC Benin; S Togo)	1
French	115
Fula (or Peulh) (Cameroon; Nigeria)	11
Fulakunda (Senegambia; Guinea Bissau)	1
Futa Jalon (NW Guinea; Sierra Leone)	1
Galician (Galicia, NW Spain)	3
Galla (see Oromo)	
Ganda (or Luganda) (S Uganda)	3
Georgian (Georgian SSR, USSR)	4
German	118
Gilaki (Gilan, NW Iran)	2
Gondi (Central India)	2
Greek (Greece)	11
Guarani (Paraguay)	4
Gujarati[1] (W and C India; S Pakistan)	36
Gusii (Kisii District, Nyanza, Kenya)	1
Hadiyya (Arusi, Ethiopia)	1
Hakka (or Kejia) (SE China)	27
Hani (S China)	1
Hausa (N Nigeria; Niger; Cameroon)	30
Hebrew (Israel)	4
Hindi[1,4]	313
Ho (West Bengal, India)	1
Hungarian (or Magyar) (Hungary)	14
Iban (Kalimantan, Indonesia; Malaysia)	1
Ibibio (see Efik)	
Ijaw (Niger River delta, Nigeria)	2
Ilocano (NW Luzon, Philippines)	6
Indonesian (see Malay-Indonesian)	
Italian (Italy)	63
Japanese	123
Javanese (Java, Indonesia)	53
Kabyle (W Kabylia, N Algeria)	2
Kalenjin (Riff Valley, Kenya)	1
Kamba (E Kenya)	2
Kannada[1] (S India)	39
Kanuri (Nigeria; Niger; Chad; Cam.)	4
Karen, Burmese (SE Burma)	1
Karo-Dairi (N Sumatra, Indonesia)	1
Kashmiri[1] (N India; NE Pakistan)	3
Kazakh (Kazakh SSR, USSR)	8
Kenuzi-Dongola (S Egypt; Sudan)	1
Khalka (see Mongolian)	
Khmer (Kampuchea; Vietnam; Thailand)	7
Khmer, Northern (Thailand)	1
Kikuyu (or Gekoyo) (W and C Kenya)	4
Kirghiz (Kirghiz SSR, USSR)	2
Kituba (Bas-Zaire, Bandundu, Zaire)	3
Kongo (W Zaire; S Congo; NW Angola)	3
Konkani (Maharashtra and SW India)	4
Korean (So., No. Korea; China; Japan)	67
Kurdish (south-west of Caspian Sea)	9
Kurukh (or Oraon) (C and E India)	2
Lao[5] (Laos)	3
Lampung-Komering (Sumatra, Indonesia)	1
Latvian (Latvian SSR, USSR)	3
Lingala (including Bangala) (Zaire)	5
Lithuanian (Lithuanian SSR, USSR)	3
Luba-Lulua (or Chiluba) (Kasai, Zaire)	5
Luba-Shaba (Shaba, Zaire)	1
Lubu (E Sumatra, Indonesia)	1
Luhya (W Kenya)	2
Luo (Kenya; Nyanza, Tanzania)	2
Luri (SW Iran; Iraq)	3
Macedonian (Macedonia, Yugoslavia)	2
Madurese (Madura, Indonesia)	9
Magindanaon (Moro Gulf, S Philippines)	1
Makassar (S Sulawesi, Indonesia)	1
Makua (S Tanzania; N Mozambique)	3
Malagasy (Madagascar)	11
Malay-Indonesian	132
Malay, Pattani (SE coast of Thailand)	1
Malayalam[1] (Kerala, India)	32
Malinke-Bambara-Dyula (W Africa)	8
Mandarin	806
Marathi[1] (Maharashtra, India)	61
Mazandarani (S Mazandaran, N Iran)	2
Mbundu (or Umbundu) (Benguela, Angola)	3
Mbundu (or Kimbundu) (Luanda, Angola)	2
Meithei (NE India; Bangladesh)	1
Mende (Central, S and E Sierra Leone)	2
Miao (or Hmong) (S China; SE Asia)	5
Min (SE China; Taiwan; Malaysia)	45
Minankabau (W Sumatra, Indonesia)	6
Moldavian (included with Romanian)	
Mongolian (Mongolia; NE China)	4
Mordvin (in and near Mord. ASSR, USSR)	1
Morê (central part of Burkina Faso)	4
Nepali (Nepal; NE India; Bhutan)	12
Ngulu (Zambezia, Mozambique; Malawi)	1
Nkole (Western Prov., Uganda)	1
Norwegian (Norway)	5
Nyamwezi-Sukuma (NW Tanzania)	2
Nyanja (Malawi; Zambia; N Zimbabwe)	4
Oriya[1] (Central and E India)	29
Oromo (W Ethiopia; N Kenya)	9
Pampangan (NW of Manila, Philippines)	1
Panay-Hiligaynon (Philippines)	5
Pangasinan (Lingayen G., Philippines)	1
Pashtu (Pakistan; Afghanistan; Iran)	20
Pedi (see Sotho, Northern)	
Persian (Iran; Afghanistan)	31
Polish (Poland)	41
Portuguese	166
Provençal (S France)	4
Punjabi[1] (Punjab, Pakistan; NW India)	74
Pushto (see Pashtu) (many spellings)	
Quechua (Peru, Bolivia)	7
Riff (N Morocco; Algerian coast)	1
Romanian (Romania; Moldavia, USSR)	24
Ruanda (Rwanda; S Uganda; E Zaire)	7
Rundi (Burundi)	5
Russian	287
Samar-Leyte (Central E Philippines)	3
Sango (Central African Republic)	2
Santali (E India; Nepal)	5
Sasak (Lombok, Alas Strait, Indonesia)	1
Serbo-Croation (Yugoslavia)	20
Shan (Shan, E Burma)	2
Shilha (W Algeria; S Morocco)	3
Sindhi[1] (SE Pakistan; W India)	13
Shona (Zimbabwe)	5
Sidamo (Sidamo, S Ethiopia)	1
Sinhalese (Sri Lanka)	12
Slovak (Czechoslovakia)	5
Slovene (Slovenia, NW Yugoslavia)	2
Soga (Busoga, Uganda)	1
Somali (Somalia; Eth.; Ken.; Djibouti)	6
Sotho, Northern (So. Africa)	3
Sotho, Southern (So. Africa; Lesotho)	4
Spanish	308
Sundanese (Sunda Strait, Indonesia)	19
Swahili (Kenya; Tanz.; Zaire; Uganda)	40
Swati (Swaziland; So. Africa)	1
Swedish (Sweden; Finland)	9
Sylhetti (Bangladesh)	1
Tagalog (Philippines)	32
Tajiki (Tajik Uzbek Kirghiz SSR, USSR)	4
Tamazight (N Morocco; W Algeria)	3
Tamil[1] (Tamil Nadu, India; Sri Lanka)	62
Tatar (Tatar SSR, USSR)	7
Telugu[1] (Andhra Pradesh, SE India)	64
Temne (central Sierra Leone)	1
Thai[5] (Thailand)	45
Thonga (Mozambique; So. Africa)	3
Tibetan (SW China; N India; Nepal)	5
Tigrinya (S Eritrea, Tigre, Ethiopia)	4
Tiv (SE Nigeria; Cameroon)	2
Tong (see Dong)	
Tonga (SW Zambia; NW Zimbabwe)	1
Tujia (SW Hubei; NW Hunan, China)	1
Tswana (Botswana; So. Africa)	3
Tulu (S India)	1
Tumbuka (N Malawi, NE Zambia)	1
Turkish (Turkey)	52
Turkmen (S USSR; NE Iran; Afghanistan)	3
Twi-Fante (see Akan)	
Uighur (Xinjiang, NW China; SC USSR)	7
Ukranian (Ukraine, USSR; Poland)	44
Urdu[1,4] (Pakistan; India)	85
Uzbek (Uzbek SSR, USSR)	11
Vietnamese (Vietnam)	53
Wolaytta (SW Ethiopia)	1
Wolof (Senegal)	5
Wu (Shanghai and nearby prov., China)	59
Xhosa (SW Cape Province, So. Africa)	6
Yao (China; Vietnam; Laos; Thailand)	1
Yi (S and SW China)	6
Yiddish[6]	
Yoruba (SW Nigeria; Zou, Benin)	17
Zande (NE Zaire; SW Sudan)	1
Zhuang (S China)	14
Zulu (N Natal, So. Africa; Lesotho)	7

(1) One of the fifteen languages of the Constitution of India. (2) See Kabyle, Riff, Shilha, and Tamazight. (3) See Mandarin, Cantonese, Wu, Min, and Hakka. The "common speech" (Putonghua) or the "national language" (Guoyu) is a standardized form of Mandarin as spoken in the area of Beijing. (4) Hindi and Urdu are essentially the same language, Hindustani. As the official language of Pakistan it is written in a modified Arabic script and called Urdu. As the official language of India it is written in the Devanagari script and called Hindi. (5) Thai includes Central, Southwestern, Northern and Northeastern Thai. The distinction between Northeastern Thai and Lao is political rather than linguistic. (6) Yiddish is usually considered a variant of German, though it has its own standard grammar, dictionaries, a highly developed literature, and is written in Hebrew characters.

American Colleges and Universities

General Information for the 1986-87 Academic Year

Source: Peterson's Guides

These listings include all accredited undergraduate degree-granting institutions in the United States and U.S. territories that have a total institutional enrollment of 600 or more. Four-year colleges (those that award a bachelor's as their highest undergraduate degree) are listed first, followed by two-year colleges (those that award an associate as their highest undergraduate degree).

All institutions are coeducational except those where the zip code is followed by: (1)–men only, (2)–primarily men, (3)–women only, (4)–primarily women.

Year is that of founding.

Governing official is the chief executive officer.

Institutional control: 1–independent (nonprofit), 2–independent-religious, 3–proprietary (profit making), 4–federal, 5–state, 7–commonwealth (Puerto Rico), 8–territory (U.S. territories), 9–county, 10–district, 11–city, 12–state and local, 13–state related.

Highest degree offered: B–bachelor's, M–master's, D–doctorate.

Enrollment is the total number of matriculated undergraduate and (if applicable) graduate students.

Faculty is the total number of faculty members teaching undergraduate and graduate courses.

Any data not reported are indicated as NR.

Four-Year Colleges

Name, address	Year	Governing official, control, and highest degree offered		Enroll-ment	Faculty
Abilene Christian U, Abilene, TX 79699	1906	Dr William J Teague	2-M	4,302	262
Acad of Art Coll, San Francisco, CA 94108	1929	Dr Donald Haight	3-M	1,840	120
Adams State Coll, Alamosa, CO 81102	1921	Dr William M Fulkerson Jr	5-M	2,193	108
Adelphi U, Garden City, NY 11530	1896	Dr Peter Diamandopoulos	1-D	10,494	1,005
Adrian Coll, Adrian, MI 49221	1859	Dr Donald S Stanton	2-B	1,186	99
Alabama Agricultural and Mechanical U, Normal, AL 35762	1875	Dr Douglas Covington	5-M	3,928	500
Alabama State U, Montgomery, AL 36195	1874	Dr Leon Howard	5-M	4,000	257
Albany Coll of Pharmacy of Union U, Albany, NY 12208	1881	Dr Kenneth W Miller	1-B	630	42
Albany State Coll, Albany, GA 31705	1903	Dr Billy C Black	5-M	1,911	136
Albion Coll, Albion, MI 49224	1835	Dr Melvin L Vulgamore	2-B	1,618	122
Albright Coll, Reading, PA 19603	1856	Dr David G Ruffer	2-B	1,326	133
Alcorn State U, Lorman, MS 39096	1871	Dr Walter Washington	5-M	2,329	162
Alderson-Broaddus Coll, Philippi, WV 26416	1871	Dr W Christian Sizemore	2-B	759	83
Alfred U, Alfred, NY 14802	1836	Dr Edward G Coll, Jr	1-D	2,491	206
Allegheny Coll, Meadville, PA 16335	1815	Dr Daniel F Sullivan	2-M	1,852	183
Allentown Coll of St Francis de Sales, Center Valley, PA 18034	1962	Very Rev Daniel G Gambet	2-M	1,053	75
Alma Coll, Alma, MI 48801	1886	Dr Gordon E Areen	2-B	1,028	86
Alvernia Coll, Reading, PA 19607	1958	Sr M Dolorey	2-B	879	79
Alverno Coll, Milwaukee, WI 53215 (3)	1887	Joel Read	1-B	1,832	143
Amber U, Garland, TX 75041	1971	Dr Douglas W Warner	1-M	926	55
American Coll of Puerto Rico, Bayamón, PR 00621	1963	Juan B Nazario Negron	1-B	3,773	186
American International Coll, Springfield, MA 01109	1885	Dr Harry J Courniotes	1-D	1,800	123
American U, Washington, DC 20016	1893	Dr Richard Berendzen	2-D	8,573	1,056
Amherst Coll, Amherst, MA 01002	1821	Peter R Pouncey	1-B	1,570	174
Anderson Coll, Anderson, IN 46012	1917	Dr Robert A Nicholson	2-M	1,921	183
Andrews U, Berrien Springs, MI 49104	1874	Dr W Richard Lesher	2-D	3,053	249
Angelo State U, San Angelo, TX 76909	1928	Dr Lloyd Drexell Vincent	5-M	5,806	211
Anna Maria Coll for Men and Women, Paxton, MA 01612	1946	Sr Bernadette Madore	2-M	1,233	138
Antillian Coll, Mayagüez, PR 00708	1957	Dr James Unger	2-B	728	61
Appalachian State U, Boone, NC 28608	1899	Dr John E Thomas	5-M	9,907	600
Aquinas Coll, Grand Rapids, MI 49506	1886	Dr Peter D O'Connor	2-M	2,648	157
Arizona State U, Tempe, AZ 85287	1885	Dr J Russell Nelson	5-D	41,540	2,248
Arkansas Coll, Batesville, AR 72501	1872	Dr Dan C West	2-B	729	59
Arkansas State U, State University, AR 72467	1909	Dr Eugene W Smith	5-M	8,526	371
Arkansas Tech U, Russellville, AR 72801	1909	Dr Kenneth G Kersh	5-M	3,406	195
Armstrong State Coll, Savannah, GA 31419	1935	Dr Robert A Burnett	5-M	2,941	160
Art Ctr Coll of Design, Pasadena, CA 91103	1930	Mr David R Brown	1-M	1,192	180
Asbury Coll, Wilmore, KY 40390	1890	Dr Dennis F Kinlaw	2-B	949	88
Ashland Coll, Ashland, OH 44805	1878	Dr Joseph Shultz	2-M	3,813	139
Assumption Coll, Worcester, MA 01609	1904	Joseph H Hagan	2-M	2,000	148
Athens State Coll, Athens, AL 35611	1822	Dr James R Chasteen	5-B	1,684	94
Atlantic Christian Coll, Wilson, NC 27893	1902	Dr James B Hemby	2-B	1,287	100
Auburn U, Auburn University, AL 36849	1856	Dr James E Martin	5-D	19,363	1,158
Auburn U at Montgomery, Montgomery, AL 36193	1967	Dr James O Williams	5-M	5,366	350
Augsburg Coll, Minneapolis, MN 55454	1869	Dr Charles S Anderson	2-M	1,827	192
Augusta Coll, Augusta, GA 30910	1925	Dr Richard S Wallace	5-M	4,113	164
Augustana Coll, Rock Island, IL 61201	1860	Dr Thomas Tredway	2-B	2,081	164
Augustana Coll, Sioux Falls, SD 57197	1860	Dr William C Nelsen	2-M	1,805	188
Aurora U, Aurora, IL 60506	1893	Dr Alan J Stone	1-M	1,790	193
Austin Coll, Sherman, TX 75090	1849	Dr Harry E Smith	2-M	1,161	87
Austin Peay State U, Clarksville, TN 37044	1927	Dr Robert O Riggs	5-M	4,943	291
Averett Coll, Danville, VA 24541	1859	Dr Frank R Campbell	2-M	972	59
Avila Coll, Kansas City, MO 64145	1916	Dr Larry Kramer	2-M	1,438	141
Azusa Pacific U, Azusa, CA 91702	1899	Dr Paul E Sago	2-M	2,587	164
Babson Coll, Babson Park, MA 02157	1919	Dr William R Dill	1-M	3,163	150
Baker Coll, Flint, MI 48507	1911	Mr Edward J Kurtz	1-B	2,548	76
Baker U, Baldwin City, KS 66006	1858	Dr Daniel M Lambert	2-M	853	56
Baldwin-Wallace Coll, Berea, OH 44017	1845	Dr Neal Malicky	2-M	4,070	208
Ball State U, Muncie, IN 47306	1918	Dr John E Worthen	5-D	17,500	1,359
Baltimore Hebrew Coll, Baltimore, MD 21215	1919	Dr Leivy Smolar	1-D	641	25
Baptist Bible Coll, Springfield, MO 65803	1950	Mr A V Henderson	2-M	839	54
Baptist Bible Coll of Pennsylvania, Clarks Summit, PA 18411	1932	Milo Thompson Jr	2-M	636	54
Baptist Coll at Charleston, Charleston, SC 29411	1964	Dr Jairy C Hunter Jr	2-M	1,646	101

Name, address	Year	Governing official, control, and highest degree offered		Enroll-ment	Faculty
Barat Coll, Lake Forest, IL 60045	1858	Dr Richard P Soter	2-B	623	80
Bard Coll, Annandale-on-Hudson, NY 12504	1860	Mr Leon Botstein	1-M	882	90
Barnard Coll, New York, NY 10027 (3)	1889	Ms Ellen Futter	1-B	2,200	266
Barry U, Miami Shores, FL 33161	1940	Sr Jeanne O'Laughlin	2-D	4,600	205
Baruch Coll of City U of NY, New York, NY 10010	1968	Dr Joel Segall	12-M	16,124	875
Bates Coll, Lewiston, ME 04240	1855	Dr Thomas H Reynolds	1-B	1,450	140
Bayamón Central U, Bayamón, PR 00619	1970	Rev Vincent A M Van Rooij OP	2-M	2,969	121
Baylor U, Waco, TX 76798	1845	Dr Herbert H Reynolds	2-D	11,556	668
Beaver Coll, Glenside, PA 19038	1853	Dr Bette E Landman	2-M	2,113	158
Belhaven Coll, Jackson, MS 39202	1883	Dr Newton Wilson	2-B	875	82
Bellarmine Coll, Louisville, KY 40205	1950	Dr Eugene V Petrik	2-M	2,644	158
Bellevue Coll, Bellevue, NE 68005	1965	Dr John B Muller	1-B	2,196	82
Belmont Abbey Coll, Belmont, NC 28012	1876	Dr John R Dempsey	2-B	936	71
Belmont Coll, Nashville, TN 37203	1951	Dr William E Troutt	2-M	2,364	202
Beloit Coll, Beloit, WI 53511	1846	Dr Roger H Hull	1-M	1,040	105
Bemidji State U, Bemidji, MN 56601	1919	Dr Lowell R Gillett	5-M	4,294	218
Benedict Coll, Columbia, SC 29204	1870	Dr Marshall C Grigsby	2-B	1,469	115
Benedictine Coll, Atchison, KS 66002	1859	Rev Gerard Senecal	2-B	865	92
Bentley Coll, Waltham, MA 02254	1917	Dr Gregory H Adamian	1-M	7,335	349
Berea Coll, Berea, KY 40404	1855	Dr John B Stephenson	1-B	1,587	127
Berklee Coll of Music, Boston, MA 02215	1945	Mr Lee Eliot Berk	1-B	2,696	269
Berry Coll, Mount Berry, GA 30149	1902	Dr Gloria M Shatto	1-M	1,528	112
Bethany Coll, Lindsborg, KS 67456	1881	Dr Peter J Ristuben	2-B	724	82
Bethany Coll, Bethany, WV 26032	1840	Dr Todd H Bullard	2-B	786	78
Bethel Coll, North Newton, KS 67117	1887	Dr Harold J Schultz	2-B	652	73
Bethel Coll, St Paul, MN 55112	1871	Dr George K Brushaber	2-B	1,722	147
Beth Medrash Govoha, Lakewood, NJ 08701 (1)	1943	NR	2-M	931	NR
Bethune-Cookman Coll, Daytona Beach, FL 32015	1904	Dr Oswald P Bronson Sr	2-B	1,815	192
Biola U, La Mirada, CA 90639	1908	Dr Clyde Cook	2-D	2,758	253
Birmingham-Southern Coll, Birmingham, AL 35254	1856	Dr Neal R Berte	2-M	1,725	94
Black Hills State Coll, Spearfish, SD 57783	1883	Dr Clifford Trump	5-M	2,139	104
Bloomfield Coll, Bloomfield, NJ 07003	1868	Dr John F Noonan	2-B	1,407	143
Bloomsburg U of Pennsylvania, Bloomsburg, PA 17815	1839	Dr Harry Ausprich	5-M	6,757	345
Bluefield State Coll, Bluefield, WV 24701	1895	Dr Jerold O Dugger	5-B	2,592	140
Bob Jones U, Greenville, SC 29614	1927	Dr Bob Jones III	2-D	4,039	311
Boise State U, Boise, ID 83725	1932	Dr John H Keiser	5-M	11,323	449
Boricua Coll, New York, NY 10032	1974	Victor G Alicea	1-B	1,140	88
Boston Architectural Ctr, Boston, MA 02115	1889	Bernard P Spring	1-B	628	133
Boston Coll, Chestnut Hill, MA 02167	1863	Rev J Donald Monan, SJ	2-D	13,003	901
Boston U, Boston, MA 02215	1839	Dr John R Silber	1-D	27,147	2,491
Bowdoin Coll, Brunswick, ME 04011	1794	Dr A LeRoy Greason	1-B	1,350	120
Bowie State Coll, Bowie, MD 20715	1865	Dr James E Lyons Sr	5-M	2,902	136
Bowling Green State U, Bowling Green, OH 43403	1910	Dr Paul J Olscamp	5-D	17,240	917
Bradley U, Peoria, IL 61625	1897	Dr Martin G Abegg	1-M	4,860	365
Brandeis U, Waltham, MA 02254	1948	Dr Evelyn E Handler	1-D	3,519	480
Brenau Professional Coll, Gainesville, GA 30501	1878	Dr John S Burd	1-M	1,222	150
Brescia Coll, Owensboro, KY 42301	1950	Sr Ruth Gehres	2-B	750	78
Brewton-Parker Coll, Mt Vernon, GA 30445	1904	Dr Y Lynn Holmes	2-B	1,242	35
Briar Cliff Coll, Sioux City, IA 51104	1930	Sister Margaret Wick	2-B	1,193	85
Bridgeport Engineering Inst, Bridgeport, CT 06606	1924	Dr William M Krummel	1-B	785	108
Bridgewater Coll, Bridgewater, VA 22812	1880	Dr Wayne F Geisert	2-B	819	68
Bridgewater State Coll, Bridgewater, MA 02324	1840	Dr Adrian Rondileau	5-M	5,717	356
Brigham Young U, Provo, UT 84602	1875	Dr Jeffrey R Holland	2-D	28,264	1,632
Brigham Young U–Hawaii Cmps, Laie, Oahu, HI 96762	1955	Dr J Elliot Cameron	2-B	1,926	116
Bristol Coll, Bristol, TN 37620	1895	Mr Ronald Cosby	3-M	[illegible]	[illegible]
Brooklyn Coll of City U of NY, Brooklyn, NY 11210	1930	Dr Robert Hess	12-M	14,426	1,136
Brooks Inst of Photography, Santa Barbara, CA 93108	1945	Mr Ernest H Brooks II	3-M	611	36
Brown U, Providence, RI 02912	1764	Howard R Swearer	1-D	7,101	527
Bryant Coll, Smithfield, RI 02917	1863	Dr William T O'Hara	1-M	5,783	179
Bryn Mawr Coll, Bryn Mawr, PA 19010 (3)	1885	Mary Patterson McPherson	1-D	1,794	197
Bucknell U, Lewisburg, PA 17837	1846	Dr Gary A Sojka	1-M	3,453	243
Buena Vista Coll, Storm Lake, IA 50588	1891	Dr Keith G Briscoe	2-B	980	70
Butler U, Indianapolis, IN 46208	1855	Mr John G Johnson	1-M	3,645	347
Cabrini Coll, Radnor, PA 19087	1957	Sr Eileen Currie MSC	2-M	1,057	75
Caguas City Coll, Caguas, PR 00626	1966	Alex A DeJorge	3-B	700	25
Caldwell Coll, Caldwell, NJ 07006	1939	Sr Vivien Jennings	2-B	700	65
California Baptist Coll, Riverside, CA 92504	1950	Dr Russell R Tuck	2-M	655	65
California Coll of Arts and Crafts, Oakland, CA 94618	1907	Mr Neil J Hoffman	1-M	1,186	130
California Inst of Tech, Pasadena, CA 91125	1891	Dr Marvin L Goldberger	1-D	1,814	283
California Inst of the Arts, Valencia, CA 91355	1961	Mr Robert J Fitzpatrick	1-M	820	178
California Lutheran U, Thousand Oaks, CA 91360	1959	Dr Jerry H Miller	2-M	2,266	176
California Polytechnic State U, San Luis Obispo, San Luis Obispo, CA 93407	1901	Dr Warren J Baker	5-M	15,849	1,016
California State Coll, Bakersfield, Bakersfield, CA 93309	1970	Dr Tomas A Arciniega	5-M	4,333	260
California State Polytechnic U, Pomona, Pomona, CA 91768	1938	Dr Hugh O La Bounty	5-M	17,679	1,009
California State U, Chico, Chico, CA 95929	1887	Dr Robin Wilson	5-M	14,900	981
California State U, Dominguez Hills, Carson, CA 90747	1960	Dr John A Brownell	5-M	7,332	452
California State U, Fresno, Fresno, CA 93740	1911	Dr Harold H Haak	5-M	17,762	1,018
California State U, Fullerton, Fullerton, CA 92634	1957	Dr Jewel Plummer Cobb	5-M	24,277	1,413
California State U, Hayward, Hayward, CA 94542	1957	Dr Ellis E McCune	5-M	12,373	615
California State U, Long Beach, Long Beach, CA 90840	1949	Dr Stephen Horn	5-M	33,588	1,739
California State U, Los Angeles, Los Angeles, CA 90032	1947	Dr James M Rosser	5-D	20,968	1,322
California State U, Northridge, Northridge, CA 91330	1958	Dr James Cleary	5-M	29,785	1,579
California State U, Sacramento, Sacramento, CA 95819	1947	Donald R Gerth	5-M	23,673	1,370
California State U, San Bernardino, San Bernardino, CA 92407	1962	Dr Anthony H Evans	5-M	7,444	272
California State U, Stanislaus, Turlock, CA 95380	1957	Dr John W Moore	5-M	4,675	280
California U of Pennsylvania, California, PA 15419	1852	Dr John Pierce Watkins	5-M	5,179	310
Calumet Coll of St Joseph, Whiting, IN 46394	1951	Rev Ronald Schiml	2-B	935	82
Calvin Coll, Grand Rapids, MI 49506	1876	Dr Anthony J Diekema	2-M	4,197	283
Cameron U, Lawton, OK 73505	1908	Dr Don Davis	5-B	5,429	325
Campbellsville Coll, Campbellsville, KY 42718	1906	Dr W Randolph Davenport	2-B	613	56
Campbell U, Buies Creek, NC 27506	1887	Dr Norman A Wiggins	2-D	3,238	162
Canisius Coll, Buffalo, NY 14208	1870	Rev James M Demske, SJ	1-M	4,250	271
Capital U, Columbus, OH 43209	1850	Mr Josiah H Blackmore	2-M	2,752	199

Name, address	Year	Governing official, control, and highest degree offered		Enroll-ment	Faculty
Capitol Coll, Laurel, MD 20708	1964	Dr G William Troxler	1-B	1,026	57
Cardinal Stritch Coll, Milwaukee, WI 53217	1937	Sr M Camille Kliebhan	2-M	2,314	147
Caribbean U Coll, Bayamón, PR 00619	1969	Dr Angel E Juan-Ortega	1-B	3,596	124
Carleton Coll, Northfield, MN 55057	1866	Dr David H Porter	1-B	1,853	156
Carlow Coll, Pittsburgh, PA 15213 (4)	1929	MaryLouise Fennell, RSM	2-M	1,120	119
Carnegie Mellon U, Pittsburgh, PA 15213	1900	Dr Richard M Cyert	1-D	6,579	607
Carroll Coll, Waukesha, WI 53186	1846	Dr Robert V Cramer	2-B	1,219	116
Carroll Coll of Montana, Helena, MT 59625	1909	Dr Francis J Kerins	2-B	1,410	113
Carson-Newman Coll, Jefferson City, TN 37760	1851	Dr J Cordell Maddox	2-B	1,681	116
Carthage Coll, Kenosha, WI 53141	1847	Dr F Gregory Campbell	2-M	1,682	97
Case Western Reserve U, Cleveland, OH 44106	1826	Dr Agnar Pytte	1-D	7,939	1,465
Castleton State Coll, Castleton, VT 05735	1787	Dr Lyle A Gray	5-M	1,998	114
Catawba Coll, Salisbury, NC 28144	1851	Dr Stephen H Wurster	2-B	886	71
Catholic U of America, Washington, DC 20064	1887	Rev William J Byron, SJ	2-D	6,717	615
Catholic U of Puerto Rico, Ponce, PR 00732	1948	Rev F Tosello Giangiacomo	2-M	11,762	579
Cedar Crest Coll, Allentown, PA 18104 (4)	1867	Dr Gene S Cesari	2-B	1,051	136
Cedarville Coll, Cedarville, OH 45314	1887	Dr Paul H Dixon	2-B	1,821	134
Centenary Coll of Louisiana, Shreveport, LA 71134	1825	Dr Donald A Webb	2-M	965	89
Ctr for Creative Studies—Coll of Art and Design, Detroit, MI 48202	1926	Jerome Grove	1-B	951	203
Central Bible Coll, Springfield, MO 65803	1922	H Maurice Lednicky	2-B	757	48
Central Connecticut State U, New Britain, CT 06050	1849	Dr John W Shumaker	5-M	13,348	644
Central Methodist Coll, Fayette, MO 65248	1854	Dr Joseph A Howell	2-B	660	62
Central Michigan U, Mount Pleasant, MI 48859	1892	Mr Arthur E Ellis	5-D	16,743	740
Central Missouri State U, Warrensburg, MO 64093	1871	Dr Ed Elliott	5-M	9,032	439
Central New England Coll, Worcester, MA 01610	1888	Edward Paul Mattar III	1-B	2,308	160
Central State U, Wilberforce, OH 45384	1887	Dr Arthur E Thomas	5-B	2,680	154
Central State U, Edmond, OK 73034	1890	Dr Bill J Lillard	5-M	13,412	480
Central U of Iowa, Pella, IA 50219	1853	Dr Kenneth J Weller	2-B	1,531	93
Central Washington U, Ellensburg, WA 98926	1891	Dr Donald L Garrity	5-M	7,163	349
Centre Coll, Danville, KY 40422	1819	Dr Richard L Morrill	2-B	814	75
Chadron State Coll, Chadron, NE 69337	1911	NR	5-M	2,250	104
Chaminade U of Honolulu, Honolulu, HI 96816	1955	Fr Raymond A Roesch, SM	2-M	2,606	75
Chapman Coll, Orange, CA 92666	1861	Dr G T Smith	2-M	2,022	153
Charter Oak Coll, Hartford, CT 06106	1973	Dr Bernard Shea	5-B	701	55
Chatham Coll, Pittsburgh, PA 15232 (3)	1869	Rebecca Stafford	1-B	683	65
Chestnut Hill Coll, Philadelphia, PA 19118 (4)	1924	Sr Matthew Anita MacDonald	2-M	913	94
Cheyney U of Pennsylvania, Cheyney, PA 19319	1837	Dr LeVerne McCummings	5-M	1,507	140
Chicago State U, Chicago, IL 60628	1867	Dr George E Ayers	5-M	7,763	443
Christian Brothers Coll, Memphis, TN 38104	1871	Br Theodore Drahmann	2-B	1,642	135
Christopher Newport Coll, Newport News, VA 23606	1961	Dr Anthony Santoro	5-B	4,089	190
The Citadel, Charleston, SC 29409 (2)	1842	Maj Gen James A Grimsley	5-M	3,339	183
City Coll of City U of NY, New York, NY 10031	1847	Bernard W Harleston	12-D	12,953	980
City U, Bellevue, WA 98008	1973	Dr Michael A Pastore	1-M	2,119	250
Claflin Coll, Orangeburg, SC 29115	1869	Dr Oscar A Rogers Jr	2-B	760	65
Claremont McKenna Coll, Claremont, CA 91711	1946	Mr Jack L Stark	1-B	833	111
Clarion U of Pennsylvania, Clarion, PA 16214	1867	Dr Thomas A Bond	5-M	6,121	361
Clark Coll, Atlanta, GA 30314	1869	Dr Elias Blake Jr	2-B	1,883	110
Clarke Coll, Dubuque, IA 52001	1843	Dr Catherine Dunn, BVM	2-M	803	60
Clarkson U, Potsdam, NY 13676	1896	Dr Allan H Clark	1-D	3,953	231
Clark U, Worcester, MA 01610	1887	Dr Richard P Traina	1-D	2,952	206
Clayton State Coll, Morrow, GA 30260	1969	Dr Harry S Downs	5-B	3,290	148
Cleary Coll, Ypsilanti, MI 48197	1883	Dr Harry Howard	1-B	917	55
Clemson U, Clemson, SC 29634	1889	Dr Max Lennon	5-D	13,062	975
Cleveland State U, Cleveland, OH 44115	1964	Dr Walter B Waetjen	5-D	18,241	763
Clinch Valley Coll of the U of Virginia, Wise, VA 24293	1954	Dr Jerry D Cardwell	5-B	1,354	58
Coe Coll, Cedar Rapids, IA 52402	1851	Dr John E Brown	2-B	1,133	121
Colby Coll, Waterville, ME 04901	1813	William R Cotter	1-B	1,730	157
Coleman Coll, La Mesa, CA 92041	1963	Dr Coleman Furr	1-M	658	48
Colgate U, Hamilton, NY 13346	1819	Dr George D Langdon Jr	1-M	2,701	264
Coll for Human Services, New York, NY 10014	1964	Audrey C Cohen	1-B	635	19
Coll Misericordia, Dallas, PA 18612	1924	Dr Joseph R Fink	2-M	1,148	129
Coll of Aeronautics, Flushing, NY 11371 (2)	1932	Dr George W Brush	1-B	1,450	68
Coll of Boca Raton, Boca Raton, FL 33431	1963	Dr Donald E Ross	1-M	1,000	65
Coll of Charleston, Charleston, SC 29424	1770	Dr Harry M Lightsey Jr	5-M	5,531	338
Coll of Great Falls, Great Falls, MT 59405	1932	Dr William A Shields	2-M	1,151	82
Coll of Idaho, Caldwell, ID 83605	1891	Dr Robert L Hendren Jr	2-M	970	104
Coll of Insurance, New York, NY 10007	1962	Linda H Lamel	1-M	1,006	93
Coll of Mount St Joseph, Mount St Joseph, OH 45051	1920	Francis Marie Thrailkill, OSU	2-M	2,219	183
Coll of Mount Saint Vincent, Riverdale, NY 10471 (4)	1847	Sr Doris Smith	1-B	1,050	82
Coll of New Rochelle, New Rochelle, NY 10805 (4)	1904	Sr Dorothy A Kelly	1-M	1,642	178
Coll of New Rochelle, New Resources Division, New Rochelle, NY 10805	1972	Sr Dorothy Ann Kelly	1-B	3,124	417
Coll of Notre Dame, Belmont, CA 94002	1851	Sr Veronica Skillin	2-M	1,053	116
Coll of Notre Dame of Maryland, Baltimore, MD 21210 (4)	1873	Sr Kathleen Feeley	2-M	1,886	72
Coll of Saint Benedict, Saint Joseph, MN 56374 (3)	1913	Sister Colman O'Connell	2-B	1,745	133
Coll of St Catherine, St Paul, MN 55105 (3)	1905	Dr Anita Pampusch	2-M	2,523	209
Coll of Saint Elizabeth, Convent Station, NJ 07961 (4)	1899	Sr Jacqueline Burns	2-B	648	94
Coll of St Francis, Joliet, IL 60435	1920	Dr John C Orr	2-M	1,788	81
Coll of Saint Mary, Omaha, NE 68124 (4)	1923	Dr Kenneth Nielsen	2-B	1,276	116
Coll of Saint Rose, Albany, NY 12203	1920	Dr Louis C Vaccaro	1-M	2,245	213
Coll of St Scholastica, Duluth, MN 55811	1906	Dr Daniel H Pilon	2-M	1,535	124
Coll of St Thomas, St Paul, MN 55105	1885	Msgr Terrence J Murphy	2-M	7,577	452
Coll of Santa Fe, Santa Fe, NM 87501	1947	James A Fries	2-M	1,463	93
Coll of Staten Island of City U of NY, Staten Island, NY 10301	1955	Dr Edmond L Volpe	12-M	10,657	672
Coll of the Holy Cross, Worcester, MA 01610	1843	Rev John E Brooks, SJ	2-B	2,646	230
Coll of the Virgin Islands, Charlotte Amalie, St Thomas, VI 00802	1962	Dr Arthur A Richards	8-M	757	220
Coll of William and Mary, Williamsburg, VA 23185	1693	Dr Paul R Verkuil	5-D	6,616	526
Coll of Wooster, Wooster, OH 44691	1866	Dr Henry J Copeland	2-B	1,786	157
Colorado Coll, Colorado Springs, CO 80903	1874	Dr Gresham Riley	1-M	1,903	175
Colorado Sch of Mines, Golden, CO 80401	1874	Dr George S Ansell	5-D	2,520	226
Colorado State U, Fort Collins, CO 80523	1870	Dr Philip E Austin	5-D	18,381	1,052
Colorado Tech Coll, Colorado Springs, CO 80907	1965	Mr David D O'Donnell	3-B	600	55
Columbia Bible Coll, Columbia, SC 29230	1923	Mr J Robertson McQuilkin	2-M	867	59
Columbia Coll, Chicago, IL 60605	1890	Mr Mirron Alexandroff	1-M	5,549	595
Columbia Coll, Columbia, MO 65216	1851	Dr Donald B Ruthenberg	2-B	660	64

Name, address	Year	Governing official, control, and highest degree offered		Enroll-ment	Faculty
Columbia Coll, New York, NY 10027	1754	NR	1-B	2,900	560
Columbia Coll, Columbia, SC 29203 (3)	1854	Dr Ralph T Mirse	2-M	1,206	77
Columbia Union Coll, Takoma Park, MD 20912	1904	Dr William A Loveless	2-B	1,015	80
Columbia U, Sch of Engineering & Applied Sci, New York, NY 10027	1864	Professor Robert A Gross	1-D	2,250	155
Columbia U, Sch of General Studies, New York, NY 10027	1947	NR	1-B	1,219	420
Columbia U, Sch of Nursing, New York, NY 10032 (4)	1935	NR	1-M	102	49
Columbus Coll, Columbus, GA 31993	1958	Francis J Brooke	5-M	3,716	220
Columbus Coll of Art and Design, Columbus, OH 43215	1879	Mr Joseph V Canzani	1-B	1,037	92
Concord Coll, Athens, WV 24712	1872	Dr Jerry L Beasley	5-B	2,356	131
Concordia Coll, River Forest, IL 60305	1864	Dr Eugene L Krentz	2-M	1,315	128
Concordia Coll, Moorhead, MN 56560	1891	Dr Paul J Dovre	2-B	2,525	179
Concordia Coll, St Paul, MN 55104	1893	Dr Alan F Harre	2-B	946	72
Concordia Coll Wisconsin, Mequon, WI 53092	1881	Dr R John Buuck	2-B	841	65
Concordia Teachers Coll, Seward, NE 68434	1894	Ralph L Reinke	2-M	812	85
Connecticut Coll, New London, CT 06320	1911	Dr Oakes Ames	1-M	1,999	204
Converse Coll, Spartanburg, SC 29301 (3)	1889	Dr Robert T Coleman Jr	1-M	1,145	85
Cooper Union for the Advancement of Science & Art, New York, NY 10003	1859	Mr Bill N Lacy	1-M	1,035	212
Coppin State Coll, Baltimore, MD 21216	1900	Dr Calvin W Burnett	5-M	2,315	172
Cornell Coll, Mount Vernon, IA 52314	1853	Dr David G Marker	2-B	1,161	96
Cornell U, Ithaca, NY 14853	1865	Dr Frank H T Rhodes	1-D	17,904	1,558
Corpus Christi State U, Corpus Christi, TX 78412	1971	Dr B Alan Sugg	5-M	3,885	157
Creighton U, Omaha, NE 68178	1878	Rev Michael G Morrison, SJ	2-D	5,903	1,075
Culver-Stockton Coll, Canton, MO 63435	1853	Dr Robert Brown	2-B	843	55
Cumberland Coll, Williamsburg, KY 40769	1889	Dr James Taylor	2-M	1,927	115
Curry Coll, Milton, MA 02186	1879	Dr William L Boyle Jr	1-M	1,350	112
Daemen Coll, Amherst, NY 14226	1947	Dr Robert S Marshall	1-B	1,598	123
Dakota State Coll, Madison, SD 57042	1881	Dr Gerald Tunheim	5-B	940	60
Dakota Wesleyan U, Mitchell, SD 57301	1885	Dr James B Beddow	2-B	621	59
Dallas Baptist U, Dallas, TX 75211	1965	Dr W Marvin Watson	2-M	1,650	98
Dartmouth Coll, Hanover, NH 03755	1769	Dr James O Freeman	1-D	5,283	1,324
Davenport Coll of Business, Grand Rapids, MI 49503	1866	Donald W Maine	1-B	4,805	150
David Lipscomb Coll, Nashville, TN 37204	1891	Dr Harold Hazelip	2-M	2,238	138
Davidson Coll, Davidson, NC 28036	1837	Dr John W Kuykendall	2-B	1,379	117
Davis & Elkins Coll, Elkins, WV 26241	1904	Dr Dorothy I MacConkey	2-B	828	69
Defiance Coll, Defiance, OH 43512	1850	Dr Marvin Ludwig	2-B	985	75
Delaware State Coll, Dover, DE 19901	1891	Dr Luna I Mishoe	5-M	2,327	162
Delaware Valley Coll of Science & Agriculture, Doylestown, PA 18901	1896	Dr William DeLauder	1-B	1,200	102
Delta State U, Cleveland, MS 38733	1925	Dr F Kent Wyatt	5-D	3,372	243
Denison U, Granville, OH 43023	1831	Dr Andrew G De Rocco	1-B	2,118	189
Denver Tech Coll, Denver, CO 80222	1945	NR	3-B	900	63
DePaul U, Chicago, IL 60604	1898	Rev John T Richardson, CM	2-D	13,132	925
DePauw U, Greencastle, IN 46135	1837	Dr Robert Bottoms	2-M	2,372	194
Detroit Coll of Business, Dearborn, MI 48126	1962	Frank Paone	1-B	3,739	105
DeVry Inst of Tech, Phoenix, AZ 85021	1967	James Dugan	3-B	3,100	63
DeVry Inst of Tech, City of Industry, CA 91744	1983	Paul R McGuirk	3-B	2,479	50
DeVry Inst of Tech, Decatur, GA 30030	1969	William N Weaver	3-B	3,023	54
DeVry Inst of Tech, Chicago, IL 60618	1931	Thomas F Davisson	3-M	3,656	56
DeVry Inst of Tech, Lombard, IL 60148	1982	Thomas F Davisson	3-B	2,740	53
DeVry Inst of Tech, Kansas City, MO 64131	1931	Mr Charles R Levalley	3-B	1,632	42
DeVry Inst of Tech, Columbus, OH 43209	1952	Mr Richard A Czerniak	3-B	2,934	68
DeVry Inst of Tech, Irving, TX 75038	1969	Mr Thomas E Colvin	3-B	2,327	46
Dickinson Coll, Carlisle, PA 17013	1773	Dr A Lee Fritschler	2-B	1,888	168
Dickinson State U, Dickinson, ND 58601	1918	Dr Albert A Watrel	5-B	1,337	90
Dillard U, New Orleans, LA 70122	1869	Dr Samuel Du Bois Cook	2-B	1,275	101
Doane Coll, Crete, NE 68333	1872	Dr Fred Brown	2-B	611	64
Dominican Coll of Blauvelt, Orangeburg, NY 10962	1952	Sr Mary E O'Brien	1-B	1,562	120
Dominican Coll of San Rafael, San Rafael, CA 94901	1890	Dr Barbara K Bundy	2-M	757	138
Dordt Coll, Sioux Center, IA 51250	1955	Dr John B Hulst	2-B	971	81
Dowling Coll, Oakdale, NY 11769	1959	Dr Victor P Meskill	1-M	3,063	232
Drake U, Des Moines, IA 50311	1881	Dr Michael Ferrari	1-D	5,537	263
Drew U, Madison, NJ 07940	1866	Dr Paul Hardin	1-D	2,272	151
Drexel U, Philadelphia, PA 19104	1891	Dr William S Gaither	1-D	12,500	858
Drury Coll, Springfield, MO 65802	1873	Dr John E Moore Jr	1-M	1,301	102
Duke U, Durham, NC 27706	1838	Dr H Keith H Brodie	2-D	9,781	1,608
Duquesne U, Pittsburgh, PA 15282	1878	Rev Donald S Nesti	2-D	6,580	492
Dyke Coll, Cleveland, OH 44115	1848	Dr John C Corfias	1-B	1,350	123
D'Youville Coll, Buffalo, NY 14201	1908	Sr Denise Roche	1-M	1,202	91
Earlham Coll, Richmond, IN 47374	1847	Dr Richard J Wood	2-M	1,114	110
East Carolina U, Greenville, NC 27858	1907	Dr Ralph Eakin	5-D	14,464	914
East Central U, Ada, OK 74820	1909	Dr Stanley P Wagner	5-M	4,113	171
Eastern Coll, St Davids, PA 19087	1932	Dr Roberta Hestenes	2-M	1,043	104
Eastern Connecticut State U, Willimantic, CT 06226	1889	Dr Charles R Webb Jr	5-M	4,150	207
Eastern Illinois U, Charleston, IL 61920	1895	Dr Stanley Rives	5-M	9,982	549
Eastern Kentucky U, Richmond, KY 40475	1906	Dr Hanly Funderburk	5-M	12,636	690
Eastern Mennonite Coll, Harrisonburg, VA 22801	1917	Mr Richard C Detweiler	2-B	774	89
Eastern Michigan U, Ypsilanti, MI 48197	1849	Dr John W Porter	5-M	21,349	944
Eastern Montana Coll, Billings, MT 59101	1927	Dr Bruce H Carpenter	5-M	3,920	236
Eastern Nazarene Coll, Quincy, MA 02170	1918	Dr Stephen W Nease	2-M	881	61
Eastern New Mexico U, Portales, NM 88130	1934	Dr Robert Matheny	5-M	3,701	200
Eastern Oregon State Coll, La Grande, OR 97850	1929	David E Gilbert	5-M	1,604	176
Eastern Washington U, Cheney, WA 99004	1882	Dr Alexander F Schilt	5-M	8,091	390
East Stroudsburg U of Pennsylvania, East Stroudsburg, PA 18301	1893	James Gilbert	5-M	4,320	232
East Tennessee State U, Johnson City, TN 37614	1911	Dr Ronald E Beller	5-D	9,765	619
East Texas Baptist U, Marshall, TX 75670	1912	Dr Robert E Craig	2-B	691	61
East Texas State U, Commerce, TX 75428	1889	Dr Charles J Austin	5-D	6,916	344
East Texas State U at Texarkana, Texarkana, TX 75501	1971	Dr John F Moss	5-M	1,144	59
Eckerd Coll, St Petersburg, FL 33733	1958	Dr Peter H Armacost	2-B	1,202	94
Edgewood Coll, Madison, WI 53711	1927	Dr James A Ebben	2-M	929	74
Edinboro U of Pennsylvania, Edinboro, PA 16444	1857	Dr Foster F Diebold	5-M	6,014	332
Edward Waters Coll, Jacksonville, FL 32209	1866	Dr Cecil W Cone	2-B	686	59
Electronic Data Processing Coll of Puerto Rico, Hato Rey, PR 00918	1968	Dr Anibal Nieves	3-B	1,570	80

Name, address	Year	Governing official, control, and highest degree offered		Enroll-ment	Faculty
Elizabeth City State U, Elizabeth City, NC 27909	1891	Dr Jimmy R Jenkins	5-B	1,613	117
Elizabethtown Coll, Elizabethtown, PA 17022	1899	Dr Gerhard E Spiegler	2-B	1,692	170
Elmhurst Coll, Elmhurst, IL 60126	1871	Dr Ivan Frick	2-B	3,306	253
Elmira Coll, Elmira, NY 14901	1855	Dr Thomas K Meier	1-M	1,502	208
Elon Coll, Elon College, NC 27244	1889	Dr J Fred Young	2-M	3,097	177
Embry-Riddle Aeronautical U, Daytona Beach, FL 32014	1926	Eric S Doten	1-M	5,000	265
Embry-Riddle Aeronautical U, Intl Cmps, Daytona Beach, FL 32014	1926	Charles S Williams	1-M	4,281	1,515
Embry-Riddle Aeronautical U, Prescott Cmps, Prescott, AZ 86302	1978	Paul Daly	1-B	1,225	55
Emerson Coll, Boston, MA 02116	1880	Dr Allen E Koenig	1-M	2,383	194
Emmanuel Coll, Boston, MA 02115 (4)	1919	Sr Janet Eisner	2-M	1,073	94
Emory & Henry Coll, Emory, VA 24327	1836	Dr Charles W Sydnor Jr	2-B	770	75
Emory U, Atlanta, GA 30322	1836	Dr James T Laney	2-D	8,791	1,397
Emporia State U, Emporia, KS 66801	1863	Dr Robert Glennen	5-M	5,230	320
Eugene Lang Coll of the New Sch, New York, NY 10011	1919	Jonathan F Fanton	1-B	200	29
Evangel Coll, Springfield, MO 65802	1955	Dr Robert H Spence	2-B	1,628	115
Evergreen State Coll, Olympia, WA 98505	1967	Dr Joseph D Olander	5-M	2,965	175
Fairfield U, Fairfield, CT 06430	1942	Rev Aloysius P Kelley	2-M	5,126	349
Fairleigh Dickinson U, Florham-Madison Cmps, Madison, NJ 07940	1958	NR	1-M	3,636	212
Fairleigh Dickinson U, Rutherford Cmps, Rutherford, NJ 07070	1942	Samuel J Raphalides	1-M	2,576	158
Fairleigh Dickinson U, Teaneck-Hackensack Cmps, Teaneck, NJ 07666	1954	Dr Robert H Donaldson	1-D	5,858	623
Fairmont State Coll, Fairmont, WV 26554	1865	Dr Wendell G Hardway	5-B	5,239	308
Fashion Inst of Tech, New York, NY 10001	1944	Dr Marvin J Feldman	12-M	11,082	735
Faulkner U, Montgomery, AL 36193	1942	Dr Ernest A Clevenger Jr	2-B	1,453	103
Fayetteville State U, Fayetteville, NC 28301	1867	Dr Charles A Lyons Jr	5-M	2,921	199
Ferris State Coll, Big Rapids, MI 49307	1884	Dr J William Wenrich	5-D	10,909	650
Ferrum Coll, Ferrum, VA 24088	1913	Dr Jerry M Boone	2-B	1,275	89
Findlay Coll, Findlay, OH 45840	1882	Dr Kenneth E Zirkle	2-B	1,499	100
Fitchburg State Coll, Fitchburg, MA 01420	1894	Dr Vincent J Mara	5-M	6,368	570
Flagler Coll, St Augustine, FL 32085	1968	Dr William L Proctor	1-B	1,128	84
Florida Agricultural and Mechanical U, Tallahassee, FL 32307	1887	Dr Frederick Humphries	5-D	5,444	327
Florida Atlantic U, Boca Raton, FL 33431	1961	Dr Helen Popovich	5-D	8,130	652
Florida Inst of Tech, Melbourne, FL 32901	1958	Dr John E Miller	1-D	6,496	536
Florida International U, Miami, FL 33199	1965	Dr Gregory B Wolfe	5-D	12,494	868
Florida Memorial Coll, Miami, FL 33054	1879	Dr W C Robinson	2-B	2,172	116
Florida Southern Coll, Lakeland, FL 33801	1885	Dr Robert A Davis	2-M	1,955	135
Florida State U, Tallahassee, FL 32306	1857	Dr Bernard F Sliger	5-D	21,577	1,410
Fontbonne Coll, St Louis, MO 63105	1917	Dr Meneve Dunham	2-M	935	130
Fordham U, Bronx, NY 10458	1841	Rev Joseph A O'Hare, SJ	2-D	12,534	865
Fort Hays State U, Hays, KS 67601	1902	Dr Edward H Hammond	5-M	5,538	235
Fort Lauderdale Coll, Fort Lauderdale, FL 33301	1940	Dr Spencer D Stolpen	3-B	860	45
Fort Lewis Coll, Durango, CO 81301	1911	NR	5-B	3,606	158
Fort Valley State Coll, Fort Valley, GA 31030	1895	Dr Luther Burse	5-M	1,811	144
Framingham State Coll, Framingham, MA 01701	1839	Dr Paul F Weller	5-M	4,303	225
Franciscan U of Steubenville, Steubenville, OH 43952	1946	Rev Michael Scanlan	2-M	1,106	70
Francis Marion Coll, Florence, SC 29501	1970	Dr Thomas C Stanton	5-M	3,687	155
Franklin and Marshall Coll, Lancaster, PA 17604	1787	Dr James L Powell	1-B	2,001	170
Franklin Coll of Indiana, Franklin, IN 46131	1834	Mr William Bryan Martin	2-B	706	68
Franklin Pierce Coll, Rindge, NH 03461	1962	Dr Walter Peterson	1-B	1,032	147
Franklin U, Columbus, OH 43215	1902	Dr Frederick J Bunte	1-B	4,239	195
Freed-Hardeman Coll, Henderson, TN 38340	1869	Dr E Claude Gardner	2-B	1,083	93
Fresno Pacific Coll, Fresno, CA 93702	1944	Mr Richard Kriegbaum	2-M	1,087	63
Friends U, Wichita, KS 67213	1898	Dr Richard Felix	2-M	1,097	60
Frostburg State Coll, Frostburg, MD 21532	1898	Dr Kenneth Jablon	5-M	3,716	185
Furman U, Greenville, SC 29613	1826	Dr John E Johns	2-M	2,605	169
Gallaudet U, Washington, DC 20002	1856	Dr Jerry C Lee	1-D	2,206	272
Gannon U, Erie, PA 16541	1944	Dr M Daniel Henry	2-M	3,959	235
Gardner-Webb Coll, Boiling Springs, NC 28017	1905	Dr M Christopher White	2-M	1,882	161
Geneva Coll, Beaver Falls, PA 15010	1848	Dr Joseph McFarland	2-B	1,256	101
George Mason U, Fairfax, VA 22030	1957	Dr George W Johnson	5-D	17,652	715
Georgetown Coll, Georgetown, KY 40324	1829	Dr W Morgan Patterson	2-M	1,362	122
Georgetown U, Washington, DC 20057	1789	Rev Timothy S Healy, SJ	2-D	11,967	1,569
George Washington U, Washington, DC 20052	1821	NR	1-D	17,545	1,717
Georgia Coll, Milledgeville, GA 31061	1889	Dr Edwin G Speir	5-M	3,983	179
Georgia Inst of Tech, Atlanta, GA 30332	1885	Dr Joseph M Pettit	5-D	11,494	506
Georgian Court Coll, Lakewood, NJ 08701 (4)	1908	Sr Barbara Williams	2-M	1,773	131
Georgia Southern Coll, Statesboro, GA 30460	1906	Dr Nicholas Henry	5-M	7,611	429
Georgia Southwestern Coll, Americus, GA 31709	1906	Dr William H Capitan	5-M	2,237	114
Georgia State U, Atlanta, GA 30303	1913	Dr William M Suttles	5-D	21,879	996
Gettysburg Coll, Gettysburg, PA 17325	1832	Dr Charles E Glassick	2-B	1,850	179
Glassboro State Coll, Glassboro, NJ 08028	1923	Dr Herman D James	5-M	8,900	534
Glenville State Coll, Glenville, WV 26351	1872	Dr William K Simmons	5-B	2,063	96
GMI Engineering & Management Inst, Flint, MI 48502	1919	Dr William B Cottingham	1-M	3,237	135
Golden Gate U, San Francisco, CA 94105	1901	Dr Otto W Butz	1-D	10,307	793
Goldey Beacom Coll, Wilmington, DE 19808	1886	Mr William R Baldt	1-B	2,500	97
Gonzaga U, Spokane, WA 99258	1887	Rev Bernard J Coughlin, SJ	2-D	3,272	342
Gordon Coll, Wenham, MA 01984	1889	Dr Richard F Gross	2-B	1,211	88
Goshen Coll, Goshen, IN 46526	1894	Dr Victor Stoltzfus	2-B	1,068	88
Goucher Coll, Baltimore, MD 21204	1885	Dr Rhoda M Dorsey	1-M	965	148
Governors State U, University Park, IL 60466	1969	Dr Leo Goodman Malamuth II	5-M	5,568	320
Grace Coll, Winona Lake, IN 46590	1948	Dr John Davis	2-B	734	49
Graceland Coll, Lamoni, IA 50140	1895	Dr Barbara J Higdon	2-B	953	70
Grambling State U, Grambling, LA 71245	1901	Dr Joseph B Johnson	5-M	5,224	200
Grand Canyon Coll, Phoenix, AZ 85061	1949	Dr William Williams	2-B	1,572	137
Grand Rapids Baptist Coll and Sem, Grand Rapids, MI 49505	1941	Dr Charles Wagner	2-M	877	62
Grand Valley State Coll, Allendale, MI 49401	1960	Mr Arend D Lubbers	5-M	7,667	391
Grand View Coll, Des Moines, IA 50316	1896	Mr Karl F Langrock	2-B	1,285	99
Grantham Coll of Engineering, Los Alamitos, CA 90720	1951	D J Grantham	3-B	678	6
Greenville Coll, Greenville, IL 62246	1892	Dr W Richard Stephens	2-B	634	49
Griffin Coll, Seattle, WA 98121	1909	J Michael Griffin	3-B	600	100

Name, address	Year	Governing official, control, and highest degree offered		Enrollment	Faculty
Grinnell Coll, Grinnell, IA 50112	1846	Dr George A Drake	1-B	1,248	125
Grove City Coll, Grove City, PA 16127	1876	Dr Charles S MacKenzie	2-B	2,133	124
Guilford Coll, Greensboro, NC 27410	1837	Dr William R Rogers	2-B	1,230	127
Gustavus Adolphus Coll, St Peter, MN 56082	1862	Dr John S Kendall	2-B	2,212	195
Gwynedd-Mercy Coll, Gwynedd Valley, PA 19437 (4)	1948	Sister Janet Baker, RSM	2-M	1,980	216
Hahnemann U, Philadelphia, PA 19102	1848	Dr Iqbal F Paroo	1-D	2,022	400
Hamilton Coll, Clinton, NY 13323	1812	Mr J Martin Carovano	1-B	1,650	146
Hamline U, St Paul, MN 55104	1854	Dr Charles J Graham	2-D	1,923	126
Hampden-Sydney Coll, Hampden-Sydney, VA 23943 (1)	1776	Dr James R Leutze	2-B	825	74
Hampshire Coll, Amherst, MA 01002	1965	Dr Adele S Simmons	1-B	1,010	109
Hampton U, Hampton, VA 23668	1868	Dr William R Harvey	1-M	4,483	297
Hannibal-LaGrange Coll, Hannibal, MO 63401	1858	Dr Larry Lewis	2-B	777	50
Hanover Coll, Hanover, IN 47243	1827	Dr John E Horner	2-B	1,088	73
Harding U, Searcy, AR 72143	1924	Dr Clifton L Ganus Jr	2-M	2,767	165
Hardin-Simmons U, Abilene, TX 79698	1891	Dr John A Davitt	2-M	1,804	124
Harris-Stowe State Coll, St Louis, MO 63103	1857	Dr Henry Givens Jr	5-B	1,374	66
Hartwick Coll, Oneonta, NY 13820	1928	Dr Philip S Wilder Jr	1-B	1,416	131
Harvard U, Cambridge, MA 02138	1636	Mr Derek Bok	1-D	16,871	1,693
Hastings Coll, Hastings, NE 68901	1882	Dr Thomas J Reeves	2-B	791	79
Haverford Coll, Haverford, PA 19041	1833	Dr Harvey C Payne	1-B	1,112	114
Hawaii Pacific Coll, Honolulu, HI 96813	1966	Mr Chatt Wright	1-M	4,071	216
Heidelberg Coll, Tiffin, OH 44883	1850	Dr William C Cassell	2-B	913	79
Henderson State U, Arkadelphia, AR 71923	1890	Dr Charles D Dunn	5-M	2,933	161
Hendrix Coll, Conway, AR 72032	1876	Dr Joe B Hatcher	2-B	1,007	71
High Point Coll, High Point, NC 27261	1924	Dr Jacob C Martinson Jr	2-B	1,392	77
Hillsdale Coll, Hillsdale, MI 49242	1844	Dr George C Roche III	1-B	1,050	92
Hiram Coll, Hiram, OH 44234	1850	Dr Russel Aiuto	2-B	1,091	85
Hobart Coll, Geneva, NY 14456 (1)	1822	Mr Carroll Brewster	2-B	1,117	160
Hofstra U, Hempstead, NY 11550	1935	Dr James M Shuart	1-D	12,067	795
Hollins Coll, Roanoke, VA 24020 (3)	1842	Dr Paula P Brownlee	1-M	965	91
Holy Family Coll, Philadelphia, PA 19114	1954	Sr M Francesca	2-B	1,549	165
Holy Names Coll, Oakland, CA 94619	1868	Sr Lois MacGillivray	2-M	600	92
Hood Coll, Frederick, MD 21701 (4)	1893	Dr Martha E Church	2-M	1,892	120
Hope Coll, Holland, MI 49423	1851	Dr John H Jacobson Jr	2-B	2,545	207
Houghton Coll, Houghton, NY 14744	1883	Dr Daniel R Chamberlain	2-B	1,268	89
Houston Baptist U, Houston, TX 77074	1960	Dr E Douglas Hodo	2-M	3,095	155
Howard Payne U, Brownwood, TX 76801	1889	Dr Ralph A Phelps Jr	2-B	980	77
Howard U, Washington, DC 20059	1867	Dr James E Cheek	1-D	11,053	2,134
Humboldt State U, Arcata, CA 95521	1913	Dr Alistair W McCrone	5-M	5,865	500
Hunter Coll of City U of NY, New York, NY 10021	1870	NR	12-M	19,577	1,341
Huntingdon Coll, Montgomery, AL 36106	1854	Dr Allen K Jackson	2-B	755	69
Husson Coll, Bangor, ME 04401	1898	Mr Delmont N Merrill	1-M	1,546	100
Idaho State U, Pocatello, ID 83209	1901	Dr Richard Bowen	5-D	9,812	443
Illinois Benedictine Coll, Lisle, IL 60532	1887	Dr Richard C Becker	2-M	2,224	192
Illinois Coll, Jacksonville, IL 62650	1829	Dr Donald C Mundinger	2-B	745	55
Illinois Inst of Tech, Chicago, IL 60616	1892	Dr Thomas L Martin Jr	1-D	6,291	485
Illinois State U, Normal, IL 61761	1857	Dr Lloyd I Watkins	5-D	22,358	1,034
Illinois Wesleyan U, Bloomington, IL 61702	1850	Dr Wayne Anderson	2-B	1,603	159
Immaculata Coll, Immaculata, PA 19345 (4)	1920	Sr Marian William	2-M	1,907	119
Incarnate Word Coll, San Antonio, TX 78209	1881	Dr Louis J Agnese, Jr	2-M	1,576	115
Indiana Inst of Tech, Fort Wayne, IN 46803	1930	Donald J Andorfer	1-B	675	46
Indiana State U, Terre Haute, IN 47809	1865	Dr Richard G Landini	5-D	11,208	670
Indiana U at Kokomo, Kokomo, IN 46902	1945	Dr Hugh L Thompson	5-M	2,857	180
Indiana U at South Bend, South Bend, IN 46634	1922	Lester M Wolfson	5-M	5,641	316
Indiana U Bloomington, Bloomington, IN 47405	1820	Kenneth R R Gros Louis	5-D	31,224	1,609
Indiana U East, Richmond, IN 47374	1971	NR	5-B	1,420	111
Indiana U Northwest, Gary, IN 46408	1959	Dr Peggy G Elliott	5-M	4,622	296
Indiana U of Pennsylvania, Indiana, PA 15705	1875	Dr John Welty	5-D	13,248	702
Indiana U–Purdue U at Fort Wayne, Fort Wayne, IN 46805	1917	Dr Edward A Nicholson	5-M	10,182	576
Indiana U–Purdue U at Indianapolis, Indianapolis, IN 46202	1969	Dr Glenn W Irwin Jr	5-D	23,468	2,021
Indiana U Southeast, New Albany, IN 47150	1941	Dr Leon Rand	5-M	4,649	250
Inter American U of PR, Aguadilla Regional Coll, Aguadilla, PR 00603	1957	Mr Juan Colon	1-B	3,601	148
Inter American U of PR, Arecibo Regional Coll, Arecibo, PR 00613	1957	Dr Maria delos A Ortiz deLeon	1-B	3,738	225
Inter Amer U of PR, Barranquitas Regional Coll, Barranquitas, PR 00615	1957	Mr Vidal Rivera-Garcia	1-B	1,335	78
Inter American U of PR, Fajardo Regional Coll, Fajardo, PR 00648	1965	Mr Jose L Larrieux Suarez	1-B	2,066	97
Inter American U of PR, Metro Cmps, Hato Rey, PR 00919	1960	Joanne Fagerburg	1-D	13,910	848
Inter American U of PR, Ponce Regional Coll, Ponce, PR 00715	1962	Mr Jose I Correa	1-B	2,665	184
Inter American U of PR, San Germán Cmps, San Germán, PR 00753	1912	Dr Federico Matheu	1-M	7,036	340
Iona Coll, New Rochelle, NY 10801	1940	Br John G Driscoll	1-M	5,976	407
Iowa State U, Ames, IA 50011	1858	Dr Gordon P Eaton	5-D	26,431	2,133
Iowa Wesleyan Coll, Mount Pleasant, IA 52641	1842	Robert J Prins	2-B	647	46
Ithaca Coll, Ithaca, NY 14850	1892	Dr James J Whalen	1-M	5,757	501
ITT Tech Inst, West Covina, CA 91790	1982	Merlyn W Cooper	3-B	810	29
ITT Tech Inst, Fort Wayne, IN 46825	1967	Jack B Cozad	3-B	1,208	32
ITT Tech Inst, Indianapolis, IN 46268	1966	Marvin L Copes	3-B	1,157	48
Jackson State U, Jackson, MS 39217	1877	Dr James A Hefner	5-D	6,425	453
Jacksonville State U, Jacksonville, AL 36265	1883	Dr Harold J McGee	5-M	6,983	548
Jacksonville U, Jacksonville, FL 32211	1934	Dr Frances B Kinne	1-M	2,214	201
James Madison U, Harrisonburg, VA 22807	1908	Dr Ronald E Carrier	5-M	9,757	600
Jersey City State Coll, Jersey City, NJ 07305	1927	Dr William J Maxwell	5-M	6,283	420
John Brown U, Siloam Springs, AR 72761	1919	Dr John E Brown III	2-B	849	57
John Carroll U, University Heights, OH 44118	1886	Rev Thomas P O'Malley, SJ	2-M	3,496	235
John F Kennedy U, Orinda, CA 94563	1964	Dr Robert M Fisher	1-M	1,820	221
John Jay Coll of Crim Justice of City U of NY, New York, NY 10019	1964	Dr Gerald Lynch	12-D	6,679	448
Johns Hopkins U, Baltimore, MD 21218	1876	Dr Steven Muller	1-D	3,600	398
Johnson & Wales Coll, Providence, RI 02903	1914	Dr Morris J Gaebe	1-M	5,389	132
Johnson C Smith U, Charlotte, NC 28216	1867	Mack L Davidson	2-B	1,130	82

Name, address	Year	Governing official, control, and highest degree offered		Enrollment	Faculty
Johnson State Coll, Johnson, VT 05656	1828	Mr Eric R Gilbertson	5-M	1,310	87
Jones Coll, Jacksonville, FL 32211	1918	James M Patch	1-B	1,437	46
Jordan Coll, Cedar Springs, MI 49319	1967	Lexie K Coxon	2-B	2,023	145
Juilliard Sch, New York, NY 10023	1905	Dr Joseph W Polisi	1-D	850	220
Juniata Coll, Huntingdon, PA 16652	1876	Dr Robert W Neff	1-B	1,117	90
Kalamazoo Coll, Kalamazoo, MI 49007	1833	Dr David Breneman	1-B	1,102	102
Kansas Newman Coll, Wichita, KS 67213	1933	Dr Robert J Giroux	2-B	765	68
Kansas State U, Manhattan, KS 66506	1863	Dr Jon Wefald	5-D	17,687	1,558
Kansas Wesleyan, Salina, KS 67401	1886	Rev Marshall P Stanton	2-B	637	51
Kean Coll of New Jersey, Union, NJ 07083	1855	Dr Nathan Weiss	5-M	12,629	713
Kearney State Coll, Kearney, NE 68849	1903	Dr William R Nester	5-M	8,816	377
Keene State Coll, Keene, NH 03431	1909	Dr Judith A Sturnick	5-M	2,981	250
Kendall Sch of Design, Grand Rapids, MI 49503	1928	Dr Phyllis I Danielson	1-B	738	64
Kennesaw Coll, Marietta, GA 30061	1966	Dr Betty L Siegel	5-M	7,300	287
Kent State U, Kent, OH 44242	1910	Dr Michael Schwartz	5-D	20,830	1,068
Kentucky State U, Frankfort, KY 40601	1886	Dr Raymond M Burse	13-M	2,205	128
Kentucky Wesleyan Coll, Owensboro, KY 42301	1858	Dr Luther W White	2-B	812	84
Kenyon Coll, Gambier, OH 43022	1824	Dr Philip H Jordan Jr	1-B	1,525	111
King's Coll, Wilkes-Barre, PA 18711	1946	Rev James Lackenmier	2-B	2,326	157
Knox Coll, Galesburg, IL 61401	1837	Dr John P McCall	1-B	967	92
Kutztown U of Pennsylvania, Kutztown, PA 19530	1866	Dr Lawrence M Stratton	5-M	6,647	337
Lafayette Coll, Easton, PA 18042	1826	Dr David W Ellis	2-B	2,032	205
LaGrange Coll, LaGrange, GA 30240	1831	Dr Walter Y Murphy	2-M	964	68
Lake Erie Coll, Painesville, OH 44077	1859	Dr Clodus R Smith	1-M	610	77
Lake Forest Coll, Lake Forest, IL 60045	1857	Dr Eugene Hotchkiss III	1-M	1,185	93
Lakeland Coll, Sheboygan, WI 53082	1862	Dr Richard E Hill	2-B	1,239	41
Lake Superior State Coll, Sault Sainte Marie, MI 49783	1946	Dr Erik Shaar	5-M	2,666	138
Lamar U, Beaumont, TX 77710	1923	Dr Bill J Franklin	5-D	14,094	545
Lambuth Coll, Jackson, TN 38301	1843	Dr Harry W Gilmer	2-B	700	80
Lander Coll, Greenwood, SC 29646	1872	Dr Larry A Jackson	5-M	2,290	144
Langston U, Langston, OK 73050	1897	Dr Ernest L Holloway	5-B	2,054	201
Laredo State U, Laredo, TX 78040	1969	Dr Manuel Pacheco	5-M	935	50
La Roche Coll, Pittsburgh, PA 15237	1963	Sr Margaret Huber	2-M	1,751	112
La Salle U, Philadelphia, PA 19141	1863	Br Patrick Ellis	2-M	6,136	242
Lawrence Inst of Tech, Southfield, MI 48075	1932	Dr Richard E Marburger	1-B	6,142	303
Lawrence U, Appleton, WI 54912	1847	Dr Richard Warch	1-B	1,072	106
Lebanon Valley Coll, Annville, PA 17003	1866	NR	2-B	1,224	105
Lee Coll, Cleveland, TN 37311	1918	Dr R Lamar Vest	2-B	1,214	100
Lehigh U, Bethlehem, PA 18015	1865	Dr Peter Likins	1-D	6,334	440
Lehman Coll of City U of NY, Bronx, NY 10468	1931	Dr Leonard Lief	12-M	9,366	669
Le Moyne Coll, Syracuse, NY 13214	1946	Rev Kevin G O'Connell	2-B	2,133	171
LeMoyne-Owen Coll, Memphis, TN 38126	1870	Dr Irving P McPhail	2-B	951	56
Lenoir-Rhyne Coll, Hickory, NC 28603	1891	Dr John E Trainer Jr	2-M	1,539	114
Lesley Coll, Cambridge, MA 02138 (3)	1909	Margaret A McKenna	1-D	3,358	206
LeTourneau Coll, Longview, TX 75607	1946	Dr Alvin O Austin	2-B	776	72
Lewis and Clark Coll, Portland, OR 97219	1867	Mr James A Gardner	1-D	2,846	309
Lewis-Clark State Coll, Lewiston, ID 83501	1894	Dr Lee A Vickers	5-B	2,176	120
Lewis U, Romeoville, IL 60441	1932	Br David Delahanty, FSC	2-M	3,268	172
Liberty U, Lynchburg, VA 24506	1971	Dr A Pierre Guillermin	2-M	6,353	220
Lincoln Memorial U, Harrogate, TN 37752	1897	Dr Gary J Burchett	1-M	1,348	77
Lincoln U, Jefferson City, MO 65101	1866	Dr Thomas Miller Jenkins	5-M	2,486	164
Lincoln U, Lincoln University, PA 19352	1854	Dr Donald L Mullett	13-M	1,500	111
Lindenwood Coll, St Charles, MO 63301	1827	Dr James I Spainhower	1-M	1,771	154
Lindsey Wilson Coll, Columbia, KY 42728	1903	Dr John B Begley	2-B	882	66
Linfield Coll, McMinnville, OR 97128	1849	Dr Charles U Walker	2-M	1,098	86
Livingstone Coll, Salisbury, NC 28144	1879	Dr William H Greene	2-B	733	63
Livingston U, Livingston, AL 35470	1835	Dr Asa N Green	5-M	1,445	95
Lock Haven U of Pennsylvania, Lock Haven, PA 17745	1870	Dr Craig Dean Willis	5-M	2,725	180
Logan Coll of Chiropractic, Chesterfield, MO 63017	1935	Dr Beatrice B Hagen	2-D	686	62
Loma Linda U, Riverside, CA 92515	1915	Dr R Dale McCune	2-D	4,390	1,870
Long Island U, Brooklyn Cmps, Brooklyn, NY 11201	1926	Dr David J Steinberg	1-D	5,985	406
Long Island U, C W Post Cmps, Brookville, NY 11548	1954	Dr Edward J Cook	1-M	9,315	705
Long Island U, Southampton Cmps, Southampton, NY 11968	1963	Dr David J Steinberg	1-M	1,224	112
Longwood Coll, Farmville, VA 23901	1839	Dr George R Healy	5-M	2,789	180
Loras Coll, Dubuque, IA 52004	1839	Dr Pasquale Di Pasquale Jr	2-M	2,009	129
Loretto Heights Coll, Denver, CO 80236	1918	Dr Thomas K Craine	1-B	715	87
Los Angeles Coll of Chiropractic, Whittier, CA 90604	1911	Dr E Maylon Drake	1-D	882	67
Louisiana Coll, Pineville, LA 71359	1906	Dr Robert L Lynn	2-B	1,038	93
Louisiana State U and A&M Coll, Baton Rouge, LA 70803	1860	Dr James H Wharton	5-D	27,704	1,495
Louisiana State U in Shreveport, Shreveport, LA 71115	1965	Dr E Grady Bogue	5-M	4,152	243
Louisiana State U Medical Ctr, New Orleans, LA 70112	1931	Dr Perry G Rigby	5-D	2,600	2,500
Louisiana Tech U, Ruston, LA 71272	1894	Dr Dan Reneau	5-D	10,053	421
Lourdes Coll, Sylvania, OH 43560	1958	Sr Ann Francis Klimkowski, OSF	2-B	805	65
Loyola Coll, Baltimore, MD 21210	1852	Rev Joseph A Sellinger	2-M	5,157	288
Loyola Marymount U, Los Angeles, CA 90045	1911	Rev James N Loughran, SJ	2-D	6,476	356
Loyola U, New Orleans, New Orleans, LA 70118	1912	Rev James C Carter, SJ	2-D	5,211	340
Loyola U of Chicago, Chicago, IL 60611	1870	Rev Raymond C Baumhart, SJ	2-D	14,158	1,322
Lubbock Christian U, Lubbock, TX 79407	1957	Dr Steven S Lemley	2-B	1,041	99
Luther Coll, Decorah, IA 52101	1861	Dr H George Anderson	2-B	2,109	168
Lycoming Coll, Williamsport, PA 17701	1812	Dr Frederick E Blumer	2-B	1,127	96
Lynchburg Coll, Lynchburg, VA 24501	1903	Dr George N Rainsford	2-M	2,188	158
Lyndon State Coll, Lyndonville, VT 05851	1911	Dr Clive C Veri	5-M	976	86
Macalester Coll, St Paul, MN 55105	1874	Dr Robert M Gavin Jr	2-B	1,768	177
MacMurray Coll, Jacksonville, IL 62650	1846	Dr Edward J Mitchell	2-B	650	76
Madonna Coll, Livonia, MI 48150	1947	Sr Mary Francilene	2-M	3,929	209
Maharishi International U, Fairfield, IA 52556	1971	Dr Bevan Morris	1-D	777	96
Malone Coll, Canton, OH 44709	1892	Dr Gordon R Werkema	2-B	1,048	74
Manchester Coll, North Manchester, IN 46962	1889	Dr William P Robinson	2-M	932	89
Manhattan Coll, Riverdale, NY 10471	1853	Br Thomas J Scanlan	1-M	4,337	338
Manhattan Sch of Music, New York, NY 10027	1917	Gideon W Waldrop	1-D	707	208
Manhattanville Coll, Purchase, NY 10577	1841	Dr Marcia Savage	1-M	1,350	170
Mankato State U, Mankato, MN 56001	1867	Dr Margaret R Preska	5-M	13,103	655

Name, address	Year	Governing official, control, and highest degree offered		Enroll-ment	Faculty
Mansfield U of Pennsylvania, Mansfield, PA 16933	1857	Mr Rod C Kelchner	5-M	2,894	205
Marian Coll, Indianapolis, IN 46222	1851	Dr Louis C Gatto	2-B	1,081	100
Marietta Coll, Marietta, OH 45750	1835	Dr Sherrill Cleland	1-M	1,320	98
Marion Coll, Marion, IN 46953	1920	NR	2-M	1,150	85
Marist Coll, Poughkeepsie, NY 12601	1949	Dr Dennis J Murray	1-M	4,471	200
Marquette U, Milwaukee, WI 53233	1881	Rev John P Raynor, SJ	2-D	11,804	958
Marshall U, Huntington, WV 25701	1837	Dr Dale F Nitzschke	5-D	11,473	514
Mars Hill Coll, Mars Hill, NC 28754	1856	Dr Fred B Bentley	2-B	1,323	114
Mary Baldwin Coll, Staunton, VA 24401 (3)	1842	Dr Cynthia Tyson	2-B	833	78
Marycrest Coll, Davenport, IA 52804	1939	NR	2-M	1,600	79
Marygrove Coll, Detroit, MI 48221	1910	Dr John E Shay Jr	2-M	1,214	64
Maryland Inst, Coll of Art, Baltimore, MD 21217	1826	Mr Fred Lazarus	1-M	856	90
Marymount Coll, Tarrytown, NY 10591 (4)	1907	Sr Brigid Driscoll	1-B	1,258	140
Marymount Coll of Kansas, Salina, KS 67401	1922	Dr Dan Johnson	2-B	640	66
Marymount Manhattan Coll, New York, NY 10021 (4)	1936	Sr Colette Mahoney	1-B	1,484	177
Marymount U, Arlington, VA 22207	1950	Sr M Majella Berg	2-M	2,408	188
Maryville Coll–Saint Louis, St Louis, MO 63141	1872	Dr Claudius H Pritchard Jr	1-M	2,631	181
Mary Washington Coll, Fredericksburg, VA 22401	1908	Dr William M Anderson Jr	5-M	3,225	169
Marywood Coll, Scranton, PA 18509	1915	Sr M Coleman Nee	2-M	3,251	213
Massachusetts Coll of Art, Boston, MA 02115	1873	Mr William F O'Neil	5-M	1,293	106
Mass Coll of Pharm & Allied Health Sciences, Boston, MA 02115	1823	Dr Raymond A Gosselin	1-D	1,088	61
Massachusetts Inst of Tech, Cambridge, MA 02139	1861	Dr Paul E Gray	1-D	9,756	1,700
Massachusetts Maritime Acad, Buzzards Bay, MA 02532 (2)	1891	Rear Adm John F Aylmer	5-B	800	74
McKendree Coll, Lebanon, IL 62254	1828	Dr Gerrit J TenBrink	2-B	952	50
McMurry Coll, Abilene, TX 79697	1923	Dr Thomas K Kim	2-B	1,703	128
McNeese State U, Lake Charles, LA 70609	1939	Dr Robert D Hebert	5-M	7,380	301
Medaille Coll, Buffalo, NY 14214	1875	Dr Leo R Downey	1-B	967	61
Medgar Evers Coll of City U of NY, Brooklyn, NY 11225	1969	Dr Leo A Corbie	12-B	2,563	323
Medical Coll of Georgia, Augusta, GA 30912	1828	Dr Jesse L Steinfeld	5-D	1,872	786
Medical U of South Carolina, Charleston, SC 29425	1824	Dr James B Edwards	5-D	1,996	513
Memphis State U, Memphis, TN 38152	1912	Dr Thomas G Carpenter	5-D	20,064	1,017
Menlo Coll, Atherton, CA 94025	1927	Dr Richard F O'Brien	1-B	650	67
Mercer U, Macon, GA 31207	1833	Dr R Kirby Godsey	2-D	2,905	143
Mercer U Atlanta, Atlanta, GA 30341	1968	Dr R Kirby Godsey	2-D	2,332	113
Mercy Coll, Dobbs Ferry, NY 10522	1951	Dr Wilbert J LeMelle	1-M	7,426	673
Mercy Coll of Detroit, Detroit, MI 48219	1941	Maureen A Fay, OP	2-M	2,404	202
Mercyhurst Coll, Erie, PA 16546	1926	Dr William P Garvey	2-M	1,848	110
Meredith Coll, Raleigh, NC 27607 (3)	1891	Dr John E Weems	2-M	1,947	147
Merrimack Coll, North Andover, MA 01845	1947	Rev John E Deegan, OSA	2-B	2,317	145
Mesa Coll, Grand Junction, CO 81502	1925	Dr John U Tomlinson	5-B	3,440	157
Messiah Coll, Grantham, PA 17027	1909	Dr D Ray Hostetter	2-B	1,916	150
Methodist Coll, Fayetteville, NC 28301	1956	Dr M Elton Hendricks	2-B	1,360	87
Metropolitan State Coll, Denver, CO 80204	1965	Dr Paul J Magelli	5-B	14,553	651
Metropolitan State U, St Paul, MN 55101	1971	Dr Reatha Clark King	5-M	3,335	482
Miami U, Oxford, OH 45056	1809	Dr Paul G Pearson	5-D	15,976	834
Michigan State U, East Lansing, MI 48824	1855	Dr John DiBiaggio	5-D	41,871	3,846
Michigan Tech U, Houghton, MI 49931	1885	Dr Dale F Stein	5-D	6,326	385
Mid-America Nazarene Coll, Olathe, KS 66061	1966	Dr Don Owens	2-B	1,040	80
Middlebury Coll, Middlebury, VT 05753	1800	Dr Olin C Robison	1-D	1,900	176
Middle Tennessee State U, Murfreesboro, TN 37132	1911	Dr Sam H Ingram	5-D	11,408	520
Midland Lutheran Coll, Fremont, NE 68025	1883	Dr Carl L Hansen	2-B	845	65
Midwestern State U, Wichita Falls, TX 76308	1922	Dr Louis J Rodriguez	5-M	4,482	179
Millersville U of Pennsylvania, Millersville, PA 17551	1854	Dr Joseph A Caputo	5-M	7,166	338
Milligan Coll, Milligan College, TN 37682	1866	Dr Marshall J Leggett	2-B	807	48
Millikin U, Decatur, IL 62522	1901	Dr J Roger Miller	2-B	1,562	137
Millsaps Coll, Jackson, MS 39210	1890	Dr George M Harmon	2-M	1,358	104
Mills Coll, Oakland, CA 94613 (3)	1852	Dr Mary S Metz	1-M	990	133
Milwaukee Sch of Engineering, Milwaukee, WI 53201 (2)	1903	Mr Robert R Spitzer	1-M	2,647	138
Minneapolis Coll of Art and Design, Minneapolis, MN 55404	1886	G Richard Slade	1-B	621	78
Minot State Coll, Minot, ND 58701	1913	Dr Gordon B Olson	5-M	3,112	155
Mississippi Coll, Clinton, MS 39058	1826	Dr Lewis Nobles	2-M	2,609	155
Mississippi State U, Mississippi State, MS 39762	1878	Dr Donald W Zacharias	5-D	11,663	864
Mississippi U for Women, Columbus, MS 39701 (4)	1884	Dr James W Strobel	5-M	2,037	117
Mississippi Valley State U, Itta Bena, MS 38941	1946	Dr Joseph L Boyer	5-M	2,002	130
Missouri Baptist Coll, St Louis, MO 63141	1968	Dr Patrick O Copley	2-B	658	39
Missouri Southern State Coll, Joplin, MO 64801	1937	Dr Julio Leon	5-B	4,610	205
Missouri Valley Coll, Marshall, MO 65340	1889	Dr Earl Reeves	2-B	800	52
Missouri Western State Coll, St Joseph, MO 64507	1915	Dr Janet Gorman Murphy	5-B	3,936	225
Mobile Coll, Mobile, AL 36613	1961	Dr Michael A Magnoli	2-M	874	78
Molloy Coll, Rockville Centre, NY 11570	1955	Dr Janet A Fitzgerald, OP	2-B	1,595	193
Monmouth Coll, Monmouth, IL 61462	1853	Dr Bruce Haywood	2-B	700	73
Monmouth Coll, West Long Branch, NJ 07764	1933	Dr Samuel H Magill	1-M	4,225	286
Montana Coll of Mineral Science and Tech, Butte, MT 59701	1893	Dr Lindsay D Norman Jr	5-M	1,850	130
Montana State U, Bozeman, MT 59717	1893	Dr William J Tietz	5-D	10,233	655
Montclair State Coll, Upper Montclair, NJ 07043	1908	Dr Donald E Walters	5-M	12,922	760
Moody Bible Inst, Chicago, IL 60610	1886	Dr Joseph Stowell	2-M	1,658	97
Moore Coll of Art, Philadelphia, PA 19103 (3)	1844	Dr Edward C McGuire	1-B	652	98
Moorhead State U, Moorhead, MN 56560	1887	Dr Roland Dille	5-M	8,121	331
Moravian Coll, Bethlehem, PA 18018	1742	Dr Roger Harry Martin	2-M	1,231	130
Morehead State U, Morehead, KY 40351	1922	Dr Herb F Reinhard	5-M	5,894	326
Morehouse Coll, Atlanta, GA 30314 (1)	1867	Dr Leroy Keith Jr	1-B	2,158	125
Morgan State U, Baltimore, MD 21239	1867	Dr Earl Richardson	5-D	3,740	295
Morningside Coll, Sioux City, IA 51106	1894	Dr Miles Tommeraasen	2-M	1,204	99
Morris Brown Coll, Atlanta, GA 30314	1881	Dr Calvert H Smith	2-B	1,257	84
Morris Coll, Sumter, SC 29150	1908	Dr Luns C Richardson	2-B	675	53
Mount Holyoke Coll, South Hadley, MA 01075 (3)	1837	Mrs Elizabeth Topham Kennan	1-B	1,944	210
Mount Ida Coll, Newton Centre, MA 02159	1899	Dr Bryan E Carlson	1-B	870	97
Mount Marty Coll, Yankton, SD 57078	1936	S Jacquelyn Ernster	2-M	778	75
Mount Mary Coll, Milwaukee, WI 53222 (3)	1913	Sr Ellen Lorenz	2-M	1,292	118
Mount Mercy Coll, Cedar Rapids, IA 52402	1928	Dr Thomas R Feld	2-B	1,325	89
Mount Saint Mary Coll, Newburgh, NY 12550	1930	Sr Ann Sakac	1-M	1,130	89
Mount St Mary's Coll, Los Angeles, CA 90049 (4)	1925	Sr Magdalen Coughlin	2-M	1,272	134
Mount Saint Mary's Coll, Emmitsburg, MD 21727	1808	Dr Robert J Wickenheiser	2-M	1,783	122
Mount Senario Coll, Ladysmith, WI 54848	1962	Dr Robert E Powless	1-B	750	54

Name, address	Year	Governing official, control, and highest degree offered	Enroll-ment	Faculty
Mount Union Coll, Alliance, OH 44601	1846	Dr Harold M Kolenbrander 2-B	1,050	90
Mount Vernon Nazarene Coll, Mount Vernon, OH 43050	1968	Dr William J Prince 2-B	1,030	76
Muhlenberg Coll, Allentown, PA 18104	1848	Dr Jonathan C Messerli 2-B	1,527	135
Multnomah Sch of the Bible, Portland, OR 97220	1936	Dr Joseph C Aldrich 2-M	662	45
Mundelein Coll, Chicago, IL 60660 (4)	1930	Sr Mary Breslin, BVM 2-M	1,182	89
Murray State U, Murray, KY 42071	1922	Dr Kala M Stroup 5-M	7,125	381
Muskegon Business Coll, Muskegon, MI 49442	1888	Mr Robert D Jewell 1-B	1,377	50
Muskingum Coll, New Concord, OH 43762	1837	Dr Arthur J De Jong 2-B	1,061	90
National Coll, Rapid City, SD 57709	1941	Mr John W Hauer 3-B	1,034	46
National Coll of Chiropractic, Lombard, IL 60148	1906	Dr Lee E Arnold 1-D	800	92
National Coll of Education, Evanston, IL 60201	1886	Dr Orley R Herron 1-D	2,350	118
National Ed Ctr–Tampa Tech Inst Cmps, Tampa, FL 33610	1948	NR 3-B	2,000	67
National U, San Diego, CA 92108	1971	Dr David Chigos 1-D	12,873	1,709
Nazareth Coll in Kalamazoo, Kalamazoo, MI 49001	1924	Dr Patrick B Smith 2-M	890	95
Nazareth Coll of Rochester, Rochester, NY 14610	1924	Dr Rose Marie Beston 1-M	2,811	222
Nebraska Wesleyan U, Lincoln, NE 68504	1887	Dr John W White Jr 2-B	1,347	118
Neumann Coll, Aston, PA 19014	1965	Sr M Margarella O'Neill 2-M	1,093	95
Newberry Coll, Newberry, SC 29108	1856	Dr John S Ammarell 2-B	606	54
New England Coll, Henniker, NH 03242	1946	William R O'Connell Jr 1-M	1,087	112
New England Conservatory of Music, Boston, MA 02115	1867	Laurence Lesser 1-M	725	178
New England Inst of Tech, Providence, RI 02907 (2)	1940	Dr Richard I Gouse 1-B	1,585	98
New Hampshire Coll, Manchester, NH 03104	1932	Mr Edward M Shapiro 1-M	3,373	79
New Jersey Inst of Tech, Newark, NJ 07102	1881	Dr Saul K Fenster 13-D	7,591	449
New Mexico Highlands U, Las Vegas, NM 87701	1893	Dr Gilbert Sanchez 5-M	2,063	125
New Mexico Inst of Mining and Tech, Socorro, NM 87801	1889	Dr Laurence H Lattman 5-D	1,211	101
New Mexico State U, Las Cruces, NM 88003	1888	Dr James E Halligan 5-D	13,718	591
New Sch for Social Research, Otis Art Inst, Los Angeles, CA 90057	1917	Jonathan F Fanton 1-M	743	168
New Sch for Social Rsrch, Parsons Sch of Design, New York, NY 10011	1896	Jonathan F Fanton 1-M	1,823	335
New Sch for Social Research, Senior Coll, New York, NY 10011	1919	NR 1-B	135	2,000
New York City Tech Coll of City U of NY, Brooklyn, NY 11201	1946	Dr Ursula C Schwerin 12-B	10,812	1,062
New York Inst of Tech, Old Westbury, NY 11568	1955	NR 1-M	12,709	1,149
New York Sch of Interior Design, New York, NY 10022	1916	Mr Arthur Satz 1-B	700	75
New York U, New York, NY 10012	1831	Dr John Brademas 1-D	32,266	5,140
Niagara U, Niagara University, NY 14109	1856	Rev Donald J Harrington, CM 1-M	3,180	250
Nicholls State U, Thibodaux, LA 70310	1948	Dr Donald J Ayo 5-M	6,950	262
Nichols Coll, Dudley, MA 01570	1815	Dr Lowell C Smith 1-M	1,349	69
Norfolk State U, Norfolk, VA 23504	1935	Dr Harrison B Wilson 5-M	6,868	483
North Adams State Coll, North Adams, MA 01247	1894	Dr Catherine Tisinger 5-M	2,500	190
North Carolina A&T State U, Greensboro, NC 27411	1891	Dr Edward B Fort 5-M	5,865	409
North Carolina Central U, Durham, NC 27707	1910	Dr Tyronza R Richmond 5-M	4,988	379
North Carolina State U at Raleigh, Raleigh, NC 27695	1862	Dr Bruce R Poulton 5-D	24,023	1,269
North Carolina Wesleyan Coll, Rocky Mount, NC 27801	1956	Dr Leslie H Garner Jr 2-B	1,333	47
North Central Bible Coll, Minneapolis, MN 55404	1930	Dr Don H Argue 2-B	1,031	46
North Central Coll, Naperville, IL 60566	1861	Mr Gael D Swing 2-M	2,108	123
North Dakota State U, Fargo, ND 58105	1890	Dr Laurel D Loftsgard 5-D	9,413	498
Northeastern Illinois U, Chicago, IL 60625	1961	Dr John Cownie 5-M	10,638	510
Northeastern State U, Tahlequah, OK 74464	1846	Dr W Roger Webb 5-D	7,043	350
Northeastern U, Boston, MA 02115	1898	Dr Kenneth Ryder 1-D	34,093	3,244
Northeast Louisiana U, Monroe, LA 71209	1931	Dr Dwight D Vines 5-D	10,227	502
Northeast Missouri State U, Kirksville, MO 63501	1867	Dr Charles J McClain 5-M	6,537	338
Northern Arizona U, Flagstaff, AZ 86011	1899	Dr Eugene M Hughes 5-D	13,208	608
Northern Illinois U, De Kalb, IL 60115	1895	Dr Clyde J Wingfield 5-D	24,311	1,244
Northern Kentucky U, Highland Heights, KY 41076	1968	Dr Leon E Boothe 5-D	8,699	480
Northern Michigan U, Marquette, MI 49855	1899	Dr James B Appleberry 5-M	7,852	323
Northern Montana Coll, Havre, MT 59501	1929	William C Merwin 5-M	1,729	120
Northern State Coll, Aberdeen, SD 57401	1901	Dr Terence Brown 5-M	2,889	118
North Georgia Coll, Dahlonega, GA 30597	1873	Dr John H Owen 5-M	2,028	108
North Park Coll, Chicago, IL 60625	1891	Dr David G Horner 2-B	954	112
Northrop U, Los Angeles, CA 90045	1942	Dr B J Shell 1-D	1,813	157
North Texas State U, Denton, TX 76203	1890	Dr Alfred F Hurley 5-D	21,271	835
Northwestern Coll, Orange City, IA 51041	1882	Dr James E Bultman 2-B	841	79
Northwestern Coll, Roseville, MN 55113	1902	Dr Donald Ericksen 2-B	967	90
Northwestern Oklahoma State U, Alva, OK 73717	1897	Dr Joe J Struckle 5-M	1,966	83
Northwestern State U of Louisiana, Natchitoches, LA 71497	1884	Dr Joseph J Orze 5-M	5,199	252
Northwestern U, Evanston, IL 60201	1851	Dr Arnold R Weber 1-D	15,951	1,598
Northwest Missouri State U, Maryville, MO 64468	1905	Dr Dean L Hubbard 5-M	4,986	236
Northwest Nazarene Coll, Nampa, ID 83651	1913	A Gordon Wetmore 2-M	1,075	88
Northwood Inst, Midland, MI 48640	1959	Dr David E Fry 1-B	1,850	70
Norwich U, Northfield, VT 05663	1819	Lt Gen W Russell Todd 1-M	2,425	218
Notre Dame Coll, Manchester, NH 03104	1950	Dr Carol J Descoteaux CSC 2-M	945	70
Notre Dame Coll of Ohio, Cleveland, OH 44121 (3)	1922	Sr Mary Marthe 2-B	802	67
Nova U, Fort Lauderdale, FL 33314	1964	Dr Abraham S Fischler 1-D	7,473	403
Nyack Coll, Nyack, NY 10960	1882	Dr David L Rambo 2-M	766	95
Oakland City Coll, Oakland City, IN 47660	1885	Dr James W Murray 2-M	646	57
Oakland U, Rochester, MI 48063	1957	Dr Joseph E Champagne 5-D	12,707	575
Oakwood Coll, Huntsville, AL 35896	1896	Dr Benjamin F Reaves 2-B	1,000	102
Oberlin Coll, Oberlin, OH 44074	1833	George H Langeler 1-M	2,845	230
Occidental Coll, Los Angeles, CA 90041	1887	Dr Richard C Gilman 1-M	1,672	140
Oglala Lakota Coll, Kyle, SD 57752	1970	Mr Elgin Badwound 12-B	737	93
Oglethorpe U, Atlanta, GA 30319	1835	Dr Manning M Pattillo Jr 1-M	1,012	55
Ohio Dominican Coll, Columbus, OH 43219	1911	Sr Mary Andrew Matesich 2-B	1,182	78
Ohio Northern U, Ada, OH 45810	1871	Dr De Bow Freed 2-D	2,367	188
Ohio State U, Columbus, OH 43210	1870	Dr Edward Jennings 5-D	53,880	3,200
Ohio State U–Lima Cmps, Lima, OH 45804	1960	Dr James S Biddle 5-B	1,154	39
Ohio State U–Mansfield Cmps, Mansfield, OH 44906	1958	Dr David W Kramer 5-B	1,141	39
Ohio State U–Marion Cmps, Marion, OH 43302	1957	Dr Francis E Hazard 5-B	983	23
Ohio State U–Newark Cmps, Newark, OH 43055	1957	Dr Julius S Greenstein 5-B	1,122	31
Ohio U, Athens, OH 45701	1804	Dr Charles J Ping 5-D	15,500	780
Ohio U–Belmont, St Clairsville, OH 43950	1957	Dr James W Newton 5-B	892	70
Ohio U–Chillicothe, Chillicothe, OH 45601	1946	Dr Ann Jones 5-B	1,162	77
Ohio U–Ironton, Ironton, OH 45638	1956	Mr Bill Dingus 5-B	1,427	80
Ohio U–Lancaster, Lancaster, OH 43130	1968	Dr Raymond Wilkes 5-M	1,595	113

Name, address	Year	Governing official, control, and highest degree offered		Enrollment	Faculty
Ohio U–Zanesville, Zanesville, OH 43701	1946	Dr Craig D Laubenthal	5-B	1,353	61
Ohio Wesleyan U, Delaware, OH 43015	1842	Dr David L Warren	2-B	1,494	154
Oklahoma Baptist U, Shawnee, OK 74801	1910	Dr Bob R Agee	2-B	1,638	134
Oklahoma Christian Coll, Oklahoma City, OK 73111	1950	Dr Terry Johnson	2-B	1,542	84
Oklahoma City U, Oklahoma City, OK 73106	1904	Dr Jerald C Walker	2-M	2,724	251
Oklahoma Panhandle State U, Goodwell, OK 73939	1909	Mr Thomas L Palmer	5-B	1,290	62
Oklahoma State U, Stillwater, OK 74078	1890	Dr Lawrence L Boger	5-D	21,176	1,135
Old Dominion U, Norfolk, VA 23508	1930	Dr Joseph M Marchello	5-D	15,463	713
Olivet Coll, Olivet, MI 49076	1844	Dr Donald A Morris	2-B	732	58
Olivet Nazarene U, Kankakee, IL 60901	1907	Dr Leslie Parrott	2-M	1,745	110
Oral Roberts U, Tulsa, OK 74171	1963	Mr G Oral Roberts	2-D	4,214	385
Oregon Health Sciences U, Portland, OR 97201	1974	Dr Leonard Laster	5-D	1,263	526
Oregon Inst of Tech, Klamath Falls, OR 97601	1947	Larry J Blake	5-B	2,995	191
Oregon State U, Corvallis, OR 97331	1868	Dr John V Byrne	5-D	15,199	1,739
Orlando Coll, Orlando, FL 32810	1918	Mrs Ovida B Kirby	1-B	746	40
Otterbein Coll, Westerville, OH 43081	1847	Dr C Brent DeVore	2-B	1,975	148
Ouachita Baptist U, Arkadelphia, AR 71923	1885	Dr Daniel R Grant	2-M	1,403	101
Our Lady of Holy Cross Coll, New Orleans, LA 70114	1916	Rev Thomas E Chambers	2-M	720	64
Our Lady of the Lake U of San Antonio, San Antonio, TX 78285	1911	Sr Elizabeth Anne Sueltenfuss	2-M	1,779	111
Pace U, New York, NY 10038	1906	Dr Edward J Mortola	1-D	8,910	588
Pace U, Pleasantville/Briarcliff Cmps, Pleasantville, NY 10570	1963	Dr Richard Podgorski	1-M	4,700	418
Pace U, White Plains Cmps, White Plains, NY 10603	1923	Dr Frank S Falcone	1-D	4,337	159
Pacific Lutheran U, Tacoma, WA 98447	1890	Dr William O Rieke	2-M	3,857	275
Pacific Union Coll, Angwin, CA 94508	1882	Dr D Malcolm Maxwell	2-M	1,499	117
Pacific U, Forest Grove, OR 97116	1849	Dr Robert F Duvall	1-D	1,275	160
Paine Coll, Augusta, GA 30910	1882	Dr William H Harris	2-B	790	59
Palm Beach Atlantic Coll, West Palm Beach, FL 33401	1968	Dr Claude Rhea	2-B	1,112	90
Pan American U, Edinburg, TX 78539	1927	Dr Miguel A Nevarez	5-M	9,166	387
Park Coll, Parkville, MO 64152	1875	Dr Donald J Breckon	2-M	655	53
Parks Coll of Saint Louis U, Cahokia, IL 62206	1927	Dr Paul A Whelan	2-B	1,067	57
Pembroke State U, Pembroke, NC 28372	1887	Dr Paul R Givens	5-M	2,481	147
Penna State U at Erie, The Behrend Coll, Erie, PA 16563	1926	Dr John M Lilley	13-M	2,378	143
Penna State U at Harrisburg—The Capital Coll, Middletown, PA 17057	1966	Dr Ruth Leventhal	13-D	2,888	153
Penna State U Univ Park Cmps, University Park, PA 16802	1855	Dr Bryce Jordan	13-D	35,261	1,846
Pepperdine U, Los Angeles, CA 90034	1937	Dr David Davenport	2-D	3,667	191
Pepperdine U, Malibu, CA 90265	1937	Dr David Davenport	2-D	3,163	271
Peru State Coll, Peru, NE 68421	1867	Dr Jerry L Gallentine	5-M	1,552	70
Pfeiffer Coll, Misenheimer, NC 28109	1885	Dr Cameron P West	2-B	851	80
Philadelphia Coll of Pharmacy and Science, Philadelphia, PA 19104	1821	Dr Allen Misher	1-D	1,390	382
Philadelphia Coll of Textiles and Science, Philadelphia, PA 19144	1884	Dr James P Gallagher	1-M	3,249	111
Philadelphia Colleges of the Arts, Philadelphia, PA 19102	1876	Peter Solmssen	1-M	1,383	374
Phillips U, Enid, OK 73702	1906	Dr Joe Jones	2-D	1,046	93
Pikeville Coll, Pikeville, KY 41501	1889	Mr William H Owens	2-B	753	41
Pittsburg State U, Pittsburg, KS 66762	1903	Dr Donald W Wilson	5-M	5,209	282
Pitzer Coll, Claremont, CA 91711	1963	Dr Frank L Ellsworth	1-B	770	78
Plymouth State Coll of the U System of NH, Plymouth, NH 03264	1871	Dr William J Farrell	5-M	3,400	189
Point Loma Nazarene Coll, San Diego, CA 92106	1902	Dr Jim L Bond	2-M	1,936	121
Point Park Coll, Pittsburgh, PA 15222	1900	Dr John V Hopkins	1-M	2,787	176
Polytechnic U, Brooklyn Cmps, Brooklyn, NY 11201	1854	Dr George Bugliarello	1-D	3,241	385
Polytechnic U, Farmingdale Cmps, Farmingdale, NY 11735	1854	Dr James J Conti	1-D	1,415	385
Pomona Coll, Claremont, CA 91711	1887	Dr David Alexander	1-B	1,350	136
Portland State U, Portland, OR 97207	1946	Dr Natale A Sicuro	5-D	15,640	671
Post Coll, Waterbury, CT 06708	1890	Dr N Patricia Yarborough	1-B	1,600	110
Prairie View A&M U, Prairie View, TX 77446	1878	Dr Percy A Pierre	5-M	4,499	267
Pratt Inst, Brooklyn, NY 11205	1887	Mr Richardson Pratt Jr	1-M	3,614	521
Presbyterian Coll, Clinton, SC 29325	1880	Dr Kenneth B Orr	2-B	1,043	82
Princeton U, Princeton, NJ 08544	1746	William G Bowen	1-D	6,199	864
Principia Coll, Elsah, IL 62028	1910	Dr John E G Boyman	2-B	673	67
Providence Coll, Providence, RI 02918	1917	Rev John F Cunningham, OP	2-D	5,621	244
Purdue U, West Lafayette, IN 47907	1869	Dr Steven C Beering	5-D	32,243	3,100
Purdue U Calumet, Hammond, IN 46323	1951	Mr Richard J Combs	5-M	7,210	389
Purdue U North Central, Westville, IN 46391	1967	Dr Dale W Alspaugh	5-M	2,783	162
Queens Coll, Charlotte, NC 28274 (4)	1857	Dr Billy O Wireman	2-M	1,342	113
Queens Coll of City U of NY, Flushing, NY 11367	1937	Dr Shirley S Kenny	12-M	16,135	1,399
Quincy Coll, Quincy, IL 62301	1860	Rev James Toal OFM	2-M	1,485	90
Quinnipiac Coll, Hamden, CT 06518	1929	Dr John L Lakey	1-M	2,769	309
Radford U, Radford, VA 24142	1910	Dr Donald N Dedmon	5-M	7,500	365
Ramapo Coll of New Jersey, Mahwah, NJ 07430	1969	Dr Robert A Scott	5-B	3,858	192
Randolph-Macon Coll, Ashland, VA 23005	1830	Dr Ladell Payne	2-B	1,013	102
Randolph-Macon Woman's Coll, Lynchburg, VA 24503 (3)	1891	Dr Linda Koch Lorimer	2-B	750	94
Reed Coll, Portland, OR 97202	1910	Mr Paul E Bragdon	1-M	1,243	113
Regis Coll, Denver, CO 80221	1877	Rev David M Clarke, SJ	2-M	3,780	95
Regis Coll, Weston, MA 02193 (3)	1927	Sr Therese Higgins	2-B	1,059	92
Rensselaer Polytechnic Inst, Troy, NY 12180	1824	Mr Stanley Landgraf	1-D	6,595	455
Rhode Island Coll, Providence, RI 02908	1854	Carol J Guardo	5-M	8,500	506
Rhode Island Sch of Design, Providence, RI 02903	1877	Dr Thomas F Schutte	1-M	1,870	190
Rhodes Coll, Memphis, TN 38112	1848	Dr James H Daughdrill Jr	2-B	1,226	133
Rice U, Houston, TX 77251	1891	Dr George Rupp	1-D	4,022	472
Rider Coll, Lawrenceville, NJ 08648	1865	Dr Frank N Elliott	1-M	5,027	285
Rio Grande Coll/Comm Coll, Rio Grande, OH 45674	1876	Dr Clodus R Smith	1-B	1,621	99
Ripon Coll, Ripon, WI 54971	1851	Dr William R Stott Jr	1-B	837	92
Rivier Coll, Nashua, NH 03060 (3)	1933	Sr Jeanne Perreault	2-M	2,264	189
Roanoke Coll, Salem, VA 24153	1842	Dr Norman D Fintel	2-B	1,541	91
Robert Morris Coll, Coraopolis, PA 15108	1921	Dr Charles L Sewall	1-M	5,429	214
Roberts Wesleyan Coll, Rochester, NY 14624	1866	Dr William C Crothers	2-B	703	92
Rochester Inst of Tech, Rochester, NY 14623	1829	Dr M Richard Rose	1-M	12,887	1,201
Rockford Coll, Rockford, IL 61108	1847	Dr Norman L Stewart	1-M	1,400	141
Rockhurst Coll, Kansas City, MO 64110	1910	Rev Robert F Weiss, SJ	2-M	3,198	177

Name, address	Year	Governing official, control, and highest degree offered		Enroll-ment	Faculty
Roger Williams Coll, Bristol, RI 02809	1948	Mr William H Rizzini	1-B	2,400	165
Rollins Coll, Winter Park, FL 32789	1885	Dr Thaddeus Seymour	1-M	1,790	141
Roosevelt U, Chicago, IL 60605	1945	Dr Rolf A Weil	1-M	6,385	497
Rosary Coll, River Forest, IL 60305	1848	Sr Jean Murray	2-M	1,536	129
Rose-Hulman Inst of Tech, Terre Haute, IN 47803 (1)	1874	Dr Samuel F Hulbert	1-M	1,320	96
Rush U, Chicago, IL 60612	1969	Dr Leo M Henikoff	1-D	1,149	825
Russell Sage Coll, Troy, NY 12180 (3)	1916	Dr William F Kahl	1-M	1,393	175
Rust Coll, Holly Springs, MS 38635	1866	Dr William A McMillan	2-B	915	60
Rutgers, State U of NJ, Camden Coll of Arts and Scis, Camden, NJ 08102	1950	Walter K Gordon	5-B	2,866	NR
Rutgers, State U of NJ, Coll of Engineering, New Brunswick, NJ 08903	1864	Dr Ellis H Dill	5-B	2,623	NR
Rutgers, State U of NJ, Coll of Nursing, Newark, NJ 07102 (4)	1956	Norman Samuels	5-B	512	39
Rutgers, State U of NJ, Coll of Pharmacy, New Brunswick, NJ 08903	1927	John Louis Colaizzi	5-B	737	NR
Rutgers, State U of NJ, Cook Coll, New Brunswick, NJ 08903	1921	Dr Stephen J Kleinschuster	5-B	3,088	NR
Rutgers, State U of NJ, Douglass Coll, New Brunswick, NJ 08903 (3)	1918	Dr Mary S Hartman	5-B	3,506	NR
Rutgers, State U of NJ, Livingston Coll, New Brunswick, NJ 08903	1969	Dr W Robert Jenkins	5-B	3,407	NR
Rutgers, State U of NJ, Mason Gross Sch of Arts, New Brunswick, NJ 08903	1976	John Bettenbender	5-M	415	NR
Rutgers, State U of NJ, Newark Coll of Arts and Scis, Newark, NJ 07102	1946	Norman Samuels	5-B	3,802	NR
Rutgers, State U of NJ, Rutgers Coll, New Brunswick, NJ 08903	1766	NR	5-B	9,116	NR
Rutgers, State U of NJ, U Coll–Camden, Camden, NJ 08102	1950	NR	5-B	986	NR
Rutgers, State U of NJ, U Coll–Newark, Newark, NJ 07102	1934	Norman Samuels	5-B	1,877	NR
Rutgers, State U of NJ, U Coll–New Brunswick, New Brunswick, NJ 08903	1934	Dr Barbara E Kovach	5-B	3,128	NR
Sacred Heart U, Bridgeport, CT 06606	1963	Dr Robert A Preston	2-M	4,831	337
Saginaw Valley State Coll, University Center, MI 48710	1963	Dr Jack M Ryder	5-M	5,377	267
St Ambrose Coll, Davenport, IA 52803	1882	Dr William J Bakrow	2-M	2,198	186
St Andrews Presbyterian Coll, Laurinburg, NC 28352	1958	Mr Alvin P Perkinson	2-B	747	71
Saint Anselm Coll, Manchester, NH 03102	1889	Br Joachim W Froehlich	2-B	1,761	160
Saint Augustine's Coll, Raleigh, NC 27611	1867	Dr Prezell R Robinson	2-B	1,701	75
St Bonaventure U, St Bonaventure, NY 14778	1854	Very Rev Mathias Doyle	2-M	2,800	213
St Cloud State U, St Cloud, MN 56301	1869	Dr Brendan McDonald	5-M	14,220	690
St Edward's U, Austin, TX 78704	1885	Dr Patricia Hayes	2-M	2,536	134
Saint Francis Coll, Fort Wayne, IN 46808	1890	Sr M JoEllen Scheetz	2-M	1,223	90
St Francis Coll, Brooklyn Heights, NY 11201	1858	Br Donald Sullivan, OSF	1-B	2,155	130
Saint Francis Coll, Loretto, PA 15940	1847	Rev Christian R Oravec	2-M	1,746	89
St John Fisher Coll, Rochester, NY 14618	1948	Rev Patrick O Braden	1-M	1,957	199
Saint John's U, Collegeville, MN 56321 (1)	1857	Fr Hilary Thimmesh, OSB	2-M	1,952	154
St John's U, Jamaica, NY 11439	1870	Rev Joseph T Cahill, CM	2-D	19,211	908
Saint Joseph Coll, West Hartford, CT 06117 (3)	1932	Dr M Paton Ryan, RSM	2-M	1,383	137
Saint Joseph's Coll, Rensselaer, IN 47978	1889	Fr Charles Banet	2-M	917	75
St Joseph's Coll, Brooklyn, NY 11205	1916	Sr George A O'Connor	1-B	872	98
St Joseph's Coll, Suffolk Cmps, Patchogue, NY 11772	1916	Sr George Aquin O'Connor	1-B	1,470	127
Saint Joseph's U, Philadelphia, PA 19131	1851	Rev Nicholas S Rashford, SJ	2-M	5,715	336
St Lawrence U, Canton, NY 13617	1856	Dr Patti McGill Peterson	1-M	2,349	183
Saint Leo Coll, Saint Leo, FL 33574	1889	Rev Monsignor Frank M Mouch	2-B	1,086	94
St Louis Coll of Pharmacy, St Louis, MO 63110	1864	Dr Sumner M Robinson	1-D	757	54
Saint Louis U, St Louis, MO 63103	1818	Rev Thomas R Fitzgerald	2-D	9,869	2,504
Saint Martin's Coll, Lacey, WA 98503	1895	Dr David Spangler	2-M	614	61
Saint Mary Coll, Leavenworth, KS 66048 (4)	1923	Sr M Janet McGilley	2-B	882	77
Saint Mary of the Plains Coll, Dodge City, KS 67801	1952	Dr Michael J McCarthy	2-B	724	87
Saint Mary-of-the-Woods Coll, Saint Mary-of-the-Woods, IN 47876 (3)	1840	Barbara Doherty, SP	2-M	850	85
Saint Mary's Coll, Notre Dame, IN 46556 (3)	1844	Dr William A Hickey	2-B	1,736	173
Saint Mary's Coll, Winona, MN 55987	1912	Br Louis DeThomasis, FSC	2-M	1,543	102
Saint Mary's Coll of California, Moraga, CA 94575	1863	Br Mel Anderson	2-M	3,276	176
St Mary's Coll of Maryland, St Mary's City, MD 20686	1839	Dr Edward T Lewis	5-B	1,396	111
St Mary's U of San Antonio, San Antonio, TX 78284	1852	Rev John A Leies, SM	2-D	3,560	209
Saint Michael's Coll, Winooski, VT 05404	1904	Dr Paul J Reiss	2-M	2,130	140
St Norbert Coll, De Pere, WI 54115	1898	Dr Thomas A Manion	2-B	1,734	140
St Olaf Coll, Northfield, MN 55057	1874	Dr Melvin George	2-B	3,094	330
Saint Paul's Coll, Lawrenceville, VA 23868	1888	Dr Marvin B Scott	2-B	736	50
Saint Peter's Coll, Jersey City, NJ 07306	1872	Rev Edward Glynn, SJ	2-M	2,280	315
St Thomas Aquinas Coll, Sparkill, NY 10976	1958	Dr Donald T McNelis	1-B	1,605	67
St Thomas U, Miami, FL 33054	1961	Rev Patrick H O'Neill	2-M	3,200	191
Saint Vincent Coll, Latrobe, PA 15650	1846	Rev John F Murtha, OSB	2-B	1,250	90
Saint Xavier Coll, Chicago, IL 60655	1847	R Champagne	2-M	2,566	160
Salem Coll, Salem, WV 26426	1888	Dr Ronald E Ohl	1-M	900	69
Salem State Coll, Salem, MA 01970	1854	Dr William E Mahaney	5-M	8,654	325
Salisbury State Coll, Salisbury, MD 21801	1925	Dr Thomas A Bellavance	5-M	4,720	243
Salve Regina–The Newport Coll, Newport, RI 02840	1934	Sr M Lucille McKillop	2-M	2,012	216
Samford U, Birmingham, AL 35229	1841	Dr Thomas E Corts	2-M	3,802	260
Sam Houston State U, Huntsville, TX 77341	1879	Dr Elliott T Bowers	5-D	10,486	369
San Diego State U, San Diego, CA 92182	1897	Dr Thomas B Day	5-D	34,677	2,200
San Francisco Art Inst, San Francisco, CA 94133	1871	Dr William O Barrett	1-M	659	63
San Francisco State U, San Francisco, CA 94132	1899	Dr Chia-Wei Woo	5-D	25,871	1,679
Sangamon State U, Springfield, IL 62794	1969	Dr Durward Long	5-M	3,485	221
San Jose State U, San Jose, CA 95192	1857	Dr Gail Fullerton	5-M	26,507	1,761
Santa Clara U, Santa Clara, CA 95053	1851	Rev William J Rewak, SJ	2-D	7,843	479
Sarah Lawrence Coll, Bronxville, NY 10708	1926	Dr Alice Stone Ilchman	1-M	1,083	132
Savannah Coll of Art and Design, Savannah, GA 31401	1976	Richard G Rowan	1-M	1,130	64
Savannah State Coll, Savannah, GA 31404	1890	Dr Wendell G Rayburn	5-M	1,900	150
Sch for Lifelong Learning of the U System of NH, Durham, NH 03824	1972	Dr Alvin L Hall	12-B	1,500	320
Sch of the Art Inst of Chicago, Chicago, IL 60603	1866	Mr Anthony Jones	1-M	1,597	211
Sch of the Museum of Fine Arts, Boston, MA 02115	1948	Bruce K MacDonald	1-M	664	93
Sch of the Ozarks, Point Lookout, MO 65726	1906	Dr Stephen G Jennings	1-B	1,241	93

Name, address	Year	Governing official, control, and highest degree offered		Enroll-ment	Faculty
Sch of Visual Arts, New York, NY 10010	1947	David Rhodes	3-M	2,394	696
Scripps Coll, Claremont, CA 91711 (3)	1926	Dr John H Chandler	1-B	600	80
Seattle Pacific U, Seattle, WA 98119	1891	Rev Msgr John J Strynkowski	2-M	2,969	205
Seattle U, Seattle, WA 98122	1891	Rev William J Sullivan, SJ	2-D	4,370	240
Seton Hall U, South Orange, NJ 07079	1856	Msgr John J Petillo	2-D	7,140	615
Seton Hill Coll, Greensburg, PA 15601 (3)	1882	Dr JoAnne Boyle	2-B	865	90
Shaw U, Raleigh, NC 27611	1865	Dr Stanley H Smith	2-B	1,402	111
Shenandoah Coll and Conservatory, Winchester, VA 22601	1875	Dr James A Davis	2-M	902	131
Shepherd Coll, Shepherdstown, WV 25443	1871	Dr James A Butcher	5-B	3,853	182
Shippensburg U of Pennsylvania, Shippensburg, PA 17257	1871	Dr Anthony F Ceddia	5-M	6,358	337
Shorter Coll, Rome, GA 30161	1873	Dr James D Jordan	2-B	736	63
Siena Coll, Loudonville, NY 12211	1937	Fr Hugh F Hines	2-B	3,617	233
Siena Heights Coll, Adrian, MI 49221	1919	Sr Cathleen Real CHM	2-M	1,550	116
Simmons Coll, Boston, MA 02115 (3)	1899	William J Holmes	1-D	3,051	280
Simpson Coll, Indianola, IA 50125	1860	Dr Robert E McBride	2-B	1,395	72
Sioux Falls Coll, Sioux Falls, SD 57105	1883	Dr Owen P Halleen	2-M	854	53
Skidmore Coll, Saratoga Springs, NY 12866	1911	Dr Joseph C Palamountain Jr	1-B	2,158	212
Slippery Rock U of Pennsylvania, Slippery Rock, PA 16057	1889	Dr Robert Aebersold	5-M	6,599	355
Smith Coll, Northampton, MA 01063 (3)	1871	Mrs Mary Maples Dunn	1-D	2,698	295
Sonoma State U, Rohnert Park, CA 94928	1961	Dr David W Benson	5-M	5,739	356
South Carolina State Coll, Orangeburg, SC 29117	1896	Dr Albert E Smith	5-D	3,855	228
South Dakota Sch of Mines and Tech, Rapid City, SD 57701	1885	Dr Richard J Gowen	5-D	2,060	130
South Dakota State U, Brookings, SD 57007	1881	Dr Robert T Wagner	5-D	6,765	338
Southeastern Coll of the Assemblies of God, Lakeland, FL 33801	1935	Dr James Hennesy	2-B	1,096	52
Southeastern Louisiana U, Hammond, LA 70402	1925	NR	5-M	7,914	294
Southeastern Massachusetts U, North Dartmouth, MA 02747	1895	Dr John R Brazil	5-M	5,816	390
Southeastern Oklahoma State U, Durant, OK 74701	1909	NR	5-M	4,269	166
Southeastern U, Washington, DC 20024	1879	Dr W Robert Higgins	1-M	1,038	103
Southeast Missouri State U, Cape Girardeau, MO 63701	1873	Dr Bill W Stacy	5-M	8,856	475
Southern Arkansas U, Magnolia, AR 71753	1909	Dr Harold T Brinson	5-M	2,065	118
Southern California Coll, Costa Mesa, CA 92626	1920	Mr Wayne E Kraiss	2-M	898	80
Southern Coll of Seventh-Day Adventists, Collegedale, TN 37315	1892	Dr Donald R Sahly	2-B	1,327	125
Southern Coll of Tech, Marietta, GA 30060	1948	Dr Stephen R Cheshier	5-M	3,795	183
Southern Connecticut State U, New Haven, CT 06515	1893	Mr Michael J Adanti	5-M	11,297	699
Southern Illinois U at Carbondale, Carbondale, IL 62901	1869	Dr John C Guyon	5-D	23,261	1,327
Southern Illinois U at Edwardsville, Edwardsville, IL 62026	1957	Earl E Lazerson	5-D	10,843	726
Southern Methodist U, Dallas, TX 75275	1911	Dr A Kenneth Pye	1-D	9,019	650
Southern Nazarene U, Bethany, OK 73008	1899	Dr Ponder W Gilliland	2-M	1,296	109
Southern Oregon State Coll, Ashland, OR 97520	1926	Dr Joseph Cox	5-M	4,552	240
Southern U and A&M Coll, Baton Rouge, LA 70813	1880	Dr Wesley C McClure	5-M	9,109	486
Southern U at New Orleans, New Orleans, LA 70126	1959	Dr Dolores Spikes	5-M	3,100	180
Southern Utah State Coll, Cedar City, UT 84720	1897	Dr Gerald R Sherratt	5-M	3,088	115
Southwest Baptist U, Bolivar, MO 65613	1878	Dr James L Sells	2-B	2,331	121
Southwestern Adventist Coll, Keene, TX 76059	1894	Dr Marvin E Anderson	2-B	795	65
Southwestern Assemblies of God Coll, Waxahachie, TX 75165	1927	Dr J Paul Savell	2-B	701	32
Southwestern Coll, Winfield, KS 67156	1885	Dr Bruce Blake	2-B	620	44
Southwestern Oklahoma State U, Weatherford, OK 73096	1903	Dr Leonard G Campbell	5-M	5,116	211
Southwestern U, Georgetown, TX 78626	1840	Dr Roy B Shilling Jr	2-B	1,119	106
Southwest Missouri State U, Springfield, MO 65804	1905	Dr Marshall Gordon	5-M	15,894	760
Southwest State U, Marshall, MN 56258	1960	Dr Douglas M Treadway	5-D	2,400	100
Southwest Texas State U, San Marcos, TX 78666	1899	Mr Robert L Hardesty	5-M	15,770	735
Spalding U, Louisville, KY 40203	1814	Sr Eileen Egan	2-D	1,175	116
Spelman Coll, Atlanta, GA 30314 (3)	1881	Ms Johnetta Cole	1-B	1,757	145
Spring Arbor Coll, Spring Arbor, MI 49283	1873	Dr Kenneth H Coffman	2-B	746	88
Springfield Coll, Springfield, MA 01109	1885	Dr Frank S Falcone	1-D	2,463	177
Spring Garden Coll, Philadelphia, PA 19119	1851	Dr Daniel N DeLucca	1-B	1,558	110
Spring Hill Coll, Mobile, AL 36608	1830	Very Rev Paul S Tipton, SJ	2-M	1,184	78
Stanford U, Stanford, CA 94305	1891	Dr James Rosse	1-D	13,272	1,315
State U of NY at Albany, Albany, NY 12222	1844	Vincent I O'Leary	5-D	13,924	926
State U of NY at Binghamton, Binghamton, NY 13901	1946	Mr Clifford D Clark	5-D	12,205	735
State U of NY at Buffalo, Buffalo, NY 14260	1846	Dr Steven B Sample	5-D	24,022	1,784
State U of NY at Stony Brook, Stony Brook, NY 11794	1957	Dr John H Marburger III	5-D	14,705	1,446
State U of NY Coll at Brockport, Brockport, NY 14420	1867	Dr John Van de Wetering	5-M	7,724	249
State U of NY Coll at Buffalo, Buffalo, NY 14222	1871	Dr D Bruce Johnstone	5-M	12,008	557
State U of NY Coll at Cortland, Cortland, NY 13045	1868	Dr James M Clark	5-M	6,491	371
State U of NY Coll at Fredonia, Fredonia, NY 14063	1867	Dr Donald A MacPhee	5-M	4,926	238
State U of NY Coll at Geneseo, Geneseo, NY 14454	1867	Dr Edward B Jakubauskas	5-M	5,190	284
State U of NY Coll at New Paltz, New Paltz, NY 12561	1828	Alice Chandler	5-M	7,568	466
State U of NY Coll at Old Westbury, Old Westbury, NY 11568	1968	Ambassador Ulric Haynes Jr	5-B	3,639	150
State U of NY Coll at Oneonta, Oneonta, NY 13820	1889	Dr Clifford J Craven	5-M	5,610	338
State U of NY Coll at Oswego, Oswego, NY 13126	1861	Dr Virginia L Radley	5-M	8,406	408
State U of NY Coll at Plattsburgh, Plattsburgh, NY 12901	1889	Dr Joseph C Burke	5-M	5,523	369
State U of NY Coll at Potsdam, Potsdam, NY 13676	1816	Dr Humphrey Tonkin	5-M	4,277	243
State U of NY Coll at Purchase, Purchase, NY 10577	1967	Dr Sheldon Grebstein	5-M	2,246	206
State U of NY Coll of A&T at Cobleskill, Cobleskill, NY 12043	1916	Dr Neal V Robbins	5-B	2,611	149
State U of NY Coll of Envir Sci & Forestry, Syracuse, NY 13210	1911	Dr Ross S Whaley	5-D	1,171	125
State U of NY Coll of Tech at Farmingdale, Farmingdale, NY 11735	1912	Dr Frank A Cipriani	5-B	11,650	561
State U of NY Coll of Tech at Utica/Rome, Utica, NY 13504	1973	Dr Peter J Cayan	5-M	2,601	163
State U of NY Empire State Coll, Saratoga Springs, NY 12866	1971	NR	5-M	5,010	338
State U of NY Health Science Ctr at Brooklyn, Brooklyn, NY 11203	1858	Dr Donald J Scherl	5-D	1,350	43
State U of NY Health Science Ctr at Syracuse, Syracuse, NY 13210	1950	Dr John Bernard Henry	5-D	926	233
State U of NY Maritime Coll, Bronx, NY 10465	1874	Rear Adm Floyd H Miller	5-M	922	70
State U of North Dakota–Mayville, Mayville, ND 58257	1889	Dr James A Schobel	5-B	761	56
Stephen F Austin State U, Nacogdoches, TX 75962	1923	Dr William R Johnson	5-D	12,350	584

Name, address	Year	Governing official, control, and highest degree offered		Enrollment	Faculty
Stephens Coll, Columbia, MO 65215 (3)	1833	Dr Patsy H Sampson	1-B	883	109
Stetson U, DeLand, FL 32720	1883	Dr H Douglas Lee	2-M	2,832	164
Stevens Inst of Tech, Hoboken, NJ 07030	1870	Dr Kenneth C Rogers	1-D	3,358	240
Stillman Coll, Tuscaloosa, AL 35403	1876	Dr Cordell Wynn	2-B	791	58
Stockton State Coll, Pomona, NJ 08240	1971	Ms Vera King Farris	5-B	5,071	181
Stonehill Coll, North Easton, MA 02357	1948	Rev Bartley MacPhaidin	2-B	1,834	153
Strayer Coll, Washington, DC 20005	1898	Charles E Palmer Jr	3-B	1,176	68
Suffolk U, Boston, MA 02114	1906	Dr Daniel H Perlman	1-M	5,778	372
Sul Ross State U, Alpine, TX 79832	1917	Dr Jack W Humphries	5-M	2,313	118
Susquehanna U, Selinsgrove, PA 17870	1858	Dr Joel L Cunningham	2-B	1,479	137
Swarthmore Coll, Swarthmore, PA 19081	1864	Dr David W Fraser	1-B	1,327	150
Sweet Briar Coll, Sweet Briar, VA 24595 (3)	1901	Dr Nenah E Fry	1-B	663	90
Syracuse U, Syracuse, NY 13244	1870	Dr Melvin A Eggers	1-D	18,353	1,379
Tampa Coll, Tampa, FL 33614	1890	Mr Donald C Jones	1-M	1,505	65
Tarkio Coll, Tarkio, MO 64491	1883	Dr Roy McIntosh	2-B	700	40
Tarleton State U, Stephenville, TX 76402	1899	Dr Barry B Thompson	5-M	4,800	177
Taylor U, Upland, IN 46989	1846	Dr Jay L Kesler	1-B	1,492	105
Temple U, Philadelphia, PA 19122	1884	Mr Peter J Liacouras	13-D	26,447	2,564
Temple U, Ambler Cmps, Ambler, PA 19002	1910	Mr James Blackhurst	13-D	3,838	363
Tennessee State U, Nashville, TN 37203	1912	Dr Otis Floyd	5-D	6,745	444
Tennessee Tech U, Cookeville, TN 38505	1915	Dr Wallace S Prescott	5-D	7,628	487
Tennessee Temple U, Chattanooga, TN 37404	1946	Dr Lee E Roberson	2-D	1,800	114
Texas A&I U, Kingsville, TX 78363	1925	Dr Steven Altman	5-D	5,012	234
Texas A&M U, College Station, TX 77843	1876	Dr Frank E Vandiver	5-D	36,570	2,170
Texas Christian U, Fort Worth, TX 76129	1873	Dr William Tucker	2-D	6,916	390
Texas Lutheran Coll, Seguin, TX 78155	1891	Dr Charles H Oestreich	2-B	1,034	87
Texas Southern U, Houston, TX 77004	1947	NR	5-D	7,246	388
Texas Tech U, Lubbock, TX 79409	1923	Lauro F Cavazos	5-D	23,589	1,444
Texas Wesleyan Coll, Fort Worth, TX 76105	1891	Dr Jerry G Bawcom	2-M	1,497	113
Texas Woman's U, Denton, TX 76204 (4)	1901	Dr Shirley Sears Chater	5-D	7,966	480
Thiel Coll, Greenville, PA 16125	1866	Dr Louis T Almen	2-B	916	87
Thomas A Edison State Coll, Trenton, NJ 08625	1972	George A Pruitt	5-B	5,034	0
Thomas Coll, Waterville, ME 04901	1894	Cyril M Joly Jr	1-M	832	45
Thomas Jefferson U, Philadelphia, PA 19107	1824	Dr Lewis W Bluemle Jr	1-D	1,636	73
Thomas More Coll, Crestview Hills, KY 41017	1921	Mr Michael Bromberg	2-B	1,120	116
Tiffin U, Tiffin, OH 44883	1888	Mr George Kidd Jr	1-B	704	40
Toccoa Falls Coll, Toccoa Falls, GA 30598	1907	Dr Paul L Alford	2-B	670	42
Tougaloo Coll, Tougaloo, MS 39174	1869	Dr J Herman Blake	2-B	739	70
Touro Coll, New York, NY 10036	1971	Dr Bernard Lander	1-D	4,901	270
Towson State U, Towson, MD 21204	1866	Dr Hoke L Smith	5-M	15,410	880
Transylvania U, Lexington, KY 40508	1780	Dr Charles L Shearer	2-B	960	89
Trenton State Coll, Trenton, NJ 08650	1855	Dr Harold Eickhoff	5-M	8,179	486
Trevecca Nazarene Coll, Nashville, TN 37203	1901	Dr Homer J Adams	2-M	1,406	104
Trinity Coll, Hartford, CT 06106	1823	James F English Jr	1-M	2,105	179
Trinity Coll, Washington, DC 20017 (3)	1897	NR	2-M	950	90
Trinity Coll, Deerfield, IL 60015	1897	Dr Kenneth M Meyer	2-B	606	56
Trinity Coll, Burlington, VT 05401 (4)	1925	Sr Janice Ryan	2-B	963	70
Trinity U, San Antonio, TX 78284	1869	Dr Ronald K Calgaard	2-M	2,700	256
Tri-State U, Angola, IN 46703	1884	Dr Beaumont Davison	1-B	1,043	78
Troy State U, Troy, AL 36082	1887	Dr Ralph W Adams	5-M	3,612	204
Troy State U at Dothan, Dothan, AL 36303	1962	Mr Thomas Harrison	5-M	1,634	67
Troy State U in Montgomery, Montgomery, AL 36195	1957	Dr Millard E Elrod	5-M	2,289	132
Tufts U, Medford, MA 02155	1852	Dr Jean Mayer	1-D	7,428	507
Tulane U, New Orleans, LA 70118	1834	Dr Eamon M Kelly	1-D	10,302	1,183
Tuskegee U, Tuskegee, AL 36088	1881	Dr Benjamin F Payton	1-D	3,300	337
Union Coll, Barbourville, KY 40906	1879	Dr Jack C Phillips	2-M	1,006	71
Union Coll, Lincoln, NE 68506	1891	John Wagner	2-B	677	77
Union Coll, Schenectady, NY 12308	1795	Dr John S Morris	1-D	2,500	197
Union for Experimenting Colleges and Universities, Cincinnati, OH 45202	1964	NR	1-D	730	91
Union U, Jackson, TN 38305	1825	Dr Robert E Craig	2-B	1,546	92
United States Air Force Acad, Colorado Springs, CO 80840	1954	LT Gen Winfield W Scott Jr	4-B	4,496	574
United States Coast Guard Acad, New London, CT 06320	1876	R Adm Richard P Cueroni	4-B	781	108
United States International U, San Diego, CA 92131	1952	Dr William C Rust	1-D	3,236	180
United States Merchant Marine Acad, Kings Point, NY 11024	1943	NR	4-B	957	76
United States Military Acad, West Point, NY 10996	1802	Lt Gen W W Scott Jr	4-B	4,524	524
United States Naval Acad, Annapolis, MD 21402	1845	R Adm Ronald F Marryott	4-B	4,500	600
Universidad del Turabo, Gurabo, PR 00658	1972	NR	1-M	7,390	180
Universidad Metropolitana, Rio Piedras, PR 00928	1980	Leonides Santos-Vargas	1-B	5,200	265
Universidad Politécnica de Puerto Rico, Hato Rey, PR 00918	1974	Ernesto Vazquez-Torres	1-B	1,895	101
U of Akron, Akron, OH 44325	1870	William V Muse	5-D	25,944	1,456
U of Alabama, University, AL 35407	1831	Dr Joab L Thomas	5-D	15,984	936
U of Alabama at Birmingham, Birmingham, AL 35294	1966	Dr Charles A McCallum	5-D	14,248	1,683
U of Alabama in Huntsville, Huntsville, AL 35899	1950	Dr John C Wright	5-D	6,194	439
U of Alaska, Anchorage, Anchorage, AK 99508	1976	Dr Marv Looney	5-M	4,330	296
U of Alaska, Fairbanks, Fairbanks, AK 99775	1917	Dr Patrick J O'Rourke	5-D	4,610	423
U of Alaska–Juneau, Juneau, AK 99801	1972	Dr Marshall Lind	5-M	2,082	124
U of Arizona, Tucson, AZ 85721	1885	Dr Henry Koffler	5-D	31,079	1,667
U of Arkansas, Fayetteville, AR 72701	1871	Dr Daniel E Ferritor	5-D	13,976	846
U of Arkansas at Little Rock, Little Rock, AR 72204	1927	Dr James H Young	5-M	10,453	664
U of Arkansas at Monticello, Monticello, AR 71655	1909	Dr Fred J Taylor	5-B	1,845	107
U of Arkansas at Pine Bluff, Pine Bluff, AR 71601	1873	Dr Johnny B Johnson	5-B	2,917	161
U of Arkansas for Medical Sciences, Little Rock, AR 72205	1879	Dr Harry P Ward	5-D	1,331	603
U of Baltimore, Baltimore, MD 21201	1925	Dr H Mebane Turner	5-M	5,020	268
U of Bridgeport, Bridgeport, CT 06601	1927	Dr Janet D Greenwood	1-D	5,615	520
U of California, Berkeley, Berkeley, CA 94720	1868	Ira Michael Heyman	5-D	31,454	3,800
U of California, Davis, Davis, CA 95616	1906	Dr Theodore L Hullar	5-D	19,809	1,421
U of California, Irvine, Irvine, CA 92717	1965	Dr Jack W Peltason	5-D	14,532	910
U of California, Los Angeles, Los Angeles, CA 90024	1919	Charles E Young	5-D	34,423	3,200
U of California, Riverside, Riverside, CA 92521	1954	Dr Rosemary S J Schraer	5-D	5,726	560
U of California, San Diego, La Jolla, CA 92093	1964	Dr Richard C Atkinson	5-D	15,940	1,005
U of California, San Francisco, San Francisco, CA 94143	1864	Dr Francis A Sooy	5-D	3,608	2,200
U of California, Santa Barbara, Santa Barbara, CA 93106	1891	Dr Barbara S Uehling	5-D	18,005	1,400
U of California, Santa Cruz, Santa Cruz, CA 95064	1965	Dr Robert B Stevens	5-D	8,593	460

Name, address	Year	Governing official, control, and highest degree offered		Enroll-ment	Faculty
U of Central Arkansas, Conway, AR 72032	1907	Dr Jefferson D Farris Jr	5-M	5,900	343
U of Central Florida, Orlando, FL 32816	1963	Dr Trevor Colbourn	5-D	16,444	836
U of Charleston, Charleston, WV 25304	1888	Dr Richard Breslin	1-M	1,400	133
U of Chicago, Chicago, IL 60637	1890	Hanna Holborn Gray	1-D	8,537	1,121
U of Cincinnati, Cincinnati, OH 45221	1819	Dr Joseph A Steger	5-D	35,322	3,086
U of Colorado at Boulder, Boulder, CO 80309	1876	William Baughn	5-D	23,126	1,152
U of Colorado at Colorado Springs, Colorado Springs, CO 80933	1965	Dr Dwayne C Nuzum	5-M	4,042	363
U of Colorado at Denver, Denver, CO 80202	1912	Dr Glendon Drake	5-D	10,601	349
U of Colorado Health Sciences Ctr, Denver, CO 80262	1883	Dr Bernard W Nelson	5-D	1,454	3,234
U of Connecticut, Storrs, CT 06268	1881	Dr John T Casteen III	5-D	23,063	1,244
U of Connecticut at Hartford, West Hartford, CT 06117	1946	Dr Russell F Farnen	5-B	849	61
U of Connecticut at Stamford, Stamford, CT 06903	1951	Ms Yakira H Frank	5-M	1,175	80
U of Dallas, Irving, TX 75062	1956	Dr Robert F Sasseen	2-D	2,540	191
U of Dayton, Dayton, OH 45469	1850	Br Raymond L Fitz, SM	2-D	10,810	720
U of Delaware, Newark, DE 19716	1743	Dr Russel C Jones	13-D	15,695	914
U of Denver, Denver, CO 80208	1864	Dr Dwight Smith	1-D	7,044	387
U of Detroit, Detroit, MI 48221	1877	Rev Robert A Mitchell, SJ	2-D	6,139	430
U of Dubuque, Dubuque, IA 52001	1852	Dr Walter F Peterson	2-D	1,262	75
U of Evansville, Evansville, IN 47722	1854	Dr James S Vinson	2-M	3,667	306
U of Florida, Gainesville, FL 32611	1853	Mr Marshall M Criser	5-D	35,094	2,784
U of Georgia, Athens, GA 30602	1785	Dr Charles B Knapp	5-D	25,698	1,788
U of Guam, Mangilao, GU 96913	1952	Dr Jose Q Cruz	8-M	3,075	210
U of Hartford, West Hartford, CT 06117	1877	Mr Stephen J Trachtenberg	1-D	7,443	598
U of Hawaii at Hilo, Hilo, HI 96720	1970	Dr Edward J Kormondy	5-B	3,300	264
U of Hawaii at Manoa, Honolulu, HI 96822	1907	Albert J Simone	5-D	18,977	1,850
U of Health Sciences/Chicago Medical Sch, North Chicago, IL 60064	1912	Dr Jerome A Gold	1-D	835	284
U of Houston, Houston, TX 77004	1927	Dr Wilbur I Meier Jr	5-D	30,000	2,100
U of Houston–Clear Lake, Houston, TX 77058	1971	Dr Thomas M Stauffer	5-M	6,691	321
U of Houston–Downtown, Houston, TX 77002	1974	NR	5-B	7,255	298
U of Houston–Victoria, Victoria, TX 77901	1973	Dr Glenn A Goerke	5-M	962	NR
U of Idaho, Moscow, ID 83843	1889	Dr Richard D Gibb	5-D	8,586	598
U of Illinois at Chicago, Chicago, IL 60680	1965	Dr Donald N Langenberg	5-D	24,560	2,467
U of Illinois at Urbana-Champaign, Urbana, IL 61801	1867	Dr Thomas E Everhart	5-D	36,330	2,692
U of Indianapolis, Indianapolis, IN 46227	1902	Dr Gene E Sease	2-M	3,039	347
U of Iowa, Iowa City, IA 52242	1847	NR	5-D	29,504	1,800
U of Kansas, Lawrence, KS 66045	1866	Gene A Budig	5-D	25,822	1,900
U of Kansas Medical Ctr, Kansas City, KS 66103	1905	D Kay Clawson, MD	5-D	2,597	706
U of Kentucky, Lexington, KY 40506	1865	Dr David P Roselle	5-D	20,795	1,855
U of La Verne, La Verne, CA 91750	1891	Dr Stephen Morgan	1-D	4,783	639
U of Louisville, Louisville, KY 40292	1798	Dr Donald C Swain	5-D	20,710	1,500
U of Lowell, Lowell, MA 01854	1894	Dr William T Hogan	5-D	14,630	830
U of Maine, Orono, ME 04469	1865	Dr Arthur M Johnson	5-D	10,954	701
U of Maine at Augusta, Augusta, ME 04330	1965	Dr George P Connick	5-B	1,580	238
U of Maine at Farmington, Farmington, ME 04938	1864	Dr Judith A Sturnick	5-B	2,261	147
U of Maine at Fort Kent, Fort Kent, ME 04743	1878	Dr Richard J Spath	5-B	725	52
U of Maine at Machias, Machias, ME 04654	1909	Mr Frederic A Reynolds	5-B	886	42
U of Maine at Presque Isle, Presque Isle, ME 04769	1903	Dr Constance H Carlson	5-B	1,351	90
U of Mary, Bismarck, ND 58501	1959	Sr Thomas Welder	2-M	1,173	95
U of Mary Hardin Baylor, Belton, TX 76513	1845	Dr Bobby E Parker	2-M	1,348	75
U of Maryland at Baltimore, Baltimore, MD 21201	1807	Dr Edward N Brandt Jr	5-D	2,634	1,103
U of Maryland Baltimore County, Catonsville, MD 21228	1963	Dr Michael K Hooker	5-B	8,541	529
U of Maryland Coll Park, College Park, MD 20742	1856	Dr John B Slaughter	5-D	38,679	2,428
U of Maryland Eastern Shore, Princess Anne, MD 21853	1886	Dr William P Hytche	5-D	1,331	120
U of Maryland U Coll, College Park, MD 20742	1947	Dr John B Slaughter	5-M	12,531	601
U of Massachusetts at Amherst, Amherst, MA 01003	1863	Joseph Duffey	5-D	27,000	1,400
U of Massachusetts at Boston, Boston, MA 02125	1964	Dr Robert A Corrigan	5-D	12,900	845
U of Miami, Coral Gables, FL 33124	1925	Dr Edward T Foote II	1-D	13,384	1,934
U of Michigan, Ann Arbor, MI 48109	1817	Dr Harold T Shapiro	5-D	34,847	2,768
U of Michigan–Dearborn, Dearborn, MI 48128	1959	Dr William A Jenkins	5-M	6,206	352
U of Michigan–Flint, Flint, MI 48502	1956	Dr Clinton B Jones	5-M	6,047	263
U of Minnesota, Duluth, Duluth, MN 55812	1948	Dr Lawrence A Ianni	5-M	7,399	537
U of Minnesota, Morris, Morris, MN 56267	1959	Dr John Q Imholte	5-B	1,775	135
U of Minnesota, Twin Cities Cmps, Minneapolis, MN 55455	1851	Dr Kenneth H Keller	5-D	45,006	5,382
U of Mississippi, University, MS 38677	1844	Dr R Gerald Turner	5-D	9,053	624
U of Mississippi Medical Ctr, Jackson, MS 39216	1955	Dr Norman C Nelson	5-D	1,508	563
U of Missouri–Columbia, Columbia, MO 65211	1839	NR	5-D	22,532	2,385
U of Missouri–Kansas City, Kansas City, MO 64110	1933	Dr George A Russell	5-D	11,583	1,033
U of Missouri–Rolla, Rolla, MO 65401	1870	Dr Martin Jischke	5-D	6,318	353
U of Missouri–St Louis, St Louis, MO 63121	1963	Dr Marguerite Ross Barnett	5-D	11,502	618
U of Montana, Missoula, MT 59812	1893	Dr Donald Habbe	5-D	8,840	484
U of Montevallo, Montevallo, AL 35115	1896	Dr James F Vickrey Jr	5-M	2,569	175
U of Nebraska at Omaha, Omaha, NE 68182	1908	Dr Del D Weber	5-M	13,907	558
U of Nebraska–Lincoln, Lincoln, NE 68588	1869	Dr Martin A Massengale	5-D	23,899	1,433
U of Nebraska Medical Ctr, Omaha, NE 68105	1869	Dr Charles E Andrews	5-D	2,188	602
U of Nevada, Las Vegas, Las Vegas, NV 89154	1957	Dr Robert Maxson	5-D	12,847	581
U of Nevada–Reno, Reno, NV 89557	1874	Dr Joseph N Crowley	5-D	8,925	421
U of New England, Biddeford, ME 04005	1939	Dr Charles W Ford	1-D	1,089	85
U of New Hampshire, Durham, NH 03824	1866	Dr Gordon A Haaland	5-D	10,503	794
U of New Haven, West Haven, CT 06516	1920	Dr Phillip S Kaplan	1-D	6,918	428
U of New Mexico, Albuquerque, NM 87131	1889	Mr Gerald May	5-D	24,108	1,239
U of New Orleans, New Orleans, LA 70148	1958	Dr Cooper R Mackin	5-D	16,083	828
U of North Alabama, Florence, AL 35632	1872	Dr Robert M Guillot	5-M	4,979	207
U of North Carolina at Asheville, Asheville, NC 28804	1927	Dr David G Brown	5-M	2,939	190
U of North Carolina at Chapel Hill, Chapel Hill, NC 27514	1795	Christopher C Fordham III	5-D	22,781	2,185
U of North Carolina at Charlotte, Charlotte, NC 28223	1946	Dr Elbert K Fretwell Jr	5-M	11,753	702
U of North Carolina at Greensboro, Greensboro, NC 27412	1891	Dr William E Moran	5-D	10,382	655
U of North Carolina at Wilmington, Wilmington, NC 28403	1947	Dr William H Wagoner	5-M	5,937	336
U of North Dakota, Grand Forks, ND 58202	1883	Dr Thomas J Clifford	5-D	11,006	541
U of Northern Colorado, Greeley, CO 80639	1890	Mr Richard O Davies	5-D	9,260	550
U of Northern Iowa, Cedar Falls, IA 50614	1876	Dr Constantine W Curris	5-D	11,577	730
U of North Florida, Jacksonville, FL 32216	1965	Dr Curtis L McCray	5-M	6,729	177
U of Notre Dame, Notre Dame, IN 46556	1842	Rev Theodore M Hesburgh	2-D	9,500	947
U of Oklahoma, Norman, OK 73019	1890	Dr Frank E Horton	5-D	20,553	826
U of Oklahoma Health Sciences Ctr, Oklahoma City, OK 73190	1890	Dr Clayton Rich	5-D	3,160	700
U of Oregon, Eugene, OR 97403	1876	Paul Olum	5-D	17,142	1,287

Name, address	Year	Governing official, control, and highest degree offered	Enroll-ment	Faculty
U of Osteopathic Medicine and Health Sciences, Des Moines, IA 50312	1898	Dr J Leonard Azneer 1-D	1,002	70
U of Pennsylvania, Philadelphia, PA 19104	1740	Dr F Sheldon Hackney 1-D	21,742	3,364
U of Phoenix, Phoenix, AZ 85040	1976	Harold J O'Donnell 3-M	4,500	537
U of Pittsburgh, Pittsburgh, PA 15260	1787	Dr Wesley W Posvar 13-D	28,449	2,827
U of Pittsburgh at Bradford, Bradford, PA 16701	1963	Dr Richard E McDowell 13-B	979	88
U of Pittsburgh at Greensburg, Greensburg, PA 15601	1963	Dr George F Chambers 13-B	1,501	57
U of Pittsburgh at Johnstown, Johnstown, PA 15904	1927	Dr Frank H Blackington III 13-B	3,258	133
U of Portland, Portland, OR 97203	1901	Rev Thomas C Oddo 2-M	2,610	176
U of Puerto Rico, Arecibo Tech U Coll, Arecibo, PR 00613	1967	Marcos Morell 7-B	3,828	183
U of Puerto Rico, Cayey U Coll, Cayey, PR 00633	1967	Dr Margarita Benitez 7-B	3,412	161
U of Puerto Rico, Humacao U Coll, Humacao, PR 00661	1962	Elsa I Berrios de Santos 7-B	3,745	235
U of Puerto Rico, Mayagüez, Mayagüez, PR 00708	1911	Dr Jose L Martinez Pico 7-D	10,203	553
U of Puerto Rico Medical Sciences Cmps, San Juan, PR 00936	1950	Dr Jose M Saldana 7-D	3,295	720
U of Puerto Rico, Ponce Tech U Coll, Ponce, PR 00732	1970	Mr Pedro E Laboy 7-B	2,136	128
U of Puerto Rico, Rio Piedras, Rio Piedras, PR 00931	1903	Jaime Rosado-Alberio 7-D	22,061	1,401
U of Puget Sound, Tacoma, WA 98416	1888	Dr Philip Monford Phibbs 2-M	2,964	222
U of Redlands, Redlands, CA 92373	1907	Dr William M Jones 1-M	2,640	202
U of Rhode Island, Kingston, RI 02881	1892	Dr Edward D Eddy 5-D	11,107	738
U of Richmond, Richmond, VA 23173	1830	Dr E Bruce Heilman 2-M	4,705	349
U of Rochester, Rochester, NY 14627	1850	G Dennis O'Brien 1-D	9,018	650
U of St Thomas, Houston, TX 77006	1947	Frank H Bredeweg, CSB 2-D	1,811	197
U of San Diego, San Diego, CA 92110	1949	Dr Author E Hughes 2-D	5,400	353
U of San Francisco, San Francisco, CA 94117	1855	Rev John J Lo Schiavo, SJ 2-D	4,976	542
U of Science and Arts of Oklahoma, Chickasha, OK 73018	1908	Dr Roy Troutt 5-B	1,325	68
U of Scranton, Scranton, PA 18510	1888	Rev J A Panuska, SJ 2-M	4,789	296
U of South Alabama, Mobile, AL 36688	1964	Dr Frederick P Whiddon 5-D	9,728	663
U of South Carolina, Columbia, SC 29208	1801	Dr James B Holderman 5-D	20,922	1,279
U of South Carolina at Aiken, Aiken, SC 29801	1961	Dr Robert E Alexander 5-B	2,069	170
U of South Carolina at Spartanburg, Spartanburg, SC 29303	1967	Dr Olin B Sansbury Jr 5-B	2,952	172
U of South Carolina–Coastal Carolina Coll, Conway, SC 29526	1954	Dr Ron G Eaglin 5-B	3,176	180
U of South Dakota, Vermillion, SD 57069	1862	Dr Joseph M McFadden 5-D	5,511	461
U of Southern California, Los Angeles, CA 90089	1880	Dr James H Zumberge 1-D	27,277	5,038
U of Southern Colorado, Pueblo, CO 81001	1933	Dr Robert Shirley 5-M	3,693	252
U of Southern Indiana, Evansville, IN 47712	1965	Dr David L Rice 5-M	4,338	224
U of Southern Maine, Portland, ME 04103	1878	Dr Robert L Woodbury 5-D	9,424	609
U of Southern Mississippi, Hattiesburg, MS 39406	1910	Dr Aubrey K Lucus 5-D	12,578	662
U of South Florida, Tampa, FL 33620	1956	Dr John Lott Brown 5-D	29,458	1,328
U of Southwestern Louisiana, Lafayette, LA 70504	1898	Dr Ray P Authement 5-D	15,610	676
U of Tampa, Tampa, FL 33606	1931	Dr Richard D Cheshire 1-M	2,597	170
U of Tennessee at Chattanooga, Chattanooga, TN 37403	1886	Dr Frederick N Obear 5-M	7,469	425
U of Tennessee at Martin, Martin, TN 38238	1927	Dr Margaret N Perry 5-M	5,000	260
U of Tennessee, Knoxville, Knoxville, TN 37996	1794	Dr Jack E Reese 5-D	25,290	1,301
U of Tennessee, Memphis, Memphis, TN 38163	1911	Dr James C Hunt 5-D	1,365	686
U of Texas at Arlington, Arlington, TX 76019	1895	Dr Wendell H Nedderman 5-D	23,243	867
U of Texas at Austin, Austin, TX 78712	1883	Dr William Cunningham 5-D	46,140	2,355
U of Texas at Dallas, Richardson, TX 75083	1969	Dr Robert H Rutford 5-D	7,324	404
U of Texas at El Paso, El Paso, TX 79968	1913	Dr Haskell M Monroe 5-D	13,753	621
U of Texas at San Antonio, San Antonio, TX 78285	1969	Dr James W Wagener 5-M	12,413	538
U of Texas at Tyler, Tyler, TX 75701	1972	Dr George F Hamm 5-M	3,651	205
U of Texas Health Science Ctr at Dallas, Dallas, TX 75235	1972	Dr Charles C Sprague 5-D	1,521	270
U of Texas Health Science Ctr at Houston, Houston, TX 77225	1943	Dr Roger J Bulger 5-D	2,664	756
U of Texas Medical Branch at Galveston, Galveston, TX 77550	1891	Dr Thomas N James 5-D	1,683	553
U of Texas of the Permian Basin, Odessa, TX 79762	1969	Dr Duane M Leach 5-M	1,828	94
U of the District of Columbia, Washington, DC 20008	1976	Dr Robert L Green 10-M	11,098	810
U of the Ozarks, Clarksville, AR 72830	1834	Dr Fritz H Ehren 2-B	670	57
U of the Pacific, Stockton, CA 95211	1851	Dr William Atchley 1-D	5,683	309
U of the Sacred Heart, Santurce, PR 00914	1939	Dr Jose Alberto Morales 2-M	8,274	353
U of the South, Sewanee, TN 37375	1858	Dr Robert M Ayres Jr 2-D	1,313	118
U of the State of New York, Regents Coll Degrees, Albany, NY 12230	1970	NR 13-B	17,000	NR
U of Toledo, Toledo, OH 43606	1872	Dr James D McComas 5-D	21,176	1,077
U of Tulsa, Tulsa, OK 74104	1894	Dr J Paschal Twyman 2-D	4,731	361
U of Utah, Salt Lake City, UT 84112	1850	Dr Chase N Peterson 5-D	24,721	3,506
U of Vermont, Burlington, VT 05401	1791	Dr Lattie F Coor 5-D	11,096	873
U of Virginia, Charlottesville, VA 22903	1819	Robert M O'Neil 13-D	17,149	1,772
U of Washington, Seattle, WA 98195	1861	William P Gerberding 5-D	33,674	2,500
U of West Florida, Pensacola, FL 32514	1963	Dr James A Robinson 5-M	6,298	344
U of West Los Angeles, Los Angeles, CA 90066	1966	Bernard Jefferson 1-D	615	26
U of Wisconsin–Eau Claire, Eau Claire, WI 54701	1916	Dr Larry Schnack 5-M	11,103	582
U of Wisconsin–Green Bay, Green Bay, WI 54301	1968	Dr Edward W Weidner 5-M	5,367	249
U of Wisconsin–La Crosse, La Crosse, WI 54601	1909	Dr Noel J Richards 5-M	9,318	425
U of Wisconsin–Madison, Madison, WI 53706	1848	Dr Donna Shalala 5-D	44,584	2,289
U of Wisconsin–Milwaukee, Milwaukee, WI 53201	1956	Norma S Rees 5-D	25,930	1,263
U of Wisconsin–Oshkosh, Oshkosh, WI 54901	1871	Dr Edward M Penson 5-M	11,735	561
U of Wisconsin–Parkside, Kenosha, WI 53141	1968	Dr Sheila Kaplan 5-M	5,157	231
U of Wisconsin–Platteville, Platteville, WI 53818	1866	Dr William W Chmurny 5-M	5,380	280
U of Wisconsin–River Falls, River Falls, WI 54022	1874	Dr Gary A Thibodeau 5-M	5,613	300
U of Wisconsin–Stevens Point, Stevens Point, WI 54481	1894	Dr Philip R Marshall 5-M	9,554	710
U of Wisconsin–Stout, Menomonie, WI 54751	1893	Dr Robert S Swanson 5-M	7,726	425
U of Wisconsin–Superior, Superior, WI 54880	1893	Dr Ralph Doty 5-M	2,179	144
U of Wisconsin–Whitewater, Whitewater, WI 53190	1868	Dr James R Connor 5-M	10,901	491
U of Wyoming, Laramie, WY 82071	1886	Dr Terry P Roark 5-D	9,985	868
Upper Iowa U, Fayette, IA 52142	1857	Dr James R Rocheleau 1-B	1,300	69
Upsala Coll, East Orange, NJ 07019	1893	NR 2-M	1,366	140
Urbana U, Urbana, OH 43078	1850	Dr Paul G Bunnell 2-B	710	94
Ursinus Coll, Collegeville, PA 19426	1869	Dr Richard P Richter 2-B	1,220	110
Ursuline Coll, Pepper Pike, OH 44124 (4)	1871	Sr Mary Kenan Dulzer 2-M	1,514	113
Utah State U, Logan, UT 84322	1888	Dr Stanford Cazier 5-D	11,690	667
Utica Coll of Syracuse U, Utica, NY 13502	1946	Dr Lansing G Baker 1-B	1,550	175
Valdosta State Coll, Valdosta, GA 31698	1906	Dr Hugh C Bailey 5-M	6,611	327
Valley City State Coll, Valley City, ND 58072	1890	Dr Charles B House Jr 5-B	1,065	67

Name, address	Year	Governing official, control, and highest degree offered		Enroll-ment	Faculty
Valparaiso U, Valparaiso, IN 46383	1859	Dr Robert V Schnabel	2-D	3,844	366
Vanderbilt U, Nashville, TN 37240	1873	Mr Joe B Wyatt	1-D	8,968	2,110
Vassar Coll, Poughkeepsie, NY 12601	1861	Frances D Fergusson	1-M	2,287	237
Villa Julie Coll, Stevenson, MD 21153	1952	Ms Carolyn Manuszak	1-B	1,141	139
Villanova U, Villanova, PA 19085	1842	Rev John M Driscoll, OSA	2-D	12,261	824
Virginia Commonwealth U, Richmond, VA 23284	1838	Dr Edmund F Ackell	5-D	19,641	1,885
Virginia Military Inst, Lexington, VA 24450 (1)	1839	Gen Sam S Walker	5-B	1,350	100
Virginia Polytechnic Inst and State U, Blacksburg, VA 24061	1872	Dr William E Lavery	5-D	22,345	2,209
Virginia State U, Petersburg, VA 23803	1882	Dr Wilbert Greenfield	5-M	3,583	263
Virginia Union U, Richmond, VA 23220	1865	Mrs Carolyn W Daughtry	2-M	1,311	98
Virginia Wesleyan Coll, Norfolk, VA 23502	1961	Dr Lambuth M Clarke	2-B	1,116	76
Viterbo Coll, La Crosse, WI 54601	1890	Dr Robert E Gibbons	2-B	1,000	85
Voorhees Coll, Denmark, SC 29042	1897	Dr John F Potts	2-B	612	39
Wabash Coll, Crawfordsville, IN 47933 (1)	1832	Dr Lewis S Salter	1-B	774	75
Wagner Coll, Staten Island, NY 10301	1883	Dr Sam Frank	1-M	2,300	166
Wake Forest U, Winston-Salem, NC 27109	1834	Dr Thomas K Hearn Jr	2-D	5,054	1,266
Walla Walla Coll, College Place, WA 99324	1892	Dr H J Bergman	2-M	1,455	145
Walsh Coll, Canton, OH 44720	1958	Dr Francis Blouin	2-M	1,316	106
Walsh Coll of Accountancy & Business Admin, Troy, MI 48084	1922	Dr Jeffery W Barry	1-M	2,250	100
Wartburg Coll, Waverly, IA 50677	1852	Dr Robert Vogel	2-B	1,329	95
Washburn U of Topeka, Topeka, KS 66621	1865	Dr John L Green Jr	11-M	6,610	270
Washington and Jefferson Coll, Washington, PA 15301	1781	Dr Howard J Burnett	1-B	1,165	91
Washington and Lee U, Lexington, VA 24450	1749	Dr John D Wilson	1-D	1,804	194
Washington Coll, Chestertown, MD 21620	1782	Mr Douglass Cater	1-M	945	84
Washington State U, Pullman, WA 99164	1892	Dr Samuel H Smith	5-D	16,063	1,017
Washington U, St Louis, MO 63130	1853	Dr William H Danforth	1-D	8,311	2,752
Wayland Baptist U, Plainview, TX 79072	1908	Dr Glenn Barnett	2-M	1,827	162
Waynesburg Coll, Waynesburg, PA 15370	1849	Dr J Thomas Mills Jr	2-M	957	63
Wayne State Coll, Wayne, NE 68787	1910	Dr Joseph Fleck	5-M	2,948	126
Wayne State U, Detroit, MI 48202	1868	Dr David Adamany	5-D	28,764	1,560
Weber State Coll, Ogden, UT 84408	1889	Dr Stephen D Nadauld	5-M	11,127	408
Webster U, St Louis, MO 63119	1915	Dr Leigh Gerdine	1-M	7,567	260
Wellesley Coll, Wellesley, MA 02181 (3)	1875	Dr Nannerl Keohane	1-B	2,257	323
Wentworth Inst of Tech, Boston, MA 02115	1904	Dr Edward T Kirkpatrick	1-B	4,020	196
Wesleyan U, Middletown, CT 06457	1831	Mr Colin Campbell	1-D	2,767	314
Wesley Coll, Dover, DE 19901	1873	Dr Reed M Stewart	2-B	1,200	86
Westbrook Coll, Portland, ME 04103 (4)	1831	Dr William D Andrews	1-B	1,000	95
West Chester U of Pennsylvania, West Chester, PA 19383	1871	Dr Kenneth L Perrin	5-M	10,385	541
West Coast U, Los Angeles, CA 90020	1909	Dr Robert M L Baker Jr	1-M	1,400	250
Western Carolina U, Cullowhee, NC 28723	1889	Dr Myron L Coulter	5-M	5,921	395
Western Connecticut State U, Danbury, CT 06810	1903	Dr Stephen Feldman	5-M	6,010	220
Western Illinois U, Macomb, IL 61455	1899	Dr Ralph H Wagoner	5-M	12,075	692
Western Kentucky U, Bowling Green, KY 42101	1906	Dr Samuel K Alexander Jr	5-M	12,257	632
Western Maryland Coll, Westminster, MD 21157	1868	Dr Robert H Chambers	1-M	1,717	119
Western Michigan U, Kalamazoo, MI 49008	1903	Dr Diether H Haenicke	5-D	21,747	903
Western Montana Coll, Dillon, MT 59725	1893	NR	5-M	1,053	44
Western New England Coll, Springfield, MA 01119	1919	Dr Beverly W Miller	1-D	4,631	305
Western New Mexico U, Silver City, NM 88061	1893	Dr Kenneth Ladner	5-M	1,565	110
Western Oregon State Coll, Monmouth, OR 97361	1856	Dr Richard S Meyers	5-D	3,394	174
Western State Coll of Colorado, Gunnison, CO 81230	1911	Dr William T Hamilton	5-M	2,123	127
Western State U Coll of Law of Orange County, Fullerton, CA 92631	1966	NR	3-D	1,060	50
Western Washington U, Bellingham, WA 98225	1893	Dr G Robert Ross	5-M	9,308	466
Westfield State Coll, Westfield, MA 01086	1838	Dr Irving H Buchen	5-M	3,741	222
West Georgia Coll, Carrollton, GA 30118	1933	Dr Maurice K Townsend	5-M	6,141	287
West Liberty State Coll, West Liberty, WV 26074	1837	Dr Clyde Campbell	5-B	2,558	131
Westminster Coll, Fulton, MO 65251	1851	Dr J Harvey Saunders	2-B	650	60
Westminster Coll, New Wilmington, PA 16172	1852	Dr Oscar E Remick	2-M	1,306	121
Westminster Coll of Salt Lake City, Salt Lake City, UT 84105	1875	Charles H Dick	1-M	1,450	79
Westmont Coll, Santa Barbara, CA 93108	1940	Dr David K Winter	2-B	1,258	118
West Texas State U, Canyon, TX 79016	1909	Dr Ed Roach	5-M	6,028	325
West Virginia Inst of Tech, Montgomery, WV 25136	1895	Dr Leonard C Nelson	5-M	2,833	200
West Virginia State Coll, Institute, WV 25112	1891	Dr Hazo W Carter	5-B	4,384	135
West Virginia U, Morgantown, WV 26506	1867	Dr Neil S Bucklew	5-D	17,175	2,395
West Virginia Wesleyan Coll, Buckhannon, WV 26201	1890	NR	2-M	1,373	101
Wheaton Coll, Wheaton, IL 60187	1860	Dr J Richard Chase	2-M	2,501	234
Wheaton Coll, Norton, MA 02766 (3)	1834	Alice F Emerson	1-B	1,050	110
Wheeling Jesuit Coll, Wheeling, WV 26003	1954	Fr Thomas S Acker, SJ	2-M	1,030	80
Wheelock Coll, Boston, MA 02215 (4)	1888	Dr Daniel S Cheever Jr	1-M	749	108
Whitman Coll, Walla Walla, WA 99362	1859	Mr Robert A Skotheim	1-B	1,169	131
Whittier Coll, Whittier, CA 90608	1887	Dr Eugene S Mills	1-M	1,579	88
Whitworth Coll, Spokane, WA 99251	1890	Dr Robert H Mounce	2-M	1,764	84
Wichita State U, Wichita, KS 67208	1895	Dr Warren B Armstrong	5-D	16,843	708
Widener U, Delaware Cmps, Wilmington, DE 19803	1965	Robert J Bruce	1-D	1,982	113
Widener U, Pennsylvania Cmps, Chester, PA 19013	1821	Mr Robert J Bruce	1-D	7,675	216
Wilberforce U, Wilberforce, OH 45384	1856	Dr Yvonne Walker-Taylor	2-B	809	62
Wilkes Coll, Wilkes-Barre, PA 18766	1933	Dr Christopher N Breiseth	1-M	3,380	200
Willamette U, Salem, OR 97301	1842	Dr Jerry E Hudson	2-D	1,948	160
William Carey Coll, Hattiesburg, MS 39401	1906	Dr James R Noonkester	2-M	1,966	128
William Jewell Coll, Liberty, MO 64068	1849	Dr J Gordon Kingsley	2-B	2,035	173
William Paterson Coll of New Jersey, Wayne, NJ 07470	1855	Dr Arnold Speert	5-M	9,232	564
Williams Coll, Williamstown, MA 01267	1793	Dr Francis C Oakley	1-M	2,089	193
William Smith Coll, Geneva, NY 14456 (3)	1908	NR	1-B	800	160
William Woods Coll, Fulton, MO 65251 (3)	1870	Dr John M Bartholomy	2-B	700	71
Wilmington Coll, New Castle, DE 19720	1967	Dr Audrey K Doberstein	1-M	1,619	79
Wilmington Coll of Ohio, Wilmington, OH 45177	1870	Neil Thorburn	2-B	779	69
Wingate Coll, Wingate, NC 28174	1895	Dr Paul R Corts	2-M	1,525	85
Winona State U, Winona, MN 55987	1858	Dr Thomas Stark	5-M	6,000	300
Winston-Salem State U, Winston-Salem, NC 27110	1892	Dr Cleon F Thompson Jr	5-B	2,590	145
Winthrop Coll, Rock Hill, SC 29733	1886	Dr Martha K Piper	5-M	5,323	356
Wittenberg U, Springfield, OH 45501	1845	Dr William A Kinnison	2-B	2,135	175
Wofford Coll, Spartanburg, SC 29301	1854	Dr Joab M Lesesne	2-B	1,103	77
Woodbury U, Burbank, CA 91504	1884	Dr Wayne Miller	1-M	725	76
Worcester Polytechnic Inst, Worcester, MA 01609	1865	Dr Jon C Strauss	1-D	4,022	327

Name, address	Year	Governing official, control, and highest degree offered		Enroll-ment	Faculty
Worcester State Coll, Worcester, MA 01602	1874	Dr Philip D Vairo	5-M	4,700	227
Wright State U, Dayton, OH 45435	1964	Dr Paige E Mulhollan	5-D	16,977	945
Xavier U, Cincinnati, OH 45207	1831	NR	2-M	6,785	343
Xavier U of Louisiana, New Orleans, LA 70125	1925	Dr Norman C Francis	2-M	1,903	183
Yale U, New Haven, CT 06520	1701	Benno C Schmidt	1-D	10,799	1,835
Yeshiva U, New York, NY 10033	1886	Dr Norman Lamm	1-D	4,361	2,905
York Coll of Pennsylvania, York, PA 17403	1787	Dr Robert V Iosue	1-M	4,633	258
York Coll of City U of NY, Jamaica, NY 11451	1967	Mr Milton G Bassin	12-B	4,276	205
Youngstown State U, Youngstown, OH 44555	1908	Dr Neil D Humphrey	5-M	15,026	827

Two-Year Colleges

The highest undergraduate degree offered for all two-year colleges is the associate degree.

Name, address	Year	Governing official, control		Enrollment	Faculty
Abraham Baldwin Agricultural Coll, Tifton, GA 31793	1933	Dr Wayne C Curtis	5	1,770	91
Adirondack Comm Coll, Glens Falls, NY 12801	1960	Dr Gordon C Blank	12	2,783	153
Aiken Tech Coll, Aiken, SC 29802	1972	Dr Paul L Blowers	12	1,350	117
Aims Comm Coll, Greeley, CO 80632	1967	Dr George R Conger	10	6,976	312
Alabama Tech Coll, Gadsden, AL 35999	1925	Mr Robert W Howard	5	833	52
Albany Jr Coll, Albany, GA 31707	1965	Dr Bill R Tilley	5	1,683	100
Alexander City State Jr Coll, Alexander City, AL 35010	1965	Dr W Byron Causey	5	1,051	88
Allan Hancock Coll, Santa Maria, CA 93454	1920	Dr Gary R Edelbrock	12	7,268	290
Allegany Comm Coll, Cumberland, MD 21502	1961	Dr Donald L Alexander	12	1,944	129
Allen County Comm Coll, Iola, KS 66749	1923	Dr Ron D Garner	12	1,119	92
Alpena Comm Coll, Alpena, MI 49707	1952	Dr Charles R Donnelly	12	1,986	122
Alvin Comm Coll, Alvin, TX 77511	1949	Dr A R Allbright	12	3,918	196
Amarillo Coll, Amarillo, TX 79178	1929	Dr George T Miller	12	5,135	321
American Acad of Art, Chicago, IL 60603	1923	Mr Clinton E Frank	3	912	26
American Inst of Banking, Boston, MA 02114	1909	NR	1	1,900	200
American Inst of Business, Des Moines, IA 50321	1921	Keith Fenton	1	1,062	54
American Samoa Comm Coll, Pago Pago, AS 96799	1969	Dr Eneliko Sofa'i	8	845	65
Anchorage Comm Coll, Anchorage, AK 99508	1954	Herbert C Lyon	5	9,452	518
Anderson Coll, Anderson, SC 29621	1911	Dr Mark L Hopkins	2	1,016	67
Angelina Coll, Lufkin, TX 75902	1968	Dr Jack W Hudgins	12	2,535	150
Anne Arundel Comm Coll, Arnold, MD 21012	1961	Dr Thomas E Florestano	12	10,037	528
Anoka-Ramsey Comm Coll, Coon Rapids, MN 55433	1965	Dr Neil Christenson	5	4,237	137
Anson Tech Coll, Ansonville, NC 28007	1962	Dr Edwin R Chapman	5	778	92
Antelope Valley Coll, Lancaster, CA 93536	1929	Dr Allan W Kurki	5	7,636	250
Arapahoe Comm Coll, Littleton, CO 80120	1965	Dr James F Weber	5	6,129	354
Arizona Western Coll, Yuma, AZ 85364	1962	Dr James R Carruthers	12	4,100	260
Arkansas State U–Beebe Branch, Beebe, AR 72012	1927	Mr William H Owen Jr	5	971	36
Art Inst of Atlanta, Atlanta, GA 30326	1949	Gerald A Murphy	3	1,031	55
Art Inst of Fort Lauderdale, Fort Lauderdale, FL 33316	1968	Ms Miryam L Drucker	3	1,299	66
Art Inst of Philadelphia, Philadelphia, PA 19103	1966	Edward R D'Allessio	3	1,250	100
Art Inst of Pittsburgh, Pittsburgh, PA 15222	1921	John T Barclay	3	1,878	80
Art Inst of Seattle, Seattle, WA 98121	1979	George L Pry	3	900	75
Asheville-Buncombe Tech Coll, Asheville, NC 28801	1959	Mr Harvey L Haynes	5	2,847	260
Asnuntuck Comm Coll, Enfield, CT 06082	1972	Dr Harvey S Irlen	5	2,007	54
Atlanta Jr Coll, Atlanta, GA 30310	1974	Dr Edwin A Thompson	5	1,300	91
Atlantic Comm Coll, Mays Landing, NJ 08330	1966	Mr Robert E Hughey	9	4,112	188
Austin Comm Coll, Austin, MN 55912	1940	Mr James Flannery	5	958	75
Austin Comm Coll, Austin, TX 78768	1972	Dr Dan Angel	10	18,340	880
Bainbridge Jr Coll, Bainbridge, GA 31717	1972	Dr Edward D Mobley	5	718	45
Bakersfield Coll, Bakersfield, CA 93305	1913	Dr Richard Wright	12	10,587	480
Barstow Coll, Barstow, CA 92311	1962	Dr Edwin Spear	12	1,927	72
Barton County Comm Coll, Great Bend, KS 67530	1969	Dr Jimmie L Downing	12	2,686	121
Bauder Fashion Coll, Atlanta, GA 30326 (4)	1963	John E Kettle	3	600	30
Bay de Noc Comm Coll, Escanaba, MI 49829	1963	Dr Dwight E Link	9	1,822	94
Bay Path Jr Coll, Longmeadow, MA 01106 (3)	1897	Dr Jeanette T Wright	1	658	29
Bay State Jr Coll, Boston, MA 02116	1946	Dr Thomas E Langford	1	768	53
Beaufort County Comm Coll, Washington, NC 27889	1968	Mr James P Blanton	5	1,364	85
Beaufort Tech Coll, Beaufort, SC 29902	1972	Dr Anne S McNutt	5	1,029	150
Beckley Coll, Beckley, WV 25802	1933	Dr John W Saunders	1	1,621	68
Bee County Coll, Beeville, TX 78102	1965	Dr Norman Wallace	9	2,143	127
Belleville Area Coll, Belleville, IL 62221	1946	Dr Bruce R Wisore	10	11,551	597
Bellevue Comm Coll, Bellevue, WA 98009	1966	Dr John B Muller	5	6,000	428
Belmont Tech Coll, St Clairsville, OH 43950	1971	Dr Steve Maradian	5	1,138	96
Bergen Comm Coll, Paramus, NJ 07652	1965	Dr Jose Lopez-Isa	9	6,786	475
Berkeley Sch, Little Falls, NJ 07424 (4)	1931	Jack R Jones	3	730	35
Berkeley Sch, New York, NY 10017 (4)	1945	Dr John E Clow	3	714	33
Berkshire Comm Coll, Pittsfield, MA 01201	1960	Dr Jonathan M Daube	5	2,129	126
Bessemer State Tech Coll, Bessemer, AL 35021	1966	Dr W Michael Bailey	5	1,765	97
Big Bend Comm Coll, Moses Lake, WA 98837	1962	Dr Peter D DeVries	5	1,841	118
Bismarck State Coll, Bismarck, ND 58501	1939	Dr Kermit Lidstrom	5	2,281	104
Black Hawk Coll–East Cmps, Kewanee, IL 61443	1967	NR	12	850	66
Black Hawk Coll–Quad-Cities Cmps, Moline, IL 61265	1946	Dr Richard J Puffer	12	4,503	215
Blackhawk Tech Inst, Janesville, WI 53547	1968	Dr James C Catania	10	1,789	130
Blair Jr Coll, Colorado Springs, CO 80915	1897	NR	3	658	43
Blinn Coll, Brenham, TX 77833	1883	Walter C Schwartz	12	4,131	166
Blue Mountain Comm Coll, Pendleton, OR 97801	1962	Mr Ronald L Daniels	9	2,061	152
Blue Ridge Comm Coll, Weyers Cave, VA 24486	1965	Dr James C Sears	5	2,378	165
Blue Ridge Tech Coll, Flat Rock, NC 28731	1969	Dr William D Killian	12	1,244	78
Borough of Manhattan Comm Coll of City U of NY, New York, NY 10007	1963	Evangelos J Gizis	12	12,911	933
Bossier Parish Comm Coll, Bossier City, LA 71111	1967	NR	12	1,849	93
Bowling Green Jr Coll of Business, Bowling Green, KY 42101	1966	Timothy E Johnson	3	601	24
Bowling Green State U–Firelands Coll, Huron, OH 44839	1968	Dr William R McGraw	5	1,123	64
Brainerd Comm Coll, Brainerd, MN 56401	1938	Sally Jane Ihne	5	998	55
Brazosport Coll, Lake Jackson, TX 77566	1948	Dr Wilbur A Bass	12	3,426	200
Brevard Comm Coll, Cocoa, FL 32922	1960	Dr Maxwell C King	5	10,696	1,110
Brewer State Jr Coll, Fayette, AL 35555	1969	Dr Tommy M Boothe	5	680	29
Bristol Comm Coll, Fall River, MA 02720	1965	Ms Eileen Farley	5	2,451	164
Bronx Comm Coll of City U of NY, Bronx, NY 10453	1959	Dr Roscoe C Brown	12	6,400	426

Name, address	Year	Governing official, control		Enroll-ment	Faculty
Brookdale Comm Coll, Lincroft, NJ 07738	1967	Dr B A Barringer	9	10,573	439
Brookhaven Coll, Farmers Branch, TX 75244	1978	Dr Patsy J Fulton	9	7,131	344
Brooks Coll, Long Beach, CA 90804	1971	Mr Steve Sotraidis	3	871	60
Broome Comm Coll, Binghamton, NY 13902	1946	Dr Murray Block	12	5,867	453
Broward Comm Coll, Fort Lauderdale, FL 33301	1960	Dr A Hugh Adams	5	19,125	848
Brunswick Jr Coll, Brunswick, GA 31523	1961	Dr John W Teel	5	1,269	62
Brunswick Tech Coll, Supply, NC 28462	1979	Joseph B Carter	5	658	45
Bryant and Stratton Business Inst, Buffalo, NY 14202	1854	Mr Francis J Gustina Jr	3	3,141	127
Bryant and Stratton Business Inst, Rochester, NY 14604 (4)	1973	Paul L Hossenloopp	3	1,198	31
Bryant and Stratton Business Inst, E Hills Cmps, Williamsville, NY 14221	1978	NR	3	1,596	103
Bucks County Comm Coll, Newtown, PA 18940	1964	Dr William E Vincent	9	9,353	389
Bunker Hill Comm Coll, Boston, MA 02129	1973	Harold E Shively	5	3,682	164
Burlington County Coll, Pemberton, NJ 08068	1966	Dr Robert Messina	9	5,879	245
Butler County Comm Coll, El Dorado, KS 67042	1927	Dr Carl L Heinrich	12	3,398	227
Butler County Comm Coll, Butler, PA 16001	1965	Dr Frederick W Woodward	9	2,458	85
Butte Coll, Oroville, CA 95965	1966	Dr Wendell L Reeder	10	6,200	330
Cabrillo Coll, Aptos, CA 95003	1959	Dr Robert F Agrella	10	11,099	300
Caldwell Comm Coll and Tech Inst, Hudson, NC 28638	1964	Dr Eric B McKeithan	5	2,627	128
California Coll for Health Sciences, National City, CA 92050	1977	NR	3	2,430	5
Camden County Coll, Blackwood, NJ 08012	1967	Dr Robert W Ramsay	12	8,127	327
Cañada Coll, Redwood City, CA 94061	1968	D Robert Stiff	10	7,363	270
Cape Cod Comm Coll, West Barnstable, MA 02668	1961	Dr James F Hall	5	1,981	135
Cape Fear Tech Inst, Wilmington, NC 28401	1959	Mr Malcolm J McLeod	5	2,000	67
Carl Albert Jr Coll, Poteau, OK 74953	1934	Dr Joe White	5	2,065	160
Carl Sandburg Coll, Galesburg, IL 61401	1967	Dr Jack W Fuller	12	2,143	117
Carteret Tech Coll, Morehead City, NC 28557	1963	Dr Donald W Bryant	5	1,265	86
Casper Coll, Casper, WY 82601	1945	Dr Lloyd H Loftin	10	1,760	221
Catawba Valley Tech Coll, Hickory, NC 28601	1960	Mr Robert E Paap	12	2,600	144
Catonsville Comm Coll, Catonsville, MD 21228	1957	Dr John M Kingsmore	9	8,937	362
Cayuga County Comm Coll, Auburn, NY 13021	1953	Dr Lawrence H Poole	12	2,697	144
Cazenovia Coll, Cazenovia, NY 13035	1824	Dr Stephen M Schneeweiss	1	820	83
Cecil Comm Coll, North East, MD 21901	1968	Dr Robert L Gell	9	1,354	97
Cedar Valley Coll, Lancaster, TX 75134	1977	Dr Floyd S Elkins	5	2,479	105
Central Arizona Coll, Coolidge, AZ 85228	1961	Dr Kathleen F Arns	9	4,515	387
Central Carolina Tech Coll, Sanford, NC 27330	1962	Dr Marvin R Joyner	12	2,611	207
Central City Business Inst, Syracuse, NY 13203	1904	Mr Donald J Nelli	3	720	57
Central Comm Coll–Grand Island Cmps, Grand Island, NE 68802	1976	Donald Nelson	12	1,917	436
Central Comm Coll–Hastings Cmps, Hastings, NE 68901	1966	Dr Carl Rolf	12	1,504	318
Central Comm Coll–Platte Cmps, Columbus, NE 68601	1968	Mr Peter Rush	12	1,979	369
Central Florida Comm Coll, Ocala, FL 32670	1957	Dr Henry E Goodlett	12	3,100	110
Centralia Coll, Centralia, WA 98531	1925	Dr Henry P Kirk	5	1,141	270
Central Ohio Tech Coll, Newark, OH 43055	1971	Dr Julius S Greenstein	5	1,334	102
Central Oregon Comm Coll, Bend, OR 97701	1949	Dr Frederick H Boyle	10	2,122	114
Central Pennsylvania Business Sch, Summerdale, PA 17093	1922	Bart A Milano	3	725	53
Central Piedmont Comm Coll, Charlotte, NC 28235	1963	Dr Ruth Shaw	12	17,114	719
Central Texas Coll, Killeen, TX 76541	1967	Dr Luis M Morton	12	6,629	224
Central Virginia Comm Coll, Lynchburg, VA 24502	1966	Dr J E Merritt	5	3,903	135
Central Wyoming Coll, Riverton, WY 82501	1966	Dr Edward L Donovan	12	1,162	68
Cerritos Coll, Norwalk, CA 90650	1956	Dr W Michael	12	18,226	582
Cerro Coso Comm Coll, Ridgecrest, CA 93555	1973	Dr Raymond McCue	5	3,865	268
Chabot Coll, Hayward, CA 94545	1961	Dr Howard B Larson	5	18,803	1,000
Chaffey Coll, Alta Loma, CA 91701	1883	Dr Jerry W Young	10	10,600	400
Chamberlayne Jr Coll, Boston, MA 02116	1892	Mr Matthew J Malloy	1	825	55
Champlain Coll, Burlington, VT 05402	1878	Dr Robert A Skiff	1	1,367	94
Charles County Comm Coll, La Plata, MD 20646	1958	Dr John Sine	12	4,550	247
Charles Stewart Mott Comm Coll, Flint, MI 48502	1923	Mr David G Moore	9	10,364	337
Chattahoochee Valley State Comm Coll, Phenix City, AL 36867	1974	Dr James E Owen	5	1,563	62
Chattanooga State Tech Comm Coll, Chattanooga, TN 37406	1965	Dr Harry D Wagner	5	4,821	158
Chemeketa Comm Coll, Salem, OR 97309	1955	William Segura	12	12,751	670
Chesapeake Coll, Wye Mills, MD 21679	1965	Dr Robert C Schleiger	12	2,023	126
Chesterfield-Marlboro Tech Coll, Cheraw, SC 29520	1967	Dr Ronald W Hampton	12	606	50
Chipola Jr Coll, Marianna, FL 32446	1947	Dr James R Richburg	5	1,669	71
Chowan Coll, Murfreesboro, NC 27855	1848	Dr Bruce E Whitaker	2	889	71
Cincinnati Tech Coll, Cincinnati, OH 45223	1966	Mr Frederick B Schlimm	5	4,058	229
Cisco Jr Coll, Cisco, TX 76437	1940	Dr Henry E McCullough	12	1,648	113
Citrus Coll, Glendora, CA 91740	1915	Dr Louis Zellers	12	9,289	386
City Coll of San Francisco, San Francisco, CA 94112	1935	Carlos Brazil Ramirez	12	23,006	996
City Colls of Chicago, Chicago City-Wide Coll, Chicago, IL 60601	1975	Dr Mark Warden	12	3,448	271
City Colls of Chicago, Harry S Truman Coll, Chicago, IL 60640	1956	Dr Wallace B Appelson	12	4,502	329
City Colls of Chicago, Kennedy-King Coll, Chicago, IL 60621	1935	Dr Harold Pates	12	4,236	293
City Colls of Chicago, Loop Coll, Chicago, IL 60601	1962	Dr Bernice Miller	12	7,684	327
City Colls of Chicago, Malcolm X Coll, Chicago, IL 60612	1911	Mr James C Griggs	12	2,868	205
City Colls of Chicago, Olive-Harvey Coll, Chicago, IL 60628	1970	Mr Homer D Franklin	12	3,717	163
City Colls of Chicago, Richard J Daley Coll, Chicago, IL 60652	1960	Dr William P Conway	12	9,217	310
City Colls of Chicago, Wilbur Wright Coll, Chicago, IL 60634	1934	Mr Raymond F LeFevour	12	5,269	256
Clackamas Comm Coll, Oregon City, OR 97045	1966	Dr John S Keyser	9	5,262	690
Clarendon Coll, Clarendon, TX 79226	1898	Mr Kenneth D Vaughan	5	744	32
Clark Coll, Vancouver, WA 98663	1933	Dr Earl P Johnson	5	7,500	300
Clark County Comm Coll, North Las Vegas, NV 89030	1971	Dr Paul Meacham	5	10,029	515
Clark Tech Coll, Springfield, OH 45501	1962	Mr Albert Salerno	5	2,024	102
Clatsop Comm Coll, Astoria, OR 97103	1958	Mr Philip L Rainer	9	2,462	136
Cleveland Inst of Electronics, Cleveland, OH 44114 (2)	1934	John D Drinko	3	4,000	63
Cleveland State Comm Coll, Cleveland, TN 37320	1967	Dr James W Ford	5	2,900	102
Cleveland Tech Coll, Shelby, NC 28150	1965	Dr James B Petty	5	1,454	00
Clinton Comm Coll, Clinton, IA 52732	1946	Dr Adelbert Purga	5	1,003	58
Clinton Comm Coll, Plattsburgh, NY 12901	1969	Dr Jay Fennell	12	1,626	103

Name, address	Year	Governing official, control		Enroll-ment	Faculty
Cloud County Comm Coll, Concordia, KS 66901	1965	Dr James P Ihrig	12	1,867	250
Coastal Carolina Comm Coll, Jacksonville, NC 28540	1964	Dr James L Henderson Jr	12	3,406	152
Coastline Comm Coll, Fountain Valley, CA 92708	1976	Mr William M Vega	12	14,153	634
Cochise Coll, Douglas, AZ 85607	1962	Mr Dan W Rehurek	12	4,673	299
Coffeyville Comm Coll, Coffeyville, KS 67337	1923	Dan Kinney	12	1,747	81
Colby Comm Coll, Colby, KS 67701	1964	Dr James H Tangeman	12	623	104
Coll of Alameda, Alameda, CA 94501	1970	Donald R Hongisto	12	5,276	157
Coll of DuPage, Glen Ellyn, IL 60137	1966	Dr Harold D McAninch	12	27,163	1,230
Coll of Eastern Utah, Price, UT 84501	1937	Dr Michael A Petersen	5	1,771	67
Coll of Lake County, Grayslake, IL 60030	1967	Dr Daniel J La Vista	12	12,056	507
Coll of San Mateo, San Mateo, CA 94402	1922	Dr Lois A Callahan	12	13,880	432
Coll of Southern Idaho, Twin Falls, ID 83301	1964	Mr Gerald R Meyerhoeffer	12	2,663	123
Coll of the Albemarle, Elizabeth City, NC 27909	1960	Dr Parker Chesson Jr	5	1,480	98
Coll of the Canyons, Valencia, CA 91355	1969	Dr Ramon F LaGrandeur	12	3,751	139
Coll of the Desert, Palm Desert, CA 92260	1959	Dr David A George	12	9,145	373
Coll of the Mainland, Texas City, TX 77591	1967	Mr Larry L Stanley	12	3,084	182
Coll of the Redwoods, Eureka, CA 95501	1964	Dr D Donald Weichert	12	7,231	393
Coll of the Sequoias, Visalia, CA 93277	1925	Dr Lincoln H Hall	12	7,909	160
Coll of the Siskiyous, Weed, CA 96094	1957	Dr Eugene Schumacher	12	2,304	150
Colorado Inst of Art, Denver, CO 80203	1952	Cheryl Murphy	3	1,150	48
Colorado Mountain Coll, Timberline Cmps, Leadville, CO 80461	1965	Dr F Dean Lillie	10	650	47
Columbia Basin Coll, Pasco, WA 99301	1955	Dr Fred L Esvelt	5	5,500	310
Columbia Coll, Columbia, CA 95310	1968	Dr Dean Cunningham	12	2,702	98
Columbia-Greene Comm Coll, Hudson, NY 12534	1969	Dr Robert K Luther	12	1,488	82
Columbia State Comm Coll, Columbia, TN 38401	1966	Dr Paul Sands	5	3,040	95
Columbus State Comm Coll, Columbus, OH 43216	1963	Dr Harold M Nestor	5	7,751	541
Comm Coll of Allegheny County Allegheny Cmps, Pittsburgh, PA 15212	1966	Dr Julius R Brown	9	6,849	455
Comm Coll of Allegheny County Boyce Cmps, Monroeville, PA 15146	1966	Dr Carl A Di Sibio	12	4,293	110
Comm Coll of Allegheny County Coll Ctr–North, Pittsburgh, PA 15237	1972	Dr Fred F Bartok	12	2,842	219
Comm Coll of Allegheny County South Cmps, West Mifflin, PA 15122	1967	Dr Thomas A Juravich	9	5,200	120
Comm Coll of Aurora, Aurora, CO 80011	1983	Larry Carter	5	2,800	173
Comm Coll of Baltimore, Baltimore, MD 21215	1947	Dr Joseph T Durham	12	6,500	440
Comm Coll of Beaver County, Monaca, PA 15061	1966	Dr William K Bauer	5	2,540	137
Comm Coll of Philadelphia, Philadelphia, PA 19130	1964	Dr Judith S Eaton	12	10,863	983
Comm Coll of Rhode Island, Flanagan Cmps, Lincoln, RI 02865	1964	Edward J Liston	5	2,800	179
Comm Coll of Rhode Island, Knight Cmps, Warwick, RI 02886	1964	Mr Edward Liston	5	4,200	519
Comm Coll of the Finger Lakes, Canandaigua, NY 14424	1965	Dr Charles J Meder	12	3,214	193
Comm Coll of Vermont, Waterbury, VT 05676	1970	Mr Ken Kalb	5	1,098	360
Compton Comm Coll, Compton, CA 90221	1927	Dr Edison O Jackson	12	3,588	338
Condie Jr Coll of Business and Tech, Campbell, CA 95008	1968	Fran Williams	3	800	45
Connors State Coll, Warner, OK 74469	1908	Dr Carl O Westbrook	5	1,576	62
Contra Costa Coll, San Pablo, CA 94806	1948	Dr D Candy Rose	12	7,459	281
Cooke County Coll, Gainesville, TX 76240	1924	Dr Luther Bud Joyner	9	2,272	105
Copiah-Lincoln Jr Coll, Wesson, MS 39191	1928	Dr Billy B Thames	10	1,666	106
Corning Comm Coll, Corning, NY 14830	1956	Dr Donald H Hangen	12	3,100	132
Cosumnes River Coll, Sacramento, CA 95823	1970	Dr Marc E Hall	10	7,867	265
County Coll of Morris, Randolph, NJ 07869	1966	Dr Edward J Yaw	9	10,057	412
Cowley County Comm Coll, Arkansas City, KS 67005	1922	Dr Gwendel Nelson	12	1,598	82
Crafton Hills Coll, Yucaipa, CA 92399	1972	Dr Donald L Singer	12	3,500	139
Craven Comm Coll, New Bern, NC 28560	1965	Dr Thurman E Brock	5	2,105	159
Crowder Coll, Neosho, MO 64850	1963	NR	12	1,366	70
Culinary Inst of America, Hyde Park, NY 12538	1946	Mr Ferdinand E Metz	1	1,852	94
Cumberland County Coll, Vineland, NJ 08360	1963	Dr Philip S Phelon	12	2,232	94
Cuyahoga Comm Coll, Eastern Cmps, Warrensville Township, OH 44122	1971	Dr David C Mitchell	9	5,695	215
Cuyahoga Comm Coll, Metropolitan Cmps, Cleveland, OH 44115	1963	Dr Curtis F Jefferson	12	6,267	391
Cuyahoga Comm Coll, Western Cmps, Parma, OH 44130	1966	Mr Ronald M Sobel	12	12,053	420
Cuyamaca Coll, El Cajon, CA 92020	1978	Dr Samuel M Ciccati	5	2,861	120
Cypress Coll, Cypress, CA 90630	1966	NR	12	13,351	440
Dabney S Lancaster Comm Coll, Clifton Forge, VA 24422	1964	Dr John F Backels	5	1,355	79
Dalton Jr Coll, Dalton, GA 30720	1963	Dr Derrell C Roberts	5	1,648	65
Danville Area Comm Coll, Danville, IL 61832	1946	Dr Ronald K Lingle	12	3,587	128
Danville Comm Coll, Danville, VA 24541	1967	Dr Arnold R Oliver	5	1,965	91
Davenport Coll of Business, Kalamazoo Cmps, Kalamazoo, MI 49007 (4)	1866	C Dexter Rohm	1	730	50
Davidson County Comm Coll, Lexington, NC 27293	1958	Dr J Bryan Brooks	12	2,250	111
Dawson Comm Coll, Glendive, MT 59330	1940	Mr Donald H Kettner	12	786	32
Daytona Beach Comm Coll, Daytona Beach, FL 32015	1958	Dr Charles H Polk	5	8,297	799
Dean Jr Coll, Franklin, MA 02038	1865	Mr Richard E Crockford	1	1,100	82
De Anza Coll, Cupertino, CA 95014	1967	Dr A Robert Dehart	12	24,426	855
DeKalb Comm Coll, Decatur, GA 30034	1964	Dr Marvin M Cole	9	8,786	505
Delaware County Comm Coll, Media, PA 19063	1967	Dr Richard D De Cosmo	10	7,837	498
Delaware Tech & Comm Coll, Southern Cmps, Georgetown, DE 19947	1967	Mr Jack F Owens	5	1,866	128
Delaware Tech & Comm Coll, Stanton/Wilmington Cmps, Newark, DE 19702	1968	Mr John H Jones	5	4,554	248
Delaware Tech & Comm Coll, Terry Cmps, Dover, DE 19901	1972	Dr Linda Jolly	5	1,516	52
Delgado Comm Coll, New Orleans, LA 70119	1921	Dr Harry J Boyer	5	7,353	489
Del Mar Coll, Corpus Christi, TX 78404	1935	Dr Edwin Biggerstaff	12	8,927	412
Delta Coll, University Center, MI 48710	1961	Mr Donald J Carlyon	9	10,132	612
Denmark Tech Coll, Denmark, SC 29042	1948	Dr Curtis E Bryan	5	689	41
Denver Inst of Tech, Denver, CO 80221 (2)	1953	R Wade Murphree	3	750	43
Des Moines Area Comm Coll, Ankeny, IA 50021	1966	Dr Joseph Borgen	12	8,667	362
Diablo Valley Coll, Pleasant Hill, CA 94523	1949	Dr Phyllis Wiedman	12	18,600	595
District One Tech Inst, Eau Claire, WI 54701	1912	Mr Norbert K Wurtzel	10	3,300	175
Dixie Coll, St George, UT 84770	1911	Dr Douglas Alder	5	2,604	73
Dodge City Comm Coll, Dodge City, KS 67801	1935	Mr Gay Dahn	12	1,407	100
Draughons Jr Coll, Memphis, TN 38116	1890	Mr Jerry F Daly	3	850	37

Name, address	Year	Governing official, control	Enrollment	Faculty
Duff's Business Inst, Pittsburgh, PA 15222 (4)	1840	Thomas W Dillenburg Jr 3	800	42
Dundalk Comm Coll, Baltimore, MD 21222	1970	Dr Philip R Day Jr 9	3,241	184
Durham Tech Comm Coll, Durham, NC 27703	1961	Dr Phail Wynn Jr 5	4,364	120
Dutchess Comm Coll, Poughkeepsie, NY 12601	1957	Dr Jerry Lee 12	6,336	432
Dyersburg State Comm Coll, Dyersburg, TN 38024	1969	Dr Karen A Bowyer 5	1,060	101
East Arkansas Comm Coll, Forrest City, AR 72335	1974	Dr Bob C Burns 5	1,244	69
East Central Coll, Union, MO 63084	1968	Dr Charles R Novak 10	2,959	120
East Central Jr Coll, Decatur, MS 39327	1928	Dr Eddie M Smith 12	946	58
Eastern Arizona Coll, Thatcher, AZ 85552	1888	Mr Gherald L Hoopes Jr 12	1,677	235
Eastern New Mexico U–Roswell, Roswell, NM 88202	1958	Dr Loyd R Hughes 5	1,349	86
Eastern Oklahoma State Coll, Wilburton, OK 74578	1907	Dr James M Miller 5	2,410	66
Eastern Wyoming Coll, Torrington, WY 82240	1948	Mr Guido Smith 12	1,283	53
Eastfield Coll, Mesquite, TX 75150	1970	NR 12	8,302	316
East Los Angeles Coll, Monterey Park, CA 91754	1945	Mr Arthur Avila 10	10,293	639
Edgecombe Tech Coll, Tarboro, NC 27886	1968	Mr Charles B McIntyre 12	1,150	68
Edison Comm Coll, Fort Myers, FL 33907	1962	Dr David G Robinson 12	6,654	227
Edison State Comm Coll, Piqua, OH 45356	1973	Mr Conrad W Burchill 5	2,487	140
Edmonds Comm Coll, Lynnwood, WA 98036	1967	Mr Thomas C Nielsen 12	7,003	269
El Camino Coll, Torrance, CA 90506	1947	Dr Sam Schauerman 10	26,708	691
El Centro Coll, Dallas, TX 75202	1966	NR 9	5,127	290
Electronic Tech Inst, Cleveland, OH 44103 (2)	1929	A Jablonski 3	1,000	25
Elgin Comm Coll, Elgin, IL 60123	1949	Dr Paul R Heath 12	6,133	441
Elizabeth Seton Coll, Yonkers, NY 10701	1960	Sr Mary Ellen Brosnan 1	1,086	126
Ellsworth Comm Coll, Iowa Falls, IA 50126	1890	Duane R Lloyd 12	920	53
El Paso Comm Coll, El Paso, TX 79998	1969	Dr Robert E Shepack 9	13,832	880
El Reno Jr Coll, El Reno, OK 73036	1938	Dr Bill S Cole 12	1,722	85
Enterprise State Jr Coll, Enterprise, AL 36331	1965	Dr J D Talmadge 5	2,091	111
Erie Comm Coll, City Cmps, Buffalo, NY 14203	1971	Dr John R Birkholz 12	2,994	189
Erie Comm Coll, North Cmps, Williamsville, NY 14221	1946	NR 12	5,374	286
Erie Comm Coll, South Cmps, Orchard Park, NY 14127	1974	Mr Vincent Rolletta 12	3,405	196
Essex Agricultural and Tech Inst, Hathorne, MA 01937	1912	Mr Raymond F Potter 9	625	29
Essex Comm Coll, Baltimore, MD 21237	1957	Dr John E Ravekes 12	9,706	481
Essex County Coll, Newark, NJ 07102	1966	Dr Zachary Yamba 9	5,546	352
Eugenio Maria de Hostos Comm Coll of City U of NY, Bronx, NY 10451	1968	Dr I Santiago 12	4,400	375
Everett Comm Coll, Everett, WA 98201	1941	Mr Robert Drewel 5	6,398	245
Evergreen Valley Coll, San Jose, CA 95135	1975	Dr Gerald H Strelitz 12	7,405	212
Fairleigh Dickinson U, Edward Williams Coll, Hackensack, NJ 07601	1964	Kenneth T Vehrkens 1	1,312	53
Fashion Inst–Design/Merchandising, SF Cmps, San Francisco, CA 94102	1969	Jane Bell 3	705	54
Fayetteville Tech Inst, Fayetteville, NC 28303	1961	Dr Craig Allen 5	6,284	545
Feather River Coll, Quincy, CA 95971	1968	Dr Joseph Brennan 12	923	85
Fergus Falls Comm Coll, Fergus Falls, MN 56537	1960	Mr Dan F True 5	1,125	65
Fiorello H LaGuardia Comm Coll of City U of NY, Long Island City, NY 11101	1971	Dr Joseph Shenker 12	7,800	368
Fisher Jr Coll, Boston, MA 02116 (3)	1903	Dr Scott A Fisher 1	610	45
Flathead Valley Comm Coll, Kalispell, MT 59901	1967	Dr Howard L Fryett PhD 12	2,004	135
Florence-Darlington Tech Coll, Florence, SC 29501	1963	Mr Fred C Fore 5	1,900	204
Florida Comm Coll at Jacksonville, Jacksonville, FL 32202	1966	Dr Charles C Spence 5	16,075	1,761
Florida Keys Comm Coll, Key West, FL 33040	1965	Dr William A Seeker 5	629	80
Floyd Jr Coll, Rome, GA 30163	1970	Dr David B McCorkle 5	1,259	63
Foothill Coll, Los Altos Hills, CA 94022	1958	Dr Thomas H Clements 12	13,906	376
Forsyth Tech Coll, Winston Salem, NC 27103	1964	Dr Bob H Greene 5	3,854	194
Fort Scott Comm Coll, Fort Scott, KS 66701	1919	Mr Richard D Hedges 12	1,700	72
Fox Valley Tech Inst, Appleton, WI 54913	1967	Dr Stanley J Spanbauer 12	4,770	700
Frank Phillips Coll, Borger, TX 79008	1948	Dr Andy Hicks 12	853	94
Frederick Comm Coll, Frederick, MD 21701	1957	Dr Lee J Betts 12	3,150	225
Fresno City Coll, Fresno, CA 93741	1910	Dr Ernest R Leach 10	14,660	378
Front Range Comm Coll, Westminster, CO 80030	1968	Dr Donald R Mankenberg 5	5,512	418
Fullerton Coll, Fullerton, CA 92634	1913	Dr Philip W Borst 12	17,304	628
Fulton-Montgomery Comm Coll, Johnstown, NY 12095	1964	Mr John G Boshart 12	1,700	100
Gadsden State Jr Coll, Gadsden, AL 35999	1965	Dr James D McEwen 5	3,044	147
Gainesville Jr Coll, Gainesville, GA 30503	1964	Dr J Foster Watkins 5	1,849	76
Galveston Coll, Galveston, TX 77550	1967	John E Pickelman 12	2,054	96
Garden City Comm Coll, Garden City, KS 67846	1919	Dr Thomas F Saffell 10	1,375	93
Garland County Comm Coll, Hot Springs, AR 71913	1973	Dr Gerald H Fisher 12	1,481	81
Gaston Coll, Dallas, NC 28034	1963	Dr W Wayne Scott 12	3,450	151
Gateway Comm Coll, Phoenix, AZ 85034	1968	Ms Myrna Harriosn 12	3,104	170
Gateway Tech Inst, Kenosha, WI 53141	1912	Dr John R Birkholz 12	12,000	473
Gavilan Coll, Gilroy, CA 95020	1919	Dr John J Holleman 12	3,376	142
Genesee Comm Coll, Batavia, NY 14020	1966	Dr Stuart Steiner 12	2,615	155
George Corley Wallace State Comm Coll, Selma, AL 36701	1966	Dr Charles L Byrd 5	1,472	46
George C Wallace State Comm Coll, Dothan, AL 36303	1949	Dr Nathan L Hodges 5	3,298	160
Georgia Military Coll, Milledgeville, GA 31061	1879	Maj Gen William P Acker 1	1,403	27
Germanna Comm Coll, Locust Grove, VA 22508	1970	Dr Marshall W Smith 5	2,000	94
Glendale Comm Coll, Glendale, AZ 85302	1965	Dr John R Waltrip 12	15,309	475
Glendale Comm Coll, Glendale, CA 91208	1927	Dr John A Davitt 12	11,169	345
Glen Oaks Comm Coll, Centreville, MI 49032	1965	Dr Philip G Ward 12	1,350	129
Gloucester County Coll, Sewell, NJ 08080	1967	NR 9	3,508	143
Gogebic Comm Coll, Ironwood, MI 49938	1932	NR 12	1,517	59
Golden West Coll, Huntington Beach, CA 92647	1966	Mr Fred Garcia 5	15,000	648
Gordon Jr Coll, Barnesville, GA 30204	1852	Dr Jerry M Williamson 5	1,510	81
Grand Rapids Jr Coll, Grand Rapids, MI 49503	1914	Mr Richard Calkins 11	10,500	333
Grays Harbor Coll, Aberdeen, WA 98520	1930	Dr Joseph A Malik 5	1,185	118
Grayson County Coll, Denison, TX 75020	1964	Dr Jim M Williams 12	3,393	146
Greater Hartford Comm Coll, Hartford, CT 06105	1967	Walter J Markiewicz 5	2,686	96
Greater New Haven State Tech Coll, North Haven, CT 06473	1977	George D Harris 5	1,000	78
Greenfield Comm Coll, Greenfield, MA 01301	1962	Dr Theodore L Provo 5	1,525	94
Green River Comm Coll, Auburn, WA 98002	1965	Richard A Rutkowski 5	5,450	274
Greenville Tech Coll, Greenville, SC 29606	1962	Dr Thomas E Barton Jr 5	6,312	393
Grossmont Coll, El Cajon, CA 92020	1961	Dr Ivan L Jones 12	15,404	565
Guam Comm Coll, Guam Main Facility, GU 96921	1977	Peter R Nelson 8	774	207

Name, address	Year	Governing official, control		Enroll-ment	Faculty
Guilford Tech Comm Coll, Jamestown, NC 27282	1958	Dr Ray Needham	12	6,247	255
Gulf Coast Comm Coll, Panama City, FL 32401	1957	Dr Lawrence W Tyree	5	4,766	387
Hagerstown Jr Coll, Hagerstown, MD 21740	1946	Dr Norman P Shea	9	2,512	150
Halifax Comm Coll, Weldon, NC 27890	1967	Dr Phillip W Taylor	12	1,051	68
Harcum Jr Coll, Bryn Mawr, PA 19010 (4)	1915	Dr Norma F Furst	1	890	84
Hardbarger Jr Coll of Business, Raleigh, NC 27602	1924	NR	3	733	32
Harford Comm Coll, Bel Air, MD 21014	1957	Dr Alfred C O'Connell	12	4,261	209
Harrisburg Area Comm Coll, Harrisburg, PA 17110	1964	Dr Kenneth B Woodbury Jr	12	6,247	257
Harry M Ayers State Tech Coll, Anniston, AL 36202	1966	Mr Pierce C Cain	5	697	49
Hartford State Tech Coll, Hartford, CT 06106	1946	Mr Kenneth E DeRego	5	603	51
Hartnell Coll, Salinas, CA 93901	1920	Dr James R Hardt	10	7,014	284
Haskell Indian Jr Coll, Lawrence, KS 66044	1884	Dr Gerald E Gipp	4	799	65
Hawkeye Inst of Tech, Waterloo, IA 50704	1967	Dr John E Hawse	12	2,149	157
Haywood Tech Coll, Clyde, NC 28721	1964	Mr Joseph H Nanney	12	1,078	68
Heald Inst of Tech, San Francisco, CA 94103 (2)	1863	Dr James Deitz	1	793	25
Henry Ford Comm Coll, Dearborn, MI 48128	1938	Dr Stuart M Bundy	10	14,595	667
Herkimer County Comm Coll, Herkimer, NY 13350	1966	Mr Ronald F Williams	12	2,019	88
Hesser Coll, Manchester, NH 03101	1900	Kenneth W Galeucia	3	1,983	143
Hibbing Comm Coll, Hibbing, MN 55746	1916	Mr Orville A Olson	5	1,051	83
Highland Comm Coll, Freeport, IL 61032	1962	Dr Joseph C Piland	10	2,954	99
Highland Comm Coll, Highland, KS 66035	1858	Dr Larry F Devane	12	1,365	63
Highland Park Comm Coll, Highland Park, MI 48203	1918	Dr Thomas Lloyd	12	2,006	112
Highline Comm Coll, Des Moines, WA 98198	1961	Dr Shirley B Gordon	5	6,500	441
Hilbert Coll, Hamburg, NY 14075	1957	Sr Edmunette Paczesny	1	680	66
Hill Jr Coll, Hillsboro, TX 76645	1923	Dr W R Auvenshine	10	1,550	71
Hillsborough Comm Coll, Tampa, FL 33622	1968	Dr Andreas A Paloumpis	5	14,555	849
Hiwassee Coll, Madisonville, TN 37354	1849	Dr Curtis Schofield	2	604	41
Hocking Tech Coll, Nelsonville, OH 45764	1968	Dr John J Light	5	4,311	210
Holyoke Comm Coll, Holyoke, MA 01040	1946	Mr David M Bartley	5	3,297	203
Horry-Georgetown Tech Coll, Conway, SC 29526	1965	Dr D Kent Sharples	12	1,468	110
Housatonic Comm Coll, Bridgeport, CT 06608	1966	Dr Vincent S Darnowski	5	2,650	94
Houston Comm Coll System, Houston, TX 77270	1971	Mr J B Whiteley	12	26,002	1,168
Howard Coll, Big Spring, TX 79720	1945	Dr Bob E Riley	12	1,333	128
Howard Comm Coll, Columbia, MD 21044	1966	Dr Dwight A Burrill	12	3,530	208
Hudson County Comm Coll, Jersey City, NJ 07306	1974	Mr Walter N Sheil	12	3,557	231
Hudson Valley Comm Coll, Troy, NY 12180	1953	Dr Joseph J Bulmer	12	8,315	350
Hutchinson Comm Coll, Hutchinson, KS 67501	1928	Dr James H Stringer	12	3,797	292
ICM Sch of Business, Pittsburgh, PA 15222	1963	Wayne R Zanardelli	3	1,100	44
ICS Ctr for Degree Studies, Scranton, PA 18515	1975	Mr David Crowther	3	6,543	43
Illinois Central Coll, East Peoria, IL 61635	1967	Dr Leon H Perley	12	7,337	559
Illinois East Comm Colls, Frontier Comm Coll, Fairfield, IL 62837	1976	Richard Mason	12	3,529	207
Illinois East Comm Colls, Lincoln Trail Coll, Robinson, IL 62454	1969	Dr Richard L Behrendt	12	1,351	89
Illinois East Comm Colls, Olney Central Coll, Olney, IL 62450	1960	Dr Stephen J. Kridelbaugh	12	2,051	130
Illinois East Comm Colls, Wabash Valley Coll, Mount Carmel, IL 62863	1960	Dr Harry K Benson	12	2,338	86
Illinois Valley Comm Coll, Oglesby, IL 61348	1924	Dr Alfred E Wisgoski	10	4,200	180
Imperial Valley Coll, Imperial, CA 92251	1922	Dr John A DePaoli	12	3,512	161
Independence Comm Coll, Independence, KS 67301	1925	Mr M Leon Foster	10	926	69
Indiana Business Coll, Indianapolis, IN 46204	1902	NR	3	900	9
Indiana Vocational Tech Coll–Central Indiana, Indianapolis, IN 46206	1963	Dr Meredith L Carter	5	4,410	265
Indiana Vocational Tech Coll–Columbus, Columbus, IN 47203	1963	Mr Harvey Poling	5	2,010	129
Indiana Vocational Tech Coll–Eastcentral, Muncie, IN 47302	1968	Mr Richard L Davidson	5	1,976	113
Indiana Vocational Tech Coll–Kokomo, Kokomo, IN 46901	1968	Mr Charles E Hefley	5	1,887	103
Indiana Vocational Tech Coll–Lafayette, Lafayette, IN 47903	1968	Dr Thomas E Reckard	5	1,548	90
Indiana Vocational Tech Coll–Northcentral, South Bend, IN 46619	1968	Dr Carl F Lutz	5	2,011	149
Indiana Vocational Tech Coll–Northeast, Fort Wayne, IN 46805	1969	Mr Jon L Rupright	5	2,768	193
Indiana Vocational Tech Coll–Northwest, Gary, IN 46409	1963	Mr Mearle R Donica	5	3,463	204
Indiana Vocational Tech Coll–Southcentral, Sellersburg, IN 47172	1968	Mr Carl F Scott	5	1,265	101
Indiana Vocational Tech Coll–Southeast, Madison, IN 47250	1963	NR	5	780	67
Indiana Vocational Tech Coll–Southwest, Evansville, IN 47710	1963	Dr H Victor Baldi	5	1,845	120
Indiana Vocational Tech Coll–Wabash Valley, Terre Haute, IN 47802	1966	Mr Sam Borden	5	1,826	107
Indiana Vocational Tech Coll–Whitewater, Richmond, IN 47374	1963	Dr Judith A Redwine	5	994	90
Indian Hills Comm Coll, Ottumwa, IA 52501	1966	Dr Lyle A Hellyer	12	2,276	118
Indian River Comm Coll, Fort Pierce, FL 33450	1960	Mr Richard A Matula	5	6,800	240
Instituto Comercial de Puerto Rico Jr Coll, Hato Rey, PR 00919	1946	Atty Enrique Pineiro	3	1,355	81
Instituto Técnico Comercial Jr Coll, Rio Piedras, PR 00926	1948	NR	3	680	46
Inter American U of PR, Guayama Regional Coll, Guayama, PR 00654	1958	Mr Pablo I Rivera Diaz	1	1,530	70
Interboro Inst, New York, NY 10019	1888	Mr Mischa Lazoff	3	900	40
International Acad of Merchandising & Design, Chicago, IL 60654	1977	Clem Stein Jr	3	721	60
Inver Hills Comm Coll, Inver Grove Heights, MN 55075	1969	Dr Patrick A Roche	5	4,218	236
Iowa Central Comm Coll, Fort Dodge, IA 50501	1966	Dr Harvey D Martin	12	2,654	97
Iowa Lakes Comm Coll, North Attendance Ctr, Estherville, IA 51334	1967	Mr Richard H Blacker	12	722	30
Iowa Lakes Comm Coll, South Attendance Ctr, Emmetsburg, IA 50536	1967	Mr Richard H Blacker	12	978	42
Iowa Western Comm Coll, Council Bluffs, IA 51502	1966	Dr Robert D Looft	10	2,739	173
Irvine Valley Coll, Irvine, CA 92720	1979	NR	12	4,766	168
Isothermal Comm Coll, Spindale, NC 28160	1965	Dr G Herman Porter	5	2,337	211
Itasca Comm Coll, Grand Rapids, MN 55744	1922	Dr Lawrence N Dukes	5	1,200	115
ITT Tech Inst, Buena Park, CA 90620	1982	Cynthia J Norman	3	725	25
ITT Tech Inst, La Mesa, CA 92041	1981	NR	3	616	25

Name, address	Year	Governing official, control		Enrollment	Faculty
ITT Tech Inst, Sacramento, CA 95827	1954	NR	3	1,500	17
ITT Tech Inst, Dayton, OH 45414 (2)	1935	Dennis W Alspaugh	3	647	21
Jackson Comm Coll, Jackson, MI 49201	1928	Dr Clyde LeTarte	9	7,000	358
Jackson State Comm Coll, Jackson, TN 38301	1967	Dr James A Hefner	5	2,458	122
James H Faulkner State Jr Coll, Bay Minette, AL 36507	1965	Dr Gary L Branch	5	2,050	85
James Sprunt Comm Coll, Kenansville, NC 28349	1964	Dr Carl D Price	5	768	57
Jamestown Comm Coll, Jamestown, NY 14701	1950	Mr Paul A Benke	12	3,765	242
Jefferson Coll, Hillsboro, MO 63050	1963	Dr B Ray Henry	12	3,289	140
Jefferson Comm Coll, Watertown, NY 13601	1961	Mr John T Henderson	12	1,870	124
Jefferson State Jr Coll, Birmingham, AL 35215	1965	Dr Judy M Merritt	5	6,095	247
Jefferson Tech Coll, Steubenville, OH 43952	1966	Dr Edward L Florak	12	1,362	80
John A Logan Coll, Carterville, IL 62918	1967	Dr Harold R O'Neil	12	3,057	142
John C Calhoun State Comm Coll, Decatur, AL 35602	1965	Dr James R Chasteen	5	6,403	294
Johnson County Comm Coll, Overland Park, KS 66210	1967	Dr Charles J Carlsen	12	8,937	389
Johnston Tech Coll, Smithfield, NC 27577	1969	Dr John L Tart	5	1,982	114
John Tyler Comm Coll, Chester, VA 23831	1967	Dr Freddie W Nicholas Sr	12	4,556	183
John Wood Comm Coll, Quincy, IL 62301	1974	NR	10	3,504	102
Joliet Jr Coll, Joliet, IL 60436	1901	NR	12	9,303	455
Jones County Jr Coll, Ellisville, MS 39437	1928	Dr T Terrell Tisdale	12	2,539	129
J Sargeant Reynolds Comm Coll, Richmond, VA 23261	1972	Dr S A Burnette	5	11,370	402
Jr Coll of Albany, Albany, NY 12208	1957	Dr William F Kahl	1	1,048	96
Kalamazoo Valley Comm Coll, Kalamazoo, MI 49009	1966	Dr Marilyn J Schlack	12	7,274	256
Kankakee Comm Coll, Kankakee, IL 60901	1966	Dr Larry D Huffman	12	3,100	109
Kansas City Kansas Comm Coll, Kansas City, KS 66112	1923	NR	9	3,614	225
Kaskaskia Coll, Centralia, IL 62801	1966	Dr Bruce G Stahl	12	3,080	95
Katharine Gibbs Sch, Boston, MA 02108 (4)	1917	NR	3	616	45
Kellogg Comm Coll, Battle Creek, MI 49016	1956	Dr Richard F Whitmore	12	5,139	200
Kent State U, Ashtabula Cmps, Ashtabula, OH 44004	1958	Dr John K Mahan	5	846	57
Kent State U, East Liverpool Cmps, East Liverpool, OH 43920	1967	Mr Richard Q King	5	600	50
Kent State U, Salem Cmps, Salem, OH 44460	1966	Dr James F Cooney	5	655	49
Kent State U, Stark Cmps, Canton, OH 44720	1967	Dr William G Bittle	5	1,689	91
Kent State U, Trumbull Cmps, Warren, OH 44483	1954	Paul A Reichert	5	1,760	81
Kent State U, Tuscarawas Cmps, New Philadelphia, OH 44663	1962	Harold D Shade	5	923	67
Keystone Jr Coll, La Plume, PA 18440	1868	Margaretta B Chamberlin	1	750	103
Kilgore Coll, Kilgore, TX 75662	1935	Dr Stewart H McLaurin	12	3,938	190
Kingsborough Comm Coll of City U of NY, Brooklyn, NY 11235	1963	Dr Leon M Goldstein	12	8,400	621
King's River Comm Coll, Reedley, CA 93654	1926	Dr Abel B Sykes Jr	12	3,605	195
Kirkwood Comm Coll, Cedar Rapids, IA 52406	1966	Mr Norm Nielsen	12	6,308	399
Kirtland Comm Coll, Roscommon, MI 48653	1966	Mr Raymond D Homer	10	1,584	103
Labette Comm Coll, Parsons, KS 67357	1923	Dr Gery C Hochanadel	12	2,921	171
Labouré Coll, Boston, MA 02124	1971	Sr Maureen St Charles	2	650	56
Lackawanna Jr Coll, Scranton, PA 18505	1894	Mr Allan P Mensky	1	1,147	77
Lake City Comm Coll, Lake City, FL 32055	1962	Dr Muriel Kay Heimer	5	2,225	170
Lake Land Coll, Mattoon, IL 61938	1966	Dr David V Schultz	12	3,708	285
Lakeland Comm Coll, Mentor, OH 44060	1967	Dr James Catanzaro	12	8,500	480
Lake Michigan Coll, Benton Harbor, MI 49022	1946	Dr Anne E Mulder	10	3,504	310
Lake Region Comm Coll, Devils Lake, ND 58301	1941	Dr William L Taylor	12	618	53
Lakeshore Tech Inst, Cleveland, WI 53015	1967	Mr Frederick J Nierode	12	2,850	123
Lake-Sumter Comm Coll, Leesburg, FL 32788	1961	Dr Robert S Palinchak	12	1,932	86
Lake Tahoe Comm Coll, South Lake Tahoe, CA 95702	1975	Dr James W Duke	12	1,400	65
Lakewood Comm Coll, White Bear Lake, MN 55110	1967	Dr Jerry Owens	5	4,494	100
Lane Comm Coll, Eugene, OR 97405	1964	Dr Richard M Turner, III	12	6,800	343
Laney Coll, Oakland, CA 94607	1953	Mr Odell Johnson	5	10,108	347
Lansing Comm Coll, Lansing, MI 48901	1957	Dr Philip J Gannon	12	23,390	1,000
Laramie County Comm Coll, Cheyenne, WY 82007	1968	Dr Timothy Davies	9	3,759	162
Laredo Jr Coll, Laredo, TX 78040	1946	Dr Roger L Worsley	12	4,000	160
Lassen Coll, Susanville, CA 96130	1925	Dr Virginia L Holten	12	1,986	200
Latter-Day Saints Business Coll, Salt Lake City, UT 84111	1886	Mr R F Kirkham	2	711	39
Lawson State Comm Coll, Birmingham, AL 35221	1965	Dr Jesse J Lewis	5	1,381	41
Lee Coll, Baytown, TX 77520	1934	Dr Vivian Bowling Blevins	10	4,566	202
Lees-McRae Coll, Banner Elk, NC 28604	1900	Dr Bradford L Crain	2	672	40
Lehigh County Comm Coll, Schnecksville, PA 18078	1967	Dr Robert L Barthlow	12	3,515	100
Lenoir Comm Coll, Kinston, NC 28502	1960	Dr Jesse L McDaniel	5	2,184	105
Lewis and Clark Comm Coll, Godfrey, IL 62035	1970	Mr J Neil Admire	10	4,914	250
Lewis Coll of Business, Detroit, MI 48235	1929	Dr Marjorie Harris	1	656	32
Lima Tech Coll, Lima, OH 45804	1971	Dr James S Biddle	5	1,795	130
Lincoln Land Comm Coll, Springfield, IL 62708	1967	Dr Robert L Poorman	10	7,538	391
Lincoln Tech Inst, Indianapolis, IN 46202	1946	James W Jackson	3	700	26
Lincoln Tech Inst, Allentown, PA 18104	1949	Donald R Frey	3	909	40
Linn-Benton Comm Coll, Albany, OR 97321	1966	Dr Thomas Gonzales	12	11,000	590
Long Beach City Coll, Long Beach, CA 90808	1927	Dr John T McCuen	5	22,698	1,320
Longview Comm Coll, Lee's Summit, MO 64063	1969	Mr Aldo W Leker	10	5,900	254
Lorain County Comm Coll, Elyria, OH 44035	1963	Dr Roy Church	12	6,013	292
Lord Fairfax Comm Coll, Middletown, VA 22645	1969	Dr William H McCoy	12	2,017	64
Los Angeles City Coll, Los Angeles, CA 90029	1929	Dr Stelle Feuers	10	16,600	560
Los Angeles Harbor Coll, Wilmington, CA 90744	1949	Mr James L Heinselman	12	8,588	275
Los Angeles Mission Coll, San Fernando, CA 91340	1974	Mr Lowell J Erickson	12	4,844	141
Los Angeles Pierce Coll, Woodland Hills, CA 91371	1947	Dr David Wolf	12	18,519	439
Los Angeles Trade-Tech Coll, Los Angeles, CA 90015	1925	Mr Thomas L Stevens Jr	10	12,000	802
Los Angeles Valley Coll, Van Nuys, CA 91401	1949	Dr Mary E Lee	12	20,123	549
Louisburg Coll, Louisburg, NC 27549	1787	Dr J Allen Norris Jr	2	804	45
Louisiana State U at Alexandria, Alexandria, LA 71302	1960	Dr James W Firnberg	5	1,901	85
Louisiana State U at Eunice, Eunice, LA 70535	1967	Dr Anthony Mumphrey	5	1,740	90
Lower Columbia Coll, Longview, WA 98632	1934	Dr Vernon R Pickett	5	3,900	150
Lurleen B Wallace State Jr Coll, Andalusia, AL 36420	1969	Dr William H McWhorter	5	1,001	49
Luzerne County Comm Coll, Nanticoke, PA 18634	1966	Thomas J Moran	9	4,609	271
MacCormac Jr Coll, Chicago, IL 60604	1904	Mr Gordon C Borchardt	1	700	50
Macomb Comm Coll, Warren, MI 48093	1954	Mr Albert L Lorenzo	10	27,017	851
Macon Jr Coll, Macon, GA 31297	1968	Dr S Aaron Hyatt	5	2,699	98
Madison Area Tech Coll, Madison, WI 53704	1911	Mr Norman P Mitby	10	9,204	1,522
Manatee Comm Coll, Bradenton, FL 33507	1957	Dr Stephen J Korcheck	5	6,376	236

Name, address	Year	Governing official, control		Enroll-ment	Faculty
Manchester Comm Coll, Manchester, CT 06040	1963	Dr William E Vincent	5	7,000	200
Maple Woods Comm Coll, Kansas City, MO 64156	1969	Dr Stephen R Brainard	12	2,647	125
Maria Coll, Albany, NY 12208	1958	Sr Laureen Fitzgerald	1	954	73
Marion Tech Coll, Marion, OH 43302	1971	Dr John Richard Bryson	13	1,427	86
Marshalltown Comm Coll, Marshalltown, IA 50158	1927	Dr Paul Kegel	10	1,301	98
Martin Comm Coll, Williamston, NC 27892	1968	Dr W Travis Martin	5	800	57
Marymount Coll, Palos Verdes, California, Rancho Palos Verdes, CA 90274	1933	Dr Thomas D Wood	2	760	69
Massachusetts Bay Comm Coll, Wellesley Hills, MA 02181	1961	Mr Roger A Van Winkle	5	4,376	136
Massasoit Comm Coll, Brockton, MA 02402	1968	Dr Gerard F Burke	5	7,805	138
Mater Dei Coll, Ogdensburg, NY 13669	1960	Rev Robert H Aucoin	2	606	77
Mattatuck Comm Coll, Waterbury, CT 06708	1967	Dr Richard L Sanders	5	3,472	148
Mayland Tech Coll, Spruce Pine, NC 28777	1971	Ms Virginia Foxx	12	770	60
McCarrie Schools of Health Sciences and Tech, Philadelphia, PA 19146	1917	Joseph Walder	3	600	50
McCook Comm Coll, McCook, NE 69001	1926	NR	12	869	55
McDowell Tech Coll, Marion, NC 28752	1964	Dr Robert M Boggs	5	640	39
McHenry County Coll, Crystal Lake, IL 60012	1967	Mr Robert C Bartlett	12	3,528	143
McIntosh Coll, Dover, NH 03820	1896	Mr Richard F Waldo	3	600	27
McLennan Comm Coll, Waco, TX 76708	1965	Dr Wilbur A Ball	9	4,827	213
Mendocino Coll, Ukiah, CA 95482	1973	Dr Leroy R Lowery	12	3,761	160
Merced Coll, Merced, CA 95348	1962	Dr Tom K Harris Jr	12	6,400	418
Mercer County Comm Coll, Trenton, NJ 08690	1966	Mr John P Hanley	12	5,583	331
Meridian Jr Coll, Meridian, MS 39305	1937	Dr William F Scaggs	12	2,285	184
Merritt Coll, Oakland, CA 94619	1953	Ms Norma J Tucker	12	6,358	325
Mesabi Comm Coll, Virginia, MN 55792	1918	Richard Kohlase	5	1,140	39
Mesa Comm Coll, Mesa, AZ 85202	1965	Dr Wallace A Simpson	12	18,244	635
Metropolitan Tech Comm Coll, Omaha, NE 68103	1974	Dr J Richard Gilliland	12	6,835	345
Miami-Dade Comm Coll, Miami, FL 33132	1960	Dr Robert H McCabe	12	41,633	1,580
Miami-Jacobs Jr Coll of Business, Dayton, OH 45401	1860	Dr Charles G Campbell	3	614	34
Miami U–Hamilton Cmps, Hamilton, OH 45011	1968	Dr Harriet Taylor	5	1,925	65
Miami U–Middletown Cmps, Middletown, OH 45042	1966	Dr C Eugene Bennett	5	1,669	137
Middle Georgia Coll, Cochran, GA 31014	1884	Dr Louis C Alderman Jr	5	1,354	94
Middlesex Comm Coll, Middletown, CT 06457	1966	Mr Robert A Chapman	5	2,789	75
Middlesex Comm Coll, Bedford, MA 01730	1970	Dr James E Houlihan Jr	5	2,597	175
Middlesex County Coll, Edison, NJ 08818	1964	Dr Flora M Edwards	9	10,445	375
Midland Coll, Midland, TX 79705	1969	Dr Jess H Parrish	12	3,658	189
Midlands Tech Coll, Columbia, SC 29202	1974	Dr James R Morris	12	5,050	361
Mid Michigan Comm Coll, Harrison, MI 48625	1965	Dr Eugene F Schorzmann	12	1,842	67
Mid-Plains Comm Coll, North Platte, NE 69101	1965	Mr Kenneth L Aten	10	2,005	74
Mid-State Tech Inst, Wisconsin Rapids, WI 54494	1967	Dr M H Schneeberg	12	1,877	87
Miles Comm Coll, Miles City, MT 59301	1939	Dr Judson H Flower	12	717	60
Milwaukee Area Tech Coll, Milwaukee, WI 53203	1912	Dr Rus F Slicker	10	16,384	1,629
Mineral Area Coll, Flat River, MO 63601	1922	Dr Dixie Kohn	10	2,080	70
Minneapolis Comm Coll, Minneapolis, MN 55403	1965	Earl W Bowman	5	3,081	161
MiraCosta Coll, Oceanside, CA 92056	1934	Dr H Deon Holt	5	8,398	347
Mission Coll, Santa Clara, CA 95054	1977	NR	12	9,777	365
Mississippi County Comm Coll, Blytheville, AR 72315	1975	Dr John P Sullins	5	1,217	85
Mississippi Delta Jr Coll, Moorhead, MS 38761	1926	Dr J T Hall	10	1,502	110
Miss Gulf Coast Jr Coll, Jackson County Cmps, Gautier, MS 39553	1965	Mr Curtis L Davis	10	1,725	122
Miss Gulf Coast Jr Coll, Jefferson Davis Cmps, Gulfport, MS 39501	1965	Mr Glen W Cadle	12	2,800	150
Miss Gulf Coast Jr Coll, Perkinston Cmps, Perkinston, MS 39573	1925	Dr Clyde E Strickland	12	878	58
Mitchell Comm Coll, Statesville, NC 28677	1852	Dr Charles C Poindexter	5	1,452	117
Moberly Area Jr Coll, Moberly, MO 65270	1927	Dr Andrew Komar Jr	12	1,100	68
Modesto Jr Coll, Modesto, CA 95350	1921	Dr Tom Van Groningen	12	7,313	369
Mohave Comm Coll, Kingman, AZ 86401	1971	Dr Charles W Hall	5	3,772	175
Mohawk Valley Comm Coll, Utica, NY 13501	1946	Dr Michael I Schafer	12	6,200	427
Mohegan Comm Coll, Norwich, CT 06360	1969	Dr Robert E Miller	5	2,146	109
Monroe Business Inst, Bronx, NY 10468	1933	Stephen J Jerome	3	1,850	95
Monroe Comm Coll, Rochester, NY 14623	1961	Dr Peter A Spina	12	11,866	545
Monroe County Comm Coll, Monroe, MI 48161	1964	Mr Gerald D Welch	9	2,990	107
Montcalm Comm Coll, Sidney, MI 48885	1965	Dr Donald C Burns	12	2,094	99
Monterey Peninsula Coll, Monterey, CA 93940	1947	Dr Samuel A Ferguson	5	8,500	315
Montgomery Coll–Germantown Cmps, Germantown, MD 20874	1975	Dr Stanley M Dahlman	12	2,611	105
Montgomery Coll–Rockville Cmps, Rockville, MD 20850	1965	Dr Robert E Parilla	12	12,792	579
Montgomery Coll–Takoma Park Cmps, Takoma Park, MD 20912	1946	Dr O Robert Brown Jr	12	3,899	200
Montgomery County Comm Coll, Blue Bell, PA 19422	1964	Dr Edmond A Watters III	9	7,047	357
Moorpark Coll, Moorpark, CA 93021	1967	Dr W Ray Hearon	9	9,362	290
Moraine Park Tech Inst, Fond du Lac, WI 54935	1967	Dr John J Shanahan	12	5,446	305
Moraine Valley Comm Coll, Palos Hills, IL 60465	1967	Dr Fred Gaskin	12	12,776	490
Morgan Comm Coll, Fort Morgan, CO 80701	1967	Dr Harold Deselms	5	616	67
Morton Coll, Cicero, IL 60650	1924	Mr Charles Ferro	12	2,645	142
Motlow State Comm Coll, Tullahoma, TN 37388	1969	Dr A Frank Glass	5	2,332	142
Mountain Empire Comm Coll, Big Stone Gap, VA 24219	1972	Dr Victor Ficker	5	3,863	90
Mountain View Coll, Dallas, TX 75211	1970	Dr William H Jordan	9	4,984	245
Mt Hood Comm Coll, Gresham, OR 97030	1966	Dr Paul Kreider	12	10,024	439
Mt San Antonio Coll, Walnut, CA 91789	1946	Dr John D Randall	10	20,657	681
Mt San Jacinto Coll, San Jacinto, CA 92383	1963	Dr Dennis M Mayer	12	3,357	130
Mount Wachusett Comm Coll, Gardner, MA 01440	1963	Dr Arthur F Haley	5	1,855	92
Murray State Coll, Tishomingo, OK 73460	1908	Dr Clyde R Kindell	5	1,341	60
Muscatine Comm Coll, Muscatine, IA 52761	1929	Dr Victor G McAvoy	5	1,012	45
Muskegon Comm Coll, Muskegon, MI 49442	1926	Dr John G Thompson	12	5,662	195
Muskingum Area Tech Coll, Zanesville, OH 43701	1969	Dr Lynn H Willett	12	1,493	99
Napa Valley Coll, Napa, CA 94558	1940	Dr William H Feddersen	12	5,708	294
Nash Tech Coll, Rocky Mount, NC 27804	1968	Dr J Reid Parrott Jr	5	1,676	86
Nashville State Tech Inst, Nashville, TN 37209	1970	Dr Howard J Lawrence	5	5,293	251
Nassau Comm Coll, Garden City, NY 11530	1959	Dr Sean A Fanelli	12	19,363	1,001
National Ed Ctr–Allentown Business Sch Cmps, Allentown, PA 18101	1869	Bettie H Thomas	3	900	18
National Ed Ctr–Bauder Coll Cmps, Fort Lauderdale, FL 33334	1964	Erik Brumme	3	1,222	55
National Ed Ctr–Brown Inst Cmps, Minneapolis, MN 55407	1946	Bill Johnson	3	1,600	64

Name, address	Year	Governing official, control		Enroll-ment	Faculty
National Ed Ctr–Kentucky Coll of Tech Cmps, Louisville, KY 40213	1946	NR	3	625	30
National Ed Ctr–National Inst of Tech Cmps, West Des Moines, IA 50265	1964	NR	3	625	19
National Ed Ctr–Spartan Sch of Aeronaut Cmps, Tulsa, OK 74158 (2)	1928	William A Orth	3	2,005	93
National Sch of Health Tech, Philadelphia, PA 19107	1963	NR	3	600	25
Navajo Comm Coll, Tsaile, AZ 86556	1968	Mr Dean Jackson	4	1,643	182
Navarro Coll, Corsicana, TX 75110	1946	Dr Kenneth P Walker	12	2,092	97
Nebraska Western Coll, Scottsbluff, NE 69361	1926	Dr John N Harms	12	1,741	75
Neosho County Comm Coll, Chanute, KS 66720	1936	Dr J C Sanders	12	1,000	83
Newbury Coll, Brookline, MA 02146	1962	Mr Edward J Tassinari	1	912	252
New Hampshire Tech Inst, Concord, NH 03301	1964	Dr David E Larrabee Sr	5	820	81
New Mexico Jr Coll, Hobbs, NM 88240	1965	Dr Robert A Anderson Jr	12	2,628	96
New Mexico State U–Alamogordo, Alamogordo, NM 88310	1958	Dr Charles R Reidlinger	5	1,541	68
New Mexico State U–Carlsbad, Carlsbad, NM 88220	1950	Dr Shelton W Marlow	5	1,050	48
New River Comm Coll, Dublin, VA 24084	1969	Dr H Randall Edwards	5	1,395	154
N F Nunnelley State Tech Coll, Childersburg, AL 35044	1965	NR	5	600	31
Niagara County Comm Coll, Sanborn, NY 14132	1962	Dr Donald J Donato	12	4,228	329
Nicolet Coll and Tech Inst, Rhinelander, WI 54501	1968	Dr Jack T Lundy	12	1,179	88
Normandale Comm Coll, Bloomington, MN 55431	1968	Mr Dale A Lorenz	5	6,966	182
Northampton County Area Comm Coll, Bethlehem, PA 18017	1967	Dr Robert J Kopecek	12	4,145	240
North Arkansas Comm Coll, Harrison, AR 72601	1974	Dr Bill Baker	12	1,025	75
North Central Michigan Coll, Petoskey, MI 49770	1958	Mr Alfred D Shankland	9	1,488	92
North Central Tech Coll, Mansfield, OH 44906	1961	Dr Byron E Kee	5	1,711	113
North Central Tech Inst, Wausau, WI 54401	1912	Dr Donald Hagon	10	2,007	171
North Country Comm Coll, Saranac Lake, NY 12983	1967	David W Petty	12	1,580	156
North Dakota State Coll of Science, Wahpeton, ND 58075	1903	Dr Clair T Blikre	5	2,583	158
Northeast Alabama State Jr Coll, Rainsville, AL 35986	1963	Dr Charles M Pendley	5	1,162	46
Northeastern Oklahoma A&M Coll, Miami, OK 74354	1919	Dr Bobby R Wright	5	2,576	110
Northeast Iowa Tech Inst–South Ctr, Peosta, IA 52068	1970	Mr James L Arneson	12	665	49
Northeast Mississippi Jr Coll, Booneville, MS 38829	1948	Harold T White	10	2,300	145
Northeast Tech Comm Coll, Norfolk, NE 68701	1973	Dr Robert P Cox	12	2,307	117
Northeast Wisconsin Tech Inst, Green Bay, WI 54307	1912	Dr Gerald D Prindiville	12	5,476	184
Northern Essex Comm Coll, Haverhill, MA 01830	1960	Dr John R Dimitry	5	6,009	381
Northern Nevada Comm Coll, Elko, NV 89801	1967	Dr William J Berg	5	2,000	125
Northern New Mexico Comm Coll, Española, NM 87532	1909	Mr Frank A Serrano III	5	1,103	73
Northern Oklahoma Coll, Tonkawa, OK 74653	1901	Dr Edwin E Vineyard	5	1,638	79
Northern Virginia Comm Coll, Annandale, VA 22003	1965	Dr Richard J Ernst	5	33,682	1,353
North Florida Jr Coll, Madison, FL 32340	1958	NR	5	1,083	116
North Harris County Coll, Houston, TX 77073	1972	Dr Joe A Airola	12	11,344	514
North Hennepin Comm Coll, Minneapolis, MN 55445	1966	Dr John Helling	5	4,912	175
North Idaho Coll, Coeur d'Alene, ID 83814	1933	Mr Carl R Bennett	12	2,305	155
North Iowa Area Comm Coll, Mason City, IA 50401	1918	Dr David Buettner	12	2,456	173
North Lake Coll, Irving, TX 75038	1977	Dr James F Horton Jr	9	5,483	206
Northland Comm Coll, Thief River Falls, MN 56701	1965	Dr T A Easton	5	766	38
Northland Pioneer Coll, Holbrook, AZ 86025	1974	Dr Marvin L Vasher	12	5,638	392
North Seattle Comm Coll, Seattle, WA 98103	1970	Dr Cecil Baxter Jr	5	6,827	248
North Shore Comm Coll, Beverly, MA 01915	1965	Dr George Traicoff	5	3,607	120
Northwest Alabama State Jr Coll, Phil Campbell, AL 35581	1961	Dr Charles W Britnell	5	1,365	83
Northwest Comm Coll, Powell, WY 82435	1946	Dr Sinclair Orendorff	12	1,788	140
Northwestern Business Coll–Tech Ctr, Lima, OH 45805	1920	Mr Loren R Jarvis	3	1,165	70
Northwestern Connecticut Comm Coll, Winsted, CT 06098	1965	Dr Booker T DeVaughn	5	2,165	63
Northwestern Electronics Inst, Columbia Heights, MN 55421	1930	David Arneson	1	690	51
Northwestern Michigan Coll, Traverse City, MI 49684	1951	Dr Phillip E Runkel	12	3,051	123
Northwest Mississippi Jr Coll, Senatobia, MS 38668	1927	Mr David Haraway	12	3,132	164
Northwest Tech Coll, Archbold, OH 43502	1968	Dr James O Miller	5	1,067	79
Norwalk Comm Coll, Norwalk, CT 06854	1961	Dr William H Schwab	5	3,430	105
Norwalk State Tech Coll, Norwalk, CT 06856	1961	Dr William M Krummel	5	614	100
Oakland Comm Coll, Bloomfield Hills, MI 48013	1964	Dr R Stephen Nicholson	12	27,827	583
Oakton Comm Coll, Des Plaines, IL 60016	1969	Dr Thomas TenHoeve	10	10,547	392
Ocean County Coll, Toms River, NJ 08753	1964	Dr Milton Shaw	9	5,642	239
Odessa Coll, Odessa, TX 79762	1946	Dr Philip T Speegle	12	4,312	265
Ohlone Coll, Fremont, CA 94539	1967	Dr Peter Blomerley	12	7,805	364
Oklahoma City Comm Coll, Oklahoma City, OK 73159	1969	Dr Donald L Newport	5	7,866	259
Oklahoma State U Tech Branch, Oklahoma City, Oklahoma City, OK 73107	1961	Dr James Hooper	5	3,142	175
Oklahoma State U Tech Branch, Okmulgee, Okmulgee, OK 74447	1946	Dr Robert Klabenes	5	2,744	160
Olympic Coll, Bremerton, WA 98310	1946	Dr Henry M Milander	5	5,874	318
Onondaga Comm Coll, Syracuse, NY 13215	1962	Dr Bruce H Leslie	12	7,115	520
Orangeburg-Calhoun Tech Coll, Orangeburg, SC 29115	1968	Mr M Rudolph Groomes	12	2,445	177
Orange Coast Coll, Costa Mesa, CA 92626	1947	Dr Donald R Bronsard	12	22,559	865
Orange County Comm Coll, Middletown, NY 10940	1950	Dr William F Messner	12	4,933	270
Otero Jr Coll, La Junta, CO 81050	1941	Dr W L McDivitt	5	754	52
Owens Tech Coll, Toledo, OH 43699	1966	Dr Jacob H See	5	4,932	370
Oxnard Coll, Oxnard, CA 93033	1975	Mr Edward W Robings	9	4,929	255
Palm Beach Jr Coll, Lake Worth, FL 33461	1933	Dr Edward M Eissey	5	12,148	619
Palomar Coll, San Marcos, CA 92069	1946	Dr George R Boggs	12	14,843	651
Palo Verde Coll, Blythe, CA 92225	1947	Mr Kirk Avery	12	720	51
Panola Jr Coll, Carthage, TX 75633	1947	Dr Gary McDaniel	12	1,380	56
Paris Jr Coll, Paris, TX 75460	1924	Dr Dennis F Michaelis	12	2,174	120
Parkersburg Comm Coll, Parkersburg, WV 26101	1971	Dr Eldon L Miller	5	3,146	166
Parks Coll, Denver, CO 80221	1895	Dr Morgan Landry	3	750	44
Pasadena City Coll, Pasadena, CA 91106	1924	Dr Jack A Scott	10	20,164	684
Pasco-Hernando Comm Coll, Dade City, FL 33525	1972	Dr Milton O Jones	5	2,864	181
Passaic County Comm Coll, Paterson, NJ 07509	1968	Kenneth E Wright	9	2,726	161
Patrick Henry Comm Coll, Martinsville, VA 24115	1962	Dr Max F Wingett	5	1,776	74
Patrick Henry State Jr Coll, Monroeville, AL 36460	1965	Mr James R Allen	5	750	32
Paul D Camp Comm Coll, Franklin, VA 23851	1971	Dr Michael B McCall	5	1,132	65
Paul Smith's Coll, Paul Smiths, NY 12970	1937	Harry K Miller Jr	1	673	73
Pearl River Jr Coll, Poplarville, MS 39470	1909	Dr Ted J Alexander	12	2,307	107
Peirce Jr Coll, Philadelphia, PA 19102	1865	Dr Raymond C Lewin	1	1,492	117
Peninsula Coll, Port Angeles, WA 98362	1961	Dr Paul G Cornaby	5	759	118
Pennco Tech, Bristol, PA 19007	1961	John Hobyak	3	745	65

Name, address	Year	Governing official, control		Enrollment	Faculty
Penna State U Altoona Cmps, Altoona, PA 16603	1929	Dr James A Duplass	13	2,354	91
Penna State U Beaver Cmps, Monaca, PA 15061	1964	David B Otto	13	1,167	53
Penna State U Berks Cmps, Reading, PA 19608	1924	Dr Frederick H Gaige	13	1,262	58
Penna State U Delaware County Cmps, Media, PA 19063	1966	Edward S J Tomezsko	13	1,566	62
Penna State U DuBois Cmps, DuBois, PA 15801	1935	Dr John D Sink	13	929	41
Penna State U Fayette Cmps, Uniontown, PA 15401	1934	Dr John D Sink	13	701	41
Penna State U Hazelton Cmps, Hazelton, PA 18201	1934	Dr William J David	13	1,123	58
Penna State U McKeesport Cmps, McKeesport, PA 15132	1947	Dr Cash J Kowalski	13	1,563	60
Penna State U Mont Alto Cmps, Mont Alto, PA 17237	1929	Vernon L Shockley	13	822	51
Penna State U New Kensington Cmps, New Kensington, PA 15068	1958	Dr Robert D Arbuckle	13	1,384	55
Penna State U Ogontz Cmps, Abington, PA 19001	1950	Dr Robert A Bernoff	13	3,418	127
Penna State U Schuylkill Cmps, Schuylkill Haven, PA 17972	1934	Dr Wayne Lammie	13	999	43
Penna State U Shenango Valley Cmps, Sharon, PA 16146	1965	Dr Vincent De Sanctis	13	1,177	47
Penna State U Wilkes-Barre Cmps, Lehman, PA 18627	1916	Dr James H Ryan	13	1,036	47
Penna State U Worthington Scranton Cmps, Dunmore, PA 18512	1923	Dr James D Gallagher	13	1,128	51
Penna State U York Cmps, York, PA 17403	1926	Dr John J Romano	13	1,294	58
Penn Valley Comm Coll, Kansas City, MO 64111	1969	Mr Andrew V Stevenson	10	5,119	240
Pensacola Jr Coll, Pensacola, FL 32504	1948	Dr Horace E Hartsell	5	8,317	958
Phillips Coll, Columbus, GA 31901	1971	NR	3	644	29
Phillips Coll, Jackson, MS 39216	1973	Ms Nan Thompson	3	605	32
Phillips County Comm Coll, Helena, AR 72342	1965	Dr John W Easley	12	1,531	90
Phoenix Coll, Phoenix, AZ 85013	1920	Dr William E Berry	12	13,146	544
Piedmont Tech Coll, Roxboro, NC 27573	1970	Dr Edward W Cox	5	901	56
Piedmont Tech Coll, Greenwood, SC 29648	1966	Dr Lex D Walters	5	1,615	115
Piedmont Virginia Comm Coll, Charlottesville, VA 22901	1972	Dr George B Vaughan	5	4,014	160
Pierce Coll, Tacoma, WA 98498	1967	Dr Robert H Stauffer	5	8,010	285
Pikes Peak Comm Coll, Colorado Springs, CO 80906	1969	Dr Cecil L Graves	5	5,362	454
Pima Comm Coll, Tucson, AZ 85702	1966	Dr S James Manilla	5	22,959	1,026
Pitt Comm Coll, Greenville, NC 27835	1961	Dr Charles E Russell	12	3,107	154
Pittsburgh Inst of Aeronautics, Pittsburgh, PA 15236 (2)	1929	Ivan D Livi	1	750	30
Polk Comm Coll, Winter Haven, FL 33880	1964	Dr Maryly VanLeer Peck	5	4,700	179
Porterville Coll, Porterville, CA 93257	1927	Dr Paul D Alcantra	5	2,502	174
Portland Comm Coll, Portland, OR 97219	1961	Dr Daniel F Moriarty	12	34,400	1,737
Potomac State Coll of West Virginia U, Keyser, WV 26726	1901	Dr James L McBee Jr	5	1,015	64
Prairie State Coll, Chicago Heights, IL 60411	1958	Dr Herbert Stoutenburg	12	4,364	348
Prince George's Comm Coll, Largo, MD 20772	1958	Dr Robert I Bickford	9	12,435	645
Pueblo Comm Coll, Pueblo, CO 81004	1979	Dr Tony Zeiss	5	1,635	156
Puerto Rico Jr Coll, Rio Piedras, PR 00928	1949	Mr Luis E Gonzalez Vales	1	4,405	366
Queensborough Comm Coll of City U of NY, Bayside, NY 11364	1958	Dr Kurt R Schmeller	12	12,194	691
Quincy Jr Coll, Quincy, MA 02169	1958	Dr O Clayton Johnson	11	1,250	173
Quinebaug Valley Comm Coll, Danielson, CT 06239	1971	Dr Robert E Miller	5	1,245	59
Quinsigamond Comm Coll, Worcester, MA 01606	1963	Dr Clifford S Peterson	5	4,269	188
Ramirez Coll of Business and Tech, Hato Rey, PR 00918	1922	NR	3	1,398	80
Rancho Santiago Coll, Santa Ana, CA 92706	1915	Dr Robert D Jensen	10	21,695	750
Randolph Tech Coll, Asheboro, NC 27203	1962	Mr Merton H Branson	5	1,247	55
Ranger Jr Coll, Ranger, TX 76470	1926	Dr Jack M Elsom	13	808	55
Rappahannock Comm Coll, Glenns, VA 23149	1970	Dr John H Upton	12	1,433	72
Reading Area Comm Coll, Reading, PA 19603	1971	Dr Gust Zogas	10	1,290	78
Red Rocks Comm Coll, Golden, CO 80401	1967	Dr Thomas K Thomas	5	3,807	161
Rend Lake Coll, Ina, IL 62846	1967	Dr Harry J Braun	5	2,372	152
RETS Electronic Inst, Birmingham, AL 35234	1974	Gene Smythe	3	680	15
Richard Bland Coll, Petersburg, VA 23805	1961	Dr Clarence Maze Jr	5	853	44
Richland Coll, Dallas, TX 75243	1972	Dr Stephen Mittelstet	12	13,610	570
Richland Comm Coll, Decatur, IL 62526	1971	Mr Howard Brown	10	3,355	167
Richmond Tech Coll, Hamlet, NC 28345	1964	Joseph W Grimsley	5	1,045	111
Ricks Coll, Rexburg, ID 83440	1888	Dr Joe J Christensen	2	6,880	293
Rio Hondo Comm Coll, Whittier, CA 90608	1960	Herbert M Sussman	12	12,536	347
Rio Salado Comm Coll, Phoenix, AZ 85003	1978	Dr Charles A Green	12	12,057	505
Riverside Comm Coll, Riverside, CA 92506	1916	Dr Charles A Kane	12	14,719	544
Roane State Comm Coll, Harriman, TN 37748	1971	Dr Cuyler A Dunbar	5	3,596	170
Robert Morris Coll, Chicago Cmps, Chicago, IL 60601	1965	Richard D Pickett	1	1,718	111
Rochester Comm Coll, Rochester, MN 55904	1915	Dr Geraldine A Evans	5	3,153	130
Rockingham Comm Coll, Wentworth, NC 27375	1964	Dr N J Owens Jr	5	1,632	138
Rockland Comm Coll, Suffern, NY 10901	1959	Dr F Thomas Clark	12	8,447	328
Rock Valley Coll, Rockford, IL 61101	1964	Dr Karl J Jacobs	10	11,500	555
Rogers State Coll, Claremore, OK 74017	1909	Dr Richard H Mosier	5	3,200	151
Rose State Coll, Midwest City, OK 73110	1971	Dr Larry Nutter	12	9,971	272
Rowan Tech Coll, Salisbury, NC 28144	1963	Dr Richard L Brownell	5	2,100	130
Sacramento City Coll, Sacramento, CA 95822	1916	Dr Carl Christian Andersen	12	13,334	450
Saddleback Coll, Mission Viejo, CA 92692	1967	Dr William O Jay	12	19,044	725
Saint Augustine Coll, Chicago, IL 60640	1980	Fr Carlos A Plazas	1	852	79
St Bernard Parish Comm Coll, Chalmette, LA 70043	1967	Dr Elizabeth Zimmermann	12	634	29
St Clair County Comm Coll, Port Huron, MI 48060	1923	Dr Richard L Norris	9	3,609	223
St Johns River Comm Coll, Palatka, FL 32077	1958	Dr R L McLendon Jr	5	2,036	117
St Louis Comm Coll at Florissant Valley, St Louis, MO 63135	1963	NR	10	10,383	377
St Louis Comm Coll at Forest Park, St Louis, MO 63110	1962	Dr Vernon O Crawley	10	6,422	331
St Louis Comm Coll at Meramec, Kirkwood, MO 63122	1963	NR	10	12,649	411
St Paul Tech Vocational Inst, St Paul, MN 55102	1922	NR	12	3,653	147
St Petersburg Jr Coll, St Petersburg, FL 33733	1927	Dr Carl M Kuttler Jr	12	16,215	613
St Philip's Coll, San Antonio, TX 78203	1898	Dr Stephen R Mitchell	10	5,816	464
Salem Comm Coll, Carneys Point, NJ 08069	1971	Dr William Wenzel	9	1,001	73
Salish Kootenai Coll, Pablo, MT 59855	1977	Dr Joe McDonald	1	803	56
Salt Lake Comm Coll, Salt Lake City, UT 84130	1948	Dr Orville D Carnahan	5	8,815	240
Sampson Tech Coll, Clinton, NC 28328	1965	Dr Clifton W Paderick	12	885	66
San Antonio Coll, San Antonio, TX 78284	1925	Dr Max Castillo	12	21,294	985
San Bernardino Valley Coll, San Bernardino, CA 92410	1926	Dr Arthur M Jensen	12	10,031	402
Sandhills Comm Coll, Pinehurst, NC 28374	1963	Dr Raymond A Stone	12	1,860	105
San Diego City Coll, San Diego, CA 92101	1914	NR	12	14,360	568
San Diego Mesa Coll, San Diego, CA 92111	1962	Dr Allen Brooks	10	21,800	890
San Diego Miramar Coll, San Diego, CA 92126	1969	Dr George F Yee	12	4,936	176

Name, address	Year	Governing official, control		Enrollment	Faculty
San Jacinto Coll–Central Cmps, Pasadena, TX 77505	1961	Dr Monte Blue	12	9,219	398
San Jacinto Coll–North Cmps, Houston, TX 77049	1974	Dr Edwin E Lehr	12	3,379	168
San Jacinto Coll–South Cmps, Houston, TX 77089	1979	Dr Parker Williams	12	4,239	188
San Joaquin Delta Coll, Stockton, CA 95207	1935	Mr Lilburn H Horton Jr	10	15,176	488
San Jose City Coll, San Jose, CA 95128	1921	Dr Byron R Skinner	10	10,203	348
San Juan Coll, Farmington, NM 87401	1958	Dr James C Henderson	9	2,608	153
Santa Barbara City Coll, Santa Barbara, CA 93109	1908	Dr Peter R MacDougall	10	10,560	445
Santa Fe Comm Coll, Gainesville, FL 32601	1966	Mr Alan J Robertson	12	8,397	430
Santa Fe Comm Coll, Santa Fe, NM 87502	1983	NR	12	751	145
Santa Monica Coll, Santa Monica, CA 90405	1929	Dr Richard L Moore	12	22,485	743
Santa Rosa Jr Coll, Santa Rosa, CA 95401	1918	Dr Roy Mikalson	12	23,282	719
Sauk Valley Comm Coll, Dixon, IL 61021	1965	NR	10	2,614	180
Schenectady County Comm Coll, Schenectady, NY 12305	1968	Dr Peter F Burnham	12	2,990	162
Schoolcraft Coll, Livonia, MI 48152	1961	Dr Richard W McDowell	10	8,750	350
Scott Comm Coll, Bettendorf, IA 52722	1966	John T Blong	12	2,907	145
S D Bishop State Jr Coll, Mobile, AL 36690	1965	Dr Yvonne Kennedy	5	1,586	51
Seattle Central Comm Coll, Seattle, WA 98122	1966	Dr Ernest A Martinez	5	8,504	570
Seminole Comm Coll, Sanford, FL 32771	1966	Dr Earl S Weldon	12	5,237	422
Seward County Comm Coll, Liberal, KS 67901	1969	Dr Theodore W Wischropp	12	1,545	106
Shasta Coll, Redding, CA 96099	1948	Kenneth B Cerreta	12	9,238	350
Shawnee Coll, Ullin, IL 62992	1967	Dr Loren E Klaus	12	2,170	219
Shawnee State U, Portsmouth, OH 45662	1975	Frank C Taylor	5	2,795	221
Shelby State Comm Coll, Memphis, TN 38174	1970	Dr Raymond C Bowen	5	3,730	212
Shelton State Comm Coll, Tuscaloosa, AL 35404	1979	Dr Leo Sumner	5	2,236	31
Sheridan Coll, Sheridan, WY 82801	1948	Dr Gordon A Ward	12	1,621	133
Shoreline Comm Coll, Seattle, WA 98133	1964	Dr Ronald E Bell	5	7,230	285
Sierra Coll, Rocklin, CA 95677	1936	Dr Gerald C Angove	5	11,374	317
Sinclair Comm Coll, Dayton, OH 45402	1887	Dr David H Ponitz	12	16,094	810
Skagit Valley Coll, Mount Vernon, WA 98273	1926	Dr James M Ford	5	2,114	309
Skyline Coll, San Bruno, CA 94066	1969	Ms Linda Graef Salter	9	7,724	311
Snead State Jr Coll, Boaz, AL 35957	1935	Dr William H Osborn	5	1,309	43
Snow Coll, Ephraim, UT 84627	1888	Dr Steven D Bennion	5	1,408	65
Solano Comm Coll, Suisun City, CA 94585	1945	Dr Marjorie K Blaha	9	8,437	313
Somerset County Coll, Somerville, NJ 08876	1905	Dr S Charles Irace	9	4,734	185
South Central Comm Coll, New Haven, CT 06511	1968	Dr Richard M Turner III	5	2,357	118
South Coll, Savannah, GA 31406	1899	Mr John T South III	3	700	58
Southeast Comm Coll, Lincoln Cmps, Lincoln, NE 68520	1973	Dr Jack Huck	10	4,109	567
Southeast Comm Coll, Milford Cmps, Milford, NE 68405	1941	Dr Thomas Stone	10	910	120
Southeastern Baptist Theological Sem, Wake Forest, NC 27587	1950	Dr W Randall Lolley	2	1,099	57
Southeastern Comm Coll, Whiteville, NC 28472	1964	Dr Dan W Moore	5	1,518	79
Southeastern Comm Coll, North Cmps, West Burlington, IA 52655	1968	Mr Carlton W Callison	12	1,637	135
Southeastern Illinois Coll, Harrisburg, IL 62946	1960	Dr Harry W Abell	5	3,400	163
Southern Arkansas U Tech, Camden, AR 71701	1968	Dr George J Brown	5	753	43
Southern Jr Coll of Business, Birmingham, AL 35203	1969	NR	3	605	30
Southern Maine Vocational-Tech Inst, South Portland, ME 04106	1946	Dr Wayne H Ross	5	1,496	144
Southern Ohio Coll, Cincinnati Cmps, Cincinnati, OH 45237	1927	Dr M Douglas Reed	3	1,122	78
Southern Ohio Coll, Fairfield Cmps, Fairfield, OH 45014	[illegible]	Duane W Hawkins	3	770	70
Southern Ohio Coll, Northeast Cmps, Akron, OH 44312	1968	Garry H Foraker	3	700	60
Southern State Comm Coll, Hillsboro, OH 45133	1975	Dr Lewis C Miller	5	1,257	82
Southern Union State Jr Coll, Wadley, AL 36276	1922	Dr Richard J Federinko	5	2,119	91
Southern U, Shreveport–Bossier City Cmps, Shreveport, LA 71107	1964	Mr Leonard C Barnes	5	757	58
Southern West Virginia Comm Coll, Logan, WV 25601	1971	Dr Gregory D Adkins	5	2,618	127
South Florida Comm Coll, Avon Park, FL 33825	1966	Dr Catherine P Cornelius	5	1,500	110
South Georgia Coll, Douglas, GA 31533	1906	Dr Edward D Jackson Jr	5	854	47
South Mountain Comm Coll, Phoenix, AZ 85040	1979	Raul Cardenas	12	2,272	120
South Plains Coll, Levelland, TX 79336	1958	Dr Marvin L Baker	12	3,598	206
South Puget Sound Comm Coll, Olympia, WA 98502	1970	Dr Kenneth Minnaert	5	4,085	188
South Seattle Comm Coll, Seattle, WA 98106	1970	Mr Jerry M Brockey	5	4,984	234
Southside Virginia Comm Coll, Alberta, VA 23821	1970	Dr John J Cavan	5	1,680	129
Southwestern Baptist Theological Sem, Fort Worth, TX 76122	1908	Dr Russell H Dilday Jr	2	4,375	198
Southwestern Coll, Chula Vista, CA 92010	1961	Mr Theodore Tilton	12	12,359	363
Southwestern Comm Coll, Creston, IA 50801	1966	Dr Richard L Byerly	5	790	48
Southwestern Michigan Coll, Dowagiac, MI 49047	1964	Mr David C Briegel	12	3,200	167
Southwestern Oregon Comm Coll, Coos Bay, OR 97420	1961	Dr Robert L Barber	12	4,316	230
Southwestern Tech Coll, Sylva, NC 28779	1964	Dr Norman K Myers	5	1,248	134
Southwest State Tech Coll, Mobile, AL 36605	1954	Mr Donald S Jefferies	5	709	37
Southwest Texas Jr Coll, Uvalde, TX 78801	1946	Dr Jimmy Goodson	12	2,116	135
Southwest Virginia Comm Coll, Richlands, VA 24641	1968	Dr Charles R King	5	5,379	190
Southwest Wisconsin Vocational-Tech Inst, Fennimore, WI 53809	1967	Mr Ronald H Anderson	12	1,400	117
Spartanburg Methodist Coll, Spartanburg, SC 29301	1911	Dr George D Fields	2	1,030	76
Spartanburg Tech Coll, Spartanburg, SC 29303	1961	Dr Jack A Powers	5	1,757	180
Spokane Comm Coll, Spokane, WA 99207	1963	Dr Terrance R Brown	5	4,530	267
Spokane Falls Comm Coll, Spokane, WA 99204	1967	Mrs Phyllis Everest	5	5,322	431
Spoon River Coll, Canton, IL 61520	1959	Felix T Haynes	5	2,100	129
Springfield Tech Comm Coll, Springfield, MA 01105	1967	Andrew M Scibelli	5	3,521	214
Stanly Tech Coll, Albemarle, NC 28001	1971	Dr Charles H Byrd	5	1,258	56
Stark Tech Coll, Canton, OH 44720	1970	Dr John J Mc Grath	12	3,363	196
State Comm Coll of East St Louis, East St Louis, IL 62201	1969	Rogers Conner	5	1,449	83
State Fair Comm Coll, Sedalia, MO 65301	1966	Dr Marvin Fielding	10	1,579	88
State Tech Inst at Knoxville, Knoxville, TN 37933	1974	Mr J L Goins	5	2,756	179
State Tech Inst at Memphis, Memphis, TN 38134	1967	Dr Charles Temple	5	7,657	349
State U of NY Coll of A&T at Morrisville, Morrisville, NY 13408	1908	Dr Thomas C Leamer	5	3,222	159
State U of NY Coll of Tech at Alfred, Alfred, NY 14802	1908	Dr John O Hunter	5	3,601	219
State U of NY Coll of Tech at Canton, Canton, NY 13617	1906	Dr Earl W MacArthur	5	2,204	120
State U of NY Coll of Tech at Delhi, Delhi, NY 13753	1913	Mr Seldon M Kruger	5	2,360	127
Stautzenberger Coll, Toledo, OH 43623	1923	Larry Mitchell & George Hawes	3	652	30
St Mary's Cmps of the Coll of St Catherine, Minneapolis, MN 55454	1964	Sr Anne Joachim Moore	2	680	90
Stratton Coll, Milwaukee, WI 53202	1863	Ms Maritza Samoorian	3	625	30

Name, address	Year	Governing official, control		Enroll-ment	Faculty
Suffolk County Comm Coll–Ammerman Cmps, Selden, NY 11784	1962	Mr Robert T Kreiling	12	11,357	512
Suffolk County Comm Coll–Eastern Cmps, Riverhead, NY 11901	1977	Steven T Kenny	12	1,837	122
Suffolk County Comm Coll–Western Cmps, Brentwood, NY 11717	1974	Salvatore J LaLima	12	4,921	250
Sullivan County Comm Coll, Loch Sheldrake, NY 12759	1962	Dr John F Walter	12	1,779	96
Sullivan Jr Coll of Business, Louisville, KY 40232	1864	David P Higley	3	1,786	73
Sumter Area Tech Coll, Sumter, SC 29150	1963	Dr James L Hudgins	5	1,586	150
Suomi Coll, Hancock, MI 49930	1896	Rev Ralph J Jalkanen	2	620	65
Surry Comm Coll, Dobson, NC 27017	1965	Dr Swanson Richards	5	2,832	75
Tacoma Comm Coll, Tacoma, WA 98465	1965	Dr Carleton Opgard	5	4,440	264
Taft Coll, Taft, CA 93268	1922	Dr David Cothrun	5	1,123	70
Tallahassee Comm Coll, Tallahassee, FL 32304	1966	Dr James H Hinson Jr	12	6,315	232
Tarrant County Jr Coll, Fort Worth, TX 76102	1967	Dr Joe B Rushing	9	24,562	839
Taylor Business Inst, New York, NY 10119	1961	Mr William N Wildish	3	1,054	92
Tech Career Institutes, New York, NY 10001	1974	George Leelike	3	1,800	90
Tech Coll of Alamance, Haw River, NC 27258	1959	Dr W Ronold McCarter	5	3,100	133
Temple Jr Coll, Temple, TX 76501	1926	Dr Marvin R Felder	10	2,031	104
Terra Tech Coll, Fremont, OH 43420	1968	Dr Richard M Simon	5	2,413	110
Texarkana Coll, Texarkana, TX 75501	1927	Dr Carl M Nelson	12	3,380	200
Texas Southmost Coll, Brownsville, TX 78520	1926	Dr Juliet V Garcia	10	5,102	200
Texas State Tech Inst–Amarillo Cmps, Amarillo, TX 79111	1970	Mr Ronald DeSpain	5	982	96
Texas State Tech Inst–Harlingen Cmps, Harlingen, TX 78550	1967	Mr J Gilbert Leal	5	2,261	165
Texas State Tech Inst–Sweetwater Cmps, Sweetwater, TX 79556	1970	Dr Herbert C Robbins	5	668	44
Texas State Tech Inst–Waco Cmps, Waco, TX 76705	1965	Dr Robert D Krienke	5	4,737	351
Thames Valley State Tech Coll, Norwich, CT 06360	1963	Dr George D Harris	5	750	47
Thomas Nelson Comm Coll, Hampton, VA 23670	1968	Dr Thomas S Kubala	5	6,355	247
Thornton Comm Coll, South Holland, IL 60473	1927	NR	5	7,462	327
Three Rivers Comm Coll, Poplar Bluff, MO 63901	1966	Dr Jack L Bottenfield	5	1,578	62
Tidewater Comm Coll, Chesapeake Cmps, Chesapeake, VA 23320	1968	Dr George B Pass	5	1,953	96
Tidewater Comm Coll, Frederick Cmps, Portsmouth, VA 23703	1968	Dr George B Pass	5	4,556	194
Tidewater Comm Coll, Virginia Beach Cmps, Virginia Beach, VA 23456	1968	Dr George B Pass	5	9,022	374
Tompkins Cortland Comm Coll, Dryden, NY 13053	1968	Eduardo J Marti	12	2,840	183
Treasure Valley Comm Coll, Ontario, OR 97914	1962	Glenn Mayle	12	1,472	73
Trenholm State Tech Coll, Montgomery, AL 36108	1965	Dr Thad McClammy	5	686	48
Trenton Jr Coll, Trenton, MO 64683	1925	Robert M Webb	10	789	64
Tri-Cities State Tech Inst, Blountville, TN 37617	1966	Dr R Wade Powers	5	1,849	97
Tri-County Comm Coll, Murphy, NC 28906	1964	Mr Vincent W Crisp	5	801	54
Tri-County Tech Coll, Pendleton, SC 29670	1962	Dr Don C Garrison	5	2,379	211
Trident Tech Coll, Charleston, SC 29411	1964	Dr Charles W Branch	12	5,218	308
Trinidad State Jr Coll, Trinidad, CO 81082	1925	Dr Thomas E Sullivan	5	1,250	98
Trinity Valley Comm Coll, Athens, TX 75751	1946	Dr William C Campion	12	3,893	154
Triton Coll, River Grove, IL 60171	1964	Richard Fonte	5	13,146	914
Trocaire Coll, Buffalo, NY 14220	1958	Sr Mary Carmina Coppola	1	802	85
Truckee Meadows Comm Coll, Reno, NV 89512	1971	Dr John Gwaltney	5	7,905	380
Tunxis Comm Coll, Farmington, CT 06032	1969	Dr Eduardo Marti	5	1,656	119
Tyler Jr Coll, Tyler, TX 75711	1926	Dr Raymond M Hawkins	12	7,227	346
Ulster County Comm Coll, Stone Ridge, NY 12484	1962	Mr Robert T Brown	12	3,150	194
Umpqua Comm Coll, Roseburg, OR 97470	1964	Dr James Kraby	12	1,718	250
Union County Coll, Cranford, NJ 07016	1933	Dr Derek Nunney	12	8,395	397
United Electronics Inst, Tampa, FL 33619 (2)	1967	Robert R DeVito	3	820	22
U of Akron, Wayne General and Tech Coll, Orrville, OH 44667	1972	Dr William V Muse	5	1,061	108
U of Alaska, Islands Comm Coll, Sitka, AK 99835	1962	Dr Jerry L Harris	5	892	62
U of Alaska, Kenai Peninsula Comm Coll, Soldotna, AK 99669	1964	Dr Les Vierra	5	1,607	91
U of Alaska, Ketchikan Comm Coll, Ketchikan, AK 99901	1954	John C Menzie	12	900	76
U of Alaska, Matanuska-Susitna Comm Coll, Palmer, AK 99645	1958	Mr Alvin S Okeson	5	1,078	93
U of Alaska, Tanana Valley Comm Coll, Fairbanks, AK 99701	1974	Michael Metty	5	2,671	170
U of Cincinnati, R Walters Gen and Tech Coll, Cincinnati, OH 45236	1967	Dr Ernest G Muntz	5	3,263	115
U of Hawaii–Honolulu Comm Coll, Honolulu, HI 96817	1920	Dr Peter R Kessinger	5	4,270	219
U of Hawaii–Kapiolani Comm Coll, Honolulu, HI 96814	1946	Mr John F Morton	5	5,422	180
U of Hawaii–Kauai Comm Coll, Lihue, HI 96766	1965	Mr David Iha	5	1,228	61
U of Hawaii–Leeward Comm Coll, Pearl City, HI 96782	1968	Dr Melvyn K Sakaguchi	5	5,645	232
U of Hawaii–Maui Comm Coll, Kahului, HI 96732	1967	Ms Alma Henderson	5	1,963	113
U of Hawaii–Windward Comm Coll, Kaneohe, HI 96744	1972	Dr Peter T Dyer	5	1,635	79
U of Kentucky, Ashland Comm Coll, Ashland, KY 41101	1937	Mr Robert L Goodpaster	5	1,991	93
U of Kentucky, Elizabethtown Comm Coll, Elizabethtown, KY 42701	1964	Dr James S Owen	5	2,091	95
U of Kentucky, Hazard Comm Coll, Hazard, KY 41701	1968	Dr G Edward Hughes	5	776	57
U of Kentucky, Henderson Comm Coll, Henderson, KY 42420	1963	Dr Patrick R Lake	5	1,071	59
U of Kentucky, Hopkinsville Comm Coll, Hopkinsville, KY 42240	1965	Dr Thomas L Riley	5	1,068	54
U of Kentucky, Lexington Comm Coll, Lexington, KY 40506	1965	Dr Sharon B Jaggard	5	2,587	165
U of Kentucky, Madisonville Comm Coll, Madisonville, KY 42431	1968	Dr Arthur D Stumpf	5	1,356	84
U of Kentucky, Maysville Comm Coll, Maysville, KY 41056	1967	Dr James C Shires	5	727	45
U of Kentucky, Paducah Comm Coll, Paducah, KY 42001	1932	Dr Donald J Clemens	5	2,047	118
U of Kentucky, Prestonsburg Comm Coll, Prestonsburg, KY 41653	1964	Dr Henry A Campbell Jr	5	1,505	43
U of Kentucky, Somerset Comm Coll, Somerset, KY 42501	1965	Dr Richard G Carpenter	5	1,327	80
U of Kentucky, Southeast Comm Coll, Cumberland, KY 40823	1960	Dr Vivian B Blevins	5	1,025	88
U of Minnesota Tech Coll, Crookston, Crookston, MN 56716	1966	Dr Donald G Sargeant	5	1,213	70
U of Minnesota Tech Coll, Waseca, Waseca, MN 56093	1971	Dr Edward C Frederick	5	805	64

Name, address	Year	Governing official, control		Enrollment	Faculty
U of New Mexico–Gallup Branch, Gallup, NM 87301	1968	Dr John M Phillips	5	1,531	100
U of New Mexico–Valencia Branch, Los Lunas, NM 87031	1981	NR	5	840	54
U of Puerto Rico, Aguadilla Regional Coll, Ramey, PR 00604	1972	Mr Paul H Benson	7	1,493	80
U of Puerto Rico, Carolina Regional Coll, Carolina, PR 00630	1974	Gilberto Moreno-Rodriguez	7	1,647	86
U of South Carolina at Beaufort, Beaufort, SC 29902	1959	Dr Ron Tuttle	5	850	54
U of South Carolina at Lancaster, Lancaster, SC 29720	1959	Mr John R Arnold	5	970	53
U of South Carolina at Sumter, Sumter, SC 29150	1966	Mr J C Anderson Jr	5	1,265	44
U of Wisconsin Ctr–Fox Valley, Menasha, WI 54952	1933	Dr Robert Young	5	1,147	53
U of Wisconsin Ctr–Marathon County, Wausau, WI 54401	1933	Dr Stephen R Portch	5	1,151	65
U of Wisconsin Ctr–Marshfield/Wood County, Marshfield, WI 54449	1964	Dr Nancy Aumann	5	617	32
U of Wisconsin Ctr–Rock County, Janesville, WI 53545	1966	Dr Thomas W Walterman	5	917	36
U of Wisconsin Ctr–Sheboygan County, Sheboygan, WI 53081	1933	Dr Barbara P Losty	5	636	36
U of Wisconsin Ctr–Washington County, West Bend, WI 53095	1968	Dr Robert Thompson	5	775	41
U of Wisconsin Ctr–Waukesha County, Waukesha, WI 53188	1966	Dr Mary S Knudten	5	2,036	88
Utah Valley Comm Coll, Orem, UT 84058	1941	Dr J Marvin Higbee	5	6,500	300
Valencia Comm Coll, Orlando, FL 32802	1967	Dr Paul C Gianini Jr	5	12,559	406
Vance-Granville Comm Coll, Henderson, NC 27536	1969	Dr Ben F Currin	5	1,527	104
Ventura Coll, Ventura, CA 93003	1925	Robert W Long	12	10,673	576
Vernon Regional Jr Coll, Vernon, TX 76384	1972	Dr Jim M Williams	12	1,801	103
Victoria Coll, Victoria, TX 77901	1925	Dr Roland E Bing	9	3,039	120
Victor Valley Coll, Victorville, CA 92392	1960	NR	5	5,009	135
Vincennes U, Vincennes, IN 47591	1801	Dr Phillip M Summers	5	4,957	182
Virginia Highlands Comm Coll, Abingdon, VA 24210	1967	Dr N DeWitt Moore Jr	5	1,717	87
Virginia Western Comm Coll, Roanoke, VA 24038	1966	Dr Charles L Downs	5	6,800	200
Vista Coll, Berkeley, CA 94704	1974	Dr Jerome A Gold	12	4,759	183
Volunteer State Comm Coll, Gallatin, TN 37066	1970	Dr Hal R Ramer	5	3,365	211
Wake Tech Coll, Raleigh, NC 27603	1958	Dr Bruce I Howell	12	5,225	285
Walker Coll, Jasper, AL 35501	1938	Dr David Rowland	1	721	36
Wallace State Comm Coll, Hanceville, AL 35077	1966	Dr James C Bailey	5	2,951	133
Walla Walla Comm Coll, Walla Walla, WA 99362	1967	Dr Steven L VanAusdle	5	4,600	240
Walters State Comm Coll, Morristown, TN 37814	1970	Dr Jack E Campbell	5	3,781	220
Washington Tech Coll, Marietta, OH 45750	1971	Dr Donald R Neff	5	711	77
Washtenaw Comm Coll, Ann Arbor, MI 48106	1965	Dr Gunder A Myran	12	8,500	574
Waterbury State Tech Coll, Waterbury, CT 06708	1964	Mr Charles A Ekstrom	5	1,480	104
Waubonsee Comm Coll, Sugar Grove, IL 60554	1966	Dr John J Swalec	10	5,304	426
Waukesha County Tech Inst, Pewaukee, WI 53072	1923	Dr Richard T Anderson	12	5,710	520
Wayne Comm Coll, Goldsboro, NC 27530	1957	Dr Clyde A Erwin Jr	12	1,864	132
Weatherford Coll, Weatherford, TX 76086	1869	Dr E W Mince	5	1,720	80
Wenatchee Valley Coll, Wenatchee, WA 98801	1939	Dr Arnie Heuchert	12	2,346	130
Westark Comm Coll, Fort Smith, AR 72913	1928	Mr Joel R Stubblefield	12	3,714	140
Westchester Business Inst, White Plains, NY 10602	1915	Ernest H Sutkowski	3	800	29
Westchester Comm Coll, Valhalla, NY 10595	1946	Dr Joseph N Hankin	12	7,763	394
Western Iowa Tech Comm Coll, Sioux City, IA 51102	1966	Dr Robert H Kiser	5	1,471	790
Western Nebraska Tech Coll, Sidney, NE 69162	1965	Gary Lund	12	766	31
Western Nevada Comm Coll, Carson City, NV 89701	1971	Dr Anthony D Calabro	5	3,944	133
Western Oklahoma State Coll, Altus, OK 73521	1926	Dr W C Burris	5	1,959	66
Western Piedmont Comm Coll, Morganton, NC 28655	1964	Dr Jim A Richardson	5	2,206	99
Western Texas Coll, Snyder, TX 79549	1969	Dr Don Newbury	12	1,207	75
Western Wisconsin Tech Inst, La Crosse, WI 54601	1911	Dr Beverly S Simone	10	2,200	883
Western Wyoming Comm Coll, Rock Springs, WY 82901	1959	Dr Terrance R Brown	12	2,584	82
West Hills Coll, Coalinga, CA 93210	1932	Mr Joseph M Conte	5	2,500	185
West Los Angeles Coll, Culver City, CA 90230	1969	Dr L M Thor	10	6,436	280
Westmoreland County Comm Coll, Youngwood, PA 15697	1970	Dr Norman P Shea	9	3,595	171
West Shore Comm Coll, Scottville, MI 49454	1967	Dr William M Anderson	10	1,092	67
West Valley Coll, Saratoga, CA 95070	1963	Dr Dale A Johnston	12	14,099	500
West Virginia Northern Comm Coll, Wheeling, WV 26003	1972	Dr Barbara Guthrie-Morse	5	2,762	142
Wharton County Jr Coll, Wharton, TX 77488	1946	Dr Elbert C Hutchins	12	2,353	119
Whatcom Comm Coll, Bellingham, WA 98226	1970	Dr Harold G Heiner	5	757	130
Wilkes Comm Coll, Wilkesboro, NC 28697	1965	Dr David E Daniel	5	2,526	165
William Rainey Harper Coll, Palatine, IL 60067	1965	Mr James J McGrath	12	13,700	611
Williamsport Area Comm Coll, Williamsport, PA 17701	1965	Dr Robert Breuder	12	3,199	237
Willmar Comm Coll, Willmar, MN 56201	1961	Harold G Conradi	5	970	62
Wilson County Tech Coll, Wilson, NC 27893	1958	Dr Frank L Eagles	5	1,352	75
Wisconsin Indianhead Tech Inst, New Richmond Cmps, New Richmond, WI 54017	1972	Marilyn McCarty	10	789	34
Wisconsin Indianhead Tech Inst, Rice Lake Cmps, Rice Lake, WI 54868	1941	Mary Ellen Filkins	10	967	47
Wisconsin Indianhead Tech Inst, Superior Cmps, Superior, WI 54880	1912	Richard Parish	10	842	43
Worthington Comm Coll, Worthington, MN 56187	1936	Dr Joanne Pertz	5	792	46
Wor-Wic Tech Comm Coll, Salisbury, MD 21801	1976	Dr Arnold H Maner	12	803	85
Wright State U, Lake Cmps, Celina, OH 45822	1969	Donald A Carlson	5	782	59
Wytheville Comm Coll, Wytheville, VA 24382	1967	Dr William F Snyder	5	2,086	123
Yakima Valley Comm Coll, Yakima, WA 98907	1928	Dr Philip R Tullar	5	4,058	267
Yavapai Coll, Prescott, AZ 86301	1966	Dr Paul Walker	12	5,531	362
York Tech Coll, Rock Hill, SC 29730	1961	Dr Baxter Hood	12	1,982	111
Yuba Coll, Marysville, CA 95901	1927	Dr Patricia L Wirth	12	8,342	267

Tuition and College Costs 1987-88

Based on the Peterson's Guides Annual Survey of Undergraduate Institutions, the average cost of tuition, mandatory fees, and college room and board at four-year private colleges is $8886. The average cost at four-year public colleges is $4052 for residents and $6381 for nonresidents. Two-year public colleges are the least expensive group of institutions and have an average cost of $2660 for resident students and $4069 for nonresidents.

The most expensive institutions, including tuition, mandatory fees, and college room and board, are Bennington College, ($17,990); Sarah Lawrence College, ($17,440); Barnard College, ($17,296); Brandeis University ($17,281); Harvard University ($17,100); Brown University ($17,035); Tufts University ($17,028); Yale University ($17,020); Massachusetts Institute of Technology ($16,970); and Princeton University ($16,918). Bennington College has the highest tuition of all undergraduate institutions ($14,850). The least expensive are the U.S. service academies, which are all free.

UNITED STATES GOVERNMENT

The Reagan Administration

As of mid-1987

Terms of office of the president and vice president, from Jan. 20, 1985 to Jan. 20, 1989. No person may be elected president of the United States for more than two 4-year terms.

President — Ronald Reagan of California receives salary of $200,000 a year taxable; in addition an expense allowance of $50,000 to assist in defraying expenses resulting from his official duties. Also there may be expended not exceeding $100,000, nontaxable, a year for travel expenses and $20,000 for official entertainment available for allocation within the Executive Office of the President. Congress has provided lifetime pensions of $69,630 a year, free mailing privileges, free office space, and up to $96,000 a year for office help for former Presidents except for the first 30 month period during which a former President is entitled to staff assistance for which an amount up to $150,000 a year may be paid, and $20,000 annually for their widows.

Vice President — George Bush of Texas receives salary of $115,000 a year and $10,000 for expenses, all of which is taxable.

For succession to presidency, see Succession in Index.

The Cabinet

(Salary: $99,500 per annum)

Secretary of State — George P. Shultz, Cal.
Secretary of Treasury — James A. Baker 3d, Tex.
Secretary of Defense — Caspar W. Weinberger, Cal.
Attorney General — Edwin Meese 3d, Cal.
Secretary of Interior — Donald P. Hodel, Ore.
Secretary of Agriculture — Richard E. Lyng, Cal.
Secretary of Commerce — C. William Verity Jr., Oh. (nominated)
Secretary of Labor — William E. Brock, Tenn.
Secretary of Health and Human Services — Otis R. Bowen, Ind.
Secretary of Housing and Urban Development — Samuel R. Pierce Jr., N.Y.
Secretary of Transportation — Elizabeth Hanford Dole, Kan.
Secretary of Energy — John S. Herrington, Cal.
Secretary of Education — William J. Bennett, N.Y.

The White House Staff

1600 Pennsylvania Ave. NW 20500

Chief of Staff — Howard H. Baker Jr.
Deputy Chief of Staff — Kenneth Duberstein.
Assistants to the President
- **Press Secy.** — James S. Brady.
- **Counsel to the President** — Arthur B. Culvahouse Jr.
- **Press Relations** — Max Marlin Fitzwater.
- **Legislative Affairs** — William L. Ball 3d.
- **Political & Intergovernmental Affairs** — Frank J. Donatelli.
- **Communications & Planning** — Thomas Griscom.
- **Domestic Affairs** — T. Kenneth Cribb Jr.
- **Operations** — Rhett B. Dawson.
- **Cabinet Secy.** — Nancy J. Risque.
- **National Security Affairs** — Frank C. Carlucci.
- **Policy Development** — Gary L. Bauer.

Executive Agencies

Council of Economic Advisers — Beryl Sprinkel.
Central Intelligence Agency — William H. Webster, dir.
Office of Management and Budget — James C. Miller 3d.
U.S. Trade Representative — Clayton Yeutter.
Office of Science and Technology Policy — William R. Graham, dir.
Council on Environmental Quality — A. Alan Hill, chmn.

Department of State

2201 C St. NW 20520

Secretary of State — George P. Shultz.
Deputy Secretary — John C. Whitehead.
Under Sec. for Political Affairs — Michael Armacost.
Under Sec. for Security Assistance, Science and Technology — Edward J. Derwinski.
Under Sec. for Economic Affairs — W. Allen Wallis.
Under Secretary for Management — Ronald I. Spiers.
Legal Advisor — Judge Abraham Sofaer.
Assistant Secretaries for:
- **Administration** — Donald Bouchard.
- **African Affairs** — Chester Crocker.
- **East Asian & Pacific Affairs** — Gaston Sigur.
- **Consular Affairs** — Joan M. Clark.
- **Diplomatic Security** — Robert E. Lamb.
- **Economic & Business Affairs** — Douglas W. McMinn.
- **European & Canadian Affairs** — Rozanne Ridgway.
- **Human Rights & Humanitarian Affairs** — Richard Schifter.
- **Inter-American Affairs** — Elliot Abrams.
- **International Narcotics Matters** — Ann B. Wrobleski.
- **International Organization Affairs** — Alan Keyes.
- **Near-Eastern & S. Asian Affairs** — Richard W. Murphy.
- **Political-Military Affairs** — H. Allen Holmes.
- **Public Affairs** — Charles E. Redman.
- **Oceans, International Environmental & Scientific Affairs** — John Negroponte.

Chief of Protocol — Selwa Roosevelt.
Dir. General, Foreign Service & Dir. of Personnel — George. S. Vest.
Dir. of Intelligence & Research — Morton Abramowitz.
Dir. of Refugee Programs — Jonathan Moore.
Inspector General — Sherman M. Funk.
Policy Planning Staff — Richard H. Solomon.
Related Agencies:
- **Arms Control & Disarmament Agency** — Kenneth Adelman, dir.
- **U.S. Information Agency** — Charles Z. Wick, dir.
- **Agency for International Development** — M. Peter McPherson.

U.S. Rep. to the UN — Gen. Vernon Walters.

Treasury Department

1500 Pennsylvania Ave. NW 20220

Secretary of the Treasury — James A. Baker 3d.
Deputy Sec. of the Treasury — M. Peter McPherson.
Under Sec. for Finance — George Gould.
General Counsel — Robert Kimmitt.
Assistant Secretaries: — Margaret Tutwiler, John Rogers, David Mulford, Charles Sethness, Francis Keating 3d, Gerald Murphy, J. Roger Mentz, J. Michael Hudson.
Bureaus:
- **Alcohol, Tobacco & Firearms** — Stephen E. Higgins, dir.
- **Comptroller of the Currency** — Robert Clarke.
- **Customs** — William von Raab.
- **Engraving & Printing** — Robert J. Leuver, dir.
- **Financial Management Service** — William E. Douglas, comm.
- **Internal Revenue Service** — vacant.
- **Mint** — Donna Pope, dir.
- **Public Debt** — W. M. Gregg, comm.
- **Treasurer of the U.S.** — Katherine Ortega.
- **U.S. Savings Bond Division** — Jerrold B. Speers, dir.
- **U.S. Secret Service** — John R. Simpson, dir.

Department of Defense

The Pentagon 20301

Secretary of Defense — Caspar W. Weinberger.
Deputy Secretary — William H. Taft IV.
Asst. to the Secy. & Deputy Secy. of Defense — Elizabeth Karabatsos.
Executive Secretariat — William M. Matz Jr.
Under Secy. for Acquisition — Richard P. Godwin.
Under Secy. for Policy — Fred C. Ikle.
Asst. Secretaries of Defense:
Products & Logistics — Robert B. Costello.
Atomic Energy — Robert B. Barker.
Command Control Communications & Intelligence — David C. Latham.
Comptroller — Robert W. Helm.
Health Affairs — Dr. William Mayer.
International Security Affairs — Richard L. Armitage.
International Security Policy — vacant.
Legislative Affairs — M. D. B. Carlisle.
Force Management & Personnel — Chapman B. Cox.
Public Affairs — Robert Sims.
Reserve Affairs — vacant.
Intelligence Oversight — Werner E. Michel.
Chairman, Joint Chiefs of Staff — Adm. William J. Crowe Jr.
General Counsel — H. Lawrence Garrett 3d.

Department of the Army

The Pentagon 20310

Secretary of the Army — John O. Marsh Jr.
Under Secretary — James R. Ambrose.
Assistant Secretaries for:
Civil Works — vacant.
Installations & Logistics — John W. Shannon.
Financial Management — Michael P. W. Stone.
Research, Development and Acquisition — Jay R. Sculley.
Manpower & Reserve Affairs — Delbert L. Spurlock Jr.
Chief of Public Affairs — Charles D. Bussey.
Chief of Staff — Gen. Carl E. Vuono.
Inspector General — Lt. Gen. Henry Doctor Jr.
Deputy Chiefs of Staff:
Logistics — Lt. Gen. Jimmy D. Ross.
Operations & Plans — Lt. Gen. H. Norman Schwarzkopf.
Personnel — Lt. Gen. Allen K. Ono.
Commanders:
U.S. Army Materiel Command — Gen. Louis C. Wagner.
U.S. Army Forces Command — Gen. Joseph T. Palastra Jr.
U.S. Army Training and Doctrine Command — Gen. Maxwell R. Thurman.
First U.S. Army — Lt. Gen. Charles D. Franklin.
Second U.S. Army — Lt. Gen. Johnny J. Johnston.
Third U.S. Army — Lt. Gen. Andrew P. Chambers.
Fourth U.S. Army — Lt. Gen. Frederic J. Brown.
Fifth U.S. Army — Lt. Gen. William H. Schneider.
Sixth U.S. Army — Lt. Gen. James E. Moore.
U.S. Army Europe & Seventh U.S. Army — Gen. Glenn K. Otis.
U.S. Forces Korea & Eighth U.S. Army — Gen. Louis Menetrey.
U.S. Army, South — Maj. Gen. Bernard Loeffke.
U.S. Army Pacific Command — Gen. Charles W. Bagnel.

Department of the Navy

The Pentagon 20350

Secretary of the Navy — James H. Webb.
Under Secretary — James F. Goodrich.
Assistant Secretaries for:
Financial Management — Robert H. Conn.
Manpower, Reserve Affairs — Chase Untermeyer.
Research, Engineering & Systems — Melvyn R. Paisley.
Shipbuilding & Logistics — Everett Pyatt.
Judge Advocate General — RADM Hugh Campbell.
Chief of Naval Operations — ADM Carlisle Trost.
Chief of Information — RADM J. B. Finkelstein.
Military Sealift Command — RADM Walter T. Piotti Jr.
Chief of Naval Personnel — VADM Dudley L. Carlson.

U.S. Marine Corps:
(Arlington Annex 20380)

Commandant — Gen. Alfred M. Gray Jr.
Asst. Commandant — Gen. T.R. Morgan.
Chief of Staff — Lt. Gen. C.D. Dean.

Department of the Air Force

The Pentagon 20330

Secretary of the Air Force — Edward C. Aldridge.
Under Secretary — James F. McGovern.
Assistant Secretaries for:
Manpower & Reserve Affairs — Richard E. Carver.
Acquisition — vacant.
Readiness Support — Tidal W. McCoy.
Public Affairs — Brig. Gen. Michael P. McRaney.
Office of Space Systems — Brig. Gen. Thomas S. Moorman Jr.
Chief of Staff — Gen. Larry D. Welch.
Inspector General — Maj. Gen. Buford R. Lary.
Deputy Chiefs of Staff:
Logistics & Engineering — Lt. Gen. Charles C. McDonald.
Programs & Resources — Lt. Gen. Michael J. Dugan.
Manpower & Personnel — Maj. Gen. Thomas J. Hickey.
Plans & Operations — Lt. Gen. Harley A. Hughes.
Major Air Commands:
AF Logistics Command — Gen. Alfred G. Hansen.
AF Systems Command — Gen. Bernard P. Randolph.
Strategic Air Command — Gen. John T. Chain.
Tactical Air Command — Gen. Robert D. Russ.
Alaskan Air Command — Lt. Gen. David L. Nichols.
Pacific Air Forces — Gen. Jacki Gregory.
USAF Europe — Gen. William Kirk.
Electronic Security Command — Maj. Gen. Paul H. Martin.
AF Communications Command — Maj. Gen. John T. Stihl.
Air Training Command — Lt. Gen. John A. Shaud.
Military Airlift Command — Gen. Duane H. Cassidy.
AF Space Command — Maj. Gen. Maurice C. Padden.

Department of Justice

Constitution Ave. & 10th St. NW 20530

Attorney General — Edwin Meese 3d.
Deputy Attorney General — Arnold I. Burns.
Solicitor General — Charles Fried.
Associate Attorney General — Stephen S. Trott.
Intelligence Policy & Review — Mary Lawton.
Professional Responsibility —Michael E. Shaheen Jr.
Assistants:
Antitrust Division — Charles Rule, act.
Civil Division — Richard K. Willard.
Civil Rights Division — Wm. Bradford Reynolds.
Criminal Division — William S. Weld.
Justice Management Division — Harry H. Flickinger.
Land & Natural Resources Division — vacant.
Legal Policy — Stephen J. Markman.
Legal Counsel — Charles J. Cooper.
Legislative Affairs — John R. Bolton.
Office of Justice Programs — Richard Abell, act.
Tax Division — Michael Durney, act.
Fed. Bureau of Investigation — William S. Sessions (nominated).
Exec. Off. for Immigration Review — David L. Milhollan, dir.

Bureau of Prisons — J. Michael Quinlan.
Comm. Relations Service — Wallace P. Warfield, act.
Exec. Off. for U.S. Trustees — Thomas Stanton, dir.
Exec. Off. for U.S. Attorneys — Laurence S. McWhorter.
Public Affairs — Terry H. Eastland, dir.
Immigration and Naturalization Service — Alan C. Nelson, comm.
Pardon Attorney — David C. Stephenson.
U.S. Parole Commission — Benjamin F. Baer, chmn.
U.S. Marshals Service — Stanley E. Morris, dir.
Foreign Claims Settlement Comm. — vacant.
Interpol, U.S. Natl. Central Bureau — Richard C. Stiener, chief.

Department of the Interior

C St. between 18th & 19th Sts. NW 20240

Secretary of the Interior — Donald P. Hodel.
Under Secretary — vacant.
Assistant Secretaries for:
- **Fish, Wildlife and Parks** — William P. Horn.
- **Water & Science** — James W. Ziglar.
- **Land & Minerals Management** — Steven Griles.
- **Policy, Budget, and Administration** — vacant.
- **Indian Affairs** — Ross Swimmer.
- **Territorial & Intl. Affairs** — Richard Montoya.

Bureau of Land Management — Bob Burford, dir.
Bureau of Mines — vacant.
Bureau of Reclamation — C. Dale Duvall, comm.
Fish & Wildlife Service — Frank H. Dunkle, dir.
Geological Survey — Dallas L. Peck, dir.
National Park Service — William Penn Mott.
Public Affairs — David Prosperi.
Office of Congressional and Legislative Affairs — Paul R. Holtz.
Solicitor — Ralph W. Tarr.

Department of Agriculture

The Mall, 12th & 14th Sts. 20250

Secretary of Agriculture — Richard E. Lyng.
Deputy Secretary — Peter C. Myers.
Administration — John Franke Jr.
Internat. Affairs & Commodity Programs — Daniel Amstutz.
Food & Consumer Services — John W. Bode.
Marketing & Inspection Services — Kenneth A. Gilles.
Small Community & Rural Development — LaVerne Ausman, act.
Economics — Ewen Wilson.
Governmental & Public Affairs — Wilmer D. Mizell.
Natural Resources & Environment — George S. Dunlop.
General Counsel — Christopher Hicks.
Science & Education — Orville G. Bentley.
Inspector General — Robert Beuley.

Department of Commerce

14th St. between Constitution & E St. NW 20230

Secretary of Commerce — C. William Verity Jr. (nom.)
Deputy Secretary — Clarence J. Brown Jr.
General Counsel — Douglas A. Riggs.
Assistant Secretaries:
- **Administration** — Kay Bulow.
- **Congressional & Intergovernmental Affairs** — Gerald J. McKiernan.
- **Economic Development Adm.** — Orson G. Swindle.
- **Intl. Economic Policy** — Louis F. Laun.
- **Natl. Tele. & Comm. Adm.** — Alfred C. Sikes.
- **Patents & Trademark Office** — Donald J. Quigg.
- **Production Tech. & Innovation** — Bruce Merrifield.
- **Trade Adminstration** — Paul Freedenberg.
- **Trade Development** — Joan McEntee, act.

Bureau of the Census — John G. Keane, dir.
Bureau of Economic Analysis — Allan H. Young, dir.
Under Secy. for International Trade — Bruce Smart.
Under Secy. for Econ. Affairs — Robert Ortner.
Natl. Oceanic & Atmospheric Admin. — Anthony Calio.
Natl. Technical Info. Service — Joseph F. Caponio, dir.
Natl. Bureau of Standards — Ernest Ambler, dir.
Minority Business Development Agency — James H. Richardson-Gonzales.
Under Secy. for U.S. Travel & Tourism Adm. — Donna F. Tuttle.
Public Affairs — B. Jay Cooper, dir.
Office Consumer Affairs — Jewell F. Duvall.

Department of Labor

200 Constitution Ave. NW 20210

Secretary of Labor — William E. Brock.
Deputy Secretary — Dennis E. Whitfield.
Assistant Secretaries for:
- **Administration and Management** — Thomas C. Komarek.
- **Employment & Training** — Roger D. Semarad.
- **Labor-Management Standards** — Salvatore Martoche.
- **Mine Safety & Health** — Alan McMillan, act.
- **Occupational Safety & Health** — John Pendergrass.
- **Pension & Welfare Benefit Programs** — vacant.
- **Policy** — Michael Baroody.
- **Veteran's Employment** — Donald E. Shasteen.

Solicitor of Labor — George Salem.
Comm. of Labor Statistics — Janet Norwood.
Dep. Under Secy. for Employment Standards — Susan R. Meisinger.
Dep. Under Secy. for Internatl. Affairs — Robert W. Searby.
Dep. Under Secy. for Congressional Affairs — William J. Maroni.
Dep. Under Secy. for Labor-Management Relations & Cooperative Programs — Stephen Schlossberg.
Dep. Under Secy. for Public & Intergovernmental Affairs — David Demarest.
Office of Information & Public Affairs — Chriss Winston.
Dir. of Women's Bureau — Shirley Dennis.
Inspector General — J. Brian Hyland.

Department of Health and Human Services

200 Independence Ave. SW 20201

Secretary of HHS — Otis R. Bowen.
Under Secretary — Donald Newman.
Assistant Secretaries for:
- **Management and Budget** — S. Anthony McCann.
- **Public Affairs** — Stephanie Lee Miller.
- **Health** — Robert E. Windom.
- **Planning and Evaluation** — Robert B. Helms.
- **Human Development Services** — Jean K. Elder.
- **Legislation** — Robert F. Docksai.
- **Personnel Administration** — Thomas McFee.

General Counsel — Ronald Robertson.
Inspector General — Richard P. Kusserow.
Civil Rights — Audrey Morton.
Health Care Financing Admin. — William L. Roper.

Department of Housing and Urban Development

451 7th St. SW 20410

Secretary of Housing & Urban Development — Samuel R. Pierce Jr.
Under Secretary — Carl D. Covitz.
- **Deputies** — Alan J. Greenwald, Timothy L. Coyle.

Assistant Secretaries for:
- **Community Planning & Development** — vacant.
- **Housing & Federal Housing Commissioner** — Thomas T. Demery.
- **Legislation & Congressional Relations** — Stephen May.
- **Public Affairs** — vacant.
- **Public & Indian Housing** — vacant.

President, Govt. Natl. Mortgage Assn. — vacant.
International Affairs — Theodore Britton Jr.
Labor Relations — Justin Logsdon.
Small & Disadvantaged Business Utilization — Bernice Williams, dir.
General Counsel — J. Michael Dorsey.
Indian & Alaska Native Programs — Raymond E. Combs.
Board of Contract Appeals — David T. Anderson.
Chief Administrative Law Judge — Alan W. Heifetz.

Department of Transportation

400 7th St. SW 20590

Secretary of Transportation — Elizabeth Hanford Dole.
Deputy Secretary — James H. Burnley 4th.
Assistant Secretaries — Matthew V. Scocozza (Policy and International Affairs); Janet Hale (Budget and Programs); John H. Seymour (Administration); Dale Petroskey (Public Affairs); Rebecca C. Range (Governmental Affairs).
National Highway Traffic Safety Admin. — Diane K. Steed.
U. S. Coast Guard Commandant — Adm. Paul A. Yost Jr.
Federal Aviation Admin. — Donald D. Engen.
Federal Highway Admin. — Ray Barnhart.
Federal Railroad Admin. — John Riley.
Maritime Admin. — John A. Gaughan.
Urban Mass Transportation Admin. — Ralph L. Stanley.
Research & Special Programs Admin. — Cindy Douglass.
Saint Lawrence Seaway Development Corp. — James L. Emery.

Department of Energy

1000 Independence Ave. SW 20585

Secretary of Energy — John S. Herrington.
Deputy Secy. — William F. Martin.
Under Secretary — Joseph Salgado.
General Counsel — J. Michael Farrell.
Assistant Secretaries — Lawrence F. Davenport (Management & Administration); Theodore Garrish (Congressional, Intergovernmental & Public Affairs); David B. Waller (International Affairs & Energy Emergencies); A. David Rossin (Nuclear Energy); Sylvester R. Foley (Defense Programs); James A. Wampler (Fossil Energy); Donna Fitzpatrick (Conservation & Renewable Energy); Mary L. Walker (Environment, Safety & Health).
Economic Regulatory Admin. — Marshall Staunton.
Energy Information Admin. — Helmut A. Merklein.
Federal Energy Regulatory Comm. — Martha O. Hesse, chmn.
Inspector General — John C. Layton.
Office of Hearings & Appeals — George B. Breznay, dir.
Office of Energy Research — James Decker, act. dir.
Office of Civilian Radioactive Waste Management — Ben C. Rusche, dir.
Office of Minority Economic Impact — Raymond G. Massie, dir.
Board of Contract Appeals — E. Barclay van Doren, chmn.

Department of Education

Wash., D.C. 20202

Secretary of Education — William J. Bennett
Under Secretary — vacant.
Deputy Under Secretaries — Peter Greer, Mary M. Rose, Bruce Carnes.
General Counsel — Wendell Willkie.
Assistant Secretaries:
- **Legislation & Public Affairs** — Frances Norris.
- **Elementary and Secondary Education** — vacant.
- **Postsecondary Education** — C. Ronald Kimberling.
- **Educational Research and Improvement** — Chester Finn.
- **Adult & Vocational Education** — vacant.
- **Special Education and Rehabilitative Services** — Madeline Will.
- **Civil Rights** — vacant.
- **Bilingual & Minority Languages** — Carol P. Whitten.
- **Regions** — George Youstra.

Judiciary of the U.S.

Data as of mid-1987

Justices of the United States Supreme Court

The Supreme Court comprises the chief justice of the United States and 8 associate justices, all appointed by the president with advice and consent of the Senate. Salaries: chief justice $115,000 annually, associate justice $110,000.

Name; apptd from *Chief Justices in italics*	Service Term	Yrs.	Born	Died
John Jay, N. Y.	1789-1795	5	1745	1829
John Rutledge, S. C.	1789-1791	1	1739	1800
William Cushing, Mass.	1789-1810	20	1732	1810
James Wilson, Pa.	1789-1798	8	1742	1798
John Blair, Va.	1789-1796	6	1732	1800
James Iredell, N. C.	1790-1799	9	1751	1799
Thomas Johnson, Md.	1791-1793	1	1732	1819
William Paterson, N. J.	1793-1806	13	1745	1806
John Rutledge, S.C.	1795(a)	—	1739	1800
Samuel Chase, Md.	1796-1811	15	1741	1811
Oliver Ellsworth, Conn.	1796-1800	4	1745	1807
Bushrod Washington, Va.	1798-1829	31	1762	1829
Alfred Moore, N. C.	1799-1804	4	1755	1810
John Marshall, Va.	1801-1835	34	1755	1835
William Johnson, S. C.	1804-1834	30	1771	1834
Henry B. Livingston, N. Y.	1806-1823	16	1757	1823
Thomas Todd, Ky.	1807-1826	18	1765	1826
Joseph Story, Mass.	1811-1845	33	1779	1845
Gabriel Duval, Md.	1811-1835	22	1752	1844
Smith Thompson, N. Y.	1823-1843	20	1768	1843
Robert Trimble, Ky.	1826-1828	2	1777	1828
John McLean, Oh.	1829-1861	32	1785	1861
Henry Baldwin, Pa.	1830-1844	14	1780	1844
James M. Wayne, Ga.	1835-1867	32	1790	1867
Roger B. Taney, Md.	1836-1864	28	1777	1864
Philip P. Barbour, Va.	1836-1841	4	1783	1841
John Catron, Tenn.	1837-1865	28	1786	1865
John McKinley, Ala.	1837-1852	15	1780	1852
Peter V. Daniel, Va.	1841-1860	19	1784	1860
Samuel Nelson, N. Y.	1845-1872	27	1792	1873
Levi Woodbury, N. H.	1845-1851	5	1789	1851
Robert C. Grier, Pa.	1846-1870	23	1794	1870
Benjamin R. Curtis, Mass.	1851-1857	6	1809	1874
John A. Campbell, Ala.	1853-1861	8	1811	1889
Nathan Clifford, Me.	1858-1881	23	1803	1881
Noah H. Swayne, Oh.	1862-1881	18	1804	1884
Samuel F. Miller, Ia.	1862-1890	28	1816	1890
David Davis, Ill.	1862-1877	14	1815	1886
Stephen J. Field, Cal.	1863-1897	34	1816	1899
Salmon P. Chase, Oh.	1864-1873	8	1808	1873
William Strong, Pa.	1870-1880	10	1808	1895
Joseph P. Bradley, N. J.	1870-1892	21	1813	1892
Ward Hunt, N. Y.	1872-1882	9	1810	1886
Morrison R. Waite, Oh.	1874-1888	14	1816	1888
John M. Harlan, Ky.	1877-1911	34	1833	1911
William B. Woods, Ga.	1880-1887	6	1824	1887
Stanley Matthews, Oh.	1881-1889	7	1824	1889
Horace Gray, Mass.	1881-1902	20	1828	1902
Samuel Blatchford, N. Y.	1882-1893	11	1820	1893
Lucius Q. C. Lamar, Miss.	1888-1893	5	1825	1893
Melville W. Fuller, Ill.	1888-1910	21	1833	1910
David J. Brewer, Kan.	1889-1910	20	1837	1910
Henry B. Brown, Mich.	1890-1906	15	1836	1913
George Shiras Jr., Pa.	1892-1903	10	1832	1924
Howell E. Jackson, Tenn.	1893-1895	2	1832	1895
Edward D. White, La.	1894-1910	16	1845	1921
Rufus W. Peckham, N. Y.	1895-1909	13	1838	1909

(continued)

Name; apptd from	Service Term	Yrs.	Born	Died
Joseph McKenna, Cal.	1898-1925	26	1843	1926
Oliver W. Holmes, Mass.	1902-1932	29	1841	1935
William R. Day, Oh.	1903-1922	19	1849	1923
William H. Moody, Mass.	1906-1910	3	1853	1917
Horace H. Lurton, Tenn.	1909-1914	4	1844	1914
Charles E. Hughes, N. Y.	1910-1916	5	1862	1948
Willis Van Devanter, Wy.	1910-1937	26	1859	1941
Joseph R. Lamar, Ga.	1910-1916	5	1857	1916
Edward D. White, La.	1910-1921	10	1845	1921
Mahlon Pitney, N. J.	1912-1922	10	1858	1924
James C. McReynolds, Tenn.	1914-1941	26	1862	1946
Louis D. Brandeis, Mass.	1916-1939	22	1856	1941
John H. Clarke, Oh.	1916-1922	5	1857	1945
William H. Taft, Conn.	1921-1930	8	1857	1930
George Sutherland, Ut.	1922-1938	15	1862	1942
Pierce Butler, Minn.	1922-1939	16	1866	1939
Edward T. Sanford, Tenn.	1923-1930	7	1865	1930
Harlan F. Stone, N. Y.	1925-1941	16	1872	1946
Charles E. Hughes, N. Y.	1930-1941	11	1862	1948
Owen J. Roberts, Pa.	1930-1945	15	1875	1955
Benjamin N. Cardozo, N.Y.	1932-1938	6	1870	1938
Hugo L. Black, Ala.	1937-1971	34	1886	1971
Stanley F. Reed, Ky.	1938-1957	19	1884	1980
Felix Frankfurter, Mass.	1939-1962	23	1882	1965
William O. Douglas, Conn.	1939-1975	36	1898	1980
Frank Murphy, Mich.	1940-1949	9	1890	1949
Harlan F. Stone, N. Y.	1941-1946	5	1872	1946
James F. Byrnes, S. C.	1941-1942	1	1879	1972
Robert H. Jackson, N. Y.	1941-1954	12	1892	1954
Wiley B. Rutledge, Ia.	1943-1949	6	1894	1949
Harold H. Burton, Oh.	1945-1958	13	1888	1964
Fred M. Vinson, Ky.	1946-1953	7	1890	1953
Tom C. Clark, Tex.	1949-1967	18	1899	1977
Sherman Minton, Ind.	1949-1956	7	1890	1965
Earl Warren, Cal.	1953-1969	16	1891	1974
John Marshall Harlan, N. Y.	1955-1971	16	1899	1971
William J. Brennan Jr., N. J.	1956 —	—	1906	—
Charles E. Whittaker, Mo.	1957-1962	5	1901	1973
Potter Stewart, Oh.	1958-1981	23	1915	1985
Byron R. White, Col.	1962 —	—	1917	—
Arthur J. Goldberg, Ill.	1962-1965	3	1908	—
Abe Fortas, Tenn.	1965-1969	4	1910	1982
Thurgood Marshall, N.Y.	1967 —	—	1908	—
Warren E. Burger, Va.	1969-1986	17	1907	—
Harry A. Blackmun, Minn.	1970 —	—	1908	—
Lewis F. Powell Jr., Va.	1972 —	—	1907	—
William H. Rehnquist, Ariz.	1972-1986	14	1924	—
John Paul Stevens, Ill.	1975 —	—	1920	—
Sandra Day O'Connor, Ariz.	1981 —	—	1930	—
William H. Rehnquist, Ariz.	1986 —	—	1924	—
Antonin Scalia, Va.	1986 —	—	1936	—

(a) Rejected Dec. 15, 1795.

U.S. Court of International Trade

New York, NY 10007 (Salaries, $89,500)

Chief Judge — Edward D. Re.

Judges — Paul P. Rao, James L. Watson, Gregory W. Carman, Jane A. Restani, Dominick L. DiCarlo, Thomas J. Aquilino Jr., Nicholas Tsoucalas.

U.S. Tax Court

Washington DC 20217 (Salaries, $89,500)

Chief Judge — Samuel B. Sterrett.

Judges — Charles R. Simpson, William A. Goffe, Herbert L. Chabot, Arthur L. Nims 3d, Edna G. Parker, Jules J. Korner 3d, Meade Whitaker, Mary Ann Cohen, Perry Shields, Charles E. Clapp 2d, Lapsley W. Hamblen Jr., Stephen J. Swift, Joel Gerber, Julien I. Jacobs, Lawrence A. Wright, Carolyn Miller Parr, B. John Williams Jr.

U.S. Courts of Appeals

(Salaries, $95,000. CJ means Chief Judge)

Federal Circuit — Howard T. Markey, CJ; Daniel M. Friedman, Giles S. Rich, Oscar H. Davis, Edward S. Smith, Helen W. Nies; Pauline Newman, Jean G. Bissell, Glenn L. Archer Jr.; Clerk's Office, Washington, DC 20439.

District of Columbia — Patricia M. Wald, CJ; Spottswood W. Robinson 3d, Abner J. Mikva, Harry T. Edwards, Ruth Bader Ginsburg, Robert H. Bork, Kenneth W. Starr, Laurence H. Silberman; James L. Buckley, Stephen F. Williams, Douglas Ginsburg; Clerk's Office, Washington, DC 20001.

First Circuit (Me., Mass., N.H., R.I., Puerto Rico) — Levin H. Campbell, CJ; Frank M. Coffin, Hugh H. Bownes, Stephen Breyer, Juan R. Torruella, Bruce M. Selya; Clerk's Office, Boston, MA 02109.

Second Circuit (Conn., N.Y., Vt.) — Wilfred Feinberg, CJ; Irving R. Kaufman, James L. Oakes, Thomas J. Meskill, Jon O. Newman, Amalya Lyle Kearse, Richard J. Cardamone, Lawrence W. Pierce, Ralph K. Winter Jr., George C. Pratt, Roger J. Miner, Frank X. Altimari, J. Daniel Mahoney; Clerk's Office, New York, NY 10007.

Third Circuit (Del., N.J., Pa., Virgin Is.) — John J. Gibbons, CJ; Collins J. Seitz, Joseph F. Weis Jr., Leonard I. Garth, A. Leon Higginbotham Jr., Dolores K. Sloviter, Edward R. Becker, Carol Los Mansmann, Walter K. Stapleton; Clerk's Office, Philadelphia, PA 19106.

Fourth Circuit (Md., N.C., S.C., Va., W.Va.) — Harrison L. Winter, CJ; Kenneth K. Hall, Donald Stuart Russell, H. Emory Widener Jr., James D. Phillips Jr., Francis D. Murnaghan Jr., James M. Sprouse, Sam J. Ervin 3d, Robert F. Chapman, J. Harvey Wilkinson 3d, William W. Wilkins Jr.; Clerk's Office, Richmond, VA 23219.

Fifth Circuit (La., Miss., Tex.) — Charles Clark, CJ; Thomas G. Gee, Alvin B. Rubin, Thomas M. Reavley, Henry A. Politz, Carolyn D. Randall, Samuel D. Johnson, Jerre S. Williams, William L. Garwood, E. Grady Jolly, Patrick E. Higginbotham, W. Eugene Davis, Robert M. Hill, Edith Hollan Jones; Clerk's Office, New Orleans, LA 70130.

Sixth Circuit (Ky., Mich., Ohio, Tenn.) — Pierce Lively, CJ; Albert J. Engel, Gilbert S. Merritt, Damon J. Keith, Boyce F. Martin Jr., Nathaniel R. Jones, Robert B. Krupansky, Harry W. Wellford, Cornelia G. Kennedy, H. Ted Milburn, Ralph B. Guy Jr., David A. Nelson, James L. Ryan, Danny J. Boggs, Alan E. Norris; Clerk's Office, Cincinnati, OH 45202.

Seventh Circuit (Ill., Ind., Wis.) — William J. Bauer, CJ; Walter J. Cummings, Harlington Wood Jr., Richard D. Cudahy, Richard A. Posner, John L. Coffey, Joel M. Flaum, Frank H. Easterbrook, Kenneth F. Ripple, Daniel A. Manion; Clerk's Office, Chicago, IL 60604.

Eighth Circuit (Ark., Ia., Minn., Mo., Neb., N.D., S.D.) — Donald P. Lay, CJ; Gerald W. Heaney, Donald R. Ross, Theodore McMillian, Richard S. Arnold, John R. Gibson, George C. Fagg, Pasco M. Bowman 2d, Roger L. Wollman, Frank J. Magill; Clerk's Office, St. Louis, MO 63101.

Ninth Circuit (Alaska, Ariz., Cal., Ha., Ida., Mont., Nev., Ore., Wash., Guam, N. Mariana Islands) — James R. Browning, CJ; Albert T. Goodwin, J. Clifford Wallace, Anthony M. Kennedy, J. Blaine Anderson, Procter Hug Jr., Thomas Tang, Joseph T. Sneed, Jerome Farris, Betty B. Fletcher, Mary M. Schroeder, Harry Pregerson, Arthur L. Alarcon, Cecil F. Poole, Dorothy W. Nelson, William C. Canby Jr., William A. Norris, Stephen Reinhardt, Robert R. Beezer, Cynthia M. Hall, Charles E. Wiggins, Melvin Brunetti, Alex Kozinski, David R. Thompson, John T. Noonan, Diarmuid F. O'Scannlain; Clerk's Office, San Francisco, CA 94101.

Tenth Circuit (Col., Kan., N.M., Okla., Ut., Wy.) — William J. Holloway Jr., CJ; James E. Barrett, Monroe G. McKay, James K. Logan, Stephanie K. Seymour, John P. Moore, Stephen H. Anderson, Deanell R. Tacha, Bobby R. Baldock; Clerk's Office, Denver, CO 80294.

Eleventh Circuit (Ala. Fla., Ga.)— Paul R. Roney, CJ; John C. Godbold, Gerald B. Tjoflat, James C. Hill, Peter T. Fay, Robert S. Vance, Phyllis A. Kravitch, Frank M. Johnson Jr., Joseph W. Hatchett, R. Lanier Anderson 3d, Thomas A. Clark, J.L. Edmondson; Clerk's Office, Atlanta GA 30303.

Temporary Emergency Court of Appeals — J. Skelly Wright, CJ; Clerk's Office, Washington, DC 20001 .

U.S. District Courts

(Salaries, $89,500. CJ means Chief Judge)

Alabama — Northern: Sam C. Pointer Jr., CJ; James Hughes Hancock, J. Foy Guin Jr., Robert B. Propst, E. B. Haltom Jr., U. W. Clemon, William M. Acker Jr.; Clerk's Office, Birmingham 35203. **Middle:** Truman M. Hobbs, CJ; Robert E. Varner, Myron H. Thompson, Joel F. Dubina; Clerk's Office, Montgomery 36101. **Southern:** William Brevard Hand, CJ; Emmett R. Cox, Alex T. Howard Jr.; Clerk's Office, Mobile 36652.

Alaska — James M. Fitzgerald, CJ; H. Russel Holland; Clerk's Office, Anchorage 99513.

Arizona — Richard M. Bilby, CJ; Vlademar A. Cordova, Charles L. Hardy, Alfredo C. Marquez, Earl H. Carroll, William D. Browning, Paul G. Rosenblat, Robert C. Bloomfield, Roger G. Strand; Clerk's Office, Phoenix 85025.

Arkansas — Eastern: Garnett Thomas Eisele, CJ; Elsijane Trimble Roy, William Ray Overton, Henry Woods, George Howard Jr.; Clerk's Office, Little Rock 72203. **Western:** H. Franklin Waters, CJ; Elsijane Trimble Roy, George Howard Jr., Morris S. Arnold; Clerk's Office, Fort Smith 72902.

California — Northern: Robert F. Peckham, CJ; Lloyd H. Burke, Samuel Conti, Spencer M. Williams, William W. Schwarzer, William A. Ingram, Robert P. Aguilar, Thelton E. Henderson, Marilyn H. Patel, Eugene F. Lynch, John P. Vukasin Jr, Charles A. Legge, D. Lowell Jensen; Clerk's Office, San Francisco 94102. **Eastern:** Lawrence K. Karlton, CJ; Milton L. Schwartz, Edward Dean Price, Raul A. Ramirez, Robert E. Coyle, Edward J. Garcia; Clerk's Office, Sacramento 95814. **Central:** Manuel L. Real, CJ; Wm. Matthew Byrne Jr., Robert M. Takasugi, Mariana R. Pfaelzer, Terry J. Hatter Jr., A. Wallace Tashima, Consuelo Bland Marshall, David V. Kenyon, Richard A. Gadbois, Edward Rafeedie, Pamela A. Rymer, Harry L. Hupp, Alicemarie H. Stotler, James M. Ideman, William J. Rea, William D. Keller, Ferdinand F. Fernandez, Stephen V. Wilson, J. Spencer Letts, Dickran M. Tevrizian Jr., John G. Davies; Clerk's Office, Los Angeles 90012. **Southern:** Gordon Thompson Jr., CJ; William B. Enright, Judith N. Keep, Earl B. Gilliam, J. Lawrence Irving, Rudi M. Brewster, John S. Rhoades Sr.; Clerk's Office, San Diego 92189.

Colorado — Sherman G. Finesilver, CJ; Richard P. Matsch, John L. Kane Jr., Jim R. Carrigan, Zita L. Weinshienk; Clerk's Office, Denver 80294.

Connecticut — T. F. Gilroy Daly, CJ; Ellen B. Burns, Warren W. Eginton, Jose A. Cabranes, Peter C. Dorsey, Alan H. Nevas; Clerk's Office, New Haven 06510.

Delaware — Murray M. Schwartz, CJ; Joseph J. Longobardi, Joseph J. Farnan Jr., Jane R. Roth; Clerk's Office, Wilmington 19801.

District of Columbia — Aubrey E. Robinson Jr., CJ; Gerhard A. Gesell, John H. Pratt, Charles R. Richey, Louis F. Oberdorfer, Harold H. Greene, John Garrett Penn, Joyce Hens Green, Norma H. Johnson, Thomas P. Jackson, Thomas F. Hogan, Stanley S. Harris, George H. Revercomb, Stanley Sporkin; Clerk's Office, Washington DC 20001.

Florida — Northern: William H. Stafford Jr. CJ; Maurice M. Paul, C. Roger Vinson; Clerk's Office, Tallahassee 32301. **Middle:** William Terrell Hodges, CJ; Howell W. Melton, George C. Carr, Susan H. Black, William J. Castagna, John H. Moore 2d, Elizabeth A. Kovachevich, George K. Sharp, Patricia C. Fawsett; Clerk's Office, Jacksonville 32201. **Southern:** James Lawrence King, CJ; Norman C. Roettger Jr.; Sidney M. Aronovitz, William M. Hoeveler, Jose A. Gonzalez Jr., James C. Paine, James W. Kehoe, Eugene P. Spellman, Edward B. Davis, Alcee L. Hastings, Lenore C. Nesbitt, Stanley Marcus, Thomas E. Scott, William J. Zloch, Kenneth L. Ryskamp; Clerk's Office, Miami 33128.

Georgia — Northern: Charles A. Moye Jr., CJ; William C.O'-Kelley, Richard C. Freeman, Harold L. Murphy, Marvin H. Shoob, G. Ernest Tidwell, Orinda Dale Evans, Robert L. Vining Jr., Robert H. Hall, Harold T. Ward, J. Owen Forrester; Clerk's Office, Atlanta 30335. **Middle:** Wilbur D. Owens Jr., CJ; J. Robert Elliott, Duross Fitzpatrick; Clerk's Office, Macon 31202. **Southern:** Anthony A. Alaimo, CJ; B. Avant Edenfield, Dudley H. Bowen Jr.; Clerk's Office, Savannah 31412.

Hawaii — Harold M. Fong, CJ, Alan C. Kay; Clerk's Office, Honolulu 96850.

Idaho — Marion J. Callister, CJ; Harold L. Ryan; Clerk's Office; Boise, 83724.

Illinois — Northern: John F. Grady, CJ; Prentice H. Marshall, Nicholas J. Bua, Stanley J. Roszkowski, James B. Moran, Marvin E. Aspen, Milton I. Shadur, Charles P. Kocoras, Susan Getzendanner, John A. Nordberg, William T. Hart, Paul E. Plunkett, Ilana Diamond Rovner, Charles R. Norgle Sr., James F. Holderman Jr., Ann C. Williams, Brian Barnett Duff, Harry D. Lienenweber; Clerk's Office, Chicago 60604. **Central:** Harold Albert Baker, CJ; Michael M. Mihm, Richard Mills; Clerk's Office, Springfield 62705. **Southern:** James L. Foreman, CJ; William L. Beatty, William D. Stiehl; Clerk's Office, Benton 62812.

Indiana — Northern: Allen Sharp, CJ; William C. Lee, James T. Moody, Michael S. Kanne, Robert L. Miller Jr.; Clerk's Office, South Bend 46601. **Southern:** Gene E. Brooks, CJ; S. Hugh Dillin, Sarah E. Barker; Clerk's Office, Indianapolis 46204.

Iowa — Northern: Donald E. O'Brien, CJ, David R. Hansen; Clerk's Office, Cedar Rapids 52407. **Southern:** Harold D. Vietor, CJ; Donald E. O'Brien; Clerk's Office, Des Moines 50309.

Kansas — Earl E. O'Connor, CJ; Richard Dean Rogers, Dale E. Saffels, Patrick F. Kelly, Sam A. Crow, Deanell Reece Tacha; Clerk's Office, Wichita 67202.

Kentucky — Eastern: Eugene E. Siler Jr., CJ; Scott Reed, William Bertelsman, G. Wix Unthank, Henry R. Wilhoit Jr.; Clerk's Office, Lexington 40586. **Western:** Edward H. Johnstone, CJ; Eugene E. Siler Jr., Thomas A. Ballantine, Ronald E. Meredith, Charles R. Simpson 3d; Clerk's Office, Louisville 40202.

Louisiana — Eastern: Frederick J. R. Heebe, CJ; Charles Schwartz Jr., Morley L. Sear, Adrian A. Duplantier, Robert F. Collins, George Arceneaux Jr., Veronica D. Wicker, Patrick E. Carr, Peter Beer, A J. McNamara, Henry A. Mentz Jr., Martin L. C. Feldman, Marcel Livaudais Jr.; Clerk's Office, New Orleans 70130. **Middle:** John V. Parker, CJ; Frank J. Polozola; Clerk's Office, Baton Rouge 70801. **Western:** Tom Stagg, CJ; Earl Ernest Veron, John M. Shaw, John M. Duhe Jr., F. A. Little Jr., Donald E. Walter; Clerk's Office, Shreveport 71101.

Maine — Conrad K. Cyr, CJ; Gene Carter; Clerk's Office, Portland 04112.

Maryland — Alexander Harvey 2d, CJ; Joseph H. Young, Herbert F. Murray, Joseph C. Howard, Norman P. Ramsey, William E. Black Jr., John R. Hargrove, J. Frederick Motz, Frederic N. Smalkin; Clerk's Office, Baltimore 21201.

Massachusetts — Frank H. Freedman, CJ; Joseph L. Tauro, Walter Jay Skinner, A. David Mazzone, Robert E. Keeton, John J. McNaught, Rya W. Zobel, David S. Nelson, Mark L. Wolf, William G. Young, Douglas P. Woodlock; Clerk's Office, Boston 02109.

Michigan — Eastern: Philip Pratt, CJ; Robert E. DeMascio, James P. Churchill, Julian A. Cook Jr., Stewart A. Newblatt, Avern Cohn, Anna Diggs Taylor, Horace W. Gilmore, George E. Woods, Richard F. Suhrheinrich, George La Plata, Barbara K. Hackett, Lawrence P. Zatkoff, Patrick J. Duggan; Clerk's Office, Detroit 48226. **Western:** Douglas W. Hillman, CJ; Benjamin F. Gibson, Richard A. Enslen; Clerk's Office, Grand Rapids 49503.

Minnesota — Donald D. Alsop, CJ; Harry H. MacLaughlin, Robert G. Renner, Diana E. Murphy, Paul A. Magnuson, James M. Rosenbaum; Clerk's Office, St. Paul 55101.

Mississippi — Northern: L. T. Senter Jr., CJ; Neal Biggers, Glen H. Davidson; Clerk's Office, Oxford 38655. **Southern:** William H. Barbour Jr., CJ; Walter L. Nixon Jr., Harry T. Wingate, Tom S. Lee, Walter J. Gex 3d; Clerk's Office, Jackson 39205.

Missouri — Eastern: John F. Nangle, CJ; Edward D. Filippine, William L. Hungate, Clyde S. Cahill Jr., Stephen N. Limbaugh, George F. Gunn Jr.; Clerk's Office, St. Louis 63101. **Western:** Scott O. Wright, CJ; Russell G. Clark, Howard F. Sachs, Joseph E. Stevens Jr., D. Brook Bartlett, Ross T. Roberts; Clerk's Office, Kansas City 64106.

Montana — James F. Battin, CJ; Paul G. Hatfield, Charles C. Lovell; Clerk's Office, Billings 59101.

Nebraska — Clarence A. Beam, CJ; Warren K. Urbom, Lyle E. Strom; Clerk's Office, Omaha 68101.

Nevada — Edward C. Reed Jr., CJ; Lloyd D. George, Howard D. McKibben; Clerk's Office, Las Vegas 89101.

New Hampshire — Shane Devine, CJ; Martin F. Loughlin; Clerk's Office, Concord 03301.

New Jersey — Clarkson S. Fisher, CJ; John F. Gerry, Stanley S. Brotman, Anne E. Thompson, D. R. Debevoise, H. Lee Sarokin, Harold A. Ackerman, John W. Bissell, Maryanne Trump Barry, Joseph H. Rodriguez, Richard E. Cowen, Garrett E. Brown Jr., Alfred J. Lechner Jr.; Clerk's Office, Newark 07102.

New Mexico — Santiago E. Campos, CJ; Juan G. Burciaga, John E. Conway; Clerk's Office, Albuquerque 87103.

New York — Northern: Howard G. Munson, CJ; Neal P. McCurn, Thomas J. McAvoy, Con G. Cholakis; Clerk's Office, Albany 12201. **Eastern:** Jack B. Weinstein, CJ; Mark A. Costantino, Thomas C. Platt Jr., Henry Bramwell, Charles P. Sifton, Eugene H. Nickerson, Joseph M. McLaughlin, Israel Leo Glasser, Raymond J. Dearie, Leonard D. Wexler, Edward R. Korman; Clerk's Office, Brooklyn 11201. **Southern:** Charles L. Brieant, CJ; David N. Edelstein, Edward Weinfeld, Whitman Knapp, Thomas P. Griesa, Robert J. Ward, Kevin Thomas Duffy, William C. Conner, Richard Owen, Leonard B. Sand, Mary Johnson Lowe, Gerard L. Goettel, Charles S. Haight Jr., Vincent L. Broderick, Pierre N. Leval, Robert W. Sweet, John E. Sprizzo, Shirley Wohl Kram, John F. Keenan, Peter K. Leisure, John M. Walker, Louis L. Stanton, Miriam G. Cedarbaum; Clerk's Office N. Y. City 10007. **Western:** John T. Curtin, CJ; John T. Elfvin, Michael A. Telesca; Clerk's Office, Buffalo 14202.

North Carolina — Eastern: W. Earl Britt, CJ; James C. Fox, Terrence W. Boyle; Clerk's Office, Raleigh 27611. **Middle:** Hiram H. Ward, CJ; Frank W. Bullock Jr., Richard C. Erwin; Clerk's Office, Greensboro 27402. **Western:** Robert D. Potter, CJ; David B. Sentelle, James B. McMillan; Clerk's Office Asheville 28802.

North Dakota — Patrick A. Conmy, CJ; Clerk's Office, Bismarck 58502.

Ohio — Northern: Frank J. Battisti, CJ; Thomas D. Lambros, John M. Manos, George W. White, Ann Aldrich, Alvin I. Krenzler, John W. Potter, David D. Dowd Jr., Sam H. Bell, Alice M. Batchelder, Richard B. McQuade Jr.; Clerk's Office, Cleveland 44114. **Southern:** Carl B. Rubin, CJ; John D. Holschuh, Walter H. Rice, S. Arthur Spiegel, Herman Jacob Weber, James L. Graham; Clerk's Office, Columbus 43215.

Oklahoma — Northern: H. Dale Cook, CJ; James O. Ellison, Thomas R. Brett, David L. Russell; Clerk's Office, Tulsa 74103. **Eastern:** Frank H. Shey, CJ; H. Dale Cook, David L. Russell; Clerk's Office, Muskogee 74401. **Western:** Ralph G. Thompson, CJ; H. Dale Cook, Wayne Alley, Lee R. West, David L. Russell; Clerk's Office, Oklahoma City 73102.

Oregon — Owen M. Panner, CJ; James M. Burns, James A. Redden, Helen J. Frye, Edward Leavy; Clerk's Office, Portland 97205.

Pennsylvania — Eastern: John P. Fullam, CJ; Charles R. Weiner, Daniel H. Huyett 3d, Clarence C. Newcomer, Clifford Scott Green, Louis Charles Bechtle, Joseph L. McGlynn Jr., Edward N. Cahn, Louis H. Pollak, Norma L. Shapiro, James T. Giles, James McGirr Kelly, Thomas N. O'Neill Jr., Marvin Katz, Anthony J. Scirica, Edmund V. Ludwig; Clerk's Office, Philadelphia 19106. **Middle:** William J. Nealon Jr., CJ; Richard P. Conaboy, Sylvia H. Rambo, William W. Caldwell, Edward M. Kosik; Clerk's Office, Scranton 18501. **Western:** Maurice B. Cohill Jr., CJ; Gerald J. Weber, Paul A. Simmons, Gustave Diamond, Donald E. Ziegler, Alan N. Bloch, Glenn E. Mencer; Clerk's Office, Pittsburgh 15230.

Rhode Island — Francis J. Boyle, CJ; Ronald R. Lagueux; Clerk's Office, Providence 02903.

South Carolina — Solomon Blatt Jr., CJ; C. Weston Houck, Falcon B. Hawkins, Matthew J. Perry Jr., George R. Anderson Jr., Clyde H. Hamilton, Karen L. Henderson, Joseph F. Anderson Jr.; Clerk's Office, Columbia 29202.

South Dakota — Donald J. Porter, CJ; Richard H. Battey, John Bailey Jones; Clerk's Office, Sioux Falls 57102.

Tennessee — Eastern: Thomas G. Hull, CJ; James H. Jarvis, R. Allan Edgar; Clerk's Office, Knoxville 37901. **Middle:** Thomas A. Wiseman Jr, CJ; Thomas A. Higgins, John T. Nixon; Clerk's Office, Nashville 37203. **Western:** Odell Horton, CJ; Julia S. Gibbons, James D. Todd; Clerk's Office, Memphis 38103.

Texas — Northern: Robert W. Porter, CJ; Eldon B. Mahon, Mary Lou Robinson, Barefoot Sanders, David O. Belew Jr., Jerry Buchmeyer, A. Joe Fish, Robert B. Maloney, Sidney A. Fitzwater; Clerk's Office, Dallas 75242. **Southern:** John V. Singleton Jr., CJ; Carl O. Bue Jr., Ross N. Sterling, Norman W. Black, James De Anda, Gabrielle K. McDonald, George P. Kazen, Hugh Gibson, Filemon B. Vela, Hayden W. Head Jr., Ricardo H. Hinojosa, Lynn N. Hughes, David Hittner; Clerk's Office, Houston 77208. **Eastern:** William Wayne Justice, CJ; William M. Steger, Robert M. Parker, Howell Cobb, Sam B. Hall Jr., Paul N. Brown; Clerk's Office, Tyler 75702. **Western:** William S. Sessions, CJ; Lucius D. Bunton 3d, Harry Lee Hudspeth, Hipolito F. Garcia, James R. Nowlin, Edward C. Prado, Walter S. Smith Jr.; Clerk's Office, San Antonio 78206.

Utah — Bruce S. Jenkins, CJ; J. Thomas Greene, David Sam, David K. Winder; Clerk's Office, Salt Lake City 84101.

Vermont — Albert W. Coffrin, CJ; Franklin S. Billings Jr.; Clerk's Office, Burlington 05402.

Virginia — Eastern: Albert V. Bryan Jr., CJ; J. Calvitt Clarke, Richard L. Williams, James C. Cacheris, Robert G. Doumar, Claude M. Hilton, James R. Spencer; Clerk's Office, Alexandria 22320. **Western:** James C. Turk, CJ; Glen M. Williams, James H. Michael Jr., Jackson L. Kiser; Clerk's Office, Roanoke 24006.

Washington — Eastern: Robert J. McNichols, CJ; Justin L. Quackenbush, Alan A. McDonald; Clerk's Office, Spokane 99210. **Western:** Walter T. McGovern, CJ; Jack E. Tanner, Barbara J. Rothstein, John C. Coughenour, Carolyn R. Dimmick, Robert J. Bryan; Clerk's Office, Seattle 98104.

West Virginia — Northern: Robert Earl Maxwell, CJ; William M. Kidd; Clerk's Office, Elkins 26241. **Southern:** Charles H. Haden 2d, CJ; Robert J. Staker, John T. Copenhaver Jr., Elizabeth V. Hallanan; Clerk's Office, Charleston 25329.

Wisconsin — Eastern: Robert W. Warren, CJ; Terence T. Evans, Thomas J. Curran; Clerk's Office, Milwaukee 53202. **Western:** Barbara B. Crabb, CJ; John C. Shabaz; Clerk's Office, Madison 53701.

Wyoming — Clarence A. Brimmer, CJ; Alan B. Johnson; Clerk's Office, Cheyenne 82001.

U.S. Territorial District Courts

Guam — Cristobal C. Duenas; Clerk's Office, Agana 96910.
Puerto Rico — Juan M. Perez-Gimenez, CJ; Gilberto Gierbolini-Ortiz, Carman Consuelo Cerezo, Jaime Pieras Jr., Raymond L. Acosta, Hector M. Laffitte, Jose Antonio Fuste; Clerk's Office, San Juan 00904.
Virgin Islands — Almeric L. Christian, CJ; David V. O'Brien; Clerk's Office, Charlotte Amalie, St. Thomas 00801.

State Officials, Salaries, Party Membership

As of mid-1987

Alabama

Governor — Guy Hunt, R., $68,838.
Lt. Gov. — Jim Folsom Jr., D., $95 per legislative day, plus annual salary of $600 per month plus $1,500 per month for expenses.
Sec. of State — Glen Browder, D., $32,940.
Atty. Gen. — Don Siegelman, D., $58,000.
Treasurer — George Wallace Jr., D., $45,000.
Legislature: meets annually the 3d Tuesday in Apr. (first year of term of office, first Tuesday in Feb. (2d and 3d years), 2d Tuesday in Jan. (4th year) at Montgomery. Members receive $600 per month, plus $95 per day during legislative sessions, and mileage of 10c per mile.
Senate — Dem., 28; Rep., 4; ind. 3. Total, 35.
House — Dem., 87; Rep., 11; ind. 6.; 1 vacancy. Total, 105.

Alaska

Governor — Steve Cowper, D., $81,648.
Lt. Gov. — Stephen McAlpine, D., $76,188.
Atty. General — Grace Berg Schaible, D., $73,620.
Legislature: meets annually in January at Juneau, for 120 days with a 10-day extension possible upon ⅔ vote. First session in odd years. Members receive $24,140 per year plus $80 a day per diem.
Senate — Dem., 9; Rep., 11. Total, 20.
House — Dem., 21; Rep., 18; Libertarians, 1. Total, 40.

Arizona

Governor — Evan Mecham, R., $75,000.
Sec. of State — Rose Mofford, D., $50,000.
Atty. Gen. — Bob Corbin, R., $70,000.
Treasurer — Ray Rottas, R., $50,000.
Legislature: meets annually in January at Phoenix. Each member receives an annual salary of $15,000.
Senate — Dem., 11; Rep., 19. Total, 30.
House — Dem., 24; Rep., 36. Total, 60.

Arkansas

Governor — Bill Clinton, D., $35,000.
Lt. Gov. — Winston Bryant, D., $14,000.
Sec. of State — W. J. "Bill" McCuen, D., $22,500.
Atty. Gen. — Steve Clark, D., $26,500.
Treasurer — Jimmie Lou Fisher, D., $22,500.
General Assembly: meets odd years in January at Little Rock. Members receive $7,500 per year, $50 a day while in regular session, plus 20½c a mile travel expense.
Senate — Dem., 31; Rep., 4. Total, 35.
House — Dem., 91; Rep., 9. Total, 100.

California

Governor — George Deukmejian, R., $85,000.
Lt. Gov. — Leo T. McCarthy, D., $72,500.
Sec. of State — March Fong Eu, D., $72,500.
Controller — Gray Davis, D., $72,500.
Atty. Gen. — John Van de Kamp, D., $77,500.
Treasurer — Jesse M. Unruh, D., $72,500.
Legislature: meets at Sacramento; regular sessions commence on the first Monday in Dec. of every even-numbered year; each session lasts 2 years. Members receive $33,732 per year plus mileage and $65 per diem.
Senate — Dem., 23; Rep., 16, one ind. Total, 40.
Assembly — Dem., 44; Rep., 36. Total, 80.

Colorado

Governor — Roy Romer, D., $70,000.
Lt. Gov. — Mike Callihan, D., $48,500.
Secy. of State — Natalie Meyer, R., $48,500.
Atty. Gen. — Duane Woodard, R., $60,000.
Treasurer — Gail Schoettler, D., $48,500.
General Assembly: meets annually in January at Denver. Members receive $17,500 annually.

Senate — Dem., 10; Rep., 25. Total, 35.
House — Dem., 25; Rep., 40. Total, 65.

Connecticut

Governor — William A. O'Neill, D., $78,000.
Lt. Gov. — Joseph J. Fauliso, D., $55,000.
Sec. of State — Julia H. Tashjian, D., $50,000.
Treasurer — Francisco Borges, D., $50,000.
Comptroller — J. Edward Caldwell, D., $50,000.
Atty. Gen. — Joseph I. Liberman, D., $60,000.
General Assembly: meets annually odd years in January and even years in February at Hartford. Salary $15,200 per year plus $4,500 (senator), $3,500 (representative) per year for expenses, plus travel allowance.
Senate — Dem., 25; Rep., 11. Total, 36.
House — Dem., 92; Rep., 59. Total, 151.

Delaware

Governor — Michael N. Castle, R., $70,000.
Lt. Gov. — S. B. Woo, D., $30,000.
Sec. of State — Michael Harkins, R., $50,000.
Atty. Gen. — Charles Oberly 3d, D., $52,320.
Treasurer — Janet C. Rzewnicki, R., $33,960.
General Assembly: meets annually at Dover from the 2d Tuesday in January to midnight June 30. Members receive $20,000 base salary.
Senate — Dem., 13; Rep., 8. Total, 21.
House — Dem., 19; Rep., 22. Total, 41.

Florida

Governor — Bob Martinez, R., $90,570.
Lt. Gov. — Bobby Brantley, R., $81,967.
Sec. of State — George Firestone, D., $81,967.
Comptroller — Gerald Lewis, D., $81,967.
Atty. Gen. — Robert Butterworth, D., $81,967.
Treasurer — Bill Gunter, D., $81,967.
Legislature: meets annually at Tallahassee. Members receive $18,900 per year plus expense allowance while on official business.
Senate — Dem., 25; Rep., 15. Total, 40.
House — Dem., 75; Rep., 45. Total, 120.

Georgia

Governor — Joe Frank Harris, D., $79,358.
Lt. Gov. — Zell Miller, D., $45,000.
Sec. of State — Max Cleland, D., $60,500.
Comptroller General — Johnnie L. Caldwell, D., $60,000.
Atty. Gen. — Michael J. Bowers, $62,000.
General Assembly: meets annually at Atlanta. Members receive $10,000 per year. During session $59 per day for expenses.
Senate — Dem., 46; Rep., 10. Total, 56.
House — Dem., 153; Rep., 27. Total, 180.

Hawaii

Governor — John Waihee, D., $59,400.
Lt. Gov. — Benjamin Cayetano, D., $53,460.
Atty. Gen. — Warren Price, $50,490.
Comptroller — Richard Rahle, $50,490.
Dir. of Budget & Finance — Yukio Takemoto, $50,490.
Legislature: meets annually on 3d Wednesday in January at Honolulu. Members receive $15,600 per year plus expenses.
Senate — Dem., 21. Rep., 4. Total, 25.
House — Dem., 40. Rep., 11. Total, 51.

Idaho

Governor — Cecil D. Andrus, D., $55,000.
Lt. Gov. — C. L. "Butch" Otter, D., $15,000.
Sec. of State — Pete T. Cenarrusa, R., $45,000.
Treasurer — Lydia Justice Edwards, R., $45,000.
Atty. Gen. — Jim Jones, R., $48,000.
Legislature: meets annually the Monday on or nearest the 9th of January at Boise. Members receive $30 per day during session, $7 per day when not in session, plus certain travel and living allowances.
Senate — Dem., 26; Rep., 26. Total, 52.
House — Dem., 20; Rep., 64. Total, 84.

Illinois

Governor — James R. Thompson, R., $93,266.
Lt. Gov. — George H. Ryan, R., $65,835.
Sec. of State — Jim Edgar, R., $82,294.
Comptroller — Roland W. Burris, D., $71,321.
Atty. Gen. — Neil F. Hartigan, D., $82,294.
Treasurer — Jerome Consentino, D., $71,321.
General Assembly: meets annually in January at Springfield. Members receive $35,661 per annum.
Senate — Dem., 31; Rep., 28. Total, 59.
House — Dem., 67; Rep., 51. Total, 118.

Indiana

Governor — Robert D. Orr, R., $66,000 plus discretionary expenses.
Lt. Gov. — John M. Mutz, R., $51,000 plus discretionary expenses.
Sec. of State — Evan Bayh, D., $46,000.
Atty. Gen. — Linley E. Pearson, R., $51,000.
Treasurer — Marjorie H. O'Laughlin, R., $46,000.
General Assembly: meets annually in January. Members receive $11,600 per year plus $75 per day while in session, $15 per day while not in session.
Senate — Dem., 20; Rep., 30. Total, 50.
House — Dem., 48; Rep., 52. Total, 100.

Iowa

Governor — Terry Branstad, R., $64,000 plus $10,000 expenses.
Lt. Gov. — Jo Ann Zimmerman, D., $21,900 plus personal expenses and travel allowances at same rate as for a senator.
Sec. of State — Elaine Baxter, D., $41,000.
Atty. Gen. — Thomas J. Miller, D., $54,000.
Treasurer — Michael L. Fitzgerald, D., $41,000.
Auditor — Richard Johnson, R., $41,000.
Secy. of Agriculture — Dale M. Cochran, D., $41,000.
General Assembly: meets annually in January at Des Moines. Members receive $14,600 annually plus maximum expense allowance of $40 per day for first 110 days of first session, and first 100 days of 2d session; mileage expenses at 24¢ a mile.
Senate — Dem., 30; Rep., 20. Total, 50.
House — Dem., 58; Rep., 42. Total, 100.

Kansas

Governor — Mike Hayden, R., $66,950.
Lt. Gov. — Jack Walker, R., $18,753.
Sec. of State — Bill Graves, R., $51,500.
Atty. Gen. — Robert T. Stephan, R., $59,225.
Treasurer — Joan Finney, D., $51,500.
Legislature: meets annually in January at Topeka. Members receive $49 a day plus $50 a day expenses while in session, plus $600 per month while not in session.
Senate — Dem., 16; Rep., 24. Total, 40.
House — Dem., 51; Rep., 74. Total, 125.

Kentucky

Governor — Martha L. Collins, D., $63,036.
Lt. Gov. — Steve Beshear, D., $55,647.
Sec. of State — Drexell R. Davis, D., $55,647.
Atty. Gen. — Dave Armstrong, D., $55,647.
Treasurer — Francis J. Mills, D., $55,647.
Auditor — Mary A. Tobin, D., $55,647.
General Assembly: meets even years in January at Frankfort. Members receive $100 per day and $100 per day during session and $950 per month for expenses for interim.
Senate — Dem., 28; Rep., 10. Total, 38.
House — Dem., 74; Rep., 26. Total, 100.

Louisiana

Governor — Edwin W. Edwards, D., $73,440.
Lt. Gov. — Robert L. Freeman, D., $63,367.
Sec. of State — James H. Brown, D., $60,169.
Atty. Gen. — William J. Guste Jr., D., $60,169.
Treasurer — Thomas D. Burbank Jr., D., $60,169.
Legislature: meets annually for 60 legislative days commencing on 3d Monday in April. Members receive $75 per day and mileage plus annual salary of $16,800.
Senate — Dem., 34; Rep., 5. Total, 39.
House — Dem., 83; Rep., 22. Total, 105.

Maine

Governor — John R. McKernan Jr., R., $70,000.
Sec. of State — Rodney Quinn, D., $45,780.
Atty. Gen. — James Tierney, D., $54,724.
Treasurer — Samuel Shapiro, D., $42,500.
Legislature: meets annually in December at Augusta. Members receive $9,000 for first regular sessions, $6,000 for second regular session plus expenses; presiding officers receive 50% more.
Senate — Dem., 20; Rep., 15. Total, 35.
House — Dem., 86; Rep., 65. Total, 151.

Maryland

Governor — William Donald Schaefer, D., $85,000.
Lt. Gov. — Melvin Steinberg, D., $72,500.
Comptroller — Louis L. Goldstein, D., $72,500.
Atty. Gen. — J. Joseph Curran Jr., D., $72,500.
Sec. of State — Winfield M. Kelly Jr., D., $52,500.
Treasurer — Lucille Maurer, D., $72,500.
General Assembly: meets 90 days annually on the 2d Wednesday

in January at Annapolis. Members receive $22,000 per year plus expenses.

Senate — Dem., 40; Rep., 7. Total, 47.
House — Dem., 124; Rep., 17. Total, 141.

Massachusetts

Governor — Michael S. Dukakis, D., $75,000.
Lt. Gov. — Evelyn Murphy, $60,000.
Sec. of State — Michael Joseph Connolly, D., $60,000.
Atty. Gen. — James M. Shannon, D., $65,000.
Treasurer — Robert Q. Crane, D., $60,000.
Auditor — A. Joseph DeNucci, D., $60,000.
General Court (Legislature): meets each January in Boston. Salaries $30,000 per annum.
Senate — Dem., 32; Rep., 8. Total, 40.
House — Dem., 126; Rep., 34. Total, 160.

Michigan

Governor — James J. Blanchard, D., $92,664.
Lt. Gov. — Martha W. Griffiths, D., $62,970.
Sec. of State — Richard H. Austin, D., $85,500.
Atty. Gen. — Frank J. Kelley, D., $89,000.
Treasurer — Robert A. Bowman, N-P, $65,700.
Legislature: meets annually in January at Lansing. Members receive $38,163 per year, plus $7,700 expense allowance.
Senate — Dem., 18; Rep., 20. Total, 38.
House — Dem., 64; Rep., 46. Total, 110.

Minnesota

Governor — Rudy Perpich, DFL, $91,460.
Lt. Gov. — Marlene Johnson, DFL, $50,305.
Sec. of State — Joan Anderson Growe, DFL., $50,305.
Atty. Gen. — Hubert H. Humphrey 3d, DFL., $71,450.
Treasurer — Michael McGrath, DFL., $47,590.
Auditor — Arnie Carlson, IR, $54,881.
Legislature: meets for a total of 120 days within every 2 years at St. Paul. Members receive $23,244 per year, plus expense allowance during session.
Senate — DFL., 47; IR, 20. Total, 67.
House — DFL., 83; IR, 51. Total, 134.
(DFL means Democratic-Farmer-Labor. IR means Independent Republican.)

Mississippi

Governor — William A. Allain, D., $63,000.
Lt. Gov. — Brad Dye, D., $34,000 per regular legislative session, plus expense allowance.
Sec. of State — Dick Molpus, D., $45,000.
Atty. Gen. — Edwin L. Pittman, D., $51,000.
Treasurer — William J. Cole 3d, D., $45,000.
Legislature: meets annually in January at Jackson. Members receive $10,100 per regular session plus travel allowance, and $500 per month while not in session.
Senate — Dem., 47; Rep., 4, 1 ind. Total, 52.
House — Dem., 115; Rep., 7. Total, 122.

Missouri

Governor — John D. Ashcroft, R., $81,000.
Lt. Gov. — Harriett Woods, D., $48,600.
Sec. of State — Roy D. Blunt, R., $64,800.
Atty. Gen. — William L. Webster, R., $70,200.
Treasurer — Wendell Bailey, R., $64,800.
State Auditor — Margaret Kelly, R., $64,800.
General Assembly: meets annually in Jefferson City on the first Wednesday after first Monday in January; adjournment in off-numbered years by June 30, in even-numbered years by May 15. Members receive $19,524 annually.
Senate — Dem., 21; Rep., 13. Total, 34.
House — Dem., 108; Rep., 55. Total, 163.

Montana

Governor — Ted Schwinden, D., $50,452.
Lt. Gov. — George Turman, D., $36,141.
Sec. of State — Jim Waltermire, R., $33,342.
Atty. Gen. — Mike Greely, D., $46,016.
Legislative Assembly: meets odd years in January at Helena. Members receive $59.12 per legislative day plus $50 per day for expenses while in session.
Senate — Dem., 25; Rep., 25. Total, 50.
House — Dem., 49; Rep., 51. Total, 100.

Nebraska

Governor — Kay Orr, R., $58,000.
Lt. Gov. — William Nichol, R., $40,000.
Sec. of State — Allen J. Beermann, R., $40,000.
Atty. Gen. — Robert Spire, R., $57,500.
Treasurer — Frank Marsh, R., $35,000.
Legislature: meets annually in January at Lincoln. Members receive salary of $4,800 annually plus travelling expenses for one round trip to and from session.
Unicameral body composed of 49 members who are elected on a nonpartisan ballot and are classed as senators.

Nevada

Governor — Richard Bryan, D., $77,500.
Lt. Gov. — Robert Miller, R., $12,500 plus $130 per day when acting as governor.
Sec. of State — Frankie Sue Del Papa, D., $50,000.
Comptroller — Darrel Daines, R., $49,000.
Atty. Gen. — Brian McKay, R., $62,500.
Treasurer — Ken Santor, R., $49,000.
Legislature: meets odd years in January at Carson City. Members receive $104 per day for 60 days (20 days for special sessions), plus per diem of $50 per day for entire length of session. Travel allowance of 20c per mile.
Senate — Dem., 13; Rep., 8. Total, 21.
Assembly — Rep., 25; Dem., 17. Total, 42.

New Hampshire

Governor — John H. Sununu, R., $66,024.
Sec. of State — William M. Gardner, D., $46,375.
Atty. Gen. — Stephen E. Merrill, $58,940.
Treasurer — Georgie A. Thomas, R., $46,375.
General Court (Legislature): meets every year in January at Concord. Members receive $200; presiding officers $250.
Senate — Dem., 8; Rep., 16. Total, 24.
House — Rep., 267; Dem., 133. Total, 400.

New Jersey

Governor — Thomas H. Kean, R., $85,000.
Sec. of State — Jane Burgio, R., $90,000.
Atty. Gen. — W. Gary Edwards, R., $90,000.
Treasurer — Feather O'Connor, $90,000.
Legislature: meets throughout the year at Trenton. Members receive $25,000 per year, except president of Senate and speaker of Assembly who receive 1/3 more.
Senate — Dem., 22; Rep., 16; 2 vacancies. Total, 40.
Assembly — Dem., 30; Rep. 50. Total, 80.

New Mexico

Governor — Garrey E. Carruthers, R., $63,000.
Lt. Gov. — Jack Stahl, R., $40,425.
Sec. of State — Rebecca Vigil-Giron, D., $40,425.
Atty. Gen. — Hal Stratton, R., $46,200.
Treasurer — James Lewis, D., $40,425.
Legislature: meets in January at Sante Fe; odd years for 60 days, even years for 30 days. Members receive $75 per day while in session.
Senate — Dem., 21; Rep., 21. Total, 42.
House — Dem., 47; Rep., 23. Total, 70.

New York

Governor — Mario M. Cuomo, D., $130,000.
Lt. Gov. — Stan Lundine, D., $110,000.
Sec. of State — Gail S. Shaffer, D., $79,218.
Comptroller — Edward V. Regan, R., $110,000.
Atty. Gen. — Robert Abrams, D., $110,000.
Legislature: meets annually in January at Albany. Members receive $43,000 per year.
Senate — Dem., 26; Rep., 35. Total, 61.
Assembly — Dem., 94; Rep., 56. Total, 150.

North Carolina

Governor — James G. Martin, R., $100,000 plus $11,500 per year expenses.
Lt. Gov. — Robert B. Jordan 3d, D., $61,044 per year, plus $11,500 per year expense allowance.
Sec. of State — Thad Eure, D., $61,044
Atty. Gen. — Lacy Thornberg, D., $61,044.
Treasurer — Harlan E. Boyles, D., $61,044.
General Assembly: meets odd years in January at Raleigh. Members receive $10,140 annual salary and $3,024 annual expense allowance, plus $79 per diem subsistence and travel allowance while in session.
Senate — Dem., 40; Rep., 10. Total, 50.
House — Dem., 86; Rep., 34. Total, 120.

North Dakota

Governor — George A. Sinner, D., $65,000.
Lt. Gov. — Lloyd B. Omdahl, D., $50,000.
Sec. of State — Ben Meier, R., $46,000.
Atty. Gen. — Nicholas Spaeth, D., $52,000.

Treasurer — Robert Hanson, D., $46,000.

Legislative Assembly: meets odd years in January at Bismarck. Members receive $90 per day expenses during session and $180 per month when not in session.

Senate — Dem., 27; Rep., 26. Total, 53.

House — Dem., 45; Rep., 60, 1 ind. Total, 106.

Ohio

Governor — Richard F. Celeste, D., $65,000.

Lt. Gov. — Paul R. Leonard, $42,542.

Sec. of State — Sherrod Brown, D., $60,775.

Atty. Gen. — Anthony J. Celebrezze Jr., D., $60,775.

Treasurer — Mary Ellen Withrow, D., $60,775.

Auditor — Thomas E. Ferguson, D., $60,775.

General Assembly: meets odd years at Columbus on first Monday in January for the 1st session, and no later than Mar. 15th of the following year for the 2d session. Members receive $30,152 per annum.

Senate — Dem., 15; Rep., 18. Total, 33.

House — Dem., 60; Rep., 39. Total, 99.

Oklahoma

Governor — Henry Bellmon, R., $70,000.

Lt. Gov. — Robert S. Kerr 3d, D., $40,000.

Sec. of State — Jeannette B. Edmondson, D., $37,000.

Atty. Gen. — Robert Henry, D., $55,000.

Treasurer — Ellis Edwards, D., $50,000.

Legislature: meets annually in January at Oklahoma City. Members receive $20,000 annually.

Senate — Dem., 30; Rep., 17; 1 vacancy. Total, 48.

House — Dem., 70; Rep., 31. Total, 101.

Oregon

Governor — Neil Goldschmidt, D., $72,050, plus $500 monthly expenses.

Sec. of State — Barbara Roberts, D., $52,826.

Atty. Gen. — David B. Frohnmayer, R., $60,000.

Treasurer — Bill Rutherford, R., $52,826.

Legislative Assembly: meets odd years in January at Salem. Members receive $775 monthly and $50 expenses per day while in session; $400 per month while not in session.

Senate — Dem., 17; Rep., 13. Total, 30.

House — Dem., 31; Rep., 29. Total, 60.

Pennsylvania

Governor — Robert Casey, D., $85,000.

Lt. Gov. — Mark S. Singel, D., $67,500.

Sec. of the Commonwealth — James J. Haggerty, D., $58,000.

Atty. Gen. — Leroy S. Zimmerman, R., $65,000.

Treasurer — G. Davis Greene, Jr., D., $58,000.

General Assembly convenes annually in January at Harrisburg. Members receive $35,000 per year plus expenses.

Senate — Dem., 23; Rep., 26; 1 ind. Total, 50.

House — Dem., 103; Rep., 100. Total, 203.

Rhode Island

Governor — Edward DiPrete, R., $69,000.

Lt. Gov. — Richard A. Licht, D., $52,000.

Sec. of State — Kathleen O'Connell, D., $52,000.

Atty. Gen. — James E. O'Neil, D., $55,000.

Treasurer — Roger N. Begin, D., $52,000.

General Assembly: meets annually in January at Providence. Members receive $5 per day for 60 days, and travel allowance of 8c per mile.

Senate — Dem., 38; Rep., 12. Total, 50.

House — Dem., 80; Rep., 20. Total, 100.

South Carolina

Governor — Carroll A. Campbell Jr., R., $81,600.

Lt. Gov. — Nick Theodore, D., $35,700.

Sec. of State — John T. Campbell, D., $69,360.

Comptroller Gen. — Earle E. Morris Jr., D., $69,360.

Atty. Gen. — T.T. Medlock, D., $69,360.

Treasurer — G.L. Patterson Jr., D., $69,360.

General Assembly: meets annually in January at Columbia. Members receive $10,000 per year and expense allowance of $68 per day, plus travel and postage allowance.

Senate — Dem., 34; Rep., 12. Total, 46.

House — Dem. 91; Rep., 32; 1 vacancy. Total, 124.

South Dakota

Governor — George S. Mickelson, R., $57,325.

Lt. Gov. — Walter B. Miller, R., $7,980 plus $75 per day during legislative session.

Sec. of State — Joyce Hazeltine, R., $38,940.

Treasurer — David Volk, R., $38,940.

Atty. Gen. — Roger Tellinghuisen, R., $48,675.

Auditor — Vernon Larson, R., $38,940.

Legislature: meets annually in January at Pierre. Members receive $3,200 for 40-day session in odd-numbered years, and $2,800 for 35-day session in even-numbered years, plus $75 per legislative day.

Senate — Dem., 11; Rep., 24. Total, 35.

House — Dem., 22; Rep., 48. Total, 70.

Tennessee

Governor — Ned Ray McWherter, D., $85,000.

Lt. Gov. — John S. Wilder, D., $12,500.

Sec. of State — Gentry Crowell, D., $65,500.

Comptroller — William Snodgrass, D., $65,000.

Atty. Gen. — Michael Cody, D., $65,650.

General Assembly: meets annually in January at Nashville. Members receive $12,500 yearly plus $75.00 expenses for each day in session.

Senate — Dem., 23; Rep., 10. Total, 33.

House — Dem., 61; Rep., 38. Total, 99.

Texas

Governor — William P. Clements, R., $91,600.

Lt. Gov. — Bill Hobby, D., $7,200, plus living quarters; $20,000 when acting as governor.

Sec. of State — Jack M. Rains, R., $63,000.

Comptroller — Bob Bullock, D., $71,100.

Atty. Gen. — Jim Mattox, D., $71,100.

Treasurer — Ann W. Richards, D., $71,100.

Legislature: meets odd years in January at Austin. Members receive annual salary not exceeding $7,200, per diem while in session, and travel allowance.

Senate — Dem., 25; Rep., 6. Total, 31.

House — Dem., 94; Rep., 56. Total, 150.

Utah

Governor — Norman Bangerter, R., $60,000.

Lt. Gov. — W. Val Oveson, R., $50,000.

Atty. Gen. — David L. Wilkinson, R., $49,000.

Treasurer — Edward T. Alter, D., $45,500.

Legislature: convenes for 60 days on 2d Monday in January each year; members receive $25 per day, $15 daily expenses, and mileage.

Senate — Dem., 8; Rep., 21. Total, 29.

House — Dem., 27; Rep., 48. Total, 75.

Vermont

Governor — Madeleine M. Kunin, D., $63,600.

Lt. Gov. — Howard Dean, D., $26,500.

Sec. of State — James H. Douglas, R., $40,000.

Atty. Gen. — Jeffrey Amestoy, R., $48,000.

Treasurer — Emory Hebard, R., $40,000.

Auditor of Accounts — Alexander V. Acebo, R., $40,000.

General Assembly: meets odd years in January at Montpelier. Members receive $320 weekly while in session, with a limit of $11,000 for a regular session and $60 per day for special session, plus specified expenses.

Senate — Dem., 19; Rep., 11. Total, 30.

House — Dem., 76; Rep., 74. Total, 150.

Virginia

Governor — Gerald L. Baliles, D., $85,000.

Lt. Gov. — L. Douglas Wilder, D., $28,000.

Atty. Gen. — Mary Sue Terry, D., $75,000.

Sec. of the Commonwealth — Sandra D. Bowen, D., $50,000.

Treasurer — William Clay Wiley, $58,613.

General Assembly: meets annually in January at Richmond. Members receive $18,000 annually plus expense and mileage allowances.

Senate — Dem., 31; Rep., 9. Total, 40.

House — Dem., 64; Rep., 34; Ind., 2. Total, 100.

Washington

Governor — Booth Gardner, D., $74,900.

Lt. Gov. — John A. Cherberg, D., $42,400.

Sec. of State — Ralph Munro, R., $42,400.

Atty. Gen. — Ken Eikenberry, R., $55,450.

Treasurer — Robert S. O'Brien, D., $46,470.

Legislature: meets annually in January at Olympia. Members receive $14,500 annually plus per diem of $50 per diem and 10¢ per mile while in session, and $50 per diem for attending meetings during interim.

Senate — Dem., 25; Rep., 24. Total, 49.

House — Dem., 61; Rep., 37. Total, 98.

West Virginia

Governor — Arch A. Moore Jr., R., $72,000
Sec. of State — Ken Hechler, D., $43,200.
Atty. Gen. — Charlie Brown, D., $50,400.
Treasurer — A. James Manchin, D., $50,400.
Comm. of Agric. — Gus R. Douglass, D., $46,800.
Auditor — Glen B. Gainer Jr., D., $46,800.
Legislature: meets annually in January at Charleston. Members receive $6,500.
Senate — Dem., 27; Rep., 7. Total, 34.
House — Dem., 78; Rep., 22. Total, 100.

Wisconsin

Governor — Tommy G. Thompson, R., $86,149.
Lt. Gov. — Scott McCollum, R., $46,360.
Sec. of State — Douglas La Follette, D., $42,089.
Treasurer — Charles P. Smith, D., $42,089.
Atty. Gen. — Donald Haraway, R., $73,930.
Superintendent of Public Instruction — Herbert J. Grover, $66,536.
Legislature: meets in January at Madison. Members receive $29,992 annually plus $45 per day expenses.
Senate — Dem., 19; Rep., 11, 3 vacancies. Total, 33.
Assembly — Dem., 54; Rep., 45. Total, 99.

Wyoming

Governor — Mike Sullivan, D., $70,000.
Sec. of State — Kathy Karpan, D., $52,500.
Atty. Gen. — Joseph Meyer, $52,500.
Treasurer — Stan Smith, R., $52,500.
Legislature: meets odd years in January, even years in February, at Cheyenne. Members receive $75 per day while in session, plus $60 per day for expenses.
Senate — Dem., 11; Rep., 19. Total, 30.
House — Dem., 20; Rep. 44. Total, 64.

Puerto Rico

Governor — Rafael Hernández-Colón.
Secretary of State — Héctor Luis Acevedo.
Secy. of Justice — Héctor Rivera-Cruz.
These officials belong to the Popular Democratic Party.
Legislature: composed of a Senate of 27 members and a House of Representatives of 51 members. Majority of the members of both chambers belongs to the Popular Democratic Party. They meet annually on the 2d Monday in January at San Juan.

U.S. Government Independent Agencies

Source: National Archives & Records Administration

Address: Washington, DC. Location and ZIP codes of agencies in parentheses; as of mid-1987.

ACTION — Donna M. Alvarado, dir. (806 Connecticut Ave., NW, 20525).
African Development Foundation — Leonard H. Robinson Jr., pres. (1625 Massachusetts Ave. NW, 20036).
Appalachian Regional Commission — Winifred A. Pizzano, federal co-chmn.; Gov. Arch A. Moore Jr. of West Virginia, states' co-chmn. (1666 Connecticut Ave. NW, 20235).
Board for International Broadcasting — Malcolm S. Forbes Jr., chmn. (1201 Connecticut Ave., 20036).
Central Intelligence Agency — Robert M. Gates, act. dir. (Wash., DC 20505).
Commission on Civil Rights — Clarence M. Pendleton Jr., chmn. (1121 Vermont Ave. NW, 20425).
Commodity Futures Trading Commission — Susan M. Phillips, chmn. (2033 K St. NW, 20581).
Consumer Product Safety Commission — Terrence Scanlon, chmn. (5401 Westbard Ave., Bethesda, MD 20207).
Environmental Protection Agency — Lee M. Thomas, adm. (401 M St., SW, 20460).
Equal Employment Opportunity Commission — Clarence Thomas, chmn. (2401 E St., NW, 20507).
Farm Credit Administration — Frank W. Naylor Jr. chmn., Federal Farm Credit Board (1501 Farm Credit Drive, McLean, VA 22102).
Federal Communications Commission — Dennis R. Patrick, chmn. (1919 M St. NW, 20554).
Federal Deposit Insurance Corporation — L. William Seidman, chmn. (550 17th St. NW, 20429).
Federal Election Commission — Scott E. Thomas, chmn. (999 E. St. NW, 20463).
Federal Emergency Management Agency — Julius W. Becton Jr., dir. (500 C St. SW, 20472).
Federal Home Loan Bank Board — Edwin J. Gray, chmn. (1700 G St. NW, 20552).
Federal Labor Relations Authority — Jerry L. Calhoun, chmn. (500 C St. SW, 20424).
Federal Mediation and Conciliation Service — Kay McMurray, dir. (2100 K St. NW, 20427).
Federal Reserve System — Chairman, board of governors: Alan Greenspan. (20th St. & Constitution Ave. NW, 20551).
Federal Trade Commission — Daniel Oliver, chmn. (Pennsylvania Ave. at 6th St. NW, 20580).
General Accounting Office — Comptroller General of the U.S.; Charles A. Bowsher (441 G St. NW, 20548).
General Services Administration — Terence C. Golden, adm. (18th & F Sts. NW, 20405).
Government Printing Office — Public printer: Ralph E. Kennickell Jr. (North Capitol and H Sts. NW, 20401).
Interstate Commerce Commission — Heather J. Gradison, chmn. (12th St. and Constitution Ave. NW, 20423).
Library of Congress — James H. Billington, librarian (101 Independence Ave. SE, 20540).
National Aeronautics and Space Administration — James C. Fletcher, adm. (600 Independence Ave., SW 20546).
National Archives & Records Administration — Frank G. Burke, act. archivist (7th & Pennsylvania Ave. NW, 20408).
National Credit Union Administration — Roger W. Jepsen, chmn. (1776 G St. NW, 20456).
National Foundation on the Arts and the Humanities — Frank S.M. Hodsoll, chmn. (arts) 1100 Pennsylvania Ave. NW, 20506; Lynne V. Cheney, act. chmn. (humanities) same address. Institute of Museum Services: Lois Burke Shepard, dir., same address.
National Labor Relations Board — Donald L. Dotson, chmn. (1717 Pennsylvania Ave. NW, 20570).
National Mediation Board — Helen M. Witt, chmn. (1425 K St. NW, 20572).
National Science Foundation — Roland W. Schmitt, chmn., National Science Board (1800 G St. NW, 20550).
National Transportation Safety Board — James E. Burnett, chmn. (800 Independence Ave. SW, 20594).
Nuclear Regulatory Commission — Lando W. Zech Jr., chmn. (1717 H St. NW, 20555).
Occupational Safety and Health Review Commission — E. Ross Buckley, chmn. (1825 K St. NW, 20006).
Office of Personnel Management — Constance Horner, dir., (1900 E St. NW, 20415).
Peace Corps — Loret Miller Ruppe, dir. (806 Connecticut Ave. NW, 20526).
Postal Rate Commission — Janet D. Steiger, chmn. (1333 H. St. NW, 20268-0001).
Railroad Retirement Board — Robert A. Gielow, chmn. (1333 H St. NW, 20268-0001), Main Office (844 Rush St., Chicago, IL 60611).
Securities and Exchange Commission — David S. Ruder, chmn. (450 5th St. NW, 20549).
Selective Service System — Wilfred Ebel, act. dir. (National Headquarters, 20435).
Small Business Administration — James Abdnor, adm. (1441 L St. NW, 20416).
Smithsonian Institution — Robert McC. Adams, secy. (1000 Jefferson Dr. SW, 20560).
United States Arms Control & Disarmament Agency — Kenneth L. Adelman, dir. (320 21st St. NW 20451).
United States Information Agency — Charles Z. Wick, dir. (301 4th St. SW, 20547).
United States International Trade Commission — Susan Wittenberg-Liebeler, chairwoman (701 E St. NW, 20436).
United States Postal Service — Preston R. Tisch, postmaster general (475 L'Enfant Plaza West SW, 20260).
Veterans Administration — Thomas K. Turnage, adm. (810 Vermont Ave. NW, 20420).

CONGRESS

The One Hundredth Congress

With 1986 Election Results

The Senate

Terms are for 6 years and end Jan. 3 of the year preceding name. Annual salary $89,500. To be eligible for the U.S. Senate a person must be at least 30 years of age, a citizen of the United States for at least 9 years, and a resident of the state from which he is chosen. The Congress must meet annually on Jan. 3, unless it has, by law, appointed a different day.

Senate officials (100th Congress): President Pro Tempore John Stennis; Majority Leader Robert C. Byrd; Majority Whip Alan Cranston; Minority Leader Bob Dole; Minority Whip Alan Simpson.

Dem., 54; Rep., 46; Total, 100. *Incumbent. Bold face denotes winner.

Official Totals (Source: News Election Service)

Term ends	Senator (Party, home)	1986 Election
	Alabama	
1991	Howell Heflin* (D, Tuscumbia)	
1993	**Richard C. Shelby** (D, Tuscaloosa)	**609,360**
	Jeremiah Denton* (R, Theodore)	602,537
	Alaska	
1991	Ted Stevens* (R, Anchorage)	
1993	**Frank Murkowski*** (R, Anchorage)	**97,674**
	Glenn Olds (D, Anchorage)	79,727
	Arizona	
1989	Dennis DeConcini* (D, Tuscon)	
1993	**John McCain** (R, Tempe)	**521,850**
	Richard Kimball (D, Phoenix)	340,965
	Arkansas	
1991	David Pryor* (D, Little Rock)	
1993	**Dale Bumpers*** (D, Charleston)	**433,092**
	Asa Hutchinson (R, Fort Smith)	262,300
	California	
1989	Pete Wilson* (R, San Diego)	
1993	**Alan Cranston*** (D, Palm Springs)	**3,646,672**
	Ed Zschau (R, Los Altos)	3,541,804
	Colorado	
1991	William L. Armstrong* (R, Aurora)	
1993	**Timothy E. Wirth** (D, Boulder)	**529,449**
	Ken Kramer (R, Colorado Springs)	512,994
	Connecticut	
1989	Lowell P. Weicker Jr.* (R, Mystic)	
1993	**Christopher J. Dodd*** (D, Norwich)	**632,695**
	Roger W. Eddy (R, Newington)	340,438
	Delaware	
1989	William V. Roth Jr.* (R, Wilmington)	
1991	Joseph R. Biden Jr.* (D, Wilmington)	
	Florida	
1989	Lawton Chiles* (D, Holmes Beach)	
1993	**Bob Graham** (D, Tallahassee)	**1,877,231**
	Paula Hawkins* (R, Winter Park)	1,551,888
	Georgia	
1991	Sam Nunn* (D, Perry)	
1993	**Wyche Fowler** (D, Atlanta)	**623,707**
	Mack Mattingly* (R, St. Simons Is.)	601,241
	Hawaii	
1989	Spark M. Matsunaga* (D, Honolulu)	
1993	**Daniel K. Inouye*** (D, Honolulu)	**241,884**
	Frank Hutchinson (R, Honolulu)	86,909
	Idaho	
1991	James A. McClure* (R, McCall)	
1993	**Steven D. Symms*** (R, Boise)	**196,958**
	John V. Evans (D, Boise)	185,066
	Illinois	
1991	Paul Simon* (D, Makanda)	
1993	**Alan J. Dixon*** (D, Belleville)	**2,033,926**
	Judy Koehler (R, Henry)	1,053,793
	Indiana	
1989	Richard G. Lugar* (R, Indianapolis)	
1993	**Dan Quayle*** (R, Huntington)	**936,143**
	Jill Lynette Long (D, Valparaiso)	595,192
	Iowa	
1991	Tom Harkin* (D, Cumming)	
1993	**Charles E. Grassley*** (R, New Hartford)	**588,880**
	John P. Roehrick (D, Des Moines)	299,406
	Kansas	
1991	Nancy Landon Kassebaum* (R, Wichita)	
1993	**Robert J. Dole*** (R, Russell)	**575,292**
	Guy MacDonald (D, Wichita)	245,499
	Kentucky	
1991	Mitch McConnell* (R, Louisville)	
1993	**Wendell H. Ford*** (D, Owensboro)	**503,775**
	Jackson M. Andrews (R, St. Matthews)	173,330
	Louisiana	
1991	J. Bennett Johnston* (D, Shreveport)	
1993	**John B. Breaux** (D, Crowley)	**723,586**
	W. Henson Moore (R, Baton Rouge)	646,311
	Maine	
1989	George J. Mitchell* (D, Waterville)	
1991	William S. Cohen* (R, Bangor)	
	Maryland	
1989	Paul S. Sarbanes* (D, Baltimore)	
1993	**Barbara A. Mikulski** (D, Baltimore)	**675,229**
	Linda Chavez (R, Bethesda)	437,419
	Massachusetts	
1989	Edward M. Kennedy* (D, Barnstable)	
1991	John Kerry* (D, Boston)	
	Michigan	
1989	Donald W. Riegle Jr.* (D, Flint)	
1991	Carl Levin* (D, Detroit)	
	Minnesota	
1989	David Durenberger* (R, Minneapolis)	
1991	Rudolph E. Boschwitz* (R, Wayzata)	
	Mississippi	
1989	John C. Stennis* (D, DeKalb)	
1991	Thad Cochran* (R, Jackson)	
	Missouri	
1989	John C. Danforth* (R, Newburg)	
1993	**Christopher "Kit" Bond** (R, Kansas City)	**777,612**
	Harriet Woods (D, University City)	699,624
	Montana	
1989	John Melcher* (D, Forsyth)	
1991	Max Baucus* (D, Helena)	
	Nebraska	
1989	Edward Zorinsky*(1) (D, Omaha)	
1991	J. James Exon* (D, Lincoln)	
	Nevada	
1989	Chic Hecht* (R, Las Vegas)	
1993	**Harry M. Reid** (D, Las Vegas)	**130,955**
	James D. Santini (R, Reno)	116,606
	New Hampshire	
1991	Gordon J. Humphrey* (R, Chichester)	
1993	**Warren Rudman*** (R, Nashua)	**154,090**
	Endicott Peabody (D, Hollis)	79,237

(1) died Mar. 6, 1987; Neb. Gov. Kay Orr appointed David Karnes, a Republican, to succeed, cutting the Democratic majority to 54-46.

Term ends	Senator (Party, home)	1986 Election
	New Jersey	
1989	Frank R. Lautenberg* (D, Montclair)	
1991	Bill Bradley* (D, Denville)	
	New Mexico	
1989	Jeff Bingaman (D, Santa Fe)	
1991	Pete V. Domenici* (R, Albuquerque)	
	New York	
1989	Daniel Patrick Moynihan* (D, Oneonta)	
1993	**Alfonse M. D'Amato*** (R, Island Park)	**2,378,197**
	Mark Green (D, New York)	1,723,216
	North Carolina	
1991	Jesse Helms* (R, Raleigh)	
1993	**Terry Sanford** (D, Durham)	**823,662**
	James T. Broyhill* (R, Lenoir)	767,668
	North Dakota	
1989	Quentin N. Burdick* (D, Fargo)	
1993	**Kent Conrad** (D, Bismark)	**143,932**
	Mark Andrews* (R, Mapleton)	141,812
	Ohio	
1989	Howard M. Metzenbaum* (D, Lyndhurst)	
1993	**John Glenn*** (D, Grandview Hts.)	**1,949,209**
	Thomas N. Kindness (R, Westchester)	1,171,893
	Oklahoma	
1991	David Boren* (D, Seminole)	
1993	**Don Nickles*** (R, Ponca City)	**493,435**
	James R. Jones (D, Tulsa)	400,230
	Oregon	
1991	Mark O. Hatfield* (R, Portland)	
1993	**Bob Packwood*** (R, Portland)	**656,317**
	Rick Bauman (D, Portland)	375,735
	Pennsylvania	
1989	John Heinz* (R, Pittsburgh)	
1993	**Arlen Specter*** (R, Philadelphia)	**1,906,537**
	Bob Edgar (D, Media)	1,448,219
	Rhode Island	
1989	John H. Chafee* (R, Warwick)	
1991	Claiborne deB. Pell* (D, Newport)	
	South Carolina	
1991	Strom Thurmond* (R, Aiken)	
1993	**Ernest Fritz Hollings*** (D, Columbia)	**465,500**
	Henry D. McMaster (R, Columbia)	262,886

Term ends	Senator (Party, home)	1986 Election
	South Dakota	
1991	Larry Pressler* (R, Humboldt)	
1993	**Thomas A. Daschle** (D, Sioux Falls)	**152,657**
	James Abdnor* (R, Sioux Falls)	143,173
	Tennessee	
1989	James R. Sasser* (D, Nashville)	
1991	Albert Gore Jr.* (D, Carthage)	
	Texas	
1989	Lloyd Bentsen* (D, Houston)	
1991	Phil Gramm* (R, Bryan)	
	Utah	
1989	Orrin G. Hatch* (R, Salt Lake City)	
1993	**E. J. "Jake" Garn*** (R, Salt Lake City)	**314,608**
	Craig S. Oliver (D, Murray)	115,523
	Vermont	
1989	Robert T. Stafford* (R, Rutland)	
1993	**Patrick J. Leahy*** (D, Burlington)	**124,123**
	Richard Snelling (R, Shelburne)	67,798
	Virginia	
1989	Paul S. Trible Jr. (R, Newport News)	
1991	John William Warner* (R, Richmond)	
	Washington	
1989	Daniel J. Evans* (R, Olympia)	
1993	**Brock Adams** (D, Seattle)	**677,471**
	Slade Gorton* (R, Olympia)	650,931
	West Virginia	
1989	Robert C. Byrd* (D, Sophia)	
1991	Jay Rockefeller* (D, Charleston)	
	Wisconsin	
1989	William Proxmire* (D, Madison)	
1993	**Robert W. Kasten Jr.*** (R, Milwaukee)	**754,573**
	Edward R. Garvey (D, Madison)	702,963
	Wyoming	
1989	Malcolm Wallop* (R, Big Horn)	
1991	Alan Kooi Simpson* (R, Cody)	

The House of Representatives

Members' terms to Jan. 3, 1989. Annual salary $89,500; house speaker $97,900. To be eligible for membership, a person must be at least 25, a U.S. citizen for at least 7 years, and a resident of the state from which he or she is chosen.

House Officials (100th Congress): Speaker James Wright; Majority Leader Thomas S. Foley; Majority Whip Tony Coelho; Minority Leader Robert H. Michel; Minority Whip Trent Lott.

C-Conservative; Com-Communist; COP-Concerns of People; D-Democrat; I-Independent; L-Liberal; Libert- Libertarian; PF-Peace and Freedom; PBP-People Before Profits; R-Republican; RTL-Right to Life; SW-Socialist Workers.

Dem., 258, Rep., 177. Total 435. *Incumbent. Bold face denotes winner.

Official Totals (Source: News Election Service)

Dist.	Representative (Party, Home)	1986 Election
	Alabama	
1.	**"H.L." Sonny Callahan*** (R, Mobile)	**Unopposed**
2.	**William L. Dickinson*** (R, Montgomery)	**115,302**
	Mercer Stone (D, Montgomery)	57,568
3.	**Bill Nichols*** (D, Sylacauga)	**115,127**
	Whit Guerin (R, Auburn)	27,769
4.	**Tom Bevel*** (D, Jasper)	**132,881**
	Al DeShazo (R, Springville)	38,588
5.	**Ronnie G. Flippo*** (D, Florence)	**125,406**
	Herb McCarley (R, Hartselle)	33,528
6.	**Ben Erdreich*** (D, Birmingham)	**139,608**
	L. Morgan Williams (R, Irondale	51,924
7.	**Claude Harris** (D, Tuscaloosa)	**108,126**
	Bill McFarland (R, Tuscaloosa)	72,777

Dist.	Representative (Party, Home)	1986 Election
	Alaska At Large	
	Don Young* (R, Fort Yukon)	**101,799**
	Pegge Begich (D, Anchorage)	74,053
	Arizona	
1.	**John J. Rhodes III** (R, Mesa)	**127,370**
	Harry Braun (D, Mesa)	51,163
2.	**Morris K. Udall*** (D, Tucson)	**77,239**
	Sheldon Clark (R, Phoenix)	24,522
3.	**Bob Stump*** (R, Tolleson)	**Unopposed**
4.	**John Kyl** (R, Phoenix)	**121,939**
	Philip R. Davis (D, Paradise Valley)	66,894
5.	**Jim Kolbe*** (R, Tucson)	**119,647**
	Joel Ireland (D, Tucson)	64,848

Dist.	Representative (Party, Home)	1986 Election
	Arkansas	
1.	**Bill Alexander*** (D, Osceola)	**105,773**
	Rick H. Albin (R, Marianna)	58,937
2.	**Tommy F. Robinson*** (D, Jacksonville)	**128,814**
	Keith Hamaker (R, Little Rock)	41,244
3.	**John Paul Hammerschmidt*** (R, Harrison)	**145,113**
	Su Sargent (D, Fayetteville)	36,726
4.	**Beryl Anthony Jr.*** (D, El Dorado)	**115,335**
	Lamar Keels (R, Camden)	22,980
	California	
1.	**Douglas H. Bosco*** (D, Santa Rosa)	**138,174**
	Floyd G. Sampson (R, Petaluma)	54,436
2.	**Wally Herger** (R, Yuba City)	**109,758**
	Stephen C. Swendiman (D, Redding)	74,602
3.	**Robert T. Matsui*** (D, Sacramento)	**158,709**
	Lowell Landowski (R, Sacramento)	50,265
4.	**Vic Fazio*** (D, Woodland)	**128,364**
	Jack D. Hite (R, Citrus Heights)	54,596
5.	**Sala Burton***[1] (D, San Francisco)	**122,688**
	Mike Garza (R, San Francisco)	36,039
6.	**Barbara Boxer*** (D, San Francisco)	**142,946**
	Franklin "Harry" Ernest III (R, Vallejo)	50,606
7.	**George Miller*** (D, Pleasant Hill)	**124,174**
	Rosemary Thakar (R, Alamo)	62,379
8.	**Ronald V. Dellums*** (D, Berkeley)	**121,790**
	Steven Eigenberg (R, Piedmont)	76,850
9.	**Fortney H. "Pete" Stark*** (D, Hayward)	**113,490**
	David M. Williams (R, Livermore)	49,300
10.	**Don Edwards*** (D, San Jose)	**84,240**
	Michael R. LaCrone (R, Freemont)	31,826
11.	**Tom Lantos*** (D, Burlingame)	**112,380**
	G.M. "Bill" Quraishi (R, El Granada)	39,315
12.	**Ernest L. Konnyu** (R, San Jose)	**111,252**
	Lance T. Weil (D, Cupertino)	69,564
13.	**Norman Y. Mineta*** (D, San Jose)	**107,696**
	Bob Nash (R, Los Gatos)	46,754
14.	**Norm Shumway*** (R, Stockton)	**146,906**
	Bill Steele (D, Nevada City)	53,597
15.	**Tony Coelho*** (D, Modesto)	**93,600**
	Carol Harner (R, Mariposa)	35,793
16.	**Leon E. Panetta*** (D, Carmel Valley)	**128,151**
	Luis Darrigo (R, Aptos)	[illegible]
17.	**Charles "Chip" Pashayan Jr.*** (R, Fresno)	**88,787**
	John Hartnett (D, Fresno)	58,682
18.	**Richard H. Lehman*** (D, Fresno)	**101,480**
	David C. Crevelt (R, Fresno)	40,907
19.	**Robert J. "Bob" Lagomarsino*** (R, Ventura)	**122,578**
	Wayne B. Norris (D, Santa Barbara)	45,619
20.	**William M. Thomas*** (R, Bakersfield)	**129,989**
	Jules H. Moquin (D, Bakersfield)	49,027
21.	**Elton Gallegly** (R, Simi Valley)	**132,100**
	Gilbert R. Saldona (R, Oxnard)	54,497
22.	**Carlos J. Moorhead*** (R, Glendale)	**141,096**
	John G. Simmons (D, Burbank)	44,036
23.	**Anthony C. Beilenson*** (D, Tarzana)	**121,468**
	George Woolverton (R, Tarzana)	58,746
24.	**Henry A. Waxman*** (D, Los Angeles)	**Unopposed**
25.	**Edward R. Roybal*** (D, Los Angeles)	**62,692**
	Gregory L. Hardy (R, Glendale)	17,558
26.	**Howard L. Berman*** (D, Panorama City)	**98,091**
	Robert M. Kerns (R, Northridge)	52,662
27.	**Mel Levine*** (D, Santa Monica)	**110,403**
	Rob Scribner (R, Santa Monica)	59,410
28.	**Julian C. Dixon*** (D, Inglewood)	**92,635**
	George Adams (R, Los Angeles)	25,858
29.	**Augustus F. "Gus" Hawkins*** (D, Los Angeles)	**78,132**
	John Van de Brooke (R, Sunnyvale)	13,432
30.	**Matthew G. "Marty" Martinez*** (D, Monterey Park)	**59,369**
	John W. Almquist (R, El Monte)	33,705
31.	**Mervyn M. Dymally*** (D, Compton)	**77,126**
	Jack McMurray (R, Torrance)	30,322
32.	**Glenn M. Anderson*** (D, Hawthorne)	**90,739**
	Joyce M. Robertson (R, Manhattan Beach)	39,003
33.	**David Dreier*** (R, Covina)	**118,541**
	Monty Hempel (D, Claremont)	44,312
34.	**Esteban E. Torres*** (D, Norwalk)	**66,404**
	Charles M. House (R, Los Angeles)	43,659
35.	**Jerry Lewis*** (R, Redlands)	**127,235**
	R. "Sarge" Hall (D, Adelonto)	38,322
36.	**George E. Brown Jr.*** (D, Riverside)	**78,118**
	Bob Henley (R, Colton)	58,660
37.	**Al McCandless*** (R, Palm Desert)	**122,416**
	David E. "Dave" Skinner (D, Riverside)	69,808
38.	**Robert K. "Bob" Dornan*** (R, Garden Grove)	**66,032**
	Richard Robinson (D, Santa Ana)	50,625
39.	**William E. "Bill" Dannemeyer*** (R, Fullerton)	**131,603**
	David D. Vest (D, Placentia)	42,377
40.	**Robert E. Badham*** (R, Newport Beach)	**119,829**
	Bruce W. Summer (D, Balboa Island)	75,664
41.	**Bill Lowery*** (R, San Diego)	**133,566**
	Dan Kripke (D, La Jolla)	59,816
42.	**Daniel Lungren*** (R, Long Beach)	**140,364**
	Michael P. Blackburn (D, Long Beach)	47,586
43.	**Ron Packard*** (R, Carlsbad)	**137,341**
	Joseph Chirra (D, Vista)	45,078
44.	**Jim Bates*** (D, San Diego)	**70,557**
	Bill Mitchell (R, San Diego)	36,359
45.	**Duncan Hunter*** (R, Coronado)	**118,900**
	Hewitt Fitts Ryan (D, San Diego)	32,800
	Colorado	
1.	**Patricia Schroeder*** (D, Denver)	**106,113**
	Joy Wood (R, Denver)	49,095
2.	**David Skaggs** (D, Boulder)	**91,223**
	Michael J. Norton (R, Golden)	86,032
3.	**Ben Nighthorse Campbell** (D, Ignacio)	**95,353**
	Mike Strang*(R, Carbondale)	88,508
4.	**Hank Brown*** (R, Greeley)	**117,089**
	David Sprague (D, Holyoke)	50,672
5.	**Joel Hefley** (R, Colorado Springs)	**121,153**
	Bill Story (D, Evergreen)	52,488
6.	**Daniel Schaefer*** (R, Lakowood)	**104,359**
	Chuck Norris (D, Littleton)	53,834
	Connecticut	
1.	**Barbara B. Kennelly*** (D, Hartford)	**128,930**
	Herschel A. Klein (R, Windsor)	44,122
2.	**Samuel Gejdenson*** (D, Bozrah)	**109,229**
	Bill Mullen (R, Niontic)	52,869
3.	**Bruce A. Morrison*** (D, Hamden)	**114,276**
	Ernest J. Diette Jr. (R, New Haven)	49,806
4.	**Stewart B. McKinney*** (R, Westport)	**77,212**
	Christine M. Niedermeier (D, Fairfield)	66,999
5.	**John G. Rowland*** (R, Waterbury)	**98,664**
	Jim Cohen (D, Waterbury)	63,371
6.	**Nancy L. Johnson*** (R, New Britain)	**111,304**
	Paul S. Amenta (D, New Britain)	62,133
	Delaware At Large	
	Thomas R. Carper* (D, New Castle)	**106,351**
	Thomas S. Neuberger (R, Wilmington)	53,767
	Florida	
1.	**Earl Hutto*** (D, Panama City)	**97,465**
	Greg Neubeck (R, Lynn Haven)	55,415
2.	**Bill Grant** (D, Madison)	**Unopposed**
3.	**Charles E. Bennett*** (D, Jacksonville)	**Unopposed**
4.	**Bill Chappell*** (D, Ormond Beach)	**Unopposed**
5.	**Bill McCollum*** (R, Altamonte Springs)	**Unopposed**

(1) Sala Burton died Feb. 1, 1987; she was succeeded by Nancy Pelosi, D, who won a special election in June.

Dist.	Representative (Party, Home)	1986 Election
6.	**Kenneth H. "Buddy" MacKay*** (D, Ocala)	**143,583**
	Larry Gallagher (R, Lecanto)	61,053
7.	**Sam M. Gibbons*** (D, Tampa)	**Unopposed**
8.	**C. W. Bill Young*** (R, Largo)	**Unopposed**
9.	**Michael Bilirakis*** (R, Palm Harbor)	**166,504**
	Gabe Cazares (D, Clearwater)	68,574
10.	**Andy Ireland*** (R, Winter Haven)	**122,368**
	David B. Higginbottom (D, Frostproof)	49,559
11.	**Bill Nelson*** (D, Melbourne)	**149,036**
	Scott Ellis (R, Melbourne)	55,904
12.	**Tom Lewis*** (R, North Palm Beach)	**Unopposed**
13.	**Connie Mack*** (R, Cape Coral)	**189,794**
	Addison S. Gilbert III (D, Sarasota)	62,694
14.	**Daniel A. Mica*** (D, Boynton Beach)	**171,961**
	Rick Martin (R, Coral Springs)	61,185
15.	**F. Clay Shaw Jr.*** (R, Fort Lauderdale)	**Unopposed**
16.	**Larry Smith*** (D, Hollywood)	**121,213**
	Mary Collins (R, N. Miami Beach)	52,807
17.	**William Lehman*** (D, Biscayne Park)	**Unopposed**
18.	**Claude Pepper*** (D, Miami)	**80,047**
	Tom Brodie (R, Miami)	28,803
19.	**Dante B. Fascell*** (D, Miami)	**99,203**
	Bill Flanagan (R, Coral Gables)	44,455

Georgia

Dist.	Representative (Party, Home)	1986 Election
1.	**Lindsay Thomas*** (D, Screven)	**Unopposed**
2.	**Charles Hatcher*** (D, Albany)	**Unopposed**
3.	**Richard Ray*** (D, Perry)	**Unopposed**
4.	**Patrick Swindall*** (R, Dunwoody)	**86,366**
	Ben Jones (D, Covington)	75,892
5.	**John Lewis** (D, Atlanta)	**93,229**
	Portia A. Scott (R, Atlanta)	30,562
6.	**Newt Gingrich*** (R, Riverdale)	**75,583**
	Crandle Bray (D, Riverdale)	51,352
7.	**George Darden*** (D, Marietta)	**88,636**
	Joe Morecraft (R, Marietta)	44,891
8.	**J. Roy Rowland*** (D, Dublin)	**82,254**
	Eddie McDowell (R, Waycross)	12,952
9.	**Ed Jenkins*** (D, Jasper)	**Unopposed**
10.	**Doug Barnard Jr.*** (D, Augusta)	**79,548**
	Jim Hill (R, Martinez)	38,714

Hawaii

Dist.	Representative (Party, Home)	1986 Election
1.	**Patricia Saiki** (R, Honolulu)	**99,683**
	Mufi Hannemann (D, Honolulu)	63,061
2.	**Daniel K. Akaka*** (D, Honolulu)	**123,830**
	Maria M. Hustace (R, Kaunakakai)	35,371

Idaho

Dist.	Representative (Party, Home)	1986 Election
1.	**Larry E. Craig*** (R, Boise)	**121,625**
	Bill Currie (D, Bonners Ferry)	59,723
2.	**Richard Stallings*** (D, Rexburg)	**103,035**
	Mel Richardson (R, Idaho Falls)	86,528

Illinois

Dist.	Representative (Party, Home)	1986 Election
1.	**Charles Hayes*** (D, Chicago)	**122,376**
	Joseph C. Faulkner (R, Chicago)	4,572
2.	**Gus Savage*** (D, Chicago)	**99,268**
	Ron Taylor (R, Chicago)	19,149
3.	**Martin Russo*** (D, South Holland)	**102,949**
	James J. Tierney (R, Chicago)	52,618
4.	**Jack Davis** (R, New Lenox)	**61,633**
	Shawn Collins (D, Joliet)	57,925
5.	**William O. Lipinski*** (D, Chicago)	**82,466**
	Daniel John Sobieski (R, Chicago)	34,738
6.	**Henry J. Hyde*** (R, Bensenville)	**98,196**
	Robert Renshaw (D, Lombard)	32,064
7.	**Cardiss Collins*** (D, Chicago)	**90,761**
	Caroline K. Kallas (R, Maywood)	21,055
8.	**Dan Rostenkowski*** (D, Chicago)	**82,873**
	Thomas J. DeFazio (R, Chicago)	22,383
9.	**Sidney R. Yates*** (D, Chicago)	**92,738**
	Herbert Sohn (R, Chicago)	36,715
10.	**John E. Porter*** (R, Winnetka)	**87,530**
	Robert A. Cleland (D, Wilmette)	28,990
11.	**Frank Annunzio*** (D, Chicago)	**106,970**
	George S. Gottlieb (R, Chicago)	44,341
12.	**Philip M. Crane*** (R, Mt. Prospect)	**89,044**
	John A. Leonardi (D, Fox River Grove)	25,536
13.	**Harris W. Fawell*** (R, Naperville)	**107,227**
	Dominick J. Jeffrey (D, LaGrange)	38,874
14.	**J. Dennis Hastert** (R, Oswego)	**77,288**
	Mary Lou Kearns (D, St. Charles)	70,293
15.	**Edward R. Madigan*** (R, Lincoln)	**Unopposed**
16.	**Lynn Morley Martin*** (R, Rockford)	**92,982**
	Kenneth F. Bohnsack (D, Freeport)	46,087
17.	**Lane Evans*** (D, Rock Island)	**85,442**
	Sam McHard (R, Rock Island)	68,101
18.	**Robert H. Michel*** (R, Peoria)	**94,308**
	Jim Dawson (D, Pekin)	56,331
19.	**Terry L. Bruce*** (D, Olney)	**111,105**
	Al Salvi (R, Champaign)	56,186
20.	**Richard J. Durbin*** (D, Springfield)	**126,556**
	Kevin B. McCarthy (R, Springfield)	59,291
21.	**Melvin Price*** (D, Belleville)	**65,722**
	Robert H. Gaffner (R, Greenville)	64,779
22.	**Kenneth J. Gray*** (D, W. Frankfort)	**97,585**
	Randy Patchett (R, Marion)	85,733

Indiana

Dist.	Representative (Party, Home)	1986 Election
1.	**Peter Visclosky*** (D, Merrillville)	**86,983**
	William Costas (R, Valparaiso)	30,395
2.	**Philip R. Sharp*** (D, Muncie)	**102,456**
	Donald J. Lynch (R, Indianapolis)	62,013
3.	**John Hiler*** (D, Knox)	**75,979**
	Thomas W. Ward (R, LaPorte)	75,932
4.	**Dan R. Coats*** (R, Fort Wayne)	**99,865**
	Gregory Alan Scher (D, Huntington)	43,105
5.	**James Jontz** (D, Brookston)	**80,772**
	James R. Butcher* (R, Kokomo)	75,507
6.	**Dan Burton*** (R, Indianapolis)	**118,363**
	Thomas F. McKenna (D, Carmel)	53,431
7.	**John T. Myers*** (R, Covington)	**104,965**
	L. Eugene Smith (D, Linton)	49,675
8.	**Francis X. McCloskey** (D, Bloomington)	**106,662**
	Richard D. McIntyre* (R, Bedford)	93,586
9.	**Lee H. Hamilton*** (D, Nashville)	**120,586**
	Robert Walker Kilroy (R, Jeffersonville)	46,398
10.	**Andrew Jacobs Jr.*** (D, Indianapolis)	**68,817**
	Jim Eynon (R, Indianapolis)	49,064

Iowa

Dist.	Representative (Party, Home)	1986 Election
1.	**Jim Leach*** (R, Davenport)	**86,834**
	John R. Whitaker (D, Hillsboro)	43,985
2.	**Thomas J. Tauke*** (R, Dubuque)	**88,708**
	Eric Tabor (D, Baldwin)	55,903
3.	**David R. Nagle** (D, Cedar Falls)	**83,504**
	John McIntee (R, Waterloo)	69,386
4.	**Neal Smith*** (D, Altoona)	**107,271**
	Bob Lockard (R, Des Moines)	49,641
5.	**Jim Ross Lightfoot*** (R, Shenandoah)	**85,025**
	Scott Hughes (D, Council Bluffs)	58,552
6.	**Fred Grandy** (R, Sioux Center)	**81,861**
	Clayton Hodgson (D, Le Mars)	78,807

Kansas

Dist.	Representative (Party, Home)	1986 Election
1.	**Pat Roberts*** (R, Dodge City)	**140,991**
	Dale Lyon (D, Athol)	43,333
2.	**Jim Slattery*** (D, Topeka)	**110,415**
	Phill Kline (R, Lawrence)	45,905
3.	**Jan Meyers*** (R, Overland Park)	**Unopposed**
4.	**Dan Glickman*** (D, Wichita)	**109,071**
	Bob Knight (R, Wichita)	60,401
5.	**Bob Whittaker*** (R, Augusta)	**116,387**
	Kim E. Myers (D, Emporia)	47,645

Kentucky

Dist.	Representative (Party, Home)	1986 Election
1.	**Carroll Hubbard Jr.*** (D, Mayfield)	**Unopposed**
2.	**William H. Natcher*** (D, Bowling Green)	**Unopposed**
3.	**Romano L. Mazzoli*** (D, Louisville)	**81,943**
	Lee Holmes (R, Louisville)	29,348
4.	**Jim Bunning** (R, Ft. Thomas)	**67,626**
	Terry L. Mann (D, Newport)	53,906
5.	**Harold Rogers*** (R, Somerset)	**Unopposed**
6.	**Larry J. Hopkins*** (R, Lexington)	**75,906**
	Jerry W. Hammond (D, Versailles)	26,315

Dist.	Representative (Party, Home)	1986 Election
7.	**Carl C. Perkins*** (D, Leburn)	**90,619**
	James T. "Jim" Polley (R, Elkhorn City)	23,209

Louisiana

Dist.	Representative (Party, Home)	1986 Election
1.	**Bob Livingston*** (R, Metairie)	
2.	**Lindy (Mrs. Hale) Boggs*** (D, New Orleans)	
3.	**W.J. "Billy" Tauzin*** (D, Thibodaux)	
4.	**Buddy Roemer III** (D, Bossier City)	
5.	**Jerry Huckaby*** (D, Ringgold)	
6.	**Richard Hugh Baker** (R, Baton Rouge)	
7.	**James A. "Jimmy" Hayes** (D, Lafayette)	**109,205**
	Margaret Laventhal (D, Lake Charles	82,293
8.	**Clyde C. Holloway** (R, Forest Hill)	**102,276**
	Faye Williams (D, Alexandria)	96,864

In Louisiana, all candidates of all parties run against each other in an open primary. All candidates who receive more than 50 percent of the primary vote run unopposed in the general election. If no candidate wins a majority, the top two finishers regardless of party oppose each other in a November runoff. This year,

Maine

Dist.	Representative (Party, Home)	1986 Election
1.	**Joseph E. Brennan** (D, Portland)	**121,848**
	H. Rollins Ives (R, Falmouth)	100,260
2.	**Olympia J. Snowe*** (R, Auburn)	**148,770**
	Richard R. Charette (D, Lewiston)	43,614

Maryland

Dist.	Representative (Party, Home)	1986 Election
1.	**Roy Dyson*** (D, Great Mills)	**88,113**
	Harley Williams (R, Elkton)	43,764
2.	**Helen Delich Bentley*** (R, Lutherville)	**96,745**
	Kathleen Kennedy Townsend (D, Towson)	68,200
3.	**Benjamin L. Cardin** (D, Baltimore)	**100,161**
	Ross Z. Pierpont (R, Baltimore)	26,452
4.	**Thomas McMillen** (D, Crofton)	**65,075**
	Robert R. Neall (R, Davidsonville)	64,651
5.	**Steny H. Hoyer*** (D, Berkshire)	**82,098**
	John Eugene Sellner (R, Ft. Washington)	18,102
6.	**Beverly B. Byron*** (D, Frederick)	**102,975**
	John Vandenberge (R, Ellicott City)	39,600
7.	**Kweisi Mfume** (D, Baltimore)	**78,228**
	St. George I.B. Crosse III (R, Baltimore)	12,170
8.	**Constance A. Morella** (R, Bethesda)	**92,917**
	Stewart Bainum Jr. (D, Silver Spring)	82,825

Massachusetts

Dist.	Representative (Party, Home)	1986 Election
1.	**Silvio O. Conte*** (R, Pittsfield)	**113,653**
	Robert S. Weiner (D, Amherst)	32,396
2.	**Edward P. Boland*** (D, Springfield)	**91,033**
	Brian P. Lees (R, Springfield)	47,022
3.	**Joseph D. Early*** (D, Worcester)	**Unopposed**
4.	**Barney Frank*** (D, Newton)	**Unopposed**
5.	**Chester Atkins*** (D, Concord)	**Unopposed**
6.	**Nicholas Mavroules*** (D, Peabody)	**Unopposed**
7.	**Edward J. Markey*** (D, Malden)	**Unopposed**
8.	**Joseph P. Kennedy II** (D, Boston)	**104,651**
	Clark C. Abt (R, Cambridge)	40,259
9.	**John Joseph Moakley*** (D, Boston)	**Unopposed**
10.	**Gerry E. Studds*** (D, Cohasset)	**121,577**
	Ricardo M. Barros (R, New Bedford)	49,451
11.	**Brian J. Donnelly*** (D, Boston)	**Unopposed**

Michigan

Dist.	Representative (Party, Home)	1986 Election
1.	**John Conyers Jr.*** (D, Detroit)	**94,307**
	Bill Ashe (R, Detroit)	10,407
2.	**Carl D. Pursell*** (R, Plymouth)	**79,567**
	Dean Baker (D, Ann Arbor)	55,204
3.	**Howard Wolpe*** (D, Lansing)	**78,720**
	Jackie McGregor (R, Lansing)	51,678
4.	**Fred Upton** (R, St. Joe)	**70,331**
	Dan Roche (D, Benton Harbor)	41,624
5.	**Paul B. Henry*** (R, Grand Rapids)	**100,577**
	Teresa S. Decker (D, Comstock Park)	40,608
6.	**Bob Carr*** (D, East Lansing)	**74,927**
	Jim Dunn (R, East Lansing)	57,283
7.	**Dale E. Kildee*** (D, Flint)	**101,225**
	Trudie Callihan (R, Clarkston)	24,848
8.	**Bob Traxler*** (D, Bay City)	**97,406**
	John A. Levi (R, Saginaw)	36,695
9.	**Guy Vander Jagt*** (R, Luther)	**89,991**
	Richard J. Anderson (D, Lake Ann)	49,702
10.	**Bill Schuette*** (R, Sanford)	**78,475**
	Donald Joseph Albosta (D, St. Charles)	74,941
11.	**Robert W. Davis*** (R, Gaylord)	**91,575**
	Robert C. Anderson (D, Marquette)	53,180
12.	**David E. Bonior*** (D, Mt. Clemens)	**87,643**
	Candice S. Miller (R, Mt. Clemens)	44,442
13.	**George W. Crockett Jr.*** (D, Detroit)	**76,435**
	Mary Griffin (R, Detroit)	12,395
14.	**Dennis M. Hertel*** (D, Detroit)	**92,328**
	Stanley T. Grot (R, Sterling Heights)	33,831
15.	**William D. Ford*** (D, Taylor)	**77,950**
	Glen Kassel (R, Westband)	25,078
16.	**John D. Dingell*** (D, Trenton)	**101,659**
	W. Frank Grzywacki (R, Monroe)	28,971
17.	**Sander Levin*** (D, Southfield)	**105,031**
	Calvin Williams (R, Detroit)	30,879
18.	**William S. Broomfield*** (R, Birmingham)	**110,099**
	Gary L. Kohut (D, Troy)	39,144

Minnesota

Dist.	Representative (Party, Home)	1986 Election
1.	**Timothy J. "Tim" Penny*** (D, New Richland)	**125,115**
	Paul H. Grawe (R, Winona)	47,750
2.	**Vin Weber*** (R, Slayton)	**100,249**
	Dave Johnson (D, Hector)	94,048
3.	**Bill Frenzel*** (R, Bloomington)	**127,434**
	Ray Stock (D, Deephaven)	54,261
4.	**Bruce F. Vento*** (D, St. Paul)	**112,662**
	Harold Stassen (R, Sunfish Lake)	41,926
5.	**Martin Olav Sabo*** (D, Minneapolis)	**105,410**
	Rick Serra (R, Bloomington)	37,583
6.	**Gerry Sikorski*** (D, Stillwater)	**110,598**
	Barbara Zwach Sykora (R, Excelsior)	57,460
7.	**Arlan Stangeland*** (R, Barnesville)	**94,024**
	Collin Peterson (D, Detroit Lakes)	93,903
8.	**James L. Oberstar*** (D, Chisholm)	**136,718**
	Dave Rueof (R, Aitkin)	51,315

Mississippi

Dist.	Representative (Party, Home)	1986 Election
1.	**Jamie L. Whitten*** (D, Charleston)	**59,870**
	Larry Cobb (R, Oxford)	30,267
2.	**Mike Espy** (D, Yazoo City)	**73,119**
	Webb Franklin* (R, Greenwood)	68,292
3.	**G. V. "Sonny" Montgomery*** (D, Meridian)	**Unopposed**
4.	**Wayne Dowdy*** (D, McComb)	**85,819**
	Gail Healy (R, Natchez)	34,190
5.	**Trent Lott*** (R, Pascagoula)	**75,288**
	Larry L. Albritton (D, Picayune)	16,143

Missouri

Dist.	Representative (Party, Home)	1986 Election
1.	**William (Bill) Clay*** (D, St. Louis)	**91,044**
	Robert J. Wittmann (R, St. Louis)	46,599
2.	**Jack Buechner** (R, Kirkwood.	**101,010**
	Robert A. Young* (D, Maryland Heights)	93,538
3.	**Richard A. Gephardt*** (D, St. Louis)	**116,403**
	Roy Amelung (R, Arnold)	52,382
4.	**Ike Skelton*** (D, Lexington)	**Unopposed**
5.	**Alan Wheat*** (D, Kansas City)	**101,030**
	Greg Fisher (R, Kansas City)	39,340
6.	**E. Thomas Coleman*** (R, Kansas City)	**95,865**
	Doug R. Hughes (D, Dawn)	73,155
7.	**Gene Taylor*** (R, Sarcoxie)	**114,210**
	Ken Young (D, Pt. Lookout)	56,291
8.	**Bill Emerson*** (R, Cape Girardeau)	**79,142**
	Wayne Cryts (D, Puxico)	71,532
9.	**Harold L. Volkmer*** (D, Hannibal)	**95,939**
	Ralph Uthlaut Jr. (R, New Florence)	70,972

Dist.	Representative (Party, Home)	1986 Election
	Montana	
1.	**Pat Williams*** (D, Helena)	**98,501**
	Don Allen (R, Claney)	61,230
2.	**Ron Marlenee*** (R, Great Falls)	**84,548**
	Buck O'Brien (D, Conrad)	73,583
	Nebraska	
1.	**Douglas K. Bereuter*** (R, Utica)	**121,772**
	Steve Burns (D, Lincolkn)	67,137
2.	**Hal Daub*** (R, Omaha)	**99,569**
	Walter M. Calinger (D, Omaha)	70,372
3.	**Virginia Smith*** (R, Chappell)	**136,985**
	Scott E. Sidwell (D, Kearney)	59,182
	Nevada	
1.	**James H. Bilbray** (D, Las Vegas)	**61,830**
	Bob Ryan (R, Las Vegas)	50,342
2.	**Barbara F. Vucanovich*** (R, Reno)	**83,479**
	Pete Sferrazza (D, Reno)	59,433
	New Hampshire	
1.	**Robert C. Smith*** (R, Dover)	**70,739**
	James M. Demers (D, Dover)	54,787
2.	**Judd Gregg*** (R, Greenfield)	**85,477**
	Lawrence Craig-Green(D, Antrim)	29,685
	New Jersey	
1.	**James J. Florio*** (D, Pine Hill)	**93,497**
	Fred A. Busch (R, Clementon)	29,175
2.	**William J. Hughes*** (D, Ocean City)	**83,821**
	Alfred J. Bennington Jr. (R, Smithville)	35,167
3.	**James J. Howard*** (D, Spring Lake Heights)	**73,743**
	Brian Kennedy (R, Bradley Beach)	51,882
4.	**Christopher H. Smith*** (R, Hamilton Square)	**78,699**
	Jeffrey Laurenti (D, Trenton)	49,290
5.	**Marge Roukema*** (R, Ridgewood)	**94,253**
	H. Vernon Jolley (D, Oradell)	32,145
6.	**Bernard J. Dwyer*** (D, Edison)	**67,460**
	John D. Scalamonti (R, Old Bridge)	28,286
7.	**Matthew J. Rinaldo*** (R, Union)	**92,254**
	June S. Fischer (D, Scotch Plains)	24,462
8.	**Robert A. Roe*** (D, Pompton Lakes)	**57,820**
	Thomas P. Zampino (R, Belleville)	34,268
9.	**Robert G. Torricelli*** (D, Hackensack)	**89,634**
	Arthur F. Jones (R, Leonia)	40,226
10.	**Peter W. Rodino Jr.*** (D, Newark)	**43,210**
11.	**Dean A. Gallo*** (R, Morris Plains)	**75,037**
	Frank Askin (D, West Orange)	35,280
12.	**Jim Courter*** (R, Hackettstown)	**72,966**
	David B. Crabiel (D, Milltown)	41,967
13.	**H. James Saxton*** (R, Vincentown)	**82,866**
	John Wydra (D, Cherry Hill)	43,920
14.	**Frank J. Guarini*** (D, Jersey City)	**63,057**
	Albio Sires (R, W. New York)	23,822
	New Mexico	
1.	**Manuel Lujan Jr.*** (R, Albuquerque)	**90,476**
	Manny Garcia (D, Tijeras)	37,138
2.	**Joe Skeen*** (R, Picacho)	**77,787**
	Mike Runnels (D, Ruidoso)	45,924
3.	**Bill Richardson*** (D, Santa Fe)	**95,760**
	David F. Cargo (R, Corrales)	38,552
	New York	
1.	**George J. Hochbrueckner** (D)	**67,139**
	Gregory J. Blass (R, Jamesport)	55,413
2.	**Thomas J. Downey*** (D, Amityville)	**69,771**
	Jeffrey A. Butzke (R, Bayport)	35,132
3.	**Robert J. Mrazek*** (D, Centerport)	**83,985**
	Joseph A. Guarino (R, Port Washington)	60,367
4.	**Norman F. Lent*** (R, East Rockaway)	**92,214**
	Patricia Sullivan (D, Seaford)	43,581
5.	**Raymond J. McGrath*** (R, Valley Stream)	**93,473**
	Michael T. Sullivan (D, Valley Stream)	49,728
6.	**Floyd H. Flake** (D, Queens)	**58,317**
	Richard Dietl (R, Queens)	27,773
7.	**Gary L. Ackerman*** (D, Queens)	**62,836**
	Edward Nelson Rodriguez (R, Queens)	18,384
8.	**James H. Scheuer*** (D, Queens)	**70,605**
	Gustave Reifenkugel (C, Fresh Meadows)	7,679
9.	**Thomas J. Manton*** (D, Queens)	**50,738**
	Salvatore J. Calise (R, Queens)	18,040
10.	**Charles E. Schumer*** (D, Brooklyn)	**76,318**
	Alice Gaffney (C, Brooklyn)	5,472
11.	**Edolphus Towns*** (D, Brooklyn)	**41,689**
	Nathaniel Hendricks (R, Brooklyn)	4,053
12.	**Major R. Owens*** (D, Brooklyn)	**42,138**
	Owen Augustin (R, Brooklyn)	2,752
13.	**Stephen J. Solarz*** (D, Brooklyn)	**61,089**
	Leon Nadrowski (R, Brooklyn)	10,941
14.	**Guy V. Molinari*** (R, Staten Island)	**64,647**
	Barbara Walla (D, Staten Island)	27,950
15.	**Bill Green*** (R, Manhattan)	**58,214**
	George A. Hirsch (D, Manhattan)	42,147
16.	**Charles B. Rangel*** (D, Manhatten)	**61,262**
	Michael T. Berns (C, Manhattan)	1,288
17.	**Ted Weiss*** (D, Manhattan)	**95,094**
	Thomas A. Chorba (R, Manhattan)	15,587
18.	**Robert Garcia*** (D, Bronx)	**43,343**
	Melanie Chase (R, Bronx)	2,479
19.	**Mario Biaggi*** (D, Bronx)	**87,774**
	Alice Farrell (C, Bronx)	6,906
20.	**Joe Dioguardi*** (R, Scarsdale)	**80,220**
	Bella S. Abzug (D, White Plains)	66,359
21.	**Hamilton Fish Jr.*** (R, Millbrook)	**102,070**
	Lawrence W. Grunberger (D, Peekskill)	28,339
22.	**Benjamin A. Gilman*** (R, Middletown)	**94,244**
	Eleanor F. Burlingham (D, Suffern)	36,852
23.	**Samuel S. Stratton*** (D, Schenectady)	**Unopposed**
24.	**Gerald B. Solomon*** (R, Glen Falls)	**117,285**
	Edward Bloch (D, Latham)	49,225
25.	**Sherwood L. Boehlert*** (R, New Hartford)	**104,216**
	Kevin J. Conway (D, Woodgate)	33,864
26.	**David O'B. Martin*** (R, Canton)	**Unopposed**
27.	**George C. Wortley*** (R, Fayetteville)	**83,430**
	Rosemary S. Pooler (D, Syracuse)	82,491
28.	**Matthew F. McHugh*** (D, Ithaca)	**103,908**
	Mark R. Masterson (R, Kingston)	48,213
29.	**Frank Horton*** (R, Rochester)	**99,704**
	James R. Vogel (D, Rochester)	34,194
30.	**Louise M. Slaughter** (D, Fairport)	**86,777**
	Fred J. Eckert* (R, Stafford)	83,402
31.	**Jack F. Kemp*** (R, Hamburg)	**92,508**
	James P. Keane (D, Buffalo)	67,574
32.	**John J. LaFalce*** (D, Buffalo)	**99,745**
	Dean L. Walker (C, Lockport)	6,234
33.	**Henry J. Nowak*** (D, Buffalo)	**109,256**
	Charles A. Walker (R, Buffalo)	19,147
34.	**Amory Houghton Jr.** (R, Corning)	**85,856**
	Larry M. Himelein (D, Gowanda)	56,898
	North Carolina	
1.	**Walter B. Jones*** (D, Farmville)	**91,122**
	Howard Moye (R, Farmville)	39,912
2.	**I.T. "Tim" Valentine Jr.*** (D, Nashville)	**95,320**
	Bud McElhaney (R, Durham)	32,515
3.	**Martin Lancaster** (D, Goldsboro)	**71,460**
	Gerald B. Hurst (R, Jacksonville)	39,408
4.	**David E. Price** (D, Chapel Hill)	**92,216**
	William Cobey Jr.* (R, Chapel Hill)	73,469
5.	**Stephen L. Neal*** (D, Winston-Salem)	**86,410**
	Stuart Epperson (R, Winston-Salem)	73,261
6.	**Howard Coble*** (R, Greensboro)	**72,329**
	Charles Robin Britt (D, Greensboro)	72,250
7.	**Charles G. Rose III***(D, Fayetteville)	**70,471**
	Thomas J. Harrelson (R, Southport)	39,289

Dist.	Representative (Party, Home)	1986 Election
8.	**W. G. "Bill" Hefner*** (D, Concord)	**80,959**
	William G. Hamby Jr. (R, Concord)	58,941
9.	**J. Alex McMillan*** (R, Charlotte)	**80,352**
	David Martin (D, Charlotte)	76,240
10.	**Cass Ballenger** (R, Hickory)	**83,902**
	Lester D. "Les" Roark (D, Shelby)	62,035
11.	**James McClure Clarke** (D, Fairview)	**91,575**
	William M. Hendon* (R, Asheville)	89,069
	North Dakota At Large	
	Byron L. Dorgan* (D, Bismarck)	**216,258**
	Syver Vinje (R, Bismark)	66,989
	Ohio	
1.	**Thomas A. Luken*** (D, Cincinnati)	**90,477**
	Fred E. Morr (R, Cincinnati)	56,100
2.	**Willis D. Gradison*** (R, Cincinnati)	**105,061**
	William F. Stineman (D, Cincinnati)	43,448
3.	**Tony P. Hall*** (D, Dayton)	**98,311**
	Ron Crutcher (R, Dayton)	35,167
4.	**Michael G. Oxley*** (R, Findlay)	**115,751**
	Clem T. Cratty (D, Wapakoneta)	26,320
5.	**Delbert L. Latta*** (R, Bowling Green)	**102,016**
	Tom Murray (D, Sandusky)	54,864
6.	**Bob McEwen*** (R, Hillsboro)	**106,354**
	Gordon R. Roberts (D, Oregonia)	42,155
7.	**Michael DeWine*** (R, Cedarville)	**Unopposed**
8.	**Donald E. Lukens** (R, Middletown)	**98,475**
	John W. Griffin (D, Eaton)	46,195
9.	**Marcy Kaptur*** (D, Toledo)	**105,646**
	Mike Shufeldt (R, Toledo)	30,643
10.	**Clarence E. Miller*** (R, Lancaster)	**106,870**
	John M. Buchanan (D, Newark)	44,847
11.	**Dennis E. Eckart*** (D, Mentor)	**104,740**
	Margaret R. Mueller (R, Novelty)	35,944
12.	**John R. Kasich*** (R, Westerville)	**117,905**
	Timothy C. Jochim (D, Columbus)	42,727
13.	**Donald J. Pease*** (D, Oberlin)	**88,612**
	William D. Nielsen Jr. (R, Valley City)	52,452
14.	**Thomas C. Sawyer** (D, Akron)	**83,257**
	Lynn Slaby (R, Bath)	71,713
15.	**Chalmers P. Wylie*** (R, Worthington)	**87,745**
	David L. Jackson (D, Columbus)	55,750
16.	**Ralph Regula*** (R, Navarre)	**118,206**
	William J. Kennick (D, Alliance)	36,639
17.	**James A. Traficant*** (D, Poland)	**112,855**
	James H. Fulks (R, Canfield)	43,334
18.	**Douglas Applegate*** (D, Steubenville)	**Unopposed**
19.	**Edward F. Feighan*** (D, Lakewood)	**97,814**
	Gary C. Suhadolnik (R, Parma Heights)	80,743
20.	**Mary Rose Oakar*** (D, Cleveland)	**110,976**
	Bill Smith (R, Middleburg Heights)	19,794
21.	**Louis Stokes*** (D, Warrensville Hts.)	**99,878**
	Frank H. Roski (R, Cleveland Heights)	22,594
	Oklahoma	
1.	**James M. Inhofe** (R, Tulsa)	**78,919**
	Gary Allison (D, Tulsa)	61,663
2.	**Mike Synar*** (D, Muskogee)	**114,543**
	Gary K. Rice (R, Catoosa)	41,795
3.	**Wes Watkins*** (D, Ada)	**114,008**
	Patrick K. Miller (R, Snow)	31,913
4.	**Dave McCurdy*** (D, Norman)	**94,984**
	Larry Humphreys (R, Velma)	29,697
5.	**Mickey Edwards*** (R, Oklahoma City)	**108,774**
	Donna Compton (D, Oklahoma City)	45,256
6.	**Glenn English*** (D, Cordell)	**Unopposed**
	Oregon	
1.	**Les AuCoin*** (D, Portland)	**141,585**
	Anthony "Tony" Meeker (R, Amity)	87,874
2.	**Bob Smith*** (R, Burns)	**113,566**
	Larry Tuttle (D, Redmond)	75,124
3.	**Ron Wyden*** (D, Portland)	**180,067**
	Thomas H. Phelan (R, Portland)	29,321
4.	**Peter A. DeFazio** (D, Springfield)	**105,697**
	Bruce Long (R, Roseburg)	89,795
5.	**Denny Smith*** (R, Salem)	**125,906**
	Barbara Ross (D, Corvallis)	82,290
	Pennsylvania	
1.	**Thomas M. Foglietta*** (D, Philadelphia)	**88,224**
	Anthony J. Mucciolo (R, Philadelphia)	29,811
2.	**William H. Gray*** (D, Philadelphia)	**Unopposed**
3.	**Robert A. Borski*** (D, Philadelphia)	**107,804**
	Robert A. Rovner (R, Philadelphia)	66,693
4.	**Joseph P. Kolter*** (D, New Brighton)	**86,133**
	Al Lindsay (R, Sarver)	55,165
5.	**Richard T. Schulze*** (R, Paoli)	**87,593**
	Tim Ringgold (D, West Chester)	45,648
6.	**Gus Yatron*** (D, Reading)	**98,142**
	Norm Bertasavage (R, Pottsville)	43,858
7.	**Curt Weldon** (R, Media)	**110,118**
	Bill Spingler (D, Wayne)	69,557
8.	**Peter H. Kostmayer*** (D, Doylestown)	**85,731**
	Dave Christian (R, Levittown)	70,047
9.	**Bud Shuster*** (R, D, Everett)	**Unopposed**
10.	**Joseph M. McDade*** (R, Scranton)	**118,603**
	Robert C. Bolus (D, Scranton)	40,248
11.	**Paul E. Kanjorski*** (D, Nanticoke)	**112,405**
	Marc Holtzman (R, Wilkes-Barre)	46,785
12.	**John P. Murtha*** (D, Johnstown)	**97,135**
	Kathy Holtzman (R, Johnstown)	46,937
13.	**Lawrence Coughlin*** (R, Norristown)	**100,701**
	Joseph M. Hoeffel (D, Roslyn)	71,381
14.	**William J. Coyne*** (D, Pittsburgh)	**104,726**
	Richard Edward Caligiuri (L, Wilkinsburg)	6,058
15.	**Don Ritter*** (R, Allentown)	**74,829**
	Joe Simonetta (D, Bethlehem)	56,972
16.	**Robert S. Walker*** (R, E. Petersburg)	**100,784**
	James D. Hagelgams (D, Lancaster)	34,399
17.	**George W. Gekas*** (R, Harrisburg)	**101,027**
	Michael S. Ogden (D, Harrisburg)	36,157
18.	**Doug Walgren*** (D, Pittsburgh)	**104,164**
	Ernie Buckman (R, Sewickley)	61,164
19.	**William F. Goodling*** (R, York)	**100,055**
	Richard F. Thornton (D, Etters)	37,223
20.	**Joseph M. Gaydos*** (D, McKeesport)	**Unopposed**
21.	**Thomas J. Ridge*** (R, Erie)	**111,148**
	Joylyn Blackwell (D, Erie)	26,324
22.	**Austin J. Murphy*** (D, R, Charleroi)	**Unopposed**
23.	**William F. Clinger Jr.*** (R, Warren)	**79,595**
	William Wachob (D, State College)	63,875
	Rhode Island	
1.	**Fernand J. St Germain*** (D, Woonsocket)	**85,077**
	John A. Holmes Jr. (R, Barrington)	62,397
2.	**Claudine Schneider*** (R, Narragansett)	**113,603**
	Donald J. Ferry (D, Johnston)	44,586
	South Carolina	
1.	**Arthur Ravenel Jr.** (R, Charleston)	**59,969**
	Jimmy Stuckney (D, Charleston)	55,262
2.	**Floyd D. Spence*** (R, Lexington)	**73,455**
	Fred Zeigler (D, Columbia)	63,592
3.	**Butler Derrick*** (D, Anderson)	**79,109**
	Richard Dickison (R, Barnwell)	36,495
4.	**Liz J. Patterson** (D, Spartanburg)	**67,012**
	Bill Workman (R, Greenville)	61,648
5.	**John Spratt*** (D, York)	**Unopposed**
6.	**Robert M. Tallon Jr.*** (D, Florence)	**92,398**
	Robbie Cunningham (R, Georgetown)	29,922
	South Dakota At Large	
1.	**Tim Johnson** (D, Sioux Falls)	**171,462**
	Dale Bell (R, Spearfish)	118,261

Dist.	Representative (Party, Home)	1986 Election
	Tennessee	
1.	**James H. "Jimmy" Quillen*** (R, Kingsport)	**80,289**
	John B. Russell (D, Jonesborough)	36,278
2.	**John J. Duncan*** (R, Knoxville)	**96,396**
	John F. Bowen (D, Knoxville)	30,088
3.	**Marilyn Lloyd*** (D, Chattanooga)	**75,034**
	Jim Golden (R, Chattanooga)	64,084
4.	**Jim Cooper*** (D, Shelbyville)	**Unopposed**
5.	**Bill Boner*** (D, Nashville)	**85,126**
	Terry Holcomb (R, Nashville)	58,701
6.	**Bart Gordon*** (D, Murfreesboro)	**102,180**
	Fred Vail (R, Brentwood)	30,823
7.	**Don Sundquist*** (R, Memphis)	**93,902**
	M. Lloyd Hiler (D, Bartlett)	35,966
8.	**Ed Jones*** (D, Yorkville)	**101,699**
	Dan H. Campbell (R, Memphis)	24,792
9.	**Harold E. Ford*** (D, Memphis)	**Unopposed**
	Texas	
1.	**Sam B. Hall Jr.*** (D, Marshall)	**Unopposed**
2.	**Charles Wilson*** (D, Lufkin)	**78,529**
	Julian Gordon (R, Liberty)	35,986
3.	**Steve Bartlett*** (R, Dallas)	**Unopposed**
4.	**Ralph M. Hall*** (D, Rockwall)	**97,540**
	Thomas Blow (R, Tyler)	38,578
5.	**John Bryant*** (D, Dallas)	**57,410**
	Tom Carter (R, Mesquite)	39,945
6.	**Joe Barton*** (R, Ennis)	**86,190**
	Pete Geren (D, Ft. Worth)	68,270
7.	**Bill Archer*** (R, Houston)	**129,673**
	Harry Kniffen (D, Houston)	17,635
8.	**Jack Fields*** (R, Humble)	**66,280**
	Blaine Mann (D, Spring)	30,617
9.	**Jack Brooks*** (D, Beaumont)	**73,285**
	Lisa D. Duperier (R, Beaumont)	45,834
10.	**J. J. "Jake" Pickle*** (D, Austin)	**135,863**
	Carole Keeton Rylander (R, Austin)	52,000
11.	**Marvin Leath*** (D, Waco)	**Unopposed**
12.	**James Wright*** (D, Fort Worth)	**84,831**
	Don McNeil (R, Fort Worth)	38,620
13.	**Beau Boulter*** (R, Amarillo)	**84,980**
	Doug Seal (D, Wellington)	45,907
14.	**Mac Sweeney*** (R, Wharton)	**74,471**
	Greg Laughlin (D, West Columbia)	67,852
15.	**E. "Kika" de la Garza*** (D, McAllen)	**Unopposed**
16.	**Ronald Coleman*** (D, El Paso)	**50,590**
	Roy Gillia (R, El Paso)	26,419
17.	**Charles W. Stenholm*** (D, Avoca)	**Unopposed**
18.	**Mickey Leland*** (D, Houston)	**Unopposed**
19.	**Larry Combest*** (R, Lubbock)	**68,695**
	Gerald McCathern (D, Hereford)	42,129
20.	**Henry B. Gonzalez*** (D, San Antonio)	**Unopposed**
21.	**Lamar Smith** (R, San Antonio)	**100,346**
	Pete Snelson (D, Midland)	63,779
22.	**Tom DeLay*** (R, Sugar Land)	**76,459**
	Susan Director (D, Houston)	30,079
23.	**Albert Bustamente*** (D, San Antonio)	**Unopposed**
24.	**Martin Frost*** (D, Dallas)	**69,368**
	Robert Burk (R, Irving)	33,819
25.	**Mike Andrews*** (D, Houston)	**Unopposed**
26.	**Dick Armey*** (R, Lewisville)	**101,735**
	George Richardson (D, Keller)	47,651
27.	**Solomon P. Ortiz*** (D, Corpus Christi)	**Unopposed**
	Utah	
1.	**James V. Hansen*** (R, Farmington)	**82,151**
	Gunn McKay (D, Huntsville)	77,178
2.	**Wayne Owens** (D, Salt Lake City)	**76,921**
	M. Tom Shimizu (R, Salt Lake City)	60,967
3.	**Howard C. Nielson*** (R, Provo)	**86,599**
	Dale F. Gardiner (D, Riverton)	42,582
	Vermont At Large	
1.	**James M. Jeffords*** (R, Montpelier)	**168,403**
	Virginia	
1.	**Herbert H. "Herb" Bateman*** (R, Newport News)	**80,713**
	Robert C. "Bobby" Scott (D, Newport News)	63,364
2.	**Owen B. Pickett** (D, Virginia Beach)	**54,491**
	A. J. "Joe" Canada Jr. (R, Virginia Beach)	46,137
3.	**Thomas J. Bliley Jr.*** (R, Richmond)	**74,525**
	Kenneth E. Powell (D, Richmond)	32,961
4.	**Norman Sisisky*** (D, Petersburg)	**Unopposed**
5.	**W. C. "Dan" Daniel*** (D, Danville)	**Unopposed**
6.	**James Olin*** (D, Roanoke)	**88,230**
	Flo Neher Trawick (R, Lynchburg)	38,051
7.	**D. French Slaughter*** (R, Culpepper)	**Unopposed**
8.	**Stan Parris*** (R, Springfield)	**72,670**
	James H. Boren (D, Falls Church)	44,965
9.	**Frederick C. "Rick" Boucher*** (D, Abingdon)	**Unopposed**
10.	**Frank G. Wolf*** (R, Vienna)	**95,724**
	John G. Milliken (D, Falls Church)	63,292
	Washington	
1.	**John Miller*** (R, Seattle)	**97,969**
	Reese M. Lindquist (D, Seattle)	92,697
2.	**Al Swift*** (D, Bellingham)	**124,840**
	Thomas S. Talman (R, Eastsound)	48,077
3.	**Don Bonker*** (D, Vancouver)	**114,775**
	Joseph R. Illing (R, Olympia)	41,275
4.	**Sid Morrison*** (R, Zillah)	**107,593**
	Robert Godecke (D, Ellersburg)	41,709
5.	**Thomas S. Foley*** (D, Spokane)	**121,732**
	Floyd Lee Wakefield (R, Colbert)	41,179
6.	**Norman D. Dicks*** (D, Bremerton)	**90,063**
	Kenneth W. Braaten, (R, Gig Harbor)	36,410
7.	**Mike Lowry*** (D, Renton)	**124,317**
	Don McDonald (R, Seattle)	46,831
8.	**Rodney Chandler*** (R, Redmond)	**107,824**
	David E. Giles (D, Issaquah)	57,545
	West Virginia	
1.	**Alan B. Mollohan*** (D, Fairmont)	**Unopposed**
2.	**Harley O. Staggers Jr.*** (D, Keyser)	**76,355**
	Michele Golden (R, Morgantown)	33,554
3.	**Bob Wise*** (D, Clendenin)	**73,669**
	Tim Sharp (R, Charleston)	39,820
4.	**Nick J. Rahall II *** (D, Beckley)	**58,217**
	Martin Miller Sr. (R, Beckley)	23,490
	Wisconsin	
1.	**Les Aspin*** (D, East Troy)	**106,288**
	Iris Peterson (R, Janesville)	34,495
2.	**Robert Kastenmeier*** (D, Sun Prairie)	**106,919**
	Ann J. Haney (R, Madison)	85,156
3.	**Steven C. Gunderson*** (R, Osseo)	**104,393**
	Leland E. Mulder (D, Holmen)	58,445
4.	**Gerald D. Kleczka*** (D, Milwaukee)	**Unopposed**
5.	**Jim Moody*** (D, Milwaukee)	**Unopposed**
6.	**Thomas E. Petri*** (R, Fond du Lac)	**Unopposed**
7.	**David R. Obey*** (D, Wausau)	**106,700**
	Kevin J. Hermening (R, Wausau)	63,408
8.	**Toby Roth*** (R, Appleton)	**118,162**
	Paul F. Willems (D, Green Bay)	57,265
9.	**F. James Sensenbrenner Jr.*** (R, Menomonee Falls)	**138,766**
	Thomas G. Popp (D, Lake Mills)	38,636
	Wyoming At Large	
	Richard B. Cheney* (R, Casper)	**111,007**
	Rick Gilmore (D, Cheyenne)	48,780

Resident Commissioner (Non-Voting)

Puerto Rico

Jaime B. Fuster* (D, San Juan)

Non-Voting Delegates

District of Columbia
Walter E. Fauntroy* (D)
Mary L. H. King (R)

Guam
Vicente G. Blaz* (R, Agana)

Virgin Islands
Ron de Lugo* (D, St. Croix)

American Samoa
Fofo I. F. Sunia* (D, Pago Pago)

Congressional Committees

Senate Standing Committees

(As of Apr. 27, 1987)

Agriculture, Nutrition, and Forestry
Chairman: Patrick L. Leahy, Vt.
Ranking Rep.: Richard G. Lugar, Ind.

Appropriations
Chairman: John C. Stennis, Miss.
Ranking Rep.: Mark O. Hatfield, Ore.

Armed Services
Chairman: Sam Nunn, Ga.
Ranking Rep.: John W. Warner, Va.

Banking, Housing, and Urban Affairs
Chairman: William Proxmire, Wis.
Ranking Rep.: Jake Garn, Utah

Budget
Chairman: Lawton Chiles, Fla.
Ranking Rep.: Pete V. Dominici, N.M.

Commerce, Science, and Transportation
Chairman: Ernest F. Hollings, S.C.
Ranking Rep.: John C. Danforth, Mo.

Energy and Natural Resources
Chairman: J. Bennett Johnston, La.
Ranking Rep.: James A. McClure, Ida.

Environment and Public Works
Chairman: Quentin N. Burdick, N.C.
Ranking Rep.: Robert T. Stafford, Vt.

Finance
Chairman: Lloyd Bentsen, Tex.
Ranking Rep.: Bob Packwood, Ore.

Foreign Relations
Chairman: Claiborne Pell, R.I.
Ranking Rep.: Jesse Helms, N.C.

Governmental Affairs
Chairman: John Glenn, Ohio
Ranking Rep.: William V. Roth, Del.

Judiciary
Chairman: Joseph R. Biden Jr., Del.
Ranking Rep.: Strom Thurmond, S.C.

Labor and Human Resources
Chairman: Edward M. Kennedy, Mass.
Ranking Rep.: Orrin G. Hatch, Utah

Rules and Administration
Chairman: Wendell H. Ford, Ky.
Ranking Rep.: Ted Stevens, Alas.

Small Business
Chairman: Dale Bumpers, Ark.
Ranking Rep.: Lowell P. Weicker Jr., Conn.

Veterans' Affairs
Chairman: Alan Cranston, Cal.
Ranking Rep.: Frank H. Murkowski, Alas.

Senate Select and Special Committees

Aging
Chairman: John Melcher, Mont.
Ranking Rep.: John Heinz, Pa.

Ethics
Chairman: Howell Heflin, Ala.
V. Chairman: Warren Rudman, N.H.

Indian Affairs
Chairman: Daniel K. Inouye, Ha.
Ranking Rep.: Daniel J. Evans, Wash.

Intelligence
Chairman: David L. Boren, Okla.
V. Chairman: William S. Cohen, Me.

Joint Committees of Congress

Economic
Chairman: Sen. Paul S. Sarbanes (D), Md.
V. Chairman: Rep. Lee H. Hamilton (D), Ind.

Library
Chairman: Sen. Claiborne Pell (D), R.I.
V. Chairman: Rep. Frank Annunzio (D), Ill.

Printing
Chairman: Rep. Frank Annunzio (D), Ill.
V. Chairman: Sen. Wendell H. Ford (D), Ky.

Taxation
Chairman: Rep. Dan Rostenkowski (D), Ill.
V. Chairman: Sen. Lloyd Bentsen (D), Tex.

House Standing Committees

(As of Mar. 3, 1987)

Agriculture
Chairman: E de la Garza, Tex.
Ranking Rep.: Edward R. Madigan, Ill.

Appropriations
Chairman: Jamie L. Whitten, Miss.
Ranking Rep.: Silvio O. Conte, Mass.

Armed Services
Chairman: Les Aspin, Wis.
Ranking Rep.: William L. Dickinson, Ala.

Banking, Finance, and Urban Affairs
Chairman: Fernand J. St. Germain, R.I.
Ranking Rep.: Chalmers P. Wylie, Ohio

Budget
Chairman: William H. Gray III, Pa.
Ranking Rep.: Delbert L. Latta, Ohio

District of Columbia
Chairman: Ronald V. Dellums, Cal.
Ranking Rep.: Stewart B. McKinney, Conn.

Education and Labor
Chairman: Augustus F. Hawkins, Cal.
Ranking Rep.: James M. Jeffords, Vt.

Energy and Commerce
Chairman: John D. Dingell, Mich.
Ranking Rep.: Norman F. Lent, N.Y.

Foreign Affairs
Chairman: Dante B. Fascell, Fla.
Ranking Rep.: William S. Broomfield, Mich.

Government Operations
Chairman: Jack Brooks, Tex.
Ranking Rep.: Frank Horton, N.Y.

House Administration
Chairman: Frank Annunzio, Ill.
Ranking Rep.: Bill Frenzel, Minn.

Interior and Insular Affairs
Chairman: Morris K. Udall, Ariz.
Ranking Rep.: Don Young, Alas.

Judiciary
Chairman: Peter W. Rodino Jr., N.J.
Ranking Rep.: Hamilton Fish Jr., N.Y.

Merchant Marine and Fisheries
Chairman: Walter B. Jones, N.C.
Ranking Rep.: Robert W. Davis, Mich.

Post Office and Civil Service
Chairman: William D. Ford, Mich.
Ranking Rep.: Gene Taylor, Mo.

Public Works and Transportation
Chairman: James J. Howard, N.J.
Ranking Rep.: John Paul Hammerschmidt, Ark.

(continued)

Rules
Chairman: Claude Pepper, Fla.
Ranking Rep.: James H. Quillen, Tenn.
Science, Space, and Technology
Chairman: Robert A. Roe, N.J.
Ranking Rep.: Manuel Lujan Jr., N. Mex.
Small Business
Chairman: John J. LaFalce, N.Y.
Ranking Rep.: Joseph M. McDade, Pa.
Standards of Official Conduct
Chairman: Julian C. Dixon, Cal.
Ranking Rep.: Floyd Spence, S.C.
Veterans' Affairs
Chairman: G.V. Montgomery, Miss.
Ranking Rep.: Gerald B. H. Solomon, N.Y.
Ways and Means
Chairman: Dan Rostenkowski, Ill.
Ranking Rep.: John J. Duncan, Tenn.

House Select Committees

Aging
Chairman: Edward R. Roybal, Cal.
Ranking Rep.: Matthew J. Rinaldo, N.J.
Children, Youth, and Families
Chairman: George Miller, Cal.
Ranking Rep.: Dan Coats, Ind.
Hunger
Chairman: Mickey Leland, Tex.
Ranking Rep.: Marge Roukema, N.J.
Intelligence
Chairman: Louis Stokes, Ohio
Ranking Rep.: Henry J. Hyde, Ill.
Narcotics Abuse and Control
Chairman: Charles B. Rangel, N.Y.
Ranking Rep.: Benjamin A. Gilman, N.Y.

Political Divisions of the U.S. Senate and House of Representatives From 1859 (36th Cong.) to 1987-1989 (100th Cong.)

Source: Clerk of the House of Representatives; Secretary of the Senate

		Senate					House of Representatives				
Congress	Years	Number of Senators	Democrats	Republicans	Other parties	Vacant	Number of Representatives	Democrats	Republicans	Other parties	Vacant
36th	1859-61	66	38	26	2		237	101	113	23	
37th	1861-63	50	11	31	7	1	178	42	106	28	2
38th	1863-65	51	12	39			183	80	103		
39th	1865-67	52	10	42			191	46	145		
40th	1867-69	53	11	42			193	49	143		1
41st	1869-71	74	11	61		2	243	73	170		
42d.	1871-73	74	17	57			243	104	139		
43d.	1873-75	74	19	54		1	293	88	203		2
44th	1875-77	76	29	46		1	293	181	107	3	2
45th	1877-79	76	36	39	1		293	156	137		
46th	1879-81	76	43	33			293	150	128	14	1
47th	1881-83	76	37	37	2		293	130	152	11	
48th	1883-85	76	36	40			325	200	119	6	
49th	1885-87	76	34	41		1	325	182	140	2	1
50th	1887-89	76	37	39			325	170	151	4	
51st	1889-91	84	37	47			330	156	173	1	
52d.	1891-93	88	39	47	2		333	231	88	14	
53d.	1893-95	88	44	38	3	3	356	220	126	10	
54th	1895-97	88	39	44	5		357	104	246	7	
55th	1897-99	90	34	46	10		357	134	206	16	1
56th	1899-1901	90	26	53	11		357	163	185	9	
57th	1901-03	90	29	56	3	2	357	153	198	5	1
58th	1903-05	90	32	58			386	178	207		1
59th	1905-07	90	32	58			386	136	250		
60th	1907-09	92	29	61		2	386	164	222		
61st	1909-11	92	32	59		1	391	172	219		
62d.	1911-13	92	42	49		1	391	228	162	1	
63d.	1913-15	96	51	44	1		435	290	127	18	
64th	1915-17	96	56	39	1		435	231	193	8	3
65th	1917-19	96	53	42	1		435	[1]210	216	9	
66th	1919-21	96	47	48	1		435	191	237	7	
67th	1921-23	96	37	59			435	132	300	1	2
68th	1923-25	96	43	51	2		435	207	225	3	
69th	1925-27	96	40	54	1	1	435	183	247	5	
70th	1927-29	96	47	48	1		435	195	237	3	
71st	1929-31	96	39	56	1		435	163	267	1	4
72d.	1931-33	96	47	48	1		435	[2]216	218	1	
73d.	1933-35	96	59	36	1		435	313	117	5	
74th	1935-37	96	69	25	2		435	322	103	10	
75th	1937-39	96	75	17	4		435	333	89	13	
76th	1939-41	96	69	23	4		435	262	169	4	
77th	1941-43	96	66	28	2		435	267	162	6	
78th	1943-45	96	57	38	1		435	222	209	4	
79th	1945-47	96	57	38	1		435	243	190	2	
80th	1947-49	96	45	51			435	188	246	1	
81st	1949-51	96	54	42			435	263	171	1	
82d.	1951-53	96	48	47	1		435	234	199	2	
83d.	1953-55	96	46	48	2		435	213	221	1	

(continued)

Congress	Years	Senate: Number of Senators	Senate: Democrats	Senate: Republicans	Senate: Other parties	Senate: Vacant	House of Representatives: Number of Representatives	House: Democrats	House: Republicans	House: Other parties	House: Vacant
84th	1955-57	96	48	47	1		435	232	203		
85th	1957-59	96	49	47			435	234	201		
86th	1959-61	98	64	34			[3]436	283	153		
87th	1961-63	100	64	36			[4]437	262	175		
88th	1963-65	100	67	33			435	258	176		1
89th	1965-67	100	68	32			435	295	140		
90th	1967-69	100	64	36			435	248	187		
91st	1969-71	100	58	42			435	243	192		
92d.	1971-73	100	54	44	2		435	255	180		
93d.	1973-75	100	56	42	2		435	242	192	1	
94th	1975-77	100	61	37	2		435	291	144		
95th	1977-79	100	61	38	1		435	292	143		
96th	1979-81	100	58	41	1		435	277	158		
97th	1981-83	100	46	53	1		435	242	190		3
98th	1983-85	100	46	54			435	269	166		
99th	1985-87	100	47	53			435	253	182		
100th. . . .	1987-89	100	54	46			435	258	177		

(1) Democrats organized House with help of other parties. (2) Democrats organized House due to Republican deaths. (3) Proclamation declaring Alaska a State issued Jan. 3, 1959. (4) Proclamation declaring Hawaii a State issued Aug. 21, 1959.

Congress: The First and the 100th

The 100th Congress began its session Jan. 6, 1987; they first met in 1789.

Members:	**First Congress**	—Representatives, 65; Senators, 26
	100th Congress	—Representatives, 435; Senators, 100
Pay Allowances:	**First Congress**	—Pay, $6 per day for each day in session; travel allowance, $6 for every 20 miles from home state or district to seat of Congress
	100th Congress	—$89,500; expenses, House, 1987, $176,853,600 for staff, $64,380,000 for offices; Senate, 1987, $104,030,000 for staff, $6,100,000 for offices
Costs:	**First Congress**	—$373,853
	100th Congress	—$3.2 billion
Average Age:	**First Congress**	—House, 43.5; Senate, 46.1
	100th Congress	—House, 50.7; Senate, 54.4
Sex:	**First Congress**	—100% Male
	100th Congress	—House, 95% Male, 5% Female —Senate, 98% Male, 2% Female
Race:	**First Congress**	—100% White
	100th Congress	—House, 92% White, 5% Black, 3% Hispanic —Senate, 100% White
Education:	**First Congress**	—House, 49% No College, 3% Some College, 48% College Graduate —Senate, 41% No College, 3% Some College, 56% College Graduate
	100th Congress	—House, 11% No College Degree, 28% College Degree, 61% Graduate Degree —Senate, 6% No College Degree, 15% College Degree, 79% Graduate Degree
Occupation:	**First Congress**	—House, 36% Planters, 38% Lawyers, 17% Merchants, 5% Ministers, 5% Office-holders —Senate, 48% Landholders/Planters, 38% Lawyers, 14% Merchants
	100th Congress	—House, 42% Law, 33% Business or Banking, 22% Public Service/Politics, 9% Education, 5% Journalism, 5% Agriculture —Senate, 62% Law, 28% Business or Banking, 20% Public Service/Politics, 12% Education, 8% Journalism, 5% Agriculture
Legislation:	**First Congress**	—143 measures introduced in House, 24 in Senate; 117 enacted
	99th Congress	—7,522 measures introduced in House, 4,080 in Senate; 664 enacted

Congressional Bills Vetoed, 1789-1986

Source: Senate Library, Sept. 1986

	Regular vetoes	Pocket vetoes	Total vetoes	Vetoes over-ridden
Washington	2	—	2	—
John Adams	—	—	—	—
Jefferson	—	—	—	—
Madison	5	2	7	—
Monroe	1	—	1	—
John Q. Adams	—	—	—	—
Jackson	5	7	12	—
Van Buren	—	1	1	—
William Harrison	—	—	—	—
Tyler	6	4	10	1
Polk	2	1	3	—
Taylor	—	—	—	—
Fillmore	—	—	—	—
Pierce	9	—	9	5
Buchanan	4	3	7	—
Lincoln	2	5	7	—
Andrew Johnson	21	8	29	15
Grant	45	48	93	4
Hayes	12	1	13	1
Garfield	—	—	—	—
Arthur	4	8	12	1
Cleveland	304	110	414	2
Benjamin Harrison	19	25	44	1
Cleveland	42	128	170	5

(continued)

	Regular vetoes	Pocket vetoes	Total vetoes	Vetoes over-ridden
McKinley	6	36	42	—
Theodore Roosevelt	42	40	82	1
Taft	30	9	39	1
Wilson	33	11	44	6
Harding	5	1	6	—
Coolidge	20	30	50	4
Hoover	21	16	37	3
Franklin Roosevelt	372	263	635	9
Truman	180	70	250	12
Eisenhower	73	108	181	2
Kennedy	12	9	21	—
Lyndon Johnson	16	14	30	—
Nixon	26	17	43	7
Ford	48	18	66	12
Carter	13	18	31	2
Reagan[1]	26	21	47	4
Total	**1,406**	**1,032**	**2,438**	**98**

(1) As of April 2, 1987, Pres. Reagan has been defeated by Congress an additional four times on legislation he vetoed, for a total of eight vetoes overridden.

Governors of States and Possessions

(as of mid-1987)

State	Capital	Governor	Party	Term years	Term expires	Annual salary
Alabama	Montgomery	Guy Hunt	Rep.	4	Jan. 1991	$63,838
Alaska	Juneau	Steve Cowper	Dem.	4	Dec. 1990	81,648
Arizona	Phoenix	Evan Mecham	Rep.	4	Jan. 1991	75,000
Arkansas	Little Rock	Bill Clinton	Dem.	4	Jan. 1991	35,000
California	Sacramento	George Deukmejian	Rep.	4	Jan. 1991	85,000
Colorado	Denver	Roy Romer	Dem.	4	Jan. 1991	70,000
Connecticut	Hartford	William O'Neill	Dem.	4	Jan. 1991	78,000
Delaware	Dover	Michael N. Castle	Rep.	4	Jan. 1989	70,000
Florida	Tallahassee	Bob Martinez	Rep.	4	Jan. 1991	90,570
Georgia	Atlanta	Joe Frank Harris	Dem.	4	Jan. 1991	79,358
Hawaii	Honolulu	John Waihee	Dem.	4	Dec. 1990	59,400
Idaho	Boise	Cecil D. Andrus	Dem.	4	Jan. 1991	55,000
Illinois	Springfield	James R. Thompson	Rep.	4	Jan. 1991	93,266
Indiana	Indianapolis	Robert D. Orr	Rep.	4	Jan. 1989	66,000
Iowa	Des Moines	Terry Branstad	Rep.	4	Jan. 1991	64,000
Kansas	Topeka	Mike Hayden	Rep.	4	Jan. 1991	66,950
Kentucky	Frankfort	Martha L. Collins	Dem.	4	Dec. 1987	63,036
Louisiana	Baton Rouge	Edwin W. Edwards	Dem.	4	May 1988	73,440
Maine	Augusta	John McKernan Jr.	Rep.	4	Jan. 1991	70,000
Maryland	Annapolis	William Donald Schaefer	Dem.	4	Jan. 1991	85,000
Massachusetts	Boston	Michael S. Dukakis	Dem.	4	Jan. 1991	75,000
Michigan	Lansing	James J. Blanchard	Dem.	4	Jan. 1991	92,664
Minnesota	St. Paul	Rudy Perpich	Dem.	4	Jan. 1991	91,460
Mississippi	Jackson	William A. Allain	Dem.	4	Jan. 1988	63,000
Missouri	Jefferson City	John D. Ashcroft	Rep.	4	Jan. 1989	81,000
Montana	Helena	Ted Schwinden	Dem.	4	Jan. 1989	50,452
Nebraska	Lincoln	Kay Orr	Rep.	4	Jan. 1991	58,000
Nevada	Carson City	Richard Bryan	Dem.	4	Jan. 1991	77,500
New Hampshire	Concord	John H. Sununu	Rep.	2	Jan. 1989	66,024
New Jersey	Trenton	Thomas H. Kean	Rep.	4	Jan. 1990	85,000
New Mexico	Santa Fe	Garrey E. Carruthers	Rep.	4	Jan. 1991	63,000
New York	Albany	Mario M. Cuomo	Dem.	4	Jan. 1991	130,000
North Carolina	Raleigh	James G. Martin	Rep.	4	Jan. 1989	100,000
North Dakota	Bismarck	George A. Sinner	Dem.	4	Jan. 1989	65,000
Ohio	Columbus	Richard F. Celeste	Dem.	4	Jan. 1991	65,000
Oklahoma	Oklahoma City	Henry Bellmon	Rep.	4	Jan. 1991	70,000
Oregon	Salem	Neil Goldschmidt	Dem.	4	Jan. 1991	72,050
Pennsylvania	Harrisburg	Robert Casey	Dem.	4	Jan. 1991	85,000
Rhode Island	Providence	Edward DiPrete	Rep.	2	Jan. 1989	69,000
South Carolina	Columbia	Carroll A. Campbell Jr.	Rep.	4	Jan. 1991	81,600
South Dakota	Pierre	George S. Mickelson	Rep.	4	Jan. 1991	57,325
Tennessee	Nashville	Ned Ray McWherter	Dem.	4	Jan. 1991	85,000
Texas	Austin	Bill Clements	Rep.	4	Jan. 1991	91,600
Utah	Salt Lake City	Norman Bangerter	Rep.	4	Jan. 1989	60,000
Vermont	Montpelier	Madeleine M. Kunin	Dem.	2	Jan. 1989	63,600
Virginia	Richmond	Gerald L. Baliles	Dem.	4	Jan. 1990	85,000
Washington	Olympia	Booth Gardner	Dem.	4	Jan. 1989	74,900
West Virginia	Charleston	Arch A. Moore Jr.	Rep.	4	Jan. 1989	72,000
Wisconsin	Madison	Tommy G. Thompson	Rep.	4	Jan. 1991	86,149
Wyoming	Cheyenne	Mike Sullivan	Dem.	4	Jan. 1991	70,000
Amer. Samoa	Pago Pago	A. P. Lutali		4	Jan. 1991	—
Guam	Agana	Joseph Ada	Dem.	4	Jan. 1991	—
Puerto Rico	San Juan	Rafael Hernandez Colón	P.D.	4	Jan. 1989	—
Virgin Islands	Charlotte Amalie	Alexander Farreley	Dem.	4	Jan. 1991	—

Mayors and City Managers of Larger North American Cities

As of mid-1987

*Asterisk before name denotes city manager. All others are mayors. For mayors, dates are those of next election; for city managers, they are dates of appointment.

D, Democrat; R, Republican; N-P, Non-Partisan

City	Name	Term
Abilene, Tex.	Dale E. Ferguson, N-P	1990, Apr.
Abington, Pa.	*Albert Herrmann	1978, May
Akron, Oh.	D.L. Plusquellic, D	1987, Nov.
Alameda, Cal.	Chuck Corica, N-P	1991, Apr.
Albany, Ga.	*Nicholas M. Meiszer	1986, Sept.
Albany, N.Y.	Thomas M. Whalen,3d,D	1989, Nov.
Albuquerque, N.M.	Ken Shultz, N-P	1989, Oct.
Alexandria, La.	Edward Randolph Jr., D.	1990, Sept.
Alexandria, Va.	*Douglas Harman	1975, Nov.
Alhambra, Cal.	*Kevin J. Murphy	1983, May
Allen Park, Mich.	Domenic Boccabella, D.	1987, Nov.
Allentown, Pa.	Joseph S. Daddona, D	1989, Nov.
Alton, Ill.	Bert J. Wuellner, R	1989, Apr.
Altoona, Pa.	David Jannetta, D	1987, Nov.
Amarillo, Tex.	*John Ward	1983, June
Ames, Ia.	*Steven L. Schainker	1982, Oct.
Anaheim, Cal.	*William O. Talley	1976, July
Anchorage, Alas.	Tony Knowles, D	1987, Oct.
Anderson, Ind.	Thomas McMahan, R	1987, Nov.
Anderson, S.C.	*Richard Burnette	1976, Sept.
Ann Arbor, Mich.	*Godfrey Collins	1982, Dec.
Appleton, Wis.	Dorothy Johnson, N-P	1988, Apr.
Arcadia, Cal.	*George J. Watts	1981, July
Arlington, Mass.	*Donald R. Marquis	1966, Nov.
Arlington, Tex.	*William Kirchhoff	1984, Oct.
Arlington Hts., Ill.	James Ryan, N-P	1989, Apr.
Arvada, Col.	*Neal G. Berlin	1986, Mar.
Asheville, N.C.	*Neal Creighton	1984, Oct.
Atlanta, Ga.	Andrew Young, D	1989, Oct.
Atlantic City, N.J.	James L. Usry, R	1990, May
Auburn, N.Y.	*Bruce Clifford	1966, Aug.
Augusta, Ga.	Charles Devaney, D.	1987, Oct.
Aurora, Col.	*James Griesemer	1984, Jan.
Aurora, Ill.	David L. Pierce, N-P	1989, Apr.
Austin, Tex.	*Jorge Carrasco	1984, Mar.
Bakersfield, Cal.	*George Caravalho	1984, Aug
Baldwin Park, Cal.	*Ralph Webb	1981, Apr.
Baltimore, Md.	William Schaefer, D	1987, Nov.
Bangor, Me.	*John W. Flynn	1977, Feb.
Baton Rouge, La.	Pat Screen, D	1988, Sept.
Battle Creek, Mich.	*Gordon Jaeger	1976, Mar.
Bay City, Mich.	*David D. Barnes	1979, May
Baytown, Tex.	*Fritz Lanham	1972, May
Beaumont, Tex.	*Albert E. Haines	1986, May
Belleville, Ill.	Richard Brauer, N-P.	1989, Apr.
Bellevue, Wash.	*Phillip Kushlaw	1985, Feb.
Bellflower, Cal.	Joseph E. Cvetko, D	1988, Apr.
Beloit, Wis.	*David Wilcox	1986, Feb.
Berkeley, Cal.	*Hal Cronkite	—
Bessemer, Ala.	Ed Porter, N-P	1990, July
Bethlehem, Pa.	Paul M. Marcincin, D	1989, Nov.
Beverly Hills, Cal.	*Edward Kreins	1979, Oct.
Billings, Mont.	*Alan Tandy	1985, May
Biloxi, Miss.	Gerald Blessey, D.	1988, June
Binghamton, N.Y.	Juanita M. Crabb, D.	1989, Nov.
Birmingham, Ala.	Richard Arrington Jr., D.	1987, Oct.
Bismarck, N.D.	Marlan Haakenson, N-P	1990, Apr.
Bloomfield, Minn.	*John Pidgeon	1967, Dec.
Bloomfield, N.J.	John Crecco, R	1989, Nov.
Bloomington, Ill.	Jesse Smart, D	1989, Apr.
Bloomington, Ind.	Tomilea Allison, D	1987, Nov.
Bloomington, Minn.	*John Pidgeon	1967, Dec.
Boca Raton, Fla.	Emil Danciu, N-P	1989, Mar.
Boise, Ida.	Dirk Kempthorne, N-P	1989, Nov.
Bossier City, La.	Don E. Jones, D	1989, Apr.
Boston, Mass.	Raymond L. Flynn, D	1987 Nov.
Boulder, Col.	*James W. Piper	1984, May
Bowie, Md.	*G. Charles Moore	1976, Mar.
Bowling Green, Ky.	*Charles W. Coates.	1977, Feb.
Bridgeport, Conn.	Thomas W. Bucci, D	1987, Nov.
Bristol, Conn.	John Leone, D	1987, Nov.
Brockton, Mass.	Carl Pitaro, D	1987, Nov.
Brooklyn Center, Minn.	*Gerald G. Splinter	1977, Oct.
Brownsville, Tex.	*Steve Fitzgibbons	1987, Jan.
Bryan, Tex.	*Ernest R. Clark	1979, Feb.
Buffalo, N.Y.	James D. Griffin, D	1989, Nov.
Burbank, Cal.	*Bud Ovrom	1985, June
Burlington, Vt.	Bernard Sanders, N-P	1989, Mar.
Calumet City, Ill.	Robert C. Stefaniak, D	1989, Apr.
Cambridge, Mass.	*Robert Healy	1974, May
Camden, N.J.	Melvin Primas Jr., D.	1989, May
Canton, Oh.	Sam Purses, D	1987, Nov.
Cape Girardeau, Mo.	*Gary A. Eide	1981, Mar.
Carson, Cal.	*John Dangleis	1984, Nov.
Casper, Wyo.	*S. Wesley McAllister Jr.	1985, Sept.
Cedar Rapids, Ia.	Donald J. Canney, N-P	1987, Nov.
Champaign, Ill.	*Steven C. Carter	1985, Feb.
Charleston, S.C.	Joseph P. Riley Jr., D	1987, Nov.
Charleston, W. Va.	James E. Roark, R	1991, Apr.
Charlotte, N.C.	Harvey Gantt, D	1987, Nov.
Charlottesville, Va.	*Cole Hendrix	1970, Jan.
Chattanooga, Tenn.	Gene Roberts, R	1991, Mar.
Chesapeake, Va.	*James W. Rein	1987, Mar.
Chester, Pa.	Willie Mae James Leake, R	1987, Nov.
Cheyenne, Wyo.	Donald Erickson, R	1988, Nov.
Chicago, Ill.	Harold Washington, D	1991, Apr.
Chicago Hts., Ill.	Charles Panici, R	1991, Apr.
Chicopee, Mass.	Richard S. Lak, D	1987, Nov.
Chino, Cal.	*Richard Rowe, N-P	1986, Feb.
Chula Vista, Cal.	*John Goss	1983, Jan.
Cincinnati, Oh.	*C. Scott Johnson	1986, Mar.
Clearwater, Fla.	*Anthony Shoemaker	1977, June
Cleveland, Oh.	George Voinovich, R	1989, Nov.
Cleveland Hgts., Oh.	*Robert Downey	1985, Jan.
Clifton, N.J.	*Joseph J. Lynn	1982, Sept.
Col. Spgs., Col.	*Larry N. Blick	1985, Oct.
Columbia, Mo.	*Raymond A. Beck	1985, Aug.
Columbia, S.C.	*Graydon V. Olive Jr.	1970, Mar.
Columbus, Ga.	James Jernigan, N-P	1990, Nov.
Columbus, Oh.	Dana Rinehart, R	1988, Nov.
Commerce, Cal.	*Robert Hinderliter	1973, Aug.
Compton, Cal.	*Laventa Montgomery	1983, Apr.
Concord, Cal.	*Michael Uberuaga	1986, May
Coon Rapids., Minn.	*Richard Thistle	1979, July
Coral Gables, Fla.	*Donald E. Lebrun	1982, Mar.
Corpus Christi, Tex.	*Craig McDowell	1986, May
Corvallis, Ore.	*Gary F. Pokorny	1976, Nov.
Costa Mesa, Cal.	*Allan L. Roeder	1985, Oct.
Council Bluffs, Ia.	*Michael G. Miller	1978, Aug.
Covington, Ky.	*Arnold Simpson	1986, Nov.
Cranston, R.I.	Michael Traficante, R	1990, Nov.
Crystal, Minn.	*John Irving	1963, Jan.
Culver City, Cal.	*Dale Jones	1967, Sept.
Cuyahoga Falls, Oh.	Don L. Robart, R	1989, Nov.
Dallas, Tex.	*Richard Knight	1986, Dec.
Daly City, Cal.	*David R. Rowe	1969, Sept.
Danbury, Conn.	James Dyer, D.	1987, Nov.
Danville, Va.	*Charles Church	1982, June
Davenport, Ia.	Thomas W. Hart, R	1987, Nov.
Dayton, Oh.	*Richard Helwig	1984, Nov.
Daytona Bch., Fla.	*Howard D. Tipton	1978, Oct.
Dearborn, Mich.	Michael Guido, N-P	1989, Nov.
Dearborn Hts., Mich.	Lyle Van Houton, R	1989, Nov.
Decatur, Ill.	*Leslie T. Allen	1972, Sept.
Denton, Tex.	*Larry Harrell	1986, Feb.
Denver, Col.	Federico Pena, D	1991, May
Des Moines, Ia.	*Cy Carney	1985, May
Des Plaines, Ill.	John Seitz, N-P	1989, Apr.
Detroit, Mich.	Coleman A. Young, N-P	1987, Nov.
Dotham, Ala.	*Don J. Marnon	1987, May
Dover, Del.	Crawford J. Carroll, N-P	1988, Apr.
Downers Grove, Ill.	*James R. Griesemer.	1972, Sept.
Downey, Cal.	*Don Davis	1985, Oct.
Dubuque, Ia.	*W. Kenneth Gearhart	1979, Aug.
Duluth, Minn.	John Fedo, N-P	1987, Nov.
Durham, N.C.	*Orville Powell	1983, Mar.
E. Chicago, Ind.	Robert A. Pastrick, D	1987, Nov.
E. Cleveland, Oh.	Darryl Pittman, D.	1987, Sept.
E. Hartford, Conn.	Robert F. McNulty, D	1987, Nov.
E. Lansing, Mich.	*Thomas Dority	1984, Nov.
E. Orange, N.J.	John Hatcher Jr., D	1989, Nov.
E. Providence, R. I.	*James Beeley Jr., act	1986, Dec.
Eau Claire, Wis.	*Eric Anderson	1984, Jan.
Edina, Minn.	*Kenneth Rosland	1977, Nov.

City	Name	Term
Edison, N.J.	Anthony Yelencsics, D	1989, Nov.
El Cajon, Cal.	*Robert Acker	1982, July
El Monte, Cal.	Don McMillen, R	1988, Apr.
El Paso, Tex.	Johnathan W. Rogers, N-P	1989, Apr.
Elgin, Ill.	*James J. Cook	1985, Oct.
Elizabeth, N.J.	Thomas G. Dunn, D	1988, Nov.
Elkhart, Ind.	James Perron, D	1987, Nov.
Elmhurst, Ill.	Robert Quinn, N-P	1989, Apr.
Elmira, N.Y.	*John Gridley	1983, Jan.
Elyria, Oh.	Michael Keys, D	1987, Nov.
Enfield, Conn.	*Robert J. Mulready	1983, Feb.
Enid, Okla.	*Lyle Smith	1979, Feb.
Erie, Pa.	Louis J. Tullio, D	1989, Nov.
Escondido, Cal.	*Vernon Hazen	1982, July
Euclid, Oh.	Anthony Giunta, D	1987, Nov.
Eugene, Ore.	*Michael Gleason	1981, Jan.
Evanston, Ill.	*Joel Asprooth	1982, May
Evansville, Ind.	Michael Vandeveer, D	1987, Nov.
Everett, Mass.	John McCarthy, D	1987, Nov.
Everett, Wash.	William Moore, N-P	1989, Nov.
Fairborn, Oh.	*Michael Hammond	1985, Dec.
Fairfield, Cal.	*B. Gale Wilson	1956, Mar.
Fair Lawn, N.J.	*Joseph Garger	1979, Oct.
Fall River, Mass.	Carlton Viveiros, N-P	1987, Nov.
Fargo, N.D.	Jon Lindgren, D	1990, Apr.
Farmington Hills, Mich.	*William M. Costick	1981, Jan.
Fayetteville, Ark.	*Donald Grimes	1972, Apr.
Fayetteville, N.C.	*John P. Smith	1981, Jan.
Fitchburg, Mass.	Bernard Chartrand, N-P	1987, Nov.
Flagstaff, Ariz.	*Frank Abeyta	1981, Jan.
Flint, Mich.	James Sharp Jr., N-P	1987, Nov.
Florissant, Mo.	James J. Eagan, N-P	1991, Apr.
Fond du Lac, Wis.	*Daniel Thompson	1983, Dec.
Ft. Collins, Col.	*Steven Burkett	1986, Apr.
Ft. Lauderdale, Fla.	*Constance Hoffmann	1980, Oct.
Ft. Lee, N.J.	Nicholas Corbiscello, R	1987, Nov.
Ft. Smith, Ark.	*William Vines, N-P	1990, Nov.
Ft. Wayne, Ind.	Win Moses, D	1987, Nov.
Ft. Worth, Tex.	*Douglas Harman	1985, Mar.
Fountain Valley, Cal.	*Judy Kelsey	1984, May
Fremont, Cal.	*Charles Kent McClain	1981, May
Fresno, Cal.	*James Aldredge	1986, July
Fullerton, Cal.	*William C. Winter	1979, Oct.
Gadsden, Ala.	David Nolen, D	1990, July
Gainesville, Fla.	*W.D. Higginbotham Jr.	1984, Sept.
Galesburg, Ill.	*Lawrence Asaro	1980, Sept.
Galveston, Tex.	*Douglas W. Matthews	1985, Mar.
Gardena, Cal.	*Kenneth Landau	1985, Apr.
Garden Grove, Cal.	*Delbert L. Powers	1980, July
Garfield Hts., Oh.	Thomas Longo, D	1989, Nov.
Garland, Tex.	*James K. Spore	1985, Mar.
Gary, Ind.	Richard G. Hatcher, D	1987, Nov.
Gastonia, N.C.	*Gary Hicks	1973, Dec.
Glendale, Ariz.	*Martin Vanacour	1985, Mar.
Glendale, Cal.	*James M. Rez	1983, Dec.
Grand Forks, N.D.	H.C. Wessman, R	1988, Apr.
Grand Island, Neb	Charles Baasch, R	1990, Nov.
Gr. Prairie, Tex.	*Bob Blodgett	1984, July
Gr. Rapids, Mich.	*G. Stevens Bernard	1981, June
Great Falls, Mont.	*G. Allen Johnson	1981, Jan.
Greeley, Col.	*Sam Sasaki	1987, Mar.
Green Bay, Wis.	Samuel Halloin, N-P	1991, Apr.
Greensboro, N.C.	*T.Z. Osborne	1973, Feb.
Greenville, Miss.	William Burnley Jr., D	1987, Oct.
Greenville, S.C.	*John Dullea	1971, Oct.
Greenwich, Conn.	John Margenot, D, first selectman	1987, Nov.
Groton, Conn.	Catherine Kolnaski, D	1989, May
Gulfport, Miss.	Leroy Urie, D	1989, Apr.
Hackensack, N.J.	*Robert F. Casey	1987, Apr.
Hamden, Conn.	John DeNicola Jr., R	1987, Nov.
Hamilton, Oh.	*J.P. Becker	1984, Dec.
Hammond, Ind.	Thomas McDermott, R	1987, Nov.
Hampton, Va.	*Robert O'Neill Jr.	1984, Oct.
Harlingen, Tex.	*G.D. Sotelo	1981, July
Harrisburg, Pa.	Stephen Reed, D	1989, Nov.
Hartford, Conn.	Thirman L. Milner, D	1987, Nov.
Hattiesburg, Miss.	G.D. Williamson, D	1989, June
Haverhill, Mass.	William H. Ryan, R	1987, Nov.
Hawthorne, Cal.	*R. Kenneth Jue	1977, Jan.
Hayward, Cal.	*Donald Blubaugh	1979, Nov.
Hialeah, Fla.	Raul Martinez, D	1987, Nov.
High Point, N.C.	*H. Lewis Price	1983, July
Hoboken, N.J.	Thomas F. Vezzetti, D	1989, May
Hollywood, Fla.	*James Chandler	1976, Nov.
Holyoke, Mass.	Ernest Proulx, D	1987, Nov.
Honolulu, Ha.	Frank Fasi, R	1988, Nov.
Hot Springs, Ark.	*Michael Wright	1986, Aug.
Houston, Tex.	Kathryn Whitmire, N-P	1987, Nov.
Huntington, W. Va.	Robert Nelson, D	1989, Nov.
Huntington Beach, Cal.	*Charles Thompson	1981, Oct.
Huntsville, Ala.	Joe W. Davis, N-P	1988, July
Hutchinson, Kan.	*George Pyle	1967, Sept.
Idaho Falls, Ida.	Thomas Campbell, N-P	1989, Nov.
Independence, Mo.	*William C. Bullard	1986, Feb.
Indianapolis, Ind.	William Hudnut, R	1987, Nov.
Inglewood, Cal.	*Paul Eckles	1975, Nov.
Inkster, Mich.	*Gregory Knowles	1984, June
Iowa City, Ia.	*Stephen Atkins	1986, July
Irving, Tex.	*Jack Huffman	1974, Jan.
Irvington, N.J.	J. Walter Jonkoski, D	1990, May
Jackson, Mich.	*William P. Buchanan	1985, Nov.
Jackson, Miss.	Dale Danks, D	1989, May
Jackson, Tenn.	Bob Conger, D	1991, May
Jacksonville, Fla.	Tommy Hazouri, D	1991, May
Jamestown, N.Y.	Steve Carlson, D	1987, Nov.
Janesville, Wis.	*Steven Sheiffer	1987, May
Jersey City, N.J.	Anthony Cucci, D	1989, May
Johnson City, Tenn.	*John G. Campbell	1984, June
Johnstown, Pa.	Herbert Pfuhl Jr., R	1989, Nov.
Joliet, Ill.	*John M. Mezera	1987, Jan.
Joplin, Mo.	*Leonard A. Martin	1986, Sept.
Kalamazoo, Mich.	*Sheryl Sculley	1984, Apr.
Kansas City, Kan.	*David Isabell	1985, June
Kansas City, Mo.	*David Olson	1984, Nov.
Kenosha, Wis.	John Bilotti, D	1988, Apr.
Kettering, Oh.	*Robert Walker	1982, Oct.
Key West, Fla.	*Joel L. Koford	1982, Oct.
Killeen, Tex.	*Robert M. Hopkins	1982, Apr.
Knoxville, Tenn.	Kyle C. Testerman, N-P	1987, Nov.
Kokomo, Ind.	Stephen Daily, D	1987, Nov.
LaCrosse, Wis.	Patrick Zielke, N-P	1989, Apr.
La Habra, Cal.	*Lee Risner	1970, Nov.
La Mesa, Cal.	*Ronald Bradley	1980, May
La Mirada, Cal.	*Gary K. Sloan	1981, Apr.
Lafayette, Ind.	James Riehle, D	1987, Nov.
Lafayette, La.	Dud Lastrapes, R	1988, Apr.
Lake Charles, La.	Edward S. Watson D	1989, June
Lakeland, Fla.	*E.S. Strickland	1986, Feb.
Lakewood, Cal.	*Howard L. Chambers	1976, June
Lakewood, Col.	*Larry Rice	1986, May
Lakewood, Oh.	Anthony Sinagra, R	1987, Nov.
Lancaster, Pa.	Arthur E. Morris, R	1989, Nov.
Lansing, Mich.	Terry John McKane, N-P	1989, Nov.
Laredo, Tex.	*Marvin Townsend	1982, June
Largo, Fla.	*D. Russell Barr	1979, Dec.
Las Cruces, N.M.	*Dana Miller	1983, Feb.
Las Vegas, Nev.	Ron Lurie, N-P	1991, June
Lawrence, Kan.	*Buford M. Watson Jr.	1970, Jan.
Lawrence, Mass.	Kevin Sullivan, N-P	1987, Nov.
Lawton, Okla.	*Melissa B. Vossmer	1986, Nov.
Lewiston, Me.	*Lucien Gosselin	1980, July
Lexington, Ky.	Scotty Baesler, N-P	1988, Nov.
Lincoln, Neb.	Bill Harris, D	1991, May
Linden, N.J.	Paul Werkmeister, D	1990, Nov.
Little Rock, Ark.	*Thomas Dalton	1986, June
Livermore, Cal.	*Leland Horner	1978, Oct.
Lombard, Ill.	*William Lichter	1985, Jan.
Long Beach, Cal.	*James Hankla	1987, May
Long Beach, N.Y.	*Edwin Eaton	1979, June
Longmont, Col.	*Geoff Dolan	1987, Jan.
Longview, Tex.	*C. Ray Jackson	1980, Apr.
Lorain, Oh.	Alex Olejko, D	1987, Nov.
Los Angeles, Cal.	Thomas Bradley, N-P	1989, June
Louisville, Ky.	Jerry Abramson, D	1989, Nov.
Lowell, Mass.	*James Campbell	1987, Jan.
L. Merion, Pa.	*Thomas B. Fulweiler	1968, Jan.
Lubbock, Tex.	*Larry Cunningham	1976, Sept.
Lynchburg, Va.	*E. Allen Culverhouse	1979, June
Lynn, Mass.	Albert DiVirgilio, D	1987, Nov.
Lynwood, Cal.	*Charles Gomez	1982, Mar.
Macon, Ga.	George Israel, R	1987, Nov.
Madison, Wis.	F.T. Sensenbrenner Jr., D	1989, Apr.
Malden, Mass.	James S. Conway, D	1987, Nov.
Manchester, Conn.	Barbara Weinberg, D	1987, Nov.
Manchester, N.H.	Robert Shaw, R	1987, Nov.
Manitowoc, Wis.	Anthony V. Dufek, D	1989, Apr.
Mansfield, Oh.	Edward Meehan, R	1987, Nov.
Marion, Oh.	Ronald Malone, D	1987, Nov.
McAllen, Tex.	Othal Brand, R	1989, Apr.
McKeesport, Pa.	Lou Washowich, D	1987, Nov.
Medford, Mass.	Marilyn Porreca, N-P	1987, Nov.
Melbourne, Fla.	*Samuel Halter	1978, July

City	Name	Term
Memphis, Tenn.	Richard C. Hackett, N-P	1987, Oct.
Mentor, Oh.	*Edward Podojil	1977, Nov.
Meriden, Conn.	*Michael Aldi, Act	1986, Nov.
Meridian, Miss.	Jimmy Kemp, D	1989, June
Mesa, Ariz.	*C.K. Luster	1979, June
Mesquite, Tex.	*C.K. Duggins	1976, Feb.
Miami, Fla.	*Cesar H. Odio	1985, Dec.
Miami Beach, Fla.	*Rob Parkins.	1982, Apr.
Middletown, Conn.	Sebastian Garafalo, R	1987, Nov.
Middletown, Oh.	*William W. Burns	1985, Oct.
Midland, Tex.	Carroll M. Thomas, N-P	1988, Apr.
Midwest City, Okla.	*Charles Johnson	1984, Nov.
Milford, Conn.	Alberta Jagoe, D	1987, Nov.
Milwaukee, Wis.	Henry W. Maier, D	1988, Apr.
Minneapolis, Minn.	Donald Fraser, D	1989, Nov.
Minnetonka, Minn.	*James F. Miller	1980, Jan.
Minot, N.D.	*Robert Schempp, R	1977, Nov.
Mobile, Ala.	Arthur Outlaw, R	1989, Aug.
Modesto, Cal.	*Garth Lipsky	1974, Jan.
Monroe, La.	Robert Powell, D	1988, Apr.
Montclair, N.J.	*Bertrand Kendall	1980, Sept.
Montebello, Cal.	*Joseph Goeden	1980, May
Monterey Park, Cal.	*Lloyd de Llamas	1976, Sept.
Montgomery, Ala.	Emory Folmar, R	1987, Nov.
Mt. Lebanon, Pa.	*James Cain	1982, Apr.
Mt. Prospect, Ill.	*John F. Dixon	1987, Mar.
Mt. Vernon, N.Y.	Roland Blackwood, D	1987, Nov.
Mountain View, Cal.	*Bruce Liedstrand	1976, June
Muncie, Ind.	James Carey, D	1987, Nov.
Muskegon, Mich.	*Robert Hagemann	1983, Sept.
Muskogee, Okla.	*Walter Beckham	1984, Feb.
Napa, Cal.	*David Finigan	1986, Sept.
Naperville, Ill.	*Ralph DeSantis.	1986, June
Nashua, N.H.	James Donchess, D	1987, Nov.
Nashville, Tenn.	Richard Fulton, D	1987, Aug.
National City, Cal.	*Tom McCabe	1979, Mar.
New Bedford, Mass.	John Bullard, D	1987, Nov.
New Britain, Conn.	William J. McNamara, D	1987, Nov.
New Brunswick, N.J.	John Lynch, D	1990, Nov.
New Castle, Pa.	Dale W. Yoho, R.	1987, Nov.
New Haven, Conn.	Biagio DiLieto, D	1987, Nov.
New London, Conn.	*C.F. Driscoll.	1969, May
New Orleans, La.	Sidney Barthelemy, D	1990, Feb.
New Rochelle, N.Y.	*C. Samuel Kissinger	1975, Apr.
New York, N.Y.	Edward Koch, D	1989, Nov.
Newark, N.J.	Sharpe James, D	1990, May
Newark, Oh.	William Moore, R	1987, Nov.
Newport, R.I.	*John Connors Jr.	1981, Mar.
Newport Beach, Cal.	*Robert L. Wynn.	1971, Aug.
Newport News, Va.	*Ed Maroney	1987, Jan.
Newton, Mass.	Theodore Mann, R	1989, Nov.
Niagara Falls, N.Y.	*Mark Palesh	1986, Mar.
Norfolk, Va.	*James B. Oliver Jr.	1987, Jan.
Norman, Okla.	*Dave Clark, act.	1986, Dec.
Norristown, Pa.	John Marberger, R	1989, Nov.
North Charleston, S.C.	John Bourne Jr., R	1990, May
No. Chicago, Ill.	Bobby Thompson, D	1989, Feb.
North Las Vegas.	*Michael Dyal	1981, May
No. Little Rock, Ark.	Terry Hartwick, D	1988, Nov.
Norwalk, Cal.	*Ray Gibbs.	1984, Feb.
Norwalk, Conn.	William Collins, D	1987, Nov.
Norwich, Conn.	*M.D. Cunningham	1986, Oct.
Novato, Cal.	*Phillip J. Brown	1974, May
Oak Lawn, Ill.	Ernest Kolb, R	1989, Apr.
Oak Park, Ill.	*J.N. Nielsen	1986, July
Oak Ridge, Tenn.	*Jeffrey J. Broughton	1986, Sept.
Oakland, Cal.	*Henry L. Gardner	1981, June
Oceanside, Cal.	*Suzanne Foucault	1982, Nov.
Odessa, Tex.	*John Harrison	1982, Aug.
Ogden, Ut.	Robert A. Madsen, N-P	1987, Nov.
Oklahoma City, Okla.	*Terry L. Childers	1986, Sept.
Omaha, Neb.	B.R. Simon, D	1989, May
Ontario, Cal.	*Roger Hughbanks, N-P	1975, July
Orange, Cal.	*J. William Little	1985, Jan.
Orange, N.J.	Paul Monacelli, D	1988, July
Orlando, Fla.	Bill Frederick, D	1988, Sept.
Oshkosh, Wis.	*W. O. Frueh.	1976, Aug.
Overland Park, Kan.	*Donald Pipes	1977, June
Owensboro, Ky.	*Max Rhoads	1959, Sept.
Oxnard, Cal.	*David Mora	1985, July
Pacifica, Cal.	*Daniel Pincetich	1985, Dec.
Palm Springs, Cal.	*Norman R. King	1979, Dec.
Palo Alto, Cal.	*William Zaner.	1979, Sept.
Park Ridge, Ill.	*George E. Hagman	1984, July
Parkersburg, W. Va.	William Nicely, R	1989, Nov.
Parma, Oh.	John Petruska, D	1987, Nov.
Pasadena, Cal.	*Donald F. McIntyre.	1973, June
Pasadena, Tex.	John Ray Harrison	1989, Apr.
Passaic, N.J.	Joseph Lipari, N-P.	1989, May
Paterson, N.J.	Frank X. Graves Jr., D	1990, May
Pawtucket, R.I.	Henry Kinch, D.	1987, Nov.
Peabody, Mass.	Peter Torigian, D	1987, Nov.
Pekin, Ill.	Larry Homerin, D	1991, Apr.
Pensacola, Fla.	*Steve Garman	1978, May
Peoria, Ill.	*Thomas Mikulecky	1987, July
Perth Amboy, N.J.	George J. Otlowski, D	1988, May
Petersburg, Va.	*Richard M. Brown	1984, Oct.
Philadelphia, Pa.	W. Wilson Goode, D.	1987, Nov.
Phoenix, Ariz.	Terry Goddard, N-P	1981, Nov.
Pico Rivera, Cal.	*Dennis Courtemarche	1984, Nov.
Pine Bluff, Ark	Carolyn Robinson, D	1988, Nov.
Pittsburgh, Pa.	Richard S. Caliguiri, D	1989, Nov.
Pittsfield, Mass.	Charles L. Smith, D.	1987, Nov.
Plainfield, N.J.	Richard Taylor, D.	1989, Nov.
Plano, Tex.	*Robert Woodruff Jr.	1985, Jan.
Pocatello, Ida.	Richard Finlayson, N-P	1989, Nov.
Pomona, Cal.	*Ora E. Lampman.	1978, July
Pompano Beach, Fla.	*James Soderlund	1984, Sept.
Pontiac, Mich.	Walter Moore, D.	1989, Nov.
Port Arthur, Tex.	*George Dibrell	1962, Oct.
Port Huron, Mich.	*Gerald R. Bouchard	1965, June
Portage, Mich.	*Donald Ziemke	1974, Aug.
Portland, Me.	*Robert Ganley	1986, Sept.
Portland, Ore.	Bud Clark, N-P.	1988, Nov.
Portsmouth, Oh.	*Barry Feldman	1977, Jan.
Portsmouth, Va.	*George Hanbury	1982, June
Poughkeepsie, N.Y.	*William J. Theysohn	1982, Mar.
Prichard, Ala.	John W. Smith, R	1988, June
Providence, R.I.	Joseph Paolino Jr., D	1990, Nov.
Provo, Ut.	Joseph Jenkins, R.	1980, Nov.
Pueblo, Col.	*Lewis A. Quigley	1987, Jan.
Quincy, Ill.	Verne Hagstrom, D	1989, Apr.
Quincy, Mass.	Francis X. McCauley, R.	1987, Nov.
Racine, Wis.	N. Owen Davies, N-P	1989, Apr.
Raleigh, N.C.	*Dempsey Benton.	1983, Dec.
Rapid City, S.D.	Keith Carlyle, N-P	1989, Apr.
Reading, Pa.	William Haggerty Jr., D.	1987, Nov.
Redding, Cal.	*Robert Christofferson	1987, Jan.
Redlands, Cal.	*John E. Holmes	1983, Apr.
Redondo Beach, Cal.	*Timothy Casey	1981, Oct.
Redwood City, Cal.	*James M. Smith	1982, Feb.
Reno, Nev.	*Harold Schilling.	1986, May
Revere, Mass.	George V. Colella, D	1987, Nov.
Richfield, Minn.	*James Prosser	1986, Sept.
Richmond, Cal.	*Larry Moore	1987, Aug.
Richmond, Ind.	Frank Waltermann, D	1987, Nov.
Richmond, Va.	*Robert C. Bobb.	1987, July
Riverside, Cal.	*Douglas Weiford	1980, Mar.
Roanoke, Va.	*W.R. Herbert	1985, Nov.
Rochester, Minn.	*Steven Kvenvold	1979, June
Rochester, N.Y.	Thomas Ryan Jr., D.	1989, Nov.
Rock Hill, S.C.	*Joe Lanford	1979, July
Rock Island, Ill.	*John Phillips	1986, Nov.
Rockford, Ill.	John McNamara, D	1989, Apr.
Rockville, Md.	*Richard Robinson	1986, Feb.
Rome, N.Y.	Carl Eilenberg, R	1987, Nov.
Roseville, Mich.	*Jeanne Riesterer, N-P	1989, Nov.
Roseville, Minn.	*James Andre	1974, May
Roswell, N.M.	*Ralph Fresquez	1986, Jan.
Royal Oak, Mich.	*William Baldridge.	1975, Sept.
Sacramento, Cal.	*Walter Slipe.	1976, Mar.
Saginaw, Mich.	*Vernon E. Stoner.	1987, Feb.
St. Clair Shores, Mich.	*Roy Stype.	1982, May
St. Cloud, Minn.	Robert Huston, N-P	1989, Nov.
St. Joseph, Mo.	*Michael Miller.	1986, Dec.
St. Louis, Mo.	Vincent Schoemehl, D	1989, Apr.
St. Louis Park, Minn.	*James Brimeyer	1980, Aug.
St. Paul, Minn.	George Latimer, D	1989, Nov.
St. Petersburg, Fla.	*Robert Obering.	1985, Oct.
Salem, Mass.	Anthony V. Salvo, D.	1987, Nov.
Salem, Ore.	*Russ Abolt	1983, Jan.
Salina, Kan.	*Rufus L. Nye	1979, May
Salt Lake City, Ut.	Palmer DePaulis, N-P.	1987, Nov.
San Angelo, Tex.	*Stephen Brown.	1982, May
San Antonio, Tex.	Henry G. Cisneros, D	1989, Apr.
San Bernardino, Cal.	Evlyn Wilcox, N-P	1989, Mar.
San Bruno, Cal.	*Gerald Minford	1971, Dec.
San Diego, Cal.	Maureen O'Connor, D	1988, Nov.
San Francisco, Cal.	Dianne Feinstein, D	1987, Nov.
San Jose, Cal.	*Gerald Newfarmer	1983, July
San Leandro, Cal.	*Richard H. Randall.	1986, July
San Mateo, Cal.	*Richard Delong.	1976, Sept.
San Rafael, Cal.	*Pamela Nicolai	1985, Dec.
Sandusky, Oh.	*Frank Link.	1972, Jan.
Sandy City, Ut.	Steve Newton, N-P	1989, Nov.
Santa Ana, Cal.	*David Ream	1986, July

City	Name	Term
Santa Barbara, Cal.	*Richard Thomas	1977, Jan.
Santa Clara, Cal.	*Jennifer Sparacino	1987, Mar.
Santa Cruz, Cal.	*Richard Wilson	1981, June
Santa Fe, N.M.	Sam Pick, D	1988, Mar.
Santa Maria, Cal.	*Robert Grogan	1963, Jan.
Santa Monica, Cal.	James Conn, D.	1988, Nov.
Santa Rosa, Cal.	*Kenneth Blackman	1970, July
Sarasota, Fla.	*David Sollenberger	1986, Dec.
Savannah, Ga.	*Arthur A. Mendonsa	1962, July
Schenectady, N.Y.	Karen Johnson, D	1987, Nov.
Scottsdale, Ariz.	*Roy Pederson	1980, Mar.
Scranton, Pa.	David Wenzel, R.	1989, Nov.
Seattle, Wash.	Charles Royer, D	1989, Nov.
Shaker Heights, Oh.	Stephen Alfred, N-P.	1987, Nov.
Sheboygan, Wis.	Richard Schneider, N-P.	1989, Apr.
Shreveport, La.	John Hussey, D	1990, Sept.
Simi Valley, Cal.	*Lin Koester	1979, Sept.
Sioux City, Ia.	*Alan Harvey	1987, Feb.
Sioux Falls, S.D.	Jack White, R	1991, Apr.
Skokie, Ill.	*Albert Rigoni	1987, Jan.
Somerville, Mass.	Eugene Brune, D	1987, Nov.
South Bend, Ind.	Roger Parent, D	1987, Nov.
South Gate, Cal.	John F. Sheehy, D.	1988, Apr.
S. San Francisco, Cal.	*Mark Lewis	1987, May
Southfield, Mich.	*Robert Block	1985, Jan.
Sparks, Nev.	*Patricia Thompson	1983, Sept.
Spartanburg, S.C.	*Wayne Bowers	1984, Sept.
Spokane, Wash.	*Terry Novak	1978, July
Springfield, Ill.	J. Michael Houston, R	1987, Apr.(1)
Springfield, Mass	Richard Neal, N-P.	1987, Nov.
Springfield, Mo.	*Don G. Busch.	1971, Oct.
Springfield, Oh.	*Gerald Seals	1986, Sept.
Springfield, Ore.	*Steven Burkett	1980, Feb.
Stamford, Conn.	Thom Serrani, D.	1987, Nov.
Sterling Hts., Mich.	*Richard Ives	1986, Feb.
Stillwater, Okla.	*Carl Weinaug	1983, Apr.
Stockton, Cal.	*S.E. Griffith	1984, Dec.
Stratford, Conn.	*Ronald Owens	1984, July
Suffolk, Va.	*John Rowe Jr.	1981, Mar.
Sunnyvale, Cal.	*Thomas Lewcock	1980, Apr.
Syracuse, N.Y.	Thomas G. Young, D	1989, Nov.
Tacoma, Wash.	*Erling O. Mork	1975, June
Tallahassee, Fla.	*Daniel A. Kleman.	1974, Aug.
Tampa, Fla.	Sandra Friedman, N-P	1991, Mar.
Taunton, Mass.	Richard Johnson, D	1987, Nov.
Taylor, Mich.	Cameron Priebe, D	1987, Nov.
Teaneck, N.J.	*Werner H. Schmid	1959, Mar.
Tempe, Ariz.	Harry E. Mitchell, D	1988, Mar.
Temple, Tex.	*Jack Parker.	1985, Apr.
Terre Haute, Ind.	P. Pete Chalos, D	1987, Nov.
Thornton, Col.	Margaret Carpenter, N-P	1987, Nov.
Thousand Oaks, Cal.	*Grant Brimhall	1978, Jan.
Titusville, Fla.	*Norman Hickey.	1974, June
Toledo, Oh.	*C.E. Riser	1985, May
Topeka, Kan.	Douglas Wright, N-P	1989, Apr.
Torrance, Cal.	*Leroy J. Jackson	1983, Jan.
Trenton, N.J.	Arthur Holland, N-P	1990, May
Troy, Mich.	*Frank Gerstenecker	1970, Feb.
Troy, N.Y.	*Steven Dworsky	1986, July

(1) Election Stayed by Federal Court.

City	Name	Term
Tucson, Ariz.	*Joel Valdez	1974, May
Tulsa, Okla.	Richard Crawford, R	1988, Apr.
Tuscaloosa, Ala.	Alvin DuPont, D	1989, June
Tyler, Tex.	*Gary Gwyn	1982, Nov.
Union City, N.J.	Robert Menendez, D	1990, May
Univ. City, Mo.	*Frank Ollendorff	1980, Mar.
Upland, Cal.	*S. Lee Travers	1974, June
Upper Arlington, Oh.	*Richard King	1984, Aug.
Urbana, Ill.	Jeffrey Markland, R	1989, Apr.
Utica, N.Y.	Louis La Polla, R	1987, Nov.
Vallejo, Cal.	*Michael Lynch	1985, Jan.
Vancouver, Wash.	*Paul Grattet.	1980, Aug.
Ventura, Cal.	*John Baker	1986, Nov.
Victoria, Tex.	*James J. Miller	1980, June
Vineland, N.J.	James E. Romano, R	1988, May
Virginia Beach, Va.	*Thomas Muelhenbeck	1982, June
Waco, Tex.	*David F. Smith Jr.	1971, Sept.
Walnut Creek, Cal.	*Thomas Dunne	1972, May
Waltham, Mass.	William Stanley, D.	1987, Nov.
Warren, Mich.	Richard Bonkowski, N-P	1987, Nov.
Warren, Oh.	Daniel Sferra, D	1991, Nov.
Warwick, R.I.	Francis X. Flaherty, D.	1988, Nov.
Wash. D.C.	Marion Barry, D	1990, Nov.
Waterbury, Conn.	Joseph Santopietro, R	1987, Nov.
Waterloo, Ia.	Bernard L. McKinley, R	1987, Nov.
Waukegan, Ill.	Robert Sabonjian, R	1989, Apr.
Waukesha, Wis.	Paul Vrakas, N-P	1988, Apr.
Wausau, Wis.	John Kannenberg, N-P	1988, Apr.
Wauwatosa, Wis.	James Brundahl, N-P	1988, Apr.
W. Allis, Wis.	Jack Barlich, N-P	1988, Apr.
W. Covina, Cal.	*Herman Fast	1976, Aug.
W. Haven, Conn.	Azelio Guerra, D.	1987, Nov.
W. New York, N.J.	Anthony DeFino, D	1991, May
W. Orange, N.J.	Samuel Spina, D	1990, May
W. Palm Beach, Fla.	*Paul Steinbrenner	1986, Jan.
Westland, Mich.	Charles T. Griffin, D	1989, Nov.
Westminster, Cal.	Elden Gillespie, N-P	1988, Nov.
Westminster, Col.	*Bill Christopher	1978, June
Wheaton, Ill.	*Donald Rose	1980, Nov.
Wheeling, W. Va.	*Michael Nau	1985, Oct.
White Plains, N.Y.	Alfred Del Vecchio, R	1989, Nov.
Whittier, Cal.	*Tom Mauk	1980, Sept.
Wichita, Kan.	*Chris Cherches.	1985, Oct.
Wichita Falls, Tex.	*James Berzina	1983, June
Wilkes-Barre, Pa.	Thomas McLaughlin, D	1987, Nov.
Williamsport, Pa.	Stephen Lucasi, R.	1987, Nov.
Wilmington, Del.	Daniel Frawley, D	1988, Nov.
Wilmington, N.C.	*William B. Farris	1983, May
Winston-Salem, N.C.	*Bryce A. Stuart	1980, Jan.
Woonsocket, R.I.	Charles Baldelli, D	1987, Nov.
Worcester, Mass.	*William Mulford	1985, Feb.
Wyandotte, Mich.	James R. DeSana, D	1989, Apr.
Wyoming, Mich.	*James Sheeran	1976, Nov.
Yakima, Wash.	*Richard Zais Jr.	1979, Jan.
Yonkers, N.Y.	*Nicholas De Santis.	1986, Nov.
York, Pa.	William Althaus, R.	1989, Nov.
Youngstown, Oh.	Patrick Ungaro, D	1989, Nov.
Yuma, Ariz.	*Doug Lowe, R	1984, Jan.
Zanesville, Oh.	Donald Lewis Mason, R	1987, Nov.

Government Employment in Selected Cities

Source: U.S. Bureau of the Census

City[1]	Full-time (1,000) 1980	Full-time (1,000) 1985	Per 10,000 population[1] 1980	Per 10,000 population[1] 1985
New York, N.Y.	302	339	427	474
Los Angeles, Cal.	40	42	136	136
Chicago, Ill.	44	43[5]	148	145[5]
Houston, Tex.	17	21	107	121
Philadelphia, Pa.	31	31	186	189
Detroit, Mich.	21	19	172	177
San Diego, Cal.	7[4]	8	83	80
Dallas, Tex.	14	14	153	152
Phoenix, Ariz.	9	9	114	104
San Antonio, Tex.	10	12	125	143
Honolulu, Hai.	9	8	115	103
Baltimore, Md.	38	29	488	378
San Francisco, Cal.	21	25	310	348
Indianapolis, Ind.	12	11	170	156
San Jose, Cal.	4	4[6]	59	61[6]
Memphis, Tenn.	21	19	329	287
Washington, D.C.	39	39	611	633
Milwaukee, Wis.	9	9	144	140
Jacksonville, Fla.	11[4]	8	202[4]	136
Boston, Mass.	24[4]	21	405[4]	360

(1) Ranked by population. (2) Includes city-operated elementary and secondary schools. (3) Includes city-operated university or college. (4) 1979 data. (5) 1982 data. (6) 1984 data.

PRESIDENTIAL ELECTIONS

Popular and Electoral Vote, 1980 and 1984

Source: News Election Service

States	1980 Electoral Vote Carter	1980 Electoral Vote Reagan	1980 Democrat Carter	1980 Republican Reagan	1980 Indep. Anderson	1984 Electoral Vote Mondale	1984 Electoral Vote Reagan	1984 Democrat Mondale	1984 Republican Reagan
Ala. . . .	0	9	636,730	654,192	16,481	0	9	551,899	872,849
Alas. . .	0	3	41,842	86,112	11,156	0	3	62,007	138,377
Ariz.. . .	0	6	246,843	529,688	76,952	0	7	333,854	681,416
Ark.. . .	0	6	398,041	403,164	22,468	0	6	338,646	534,774
Cal.. . .	0	45	3,083,652	4,524,858	739,832	0	47	3,815,947	5,305,410
Col.. . .	0	7	367,973	652,264	130,633	0	8	454,975	821,817
Conn.. .	0	8	541,732	677,210	171,807	0	8	569,597	890,877
Del.. . .	0	3	105,754	111,252	16,288	0	3	101,656	152,190
D.C.. . .	3	0	130,231	23,313	16,131	3	0	180,408	29,009
Fla. . . .	0	17	1,419,475	2,046,951	189,692	0	21	1,448,344	2,728,775
Ga. . . .	12	0	890,955	654,168	36,055	0	12	706,628	1,068,722
Ha. . . .	4	0	135,879	130,112	32,021	0	4	147,098	184,934
Ida. . . .	0	4	110,192	290,699	27,058	0	4	108,510	297,523
Ill.. . . .	0	26	1,981,413	2,358,049	346,754	0	24	2,086,499	2,707,103
Ind. . . .	0	13	844,197	1,255,656	111,639	0	12	841,481	1,377,230
Ia.. . . .	0	8	508,672	676,026	115,633	0	8	605,620	703,088
Kan. . .	0	7	326,150	566,812	68,231	0	7	332,471	674,646
Ky. . . .	0	9	616,417	635,274	31,127	0	9	536,756	815,345
La. . . .	0	10	708,453	792,853	26,345	0	10	651,586	1,037,299
Me. . . .	0	4	220,974	238,522	53,327	0	4	214,515	336,500
Md. . . .	10	0	726,161	680,606	119,537	0	10	787,935	879,918
Mass.. .	0	14	1,057,631	1,056,223	382,539	0	13	1,239,606	1,310,936
Mich. . .	0	21	1,661,532	1,915,225	275,223	0	20	1,529,638	2,251,571
Minn. . .	10	0	954,173	873,268	174,997	10	0	1,036,364	1,032,603
Miss. . .	0	7	429,281	441,089	12,036	0	7	352,192	582,377
Mo. . . .	0	12	931,182	1,074,181	77,920	0	11	848,583	1,274,188
Mon. . .	0	4	118,032	206,814	29,281	0	4	146,742	232,450
Neb. . .	0	5	166,424	419,214	44,854	0	5	187,475	459,135
Nev. . .	0	3	66,666	155,017	17,651	0	4	91,655	188,770
N.H.. . .	0	4	108,864	221,705	49,693	0	4	120,377	267,051
N.J.. . .	0	17	1,147,364	1,546,557	234,632	0	16	1,261,323	1,933,630
N.M. . .	0	4	167,826	250,779	29,459	0	5	201,769	307,101
N.Y.. . .	0	41	2,728,372	2,893,831	467,801	0	36	3,119,609	3,664,763
N.C.. . .	0	13	875,635	915,018	52,800	0	13	824,287	1,346,481
N.D.. . .	0	3	79,189	193,695	23,640	0	3	104,429	200,336
Oh. . . .	0	25	1,752,414	2,206,545	254,472	0	23	1,825,440	2,678,559
Okla. . .	0	8	402,026	695,570	38,284	0	8	385,080	861,530
Ore.. . .	0	6	456,890	571,044	112,389	0	7	536,479	685,700
Pa. . . .	0	27	1,933,740	2,261,872	292,921	0	25	2,228,131	2,584,323
R.I. . . .	4	0	198,342		59,819	0	4	197,106	212,080
S.C.. . .	0	8	428,220	439,277	13,868	0	8	344,459	615,539
S.D.. . .	0	4	103,855	198,343	21,431	0	3	116,113	200,267
Tenn.. .	0	10	783,051	787,761	35,991	0	11	711,714	990,212
Tex.. . .	0	26	1,881,147	2,510,705	111,613	0	29	1,949,276	3,433,428
Ut. . . .	0	4	124,266	439,687	30,284	0	5	155,369	469,105
Vt.. . . .	0	3	81,891	94,628	31,761	0	3	95,730	135,865
Va. . . .	0	12	752,174	989,609	95,418	0	12	796,250	1,337,078
Wash. .	0	9	650,193	865,244	185,073	0	10	798,352	1,051,670
W.Va.. .	6	0	367,462	334,206	31,691	0	6	328,125	405,483
Wis.. . .	0	11	981,584	1,088,845	160,657	0	11	995,740	1,198,584
Wyo. . .	0	3	49,427	110,700	12,072	0	3	53,370	133,241
Total . .	**49**	**489**	**35,481,435**	**43,899,248**	**5,719,437**	**13**	**525**	**37,457,215**	**54,281,858**

Presidential Election Returns by Counties

All results are official. Results for New England states are for selected cities or towns due to unavailability of county results. Totals are always statewide.

Source: News Election Service

Alabama

	1980			1984	
County	Carter (D)	Reagan (R)	Anderson (I)	Mondale (D)	Reagan (R)
Autauga	4,295	6,292	125	3,366	8,350
Baldwin	8,448	18,652	414	7,272	24,964
Barbour	4,458	4,171	65	4,591	5,459
Bibb	3,097	2,491	22	2,167	3,487
Blount	5,656	6,819	75	3,738	8,508
Bullock	3,960	1,446	29	3,537	1,697
Butler	4,156	3,810	,59	3,641	4,941
Calhoun	17,017	17,475	433	12,752	23,291
Chambers	6,649	4,864	122	5,302	8,024
Cherokee	3,764	2,482	63	3,029	3,225
Chilton	4,706	6,615	60	3,924	8,243
Choctaw	3,680	2,859	22	3,373	3,960
Clarke	5,249	5,059	55	4,452	6,282
Clay	2,858	2,764	34	1,456	3,432
Cleburne	2,050	2,389	34	1,238	3,259
Coffee	6,140	6,760	189	4,370	10,558
Colbert	12,550	6,619	209	11,008	9,530
Conecuh	3,102	2,948	29	2,737	3,538
Coosa	2,383	1,714	19	1,781	2,585
Covington	6,305	7,014	110	3,812	9,944
Crenshaw	2,704	2,478	39	1,904	3,261
Cullman	11,525	10,212	228	7,989	14,782
Dale	4,936	7,247	134	3,215	10,319
Dallas	9,770	7,647	131	10,955	9,585
DeKalb	8,820	9,673	107	7,212	12,098
Elmore	5,947	8,688	171	4,198	11,694
Escambia	5,148	6,513	87	3,853	8,694
Etowah	20,790	16,177	358	19,074	19,243
Fayette	3,389	3,315	47	2,533	4,654
Franklin	6,136	4,448	51	4,601	5,304
Geneva	4,703	4,747	67	2,330	6,308
Greene	3,474	1,034	16	3,675	1,361
Hale	3,583	2,074	56	3,289	2,691
Henry	2,973	2,813	18	2,231	3,952
Houston	7,848	14,884	184	6,488	20,834
Jackson	8,776	4,897	156	7,635	6,730
Jefferson	113,069	132,612	3,509	107,506	158,362
Lamar	3,366	2,778	16	1,910	3,943
Lauderdale	15,379	10,467	431	12,907	15,354
Lawrence	6,112	2,456	64	4,866	4,466
Lee	9,606	10,982	643	9,077	16,757
Limestone	8,180	4,574	183	5,410	8,423
Lowndes	3,577	1,524	15	3,567	1,629
Macon	7,028	1,259	36	7,857	1,543
Madison	30,469	30,604	2,246	26,889	50,428
Marengo	5,178	4,048	35	4,811	5,261
Marion	5,450	5,182	61	3,918	6,771
Marshall	10,854	8,159	283	7,704	12,330
Mobile	46,180	67,515	1,333	47,252	81,923
Monroe	4,262	4,615	43	3,725	5,917
Montgomery	28,018	35,745	985	31,206	43,328
Morgan	14,703	13,214	457	11,324	24,103
Perry	4,208	2,262	28	3,731	2,600
Pickens	4,504	3,582	61	3,586	4,685
Pike	4,417	5,220	83	3,541	6,231
Randolph	3,378	3,279	58	2,439	4,940
Russell	8,123	4,485	137	7,610	6,654
St. Clair	5,236	7,768	121	4,000	10,408
Shelby	7,396	14,957	407	5,884	21,858
Sumter	5,015	2,104	45	4,478	2,493
Talladega	10,159	9,902	140	8,490	14,067
Tallapoosa	7,260	5,958	96	4,458	9,045
Tuscaloosa	19,103	19,750	789	16,066	28,075
Walker	13,616	8,795	82	10,591	12,852
Washington	3,520	3,045	24	3,081	4,434
Wilcox	4,951	2,280	13	2,663	2,337
Winston	3,368	4,981	39	2,624	6,845
Totals	**636,730**	**654,192**	**16,481**	**551,899**	**872,849**

Alabama Vote Since 1936

1936, Roosevelt, Dem., 238,195; Landon, Rep., 35,358; Colvin, Proh., 719; Browder, Com., 679; Lemke, Union, 549; Thomas, Soc., 242.

1940, Roosevelt, Dem., 250,726; Willkie, Rep., 42,174; Babson, Proh., 698; Browder, Com., 509; Thomas, Soc., 100.

1944, Roosevelt, Dem., 198,918; Dewey, Rep., 44,540; Watson, Proh., 1,095; Thomas, Soc., 190.

1948, Thurmond, States' Rights, 171,443; Dewey, Rep., 40,930; Wallace, Prog., 1,522; Watson, Proh., 1,085.

1952, Eisenhower, Rep., 149,231; Stevenson, Dem., 275,075; Hamblen, Proh., 1,814.

1956, Stevenson, Dem., 290,844; Eisenhower, Rep. 195,694; Independent electors, 20,323.

1960, Kennedy, Dem., 324,050; Nixon, Rep., 237,981; Faubus, States' Rights, 4,367; Decker, Proh., 2,106; King, Afro-Americans, 1,485; scattering, 236.

1964, Dem. 209,848 (electors unpledged); Goldwater, Rep., 479,085; scattering, 105.

1968, Nixon, Rep., 146,923; Humphrey, Dem., 196,579; Wallace, 3d party, 691,425; Munn, Proh., 4,022.

1972, Nixon, Rep., 728,701; McGovern, Dem., 219,108 plus 37,815 Natl. Demo. Party of Alabama; Schmitz, Conservative, 11,918; Munn., Proh., 8,551.

1976, Carter, Dem., 659,170; Ford, Rep., 504,070; Maddox, Am. Ind., 9,198; Bubar, Proh., 6,669; Hall, Com., 1,954; MacBride, Libertarian, 1,481.

1980, Reagan, Rep., 654,192; Carter, Dem., 636,730; Anderson, Independent, 16,481; Rarick, Amer. Ind., 15,010; Clark, Libertarian, 13,318; Bubar, Statesman, 1,743; Hall, Com., 1,629; DeBerry, Soc. Work., 1,303; McReynolds, Socialist, 1,006; Commoner, Citizens, 517.

1984, Reagan, Rep., 872,849; Mondale, Dem., 551,899; Bergland, Libertarian, 9,504.

Alaska

	1980			1984	
Election District	Carter (D)	Reagan (R)	Anderson (I)	Mondale (D)	Reagan (R)
No. 1	1,772	3,473	440	2,937	5,256
No. 2	1,256	1,612	329	1,857	2,645
No. 3	1,354	2,019	346	1,561	2,540
No. 4	3,899	5,345	1,282	5,293	7,322
No. 5	973	2,847	288	2,896	8,188
No. 6	1,316	5,008	402	1,261	2,883
No. 7	2,620	4,311	676	1,539	4,363
No. 8	2,860	7,432	737	2,752	8,603
No. 9	1,164	2,363	342	3,186	8,361
No. 10	2,778	7,659	849	3,034	7,634
No. 11	3,308	9,741	1,016	2,621	5,176
No. 12	2,456	7,450	829	4,063	5,348
No. 13	1,806	6,170	479	2,616	6,106
No. 14	844	1,473	254	2,843	7,465
No. 15	710	832	213	2,749	8,993
No. 16	1,083	869	204	2,935	9,942
No. 17	1,623	720	280	1,014	3,793
No. 18	1,327	769	193	967	4,858
No. 19	1,168	2,255	267	1,905	3,880
No. 20	5,310	11,673	1,304	2,914	6,538
No. 21	1,022	1,010	223	2,433	3,629
No. 22	1,193	1,081	202	1,319	2,075
No. 23	—	—	—	1,546	2,165
No. 24	—	—	—	1,473	2,321
No. 25	—	—	—	1,825	2,004
No. 26	—	—	—	1,216	3,019
No. 27	—	—	—	1,252	3,270
Totals	**41,842**	**86,112**	**11,155**	**62,007**	**138,377**

Alaska Vote Since 1960

1960, Kennedy, Dem., 29,809; Nixon, Rep. 30,953.

1964, Johnson, Dem., 44,329; Goldwater, Rep., 22,930.

1968, Nixon, Rep., 37,600; Humphrey, Dem., 35,411; Wallace, 3d party, 10,024.

1972, Nixon, Rep., 55,349; McGovern, Dem., 32,967; Schmitz, American, 6,903.

1976, Carter, Dem., 44,058; Ford, Rep., 71,555; MacBride, Libertarian, 6,785.

1980, Reagan, Rep., 86,112; Carter, Dem., 41,842; Clark, Libertarian, 18,479; Anderson, Ind., 11,155; Write-in, 857.

1984, Reagan, Rep., 138,377; Mondale, Dem., 62,007; Bergland, Libertarian, 6,378.

Arizona

	1980			1984	
County	Carter (D)	Reagan (R)	Anderson (I)	Mondale (D)	Reagan (R)
Apache	3,917	5,991	495	7,277	5,638
Cochise	7,028	13,351	1,656	9,671	16,405
Coconino	7,832	14,613	2,815	11,528	17,581

Gila	5,068	7,405	656	6,509	8,543
Graham	2,801	4,765	268	3,080	5,247
Greenlee	2,043	1,537	150	1,963	1,801
La Paz	—	—	—	1,502	2,757
Maricopa	119,752	316,287	38,975	154,833	411,902
Mohave	4,900	13,809	978	7,436	17,364
Navajo	5,110	10,790	710	8,017	11,379
Pima	64,418	93,055	25,294	91,585	123,830
Pinal	9,207	12,195	1,346	11,923	16,464
Santa Cruz	2,089	2,674	482	2,463	3,855
Yavapai	6,664	19,823	1,754	9,609	24,802
Yuma	6,014	13,393	1,373	6,458	13,848
Totals	**246,843**	**529,688**	**76,952**	**333,854**	**681,416**

Arizona Vote Since 1936

1936, Roosevelt, Dem., 86,722; Landon, Rep., 33,433; Lemke, Union, 3,307; Colvin, Proh., 384; Thomas, Soc., 317.

1940, Roosevelt, Dem., 95,267; Willkie, Rep., 54,030; Babson, Proh., 742.

1944, Roosevelt, Dem., 80,926; Dewey, Rep., 56,287; Watson, Proh., 421.

1948, Truman, Dem., 95,251; Dewey, Rep., 77,597; Wallace, Prog., 3,310; Watson, Proh., 786; Teichert, Soc. Labor, 121.

1952, Eisenhower, Rep., 152,042; Stevenson, Dem., 108,528.

1956, Eisenhower, Rep., 176,990; Stevenson, Dem., 112,880; Andrews, Ind. 303.

1960, Kennedy, Dem., 176,781; Nixon, Rep., 221,241; Hass, Soc. Labor, 469.

1964, Johnson, Dem., 237,753; Goldwater, Rep., 242,535; Hass, Soc. Labor, 482.

1968, Nixon, Rep., 266,721; Humphrey, Dem., 170,514; Wallace, 3d party, 46,573; McCarthy, New Party, 2,751; Halstead, Soc. Worker, 85; Cleaver, Peace and Freedom, 217; Blomen, Soc. Labor, 75.

1972, Nixon, Rep., 402,812; McGovern, Dem., 198,540; Schmitz, Amer., 21,208; Soc. Workers, 30,945. (Due to ballot peculiarities in 3 counties (particularly Pima), thousands of voters cast ballots for the Socialist Workers Party *and* one of the major candidates. Court ordered both votes counted as official.

1976, Carter, Dem., 295,602; Ford, Rep., 418,642; McCarthy, Ind., 19,229; MacBride, Libertarian, 7,647; Camejo, Soc. Workers, 928; Anderson, Amer., 564; Maddox, Am. Ind., 85.

1980, Reagan, Rep., 529,688; Carter, Dem., 246,843; Anderson, Ind., 76,952; Clark, Libertarian, 18,784; De Berry, Soc. Workers, 1,100; Commoner, Citizens, 551; Hall, Com., 25; Griswold, Workers World, 2.

1984, Reagan, Rep., 681,416; Mondale, Dem., 333,854; Bergland, Libertarian, 10,585.

Arkansas

	1980			1984	
County	Carter (D)	Reagan (R)	Anderson (I)	Mondale (D)	Reagan (R)
Arkansas	4,303	3,409	193	3,153	4,804
Ashley	4,552	3,960	130	3,373	5,675
Baxter	4,709	9,684	494	4,528	10,870
Benton	9,231	18,830	1,018	7,306	24,296
Boone	4,576	6,778	429	3,356	7,961
Bradley	3,139	1,650	66	2,313	2,690
Calhoun	1,438	896	52	1,058	1,474
Carroll	2,977	4,273	298	2,263	5,041
Chicot	3,445	2,239	26	3,407	2,502
Clark	6,122	2,743	215	4,638	4,185
Clay	3,985	3,091	121	3,279	3,767
Cleburne	4,021	4,042	204	3,172	5,769
Cleveland	1,856	1,124	36	1,378	1,773
Columbia	4,445	5,259	107	3,680	6,526
Conway	4,698	4,145	232	3,742	5,049
Craighead	9,231	11,010	708	8,035	14,047
Crawford	3,948	8,542	245	3,071	9,551
Crittenden	7,022	6,248	185	6,520	6,663
Cross	3,471	2,895	89	2,701	3,917
Dallas	2,838	1,596	74	2,035	2,361
Desha	3,748	2,057	77	2,918	2,696
Drew	3,757	2,272	117	2,638	3,407
Faulkner	8,528	7,544	769	7,169	11,595
Franklin	2,716	3,448	197	2,399	4,382
Fulton	2,037	2,101	83	1,864	2,329
Garland	12,515	15,739	1,042	11,484	21,213
Grant	3,078	2,007	102	2,148	3,167
Greene	5,996	4,514	219	4,730	6,179
Hempstead	4,671	3,852	72	3,327	4,904
Hot Spring	6,897	3,561	244	5,836	5,629
Howard	2,564	2,386	63	1,746	3,079
Independence	5,683	5,076	276	4,415	7,428
Izard	2,750	2,266	160	2,346	2,726
Jackson	4,651	3,191	174	4,038	3,901
Jefferson	17,292	10,697	802	18,082	14,514
Johnson	3,709	3,619	187	3,056	4,720
Lafayette	1,947	1,756	47	1,695	2,290
Lawrence	3,547	3,245	117	2,594	4,039
Lee	3,103	1,711	47	2,541	2,101
Lincoln	2,517	1,243	56	2,406	1,860
Little River	2,631	2,272	41	2,090	3,155
Logan	4,098	4,511	166	3,206	5,663
Lonoke	5,605	5,619	246	4,636	8,425
Madison	2,434	3,180	126	2,133	3,516
Marion	2,046	3,059	160	1,945	3,545
Miller	5,996	6,770	105	4,686	8,302
Mississippi	8,908	7,170	234	7,548	10,180
Monroe	2,686	2,027	82	2,413	2,508
Montgomery	1,878	1,585	86	1,497	2,221
Nevada	2,631	1,697	50	1,783	2,352
Newton	1,436	2,423	100	1,414	2,749
Ouachita	7,152	4,329	248	5,858	6,700
Perry	1,606	1,459	73	1,404	2,047
Phillips	6,642	4,270	163	5,946	4,686
Pike	2,094	1,916	58	1,443	2,665
Poinsett	4,894	4,040	153	3,906	5,622
Polk	2,617	3,993	139	2,101	5,181
Pope	6,364	7,217	471	5,082	10,667
Prairie	1,928	1,855	64	1,437	2,407
Pulaski	54,839	52,125	4,657	54,237	77,651
Randolph	3,070	2,579	125	2,507	3,188
St. Francis	5,816	4,485	132	4,866	5,378
Saline	10,368	8,330	643	5,977	11,709
Scott	2,236	2,228	92	1,609	3,066
Searcy	1,536	2,459	101	1,313	2,819
Sebastian	10,141	23,403	1,023	8,688	27,595
Sevier	2,854	2,502	97	1,942	3,302
Sharp	2,774	3,420	160	2,492	4,392
Stone	1,968	1,793	133	1,654	2,325
Union	6,852	9,401	313	6,208	12,333
Van Buren	2,968	3,090	153	2,529	4,060
Washington	12,276	20,788	1,737	11,319	24,993
White	8,750	8,079	309	6,603	12,666
Woodruff	2,452	1,204	74	2,055	1,675
Yell	3,702	3,187	181	2,679	4,051
Totals	**398,041**	**403,164**	**22,468**	**338,646**	**534,774**

Arkansas Vote Since 1936

1936, Roosevelt, Dem. 146,765; Landon, Rep., 32,039; Thomas, Soc., 446; Browder, Com., 164; Lemke, Union, 4.

1940, Roosevelt, Dem., 158,622; Willkie, Rep., 42,121; Babson, Proh., 793; Thomas, Soc., 305.

1944, Roosevelt, Dem., 148,965; Dewey, Rep., 63,551; Thomas, Soc. 438.

1948, Truman, Dem., 149,659; Dewey, Rep., 50,959; Thurmond, States' Rights, 40,068; Thomas, Soc., 1,037; Wallace, Prog., 751; Watson, Proh., 1.

1952, Eisenhower, Rep., 177,155; Stevenson, Dem., 226,300; Hamblen, Proh., 886; MacArthur, Christian Nationalist, 458; Hass, Soc. Labor, 1.

1956, Stevenson, Dem., 213,277; Eisenhower, Rep., 186,287; Andrews, Ind., 7,008.

1960, Kennedy, Dem., 215,049; Nixon, Rep., 184,508; Nat'l. States' Rights, 28,952.

1964, Johnson, Dem., 314,197; Goldwater, Rep., 243,264; Kasper, Nat'l. States Rights, 2,965.

1968, Nixon, Rep., 189,062; Humphrey, Dem., 184,901; Wallace, 3d party, 235,627.

1972, Nixon, Rep., 445,751; McGovern, Dem., 198,899; Schmitz, Amer., 3,016.

1976, Carter, Dem., 498,604; Ford, Rep., 267,903; McCarthy, Ind., 639; Anderson, Amer., 389.

1980, Reagan, Rep., 403,164; Carter, Dem., 398,041; Anderson, Ind., 22,468; Clark, Libertarian, 8,970; Commoner, Citizens, 2,345; Bubar, Statesman, 1,350; Hall, Comm., 1,244.

1984, Reagan, Rep., 534,774; Mondale, Dem., 338,646; Bergland, Libertarian, 2,220.

California

	1980			1984	
County	Carter (D)	Reagan (R)	Anderson (I)	Mondale (D)	Reagan (R)
Alameda	201,720	158,531	40,834	279,281	190,029
Alpine	[illegible]	[illegible]	[illegible]	154	264
Amador	3,191	5,401	788	4,166	6,970
Butte	19,520	38,188	6,108	25,126	44,836
Calaveras	3,076	6,054	776	3,919	7,339
Colusa	1,605	2,897	325	1,715	3,362
Contra Costa	107,398	144,112	28,209	137,941	167,797
Del Norte	2,338	4,016	486	2,693	3,989

El Dorado	10,765	21,238	3,287	13,969	26,900
Fresno	65,254	82,515	10,727	83,416	101,156
Glenn	2,227	5,386	537	2,480	5,994
Humboldt	17,113	24,047	5,440	24,870	27,495
Imperial	7,961	12,068	1,203	8,231	13,816
Inyo	2,080	5,201	515	2,348	5,811
Kern	41,097	72,842	5,799	44,523	85,872
Kings	7,299	10,531	901	7,317	13,357
Lake	5,978	8,934	1,157	8,292	10,291
Lassen	2,941	4,464	543	3,253	5,338
Los Angeles	979,830	1,224,533	175,882	1,114,578	1,370,813
Madera	7,783	10,599	1,013	8,701	13,853
Marin	39,231	49,678	13,805	56,796	55,845
Mariposa	1,889	3,082	458	2,121	3,571
Mendocino	10,784	12,432	2,747	14,172	16,107
Merced	15,886	18,043	2,316	16,875	25,003
Modoc	1,046	2,579	293	1,219	2,995
Mono	865	2,132	302	944	2,630
Monterey	29,086	47,452	8,008	39,676	54,440
Napa	14,898	23,632	4,218	18,234	25,715
Nevada	7,605	15,207	2,235	10,941	19,440
Orange	176,704	529,797	55,299	200,477	615,099
Placer	17,311	28,179	4,356	20,527	36,565
Plumas	2,911	4,182	783	3,709	5,079
Riverside	76,650	145,642	16,362	99,853	178,397
Sacramento	130,031	153,721	29,655	153,450	197,957
San Benito	2,749	4,054	552	3,454	5,530
San Bernardino	91,790	172,957	19,106	114,710	217,556
San Diego	195,410	435,910	67,491	251,134	487,362
San Francisco	133,184	80,967	29,365	190,396	88,683
San Joaquin	41,551	64,718	8,416	53,441	81,084
San Luis Obispo	20,508	38,631	8,407	26,626	48,331
San Mateo	87,335	116,491	27,985	120,853	133,912
Santa Barbara	40,650	69,629	14,786	49,505	85,458
Santa Clara	166,995	229,048	65,481	224,032	280,425
Santa Cruz	32,346	37,347	10,590	47,240	39,862
Shasta	15,364	27,547	3,220	19,178	32,854
Sierra	651	855	156	781	1,078
Siskiyou	5,664	9,331	1,269	7,130	10,544
Solano	30,952	40,919	6,713	41,435	50,867
Sonoma	45,596	60,722	14,068	69,383	74,014
Stanislaus	33,683	41,595	7,134	36,599	54,085
Sutter	5,103	11,778	1,089	5,526	14,425
Tehama	4,832	9,140	1,014	6,511	11,536
Trinity	1,734	3,048	506	2,204	3,525
Tulare	25,155	41,317	3,244	27,707	50,262
Tuolumne	5,449	8,810	1,390	7,212	10,376
Ventura	56,311	114,930	14,887	64,623	146,647
Yolo	21,527	19,603	6,669	25,264	23,604
Yuba	4,896	7,942	878	4,996	9,265
Totals	**3,083,661**	**4,524,858**	**739,833**	**3,815,947**	**5,305,410**

California Vote Since 1936

1936, Roosevelt, Dem., 1,766,836; Landon, Rep., 836,431; Colvin, Proh., 12,917; Thomas, Soc., 11,325; Browder, Com., 10,877.

1940, Roosevelt, Dem., 1,877,618; Willkie, Rep., 1,351,419; Thomas, Prog., 16,506; Browder, Com., 13,586; Babson, Proh., 9,400.

1944, Roosevelt, Dem., 1,988,564; Dewey, Rep., 1,512,965; Watson, Proh., 14,770; Thomas, Soc., 3,923; Teichert, Soc. Labor, 327.

1948, Truman, Dem., 1,913,134; Dewey, Rep., 1,895,269; Wallace, Prog., 190,381; Watson, Proh., 16,926; Thomas, Soc., 3,459; Thurmond, States' Rights, 1,228; Teichert, Soc. Labor, 195; Dobbs, Soc. Workers, 133.

1952, Eisenhower, Rep., 2,897,310; Stevenson, Dem., 2,197,548; Hallinan, Prog., 24,106; Hamblen, Proh., 15,653; MacArthur, (Tenny Ticket), 3,326; (Kellems Ticket) 178; Hass, Soc. Labor, 273; Hoopes, Soc., 206; scattered, 3,249.

1956, Eisenhower, Rep., 3,027,668; Stevenson, Dem., 2,420,136; Holtwick, Proh., 11,119; Andrews, Constitution, 6,087; Hass, Soc. Labor, 300; Hoopes, Soc., 123; Dobbs, Soc. Workers, 96; Smith, Christian Nat'l., 8.

1960, Kennedy, Dem., 3,224,099; Nixon, Rep., 3,259,722; Decker, Proh., 21,706; Hass, Soc. Labor, 1,051.

1964, Johnson, Dem., 4,171,877; Goldwater, Rep., 2,879,108; Hass, Soc. Labor, 489; DeBerry, Soc. Worker, 378; Munn, Proh., 305; Hensley, Universal, 19.

1968, Nixon, Rep., 3,467,664; Humphrey, Dem., 3,244,318; Wallace, 3d party, 487,270; Peace and Freedom party, 27,707; McCarthy, Alternative, 20,721; Gregory, write-in, 3,230; Mitchell, Com., 260; Munn, Proh., 59; Blomen, Soc. Labor, 341; Soeters, Defense, 17.

1972, Nixon, Rep., 4,602,096; McGovern, Dem., 3,475,847; Schmitz, Amer., 232,554; Spock, Peace and Freedom, 55,167; Hall, Com., 373; Hospers, Libertarian, 980; Munn, Proh., 53; Fisher, Soc. Labor, 197; Jenness, Soc. Workers, 574; Green, Universal, 21.

1976, Carter, Dem., 3,742,284; Ford, Rep., 3,882,244; MacBride, Libertarian, 56,388; Maddox, Am. Ind., 51,098; Wright, People's, 41,731; Camejo, Soc. Workers, 17,259; Hall, Com., 12,766; write-in, McCarthy, 58,412; other write-in, 4,935.

1980, Reagan, Rep. 4,524,858; Carter, Dem., 3,083,661; Anderson, Ind., 739,833; Clark, Libertarian, 148,434; Commoner, Ind. 61,063; Smith, Peace & Freedom, 18,116; Rarick, Amer. Ind., 9,856.

1984, Reagan, Rep. 5,305,410; Mondale, Dem., 3,815,947; Bergland, Libertarian, 48,400.

Colorado

County	1980 Carter (D)	1980 Reagan (R)	1980 Anderson (I)	1984 Mondale (D)	1984 Reagan (R)
Adams	31,357	42,916	8,342	35,285	55,092
Alamosa	1,821	2,601	289	1,720	2,953
Arapahoe	30,148	79,594	15,329	39,891	107,556
Archuleta	532	1,252	83	584	1,557
Baca	551	1,999	106	580	1,903
Bent	894	1,206	164	859	1,314
Boulder	28,422	40,698	13,712	42,195	53,535
Chaffee	1,583	3,327	432	1,779	3,680
Cheyenne	322	816	76	307	892
Clear Creek	837	1,784	402	1,089	2,151
Conejos	1,503	1,597	90	1,553	1,669
Costilla	1,036	489	38	997	621
Crowley	472	926	57	517	993
Custer	231	674	59	241	832
Delta	2,348	6,179	455	2,835	6,678
Denver	85,903	88,398	28,610	110,200	105,096
Dolores	157	615	32	173	667
Douglas	2,108	8,126	1,058	3,011	12,249
Eagle	1,608	3,061	906	2,032	4,500
Elbert	698	2,107	238	802	2,605
El Paso	27,463	66,199	7,886	28,185	88,377
Fremont	3,952	7,162	731	3,895	8,250
Garfield	2,639	5,416	978	3,076	7,111
Gilpin	441	694	175	634	896
Grand	820	2,133	413	1,017	2,865
Gunnison	1,297	2,756	704	1,424	3,100
Hinsdale	76	232	13	98	310
Huerfano	1,574	1,258	146	1,602	1,581
Jackson	283	673	80	191	722
Jefferson	41,525	97,008	19,530	53,700	124,496
Kiowa	331	754	61	265	850
Kit Carson	790	2,622	185	778	2,762
Lake	1,213	1,375	289	1,324	1,364
La Plata	3,034	7,291	1,537	4,040	8,719
Larimer	17,072	36,240	8,887	23,896	49,883
Las Animas	4,117	2,917	278	3,670	2,992
Lincoln	602	1,535	175	587	1,661
Logan	2,332	5,238	588	2,155	5,883
Mesa	7,549	22,686	2,004	9,938	23,736
Mineral	125	271	41	117	333
Moffat	1,079	3,344	329	1,228	3,630
Montezuma	1,467	4,120	275	1,665	4,753
Montrose	2,232	6,685	635	2,864	7,162
Morgan	2,246	5,209	693	2,331	6,097
Otero	3,294	4,801	572	3,005	5,373
Ouray	237	813	129	366	914
Park	674	1,623	293	782	2,041
Philips	640	1,488	193	651	1,689
Pitkin	1,760	2,153	1,128	2,293	3,117
Prowers	1,669	3,115	340	1,467	3,501
Pueblo	21,874	20,770	3,102	27,126	24,634
Rio Blanco	462	1,971	143	484	2,131
Rio Grande	1,370	2,844	185	1,104	3,122
Routt	1,944	3,574	920	2,051	4,239
Saguache	893	1,124	71	867	1,201
San Juan	146	268	94	183	320
San Miguel	651	774	297	654	833
Sedgwick	438	1,151	100	429	1,146
Summit	1,285	2,027	845	1,588	3,253
Teller	802	2,457	322	1,043	3,460
Washington	568	2,007	160	568	2,080
Weld	11,433	23,901	4,309	13,863	31,293
Yuma	1,043	3,220	319	1,121	3,394
Total	**367,973**	**652,264**	**130,633**	**454,975**	**821,817**

Colorado Vote Since 1936

1936, Roosevelt, Dem., 295,081; Landon, Rep., 181,267; Lemke, Union, 9,962; Thomas, Soc., 1,593; Browder, Com., 497; Aiken, Soc. Labor, 336.

1940, Roosevelt, Dem., 265,554; Willkie, Rep., 279,576; Thomas, Soc., 1,899; Babson, Proh., 1,597; Browder, Com., 378.

1944, Roosevelt, Dem., 234,331; Dewey, Rep., 268,731; Thomas, Soc., 1,977.

1948, Truman, Dem., 267,288; Dewey, Rep., 239,714; Wallace, Prog., 6,115; Thomas, Soc., 1,678; Dobbs, Soc. Workers, 228; Teichert, Soc. Labor, 214.

1952, Eisenhower, Rep., 379,782; Stevenson, Dem., 245,504; MacArthur, Constitution, 2,181; Hallinan, Prog., 1,919; Hoopes, Soc., 365; Hass, Soc. Labor, 352.

1956, Eisenhower, Rep., 394,479; Stevenson, Dem., 263,997; Hass, Soc. Lab., 3,308; Andrews, Ind., 759; Hoopes, Soc., 531.

1960, Kennedy, Dem., 330,629; Nixon, Rep., 402,242; Hass, Soc. Labor, 2,803; Dobbs, Soc. Workers, 572.

1964, Johnson, Dem., 476,024; Goldwater, Rep., 296,767; Hass, Soc. Labor, 302; DeBerry, Soc. Worker, 2,537; Munn, Proh., 1,356.

1968, Nixon, Rep., 409,345; Humphrey, Dem., 335,174; Wallace, 3d party, 60,813; Blomen, Soc. Labor, 3,016; Gregory, New-party, 1,393; Munn, Proh., 275; Halstead, Soc. Worker, 235.

1972, Nixon, Rep., 597,189; McGovern, Dem., 329,980; Fisher, Soc. Labor, 4,361; Hospers, Libertarian, 1,111; Hall, Com., 432; Jenness, Soc. Workers, 555; Munn, Proh., 467; Schmitz, Amer., 17,269; Spock, Peoples, 2,403.

1976, Carter, Dem., 460,353; Ford, Rep., 584,367; McCarthy, Ind., 26,107; MacBride, Libertarian, 5,330; Bubar, Proh., 2,882.

1980, Reagan, Rep., 652,264; Carter, Dem., 367,973; Anderson, Ind., 130,633; Clark, Libertarian, 25,744; Commoner, Citizens, 5,614; Bubar, Statesman, 1,180; Pulley, Socialist, 520; Hall, Com., 487.

1984, Reagan, Rep., 821,817; Mondale, Dem., 454,975; Bergland, Libertarian, 11,257.

Connecticut

City	1980 Carter (D)	1980 Reagan (R)	1980 Anderson (I)	1984 Mondale (D)	1984 Reagan (R)
Bridgeport	23,505	19,185	2,793	24,332	24,256
Hartford	27,657	8,138	3,441	29,327	11,621
New Britain	15,649	10,292	3,203	14,608	13,723
New Haven	26,646	14,388	3,930	32,518	16,483
Norwalk	11,785	16,696	3,284	12,509	22,447
Stamford	17,633	23,250	4,669	19,432	29,167
Waterbury	17,992	19,461	3,853	18,217	24,764
West Hartford	14,660	[illegible]	[illegible]	18,883	20,817
Totals	541,732	677,210	171,807	569,597	890,877

Connecticut Vote Since 1936

1936, Roosevelt, Dem., 382,129; Landon, Rep., 278,685; Lemke, Union, 21,805; Thomas, Soc., 5,683; Browder, Com., 1,193.

1940, Roosevelt, Dem., 417,621; Willkie, Rep., 361,021; Browder, Com., 1,091; Aiken, Soc. Labor, 971; Willkie, Union, 798.

1944, Roosevelt, Dem., 435,146; Dewey, Rep., 390,527; Thomas, Soc., 5,097; Teichert, Soc. Labor, 1,220.

1948, Truman, Dem., 423,297; Dewey, Rep., 437,754; Wallace, Prog., 13,713; Thomas, Soc., 6,964; Teichert, Soc. Labor, 1,184; Dobbs, Soc. Workers, 606.

1952, Eisenhower, Rep., 611,012; Stevenson, Dem., 481,649; Hoopes, Soc., 2,244; Hallinan, Peoples, 1,466; Hass, Soc. Labor, 535; write-in, 5.

1956, Eisenhower, Rep., 711,837; Stevenson, Dem., 405,079; scattered, 205.

1960, Kennedy, Dem., 657,055; Nixon, Rep., 565,813.

1964, Johnson, Dem., 826,269; Goldwater, Rep., 390,996; scattered, 1,313.

1968, Nixon, Rep., 556,721; Humphrey, Dem., 621,561; Wallace, 3d party, 76,650; scattered, 1,300.

1972, Nixon, Rep., 810,763; McGovern, Dem., 555,498; Schmitz, Amer., 17,239; scattered, 777.

1976, Carter, Dem., 647,895; Ford, Rep., 719,261; Maddox, George Wallace Party, 7,101; LaRouche, U.S. Labor, 1,789.

1980, Reagan, Rep., 677,210; Carter, Dem., 541,732; Anderson, Ind., 171,807; Clark, Libertarian, 8,570; Commoner, Citizens, 6,130; scattered, 836.

1984, Reagan, Rep., 890,877; Mondale, Dem., 569,597.

Delaware

County	1980 Carter (D)	1980 Reagan (R)	1980 Anderson (I)	1984 Mondale (D)	1984 Reagan (R)
Kent	12,884	14,882	1,831	11,789	21,531
New Castle	76,897	76,898	12,828	76,238	102,322
Sussex	15,973	19,472	1,629	13,629	28,337
Totals	105,754	111,252	16,288	101,656	152,190

Delaware Vote Since 1936

1936, Roosevelt, Dem., 69,702; Landon, Rep. 54,014; Lemke, Union, 442; Thomas, Soc., 179; Browder, Com., 52.

1940, Roosevelt, Dem., 74,559; Willkie, Rep., 61,440; Babson, Proh., 220; Thomas, Soc., 115.

1944, Roosevelt, Dem., 68,166; Dewey, Rep., 56,747; Watson, Proh., 294; Thomas, Soc., 154.

1948, Truman, Dem., 67,813; Dewey, Rep., 69,688; Wallace, Prog., 1,050; Watson, Proh., 343; Thomas, Soc., 250; Teichert, Soc. Labor, 29.

1952, Eisenhower, Rep., 90,059; Stevenson, Dem., 83,315; Hass, Soc. Labor, 242; Hamblen, Proh., 234; Hallinan, Prog., 155; Hoopes, Soc., 20.

1956, Eisenhower, Rep., 98,057; Stevenson, Dem., 79,421; Oltwick, Proh., 400; Hass, Soc. Labor, 110.

1960, Kennedy, Dem., 99,590; Nixon, Rep., 96,373; Faubus, States' Rights, 354; Decker, Proh., 284; Hass, Soc. Labor, 82.

1964, Johnson, Dem., 122,704; Goldwater, Rep., 78,078; Hass, Soc. Labor, 113; Munn, Proh., 425.

1968, Nixon, Rep., 96,714; Humphrey, Dem., 89,194; Wallace, 3d party, 28,459.

1972, Nixon, Rep., 140,357; McGovern, Dem., 92,283; Schmitz, Amer., 2,638; Munn, Proh., 238.

1976, Carter, Dem., 122,596; Ford, Rep., 109,831; McCarthy, non-partisan, 2,437; Anderson, Amer., 645; LaRouche, U.S. Labor, 136; Bubar, Proh., 103; Levin, Soc. Labor, 86.

1980, Reagan, Rep., 111,252; Carter, Dem., 105,754; Anderson, Ind., 16,288; Clark, Libertarian, 1,974; Greaves, American, 400.

1984, Reagan, Rep., 152,190, Mondale, Dem., 101,656; Bergland, Libertarian, 268.

District of Columbia

County	1980 Carter (D)	1980 Reagan (R)	1980 Anderson (I)	1984 Mondale (D)	1984 Reagan (R)
Totals	130,231	23,313	16,131	180,408	29,009

District of Columbia Vote Since 1964

1964, Johnson, Dem., 169,796; Goldwater, Rep., 28,801.

1968, Nixon, Rep., 31,012; Humphrey, Dem., 139,566.

1972, Nixon, Rep., 35,226; McGovern, Dem., 127,627; Reed, Soc. Workers, 316; Hall, Com., 252.

1976, Carter, Dem., 137,818; Ford, Rep., 27,873; Camejo, Soc. Workers, 545; MacBride, Libertarian, 274; Hall, Com., 219; LaRouche, U.S. Labor, 157.

1980, Reagan, Rep., 23,313; Carter, Dem., 130,231; Anderson, Ind., 16,131; Commoner, Citizens, 1,826; Clark, Libertarian, 1,104; Hall, Com., 369; De Berry, Soc. Work., 173; Griswold, Workers World, 52; write-ins, 690.

1984, Mondale, Dem., 180,408; Reagan, Rep., 29,009; Bergland, Libertarian, 279.

Florida

County	1980 Carter (D)	1980 Reagan (R)	1980 Anderson (I)	1984 Mondale (D)	1984 Reagan (R)
Alachua	26,817	19,771	4,167	26,551	30,582
Baker	2,606	2,271	56	1,381	3,485
Bay	12,338	20,815	720	9,381	29,322
Bradford	3,340	2,771	89	2,341	4,128
Brevard	38,915	69,228	5,820	36,963	102,339
Broward	146,322	229,693	31,553	194,542	254,501
Calhoun	2,295	1,504	52	1,312	2,493
Charlotte	9,750	20,433	1,204	11,303	27,464
Citrus	9,148	14,276	784	10,463	20,754
Clay	7,589	15,497	679	5,488	21,545
Collier	7,735	23,878	1,675	9,065	33,603
Columbia	5,677	5,638	246	4,261	8,807
Dade	210,683	265,550	44,723	223,793	324,216
De Soto	2,709	3,340	155	2,302	4,822

Dixie	2,007	1,098	45	1,224	2,204
Duval	90,330	98,389	5,153	77,459	128,653
Escambia	33,378	51,443	2,595	26,798	66,638
Flagler	2,494	2,876	153	2,999	4,907
Franklin	1,772	1,500	53	1,089	2,218
Gadsden	8,207	3,708	201	7,399	5,805
Gilchrist	1,625	1,089	55	1,051	2,056
Glades	1,203	1,096	61	1,070	1,987
Gulf	2,680	2,116	56	1,783	3,573
Hamilton	1,921	1,301	40	1,401	1,921
Hardee	2,597	2,595	83	1,536	3,957
Hendry	2,540	2,696	130	2,018	4,524
Hemando	8,835	12,099	852	12,204	21,273
Highlands	6,685	11,914	531	7,217	16,465
Hillsborough	88,221	106,080	8,939	86,189	157,827
Holmes	2,767	3,208	68	1,231	4,547
Indian River	7,748	15,545	1,184	8,731	23,694
Jackson	7,549	6,331	158	4,956	9,086
Jefferson	2,366	1,621	96	2,055	2,244
Lafayette	1,034	795	22	862	1,513
Lake	13,121	26,775	1,240	12,215	35,304
Lee	28,007	60,717	4,191	30,011	85,006
Leon	28,420	24,840	3,181	29,654	36,301
Levy	4,170	3,203	175	3,103	5,561
Liberty	1,111	895	24	649	1,409
Madison	3,129	2,275	65	2,101	2,816
Manatee	21,660	40,506	2,921	20,887	55,775
Marion	15,362	23,668	1,173	16,221	37,796
Martin	8,078	20,493	1,317	8,976	28,897
Monroe	7,875	11,546	1,914	7,771	16,316
Nassau	5,051	5,414	178	3,483	8,033
Okaloosa	10,738	27,665	1,080	7,289	36,963
Okeechobee	3,226	2,778	156	2,226	4,447
Orange	48,732	87,375	5,389	48,737	122,007
Osceola	6,594	10,839	560	6,627	18,344
Palm Beach	91,932	143,491	15,178	116,071	186,755
Pasco	34,045	50,080	3,565	40,961	66,609
Pinellas	138,307	185,482	17,789	128,547	240,535
Polk	43,291	59,600	2,618	35,505	84,174
Putnam	8,898	8,258	410	7,821	11,424
St. Johns	6,879	11,179	546	6,652	16,493
St. Lucie	10,341	18,107	1,109	13,039	28,189
Santa Rosa	6,964	13,802	606	4,646	21,237
Sarasota	25,557	67,946	4,773	30,512	87,713
Seminole	17,431	39,970	2,451	17,789	56,229
Sumter	4,378	3,666	141	3,460	6,252
Suwannee	4,345	3,894	135	2,788	6,079
Taylor	2,955	2,772	78	1,728	4,030
Union	1,235	1,120	45	761	1,804
Volusia	44,476	52,598	3,296	43,811	68,317
Wakulla	2,078	2,014	111	1,469	3,087
Walton	4,323	4,651	194	2,500	7,117
Washington	3,095	3,222	92	1,916	4,603
Totals	**1,419,475**	**2,046,951**	**189,692**	**1,448,344**	**2,728,775**

Florida Vote Since 1936

1936, Roosevelt, Dem., 249,117; Landon, Rep., 78,248.

1940, Roosevelt, Dem., 359,334; Willkie, Rep., 126,158.

1944, Roosevelt, Dem., 339,377; Dewey, Rep., 143,215.

1948, Truman, Dem., 281,988; Dewey, Rep., 194,280; Thurmond, States' Rights, 89,755; Wallace, Prog., 11,620.

1952, Eisenhower, Rep., 544,036; Stevenson, Dem., 444,950; scattered, 351.

1956, Eisenhower, Rep., 643,849; Stevenson, Dem., 480,371.

1960, Kennedy, Dem., 748,700; Nixon, Rep., 795,476.

1964, Johnson, Dem., 948,540; Goldwater, Rep., 905,941.

1968, Nixon, Rep., 886,804; Humphrey, Dem., 676,794; Wallace, 3d party, 624,207.

1972, Nixon, Rep., 1,857,759; McGovern, Dem., 718,117; scattered, 7,407.

1976, Carter, Dem., 1,636,000; Ford, Rep., 1,469,531; McCarthy, Ind., 23,643; Anderson, Amer., 21,325.

1980, Reagan, Rep., 2,046,951; Carter, Dem., 1,419,475; Anderson, Ind., 189,692; Clark, Libertarian, 30,524; write-ins, 285.

1984, Reagan, Rep., 2,728,775; Mondale, Dem., 1,448,344.

Georgia

	1980			1984	
County	Carter (D)	Reagan (R)	Anderson (I)	Mondale (D)	Reagan (R)
Appling	2,985	1,961	41	1,958	2,929
Atkinson	1,449	747	16	901	944
Bacon	1,622	1,427	32	1,010	1,778
Baker	1,035	510	11	691	675
Baldwin	4,368	3,639	230	3,853	5,717
Banks	2,091	746	18	1,063	1,549
Barrow	3,876	2,284	99	2,367	4,123
Bartow	7,490	3,135	135	4,780	7,104
Ben Hill	2,544	1,459	41	1,859	2,313
Berrien	2,869	1,487	24	1,670	2,395
Bibb	31,770	15,175	848	26,427	24,170
Bleckley	2,014	1,261	47	1,465	1,912
Brantley	2,066	882	17	1,517	1,679
Brooks	2,230	1,546	39	1,661	2,229
Bryan	1,966	1,212	51	1,398	2,265
Bulloch	4,921	3,750	160	3,644	6,117
Burke	3,047	1,871	56	3,127	3,137
Butts	2,574	1,210	38	1,820	2,141
Calhoun	1,414	652	16	1,077	776
Camden	2,924	1,439	62	2,164	2,841
Candler	1,358	1,030	24	1,014	1,497
Carroll	8,202	5,815	294	5,590	11,436
Catoosa	4,921	5,962	121	3,089	7,908
Charlton	1,469	779	26	1,111	1,368
Chatham	28,635	26,499	1,244	28,271	38,482
Chattahoochee	476	256	16	428	459
Chattooga	4,279	1,946	61	2,576	2,953
Cherokee	6,020	5,250	230	3,499	11,146
Clarke	10,519	8,094	1,060	10,132	11,503
Clay	909	316	9	750	419
Clayton	17,540	19,160	923	11,763	31,553
Clinch	1,325	513	18	625	862
Cobb	39,157	51,977	3,229	28,414	97,429
Coffee	4,038	2,499	58	2,633	4,200
Colquitt	5,353	3,593	80	3,208	5,815
Columbia	5,335	6,293	248	3,727	12,294
Cook	2,461	1,188	25	1,510	1,860
Coweta	5,697	4,480	161	3,650	7,981
Crawford	1,673	642	35	1,423	1,298
Crisp	3,403	1,861	54	2,128	2,895
Dade	1,735	2,114	62	1,150	2,750
Dawson	1,072	729	23	643	1,322
Decatur	3,242	2,919	54	2,656	4,134
DeKalb	82,743	74,904	7,241	77,329	104,697
Dodge	4,635	1,719	56	2,513	2,765
Dooly	2,364	1,083	31	1,726	1,435
Dougherty	13,430	12,726	326	12,904	16,920
Douglas	6,807	6,945	304	4,371	12,428
Early	2,110	1,538	23	1,494	2,239
Echols	515	259	8	227	453
Effingham	2,783	2,528	38	2,055	4,266
Elbert	4,014	1,967	50	2,670	3,366
Emanuel	3,971	2,199	45	2,458	3,920
Evans	1,456	1,090	20	1,193	1,601
Fannin	2,526	3,196	61	1,965	4,159
Fayette	3,798	6,351	272	2,861	12,575
Floyd	13,710	9,220	398	8,873	15,437
Forsyth	4,325	3,157	160	2,275	6,841
Franklin	3,528	1,387	30	1,838	2,549
Fulton	118,748	64,909	6,738	125,567	95,149
Gilmer	2,246	2,170	72	1,234	2,972
Glascock	614	510	7	317	827
Glynn	7,540	7,214	296	6,574	11,724
Gordon	5,199	3,107	141	2,607	5,566
Grady	3,023	2,018	56	2,261	3,886
Greene	2,571	961	29	1,992	1,599
Gwinnett	21,958	27,185	1,497	14,139	54,749
Habersham	4,394	2,224	100	2,125	4,647
Hall	12,124	7,760	463	7,421	15,076
Hancock	2,205	573	23	2,109	644
Haralson	3,606	2,229	71	1,938	3,945
Harris	2,807	2,001	100	2,096	3,138
Hart	4,539	1,577	59	2,496	2,842
Heard	1,348	875	35	810	1,492
Henry	5,635	5,326	163	4,096	9,142
Houston	10,915	9,005	536	9,226	14,255
Irwin	1,555	1,056	11	905	1,330
Jackson	4,591	2,209	107	2,717	4,202
Jasper	1,546	879	38	1,122	1,431
Jeff Davis	2,059	1,191	40	1,380	2,233
Jefferson	3,305	1,605	44	2,816	2,999
Jenkins	1,632	824	24	1,108	1,399
Johnson	1,854	1,123	29	1,199	1,733
Jones	3,239	1,828	112	2,781	3,401
Lamar	2,453	1,298	42	1,605	2,198
Lanier	1,116	470	9	741	852
Laurens	7,860	4,392	147	5,471	7,181
Lee	1,670	1,942	26	1,284	2,972
Liberty	3,099	1,507	49	2,803	3,229
Lincoln	1,617	806	10	1,115	1,357
Long	1,202	514	23	816	1,099
Lowndes	5,989	6,622	214	6,167	10,437
Lumpkin	1,951	1,024	83	1,110	1,991
McDuffie	2,667	1,928	59	2,006	3,284
McIntosh	2,104	876	38	1,796	1,512
Macon	3,025	894	39	2,521	1,515
Madison	2,980	2,330	59	1,690	3,768
Marion	1,174	567	16	951	846
Meriwether	3,876	1,838	59	2,864	3,195
Miller	1,127	900	19	526	1,348
Mitchell	3,566	2,231	40	2,791	2,737
Monroe	2,542	1,242	43	2,189	2,420
Montgomery	1,663	948	23	950	1,365
Morgan	2,276	1,323	57	1,714	2,301
Murray	3,094	1,538	42	1,649	3,521
Muscogee	23,272	15,203	811	20,835	23,816
Newton	5,611	3,206	150	3,389	5,810
Oconee	2,141	2,065	106	1,467	3,471
Oglethorpe	1,611	1,187	44	1,238	2,122
Paulding	4,686	2,845	97	2,621	6,048
Peach	3,415	1,642	68	3,369	2,652
Pickens	2,358	1,612	73	1,329	2,801

County	Carter (D) 1980	Reagan (R) 1980	Anderson (I) 1980	Mondale (D) 1984	Reagan (R) 1984
Pierce	1,918	1,027	21	1,501	1,978
Pike	1,755	1,271	45	1,203	1,855
Polk	5,421	2,949	116	3,262	5,435
Pulaski	1,997	1,153	54	1,440	1,509
Putnam	1,951	1,166	35	1,336	1,830
Quitman	589	240	2	490	361
Rabun	2,327	1,070	67	1,267	2,191
Randolph	1,861	879	1	1,454	1,578
Richmond	24,104	19,619	887	21,208	29,869
Rockdale	4,395	5,300	219	3,291	10,121
Schley	613	453	9	403	614
Screven	2,117	1,490	36	1,747	2,583
Seminole	1,794	1,117	16	1,350	1,636
Spalding	7,176	4,809	248	4,878	8,571
Stephens	4,529	2,045	69	2,272	4,057
Stewart	1,440	611	23	1,308	805
Sumter	4,956	2,957	103	3,725	4,607
Talbot	1,635	572	20	1,494	778
Taliaferro	670	270	8	550	318
Tattnall	2,864	2,082	37	1,954	3,641
Taylor	1,845	815	19	1,340	1,292
Telfair	2,700	1,173	41	2,049	1,980
Terrell	2,010	1,378	21	1,598	1,744
Thomas	5,695	4,294	117	4,039	6,427
Tift	4,572	3,280	99	2,736	4,429
Toombs	3,255	2,835	68	2,385	4,470
Towns	1,510	1,475	57	1,007	1,960
Treutlen	1,307	668	21	843	1,086
Troup	7,716	5,398	191	5,272	9,340
Turner	1,990	898	16	1,270	1,329
Twiggs	2,213	747	8	1,755	1,143
Union	1,700	1,546	43	1,112	1,914
Upson	4,713	2,788	77	2,943	4,803
Walker	6,809	7,088	171	5,000	10,734
Walton	4,525	2,618	112	2,481	4,995
Ware	6,307	3,715	77	4,435	5,547
Warren	1,517	779	20	1,258	1,087
Washington	3,452	1,822	60	3,034	2,887
Wayne	3,843	2,213	52	2,434	3,698
Webster	608	312	8	534	402
Wheeler	1,599	550	28	774	833
White	2,017	1,175	58	1,090	2,369
Whitfield	0,601	0,404	229	5,284	11,957
Wilcox	1,780	827	13	1,212	1,218
Wilkes	2,350	1,212	31	1,586	1,837
Wilkinson	2,365	1,116	31	2,103	1,766
Worth	2,567	2,076	35	1,685	2,910
Totals	890,955	654,168	36,055	706,628	1,068,722

Georgia Vote Since 1936

1936, Roosevelt, Dem., 255,364; Landon, Rep., 36,942; Colvin, Proh., 660, Lemke, Union, 141; Thomas, Soc., 68.

1940, Roosevelt, Dem., 265,194; Willkie, Rep., 23,934; Ind. Dem., 22,428; total, 46,362; Babson, Proh., 983.

1944, Roosevelt, Dem., 268,187; Dewey, Rep., 56,506; Watson, Proh., 36.

1948, Truman, Dem., 254,646; Dewey, Rep., 76,691; Thurmond, States' Rights, 85,055; Wallace, Prog., 1,636; Watson, Proh., 732.

1952, Eisenhower, Rep., 198,979; Stevenson, Dem., 456,823; Liberty Party, 1.

1956, Stevenson, Dem., 444,388; Eisenhower, Rep., 222,778; Andrews, Ind., write-in, 1,754.

1960, Kennedy, Dem., 458,638; Nixon, Rep., 274,472; write-in, 239.

1964, Johnson, Dem., 522,557; Goldwater, Rep., 616,600.

1968, Nixon, Rep., 380,111; Humphrey, Dem., 334,440; Wallace, 3d party, 535,550; write-in, 162.

1972, Nixon, Rep., 881,496; McGovern, Dem., 289,529; Schmitz, Amer., 2,288; scattered.

1976, Carter, Dem., 979,409; Ford, Rep., 483,743; write-in, 4,306.

1980, Reagan, Rep., 654,168; Carter, Dem., 890,955; Anderson, Ind., 36,055; Clark, Libertarian, 15,627.

1984, Reagan, Rep., 1,068,722; Mondale, Dem., 706,628.

Hawaii

County	Carter (D) 1980	Reagan (R) 1980	Anderson (I) 1980	Mondale (D) 1984	Reagan (R) 1984
Hawaii	17,630	14,247	3,091	17,866	20,707
Kauai	9,081	5,883	1,352	8,862	9,249
Maui	12,674	10,359	2,237	12,966	14,720
Oahu	96,472	99,596	25,331	107,404	140,258
Absentees	22	27	10	NA	NA
Totals	135,879	130,112	32,021	147,098	184,934

Hawaii Vote Since 1960

1960, Kennedy, Dem., 92,410; Nixon, Rep., 92,295.

1964, Johnson, Dem., 163,249; Goldwater, Rep., 44,022.

1968, Nixon, Rep., 91,425; Humphrey, Dem., 141,324; Wallace, 3d party, 3,469.

1972, Nixon, Rep., 168,865; McGovern, Dem., 101,409.

1976, Carter, Dem., 147,375; Ford, Rep., 140,003; MacBride, Libertarian, 3,923.

1980, Reagan, Rep., 130,112; Carter, Dem., 135,879; Anderson, Ind., 32,021; Clark, Libertarian, 3,269; Commoner, Citizens, 1,548; Hall, Com., 458.

1984, Reagan, Rep., 184,934; Mondale, Dem., 147,098; Bergland, Libertarian, 2,167.

Idaho

County	Carter (D) 1980	Reagan (R) 1980	Anderson (I) 1980	Mondale (D) 1984	Reagan (R) 1984
Ada	21,324	55,205	7,987	21,760	60,036
Adams	590	1,189	88	540	1,381
Bannock	8,639	18,477	1,896	9,399	18,742
Bear Lake	508	2,941	63	481	2,760
Benewah	1,361	2,111	286	1,447	2,039
Bingham	2,933	11,781	489	3,064	11,900
Blaine	1,840	2,716	775	1,971	3,603
Boise	518	1,134	86	436	1,249
Bonner	4,060	6,727	[illegible]	4,628	8,889
Bonneville	5,052	24,715	1,355	4,877	24,392
Boundary	1,087	2,088	225	1,158	2,159
Butte	424	1,275	35	429	1,245
Camas	145	360	16	123	364
Canyon	9,172	24,375	1,798	7,527	24,613
Caribou	481	3,234	106	535	3,032
Cassias	1,309	6,511	212	1,036	6,503
Clark	87	379	11	59	353
Clearwater	1,699	2,178	291	1,608	2,176
Custer	398	1,398	64	461	1,653
Elmore	1,760	3,994	311	1,458	4,595
Franklin	511	3,669	61	439	3,261
Fremont	926	4,167	108	818	4,006
Gem	1,613	3,766	218	1,607	3,644
Gooding	1,481	3,897	218	1,247	3,819
Idaho	2,078	4,425	409	1,996	4,219
Jefferson	833	5,860	135	743	5,770
Jerome	1,308	4,802	178	1,284	4,913
Kootenai	7,521	17,022	1,808	9,004	17,330
Latah	6,037	6,907	2,405	5,571	7,709
Lemhi	794	2,646	167	852	2,810
Lewis	774	1,088	160	648	1,000
Lincoln	462	1,294	83	386	1,211
Madison	728	[illegible]	64	483	[illegible]
Minidoka	1,689	6,035	260	1,398	5,938
Nez Perce	6,565	7,495	1,344	5,981	8,153
Oneida	434	1,461	50	360	1,528
Owyhee	702	2,257	[illegible]	574	2,141
Payette	1,828	4,508	253	1,410	4,605
Power	727	2,235	119	678	2,298
Shoshone	3,102	3,994	407	3,033	3,156
Teton	360	1,227	67	370	1,242
Twin Falls	4,835	17,425	976	4,567	16,974
Valley	926	2,041	245	945	2,299
Washington	1,421	2,915	172	1,119	3,015
Totals	110,192	290,699	27,058	108,510	297,523

Idaho Vote Since 1936

1936, Roosevelt, Dem., 125,683; Landon, Rep., 66,256; Lemke, Union, 7,684.

1940, Roosevelt, Dem., 127,842; Willkie, Rep., 106,553; Thomas, Soc., 497; Browder, Com., 276.

1944, Roosevelt, Dem., 107,399; Dewey, Rep., 100,137; Watson, Proh., 503; Thomas, Soc., 282.

1948, Truman, Dem., 107,370; Dewey, Rep., 101,514; Wallace, Prog., 4,972; Watson, Proh., 628; Thomas, Soc., 332.

1952, Eisenhower, Rep., 180,707; Stevenson Dem., 95,081; Hallinan, Prog., 443; write-in, 23.

1956, Eisenhower, Rep., 166,979; Stevenson, Dem., 105,868; Andrews, Ind., 126; write-in, 16.

1960, Kennedy, Dem., 138,853; Nixon, Rep., 161,597.

1964, Johnson, Dem., 148,920; Goldwater, Rep., 143,557.

1968, Nixon, Rep., 165,369; Humphrey, Dem., 89,273; Wallace, 3d party, 36,541.

1972, Nixon, Rep., 199,384; McGovern, Dem., 80,826; Schmitz, Amer., 28,869; Spock, Peoples, 903.

1976, Carter, Dem., 126,549; Ford, Rep., 204,151; Maddox, Amer., 5,935; MacBride, Libertarian, 3,558; LaRouche, U.S. Labor, 739.

1980, Reagan, Rep., 290,699; Carter, Dem., 110,192; Anderson, Ind., 27,058; Clark, Libertarian, 8,425; Rarick, Amer., 1,057.

1984, Reagan, Rep., 297,523; Mondale, Dem., 108,510; Bergland, Libertarian, 2,823.

Illinois

	1980			1984	
County	Carter (D)	Reagan (R)	Anderson (I)	Mondale (D)	Reagan (R)
Adams	10,606	19,842	1,202	10,336	20,225
Alexander	2,925	2,650	74	2,872	2,574
Bond	2,834	4,398	244	2,870	4,240
Boone	3,175	6,697	1,578	3,717	7,536
Brown	950	1,660	59	959	1,478
Bureau	5,753	11,484	1,093	6,925	11,741
Calhoun	1,208	1,591	76	1,443	1,648
Carroll	2,154	5,084	705	2,398	5,237
Cass	2,543	3,965	199	2,937	3,435
Champaign	21,017	33,329	9,972	27,266	39,224
Christian	6,625	8,770	499	7,541	8,534
Clark	2,855	5,476	243	3,032	5,318
Clay	2,587	4,447	187	2,524	4,562
Clinton	4,470	8,500	528	4,628	9,233
Coles	6,743	11,994	1,726	7,156	14,044
Cook	1,124,584	856,574	149,712	1,112,641	1,055,558
Crawford	3,372	5,894	341	3,130	6,261
Cumberland	1,892	3,159	190	1,733	3,002
DeKalb	8,913	16,370	4,526	10,942	20,294
DeWitt	2,262	4,648	368	2,352	4,534
Douglas	2,564	5,330	344	2,886	5,691
DuPage	68,991	182,308	29,810	71,430	227,141
Edgar	3,394	6,639	400	3,241	6,821
Edwards	1,041	2,556	118	1,057	2,778
Effingham	4,229	9,104	393	3,841	9,617
Fayette	3,614	6,523	229	3,844	6,607
Ford	1,803	5,024	328	1,763	4,871
Franklin	9,425	9,731	558	10,667	9,656
Fulton	7,481	10,316	838	9,131	9,147
Gallatin	1,678	1,700	78	2,164	1,939
Greene	2,607	4,224	220	2,563	4,057
Grundy	3,970	8,397	701	4,671	9,595
Hamilton	1,990	3,254	171	2,251	3,074
Hancock	3,522	6,597	383	3,713	6,251
Hardin	1,314	1,721	56	1,205	1,689
Henderson	1,609	2,443	143	1,969	2,289
Henry	7,977	14,506	1,440	10,679	14,504
Iroquois	3,362	11,247	592	3,300	11,327
Jackson	10,291	10,505	2,526	12,105	13,609
Jasper	1,846	3,548	157	1,750	3,673
Jefferson	6,761	8,972	506	7,200	9,642
Jersey	3,324	5,266	314	3,762	5,146
JoDaviess	2,678	5,186	983	3,348	5,877
Johnson	1,586	3,201	84	1,647	3,424
Kane	29,015	64,106	9,179	31,875	72,655
Kankakee	14,626	23,810	1,802	15,246	23,807
Kendall	3,143	10,028	979	3,789	10,872
Knox	8,749	14,907	2,069	12,027	14,974
Lake	48,287	96,350	17,726	53,947	118,401
LaSalle	16,818	27,323	3,041	20,532	27,388
Lawrence	3,030	4,453	293	2,924	4,686
Lee	3,170	11,373	781	3,919	11,178
Livingston	4,111	11,544	980	4,567	12,291
Logan	3,916	9,681	650	4,052	9,932
McDonough	4,093	8,995	1,230	4,561	9,383
McHenry	14,540	40,045	5,871	14,420	47,282
McLean	13,587	30,096	4,961	15,880	32,221
Macon	22,325	28,298	2,804	25,463	30,457
Macoupin	9,116	12,131	901	10,602	12,282
Madison	43,860	51,160	4,206	48,352	57,021
Marion	6,990	10,969	567	7,599	11,300
Marshall	1,903	4,349	336	2,386	4,060
Mason	2,680	4,644	267	3,354	4,109
Massac	2,821	4,284	124	3,194	3,827
Menard	1,589	3,622	274	1,826	3,925
Mercer	3,361	5,144	540	3,982	4,907
Monroe	3,121	6,315	405	3,256	6,936
Montgomery	5,721	8,947	611	6,360	8,191
Morgan	5,483	10,406	900	5,361	10,683
Moultrie	2,332	3,495	280	2,458	3,593
Ogle	4,067	12,533	2,042	4,803	13,503
Peoria	28,276	47,815	6,169	36,830	45,607
Perry	4,337	5,888	319	4,584	5,852
Piatt	2,421	4,867	447	2,840	5,000
Pike	3,695	5,301	303	3,965	5,295
Pope	880	1,501	58	940	1,545
Pulaski	1,955	2,083	49	1,724	1,923
Putnam	1,158	1,959	235	1,487	1,912
Randolph	6,052	8,810	514	6,355	9,415
Richland	2,463	5,241	358	2,182	5,665
Rock Island	30,045	34,788	5,818	40,208	35,121
St. Clair	50,046	46,063	3,879	52,294	51,046
Saline	5,683	7,157	321	6,038	7,176
Sangamon	29,354	49,372	5,439	34,059	54,086
Schuyler	1,445	2,799	155	1,533	2,515
Scott	941	1,990	80	943	1,976
Shelby	3,988	6,441	381	4,317	6,372
Stark	806	2,358	147	1,072	2,228
Stephenson	6,195	10,779	3,145	6,723	14,237
Tazewell	16,924	35,481	3,206	23,095	33,782
Union	3,781	4,289	291	3,815	4,721
Vermilion	14,498	22,579	2,110	16,530	22,932
Wabash	1,975	3,571	230	1,795	3,639
Warren	2,756	5,667	489	3,318	5,846
Washington	2,158	5,354	205	2,363	5,129
Wayne	3,258	6,013	222	2,621	6,298
White	3,463	5,279	274	3,457	5,500
Whiteside	7,191	17,389	1,242	11,226	16,743
Will	41,975	69,310	7,855	45,193	78,684
Williamson	10,779	14,451	793	11,614	14,930
Winnebago	32,384	48,825	22,596	44,629	64,203
Woodford	3,552	10,791	711	4,425	10,758
Totals	**1,981,413**	**2,358,049**	**346,754**	**2,086,499**	**2,707,103**

Illinois Vote Since 1936

1936, Roosevelt, Dem., 2,282,999; Landon, Rep., 1,570,393; Lemke, Union, 89,439; Thomas, Soc., 7,530; Colvin, Proh., 3,439; Aiken, Soc. Labor, 1,921.

1940, Roosevelt, Dem., 2,149,934; Willkie, Rep., 2,047,240; Thomas, Soc., 10,914; Babson, Proh., 9,190.

1944, Roosevelt, Dem., 2,079,479; Dewey, Rep., 1,939,314; Teichert, Soc. Labor, 9,677; Watson, Proh., 7,411; Thomas, Soc., 180.

1948, Truman, Dem., 1,994,715; Dewey, Rep., 1,961,103; Watson, Proh., 11,959; Thomas, Soc., 11,522; Teichert, Soc. Labor, 3,118.

1952, Eisenhower, Rep., 2,457,327; Stevenson, Dem., 2,013,920; Hass, Soc. Labor, 9,363; write-in, 448.

1956, Eisenhower, Rep., 2,623,327; Stevenson, Dem., 1,775,682; Hass, Soc. Labor, 8,342; write-in, 56.

1960, Kennedy, Dem., 2,377,846; Nixon, Rep., 2,368,988; Hass, Soc. Labor, 10,560; write-in, 15.

1964, Johnson, Dem., 2,796,833; Goldwater, Rep., 1,905,946; write-in, 62.

1968, Nixon, Rep., 2,174,774; Humphrey, Dem., 2,039,814; Wallace, 3d party, 390,958; Blomen, Soc. Labor, 13,878; write-in, 325.

1972, Nixon, Rep. 2,788,179; McGovern, Dem., 1,913,472; Fisher, Soc. Labor, 12,344; Schmitz, Amer., 2,471; Hall, Com., 4,541; others, 2,229.

1976, Carter, Dem., 2,271,295; Ford, Rep., 2,364,269; McCarthy, Ind., 55,939; Hall, Com., 9,250; MacBride, Libertarian, 8,057; Camejo, Soc. Workers, 3,615; Levin, Soc. Labor, 2,422; LaRouche, U.S. Labor, 2,018; write-in, 1,968.

1980, Reagan, Rep., 2,358,049; Carter, Dem., 1,981,413; Anderson, Ind., 346,754; Clark, Libertarian, 38,939; Commoner, Citizens, 10,692; Hall, Com., 9,711; Griswold, Workers World, 2,257; DeBerry, Socialist Workers, 1,302; write-ins, 604.

1984, Reagan, Rep., 2,707,103; Mondale, Dem., 2,086,499; Bergland, Libertarian, 10,086.

Indiana

	1980			1984	
County	Carter (D)	Reagan (R)	Anderson (I)	Mondale (D)	Reagan (R)
Adams	4,673	6,368	767	3,923	7,958
Allen	37,765	68,524	10,368	38,462	75,505
Bartholomew	9,260	15,801	1,604	8,075	18,704
Benton	1,520	3,189	187	1,357	3,281
Blackford	2,431	3,168	258	2,395	3,787
Boone	4,535	10,484	681	3,982	11,790
Brown	2,014	2,884	237	2,657	3,517
Carroll	2,966	5,262	338	2,774	5,528
Cass	5,838	11,500	696	5,521	12,355
Clark	14,137	15,508	1,102	14,138	19,419
Clay	4,363	6,980	311	3,707	6,957
Clinton	5,258	8,158	427	4,329	8,969
Crawford	2,130	2,554	124	2,256	2,633
Daviess	4,057	7,022	345	3,545	7,721
Dearborn	5,135	7,467	464	4,920	9,149
Decatur	3,646	5,819	377	2,766	6,551
Dekalb	4,911	7,886	883	4,617	8,769
Delaware	20,923	28,342	2,743	19,791	30,092
Dubois	6,700	6,775	578	5,423	9,391
Elkhart	14,883	30,081	3,256	13,240	34,621
Fayette	4,304	6,004	293	4,122	7,142
Floyd	11,543	12,456	1,047	10,616	15,466
Fountain	2,845	5,289	280	2,897	5,450
Franklin	2,834	4,551	234	2,225	5,202
Fulton	2,788	5,458	349	2,527	6,057
Gibson	6,834	7,643	591	7,082	8,618
Grant	10,390	19,078	1,043	9,986	20,482
Greene	6,027	7,452	299	5,267	8,438
Hamilton	7,036	26,218	1,736	6,364	30,254
Hancock	5,124	12,093	746	4,550	12,880
Harrison	4,865	6,287	341	4,634	7,255
Hendricks	7,412	19,366	1,048	6,659	21,307
Henry	7,626	12,724	562	7,064	11,926

Howard	12,916	21,272	1,325	10,458	22,386
Huntington	5,415	9,497	824	4,598	10,805
Jackson	6,425	8,903	430	5,163	9,879
Jasper	2,544	6,316	283	2,821	6,537
Jay	3,256	5,351	484	3,174	5,975
Jefferson	5,496	6,831	477	4,952	7,482
Jennings	3,931	5,498	281	3,264	6,356
Johnson	8,445	20,018	1,348	7,715	23,482
Knox	7,829	10,083	617	6,417	10,872
Kosciusko	5,684	15,633	1,164	4,877	17,560
LaGrange	2,095	4,259	377	1,884	4,772
Lake	101,145	95,408	8,275	117,984	94,870
LaPorte	15,387	22,424	2,080	15,904	23,346
Lawrence	5,826	10,846	380	5,608	11,440
Madison	23,554	35,582	2,389	22,254	36,510
Marion	126,103	168,680	15,709	130,185	184,880
Marshall	5,113	10,209	836	4,931	11,100
Martin	2,479	3,082	149	1,937	3,363
Miami	4,927	8,672	508	4,224	9,551
Monroe	13,316	18,233	3,921	14,719	21,772
Montgomery	4,158	9,936	622	3,626	11,119
Morgan	5,439	13,321	498	4,627	14,884
Newton	1,649	3,850	194	1,596	3,560
Noble	4,721	7,624	749	4,237	8,459
Ohio	1,074	1,264	57	1,068	1,503
Orange	3,228	5,073	181	2,571	5,909
Owen	2,325	3,632	188	2,082	4,204
Parke	2,432	4,595	194	2,205	5,052
Perry	4,540	4,350	448	4,760	4,785
Pike	3,346	3,343	190	3,231	3,089
Porter	12,869	30,055	3,061	17,862	32,505
Posey	4,465	6,096	667	4,452	6,472
Pulaski	2,092	3,916	175	2,008	4,167
Putnam	3,996	7,090	501	3,392	7,820
Randolph	4,025	7,762	426	3,805	7,793
Ripley	4,022	5,770	303	3,336	7,143
Rush	2,388	4,829	224	2,307	5,429
St. Joseph	44,218	50,607	6,962	47,513	54,404
Scott	3,694	3,432	139	3,460	4,110
Shelby	5,861	10,496	614	5,357	11,056
Spencer	4,153	5,284	196	4,005	5,816
Starke	3,615	5,035	297	3,674	5,104
Steuben	2,606	5,670	602	2,441	6,424
Sullivan	4,335	4,465	212	4,006	4,771
Switzerland	1,704	1,584	38	1,484	1,857
Tippecanoe	14,636	27,589	5,141	15,789	29,706
Tipton	2,547	5,150	285	2,328	5,687
Union	898	1,766	92	816	1,970
Vanderburgh	29,930	36,248	4,150	31,049	40,994
Vermillion	3,793	4,195	269	3,666	4,428
Vigo	19,261	24,133	2,484	18,429	26,259
Wabash	4,620	8,738	797	4,077	9,862
Warren	1,287	2,665	145	1,309	2,525
Warrick	6,845	8,681	890	6,345	10,203
Washington	3,663	5,234	191	3,334	5,874
Wayne	9,599	16,981	1,174	10,173	18,955
Wells	3,760	5,864	717	3,274	7,579
White	3,247	6,999	466	3,157	7,079
Whitley	4,497	7,146	928	3,690	7,763
Totals	844,197	1,255,656	111,639	841,481	1,377,230

Indiana Vote Since 1936

1936, Roosevelt, Dem., 943,974; Landon, Rep., 691,570; Lemke, Union, 19,407; Thomas, Soc., 3,856; Browder, Com., 1,090.

1940, Roosevelt, Dem., 874,063; Willkie, Rep., 899,466; Babson, Proh., 6,437; Thomas, Soc., 2,075; Aiken, Soc. Labor, 706.

1944, Roosevelt, Dem., 781,403; Dewey, Rep., 875,891; Watson, Proh., 12,574; Thomas, Soc., 2,223.

1948, Truman, Dem., 807,833; Dewey, Rep., 821,079; Watson, Proh., 14,711; Wallace, Prog., 9,649; Thomas, Soc., 2,179; Teichert, Soc. Labor, 763.

1952, Eisenhower, Rep., 1,136,259; Stevenson, Dem., 801,530; Hamblen, Proh., 15,335; Hallinan, Prog., 1,222; Hass, Soc. Labor, 979.

1956, Eisenhower, Rep., 1,182,811; Stevenson, Dem., 783,908; Holtwick, Proh., 6,554; Hass, Soc. Labor, 1,334.

1960, Kennedy, Dem., 952,358; Nixon, Rep., 1,175,120; Decker, Proh., 6,746; Hass, Soc. Labor, 1,136.

1964, Johnson, Dem. 1,170,848; Goldwater, Rep., 911,118; Munn, Proh., 8,266; Hass, Soc. Labor, 1,374.

1968, Nixon, Rep., 1,067,885; Humphrey, Dem., 806,659; Wallace, 3d party, 243,108; Munn, Proh., 4,616; Halstead, Soc. Worker, 1,293; Gregory, write-in, 36.

1972, Nixon, Rep., 1,405,154; McGovern, Dem., 708,568; Reed, Soc. Workers, 5,575; Fisher, Soc. Labor, 1,688; Spock, Peace & Freedom, 4,544.

1976, Carter, Dem., 1,014,714; Ford, Rep., 1,185,958; Anderson, Amer., 14,048; Camejo, Soc. Workers, 5,695; LaRouche, U.S. Labor, 1,947.

1980 Reagan, Rep., 1,255,656; Carter, Dem., 844,197; Anderson, Ind., 111,639; Clark, Libertarian, 19,627; Commoner, Citizens, 4,852; Greaves, American, 4,750; Hall, Com., 702; DeBerry, Soc., 610.

1984 Reagan, Rep., 1,377,230; Mondale, Dem., 841,481; Bergland, Libertarian, 6,741.

Iowa

County	1980 Carter (D)	1980 Reagan (R)	1980 Anderson (I)	1984 Mondale (D)	1984 Reagan (R)
Adair	1,454	2,821	356	1,979	2,615
Adams	940	1,779	214	1,221	1,706
Allamakee	2,170	4,000	343	2,282	3,997
Appanoose	2,769	3,544	353	3,289	3,412
Audubon	1,546	2,523	251	1,854	2,306
Benton	4,223	5,329	948	4,993	5,566
Black Hawk	27,443	29,627	5,847	31,467	32,262
Boone	5,126	5,732	1,081	6,485	5,746
Bremer	3,527	6,706	970	4,084	6,895
Buchanan	3,605	5,041	689	4,129	4,965
Buena Vista	3,468	5,272	771	4,109	5,193
Butler	1,990	4,730	392	2,323	4,570
Calhoun	2,150	3,633	407	2,541	3,311
Carroll	3,885	5,017	736	4,960	5,021
Cass	2,176	5,391	475	2,417	5,053
Cedar	2,589	4,398	697	3,086	4,617
Cerro Gordo	9,363	11,189	2,024	11,570	11,214
Cherokee	2,719	4,087	599	3,349	4,046
Chickasaw	2,935	3,929	500	3,186	3,661
Clarke	1,614	2,417	310	2,030	2,262
Clay	3,179	4,479	991	3,774	4,450
Clayton	3,297	5,115	669	3,446	5,029
Clinton	9,698	13,025	2,140	11,240	13,914
Crawford	2,500	4,883	509	3,396	4,552
Dallas	5,310	6,296	1,200	6,564	6,080
Davis	1,689	2,003	200	2,187	1,956
Decatur	2,048	2,212	318	2,098	2,104
Delaware	2,671	4,316	727	3,158	4,760
Des Moines	9,977	9,158	1,041	11,173	9,559
Dickinson	2,620	4,028	687	3,025	4,064
Dubuque	18,689	18,640	3,700	21,070	19,239
Emmet	2,153	3,062	446	2,746	2,946
Fayette	4,377	6,374	647	4,677	6,505
Floyd	3,634	4,665	728	4,154	4,341
Franklin	1,920	3,290	406	2,349	3,129
Fremont	1,203	2,693	191	1,426	2,686
Greene	2,210	3,154	510	2,831	2,579
Grundy	1,869	4,644	440	1,915	4,527
Guthrie	1,866	3,214	384	2,517	2,783
Hamilton	2,741	4,745	679	3,330	4,279
Hancock	1,918	3,681	462	2,639	3,362
Hardin	3,757	5,329	730	4,477	5,195
Harrison	2,152	4,502	311	2,495	4,352
Henry	3,317	4,430	629	3,377	4,616
Howard	2,214	2,975	336	2,135	2,718
Humboldt	1,840	3,575	394	2,408	3,398
Ida	1,235	2,825	254	1,559	2,618
Iowa	2,606	4,153	667	2,815	4,352
Jackson	3,510	4,479	622	4,400	4,811
Jasper	7,258	8,286	1,221	8,023	8,576
Jefferson	2,577	4,099	505	2,961	4,727
Johnson	20,122	13,642	8,101	26,000	18,677
Jones	3,521	4,506	759	3,825	4,907
Keokuk	2,390	3,145	369	2,649	2,913
Kossuth	3,810	5,568	775	4,838	4,872
Lee	8,204	8,793	1,047	8,912	8,756
Linn	31,950	36,254	8,773	38,528	41,061
Louisa	1,700	2,530	291	1,927	2,623
Lucas	1,989	2,593	291	2,422	2,630
Lyon	1,431	4,349	375	1,401	4,178
Madison	2,496	3,320	505	3,067	3,168
Mahaska	3,968	5,650	603	4,107	6,086
Marion	5,490	6,665	1,232	6,313	7,259
Marshall	7,114	10,707	1,541	8,809	10,839
Mills	1,244	3,581	281	1,434	3,994
Mitchell	2,040	3,401	361	2,531	3,144
Monona	1,660	3,268	275	2,159	2,746
Monroe	1,866	2,003	216	2,342	1,927
Montgomery	1,556	4,115	301	1,661	4,224
Muscatine	5,597	7,829	1,522	5,986	9,069
O'Brien	2,210	4,937	536	2,479	5,008
Osceola	1,051	2,177	234	1,146	2,285
Page	1,772	5,618	356	1,914	5,876
Palo Alto	2,463	3,025	412	3,018	2,715
Plymouth	2,965	6,515	756	3,464	6,482
Pocahontas	1,959	3,194	397	2,481	2,627
Polk	61,984	64,156	15,819	75,413	71,413
Pottawattamie	10,709	20,222	1,870	12,329	21,527
Poweshiek	3,529	4,598	821	4,103	4,715
Ringgold	1,150	1,884	191	1,593	1,512
Sac	1,976	3,725	467	2,363	3,298
Scott	26,391	34,701	5,760	32,550	38,034
Shelby	1,892	4,147	372	2,291	4,200
Sioux	2,698	10,768	610	2,585	11,665
Story	13,529	15,829	7,252	18,277	19,804
Tama	3,049	4,840	593	4,061	4,882

Taylor	1,226	2,715	240	1,499	2,496
Union	2,182	3,372	368	2,875	3,583
Van Buren	1,311	2,142	183	1,606	2,138
Wapello	8,923	7,475	1,050	10,545	7,098
Warren	6,610	7,360	1,369	8,171	8,277
Washington	2,877	3,967	703	3,079	4,613
Wayne	1,627	2,221	218	1,927	2,061
Webster	9,001	10,438	1,386	9,930	9,619
Winnebago	2,208	3,808	417	2,669	3,616
Winneshiek	3,201	5,033	938	3,724	5,277
Woodbury	15,930	23,553	3,184	18,951	23,002
Worth	1,721	2,247	301	2,263	1,985
Wright	2,645	3,936	497	2,980	3,675
Totals	**508,672**	**676,026**	**115,633**	**605,620**	**703,088**

Iowa Vote Since 1936

1936, Roosevelt, Dem., 621,756; Landon, Rep., 487,977; Lemke, Union, 29,687; Thomas, Soc., 1,373; Colvin, Proh., 1,182; Browder, Com., 506; Aiken, Soc. Labor, 252.

1940, Roosevelt, Dem., 578,800; Willkie, Rep., 632,370; Babson, Proh., 2,284; Browder, Com., 1,524; Aiken, Soc. Labor, 452.

1944, Roosevelt, Dem., 499,876; Dewey, Rep., 547,267; Watson, Proh., 3,752; Thomas, Soc., 1,511; Teichert, Soc. Labor, 193.

1948, Truman, Dem., 522,380; Dewey, Rep., 494,018; Wallace, Prog., 12,125; Teichert, Soc. Labor, 4,274; Watson, Proh., 3,382; Thomas, Soc., 1,829; Dobbs, Soc. Workers, 26.

1952, Eisenhower, Rep., 808,906; Stevenson, Dem., 451,513; Hallinan, Prog., 5,085; Hamblen, Proh., 2,882; Hoopes, Soc., 219; Hass, Soc. Labor, 139; scattering 29.

1956, Eisenhower, Rep., 729,187; Stevenson, Dem., 501,858; Andrews (A.C.P. of Iowa), 3,202; Hoopes, Soc., 192; Hass, Soc. Labor, 125.

1960, Kennedy, Dem., 550,565; Nixon, Rep., 722,381; Hass, Soc. Labor, 230; write-in, 634.

1964, Johnson, Dem., 733,030; Goldwater, Rep., 449,148; Hass, Soc. Labor, 182; DeBerry, Soc. Worker, 159; Munn, Proh., 1,902.

1968, Nixon, Rep., 619,106; Humphrey, Dem., 476,699; Wallace, 3d party, 66,422; Munn, Proh., 362; Halstead, Soc. Worker, 3,377; Cleaver, Peace and Freedom, 1,332; Blomen, Soc. Labor, 241.

1972, Nixon, Rep., 706,207; McGovern, Dem., 496,206; Schmitz, Amer., 22,056; Jenness, Soc. Workers, 488; Fisher, Soc. Labor, 195; Hall, Com. 272; Green, Universal, 199; scattered, 321.

1976, Carter, Dem., 619,931; Ford, Rep., 632,863; McCarthy, Ind., 20,051; Anderson, Amer., 3,040; MacBride, Libertarian, 1,452.

1980, Reagan, Rep., 676,026; Carter, Dem., 508,672; Anderson, Ind., 115,633; Clark, Libertarian, 13,123; Commoner, Citizens, 2,273; McReynolds, Socialist, 534; Hall Com., 298; DeBerry, Soc. Work., 244; Greaves, American, 189; Bubar, Statesman, 150; scattering, 519.

1984, Reagan, Rep., 703,088; Mondale, Dem., 605,620; Bergland, Libertarian, 1,844.

Kansas

	1980			1984	
County	Carter (D)	Reagan (R)	Anderson (I)	Mondale (D)	Reagan (R)
Allen	2,009	3,811	380	1,779	4,266
Anderson	1,170	2,363	184	1,155	2,462
Atchison	3,063	4,084	345	2,641	4,536
Barber	914	1,872	168	805	2,111
Barton	3,663	9,147	793	3,111	10,234
Bourbon	2,605	4,263	251	2,174	4,856
Brown	1,370	3,598	286	1,303	3,894
Butler	6,875	10,210	1,015	6,352	12,920
Chase	413	1,073	92	393	1,162
Chautauqua	543	1,566	57	497	1,688
Cherokee	3,969	5,296	282	3,663	5,081
Cheyenne	358	1,330	81	356	1,442
Clark	430	901	67	324	1,075
Clay	932	3,449	217	919	3,559
Cloud	1,793	3,581	344	1,878	3,856
Coffey	938	2,491	128	1,037	3,063
Comanche	393	877	50	285	993
Cowley	5,474	8,749	866	5,153	9,930
Crawford	7,658	8,058	847	6,722	9,518
Decatur	443	1,642	125	467	1,769
Dickinson	2,108	5,654	469	2,168	6,487
Doniphan	1,001	2,523	146	962	2,818
Douglas	9,360	14,106	4,770	12,877	18,804
Edwards	616	1,409	127	606	1,352
Elk	482	1,280	54	452	1,301
Ellis	3,940	5,634	923	3,457	7,509
Ellsworth	886	2,155	167	905	2,353
Finney	2,689	4,831	531	2,398	6,943
Ford	3,194	5,686	622	2,914	6,738
Franklin	2,726	5,525	432	2,524	6,283
Geary	2,357	3,534	332	2,301	4,475
Gove	396	1,263	91	426	1,310
Graham	473	1,450	98	480	1,423
Grant	683	1,711	150	615	2,043
Gray	583	1,310	123	514	1,580
Greeley	235	600	85	227	699
Greenwood	1,241	2,685	170	1,173	2,900
Hamilton	402	889	66	408	1,037
Harper	990	2,254	182	893	2,696
Harvey	4,173	7,045	1,356	4,599	8,507
Haskell	374	1,014	84	281	1,151
Hodgeman	339	831	69	306	939
Jackson	1,537	3,211	234	1,667	3,464
Jefferson	1,776	4,046	364	1,990	4,524
Jewell	578	2,074	153	583	1,992
Johnson	33,210	78,048	10,947	37,782	101,042
Kearny	375	924	62	321	1,214
Kingman	1,133	2,610	286	1,047	2,826
Kiowa	438	1,433	88	361	1,537
Labette	3,947	5,244	588	3,631	6,542
Lane	321	924	100	282	1,008
Leavenworth	6,354	9,157	955	6,583	11,018
Lincoln	528	1,685	96	551	1,723
Linn	1,157	2,407	103	1,152	2,794
Logan	358	1,261	66	331	1,235
Lyon	4,680	8,431	1,216	4,188	9,796
McPherson	3,340	6,843	1,222	3,185	8,630
Marion	1,569	3,960	488	1,633	4,407
Marshall	1,555	4,127	330	1,813	4,097
Meade	482	1,618	121	491	1,804
Miami	3,071	4,740	368	3,076	5,877
Mitchell	876	2,821	197	919	3,036
Montgomery	5,282	10,856	488	4,933	12,023
Morris	810	1,933	166	820	2,240
Morton	414	1,157	71	322	1,353
Nemaha	1,600	3,546	243	1,761	3,653
Neosho	2,923	4,613	432	2,679	4,968
Ness	616	1,657	136	539	1,779
Norton	666	2,625	151	611	2,515
Osage	2,088	3,817	330	2,072	4,288
Osborne	620	2,188	125	686	2,171
Ottawa	630	2,118	150	698	2,343
Pawnee	1,184	2,170	281	1,092	2,570
Phillips	748	2,731	143	626	2,810
Pottawatomie	1,724	3,895	444	1,798	4,596
Pratt	1,369	2,866	329	1,253	3,240
Rawlins	427	1,524	87	412	1,625
Reno	9,615	13,804	2,225	9,229	16,621
Republic	850	3,031	183	966	2,974
Rice	1,847	3,211	426	1,559	3,598
Riley	5,224	8,904	2,443	5,974	11,306
Rooks	725	2,275	144	699	2,604
Rush	557	1,840	144	718	1,758
Russell	910	3,241	229	1,055	3,673
Saline	6,382	12,758	1,706	6,527	15,242
Scott	456	1,829	99	427	2,017
Sedgwick	55,105	75,317	10,222	55,060	95,972
Seward	1,460	4,385	250	1,198	5,047
Shawnee	24,852	36,290	5,524	26,307	43,435
Sheridan	391	1,202	68	429	1,274
Sherman	779	2,315	215	714	2,702
Smith	719	2,415	183	684	2,330
Stafford	872	1,865	184	844	2,062
Stanton	231	672	62	205	783
Stevens	478	1,502	67	386	1,862
Summer	3,761	6,038	486	3,713	6,942
Thomas	1,045	2,789	269	887	3,106
Trego	523	1,340	138	598	1,491
Wabaunsee	853	2,255	173	805	2,276
Wallace	167	811	36	152	838
Washington	784	3,058	195	889	2,979
Wichita	303	880	60	232	916
Wilson	1,205	3,328	208	1,343	3,660
Woodson	646	1,435	89	596	1,408
Wyandotte	32,763	23,012	3,018	35,887	27,267
Totals	**326,150**	**566,812**	**68,231**	**332,471**	**674,646**

Kansas Vote Since 1936

1936, Roosevelt, Dem., 464,520; Landon, Rep., 397,727; Thomas, Soc., 2,766; Lemke, Union, 494.

1940, Roosevelt, Dem., 364,725; Willkie, Rep., 489,169; Babson, Proh., 4,056; Thomas, Soc., 2,347.

1944, Roosevelt, Dem., 287,458; Dewey, Rep., 442,096; Watson, Proh., 2,609; Thomas, Soc., 1,613.

1948, Truman, Dem., 351,902; Dewey, Rep., 423,039; Watson, Proh., 6,468; Wallace, Prog., 4,603; Thomas, Soc., 2,807.

1952, Eisenhower, Rep., 616,302; Stevenson, Dem., 273,296; Hamblen, Proh., 6,038; Hoopes, Soc., 530.

1956, Eisenhower, Rep., 566,878; Stevenson. Dem., 296,317; Holtwick, Proh., 3,048.

1960, Kennedy, Dem., 363,213; Nixon, Rep., 561,474; Decker, Proh., 4,138.

1964, Johnson, Dem., 464,028; Goldwater, Rep., 386,579; Munn, Proh., 5,393; Hass, Soc. Labor, 1,901.

1968, Nixon, Rep., 478,674; Humphrey, Dem., 302,996; Wallace, 3d, 88,921; Munn, Proh., 2,192.

1972, Nixon, Rep., 619,812; McGovern, Dem., 270,287; Schmitz, Cons., 21,808; Munn, Proh., 4,188.

1976, Carter, Dem., 430,421; Ford, Rep., 502,752; McCarthy, Ind., 13,185; Anderson, Amer., 4,724; MacBride, Libertarian, 3,242; Maddox, Cons., 2,118; Bubar, Proh., 1,403.

1980, Reagan, Rep., 566,812; Carter, Dem., 326,150; Anderson, Ind., 68,231; Clark, Libertarian, 14,470; Shelton, American, 1,555; Hall, Com., 967; Bubar, Statesman, 821; Rarick, Conservative, 789.

1984, Reagan, Rep., 674,646; Mondale, Dem., 332,471; Bergland, Libertarian, 3,585.

Kentucky

	1980			1984	
County	Carter (D)	Reagan (R)	Anderson (I)	Mondale (D)	Reagan (R)
Adair	2,285	4,051	53	1,812	4,600
Allen	2,010	3,106	54	1,521	3,427
Anderson	2,567	2,052	90	1,717	3,425
Ballard	2,583	1,190	23	2,002	1,663
Barren	5,285	6,405	164	4,503	7,717
Bath	2,174	1,463	47	1,781	2,020
Bell	6,362	5,433	150	5,490	7,249
Boone	5,374	8,263	383	4,853	12,690
Bourbon	3,641	2,475	153	2,649	3,836
Boyd	10,702	10,367	496	9,601	10,925
Boyle	4,429	3,848	254	3,378	5,675
Bracken	1,420	1,154	36	1,136	1,812
Breathitt	3,916	1,532	68	3,435	2,055
Breckinridge	3,163	3,629	72	2,669	4,432
Bulliitt	5,884	6,364	202	5,005	9,566
Butler	1,274	3,129	28	1,055	3,121
Caldwell	2,924	2,609	66	2,427	3,162
Calloway	6,809	4,498	318	5,028	6,442
Campbell	11,059	16,743	943	9,068	21,473
Carlisle	1,542	975	8	1,277	1,308
Carroll	2,127	1,076	82	1,564	1,824
Carter	3,782	3,934	86	3,985	4,056
Casey	1,298	4,239	38	1,122	4,356
Christian	7,048	8,209	190	5,432	10,708
Clark	5,071	4,302	242	3,595	6,130
Clay	2,121	4,594	37	1,634	4,772
Clinton	1,000	3,539	34	838	3,459
Crittenden	1,508	2,219	28	1,483	2,167
Cumberland	821	2,216	27	766	2,729
Daviess	14,902	14,643	752	13,347	19,495
Edmonson	1,252	2,913	28	1,200	3,001
Elliott	1,668	551	15	1,683	601
Estill	1,905	2,818	45	1,593	3,512
Fayette	30,511	35,349	4,933	28,961	51,993
Fleming	2,051	2,189	54	1,616	2,824
Floyd	10,975	4,179	171	10,259	5,218
Franklin	11,193	6,455	610	7,790	11,057
Fulton	2,016	1,462	31	1,534	1,780
Gallatin	988	684	20	1,042	1,042
Garrard	1,774	2,585	62	1,566	3,284
Grant	2,272	1,779	76	1,685	2,840
Graves	6,999	6,556	135	6,759	7,287
Grayson	2,788	5,084	78	2,200	5,524
Green	1,758	2,775	39	1,611	3,210
Greenup	7,126	6,857	220	6,923	7,451
Hancock	1,530	1,367	52	1,287	1,967
Hardin	8,339	9,779	452	6,329	14,293
Harlan	8,798	5,460	131	7,663	6,959
Harrison	3,319	2,184	107	2,405	3,467
Hart	3,005	3,129	42	2,278	3,065
Henderson	8,082	5,074	354	6,795	7,389
Henry	2,999	1,723	69	2,279	2,802
Hickman	1,456	1,143	28	1,049	1,380
Hopkins	8,810	6,238	213	6,743	9,368
Jackson	702	3,379	29	542	3,806
Jefferson	125,844	127,254	9,686	119,350	161,283
Jessamine	3,310	4,809	278	2,379	7,081
Johnson	3,142	5,039	96	3,078	5,225
Kenton	17,907	25,965	1,583	14,642	34,304
Knott	5,405	1,602	25	4,487	1,728
Knox	3,543	5,539	113	2,932	5,730
Larue	2,183	2,000	43	1,514	2,873
Laurel	3,969	8,868	114	3,267	9,621
Lawrence	2,362	2,564	32	2,223	2,713
Lee	1,017	1,650	41	768	1,862
Leslie	1,327	3,536	40	1,075	3,385
Letcher	4,280	3,426	78	4,153	3,676
Lewis	1,543	2,802	34	1,484	3,445
Lincoln	2,991	3,034	58	2,498	3,996
Livingston	2,287	1,670	30	2,007	1,866
Logan	4,264	3,366	85	3,347	4,889
Lyon	1,496	968	26	1,272	969
McCracken	13,365	10,281	369	12,535	12,903
McCreary	1,377	3,786	40	1,609	4,028
McLean	2,147	1,497	44	1,917	1,942
Madison	8,208	8,437	739	6,509	11,309
Magoffin	2,986	2,265	25	2,942	2,343
Marion	3,577	2,126	87	2,835	3,305
Marshall	6,231	4,403	96	5,725	5,152
Martin	1,567	2,793	51	1,471	3,248
Mason	3,181	2,926	127	2,663	2,751
Meade	3,205	2,740	90	2,503	3,820
Menifee	966	547	11	956	785
Mercer	3,528	3,275	92	2,516	4,592
Metcalfe	1,628	2,013	39	1,575	2,349
Monroe	1,156	4,592	47	1,052	4,670
Montgomery	3,391	2,869	117	2,490	3,864
Morgan	2,698	1,450	31	2,481	1,834
Muhlenberg	6,616	4,893	148	6,157	6,094
Nelson	5,514	3,349	162	4,199	6,044
Nicholas	1,349	915	56	1,107	1,535
Ohio	3,486	5,272	103	3,253	5,119
Oldham	3,487	5,586	351	2,857	8,112
Owen	2,323	944	43	1,575	1,735
Owsley	437	1,250	7	375	1,466
Pendleton	1,992	1,757	69	1,529	2,767
Perry	6,031	4,226	72	5,250	5,218
Pike	14,878	10,550	204	15,817	11,009
Powell	2,006	1,716	33	1,575	2,269
Pulaski	6,570	12,970	257	4,384	14,434
Robertson	562	416	14	467	567
Rockcastle	1,345	3,543	37	1,089	4,328
Rowan	2,975	2,758	191	2,748	3,698
Russell	1,693	3,804	29	1,448	4,476
Scott	3,531	2,868	197	2,606	4,461
Shelby	4,429	3,423	178	3,326	5,390
Simpson	2,713	2,020	59	2,140	3,073
Spencer	1,216	935	27	910	1,456
Taylor	3,400	4,243	84	3,286	5,932
Todd	1,956	1,945	44	1,505	2,364
Trigg	2,619	1,913	56	1,905	2,512
Trimble	1,478	824	49	1,088	1,389
Union	3,479	1,847	68	3,090	2,524
Warren	9,643	12,184	602	7,937	16,167
Washington	2,147	2,008	43	1,786	2,804
Wayne	2,073	3,972	50	2,277	4,449
Webster	3,506	1,939	52	3,042	2,504
Whitley	3,889	7,007	125	3,575	7,851
Wolfe	1,814	951	19	1,394	1,257
Woodford	3,122	3,105	213	2,290	4,746
Totals	616,417	635,274	31,127	536,756	815,345

Kentucky Vote Since 1936

1936, Roosevelt, Dem., 541,944; Landon, Rep., 369,702; Lemke, Union, 12,501; Colvin, Proh., 929; Thomas, Soc., 627; Aiken, Soc. Labor, 294; Browder, Com., 204.

1940, Roosevelt, Dem., 557,222; Willkie, Rep., 410,384; Babson, Proh., 1,443; Thomas, Soc., 1,014.

1944, Roosevelt, Dem., 472,589; Dewey, Rep., 392,448; Watson, Proh., 2,023; Thomas, Soc., 535; Teichert, Soc. Labor, 326.

1948, Truman, Dem., 466,756; Dewey, Rep., 341,210; Thurmond, States' Rights, 10,411; Wallace, Prog., 1,567; Thomas, Soc., 1,284; Watson, Proh., 1,245; Teichert, Soc. Labor, 185.

1952, Eisenhower, Rep., 495,029; Stevenson, Dem., 495,729; Hamblen, Proh., 1,161; Hass, Soc. Labor, 893; Hallinan, Proh., 336.

1956, Eisenhower, Rep., 572,192; Stevenson, Dem., 476,453; Byrd, States' Rights, 2,657; Holtwick, Proh., 2,145; Hass, Soc. Labor, 358.

1960, Kennedy, Dem., 521,855; Nixon, Rep., 602,607.

1964, Johnson, Dem., 669,659; Goldwater, Rep., 372,977; John Kasper, Nat'l. States Rights, 3,469.

1968, Nixon, Rep., 462,411; Humphrey, Dem., 397,547; Wallace, 3d p., 193,098; Halstead, Soc. Worker, 2,843.

1972, Nixon, Rep., 676,446; McGovern, Dem., 371,159; Schmitz, Amer., 17,627; Jenness, Soc. Workers, 685; Hall, Com., 464; Spock, Peoples, 1,118.

1976, Carter, Dem., 615,717; Ford, Rep., 531,852; Anderson, Amer., 8,308; McCarthy, Ind., 6,837; Maddox, Amer. Ind., 2,328; MacBride, Libertarian, 814.

1980, Reagan, Rep., 635,274; Carter, Dem., 616,417; Anderson, Ind., 31,127; Clark, Libertarian, 5,531; McCormack, Respect For Life, 4,233; Commoner, Citizens, 1,304; Pulley, Socialist, 393; Hall, Com., 348.

1984, Reagan, Rep., 815,345; Mondale, Dem., 536,756.

Louisiana

Parish	1980 Carter (D)	1980 Reagan (R)	1980 Anderson (I)	1984 Mondale (D)	1984 Reagan (R)
Acadia	9,948	11,533	416	9,262	14,906
Allen	6,057	3,328	110	4,842	4,474
Ascension	12,381	7,238	286	11,048	11,945
Assumption	4,679	4,001	153	4,660	5,433
Avoyelles	7,174	8,216	190	6,808	9,402
Beauregard	5,556	5,250	163	4,199	7,353
Bienville	4,123	3,508	51	3,530	4,587
Bossier	9,377	16,515	327	7,006	22,638
Caddo	36,422	51,202	1,128	35,727	63,429
Calcasieu	35,446	27,600	1,259	33,214	35,566
Caldwell	1,786	2,653	43	1,348	3,341
Cameron	2,221	1,449	82	1,608	2,265
Catahoula	2,414	2,942	38	1,649	3,640
Claiborne	3,443	3,538	53	2,788	4,349
Concordia	3,956	4,933	52	3,332	6,177
DeSoto	5,861	4,349	49	4,642	5,989
E. Baton Rouge	57,442	71,063	3,312	56,673	95,704
East Carroll	2,283	1,867	24	2,089	1,974
East Feliciana	4,033	2,650	53	4,122	4,166
Evangeline	6,722	7,412	160	6,981	8,680
Franklin	4,177	5,301	65	2,937	6,708
Grant	3,290	3,611	77	2,588	5,334
Iberia	9,681	14,273	410	10,170	17,727
Iberville	9,361	4,463	172	8,587	6,455
Jackson	3,609	3,923	56	2,568	5,034
Jefferson	50,870	99,403	3,578	41,183	123,997
Jefferson Davis	6,140	5,667	201	5,962	8,296
Lafayette	19,694	31,429	1,263	19,265	44,344
Lafourche	14,222	14,951	675	10,186	20,930
LaSalle	2,665	3,792	61	1,318	5,404
Lincoln	5,598	7,515	177	5,432	9,087
Livingston	11,319	10,666	287	8,913	17,465
Madison	3,264	2,531	16	2,906	2,849
Morehouse	4,856	7,254	65	4,829	8,585
Natchitoches	7,102	6,668	158	5,806	8,836
Orleans	106,858	74,302	4,246	119,478	86,316
Ouachita	16,306	29,799	495	15,525	37,270
Plaquemines	4,318	5,489	154	3,261	7,655
Pointe Coupee	6,395	3,667	105	6,732	5,477
Rapides	19,436	25,576	530	16,121	32,879
Red River	2,776	2,147	29	1,958	3,060
Richland	3,745	4,772	48	2,918	5,980
Sabine	5,100	4,265	74	2,980	6,295
St. Bernard	11,367	19,410	616	8,076	24,428
St. Charles	7,898	6,779	283	6,784	10,185
St. Helena	3,183	1,531	42	2,956	2,366
St. James	6,206	3,429	113	5,989	4,627
St. John The Baptist	7,647	5,819	261	7,646	9,093
St. Landry	17,125	14,940	332	17,950	19,055
St. Martin	7,760	6,701	261	8,589	9,698
St. Mary	10,506	10,378	339	9,411	15,275
St. Tammany	14,161	27,214	872	11,719	38,664
Tangipahoa	15,272	15,187	491	12,799	19,580
Tensas	2,046	1,645	25	1,628	1,956
Terrebonne	10,804	16,644	559	9,640	23,696
Union	3,841	5,130	60	2,916	6,585
Vermilion	9,743	10,481	473	9,033	12,721
Vernon	7,198	5,869	167	4,076	9,035
Washington	10,413	8,681	170	7,680	11,185
Webster	8,568	8,866	118	6,509	12,055
W. Baton Rouge	4,739	2,828	117	4,631	4,189
West Carroll	2,118	3,430	38	1,474	3,874
West Feliciana	2,341	1,237	40	2,296	2,097
Winn	3,411	3,944	57	2,633	4,934
Totals	708,453	792,853	26,345	651,586	1,037,299

Louisiana Vote Since 1936

1936, Roosevelt, Dem., 292,894; Landon, Rep., 36,791.

1940, Roosevelt, Dem., 319,751; Willkie, Rep., 52,446.

1944, Roosevelt, Dem., 281,564; Dewey, Rep., 67,750.

1948, Thurmond, States' Rights, 204,290; Truman, Dem., 136,344; Dewey, Rep., 72,657; Wallace, Prog., 3,035.

1952, Eisenhower, Rep., 306,925, Stevenson, Dem., 345,027.

1956, Eisenhower, Rep., 329,047; Stevenson, Dem., 243,977; Andrews, States' Rights, 44,520.

1960, Kennedy, Dem., 407,339; Nixon, Rep., 230,890; States' Rights (unpledged) 169,572.

1964, Johnson, Dem., 387,068; Goldwater, Rep., 509,225.

1968, Nixon, Rep., 257,535; Humphrey, Dem., 309,615; Wallace, 3d party, 530,300.

1972, Nixon, Rep., 686,852; McGovern, Dem., 298,142; Schmitz, Amer., 52,099; Jenness, Soc. Workers, 14,398.

1976, Carter, Dem., 661,365; Ford, Rep., 587,446; Maddox, Amer., 10,058; Hall, Com., 7,417; McCarthy, Ind., 6,588; MacBride, Libertarian, 3,325.

1980, Reagan, Rep., 792,853; Carter, Dem., 708,453; Anderson, Ind., 26,345; Rarick, Amer. Ind., 10,333; Clark, Libertarian, 8,240; Commoner, Citizens, 1,584; DeBerry, Soc. Work., 783.

1984, Reagan, Rep., 1,037,299; Mondale, Dem., 651,586; Bergland, Libertarian, 1,876.

Maine

City	1980 Carter (D)	1980 Reagan (R)	1980 Anderson (I)	1984 Mondale (D)	1984 Reagan (R)
Auburn	5,071	4,886	1,136	4,430	6,994
Augusta	4,470	4,271	1,262	4,451	5,995
Bangor	6,032	6,082	1,562	6,155	8,389
Bath	2,173	2,005	398	1,714	2,899
Bidderford	5,788	2,738	888	5,489	4,147
Brewer	1,767	2,526	435	1,461	3,093
Gardiner	1,325	1,265	415	1,216	1,942
Lewiston	11,365	6,205	1,875	9,853	9,480
Old Town	2,454	1,480	466	2,217	2,087
Portland	14,815	9,122	3,325	17,543	13,315
Rockland	1,140	1,366	292	1,051	2,169
Saco	3,240	2,583	695	3,094	3,761
Sanford	4,020	3,124	695	3,517	4,578
South Portland	5,371	4,519	1,280	5,377	6,653
Waterville	4,125	2,952	877	4,075	3,873
Westbrook	3,882	2,952	693	3,345	4,456
Totals	220,974	238,522	53,327	214,515	336,500

Maine Vote Since 1936

1936, Landon, Rep., 168,823; Roosevelt, Dem., 126,333; Lemke, Union, 7,581; Thomas, Soc., 783; Colvin, Proh., 334; Browder, Com., 257; Aiken, Soc. Labor, 129.

1940, Roosevelt, Dem., 156,478; Willkie, Rep., 165,951; Browder, Com., 411.

1944, Roosevelt, Dem., 140,631; Dewey, Rep., 155,434; Teichert, Soc. Labor, 335.

1948, Truman, Dem., 111,916; Dewey, Rep., 150,234; Wallace, Prog., 1,884; Thomas, Soc., 547; Teichert, Soc. Labor, 206.

1952, Eisenhower, Rep., 232,353; Stevenson, Dem., 118,806; Hallinan, Prog., 332; Hass, Soc. Labor, 156; Hoopes, Soc., 138; scattered, 1.

1956, Eisenhower, Rep., 249,238; Stevenson, Dem., 102,468.

1960, Kennedy, Dem., 181,159; Nixon, Rep., 240,608.

1964, Johnson, Dem., 262,264; Goldwater, Rep., 118,701.

1968, Nixon, Rep., 169,254; Humphrey, Dem., 217,312; Wallace, 3d party, 6,370.

1972, Nixon, Rep., 256,458; McGovern, Dem., 160,584; scattered, 229.

1976, Carter, Dem., 232,279; Ford, Rep., 236,320; McCarthy, Ind., 10,874; Bubar, Proh., 3,495.

1980, Reagan, Rep., 238,522; Carter, Dem., 220,974; Anderson, Ind., 53,327; Clark, Libertarian, 5,119; Commoner, Citizens, 4,394; Hall, Com., 591; write-ins, 84.

1984, Reagan, Rep., 336,500; Mondale, Dem., 214,515.

Maryland

County	1980 Carter (D)	1980 Reagan (R)	1980 Anderson (I)	1984 Mondale (D)	1984 Reagan (R)
Allegany	12,167	17,512	1,486	11,143	19,763
Anne Arundel	50,780	69,443	10,020	47,565	94,171
Baltimore	121,280	132,490	23,096	106,908	171,929
Calvert	4,745	5,440	590	5,455	8,303
Caroline	2,833	3,582	291	2,198	4,876
Carroll	10,393	19,859	2,243	8,898	27,230
Cecil	7,937	9,673	1,037	6,681	13,111
Charles	8,887	11,807	1,153	10,264	16,132
Dorchester	4,908	5,160	360	3,160	6,899
Frederick	13,629	22,033	2,891	13,411	29,606
Garrett	2,708	5,475	270	2,386	7,042
Harford	20,042	26,713	3,761	17,133	37,382
Howard	20,702	24,272	6,028	25,713	35,641
Kent	2,986	2,889	371	2,390	3,897
Montgomery	105,822	125,515	32,730	146,036	146,924
Prince George's	98,757	78,977	14,574	136,063	95,121
Queen Anne's	3,820	4,749	480	2,938	6,784
St. Mary's	6,773	8,267	892	6,420	11,201
Somerset	3,342	3,312	215	2,439	4,508
Talbot	3,995	6,044	570	3,198	8,028
Washington	14,118	22,901	1,689	13,329	27,118
Wicomico	9,431	11,229	1,092	8,160	16,124
Worcester	4,195	5,362	586	3,770	8,208
BALTIMORE CITY	191,911	57,902	13,112	202,277	80,120
Totals	726,161	680,606	119,537	787,935	879,918

Maryland Vote Since 1936

1936, Roosevelt, Dem., 389,612; Landon, Rep., 231,435; Thomas, Soc., 1,629; Aiken, Soc. Labor, 1,305; Browder, Com., 915.

1940, Roosevelt, Dem., 384,546; Willkie, Rep., 269,534; Thomas, Soc., 4,093; Browder, Com., 1,274; Aiken, Soc. Labor, 657.

1944, Roosevelt, Dem., 315,490; Dewey, Rep., 292,949.

1948, Truman, Dem., 286,521; Dewey, Rep., 294,814; Wallace, Prog., 9,983; Thomas, Soc., 2,941; Thurmond, States' Rights, 2,476; Wright, write-in, 2,294.

1952, Eisenhower, Rep., 499,424; Stevenson, Dem., 395,337; Hallinan, Prog., 7,313.

1956, Eisenhower, Rep., 559,738; Stevenson, Dem., 372,613.

1960, Kennedy, Dem., 565,800; Nixon, Rep., 489,538.

1964, Johnson, Dem., 730,912; Goldwater, Rep., 385,495; write-in, 50.

1968, Nixon, Rep., 517,995; Humphrey, Dem., 538,310; Wallace, 3d party, 178,734.

1972, Nixon, Rep., 829,305; McGovern, Dem., 505,781; Schmitz, Amer., 18,726.

1976, Carter, Dem., 759,612; Ford, Rep., 672,661.

1980, Reagan, Rep., 680,606; Carter, Dem., 726,161; Anderson, Ind., 119,537; Clark, Libertarian, 14,192.

1984, Reagan, Rep., 879,918; Mondale, Dem., 787,935; Bergland, Libertarian, 5,721.

Massachusetts

City	1980 Carter (D)	1980 Reagan (R)	1980 Anderson (I)	1984 Mondale (D)	1984 Reagan (R)
Boston	95,133	58,656	22,577	131,745	75,311
Brockton	12,751	15,350	4,633	14,130	17,161
Cambridge	24,337	7,952	6,694	32,582	10,007
Fall River	19,644	9,958	3,694	20,722	11,463
Framingham	12,275	11,979	4,940	14,368	15,074
Lawrence	12,145	8,020	2,341	10,986	9,877
Lowell	16,353	12,668	3,791	15,042	16,834
Lynn	15,777	11,966	3,911	17,103	14,445
New Bedford	18,014	13,217	3,843	22,070	13,147
Newton	20,173	15,621	7,778	27,343	16,184
Quincy	17,977	18,038	5,328	18,971	20,123
Somerville	16,931	9,533	4,143	21,065	11,318
Springfield	26,414	17,694	6,327	29,376	21,431
Worcester	31,146	23,305	8,411	32,525	27,348
Totals	**1,053,802**	**1,057,631**	**382,539**	**1,239,606**	**1,310,936**

Massachusetts Vote Since 1936

1936, Roosevelt, Dem., 942,716; Landon, Rep., 768,613; Lemke, Union, 118,639; Thomas, Soc., 5,111; Browder, Com., 2,930; Aiken, Soc. Labor, 1,305; Colvin, Proh., 1,032.

1940, Roosevelt, Dem., 1,076,522; Willkie, Rep., 939,700; Thomas, Soc., 4,091; Browder, Com., 3,806; Aiken, Soc. Labor, 1,492; Babson, Proh., 1,370.

1944, Roosevelt, Dem., 1,035,296; Dewey, Rep., 921,350; Teichert, Soc. Labor, 2,780; Watson, Proh., 973.

1948, Truman, Dem., 1,151,788; Dewey, Rep., 909,370; Wallace, Prog., 38,157; Teichert, Soc. Labor, 5,535; Watson, Proh., 1,663.

1952, Eisenhower, Rep., 1,292,325; Stevenson, Dem., 1,083,525; Hallinan, Prog., 4,636; Hass, Soc. Labor, 1,957; Hamblen, Proh., 886; scattered, 69; blanks, 41,150.

1956, Eisenhower, Rep., 1,393,197; Stevenson, Dem., 948,190; Hass, Soc. Labor, 5,573; Holtwick, Proh., 1,205; others, 341.

1960, Kennedy, Dem., 1,487,174; Nixon, Rep., 976,750; Hass, Soc. Labor, 3,892; Decker, Proh., 1,633; others, 31; blank and void, 26,024.

1964, Johnson, Dem., 1,786,422; Goldwater, Rep., 549,727; Hass, Soc. Labor, 4,755; Munn, Proh., 3,735; scattered, 159; blank, 48,104.

1968, Nixon, Rep., 766,844; Humphrey, Dem., 1,469,218; Wallace, 3d party, 87,088; Blomen, Soc. Labor, 6,180; Munn, Proh., 2,369; scattered, 53; blanks, 25,394.

1972, Nixon, Rep., 1,112,078; McGovern, Dem., 1,332,540; Jenness, Soc. Workers, 10,600; Fisher, Soc. Labor, 129; Schmitz, Amer., 2,877; Spock, Peoples, 101; Hall, Com., 46; Hospers, Libertarian, 43; scattered, 342.

1976, Carter, Dem., 1,429,475; Ford, Rep., 1,030,276; McCarthy, Ind., 65,637; Camejo, Soc. Workers, 8,138; Anderson, Amer., 7,555; La Rouche, U.S. Labor, 4,922; MacBride, Libertarian, 135.

1980, Reagan, Rep., 1,057,631; Carter, Dem., 1,053,802; Anderson, Ind., 382,539; Clark, Libertarian, 22,038; DeBerry, Soc. Workers, 3,735; Commoner, Citizens, 2,056; McReynolds, Socialist, 62; Bubar, Statesman, 34; Griswold, Workers World, 19; scattered, 2,382.

1984, Reagan, Rep., 1,310,936; Mondale, Dem., 1,239,606.

Michigan

County	1980 Carter (D)	1980 Reagan (R)	1980 Anderson (I)	1984 Mondale (D)	1984 Reagan (R)
Alcona	1,857	2,905	247	1,616	3,223
Alger	2,242	2,059	263	2,018	2,175
Allegan	9,877	20,560	1,984	8,389	23,762
Alpena	5,834	6,901	913	5,136	8,212
Antrim	2,909	4,706	602	2,507	5,726
Arenac	2,547	3,436	333	2,436	3,483
Baraga	1,609	2,046	201	1,818	1,965
Barry	6,857	12,006	1,399	5,898	14,245
Bay	24,517	25,331	3,886	22,597	26,198
Benzie	1,842	3,054	455	1,866	3,590
Berrien	22,152	41,458	3,422	21,228	43,160
Branch	4,635	10,224	1,102	3,860	11,004
Calhoun	23,022	30,912	4,408	20,313	34,470
Cass	7,058	11,206	1,156	6,634	11,647
Charlevoix	3,741	5,053	816	3,175	6,355
Cheboygan	3,938	5,221	638	3,358	6,053
Chippewa	5,268	7,059	951	4,575	8,135
Clare	4,164	5,719	663	3,764	6,587
Clinton	7,539	14,968	1,736	6,226	17,387
Crawford	1,826	2,652	390	1,558	3,303
Delta	8,475	8,146	849	7,934	8,952
Dickinson	5,694	6,614	596	5,614	6,880
Eaton	12,742	22,927	3,533	10,290	27,720
Emmet	3,724	5,930	1,134	3,254	7,760
Genesee	90,393	78,572	12,274	89,491	92,943
Gladwin	3,733	4,509	463	3,368	5,401
Gogebic	5,254	4,388	493	5,554	4,006
Grand Traverse	7,150	14,484	2,568	7,271	18,036
Gratiot	4,916	9,294	1,193	4,000	10,456
Hillsdale	4,375	10,951	882	3,616	12,063
Houghton	6,858	7,926	1,423	6,434	8,652
Huron	4,434	10,553	976	3,966	11,073
Ingham	48,278	56,777	17,139	46,411	68,753
Ionia	7,039	12,040	1,539	5,735	14,162
Iosco	4,255	6,680	739	3,850	7,907
Iron	3,742	3,507	371	3,559	3,468
Isabella	7,293	10,407	2,511	6,435	12,215
Jackson	23,685	33,749	4,165	18,340	40,133
Kalamazoo	34,528	48,669	10,833	32,460	58,327
Kalkaska	1,807	2,802	260	1,595	3,623
Kent	72,790	112,004	17,813	66,238	137,417
Keweenaw	570	583	87	628	599
Lake	2,041	1,730	187	1,845	2,125
Lapeer	9,671	15,996	1,868	7,800	19,222
Leelanau	2,348	4,585	830	2,400	5,050
Lenawee	12,935	20,366	2,230	11,012	22,409
Livingston	12,626	25,012	3,247	10,720	31,846
Luce	992	1,659	177	833	1,715
Mackinac	2,262	3,021	415	1,949	3,627
Macomb	120,125	154,155	18,975	97,816	194,300
Manistee	4,164	5,662	699	3,917	6,328
Marquette	13,312	13,181	2,481	14,074	14,196
Mason	4,134	7,137	825	3,803	8,202
Mecosta	5,228	7,754	1,322	4,048	9,023
Menominee	4,962	6,170	452	4,425	6,618
Midland	12,019	17,828	3,152	10,769	21,521
Missaukee	1,563	3,221	230	1,256	3,970
Monroe	20,578	25,612	3,111	19,617	29,419
Montcalm	6,706	10,822	1,309	5,401	10,109
Montmorency	1,654	2,400	195	1,387	2,913
Muskegon	26,645	36,512	4,094	25,247	39,355
Newaygo	5,236	8,918	850	4,496	10,636
Oakland	164,869	253,211	38,273	150,286	306,050
Oceana	3,386	5,465	570	2,865	6,405
Ogemaw	3,426	4,169	425	3,132	4,901
Ontonagon	2,375	2,569	237	2,350	2,464
Osceola	2,650	4,902	466	2,127	5,923
Oscoda	1,325	1,915	183	951	2,239
Otsego	2,666	3,771	493	2,117	4,639
Ottawa	18,435	51,217	4,903	15,000	60,142
Presque Isle	2,952	3,486	382	2,481	4,207
Roscommon	3,763	5,280	508	3,359	6,419
Saginaw	41,650	45,233	5,677	38,420	51,495
St. Clair	20,410	31,021	3,592	16,998	36,114
St. Joseph	6,318	13,631	1,283	5,795	15,405
Sanilac	4,898	12,158	863	4,126	12,627
Schoolcraft	1,964	2,097	243	1,920	2,139
Shiawassee	11,985	15,756	2,121	9,514	18,756
Tuscola	7,632	13,306	1,266	6,212	14,698
Van Buren	9,248	14,451	1,691	8,853	16,426
Washtenaw	51,013	48,699	13,463	55,084	58,736
Wayne	522,024	315,532	43,608	496,632	367,391

Wexford	4,173	6,027	752	3,398	7,279
Totals	1,661,532	1,915,225	275,223	1,529,638	2,251,571

Michigan Vote Since 1936

1936, Roosevelt, Dem., 1,016,794; Landon, Rep., 699,733; Lemke, Union, 75,795; Thomas, Soc., 8,208; Browder, Com., 3,384; Aiken, Soc. Labor, 600; Colvin, Proh., 579.

1940, Roosevelt, Dem., 1,032,991; Willkie, Rep., 1,039,917; Thomas, Soc., 7,593; Browder, Com., 2,834; Babson, Proh., 1,795; Aiken, Soc. Labor, 795.

1944, Roosevelt, Dem., 1,106,899; Dewey, Rep., 1,084,423; Watson, Proh., 6,503; Thomas, Soc., 4,598; Smith, America First, 1,530; Teichert, Soc. Labor, 1,264.

1948, Truman, Dem., 1,003,448; Dewey, Rep., 1,038,595; Wallace, Prog., 46,515; Watson, Proh., 13,052; Thomas, Soc. 6,063; Teichert, Soc. Labor, 1,263; Dobbs, Soc. Workers, 672.

1952, Eisenhower, Rep., 1,551,529; Stevenson, Dem., 1,230,657; Hamblen, Proh., 10,331; Hallinan, Prog., 3,922; Hass, Soc. Labor, 1,495; Dobbs, Soc. Workers, 655; scattered, 3.

1956, Eisenhower, Rep., 1,713,647; Stevenson, Dem., 1,359,898; Holtwick, Proh., 6,923.

1960, Kennedy, Dem., 1,687,269; Nixon, Rep., 1,620,428; Dobbs, Soc. Workers, 4,347; Decker, Proh., 2,029; Daly, Tax Cut, 1,767; Hass, Soc. Labor, 1,718; Ind. American, 539.

1964, Johnson, Dem., 2,136,615; Goldwater, Rep., 1,060,152; DeBerry, Soc. Workers, 3,817; Hass, Soc. Labor, 1,704; Proh. (no candidate listed), 699, scattering, 145.

1968, Nixon, Rep., 1,370,665; Humphrey, Dem., 1,593,082; Wallace, 3d party, 331,968; Halstead, Soc. Worker, 4,099; Blomen, Soc. Labor, 1,762; Cleaver, New Politics, 4,585; Munn, Proh., 60; scattering, 29.

1972, Nixon, Rep., 1,961,721; McGovern, Dem., 1,459,435; Schmitz, Amer., 63,321; Fisher, Soc. Labor, 2,437; Jenness, Soc. Workers, 1,603; Hall, Com., 1,210.

1976, Carter, Dem., 1,696,714; Ford, Rep., 1,893,742; McCarthy, Ind., 47,905; MacBride, Libertarian, 5,406; Wright, People's, 3,504, Camejo, Soc. Workers, 1,804; LaRouche, U.S. Labor, 1,366; Levin, Soc. Labor, 1,148; scattering, 2,160.

1980, Reagan, Rep., 1,915,225; Carter, Dem., 1,661,532; Anderson, Ind., 275,223; Clark, Libertarian, 41,597; Commoner, Citizens, 11,930; Hall, Com., 3,262; Griswold, Workers World, 30; Greaves, American, 21; Bubar, Statesman, 9.

1984, Reagan, Rep., 2,251,571; Mondale, Dem., 1,529,638; Bergland, Libertarian, 10,055.

Minnesota

	1980			1984	
County	Carter (D)	Reagan (R)	Anderson (I)	Mondale (D)	Reagan (R)
Aitkin	3,677	3,396	380	3,943	3,422
Anoka	45,532	33,100	6,828	50,305	46,578
Becker	5,221	6,848	866	5,456	7,553
Beltrami	7,432	6,481	1,254	7,481	7,414
Benton	5,272	5,513	646	4,922	6,830
Big Stone	1,814	1,950	249	1,994	1,821
Blue Earth	10,930	11,966	2,698	11,877	14,298
Brown	4,915	8,051	842	4,469	8,399
Carlton	8,822	4,760	883	9,189	4,877
Carver	6,621	9,909	1,496	6,725	11,963
Cass	4,717	6,119	434	4,773	6,619
Chippewa	3,164	4,252	532	3,047	3,964
Chisago	6,240	5,017	939	6,683	6,279
Clay	8,940	10,447	2,773	10,294	11,565
Clearwater	1,955	1,919	185	1,917	2,066
Cook	871	1,174	182	1,129	1,219
Cottonwood	2,958	4,258	535	3,073	4,275
Crow Wing	9,323	10,844	1,046	8,719	11,362
Dakota	43,433	40,708	8,588	49,125	55,119
Dodge	2,698	3,900	367	2,786	4,428
Douglas	5,530	7,778	844	5,444	9,005
Faribault	3,620	6,206	525	3,993	5,690
Fillmore	4,010	6,452	650	4,351	6,342
Freeborn	8,212	8,475	808	9,338	8,413
Goodhue	8,566	9,329	1,964	8,679	11,171
Grant	1,822	2,054	333	1,867	2,111
Hennepin	239,592	194,998	56,390	272,401	253,921
Houston	3,218	5,582	477	3,512	5,645
Hubbard	2,840	4,172	365	2,806	4,621
Isanti	5,457	4,480	641	5,378	5,660
Itasca	12,138	8,368	1,080	11,455	9,306
Jackson	3,062	3,391	463	3,437	3,131
Kanabec	2,654	2,500	269	2,660	3,027
Kandiyohi	8,038	8,480	1,244	8,402	9,539
Kittson	1,407	1,875	243	1,610	1,716
Koochiching	4,181	3,433	496	4,238	3,466
LacQuiParle	2,457	2,981	334	2,685	2,731
Lake	3,864	2,414	443	4,468	2,003
Lake O'Woods	763	1,052	128	824	1,094
Le Sueur	5,161	5,478	731	5,070	6,033
Lincoln	1,640	2,122	295	1,827	1,905
Lyon	5,626	5,852	1,129	5,389	7,170
McLeod	4,987	7,819	852	4,864	8,728
Mahnomen	1,175	1,275	153	1,241	1,328
Marshall	2,636	3,638	397	2,705	3,433
Martin	4,301	7,057	751	4,673	7,308
Meeker	4,238	5,032	668	4,156	5,511
Mille Lacs	4,443	3,860	550	4,011	4,307
Morrison	6,930	6,296	559	6,225	7,556
Mower	10,538	7,908	1,465	12,498	8,054
Murray	2,714	3,004	359	2,741	2,780
Nicollet	5,400	6,436	1,519	5,789	7,472
Nobles	4,703	4,706	657	4,619	4,876
Norman	2,253	2,192	369	2,202	2,152
Olmsted	13,983	22,704	3,638	16,335	28,129
Otter Tail	9,108	15,091	1,538	9,714	15,664
Pennington	3,101	3,715	472	2,913	3,536
Pine	5,121	3,899	467	5,223	4,493
Pipestone	2,392	3,207	561	2,391	3,043
Polk	7,151	9,036	1,207	7,033	8,617
Pope	2,527	3,159	354	2,757	3,064
Ramsey	124,774	78,860	23,222	141,623	95,667
Red Lake	1,318	1,223	116	1,294	1,184
Redwood	2,952	5,993	548	2,957	6,020
Renville	4,058	5,544	653	3,972	5,571
Rice	9,531	8,168	2,414	10,880	10,456
Rock	2,089	3,164	397	2,188	2,971
Roseau	2,616	3,358	259	2,319	3,445
St. Louis	69,403	33,407	8,719	77,683	34,162
Scott	9,115	9,018	1,475	9,452	12,573
Sherburne	6,229	6,035	985	6,140	7,738
Sibley	2,521	4,460	509	2,761	4,638
Stearns	21,862	24,888	3,555	20,944	30,216
Steele	5,095	7,805	1,087	5,060	8,780
Stevens	2,559	3,283	524	2,451	3,251
Swift	3,245	2,943	511	3,531	2,893
Todd	4,975	6,451	451	4,657	6,585
Traverse	1,258	1,574	159	1,325	1,399
Wabasha	3,712	4,886	549	3,872	5,299
Wadena	2,635	4,089	265	2,454	4,306
Waseca	3,535	4,801	777	3,527	5,509
Washington	25,634	22,718	5,050	28,527	29,046
Watonwan	2,442	3,629	415	2,425	3,526
Wilkin	1,496	2,224	318	1,410	2,367
Winona	9,814	10,332	1,780	9,577	11,981
Wright	12,383	12,293	1,692	12,486	15,399
Yellow Med	2,833	4,004	456	3,018	3,819
Totals	954,173	873,268	174,997	1,036,364	1,032,603

Minnesota Vote Since 1936

1936, Roosevelt, Dem., 698,811; Landon, Rep., 350,461; Lemke, Union, 74,296; Thomas, Soc., 2,872; Browder, Com., 2,574; Aiken, Soc. Labor, 961.

1940, Roosevelt, Dem., 644,196; Willkie, Rep., 596,274; Thomas, Soc., 5,454; Browder, Com., 2,711; Aiken, Ind., 2,553.

1944, Roosevelt, Dem., 589,864; Dewey, Rep., 527,416; Thomas, Soc., 5,073; Teichert, Ind. Gov't., 3,176.

1948, Truman, Dem., 692,966; Dewey, Rep., 483,617; Wallace, Prog., 27,866; Thomas, Soc., 4,646; Teichert, Soc. Labor, 2,525; Dobbs, Soc. Workers, 606.

1952, Eisenhower, Rep., 763,211; Stevenson, Dem., 608,458; Hallinan, Prog., 2,666; Hass, Soc. Labor, 2,383; Hamblen, Proh., 2,147; Dobbs, Soc. Workers, 618.

1956, Eisenhower, Rep., 719,302; Stevenson, Dem., 617,525; Hass, Soc. Labor (Ind. Gov.), 2,080; Dobbs, Soc. Workers, 1,098.

1960, Kennedy, Dem., 779,933; Nixon, Rep., 757,915; Dobbs, Soc. Workers, 3,077; Industrial Gov., 962.

1964, Johnson, Dem., 991,117; Goldwater, Rep., 559,624; DeBerry, Soc. Workers, 1,177; Hass, Industrial Gov., 2,544.

1968, Nixon, Rep., 658,643; Humphrey, Dem., 857,738; Wallace, 3d party, 68,931; scattered, 2,443; Halstead, Soc. Worker, 808; Blomen, Ind. Gov't., 285; Mitchell, Com., 415; Cleaver, Peace, 935; McCarthy, write-in, 585; scattered, 170.

1972, Nixon, Rep., 898,269; McGovern, Dem., 802,346; Schmitz, Amer., 31,407; Spock, Peoples, 2,805; Fisher, Soc. Labor, 4,261; Jenness, Soc. Workers, 940; Hall, Com., 662; scattered, 962.

1976, Carter, Dem., 1,070,440; Ford, Rep., 819,395; McCarthy, Ind., 35,490; Anderson, Amer., 13,592; Camejo, Soc. Workers, 4,149; MacBride, Libertarian, 3,529; Hall, Com., 1,092.

1980, Reagan, Rep., 873, 268; Carter, Dem., 954,173; Anderson, Ind., 174,997; Clark, Libertarian, 31,593; Commoner, Citizens, 8,406; Hall, Com., 1,117; DeBerry, Soc. Workers, 711; Griswold, Workers World, 698; McReynolds, Socialist, 536; write-ins, 281.

1984, Mondale, Dem., 1,036,364; Reagan, Rep., 1,032,603; Bergland, Libertarian, 2,996.

Mississippi

	1980			1984	
County	Carter (D)	Reagan (R)	Anderson (I)	Mondale (D)	Reagan (R)
Adams	7,228	7,523	151	7,849	9,440
Alcorn	6,242	5,196	898	4,862	7,203
Amite	3,229	2,653	43	2,569	3,463
Attala	4,117	3,975	71	3,327	4,870
Benton	2,094	1,254	35	1,715	1,737
Bolivar	8,839	5,148	280	8,769	6,939
Calhoun	3,295	2,579	64	1,749	3,579
Carroll	2,037	2,153	22	1,462	2,823
Chickasaw	3,622	2,540	71	2,329	3,605
Choctaw	1,729	1,927	26	1,166	2,491
Claiborne	3,032	1,129	22	3,179	1,294
Clarke	3,303	3,303	41	2,262	4,551
Clay	4,275	3,439	124	4,046	4,112
Coahoma	7,030	4,592	256	6,839	5,759
Copiah	5,517	4,461	76	4,591	5,806
Covington	2,956	3,471	39	2,219	4,165
DeSoto	6,344	9,655	237	4,369	12,576
Forrest	8,274	12,656	275	6,786	15,719
Franklin	2,040	2,026	23	1,494	2,564
George	2,757	3,052	64	1,655	4,346
Greene	1,740	1,772	23	1,297	2,744
Grenada	4,182	3,993	59	3,325	5,181
Hancock	3,544	5,088	159	2,630	7,662
Harrison	16,318	25,175	822	12,495	33,995
Hinds	39,369	48,135	1,414	42,373	56,953
Holmes	5,463	2,693	57	5,641	3,102
Humphreys	2,970	1,841	68	2,596	2,309
Issaquena	598	349	5	501	512
Itawamba	4,852	2,906	57	2,674	4,587
Jackson	12,226	22,498	653	8,821	29,585
Jasper	3,813	2,781	34	3,104	3,727
Jefferson	2,871	751	41	3,049	856
Jefferson Davis	3,831	2,280	24	2,644	2,884
Jones	11,117	12,900	155	7,298	17,586
[illegible]	4,601	[illegible]	[illegible]	[illegible]	2,354
Lafayette	4,887	4,366	243	3,646	6,006
Lamar	3,005	5,395	84	1,964	7,929
Lauderdale	9,918	14,727	784	7,534	18,807
Lawrence	[illegible]	[illegible]	49	[illegible]	[illegible]
Leake	4,033	3,624	40	2,845	4,663
Lee	10,047	8,326	321	6,208	13,312
Leflore	7,498	5,798	166	7,443	7,550
Lincoln	5,213	7,286	75	4,458	8,898
Lowndes	6,187	9,973	140	6,078	12,049
Madison	7,621	6,024	276	8,002	9,298
Marion	5,366	5,218	62	3,757	7,355
Marshall	7,153	3,455	121	5,845	4,389
Monroe	6,998	4,793	177	4,437	7,387
Montgomery	2,730	2,479	42	1,881	3,093
Neshoba	3,872	5,165	72	2,630	6,715
Newton	3,455	4,317	86	2,127	5,911
Noxubee	3,434	1,970	47	2,928	2,123
Oktibbeha	6,039	6,300	258	5,097	7,574
Panola	6,179	4,219	149	5,465	5,850
Pearl River	5,028	6,822	161	3,085	9,978
Perry	1,957	2,255	25	1,415	3,098
Pike	6,694	6,661	129	6,137	8,254
Pontotoc	4,499	3,198	58	2,434	5,182
Prentiss	4,832	3,264	40	2,897	4,821
Quitman	2,926	1,691	83	2,343	2,198
Rankin	8,047	16,650	296	5,874	22,393
Scott	4,043	4,645	72	3,274	5,763
Sharkey	1,957	996	28	1,723	1,487
Simpson	4,015	5,190	70	2,894	5,983
Smith	2,474	3,772	46	1,573	5,116
Stone	1,821	1,888	53	1,185	2,980
Sunflower	5,035	3,728	82	4,913	5,178
Tallahatchie	3,467	2,183	45	2,725	2,901
Tate	3,892	3,343	80	2,846	4,677
Tippah	3,878	3,338	116	2,566	4,706
Tishomingo	4,595	2,489	79	2,879	3,527
Tunica	2,198	954	24	1,621	1,109
Union	5,001	3,545	94	2,766	5,837
Walthall	2,960	2,703	34	2,219	3,305
Warren	7,489	10,151	274	8,054	12,959
Washington	10,722	8,978	186	10,617	12,454
Wayne	3,494	3,844	26	2,818	5,000
Webster	2,178	2,386	75	1,397	3,390
Wilkinson	2,981	1,442	25	2,627	1,722
Winston	4,416	3,998	65	3,543	5,192
Yalobusha	3,432	2,224	78	2,337	2,934
Yazoo	5,468	4,819	99	5,037	6,275
Totals	**429,281**	**441,089**	**12,036**	**352,192**	**582,377**

Mississippi Vote Since 1936

1936, Roosevelt, Dem., 157,318; Landon, Rep., Howard faction, 2,760; Rowlands faction, 1,675 total 4,435; Thomas, Soc., 329.

1940, Roosevelt, Dem., 168,252; Willkie, Ind. Rep., 4,550; Rep., 2,814; total, 7,364; Thomas, Soc., 103.

1944, Roosevelt, Dem., 158,515; Dewey, Rep., 3,742; Reg. Dem., 9,964; Ind. Rep., 7,859.

1948, Thurmond, States'. Rights, 167,538; Truman, Dem., 19,384; Dewey, Rep., 5,043; Wallace, Prog., 225.

1952, Eisenhower, Ind. vote pledged to Rep. candidate, 112,966; Stevenson, Dem., 172,566.

1956, Stevenson, Dem., 144,498; Eisenhower, Rep., 56,372; Black and Tan Grand Old Party, 4,313; total, 60,685; Byrd, Ind., 42,966.

1960, Democratic unpledged electors, 116,248; Kennedy, Dem., 108,362; Nixon, Rep., 73,561. Mississippi's victorious slate of 8 unpledged Democratic electors cast their votes for Sen. Harry F. Byrd (D-Va.).

1964, Johnson, Dem., 52,618; Goldwater, Rep., 356,528.

1968, Nixon, Rep., 88,516; Humphrey, Dem., 150,644; Wallace, 3d party, 415,349.

1972, Nixon, Rep., 505,125; McGovern, Dem., 126,782; Schmitz, Amer., 11,598; Jenness, Soc. Workers, 2,458.

1976, Carter, Dem., 381,309; Ford, Rep., 366,846; Anderson, Amer., 6,678; McCarthy, Ind., 4,074; Maddox, Ind., 4,049; Camejo, Soc. Workers, 2,805; MacBride, Libertarian, 2,609.

1980, Reagan, Rep., 441,089; Carter, Dem., 429,281; Anderson, Ind., 12,036; Clark, Libertarian, 5,465; Griswold, Workers World, 2,402; Pulley, Soc. Worker, 2,347.

1984, Reagan, Rep., 582,377; Mondale, Dem., 352,192; Bergland, Libertarian, 2,336.

Missouri

	1980			1984	
County	Carter (D)	Reagan (R)	Anderson (I)	Mondale (D)	Reagan (R)
Adair	3,507	5,513	414	3,119	6,430
Andrew	2,575	3,690	245	2,457	4,252
[illegible]	[illegible]	[illegible]	151	1,210	2,277
Audrain	5,168	6,347	233	4,662	7,261
Barry	4,193	7,038	150	3,483	7,683
Barton	1,901	3,337	115	1,348	3,996
[illegible]	[illegible]	4,061	114	2,009	4,223
Benton	2,241	3,451	126	2,251	3,805
Bollinger	2,160	2,863	35	1,923	2,778
Boone	18,527	16,313	3,519	19,364	26,600
Buchanan	16,967	16,551	1,301	15,369	19,735
Butler	5,605	8,342	181	4,699	8,712
Caldwell	1,541	2,551	108	1,382	2,678
Callaway	5,560	6,755	420	4,327	8,262
Camden	3,416	6,541	218	3,088	8,057
Cape Girardeau	8,625	14,861	873	7,346	17,404
Carroll	2,130	3,291	130	1,980	3,495
Carter	1,087	1,218	37	916	1,402
Cass	8,198	10,105	667	7,517	14,456
Cedar	1,703	3,469	86	1,440	3,530
Chariton	2,250	2,641	63	2,244	2,744
Christian	3,502	6,487	205	3,223	7,634
Clark	1,494	2,042	56	1,627	2,068
Clay	24,250	28,521	2,782	22,586	36,529
Clinton	3,001	3,599	184	2,778	4,226
Cole	9,210	16,373	691	6,702	20,366
Cooper	2,687	3,996	130	2,219	4,603
Crawford	2,710	4,081	170	2,610	4,716
Dade	1,283	2,410	61	1,100	2,600
Dallas	2,011	3,297	114	1,902	3,577
Daviess	1,770	2,125	61	1,526	2,414
DeKalb	1,677	2,062	111	1,464	2,188
Dent	2,528	3,477	86	2,544	3,490
Douglas	1,677	3,440	93	1,536	3,662
Dunklin	6,120	5,253	128	4,967	6,092
Franklin	10,480	15,210	863	8,319	18,669
Gasconade	1,550	4,481	136	1,130	4,678
Gentry	1,720	2,005	117	1,600	2,047
Greene	30,408	43,116	3,261	27,985	37,250
Grundy	2,064	2,890	110	1,861	3,156
Harrison	1,732	2,734	140	1,649	2,844
Henry	4,648	4,807	238	3,741	5,419
Hickory	1,248	1,893	52	1,212	2,190
Holt	1,119	1,993	59	1,026	2,087
Howard	2,243	2,179	114	2,014	2,360
Howell	4,472	7,149	311	3,767	[illegible]
Iron	2,226	2,205	94	2,023	2,316
Jackson	135,805	106,156	12,260	135,067	132,271
Jasper	11,953	21,664	785	9,259	23,066

Jefferson	24,042	28,546	1,753	20,026	34,525
Johnson	5,441	6,449	571	4,238	8,413
Knox	1,187	1,475	36	1,097	1,513
Laclede	3,443	5,642	153	2,665	6,406
Lafayette	5,792	7,271	339	4,848	8,581
Lawrence	4,670	7,921	184	3,720	8,370
Lewis	2,314	2,350	102	1,977	2,438
Lincoln	4,110	4,963	182	3,290	6,137
Linn	3,467	3,585	139	3,112	3,822
Livingston	3,368	3,654	205	2,699	4,090
McDonald	2,485	4,114	124	2,109	4,521
Macon	3,578	4,430	135	3,037	4,542
Madison	2,231	2,618	70	1,862	2,808
Maries	1,732	1,985	39	1,388	2,267
Marion	5,890	6,036	192	4,666	6,831
Mercer	821	1,266	54	875	1,229
Miller	2,469	5,560	115	2,054	6,706
Mississippi	3,040	2,459	64	2,524	2,502
Moniteau	2,284	3,430	98	1,614	4,197
Monroe	2,445	2,026	53	1,992	2,163
Montgomery	2,007	3,061	124	1,668	3,261
Morgan	2,460	3,577	114	2,169	4,392
New Madrid	4,171	4,041	64	3,776	4,323
Newton	5,621	10,515	341	4,623	11,709
Nodaway	4,257	4,544	414	3,615	5,471
Oregon	2,326	1,523	26	2,026	1,979
Osage	2,045	3,679	72	1,343	4,381
Ozark	1,242	2,434	63	1,110	2,614
Pemiscot	4,140	3,519	52	3,293	3,733
Perry	2,416	5,053	178	1,837	4,493
Pettis	6,475	8,833	435	5,413	10,991
Phelps	5,470	7,366	620	5,074	9,012
Pike	3,454	3,932	158	3,313	3,933
Platte	7,342	10,092	1,107	7,668	12,859
Polk	3,336	4,842	135	2,819	5,467
Pulaski	3,707	3,998	128	2,865	5,330
Putnam	871	1,722	44	797	1,540
Ralls	2,069	1,968	75	2,011	2,067
Randolph	4,884	5,141	213	4,471	5,735
Ray	4,518	4,064	215	3,979	4,875
Reynolds	1,919	1,271	44	2,026	1,330
Ripley	2,156	2,524	61	1,883	2,927
St. Charles	20,668	36,050	2,494	17,617	47,784
St. Clair	1,706	2,419	60	1,655	2,667
St. Francois	7,495	8,914	397	7,137	9,792
Ste. Genevieve	3,324	2,768	151	2,723	3,245
St. Louis	192,796	263,518	25,032	173,144	307,684
Saline	4,943	5,218	353	4,281	6,042
Schuyler	1,114	1,386	48	1,141	1,250
Scotland	1,200	1,592	63	1,075	1,485
Scott	6,854	8,227	203	5,569	8,727
Shannon	1,818	1,523	44	1,580	1,779
Shelby	1,849	2,151	60	1,573	2,243
Stoddard	5,128	6,199	132	4,294	6,701
Stone	2,210	4,780	180	2,119	5,706
Sullivan	1,824	2,412	76	1,784	2,306
Taney	3,389	6,230	195	2,912	7,082
Texas	4,261	4,879	125	3,662	5,591
Vernon	3,704	4,391	285	2,984	5,181
Warren	2,132	4,366	192	1,964	5,150
Washington	2,873	3,439	89	2,987	3,755
Wayne	2,549	2,823	44	2,363	2,867
Webster	3,409	5,121	149	2,982	5,529
Worth	760	833	47	734	921
Wright	2,182	4,451	56	1,973	4,687
ST. LOUIS CITY	113,697	50,333	5,656	112,318	61,020
Totals	**931,182**	**1,074,181**	**77,920**	**848,583**	**1,274,188**

Missouri Vote Since 1936

1936, Roosevelt, Dem., 1,111,403; Landon, Rep., 697,891; Lemke, Union, 14,630; Thomas, Soc., 3,454; Colvin, Proh., 908; Browder, Com., 417; Aiken, Soc. Labor, 292.

1940, Roosevelt, Dem., 958,476; Willkie, Rep., 871,009; Thomas, Soc., 2,226; Babson, Proh., 1,809; Aiken, Soc. Labor, 209.

1944, Roosevelt, Dem., 807,357; Dewey, Rep., 761,175; Thomas, Soc., 1,750; Watson, Proh., 1,175; Teichert, Soc. Labor, 221.

1948, Truman, Dem., 917,315; Dewey, Rep., 655,039; Wallace, Prog., 3,998; Thomas, Soc., 2,222.

1952, Eisenhower, Rep., 959,429; Stevenson, Dem., 929,830; Hallinan, Prog., 987; Hamblen, Proh., 885; MacArthur, Christian Nationalist, 302; America First, 233; Hoopes, Soc., 227; Hass, Soc. Labor, 169.

1956, Stevenson, Dem., 918,273; Eisenhower, Rep., 914,299.

1960, Kennedy, Dem., 972,201; Nixon, Rep., 962,221.

1964, Johnson, Dem., 1,164,344; Goldwater, Rep., 653,535.

1968, Nixon, Rep., 811,932; Humphrey, Dem., 791,444; Wallace, 3d party, 206,126.

1972, Nixon, Rep., 1,154,058; McGovern, Dem., 698,531.

1976, Carter, Dem., 999,163; Ford, Rep., 928,808; McCarthy, Ind., 24,329.

1980, Reagan, Rep., 1,074,181; Carter, Dem., 931,182; Anderson, Ind., 77,920; Clark, Libertarian, 14,422; DeBerry, Soc. Workers, 1,515; Commoner, Citizens, 573; write-ins, 31.

1984, Reagan, Rep., 1,274,188; Mondale, Dem., 848,583.

Montana

	1980			1984	
County	Carter (D)	Reagan (R)	Anderson (I)	Mondale (D)	Reagan (R)
Beaverhead	842	2,955	205	942	3,044
Big Horn	1,644	1,730	308	2,681	2,390
Blaine	1,107	1,686	163	1,229	1,736
Broadwater	401	1,052	69	458	1,345
Carbon	1,468	2,471	331	1,657	2,877
Carter	237	766	37	194	823
Cascade	11,105	17,664	2,655	14,252	19,846
Chouteau	853	2,448	216	896	2,425
Custer	1,822	3,533	369	1,982	3,879
Daniels	483	1,086	77	473	984
Dawson	1,543	3,045	424	1,776	3,468
Deer Lodge	3,077	1,905	474	3,539	1,901
Fallon	512	1,286	94	569	1,237
Fergus	1,840	4,455	388	1,804	4,585
Flathead	6,349	15,102	1,621	8,310	17,012
Gallatin	5,747	12,738	2,432	8,163	15,643
Garfield	169	760	29	134	770
Glacier	1,394	2,283	297	2,167	2,228
Golden Valley	155	362	28	211	384
Granite	439	811	76	417	880
Hill	2,875	4,448	604	3,657	4,635
Jefferson	1,055	1,841	216	1,324	2,226
Judith Basin	480	1,030	93	483	1,050
Lake	2,615	5,083	573	3,473	5,754
Lewis & Clark	6,815	12,128	1,793	8,768	13,569
Liberty	283	872	71	323	895
Lincoln	2,422	4,202	485	2,959	4,080
Madison	676	2,220	174	708	2,308
McCone	349	1,000	86	459	1,015
Meagher	247	689	41	283	771
Mineral	660	800	138	718	943
Missoula	13,115	16,161	3,847	16,540	19,777
Musselshell	784	1,279	106	781	1,541
Park	1,663	3,929	459	2,387	4,115
Petroleum	90	225	15	86	258
Phillips	745	1,723	146	787	1,934
Pondera	897	2,270	207	1,039	2,239
Powder River	336	985	94	346	1,066
Powell	883	1,770	198	1,066	1,877
Prairie	283	580	57	289	693
Ravalli	3,063	7,268	743	3,825	8,161
Richland	1,252	3,348	343	1,382	3,847
Roosevelt	1,504	2,298	304	1,962	2,431
Rosebud	1,167	1,875	265	1,920	2,413
Sanders	1,395	2,194	291	1,654	2,467
Sheridan	955	1,658	247	1,087	1,774
Silver Bow	9,721	7,301	1,752	11,095	6,637
Stillwater	919	1,828	181	1,100	2,118
Sweet Grass	440	1,169	98	378	1,417
Teton	902	2,415	186	1,102	2,257
Toole	634	2,000	154	789	1,949
Treasure	181	321	34	209	353
Valley	1,567	3,242	264	1,849	3,123
Wheatland	381	742	88	407	753
Wibaux	219	450	45	216	423
Yellowstone	15,272	27,332	4,590	19,437	34,124
Totals	**118,032**	**206,814**	**29,281**	**146,742**	**232,450**

Montana Vote Since 1936

1936, Roosevelt, Dem., 159,690; Landon, Rep., 63,598; Lemke, Union, 5,549; Thomas, Soc., 1,066; Browder, Com., 385; Colvin, Proh., 224.

1940, Roosevelt, Dem., 145,698; Willkie, Rep., 99,579; Thomas, Soc., 1,443; Babson, Proh., 664; Browder, Com., 489.

1944, Roosevelt, Dem., 112,556; Dewey, Rep., 93,163; Thomas, Soc., 1,296; Watson, Proh., 340.

1948, Truman, Dem., 119,071; Dewey, Rep., 96,770; Wallace, Prog., 7,313; Thomas, Soc., 695; Watson, Proh., 429.

1952, Eisenhower, Rep., 157,394; Stevenson, Dem., 106,213; Hallinan, Prog., 723; Hamblen, Proh., 548; Hoopes, Soc., 159.

1956, Eisenhower, Rep., 154,933; Stevenson, Dem., 116,238.

1960, Kennedy, Dem., 134,891; Nixon, Rep., 141,841; Decker, Proh., 456; Dobbs, Soc. Workers, 391.

1964, Johnson, Dem., 164,246; Goldwater, Rep., 113,032; Kasper, Nat'l States Rights, 519; Munn, Proh., 499; DeBerry, Soc. Worker, 332.

1968, Nixon, Rep., 138,835; Humphrey, Dem., 114,117; Wallace, 3d party, 20,015; Halstead, Soc. Worker, 457; Munn, Proh., 510; Caton, New Reform, 470.

1972, Nixon, Rep., 183,976; McGovern, Dem., 120,197; Schmitz, Amer., 13,430.

1976, Carter, Dem., 149,259; Ford, Rep., 173,703; Anderson, Amer., 5,772.

1980, Reagan, Rep., 206,814; Carter, Dem., 118,032; Anderson, Ind., 29,281; Clark, Libertarian, 9,825.

1984, Reagan, Rep., 232,450; Mondale, Dem., 146,742; Bergland, Libertarian, 5,185.

Nebraska

County	1980 Carter (D)	1980 Reagan (R)	1980 Anderson (I)	1984 Mondale (D)	1984 Reagan (R)
Adams	3,361	8,469	879	2,940	9,092
Antelope	659	3,192	150	697	3,222
Arthur	55	242	9	33	248
Banner	33	481	14	58	457
Blaine	63	361	15	48	363
Boone	769	2,598	176	690	2,508
Box Butte	1,206	3,898	307	1,471	4,011
Boyd	376	1,261	62	308	1,173
Brown	341	1,614	105	312	1,513
Buffalo	3,162	9,764	1,028	3,083	11,343
Burt	814	2,806	232	1,054	2,645
Butler	1,112	2,590	159	1,192	2,555
Cass	2,007	5,180	487	2,495	5,451
Cedar	1,265	3,257	273	1,201	3,298
Chase	324	1,593	91	367	1,687
Cherry	489	2,517	105	463	2,720
Cheyenne	776	3,073	196	857	3,159
Clay	840	2,739	190	811	2,919
Colfax	892	3,259	230	901	2,998
Cuming	803	3,999	266	779	3,931
Custer	1,011	4,562	285	1,090	4,749
Dakota	1,928	3,165	317	2,510	3,487
Dawes	703	3,281	228	864	3,325
Dawson	1,462	6,687	357	1,487	6,878
Deuel	192	943	63	198	961
Dixon	822	2,020	200	985	2,154
Dodge	3,556	9,514	988	4,259	10,167
Douglas	51,504	96,741	13,198	58,867	112,557
Dundy	192	1,135	55	225	002
Fillmore	1,025	2,435	221	1,009	2,474
Franklin	441	1,672	109	522	1,597
Frontier	259	1,345	84	258	1,351
Furnas	536	2,403	113	579	2,363
Gage	2,268	6,072	722	2,699	6,102
Garden	202	1,297	63	180	1,158
Garfield	238	811	42	196	899
Gosper	181	783	47	201	802
Grant	76	373	13	51	404
Greeley	495	1,028	78	485	918
Hall	4,201	12,083	001	4,015	13,082
Hamilton	777	3,199	245	840	3,417
Harlan	486	1,690	109	493	1,692
Hayes	82	617	21	100	591
Hitchcock	328	1,471	115	341	1,391
Holt	1,016	4,488	243	893	4,611
Hooker	63	386	18	55	433
Howard	788	1,969	170	887	1,899
Jefferson	1,125	3,090	297	1,366	3,114
Johnson	623	1,716	180	821	1,536
Kearney	726	2,510	227	726	2,505
Keith	710	3,373	199	631	3,423
Keya Paha	130	524	27	126	505
Kimball	385	1,615	97	339	1,732
Knox	1,057	3,404	245	1,149	3,364
Lancaster	27,040	38,630	9,221	32,780	48,627
Lincoln	3,762	9,631	841	4,483	10,692
Logan	71	442	17	66	445
Loup	74	368	21	79	323
McPherson	49	285	5	57	295
Madison	1,924	9,715	552	1,755	9,786
Merrick	712	2,710	212	818	2,696
Morrill	512	1,887	96	463	1,888
Nance	561	1,439	100	524	1,391
Nemaha	929	2,693	221	1,004	2,752
Nuckolls	899	2,180	159	947	2,132
Otoe	1,471	4,611	391	1,868	4,679
Pawnee	431	1,418	122	552	1,306
Perkins	313	1,338	81	307	1,418
Phelps	734	3,465	192	739	3,739
Pierce	517	2,935	155	545	3,016
Platte	2,385	8,781	546	2,057	10,035
Polk	538	2,206	149	610	2,149
Red Willow	892	4,019	254	1,022	4,101
Richardson	1,350	3,634	264	1,422	3,634
Rock	145	855	39	147	873
Saline	1,908	2,934	480	2,385	2,941
Sarpy	5,678	15,523	1,685	6,831	20,155
Saunders	2,034	5,222	516	2,467	5,217
Scotts Bluff	2,851	9,485	677	3,060	10,676
Seward	1,799	3,525	533	1,905	3,969
Sheridan	369	2,747	121	377	2,661
Sherman	576	1,253	116	701	1,144
Sioux	120	759	32	121	732
Stanton	361	1,942	118	410	2,080
Thayer	925	2,514	178	946	2,578
Thomas	65	306	26	73	298
Thurston	724	1,454	140	1,077	1,410
Valley	654	2,100	124	739	2,052
Washington	1,445	4,560	356	1,561	5,163
Wayne	733	2,844	300	833	3,075
Webster	547	1,676	138	645	1,694
Wheeler	93	371	22	97	365
York	1,118	5,065	323	1,114	5,012
Totals	**166,424**	**419,214**	**44,854**	**187,475**	**459,135**

Nebraska Vote Since 1936

1936, Roosevelt, Dem., 347,454; Landon, Rep., 248,731; Lemke, Union, 12,847.

1940, Roosevelt, Dem., 263,677; Willkie, Rep., 352,201.

1944, Roosevelt, Dem., 233,246; Dewey, Rep., 329,880.

1948, Truman, Dem., 224,165; Dewey, Rep., 264,774.

1952, Eisenhower, Rep., 421,603; Stevenson Dem., 188,057.

1956, Eisenhower, Rep., 378,108; Stevenson, Dem., 199,029.

1960, Kennedy, Dem., 232,542; Nixon, Rep., 380,553.

1964, Johnson, Dem., 307,307; Goldwater, Rep., 276,847.

1968, Nixon, Rep., 321,163; Humphrey, Dem., 170,784; Wallace, 3d party, 44,904.

1972, Nixon, Rep., 406,298; McGovern, Dem., 169,991; scattered 817.

1976, Carter, Dem., 233,287; Ford, Rep., 359,219; McCarthy, Ind., 9,383; Maddox, Amer. Ind., 3,378; MacBride, Libertarian, 1,476.

1980, Reagan, Rep., 419,214; Carter, Dem., 166,424; Anderson, Ind., 44,854; Clark, Libertarian, 9,041.

1984, Reagan, Rep., 459,135; Mondale, Dem., 187,475; Bergland, Libertarian, 2,075.

Nevada

County	1980 Carter (D)	1980 Reagan (R)	1980 Anderson (I)	1984 Mondale (D)	1984 Reagan (R)
Churchill	1,055	3,841	257	1,304	4,479
Clark	38,313	76,194	8,702	53,386	94,133
Douglas	1,352	5,254	511	1,877	6,385
Elko	1,296	4,393	301	1,566	5,110
Esmeralda	110	311	29	158	453
Eureka	103	430	13	124	439
Humboldt	684	1,980	126	002	2,498
Lander	361	935	64	301	1,222
Lincoln	396	1,087	38	397	1,175
Lyon	1,288	3,709	271	1,673	4,370
Mineral	631	1,620	147	788	1,645
Nye	973	2,387	204	1,269	3,573
Pershing	311	877	60	333	956
Storey	222	460	62	252	570
Washoe	15,621	41,276	5,705	22,321	50,418
White Pine	1,181	1,896	195	1,276	1,917
CARSON CITY	2,769	8,389	964	3,790	9,477
Totals	**66,666**	**155,017**	**17,651**	**91,655**	**188,770**

Nevada Vote Since 1936

1936, Roosevelt, Dem., 31,925; Landon, Rep., 11,923.

1940, Roosevelt, Dem., 31,945; Willkie, Rep., 21,229.

1944, Roosevelt, Dem., 29,623; Dewey, Rep., 24,611.

1948, Truman, Dem., 31,291; Dewey, Rep., 29,357; Wallace, Prog., 1,469.

1952, Eisenhower, Rep., 50,502; Stevenson, Dem., 31,688.

1956, Eisenhower, Rep., 56,049; Stevenson, Dem., 40,640.

1960, Kennedy, Dem., 54,880; Nixon, Rep., 52,387.

1964, Johnson, Dem., 79,339; Goldwater, Rep., 56,094.

1968, Nixon, Rep., 73,188; Humphrey, Dem., 60,598; Wallace, 3d party, 20,432.

1972, Nixon, Rep., 115,750; McGovern, Dem. 66,016.

1976, Carter Dem., 92,479; Ford, Rep., 101,273; MacBride, Libertarian, 1,519; Maddox, Amer. Ind., 1,497; scattered 5,108.

1980, Reagan, Rep., 155,017; Carter, Dem., 66,666; Anderson, Ind., 17,651; Clark, Libertarian, 4,358.

1984, Reagan, Rep., 108,770; Mondale, Dem., 91,655; Bergland, Libertarian, 2,292.

New Hampshire

City	1980 Carter (D)	1980 Reagan (R)	1980 Anderson (I)	1984 Mondale (D)	1984 Reagan (R)
Berlin City	2,202	2,847	347	1,863	3,261
Claremont	2,171	2,365	506	2,006	2,868
Concord	4,330	6,092	2,204	5,172	7,190
Dover	3,344	4,497	1,517	3,826	5,397
Keene	2,875	4,317	1,650	3,238	4,975
Laconia	1,635	3,529	628	1,552	4,151
Manchester	10,919	23,557	3,178	10,283	24,780
Nashua	9,156	13,874	3,391	9,305	16,961
Portsmith	3,666	4,023	1,467	4,418	4,967
Rochester	2,566	4,495	650	2,622	5,457
Totals	**108,864**	**221,705**	**49,693**	**120,377**	**267,051**

New Hampshire Vote Since 1936

1936, Roosevelt, Dem., 108,640; Landon, Rep., 104,642; Lemke, Union, 4,819; Browder, Com., 193.

1940, Roosevelt, Dem., 125,292; Willkie, Rep., 110,127.

1944, Roosevelt, Dem., 119,663; Dewey, Rep., 109,916; Thomas, Soc., 46.

1948, Truman, Dem., 107,995; Dewey, Rep., 121,299; Wallace, Prog., 1,970; Thomas, Soc., 86; Teichert, Soc. Labor, 83; Thurmond, States' Rights, 7.

1952, Eisenhower, Rep., 166,287; Stevenson, Dem., 106,663.

1956, Eisenhower, Rep., 176,519; Stevenson, Dem., 90,364; Andrews, Const., 111.

1960, Kennedy, Dem., 137,772; Nixon, Rep., 157,989.

1964, Johnson, Dem., 182,065; Goldwater, Rep., 104,029.

1968, Nixon, Rep., 154,903; Humphrey, Dem., 130,589; Wallace, 3d party, 11,173; New Party, 421; Halstead, Soc. Worker, 104.

1972, Nixon, Rep., 213,724; McGovern, Dem., 116,435; Schmitz, Amer., 3,386; Jenness, Soc. Workers, 368; scattered, 142.

1976, Carter, Dem., 147,645; Ford, Rep., 185,935; McCarthy, Ind., 4,095; MacBride, Libertarian, 936; Reagan, write-in, 388; La Rouche, U.S. Labor, 186; Camejo, Soc. Workers, 161, Levin, Soc. Labor, 66; scattered, 215.

1980, Reagan, Rep., 221,705; Carter, Dem., 108,864; Anderson, Ind., 49,693; Clark, Libertarian, 2,067; Commoner, Citizens, 1,325; Hall, Com., 129; Griswold, Workers World, 76; DeBerry, Soc. Workers, 72; scattered, 68.

1984, Reagan, Rep., 267,051; Mondale, Dem., 120,377; Bergland, Libertarian, 735.

New Jersey

County	1980 Carter (D)	1980 Reagan (R)	1980 Anderson (I)	1984 Mondale (D)	1984 Reagan (R)
Atlantic	31,286	37,973	5,582	33,240	49,158
Bergen	139,474	232,043	38,242	155,039	268,507
Burlington	50,083	68,415	11,314	57,467	89,815
Camden	80,033	87,939	16,125	90,233	109,749
Cape May	12,708	22,729	2,550	13,378	28,768
Cumberland	19,356	23,242	3,253	21,141	29,398
Essex	145,281	117,222	21,271	173,295	136,798
Gloucester	29,804	40,306	7,533	32,702	54,041
Hudson	95,622	91,207	8,941	94,304	112,834
Hunterdon	10,029	21,403	3,610	10,972	29,737
Mercer	60,888	53,450	12,117	66,398	71,195
Middlesex	97,304	122,354	17,463	104,905	160,221
Monmouth	71,328	120,173	17,444	79,382	152,595
Morris	48,965	105,260	17,181	53,201	137,719
Ocean	46,923	98,433	10,073	51,012	124,391
Passaic	61,486	82,531	9,385	69,590	101,951
Salem	10,209	13,000	1,800	8,935	17,368
Somerset	29,470	52,591	8,346	31,924	66,303
Sussex	10,531	27,063	3,988	11,502	35,680
Union	86,074	112,288	15,586	92,056	135,446
Warren	10,510	16,935	2,828	10,647	21,938
Totals	**1,147,364**	**1,546,557**	**234,632**	**1,261,323**	**1,933,630**

New Jersey Vote Since 1936

1936, Roosevelt, Dem., 1,083,549; Landon, Rep., 719,421; Lemke, Union, 9,405; Thomas, Soc., 3,895; Browder, Com., 1,590; Colvin, Proh., 916; Aiken, Soc. Labor, 346.

1940, Roosevelt, Dem., 1,016,404; Willkie, Rep., 944,876; Browder, Com., 8,814; Thomas, Soc., 2,823; Babson, Proh., 851; Aiken, Soc. Labor, 446.

1944, Roosevelt, Dem., 987,874; Dewey, Rep., 961,335; Teichert, Soc. Labor, 6,939; Watson, Nat'l. Proh., 4,255; Thomas, Soc., 3,385.

1948, Truman, Dem., 895,455; Dewey, Rep., 981,124; Wallace, Prog., 42,683; Watson, Proh., 10,593; Thomas, Soc., 10,521; Dobbs, Soc. Workers, 5,825; Teichert, Soc. Labor, 3,354.

1952, Eisenhower, Rep., 1,373,613; Stevenson, Dem., 1,015,902; Hoopes, Soc., 8,593; Hass, Soc. Labor, 5,815; Hallinan, Prog., 5,589; Krajewski, Poor Man's, 4,203; Dobbs, Soc. Workers, 3,850; Hamblen, Proh., 989.

1956, Eisenhower, Rep., 1,606,942; Stevenson Dem., 850,337; Holtwick, Proh., 9,147; Hass, Soc. Labor, 6,736; Andrews, Conservative, 5,317; Dobbs, Soc. Workers, 4,004; Krajewski, American Third Party, 1,829.

1960, Kennedy, Dem., 1,385,415; Nixon, Rep., 1,363,324; Dobbs, Soc. Workers, 11,402; Lee, Conservative, 8,708; Hass, Soc. Labor, 4,262.

1964, Johnson, Dem., 1,867,671; Goldwater, Rep., 963,843; DeBerry, Soc. Workers, 8,181; Hass, Soc. Labor, 7,075.

1968, Nixon, Rep., 1,325,467; Humphrey, Dem., 1,264,206; Wallace, 3d party, 262,187; Halstead, Soc. Worker, 8,667; Gregory, Peace Freedom, 8,084; Blomen, Soc. Labor, 6,784.

1972, Nixon, Rep., 1,845,502; McGovern, Dem., 1,102,211; Schmitz, Amer., 34,378; Spock, Peoples, 5,355; Fisher, Soc. Labor, 4,544; Jenness, Soc. Workers, 2,233; Mahalchik, Amer. First, 1,743; Hall, Com., 1,263.

1976, Carter, Dem., 1,444,653; Ford, Rep., 1,509,688; McCarthy, Ind., 32,717; MacBride, Libertarian, 9,449; Maddox, Amer., 7,716; Levin, Soc. Labor, 3,686; Hall, Com., 1,662; LaRouche, U.S. Labor, 1,650; Camejo, Soc. Workers, 1,184; Wright, People's, 1,044; Bubar, Proh., 554; Zeidler, Soc., 469.

1980, Reagan, Rep., 1,546,557; Carter, Dem., 1,147,364; Anderson, Ind., 234,632; Clark, Libertarian, 20,652; Commoner, Citizens, 8,203; McCormack, Right to Life, 3,927; Lynen, Middle Class, 3,694; Hall, Com., 2,555; Pulley, Soc. Workers, 2,198; McReynolds, Soc., 1,973; Gahres, Down With Lawyers, 1,718; Griswold, Workers World, 1,288; Wendelken, Ind., 923.

1984, Reagan, Rep., 1,933,630; Mondale, Dem., 1,261,323; Bergland, Libertarian, 6,416.

New Mexico

County	1980 Carter (D)	1980 Reagan (R)	1980 Anderson (I)	1984 Mondale (D)	1984 Reagan (R)
Bernalillo	54,841	83,956	15,118	67,789	104,694
Catron	466	906	40	418	970
Chaves	5,350	12,502	543	5,332	15,248
Ciboia				3,140	3,578
Colfax	2,266	2,537	199	2,435	2,994
Curry	3,622	8,132	183	3,108	9,188
De Baca	484	655	14	386	756
Dona Ana	10,839	15,539	1,863	13,878	22,153
Eddy	7,028	9,817	326	7,364	11,810
Grant	4,600	4,628	349	5,755	4,979
Guadalupe	980	1,065	58	946	990
Harding	225	356	14	224	401
Hidalgo	840	1,059	59	860	1,282
Lea	5,006	10,727	298	4,558	14,569
Lincoln	1,127	3,009	172	1,134	3,992
Los Alamos	2,368	5,460	1,388	2,859	6,882
Luna	2,443	3,636	157	2,557	4,145
McKinley	4,869	7,329	498	7,915	6,557
Mora	1,274	1,037	44	1,235	1,017
Otero	4,111	7,210	478	4,167	9,751
Quay	1,422	2,499	58	1,368	2,842
Rio Arriba	6,245	3,794	379	6,938	4,116
Roosevelt	2,240	3,950	208	1,696	4,598
Sandoval	4,740	6,762	789	7,080	9,005
San Juan	6,705	15,579	741	8,963	18,690
San Miguel	4,514	3,292	416	5,227	3,485
Santa Fe	12,658	12,361	3,123	18,262	15,886
Sierra	1,169	2,222	117	1,335	2,663
Socorro	2,226	2,685	387	2,541	3,403
Taos	4,346	3,584	482	5,144	4,154
Torrance	1,261	1,907	101	1,274	2,326
Union	675	1,407	32	488	1,503
Valencia	6,886	11,177	825	5,393	8,474
Totals	**167,826**	**250,779**	**29,459**	**201,769**	**307,101**

New Mexico Vote Since 1936

1936, Roosevelt, Dem., 105,838; Landon, Rep., 61,710; Lemke, Union, 942; Thomas, Soc., 343; Browder, Com., 43.

1940, Roosevelt, Dem., 103,699; Willkie, Rep., 79,315.

1944, Roosevelt, Dem., 81,389; Dewey, Rep., 70,688; Watson, Proh., 148.

1948, Truman, Dem., 105,464; Dewey, Rep., 80,303; Wallace, Prog., 1,037; Watson, Proh., 127; Thomas, Soc., 83; Teichert, Soc. Labor, 49.

1952, Eisenhower, Rep., 132,170; Stevenson, Dem., 105,661; Hamblen, Proh., 297; Hallinan, Ind. Prog., 225; MacArthur, Christian National, 220; Hass, Soc. Labor, 35.

1956, Eisenhower, Rep., 146,788; Stevenson, Dem., 106,098; Holtwick, Proh., 607; Andrews, Ind., 364; Hass, Soc. Labor, 69.

1960, Kennedy, Dem., 156,027; Nixon, Rep., 153,733; Decker, Proh., 777; Hass, Soc. Labor, 570.

1964, Johnson, Dem., 194,017; Goldwater, Rep., 131,838; Hass, Soc. Labor, 1,217; Munn, Proh., 543.

1968, Nixon, Rep., 169,692; Humphrey, Dem., 130,081; Wallace, 3d party, 25,737; Chavez, 1,519; Halstead, Soc. Worker, 252.

1972, Nixon, Rep., 235,606; McGovern, Dem., 141,084; Schmitz, Amer., 8,767; Jenness, Soc. Workers, 474.

1976, Carter, Dem., 201,148; Ford, Rep., 211,419; Camejo, Soc. Workers, 2,462; MacBride, Libertarian, 1,110; Zeidler, Soc., 240; Bubar, Proh., 211.

1980, Reagan, Rep., 250,779; Carter, Dem., 167,826; Anderson, Ind., 29,459; Clark, Libertarian, 4,365; Commoner, Citizens, 2,202; Bubar, Statesman, 1,281; Pulley, Soc. Worker, 325.

1984, Reagan, Rep., 307,101; Mondale, Dem., 201,769; Bergland, Libertarian, 4,459.

New York

County	1980 Carter (D)	1980 Reagan (R-C**)	1980 Anderson (L)	1984 Mondale (D)	1984 Reagan (R)
Albany	74,429	52,354	14,563	75,447	74,542
Allegany	5,879	10,423	973	4,720	14,527
Bronx	181,090	86,843	11,286	223,112	109,308
Broome	37,013	39,275	11,388	37,658	58,109
Cattaraugus	12,917	17,222	1,848	10,194	24,162
Cayuga	11,708	17,945	2,539	12,207	21,451
Chautauqua	22,871	30,081	4,600	[illegible]	[illegible]
Chemung	14,565	19,674	2,465	14,638	24,909
Chenango	6,917	10,400	1,908	6,343	14,254
Clinton	11,498	13,120	1,904	10,804	19,549
Columbia	9,500	13,946	2,204	8,960	18,814
Cortland	6,176	9,885	1,603	6,438	13,691
Delaware	6,333	10,609	1,865	5,745	14,003
Dutchess	28,616	53,616	8,824	32,867	70,324
Erie	215,283	169,209	29,580	237,631	222,882
Essex	6,443	9,025	1,213	5,119	12,114
Franklin	7,281	7,620	1,182	6,400	10,617
Fulton	8,105	11,440	1,500	7,644	14,887
Genesee	10,677	11,650	1,651	8,549	16,582
Greene	6,488	11,286	1,338	5,858	14,150
Hamilton	925	2,038	176	737	2,637
Herkimer	11,497	14,105	1,830	10,346	18,827
Jefferson	13,271	16,455	2,834	10,960	23,445
Kings	288,893	200,306	24,341	368,518	230,064
Lewis	3,973	4,937	716	2,757	7,069
Livingston	9,030	11,193	1,694	7,399	16,389
Madison	7,843	13,369	2,122	8,291	17,568
Monroe	142,423	128,615	29,118	132,109	182,696
Montgomery	9,645	11,917	2,080	9,044	14,398
Nassau	207,602	333,567	44,758	240,697	392,017
New York	275,742	115,911	38,597	379,521	144,281
Niagara	40,405	38,760	6,014	41,368	51,289
Oneida	44,292	51,968	6,929	42,603	65,377
Onondaga	73,453	97,887	18,805	81,777	121,857
Ontario	14,477	17,036	3,147	12,844	24,507
Orange	30,022	51,268	7,656	32,663	69,413
Orleans	5,767	7,536	977	4,429	10,453
Oswego	15,343	22,816	3,333	14,437	31,481
Otsego	8,795	11,814	2,874	9,582	16,777
Putnam	8,691	20,193	2,340	9,473	25,707
Queens	269,147	251,333	32,566	328,379	285,477
Rensselaer	29,880	32,005	6,443	26,755	43,892
Richmond	37,306	64,885	7,055	44,345	83,187
Rockland	35,277	59,068	8,709	44,687	70,020
St. Lawrence	17,006	18,437	3,544	15,963	26,062
Saratoga	23,641	34,184	6,201	22,166	47,394
Schenectady	29,932	32,003	7,146	30,612	42,808
Schoharie	4,715	6,382	940	3,996	8,692
Schuyler	2,514	3,838	476	2,422	5,207
Seneca	5,010	7,174	1,205	4,825	9,420
Steuben	12,826	22,418	2,257	10,471	28,848
Suffolk	149,945	256,294	34,743	171,295	335,485
Sullivan	9,553	15,089	2,095	10,475	18,037
Tioga	6,690	10,391	1,051	[illegible]	[illegible]
Tompkins	11,970	12,448	4,081	19,357	18,255
Ulster	22,179	36,709	5,995	26,445	47,372
Warren	6,971	13,264	1,766	5,886	17,616
Washington	7,144	12,835	1,501	5,909	16,580
Wayne	12,590	16,498	2,623	9,700	24,171
Westchester	130,136	198,552	30,119	160,225	229,005
Wyoming	5,234	8,108	855	4,381	11,199
Yates	2,828	4,694	690	2,670	6,367
Totals	**2,728,372**	**2,893,831**	**467,801**	**3,119,609**	**3,664,763**

New York Vote Since 1936

1936, Roosevelt, Dem., 3,018,298; American Lab., 274,924; total 3,293,222; Landon, Rep., 2,180,670; Thomas, Soc., 86,879; Browder, Com., 35,609.

1940, Roosevelt, Dem., 2,834,500; American Lab., 417,418; total, 3,251,918; Willkie, Rep., 3,027,478; Thomas, Soc., 18,950; Babson, Proh., 3,250.

1944, Roosevelt, Dem., 2,478,598; American Lab., 496,405; Liberal, 329,325; total, 3,304,238; Dewey, Rep., 2,987,647; Teichert, Ind. Gov't., 14,352; Thomas, Soc., 10,553.

1948, Truman, Dem., 2,557,642; Liberal, 222,562; total, 2,780,204; Dewey, Rep., 2,841,163; Wallace, Amer. Lab., 509,559; Thomas, Soc., 40,879; Teichert, Ind. Gov't., 2,729; Dobbs, Soc. Workers, 2,675.

1952, Eisenhower, Rep., 3,952,815; Stevenson, Dem., 2,687,890, Liberal, 416,711; total, 3,104,601; Hallinan, American Lab., 64,211; Hoopes, Soc., 2,664; Dobbs, Soc. Workers, 2,212; Hass, Ind. Gov't., 1,560; scattering, 178; blank and void, 87,813.

1956, Eisenhower, Rep., 4,340,340; Stevenson, Dem., 2,458,212; Liberal, 292,557; total, 2,750,769; write-in votes for Andrews, 1,027; Werdel, 492; Hass, 150; Hoopes, 82; others, 476.

1960, Kennedy, Dem., 3,423,909; Liberal, 406,176; total, 3,830,085; Nixon, Rep., 3,446,419; Dobbs, Soc. Workers, 14,319; scattering, 256; blank and void, 88,896.

1964, Johnson, Dem., 4,913,156; Goldwater, Rep., 2,243,559; Hass, Soc. Labor, 6,085; DeBerry, Soc. Workers, 3,215; scattering, 188; blank and void, 151,383.

1968, Nixon, Rep., 3,007,932; Humphrey, Dem., 3,378,470; Wallace, 3d party, 358,864; Blomen, Soc. Labor, 8,432; Halstead, Soc. Worker, 11,851; Gregory, Freedom and Peace, 24,517; blank, void, and scattering, 171,624.

1972, Nixon, Rep., 3,824,642; Conservative, 368,136; McGovern, Dem., 2,767,956; Liberal, 183,128; Reed, Soc. Workers, 7,797; Fisher, Soc. Labor, 4,530; Hall, Com., 5,641; blank, void, or scattered, 161,641.

1976, Carter, Dem., 3,389,558; Ford, Rep., 3,100,791; MacBride, Libertarian, 12,197; Hall, Com., 10,270; Camejo, Soc. Workers, 6,996; LaRouche, U.S. Labor, 5,413; blank, void, or scattered, 143,037.

1980, Reagan, Rep., 2,893,831; Carter, Dem., 2,728,372; Anderson, Lib., 467,801; Clark, Libertarian, 52,648; McCormack, Right To Life, 24,159; Commoner, Citizens, 23,186; Hall, Com., 7,414; DeBerry, Soc. Workers, 2,068; Griswold, Workers World, 1,416; scattering, 1,064.

1984, Reagan, Rep., 3,664,763; Mondale, Dem., 3,119,609; Bergland, Libertarian, 11,949.

North Carolina

County	1980 Carter (D)	1980 Reagan (R)	1980 Anderson (I)	1984 Mondale (D)	1984 Reagan (R)
Alamance	15,042	18,077	760	11,230	26,063
Alexander	4,546	6,376	137	3,581	8,502
Alleghany	2,198	1,995	91	2,013	2,589
Anson	4,973	1,968	111	5,015	3,719
Ashe	4,461	5,643	154	4,009	6,611
Avery	1,527	3,480	147	1,159	4,702
Beaufort	6,024	6,773	186	5,987	9,284
Bertie	3,863	1,695	45	3,953	2,879
Bladen	6,104	2,745	64	5,064	4,701
Brunswick	6,761	5,897	265	6,774	9,673
Buncombe	24,837	26,124	2,153	23,337	37,698
Burke	11,680	12,956	558	10,353	18,766
Cabarrus	9,768	15,143	562	8,477	22,528
Caldwell	8,738	12,965	440	7,311	17,024
Camden	1,212	813	45	1,075	1,282
Carteret	6,485	7,733	460	5,882	11,637
Caswell	3,529	2,156	66	4,157	3,992
Catawba	13,873	22,873	866	11,700	31,476
Chatham	7,144	5,414	481	7,458	8,595
Cherokee	3,114	3,849	80	2,776	4,894
Chowan	2,146	1,424	71	1,736	2,171
Clay	1,324	2,136	53	1,340	2,259
Cleveland	12,210	[illegible]	[illegible]	10,288	17,095
Columbus	10,212	5,522	148	8,728	9,150
Craven	7,781	8,554	356	7,186	12,893

Cumberland	22,073	21,540	1,261	22,614	31,602
Currituck	1,980	1,668	97	1,668	2,885
Dare	2,497	2,794	260	1,839	4,738
Davidson	14,579	22,794	679	11,469	30,471
Davie	3,289	6,302	223	2,911	8,201
Duplin	7,524	5,403	109	6,830	7,708
Durham	24,969	19,276	3,052	32,244	29,185
Edgecombe	7,945	5,916	148	10,545	9,635
Forsyth	38,870	42,389	2,897	36,814	59,208
Franklin	5,427	3,508	104	4,766	5,984
Gaston	19,016	25,139	823	14,142	39,167
Gates	2,435	957	61	2,225	1,694
Graham	1,608	1,961	36	1,494	2,514
Granville	5,556	3,513	133	5,217	6,302
Greene	2,835	2,221	34	2,772	3,195
Guilford	44,516	53,291	4,019	46,027	73,096
Halifax	8,364	6,033	180	9,278	8,832
Harnett	8,791	7,284	165	7,106	11,198
Haywood	9,814	7,217	349	7,958	10,146
Henderson	7,578	13,573	901	7,222	19,369
Hertford	4,102	1,854	80	4,498	3,176
Hoke	3,376	1,168	56	3,214	2,449
Hyde	1,221	807	37	1,004	1,195
Iredell	12,067	14,926	624	9,999	23,641
Jackson	4,857	4,140	246	4,367	5,582
Johnston	9,601	10,444	271	7,833	16,210
Jones	2,198	1,401	18	2,025	2,062
Lee	5,426	4,847	251	3,925	8,198
Lenoir	7,546	9,832	263	8,556	13,321
Lincoln	7,796	9,009	299	5,996	12,621
McDowell	4,703	5,680	175	4,076	7,639
Macon	4,105	4,727	153	3,570	6,661
Madison	3,202	2,629	108	2,988	3,666
Martin	4,750	2,564	81	3,870	4,266
Mecklenburg	66,995	68,384	6,560	63,190	106,754
Mitchell	1,765	4,322	146	1,286	4,737
Montgomery	4,129	3,587	99	3,831	5,109
Moore	8,084	10,158	563	7,063	14,681
Nash	8,184	11,043	293	8,588	17,295
New Hanover	13,670	17,243	1,114	12,591	23,771
Northampton	4,933	1,847	62	5,094	3,198
Onslow	7,371	8,861	400	5,713	13,928
Orange	15,226	9,261	3,364	20,564	15,585
Pamlico	2,224	1,504	48	2,152	2,554
Pasquotank	4,128	3,340	179	3,854	4,646
Pender	4,382	3,018	103	4,354	5,079
Perquimans	1,560	1,210	63	1,441	1,939
Person	4,111	3,281	104	3,528	5,854
Pitt	12,590	12,816	827	13,481	18,983
Polk	2,375	3,021	160	2,169	4,046
Randolph	10,107	19,881	563	7,511	25,759
Richmond	7,416	3,911	224	7,494	6,807
Robeson	17,618	6,982	331	15,257	12,947
Rockingham	11,708	11,205	463	10,605	17,895
Rowan	11,671	18,566	707	10,643	25,207
Rutherford	8,315	8,363	203	6,862	11,369
Sampson	9,090	8,097	308	9,115	10,665
Scotland	4,446	2,133	155	4,028	4,077
Stanly	7,784	9,734	248	6,138	13,116
Stokes	5,764	7,275	151	4,950	9,515
Surry	8,987	10,065	256	7,188	13,340
Swain	1,987	1,457	70	2,000	2,012
Transylvania	4,008	4,826	274	3,733	6,956
Tyrrell	887	466	14	807	774
Union	10,073	9,012	487	7,048	16,885
Vance	5,415	4,217	101	5,880	6,836
Wake	49,003	49,768	5,455	50,323	81,251
Warren	3,750	1,582	74	3,946	2,664
Washington	3,008	1,943	68	3,114	2,731
Watauga	5,022	6,149	645	5,163	9,370
Wayne	9,586	12,860	322	10,011	17,961
Wilkes	8,184	14,462	282	6,852	18,670
Wilson	8,042	8,329	243	8,343	12,243
Yadkin	3,850	7,530	136	3,075	8,976
Yancey	4,010	3,363	110	3,651	4,296
Totals	**875,635**	**915,018**	**52,800**	**824,287**	**1,346,481**

North Carolina Vote Since 1936

1936, Roosevelt, Dem., 616,141; Landon, Rep., 223,283; Thomas, Soc., 21; Browder, Com., 11; Lemke, Union 2.

1940, Roosevelt, Dem., 609,015; Willkie, Rep., 213,633.

1944, Roosevelt, Dem., 527,399; Dewey, Rep., 263,155.

1948, Truman, Dem., 459,070; Dewey, Rep., 258,572; Thurmond, States' Rights, 69,652; Wallace, Prog., 3,915.

1952, Eisenhower, Rep., 558,107; Stevenson, Dem., 652,803.

1956, Eisenhower, Rep., 575,062; Stevenson, Dem., 590,530.

1960, Kennedy, Dem., 713,136; Nixon, Rep., 655,420.

1964, Johnson, Dem., 800,139; Goldwater Rep., 624,844.

1968, Nixon, Rep., 627,192; Humphrey, Dem., 464,113; Wallace, 3d party, 496,188.

1972, Nixon, Rep., 1,054,889; McGovern, Dem., 438,705; Schmitz, Amer., 25,018.

1976, Dem., 927,365; Ford, Rep., 741,960; Anderson, Amer., 5,607; MacBride, Libertarian, 2,219; LaRouche, U.S. Labor, 755.

1980, Reagan, Rep., 915,018; Carter, Dem., 875,635; Anderson, Ind., 52,800; Clark, Libertarian, 9,677; Commoner, Citizens, 2,287; DeBerry, Soc. Workers, 416.

1984, Reagan, Rep., 1,346,481; Mondale, Dem., 824,287; Bergland, Libertarian, 3,794.

North Dakota

	1980			1984	
County	Carter (D)	Reagan (R)	Anderson (I)	Mondale (D)	Reagan (R)
Adams	470	1,334	107	530	1,343
Barnes	2,128	4,392	705	2,507	4,348
Benson	1,119	2,149	262	1,599	1,729
Billings	122	524	33	133	505
Bottineau	1,090	3,394	267	1,279	3,356
Bowman	454	1,507	142	562	1,559
Burke	418	1,442	82	543	1,298
Burleigh	6,129	18,437	2,109	8,781	19,913
Cass	13,562	23,886	5,421	18,054	29,221
Cavalier	1,105	2,582	238	1,110	2,661
Dickey	917	2,455	161	1,051	2,460
Divide	509	1,267	109	626	1,165
Dunn	532	1,706	115	716	1,583
Eddy	539	1,153	145	796	1,049
Emmons	502	2,369	132	620	1,885
Foster	586	1,534	152	765	1,422
Golden Valley	259	1,006	62	325	964
Grand Forks	6,997	14,257	2,932	10,050	15,898
Grant	317	1,891	110	507	1,607
Griggs	636	1,342	158	828	1,254
Hettinger	434	1,699	104	524	1,646
Kidder	326	1,474	85	506	1,240
La Moure	850	2,136	254	1,086	1,978
Logan	283	1,474	69	401	1,222
McHenry	939	2,922	190	1,283	2,485
McIntosh	308	2,471	72	427	2,047
McKenzie	867	2,265	182	974	2,610
McLean	1,613	4,234	318	2,062	3,673
Mercer	1,209	3,224	204	1,729	3,705
Morton	2,861	7,659	742	3,996	7,146
Mountrail	1,183	2,165	182	1,565	1,959
Nelson	726	1,611	226	1,026	1,445
Oliver	270	966	55	419	915
Pembina	1,239	3,101	303	1,367	2,895
Pierce	517	2,273	168	691	1,883
Ramsey	1,607	4,078	514	2,304	4,150
Ransom	974	1,883	237	1,222	1,706
Renville	570	1,154	98	592	1,163
Richland	2,698	5,711	750	3,047	5,980
Rolette	1,660	1,599	265	2,179	1,479
Sargent	1,048	1,565	174	1,295	1,385
Sheridan	208	1,326	65	306	1,075
Sioux	383	620	72	655	442
Slope	128	462	45	174	419
Stark	2,016	6,312	512	2,759	7,641
Steele	617	997	229	781	941
Stutsman	2,573	6,545	960	3,495	6,591
Towner	568	1,375	152	789	1,242
Traill	1,428	3,092	512	1,580	3,037
Walsh	1,850	4,488	485	2,264	4,347
Ward	5,554	14,997	1,234	7,336	16,077
Wells	746	2,660	148	1,036	2,426
Williams	2,545	6,530	592	3,177	8,166
Totals	**79,189**	**193,695**	**23,640**	**104,429**	**200,336**

North Dakota Vote Since 1936

1936, Roosevelt, Dem., 163,148; Landon, Rep., 72,751; Lemke, Union, 36,708; Thomas, Soc., 552; Browder, Com., 360; Colvin, Proh., 197.

1940, Roosevelt, Dem., 124,036; Willkie, Rep., 154,590; Thomas, Soc., 1,279; Knutson, Com., 545; Babson, Proh., 325.

1944, Roosevelt, Dem., 100,144; Dewey, Rep., 118,535; Thomas, Soc., 943, Watson, Proh., 549.

1948, Truman, Dem., 95,812; Dewey, Rep., 115,139; Wallace, Prog., 8,391; Thomas, Soc., 1,000, Thurmond, States' Rights, 374.

1952, Eisenhower, Rep., 191,712; Stevenson, Dem., 76,694; MacArthur, Christian Nationalist, 1,075; Hallinan, Prog., 344; Hamblen, Proh., 302.

1956, Eisenhower, Rep., 156,766; Stevenson, Dem., 96,742; Andrews, Amer., 483.

1960, Kennedy, Dem., 123,963; Nixon, Rep., 154,310; Dobbs, Soc. Workers, 158.

1964, Johnson, Dem., 149,784; Goldwater, Rep., 108,207; DeBerry, Soc. Worker, 224; Munn, Proh., 174.

1968, Nixon, Rep., 138,669; Humphrey, Dem., 94,769; Wallace, 3d party, 14,244; Halstead, Soc. Worker, 128; Munn, Prohibition, 38; Troxell, Ind., 34.

1972, Nixon, Rep., 174,109; McGovern, Dem., 100,384; Jenness, Soc. Workers, 288; Hall, Com., 87; Schmitz, Amer., 5,646.

1976, Carter, Dem., 136,078; Ford, Rep., 153,470; Anderson, Amer., 3,698; McCarthy, Ind., 2,952; Maddox, Amer. Ind., 269; MacBride, Libertarian, 256; scattering, 371.

1980, Reagan, Rep., 193,695; Carter, Dem., 79,189; Anderson, Ind., 23,640; Clark, Libertarian, 3,743; Commoner, Libertarian, 429; McLain, Nat'l People's League, 296; Greaves, American, 235; Hall, Com., 93; DeBerry, Soc. Workers, 89; McReynolds, Soc., 82; Bubar, Statesman, 54.

1984, Reagan, Rep., 200,336; Mondale, Dem., 104,429; Bergland, Libertarian, 703.

Ohio

County	1980 Carter (D)	Reagan (R)	Anderson (I)	1984 Mondale (D)	Reagan (R)
Adams	4,161	5,336	303	3,534	6,113
Allen	13,140	29,070	1,439	12,176	33,506
Ashland	5,142	11,691	1,128	4,786	14,339
Ashtabula	17,363	19,847	2,481	19,344	21,669
Athens	9,514	8,170	1,544	10,201	11,548
Auglaize	5,022	11,537	785	4,102	14,766
Belmont	16,653	13,601	1,432	19,458	15,170
Brown	4,706	6,065	339	4,067	8,221
Butler	31,796	61,231	4,717	27,700	76,216
Carroll	3,476	5,806	406	3,771	6,703
Champaign	4,109	7,356	596	3,544	9,935
Clark	22,630	27,237	3,414	21,154	35,831
Clermont	13,199	26,674	1,697	11,713	35,316
Clinton	3,967	7,675	608	3,332	9,603
Columbiana	17,459	20,798	2,320	20,155	24,552
Coshocton	4,725	8,359	525	4,392	9,842
Crawford	6,058	12,424	915	4,932	14,682
Cuyahoga	307,448	254,883	40,750	362,636	201,091
Darke	7,635	12,773	1,198	5,904	16,379
Defiance	5,096	9,358	896	5,004	10,951
Delaware	6,417	14,740	1,278	5,773	19,050
Erie	12,343	15,628	1,908	13,508	19,174
Fairfield	13,144	24,096	1,689	9,817	30,843
Fayette	2,810	5,827	327	2,126	6,838
Franklin	143,932	200,948	21,269	131,530	250,360
Fulton	3,972	9,519	1,026	4,217	11,412
Gallia	4,406	6,469	401	4,251	8,194
Geauga	9,542	17,762	2,359	9,061	22,060
Greene	20,068	24,922	3,160	17,129	34,267
Guernsey	5,121	8,100	604	4,967	10,252
Hamilton	129,114	206,979	17,898	140,350	246,288
Hancock	6,843	18,264	1,467	5,758	22,169
Hardin	3,003	7,457	528	3,813	8,722
Harrison	2,848	3,639	331	3,370	4,276
Henry	3,059	7,584	691	2,779	9,317
Highland	4,363	7,359	454	3,784	9,000
Hocking	3,765	4,588	312	3,280	6,071
Holmes	2,094	3,860	329	1,737	5,146
Huron	6,537	11,173	1,110	6,609	14,388
Jackson	4,409	5,902	274	4,369	7,411
Jefferson	20,382	15,777	1,797	22,832	17,105
Knox	6,586	10,384	987	5,730	14,062
Lake	35,246	43,485	5,925	36,711	54,587
Lawrence	11,366	13,799	813	11,431	14,973
Licking	17,208	28,425	2,419	13,995	37,560
Logan	4,319	9,727	718	3,645	12,230
Lorain	40,919	51,034	7,324	52,970	57,370
Lucas	85,341	86,653	16,636	97,293	100,285
Madison	3,565	7,166	438	2,928	8,979
Mahoning	63,677	50,153	9,490	76,514	53,424
Marion	9,419	14,605	1,255	8,827	17,392
Medina	13,573	24,723	2,965	15,897	30,690
Meigs	3,827	4,911	294	3,549	6,307
Mercer	5,506	8,673	941	4,422	11,542
Miami	12,893	19,928	2,429	9,695	26,300
Monroe	3,166	2,870	266	3,611	3,302
Montgomery	105,110	101,443	13,817	94,016	137,053
Morgan	1,875	3,236	156	1,868	3,994
Morrow	3,239	6,179	383	2,839	8,116
Muskingum	12,584	17,921	1,329	10,037	21,821
Noble	1,944	3,025	208	1,777	3,853
Ottawa	6,753	8,641	1,281	7,053	10,920
Paulding	2,778	4,971	550	2,811	5,545
Perry	4,383	5,725	369	3,961	7,548
Pickaway	5,052	9,289	515	4,110	11,942
Pike	4,938	4,426	257	4,895	6,318
Portage	20,570	22,829	3,798	21,719	29,536
Preble	5,416	8,376	687	4,198	11,065
Putnam	3,742	9,752	533	3,194	11,936
Richland	18,253	29,213	2,586	16,141	35,299
Ross	9,355	13,251	812	8,020	17,015
Sandusky	8,482	13,420	1,851	8,564	17,214
Scioto	15,552	15,881	816	14,120	18,818
Seneca	7,303	14,172	1,415	7,905	16,520
Shelby	6,425	8,988	895	4,315	13,509
Stark	59,005	87,769	8,030	65,157	98,434
Summit	102,459	92,299	15,002	109,569	115,637
Trumbull	44,366	41,056	6,281	56,902	45,623
Tuscarawas	12,117	15,708	1,779	13,149	19,366
Union	3,038	7,576	421	2,579	9,336
Van Wert	4,070	7,866	741	3,338	9,570
Vinton	2,381	2,484	138	1,990	3,041
Warren	11,306	22,430	1,348	9,031	29,848
Washington	7,936	14,310	1,121	7,920	16,529
Wayne	12,129	18,962	2,313	11,323	24,475
Williams	4,015	9,146	872	3,624	10,804
Wood	14,139	23,315	4,156	15,907	29,750
Wyandot	2,757	5,786	407	2,342	7,204
Totals	**1,752,414**	**2,206,545**	**254,472**	**1,825,440**	**2,678,559**

Ohio Vote Since 1936

1936, Roosevelt, Dem., 1,747,122; Landon, Rep., 1,127,709; Lemke, Union, 132,212; Browder, Com., 5,251; Thomas, Soc., 117; Aiken, Soc. Labor, 14.

1940, Roosevelt, Dem., 1,733,139; Willkie, Rep., 1,586,773.

1944, Roosevelt, Dem., 1,570,763; Dewey, Rep., 1,582,293.

1948, Truman, Dem., 1,452,791; Dewey, Rep., 1,445,684; Wallace, Prog., 37,596.

1952, Eisenhower, Rep., 2,100,391; Stevenson, Dem., 1,600,367.

1956, Eisenhower, Rep., 2,262,610; Stevenson, Dem., 1,439,655.

1960, Kennedy, Dem., 1,944,248; Nixon, Rep., 2,217,611.

1964, Johnson, Dem., 2,498,331; Goldwater, Rep., 1,470,865.

1968, Nixon, Rep., 1,791,014; Humphrey, Dem., 1,700,586; Wallace, 3d party, 467,495; Gregory, 372; Munn, Proh., 19; Blomen, Soc. Labor, 120; Halstead, Soc. Worker, 69; Mitchell, Com., 23.

1972, Nixon, Rep., 2,441,827; McGovern, Dem., 1,558,889; Fisher, Soc. Labor, 7,107; Hall, Com., 6,437; Schmitz, Amer., 80,067; Wallace, Ind., 460.

1976, Carter, Dem., 2,011,621; Ford, Rep., 2,000,505; McCarthy, Ind., 58,258; Maddox, Amer. Ind., 15,529; MacBride, Libertarian, 8,961; Hall, Com., 7,817; Camejo, Soc. Workers, 4,717; LaRouche, U.S. Labor, 4,335; scattered, 130.

1980, Reagan, Rep., 2,206,545, Carter, Dem., 1,752,414; Anderson, Ind., 254,472; Clark, Libertarian, 49,033; Commoner, Citizens, 8,564; Hall, Com., 4,729; Congress, Ind. 4,029; Griswold, Workers World, 3,790; Bubar, Statesman, 27.

1984, Reagan, Rep., 2,678,559; Mondale, Dem., 1,825,440; Bergland, Libertarian, 5,886.

Oklahoma

County	1980 Carter (D)	Reagan (R)	Anderson (I)	1984 Mondale (D)	Reagan (R)
Adair	2,761	3,429	107	2,266	4,423
Alfalfa	899	2,628	86	866	2,715
Atoka	2,505	1,613	66	2,047	2,361
Beaver	696	2,430	58	536	2,689
Beckham	3,298	3,637	123	2,601	5,005
Blaine	1,399	3,708	103	1,484	4,037
Bryan	6,410	3,880	129	5,475	6,246
Caddo	4,695	5,945	232	4,463	6,811
Canadian	4,889	15,272	642	5,245	20,929
Carter	6,509	9,262	258	6,161	11,578
Cherokee	5,215	5,594	362	5,307	7,614
Choctaw	3,507	2,394	73	2,801	3,155
Cimarron	373	1,404	23	359	1,420
Cleveland	14,536	31,178	3,910	16,512	42,806
Coal	1,442	926	47	1,284	1,259
Comanche	9,972	16,609	1000	8,890	21,382
Cotton	1,410	1,702	63	1,264	1,796
Craig	2,801	2,956	156	2,515	3,629
Creek	7,339	11,749	460	7,465	15,011
Custer	3,008	6,469	290	2,700	8,191
Delaware	4,244	5,302	177	3,789	6,690
Dewey	826	1,943	70	664	2,098
Ellis	561	1,908	54	562	1,881
Garfield	5,718	17,989	846	5,730	19,642
Garvin	5,033	5,520	210	4,215	7,505
Grady	5,330	8,131	351	4,846	11,042
Grant	927	2,411	84	825	2,470
Greer	1,492	1,535	48	1,220	1,664
Harmon	961	676	21	785	1,009

County	Carter (D) 1980	Reagan (R) 1980	Anderson (I) 1980	Mondale (D) 1984	Reagan (R) 1984
Harper	517	1,652	40	373	1,748
Haskell	2,874	2,024	65	2,535	2,417
Hughes	3,211	2,170	85	2,901	2,663
Jackson	4,031	4,327	144	2,996	5,773
Jefferson	1,812	1,440	55	1,496	1,656
Johnston	2,066	1,701	57	1,820	2,195
Kay	6,449	15,004	665	6,044	16,731
Kingfisher	1,282	4,962	122	1,125	5,528
Kiowa	2,372	2,636	88	2,016	2,951
Latimer	2,105	1,737	71	1,858	2,210
Le Flore	6,668	6,807	174	5,990	8,604
Lincoln	3,231	6,064	204	3,020	8,088
Logan	3,246	6,311	259	3,551	8,356
Love	1,578	1,449	31	1,359	1,833
McClain	2,990	4,284	185	2,549	6,056
McCurtain	6,963	5,189	149	3,994	6,381
McIntosh	3,654	2,925	118	3,479	3,646
Major	584	3,059	62	619	3,385
Marshall	2,157	1,961	52	2,039	2,488
Mayes	5,344	6,633	256	5,154	8,585
Murray	2,384	2,494	126	2,229	3,073
Muskogee	13,341	11,511	633	12,343	14,652
Noble	1,398	3,663	124	1,238	4,018
Nowata	1,694	2,640	75	1,687	3,030
Okfuskee	2,177	2,126	58	1,684	2,443
Oklahoma	58,765	139,538	9,190	60,235	159,974
Okmulgee	7,236	6,652	286	7,380	8,704
Osage	5,687	8,044	363	6,095	10,083
Ottawa	6,143	6,362	317	5,781	7,666
Pawnee	2,020	3,902	161	2,165	4,699
Payne	7,466	15,955	1,812	7,653	20,811
Pittsburg	8,292	7,062	339	6,860	9,778
Pontotoc	5,942	6,232	335	5,526	8,301
Pottawatomie	8,526	12,466	625	6,966	16,143
Pushmataha	2,666	1,969	65	2,079	2,499
Roger Mills	877	1,221	50	680	1,550
Rogers	6,399	11,581	461	6,013	16,137
Seminole	4,726	5,067	224	3,957	6,009
Sequoyah	4,983	5,987	178	4,202	7,042
Stephens	7,191	10,199	310	6,359	12,871
Texas	1,451	5,503	93	1,033	5,968
Tillman	2,144	2,450	69	1,674	2,637
Tulsa	53,438	124,643	7,802	58,274	159,549
Wagoner	5,235	8,969	369	5,271	12,534
Washington	5,854	16,563	851	5,476	19,043
Washita	2,044	3,206	71	1,547	3,847
Woods	1,364	3,592	191	1,231	3,741
Woodward	1,703	5,318	175	1,647	6,376
Totals	**402,026**	**695,570**	**38,284**	**385,080**	**861,530**

Oklahoma Vote Since 1936

1936, Roosevelt, Dem., 501,069; Landon, Rep., 245,122; Thomas, Soc., 2,221; Colvin, Proh., 1,328.

1940, Roosevelt, Dem., 474,313; Willkie, Rep., 348,872; Babson, Proh., 3,027.

1944, Roosevelt, Dem., 401,549; Dewey, Rep., 319,424; Watson, Proh., 1,663.

1948, Truman, Dem., 452,782; Dewey, Rep., 268,817.

1952, Eisenhower, Rep., 518,045; Stevenson, Dem., 430,939.

1956, Eisenhower, Rep., 473,769; Stevenson, Dem., 385,581.

1960, Kennedy, Dem., 370,111; Nixon, Rep., 533,039.

1964, Johnson, Dem., 519,834; Goldwater, Rep. 412,665.

1968, Nixon, Rep., 449,697; Humphrey, Dem., 301,658; Wallace, 3d party, 191,731.

1972, Nixon, Rep. 759,025; McGovern, Dem., 247,147; Schmitz, Amer., 23,728.

1976, Carter, Dem., 532,442; Ford, Rep., 545,708; McCarthy, Ind., 14,101.

1980, Reagan, Rep., 695,570; Carter, Dem., 402,026; Anderson, Ind., 38,284; Clark, Libertarian, 13,828.

1984, Reagan, Rep., 861,530; Mondale, Dem., 385,080; Bergland, Libertarian, 9,066.

Oregon

County	1980 Carter (D)	1980 Reagan (R)	1980 Anderson (I)	1984 Mondale (D)	1984 Reagan (R)
Baker	2,515	4,747	487	2,591	5,204
Benton	13,150	14,982	4,950	16,073	17,836
Clackamas	40,462	54,111	11,386	47,254	68,630
Clatsop	6,482	6,124	1,854	7,525	7,522
Columbia	7,124	6,623	1,158	8,219	7,811
Coos	11,817	13,041	2,428	13,582	13,637
Crook	2,162	3,113	435	2,268	3,773
Curry	2,656	4,910	652	3,423	5,363
Deschutes	9,641	15,186	2,909	11,671	19,323
Douglas	12,564	23,101	2,529	14,609	25,243
Gilliam	394	622	85	369	700
Grant	1,274	2,519	273	1,344	2,695
Harney	1,110	2,313	255	1,290	2,197
Hood River	2,924	3,450	530	3,022	4,531
Jackson	19,903	32,879	4,019	22,230	37,895
Jefferson	1,654	2,523	431	1,920	3,283
Josephine	7,116	16,827	1,401	8,539	19,470
Klamath	7,371	16,060	1,427	7,575	17,686
Lake	1,147	2,234	201	1,184	2,466
Lane	52,240	54,750	12,076	63,999	61,493
Lincoln	7,009	7,637	1,637	8,637	9,110
Linn	13,516	18,943	2,823	16,161	23,463
Malheur	2,937	7,705	472	2,611	8,441
Marion	32,134	42,191	8,755	36,440	54,535
Morrow	1,077	1,728	239	1,254	2,130
Multnomah	120,487	101,606	27,572	144,179	119,932
Polk	7,833	10,006	2,026	8,709	12,678
Sherman	389	677	62	398	828
Tillamook	4,521	4,123	931	4,988	5,267
Umatilla	7,382	12,950	1,531	8,246	14,211
Union	3,677	6,514	763	4,134	6,645
Wallowa	995	2,485	216	1,204	2,619
Wasco	4,336	4,703	819	5,526	6,905
Washington	37,915	57,165	13,076	44,602	75,877
Wheeler	282	442	62	253	504
Yamhill	8,694	12,054	1,919	9,450	15,797
Totals	**456,890**	**571,044**	**112,389**	**536,479**	**685,700**

Oregon Vote Since 1936

1936, Roosevelt, Dem., 266,733; Landon, Rep., 122,706; Lemke, Union, 21,831; Thomas, Soc., 2,143; Aiken, Soc. Labor, 500; Browder, Com., 104; Colvin, Proh., 4.

1940, Roosevelt, Dem., 258,415; Willkie, Rep., 219,555; Aiken, Soc. Labor, 2,487; Thomas, Soc., 398; Browder, Com., 191; Babson, Proh., 154.

1944, Roosevelt, Dem., 248,635; Dewey, Rep., 225,365; Thomas, Soc., 3,785; Watson, Proh., 2,362.

1948, Truman, Dem., 243,147; Dewey, Rep., 260,904; Wallace, Prog., 14,978; Thomas, Soc., 5,051.

1952, Eisenhower, Rep., 420,815; Stevenson, Dem., 270,579; Hallinan, Ind., 3,665.

1956, Eisenhower, Rep., 406,393; Stevenson, Dem., 329,204.

1960, Kennedy, Dem., 367,402; Nixon, Rep., 408,060.

1964, Johnson, Dem., 501,017; Goldwater, Rep., 282,779; write-in, 2,509.

1968, Nixon, Rep., 408,433; Humphrey, Dem., 358,866; Wallace, 3d party, 49,683; write-in, McCarthy, 1,496; N. Rockefeller, 69; others, 1,075.

1972, Nixon, Rep., 486,686; McGovern, Dem., 392,760, Schmitz, Amer., 46,211; write-in, 2,289.

1976, Carter, Dem., 490,407; Ford, Rep., 492,120; McCarthy, Ind., 40,207; write-in, 7,142.

1980, Reagan, Rep., 571,044; Carter, Dem., 456,890; Anderson, Ind., 112,389; Clark, Libertarian, 25,838; Commoner, Citizens, 13,642; scattered, 1,713.

1984, Reagan, Rep., 658,700; Mondale, Dem., 536,479.

Pennsylvania

County	1980 Carter (D)	1980 Reagan (R)	1980 Anderson (I)	1984 Mondale (D)	1984 Reagan (R)
Adams	7,266	13,760	1,139	7,289	16,786
Allegheny	297,464	271,850	38,710	372,576	284,692
Armstrong	12,718	12,955	1,153	14,525	13,709
Beaver	43,955	30,496	4,549	54,765	32,052
Bedford	4,950	10,930	416	5,424	13,085
Berks	36,449	60,576	8,863	37,849	74,605
Blair	15,014	28,931	2,011	15,651	30,104
Bradford	6,439	13,139	1,068	5,474	14,808
Bucks	59,120	100,536	18,107	74,568	130,119
Butler	19,711	28,821	3,453	24,735	31,676
Cambria	36,121	33,072	2,398	39,865	32,173
Cameron	1,112	1,795	92	990	2,031
Carbon	8,009	10,042	956	8,836	10,701
Centre	15,987	20,605	5,247	16,194	27,802
Chester	34,307	73,046	10,911	38,870	92,221
Clarion	5,472	8,812	678	5,407	9,836
Clearfield	11,647	15,299	944	11,963	18,653
Clinton	4,842	6,288	733	4,525	6,678
Columbia	9,449	12,426	1,197	8,254	14,402
Crawford	11,778	16,552	2,095	12,792	20,181
Cumberland	19,789	41,152	5,437	21,374	49,282
Dauphin	27,252	44,039	6,034	33,576	54,330
Delaware	88,314	143,282	20,907	98,207	161,754
Elk	5,898	7,175	472	5,486	8,470
Erie	45,946	48,918	6,349	52,471	55,860
Fayette	27,963	19,252	1,348	35,098	21,314
Forest	819	1,206	93	839	1,468
Franklin	12,061	22,716	1,724	11,480	27,243
Fulton	1,342	2,740	107	1,309	3,254
Greene	8,193	5,336	450	9,365	6,376
Huntingdon	5,094	8,140	567	4,430	10,220
Indiana	13,828	15,607	1,708	15,791	18,845
Jefferson	6,296	9,628	687	5,950	11,334
Juniata	2,696	4,139	280	2,624	5,059
Lackawanna	45,257	44,242	4,209	45,851	48,132
Lancaster	30,026	79,963	7,442	31,308	99,090

Lawrence.	19,506	18,404	1,908	23,981	19,277
Lebanon	8,281	24,495	2,314	10,520	27,008
Lehigh	34,827	50,782	8,977	41,089	61,799
Luzerne.	59,976	67,822	4,947	58,482	69,169
Lycoming.	14,609	23,415	2,034	13,147	28,498
McKean.	5,064	9,229	661	4,818	10,963
Mercer	19,716	22,372	3,247	24,658	24,211
Mifflin	5,226	7,541	578	5,178	9,106
Monroe	7,551	12,357	1,967	8,193	16,109
Montgomery	84,289	156,996	26,133	99,741	181,426
Montour	2,272	3,399	375	2,055	4,174
Northampton. . . .	31,920	35,787	6,823	37,979	44,648
Northumberland . .	13,750	20,608	1,515	13,748	22,109
Perry	3,681	8,026	717	3,692	9,365
Philadelphia	421,253	244,108	42,967	501,369	267,178
Pike	2,132	5,249	452	2,503	6,343
Potter.	2,299	4,073	225	1,789	5,164
Schuylkill	24,968	36,273	3,079	25,758	37,330
Snyder	2,418	7,634	451	2,383	8,968
Somerset.	11,695	17,729	815	13,900	19,502
Sullivan.	1,074	1,676	130	952	1,926
Susquehanna . . .	4,660	8,994	786	4,471	10,566
Tioga	4,273	8,770	664	4,060	10,532
Union	2,687	6,798	628	2,747	7,792
Venango	7,800	11,547	1,015	9,114	13,507
Warren	5,560	9,165	922	6,244	10,838
Washington	45,295	32,532	3,413	50,911	34,782
Wayne	3,375	8,468	496	3,155	10,061
Westmoreland. . .	68,627	63,140	5,985	79,906	71,377
Wyoming	2,766	5,919	384	2,518	7,230
York.	33,406	61,098	5,779	33,359	75,020
Totals	**1,937,540**	**2,261,872**	**292,921**	**2,228,131**	**2,584,323**

Pennsylvania Vote Since 1936

1936, Roosevelt, Dem., 2,353,788; Landon, Rep., 1,690,300; Lemke, Royal Oak, 67,467; Thomas, Soc., 14,375; Colvin, Proh., 6,691; Browder, Com., 4,060; Aiken, Ind. Lab., 1,424.

1940, Roosevelt, Dem., 2,171,035; Willkie, Rep., 1,889,848; Thomas, Soc., 10,967; Browder, Com., 4,519; Aiken, Ind. Gov., 1,518.

1944, Roosevelt, Dem., 1,940,479; Dewey, Rep., 1,835,054; Thomas, Soc., 11,721; Watson, Proh., 5,750; Teichert, Ind. Gov., 1,789.

1948, Truman, Dem., 1,752,426; Dewey, Rep., 1,902,197; Wallace, Prog., 55,161; Thomas, Soc., 11,325; Watson, Proh., 10,338; Dobbs, Militant Workers, 2,133; Teichert, Ind. Gov., 1,461.

1952, Eisenhower, Rep., 2,415,789; Stevenson, Dem., 2,146,269; Hamblen, Proh., 8,771; Hallinan, Prog., 4,200; Hoopes, Soc., 2,684; Dobbs, Militant Workers, 1,502; Hass, Ind. Gov., 1,347; scattered, 155.

1956, Eisenhower, Rep., 2,585,252; Stevenson, Dem., 1,981,769; Hass, Soc. Labor, 7,447; Dobbs, Militant Workers, 2,035.

1960, Kennedy, Dem., 2,556,282; Nixon, Rep., 2,439,956; Hass, Soc. Labor, 7,185; Dobbs, Soc. Workers, 2,678; scattering, 440.

1964, Johnson, Dem., 3,130,954; Goldwater, Rep., 1,673,657; DeBerry, Soc. Workers, 10,456; Hass, Soc. Labor, 5,092; scattering, 2,531.

1968, Nixon, Rep., 2,090,017; Humphrey, Dem., 2,259,405; Wallace, 3d party, 378,582; Blomen, Soc. Labor, 4,977; Halstead, Soc. Workers, 4,862; Gregory, 7,821; others, 2,264.

1972, Nixon, Rep., 2,714,521; McGovern, Dem., 1,796,951; Schmitz, Amer., 70,593; Jenness, Soc. Workers, 4,639; Hall, Com., 2,686; others, 2,715.

1976, Carter, Dem., 2,328,677; Ford, Rep., 2,205,604; McCarthy, Ind., 50,584; Maddox, Constitution, 25,344; Camejo, Soc. Workers, 3,009; LaRouche, U.S. Labor, 2,744; Hall, Com., 1,891; others, 2,934.

1980, Reagan, Rep., 2,261,872; Carter, Dem., 1,937,540; Anderson, Ind., 292,921; Clark, Libertarian, 33,263; DeBerry, Soc. Workers, 20,291; Commoner, Consumer, 10,430; Hall, Com., 5,184.

1984, Reagan, Rep., 2,584,323; Mondale, Dem., 2,228,131; Bergland, Libertarian, 6,982.

Rhode Island

City	1980 Carter (D)	1980 Reagan (R)	1980 Anderson (I)	1984 Mondale (D)	1984 Reagan (R)
Cranston	17,293	14,781	5,420	17,742	19,517
East Providence . .	11,440	7,566	3,094	11,064	10,332
Pawtucket	14,455	8,402	3,644	14,109	12,460
Providence	36,249	16,689	7,932	35,751	19,748
Warwick	18,424	15,890	6,498	19,278	22,276
Totals	**198,342**	**154,793**	**59,819**	**197,106**	**212,080**

Rhode Island Vote Since 1936

1936, Roosevelt, Dem., 165,238; Landon, Rep., 125,031; Lemke, Union, 19,569; Aiken, Soc. Labor, 929; Browder, Com., 411.

1940, Roosevelt, Dem., 182,182; Willkie, Rep., 138,653; Browder, Com., 239; Babson, Proh., 74.

1944, Roosevelt, Dem., 175,356; Dewey, Rep., 123,487; Watson, Proh., 433.

1948, Truman, Dem., 188,736; Dewey, Rep., 135,787; Wallace, Prog., 2,619; Thomas, Soc., 429; Teichert, Soc. Labor, 131.

1952, Eisenhower, Rep., 210,935; Stevenson, Dem., 203,293; Hallinan, Prog., 187; Hass, Soc. Labor, 83.

1956, Eisenhower, Rep., 225,819; Stevenson, Dem., 161,790.

1960, Kennedy, Dem., 258,032; Nixon, Rep., 147,502.

1964, Johnson, Dem., 315,463; Goldwater, Rep., 74,615.

1968, Nixon, Rep., 122,359; Humphrey, Dem., 246,518; Wallace, 3d party, 15,678; Halstead, Soc. Worker, 383.

1972, Nixon, Rep., 220,383; McGovern, Dem., 194,645; Jenness, Soc. Workers, 729.

1976, Carter, Dem., 227,636; Ford, Rep., 181,249; MacBride, Libertarian, 715; Camejo, Soc. Workers, 462; Hall, Com., 334; Levin, Soc. Labor, 188.

1980, Reagan, Rep., 154,793; Carter, Dem., 198,342; Anderson, Ind., 59,819; Clark, Libertarian, 2,458; Hall, Com., 218; McReynolds, Socialist, 170; DeBerry, Soc. Worker, 90; Griswold, Workers World, 77.

1984, Reagan, Rep., 212,080; Mondale, Dem., 197,106; Bergland, Libertarian, 277.

South Carolina

County	1980 Carter (D)	1980 Reagan (R)	1980 Anderson (I)	1984 Mondale (D)	1984 Reagan (R)
Abbeville	4,049	2,261	111	2,051	2,709
Aiken	13,014	18,568	601	9,872	25,872
Allendale	2,775	1,181	18	2,170	1,570
Anderson.	18,796	15,666	474	10,324	24,123
Bamberg	3,294	2,098	18	2,892	2,908
Barnwell	3,399	3,228	64	2,811	4,346
Beaufort	7,415	[illegible]	[illegible]	[illegible]	[illegible]
Berkeley	9,850	12,790	17	7,380	16,972
Calhoun	2,043	1,767	31	2,315	2,742
Charleston	32,744	44,006	2,213	29,470	53,779
Cherokee.	6,801	5,378	[illegible]	4,101	[illegible]
Chester.	5,145	3,104	87	3,559	4,441
Chesterfield	6,393	3,477	65	4,593	5,451
Clarendon	5,980	4,158	28	5,591	5,102
Colleton	5,745	4,719	58	4,910	6,200
Darlington	9,009	8,289	219	7,456	11,100
Dillon	4,518	3,384	59	3,360	4,846
Dorchester	7,237	10,893	140	7,037	15,289
Edgefield	3,465	2,415	30	3,227	3,224
Fairfield.	4,153	2,098	37	4,117	3,147
Florence	16,391	17,069	348	14,639	22,753
Georgetown	6,701	5,151	148	6,392	7,370
Greenville	32,135	46,168	1,600	24,137	66,766
Greenwood.	9,283	7,287	230	6,339	10,887
Hampton	4,329	2,217	35	3,736	3,464
Horry	13,885	14,322	530	8,940	20,396
Jasper	3,316	1,617	33	3,753	3,102
Kershaw	5,103	6,652	145	4,323	8,822
Lancaster.	8,282	6,409	331	5,804	10,383
Laurens.	7,858	6,034	129	5,312	9,729
Lee	4,816	2,952	18	3,912	3,548
Lexington.	12,334	28,313	762	8,828	38,628
McCormick.	5,378	2,585	52	1,526	1,186
Marion	1,774	797	22	5,043	4,698
Marlboro	5,377	3,318	80	4,294	3,951
Newberry.	4,825	5,568	80	3,790	7,176
Oconee.	7,677	5,652	188	3,333	8,625
Orangeburg	16,178	11,313	141	15,121	14,286
Pickens.	7,789	9,574	402	4,481	15,155
Richland	33,298	35,843	1,808	32,212	46,773
Saluda	2,649	2,451	38	1,962	3,515
Spartanburg	27,238	28,820	933	20,130	41,553
Sumter	9,205	10,655	250	9,566	12,909
Union	6,274	4,035	93	4,424	6,331
Williamsburg	8,135	5,110	64	7,586	6,492
York.	12,075	11,265	539	9,273	20,008
Totals	**428,220**	**439,277**	**13,868**	**344,459**	**615,539**

South Carolina Vote Since 1936

1936, Roosevelt, Dem., 113,791; Landon, Rep., Tolbert faction 953, Hambright faction 693, total, 1,646.

1940, Roosevelt, Dem., 95,470; Willkie, Rep., 1,727.

1944, Roosevelt, Dem., 90,601; Dewey, Rep., 4,547; Southern Democrats, 7,799; Watson, Proh., 365; Rep. Tolbert faction, 63.

1948, Thurmond, States' Rights, 102,607; Truman, Dem., 34,423; Dewey, Rep., 5,386; Wallace, Prog., 154; Thomas, Soc., 1.

1952, Eisenhower ran on two tickets. Under state law vote cast for two Eisenhower slates of electors could not be combined. Eisenhower, Ind., 158,289; Rep., 9,793; total, 168,082; Stevenson, Dem., 173,004; Hamblen, Proh., 1.

1956, Stevenson, Dem., 136,372; Byrd, Ind., 88,509; Eisenhower, Rep., 75,700; Andrews, Ind., 2.

1960, Kennedy, Dem., 198,129; Nixon, Rep., 188,558; write-in, 1.

1964, Johnson, Dem., 215,700; Goldwater, Rep., 309,048; write-ins: Nixon, 1, Wallace, 5; Powell, 1; Thurmond, 1.

1968, Nixon, Rep., 254,062; Humphrey, Dem., 197,486; Wallace, 3d party, 215,430.

1972, Nixon, Rep., 477,044; McGovern, Dem., 184,559, United Citizens, 2,265; Schmitz, Amer., 10,075; write-in, 17.

1976, Carter, Dem., 450,807; Ford, Rep., 346,149; Anderson, Amer., 2,996; Maddox, Amer. Ind., 1,950; write-in, 681.

1980, Reagan, Rep., 439,277; Carter, Dem., 428,220; Anderson, Ind., 13,868; Clark, Libertarian, 4,807; Rarick, Amer. Ind., 2,086.

1984, Reagan, Rep., 615,539; Mondale, Dem., 344,459; Bergland, Libertarian, 4,359.

South Dakota

County	1980 Carter (D)	1980 Reagan (R)	1980 Anderson (I)	1984 Mondale (D)	1984 Reagan (R)
Aurora	709	1,251	125	840	1,029
Beadle	3,521	5,921	545	3,523	5,876
Bennett	350	919	42	453	856
Bon Homme	1,191	2,794	214	1,408	2,478
Brookings	3,934	5,727	1,169	4,089	6,679
Brown	6,050	10,550	1,143	6,852	10,541
Brule	925	1,674	153	961	1,578
Buffalo	147	272	26	236	253
Butte	843	2,850	150	784	2,865
Campbell	182	1,271	39	214	1,035
Chas. Mix	1,741	2,608	203	1,879	2,660
Clark	774	1,963	151	960	1,748
Clay	2,271	3,004	906	2,711	3,057
Codington	3,353	5,903	638	3,528	6,108
Corson	522	1,233	82	792	955
Custer	708	2,057	129	858	2,183
Davison	3,107	4,743	568	3,248	4,783
Day	1,720	2,507	259	1,932	2,150
Deuel	891	1,657	169	941	1,537
Dewey	600	1,045	109	772	941
Douglas	508	1,855	91	536	1,713
Edmunds	883	1,881	125	1,007	1,553
Fall River	982	2,831	184	1,135	2,748
Faulk	520	1,300	110	579	1,124
Grant	1,602	2,691	254	1,606	2,738
Gregory	883	2,283	121	780	1,777
Haakon	255	1,162	38	237	1,168
Hamlin	903	1,885	197	963	1,782
Hand	803	2,066	159	846	2,030
Hanson	598	1,015	93	625	898
Harding	205	727	28	186	723
Hughes	1,751	4,652	554	2,072	4,985
Hutchinson	1,145	3,789	228	1,237	3,372
Hyde	273	864	60	350	797
Jackson	354	929	50	365	903
Jerauld	595	1,018	103	542	1,012
Jones	189	689	37	206	689
Kingsbury	1,132	2,376	258	1,249	2,121
Lake	2,207	3,093	504	2,367	3,027
Lawrence	2,259	5,306	574	2,565	5,949
Lincoln	2,261	3,848	524	2,626	3,988
Lyman	486	1,256	106	478	1,120
McCook	1,223	2,014	269	1,448	1,902
McPherson	287	2,056	54	418	1,813
Marshall	1,120	1,710	147	1,111	1,529
Meade	1,721	5,349	342	2,093	5,908
Mellette	279	624	46	303	616
Miner	833	1,172	148	960	1,004
Minnehaha	20,008	26,256	4,658	23,042	29,908
Moody	1,364	1,807	279	1,586	1,633
Pennington	7,121	18,991	1,650	8,224	21,947
Perkins	595	1,931	93	714	1,686
Potter	436	1,633	81	482	1,551
Roberts	1,829	2,904	235	2,063	2,767
Sanborn	628	1,178	107	611	1,080
Shannon	1,132	438	91	1,489	324
Spink	1,572	2,915	294	1,680	2,627
Stanley	339	892	55	351	942
Sully	220	852	60	266	836
Todd	972	803	112	1,022	679
Tripp	947	2,669	130	935	2,483
Turner	1,369	3,343	281	1,486	3,086
Union	1,830	2,788	359	2,221	2,431
Walworth	753	2,675	139	779	2,396
Yankton	2,698	5,355	553	2,932	5,161
Ziebach	246	523	30	359	429
Totals	**103,855**	**198,343**	**21,431**	**116,113**	**200,267**

South Dakota Vote Since 1936

1936, Roosevelt, Dem., 160,137; Landon, Rep., 125,977; Lemke, Union, 10,338.

1940, Roosevelt, Dem., 131,862; Willkie, Rep., 177,065.

1944, Roosevelt, Dem., 96,711; Dewey, Rep., 135,365.

1948, Truman, Dem., 117,653; Dewey, Rep., 129,651; Wallace, Prog., 2,801.

1952, Eisenhower, Rep., 203,857; Stevenson, Dem., 90,426.

1956, Eisenhower, Rep., 171,569; Stevenson, Dem., 122,288.

1960, Kennedy, Dem., 128,070; Nixon, Rep., 178,417.

1964, Johnson, Dem., 163,010; Goldwater, Rep., 130,108.

1968, Nixon, Rep., 149,841; Humphrey, Dem., 118,023; Wallace, 3d party, 13,400.

1972, Nixon, Rep., 166,476; McGovern, Dem., 139,945; Jenness, Soc. Workers, 994.

1976, Carter, Dem., 147,068; Ford, Rep., 151,505; MacBride, Libertarian, 1,619; Hall, Com., 318; Camejo, Soc. Workers, 168.

1980, Reagan, Rep., 198,343; Carter, Dem., 103,855; Anderson, Ind., 21,431; Clark, Libertarian, 3,824; Pulley, Soc. Workers, 250.

1984, Reagan, Rep., 200,267; Mondale, Dem., 116,113.

Tennessee

County	1980 Carter (D)	1980 Reagan (R)	1980 Anderson (I)	1984 Mondale (D)	1984 Reagan (R)
Anderson	10,194	14,235	1,161	10,415	16,783
Bedford	5,987	3,377	159	4,499	4,699
Benton	3,811	2,281	71	3,398	2,481
Bledsoe	1,585	1,970	26	1,316	1,950
Blount	9,412	17,959	620	9,188	20,525
Bradley	7,638	11,869	316	6,085	16,322
Campbell	4,752	5,537	120	4,692	5,685
Cannon	2,351	1,403	41	1,846	1,669
Carroll	5,277	5,681	125	4,568	6,017
Carter	6,006	11,648	326	4,642	13,153
Cheatham	3,771	2,296	90	3,007	4,109
Chester	2,123	2,751	52	1,854	2,793
Claiborne	2,844	4,289	94	2,870	4,474
Clay	1,376	1,344	27	1,281	1,338
Cocke	2,139	6,802	139	2,068	6,665
Coffee	7,612	5,454	239	5,691	7,695
Crockett	2,422	2,117	27	1,937	2,479
Cumberland	3,775	6,354	227	3,605	7,083
Davidson	103,741	65,772	4,834	89,498	98,115
Decatur	2,139	2,095	35	2,031	2,390
De Kalb	2,948	1,841	48	2,645	2,337
Dickson	6,622	3,636	157	5,809	5,846
Dyer	5,713	5,475	158	3,991	6,610
Fayette	4,141	2,944	75	3,634	3,733
Fentress	1,543	2,493	49	1,755	2,922
Franklin	6,760	3,995	251	5,846	5,705
Gibson	9,829	6,792	227	8,334	9,484
Giles	4,653	2,757	85	3,812	3,875
Grainger	1,495	3,254	66	1,565	3,212
Greene	5,822	10,704	338	4,763	13,215
Grundy	2,837	1,139	33	2,596	1,396
Hamblen	5,890	9,741	336	4,922	11,144
Hamilton	41,913	57,575	2,087	41,449	69,626
Hancock	704	1,734	32	619	1,491
Hardeman	4,153	2,931	73	3,797	3,712
Hardin	3,164	4,152	76	3,051	4,632
Hawkins	5,283	7,836	310	4,802	9,863
Haywood	3,445	2,435	49	3,308	2,839
Henderson	2,702	5,108	78	2,426	5,362
Henry	6,601	4,299	200	5,407	5,376
Hickman	3,225	1,903	78	2,941	2,370
Houston	1,757	738	31	1,716	882
Humphreys	3,974	1,897	74	3,668	2,249
Jackson	2,480	995	27	2,894	1,544
Jefferson	3,180	6,944	201	3,185	7,721
Johnson	1,141	3,716	66	999	3,853
Knox	45,634	66,153	4,801	43,448	76,965
Lake	1,718	823	11	1,191	878
Lauderdale	4,318	2,818	73	3,506	3,566
Lawrence	6,082	6,532	212	5,458	6,034
Lewis	2,190	1,076	33	1,556	1,733
Lincoln	5,387	2,856	119	4,103	3,982

Loudon	3,699	6,382	235	3,227	7,113
McMinn	5,460	7,825	200	5,141	9,604
McNairy	3,801	4,603	76	3,825	4,776
Macon	1,947	2,925	65	1,747	3,330
Madison	12,986	13,667	363	12,006	17,819
Marion	4,623	3,902	93	3,942	4,337
Marshall	4,277	2,282	78	2,935	3,416
Maury	7,957	6,637	225	6,950	9,008
Meigs	999	1,278	31	1,012	1,575
Monroe	4,612	6,246	125	4,223	6,665
Montgomery	11,573	8,503	490	9,939	13,228
Moore	993	551	34	808	863
Morgan	2,094	2,823	70	2,121	2,903
Obion	5,766	5,397	138	4,769	6,384
Overton	3,343	1,869	38	2,749	2,054
Perry	1,401	783	32	1,316	948
Pickett	758	1,319	12	706	1,246
Polk	2,470	2,414	45	2,112	2,785
Putnam	8,084	6,235	342	7,443	8,999
Rhea	3,070	4,689	93	2,804	5,692
Roane	6,473	11,096	481	6,623	11,882
Robertson	7,381	3,560	127	5,756	5,445
Rutherford	15,213	11,208	703	11,618	19,503
Scott	1,724	3,014	63	1,810	3,107
Sequatchie	1,509	1,512	23	1,238	1,785
Sevier	3,450	10,576	338	3,384	12,517
Shelby	159,240	140,157	7,180	169,717	165,947
Smith	3,674	1,755	69	3,258	2,393
Stewart	2,274	985	42	2,174	1,285
Sullivan	22,341	25,963	1,874	16,925	36,516
Sumner	14,150	11,876	540	11,535	18,442
Tipton	4,934	4,339	109	3,895	5,945
Trousdale	1,674	629	30	1,142	781
Unicoi	1,880	3,828	97	1,696	4,249
Union	1,435	2,453	45	1,495	2,447
Van Buren	886	499	11	810	718
Warren	6,021	3,680	148	4,813	4,811
Washington	11,599	17,457	934	9,452	21,762
Wayne	1,633	3,418	78	1,534	3,332
Weakley	5,910	5,668	136	4,752	6,480
White	3,415	2,100	64	3,033	2,895
Williamson	8,815	11,597	551	6,929	17,975
Wilson	11,248	7,535	380	8,433	12,858
Totals	**783,051**	**787,761**	**35,991**	**711,714**	**990,212**

Tennessee Vote Since 1936

1936, Roosevelt, Dem., 327,083; Landon, Rep., 146,516; Thomas, Soc., 685; Colvin, Proh., 632; Browder, Com., 319; Lemke, Union, 296.

1940, Roosevelt, Dem., 351,601; Willkie, Rep., 169,153; Babson, Proh., 1,606; Thomas, Soc., 463.

1944, Roosevelt, Dem., 308,707; Dewey, Rep., 200,311; Watson, Proh., 882; Thomas, Soc., 892.

1948, Truman, Dem., 270,402; Dewey, Rep., 202,914; Thurmond, States' Rights, 73,815; Wallace, Prog., 1,864; Thomas, Soc., 1,288.

1952, Eisenhower, Rep., 446,147; Stevenson, Dem., 443,710; Hamblen, Proh., 1,432; Hallinan, Prog., 885; MacArthur, Christian Nationalist, 379.

1956, Eisenhower, Rep., 462,288; Stevenson, Dem., 456,507; Andrews, Ind., 19,820; Holtwick, Proh., 789.

1960, Kennedy, Dem., 481,453; Nixon, Rep., 556,577; Faubus, States' Rights, 11,304; Decker, Proh., 2,458.

1964, Johnson, Dem. 635,047; Goldwater, Rep., 508,965; write-in, 34.

1968, Nixon, Rep., 472,592; Humphrey, Dem., 351,233; Wallace, 3d party, 424,792.

1972, Nixon, Rep., 813,147; McGovern, Dem., 357,293; Schmitz, Amer., 30,373; write-in, 369.

1976, Carter, Dem., 825,879; Ford, Rep., 633,969; Anderson, Amer., 5,769; McCarthy, Ind., 5,004; Maddox, Am. Ind., 2,303; MacBride, Libertarian, 1,375; Hall, Com., 547; LaRouche, U.S. Labor, 512; Bubar, Proh., 442; Miller, Ind., 316; write-in, 230.

1980, Reagan, Rep., 787,761; Carter, Dem., 783,051; Anderson, Ind., 35,991; Clark, Libertarian, 7,116; Commoner, Citizens, 1,112; Bubar, Statesman, 521; McReynolds, Socialist, 519; Hall, Com., 503; DeBerry, Soc. Worker, 490; Griswold, Workers World, 400; write-ins, 152.

1984, Reagan, Rep., 990,212; Mondale, Dem., 711,714; Bergland, Libertarian, 3,072.

Texas

County	1980 Carter (D)	1980 Reagan (R)	1980 Anderson (I)	1984 Mondale (D)	1984 Reagan (R)
Anderson	5,163	5,970	137	4,747	8,634
Andrews	1,155	2,800	39	820	3,918
Angelina	10,140	9,900	232	9,054	14,685
Aransas	1,800	3,081	134	1,696	4,352
Archer	1,444	1,804	30	1,089	2,487
Armstrong	333	709	9	238	791
Atascosa	3,980	4,364	93	3,547	5,279
Austin	1,893	3,734	87	1,941	4,872
Bailey	800	1,809	26	684	1,888
Bandera	894	2,373	64	771	3,152
Bastrop	4,716	3,768	205	4,744	6,439
Baylor	1,183	1,098	14	1,019	1,314
Bee	3,606	4,171	125	3,659	5,377
Bell	15,823	20,729	934	13,322	31,117
Bexar	137,729	159,578	9,467	136,947	203,319
Blanco	794	1,434	52	700	1,957
Borden	131	279	3	140	325
Bosque	2,431	2,908	62	2,046	3,923
Bowie	11,339	13,942	244	10,077	18,244
Brazoria	18,253	27,614	1,205	18,609	39,166
Brazos	9,856	17,798	1,453	12,348	34,733
Brewster	1,271	1,496	89	1,462	2,066
Briscoe	561	562	13	471	538
Brooks	2,488	780	43	2,702	896
Brown	4,867	6,515	102	4,070	8,468
Burleson	2,615	1,943	33	2,578	3,076
Burnet	3,711	4,033	132	2,983	5,895
Caldwell	3,155	2,879	112	3,401	4,315
Calhoun	3,034	3,312	136	2,586	4,434
Callahan	2,002	2,284	29	1,305	3,538
Cameron	23,200	22,041	801	26,394	29,545
Camp	2,052	1,531	19	1,917	2,238
Carson	1,006	1,888	26	826	2,412
Cass	5,578	4,993	60	5,053	6,677
Castro	1,199	1,955	44	1,009	2,026
Chambers	2,517	3,140	96	2,632	4,322
Cherokee	5,726	5,629	92	4,494	8,187
Childress	1,222	1,443	33	900	1,574
Clay	2,233	1,824	40	1,844	2,569
Cochran	513	1,064	23	557	1,117
Coke	808	700	10	532	1,080
Coleman	1,719	2,228	33	1,420	2,790
Collin	15,187	36,559	1,559	13,604	61,095
Collingsworth	798	1,020	18	742	1,398
Colorado	2,377	3,520	50	2,428	4,528
Comal	3,554	9,758	324	4,179	13,452
Comanche	2,550	1,977	40	2,248	2,678
Concho	702	700	8	580	821
Cooke	3,842	6,760	129	3,278	8,260
Coryell	4,097	5,494	228	3,113	9,056
Cottle	732	511	9	637	607
Crane	607	1,310	23	392	1,473
Crockett	595	885	10	589	1,094
Crosby	1,408	1,361	17	1,212	1,376
Culberson	423	541	7	407	509
Dallam	632	965	33	496	1,594
Dallas	190,459	306,680	14,071	200,502	405,444
Dawson	1,867	3,267	55	1,781	3,685
Deaf Smith	1,666	4,073	77	1,465	4,762
Delta	1,347	767	18	973	1,024
Denton	17,381	29,908	1,953	16,772	52,865
DeWitt	2,044	3,450	66	1,882	4,401
Dickens	912	554	13	692	594
Dimmit	2,102	1,173	25	2,546	1,338
Donley	751	1,106	22	529	1,297
Duval	3,706	1,012	20	3,748	1,201
Eastland	3,346	3,442	37	2,522	4,841
Ector	9,069	26,188	636	8,913	31,228
Edwards	237	575	11	159	626
Ellis	9,219	10,046	214	8,029	16,873
El Paso	40,082	53,276	5,096	51,917	66,114
Erath	4,156	3,981	92	3,234	6,122
Falls	3,328	2,606	51	2,834	3,133
Fannin	5,284	3,196	74	4,399	4,692
Fayette	2,590	4,104	77	2,379	5,711
Fisher	1,564	838	23	1,384	965
Floyd	1,477	2,043	24	1,023	2,092
Foard	617	349	7	448	472
Fort Bend	11,583	25,366	1,005	18,729	41,370
Franklin	1,487	1,105	14	1,104	1,836
Freestone	2,739	2,468	33	2,489	3,624
Frio	2,849	1,753	47	2,656	2,003
Gaines	1,182	2,390	46	797	2,714
Galveston	30,778	29,527	1,955	36,092	40,262
Garza	677	1,188	22	521	1,219
Gillespie	1,170	4,736	90	1,137	5,496
Glasscock	116	416	2	128	403
Goliad	1,081	1,170	22	836	1,540
Gonzales	2,896	2,931	61	2,196	3,962
Gray	2,786	7,187	103	2,003	8,955
Grayson	13,807	16,811	532	11,803	22,554
Gregg	10,219	23,399	311	10,700	29,697
Grimes	2,440	2,087	42	2,370	3,365
Guadalupe	5,049	9,901	407	5,060	14,382
Hale	3,610	7,277	123	3,202	7,670
Hall	1,057	1,141	13	984	1,058
Hamilton	1,526	1,683	30	1,130	2,118
Hansford	518	2,046	17	259	2,213
Hardeman	1,174	1,056	28	927	1,238
Hardin	7,358	6,087	200	6,782	8,380
Harris	274,061	416,555	22,917	334,135	536,029
Harrison	7,746	9,328	125	7,773	12,618
Hartley	470	1,248	28	356	1,419
Haskell	1,951	1,447	22	1,434	1,701
Hays	6,013	6,517	590	6,663	12,467

Hemphill	592	1,152	21	413	1,650
Henderson	8,199	7,903	134	7,302	12,725
Hidalgo	34,542	25,808	1,063	44,147	35,059
Hill	4,688	4,113	73	3,420	5,344
Hockley	2,447	4,599	90	2,044	5,462
Hood	3,001	3,755	109	3,063	6,817
Hopkins	4,344	3,834	93	3,707	5,772
Houston	4,181	2,889	47	3,275	4,542
Howard	4,451	6,658	158	4,115	7,519
Hudspeth	394	471	14	362	557
Hunt	8,773	9,283	327	6,971	14,303
Hutchinson	2,935	7,439	170	2,052	9,078
Irion	239	427	2	199	619
Jack	1,349	1,482	29	945	1,825
Jackson	1,826	2,540	66	1,804	3,661
Jasper	5,707	4,396	98	5,787	5,965
Jeff Davis	300	409	10	299	511
Jefferson	45,642	36,763	1,664	54,846	45,124
Jim Hogg	1,437	535	23	1,703	608
Jim Wells	7,267	4,606	102	7,795	5,896
Johnson	10,542	11,411	333	9,148	18,254
Jones	3,043	2,765	45	2,343	4,017
Karnes	2,284	2,719	52	1,802	3,068
Kaufman	6,266	5,852	110	5,554	9,343
Kendall	1,075	3,890	88	938	4,568
Kenedy	106	76	2	110	96
Kent	351	339	0	253	332
Kerr	3,387	9,090	259	3,102	11,829
Kimble	608	1,011	22	442	1,333
King	55	144	5	53	141
Kinney	472	543	23	486	774
Kleberg	5,125	4,608	231	4,924	5,712
Knox	1,163	783	17	921	1,027
Lamar	7,178	6,094	148	5,504	9,273
Lamb	2,132	3,723	51	1,919	3,892
Lampasas	1,979	2,323	56	1,356	3,285
LaSalle	1,442	773	19	1,504	1,007
Lavaca	2,678	3,254	54	2,464	5,058
Lee	1,581	1,803	59	1,659	2,967
Leon	2,190	1,821	19	1,821	3,207
Liberty	6,810	6,470	163	6,292	10,504
Limestone	3,403	2,835	45	3,228	4,063
Lipscomb	338	1,343	28	241	1,461
Live Oak	1,380	2,193	32	1,260	2,481
Llano	2,130	2,866	72	1,894	4,042
Loving	22	50	0	16	57
Lubbock	18,732	46,711	1,952	18,793	57,151
Lynn	1,236	1,603	28	1,009	1,617
McCulloch	1,750	1,572	24	1,433	2,060
McLennan	26,305	31,968	964	23,206	42,232
McMullen	122	271	4	61	337
Madison	1,583	1,389	32	1,384	2,158
Marion	2,015	1,666	28	2,111	2,336
Martin	605	1,093	15	512	1,218
Mason	630	966	17	570	1,168
Matagorda	4,585	5,545	146	5,201	8,452
Maverick	2,932	1,370	39	3,063	1,783
Medina	3,034	4,742	84	3,053	5,737
Menard	489	548	11	394	725
Midland	6,839	25,027	586	7,214	33,706
Milam	4,230	3,251	111	3,734	4,384
Mills	1,028	985	24	688	1,262
Mitchell	1,446	1,455	12	1,332	2,007
Montague	3,233	3,143	59	2,602	4,406
Montgomery	12,593	26,237	819	13,293	41,230
Moore	1,743	3,736	67	1,129	4,649
Morris	3,105	2,133	27	2,925	2,778
Motley	341	573	7	282	533
Nacogdoches	5,981	8,626	422	5,694	13,063
Navarro	6,988	5,400	126	5,672	7,816
Newton	3,284	1,379	24	3,296	2,123
Nolan	2,796	2,781	87	2,524	3,608
Nueces	43,424	40,586	2,045	46,721	54,333
Ochiltree	594	3,032	52	419	3,492
Oldham	290	557	9	226	762
Orange	14,928	12,389	395	16,816	15,386
Palo Pinto	4,244	4,068	98	3,349	5,701
Panola	3,637	4,022	58	3,179	5,676
Parker	7,336	8,505	189	6,050	13,647
Parmer	707	2,640	30	567	2,524
Pecos	1,602	2,723	37	1,596	3,451
Polk	4,213	3,771	80	3,898	5,987
Potter	9,633	16,327	545	8,365	20,396
Presidio	1,039	723	22	992	837
Rains	1,174	813	18	1,027	1,560
Randall	7,323	23,136	677	6,044	30,249
Reagan	414	917	14	243	1,079
Real	603	832	14	360	1,004
Red River	3,501	2,225	31	2,518	2,979
Reeves	2,138	2,315	52	2,396	2,461
Refugio	2,224	1,944	57	1,559	2,421
Roberts	150	482	4	106	539
Robertson	3,572	1,661	33	3,339	2,663
Rockwall	1,985	4,036	113	1,639	6,688
Runnels	1,648	2,532	36	1,179	2,968
Rusk	5,582	8,705	116	4,599	11,081
Sabine	1,983	1,387	15	1,940	2,045
San Augustine	1,674	1,397	14	1,583	1,937
San Jacinto	2,376	1,726	42	2,466	3,174
San Patricio	8,627	8,326	280	8,838	11,074
San Saba	1,405	948	23	1,070	1,566
Schleicher	444	672	6	326	854
Scurry	2,003	3,745	53	1,564	5,028
Shackelford	606	959	9	415	1,181
Shelby	4,215	3,500	71	3,610	4,863
Sherman	286	1,128	28	246	1,269
Smith	14,838	28,236	414	15,227	40,740
Somervell	1,015	792	21	635	1,422
Starr	4,782	1,389	50	5,047	1,658
Stephens	1,372	2,161	34	1,046	2,898
Sterling	218	364	2	129	577
Stonewall	719	488	6	643	599
Sutton	485	1,000	13	465	1,251
Swisher	1,854	1,450	50	1,642	1,611
Tarrant	121,068	173,466	7,818	120,147	248,050
Taylor	13,245	22,961	620	9,628	34,444
Terrell	260	411	14	289	407
Terry	1,945	3,178	45	1,535	3,181
Throckmorton	455	444	7	388	586
Titus	3,872	3,747	44	3,631	5,069
Tom Green	9,892	16,555	661	8,981	23,847
Travis	75,028	73,151	9,796	94,124	124,944
Trinity	2,510	1,503	32	2,115	2,599
Tyler	3,540	2,545	70	3,119	3,638
Upshur	4,894	4,836	78	4,614	7,325
Upton	485	1,169	13	380	1,603
Uvalde	2,402	3,887	62	2,482	4,790
Val Verde	4,116	5,055	145	3,857	5,909
Van Zandt	5,707	5,495	78	4,506	8,474
Victoria	7,382	13,392	347	7,037	18,787
Walker	4,869	5,657	274	4,263	8,809
Waller	3,329	3,019	76	3,828	4,116
Ward	1,405	2,912	50	1,188	3,474
Washington	2,518	4,821	95	2,483	6,506
Webb	11,856	5,421	242	12,308	8,582
Wharton	5,138	6,598	160	5,072	8,495
Wheeler	1,090	1,626	16	805	2,251
Wichita	17,657	22,884	847	16,009	28,932
Wilbarger	2,347	3,031	53	2,011	3,644
Willacy	3,047	1,995	38	3,037	2,340
Williamson	10,408	15,035	946	9,911	25,774
Wilson	3,097	3,443	73	2,829	4,588
Winkler	1,021	2,160	35	752	2,213
Wise	4,674	4,350	108	3,856	6,958
Wood	4,033	4,515	74	3,449	7,144
Yoakum	715	1,937	28	456	2,204
Young	2,740	4,153	84	2,203	5,282
Zapata	1,218	874	19	1,577	1,214
Zavala	2,621	831	69	2,937	924
Totals	**1,881,147**	**2,510,705**	**111,613**	**1,949,276**	**3,433,428**

Texas Vote Since 1936

1936, Roosevelt, Dem., 734,485; Landon, Rep., 103,874; Lemke, Union, 3,281; Thomas, Soc., 1,075; Colvin, Proh., 514; Browder, Com., 253.

1940, Roosevelt, Dem., 840,151; Willkie, Rep., 199,152; Babson, Proh., 925; Thomas, Soc., 728; Browder, Com., 212.

1944, Roosevelt, Dem., 821,605; Dewey, Rep., 191,425; Texas Regulars, 135,439; Watson, Proh., 1,017; Thomas, Soc., 594; America First, 250.

1948, Truman, Dem., 750,700; Dewey, Rep., 282,240; Thurmond, States' Rights, 106,909; Wallace, Prog., 3,764; Watson, Proh., 2,758; Thomas, Soc., 874.

1952, Eisenhower, Rep., 1,102,878; Stevenson, Dem., 969,228; Hamblen, Proh., 1,983; MacArthur, Christian Nationalist, 833; MacArthur, Constitution, 730; Hallinan, Prog., 294.

1956, Eisenhower, Rep., 1,080,619; Stevenson, Dem., 859,958; Andrews, Ind., 14,591.

1960, Kennedy, Dem., 1,167,932; Nixon, Rep., 1,121,699; Sullivan, Constitution, 18,169; Decker, Proh., 3,870; write-in, 15.

1964, Johnson, Dem., 1,663,185; Goldwater, Rep., 958,566; Lightburn, Constitution, 5,060.

1968, Nixon, Rep., 1,227,844; Humphrey, Dem., 1,266,804; Wallace, 3d party, 584,269; write-in, 489.

1972, Nixon, Rep., 2,298,896; McGovern, Dem., 1,154,289; Schmitz, Amer., 6,039; Jenness, Soc. Workers, 8,664; others, 3,393.

1976, Carter, Dem., 2,082,319; Ford, Rep., 1,953,300; McCarthy, Ind., 20,118; Anderson, Amer., 11,442; Camejo, Soc. Workers, 1,723; write-in, 2,982.

1980, Reagan, Rep., 2,510,705; Carter, Dem., 1,881,147; Anderson, Ind., 111,613; Clark, Libertarian, 37,643; write-in, 528.

1984, Reagan, Rep., 3,433,428; Mondale, Dem., 1,949,276.

Utah

County	1980 Carter (D)	1980 Reagan (R)	1980 Anderson (I)	1984 Mondale (D)	1984 Reagan (R)
Beaver	621	1,477	43	708	1,516
Box Elder	2,142	12,500	306	1,983	13,243
Cache	3,639	20,251	1,494	4,123	22,127
Carbon	4,317	4,320	309	4,357	4,393
Daggett	109	290	10	227	296
Davis	9,065	45,695	2,253	11,727	49,863
Duchesne	854	3,827	87	746	4,437
Emery	1,315	3,076	90	1,326	3,081
Garfield	375	1,578	50	315	1,609
Grand	703	2,362	205	876	2,463
Iron	1,242	6,207	240	1,342	6,856
Juab	720	1,872	51	917	1,902
Kane	256	1,492	59	294	1,710
Millard	795	3,620	72	1,192	4,345
Morgan	373	1,985	42	481	1,934
Piute	157	551	3	151	606
Rich	143	762	18	131	797
Salt Lake	58,472	169,411	19,547	78,488	183,536
San Juan	763	2,774	72	1,145	2,598
Sanpete	1,260	5,143	112	1,227	5,507
Sevier	1,112	5,614	117	1,072	5,736
Summit	1,184	3,330	480	1,539	4,093
Tooele	3,132	6,024	391	3,584	6,478
Uintah	1,049	6,045	155	1,186	7,337
Utah	12,166	71,859	1,264	14,801	72,284
Wasatch	994	2,799	113	1,015	2,789
Washington	1,678	10,181	185	1,846	12,049
Wayne	226	835	15	224	930
Weber	15,404	43,807	2,501	18,346	44,590
Totals	**124,266**	**439,687**	**30,284**	**155,369**	**469,105**

Utah Vote Since 1936

1936, Roosevelt, Dem., 150,246; Landon, Rep., 64,555; Lemke, Union, 1,121; Thomas, Soc., 432; Browder, Com., 280; Colvin, Proh., 43.

1940, Roosevelt, Dem., 154,277; Willkie, Rep., 93,151; Thomas, Soc., 200; Browder, Com., 191.

1944, Roosevelt, Dem., 150,088; Dewey, Rep., 97,891; Thomas, Soc., 340.

1948, Truman, Dem., 149,151; Dewey, Rep., 124,402; Wallace, Prog., 2,679; Dobbs, Soc. Workers, 73.

1952, Eisenhower, Rep., 194,190; Stevenson, Dem., 135,364.

1956, Eisenhower, Rep., 215,631; Stevenson, Dem., 118,364.

1960, Kennedy, Dem., 169,248; Nixon, Rep., 205,361; Dobbs, Soc. Workers, 100.

1964, Johnson, Dem., 219,628; Goldwater, Rep., 181,785.

1968, Nixon, Rep., 238,728; Humphrey, Dem., 156,665; Wallace, 3d party, 26,906; Halstead, Soc. Worker, 89; Peace and Freedom, 180.

1972, Nixon, Rep., 323,643; McGovern, Dem., 126,284; Schmitz, Amer., 28,549.

1976, Carter, Dem., 182,110; Ford, Rep., 337,908; Anderson, Amer., 13,304; McCarthy, Ind., 3,907; MacBride, Libertarian, 2,438; Maddox, Am. Ind., 1,162; Camejo, Soc. Workers, 268; Hall, Com., 121.

1980, Reagan, Rep., 439,687; Carter, Dem., 124,266; Anderson, Ind., 30,284; Clark, Libertarian, 7,226; Commoner, Citizens, 1,009; Greaves, American, 965; Rarick, Amer. Ind., 522; Hall, Com., 139; DeBerry, Soc. Worker, 124.

1984, Reagan, Rep., 469,105; Mondale, Dem., 155,369; Bergland, Libertarian, 2,447.

Vermont

City	1980 Carter (D)	1980 Reagan (R)	1980 Anderson (I)	1984 Mondale (D)	1984 Reagan (R)
Barre City	1,857	1,603	461	1,903	2,195
Bennington	2,528	2,059	828	2,879	3,237
Brattleboro	1,877	1,890	1,021	2,741	2,645
Burlington	6,752	4,506	2,796	10,080	7,857
Montpelier	1,575	1,824	656	2,120	2,257
Rutland City	3,284	2,921	991	3,298	3,970
St. Albans City	1,395	1,381	299	1,346	1,748
St. Johnsbury	1,055	1,918	300	915	2,152
South Burlington	2,044	2,324	1,025	2,728	3,443
Winooski	1,425	686	251	1,361	1,264
Totals	**81,891**	**94,598**	**31,760**	**95,730**	**135,865**

Vermont Vote Since 1936

1936, Landon, Rep., 81,023; Roosevelt, Dem., 62,124; Browder, Com., 405.

1940, Roosevelt, Dem., 64,269; Willkie, Rep., 78,371; Browder, Com., 411.

1944, Roosevelt, Dem., 53,820; Dewey, Rep., 71,527.

1948, Truman, Dem., 45,557; Dewey, Rep., 75,926; Wallace, Prog., 1,279; Thomas, Soc., 585.

1952, Eisenhower, Rep., 109,717; Stevenson, Dem., 43,355; Hallinan, Prog., 282; Hoopes, Soc., 185.

1956, Eisenhower, Rep., 110,390; Stevenson, Dem., 42,549; scattered, 39.

1960, Kennedy, Dem., 69,186; Nixon, Rep., 98,131.

1964, Johnson, Dem., 107,674; Goldwater, Rep., 54,868.

1968, Nixon, Rep., 85,142; Humphrey, Dem., 70,255; Wallace, 3d party, 5,104; Halstead, Soc. Worker, 295; Gregory, New Party, 579.

1972, Nixon, Rep., 117,149; McGovern, Dem., 68,174; Spock, Liberty Union, 1,010; Jenness, Soc. Workers, 296; scattered, 318.

1976, Carter, Dem., 77,798; Carter, Ind. Vermonter, 991; Ford, Rep., 100,387; McCarthy, Ind., 4,001; Camejo, Soc. Workers, 430; LaRouche, U.S. Labor, 196; scattered, 99.

1980, Reagan, Rep., 94,598; Carter, Dem., 81,891; Anderson, Ind., 31,760; Commoner, Citizens, 2,316; Clark, Libertarian, 1,900; McReynolds, Liberty Union, 136; Hall, Com. 118; DeBerry, Soc. Worker, 75; scattering, 413.

1984, Reagan, Rep., 135,865; Mondale, Dem., 95,730; Bergland, Libertarian, 1,002.

Virginia

County	1980 Carter (D)	1980 Reagan (R)	1980 Anderson (I)	1984 Mondale (D)	1984 Reagan (R)
Accomack	4,872	5,371	292	4,355	8,047
Albemarle	7,293	10,424	1,435	7,982	14,455
Alleghany	2,411	2,185	116	1,932	3,067
Amelia	1,643	1,969	52	1,432	2,336
Amherst	3,476	5,088	208	3,409	7,004
Appomattox	1,492	2,548	85	1,498	3,386
Arlington	26,502	30,854	8,042	37,031	34,848
Augusta	5,202	11,011	539	3,899	15,308
Bath	999	921	70	727	1,434
Bedford	4,721	6,608	336	4,754	10,371
Bland	1,002	1,278	35	867	1,812
Botetourt	3,698	4,408	329	3,243	5,959
Brunswick	3,430	2,310	70	3,040	2,950
Buchanan	5,768	4,554	95	7,828	5,053
Buckingham	1,933	1,864	77	1,879	2,627
Campbell	4,473	9,592	396	4,380	13,388
Caroline	2,924	2,071	116	3,111	2,949
Carroll	3,437	5,905	183	2,914	7,056
Charles City	1,564	506	39	1,776	776
Charlotte	2,108	2,322	59	1,811	2,999
Chesterfield	13,080	37,904	2,182	13,730	54,806
Clarke	1,156	1,876	177	1,215	2,529
Craig	946	768	41	845	1,173
Culpeper	2,519	4,312	231	2,255	5,596
Cumberland	1,355	1,515	51	1,237	2,027
Dickenson	4,177	3,687	77	4,848	3,921
Dinwiddie	3,475	3,369	107	3,485	4,547
Essex	1,280	1,581	76	1,300	2,120
Fairfax	73,734	137,620	24,605	107,295	183,181
Fauquier	4,119	6,782	548	4,056	10,319
Floyd	1,642	2,447	131	1,599	3,431
Fluvanna	1,424	1,605	108	1,332	2,247
Franklin	5,685	4,993	304	4,903	7,684
Frederick	2,948	7,293	455	2,671	9,542
Giles	3,627	2,978	211	3,047	4,340
Gloucester	3,138	4,261	354	2,830	7,109
Goochland	2,290	2,423	113	2,178	3,404
Grayson	2,875	3,494	106	2,319	4,508
Greene	925	1,702	105	760	2,216
Greensville	2,142	1,583	39	2,352	2,304
Halifax	4,528	5,088	125	4,231	6,726
Hanover	5,383	14,262	589	4,831	18,800
Henrico	21,023	50,505	2,956	21,336	63,864
Henry	8,800	8,258	355	6,976	12,693
Highland	487	751	25	398	997
Isle of Wight	3,951	3,526	197	3,650	5,664
James City	3,068	4,289	551	3,486	7,104
King George	1,318	1,784	185	1,450	2,356
King and Queen	1,128	949	43	1,201	1,449
King William	1,446	2,036	80	1,448	2,803
Lancaster	1,567	2,780	106	1,559	3,416
Lee	4,758	4,417	137	5,085	5,365
Loudoun	6,694	12,076	1,312	8,227	17,765
Louisa	2,809	2,633	160	2,703	3,789
Lunenburg	1,958	2,045	59	1,754	2,713
Madison	1,351	1,959	156	1,302	2,723
Mathews	1,300	2,204	148	1,106	2,868
Mecklenburg	3,790	4,853	142	3,438	6,777
Middlesex	1,395	1,810	90	1,206	2,612
Montgomery	7,455	8,222	1,400	7,303	12,408
Nelson	2,410	1,866	143	2,021	2,777
New Kent	1,204	1,739	68	1,204	2,679
Northampton	2,363	2,165	114	2,226	2,906

Northumberland	1,551	2,598	109	1,407	3,166
Nottoway	2,593	2,813	113	2,296	3,418
Orange	2,420	3,381	241	2,285	4,483
Page	2,607	4,297	161	2,437	5,021
Patrick	2,382	3,436	105	1,908	4,703
Pittsylvania	7,653	12,022	250	7,791	15,743
Powhatan	1,484	2,933	98	1,381	3,921
Prince Edward	2,553	2,774	137	2,589	3,454
Prince George	2,310	3,389	130	2,136	4,999
Prince William	12,787	23,061	2,676	15,631	34,992
Pulaski	5,769	5,747	343	4,364	8,242
Rappahannock	1,055	1,179	99	999	1,696
Richmond	854	1,567	49	830	1,869
Roanoke	12,114	17,182	1,286	10,569	23,348
Rockbridge	2,475	2,784	296	2,098	4,067
Rockingham	5,294	11,397	771	4,220	13,480
Russell	5,764	4,778	125	6,760	5,738
Scott	4,314	4,744	153	3,904	5,804
Shenandoah	3,137	7,517	385	2,771	9,048
Smyth	5,335	6,033	224	4,102	8,593
Southampton	3,347	2,997	163	3,300	4,669
Spotsylvania	4,039	5,385	464	4,012	8,207
Stafford	4,211	7,106	623	4,429	10,283
Surry	1,756	962	63	1,875	1,462
Sussex	2,447	1,664	86	2,408	2,183
Tazewell	7,003	7,021	225	8,014	9,645
Warren	2,597	3,861	297	2,551	5,016
Washington	6,390	8,402	382	5,573	12,132
Westmoreland	2,271	2,510	133	2,363	3,219
Wise	6,779	5,767	258	7,303	7,909
Wythe	3,677	4,758	164	2,996	6,773
York	4,532	6,744	723	4,063	10,214
	City				
Alexandria	17,134	17,865	4,546	23,552	21,166
Bedford	1,149	1,145	75	997	1,553
Bristol	2,889	3,432	160	2,429	5,012
Buena Vista	1,031	942	59	724	1,335
Charlottesville	6,866	5,907	1,377	7,317	6,947
Chesapeake	17,155	17,888	1,189	16,740	27,542
Clifton Forge	1,012	716	68	896	965
Colonial Heights	1,692	5,012	219	1,218	6,387
Covington	1,813	1,187	101	1,391	1,722
Danville	6,138	10,665	296	5,846	12,141
Emporia	855	988	41	807	1,252
Fairfax	2,614	4,475	800	3,263	6,234
Falls Church	1,703	2,485	497	2,398	2,684
Franklin	1,324	1,045	62	1,537	1,561
Fredericksburg	2,174	2,502	245	2,439	3,500
Galax	1,061	1,188	31	814	1,548
Hampton	18,517	17,023	1,598	18,180	25,537
Harrisonburg	1,896	3,388	403	2,384	5,221
Hopewell	3,102	4,423	178	2,564	5,661
Lexington	963	956	129	946	1,197
Lynchburg	7,783	15,245	854	8,542	17,447
Manassas	1,565	3,009	318	1,824	4,615
Manassas Park	447	729	52	375	975
Martinsville	3,337	3,433	162	2,942	4,234
Newport News	22,066	22,423	2,068	21,834	33,614
Norfolk	35,118	27,506	3,333	38,913	36,360
Norton	762	572	42	842	806
Petersburg	7,931	5,001	254	9,248	5,753
Poquoson	877	2,338	158	647	3,667
Portsmouth	20,900	13,660	1,124	21,623	18,940
Radford	2,225	1,964	233	1,781	2,855
Richmond	47,975	34,629	3,502	49,408	38,754
Roanoke	18,139	15,164	1,350	17,300	19,008
Salem	4,091	4,862	359	3,347	6,419
South Boston	971	1,615	51	974	1,899
Staunton	2,658	4,819	311	2,012	6,137
Suffolk	9,064	7,179	360	8,842	10,128
Virginia Beach	24,895	47,936	4,830	24,703	72,571
Waynesboro	1,926	3,697	255	1,579	4,465
Williamsburg	1,199	1,344	340	1,469	1,913
Winchester	2,006	4,240	320	2,064	5,055
Total	**752,174**	**989,609**	**95,418**	**796,250**	**1,337,078**

Virginia Vote Since 1936

1936, Roosevelt, Dem., 234,980; Landon, Rep., 98,366; Colvin, Proh., 594; Thomas, Soc., 313; Lemke, Union, 233; Browder, Com., 98.

1940, Roosevelt, Dem., 235,961; Willkie, Rep., 109,363; Babson, Proh., 882; Thomas, Soc., 282; Browder, Com., 71; Aiken, Soc. Labor, 48.

1944, Roosevelt, Dem., 242,276; Dewey, Rep., 145,243; Watson, Proh., 459; Thomas, Soc., 417; Teichert, Soc. Labor, 90.

1948, Truman, Dem., 200,786; Dewey, Rep., 172,070; Thurmond, States' Rights, 43,393; Wallace, Prog., 2,047; Thomas, Soc., 726; Teichert, Soc. Labor, 234.

1952, Eisenhower, Rep., 349,037; Stevenson, Dem., 268,677; Hass, Soc. Labor, 1,160; Hoopes, Social Dem., 504; Hallinan, Prog., 311.

1956, Eisenhower, Rep., 386,459; Stevenson, Dem., 267,760; Andrews, States' Rights, 42,964; Hoopes, Soc. Dem., 444; Hass, Soc. Labor, 351.

1960, Kennedy, Dem., 362,327; Nixon, Rep., 404,521; Coiner, Conservative, 4,204; Hass, Soc. Labor, 397.

1964, Johnson, Dem., 558,038; Goldwater, Rep., 481,334; Hass, Soc. Labor, 2,895.

1968, Nixon, Rep., 590,319; Humphrey, Dem., 442,387; Wallace, 3d party, *320,272; Blomen, Soc. Labor, 4,671; Munn, Proh., 601; Gregory, Peace and Freedom, 1,680.

*10,561 votes for Wallace were omitted in the count.

1972, Nixon, Rep., 988,493; McGovern, Dem., 438,887; Schmitz, Amer., 19,721; Fisher, Soc. Labor, 9,918.

1976, Carter, Dem., 813,896; Ford, Rep., 836,554; Camejo, Soc. Workers, 17,802; Anderson, Amer., 16,686; LaRouche, U.S. Labor, 7,508; MacBride, Libertarian, 4,648.

1980, Reagan, Rep., 989,609; Carter, Dem., 752,174; Anderson, Ind., 95,418; Commoner, Citizens, 14,024; Clark, Libertarian, 12,821; DeBerry, Soc. Worker, 1,986.

1984, Reagan, Rep., 1,337,078; Mondale, Dem., 796,250.

Washington

County	1980 Carter (D)	1980 Reagan (R)	1980 Anderson (I)	1984 Mondale (D)	1984 Reagan (R)
Adams	1,223	3,248	255	1,311	3,449
Asotin	2,724	3,275	539	3,042	3,876
Benton	11,561	28,728	3,301	13,784	32,307
Chelan	6,483	11,299	1,608	6,978	13,667
Clallam	8,029	11,515	2,172	9,701	13,605
Clark	30,584	33,223	6,445	35,248	40,681
Columbia	587	1,349	119	673	1,404
Cowlitz	12,560	13,154	2,336	15,361	14,858
Douglas	2,833	5,171	564	3,127	6,443
Ferry	802	1,108	127	935	1,232
Franklin	3,719	7,327	699	4,328	7,724
Garfield	509	875	122	493	913
Grant	5,673	11,152	1,091	6,298	12,888
Grays Harbor	11,290	10,226	3,267	14,050	11,286
Island	5,422	10,926	1,800	6,850	13,548
Jefferson	3,279	3,645	876	4,602	4,543
King	235,046	272,567	76,119	289,620	332,987
Kitsap	20,893	29,420	8,525	29,681	36,101
Kittitas	4,075	5,359	1,066	4,830	6,580
Klickitat	2,596	3,113	423	2,712	3,910
Lewis	6,962	13,636	1,603	7,634	15,846
Lincoln	1,597	3,324	357	1,671	3,474
Mason	5,241	6,745	1,353	7,007	8,410
Okanogan	4,634	6,460	1,030	5,330	7,476
Pacific	3,727	3,132	945	4,679	3,613
Pend Oreille	1,399	2,136	221	1,655	2,374
Pierce	64,444	90,247	18,345	79,498	112,877
San Juan	1,666	2,363	728	2,514	2,900
Skagit	11,299	15,520	2,854	13,947	18,840
Skamania	1,373	1,416	218	1,552	1,736
Snohomish	52,003	66,153	14,465	66,728	90,362
Spokane	49,263	78,096	11,258	59,620	88,043
Stevens	3,584	7,094	601	4,304	8,211
Thurston	20,508	26,369	5,993	26,840	34,442
Wahkiakum	751	828	148	930	776
Walla Walla	5,825	11,223	1,591	6,804	12,361
Whatcom	18,430	21,371	4,906	22,670	27,228
Whitman	5,726	8,636	2,331	6,621	10,021
Yakima	21,873	33,815	4,672	24,724	40,678
Totals	**650,193**	**865,244**	**185,073**	**798,352**	**1,051,670**

Washington Vote Since 1936

1936, Roosevelt, Dem., 459,579; Landon, Rep., 206,892; Lemke, Union, 17,463; Thomas, Soc., 3,496; Browder, Com., 1,907; Pellsy, Christian, 1,598; Colvin, Proh., 1,041; Aiken, Soc. Labor, 362.

1940, Roosevelt, Dem., 462,145; Willkie, Rep., 322,123; Thomas, Soc., 4,586; Browder, Com., 2,626; Babson, Proh., 1,686; Aiken, Soc. Labor, 667.

1944, Roosevelt, Dem., 486,774; Dewey, Rep., 361,689; Thomas, Soc., 3,824; Watson, Proh., 2,396; Teichert, Soc. Labor, 1,645.

1948, Truman, Dem., 476,165; Dewey, Rep., 386,315; Wallace, Prog., 31,692; Watson, Proh., 6,117; Thomas, Soc., 3,534; Teichert, Soc. Labor, 1,133; Dobbs, Soc. Workers, 103.

1952, Eisenhower, Rep., 599,107; Stevenson, Dem., 492,845; MacArthur, Christian Nationalist, 7,290; Hallinan, Prog., 2,460; Hass, Soc. Labor, 633; Hoopes, Soc., 254; Dobbs, Soc. Workers, 119.

1956, Eisenhower, Rep., 620,430; Stevenson, Dem., 523,002; Hass, Soc. Labor, 7,457.

1960, Kennedy, Dem., 599,298; Nixon, Rep., 629,273; Hass, Soc. Labor, 10,895; Curtis, Constitution, 1,401; Dobbs, Soc. Workers, 705.

1964, Johnson, Dem., 779,699; Goldwater, Rep., 470,366; Hass, Soc. Labor, 7,772; DeBerry, Freedom Soc., 537.

1968, Nixon, Rep., 588,510; Humphrey, Dem., 616,037; Wallace, 3d party, 96,990; Blomen, Soc. Labor, 488; Cleaver, Peace and Freedom, 1,609; Halstead, Soc. Worker, 270; Mitchell, Free Ballot, 377.

1972, Nixon, Rep., 837,135; McGovern, Dem., 568,334; Schmitz, Amer., 58,906; Spock, Ind., 2,644; Fisher, Soc. Labor, 1,102; Jenness, Soc. Worker, 623; Hall, Com., 566; Hospers, Libertarian, 1,537.

1976, Carter, Dem., 717,323; Ford, Rep., 777,732; McCarthy, Ind., 36,986; Maddox, Amer. Ind., 8,585; Anderson, Amer., 5,046; MacBride, Libertarian, 5,042; Wright, People's, 1,124; Camejo, Soc. Workers, 905; LaRouche, U.S. Labor, 903; Hall, Com., 817; Levin, Soc. Labor, 713; Zeidler, Soc., 358.

1980, Reagan, Rep., 865,244; Carter, Dem., 650,193; Anderson, Ind., 185,073; Clark, Libertarian, 29,213; Commoner, Citizens, 9,403; DeBerry, Soc. Worker, 1,137; McReynolds, Socialist, 956; Hall, Com., 834; Griswold, Workers World, 341.

1984, Reagan, Rep., 1,051,670; Mondale, Dem., 798,352; Bergland, Libertarian, 8,844.

West Virginia

County	1980 Carter (D)	1980 Reagan (R)	1980 Anderson (I)	1984 Mondale (D)	1984 Reagan (R)
Barbour	3,451	3,311	292	3,108	3,877
Berkeley	6,783	9,955	625	6,181	12,887
Boone	7,515	4,104	268	7,121	4,656
Braxton	3,795	2,403	173	3,350	2,902
Brooke	6,430	4,622	634	6,636	4,819
Cabell	17,732	19,482	2,146	15,513	21,815
Calhoun	1,717	1,606	92	1,473	1,765
Clay	2,185	1,452	102	2,117	1,667
Doddridge	1,043	1,888	120	836	2,343
Fayette	13,175	5,784	725	11,650	7,360
Gilmer	1,854	1,452	153	1,494	1,953
Grant	1,041	3,452	87	828	3,715
Greenbrier	7,128	6,221	546	5,599	7,337
Hampshire	2,522	2,879	157	2,102	4,065
Hancock	8,784	6,610	917	8,708	7,326
Hardy	2,050	2,329	99	1,641	2,938
Harrison	18,813	14,251	1,339	14,969	19,400
Jackson	4,120	6,041	352	4,147	7,117
Jefferson	4,679	4,464	672	4,216	5,884
Kanawha	42,829	42,604	5,838	37,832	51,499
Lewis	3,455	3,747	359	2,693	5,297
Lincoln	5,317	4,009	128	5,467	4,405
Logan	12,024	4,945	301	10,892	6,425
McDowell	9,822	3,862	216	8,546	4,284
Marion	14,189	10,952	1,171	13,833	13,106
Marshall	7,832	7,252	725	7,947	8,615
Mason	5,683	6,040	312	5,701	6,648
Mercer	11,804	12,273	563	9,164	13,910
Mineral	4,671	6,125	386	3,832	7,291
Mingo	9,328	3,716	208	8,434	4,275
Monongalia	12,883	11,972	2,745	13,236	14,972
Monroe	2,877	2,999	166	2,333	3,612
Morgan	1,594	2,833	172	1,457	3,469
Nicholas	5,265	3,885	322	4,588	4,656
Ohio	10,973	11,414	1,334	10,163	13,447
Pendleton	1,724	1,677	80	1,464	2,047
Pleasants	1,494	1,852	84	1,458	2,255
Pocahontas	2,170	2,011	150	1,903	2,479
Preston	4,317	5,828	515	4,054	6,955
Putnam	6,409	7,561	632	5,208	9,238
Raleigh	16,955	10,713	1,046	14,442	14,571
Randolph	5,937	4,374	518	4,839	6,100
Ritchie	1,450	3,081	128	1,231	3,355
Roane	2,498	3,219	184	2,468	3,751
Summers	3,114	2,456	201	2,670	2,975
Taylor	3,216	3,010	233	2,754	4,007
Tucker	1,862	1,798	153	1,766	2,240
Tyler	1,482	2,707	163	1,395	3,170
Upshur	2,867	4,751	415	2,468	5,951
Wayne	8,687	7,541	441	8,378	8,811
Webster	2,578	1,262	117	2,355	1,565
Wetzel	4,035	3,588	327	3,549	4,626
Wirt	1,058	1,176	44	868	1,450
Wood	13,622	20,080	1,536	11,357	24,821
Wyoming	6,624	4,537	299	5,691	5,379
Totals	367,462	334,206	31,691	328,125	405,483

West Virginia Vote Since 1936

1936, Roosevelt, Dem., 502,582; Landon, Rep., 325,358; Colvin, Prog., 1,173; Thomas, Soc., 832.

1940, Roosevelt, Dem., 495,662; Willkie, Rep., 372,414.

1944, Roosevelt, Dem., 392,777; Dewey, Rep., 322,819.

1948, Truman, Dem., 429,188; Dewey, Rep., 316,251; Wallace, Prog., 3,311.

1952, Eisenhower, Rep., 419,970; Stevenson, Dem., 453,578.

1956, Eisenhower, Rep., 449,297; Stevenson, Dem., 381,534.

1960, Kennedy, Dem., 441,786; Nixon, Rep., 395,995.

1964, Johnson, Dem., 538,087; Goldwater, Rep., 253,953.

1968, Nixon, Rep., 307,555; Humphrey, Dem., 374,091; Wallace, 3d party, 72,560.

1972, Nixon, Rep., 484,964; McGovern, Dem., 277,435.

1976, Carter, Dem., 435,864; Ford, Rep., 314,726.

1980, Reagan, Rep., 334,206; Carter, Dem., 367,462; Anderson, Ind., 31,691; Clark, Libertarian, 4,356.

1984, Reagan, Rep., 405,483; Mondale, Dem., 328,125.

Wisconsin

County	1980 Carter (D)	1980 Reagan (R)	1980 Anderson (I)	1984 Mondale (D)	1984 Reagan (R)
Adams	2,773	3,304	318	2,713	3,644
Ashland	4,469	3,262	685	4,680	3,517
Barron	8,654	8,791	883	8,060	9,587
Dayfield	3,705	3,278	554	4,034	3,474
Brown	29,796	47,067	4,680	30,208	51,186
Buffalo	3,276	3,569	404	2,921	3,325
Burnet	3,200	3,027	393	3,328	3,528
Calumet	5,036	7,885	1,064	4,735	8,969
Chippewa	9,836	10,531	1,160	10,200	10,983
Clark	6,091	7,921	679	5,647	8,098
Columbia	8,715	10,478	1,373	8,124	11,658
Crawford	3,392	3,934	371	3,435	4,411
Dane	85,609	57,545	19,772	94,638	74,009
Dodge	11,966	19,435	1,709	11,052	20,455
Door	4,961	7,170	855	3,915	8,264
Douglas	11,703	7,258	1,728	14,290	7,066
Dunn	7,743	7,428	1,565	7,709	8,472
Eau Claire	17,602	17,304	3,486	19,344	20,394
Florence	943	1,187	86	870	1,227
Fond duLac	15,293	24,196	2,191	13,982	26,067
Forest	[illegible]	[illegible]	141	[illegible]	[illegible]
Grant	8,406	13,298	1,690	7,890	13,427
Green	5,336	7,714	947	4,367	7,826
Green Lake	2,851	5,868	368	2,441	6,198
Iowa	4,154	4,068	546	3,842	4,982
Iron	1,941	1,811	219	1,967	1,667
Jackson	3,629	4,327	413	3,427	4,383
Jefferson	11,335	16,174	1,925	10,768	17,779
Juneau	3,884	5,591	463	3,151	5,627
Kenosha	26,738	24,481	3,802	29,233	26,112
Kewaunee	[illegible]	[illegible]	[illegible]	3,444	[illegible]
La Crosse	17,304	23,427	3,652	17,787	25,717
La Fayette	3,598	4,421	450	2,959	4,582
Langlade	4,498	4,866	369	3,675	5,828
Lincoln	5,438	6,473	630	5,352	6,681
Manitowoc	17,330	18,591	2,014	17,249	19,635
Marathon	23,281	25,868	3,257	20,126	27,077
Marinette	7,718	10,444	683	6,798	11,439
Marquette	2,180	3,166	270	2,031	3,404
Menominee	544	302	57	832	392
Milwaukee	240,174	183,450	34,281	259,134	196,259
Monroe	6,521	8,136	780	5,564	8,225
Oconto	5,352	8,292	440	5,288	8,713
Oneida	7,008	8,602	832	6,416	9,782
Outagamie	[illegible]	[illegible]	[illegible]	[illegible]	[illegible]
Ozaukee	10,779	21,371	2,463	10,763	23,896
Pepin	1,673	1,541	183	1,629	1,555
Pierce	7,312	6,209	1,752	7,285	7,611
Polk	7,607	7,207	1,102	8,033	8,101
Portage	16,443	10,465	2,851	14,399	13,603
Price	3,595	4,028	394	3,479	4,286
Racine	33,565	39,683	5,167	36,953	42,085
Richland	3,413	4,601	413	2,844	4,857
Rock	24,740	30,960	4,408	26,430	32,483
Rusk	3,584	3,704	340	3,843	4,061
St. Croix	10,203	9,265	1,867	10,126	11,365
Sauk	8,456	9,992	1,405	7,157	11,067
Sawyer	3,065	3,548	323	2,981	3,911
Shawano	5,410	9,922	652	5,469	10,635
Sheboygan	20,974	23,036	3,859	21,111	26,343
Taylor	3,739	4,596	403	3,271	4,918
Trempealeau	5,390	5,992	558	5,405	6,007
Vernon	5,501	6,528	494	5,051	6,468
Vilas	3,293	6,034	421	2,940	5,963
Walworth	11,344	19,194	2,581	9,876	20,590
Washburn	3,172	3,193	355	3,188	3,847
Washington	12,944	23,213	2,654	12,966	25,278
Waukesha	46,612	81,059	9,778	47,308	92,415
Waupaca	6,401	12,568	1,072	5,894	13,097
Waushara	2,987	5,576	335	2,782	5,768
Winnebago	24,203	34,286	4,779	22,791	39,014
Wood	13,804	17,987	2,010	12,118	20,525
Totals	981,584	1,088,845	160,657	995,740	1,198,584

Wisconsin Vote Since 1936

1936, Roosevelt, Dem., 802,984; Landon, Rep., 380,828; Lemke, Union, 60,297; Thomas, Soc., 10,626; Browder, Com., 2,197; Colvin, Proh., 1,071; Aiken, Soc. Labor, 557.

1940, Roosevelt, Dem., 704,821; Willkie, Rep., 679,260; Thomas, Soc., 15,071; Browder, Com., 2,394; Babson, Proh., 2,148; Aiken, Soc. Labor, 1,882.

1944, Roosevelt, Dem., 650,413; Dewey, Rep., 674,532; Thomas, Soc., 13,205; Teichert, Soc. Labor, 1,002.

1948, Truman, Dem., 647,310; Dewey, Rep., 590,959; Wallace, Prog., 25,282; Thomas, Soc., 12,547; Teichert, Soc. Labor, 399; Dobbs, Soc. Workers, 303.

1952, Eisenhower, Rep., 979,744; Stevenson, Dem., 622,175; Hallinan, Ind., 2,174; Dobbs, Ind., 1,350; Hoopes, Ind., 1,157; Hass, Ind., 770.

1956, Eisenhower, Rep., 954,844; Stevenson, Dem., 586,768; Andrews, Ind., 6,918; Hoopes, Soc., 754; Hass, Soc. Labor, 710; Dobbs, Soc. Workers, 564.

1960, Kennedy, Dem., 830,805; Nixon, Rep., 895,175; Dobbs, Soc. Workers, 1,792; Hass, Soc. Labor, 1,310.

1964, Johnson, Dem., 1,050,424; Goldwater, Rep., 638,495; DeBerry, Soc. Worker, 1,692; Hass, Soc. Labor, 1,204.

1968, Nixon, Rep., 809,997; Humphrey, Dem., 748,804; Wallace, 3d party, 127,835; Blomen, Soc. Labor, 1,338; Halstead, Soc. Worker, 1,222; scattered, 2,342.

1972 Nixon, Rep., 989,430; McGovern, Dem., 810,174; Schmitz, Amer., 47,525; Spock, Ind., 2,701; Fisher, Soc. Labor, 998; Hall, Com., 663; Reed, Ind., 506; scattered, 893.

1976, Carter, Dem., 1,040,232; Ford, Rep., 1,004,987; McCarthy, Ind., 34,943; Maddox, Amer. Ind., 8,552; Zeidler, Soc., 4,298; MacBride, Libertarian, 3,814; Camejo, Soc. Workers, 1,691; Wright, People's, 943; Hall, Com., 749; LaRouche, U.S. Lab., 738; Levin, Soc. Labor, 389; scattered, 2,839.

1980, Reagan, Rep., 1,088,845; Carter, Dem., 981,584; Anderson, Ind., 160,657; Clark, Libertarian, 29,135; Commoner, Citizens, 7,767; Rarick, Constitution, 1,519; McReynolds, Socialist, 808; Hall, Com., 772; Griswold, Workers World, 414; DeBerry, Soc. Workers, 383; scattering, 1,337.

1984, Reagan, Rep., 1,198,584; Mondale, Dem., 995,740; Bergland, Libertarian, 4,883.

Wyoming

County	1980 Carter (D)	1980 Reagan (R)	1980 Anderson (I)	1984 Mondale (D)	1984 Reagan (R)
Albany	3,772	5,830	1,630	4,708	7,452
Big Horn	1,212	3,709	209	1,175	4,019
Campbell	1,400	5,613	460	1,525	8,387
Carbon	2,272	4,337	493	2,295	4,557
Converse	922	2,987	215	929	3,542
Crook	413	1,909	70	450	2,286
Fremont	3,307	9,077	731	3,969	9,885
Goshen	1,373	3,572	269	1,364	3,776
Hot Springs	745	1,602	136	672	1,943
Johnson	635	2,291	139	558	2,634
Laramie	9,512	15,361	2,225	10,110	19,348
Lincoln	1,063	3,412	120	1,021	3,854
Natrona	7,111	16,801	1,768	7,598	18,488
Niobrara	270	1,075	38	239	1,098
Park	1,718	6,435	496	1,965	7,994
Platte	1,555	2,642	262	1,232	2,813
Sheridan	3,034	5,649	641	3,648	7,460
Sublette	357	1,538	139	389	1,976
Sweetwater	4,728	6,265	826	5,230	8,308
Teton	1,361	3,004	664	1,565	3,487
Uinta	1,138	2,738	189	1,276	4,075
Washakie	945	2,634	230	970	3,245
Weston	583	2,219	122	482	2,614
Totals	**49,427**	**110,700**	**12,072**	**53,370**	**133,241**

Wyoming Vote Since 1936

1936, Roosevelt, Dem., 62,624; Landon, Rep., 38,739; Lemke, Union, 1,653; Thomas, Soc., 200; Browder, Com., 91; Colvin, Proh., 75.

1940, Roosevelt, Dem., 59,287; Willkie, Rep., 52,633; Babson, Proh., 172; Thomas, Soc., 148.

1944, Roosevelt, Dem., 49,419; Dewey, Rep., 51,921.

1948, Truman, Dem., 52,354; Dewey, Rep., 47,947; Wallace, Prog., 931; Thomas, Soc., 137; Teichert, Soc. Labor, 56.

1952, Eisenhower, Rep., 81,047; Stevenson, Dem., 47,934; Hamblen, Proh., 194; Hoopes, Soc., 40; Haas, Soc. Labor, 36.

1956, Eisenhower, Rep., 74,573; Stevenson, Dem., 49,554.

1960, Kennedy, Dem., 63,331; Nixon, Rep., 77,451.

1964, Johnson, Dem., 80,718; Goldwater, Rep., 61,998.

1968, Nixon, Rep., 70,927; Humphrey, Dem., 45,173; Wallace, 3d party, 11,105.

1972, Nixon, Rep., 100,464; McGovern, Dem., 44,358; Schmitz, Amer., 748.

1976, Carter, Dem., 62,239; Ford, Rep., 92,717; McCarthy, Ind., 624; Reagan, Ind., 307; Anderson, Amer., 290; MacBride, Libertarian, 89; Brown, Ind., 47; Maddox, Amer. Ind., 30.

1980, Reagan, Rep., 110,700; Carter, Dem., 49,427; Anderson, Ind., 12,072; Clark, Libertarian, 4,514.

1984, Reagan, Rep., 133,241; Mondale, Dem., 53,370; Bergland, Libertarian, 2,357.

Law on Succession to the Presidency

If by reason of death, resignation, removal from office, inability, or failure to qualify there is neither a president nor vice president to discharge the powers and duties of the office of president, then the speaker of the House of Representatives shall upon his resignation as speaker and as representative, act as president. The same rule shall apply in the case of the death, resignation, removal from office, or inability of an individual acting as president.

If at the time when a speaker is to begin the discharge of the powers and duties of the office of president there is no speaker, or the speaker fails to qualify as acting president, then the president pro tempore of the Senate, upon his resignation as president pro tempore and as senator, shall act as president.

An individual acting as president shall continue to act until the expiration of the then current presidential term, except that (1) if his discharge of the powers and duties of the office is founded in whole or in part in the failure of both the president-elect and the vice president-elect to qualify, then he shall act only until a president or vice president qualifies, and (2) if his discharge of the powers and duties of the office is founded in whole or in part on the inability of the president or vice president, then he shall act only until the removal of the disability of one of such individuals.

If, by reason of death, resignation, removal from office, or failure to qualify, there is no president pro tempore to act as president, then the officer of the United States who is highest on the following list, and who is not under any disability to discharge the powers and duties of president shall act as president; the secretaries of state, treasury, defense, attorney general; secretaries of interior, agriculture, commerce, labor, health and human services, housing and urban development, transportation, energy, education.

(Legislation approved July 18, 1947; amended Sept. 9, 1965, Oct. 15, 1966, Aug. 4, 1977, and Sept. 27, 1979. (See also Constitutional Amendment XXV.)

The Electoral College

The president and the vice president of the United States are the only elective federal officials not elected by direct vote of the people. They are elected by the members of the Electoral College, an institution that has survived since the founding of the nation despite repeated attempts in Congress to alter or abolish it. In the elections of 1824, 1876 and 1888 the presidential candidate receiving the largest popular vote failed to win a majority of the electoral votes.

On presidential election day, the first Tuesday after the first Monday in November of every 4th year, each state chooses as many electors as it has senators and representatives in Congress. In 1964, for the first time, as provided by the 23d Amendment to the Constitution, the District of Columbia voted for 3 electors. Thus, with 100 senators and 435 representatives, there are 538 members of the Electoral College, with a majority of 270 electoral votes needed to elect the president and vice president.

Political parties customarily nominate their lists of electors at their respective state conventions. An elector cannot be a member of Congress or any person holding federal office.

Some states print the names of the candidates for president and vice president at the top of the November ballot while others list only the names of the electors. In either case, the electors of the party receiving the highest vote are elected. The electors meet on the first Monday after the 2d Wednesday in December in their respective state capitals or in some other place prescribed by state legislatures. By long-established custom they vote for their party nominees, although the Constitution does not require them to do so. All of the state's electoral votes are then awarded to the winners. The only Constitutional requirement is that at least one of the persons each elector votes for shall not be an inhabitant of that elector's home state.

Certified and sealed lists of the votes of the electors in each state are mailed to the president of the U.S. Senate. He opens them in the presence of the members of the Senate and House of Representatives in a joint session held on Jan. 6 (the next day if that falls on a Sunday), and the electoral votes of all the states are then counted. If no candidate for president has a majority, the House of Representatives chooses a president from among the 3 highest candidates, with all representatives from each state combining to cast one vote for that state. If no candidate for vice president has a majority, the Senate chooses from the top 2, with the senators voting as individuals.

Voting for President

Source: Federal Election Commission; Commission for Study of American Electorate

	Candidates	Voter Participation (% of voting-age population)
1932	Roosevelt-Hoover	52.4
1936	Roosevelt-Landon	56.0
1940	Roosevelt-Wilkie	58.9
1944	Roosevelt-Dewey	56.0
1948	Truman-Dewey	51.1
1952	Stevenson-Eisenhower	61.6
1956	Stevenson-Eisenhower	59.3
1960	Kennedy-Nixon	62.8
1964	Johnson-Goldwater	61.9
1968	Humphrey-Nixon	60.9
1972	McGovern-Nixon	55.2
1976	Carter-Ford	53.5
1980	Carter-Reagan	54.0
1984	Mondale-Reagan	53.3

Americans voted in record numbers in the 1984 Presidential election, according to a state-by-state tabulation of votes compiled by the Federal Election Commission.

The report, which is based on official counts provided to the FEC by voting authorities of each of the 50 states and the District of Columbia, shows 92,652,842 votes were cast for the President out of the 1984 estimated voting age population of 173,936,000. The votes went to 17 Presidential candidates plus write-ins.

In 1980, there were 86,495,678 votes cast for 21 Presidential candidates appearing on various state ballots, plus write-ins.

Because of the variety of state laws governing registration, there is no official record of total registered voters in the United States. Estimated voting age population figures, upon which the FEC bases its statistics, are provided each year by the Bureau of the Census.

Also, because the FEC figures are obtained from official state election sources, the counts are based on individual state definitions of a valid vote cast and counted for a candidate.

Characteristics of the Voting-Age Population: November 1984 and 1980

Source: U.S. Bureau of the Census

Characteristic	1984 Number of persons (thousands)	1984 Percent registered	1984 Percent voted	1980 Number of persons (thousands)	1980 Percent registered	1980 Percent voted
Total, 18 years and over	**169,963**	**68.3**	**59.9**	**157,085**	**66.9**	**59.2**
White	146,761	69.6	61.4	137,676	68.4	60.9
Black	18,432	66.3	55.8	16,423	60.0	50.5
Spanish origin[1]	9,471	40.1	32.6	8,210	36.3	29.9
Male	80,327	67.3	59.0	74,082	66.6	59.1
Female	89,636	69.3	60.8	83,003	67.1	59.4
18 to 24 years	27,976	51.3	40.8	28,138	49.2	39.9
25 to 44 years	71,023	66.6	58.4	61,285	65.6	58.7
45 to 64 years	44,307	76.6	69.8	43,569	75.8	69.3
65 years and over	26,658	76.9	67.7	24,094	74.6	65.1
Northeast	36,868	66.6	59.7	35,500	64.8	58.5
Midwest	42,136	74.6	65.7	41,542	73.8	65.8
South	57,587	66.9	56.8	50,561	64.8	55.6
West	33,372	64.7	58.5	29,483	63.3	57.2
Years of school completed:						
Elementary: 0 to 8 years	20,580	53.4	42.9	22,656	53.0	42.6
High school: 1 to 3 years	22,068	54.9	44.4	22,477	54.6	45.6
4 years	67,807	67.3	58.7	61,165	66.4	58.9
College: 1 to 3 years	30,915	75.7	67.5	26,747	74.4	67.2
4 years or more	28,593	83.8	79.1	24,040	84.3	79.9
Family income:[2]						
Under $5,000	7,843	49.8	37.5	8,567	50.4	39.4
$10,000 to $14,999	18,131	62.9	53.5	21,746	63.6	54.8
$20,000 to $24,999	14,790	68.7	61.1	19,100	73.5	67.2
$35,000 and over	35,218	80.7	74.2			

(1) Persons of Spanish origin may be of any race. (2) Restricted to members of families. Income in current dollars.

Major Parties' Popular and Electoral Vote for President

(F) Federalist; (D) Democrat; (R) Republican; (DR) Democrat Republican; (NR) National Republican; (W) Whig; (P) People's; (PR) Progressive; (SR) States' Rights; (LR) Liberal Republican; Asterisk (*)—See notes.

Year	President elected	Popular	Elec.	Losing candidate	Popular	Elec.
1789	George Washington (F)	Unknown	69	No opposition	—	—
1792	George Washington (F)	Unknown	132	No opposition	—	—
1796	John Adams (F)	Unknown	71	Thomas Jefferson (DR)	Unknown	68
1800*	Thomas Jefferson (DR)	Unknown	73	Aaron Burr (DR)	Unknown	73
1804	Thomas Jefferson (DR)	Unknown	162	Charles Pinckney (F)	Unknown	14
1808	James Madison (DR)	Unknown	122	Charles Pinckney (F)	Unknown	47
1812	James Madison (DR)	Unknown	128	DeWitt Clinton (F)	Unknown	89
1816	James Monroe (DR)	Unknown	183	Rufus King (F)	Unknown	34
1820	James Monroe (DR)	Unknown	231	John Quincy Adams (DR)	Unknown	1
1824*	John Quincy Adams (DR)	105,321	84	Andrew Jackson (DR)	155,872	99
				Henry Clay (DR)	46,587	37
				William H. Crawford (DR)	44,282	41
1828	Andrew Jackson (D)	647,231	178	John Quincy Adams (NR)	509,097	83
1832	Andrew Jackson (D)	687,502	219	Henry Clay (NR)	530,189	49
1836	Martin Van Buren (D)	762,678	170	William H. Harrison (W)	548,007	73
1840	William H. Harrison (W)	1,275,017	234	Martin Van Buren (D)	1,128,702	60
1844	James K. Polk (D)	1,337,243	170	Henry Clay (W)	1,299,068	105
1848	Zachary Taylor (W)	1,360,101	163	Lewis Cass (D)	1,220,544	127
1852	Franklin Pierce (D)	1,601,474	254	Winfield Scott (W)	1,386,578	42
1856	James C. Buchanan (D)	1,927,995	174	John C. Fremont (R)	1,391,555	114
1860	Abraham Lincoln (R)	1,866,352	180	Stephen A. Douglas (D)	1,375,157	12
				John C. Breckinridge (D)	845,763	72
				John Bell (Const. Union)	589,581	39
1864	Abraham Lincoln (R)	2,216,067	212	George McClellan (D)	1,808,725	21
1868	Ulysses S. Grant (R)	3,015,071	214	Horatio Seymour (D)	2,709,615	80
1872*	Ulysses S. Grant (R)	3,597,070	286	Horace Greeley (D-LR)	2,834,079	—
1876*	Rutherford B. Hayes (R)	4,033,950	185	Samuel J. Tilden (D)	4,284,757	184
1880	James A. Garfield (R)	4,449,053	214	Winfield S. Hancock (D)	4,442,030	155
1884	Grover Cleveland (D)	4,911,017	219	James G. Blaine (R)	4,848,334	182
1888*	Benjamin Harrison (R)	5,444,337	233	Grover Cleveland (D)	5,540,050	168
1892	Grover Cleveland (D)	5,554,414	277	Benjamin Harrison (R)	5,190,802	145
				James Weaver (P)	1,027,329	22
1896	William McKinley (R)	7,035,638	271	William J. Bryan (D-P)	6,467,946	176
1900	William McKinley (R)	7,219,530	292	William J. Bryan (D)	6,358,071	155
1904	Theodore Roosevelt (R)	7,628,834	336	Alton B. Parker (D)	5,084,491	140
1908	William H. Taft (R)	7,679,006	321	William J. Bryan (D)	6,409,106	162
1912	Woodrow Wilson (D)	6,286,214	435	Theodore Roosevelt (PR)	4,216,020	88
				William H. Taft (R)	3,483,922	8
1916	Woodrow Wilson (D)	9,129,606	277	Charles E. Hughes (R)	8,538,221	254
1920	Warren G. Harding (R)	16,152,200	404	James M. Cox (D)	9,147,353	127
1924	Calvin Coolidge (R)	15,725,016	382	John W. Davis (D)	8,385,586	136
				Robert M. LaFollette (PR)	4,822,856	13
1928	Herbert Hoover (R)	21,392,190	444	Alfred E. Smith (D)	15,016,443	87
1932	Franklin D. Roosevelt (D)	22,821,857	472	Herbert Hoover (R)	15,761,841	59
				Norman Thomas (Socialist)	884,781	—
1936	Franklin D. Roosevelt (D)	27,751,597	523	Alfred Landon (R)	16,679,583	8
1940	Franklin D. Roosevelt (D)	27,243,466	449	Wendell Willkie (R)	22,304,755	82
1944	Franklin D. Roosevelt (D)	25,602,505	432	Thomas E. Dewey (R)	22,006,278	99
1948	Harry S Truman (D)	24,105,812	303	Thomas E. Dewey (R)	21,970,065	189
				J. Strom Thurmond (SR)	1,169,021	39
				Henry A. Wallace (PR)	1,157,172	—
1952	Dwight D. Eisenhower (R)	33,936,252	442	Adlai E. Stevenson (D)	27,314,992	89
1956*	Dwight D. Eisenhower (R)	35,585,316	457	Adlai E. Stevenson (D)	26,031,322	73
1960*	John F. Kennedy (D)	34,227,096	303	Richard M. Nixon (R)	34,108,546	219
1964	Lyndon B. Johnson (D)	43,126,506	486	Barry M. Goldwater (R)	27,176,799	52
1968	Richard M. Nixon (R)	31,785,480	301	Hubert H. Humphrey (D)	31,275,166	191
				George C. Wallace (3d party)	9,906,473	46
1972*	Richard M. Nixon (R)	47,165,234	520	George S. McGovern (D)	29,170,774	17
1976*	Jimmy Carter (D)	40,828,929	297	Gerald R. Ford (R)	39,148,940	240
1980	Ronald Reagan (R)	43,899,248	489	Jimmy Carter (D)	35,481,435	49
				John B. Anderson (independent)	5,719,437	—
1984	Ronald Reagan (R)	54,281,858	525	Walter F. Mondale (D)	37,457,215	13

1800—Elected by House of Representatives because of tied electoral vote.

1824—Elected by House of Representatives. No candidate polled a majority. In 1824, the Democrat Republicans had become a loose coalition of competing political groups. By 1828, the supporters of Jackson were known as Democrats, and the J.Q. Adams and Henry Clay supporters as National Republicans.

1872—Greeley died Nov. 29, 1872. His electoral votes were split among 4 individuals.

1876—Fla., La., Ore., and S. C. election returns were disputed. Congress in joint session (Mar. 2, 1877) declared Hayes and Wheeler elected President and Vice-President.

1888—Cleveland had more votes than Harrison but the 233 electoral votes cast for Harrison against the 168 for Cleveland elected Harrison president.

1956—Democrats elected 74 electors but one from Alabama refused to vote for Stevenson.

1960—Sen. Harry F. Byrd (D-Va.) received 15 electoral votes.

1972—John Hospers of Cal. and Theodora Nathan of Ore. received one vote from an elector of Virginia.

1976—Ronald Reagan of Cal. received one vote from an elector of Washington.

Electoral Votes for President

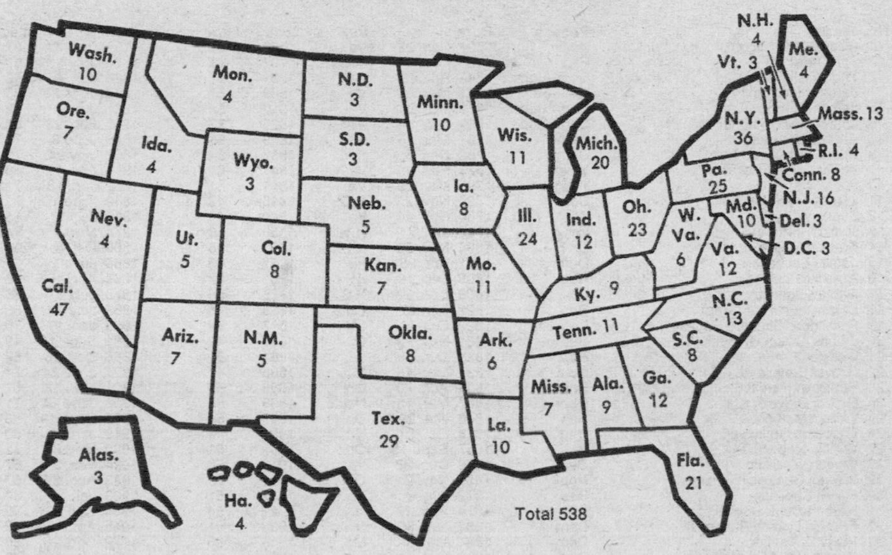

Voter Turnout in Presidential Elections

Source: Committee for the Study of the American Electorate

National average of voting age population that voted: 1960—63.1; 1964—61.9; 1968—60.6; 1972—55.2; 1976—53.5; 1980—52.6; 1984—53.3. The sharp drop in 1972 reflects the expansion of eligibility with the enfranchisement of 18 to 21 year olds.

	1984 Registered voters voting	1984 Voting age population voting	1980 Voting age population voting		1984 Registered voters voting	1984 Voting age population voting	1980 Voting age population voting		1984 Registered voters voting	1984 Voting age population voting	1980 Voting age population voting
Ala.	61.5%	50.2%	40.7%	Ky.	67.7	50.7	49.9	N.D.	n/a	62.9	64.7
Alas.	68.0	60.2	57.4	La.	75.5	54.2	53.1	Oh.	71.8	58.2	55.4
Ariz.	70.1	46.6	44.5	Me.	68.2	65.2	64.6	Okla.	64.4	51.2	52.2
Ark.	69.8	53.2	51.6	Md	74.4	51.4	50.0	Ore.	70.2	62.0	61.3
Cal.	72.7	49.9	49.0	Mass.	78.7	57.9	59.0	Pa.	78.2	53.9	51.9
Col.	80.0	54.8	55.8	Mich.	64.6	58.2	59.9	R.I.	75.7	56.0	58.7
Conn.	81.2	61.0	61.0	Minn.	72.1	68.5	70.0	S.C.	69.4	40.6	40.4
Del.	81.1	55.7	54.7	Miss.	56.4	52.0	51.8	S.D.	71.8	63.8	67.3
D.C.	76.9	43.8	35.5	Mo.	71.5	57.7	58.7	Tenn.	66.4	49.3	48.7
Fla.	75.0	49.0	48.7	Mon.	73.0	65.0	65.0	Tex.	68.3	47.0	44.9
Ga.	65.0	42.2	41.2	Neb.	72.2	56.1	56.7	Ut.	74.9	60.5	64.4
Ha.	80.2	44.5	43.6	Nev.	80.4	41.6	41.2	Vt.	72.8	60.0	57.6
Ida.	70.6	60.4	67.8	N.H.	71.5	53.9	57.2	Va.	84.1	51.1	47.6
Ill. .	74.5	57.3	57.7	N.J.	79.0	56.9	54.9	Wash.	76.3	58.5	57.4
Ind.	73.1	56.3	57.6	N.M.	79.0	51.6	50.8	W.Va.	71.8	51.3	52.8
Ia.	76.3	62.3	62.8	N.Y.	75.3	51.1	48.0	Wis.	n/a	63.4	67.4
Kan.	79.1	57.0	56.7	N.C.	66.5	47.7	43.4	Wy.	78.8	51.8	53.2

n/a—not available.

Party Nominees for President and Vice President

Asterisk (*) denotes winning ticket

Year	Democratic President	Democratic Vice President	Republican President	Republican Vice President
1920	James M. Cox	Franklin D. Roosevelt	Warren G. Harding*	Calvin Coolidge
1924	John W. Davis	Charles W. Bryan	Calvin Coolidge*	Charles G. Dawes
1928	Alfred E. Smith	Joseph T. Robinson	Herbert Hoover*	Charles Curtis
1932	Franklin D. Roosevelt*	John N. Garner	Herbert Hoover	Charles Curtis
1936	Franklin D. Roosevelt*	John N. Garner	Alfred M. Landon	Frank Knox
1940	Franklin D. Roosevelt*	Henry A. Wallace	Wendell L. Willkie	Charles McNary
1944	Franklin D. Roosevelt*	Harry S. Truman	Thomas E. Dewey	John W. Bricker
1948	Harry S. Truman*	Alben W. Barkley	Thomas E. Dewey	Earl Warren
1952	Adlai E. Stevenson	John J. Sparkman	Dwight D. Eisenhower*	Richard M. Nixon
1956	Adlai E. Stevenson	Estes Kefauver	Dwight D. Eisenhower*	Richard M. Nixon
1960	John F. Kennedy*	Lyndon B. Johnson	Richard M. Nixon	Henry Cabot Lodge
1964	Lyndon B. Johnson*	Hubert H. Humphrey	Barry M. Goldwater	William E. Miller
1968	Hubert H. Humphrey	Edmund S. Muskie	Richard M. Nixon*	Spiro T. Agnew
1972	George S. McGovern	R. Sargent Shriver Jr.	Richard M. Nixon*	Spiro T. Agnew
1976	Jimmy Carter*	Walter F. Mondale	Gerald R. Ford	Robert J. Dole
1980	Jimmy Carter	Walter F. Mondale	Ronald Reagan*	George Bush
1984	Walter F. Mondale	Geraldine Ferraro	Ronald Reagan*	George Bush

Presidents of the U.S.

No.	Name	Politics	Born	in	Inaug.	at age	Died	at age
1	George Washington	Fed.	1732, Feb. 22	Va.	1789	57	1799, Dec. 14	67
2	John Adams	Fed.	1735, Oct. 30	Mass.	1797	61	1826, July 4	90
3	Thomas Jefferson	Dem.-Rep.	1743, Apr. 13	Va.	1801	57	1826, July 4	83
4	James Madison	Dem.-Rep.	1751, Mar. 16	Va.	1809	57	1836, June 28	85
5	James Monroe	Dem.-Rep.	1758, Apr. 28	Va.	1817	58	1831, July 4	73
6	John Quincy Adams	Dem.-Rep.	1767, July 11	Mass.	1825	57	1848, Feb. 23	80
7	Andrew Jackson	Dem.	1767, Mar. 15	S.C.	1829	61	1845, June 8	78
8	Martin Van Buren	Dem.	1782, Dec. 5	N.Y.	1837	54	1862, July 24	79
9	William Henry Harrison	Whig	1773, Feb. 9	Va.	1841	68	1841, Apr. 4	68
10	John Tyler	Whig	1790, Mar. 29	Va.	1841	51	1862, Jan. 18	71
11	James Knox Polk	Dem.	1795, Nov. 2	N.C.	1845	49	1849, June 15	53
12	Zachary Taylor	Whig	1784, Nov. 24	Va.	1849	64	1850, July 9	65
13	Millard Fillmore	Whig	1800, Jan. 7	N.Y.	1850	50	1874, Mar. 8	74
14	Franklin Pierce	Dem.	1804, Nov. 23	N.H.	1853	48	1869, Oct. 8	64
15	James Buchanan	Dem.	1791, Apr. 23	Pa.	1857	65	1868, June 1	77
16	Abraham Lincoln	Rep.	1809, Feb. 12	Ky.	1861	52	1865, Apr. 15	56
17	Andrew Johnson	(1)	1808, Dec. 29	N.C.	1865	56	1875, July 31	66
18	Ulysses Simpson Grant	Rep.	1822, Apr. 27	Oh.	1869	46	1885, July 23	63
19	Rutherford Birchard Hayes	Rep.	1822, Oct. 4	Oh.	1877	54	1893, Jan. 17	70
20	James Abram Garfield	Rep.	1831, Nov. 19	Oh.	1881	49	1881, Sept. 19	49
21	Chester Alan Arthur	Rep.	1829, Oct. 5	Vt.	1881	51	1886, Nov. 18	57
22	Grover Cleveland	Dem.	1837, Mar. 18	N.J.	1885	47	1908, June 24	71
23	Benjamin Harrison	Rep.	1833, Aug. 20	Oh.	1889	55	1901, Mar. 13	67
24	Grover Cleveland	Dem.	1837, Mar. 18	N.J.	1893	55	1908, June 24	71
25	William McKinley	Rep.	1843, Jan. 29	Oh.	1897	54	1901, Sept. 14	58
26	Theodore Roosevelt	Rep.	1858, Oct. 27	N.Y.	1901	42	1919, Jan. 6	60
27	William Howard Taft	Rep.	1857, Sept. 15	Oh.	1909	51	1930, Mar. 8	72
28	Woodrow Wilson	Dem.	1856, Dec. 28	Va.	1913	56	1924, Feb. 3	67
29	Warren Gamaliel Harding	Rep.	1865, Nov. 2	Oh.	1921	55	1923, Aug. 2	57
30	Calvin Coolidge	Rep.	1872, July 4	Vt.	1923	51	1933, Jan. 5	60
31	Herbert Clark Hoover	Rep.	1874, Aug. 10	Ia.	1929	54	1964, Oct. 20	90
32	Franklin Delano Roosevelt	Dem.	1882, Jan. 30	N.Y.	1933	51	1945, Apr. 12	63
33	Harry S. Truman	Dem.	1884, May 8	Mo.	1945	60	1972, Dec. 26	88
34	Dwight David Eisenhower	Rep.	1890, Oct. 14	Tex.	1953	62	1969, Mar. 28	78
35	John Fitzgerald Kennedy	Dem.	1917, May 29	Mass.	1961	43	1963, Nov. 22	46
36	Lyndon Baines Johnson	Dem.	1908, Aug. 27	Tex.	1963	55	1973, Jan. 22	64
37	Richard Milhous Nixon (2)	Rep.	1913, Jan. 9	Cal.	1969	56		
38	Gerald Rudolph Ford	Rep.	1913, July 14	Neb.	1974	61		
39	Jimmy (James Earl) Carter	Dem.	1924, Oct. 1	Ga.	1977	52		
40	Ronald Reagan	Rep.	1911, Feb. 6	Ill.	1981	69		

(1) Andrew Johnson — a Democrat, nominated vice president by Republicans and elected with Lincoln on National Union ticket. (2) Resigned Aug. 9, 1974.

Presidents, Vice Presidents, Congresses

	President	Service		Vice President	Congress
1	George Washington	Apr. 30, 1789—Mar. 3, 1797	1	John Adams	1, 2, 3, 4
2	John Adams	Mar. 4, 1797—Mar. 3, 1801	2	Thomas Jefferson	5, 6
3	Thomas Jefferson	Mar. 4, 1801—Mar. 3, 1805	3	Aaron Burr	7, 8
	"	Mar. 4, 1805—Mar. 3, 1809	4	George Clinton	9, 10
4	James Madison	Mar. 4, 1809—Mar. 3, 1813		"(1)	11, 12
	"	Mar. 4, 1813—Mar. 3, 1817	5	Elbridge Gerry (2)	13, 14
5	James Monroe	Mar. 4, 1817—Mar. 3, 1825	6	Daniel D. Tompkins	15, 16, 17, 18
6	John Quincy Adams	Mar. 4, 1825—Mar. 3, 1829	7	John C. Calhoun	19, 20
7	Andrew Jackson	Mar. 4, 1829—Mar. 3, 1833		"(3)	21, 22
	"	Mar. 4, 1833—Mar. 3, 1837	8	Martin Van Buren	23, 24
8	Martin Van Buren	Mar. 4, 1837—Mar. 3, 1841	9	Richard M. Johnson	25, 26
9	William Henry Harrison (4)	Mar. 4, 1841—Apr. 4, 1841	10	John Tyler	27
10	John Tyler	Apr. 6, 1841—Mar. 3, 1845			27, 28
11	James K. Polk	Mar. 4, 1845—Mar. 3, 1849	11	George M. Dallas	29, 30
12	Zachary Taylor (4)	Mar. 5, 1849—July 9, 1850	12	Millard Fillmore	31
13	Millard Fillmore	July 10, 1850—Mar. 3, 1853			31, 32
14	Franklin Pierce	Mar. 4, 1853—Mar. 3, 1857	13	William R. King (5)	33, 34
15	James Buchanan	Mar. 4, 1857—Mar. 3, 1861	14	John C. Breckinridge	35, 36
16	Abraham Lincoln	Mar. 4, 1861—Mar. 3, 1865	15	Hannibal Hamlin	37, 38
	"(4)	Mar. 4, 1865—Apr. 15, 1865	16	Andrew Johnson	39
17	Andrew Johnson	Apr. 15, 1865—Mar. 3, 1869			39, 40
18	Ulysses S. Grant	Mar. 4, 1869—Mar. 3, 1873	17	Schuyler Colfax	41, 42
	"	Mar. 4, 1873—Mar. 3, 1877	18	Henry Wilson (6)	43, 44
19	Rutherford B. Hayes	Mar. 4, 1877—Mar. 3, 1881	19	William A. Wheeler	45, 46
20	James A. Garfield (4)	Mar. 4, 1881—Sept. 19, 1881	20	Chester A. Arthur	47
21	Chester A. Arthur	Sept. 20, 1881—Mar. 3, 1885			47, 48
22	Grover Cleveland (7)	Mar. 4, 1885—Mar. 3, 1889	21	Thomas A. Hendricks (8)	49, 50
23	Benjamin Harrison	Mar. 4, 1889—Mar. 3, 1893	22	Levi P. Morton	51, 52
24	Grover Cleveland (7)	Mar. 4, 1893—Mar. 3, 1897	23	Adlai E. Stevenson	53, 54
25	William McKinley	Mar. 4, 1897—Mar. 3, 1901	24	Garret A. Hobart (9)	55, 56
	"(4)	Mar. 4, 1901—Sept. 14, 1901	25	Theodore Roosevelt	57
26	Theodore Roosevelt	Sept. 14, 1901—Mar. 3, 1905			57, 58
	"	Mar. 4, 1905—Mar. 3, 1909	26	Charles W. Fairbanks	59, 60

	President	Service		Vice President	Congress
27	William H. Taft	Mar. 4, 1909—Mar. 3, 1913	27	James S. Sherman (10)	61, 62
28	Woodrow Wilson	Mar. 4, 1913—Mar. 3, 1921	28	Thomas R. Marshall	63, 64, 65, 66
29	Warren G. Harding (4)	Mar. 4, 1921—Aug. 2, 1923	29	Calvin Coolidge	67
30	Calvin Coolidge	Aug. 3, 1923—Mar. 3, 1925			68
	"	Mar. 4, 1925—Mar. 3, 1929	30	Charles G. Dawes	69, 70
31	Herbert C. Hoover	Mar. 4, 1929—Mar. 3, 1933	31	Charles Curtis	71, 72
32	Franklin D. Roosevelt (16)	Mar. 4, 1933—Jan. 20, 1941	32	John N. Garner	73, 74, 75, 76
	"	Jan. 20, 1941—Jan. 20, 1945	33	Henry A. Wallace	77, 78
	"(4)	Jan. 20, 1945—Apr. 12, 1945	34	Harry S. Truman	79
33	Harry S. Truman	Apr. 12, 1945—Jan. 20, 1949			79, 80
	"	Jan. 20, 1949—Jan. 20, 1953	35	Alben W. Barkley	81, 82
34	Dwight D. Eisenhower	Jan. 20, 1953—Jan. 20, 1961	36	Richard M. Nixon	83, 84, 85, 86
35	John F. Kennedy (4)	Jan. 20, 1961—Nov. 22, 1963	37	Lyndon B. Johnson	87, 88
36	Lyndon B. Johnson	Nov. 22, 1963—Jan. 20, 1965			88
	"	Jan. 20, 1965—Jan. 20, 1969	38	Hubert H. Humphrey	89, 90
37	Richard M. Nixon	Jan. 20, 1969—Jan. 20, 1973	39	Spiro T. Agnew (11)	91, 92, 93
	"(12)	Jan. 20, 1973—Aug. 9, 1974	40	Gerald R. Ford (13)	93
38	Gerald R. Ford (14)	Aug. 9, 1974—Jan. 20, 1977	41	Nelson A. Rockefeller (15)	93, 94
39	Jimmy (James Earl) Carter	Jan. 20, 1977—Jan. 20, 1981	42	Walter F. Mondale	95, 96
40	Ronald Reagan	Jan. 20, 1981—	43	George Bush	97, 98, 99, 100

(1) Died Apr. 20, 1812. (2) Died Nov. 23, 1814. (3) Resigned Dec. 28, 1832, to become U.S. Senator. (4) Died in office. (5) Died Apr. 18, 1853. (6) Died Nov. 22, 1875. (7) Terms not consecutive. (8) Died Nov. 25, 1885. (9) Died Nov. 21, 1899. (10) Died Oct. 30, 1912. (11) Resigned Oct. 10, 1973. (12) Resigned Aug. 9, 1974. (13) First non-elected vice president, chosen under 25th Amendment procedure. (14) First non-elected president. (15) 2d non-elected vice president. (16) First president to be inaugurated under 20th Amendment, Jan. 20, 1937.

Vice Presidents of the U.S.

The numerals given vice presidents do not coincide with those given presidents, because some presidents had none and some had more than one.

	Name	Birthplace	Year	Home	Inaug.	Politics	Place of death	Year	Age
1	John Adams	Quincy, Mass.	1735	Mass.	1789	Fed.	Quincy, Mass.	1826	90
2	Thomas Jefferson	Shadwell, Va.	1743	Va.	1797	Dem.-Rep.	Monticello, Va.	1826	83
3	Aaron Burr	Newark, N.J.	1756	N.Y.	1801	Dem.-Rep.	Staten Island, N.Y.	1836	80
4	George Clinton	Ulster Co., N.Y.	1739	N.Y.	1805	Dem.-Rep.	Washington, D.C.	1812	73
5	Elbridge Gerry	Marblehead, Mass.	1744	Mass.	1813	Dem.-Rep.	Washington, D.C.	1814	70
6	Daniel D. Tompkins	Scarsdale, N.Y.	1774	N.Y.	1817	Dem.-Rep.	Staten Island, N.Y.	1825	51
7	John C. Calhoun (1)	Abbeville, S.C.	1782	S.C.	1825	Dem.-Rep.	Washington, D.C.	1850	68
8	Martin Van Buren	Kinderhook, N.Y.	1782	N.Y.	1833	Dem.	Kinderhook, N.Y.	1862	79
9	Richard M. Johnson	Louisville, Ky.	1780	Ky.	1837	Dem.	Frankfort, Ky.	1850	70
10	John Tyler	Greenway, Va.	1790	Va.	1841	Whig	Richmond, Va.	1862	71
11	George M. Dallas	Philadelphia, Pa.	1792	Pa.	1845	Dem.	Philadelphia, Pa.	1864	72
12	Millard Fillmore	Summerhill, N.Y.	1800	N.Y.	1849	Whig	Buffalo, N.Y.	1874	74
13	William R. King	Sampson Co., N.C.	1786	Ala.	1853	Dem.	Dallas Co., Ala.	1853	67
14	John C. Breckinridge	Lexington, Ky.	1821	Ky.	1857	Dem.	Lexington, Ky.	1875	54
15	Hannibal Hamlin	Paris, Me.	1809	Me.	1861	Rep.	Bangor, Me.	1891	81
16	Andrew Johnson	Raleigh, N.C.	1808	Tenn.	1865	(2)	Carter Co., Tenn.	1875	66
17	Schuyler Colfax	New York, N.Y.	1823	Ind.	1869	Rep.	Mankato, Minn.	1885	62
18	Henry Wilson	Farmington, N.H.	1812	Mass.	1873	Rep.	Washington, D.C.	1875	63
19	William A. Wheeler	Malone, N.Y.	1819	N.Y.	1877	Rep.	Malone, N.Y.	1887	68
20	Chester A. Arthur	Fairfield, Vt.	1829	N.Y.	1881	Rep.	New York, N.Y.	1886	57
21	Thomas A. Hendricks	Muskingum Co., Oh.	1819	Ind.	1885	Dem.	Indianapolis, Ind.	1885	66
22	Levi P. Morton	Shoreham, Vt.	1824	N.Y.	1889	Rep.	Rhinebeck, N.Y.	1920	96
23	Adlai E. Stevenson (3)	Christian Co., Ky.	1835	Ill.	1893	Dem.	Chicago, Ill.	1914	78
24	Garret A. Hobart	Long Branch, N.J.	1844	N.J.	1897	Rep.	Paterson, N.J.	1899	55
25	Theodore Roosevelt	New York, N.Y.	1858	N.Y.	1901	Rep.	Oyster Bay, N.Y.	1919	60
26	Charles W. Fairbanks	Unionville Centre, Oh.	1852	Ind.	1905	Rep.	Indianapolis, Ind.	1918	66
27	James S. Sherman	Utica, N.Y.	1855	N.Y.	1909	Rep.	Utica, N.Y.	1912	57
28	Thomas R. Marshall	N. Manchester, Ind.	1854	Ind.	1913	Dem.	Washington, D.C.	1925	71
29	Calvin Coolidge	Plymouth, Vt.	1872	Mass.	1921	Rep.	Northampton, Mass.	1933	60
30	Charles G. Dawes	Marietta, Oh.	1865	Ill.	1925	Rep.	Evanston, Ill.	1951	85
31	Charles Curtis	Topeka, Kan.	1860	Kan.	1929	Rep.	Washington, D.C.	1936	76
32	John Nance Garner	Red River Co., Tex.	1868	Tex.	1933	Dem.	Uvalde, Tex.	1967	98
33	Henry Agard Wallace	Adair County, Ia.	1888	Iowa	1941	Dem.	Danbury, Conn.	1965	77
34	Harry S. Truman	Lamar, Mo.	1884	Mo.	1945	Dem.	Kansas City, Mo.	1972	88
35	Alben W. Barkley	Graves County, Ky.	1877	Ky.	1949	Dem.	Lexington, Va.	1956	78
36	Richard M. Nixon	Yorba Linda, Cal.	1913	Cal.	1953	Rep.			
37	Lyndon B. Johnson	Johnson City, Tex.	1908	Tex.	1961	Dem.	San Antonio, Tex.	1973	64
38	Hubert H. Humphrey	Wallace, S.D.	1911	Minn.	1965	Dem.	Waverly, Minn.	1978	66
39	Spiro T. Agnew	Baltimore, Md.	1918	Md.	1969	Rep.			
40	Gerald R. Ford	Omaha, Neb.	1913	Mich.	1973	Rep.			
41	Nelson A. Rockefeller	Bar Harbor, Me.	1908	N.Y.	1974	Rep.	New York, N.Y.	1979	70
42	Walter F. Mondale	Ceylon, Minn.	1928	Minn.	1977	Dem.			
43	George Bush	Milton, Mass.	1924	Tex.	1981	Rep.			

(1) John C. Calhoun resigned Dec. 28, 1832, having been elected to the Senate to fill a vacancy. (2) Andrew Johnson — a Democrat nominated by Republicans and elected with Lincoln on the National Union Ticket. (3) Adlai E. Stevenson, 23d vice president, was grandfather of Democratic candidate for president, 1952 and 1956.

The Continental Congress: Meetings, Presidents

Meeting places	Dates of meetings	Congress presidents	Date elected
Philadelphia	Sept. 5 to Oct. 26, 1774	Peyton Randolph, Va. (1)	Sept. 5, 1774
"	"	Henry Middleton, S.C.	Oct. 22, 1774
Philadelphia	May 10, 1775 to Dec. 12, 1776	Peyton Randolph, Va.	May 10, 1775
"	"	John Hancock, Mass.	May 24, 1775
Baltimore	Dec. 20, 1776 to Mar. 4, 1777	"	
Philadelphia	Mar. 5 to Sept. 18, 1777	"	
Lancaster, Pa.	Sept. 27, 1777 (one day)	"	
York, Pa.	Sept. 30, 1777 to June 27, 1778	Henry Laurens, S.C.	Nov. 1, 1777(4)
Philadelphia	July 2, 1778 to June 21, 1783	John Jay, N.Y.	Dec. 10, 1778
"	"	Samuel Huntington, Conn.	Sept. 28, 1779
"	"	Thomas McKean, Del.	July 10, 1781
"	"	John Hanson, Md. (2)	Nov. 5, 1781
"	"	Elias Boudinot, N.J.	Nov. 4, 1782
Princeton, N.J.	June 30 to Nov. 4, 1783	Thomas Mifflin, Pa.	Nov. 3, 1783
Annapolis, Md.	Nov. 26, 1783 to June 3, 1784	"	
Trenton, N.J.	Nov. 1 to Dec. 24, 1784	Richard Henry Lee, Va.	Nov. 30, 1784
New York City	Jan. 11 to Nov. 4, 1785	"	
"	Nov. 7, 1785 to Nov. 3, 1786	John Hancock, Mass. (3)	Nov. 23, 1785
"	"	Nathaniel Gorham, Mass.	June 6, 1786
"	Nov. 6, 1786 to Oct. 30, 1787	Arthur St. Clair, Pa.	Feb. 2, 1787
"	Nov. 5, 1787 to Oct. 21, 1788	Cyrus Griffin, Va.	Jan. 22, 1788
"	Nov. 3, 1788 to Mar. 2, 1789	"	

(1) Resigned Oct. 22, 1774. (2) Titled "President of the United States in Congress Assembled," John Hanson is considered by some to be the first U.S. President as he was the first to serve under the Articles of Confederation. He was, however, little more than presiding officer of the Congress, which retained full executive power. He could be considered the head of government, but not head of state. (3) Resigned May 29, 1786, without serving, because of illness. (4) Articles of Confederation agreed upon, Nov. 15, 1777; last ratification from Maryland, Mar. 1, 1781.

Cabinets of the U. S.

Secretaries of State

The Department of Foreign Affairs was created by act of Congress July 27, 1789, and the name changed to Department of State on Sept. 15.

President	Secretary	Home	Apptd.
Washington	Thomas Jefferson	Va.	1789
"	Edmund Randolph	"	1794
"	Timothy Pickering	Pa.	1795
Adams, J.	"	"	1797
"	John Marshall	Va.	1800
Jefferson	James Madison	"	1801
Madison	Robert Smith	Md.	1809
"	James Monroe	Va.	1811
Monroe	John Quincy Adams	Mass.	1817
Adams, J.Q.	Henry Clay	Ky.	1825
Jackson	Martin Van Buren	N.Y.	1829
"	Edward Livingston	La.	1831
"	Louis McLane	Del.	1833
"	John Forsyth	Ga.	1834
Van Buren	"	"	1837
Harrison, W.H.	Daniel Webster	Mass.	1841
Tyler	"	"	1841
"	Abel P. Upshur	Va.	1843
"	John C. Calhoun	S.C.	1844
Polk	"	"	1845
"	James Buchanan	Pa.	1845
Taylor	"	"	1849
"	John M. Clayton	Del.	1849
Fillmore	"	"	1850
"	Daniel Webster	Mass.	1850
"	Edward Everett	"	1852
Pierce	William L. Marcy	N.Y.	1853
Buchanan	"	"	1857
"	Lewis Cass	Mich.	1857
"	Jeremiah S. Black	Pa.	1860
Lincoln	"	"	1861
"	William H. Seward	N.Y.	1861
Johnson, A.	"	"	1865
Grant	Elihu B. Washburne	Ill.	1869
"	Hamilton Fish	N.Y.	1869
Hayes	"	"	1877
"	William M. Evarts	"	1877
Garfield	"	"	1881
"	James G. Blaine	Me.	1881
Arthur	"	"	1881
"	F.T. Frelinghuysen	N.J.	1881
Cleveland	"	"	1885
"	Thomas F. Bayard	Del.	1885
Harrison, B.	"	"	1889
"	James G. Blaine	Me.	1889
"	John W. Foster	Ind.	1892
Cleveland	Walter Q. Gresham	Ill.	1893
"	Richard Olney	Mass.	1895
McKinley	"	"	1897
"	John Sherman	Oh.	1897
"	William R. Day	"	1898
"	John Hay	D.C.	1898
Roosevelt, T.	"	"	1901
"	Elihu Root	N.Y.	1905
"	Robert Bacon	"	1909
Taft	"	"	1909
"	Philander C. Knox	Pa.	1909
Wilson	"	"	1913
"	William J. Bryan	Neb.	1913
"	Robert Lansing	N.Y.	1915
"	Bainbridge Colby	"	1920
Harding	Charles E. Hughes	"	1921
Coolidge	"	"	1923
"	Frank B. Kellogg	Minn.	1925
Hoover	"	"	1929
"	Henry L. Stimson	N.Y.	1929
Roosevelt, F.D.	Cordell Hull	Tenn.	1933
"	E.R. Stettinius Jr.	Va.	1944
Truman	"	"	1945
"	James F. Byrnes	S.C.	1945
"	George C. Marshall	Pa.	1947
"	Dean G. Acheson	Conn.	1949
Eisenhower	John Foster Dulles	N.Y.	1953
"	Christian A. Herter	Mass.	1959
Kennedy	Dean Rusk	N.Y.	1961
Johnson, L.B.	"	"	1963
Nixon	William P. Rogers	N.Y.	1969
"	Henry A. Kissinger	D.C.	1973
Ford	"	"	1974
Carter	Cyrus R. Vance	N.Y.	1977
"	Edmund S. Muskie	Me.	1980
Reagan	Alexander M. Haig Jr.	Conn.	1981
"	George P. Shultz	Cal.	1982

Secretaries of the Treasury

The Treasury Department was organized by act of Congress Sept. 2, 1789.

President	Secretary	Home	Apptd.
Washington	Alexander Hamilton	N.Y.	1789
"	Oliver Wolcott	Conn.	1795
Adams, J.	Oliver Wolcott	Conn.	1797
"	Samuel Dexter	Mass.	1801

President	Secretary	Home	Apptd.
Jefferson	Samuel Dexter	Mass.	1801
"	Albert Gallatin	Pa.	1801
Madison	"	Pa	1809
"	George W. Campbell	Tenn.	1814
"	Alexander J. Dallas	Pa.	1814
"	William H. Crawford	Ga.	1816
Monroe	"	"	1817
Adams, J.Q.	Richard Rush	Pa.	1825
Jackson	Samuel D. Ingham	"	1829
"	Louis McLane	Del.	1831
"	William J. Duane	Pa.	1833
"	Roger B. Taney	Md.	1833
"	Levi Woodbury	N.H.	1834
Van Buren	"	"	1837
Harrison, W.H.	Thomas Ewing	Oh.	1841
Tyler	"	"	1841
"	Walter Forward	Pa.	1841
"	John C. Spencer	N.Y.	1843
Tyler	George M. Bibb	Ky.	1844
Polk	Robert J. Walker	Miss.	1845
Taylor	William M. Meredith	Pa.	1849
Fillmore	Thomas Corwin	Oh.	1850
Pierce	James Guthrie	Ky.	1853
Buchanan	Howell Cobb	Ga.	1857
"	Phillip F. Thomas	Md.	1860
"	John A. Dix	N.Y.	1861
Lincoln	Salmon P. Chase	Oh.	1861
"	William P. Fessenden	Me.	1864
"	Hugh McCulloch	Ind.	1865
Johnson, A.	"	"	1865
Grant	George S. Boutwell	Mass.	1869
"	William A. Richardson	Mass.	1873
"	Benjamin H. Bristow	Ky.	1874
"	Lot M. Morrill	Me.	1876
Hayes	John Sherman	Oh.	1877
Garfield	William Windom	Minn.	1881
Arthur	Charles J. Folger	N.Y.	1881
"	Walter Q. Gresham	Ind.	1884
Arthur	Hugh McCulloch	Ind.	1884
Cleveland	Daniel Manning	N.Y.	1885
Cleveland	Charles S. Fairchild	"	1887
Harrison, B.	William Windom	Minn.	1889
"	Charles Foster	Oh.	1891
Cleveland	John G. Carlisle	Ky.	1893
McKinley	Lyman J. Gage	Ill.	1897
Roosevelt, T.	"	"	1901
"	Leslie M. Shaw	Ia.	1902
"	George B. Cortelyou	N.Y.	1907
Taft	Franklin MacVeagh	Ill.	1909
Wilson	William G. McAdoo	N.Y.	1913
"	Carter Glass	Va.	1918
"	David F. Houston	Mo.	1920
Harding	Andrew W. Mellon	Pa.	1921
Coolidge	"	"	1923
Hoover	"	"	1929
"	Ogden L. Mills	N.Y.	1932
Roosevelt, F.D.	William H. Woodin	"	1933
"	Henry Morgenthau, Jr.	"	1934
Truman	Fred M. Vinson	Ky.	1945
"	John W. Snyder	Mo.	1946
Eisenhower	George M. Humphrey	Oh.	1953
"	Robert B. Anderson	Conn.	1957
Kennedy	C. Douglas Dillon	N.J.	1961
Johnson, L.B.	"	"	1963
"	Henry H. Fowler	Va.	1965
"	Joseph W. Barr	Ind.	1968
Nixon	David M. Kennedy	Ill.	1969
"	John B. Connally	Tex.	1971
"	George P. Shultz	Ill.	1972
"	William E. Simon	N.J.	1974
Ford	"	"	1974
Carter	W. Michael Blumenthal	Mich.	1977
"	G. William Miller	R.I.	1979
Reagan	Donald T. Regan	N.Y.	1981
"	James A. Baker 3d	Tex.	1985

Secretaries of Defense

The Department of Defense, originally designated the National Military Establishment, was created Sept. 18, 1947. It is headed by the secretary of defense, who is a member of the president's cabinet.

The departments of the army, of the navy, and of the air force function within the Department of Defense, and their respective secretaries are no longer members of the president's cabinet.

President	Secretary	Home	Apptd.
Truman	James V. Forrestal	N.Y.	1947
"	Louis A. Johnson	W.Va.	1949
"	George C. Marshall	Pa.	1950
"	Robert A. Lovett	N.Y.	1951
Eisenhower	Charles E. Wilson	Mich.	1953
"	Neil H. McElroy	Oh.	1957
"	Thomas S. Gates Jr.	Pa.	1959
Kennedy	Robert S. McNamara	Mich.	1961
Johnson, L.B.	Robert S. McNamara	Mich.	1963
"	Clark M. Clifford	Md.	1968
Nixon	Melvin R. Laird	Wis.	1969
"	Elliot L. Richardson	Mass.	1973
"	James R. Schlesinger	Va.	1973
Ford	"	"	1974
"	Donald H. Rumsfeld	Ill.	1975
Carter	Harold Brown	Cal.	1977
Reagan	Caspar W. Weinberger	Cal.	1981

Secretaries of War

The War (and Navy) Department was created by act of Congress Aug. 7, 1789, and Gen. Henry Knox was commissioned secretary of war under that act Sept. 12, 1789.

President	Secretary	Home	Apptd.
Washington	Henry Knox	Mass.	1789
"	Timothy Pickering	Pa.	1795
"	James McHenry	Md.	1796
Adams, J.	"	"	1797
"	Samuel Dexter	Mass.	1800
Jefferson	Henry Dearborn	"	1801
Madison	William Eustis	Mass.	1809
"	John Armstrong	N.Y.	1813
Madison	James Monroe	Va.	1814
"	William H. Crawford	Ga.	1815
Monroe	John C. Calhoun	S.C.	1817
Adams, J.Q.	James Barbour	Va.	1825
"	Peter B. Porter	N.Y.	1828
Jackson	John H. Eaton	Tenn.	1829
"	Lewis Cass	Mich.	1831
"	Benjamin F. Butler	N.Y.	1837
Van Buren	Joel R. Poinsett	S.C.	1837
Harrison, W.H.	John Bell	Tenn.	1841
Tyler	John Bell	Tenn	1841
Tyler	John C. Spencer	N.Y.	1841
"	James M. Porter	Pa.	1843
"	William Wilkins	"	1844
Polk	William L. Marcy	N.Y.	1845
Taylor	George W. Crawford	Ga.	1849
Fillmore	Charles M. Conrad	La.	1850
Pierce	Jefferson Davis	Miss.	1853
Buchanan	John B. Floyd	Va.	1857
"	Joseph Holt	Ky.	1861
Lincoln	Simon Cameron	Pa.	1861
"	Edwin M. Stanton	Pa.	1862
Johnson, A.	"	"	1865
"	John M. Schofield	Ill.	1868
Grant	John A. Rawlins	Ill.	1869
"	William T. Sherman	Oh.	1869
"	William W. Belknap	Ia.	1869
"	Alphonso Taft	Oh.	1876
"	James D. Cameron	Pa.	1876
Hayes	George W. McCrary	Ia.	1877
"	Alexander Ramsey	Minn.	1879
Garfield	Robert T. Lincoln	Ill.	1881
Arthur	"	"	1881
Cleveland	William C. Endicott	Mass.	1885
Harrison, B.	Redfield Proctor	Vt.	1889
"	Stephen B. Elkins	W.Va.	1891
Cleveland	Daniel S. Lamont	N.Y.	1893
McKinley	Russel A. Alger	Mich.	1897
"	Elihu Root	N.Y	1899
Roosevelt, T.	"	"	1901

(continued)

President	Secretary	Home	Apptd.
Roosevelt, T.	William H. Taft	Oh.	1904
"	Luke E. Wright	Tenn.	1908
Taft	Jacob M. Dickinson	Tenn.	1909
"	Henry L. Stimson	N.Y.	1911
Wilson	Lindley M. Garrison	N.J.	1913
"	Newton D. Baker	Oh.	1916
Harding	John W. Weeks	Mass.	1921
Coolidge	"	"	1923
Coolidge	Dwight F. Davis	Mo.	1925
Hoover	James W. Good	Ill.	1929
Hoover	Patrick J. Hurley	Okla.	1929
Roosevelt, F.D.	George H. Dern	Ut.	1933
"	Harry H. Woodring	Kan.	1937
Roosevelt, F.D.	Henry L. Stimson	N.Y.	1940
Truman	Robert P. Patterson	N.Y.	1945
"	*Kenneth C. Royall	N.C.	1947

Secretaries of the Navy

The Navy Department was created by act of Congress Apr. 30, 1798.

President	Secretary	Home	Apptd.
Adams, J.	Benjamin Stoddert	Md.	1798
Jefferson	"	"	1801
"	Robert Smith	"	1801
Madison	Paul Hamilton	S.C.	1809
"	William Jones	Pa.	1813
"	Benjamin Williams Crowninshield	Mass.	1814
Monroe	"	"	1817
"	Smith Thompson	N.Y.	1818
"	Samuel L. Southard	N.J.	1823
Adams, J.Q.	"	"	1825
Jackson	John Branch	N.C.	1829
"	Levi Woodbury	N.H.	1831
"	Mahlon Dickerson	N.J.	1834
Van Buren	"	"	1837
"	James K. Paulding	N.Y.	1838
Harrison, W.H.	George E. Badger	N.C.	1841
Tyler	"	"	1841
"	Abel P. Upshur	Va.	1841
"	David Henshaw	Mass.	1843
"	Thomas W. Gilmer	Va.	1844
"	John Y. Mason	"	1844
Polk	George Bancroft	Mass.	1845
"	John Y. Mason	Va.	1846
Taylor	William B. Preston	"	1849
Fillmore	William A. Graham	N.C.	1850
"	John P. Kennedy	Md.	1852
Pierce	James C. Dobbin	N.C.	1853
Buchanan	Isaac Toucey	Conn.	1857
Lincoln	Gideon Welles	Conn.	1861
Johnson, A.	"	"	1865
Grant	Adolph E. Borie	Pa.	1869
"	George M. Robeson	N.J.	1869
Hayes	Richard W. Thompson	Ind.	1877
"	Nathan Goff Jr.	W.Va.	1881
Garfield	William H. Hunt	La.	1881
Arthur	William E. Chandler	N.H.	1882
Cleveland	William C. Whitney	N.Y.	1885
Harrison, B.	Benjamin F. Tracy	N.Y.	1889
Cleveland	Hilary A. Herbert	Ala.	1893
McKinley	John D. Long	Mass.	1897
Roosevelt, T.	"	"	1901
"	William H. Moody	"	1902
"	Paul Morton	Ill.	1904
"	Charles J. Bonaparte	Md.	1905
"	Victor H. Metcalf	Cal.	1906
"	Truman H. Newberry	Mich.	1908
Taft	George von L. Meyer	Mass.	1909
Wilson	Josephus Daniels	N.C.	1913
Harding	Edwin Denby	Mich.	1921
Coolidge	"	"	1923
"	Curtis D. Wilbur	Cal.	1924
Hoover	Charles Francis Adams	Mass.	1929
Roosevelt, F.D.	Claude A. Swanson	Va.	1933
"	Charles Edison	N.J.	1940
"	Frank Knox	Ill.	1940
"	*James V. Forrestal	N.Y.	1944
Truman	"	"	1945

*Last members of Cabinet. The War Department became the Department of the Army and it and the Navy Department became branches of the Department of Defense, created Sept. 18, 1947.

Attorneys General

The office of attorney general was organized by act of Congress Sept. 24, 1789. The Department of Justice was created June 22, 1870.

President	Attorney General	Home	Apptd.
Washington	Edmund Randolph	Va.	1789
"	William Bradford	Pa.	1794
"	Charles Lee	Va.	1795
Adams, J.	"	"	1797
Jefferson	Levi Lincoln	Mass.	1801
"	John Breckenridge	Ky.	1805
"	Caesar A. Rodney	Del.	1807
Madison	"	"	1809
"	William Pinkney	Md.	1811
"	Richard Rush	Pa.	1814
Monroe	"	"	1817
"	William Wirt	Va.	1817
Adams, J.Q.	"	"	1825
Jackson	John M. Berrien	Ga.	1829
"	Roger B. Taney	Md.	1831
"	Benjamin F. Butler	N.Y.	1833
Van Buren	"	"	1837
"	Felix Grundy	Tenn.	1838
"	Henry D. Gilpin	Pa.	1840
Harrison, W.H.	John J. Crittenden	Ky.	1841
Tyler	"	"	1841
"	Hugh S. Legare	S.C.	1841
"	John Nelson	Md.	1843
Polk	John Y. Mason	Va.	1845
"	Nathan Clifford	Me.	1846
"	Isaac Toucey	Conn.	1848
Taylor	Reverdy Johnson	Md.	1849
Fillmore	John J. Crittenden	Ky.	1850
Pierce	Caleb Cushing	Mass.	1853
Buchanan	Jeremiah S. Black	Pa.	1857
"	Edwin M. Stanton	Pa.	1860
Lincoln	Edward Bates	Mo.	1861
"	James Speed	Ky.	1864
Johnson, A.	"	"	1865
"	Henry Stanbery	Oh.	1866
"	William M. Evarts	N.Y.	1868
Grant	Ebenezer R. Hoar	Mass.	1869
Grant	Amos T. Akerman	Ga.	1870
"	George H. Williams	Ore.	1871
"	Edwards Pierrepont	N.Y.	1875
"	Alphonso Taft	Oh.	1876
Hayes	Charles Devens	Mass.	1877
Garfield	Wayne MacVeagh	Pa.	1881
Arthur	Benjamin H. Brewster	",4	1881
Cleveland	Augustus Garland	Ark.	1885
Harrison, B.	William H. H. Miller	Ind.	1889
Cleveland	Richard Olney	Mass.	1893
"	Judson Harmon	Oh.	1895
McKinley	Joseph McKenna	Cal.	1897
"	John W. Griggs	N.J.	1898
"	Philander C. Knox	Pa.	1901
Roosevelt, T.	"	"	1901
"	William H. Moody	Mass.	1904
"	Charles J. Bonaparte	Md.	1906
Taft	George W. Wickersham	N.Y.	1909
Wilson	J.C. McReynolds	Tenn.	1913
"	Thomas W. Gregory	Tex.	1914
"	A. Mitchell Palmer	Pa.	1919
Harding	Harry M. Daugherty	Oh.	1921
Coolidge	"	"	1923
"	Harlan F. Stone	N.Y.	1924
"	John G. Sargent	Vt.	1925
Hoover	William D. Mitchell	Minn.	1929
Roosevelt, F.D.	Homer S. Cummings	Conn.	1933
"	Frank Murphy	Mich.	1939
"	Robert H. Jackson	N.Y.	1940
"	Francis Biddle	Pa.	1941
Truman	Thomas C. Clark	Tex.	1945
"	J. Howard McGrath	R.I.	1949
"	J.P. McGranery	Pa.	1952
Eisenhower	Herbert Brownell Jr.	N.Y.	1953
"	William P. Rogers	Md.	1957
Kennedy	Robert F. Kennedy	Mass.	1961
Johnson, L.B.	"	"	1963

President	Attorney General	Home	Apptd.
Johnson, L.B.	N. de B. Katzenbach	Ill.	1964
"	Ramsey Clark	Tex.	1967
Nixon	John N. Mitchell	N.Y.	1969
"	Richard G. Kleindienst	Ariz.	1972
"	Elliot L. Richardson	Mass.	1973
"	William B. Saxbe	Oh.	1974
Ford	William B. Saxbe	Oh.	1974
"	Edward H. Levi	Ill.	1975
Carter	Griffin B. Bell	Ga.	1977
"	Benjamin R. Civiletti	Md.	1979
Reagan	William French Smith	Cal.	1981
"	Edwin Meese 3d	Cal.	1985

Secretaries of the Interior

The Department of Interior was created by act of Congress Mar. 3, 1849

President	Secretary	Home	Apptd.
Taylor	Thomas Ewing	Oh.	1849
Fillmore	Thomas M. T. McKennan	Pa.	1850
Fillmore	Alex H. H. Stuart	Va.	1850
Pierce	Robert McClelland	Mich.	1853
Buchanan	Jacob Thompson	Miss.	1857
Lincoln	Caleb B. Smith	Ind.	1861
"	John P. Usher	"	1863
Johnson, A.	"	"	1865
"	James Harlan	Ia.	1865
"	Orville H. Browning	Ill.	1866
Grant	Jacob D. Cox	Oh.	1869
"	Columbus Delano	"	1870
"	Zachariah Chandler	Mich.	1875
Hayes	Carl Schurz	Mo.	1877
Garfield	Samuel J. Kirkwood	Ia.	1881
Arthur	Henry M. Teller	Col.	1882
Cleveland	Lucius Q.C. Lamar	Miss.	1885
"	William F. Vilas	Wis.	1888
Harrison, B.	John W. Noble	Mo.	1889
Cleveland	Hoke Smith	Ga.	1893
"	David R. Francis	Mo.	1896
McKinley	Cornelius N. Bliss	N.Y.	1897
"	Ethan A. Hitchcock	Mo.	1898
Roosevelt, T.	"	"	1901
"	James R. Garfield	Oh.	1907
Taft	Richard A. Ballinger	Wash.	1909
"	Walter L. Fisher	Ill.	1911
Wilson	Franklin K. Lane	Cal.	1913
"	John B. Payne	Ill.	1920
Harding	Albert B. Fall	N.M.	1921
"	Hubert Work	Col.	1923
Coolidge	"	"	1923
"	Roy O. West	Ill.	1929
Hoover	Ray Lyman Wilbur	Cal.	1929
Roosevelt, F.D.	Harold L. Ickes	Ill.	1933
Truman	"	"	1945
"	Julius A. Krug	Wis.	1946
"	Oscar L. Chapman	Col.	1949
Eisenhower	Douglas McKay	Ore.	1953
"	Fred A Seaton	Neb.	1956
Kennedy	Stewart L. Udall	Ariz.	1961
Johnson, L.B.	"	"	1963
Nixon	Walter J. Hickel	Alas.	1969
"	Rogers C.B. Morton	Md.	1971
Ford	"	"	1974
"	Stanley K. Hathaway	Wyo.	1975
"	Thomas S. Kleppe	N.D.	1975
Carter	Cecil D. Andrus	Ida.	1977
Reagan	James G. Watt	Col.	1981
"	William P. Clark	Cal.	1983
"	Donald P. Hodel	Ore.	1985

Secretaries of Agriculture

The Department of Agriculture was created by act of Congress May 15, 1862. On Feb. 8, 1889, its commissioner was renamed secretary of agriculture and became a member of the cabinet.

President	Secretary	Home	Apptd.
Cleveland	Norman J. Colman	Mo.	1889
Harrison, B.	Jeremiah M. Rusk	Wis.	1889
Cleveland	J. Sterling Morton	Neb.	1893
McKinley	James Wilson	Ia.	1897
Roosevelt, T.	"	"	1901
Taft	"	"	1909
Wilson	David F. Houston	Mo.	1913
"	Edwin T. Meredith	Ia.	1920
Harding	Henry C. Wallace	Ia.	1921
Coolidge	"	"	1923
"	Howard M. Gore	W.Va.	1924
"	William M. Jardine	Kan.	1925
Hoover	Arthur M. Hyde	Mo.	1929
Roosevelt, F.D.	Henry A. Wallace	Ia.	1933
"	Claude R. Wickard	Ind.	1940
Truman	Clinton P. Anderson	N.M.	1945
"	Charles F. Brannan	Col.	1948
Eisenhower	Ezra Taft Benson	Ut.	1953
Kennedy	Orville L. Freeman	Minn.	1961
Johnson, L.B.	"	"	1963
Nixon	Clifford M. Hardin	Ind.	1969
"	Earl L. Butz	Ind.	1971
Ford	"	"	1974
"	John A. Knebel	Va.	1976
Carter	Bob Bergland	Minn.	1977
Reagan	John R. Block	Ill.	1981
"	Richard E. Lyng	Cal.	1986

Secretaries of Commerce and Labor

The Department of Commerce and Labor, created by Congress Feb. 14, 1903, was divided by Congress Mar. 4, 1913, into separate departments of Commerce and Labor. The secretary of each was made a cabinet member.

President	Secretary	Home	Apptd.
	Secretaries of Commerce and Labor		
Roosevelt, T.	George B. Cortelyou	N.Y.	1903
"	Victor H. Metcalf	Cal.	1904
"	Oscar S. Straus	N.Y.	1906
Taft	Charles Nagel	Mo.	1909
	Secretaries of Labor		
Wilson	William B. Wilson	Pa.	1913
Harding	James J. Davis	Pa.	1921
Coolidge	"	"	1923
Hoover	"	"	1929
"	William N. Doak	Va.	1930
Roosevelt, F.D.	Frances Perkins	N.Y.	1933
Truman	L.B. Schwellenbach	Wash.	1945
"	Maurice J. Tobin	Mass.	1949
Eisenhower	Martin P. Durkin	Ill.	1953
Eisenhower	James P. Mitchell	N.J.	1953
Kennedy	Arthur J. Goldberg	Ill.	1961
"	W. Willard Wirtz	Ill.	1962
Johnson, L.B.	"	Ill.	1963
Nixon	George P. Shultz	Ill.	1969
"	James D. Hodgson	Cal.	1970
	Peter J. Brennan	N.Y.	1973
Ford	Peter J. Brennan	N.Y.	1974
"	John T. Dunlop	Cal.	1975
"	W.J. Usery Jr.	Ga.	1976
Carter	F. Ray Marshall	Tex.	1977
Reagan	Raymond J. Donovan	N.J.	1981
"	William E. Brock	Tenn.	1985
	Secretaries of Commerce		
Wilson	William C. Redfield	N.Y.	1913
"	Joshua W. Alexander	Mo.	1919
Harding	Herbert C. Hoover	Cal.	1921
Coolidge	"	"	1923
"	William F. Whiting	Mass.	1928
Hoover	Robert P. Lamont	Ill.	1929
"	Roy D. Chapin	Mich.	1932
Roosevelt, F.D.	Daniel C. Roper	S.C.	1933
"	Harry L. Hopkins	N.Y.	1939
"	Jesse Jones	Tex.	1940
"	Henry A. Wallace	Ia.	1945
Truman	"	"	1945
"	W. Averell Harriman	N.Y.	1947
"	Charles Sawyer	Oh.	1948

(continued)

President	Secretary	Home	Apptd.
Eisenhower	Sinclair Weeks	Mass.	1953
"	Lewis L. Strauss	N.Y.	1958
"	Frederick H. Mueller	Mich.	1959
Kennedy	Luther H. Hodges	N.C.	1961
Johnson, L.B.	"	10 "	1963
"	John T. Connor	N.J.	1965
"	Alex B. Trowbridge	N.J.	1967
"	Cyrus R. Smith	N.Y.	1968
Nixon	Maurice H. Stans	Minn.	1969
Nixon	Peter G. Peterson	Ill.	1972
"	Frederick B. Dent	S.C.	1973
Ford	"	"	1974
"	Rogers C.B. Morton	Md.	1975
"	Elliot L. Richardson	Mass.	1975
Carter	Juanita M. Kreps	N.C.	1977
"	Philip M. Klutznick	Ill.	1979
Reagan	Malcolm Baldrige	Conn.	1981
"	C. William Verity Jr.	Oh.	1987

Secretaries of Housing and Urban Development

The Department of Housing and Urban Development was created by act of Congress Sept. 9, 1965.

President	Secretary	Home	Apptd.
Johnson, L.B.	Robert C. Weaver	Wash.	1966
"	Robert C. Wood	Mass.	1969
Nixon	George W. Romney	Mich.	1969
"	James T. Lynn	Oh.	1973
Ford	"	"	1974
"	Carla Anderson Hills	Cal.	1975
Carter	Patricia Roberts Harris	D.C.	1977
"	Moon Landrieu	La.	1979
Reagan	Samuel R. Pierce Jr.	N.Y.	1981

Secretaries of Transportation

The Department of Transportation was created by act of Congress Oct. 15, 1966.

President	Secretary	Home	Apptd.
Johnson, L.B.	Alan S. Boyd	Fla.	1966
Nixon	John A. Volpe	Mass.	1969
"	Claude S. Brinegar	Cal.	1973
Ford	Claude S. Brinegar	Cal.	1974
"	William T. Coleman Jr.	Pa.	1975
Carter	Brock Adams	Wash.	1977
"	Neil E. Goldschmidt	Ore.	1979
Reagan	Andrew L. Lewis Jr.	Pa.	1981
"	Elizabeth Hanford Dole	Kan.	1983

Secretaries of Energy

The Department of Energy was created by federal law Aug. 4, 1977.

President	Secretary	Home	Apptd.
Carter	James R. Schlesinger	Va.	1977
"	Charles Duncan Jr.	Wyo.	1979
Reagan	James B. Edwards	S.C.	1981
"	Donald P. Hodel	Ore.	1982
"	John S. Herrington	Cal.	1985

Secretaries of Health, Education, and Welfare

The Department of Health, Education and Welfare, created by Congress Apr. 11, 1953, was divided by Congress Sept. 27, 1979, into separate departments of Education, and Health and Human Services. The secretary of each is a cabinet member.

President	Secretary	Home	Apptd.
Eisenhower	Oveta Culp Hobby	Tex.	1953
"	Marion B. Folsom	N.Y.	1955
"	Arthur S. Flemming	Oh.	1958
Kennedy	Abraham A. Ribicoff	Conn.	1961
"	Anthony J. Celebrezze	Oh.	1962
Johnson, L.B.	"	"	1963
"	John W. Gardner	N.Y.	1965
Johnson, L.B.	Wilbur J. Cohen	Mich.	1968
Nixon	Robert H. Finch	Cal.	1969
"	Elliot L. Richardson	Mass.	1970
"	Caspar W. Weinberger	Cal.	1973
Ford	"	"	1974
"	Forrest D. Mathews	Ala.	1975
Carter	Joseph A. Califano, Jr.	D.C.	1977
"	Patricia Roberts Harris	D.C.	1979

Secretaries of Health and Human Services

President	Secretary	Home	Apptd.
Carter	Patricia Roberts Harris	D.C.	1979
Reagan	Richard S. Schweiker	Pa.	1981
"	Margaret M. Heckler	Mass.	1983
"	Otis R. Bowen	Ind.	1985

Secretaries of Education

President	Secretary	Home	Apptd.
Carter	Shirley Hufstedler	Cal.	1979
Reagan	Terrel Bell	Ut.	1981
"	William J. Bennett	N.Y.	1985

Federal Bureau of Investigation

The Federal Bureau of Investigation was created July 26, 1908 and was referred to as Office of Chief Examiner. It became the Bureau of Investigation (Mar. 26, 1909), United States Bureau of Investigation (July 1, 1932), Division of Investigation (Aug. 10, 1933), and Federal Bureau of Investigation (July 1, 1935).

Director	Date of assumed office
Stanley W. Finch	July 26, 1908
A(lexander) Bruce Bielaski	Apr. 30, 1912
William E. Allen, act.	Feb. 10, 1919
William J. Flynn	July 1, 1919
William J. Burns	Aug. 22, 1921
J. Edgar Hoover, act.	May 10, 1924
J. Edgar Hoover	Dec. 10, 1924
L. Patrick Gray, act.	May 3, 1972
William D. Ruckelshaus, act.	Apr. 27, 1973
Clarence M. Kelley	July 9, 1973
William H. Webster	Feb. 23, 1978
John E. Otto, act.	May 27, 1987

Central Intelligence Agency

On June 13, 1942 President Roosevelt established the Office of Strategic Services (OSS) and maned William J. Donovan as its director. The OSS was disbanded Oct. 1, 1945 and its functions absorbed by the State and War departments. President Truman, Jan. 22, 1946, established the Central Intelligence Agency Group (CIG) to operate under the direction of the National Intelligence Authority (NIA). The National Security Act of 1947 replaced the NIA with the National Security Council and the CIG with the Central Intelligence Agency.

Director	Served	Appointed by President
Adm. Sidney W. Souers	1946	Truman
Gen. Hoyt S. Vandenberg	1946-1947	Truman
Adm. Roscoe H. Hillenkoetter	1947-1950	Truman
Gen. Walter Bedell Smith	1950-1953	Truman
Allen W. Dulles	1953-1961	Eisenhower
John A. McCone	1961-1965	Kennedy
Adm. William F. Raborn Jr.	1965-1966	Johnson
Richard Helms	1966-1973	Johnson
James R. Schlesinger	1973	Nixon
William E. Colby	1973-1976	Nixon
George Bush	1976-1977	Ford
Adm. Stansfield Turner	1977-1981	Carter
William J. Casey	1981-1987	Reagan
William H. Webster	1987-	Reagan

Librarians of Congress

Librarian	Served	Appointed by President
John J. Beckley	1802-1807	Jefferson
Patrick Magruder	1807-1815	Jefferson
George Watterston	1815-1829	Madison
John Silva Meehan	1829-1861	Jackson
John G. Stephenson	1861-1864	Lincoln
Ainsworth Rand Spofford	1864-1897	Lincoln
John Russell Young	1897-1899	McKinley
Herbert Putnam	1899-1939	McKinley
Archibald MacLeish	1939-1944	F. Roosevelt
Luther H. Evans	1945-1953	Truman
L. Quincy Mumford	1954-1974	Eisenhower
Daniel J. Boorstin	1975-1987	Carter
James H. Billington	1987-	Reagan

Presidents Pro Tempore of the Senate

Until 1890, presidents "pro tem" were named "for the occasion only." Beginning with that year, they have served "until the Senate otherwise ordered." Sen. John J. Ingalls, chosen under the old rule in 1887, was again elected, under the new rule, in 1890. Party designations are D, Democrat; R, Republican.

Name	Party	State	Elected
John J. Ingalls	R	Kan.	Apr. 3, 1890
Charles F. Manderson	R	Neb.	Mar. 2, 1891
Isham G. Harris	D	Tenn.	Mar. 22, 1893
Matt W. Ransom	D	N.C.	Jan. 7, 1895
Isham G. Harris	D	Tenn.	Jan. 10, 1895
William P. Frye	R	Me.	Feb. 7, 1896
Charles Curtis	R	Kan.	Dec. 4, 1911
Augustus O. Bacon	D	Ga.	Jan. 15, 1912
Jacob H. Gallinger	R	N.H.	Feb. 12, 1912
Henry Cabot Lodge	R	Mass.	Mar. 25, 1912
Frank R. Brandegee	R	Conn.	May 25, 1912
James P. Clarke	D	Ark.	Mar. 13, 1913
Willard Saulsbury	D	Del.	Dec. 14, 1916
Albert B. Cummins	R	Ia.	May 19, 1919
George H. Moses	R	N.H.	Mar. 6, 1925
Key Pittman	D	Nev.	Mar. 9, 1933
William H. King	D	Ut.	Nov. 19, 1940
Pat Harrison	D	Miss.	Jan. 6, 1941
Carter Glass	D	Va.	July 10, 1941
Kenneth McKellar	D	Tenn.	Jan. 6, 1945
Arthur H. Vandenberg	R	Mich.	Jan. 4, 1947
Kenneth McKellar	D	Tenn.	Jan. 3, 1949
Styles Bridges	R	N.H.	Jan. 3, 1953
Walter F. George	D	Ga.	Jan. 5, 1955
Carl Hayden	D	Ariz.	Jan. 3, 1957
Richard B. Russell	D	Ga.	Jan. 3, 1969
Allen J. Ellender	D	La.	Jan. 22, 1971
James O. Eastland	D	Miss.	July 28, 1972
Warren G. Magnuson	D	Wash.	Jan. 23, 1979
Strom Thurmond	R	S.C.	Jan. 5, 1981
John C. Stennis	D	Miss.	Jan. 6, 1987

Speakers of the House of Representatives

Party designations: A, American; D, Democratic; DR, Democratic Republican; F, Federalist; R, Republican; W, Whig. *Served only one day.

Name	Party	State	Tenure
Frederick Muhlenberg	F	Pa.	1789-1791
Jonathan Trumbull	F	Conn.	1791-1793
Frederick Muhlenberg	F	Pa.	1793-1795
Jonathan Dayton	F	N.J.	1795-1799
Theodore Sedgwick	F	Mass.	1799-1801
Nathaniel Macon	DR	N.C.	1801-1807
Joseph B. Varnum	DR	Mass.	1807-1811
Henry Clay	DR	Ky.	1811-1814
Langdon Cheves	DR	S.C.	1814-1815
Henry Clay	DR	Ky.	1815-1820
John W. Taylor	DR	N.Y.	1820-1821
Philip P. Barbour	DR	Va.	1821-1823
Henry Clay	DR	Ky.	1823-1825
John W. Taylor	D	N.Y.	1825-1827
Andrew Stevenson	D	Va.	1827-1834
John Bell	D	Tenn.	1834-1835
James K. Polk	D	Tenn.	1835-1839
Robert M. T. Hunter	D	Va.	1839-1841
John White	W	Ky.	1841-1843
John W. Jones	D	Va.	1843-1845
John W. Davis	D	Ind.	1845-1847
Robert C. Winthrop	W	Mass.	1847-1849
Howell Cobb	D	Ga.	1849-1851
Linn Boyd	D	Ky.	1851-1855
Nathaniel P. Banks	A	Mass.	1856-1857
James L. Orr	D	S.C.	1857-1859
William Pennington	R	N.J.	1860-1861
Galusha A. Grow	R	Pa.	1861-1863
Schuyler Colfax	R	Ind.	1863-1869
*Theodore M. Pomeroy	R	N.Y.	1869-1869
James G. Blaine	R	Me.	1869-1875
Michael C. Kerr	D	Ind.	1875-1876
Samuel J. Randall	D	Pa.	1876-1881
Joseph W. Keifer	R	Oh.	1881-1883
John G. Carlisle	D	Ky.	1883-1889
Thomas B. Reed	R	Me.	1889-1891
Charles F. Crisp	D	Ga.	1891-1895
Thomas B. Reed	R	Me.	1895-1899
David B. Henderson	R	Ia.	1899-1903
Joseph G. Cannon	R	Ill.	1903-1911
Champ Clark	D	Mo.	1911-1919
Frederick H. Gillett	R	Mass.	1919-1925
Nicholas Longworth	R	Oh.	1925-1931
John N. Garner	D	Tex.	1931-1933
Henry T. Rainey	D	Ill.	1933-1935
Joseph W. Byrns	D	Tenn.	1935-1936
William B. Bankhead	D	Ala.	1936-1940
Sam Rayburn	D	Tex.	1940-1947
Joseph W. Martin Jr.	R	Mass.	1947-1949
Sam Rayburn	D	Tex.	1949-1953
Joseph W. Martin Jr.	R	Mass.	1953-1955
Sam Rayburn	D	Tex.	1955-1961
John W. McCormack	D	Mass.	1962-1971
Carl Albert	D	Okla.	1971-1977
Thomas P. O'Neill Jr.	D	Mass.	1977-1987
James Wright	D	Tex.	1987-

National Political Parties

As of mid-1987

Republican Party

National Headquarters—310 First St., SE, Washington, DC 20003.
Chairman—Frank J. Fahrenkopf Jr.
Co-Chairman—Maureen Reagan.
Vice Chairmen—Bernard M. Shanley, Shelia Roberge, Jack Londen, Martha Moore, Peter Secchia, Nelda Barton, Ernest Angelo Jr., Jennifer Dunn.
Secretary—Kit Mehrtens.
Treasurer—William J. McManus.
General Counsel—Roger Allan Moore.

Democratic Party

National Headquarters—430 South Capitol St., SE, Washington, DC 20003.
Chairman—Paul G. Kirk Jr.
Vice Chairpersons—Roland Burris, Polly Baca, Lynn Cutler.
Secretary—Dorothy V. Bush.
Treasurer—Sharon Pratt Dixon.
Finance Chairman—C. Victor Raiser 2d.

Other Major Political Organizations

American Party of the United States

(P.O. Box 22382, Lexington, KY 40522)
National Chairman—Dr. Wasley Krogdahl.
Secretary—Doris Feimer.
Treasurer—Jewell Addison.

Americans For Democratic Action

(815 15th St. NW, Washington, DC 20005)
President—Ted Weiss.
National Director—Ann F. Lewis.
Chairperson Exec. Comm.—Tom Kerr.

Comm. on Political Education, AFL-CIO

(AFL-CIO Building, 815 16th St., Wash., DC 20006)
Chairman—Lane Kirkland.

Communist Party U.S.A.

(235 W. 23d St., New York, NY 10011)
General Secretary—Gus Hall.

Conservative Party of the State of N.Y.

(45 E. 29th St., New York, NY 10016)
Chairman—Serphin R. Maltese.
Executive Director—Anthony Rudmann.
Secretary—John J. Flynn.

Liberal Party of New York State

(18 W. 56th St., New York, NY 10019)
Chairman—Frank Marin.
Exec. Director—Carl F. Grillo.

Libertarian National Committee

(301 W. 21st., Houston, TX 77008.)
Chair—James B. Turney.
Vice-Chair—Sharon A. Ayres.
Secretary—Imad A. Ahmad.
National Director—Terry Von Mitchell.

Prohibition National Committee

(P.O. Box 2635, Denver, CO 80201)
National Chairman—Earl F. Dodge.
National Secretary—Rayford G. Feather.

Socialist Party USA

(7109 N. Glenwood Ave. #704, Chicago, IL 60626)

Socialist Labor Party

In Minnesota: Industrial Gov't. Party
(914 Industrial Ave., Palo Alto, CA 94303)
National Secretary—Robert Bills.
Financial Secretary—Genevieve Gunderson.

Socialist Workers Party

(14 Charles Lane, New York, NY 10014)
National Secretary—Jack Barnes.

America's Third Parties

Since 1860, there have been only 4 presidential elections in which all third parties together polled more than 10% of the vote: the Populists (James Baird Weaver) in 1892, the National Progressives (Theodore Roosevelt) in 1912, the La Follette Progressives in 1924, and George Wallace's American Party in 1968. In 1948, the combined third parties (Henry Wallace's Progessives, Strom Thurmond's States' Rights party or Dixiecrats, Prohibition, Socialists, and others) received only 5.75% of the vote. In most elections since 1860, fewer than one vote in 20 has been cast for a third party. The only successful third party in American history was the Republican Party in the election of Abraham Lincoln in 1860.

Notable Third Parties

Party	Presidential nominee	Election	Issues	Strength in
Anti-Masonic	William Wirt	1832	Against secret societies and oaths	Pa., Vt.
Liberty	James G. Birney	1844	Anti-slavery	North
Free Soil	Martin Van Buren	1848	Anti-slavery	New York, Ohio
American (Know Nothing)	Millard Fillmore	1856	Anti-immigrant	Northeast, South
Greenback	Peter Cooper	1876	For "cheap money,"	
Greenback	James B. Weaver	1880	labor rights	National
Prohibition	John P. St. John	1884	Anti-liquor	National
Populist	James B. Weaver	1892	For "cheap money," end of national banks	South, West
Socialist	Eugene V. Debs	1900-20	For public ownership	National
Progressive (Bull Moose)	Theodore Roosevelt	1912	Against high tariffs	Midwest, West
Progressive	Robert M. LaFollette	1924	Farmer & labor rights	Midwest, West
Socialist	Norman Thomas	1928-48	Liberal reforms	National
Union	William Lemke	1936	Anti "New Deal"	National
States' Rights	Strom Thurmond	1948	For states' rights	South
Progressive	Henry Wallace	1948	Anti-cold war	New York, California
American Independent	George Wallace	1968	For states' rights	South
American	John G. Schmitz	1972	For "law and order"	Far West, Oh., La.
None (Independent)	John B. Anderson	1980	A 3d choice	National

NATIONAL DEFENSE

Data as of July, 1987

Chairman, Joint Chiefs of Staff
Adm. William J. Crowe, Jr.

The Joint Chiefs of Staff consists of the Chairman and Vice Chairman of the Joint Chiefs of Staff; the Chief of Staff, U.S. Army; the Chief of Naval Operations; the Chief of Staff, U.S. Air Force; and the Commandant of the Marine Corps.

Army

Chief of Staff—Carl E. Vuono

Generals

Name	Date of Rank
Brown, Arthur E.	June 24, 1986
Galvin, John R.	Feb. 25, 1985
Lindsay, James J.	Oct. 10, 1986
Menetrey, Louis C.	June 24, 1987
Merritt, Jack N.	Dec. 1, 1985
Otis, Glenn K.	Aug. 1, 1981
Palastra, Joseph T. Jr.	July 1, 1986
Thurman, Maxwell R.	June 23, 1983
Vuono, Carl E.	July 1, 1986
Wagner, Louis C.	Apr. 13, 1987
Woerner, Frederick F.	June 6, 1986

Air Force

Chief of Staff—Larry D. Welch

Generals

Name	Date of Rank
Abrahamson, James A.	—
Cassidy, Duane H.	Nov. 8, 1985
Chain, John T., Jr.	July 1, 1985
Gregory, Jack I.	Jan. 1, 1987
Hatch, Monroe W. Jr.	Jan. 29, 1987
Herres, Robert T.	Aug. 1, 1984
Kirk, William L.	May 1, 1987
O'Loughlin, Earl T.	Nov. 1, 1984
Piotrowski, John L.	Aug. 1, 1985
Randolph, Bernard P.	(nominated)
Reed, Robert H.	July 1, 1986
Richards, Thomas C.	Dec. 1, 1986
Russ, Robert D.	May 22, 1985
Welch, Larry D.	Aug. 1, 1984

Navy

Chief of Naval Operations
Admiral Carlisle A.H. Trost (submariner)

Admirals

Name	Date of Rank
Baggett, Lee, Jr. (surface warfare)	May 30, 1985
Busey, James B. (aviator)	Oct. 17, 1985
Crowe, William J., Jr. (submariner)	May 30, 1980
Hays, Ronald J. (aviator)	April 29, 1983
Kelso, Frank B., II (submariner)	June 30, 1986
Lyons, James A. (surface warfare)	Sept. 16, 1985
McKee, Kinnaird R. (submariner)	Mar. 2, 1982
Trost, Carlisle A.H. (submariner)	Oct. 4, 1985

Marine Corps

Corps Commandant, with rank of General

Alfred M. Gray . . . . July 1, 1987

Chief of Staff, with rank of Lt. Gen.

Clyde D. Dean . . . . June 1, 1986

Coast Guard

Commandant, with rank of Admiral

P. A. Yost, Jr. . . . . May 30, 1986

Vice Commandant, with rank of Vice Admiral

J.C. Irwin . . . . May 30, 1986

United States Unified and Specified Commands

Atlantic Command—Admiral Lee Baggett Jr., USN
HQ Aerospace Defense Command—General John L. Piotrowski, USAF
U.S. European Command—General John R. Galvin, USA
Pacific Command—Admiral Ronald J. Hays, USN
U.S. Southern Command—Lt. Gen. Frederick F. Woerner, Jr., USA
Strategic Air Command—General John T. Chain, USAF
U.S. Central Command—Gen. George B. Crist, USMC
U.S. Readiness Command—General John J. Lindsey, USA
Military Air Lift Command—General Duane H. Cassidy, USAF
Military Sea Lift Command—RADM Walter T. Piotti, Jr., USN

North Atlantic Treaty Organization International Commands

Supr. Allied Commander, Europe (SACEUR)—Gen. John R. Galvin, USA
Deputy SACEUR—Gen. Hans-Joachim Mack (German)
Deputy SACEUR—Gen. Sir John Akehurst, UK
C-in-C SACEUR—Gen. John R. Galvin, USA
C-in-C Allied Forces, Northern Europe—Gen. Sir Geoffrey Howlett, UK Army
C-in-C Allied Forces, Central Europe—Gen. Leopold Chalupa, German Army
C-in-C Allied Forces, Southern Europe—Adm. James B. Busey, USN
Supr. Allied Commander Atlantic (SACLANT)—Adm. Lee Baggett, Jr., USN
Deputy SACLANT—VADM W.R.S. Thomas, UK
Chief of Staff (SACLANT)—RADM Warren E. Aut, USN
Commander Strike Force South—VADM Kendall E. Moranville, USN
Allied Commander in Chief, Channel—Adm. Sir Nicholas Hunt, UK

Principal U.S. Military Training Centers

Army

Name, P.O. address	Zip	Nearest city
Aberdeen Proving Ground, MD	21005	Aberdeen
Carlisle Barracks, PA	17013	Carlisle
Fort Belvoir, VA	22060	Alexandria
Fort Benning, GA	31905	Columbus
Fort Bliss, TX	79916	El Paso
Fort Bragg, NC	28307	Fayetteville
Fort Devens, MA	01433	Ayer
Fort Dix, NJ	08640	Trenton
Fort Eustis, VA	23604	Newport News
Fort Gordon, GA	30905	Augusta
Fort Benjamin Harrison, IN	46216	Indianapolis
Fort Sam Houston, TX	78234	San Antonio
Fort Huachuca, AZ	85613	Sierra Vista
Fort Jackson, SC	29207	Columbia
Fort Knox, KY	40121	Louisville
Fort Leavenworth, KS	66027	Leavenworth
Fort Lee, VA	23801	Petersburg
Fort McClellan, AL	36205	Anniston
Fort Monmouth, NJ	07703	Red Bank
Fort Rucker, AL	36362	Dothan
Fort Sill, OK	73503	Lawton
Fort Leonard Wood, MO	65473	Rolla
National Training Center	92311	Barstow, CA
Redstone Arsenal, AL	35809	Huntsville
The Judge Advocate General School, VA	22901	Charlottesville
U.S. Military Acad., NY	10996	West Point

Navy Recruit Training Centers

Name, P.O. address	Zip	Nearest city
Great Lakes, IL	60088	North Chicago
San Diego, CA	92133	San Diego
Orlando, FL	32813	Orlando

Major Marine Corps Facilities

Name, P.O. address	Zip	Nearest city
MCB Camp Lejeune, NC	28542	Jacksonville
MCB Camp Pendleton, CA	92055	Oceanside
MCB Camp Butler, Okinawa	FPO Seattle 98773	Futenma, Okinawa
MCAGCC Twentynine Palms, CA	92278	Palm Springs
MCDEC Quantico, VA	22134	Quantico
MCRD Parris Island, SC	29905	Beaufort
MCRD San Diego, CA	92140	San Diego
MCAS Cherry Point, NC	28533	Cherry Point
MCAS El Toro, CA	92709	Santa Ana
MCAS Tustin, CA	92780	Santa Ana
MCAS New River, NC	28540	Jacksonville
MCAS Iwakuni, Japan	FPO Seattle 98764	Iwakuni
MCAS Kaneohe Bay, Oahu, HI	FPO San Francisco 96615	Kailua
MCAS (Helo) Futenma, Okinawa FPO Seattle	98772	Futenma
MCAS Beaufort, SC	29904	Beaufort
MCAS Yuma, AZ	85364	Yuma
MCMWTC Bridgeport, CA	93517	Bridgeport
MCLB Albany, GA	31704	Albany
MCLB Barstow, CA	92311	Barstow

MCB = Marine Corps Base. MCDEC = Marine Corps Development & Education Command. MCAS = Marine Corps Air Station. Helo = Helicopter. MCAGCC = Marine Corps Air-Ground Combat Center. MCMWTC = Marine Corps Mountain Warfare Training Center. MCLB = Marine Corps Logistics Base.

Air Force*

Name	Zip	Nearest city
Chanute AFB, IL	61868	Rantoul
Columbus AFB, MS	39701	Columbus
Goodfellow AFB, TX	76903	San Angelo
Gunter AFS, AL**	36114	Montgomery
Keesler AFB, MS	39534	Biloxi
Lackland AFB, TX	78236	San Antonio
Laughlin AFB, TX	78843	Del Rio
Lowry AFB, CO	80230	Denver
Mather AFB, CA	95655	Sacramento
Maxwell AFB, AL**	36112	Montgomery
Randolph AFB, TX	78150	San Antonio
Reese AFB, TX	79489	Lubbock
Sheppard AFB, TX	76311	Wichita Falls
Vance AFB, OK	73702	Enid
Williams AFB, AZ	85224	Phoenix

*Air Training Command Bases. **Air University Bases.

Personal Salutes and Honors

The United States national salute, 21 guns, is also the salute to a national flag. The independence of the United States is commemorated by the salute to the union — one gun for each state — fired at noon on July 4 at all military posts provided with suitable artillery.

A-21-gun salute on arrival and departure, with 4 ruffles and flourishes, is rendered to the President of the United States, to an ex-President and to a President-elect. The national anthem or *Hail to the Chief,* as appropriate, is played for the President, and the national anthem for the others. A 21-gun salute on arrival and departure with 4 ruffles and flourishes, also is rendered to the sovereign or chief of state of a foreign country or a member of a reigning royal family; the national anthem of his or her country is played. The music is considered an inseparable part of the salute and will immediately follow the ruffles and flourishes without pause.

Rank	Salute—guns Arrive	Leave	Ruffles, flourishes	Music
Vice President of United States	19		4	Hail Columbia
Speaker of the House	19		4	March
American or foreign ambassador	19		4	Nat. anthem of official
Premier or prime minister	19		4	Nat. anthem of official
Secretary of Defense, Army, Navy or Air Force	19	19	4	March
Other Cabinet members, Senate President pro tempore, Governor, or Chief Justice of U.S.	19		4	March
Chairman, Joint Chiefs of Staff	19	19	4	
Army Chief of Staff, Chief of Naval Operations, Air Force Chief of Staff, Marine Commandant	19	19	4	General's or Admiral's March
General of the Army, General of the Air Force, Fleet Admiral	19	19	4	
Generals, Admirals	17	17	4	
Assistant Secretaries of Defense, Army, Navy or Air Force	17	17	4	March
Chairman of a Committee of Congress	17		4	March

Other salutes (on arrival only) include 15 guns for American envoys or ministers and foreign envoys or ministers accredited to the United States; 15 guns for a lieutenant general or vice admiral; 13 guns for a major general or rear admiral (upper half); 13 guns for American ministers resident and ministers resident accredited to the U.S.; 11 guns for a brigadier general or rear admiral (lower half); 11 guns for American charges d'affaires and like officials accredited to U.S.; and 11 guns for consuls general accredited to U.S.

Military Units, U.S. Army and Air Force

Army units. Squad. In infantry usually ten men under a staff sergeant. **Platoon.** In infantry 4 squads under a lieutenant. **Company.** Headquarters section and 4 platoons under a captain. (Company in the artillery is a battery; in the cavalry, a troop.) **Battalion.** Hdqts. and 4 or more companies under a lieutenant colonel. (Battalion size unit in the cavalry is a squadron.) **Brigade.** Hdqts. and 3 or more battalions under a colonel. **Division.** Hdqts. and 3 brigades with artillery, combat support, and combat service support units under a major general. **Army Corps.** Two or more divisions with corps troops under a lieutenant general. **Field Army.** Hdqts. and two or more corps with field Army troops under a general.

Air Force Units. Flight. Numerically designated flights are the lowest level unit in the Air Force. They are used primarily where there is a need for small mission elements to be incorporated into an organized unit. **Squadron.** A squadron is the basic unit in the Air Force. It is used to designate the mission units in operational commands. **Group.** The group is a flexible unit composed of two or more squadrons whose functions may be either tactical, support or administrative in nature. **Wing.** An operational wing normally has two or more assigned mission squadrons in an area such as combat, flying training or airlift. **Air Division.** The organization of the air division may be similar to that of the numbered air force, though on a much smaller scale. Functions are usually limited to operations and logistics. **Numbered Air Forces.** Normally an operationally oriented agency, the numbered air force is designed for the control of two or more air divisions or units of comparable strength. It is a flexible organization and may be of any size. Its wings may be assigned to air divisions or directly under the numbered air force. **Major Command.** A major subdivision of the Air Force that is assigned a major segment of the USAF mission.

U.S. Army Insignia and Chevrons

Source: Department of the Army

Grade | **Insignia**

General of the Armies

General John J. Pershing, the only person to have held this rank, was authorized to prescribe his own insignia, but never wore in excess of four stars. The rank originally was established by Congress for George Washington in 1799, and he was promoted to the rank by joint resolution of Congress, approved by Pres. Ford Oct. 19, 1976.

General of Army... Five silver stars fastened together in a circle and the coat of arms of the United States in gold color metal with shield and crest enameled.

General	Four silver stars
Lieutenant General	Three silver stars
Major General	Two silver stars
Brigadier General	One silver star
Colonel	Silver eagle
Lieutenant Colonel	Silver oak leaf
Major	Gold oak leaf
Captain	Two silver bars
First Lieutenant	One silver bar
Second Lieutenant	One gold bar

Warrant officers

Grade Four—Silver bar with 4 enamel black squares.
Grade Three—Silver bar with 3 enamel black squares.
Grade Two—Silver bar with 2 enamel black squares.
Grade One—Silver bar with 1 enamel black squares.

Non-commissioned Officers

Sergeant Major of the Army (E-9). Same as Command Sergeant Major (below) but with 2 stars. Also wears distinctive red and white shield on lapel.

Command Sergeant Major (E-9). Three chevrons above three arcs with a 5-pointed star with a wreath around the star between the chevrons and arcs.

Sergeant Major (E-9). Three chevrons above three arcs with a five-pointed star between the chevrons and arcs.

First Sergeant (E-8). Three chevrons above three arcs with a lozenge between the chevrons and arcs.

Master Sergeant (E-8). Three chevrons above three arcs.

Platoon Sergeant or Sergeant First Class (E-7). Three chevrons above two arcs.

Staff Sergeant (E-6). Three chevrons above one arc.

Sergeant (E-5). Three chevrons.

Corporal (E-4). Two chevrons.

Specialists

Specialist Six (E-6). Two arcs above the eagle device.
Specialist Five (E-5). One arc above the eagle device.
Specialist Four (E-4). Eagle device only.

Other enlisted

Private First Class (E-3). One chevron above one arc.
Private (E-2). One chevron.
Private (E-1). None.

U.S. Army

Source: Department of the Army

Army Military Personnel on Active Duty[1]

June 30[2]	Total strength	Commissioned officers			Warrant officers		Enlisted personnel		
		Total	Male	Female[3]	Male[4]	Female	Total	Male	Female
1940	267,767	17,563	16,624	939	763	—	249,441	249,441	—
1942	3,074,184	203,137	190,662	12,475	3,285	—	2,867,762	2,867,762	—
1943	6,993,102	557,657	521,435	36,222	21,919	0	6,413,526	6,358,200	55,325
1944	7,992,868	740,077	692,351	47,726	36,893	10	7,215,888	7,144,601	71,287
1945	8,266,373	835,403	772,511	62,892	56,216	44	7,374,710	7,283,930	90,780
1946	1,889,690	257,300	240,643	16,657	9,826	18	1,622,546	1,605,847	16,699
1950	591,487	67,784	63,375	4,409	4,760	22	518,921	512,370	6,551
1955	1,107,606	111,347	106,173	5,174	10,552	10	985,650	977,943	7,710
1960	871,348	91,056	86,832	4,224	10,141	39	770,112	761,833	8,279
1965	967,049	101,812	98,029	3,783	10,285	23	854,929	846,409	8,520
1969	1,509,637	148,836	143,699	5,137	23,734	20	1,327,047	1,316,326	10,721
1970	1,310,735	140,704	100,409	5,295	23,005	13	1,153,013	1,141,537	11,476
1975	781,316	89,756	85,184	4,572	13,214	22	678,324	640,621	37,703
1980 (Sept 30)	772,661	85,339	77,843	7,496	13,265	113	673,944	612,593	61,351
1982 (Sept. 30)	775,808	88,669	79,796	8,873	14,280	160	672,699	609,077	63,622
1983 (Sept. 30)	775,038	90,750	81,446	9,304	14,738	186	669,304	603,332	66,032
1984 (Sept. 30)	775,594	92,484	82,497	9,987	15,156	243	667,711	601,695	66,616
1985 (Sept. 30)	776,244	94,103	83,563	10,540	15,296	288	666,557	598,639	67,918
1987 (Mar. 30)	770,075	105,060	93,973	11,087	15,225	322	731,905	660,847	71,058

(1) Represents strength of the active Army, including Philippine Scouts, retired Regular Army personnel on extended active duty, and National Guard and Reserve personnel on extended active duty; excludes U.S. Military Academy cadets, contract surgeons, and National Guard and Reserve personnel not on extended active duty.
(2) Data for 1940 to 1947 include personnel in the Army Air Forces and its predecessors (Air Service and Air Corps).
(3) Includes: women doctors, dentists, and Medical Service Corps officers for 1946 and subsequent years, women in the Army Nurse Corps for all years, and the Women's Army Corps and Women's Medical Specialists Corps (dieticians, physical therapists, and occupational specialists) for 1943 and subsequent years.
(4) Act of Congress approved April 27, 1926, directed the appointment as warrant officers of field clerks still in active service. Includes flight officers as follows: 1943, 5,700; 1944, 13,615; 1945, 31,117; 1946, 2,580.

The Federal Service Academies

U.S. Military Academy, West Point, N.Y. Founded 1802. Awards B.S. degree and Army commission for a 5-year service obligation. For admissions information, write Admissions Office, USMA, West Point, NY 10996.

U.S. Naval Academy, Annapolis, Md. Founded 1845. Awards B.S. degree and Navy or Marine Corps commission for a 5-year service obligation. For admissions information, write Dean of Admissions, Naval Academy, Annapolis, MD 21402.

U.S. Air Force Academy, Colorado Springs, Colo. Founded 1954. Awards B.S. degree and Air Force commission for a 5-year service obligation. For admissions information, write Registrar, U.S. Air Force Academy, CO 80840.

U.S. Coast Guard Academy, New London, Conn. Founded 1876. Awards B.S. degree and Coast Guard commission for a 5-year service obligation. For admissions information, write Director of Admissions, Coast Guard Academy, New London, CT 06320.

U.S. Merchant Marine Academy, Kings Point, N.Y. Founded 1943. Awards B.S. degree, a license as a deck, engineer, or dual officer, and a U.S. Naval Reserve commission. Service obligations vary according to options taken by the graduate. For admissions information, write Admission Office, U.S. Merchant Marine Academy, Kings Point, NY 11024.

U.S. Navy Insignia

Source: Department of the Navy

Navy

Stripes and corps device are of gold embroidery.

	Stripes
Fleet Admiral	1 two inch with 4 one-half inch.
Admiral	1 two inch with 3 one-half inch.
Vice Admiral.	1 two inch with 2 one-half inch.
Rear Admiral (upper half)	1 two inch with 1 one-half inch.
Rear Admiral (lower half)	1 two inch.
Captain.	4 one-half inch.
Commander	3 one-half inch.
Lieut. Commander	2 one-half inch, with 1 one-quarter inch between.
Lieutenant	2 one-half inch.
Lieutenant (j.g.)	1 one-half inch with one-quarter inch above.
Ensign	1 one-half inch.

Warrant Officers—One 1/2" broken with 1/2" intervals of blue as follows:

Warrant Officer W-4—1 break

Warrant Officer W-3—2 breaks, 2" apart

Warrant Officer W-2—3 breaks, 2" apart

The breaks are symmetrically centered on outer face of the sleeve.

Enlisted personnel (non-Commissioned petty officers). . .A rating badge worn on the upper left arm, consisting of a spread eagle, appropriate number of chevrons, and centered specialty mark.

Marine Corps

Marine Corps and Army officer insignia are similar. Marine Corps and Army enlisted insignia, although basically similar, differ in color, design, and fewer Marine Corps subdivisions. The Marine Corps' distinctive cap and collar ornament is a combination of the American eagle, globe, and anchor.

Coast Guard

Coast Guard insignia follow Navy custom, with certain minor changes such as the officer cap insignia. The Coast Guard shield is worn on both sleeves of officers and on the right sleeve of all enlisted personnel.

U.S. Navy Personnel on Active Duty

June 30	Officers[1]	Nurses	Enlisted[2]	Off. Cand.	Total
1940	13,162	442	144,824	2,569	160,997
1945	320,293	11,086	2,988,207	61,231	3,380,817
1950	42,687	1,964	331,860	5,037	381,538
1960	67,456	2,103	544,040	4,385	617,984
1970	78,488	2,273	605,899	6,000	692,660
1980	63,100	—	464,100	—	527,200
1985 (Jan.)	70,291	—	500,810	—	571,101
1986 (Jan.)	70,258	3,012	494,412	5,928	570,598
1987 (Jan.)	73,530	—	522,639	5,765	601,934

(1) Nurses are included after 1973. (2) Officer candidates are included after 1973.

Marine Corps Personnel On Active Duty

Yr.	Officers	Enl.	Total	Yr.	Officers	Enl.	Total	Yr.	Officers	Enl.	Total
1955	18,417	186,753	205,170	1970	24,941	234,796	259,737	1985	20,175	177,850	198,025
1960	16,203	154,418	170,621	1980	18,198	170,271	188,469	1986	21,099	178,615	199,714
1965	17,258	172,955	190,213	1984	20,000	174,000	197,000				

Armed Services Senior Enlisted Adviser

The U.S. Army, Navy and Air Force in 1966-67 each created a new position of senior enlisted adviser whose primary job is to represent the point of view of his services' enlisted men and women on matters of welfare, morale, and any problems concerning enlisted personnel. The senior adviser will have direct access to the military chief of his branch of service and policy-making bodies.

The senior enlisted adviser for each Dept. is:

Army—Sgt. Major of the Army Julius W. Gates.

Navy—Master Chief Petty Officer of the Navy William H. Plackett.

Air Force—Chief Master Sgt. of the AF James C. Binnicker.

Marines—Sgt. Major of the Marine Corps David W. Sommers.

Veteran Population

Source: Veterans Administration

	March 1987
Veterans in civil life, end of month — Total	**27,567,000**
War Veterans — Total	**21,835,000**
Vietnam Era — Total	8,269,000
And service in Korean Conflict	624,000
No service in Korean Conflict	7,645,000
Korean Conflict — Total	5,071,000
And service in WW II.	958,000
No service in WW II	4,112,000
World War II	9,923,000
World War I	154,000
Spanish-American War	6
Peacetime Veterans — Total	5,732,000
Post-Vietnam Era	2,366,000
Peacetime service between Korean Conflict and Vietnam Era only	2,996,000
Peactime Service — other	370,000

Compensation and Pension Case Payments

Fiscal year	Living veteran cases No.	Deceased veteran cases No.	Total cases No.	Total disbursement Dollars	Fiscal year	Living veteran cases No.	Deceased veteran cases No.	Total cases No.	Total disbursement Dollars
1900	752,510	241,019	993,529	138,462,130	1950	2,368,238	658,123	3,026,361	2,009,462,298
1910	602,622	318,461	921,083	159,974,056	1960	3,008,935	950,802	3,959,737	3,314,761,383
1920	419,627	349,916	769,543	316,418,029	1970	3,127,338	1,487,176	4,614,514	5,113,649,490
1930	542,610	298,223	840,833	418,432,808	1980	3,195,395	1,450,785	4,646,180	11,045,412,000
1940	610,122	239,176	849,298	429,138,465	1986	2,883,395	1,016,386	3,899,781	14,264,164,924

USAF and Air Reserve Forces Personnel by Categories

Category	FY '83[2]	FY '84[2]	FY '85[2]	FY '86[2]	FY '87[2]	FY '88
Air Force Military						
Officers	104,600	106,200	108,400	109,400	109,400	109,000
Airmen	483,000	486,400	488,600	494,700	493,000	484,400
Cadets	4,500	4,500	4,500	4,500	4,400	4,400
Total, Air Force Military	**592,100**	**597,100**	**601,500**	**608,200**	**606,800**	**597,800**
Career Reenlistments	43,500	38,000	36,000	38,900	43,000	37,000
Rate	92%	90%	89%	88%	88%	88%
First-Term Reenlistments	31,100	24,700	25,700	23,500	22,100	21,700
Rate	66%	62%	54%	58%	58%	58%
Civilian Personnel						
Direct Hire (including Technicians)	230,000	239,800	250,400	249,604	250,266	251,674
Indirect Hire—Foreign Nationals	13,000	13,000	13,468	13,644	13,496	13,443
Total, Civilian Personnel	**243,000**	**252,800**	**263,868**	**263,248**	**263,762**	**265,117**
Total, Military and Civilian[1]	**835,100**	**849,900**	**865,368**	**871,448**	**870,562**	**862,917**
Technicians (including above as Direct Hire Civilians)						
AFRES Technicians	7,984	7,634	8,064	8,866	9,178	9,830
ANG Technicians	21,949	22,160	22,671	22,497	23,221	23,252
Air Reserve Forces						
Air National Guard, Selected Reserve	102,200	104,104	109,398	112,592	113,767	116,700
Air Force Reserve, Paid	67,227	70,318	75,214	78,519	79,562	83,300
Air Force Reserve, Nonpaid	42,864	40,000	42,371	47,153	49,941	48,291
Total, Ready Reserve	**212,291**	**214,422**	**226,983**	**238,264**	**243,270**	**248,291**
Standby	28,939	29,121	28,321	25,823	28,325	28,325
Total, Air Reserve Forces[3]	**241,230**	**243,543**	**255,304**	**264,087**	**271,595**	**276,616**

Note: Totals may not add due to rounding. (1) President's budget request. (2) FY '83-86 are actual figures; FY '87-88 are estimates; excludes nonchargeable personnel. (3) Excludes Retired Air Force Reserve.

U.S. Air Force Personnel Strength: 1907–1988

Year[2]	Strength	Year	Strength	Year	Strength	Year	Strength
1907	3	1941	152,125	1945	2,282,259	1980	557,969
1918	195,023	1942	764,415	1950	411,277	1986	608,199
1920	9,050	1943	2,197,114	1960	814,213	1987	606,850[1]
1930	13,531	1944	2,372,292	1970	791,078	1988	597,753[1]
1940	51,165						

(1) Programmed. (2) Prior to 1947, data are for U.S. Army Air Corps and Air Service of the Signal Corps.

Women in the Armed Forces

Women in the Army, Navy, Air Force, Marines, and Coast Guard are all fully integrated with male personnel. Expansion of military women's programs began in the Department of Defense in fiscal year 1973.

Although women are prohibited by law and directives based on law from serving in combat positions, policy changes in the Department of Defense have made possible the assignment of women to almost all other career fields. Career progression for women is now comparable to that for male personnel. Women are routinely assigned to overseas locations formerly closed to female personnel. Women are in command of activities and units that have missions other than administration of women.

Admission of women to the service academies began in the fall of 1976. The academies provide single-track education, allowing only for minor variations in the cadet program based on physiological differences between men and women.

Army — Information: Chief, Office of Public Affairs, Dept. of Army, Wash., DC 20310; (as of Dec. 1986): 82,824 women, 71,354 enlisted women, 11,106 women commissioned officers, 364 women warrant officers.

Army Nurse Corps — Brig. Gen. Connie L. Slewitzke, Chief Army Nurse Corps, Office of the Surgeon General, Dept. of Army, 5111 Leesburg Pike, Falls Church, VA 22041.

Navy — Information: Chief of Information, Dept. of Navy, Wash., DC 20350-1200; 7,342 women officers; 47,369 enlisted women; officer candidates, 449.

Navy Nurse Corps — Rear Adm. Mary J. Nielubowicz, Dir., Navy Nurse Corps, Dept. of Navy, Wash., DC 20372-2000; 2,282 women officers; 776 men. (As of 2/28/87).

Air Force — Information: Office of Public Affairs, Dept. of the Air Force, Wash., DC 20330; 12,377 women officers; 60,694 enlisted women.

Air Force Nurse Corps — Brig. Gen. Carmelita Schimmenti, Chief, Air Force Nurse Corps, Office of the Surgeon Gen., USAF, Bolling AFB, Wash., DC 20332.

Marine Corps — Information: Commandant of the Marine Corps (Code PA), Headquarters, Marine Corps, Wash., DC 20380-0001; 654 women officers; 9,041 enlisted women.

Coast Guard — Information: Commandant (G-BPA), U.S. Coast Guard, 2100 Second St., SW, Wash., DC 20593; 130 women commissioned officers; 3 woman warrant officer; 2,304 enlisted women.

Generals of the U.S. Army

Ulysses S. Grant	Jul. 1866-Mar. 1869
William T. Sherman	May 1869-Feb. 1884
Philip H. Sheridan	Jun. 1888-Aug. 1888
George C. Marshall	Dec. 1944-Feb. 1947
Douglas MacArthur	Dec. 1944-Apr. 1964
Dwight D. Eisenhower	Dec. 1944-Jul. 1952 Mar. 1961-Mar. 1969
Henry H. Arnold	Dec. 1944-Jun. 1946
Omar N. Bradley	Sept. 1950-1981

General of the Armies

John J. Pershing Sept. 1919-Sept. 1924

Monthly Pay Scale of

Effective

Commissioned Officers

Pay grade	Army rank	Navy rank	Under 2	2	3	4	6	8
	Rank or pay grade		Cumulative years of service					
0-10[1]	General*	Admiral	$5,378.10	$5,567.70	$5,567.70	$5,567.70	$5,567.70	$5,781.00
0-9	Lieutenant General	Vice Admiral	4,766.70	4,891.50	4,995.60	4,995.60	4,995.60	5,122.50
0-8	Major General	Rear Admiral	4,317.30	4,446.60	4,552.20	4,552.20	4,552.20	4,891.50
0-7	Brigadier General	Commodore	3,587.40	3,831.30	3,831.30	3,831.30	4,002.90	4,002.90
0-6	Colonel	Captain	2,658.90	2,921.40	3,112.50	3,112.50	3,112.50	3,112.50
0-5	Lieutenant Colonel	Commander	2,126.40	2,497.20	2,669.70	2,669.70	2,669.70	2,669.70
0-4	Major	Lieutenant Comdr.	1,792.50	2,182.80	2,328.30	2,328.30	2,371.50	2,476.20
0-3	Captain	Lieutenant	1,665.90	1,862.40	1,990.80	2,202.90	2,308.20	2,391.30
0-2	First Lieutenant	Lieutenant (J.G.)	1,452.60	1,586.40	1,905.60	1,969.80	2,011.20	2,011.20
0-1	Second Lieutenant	Ensign	1,260.90	1,312.80	1,586.40	1,586.40	1,586.40	1,586.40
Commissioned officers with over 4 years active duty as an enlisted member or warrant officer								
0-3E	Captain	Lieutenant	0.00	0.00	0.00	2,202.90	2,308.20	2,391.30
0-2E	First Lieutenant	Lieutenant (J.G.)	0.00	0.00	0.00	1,969.80	2,011.20	2,074.80
0-1E	Second Lieutenant	Ensign	0.00	0.00	0.00	1,586.40	1,694.70	1,755.10

Warrant Officers

Pay grade	Army rank	Navy rank	Under 2	2	3	4	6	8
W-4	Chief Warrant	Comm. Warrant	1,697.10	1,820.70	1,820.70	1,862.40	1,947.00	2.032.80
W-3	Chief Warrant	Comm. Warrant	1,542.30	1,673.10	1,673.10	1,694.70	1,714.50	1,839.90
W-2	Chief Warrant	Comm. Warrant	1,350.90	1,461.60	1,461.60	1,504.20	1,586.40	1,673.10
W-1	Warrant Officer	Warrant Officer	1,125.60	1,290.60	1,290.60	1,398.30	1,461.60	1,524.30

Enlisted Personnel[2]

Pay grade	Army rank	Navy rank	Under 2	2	3	4	6	8
E-9[3]	Sergeant Major**	Master C.P.O.	0.00	0.00	0.00	0.00	0.00	0.00
E-8[3]	Master Sergeant	Senior C.P.O.	0.00	0.00	0.00	0.00	0.00	1,655.70
E-7	Sgt. 1st Class	Chief Petty Officer	1,155.90	1,247.70	1,294.20	1,339.20	1,385.10	1,429.20
E-6	Staff Sergeant	Petty Officer 1st Class	994.50	1,083.90	1,129.20	1,117.20	1,221.00	1,265.40
E-5	Sergeant	Petty Officer 2nd Cl.	872.70	950.10	996.00	1,039.50	1,107.60	1,152.60
E-4	Corporal	Petty Officer 3rd Cl.	814.20	859.50	909.90	980.70	1,019.40	1,019.40
E-3	Private 1st Class	Seaman	766.80	808.80	841.50	874.80	874.80	874.80
E-2	Private	Seaman Apprentice	738.00	738.00	738.00	738.00	738.00	738.00
E-1 > 4	Private	Seaman Recruit	658.20	658.20	658.20	658.20	658.20	658.20
E-1 < 4			608.40	608.40	608.40	608.40	608.40	608.40

The pay scale also applies to: Coast Guard and Marine Corps, National Oceanic and Atmospheric Administration, Public Health Service, National Guard, and the organized reserves.

*Basic pay is limited to $5,900 by Level V of the Executive Schedule and further limited by Sec. 101C, P.L. 96-86 to $4,176.00 max. Four star General or Admiral—personal money allowances of $2,200 per annum, or $4,000 if Chief of Staff of the Army, Chief of Staff of the Air Force, Chief of Naval Operations, Commandant of the Marine Corps, or Commandant of the Coast Guard. Three star General or Admiral—personal money allowance of $500 per annum.

**A title of Chief Master Sergeant rates E-9 classification.

(1) While serving as Chairman of Joint Chiefs of Staff, Chief of Staff of the Army, Chief of Naval Operations, Chief of Staff of the Air Forces, or Commandant of the Marine Corps, basic pay for this grade is $6,988.50 regardless of years of service.

(2) Air Force enlisted personnel pay grades, E-9, Chief Master Sergeant; E-8, Sr. Master Sergeant; E-7, Master Sergeant; E-6, Technical Sergeant; E-5, Staff Sergeant; E-4, Sergeant; E-3, Airman 1st Class; E-2, Airman; E-1, Basic Airman.

Marine Corps enlisted ranks are as follows: E-9, Sergeant Major and Master Gunnery Sergeant; E-8, First Sergeant and Master Sergeant: E-7, Gunnery Sergeant; E-6, Staff Sergeant; E-5, Sergeant; E-4, Corporal; E-3, Lance Corporal; E-2, Private, First Class Marine; E-1, Private.

Marine Corps and Air Force officer ranks are same as Army.

(3) While serving as Sergeant Major of the Army, Master Chief Petty Officer of the Navy, Chief Master Sergeant of the Air Force, or Sergeant Major of the Marine Corps, basic pay for this grade is $2,692.50 regardless of years of service.

U.S. Military Personnel Strengths—Worldwide[1]

(As of Dec. 12, 1986)

Source: U.S. Department of Defense

U.S. Territory & Special Locations	**1,677,787**	Japan	49,218	**Antarctica**	**115**
Continental U.S.	1,328,956	Rep. of Korea	43,004	**Eastern Europe**	**202**
Hawaii	47,256	Philippines	15,632	USSR	53
Guam	8,850	Afloat	21,566	**Total foreign countries**	**500,058**
Afloat	187,361	**Africa, Near East & South Asia**	**7,632**	Ashore[3]	450,408
Western & Southern Europe	**344,799**	Egypt	1,365	Afloat	49,650
W. Germany[2]	246,852	British Indian Ocean Terr.	1,232		
United Kingdom[2]	29,458	Saudi Arabia	442	**Total Worldwide**	**2,177,845**
Italy[2]	15,082	Afloat	3,688	Ashore[3]	1,940,834
Spain[2]	9,136	**Western Hemisphere**	**16,646**	Afloat	237,011
Afloat	23,892	Panama	10,046		
East Asia & Pacific	**130,500**	Cuba (Guantanamo)	2,244		
		Afloat	504		

(1) Totals and selected nations. (2) European NATO. (3) Includes temporarily shore-based.

the Uniformed Services
January 1987

Commissioned Officers

Cumulative years of service 10	12	14	16	18	20	22	26	Monthly basic allowances for quarters rates: Without dependents, Full Rate	Without dependents, Partial Rate	With Dependents
$5,781.00	$6,223.50	$6,223.50	$6,668.70	$6,668.70	$7,115.10	$7,115.10	$7,558.50	$570.00	$50.70	$701.10
5,122.50	5,335.80	5,335.80	5,781.00	5,781.00	6,223.50	6,223.50	6,668.70	570.00	50.70	701.10
4,891.50	5,122.50	5,122.50	5,335.80	5,567.70	5,781.00	6,012.90	6,012.90	570.00	50.70	701.10
4,235.10	4,235.10	4,446.60	4,891.50	5,227.80	5,227.80	5,227.80	5,227.80	570.00	50.70	701.10
3,112.50	3,112.50	3,218.10	3,727.20	3,917.70	4,002.90	4,235.10	4,593.30	523.20	39.60	636.00
2,750.70	2,898.30	3,092.70	3,324.00	3,514.80	3,621.30	3,747.60	3,747.60	493.80	33.00	585.90
2,645.10	2,793.90	2,921.40	3,049.50	3,133.80	3,133.80	3,133.80	3,133.80	452.70	26.70	535.50
2,520.60	2,645.10	2,710.20	2,710.20	2,710.20	2,710.20	2,710.20	2,710.20	366.60	22.20	446.40
2,011.20	2,011.20	2,011.20	2,011.20	2,011.20	2,011.20	2,011.20	2,011.20	295.20	17.70	382.80
1,586.40	1,586.40	1,586.40	1,586.40	1,586.40	1,586.40	1,586.40	1,586.40	253.20	13.20	343.20
2,520.60	2,645.10	2,750.70	2,750.70	2,750.70	2,750.70	2,750.70	2,750.70			
2,182.80	2,266.20	2,328.30	2,328.30	2,328.30	2,328.30	2,328.30	2,328.30			
1,820.70	1,884.00	1,969.80	1,969.80	1,969.80	1,969.80	1,969.80	1,969.80			

Warrant Officers

2,118.30	2,266.20	2,371.50	2,454.60	2,520.60	2,601.90	2,688.90	2,898.30	414.90	25.20	481.50
1,947.00	2,011.20	2,074.80	2,136.60	2,202.90	2,288.40	2,371.50	2,454.60	350.40	20.70	430.80
1,736.70	1,800.30	1,862.40	1,927.50	1,990.80	2,053.80	2,136.60	2,136.60	315.30	15.90	402.60
1,586.40	1,652.10	1,714.50	1,778.10	1,839.90	1,905.60	1,905.60	1,905.60	266.70	13.80	351.00

Enlisted Personnel

1,974.00	2,018.70	2,064.30	2,111.70	2,158.80	2,200.80	2,316.60	2,541.90	334.50	18.60	456.00
1,702.80	1,747.50	1,793.10	1,840.20	1,882.80	1,929.00	2,042.40	2,270.10	309.90	15.30	424.80
1,474.80	1,520.70	1,589.40	1,634.70	1,680.30	1,702.20	1,816.50	2,042.40	264.60	12.00	395.10
1,311.90	1,379.40	1,422.60	1,468.50	1,491.00	1,491.00	1,491.00	1,491.00	234.90	9.90	358.50
1,198.50	1,242.60	1,265.40	1,265.40	1,265.40	1,265.40	1,265.40	1,265.40	217.20	8.70	318.60
1,019.40	1,019.40	1,019.40	1,019.40	1,019.40	1,019.40	1,019.40	1,019.40	188.40	8.10	275.40
874.80	874.80	874.80	874.80	874.80	874.80	874.80	874.80	183.00	7.80	253.20
738.00	738.00	738.00	738.00	738.00	738.00	738.00	738.00	155.40	7.20	253.20
658.20	658.20	658.20	658.20	658.20	658.20	658.20	658.20	141.60	6.90	253.20
608.40	608.40	608.40	608.40	608.40	608.40	608.40	608.40			

Basic Allowance for Subsistence

This allowance, the quarters allowance, and any other allowance are not subject to income tax.

Officers — Subsistence (food) is paid to all officers regardless of rank $112.65/month

Enlisted members: When on leave or authorized to mess separately $5.37/day

When rations in kind are not available. $6.07/day

When assigned to duty under emergency conditions where no government messing facilities are available $8.03/day

Family Separation Allowance

Under certain conditions of family separation of more than 30 days, a member in Pay Grades E-4 (with over 4 years' service) and above will be allowed $30 a month in addition to any other allowances to which he is entitled. When separated from family and required to maintain a home for his family and one for himself, the member is entitled to an additional monthly basic allowance for quarters at the "without dependents" rate for his grade.

The Medal of Honor

The Medal of Honor is the highest military award for bravery that can be given to any individual in the United States. The first Army Medals were awarded on March 25, 1863, and the first Navy Medals went to sailors and Marines on April 3, 1863.

The Medal of Honor, established by Joint Resolution of Congress, 12 July 1862 (amended by Act of 9 July 1918 and Act of 25 July 1963) is awarded in the name of Congress to a person who, while a member of the Armed Forces, distinguishes himself conspicuously by gallantry and intrepidity at the risk of his life above and beyond the call of duty while engaged in an action against any enemy of the United States; while engaged in military operations involving conflict with an opposing foreign force; or while serving with friendly foreign forces engaged in an armed conflict against an opposing armed force in which the United States is not a belligerent party. The deed performed must have been one of personal bravery or self-sacrifice so conspicuous as to clearly distinguish the individual above his comrades and must have involved risk of life. Incontestable proof of the performance of service is exacted and each recommendation for award of this decoration is considered on the standard of extraordinary merit.

Prior to World War I, the 2,625 Army Medal of Honor awards up to that time were reviewed to determine which past awards met new stringent criteria. The Army removed 911 names from the list, most of them former members of a volunteer infantry group during the Civil War who had been induced to extend their enlistments when they were promised the Medal.

Since that review Medals of Honor have been awarded in the following numbers:

World War I . . . . . . 123 Korean War 131
World War II . . . . . . 433 Vietnam (to date) 239

Casualties in Principal Wars of the U.S.

Data on Revolutionary War casualties is from **The Toll of Independence,** Howard H. Peckham, ed., U. of Chicago Press, 1974.

Data prior to World War I are based on incomplete records in many cases. Casualty data are confined to dead and wounded personnel and therefore exclude personnel captured or missing in action who were subsequently returned to military control. Dash (—) indicates information is not available.

			Casualties			
Wars	Branch of service	Number serving	Battle deaths	Other deaths	Wounds not mortal[8]	Total
Revolutionary War	**Total**	**—**	**6,824**	**18,500**	**8,445**	**33,769**
1775-1783	Army	184,000	5,992	—	7,988	13,980
	Navy &	to	—	—	—	—
	Marines	250,000	832	—	457	1,289
War of 1812	**Total**	**[9]286,730**	**2,260**	**—**	**4,505**	**6,765**
1812-1815	Army	—	1,950	—	4,000	5,950
	Navy	—	265	—	439	704
	Marines	—	45	—	66	111
Mexican War	**Total**	**[9]78,718**	**1,733**	**11,550**	**4,152**	**17,435**
1846-1848	Army	—	1,721	11,500	4,102	17,373
	Navy	—	1	—	3	4
	Marines	—	11	—	47	58
Civil War	**Total**	**[9]2,213,363**	**140,414**	**224,097**	**281,881**	**646,392**
(Union forces only)	Army	2,128,948	138,154	221,374	280,040	639,568
1861-1865	Navy	—	2,112	2,411	1,710	6,233
	Marines	84,415	148	312	131	591
Confederate forces	**Total**	**—**	**74,524**	**59,297**	**—**	**133,821**
(estimate)[1]	Army	600,000	—	—	—	—
1863-1866	Navy	to	—	—	—	—
	Marines	1,500,000	—	—	—	—
Spanish-American War	**Total**	**306,760**	**385**	**2,061**	**1,662**	**4,108**
1898	Army[4]	280,564	369	2,061	1,594	4,024
	Navy	22,875	10	0	47	57
	Marines	3,321	6	0	21	27
World War I	**Total**	**4,743,826**	**53,513**	**63,195**	**204,002**	**320,710**
April 6, 1917-	Army[5]	4,057,101	50,510	55,868	193,663	300,041
Nov. 11, 1918	Navy	599,051	431	6,856	819	8,106
	Marines	78,839	2,461	390	9,520	12,371
	Coast Gd.	8,835	111	81	—	192
World War II	**Total**	**16,353,659**	**292,131**	**115,185**	**670,846**	**1,078,162**
Dec. 7, 1941-	Army[6]	11,260,000	234,874	83,400	565,861	884,135
Dec. 31, 1946[2]	Navy[7]	4,183,466	36,950	25,664	37,778	100,392
	Marines	669,100	19,733	4,778	67,207	91,718
	Coast Gd.	241,093	574	1,343	—	1,917
Korean War	**Total**	**5,764,143**	**33,629**	**20,617**	**103,284**	**157,530**
June 25, 1950-	Army	2,834,000	27,704	9,429	77,596	114,729
July 27, 1953[3]	Navy	1,177,000	458	4,043	1,576	6,077
	Marines	424,000	4,267	1,261	23,744	29,272
	Air Force	1,285,000	1,200	5,884	368	7,452
	Coast Gd.	44,143	—	—	—	—
Vietnam (preliminary)[10]	**Total**	**8,744,000**	**47,321**	**10,700**	**153,303**	**211,324**
Aug. 4, 1964-	Army	4,368,000	30,899	7,271	96,802	134,972
Jan. 27, 1973	Navy	1,842,000	1,606	913	4,178	6,697
	Marines	794,000	13,073	1,748	51,392	66,213
	Air Force	1,740,000	1,738	766	931	3,435
	Coast Gd.	—	5	2	—	7

(1) Authoritative statistics for the Confederate Forces are not available. An estimated 26,000-31,000 Confederate personnel died in Union prisons.

(2) Data are for the period Dec. 1, 1941 through Dec. 31, 1946 when hostilities were officially terminated by Presidential Proclamation, but few battle deaths or wounds not mortal were incurred after the Japanese acceptance of Allied peace terms on Aug. 14, 1945. Numbers serving from Dec. 1, 1941-Aug. 31, 1945 were: Total—14,903,213; Army—10,420,000; Navy—3,883,520; and Marine Corps—599,693.

(3) Tentative final data based upon information available as of Sept. 30, 1954, at which time 24 persons were still carried as missing in action.

(4) Number serving covers the period April 21-Aug. 13, 1898, while dead and wounded data are for the period May 1-Aug. 31, 1898. Active hostilities ceased on Aug. 13, 1898, but ratifications of the treaty of peace were not exchanged between the United States and Spain until April 11, 1899.

(5) Includes Air Service Battle deaths and wounds not mortal include casualties suffered by American forces in Northern Russia to Aug. 25, 1919 and in Siberia to April 1, 1920. Other deaths covered the period April 1, 1917-Dec. 31, 1918.

(6) Includes Army Air Forces.

(7) Battle deaths and wounds not mortal include casualties incurred in Oct. 1941 due to hostile action.

(8) Marine Corps data for World War II, the Spanish-American War and prior wars represent the number of individuals wounded, whereas all other data in this column represent the total number (incidence) of wounds.

(9) As reported by the Commissioner of Pensions in his Annual Report for Fiscal Year 1903.

(10) Number serving covers the period Aug. 4 1964-Jan. 27, 1973 (date of ceasefire). Number of casualties incurred in connection with the conflict in Vietnam from Jan. 1, 1961-Sept. 30, 1977. Includes casualties incurred in Mayaguez Incident. Wounds not mortal exclude 150,375 persons not requiring hospital care.

Nuclear Arms Treaties and Negotiations: An Historical Overview

Aug. 4, 1963—Nuclear Test Ban Treaty, signed in Moscow by the U.S., USSR, and Great Britain, prohibited testing of nuclear weapons in space, above ground, and under water.

1966—Outer Space Treaty banned the introduction of nuclear weapons into space.

1968—Non-proliferation of Nuclear Weapons Treaty, with U.S., USSR, and Great Britain as major signers, limited the spread of military nuclear technology by agreement not to assist nonnuclear nations in getting or making nuclear weapons.

May 26, 1972—SALT I (Strategic Arms Limitations Talks) agreement, in negotiation since Nov. 17, 1969, signed in Moscow by U.S. and USSR. In the area of defensive nuclear weapons, the treaty limited antiballistic missiles to 2 sites of 100 antiballistic missile launchers in each country (amended in 1974 to one site in each country). The treaty also imposed a 5-year freeze on testing and deployment of intercontinental ballistic missiles and submarine-launched ballistic missiles (U.S.: 1,054 ICBMs and 656 SLBMs; USSR: 1,400 ICBMs and 950 SLBMs). An interim short-term agreement putting a ceiling on numbers of offensive nuclear weapons was also signed. SALT I was in effect until Oct. 3, 1977.

July 3, 1974—Protocol on antiballistic missile systems and a treaty and protocol on limiting underground testing of nuclear weapons was signed by U.S. and USSR in Moscow.

Nov. 24, 1974—Vladivostok Agreement announced establishing the framework for a more comprehensive agreement on offensive nuclear arms, setting the guidelines of a second SALT treaty.

Sept. 1977—U.S. and USSR agreed to continue to abide by SALT I, despite its expiration date.

June 18, 1979—SALT II, signed in Vienna by the U.S. and USSR, constrained offensive nuclear weapons, limiting each side to 2,400 missile launchers and heavy bombers with that ceiling to apply until Jan. 1, 1985. The treaty also set a combined total of 1,320 ICBMs and SLBMs with multiple warheads on each side. Although approved by the U.S. Senate Foreign Relations Committee, the treaty never reached the Senate floor because Pres. Jimmy Carter withdrew his support for the treaty following the December 1979 invasion of Afghanistan by Soviet troops.

Nov. 18, 1981—U.S. Pres. Ronald Reagan proposed his controversial "zero option" to cancel deployment of new U.S. intermediate-range missiles in Western Europe in return for Soviet dismantling of comparable forces (600 SS-20, SS-4, and SS-5 missiles already stationed in the European part of its territory).

Nov. 30, 1981—Geneva talks on limiting intermediate nuclear forces based in and around Europe began.

May 9, 1982—U.S. Pres. Ronald Reagan proposed 2-step plan for strategic arms reductions and announced that he had proposed to the USSR that START (Strategic Arms Reduction Talks) begin in June.

May 18, 1982—Soviet Pres. Leonid Brezhnev rejected Reagan's plan as one-sided, but responded positively to the call for arms reduction talks.

June 29, 1982—START (Strategic Arms Reduction Talks) began in Geneva.

1985-1987—Disarmament talks between the U.S. and the USSR began in Geneva, Switzerland on March 12, 1985.

(For details and events after Aug. 15, 1987, see Index and Chronology.)

Estimates of Total Dollar Costs of American Wars

(In millions of dollars, except percent)

Source: *The Military Budget and National Economic Priorities,* revised and updated by James L. Clayton, Univ. of Utah.

Item	World War II	Vietnam Conflict	Korean Conflict	World War I	Civil War: Union	Civil War: Confederacy	Spanish American War	American Revolution	War of 1812	Mexican War
Original increment, direct costs:[1]										
Current dollars	360,000	140,600	50,000	32,700	[illegible],000	1,000	270	100-140	87	82
Constant (1967) dollars	816,300	148,800	69,300	100,000	8,500	3,700	1,100	400-680	170	300
Percent 1 year's GNP	188	14	15	43	74	123	2	104	14	4
Service-connected veterans' benefits[2]	69,034	15,497	12,447	14,098	3,289	—	2,111	28	20	26
Interest, pmts. on war loans[3]	220,000	(5)	(5)	11,000	1,200	(5)	60	20	14	10
Current cost to 1983[4]	649,600	156,100	62,400	57,800	6,800	(5)	2,441	170	120	120

(1) Figures are rounded and taken from Claudia D. Goldin, *Encyclopedia of American Economic History.* (2) Total cost to Oct. 1, 1982. For World War I and later wars, benefits are actual service-connected figures from 1981 *Annual Report* of Veterans Administration. For earlier wars, service-connected veterans' benefits are estimated at 40 percent of total, the approximate ratio of service-connected to total benefits since World War I. (3) Total cost to 1983. Interest payments are a very rough approximation based on the percentage of the original costs of each war financed by money creation and debt, the difference between the level of public debt at the beginning of the war and at its end, and the approximate time required to pay off the war debts. (4) Figures are rounded estimates. (5) Unknown.

Armed Forces Personnel—Number and Rate, 1986

Source: U.S. Arms Control and Disarmament Agency
(Number (1,000), Rate per 1,000 population)

Armed forces refer to active-duty military personnel, including paramilitary forces where those forces resemble regular units in their organization, equipment, training or mission. Reserve forces are not included.

	Number	Rate		Number	Rate		Number	Rate
United States	2,224	9.5	Germany, Fed. Rep.	487	8.0	Nigeria	144	1.4
Argentina	174	5.8	Greece	197	19.9	Pakistan	646	6.7
Brazil	459	3.4	India	1,380	1.8	Poland	430	11.6
Bulgaria	177	19.8	Indonesia	281	1.7	Romania	244	10.8
Chile	123	10.4	Iran	335	7.6	Soviet Union	4,500	16.4
China	4,100	4.0	Iraq	788	52.5	Spain	411	10.7
Cuba	297	29.7	Israel	205	50.6	Syria	402	39.6
Czechoslovakia	213	13.8	Italy	508	8.9	Taiwan	470	24.7
Egypt	466	9.8	Japan	241	2.0	Thailand	250	4.9
El Salvador	45	9.2	Korea, Dem. People's Rep. of	784	39.9	Turkey	815	16.5
France	571	10.4	Korea, Rep. of	602	14.3	United Kingdom	336	6.0
German Dem. Rep.	240	14.4	Nicaragua	67	21.4	Vietnam	1,000	16.9

Nuclear Weapon Tests

Source: Natural Resources Defense Council

(Known nuclear tests, 1945-1985)

	United States	Soviet Union	Britain	France	China
1945-49	8	1	0	0	0
1950-59[1]	188	89	21	0	0
1960-69[2]	344	168	4	30	10
1970-79[3]	162	198	5	57	15
1980-85	97	135	9	54	5
Total	799	604	39	141	30

(1) Stockholm International Peace Research Institute and the Swedith National Defense Research Institute report 18 additional Soviet tests conducted between 1956 and 1958. (2) Since 1962, British underground nuclear tests have been conducted jointly with the United States in Nevada. (3) French Ministry of Defense reports 16 additional Soviet tests conducted between 1963 and 1977. India reported one test in 1974.

During 1987 (through August), the Soviet Union reported one test, its first since 7/25/85, and the U.S. reported 9 tests.

Strategic Nuclear Armaments: U.S. and USSR

Source: International Institute for Strategic Services, London, England

United States

		Range[2] (km)	Estimated warhead yield[3]	Deployed (July 1986)
Land-based missiles[1]				
ICBM	Titan 2	15,000	9 MT	10
	Minuteman 2	11,300	1-2 MT	450
	Minuteman 3	13,000	3x170 KT	550
Sea-based missiles				
SLBM (nuclear subs)	Poseidon C3	4,600	10x50 KT	272
	Trident C4	7,400	8x100 KT	384

		Range[9] (km)	Weapons load (lb)	Deployed (July 1986)
Aircraft[8]				
Long-range	B-52G	12,000	70,000	99
	B-52H	16,000	70,000	90
Medium-range	FB-111A	4,700	37,500	55
Strike aircraft: land-based	F-4-E	2,200	16,000	(96)[11]
	F-111E/F	4,700	28,000	(150)[11]
Strike aircraft: carrier-based	A-6E	3,200	18,000	(20)[11]
	A-7E/F/A-18	2,800	20,000	(48)[11]

Soviet Union

		Range[2] (km)	Estimated warhead yield[3]	Deployed (July 1986)
Land-based missiles[1]				
ICBM	SS-11 Sego	10,500	1 MT[4]	448
	SS-13 Savage	10,000	1x750 KT	60
	SS-17	10,000	4x200 KT[5]	150
	SS-18	10,000	1x20 MT[6]	308
	SS-19	10,000	6x550 KT	360
Sea-based missiles				
SLBM (nuclear subs)	SS-N-5-Serb	1,400	1x1 MT	39
	SS-N-6-Sawfly	3,000	1x1 MT[7]	304
	SS-N-8	7,800	1x1 MT[8]	292
	SS-N-17	3,900	1x1 MT	12
	SS-N-18	6,500	5x200 KT MIRV	224
	SS-N-20	8,300	9x100 KT MIRV	80

	Range[10] (km)	Weapons load (lb)	Deployed (July 1986)
Aircraft[9]			
Tu-95 Bear	12,800	40,000	140
Mya-4 Bison	11,200	20,000	20
Tu-16 Badger	4,800	20,000	480
Tu22-Blinder	4,000	12,000	165
Tu22M-26 Backfire	8,000	17,500	260
Su-7 Fitter A	1,400	5,500	80
MiG-21 Fishbed L	1,100	2,000	135
MiG-27 Flogger D J	1,400	7,500	760
Su-17 Fitter D/H	1,800	11,000	900
Su-24 Fencer	4,000	8,000	750

(1) ICBM = intercontinental ballistic missile; SLBM = submarine-launched ballistic missile. (2) Operation range depends upon the payload carried; use of maximum payload may reduce missile range by up to 25%. (3) MT = megaton range = 1,000,000 tons of TNT equivalent or over; KT = kiloton range = 1,000 tons of TNT equivalent or more, but less than 1 MT. (4) Some 420 SS-11 missiles carry 3x100 to 300 KT warheads. (5) Some SS-17 carry 1x3.6 MT warheads. (6) Three SS-18 warhead variants: 10x500 KT, 8x900KT. (7) SS-N-6, 1x1 MT or 2x200 KT MIRV warheads. (8) 85-N-8 variant; 1x800 KT to 9,000 KA. (9) All aircraft listed are dual-capable and many, especially in the categories of strike aircraft, would be more likely to carry conventional than nuclear weapons. (10) Theoretical maximum range, with internal fuel only, at optimum altitude and speed. Ranges for strike aircraft assume no weapons load. Especially in the case of strike aircraft, therefore, range falls sharply for flights at lower altitude, at higher speed, or with full weapons load. (11) Figures in parentheses are estimates of Europe-based systems only.

Leading Arms Exporting Countries, 1984

Source: U.S. Arms Control and Disarmament Agency

(millions of dollars)

Soviet Union	11,100	China	1,900	Poland	775	Korea, South	525
United States	10,200	United Kingdom	1,500	Czechoslovakia	725	Brazil	500
France	3,600	Italy	1,000	Bulgaria	700	Germany, East	380
Germany, West	2,800	Spain	1,000	Yugoslavia	575	Korea, North	380

Leading Arms Importing Countries, 1984

Source: U.S. Arms Control and Disarmament Agency

(millions of dollars)

Iraq	7,700	Egypt	1,600	Japan	925	Cuba	700
Saudi Arabia	2,600	Syria	1,500	India	800	Colombia	675
Iran	2,200	Angola	1,100	United Kingdom	800	Israel	675
Libya	1,800	Soviet Union	1,000	Vietnam	800	Australia	600

AWARDS — MEDALS — PRIZES

The Alfred B. Nobel Prize Winners

Alfred B. Nobel, inventor of dynamite, bequeathed $9,000,000, the interest to be distributed yearly to those who had most benefited mankind in physics, chemistry, medicine-physiology, literature, and peace. The first Nobel Memorial Prize in Economics was awarded in 1969. No awards given for years omitted. In 1986, each prize was worth approximately $290,000.

Physics

1986 Ernest Ruska, German, Gerd Binnig, W. German, Heinrich Rohrer, Swiss
1985 Klaus von Klitzing, W. German
1984 Carlo Rubbia, Italian, Simon van der Meere, Dutch
1983 Subrahmanyan Chandrasekhar, William A. Fowler, both U.S.
1982 Kenneth G. Wilson, U.S.
1981 Nicolass Boembergen, Arthur Schlawlow, both U.S.; Kai M. Siegbahn, Swedish
1980 James W. Cronin, Val L. Fitch, U.S.
1979 Steven Weinberg, Sheldon L. Glashow, both U.S.; Abdus Salam, Pakistani
1978 Pyotr Kapitsa, USSR; Arno Penzias, Robert Wilson, both U.S.
1977 John H. Van Vleck, Philip W. Anderson, both U.S.; Nevill F. Mott, British
1976 Burton Richter, U.S.
Samuel C.C. Ting, U.S.
1975 James Rainwater, U.S.
Ben Mottelson, U.S.-Danish,
Aage Bohr, Danish
1974 Martin Ryle, British
Antony Hewish, British
1973 Ivar Giaever, U.S.
Leo Esaki, Japan
Brian D. Josephson, British
1972 John Bardeen, U.S.
Leon N. Cooper, U.S.
John R. Schrieffer, U.S.
1971 Dennis Gabor, British
1970 Louis Neel, French
Hannes Alfven, Swedish
1969 Murray Gell-Mann, U.S.
1968 Luis W. Alvarez, U.S.
1967 Hans A. Bethe, U.S.
1966 Alfred Kastler, French
1965 Richard P. Feynman, U.S.
Julian S. Schwinger, U.S.
Shinichiro Tomonaga, Japanese
1964 Nikolai G. Basov, USSR
Aleksander M. Prochorov, USSR
Charles H. Townes, U.S.
1963 Maria Goeppert-Mayer, U.S.
J. Hans D. Jensen, German
Eugene P. Wigner, U.S.
1962 Lev. D. Landau, USSR
1961 Robert Hofstadter, U.S.
Rudolf L. Mossbauer, German
1960 Donald A. Glaser, U.S.
1959 Owen Chamberlain, U.S.
Emilio G. Segre, U.S.
1958 Pavel Cherenkov, Ilya Frank, Igor Y. Tamm, all USSR
1957 Tsung-dao Lee,
Chen Ning Yang, both U.S.
1956 John Bardeen, U.S.
Walter H. Brattain, U.S.
William Shockley, U.S.
1955 Polykarp Kusch, U.S.
Willis E. Lamb, U.S.
1954 Max Born, British
Walter Bothe, German
1953 Frits Zernike, Dutch
1952 Felix Bloch, U.S.
Edward M. Purcell, U.S.
1951 Sir John D. Cockroft, British
Ernest T. S. Walton, Irish
1950 Cecil F. Powell, British
1949 Hideki Yukawa, Japanese
1948 Patrick M. S. Blackett, British
1947 Sir Edward V. Appleton, British
1946 Percy Williams Bridgman, U.S.
1945 Wolfgang Pauli, U.S.
1944 Isidor Isaac Rabi, U.S.
1943 Otto Stern, U.S.
1939 Ernest O. Lawrence, U.S.
1938 Enrico Fermi, U.S.
1937 Clinton J. Davisson, U.S.
Sir George P. Thomson, British
1936 Carl D. Anderson, U.S.
Victor F. Hess, Austrian
1935 Sir James Chadwick, British
1933 Paul A. M. Dirac, British
Erwin Schrodinger, Austrian
1932 Werner Heisenberg, German
1930 Sir Chandrasekhara V. Raman, Indian
1929 Prince Louis-Victor de Broglie, French
1928 Owen W. Richardson, British
1927 Arthur H. Compton, U.S.
Charles T. R. Wilson, British
1926 Jean B. Perrin, French
1925 James Franck,
Gustav Hertz, both German
1924 Karl M. G. Siegbahn, Swedish
1923 Robert A. Millikan, U.S.
1922 Niels Bohr, Danish
1921 Albert Einstein, Ger.-U.S.
1920 Charles E. Guillaume, French
1919 Johannes Stark, German
1918 Max K. E. L. Planck, German
1917 Charles G. Barkla, British
1915 Sir William H. Bragg, British
Sir William L. Bragg, British
1914 Max von Laue, German
1913 Heike Kamerlingh-Onnes, Dutch
1912 Nils G. Dalen, Swedish
1911 Wilhelm Wien, German
1910 Johannes D. van der Waals, Dutch
1909 Carl F. Braun, German
Guglielmo Marconi, Italian
1908 Gabriel Lippmann, French
1907 Albert A. Michelson, U.S.
1906 Sir Joseph J. Thomson, British
1905 Philipp E. A. von Lenard, Ger.
1904 John W. Strutt, Lord Rayleigh, British
1903 Antoine Henri Becquerel, French
Marie Curie, Polish-French
Pierre Curie, French
1902 Hendrik A. Lorentz,
Pieter Zeeman, both Dutch
1901 Wilhelm C. Roentgen, German

Chemistry

1986 Dudley Herschbach, Yuan T. Lee, both U.S.; John C. Polanyi, Canadian
1985 Herbert A. Hauptman, Jerome Karle, both U.S.
1984 Bruce Merrifield, U.S.
1983 Henry Taube, Canadian
1982 Aaron Klug, S. African
1981 Kenichi Fukui, Japan.,
Roald Hoffmann, U.S.
1980 Paul Berg., U.S.;
Walter Gilbert, U.S.,
Frederick Sanger, U.K.
1979 Herbert C. Brown, U.S.
George Wittig, German
1978 Peter Mitchell, British
1977 Ilya Prigogine, Belgian
1976 William N. Lipscomb, U.S.
1975 John Cornforth, Austral.-Brit.,
Vladimir Prelog, Yugo.-Switz.
1974 Paul J. Flory, U.S.
1973 Ernst Otto Fischer, W. German
Geoffrey Wilkinson, British
1972 Christian B. Anfinsen, U.S.
Stanford Moore, U.S.
William H. Stein, U.S.
1971 Gerhard Herzberg, Canadian
1970 Luis F. Leloir, Arg.
1969 Derek H. R. Barton, British
Odd Hassel, Norwegian
1968 Lars Onsager, U.S.
1967 Manfred Eigen, German
Ronald G. W. Norrish, British
George Porter, British
1966 Robert S. Mulliken, U.S.
1965 Robert B. Woodward, U.S.
1964 Dorothy C. Hodgkin, British
1963 Giulio Natta, Italian
Karl Ziegler, German
1962 John C. Kendrew, British
Max F. Perutz, British
1961 Melvin Calvin, U.S.
1960 Willard F. Libby, U.S.
1959 Jaroslav Heyrovsky, Czech
1958 Frederick Sanger, British
1957 Sir Alexander R. Todd, British
1956 Sir Cyril N. Hinshelwood, British
Nikolai N. Semenov, USSR
1955 Vincent du Vigneaud, U.S.
1954 Linus C. Pauling, U.S.
1953 Hermann Staudinger, German
1952 Archer J. P. Martin, British
Richard L. M. Synge, British
1951 Edwin M. McMillan, U.S.
Glenn T. Seaborg, U.S.
1950 Kurt Alder, German
Otto P. H. Diels, German
1949 William F. Giauque, U.S.
1948 Arne W. K. Tiselius, Swedish
1947 Sir Robert Robinson, British
1946 James B. Sumner, John H. Northrop, Wendell M. Stanley, U.S.
1945 Artturi I. Virtanen, Finnish
1944 Otto Hahn, German
1943 Georg de Hevesy, Hungarian
1939 Adolf F. J. Butenandt, German
Leopold Ruzicka, Swiss
1938 Richard Kuhn, German
1937 Walter N. Haworth, British
Paul Karrer, Swiss
1936 Peter J. W. Debye, Dutch
1935 Frederic Joliot-Curie, French
Irene Joliot-Curie, French
1934 Harold C. Urey, U.S.
1932 Irving Langmuir, U.S.
1931 Friedrich Bergius, German
Karl Bosch, German
1930 Hans Fischer, German
1929 Sir Arthur Harden, British
Hans von Euler-Chelpin, Swed.
1928 Adolf O. R. Windaus, German
1927 Heinrich O. Wieland, German
1926 Theodor Svedberg, Swedish
1925 Richard A. Zsigmondy, German
1923 Fritz Pregl, Austrian
1922 Francis W. Aston, British
1921 Frederick Soddy, British
1920 Walther H. Nernst, German
1918 Fritz Haber, German
1915 Richard M. Willstatter, German
1914 Theodore W. Richards, U.S.
1913 Alfred Werner, Swiss
1912 Victor Grignard, French
Paul Sabatier, French
1911 Marie Curie, Polish-French
1910 Otto Wallach, German
1909 Wilhelm Ostwald, German
1908 Ernest Rutherford, British
1907 Eduard Buchner, German
1906 Henri Moissan, French
1905 Adolf von Baeyer, German
1904 Sir William Ramsay, British
1903 Svante A. Arrhenius, Swedish
1902 Emil Fischer, German
1901 Jacobus H. van't Hoff, Dutch

Physiology or Medicine

1986 Rita Levi-Montalcini, It.-U.S., Stanley Cohen, U.S.
1985 Michael S. Brown, Joseph L. Goldstein, both U.S.
1984 Cesar Milstein, Brit.-Argentina; Georges J. F. Koehler, German; Niels K. Jerne, Brit.-Danish
1983 Barbara McClintock, U.S.
1982 Sune Bergstrom, Bengt Samuelsson, both Swedish; John R. Vane, British.
1981 Roger W. Sperry, David H. Hubel, Tosten N. Wiesel, all U.S.
1980 Baruj Benacerraf, George Snell, both U.S.; Jean Dausset, France
1979 Allan M. Cormack, U.S. Geoffrey N. Hounsfield, British
1978 Daniel Nathans, Hamilton O. Smith, both U.S.; Werner Arber, Swiss
1977 Rosalyn S. Yalow, Roger C.L. Guillemin, Andrew V. Schally, U.S.
1976 Baruch S. Blumberg, U.S. Daniel Carleton Gajdusek, U.S.
1975 David Baltimore, Howard Temin, both U.S.; Renato Dulbecco, Ital.-U.S.
1974 Albert Claude, Lux.-U.S.; George Emil Palade, Rom.-U.S.; Christian Rene de Duve, Belg.
1973 Karl von Frisch, Ger.; Konrad Lorenz, Ger.-Austrian; Nikolaas Tinbergen, Brit.
1972 Gerald M. Edelman, U.S. Rodney R. Porter, British
1971 Earl W. Sutherland Jr., U.S.
1970 Julius Axelrod, U.S. Sir Bernard Katz, British Ulf von Euler, Swedish
1969 Max Delbruck, Alfred D. Hershey, Salvador Luria, all U.S.
1968 Robert W. Holley, H. Gobind Khorana, Marshall W. Nirenberg, all U.S.
1967 Ragnar Granit, Swedish Haldan Keffer Hartline, U.S. George Wald, U.S.
1966 Charles B. Huggins, Francis Peyton Rous, both U.S.
1965 Francois Jacob, Andre Lwoff, Jacques Monod, all French
1964 Konrad E. Bloch, U.S. Feodor Lynen, German
1963 Sir John C. Eccles, Australian Alan L. Hodgkin, British Andrew F. Huxley, British
1962 Francis H. C. Crick, British James D. Watson, U.S. Maurice H. F. Wilkins, British
1961 Georg von Bekesy, U.S.
1960 Sir F. MacFarlane Burnet, Australian Peter B. Medawar, British
1959 Arthur Kornberg, U.S. Severo Ochoa, U.S.
1958 George W. Beadle, U.S. Edward L. Tatum, U.S. Joshua Lederberg, U.S.
1957 Daniel Bovet, Italian
1956 Andre F. Cournand, U.S. Werner Forssmann, German Dickinson W. Richards, Jr., U.S.
1955 Alex H. T. Theorell, Swedish
1954 John F. Enders, Frederick C. Robbins, Thomas H. Weller, all U.S.
1953 Hans A. Krebs, British Fritz A. Lipmann, U.S.
1952 Selman A. Waksman, U.S.
1951 Max Theiler, U.S.
1950 Philip S. Hench, Edward C. Kendall, both U.S. Tadeus Reichstein, Swiss
1949 Walter R. Hess, Swiss Antonio Moniz, Portuguese
1948 Paul H. Müller, Swiss
1947 Carl F. Cori, Gerty T. Cori, both U.S. Bernardo A. Houssay, Arg.
1946 Hermann J. Muller, U.S.
1945 Ernst B. Chain, British Sir Alexander Fleming, British Sir Howard W. Florey, British
1944 Joseph Erlanger, U.S. Herbert S. Gasser, U.S.
1943 Henrik C. P. Dam, Danish Edward A. Doisy, U.S.
1939 Gerhard Domagk, German
1938 Corneille J. F. Heymans, Belg.
1937 Albert Szent-Gyorgyi, Hung.-U.S.
1936 Sir Henry H. Dale, British Otto Loewi, U.S.
1935 Hans Spemann, German
1934 George R. Minot, Wm. P. Murphy, G. H. Whipple, all U.S.
1933 Thomas H. Morgan, U.S.
1932 Edgar D. Adrian, British Sir Charles S. Sherrington, Brit.
1931 Otto H. Warburg, German
1930 Karl Landsteiner, U.S.
1929 Christiaan Eijkman, Dutch Sir Frederick G. Hopkins, British
1928 Charles J. H. Nicolle, French
1927 Julius Wagner-Jauregg, Aus.
1926 Johannes A. G. Fibiger, Danish
1924 Willem Einthoven, Dutch
1923 Frederick G. Banting, Canadian John J. R. Macleod, Scottish
1922 Archibald V. Hill, British Otto F. Meyerhof, German
1920 Schack A. S. Krogh, Danish
1919 Jules Bordet, Belgian
1914 Robert Barany, Austrian
1913 Charles R. Richet, French
1912 Alexis Carrel, French
1911 Allvar Gullstrand, Swedish
1910 Albrecht Kossel, German
1909 Emil T. Kocher, Swiss
1908 Paul Ehrlich, German Elie Metchnikoff, French
1907 Charles L. A. Laveran, French
1906 Camillo Golgi, Italian Santiago Ramon y Cajal, Sp.
1905 Robert Koch, German
1904 Ivan P. Pavlov, Russian
1903 Niels R. Finsen, Danish
1902 Sir Ronald Ross, British
1901 Emil A. von Behring, German

Literature

1986 Wole Soyinka, Nigerian
1985 Claude Simon, French
1984 Jaroslav Siefert, Czech.
1983 William Golding, British
1982 Gabriel Garcia Marquez, Colombian-Mex.
1981 Elias Canetti, Bulgarian-British
1980 Czeslaw Milosz, Polish-U.S.
1979 Odysseus Elytis, Greek
1978 Isaac Bashevis Singer, U.S. (Yiddish)
1977 Vicente Aleixandre, Spanish
1976 Saul Bellow, U.S.
1975 Eugenio Montale, Ital.
1974 Eyvind Johnson, Harry Edmund Martinson, both Swedish
1973 Patrick White, Australian
1972 Heinrich Boll, W. German
1971 Pablo Neruda, Chilean
1970 Aleksandr I. Solzhenitsyn, Russ.
1969 Samuel Beckett, Irish
1968 Yasunari Kawabata, Japanese
1967 Miguel Angel Asturias, Guate.
1966 Samuel Joseph Agnon, Israeli Nelly Sachs, Swedish
1965 Mikhail Sholokhov, Russian
1964 Jean Paul Sartre, French (Prize declined)
1963 Giorgos Seferis, Greek
1962 John Steinbeck, U.S.
1961 Ivo Andric, Yugoslavian
1960 Saint-John Perse, French
1959 Salvatore Quasimodo, Italian
1958 Boris L. Pasternak, Russian (Prize declined)
1957 Albert Camus, French
1956 Juan Ramon Jimenez, Puerto Rican-Span.
1955 Halldor K. Laxness, Icelandic
1954 Ernest Hemingway, U.S.
1953 Sir Winston Churchill, British
1952 Francois Mauriac, French
1951 Par F. Lagerkvist, Swedish
1950 Bertrand Russell, British
1949 William Faulkner, U.S.
1948 T.S. Eliot, British
1947 Andre Gide, French
1946 Hermann Hesse, Swiss
1945 Gabriela Mistral, Chilean
1944 Johannes V. Jensen, Danish
1939 Frans E. Sillanpaa, Finnish
1938 Pearl S. Buck, U.S.
1937 Roger Martin du Gard, French
1936 Eugene O'Neill, U.S.
1934 Luigi Pirandello, Italian
1933 Ivan A. Bunin, French
1932 John Galsworthy, British
1931 Erik A. Karlfeldt, Swedish
1930 Sinclair Lewis, U.S.
1929 Thomas Mann, German
1928 Sigrid Undset, Norwegian
1927 Henri Bergson, French
1926 Grazia Deledda, Italian
1925 George Bernard Shaw, British
1924 Wladyslaw S. Reymont, Polish
1923 William Butler Yeats, Irish
1922 Jacinto Benavente, Spanish
1921 Anatole France, French
1920 Knut Hamsun, Norwegian
1919 Carl F. G. Spitteler, Swiss
1917 Karl A. Gjellerup, Danish Henrik Pontoppidan, Danish
1916 Verner von Heidenstam, Swed.
1915 Romain Rolland, French
1913 Rabindranath Tagore, Indian
1912 Gerhart Hauptmann, German
1911 Maurice Maeterlinck, Belgian
1910 Paul J. L. Heyse, German
1909 Selma Lagerlof, Swedish
1908 Rudolf C. Eucken, German
1907 Rudyard Kipling, British
1906 Giosue Carducci, Italian
1905 Henryk Sienkiewicz, Polish
1904 Frederic Mistral, French Jose Echegaray, Spanish
1903 Bjornsterne Bjornson, Norw.
1902 Theodor Mommsen, German
1901 Rene F. A Sully Prudhomme, French

Nobel Memorial Prize in Economics

1986 James M. Buchanon, U.S.
1985 Franco Modigliani, It.-U.S.
1984 Richard Stone, British
1983 Gerard Debreu, Fr.-U.S.
1982 George J. Stigler, U.S.
1981 James Tobin, U.S.
1980 Lawrence R. Klein, U.S.
1979 Theodore W. Schultz, U.S., Sir Arthur Lewis, British
1978 Herbert A. Simon, U.S.
1977 Bertil Ohlin, Swedish James E. Meade, British

1976 Milton Friedman, U.S.
1975 Tjalling Koopmans, Dutch-U.S., Leonid Kantorovich, USSR
1974 Gunnar Myrdal, Swed., Friedrich A. von Hayek, Austrian
1973 Wassily Leontief, U.S.
1972 Kenneth J. Arrow, U.S. John R. Hicks, British
1971 Simon Kuznets, U.S.
1970 Paul A. Samuelson, U.S.
1969 Ragnar Frisch, Norwegian Jan Tinbergen, Dutch

Peace

1986 Elie Wiesel, Romania-U.S.
1985 Intl. Physicians for the Prevention of Nuclear War, U.S.
1984 Bishop Desmond Tutu, So. African
1983 Lech Walesa, Polish
1982 Alva Myrdal, Swedish; Alfonso Garcia Robles, Mexican
1981 Office of U.N. High Commissioner for Refugees
1980 Adolfo Perez Esquivel, Argentine
1979 Mother Teresa of Calcutta, Albanian-Indian
1978 Anwar Sadat, Egyptian Menachem Begin, Israeli
1977 Amnesty International
1976 Mairead Corrigan, Betty Williams, N. Irish
1975 Andrei Sakharov, USSR
1974 Eisaku Sato, Japanese, Sean MacBride, Irish
1973 Henry Kissinger, U.S. Le Duc Tho, N. Vietnamese (Tho declined)
1971 Willy Brandt, W. German
1970 Norman E. Borlaug, U.S.
1969 Intl. Labor Organization
1968 Rene Cassin, French
1965 U.N. Children's Fund (UNICEF)
1964 Martin Luther King Jr., U.S.
1963 International Red Cross, League of Red Cross Societies
1962 Linus C. Pauling, U.S.
1961 Dag Hammarskjold, Swedish
1960 Albert J. Luthuli, South African
1959 Philip J. Noel-Baker, British
1958 Georges Pire, Belgian
1957 Lester B. Pearson, Canadian
1954 Office of the UN High Commissioner for Refugees
1953 George C. Marshall, U.S.
1952 Albert Schweitzer, French
1951 Leon Jouhaux, French
1950 Ralph J. Bunche, U.S.
1949 Lord John Boyd Orr of Brechin Mearns, British
1947 Friends Service Council, Brit. Amer. Friends Service Com.
1946 Emily G. Balch, John R. Mott, both U.S.
1945 Cordell Hull, U.S.
1944 International Red Cross
1938 Nansen International Office for Refugees
1937 Viscount Cecil of Chelwood, Brit.
1936 Carlos de Saavedra Lamas, Arg.
1935 Carl von Ossietzky, German
1934 Arthur Henderson, British
1933 Sir Norman Angell, British
1931 Jane Addams, U.S. Nicholas Murray Butler, U.S.
1930 Nathan Soderblom, Swedish
1929 Frank B. Kellogg, U.S.
1927 Ferdinand E. Buisson, French Ludwig Quidde, German
1926 Aristide Briand, French Gustav Stresemann, German
1925 Sir J. Austen Chamberlain, Brit. Charles G. Dawes, U.S.
1922 Fridtjof Nansen, Norwegian
1921 Karl H. Branting, Swedish Christian L. Lange, Norwegian
1920 Leon V.A. Bourgeois, French
1919 Woodrow Wilson, U.S.
1917 International Red Cross
1913 Henri La Fontaine, Belgian
1912 Elihu Root, U.S.
1911 Tobias M.C. Asser, Dutch Alfred H. Fried, Austrian
1910 Permanent Intl. Peace Bureau
1909 Auguste M. F. Beernaert, Belg. Paul H. B. B. d'Estournelles de Constant, French
1908 Klas P. Arnoldson, Swedish Fredrik Bajer, Danish
1907 Ernesto T. Moneta, Italian Louis Renault, French
1906 Theodore Roosevelt, U.S.
1905 Baroness Bertha von Suttner, Austrian
1904 Institute of International Law
1903 Sir William R. Cremer, British
1902 Elie Ducommun, Charles A. Gobat, both Swiss
1901 Jean H. Dunant, Swiss Frederic Passy, French

Pulitzer Prizes in Journalism, Letters, and Music

The Pulitzer Prizes were endowed by Joseph Pulitzer (1847-1911), publisher of The World, New York, N.Y., in a bequest to Columbia University, and are awarded annually by the president of the university on recommendation of the Pulitzer Prize Board for work done during the preceding year. The administrator is Robert C. Christopher of Columbia Univ. All prizes are $1,000 (originally $500) in each category, except Meritorious Public Service for which a gold medal is given.

Journalism

Meritorious Public Service

For distinguished and meritorious public service by a United States newspaper.

1918—New York Times. Also special award to Minna Lewinson and Henry Beetle Hough.
1919—Milwaukee Journal.
1921—Boston Post.
1922—New York World.
1923—Memphis (Tenn.) Commercial Appeal.
1924—New York World.
1926—Enquirer-Sun, Columbus, Ga.
1927—Canton (Oh.) Daily News.
1928—Indianapolis Times.
1929—Evening World, New York.
1931—Atlanta (Ga.) Constitution.
1932—Indianapolis (Ind.) News.
1933—New York World-Telegram.
1934—Medford (Ore.) Mail-Tribune.
1935—Sacramento (Cal.) Bee.
1936—Cedar Rapids (Ia.) Gazette.
1937—St.Louis Post-Dispatch.
1938—Bismarck (N.D.) Tribune.
1939—Miami (Fla.) Daily News.
1940—Waterbury (Conn.) Republican and American.
1941—St.Louis Post-Dispatch.
1942—Los Angeles Times.
1943—Omaha World Herald.
1944—New York Times.
1945—Detroit Free Press.
1946—Scranton (Pa.) Times.
1947—Baltimore Sun.
1948—St. Louis Post-Dispatch.
1949—Nebraska State Journal.
1950—Chicago Daily News; St. Louis Post-Dispatch.
1951—Miami (Fla.) Herald and Brooklyn Eagle.
1952—St. Louis Post-Dispatch.
1953—Whiteville (N.C.) News Reporter; Tabor City (N.C.) Tribune.
1954—Newsday (Long Island, N.Y.)
1955—Columbus (Ga.) Ledger and Sunday Ledger-Enquirer.
1956—Watsonville (Cal.) Register-Pajaronian.
1957—Chicago Daily News.
1958—Arkansas Gazette, Little Rock.
1959—Utica (N.Y.) Observer-Dispatch and Utica Daily Press.
1960—Los Angeles Times.
1961—Amarillo (Tex.) Globe-Times.
1962—Panama City (Fla.) News-Herald.
1963—Chicago Daily News.
1964—St.Petersburg (Fla.) Times.
1965—Hutchinson (Kan.) News.
1966—Boston Globe.
1967—The Louisville Courier-Journal; The Milwaukee Journal.
1968—Riverside (Cal.) Press-Enterprise.
1969—Los Angeles Times.
1970—Newsday (Long Island, N.Y.).
1971—Winston Salem (N.C.) Journal & Sentinel.
1972—New York Times.
1973—Washington Post.
1974—Newsday (Long Island, N.Y.).
1975—Boston Globe.
1976—Anchorage Daily News.
1977—Lufkin (Tex.) News.
1978—Philadelphia Inquirer.
1979—Point Reyes (Cal.) Light.
1980—Gannett News Service.
1981—Charlotte (N.C.) Observer.
1982—Detroit News.
1983—Jackson (Miss.) Clarion-Ledger.
1984—Los Angeles Times.
1985—Ft. Worth (Tex.) Star-Telegram.
1986—Denver Post.
1987—Pittsburgh Press.

Reporting

This category originally embraced all fields, local, national, and international. Later separate categories were created for the different fields of reporting.

1917—Herbert Bayard Swope, New York World.
1918—Harold A. Littledale, New York Evening Post.
1920—John J. Leary, Jr., New York World.
1921—Louis Seibold, New York World.
1922—Kirke L. Simpson, Associated Press.
1923—Alva Johnston, New York Times.
1924—Magner White, San Diego Sun.
1925—James W. Mulroy and Alvin H. Goldstein, Chicago Daily News.
1926—William Burke Miller, Louisville Courier-Journal.
1927—John T. Rogers, St. Louis Post-Dispatch.
1929—Paul Y. Anderson, St. Louis Post-Dispatch.

1930—Russell D. Owens, New York Times. Also $500 to W.O. Dapping, Auburn (N.Y.) Citizen.
1931—A.B. MacDonald, Kansas City (Mo.) Star.
1932—W.C. Richards, D.D. Martin, J.S. Pooler, F.D. Webb, J.N.W. Sloan, Detroit Free Press.
1933—Francis A. Jamieson, Associated Press.
1934—Royce Brier, San Francisco Chronicle.
1935—William H.Taylor, New York Herald Tribune.
1936—Lauren D.Lyman, New York Times.
1937—John J. O'Neill, N.Y.Herald Tribune; William L. Laurence, N.Y Times; Howard W. Blakeslee, A.P.; Gobind Behan Lal, University Service; and David Dietz, Scripps-Howard Newspapers.
1938—Raymond Sprigle, Pittsburgh Post-Gazette.
1939—Thomas L. Stokes, Scripps-Howard Newspaper Alliance.
1940—S.Burton Heath, New York World-Telegram.
1941—Westbrook Pegler, New York World-Telegram.
1942—Stanton Delaplane, San Francisco Chronicle.
1943—George Weller, Chicago Daily News.
1944—Paul Schoenstein, N.Y.Journal-American.
1945—Jack S. McDowell, San Francisco Call-Bulletin.
1946—William L. Laurence, New York Times.
1947—Frederick Woltman, N.Y.World-Telegram.
1948—George E. Goodwin, Atlanta Journal.
1949—Malcolm Johnson, New York Sun.
1950—Meyer Berger, New York Times.
1951—Edward S. Montgomery, San Francisco Examiner.
1952—Geo. de Carvalho, San Francisco Chronicle.

(1) General or Spot; (2) Special or Investigative

1953—(1) Providence (R.I.) Journal and Evening Bulletin; (2) Edward J. Mowery, N.Y.World-Telegram & Sun.
1954—(1) Vicksburg (Miss.) Sunday Post-Herald; (2) Alvin Scott McCoy, Kansas City (Mo.) Star.
1955—(1) Mrs. Caro Brown, Alice (Tex.) Daily Echo; (2) Roland K. Towery, Cuero (Tex.) Record.
1956—(1) Lee Hills, Detroit Free Press; (2) Arthur Daley, New York Times.
1957—(1) Salt Lake Tribune, Salt Lake City, Ut.; (2) Wallace Turner and William Lambert, Portland Oregonian.
1958—(1) Fargo, (N.D.) Forum; (2) George Beveridge, Evening Star, Washington, D.C.
1959—(1) Mary Lou Werner, Washington Evening Star; (2) John Harold Brislin, Scranton (Pa.) Tribune, and The Scrantonian.
1960—(1) Jack Nelson, Atlanta Constitution; (2) Miriam Ottenberg, Washington Evening Star.
1961—(1) Sanche de Gramont, N.Y.Herald Tribune; (2) Edgar May, Buffalo Evening News.
1962—(1) Robert D.Mullins, Deseret News, Salt Lake City; (2) George Bliss, Chicago Tribune.
1963—(1) Shared by Sylvan Fox, William Longgood, and Anthony Shannon, N.Y.World-Telegram & Sun; (2) Oscar Griffin, Jr., Pecos (Tex.) Independent and Enterprise.

(1) General Reporting; (2) Special Reporting.

1964—(1) Norman C.Miller, Wall Street Journal; (2) Shared by James V. Magee, Albert V. Gaudiosi, and Frederick A. Meyer, Philadelphia Bulletin.
1965—(1) Melvin H.Ruder, Hungry Horse News (Columbia Falls, Mon.); (2) Gene Goltz, Houston Post.
1966—(1) Los Angeles Times Staff; (2) John A. Frasca, Tampa (Fla.) Tribune.
1967—(1) Robert V.Cox, Chambersburg (Pa.) Public Opinion; (2) Gene Miller, Miami Herald.
1968—Detroit Free Press Staff; (2) J. Anthony Lukas, N.Y. Times.
1969—(1) John Fetterman, Louisville Courier-Journal and Times; (2) Albert L.Delugach, St.Louis Globe Democrat, and Denny Walsh, Life.
1970—(1) Thomas Fitzpatrick, Chicago Sun-Times; (2) Harold Eugene Martin, Montgomery Advertiser & Alabama Journal.
1971—(1) Akron Beacon Journal Staff, (2) William Hugh Jones, Chicago Tribune.
1972—(1) Richard Cooper and John Machacek, Rochester Times-Union; (2) Timothy Leland, Gerard M. O'Neill, Stephen A. Kurkjian and Anne De Santis, Boston Globe.
1973—(1) Chicago Tribune; (2) Sun Newspapers of Omaha.
1974—(1) Hugh F. Hough, Arthur M. Petacque, Chicago Sun-Times; (2) William Sherman, N.Y. Daily News.
1975—(1) Xenia (Oh.) Daily Gazette; (2) Indianapolis Star.
1976—(1) Gene Miller, Miami Herald; (2) Chicago Tribune.
1977—(1) Margo Huston, Milwaukee Journal; (2) Acel Moore, Wendell Rawls Jr., Philadelphia Inquirer.
1978—(1) Richard Whitt, Louisville Courier-Journal; (2) Anthony R. Dolan, Stamford (Conn.) Advocate.
1979—(1) San Diego (Cal.) Evening Tribune; (2) Gilbert M. Gaul, Elliot G.Jaspin, Pottsville (Pa.) Republican.
1980—(1) Philadelphia Inquirer; (2) Stephen A. Kurkjian, Alexander B.Hawes Jr., Nils Bruzelius, Joan Vennochi, Robert M. Porterfield, Boston Globe.
1981—(1) Longview (Wash.) Daily News staff; (2) Clark Hallas and Robert B. Lowe, Arizona Daily Star.
1982—(1) Kansas City Star, Kansas City Times; (2) Paul Henderson, Seattle Times.
1983—(1) Fort Wayne (Ind.) News-Sentinel; (2) Loretta Tofani, Washington Post.
1984—(1) Newsday (N.Y.); (2) Boston Globe.
1985—(1) Thomas Turcol, Virginian-Pilot and Ledger-Star, Norfolk, Va.; (2) William K.Marimow, Philadelphia Inquirer.
1986—(1) Edna Buchanan, Miami Herald; (2) Jeffrey A. Marx & Michael M. York, Lexington (Ky.) Herald-Leader.
1987—(1) Akron Beacon Journal; (2) Daniel R. Biddle, H.G. Bissinger, Fredric N. Tulsky, Philadelphia Inquirer; John Woestendiek, Philadelphia Inquirer.

Criticism or Commentary

(1) Criticism; (2) Commentary

1970—(1) Ada Louise Huxtable, N.Y. Times; (2) Marquis W. Childs, St.Louis Post-Dispatch.
1971—(1) Harold C.Schonberg, N.Y. Times; (2) William A. Caldwell, The Record, Hackensack, N.J.
1972—(1) Frank Peters Jr., St. Louis Post-Dispatch; (2) Mike Royko, Chicago Daily News.
1973—(1) Ronald Powers, Chicago Sun-Times; (2) David S. Broder, Washington Post.
1974—(1) Emily Genauer, Newsday, (N.Y.); (2) Edwin A. Roberts, Jr., National Observer.
1975—(1) Roger Ebert, Chicago Sun Times; (2) Mary McGrory, Washington Star.
1976—(1) Alan M.Kriegsman, Washington Post; (2) Walter W. (Red) Smith, N.Y. Times.
1977—(1) William McPherson, Washington Post; (2) George F. Will, Wash. Post Writers Group.
1978—(1) Walter Kerr, New York Times; (2) William Safire, New York Times.
1979—(1) Paul Gapp, Chicago Tribune; (2) Russell Baker, New York Times.
1980—(1) William A. Henry III, Boston Globe; (2) Ellen Goodman, Boston Globe.
1981—(1) Jonathan Yardley, Washington Star; (2) Dave Anderson, New York Times.
1982—(1) Martin Bernheimer, Los Angeles Times; (2) Art Buchwald, Los Angeles Times Syndicate.
1983—(1) Manuela Hoelterhoff, Wall St. Journal; (2) Claude Sitton, Raleigh (N.C.) News & Observer.
1984—Paul Goldberger, New York Times; (2) Vermont Royster, Wall St. Journal
1985—(1) Howard Rosenberg, Los Angeles Times; (2) Murray Kempton, Newsday (N.Y.).
1986—(1) Donal J. Henahan, New York Times; (2) Jimmy Breslin, N.Y. Daily News.
1987—(1) Richard Eder, Los Angeles Times; (2) Charles Krauthammer, Washington Post.

National Reporting

1942—Louis Stark, New York Times.
1944—Dewey L. Fleming, Baltimore Sun.
1945—James B. Reston, New York Times.
1946—Edward A. Harris, St. Louis Post-Dispatch.
1947—Edward T. Folliard, Washington Post.
1948—Bert Andrews, New York Herald Tribune; Nat S. Finney, Minneapolis Tribune.
1949—Charles P. Trussell, New York Times.
1950—Edwin O. Guthman, Seattle Times.
1952—Anthony Leviero, New York Times.
1953—Don Whitehead, Associated Press.
1954—Richard Wilson, Des Moines Register.
1955—Anthony Lewis, Washington Daily News.
1956—Charles L. Bartlett, Chattanooga Times.
1957—James Reston, New York Times.
1958—Relman Morin, AP; Clark Mollenhoff, Des Moines Register & Tribune.
1959—Howard Van Smith, Miami (Fla.) News.
1960—Vance Trimble, Scripps-Howard, Washington, D.C.
1961—Edward R. Cony, Wall Street Journal.
1962—Nathan G. Caldwell and Gene S. Graham, Nashville Tennessean.
1963—Anthony Lewis, New York Times.
1964—Merriman Smith, UPI.
1965—Louis M. Kohlmeier, Wall Street Journal.
1966—Haynes Johnson, Washington Evening Star.
1967—Monroe Karmin and Stanley Penn, Wall Street Journal.
1968—Howard James, Christian Science Monitor; Nathan K. Kotz, Des Moines Register.
1969—Robert Cahn, Christian Science Monitor.
1970—William J. Eaton, Chicago Daily News.
1971—Lucinda Franks & Thomas Powers, UPI.
1972—Jack Anderson, United Features.
1973—Robert Boyd and Clark Hoyt, Knight Newspapers.
1974—James R. Polk, Washington Star-News; Jack White, Providence Journal-Bulletin.
1975—Donald L. Barlett and James B. Steele, Philadelphia Inquirer.
1976—James Risser, Des Moines Register.
1977—Walter Mears, Associated Press.
1978—Gaylord D. Shaw, Los Angeles Times.
1979—James Risser, Des Moines Register.
1980—Charles Stafford, Bette Swenson Orsini, St. Petersburg (Fla.) Times.
1981—John M. Crewdson, New York Times.
1982—Rick Atkinson, Kansas City Times.
1983—Boston Globe.
1984—John Noble Wilford, New York Times.
1985—Thomas J. Knudson, Des Moines (Ia.) Register.
1986—Craig Flournoy & George Rodrigue, Dallas Morning News; Arthur Howe, Philadelphia Inquirer.
1987—Miami Herald; and New York Times.

International Reporting

1942—Laurence Edmund Allen, Associated Press.
1943—Ira Wolfert, No. Am. Newspaper Alliance.
1944—Daniel DeLuce, Associated Press.
1945—Mark S. Watson, Baltimore Sun.
1946—Homer W. Bigart, New York Herald Tribune.

1947—Eddy Gilmore, Associated Press.
1948—Paul W. Ward, Baltimore Sun.
1949—Price Day, Baltimore Sun.
1950—Edmund Stevens, Christian Science Monitor.
1951—Keyes Beech and Fred Sparks, Chicago Daily News; Homer Bigart and Marguerite Higgins, New York Herald Tribune; Relman Morin and Don Whitehead, AP.
1952—John M. Hightower, Associated Press.
1953—Austin C. Wehrwein, Milwaukee Journal.
1954—Jim G. Lucas, Scripps-Howard Newspapers.
1955—Harrison Salisbury, New York Times.
1956—William Randolph Hearst, Jr., Frank Conniff, Hearst Newspapers; Kingsbury Smith, INS.
1957—Russell Jones, United Press.
1958—New York Times.
1959—Joseph Martin and Philip Santora, N.Y. News.
1960—A.M. Rosenthal, New York Times.
1961—Lynn Heinzerling, Associated Press.
1962—Walter Lippmann, N.Y. Herald Tribune Synd.
1963—Hal Hendrix, Miami (Fla.) News.
1964—Malcolm W. Browne, AP; David Halberstam, N.Y. Times.
1965—J.A. Livingston, Philadelphia Bulletin.
1966—Peter Arnett, AP.
1967—R. John Hughes, Christian Science Monitor.
1968—Alfred Friendly, Washington Post.
1969—William Tuohy, L.A. Times.
1970—Seymour M. Hersh, Dispatch News Service.
1971—Jimmie Lee Hoagland, Washington Post.
1972—Peter R. Kann, Wall Street Journal.
1973—Max Frankel, N.Y. Times.
1974—Hedrick Smith, N.Y. Times.
1975—William Mullen and Ovie Carter, Chicago Tribune.
1976—Sydney H. Schanberg, N.Y. Times.
1978—Henry Kamm, N.Y. Times.
1979—Richard Ben Cramer, Philadelphia Inquirer.
1980—Joel Brinkley, Jay Mather, Louisville (Ky.) Courier-Journal.
1981—Shirley Christian, Miami Herald.
1982—John Darnton, New York Times.
1983—Thomas L. Friedman, New York Times; Loren Jenkins, Washington Post.
1984—Karen Elliot House, Wall St. Journal
1985—Josh Friedman, Dennis Bell, Ozier Muhammad, Newsday (N.Y.).
1986—Lewis M. Simons, Pete Carey, Katherine Ellison, San Jose (Calif.) Mercury News.
1987—Michael Parks, Los Angeles Times.

Correspondence

For Washington or foreign correspondence. Category was merged with those in national and international reporting in 1948.

1929—Paul Scott Mowrer, Chicago Daily News.
1930—Leland Stowe, New York Herald Tribune.
1931—H.R. Knickerbocker, Philadelphia Public Ledger and New York Evening Post.
1932—Walter Duranty, New York Times, and Charles G. Ross, St. Louis Post-Dispatch.
1933—Edgar Ansel Mowrer, Chicago Daily News.
1934—Frederick T. Birchall, New York Times.
1935—Arthur Krock, New York Times.
1936—Wilfred C. Barber, Chicago Tribune.
1937—Anne O'Hare McCormick, New York Times.
1938—Arthur Krock, New York Times.
1939—Louis P. Lochner, Associated Press.
1940—Otto D. Tolischus, New York Times.
1941—Bronze plaque to commemorate work of American correspondents on war fronts.
1942—Carlos P. Romulo, Philippines Herald.
1943—Hanson W. Baldwin, New York Times.
1944—Ernest Taylor Pyle, Scripps-Howard Newspaper Alliance.
1945—Harold V. (Hal) Boyle, Associated Press.
1946—Arnaldo Cortesi, New York Times.
1947—Brooks Atkinson, New York Times.

Editorial Writing

1917—New York Tribune.
1918—Louisville (Ky.) Courier-Journal.
1920—Harvey E. Newbranch, Omaha Evening World-Herald.
1922—Frank M. O'Brien, New York Herald.
1923—William Allen White, Emporia Gazette.
1924—Frank Buxton, Boston Herald, Special Prize. Frank I. Cobb, New York World.
1925—Robert Lathan, Charleston (S.C.) News and Courier.
1926—Edward M. Kingsbury, N. Y. Times.
1927—F. Lauriston Bullard, Boston Herald.
1928—Grover C. Hall, Montgomery Advertiser.
1929—Louis Isaac Jaffe, Norfolk Virginian-Pilot.
1931—Chas. Ryckman, Fremont (Neb.) Tribune.
1933—Kansas City (Mo.) Star.
1934—E. P. Chase, Atlantic (Ia.) News Telegraph.
1936—Felix Morley, Washington Post. George B. Parker, Scripps-Howard Newspapers.
1937—John W. Owens, Baltimore Sun.
1938—W.W. Waymack, Des Moines (Ia.) Register and Tribune.
1939—Ronald G. Callvert, Portland Oregonian.
1940—Bart Howard, St. Louis Post-Dispatch.
1941—Reuben Maury, Daily News, N.Y.
1942—Geoffrey Parsons, New York Herald Tribune.
1943—Forrest W. Seymour, Des Moines (Ia.) Register and Tribune.
1944—Henry J. Haskell, Kansas City (Mo.) Star.
1945—George W. Potter, Providence (R.I.) Journal-Bulletin.
1946—Hodding Carter, Greenville (Miss.) Delta Democrat-Times.
1947—William H. Grimes, Wall Street Journal.
1948—Virginius Dabney, Richmond (Va.) Times-Dispatch.
1949—John H. Crider, Boston (Mass.) Herald, Herbert Elliston, Washington Post.
1950—Carl M. Saunders, Jackson (Mich.) Citizen-Patriot.
1951—William H. Fitzpatrick, New Orleans States.
1952—Louis LaCoss, St. Louis Globe Democrat.
1953—Vermont C. Royster, Wall Street Journal.
1954—Don Murray, Boston Herald.
1955—Royce Howes, Detroit Free Press.
1956—Lauren K. Soth, Des Moines (Ia.) Register and Tribune.
1957—Buford Boone, Tuscaloosa (Ala.) News.
1958—Harry S. Ashmore, Arkansas Gazette.
1959—Ralph McGill, Atlanta Constitution.
1960—Lenoir Chambers, Norfolk Virginian-Pilot.
1961—William J. Dorvillier, San Juan (Puerto Rico) Star.
1962—Thomas M. Storke, Santa Barbara (Cal.) News-Press.
1963—Ira B. Harkey, Jr., Pascagoula (Miss.) Chronicle.
1964—Hazel Brannon Smith, Lexington (Miss.) Advertiser.
1965—John R. Harrison, The Gainesville (Fla.) Sun.
1966—Robert Lasch, St. Louis Post-Dispatch.
1967—Eugene C. Patterson, Atlanta Constitution.
1968—John S. Knight, Knight Newspapers.
1969—Paul Greenberg, Pine Bluff (Ark.) Commercial.
1970—Philip L. Geyelin, Washington Post.
1971—Horance G. Davis, Jr., Gainesville (Fla.) Sun.
1972—John Strohmeyer, Bethlehem (Pa.) Globe-Times.
1973—Roger B. Linscott, Berkshire Eagle, Pittsfield, Mass.
1974—F. Gilman Spencer, Trenton (N.J.) Trentonian.
1975—John D. Maurice, Charleston (W. Va.) Daily Mail.
1976—Philip Kerby, Los Angeles Times.
1977—Warren L. Lerude, Foster Church, and Norman F. Cardoza, Reno (Nev.) Evening Gazette and Nevada State Journal.
1978—Meg Greenfield, Washington Post.
1979—Edwin M. Yoder, Washington Star.
1980—Robert L. Bartley, Wall Street Journal.
1982—Jack Rosenthal, New York Times.
1983—Editorial board, Miami Herald.
1984—Albert Scardino, Georgia Gazette.
1985—Richard Aregood, Philadelphia Daily News.
1986—Jack Fuller, Chicago Tribune.
1987—Janathan Freedman, The Tribune (San Diego).

Editorial Cartooning

1922—Rollin Kirby, New York World.
1924—Jay N. Darling, Des Moines Register.
1925—Rollin Kirby, New York World.
1926—D. R. Fitzpatrick, St. Louis Post-Dispatch.
1927—Nelson Harding, Brooklyn Eagle.
1928—Nelson Harding, Brooklyn Eagle.
1929—Rollin Kirby, New York World.
1930—Charles Macauley, Brooklyn Eagle.
1931—Edmund Duffy, Baltimore Sun.
1932—John T. McCutcheon, Chicago Tribune.
1933—H. M. Talburt, Washington Daily News.
1934—Edmund Duffy, Baltimore Sun.
1935—Ross A. Lewis, Milwaukee Journal.
1937—C. D. Batchelor, New York Daily News.
1938—Vaughn Shoemaker, Chicago Daily News.
1939—Charles G. Werner, Daily Oklahoman.
1940—Edmund Duffy, Baltimore Sun.
1941—Jacob Burck, Chicago Times.
1942—Herbert L. Block, Newspaper Enterprise Assn.
1943—Jay N. Darling, Des Moines Register.
1944—Clifford K. Berryman, Washington Star.
1945—Bill Mauldin, United Feature Syndicate.
1946—Bruce Alexander Russell, Los Angeles Times.
1947—Vaughn Shoemaker, Chicago Daily News.
1948—Reuben L. (Rube) Goldberg, N. Y. Sun.
1949—Lute Pease, Newark (N.J.) Evening News.
1950—James T. Berryman, Washington Star.
1951—Reginald W. Manning, Arizona Republic.
1952—Fred L. Packer, New York Mirror.
1953—Edward D. Kuekes, Cleveland Plain Dealer.
1954—Herbert L. Block, Washington Post & Times-Herald.
1955—Daniel R. Fitzpatrick, St. Louis Post-Dispatch.
1956—Robert York, Louisville (Ky.) Times.
1957—Tom Little, Nashville Tennessean.
1958—Bruce M. Shanks, Buffalo Evening News.
1959—Bill Mauldin, St. Louis Post-Dispatch.
1961—Carey Orr, Chicago Tribune.
1962—Edmund S. Valtman, Hartford Times.
1963—Frank Miller, Des Moines Register.
1964—Paul Conrad, Denver Post.
1966—Don Wright, Miami News.
1967—Patrick B. Oliphant, Denver Post.
1968—Eugene Gray Payne, Charlotte Observer.
1969—John Fischetti, Chicago Daily News.
1970—Thomas F. Darcy, Newsday.
1971—Paul Conrad, L. A. Times.
1972—Jeffrey K. MacNelly, Richmond News-Leader.
1974—Paul Szep, Boston Globe.
1975—Garry Trudeau, Universal Press Syndicate.
1976—Tony Auth, Philadelphia Inquirer.
1977—Paul Szep, Boston Globe.
1978—Jeffrey K. MacNelly, Richmond News Leader.
1979—Herbert L. Block, Washington Post.
1980—Don Wright, Miami (Fla.) News.
1981—Mike Peters, Dayton (Oh.) Daily News.

1982—Ben Sargent, Austin American-Statesman.
1983—Richard Lochner, Chicago Tribune.
1984—Paul Conrad, Los Angeles Times.
1985—Jeffrey K. MacNelly, Chicago Tribune.
1986—Jules Feiffer, Village Voice (N.Y. City)
1987—Berke Breathed, Washington Post.

Spot News Photography

1942—Milton Brooks, Detroit News.
1943—Frank Noel, Associated Press.
1944—Frank Filan, AP; Earl L. Bunker, Omaha World-Herald.
1945—Joe Rosenthal, Associated Press, for photograph of planting American flag on Iwo Jima.
1947—Arnold Hardy, amateur, Atlanta, Ga.
1948—Frank Cushing, Boston Traveler.
1949—Nathaniel Fein, New York Herald Tribune.
1950—Bill Crouch, Oakland (Cal.) Tribune.
1951—Max Desfor, Associated Press.
1952—John Robinson and Don Ultang, Des Moines Register and Tribune.
1953—William M. Gallagher, Flint (Mich.) Journal.
1954—Mrs. Walter M. Schau, amateur.
1955—John L. Gaunt, Jr., Los Angeles Times.
1956—New York Daily News.
1957—Harry A. Trask, Boston Traveler.
1958—William C. Beall, Washington Daily News.
1959—William Seaman, Minneapolis Star.
1960—Andrew Lopez, UPI.
1961—Yasushi Nagao, Mainichi Newspapers, Tokyo.
1962—Paul Vathis, Associated Press.
1963—Hector Rondon, La Republica, Caracas, Venezuela.
1964—Robert H. Jackson, Dallas Times-Herald.
1965—Horst Faas, Associated Press.
1966—Kyoichi Sawada, UPI.
1967—Jack R. Thornell, Associated Press.
1968—Rocco Morabito, Jacksonville Journal.
1969—Edward Adams, AP.
1970—Steve Starr, AP.
1971—John Paul Filo, Valley Daily News & Daily Dispatch of Tarentum & New Kensington, Pa.
1972—Horst Faas and Michel Laurent, AP.
1973—Huynh Cong Ut, AP.
1974—Anthony K. Roberts, AP.
1975—Gerald H. Gay, Seattle Times.
1976—Stanley Forman, Boston Herald American.
1977—Neal Ulevich, Associated Press; Stanley Forman, Boston Herald American.
1978—John H. Blair, UPI.
1979—Thomas J. Kelly III, Pottstown (Pa.) Mercury.
1980—UPI.
1981—Larry C. Price, Ft. Worth (Tex.) Star-Telegram.
1982—Ron Edmonds, Associated Press.
1983—Bill Foley, AP.
1984—Stan Grossfeld, Boston Globe.
1985—The Register, Santa Ana, Calif.
1986—Carol Guzy & Michel duCille, Miami Herald.
1987—Kim Komenich, San Francisco Examiner.

Feature Photography

1968—Toshio Sakai, UPI.
1969—Moneta Sleet Jr., Ebony.
1970—Dallas Kinney, Palm Beach Post.
1971—Jack Dykinga, Chicago Sun-Times.
1972—Dave Kennerly, UPI.
1973—Brian Lanker, Topeka Capitol-Journal.
1974—Slava Veder, AP.
1975—Matthew Lewis, Washington Post.
1976—Louisville Courier-Journal and Louisville Times.
1977—Robin Hood, Chattanooga News-Free Press.
1978—J. Ross Baughman, AP.
1979—Staff Photographers, Boston Herald American.
1980—Erwin H. Hagler, Dallas Times-Herald.
1981—Taro M. Yamasaki, Detroit Free Press.
1982—John H. White, Chicago Sun-Times.
1983—James B. Dickman, Dallas Times-Herald.
1984—Anthony Suad, Denver Post.
1985—Stan Grossfeld, Boston Globe; Larry C. Price, Philadelphia Inquirer.
1986—Tom Gralish, Philadelphia Inquirer.
1987—David Peterson, Des Moines Register.

Special Citation

1938—Edmonton (Alberta) Journal, bronze plaque.
1941—New York Times.
1944—Byron Price and Mrs. William Allen White. Also to Richard Rodgers and Oscar Hammerstein 2d, for musical, Oklahoma!
1945—Press cartographers for war maps.
1947—(Pulitzer centennial year.) Columbia Univ. and the Graduate School of Journalism, and St. Louis Post-Dispatch.
1948—Dr. Frank Diehl Fackenthal.
1951—Cyrus L. Sulzberger, New York Times.
1952—Max Kase, New York Journal-American, Kansas City Star.
1953—The New York Times; Lester Markel.
1957—Kenneth Roberts, for his historical novels.
1958—Walter Lippmann, New York Herald Tribune.
1960—Garrett Mattingly, for The Armada.
1961—American Heritage Picture History of the Civil War.
1964—The Gannett Newspapers.
1973—James T. Flexner, for biography of George Washington.
1976—John Hohenberg, for services to American journalism.
1977—Alex Haley, for Roots.
1978—Richard Lee Strout, Christian Science Monitor and New Republic.
—E.B. White.
1984—Theodore Geisel ("Dr. Seuss").
1985—William Schuman, composer, educational leader.
1987—Joseph Pulitzer Jr.

Feature Writing

1979—Jon D. Franklin, Baltimore Evening Sun.
1980—Madeleine Blais, Miami Herald Tropic Magazine.
Janet Cooke, Washington Post.
1981—Teresa Carpenter, Village Voice, New York City.
1982—Saul Pett, Associated Press.
1984—Peter M. Rinearson, Seattle Times.
1985—Alice Steinbach, Baltimore Sun.
1986—John Camp, St. Paul Pioneer Press & Dispatch
1987—Steve Twomey, Philadephia Inquirer.

Explanatory Journalism

1985—Jon Franklin, Baltimore Evening Sun.
1986—New York Times Staff.
1987—Jeff Lyon & Peter Gorner, Chicago Tribune.

Specialized Reporting

1985—Randall Savage, Jackie Crosby, Macon (Ga.) Telegraph and News.
1986—Andrew Schneider & Mary Pat Flaherty, Pittsburgh Press.
1987—Alex S. Jones, New York Times.

Letters

Fiction

For fiction in book form by an American author, preferably dealing with American life.

1918—Ernest Poole, His Family.
1919—Booth Tarkington, The Magnificent Ambersons.
1921—Edith Wharton, The Age of Innocence.
1922—Booth Tarkington, Alice Adams.
1923—Willa Cather, One of Ours.
1924—Margaret Wilson, The Able McLaughlins.
1925—Edna Ferber, So Big.
1926—Sinclair Lewis, Arrowsmith. (Refused prize.)
1927—Louis Bromfield, Early Autumn.
1928—Thornton Wilder, Bridge of San Luis Rey.
1929—Julia M. Peterkin, Scarlet Sister Mary.
1930—Oliver LaFarge, Laughing Boy.
1931—Margaret Ayer Barnes, Years of Grace.
1932—Pearl S. Buck, The Good Earth.
1933—T. S. Stribling, The Store.
1934—Caroline Miller, Lamb in His Bosom.
1935—Josephine W. Johnson, Now in November.
1936—Harold L. Davis, Honey in the Horn.
1937—Margaret Mitchell, Gone with the Wind.
1938—John P. Marquand, The Late George Apley.
1939—Marjorie Kinnan Rawlings, The Yearling.
1940—John Steinbeck, The Grapes of Wrath.
1942—Ellen Glasgow, In This Our Life.
1943—Upton Sinclair, Dragon's Teeth.
1944—Martin Flavin, Journey in the Dark.
1945—John Hersey, A Bell for Adano.
1947—Robert Penn Warren, All the King's Men.
1948—James A Michener, Tales of the South Pacific.
1949—James Gould Cozzens, Guard of Honor.
1950—A. B. Guthrie Jr., The Way West.
1951—Conrad Richter, The Town.
1952—Herman Wouk, The Caine Mutiny.
1953—Ernest Hemingway, The Old Man and the Sea.
1955—William Faulkner, A Fable.
1956—MacKinlay Kantor, Andersonville.
1958—James Agee, A Death in the Family.
1959—Robert Lewis Taylor, The Travels of Jaimie McPheeters.
1960—Allen Drury, Advise and Consent.
1961—Harper Lee, To Kill a Mockingbird.
1962—Edwin O'Connor, The Edge of Sadness.
1963—William Faulkner, The Reivers.
1965—Shirley Ann Grau, The Keepers of the House.
1966—Katherine Anne Porter, Collected Stories of Katherine Anne Porter.
1967—Bernard Malamud, The Fixer.
1968—William Styron, The Confessions of Nat Turner.
1969—N. Scott Momaday, House Made of Dawn.
1970—Jean Stafford, Collected Stories.
1972—Wallace Stegner, Angle of Repose.
1973—Eudora Welty, The Optimist's Daughter.
1975—Michael Shaara, The Killer Angels.
1976—Saul Bellow, Humboldt's Gift.
1978—James Alan McPherson, Elbow Room.
1979—John Cheever, The Stories of John Cheever.
1980—Norman Mailer, The Executioner's Song.
1981—John Kennedy Toole, A Confederacy of Dunces.
1982—John Updike, Rabbit is Rich.
1983—Alice Walker, The Color Purple.

1984—William Kennedy, Ironweed.
1985—Alison Lurie, Foreign Affairs.
1986—Larry McMurtry, Lonesome Dove.
1987—Peter Taylor, A Summons to Memphis.

Drama

For an American play, preferably original and dealing with American life.

1918—Jesse Lynch Williams, Why Marry?
1920—Eugene O'Neill, Beyond the Horizon.
1921—Zona Gale, Miss Lulu Bett.
1922—Eugene O'Neill, Anna Christie.
1923—Owen Davis, Icebound.
1924—Hatcher Hughes, Hell-Bent for Heaven.
1925—Sidney Howard, They Knew What They Wanted.
1926—George Kelly, Craig's Wife.
1927—Paul Green, In Abraham's Bosom.
1928—Eugene O'Neill, Strange Interlude.
1929—Elmer Rice, Street Scene.
1930—Marc Connolly, The Green Pastures.
1931—Susan Glaspell, Alison's House.
1932—George S. Kaufman, Morrie Ryskind and Ira Gershwin, Of Thee I Sing.
1933—Maxwell Anderson, Both Your Houses.
1934—Sidney Kingsley, Men in White.
1935—Zoe Akins, The Old Maid.
1936—Robert E. Sherwood, Idiot's Delight.
1937—George S. Kaufman and Moss Hart, You Can't Take It With You.
1938—Thornton Wilder, Our Town.
1939—Robert E. Sherwood, Abe Lincoln in Illinois.
1940—William Saroyan, The Time of Your Life.
1941—Robert E. Sherwood, There Shall Be No Night.
1943—Thornton Wilder, The Skin of Our Teeth.
1945—Mary Chase, Harvey.
1946—Russel Crouse and Howard Lindsay, State of the Union.
1948—Tennessee Williams, A Streetcar Named Desire.
1949—Arthur Miller, Death of a Salesman.
1950—Richard Rodgers, Oscar Hammerstein 2d, and Joshua Logan, South Pacific.
1952—Joseph Kramm, The Shrike.
1953—William Inge, Picnic.
1954—John Patrick, Teahouse of the August Moon.
1955—Tennessee Williams, Cat on a Hot Tin Roof.
1956—Frances Goodrich and Albert Hackett, The Diary of Anne Frank.
1957—Eugene O'Neill, Long Day's Journey Into Night.
1958—Ketti Frings, Look Homeward, Angel.
1959—Archibald MacLeish, J. B.
1960—George Abbott, Jerome Weidman, Sheldon Harnick and Jerry Bock, Fiorello.
1961—Tad Mosel, All the Way Home.
1962—Frank Loesser and Abe Burrows, How To Succeed In Business Without Really Trying.
1965—Frank D. Gilroy, The Subject Was Roses.
1967—Edward Albee, A Delicate Balance.
1969—Howard Sackler, The Great White Hope.
1970—Charles Gordone, No Place to Be Somebody.
1971—Paul Zindel, The Effect of Gamma Rays on Man-in-the-Moon Marigolds.
1973—Jason Miller, That Championship Season.
1975—Edward Albee, Seascape.
1976—Michael Bennett, James Kirkwood, Nicholas Dante, Marvin Hamlisch, Edward Kleban, A Chorus Line.
1977—Michael Cristofer, The Shadow Box.
1978—Donald L. Coburn, The Gin Game.
1979—Sam Shepard, Buried Child.
1980—Lanford Wilson, Talley's Folly.
1981—Beth Henley, Crimes of the Heart.
1982—Charles Fuller, A Soldier's Play.
1983—Marsha Norman, 'night, Mother.
1984—David Mamet, Glengarry Glen Ross.
1985—Stephen Sondheim, James Lapine, Sunday in the Park with George.
1987—August Wilson, Fences

History

For a book on the history of the United States.

1917—J. J. Jusserand, With Americans of Past and Present Days.
1918—James Ford Rhodes, History of the Civil War.
1920—Justin H. Smith, The War with Mexico.
1921—William Sowden Sims, The Victory at Sea.
1922—James Truslow Adams, The Founding of New England.
1923—Charles Warren, The Supreme Court in United States History.
1924—Charles Howard McIlwain, The American Revolution: A Constitutional Interpretation.
1925—Frederick L. Paxton, A History of the American Frontier.
1926—Edward Channing, A History of the U.S..
1927—Samuel Flag Bemis, Pinckney's Treaty.
1928—Vernon Louis Parrington, Main Currents in American Thought.
1929—Fred A. Shannon, The Organization and Administration of the Union Army, 1861-65.
1930—Claude H. Van Tyne, The War of Independence.
1931—Bernadotte E. Schmitt, The Coming of the War, 1914.
1932—Gen. John J. Pershing, My Experiences in the World War.
1933—Frederick J. Turner, The Significance of Sections in American History.
1934—Herbert Agar, The People's Choice.
1935—Charles McLean Andrews, The Colonial Period of American History.
1936—Andrew C. McLaughlin, The Constitutional History of the United States.
1937—Van Wyck Brooks, The Flowering of New England.
1938—Paul Herman Buck, The Road to Reunion, 1865-1900.
1939—Frank Luther Mott, A History of American Magazines.
1940—Carl Sandburg, Abraham Lincoln: The War Years.
1941—Marcus Lee Hansen, The Atlantic Migration, 1607-1860.
1942—Margaret Leech, Reveille in Washington.
1943—Esther Forbes, Paul Revere and the World He Lived In.
1944—Merle Curti, The Growth of American Thought.
1945—Stephen Bonsal, Unfinished Business.
1946—Arthur M. Schlesinger Jr., The Age of Jackson.
1947—James Phinney Baxter 3d, Scientists Against Time.
1948—Bernard De Voto, Across the Wide Missouri.
1949—Roy F. Nichols, The Disruption of American Democracy.
1950—O. W. Larkin, Art and Life in America.
1951—R. Carlyle Buley, The Old Northwest: Pioneer Period 1815-1840.
1952—Oscar Handlin, The Uprooted.
1953—George Dangerfield, The Era of Good Feelings.
1954—Bruce Catton, A Stillness at Appomattox.
1955—Paul Horgan, Great River: The Rio Grande in North American History.
1956—Richard Hofstadter, The Age of Reform.
1957—George F. Kennan, Russia Leaves the War.
1958—Bray Hammond, Banks and Politics in America—From the Revolution to the Civil War.
1959—Leonard D. White and Jean Schneider, The Republican Era; 1869-1901.
1960—Margaret Leech, In the Days of McKinley.
1961—Herbert Feis, Between War and Peace: The Potsdam Conference.
1962—Lawrence H. Gibson, The Triumphant Empire: Thunderclouds Gather in the West.
1963—Constance McLaughlin Green, Washington: Village and Capital, 1800-1878.
1964—Sumner Chilton Powell, Puritan Village: The Formation of A New England Town.
1965—Irwin Unger, The Greenback Era.
1966—Perry Miller, Life of the Mind in America.
1967—William H. Goetzmann, Exploration and Empire: the Explorer and Scientist in the Winning of the American West.
1968—Bernard Bailyn, The Ideological Origins of the American Revolution.
1969—Leonard W. Levy, Origin of the Fifth Amendment.
1970—Dean Acheson, Present at the Creation: My Years in the State Department.
1971—James McGregor Burns, Roosevelt: The Soldier of Freedom.
1972—Carl N. Degler, Neither Black Nor White.
1973—Michael Kammen, People of Paradox: An Inquiry Concerning the Origins of American Civilization.
1974—Daniel J. Boorstin, The Americans: The Democratic Experience.
1975—Dumas Malone, Jefferson and His Time.
1976—Paul Horgan, Lamy of Santa Fe.
1977—David M. Potter, The Impending Crisis.
1978—Alfred D. Chandler, Jr., The Visible Hand: The Managerial Revolution in American Business.
1979—Don E. Fehrenbacher, The Dred Scott Case: Its Significance in American Law and Politics.
1980—Leon F. Litwack, Been in the Storm So Long.
1981—Lawrence A. Cremin, American Education: The National Experience, 1783-1876.
1982—C. Vann Woodward, ed., Mary Chestnut's Civil War.
1983—Rhys L. Issac, The Transformation of Virginia, 1740-1790.
1985—Thomas K. McCraw, Prophets of Regulation.
1986—Walter A. McDougall, . . . The Heavens and the Earth.
1987—Bernard Bailyn, Voyagers to the West.

Biography or Autobiography

For a distinguished biography or autobiography by an American author.

1917—Laura E. Richards and Maude Howe Elliott, assisted by Florence Howe Hall, Julia Ward Howe.
1918—William Cabell Bruce, Benjamin Franklin, Self-Revealed.
1919—Henry Adams, The Education of Henry Adams.
1920—Albert J. Beveridge, The Life of John Marshall.
1921—Edward Bok, The Americanization of Edward Bok.
1922—Hamlin Garland, A Daughter of the Middle Border.
1923—Burton J. Hendrick, The Life and Letters of Walter H. Page.
1924—Michael Pupin, From Immigrant to Inventor.
1925—M. A. DeWolfe Howe, Barrett Wendell and His Letters.
1926—Harvey Cushing, Life of Sir William Osler.
1927—Emory Holloway, Whitman: An Interpretation in Narrative.
1928—Charles Edward Russell, The American Orchestra and Theodore Thomas.
1929—Burton J. Hendrick, The Training of an American: The Earlier Life and Letters of Walter H. Page.
1930—Marquis James, The Raven (Sam Houston).
1931—Henry James, Charles W. Eliot.
1932—Henry F. Pringle, Theodore Roosevelt.
1933—Allan Nevins, Grover Cleveland.
1934—Tyler Dennett, John Hay.
1935—Douglas Southall Freeman, R. E. Lee
1936—Ralph Barton Perry, The Thought and Character of William James.
1937—Allan Nevins, Hamilton Fish: The Inner History of the Grant Administration.
1938—Divided between Odell Shepard, Pedlar's Progress; Marquis James, Andrew Jackson.
1939—Carl Van Doren, Benjamin Franklin.
1940—Ray Stannard Baker, Woodrow Wilson, Life and Letters.
1941—Ola Elizabeth Winslow, Jonathan Edwards.

1942—Forrest Wilson, Crusader in Crinoline.
1943—Samuel Eliot Morison, Admiral of the Ocean Sea (Columbus).
1944—Carleton Mabee, The American Leonardo: The Life of Samuel F. B. Morse.
1945—Russell Blaine Nye, George Bancroft; Brahmin Rebel.
1946—Linny Marsh Wolfe, Son of the Wilderness.
1947—William Allen White, The Autobiography of William Allen White.
1948—Margaret Clapp, Forgotten First Citizen: John Bigelow.
1949—Robert E. Sherwood, Roosevelt and Hopkins.
1950—Samuel Flag Bemis, John Quincy Adams and the Foundations of American Foreign Policy.
1951—Margaret Louise Colt, John C. Calhoun: American Portrait.
1952—Merlo J. Pusey, Charles Evans Hughes.
1953—David J. Mays, Edmund Pendleton, 1721-1803.
1954—Charles A. Lindbergh, The Spirit of St. Louis.
1955—William S. White, The Taft Story.
1956—Talbot F. Hamlin, Benjamin Henry Latrobe.
1957—John F. Kennedy, Profiles in Courage.
1958—Douglas Southall Freeman (decd. 1953), George Washington, Vols. I-VI: John Alexander Carroll and Mary Wells Ashworth, Vol. VII.
1959—Arthur Walworth, Woodrow Wilson: American Prophet.
1960—Samuel Eliot Morison, John Paul Jones.
1961—David Donald, Charles Sumner and The Coming of the Civil War.
1963—Leon Edel, Henry James: Vol. II, The Conquest of London, 1870-1881; Vol. III, The Middle Years, 1881-1895.
1964—Walter Jackson Bate, John Keats.
1965—Ernest Samuels, Henry Adams.
1966—Arthur M. Schlesinger Jr., A Thousand Days.
1967—Justin Kaplan, Mr. Clemens and Mark Twain.
1968—George F. Kennan, Memoirs (1925-1950).
1969—B. L. Reid, The Man from New York: John Quinn and his Friends.
1970—T. Harry Williams, Huey Long.
1971—Lawrence Thompson, Robert Frost: The Years of Triumph, 1915-1938.
1972—Joseph P. Lash, Eleanor and Franklin.
1973—W. A. Swanberg, Luce and His Empire.
1974—Louis Sheaffer, O'Neill, Son and Artist.
1975—Robert A. Caro, The Power Broker: Robert Moses and the Fall of New York.
1976—R.W.B. Lewis, Edith Wharton: A Biography.
1977—John E. Mack, A Prince of Our Disorder, The Life of T.E. Lawrence.
1978—Walter Jackson Bate, Samuel Johnson.
1979—Leonard Baker, Days of Sorrow and Pain: Leo Baeck and the Berlin Jews.
1980—Edmund Morris, The Rise of Theodore Roosevelt.
1981—Robert K. Massie, Peter the Great: His Life and World.
1982—William S. McFeely, Grant: A Biography.
1983—Russell Baker, Growing Up.
1984—Louis R. Harlan, Booker T. Washington.
1985—Kenneth Silverman, The Life and Times of Cotton Mather.
1986—Elizabeth Frank, Louise Bogan: A Portrait.
1987—David J. Garrow, Bearing the Cross: Martin Luther King Jr. and the Southern Christian Leadership Conference.

American Poetry

Before this prize was established in 1922, awards were made from gifts provided by the Poetry Society: 1918—Love Songs, by Sara Teasdale. 1919—Old Road to Paradise, by Margaret Widemer; Corn Huskers, by Carl Sandburg.

1922—Edwin Arlington Robinson, Collected Poems.
1923—Edna St. Vincent Millay, The Ballad of the Harp-Weaver; A Few Figs from Thistles; Eight Sonnets in American Poetry, 1922; A Miscellany.
1924—Robert Frost, New Hampshire: A Poem with Notes and Grace Notes.
1925—Edwin Arlington Robinson, The Man Who Died Twice.
1926—Amy Lowell, What's O'Clock.
1927—Leonora Speyer, Fiddler's Farewell.
1928—Edwin Arlington Robinson, Tristram.
1929—Stephen Vincent Benet, John Brown's Body.
1930—Conrad Aiken, Selected Poems.
1931—Robert Frost, Collected Poems.
1932—George Dillon, The Flowering Stone.
1933—Archibald MacLeish, Conquistador.
1934—Robert Hillyer, Collected Verse.
1935—Audrey Wurdemann, Bright Ambush.
1936—Robert P. Tristram Coffin, Strange Holiness.
1937—Robert Frost, A Further Range.
1938—Marya Zaturenska, Cold Morning Sky.
1939—John Gould Fletcher, Selected Poems.
1940—Mark Van Doren, Collected Poems.
1941—Leonard Bacon, Sunderland Capture.
1942—William Rose Benet, The Dust Which Is God.
1943—Robert Frost, A Witness Tree.
1944—Stephen Vincent Benet, Western Star.
1945—Karl Shapiro, V-Letter and Other Poems.
1947—Robert Lowell, Lord Weary's Castle.
1948—W. H. Auden, The Age of Anxiety.
1949—Peter Viereck, Terror and Decorum.
1950—Gwendolyn Brooks, Annie Allen.
1951—Carl Sandburg, Complete Poems.
1952—Marianne Moore, Collected Poems.
1953—Archibald MacLeish, Collected Poems.
1954—Theodore Roethke, The Waking.
1955—Wallace Stevens, Collected Poems.
1956—Elizabeth Bishop, Poems, North and South.
1957—Richard Wilbur, Things of This World.
1958—Robert Penn Warren, Promises: Poems 1954-1956.
1959—Stanley Kunitz, Selected Poems 1928-1958.
1960—W. D. Snodgrass, Heart's Needle.
1961—Phyllis McGinley, Times Three: Selected Verse from Three Decades.
1962—Alan Dugan, Poems.
1963—William Carlos Williams, Pictures From Breughel.
1964—Louis Simpson, At the End of the Open Road.
1965—John Berryman, 77 Dream Songs.
1966—Richard Eberhart, Selected Poems.
1967—Anne Sexton, Live or Die.
1968—Anthony Hecht, The Hard Hours.
1969—George Oppen, Of Being Numerous.
1970—Richard Howard, Untitled Subjects.
1971—William S. Merwin, The Carrier of Ladders.
1972—James Wright, Collected Poems.
1973—Maxine Winokur Kumin, Up Country.
1975—Gary Snyder, Turtle Island.
1976—John Ashbery, Self-Portrait in a Convex Mirror.
1977—James Merrill, Divine Comedies.
1978—Howard Nemerov, Collected Poems.
1979—Robert Penn Warren, Now and Then: Poems 1976-1978.
1980—Donald Justice, Selected Poems.
1981—James Schuyler, The Morning of the Poem.
1982—Sylvia Plath, The Collected Poems.
1983—Galway Kinnell, Selected Poems.
1984—Mary Oliver, American Primitive.
1985—Carolyn Kizer, Yin.
1986—Henry Taylor, The Flying Change.
1987—Rita Dove, Thomas and Beulah.

General Non-Fiction

1962—Theodore H. White, The Making of the President 1960.
1963—Barbara W. Tuchman, The Guns of August.
1964—Richard Hofstadter, Anti-Intellectualism in American Life.
1965—Howard Mumford Jones, O Strange New World.
1966—Edwin Way Teale, Wandering Through Winter.
1967—David Brion Davis, The Problem of Slavery in Western Culture.
1968—Will and Ariel Durant, Rousseau and Revolution.
1969—Norman Mailer, The Armies of the Night; and Rene Jules Dubos, So Human an Animal: How We Are Shaped by Surroundings and Events.
1970—Eric H. Erikson, Gandhi's Truth.
1971—John Toland, The Rising Sun.
1972—Barbara W. Tuchman, Stilwell and the American Experience in China, 1911-1945.
1973—Frances FitzGerald, Fire in the Lake: The Vietnamese and the Americans in Vietnam; and Robert Coles, Children of Crisis, Volumes II and III.
1974—Ernest Becker, The Denial of Death.
1975—Annie Dillard, Pilgrim at Tinker Creek.
1976—Robert N. Butler, Why Survive? Being Old in America.
1977—William W. Warner, Beautiful Swimmers.
1978—Carl Sagan, The Dragons of Eden.
1979—Edward O. Wilson, On Human Nature.
1980—Douglas R. Hofstadter, Gödel, Escher, Bach: An Eternal Golden Braid.
1981—Carl E. Schorske, Fin-de-Siecle Vienna: Politics and Culture.
1982—Tracy Kidder, The Soul of a New Machine.
1983—Susan Sheehan, Is There No Place on Earth for Me?
1984—Paul Starr, Social Transformation of American Medicine.
1985—Studs Terkel, The Good War.
1986—Joseph Lelyveld, Move Your Shadow; J. Anthony Lukas, Common Ground.
1987—David K. Shipler, Arab and Jew.

Music

For composition by an American (before 1977, by a composer resident in the U.S.), in the larger forms of chamber, orchestra or choral music or for an operatic work including ballet. A special posthumous award was granted in 1976 to Scott Joplin.

1943—William Schuman, Secular Cantata No. 2, A Free Song.
1944—Howard Hanson, Symphony No. 4, Op. 34.
1945—Aaron Copland, Appalachian Spring.
1946—Leo Sowerby, The Canticle of the Sun.
1947—Charles E. Ives, Symphony No. 3.
1948—Walter Piston, Symphony No. 3.
1949—Virgil Thomson, Louisiana Story.
1950—Gian-Carlo Menotti, The Consul.
1951—Douglas Moore, Giants in the Earth.
1952—Gail Kubik, Symphony Concertante.
1954—Quincy Porter, Concerto for Two Pianos and Orchestra.
1955—Gian-Carlo Menotti, The Saint of Bleecker Street.
1956—Ernest Toch, Symphony No. 3.
1957—Norman Dello Joio, Meditations on Ecclesiastes.
1958—Samuel Barber, Vanessa.
1959—John La Montaine, Concerto for Piano and Orchestra.
1960—Elliott Carter, Second String Quartet.
1961—Walter Piston, Symphony No. 7.
1962—Robert Ward, The Crucible.
1963—Samuel Barber, Piano Concerto No. 1.
1966—Leslie Bassett, Variations for Orchestra.
1967—Leon Kirchner, Quartet No. 3.
1968—George Crumb, Echoes of Time and The River.
1969—Karel Husa, String Quartet No. 3.

1970—Charles W. Wuorinen, Time's Encomium.
1971—Mario Davidovsky, Synchronisms No. 6.
1972—Jacob Druckman, Windows.
1973—Elliott Carter, String Quartet No. 3.
1974—Donald Martino, Notturno. (Special citation) Roger Sessions.
1975—Dominick Argento, From the Diary of Virginia Woolf.
1976—Ned Rorem, Air Music.
1977—Richard Wernick, Visions of Terror and Wonder.
1978—Michael Colgrass, Deja Vu for Percussion and Orchestra.
1979—Joseph Schwantner, Aftertones of Infinity.
1980—David Del Tredici, In Memory of a Summer Day.
1982—Roger Sessions, Concerto For Orchestra. (Special Citation) Milton Babbitt.
1983—Ellen T. Zwilich, Three Movements for Orchestra.
1984—Bernard Rands, Canti del Sole.
1985—Stephen Albert, Symphony, RiverRun.
1986—George Perle, Wind Quintet IV.
1987—John Harbison, The Flight Into Egypt.

Special Awards

Awarded in 1986 unless otherwise noted

Books, Allied Arts

Academy of American Poets awards: fellowship for distinquished achievement, $10,000: Howard Moss; Landon Translation Award, $1,000: Mark Anderson, *The Storm of Roses* by Ingeborg Bachmann; Lavan Younger Poet Awards, $1,000 each: Rita Dove, Rodney Jones, Timothy Steele.

American Academy and Institute of Arts and Letters awards: gold medal for belles lettres: Jacques Barzun; new Academy literary members: Renata Adler, Robert Bly, Amy Clampitt, Robert Coover, Robert Creeley, Emily Hahn, Gary Snyder; literary awards, $1,500 to $5,000 each: Antler, Wendell Berry, Evan S. Connell, Ernest J. Gaines, Stephen Jay Gould, A.R. Gurney Jr., Jeannette Haien, Ralph Manheim, Sandra McPherson, Paul Metcalf, Steven Millhauser, Robert Phillips, Padgett Powell, Norman Rush, Roger Shattuck.

American Book Awards, $10,000 each & Louise Nevelson plaque: fiction: E.L. Doctorow, *World's Fair;* non-fiction: Barry Lopez, *Arctic Dreams.*

Anhinga Prize for Poetry, by Anhinga Press: Robert J. Levy, *Whistle Maker.*

Bancroft Prizes, by Columbia Univ., for American history book, $4,000 each: Thomas M. Doerflinger, *A Vigorous Spirit of Enterprise;* Roger Lane, *Roots of Violence in Black Philadelphia, 1860-1900.*

Caldecott Medal, by American Library Assn., for children's book illustration: Richard Egielski, *Hey, Al.*

Carey-Thomas Award, by *Publishers Weekly,* for creative publishing: Elizabeth Sifton, Viking Press.

Christopher Awards, by Christopher Foundation, for affirmation of human values, bronze medallions: books for adults: *Arctic Dreams,* Barry Lopez, *Beyond Survival,* Theresa Saldana; *Decision in Philadelphia,* Christopher Collier and James Lincoln Collier; *Faith of a People,* Pablo Galdamez, trans. Robert A. Barr; *Kaffir Boy,* Mark Mathabane, *A Loss for Words,* Lou Ann Walker; *A Testament of Hope,* ed. James M. Washington; *Through the Gospel with Dom Helder Camara,* trans. Alan Neame; *When All You've Wanted Isn't Enough,* Harold S. Kushner; books for young people: *Duncan and Dolores,* Barbara Samuels; *The Purple Coat,* Amy Hest, il. Amy Schwartz; *Borrowed Summer,* Marion Walker Doren; *Class Dismissed II,* Mel Glenn, photos by Michael J. Bernstein.

General Electric Foundation Awards for Younger Writers: Julia Alvarez, in *new renaissance;* Sandra Joy Jackson-Opoku, in *Heresies;* Rodney Jones, in *River Styx;* Ewa Kuryluk, in *Formations;* Jim Powell, in *The Paris Review;* Eliot Weinberger, in *Sulfur.*

Golden Kite Awards, by Society of Children's Book Writers: fiction: Margaret Rostkowski, *After the Dancing Days;* non-fiction: Milton Meltzer, *Poverty in America;* picture-illustration: Suse MacDonald, *Alphabatics.*

Los Angeles Times Book Prizes: Margaret Atwood, *The Handmaid's Tale;* Geoffrey Hosking, *The First Socialist Society;* Joseph Lelyveld, *Move Your Shadow;* Maynard Mack, *Alexander Pope;* Derek Walcott, *Collected Poems, 1948-1984;* Kirsch Award, for body of work by writer on or in the West: Kay Boyle.

National Arts Club Medal of Honor for Literature: Robertson Davies.

National Book Critics Circle Prizes: fiction: *Kate Vaiden,* Reynolds Price; nonfiction: *War Without Mercy,* John W. Dower; biography: *Tombee,* Theodore Rosengarten, poetry: *Wild Gratitude,* Edward Hirsch; criticism: *Less Than One,* Joseph Brodsky; citation for excellence in reviewing: Richard Eder, Los Angeles Times.

Newbery Medal: by American Library Assn., for children's literature: Sid Fleischman, *The Whipping Boy.*

New York Times Best Illustrated Children's Books: *The Stranger,* Chris Van Allsburg; *The Ugly Duckling,* by Hans Christian Andersen, il. Robert Van Nutt; *Flying,* Donald Crews; *The Owl Scatterer,* Howard Norman, il. Michael McCurdy; *Rembrandt Takes a Walk,* Mark Strand, il. Red Grooms; *Cherries and Cherry Pits,* Vera B. Williams; *Molly's New Washing Machine,* Laura Geringer, il. Peter Mathers; *Brave Irene,* William Steig; *One Morning,* Canna Funakoshi, il. Yohji Izawa, *Pigs from A to Z,* Arthur Geisert.

O'Dell Award, for juvenile historical fiction, $5,000: Scott O'Dell, *Streams to the River.*

Poe Awards, by Mystery Writers of America: novel: *A Dark-Adapted Eye,* Barbara Vine; first novel: *No One Rides for Free,* Larry Beinhart; critical autobiographical: *Here Lies,* Eric Ambler; paperback: *The Junkyard Dog,* Robert Campbell; fact crime: *Careless Whispers,* Carlton Stowers; juvenile: *The Other Side of the Dark,* Joan Lowery Nixon; grand master: Michael Gilbert.

Rhea Award, by Dungannon Foundation, for short story contribution, $25,000: Robert Coover.

Ritz-Hemingway Award, for novel, $50,000: Peter Taylor, *A Summons to Memphis.*

Taylor Award for Modern American Poetry, for distinguished career, $10,000: Howard Nemerov.

Whitman Award, $1,000: Judith Baumel, *The Weight of Numbers.*

Whitman Citation of Merit for Poets, $10,000 and 2-year title, New York State Poet: Stanley Kunitz.

Whiting Writers Awards, Whiting Foundation, for emerging talent, $25,000 each: Hayden Carruth, August Wilson, John Ash, Kent Haruf, Denis Johnson, Darryl Pinkney, Padgett Powell, Mona Simpson, Frank Stewart, Ruth Stone.

Journalism Awards

Catholic Press Assn. Awards: short story: *U.S. Catholic,* "Whose Child Is This?" Garrison Keillor; *Commonweal,* "The Force of Cardinal Lustiger," Steven Englund; editorial: *U.S. Catholic,* "Property Values," Robert E. Burns; column: *Commonweal,* "Of Several Minds," John Garvey; poetry: *New Catholic World,* "Asymmetry," Ruth de Menezes.

International Center Award (New York City), for achievement in journalism: A.M. Rosenthal, *New York Times.*

National Journalism Awards, by Scripps-Howard Foundation, $41,000: Pyle Award, for human interest reporting: Greta Tilley, *Greensboro* (N.C.) *News & Record,* Stone Award, for editorial writing: Mary Cantwell, *New York Times;* Meeman Award, for conservation journalism: Eric Nalder, Dick Clever, Elouise Shumacher, Tom Brown, Eric Pryner, *Seattle Times;* Bob Anderson, Michael P. Dunne, *Morning Advocate* (Baton Rouge, La.); E.W. Scripps Award, for First Amendment service: Douglass T. Davidoff, Kathleen M. Johnston, Hugh M. Rutledge, *Indianapolis News;* Howard Award, for public service journalism; Matthew Brelis, Andrew Schneider, *Pittsburgh Press;* Louis M. Perez, Dave Schultz, Terrence Tomalin, Tom Arthur, *The Ledger* (Lakeland, Fla.); Schulz Award, for promising cartoonist: V. Gene Myers; Charles E. Scripps Award, for newspaper promoting literacy. *El Paso Herald-Post.*

National Magazine Awards, by Amer. Society of Magazine Editors: public interest: *Money*, Andrea Rock, Martha Mader; reporting: *Life*, Anne Fadiman; personal service: *Consumer Reports*, Trudy Lieberman; special interests: *Sports Afield:* design: *Elle;* photography: *National Geographic;* fiction: *Esquire*, Louis Erdrich, John Edgar Wideman, Tim O'Brien; essays & criticism: *Outside*, David Quammen; single-topic issue: *The Bulletin of the Atomic Scientists*, "Chernobyl: The Emerging Story"; general excellence: *New England Monthly*, *Common Cause*, *Elle*, *People*.

Olive Branch Awards, by Writers' and Publishers' Alliance for Nuclear Disarmament & N.Y.U. Center for War, Peace, and the News Media, for magazine coverage of nuclear arms issue: *Bulletin of the Atomic Scientists*, *People*, *The Sciences*, *Harper's*, *The Atlantic*, *The New Republic*, *U.S.A. Today Magazine*, *World Policy Journal*, *National Journal*, *Science;* newspaper: Los Angeles Times, Washington Post/Fred Hiatt.

Polk Awards, by Long Island Univ.: citation for life's work: James Reston, *New York Times;* science reporting: "Science Times," *New York Times*, Richard Flaste, ed.; foreign reporting: *Newsweek*, for coverage of terrorism in Middle East; national reporting: Andrew Wolfson, Daniel Rubin, *Louisville Courier-Journal;* local reporting, Sally Jacobs, *Raleigh News and Observer;* regional reporting: Alex Beasley, Rosemary Goudreau, *Orlando Sentinel;* financial reporting: Peter G. Gosselin, *Boston Globe;* environmental reporting: High Country News, Paonia, Col.

Theater and Broadcasting Awards

Astaire Award, for best dancers of theater season: Robert Lindsay, "Me and My Girl"; special lifetime achievement award: Hanya Holm.

Blackburn Prize, for woman playwright, de Kooning print & $2,000 each: Ellen McLaughlin, "How to Say Goodbye"; Mary Gallagher, "A Narrow Bed."

Drama Desk Awards: new play: "Fences," August Wilson; new musical: "Les Miserables"; actor: James Earl Jones, "Fences"; actress: Linda Lavin, "Broadway Bound"; musical actor: Robert Lindsay, "Me and My Girl"; musical actress: Teresa Stratas, "Rags."

Emmy Awards, by Academy of Television Arts and Sciences, for nighttime programs, 1985-86: Dramatic series: *Cagney & Lacey*, CBS: actress, drama: Sharon Gless, *Cagney & Lacey;* actor, drama: William Daniels, *St. Elsewhere*, NBC; supporting actress: Bonnie Bartlett, *St. Elsewhere;* supporting actor: John Karlen, *Cagney & Lacey*. Comedy series: *Golden Girls*, NBC; actress, comedy: Betty White, *Golden Girls;* actor, comedy: Michael J. Fox, *Family Ties*, NBC; supporting actress: Rhea Perlman, *Cheers*, NBC; supporting actor: John Larroquette, *Night Court*, NBC; series guest performer: John Lithgow, "The Doll," *Amazing Stories*, NBC; series direction: Georg Stanford Brown, *Cagney & Lacey*. Special: "Love is Never Silent," NBC; mini-series: "Peter the Great," NBC; actress: Marlo Thomas, "Nobody's Child," CBS; actor: Dustin Hoffman, "Death of a Salesman," CBS.

Hayes Awards, for Washington, D.C. theater: resident shows: play: "The Miser," Shakespeare Theater at the Folger; musical: "Quilters," Castle Arts Center; new play: "New York Mets," T.J. Edwards; actress: Tana Hicken, "The Wild Duck"; actor: Howie Seago, "Ajax"; supporting actress: Pat Carroll, "Romeo and Juliet"; supporting actor: Stanley Anderson, "The Piggy Bank"; musical performer: Frank Kopyc, "Hot Mikado"; director: John Going, "The Miser."

Nathan Award, for drama criticism, $5,000: Gordon Rogoff, *The Village Voice*.

National Journalism Awards, by Scripps-Howard Foundation, for broadcast journalism: Charles E. Scripps Award, for promotion of literacy: Jeanne Findlater, Mimmi Mathis, Larry Alt, WXYZ-TV, Detroit; Howard Award, for public service, radio: Leonard Marcotte, John O. Reynolds, Edward W. Brouder Jr., Jerry Little, WJYY, Concord, N.H.; public service, TV: Mark Lagervist, WXFL, Tampa.

Outer Critics Circle Awards, by non-New York City critics: Broadway play: "Fences," August Wilson; Broadway musical: "Les Miserables"; Off-Broadway play: "The Common Pursuit"; Off-Broadway musical: "Stardust"; Gasner Award, for playwright: August Wilson, "Fences"; Broadway actor: James Earl Jones, "Fences"; Broadway actress: Linda Lavin, "Broadway Bound"; special award: Jackie Mason, "The World According to Me!"

Polk Awards, by Long Island University, for national TV reporting: Bill Moyers, "CBS Reports: The Vanishing Family—Crisis in Black America"; local TV reporting: Lee Coppola, WKBW-TV, Buffalo, "A Lesson in Deceit."

Peabody Awards, by Univ. of Georgia School of Journalism & Mass Communications, for broadcasting: "The Cosby Show," NBC; Jim Henson's Muppets; "This Week with David Brinkley," ABC; "Newsmark: Where in the World Are We?", CBS News; "CBS Reports: The Vanishing Family—Crisis in Black America"; "Sunday Morning: Vladimir Horowitz," CBS News.

Tony (Antoinette Perry) Awards: musical: "Les Miserables"; play: "Fences"; musical actor: Robert Lindsay, "Me and My Girl"; musical actress: Maryann Plunkett, "Me and My Girl"; actor, play: James Earl Jones, "Fences"; actress, play: Linda Lavin, "Broadway Bound"; featured actor, musical: Michael Maguire, "Les Miserables"; featured actress, musical: Frances Ruffelle, "Les Miserables"; featured actor, play: John Randolph, "Broadway Bound"; featured actress, play: Mary Alice, "Fences"; book, musical: Alain Boublil and Claude-Michel Schonberg, "Les Miserables"; direction, play: Lloyd Richards, "Fences"; direction, musical: Trevor Nunn and John Caird, "Les Miserables"; scenic design: John Napier, "Les Miserables"; costume design: John Napier, "Starlight Express"; lighting design: David Hersey, "Les Miserables"; choreography: Gillian Gregory, "Me and My Girl"; reproduction: "All My Sons."

Miscellaneous Awards

Academy of Country Music Awards: new female vocalist: Holly Dunn; new male vocalist: Dwight Yoakom; group: The Forester Sisters; duet: The Judds; female vocalist: Reba McEntire; male vocalist: Randy Travis; entertainer of the year: Hank Williams Jr.: album of the year: "Storms of Life," Randy Travis; song of the year: "On the Other Hand," by Paul Overstreet & Don Schlitz; single of the year: "On the Other Hand," Randy Travis; video: "Whoever's in New England," Reba McEntire; pioneer award: Minnie Pearl; career achievement: Carl Perkins.

American Academy and Institute of Arts and Letters Awards, $50,000: distinguished service: Isaac Stern; gold medal for painting: Isabel Bishop; Brunner Memorial Prize in Architecture: James Ingo Freed; new Institute members: Frank Gehry, Anne Poor, James Rosenquist, Cy Twombly; new Academy members: Robert Motherwell, Milton Babbitt.

Capezio Dance Awards, $5,000 each: Fred Astaire, Bob Fosse, Rudolf Nureyev, Jac Venza of "Dance in America."

Christopher Awards: films: "The Mission" & "Mother Teresa"; special award: Elie Wiesel; youth award: Trevor Ferrell.

Directors Guild of America Award: Oliver Stone, "Platoon"; Griffith Award, for lifetime achievement, Elia Kazan.

National High School Band Institute Awards: band of the year: Harlingen H.S. Band Wind Ensemble, Harlingen, Tex.; band directors of the year: Larry Guilliouma, Harlingen H.S. Band; William P. Foster, McDonald's All-American H.S. Marching Band, Tallahassee, Fla.; Band Directors' Hall of Fame: William P. Foster.

Rock and Roll Hall of Fame: new members: B.B. King, Muddy Waters, Big Joe Turner, The Coasters, Clyde McPhatter, Jackie Wilson, Smokey Robinson, Marvin Gaye, Aretha Franklin, Bo Diddley, Bill Haley, Carl Perkins, Roy Orbison, Eddie Cochran, Rick Nelson.

Scripps American Dance Festival Award, for lifetime contribution to American modern dance $25,000: Alvin Ailey.

Tyler Prize, by Univ. of Southern California, for environmental science research, $150,000: Richard Evans Schultes, botanist; Gilbert F. White, geographer.

Weekly Reader Invention Contest Winner: Suzanna Goodlin, for "edible pet food server."

Motion Picture Academy Awards (Oscars)

1927-28

Actor: Emil Jannings, *The Way of All Flesh.*
Actress: Janet Gaynor, *Seventh Heaven.*
Director: Frank Borzage, *Seventh Heaven;* Lewis Milestone, *Two Arabian Knights.*
Picture: *Wings,* Paramount.

1928-29

Actor: Warner Baxter, *In Old Arizona.*
Actress: Mary Pickford, *Coquette.*
Director: Frank Lloyd, *The Divine Lady.*
Picture: *Broadway Melody,* MGM.

1929-30

Actor: George Arliss, *Disraeli.*
Actress: Norma Shearer, *The Divorcee.*
Director: Lewis Milestone, *All Quiet on the Western Front.*
Picture: *All Quiet on the Western Front,* Univ.

1930-31

Actor: Lionel Barrymore, *Free Soul.*
Actress: Marie Dressler, *Min and Bill.*
Director: Norman Taurog, *Skippy.*
Picture: *Cimarron,* RKO.

1931-32

Actor: Fredric March, *Dr. Jekyll and Mr. Hyde;* Wallace Beery, *The Champ* (tie).
Actress: Helen Hayes, *Sin of Madelon Claudet.*
Director: Frank Borzage, *Bad Girl.*
Picture: *Grand Hotel,* MGM.
Special: Walt Disney, *Mickey Mouse.*

1932-33

Actor: Charles Laughton, *Private Life of Henry VIII.*
Actress: Katharine Hepburn, *Morning Glory.*
Director: Frank Lloyd, *Cavalcade.*
Picture: *Cavalcade,* Fox.

1934

Actor: Clark Gable, *It Happened One Night.*
Actress: Claudette Colbert, same.
Director: Frank Capra, *It Happened One Night.*
Picture: *It Happened One Night,* Columbia.

1935

Actor: Victor McLaglen, *The Informer.*
Actress: Bette Davis, *Dangerous.*
Director: John Ford, *The Informer.*
Picture: *Mutiny on the Bounty,* MGM.

1936

Actor: Paul Muni, *Story of Louis Pasteur.*
Actress: Luise Rainer, *The Great Ziegfeld.*
Sup. Actor: Walter Brennan, *Come and Get It.*
Sup. Actress: Gale Sondergaard, *Anthony Adverse.*
Director: Frank Capra, *Mr. Deeds Goes to Town.*
Picture: *The Great Ziegfeld,* MGM.

1937

Actor: Spencer Tracy, *Captains Courageous.*
Actress: Luise Rainer, *The Good Earth.*
Sup. Actor: Joseph Schildkraut, *Life of Emile Zola.*
Sup. Actress: Alice Brady, *In Old Chicago.*
Director: Leo McCarey, *The Awful Truth.*
Picture: *Life of Emile Zola,* Warner.

1938

Actor: Spencer Tracy, *Boys Town.*
Actress: Bette Davis, *Jezebel.*
Sup. Actor: Walter Brennan, *Kentucky.*
Sup. Actress: Fay Bainter, *Jezebel.*
Director: Frank Capra, *You Can't Take It With You.*
Picture: *You Can't Take It With You,* Columbia.

1939

Actor: Robert Donat, *Goodbye Mr. Chips.*
Actress: Vivien Leigh, *Gone With the Wind.*
Sup. Actor: Thomas Mitchell, *Stage Coach.*
Sup. Actress: Hattie McDaniel, *Gone With the Wind.*
Director: Victor Fleming, *Gone With the Wind.*
Picture: *Gone With the Wind,* Selznick International.

1940

Actor: James Stewart, *The Philadelphia Story.*
Actress: Ginger Rogers, *Kitty Foyle.*
Sup. Actor: Walter Brennan, *The Westerner.*
Sup. Actress: Jane Darwell, *The Grapes of Wrath.*
Director: John Ford, *The Grapes of Wrath.*
Picture: *Rebecca,* Selznick International.

1941

Actor: Gary Cooper, *Sergeant York.*
Actress: Joan Fontaine, *Suspicion.*
Sup. Actor: Donald Crisp, *How Green Was My Valley.*
Sup. Actress: Mary Astor, *The Great Lie.*
Director: John Ford, *How Green Was My Valley.*
Picture: *How Green Was My Valley,* 20th Cent.-Fox.

1942

Actor: James Cagney, *Yankee Doodle Dandy.*
Actress: Greer Garson, *Mrs. Miniver.*
Sup. Actor: Van Heflin, *Johnny Eager.*
Sup. Actress: Teresa Wright, *Mrs. Miniver.*
Director: William Wyler, *Mrs. Miniver.*
Picture: *Mrs. Miniver,* MGM.

1943

Actor: Paul Lukas, *Watch on the Rhine.*
Actress: Jennifer Jones, *The Song of Bernadette.*
Sup. Actor: Charles Coburn, *The More the Merrier.*
Sup. Actress: Katina Paxinou, *For Whom the Bell Tolls.*
Director: Michael Curtiz, *Casablanca.*
Picture: *Casablanca,* Warner.

1944

Actor: Bing Crosby, *Going My Way.*
Actress: Ingrid Bergman, *Gaslight.*
Sup. Actor: Barry Fitzgerald, *Going My Way.*
Sup. Actress: Ethel Barrymore, *None But the Lonely Heart.*
Director: Leo McCarey, *Going My Way.*
Picture: *Going My Way,* Paramount.

1945

Actor: Ray Milland, *The Lost Weekend.*
Actress: Joan Crawford, *Mildred Pierce.*
Sup. Actor: James Dunn, *A Tree Grows in Brooklyn.*
Sup. Actress: Anne Revere, *National Velvet.*
Director: Billy Wilder, *The Lost Weekend.*
Picture: *The Lost Weekend,* Paramount.

1946

Actor: Fredric March, *Best Years of Our Lives.*
Actress: Olivia de Havilland, *To Each His Own.*
Sup. Actor: Harold Russell, *The Best Years of Our Lives.*
Sup. Actress: Anne Baxter, *The Razor's Edge.*
Director: William Wyler, *The Best Years of Our Lives.*
Picture: *The Best Years of Our Lives,* Goldwyn, RKO.

1947

Actor: Ronald Colman, *A Double Life.*
Actress: Loretta Young, *The Farmer's Daughter.*
Sup. Actor: Edmund Gwenn, *Miracle on 34th Street.*
Sup. Actress: Celeste Holm, *Gentleman's Agreement.*
Director: Elia Kazan, *Gentleman's Agreement.*
Picture: *Gentleman's Agreement,* 20th Cent.-Fox.

1948

Actor: Laurence Olivier, *Hamlet.*
Actress: Jane Wyman, *Johnny Belinda.*
Sup. Actor: Walter Huston, *Treasure of Sierra Madre.*
Sup. Actress: Claire Trevor, *Key Largo.*
Director: John Huston, *Treasure of Sierra Madre.*
Picture: *Hamlet,* Two Cities Film, Universal International.

1949

Actor: Broderick Crawford, *All the King's Men.*
Actress: Olivia de Havilland, *The Heiress.*
Sup. Actor: Dean Jagger, *Twelve O'Clock High.*
Sup. Actress: Mercedes McCambridge, *All the King's Men.*
Director: Joseph L. Mankiewicz, *Letter to Three Wives.*
Picture: *All the King's Men,* Columbia.

1950

Actor: Jose Ferrer, *Cyrano de Bergerac.*
Actress: Judy Holliday, *Born Yesterday.*
Sup. Actor: George Sanders, *All About Eve.*
Sup. Actress: Josephine Hull, *Harvey.*
Director: Joseph L. Mankiewicz, *All About Eve.*
Picture: *All About Eve,* 20th Century-Fox.

1951

Actor: Humphrey Bogart, *The African Queen.*
Actress: Vivien Leigh, *A Streetcar Named Desire.*
Sup. Actor: Karl Malden, *A Streetcar Named Desire.*
Sup. Actress: Kim Hunter, *A Streetcar Named Desire.*
Director: George Stevens, *A Place in the Sun.*
Picture: *An American in Paris,* MGM.

1952

Actor: Gary Cooper, *High Noon.*
Actress: Shirley Booth, *Come Back, Little Sheba.*
Sup. Actor: Anthony Quinn, *Viva Zapata!*
Sup. Actress: Gloria Grahame, *The Bad and the Beautiful.*
Director: John Ford, *The Quiet Man.*
Picture: *Greatest Show on Earth,* C.B. DeMille, Paramount.

1953

Actor: William Holden, *Stalag 17.*
Actress: Audrey Hepburn, *Roman Holiday.*
Sup. Actor: Frank Sinatra, *From Here to Eternity.*
Sup. Actress: Donna Reed, *From Here to Eternity.*
Director: Fred Zinnemann, *From Here to Eternity.*
Picture: *From Here to Eternity,* Columbia.

1954

Actor: Marlon Brando, *On the Waterfront.*
Actress: Grace Kelly, *The Country Girl.*
Sup. Actor: Edmond O'Brien, *The Barefoot Contessa.*
Sup. Actress: Eva Marie Saint, *On the Waterfront.*

(continued)

Director: Elia Kazan, *On the Waterfront.*
Picture: *On the Waterfront*, Horizon-American, Colum.

1955

Actor: Ernest Borgnine, *Marty.*
Actress: Anna Magnani, *The Rose Tattoo.*
Sup. Actor: Jack Lemmon, *Mister Roberts.*
Sup. Actress: Jo Van Fleet, *East of Eden.*
Director: Delbert Mann, *Marty.*
Picture: *Marty*, Hecht and Lancaster's Steven Prods., U.A.

1956

Actor: Yul Brynner, *The King and I.*
Actress: Ingrid Bergman, *Anastasia.*
Sup. Actor: Anthony Quinn, *Lust for Life.*
Sup. Actress: Dorothy Malone, *Written on the Wind.*
Director: George Stevens, *Giant.*
Picture: *Around the World in 80 Days*, Michael Todd, U.A.

1957

Actor: Alec Guinness, *The Bridge on the River Kwai.*
Actress: Joanne Woodward, *The Three Faces of Eve.*
Sup. Actor: Red Buttons, *Sayonara.*
Sup. Actress: Miyoshi Umeki, *Sayonara.*
Director: David Lean, *The Bridge on the River Kwai.*
Picture: *The Bridge on the River Kwai*, Columbia.

1958

Actor: David Niven, *Separate Tables.*
Actress: Susan Hayward, *I Want to Live.*
Sup. Actor: Burl Ives, *The Big Country.*
Sup. Actress: Wendy Hiller, *Separate Tables.*
Director: Vincente Minnelli, *Gigi.*
Picture: *Gigi*, Arthur Freed Production, MGM.

1959

Actor: Charlton Heston, *Ben-Hur.*
Actress: Simone Signoret, *Room at the Top.*
Sup. Actor: Hugh Griffith, *Ben-Hur.*
Sup. Actress: Shelley Winters, *Diary of Anne Frank.*
Director: William Wyler, *Ben-Hur.*
Picture: *Ben-Hur*, MGM.

1960

Actor: Burt Lancaster, *Elmer Gantry.*
Actress: Elizabeth Taylor, *Butterfield 8.*
Sup. Actor: Peter Ustinov, *Spartacus.*
Sup. Actress: Shirley Jones, *Elmer Gantry.*
Director: Billy Wilder, *The Apartment.*
Picture: *The Apartment*, Mirisch Co., U.A.

1961

Actor: Maximilian Schell, *Judgment at Nuremberg.*
Actress: Sophia Loren, *Two Women.*
Sup. Actor: George Chakiris, *West Side Story.*
Sup. Actress: Rita Moreno, *West Side Story.*
Director: Jerome Robbins, Robert Wise, *West Side Story.*
Picture: *West Side Story*, United Artists.

1962

Actor: Gregory Peck, *To Kill a Mockingbird.*
Actress: Anne Bancroft, *The Miracle Worker.*
Sup. Actor: Ed Begley, *Sweet Bird of Youth.*
Sup. Actress: Patty Duke, *The Miracle Worker.*
Director: David Lean, *Lawrence of Arabia.*
Picture: *Lawrence of Arabia*, Columbia.

1963

Actor: Sidney Poitier, *Lilies of the Field.*
Actress: Patricia Neal, *Hud.*
Sup. Actor: Melvyn Douglas, *Hud.*
Sup. Actress: Margaret Rutherford, *The V.I.P.s.*
Director: Tony Richardson, *Tom Jones.*
Picture: *Tom Jones*, Woodfall Prod., UA-Lopert Pictures.

1964

Actor: Rex Harrison, *My Fair Lady.*
Actress: Julie Andrews, *Mary Poppins.*
Sup. Actor: Peter Ustinov, *Topkapi.*
Sup. Actress: Lila Kedrova, *Zorba the Greek.*
Director: George Cukor, *My Fair Lady.*
Picture: *My Fair Lady*, Warner Bros.

1965

Actor: Lee Marvin, *Cat Ballou.*
Actress: Julie Christie, *Darling.*
Sup. Actor: Martin Balsam, *A Thousand Clowns.*
Sup. Actress: Shelley Winters, *A Patch of Blue.*
Director: Robert Wise, *The Sound of Music.*
Picture: *The Sound of Music*, 20th Century-Fox.

1966

Actor: Paul Scofield, *A Man for All Seasons.*
Actress: Elizabeth Taylor, *Who's Afraid of Virginia Woolf?*
Sup. Actor: Walter Matthau, *The Fortune Cookie.*
Sup. Actress: Sandy Dennis, *Who's Afraid of Virginia Woolf?*
Director: Fred Zinnemann, *A Man for All Seasons.*
Picture: *A Man for All Seasons*, Columbia.

1967

Actor: Rod Steiger, *In the Heat of the Night.*
Actress: Katharine Hepburn, *Guess Who's Coming to Dinner.*
Sup. Actor: George Kennedy, *Cool Hand Luke.*
Sup. Actress: Estelle Parsons, *Bonnie and Clyde.*
Director: Mike Nichols, *The Graduate.*
Picture: *In the Heat of the Night.*

1968

Actor: Cliff Robertson, *Charly.*
Actress: Katharine Hepburn, *The Lion in Winter;* Barbra Streisand, *Funny Girl* (tie).
Sup. Actor: Jack Albertson, *The Subject Was Roses.*
Sup. Actress: Ruth Gordon, *Rosemary's Baby.*
Director: Sir Carol Reed, *Oliver!*
Picture: *Oliver!*

1969

Actor: John Wayne, *True Grit.*
Actress: Maggie Smith, *The Prime of Miss Jean Brodie.*
Sup. Actor: Gig Young, *They Shoot Horses, Don't They?*
Sup. Actress: Goldie Hawn, *Cactus Flower.*
Director: John Schlesinger, *Midnight Cowboy.*
Picture: *Midnight Cowboy.*

1970

Actor: George C. Scott, *Patton* (refused).
Actress: Glenda Jackson, *Women in Love.*
Sup. Actor: John Mills, *Ryan's Daughter.*
Sup. Actress: Helen Hayes, *Airport.*
Director: Franklin Schaffner, *Patton.*
Picture: *Patton.*

1971

Actor: Gene Hackman, *The French Connection.*
Actress: Jane Fonda, *Klute.*
Sup. Actor: Ben Johnson, *The Last Picture Show.*
Sup. Actress: Cloris Leachman, *The Last Picture Show.*
Director: William Friedkin, *The French Connection.*
Picture: *The French Connection.*

1972

Actor: Marlon Brando, *The Godfather* (refused).
Actress: Liza Minnelli, *Cabaret.*
Sup. Actor: Joel Grey, *Cabaret.*
Sup. Actress: Eileen Heckart, *Butterflies are Free.*
Director: Bob Fosse, *Cabaret.*
Picture: *The Godfather.*

1973

Actor: Jack Lemmon, *Save the Tiger.*
Actress: Glenda Jackson, *A Touch of Class.*
Sup. Actor: John Houseman, *The Paper Chase.*
Sup. Actress: Tatum O'Neal, *Paper Moon.*
Director: George Roy Hill, *The Sting.*
Picture: *The Sting.*

1974

Actor: Art Carney, *Harry and Tonto.*
Actress: Ellen Burstyn, *Alice Doesn't Live Here Anymore.*
Sup. Actor: Robert DeNiro, *The Godfather, Part II.*
Sup. Actress: Ingrid Bergman, *Murder on the Orient Express.*
Director: Francis Ford Coppola, *The Godfather, Part II.*
Picture: *The Godfather, Part II.*

1975

Actor: Jack Nicholson, *One Flew Over the Cuckoo's Nest.*
Actress: Louise Fletcher, *One Flew Over the Cuckoo's Nest.*
Sup. Actor: George Burns, *The Sunshine Boys.*
Sup. Actress: Lee Grant, *Shampoo.*
Director: Milos Forman, *One Flew Over the Cuckoo's Nest.*
Picture: *One Flew Over the Cuckoo's Nest.*

1976

Actor: Peter Finch, *Network.*
Actress: Faye Dunaway, *Network.*
Sup. Actor: Jason Robards, *All the President's Men.*
Sup. Actress: Beatrice Straight, *Network.*
Director: John G. Avildsen, *Rocky.*
Picture: *Rocky.*

1977

Actor: Richard Dreyfuss, *The Goodbye Girl.*
Actress: Diane Keaton, *Annie Hall.*
Sup. Actor: Jason Robards, *Julia.*
Sup. Actress: Vanessa Redgrave, *Julia.*
Director: Woody Allen, *Annie Hall.*
Picture: *Annie Hall.*

1978

Actor: Jon Voight, *Coming Home.*
Actress: Jane Fonda, *Coming Home.*
Sup. Actor: Christopher Walken, *The Deer Hunter.*
Sup. Actress: Maggie Smith, *California Suite.*
Director: Michael Cimino, *The Deer Hunter.*
Picture: *The Deer Hunter.*

1979

Actor: Dustin Hoffman, *Kramer vs. Kramer.*
Actress: Sally Field, *Norma Rae.*
Sup. Actor: Melvyn Douglas, *Being There.*
Sup. Actress: Meryl Streep, *Kramer vs. Kramer.*

Director: Robert Benton, *Kramer vs. Kramer.*
Picture: *Kramer vs. Kramer.*

1980

Actor: Robert DeNiro, *Raging Bull.*
Actress: Sissy Spacek, *Coal Miner's Daughter.*
Sup. Actor: Timothy Hutton, *Ordinary People.*
Sup. Actress: Mary Steenburgen, *Melvin & Howard.*
Director: Robert Redford, *Ordinary People.*
Picture: *Ordinary People.*

1981

Actor: Henry Fonda, *On Golden Pond.*
Actress: Katharine Hepburn, *On Golden Pond.*
Sup. Actor: John Gielgud, *Arthur.*
Sup. Actress: Maureen Stapleton, *Reds.*
Director: Warren Beatty, *Reds.*
Picture: *Chariots of Fire.*

1982

Actor: Ben Kingsley, *Gandhi.*
Actress: Meryl Streep, *Sophie's Choice.*
Sup. Actor: Louis Gossett, Jr., *An Officer and a Gentleman.*
Sup. Actress: Jessica Lange, *Tootsie.*
Director: Richard Attenborough, *Gandhi.*
Picture: *Gandhi.*

1983

Actor: Robert Duvall, *Tender Mercies.*
Actress: Shirley MacLaine, *Terms of Endearment.*
Supporting Actor: Jack Nicholson, *Terms of Endearment.*
Supporting Actress: Linda Hunt, *The Year of Living Dangerously.*
Director: James L. Brooks, *Terms of Endearment.*
Picture: *Terms of Endearment.*

1984

Actor: F. Murray Abraham, *Amadeus.*
Actress: Sally Field, *Places in the Heart.*
Supporting Actor: Haing S. Ngor, *The Killing Fields.*
Supporting Actress: Peggy Ashcroft, *A Passage to India.*
Director: Milos Forman, *Amadeus.*
Picture: *Amadeus.*

1985

Actor: William Hurt, *Kiss of the Spider Woman.*
Actress: Geraldine Page, *The Trip to Bountiful.*
Supporting Actor: Don Ameche, *Cocoon.*
Supporting Actress: Anjelica Huston, *Prizzi's Honor.*
Director: Sydney Pollack, *Out of Africa.*
Picture: *Out of Africa.*

1986

Picture: *Platoon.*
Actor: Paul Newman, *The Color of Money.*
Actress: Marlee Matlin, *Children of a Lesser God.*
Supporting Actor: Michael Caine, *Hannah and Her Sisters.*
Supporting Actress: Dianne Wiest, *Hannah and Her Sisters.*
Director: Oliver Stone, *Platoon.*
Foreign Film: *The Assault* (The Netherlands).
Original Screenplay: Woody Allen, *Hannah and Her Sisters.*
Screenplay Adaptation: Ruth Prawler Jhabvala, *A Room With a View.*
Original Score: Herbie Hancock, *'Round Midnight.*
Original Song: "Take My Breath Away" (*Top Gun*).
Cinematography: *The Mission.*
Art Direction: *A Room With a View.*
Costume Design: *A Room With a View.*
Documentary Feature: Tie—*Artie Shaw: Time is All You've Got; Down and Out in America.*
Documentary Short: Women—*For America, for the World.*
Film Editing: *Platoon.*
Animated Short: *A Greek Tragedy.*
Live Action Short: *Precious Images.*
Sound: *Platoon.*
Sound Effects: *Aliens.*
Visual Effects: *Aliens.*
Makeup: *The Fly.*
Irving Thalberg Award: Steven Spielberg.
Honorary Award: Ralph Bellamy.

The Spingarn Medal

The Spingarn Medal has been awarded annually since 1914 by the National Association for the Advancement of Colored People for the highest achievement by a black American.

1946 Dr. Percy L. Julian
1947 Channing H. Tobias
1948 Ralph J. Bunche
1949 Charles Hamilton Houston
1950 Mabel Keaton Staupers
1951 Harry T. Moore
1952 Paul R. Williams
1953 Theodore K. Lawless
1954 Carl Murphy
1955 Jack Roosevelt Robinson
1956 Martin Luther King Jr.
1957 Mrs. Daisy Bates and the Little Rock Nine
1958 Edward Kennedy (Duke) Ellington
1959 Langston Hughes
1960 Kenneth B. Clark
1961 Robert C. Weaver
1962 Medgar Wiley Evers
1963 Roy Wilkins
1964 Leontyne Price
1965 John H. Johnson
1966 Edward W. Brooke
1967 Sammy Davis Jr.
1968 Clarence M. Mitchell Jr.
1969 Jacob Lawrence
1970 Leon Howard Sullivan
1971 Gordon Parks
1972 Wilson C. Riles
1973 Damon Keith
1974 Henry (Hank) Aaron
1975 Alvin Ailey
1976 Alex Haley
1977 Andrew Young
1978 Mrs. Rosa L. Parks
1979 Dr. Rayford W. Logan
1980 Coleman Young
1981 Dr. Benjamin Elijah Mays
1982 Lena Horne
1983 Thomas Bradley
1984 Bill Cosby
1985 Dr. Benjamin L. Hooks
1986 Percy E. Sutton

Miss America Winners

1921 Margaret Gorman, Washington, D.C.
1922-23 Mary Campbell, Columbus, Ohio
1924 Ruth Malcolmson, Philadelphia, Pennsylvania
1925 Fay Lamphier, Oakland, California
1926 Norma Smallwood, Tulsa, Oklahoma
1927 Lois Delaner, Joliet, Illinois
1933 Marion Bergeron, West Haven, Connecticut
1935 Henrietta Leaver, Pittsburgh, Pennsylvania
1936 Rose Coyle, Philadelphia, Pennsylvania
1937 Bette Cooper, Bertrand Island, New Jersey
1938 Marilyn Meseke, Marion, Ohio
1939 Patricia Donnelly, Detroit, Michigan
1940 Frances Marie Burke, Philadelphia, Pennsylvania
1941 Rosemary LaPlanche, Los Angeles, California
1942 Jo-Caroll Dennison, Tyler, Texas
1943 Jean Bartel, Los Angeles, California
1944 Venus Ramey, Washington, D.C.
1945 Bess Myerson, New York City, N.Y.
1946 Marilyn Buferd, Los Angeles, California
1947 Barbara Walker, Memphis, Tennessee
1948 BeBe Shopp, Hopkins, Minnesota
1949 Jacque Mercer, Litchfield, Arizona
1951 Yolande Betbeze, Mobile, Alabama
1952 Coleen Kay Hutchins, Salt Lake City, Utah
1953 Neva Jane Langley, Macon, Georgia
1954 Evelyn Margaret Ay, Ephrata, Pennsylvania
1955 Lee Meriwether, San Francisco, California
1956 Sharon Ritchie, Denver, Colorado
1957 Marian McKnight, Manning, South Carolina
1958 Marilyn Van Derbur, Denver, Colorado
1959 Mary Ann Mobley, Brandon, Mississippi
1960 Lynda Lee Mead, Natchez, Mississippi
1961 Nancy Fleming, Montague, Michigan
1962 Maria Fletcher, Asheville, North Carolina
1963 Jacquelyn Mayer, Sandusky, Ohio
1964 Donna Axum, El Dorado, Arkansas
1965 Vonda Kay Van Dyke, Phoenix, Arizona
1966 Deborah Irene Bryant, Overland Park, Kansas
1967 Jane Anne Jayroe, Laverne, Oklahoma
1968 Debra Dene Barnes, Moran, Kansas
1969 Judith Anne Ford, Belvidere, Illinois
1970 Pamela Anne Eldred, Birmingham, Michigan
1971 Phyllis Ann George, Denton, Texas
1972 Laurie Lea Schaefer, Columbus, Ohio
1973 Terry Anne Meeuwsen, DePere, Wisconsin
1974 Rebecca Ann King, Denver, Colorado
1975 Shirley Cothran, Fort Worth, Texas
1976 Tawney Elaine Godin, Yonkers, N.Y.
1977 Dorothy Kathleen Benham, Edina, Minnesota
1978 Susan Perkins, Columbus, Ohio
1979 Kylene Baker, Galax, Virginia
1980 Cheryl Prewitt, Ackerman, Mississippi
1981 Susan Powell, Elk City, Oklahoma
1982 Elizabeth Ward, Russellville, Arkansas
1983 Debra Maffett, Anaheim, California
1984 Vanessa Williams, Milwood, New York*
Suzette Charles, Mays Landing, New Jersey
1985 Sharlene Wells, Salt Lake City, Utah
1986 Susan Akin, Meridian, Mississippi
1987 Kellye Cash, Tennessee

*Resigned July 23, 1984.

Grammy Awards

Source: National Academy of Recording Arts & Sciences

1962
Record: Tony Bennett, *I Left My Heart in San Francisco.*
Album: Vaughn Meader, *The First Family.*
Male vocalist: Tony Bennett, *I Left My Heart in San Francisco.*
Female vocalist: Ella Fitzgerald, *Ella Swings Brightly with Nelson Riddle* (album).
Group: Peter, Paul and Mary, *If I Had a Hammer.*
1963
Record: Henry Mancini, *The Days of Wine and Roses.*
Album: *The Barbra Streisand Album.*
Male vocalist: Jack Jones, *Wives and Lovers.*
Female vocalist: *The Barbra Streisand Album.*
Group: Peter, Paul and Mary, *Blowin' in the Wind.*
1964
Record: Stan Getz and Astrud Gilberto, *The Girl From Ipanema.*
Album: *Getz/Gilberto.*
Male vocalist: Louis Armstrong, *Hello, Dolly!*
Female vocalist: Barbra Streisand, *People.*
Group: The Beatles, *A Hard Day's Night.*
1965
Record: Herb Alpert, *A Taste Of Honey.*
Album: Frank Sinatra, *September of My Years.*
Male vocalist: Frank Sinatra, *It Was a Very Good Year.*
Female vocalist: Barbra Streisand, *My Name is Barbra* (album).
Group: Anita Kerr Singers, *We Dig Mancini* (album).
1966
Record: Frank Sinatra, *Strangers in the Night.*
Album: Frank Sinatra, *A Man and His Music.*
Male vocalist: Frank Sinatra, *Strangers in the Night.*
Female vocalist: Eydie Gorme, *If He Walked into My Life.*
Group: Anita Kerr Singers, *A Man and A Woman.*
1967
Record: 5th Dimension, *Up, Up and Away.*
Album: The Beatles, *Sgt. Pepper's Lonely Hearts Club Band.*
Male vocalist: Glen Campbell, *By the Time I Get to Phoenix.*
Female vocalist: Bobbie Gentry, *Ode to Billie Joe.*
Group: 5th Dimension, *Up, Up and Away.*
1968
Record: Simon & Garfunkel, *Mrs. Robinson.*
Album: Glen Campbell, *By the Time I Get to Phoenix.*
Male pop vocalist: Jose Feliciano, *Light My Fire.*
Female pop vocalist: Dionne Warwick, *Do You Know the Way to San Jose.*
Pop group: Simon & Garfunkel, *Mrs. Robinson.*
1969
Record: 5th Dimension, *Aquarius/Let the Sunshine In.*
Album: *Blood, Sweat and Tears.*
Male pop vocalist: Harry Nilsson, *Everybody's Talkin'.*
Female pop vocalist: Peggy Lee, *Is That All There Is.*
Pop group: 5th Dimension, *Aquarius/Let the Sunshine In.*
1970
Record: Simon & Garfunkel, *Bridge Over Troubled Waters.*
Album: *Bridge Over Troubled Waters.*
Male pop vocalist: Ray Stevens, *Everything is Beautiful.*
Female pop vocalist: Dionne Warwick, *I'll Never Fall in Love Again.*
Pop group: The Carpenters, *Close to You.*
1971
Record: Carole King, *It's Too Late.*
Album: Carole King, *Tapestry.*
Male pop vocalist: James Taylor, *You've Got a Friend.*
Female pop vocalist: Carole King, *Tapestry (album).*
Pop group: *The Carpenters (album).*
1972
Record: Roberta Flack, *The First Time Ever I Saw Your Face.*
Album: *The Concert For Bangla Desh.*
Male pop vocalist: Harry Nilsson, *Without You.*
Female pop vocalist: Helen Reddy, *I Am Woman.*
Pop group: Roberta Flack, Donny Hathaway, *Where is the Love.*
1973
Record: Roberta Flack, *Killing Me Softly with His Song.*
Album: Stevie Wonder, *Innervisions.*
Male pop vocalist: Stevie Wonder, *You Are the Sunshine of My Life.*
Female pop vocalist: Roberta Flack, *Killing Me Softly with His Song.*
Pop group: Gladys Knight & The Pips, *Neither One of Us (Wants to Be the First to Say Goodbye).*
1974
Record: Olivia Newton-John, *I Honestly Love You.*
Album: Stevie Wonder, *Fulfullingness' First Finale.*
Male pop vocalist: Stevie Wonder, *Fulfillingness' First Finale* (album).
Female pop vocalist: Olivia Newton-John, *I Honestly Love You.*
Pop group: Paul McCartney & Wings, *Band on the Run.*
1975
Record: Captain & Tennille, *Love Will Keep Us Together.*
Album: Paul Simon, *Still Crazy After All These Years.*
Male pop vocalist: Paul Simon, *Still Crazy After All These Years* (album).
Female pop vocalist: Janis Ian, *At Seventeen.*
Pop group: Eagles, *Lyin' Eyes.*
1976
Record: George Benson, *This Masquerade.*
Album: Stevie Wonder, *Songs in the Key of Life.*
Male pop vocalist: Stevie Wonder, *Songs in the Key of Life* (album).
Female pop vocalist: Linda Ronstadt, *Hasten Down the Wind* (album).
Pop group: Chicago, *If You Leave Me Now.*
1977
Record: Eagles, *Hotel California.*
Album: Fleetwood Mac, *Rumours.*
Male pop vocalist: James Taylor, *Handy Man.*
Female pop vocalist: Barbra Streisand, *Evergreen.*
Pop group: Bee Gees, *How Deep is Your Love.*
1978
Record: Billy Joel, *Just the Way You Are.*
Album: Bee Gees, *Saturday Night Fever.*
Male pop vocalist: Barry Manilow, *Copacabana.*
Female pop vocalist: Anne Murray, *You Needed Me.*
Pop group: Bee Gees, *Saturday Night Fever* (album).
1979
Record: The Doobie Brothers, *What a Fool Believes.*
Album: Billy Joel, *52nd Street.*
Male pop vocalist: Billy Joel, *52nd Street* (album).
Female pop vocalist: Dionne Warwick, *I'll Never Love This Way Again.*
Pop group: The Doobie Brothers, *Minute by Minute* (album).
1980
Record: Christopher Cross, *Sailing.*
Album: Christopher Cross, *Christopher Cross.*
Male pop vocalist: Kenny Loggins, *This Is It.*
Female pop vocalist: Bette Midler, *The Rose.*
Pop group: Barbra Streisand & Barry Gibb, *Guilty* (album).
1981
Record: Kim Carnes, *Bette Davis Eyes.*
Album: John Lennon, Yoko Ono, *Double Fantasy.*
Male pop vocalist: Al Jarreau, *Breaking Away* (album).
Female pop vocalist: Lena Horne, *Lena Horne: The Lady and Her Music,* Live on Broadway (album).
Pop group: Manhattan Transfer, *Boy from New York City.*
1982
Record: Toto, *Rosanna.*
Album: Toto, *Toto IV.*
Male pop vocalist: Lionel Richie, *Truly.*
Female pop vocalist: Melissa Manchester, *You Should See How She Talks About You.*
Pop group: Joe Cocker & Jennifer Warnes, *Up Where We Belong.*
1983
Record: Michael Jackson, *Beat It.*
Album: Michael Jackson, *Thriller.*
Male pop vocalist: Michael Jackson, *Thriller.*
Female pop vocalist: Irene Cara, *Flashdance.*
Pop group: Police, *Every Breath You Take.*
1984
Record: Tina Turner, *What's Love Got to Do With It.*
Album: Lionel Richie, *Can't Slow Down.*
Male pop vocalist: Phil Collins, *Against All Odds.*
Female pop vocalist: Tina Turner, *What's Love Got to Do With It.*
Pop group: Pointer Sisters, *Jump.*
1985
Record: USA for Africa, *We Are the World.*
Album: Phil Collins, *No Jacket Required.*
Male pop vocalist: Phil Collins, *No Jacket Required.*
Female pop vocalist: Whitney Houston, *Saving All My Love For You.*
Pop group: USA for Africa, *We Are the World.*
1986
Record: Steve Winwood, *Higher Love.*
Album: Paul Simon, *Graceland.*
Male pop vocalist: Steve Winwood, *Higher Love.*
Female pop vocalist: Barbra Streisand, *The Broadway Album.*
Pop group: Dionne Warwick & Friends, *That's What Friends Are For.*

ARTS AND MEDIA

Notable New York Theater Openings, 1986-87 Season

A Man for All Seasons, revival of the 1960 Robert Bolt play; with Philip Bosco, Robert Stattel, Charles Keating, and Maria Tucci.

A Month of Sundays, play by Bob Larbey; with Jason Robarts and Lynne Thigpen.

A Raisin in the Sun, revival of the 1959 Lorraine Hansberry drama; with Olivia Cole, James Pickens Jr., Starletta DuPois, Kim Yancey, and John Fiedler.

Blithe Spirit, revival of the 1941 Noel Coward comedy; with Blythe Danner, Richard Chamberlain, Geraldine Page, and Judith Ivey.

Broadway Bound, play by Neil Simon; with Linda Lavin, Jonathan Silverman, John Randolph, and Phyllis Newman.

Coastal Disturbances, play by Tina Howe; with Joanne Camp, Heather MacRae, Annette Bening, and Timothy Daly.

Danger: Memory!, 2 one-act plays by Arthur Miller; with Geraldine Fitzgerald, Mason Adams, Kenneth McMillan, and James Tolkan.

Death and the King's Horseman; drama by Wole Soyinka; with Earle Hyman, Ben Halley Jr., and Alan Coates.

Educating Rita, play by Willy Russell; with Laurie Metcalf and Austin Pendleton.

Fences, play by August Wilson; with James Earl Jones, Mary Alice, Frankie R. Faison, and Courtney B. Vance.

Hunting Cockroaches, comedy by Janusz Glowacki; with Dianne Wiest and Ron Silver.

Into the Light, musical by Lee Holdridge and John Forster; with Dean Jones, Susan Bigelow, William Parry, and Alan Mintz.

Les Liaisons Dangereuses, the Royal Shakespeare production of Christopher Hampton's play, which is based on the 1782 novel by Choderlos de Laclos; with Lindsay Duncan and Suzanne Burden.

Les Miserables, musical by Claude-Michel Schonberg, Alain Boublil and Herbert Kretzmer, based on the Victor Hugo classic; with Colm Wilkinson, Terrence Mann, and Frances Ruffelle.

Lily Dale, drama by Horton Foote; with Don Bloomfield, Molly Ringwald, and Julie Heberlein.

Little Murders, revival of Jules Feiffer's 1967 play; with Frances Sternhagen, MacIntyre Dixon, Fisher Stevens, and Christine Lahti.

Me and My Girl, musical by Noel Gay, L. Arthur Rose, and Douglas Furber; with Robert Lindsay, Maryann Plunkett, George S. Irving, and Jane Connell.

Moms, musical-play by Alice Childress based on the career of Moms Mabley; with Clarice Taylor.

My Gene, play by Barbara Gelb about Carlotta Monterey and Eugene O'Neill; with Colleen Dewhurst.

Oh Coward!, songs and excerpts from the plays and books of Noel Coward; with Roderick Cook, Catherine Cox, and Patrick Quinn.

Pygmalion, revival of the George Bernard Shaw classic; with Peter O'Toole, Amanda Plummer, John Mills, Lionel Jeffries, and Dora Bryan.

Raggedy Ann, musical by Joe Raposo; with Ivy Austin, Lisa Rieffel, and Leo Burmester.

Rags, musical by Charles Strouse and Stephen Schwartz; with Teresa Stratas, Larry Kert, and Terrence Mann.

Road Show, play by Murray Schisgal; with David Groh, Anita Gillette, Trish Hawkins, and Jonathan Hadary.

Rosencrantz and Guildenstern Are Dead; revival of Tom Stoppard's 1967 drama; with John Wood, John Rubinstein, and Stephen Lang.

Safe Sex, 3 one-act plays by and with Harvey Fierstein.

Smile, musical by Marvin Hamlisch and Howard Ashman based on the 1975 film; with Jeff McCarthy, Marsha Waterbury, Michael O'Gorman, and Jodi Benson.

Starlight Express, musical by Andrew Lloyd Webber and Richard Stilgoe; with Robert Torti, Greg Mowry, Reva Rice, and Braden Danner.

Sweet Sue, play by A.R. Gurney Jr.; with Mary Tyler Moore and Lynn Redgrave.

Talk Radio, play by Eric Bogosian; with Eric Bogosian, John C. McGinley, and Robyn Peterson.

The Common Pursuit, play by Simon Gray; with Judy Geeson, Kristoffer Tabori, Michael Countryman, and Nathan Lane.

The Front Page, revival of the Ben Hecht and Charles MacArthur 1928 play; with John Lithgow, Richard Thomas, Richard B. Shull, Ed Lauter, and Julie Hagerty.

The Johnstown Vindicator, play by Quincy Long; with James Harper, Patty Heaton, Elizabeth Owens, and David Thornton.

The Knife, musical by Nick Bicat and Tim Rose Price; with Mandy Patinkin, Mary Elizabeth Mastrantonio, and Cass Morgan.

The Life and Adventures of Nicholas Nickleby, the Royal Shakespeare Co. production of the Dickens novel; with John Lynch, Michael Siberry, John Carlisle, David Delve, and DeNica Fairman.

The Lucky Spot, play by Beth Henley; with Amy Madigan, Mary Stuart Masterson, and Belinda Moreno.

The Miracle Worker, revival of the 1959 play by William Gibson about the early years of Helen Keller; with Karen Allen and Eevin Hartsough.

The Nerd, comedy by Larry Shue; with Robert Joy, Mark Hamill, and Patricia Kalember.

Widow Claire, play by Horton Foote; with Matthew Broderick, Hallie Foote, and Dan Butler.

Wild Honey, play by Michael Frayn from an untitled play by Anton Chekhov; with Ian McKellen, Kate Burton, Kathryn Walker, and Kim Cattrall.

You Can Never Tell, revival of the George Bernard Shaw comedy; with Victor Garber, Uta Hagen, Philip Bosco, and Amanda Plummer.

Record Long Run Broadway Plays[1]

*Chorus Line	4,950	Hair	1,750	Oh! Calcutta! (original)	1,314
*Oh, Calcutta (revival)	4,818	The Wiz	1,672	Angel Street	1,295
Grease	3,388	Born Yesterday	1,642	Lightnin'	1,291
Fiddler on the Roof	3,242	*La Cage aux Folles	1,607	Promises, Promises	1,281
Life With Father	3,224	Ain't Misbehavin'	1,604	The King and I	1,246
Tobacco Road	3,182	Best Little Whorehouse in Texas	1,584	Cactus Flower	1,234
*42d Street	2,851	Mary, Mary	1,572	Sleuth	1,222
Hello Dolly	2,844	Evita	1,567	"1776"	1,217
My Fair Lady	2,717	Voice of the Turtle	1,557	Equus	1,209
Annie	2,377	Barefoot in the Park	1,530	Sugar Babies	1,208
Man of La Mancha	2,328	Dreamgirls	1,522	Guys and Dolls	1,200
Abie's Irish Rose	2,327	Mame	1,508	Torch Song Trilogy	1,166
Oklahoma!	2,212	Same Time, Next Year	1,453	Cabaret	1,165
Pippin	1,994	Arsenic and Old Lace	1,444	Mister Roberts	1,157
*Cats	1,972	The Sound of Music	1,443	Amadeus	1,155
South Pacific	1,925	How To Succeed in Business Without Really Trying	1,417	Annie Get Your Gun	1,147
Magic Show	1,920	Hellzapoppin	1,404	Seven Year Itch	1,141
Deathtrap	1,792	The Music Man	1,375	Butterflies Are Free	1,128
Gemini	1,788	Funny Girl	1,348	Pins and Needles	1,108
Harvey	1,775	Mumenschanz	1,326	Plaza Suite	1,097
Dancin'	1,774				

(1) Number of performances through June 30, 1987. *Still running July 1, 1987

Notable Movies of the Year (Aug. 1986 to Aug. 1987)

Movie	Stars	Director
A Man and a Woman: 20 Years Later	Anouk Aimee, Jean-Louis Trintignant	Claude Lelouch
Aliens	Sigourney Weaver, Carrie Henn, Michael Biehn	James Cameron
An American Tail	(voices) Dom De Luise, Madeleine Kahn, Philip Glasser	Don Bluth
Angel Heart	Mickey Rourke, Lisa Bonet, Robert DeNiro	Alan Parker
Beverly Hills Cop 2	Eddie Murphy, Judge Reinhold, Brigitte Nielsen	Tony Scott
Black Widow	Debra Winger, Theresa Russell, Dennis Hopper	Bob Rafaelson
Blind Date	Kim Basinger, Bruce Willis, William Daniels, John Larroquette	Blake Edwards
Blue Velvet	Kyle MacLachlan, Isabella Rossellini, Dennis Hopper	David Lynch
Brighton Beach Memoirs	Blythe Danner, Jonathan Silverman, Judith Ivey	Gene Saks
Children of a Lesser God	William Hurt, Marlee Matlin	Randa Haines
Crimes of the Heart	Diane Keaton, Jessica Lange, Sissy Spacek, Sam Shepard	Bruce Beresford
Crocodile Dundee	Paul Hogan	Peter Faiman
Dead of Winter	Mary Steenburgen, Roddy McDowell, Jan Rubes	Arthur Penn
Dragnet	Dan Aykroyd, Tom Hanks, Christopher Plummer, Dabney Coleman	Tom Mankiewicz
Duet for One	Julie Andrews, Max von Sydow, Alan Bates	Andrei Konchalovsky
84 Charing Cross Road	Anne Bancroft, Anthony Hopkins	David Jones
Extremities	Farrah Fawcett, James Russo, Alfre Woodard	Robert M. Young
Firewalker	Chuck Norris, Lou Gossett, Melody Anderson	J. Lee Thompson
From the Hip	Judd Nelson, John Hurt, Elizabeth Perkins	Bob Clark
Full Metal Jacket	Matthew Modine, Adam Baldwin, Lee Ermey	Stanley Kubrick
Gardens of Stone	James Caan, Anjelica Huston, James Earl Jones	Francis Coppola
Half Moon Street	Michael Caine, Sigourney Weaver	Bob Swaim
Heartbreak Ridge	Clint Eastwood, Marsha Mason	Clint Eastwood
Heartburn	Meryl Streep, Jack Nicholson	Mike Nichols
Heat	Burt Reynolds, Karen Young, Howard Hesseman	R. M. Richards
Hollywood Shuffle	Robert Townsend	Robert Townsend
Hoosiers	Gene Hackman, Dennis Hopper, Barbara Hershey	David Anspaugh
Howard the Duck	Lea Thompson, Jeffrey Jones, Tim Robbins	Willard Huyck
Innerspace	Dennis Quaid, Martin Short, Meg Ryan	Joe Dante
Ishtar	Warren Beatty, Dustin Hoffman	Elaine May
Jaws: The Revenge	Michael Caine, Lorraine Gray, Mario Van Peeples	Joseph Sargent
Jumpin' Jack Flash	Whoopi Goldberg, Jim Belushi, Carol Kane	Penny Marshall
La Bamba	Lou Diamond Phillips, Esai Morales	Luis Valdez
Lethal Weapon	Mel Gibson, Danny Glover	Richard Donner
Light of Day	Michael J. Fox, Joan Jett, Gena Rowlands	Paul Schrader
Little Shop of Horrors	Rick Moranis, Ellen Greene, Vincent Gardenia	Frank Oz
Making Mr. Right	John Malkovich, Ann Magnuson	Susan Seidelman
Maximum Overdrive	Emilio Estevez, Pat Hingle, Laura Harrington	Stephen King
Native Son	Oprah Winfrey, Victor Love, Matt Dillon, Elizabeth McGovern	Jerrold Freedman
'Night, Mother	Anne Bancroft, Sissy Spacek	Tom Moore
No Mercy	Richard Gere, Kim Basinger	Richard Pearce
Nothing in Common	Tom Hanks, Jackie Gleason, Eva Marie Saint	Garry Marshall
Outrageous Fortune	Shelley Long, Bette Midler	Arthur Hiller
Over the Top	Sylvester Stallone, Robert Loggia, Susan Blakely	Menahem Golan
Peggy Sue Got Married	Kathleen Turner, Nicolas Cage	Francis Coppola
Platoon	Tom Berenger, Charlie Sheen, Willem Dafoe	Oliver Stone
Project X	Matthew Broderick, Helen Hunt	Jonathan Kaplan
Radio Days	Mia Farrow, Danny Aiello, Dianne Wiest, Diane Keaton	Woody Allen
Raising Arizona	Nicolas Cage, Holly Hunter	Joel Coen
Robocop	Peter Weller, Nancy Allen, Ronny Cox	Peter Verhoeven
'Round Midnight	Dexter Gordon, Francois Cluzet, Lonette McKee	Bertrand Tavernier
Roxanne	Steve Martin, Daryl Hannah	Fred Schepsi
Shanghai Surprise	Sean Penn, Madonna	Jim Goddard
Something Wild	Melanie Griffith, Jeff Daniels	Jonathan Demme
Soul Man	C. Thomas Howell, Rae Dawn Chong, James Earl Jones	Steve Minor
Spaceballs	Mel Brooks, John Candy, Rick Moranis	Mel Brooks
Square Dance	Jane Alexander, Jason Robards, Rob Lowe	Daniel Petrie
Stand By Me	Will Wheaton, River Phoenix, Jerry O'Connell, Corey Feldman	Rob Reiner
Star Trek IV: The Voyage Home	William Shatner, Leonard Nimoy, DeForest Kelley, Catherine Hicks	Leonard Nimoy
Summer	Marie Riviere, Lisa Heredia	Eric Rohmer
Superman IV: The Quest For Peace	Christopher Reeve, Gene Hackman, Margot Kidder	Sidney J. Furie
That's Life	Jack Lemmon, Julie Andrews, Robert Loggia	Blake Edwards
The Bedroom Window	Steve Guttenberg, Elizabeth McGovern, Isabelle Huppert	Curtis Hanson
The Color of Money	Paul Newman, Tom Cruise	Martin Scorsese
The Believers	Martin Sheen, Helen Shaver, Robert Loggia	John Schlesinger
The Fly	Jeff Goldblum, Geena Davis	David Cronenberg
The Golden Child	Eddie Murphy	Michael Ritchie
The Hanoi Hilton	Michael Moriarty, Paul Le Mat, Jeffrey Jones, David Soul	Lionel Chetwynd
The Living Daylights	Timothy Dalton, Maryam d'Abo, Joe Don Baker	John Glen
The Lost Boys	Keifer Sutherland, Barnard Hughes, Edward Hermann, Dianne Wiest	Joel Schumacher
The Mission	Robert DeNiro, Jeremy Irons	Roland Joffe
The Morning After	Jane Fonda, Jeff Bridges, Raul Julia	Sidney Lumet
The Mosquito Coast	Harrison Ford, River Phoenix	Peter Weir
The Name of the Rose	Sean Connery, F. Murray Abraham	Jean-Jacques Annaud
The Secret of My Success	Michael J. Fox, Helen Slater	Herbert Ross
The Squeeze	Michael Keaton, Rae Dawn Chong	Roger Young
The Three Amigos	Steve Martin, Chevy Chase, Martin Short	John Landis
The Untouchables	Robert DeNiro, Kevin Costner, Sean Connery	Brian De Palma
The Whistle Blower	Michael Caine, James Fox, Felicity Dean, John Gielgud	Simon Langton
The Witches of Eastwick	Jack Nicholson, Susan Sarandon, Michelle Pfeiffer, Cher	George Miller
Tin Men	Richard Dreyfuss, Barbara Hershey, Danny DeVito	Barry Levinson
Touch and Go	Michael Keaton, Maria Conchita Alonso	Robert Mandel
Tough Guys	Burt Lancaster, Kirk Douglas	Jeff Kenew

All-Time Top 50 Films

Source: *Variety*, January, 1987

Rental figures are in absolute dollars, reflecting actual amounts received by the distributors (estimated for movies in current release). Ticket price inflation favors recent films, but older films have the advantage of numerous reissues adding to their totals.

	Title	Total Rentals
1.	E.T. The Extra-Terrestrial; 1982	$228,379,346
2.	Star Wars; 1977	193,500,000
3.	Return of the Jedi; 1983	168,002,414
4.	The Empire Strikes Back; 1980	141,600,000
5.	Jaws; 1975	129,961,081
6.	Ghostbusters; 1984	128,264,005
7.	Raiders of the Lost Ark; 1981	115,598,000
8.	Indiana Jones and the Temple of Doom; 1984	109,000,000
9.	Beverly Hills Cop; 1984	108,000,000
10.	Back to the Future; 1985	101,955,795
11.	Grease; 1978	96,300,000
12.	Tootsie; 1982	95,268,806
13.	The Exorcist; 1973	89,000,000
14.	The Godfather; 1972	86,275,000
15.	Superman; 1978	82,800,000
16.	Close Encounters of the Third Kind; 1977/1980	82,750,000
17.	Top Gun; 1986	82,000,000
18.	Rambo: First Blood Part II; 1985	$80,000,000
19.	The Sound of Music; 1965	79,748,000
20.	Gremlins; 1984	79,500,000
21.	The Sting; 1973	78,198,608
22.	Gone with the Wind; 1939	76,700,000
23.	Rocky IV; 1985	75,782,000
24.	Saturday Night Fever; 1977	74,100,000
25.	National Lampoon's Animal House; 1978	70,778,176
26.	Rocky III; 1982	65,715,000
27.	Superman II; 1981	65,100,000
28.	On Golden Pond; 1981	63,990,088
29.	Kramer Vs. Kramer, 1979	59,986,335
30.	Smokey and the Bandit; 1977	59,859,515
31.	One Flew Over the Cuckoo's Nest; 1975	59,220,000
32.	Nine To Five; 1980	59,100,000
33.	Stir Crazy; 1980	58,364,420
34.	The Karate Kid Part II; 1986	56,936,752
35.	Star Trek; 1979	56,000,000
36.	Rocky; 1976	$55,925,000
37.	American Graffiti; 1973	55,692,940
38.	An Officer and a Gentleman; 1982	55,223,000
39.	Porky's; 1982	54,000,000
40.	Jaws II; 1978	52,442,396
41.	The Towering Inferno; 1975	52,000,000
42.	Every Which Way But Loose; 1978	51,900,000
43.	Crocodile Dundee; 1986	51,000,000
44.	Terms of Endearment; 1983	
45.	Love Story; 1970	50,000,000
46.	Heaven Can Wait; 1978	49,400,000
47.	The Color Purple; 1985	47,900,000
48.	Blazing Saddles; 1974	47,800,000
49.	The Best Little Whorehouse In Texas; 1982	47,549,136
50.	Doctor Zhivago; 1965	47,073,000

Best-Selling Books of 1986

Source: *New York Times;* numbers in parentheses show rank on *Publishers Weekly* bestseller lists.

Hardcover Fiction

1. *It*, Stephen King (1).
2. *Red Storm Rising*, Tom Clancy (2).
3. *The Bourne Supremacy*, Robert Ludlum (4).
4. *The Mammoth Hunters*, Jean M. Auel.
5. *Whirlwind*, James Clavell (3).
6. *Wanderlust*, Danielle Steel (6).
7. *Lake Wobegon Days*, Garrison Keillor.
8. *A Perfect Spy*, John le Carre (10).
9. *Last of the Breed*, Louis L'Amour (8).
10. *I'll Take Manhattan*, Judith Krantz (7).

Hardcover Nonfiction

1. *Fatherhood*, Bill Cosby (1).
2. *You're Only Old Once*, Dr. Suess (5).
3. *His Way*, Kitty Kelly (3).
4. *James Herriot's Dog Stories*, James Herriot (10).
5. *A Day in the Life of America*.
6. *Bus 9 to Paradise*, Leo Buscaglia.
7. *McMahon!*, Jim McMahon with Bob Verdi.
8. *Necessary Losses*, Judith Viorst.
9. *Word for Word*, Andrew A. Rooney (9).
10. *Yeager*, by Chuck Yeager and Leo Janos.

Hardcover How-to, Advice, Other

1. *Fit for Life*, Harvey Diamond and Marilyn Diamond.
2. *Callanetics*, Callan Pinckney with Sallie Batson.
3. *The Rotation Diet*, Martin Katahn.
4. *Webster's Ninth New Collegiate Dictionary*.
5. *The Frugal Gourmet*, Jeff Smith.

Paperback Fiction

1. *The Color Purple*, Alice Walker.
2. *The Hunt for Red October*, Tom Clancy.
3. *Lake Wobegon Days*, Garrison Keillor.
4. *If Tomorrow Comes*, Sidney Sheldon.
5. *Family Album*, Danielle Steel.
6. *The Clan of the Cave Bear*, Jean M. Auel.
7. *Skeleton Crew*, Stephen King.
8. *The Mammoth Hunters*, Jean M. Auel.
9. *Secrets*, Danielle Steel.
10. *Lonesome Dove*, Larry McMurtry.

Paperback Nonfiction

1. *Out of Africa & Shadows on the Grass*, Isak Dinesen.
2. *The Road Less Traveled*, M. Scott Peck.
3. *Iacocca*, Lee Iacocca with William Novak.
4. *The Bridge Across Forever*, Richard Bach.
5. *Smart Women, Foolish Choices*, Connell Cowan and Melvin Kinder.
6. *Isak Dinesen*, Judith Thurman.
7. *West With the Night*, Beryl Markham.

Paperback How-to, Advice, Other

1. *Women Who Love Too Much*, Robin Norwood.
2. *Rand McNally Road Atlas: U.S., Canada, Mexico*.
3. *Bloom County Babylon*, Berke Breathed.
4. *It Came from the Far Side*, Gary Larson.
5. *The Far Side Gallery*, Gary Larson.
6. *The Far Side Gallery 2*, Gary Larson.
7. *Adult Children of Alcoholics*, Janet Geringer Woititz.
8. *What Color Is Your Parachute?*, Richard Nelson Bolles.

American Book Production

Source: Publishers Weekly, Mar. 13, 1987

Category	Hardcover and Paperback, 1985	Hardcover and Paperback, 1986p	Category	Hardcover and Paperback, 1985	Hardcover and Paperback, 1986p
Agriculture	536	445	Literature	1,964	1,800
Art	1,545	1,316	Medicine	3,579	2,731
Biography	1,953	1,729	Music	364	292
Business	1,518	1,349	Philosophy, Psychology	1,559	1,369
Education	1,085	841	Poetry, Drama	1,166	1,056
Fiction	5,105	4,877	Religion	2,564	2,212
General Works	2,905	1,970	Science	3,304	2,570
History	2,327	1,936	Sociology, Economics	7,441	6,471
Home Economics	1,228	894	Sports, Recreation	1,154	962
Juveniles	3,801	3,812	Technology	2,526	2,110
Language	632	562	Travel	465	412
Law	1,349	1,077	**Total**	**50,070**	**42,793**

(p) = preliminary

Notable Books of 1986

Source: American Library Association

Atwood, Margaret, *The Handmaid's Tale.*
Baker, Will, *Mountain Blood.*
Beschloss, Michael R., *Mayday.*
Carillo, Charles, *Shepherd Avenue.*
Carter, Angela, *Saints and Strangers.*
Charyn, Jerome, *Metropolis.*
Critchfield, Richard, *Those Days.*
Denby, Edwin, *The Complete Poems.*
Dubus, Andre, *The Last Worthless Evening.*
Duras, Marguerite, *The War.*
Erdrich, Louise, *The Beet Queen.*
Goldberg, Vicki, *Margaret Bourke-White.*
Grooms, Red, *Red Grooms.*
Henley, Patricia, *Friday Night at Silver Star.*
Hersh, Seymour M., *"The Target Is Destroyed."*
Hochschild, Adam, *Half the Way Home.*
Hugo, Richard, *The Real West Marginal Way.*
Ishiguro, Kazuo, *An Artist of the Floating World.*
Jhabvala, Ruth Prawer, *Out of India.*
Lopez, Barry, *Arctic Dreams.*
McFadden, Cyra, *Rain or Shine.*
Malone, Michael, *Handling Sin.*
Maslow, Jonathan Evan, *Bird of Life, Bird of Death.*
Mathiessen, Peter, *Men's Lives.*
Mehta, Ved, *Sound-shadows of the New World.*
Parfit, Michael, *South Light.*
Pratt, Charles, W., *In the Orchard.*
Price, Reynolds, *Kate Vaiden.*
Rivabella, Omar, *Requiem for a Woman's Soul.*
Rosengarten, Theodore, *Tombee.*
Roszak, Theodore, *The Cult of Information.*
Rush, Norman, *Whites.*
Shipler, David K., *Arab and Jew.*
Sperber, A.M., *Murrow.*
Stone, Robert, *Children of Light.*
Szulc, Tad, *Fidel.*
Taylor, Peter, *A Summons to Memphis.*

Circulation of Leading U.S. Magazines

Source: Audit Bureau of Circulations, Schaumburg, IL

General magazines, exclusive of groups and comics. Based on total average paid cirulation during the 6 months prior to Dec. 31, 1986.

Magazine	Circulation	Magazine	Circulation	Magazine	Circulation
TV Guide	16,800,441	Penthouse	2,379,333	Sunset	1,442,478
Reader's Digest	16,609,847	Smithsonian	2,310,970	Bon Appetit	1,431,047
Modern Maturity	14,973,019	U.S. News & World Report	2,287,016	The American Hunter	1,412,723
National Geographic	10,764,998	Southern Living	2,263,922	True Story	1,405,087
Better Homes & Gardens	8,091,751	Field & Stream	2,007,479	Changing Times	1,379,781
Family Circle	6,261,519	VFW	1,951,004	The American Rifleman	1,362,225
Woman's Day	5,744,842	Money	1,862,106	Woman's World	1,348,098
Good Housekeeping	5,221,575	Seventeen	1,853,314	Discover	1,328,534
McCall's	5,186,393	Popular Science	1,843,067	Boys' Life	1,306,172
Ladies' Home Journal	5,020,551	The Workbasket	1,779,463	Mademoiselle	1,297,938
Time	4,720,159	Home & Away	1,749,083	Vogue	1,281,597
National Enquirer	4,381,242	Parents	1,721,816	Golf Digest	1,239,045
Guideposts	4,260,697	Life	1,718,726	New Woman	1,234,726
Redbook	4,009,450	Ebony	1,703,019	Rodale's Organic Gardening	1,212,151
Star	3,706,131	Motorland	1,692,501	Home Mechanics	1,201,584
Playboy	3,447,324	Popular Mechanics	1,634,930	The Family Handyman	1,201,581
Newsweek	3,101,152	Country Living	1,619,121	'Teen	1,181,862
People	3,038,363	Globe	1,600,963	Sesame Street	1,156,119
Sports Illustrated	2,895,131	Elks	1,577,302	Travel & Leisure	1,118,132
Cosmopolitan	2,873,071	Adventure Road	1,569,951	Rolling Stone	1,109,812
Prevention	2,820,748	1,001 Home Ideas	1,540,428	Self	1,090,027
American Legion	2,648,627	Outdoor Life	1,520,915		
Glamour	2,386,150	Discovery	1,448,446		

(continued)

Magazine	Circulation
National Examiner	1,066,066
Us	1,021,288
Yankee	1,018,245
Weekly World News	1,016,555
Health	1,016,410
Scouting	956,258
Good Food	952,134
Sport	932,084
Car and Driver	905,492
Weight Watchers	902,525
Consumer's Digest	901,670
Michigan Living	893,852
Workbench	887,180
Touring & Travel	884,240
Nation's Business	862,410
Omni	857,614
Golf	850,893
Soap Opera Digest	849,385
Traveler	847,749
Popular Photography	838,844
House Beautiful	837,938
Jet	831,543
Country Home	828,473
Signature	810,647
Home	808,917
YM	808,168
Essence	800,064
Hot Rod	794,996
National News	790,625
Business Week, N.A.	788,205
Creative Ideas for Living	778,191
Working Woman	775,512
Motor Trend	745,363
Junior Scholastic	737,206
Forbes	733,255
VFW Auxiliary	730,298
Metropolitan Home	729,158
Harper's Bazaar	727,740
The Sporting News	722,977
Food & Wine	712,918
Practical Homeowner	708,363
Road & Track	707,534
Esquire	702,512
Mother Earth News	702,372
The Homeowner	695,397
Modern Photography	666,983
Fortune, N.A.	641,239
Flower & Garden	631,258
Gentlemen's Quarterly	662,801
Games	662,379
McCall's Needlework & Crafts	616,736
Architectural Digest	615,123
Inc.	606,577
The Saturday Evening Post	602,730
Elle	600,775
Shape	598,705
Catholic Digest	583,996
The New Yorker	560,070
Working Mother	554,972
Colonial Homes	551,187
Grit	551,131
Stereo Review	550,430
House & Garden	547,177
Muscle & Fitness	538,135
Sports Afield	516,227
Tennis	512,204
Endless Vacation	506,839
Natural History	502,751
Satellite Orbit	501,104
The Rotarian	498,404
Guns & Ammo	495,949
Woman	486,726
Ms	482,921
Personal Computing	477,129
Westways	463,976
Crafts	462,552
Ski	458,264
The Atlantic Monthly	456,927
Skiing	454,266
Video Review	443,147
Sun	418,067
Vanity Fair	417,904
Gallery	413,462
Town & Country	412,908
Cycle	412,649
Pillsbury Classics	409,826
Success!	407,447
3-2-1 Contact	379,505
World Tennis	378,452
Video	356,560
Country Music	355,593
High Fidelity	353,784
Sylvia Porter's Personal Finance	350,819
Club	337,890
Country Journal	334,288
Connoisseur	330,499
Venture	330,277
Flying	330,102
Compute!	329,867
Early American Life	329,168

25 Top Newspaper Companies

Source: *New York Times;* as of July 31, 1986.

Company	Circulation	% of circulation of all dailies*	Number of dailies
1. Gannett	5,724,738	8.8	91
2. Knight-Ridder	3,641,488	5.6	27
3. Newhouse Newspapers	2,987,942	4.6	26
4. Times Mirror	2,643,519	4.1	9
5. Tribune	2,622,533	4.0	7
6. Dow Jones	2,537,494	3.9	23
7. New York Times	1,620,000	2.5	26
8. Scripps Howard	1,516,138	2.3	20
9. Thomson Newspapers	1,481,755	2.3	94
10. Cox Enterprises	1,297,244	2.0	21
11. News America Publishing	1,278,621	2.0	3
12. Hearst Newspapers	1,039,759	1.6	14
13. Capital Cities/ABC	945,120	1.5	9
14. Freedom Newspapers	933,024	1.4	29
15. Central Newspapers	858,241	1.3	7
16. Washington Post	837,408	1.3	2
17. Copley Newspapers	738,657	1.1	11
18. Donrey Media Group	700,968	1.1	54
19. Ingersoll Newspapers	692,376	1.1	26
20. Media News Group	660,000	1.0	21
21. Chronicle Publishing	607,868	0.9	2
22. Media General	571,309	0.9	4
23. McClatchy Newspapers	549,435	0.8	7
24. Lee Enterprises	547,360	0.8	18
25. Morris Communications	547,234	0.8	14
Totals	**37,884,766**	**58.6**	**565**

*Total circulation of the nation's 1,675 dailies is 64,643,012. Column may not add up to total because of rounding.

Top 100 U.S. Daily Newspapers

Source: Editor & Publisher Intl. Yearbook 1987; circulation for 6-month period ending Sept. 30, 1986.

In 1986, 12 daily newspapers merged with other dailies, 17 discontinued daily publication, and 10 new dailies started, for a net loss of 19 (1,657 dailies vs. 1985's 1,676). Total daily circulation was 62,766,232, 0.4% less than in 1985. Twenty evening newspapers switched to morning distribution, bringing the a.m. total to 499 vs. 1985's 482; evening newspapers fell from 1,220 to 1,188; all-day newspapers grew to 30 from 26. Morning circulation was 37,441,125 vs. 1985's 36,361,561; evening circulation was 26,404,671 vs. 1985's 25,060,911. Sunday newspapers published in conjunction with dailies grew to 802 from 798, circulation to 58,924,518 from 58,825,978.

Newspaper		Circulation
New York (NY) *Wall Street Journal*	(m)	1,952,283
Washington (DC) *USA Today*	(m)	*1,459,049
New York (NY) *Daily News*	(mS)	1,270,926
Los Angeles (CA) *Times*	(mS)	1,086,383
New York (NY) *Times*	(mS)	1,001,694
Washington (DC) *Post*	(mS)	748,019
Chicago (IL) *Tribune*	(mS)	744,969
New York (NY) *Post*	(all day)	731,668
Detroit (MI) *News*	(all day, S)	680,800
Detroit (MI) *Free Press*	(mS)	656,477
Chicago (IL) *Sun-Times*	(mS)	612,686
Long Island (NY) *Newsday*	(eS)	603,172
San Francisco (CA) *Chronicle*	(m)	551,545
Boston (MA) *Globe*	(m)	516,284
Philadelphia (PA) *Inquirer*	(mS)	504,946
Newark (NJ) *Star-Ledger*	(mS)	460,330
Cleveland (OH) *Plain Dealer*	(mS)	452,343
Miami (FL) *Herald*	(mS)	432,993
Houston (TX) *Chronicle*	(all day, S)	425,434
Dallas (TX) *Morning News*	(mS)	390,987
Minneapolis (MN) *Star and Tribune*	(mS)	378,981

(continued)

Boston (MA) *Herald*	(mS)	359,527
Denver (CO) *Rocky Mountain News*	(mS)	327,357
Houston (TX) *Post*	(mS)	319,389
Buffalo (NY) *News*	(all day, S)	317,651
Portland (OR) *Oregonian*	(all day, S)	317,162
St. Louis (MO) *Post-Dispatch*	(mS)	308,279
Orange Co.-Santa Ana (CA) *Register*	(all day, S)	307,776
Milwaukee (WI) *Journal*	(eS)	293,384
St. Petersburg (FL) *Times*	(mS)	291,202
Phoenix (AZ) *Arizona Republic*	(mS)	290,162
New Orleans (LA) *Times-Picayune*	(all day, S)	277,113
Kansas City (MO) *Times*	(m)	272,734
San Jose (CA) *Mercury-News*	(all day, S)	264,492
Atlanta (GA) *Constitution*	(m)	255,636
Orlando (FL) *Sentinel*	(all day, S)	253,310
Philadelphia (PA) *Daily News*	(e)	252,150
Columbus (OH) *Dispatch*	(mS)	248,121
Dallas (TX) *Times Herald*	(all day, S)	246,370
San Diego (CA) *Union*	(mS)	243,158
Los Angeles (CA) *Herald Examiner*	(mS)	241,454
Sacramento (CA) *Bee*	(mS)	233,290
Pittsburgh (PA) *Press*	(eS)	233,132
Oklahoma City (OK) *Daily Oklahoman*	(m)	231,993
Seattle (WA) *Times*	(e)	230,094
Indianapolis (IN) *Star*	(mS)	229,595
Denver (CO) *Post*	(mS)	227,105
Memphis (TN) *Commercial Appeal*	(mS)	225,224
Hartford (CT) *Courant*	(mS)	222,749
Baltimore (MD) *Sun*	(m)	221,941
*Des Moines (IA) *Register*	(m)	221,869
Kansas City (MO) *Star*	(eS)	220,758
Tampa (FL) *Tribune*	(m)	218,189
Charlotte (NC) *Observer*	(mS)	214,700
Dayton (OH) *News/Journal Herald*	(all day, S)	211,462
Seattle (WA) *Post-Intelligencer*	(m)	206,851
Milwaukee (WI) *Sentinel*	(m)	196,068
Cincinnati (OH) *Enquirer*	(mS)	188,927
St. Paul (MN) *Pioneer Press & Dispatch*	(all day, S)	187,505
Atlanta (GA) *Journal*	(e)	185,375
Baltimore (MD) *Evening Sun*	(e)	175,643
Pittsburgh (PA) *Post-Gazette*	(m)	168,961
Austin (TX) *American-Statesman*	(all day, S)	166,860
Birmingham (AL) *News*	(eS)	166,554
Louisville (KY) *Courier-Journal*	(all day, S)	166,182
San Antonio (TX) *Express-News*	(all day, S)	165,746
Hackensack (NJ) *Record*	(e)	161,327
Toledo (OH) *Blade*	(eS)	160,606
Jacksonville (FL) *Times-Union*	(m)	160,396
Akron (OH) *Beacon Journal*	(eS)	155,023
Los Angeles (CA) *Daily News*	(mS)	153,441
Oakland (CA) *Tribune*	(mS)	152,739
Boston (MA) *Christian Science Monitor*	(m)	150,807
Fort Lauderdale (FL) *Sun-Sentinel*	(m)	146,186
San Francisco (CA) *Examiner*	(e)	145,014
Norfolk (VA) *Virginian-Pilot*	(m)	144,809
Fresno (CA) *Bee*	(mS)	139,689
Asbury Park (NJ) *Press*	(eS)	139,585
San Antonio (TX) *Light*	(all day, S)	138,125
Richmond (VA) *Times-Dispatch*	(mS)	137,801
Raleigh (NC) *News & Observer*	(mS)	137,746
Grand Rapids (MI) *Press*	(eS)	135,998
Riverside (CA) *Press-Enterprise*	(mS)	132,935
Allentown (PA) *Morning Call*	(mS)	132,806
Tulsa (OK) *World*	(mS)	131,816
Fort Worth (TX) *Star-Telegram*	(e)	130,309
Rochester (NY) *Democrat & Chronicle*	(mS)	128,869
Fort Worth (TX) *Star-Telegram*	(m)	127,682
Little Rock (AR) *Gazette*	(mS)	126,346
Long Beach (CA) *Press-Telegram*	(meS)	124,488
Louisville (KY) *Courier-Journal*	(all day, S)	124,386
Indianapolis (IN) *News*	(e)	124,292
Wichita (KA) *Eagle-Beacon*	(mS)	122,622
San Diego (CA) *Tribune*	(e)	122,577
Omaha (NE) *World-Herald*	(meS)	119,428
Nashville (TN) *Tennessean*	(mS)	119,120
Cincinnati (OH) *Post*	(e)	117,216
Columbia (SC) *State*	(mS)	116,342
Providence (RI) *Bulletin*	(e)	115,127

*Includes 279,997 copies sold in bulk; m = morning, e = evening, S = Sunday.

Selected U.S. Daily Newspaper Circulation

Source: Audit Bureau of Circulations' FAS-FAX Report of average paid circulation for 6 months to Mar. 31, 1987.

Newspaper	Daily
Akron Beacon Journal(e)	153,581
Albuquerque Journal(m)	†111,331
Albuquerque Tribune(e)	†42,283
Amarillo News(m)	44,147
Amarillo Globe-Times(e)	†26,033
Anchorage Times(e)	35,696
Ann Arbor News(e)	48,910
Asbury Park (N.J.) Press(e)	139,954
Athens (Ga.) News(m)	*10,421
Athens (Ga.) Banner-Herald(e)	*12,667
Augusta (Ga.) Chronicle(m)	*63,536
Augusta (Ga.) Herald(e)	*17,249
Bakersfield Californian(m)	†81,831
Bangor (Me.) News(m)	*77,795
Baton Rouge Advocate(m)	83,676
Baton Rouge State-Times(e)	33,188
Bergen Co. (N.J.) Record(e)	*†159,151
Billings (Mont.) Gazette(m)	57,001
Binghamton (N.Y.) Press & Sun Bulletin(m)	65,738
Birmingham Post-Herald(m)	*62,318
Bismark (N.D.) Tribune(e)	28,341
Bloomington (Ill.) Pantagraph(m)	52,022
Bridgeport (Conn.) Post(e)	*†61,028
Bristol (Va.) Herald-Courier(m)	*41,885
Camden (N.J.) Courier-Post(e)	*99,419
Casper (Wyo.) Star Tribune(m)	34,993
Charleston Gazette(m)	55,151
Chattanooga News-Free Press(e)	*57,320
Christian Science Monitor(m)	*186,195
Columbia (S.C.) Record(e)	29,484
Columbus (Ga.) Enquirer(m)	*35,940
Columbus (Ga.) Ledger(e)	*25,120
Corpus Christi Caller(m)	*†60,940
Corpus Christi Times(e)	*†21,509
Daytona Beach News Journal(m)	82,935
Dubuque Telegraph-Herald(e)	*34,406
El Paso Herald-Post(e)	†31,178
Evansville Courier(m)	63,219
Evansville Press(e)	38,219
Everett (Wash.) Herald(e)	55,170
Ft. Lauderdale Sun Sentinel(m)	*176,093
Ft. Lauderdale News(e)	*66,622
Ft. Myers News-Press(m)	83,487
Ft. Wayne Journal-Gazette(m)	†60,248
Fresno Bee(m)	†139,888
Gary Post-Tribune(e)	74,185
Greenville (S.C.) News(m)	*87,020
Greenville (S.C.) Piedmont(e)	*25,394
Honolulu Advertiser(m)	91,916
Honolulu Star-Bulletin(e)	99,963
Huntington (W.Va.) Herald-Dispatch(m)	†41,256
Hyannis: Cape Cod Times(m)	39,262
Jackson (Miss.) Clarion-Ledger(m)	†69,079
Jacksonville Times-Union(m)	*160,405
Kalamazoo Gazette(e)	62,956
Knoxville News-Sentinel(e)	100,452
Las Vegas Review-Journal(m&e)	*114,269
Lexington Herald-Leader(m)	116,720
Lubbock (Tex.) Avalanche Journal(m)	*59,685
Lynchburg (Va.) Advance(e)	*†4,434
Lynchburg (Va.) News(m)	*†33,492
Macon (Ga.) Telegraph & News(m)	72,601
Madison (Wis.) State Journal(m)	*78,568
Miami News(e)	56,590
Middletown (N.Y.) Times Herald Record(m)	81,638
Mobile Press(e)	*†47,031
Mobile Register(m)	*†54,421
Modesto (Cal.) Bee(m)	†75,675
Montgomery Advertiser(m)	*50,682
Montgomery Journal(e)	*18,122
Nashville Banner(e)	67,408
New London (Conn.) Day(m)	37,363
Newport News Press(m)	†69,529
Newport News Times Herald(e)	*†36,229
Oakland Tribune(m)	*150,482
Omaha World-Herald(m&e)	222,053
Pensacola News-Journal(m)	†60,592
Peoria Journal Star(m&e)	98,318
Phoenix Gazette(e)	†111,253
Portland (Me.) Press Herald(m)	59,008
Providence Journal(m)	*93,578
Reno Gazette Journal(m)	60,402
Roanoke Times & World News(m&e)	123,739
Rochester Democrat-Chronicle(m)	*124,993
Rochester Times-Union(e)	97,644
Rockford (Ill.) Register-Star(m)	69,909
Salem (Ore.) Statesman-Journal(m)	53,655
Salt Lake City Tribune(m)	112,625
San Bernardino Sun(m)	82,573
San Juan (P.R.) Star(m)	†36,751
Sarasota Herald-Tribune(m)	†125,307
Savannah News(m)	55,931
Savannah Press(e)	20,153
Scranton Times(e)	58,062
Scranton Tribune(m)	37,222
Sioux City Journal(m)	*52,003
Sioux Falls Argus-Leader(m)	44,395
Spokane Daily Chronicle(e)	*34,671
Springfield (Ill.) State Journal Register(m&e)	68,339
Springfield (Mass.) News(e)	63,575
Springfield (Mass.) Union(m&e)	67,218
Stockton (Cal.) Record(m)	52,582
Syracuse Herald-Journal(e)	99,981
Syracuse Post-Standard(m)	84,393
Tacoma News Tribune(e)	110,184
Tallahassee Democrat(m)	55,429
Terre Haute Tribune Star(m)	36,323
Toledo Blade(e)	158,047
Topeka Capital-Journal(m)	67,677
Tucson Daily Star(m)	†87,571
Tulsa Tribune(e)	†75,106
West Palm Beach Post(m)	*130,033
West Palm Beach Times(e)	*19,032
Wilmington News(m)	*†67,384
Winston-Salem Journal(m)	91,571
Worcester Gazette(e)	†79,109
Worcester Telegram(m)	†55,616
Yakima (Wash.) Herald Republic(m&e)	†38,895
Youngstown Vindicator(e)	†93,929

(m) morning; (e) evening; *Mon.-Fri. average; †3 months.

Average Television Viewing Time

Source: A.C. Nielsen estimates, Nov. 1986 (hours: minutes, per week)

		Total	Mon.-Fri. 10am-4:30pm	Mon.-Fri. 4:30pm-7:30pm	Mon.-Sun. 8-11pm	Sat. 7am-1pm	Mon.-Fri. 11:30pm-1am
Avg. all persons		30:20	4:29	4:35	8:46	:55	1:37
Women	Total 18+	34:56	6:20	4:56	10:16	:47	1:24
	18-24	26:05	5:24	3:25	7:06	:51	1:14
	55+	43:58	8:04	7:13	12:25	:49	1:38
Men	Total 18+	29:21	3:09	4:07	8:58	:39	1:20
	18-24	20:20	3:38	2:44	5:00	:42	:57
	55+	39:14	5:06	6:36	11:24	:44	1:30
Teens	Female	20:33	2:38	3:56	6:33	:49	:23
	Male	22:38	2:03	4:11	6:41	:59	:30
Kids	2-5	28:06	6:20	5:00	4:44	2:11	:16
	6-11	23:31	2:19	5:04	6:03	2:01	:13

America's Favorite Television Programs

Source: A.C. Nielsen
(Percent of TV households and persons in TV households)

Network Programs (December 1986)

(Nielsen Average Audience Estimates)

	TV Households	Women	Men	Teens	Children
Bill Cosby Show	34.0	31.2	23.4	30.9	29.5
Family Ties	31.8	29.1	21.4	31.3	25.7
Cheers	26.7	22.9	19.9	20.3	
Night Court	25.6	21.6	18.3	19.0	
Golden Girls	24.2	21.5	13.7	12.9	
Murder, She Wrote	23.5	19.6	15.2		
60 Minutes	23.4	16.9	18.1		
Who's The Boss?	21.3	17.6	12.4	18.6	15.0
Dallas	21.3	19.0			
Moonlighting	21.2	18.7	13.1	14.9	
Growing Pains	21.2	18.1		21.2	16.7
Newhart	20.2	16.7			
NFL Monday Night Football	19.4		17.9		
Amen	19.4	16.8			
NBC Monday Night Movies	18.9	16.6			
Falcon Crest		16.0			

	TV Households	Women	Men	Teens	Children
NFL Football Game 2-NBC			15.7		
CBS NFL Football Game 1			13.5		
CBS NFL Football Game 2			13.3		
Miami Vice			12.9		
Magnum, P.I.			12.7		
Alf				14.5	19.8
Amazing Stories				14.1	
Disney Sunday Movie				13.6	16.9
Head of the Class				13.2	
Sidekicks				13.1	
Hunter				12.9	
Perfect Strangers				12.7	
Foofur					19.9

Syndicated Programs (Nov. 1985)*

(Average Ratings for Total U.S.)

	TV households	Women	Men	Teens	Children
Wheel of Fortune	19.3	16.3	11.7	6.5	7.1
Jeopardy	12.3	10.1	6.5	4.0	3.0
PM Magazine	9.7	7.3	5.8	3.3	2.7
New Newlywed Game	8.9	7.2	5.1	5.2	4.1
M*A*S*H	8.7	5.7	6.0	4.6	3.0
Peoples Court	8.2	6.2	4.4	2.7	1.4
Three's Company	7.9	4.9	3.7	9.1	7.3
Oprah Winfrey	7.7	6.5	2.2	1.0	0.8
Phil Donahue Show	7.6	6.0	2.6	0.8	0.5
National Geographic	7.6	5.3	5.4	2.9	3.3

	TV households	Women	Men	Teens	Children
Entertainment Tonight	7.5	5.7	4.3	2.4	1.6
Best of National Geographic Spc.	7.5	5.3	5.6	2.9	3.6
Hollywood Squares	7.2	5.5	3.5	4.1	3.4
Hee Haw	7.1	5.4	5.0	1.8	2.6
Card Sharks	6.6	5.0	3.2	2.8	2.2
Facts of Life	6.5	3.7	2.1	9.7	8.5
Magnum, P.I.	6.4	4.5	3.4	3.3	2.1
Gimme A Break	6.2	3.8	2.1	8.5	8.6
Small Wonder	6.2	4.1	2.4	6.6	9.1
Benson	6.0	4.0	3.1	5.1	4.5

*Programs that cleared in 20+ markets.

Network TV Program Ratings

Source: A. C. Nielsen, December, 1986

Program or type	TV Households Rating %	TV Households No. (000)	Audience Composition (thousands) Men (18+)	Women (18+)	Teens 12-17	Children 2-11
Today (7:30-8:00)	4.8	4,200	1,960	3,210	90	170
Morning (7:30-8:00)	2.7	2,360	1,030	1,580	80	100
Good Morning Am. (7:30-8:00)	4.4	3,850	1,410	2,770	210	220
Daytime Drama (Soaps)	5.9	5,180	1,360	4,770	320	370
Quiz & Aud. Participation	4.4	3,860	1,330	2,940	170	310
All 10am-4:30pm	5.3	4,660	1,310	4,100	270	350
Evening						
Informational	11.8	10,310	6,440	7,460	640	790
General Drama	16.2	14,140	7,060	12,810	1,240	1,340
Susp. & Mystery	14.9	13,040	8,070	10,350	1,490	1,550
Sitcom Comedy	18.5	16,170	8,990	14,220	2,770	3,720
Feature Film	14.7	12,850	7,730	10,510	1,710	2,150
All 7-11pm Regular	15.9	13,890	8,260	11,330	1,710	2,030

All-time Top Television Programs

Source: A.C. Nielsen estimates, July 1960-Jan. 26, 1987, excluding unsponsored or joint network telecasts or programs under 30 minutes long.

Ranked by percent of average audience.

	Program	Date	Network	Households
1	M*A*S*H Special	2/28/83	CBS	50,150,000
2	Dallas	11/21/80	CBS	41,470,000
3	Roots Pt. VIII	1/30/77	ABC	36,380,000
4	Super Bowl XVI	1/24/82	CBS	40,020,000
5	Super Bowl XVII	1/30/83	NBC	40,480,000
6	Super Bowl XX	1/26/86	NBC	41,490,000
7	Gone With The Wind-Pt. 1	11/7/76	NBC	33,960,000
8	Gone With The Wind-Pt. 2	11/8/76	NBC	33,750,000
9	Super Bowl XII	1/15/78	CBS	34,410,000
10	Super Bowl XIII	1/21/79	NBC	35,090,000
11	Bob Hope Christmas Show	1/15/70	NBC	27,260,000
12	Super Bowl XVIII	1/22/84	CBS	38,800,000
12	Super Bowl XIX	1/20/85	ABC	39,390,000
14	Super Bowl XIV	1/20/80	CBS	35,330,000
15	The Day After	11/20/83	ABC	38,550,000
16	Roots Pt. VI	1/28/77	ABC	32,680,000
16	The Fugitive	8/29/67	ABC	25,700,000
18	Super Bowl XXI	1/25/87	CBS	40,030,000
19	Roots Pt. V	1/27/77	ABC	32,540,000
20	Ed Sullivan	2/9/64	CBS	23,240,000
21	Bob Hope Christmas Show	1/14/71	NBC	27,050,000
22	Roots Pt. III	1/25/77	ABC	31,900,000
23	Super Bowl XI	1/9/77	NBC	31,610,000
23	Super Bowl XV	1/25/81	NBC	34,540,000
25	Super Bowl VI	1/16/72	CBS	27,450,000
26	Roots Pt. II	1/24/77	ABC	31,400,000
27	Beverly Hillbillies	1/8/64	CBS	22,570,000
28	Roots Pt. IV	1/26/77	ABC	31,190,000
28	Ed Sullivan	2/16/64	CBS	22,445,000
30	Academy Awards	4/7/70	ABC	25,390,000
31	Thorn Birds Pt. III	3/29/83	ABC	35,990,000
32	Thorn Birds Pt. IV	3/30/83	ABC	35,900,000
33	NFC Championship Game	1/10/82	CBS	34,960,000
34	Beverly Hillbillies	1/15/64	CBS	21,960,000
35	Super Bowl VII	1/14/73	NBC	27,670,000

U.S. Television Sets and Stations Received

Set Ownership
(Nielsen est. as of Jan. 1, 1987)

		%
Total TV homes	89,130,000	
(98% of U.S. homes own at least one TV set)		
Homes with:		
Color TV sets	82,680,000	91
B&W only	4,720,000	10
2 or more sets	51,400,000	57
One set	36,000,000	45
Cable (Feb. 1986)	42,820,780	44.6

Number of Stations
(FCC, Jan. 1, 1987)

Commercial 941

Educational 300

Total 1,241

Stations Receivable
(Nielsen, Sept. 1986)
% of TV homes receiving:

Stations	%
1-4 stations	3
5	4
6	5
7	7
8	10
9	11
10	11
11+	49

Total TV Households—87.4 million, 18+ women—90,830,000; 18+ men—81,980,000; teens 12–17 20,250,000; children 2–11 34,010,000.

Television Network Addresses and Phone Numbers

American Broadcasting Company (ABC)
1330 Avenue of Americas
New York, NY 10019
(212) 887-7777

CBS, Inc.
51 W. 52nd St.
New York, NY 10019
(212) 975-4321

National Broadcasting Company (NBC)
30 Rockefeller Plaza
New York, NY 10112
(212) 664-4444

Westinghouse Broadcasting and Cable Inc.
888 7th Ave.
New York, NY 10106
(212) 307-3000

Fox Television (WNYW-TV)
205 E. 67 St.
New York, NY 10021
(212) 535-1000

Public Broadcasting Service (PBS)
609 Fifth Ave.
New York, NY 10017
(212) 753-7373

Symphony Orchestras of the U.S.

Source: American Symphony Orchestra League (as of June, 1987)

Classifications are based on annual incomes or budgets of orchestras.

Major Orchestras	Music Director
Atlanta Symphony	Robert Shaw[1]
Baltimore Symphony	David Zinman
Boston Symphony	Seiji Ozawa
Buffalo Philharmonic	Semyon Bychkov
Chicago Symphony	Sir Georg Solti
Cincinnati Symphony	Jesus Lopez-Cobos
Cleveland Orchestra	Christoph von Dohnanyi
Dallas Symphony	Eduardo Mata
Denver Symphony	Philippe Entremont
Detroit Symphony	Gunther Herbig
Houston Symphony	Sergiu Comissiona
Indianapolis Symphony	John Nelson
Los Angeles Philharmonic	Andre Previn
Milwaukee Symphony	Zdenek Macal
Minnesota Orchestra	Edo de Waart
National Arts Centre Orchestra	Franco Mannino[2]
National Symphony	Mstislav Rostropovich
New Orleans Symphony	Maxim Shostakovich
New York Philharmonic	Zubin Mehta
Oregon Symphony	James DePriest[1]
Philadelphia Orchestra	Riccardo Muti[1]
Phoenix Symphony	Theo Alcantara[3]
Pittsburgh Symphony	Lorin Maazel[4]
Rochester Philharmonic	Jerzy Semkow[5]
St. Louis Symphony	Leonard Slatkin[1]
St. Paul Chamber Orchestra	Stanley Skrowaczewski[6]
San Antonio Symphony	Sixten Ehrling
San Diego Symphony	vacant
San Francisco Symphony	Herbert Blomstedt[1]
Seattle Symphony	Gerard Schwarz
Syracuse Symphony	Kazuyoshi Akiyama
Utah Symphony	Joseph Silverstein

Regional Orchestras	Music Director
Alabama Symphony	Paul Polivnick[1]
American Symphony	John Mauceri[3]
Austin Symphony	Sung Kwak
Brooklyn Philharmonic	Lukas Foss[1]
Charlotte Symphony	Leo B. Driehuys
Colorado Springs Symphony	Charles Ansbacher[8]
Columbus Symphony	Christian Badea[9]
Concerto Soloists Chamber	Marc S. Mostovoy[1]
Dayton Philharmonic	Charles Wendelken-Wilson[1]
Philharmonic of Florida	James Judd
Florida Orchestra	Irwin Hoffman
Florida Symphony	Kenneth Jean
Fort Worth Symphony	John Giordano
Grand Rapids Symphony	Catherine Comet
Hartford Symphony	Michael Lankester
Honolulu Symphony	Donald Johanos
Hudson Valley Philharmonic	Imre Pallo
Jacksonville Symphony	Roger Nierenberg
Kansas City Symphony	William McGlaughlin
Long Beach Symphony	Murry Sidlin[1]
Long Island Philharmonic	Christopher Keene
Los Angeles Chamber	Iona Brown
Louisville Orchestra	Lawrence Leighton Smith
Memphis Symphony	Alan Balter[1]
Nashville Symphony	Kenneth D. Schermerhorn
New Haven Symphony	Murry Sidlin[1]
New Jersey Symphony	Hugh Wolff
New Mexico Symphony	Neal H. Stulberg[8]
North Carolina Symphony	Gerhardt Zimmerman[1]
Oklahoma Symphony	Luis Herrera de la Fuente[1]
Omaha Symphony	Bruce Hangen
Orange County Pacific Symphony	Keith Steward Clark
Phoenix Symphony	Theo Alcantara[7]
Puerto Rico Symphony	Odon Alonso
Richmond Symphony	Peter Bay[6]
Sacramento Symphony	Carter Nice[1]
San Jose Symphony	George Cleve[1]
Spokane Symphony	Bruce Ferden
Springfield Symphony	Raymond C. Harvey[1]
Toledo Symphony	Yuval Zaliouk[1]
Tucson Symphony	Robert E. Bernhardt
Tulsa Philharmonic	Bernard Rubenstein
Virginia Symphony	Winston Dan Vogel[1]
Wichita Symphony	Michael Palmer[1]

(1) Music Director & Conductor (2) Principal Conductor (3) Music Director & Principal Conductor (4) Principal Guest Conductor & Music Advisor (5) Music Advisor & Principal Conductor (6) Music Advisor (7) Artistic Advisor (8) Music Director & Conductor-Designate (9) Artistic Director & Principal Conductor

Metropolitan Orchestras

Akron Symphony OH
Albany Symphony NY
Amarillo Symphony TX
American Composers NY
Anchorage Symphony AK
Arkansas Symphony AR
B.C. Pops, Inc. NY
Baton Rouge Symphony LA
Binghampton Symphony & Choral Society NY
Boca Raton Symphonic Pops FL
Boise Philharmonic ID
Brevard Symphony FL
Cabrillo Music Festival CA
Canton Symphony OH
Cathedral Symphony NJ
Cedar Rapids Symphony IA
Charleston Symphony SC
Charleston Symphony WV
Chattanooga Symphony & Opera Assn. TN
Colorado Music Festival CO
Corpus Christi Symphony TX
Delaware Symphony DE
Des Moines Symphony IA
Duluth-Superior Symphony MN
Eastern Philharmonic NC
El Paso Symphony TX
Elgin Symphony IL
Erie Philharmonic PA
Eugene Symphony OR
Evansville Philharmonic IN
Fairbanks Symphony/Arctic Chamber Orch. AK
Flint Symphony MI
Florida West Coast Symphony FL
Fort Wayne Philharmonic IN
Fresno Philharmonic CA
Glendale Symphony CA
Greensboro Symphony NC
Handel and Haydn Society MA
Harrisburg Symphony PA
Orchestra of Illinois IL
Jackson Symphony MS
Kalamazoo Symphony MI
Knoxville Symphony TN
Lake Forest Symphony Association IL
Lansing Symphony MI
Lexington Philharmonic KY
Lincoln Symphony NE
Little Orchestra Society of New York NY
Los Angeles Pops CA
Lubbock Symphony TX
Madison Symphony WI
Marin Symphony CA
Midland-Odessa Symphony & Chorale TX
Monterey County Symphony CA
National Repertory
Orchestra New England CT
New Hampshire Symphony NH
Northeastern Pennsylvania Philharmonic PA
Northwest Chamber WA
Ohio Chamber OH
Pasadena Symphony CA
Peoria Symphony IL
Philharmonia Virtuosi NY
Portland Symphony ME
Quad City Symphony IA
Queens Symphony NY
Reading Symphony PA
Rhode Island Philharmonic RI
Rochester Symphony MN
Saginaw Symphony MI
Santa Barbara Symphony CA
Santa Rosa Symphony CA
Savannah Symphony GA
Shreveport Symphony LA
Sioux City Symphony IA
South Bend Symphony IN
South Dakota Symphony SD
South Florida Symphony FL
Springfield Symphony IL
Springfield Symphony MO
Stockton Symphony CA
Summer of Music on the Hudson NY
Tacoma Symphony WA
Ventura Symphony CA
Vermont Symphony VT
Virginia Beach Pops VA
Wheeling Symphony WV
New Orchestra of Westchester NY
White Plains Symphony NY
Winston-Salem Symphony NC
Youngstown Symphony OH

Recordings

The Recording Industry of America, Inc. confers Gold Record Awards on single records that sell one million units, Platinum Awards to those selling two million, Gold Awards to albums and their tape equivalents that sell 500,000 units, Platinum Awards to those selling one million, and Multi-Platinum Awards to those selling two million or more. There were no Platinum Awards for single records in 1986. Multi-Platinum Awards for albums, Platinum Awards for albums, and Gold Awards for singles conferred in 1986 on records released in 1985 or 1986 follow.

Artists, Recording Titles

Albums, Multi-Platinum

(number in parentheses indicates millions of albums sold)

Bon Jovi: *Slippery When Wet* (3).
Boston: *Third Stage* (3).
Phil Collins: *No Jacket Required.* (5).
John Cougar Mellencamp: *Scarecrow* (3).
Dire Straits: *Brothers in Arms* (5).
John Fogerty: *Centerfield* (2).
Genesis: *Invisible Touch* (2).
Heart: *Heart* (4).
Whitney Houston: *Whitney Houston* (7).
Janet Jackson: *Control* (3).
Billy Joel: *Greatest Hits, I & II* (2).
Huey Lewis & The News: *Fore!* (2).
Madonna: *True Blue* (3).
Motley Crüe: *Theatre of Pain* (2).
Billy Ocean: *Love Zone* (2).
Lionel Richie: *Dancing on the Ceiling* (3).
Run-D.M.C.: *Raising Hell* (2).
Sade: *Promise* (2).
Soundtrack: *Miami Vice* (4).
Soundtrack: *Top Gun* (3).
Sting: *The Dream of the Blue Turtles* (2).
Barbra Streisand: *The Broadway Album* (3).
Tears for Fears: *Songs from the Big Chair* (4).
Van Halen: *5150* (3).
ZZ Top: *Afterburner* (3).

Albums, Platinum

A-Ha: *Hunting High and Low.*
Alabama: *Greatest Hits.*
Arcadia: *So Red the Rose.*
Anita Baker: *Rapture.*
Bangles: *Different Light.*
Cameo: *Word Up.*
The Cars: *Greatest Hits.*
Cinderella: *Night Songs.*
Peter Gabriel: *So.*
Amy Grant: *Unguarded.*
The Hooters: *Nervous Night.*
Bruce Hornsby and the Range: *The Way It Is.*
Billy Joel: *The Bridge.*
Journey: *Raised on Radio.*
The Judds: *Rockin' with the Rhythm.*
Patti Labelle: *Winner in You.*
Cyndi Lauper: *True Colors.*
Miami Sound Machine: *Primitive Love.*
New Edition: *All for Love.*
Stevie Nicks: *Rock a Little.*
Ozzy Osbourne: *The Ultimate Sin.*
The Outfield: *Play Deep.*
Robert Palmer: *Riptide.*
Pet Shop Boys: *Please.*
Prince & the Revolution: *Parade.*
Ready for the World: *Ready for the World.*
Rolling Stones: *Dirty Work.*
David Lee Roth: *Eat 'Em and Smile.*
Rush: *Power Windows.*
Scorpions: *World Wide Live.*
Bob Seger/Silver Bullet Band: *Like a Rock.*
Paul Simon: *Graceland.*
Soundtrack: *Rocky IV.*
Tina Turner: *Break Every Rule.*
Luther Vandross: *Give Me the Reason.*
Wham!: *Music from the Edge of Heaven.*
Steve Winwood: *Back in the High Life.*

Singles, Gold

Dionne Warwick & Friends: *That's What Friends Are For.*
Doug E. Fresh & the Get Fresh Crew: *The Show* (12").
P. Labelle and M. McDonald: *On My Own.*
Elvis Presley: *Crying in the Chapel.*
Prince & the Revolution: *Kiss.*
Lionel Richie: *Say You, Say Me.*
The Chicago Bears Shufflin' Crew: *Superbowl Shuffle.*

Notable U.S. Dance Companies

Source: Dance/USA; June 30, 1987

(**Note:** Artistic director named only if not in company title.)

Dance Company/City, State	Artistic Director
Alvin Ailey American Dance Theatre; N.Y., NY	
Aman Folk Ensemble; Los Angeles, CA	Barry Glass
American Ballet Theatre; N.Y., NY	Mikhail Baryshnikov
Atlanta Ballet; Atlanta, GA	Robert Barnett
Ballet Arizona; Phoenix, AZ	Malcolm Burn, Jean Paul Comelin
Ballet Hispanico of New York; N.Y., NY	Tina Ramirez
Tandy Beal and Company; Santa Cruz, CA	
Boston Ballet; Boston, MA	Bruce Marks
Trisha Brown Co.; N.Y., NY	
Caribbean Dance Company; St. Croix, VI	Montgomery Thompson
Lucinda Childs Dance Company, N.Y., NY	
Cincinnati/New Orleans Ballet; Cincinnati, OH	Ivan Nagy
Cleveland Ballet, OH	Dennis Nahat
Merce Cunningham Dance Company, N.Y., NY	
Dance Exchange; Washington, DC	Liz Lerman
Laura Dean Dancers and Musicians; N.Y., NY	
Dinosaur Dance Company; N.Y., NY	Michael Mao
Garth Fagan's Bucket Dance Theater; Rochester, NY	
Feld Ballet; N.Y., NY	
David Gordon/Pick Up Co.; N.Y., NY	
Harry; N.Y., NY	Senta Driver
Hartford Ballet; Hartford, CT	Michael Uthoff
Houston Ballet; Houston, TX	Ben Stevenson
Hubbard Street Dance Company; Chicago, IL	Lou Conte
Jazz Tap Ensemble; No. Hollywood	Lynn Dally
Margaret Jenkins Dance Company; San Francisco, CA	
Bill T. Jones/Arnie Zane Company; N.Y., NY	
Bella Lewitzky Dance Company; Los Angeles, CA	
Jose Limon Dance Company; N.Y., NY	
Elisa Monte Dance Company; N.Y., NY	
Mordine & Co.; Chicago, IL	
Jennifer Muller and the Works; N.Y., NY	
New Dance Ensemble; Minneapolis, MN	Linda Shapiro

Rosalind Newman and Dancers; N.Y., NY	
New York City Ballet; N.Y., NY	Peter Martins, Jerome Robbins
No. Carolina Dance Theater; Winston Salem, NC	Salvatore Aiello
Oakland Ballet; Oakland, CA	Ronn Guidi
ODC/San Francisco; San Francisco, CA	Salvatore Aiello
Ohio Ballet; Akron, OH	Heinz Poll
Pacific Northwest Ballet; Seattle, WA	Francis Russell
Pennsylvania Ballet; Philadelphia, PA	Robert Weiss
Phildanco; Philadelphia, PA	Joan Myers Brown
Pilobus; Washington, CT	Robby Barnett, Alison Chase, Moses Pendleton, Michael Tracy, Jonathan Wolken
Murray Louis Dance Company; N.Y., NY	
Louisville Ballet; Louisville, KY	Alun Jones
Miami City Ballet; Miami Beach, FL	Edward Villela
Milwaukee Ballet; Milwaukee, WI	Basil Thompson
Pittsburgh Ballet Theatre; Pittsburgh, PA	Patricia Wilde
Ram Island Dance Company; Portland, ME	Daniel McCusker
Repertory Dance Theatre; Salt Lake City, UT	Linda C. Smith
Ririe-Woodbury Dance Company; Salt Lake City, UT	
San Francisco Ballet; San Francisco, CA	Helgi Tomasson
Solomons Company/Dance; N.Y., NY	
Sounds in Motion; N.Y., NY	Dianne McIntyre
Paul Taylor Dance Company; N.Y., NY	
Twyla Tharp Dance; N.Y., NY	
Joyce Trisler Dance Company; N.Y., NY	
Tulsa Ballet Theater; Tulsa, OK	Toman Jasinski, Moscelyne Larkin
Dan Wagoner and Dancers; N.Y., NY	
Washington Ballet; Washington, DC	Mary Day, Choo San Goh
Nina Wiener and Dancers; N.Y., NY	
ZeroMoving Dance Company; Philadelphia, PA	Hellmut Gottschild
Zivili Kolo Ensemble; Granville, OH	Pamela Lacko Kelly

U.S. Opera Companies with Budgets of $500,000 or More

Source: Central Opera Service, New York, N.Y.; June, 1987

Anchorage Opera; James Wright, gen. mgr.
Arizona Opera Co. (Tucson); Glynn Ross, gen. dir.
Fullerton Civic Light Opera (Calif.); Griff Duncan, gen. mgr.
Long Beach Opera (Calif.); Micheal Milenski, gen. dir.
Long Beach Civic Light Opera (Calif.), Harvey Waggoner, exec. dir.
Los Angeles Music Center Opera Assn.; Peter Hemmings, exec. dir.
Opera Pacific (Irvine, Calif.); David DiChiera, gen. dir.
San Diego Civic Light Opera; Leon Drew, gen mgr.
San Diego Opera Assn.; Ian Campbell, gen. mgr.
San Francisco Opera; Terence McEwen, gen. dir.
San Francisco Opera Center (inc. Western Opera Theater), Christine Bullin, mgr.
Central City Opera (Denver); Daniel Rule, gen. mgr.
Opera Colorado (Denver); Nathaniel Merrill, art. dir.
Connecticut Opera (Hartford); George Osborne, gen. dir.
Goodspeed Opera House (E. Haddam, Conn.); Michael Price, exec. dir.
Washington Opera (D.C.); Martin Feinstein, gen. dir.
Greater Miami Opera Assn.; Robert Hever, gen. mgr.
Orlando Opera Co. (Fla.); Richard Owens, gen. mgr.
Palm Beach Opera; Joseph Conlin, gen. dir.
Sarasota Opera Assn. (Fla.); Deane Allyn, exec. dir.
Hawaii Opera Theatre; Beebe Freitas, art. dir.
Chicago Opera Theatre; Alan Stone, art. dir.
Lyric Opera of Chicago; Ardis Krainik, gen. mgr.
Indianapolis Opera; Robert Driver, art. dir.
Des Moines Metro Opera (Indianola); Robert Larsen, art. dir.
Music Theatre of Wichita; John Holly, prod. dir.
Kentucky Opera Assn. (Louisville); Thomson Smillie, gen. dir.
New Orleans Opera Assn.; Arthur Cosenza, gen. dir.
Baltimore Opera Co.; Jay Holbrook, gen. mgr.
Opera Company of Boston; Sarah Caldwell, art. dir.
Michigan Opera Theatre (Detroit); David DiChiera, gen. dir.
Minnesota Opera Co. (St. Paul); Kevin Smith, gen. mgr.
Lyric Opera of Kansas City (Missouri); Russell Patterson gen. dir. & art. dir.
Opera Theatre of St. Louis (Missouri); Charles MacKay, gen. dir.
Opera/Omaha (Neb.); Mary Robert, gen. dir.
Nevada Opera (Reno); Ted Puffer, gen. dir.
New Jersey State Opera (Newark); Alfredo Silipigni, art. dir.
Santa Fe Opera (New Mexico); John Crosby, gen. dir.
Tri-Cities Opera (Binghamton, N.Y.); Gerald Blount-Bierly, exec. dir.
Lake George Opera Festival (Glens Falls, N.Y.); Brian Lingham, gen. dir.
Syracuse Opera; vacancy, gen. dir.
Metropolitan Opera Assn. (New York City); Bruce Crawford, gen. mgr.
New York City Opera; Beverly Sills, gen. dir.
New York City Opera Natl. Co.; Nancy Kelly, adm. dir.
Opera Orchestra of N.Y. (N.Y.C.); Eve Queler, art dir.
Carolina Opera Assn. (Charlotte, N.C.); Bruce Chalmers, gen. dir.
Cincinnati Opera Assn.; James deBlasis, art. dir.
Cleveland Opera; David Bamberger, gen. mgr. & art. dir.
Opera Columbus (Oh.); Michael Harrison, gen. dir.
Dayton Opera Assn. (Oh.); Dennis Hanthorn, mng. dir.
Tulsa Opera (Oklahoma); vacancy, gen. dir.
Portland Opera Assn. (Oregon); Robert Bailey, exec. dir.
American Music Theatre Festival (Phila.); Marjorie Samoff, prod. dir.
Opera Company of Philadelphia; Margaret Anne Everitt, gen. dir.
Pennsylvania Opera Theater (Phila.); Barbara Silverstein, art dir. & gen. mgr.
Pittsburgh Civic Light Opera; Charles Gray, exec. dir.
Pittsburgh Opera Co.; Tito Capobianco, gen. dir.
Opera/Memphis (Tenn.); Robert Driver, gen. & art. dir.
Dallas Opera; Plato Karayanis, gen. dir.
Fort Worth Opera; J. Mano Ramos, mng. dir.
Houston Grand Opera Assn.; R. David Gockley, gen. dir.
Texas Opera Theater (Houston); M. Jane Weaver, gen. mgr.
Theatre Under the Stars (Houston); Vivian Flynn, gen. mgr.
Utah Opera Company (Salt Lake City); Glade Peterson, gen. dir.
Virginia Opera (Norfolk); Peter Mark, gen. dir.
Seattle Opera Assn.; Speight Jenkins, gen. dir.
Florentine Opera of Milwaukee; John Gage, gen. mgr.
Skylight Comic Opera (Milwaukee); Colin Cabot, mng. dir.

50 Leading U.S. Advertisers, 1985

Source: Advertising Age, Sept. 4, 1986; copyright © Crain Communications Inc. 1986.

Rank	Company	U.S. Ad Costs (000)	U.S. Sales (000)	Ads as % sales
	Automotive			
5	General Motors Corp.	$779,000	$89,099,000	0.9
7	Ford Motor Co.	614,600	43,526,000	1.4
22	Chrysler Corp.	393,400	18,767,200	2.1
45	Toyota Motor Corp.	172,035	NA	NA
49	Nissan Motor Co.	162,566	NA	NA
	Chemicals & Petroleum			
31	American Cyanamid Co.	266,189	2,489,100	10.7
40	Mobil Corp.	195,262	16,601,000	1.2
	Electronics			
24	GE/RCA	373,336	35,060,300	1.1
27	Inter. Business Machines	327,834	28,511,000	1.1
35	Eastman Kodak Co.	247,300	7,392,000	3.3
41	Tandy Corp.	186,861	NA	NA
	Entertainment, Communications			
39	CBS, Inc.	208,000	4,201,000	5.0
	Food			
3	RJR/Nabisco	1,093,000	12,557,000	8.7
6	Beatrice Cos.	684,000	8,662,000	7.9
9	McDonald's Corp.	500,000	2,863,826	19.2
12	Ralston Purina Co.	508,365	NA	NA
13	Dart & Kraft	489,349	7,316,900	6.7
14	General Mills	484,146	NA	NA
17	Pillsbury Co.	473,220	5,373,700	8.8
25	Kellogg Co.	364,299	2,074,900	17.6
29	Sara Lee Corp.	285,956	6,631,000	8.7
38	Campbell Soup Co.	215,059	3,344,702	6.4
46	IC Industries	171,000	3,943,900	4.3
	Gum, Candy			
30	Mars Inc.	275,504	NA	NA
	Miscellaneous			
33	U.S. Government	259,050	NA	NA
47	American Express	169,868	9,434,000	1.8
	Pharmaceuticals			
18	Warner-Lambert Co.	469,339	1,670,000	28.1
20	Johnson & Johnson	401,217	3,989,900	10.1
21	American Home Prods.	399,516	3,636,900	11.0
26	Bristol-Myers Co.	344,293	3,380,200	10.2
37	Sterling Drug	224,940	1,143,575	19.7
48	Schering-Plough	169,383	1,123,700	15.1
	Retail			
4	Sears, Rosebuck Co.	800,000	NA	NA
8	K mart Corp.	567,000	NA	NA
15	J.C. Penney Co.	478,892	13,228,000	3.6
	Soaps, Cleaners			
1	Procter & Gamble	1,600,000	10,243,000	15.6
19	Unilever U.S.	413,623	4,188,000	9.9
34	Colgate-Palmolive	253,495	2,169,988	11.7
	Soft Drinks			
16	PepsiCo. Inc.	478,372	7,105,000	6.7
23	Coca-Cola Inc.	390,000	4,909,000	7.9
	Telephone			
11	Amer. Telephone & Telegraph	521,318	NA	NA
	Tobacco			
2	Philip Morris Cos.	1,400,000	11,496,000	12.2
43	Grand Metropolitan	176,749	2,269,900	7.8
44	Batus Inc.	175,420	NA	NA
	Toiletries, Cosmetics			
42	Beecham Group	186,322	1,007,500	18.5
	Wine, Beer, Liquor			
10	Anheuser-Busch Cos.	522,900	NA	NA

30 Top U.S. Advertisers: 1985 Expenditures by Type of Media

Source: Advertising Age, Sept. 4, 1986; copyright © Crain Communications Inc., 1986.

(thousands of dollars)

Rank	Company	Newspaper	Magazine	Network tv	Spot tv	Network cable	Network radio
1	Procter & Gamble	$7,345	$93,144	$488,756	$285,118	$31,404	$12,770
2	Philip Morris Cos.	78,031	215,038	348,281	138,970	21,261	2,076
3	RJR/Nabisco	73,321	164,137	179,254	81,686	8,736	9,334
4	Sears, Roebuck & Co.	0	19,190	122,657	34,421	4,340	20,803
5	General Motors Corp.	140,979	107,524	209,898	49,067	4,724	9,034
6	Beatrice Cos.	8,773	43,113	111,640	53,381	2,260	5,456
7	Ford Motor Co.	77,295	114,739	191,373	37,087	6,068	7,625
8	K mart Corp.	0	10,724	16,222	23,257	513	4,435
9	McDonald's Corp.	0	892	184,882	118,046	1,425	195
10	Anheuser-Busch Cos.	5,611	13,956	154,503	70,747	16,395	8,929
11	AT&T	57,210	88,137	167,728	29,700	3,696	24,853
12	Ralston Purina Co.	2,345	21,719	102,617	58,471	2,550	1,408
13	Dart & Kraft	6,433	35,723	111,182	64,033	1,584	652
14	General Mills	1,592	24,804	114,372	122,674	12,792	2,030
15	J.C. Penney Co.	0	9,280	44,552	17,640	358	0
16	PepsiCo Inc.	5,926	2,668	82,456	183,220	4,515	5,296
17	Pillsbury Co.	769	4,675	115,861	112,374	728	0
18	Warner-Lambert Co.	1,150	13,585	83,352	39,281	3,474	16,268
19	Unilever U.S.	2,398	18,252	153,754	56,415	2,363	1,255
20	Johnson & Johnson	113	29,419	154,964	10,618	3,411	790
21	American Home	89	16,235	183,394	20,233	4,720	925
22	Chrysler Corp.	42,000	73,579	96,194	63,133	5,126	4,269
23	Coca-Cola Co.	6,941	9,059	114,708	76,188	4,375	791
24	GE/RCA	29,870	55,288	49,173	11,953	2,520	1,668
25	Kellogg Co.	460	300	156,431	51,050	4,725	0
26	Bristol-Myers Co.	1,995	28,435	127,642	17,092	4,456	291
27	IBM	30,610	52,535	62,749	2,227	832	3,014
28	Nestle SA	1,250	21,777	76,754	54,327	3,400	4,004
29	Sara Lee Corp.	3,350	27,940	64,129	26,196	1,974	2,313
30	Mars Inc.	377	5,820	87,216	40,304	11,605	3,991

NOTED PERSONALITIES

Widely Known Americans of the Present

Statesmen, authors of nonfiction, military men, and other prominent persons not listed in other categories; as of mid-1987.

Name (Birthplace)	Birthdate
Abel, I. W. (Magnolia, Oh.)	8/11/08
Arledge, Roone (Forest Hills, N.Y.)	7/8/31
Armstrong, William L. (Fremont, Neb.)	1937
Anderson, Jack (Long Beach, Cal.)	10/19/22
Armstrong, Neil (Wapakoneta, Oh.)	8/5/30
Ash, Mary Kay (Hot Wells, Tex.)	—
Bailey, F. Lee (Waltham, Mass.)	6/10/33
Baker, Howard (Huntsville, Tenn.)	11/15/25
Baker, James A. (Houston, Tex.)	4/28/30
Baker, Russell (Loudoun Co., Va.)	8/14/25
Barthelmy, Sidney K. (New Orleans, La.)	3/17/42
Belli, Melvin (Sonora, Cal.)	7/29/07
Bennett, William J. (Salem, Oh.)	5/4/38
Biden, Joseph R. Jr. (Scranton, Pa.)	11/20/42
Blackmun, Harry (Nashville, Ill.)	11/12/08
Blass, Bill (Ft. Wayne, Ind.)	6/22/22
Bombeck, Erma (Dayton, Oh.)	2/21/27
Bond, Julian (Nashville, Tenn.)	1/14/40
Borman, Frank (Gary, Ind.)	3/14/28
Boorstin, Daniel (Atlanta, Ga.)	10/1/14
Bradlee, Ben (Boston, Mass.)	8/26/21
Bradley, Bill (Crystal City, Mo.)	7/28/43
Bradley, Ed (Philadelphia, Pa.)	6/22/41
Bradley, Thomas (Calvert, Tex.)	12/29/17
Brennan, William J. (Newark, N.J.)	4/25/06
Breslin, Jimmy (Jamaica, N.Y.)	10/17/30
Brinkley, David (Wilmington, N.C.)	7/10/20
Brock, William (Chattanooga, Tenn.)	11/23/30
Brody, Jane (Brooklyn, N.Y.)	5/19/41
Brokaw, Tom (Webster, S. Dak.)	2/6/40
Brothers, Joyce (New York, N.Y.)	—
Brown, Helen Gurley (Green Forest, Ark.)	2/18/22
Buchwald, Art (Mt. Vernon, N.Y.)	10/20/25
Buckley, William F. (New York, N.Y.)	11/24/25
Bumpers, Dale (Charleston, Ark.)	8/12/25
Bush, George (Milton, Mass.)	6/12/24
Byrd, Robert (N. Wilkesboro, N.C.)	11/20/17
Calderone, Mary (New York, N.Y.)	7/1/04
Carter, Jimmy (Plains, Ga.)	10/1/24
Carter, Rosalynn (Plains, Ga.)	8/18/27
Chancellor, John (Chicago, Ill.)	7/14/27
Chavez, Cesar (Yuma, Ariz.)	3/31/27
Child, Julia (Pasadena, Cal.)	8/15/12
Chisholm, Shirley (Brooklyn, N.Y.)	11/30/24
Chung, Connie (Washington, D.C.)	8/20/46
Cisneros, Henry (San Antonio, Tex.)	6/11/47
Claiborne, Craig (Sunflower, Miss.)	9/4/20
Clark, William (Dallas, Tex.)	12/11/30
Coelho, Tony (Los Banos, Cal.)	6/15/42
Collins, Martha (Shelby Cty, Ky.)	12/7/36
Commager, Henry Steele (Pittsburgh, Pa.)	10/25/02
Cooney, Joan Ganz (Phoenix, Ariz.)	10/30/29
Cosell, Howard (Winston-Salem, N.C.)	3/25/20
Cousins, Norman (Union Hill, N.J.)	6/24/12
Cranston, Alan (Palo Alto, Cal.)	6/19/14
Crist, Judith (New York, N.Y.)	5/22/22
Cronkite, Walter (St. Joseph, Mo.)	11/4/16
Cuomo, Mario (Queens, N.Y.)	6/15/32
Dellums, Ronald (Oakland, Cal.)	11/24/35
Dodd, Christopher (Willimantic, Conn.)	5/27/44
Dole, Elizabeth (Salisbury, N.C.)	7/29/36
Dole, Robert (Russell, Kan.)	7/22/23
Domenici, Pete (Albuquerque, N.M.)	5/7/32
Donaldson, Sam (El Paso, Tex.)	3/11/34
Doolittle, James H. (Alameda, Cal.)	12/14/96
Dukakis, Michael S. (Boston, Mass.)	11/3/33
Du Pont, Pierre S. IV (Wilmington, Del.)	1/22/35
Dymally, Mervyn (Trinidad, W.I.)	5/12/26
Ephron, Nora (New York, N.Y.)	5/19/41
Falwell, Jerry (Lynchburg, Va.)	8/11/33
Feinstein, Dianne (San Francisco, Cal.)	6/22/33
Feldstein, Martin (New York, N.Y.)	11/25/39
Ferraro, Geraldine (Newburgh, N.Y.)	8/26/35
Foley, Thomas S. (Spokane, Wash.)	3/6/29
Ford, Betty (Chicago, Ill.)	4/8/18
Ford, Gerald R. (Omaha, Neb.)	7/14/13
Friedan, Betty (Peoria, Ill.)	2/4/21
Friedman, Milton (Brooklyn, N.Y.)	7/31/12
Fulbright, J. William (Sumner, Mo.)	4/9/05
Galbraith, John Kenneth (Ontario, Can.)	10/15/08
Gephardt, Richard (St. Louis, Mo.)	1/31/41
Giamatti, A. Bartlett (Boston, Mass.)	4/4/38
Gifford, Frank (Santa Monica, Cal.)	8/16/30
Ginsberg, Allen (Paterson, N.J.)	6/3/21
Glenn, John (Cambridge, Oh.)	7/18/21
Goldwater, Barry M. (Phoenix, Ariz.)	1/1/09
Goodman, Ellen (Newton, Mass.)	4/11/41
Gottlieb, Robert A. (New York)	4/9/31
Graham, Billy (Charlotte, N.C.)	11/7/18
Graham, Katharine (New York, N.Y.)	6/16/17
Gray, William H. III (Baton Rouge, La.)	9/20/41
Greenspan, Alan (New York, N.Y.)	3/6/26
Gumble, Bryant (New Orleans, La.)	9/29/48
Haig, Alexander (Philadelphia, Pa.)	12/2/24
Hammer, Armand (New York, N.Y.)	5/21/98
Hart, Gary (Ottawa, Kan.)	11/28/37
Harvey, Paul (Tulsa, Okla.)	9/4/18
Hatch, Orrin (Homestead, Pa.)	3/22/34
Hatfield, Mark O. (Dallas, Ore.)	7/12/22
Hefner, Hugh (Chicago, Ill.)	4/9/26
Heller, Walter (Buffalo, N.Y.)	8/27/15
Helms, Jesse (Monroe, N.C.)	10/18/21
Heloise (Waco, Tex.)	4/15/51
Hershey, Lenore (New York, N.Y.)	3/20/20
Hollings, Ernest (Charleston, S.C.)	1/1/22
Iacocca, Lee A. (Allentown, Pa.)	10/15/24
Jackson, Jesse (Greenville, N.C.)	10/8/41
Jennings, Peter (Toronto, Ont.)	8/29/38
Johnson, Lady Bird (Karnack, Tex.)	12/22/12
Jordan, Barbara (Houston, Tex.)	2/21/36
Kael, Pauline (Petaluma, Calif.)	6/19/19
Kaufman, Henry (Wenings, Germany)	10/20/27
Keillor, Garrison (Anoka, Minn.)	8/7/42
Kemp, Jack (Los Angeles, Cal.)	7/13/35
Kennedy, Edward M. (Brookline, Mass.)	2/22/32
Kennedy, Rose (Boston, Mass.)	7/22/90
Kerr, Walter (Evanston, Ill.)	7/8/13
King, Coretta (Mrs. Martin L.) (Marion, Ala.)	4/27/27
King, Larry (Brooklyn, N.Y.)	11/19/34
Kirkland, Lane (Camden, S.C.)	3/12/22
Kirkpatrick, Jeane (Duncan, Okla.)	11/19/26
Kissinger, Henry (Fuerth, Germany)	5/27/23
Klein, Calvin (New York, N.Y.)	11/19/42
Koch, Edward I. (New York, N.Y.)	12/12/24
Koppel, Ted (Lancashire, Eng.)	2/8/40
Kuhn, Maggie (Buffalo, N.Y.)	1905
Landers, Ann (Sioux City, Ia.)	7/4/18
Lauder, Estée (New York, N.Y.)	—
Lauren, Ralph (Bronx, N.Y.)	10/14/39
Laxalt, Paul (Reno, Nev.)	8/2/22
Leland, Mickey (Lubbock, Tex.)	11/27/44
Lindbergh, Anne Morrow (Englewood, N.J.)	1906
Long, Russell B. (Shreveport, La.)	11/3/18
Lott, Trent (Grenada, Miss.)	10/9/41
Luce, Clare Boothe (New York, N.Y.)	4/10/03
Lugar, Richard G. (Indianapolis, Ind.)	4/4/32
Madden, John (Austin, Minn.)	1936
Manchester, William (Attleboro, Mass.)	4/1/22
Mansfield, Mike (New York, N.Y.)	3/16/03
Marshall, Thurgood (Baltimore, Md.)	7/2/08
McCarthy, Eugene (Watkins, Minn.)	3/29/16
McCarver, Tim (Memphis, Tenn.)	10/16/41
McGovern, George (Avon, S.D.)	7/19/22
McNamara, Robert S. (San Francisco, Cal.)	6/9/16
Meese, Edwin (Oakland, Cal.)	12/2/31
Metzenbaum, Howard (Cleveland, Oh.)	6/4/17
Michel, Robert H. (Peoria, Ill.)	3/2/23
Mikulski, Barbara (Baltimore, Md.)	7/20/36
Mondale, Walter (Ceylon, Minn.)	1/5/28
Moyers, Bill (Hugo, Okla.)	6/5/34
Moynihan, Daniel P. (Tulsa, Okla.)	3/16/27
Mudd, Roger (Washington, D.C.)	2/9/28
Murdoch, Rupert (Melbourne, Austr.)	5/11/31
Muskie, Edmund (Rumford, Me.)	3/28/14
Nader, Ralph (Winsted, Conn.)	2/27/34
Nidetch, Jean (Brooklyn, N.Y.)	10/12/23
Nixon, Pat (Ely, Nev.)	3/16/12
Nixon, Richard (Yorba Linda, Cal.)	1/9/13
Nizer, Louis (London, England)	2/6/02
Norton, Eleanor Holmes (Washington, D.C.)	6/13/37

Name (Birthplace)	Birthdate
Nunn, Sam (Perry, Ga.)	9/8/38
O'Connor, Cardinal John (Phila., Pa.)	1/15/20
O'Connor, Sandra Day (nr. Duncan, Ariz.)	3/26/30
Onassis, Jacqueline (Southampton, N.Y.)	7/28/29
O'Neill, Thomas P. (Cambridge, Mass.)	12/9/12
Packwood, Bob (Portland, Ore.)	9/11/32
Paley, William S. (Chicago, Ill.)	9/28/01
Pauley, Jane (Indianapolis, Ind.)	10/31/50
Pauling, Linus (Portland, Ore.)	2/28/01
Peale, Norman Vincent (Bowersville, Oh.)	5/31/98
Pepper, Claude (Dudleyville, Ala.)	9/8/00
Pickens, T. Boone (Holdenville, Okla.)	5/22/28
Porter, Sylvia (Patchogue, N.Y.)	6/18/13
Powell, Lewis F. (Suffolk, Va.)	9/19/07
Proxmire, William (Lake Forest, Ill.)	1/11/15
Quinn, Jane Bryant (Niagara Falls, N.Y.)	2/5/39
Rather, Dan (Wharton, Tex.)	10/31/31
Reagan, Nancy (New York, N.Y.)	7/6/23
Reasoner, Harry (Dakota City, Ia.)	4/17/23
Regan, Donald T. (Cambridge, Mass.)	12/21/18
Rehnquist, William (Milwaukee, Wis.)	10/1/24
Reston, James (Clydebank, Scotland)	11/3/09
Ride, Sally K. (Encino, Calif.)	1952
Roberts, Oral (nr. Ada, Okla.)	1/24/18
Rockefeller, David (New York, N.Y.)	6/12/15
Rockefeller, John D. 4th "Jay" (New York, N.Y.)	6/18/37
Rockefeller, Laurance S. (New York, N.Y.)	5/26/10
Rodino, Peter (Newark, N.J.)	6/7/09
Rooney, Andy (Albany, N.Y.)	1/14/19
Rostenkowski, Dan (Chicago, Ill.)	1/2/28
Rozelle, Pete (S. Gate, Calif.)	3/1/26
Ruckelshaus, William D. (Indianapolis, Ind.)	7/24/32
Rukeyser, Louis (New York, N.Y.)	1/30/33
Safer, Morley (Toronto, Ontario)	11/8/31
Safire, William (New York, N.Y.)	12/17/29
Sagan, Carl (New York, N.Y.)	11/9/34
Salk, Jonas (New York, N.Y.)	10/28/14
Salk, Lee (New York, N.Y.)	12/27/26
Sawyer, Diane (Glasgow, Ky.)	12/22/45
Schlesinger, Arthur Jr. (Columbus, Oh.)	10/15/17
Schroeder, Patricia (Portland, Ore.)	7/30/40
Schuller, Robert (Alton, Ia.)	9/16/26
Seaborg, Glenn T. (Ishpeming, Mich.)	4/19/12
Shanker, Albert (New York, N.Y.)	9/14/28
Shirer, William L. (Chicago, Ill.)	2/23/04
Shultz, George P. (New York, N.Y.)	12/13/20
Silverstein, Shel (Chicago, Ill.)	1932
Simmons, Richard (New Orleans, La.)	7/12/48
Smith, Howard K. (Ferriday, La.)	5/12/14
Smith, Margaret Chase (Skowhegan, Me.)	12/14/97
Speakes, Larry (Cleveland, Miss.)	9/13/39
Spock, Benjamin (New Haven, Conn.)	5/2/03
Stahl, Leslie (Lynn, Mass.)	12/16/41
Steinbrenner, George (Rocky River, Oh.)	7/4/30
Steinem, Gloria (Toledo, Oh.)	3/25/34
Stennis, John (Kamper City, Miss.)	8/3/01
Stern, David J. (New York, N.Y.)	9/22/42
Stevens, John Paul (Chicago, Ill.)	4/20/20
Sulzberger, Arthur Ochs (New York, N.Y.)	2/5/26
Taft, Robert Jr. (Cincinnati, Oh.)	2/26/17
Terkel, Studs (New York, N.Y.)	5/16/12
Thomas, Helen (Winchester, Ky.)	8/4/20
Thurmond, J. Strom (Edgefield, S.C.)	12/5/02
Tinker, Grant (Stamford, Conn.)	1/11/26
Tower, John (Houston, Tex.)	9/29/25
Trillin, Calvin (Kansas City, Mo.)	12/5/35
Truman, Margaret (Independence, Mo.)	2/17/24
Trump, Donald (New York, N.Y.)	1946
Tuchman, Barbara (New York, N.Y.)	1/30/12
Turner, Ted (Cincinnati, Oh.)	1938
Udall, Morris K. (St. Johns, Ariz.)	6/15/22
Ueberroth, Peter (Chicago, Ill.)	9/2/37
Van Buren, Abigail (Sioux City, Ia.)	7/4/18
Vance, Cyrus R. (Clarksburg, W. Va.)	3/27/17
Vanderbilt, Gloria (New York, N.Y.)	2/20/24
Volcker, Paul A. (Cape May, N.J.)	9/5/27
Wallace, George (Clio, Ala.)	8/25/19
Wallace, Mike (Brookline, Mass.)	5/9/18
Walters, Barbara (Boston, Mass.)	9/25/31
Walters, Vernon (New York, N.Y.)	1/3/17
Washington, Harold (Chicago, Ill.)	4/15/22
Webster, William H. (St. Louis, Mo.)	3/6/24
Weicker, Lowell (Paris, France)	5/16/31
Weinberger, Caspar (San Francisco, Cal.)	8/18/17
Westheimer, Ruth (Germany)	1928
Williams, Edward Bennett (Hartford, Conn.)	5/31/20
Wolfe, Tom (Richmond, Va.)	3/2/31
Woodcock, Leonard (Providence, R.I.)	2/15/11
Woodruff, Judy (Tulsa, Okla.)	11/20/46
Woodward, Robert (Geneva, Ill.)	3/26/43
Wright, James C. Jr. (Ft. Worth, Tex.)	12/22/22
Young, Andrew (New Orleans, La.)	3/12/32
Young, Coleman (Tuscaloosa, Ala.)	5/24/18

Noted Black Americans

Names of black athletes and entertainers are not included here as they are listed elsewhere in The World Almanac.

The Rev. Dr. Ralph David Abernathy, b. 1926, organizer, 1957, and president, 1968, of the Southern Christian Leadership Conference.

Crispus Attucks, c. 1723-1770, agitator led group that precipitated the "Boston Massacre," Mar. 5, 1770.

James Baldwin, b. 1924, author, playwright; *The Fire Next Time, Blues for Mister Charlie, Just Above My Head.*

Benjamin Banneker, 1731-1806, inventor, astronomer, mathematician, and gazeteer; served on commission that surveyed and laid out Washington, D. C.

Imamu Amiri Baraka, b. LeRoi Jones, 1934, poet, playwright.

James P. Beckwourth, 1798-c. 1867, western fur-trader, scout, after whom Beckwourth Pass in northern California is named.

Dr. Mary McCleod Bethune, 1875-1955, adviser to presidents Roosevelt, Truman; division administrator, Natl. Youth Administration, 1935; founder, pres. Bethune-Cookman College.

Henry Blair, 19th century, obtained patents (believed the first issued to a black) for a corn-planter, 1834, and for a cotton-planter, 1836.

Julian Bond, b. 1940, civil rights leader first elected to the Georgia state legislature, 1965; helped found Student Nonviolent Coordinating Committee.

Edward Bouchet, 1852-1918, first black to earn a Ph.D., Yale, 1876, at a U. S. university; first black elected to Phi Beta Kappa.

Thomas Bradley, b. 1917, elected mayor of Los Angeles, 1973.

Andrew F. Brimmer, b. 1926, first black member, 1966, Federal Reserve Board.

Edward W. Brooke, b. 1919, attorney general, 1962, of Massachusetts; first black elected to U. S. Senate, 1967, since 19th century Reconstruction.

Gwendolyn Brooks, b. 1917, poet, novelist; first black to win a Pulitzer Prize, 1950, for *Annie Allen.*

William Wells Brown, 1815-1884, novelist, dramatist; first American black to publish a novel.

Dr. Ralph Bunche, 1904-1971, first black to win the Nobel Peace Prize, 1950; undersecretary of the UN, 1950.

George E. Carruthers, b. 1940, physicist developed the Apollo 16 lunar surface ultraviolet camera/spectograph.

George Washington Carver, 1861-1943, botanist, chemurgist, and educator; his extensive experiments in soil building and plant diseases revolutionized the economy of the South.

Charles Waddell Chestnutt, 1858-1932, author known primarily for his short stories, including *The Conjure Woman.*

Shirley Chisholm, b. 1924, first black woman elected to House of Representatives, Brooklyn, N. Y., 1968.

Bishop Philip R. Cousin, b. 1933, Pres., Natl. Council of Churches of Christ in the USA, 1985-.

Countee Cullen, 1903-1946, poet; won many literary prizes.

Lt. Gen. Benjamin O. Davis Jr. b. 1912, West Point, 1936, first black Air Force general, 1954.

Brig. Gen. Benjamin O. Davis Sr., 1877-1970, first black general, 1940, in U. S. Army.

William L. Dawson, 1886-1970, Illinois congressman, first black chairman of a major House of Representatives committee.

Isaiah Dorman, 19th century, U. S. Army interpreter, killed with Custer, 1876, at Battle of the Little Big Horn.

Aaron Douglas, 1900-1979, painter; called father of black American art.

Frederick Douglass, 1817-1895, author, editor, orator, diplomat; edited the abolitionist weekly, The North Star, in Rochester, N. Y.; U.S. minister and consul general to Haiti.

Dr. Charles Richard Drew, 1904-1950, pioneer in development of blood banks; director of American Red Cross blood donor project in World War II.

William Edward Burghardt Du Bois, 1868-1963, historian, sociologist; a founder of the National Association for the Advancement of Colored People (NAACP), 1909, and founder of its magazine The Crisis; author, *The Souls of Black Folk.*

Paul Laurence Dunbar, 1872-1906, poet, novelist; won fame with *Lyrics of Lowly Life,* 1896.

Jean Baptiste Point du Sable, c. 1750-1818, pioneer trader and first settler of Chicago, 1779.

Ralph Ellison, b. 1914, novelist, *Invisible Man.*

Estevanico, explorer led Spanish expedition of 1538 into the American Southwest.

James Farmer, b. 1920, a founder of the Congress of Racial Equality, 1942; asst. secretary, Dept. of HEW, 1969.

Henry O. Flipper, 1856-1940, first black to graduate, 1877, from West Point.

Charles Fuller, b. 1939, Pulitzer Prize-winning playwright; *A Soldier's Play.*

Mary Hatwood Futrell, b. 1940, president, Natl. Education Assn., 1983-.

Marcus Garvey, 1887-1940, founded Universal Negro Improvement Assn., 1911.

Kenneth Gibson, b. 1932, Newark, N.J., mayor, 1970-1986.

Charles Gordone, b. 1925, won 1970 Pulitzer Prize in Drama, with *No Place to Be Somebody.*

Vice Adm. Samuel L. Gravely Jr. b. 1922, first black admiral, 1971, served in World War II, Korea, and Vietnam; commander, Third Fleet.

Alex Haley, b. 1921, Pulitzer Prize-winning author; *Roots, The Autobiography of Malcolm X.*

Jupiter Hammon, c. 1720-1800, poet; the first black American to have his works published, 1761.

Lorraine Hansberry, 1930-1965, playwright; won New York Drama Critics Circle Award, 1959, with *Raisin in the Sun.*

Patricia Roberts Harris, 1924-1985, U. S. ambassador to Luxembourg, 1965-67, secretary; Dept. of HUD, 1977-1979, Dept. of HHS, 1979-1981.

William H. Hastie, 1904-1976 first black federal judge, appointed 1937; governor of Virgin Islands, 1946-49; judge, U.S. Circuit Court of Appeals, 1949.

Chester Himes, 1909-1984, novelist, *Cotton Comes to Harlem.*

Matthew A. Henson, 1866-1955, member of Peary's 1909 expedition to the North Pole; placed U.S. flag at the Pole.

Dr. William A. Hinton, 1883-1959, developed the Hinton and Davies-Hinton tests for detection of syphilis; first black professor, 1949, at Harvard Medical School.

Benjamin L. Hooks, b. 1925, first black member, 1972-1979, Federal Communications Comm.; exec. dir., 1977, NAACP.

Langston Hughes, 1902-1967, poet; story, song lyric author.

The Rev. Jesse Jackson, b. 1941, national director, Operation Bread Basket; campaigned for Democratic presidential nomination, 1984.

Maynard Jackson, b. 1938, elected mayor of Atlanta, 1973.

Gen. Daniel James Jr. 1920-1978, first black 4-star general, 1975; Commander, North American Air Defense Command.

Pvt. Henry Johnson, 1897-1929, the first American decorated by France in World War I with the Croix de Guerre.

James Weldon Johnson, 1871-1938, poet, lyricist, novelist; first black admitted to Florida bar; U.S. consul in Venezuela and Nicaragua.

John H. Johnson, b. 1918, publisher, editor of Ebony, Jet, Ebony Jr. magazines, from 1942.

Barbara Jordan, b. 1936, former congresswoman from Texas; member, House Judiciary Committee.

Vernon E. Jordan, b. 1935, exec. dir. Natl. Urban League, 1972.

Ernest E. Just, 1883-1941, marine biologist, studied egg development; author, *Biology of Cell Surfaces,* 1941.

The Rev. Dr. Martin Luther King Jr., 1929-1968, led 382-day, Montgomery, Ala., boycott that brought 1956 U.S. Supreme Court decision holding segregation on buses unconstitutional; founder, president, of the Southern Christian Leadership Conference, 1957; won Nobel Peace Prize, 1964.

Lewis H. Latimer, 1848-1928, associate of Edison; supervised installation of first electric street lighting in N.Y.C.

Malcolm X, 1925-1965, leading spokesman for black pride, founded, 1963, Organization of Afro-American Unity.

Thurgood Marshall, b. 1908, first black U.S. solicitor general 1965; first black justice of the U. S. Supreme Court, 1967; as a lawyer led the legal battery that won the historic decision from the Supreme Court declaring racial segregation of public schools unconstitutional, 1954.

Jan Matzeliger, 1852-1889, invented lasting machine, patented 1883, which revolutionized the shoe industry.

Benjamin Mays, 1895-1984, educator, civil rights leader; headed Morehouse College, 1940-1967.

Wade H. McCree Jr., b. 1920, solicitor general of the U.S., 1977-1981.

Donald E. McHenry, b. 1936, U.S. ambassador to the United Nations, 1979-1981.

Ronald McNair, 1950-1986, physicist, first black astronaut; killed in *Challenger* explosion.

Dorie Miller, 1919-1943, Navy hero of Pearl Harbor attack; awarded the Navy Cross.

Ernest N. Morial, b. 1929, elected first black mayor of New Orleans, 1977.

Toni Morrison, novelist; *Song of Solomon, Tar Baby.*

Willard Motley, 1912-1965, novelist; *Knock on Any Door.*

Elijah Muhammad, 1897-1975, founded Black Muslims, 1931.

Pedro Alonzo Nino, navigator of the Nina, one of Columbus' 3 ships on his first voyage of discovery to the New World, 1492.

Rosa Parks, b. 1913, Montgomery Ala. Citizen arrested for refusing to move to the back of the bus, Dec. 1, 1955, bringing a 382-day bus boycott led by Martin Luther King Jr.

Adam Clayton Powell, 1908-1972, early civil rights leader, congressman, 1945-1969; chairman, House Committee on Education and Labor, 1960-1967.

Joseph H. Rainey, 1832-1887, first black elected to House of Representatives, 1869, from South Carolina.

A. Philip Randolph, 1889-1979, organized the Brotherhood of Sleeping Car Porters, 1925; organizer of 1941 and 1963 March on Washington movements; vice president, AFL-CIO.

Charles Rangel, b. 1930, congressman from N.Y.C. from 1970; member, Ways and Means Committee; chairman, Select Committee on Narcotics Abuse & Control.

Hiram R. Revels, 1822-1901, first black U.S. senator, elected in Mississippi, served 1870-1871.

Wilson C. Riles, b. 1917, elected, 1970, California State Superintendent of Public Instruction.

Norbert Rillieux, 1806-1894; invented a vacuum pan evaporator, 1846, revolutionizing the sugar-refining industry.

Paul Robeson, 1898-1976, actor and concert singer, graduated 1st in class at Rutgers, 1918, Phi Beta Kappa; grad. Columbia Univ. law school, 1923; associated with communist causes.

Carl T. Rowan, b. 1925, prize-winning journalist; director of the U.S. Information Agency, 1964, the first black to sit on the National Security Council; U. S. ambassador to Finland, 1963.

John B. Russwurm, 1799-1851, with **Samuel E. Cornish,** 1793-1858, founded, 1827, the nation's first black newspaper, Freedom's Journal, in N.Y.C.

Bayard Rustin, b. 1910, organizer of the 1963 March on Washington; executive director, A. Philip Randolph Institute.

Peter Salem, at the Battle of Bunker Hill, June 17, 1775, shot and killed British commander Maj. John Pitcairn.

Ntozake Shange, b. 1948, writer, *For Colored Girls Who Have Considered Suicide/When the Rainbow is Enuf.*

Bishop Stephen Spottswood, 1897-1974, board chairman of NAACP, 1961-1974.

The Rev. Leon H. Sullivan, b. 1922, economic development planner, first black on General Motors Bd. of Directors.

Willard Townsend, 1895-1957, organized the United Transport Service Employees, 1935 (redcaps, etc.); vice pres. AFL-CIO.

Sojourner Truth, 1797-1883, born Isabella Baumfree; preacher, abolitonist; raised funds for Union in Civil War; worked for black educational opportunities.

Harriet Tubman, 1823-1913, Underground Railroad conductor served as nurse and spy for Union Army in the Civil War.

Nat Turner, 1800-1831, led the most significant of over 200 slave revolts in U.S., in Southampton, Va.; hanged.

Alice Walker, b. 1944, novelist, *The Color Purple.*

Booker T. Washington, 1856-1915, founder, 1881, and first president of Tuskegee Institute; author, *Up From Slavery.*

Dr. Robert C. Weaver, b. 1907, first black member of the U.S. Cabinet, secretary, Dept. of HUD, 1966.

Phillis Wheatley, c. 1753-1784, poet; 2d American woman and first black woman to have her works published, 1770.

Walter White, 1893-1955, exec. secretary, NAACP, 1931-1955.

Roy Wilkins, 1901-1981, exec. director, NAACP, 1955-1977.

Dr. Daniel Hale Williams, 1858-1931, performed one of first 2 open-heart operations, 1893; founded Provident, Chicago's first Negro hospital; first black elected a fellow of the American College of Surgeons.

August Wilson, b. 1945, playwright, won 1987 Pulitzer Prize, Tony Award for *Fences.*

Granville T. Woods, 1856-1910, invented the third-rail system now used in subways, a complex railway telegraph device that helped reduce train accidents, and an automatic air brake.

Dr. Carter G. Woodson, 1875-1950, historian; founded Assn. for the Study of Negro Life and History, 1915, and Journal of Negro History, 1916.

Richard Wright, 1908-1960, novelist; *Native Son, Black Boy.*

Frank Yerby, b. 1916, first best-selling American black novelist; *The Foxes of Harrow, Vixen.*

Andrew Young, b. 1932, civil rights leader, congressman from Georgia, U.S. ambassador to the United Nations, 1977-79; mayor of Atlanta, 1982-.

Whitney M. Young Jr., 1921-1971, exec. director, 1961, National Urban League; author, lecturer, newspaper columnist.

About 5,000 blacks served in the Continental Army during the **American Revolution,** mostly in integrated units, some in all-black combat units. Some 200,000 blacks served in the Union Army during the **Civil War;** 38,000 gave their lives; 22 won the Medal of Honor, the nation's highest award. Of 367,000 blacks in the armed forces during **World War I,** 100,000 served in France. More than 1,000,000 blacks served in the armed forces during **World War II;** all-black fighter and bomber AAF units and infantry divisions gave distinguished service. In 1954 the policy of all-black units was finally abolished. Of 274,937 blacks who served in the armed forces during the **Vietnam War** (1965-1974), 5,681 were killed in combat.

As of Jan., 1987, there were 303 black mayors, 2,485 members of municipal governing boards, 311 state legislators, and 23 U.S. representatives. There are now 6,681 blacks holding elected office in the U.S. and Virgin Islands, an increase of 4.0% over the previous year, according to a survey by the Joint Center for Political Studies, Washington, D.C.,

Notable American Fiction Writers and Playwrights

Name (Birthplace)	Birthdate
Adams, Alice (Fredericksburg, Va.)	8/14/26
Albee, Edward (Washington, D.C.)	3/12/28
Anderson, Robert (New York, N.Y.)	4/28/17
Asimov, Isaac (Petrovichi, Russia)	1/2/20
Atwood, Margaret (Ottawa, Ont., Canada)	11/18/39
Auchincloss, Louis (Lawrence, N.Y.)	9/27/17
Baldwin, James (New York, N.Y.)	8/2/24
Barth, John (Cambridge, Md.)	5/27/30
Barthelme, Donald (Philadelphia, Pa.)	1931
Beattie, Ann (Washington, D.C.)	9/7/47
Bellow, Saul (Quebec, Canada)	7/10/15
Benchley, Peter (New York, N.Y.)	5/8/40
Blume, Judy (Elizabeth, N.J.)	2/12/38
Bradbury, Ray (Waukegan, Ill.)	8/22/20
Brooks, Gwendolyn (Topeka, Kan.)	6/7/17
Calisher, Hortense (New York, N.Y.)	12/20/11
Carver, Raymond (Clatskanie, Ore.)	5/25/38
Clavell, James (England)	10/10/24
Cleary, Beverly (McMinnville, Ore.)	1916
Conroy, Pat (Atlanta, Ga.)	10/26/45
Crews, Harry (Alma, Ga.)	6/6/35
Crichton, Michael (Chicago, Ill.)	10/23/42
De Vries, Peter (Chicago, Ill.)	2/27/10
Dickey, James (Atlanta, Ga.)	2/2/23
Didion, Joan (Sacramento, Cal.)	12/5/34
Doctorow, E. L. (New York, N.Y.)	1/6/31
Drury, Allen (Houston, Tex.)	9/2/18
Dunne, John Gregory (Hartford, Conn.)	5/25/32
Elkin, Stanley (New York, N.Y.)	5/11/30
Ellison, Ralph (Oklahoma City, Okla.)	3/1/14
Fast, Howard (New York, N.Y.)	11/11/14
Fuller, Charles (Philadelphia, Pa.)	3/5/39
Gaddis, William (New York, N.Y.)	1922
Geisel, Theodore ("Dr. Seuss," Springfield, Mass.)	3/2/04
Gibson, William (New York, N.Y.)	11/13/14
Gilroy, Frank (New York, N.Y.)	10/13/25
Godwin, Gail (Birmingham, Ala.)	6/18/37
Goldman, William (Chicago, Ill.)	8/12/31
Gordon, Mary (Long Island, N.Y.)	12/8/49
Grau, Shirley Ann (New Orleans, La.)	7/8/29
Guare, John (New York, N.Y.)	2/5/38
Hailey, Arthur (Luton, England)	4/5/20
Haley, Alex (Ithaca, N.Y.)	8/11/21
Hawkes, John (Stamford, Conn.)	8/17/25
Heinlein, Robert (Butler, Mon.)	7/7/07
Heller, Joseph (Brooklyn, N.Y.)	5/1/23
Helprin, Mark (New York, N.Y.)	6/28/47
Hersey, John (Tientsin, China)	6/17/14
Irving, John (Exeter, N.H.)	3/2/42
Jaffe, Rona (New York, N.Y.)	6/12/32
Jong, Erica (New York, N.Y.)	3/26/42
Kennedy, William (Albany, N.Y.)	1/16/28
Kerr, Jean (Scranton, Pa.)	7/?/23
Kesey, Ken (La Junta, Col.)	9/17/35
King, Stephen (Portland, Me.)	9/21/47
Knowles, John (Fairmont, W. Va.)	9/16/26
Kosinski, Jerzy (Lódz, Poland)	6/14/33
Krantz, Judith (New York, N.Y.)	1/9/28
L'Amour, Louis (Jamestown, N.D.)	—
LeGuin, Ursula (Berkeley, Cal.)	10/21/29
L'Engle, Madeleine (New York, N.Y.)	11/29/18
Leonard, Elmore (New Orleans, La.)	10/11/25
Levin, Ira (New York, N.Y.)	8/27/29
Ludlum, Robert (New York, N.Y.)	5/25/27
Lurie, Alison (Chicago, Ill.)	9/3/26
Mailer, Norman (Long Branch, N.J.)	1/31/23
Mamet, David (Chicago, Ill.)	11/30/47
McCarthy, Mary (Seattle, Wash.)	6/21/12
McMurtry, Larry (Wichita Falls, Tex.)	6/3/36
Michener, James A. (New York, N.Y.)	2/3/07
Miller, Arthur (New York, N.Y.)	10/17/15
Morris, Wright (Central City, Neb.)	1/6/10
Morrison, Toni (Lorain, Oh.)	—
Munro, Alice (Wingham, Ont., Canada)	7/10/31
Oates, Joyce Carol (Lockport, N.Y.)	6/16/38
Ozick, Cynthia (New York, N.Y.)	4/17/28
Paley, Grace (New York, N.Y.)	12/11/22
Percy, Walker (Birmingham, Ala.)	5/28/16
Piercy, Marge (Detroit, Mich.)	3/31/36
Potok, Chaim (New York, N.Y.)	2/17/29
Price, Reynolds (Macon, N.C.)	2/1/33
Puzo, Mario (New York, N.Y.)	10/15/20
Pynchon, Thomas (Glen Cove, N.Y.)	5/8/37
Rabe, David (Dubuque, Ia.)	3/10/40
Reed, Ishmael (Chattanooga, Tenn.)	2/22/38
Roth, Henry (Austria-Hungary)	2/8/06
Roth, Philip (Newark, N.J.)	3/19/33
Salinger, J. D. (New York, N.Y.)	1/1/19
Sanders, Lawrence (New York, N.Y.)	1920
Schulberg, Budd (New York, N.Y.)	3/27/14
Segal, Erich (Brooklyn, N.Y.)	6/16/37
Sendak, Maurice (New York, N.Y.)	6/10/28
Shepard, Sam (Ft. Sheridan, Fla.)	11/5/42
Simon, Neil (New York, N.Y.)	7/4/27
Singer, Isaac Bashevis (Radzymin, Poland)	7/14/04
Slaughter, Frank (Washington, D.C.)	2/25/08
Spillane, Mickey (Brooklyn, N.Y.)	3/9/18
Stegner, Wallace (Lake Mills, Ia.)	2/18/09
Stone, Irving (San Francisco, Cal.)	7/14/03
Styron, William (Newport News, Va.)	6/11/25
Taylor, Peter (Trenton, Tenn.)	1/8/17
Theroux, Paul (Medford, Mass.)	4/10/41
Tyler, Anne (Minneapolis, Minn.)	10/25/41
Updike, John (Shillington, Pa.)	3/18/32
Uris, Leon (Baltimore, Md.)	8/3/24
Vidal, Gore (West Point, N.Y.)	10/3/25
Vonnegut, Kurt Jr. (Indianapolis, Ind.)	11/11/22
Walker, Alice (Eatonton, Ga.)	1944
Wallace, Irving (Chicago, Ill.)	3/18/16
Wambaugh, Joseph (East Pittsburgh, Pa.)	1/22/37
Warren, Robert Penn (Guthrie, Ky.)	4/24/05
Welty, Eudora (Jackson, Miss.)	4/13/09
Wilson, August (Pittsburgh, Pa.)	4/27/45
Wilson, Lanford (Lebanon, Mo.)	4/13/37
Wouk, Herman (New York, N.Y.)	5/27/15
Yerby, Frank (Augusta, Ga.)	9/5/16
Zindel, Paul (New York, N.Y.)	5/15/36

American Architects and Some of Their Achievements

Max Abramovitz, b. 1908, Avery Fisher Hall, Lincoln Center, N.Y.C.

Henry Bacon, 1866-1924, Lincoln Memorial.

Pietro Belluschi, b. 1899, Juilliard School of Music, Lincoln Center, N.Y.C.

Marcel Breuer, 1902-1981, Whitney Museum of American Art, N.Y.C. (with Hamilton Smith).

Charles Bulfinch, 1763-1844, State House, Boston; Capitol, Wash. D.C., (part).

Daniel H. Burnham, 1846-1912, Union Station, Wash. D.C.; Flatiron, N.Y.C.

Ralph Adams Cram, 1863-1942, Cathedral of St. John the Divine, N.Y.C.; U.S. Military Academy (part).

R. Buckminster Fuller, 1895-1983, U.S. Pavilion, Expo 67, Montreal (geodesic domes).

Cass Gilbert, 1859-1934, Custom House, Woolworth Bldg., N.Y.C.; Supreme Court bldg., Wash., D.C.

Bertram G. Goodhue, 1869-1924, Capitol, Lincoln, Neb.; St. Thomas, St. Bartholomew, N.Y.C.

Walter Gropius, 1883-1969, Pan Am Building, N.Y.C. (with Pietro Belluschi).

Peter Harrison, 1716-1775, Touro Synagogue, Redwood Library, Newport, R.I.

Wallace K. Harrison, 1895-1981, Metropolitan Opera House, Lincoln Center, N.Y.C.

Thomas Hastings, 1860-1929, Public Library, Frick Mansion, N.Y.C.

James Hoban, 1762-1831, The White House.

Raymond Hood, 1881-1934, Rockefeller Center, N.Y.C. (part); Daily News, N.Y.C.; Tribune, Chicago.

Richard M. Hunt, 1827-1895, Metropolitan Museum, N.Y.C. (part); Natl. Observatory, Wash., D.C.

William Le Baron Jenney, 1832-1907, Home Insurance, Chicago (demolished 1931).

Philip C. Johnson, b. 1906, N.Y. State Theater, Lincoln Center, N.Y.C.

Albert Kahn, 1869-1942, Athletic Club Bldg., General Motors Bldg., Detroit.

Louis Kahn, 1901-1974, Salk Laboratory, La Jolla, Cal.; Yale Art Gallery.

Christopher Grant LaFarge, 1862-1938, Roman Catholic Chapel, West Point.

Benjamin H. Latrobe, 1764-1820, U.S. Capitol (part).

William Lescaze, 1896-1969, Philadelphia Savings Fund Society; Borg-Warner Bldg., Chicago.

Charles F. McKim, 1847-1909, Public Library, Boston, Columbia Univ., N.Y.C. (part).

Charles M. McKim, b. 1920, KUHT-TV Transmitter Building, Houston; Lutheran Church of the Redeemer, Houston.

Ludwig Mies van der Rohe, 1886-1969, Seagram Building, N.Y.C. (with Philip C. Johnson); National Gallery, Berlin.

Robert Mills, 1781-1855, Washington Monument.

Richard J. Neutra, 1892-1970, Mathematics Park, Princeton; Orange Co. Courthouse, Santa Ana, Cal.

Gyo Obata, b. 1923, Natl. Air & Space Mus., Smithsonian Institution; Dallas-Ft. Worth Airport.

Frederick L. Olmsted, 1822-1903, Central Park, N.Y.C.; Fairmount Park, Philadelphia.

Ieoh Ming Pei, b. 1917, National Center for Atmospheric Research, Boulder, Col.

William Pereira, 1909-1985, Cape Canaveral; Transamerica Bldg., San Francisco.

John Russell Pope, 1874-1937, National Gallery.

John Portman, b. 1924, Peachtree Center, Atlanta.

James Renwick Jr., 1818-1895, Grace Church, St. Patrick's Cathedral, N.Y.C.; Smithsonian, Corcoran Galleries, Wash., D.C.

Henry H. Richardson, 1838-1886, Trinity Church, Boston.

Kevin Roche, b. 1922, Oakland Cal. Museum; Fine Arts Center, U. of Mass.

James Gamble Rogers, 1867-1947, Columbia-Presbyterian Medical Center, N.Y.C.; Northwestern Univ., Chicago.

John Wellborn Root, 1887-1963, Palmolive Building, Chicago; Hotel Statler, Washington; Hotel Tamanaco, Caracas.

Paul Rudolph, b. 1918, Jewitt Art Center, Wellesley College; Art & Architecture Bldg., Yale.

Charles M. Russell, 1866-1926, Western life.

Eero Saarinen, 1910-1961, Gateway to the West Arch, St. Louis; Trans World Flight Center, N.Y.C.

Louis Skidmore, 1897-1962, AEC town site, Oak Ridge, Tenn.; Terrace Plaza Hotel, Cincinnati.

Clarence S. Stein, 1882-1975, Temple Emanu-El, N.Y.C.

Edward Durell Stone, 1902-1978, U.S. Embassy, New Delhi, India; (H. Hartford) Gallery of Modern Art, N.Y.C.

Louis H. Sullivan, 1856-1924, Auditorium, Chicago.

Richard Upjohn, 1802-1878, Trinity Church, N.Y.C.

Ralph T. Walker, 1889-1973, N.Y. Telephone Hdqrs., N.Y.C.; IBM Research Lab., Poughkeepsie, N.Y.

Roland A. Wank, 1898-1970, Cincinnati Union Terminal; head architect TVA, 1933-44.

Stanford White, 1853-1906, Washington Arch; first Madison Square Garden, N.Y.C.

Frank Lloyd Wright, 1867 or 1869-1959, Imperial Hotel, Tokyo; Guggenheim Museum, N.Y.C.

William Wurster, 1895-1973, Ghirardelli Sq., San Francisco; Cowell College, U. Cal., Berkeley.

Minoru Yamasaki, 1912-1986, World Trade Center, N.Y.C.

Noted American Cartoonists

Charles Addams, b. 1912, macabre cartoons.

Peter Arno, 1904-1968, urban characterizations.

Tex Avery, b. 1908, **Friz Freleng,** b. 1905?, **Chuck Jones,** b. 1912, animators of Bugs Bunny, Porky Pig, Daffy Duck.

George Baker, 1915-1975, The Sad Sack.

C. C. Beck, b. 1910, Captain Marvel.

Herb Block (Herblock), b. 1909, leading political cartoonist.

Clare Briggs, 1875-1930, Mr. & Mrs.

Dik Browne, b. 1917, Hi & Lois, Hagar the Horrible.

Ernie Bushmiller, 1905-1982, Nancy.

Milton Caniff, b. 1907, Terry & the Pirates; Steve Canyon.

Al Capp, 1909-1979, Li'l Abner.

Paul Conrad, 1924, political cartoonist.

Roy Crane, 1901-1977, Captain Easy; Buz Sawyer.

Robert Crumb, b. 1943, "Underground" cartoonist.

Jay N. Darling (Ding), 1876-1962, political cartoonist.

Jim Davis, b. 1945, Garfield.

Billy DeBeck, 1890-1942, Barney Google.

Rudolph Dirks, 1877-1968, The Katzenjammer Kids.

Walt Disney, 1901-1966, producer of animated cartoons; created Mickey Mouse & Donald Duck.

Jules Feiffer, b. 1929, satirical *Village Voice* cartoonist.

Bud Fisher, 1884-1954, Mutt & Jeff.

Ham Fisher, 1900-1955, Joe Palooka.

James Montgomery Flagg, 1877-1960, illustrator; created the famous Uncle Sam recruiting poster during WWI.

Max Fleischer, 1883-1972, creator of Betty Boop, Popeye cartoons.

Hal Foster, 1892-1982, Tarzan; Prince Valiant.

Fontaine Fox, 1884-1964, Toonerville Folks.

Rube Goldberg, 1883-1970, Boob McNutt.

Chester Gould, 1900-1985, Dick Tracy.

Harold Gray, 1894-1968, Little Orphan Annie.

Bill Hanna, b. 1910, & **Joe Barbera,** b. 1911, animators of Tom & Jerry, Huckleberry Hound, Yogi Bear, Flintstones.

Johnny Hart, b. 1931, BC, Wizard of Id.

Jimmy Hatlo, 1898-1963, Little Iodine.

John Held Jr., 1889-1958, "Jazz Age" cartoonist.

George Herriman, 1881-1944, Krazy Kat.

Harry Hershfield, 1885-1974, Abie the Agent.

Al Hirschfeld, b. 1903, N.Y. Times theater caricaturist.

Burne Hogarth, b. 1911, Tarzan.

Helen Hokinson, 1900-1949, satirized clubwomen.

Bil Keane, b. 1922, The Family Circus.

Walt Kelly, 1913-1973, Pogo.

Hank Ketcham, b. 1920, Dennis the Menace.

Ted Key, b. 1912, Hazel.

Frank King, 1883-1969, Gasoline Alley.

Jack Kirby, b. 1917, Captain America.

Rollin Kirby, 1875-1952, political cartoonist.

Edward Koren, b. 1935, New Yorker woolly characters.

Walter Lantz, b. 1900, Woody Woodpecker.

Mell Lazarus, b. 1929, Momma, Miss Peach.

Stan Lee, b. 1922, Spiderman, Incredible Hulk.

Bill Mauldin, b. 1921, depicted squalid life of the G.I. in WWII.

Jeff MacNelly, b. 1947, political cartoonist, and strip Shoe.

Winsor McCay, 1872-1934, Little Nemo.

John T. McCutcheon, 1870-1949, midwestern rural life.

George McManus, 1884-1954, Maggie & Jiggs.

Dale Messick, b. 1906, Brenda Starr.

Norman Mingo, b. 1896, Alfred E. Neuman.

Bob Montana, 1920-1975, Archie.

Dick Moores, b. 1909, Gasoline Alley.

Willard Mullin, 1902-1978, sports cartoonist; created Dodgers "Bum" and Mets "Kid".

Russel Myers, b. 1938, Broom Hilda.

Thomas Nast, 1840-1902, political cartoonist; created the Democratic donkey and Republican elephant.

Pat Oliphant, b. 1935, political cartoonist.

Frederick Burr Opper, 1857-1937, Happy Hooligan.

Richard Outcault, 1863-1928, Yellow Kid; Buster Brown.

Mike Peters, b. 1943, editorial cartoonist.

George Price, b. 1901, New Yorker lower-class life.

Alex Raymond, 1909-1956, Flash Gordon; Jungle Jim.

Charles Schulz, b. 1922, Peanuts.

Elzie C. Segar, 1894-1938, Popeye.

Jerry Siegel, b. 1914, & **Joe Shuster,** b. 1914, Superman.

Sydney Smith, 1887-1935, The Gumps.

Otto Soglow, 1900-1975, Little King; Canyon Kiddies.

William Steig, b. 1907, *New Yorker* cartoonist.

James Swinnerton, 1875-1974, Little Jimmy.

Paul Terry, 1887-1971, animator of Mighty Mouse.

James Thurber, 1894-1961, *New Yorker* cartoonist.

Garry Trudeau, b. 1948, Doonesbury.

Mort Walker, b. 1923, Beetle Bailey.

Russ Westover, 1887-1966, Tillie the Toiler.

Frank Willard, 1893-1958, Moon Mullins.

J. R. Williams, 1886-1957, The Willets Family; Out Our Way.

Gahan Wilson, b. 1930, cartoonist of the macabre.

Tom Wilson, b. 1931, Ziggy.

Art Young, 1866-1943, political radical and satirist.

Chic Young, 1901-1973, Blondie.

Noted Political Leaders of the Past

(U.S. presidents and most vice presidents, Supreme Court justices, signers of Declaration of Independence, listed elsewhere.)

Abu Bakr, 573-634, Mohammedan leader, first caliph, chosen successor to Mohammed.

Dean Acheson, 1893-1971, (U.S.) secretary of state, chief architect of cold war foreign policy.

Samuel Adams, 1722-1803, (U.S.) patriot, Boston Tea Party firebrand.

Konrad Adenauer, 1876-1967, (G.) West German chancellor.

Emilio Aguinaldo, 1869-1964, (Philip.) revolutionary, fought against Spain and the U.S.

Akbar, 1542-1605, greatest Mogul emperor of India.

Salvador Allende Gossens, 1908-1973, (Chil.) president, advocate of democratic socialism.

Herbert H. Asquith, 1852-1928, (Br.) Liberal prime minister, instituted an advanced program of social reform.

Atahualpa, ?-1533, Inca (ruling chief) of Peru.

Kemal Atatürk, 1881-1938, (Turk.) founded modern Turkey.

Clement Attlee, 1883-1967, (Br.) Labour party leader, prime minister, enacted national health, nationalized many industries.

Stephen F. Austin, 1793-1836, (U.S.) led Texas colonization.

Mikhail Bakunin, 1814-1876, (R.) revolutionary, leading exponent of anarchism.

Arthur J. Balfour, 1848-1930, (Br.) as foreign secretary under Lloyd George issued Balfour Declaration expressing official British approval of Zionism.

Bernard M. Baruch, 1870-1965, (U.S.) financier, gvt. adviser.

Fulgencio Batista y Zaldivar, 1901-1973, (Cub.) ruler overthrown by Castro.

Lord Beaverbrook, 1879-1964, (Br.) financier, statesman, newspaper owner.

Eduard Benes, 1884-1948, (Czech.) president during interwar and post-WW II eras.

David Ben-Gurion, 1886-1973, (Isr.) first premier of Israel.

Thomas Hart Benton, 1782-1858, (U.S.) Missouri senator, championed agrarian interests and westward expansion.

Lavrenti Beria, 1899-1953, (USSR) Communist leader prominent in political purges under Stalin.

Aneurin Bevan, 1897-1960, (Br.) Labour party leader.

Ernest Bevin, 1881-1951, (Br.) Labour party leader, foreign minister, helped lay foundation for NATO.

Otto von Bismarck, 1815-1898, (G.) statesman known as the Iron Chancellor, uniter of Germany, 1870.

James G. Blaine, 1830-1893, (U.S.) Republican politician, diplomat, influential in launching Pan-American movement.

Léon Blum, 1872-1950, (F.) socialist leader, writer, headed first Popular Front government.

Simón Bolívar, 1783-1830, (Venez.) South American revolutionary who liberated much of the continent from Spanish rule.

William E. Borah, 1865-1940, (U.S.) isolationist senator, instrumental in blocking U.S. membership in League of Nations and the World Court.

Cesare Borgia, 1476-1507, (It.) soldier, politician, an outstanding figure of the Italian Renaissance.

Leonid Brezhnev, 1906-1982, (USSR) leader of the Soviet Union, 1964-82.

Aristide Briand, 1862-1932, (F.) foreign minister, chief architect of Locarno Pact and anti-war Kellogg-Briand Pact.

William Jennings Bryan, 1860-1925, (U.S.) Democratic, populist leader, orator, 3 times lost race for presidency.

Nikolai Bukharin, 1888-1938, (USSR) communist leader.

William C. Bullitt, 1891-1967, (U.S.) diplomat, first ambassador to USSR, ambassador to France.

Ralph Bunche, 1904-1971, (U.S.) a founder and key diplomat of United Nations for more than 20 years.

John C. Calhoun, 1782-1850, (U.S.) political leader, champion of states' rights and a symbol of the Old South.

Robert Castlereagh, 1769-1822, (Br.) foreign secy, guided Grand Alliance against Napoleon.

Camillo Benso Cavour, 1810-1861, (It.) statesman, largely responsible for uniting Italy under the House of Savoy.

Austen Chamberlain, 1863-1937, (Br.) Conservative party leader, largely responsible for Locarno Pact of 1925.

Neville Chamberlain, 1869-1940, (Br.) Conservative prime minister whose appeasement of Hitler led to Munich Pact.

Salmon P. Chase, 1808-1873, (U.S.) public official, abolitionist, jurist, 6th Supreme Court chief justice.

Chiang Kai-shek, 1887-1975, (Chin.) Nationalist Chinese president whose govt. was driven from mainland to Taiwan.

Chou En-lai, 1898-1976, (Chin.) diplomat, prime minister, a leading figure of the Chinese Communist party.

Winston Churchill, 1874-1965, (Br.) prime minister, soldier, author, guided Britain through WW II.

Galeazzo Ciano, 1903-1944, (It.) fascist foreign minister, helped create Rome-Berlin Axis, executed by Mussolini.

Henry Clay, 1777-1852, (U.S.) "The Great Compromiser," one of most influential pre-Civil War political leaders.

Georges Clemenceau, 1841-1929, (F.) twice premier, Wilson's chief antagonist at Paris Peace Conference after WW I.

DeWitt Clinton, 1769-1828, (U.S.) political leader, responsible for promoting idea of the Erie Canal.

Robert Clive, 1725-1774, (Br.) first administrator of Bengal, laid foundation for British Empire in India.

Jean Baptiste Colbert, 1619-1683, (F.) statesman, influential under Louis XIV, created the French navy.

Oliver Cromwell, 1599-1658, (Br.) Lord Protector of England, led parliamentary forces during Civil War.

Curzon of Kedleston, 1859-1925, (Br.) viceroy of India, foreign secretary, major force in dealing with post-WW I problems in Europe and Far East.

Édouard Daladier, 1884-1970, (F.) radical socialist politician, arrested by Vichy, interned by Germans until liberation in 1945.

Georges Danton, 1759-1794, (F.) a leading figure in the French Revolution.

Jefferson Davis, 1808-1889, (U.S.) president of the Confederate States of America.

Charles G. Dawes, 1865-1951, (U.S.) statesman, banker, advanced Dawes Plan to stabilize post-WW I German finances.

Alcide De Gasperi, 1881-1954, (It.) premier, founder of the Christian Democratic party.

Charles DeGaulle, 1890-1970, (F.) general, statesman, and first president of the Fifth Republic.

Eamon De Valera, 1882-1975, (Ir.-U.S.) statesman, led fight for Irish independence.

Thomas E. Dewey, 1902-1971, (U.S.) New York governor, twice loser in try for presidency.

Ngo Dinh Diem, 1901-1963, (Viet.) South Vietnamese president, assassinated in government take-over.

Everett M. Dirksen, 1896-1969, (U.S.) Senate Republican minority leader, orator.

Benjamin Disraeli, 1804-1881, (Br.) prime minister, considered founder of modern Conservative party.

Engelbert Dollfuss, 1892-1934, (Aus.) chancellor, assassinated by Austrian Nazis.

Andrea Doria, 1466-1560, (It.) Genoese admiral, statesman, called "Father of Peace" and "Liberator of Genoa."

Stephen A. Douglas, 1813-1861, (U.S.) Democratic leader, orator, opposed Lincoln for the presidency.

John Foster Dulles, 1888-1959, (U.S.) secretary of state under Eisenhower, cold war policy maker.

Friedrich Ebert, 1871-1925, (G.) Social Democratic movement leader, instrumental in bringing about Weimar constitution.

Sir Anthony Eden, 1897-1977, (Br.) foreign secretary, prime minister during Suez invasion of 1956.

Ludwig Erhard, 1897-1977, (G.) economist, West German chancellor, led nation's economic rise after WW II.

Hamilton Fish, 1808-1893, (U.S.) secretary of state, successfully mediated disputes with Great Britain, Latin America.

James V. Forrestal, 1892-1949, (U.S.) secretary of navy, first secretary of defense.

Francisco Franco, 1892-1975, (Sp.) leader of rebel forces during Spanish Civil War and dictator of Spain.

Benjamin Franklin, 1706-1790, (U.S.) printer, publisher, author, inventor, scientist, diplomat.

Louis de Frontenac, 1620-1698, (F.) governor of New France (Canada); encouraged explorations, fought Iroquois.

Hugh Gaitskell, 1906-1963, (Br.) Labour party leader, major force in reversing its stand for unilateral disarmament.

Albert Gallatin, 1761-1849, (U.S.) secretary of treasury who was instrumental in negotiating end of War of 1812.

Léon Gambetta, 1838-1882, (F.) statesman, politician, one of the founders of the Third Republic.

Indira Gandhi, 1917-1984, (Ind.) succeeded father, Jawaharlal Nehru, as prime minister, assassinated.

Mohandas K. Gandhi, 1869-1948, (Ind.) political leader, ascetic, led nationalist movement against British rule.

Giuseppe Garibaldi, 1807-1882, (It.) patriot, soldier, a leading figure in the Risorgimento, the Italian unification movement.

Genghis Khan, c. 1167-1227, brilliant Mongol conqueror, ruler of vast Asian empire.

William E. Gladstone, 1809-1898, (Br.) prime minister 4 times, dominant force of Liberal party from 1868 to 1894.

Paul Joseph Goebbels, 1897-1945, (G.) Nazi propagandist, master of mass psychology.

Klement Gottwald, 1896-1953, (Czech.) communist leader ushered communism into his country.

Che (Ernesto) Guevara, 1928-1967, (Arg.) guerilla leader, prominent in Cuban revolution, killed in Bolivia.

Haile Selassie, 1891-1975, (Eth.) emperor, maintained monarchy through invasion, occupation, internal resistance.

Alexander Hamilton, 1755-1804, (U.S.) first treasury secretary, champion of strong central government.

Dag Hammarskjold, 1905-1961, (Swed.) statesman, UN secretary general.

John Hancock, 1737-1793, (U.S.) revolutionary leader, first signer of Declaration of Independence.

John Hay, 1838-1905, (U.S.) secretary of state, primarily associated with Open Door Policy toward China.

Patrick Henry, 1736-1799, (U.S.) major revolutionary figure, remarkable orator.

Édouard Herriot, 1872-1957, (F.) Radical Socialist leader, twice premier, president of National Assembly.

Theodor Herzl, 1860-1904, (Aus.) founder of modern Zionism.

Heinrich Himmler, 1900-1945, (G.) chief of Nazi SS and Gestapo, primarily responsible for the Holocaust.

Paul von Hindenburg, 1847-1934, (G.) field marshal, president.

Adolf Hitler, 1889-1945, (G.) dictator, founder of National Socialism.

Ho Chi Minh, 1890-1969, (Viet.) North Vietnamese president, Vietnamese Communist leader, national hero.

Harry L. Hopkins, 1890-1946, (U.S.) New Deal administrator, closest adviser to FDR during WW II.

Edward M. House, 1858-1938, (U.S.) diplomat, confidential adviser to Woodrow Wilson.

Samuel Houston, 1793-1863, (U.S.) leader of struggle to win control of Texas from Mexico.

Cordell Hull, 1871-1955, (U.S.) secretary of state, initiated reciprocal trade to lower tariffs, helped organize UN.

Hubert H. Humphrey, 1911-1978, (U.S.) Minnesota Democrat, senator, vice president, spent 32 years in public service.

Ibn Saud, c. 1888-1953, (S. Arab.) founder of Saudi Arabia and its first king.

Jacob Javits, 1904-1986 (U.S.) U.S. senator from New York for 24 years.

Benito Juarez, 1806-1872, (Mex.) rallied countrymen against foreign threats, sought to create democratic, federal republic.

Frank B. Kellogg, 1856-1937, (U.S.) secretary of state, negotiated Kellogg-Briand Pact to outlaw war.

Robert F. Kennedy, 1925-1968, (U.S.) attorney general, senator, assassinated while seeking presidential nomination.

Aleksandr Kerensky, 1881-1970, (R.) revolutionary, served as premier after Feb. 1917 revolution until Bolshevik overthrow.

Nikita Khrushchev, 1894-1971, (USSR) premier, first secretary of Communist party, initiated de-Stalinization.

Lajos Kossuth, 1802-1894, (Hung.) principal figure in 1848 Hungarian revolution.

Pyotr Kropotkin, 1842-1921, (R.) anarchist, championed the peasants but opposed Bolshevism.

Kublai Khan, c. 1215-1294, Mongol emperor, founder of Yüan dynasty in China.

Béla Kun, 1886-c.1939, (Hung.) communist, member of 3d International, tried to foment worldwide revolution.

Robert M. LaFollette, 1855-1925, (U.S.) Wisconsin public official, leader of progressive movement.

Pierre Laval, 1883-1945, (F.) politician, Vichy foreign minister, executed for treason.

Andrew Bonar Law, 1858-1923, (Br.) Conservative party politician, led opposition to Irish home rule.

Vladimir Ilyich Lenin (Ulyanov), 1870-1924, (USSR) revolutionary, founder of Bolshevism, Soviet leader 1917-1924.

Ferdinand de Lesseps, 1805-1894, (F.) diplomat, engineer, conceived idea of Suez Canal.

Liu Shao-ch'i, c.1898-1974, (Chin.) communist leader, fell from grace during "cultural revolution."

Maxim Litvinov, 1876-1951, (USSR) revolutionary, commissar of foreign affairs, favored cooperation with Western powers.

David Lloyd George, 1863-1945, (Br.) Liberal party prime minister, laid foundations for modern welfare state.

Henry Cabot Lodge, 1850-1924, (U.S.) Republican senator, led opposition to participation in League of Nations.

Huey P. Long, 1893-1935, (U.S.) Louisiana political demagogue, governor, assassinated.

Rosa Luxemburg, 1871-1919, (G.) revolutionary, leader of the German Social Democratic party and Spartacus party.

J. Ramsay MacDonald, 1866-1937, (Br.) first Labour party prime minister of Great Britain.

Joseph R. McCarthy, 1908-1957, (U.S.) senator notorious for his witch hunt for communists in the government.

Makarios III, 1913-1977, (Cypr.) Greek Orthodox archbishop, first president of Cyprus.

Malcolm X (Malcolm Little), 1925-1965, (U.S.) black separatist leader, assassinated.

Mao Tse-tung, 1893-1976, (Chin.) chief Chinese Marxist theorist, soldier, led Chinese revolution establishing his nation as an important communist state.

Jean Paul Marat, 1743-1793, (F.) revolutionary, politician, identified with radical Jacobins, assassinated.

José Marti, 1853-1895, (Cub.) patriot, poet, leader of Cuban struggle for independence.

Jan Masaryk, 1886-1948, (Czech.) foreign minister, died by mysterious suicide following communist coup.

Thomas G. Masaryk, 1850-1937, (Czech.) statesman, philosopher, first president of Czechoslovak Republic.

Jules Mazarin, 1602-1661, (F.) cardinal, statesman, prime minister under Louis XIII and queen regent Anne of Austria.

Tom Mboya, 1930-1969, (Kenyan) political leader, instrumental in securing independence for his country.

Cosimo I de' Medici, 1519-1574, (It.) Duke of Florence, grand duke of Tuscany.

Lorenzo de' Medici, the Magnificent, 1449-1492, (It.) merchant prince, a towering figure in Italian Renaissance.

Catherine de Medicis, 1519-1589, (F.) queen consort of Henry II, regent of France, influential in Catholic-Huguenot wars.

Golda Meir, 1898-1979, (Isr.) prime minister, 1969-74.

Klemens W.N.L. Metternich, 1773-1859, (Aus.) statesman, arbiter of post-Napoleonic Europe.

Anastas Mikoyan, 1895-1978, (USSR) prominent Soviet leader from 1917; president 1964-65.

Guy Mollet, 1905-1975, (F.) social politician, resistance leader.

Henry Morgenthau Jr., 1891-1967, (U.S.) secretary of treasury, raised funds to finance New Deal and U.S. WW II activities.

Gouverneur Morris, 1752-1816, (U.S.) statesman, diplomat, financial expert who helped plan decimal coinage system.

Wayne Morse, 1900-1974, (U.S.) senator, long-time critic of Vietnam War.

Muhammad Ali, 1769?-1849, (Egypt), pasha, founder of dynasty that encouraged emergence of modern Egyptian state.

Benito Mussolini, 1883-1945, (It.) dictator and leader of the Italian fascist state.

Imre Nagy, c. 1895-1958, (Hung.) communist premier, assassinated after Soviets crushed 1956 uprising.

Gamal Abdel Nasser, 1918-1970, (Egypt.) leader of Arab unification, second Egyptian president.

Jawaharlal Nehru, 1889-1964, (Ind.) prime minister, guided India through its early years of independence.

Kwame Nkrumah, 1909-1972, (Ghan.) dictatorial prime minister, deposed in 1966.

Frederick North, 1732-1792, (Br.) prime minister, his inept policies led to loss of American colonies.

Daniel O'Connell, 1775-1847, (Ir.) political leader, known as The Liberator.

Omar, c.581-644, Mohammedan leader, 2d caliph, led Islam to become an imperial power.

Ignace Paderewski, 1860-1941, (Pol.) statesman, pianist, composer, briefly prime minister, an ardent patriot.

Viscount Palmerston, 1784-1865, (Br.) Whig-Liberal prime minister, foreign minister, embodied British nationalism.

George Papandreou, 1888-1968, (Gk.) Republican politician, served three times as prime minister.

Franz von Papen, 1879-1969, (G.) politician, played major role in overthrow of Weimar Republic and rise of Hitler.

Charles Stewart Parnell, 1846-1891, (Ir.) nationalist leader, "uncrowned king of Ireland."

Lester Pearson, 1897-1972, (Can.) diplomat, Liberal party leader, prime minister.

Robert Peel, 1788-1850, (Br.) reformist prime minister, founder of Conservative party.

Juan Perón, 1895-1974, (Arg.) president, dictator.

Joseph Pilsudski, 1867-1935, (Pol.) statesman, instrumental in re-establishing Polish state in the 20th century.

Charles Pinckney, 1757-1824, (U.S.) founding father, his Pinckney plan was largely incorporated into constitution.

William Pitt, the Elder, 1708-1778, (Br.) statesman, called the "Great Commoner," transformed Britain into imperial power.

William Pitt, the Younger, 1759-1806, (Br.) prime minister during French Revolutionary wars.

Georgi Plekhanov, 1857-1918, (R.) revolutionary, social philosopher, called "father of Russian Marxism."

Raymond Poincaré, 1860-1934, (F.) 9th president of the Republic, advocated harsh punishment of Germany after WW I.

Georges Pompidou, 1911-1974, (F.) Gaullist political leader, president from 1969 to 1974.

Grigori Potemkin, 1739-1791, (R.) field marshal, favorite of Catherine II.

Edmund Randolph, 1753-1813, (U.S.) attorney, prominent in drafting, ratification of constitution.

John Randolph, 1773-1833, (U.S.) southern planter, strong advocate of states' rights.

Jeannette Rankin, 1880-1973, (U.S.) pacifist, first woman member of U.S. Congress.

Walter Rathenau, 1867-1922, (G.) industrialist, social theorist, statesman.
Sam Rayburn, 1882-1961, (U.S.) Democratic leader, representative for 47 years, House speaker for 17.
Paul Reynaud, 1878-1966, (F.) statesman, premier in 1940 at the time of France's defeat by Germany.
Syngman Rhee, 1875-1965, (Kor.) first president of the Republic of Korea.
Cecil Rhodes, 1853-1902, (Br.) imperialist, industrial magnate, established Rhodes scholarships in his will.
Cardinal de Richelieu, 1585-1642, (F.) statesman, known as "red eminence," chief minister to Louis XIII.
Maximilien Robespierre, 1758-1794, (F.) leading figure of French Revolution, responsible for much of Reign of Terror.
Nelson Rockefeller, 1908-1979, (U.S.) Republican gov. of N.Y., 1959-73; U.S. vice president, 1974-77.
Eleanor Roosevelt, 1884-1962, (U.S.) humanitarian, United Nations diplomat.
Elihu Root, 1845-1937, (U.S.) lawyer, statesman, diplomat, leading Republican supporter of the League of Nations.
John Russell, 1792-1878, (Br.) Liberal prime minister during the Irish potato famine.
Anwar el-Sadat, 1918-1981, (Egypt) president, 1970-1981, promoted peace with Israel.
António de O. Salazar, 1899-1970, (Port.) statesman, longtime dictator.
José de San Martin, 1778-1850, South American revolutionary, protector of Peru.
Eisaku Sato, 1901-1975, (Jap.) prime minister, presided over Japan's post-WW II emergence as major world power.
Philipp Scheidemann, 1865-1939, (G.) Social Democratic leader, first chancellor of the German republic.
Robert Schuman, 1886-1963, (F.) statesman, founded European Coal and Steel Community.
Carl Schurz, 1829-1906, (U.S.) German-American political leader, journalist, orator, dedicated reformer.
Kurt Schuschnigg, 1897-1977, (Aus.) chancellor, unsuccessful in stopping his country's annexation by Germany.
William H. Seward, 1801-1872, (U.S.) anti-slavery activist, as Lincoln's secretary of state purchased Alaska.
Carlo Sforza, 1872-1952, (It.) foreign minister, anti-fascist.
Alfred E. Smith, 1873-1944, (U.S.) New York Democratic governor, first Roman Catholic to run for presidency.
Jan C. Smuts, 1870-1950, (S.Af.) statesman, philosopher, soldier, prime minister.
Paul Henri Spaak, 1899-1972, (Belg.) statesman, socialist leader.
Joseph Stalin, 1879-1953, (USSR) Soviet dictator, 1924-53.
Edwin M. Stanton, 1814-1869, (U.S.) Lincoln's secretary of war during the Civil War.
Edward R. Stettinius Jr., 1900-1949, (U.S.) industrialist, secretary of state who coordinated aid to WW II allies.
Adlai E. Stevenson, 1900-1965, (U.S.) Democratic leader, diplomat, Illinois governor, presidential candidate.
Henry L. Stimson, 1867-1950, (U.S.) statesman, served in 5 administrations, influenced foreign policy in 1930s and 1940s.
Gustav Stresemann, 1878-1929, (G.) chancellor, foreign minister, dedicated to regaining friendship for post-WW I Germany.
Sukarno, 1901-1970, (Indon.) dictatorial first president of the Indonesian republic.
Sun Yat-sen, 1866-1925, (Chin.) revolutionary, leader of Kuomintang, regarded as the father of modern China.
Robert A. Taft, 1889-1953, (U.S.) conservative Senate leader, called "Mr. Republican."
Charles de Talleyrand, 1754-1838, (F.) statesman, diplomat, the major force of the Congress of Vienna of 1814-15.
U Thant, 1909-1974 (Bur.) statesman, UN secretary-general.
Norman M. Thomas, 1884-1968, (U.S.) social reformer, 6 times unsuccessful Socialist party presidential candidate.
Josip Broz Tito, 1892-1980, (Yug.) president of Yugoslavia from 1953, World War II guerrilla chief, postwar rival of Stalin, leader of 3d world movement.
Palmiro Togliatti, 1893-1964, (It.) major leader of Italian Communist party.
Hideki Tojo, 1885-1948, (Jap.) statesman, soldier, prime minister during most of WW II.
François Toussaint L'Ouverture, c. 1744-1803, (Hait.) patriot, martyr, thwarted French colonial aims.
Leon Trotsky, 1879-1940, (USSR) revolutionary, founded Red Army, expelled from party in conflict with Stalin.
Rafael L. Trujillo Molina, 1891-1961, (Dom.) absolute dictator, assassinated.
Moise K. Tshombe, 1919-1969, (Cong.) politician, president of secessionist Katanga, premier of Republic of Congo (Zaire).
William M. Tweed, 1823-1878, (U.S.) politician, absolute leader of Tammany Hall, NYC's Democratic political machine.
Walter Ulbricht, 1893-1973, (G.) communist leader of German Democratic Republic.
Arthur H. Vandenberg, 1884-1951, (U.S.) senator, proponent of anti-communist bipartisan foreign policy after WW II.
Eleutherios Venizelos, 1864-1936, (Gk.) most prominent Greek statesman in early 20th century; expanded territory.
Hendrik F. Verwoerd, 1901-1966, (S.Af.) prime minister, rigorously applied apartheid policy despite protest.
Robert Walpole, 1676-1745, (Br.) statesman, generally considered Britain's first prime minister.
Daniel Webster, 1782-1852, (U.S.) orator, politician, advocate of business interests during Jacksonian agrarianism.
Chaim Weizmann, 1874-1952, Zionist leader, scientist, first Israeli president.
Wendell L. Willkie, 1892-1944, (U.S.) Republican who tried to unseat FDR when he ran for his 3d term.
Emiliano Zapata, c. 1879-1919, (Mex.) revolutionary, major influence on modern Mexico.

Notable Military and Naval Leaders of the Past

Creighton Abrams, 1914-1974, (U.S.) commanded forces in Vietnam, 1968-72.
Harold Alexander, 1891-1969, (Br.) led Allied invasion of Italy, 1943.
Ethan Allen, 1738-1789, (U.S.) headed Green Mountain Boys; captured Ft. Ticonderoga, 1775.
Edmund Allenby, 1861-1936, (Br.) in Boer War, WW1; led Egyptian expeditionary force, 1917-18.
Benedict Arnold, 1741-1801, (U.S.) victorious at Saratoga; tried to betray West Point to British.
Henry "Hap" Arnold, 1886-1950, (U.S.) commanded Army Air Force in WW2.
Petr Bagration, 1765-1812, (R.) hero of Napoleonic wars.
John Barry, 1745-1803, (U.S.) won numerous sea battles during revolution.
Pierre Beauregard, 1818-1893, (U.S.) Confederate general ordered bombardment of Ft. Sumter that began the Civil War.
Gebhard v. Blücher, 1742-1819, (G.) helped defeat Napoleon at Waterloo.
Napoleon Bonaparte, 1769-1821, (F.) defeated Russia and Austria at Austerlitz, 1805; invaded Russia, 1812; defeated at Waterloo, 1815.
Edward Braddock, 1695-1755, (Br.) commanded forces in French and Indian War.
Omar N. Bradley, 1893-1981, (U.S.) headed U.S. ground troops in Normandy invasion, 1944.
John Burgoyne, 1722-1792, (Br.) defeated at Saratoga.
Claire Chennault, 1890-1958, (U.S.) headed Flying Tigers in WW2.
Mark Clark, 1896-1984, (U.S.) led forces in WW2 and Korean War.
Karl v. Clausewitz, 1780-1831, (G.) wrote books on military theory.
Henry Clinton, 1738-1795, (Br.) commander of forces in America, 1778-81.
Lucius D. Clay, 1897-1978, (U.S.) led Berlin airlift, 1948-49.
Charles Cornwallis, 1738-1805, (Br.) victorious at Brandywine, 1777; surrendered at Yorktown.
Crazy Horse, 1849-1877, (U.S.) Sioux war chief victorious at Little Big Horn.
George A. Custer, 1839-1876, (U.S.) defeated and killed at Little Big Horn.
Moshe Dayan, 1915-1981, (Isr.) directed campaigns in the 1967, 1973 wars.
Stephen Decatur, 1779-1820, (U.S.) naval hero of Barbary wars, War of 1812.
Anton Denikin, 1872-1947, (R.) led White forces in Russian civil war.
George Dewey, 1837-1917, (U.S.) destroyed Spanish fleet at Manila, 1898.
Hugh C. Dowding, 1883-1970, (Br.) headed RAF, 1936-40.
Jubal Early, 1816-1894, (U.S.) Confederate general led raid on Washington, 1864.
Dwight D. Eisenhower, 1890-1969, (U.S.) commanded Allied forces in Europe, WW2.
David Farragut, 1801-1870, (U.S.) Union admiral captured New Orleans, Mobile Bay.
Ferdinand Foch, 1851-1929, (F.) headed victorious Allied armies, 1918.
Nathan Bedford Forrest, 1821-1877, (U.S.) Confederate general led cavalry raids against Union supply lines.

Frederick the Great, 1712-1786, (G.) led Prussia in The Seven Years War.

Nathanael Greene, 1742-1786, (U.S.) defeated British in Southern campaign, 1780-81.

Charles G. Gordon, 1833-1885, (Br.) led forces in China; killed at Khartoum.

Horatio Gates, 1728-1806, (U.S.) commanded army at Saratoga.

Ulysses S. Grant, 1822-1885, (U.S.) headed Union army, 1864-65; forced Lee's surrender, 1865.

Heinz Guderian, 1888-1953, (G.) tank theorist led panzer forces in Poland, France, Russia.

Douglas Haig, 1861-1928, (Br.) led British armies in France, 1915-18.

William F. Halsey, 1882-1959, (U.S.) defeated Japanese fleet at Leyte Gulf, 1944.

Sir Arthur Travers Harris, 1895-1984, (Br.) led Britain's WWII bomber command.

Richard Howe, 1726-1799, (Br.) commanded navy in America, 1776-78; first of June victory against French, 1794.

William Howe, 1729-1814, (Br.) commanded forces in America, 1776-78.

Isaac Hull, 1773-1843, (U.S.) sunk British frigate Guerriere, 1812.

Thomas (Stonewall) Jackson, 1824-1863, (U.S.) Confederate general led forces in the Shenandoah Valley campaign.

Joseph Joffre, 1852-1931, (F.) headed Allied armies, won Battle of the Marne, 1914.

John Paul Jones, 1747-1792, (U.S.) raided British coast; commanded *Bonhomme Richard* in victory over Serapis, 1779.

Stephen Kearny, 1794-1848, (U.S.) headed Army of the West in Mexican War.

Ernest J. King, 1878-1956, (U.S.) chief naval strategist in WW2.

Horatio H. Kitchener, 1850-1916, (Br.) led forces in Boer War; victorious at Khartoum; organized army in WW1.

Lavrenti Kornilov, 1870-1918, (R.) Commander-in-Chief, 1917; led counter-revolutionary march on Petrograd.

Thaddeus Kosciusko, 1746-1817, (P.) aided American cause in revolution.

Mikhail Kutuzov, 1745-1813, (R.) fought French at Borodino, 1812; abandoned Moscow; forced French retreat.

Marquis de Lafayette, 1757-1834, (F.) aided American cause in the revolution.

Thomas E. Lawrence (of Arabia), 1888-1935, (Br.) organized revolt of Arabs against Turks in WW1.

Henry (Light-Horse Harry) Lee, 1756-1818, (U.S.) cavalry officer in revolution.

Robert E. Lee, 1807-1870, (U.S.) Confederate general defeated at Gettysburg; surrendered to Grant, 1865.

James Longstreet, 1821-1904, (U.S.) aided Lee at Gettysburg.

Douglas MacArthur, 1880-1964, (U.S.) commanded forces in SW Pacific in WW2; headed occupation forces in Japan, 1945-51; UN commander in Korean War.

Francis Marion, 1733-1795, (U.S.) led guerrilla actions in S.C. during revolution.

Duke of Marlborough, 1650-1722, (Br.) led forces against Louis XIV in War of the Spanish Sucession.

George C. Marshall, 1880-1959, (U.S.) chief of staff in WW2; authored Marshall Plan.

George B. McClellan, 1826-1885, (U.S.) Union general commanded Army of the Potomac, 1861-62.

George Meade, 1815-1872; (U.S.) commanded Union forces at Gettysburg.

Billy Mitchell, 1879-1936, (U.S.) air-power advocate; court-martialed for insubordination, later vindicated.

Helmuth v. Moltke, 1800-1891; (G.) victorious in Austro-Prussian, Franco-Prussian wars.

Louis de Montcalm, 1712-1759, (F.) headed troops in Canada; defeated at Quebec, 1759.

Bernard Law Montgomery, 1887-1976, (Br.) stopped German offensive at Alamein, 1942; helped plan Normandy invasion.

Daniel Morgan, 1736-1802, (U.S.) victorious at Cowpens, 1781.

Louis Mountbatten, 1900-1979, (Br.) Supreme Allied Commander of SE Asia, 1943-46.

Joachim Murat, 1767-1815, (F.) leader of cavalry at Marengo, 1800; Austerlitz, 1805; and Jena, 1806.

Horatio Nelson, 1758-1805, (Br.) naval commander destroyed French fleet at Trafalgar.

Michel Ney, 1769-1815, (F.) commanded forces in Switzerland, Austria, Russia; defeated at Waterloo.

Chester Nimitz, 1885-1966, (U.S.) commander of naval forces in Pacific in WW2.

George S. Patton, 1885-1945, (U.S.) led assault on Sicily, 1943; headed 3d Army invasion of German-occupied Europe.

Oliver Perry, 1785-1819, (U.S.) won Battle of Lake Erie in War of 1812.

John Pershing, 1860-1948, (U.S.) commanded Mexican border campaign, 1916; American expeditionary forces in WW1.

Henri Philippe Pétain, 1856-1951, (F.) defended Verdun, 1916; headed Vichy government in WW2.

George E. Pickett, 1825-1875, (U.S.) Confederate general famed for "charge" at Gettysburg.

Hyman Rickover, 1900-1986 (U.S.) father of the nuclear navy.

Erwin Rommel, 1891-1944, (G.) headed Afrika Korps.

Karl v. Rundstedt, 1875-1953, (G.) supreme commander in West, 1943-45.

Aleksandr Samsonov, 1859-1914, (R.) led invasion of E. Prussia, defeated at Tannenberg, 1914.

Winfield Scott, 1786-1866, (U.S.) hero of War of 1812; headed forces in Mexican war, took Mexico City.

Philip Sheridan, 1831-1888, (U.S.) Union cavalry officer headed Army of the Shenandoah, 1864-65.

William T. Sherman, 1820-1891, (U.S.) Union general sacked Atlanta during "march to the sea," 1864.

Carl Spaatz, 1891-1974, (U.S.) directed strategic bombing against Germany, later Japan, in WW2.

Raymond Spruance, 1886-1969, (U.S.) victorious at Midway Island, 1942.

Joseph W. Stilwell, 1883-1946, (U.S.) headed forces in the China, Burma, India theater in WW2.

J.E.B. Stuart, 1833-1864, (U.S.) Confederate cavalry commander.

George H. Thomas, 1816-1870, (U.S.) saved Union army at Chattanooga, 1863; victorious at Nashville, 1864.

Semyon Timoshenko, 1895-1970, (USSR) defended Moscow, Stalingrad; led winter offensive, 1942-43.

Alfred v. Tirpitz, 1849-1930, (G.) responsible for submarine blockade in WW1.

Jonathan M. Wainwright, 1883-1953, (U.S.) forced to surrender on Corregidor, 1942.

George Washington, 1732-1799, (U.S.) led Continental army, 1775-83.

Archibald Wavell, 1883-1950, (Br.) commanded forces in N. and E. Africa, and SE Asia in WW2.

Anthony Wayne, 1745-1796, (U.S.) captured Stony Point, 1779; defeated Indians at Fallen Timbers, 1794.

Duke of Wellington, 1769-1852, (Br.) defeated Napoleon at Waterloo.

James Wolfe, 1727-1759, (Br.) captured Quebec from French, 1759.

Georgi Zhukov, 1895-1974, (USSR) defended Moscow, 1941; led assault on Berlin.

Poets Laureate of England

There is no authentic record of the origin of the office of Poet Laureate of England. According to Warton, there was a Versificator Regis, or King's Poet, in the reign of Henry III (1216-1272), and he was paid 100 shillings a year. Geoffrey Chaucer (1340-1400) assumed the title of Poet Laureate, and in 1389 got a royal grant of a yearly allowance of wine. In the reign of Edward IV (1461-1483), John Kay held the post. Under Henry VII (1485-1509), Andrew Bernard was the Poet Laureate, and was succeeded under Henry VIII (1509-1547) by John Skelton. Next came Edmund Spenser, who died in 1599; then Samuel Daniel, appointed 1599, and then Ben Jonson, 1619. Sir William D'Avenant was appointed in 1637. He was a godson of William Shakespeare.

Others were John Dryden, 1670; Thomas Shadwell, 1688; Nahum Tate, 1692; Nicholas Rowe, 1715; the Rev. Laurence Eusden, 1718; Colley Cibber, 1730; William Whitehead, 1757, on the refusal of Gray; Rev. Thomas Warton, 1785, on the refusal of Mason; Henry J. Pye, 1790; Robert Southey, 1813, on the refusal of Sir Walter Scott; William Wordsworth, 1843; Alfred, Lord Tennyson, 1850; Alfred Austin, 1896; Robert Bridges, 1913; John Masefield, 1930; Cecil Day Lewis, 1967; Sir John Betjeman, 1972; Ted Hughes, 1984.

U.S. Poet Laureate

Robert Penn Warren, the poet, novelist, and essayist, was named the country's first official Poet Laureate on Feb. 26, 1986. The only writer to have won the Pulitzer Prize for fiction and poetry (twice), Warren was chosen by Daniel J. Boorstin, the Librarian of Congress. The appointment, which would reportedly pay $36,000 a year, began in September, 1986. On April 17, 1987, Richard Wilbur was named the second Poet Laureate.

Noted Writers of the Past

Henry Adams, 1838-1918, (U.S.) historian, philosopher. *The Education of Henry Adams.*

George Ade, 1866-1944, (U.S.) humorist. *Fables in Slang.*

Conrad Aiken, 1889-1973, (U.S.) poet, critic.

Louisa May Alcott, 1832-1888, (U.S.) novelist. *Little Women.*

Sholom Aleichem, 1859-1916. (R.) Yiddish writer. *Tevye's Daughter, The Great Fair.*

Vicente Aleixandre, 1898-1984, (Sp.) poet. 1977 Nobel Prize winner.

Horatio Alger, 1832-1899, (U.S.) "rags-to-riches" books.

Hans Christian Andersen, 1805-1875, (Den.) author of fairy tales. *The Princess and the Pea, The Ugly Duckling.*

Maxwell Anderson, 1888-1959, (U.S.) playwright. *What Price Glory?, High Tor, Winterset, Key Largo.*

Sherwood Anderson, 1876-1941, (U.S.) author. *Winesburg, Ohio.*

Matthew Arnold, 1822-1888, (Br.) poet, critic. "Thrysis," "Dover Beach."

Jane Austen, 1775-1817, (Br.) novelist. *Pride and Prejudice, Sense and Sensibility, Emma, Mansfield Park.*

Isaac Babel, 1894-1941, (R.) short-story writer, playwright. *Odessa Tales, Red Cavalry.*

Enid Bagnold, 1890-1981, (Br.) playwright, novelist. *National Velvet.*

James M. Barrie, 1860-1937, (Br.) playwright, novelist. *Peter Pan, Dear Brutus, What Every Woman Knows.*

Honoré de Balzac, 1799-1850, (Fr.) novelist. *Le Père Goriot, Cousine Bette, Eugénie Grandet, The Human Comedy.*

Charles Baudelaire, 1821-1867, (Fr.) symbolist poet. *Les Fleurs du Mal.*

L. Frank Baum, 1856-1919, (U.S.) children's author. Wizard of Oz series.

Simone de Beauvoir, 1980-1986, (Fr.) novelist, essayist. *The Second Sex.*

Brendan Behan, 1923-1964, (Ir.) playwright. *The Quare Fellow, The Hostage, Borstal Boy.*

Robert Benchley, 1889-1945, (U.S.) humorist. *From Bed to Worse, My Ten Years in a Quandary.*

Stephen Vincent Benét, 1898-1943, (U.S.) poet, novelist. *John Brown's Body.*

John Berryman, 1914-1972, (U.S.) poet. *Homage to Mistress Bradstreet.*

Ambrose Bierce, 1842-1914, (U.S.) short-story writer, journalist. *In the Midst of Life, The Devil's Dictionary.*

William Blake, 1757-1827, (Br.) poet, mystic, artist. *Songs of Innocence, Songs of Experience.*

Giovanni Boccaccio, 1313-1375, (It.) poet, storyteller. *Decameron, Filostrato.*

Jorge Luis Borges, 1900-1986 (Arg.) short-story writer, poet, essayist, *Labyrinths.*

James Boswell, 1740-1795, (Sc.) author. *The Life of Samuel Johnson.*

Anne Bradstreet, c. 1612-1672, (U.S.) poet. *The Tenth Muse Lately Sprung Up in America.*

Bertolt Brecht, 1898-1956, (G.) dramatist, poet. *The Threepenny Opera, Mother Courage and Her Children.*

Charlotte Brontë, 1816-1855, (Br.) novelist. *Jane Eyre.*

Emily Brontë, 1818-1848, (Br.) novelist. *Wuthering Heights.*

Elizabeth Barrett Browning, 1806-1861, (Br.) poet. *Sonnets from the Portuguese.*

Robert Browning, 1812-1889, (Br.) poet. "My Last Duchess," "Soliloquy of the Spanish Cloister."

Pearl Buck, 1892-1973, (U.S.) novelist. *The Good Earth.*

Mikhail Bulgakov, 1891-1940, (R.) novelist, playwright. *The Heart of a Dog, The Master and Margarita.*

John Bunyan, 1628-1688, (Br.) writer. *Pilgrim's Progress.*

Robert Burns, 1759-1796, (Sc.) poet. "Flow Gently, Sweet Afton," "My Heart's in the Highlands," "Auld Lang Syne."

Edgar Rice Burroughs, 1875-1950, (U.S.) novelist. *Tarzan of the Apes.*

George Gordon Lord Byron, 1788-1824, (Br.) poet. *Don Juan, Childe Harold.*

Italo Calvino, 1923-1985 (It.) novelist, short story writer. *If on a Winter's Night a Traveler . . .*

Albert Camus, 1913-1960, (F.) novelist. *The Plague, The Stranger, Caligula, The Fall.*

Lewis Carroll, 1832-1898, (Br.) writer, mathematician. *Alice's Adventures in Wonderland, Through the Looking Glass.*

Karel Capek, 1890-1938, (Czech.) playwright, novelist, essayist. *R.U.R. (Rossum's Universal Robots).*

Giacomo Casanova, 1725-1798, (It.) Venetian adventurer, author, world famous for his memoirs.

Willa Cather, 1876-1947, (U.S.) novelist, essayist. *O Pioneers!, My Antonia.*

Miguel de Cervantes Saavedra, 1547-1616, (Sp.) novelist, dramatist, poet. *Don Quixote de la Mancha.*

Raymond Chandler, 1888-1959, (U.S.) writer of detective fiction. Philip Marlowe series.

Geoffrey Chaucer, c. 1340-1400, (Br.) poet. *The Canterbury Tales.*

John Cheevers, 1912-1983, (U.S.) short story writer, novelist. *The Wapshot Scandal.*

Anton Chekhov, 1860-1904, (R.) short-story writer, dramatist. *Uncle Vanya, The Cherry Orchard, The Three Sisters.*

G.K. Chesterton, 1874-1936, (Br.) author, Fr. Brown series.

Agatha Christie, 1891-1976, (Br.) mystery writer. *And Then There Were None, Murder on the Orient Express.*

Jean Cocteau, 1889-1963, (F.) writer, visual artist, filmmaker. *The Beauty and the Beast, Enfants Terribles.*

Samuel Taylor Coleridge, 1772-1834, (Br.) poet, man of letters. "Kubla Khan," "The Rime of the Ancient Mariner."

Sidonie Colette, 1873-1954, (F.) novelist. *Claudine, Gigi.*

Joseph Conrad, 1857-1924, (Br.) novelist. *Lord Jim, Heart of Darkness, The Nigger of the Narcissus.*

James Fenimore Cooper, 1789-1851, (U.S.) novelist. *Leather-Stocking Tales.*

Pierre Corneille, 1606-1684, (F.) Dramatist. *Medeé, Le Cid, Horace, Cinna, Polyeucte.*

Hart Crane, 1899-1932, (U.S.) poet. "The Bridge."

Stephen Crane, 1871-1900, (U.S.) novelist. *The Red Badge of Courage.*

e.e. cummings, 1894-1962, (U.S.) poet. *Tulips and Chimneys.*

Gabriele D'Annunzio, 1863-1938, (It.) poet, novelist, dramatist. *The Child of Pleasure, The Intruder, The Victim.*

Dante Alighieri, 1265-1321, (It.) poet. *The Divine Comedy.*

Daniel Defoe, 1660-1731, (Br.) writer. *Robinson Crusoe, Moll Flanders, Journal of the Plague Year.*

Charles Dickens, 1812-1870, (Br.) novelist. *David Copperfield, Oliver Twist, Great Expectations, The Pickwick Papers.*

Emily Dickinson, 1830-1886, (U.S.) poet.

Isak Dinesen (Karen Blixen), 1885-1962, (Dan.) author. *Out of Africa, Seven Gothic Tales, Winter's Tales.*

John Donne, 1573-1631, (Br.) poet. *Songs and Sonnets, Holy Sonnets,* "Death Be Not Proud."

John Dos Passos, 1896-1970, (U.S.) author. *U.S.A.*

Fyodor Dostoyevsky, 1821-1881, (R.) author. *Crime and Punishment, The Brothers Karamazov, The Possessed.*

Arthur Conan Doyle, 1859-1930, (Br.) author, created Sherlock Holmes.

Theodore Dreiser, 1871-1945, (U.S.) novelist. *An American Tragedy, Sister Carrie.*

John Dryden, 1631-1700, (Br.) poet, dramatist, critic. *Fables, Ancient and Modern.*

Alexandre Dumas, 1802-1870, (F.) novelist, dramatist. *The Three Musketeers, The Count of Monte Cristo.*

Alexandre Dumas (fils), 1824-1895, (F.) dramatist, novelist. *La Dame aux camélias, Le Demi-Monde.*

Ilya G. Ehrenburg, 1891-1967, (R.) novelist, journalist. *The Thaw.*

George Eliot, 1819-1880, (Br.) novelist. *Adam Bede, Silas Marner, The Mill on the Floss.*

T.S. Eliot, 1888-1965, (Br.) poet, critic. *The Waste Land,* "The Love Song of J. Alfred Prufrock," *Murder in the Cathedral.*

Ralph Waldo Emerson, 1803-1882, (U.S.) poet, essayist. "The Concord Hymn," "Brahma," *Nature.*

James T. Farrell, 1904-1979, (U.S.) novelist. Studs Lonigan trilogy.

William Faulkner, 1897-1962, (U.S.) novelist. *Sanctuary, Light in August, The Sound and the Fury, Absalom, Absalom!*

Edna Ferber, 1885-1968, (U.S.) novelist, dramatist. *Show Boat, Saratoga Trunk, Giant, Dinner at Eight.*

Henry Fielding, 1707-1754, (Br.) novelist. *Tom Jones.*

F. Scott Fitzgerald, 1896-1940, (U.S.) short-story writer, novelist. *The Great Gatsby, Tender is the Night.*

Gustave Flaubert, 1821-1880, (F.) novelist. *Madame Bovary.*

C.S. Forester, 1899-1966, (Br.) novelist. Horatio Hornblower series.

E.M. Forster, 1879-1970, (Br.) novelist. *A Passage to India.*

Anatole France, 1844-1924. (F.) writer. *Penguin Island, My Friend's Book, Le Crime de Sylvestre Bonnard.*

Robert Frost, 1874-1963, (U.S.) poet. "Birches," "Fire and Ice," "Stopping by Woods on a Snowy Evening."

John Galsworthy, 1867-1933, (Br.) novelist, dramatist. *The Forsyte Saga, A Modern Comedy.*

Erle Stanley Gardner, 1889-1970, (U.S.) author, lawyer. Perry Mason series.

Jean Genet, 1911-1986, (Fr.) playwright, novelist. "The Blacks."

André Gide, 1869-1951, (F.) writer, *The Immoralist, The Pastoral Symphony, Strait is the Gate.*

Jean Giraudoux, 1882-1944, (F.) novelist, dramatist. *Electra, The Madwoman of Chaillot, Ondine, Tiger at the Gate.*

Johann W. von Goethe, 1749-1832, (G.) poet, dramatist, novelist. *Faust.*

Nikolai Gogol, 1809-1852, (R.) short-story writer, dramatist, novelist. *Dead Souls, The Inspector General.*

Oliver Goldsmith, 1730?-1774, (Br.-Ir.) writer. *The Vicar of Wakefield, She Stoops to Conquer.*

Maxim Gorky, 1868-1936, (R.) writer, founder of Soviet realism. *Mother, The Lower Depths.*

Robert Graves, 1895-1985, (Br.) poet, classical scholar, novelist. *The White Goddess.*

Thomas Gray, 1716-1771, (Br.) poet. "Elegy Written in a Country Churchyard."

Zane Grey, 1875-1939, (U.S.) writer of western stories.

Jakob Grimm, 1785-1863, (G.) philologist, folklorist. *German Methodology, Grimm's Fairy Tales.*

Wilhelm Grimm, 1786-1859, (G.) philologist, folklorist. *Grimm's Fairy Tales.*

Edgar A. Guest, 1881-1959, (U.S.) poet. *A Heap of Livin!*

Dashiell Hammett, 1894-1961, (U.S.) writer of detective fiction, created Sam Spade.

Knute Hamsun, 1859-1952 (Nor.) novelist. *Hunger.*

Thomas Hardy, 1840-1928, (Br.) novelist, poet. *The Return of the Native, Tess of the D'Urbervilles, Jude the Obscure.*

Joel Chandler Harris, 1848-1908, (U.S.) short-story writer. Uncle Remus series.

Moss Hart, 1904-1961, (U.S.) playwright. *Once in a Lifetime, You Can't Take It With You.*

Bret Harte, 1836-1902, (U.S.) short-story writer, poet. *The Luck of Roaring Camp.*

Jaroslav Hasek, 1883-1923, (Czech.) writer. *The Good Soldier Schweik.*

Nathaniel Hawthorne, 1804-1864, (U.S.) novelist, short story writer. *The Scarlet Letter, The House of the Seven Gables.*

Heinrich Heine, 1797-1856, (G.) poet. *Book of Songs.*

Lillian Hellman, 1907-1984, (U.S.) playwright, author of memoirs, "The Little Foxes," *An Unfinished Woman.*

Ernest Hemingway, 1899-1961, (U.S.) novelist, short-story writer. *A Farewell to Arms, For Whom the Bell Tolls.*

O. Henry (W.S. Porter), 1862-1910, (U.S.) short-story writer. "The Gift of the Magi."

Hermann Hesse, 1877-1962, (G.) novelist, poet. *Death and the Lover, Steppenwolf, Siddhartha.*

Oliver Wendell Holmes, 1809-1894, (U.S.) poet, novelist. *The Autocrat of the Breakfast-Table.*

Alfred E. Housman, 1859-1936, (Br.) poet. *A Shropshire Lad.*

William Dean Howells, 1837-1920, (U.S.) novelist, critic, dean of late 19th century American letters.

Langston Hughes, 1902-1967, (U.S.) poet, playwright. *The Weary Blues, One-Way Ticket, Shakespeare in Harlem.*

Victor Hugo, 1802-1885, (F.) poet, dramatist, novelist. *Notre Dame de Paris, Les Misérables.*

Aldous Huxley 1894-1963, (Br.) author. *Point Counter Point, Brave New World.*

Henrik Ibsen, 1828-1906, (Nor.) dramatist, poet. *A Doll's House, Ghosts, The Wild Duck, Hedda Gabler.*

William Inge, 1913-1973, (U.S.) playwright. *Come Back Little Sheba, Bus Stop, The Dark at the Top of the Stairs, Picnic.*

Washington Irving, 1783-1859, (U.S.) essayist, author. "Rip Van Winkle," "The Legend of Sleepy Hollow."

Shirley Jackson, 1919-1965, (U.S.) writer. "The Lottery."

Henry James, 1843-1916, (U.S.) novelist, critic. *Washington Square, Portrait of a Lady, The American.*

Robinson Jeffers, 1887-1962, (U.S.) poet, dramatist. *Tamar and Other Poems, Medea.*

Samuel Johnson, 1709-1784, (Br.) author, scholar, critic. *Dictionary of the English Language.*

Ben Jonson, 1572-1637, (Br.) dramatist, poet. *Volpone.*

James Joyce, 1882-1941, (Ir.) novelist. *Ulysses, A Portrait of the Artist as a Young Man, Finnegans Wake.*

Franz Kafka, 1883-1924, (G.) novelist, short story writer. *The Trial, Amerika, The Castle.*

George S. Kaufman, 1889-1961, (U.S.) playwright. *The Man Who Came to Dinner, You Can't Take It With You, Stage Door.*

Nikos Kazantzakis, 1883?-1957, (Gk.) novelist. *Zorba the Greek, A Greek Passion.*

John Keats, 1795-1821, (Br.) poet. *On a Grecian Urn, La Belle Dame Sans Merci.*

Joyce Kilmer, 1886-1918, (U.S.) poet, "Trees."

Rudyard Kipling, 1865-1936, (Br.) author, poet. "The White Man's Burden," "Gunga Din," *The Jungle Book.*

Jean de la Fontaine, 1621-1695, (F.) poet. *Fables choisies.*

Pär Lagerkvist, 1891-1974, (Swed.) poet, dramatist, novelist. *Barabbas, The Sybil.*

Selma Lagerlöf, 1858-1940, (Swed.) novelist. *Jerusalem, The Ring of the Lowenskolds.*

Alphonse de Lamartine, 1790-1869, (F.) poet, novelist, statesman. *Méditations poétiques.*

Charles Lamb, 1775-1834, (Br.) essayist. *Specimens of English Dramatic Poets, Essays of Elia.*

Giuseppe di Lampedusa, 1896-1957, (It.) novelist. *The Leopard.*

Ring Lardner, 1885-1933, (U.S.) short story writer, humorist. *You Know Me, Al.*

D. H. Lawrence, 1885-1930, (Br.) novelist. *Women in Love, Lady Chatterley's Lover, Sons and Lovers.*

Mikhail Lermontov, 1814-1841, (R.) novelist, poet. "Demon," *Hero of Our Time.*

Alain-René Lesage, 1668-1747, (F.) novelist. *Gil Blas de Santillane.*

Gotthold Lessing, 1729-1781, (G.) dramatist, philosopher, critic. *Miss Sara Sampson, Minna von Barnhelm.*

Sinclair Lewis, 1885-1951, (U.S.) novelist, playwright. *Babbitt, Arrowsmith, Dodsworth, Main Street.*

Vachel Lindsay, 1879-1931, (U.S.) poet. *General William Booth Enters into Heaven, The Congo.*

Hugh Lofting, 1886-1947, (Br.) Dr. Doolittle series.

Jack London, 1876-1916, (U.S.) novelist, journalist. *Call of the Wild, The Sea-Wolf.*

Henry Wadsworth Longfellow, 1807-1882, (U.S.) poet. *Evangeline, The Song of Hiawatha.*

Amy Lowell, 1874-1925, (U.S.) poet, critic. "Lilacs."

James Russell Lowell, 1819-1891, (U.S.) poet, editor. *Poems, The Bigelow Papers.*

Robert Lowell, 1917-1977, (U.S.) poet. "Lord Weary's Castle," "For the Union Dead."

Emil Ludwig, 1881-1948, (G.) biographer. *Goethe, Beethoven, Napoleon, Bismarck.*

Niccolò Machiavelli, 1469-1527, (It.) author, statesman. *The Prince, Discourses on Livy.*

Bernard Malamud, 1915-1986, (U.S.) short story writer, novelist, "The Magic Barrel," *The Assistant, The Fixer.*

Stéphane Mallarmé, 1842-1898, (F.) poet. *The Afternoon of a Faun.*

Thomas Malory, ?-1471, (Br.) writer. *Morte d'Arthur.*

André Malraux, 1901-1976, (F.) novelist. *Man's Fate.*

Osip Mandelstam, 1891-1938, (R.) Acmeist poet.

Thomas Mann, 1875-1955, (G.) novelist, essayist. *Buddenbrooks, Death in Venice, The Magic Mountain.*

Katherine Mansfield, 1888-1923, (Br.) short story writer. "Bliss," "The Garden Party."

Christopher Marlowe, 1564-1593, (Br.) dramatist, poet. *Tamburlaine the Great, Dr. Faustus, The Jew of Malta.*

John Masefield, 1878-1967, (Br.) poet. "Sea Fever," "Cargoes," *Salt Water Ballads.*

Edgar Lee Masters, 1869-1950, (U.S.) poet, biographer. *Spoon River Anthology.*

W. Somerset Maugham, 1874-1965, (Br.) author. *Of Human Bondage, The Razor's Edge, The Moon and Sixpence.*

Guy de Maupassant, 1850-1893, (F.) novelist, short-story writer. "A Life," "Bel-Ami," "The Necklace."

François Mauriac, 1885-1970, (F.) novelist, dramatist. *Viper's Tangle, The Kiss to the Leper.*

Vladimir Mayakovsky, 1893-1930, (R.) poet, dramatist. *The Cloud in Trousers.*

Carson McCullers, 1917-1967, (U.S.) novelist. *The Heart is a Lonely Hunter, Member of the Wedding.*

Herman Melville, 1819-1891, (U.S.) novelist, poet. *Moby Dick, Typee, Billy Budd, Omoo.*

H.L. Mencken, 1880-1956, (U.S.) author, critic, editor. *Prejudices, The American Language.*

George Meredith, 1828-1909, (Br.) novelist, poet. *The Ordeal of Richard Feverel, The Egoist.*

Prosper Mérimée, 1803-1870, (F.) author. *Carmen.*

Edna St. Vincent Millay, 1892-1950, (U.S.) poet. *The Harp Weaver and Other Poems, A Few Figs from Thistles.*

A.A. Milne, 1882-1956, (Br.) author. *Winnie the Pooh.*

John Milton, 1608-1674, (Br.) poet. *Paradise Lost.*

Gabriela Mistral, 1889-1957, (Chil.) poet. *Sonnets of Death, Desolación, Tala, Lagar.*

Margaret Mitchell, 1900-1949, (U.S.) novelist. *Gone With the Wind.*

Jean Baptiste Molière, 1622-1673, (F.) dramatist. *Le Tartuffe, Le Misanthrope, Le Bourgeois Gentilhomme.*

Ferenc Molnár, 1878-1952, (Hung.) dramatist, novelist. *Liliom, The Guardsman, The Swan.*

Michel de Montaigne, 1533-1592, (F.) essayist. *Essais.*

Eugenio Montale, 1896-1981, (It.) poet.

Clement C. Moore, 1779-1863, (U.S.) poet, educator. "A Visit from Saint Nicholas."

Marianne Moore, 1887-1972, (U.S.) poet. *O to Be a Dragon.*

Thomas More, 1478-1535, (Br.) author. *Utopia.*

H.H. Munro (Saki), 1870-1916, (Br.) author. *Reginald, The Chronicles of Clovis, Beasts and Super-Beasts.*

Alfred de Musset, 1810-1857, (F.) poet, dramatist. *Confession d'un enfant du siècle.*

Vladimir Nabokov, 1899-1977, (Rus.-U.S.) author. *Lolita.*

Ogden Nash, 1902-1971, (U.S.) poet. *Hard Lines, I'm a Stranger Here Myself, The Private Dining Room.*

Pablo Neruda, 1904-1973, (Chil.) poet. *Twenty Love Poems and One Song of Despair, Toward the Splendid City.*

Sean O'Casey, 1884-1964, (Ir.) dramatist. *Juno and the Paycock, The Plough and the Stars.*

Flannery O'Connor, 1925-1964, (U.S.) novelist, short story writer. *Wise Blood,* "A Good Man Is Hard to Find."

Clifford Odets, 1906-1963, (U.S.) playwright. *Waiting for Lefty, Awake and Sing, Golden Boy, The Country Girl.*

John O'Hara, 1905-1970, (U.S.) novelist. *From the Terrace, Appointment in Samarra.*

Omar Khayyam, c. 1028-1122, (Per.) poet. *Rubaiyat.*

Eugene O'Neill, 1888-1953, (U.S.) playwright. *Emperor Jones, Anna Christie, Long Day's Journey into Night.*

George Orwell, 1903-1950, (Br.) novelist, essayist. *Animal Farm, Nineteen Eighty-Four.*

Thomas (Tom) Paine, 1737-1809, (U.S.) author, political theorist. *Common Sense.*

Dorothy Parker, 1893-1967, (U.S.) poet, short-story writer. *Enough Rope, Laments for the Living.*

Boris Pasternak, 1890-1960, (R.) poet, novelist. *Doctor Zhivago, My Sister, Life.*

Samuel Pepys, 1633-1703, (Br.) public official, author of the greatest diary in the English language.

S. J. Perelman, 1904-1979, (U.S.) humorist. *The Road to Miltown, Under the Spreading Atrophy.*

Francesco Petrarca, 1304-1374, (It.) poet, humanist. *Africa, Trionfi, Canzoniere, On Solitude.*

Luigi Pirandello, 1867-1936, (It.) novelist, dramatist. *Six Characters in Search of an Author.*

Edgar Allan Poe, 1809-1849, (U.S.) poet, short-story writer, critic. "Annabel Lee," "The Raven," "The Purloined Letter."

Alexander Pope, 1688-1744, (Br.) poet. *The Rape of the Lock, An Essay on Man.*

Katherine Anne Porter, 1890-1980, (U.S.) novelist, short story writer. *Ship of Fools.*

Ezra Pound, 1885-1972, (U.S.) poet. *Cantos.*

Marcel Proust, 1871-1922, (F.) novelist. *A la recherche du temps perdu (Remembrance of Things Past).*

Aleksandr Pushkin, 1799-1837, (R.) poet, prose writer. *Boris Godunov, Eugene Onegin, The Bronze Horseman.*

François Rabelais, 1495-1553, (F.) writer, physician. Gargantua, Pantagruel.

Jean Racine, 1639-1699, (F.) dramatist. *Andromaque, Phèdre, Bérénice, Britannicus.*

Ayn Rand, 1905-1982 (Rus.-U.S.) novelist, philosopher. *The Fountainhead, Atlas Shrugged.*

Erich Maria Remarque, 1898-1970, (Ger.-U.S.) novelist. *All Quiet on the Western Front.*

Samuel Richardson, 1689-1761, (Br.) novelist. *Clarissa Harlowe, Pamela; or, Virtue Rewarded.*

James Whitcomb Riley, 1849-1916, (U.S.) poet. "When the Frost is on the Pumpkin," "Little Orphant Annie."

Rainer Maria Rilke, 1875-1926, (G.) poet. *Life and Songs, Divine Elegies, Sonnets to Orpheus.*

Arthur Rimbaud, 1854-1891, (F.) *A Season in Hell.*

Edwin Arlington Robinson, 1869-1935, (U.S.) poet. "Richard Cory," "Miniver Cheevy."

Theodore Roethke, 1908-1963, (U.S.) poet. *Open House, The Waking, The Far Field.*

Romain Rolland, 1866-1944, (F.) novelist, biographer. *Jean-Christophe.*

Pierre de Ronsard, 1524-1585, (F.) poet. *Sonnets pour Hélène.*

Edmond Rostand, 1868-1918, (F.) poet, dramatist. *Cyrano de Bergerac.*

Damon Runyon, 1880-1946, (U.S.) short-story writer, journalist. *Guys and Dolls, Blue Plate Special.*

John Ruskin, 1819-1900, (Br.) critic, social theorist. *Modern Painters, The Seven Lamps of Architecture.*

Antoine de Saint-Exupery, 1900-1944, (F.) writer, aviator. *Wind, Sand and Stars, Le Petit Prince.*

George Sand, 1804-1876, (F.) novelist. *Consuelo, The Haunted Pool, Les Maitres sonneurs.*

Carl Sandburg, 1878-1967, (U.S.) poet. *Chicago Poems, Smoke and Steel, Harvest Poems.*

George Santayana, 1863-1952, (U.S.) poet, essayist, philosopher. *The Sense of Beauty, The Realms of Being.*

William Saroyan, 1908-1981, (U.S.) playwright, novelist. *The Time of Your Life, The Human Comedy.*

Jean-Paul Sartre, 1905-1980, (Fr.) philosopher, novelist, playwright. *Nausea, No Exit.*

Friedrich von Schiller, 1759-1805, (G.) dramatist, poet, historian. *Don Carlos, Maria Stuart, Wilhelm Tell.*

Sir Walter Scott, 1771-1832, (Sc.) novelist, poet. *Ivanhoe, Rob Roy, The Bride of Lammermoor.*

Jaroslav Seifert, 1902-1986, (Cz.) poet.

William Shakespeare, 1564-1616, (Br.) dramatist, poet. *Romeo and Juliet, Hamlet, King Lear, The Merchant of Venice.*

George Bernard Shaw, 1856-1950, (Ir.) playwright, critic. *St. Joan, Pygmalion, Major Barbara, Man and Superman.*

Mary Wollstonecraft Shelley, 1797-1851, (Br.) author. *Frankenstein.*

Percy Bysshe Shelley, 1792-1822, (Br.) poet. *Prometheus Unbound, Adonais,* "Ode to the West Wind," "To a Skylark."

Richard B. Sheridan, 1751-1816, (Br.) dramatist. *The Rivals, School for Scandal.*

Robert Sherwood, 1896-1955, (U.S.) playwright. *The Petrified Forest, Abe Lincoln in Illinois, Reunion in Vienna.*

Mikhail Sholokhov, 1906-1984 (U.S.S.R.) author, 1965 Nobel laureate. *And Quiet Flows the Don.*

Upton Sinclair, 1878-1968, (U.S.) novelist. *The Jungle.*

Edmund Spenser, 1552-1599, (Br.) poet. *The Faerie Queen.*

Christina Stead, 1903-1983 (Austral.) novelist, short-story writer. *The Man Who Loved Children.*

Richard Steele, 1672-1729, (Br.) essayist, playwright, began the Tatler and Spectator. *The Conscious Lovers.*

Lincoln Steffens, 1866-1936, (U.S.) editor, author. *The Shame of the Cities.*

Gertrude Stein, 1874-1946, (U.S.) author. *Three Lives.*

John Steinbeck, 1902-1968, (U.S.) novelist. *Grapes of Wrath, Of Mice and Men, Winter of Our Discontent.*

Stendhal (Marie Henri Beyle), 1783-1842, (F.) poet, novelist. *The Red and the Black, The Charterhouse of Parma.*

Laurence Sterne, 1713-1768, (Br.) novelist. *Tristram Shandy.*

Wallace Stevens, 1879-1955, (U.S.) poet. *Harmonium, The Man With the Blue Guitar, Transport to Summer.*

Robert Louis Stevenson, 1850-1894, (Br.) novelist, poet, essayist. *Treasure Island, A Child's Garden of Verses.*

Rex Stout, 1886-1975, (U.S.) novelist, created Nero Wolfe.

Harriet Beecher Stowe, 1811-1896, (U.S.) novelist. *Uncle Tom's Cabin.*

Lytton Strachey, 1880-1932, (Br.) biographer, critic. *Eminent Victorians, Queen Victoria, Elizabeth and Essex.*

August Strindberg, 1849-1912, (Swed.) dramatist, novelist. *The Father, Miss Julie, The Creditors.*

Jonathan Swift, 1667-1745, (Br.) author. *Gulliver's Travels.*

Algernon C. Swinburne, 1837-1909, (Br.) poet, critic. *Songs Before Sunrise.*

John M. Synge, 1871-1909, (Ir.) poet, dramatist. *Riders to the Sea, The Playboy of the Western World.*

Rabindranath Tagore, 1861-1941, (Ind.), author, poet. *Sadhana, The Realization of Life, Gitanjali.*

Booth Tarkington, 1869-1946, (U.S.) novelist. *Seventeen, Alice Adams, Penrod.*

Sara Teasdale, 1884-1933, (U.S.) poet. *Helen of Troy and Other Poems, Rivers to the Sea, Flame and Shadow.*

Alfred Lord Tennyson, 1809-1892, (Br.) poet. *Idylls of the King, In Memoriam,* "The Charge of the Light Brigade."

William Makepeace Thackeray, 1811-1863, (Br.) novelist. *Vanity Fair.*

Dylan Thomas, 1914-1953, (Welsh) poet. *Under Milk Wood, A ChilJ's Christmas in Wales.*

Henry David Thoreau, 1817-1862, (U.S.) transcendentalist thinker, writer. *Walden.*

James Thurber, 1894-1961, (U.S.) humorist, artist. *The New Yorker, The Owl in the Attic, Thurber Carnival.*

J.R.R. Tolkien, 1892-1973, (Br.) author. *The Hobbit, Lord of the Rings.*

Leo Tolstoy, 1828-1910, (R.) novelist. *War and Peace, Anna Karenina.*

Anthony Trollope, 1815-1882, (Br.) novelist. *The Warden, Barchester Towers,* The Palliser novels.

Ivan Turgenev, 1818-1883, (R.) novelist, short-story writer. *Fathers and Sons, First Love, A Month in the Country.*

Mark Twain (Samuel Clemens), 1835-1910, (U.S.) novelist, humorist. *The Adventures of Huckleberry Finn, Tom Sawyer.*

Sigrid Undset, 1881-1949, (Nor.) novelist, poet. *Kristin Lavransdatter.*

Paul Valéry, 1871-1945, (F.) poet, critic. *La Jeune Parque, The Graveyard by the Sea.*

Jules Verne, 1828-1905, (F.) novelist, originator of modern science fiction. *Twenty Thousand Leagues Under the Sea.*

François Villon, 1431-1463?, (F.) poet. *Le petit et le Grand, Testament.*

Evelyn Waugh, 1903-1966, (Br.) satirist. *The Loved One.*

H.G. Wells, 1866-1946, (Br.) author. *The Time Machine, The Invisible Man, The War of the Worlds.*

Rebecca West, 1893-1983 (Br.) author. *Black Lamb and Grey Falcon.*

Edith Wharton, 1862-1937, (U.S.) novelist. *The Age of Innocence, The House of Mirth.*

E.B. White, 1899-1985 (U.S.), essayist, children's book author. *Here is New York, Charlotte's Web, Stuart Little.*

T.H. White, 1906-1964, (Br.) author. *The Once and Future King.*

Walt Whitman, 1819-1892, (U.S.) poet. *Leaves of Grass.*

John Greenleaf Whittier, 1807-1892, (U.S.) poet, journalist. *Snow-bound.*

Oscar Wilde, 1854-1900, (Ir.) author, wit. *The Picture of Dorian Gray, The Importance of Being Earnest.*

Thornton Wilder, 1897-1975, (U.S.) playwright. *Our Town, The Skin of Our Teeth, The Matchmaker.*

Tennessee Williams, 1912-1983 (U.S.) playwright. *A Streetcar Named Desire, Cat on a Hot Tin Roof, The Glass Menagerie.*

William Carlos Williams, 1883-1963, (U.S.) poet, physician. *Tempers, Al Que Quiere!, Paterson.*

Edmund Wilson, 1895-1972, (U.S.) author, literary and social critic. *Axel's Castle, To the Finland Station.*

P.G. Wodehouse, 1881-1975, (U.S.) poet, dramatist. The "Jeeves" novels, *Anything Goes.*

Thomas Wolfe, 1900-1938, (U.S.) novelist. *Look Homeward, Angel, You Can't Go Home Again, Of Time and the River.*

Virginia Woolf, 1882-1941, (Br.) novelist, essayist. *Mrs. Dalloway, To the Lighthouse, The Waves.*

William Wordsworth, 1770-1850, (Br.) poet. "Tintern Abbey," "Ode: Intimations of Immortality."

William Butler Yeats, 1865-1939, (Ir.) poet, playwright. *The Wild Swans at Coole, The Tower, Last Poems.*

Émile Zola, 1840-1902, (F.) novelist. *Nana, The Dram Shop.*

Noted Artists and Sculptors of the Past

Artists are painters unless otherwise indicated.

Washington Allston, 1779-1843, (U.S.) landscapist. Belshazzar's Feast.

Albrecht Altdorfer, 1480-1538, (Ger.) landscapist. Battle of Alexander.

Andrea del Sarto, 1486-1530, frescoes. Madonna of the Harpies.

Fra Angelico, c. 1400-1455, (It.) Renaissance muralist. Madonna of the Linen Drapers' Guild.

Alexsandr Archipenko, 1887-1964, (U.S.) sculptor. Boxing Match, Medranos.

John James Audubon, 1785-1851, (U.S.) Birds of America.

Hans Baldung Grien, 1484-1545, (Ger.) Todentanz.

Ernst Barlach, 1870-1938, (Ger.) Expressionist sculptor. Man Drawing a Sword.

Frederic-Auguste Bartholdi, 1834-1904, (Fr.) Liberty Enlightening the World, Lion of Belfort.

Fra Bartolommeo, 1472-1517, (It.) Vision of St. Bernard.

Aubrey Beardsley, 1872-1898, (Br.) illustrator. Salome, Lysistrata.

Max Beckmann, 1884-1950, (Ger.) Expressionist. The Descent from the Cross.

Gentile Bellini, 1426-1507, (It.) Renaissance. Procession in St. Mark's Square.

Giovanni Bellini, 1428-1516, (It.) St. Francis in Ecstasy.

Jacopo Bellini, 1400-1470, (It.) Crucifixion.

George Wesley Bellows, 1882-1925, (U.S.) sports artist. Stag at Sharkey's.

Thomas Hart Benton, 1889-1975, (U.S.) American regionalist. Threshing Wheat, Arts of the West.

Gianlorenzo Bernini, 1598-1680, (It.) Baroque sculpture. The Assumption.

Albert Bierstadt, 1830-1902, (U.S.) landscapist. The Rocky Mountains, Mount Corcoran.

George Caleb Bingham, 1811-1879, (U.S.) Fur Traders Descending the Missouri.

William Blake, 1752-1827, (Br.) engraver. Book of Job, Songs of Innocence, Songs of Experience.

Rosa Bonheur, 1822-1899, (Fr.) The Horse Fair.

Pierre Bonnard, 1867-1947, (Fr.) Intimist. The Breakfast Room.

Gutzon Borglum, 1871-1941, (U.S.) sculptor. Mt. Rushmore Memorial.

Hieronymus Bosch, 1450-1516, (Flem.) religious allegories. The Crowning with Thorns.

Sandro Botticelli, 1444-1510, (It.) Renaissance. Birth of Venus.

Constantin Brancusi, 1876-1957, (Rum.) Nonobjective sculptor. Flying Turtle, The Kiss.

Georges Braque, 1882-1963, (Fr.) Cubist. Violin and Palette.

Pieter Bruegel the Elder, c. 1525-1569, (Flem.) The Peasant Dance.

Pieter Bruegel the Younger, 1564-1638, (Flem.) Village Fair, The Crucifixion.

Edward Burne-Jones, 1833-1898, (Br.) Pre-Raphaelite artist-craftsman. The Mirror of Venus.

Alexander Calder, 1898-1976, (U.S.) sculptor. Lobster Trap and Fish Tail.

Michelangelo Merisi da Caravaggio, 1573-1610, (It.) Baroque. The Supper at Emmaus.

Emily Carr, 1871-1945, (Can.) landscapist. Blunden Harbour, Big Raven.

Carlo Carra, 1881-1966, (It.) Metaphysical school. Lot's Daughters.

Mary Cassatt, 1845-1926, (U.S.) Impressionist. Woman Bathing.

George Catlin, 1796-1872, (U.S.) American Indian life. Gallery of Indians.

Benvenuto Cellini, 1500-1571, (It.) Mannerist sculptor, goldsmith. Perseus.

Paul Cezanne, 1839-1906, (Fr.) Card Players, Mont-Sainte-Victoire with Large Pine Trees.

Marc Chagall, 1898-1985, (Rus.) Jewish life and folklore. I and the Village.

Jean Simeon Chardin, 1699-1779, (Fr.) still lifes. The Kiss, The Grace.

Frederic Church, 1826-1900, (U.S.) Hudson River school. Niagara, Andes of Ecuador.

Giovanni Cimabue, 1240-1302, (It.) Byzantine mosaicist. Madonna Enthroned with St. Francis.

Claude Lorrain, 1600-1682, (Fr.) ideal-landscapist. The Enchanted Castle.

Thomas Cole, 1801-1848, (U.S.) Hudson River school. The Ox-Bow.

John Constable, 1776-1837, (Br.) landscapist. Salisbury Cathedral from the Bishop's Grounds.

John Singleton Copley, 1738-1815, (U.S.) portraitist. Samuel Adams, Watson and the Shark.

Lovis Corinth, 1858-1925, (Ger.) Expressionist. Apocalypse.

Jean-Baptiste-Camille Corot, 1796-1875, (Fr.) landscapist. Souvenir de Mortefontaine, Pastorale.

Correggio, 1494-1534, (It.) Renaissance muralist. Mystic Marriages of St. Catherine.

Gustave Courbet, 1819-1877, (Fr.) Realist. The Artist's Studio.

Lucas Cranach the Elder, 1472-1553, (Ger.) Protestant Reformation portraitist. Luther.

Nathaniel Currier, 1813-1888, and **James M. Ives,** 1824-1895, (both U.S.) lithographers. A Midnight Race on the Mississippi.

John Steuart Curry, 1897-1946, (U.S.) Americana, murals. Baptism in Kansas.

Honore Daumier, 1808-1879, (Fr.) caricaturist. The Third-Class Carriage.

Jacques-Louis David, 1748-1825, (Fr.) Neoclassicist. The Oath of the Horatii.

Arthur Davies, 1862-1928, (U.S.) Romantic landscapist. Unicorns.

Edgar Degas, 1834-1917, (Fr.) The Ballet Class.

Eugene Delacroix, Co. 1400-1455, (Fr.) Romantic. Massacre at Chios.

Paul Delaroche, 1797-1856, (Fr.) historical themes. Children of Edward IV.

Luca Della Robbia, 1400-1482, (It.) Renaissance terracotta artist. Cantoria (singing gallery), Florence cathedral.

Donatello, 1386-1466, (It.) Renaissance sculptor. David, Gattamelata.

Jean Dubuffet, 1902-1985, (Fr.) painter, sculpter, printmaker. Group of Four Trees.

Marcel Duchamp, 1887-1968, (Fr.) Nude Descending a Staircase.

Raoul Dufy, 1877-1953, (Fr.) Fauvist. Chateau and Horses.

Asher Brown Durand, 1796-1886, (U.S.) Hudson River school. Kindred Spirits.

Albrecht Durer, 1471-1528, (Ger.) Renaissance engraver, woodcuts. St. Jerome in His Study, Melancholia I, Apocalypse.

Anthony van Dyck, 1599-1641, (Flem.) Baroque portraitist. Portrait of Charles I Hunting.

Thomas Eakins, 1844-1916, (U.S.) Realist. The Gross Clinic.

Jacob Epstein, 1880-1959, (Br.) religious and allegorical sculptor. Genesis, Ecce Homo.

Jan van Eyck, 1380-1441, (Flem.) naturalistic panels. Adoration of the Lamb.
Anselm Feuerbach, 1829-1880, (Ger.) Romantic Classicism. Judgement of Paris, Iphigenia.
John Bernard Flannagan, 1895-1942, (U.S.) animal sculptor. Triumph of the Egg.
Jean-Honore Fragonard, 1732-1806, (Fr.) Rococo. The Swing.
Daniel Chester French, 1850-1931, (U.S.) The Minute Man of Concord; seated Lincoln, Lincoln Memorial, Washington, D.C.
Caspar David Friedrich, 1774-1840, (Ger.) Romantic landscapes. Man and Woman Gazing at the Moon.
Thomas Gainsborough, 1727-1788, (Br.) portraitist. The Blue Boy.
Paul Gauguin, 1848-1903, (Fr.) Post-impressionist. The Tahitians.
Lorenzo Ghiberti, 1378-1455, (It.) Renaissance sculptor. Gates of Paradise baptistry doors, Florence.
Alberto Giacometti, 1901-1966, (It.) attenuated sculptures of solitary figures. Man Pointing.
Giorgione, c. 1477-1510, (It.) Renaissance. The Tempest.
Giotto di Bondone, 1267-1337, (It.) Renaissance. Presentation of Christ in the Temple.
Francois Girardon, 1628-1715, (Fr.) Baroque sculptor of classical themes. Apollo Tended by the Nymphs.
Vincent van Gogh, 1853-1890, (Dutch) The Starry Night, L'Arlesienne.
Arshile Gorky, 1905-1948, (U.S.) Surrealist. The Liver Is the Cock's Comb.
Francisco de Goya y Lucientes, 1746-1828, (Sp.) The Naked Maja, The Disasters of War (etchings).
El Greco, 1541-1614, View of Toledo.
Horatio Greenough, 1805-1852, (U.S.) Neo-classical sculptor. George Washington.
Matthias Grünewald, 1480-1528, (Ger.) mystical religious themes. The Resurrection.
Frans Hals, c. 1580-1666, (Dutch) portraitist. Laughing Cavalier, Gypsy Girl.
Childe Hassam, 1859-1935, (U.S.) Impressionist. Southwest Wind.
Edward Hicks, 1780-1849, (U.S.) folk painter. The Peaceable Kingdom.
Hans Hofmann, 1880-1966, (U.S.) early Abstract Expressionist. Spring, The Gate.
William Hogarth, 1697-1764, (Br.) caricaturist. The Rake's Progress.
Katsushika Hokusai, 1760-1849, (Jap.) printmaker. Crabs.
Hans Holbein the Elder, 1460-1524, (Ger.) late Gothic. Presentation of Christ in the Temple.
Hans Holbein the Younger, 1497-1543, (Ger.) portraitist. Henry VIII.
Winslow Homer, 1836-1910, (U.S.) marine themes. Marine Coast, High Cliff.
Edward Hopper, 1882-1967, (U.S.) realistic urban scenes. Sunlight in a Cafeteria.
Jean-Auguste-Dominique Ingres, 1780-1867, (Fr.) Classicist. Valpincon Bather.
George Inness, 1825-1894, (U.S.) luminous landscapist. Delaware Water Gap.
Vasily Kandinsky, 1866-1944, (Rus.) Abstractionist. Capricious Forms.
Paul Klee, 1879-1940, (Swiss) Abstractionist. Twittering Machine.
Oscar Kokoschka, 1886-1980, (Aus.) Expressionist. View of Prague.
Kathe Kollwitz, 1867-1945, (Ger.) printmaker, social justice themes. The Peasant War.
Gaston Lachaise, 1882-1935, (U.S.) figurative sculptor. Standing Woman.
John La Farge, 1835-1910, (U.S.) muralist. Red and White Peonies.
Fernand Leger, 1881-1955, (Fr.) machine art. The Cyclists.
Leonardo da Vinci, 1452-1519, (It.) Mona Lisa, Last Supper, The Annunciation.
Emanuel Leutze, 1816-1868, (U.S.) historical themes. Washington Crossing the Delaware.
Jacques Lipchitz, 1891-1973, (Fr.) Cubist sculptor. Harpist.
Filippino Lippi, 1457-1504, (It.) Renaissance. The Vision of St. Bernard.
Fra Filippo Lippi, 1406-1469, (It.) Renaissance. Coronation of the Virgin.
Morris Louis, 1912-1962, (U.S.) Abstract Expressionist. Signa, Stripes.
Aristide Maillol, 1861-1944, (Fr.) sculptor. The Mediterranean.
Edouard Manet, 1832-1883, (Fr.) forerunner of Impressionism. Luncheon on the Grass, Olympia.
Andrea Mantegna, 1431-1506, (It.) Renaissance frescoes. Triumph of Caesar.
Franz Marc, 1880-1916, (Ger.) Expressionist. Blue Horses.
John Marin, 1870-1953, (U.S.) expressionist seascapes. Maine Island.
Reginald Marsh, 1898-1954, (U.S.) satirical artist. Tattoo and Haircut.
Masaccio, 1401-1428, (It.) Renaissance. The Tribute Money.
Henri Matisse, 1869-1954, (Fr.) Fauvist. Woman with the Hat.
Michelangelo Buonarroti, 1475-1564, (It.) Pieta, David, Moses, The Last Judgment, Sistine Ceiling.
Jean-Francois Millet, 1814-1875, (Fr.) painter of peasant subjects. The Gleaners, The Man with a Hoe.
Amedeo Modigliani, 1884-1920, (It.) Reclining Nude.
Piet Mondrian, 1872-1944, (Dutch) Abstractionist. Composition.
Claude Monet, 1840-1926, (Fr.) Impressionist. The Bridge at Argenteuil, Haystacks.
Henry Moore, 1898-1986, (Br.) sculptor of large-scale, abstract works. Reclining Figure (several).
Gustave Moreau, 1826-1898, (Fr.) Symbolist. The Apparition, Dance of Salome.
James Wilson Morrice, 1865-1924, (Can.) landscapist. The Ferry, Quebec, Venice, Looking Over the Lagoon.
Grandma Moses, 1860-1961, (U.S.) folk painter. Out for the Christmas Trees.
Edvard Munch, 1863-1944, (Nor.) Expressionist. The Cry.
Bartolome Murillo, 1618-1682, (Sp.) Baroque religious artist. Vision of St. Anthony. The Two Trinities.
Barnett Newman, 1905-1970, (U.S.) Abstract Expressionist. Stations of the Cross.
Georgia O'Keeffe, 1887-1986, (U.S.) Southwest motifs. Cow's Skull.
Jose Clemente Orozco, 1883-1949, (Mex.) frescoes. House of Tears.
Charles Willson Peale, 1741-1827, (U.S.) American Revolutionary portraitist. Washington, Franklin, Jefferson, John Adams.
Rembrandt Peale, 1778-1860, (U.S.) portraitist. Thomas Jefferson.
Pietro Perugino, 1446-1523, (It.) Renaissance. Delivery of the Keys to St. Peter.
Pablo Picasso, 1881-1973, (Sp.) Guernica, Dove, Head of a Woman.
Piero della Francesca, c. 1415-1492, (It.) Renaissance. Duke of Urbino, Flagellation of Christ.
Camille Pissarro, 1830-1903, (Fr.) Impressionist. Morning Sunlight.
Jackson Pollock, 1912-1956, (U.S.) Abstract Expressionist. Autumn Rhythm.
Nicolas Poussin, 1594-1665, (Fr.) Baroque pictorial classicism. St. John on Patmos.
Maurice B. Prendergast, c. 1860-1924, (U.S.) Post-impressionist water colorist. Umbrellas in the Rain.
Pierre-Paul Prud'hon, 1758-1823, (Fr.) Romanticist. Crime pursued by Vengeance and Justice.
Pierre Cecile Puvis de Chavannes, 1824-1898, (Fr.) muralist. The Poor Fisherman.
Raphael Sanzio, 1483-1520, (It.) Renaissance. Disputa, School of Athens, Sistine Madonna.
Man Ray, 1890-1976, (U.S.) Dadaist. Observing Time, The Lovers.
Odilon Redon, 1840-1916, (Fr.) Symbolist lithographer. In the Dream.
Rembrandt van Rijn, 1606-1669, (Dutch) The Bridal Couple, The Night Watch.
Frederic Remington, 1861-1909, (U.S.) painter, sculptor, portrayer of the American West. Bronco Buster.
Pierre-Auguste Renoir, 1841-1919, (Fr.) Impressionist. The Luncheon of the Boating Party.
Joshua Reynolds, 1723-1792, (Br.) portraitist. Mrs. Siddons as the Tragic Muse.
Diego Rivera, 1886-1957, (Mex.) frescoes. The Fecund Earth.
Norman Rockwell, 1894-1978, (U.S.) illustrator. Saturday Evening Post covers.
Auguste Rodin, 1840-1917, (Fr.) sculptor. The Thinker, The Burghers of Calais.
Mark Rothko, 1903-1970, (U.S.) Abstract Expressionist. Light, Earth and Blue.
Georges Rouault, 1871-1958, (Fr.) Expressionist. The Old King.
Henri Rousseau, 1844-1910, (Fr.) primitive exotic themes. The Snake Charmer.
Theodore Rousseau, 1812-1867, (Swiss-Fr.) landscapist. Under the Birches, Evening.
Peter Paul Rubens, 1577-1640, (Flem.) Baroque. Mystic Marriage of St. Catherine.
Jacob van Ruisdael, c. 1628-1682, (Dutch) landscapist. Jewish Cemetery.
Salomon van Ruysdael, c. 1600-1670, (Dutch) landscapist. River with Ferry-Boat.
Albert Pinkham Ryder, 1847-1917, (U.S.) seascapes and allegories. Toilers of the Sea.

Augustus Saint-Gaudens, 1848-1907, (U.S.) memorial statues. Farragut, Mrs. Henry Adams (Grief).

Andrea Sansovino, 1460-1529, (It.) Renaissance sculptor. Baptism of Christ.

Jacopo Sansovino, 1486-1570, (It.) Renaissance sculptor. St. John the Baptist.

John Singer Sargent, 1856-1925, (U.S.) Edwardian society portraitist. The Wyndham Sisters, Madam X.

Georges Seurat, 1859-1891, (Fr.) Pointillist. Sunday Afternoon on the Island of Grande Jatte.

Gino Severini, 1883-1966, (It.) Futurist and Cubist. Dynamic Hieroglyph of the Bal Tabarin.

Ben Shahn, 1898-1969, (U.S.) social and political themes. Sacco and Vanzetti series, Seurat's Lunch, Handball.

Charles Sheeler, 1883-1965, (U.S.) Abstractionist. Upper Deck.

David Alfaro Siqueiros, 1896-1974, (Mex.) political muralist. March of Humanity.

John F. Sloan, 1871-1951, (U.S.) depictions of New York City. Wake of the Ferry.

David Smith, 1906-1965, (U.S.) welded metal sculpture. Hudson River Landscape, Zig, Cubi series.

Gilbert Stuart, 1755-1828, (U.S.) portraitist. George Washington.

Thomas Sully, 1783-1872, (U.S.) portraitist. Col. Thomas Handasyd Perkins, The Passage of the Delaware.

Yves Tanguy, 1900-1955, (Fr.) Surrealist. Rose of the Four Winds.

Giovanni Battista Tiepolo, 1696-1770, (It.) Rococo frescoes. The Crucifixion.

Jacopo Tintoretto, 1518-1594, (It.) Mannerist. The Last Supper.

Titian, c. 1485-1576, (It.) Renaissance. Venus and the Lute Player, The Bacchanal.

Henri de Toulouse-Lautrec, 1864-1901, (Fr.) At the Moulin Rouge.

John Trumbull, 1756-1843, (U.S.) historical themes. The Declaration of Independence.

Joseph Mallord William Turner, 1775-1851, (Br.) Romantic landscapist. Snow Storm.

Paolo Uccello, 1397-1475, (It.) Gothic-Renaissance. The Rout of San Romano.

Maurice Utrillo, 1883-1955, (Fr.) Impressionist. Sacre-Coeur de Montmartre.

John Vanderlyn, 1775-1852, (U.S.) Neo-classicist. Ariadne Asleep on the Island of Naxos.

Diego Velazquez, 1599-1660, (Sp.) Baroque. Las Meninas, Portrait of Juan de Pareja.

Jan Vermeer, 1632-1675, (Dutch) interior genre subjects. Young Woman with a Water Jug.

Paolo Veronese, 1528-1588, (It.) devotional themes, vastly peopled canvases. The Temptation of St. Anthony.

Andrea del Verrocchio, 1435-1488, (It.) Florentine sculptor. Colleoni.

Maurice de Vlaminck, 1876-1958, (Fr.) Fauvist landscapist. The Storm.

Antoine Watteau, 1684-1721, (Fr.) Rococo painter of "scenes of gallantry". The Embarkation for Cythera.

George Frederic Watts, 1817-1904, (Br.) painter and sculptor of grandiose allegorical themes. Hope, Physical Energy.

Benjamin West, 1738-1820, realistic historical themes. Death of General Wolfe.

James Abbott McNeill Whistler, 1834-1903, (U.S.) Arrangement in Grey and Black, No. 1: The Artist's Mother.

Archibald M. Willard, 1836-1918, (U.S.) The Spirit of '76.

Grant Wood, 1891-1942, (U.S.) Midwestern regionalist. American Gothic, Daughters of Revolution.

Ossip Zadkine, 1890-1967, (Rus.) School of Paris sculptor. The Destroyed City, Musicians, Christ.

Noted Philosophers and Religionists of the Past

Lyman Abbott, 1835-1922, (U.S.) clergyman, reformer; advocate of Christian Socialism.

Pierre Abelard, 1079-1142, (F.) philosopher, theologian, and teacher, used dialectic method to support Christian dogma.

Felix Adler, 1851-1933, (U.S.) German-born founder of the Ethical Culture Society.

St. Augustine, 354-430, Latin bishop considered the founder of formalized Christian theology.

Averroes, 1126-1198, (Sp.) Islamic philosopher.

Roger Bacon, c.1214-1294, (Br.) philosopher and scientist.

Karl Barth, 1886-1968, (Sw.) theologian, a leading force in 20th-century Protestantism.

St. Benedict, c.480-547, (It.) founded the Benedictines.

Jeremy Bentham, 1748-1832, (Br.) philosopher, reformer, founder of Utilitarianism.

Henri Bergson, 1859-1941, (F.) philosopher of evolution.

George Berkeley, 1685-1753, (Ir.) philosopher, churchman.

John Biddle, 1615-1662, (Br.) founder of English Unitarianism.

Jakob Boehme, 1575-1624, (G.) theosophist and mystic.

William Brewster, 1567-1644, (Br.) headed Pilgrims, signed Mayflower Compact.

Emil Brunner, 1889-1966, (Sw.) theologian.

Giordano Bruno, 1548-1600, (It.) philosopher.

Martin Buber, 1878-1965, (G.) Jewish philosopher, theologian, wrote *I and Thou.*

Buddha (Siddhartha Gautama), c.563-c.483 BC, (Ind.) philosopher, founded Buddhism.

John Calvin, 1509-1564, (F.) theologian, a key figure in the Protestant Reformation.

Rudolph Carnap, 1891-1970, (U.S.) German-born philosopher, a founder of logical positivism.

William Ellery Channing, 1780-1842, (U.S.) clergyman, early spokesman for Unitarianism.

Auguste Comte, 1798-1857, (F.) philosopher, the founder of positivism.

Confucius, 551-479 BC, (Chin.) founder of Confucianism.

John Cotton, 1584-1652, (Br.) Puritan theologian.

Thomas Cranmer, 1489-1556, (Br.) churchman, wrote much of *Book of Common Prayer;* promoter of English Reformation.

René Descartes, 1596-1650, (F.) philosopher, mathematician.

John Dewey, 1859-1952, (U.S.) philosopher, educator; helped inaugurate the progressive education movement.

Denis Diderot, 1713-1784, (F.) philosopher, creator of first modern encyclopedia.

Mary Baker Eddy, 1821-1910, (U.S.) founder of Christian Science.

Jonathan Edwards, 1703-1758, (U.S.) preacher, theologian.

(Desiderius) Erasmus, c.1466-1536, (Du.) Renaissance humanist.

Johann Fichte, 1762-1814, (G.) philosopher, the first of the Transcendental Idealists.

George Fox, 1624-1691, (Br.) founder of Society of Friends.

St. Francis of Assisi, 1182-1226, (It.) founded Franciscans.

al Ghazali, 1058-1111, Islamic philosopher.

Georg W. Hegel, 1770-1831, (G.) Idealist philosopher.

Martin Heidegger, 1889-1976, (G.) existentialist philosopher, affected fields ranging from physics to literary criticism.

Johann G. Herder, 1744-1803, (G.) philosopher, cultural historian; a founder of German Romanticism.

David Hume, 1711-1776, (Sc.) philosopher, historian.

Jan Hus, 1369-1415, (Czech.) religious reformer.

Edmund Husserl, 1859-1938, (G.) philosopher, founded the Phenomenological movement.

Thomas Huxley, 1825-1895, (Br.) philosopher, educator.

Ignatius of Loyola, 1491-1556, (Sp.) founder of the Jesuits.

William Inge, 1860-1954, (Br.) theologian, explored the mystic aspects of Christianity.

William James, 1842-1910, (U.S.) philosopher, psychologist; advanced theory of the pragmatic nature of truth.

Karl Jaspers, 1883-1969, (G.) existentialist philosopher.

Immanuel Kant, 1724-1804, (G.) metaphysician, preeminent founder of modern critical philosophy.

Soren Kierkegaard, 1813-1855, (Den.) philosopher, considered the father of Existentialism.

John Knox, 1505-1572, (Sc.) leader of the Protestant Reformation in Scotland.

Lao-Tzu, 604-531 BC, (Chin.) philosopher, considered the founder of the Taoist religion.

Gottfried von Leibniz, 1646-1716, (G.) philosopher, mathematician.

Martin Luther, 1483-1546, (G.) leader of the Protestant Reformation, founded Lutheran church.

Maimonides, 1135-1204, (Sp.) Jewish philosopher.
Jacques Maritain, 1882-1973, (F.) Neo-Thomist philosopher.
Cotton Mather, 1663-1728, (U.S.) defender of orthodox Puritanism; founded Yale, 1703.
Philipp Melanchthon, 1497-1560, (G.) theologian, humanist; an important voice in the Reformation.
Mohammed, c.570-632, Arab prophet of the religion of Islam.
Dwight Moody, 1837-1899, (U.S.) evangelist.
George E. Moore, 1873-1958, (Br.) ethical theorist.
Elijah Muhammad, 1897-1975, (U.S.) leader of the Black Muslim sect.
Heinrich Muhlenberg, 1711-1787, (G.) organized the Lutheran Church in America.
John H. Newman, 1801-1890, (Br.) Roman Catholic cardinal, led Oxford Movement.
Reinhold Niebuhr, 1892-1971, (U.S.) Protestant theologian, social and political critic.
Friedrich Nietzsche, 1844-1900, (G.) moral philosopher.
Blaise Pascal, 1623-1662, (F.) philosopher and mathematician.
St. Patrick, c.389-c.461, brought Christianity to Ireland.
St. Paul, ?-c.67, a founder of the Christian religion.
Charles S. Peirce, 1839-1914, (U.S.) philosopher, logician; originated concept of Pragmatism, 1878.
Josiah Royce 1855-1916, (U.S.) Idealist philosopher.
Charles T. Russell, 1852-1916, (U.S.) founder of Jehovah's Witnesses.
Fredrich von Schelling, 1775-1854, (G.) philosopher.
Friedrich Schleiermacher, 1768-1834, (G.) theologian, a founder of modern Protestant theology.
Arthur Schopenhauer, 1788-1860, (G.) philosopher.
Joseph Smith, 1805-1844, (U.S.) founded Latter Day Saints (Mormon) movement, 1830.
Herbert Spencer, 1820-1903, (Br.) philosopher of evolution.
Baruch Spinoza, 1632-1677, (Du.) rationalist philosopher.
Billy Sunday, 1862-1935, (U.S.) evangelist.
Daisetz Teitaro Suzuki, 1870-1966, (Jap.) Buddhist scholar.
Emanuel Swedenborg, 1688-1722, (Swed.) philosopher, mystic.
Thomas à Becket, 1118-1170, (Br.) archbishop of Canterbury, opposed Henry II.
Thomas à Kempis, c.1380-1471, (G.) theologian probably wrote *Imitation of Christ.*
Thomas Aquinas, 1225-1274, (It.) theologian, philosopher.
Paul Tillich, 1886-1965, (U.S.) German-born philosopher and theologian.
John Wesley, 1703-1791, (Br.) theologian, evangelist; founded Methodism.
Alfred North Whitehead, 1861-1947, (Br.) philosopher, mathematician.
William of Occam, c.1285-c.1349 (Br.) philosopher.
Roger Williams, c.1603-1683, (U.S.) clergyman, championed religious freedom and separation of church and state.
Ludwig Wittgenstein, 1889-1951, (Aus.) philosopher.
John Wycliffe, 1320-1384, (Br.) theologian, reformer.
Brigham Young, 1801-1877, (U.S.) Mormon leader, colonized Utah.
Huldrych Zwingli, 1484-1531, (Sw.) theologian, led Swiss Protestant Reformation.

Noted Social Reformers and Educators of the Past

Jane Addams, 1860-1935, (U.S.) co-founder of Hull House; won Nobel Peace Prize, 1931.
Susan B. Anthony, 1820-1906, (U.S.) a leader in temperance, anti-slavery, and women's suffrage movements.
Henry Barnard, 1811-1900, (U.S.) public school reformer.
Thomas Barnardo, 1845-1905, (Br.) social reformer, pioneered in the care of destitute children.
Clara Barton, 1821-1912, (U.S.) organizer of the American Red Cross.
Henry Ward Beecher, 1813-1887, (U.S.) clergyman, abolitionist.
Sarah G. Blanding, 1899-1985, (U.S.), head of Vassar College, 1946-64.
Amelia Bloomer, 1818-1894, (U.S.) social reformer, women's rights advocate.
William Booth, 1829-1912, (Br.) founded the Salvation Army.
Nicholas Murray Butler, 1862-1947, (U.S.) educator headed Columbia Univ., 1902-45; won Nobel Peace Prize, 1931.
Frances X. (Mother) Cabrini, 1850-1917, (U.S.) Italian-born nun founded charitable institutions; first American canonized.
Carrie Chapman Catt, 1859-1947, (U.S.) suffragette, helped win passage of the 19th amendment.
Dorothy Day, 1897-1980, (U.S.) founder of Catholic Worker Movement.
Eugene V. Debs, 1855-1926, (U.S.) labor leader, led Pullman strike, 1894; 4-time Socialist presidential candidate.
Melvil Dewey, 1851-1931, (U.S.) devised decimal system of library-book classification.
Dorothea Dix, 1802-1887, (U.S.) crusader for humane care of mentally ill.
Frederick Douglass, 1817-1895, (U.S.) abolitionist.
W.E.B. DuBois, 1868-1963, (U.S.) Negro-rights leader, educator, and writer.
William Lloyd Garrison, 1805-1879, (U.S.) abolitionist, reformer.
Giovanni Gentile, 1875-1944, (It.) philosopher, educator; reformed Italian educational system.
Samuel Gompers, 1850-1924, (U.S.) labor leader; a founder and president of AFL.
William Green, 1873-1952, (U.S.) president of AFL, 1924-52.
Sidney Hillman, 1887-1946, (U.S.) labor leader, helped organize CIO.
John Holt, 1924-1986, (U.S.) educator and author, *How Children Fail.*
Samuel G. Howe, 1801-1876, (U.S.) social reformer, changed public attitudes toward the handicapped.
Helen Keller, 1880-1968, (U.S.) crusader for better treatment for the handicapped.
Martin Luther King Jr., 1929-1968, (U.S.) civil rights leader; won Nobel Peace Prize, 1964.
John L. Lewis, 1880-1969, (U.S.) labor leader, headed United Mine Workers, 1920-60.
Horace Mann, 1796-1859, (U.S.) pioneered modern public school system.
William H. McGuffey, 1800-1873, (U.S.) author of *Reader,* the mainstay of 19th century U.S. public education.
Alexander Meiklejohn, 1872-1964, (U.S.) British-born educator, championed academic freedom and experimental curricula.
Lucretia Mott, 1793-1880, (U.S.) reformer, pioneer feminist.
Philip Murray, 1886-1952, (U.S.) Scotch-born labor leader.
Florence Nightingale, 1820-1910, (Br.) founder of modern nursing.
Emmeline Pankhurst, 1858-1928, (Br.) woman suffragist.
Elizabeth P. Peabody, 1804-1894, (U.S.) education pioneer, founded 1st kindergarten in U.S., 1860.
Walter Reuther, 1907-1970, (U.S.) labor leader, headed UAW.
Jacob Riis, 1849-1914, (U.S.) crusader for urban reforms.
Margaret Sanger, 1883-1966, (U.S.) social reformer, pioneered the birth control movement.
Elizabeth Seton, 1774-1821, (U.S.) established parochial school education in U.S.
Earl of Shaftesbury (A.A. Cooper), 1801-1885, (Br.) social reformer.
Elizabeth Cady Stanton, 1815-1902, (U.S.) women's suffrage pioneer.
Lucy Stone, 1818-1893, (U.S.) feminist, abolitionist.
Harriet Tubman, c.1820-1913, (U.S.) abolitionist, ran Underground Railroad.
Booker T. Washington, 1856-1915, (U.S.) educator, reformer; championed vocational training for blacks.
Walter F. White, 1893-1955, (U.S.) headed NAACP, 1931-55.
William Wilberforce, 1759-1833, (Br.) social reformer, prominent in struggle to abolish the slave trade.
Emma Hart Willard, 1787-1870, (U.S.) pioneered higher education for women.
Frances E. Willard, 1839-1898, (U.S.) temperance, woman's rights leader.
Whitney M. Young Jr., 1921-1971, (U.S.) civil rights leader, headed National Urban League, 1961-71.

Noted Historians, Economists, and Social Scientists of the Past

Brooks Adams, 1848-1927, (U.S.) historian, political theoretician.
Francis Bacon, 1561-1626, (Br.) philosopher, essayist, and statesman.
George Bancroft, 1800-1891, (U.S.) historian, wrote 10-volume *History of the United States.*
Charles A. Beard, 1874-1948, (U.S.) historian, attacked motives of the Founding Fathers.
Bede (the Venerable), c.673-735, (Br.) scholar, historian.
Ruth Benedict, 1887-1948, (U.S.) anthropologist, studied Indian tribes of the Southwest.

Louis Blanc, 1811-1882, (F.) Socialist leader and historian whose ideas were a link between utopian and Marxist socialism.
Leonard Bloomfield, 1887-1949, (U.S.) linguist. *Language.*
Franz Boas, 1858-1942, (U.S.) German-born anthropologist, studied American Indians.
Van Wyck Brooks, 1886-1963, (U.S.) cultural historian, critic.
Edmund Burke, 1729-1797, (Ir.) British parliamentarian and political philosopher; influenced many Federalists.
Thomas Carlyle, 1795-1881, (Sc.) philosopher, historian, and critic.
Edward Channing, 1856-1931, (U.S.) historian wrote 6-volume *A History of the United States.*
John R. Commons, 1862-1945, (U.S.) economist, labor historian.
Benedetto Croce, 1866-1952, (It.) philosopher, statesman, and historian.
Bernard A. De Voto, 1897-1955, (U.S.) historian, won Pulitzer prize in 1948 for *Across the Wide Missouri.*
Ariel Durant, 1898-1981, (U.S.) historian, collaborated with husband on 11-volume *The Story of Civilization.*
Will Durant, 1885-1981, (U.S.) historian. *The Story of Civilization, The Story of Philosophy.*
Emile Durkheim, 1858-1917, (F.) a founder of modern sociology.
Friedrich Engels, 1820-1895, (G.) political writer, with Marx wrote the *Communist Manifesto.*
Irving Fisher, 1867-1947, (U.S.) economist, contributed to the development of modern monetary theory.
John Fiske, 1842-1901, (U.S.) historian and lecturer, popularized Darwinian theory of evolution.
Charles Fourier, 1772-1837, (F.) utopian socialist.
Henry George, 1839-1897, (U.S.) economist, reformer, led single-tax movement.
Edward Gibbon, 1737-1794, (Br.) historian, wrote *The History of the Decline and Fall of the Roman Empire.*
Francesco Guicciardini, 1483-1540, (It.) historian, wrote *Storia d'Italia,* principal historical work of the 16th-century.
Alvin Hansen, 1887-1975, (U.S.) economist.
Thomas Hobbes, 1588-1679, (Br.) social philosopher.
Richard Hofstadter, 1916-1970, (U.S.) historian, wrote *The Age of Reform.*
John Maynard Keynes, 1883-1946, (Br.) economist, principal advocate of deficit spending.
Alfred L. Kroeber, 1876-1960, (U.S.) cultural anthropologist, studied Indians of North and South America.
James L. Laughlin, 1850-1933, (U.S.) economist, helped establish Federal Reserve System.
Lucien Lévy-Bruhl, 1857-1939, (F.) philosopher, studied the psychology of primitive societies.
Kurt Lewin, 1890-1947, (U.S.) German-born psychologist, studied human motivation and group dynamics.
John Locke, 1632-1704, (Br.) political philosopher.
Thomas B. Macaulay, 1800-1859, (Br.) historian, statesman.
Bronislaw Malinowski, 1884-1942, (Pol.) anthropologist, considered the father of social anthropology.
Thomas R. Malthus, 1766-1834, (Br.) economist, famed for *Essay on the Principle of Population.*
Karl Mannheim, 1893-1947, (Hung.) sociologist, historian.
Karl Marx, 1818-1883, (G.) political philosopher, proponent of modern communism.
Giuseppe Mazzini, 1805-1872, (It.) political philosopher.
George H. Mead, 1863-1931, (U.S.) philosopher and social psychologist.
Margaret Mead, 1901-1978, (U.S.) cultural anthropologist, popularized field.
James Mill, 1773-1836, (Sc.) philosopher, historian, and economist; a proponent of Utilitarianism.
John Stuart Mill, 1806-1873, (Br.) philosopher, political economist.
Perry G. Miller, 1905-1963, (U.S.) historian, interpreted 17th-century New England.
Theodor Mommsen, 1817-1903, (G.) historian, wrote *The History of Rome.*
Charles-Louis Montesquieu, 1689-1755, (F.) social philosopher.
Samuel Eliot Morison, 1887-1976, (U.S.) historian, chronicled voyages of early explorers.
Gunnar Myrdal, 1899-1987 (Swe.) economist, social scientist; *An American Dilemna* helped destroy the "separate but equal" U.S. racial policy.
Allan Nevins, 1890-1971, (U.S.) historian, biographer; twice won Pulitzer prize.
Jose Ortega y Gasset, 1883-1955, (Sp.) philosopher and humanist; advocated control by an elite.
Robert Owen, 1771-1858, (Br.) political philosopher, reformer.
Vilfredo Pareto, 1848-1923, (It.) economist, sociologist.
Francis Parkman, 1823-1893, (U.S.) historian, wrote 8-volume *France and England in North America, 1851-92.*
Marco Polo, c.1254-1324, (It.) narrated an account of his travels to China.
William Prescott, 1796-1859, (U.S.) early American historian.
Pierre Joseph Proudhon, 1809-1865, (F.) social theorist, regarded as the father of anarchism.
Francois Quesnay, 1694-1774, (F.) economic theorist, demonstrated circular flow of economic activity through society.
David Ricardo, 1772-1823, (Br.) economic theorist, advocated free international trade.
James H. Robinson, 1863-1936, (U.S.) historian, educator.
Carl Rogers, 1902-1987, (U.S.) psychotherapist, author.
Jean-Jacques Rousseau, 1712-1778, (F.) social philosopher, author.
Edward Sapir, 1884-1939 (Ger.-U.S.) anthropologist, studied ethnology and linguistics of some U.S. Indian groups.
Ferdinand de Saussure, 1857-1913, (Swiss) a founder of modern lingustics.
Hjalmar Schacht, 1877-1970, (G.) economist.
Joseph Schumpeter, 1883-1950, (U.S.) Czech.-born economist, championed big business, capitalism.
Albert Schweitzer, 1875-1965, (Alsatian) social philosopher, theologian, and humanitarian.
George Simmel, 1858-1918, (G.) sociologist, philosopher.
Adam Smith, 1723-1790, (Br.) economist, advocated laissez faire economy and free trade.
Jared Sparks, 1789-1866, (U.S.) historian, among first to do research from original documents.
Oswald Spengler, 1880-1936, (G.) philosopher and historian, wrote *The Decline of the West.*
William G. Sumner, 1840-1910, (U.S.) social scientist, economist; championed laissez-faire economy, Social Darwinism.
Hippolyte Taine, 1828-1893, (F.) historian.
Frank W. Taussig, 1859-1940, (U.S.) economist, educator.
Alexis de Tocqueville, 1805-1859, (F.) political scientist, historian.
Francis E. Townsend, 1867-1960, (U.S.) author of old age pension plan.
Arnold Toynbee, 1889-1975, (Br.) historian, wrote 10-volume *A Study of History.*
Heinrich von Treitschke, 1834-1896, (G.) historian, political writer.
George Trevelyan, 1838-1928, (Br.) historian, statesman.
Frederick J. Turner, 1861-1932, (U.S.) historian, educator.
Thorstein B. Veblen, 1857-1929, (U.S.) economist, social philosopher.
Giovanni Vico, 1668-1744, (It.) historian, philosopher.
Voltaire (F.M. Arouet), 1694-1778, (F.) philosopher, historian, and poet.
Izaak Walton, 1593-1683, (Br.) author, wrote first biographical works in English literature.
Sidney J., 1859-1947, and wife **Beatrice,** 1858-1943, **Webb** (Br.) leading figures in Fabian Society and British Labour Party.
Walter P. Webb, 1888-1963, (U.S.) historian of the West.
Max Weber, 1864-1920, (G.) sociologist. *The Protestant Ethic and the Spirit of Capitalism.*

Noted Scientists of the Past

Howard H. Aiken, 1900-1973, (U.S.) mathematician, credited with designing forerunner of digital computer.
Albertus Magnus, 1193-1280, (G.) theologian, philosopher, scientist, established medieval Christian study of natural science.
Andre-Marie Ampère, 1775-1836, (F.) scientist known for contributions to electrodynamics.
Amedeo Avogadro, 1776-1856, (It.) chemist, physicist, advanced important theories on properties of gases.
A.C. Becquerel, 1788-1878, (F.) physicist, pioneer in electrochemical science.
A.H. Becquerel, 1852-1908, (F.) physicist, discovered radioactivity in uranium.
Alexander Graham Bell, 1847-1922, (U.S.) inventor, first to patent and commercially exploit the telephone, 1876.
Daniel Bernoulli, 1700-1782, (Swiss) mathematician, advanced kinetic theory of gases and fluids.
Jöns Jakob Berzelius, 1779-1848, (Swed.) chemist, developed modern chemical symbols and formulas.
Henry Bessemer, 1813-1898, (Br.) engineer, invented Bessemer steel-making process.
Louis Blériot, 1872-1936, (F.) engineer, pioneer aviator, invented and constructed monoplanes.
Niels Bohr, 1885-1962, (Dan.) physicist, leading figure in the development of quantum theory.
Max Born, 1882-1970, (G.) physicist known for research in quantum mechanics.

Satyendranath Bose, 1894-1974, (In.) physicist, chemist, mathematician known for Bose statistics, forerunner of modern quantum theory.

Robert Bunsen, 1811-1899, (G.) chemist, invented Bunsen burner.

Luther Burbank, 1849-1926, (U.S.) plant breeder whose work developed plant breeding into a modern science.

Vannevar Bush, 1890-1974, (U.S.) electrical engineer, developed differential analyzer, first electronic analogue computer.

Alexis Carrel, 1873-1944, (F.) surgeon, biologist, developed methods of suturing blood vessels and transplanting organs.

George Washington Carver, 1860?-1943, (U.S.) agricultural chemist, experimenter, benefactor of South, a black hero.

Henry Cavendish, 1731-1810, (Br.) chemist, physicist, discovered hydrogen.

James Chadwick, 1891-1974, (Br.) physicist, discovered the neutron.

Jean M. Charcot, 1825-1893, (F.) neurologist known for work on hysteria, hypnotism, sclerosis.

Albert Claude, 1899-1983, (Belg.) a founder of modern cell biology.

John D. Cockcroft, 1897-1967, (Br.) nuclear physicist, constructed first atomic particle accelerator with E.T.S. Walton.

William Crookes, 1832-1919, (Br.) physicist, chemist, discovered thallium, invented a cathode-ray tube, radiometer.

Marie Curie, 1867-1934, (Pol.-F.) physical chemist known for work on radium and its compounds.

Pierre Curie, 1859-1906, (F.) physical chemist known for work with his wife on radioactivity.

Gottlieb Daimler, 1834-1900, (G.) engineer, inventor, pioneer automobile manufacturer.

John Dalton, 1766-1844, (Br.) chemist, physicist, formulated atomic theory, made first table of atomic weights.

Charles Darwin, 1809-1882, (Br.) naturalist, established theory of organic evolution.

Humphry Davy, 1778-1829, (Br.) chemist, research in electrochemistry led to isolation of potassium, sodium, calcium, barium, boron, magnesium, and strontium.

Lee De Forest, 1873-1961, (U.S.) inventor, pioneer in development of wireless telegraphy, sound pictures, television.

Max Delbruck, 1907-1981, (U.S.) pioneer in modern molecular genetics.

Rudolf Diesel, 1858-1913, (G.) mechanical engineer, patented Diesel engine.

Thomas Dooley, 1927-1961, (U.S.) "jungle doctor," noted for efforts to supply medical aid to underdeveloped countries.

Christian Doppler, 1803-1853, (Aus.) physicist, demonstrated Doppler effect (change in energy wavelengths caused by motion).

Thomas A. Edison, 1847-1931, (U.S.) inventor, held over 1,000 patents, including incandescent electric lamp, phonograph.

Paul Ehrlich, 1854-1915, (G.) bacteriologist, pioneer in modern immunology and bacteriology.

Albert Einstein, 1879-1955, (Ger.-U.S.) theoretical physicist, known for formulation of relativity theory.

John F. Enders, 1898-1986, (U.S.) virologist who helped discover vaccines against polio, measles, and mumps.

Leonhard Euler, 1707-1783, (Swiss), mathematician, physicist, authored first calculus book.

Gabriel Fahrenheit, 1686-1736, (G.) physicist, introduced Fahrenheit scale for thermometers.

Michael Faraday, 1791-1867, (Br.) chemist, physicist, known for work in field of electricity.

Pierre de Fermat, 1601-1665, (F.) mathematician, discovered analytic geometry, founded modern theory of numbers and calculus of probabilities.

Enrico Fermi, 1901-1954, (It.) physicist, one of chief architects of the nuclear age.

Galileo Ferraris, 1847-1897, (It.) physicist, electrical engineer, discovered principle of rotary magnetic field.

Camille Flammarion, 1842-1925, (F.) astronomer, popularized study of astronomy.

Alexander Fleming, 1881-1955, (Br.) bacteriologist, discovered penicillin.

Jean B.J. Fourier, 1768-1830, (F.) mathematician, discovered theorem governing periodic oscillation.

James Franck, 1882-1964, (G.) physicist, proved value of quantum theory.

Sigmund Freud, 1856-1939, (Aus.) psychiatrist, founder of psychoanalysis.

Galileo Galilei, 1564-1642, (It.) astronomer, physicist, a founder of the experimental method.

Luigi Galvani, 1737-1798, (It.) physician, physicist, known as founder of galvanism.

Carl Friedrich Gauss, 1777-1855, (G.) mathematician, astronomer, physicist, made important contributions to almost every field of physical science, founded a number of new fields.

Joseph Gay-Lussac, 1778-1850, (F.) chemist, physicist, investigated behavior of gases, discovered law of combining volumes.

Josiah W. Gibbs, 1839-1903, (U.S.) theoretical physicist, chemist, founded chemical thermodynamics.

Robert H. Goddard, 1882-1945 (U.S.) physicist, father of modern rocketry.

George W. Goethals, 1858-1928, (U.S.) army engineer, built the Panama Canal.

William C. Gorgas, 1854-1920, (U.S.) sanitarian, U.S. army surgeon-general, his work to prevent yellow fever, malaria helped insure construction of Panama Canal.

Ernest Haeckel, 1834-1919, (G.) zoologist, evolutionist, a strong proponent of Darwin.

Otto Hahn, 1879-1968, (G.) chemist, worked on atomic fission.

J.B.S. Haldane, 1892-1964, (Sc.) scientist, known for work as geneticist and application of mathematics to science.

James Hall, 1761-1832, (Br.) geologist, chemist, founded experimental geology, geochemistry.

Edmund Halley, 1656-1742, (Br.) astronomer, calculated the orbits of many planets.

William Harvey, 1578-1657, (Br.) physician, anatomist, discovered circulation of the blood.

Hermann v. Helmholtz, 1821-1894, (G.) physicist, anatomist, physiologist, made fundamental contributions to physiology, optics, electrodynamics, mathematics, meteorology.

William Herschel, 1738-1822, (Br.) astronomer, discovered Uranus.

Heinrich Hertz, 1857-1894, (G.) physicist, his discoveries led to wireless telegraphy.

David Hilbert, 1862-1943, (G.) mathematician, formulated first satisfactory set of axioms for modern Euclidean geometry.

Edwin P. Hubble, 1889-1953, (U.S.) astronomer, produced first observational evidence of expanding universe.

Alexander v. Humboldt, 1769-1859, (G.) explorer, naturalist, propagator of earth sciences, originated ecology, geophysics.

Julian Huxley, 1887-1975, (Br.) biologist, a gifted exponent and philosopher of science.

Edward Jenner, 1749-1823, (Br.) physician, discovered vaccination.

William Jenner, 1815-1898, (Br.) physician, pathological anatomist.

Frederic Joliot-Curie, 1900-1958, (F.) physicist, with his wife continued work of Curies on radioactivity.

Irene Joliot-Curie, 1897-1956, (F.) physicist, continued work of Curies in radioactivity.

James P. Joule, 1818-1889, (Br.) physicist, determined relationship between heat and mechanical energy (conservation of energy).

Carl Jung, 1875-1961, (Sw.) psychiatrist, founder of analytical psychology.

Wm. Thomson Kelvin, 1824-1907, (Br.) mathematician, physicist, known for work on heat and electricity.

Sister Elizabeth Kenny, 1886-1952, (Austral.) nurse, developed method of treatment for polio.

Johannes Kepler, 1571-1630, (G.) astronomer, discovered important laws of planetary motion.

Joseph Lagrange, 1736-1813, (F.) geometer, astronomer, worked in all fields of analysis, and number theory, and analytical and celestial mechanics.

Jean B. Lamarck, 1744-1829, (F.) naturalist, forerunner of Darwin in evolutionary theory.

Irving Langmuir, 1881-1957, (U.S.) physical chemist, his studies of molecular films on solid and liquid surfaces opened new fields in colloid research and biochemistry.

Pierre S. Laplace, 1749-1827, (F.) astronomer, physicist, put forth nebular hypothesis of origin of solar system.

Antoine Lavoisier, 1743-1794, (F.) chemist, founder of modern chemistry.

Ernest O. Lawrence, 1901-1958, (U.S.) physicist, invented the cyclotron.

Louis Leakey, 1903-1972, (Br.) anthropologist, discovered important fossils, remains of early hominids.

Anton van Leeuwenhoek, 1632-1723, (Du.) microscopist, father of microbiology.

Gottfried Wilhelm Leibniz, 1646-1716, (G.) mathematician, developed theories of differential and integral calculus.

Justus von Liebig, 1803-1873, (G.) chemist, established quantitative organic chemical analysis.

Joseph Lister, 1827-1912, (Br.) pioneer of antiseptic surgery.

Percival Lowell, 1855-1916, (U.S.) astronomer, predicted the existence of Pluto.

Guglielmo Marconi, 1874-1937, (It.) physicist, known for his development of wireless telegraphy.

James Clerk Maxwell, 1831-1879, (Sc.) physicist, known especially for his work in electricity and magnetism.

Maria Goeppert Mayer, 1906-1972, (G.-U.S.) physicist, independently developed theory of structure of atomic nuclei.
Lise Meitner, 1878-1968, (Aus.) physicist whose work contributed to the development of the atomic bomb.
Gregor J. Mendel, 1822-1884, (Aus.) botanist, known for his experimental work on heredity.
Franz Mesmer, 1734-1815, (G.) physician, developed theory of animal magnetism.
Albert A. Michelson, 1852-1931, (U.S.) physicist, established speed of light as a fundamental constant.
Robert A. Millikan, 1868-1953, (U.S.) physicist, noted for study of elementary electronic charge and photoelectric effect.
Thomas Hunt Morgan, 1866-1945, (U.S.) geneticist, embryologist, established chromosome theory of heredity.
Isaac Newton, 1642-1727, (Br.) natural philosopher, mathematician, discovered law of gravitation, laws of motion.
J. Robert Oppenheimer, 1904-1967, (U.S.) physicist, director of Los Alamos during development of the atomic bomb.
Wilhelm Ostwald, 1853-1932, (G.) physical chemist, philosopher, chief founder of physical chemistry.
Louis Pasteur, 1822-1895, (F.) chemist, originated process of pasteurization.
Max Planck, 1858-1947, (G.) physicist, originated and developed quantum theory.
Henri Poincaré, 1854-1912, (F.) mathematician, physicist, influenced cosmology, relativity, and topology.
Joseph Priestley, 1733-1804, (Br.) chemist, one of the discoverers of oxygen.
Walter S. Reed, 1851-1902, (U.S.) army pathologist, bacteriologist, proved mosquitos transmit yellow fever.
Bernhard Riemann, 1826-1866, (G.) mathematician, contributed to development of calculus, complex variable theory, and mathematical physics.
Wilhelm Roentgen, 1845-1923, (G.) physicist, discovered X-rays.
Bertrand Russell, 1872-1970, (Br.) logician, philosopher, one of the founders of modern logic, wrote *Principia Mathematica*.
Ernest Rutherford, 1871-1937, (Br.) physicist, discovered the atomic nucleus.
Giovanni Schiaparelli, 1835-1910, (It.) astronomer, hypothesized canals on the surface of Mars.
Angelo Secchi, 1818-1878, (It.) astronomer, pioneer in classifying stars by their spectra.
Harlow Shapley, 1885-1972, (U.S.) astronomer, noted for his studies of the galaxy.
Charles P. Steinmetz, 1865-1923, (G.-U.S.) electrical engineer, developed basic ideas on alternating current systems.
Leo Szilard, 1898-1964, (Hung.-U.S.) physicist, helped create first sustained nuclear reaction.
Nikola Tesla, 1856-1943, (Croatia-U.S.) electrical engineer, contributed to most developments in electronics.
Rudolf Virchow, 1821-1902, (G.) pathologist, a founder of cellular pathology.
Alessandro Volta, 1745-1827, (It.) physicist, pioneer in electricity.
Alfred Russell Wallace, 1823-1913, (Br.) naturalist, proposed concept of evolution similar to Darwin.
August v. Wasserman, 1866-1925, (G.) bacteriologist, discovered reaction used as test for syphilis.
James E. Watt, 1736-1819, (Sc.) mechanical engineer, inventor, invented modern steam condensing engine.
Alfred L. Wegener, 1880-1930, (G.) meteorologist, geophysicist, postulated theory of continental drift.
Norbert Wiener, 1894-1964, (U.S.) mathematician, founder of the science of cybernetics.
Ferdinand v. Zeppelin, 1838-1917 (G.) soldier, aeronaut, airship designer.

Noted Business Leaders, Industrialists, and Philanthropists of the Past

Elizabeth Arden (F.N. Graham), 1884-1966, (U.S.) Canadian-born businesswoman founded and headed cosmetics empire.
Philip D. Armour, 1832-1901, (U.S.) industrialist, streamlined meat packing.
John Jacob Astor, 1763-1848, (U.S.) German-born fur trader, banker, real estate magnate; at death, richest in U.S.
Francis W. Ayer, 1848-1923, (U.S.) ad industry pioneer.
August Belmont, 1816-1890, (U.S.) German-born financier.
James B. (Diamond Jim) Brady, 1856-1917, (U.S.) financier, philanthropist, legendary bon vivant.
Adolphus Busch, 1839-1913, (U.S.) German-born businessman, established brewery empire.
Asa Candler, 1851-1929, (U.S.) founded Coca-Cola Co.
Andrew Carnegie, 1835-1919, (U.S.) Scots-born industrialist, founded U.S. Steel; financed over 2,800 libraries.
William Colgate, 1783-1857, (U.S.) British-born businessman, philanthropist; founded soap-making empire.
Jay Cooke, 1821-1905, (U.S.) financier, sold $1 billion in Union bonds during Civil War.
Peter Cooper, 1791-1883, (U.S.) industrialist, inventor, philanthropist.
Ezra Cornell, 1807-1874, (U.S.) businessman, philanthropist; headed Western Union, established univ.
Erastus Corning, 1794-1872, (U.S.) financier, headed N.Y. Central.
Charles Crocker, 1822-1888, (U.S.) railroad builder, financier.
Samuel Cunard, 1787-1865, (Can.) pioneered trans-Atlantic steam navigation.
Marcus Daly, 1841-1900, (U.S.) Irish-born copper magnate.
Walt Disney, 1901-1966, (U.S.) pioneer in cinema animation, built entertainment empire.
Herbert H. Dow, 1866-1930, (U.S.) Canadian-born founder of chemical co.
James Duke, 1856-1925, (U.S.) founded American Tobacco, Duke Univ.
Eleuthere I. du Pont, 1771-1834, (U.S.) French-born gunpowder manufacturer; founded one of world's largest business empires.
Thomas C. Durant, 1820-1885, (U.S.) railroad official, financier.
William C. Durant, 1861-1947, (U.S.) industrialist, formed General Motors.
George Eastman, 1854-1932, (U.S.) inventor, manufacturer of photographic equipment.
Marshall Field, 1834-1906, (U.S.) merchant, founded Chicago's largest department store.
Harvey Firestone, 1868-1938, (U.S.) industrialist, founded tire co.
Henry M. Flagler, 1830-1913, (U.S.) financier, helped form Standard Oil; developed Florida as resort state.
Henry Ford, 1863-1947, (U.S.) auto maker, developed first popular low-priced car.
Henry C. Frick, 1849-1919, (U.S.) industrialist, helped organize U.S. Steel.
Jakob Fugger (Jakob the Rich), 1459-1525, (G.) headed leading banking house, trading concern, in 16th-century Europe.
Alfred C. Fuller, 1885-1973, (U.S.) Canadian-born businessman, founded brush co.
Elbert H. Gary, 1846-1927, (U.S.) U.S. Steel head, 1903-27.
Amadeo P. Giannini, 1870-1949, (U.S.) founded Bank of America.
Stephen Girard, 1750-1831, (U.S.) French-born financier, philanthropist; richest man in U.S. at his death.
Jean Paul Getty, 1892-1976, (U.S.) founded oil empire.
Jay Gould, 1836-1892, (U.S.) railroad magnate, financier, speculator.
Hetty Green, 1834-1916, (U.S.) financier, the "witch of Wall St."; richest woman in U.S in her day.
William Gregg, 1800-1867, (U.S.) launched textile industry in the South.
Meyer Guggenheim, 1828-1905, (U.S.) Swiss-born merchant, philanthropist; built merchandising, mining empires.
Edward H. Harriman, 1848-1909, (U.S.) railroad financier, administrator; headed Union Pacific.
William Randolph Hearst, 1863-1951, (U.S.) a dominant figure in American journalism; built vast publishing empire.
Henry J. Heinz, 1844-1919, (U.S.) founded food empire.
James J. Hill, 1838-1916, (U.S.) Canadian-born railroad magnate, financier; founded Great Northern Railway.
Conrad N. Hilton, 1888-1979, (U.S.) intl. hotel chain founder.
Howard Hughes, 1905-1976, (U.S.) industrialist, financier, movie maker.
H.L. Hunt, 1889-1974, (U.S.) oil magnate.
Collis P. Huntington, 1821-1900, (U.S.) railroad magnate.
Henry E. Huntington, 1850-1927, (U.S.) railroad builder, philanthropist.
Walter L. Jacobs, 1898-1986, (U.S.) founder of the first rental car agency, which later became Hertz.
Howard Johnson, 1896-1972, (U.S.) founded restaurant chain.
Henry J. Kaiser, 1882-1967, (U.S.) industrialist, built empire in steel, aluminum.
Minor C. Keith, 1848-1929, (U.S.) railroad magnate; founded United Fruit Co.
Will K. Kellogg, 1860-1951, (U.S.) businessman, philanthropist, founded breakfast food co.
Richard King, 1825-1885, (U.S.) cattleman, founded half-million acre King Ranch in Texas.
William S. Knudsen, 1879-1948, (U.S.) Danish-born auto industry executive.

Samuel H. Kress, 1863-1955, (U.S.) businessman, art collector, philanthropist; founded "dime store" chain.
Ray A. Kroc, 1902-1984, (U.S.) builder of McDonald's fast food empire; owner, San Diego Padres baseball team.
Alfred Krupp, 1812-1887, (G.) armaments magnate.
Albert Lasker, 1880-1952, (U.S.) businessman, philanthropist.
Thomas Lipton, 1850-1931, (Ir.) merchant, built tea empire.
James McGill, 1744-1813, (Can.) Scots-born fur trader, founded univ.
Andrew W. Mellon, 1855-1937, (U.S.) financier, industrialist; benefactor of National Gallery of Art.
Charles E. Merrill, 1885-1956, (U.S.) financier, developed firm of Merrill Lynch.
John Pierpont Morgan, 1837-1913, (U.S.) most powerful figure in finance and industry at the turn-of-the-century.
Malcolm Muir, 1885-1979, (U.S.) created *Business Week* magazine; headed *Newsweek*, 1937-61.
Samuel Newhouse, 1895-1979, (U.S.) publishing and broadcasting magnate, built communications empire.
Aristotle Onassis, 1900-1975, (Gr.) shipping magnate.
George Peabody, 1795-1869, (U.S.) merchant, financier, philanthropist.
James C. Penney, 1875-1971, (U.S.) businessman, developed department store chain.
William C. Procter, 1862-1934, (U.S.) headed soap co.
John D. Rockefeller, 1839-1937, (U.S.) industrialist, established Standard Oil; became world's wealthiest person.
John D. Rockefeller Jr., 1874-1960, (U.S.) philanthropist, established foundation; provided land for United Nations.
Meyer A. Rothschild, 1743-1812, (G.) founded international banking house.
Thomas Fortune Ryan, 1851-1928, (U.S.) financier, dominated N.Y. City public transportation; helped found American Tobacco.
Russell Sage, 1816-1906, (U.S.) financier.
David Sarnoff, 1891-1971, (U.S.) broadcasting pioneer, established first radio network, NBC.
Richard W. Sears, 1863-1914, (U.S.) founded mail-order co.
(Ernst) Werner von Siemens, 1816-1892, (G.) industrialist, inventor.
Alfred P. Sloan, 1875-1966, (U.S.) industrialist, philanthropist; headed General Motors.
A. Leland Stanford, 1824-1893, (U.S.) railroad official, philanthropist; founded univ.
Nathan Strauss, 1848-1931, (U.S.) German-born merchant, philanthropist; headed Macy's.
Levi Strauss, c.1829-1902, (U.S.) pants manufacturer.
Clement Studebaker, 1831-1901, (U.S.) wagon, carriage manufacturer.
Gustavus Swift, 1839-1903, (U.S.) pioneer meat-packer; promoted refrigerated railroad cars.
Gerard Swope, 1872-1957, (U.S.) industrialist, economist; headed General Electric.
James Walter Thompson, 1847-1928, (U.S.) ad executive.
Theodore N. Vail, 1845-1920, (U.S.) organized Bell Telephone system, headed ATT.
Cornelius Vanderbilt, 1794-1877, (U.S.) financier, established steamship, railroad empires.
Henry Villard, 1835-1900, (U.S.) German-born railroad executive, financier.
Charles R. Walgreen, 1873-1939, (U.S.) founded drugstore chain.
DeWitt Wallace, 1890-1981, (U.S.) and **Lila Wallace**, 1890-1984, (U.S.) co-founders of *Reader's Digest* magazine, philanthropists.
John Wanamaker, 1838-1922, (U.S.) pioneered department-store merchandising.
Aaron Montgomery Ward, 1843-1913, (U.S.) established first mail-order firm.
Thomas J. Watson, 1874-1956, (U.S.) headed IBM, 1924-49.
John Hay Whitney, 1905-1982, (U.S.) publisher, sportsman, philanthropist.
Charles E. Wilson, 1890-1961, (U.S.) auto industry executive; public official.
Frank W. Woolworth, 1852-1919, (U.S.) created 5 & 10 chain.
William Wrigley Jr., 1861-1932, (U.S.) founded chewing gum co.

Composers of the Western World

Carl Philipp Emanuel Bach, 1714-1788, (G.) Prussian and Wurtembergian Sonatas.
Johann Christian Bach, 1735-1782, (G.) Concertos; sonatas.
Johann Sebastian Bach, 1685-1750, (G.) St. Matthew Passion, The Well-Tempered Clavichord.
Samuel Barber, 1910-1981, (U.S.) Adagio for Strings, Vanessa.
Bela Bartok, 1881-1945, (Hung.) Concerto for Orchestra, The Miraculous Mandarin.
Ludwig Van Beethoven, 1770-1827, (G.) Concertos (Emperor); sonatas (Moonlight, Pastorale, Pathetique); symphonies (Eroica).
Vincenzo Bellini, 1801-1835, (It.) La Sonnambula, Norma, I Puritani.
Alban Berg, 1885-1935, (Aus.) Wozzeck, Lulu.
Hector Berlioz, 1803-1869, (F.) Damnation of Faust, Symphonie Fantastique, Requiem.
Leonard Bernstein, b. 1918, (U.S.) Jeremiah, West Side Story.
Georges Bizet, 1838-1875, (F.) Carmen, Pearl Fishers.
Ernest Bloch, 1880-1959, (Swiss) Schelomo, Voice in the Wilderness, Sacred Service.
Luigi Boccherini, 1743-1805, (It.) Cello Concerto in B Flat, Symphony in C.
Alexander Borodin, 1833-1887, (R.) Prince Igor, In the Steppes of Central Asia.
Johannes Brahms, 1833-1897, (G.) Liebeslieder Waltzes, Rhapsody in E Flat Major, Opus 119 for Piano, Academic Festival Overture; symphonies; quartets.
Benjamin Britten, 1913-1976, (Br.) Peter Grimes, Turn of the Screw, Ceremony of Carols, War Requiem.
Anton Bruckner, 1824-1896, (Aus.) Symphonies (Romantic), Intermezzo for String Quintet.
Ferruccio Busoni, 1866-1924, (It.) Doctor Faust, Comedy Overture.
Dietrich Buxtehude, 1637-1707, (D.) Cantatas, trio sonatas.
William Byrd, 1543-1623, (Br.) Masses, sacred songs.
(Alexis-) Emmanuel Chabrier, 1841-1894, (Fr.) Le Roi Malgre Lui, Espana.
Gustave Charpentier, 1860-1956, (F.) Louise.
Frederic Chopin, 1810-1849, (P.) Polonaises, mazurkas, waltzes, etudes, nocturnes. Polonaise No. 6 in A Flat Major (Heroic); sonatas.
Aaron Copland, b. 1900, (U.S.) Appalachian Spring.
(Achille-) Claude Debussy, 1862-1918, (F.) Pelleas et Melisande, La Mer, Prelude to the Afternoon of a Faun.
C.P. Leo Delibes, 1836-1891, (F.) Lakme, Coppelia, Sylvia.
Norman Dello Joio, b. 1913, (U.S.), Triumph of St. Joan, Psalm of David.
Gaetano Donizetti, 1797-1848, (It.) Elixir of Love, Lucia Di Lammermoor, Daughter of the Regiment.
Paul Dukas, 1865-1935, (Fr.) Sorcerer's Apprentice.
Antonin Dvorak, 1841-1904, (C.) Symphony in E Minor (From the New World).
Edward Elgar, 1857-1934, (Br.) Pomp and Circumstance.
Manuel de Falla, 1876-1946, (Sp.) La Vide Breve, El Amor Brujo.
Gabriel Faure, 1845-1924, (Fr.) Requiem, Ballade.
Friedrich von Flotow, 1812-1883, (G.) Martha.
Cesar Franck, 1822-1890, (Belg.) D Minor Symphony.
George Gershwin, 1898-1937, (U.S.) Rhapsody in Blue, American in Paris, Porgy and Bess.
Umberto Giordano, 1867-1948, (It.) Andrea Chenier.
Alexander K. Glazunoff, 1865-1936, (R.) Symphonies, Stenka Razin.
Mikhail Glinka, 1804-1857, (R.) Ruslan and Ludmilla.
Christoph W. Gluck, 1714-1787, (G.) Alceste, Iphigenie en Tauride.
Charles Gounod, 1818-1893, (F.) Faust, Romeo and Juliet.
Edvard Grieg, 1843-1907, (Nor.) Peer Gynt Suite, Concerto in A Minor.
George Frederick Handel, 1685-1759, (G., Br.) Messiah, Xerxes, Berenice.
Howard Hanson, 1896-1981, (U.S.) Symphonies No. 1 (Nordic) and 2 (Romantic).
Roy Harris, 1898-1979, (U.S.) Symphonies, Amer. Portraits.
Joseph Haydn, 1732-1809, (Aus.) Symphonies (Clock); oratorios; chamber music.
Paul Hindemith, 1895-1963, (U.S.) Mathis Der Maler.
Gustav Holst, 1874-1934, (Br.) The Planets.
Arthur Honegger, 1892-1955, (Swiss) Judith, Le Roi David, Pacific 231.
Alan Hovhaness, b. 1911, (U.S.) Symphonies, Magnificat.
Engelbert Humperdinck, 1854-1921, (G.) Hansel and Gretel.
Charles Ives, 1874-1954, (U.S.) Third Symphony.
Aram Khachaturian, 1903-1978, (Armen.) Gayane (ballet), symphonies.
Zoltan Kodaly, 1882-1967, (Hung.) Hary Janos, Psalmus Hungaricus.
Fritz Kreisler, 1875-1962, (Aus.) Caprice Viennois, Tambourin Chinois.

Rodolphe Kreutzer, 1766-1831, (F.) 40 etudes for violin.
Edouard V.A. Lalo, 1823-1892, (F.) Symphonie Espagnole.
Ruggiero Leoncavallo, 1857-1919, (It.) Pagliacci.
Franz Liszt, 1811-1886, (Hung.) 20 Hungarian rhapsodies; symphonic poems.
Edward MacDowell, 1861-1908, (U.S.) To a Wild Rose.
Gustav Mahler, 1860-1911, (Aus.) Lied von der Erde.
Pietro Mascagni, 1863-1945, (It.) Cavalleria Rusticana.
Jules Massenet, 1842-1912, (F.) Manon, Le Cid, Thais.
Felix Mendelssohn, 1809-1847, (G.) Midsummer Night's Dream, Songs Without Words.
Gian-Carlo Menotti, b. 1911, (It.-U.S.) The Medium, The Consul, Amahl and the Night Visitors.
Giacomo Meyerbeer, 1791-1864, (G.) Robert le Diable, Les Huguenots.
Claudio Monteverdi, 1567-1643, (It.) Opera; masses; madrigals.
Wolfgang Amadeus Mozart, 1756-1791, (Aus.) Magic Flute, Marriage of Figaro; concertos; symphonies, etc.
Modest Moussorgsky, 1835-1881, (R.) Boris Godunov, Pictures at an Exhibition.
Jacques Offenbach, 1819-1880, (F.) Tales of Hoffmann.
Carl Orff, 1895-1982, (G.) Carmina Burana.
Ignace Paderewski, 1860-1941, (P.) Minuet in G.
Giovanni P. da Palestrina, c. 1525-1594, (It.) Masses; madrigals.
Amilcare Ponchielli, 1834-1886, (It.) La Gioconda.
Francis Poulenc, 1899-1963, (F.) Dialogues des Carmelites.
Serge Prokofiev, 1891-1953, (R.) Love for Three Oranges, Lt. Kije, Peter and the Wolf.
Giacomo Puccini, 1858-1924, (It.) La Boheme, Manon Lescaut, Tosca, Madame Butterfly.
Sergei Rachmaninov, 1873-1943, (R.) 24 preludes, E concerti, 4 symphonies. Prelude in C Sharp Minor.
Maurice Ravel, 1875-1937, (Fr.) Bolero, Daphnis et Chloe, Rapsodie Espagnole.
Nikolai Rimsky-Korsakov, 1844-1908, (R.) Golden Cockerel, Capriccio Espagnol, Scheherazade, Russian Easter Overture.
Gioacchino Rossini, 1792-1868, (It.) Barber of Seville, Semiramide, William Tell.
Chas. Camille Saint-Saens, 1835-1921, (F.) Samson and Delilah, Danse Macabre.
Alessandro Scarlatti, 1660-1725, (It.) Cantatas; concertos.
Domenico Scarlatti, 1685-1757, (It.) Harpsichord sonatas.
Arnold Schoenberg, 1874-1951, (Aus.) Pelleas and Melisande, Transfigured Night, De Profundis.
Franz Schubert, 1797-1828, (A.) Lieder; symphonies (Unfinished); overtures (Rosamunde).
William Schuman, b. 1910, (U.S.) Credendum, New England Triptych.
Robert Schumann, 1810-1856, (G.) Symphonies, songs.
Aleksandr Scriabin, 1872-1915, (R.) Prometheus.
Dimitri Shostakovich, 1906-1975, (R.) Symphonies, Lady Macbeth of Mzensk, The Nose.
Jean Sibelius, 1865-1957, (Finn.) Finlandia, Karelia.
Bedrich Smetana, 1824-1884, (Cz.). The Bartered Bride.
Karlheinz Stockhausen, b. 1928, (G.) Kontrapunkte, Kontakte.
Richard Strauss, 1864-1949, (G.) Salome, Elektra, Der Rosenkavalier, Thus Spake Zarathustra.
Igor F. Stravinsky, 1882-1971, (R.-U.S.) Oedipus Rex, Le Sacre du Printemps, Petrushka.
Peter I. Tchaikovsky, 1840-1893, (R.) Nutcracker Suite, Swan Lake, Eugene Onegin.
Ambroise Thomas, 1811-1896, (F.) Mignon.
Virgil Thomson, b. 1896, (U.S.) Opera, ballet; Four Saints in Three Acts.
Ralph Vaughan Williams, 1872-1958, (Br.) Job, London Symphony, Symphony No. 7 (Antartica).
Giuseppe Verdi, 1813-1901, (It.) Aida, Rigoletto, Don Carlo, Il Trovatore, La Traviata, Falstaff, Macbeth.
Heitor Villa-Lobos, 1887-1959, (Brazil) Choros.
Antonio Vivaldi, 1678-1741, (It.) Concerti, The Four Seasons.
Richard Wagner, 1813-1883, (G.) Rienzi, Tannhauser, Lohengrin, Tristan und Isolde.
Carl Maria von Weber, 1786-1826, (G.) Der Freischutz.

Composers of Operettas, Musicals, and Popular Music

Richard Adler, b. 1921, (U.S.) *Pajama Game; Damn Yankees.*
Milton Ager, 1893-1979, (U.S.) I Wonder What's Become of Sally; Hard Hearted Hannah; Ain't She Sweet?
Leroy Anderson, 1908-1975, (U.S.) Syncopated Clock.
Paul Anka, b. 1941, (Can.) My Way; She's a Lady; Tonight Show theme.
Harold Arlen, 1905-1986, (U.S.) Stormy Weather; Over the Rainbow; Blues in the Night; That Old Black Magic.
Burt Bacharach, b. 1928, (U.S.) Raindrops Keep Fallin' on My Head; Walk on By; What the World Needs Now is Love.
Ernest Ball, 1878-1927, (U.S.) Mother Machree; When Irish Eyes Are Smiling.
Irving Berlin, b. 1888, (U.S.) *This is the Army; Annie Get Your Gun; Call Me Madam;* God Bless America; White Christmas.
Leonard Bernstein, b. 1918, (U.S.) *On the Town; Wonderful Town; Candide; West Side Story.*
Eubie Blake, 1883-1983, (U.S.) *Shuffle Along;* I'm Just Wild about Harry.
Jerry Bock, b. 1928, (U.S.) *Mr. Wonderful; Fiorello; Fiddler on the Roof; The Rothschilds.*
Carrie Jacobs Bond, 1862-1946, (U.S.) I Love You Truly.
Nacio Herb Brown, 1896-1964, (U.S.) Singing in the Rain; You Were Meant for Me; All I Do Is Dream of You.
Hoagy Carmichael, 1899-1981, (U.S.) Stardust; Georgia on My Mind; Old Buttermilk Sky.
George M. Cohan, 1878-1942, (U.S.) Give My Regards to Broadway; You're A Grand Old Flag; Over There.
Cy Coleman, b. 1929, (U.S.) *Sweet Charity;* Witchcraft.
Noel Coward, 1899-1973 (Br.) *Bitter Sweet;* Mad Dogs and Englishmen; Mad About the Boy.
Walter Donaldson, 1893-1947, (U.S.) My Buddy; Carolina in the Morning; You're Driving Me Crazy; Makin' Whoopee.
Neil Diamond, b. 1941, (U.S.) I'm a Believer; Sweet Caroline.
Vernon Duke, 1903-1969, (U.S.) April in Paris.
Bob Dylan, b. 1941, (U.S.) Blowin' in the Wind.
Gus Edwards, 1879-1945, (U.S.) School Days; By the Light of the Silvery Moon; In My Merry Oldsmobile.
Sherman Edwards, 1919-1981, (U.S.) See You in September; Wonderful! Wonderful!
Duke Ellington, 1899-1974, (U.S.) Sophisticated Lady; Satin Doll; It Don't Mean a Thing; Solitude.
Sammy Fain, b. 1902, I'll Be Seeing You; Love Is a Many-Splendored Thing.
Fred Fisher, 1875-1942, (U.S.) Peg O' My Heart; Chicago.
Stephen Collins Foster, 1826-1864, (U.S.) My Old Kentucky Home; Old Folks At Home.
Rudolf Friml, 1879-1972, (naturalized U.S.) *The Firefly; Rose Marie; Vagabond King; Bird of Paradise.*
John Gay, 1685-1732, (Br.) *The Beggar's Opera.*
George Gershwin, 1898-1937, (U.S.) Someone to Watch Over Me; I've Got a Crush on You; Embraceable You.
Ferde Grofe, 1892-1972, (U.S.) Grand Canyon Suite.
W. C. Handy, 1873-1958, (U.S.) St. Louis Blues.
Ray Henderson, 1896-1970, (U.S.) *George White's Scandals;* That Old Gang of Mine; Five Foot Two, Eyes of Blue.
Victor Herbert, 1859-1924, (Ir.-U.S.) *Mlle. Modiste; Babes in Toyland, The Red Mill; Naughty Marietta; Sweethearts.*
Jerry Herman, b. 1932, (U.S.) *Hello Dolly; Mame.*
Brian Holland, b. 1941, **Lamont Dozier,** b. 1941, **Eddie Holland,** b. 1939, (all U.S.) Heat Wave; Stop! In the Name of Love; Baby, I Need Your Loving.
Scott Joplin, 1868-1917, (U.S.) *Treemonisha.*
John Kander, b. 1927, (U.S.) *Cabaret; Chicago; Funny Lady.*
Jerome Kern, 1885-1945, (U.S.) *Sally; Sunny; Show Boat.*
Carole King, b. 1942, (U.S.) Will You Love Me Tomorrow?; Natural Woman; One Fine Day; Up on the Roof.
Burton Lane, b. 1912, (U.S.) *Finian's Rainbow.*
Franz Lehar, 1870-1948, (Hung.) *Merry Widow.*
Jerry Leiber, & Mike Stoller, both b. 1942, (both U.S.) Hound Dog; Searchin'; Yakety Yak; Love Me Tender.
Mitch Leigh, b. 1928, (U.S.) *Man of La Mancha.*
John Lennon, 1940-1980, & **Paul McCartney,** b. 1942, (both Br.) I Want to Hold Your Hand; She Loves You; Hard Day's Night; Can't Buy Me Love; And I Love Her.
Frank Loesser, 1910-1969, (U.S.) *Guys and Dolls; Where's Charley?; The Most Happy Fella; How to Succeed . . .*
Frederick Loewe, b. 1901, (Aust.-U.S.) *The Day Before Spring; Brigadoon; Paint Your Wagon; My Fair Lady; Camelot.*
Henry Mancini, b. 1924, (U.S.) Moon River; Days of Wine and Roses; Pink Panther Theme.
Barry Mann, b. 1939, & **Cynthia Weil,** b. 1937, (both U.S.) You've Lost That Loving Feeling, Saturday Night at the Movies.
Jimmy McHugh, 1894-1969 (U.S.) Don't Blame Me; I'm in the Mood for Love; I Feel a Song Coming On.
Joseph Meyer, b. 1894, (U.S.) If You Knew Susie; California, Here I Come, Crazy Rhythm.
Chauncey Olcott, 1860-1932, (U.S.) Mother Machree.
Cole Porter, 1893-1964, (U.S.) *Anything Goes; Kiss Me Kate; Can Can; Silk Stockings.*

Richard Rodgers, 1902-1979, (U.S.) *Connecticut Yankee; Oklahoma!; Carousel; South Pacific; The King and I; The Sound of Music.*
Smokey Robinson, b. 1959, (U.S.) Shop Around; My Guy; My Girl; Get Ready.
Sigmund Romberg, 1887-1951, (Hung.) *Maytime; The Student Prince; Desert Song; Blossom Time.*
Harold Rome, b. 1908, (U.S.) *Pins and Needles; Call Me Mister; Wish You Were Here; Fanny; Destry Rides Again.*
Vincent Rose, b. 1880-1944, (U.S.) Avalon; Whispering; Blueberry Hill.
Harry Ruby, 1895-1974, (U.S.) Three Little Words; Who's Sorry Now?
Arthur Schwartz, 1900-1984, (U.S.) *The Band Wagon;* Dancing in the Dark; By Myself; That's Entertainment.
Neil Sedaka, b. 1939, (U.S.) Breaking Up Is Hard to Do.
Paul Simon, b. 1942, (U.S.) Sounds of Silence; I Am a Rock; Mrs. Robinson; Bridge Over Troubled Waters.
Stephen Sondheim, b. 1930, (U.S.) *A Little Night Music; Company; Sweeney Todd; Sunday in the Park with George.*
John Philip Sousa. 1854-1932, (U.S.) *El Capitan;* Stars and Stripes Forever.
Oskar Straus, 1870-1954, (Aus.) *Chocolate Soldier.*
Johann Strauss, 1825-1899, (Aus.) *Gypsy Baron; Die Fledermaus;* waltzes: Blue Danube, Artist's Life.
Charles Strouse, b. 1928, (U.S.) *Bye Bye, Birdie; Annie.*
Jule Styne, b. 1905, (b. Br.-U.S.) *Gentlemen Prefer Blondes; Bells Are Ringing; Gypsy; Funny Girl.*
Arthur S. Sullivan, 1842-1900, (Br.) *H.M.S. Pinafore, Pirates of Penzance; The Mikado.*
Deems Taylor, 1885-1966, (U.S.) *Peter Ibbetson.*
Egbert van Alstyne, 1882-1951, (U.S.) In the Shade of the Old Apple Tree; Memories; Pretty Baby.
James Van Heusen, b. 1913, (U.S.) Moonlight Becomes You; Swinging on a Star; All the Way; Love and Marriage.
Albert von Tilzer, 1878-1956, (U.S.) I'll Be With You in Apple Blossom Time; Take Me Out to the Ball Game.
Harry von Tilzer, 1872-1946, (U.S.) Only a Bird in a Gilded Cage; On a Sunday Afternoon.
Fats Waller, 1904-1943, (U.S.) Honeysuckle Rose; Ain't Misbehavin'.
Harry Warren, 1893-1981, (U.S.) You're My Everything; We're in the Money; I Only Have Eyes for You.
Jimmy Webb, b. 1946, (U.S.) Up, Up and Away; By the Time I Get to Phoenix; Didn't We?; Wichita Lineman.
Kurt Weill, 1900-1950, (G.-U.S.) *Threepenny Opera; Lady in the Dark; Knickerbocker Holiday; One Touch of Venus.*
Percy Wenrich, 1887-1952, (U.S.) When You Wore a Tulip; Moonlight Bay; Put On Your Old Gray Bonnet.
Richard A. Whiting, 1891-1938, (U.S.) Till We Meet Again; Sleepytime Gal; Beyond the Blue Horizon; My Ideal.
Meredith Willson, 1902-1984, (U.S.) *The Music Man.*
Stevie Wonder, b. 1950, (U.S.) You Are the Sunshine of My Life; Signed, Sealed, Delivered, I'm Yours.
Vincent Youmans, 1898-1946, (U.S.) *Two Little Girls in Blue; Wildflower; No, No, Nanette; Hit the Deck; Rainbow; Smiles.*

Lyricists

Johnny Burke, 1908-1924, (U.S.) What's New?; Misty; Imagination; Polka Dots and Moonbeams.
Sammy Cahn, b. 1913, (U.S.) High Hopes; Love and Marriage; The Second Time Around; It's Magic.
Betty Comden, b. 1919 (U.S.) and **Adolph Green,** b. 1915 (U.S.) The Party's Over; Just in Time; New York, New York.
Buddy De Sylva, 1895-1950, (U.S.) When Day is Done; Look for the Silver Lining; April Showers.
Hal David, b. 1921 (U.S.) What the World Needs Now Is Love; Close to You.
Howard Dietz, b. 1896, (U.S.) Dancing in the Dark; You and the Night and the Music; That's Entertainment.
Al Dubin, 1891-1945, (U.S.) Tiptoe Through the Tulips; Anniversary Waltz; Lullaby of Broadway.
Fred Ebb, b. 1936 (U.S.) *Cabaret, Zorba, Woman of the Year.*
Dorothy Fields, 1905-1974, (U.S.) On the Sunny Side of the Street; Don't Blame Me; The Way You Look Tonight.
Ira Gershwin, 1896-1983, (U.S.) The Man I Love; Fascinating Rhythm; S'Wonderful; Embraceable You.
Wm. S. Gilbert, 1836-1911, (Br.) *The Mikado; H.M.S. Pinafore.*
Mack Gordon, 1905-1959, (Pol.-U.S.) You'll Never Know; The More I See You; Chattanooga Choo-Choo; You Make Me Feel So Young.
Oscar Hammerstein II, 1895-1960, (U.S.) Ol' Man River; *Oklahoma; Carousel.*
E. Y. (Yip) Harburg, 1898-1981, (U.S.) Brother, Can You Spare a Dime; April in Paris; Over the Rainbow.
Lorenz Hart, 1895-1943, (U.S.) Isn't It Romantic; Blue Moon; Lover; Manhattan; My Funny Valentine; Mountain Greenery.
DuBose Heyward, 1885-1940, (U.S.) Summertime; A Woman Is A Sometime Thing.
Gus Kahn, 1886-1941, (U.S.) Memories; Ain't We Got Fun.
Alan J. Lerner, 1918-1986, (U.S.) *Brigadoon; My Fair Lady; Camelot; Gigi.; On a Clear Day You Can See Forever.*
Johnny Mercer, 1909-1976, (U.S.) Blues in the Night; Come Rain or Come Shine; Laura; That Old Black Magic.
Bob Merrill, b. 1921, (U.S.) People; Don't Rain on My Parade.
Jack Norworth, 1879-1959, (U.S.) Take Me Out to the Ball Game; Shine On Harvest Moon.
Mitchell Parish, b. 1901, (U.S.) Stairway to the Stars; Stardust.
Leo Robin, 1900-1981, (U.S.) Thanks for the Memory; Hooray for Love; Diamonds are a Girl's Best Friend.
Jack Yellen, b. 1892, (U.S.) Down by the O-Hi-O; Ain't She Sweet; Happy Days Are Here Again.

Noted Jazz Artists

Jazz has been called America's only completely unique contribution to Western culture. The following individuals have made major contributions in this field:

Julian "Cannonball" Adderley, 1928-1975: alto sax.
Louis "Satchmo" Armstrong, 1900-1971: trumpet, singer; originated the "scat" vocal.
Mildred Bailey, 1907-1951: blues singer.
Chet Baker, b. 1929: trumpet.
Count Basie, 1904-1984: orchestra leader, piano.
Sidney Bechet, 1897-1950: early innovator, soprano sax.
Bix Beiderbecke, 1903-1931: cornet, piano, composer.
Bunny Berrigan, 1909-1942: trumpet, singer.
Barney Bigard, 1906-1980: clarinet.
Art Blakey, b. 1919: drums, leader.
Jimmy Blanton, 1921-1942: bass.
Charles "Buddy" Bolden, 1868-1931: cornet; formed the first jazz band in the 1890s.
Big Bill Broonzy, 1893-1958: blues singer, guitar.
Clifford Brown, 1930-1956: trumpet.
Ray Brown, b. 1926: bass.
Dave Brubeck, b. 1920: piano, combo leader.
Don Byas, b. 1912: tenor sax.
Harry Carney, 1910-1974: baritone sax.
Benny Carter, b. 1907: alto sax, trumpet, clarinet.
Ron Carter, b. 1937: bass, cello.
Sidney Catlett, 1910-1951: drums.
Charlie Christian, 1919-1942: guitar.
Kenny Clarke, 1914-1985: pioneer of modern drums.
Buck Clayton, b. 1911: trumpet, arranger.
Al Cohn, b. 1925: tenor sax, composer.
Cozy Cole, 1909-1981: drums.
Ornette Coleman, b. 1930: saxophone; unorthodox style.
John Coltrane, 1926-1967: tenor sax innovator.
Eddie Condon, 1904-1973: guitar, band leader; promoter of Dixieland.
Chick Corea, b. 1941: pianist, composer.
Miles Davis, b. 1926: trumpet; pioneer of cool jazz.
Tadd Dameron, 1917-1965: piano, composer.
Wild Bill Davison, b. 1906: cornet, leader; prominent in early Chicago jazz.
Buddy De Franco, b. 1933: clarinet.
Paul Desmond, 1924-1977: alto sax.
Vic Dickenson, 1906-1984: trombone, composer.
Warren "Baby" Dodds, 1898-1959: Dixieland drummer.
Johnny Dodds, 1892-1940: clarinet.
Eric Dolphy, 1928-1964: alto sax, composer.
Jimmy Dorsey, 1904-1957: clarinet, alto sax; band leader.
Tommy Dorsey, 1905-1956: trombone; band leader.
Roy Eldridge, b. 1911: trumpet, drums, singer.
Duke Ellington, 1899-1974: piano, band leader, composer.
Bill Evans, 1929-1980: piano.
Gil Evans, b. 1912: composer, arranger, piano.
Ella Fitzgerald, b. 1918: singer.
"Red" Garland, 1923-1984: piano.
Erroll Garner, 1921-1977: piano, composer, "Misty."
Stan Getz, b. 1927: tenor sax.
Dizzy Gillespie, b. 1917: trumpet, composer; bop developer.
Benny Goodman, 1909-1986: clarinet, band and combo leader.

Dexter Gordon, b. 1923: tenor sax; bop-derived style.
Stephane Grappelli, b. 1908: violin.
Bobby Hackett, 1915-1976: trumpet, cornet.
Lionel Hampton, b. 1913: vibes, drums, piano, combo leader.
Herbie Hancock, b. 1940: piano, composer.
W. C. Handy, 1873-1958: composer, "St. Louis Blues."
Coleman Hawkins, 1904-1969: tenor sax; 1939 recording of "Body and Soul", a classic.
Roy Haynes, b. 1926: drums.
Fletcher Henderson, 1898-1952: orchestra leader, arranger; pioneered jazz and dance bands of the 30s.
Woody Herman, b. 1913: clarinet, alto sax, band leader.
Jay C. Higginbotham, 1906-1973: trombone.
Earl "Fatha" Hines, 1905-1983: piano, songwriter.
Johnny Hodges, 1906-1971: alto sax.
Billie Holiday, 1915-1959: blues singer, "Strange Fruit."
Sam "Lightnin' " Hopkins, 1912-1982: blues singer, guitar.
Mahalia Jackson, 1911-1972: gospel singer.
Milt Jackson, b. 1923: vibes, piano, guitar.
Illinois Jacquet, b. 1922: tenor sax.
Keith Jarrett, b. 1945: technically phenomenal pianist.
Blind Lemon Jefferson, 1897-1930: blues singer, guitar.
Bunk Johnson, 1879-1949: cornet, trumpet.
James P. Johnson, 1891-1955: piano, composer.
J. J. Johnson, b. 1924: trombone, composer.
Elvin Jones, b. 1927: drums.
Jo Jones, 1911-1985: drums.
Philly Joe Jones, 1923-1985: drums.
Quincy Jones, b. 1933: arranger.
Thad Jones, 1923-1986: trumpet, cornet.
Scott Joplin, 1868-1917: composer; "Maple Leaf Rag."
Stan Kenton, 1912-1979: orchestra leader, composer, piano.
Barney Kessel, b. 1923: guitar.
Lee Konitz, b. 1927: alto sax.
Gene Krupa, 1909-1973: drums, band and combo leader.
Scott LaFaro, 1936-1961: bass.
Huddie Ledbetter (Leadbelly), 1888-1949: blues singer, guitar.
John Lewis, b. 1920: composer, piano, combo leader.
Jimmie Lunceford, 1902-1947: band leader, sax.
Herbie Mann, b. 1930: flute.
Wynton Marsalis, b. 1961: trumpet.
Jimmy McPartland, b. 1907: trumpet.
Marian McPartland, b. 1920: piano.
Glenn Miller, 1904-1944: trombone, dance band leader.
Charles Mingus, 1922-1979: bass, composer, combo leader.
Thelonious Monk, 1920-1982: piano, composer, combo leader; a developer of bop.
Wes Montgomery, 1925-1968: guitar.
"Jelly Roll" Morton, 1885-1941: composer, piano, singer.
Bennie Moten, 1894-1935: piano; an early organizer of large jazz orchestras.
Gerry Mulligan, b. 1927: baritone sax, arranger, leader.
Turk Murphy, 1915-1987: trombone, band leader.
Theodore "Fats" Navarro, 1923-1950: trumpet.
Red Nichols, 1905-1965: cornet, combo leader.
Red Norvo, b. 1908: vibes, band leader.
Anita O'Day, b. 1919: singer.
King Oliver, 1885-1938: cornet, band leader; teacher of Louis Armstrong.
Kid Ory, 1886-1973: trombone, "Muskrat Ramble".
Charlie "Bird" Parker, 1920-1955: alto sax, composer; rated by many as the greatest jazz improviser.
Art Pepper, 1925-1983: alto sax.
Oscar Peterson, b. 1925: piano, composer, combo leader.
Oscar Pettiford, 1922-1960: a leading bassist in the bop era.
Bud Powell, 1924-1966: piano; modern jazz pioneer.
Sun Ra, b. 1915?: big band leader, pianist, composer.
Gertrude "Ma" Rainey, 1886-1939: blues singer.
Don Redman, 1900-1964: composer, arranger; pioneer in the evolution of the large orchestra.
Django Reinhardt, 1910-1953: guitar; Belgian gypsy, first European to influence American jazz.
Buddy Rich, b. 1917: drums, band leader.
Max Roach, b. 1925: drums.
Sonny Rollins, b. 1929: tenor sax.
Frank Rosollino, 1926-1978: trombone.
Jimmy Rushing, 1903-1972: blues singer.
George Russell, b. 1923: composer, piano.
Pee Wee Russell, 1906-1969: clarinet.
Artie Shaw, b. 1910: clarinet, combo leader.
George Shearing, b. 1919: piano, composer, "Lullaby of Birdland."
Horace Silver, b. 1928: piano, combo leader.
Zoot Sims, 1925-1985: tenor, alto sax; clarinet.
Zutty Singleton, 1898-1975: Dixieland drummer.
Bessie Smith, 1894-1937: blues singer.
Clarence "Pinetop" Smith, 1904-1929: piano, singer; pioneer of boogie woogie.
Willie "The Lion" Smith, 1897-1973: stride style pianist.
Muggsy Spanier, 1906-1967: cornet, band leader.
Billy Strayhorn, 1915-67: composer, piano.
Sonny Stitt, 1924-1982: alto, tenor sax.
Art Tatum, 1910-1956: piano; technical virtuoso.
Billy Taylor, b. 1921: piano, composer.
Cecil Taylor, b. 1933: piano, composer.
Jack Teagarden, 1905-1964: trombone, singer.
Dave Tough, 1908-1948: drums.
Lennie Tristano, 1919-1978: piano, composer.
Joe Turner, 1911-1985: blues singer.
McCoy Tyner, b. 1938: piano, composer.
Sarah Vaughan, b. 1924: singer.
Joe Venuti, 1904-1978: first great jazz violinist.
Thomas "Fats" Waller, 1904-1943: piano, singer, composer. "Ain't Misbehavin' ".
Dinah Washington, 1924-1963: singer.
Chick Webb, 1902-1939: band leader, drums.
Ben Webster, 1909-1973: tenor sax.
Paul Whiteman, 1890-1967: orchestra leader; a major figure in the introduction of jazz to a large audience.
Charles "Cootie" Williams, 1908-1985: trumpet, band leader.
Mary Lou Williams, 1914-1981: piano, composer.
Teddy Wilson, 1912-1986: piano, composer.
Kai Winding, 1922-1983: trombone, composer.
Jimmy Yancey, 1894-1951: piano.
Lester "Pres" Young, 1909-1959: tenor sax, composer; a bop pioneer.

Rock & Roll Notables

For more than a quarter of a century, rock & roll has been an important force in American popular culture. The following individuals or groups have made a significant impact. Next to each is an associated single record or record album.

Alabama: "Tennessee River"
The Allman Brothers Band: "Ramblin' Man"
The Animals: "House of the Rising Sun"
Paul Anka: "Lonely Boy"
The Association: "Cherish"
Frankie Avalon: "Venus"
The Band: "The Weight"
The Beach Boys: "Surfin' U.S.A."
The Beastie Boys: "(You've Got to) Fight for Your Right to Party"
The Beatles: "Hey Jude"
The Bee Gees: "Stayin' Alive"
Pat Benatar: "Hit Me With Your Best Shot"
Chuck Berry: "Johnny B. Goode"
The Big Bopper: "Chantilly Lace"
Black Sabbath: "Paranoid"
Blind Faith: "Can't Find My Way Home"
Blondie: "Heart of Glass"
Blood, Sweat and Tears: "Spinning Wheel"
Bon Jovi: "You Give Love a Bad Name"
Gary "U.S." Bonds: "Quarter to Three"
Booker T. and the MGs: "Green Onions"
David Bowie: "Let's Dance"
James Brown: "Papa's Got a Brand New Bag"
Jackson Browne: "Doctor My Eyes"
Buffalo Springfield: "For What It's Worth"
The Byrds: "Turn! Turn! Turn!
Canned Heat: "Going Up the Country"
The Cars: "Shake It Up"
Ray Charles: "Georgia on My Mind"
Chubby Checker: "The Twist"
Chicago: "Hard Habit to Break"
Eric Clapton: "Layla"
The Coasters: "Yakety Yak"
Eddie Cochran: "Summertime Blues"
Phil Collins: "Against All Odds"
Sam Cooke: "You Send Me"
Alice Cooper: "School's Out"
Elvis Costello: "Allison"
John Cougar: "Hurt So Good"
Cream: "Sunshine of Your Love"
Credence Clearwater Revival: "Proud Mary"
Crosby, Stills, Nash and Young: "Suite: Judy Blue Eyes"
The Crystals: "Da Doo Ron Ron"
Culture Club: *Colour by Numbers*
Danny and the Juniors: "At the Hop"
Bobby Darin: "Splish Splash"
Spencer Davis Group: "Gimme Some Lovin' "

Bo Diddley: "Who Do You Love?"
Dion and the Belmonts: "A Teenager in Love"
Dire Straits: *Brothers in Arms*
Fats Domino: "Blueberry Hill"
The Doobie Brothers: "What a Fool Believes"
The Doors: "Light My Fire"
The Drifters: "Save the Last Dance for Me"
Duran Duran: "Hungry Like the Wolf"
Bob Dylan: "Like a Rolling Stone"
The Eagles: "Hotel California"
Earth, Wind and Fire: "Shining Star"
Emerson, Lake and Palmer: "From the Beginning"
The Eurythmics: "Sweet Dreams (Are Made of This)"
Everly Brothers: "Wake Up Little Susie"
Jose Feliciano: "Light My Fire"
The Five Satins: "In the Still of the Night"
Fleetwood Mac: *Rumours*
Dan Fogelberg: "Missing You"
The Four Seasons: "Sherry"
The Four Tops: "I Can't Help Myself"
Aretha Franklin: "Respect"
Marvin Gaye: "I Heard It through the Grapevine"
Genesis: "Land of Confusion"
The J. Geils Band: *Freeze-Frame*
Grand Funk Railroad: "We're an American Band"
The Grateful Dead: "Truckin' "
Bill Haley and the Comets: "Rock Around the Clock"
Hall and Oates: "Rich Girl"
Jimi Hendrix: *Are You Experienced?*
Buddy Holly and the Crickets: "That'll Be the Day"
Janis Ian: "At Seventeen"
The Isley Brothers: "It's Your Thing"
The Jackson 5/The Jacksons: "ABC"
Janet Jackson: "Control"
Michael Jackson: "Beat It"
Jay and the Americans: "This Magic Moment"
The Jefferson Airplane/Jefferson Starship: "White Rabbit"
Jethro Tull: *Aqualung*
Joan Jett: "I Love Rock' n' Roll"
Billy Joel: "Uptown Girl"
Elton John: "Sad Songs"
Janis Joplin: "Me and Bobby McGee"
Chaka Khan: "I Feel for You"
B.B. King: "The Thrill Is Gone"
Carole King: *Tapestry*
The Kinks: "You Really Got Me"
Kiss: "Rock' n' Roll All Night"
Gladys Knight and the Pips: "Midnight Train to Georgia"
Cyndi Lauper: "Girls Just Want to Have Fun"
Led Zeppelin: "Stairway to Heaven"
Brenda Lee: "I'm Sorry"
Huey Lewis and the News: *Sports*
Jerry Lee Lewis: "Whole Lotta Shakin' Going On"
Little Anthony and the Imperials: "Tears on My Pillow"
Little Richard: "Tutti Frutti"
Lovin Spoonful: "Do You Believe in Magic?"
Frankie Lymon: "Why Do Fools Fall in Love?"
Lynyrd Skynyrd: "Freebird"
Madonna: "Material Girl"
The Mamas and the Papas: "Monday, Monday"
Bob Marley: "Jamming"
Martha and the Vandellas: "Dancin' in the Streets"
The Marvelettes: "Please Mr. Postman"
Clyde McPhatter: "Money Honey"
Steve Miller Band: "Abracadabra"
Joni Mitchell: "Big Yellow Taxi"
The Monkees: "I'm a Believer"
Moody Blues: "Nights in White Satin"
Rick Nelson: "Hello Mary Lou"
Roy Orbison: "Oh Pretty Woman"
Ozzy Osbourne: "You Can't Kill Rock 'n' Roll"
Carl Perkins: "Blue Suede Shoes"
Tom Petty and the Heartbreakers: "Refugee"
Pink Floyd: *Dark Side of the Moon*
Poco: *Deliverin'*
The Police: "Every Breath You Take"
Iggy Pop: "Lust for Life"
Elvis Presley: "Love Me Tender"
The Pretenders: *Learning to Crawl*
Lloyd Price: "Stagger Lee"
Prince: "Purple Rain"
Procul Harum: "A Whiter Shade of Pale"
Gary Puckett and the Union Gap: "Young Girl"
Queen: "Bohemian Rhapsody"
The Rascals: "Good Lovin' "
Otis Redding: "The Dock of the Bay"
Lou Reed: "Walk on the Wild Side"
REO Speedwagon: "Keep on Lovin' You"
Righteous Brothers: "You've Lost that Lovin' Feeling"
Johnny Rivers: "Poor Side of Town"
Smokey Robinson and the Miracles: "Ooh Baby Baby"
The Rolling Stones: "Satisfaction"
The Ronettes: "Be My Baby"
Linda Ronstadt: "You're No Good"
Run D.M.C.: "Raisin' Hell"
Sam and Dave: "Soul Man"
Santana: "Black Magic Woman"
Neil Sedaka: "Breaking Up is Hard to Do"
Bob Seger: "Old Time Rock and Roll"
Del Shannon: "Runaway"
The Shirelles: "Soldier Boy"
Simon and Garfunkel: "Bridge Over Troubled Water"
Carly Simon: "You're So Vain"
Sly and the Family Stone: "Everyday People"
Patti Smith: "Because the Night"
Southside Johnny and the Asbury Jukes: *This Time*
Dusty Springfield: "You Don't Have to Say You Love Me"
Bruce Springsteen: "Born in the U.S.A."
Steely Dan: "Rikki Don't Lose That Number"
Steppenwolf: "Born to Be Wild"
Cat Stevens: "Wild World"
Rod Stewart: "Maggie Mae"
Sting: "If You Love Somebody, Set Them Free"
Donna Summer: "Bad Girls"
The Supremes: "Stop! In the Name of Love"
Talking Heads: "Wild Wild Life"
James Taylor: "You've Got a Friend"
The Temptations: "My Girl"
Three Dog Night: "Joy to the World"
Traffic: "Feelin' Alright"
Big Joe Turner: "Shake, Rattle & Roll"
Tina Turner: "What's Love Got to Do with It?"
U2: "With or Without You"
Van Halen: "Jump"
Dionne Warwick: "I'll Never Fall in Love Again"
Muddy Waters: "Rollin' Stone"
Mary Wells: "My Guy"
The Who: "My Generation"
Jackie Wilson: "That's Why"
Stevie Wonder: "You Are the Sunshine of My Life"
The Yardbirds: "For Your Love"
Yes: "Owner of a Lonely Heart"
Frank Zappa/Mothers of Invention: *Sheik Yerbouti*

Entertainment Personalities — Where and When Born

Actors, Actresses, Dancers, Musicians, Producers, Radio-TV Performers, Singers

(As of June 30, 1987)

Name	Birthplace	Born
Abbado, Claudio	Milan, Italy	6/26/33
Abbott, George	Forestville, N.Y.	6/25/87
Abraham, F. Murray	Pittsburgh, Pa.	10/24/39
Acuff, Roy	Maynardville, Tenn.	9/15/03
Adams, Don	New York, N.Y.	4/19/26
Adams, Edie	Kingston, Pa.	4/16/29
Adams, Joey	New York, N.Y.	1/6/11
Adams, Mason	New York, N.Y.	2/26/19
Adams, Maud	Lulea, Sweden	2/12/45
Adler, Larry	Baltimore, Md.	2/10/14
Agutter, Jenny	London, England	12/20/52
Aiello, Danny	New York, N.Y.	6/20/33
Ailey, Alvin	Rogers, Tex.	1/5/31
Aimee, Anouk	Paris, France	4/27/32
Akins, Christopher	Rye, N.Y.	2/21/61
Akins, Claude	Nelson, Ga.	5/25/18
Albanese, Licia	Bari, Italy	7/22/13
Alberghetti, Anna Maria	Pesaro, Italy	5/15/36
Albert, Eddie	Rock Island, Ill.	4/22/08
Albert, Edward	Los Angeles, Cal.	2/20/51
Albright, Lola	Akron, Oh.	7/20/24
Alda, Alan	New York, N.Y.	1/28/36
Alexander, Jane	Boston, Mass.	10/28/39
Allen, Debbie	Houston, Tex.	1/16/52
Allen, Karen	Carrollton, Ill.	10/5/51
Allen, Mel	Birmingham, Ala.	2/14/13

Name	Birthplace	Born
Allen, Nancy	New York, N.Y.	6/24/50
Allen, Peter	Tenderfield, Australia	2/10/44
Allen, Steve	New York, N.Y.	12/26/21
Allen, Woody	Brooklyn, N.Y.	12/1/35
Allison, Fran	LaPorte City, Ia.	—
Allman, Gregg	Nashville, Tenn.	12/7/47
Allyson, June	New York, N.Y.	10/7/17
Alpert, Herb	Los Angeles, Cal.	3/31/35
Altman, Robert	Kansas City, Mo.	2/20/25
Ameche, Don	Kenosha, Wis.	5/31/08
Ames, Ed	Boston, Mass.	7/9/27
Ames, Leon	Portland, Ind.	1/20/03
Amos, John	Newark, N.J.	12/27/39
Amsterdam, Morey	Chicago, Ill.	12/14/14
Anderson, Harry	Newport, R.I.	10/14/52
Anderson, Ian	Dunfermline, Scotland	8/10/47
Anderson, Judith	Adelaide, Australia	2/10/98
Anderson, Loni	St. Paul, Minn.	8/7/44
Anderson, Lynn	Grand Forks, N.D.	9/26/47
Anderson, Marian	Philadelphia, Pa.	2/17/02
Anderson, Melissa Sue	Berkeley, Cal.	9/26/62
Anderson, Richard	Long Branch, N.J.	8/8/26
Anderson, Richard Dean	Minneapolis, Minn.	1/23/53
Andersson, Bibi	Stockholm, Sweden	11/11/35
Andress, Ursula	Switzerland	3/19/36
Andrews, Anthony	London, England	1948
Andrews, Dana	Collins, Miss.	1/1/09
Andrews, Julie	Walton, England	10/1/35
Andrews, Maxene	Minneapolis, Minn.	1/3/18
Andrews, Patty	Minneapolis, Minn.	2/16/20
Anka, Paul	Ottawa, Ont.	7/30/41
Ann-Margret	Stockholm, Sweden	4/28/41
Ant, Adam	London, England	11/3/54
Archer, Anne	Los Angeles, Cal.	8/25/50
Arden, Eve	Mill Valley, Cal.	4/30/12
Arkin, Alan	New York, N.Y.	3/26/34
Arnaz, Desi Jr.	Los Angeles, Cal.	1/19/53
Arnaz, Lucie	Hollywood, Cal.	7/17/51
Arness, James	Minneapolis, Minn.	5/26/23
Arnold, Eddy	Henderson, Tenn.	5/15/18
Arrau, Claudio	Chillau, Chile	2/6/03
Arroyo, Martina	New York, N.Y.	2/2/37
Arthur, Beatrice	New York, N.Y.	5/13/26
Arthur, Jean	New York, N.Y.	10/17/08
Ashcroft, Peggy	England	12/22/07
Ashley, Elizabeth	Ocala, Fla.	8/30/39
Asner, Ed	Kansas City, Mo.	11/15/29
Assante, Armand	New York, N.Y.	10/4/49
Astin, John	Baltimore, Md.	3/30/30
Astor, Mary	Quincy, Ill.	5/3/06
Atherton, William	New Haven, Conn.	1947
Atkins, Chet	Luttrell, Tenn.	6/20/24
Attenborough, Richard	Cambridge, England	8/29/23
Auberjonois, Rene	New York, N.Y.	6/1/40
Aumont, Jean-Pierre	Paris, France	1/5/11
Autry, Gene	Tioga, Tex.	9/29/11
Avalon, Frankie	Philadelphia, Pa.	9/8/40
Ax, Emmanuel	Lvov, USSR	6/8/49
Aykroyd, Dan	Ottawa, Ont.	7/1/52
Ayres, Lew	Minneapolis, Minn.	12/28/08
Aznavour, Charles	Paris, France	5/22/24
Bacall, Lauren	New York, N.Y.	9/16/24
Backus, Jim	Cleveland, Oh.	2/25/13
Bacon, Kevin	Philadelphia, Pa.	1958
Baez, Joan	Staten Island, N.Y.	1/9/41
Bailey, Pearl	Newport News, Va.	3/29/18
Bain, Conrad	Lethbridge, Alta.	2/4/23
Baio, Scott	Brooklyn, N.Y.	9/22/61
Baker, Anita	Detroit, Mich.	1957
Baker, Carroll	Johnstown, Pa.	5/28/31
Baker, Joe Don	Groesbeck, Tex.	2/12/36
Ball, Lucille	Jamestown, N.Y.	8/6/11
Ballard, Kaye	Cleveland, Oh.	11/20/26
Balsam, Martin	New York, N.Y.	11/4/19
Bancroft, Anne	New York, N.Y.	9/17/31
Barber, Red	Columbus, Miss.	2/17/08
Bardot, Brigitte	Paris, France	9/28/34
Bari, Lynn	Roanoke, Va.	12/18/17
Barker, Bob	Darrington, Wash.	12/12/23
Barnes, Priscilla	Ft. Dix, N.J.	12/7/56
Barrault, Jean-Louis	Vesinet, France	9/8/10
Barrie, Barbara	Chicago, Ill.	5/23/31
Barrie, Mona	London, England	12/18/09
Barry, Gene	New York, N.Y.	6/4/22
Bartholomew, Freddie	London, England	3/28/24
Bartok, Eva	Budapest, Hungary	6/18/29
Baryshnikov, Mikhail	Riga, Latvia	1/28/48
Basinger, Kim	Athens, Ga.	12/8/53
Bassey, Shirley	Cardiff, Wales	1/8/37
Bateman, Justine	Rye, N.Y.	2/19/66
Bates, Alan	Allestree, England	2/17/34
Baxter-Birney, Meredith	Los Angeles, Cal.	6/21/47
Beal, John	Joplin, Mo.	8/13/09
Bean, Orson	Burlington, Vt.	7/22/28
Beasley, Allyce	New York, N.Y.	7/6/54
Beatty, Ned	Louisville, Ky.	7/6/37
Beatty, Robert	Hamilton, Ont.	10/19/09
Beatty, Warren	Richmond, Va.	3/30/37
Beck, John	Chicago, Ill.	1943
Bedelia, Bonnie	New York, N.Y.	3/25/52
Bee Gees		
Gibb, Barry	Manchester, England	9/1/46
Gibb, Robin	" "	12/22/49
Gibb, Maurice	" "	12/22/49
Beery, Noah Jr.	New York, N.Y.	8/10/16
Begley, Ed Jr.	Los Angeles, Cal.	9/16/49
Belafonte, Harry	New York, N.Y.	3/1/27
Belafonte-Harper, Shari	New York, N.Y.	9/22/54
Bel Geddes, Barbara	New York, N.Y.	10/31/22
Bellamy, Ralph	Chicago, Ill.	6/17/04
Bellwood, Pamela	New York, N.Y.	6/26/-
Belmondo, Jean-Paul	Neuilly-sur-Seine, France	4/9/33
Benatar, Pat	Brooklyn, N.Y.	1/10/53
Benedict, Dirk	Helena, Mont.	3/1/45
Benjamin, Richard	New York, N.Y.	5/22/38
Bennett, Joan	Palisades, N.J.	2/27/10
Bennett, Tony	New York, N.Y.	8/3/26
Benson, George	Pittsburgh, Pa.	3/22/43
Benson, Robby	Dallas, Tex.	1/21/55
Bentley, John	Warwickshire, England	12/2/16
Beradino, John	Los Angeles, Cal.	5/1/17
Beranger, Tom	Chicago, Ill.	5/31/50
Bergen, Candice	Beverly Hills, Cal.	5/9/46
Bergen, Polly	Knoxville, Tenn.	7/4/30
Bergerac, Jacques	Biarritz, France	5/26/27
Bergman, Ingmar	Uppsala, Sweden	7/14/18
Berle, Milton	New York, N.Y.	7/12/08
Berlinger, Warren	Brooklyn, N.Y.	8/31/37
Berman, Lazar	Leningrad, USSR	2/26/30
Berman, Shelley	Chicago, Ill.	2/3/26
Bernsen, Corbin	No. Hollywood, Cal.	9/7/54
Bernstein, Leonard	Lawrence, Mass.	8/25/18
Berry, Chuck	San Jose, Cal.	1/15/26
Berry, Ken	Moline, Ill.	11/3/33
Bertinelli, Valerie	Wilmington, Del.	4/23/60
Bikel, Theodore	Vienna, Austria	5/2/24
Birney, David	Washington, D.C.	4/23/39
Bishop, Joey	Bronx, N.Y.	2/3/18
Bisoglio, Val	New York, N.Y.	5/7/26
Bisset, Jacqueline	Weybridge, England	9/13/44
Bixby, Bill	San Francisco, Cal.	1/22/34
Black, Karen	Park Ridge, Ill.	7/1/42
Blackstone Jr., Harry	Three Rivers, Mich.	6/30/34
Blaine, Vivian	Newark, N.J.	11/21/23
Blair, Linda	St. Louis, Mo.	1/22/59
Blake, Amanda	Buffalo, N.Y.	2/20/29
Blake, Robert	Nutley, N.J.	9/18/34
Blanc, Mel	San Francisco, Cal.	5/30/08
Bledsoe, Tempestt	Chicago, Ill.	8/1/73
Bloom, Claire	London, England	2/15/31
Blyth, Ann	Mt. Kisco, N.Y.	8/16/28
Bogarde, Dirk	London, England	3/28/20
Bogdanovich, Peter	Kingston, N.Y.	7/30/39
Bonet, Lisa	San Francisco, Cal.	11/16/67
Bono, Sonny	Detroit, Mich.	2/16/40
Booke, Sorrell	Buffalo, N.Y.	1/4/30
Boone, Debby	Hackensack, N.J.	9/22/56
Boone, Pat	Jacksonville, Fla.	6/1/34
Booth, Shirley	New York, N.Y.	8/30/07
Borge, Victor	Copenhagen, Denmark	1/3/09
Borgnine, Ernest	Hamden, Conn.	1/24/17
Bosley, Tom	Chicago, Ill.	10/1/27
Bosson, Barbara	Charleroi, Pa.	11/1/39
Bostwick, Barry	San Mateo, Cal.	2/24/46
Bottoms, Joseph	Santa Barbara, Cal.	4/22/54
Bottoms, Timothy	Santa Barbara, Cal.	8/30/51
Bowie, David	London, England	1/8/47
Boxleitner, Bruce	Elgin, Ill.	5/12/50
Boy George	London, England	1961
Boyle, Peter	Philadelphia, Pa.	10/18/33
Bracken, Eddie	New York, N.Y.	2/7/20
Brand, Neville	Kewanee, Ill.	8/13/21
Brando, Marlon	Omaha, Neb.	4/3/24
Brazzi, Rossano	Bologna, Italy	9/18/16
Brendel, Alfred	Wiesenberg, Austria	1/5/01
Brennan, Eileen	Los Angeles, Cal.	9/3/35

Name	Birthplace	Born
Brenner, David	Philadelphia, Pa.	1945
Brewer, Teresa	Toledo, Oh.	5/7/31
Brian, David	New York, N.Y.	8/5/14
Bridges, Beau	Hollywood, Cal.	12/9/41
Bridges, Jeff	Los Angeles, Cal.	12/4/49
Bridges, Lloyd	San Leandro, Cal.	1/15/13
Bridges, Todd	San Francisco, Cal.	5/27/65
Brimley, Wilford	Salt Lake City, Ut.	9/27/34
Broderick, Matthew	New York, N.Y.	3/21/53
Brolin, James	Los Angeles, Cal.	7/18/40
Bronson, Charles	Scooptown, Pa.	11/3/22
Brooks, Albert	Beverly Hills, Cal.	7/22/47
Brooks, Avery	Evansville, Ind.	10/2/-
Brooks, Mel	New York, N.Y.	6/28/26
Brooks, Stephen	Columbus, Oh.	1942
Brosnan, Pierce	Co. Meath, Ireland	5/16/52
Brown, Blair	Washington, D.C.	1948
Brown, James	Pulaski, Tenn.	6/17/28
Brown, Jim	St. Simons Island, Ga.	2/17/36
Brown, Les	Reinerton, Pa.	3/14/12
Brown, Ray	Pittsburgh, Pa.	10/13/26
Browne, Roscoe Lee	Woodbury, N.J.	1925
Bruce, Carol	Great Neck, N.Y.	11/15/19
Bryant, Anita	Barnsdall, Okla.	3/25/40
Bujold, Genevieve	Montreal, Que.	7/1/42
Bumbry, Grace	St. Louis, Mo.	1/4/37
Burghoff, Gary	Bristol, Conn.	5/24/43
Burke, Paul	New Orleans, La.	7/21/26
Burnett, Carol	San Antonio, Tex.	4/26/36
Burns, George	New York, N.Y.	1/20/96
Burr, Raymond	New Westminster, B.C.	5/21/17
Burstyn, Ellen	Detroit, Mich.	12/7/32
Burton, LeVar	Landsthul, W. Germany	2/16/57
Bushell, Anthony	Kent, England	5/19/04
Busey, Gary	Goose Creek, Tex.	6/29/44
Buttons, Red	New York, N.Y.	2/5/19
Buzzi, Ruth	Westerly, R.I.	7/24/36
Byrne, David	Dumbarton, Scotland	5/14/52
Caan, James	New York, N.Y.	3/26/39
Caballe, Montserrat	Barcelona, Spain	4/12/33
Caesar, Sid	Yonkers, N.Y.	9/8/22
Cage, Nicolas	Long Beach, Cal.	1965
Caine, Michael	London, England	3/14/33
Caldwell, Sarah	Maryville, Mo.	3/6/24
Caldwell, Zoe	Melbourne, Australia	9/14/33
Calhoun, Rory	Los Angeles, Cal.	8/8/22
Callas, Charlie	Brooklyn, N.Y.	12/20/-
Calloway, Cab	Rochester, N.Y.	12/25/07
Cameron, Kirk	San Fernando Valley, Cal.	1971
Campanella, Joseph	New York, N.Y.	11/21/27
Campbell, Glen	Billstown, Ark.	4/22/36
Candy, John	Toronto, Ont.	10/11/50
Cannon, Dyan	Tacoma, Wash.	1/4/37
Cantrell, Lana	Sydney, Australia	8/7/43
Capra, Frank	Palermo, Italy	5/18/97
Cara, Irene	New York, N.Y.	3/18/58
Carey, Macdonald	Sioux City, Ia.	3/15/13
Carey, Phil	Hackensack, N.J.	7/15/25
Carey, Ron	Newark, N.J.	12/11/35
Cariou, Len	Winnipeg, Canada	9/30/39
Carle, Frankie	Providence, R.I.	3/25/03
Carlin, George	New York, N.Y.	5/12/38
Carlisle, Kitty	New Orleans, La	9/3/15
Carmen, Eric	Cleveland, Oh.	8/11/49
Carmichael, Ian	Hull, England	6/18/20
Carnes, Kim	California	1948
Carney, Art	Mt. Vernon, N.Y.	11/4/18
Carnovsky, Morris	St. Louis, Mo.	9/5/97
Caron, Leslie	Boulogne, France	7/1/31
Carpenter, John	Carthage, N.Y.	1/16/48
Carr, Vikki	El Paso, Tex.	7/19/41
Carradine, David	Hollywood, Cal.	10/8/36
Carradine, John	New York, N.Y.	2/5/06
Carradine, Keith	San Mateo, Cal.	8/8/49
Carreras, Jose	Barcelona, Spain	12/5/47
Carroll, Diahann	Bronx, N.Y.	7/17/35
Carroll, Madeleine	W. Bromwich, England	2/26/06
Carroll, Pat	Shreveport, La.	5/5/27
Carson, Johnny	Corning, Ia.	10/23/25
Carter, Dixie	McLemoresville, Tenn.	5/25/-
Carter, Jack	New York, N.Y.	6/24/23
Carter, June	Maces Spring, Va.	6/23/29
Carter, Lynda	Phoenix, Ariz.	7/24/51
Carter, Nell	Birmingham, Ala.	9/13/48
Casadesus, Gaby	Marseilles, France	1902
Cash, Johnny	Kingsland, Ark.	2/26/32
Cash, Rosanne	Memphis, Tenn.	5/24/55
Cass, Peggy	Boston, Mass.	5/21/24
Cassavetes, John	New York, N.Y.	12/9/29
Cassidy, David	New York, N.Y.	4/12/50
Cassidy, Shaun	Los Angeles, Cal.	9/27/58
Castellano, Richard	New York, N.Y.	9/4/33
Cates, Phoebe	New York, N.Y.	1963
Caulfield, Joan	West Orange, N.J.	6/1/22
Cavallaro, Carmen	New York, N.Y.	5/6/13
Cavett, Dick	Gibbon, Neb.	11/19/36
Chamberlain, Richard	Beverly Hills, Cal.	3/31/35
Champion, Marge	Los Angeles, Cal.	9/2/23
Channing, Carol	Seattle, Wash.	1/31/23
Channing, Stockard	New York, N.Y.	2/13/44
Chaplin, Geraldine	Santa Monica, Cal.	7/31/44
Chaplin, Sydney	Beverly Hills, Cal.	3/31/26
Charisse, Cyd	Amarillo, Tex.	3/8/21
Charles, Ray	Albany, Ga.	9/23/30
Charo	Murcia, Spain	1/15/51
Chase, Chevy	New York, N.Y.	10/8/43
Checker, Chubby	Philadelphia, Pa.	10/3/41
Cher	El Centro, Cal.	5/20/46
Chong, Thomas	Edmonton, Alta.	5/24/38
Christie, Julie	Assam, India	4/14/40
Christopher, William	Evanston, Ill.	10/20/32
Christy, June	Springfield, Ill.	11/20/25
Clapton, Eric	Surrey, England	3/30/45
Clark, Dane	New York, N.Y.	2/18/13
Clark, Dick	Mt. Vernon, N.Y.	11/30/29
Clark, Petula	Ewell, Surrey, England	11/15/32
Clark, Roy	Meherrin, Va.	4/5/33
Clark, Susan	Sarnia, Ont.	3/8/40
Clary, Robert	Paris, France	3/1/26
Clayburgh, Jill	New York, N.Y.	4/30/44
Cleese, John	England	1939
Cliburn, Van	Shreveport, La.	7/12/34
Clooney, Rosemary	Maysville, Ky.	5/23/28
Close, Glenn	Greenwich, Conn.	3/19/47
Coburn, James	Laurel, Neb.	8/31/28
Coca, Imogene	Philadelphia, Pa.	11/18/08
Cohn, Mindy	Los Angeles, Cal.	5/20/66
Colbert, Claudette	Paris, France	9/18/05
Cole, Natalie	Los Angeles, Cal.	2/6/50
Coleman, Dabney	Austin, Tex.	1/3/32
Coleman, Gary	Zion, Ill.	2/8/68
Collins, Dorothy	Windsor, Ont.	11/18/26
Collins, Joan	London, England	5/23/33
Collins, Judy	Seattle, Wash.	5/1/39
Collins, Phil	London, England	1/30/51
Comden, Betty	Brooklyn, N.Y.	5/3/19
Como, Perry	Canonsburg, Pa.	5/18/12
Compton, Forrest	Reading, Pa.	9/15/25
Conner, Nadine	Compton, Cal.	2/20/13
Connery, Sean	Edinburgh, Scotland	8/25/30
Conniff, Ray	Attleboro, Mass.	11/6/16
Connors, Chuck	Brooklyn, N.Y.	4/10/21
Connors, Mike	Fresno, Cal.	8/15/25
Conrad, Robert	Chicago, Ill.	3/1/35
Constantine, Michael	Reading, Pa.	5/22/27
Conti, Tom	Paisley, Scotland	11/22/41
Convy, Bert	St. Louis, Mo.	6/23/33
Conway, Tim	Willoughby, Oh.	12/15/33
Cook, Barbara	Atlanta, Ga.	10/25/27
Cook, Peter	Torquay, England	11/17/37
Cooke, Alistair	Manchester, England	11/20/08
Coolidge, Rita	Nashville, Tenn.	5/1/45
Cooper, Alice	Detroit, Mich.	2/4/48
Cooper, Jackie	Los Angeles, Cal.	9/15/21
Coppola, Francis	Detroit, Mich.	4/7/39
Corby, Ellen	Racine, Wis.	6/3/13
Cord, Alex	New York, N.Y.	8/3/31
Corea, Chick	Chelsea, Mass.	6/12/41
Corelli, Franco	Ancona, Italy	4/8/23
Corey, Jeff	New York, N.Y.	8/10/14
Cosby, Bill	Philadelphia, Pa.	7/12/37
Costello, Elvis	London, England	8/25/54
Cotten, Joseph	Petersburg, Va.	5/15/05
Cougar, John	Seymour, Ind.	10/7/51
Courtenay, Tom	Hull, England	2/25/37
Craddock, Crash	Greensboro, N.C.	6/16/40
Crain, Jeanne	Barstow, Cal.	5/25/25
Crenna, Richard	Los Angeles, Cal.	11/30/26
Crespin, Regine	Marseilles, France	2/23/26
Cronyn, Hume	London, Ont.	7/18/11
Crosby, Bob	Spokane, Wash.	8/25/13
Crosby, Cathy Lee	Los Angeles, Cal.	12/2/-
Crosby, David	Los Angeles, Cal.	8/14/41
Crosby, Kathryn	Houston, Tex.	11/25/33

Name	Birthplace	Born
Crosby, Norm	Boston, Mass.	1/15/27
Cross, Christopher	San Antonio, Tex.	5/3/51
Cruise, Tom	Glen Ridge, N.J.	1962
Crystal, Billy	Long Beach, N.Y.	3/14/47
Cugat, Xavier	Barcelona, Spain	1/1/00
Cullen, Bill	Pittsburgh, Pa.	2/18/20
Cullum, John	Knoxville, Tenn.	3/2/30
Culp, Robert	Oakland, Cal.	8/16/30
Cummings, Constance	Seattle, Wash.	5/15/10
Cummings, Robert	Joplin, Mo.	6/9/10
Curtin, Jane	Cambridge, Mass.	9/6/47
Curtin, Phyllis	Clarksburg, W.Va.	12/3/30
Curtis, Jamie Lee	Los Angeles, Cal.	11/22/58
Curtis, Keene	Salt Lake City, Ut.	2/15/23
Curtis, Ken	Lamar, Col.	7/2/16
Curtis, Tony	New York, N.Y.	6/3/25
Cusack, Cyril	Durban, S. Africa	11/26/10
Cushing, Peter	Surrey, England	5/26/13
Dafoe, Willem	Milwaukee, Wis.	1955
Dahl, Arlene	Minneapolis, Minn.	8/11/28
Dailey, Irene	New York, N.Y.	9/12/20
Dale, Jim	Rothwell, England	8/15/35
Dalton, Abby	Las Vegas, Nev.	8/15/35
Daly, John	Johannesburg, S. Africa	2/20/14
Daly, Tyne	Madison, Wis.	2/21/47
Damone, Vic	Brooklyn, N.Y.	6/12/28
Dangerfield, Rodney	Babylon, N.Y.	11/22/21
Daniels, Charlie	Wilmington, N.C.	10/28/36
Daniels, William	Brooklyn, N.Y.	3/31/27
Danilova, Alexandra	Peterhof, Russia	11/20/07
Danner, Blythe	Philadelphia, Pa.	2/3/43
Danson, Ted	San Diego, Cal.	12/29/47
Danza, Tony	New York, N.Y.	4/21/50
Darby, Kim	Hollywood, Cal.	7/8/48
Darcel, Denise	Paris, France	9/8/25
Darren, James	Philadelphia, Pa.	6/8/36
Davidson, John	Pittsburgh, Pa.	12/13/41
Davis, Ann B.	Schenectady, N.Y.	5/5/26
Davis, Bette	Lowell, Mass.	4/5/08
Davis, Brad	Florida	11/6/49
Davis, Clifton	Chicago, Ill.	10/4/45
Davis, Geena	Ware, Mass.	1957
Davis, Judy	Perth, Australia	1956
Davis, Mac	Lubbock, Tex.	1/21/42
Davis, Ossie	Cogdell, Ga.	12/18/17
Davis, Sammy Jr.	New York, N.Y.	12/8/25
Davis, Skeeter	Dry Ridge, Ky.	12/30/31
Dawber, Pam	Detroit, Mich.	10/10/51
Dawn, Hazel	Ogden, Ut.	3/23/98
Dawson, Richard	Hampshire, England	11/20/02
Day, Dennis	New York, N.Y.	5/21/17
Day, Doris	Cincinnati, Oh.	4/3/24
Day, Laraine	Roosevelt, Ut.	10/13/17
Dean, Jimmy	Plainview, Tex.	8/10/28
De Camp, Rosemary	Prescott, Ariz.	11/14/10
DeCarlo, Yvonne	Vancouver, B.C.	9/1/22
Dee, Frances	Los Angeles, Cal.	11/26/07
Dee, Ruby	Cleveland, Oh.	10/27/23
Dee, Sandra	Bayonne, N.J.	4/29/42
Defore, Don	Cedar Rapids, Ia.	8/25/17
DeHaven, Gloria	Los Angeles, Cal.	7/23/25
De Havilland, Olivia	Tokyo, Japan	7/1/16
Dell, Gabriel	Barbados, BWI	10/7/19
Della Chiesa, Vivienne	Chicago, Ill.	10/9/20
Delon, Alain	Sceaux, France	11/8/35
DeLuise, Dom	Brooklyn, N.Y.	8/1/33
De Mille, Agnes	New York, N.Y.	1905
De Mornay, Rebecca	California	1963
Deneuve, Catherine	Paris, France	10/22/43
De Niro, Robert	New York, N.Y.	8/17/45
Dennehy, Brian	Bridgeport, Conn.	1938
Denning, Richard	Poughkeepsie, N.Y.	3/27/14
Dennis, Sandy	Hastings, Neb.	4/27/37
Denver, Bob	New Rochelle, N.Y.	1/9/35
Denver, John	Roswell, N.M.	12/31/43
DePalma, Brian	Newark, N.J.	9/11/40
Derek, Bo	Long Beach, Cal.	11/20/56
Derek, John	Hollywood, Cal.	8/12/26
Dern, Bruce	Chicago, Ill.	6/4/36
Devane, William	Albany, N.Y.	9/5/37
DeVito, Danny	Neptune, N.J.	11/17/44
Dewhurst, Colleen	Montreal, Que.	6/3/26
DeWitt, Joyce	Wheeling, W.Va.	4/23/49
Dey, Susan	Pekin, Ill.	12/10/52
Diamond, Neil	Brooklyn, N.Y.	1/24/41
Dickinson, Angie	Kulm, N.D.	9/30/31
Dietrich, Marlene	Berlin, Germany	12/27/01
Diller, Phyllis	Lima, Oh.	7/17/17
Dillman, Bradford	San Francisco, Cal.	4/14/30
Dillon, Matt	Westchester Co., N.Y.	2/18/64
Dixon, Ivan	New York, N.Y.	4/6/31
Dobson, Kevin	New York, N.Y.	3/18/44
Domingo, Placido	Madrid, Spain	1/21/41
Domino, Fats	New Orleans, La.	2/26/28
Donahue, Phil	Cleveland, Oh.	12/21/35
Donahue, Troy	New York, N.Y.	1/27/36
Donald, James	Aberdeen, Scotland	5/18/17
Donovan	Glasgow, Scotland	5/10/43
Dorati, Antol	Budapest, Hungary	4/9/06
Douglas, Kirk	Amsterdam, N.Y.	12/9/18
Douglas, Michael	New Brunswick, N.J.	9/25/44
Douglas, Mike	Chicago, Ill.	8/11/25
Down, Leslie-Ann	London, England	3/17/54
Downs, Hugh	Akron, Oh.	2/14/21
Doyle, David	Lincoln, Neb.	12/1/29
Dragon, Daryl	Los Angeles, Cal.	8/27/42
Drake, Alfred	Bronx, N.Y.	10/7/14
Drew, Ellen	Kansas City, Mo.	11/23/15
Dryer, Fred	Hawthorne, Cal.	7/6/46
Dreyfuss, Richard	Brooklyn, N.Y.	10/29/47
Dru, Joanne	Logan, W.Va.	1/31/23
Duchin, Peter	New York, N.Y.	7/28/37
Duff, Howard	Bremerton, Wash.	11/24/17
Duffy, Julia	Minneapolis, Minn.	6/27/52
Duffy, Patrick	Townsend, Mont.	3/17/49
Dufour, Val	New Orleans, La.	2/5/27
Duke, Patty	New York, N.Y.	12/14/46
Dullea, Keir	Cleveland, Oh.	5/30/36
Dunaway, Faye	Bascom, Fla.	1/14/41
Duncan, Sandy	Henderson, Tex.	2/20/46
Duncan, Todd	Danville, Ky.	2/12/00
Duncan, Vivian	Los Angeles, Cal.	6/17/02
Dunham, Katherine	Joliet, Ill.	6/22/10
Dunne, Irene	Louisville, Ky.	12/20/98
Dunnock, Mildred	Baltimore, Md.	1/25/04
Durbin, Deanna	Winnipeg, Man.	12/4/21
Durning, Charles	Highland Falls, N.Y.	2/28/23
Dussault, Nancy	Pensacola, Fla.	6/30/36
Duvall, Robert	San Diego, Cal.	1/5/31
Duvall, Shelley	Houston, Tex.	1949
Dylan, Bob	Duluth, Minn.	5/24/41
Dysart, Richard	Brighton, Me.	3/30/-
Easton, Sheena	Glascow, Scotland	4/27/59
Eastwood, Clint	San Francisco, Cal.	5/31/30
Ebson, Buddy	Belleville, Ill.	4/2/08
Eckstine, Billy	Pittsburgh, Pa.	7/8/14
Edelman, Herb	Brooklyn, N.Y.	11/5/33
Eden, Barbara	Tucson, Ariz.	8/23/31
Edwards, Blake	Tulsa, Okla.	7/26/22
Edwards, Ralph	Merino, Col.	6/13/13
Edwards, Vincent	Brooklyn, N.Y.	7/7/28
Egan, Richard	San Francisco, Cal.	7/29/21
Eggar, Samantha	London, England	3/5/39
Eichhorn, Lisa	Reading, Pa.	2/4/52
Eikenberry, Jill	New Haven, Conn.	2/21/47
Ekberg, Anita	Malmo, Sweden	9/29/31
Ekland, Britt	Stockholm, Sweden	10/6/42
Elam, Jack	Miami, Ariz.	11/13/16
Eldridge, Florence	Brooklyn, N.Y.	9/5/01
Elgart, Larry	New London, Conn.	3/20/22
Elgart, Les	New Haven, Conn.	1918
Elliott, Bob	Boston, Mass.	3/26/23
Elliott, Sam	Sacramento, Cal.	8/9/44
Estevez, Emelio	New York, N.Y.	1963
Estrada, Erik	New York, N.Y.	3/16/49
Evans, Dale	Uvalde, Tex.	10/31/12
Evans, Gene	Holbrook, Ariz.	7/11/24
Evans, Linda	Hartford, Conn.	11/18/42
Evans, Maurice	Dorchester, England	6/3/01
Evans, Robert	New York, N.Y.	6/29/30
Everett, Chad	South Bend, Ind.	6/11/36
Everly, Don	Brownie, Ky.	2/1/37
Everly, Phil	Brownie, Ky.	1/19/38
Ewell, Tom	Owensboro, Ky.	4/29/09
Fabares, Shelley	Santa Monica, Cal.	1/19/42
Fabian (Forte)	Philadelphia, Pa.	2/6/43
Fabray, Nanette	San Diego, Cal.	10/27/20
Fairbanks, Douglas Jr.	New York, N.Y.	12/9/09
Fairchild, Morgan	Dallas, Tex.	2/3/50
Falana, Lola	Philadelphia, Pa.	9/11/46
Falk, Peter	New York, N.Y.	9/16/27
Farentino, James	Brooklyn, N.Y.	2/24/38
Fargo, Donna	Mt. Airy, N.C.	11/10/45
Farr, Jamie	Toledo, Oh.	7/1/34
Farrell, Charles	Onset Bay, Mass.	1901
Farrell, Eileen	Willimantic, Conn.	2/13/20

Name	Birthplace	Born
Farrell, Mike	St. Paul, Minn.	2/6/39
Farrow, Mia	Los Angeles, Cal.	2/9/45
Fawcett, Farrah	Corpus Christi, Tex.	2/2/47
Faye, Alice	New York, N.Y.	5/5/12
Feld, Fritz	Berlin, Germany	10/15/00
Feldon, Barbara	Pittsburgh, Pa.	3/12/41
Feldshuh, Tovah	New York, N.Y.	12/27/52
Feliciano, Jose	Lares, Puerto Rico	9/10/45
Fell, Norman	Philadelphia, Pa.	3/24/24
Fellini, Federico	Rimini, Italy	1/20/20
Fellows, Edith	Boston, Mass.	5/20/23
Fender, Freddy	San Benito, Tex.	6/4/37
Ferrer, Jose	Santurce, P.R.	1/8/12
Ferrer, Mel	Elberon, N.J.	8/25/17
Ferrigno, Lou	Brooklyn, N.Y.	11/9/52
Field, Sally	Pasadena, Cal.	11/6/46
Fields, Kim	Los Angeles, Cal.	5/12/69
Finney, Albert	Salford, England	5/9/36
Firkusny, Rudolf	Napajedla, Czechoslovakia	2/11/12
Firth, Peter	Yorkshire, England	10/27/53
Fischer-Dieskau, Dietrich	Berlin, Germany	5/28/25
Fisher, Carrie	Beverly Hills, Cal.	10/21/56
Fisher, Eddie	Philadelphia, Pa.	8/10/28
Fitzgerald, Ella	Newport News, Va.	4/25/18
Fitzgerald, Geraldine	Dublin, Ireland	11/24/13
Flack, Roberta	Black Mountain, N.C.	2/10/39
Flanders, Ed	Minneapolis, Minn.	12/29/34
Fleming, Rhonda	Hollywood, Cal.	8/10/23
Fletcher, Louise	Birmingham, Ala.	1936
Foch, Nina	Leyden, Netherlands	4/20/24
Fogelberg, Dan	Peoria, Ill.	8/13/51
Fonda, Jane	New York, N.Y.	12/21/37
Fonda, Peter	New York, N.Y.	2/23/39
Fontaine, Joan	Tokyo, Japan	10/22/17
Fonteyn, Margot	Reigate, England	5/18/19
Ford (Tenn.), Ernie	Bristol, Tenn.	2/13/19
Ford, Glenn	Quebec, Canada	5/1/16
Ford, Harrison	Chicago, Ill.	7/13/42
Ford, Ruth	Brookhaven, Miss.	1920
Forrest, Steve	Huntsville, Tex.	9/29/24
Forsythe, Henderson	Macon, Mo.	9/11/17
Forsythe, John	Penns Grove, N.J.	1/29/18
Fosse, Bob	Chicago, Ill.	6/23/27
Foster, Jodie	Los Angeles, Cal.	11/19/62
Fox, James	London, England	5/19/39
Fox, Michael J.	Edmonton, Alta.	6/9/61
Foxworth, Robert	Houston, Tex.	11/1/41
Foxx, Redd	St. Louis, Mo.	12/9/22
Frampton, Peter	Kent, England	4/22/50
Francescatti, Zino	Marseilles, France	8/9/05
Franciosa, Anthony	New York, N.Y.	10/25/28
Francis, Anne	Ossining, N.Y.	9/16/30
Francis, Arlene	Boston, Mass.	10/20/08
Francis, Connie	Newark, N.J.	12/12/38
Francis, Genie	Los Angeles, Cal.	5/26/62
Franciscus, James	Clayton, Mo.	1/31/34
Frankenheimer, John	Malba, N.Y.	2/19/30
Franklin, Aretha	Memphis, Tenn.	3/25/42
Franklin, Bonnie	Santa Monica, Cal.	1/6/44
Franklin, Joe	New York, N.Y.	1929
Frann, Mary	St. Louis, Mo.	2/27/43
Franz, Dennis	Chicago, Ill.	10/28/-
Freberg, Stan	Pasadena, Cal.	8/7/26
Freed, Bert	New York, N.Y.	11/3/19
Freeman Jr., Al	San Antonio, Tex.	3/21/34
French, Victor	Santa Barbara, Cal.	12/4/34
Frey, Leonard	New York, N.Y.	9/14/38
Frick, Mr. (W. Groebli)	Basel, Switzerland	4/21/15
Friedkin, William	Chicago, Ill.	8/29/39
Frost, David	Tenterden, England	4/7/39
Frye, David	Brooklyn, N.Y.	1934
Funicello, Annette	Utica, N.Y.	10/22/42
Funt, Allen	New York, N.Y.	9/16/14
Gabor, Eva	Hungary	1921
Gabor, Zsa Zsa	Hungary	—
Gabriel, John	Niagara Falls, N.Y.	5/25/31
Gail, Max	Detroit, Mich.	4/5/43
Galloway, Don	Brooksville, Ky.	7/27/37
Galway, James	Belfast, Ireland	12/8/39
Garagiola, Joe	St. Louis, Mo.	2/12/26
Garbo, Greta	Stockholm, Sweden	9/18/05
Gardenia, Vincent	Naples, Italy	1/7/22
Gardner, Ava	Smithfield, N.C.	12/24/22
Garfunkel, Art	New York, N.Y.	10/13/41
Garland, Beverly	Santa Cruz, Cal.	10/17/26
Garner, James	Norman, Okla.	4/7/28
Garr, Terri	Los Angeles, Cal.	—
Garrett, Betty	St. Joseph, Mo.	5/23/19
Garrett, Leif	Hollywood, Cal.	11/8/61
Garson, Greer	Co. Down, N. Ireland	9/29/08
Gatlin, Larry	Seminole, Tex.	5/2/48
Gavin, John	Los Angeles, Cal.	4/8/32
Gayle, Crystal	Paintsville, Ky.	1/9/51
Gaynor, Mitzi	Chicago, Ill.	9/4/30
Gazzara, Ben	New York, N.Y.	8/28/30
Geary, Anthony	Coalsville, Ut.	5/29/47
Gedda, Nicolai	Stockholm, Sweden	7/11/25
Geldof, Bob	Co. Dublin, Ire.	10/5/51
Gennaro, Peter	Metairie, La.	1924
Gentry, Bobbie	Chickasaw Co., Miss.	7/27/44
Gerard, Gil	Little Rock, Ark.	1/23/43
Gere, Richard	Philadelphia, Pa.	8/31/49
Getty, Estelle	New York, N.Y.	7/25/-
Ghostley, Alice	Eve, Mo.	8/14/26
Giannini, Giancarlo	Spezia, Italy	8/1/42
Gibb, Andy	Manchester, England	3/5/58
Gibbs, Marla	Chicago, Ill.	6/14/31
Gibson, Henry	Germantown, Pa.	9/21/35
Gibson, Mel	New York, N.Y.	1/3/51
Gielgud, John	London, England	4/14/04
Gilbert, Melissa	Los Angeles, Cal.	5/8/64
Gilberto, Astrud	Salvador, Brazil	3/30/40
Gilford, Jack	New York, N.Y.	7/25/07
Gillette, Anita	Baltimore, Md.	8/16/36
Gilley, Mickey	Natchez, Miss.	3/9/36
Ginty, Robert	New York, N.Y.	11/14/48
Gish, Lillian	Springfield, Oh.	10/14/96
Glaser, Paul Michael	Cambridge, Mass.	3/25/43
Glass, Ron	Evansville, Ind.	7/10/45
Gless, Sharon	Los Angeles, Cal.	5/31/43
Glover, Danny	San Francisco, Cal.	1948
Glynn, Carlin	Cleveland, Oh.	2/19/40
Gobel, George	Chicago, Ill.	5/20/19
Godard, Jean Luc	Paris, France	12/3/30
Goddard, Paulette	Great Neck, N.Y.	6/3/11
Godunov, Alexander	Sakhalin Is., USSR	11/28/49
Goldberg, Whoopi	New York, N.Y.	1950
Goldblum, Jeff	Pittsburgh, Pa.	10/22/52
Goldsboro, Bobby	Marianna, Fla.	1/11/41
Goldthwait, Bob	Syracuse, N.Y.	1962
Gordon, Gale	New York, N.Y.	2/2/06
Gorman, Cliff	New York, N.Y.	10/13/36
Gorme, Eydie	Bronx, N.Y.	8/16/32
Gorshin, Frank	Pittsburgh, Pa.	4/5/34
Gossett Jr., Louis	Brooklyn, N.Y.	5/27/36
Gould, Elliott	Brooklyn, N.Y.	8/29/38
Gould, Harold	Schenectady, N.Y.	12/10/23
Gould, Morton	Richmond Hill, N.Y.	12/10/13
Goulding, Ray	Lowell, Mass.	3/20/22
Goulet, Robert	Lawrence, Mass.	11/26/33
Gowdy, Curt	Green River, Wyo.	7/31/19
Graham, Martha	Pittsburgh, Pa.	5/11/94
Graham, Virginia	Chicago, Ill.	7/4/12
Granger, Farley	San Jose, Cal.	7/1/25
Granger, Stewart	London, England	5/6/13
Granville, Bonita	New York, N.Y.	2/2/23
Grant, Lee	New York, N.Y.	10/31/29
Graves, Peter	Minneapolis, Minn.	3/18/25
Gray, Coleen	Staplehurst, Neb.	10/23/22
Gray, Erin	Honolulu, Ha.	1/7/-
Gray, Linda	Santa Monica, Cal.	9/12/40
Grayson, Kathryn	Winston-Salem, N.C.	2/9/22
Graziano, Rocky	New York, N.Y.	6/7/22
Greco, Buddy	Philadelphia, Pa.	8/14/26
Greco, Jose	Abruzzi, Italy	12/23/18
Green, Adolph	New York, N.Y.	12/2/15
Green, Al	Forest City, Ark.	4/13/46
Greene, Ellen	New York, N.Y.	1950
Greene, Lorne	Ottawa, Ont.	2/12/15
Greene, Shecky	Chicago, Ill.	4/8/26
Gregory, Cynthia	Los Angeles, Cal.	7/8/46
Gregory, Dick	St. Louis, Mo.	10/12/32
Gregory, James	Bronx, N.Y.	12/23/11
Grey, Joel	Cleveland, Oh.	4/11/32
Griffin, Merv	San Mateo, Cal.	7/6/25
Griffith, Andy	Mount Airy, N.C.	6/1/26
Grimes, Tammy	Lynn, Mass.	1/30/36
Grizzard, George	Roanoke Rapids, N.C.	4/1/28
Grodin, Charles	Pittsburgh, Pa.	4/21/35
Groh, David	New York, N.Y.	5/2/41
Grosbard, Ulu	Antwerp, Belgium	1/19/29
Gross, Mary	Chicago, Ill.	3/25/53
Gross, Michael	Chicago, Ill.	6/21/47
Grouch, Andrae	Los Angeles, Cal.	7/1/42
Guardino, Harry	New York, N.Y.	12/23/25

Name	Birthplace	Born
Guillaume, Robert	St. Louis, Mo.	11/30/28
Guinness, Alec	London, England	4/2/14
Gunn, Moses	St. Louis, Mo.	10/2/29
Guthrie, Arlo	New York, N.Y.	7/10/47
Guttenberg, Steve	New York, N.Y.	8/24/58
Gwynne, Fred	New York, N.Y.	7/10/26
Hackett, Buddy	Brooklyn, N.Y.	8/31/24
Hackman, Gene	San Bernardino, Cal.	1/30/30
Hagen, Uta	Gottingen, Germany	6/12/19
Haggard, Merle	Bakersfield, Cal.	4/6/37
Haggerty, Dan	Hollywood, Cal.	11/19/41
Hagman, Larry	Ft. Worth, Tex.	9/21/31
Haid, Charles	San Francisco, Cal.	6/2/43
Hale, Barbara	DeKalb, Ill.	4/18/22
Hall, Daryl	Pottstown, Pa.	10/11/49
Hall, Deidre	Milwaukee, Wis.	—
Hall, Huntz	New York, N.Y.	8/15/19
Hall, Monty	Winnipeg, Man.	8/25/23
Hall, Tom T.	Olive Hill, Ky.	5/25/36
Hamel, Veronica	Philadelphia, Pa.	11/20/43
Hamill, Mark	Oakland, Cal.	9/25/51
Hamilton, George	Memphis, Tenn.	8/12/39
Hamlin, Harry	Pasadena, Cal.	10/30/51
Hampshire, Susan	London, England	5/12/38
Hampton, Lionel	Birmingham, Ala.	4/12/13
Hancock, Herbie	Chicago, Ill.	4/12/40
Hanks, Tom	Oakland, Cal.	1956
Hannah, Daryl	Chicago, Ill.	1961
Harmon, Mark	Burbank, Cal.	9/2/51
Harper, Jessica	Chicago, Ill.	1949
Harper, Tess	Mommoth Springs, Ark.	1952
Harper, Valerie	Suffern, N.Y.	8/22/40
Harrington, Pat Jr.	New York, N.Y.	8/13/29
Harris, Barbara	Evanston, Ill.	7/25/35
Harris, Ed	Tenafly, N.J.	1950
Harris, Emmylou	Birmingham, Ala.	4/2/47
Harris, Julie	Grosse Pte. Park, Mich.	12/2/25
Harris, Phil	Linton, Ind.	6/24/04
Harris, Richard	Co. Limerick, Ireland	10/1/33
Harris, Rosemary	Ashby, England	9/19/30
Harrison, George	Liverpool, England	2/25/43
Harrison, Gregory	Avalon, Cal.	5/31/50
Harrison, Rex	Huyton, England	3/5/08
Harry, Deborah	Miami, Fla.	7/1/45
Harry, Jackee	Winston-Salem, N.C.	8/14/-
Hartley, Mariette	New York, N.Y.	6/21/40
Hartman, David	Pawtucket, R.I.	5/19/35
Hartman, Lisa	Houston, Tex.	1957
Hasselhoff, David	Baltimore, Md.	7/17/52
Hasso, Signe	Stockholm, Sweden	8/15/15
Haver, June	Rock Island, Ill.	6/10/26
Havoc, June	Vancouver, B.C.	11/0/10
Hawn, Goldie	Washington, D.C.	11/21/45
Hayden, Melissa	Toronto, Ont.	4/25/23
Hayes, Helen	Washington, D.C.	10/10/00
Hayes, Isaac	Covington, Tenn.	8/20/42
Hayes, Peter Lind	San Francisco, Cal.	6/25/15
Hays, Robert	Bethesda, Md.	7/24/47
Healy, Mary	New Orleans, La.	4/14/18
Heatherton, Joey	Rockville Centre, N.Y.	9/14/44
Heckart, Eileen	Columbus, Oh.	3/29/19
Heifetz, Jascha	Vilna, Lithuania	2/2/01
Helmond, Katherine	Galveston, Tex.	7/5/34
Hemingway, Margaux	Portland, Ore.	2/19/55
Hemingway, Mariel	Ketchum, Ida.	11/22/61
Hemmings, David	Guildford, England	11/18/41
Hemsley, Sherman	Philadelphia, Pa.	2/1/38
Henderson, Florence	Dale, Ind.	2/14/34
Henderson, Skitch	Halstad, Minn.	1/27/18
Henner, Marilu	Chicago, Ill.	4/6/52
Henning, Doug	Ft. Garry, Man., Canada	5/3/47
Henreid, Paul	Trieste, Austria	1/10/08
Hensley, Pamela	Los Angeles, Cal.	10/3/50
Henson, Jim	Greenville, Miss.	9/24/36
Hepburn, Audrey	Brussels, Belgium	5/4/29
Hepburn, Katharine	Hartford, Conn.	11/8/09
Herman, Pee-wee	Peekskill, N.Y.	1952
Herrmann, Edward	Washington, D.C.	7/21/43
Hershey, Barbara	Los Angeles, Cal.	2/5/48
Hesseman, Howard	Lebanon, Ore.	2/27/40
Heston, Charlton	Evanston, Ill.	10/4/23
Higgins, Joel	Bloomington, Ill.	9/28/46
Hildegarde	Adell, Wis.	2/1/06
Hill, Arthur	Melfort, Sask.	8/1/22
Hill, Benny	Southampton, England	1/21/25
Hill, George Roy	Minneapolis, Minn.	12/20/22
Hiller, Wendy	Stockport, England	8/15/12

Name	Birthplace	Born
Hillerman, John	Denison, Tex.	12/30/32
Hines, Gregory	New York, N.Y.	2/14/46
Hines, Jerome	Hollywood, Cal.	11/8/21
Hingle, Pat	Denver, Col.	7/19/23
Hirsch, Judd	Bronx, N.Y.	3/15/35
Hirt, Al	New Orleans, La.	11/7/22
Ho, Don	Kakaako, Oahu, Ha.	8/13/30
Hoffman, Dustin	Los Angeles, Cal.	8/8/37
Hogan, Paul	Sydney, Australia	1939
Holbrook, Hal	Cleveland, Oh.	2/17/25
Holder, Geoffrey	Trinidad	8/1/30
Holliday, Polly	Jasper, Ala.	7/2/37
Holliman, Earl	Delhi, La.	9/11/28
Holloway, Sterling	Cedartown, Ga.	1/4/05
Holm, Celeste	New York, N.Y.	4/29/19
Hooks, Robert	Washington, D.C.	4/18/37
Hope, Bob	London, England	5/29/03
Hopkins, Anthony	Wales	12/31/37
Hopkins, Telma	Louisville, Ky.	10/28/48
Hopper, Dennis	Dodge City, Kan.	5/17/36
Horne, Lena	Brooklyn, N.Y.	6/30/17
Horne, Marilyn	Bradford, Pa.	1/16/34
Horowitz, Vladimir	Kiev, Russia	10/1/04
Horsley, Lee	Muleshoe, Tex.	5/15/55
Horton, Robert	Los Angeles, Cal.	7/29/24
Hoskins, Bob	Suffolk, England	10/20/42
Houseman, John	Bucharest, Romania	9/22/02
Houston, Whitney	Newark, N.J.	1963
Howard, Ken	El Centro, Cal.	3/28/44
Howard, Ron	Duncan, Okla.	3/1/54
Howard, Susan	Marshall, Tex.	1/28/-
Howard, Trevor	Kent, England	9/29/16
Howes, Sally Ann	London, England	7/20/30
Hughes, Barnard	Bedford Hills, N.Y.	7/16/15
Hulce, Tom	White Water, Wis.	1953
Humperdinck, Engelbert	Madras, India	5/3/36
Hunt, Linda	Morristown, N.J.	1945
Hunter, Kim	Detroit, Mich.	11/12/22
Hunter, Ross	Cleveland, Oh.	5/6/21
Hunter, Tab	New York, N.Y.	7/11/31
Hurt, John	Chesterfield, England	1/22/40
Hurt, Mary Beth	Marshalltown, Ia.	9/26/48
Hurt, William	Washington, D.C.	3/20/50
Hussey, Olivia	Buenos Aires, Argentina	4/17/51
Hussey, Ruth	Providence, R.I.	10/30/14
Huston, John	Nevada, Mo.	8/5/06
Hutchinson, Josephine	Seattle, Wash.	10/12/09
Hutton, Betty	Battle Creek, Mich.	2/26/21
Hutton, Lauren	Charleston, S.C.	11/17/43
Hutton, Timothy	Malibu, Cal.	8/16/60
Hyde-White, Wilfrid	Gloucester, England	5/12/03
Hyman, Earle	Rocky Mount, N.C.	11/11/26
Ian, Janis	New York, N.Y.	4/7/50
Iglesias, Julio	Spain	9/23/43
Ireland, Jill	London, England	4/24/36
Ireland, John	Vancouver, B.C.	1/30/14
Irons, Jeremy	Cowes, England	9/19/48
Irving, Amy	Palo Alto, Cal.	9/10/53
Irving, George S.	Springfield, Mass.	11/1/22
Ives, Burl	Hunt Township, Ill.	6/14/09
Ivey, Judith	El Paso, Tex.	9/4/51
Jackson, Anne	Allegheny, Pa.	9/3/26
Jackson, Glenda	Liverpool, England	5/9/38
Jackson, Jermaine	Gary, Ind.	12/11/54
Jackson, Kate	Birmingham, Ala.	10/29/48
Jackson, Michael	Gary, Ind.	8/29/58
Jacobi, Derek	London, England	10/22/38
Jaeckel, Richard	Long Beach, Cal.	10/10/26
Jagger, Dean	Columbus Grove, Oh.	11/7/03
Jagger, Mick	Dartford, England	7/26/43
James, Dennis	Jersey City, N.J.	8/24/17
James, John	Minneapolis, Minn.	4/18/-
Janis, Conrad	New York, N.Y.	2/11/28
Jarreau, Al	Milwaukee, Wis.	3/12/40
Jeanmaire, Renee	Paris, France	4/29/24
Jeffreys, Anne	Goldsboro, N.C.	1/26/23
Jeffries, Fran	San Jose, Cal.	1939
Jenner, Bruce	Mt. Kisco, N.Y.	10/28/49
Jennings, Waylon	Littlefield, Tex.	6/15/37
Jett, Joan	Philadelphia, Pa.	9/22/60
Jillian, Ann	Cambridge, Mass.	1/29/51
Joel, Billy	Bronx, N.Y.	5/9/49
John, Elton	Middlesex, England	3/25/47
Johns, Glynis	Durban, S. Africa	10/5/23
Johnson, Arte	Benton Harbor, Mich.	1/20/29
Johnson, Ben	Foeaker, Okla.	6/13/18
Johnson, Don	Flatt Creek, Mo.	12/15/49

Name	Birthplace	Born
Johnson, Van	Newport, R.I.	8/25/16
Jones, Allan	Scranton, Pa.	10/14/07
Jones, Chris	Jackson, Tenn.	8/18/41
Jones, Dean	Morgan City, Ala.	1/25/35
Jones, George	Saratoga, Tex.	9/12/31
Jones, Grace	Spanishtown, Jamaica	5/19/52
Jones, Grandpa	Niagara, Ky.	10/20/13
Jones, Henry	Philadelphia, Pa.	8/1/12
Jones, Jack	Hollywood, Cal.	1/14/38
Jones, James Earl	Tate Co., Miss.	1/17/31
Jones, Jennifer	Tulsa, Okla.	3/2/19
Jones, Shirley	Smithton, Pa.	3/31/34
Jones, Tom	Pontypridd, Wales	6/7/40
Jones, Tommy Lee	San Saba, Tex.	9/15/46
Jourdan, Louis	Marseilles, France	6/19/19
Julia, Raul	San Juan, P.R.	3/9/40
Jurado, Katy	Guadalajara, Mexico	1/16/24
Kahn, Madeline	Boston, Mass.	9/29/42
Kanaly, Steve	Burbank, Cal.	3/14/46
Kane, Carol	Cleveland, Oh.	6/18/52
Kaplan, Gabe	Brooklyn, N.Y.	3/31/45
Karlen, John	New York, N.Y.	5/28/-
Karras, Alex	Gary, Ind.	7/15/35
Katt, William	Los Angeles, Cal.	2/16/55
Kavner, Julie	Los Angeles, Cal.	9/7/51
Kazan, Elia	Istanbul, Turkey	9/7/09
Kazan, Lainie	New York, N.Y.	5/15/42
Keach, Stacy	Savannah, Ga.	6/2/41
Keaton, Diane	Santa Ana, Cal.	1/5/46
Keel, Howard	Gillespie, Ill.	4/13/17
Keeler, Ruby	Halifax, N.S.	8/25/09
Keeshan, Bob	Lynbrook, N.Y.	6/27/27
Keitel, Harvey	Brooklyn, N.Y.	1947
Keith, Brian	Bayonne, N.J.	11/14/21
Keith, David	Knoxville, Tenn.	1955
Keller, Marthe	Basel, Switzerland	1945
Kellerman, Sally	Long Beach, Cal.	6/2/37
Kelley, DeForest	Atlanta, Ga.	1/20/20
Kelly, Gene	Pittsburgh, Pa.	8/23/12
Kelly, Jack	Astoria, N.Y.	9/16/27
Kelly, Nancy	Lowell, Mass.	3/25/21
Kennedy, Arthur	Worcester, Mass.	2/17/14
Kennedy, George	New York, N.Y.	2/18/26
Kennedy, Jayne	Washington, D.C.	11/27/51
Kennedy, Tom	Louisville, Ky.	2/26/-
Kent, Allegra	Los Angeles, Cal.	8/11/37
Kercheval, Ken	Wolcottville, Ind.	7/15/35
Kerr, Deborah	Helensburgh, Scotland	9/30/21
Kerr, John	New York, N.Y.	11/15/31
Khan, Chaka	Great Lakes, Ill.	3/23/53
Kidd, Michael	New York, N.Y.	8/12/19
Kidder, Margot	Yellowknife, N.W.T.	10/17/48
Kiley, Richard	Chicago, Ill.	3/31/22
King, Alan	Brooklyn, N.Y.	12/26/27
King, B. B.	Itta Bena, Miss.	9/16/25
King, Carole	Brooklyn, N.Y.	2/9/42
King, Perry	Alliance, Oh.	4/30/48
Kingsley, Ben	Yorkshire, England	12/31/43
Kinski, Klaus	Berlin, Germany	1926
Kinski, Nastassia	Berlin, W. Germany	1/24/60
Kirby, Durward	Covington, Ky.	8/24/12
Kirkland, Gelsey	Bethlehem, Pa.	12/29/52
Kirsten, Dorothy	Montclair, N.J.	7/6/19
Kitt, Eartha	North, S.C.	1/26/28
Klein, Robert	New York, N.Y.	2/8/42
Klemperer, Werner	Cologne, Germany	3/22/19
Kline, Kevin	St. Louis, Mo.	10/24/47
Klugman, Jack	Philadelphia, Pa.	4/27/22
Knight, Gladys	Atlanta, Ga.	5/28/44
Knotts, Don	Morgantown, W. Va.	7/21/24
Knox, Alexander	Strathroy, Ont., Canada	1/16/07
Kopell, Bernie	New York, N.Y.	6/21/33
Korman, Harvey	Chicago, Ill.	2/15/27
Kotero, Apollonia	Santa Monica, Cal.	8/2/-
Kotto, Yaphet	New York, N.Y.	11/15/37
Kramer, Stanley	New York, N.Y.	9/29/13
Kramer, Stephanie	Los Angeles, Cal.	8/6/-
Kristofferson, Kris	Brownsville, Tex.	6/22/36
Kubelik, Rafael	Bychori, Czechoslovakia	6/29/14
Kubrick, Stanley	Bronx, N.Y.	7/26/28
Kulp, Nancy	Harrisburg, Pa.	8/28/21
Kurtz, Swoosie	Omaha, Neb.	9/6/44
LaBelle, Patti	Philadelphia, Pa.	10/4/44
Ladd, Cheryl	Huron, S.D.	7/12/51
Ladd, Diane	Meridian, Miss.	11/29/39
Lahti, Christine	Detroit, Mich.	4/4/50
Laine, Frankie	Chicago, Ill.	3/30/13

Name	Birthplace	Born
Lamarr, Hedy	Vienna, Austria	9/11/14
Lamas, Lorenzo	Los Angeles, Cal.	1/20/58
Lamb, Gil	Minneapolis, Minn.	6/14/06
Lamour, Dorothy	New Orleans, La.	12/10/14
Lancaster, Burt	New York, N.Y.	11/2/13
Landau, Martin	New York, N.Y.	1933
Landesberg, Steve	New York, N.Y.	11/23/-
Landis, John	Chicago, Ill.	8/30/50
Landon, Michael	Forest Hills, N.Y.	10/31/36
Lane, Abbe	Brooklyn, N.Y.	12/14/32
Lane, Priscilla	Indianola, Ia.	6/12/17
Lange, Hope	Redding Ridge, Conn.	11/28/31
Lange, Jessica	Cloquet, Minn.	4/20/49
Langella, Frank	Bayonne, N.J.	1/1/40
Langford, Frances	Lakeland, Fla.	4/4/13
Lansbury, Angela	London, England	10/16/25
Lansing, Robert	San Diego, Cal.	6/5/29
Laredo, Ruth	Detroit, Mich.	11/20/37
Larroquette, John	New Orleans, La.	11/25/57
Lasser, Louise	New York, N.Y.	4/11/39
Lauper, Cyndi	New York, N.Y.	6/20/53
Laurie, Piper	Detroit, Mich.	1/22/32
Lauter, Ed	Long Beach, N.Y.	10/30/40
Lavin, Linda	Portland, Me.	10/15/37
Lawrence, Carol	Melrose Park, Ill.	9/5/34
Lawrence, Steve	Brooklyn, N.Y.	7/8/35
Lawrence, Vicki	Inglewood, Cal.	3/26/49
Leachman, Cloris	Des Moines, Ia.	4/4/26
Lean, David	Croydon, England	3/25/08
Lear, Norman	New Haven, Conn.	7/27/22
Learned, Michael	Washington, D.C.	4/9/39
LeBon, Simon	Bushey, England	10/27/58
Lederer, Francis	Prague, Czechoslovakia	11/6/06
Lee, Brenda	Atlanta, Ga.	12/11/44
Lee, Christopher	London, England	5/27/22
Lee, Michele	Los Angeles, Cal.	6/24/42
Lee, Peggy	Jamestown, N.D.	5/26/20
Le Gallienne, Eva	London, England	1/11/99
Legrand, Michel	Paris, France	2/24/32
Leibman, Ron	New York, N.Y.	10/11/37
Leigh, Janet	Merced, Cal.	7/6/27
Leinsdorf, Erich	Vienna, Austria	2/4/12
Lemmon, Jack	Boston, Mass.	2/8/25
Lennon, Dianne	Los Angeles, Cal.	12/1/39
Lennon, Janet	Culver City, Cal.	11/15/46
Lennon, Julian	Liverpool, England	4/8/63
Lennon, Kathy	Santa Monica, Cal.	8/22/42
Lennon, Peggy	Los Angeles, Cal.	4/8/41
Leonard, Sheldon	New York, N.Y.	2/22/07
Leontovich, Eugenie	Moscow, Russia	3/21/00
LeRoy, Mervyn	San Francisco, Cal.	10/15/00
Leslie, Joan	Detroit, Mich.	1/26/25
Lester, Jerry	Chicago, Ill.	1911
Letterman, David	Indianapolis, Ind.	4/12/47
Levine, James	Cincinnati, Oh.	6/23/43
Lewis, Emmanuel	New York, N.Y.	3/9/71
Lewis, Huey	New York, N.Y.	1952
Lewis, Jerry	Newark, N.J.	3/16/26
Lewis, Jerry Lee	Ferriday, La.	9/29/35
Lewis, Shari	New York, N.Y.	1/17/34
Light, Judith	Trenton, N.J.	2/9/50
Lightfoot, Gordon	Orillia, Ont.	11/17/38
Lillie, Beatrice	Toronto, Ont.	5/29/94
Linden, Hal	New York, N.Y.	3/20/31
Lindfors, Viveca	Uppsala, Sweden	12/29/20
Lindsey, Mort	Newark, N.J.	3/21/23
Linkletter, Art	Saskatchewan, Canada	7/17/12
Lithgow, John	Rochester, N.Y.	10/19/45
Little, Cleavon	Chickasha, Okla.	6/1/39
Little, Rich	Ottawa, Ont.	11/26/38
Little Richard	Macon, Ga.	12/25/35
Lloyd, Christopher	Stamford, Conn.	10/22/38
Locke, Sondra	Shelbyville, Tenn.	5/28/47
Lockhart, June	New York, N.Y.	6/25/25
Locklear, Heather	Los Angeles, Cal.	9/25/61
Lockwood, Margaret	Karachi, India	9/15/16
Loder, John	London, England	1/3/98
Logan, Joshua	Texarkana, Tex.	10/5/08
Loggia, Robert	New York, N.Y.	1/3/30
Loggins, Kenny	Everett, Wash.	1/7/48
Lollobrigida, Gina	Subiaco, Italy	7/4/28
Lom, Herbert	Prague, Czechoslovakia	1/9/17
London, Julie	Santa Rosa, Cal.	9/26/26
Long, Shelley	Ft. Wayne, Ind.	8/23/49
Lopez, Priscilla	New York, N.Y.	2/26/48
Lopez, Trini	Dallas, Tex.	5/15/37
Lord, Jack	New York, N.Y.	—
Loren, Sophia	Rome, Italy	9/20/34

Name	Birthplace	Born
Loring, Gloria	New York, N.Y.	12/10/46
Loudon, Dorothy	Boston, Mass.	9/17/33
Louise, Tina	New York, N.Y.	3/11/34
Lowe, Rob	Virginia	1964
Loy, Myrna	Helena, Mon.	8/2/05
Lucas, George	Modesto, Cal.	5/14/44
Lucci, Susan	Westchester Co., N.Y.	12/23/49
Luckinbill, Laurence	Ft. Smith, Ark.	11/21/34
Ludwig, Christa	Berlin, Germany	3/16/28
Luke, Keye	Canton, China	1904
Lumet, Sidney	Philadelphia, Pa.	6/25/24
Lund, John	Rochester, N.Y.	2/6/13
Lupino, Ida	London, England	2/4/18
LuPone, Patti	Northport, N.Y.	4/21/49
Lynley, Carol	New York, N.Y.	2/13/42
Lynn, Jeffrey	Auburn, Mass.	2/16/09
Lynn, Loretta	Butcher Hollow, Ky.	4/14/35
Maazel, Lorin	Paris, France	3/6/30
MacArthur, James	Los Angeles, Cal.	12/8/37
MacCorkindale, Simon	Cambridge, England	2/12/52
MacGraw, Ali	Pound Ridge, N.Y.	4/1/39
MacKenzie, Gisele	Winnipeg, Man.	1/10/27
MacLaine, Shirley	Richmond, Va.	4/24/34
MacLeod, Gavin	Mt. Kisco, N.Y.	2/28/30
MacMurray, Fred	Kankakee, Ill.	8/30/08
MacNee, Patrick	England	1922
MacNeil, Cornell	Minneapolis, Minn.	9/24/22
Macchio, Ralph	Long Island, N.Y.	1961
Macy, Bill	Revere, Mass.	5/18/22
Madden, John	Austin, Minn.	4/10/36
Madonna (Ciccone)	Bay City, Mich.	8/16/58
Majors, Lee	Wyandotte, Mich.	4/23/40
Makarova, Natalia	Leningrad, USSR	11/21/40
Malbin, Elaine	New York, N.Y.	5/24/32
Malden, Karl	Chicago, Ill.	3/22/13
Malfitano, Catherine	New York, N.Y.	4/18/48
Malkovich, John	Christopher, Ill.	12/9/53
Malle, Louis	Thumeries, France	10/30/32
Malone, Dorothy	Chicago, Ill.	1/30/25
Manchester, Melissa	Bronx, N.Y.	2/15/51
Mancini, Henry	Cleveland, Oh.	4/16/24
Mandel, Howie	Toronto, Ont.	11/29/
Mandrell, Barbara	Houston, Tex.	12/25/48
Mangione, Chuck	Rochester, N.Y.	11/29/40
Manilow, Barry	New York, N.Y.	6/17/46
Mann, Herbie	New York, N.Y.	4/16/30
Marceau, Marcel	Strasbourg, France	3/22/23
Marchand, Nancy	Buffalo, N.Y.	6/19/28
Margolin, Janet	New York, N.Y.	7/25/43
Marin, Cheech	Los Angeles, Cal.	7/13/46
Markova, Alicia	London, England	12/1/10
Marriner, Neville	Lincoln, England	4/15/24
Marsh, Jean	London, England	7/1/34
Marshall, E. G.	Owatonna, Minn.	6/18/10
Marshall, Penny	New York, N.Y.	10/15/43
Marshall, Peter	Huntington, W.Va.	3/30/-
Martin, Dean	Steubenville, Oh.	6/17/17
Martin, Dick	Detroit, Mich.	1/30/23
Martin, Mary	Weatherford, Tex.	12/1/13
Martin, Pamela Sue	Westport, Conn.	1/5/54
Martin, Steve	Waco, Tex.	1945
Martin, Tony	San Francisco, Cal.	12/25/13
Martins, Peter	Copenhagen, Denmark	10/27/46
Martino, Al	Philadelphia, Pa.	10/7/27
Marvin, Lee	New York, N.Y.	2/19/24
Mason, Jackie	Sheboygan, Wis.	1931
Mason, Marsha	St. Louis, Mo.	4/3/42
Mason, Pamela	London, England	3/10/22
Mastroianni, Marcello	Rome, Italy	9/28/24
Matheson, Tim	Glendale, Cal.	12/31/47
Mathis, Johnny	San Francisco, Cal.	9/30/35
Matthau, Walter	New York, N.Y.	10/1/20
Mature, Victor	Louisville, Ky.	1/29/16
May, Elaine	Philadelphia, Pa.	4/21/32
Mayo, Virginia	St. Louis, Mo.	11/30/20
Mazurki, Mike	Austria	12/25/09
Mazursky, Paul	Brooklyn, N.Y.	4/25/30
McArdle, Andrea	Philadelphia, Pa.	11/5/63
McBride, Patricia	Teaneck, N.J.	8/23/42
McCallum, David	Glasgow, Scotland	9/19/33
McCambridge, Mercedes	Joliet, Ill.	3/17/18
McCarthy, Andrew	New York, N.Y.	1963
McCarthy, Kevin	Seattle, Wash.	2/15/14
McCartney, Paul	Liverpool, England	6/18/42
McClanahan, Rue	Healdton, Okla.	2/21/36
McClure, Doug	Glendale, Cal.	5/11/35
McCoo, Marilyn	Jersey City, N.J.	9/30/43
McCord, Kent	Los Angeles, Cal.	9/26/42
McCrea, Joel	Los Angeles, Cal.	11/5/05
McDowall, Roddy	London, England	9/17/28
McDowell, Malcolm	Leeds, England	6/19/43
McEntire, Reba	Chockie, Okla.	3/28/54
McFarland, Spanky	Dallas, Tex.	10/2/28
McGavin, Darren	San Joaquin, Cal.	5/7/22
McGee, Fibber	Peoria, Ill.	11/6/96
McGoohan, Patrick	New York, N.Y.	3/19/28
McGovern, Elizabeth	Evanston, Ill.	7/18/61
McGovern, Maureen	Youngstown, Oh.	7/27/49
McGuire, Dorothy	Omaha, Neb.	6/14/19
McIntire, John	Spokane, Wash.	6/27/07
McKechnie, Donna	Pontiac, Mich.	11/16/42
McKee, Lonette	Detroit, Mich.	1954
McKellen, Ian	Burnley, England	5/25/39
McKeon, Nancy	Westbury, N.Y.	4/4/66
McLean, Don	New Rochelle, N.Y.	10/2/45
McLerie, Allyn	Grand Mere, Que.	12/1/26
McMahon, Ed	Detroit, Mich.	3/6/23
McMillan, Kenneth	New York, N.Y.	7/2/32
McNair, Barbara	Racine, Wis.	3/4/39
McNichol, Jimmy	Los Angeles, Cal.	7/2/61
McNichol, Kristy	Los Angeles, Cal.	9/11/62
McQueen, Butterfly	Tampa, Fla.	1/7/11
McRaney, Gerald	Collins, Miss.	8/19/47
Meadows, Audrey	Wu Chang, China	1924
Meadows, Jayne	Wu Chang, China	9/27/20
Meara, Anne	New York, N.Y.	9/20/29
Meeker, Ralph	Minneapolis, Minn.	11/21/20
Mehta, Zubin	Bombay, India	4/29/36
Melanie	New York, N.Y.	2/3/47
Mendes, Sergio	Nitero, Brazil	2/11/41
Menuhin, Yehudi	New York, N.Y.	4/22/16
Mercouri, Melina	Athens, Greece	10/18/25
Meredith, Burgess	Cleveland, Oh.	11/16/08
Merrick, David	Hong Kong	11/27/12
Merrill, Dina	New York, N.Y.	12/9/25
Merrill, Gary	Hartford, Conn.	8/2/15
Merrill, Robert	Brooklyn, N.Y.	6/4/19
Messina, Jim	Maywood, Cal.	12/5/47
Midler, Bette	Paterson, N.J.	12/1/45
Milanov, Zinka	Zagreb, Yugoslavia	5/17/08
Miles, Joanna	Nice, France	3/6/40
Miles, Sarah	Ingatestone, England	12/31/41
Miles, Vera	near Boise City, Okla.	8/23/30
Miller, Ann	Houston, Tex.	4/12/23
Miller, Jason	New York, N.Y.	4/22/39
Miller, Mitch	Rochester, N.Y.	7/4/11
Miller, Roger	Ft. Worth, Tex.	1/2/36
Mills, Donna	Chicago, Ill.	12/11/43
Mills, Hayley	London, England	4/18/46
Mills, John	Suffolk, England	2/22/08
Mills, Juliet	London, England	11/21/41
Mills Brothers.		
Mills, Herbert	Piqua, Oh.	4/12/12
Mills, Donald	Piqua, Oh.	4/29/15
Milner, Martin	Detroit, Mich.	12/28/31
Milnes, Sherrill	Downers Grove, Ill.	1/10/35
Milsap, Ronnie	Robinsville, N.C.	1/16/43
Milstein, Nathan	Odessa, Russia	12/31/04
Mimieux, Yvette	Hollywood, Cal.	1/8/39
Minnelli, Liza	Los Angeles, Cal.	3/12/46
Mitchell, Cameron	Dallastown, Pa.	11/4/18
Mitchell, James	Sacramento, Cal.	2/29/20
Mitchell, Joni	McLeod, Alta.	11/7/43
Mitchum, Robert	Bridgeport, Conn.	8/6/17
Moffat, Donald	Plymouth, England	12/26/30
Moffo, Anna	Wayne, Pa.	6/27/34
Molinaro, Al	Kenosha, Wis.	6/24/19
Montalban, Ricardo	Mexico City, Mexico	11/25/20
Montand, Yves	Monsumagno, Italy	10/13/21
Montgomery, Elizabeth	Hollywood, Cal.	4/15/33
Montgomery, George	Brady, Mon.	8/29/16
Moody, Ron	London, England	1/8/24
Moore, Clayton	Chicago, Ill.	9/14/14
Moore, Constance	Sioux City, Ia.	1/18/22
Moore, Dudley	London, England	4/19/35
Moore, Garry	Baltimore, Md.	1/31/15
Moore, Mary Tyler	Brooklyn, N.Y.	12/29/37
Moore, Melba	New York, N.Y.	10/29/45
Moore, Roger	London, England	10/14/27
Moore, Terry	Los Angeles, Cal.	1/1/32
Moran, Erin	Los Angeles, Cal.	10/18/61
Moreau, Jeanne	Paris, France	1/23/28
Moreno, Rita	Humacao, P.R.	12/11/31
Morgan, Dennis	Prentice, Wis.	12/10/10

Name	Birthplace	Born
Morgan, Harry	Detroit, Mich.	4/10/15
Morgan, Henry	New York, N.Y.	3/31/15
Morgan, Jane	Boston, Mass.	1920
Morgan, Jaye P.	Mancos, Col.	12/3/31
Moriarty, Michael	Detroit, Mich.	4/5/41
Morini, Erika	Vienna, Austria	1/5/10
Morley, Robert	Wiltshire, England	5/26/08
Morris, Greg	Cleveland, Oh.	9/27/34
Morris, Howard	New York, N.Y.	9/4/25
Morse, Robert	Newton, Mass.	5/18/31
Mulgrew, Kate	Dubuque, Ia.	4/29/55
Mulhare, Edward	Ireland	4/8/23
Mull, Martin	Chicago, Ill.	8/18/43
Mulligan, Richard	New York, N.Y.	11/13/32
Munsel, Patrice	Spokane, Wash.	5/14/25
Murphy, Ben	Jonesboro, Ark.	3/6/42
Murphy, Eddie	Brooklyn, N.Y.	4/3/61
Murphy, George	New Haven, Conn.	7/4/02
Murphy, Michael	Los Angeles, Cal.	5/5/38
Murray, Anne	Springhill, Nova Scotia	6/20/45
Murray, Arthur	New York, N.Y.	4/4/95
Murray, Bill	Evanston, Ill.	9/21/50
Murray, Don	Hollywood, Cal.	7/31/29
Murray, Kathryn	Jersey City, N.J.	9/15/06
Murray, Ken	New York, N.Y.	7/14/03
Musante, Tony	Bridgeport, Conn.	6/30/36
Musburger, Brent	Portland, Ore.	5/26/39
Muti, Riccardo	Naples, Italy	7/28/41
Nabors, Jim	Sylacauga, Ala.	6/12/33
Nash, Graham	Blackpool, England	2/2/42
Natwick, Mildred	Baltimore, Md.	6/19/08
Neal, Patricia	Packard, Ky.	1/20/26
Neff, Hildegarde	Ulm, Germany	12/28/25
Negri, Pola	Lipno, Poland	1899
Nelligan, Kate	London, Ontario	3/16/51
Nelson, Barry	San Francisco, Cal.	4/16/20
Nelson, Craig T.	Spokane, Wash.	1944
Nelson, David	New York, N.Y.	10/24/36
Nelson, Ed	New Orleans, La.	12/21/28
Nelson, Gene	Seattle, Wash.	3/24/20
Nelson, Harriet (Hilliard)	Des Moines, Ia.	7/18/14
Nelson, Willie	Abbott, Tex.	4/30/33
Nero, Peter	New York, N.Y.	5/22/34
Newhart, Bob	Oak Park, Ill.	9/5/29
Newley, Anthony	Hackney, England	9/24/31
Newman, Barry	Boston, Mass.	11/7/38
Newman, Laraine	Los Angeles, Cal.	3/2/-
Newman, Paul	Cleveland, Oh.	1/26/25
Newman, Phyllis	Jersey City, N.J.	3/19/35
Newman, Randy	Los Angeles, Cal.	11/28/43
Newton, Wayne	Norfolk, Va.	4/3/42
Newton-John, Olivia	Cambridge, England	9/26/48
Nichols, Mike	Berlin, Germany	11/6/31
Nicholson, Jack	Neptune, N.J.	4/28/37
Nicks, Stevie	California	5/26/48
Nielsen, Leslie	Regina, Sask	2/11/26
Nilsson, Birgit	Karup, Sweden	5/17/18
Nimoy, Leonard	Boston, Mass.	3/26/31
Noble, James	Dallas, Tex.	3/5/22
Nolte, Nick	Omaha, Neb.	2/8/40
Norman, Jessye	Augusta, Ga.	9/15/45
Norris, Chuck	Ryan, Okla.	1939
North, Sheree	Los Angeles, Cal.	1/17/33
Norton-Taylor, Judy	Santa Monica, Cal.	1/29/58
Novak, Kim	Chicago, Ill.	2/18/33
Novello, Don	Ashabula, Oh.	1/1/43
Nureyev, Rudolf	Russia	3/17/38
Oates, John	New York, N.Y.	4/7/48
O'Brian, Hugh	Rochester, N.Y.	4/19/30
O'Brien, Margaret	San Diego, Cal.	1/15/37
O'Connell, Helen	Lima, Oh.	1920
O'Connor, Carroll	New York, N.Y.	8/2/24
O'Connor, Donald	Chicago, Ill.	8/28/25
Odetta	Birmingham, Ala.	12/31/30
O'Hara, Maureen	Dublin, Ireland	8/17/21
O'Herlihy, Dan	Wexford, Ireland	5/1/19
O'Keefe, Michael	Paulland, N.J.	1955
Olin, Ken	Chicago, Ill.	7/30/54
Olivier, Laurence	Dorking, England	5/22/07
Olmos, Edward James	E. Los Angeles, Cal.	2/24/-
Olsen, Merlin	Logan, Ut.	9/15/40
O'Neal, Patrick	Ocala, Fla.	9/26/27
O'Neal, Ryan	Los Angeles, Cal.	4/20/41
O'Neal, Tatum	Los Angeles, Cal.	11/5/63
O'Neill, Jennifer	Brazil	2/20/48
Ontkean, Michael	Canada	1946
Opatoshu, David	New York, N.Y.	1/30/18
Orbach, Jerry	New York, N.Y.	10/20/35
Orlando, Tony	New York, N.Y.	4/3/44
Osbourne, Ozzy	Birmingham, England	12/3/48
Osmond, Donny	Ogden, Ut.	12/9/57
Osmond, Marie	Ogden, Ut.	10/13/59
O'Sullivan, Maureen	Boyle, Ireland	5/17/11
O'Toole, Annette	Houston, Tex.	4/1/52
O'Toole, Peter	Connemara, Ireland	8/2/32
Owens, Buck	Sherman, Tex.	8/12/29
Owens, Gary	Mitchell, S.D.	5/10/36
Ozawa, Seiji	Shenyang, China	9/1/35
Paar, Jack	Canton, Oh.	5/1/18
Pacino, Al	New York, N.Y.	4/25/40
Page, LaWanda	Cleveland, Oh.	10/19/20
Page, Patti	Claremore, Okla.	11/8/27
Paige, Janis	Tacoma, Wash.	9/16/22
Palance, Jack	Lattimer, Pa.	2/18/20
Palin, Michael	England	1943
Palmer, Betsy	East Chicago, Ind.	11/1/29
Papas, Irene	Greece	1926
Papp, Joseph	Brooklyn, N.Y.	6/22/21
Parker, Alan	London, England	2/14/44
Parker, Eleanor	Cedarville, Oh.	6/26/22
Parker, Fess	Ft. Worth, Tex.	8/16/25
Parker, Jameson	Baltimore, Md.	11/18/50
Parker, Jean	Deer Lodge, Mon.	8/11/12
Parks, Bert	Atlanta, Ga.	12/30/14
Parsons, Estelle	Lynn, Mass.	11/20/27
Parton, Dolly	Sevierville, Tenn.	1/19/46
Pasternak, Joseph	Hungary	9/19/01
Patane, Giuseppe	Napoli, Italy	1/1/32
Patinkin, Mandy	Chicago, Ill.	11/30/52
Pavarotti, Luciano	Modena, Italy	10/12/35
Paycheck, Johnny	Greenfield, Oh.	5/31/38
Payne, John	Roanoke, Va.	5/23/12
Pearl, Minnie	Centerville, Tenn.	10/25/12
Peck, Gregory	La Jolla, Cal.	4/5/16
Pendergrass, Teddy	Philadelphia, Pa.	3/26/50
Penn, Arthur	Philadelphia, Pa.	9/27/22
Penn, Sean	Santa Monica, Cal.	8/17/60
Peppard, George	Detroit, Mich.	10/1/28
Perkins, Anthony	New York, N.Y.	4/4/32
Perlman, Itzhak	Tel Aviv, Israel	8/31/45
Perlman, Rhea	Brooklyn, N.Y.	3/31/-
Perrine, Valerie	Galveston, Tex.	9/3/43
Persoff, Nehemiah	Jerusalem, Palestine	8/14/20
Peters, Bernadette	New York, N.Y.	2/28/48
Peters, Brock	New York, N.Y.	7/2/27
Peters, Jean	Canton, Oh.	10/15/26
Peters, Roberta	New York, N.Y.	5/4/30
Petit, Pascale	Paris, France	2/27/38
Pfeiffer, Michelle	Santa Ana, Cal.	1957
Phillips, MacKenzie	Alexandria, Va.	11/10/59
Phillips, Michelle	Long Beach, Cal.	4/6/44
Piazza, Marguerite	New Orleans, La.	5/6/26
Picon, Molly	New York, N.Y.	6/1/98
Pinchot, Bronson	New York, N.Y.	5/20/59
Piscopo, Joe	Passaic, N.J.	6/17/51
Pleasence, Donald	Worksop, England	10/5/19
Pleshette, Suzanne	New York, N.Y.	1/31/37
Plowright, Joan	Brigg, England	10/28/29
Plummer, Amanda	New York, N.Y.	3/23/57
Plummer, Christopher	Toronto, Ont.	12/13/29
Poitier, Sidney	Miami, Fla.	2/20/27
Polanski, Roman	Paris, France	8/18/33
Ponti, Carlo	Milan, Italy	12/11/13
Post, Markie	Walnut Creek, Cal.	11/4/-
Poston, Tom	Columbus, Oh.	10/17/21
Potts, Annie	Nashville, Tenn.	10/28/-
Powell, Jane	Portland, Ore.	4/1/28
Powers, Stefanie	Hollywood, Cal.	11/12/43
Prentiss, Paula	San Antonio, Tex.	3/4/39
Presley, Priscilla	New York, N.Y.	5/24/45
Preston, Billy	Houston, Tex.	9/9/46
Previn, Andre	Berlin, Germany	4/6/29
Price, Leontyne	Laurel, Miss.	2/10/27
Price, Ray	Perryville, Tex.	1/12/26
Price, Vincent	St. Louis, Mo.	5/27/11
Pride, Charlie	Sledge, Miss.	3/18/39
Prince	Minneapolis, Minn.	6/7/58
Principal, Victoria	Japan	1/30/46
Prosky, Robert	Philadelphia, Pa.	12/13/30
Prowse, Juliet	Bombay, India	9/25/37
Pryor, Richard	Peoria, Ill.	12/1/40
Pulliam, Keshia Knight	Newark, N.J.	4/9/79
Pyle, Denver	Bethune, Col.	5/11/20
Quaid, Dennis	Houston, Tex.	4/9/54
Quaid, Randy	Houston, Tex.	1950

Name	Birthplace	Born
Quayle, Anthony	Lancashire, England	9/7/13
Quillan, Eddie	Philadelphia, Pa.	3/31/07
Quinlan, Kathleen	Pasadena, Cal.	11/19/54
Quinn, Anthony	Chihuahua, Mexico	4/21/15
Rabb, Ellis	Memphis, Tenn.	6/20/30
Rabbitt, Eddie	Brooklyn, N.Y.	11/27/41
Radner, Gilda	Detroit, Mich.	6/28/46
Rae, Charlotte	Milwaukee, Wis.	4/22/26
Raffin, Deborah	Los Angeles, Cal.	3/13/53
Rainer, Luise	Vienna, Austria	1/12/10
Raines, Ella	Snoqualmie Falls, Wash.	8/6/21
Raitt, John	Santa Ana, Cal.	1/19/17
Ralston, Esther	Bar Harbor, Me.	9/17/02
Ralston, Vera Hruba	Prague, Czechoslovakia	6/12/19
Rambo, Dack	Delano, Cal.	11/13/-
Rampal, Jean-Pierre	Marseilles, France	1/7/22
Randall, Tony	Tulsa, Okla.	2/26/20
Randolph, John	New York, N.Y.	1/1/15
Rashad, Phylicia	Houston, Tex.	6/17/48
Ratzenberger, John	Bridgeport, Conn.	4/6/47
Rawls, Lou	Chicago, Ill.	12/1/36
Ray, Aldo	Pen Argyl, Pa.	9/25/26
Ray, Gene Anthony	New York, N.Y.	5/24/63
Ray, Johnnie	Dallas, Ore.	1/10/27
Rayburn, Gene	Christopher, Ill.	12/22/17
Raye, Martha	Butte, Mon.	8/27/16
Raymond, Gene	New York, N.Y.	8/13/08
Reddy, Helen	Melbourne, Australia	10/25/41
Redford, Robert	Santa Monica, Cal.	8/18/37
Redgrave, Lynn	London, England	3/8/43
Redgrave, Vanessa	London, England	1/30/37
Reed, Jerry	Atlanta, Ga.	3/20/37
Reed, Oliver	London, England	2/13/38
Reed, Rex	Ft. Worth, Tex.	10/2/38
Reed, Robert	Highland Park, Ill.	10/19/32
Reese, Della	Detroit, Mich	7/6/31
Reeve, Christopher	New York, N.Y.	9/25/52
Reeves, Dell	Sparta, N.C.	7/14/33
Regan, Phil	Brooklyn, N.Y.	5/28/06
Reid, Kate	London, England	11/4/30
Reid, Tim	Norfolk, Va	12/19/44
Reilly, Charles Nelson	New York, N.Y.	1/13/31
Reiner, Carl	Bronx, N.Y.	3/20/22
Reiner, Rob	Bronx, N.Y.	3/6/45
Reinking, Ann	Seattle, Wash.	11/10/49
Remick, Lee	Boston, Mass.	12/14/35
Resnik, Regina	New York, N.Y.	8/30/24
Reynolds, Burt	Waycross, Ga.	2/11/36
Reynolds, Debbie	El Paso, Tex.	4/1/32
Reynolds, Marjorie	Buhl, Ida.	8/12/21
Rich, Charlie	Forest City, Ark.	12/14/32
Rich, Irene	Buffalo, N.Y.	10/13/97
Richards, Keith	Kent, England	12/18/43
Richardson, Tony	Shipley, England	6/5/28
Richie, Lionel	Tuskegee, Ala.	6/20/50
Rickles, Don	New York, N.Y.	5/8/26
Rigg, Diana	Doncaster, England	7/20/38
Ringwald, Molly	Rosewood, Cal.	2/14/68
Ritter, John	Burbank, Cal.	9/17/48
Rivera, Chita	Washington, D.C.	1/23/33
Rivers, Joan	Brooklyn, N.Y.	6/8/33
Robards, Jason Jr.	Chicago, Ill.	7/26/22
Robbins, Jerome	New York, N.Y.	10/11/18
Roberts, Doris	St. Louis, Mo.	11/4/30
Roberts, Eric	Biloxi, Miss.	4/18/56
Roberts, Pernell	Waycross, Ga.	5/18/30
Roberts, Tony	New York, N.Y.	10/22/39
Robertson, Cliff	La Jolla, Cal.	9/9/25
Robertson, Dale	Oklahoma City, Okla.	7/14/23
Robinson, Smokey	Detroit, Mich.	2/19/40
Roche, Eugene	Boston, Mass.	9/22/28
Rodgers, Jimmie	Camas, Wash.	1933
Rodriquez, Johnny	Sabinal, Tex.	12/10/51
Rogers, Chas. (Buddy)	Olathe, Kan.	8/13/04
Rogers, Fred	Latrobe, Pa.	3/20/28
Rogers, Ginger	Independence, Mo.	7/16/11
Rogers, Kenny	Houston, Tex.	8/21/38
Rogers, Roy	Cincinnati, Oh.	11/5/12
Rogers, Wayne	Birmingham, Ala.	4/7/33
Roland, Gilbert	Juarez, Mexico	12/11/05
Rolle, Esther	Pompano Beach, Fla.	11/8/33
Romero, Cesar	New York, N.Y.	2/15/07
Ronstadt, Linda	Tucson, Ariz.	7/15/46
Rooney, Mickey	Brooklyn, N.Y.	9/23/20
Rose, George	Bicester, England	2/19/20
Rose Marie	New York, N.Y.	8/15/25
Ross, Diana	Detroit, Mich.	3/26/44
Ross, Katharine	Hollywood, Cal.	1/29/43
Ross, Lanny	Seattle, Wash.	1/19/06
Ross, Marion	Albert Lea, Minn.	10/25/28
Rostropovich, Mstislav	Baku USSR	3/12/27
Roth, David Lee	Bloomington, Ind.	10/10/55
Rourke, Mickey	Schenectady, N.Y.	1956
Rowan, Dan	Beggs, Okla.	7/2/22
Rowlands, Gena	Cambria, Wis.	6/19/36
Rubinstein, John	Los Angeles, Cal.	12/8/46
Rudolf, Max	Frankfurt, Germany	6/15/02
Rule, Janice	Norwood, Oh.	8/15/31
Rush, Barbara	Denver, Col.	1/4/30
Russell, Jane	Bemidji, Minn.	6/21/21
Russell, Ken	Southampton, England	7/3/27
Russell, Kurt	Springfield, Mass.	3/17/51
Russell, Mark	Buffalo, N.Y.	8/23/32
Russell, Nipsey	Atlanta, Ga.	10/13/24
Russell, Theresa	San Diego, Cal.	1957
Rutherford, Ann	Toronto, Ont.	11/2/20
Ryan, Peggy	Long Beach, Cal.	8/28/24
Ryan, Roz	Detroit, Mich.	7/7/51
Rydell, Bobby	Philadelphia, Pa.	4/26/42
Sahl, Mort	Montreal, Que.	5/11/27
Saint, Eva Marie	Newark, N.J.	7/4/24
St. James, Susan	Los Angeles, Cal	8/14/46
St. John, Jill	Los Angeles, Cal.	8/19/40
Sainte-Marie, Buffy	Maine	2/20/41
Sajac, Pat	Chicago, Ill.	10/26/-
Saks, Gene	New York, N.Y.	11/8/21
Sales, Soupy	Franklinton, N.C.	1/8/26
Samms, Emma	London, England	8/28/-
Sanderson, William	Memphis, Tenn.	1/10/-
Sandy, Gary	Dayton, Oh.	12/25/45
Sanford, Isabel	New York, N.Y.	8/29/17
Santana, Carlos	Mexico	7/20/47
Sarandon, Chris	Beckley, W.Va.	7/24/42
Sarandon, Susan	New York, N.Y.	10/4/46
Sarnoff, Dorothy	New York, N.Y.	5/25/17
Sarrazin, Michael	Quebec City, Que.	5/22/40
Savalas, Telly	Garden City, N.Y.	1/21/24
Saxon, John	Brooklyn, N.Y.	8/5/35
Sayao, Bidu	Rio de Janeiro, Brazil	5/11/02
Scaggs, Boz	Dallas, Tex.	6/8/44
Schallert, William	Los Angeles, Cal.	7/6/22
Scheider, Roy	Orange, N.J.	11/10/32
Schell, Maria	Vienna, Austria	1/15/26
Schell, Maximilian	Vienna, Austria	12/8/30
Schell, Ronnie	Richmond, Cal.	12/23/31
Schenkel, Chris	Bippus, Ind.	1924
Schnabel, Stefan	Berlin, Germany	2/2/12
Schneider, Alexander	Vilna, Poland	10/21/08
Schneider, John	Mt. Kisco, N.Y.	4/8/54
Schreiber, Avery	Chicago, Ill.	1935
Schroder, Ricky	Staten Island, N.Y.	4/13/70
Schwarzenegger, Arnold	Braz, Austria	7/30/47
Schwarzkopf, Elisabeth	Jarotschin, Poland	12/9/15
Scofield, Paul	Hurst, Pierpont, England	1/21/22
Scolari, Peter	New Rochelle, Ill.	9/12/-
Scorsese, Martin	New York, N.Y.	11/17/42
Scott, George C.	Wise, Va.	10/18/27
Scott, Lizabeth	Scranton, Pa.	9/29/22
Scott, Martha	Jamesport, Mo.	9/22/14
Scotto, Renata	Savona, Italy	2/24/35
Scully, Vin	New York, N.Y.	11/29/27
Sebastian, John	New York N.Y.	3/17/44
Sedaka, Neil	New York, N.Y.	3/13/39
Seeger, Pete	New York, N.Y.	5/3/19
Segal, George	Great Neck, N.Y.	2/13/34
Segal, Vivienne	Philadelphia, Pa.	4/19/97
Sellacca, Connie	New York, N.Y.	5/25/55
Selleck, Tom	Detroit, Mich.	1/29/45
Serkin, Rudolf	Eger, Austria	3/28/03
Severinsen, Doc	Arlington, Ore.	7/7/27
Seymour, Jane	Middlesex, England	2/15/51
Shackelford, Ted	Oklahoma City, Okla.	6/23/46
Shandling, Garry	Tucson, Ariz.	1950
Shankar, Ravi	India	4/7/20
Sharif, Omar	Alexandria, Egypt	4/10/32
Shatner, William	Montreal, Que.	3/22/31
Shaw, Robert	Red Bluff, Cal.	4/30/16
Shearer, Moira	Scotland	1/17/26
Sheedy, Ally	New York, N.Y.	6/12/62
Sheen, Charlie	New York, N.Y.	1961
Sheen, Martin	Dayton, Oh	8/3/40
Sheldon, Jack	Jacksonville, Fla.	1931
Shelley, Carole	London, England	8/16/39

Name	Birthplace	Born
Shepard, Sam	Ft. Sheridan, Ill.	11/5/43
Shepherd, Cybill	Memphis, Tenn.	2/18/50
Shera, Mark	Bayonne, N.J.	7/10/49
Shields, Brooke	New York, N.Y.	5/31/65
Shire, Talia	New York, N.Y.	4/25/46
Shirley, Ann	New York, N.Y.	4/17/18
Shore, Dinah	Winchester, Tenn.	3/1/17
Short, Bobby	Danville, Ill.	9/15/24
Shull, Richard	Evanston, Ill.	2/24/29
Sidney, Sylvia	New York, N.Y.	8/8/10
Siepi, Cesare	Milan, Italy	2/10/23
Sikking, James B.	Los Angeles, Cal.	3/5/34
Sills, Beverly	Brooklyn, N.Y.	5/25/29
Simmons, Gene	Haifa, Israel	8/25/49
Simmons, Jean	London, England	1/31/29
Simon, Carly	New York, N.Y.	6/25/45
Simon, Paul	Newark, N.J.	11/5/42
Simone, Nina	Tyron, N.C.	2/21/33
Sinatra, Frank	Hoboken, N.J.	12/12/15
Sinatra, Nancy	Jersey City, N.J.	6/8/40
Singer, Lori	Corpus Christie, Tex.	5/6/62
Singer, Marc	Vancouver, B.C.	1/29/-
Skelton, Red (Richard)	Vincennes, Ind.	7/18/10
Skerritt, Tom	Detroit, Mich.	8/25/33
Slezak, Erika	Hollywood, Cal.	8/5/-
Slick, Grace	Chicago, Ill.	10/30/39
Smith, Alexis	Penticton, B.C.	6/8/21
Smith, Buffalo Bob	Buffalo, N.Y.	11/27/17
Smith, Connie	Elkhart, Ind.	8/14/41
Smith, Jaclyn	Houston, Tex.	10/26/48
Smith, Keely	Norfolk, Va.	3/9/35
Smith, Maggie	Ilford, England	12/28/34
Smith, Roger	South Gate, Cal.	12/18/32
Smits, Jimmy	New York, N.Y.	7/9/58
Smothers, Dick	New York, N.Y.	11/20/39
Smothers, Tom	New York, N.Y.	2/2/37
Snodgress, Carrie	Park Ridge, Ill.	10/27/45
Snow, Hank	Nova Scotia, Canada	5/9/14
Snyder, Jimmy "Greek"	Steubenville, Oh.	9/9/19
Snyder, Tom	Milwaukee, Wis.	5/12/36
Solti, Georg	Budapest, Hungary	10/21/12
Somers, Suzanne	San Bruno, Cal.	10/16/46
Somes, Michael	nr. Stroud, England	9/28/17
Sommer, Elke	Berlin, Germany	11/5/41
Sorvino, Paul	New York, N.Y.	1939
Sothern, Ann	Valley City, N.D.	1/22/09
Soul, David	Chicago, Ill.	8/28/43
Spacek, Sissy	Quitman, Tex.	12/25/49
Spano, Joe	San Francisco, Cal.	7/7/46
Spelling, Aaron	Dallas, Tex.	4/22/28
Spielberg, Steven	Cincinnati, Oh.	12/18/47
Springfield, Dusty	London, England	4/16/39
Springfield, Rick	Sydney, Australia	8/23/49
Springsteen, Bruce	Freehold, N.J.	9/23/49
Stack, Robert	Los Angeles, Cal.	1/13/19
Stafford, Jo	Coalinga, Cal.	11/12/18
Stallone, Sylvester	New York, N.Y.	7/6/46
Stamp, Terence	Stepney, England	7/22/39
Stander, Lionel	New York, N.Y.	1/11/08
Stang, Arnold	Chelsea, Mass.	9/28/25
Stanley, Kim	Tularosa, N.M.	2/11/25
Stanton, Harry Dean	Kentucky	7/14/26
Stanwyck, Barbara	Brooklyn, N.Y.	7/16/07
Stapleton, Jean	New York, N.Y.	1/19/23
Stapleton, Maureen	Troy, N.Y.	6/21/25
Starr, Kay	Dougherty, Okla.	7/21/22
Starr, Ringo	Liverpool, England	7/7/40
Steber, Eleanor	Wheeling, W. Va.	7/17/16
Steenburgen, Mary	Newport, Ark.	1953
Steiger, Rod	W. Hampton, N.Y.	4/14/25
Steinberg, David	Winnipeg, Man.	8/9/42
Stephens, James	Mt. Kisco, N.Y.	5/18/51
Sterling, Jan	New York, N.Y.	4/3/23
Sterling, Robert	New Castle, Pa.	11/13/17
Stern, Isaac	Kreminiecz, Russia	7/21/20
Sternhagen, Frances	Washington, D.C.	1/13/30
Stevens, Andrew	Memphis, Tenn.	6/10/55
Stevens, Cat	London, England	7/21/48
Stevens, Connie	Brooklyn, N.Y.	8/8/38
Stevens, Kaye	E. Cleveland, Oh.	7/21/35
Stevens, Rise	New York, N.Y.	6/11/13
Stevens, Stella	Yazoo City, Miss.	10/1/36
Stevens, Warren	Clark's Summit, Pa.	11/2/19
Stevenson, McLean	Normal, Ill.	11/14/29
Stevenson, Parker	Philadelphia, Pa.	6/4/53
Stewart, James	Indiana, Pa.	5/20/08
Stewart, Rod	London, England	1/10/45

Name	Birthplace	Born
Stickney, Dorothy	Dickinson, N.D.	6/21/00
Stiers, David Ogden	Peoria, Ill.	10/31/42
Stiller, Jerry	New York, N.Y.	6/8/29
Stills, Stephen	Dallas, Tex.	1/3/45
Sting (G. Sumner)	Newcastle, England	10/2/51
Stockwell, Dean	Hollywood, Cal.	3/5/36
Stookey, Paul	Baltimore, Md.	12/30/37
Storch, Larry	New York, N.Y.	1/8/25
Storm, Gale	Bloomington, Tex.	4/5/21
Straight, Beatrice	Old Westbury, N.Y.	8/2/18
Strasberg, Susan	New York, N.Y.	5/22/38
Strasser, Robin	New York, N.Y.	5/7/45
Stratas, Teresa	Toronto, Ont.	5/26/38
Strauss, Peter	New York, N.Y.	2/20/47
Streep, Meryl	Summit, N.J.	6/22/49
Streisand, Barbra	Brooklyn, N.Y.	4/24/42
Stritch, Elaine	Detroit, Mich.	2/2/26
Struthers, Sally	Portland, Ore.	7/28/48
Stuarti, Enzo	Rome, Italy	3/3/25
Sullivan, Barry	New York, N.Y.	8/29/12
Sullivan, Susan	New York, N.Y.	11/18/43
Sullivan, Tom	Boston, Mass.	3/27/47
Sumac, Yma	Ichocan, Peru	9/10/27
Summer, Donna	Boston, Mass.	12/31/48
Sutherland, Donald	St. John, New Brunswick	7/17/34
Sutherland, Joan	Sydney, Australia	11/7/26
Suzuki, Pat	Cressey, Cal	1931
Swenson, Inga	Omaha, Neb.	12/29/34
Swit, Loretta	Passaic, N.J.	11/4/37
Mr. T (Lawrence Tero)	Chicago, Ill.	5/21/52
Talbot, Lyle	Pittsburgh, Pa.	2/8/02
Tallchief, Maria	Fairfax, Okla.	1/24/25
Tambor, Jeffrey	San Francisco, Cal.	7/8/-
Tandy, Jessica	London, England	6/7/09
Tarkenton, Fran	Richmond, Va.	2/3/40
Tayback, Vic	New York, N.Y.	1/6/29
Taylor, Elizabeth	London, England	2/27/32
Taylor, James	Boston, Mass.	3/12/48
Taylor, Rod	Sydney, Australia	1/11/29
Te Kanawa, Kiri	Gisborne, New Zealand	3/6/44
Tebaldi, Renata	Pesaro, Italy	2/1/22
Temple, Shirley	Santa Monica, Cal.	4/23/28
Tennille, Toni	Montgomery, Ala.	5/8/43
Terry-Thomas	London, England	7/14/11
Tharp, Twyla	Portland, Ind.	7/1/41
Thaxter, Phyllis	Portland, Me.	11/20/21
Thicke, Alan	Kirkland Lake, Ont.	3/1/-
Thinnes, Roy	Chicago, Ill.	4/6/38
Thomas, B.J.	Houston, Tex.	8/7/42
Thomas, Betty	St. Louis, Mo.	7/27/47
Thomas, Danny	Deerfield, Mich.	1/6/14
Thomas, Heather	Greenwich, Conn.	9/8/57
Thomas, Marlo	Detroit, Mich.	11/21/43
Thomas, Philip Michael	Columbus, Oh.	5/26/49
Thomas, Richard	New York, N.Y.	6/13/51
Thompson, Jack	Sydney, Australia	8/31/40
Thompson, Marshall	Peoria, Ill.	11/27/26
Thompson, Sada	Des Moines, Ia.	9/27/29
Thulin, Ingrid	Sweden	1/27/29
Tiegs, Cheryl	Minnesota	9/27/47
Tierney, Gene	Brooklyn, N.Y.	11/20/20
Tillis, Mel	Tampa, Fla.	8/8/32
Tiny Tim	New York, N.Y.	4/12/23
Todd, Richard	Dublin, Ireland	6/11/19
Tomlin, Lily	Detroit, Mich.	9/1/39
Tomlinson, David	Scotland	5/7/17
Toomey, Regis	Pittsburgh, Pa.	8/13/02
Torme, Mel	Chicago, Ill.	9/13/25
Torn, Rip	Temple, Tex.	2/6/31
Tracy, Arthur	Russia	6/25/03
Travanti, Daniel J.	Kenosha, Wis.	3/7/40
Travers, Mary	Louisville, Ky.	11/9/36
Travis, Randy	No. Carolina	1963
Travolta, John	Englewood, N.J.	2/18/54
Trevor, Claire	New York, N.Y.	3/8/09
Troyanos, Tatiana	New York, N.Y.	9/12/38
Tucker, Forrest	Plainfield, Ind.	2/12/19
Tucker, Tanya	Seminole, Tex.	10/10/58
Tune, Tommy	Wichita Falls, Tex.	2/28/39
Turner, Ike	Clarksdale, Miss.	11/5/31
Turner, Kathleen	Springfield, Mo.	6/19/54
Turner, Lana	Wallace, Ida.	2/8/20
Turner, Tina	Nutbush, Tenn.	11/26/38
Tushingham, Rita	Liverpool, England	3/14/40
Twiggy (Leslie Hornby)	London, England	9/19/49
Twitty, Conway	Friar's Point, Miss.	9/1/33
Tyson, Cicely	New York, N.Y.	12/19/33

Name	Birthplace	Born
Uecker, Bob	Milwaukee, Wis.	1/26/35
Uggams, Leslie	New York, N.Y.	5/25/43
Ullmann, Liv	Tokyo, Japan	12/16/39
Urich, Robert	Toronto, Oh.	12/19/47
Ustinov, Peter	London, England	4/16/21
Vaccaro, Brenda	Brooklyn, N.Y.	11/18/39
Vale, Jerry	New York, N.Y.	7/8/31
Valente, Caterina	Paris, France	1/14/31
Valentine, Karen	Santa Rosa, Cal.	5/25/47
Valli, Frankie	Newark, N.J.	5/3/37
Van Ark, Joan	New York, N.Y.	6/16/46
Van Cleef, Lee	Somerville, N.J.	1/9/25
Van Devere, Trish	Tenafly, N.J.	3/9/44
Van Doren, Mamie	Rowena, S.D.	2/6/33
Van Dyke, Dick	West Plains, Mo.	12/13/25
Van Dyke, Jerry	Danville, Ill.	7/27/32
Van Fleet, Jo	Oakland, Cal.	12/30/19
Van Pallandt, Nina	Copenhagen, Denmark	7/15/32
Van Patten, Dick	New York, N.Y.	12/9/28
Vaughan, Sarah	Newark, N.J.	3/27/24
Vaughn, Robert	New York, N.Y.	11/22/32
Venuta, Benay	San Francisco, Cal.	1/27/11
Verdon, Gwen	Los Angeles, Cal.	1/13/25
Vereen, Ben	Miami, Fla.	10/10/46
Verrett, Shirley	New Orleans, La.	5/31/31
Vickers, Jon	Prince Albert, Sask.	10/26/26
Vigoda, Abe	New York, N.Y.	2/24/21
Villechaize, Herve	Paris, France	4/23/43
Villella, Edward	Long Island, N.Y.	10/1/36
Vincent, Jan-Michael	Denver, Col.	7/15/44
Vinson, Helen	Beaumont, Tex.	9/17/07
Vinton, Bobby	Canonsburg, Pa.	4/16/35
Voight, Jon	Yonkers, N.Y.	12/29/38
Von Stade, Frederica	Somerville, N.J.	6/1/45
Von Sydow, Max	Lund, Sweden	4/10/29
Voorhees, Donald	Allentown, Pa.	7/26/03
Waggoner, Lyle	Kansas City, Kan.	4/13/35
Wagner, Lindsay	Los Angeles, Cal.	6/22/49
Wagner, Robert	Detroit, Mich.	2/10/30
Wagoner, Porter	West Plains, Mo.	8/12/27
Wain, Bea	Bronx, N.Y.	4/30/17
Waite, Ralph	White Plains, N.Y.	6/22/29
Walden, Robert	New York, N.Y.	9/25/43
Walken, Christopher	New York, N.Y.	3/31/43
Walker, Clint	Hartford, Ill.	5/30/27
Walker, Nancy	Philadelphia, Pa.	5/10/21
Wallach, Eli	Brooklyn, N.Y.	12/7/15
Walston, Roy	Laurel, Miss.	12/2/14
Walter, Jessica	New York, N.Y.	1/31/44
Wanamaker, Sam	Chicago, Ill.	6/14/19
Ward, Rachel	London, England	1957
Ward, Simon	London, England	10/19/41
Warden, Jack	Newark, N.J.	9/18/20
Warfield, William	W. Helena, Ark.	1/22/20
Warner, Malcolm-Jamal	Jersey City, N.J.	8/18/70
Warren, Leslie Ann	New York, N.Y.	1946
Warren, Michael	So. Bend, Ind.	3/5/46
Warrick, Ruth	St. Joseph, Mo.	6/29/15
Warwick, Dionne	E. Orange, N.J.	12/12/41
Washington, Denzel	Mt. Vernon, N.Y.	12/28/-
Waterston, Sam	Cambridge, Mass.	11/15/40
Watson, Mills	Oakland, Cal.	7/10/40
Watts, Andre	Nuremberg, Germany	6/20/46
Wayne, David	Traverse City, Mich.	1/30/14
Waxman, Al	Toronto, Ont.	3/2/35
Weaver, Dennis	Joplin, Mo.	6/4/24
Weaver, Fritz	Pittsburgh, Pa.	1/19/26
Weaver, Sigourney	New York, N.Y.	10/8/49
Webber, Robert	Santa Ana, Cal.	10/14/28
Weir, Peter	Sydney, Australia	8/8/44
Welch, Raquel	Chicago, Ill.	9/5/40
Weld, Tuesday	New York, N.Y.	8/27/43
Welk, Lawrence	nr. Strasburg, N.D.	3/11/03
Wells, Kitty	Nashville, Tenn.	8/30/19
Wendt, George	Chicago, Ill.	10/17/48
Weston, Jack	Cleveland, Oh.	1915
Whelchel, Lisa	Ft. Worth, Tex.	5/29/63

Name	Birthplace	Born
White, Barry	Galveston, Tex.	9/12/44
White, Betty	Oak Park, Ill.	1/17/24
White, Jesse	Buffalo, N.Y.	1/3/19
Whiting, Margaret	Detroit, Mich.	7/22/24
Whitmore, James	White Plains, N.Y.	10/1/21
Widmark, Richard	Sunrise, Minn.	12/26/14
Wiest, Diane	Kansas City, Mo.	—
Wilcox, Larry	San Diego, Cal.	8/8/47
Wilde, Cornel	New York, N.Y.	10/13/15
Wilder, Billy	Vienna, Austria	6/22/06
Wilder, Gene	Milwaukee, Wis.	6/11/35
Williams, Andy	Wall Lake, Ia.	12/3/30
Williams, Billy Dee	New York, N.Y.	4/6/37
Williams, Cindy	Van Nuys, Cal.	8/22/47
Williams, Emlyn	Mostyn, Wales	11/26/05
Williams, Esther	Los Angeles, Cal.	8/8/23
Williams, Hal	Columbus, Oh.	12/14/-
Williams Jr., Hank	Shreveport, La.	5/26/49
Williams, Joe	Cordele, Ga.	12/12/18
Williams, JoBeth	Houston, Tex.	1953
Williams, Paul	Omaha, Neb.	9/19/40
Williams, Robin	Chicago, Ill.	7/21/52
Williams, Roger	Omaha, Neb.	1926
Williams, Treat	Stamford, Conn.	12/1/51
Williamson, Nicol	Hamilton, Scotland	9/14/38
Willis, Bruce	Penns Grove, N.J.	3/19/55
Wilson, Demond	Valdosta, Ga.	1946
Wilson, Dolores	Philadelphia, Pa.	1929
Wilson, Elizabeth	Grand Rapids, Mich.	4/4/25
Wilson, Flip	Jersey City, N.J.	12/8/33
Wilson, Nancy	Chillicothe, Oh.	2/20/37
Winchell, Paul	New York, N.Y.	12/21/22
Windom, William	New York, N.Y.	9/28/23
Winfield, Paul	Los Angeles, Cal.	5/22/41
Winfrey, Oprah	Kosciusko, Miss.	1953
Winger, Debra	Columbus, Oh.	5/16/55
Winkler, Henry	New York, N.Y.	10/30/45
Winters, Jonathan	Dayton, Oh.	11/11/25
Winters, Shelley	St. Louis, Mo.	8/18/22
Wiseman, Joseph	Montreal, Que.	5/15/18
Withers, Jane	Atlanta, Ga.	4/12/26
Wonder, Stevie	Saginaw, Mich.	5/13/50
Woodard, Alfre	Tulsa, Okla.	11/2/-
Woods, James	Vernal, N.J.	4/18/47
Woodward, Edward	Croyden, England	1930
Woodward, Joanne	Thomasville, Ga.	2/27/30
Wopat, Tom	Lodi, Wis.	9/9/51
Worth, Irene	Nebraska	6/23/16
Wray, Fay	Alberta, Canada	9/10/07
Wright, Martha	Seattle, Wash.	3/23/26
Wright, Max	Detroit, Mich.	8/2/-
Wright, Teresa	New York, N.Y.	10/27/18
Wrightson, Earl	Baltimore, Md.	1916
Wyatt, Jane	Campgaw, N.J.	8/10/11
Wyman, Jane	St. Joseph, Mo.	1/4/14
Wynette, Tammy	Red Bay, Ala.	5/5/42
Wynter, Dana	London, England	6/8/30
Yarborough, Glenn	Milwaukee, Wis.	1/12/30
Yarrow, Peter	New York, N.Y.	5/31/38
York, Dick	Ft. Wayne, Ind.	9/4/28
York, Michael	Fulmer, England	3/27/42
York, Susannah	London, England	1/9/41
Yothers, Tina	Whittier, Cal.	9/5/73
Young, Alan	Northumberland, England	11/19/19
Young, Burt	New York, N.Y.	4/30/40
Young, Loretta	Salt Lake City, Ut.	1/6/12
Young, Neil	Toronto, Ont.	11/12/45
Young, Robert	Chicago, Ill.	2/22/07
Youngman, Henny	Liverpool, England	1906
Zadora, Pia	Hoboken, N.J.	1957
Zappa, Frank	Baltimore, Md.	12/21/40
Zeffirelli, Franco	Florence, Italy	2/12/23
Zeman, Jacklyn	Englewood, N.J.	3/6/-
Zimbalist, Efrem Jr.	New York, N.Y.	11/30/23
Zimbalist, Stephanie	New York, N.Y.	10/6/56
Zmed, Adrian	Chicago, Ill.	3/14/54
Zukerman, Pinchas	Tel Aviv, Israel	7/16/48

Entertainment Personalities of the Past

(as of June 30, 1987)

Born	Died	Name
1895	1974	Abbott, Bud
1872	1953	Adams, Maude
1855	1926	Adler, Jacob P.
1898	1933	Adoree, Renee
1902	1986	Aherne, Brian
1909	1964	Albertson, Frank
1910	1981	Albertson, Jack
1885	1952	Alda, Frances
1894	1956	Allen, Fred

Born	Died	Name
1906	1964	Allen, Gracie
1883	1950	Allgood, Sara
1886	1954	Anderson, John Murray
1915	1967	Andrews, Laverne
1933	1971	Angeli, Pier
1876	1958	Anglin, Margaret
1887	1933	Arbuckle, Fatty (Roscoe)
1900	1976	Arlen, Richard
1868	1946	Arliss, George
1888	1945	Armetta, Henry
1900	1971	Armstrong, Louis
1917	1986	Arnaz, Desi
1890	1956	Arnold, Edward
1905	1974	Arquette, Cliff
1899	1987	Astaire, Fred
1885	1946	Atwill, Lionel
1845	1930	Auer, Leopold
1905	1967	Auer, Mischa
1900	1972	Austin, Gene
1898	1940	Ayres, Agnes
1864	1922	Bacon, Frank
1891	1968	Bainter, Fay
1895	1957	Baker, Belle
1906	1975	Baker, Josephine
1898	1963	Baker, Phil
1904	1983	Balanchine, George
1882	1956	Bancroft, George
1903	1968	Bankhead, Tallulah
1890	1952	Banks, Leslie
1890	1955	Bara, Theda
1810	1891	Barnum, Phineas T.
1912	1978	Barrie, Wendy
1879	1959	Barrymore, Ethel
1882	1942	Barrymore, John
1878	1954	Barrymore, Lionel
1848	1905	Barrymore, Maurice
1897	1963	Barthelmess, Richard
1890	1962	Barton, James
1914	1984	Basehart, Richard
1904	1984	Basie, Count
1873	1951	Bauer, Harold
1923	1985	Baxter, Anne
1893	1951	Baxter, Warner
1880	1928	Bayes, Nora
1904	1965	Beatty, Clyde
1902	1962	Beavers, Louise
1884	1946	Beery, Noah
1889	1949	Beery, Wallace
1901	1970	Begley, Ed
1854	1931	Belasco, David
1949	1982	Belushi, John
1906	1968	Benaderet, Bea
1906	1964	Bendix, William
1904	1965	Bennett, Constance
1943	1987	Bennett, Michael
1873	1944	Bennett, Richard
1894	1974	Benny, Jack
1924	1970	Benzell, Mimi
1899	1966	Berg, Gertrude
1903	1978	Bergen, Edgar
1915	1982	Bergman, Ingrid
1895	1976	Berkeley, Busby
1863	1927	Bernard, Sam
1923	1986	Bernardi, Herschel
1844	1923	Bernhardt, Sarah
1893	1943	Bernie, Ben
1889	1967	Bickford, Charles
1911	1960	Bjoerling, Jussi
1898	1973	Blackmer, Sidney
1882	1951	Blaney, Charles E.
1900	1943	Bledsoe, Jules
1928	1972	Blocker, Dan
1909	1979	Blondell, Joan
1888	1959	Blore, Eric
1901	1975	Blue, Ben
1899	1957	Bogart, Humphrey
1880	1965	Boland, Mary
1897	1969	Boles, John
1904	1987	Bolger, Ray
1903	1960	Bond, Ward
1892	1981	Bondi, Beulah
1917	1981	Boone, Richard
1833	1893	Booth, Edwin
1796	1852	Booth, Junius Brutus
1894	1953	Bordoni, Irene
1888	1960	Bori, Lucrezia
1905	1965	Bow, Clara
1874	1946	Bowes, Maj. Edward
1928	1977	Boyd, Stephen
1898	1972	Boyd, William
1899	1978	Boyer, Charles
1893	1939	Brady, Alice
1871	1936	Breese, Edmund
1898	1964	Brendel, El
1894	1974	Brennan, Walter
1904	1979	Brent, George
1875	1948	Brian, Donald
1891	1951	Brice, Fanny
1891	1959	Broderick, Helen
1904	1951	Bromberg, J. Edward
1892	1973	Brown, Joe E.
1926	1966	Bruce, Lenny
1895	1953	Bruce, Nigel
1910	1982	Bruce, Virginia
1920	1985	Brynner, Yul
1903	1979	Buchanan, Edgar
1891	1957	Buchanan, Jack
1885	1957	Buck, Gene
1938	1982	Buono, Victor
1885	1970	Burke, Billie
1912	1967	Burnette, Smiley
1896	1956	Burns, Bob
1902	1971	Burns, David
1882	1941	Burr, Henry
1925	1984	Burton, Richard
1897	1946	Busch, Mae
1883	1966	Bushman, Francis X.
1896	1946	Butterworth, Charles
1893	1971	Byington, Spring
1905	1972	Cabot, Bruce
1918	1977	Cabot, Sebastian
1899	1986	Cagney, James
1895	1956	Calhern, Louis
1923	1977	Callas, Maria
1853	1942	Calve, Emma
1933	1976	Cambridge, Godfrey
1865	1940	Campbell, Mrs. Patrick
1892	1964	Cantor, Eddie
1878	1947	Carey, Harry
1950	1983	Carpenter, Karen
1880	1961	Carrillo, Leo
1892	1972	Carroll, Leo G.
1905	1965	Carroll, Nancy
1910	1963	Carson, Jack
1862	1937	Carter, Mrs. Leslie
1873	1921	Caruso, Enrico
1876	1973	Casals, Pablo
1927	1976	Cassidy, Jack
1893	1969	Castle, Irene
1887	1918	Castle, Vernon
1889	1960	Catlett, Walter
1887	1950	Cavanaugh, Hobart
1873	1938	Chaliapin, Feodor
1919	1980	Champion, Gower
1918	1961	Chandler, Jeff
1883	1930	Chaney, Lon
1905	1973	Chaney Jr., Lon
1889	1977	Chaplin, Charles
1893	1940	Chase, Charlie
1893	1961	Chatterton, Ruth
1888	1972	Chevalier, Maurice
1888	1960	Clark, Bobby
1914	1968	Clark, Fred
1887	1950	Clayton, Lou
1920	1966	Clift, Montgomery
1932	1963	Cline, Patsy
1900	1937	Clive, Colin
1892	1967	Clyde, Andy
1911	1976	Cobb, Lee J.
1877	1961	Coburn, Charles
1887	1934	Cody, Lew
1878	1942	Cohan, George M.
1919	1965	Cole, Nat (King)
1878	1955	Collier, Constance
1890	1965	Collins, Ray
1891	1958	Colman, Ronald
1908	1934	Columbo, Russ
1907	1944	Compton, Betty
1887	1940	Connolly, Walter
1917	1982	Conried, Hans
1855	1909	Conried, Henrich
1914	1975	Conte, Richard
1914	1984	Coogan, Jackie
1935	1964	Cooke, Sam
1901	1961	Cooper, Gary
1891	1971	Cooper, Gladys
1896	1973	Cooper, Melville
1914	1968	Corey, Wendell
1893	1974	Cornell, Katherine
1890	1972	Correll, Charles (Andy)
1905	1979	Costello, Dolores
1904	1957	Costello, Helene
1908	1959	Costello, Lou
1877	1950	Costello, Maurice
1899	1973	Coward, Noel
1890	1950	Cowl, Jane
1924	1973	Cox, Wally
1908	1983	Crabbe, Buster
1847	1924	Crabtree, Lotta
1928	1978	Crane, Bob
1875	1945	Craven, Frank
1911	1986	Crawford, Broderick
1908	1977	Crawford, Joan
1916	1944	Cregar, Laird
1880	1942	Crews, Laura Hope
1880	1974	Crisp, Donald
1942	1973	Croce, Jim
1910	1960	Cromwell, Richard
1903	1977	Crosby, Bing
1897	1975	Cross, Milton
1910	1986	Crothers, Scatman
1878	1968	Currie, Finlay
1816	1876	Cushman, Charlotte
1917	1978	Dailey, Dan
1899	1981	Chief Dan George
1923	1965	Dandridge, Dorothy
1869	1941	Danforth, William
1894	1963	Daniell, Henry
1901	1971	Daniels, Bebe
1860	1935	Daniels, Frank
1936	1973	Darin, Bobby
1921	1965	Darnell, Linda
1879	1967	Darwell, Jane
1909	1986	Da Silva, Howard
1866	1949	Davenport, Harry
1897	1961	Davies, Marion
1907	1961	Davis, Joan
1931	1955	Dean, James
1881	1950	DeCordoba, Pedro
1905	1968	Dekker, Albert
1908	1983	Del Rio, Dolores
1881	1959	DeMille, Cecil B.
1891	1967	Denny, Reginald
1901	1974	DeSica, Vittorio
1905	1977	Devine, Andy
1942	1972	De Wilde, Brandon
1907	1974	De Wolfe, Billy
1865	1950	De Wolfe, Elsie
1921	1985	Diamond, Selma
1879	1947	Digges, Dudley
1901	1966	Disney, Walt
1894	1949	Dix, Richard
1856	1924	Dockstader, Lew
1892	1941	Dolly, Jennie
1892	1970	Dolly, Rosie
1905	1958	Donat, Robert
1903	1972	Donlevy, Brian
1901	1981	Douglas, Melvyn
1907	1959	Douglas, Paul
—	1980	Dragonette, Jessica
1889	1956	Draper, Ruth
1881	1965	Dresser, Louise
1869	1934	Dressler, Marie
1820	1897	Drew, Mrs. John
1853	1927	Drew, John (son)
1909	1951	Duchin, Eddy
1890	1974	Dumbrille, Douglas
1890	1965	Dumont, Margaret
1878	1927	Duncan, Isadora
1905	1967	Dunn, James
1935	1973	Dunn, Michael
1893	1980	Durante, Jimmy
1907	1968	Duryea, Dan
1858	1924	Duse, Eleanora
1894	1929	Eagels, Jeanne
1896	1930	Eames, Clare
1865	1952	Eames, Emma
1901	1967	Eddy, Nelson
1897	1971	Edwards, Cliff

Born	Died	Name
1879	1945	Edwards, Gus
1899	1974	Ellington, Duke
1941	1974	Elliot, Cass
1871	1940	Elliott, Maxine
1891	1967	Elman, Mischa
1881	1951	Errol, Leon
1903	1967	Erwin, Stuart
1888	1976	Evans, Edith
1913	1967	Evelyn, Judith
1883	1939	Fairbanks, Douglas
1915	1970	Farmer, Frances
1870	1929	Farnum, Dustin
1876	1953	Farnum, William
1882	1967	Farrar, Geraldine
1904	1971	Farrell, Glenda
1868	1940	Faversham, William
1861	1939	Fawcett, George
1897	1961	Fay, Frank
1895	1962	Fazenda, Louise
1933	1982	Feldman, Marty
1902	1985	Fetchit, Stepin
1894	1979	Fiedler, Arthur
1918	1973	Field, Betty
1898	1979	Fields, Gracie
1867	1941	Fields, Lew
1879	1946	Fields, W.C.
1931	1978	Fields, Totie
1916	1977	Finch, Peter
1865	1932	Fiske, Minnie Maddern
1888	1961	Fitzgerald, Barry
1895	1962	Flagstad, Kirsten
1900	1971	Flippen, Jay C.
1909	1959	Flynn, Errol
1925	1974	Flynn, Joe
1880	1942	Fokine, Michel
1910	1968	Foley, Red
1905	1982	Fonda, Henry
1920	1978	Fontaine, Frank
1887	1983	Fontanne, Lynn
1853	1937	Forbes-Robertson, J.
1895	1973	Ford, John
1901	1976	Ford, Paul
1899	1966	Ford, Wallace
1806	1872	Forrest, Edwin
1902	1970	Foster, Preston
1857	1928	Foy, Eddie
1903	1968	Francis, Kay
1887	1966	Frawley, William
1885	1938	Frederick, Pauline
1870	1955	Friganza, Trixie
1890	1958	Frisco, Joe
1860	1915	Frohman, Charles
1851	1940	Frohman, Daniel
1885	1947	Fyffe, Will
1901	1960	Gable, Clark
1889	1963	Galli-Curci, Amelita
1877	1967	Garden, Mary
1913	1952	Garfield, John
1922	1969	Garland, Judy
1893	1963	Gaxton, William
1939	1984	Gaye, Marvin
1906	1984	Gaynor, Janet
1902	1978	Geer, Will
1904	1954	George, Gladys
1892	1962	Gibson, Hoot
1890	1957	Gigli, Beniamino
1894	1971	Gilbert, Billy
1899	1936	Gilbert, John
1855	1937	Gillette, William
1867	1943	Gillmore, Frank
1879	1939	Gilpin, Charles
1897	1987	Gingold, Hermione
1898	1968	Gish, Dorothy
1916	1987	Gleason, Jackie
1886	1959	Gleason, James
1884	1938	Gluck, Alma
1903	1983	Godfrey, Arthur
1874	1955	Golden, John
1882	1974	Goldwyn, Samuel
1917	1969	Gorcey, Leo
1884	1940	Gordon, C. Henry
1896	1985	Gordon, Ruth
1899	1982	Gordon, Freeman (Amos)
1869	1944	Gottschalk, Ferdinand
1829	1869	Gottschalk, Louis
1916	1973	Grable, Betty

Born	Died	Name
1929	1981	Grahame, Gloria
1904	1986	Grant, Cary
1901	1959	Gray, Gilda
1879	1954	Greenstreet, Sydney
1893	1978	Greenwood, Charlotte
1874	1948	Griffith, David Wark
1912	1980	Griffith, Hugh
1912	1967	Guthrie, Woody
1875	1959	Gwenn, Edmund
1888	1942	Hackett, Charles
1902	1958	Hackett, Raymond
1870	1943	Haines, Robert T.
1892	1950	Hale, Alan
1927	1981	Haley, Bill
1899	1979	Haley, Jack
1902	1985	Hamilton, Margaret
1847	1919	Hammerstein, Oscar
1879	1955	Hampden, Walter
1924	1964	Haney, Carol
1893	1964	Hardwicke, Sir Cedric
1892	1957	Hardy, Oliver
1883	1939	Hare, T.E. (Ernie)
1911	1937	Harlow, Jean
1872	1946	Harned, Virginia
1844	1911	Harrigan, Edward
1870	1946	Hart, William S.
1907	1955	Hartman, Grace
1928	1973	Harvey, Laurence
1910	1973	Hawkins, Jack
1890	1973	Hayakawa, Sessue
1885	1969	Hayes, Gabby
1918	1980	Haymes, Dick
1902	1971	Hayward, Leland
1917	1975	Hayward, Susan
1918	1987	Hayworth, Rita
1896	1937	Healy, Ted
1910	1971	Heflin, Van
1879	1936	Heggie, O.P.
1873	1918	Held, Anna
1942	1970	Hendrix, Jimi
1913	1969	Henie, Sonja
1879	1942	Herbert, Henry
1887	1951	Herbert, Hugh
1886	1956	Hersholt, Jean
1895	1942	Hibbard, Edna
1899	1980	Hitchcock, Alfred
1914	1955	Hodiak, John
1894	1973	Holden, Fay
1918	1981	Holden, William
1922	1965	Holliday, Judy
1936	1959	Holly, Buddy
1888	1951	Holt, Jack
1918	1973	Holt, Tim
1871	1947	Homer, Louise
1898	1978	Homolka, Oscar
1902	1972	Hopkins, Miriam
1858	1935	Hopper, DeWolf
1874	1959	Hopper, Edna Wallace
1915	1969	Hopper, William
1888	1970	Horton, Edward Everett
1874	1926	Houdini, Harry
1881	1965	Howard, Eugene
1867	1961	Howard, Joe
1893	1943	Howard, Leslie
1885	1955	Howard, Tom
1885	1949	Howard, Willie
1914	1972	Hudson, Rochelle
1925	1985	Hudson, Rock
1890	1977	Hull, Henry
1886	1957	Hull, Josephine
1895	1958	Humphrey, Doris
1895	1945	Hunter, Glenn
1925	1969	Hunter, Jeffrey
1901	1962	Husing, Ted
1884	1950	Huston, Walter
1892	1950	Ingram, Rex
1895	1969	Ingram, Rex
1895	1980	Iturbi, Jose
1838	1905	Irving, Henry
1871	1944	Irving, Isabel
1872	1914	Irving, Laurence
1875	1942	Jackson, Joe
1911	1972	Jackson, Mahalia
1891	1984	Jaffe, Sam
1916	1983	James, Harry
1889	1956	Janis, Elsie

Born	Died	Name
1886	1950	Jannings, Emil
1930	1980	Janssen, David
1829	1905	Jefferson, Joseph
1859	1923	Jefferson, Thomas
1900	1974	Jenkins, Allen
1898	1981	Jessel, George
1862	1930	Jewett, Henry
1892	1962	Johnson, Chic
1878	1952	Johnson, Edward
1886	1950	Jolson, Al
1889	1942	Jones, Buck
1933	1983	Jones, Carolyn
1911	1965	Jones, Spike
1943	1970	Joplin, Janis
1897	1961	Jordan, Marian (Molly McGee)
1905	1981	Joslyn, Allyn
1890	1955	Joyce, Alice
1910	1966	Kane, Helen
1887	1969	Karloff, Boris
1893	1970	Karns, Roscoe
1913	1987	Kaye, Danny
1913	1987	Kaye, Sammy
1811	1868	Kean, Charles
1806	1880	Kean, Mrs. Charles
1787	1833	Kean, Edmund
1895	1966	Keaton, Buster
1830	1873	Keene, Laura
1841	1893	Keene, Thomas W.
1899	1960	Keith, Ian
1894	1973	Kellaway, Cecil
1898	1979	Kelly, Emmett
1929	1982	Kelly, Grace
1910	1981	Kelly, Patsy
1899	1956	Kelly, Paul
1873	1939	Kelly, Walter C.
1909	1968	Kelton, Pert
1823	1895	Kemble, Agnes
1775	1854	Kemble, Charles
1809	1893	Kemble, Fannie
1848	1935	Kendal, Dame Madge
1843	1917	Kendal, William H.
1926	1959	Kendall, Kay
1890	1948	Kennedy, Edgar
1886	1945	Kent, William
1880	1947	Kerrigan, J. Warren
1886	1956	Kibbee, Guy
1902	1966	Kiepura, Jan
1888	1964	Kilbride, Percy
1863	1933	Kilgour, Joseph
1894	1944	King, Charles
1897	1971	King, Dennis
1923	1986	Knight, Ted
1901	1980	Kostelanetz, Andre
1919	1962	Kovacs, Ernie
1885	1974	Kruger, Otto
1913	1964	Ladd, Alan
1895	1967	Lahr, Bert
1919	1973	Lake, Veronica
1925	1982	Lamas, Fernando
1919	1948	Landis, Carole
1904	1972	Landis, Jessie Royce
1884	1944	Langdon, Harry
1853	1929	Langtry, Lillie
1921	1959	Lanza, Mario
1870	1950	Lauder, Harry
1899	1962	Laughton, Charles
1890	1965	Laurel, Stan
1923	1984	Lawford, Peter
1898	1952	Lawrence, Gertrude
1890	1929	Lawrence, Margaret
1940	1973	Lee, Bruce
1907	1952	Lee, Canada
1914	1970	Lee, Gypsy Rose
1848	1929	Lehmann, Lilli
1888	1976	Lehmann, Lotte
1896	1950	Lehr, Lew
1913	1967	Leigh, Vivien
1852	1908	Leighton, Margaret
1922	1976	Leighton, Margaret
1894	1931	Leitzel, Lillian
1940	1980	Lennon, John
1900	1981	Lenya, Lotte
1870	1941	Leonard, Eddie
1911	1973	Leonard, Jack E.
1906	1972	Levant, Oscar

Born	Died	Name
1905	1980	Levene, Sam
1911	1980	Levenson, Sam
1881	1955	Levy, Ethel
1902	1971	Lewis, Joe E.
1892	1971	Lewis, Ted
1874	1944	Lhevinne, Josef
1919	1987	Liberace
1889	1952	Lincoln, Elmo
1820	1887	Lind, Jenny
1889	1968	Lindsay, Howard
1869	1952	Lipman, Clara
1893	1971	Lloyd, Harold
1870	1922	Lloyd, Marie
1891	1957	Lockhart, Gene
1913	1969	Logan, Ella
1909	1942	Lombard, Carole
1902	1977	Lombardo, Guy
1927	1974	Long, Richard
1903	1983	Loo, Richard
1895	1975	Lopez, Vincent
1888	1968	Lorne, Marion
1904	1964	Lorre, Peter
1912	1962	Lovejoy, Frank
1890	1971	Lowe, Edmund
1892	1947	Lubitsch, Ernst
1882	1956	Lugosi, Bela
1895	1971	Lukas, Paul
1892	1977	Lunt, Alfred
1853	1932	Lupino, George
1893	1942	Lupino, Stanley
1897	1957	Lyman, Abe
1926	1982	Lynde, Paul
1926	1971	Lynn, Diana
1885	1954	Lytell, Bert
1867	1936	Lytton, Henry
1907	1965	MacDonald, Jeanette
1902	1969	MacLane, Barton
1921	1986	MacRae, Gordon
1909	1973	Macready, George
1861	1946	Macy, George Carleton
1908	1973	Magnani, Anna
1896	1967	Mahoney, Will
1890	1975	Main, Marjorie
1933	1967	Mansfield, Jayne
1854	1907	Mansfield, Richard
1905	1980	Mantovani, Annunzio
1897	1975	March, Fredric
1945	1981	Marley, Bob
1865	1950	Marlowe, Julia
1890	1966	Marshall, Herbert
1864	1943	Marshall, Tully
1920	1981	Martin, Ross
1885	1969	Martinelli, Giovanni
1888	1964	Marx, Arthur (Harpo)
1890	1977	Marx, Julius (Groucho)
1887	1961	Marx, Leonard (Chico)
1909	1984	Mason, James
1896	1983	Massey, Raymond
1862	1951	Maude, Cyril
1922	1972	Maxwell, Marilyn
1879	1948	May, Edna
1885	1957	Mayer, Louis B.
1895	1973	Maynard, Ken
1884	1945	McCormack, John
1907	1962	McCormick, Myron
1888	1931	McCoy, Bessie
1891	1978	McCoy, Tim
1895	1952	McDaniel, Hattie
1924	1965	McDonald, Marie
1913	1975	McGiver, John
1899	1981	McHugh, Frank
1879	1949	McIntyre, Frank J.
1857	1937	McIntyre, James
1879	1937	McKinley, Mabel
1883	1959	McLaglen, Victor
1907	1971	McMahon, Horace
1930	1980	McQueen, Steve
1920	1980	Medford, Kay
1880	1946	Meek, Donald
1879	1936	Meighan, Thomas
1861	1931	Melba, Nellie
1890	1973	Melchior, Lauritz
1904	1961	Melton, James
1890	1963	Menjou, Adolphe
1902	1966	Menken, Helen
1908	1984	Merman, Ethel
1908	1986	Milland, Ray
1904	1944	Miller, Glenn
1860	1926	Miller, Henry
1898	1936	Miller, Marilyn
1895	1927	Mills, Florence
1939	1976	Mineo, Sal
1903	1955	Minnevitch, Borrah
1913	1955	Miranda, Carmen
1892	1962	Mitchell, Thomas
1880	1940	Mix, Tom
1845	1909	Modjeska, Helena
1926	1962	Monroe, Marilyn
1911	1973	Monroe, Vaughn
1875	1964	Monteux, Pierre
1917	1951	Montez, Maria
1904	1981	Montgomery, Robert
1901	1947	Moore, Grace
1885	1955	Moore, Tom
1876	1962	Moore, Victor
1906	1974	Moorehead, Agnes
1882	1949	Moran, George
1884	1952	Moran, Polly
1890	1949	Morgan, Frank
1900	1941	Morgan, Helen
1888	1956	Morgan, Ralph
1901	1970	Morris, Chester
1849	1925	Morris, Clara
1914	1959	Morris, Wayne
1943	1971	Morrison, Jim
1932	1982	Morrow, Vic
1915	1977	Mostel, Zero
1897	1969	Mowbray, Alan
1895	1967	Muni, Paul
1894	1953	Munn, Frank
1915	1970	Munshin, Jules
1924	1971	Murphy, Audie
1885	1965	Murray, Mae
1896	1970	Nagel, Conrad
1900	1973	Naish, J. Carroll
1898	1961	Naldi, Nita
1888	1950	Nash, Florence
1865	1945	Nash, George
1879	1945	Nazimova, Alla
1846	1905	Neilson, Ada
1848	1880	Neilson, Adelaide
1868	1957	Neilson-Terry, Julia
1907	1975	Nelson, Ozzie
1940	1985	Nelson, Rick
1885	1967	Nesbit, Evelyn
1870	1951	Nethersole, Olga
1910	1983	Niven, David
1874	1948	Niblo, Fred
1890	1950	Nijinsky, Vaslav
1893	1974	Nilsson, Anna Q.
1902	1985	Nolan, Lloyd
1898	1930	Normand, Mabel
1879	1959	Norworth, Jack
1905	1968	Novarro, Ramon
1893	1951	Novello, Ivor
1903	1978	Oakie, Jack
1860	1926	Oakley, Annie
1928	1982	Oates, Warren
1911	1979	Oberon, Merle
1915	1985	O'Brien, Edmond
1899	1983	O'Brien, Pat
1908	1981	O'Connell, Arthur
1898	1943	O'Connell, Hugh
1880	1959	O'Connor, Una
1878	1945	O'Hara, Fiske
1908	1968	O'Keefe, Dennis
1880	1938	Oland, Warner
1860	1932	Olcott, Chauncey
1883	1942	Oliver, Edna May
1892	1963	Olsen, Ole
1849	1920	O'Neill, James
1899	1985	Ormandy, Eugene
1876	1949	Ouspenskaya, Maria
1887	1972	Owen, Reginald
1860	1941	Paderewski, Ignace
1924	1987	Page, Geraldine
1889	1954	Pallette, Eugene
1914	1986	Palmer, Lilli
1894	1958	Pangborn, Franklin
1914	1975	Parks, Larry
1881	1940	Pasternack, Josef A.
1837	1908	Pastor, Tony
1843	1919	Patti, Adelina
1840	1889	Patti, Carlotta
1885	1931	Pavlova, Anna
1900	1973	Paxinou, Katina
1904	1984	Peerce, Jan
1885	1950	Pemberton, Brock
1899	1967	Pendleton, Nat
1905	1941	Penner, Joe
1892	1937	Perkins, Osgood
1893	1956	Peters, Brandon
1915	1963	Piaf, Edith
1893	1979	Pickford, Mary
1897	1984	Pidgeon, Walter
1892	1957	Pinza, Ezio
1898	1963	Pitts, Zasu
1904	1976	Pons, Lily
1897	1981	Ponselle, Rosa
1903	1969	Portman, Eric
1904	1963	Powell, Dick
1912	1982	Powell, Eleanor
1892	1984	Powell, William
1913	1958	Power, Tyrone
1872	1935	Powers, Eugene
1905	1986	Preminger, Otto
1935	1977	Presley, Elvis
1918	1987	Preston, Robert
1911	1978	Prima, Louis
1856	1919	Primrose, George
1954	1977	Prinze, Freddie
1879	1956	Prouty, Jed
1871	1942	Pryor, Arthur
1895	1980	Raft, George
1890	1967	Rains, Claude
1889	1970	Rambeau, Marjorie
1900	1947	Rankin, Arthur
1892	1967	Rathbone, Basil
1897	1960	Ratoff, Gregory
1883	1953	Rawlinson, Herbert
1891	1943	Ray, Charles
1941	1967	Redding, Otis
1908	1985	Redgrave, Michael
1921	1986	Reed, Donna
1914	1959	Reeves, George
1923	1964	Reeves, Jim
1860	1916	Rehan, Ada
1892	1923	Reid, Wallace
1873	1943	Reinhardt, Max
1909	1971	Rennie, Michael
1902	1983	Richardson, Ralph
1870	1940	Richman, Charles
1895	1972	Richman, Harry
1921	1985	Riddle, Nelson
1872	1961	Ring, Blanche
1898	1977	Ritchard, Cyril
1907	1974	Ritter, Tex
1905	1969	Ritter, Thelma
1903	1966	Ritz, Al
1925	1982	Robbins, Marty
1898	1976	Robeson, Paul
1878	1949	Robinson, Bill
1893	1973	Robinson, Edward G.
1865	1942	Robson, May
1905	1977	Rochester (E. Anderson)
1897	1933	Rodgers, Jimmy
1894	1958	Rodzinsky, Artur
1879	1935	Rogers, Will
1897	1937	Roland, Ruth
1880	1962	Rooney, Pat
1899	1966	Rose, Billy
1910	1980	Roth, Lillian
1882	1936	Rothafel, S. L. (Roxy)
1887	1982	Rubinstein, Artur
1878	1953	Ruffo, Titta
1892	1970	Ruggles, Charles
1864	1936	Russell, Annie
1924	1961	Russell, Gail
1861	1922	Russell, Lillian
1911	1976	Russell, Rosalind
1892	1972	Rutherford, Margaret
1902	1973	Ryan, Irene
1909	1973	Ryan, Robert
1924	1963	Sabu (Dastagir)
1877	1968	St. Denis, Ruth
1884	1955	Sakall, S.Z.
1885	1936	Sale (Chic), Charles
1906	1972	Sanders, George

Born	Died	Name
1934	1973	Sands, Diana
1896	1960	Savo, Jimmy
1879	1954	Scheff, Fritzi
1892	1930	Schenck, Joe
1895	1964	Schildkraut, Joseph
1865	1930	Schildkraut, Rudolph
1889	1965	Schipa, Tito
1882	1951	Schnabel, Artur
1938	1982	Schneider, Romy
1910	1949	Schumann, Henrietta
1861	1936	Schumann-Heink, E.
1866	1945	Scott, Cyril
1920	1983	Scott, Hazel
1898	1987	Scott, Randolph
1914	1965	Scott, Zachary
1843	1896	Scott-Siddons, Mrs.
1938	1979	Seberg, Jean
1892	1974	Seeley, Blossom
1893	1987	Segovia, Andres
1925	1980	Sellers, Peter
1902	1965	Selznick, David O.
1858	1935	Sembrich, Marcella
1880	1960	Sennett, Mack
1881	1951	Shattuck, Arthur
1860	1929	Shaw, Mary
1927	1978	Shaw, Robert
1891	1972	Shawn, Ted
1868	1949	Shean, Al
1902	1983	Shearer, Norma
1915	1967	Sheridan, Ann
1885	1934	Sherman, Lowell
1918	1970	Shriner, Herb
1875	1953	Shubert, Lee
1755	1831	Siddons, Mrs. Sarah
1921	1985	Signoret, Simone
1882	1930	Sills, Milton
1912	1985	Silvers, Phil
1900	1976	Sim, Alastair
1891	1934	Skelly, Hal
1858	1942	Skinner, Otis
1870	1952	Skipworth, Alison
1863	1948	Smith, C. Aubrey
1917	1979	Soo, Jack
1826	1881	Sothern, Edward A.
1859	1933	Sothern, Edward H.
1884	1957	Sothern, Harry
1854	1932	Sousa, John Philip
1884	1967	Sparks, Ned
1876	1948	Speaks, Oley
1890	1970	Spitalny, Phil
1873	1937	Standing, Guy
1900	1941	Stephenson, James
1883	1939	Sterling, Ford
1882	1928	Stevens, Emily A.
1934	1970	Stevens, Inger
1896	1961	Stewart, Anita
1882	1977	Stokowski, Leopold
1873	1959	Stone, Fred
1879	1953	Stone, Lewis
1904	1980	Stone, Milburn
1898	1959	Sturges, Preston
1911	1960	Sullavan, Margaret
1902	1974	Sullivan, Ed
1903	1956	Sullivan, Francis L.
1892	1946	Summerville, Slim
1899	1983	Swanson, Gloria
1904	1969	Swarthout, Gladys
1893	1957	Talmadge, Norma
1900	1972	Tamiroff, Akim
1878	1947	Tanguay, Eva
1899	1934	Tashman, Lilyan
1885	1966	Taylor, Deems
1899	1958	Taylor, Estelle
1887	1946	Taylor, Laurette
1911	1969	Taylor, Robert
1878	1938	Tearle, Conway
1884	1953	Tearle, Godfrey
1892	1937	Tell, Alma
1864	1942	Tempest, Marie
1910	1963	Templeton, Alec
1847	1928	Terry, Ellen
1871	1940	Tetrazzini, Luisa
1899	1936	Thalberg, Irving
1857	1914	Thomas, Brandon
1892	1960	Thomas, John Charles
1882	1976	Thorndike, Sybil
		(Three Stooges)
1902	1975	Fine, Larry
1906	1952	Howard, Curly
1897	1975	Howard, Moe
1869	1936	Thurston, Howard
1896	1960	Tibbett, Lawrence
1887	1940	Tinney, Frank
1909	1958	Todd, Michael
1906	1935	Todd, Thelma
1874	1947	Toler, Sidney
1905	1968	Tone, Franchot
1867	1957	Toscanini, Arturo
1898	1968	Tracy, Lee
1900	1967	Tracy, Spencer
1903	1972	Traubel, Helen
1894	1975	Treacher, Arthur
1853	1917	Tree, Herbert Beerbohm
1889	1973	Truex, Ernest
1932	1984	Truffaut, Francois
1916	1976	Tucker, Richard
1884	1966	Tucker, Sophie
1874	1940	Turpin, Ben
1908	1959	Twelvetrees, Helen
1894	1970	Ulric, Lenore
1933	1975	Ure, Mary
1895	1926	Valentino, Rudolph
1870	1950	Van, Billy B.
1912	1979	Vance, Vivian
1893	1943	Veidt, Conrad
1926	1981	Vera-Ellen
1885	1957	Von Stroheim, Erich
1906	1981	Von Zell, Harry
1887	1969	Walburn, Raymond
1874	1946	Waldron, Charles D.
1904	1966	Walker, June
1914	1951	Walker, Robert
1898	1983	Wallenstein, Alfred
1887	1980	Walsh, Raoul
1876	1962	Walter, Bruno
1878	1936	Walthall, Henry B.
1872	1952	Ward, Fannie
1866	1951	Warfield, David
1900	1984	Waring, Fred
1876	1958	Warner, H. B.
1878	1964	Warwick, Robert
1924	1963	Washington, Dinah
1900	1977	Waters, Ethel
1887	1945	Watson, Billy
1907	1979	Wayne, John
1896	1966	Webb, Clifton
1920	1982	Webb, Jack
1867	1942	Weber, Joe
1905	1973	Webster, Margaret
1915	1985	Welles, Orson
1896	1975	Wellman, William
1922	1984	Werner, Oskar
1892	1980	West, Mae
1895	1968	Wheeler, Bert
1889	1938	White, Pearl
1891	1967	Whiteman, Paul
1865	1948	Whitty, Dame May
1912	1979	Wilding, Michael
1895	1948	William, Warren
1877	1922	Williams, Bert
1867	1918	Williams, Evan
1923	1953	Williams, Hank
1905	1975	Wills, Bob
1902	1978	Wills, Chill
1894	1953	Wilson, Dooley
1917	1972	Wilson, Marie
1884	1969	Winninger, Charles
1904	1959	Withers, Grant
1881	1931	Wolheim, Louis
1907	1961	Wong, Anna May
1938	1981	Wood, Natalie
1892	1978	Wood, Peggy
1888	1963	Woolley, Monty
1881	1956	Wycherly, Margaret
1902	1981	Wyler, William
1886	1966	Wynn, Ed
1916	1986	Wynn, Keenan
1906	1964	Wynyard, Diana
1890	1960	Young, Clara Kimball
1917	1970	Young, Gig
1887	1953	Young, Roland
1902	1979	Zanuck, Darryl F.
1869	1932	Ziegfeld, Florenz
1873	1976	Zukor, Adolph

Original Names of Selected Entertainers

Edie Adams: Elizabeth Edith Enke
Eddie Albert: Edward Albert Heimberger
Alan Alda: Alphonso D'Abruzzo
Jane Alexander: Jane Quigley
Fred Allen: John Sullivan
Woody Allen: Allen Konigsberg
Julie Andrews: Julia Wells
Eve Arden: Eunice Quedens
Beatrice Arthur: Bernice Frankel
Jean Arthur: Gladys Greene
Fred Astaire: Frederick Austerlitz

Lauren Bacall: Betty Joan Perske
Anne Bancroft: Anna Maria Italiano
Brigitte Bardot: Camille Javal
Gene Barry: Eugene Klass
Orson Bean: Dallas Burrows
Pat Benatar: Patricia Andrejewski
Robbie Benson: Robert Segal
Tony Bennett: Anthony Benedetto
Busby Berkeley: William Berkeley Enos
Jack Benny: Benjamin Kubelsky
Joey Bishop: Joseph Gottlieb
Robert Blake: Michael Gubitosi
Victor Borge: Borge Rosenbaum
David Bowie: David Robert Jones
Boy George: George Alan O'Dowd
Fanny Brice: Fanny Borach
Morgan Brittany: Suzanne Cupito
Charles Bronson: Charles Buchinski
Mel Brooks: Melvin Kaminsky
George Burns: Nathan Birnbaum
Ellen Burstyn: Edna Gilhooley
Richard Burton: Richard Jenkins
Red Buttons: Aaron Chwatt
Michael Caine: Maurice Micklewhite
Maria Callas: Maria Kalogeropoulos
Diahann Carroll: Carol Diahann Johnson
Cyd Charisse: Tula Finklea
Ray Charles: Ray Charles Robinson
Cher: Cherilyn Sarkisian
Patsy Cline: Virginia Patterson Hensley
Lee J. Cobb: Leo Jacoby
Claudette Colbert: Lily Chauchoin
Michael Connors: Kreker Ohanian
Robert Conrad: Conrad Robert Falk
Alice Cooper: Vincent Furnier
Howard Cosell: Howard Cohen

Elvis Costello: Declan Patrick McManus
Lou Costello: Louis Cristillo
Joan Crawford: Lucille Le Sueur
Tony Curtis: Bernard Schwartz

Vic Damone: Vito Farinola
Rodney Dangerfield: Jacob Cohen
Bobby Darin: Walden Waldo Cassotto
Doris Day: Doris von Kappelhoff
Yvonne De Carlo: Peggy Middleton
Sandra Dee: Alexandra Zuck
John Denver: Henry John Deutschendorf Jr.
Bo Derek: Cathleen Collins
John Derek: Derek Harris
Angie Dickinson: Angeline Brown
Phyllis Diller: Phyllis Driver
Diana Dors: Diana Fluck
Melvyn Douglas: Melvyn Hesselberg
Bob Dylan: Robert Zimmerman

Barbara Eden: Barbara Huffman
Ron Ely: Ronald Pierce
Chad Everett: Raymond Cramton
Tom Ewell: S. Yewell Tompkins

Douglas Fairbanks: Douglas Ullman
Morgan Fairchild: Patsy McClenny
Alice Faye: Ann Leppert
Stepin Fetchit: Lincoln Perry
W.C. Fields: William Claude Dukenfield
Peter Finch: William Mitchell
Barry Fitzgerald: William Joseph Shields
Joan Fontaine: Joan de Havilland
John Ford: Sean O'Fearna
John Forsythe: John Freund
Redd Foxx : John Sanford
Anthony Franciosa: Anthony Papaleo
Arlene Francis: Arlene Kazanjian
Connie Francis: Concetta Franconero

Greta Garbo: Greta Gustafsson
John Garfield: Julius Garfinkle
Judy Garland: Frances Gumm
James Garner: James Baumgardner
Crystal Gayle: Brenda Gayle Webb
Bobbie Gentry: Roberta Streeter
Eydie Gorme: Edith Gormezano
Stewart Granger: James Stewart
Cary Grant: Archibald Leach
Lee Grant: Lyova Rosenthal
Joel Grey: Joe Katz

Buddy Hackett: Leonard Hacker
Jean Harlow: Harlean Carpentier
Rex Harrison: Reginald Carey
Lawrence Harvey: Larushka Skikne
Helen Hayes: Helen Brown
Susan Hayward: Edythe Marriner
Rita Hayworth: Margarita Cansino
Pee-Wee Herman: Paul Rubenfeld
Barbara Hershey: Barbara Herzstine
William Holden: William Beedle
Judy Holliday: Judith Tuvim
Harry Houdini: Ehrich Weiss
Leslie Howard: Leslie Stainer
Moe Howard: Moses Horowitz
Rock Hudson: Roy Scherer Jr. (later Fitzgerald)
Engelbert Humperdinck: Arnold Dorsey
Kim Hunter: Janet Cole
Mary Beth Hurt: Mary Supinger
Betty Hutton: Betty Thornberg

David Janssen: David Meyer
Elton John: Reginald Dwight
Don Johnson: Donald Wayne
Jennifer Jones: Phyllis Isley
Tom Jones: Thomas Woodward
Louis Jourdan: Louis Gendre

Boris Karloff: William Henry Pratt
Danny Kaye: David Kaminsky
Diane Keaton: Diane Hall
Michael Keaton: Michael Douglas
Howard Keel: Harold Leek
Chaka Khan: Yvette Stevens
Carole King: Carole Klein
Ben Kingsley: Krishna Banji
Nastassja Kinski: Nastassja Naksyznyski
Ted Knight: Tadeus Wladyslaw Konopka

Cheryl Ladd: Cheryl Stoppelmoor
Veronica Lake: Constance Ockleman
Dorothy Lamour: Mary Kaumeyer
Michael Landon: Eugene Orowitz
Mario Lanza: Alfredo Cocozza
Stan Laurel: Arthur Jefferson
Steve Lawrence: Sidney Leibowitz
Brenda Lee: Brenda Mae Tarpley
Gypsy Rose Lee: Rose Louise Hovick
Michelle Lee: Michelle Dusiak
Peggy Lee: Norma Egstrom
Janet Leigh: Jeanette Morrison
Vivien Leigh: Vivien Hartley
Huey Lewis: Hugh Cregg
Jerry Lewis: Joseph Levitch
Hal Linden: Harold Lipshitz
Carole Lombard: Jane Peters
Jack Lord: John Joseph Ryan
Sophia Loren: Sophia Scicoloni
Peter Lorre: Laszio Lowenstein
Myrna Loy: Myrna Williams
Bela Lugosi: Bela Ferenc Blasko

Moms Mabley: Loretta Mary Aitken
Shirley MacLaine: Shirley Beaty
Madonna: Madonna Louise Ciccone
Lee Majors: Harvey Lee Yeary 2d
Karl Malden: Malden Sekulovich
Jayne Mansfield: Vera Jane Palmer
Fredric March: Frederick Bickel
Peter Marshall: Pierre LaCock
Dean Martin: Dino Crocetti
Ethel Merman: Ethel Zimmerman
Ray Milland: Reginald Truscott-Jones
Ann Miller: Lucille Collier
Joni Mitchell: Roberta Joan Anderson
Marilyn Monroe: Norma Jean Mortenson, (later) Baker
Yves Montand: Ivo Levi
Ron Moody: Ronald Moodnick
Garry Moore: Thomas Garrison Morfit
Rita Moreno: Rosita Alverio
Harry Morgan: Harry Bratsburg
Paul Muni: Muni Weisenfreund

Mike Nichols: Michael Igor Peschowsky
Sheree North: Dawn Bethel

Hugh O'Brian: Hugh Krampke
Maureen O'Hara: Maureen Fitzsimmons

Patti Page: Clara Ann Fowler
Jack Palance: Walter Palanuik
Lilli Palmer: Lilli Peiser
Bert Parks: Bert Jacobson
Minnie Pearl: Sarah Ophelia Cannon
Bernadette Peters: Bernadette Lazzaro
Edith Piaf: Edith Gassion
Slim Pickens: Louis Lindley
Mary Pickford: Gladys Smith
Stephanie Powers: Stefania Federkiewcz
Paula Prentiss: Paula Ragusa
Robert Preston: Robert Preston Meservey
Prince: Prince Rogers Nelson

Tony Randall: Leonard Rosenberg
Martha Raye: Margaret O'Reed
Donna Reed: Donna Belle Mullenger
Della Reese: Delloreese Patricia Early
Joan Rivers: Joan Sandra Molinsky
Edward G. Robinson: Emanual Goldenberg
Ginger Rogers: Virginia McMath
Roy Rogers: Leonard Slye
Mickey Rooney: Joe Yule Jr.
Lillian Russell: Helen Leonard

Susan St. James: Susan Miller
Soupy Sales: Milton Hines
Susan Sarandon: Susan Tomaling
Randolph Scott: George Randolph Crane
Jane Seymour: Joyce Frankenberg
Omar Sharif: Michael Shalhoub
Martin Sheen: Ramon Estevez
Beverly Sills: Belle Silverman
Talia Shire: Talia Coppola
Phil Silvers: Philip Silversmith
Suzanne Somers: Suzanne Mahoney
Ann Sothern: Harriette Lake
Barbara Stanwyck: Ruby Stevens
Jean Stapleton: Jeanne Murray

Ringo Starr: Richard Starkey
Connie Stevens: Concetta Ingolia
Donna Summers: LaDonna Gaines

Robert Taylor: Spangler Arlington Brugh
Danny Thomas: Amos Jacobs
Sophie Tucker: Sophia Kalish
Tina Turner: Annie Mae Bullock
Conway Twitty: Harold Lloyd Jenkins
Rudolph Valentino: Rudolpho D'Antonguolla
Frankie Valli: Frank Castelluccio

Nancy Walker: Myrtle Swoyer
David Wayne: Wayne McMeekan
John Wayne: Marion Morrison
Clifton Webb: Webb Parmalee Hollenbeck
Raquel Welch: Raquel Tejada
Gene Wilder: Jerome Silberman
Shelly Winters: Shirley Schrift
Stevie Wonder: Stevland Morris
Natalie Wood: Natasha Gurdin
Jane Wyman: Sarah Jane Fulks
Gig Young: Byron Barr

Figures in American Folklore

Johnny Appleseed: John Chapman, 1774-1845; according to legend, wandered through Ohio, Indiana, and W. Pennsylvania for 40 years, sowing seeds that produced the Midwest orchards.

P(hineas) T. Barnum: 1810-1891; showman known for extravagant ads and exhibits of "freaks," including Tom Thumb and the original Siamese Twins; his circus, "The Greatest Show on Earth," opened in 1871, in 1881 merged with its chief competitor to become Barnum & Bailey.

Judge Roy Bean: c. 1825-1903; frontier trader, cattle rustler, gambler, saloon keeper; in 1882 in Texas he named himself justice of the peace and set up court in his saloon, rendering unorthodox decisions with one law book and a six-shooter, wit, and common sense.

Billy the Kid: William H. Bonney, 1859-1881; range war gunman and cattle rustler accused of 21 murders, the first before he reached his teens.

Nellie Bly: Elizabeth Seaman, 1867-1922; *New York World* reporter who traveled around the world in 72 days, 6 hours, 11 minutes in 1889-90, beating the record of the fictional Phileas Fogg.

Bonnie & Clyde: Clyde Barrow, 1909-1934, and Bonnie Parker, 1910-1934; outlaws accused of 12 murders during a 2-year robbery spree in the Southwest.

Lizzie Borden: 1860-1927; 32-year-old spinster accused of killing her stepmother and father by hacking them with an ax; tried and found not guilty; she was popularly believed guilty.

Daniel Boone: 1734-1820; frontiersman who blazed the Wilderness Road and founded Boonesboro, Kentucky, which he helped defend against the Indians in 1779; many legendary adventures were disproved.

Jim Bowie: 1796-1836; frontiersman, soldier, and popular hero of the Texas Revolution, killed at the Alamo; either he or his brother Rezin invented the Bowie knife.

Diamond Jim Brady: James Buchanan Brady, 1856-1917; financier and bon vivant, noted for ample girth and lavish life-style.

John Brown: 1800-1859; abolitionist who led a raid on the federal arsenal at Harper's Ferry, Virginia, 1859; captured and tried for treason, his dignity and high moral tone in court won Northern sympathy and when convicted and hanged he became a martyr to the antislavery cause.

Buffalo Bill: William Cody, 1846-1917; army scout, buffalo hunter, Indian fighter, and showman who organized Buffalo Bill's Wild West Show, featuring fancy shooting, a buffalo hunt, Annie Oakley, and Chief Sitting Bull.

Paul Bunyan: legendary lumberjack of fantastic size and strength, the hero of many tall tales popular in the Western timber country.

Kit Carson: Christopher Carson, 1809-1868; frontiersman, soldier, and Indian agent who guided John C. Fremont's expeditions into Wyoming and California, 1842-46.

Calamity Jane: Martha Jane Canary, 1852-1903; frontier character who in 1876 appeared in Deadwood, S. Dakota dressed in men's clothes, boasting of her exploits as a pony express rider and Army scout.

Casey Jones: John Luther Jones, 1864-1900; locomotive engineer celebrated in song, who got his nickname from his Cayce, Kentucky workplace; driving the Cannon Ball express from Memphis to Canton, Mississippi, he applied the brakes in time to save the lives of the passengers in a wreck at Vaughn, Mississippi, but he was killed.

Davey Crockett: 1786-1836; a hero of frontier America, he fought in the Creek War under Andrew Jackson, was elected to the Tennessee legislature and the U.S. Congress, joined the Texas independence forces, and was killed at the Alamo.

Wyatt Earp: 1848-1929; law officer and gunfighter who was involved with his brothers and Doc Holliday in the controversial shootout at the OK Corral, 1881, Tombstone, Arizona.

Wild Bill Hickok: James Butler Hickok, 1837-1876; frontier marshal in Hays and Abilene, Kansas, who gained repute as a marksman and became a legend after his murder in Deadwood, S. Dakota by outlaw Jack McCall.

John Henry: legendary black man celebrated for his strength in ballads and tales; in one version of his story, he succeeded in outworking a steam drill but died from the strain.

Hiawatha: c. 1550; chief of the Onandaga Indians, credited with founding the Iroquois Confederacy, and the hero of a well-known poem by Henry Wadsworth Longfellow.

Jesse James: 1847-1882; outlaw who led his gang in daring bank and train robberies in the Midwest from 1866. He was murdered by Robert Ford, one of his gang.

Annie Oakley: Phoebe Anne Oakley Mozee, 1860-1926; rifle and shotgun markswoman who was the star attraction of Buffalo Bill's Wild West Show, 1885-1902.

Pocahontas: c. 1595-1617; daughter of Chief Powhatan, she was said to have saved the life of Capt. John Smith at Jamestown as Powhatan was about to execute him. Later held hostage at Jamestown for the return of her father's English prisoners, she became a Christian and in 1614 married a settler, John Rolfe; in 1616 Rolfe took her to England, where she was received as a princess; she died during the trip home, and was buried at Gravesend, England.

Betsy Ross: 1752-1846; seamstress who made flags during the American Revolution; however, the legend that she designed and made the first American national flag is generally discredited.

Uncle Remus: main character in *Uncle Remus: His Songs and His Sayings*, by Joel Chandler Harris, 1880, based on oral tales of southern blacks. Uncle Remus is depicted as a benign autocratic figure spinning animal fables to a white boy on a plantation.

Squanto: d. 1622; Indian of the Pawtuxet tribe who was kidnapped by Capt. Thomas Hunt in 1615, lived in England, and returned in 1619; he later acted as interpretor in concluding a treaty between the Pilgrim settlers and Massasoit, became friendly with the Plymouth colonists, and helped them, especially with planting and fishing.

Belle Starr: Myra Belle Shirley, 1848-1889; woman who led a band of cattle rustlers and horse thieves that made regular raids on Oklahoma ranches.

BIOGRAPHIES OF U.S. PRESIDENTS

George Washington (1789-1797)

George Washington, first president, was born Feb. 22, 1732 (Feb. 11, 1731, old style), the son of Augustine Washington and Mary Ball, at Wakefield on Pope's Creek, Westmoreland Co., Va. His early childhood was spent on the Ferry farm, near Fredericksburg. His father died when George was 11. He studied mathematics and surveying and when 16 went to live with his half brother Lawrence, who built and named Mount Vernon. George surveyed the lands of William Fairfax in the Shenandoah Valley, keeping a diary. He accompanied Lawrence to Barbados, West Indies, contracted small pox, and was deeply scarred. Lawrence died in 1752 and George acquired his property by inheritance. He valued land and when he died owned 70,000 acres in Virginia and 40,000 acres in what is now West Virginia.

Washington's military service began in 1753 when Gov. Dinwiddie of Virginia sent him on missions deep into Ohio country. He clashed with the French and had to surrender Fort Necessity July 3, 1754. He was an aide to Braddock and at his side when the army was ambushed and defeated on a march to Ft. Duquesne, July 9, 1755. He helped take Fort Duquesne from the French in 1758.

After his marriage to Martha Dandridge Custis, a widow, in 1759, Washington managed his family estate at Mount Vernon. Although not at first for independence, he opposed British exactions and took charge of the Virginia troops before war broke out. He was made commander-in-chief by the Continental Congress June 15, 1775.

The successful issue of a war filled with hardships was due to his leadership. He was resourceful, a stern disciplinarian, and the one strong, dependable force for unity. He favored a federal government and became chairman of the Constitutional Convention of 1787. He helped get the Constitution ratified and was unanimously elected president by the electoral college and inaugurated, Apr. 30, 1789, on the balcony of New York's Federal Hall.

He was reelected 1792, but refused to consider a 3d term and retired to Mount Vernon. He suffered acute laryngitis after a ride in snow and rain around his estate, was bled profusely, and died Dec. 14, 1799.

John Adams (1797-1801)

John Adams, 2d president, Federalist, was born in Braintree (Quincy), Mass., Oct. 30, 1735 (Oct. 19, o. s.), the son of John Adams, a farmer, and Susanna Boylston. He was a great-grandson of Henry Adams who came from England in 1636. He was graduated from Harvard, 1755, taught school, studied law. In 1765 he argued against taxation without representation before the royal governor. In 1770 he defended in court the British soldiers who fired on civilians in the "Boston Massacre." He was a delegate to the first Continental Congress, and signed the Declaration of Independence. He was a commissioner to France, 1778, with Benjamin Franklin and Arthur Lee; won recognition of the U.S. by The Hague, 1782; was first American minister to England, 1785-1788, and was elected vice president, 1788 and 1792.

In 1796 Adams was chosen president by the electors. Intense antagonism to America by France caused agitation for war, led by Alexander Hamilton. Adams, breaking with Hamilton, opposed war.

To fight alien influence and muzzle criticism Adams supported the Alien and Sedition laws of 1798, which led to his defeat for reelection. He died July 4, 1826, on the same day as Jefferson (the 50th anniversary of the Declaration of Independence).

Thomas Jefferson (1801-1809)

Thomas Jefferson, 3d president, was born Apr. 13, 1743 (Apr. 2, o. s.), at Shadwell, Va., the son of Peter Jefferson, a civil engineer of Welsh descent who raised tobacco, and Jane Randolph. His father died when he was 14, leaving him 2,750 acres and his slaves. Jefferson attended the College of William and Mary, 1760-1762, read classics in Greek and Latin and played the violin. In 1769 he was elected to the House of Burgesses. In 1770 he began building Monticello, near Charlottesville. He was a member of the Virginia Committee of Correspondence and the Continental Congress. Named a member of the committee to draw up a Declaration of Independence, he wrote the basic draft. He was a member of the Virginia House of Delegates, 1776-79, elected governor to succeed Patrick Henry, 1779, reelected 1780, resigned June 1781, amid charges of ineffectual military preparation. During his term he wrote the statute on religious freedom. In the Continental Congress, 1783, he drew up an ordinance for the Northwest Territory, forbidding slavery after 1800; its terms were put into the Ordinance of 1787. He was sent to Paris with Benjamin Franklin and John Adams to negotiate commercial treaties, 1784; made minister to France, 1785.

Washington appointed him secretary of state, 1789. Jefferson's strong faith in the consent of the governed, as opposed to executive control favored by Hamilton, secretary of the treasury, often led to conflict: Dec. 31, 1793, he resigned. He was the Democrat Republican candidate for president in 1796; beaten by John Adams, he became vice president. In 1800, Jefferson and Aaron Burr received equal electoral college votes for president. The House of Representatives elected Jefferson. Major events of his administration were the Louisiana Purchase, 1803, and the Lewis and Clark Expedition. He established the Univ. of Virginia and designed its buildings. He died July 4, 1826, on the same day as John Adams.

James Madison (1809-1817)

James Madison, 4th president, Democrat Republican, was born Mar. 16, 1751 (Mar. 5, 1750, o. s.) at Port Conway, King George Co., Va., eldest son of James Madison and Eleanor Rose Conway. Madison was graduated from Princeton, 1771; studied theology, 1772; sat in the Virginia Constitutional Convention, 1776. He was a member of the Continental Congress. He was chief recorder at the Constitutional Convention in 1787, and supported ratification in the Federalist Papers, written with Alexander Hamilton and John Jay. He was elected to the House of Representatives in 1789, helped frame the Bill of Rights and fought the Alien and Sedition Acts. He became Jefferson's secretary of state, 1801.

Elected president in 1808, Madison was a "strict constructionist," opposed to the free interpretation of the Constitution by the Federalists. He was reelected in 1812 by the votes of the agrarian South and recently admitted western states. Caught between British and French maritime restrictions, the U.S. drifted into war, declared June 18, 1812. The war ended in a stalemate. He retired in 1817 to his estate at Montpelier. There he edited his famous papers on the Constitutional Convention. He became rector of the Univ. of Virginia, 1826. He died June 28, 1836.

James Monroe (1817-1825)

James Monroe, 5th president, Democrat Republican, was born Apr. 28, 1758, in Westmoreland Co., Va., the son of Spence Monroe and Eliza Jones, who were of Scottish and Welsh descent, respectively. He attended the College of William and Mary, fought in the 3d Virginia Regiment at White Plains, Brandywine, Monmouth, and was wounded at Trenton. He studied law with Thomas Jefferson, 1780, was a member of the Virginia House of Delegates and of Congress, 1783-86. He opposed ratification of the Constitution because it lacked a bill of rights; was U.S. senator, 1790; minister to France, 1794-96; governor of Virginia, 1799-1802, and 1811. Jefferson sent him to France as minister, 1803. He helped Robert Livingston negotiate the Louisiana Purchase, 1803. He ran against Madison for president in 1808. He was elected to the Virginia Assembly, 1810-1811; was secretary of state under Madison, 1811-1817.

In 1816 Monroe was elected president; in 1820 reelected with all but one electoral college vote. Monroe's administration became the "Era of Good Feeling." He obtained Florida from Spain; settled boundaries with Canada, and eliminated border forts. He supported the anti-slavery position that led to the Missouri Compromise. His most significant contribution was the "Monroe Doctrine," which became a cornerstone of U.S. foreign policy. Monroe retired to Oak Hill, Va. Financial problems forced him to sell his property.

He moved to New York City to live with a daughter. He died there July 4, 1831.

John Quincy Adams (1825-1829)

John Quincy Adams, 6th president, independent Federalist, was born July 11, 1767, at Braintree (Quincy), Mass., the son of John and Abigail Adams. His father was the 2d president. He was educated in Paris, Leyden, and Harvard, graduating in 1787. He served as American minister in various European capitals, and helped draft the War of 1812 peace treaty. He was U.S. Senator, 1803-08. President Monroe made him secretary of state, 1817, and he negotiated the cession of the Floridas from Spain, supported exclusion of slavery in the Missouri Compromise, and helped formulate the Monroe Doctrine. In 1824 he was elected president by the House after he failed to win an electoral college majority. His expansion of executive powers was strongly opposed and he was beaten in 1828 by Jackson. In 1831 he entered Congress and served 17 years with distinction. He opposed slavery, the annexation of Texas, and the Mexican War. He helped establish the Smithsonian Institution. He had a stroke in the House and died in the Speaker's Room, Feb. 23, 1848.

Andrew Jackson (1829-1837)

Andrew Jackson, 7th president, was a Jeffersonian-Republican, later a Democrat. He was born in the Waxhaws district, New Lancaster Co., S.C., Mar. 15, 1767, the posthumous son of Andrew Jackson and Elizabeth Hutchinson, who were Irish immigrants. At 13, he joined the militia in the Revolution and was captured.

He read law in Salisbury, N.C., moved to Nashville, Tenn., speculated in land, married, and practiced law. In 1796 he helped draft the constitution of Tennessee and for a year occupied its one seat in Congress. He was in the Senate in 1797, and again in 1823. He defeated the Creek Indians at Horseshoe Bend, Ala., 1814. With 6,000 backwoods fighters he defeated Packenham's 12,000 British troops at the Chalmette, outside New Orleans, Jan. 8, 1815. In 1818 he briefly invaded Spanish Florida to quell Seminoles and outlaws who harassed frontier settlements. In 1824 he ran for president against John Quincy Adams and had the most popular and electoral votes but not a majority; the election was decided by the House, which chose Adams. In 1828 he defeated Adams, carrying the West and South. He was a noisy debater and a duelist and introduced rotation in office called the "spoils system." Suspicious of privilege, he ruined the Bank of the United States by depositing federal funds with state banks. Though "Let the people rule" was his slogan, he at times supported strict constructionist policies against the expansionist West. He killed the congressional caucus for nominating presidential candidates and substituted the national convention, 1832. When South Carolina refused to collect imports under his protective tariff he ordered army and naval forces to Charleston. Jackson recognized the Republic of Texas, 1836. He died at the Hermitage, June 8, 1845.

Martin Van Buren (1837-1841)

Martin Van Buren, 8th president, Democrat, was born Dec. 5, 1782, at Kinderhook, N.Y., the son of Abraham Van Buren, a Dutch farmer, and Mary Hoes. He was surrogate of Columbia County, N.Y., state senator and attorney general. He was U.S. senator 1821, reelected, 1827, elected governor of New York, 1828. He helped swing eastern support to Jackson in 1828 and was his secretary of state 1829-31. In 1832 he was elected vice president. He was a consummate politician, known as "the little magician," and influenced Jackson's policies. In 1836 he defeated William Henry Harrison for president and took office as the Panic of 1837 initiated a 5-year nationwide depression. He inaugurated the independent treasury system. His refusal to spend land revenues led to his defeat by Harrison in 1840. He lost the Democratic nomination in 1844 to Polk. In 1848 he ran for president on the Free Soil ticket and lost. He died July 24, 1862, at Kinderhook.

William Henry Harrison (1841)

William Henry Harrison, 9th president, Whig, who served only 31 days, was born in Berkeley, Charles City Co., Va., Feb. 9, 1773, the 3d son of Benjamin Harrison, signer of the Declaration of Independence. He attended Hampden Sydney College. He was secretary of the Northwest Territory, 1798; its delegate in Congress, 1799; first governor of Indiana Territory, 1800; and superintendent of Indian affairs. With 900 men he routed Tecumseh's Indians at Tippecanoe, Nov. 7, 1811. A major general, he defeated British and Indians at Battle of the Thames, Oct. 5, 1813. He served in Congress, 1816-19; Senate, 1825-28. In 1840, when 68, he was elected president with a "log cabin and hard cider" slogan. He caught pneumonia during the inauguration and died Apr. 4, 1841.

John Tyler (1841-1845)

John Tyler, 10th president, independent Whig, was born Mar. 29, 1790, in Greenway, Charles City Co., Va., son of John Tyler and Mary Armistead. His father was governor of Virginia, 1808-11. Tyler was graduated from William and Mary, 1807; member of the House of Delegates, 1811; in congress, 1816-21; in Virginia legislature, 1823-25; governor of Virginia, 1825-26; U.S. senator, 1827-36. In 1840 he was elected vice president and, on Harrison's death, succeeded him. He favored pre-emption, allowing settlers to get government land; rejected a national bank bill and thus alienated most Whig supporters; refused to honor the spoils system. He signed the resolution annexing Texas, Mar. 1, 1845. He accepted renomination, 1844, but withdrew before election. In 1861, he chaired an unsuccessful Washington conference called to avert civil war. After its failure he supported secession, sat in the provisional Confederate Congress, became a member of the Confederate House, but died in Richmond, Jan. 18, 1862, before it met.

James Knox Polk (1845-1849)

James Knox Polk, 11th president, Democrat, was born in Mecklenburg Co., N.C., Nov. 2, 1795, the son of Samuel Polk, farmer and surveyor of Scotch-Irish descent, and Jane Knox. He graduated from the Univ. of North Carolina, 1818; member of the Tennessee state legislature, 1823-25. He served in Congress 1825-39 and as speaker 1835-39. He was governor of Tennessee 1839-41, but was defeated 1841 and 1843. In 1844, when both Clay and Van Buren announced opposition to annexing Texas, the Democrats made Polk the first dark horse nominee because he demanded control of all Oregon and annexation of Texas. Polk reestablished the independent treasury system originated by Van Buren. His expansionist policy was opposed by Clay, Webster, Calhoun; he sent troops under Zachary Taylor to the Mexican border and, when Mexicans attacked, declared war existed. The Mexican war ended with the annexation of California and much of the Southwest as part of America's "manifest destiny." He compromised on the Oregon boundary ("54-40 or fight!") by accepting the 49th parallel and giving Vancouver to the British. Polk died in Nashville, June 15, 1849.

Zachary Taylor (1849-1850)

Zachary Taylor, 12th president, Whig, who served only 16 months, was born Nov. 24, 1784, in Orange Co., Va., the son of Richard Taylor, later collector of the port of Louisville, Ky., and Sarah Strother. Taylor was commissioned first lieutenant, 1808; fought in the War of 1812; the Black Hawk War, 1832; and the second Seminole War, 1837. He was called Old Rough and Ready. He settled on a plantation near Baton Rouge, La. In 1845 Polk sent him with an army to the Rio Grande. When the Mexicans attacked him, Polk declared war. Taylor was successful at Palo Alto and Resaca de la Palma, 1846; occupied Monterrey. Polk made him major general but sent many of his troops to Gen. Winfield Scott. Outnumbered 4-1, he defeated Santa Anna at Buena Vista, 1847. A national hero, he received the Whig nomination in 1848, and was elected president. He resumed the spoils system and though once a slave-holder worked to have California admitted as a free state. He died in office July 9, 1850.

Millard Fillmore (1850-1853)

Millard Fillmore, 13th president, Whig, was born Jan. 7, 1800, in Cayuga Co., N.Y., the son of Nathaniel Fillmore and Phoebe Millard. He taught school and studied law; admitted to the bar, 1823. He was a member of the state assembly, 1829-32; in Congress, 1833-35 and again 1837-43.

He opposed the entrance of Texas as slave territory and voted for a protective tariff. In 1844 he was defeated for governor of New York. In 1848 he was elected vice president and succeeded as president July 10, 1850, after Taylor's death. Fillmore favored the Compromise of 1850 and signed the Fugitive Slave Law. His policies pleased neither expansionists nor slave-holders and he was not renominated in 1852. In 1856 he was nominated by the American (Know-Nothing) party and accepted by the Whigs, but defeated by Buchanan. He died in Buffalo, Mar. 8, 1874.

Franklin Pierce (1853-1857)

Franklin Pierce, 14th president, Democrat, was born in Hillsboro, N. H., Nov. 23, 1804, the son of Benjamin Pierce, veteran of the Revolution and governor of New Hampshire, 1827. He graduated from Bowdoin, 1824. A lawyer, he served in the state legislature 1829-33; in Congress, supporting Jackson, 1833-37; U.S. senator, 1837-42. He enlisted in the Mexican War, became brigadier general under Gen. Winfield Scott. In 1852 Pierce was nominated on the 49th ballot over Lewis Cass, Stephen A. Douglas, and James Buchanan, and defeated Gen. Scott, Whig. Though against slavery, Pierce was influenced by pro-slavery Southerners. He ignored the Ostend Manifesto that the U.S. either buy or take Cuba. He approved the Kansas-Nebraska Act, leaving slavery to popular vote ("squatter sovereignty"), 1854. He signed a reciprocity treaty with Canada and approved the Gadsden Purchase from Mexico, 1853. Denied renomination by the Democrats, he spent most of his remaining years in Concord, N.H., where he died Oct. 8, 1869.

James Buchanan (1857-1861)

James Buchanan, 15th president, Federalist, later Democrat, was born of Scottish descent near Mercersburg, Pa., Apr. 23, 1791. He graduated from Dickinson, 1809; was a volunteer in the War of 1812; member, Pennsylvania legislature, 1814-16, Congress, 1820-31; Jackson's minister to Russia, 1831-33; U.S. senator 1834-45. As Polk's secretary of state, 1845-49, he ended the Oregon dispute with Britain, supported the Mexican War and annexation of Texas. As minister to Britain, 1853, he signed the Ostend Manifesto. Nominated by Democrats, he was elected, 1856, over John C. Fremont (Republican) and Millard Fillmore (American Know-Nothing and Whig tickets). On slavery he favored popular sovereignty and choice by state constitutions; he accepted the pro-slavery Dred Scott decision as binding. He denied the right of states to secede. A strict constructionist, he desired to keep peace and found no authority for using force. He died at Wheatland, near Lancaster, Pa., June 1, 1868.

Abraham Lincoln (1861-1865)

Abraham Lincoln, 16th president, Republican, was born Feb. 12, 1809, in a log cabin on a farm then in Hardin Co., Ky., now in Larue. He was the son of Thomas Lincoln, a carpenter, and Nancy Hanks.

The Lincolns moved to Spencer Co., Ind., near Gentryville, when Abe was 7. When his mother died his father married Mrs. Sarah Bush Johnston, 1819; she had a favorable influence on Abe. In 1830 the family moved to Macon Co., Ill. Lincoln lost election to the Illinois General Assembly, 1832, but later won 4 times, beginning in 1834. He enlisted in the militia for the Black Hawk War, 1832. In New Salem he ran a store, surveyed land, and was postmaster.

In 1837 Lincoln was admitted to the bar and became partner in a Springfield, Ill., law office. He was elected to Congress, 1847-49. He opposed the Mexican War. He supported Zachary Taylor, 1848. He opposed the Kansas-Nebraska Act and extension of slavery, 1854. He failed, in his bid for the Senate, 1855. He supported John C. Fremont, 1856.

In 1858 Lincoln had Republican support in the Illinois legislature for the Senate but was defeated by Stephen A. Douglas, Dem., who had sponsored the Kansas-Nebraska Act.

Lincoln was nominated for president by the Republican party on an anti-slavery platform, 1860. He ran against Douglas, a northern Democrat; John C. Breckinridge, southern pro-slavery Democrat; John Bell, Constitutional Union party. When he won the election, South Carolina seceded from the Union Dec. 20, 1860, followed in 1861 by 10 Southern states.

The Civil War erupted when Fort Sumter was attacked Apr. 12, 1861. On Sept. 22, 1862, 5 days after the battle of Antietam, he announced that slaves in territory then in rebellion would be free Jan. 1, 1863, date of the Emancipation Proclamation. His speeches, including his Gettysburg and Inaugural addresses, are remembered for their eloquence.

Lincoln was reelected, 1864, over Gen. George B. McClellan, Democrat. Lee surrendered Apr. 9, 1865. On Apr. 14, Lincoln was shot by actor John Wilkes Booth in Ford's Theatre, Washington. He died the next day.

Andrew Johnson (1865-1869)

Andrew Johnson, 17th president, Democrat, was born in Raleigh, N.C., Dec. 29, 1808, the son of Jacob Johnson, porter at an inn and church sexton, and Mary McDonough. He was apprenticed to a tailor but ran away and eventually settled in Greeneville, Tenn. He became an alderman, 1828; mayor, 1830; state representative and senator, 1835-43; member of Congress, 1843-53; governor of Tennessee, 1853-57; U.S. senator, 1857-62. He supported John C. Breckinridge against Lincoln in 1860. He had held slaves, but opposed secession and tried to prevent his home state, Tennessee, from seceding. In Mar. 1862, Lincoln appointed him military governor of occupied Tennessee. In 1864 he was nominated for vice president with Lincoln on the National Union ticket to win Democratic support. He succeeded Lincoln as president Apr. 15, 1865. In a controversy with Congress over the president's power over the South, he proclaimed, May 26, 1865, an amnesty to all Confederates except certain leaders if they would ratify the 13th Amendment abolishing slavery. States doing so added anti-Negro provisions that enraged Congress, which restored military control over the South. When Johnson removed Edwin M. Stanton, secretary of war, without notifying the Senate, thus repudiating the Tenure of Office Act, the House impeached him for this and other reasons. He was tried by the Senate, and acquitted by only one vote, May 26, 1868. He returned to the Senate in 1875. Johnson died July 31, 1875.

Ulysses Simpson Grant (1869-1877)

Ulysses S. Grant, 18th president, Republican, was born at Point Pleasant, Oh., Apr. 27, 1822, son of Jesse R. Grant, a tanner, and Hannah Simpson. The next year the family moved to Georgetown, Oh. Grant was named Hiram Ulysses, but on entering West Point, 1839, his name was entered as Ulysses Simpson and he adopted it. He was graduated in 1843; served under Gens. Taylor and Scott in the Mexican War; resigned, 1854; worked in St. Louis until 1860, then went to Galena, Ill. With the start of the Civil War, he was named colonel of the 21st Illinois Vols., 1861, then brigadier general; took Forts Henry and Donelson; fought at Shiloh, took Vicksburg. After his victory at Chattanooga, Lincoln placed him in command of the Union Armies. He accepted Lee's surrender at Appomattox, Apr., 1865. President Johnson appointed Grant secretary of war when he suspended Stanton, but Grant was not confirmed. He was nominated for president by the Republicans in 1868 and elected over Horatio Seymour, Democrat. The 15th Amendment, amnesty bill, and civil service reform were events of his administration. The Liberal Republicans and Democrats opposed him with Horace Greeley, 1872, but he was reelected. An attempt by the Stalwarts (Old Guard) to nominate him in 1880 failed. In 1884 the collapse of Grant & Ward, investment house, left him penniless. He wrote his personal memoirs while ill with cancer and completed them 4 days before his death at Mt. McGregor, N.Y., July 23, 1885. The book realized over $450,000.

Rutherford Birchard Hayes (1877-1881)

Rutherford B. Hayes, 19th president, Republican, was born in Delaware, Oh., Oct. 4, 1822, the posthumous son of Rutherford Hayes, a farmer, and Sophia Birchard. He was raised by his uncle Sardis Birchard. He graduated from Kenyon College, 1842, and Harvard Law School, 1845. He practiced law in Lower Sandusky, Oh., now Fremont; was city solicitor of Cincinnati, 1858-61. In the Civil War, he was major of the 23d Ohio Vols., was wounded several times, and rose to the rank of brevet major general, 1864. He served in Congress 1864-67, supporting Reconstruction and Johnson's impeachment. He was elected governor of Ohio, 1867 and 1869; beaten in the race for Congress, 1872; reelected governor, 1875. In 1876 he was nominated for president and believed he had lost the election to Samuel J. Tilden, Democrat. But a few Southern states submitted 2 different sets of electoral votes and the result was in dispute. An electoral commission, appointed by Congress, 8 Republicans and 7 Democrats, awarded all disputed votes to Hayes allowing him to become president by one electoral vote. Hayes, keeping a promise to southerners, withdrew troops from areas still occupied in the South, ending the era of Reconstruction. He proceeded to reform the civil service, alienating political spoilsmen. He advocated repeal of the Tenure of Office Act. He supported sound money and specie payments. Hayes died in Fremont, Oh., Jan. 17, 1893.

James Abram Garfield (1881-1881)

James A. Garfield, 20th president, Republican, was born Nov. 19, 1831, in Orange, Cuyahoga Co., Oh., the son of Abram Garfield and Eliza Ballou. His father died in 1833. He worked as a canal bargeman, farmer, and carpenter; attended Western Reserve Eclectic, later Hiram College, and was graduated from Williams in 1856. He taught at Hiram, and later became principal. He was in the Ohio senate in 1859. Anti-slavery and anti-secession, he volunteered for the war, became colonel of the 42d Ohio Infantry and brigadier in 1862. He fought at Shiloh, was chief of staff for Rosecrans and was made major general for gallantry at Chickamauga. He entered Congress as a radical Republican in 1863; supported specie payment as against paper money (greenbacks). On the electoral commission in 1877 he voted for Hayes against Tilden on strict party lines. He was senator-elect in 1880 when he became the Republican nominee for president. He was chosen as a compromise over Gen. Grant, James G. Blaine, and John Sherman. This alienated the Grant following but Garfield was elected. On July 2, 1881, Garfield was shot by mentally disturbed office-seeker, Charles J. Guiteau, while entering a railroad station in Washington. He died Sept. 19, 1881, at Elberon, N.J.

Chester Alan Arthur (1881-1885)

Chester A. Arthur, 21st president, Republican, was born at Fairfield, Vt., Oct. 5, 1829, the son of the Rev. William Arthur, from County Antrim, Ireland, and Malvina Stone. He graduated from Union College, 1848, taught school at Pownall, Vt., studied law in New York. In 1853 he argued in a fugitive slave case that slaves transported through N.Y. State were thereby freed. He was made collector of the Port of New York, 1871. President Hayes, reforming the civil service, forced Arthur to resign, 1879. This made the New York machine stalwarts enemies of Hayes. Arthur and the stalwarts tried to nominate Grant for a 3d term in 1880. When Garfield was nominated, Arthur received 2d place in the interests of harmony. When Garfield died, Arthur became president. He supported civil service reform and the tariff of 1883. He was defeated for renomination by James G. Blaine. He died in New York City Nov. 18, 1886.

Grover Cleveland (1885-1889) (1893-1897)

(According to a ruling of the State Dept., Grover Cleveland is both the 22d and the 24th president, because his 2 terms were not consecutive. By individuals, he is only the 22d.)

Grover Cleveland, 22d and 24th president, Democrat, was born in Caldwell, N.J. Mar. 18, 1837, the son of Richard F. Cleveland, a Presbyterian minister, and Ann Neale. He was named Stephen Grover, but dropped the Stephen. He clerked in Clinton and Buffalo, N.Y., taught at the N.Y. City Institution for the Blind; was admitted to the bar in Buffalo, 1859; became assistant district attorney, 1863; sheriff, 1871; mayor, 1881; governor of New York, 1882. He was an independent, honest administrator who hated corruption. He was nominated for president over Tammany Hall opposition, 1884, and defeated Republican James G. Blaine. He enlarged the civil service, vetoed many pension raids on the Treasury. In 1888 he was defeated by Benjamin Harrison, although his popular vote was larger. Reelected over Harrison in 1892, he faced a money crisis brought about by lowering of the gold reserve, circulation of paper and exorbitant silver purchases under the Sherman Act; obtained a repeal of the latter and a reduced tariff. A severe depression and labor troubles racked his administration but he refused to interfere in business matters and rejected Jacob Coxey's demand for unemployment relief. He broke the Pullman strike, 1894. In 1896, the Democrats repudiated his administration and chose silverite William Jennings Bryan as their candidate. Cleveland died in Princeton, N.J., June 24, 1908.

Benjamin Harrison (1889-1893)

Benjamin Harrison, 23d president, Republican, was born at North Bend, Oh., Aug. 20, 1833. His great-grandfather, Benjamin Harrison, was a signer of the Declaration of Independence; his grandfather, William Henry Harrison, was 9th President; his father, John Scott Harrison, was a member of Congress. His mother was Elizabeth F. Irwin. He attended school on his father's farm; graduated from Miami Univ. at Oxford, Oh., 1852; admitted to the bar, 1853, and practiced in Indianapolis. In the Civil War, he rose to the rank of brevet brigadier general, fought at Kennesaw Mountain, Peachtree Creek, Nashville, and in the Atlanta campaign. He failed to be elected governor of Indiana, 1876; but became senator, 1881. In 1888 he defeated Cleveland for president despite having fewer popular votes. He expanded the pension list, signed the McKinley high tariff bill, and the Sherman Silver Purchase Act. During his administration, 6 states were admitted to the union. He was defeated for reelection, 1892. He represented Venezuela in a boundary arbitration with Great Britain in Paris, 1899. He died in Indianapolis, Mar. 13, 1901.

William McKinley (1897-1901)

William McKinley, 25th president, Republican, was born in Niles, Oh., Jan. 29, 1843, the son of William McKinley, an ironmaker, and Nancy Allison. McKinley attended school in Poland, Oh., and Allegheny College, Meadville, Pa., and enlisted for the Civil War at 18 in the 23d Ohio, in which Rutherford B. Hayes was a major. He rose to captain and in 1865 was made brevet major. He studied law in the Albany, N.Y., law school; opened an office in Canton, Oh., in 1867, and campaigned for Grant and Hayes. He served in the House of Representatives, 1877-83, 1885-91, and led the fight for passage of the McKinley Tarriff, 1890. Defeated for reelection on the issue in 1890, he was governor of Ohio, 1892-96. He had support for president in the convention that nominated Benjamin Harrison in 1892. In 1896 he was elected president on a protective tariff, sound money (gold standard) platform over William Jennings Bryan, Democratic proponent of free silver. McKinley was reluctant to intervene in Cuba but the loss of the battleship Maine at Havana crystallized opinion. He demanded Spain's withdrawal from Cuba; Spain made some concessions but Congress announced state of war as of Apr. 21. He was reelected in the 1900 campaign, defeating Bryan's anti-imperialist arguments with the promise of a "full dinner pail." McKinley was respected for his conciliatory nature, but conservative on business issues. On Sept. 6, 1901, while welcoming citizens at the Pan-American Exposition, Buffalo, N.Y., he was shot by Leon Czolgosz, an anarchist. He died Sept. 14.

Theodore Roosevelt (1901-1909)

Theodore Roosevelt, 26th president, Republican, was born in N.Y. City, Oct. 27, 1858, the son of Theodore Roosevelt, a glass importer, and Martha Bulloch. He was a 5th cousin of Franklin D. Roosevelt and an uncle of Eleanor Roosevelt. Roosevelt graduated from Harvard, 1880; attended Columbia Law School briefly; sat in the N.Y. State Assembly, 1882-84; ranched in North Dakota, 1884-86; failed election as mayor of N.Y. City, 1886; member of U.S. Civil Service Commission, 1889; president, N.Y. Police Board, 1895, supporting the merit system; assistant secretary of the Navy under McKinley, 1897-98. In the war with Spain, he organized the 1st U.S. Volunteer Cavalry (Rough Riders) as lieutenant colonel; led the charge up Kettle Hill at San Juan. Elected New York governor, 1898-1900, he fought the spoils system and achieved taxation of corporation franchises. Nominated for vice president, 1900, he became nation's youngest president when McKinley died. As president he fought corruption of politics by big business; dissolved Northern Securities Co. and others for violating anti-trust laws; intervened in coal strike on behalf of the public, 1902; obtained Elkins Law forbidding rebates to favored corporations, 1903; Hepburn Law regulating railroad rates, 1906; Pure Food and Drugs Act, 1906, Reclamation Act and employers' liability laws. He organized conservation, mediated the peace between Japan and Russia, 1905; won the Nobel Peace Prize. He was the first to use the Hague Court of International Arbitration. By recognizing the new Republic of Panama he made Panama Canal possible. He was reelected in 1904.

In 1908 he obtained the nomination of William H. Taft, who was elected. Feeling that Taft had abandoned his policies, Roosevelt unsuccessfully sought the nomination in 1912. He bolted the party and ran on the Progressive "Bull Moose", ticket against Taft and Woodrow Wilson, splitting the Republicans and insuring Wilson's election. He was shot during the campaign but recovered. In 1916 he supported Charles E. Hughes, Republican. A strong friend of Britain, he fought American isolation in World War I. He wrote some 40 books on many topics; his *Winning of the West* is best known. He died Jan. 6, 1919, at Sagamore Hill, Oyster Bay, N.Y.

William Howard Taft (1909-1913)

William Howard Taft, 27th president, Republican, was born in Cincinnati, Oh., Sept. 15, 1857, the son of Alphonso Taft and Louisa Maria Torrey. His father was secretary of war and attorney general in Grant's cabinet; minister to Austria and Russia under Arthur. Taft was graduated from Yale, 1878; Cincinnati Law School, 1880; became law reporter for Cincinnati newspapers; was assistant prosecuting attorney, 1881-83; assistant county solicitor, 1885; judge, superior court, 1887; U.S. solicitor-general, 1890; federal circuit judge, 1892. In 1900 he became head of the U.S. Philippines Commission and was first civil governor of the Philippines, 1901-04; secretary of war, 1904; provisional governor of Cuba, 1906. He was groomed for president by Roosevelt and elected over Bryan, 1908. His administration dissolved Standard Oil and tobacco trusts; instituted Dept. of Labor; drafted direct election of senators and income tax amendments. His tariff and conservation policies angered progressives; though renominated he was opposed by Roosevelt; the result was Democrat Woodrow Wilson's election. Taft, with some reservations, supported the League of Nations. He was professor of constitutional law, Yale, 1913-21; chief justice of the U.S. Supreme Court, 1921-30; illness forced him to resign. He died in Washington, Mar. 8, 1930.

Woodrow Wilson (1913-1921)

Woodrow Wilson, 28th president, Democrat, was born at Staunton, Va., Dec. 28, 1856, as Thomas Woodrow Wilson, son of a Presbyterian minister, the Rev. Joseph Ruggles Wilson and Janet (Jessie) Woodrow. In his youth Wilson lived in Augusta, Ga., Columbia, S.C., and Wilmington, N.C. He attended Davidson College, 1873-74; was graduated from Princeton, A.B., 1879; A.M., 1882; read law at the Univ. of Virginia, 1881; practiced law, Atlanta, 1882-83; Ph.D., Johns Hopkins, 1886. He taught at Bryn Mawr, 1885-88; at Wesleyan, 1888-90; was professor of jurisprudence and political economy at Princeton, 1890-1910; president of Princeton, 1902-1910; governor of New Jersey, 1911-13. In 1912 he was nominated for president with the aid of William Jennings Bryan, who sought to block James "Champ" Clark and Tammany Hall. Wilson won the election because the Republican vote for Taft was split by the Progressives under Roosevelt.

Wilson protected American interests in revolutionary Mexico and fought for American rights on the high seas. His sharp warnings to Germany led to the resignation of his secretary of state, Bryan, a pacifist. In 1916 he was reelected by a slim margin with the slogan, "He kept us out of war." Wilson's attempts to mediate in the war failed. After 4 American ships had been sunk by the Germans, he secured a declaration of war against Germany on Apr. 6, 1917.

Wilson proposed peace Jan. 8, 1918, on the basis of his "Fourteen Points," a state paper with worldwide influence. His doctrine of self-determination continues to play a major role in territorial disputes. The Germans accepted his terms and an armistice, Nov. 11.

Wilson went to Paris to help negotiate the peace treaty, the crux of which he considered the League of Nations. The Senate demanded reservations that would not make the U.S. subordinate to the votes of other nations in case of war. Wilson refused to consider any reservations and toured the country to get support. He suffered a stroke, Oct., 1919. An invalid for months, he clung to his executive powers while his wife and doctor sought to shield him from affairs which would tire him.

He was awarded the 1919 Nobel Peace Prize, but the treaty embodying the League of Nations was rejected by the Senate, 1920. He died in Washington, Feb. 3, 1924.

Warren Gamaliel Harding (1921-1923)

Warren Gamaliel Harding, 29th president, Republican, was born near Corsica, now Blooming Grove, Oh., Nov. 2, 1865, the son of Dr. George Tyron Harding, a physician, and Phoebe Elizabeth Dickerson. He attended Ohio Central College. He was state senator, 1900-04; lieutenant governor, 1904-06; defeated for governor, 1910; chosen U.S. senator, 1915. He supported Taft, opposed federal control of food and fuel; voted for anti-strike legislation, woman's suffrage, and the Volstead prohibition enforcement act over President Wilson's veto; and opposed the League of Nations. In 1920 he was nominated for president and defeated James M. Cox in the election. The Republicans capitalized on war weariness and fear that Wilson's League of Nations would curtail U.S. sovereignty. Harding stressed a return to "normalcy"; worked for tariff revision and repeal of excess profits law and high income taxes. Two Harding appointees, Albert B. Fall (interior) and Harry Daugherty (attorney general), became involved in the Teapot Dome scandal that embittered Harding's last days. He called the International Conference on Limitation of Armaments, 1921-22. Returning from a trip to Alaska he became ill and died in San Francisco, Aug. 2, 1923.

Calvin Coolidge (1923-1929)

Calvin Coolidge, 30th president, Republican, was born in Plymouth, Vt., July 4, 1872, the son of John Calvin Coolidge, a storekeeper, and Victoria J. Moor, and named John Calvin Coolidge. Coolidge graduated from Amherst in 1895. He entered Republican state politics and served as mayor of Northampton, Mass., state senator, lieutenant governor, and, in 1919, governor. In Sept., 1919, Coolidge attained national prominence by calling out the state guard in the Boston police strike. He declared: "There is no right to strike against the public safety by anybody, anywhere, anytime." This brought his name before the Republican convention of 1920, where he was nominated for vice president. He succeeded to the presidency on Harding's death. He opposed the League of Nations; approved the World Court; vetoed the soldiers' bonus bill, which was passed over his veto. In 1924 he was elected by a huge majority. He reduced the national debt by $2 billion in 3 years. He twice vetoed the McNary-Haugen farm bill, which would have provided relief to financially hard-pressed farmers. With Republicans eager to renominate him he announced, Aug. 2, 1927: "I do not choose to run for president in 1928." He died in Northampton, Jan. 5, 1933.

Herbert Clark Hoover (1929-1933)

Herbert C. Hoover, 31st president, Republican, was born at West Branch, Ia., Aug. 10, 1874, son of Jesse Clark Hoover, a blacksmith, and Hulda Randall Minthorn. Hoover grew up in Indian Territory (now Oklahoma) and Oregon; won his A.B. in engineering at Stanford, 1891. He worked briefly with U.S. Geological Survey and western mines; then was a mining engineer in Australia, Asia, Europe, Africa, U.S. While chief engineer, imperial mines, China, he directed food relief for victims of Boxer Rebellion, 1900. He directed American Relief Committee, London, 1914-15; U.S. Comm. for Relief in Belgium, 1915-1919; was U.S. Food Administrator, 1917-1919; American Relief Administrator, 1918-1923, feeding children in defeated nations; Russian Relief, 1918-1923. He was secy. of commerce, 1921-28. He was elected president over Alfred E. Smith, 1928. In 1929 the stock market crashed and the economy collapsed. During the depression, Hoover opposed federal aid to the unemployed. He was defeated in the 1932 election by Franklin D. Roosevelt. President Truman made him coordinator of European Food Program, 1947, chairman of the Commission for Reorganization of the Executive Branch, 1947-49. He founded the Hoover Institution on

War, Revolution, and Peace at Stanford Univ. He died in N.Y. City, Oct. 20, 1964.

Franklin Delano Roosevelt (1933-1945)

Franklin D. Roosevelt, 32d president, Democrat, was born near Hyde Park, N.Y., Jan. 30, 1882, the son of James Roosevelt and Sara Delano. He graduated from Harvard, 1904; attended Columbia Law School; was admitted to the bar. He went to the N.Y. Senate, 1910 and 1913. In 1913 President Wilson made him assistant secretary of the navy.

Roosevelt ran for vice president, 1920, with James Cox and was defeated. From 1920 to 1928 he was a N.Y. lawyer and vice president of Fidelity & Deposit Co. In Aug., 1921, polio paralyzed his legs. He learned to walk with leg braces and a cane.

Roosevelt was elected governor of New York, 1928 and 1930. In 1932, W. G. McAdoo, pledged to John N. Garner, threw his votes to Roosevelt, who was nominated. The depression and the promise to repeal prohibition insured his election. He asked emergency powers, proclaimed the New Deal, and put into effect a vast number of administrative changes. Foremost was the use of public funds for relief and public works, resulting in deficit financing. He greatly expanded the controls of the central government over business, and by an excess profits tax and progressive income taxes produced a redistribution of earnings on an unprecedented scale. The Wagner Act gave labor many advantages in organizing and collective bargaining. He was the last president inaugurated on Mar. 4 (1933) and the first inaugurated on Jan. 20 (1937).

Roosevelt was the first president to use radio for "fireside chats." When the Supreme Court nullified some New Deal laws, he sought power to "pack" the court with additional justices, but Congress refused to give him the authority. He was the first president to break the "no 3d term" tradition (1940) and was elected to a 4th term, 1944, despite failing health. He was openly hostile to fascist governments before World War II and launched a lend-lease program on behalf of the Allies. He wrote the principles of fair dealing into the Atlantic Charter, Aug. 14, 1941 (with Winston Churchill), and urged the Four Freedoms (freedom of speech, of worship, from want, from fear) Jan. 6, 1941. When Japan attacked Pearl Harbor, Dec. 7, 1941, the U.S. entered the war. He conferred with allied heads of state at Casablanca, Jan., 1943; Quebec, Aug., 1943; Teheran, Nov.-Dec., 1943; Cairo, Dec., 1943; Yalta, Feb., 1945. He died at Warm Springs, Ga., Apr. 12, 1945.

Harry S. Truman (1945-1953)

Harry S. Truman, 33d president, Democrat, was born at Lamar, Mo., May 8, 1884, the son of John Anderson Truman and Martha Ellen Young. A family disagreement on whether his middle name was Shippe or Solomon, after names of 2 grandfathers, resulted in his using only the middle initial S. He attended public schools in Independence, Mo., worked for the Kansas City Star, 1901, and as railroad timekeeper, and helper in Kansas City banks up to 1905. He ran his family's farm, 1906-17. He was commissioned a first lieutenant and took part in the Vosges, Meuse-Argonne, and St. Mihiel actions in World War I. After the war he ran a haberdashery, became judge of Jackson Co. Court, 1922-24; attended Kansas City School of Law, 1923-25.

Truman was elected U.S. senator in 1934; reelected 1940. In 1944 with Roosevelt's backing he was nominated for vice president and elected. On Roosevelt's death Truman became president. In 1948 he was elected president.

Truman authorized the first uses of the atomic bomb (Hiroshima and Nagasaki, Aug. 6 and 9, 1945), bringing World War II to a rapid end. He was responsible for creating NATO, the Marshall Plan, and what came to be called the Truman Doctrine (to aid nations such as Greece and Turkey, threatened by Russian or other communist takeover). He broke a Russian blockade of West Berlin with a massive airlift, 1948-49. When communist North Korea invaded South Korea, June, 1950, he won UN approval for a "police action" and sent in forces under Gen. Douglas MacArthur. When MacArthur opposed his policy of limited objectives, Truman removed him from command.

Truman was responsible for higher minimum-wage, increased social-security, and aid-for-housing laws. Truman died Dec. 26, 1972, in Kansas City, Mo.

Dwight David Eisenhower (1953-1961)

Dwight D. Eisenhower, 34th president, Republican, was born Oct. 14, 1890, at Denison, Tex., the son of David Jacob Eisenhower and Ida Elizabeth Stover. The next year, the family moved to Abilene, Kan. He graduated from West Point, 1915. He was on the American military mission to the Philippines, 1935-39 and during 4 of those years on the staff of Gen. Douglas MacArthur. He was made commander of Allied forces landing in North Africa, 1942, full general, 1943. He became supreme Allied commander in Europe, 1943, and as such led the Normandy invasion June 6, 1944. He was given the rank of general of the army Dec. 20, 1944, made permanent in 1946. On May 7, 1945, he received the surrender of the Germans at Rheims. He returned to the U.S. to serve as chief of staff, 1945-1948. In 1948, Eisenhower published *Crusade in Europe*, his war memoirs, which quickly became a best seller. From 1948 to 1953, he was president of Columbia Univ., but took leave of absence in 1950, to command NATO forces.

Eisenhower resigned from the army and was nominated for president by the Republicans, 1952. He defeated Adlai E. Stevenson in the election. He again defeated Stevenson, 1956. He called himself a moderate, favored "free market system" vs. government price and wage controls; kept government out of labor disputes; reorganized defense establishment; promoted missile programs. He continued foreign aid; sped end of Korean fighting; endorsed Taiwan and SE Asia defense treaties; backed UN in condemning Anglo-French raid on Egypt; advocated "open skies" policy of mutual inspection to USSR. He sent U.S. troops into Little Rock, Ark., Sept., 1957, during the segregation crisis and ordered Marines into Lebanon July-Aug., 1958.

During his retirement at his farm near Gettysburg, Pa., Eisenhower took up the role of elder statesman, counseling his 3 successors in the White House. He died Mar. 28, 1969, in Washington.

John Fitzgerald Kennedy (1961-1963)

John F. Kennedy, 35th president, Democrat, was born May 29, 1917, in Brookline, Mass., the son of Joseph P. Kennedy, financier, who later became ambassador to Great Britain, and Rose Fitzgerald. He entered Harvard, attended the London School of Economics briefly in 1935, received a B.S., from Harvard, 1940. He served in the Navy, 1941-1945, commanded a PT boat in the Solomons and won the Navy and Marine Corps Medal. He wrote *Profiles in Courage*, which won a Pulitzer prize. He served as representative in Congress, 1947-1953; was elected to the Senate in 1952, reelected 1958. He nearly won the vice presidential nomination in 1956.

In 1960, Kennedy won the Democratic nomination for president and defeated Richard M. Nixon, Republican. He was the first Roman Catholic president.

In Apr. 1961, Kennedy's new administration suffered a severe setback when an invasion force of anti-Castro Cubans, trained and directed by the U.S. Central Intelligence Agency, failed to establish a beachhead at the Bay of Pigs in Cuba.

Kennedy's most important act was his successful demand Oct. 22, 1962, that the Soviet Union dismantle its missile bases in Cuba. He established a quarantine of arms shipments to Cuba and continued surveillance by air. He defied Soviet attempts to force the Allies out of Berlin. He made the steel industry rescind a price rise. He backed civil rights, a mental health program, arbitration of railroad disputes, and expanded medical care for the aged. Astronaut flights and satellite orbiting were greatly developed during his administration.

On Nov. 22, 1963, Kennedy was assassinated in Dallas, Tex.

Lyndon Baines Johnson (1963-1969)

Lyndon B. Johnson, 36th president, Democrat, was born near Stonewall, Tex., Aug. 27, 1908, son of Sam Ealy Johnson and Rebekah Baines. He received a B.S. degree at Southwest Texas State Teachers College, 1930, attended Georgetown Univ. Law School, Washington, 1935. He taught public speaking in Houston, 1930-32; served as secretary to Rep. R. M. Kleberg, 1932-35. In 1937 Johnson won a contest to fill the vacancy caused by the death of a representative and in 1938 was elected to the full term, after which he returned for 4 terms. He was elected U.S. senator in 1948 and reelected in 1954. He became Democratic leader, 1953. Johnson was Texas' favorite son for the Democratic presidential nomination in 1956 and had strong support in the 1960 convention, where the nominee, John F. Kennedy, asked him to run for vice president. His campaigning helped overcome religious bias against Kennedy in the South.

Johnson became president on the death of Kennedy. Johnson worked hard for welfare legislation, signed civil rights, anti-proverty, and tax reduction laws, and averted strikes on railroads. He was elected to a full term, 1964. The war in Vietnam overshadowed other developments during his administration.

In face of increasing division in the nation and his own party over his handling of the war, Johnson announced that he would not seek another term, Mar. 31, 1968.

Retiring to his ranch near Johnson City, Tex., Johnson wrote his memoirs and oversaw the construction of the Lyndon Baines Johnson Library. He died Jan. 22, 1973.

Richard Milhous Nixon (1969-1974)

Richard M. Nixon, 37th president, Republican, was the only president to resign without completing an elected term. He was born in Yorba Linda, Cal., Jan. 9, 1913, the son of Francis Anthony Nixon and Hannah Milhous. Nixon graduated from Whittier College, 1934; Duke Univ. Law School, 1937. After practicing law in Whittier and serving briefly in the Office of Price Administration in 1942, he entered the navy, and served in the South Pacific.

Nixon was elected to the House of Representatives in 1946 and 1948. He achieved prominence as the House Un-American Activities Committee member who forced the showdown that resulted in the Alger Hiss perjury conviction. In 1950 Nixon was elected to the Senate.

He was elected vice president in the Eisenhower landslides of 1952 and 1956. With Eisenhower's endorsement, Nixon won the Republican nomination in 1960. He was defeated by Democrat John F. Kennedy, returned to Cal. and was defeated in his race for governor, 1962.

In 1968, he won the presidential nomination and went on to defeat Democrat Hubert H. Humphrey.

Nixon was the first U.S. president to visit China and Russia (1972). He and his foreign affairs advisor, Henry A. Kissinger, achieved a detente with China. Nixon appointed 4 Supreme Court justices, including the chief justice, thus altering the court's balance in favor of a more conservative view.

Reelected 1972, Nixon secured a cease-fire agreement in Vietnam and completed the withdrawal of U.S. troops.

Nixon's 2d term was cut short by a series of scandals beginning with the burglary of Democratic party national headquarters in the Watergate office complex on June 17, 1972. Nixon denied any White House involvement in the Watergate break-in. On July 16, 1973, a White House aide, under questioning by a Senate committee, revealed that most of Nixon's office conversations and phone calls had been recorded. Nixon claimed executive privilege to keep the tapes secret and the courts and Congress sought the tapes for criminal proceedings against former White House aides and for a House inquiry into possible impeachment.

On Oct. 10, 1973, Nixon fired the Watergate special prosecutor and the attorney general resigned in protest. The public outcry which followed caused Nixon to appoint a new special prosecutor and to turn over to the courts a number of subpoenaed tape recordings. Public reaction also brought the initiation of a formal inquiry into impeachment.

On July 24, 1974, the Supreme Court ruled that Nixon's claim of executive privilege must fall before the special prosecutor's subpoenas of tapes relevant to criminal trial proceedings. That same day, the House Judiciary Committee opened debate on impeachment. On July 30, the committee recommended House adoption of 3 articles of impeachment charging Nixon with obstruction of justice, abuse of power, and contempt of Congress.

On Aug. 5, Nixon released transcripts of conversations held 6 days after the Watergate break-in showing that Nixon had known of, approved, and directed Watergate cover-up activities. Nixon resigned from office Aug. 9.

Gerald Rudolph Ford (1974-1977)

Gerald R. Ford, 38th president, Republican, was born July 14, 1913, in Omaha, Neb., son of Leslie King and Dorothy Gardner, and was named Leslie Jr. When he was 2, his parents were divorced and his mother moved with the boy to Grand Rapids, Mich. There she met and married Gerald R. Ford, who formally adopted the boy and gave him his own name.

He graduated from the Univ. of Michigan, 1935 and Yale Law School, 1941.

He began practicing law in Grand Rapids, but in 1942 joined the navy and served in the Pacific, leaving the service in 1946 as a lieutenant commander.

He entered congress in 1949 and spent 25 years in the House, 8 of them as Republican leader.

On Oct. 12, 1973, after Vice President Spiro T. Agnew resigned, Ford was nominated by President Nixon to replace him. It was the first use of the procedures set out in the 25th Amendment.

When Nixon resigned Aug. 9, 1974, Ford became president, the first to serve without being chosen in a national election. On Sept. 8 he pardoned Nixon for any federal crimes he might have committed as president. Ford veoted 48 bills in his first 21 months in office, saying most would prove too costly. He visited China. In 1976, he was defeated in the election by Democrat Jimmy Carter.

Jimmy (James Earl) Carter (1977-1981)

Jimmy (James Earl) Carter, 39th president, Democrat, was the first president from the Deep South since before the Civil War. He was born Oct. 1, 1924, at Plains, Ga., where his parents, James and Lillian Gordy Carter, had a farm and several businesses.

He attended Georgia Tech, and graduated from the U.S. Naval Academy. He entered the Navy's nuclear submarine program as an aide to Adm. Hyman Rickover, and studied nuclear physics at Union College.

His father died in 1953 and Carter left the Navy to take over the family businesses — peanut-raising, warehousing, and cotton-ginning. He was elected to the Georgia state senate, was defeated for governor, 1966, but elected in 1970.

Carter won the Democratic nomination and defeated President Gerald R. Ford in the election of 1976. He played a major role in the peace negotiations between Israel and Egypt. In Nov. 1979, Iranian student militants attacked the U.S. embassy in Teheran and held members of the embassy staff hostage.

Carter was widely criticized for the poor state of the economy and high inflation. He was also viewed as weak in his handling of foreign policy. He reacted to the Soviet invasion of Afghanistan by imposing a grain embargo and boycotting the Moscow Olympic games. His failure to obtain the release of the remaining 52 hostages held in Iran plagued Carter to the end of his term. He was defeated by Ronald Reagan in the 1980 election. Carter finally succeeded in obtaining the release of the hostages on Inauguration Day, as the new president was taking the oath of office.

Ronald Wilson Reagan (1981-)

Ronald Wilson Reagan, 40th president, Republican, was born Feb. 6, 1911, in Tampico, Ill., the son of John Edward Reagan and Nellie Wilson. Reagan graduated from Eureka (Ill.) College in 1932. Following his graduation, he worked for 5 years as a sports announcer in Des Moines, Ia.

Reagan began a successful career as a film actor in 1937, and starred in numerous movies, and later television, until the 1960s. He was a captain in the Army Air Force during World War II.

He served as president of the Screen Actors Guild from 1947 to 1952, and in 1959.

Once a liberal Democrat, Reagan became active in Republican politics during the 1964 presidential campaign of Barry Goldwater. He was elected governor of California in 1966, and reelected in 1970.

Following his retirement as governor, Reagan became the

leading spokesman for the conservative wing of the Republican Party, and made a strong bid for the party's 1976 presidential nomination.

In 1980, he gained the Republican nomination and won a landslide victory over Jimmy Carter. He was easily reelected in 1984. Reagan, at 73, was the oldest man ever elected president.

Reagan successfully forged a bipartisan coalition in Congress which led to enactment of an economic program which included the largest budget and tax cuts in U.S. history, and a Social Security reform bill designed to insure the long-term solvency of the system. In 1986, he signed into law a revolutionary tax-reform bill. He was shot in an assassination attempt in 1981, and had major surgery in 1985 and 1987.

The nation was plagued by a severe recession, causing a 9.7% unemployment rate in 1982, the highest since 1941.

In 1983, Reagan sent a task force to lead the invasion of Grenada, and joined 3 European nations in maintaining a peacekeeping force in Beirut, Lebanon. His opposition to international terrorism led to the U.S. bombing of Lybian military installations in 1986. He has strongly supported El Salvador, the Nicaraguan contras, and other anti-communist governments and forces in Central America.

Reagan held summit meetings with Soviet leader Gorbachev in Nov. 1985 in Geneva, and Oct. 1986 in Iceland to discuss arms control, human rights, and other issues.

By his second term, Reagan was considered one of the most popular presidents in history because of the strong economy and low unemployment, spurred by lower interest rates, energy costs, and inflation. He remained unable to control the high budget deficits while resisting all calls for additional taxes or smaller increases in military spending.

Reagan faced a major crisis in 1986-1987, when it was revealed that the U.S. had sold weapons to Iran in exchange for the release of U.S. hostages being held in Lebanon; and that subsequently some of the money was diverted to the Nicaraguan contras. (*See Chronology*)

Wives and Children of the Presidents

Listed in order of presidential administrations.

Name (Born–died, married)	State	Sons/ daughters
Martha Dandridge Custis Washington (1732-1802, 1759)	Va.	None
Abigail Smith Adams (1744-1818, 1764)	Mass.	3/2
Martha Wayles Skelton Jefferson (1748-1782, 1772)	Va.	1/5
Dorothea "Dolley" Payne Todd Madison (1768-1849, 1794)	N.C.	None
Elizabeth Kortright Monroe (1768-1830, 1786)	N.Y.	.../2 (A)
Louise Catherine Johnson Adams (1775-1852, 1797)	Md.(B)	3/1
Rachel Donelson Robards Jackson (1767-1828, 1791)	Va.	None
Hannah Hoes Van Buren (1783-1819, 1807)	N.Y.	4/...
Anna Symmes Harrison (1775-1864, 1795)	N.J.	6/4
Letitia Christian Tyler (1790-1842, 1813)	Va.	3/5
Julia Gardiner Tyler (1820-1889, 1844)	N.Y.	5/2
Sarah Childress Polk (1803-1891, 1824)	Tenn.	None
Margaret Smith Taylor (1788-1852, 1810)	Md.	1/5
Abigail Powers Fillmore (1798-1853, 1826)	N.Y.	1/1
Caroline Carmichael McIntosh Fillmore (1813-1881, 1858)	N.J.	None
Jane Means Appleton Pierce (1806-1863, 1834)	N.H.	3/...
Mary Todd Lincoln (1818-1882, 1842)	Ky.	4/...
Eliza McCardle Johnson (1810-1876, 1827)	Tenn.	3/2
Julia Dent Grant (1826-1902, 1848)	Mo.	3/1
Lucy Ware Webb Hayes (1831-1889, 1852)	Oh.	7/1
Lucretia Rudolph Garfield (1832-1918, 1858)	Oh.	4/1
Ellen Lewis Herndon Arthur (1837-1880, 1859)	Va.	2/1
Frances Folsom Cleveland (1864-1947, 1886)	N.Y.	2/3
Caroline Lavinia Scott Harrison (1832-1892, 1853)	Oh.	1/1
Mary Scott Lord Dimmick Harrison (1858-1948, 1896)	Pa.	.../1
Ida Saxton McKinley (1847-1907, 1871)	Oh.	.../2
Alice Hathaway Lee Roosevelt (1861-1884, 1880)	Mass.	.../1
Edith Kermit Carow Roosevelt (1861-1948, 1886)	Conn.	4/1
Helen Herron Taft (1861-1943, 1886)	Oh.	2/1
Ellen Louise Axson Wilson (1860-1914, 1885)	Ga.	.../3
Edith Bolling Galt Wilson (1872-1961, 1915)	Va.	None
Florence Kling De Wolfe Harding (1860-1924, 1891)	Oh.	None
Grace Anna Goodhue Coolidge (1879-1957, 1905)	Vt.	2/...
Lou Henry Hoover (1875-1944, 1899)	Ia.	2/...
Anna Eleanor Roosevelt Roosevelt (1884-1962, 1905)	N.Y.	4/1 (A)
Bess Wallace Truman (1885-1982, 1919)	Mo.	.../1
Mamie Geneva Doud Eisenhower (1896-1979, 1916)	Ia.	1/...(A)
Jacqueline Lee Bouvier Kennedy (b. 1929, 1953)	N.Y.	1/1 (A)
Claudia "Lady Bird" Alta Taylor Johnson (b. 1912, 1934)	Tex.	.../2
Thelma Catherine Patricia Ryan Nixon (b. 1912, 1940)	Nev.	.../2
Elizabeth Bloomer Warren Ford (b. 1918, 1948)	Ill.	3/1
Rosalynn Smith Carter (b. 1927, 1946)	Ga.	3/1
Anne Frances "Nancy" Robbins Davis Reagan (b. 1923, 1952)	N.Y.	1/1 (C)

James Buchanan, 15th president, was unmarried. (A) plus one infant, deceased. (B) Born London, father a Md. citizen. (C) President Reagan has a son and daughter from a former marriage.

Burial Places of the Presidents

President	Burial place
Washington	Mt. Vernon, Va.
J. Adams	Quincy, Mass.
Jefferson	Charlottesville, Va.
Madison	Montpelier Station, Va.
Monroe	Richmond, Va.
J.Q. Adams	Quincy, Mass.
Jackson	Nashville, Tenn.
Van Buren	Kinderhook, N.Y.
W.H. Harrison	North Bend, Oh.
Tyler	Richmond, Va.
Polk	Nashville, Tenn.
Taylor	Louisville, Ky.
Fillmore	Buffalo, N.Y.
Pierce	Concord, N.H.
Buchanan	Lancaster, Pa.
Lincoln	Springfield, Ill.
A. Johnson	Greeneville, Tenn.
Grant	New York City
Hayes	Fremont, Oh.
Garfield	Cleveland, Oh.
Arthur	Albany, N.Y.
Cleveland	Princeton, N.J.
B. Harrison	Indianapolis, Ind.
McKinley	Canton, Oh.
T. Roosevelt	Oyster Bay, N.Y.
Taft	Arlington Nat'l. Cem'y.
Wilson	Washington Cathedral
Harding	Marion, Oh.
Coolidge	Plymouth, Vt.
Hoover	West Branch, Ia.
F.D. Roosevelt	Hyde Park, N.Y.
Truman	Independence, Mo.
Eisenhower	Abilene, Kan.
Kennedy	Arlington Nat'l. Cem'y.
L.D. Johnson	Stonewall, Tex.

UNITED STATES FACTS

Superlative U.S. Statistics

Source: Geological Survey, U.S. Interior Department

Area for 50 states	Total Land 3,543,883 sq. mi.—Water 79,537 sq. mi.	3,623,420 sq. mi.
Largest state	Alaska	589,757 sq. mi.
Smallest state	Rhode Island	1,214 sq. mi.
Largest county	San Bernardino County, California	20,102 sq. mi.
Smallest county	New York, New York	22 sq. mi.
Northernmost city	Barrow, Alaska	71°17'N.
Northernmost point	Point Barrow, Alaska	71°23'N.
Southernmost city	Hilo, Island of Hawaii	19°43'N.
Southernmost town	Naalehu, Island of Hawaii	19°03'N.
Southernmost point	Ka Lae (South Cape), Island of Hawaii	18°56'N. (155°41'W.)
Easternmost city	Eastport, Maine	66°59'02"W.
Easternmost town	Lubec, Maine	66°58'49"W.
Easternmost point	West Quoddy Head, Maine	66°57'W.
Westernmost city	Lihue, Island of Kauai, Hawaii	159°22'W.
Westernmost town	Adak, Aleutians, Alaska	176°45'W.
Westernmost point	Cape Wrangell, Attu Island, Aleutians, Alaska	172°27'E.
Highest city	Climax, Colorado	11,560 ft.
Lowest town	Calipatria, California	−184 ft.
Highest point on Atlantic coast	Cadillac Mountain, Mount Desert Is., Maine	1,530 ft.
Oldest national park	Yellowstone National Park (1872), Wyoming, Montana, Idaho	3,468 sq. mi.
Largest national park	Wrangell-St. Elias, Alaska	12,730 sq. mi.
Largest national monument	Death Valley, California, Nevada	3,231 sq. mi.
Highest waterfall	Yosemite Falls—Total in three sections	2,425 ft.
	Upper Yosemite Fall	1,430 ft.
	Cascades in middle section	675 ft.
	Lower Yosemite Fall	320 ft.
Longest river	Mississippi-Missouri	3,710 mi.
Highest mountain	Mount McKinley, Alaska	20,320 ft.
Lowest point	Death Valley, California	−282 ft.
Deepest lake	Crater Lake, Oregon	1,932 ft.
Rainiest spot	Mt. Waialeale, Hawaii	Annual aver. rainfall 460 inches
Largest gorge	Grand Canyon, Colorado River, Arizona	277 miles long, 600 ft. to 18 miles wide, 1 mile deep
Deepest gorge	Hell's Canyon, Snake River, Idaho-Oregon	7,900 ft.
Strongest surface wind	Mount Washington, New Hampshire recorded 1934	231 mph
Biggest dam	New Cornelia Tailings, Ten Mile Wash, Arizona	274,026,000 cu. yds. material used
Tallest building	Sears Tower, Chicago, Illinois	1,454 ft.
Largest building	Boeing 747 Manufacturing Plant, Everett, Washington	205,600,000 cu. ft.; covers 47 acres.
Tallest structure	TV tower, Blanchard, North Dakota	2,063 ft.
Longest bridge span	Verrazano-Narrows, New York	4,260 ft.
Highest bridge	Royal Gorge, Colorado	1,053 ft. above water
Deepest well	Gas well, Washita County, Oklahoma	31,441 ft.

The 49 States, Including Alaska

Area for 49 states	Total Land 3,537,458 sq. mi.—Water 79,491 sq. mi.	3,616,949 sq. mi.

The 48 Contiguous States

Area for 48 states	Total Land 2,966,625 sq. mi.—Water 59,320 sq. mi.	3,025,945 sq. mi.
Largest state	Texas	267,338 sq. mi
Northernmost town	Angle Inlet, Minnesota	49°22'N.
Northernmost point	Northwest Angle, Minnesota	49°23'N.
Southernmost city	Key West, Florida	24°33'N.
Southernmost mainland city	Florida City, Florida	25°27'N.
Southernmost point	Key West, Florida	24°33'N.
Westernmost town	La Push, Washington	124°38'W.
Westernmost point	Cape Alava, Washington	124°44'W.
Highest mountain	Mount Whitney, California	14,494 ft.

Note to users: The distinction between cities and towns varies from state to state. In this table the U.S. Bureau of the Census usage was followed.

Geodetic Datum Point of North America

The geodetic datum point of the U.S., for the North American Datum of 1927, is the National Ocean Service's triangulation station Meades Ranch in Osborne County, Kansas, at latitude 39° 13'26". 686 N and longitude 98° 32'30". 506 W. This geodetic datum point is a fundamental point from which all latitude and longitude computations originate for North America and Central America.

Statistical Information about the U.S.

In the *Statistical Abstract of the United States* the Bureau of the Census, U.S. Dept. of Commerce, annually publishes a summary of social, political, and economic information. A book of more than 1,000 pages, it presents in 32 sections comprehensive data on population, housing, health, education, employment, income, prices, business, banking, energy, science, defense, trade, government finance, foreign country comparison, and other subjects. Special features include sections on State Rankings and Metropolitan Statistical Areas and a new section with telephone contacts. The book is prepared under the direction of Glenn W. King, Chief, Statistical Compendia Staff, Bureau of the Census. Supplements to the *Statistical Abstract* are *Pocket Data Book USA, 1979; County and City Data Book, 1983* (1988 in process); *Historical Statistics of the United States, Colonial Times to 1970;* and *State and Metropolitan Area Data Book, 1986.* Information concerning these and other publications may be obtained from the Supt. of Documents, Government Printing Office, Wash., D.C. 20402, or from the U.S. Bureau of the Census, Data User Services Division, Wash., D.C. 20233.

Highest and Lowest Altitudes in the U.S. and Territories

Source: Geological Survey, U.S. Interior Department. (Minus sign means below sea level; elevations are in feet.)

State	Highest Point Name	Highest Point County	Elev.	Lowest Point Name	Lowest Point County	Elev.
Alabama	Cheaha Mountain	Cleburne	2,407	Gulf of Mexico		Sea level
Alaska	Mount McKinley		20,320	Pacific Ocean		Sea level
Arizona	Humphreys Peak	Coconino	12,633	Colorado R.	Yuma	70
Arkansas	Magazine Mountain	Logan	2,753	Ouachita R.	Ashley/Union	55
California	Mount Whitney	Inyo-Tulare	14,494	Death Valley	Inyo	−282
Colorado	Mount Elbert	Lake	14,433	Arkansas R.	Prowers	3,350
Connecticut	Mount Frissell	Litchfield	2,380	L.I. Sound		Sea level
Delaware	On Ebright Road	New Castle	442	Atlantic Ocean		Sea level
Dist. of Col.	Tenleytown	N. W. part	410	Potomac R.		1
Florida	Sec. 30, T 6N, R 20W	Walton	345	Atlantic Ocean		Sea level
Georgia	Brasstown Bald	Towns-Union	4,784	Atlantic Ocean		Sea level
Guam	Mount Lamlam	Agat District	1,329	Pacific Ocean		Sea level
Hawaii	Mauna Kea	Hawaii	13,796	Pacific Ocean		Sea level
Idaho	Borah Peak	Custer	12,662	Snake R.	Nez Perce	710
Illinois	Charles Mound	Jo Daviess	1,235	Mississippi R.	Alexander	279
Indiana	Franklin Township	Wayne	1,257	Ohio R.	Posey	320
Iowa	Sec. 29, T 100N, R 41W	Osceola	1,670	Mississippi R.	Lee	480
Kansas	Mount Sunflower	Wallace	4,039	Verdigris R.	Montgomery	680
Kentucky	Black Mountain	Harlan	4,145	Mississippi R.	Fulton	257
Louisiana	Driskill Mountain	Bienville	535	New Orleans	Orleans	−5
Maine	Mount Katahdin	Piscataquis	5,268	Atlantic Ocean		Sea level
Maryland	Backbone Mountain	Garrett	3,360	Atlantic Ocean		Sea level
Massachusetts	Mount Greylock	Berkshire	3,491	Atlantic Ocean		Sea level
Michigan	Mount Curwood	Baraga	1,980	Lake Erie	Monroe	572
Minnesota	Eagle Mountain	Cook	2,301	Lake Superior		602
Mississippi	Woodall Mountain	Tishomingo	806	Gulf of Mexico		Sea level
Missouri	Taum Sauk Mt.	Iron	1,772	St. Francis R.	Dunklin	230
Montana	Granite Peak	Park	12,799	Kootenai R.	Lincoln	1,800
Nebraska	Johnson Township	Kimball	5,426	S.E. cor. State	Richardson	840
Nevada	Boundary Peak	Esmeralda	13,143	Colorado R.	Clark	470
New Hamp.	Mt. Washington	Coos	6,288	Atlantic Ocean	Rockingham	Sea level
New Jersey	High Point	Sussex	1,803	Atlantic Ocean		Sea level
New Mexico	Wheeler Peak	Taos	13,161	Red Bluff Res.	Eddy	2,817
New York	Mount Marcy	Essex	5,344	Atlantic Ocean		Sea level
North Carolina	Mount Mitchell	Yancey	6,684	Atlantic Ocean		Sea level
North Dakota	White Butte	Slope	3,506	Red R.	Pembina	750
Ohio	Campbell Hill	Logan	1,550	Ohio R.	Hamilton	433
Oklahoma	Black Mesa	Cimarron	4,973	Little R.	McCurtain	287
Oregon	Mount Hood	Clackamas-Hood R.	11,239	Pacific Ocean		Sea level
Pennsylvania	Mt. Davis	Somerset	3,213	Delaware R.	Delaware	Sea level
Puerto Rico	Cerro de Punta	Ponce District	4,389	Atlantic Ocean		Sea level
Rhode Island	Jerimoth Hill	Providence	812	Atlantic Ocean		Sea level
Samoa	Lata Mountain	Tau Island	3,160	Pacific Ocean		Sea level
South Carolina	Sassafras Mountain	Pickens	3,560	Atlantic Ocean		Sea level
South Dakota	Harney Peak	Pennington	7,242	Big Stone Lake	Roberts	962
Tennessee	Clingmans Dome	Sevier	6,643	Mississippi R.	Shelby	182
Texas	Guadalupe Peak	Culberson	8,749	Gulf of Mexico		Sea level
Utah	Kings Peak	Duchesne	13,528	Beaverdam Cr.	Washington	2,000
Vermont	Mount Mansfield	Lamoille	4,393	Lake Champlain	Franklin	95
Virginia	Mount Rogers	Grayson-Smyth	5,729	Atlantic Ocean		Sea level
Virgin Islands	Crown Mountain	St. Thomas Island	1,556	Atlantic Ocean		Sea level
Washington	Mount Rainier	Pierce	14,410	Pacific Ocean		Sea level
West Virginia	Spruce Knob	Pendleton	4,863	Potomac R.	Jefferson	240
Wisconsin	Timms Hill	Price	1,951	Lake Michigan		581
Wyoming	Gannett Peak	Fremont	13,804	B. Fourche R.	Crook	3,100

U.S. Coastline by States

Source: NOAA, U.S. Commerce Department
(statute miles)

State	Coastline[1]	Shoreline[2]
Atlantic coast	**2,069**	**28,673**
Connecticut	0	618
Delaware	28	381
Florida	580	3,331
Georgia	100	2,344
Maine	228	3,478
Maryland	31	3,190
Massachusetts	192	1,519
New Hampshire	13	131
New Jersey	130	1,792
New York	127	1,850
North Carolina	301	3,375
Pennsylvania	0	89
Rhode Island	40	384
South Carolina	187	2,876
Virginia	112	3,315

State	Coastline[1]	Shoreline[2]
Gulf coast	**1,631**	**17,141**
Alabama	53	607
Florida	770	5,095
Louisiana	397	7,721
Mississippi	44	359
Texas	367	3,359
Pacific coast	**7,623**	**40,298**
Alaska	5,580	31,383
California	840	3,427
Hawaii	750	1,052
Oregon	296	1,410
Washington	157	3,026
Arctic coast, Alaska	**1,060**	**2,521**
United States	**12,383**	**88,633**

(1) Figures are lengths of general outline of seacoast. Measurements were made with a unit measure of 30 minutes of latitude on charts as near the scale of 1:1,200,000 as possible. Coastline of sounds and bays is included to a point where they narrow to width of unit measure, and includes the distance across at such point. (2) Figures obtained in 1939-40 with a recording instrument on the largest-scale charts and maps then available. Shoreline of outer coast, offshore islands, sounds, bays, rivers, and creeks is included to the head of tidewater or to a point where tidal waters narrow to a width of 100 feet.

States: Settled, Capitals, Entry into Union, Area, Rank

The original 13 states—The 13 colonies that seceded from Great Britain and fought the War of Independence (American Revolution) became the 13 original states. They were: Delaware, Pennsylvania, New Jersey, Georgia, Connecticut, Massachusetts, Maryland, South Carolina, New Hampshire, Virginia, New York, North Carolina, and Rhode Island. The order for the original 13 states is the order in which they ratified the Constitution.

State	Settled*	Capital	Entered Union Date	Order	Extent in miles Long (approx.)	Wide (mean)	Area in square miles Land	Inland water	Total	Rank in area
Ala.	1702	Montgomery	Dec. 14, 1819	22	330	190	50,708	901	51,609	29
Alas.	1784	Juneau	Jan. 3, 1959	49	(a)1,480	810	569,600	20,157	589,757	1
Ariz.	1776	Phoenix	Feb. 14, 1912	48	400	310	113,417	492	113,909	6
Ark.	1686	Little Rock	June 15, 1836	25	260	240	51,945	1,159	53,104	27
Cal.	1769	Sacramento	Sept. 9, 1850	31	770	250	156,361	2,332	158,693	3
Col.	1858	Denver	Aug. 1, 1876	38	380	280	103,766	481	104,247	8
Conn.	1634	Hartford	Jan. 9, 1788	5	110	70	4,862	147	5,009	48
Del.	1638	Dover	Dec. 7, 1787	1	100	30	1,982	75	2,057	49
D.C.	...	Washington	...		...	...	61	6	67	51
Fla.	1565	Tallahassee	Mar. 3, 1845	27	500	160	54,090	4,470	58,560	22
Ga.	1733	Atlanta	Jan. 2, 1788	4	300	230	58,073	803	58,876	21
Ha.	1820	Honolulu	Aug. 21, 1959	50	...	...	6,425	25	6,450	47
Ida.	1842	Boise	July 3, 1890	43	570	300	82,677	880	83,557	13
Ill.	1720	Springfield	Dec. 3, 1818	21	390	210	55,748	652	56,400	24
Ind.	1733	Indianapolis	Dec. 11, 1816	19	270	140	36,097	194	36,291	38
Ia.	1788	Des Moines	Dec. 28, 1846	29	310	200	55,941	349	56,290	25
Kan.	1727	Topeka	Jan. 29, 1861	34	400	210	81,787	477	82,264	14
Ky.	1774	Frankfort	June 1, 1792	15	380	140	39,650	745	40,395	37
La.	1699	Baton Rouge	Apr. 30, 1812	18	380	130	44,930	3,593	48,523	31
Me.	1624	Augusta	Mar. 15, 1820	23	320	190	30,920	2,295	33,215	39
Md.	1634	Annapolis	Apr. 28, 1788	7	250	90	9,891	686	10,577	42
Mass.	1620	Boston	Feb. 6, 1788	6	190	50	7,826	431	8,257	45
Mich.	1668	Lansing	Jan. 26, 1837	26	490	240	56,817	1,399	58,216	23
Minn.	1805	St. Paul	May 11, 1858	32	400	250	79,289	4,779	84,068	12
Miss.	1699	Jackson	Dec. 10, 1817	20	340	170	47,296	420	47,716	32
Mo.	1735	Jefferson City	Aug. 10, 1821	24	300	240	68,995	691	69,686	19
Mon.	1809	Helena	Nov. 8, 1889	41	630	280	145,587	1,551	147,138	4
Neb.	1823	Lincoln	Mar. 1, 1867	37	430	210	76,483	744	77,227	15
Nev.	1849	Carson City	Oct. 31, 1864	36	490	320	109,889	651	110,540	7
N.H.	1623	Concord	June 21, 1788	9	190	70	9,027	277	9,304	44
N.J.	1664	Trenton	Dec. 18, 1787	3	150	70	7,521	315	7,836	46
N.M.	1610	Santa Fe	Jan. 6, 1912	47	370	343	121,412	254	121,666	5
N.Y.	1614	Albany	July 26, 1788	11	330	283	47,831	1,745	49,576	30
N.C.	1660	Raleigh	Nov. 21, 1789	12	500	150	48,798	3,788	52,586	28
N.D.	1812	Bismarck	Nov. 2, 1889	39	340	211	69,273	1,392	70,665	17
Oh.	1788	Columbus	Mar. 1, 1803	17	220	220	40,975	247	41,222	35
Okla.	1889	Oklahoma City	Nov. 16, 1907	46	400	220	68,782	1,137	69,919	18
Ore.	1811	Salem	Feb. 14, 1859	33	360	261	96,184	797	96,981	10
Pa.	1682	Harrisburg	Dec. 12, 1787	2	283	160	44,966	367	45,333	33
R.I.	1636	Providence	May 29, 1790	13	40	30	1,049	165	1,214	50
S.C.	1670	Columbia	May 23, 1788	8	260	200	30,225	830	31,055	40
S.D.	1859	Pierre	Nov. 2, 1889	40	380	210	75,955	1,092	77,047	16
Tenn.	1769	Nashville	June 1, 1796	16	440	120	41,328	916	42,244	34
Tex.	1682	Austin	Dec. 29, 1845	28	790	660	262,134	5,204	267,338	2
Ut.	1847	Salt Lake City	Jan. 4, 1896	45	350	270	82,096	2,820	84,916	11
Vt.	1724	Montpelier	Mar. 4, 1791	14	160	80	9,267	342	9,609	43
Va.	1607	Richmond	June 25, 1788	10	430	200	39,780	1,037	40,817	36
Wash.	1811	Olympia	Nov. 11, 1889	42	360	240	66,570	1,622	68,192	20
W.Va.	1727	Charleston	June 20, 1863	35	240	130	24,070	111	24,181	41
Wis.	1766	Madison	May 29, 1848	30	310	260	54,464	1,690	56,154	26
Wy.	1834	Cheyenne	July 10, 1890	44	360	280	97,203	711	97,914	9

*First European permanent settlement. (a) Aleutian Islands and Alexander Archipelago are not considered in these lengths.

The Continental Divide

Source: Geological Survey, U.S. Interior Department

The Continental Divide: watershed, created by mountain ranges or table-lands of the Rocky Mountains, from which the drainage is easterly or westerly; the easterly flowing waters reaching the Atlantic Ocean chiefly through the Gulf of Mexico, and the westerly flowing waters reaching the Pacific Ocean through the Columbia River, or through the Colorado River, which flows into the Gulf of California.

The location and route of the Continental Divide across the United States may briefly be described as follows:

Beginning at point of crossing the United States-Mexican boundary, near long. 108°45'W., the Divide, in a northerly direction, crosses New Mexico along the western edge of the Rio Grande drainage basin, entering Colorado near long. 106°41'W.

Thence by a very irregular route northerly across Colorado along the western summits of the Rio Grande and of the Arkansas, the South Platte, and the North Platte River basins, and across Rocky Mountain National Park, entering Wyoming near long. 106°52'W.

Thence in a northwesterly direction, forming the western rims of the North Platte, Big Horn, and Yellowstone River basins, crossing the southwestern portion of Yellowstone National Park.

Thence in a westerly and then a northerly direction forming the common boundary of Idaho and Montana, to a point on said boundary near long. 114°00'W.

Thence northeasterly and northwesterly through Montana and the Glacier National Park, entering Canada near long. 114°04'W.

Chronological List of Territories

Source: National Archives and Records Service

Name of territory	Date of Organic Act	Organic Act effective	Admission as state	Yrs. terr.
Northwest Territory(a)	July 13, 1787	No fixed date	Mar. 1, 1803(b)	16
Territory southwest of River Ohio	May 26, 1790	No fixed date	June 1, 1796(c)	6
Mississippi	Apr. 7, 1798	When president acted	Dec. 10, 1817	19
Indiana	May 7, 1800	July 4, 1800	Dec. 11, 1816	16
Orleans	Mar. 26, 1804	Oct. 1, 1804	Apr. 30, 1812(d)	7
Michigan	Jan. 11, 1805	June 30, 1805	Jan. 26, 1837	31
Louisiana-Missouri(e)	Mar. 3, 1805	July 4, 1805	Aug. 10, 1821	16
Illinois	Feb. 3, 1809	Mar. 1, 1809	Dec. 3, 1818	9
Alabama	Mar. 3, 1817	When Miss. became a state	Dec. 14, 1819	2
Arkansas	Mar. 2, 1819	July 4, 1819	June 15, 1836	17
Florida	Mar. 30, 1822	No fixed date	Mar. 3, 1845	23
Wisconsin	Apr. 20, 1836	July 3, 1836	May 29, 1848	12
Iowa	June 12, 1838	July 3, 1838	Dec. 28, 1846	7
Oregon	Aug. 14, 1848	Date of act	Feb. 14, 1859	10
Minnesota	Mar. 3, 1849	Date of act	May 11, 1858	9
New Mexico	Sept. 9, 1850	On president's proclamation	Jan. 6, 1912	61
Utah	Sept. 9, 1850	Date of act	Jan. 4, 1896	44
Washington	Mar. 2, 1853	Date of act	Nov. 11, 1889	36
Nebraska	May 30, 1854	Date of act	Mar. 1, 1867	12
Kansas	May 30, 1854	Date of act	Jan. 29, 1861	6
Colorado	Feb. 28, 1861	Date of act	Aug. 1, 1876	15
Nevada	Mar. 2, 1861	Date of act	Oct. 31, 1864	3
Dakota	Mar. 2, 1861	Date of act	Nov. 2, 1889	28
Arizona	Feb. 24, 1863	Date of act	Feb. 14, 1912	49
Idaho	Mar. 3, 1863	Date of act	July 3, 1890	27
Montana	May 26, 1864	Date of act	Nov. 8, 1889	25
Wyoming	July 25, 1868	When officers were qualified	July 10, 1890	22
Alaska(f)	May 17, 1884	No fixed date	Jan. 3, 1959	75
Oklahoma	May 2, 1890	Date of act	Nov. 16, 1907	17
Hawaii	Apr. 30, 1900	June 14, 1900	Aug. 21, 1959	59

(a) Included Ohio, Indiana, Illinois, Michigan, Wisconsin, eastern Minnesota; (b) as the state of Ohio; (c) as the state of Tennessee; (d) as the state of Louisiana; (e) organic act for Missouri Territory of June 4, 1812, became effective Dec. 7, 1812; (f) Although the May 17, 1884 act actually constituted Alaska as a district, it was often referred to as a territory, and unofficially administered as such. The Territory of Alaska was legally and formally organized by an act of Aug. 24, 1912.

Geographic Centers, U.S. and Each State

Source: Geological Survey, U.S. Interior Department

United States, including Alaska and Hawaii — South Dakota; Butte County, W of Castle Rock, Approx. lat. 44°58'N. long. 103°46'W.

Contiguous U. S. (48 states) — Near Lebanon, Smith Co., Kansas, lat. 39°50'N. long. 98°35'W.

North American continent — The geographic center is in Pierce County, North Dakota, 6 miles W of Balta, latitude 48°10', longitude 100°10'W.

State—county, locality

Alabama—Chilton, 12 miles SW of Clanton.
Alaska—lat. 63°50'N. long. 152°W. Approx. 60 mi. NW of Mt. McKinley.
Arizona—Yavapai, 55 miles ESE of Prescott.
Arkansas—Pulaski, 12 miles NW of Little Rock.
California—Madera, 38 miles E of Madera.
Colorado—Park, 30 miles NW of Pikes Peak.
Connecticut—Hartford, at East Berlin.
Delaware—Kent, 11 miles S of Dover.
District of Columbia—Near 4th and L Sts., NW.
Florida—Hernando, 12 miles NNW of Brooksville.
Georgia—Twiggs, 18 miles SE of Macon.
Hawaii—Hawaii, 20°15'N, 156°20'W, off Maui Island.
Idaho—Custer, at Custer, SW of Challis.
Illinois—Logan, 28 miles NE of Springfield.
Indiana—Boone, 14 miles NNW of Indianapolis.
Iowa—Story, 5 miles NE of Ames.
Kansas—Barton, 15 miles NE of Great Bend.
Kentucky—Marion, 3 miles NNW of Lebanon.
Louisiana—Avoyelles, 3 miles SE of Marksville.
Maine—Piscataquis, 18 miles north of Dover.
Maryland—Prince Georges, 4.5 miles NW of Davidsonville.
Massachusetts—Worcester, north part of city.
Michigan—Wexford, 5 miles NNW of Cadillac.
Minnesota—Crow Wing, 10 miles SW of Brainerd.
Mississippi—Leake, 9 miles WNW of Carthage.
Missouri—Miller, 20 miles SW of Jefferson City.
Montana—Fergus, 12 miles west of Lewistown.
Nebraska—Custer, 10 miles NW of Broken Bow.
Nevada—Lander, 26 miles SE of Austin.
New Hampshire—Belknap, 3 miles E of Ashland.
New Jersey—Mercer, 5 miles SE of Trenton.
New Mexico—Torrance, 12 miles SSW of Willard.
New York—Madison, 12 miles S of Oneida and 26 miles SW of Utica.
North Carolina—Chatham, 10 miles NW of Sanford.
North Dakota—Sheridan, 5 miles SW of McClusky.
Ohio—Delaware, 25 miles NNE of Columbus.
Oklahoma—Oklahoma, 8 miles N of Oklahoma City.
Oregon—Crook, 25 miles SSE of Prineville.
Pennsylvania—Centre, 2.5 miles SW of Bellefonte.
Rhode Island—Kent, 1 mile SSW of Crompton.
South Carolina—Richland, 13 miles SE of Columbia.
South Dakota—Hughes, 8 miles NE of Pierre.
Tennessee—Rutherford, 5 mi. NE of Murfreesboro.
Texas—McCulloch, 15 miles NE of Brady.
Utah—Sanpete, 3 miles N of Manti.
Vermont—Washington, 3 miles E of Roxbury.
Virginia—Buckingham, 5 miles SW of Buckingham.
Washington—Chelan, 10 mi. WSW of Wenatchee.
West Virginia—Braxton, 4 miles E of Sutton.
Wisconsin—Wood, 9 miles SE of Marshfield.
Wyoming—Fremont, 58 miles ENE of Lander.

There is no generally accepted definition of geographic center, and no satisfactory method for determining it. The geographic center of an area may be defined as the center of gravity of the surface, or that point on which the surface of the area would balance if it were a plane of uniform thickness.

No marked or monumented point has been established by any government agency as the geographic center of either the 50 states, the contiguous United States, or the North American continent. A monument was erected in Lebanon, Kan., contiguous U.S. center, by a group of citizens. A cairn in Rugby, N.D. marks the center of the North American continent.

International Boundary Lines of the U.S.

The length of the northern boundary of the contiguous U.S. — the U.S.-Canadian border, excluding Alaska — is 3,987 miles according to the U.S. Geological Survey, Dept. of the Interior. The length of the Alaskan-Canadian border is 1,538 miles. The length of the U.S.-Mexican border, from the Gulf of Mexico to the Pacific Ocean, is approximately 1,933 miles (1963 boundary agreement).

Origin of the Names of U.S. States

Source: State officials, the Smithsonian Institution, and the Topographic Division, U.S. Geological Survey.

Alabama—Indian for tribal town, later a tribe (Alabamas or Alibamons) of the Creek confederacy.

Alaska—Russian version of Aleutian (Eskimo) word, alakshak, for "peninsula," "great lands," or "land that is not an island."

Arizona—Spanish version of Pima Indian word for "little spring place," or Aztec arizuma, meaning "silver-bearing."

Arkansas—French variant of Quapaw, a Siouan people meaning "downstream people."

California—Bestowed by the Spanish conquistadors (possibly by Cortez). It was the name of an imaginary island, an earthly paradise, in "Las Serges de Esplandian," a Spanish romance written by Montalvo in 1510. Baja California (Lower California, in Mexico) was first visited by Spanish in 1533. The present U.S. state was called Alta (Upper) California.

Colorado—Spanish, red, first applied to Colorado River.

Connecticut—From Mohican and other Algonquin words meaning "long river place."

Delaware—Named for Lord De La Warr, early governor of Virginia; first applied to river, then to Indian tribe (Lenni-Lenape), and the state.

District of Columbia—For Columbus, 1791.

Florida—Named by Ponce de Leon on Pascua Florida, "Flowery Easter," on Easter Sunday, 1513.

Georgia—For King George II of England by James Oglethorpe, colonial administrator, 1732.

Hawaii—Possibly derived from native world for homeland, Hawaiki or Owhyhee.

Idaho—A coined name with an invented Indian meaning: "gem of the mountains;" originally suggested for the Pike's Peak mining territory (Colorado), then applied to the new mining territory of the Pacific Northwest. Another theory suggests Idaho may be a Kiowa Apache term for the Comanche.

Illinois—French for Illini or land of Illini, Algonquin word meaning men or warriors.

Indiana—Means "land of the Indians."

Iowa—Indian word variously translated as "one who puts to sleep" or "beautiful land."

Kansas—Sioux word for "south wind people."

Kentucky—Indian word variously translated as "dark and bloody ground," "meadow land" and "land of tomorrow."

Louisiana—Part of territory called Louisiana by Sieur de La Salle for French King Louis XIV.

Maine—From Maine, ancient French province. Also: descriptive, referring to the mainland as distinct from the many coastal islands.

Maryland—For Queen Henrietta Maria, wife of Charles I of England.

Massachusetts—From Indian tribe named after "large hill place" identified by Capt. John Smith as being near Milton, Mass.

Michigan—From Chippewa words mici gama meaning "great water," after the lake of the same name.

Minnesota—From Dakota Sioux word meaning "cloudy water" or "sky-tinted water" of the Minnesota River.

Mississippi—Probably Chippewa; mici zibi, "great river" or "gathering-in of all the waters." Also: Algonquin word, "Messipi."

Missouri—Algonquin Indian tribe named after Missouri River, meaning "muddy water."

Montana—Latin or Spanish for "mountainous."

Nebraska—From Omaha or Otos Indian word meaning "broad water" or "flat river," describing the Platte River.

Nevada—Spanish, meaning snow-clad.

New Hampshire—Named 1629 by Capt. John Mason of Plymouth Council for his home county in England.

New Jersey—The Duke of York, 1664, gave a patent to John Berkeley and Sir George Carteret to be called Nova Caesaria, or New Jersey, after England's Isle of Jersey.

New Mexico—Spaniards in Mexico applied term to land north and west of Rio Grande in the 16th century.

New York—For Duke of York and Albany who received patent to New Netherland from his brother Charles II and sent an expedition to capture it, 1664.

North Carolina—In 1619 Charles I gave a large patent to Sir Robert Heath to be called Province of Carolana, from Carolus, Latin name for Charles. A new patent was granted by Charles II to Earl of Clarendon and others. Divided into North and South Carolina, 1710.

North Dakota—Dakota is Sioux for friend or ally.

Ohio—Iroquois word for "fine or good river."

Oklahoma—Choctaw coined word meaning red man, proposed by Rev. Allen Wright, Choctaw-speaking Indian.

Oregon—Origin unknown. One theory holds that the name may have been derived from that of the Wisconsin River shown on a 1715 French map as "Ouaricon-sint."

Pennsylvania—William Penn, the Quaker, who was made full proprietor by King Charles II in 1681, suggested Sylvania, or woodland, for his tract. The king's government owed Penn's father, Admiral William Penn, £16,000, and the land was granted as partial settlement. Charles II added the Penn to Sylvania, against the desires of the modest proprietor, in honor of the admiral.

Puerto Rico—Spanish for Rich Port.

Rhode Island—Exact origin is unknown. One theory notes that Giovanni de Verrazano recorded an island about the size of Rhodes in the Mediterranean in 1524, but others believe the state was named Roode Eylandt by Adriaen Block, Dutch explorer, because of its red clay.

South Carolina—See North Carolina.

South Dakota—See North Dakota.

Tennessee—Tanasi was the name of Cherokee villages on the Little Tennessee River. From 1784 to 1788 this was the State of Franklin, or Frankland.

Texas—Variant of word used by Caddo and other Indians meaning friends or allies, and applied to them by the Spanish in eastern Texas. Also written texias, tejas, teysas.

Utah—From a Navajo word meaning upper, or higher up, as applied to a Shoshone tribe called Ute. Spanish form is Yutta, English Uta or Utah. Proposed name Deseret, "land of honeybees," from Book of Mormon, was rejected by Congress.

Vermont—From French words vert (green) and mont (mountain). The Green Mountains were said to have been named by Samuel de Champlain. The Green Mountain Boys were Gen. Stark's men in the Revolution. When the state was formed, 1777, Dr. Thomas Young suggested combining vert and mont into Vermont.

Virginia—Named by Sir Walter Raleigh, who fitted out the expedition of 1584, in honor of Queen Elizabeth, the Virgin Queen of England.

Washington—Named after George Washington. When the bill creating the Territory of Columbia was introduced in the 32d Congress, the name was changed to Washington because of the existence of the District of Columbia.

West Virginia—So named when western counties of Virginia refused to secede from the United States, 1863.

Wisconsin—An Indian name, spelled Ouisconsin and Mesconsing by early chroniclers. Believed to mean "grassy place" in Chippewa. Congress made it Wisconsin.

Wyoming—The word was taken from Wyoming Valley, Pa., which was the site of an Indian massacre and became widely known by Campbell's poem, "Gertrude of Wyoming." In Algonquin it means "large prairie place."

Accession of Territory by the U.S.

Source: Statistical Abstract of the United States

Division	Year	Sq. mi.[1]	Division	Year	Sq. mi.[1]	Division	Year	Sq. mi.[1]
Total U.S.	**1970**	**3,630,854**	Oregon	1846	285,580	American Samoa	1900	76
50 states & D.C.		3,618,467	Mexican Cession	1848	529,017	Corn Islands[4]	1914	4
Territory in 1790[2]		888,685	Gadsden Purchase	1853	29,640	Virgin Islands, U.S.	1917	133
Louisiana Purchase	1803	827,192	Alaska	1867	589,757	Trust Territory of the Pacific Is.	1947	8,489
By treaty with Spain:			Hawaii	1898	6,450	All other[5]	...	42
Florida	1819	58,560	The Philippines[3]	1898	115,600			
Other areas	1819	13,443	Puerto Rico	1899	3,435			
Texas	1845	390,143	Guam	1899	212			

(1) Gross area (land and water). (2) Includes drainage basin of Red River on the north, south of 49th parallel, sometimes considered a part of the Louisiana Purchase. (3) Area not included in total; became Republic of the Philippines July 4, 1946. (4) Leased from Nicaragua for 99 years but returned Apr. 25, 1971; area not included in total. (5) See index for Outlying Areas, U.S.

Public Lands of the U. S.

Source: Bureau of Land Management, U.S. Interior Department

Acquisition of the Public Domain 1781-1867

Acquisition Area* (acres)	Land	Water	Total	Cost[1]
State Cessions (1781-1802)	233,415,680	3,409,920	236,825,600	[2]$6,200,000
Louisiana Purchase (1803)[3]	523,446,400	6,465,280	529,911,680	[5]23,213,568
Red River Basin[4]	29,066,880	535,040	29,601,920	
Cession from Spain (1819)	43,342,720	2,801,920	46,144,640	6,674,057
Oregon Compromise (1846)	180,644,480	2,741,760	183,386,240	
Mexican Cession (1848)	334,479,360	4,201,600	338,680,960	16,295,149
Purchase from Texas (1850)	78,842,880	83,840	78,926,720	15,496,448
Gadsden Purchase (1853)	18,961,920	26,880	18,988,800	10,000,000
Alaska Purchase (1867)	362,333,120	12,909,440	378,242,560	7,200,000
Total	**1,807,533,440**	**33,175,680**	**1,840,709,120**	**$85,079,222**

*All areas except Alaska were computed in 1912, and have not been adjusted for the recomputation of the area of the United States which was made for the 1950 Decennial Census. (1) Cost data for all except "State Cessions" obtained from U.S. Geological Survey. (2) Paid by federal government for Georgia cession, 1802 (56,689,920 acres). (3) Excludes areas eliminated by Treaty of 1819 with Spain. (4) Basin of the Red River of the North, south of the 49th parallel. (5) Includes $8,221,321 in interest paid on bonds floated by U.S to France.

Disposition of Public Lands 1781 to 1982

Disposition by methods not elsewhere classified[1]	Acres
Disposition by methods not elsewhere classified[1]	303,500,000
Granted or sold to homesteaders	287,500,000
Granted to railroad corporations	94,400,000
Granted to veterans as military bounties	61,000,000
Confirmed as private land claims[2]	34,000,000
Sold under timber and stone law[3]	13,900,000
Granted or sold under timber culture law[4]	10,900,000
Sold under desert land law[5]	10,700,000

Granted to states for:	Acres
Support of common schools	77,630,000
Reclamation of swampland	64,920,000
Construction of railroads	37,130,000
Support of misc. institutions[6]	21,700,000
Purposes not elsewhere classified[7]	117,600,000
Canals and rivers	6,100,000
Construction of wagon roads	3,400,000
Total granted to states	**328,480,000**

(1) Chiefly public, private, and preemption sales, but includes mineral entries, script locations, sales of townsites and townlots. (2) The Government has confirmed title to lands claimed under valid grants made by foreign governments prior to the acquisition of the public domain by the United States. (3) The law provided for the sale of lands valuable for timber or stone and unfit for cultivation. (4) The law provided for the granting of public lands to settlers on condition that they plant and cultivate trees on the lands granted. (5) The law provided for the sale of arid agricultural public lands to settlers who irrigate them and bring them under cultivation. (6) Universities, hospitals, asylums, etc. (7) For construction of various public improvements (individual items not specified in the granting act) reclamation of desert lands, construction of water reservoirs, etc.

Public Lands Administered by Federal Agencies

Agency (Acres, Sept. 30, 1985)	Public domain	Acquired	Total
Forest Service	161,038,854.3	28,369,069.5	189,407,923.8
Bureau of Land Management	334,029,039.4	2,362,420.5	336,391,402.9
Bureau of Reclamation	4,186,782.1	2,038,978.6	6,225,760.7
Fish and Wildlife Service	81,007,067.7	4,930,513.4	85,937,581.1
National Park Service	59,648,050.3	8,586,040.1	68,234,000.7
Tennessee Valley Authority	—	1,015,879.8	1,015,879.8
Corps of Engineers	652,496.7	7,727,129.1	8,379,625.8
U.S. Army	2,679,321.0	10,040,206.0	12,719,527.0
U.S. Navy	1,666,612.6	2,203,317.7	3,869,930.3
Department of Energy	1,467,313.7	1,005,283.2	2,472,596.9
Bureau of Indian Affairs	2,554,358.7	393,076.8	2,947,435.5
Total, all agencies (incl. those not shown)	**665,438,167.4**	**75,445,358.9**	**740,885,157.6**

National Parks, Other Areas Administered by Nat'l Park Service

Figures given are date area initially protected by Congress or presidential proclamation, date given current designation, and gross area in acres 12/31/86.

National Parks

Acadia, Me. (1916/1929) 41,231. Includes Mount Desert Island, half of Isle au Haut, Schoodic Point on mainland. Highest elevation on Eastern seaboard.

Arches, Ut. (1929/1978) 73,379. Contains giant red sandstone arches and other products of erosion.

Badlands, S.D. (1929/1978) 243,302; eroded prairie, bison, bighorn and antelope. Contains animal fossils of 40 million years ago.

Big Bend, Tex. (1935/1944) 735,416. Rio Grande, Chisos Mts.

Biscayne, Fla. (1968/1980) 173,039. Aquatic park encompasses chain of islands south of Miami.

Bryce Canyon, Ut. (1923/1928) 35,835. Spectacularly colorful and unusual display of erosion effects.

Canyonlands, Ut. (1964) 337,570. At junction of Colorado and Green rivers, extensive evidence of prehistoric Indians.

Capitol Reef, Ut. (1937/1971) 241,904. A 60-mile uplift of sandstone cliffs dissected by high-walled gorges.

Carlsbad Caverns, N.M. (1923/1930) 46,755. Largest known caverns; not yet fully explored.

Channel Islands, Cal. (1938/1980) 249,354. Seal lion breeding place, nesting sea birds, unique plants.

Crater Lake, Ore. (1902) 183,227. Extraordinary blue lake in crater of extinct volcano encircled by lava walls 500 to 2,000 feet high.

Denali, Alas. (1917/1980) 4,700,000. Name changed from Mt. McKinley NP. Contains highest mountain in U.S.; wildlife.

Everglades, Fla. (1934) 1,398,937. Largest remaining subtropical wilderness in continental U.S.

Gates of the Arctic, Alas. (1978/1980) 7,500,000. Vast wilderness in north central region.

Glacier, Mon. (1910) 1,013,572. Superb Rocky Mt. scenery, numerous glaciers and glacial lakes. Part of Waterton-Glacier Intl. Peace Park established by U.S. and Canada in 1932.

Glacier Bay, Alas. (1925/1980) 3,225,198. Great tidewater glaciers that move down mountain sides and break up into the sea; much wildlife.

Grand Canyon, Ariz. (1908/1919) 1,218,375. Most spectacular part of Colorado River's greatest canyon.

Grand Teton, Wy. (1929) 310,521. Most impressive part of the Teton Mountains, winter feeding ground of largest American elk herd.

Great Basin, Nev. (1986) 76,800. Wide basins and high mountain ranges.

Great Smoky Mountains, N.C.-Tenn. (1926) 520,269. Largest eastern mountain range, magnificent forests.

Guadalupe Mountains, Tex. (1966/1972) 76,293. Extensive

Permian limestone fossil reef; tremendous earth fault.

Haleakala, Ha. (1916/1960) 28,655. Dormant volcano on Maui with large colorful craters.

Hawaii Volcanoes, Ha. (1916/1961) 229,177. Contains Kilauea and Mauna Loa, active volcanoes.

Hot Springs, Ark. (1832/1921) 5,839. Government supervised bath houses use waters of 45 of the 47 natural hot springs.

Isle Royale, Mich. (1931) 571,790. Largest island in Lake Superior, noted for its wilderness area and wildlife.

Katmai, Alas. (1918/1980) 3,716,000. Valley of Ten Thousand Smokes, scene of 1917 volcanic eruption.

Kenai Fjords, Alas. (1978/1980) 670,000. Abundant mountain goats, marine mammals, birdlife; the Harding Icefield, one of the major icecaps in U.S.

Kings Canyon, Cal. (1890/1940) 461,901. Mountain wilderness, dominated by Kings River Canyons and High Sierra; contains giant sequoias.

Kobuk Valley, Alas. (1978/1980) 1,750,000. Broad river is core of native culture.

Lake Clark, Alas. (1978/1980) 2,874,000. Across Cook Inlet from Anchorage. A scenic wilderness rich in fish and wildlife.

Lassen Volcanic, Cal. (1907/1916) 106,372. Contains Lassen Peak, recently active volcano, and other volcanic phenomena.

Mammoth Cave, Ky. (1926) 52,420. 144 miles of surveyed underground passages, beautiful natural formations, river 300 feet below surface.

Mesa Verde, Col. (1906) 52,085. Most notable and best preserved prehistoric cliff dwellings in the United States.

Mount Rainier, Wash. (1899) 235,404. Greatest single-peak glacial system in the lower 48 states.

North Cascades, Wash. (1968) 504,781. Spectacular mountainous region with many glaciers, lakes.

Olympic, Wash. (1909/1938) 914,816. Mountain wilderness containing finest remnant of Pacific Northwest rain forest, active glaciers, Pacific shoreline, rare elk.

Petrified Forest, Ariz. (1906/1962) 93,533. Extensive petrified wood and Indian artifacts. Contains part of Painted Desert.

Redwood, Cal. (1968) 110,178. Forty miles of Pacific coastline, groves of ancient redwoods and world's tallest trees.

Rocky Mountain, Col. (1915) 265,200. On the continental divide, includes 107 named peaks over 11,000 feet.

Sequoia, Cal. (1890) 402,482. Groves of giant sequoias, highest mountain in contiguous United States — Mount Whitney (14,494 feet). World's largest tree.

Shenandoah, Va. (1926/1935) 195,347. Portion of the Blue Ridge Mountains; overlooks Shenandoah Valley; Skyline Drive.

Theodore Roosevelt, N.D. (1947/1978) 70,416. Contains part of T.R.'s ranch and scenic badlands.

Virgin Islands, V.I. (1956) 14,695. Covers 75% of St. John Island, lush growth, lovely beaches, Indian relics, evidence of colonial Danes.

Voyageurs, Minn. (1971/1975) 215,059. Abundant lakes, forests, wildlife, canoeing, boating.

Wind Cave, S.D. (1903) 28,292. Limestone caverns in Black Hills. Extensive wildlife includes a herd of bison.

Wrangell-St. Elias, Alas. (1978/1980) 8,945,000. Largest area in park system, most peaks over 16,000 feet, abundant wildlife; day's drive east of Anchorage.

Yellowstone, Ida., Mon., Wy., (1872) 2,219,785. Oldest national park. World's greatest geyser area has about 3,000 geysers and hot springs; spectacular falls and impressive canyons of the Yellowstone River; grizzly bear, moose, and bison.

Yosemite, Cal. (1890) 761,170. Yosemite Valley, the nation's highest waterfall, 3 groves of sequoias, and mountainous.

Zion, Ut. (1909/1919) 146,598. Unusual shapes and landscapes have resulted from erosion and faulting; Zion Canyon, with sheer walls ranging up to 2,500 feet, is readily accessible.

National Historical Parks

Appomattox Court House, Va. (1930/1954) 1,325. Where Lee surrendered to Grant.

Boston, Mass. (1974) 41. Includes Faneuil Hall, Old North Church, Bunker Hill, Paul Revere House.

Chaco Culture, N.M. (1907/1980) 33,974. Ruins of pueblos built by prehistoric Indians.

Chesapeake and Ohio Canal, Md.-W.Va.-D.C. (1961/1971) 20,781. 185 mile historic canal; D.C. to Cumberland, Md.

Colonial, Va. (1930/1936) 9,327. Includes most of Jamestown Island, site of first successful English colony; Yorktown, site of Cornwallis' surrender to George Washington; and the Colonial Parkway.

Cumberland Gap, Ky.-Tenn.-Va. (1940) 20,274. Mountain pass of the Wilderness Road which carried the first great migration of pioneers into America's interior.

George Rogers Clark, Vincennes, Ind. (1966) 25. Commemorates American defeat of British in west during Revolution.

Harpers Ferry, Md., W. Va. (1944/1963) 2,238. At the confluence of the Shenandoah and Potomac rivers, the site of John Brown's 1859 raid on the Army arsenal.

Independence, Pa. (1948/1956) 45. Contains several properties in Philadelphia associated with the Revolutionary War and the founding of the U.S.

Jean Laffite (and preserve), La. (1939/1978) 20,000. Includes Chalmette, site of 1814 Battle of New Orleans; French Quarter.

Kalaupapa, Ha. (1980) 10,902. Molokai's former leper colony site and other historic areas.

Kaloko-Honokohau, Ha. (1978) 1,161. Culture center has 234 historic features and grave of first king, Kamehameha.

Klondike Gold Rush, Alas.-Wash. (1976) 13,191. Alaskan Trails in 1898 Gold Rush. Museum in Seattle.

Lowell, Mass. (1978) 136. Seven mills, canal, 19th C. structures, park to show planned city of Industrial Revolution.

Lyndon B. Johnson, Tex. (1969/1980) 1,571. President's birthplace, boyhood home, ranch.

Minute Man, Mass. (1959) 749. Where the colonial Minute Men battled the British, April 19, 1775. Also contains Nathaniel Hawthorne's home.

Morristown, N.J. (1933) 1,671. Sites of important military encampments during the Revolutionary War; Washington's headquarters 1777, 1779-80.

Nez Perce, Ida. (1965) 2,109. Illustrates the history and culture of the Nez Perce Indian country. 22 separate sites.

Pu'uhonua o Honaunau, Ha. (1955/1978) 182. Until 1819, a sanctuary for Hawaiians vanquished in battle, and those guilty of crimes or breaking taboos.

San Antonio Missions, Tex. (1978) 477. Four of finest Spanish missions in U.S., 18th C. irrigation system.

San Juan Island, Wash. (1966) 1,752. Commemorates peaceful relations of the U.S., Canada and Great Britain since the 1872 boundary disputes.

Saratoga, N.Y. (1938) 3,389. Scene of a major battle which became a turning point in the War of Independence.

Sitka, Alas. (1910/1972) 107. Scene of last major resistance of the Tlingit Indians to the Russians, 1804.

Valley Forge, Pa. (1976) 3,468. Continental Army campsite in 1777-78 winter.

War in the Pacific, Guam (1978) 1,960. Scenic park memorial for WWII combatants in Pacific.

Women's Rights, N.Y. (1980) 5. Seneca Falls site where Susan B. Anthony, Elizabeth Cady Stanton began rights movement in 1848.

National Battlefields

Antietam, Md. (1890) 3,244. Battle ended first Confederate invasion of North, Sept. 17, 1862.

Big Hole, Mon. (1910/1963) 656. Site of major battle with Nez Perce Indians.

Cowpens, S.C. (1929/1972) 842. Revolutionary War battlefield.

Fort Donelson, Tenn. (1928) 537. Site of first major Union victory.

Fort Necessity, Pa. (1931/1961) 903. First battle of French and Indian War.

Monocacy, Md. (1934/1976) 1,647. Civil War battle in defense of Wash., D.C., July 9, 1864.

Moores Creek, N.C. (1926) 87. Pre-Revolutionary War battle.

Petersburg, Va. (1926/1962) 2,735. Scene of 10-month Union campaign 1864-65.

Stones River, Tenn. (1927/1960) 331. Civil War battle leading to Sherman's "March to the Sea."

Tupelo, Miss. (1929/1961) 1. Crucial battle over Sherman's supply line.

Wilson's Creek, Mo. (1960/1970) 1,750. Civil War battle for control of Missouri.

National Battlefield Parks

Kennesaw Mountain, Ga. (1917/1935) 2,884. Two major battles of Atlanta campaign in Civil War.

Manassas, Va. (1940) 4,513. Two battles of Bull Run in Civil War, 1861 and 1862.

Richmond, Va. (1936) 771. Site of battles defending Confederate capital.

National Battlefield Site

Brices Cross Roads, Miss. (1929) 1. Civil War battlefield.

National Military Parks

Chickamauga and Chattanooga, Ga.-Tenn. (1890) 8,103. Four Civil War battlefields.

Fredericksburg and Spotsylvania County, Va. (1927) 5,909. Sites of several major Civil War battles and campaigns.

Gettysburg, Pa. (1895) 3,865. Site of decisive Confederate defeat in North. Gettysburg Address.

Guilford Courthouse, N.C. (1917) 220. Revolutionary War battle site.

Horseshoe Bend, Ala. (1956) 2,040. On Tallapoosa River, where Gen. Andrew Jackson broke the power of the Creek Indian Confederacy.

Kings Mountain, S.C. (1931) 3,945. Revolutionary War battle.

Pea Ridge, Ark. (1956) 4,300. Civil War battle.

Shiloh, Tenn. (1894) 3,838. Major Civil War battle; site includes some well-preserved Indian burial mounds.

Vicksburg, Miss. (1899) 1,620. Union victory gave North control of the Mississippi and split the Confederacy in two.

National Memorials

Arkansas Post, Ark. (1960) 389. First permanent French settlement in the lower Mississippi River valley.

Arlington House, the Robert E. Lee Memorial, Va. (1925/1972) 28. Lee's home overlooking the Potomac.

Chamizal, El Paso, Tex. (1964/1966) 55. Commemorates 1963 settlement of 99-year border dispute with Mexico.

Coronado, Ariz. (1941/1952) 4,750. Commemorates first European exploration of the Southwest.

DeSoto, Fla. (1948) 27. Commemorates 16th-century Spanish explorations.

Federal Hall, N.Y. (1939/1955) 0.45. First seat of U.S. government under the Constitution.

Fort Caroline, Fla. (1950) 138. On St. Johns River, overlooks site of second attempt by French Huguenots to colonize North America.

Fort Clatsop, Ore. (1958) 125. Lewis and Clark encampment 1805-06.

General Grant, N.Y. (1958) 0.76. Tombs of Pres. and wife.

Hamilton Grange, N.Y. (1962) 0.71. Home of Alexander Hamilton.

John F. Kennedy Center for the Performing Arts, D.C. (1958/1964) 18.

Johnstown Flood, Pa. (1964) 163. Commemorates tragic flood of 1889.

Lincoln Boyhood, Ind. (1962) 200. Lincoln grew up here.

Lincoln Memorial, D.C. (1911) 110.

Lyndon B. Johnson Grove on the Potomac, D.C. (1973) 17.

Mount Rushmore, S.D. (1925) 1,278. World famous sculpture of 4 presidents.

Roger Williams, R.I. (1965) 5. Memorial to founder of Rhode Island.

Thaddeus Kosciuszko, Pa. (1972) 0.02. Memorial to Polish hero of American Revolution.

Theodore Roosevelt Island, D.C. (1932) 89.

Thomas Jefferson Memorial, D.C. (1934) 18.

USS Arizona, Ha. (1980). 00. Memorializes American losses at Pearl Harbor.

Washington Monument, D.C. (1848) 106.

Wright Brothers, N.C. (1927/1953) 431. Site of first powered flight.

National Historic Sites

Abraham Lincoln Birthplace, Hodgenville, Ky. (1916/1959) 117.

Adams, Quincy, Mass. (1946/1952) 10. Home of Presidents John Adams, John Quincy Adams, and celebrated descendants.

Allegheny Portage Railroad, Pa. (1964) 1,135. Part of the Pennsylvania Canal system.

Andersonville, Andersonville, Ga. (1970) 476. Noted Civil War prison.

Andrew Johnson, Greeneville, Tenn. (1935/1963) 17. Home of the President.

Bent's Old Fort, Col. (1960) 800. Old West fur-trading post.

Carl Sandburg Home, N.C. (1968/1972) 264. Poet's home.

Christiansted, St. Croix; V.I. (1952/1961) 27. Commemorates Danish colony.

Clara Barton, Md. (1974) 9. Home of founder of American Red Cross.

Edgar Allan Poe, Pa. (1978/1980) 1. Poet's home.

Edison, West Orange, N.J. (1955/1962) 21. Home and laboratory.

Eisenhower, Gettysburg, Pa. (1967/1969) 690. Home of 34th president.

Eleanor Roosevelt, Hyde Park, N.Y. (1977) 181.

Eugene O'Neill, Danville, Cal. (1976) 13. Playwright's home.

Ford's Theatre, Washington, D.C. (1866/1970) 0.29. Includes theater, now restored, where Lincoln was assassinated, house where he died, and Lincoln Museum.

Fort Bowie, Ariz. (1964/1972) 1,000. Focal point of operations against Geronimo and the Apaches.

Fort Davis, Tex. (1961) 460. Frontier outpost battled Comanches and Apaches.

Fort Laramie, Wy. (1938/1960) 832. Military post on Oregon Trail.

Fort Larned, Kan. (1964) 718. Military post on Santa Fe Trail.

Fort Point, San Francisco, Cal. (1970) 29. Largest West Coast fortification.

Fort Raleigh, N.C. (1941) 157. First English settlement.

Fort Scott, Kan. (1978) 17. Commemorates events of Civil War period.

Fort Smith, Ark. (1961) 73. Active post from 1817 to 1890.

Fort Union Trading Post, Mon., N.D. (1966) 434. Principal fur-trading post on upper Missouri, 1828-1867.

Fort Vancouver, Wash. (1948/1961) 209. Hdqts. for Hudson's Bay Company in 1825. Early military and political seat.

Frederick Law Olmsted, Mass. (1979) 2. Home of famous park planner (1822-1903).

Friendship Hill, Pa. (1978) 675. Home of Albert Gallatin, Jefferson's Sec'y of Treasury. Not open to public.

Golden Spike, Utah (1957) 2,735. Commemorates completion of first transcontinental railroad in 1869.

Grant-Kohrs Ranch, Mon. (1972) 1,499. Ranch house and part of 19th century ranch.

Hampton, Md. (1948) 59. 18th-century Georgian mansion.

Harry S Truman, Mo. (1980/1982). 0.78. Home of Pres. Truman after 1919.

Herbert Hoover, West Branch, Ia. (1965) 187. Birthplace and boyhood home of 31st president.

Home of Franklin D. Roosevelt, Hyde Park, N.Y. (1944) 290. Birthplace, home and "Summer White House".

Hopewell Furnace, Pa. (1938) 848. 19th-century iron making village.

Hubbell Trading Post, Ariz. (1965) 160. Indian trading post.

James A. Garfield, Mentor, Oh. (1980) 8. President's home.

Jefferson National Expansion Memorial, St. Louis, Mo. (1935/1954) 191. Commemorates westward expansion.

John Fitzgerald Kennedy, Brookline, Mass. (1967) 0.09. Birthplace and childhood home of the President.

John Muir, Martinez, Cal. (1964) 9. Home of early conservationist and writer.

Knife River Indian Villages, N.D. (1974) 1,293. Remnants of 5 Hidatsa villages.

Lincoln Home, Springfield, Ill. (1971) 12. Lincoln's residence when he was elected President, 1860.

Longfellow, Cambridge, Mass. (1972) 2. Longfellow's home, 1837-82, and Washington's hq. during Boston Siege, 1775-76. No federal facilities.

Maggie L. Walker, Va. (1978) 1. Richmond home of black leader and 1903 founder of bank.

Martin Luther King, Jr., Atlanta, Ga. (1980) 23. Birthplace, grave.

Martin Van Buren, N.Y. (1974) 40. Lindenwald, home of 8th president, near Kinderhook.

Ninety Six, S.C. (1976) 989. Colonial trading village.

Palo Alto Battlefield, Tex. (1978) 50. One of 2 Mexican War battles fought in U.S.

Puukohola Heiau, Ha. (1972) 80. Ruins of temple built by King Kamehameha.

Sagamore Hill, Oyster Bay, N.Y. (1962) 83. Home of President Theodore Roosevelt from 1885 until his death in 1919.

Saint-Gaudens, Cornish, N.H. (1964/1977) 148. Home, studio and gardens of American sculptor Augustus Saint-Gaudens.

Salem Maritime, Mass. (1938) 9. Only port never seized from the patriots by the British. Major fishing and whaling port.

San Juan, P.R. (1949) 75. 16th-century Spanish fortifications.

Saugus Iron Works, Mass. (1968) 9. Reconstructed 17th century colonial ironworks.

Sewall-Belmont House, D.C. (1974) 0.35. National Women's Party headquarters 1929-74.

Springfield Armory, Mass. (1974) 55. Small arms manufacturing center for nearly 200 years.

Steamtown, Scranton, Pa. (1986) 40. Railroad yard with 120 steam locomotives with 20 miles of track.

Theodore Roosevelt Birthplace, N.Y., N.Y. (1962) 0.11.

Theodore Roosevelt Inaugural, Buffalo, N.Y. (1966) 1. Wilcox House where he took oath of office, 1901.

Thomas Stone, Md. (1978) 328. Home of signer of Declaration, built in 1771. Not open to public.

Tuskegee Institute, Ala. (1974) 74. College founded by Booker T. Washington in 1881 for blacks, includes student-made brick buildings.

Vanderbilt Mansion, Hyde Park, N.Y. (1940) 212. Mansion of 19th-century financier.

Whitman Mission, Wash. (1936/1963) 98. Site where Dr. and Mrs. Marcus Whitman ministered to the Indians until slain by them in 1847.

William Howard Taft, Cincinnati, Oh. (1969) 3. Birthplace and early home of the 27th president.

National Monuments

Name	State	Year	Acreage
Agate Fossil Beds	Neb.	1965	3,055
Alibates Flint Quarries	N.M.-Tex..	1965	1,371
Aniakchak	Alas.	1978	137,176
Aztec Ruins	N.M..	1923	27
Bandelier	N.M..	1916	36,917
Black Canyon of the Gunnison	Col.	1933	20,766
Booker T. Washington	Va.	1956	224
Buck Island Reef	V.I.	1961	880
Cabrillo	Cal.	1913	144
Canyon de Chelly	Ariz..	1931	83,840
Cape Krusenstern	Alas.	1978	59,807
Capulin Mountain	N.M..	1916	775
Casa Grande Ruins	Ariz..	1892	473

Name	State	Year	Acreage
Castillo de San Marcos	Fla.	1924	20
Castle Clinton	N.Y.	1946	1
Cedar Breaks	Ut.	1933	6,155
Chiricahua	Ariz.	1924	11,985
Colorado	Col.	1911	20,454
Congaree Swamp	S.C.	1976	15,138
Craters of the Moon	Ida.	1924	53,545
Custer Battlefield	Mon.	1879	765
Death Valley	Cal.-Nev.	1933	2,067,628
Devils Postpile	Cal.	1911	798
Devils Tower	Wy.	1906	1,347
Dinosaur	Col.-Ut.	1915	211,142
Effigy Mounds	Ia.	1949	1,481
El Morro	N.M.	1906	1,279
Florissant Fossil Beds**	Col.	1969	5,998
Fort Frederica	Ga.	1936	216
Fort Jefferson	Fla.	1935	64,700
Fort Matanzas	Fla.	1924	228
Fort McHenry National Monument and Historic Shrine	Md.	1925	43
Fort Pulaski	Ga.	1924	5,623
Fort Stanwix	N.Y.	1935	16
Fort Sumter	S.C.	1948	198
Fort Union	N.M.	1954	721
Fossil Butte	Wy.	1972	8,198
G. Washington Birthplace	Va.	1930	538
George Washington Carver	Mo.	1943	210
Gila Cliff Dwellings	N.M.	1907	533
Grand Portage	Minn.	1951	710
Great Sand Dunes	Col.	1932	38,662
Hohokam Pima*	Ariz.	1972	1,690
Homestead Nat'l. Monument of America	Neb.	1936	195
Hovenweep	Col.-Ut.	1923	785
Jewel Cave	S.D.	1908	1,274
John Day Fossil Beds	Ore.	1974	14,014
Joshua Tree	Cal.	1936	559,960
Lava Beds	Cal.	1925	46,560
Montezuma Castle	Ariz.	1906	858
Mound City Group	Oh.	1923	270
Muir Woods	Cal.	1908	554
Natural Bridges	Ut.	1908	7,636
Navajo	Ariz.	1909	360
Ocmulgee	Ga.	1934	683
Oregon Caves	Ore.	1909	488
Organ Pipe Cactus	Ariz.	1937	330,689
Pecos	N.M.	1965	365
Pinnacles	Cal.	1908	16,265
Pipe Spring	Ariz.	1923	40
Pipestone	Minn.	1937	282
Rainbow Bridge	Ut.	1910	160
Russell Cave	Ala.	1961	310
Saguaro	Ariz.	1933	83,574
Saint Croix Island**	Me.	1949	35
Salinas	N.M.	1909	1,077
Scotts Bluff	Neb.	1919	2,997
Statue of Liberty	N.J.-N.Y.	1924	58
Sunset Crater	Ariz.	1930	3,040
Timpanogos Cave	Ut.	1922	250
Tonto	Ariz.	1907	1,120
Tumacacori	Ariz.	1908	17
Tuzigoot	Ariz.	1939	801
Walnut Canyon	Ariz.	1915	2,249
White Sands	N.M.	1933	143,733
Wupatki	Ariz.	1924	35,253
Yucca House*	Col.	1919	10

National Preserves

Name	State	Year	Acreage
Aniakchak	Alas.	1978	465,603
Bering Land Bridge	Alas.	1978	2,784,760
Big Cypress	Fla.	1974	570,000
Big Thicket	Tex.	1974	85,774
Denali	Alas.	1917	1,330,000
Gates of the Arctic	Alas.	1978	940,000
Glacier Bay	Alas.	1925	55,000
Katmai	Alas.	1918	374,000
Lake Clark	Alas.	1978	1,171,000
Noatak	Alas.	1978	6,560,000
Wrangell-St. Elias	Alas.	1978	4,255,000
Yukon-Charley Rivers	Alas.	1978	2,520,000

National Seashores

Name	State	Year	Acreage
Assateague Island	Md.-Va.	1965	39,631
Canaveral	Fla.	1975	57,627
Cape Cod	Mass.	1961	43,526
Cape Hatteras	N.C.	1937	30,319
Cape Lookout**	N.C.	1966	28,415
Cumberland Island	Ga.	1972	36,415
Fire Island	N.Y.	1964	19,579
Gulf Islands	Fla.-Miss.	1971	139,775
Padre Island	Tex.	1962	130,697
Point Reyes	Cal.	1962	71,046

National Parkways

Name	State	Year	Acreage
Blue Ridge	Va.-N.C.	1936	82,117
George Washington Memorial	Va.-Md.	1930	7,146
John D. Rockefeller Jr. Mem.	Wy.	1972	23,777
Natchez Trace	Ala.-Miss.-Tenn.	1938	50,189

National Lakeshores

Name	State	Year	Acreage
Apostle Islands	Wis.	1970	8,085
Indiana Dunes	Ind.	1966	12,857
Pictured Rocks	Mich.	1966	72,899
Sleeping Bear Dunes	Mich.	1970	71,132

National Rivers

Name	State	Year	Acreage
Big South Fork	Ky.-Tenn.	1976	122,960
Buffalo	Ark.	1972	94,219
New River Gorge	W.Va.	1978	62,024

National Scenic Rivers and Riverways

Name	State	Year	Acreage
Alagnak Wild	Alas.	1980	24,038
Delaware	N.Y.-N.J.-Pa.	1978	1,973
Lower Saint Croix	Minn.-Wis.	1972	9,472
Missouri Natl. Recreational River	Neb.	1978	14,941
Obed Wild	Tenn.	1976	5,006
Ozark	Mo.	1964	80,788
Rio Grande	Tex.	1978	9,600
Saint Croix	Minn.-Wis.	1968	68,793
Upper Delaware	N.Y.-N.J.	1978	75,000

Parks (no other classification)

Name	State	Year	Acreage
Catoctin Mountain	Md.	1954	5,770
Constitution Gardens	D.C.	1978	52
Fort Washington	Md.	1930	341
Frederick Douglass Home	D.C.	1962	8
Greenbelt	Md.	1950	1,176
Perry's Victory	Oh.	1936	25
Piscataway	Md.	1961	4,263
Prince William Forest	Va.	1948	18,572
Rock Creek	D.C.	1890	1,754
Vietnam Veterans	D.C.	1980	2
Wolf Trap Farm Park for the Performing Arts	Va.	1966	130

National Recreation Areas

Name	State	Year	Acreage
Amistad	Tex.	1965	57,292
Bighorn Canyon	Mon.-Wy.	1966	120,296
Chattahoochee R.	Ga.	1978	9,200
Chickasaw	Okla.	1902	9,522
Coulee Dam	Wash.	1946	100,390
Curecanti	Col.	1965	42,114
Cuyahoga Valley	Oh.	1974	32,460
Delaware Water Gap	N.J.-Pa.	1965	66,192
Gateway	N.Y.-N.J.	1972	26,311
Glen Canyon	Ariz.-Ut.	1958	1,236,880
Golden Gate	Cal.	1972	73,117
Lake Chelan	Wash.	1968	61,890
Lake Mead	Ariz.-Nev.	1936	1,495,666
Lake Meredith	Tex.	1965	44,978
Ross Lake	Wash.	1968	117,574
Santa Monica Mts.	Cal.	1978	150,000
Whiskeytown	Cal.	1965	42,503

National Mall

Name	State	Year	Acreage
National Mall	D.C.	1933	146

National Scenic Trails

Name	State	Year	Acreage
Appalachian	Me. to Ga.	1968	143,162
Natchez Trace	Ga.-Ala.-Tenn.	1983	10,995
Potomac Heritage	Md.-D.C.-Va.-Pa.	1983	***

*Not open to the public. **No federal facilities. ***Undetermined.

National Recreation Areas Administered by Forest Service

Name	State	Year	Acreage
Allegheny	Pa.	1984	23,063
Arapaho	Col.	1978	35,697
Flaming Gorge	Ut.-Wyo.	1968	201,114
Hell's Canyon	Ida.-Ore.	1975	538,104
Mount Rogers	Va.	1966	154,770
Oregon Dunes	Ore.	1972	31,566
Rattlesnake	Mon.	1980	61,000
Sawtooth	Ida.	1972	756,019
Spruce Knob-Seneca Rocks	W. Va.	1965	100,000
Whiskeytown Shasta-Trinity	Cal.	1965	203,587
White Rocks	Vt.	1984	36,400

Federal Indian Reservations[1]

Source: Bureau of Indian Affairs, U.S. Interior Department (data for persons and unemployment as of 1985, other data as of 1984)
The total American Indian population according to the 1980 Census is 1.534 million.

State	No. of reser.	Tribally-owned acreage[2]	Allotted acreage[2]	No. of tribes[3]	No. of persons[4]	Avg. (%) unemp. rate[5]	Major tribes and/or natives
Alaska	1[6]	90,077	822,278	6	69,410	51	Aleut, Eskimo, Athapascan[7], Haida, Tlingit, Tsimpshian
Arizona	20	19,695,448	252,666	13	166,330	43	Navajo, Apache, Papago, Hopi, Yavapai, Pima
California	78	501,484	67,811	—[8]	25,263	55	Hoopa, Paiute, Yurok, Karok, Mission Bands
Colorado	2	784,062	3,042	1	2,427	47	Ute
Florida	3	155,832	—	1	1,873	26	Seminole, Miccosukee[9]
Idaho	4	463,456	328,402		7,218	46	Shoshone, Bannock, Nez Perce
Iowa	1	4,164	—		745	66	Sac and Fox[10]
Kansas	4	7,459	22,217		2,254	28	Potawatomi, Kickapoo, Iowa
Louisiana	2	436	—		781	18	Chitimacha, Coushatta
Maine	3	221,632	—		2,421	22	Passamaquoddy, Penobscot, Maliseet
Michigan	5	12,367	9,223		6,498	58	Chippewa, Potawatomi, Ottawa
Minnesota	14	714,196	51,010		17,886	59	Chippewa, Sioux
Mississippi	1	17,715	18		4,599	26	Choctaw
Montana	7	2,273,434	2,945,551		28,963	39	Blackfeet, Crow, Sioux, Assiniboine, Cheyenne
Nebraska	3	23,468	41,145		4,415	60	Omaha, Winnebago, Santee Sioux
Nevada	23	1,145,252	78,567		8,410	44	Paiute, Shoshone, Washoe
New Mexico	24	6,991,858	675,968		110,172	32	Zuni, Apache, Navajo
New York	6	—	—		11,070	50	Seneca, Mohawk, Onondaga, Oneida[11]
North Carolina	1	56,460	—		6,110	39	Cherokee
North Dakota	5	214,260	636,719		21,835	50	Sioux, Chippewa, Mandan, Arikara, Hidatsa
Oklahoma	—[12]	88,526	1,024,224		159,587	18	Cherokee, Creek, Choctaw, Chickasaw, Osage, Cheyenne, Arapahoe, Kiowa, Comanche
Oregon	5	632,514	136,000		4,856	37	Warm Springs, Wasco, Paiute, Umatilla, Siletz
South Dakota	9	2,652,306	2,433,563		49,832	64	Sioux
Utah	6	2,286,350	33,423		7,400	25	Ute, Goshute, Southern Paiute
Washington	26	2,077,114	472,512		40,521	52	Yakima, Lummi, Quinault
Wisconsin	15	332,478	80,676		19,334	49	Chippewa, Oneida, Winnebago
Wyoming	1	1,793,284	93,979		5,254	65	Shoshone, Arapahoe

(1) As of 1985 the federal government recognized and acknowledged that it had a special relationship with, and a trust responsibility for, 506 Federally recognized Indian entities in the U.S., including Alaska. The term "Indian entities" encompasses Indian tribes, bands, villages, groups, pueblos, Eskimos, and Aleuts, eligible for federal services and classified in the following 3 categories: (a) Officially approved Indian organizations pursuant to federal statutory authority (Indian Reorganization Act; Oklahoma Indian Welfare Act and Alaska Native Act.) (b) Officially approved Indian organizations outside of specified federal statutory authority. (c) Traditional Indian organizations recognized without formal federal approval of organizational structure.

(2) The acreages refer only to Indian lands which are either owned by the tribes or individual Indians, and held in trust by the U.S. government.

(3) "Tribe" among the North American Indians originally meant a body of persons bound together by blood ties who were socially, politically, and religiously organized, and who lived together, occupying a definite territory and having a common language or dialect. With the relegation of Indians to reservations, the word "tribe" developed a number of different meanings. Today, it can be a distinct group within an Indian village or community, the entire community, a large number of communities, several different groups or villages speaking different languages but sharing a common government, or a widely scattered number of villages with a common language but no common government.

(4) Number of Indians living on or adjacent to federally recognized reservations comprising the BIA service population.

(5) Unemployment rate of Indian work force consisting of all those 16 years old and over who are able and actively seeking work.

(6) Alaskan Indian Affairs are carried out under the Alaska Native Claims Settlement Act (Dec. 18, 1971). The Act provided for the establishment of regional and village corporations to conduct business for profit and non-profit purposes. There are 13 such regional corporations, each one with organized village corporations. The Metlakatla Reservation remains the only federally recognized reservation in Alaska in the sense of specific reservation boundaries, trust lands, etc.

(7) Aleuts and Eskimos are racially and linguistically related. Athapascans are related to the Navaho and Apache Indians.

(8) Some 62 distinct tribes are known to have lived in or wandered through what is now California at some time in the past. Many of these were village groups and are historically associated with bands which settled near Spanish missions where much of the traditional culture was destroyed. Many of these bands, however, still retain some of their Indian language and customs. Excluding the 30 mission bands, who are primarily of the Cahuilla, Diegueno, or Luiseno, there are some 22 tribes represented on the California reservations.

(9) "Seminole" means "runaways" and these Indians from various tribes were originally refugees from whites in the Carolinas and Georgia. Later joined by runaway slaves, the Seminole were united by their hostility to the United States. Formal peace with the Seminoles in Florida was not achieved until 1934. The Miccosukee are a branch of the Seminole; they retain their Indian religion and have not made formal peace with the United States.

(10) Once two tribes, the Sac and Fox formed a political alliance in 1734.

(11) These 4 tribes along with the Cayuga and Tuscarora made up the Iroquois League, which ruled large portions of New York, New England and Pennsylvania and ranged into the Midwest and South. The Onondaga, who traditionally provide the president of the league, maintain that they are a foreign nation within New York and the United States.

(12) Indian land status in Oklahoma is unique and there are no reservations in the sense that the term is used elsewhere in the U.S. Likewise, many of the Oklahoma tribes are unique in their high degree of assimilation to the white culture.

Declaration of Independence

The Declaration of Independence was adopted by the Continental Congress in Philadelphia, on July 4, 1776. John Hancock was president of the Congress and Charles Thomson was secretary. A copy of the Declaration, engrossed on parchment, was signed by members of Congress on and after Aug. 2, 1776. On Jan. 18, 1777, Congress ordered that "an authenticated copy, with the names of the members of Congress subscribing the same, be sent to each of the United States, and that they be desired to have the same put upon record." Authenticated copies were printed in broadside form in Baltimore, where the Continental Congress was then in session. The following text is that of the original printed by John Dunlap at Philadelphia for the Continental Congress.

IN CONGRESS, July 4, 1776.

A DECLARATION

By the REPRESENTATIVES of the

UNITED STATES OF AMERICA,

In GENERAL CONGRESS assembled

When in the Course of human Events, it becomes necessary for one People to dissolve the Political Bands which have connected them with another, and to assume among the Powers of the Earth, the separate and equal Station to which the Laws of Nature and of Nature's God entitle them, a decent Respect to the Opinions of Mankind requires that they should declare the causes which impel them to the Separation.

We hold these Truths to be self-evident, that all Men are created equal, that they are endowed by their Creator with certain unalienable Rights, that among these are Life, Liberty, and the Pursuit of Happiness—That to secure these Rights, Governments are instituted among Men, deriving their just Powers from the Consent of the Governed, that whenever any Form of Government becomes destructive of these Ends, it is the Right of the People to alter or to abolish it, and to institute new Government, laying its Foundation on such Principles, and organizing its Powers in such Form, as to them shall seem most likely to effect their Safety and Happiness. Prudence, indeed, will dictate that Governments long established should not be changed for light and transient Causes; and accordingly all Experience hath shewn, that Mankind are more disposed to suffer, while Evils are sufferable, than to right themselves by abolishing the Forms to which they are accustomed. But when a long Train of Abuses and Usurpations, pursuing invariably the same Object, evinces a Design to reduce them under absolute Despotism, it is their Right, it is their Duty, to throw off such Government, and to provide new Guards for their future Security. Such has been the patient Sufferance of these Colonies; and such is now the Necessity which constrains them to alter their former Systems of Government. The History of the present King of Great-Britain is a History of repeated Injuries and Usurpations, all having in direct Object the Establishment of an absolute Tyranny over these States. To prove this, let Facts be submitted to a candid World.

He has refused his Assent to Laws, the most wholesome and necessary for the public Good.

He has forbidden his Governors to pass Laws of immediate and pressing Importance, unless suspended in their Operation till his Assent should be obtained; and when so suspended, he has utterly neglected to attend to them.

He has refused to pass other Laws for the Accommodation of large Districts of People, unless those People would relinquish the Right of Representation in the Legislature, a Right inestimable to them, and formidable to Tyrants only.

He has called together Legislative Bodies at Places unusual, uncomfortable, and distant from the Depository of their Public Records, for the sole Purpose of fatiguing them into Compliance with his Measures.

He has dissolved Representative Houses repeatedly, for opposing with manly Firmness his Invasions on the Rights of the People.

He has refused for a long Time, after such Dissolutions, to cause others to be elected; whereby the Legislative Powers, incapable of Annihilation, have returned to the People at large for their exercise; the State remaining in the mean time exposed to all the Dangers of Invasion from without, and Convulsions within.

He has endeavoured to prevent the Population of these States; for that Purpose obstructing the Laws for Naturalization of Foreigners; refusing to pass others to encourage their Migrations hither, and raising the Conditions of new Appropriations of Lands.

He has obstructed the Administration of Justice, by refusing his Assent to Laws for establishing Judiciary Powers.

He has made Judges dependent on his Will alone, for the Tenure of their Offices, and the Amount and payment of their Salaries.

He has erected a Multitude of new Offices, and sent hither Swarms of Officers to harrass our People, and eat out their Substance.

He has kept among us, in Times of Peace, Standing Armies, without the consent of our Legislatures.

He has affected to render the Military independent of, and superior to the Civil Power.

He has combined with others to subject us to a Jurisdiction foreign to our Constitution, and unacknowledged by our Laws; giving his Assent to their Acts of pretended Legislation:

For quartering large Bodies of Armed Troops among us:

For protecting them, by a mock Trial, from Punishment for any Murders which they should commit on the Inhabitants of these States:

For cutting off our Trade with all Parts of the World:

For imposing Taxes on us without our Consent:

For depriving us, in many Cases, of the Benefits of Trial by Jury:

For transporting us beyond Seas to be tried for pretended Offences:

For abolishing the free System of English Laws in a neighbouring Province, establishing therein an arbitrary Government, and enlarging its Boundaries, so as to render it at once an Example and fit Instrument for introducing the same absolute Rule into these Colonies:

For taking away our Charters, abolishing our most valuable Laws, and altering fundamentally the Forms of our Governments:

For suspending our own Legislatures, and declaring themselves invested with Power to legislate for us in all Cases whatsoever.

He has abdicated Government here, by declaring us out of his Protection and waging War against us.

He has plundered our Seas, ravaged our Coasts, burnt our towns, and destroyed the Lives of our People.

He is, at this Time, transporting large Armies of foreign Mercenaries to compleat the works of Death, Desolation, and Tyranny, already begun with circumstances of Cruelty and Perfidy, scarcely paralleled in the most barbarous Ages, and totally unworthy the Head of a civilized Nation.

He has constrained our fellow Citizens taken Captive on the high Seas to bear Arms against their Country, to become the Executioners of their Friends and Brethren, or to fall themselves by their Hands.

He has excited domestic Insurrections amongst us, and has endeavoured to bring on the Inhabitants of our Frontiers, the merciless Indian Savages, whose known Rule of Warfare, is an undistinguished Destruction, of all Ages, Sexes and Conditions.

In every stage of these Oppressions we have Petitioned for Redress in the most humble Terms: Our repeated Petitions have been answered only by repeated Injury. A Prince, whose Character is thus marked by every act which may define a Tyrant, is unfit to be the Ruler of a free People.

Nor have we been wanting in Attentions to our British Brethren. We have warned them from Time to Time of Attempts by their Legislature to extend an unwarrantable Jurisdiction over us. We have reminded them of the Circumstances of our Emigration and Settlement here. We have appealed to their native Justice and Magnanimity, and we have conjured them by the Ties of our common Kindred to disavow these Usurpations, which, would inevitably interrupt our Connections and Correspondence. They too have been deaf to the Voice of Justice and of Consanguinity. We must, therefore, acquiesce in the Necessity, which denounces our Separation, and hold them, as we hold the rest of Mankind, Enemies in War, in Peace, Friends.

We, therefore, the Representatives of the UNITED STATES OF AMERICA, in General Congress, Assembled, appealing to the Supreme Judge of the World for the Rectitude of our Intentions, do, in the Name, and by Authority of the good People of these Colonies, solemnly Publish and Declare, That these United Colonies are, and of Right ought to be, Free and Independent States; that they are absolved from all Allegiance to the British Crown, and that all political Connection between them and the State of Great-Britain, is and ought to be totally dissolved; and that as Free and Independent States, they have full Power to levy War, conclude Peace, contract Alliances, establish Commerce, and to do all other Acts and Things which Independent States may of right do. And for the support of this declaration, with a firm Reliance on the Protection of divine Providence, we mutually pledge to each other our lives, our Fortunes, and our sacred Honor.

JOHN HANCOCK, President

Attest.
CHARLES THOMSON, Secretary.

Signers of the Declaration of Independence

Delegate and state	Vocation	Birthplace	Born	Died
Adams, John (Mass.)	Lawyer	Braintree (Quincy), Mass.	Oct. 30, 1735	July 4, 1826
Adams, Samuel (Mass.)	Political leader	Boston, Mass.	Sept. 27, 1722	Oct. 2, 1803
Bartlett, Josiah (N.H.)	Physician, judge	Amesbury, Mass.	Nov. 21, 1729	May 19, 1795
Braxton, Carter (Va.)	Farmer	Newington Plantation, Va.	Sept. 10, 1736	Oct. 10, 1797
Carroll, Chas. of Carrollton (Md.)	Lawyer	Annapolis, Md.	Sept. 19, 1737	Nov. 14, 1832
Chase, Samuel (Md.)	Judge	Princess Anne, Md.	Apr. 17, 1741	June 19, 1811
Clark, Abraham (N.J.)	Surveyor	Roselle, N.J.	Feb. 15, 1726	Sept. 15, 1794
Clymer, George (Pa.)	Merchant	Philadelphia, Pa.	Mar. 16, 1739	Jan. 23, 1813
Ellery, William (R.I.)	Lawyer	Newport, R.I.	Dec. 22, 1727	Feb. 15, 1820
Floyd, William (N.Y.)	Soldier	Brookhaven, N.Y.	Dec. 17, 1734	Aug. 4, 1821
Franklin, Benjamin (Pa.)	Printer, publisher	Boston, Mass.	Jan. 17, 1706	Apr. 17, 1790
Gerry, Elbridge (Mass.)	Merchant	Marblehead, Mass.	July 17, 1744	Nov. 23, 1814
Gwinnett, Button (Ga.)	Merchant	Down Hatherly, England	c. 1735	May 19, 1777
Hall, Lyman (Ga.)	Physician	Wallingford, Conn.	Apr. 12, 1724	Oct. 19, 1790
Hancock, John (Mass.)	Merchant	Braintree (Quincy), Mass.	Jan. 12, 1737	Oct. 8, 1793
Harrison, Benjamin (Va.)	Farmer	Berkeley, Va.	Apr. 5, 1726	Apr. 24, 1791
Hart, John (N.J.)	Farmer	Stonington, Conn.	c. 1711	May 11, 1779
Hewes, Joseph (N.C.)	Merchant	Princeton, N.J.	Jan. 23, 1730	Nov. 10, 1779
Heyward, Thos. Jr. (S.C.)	Lawyer, farmer	St. Luke's Parish, S.C.	July 28, 1746	Mar. 6, 1809
Hooper, William (N.C.)	Lawyer	Boston, Mass.	June 28, 1742	Oct. 14, 1790
Hopkins, Stephen (R.I.)	Judge, educator	Providence, R.I.	Mar. 7, 1707	July 13, 1785
Hopkinson, Francis (N.J.)	Judge, author	Philadelphia, Pa.	Sept. 21, 1737	May 9, 1791
Huntington, Samuel (Conn.)	Judge	Windham County, Conn.	July 3, 1731	Jan. 5, 1796
Jefferson, Thomas (Va.)	Lawyer	Shadwell, Va.	Apr. 13, 1743	July 4, 1826
Lee, Francis Lightfoot (Va.)	Farmer	Westmoreland County, Va.	Oct. 14, 1734	Jan. 11, 1797
Lee, Richard Henry (Va.)	Farmer	Westmoreland County, Va.	Jan. 20, 1732	June 19, 1794
Lewis, Francis (N.Y.)	Merchant	Llandaff, Wales	Mar., 1713	Dec. 31, 1802
Livingston, Philip (N.Y.)	Merchant	Albany, N.Y.	Jan. 15, 1716	June 12, 1778
Lynch, Thomas Jr. (S.C.)	Farmer	Winyah, S.C.	Aug. 5, 1749	(at sea) 1779
McKean, Thomas (Del.)	Lawyer	New London, Pa.	Mar. 19, 1734	June 24, 1817
Middleton, Arthur (S.C.)	Farmer	Charleston, S.C.	June 26, 1742	Jan. 1, 1787
Morris, Lewis (N.Y.)	Farmer	Morrisania (Bronx County), N.Y.	Apr. 8, 1726	Jan. 22, 1798
Morris, Robert (Pa.)	Merchant	Liverpool, England	Jan. 20, 1734	May 9, 1806
Morton, John (Pa.)	Judge	Ridley, Pa.	1724	Apr., 1777
Nelson, Thos. Jr. (Va.)	Farmer	Yorktown, Va.	Dec. 26, 1738	Jan. 4, 1789
Paca, William (Md.)	Judge	Abingdon, Md.	Oct. 31, 1740	Oct. 23, 1799
Paine, Robert Treat (Mass.)	Judge	Boston, Mass.	Mar. 11, 1731	May 12, 1814
Penn, John (N.C.)	Lawyer	Near Port Royal, Va.	May 17, 1741	Sept. 14, 1788
Read, George (Del.)	Judge	Near North East, Md.	Sept. 18, 1733	Sept. 21, 1798
Rodney, Caesar (Del.)	Judge	Dover, Del.	Oct. 7, 1728	June 29, 1784
Ross, George (Pa.)	Judge	New Castle, Del.	May 10, 1730	July 14, 1779
Rush, Benjamin (Pa.)	Physician	Byberry, Pa. (Philadelphia)	Dec. 24, 1745	Apr. 19, 1813
Rutledge, Edward (S.C.)	Lawyer	Charleston, S.C.	Nov. 23, 1749	Jan. 23, 1800
Sherman, Roger (Conn.)	Lawyer	Newton, Mass.	Apr. 19, 1721	July 23, 1793
Smith, James (Pa.)	Lawyer	Dublin, Ireland	c. 1719	July 11, 1806
Stockton, Richard (N.J.)	Lawyer	Near Princeton, N.J.	Oct. 1, 1730	Feb. 28, 1781
Stone, Thomas (Md.)	Lawyer	Charles County, Md.	1743	Oct. 5, 1787
Taylor, George (Pa.)	Ironmaster	Ireland	1716	Feb. 23, 1781
Thornton, Matthew (N.H.)	Physician	Ireland	1714	June 24, 1803
Walton, George (Ga.)	Judge	Prince Edward County, Va.	1741	Feb. 2, 1804
Whipple, William (N.H.)	Merchant, judge	Kittery, Me.	Jan. 14, 1730	Nov. 28, 1785
Williams, William (Conn.)	Merchant	Lebanon, Conn.	Apr. 23, 1731	Aug. 2, 1811
Wilson, James (Pa.)	Judge	Carskerdo, Scotland	Sept. 14, 1742	Aug. 28, 1798
Witherspoon, John (N.J.)	Clergyman, educator	Gifford, Scotland	Feb. 5, 1723	Nov. 15, 1794
Wolcott, Oliver (Conn.)	Judge	Windsor, Conn.	Dec. 1, 1726	Dec. 1, 1797
Wythe, George (Va.)	Lawyer	Elizabeth City Co. (Hampton), Va.	1726	June 8, 1806

Constitution of the United States

The Original 7 Articles

PREAMBLE

We, the people of the United States, in order to form a more perfect Union, establish justice, insure domestic tranquility, provide for the common defense, promote the general welfare, and secure the blessings of liberty to ourselves and our posterity do ordain and establish this Constitution for the United States of America.

ARTICLE I.

Section 1—Legislative powers; in whom vested:

All legislative powers herein granted shall be vested in a Congress of the United States, which shall consist of a Senate and House of Representatives.

Section 2—House of Representatives, how and by whom chosen. Qualifications of a Representative. Representatives and direct taxes, how apportioned. Enumeration. Vacancies to be filled. Power of choosing officers, and of impeachment.

1. The House of Representatives shall be composed of members chosen every second year by the people of the several States, and the electors in each State shall have the qualifications requisite for electors of the most numerous branch of the State Legislature.

2. No person shall be a Representative who shall not have attained to the age of twenty-five years, and been seven years a citizen of the United States, and who shall not, when elected, be an inhabitant of that State in which he shall be chosen.

3. *(Representatives and direct taxes shall be apportioned among the several States which may be included within this Union, according to their respective numbers, which shall be determined by adding to the whole number of free persons, including those bound to service for a term of years, and excluding Indians not taxed, three-fifths of all other persons.) (The previous sentence was superseded by Amendment XIV, section 2.)* The actual enumeration shall be made within three years after the first meeting of the Congress of the United States, and within every subsequent term of ten years, in such manner as they shall by law direct. The number of Representatives shall not exceed one for every thirty thousand, but each State shall have at least one Representative; and until such enumeration shall be made, the State of New Hampshire shall be entitled to choose three, Massachusetts eight, Rhode Island and Providence Plantations one, Connecticut five, New York six, New Jersey four, Pennsylvania eight, Delaware one, Maryland six, Virginia ten, North Carolina five, South Carolina five, and Georgia three.

4. When vacancies happen in the representation from any State, the Executive Authority thereof shall issue writs of election to fill such vacancies.

5. The House of Representatives shall choose their Speaker and other officers; and shall have the sole power of impeachment.

Section 3—Senators, how and by whom chosen. How classified. Qualifications of a Senator. President of the Senate, his right to vote. President pro tem., and other officers of the Senate, how chosen. Power to try impeachments. When President is tried, Chief Justice to preside. Sentence.

1. The Senate of the United States shall be composed of two Senators from each State, *(chosen by the Legislature thereof), (The preceding five words were superseded by Amendment XVII, section 1.)* for six years; and each Senator shall have one vote.

2. Immediately after they shall be assembled in consequence of the first election, they shall be divided as equally as may be into three classes. The seats of the Senators of the first class shall be vacated at the expiration of the second year, of the second class at the expiration of the fourth year, and of the third class at the expiration of the sixth year, so that one-third may be chosen every second year; *(and if vacancies happen by resignation, or otherwise, during the recess of the Legislature of any State, the Executive thereof may make temporary appointments until the next meeting of the Legislature, which shall then fill such vacancies.) (The words in parentheses were superseded by Amendment XVII, section 2.)*

3. No person shall be a Senator who shall not have attained to the age of thirty years, and been nine years a citizen of the United States, and who shall not, when elected, be an inhabitant of that State for which he shall be chosen.

4. The Vice President of the United States shall be President of the Senate, but shall have no vote, unless they be equally divided.

5. The Senate shall choose their other officers, and also a President pro tempore, in the absence of the Vice President, or when he shall exercise the office of President of the United States.

6. The Senate shall have the sole power to try all impeachments. When sitting for that purpose, they shall be on oath or affirmation. When the President of the United States is tried, the Chief Justice shall preside: and no person shall be convicted without the concurrence of two-thirds of the members present.

7. Judgment in cases of impeachment shall not extend further than to removal from office, and disqualification to hold and enjoy any office of honor, trust or profit under the United States: but the party convicted shall nevertheless be liable and subject to indictment, trial, judgment and punishment, according to law.

Section 4—Times, etc., of holding elections, how prescribed. One session each year.

1. The times, places and manner of holding elections for Senators and Representatives, shall be prescribed in each State by the Legislature thereof; but the Congress may at any time by law make or alter such regulations, except as to the places of choosing Senators.

2. The Congress shall assemble at least once in every year, and such meeting shall *(be on the first Monday in December,) (The words in parentheses were superseded by Amendment XX, section 2).* unless they shall by law appoint a different day.

Section 5—Membership, quorum, adjournments, rules. Power to punish or expel. Journal. Time of adjournments, how limited, etc.

1. Each House shall be the judge of the elections, returns and qualifications of its own members, and a majority of each shall constitute a quorum to do business; but a smaller number may adjourn from day to day, and may be authorized to compel the attendance of absent members, in such manner, and under such penalties as each House may provide.

2. Each House may determine the rules of its proceedings, punish its members for disorderly behavior, and, with the concurrence of two-thirds, expel a member.

3. Each House shall keep a journal of its proceedings, and from time to time publish the same, excepting such parts as may in their judgment require secrecy; and the yeas and nays of the members of either House on any question shall, at the desire of one-fifth of those present, be entered on the journal.

4. Neither House, during the session of Congress, shall, without the consent of the other, adjourn for more than three days, nor to any other place than that in which the two Houses shall be sitting.

Section 6—Compensation, privileges, disqualifications in certain cases.

1. The Senators and Representatives shall receive a compensation for their services, to be ascertained by law, and paid out of the Treasury of the United States. They shall in all cases, except treason, felony and breach of the peace, be privileged from arrest during their attendance at the session of their respective Houses, and in going to and returning from the same; and for any speech or debate in either House, they shall not be questioned in any other place.

2. No Senator or Representative shall, during the time for which he was elected, be appointed to any civil office under the authority of the United States, which shall have been created, or the emoluments whereof shall have been increased during such time; and no person holding any office under the United States, shall be a member of either House

during his continuance in office.

Section 7—House to originate all revenue bills. Veto. Bill may be passed by two-thirds of each House, notwithstanding, etc. Bill, not returned in ten days, to become a law. Provisions as to orders, concurrent resolutions, etc.

1. All bills for raising revenue shall originate in the House of Representatives; but the Senate may propose or concur with amendments as on other bills.

2. Every bill which shall have passed the House of Representatives and the Senate, shall, before it becomes a law, be presented to the President of the United States; if he approves he shall sign it, but if not he shall return it, with his objections to that House in which it shall have originated, who shall enter the objections at large on their journal, and proceed to reconsider it. If after such reconsideration two-thirds of that House shall agree to pass the bill, it shall be sent, together with the objections, to the other House, by which it shall likewise be reconsidered, and if approved by two-thirds of that House, it shall become a law. But in all such cases the votes of both Houses shall be determined by yeas and nays, and the names of the persons voting for and against the bill shall be entered on the journal of each House respectively. If any bill shall not be returned by the President within ten days (Sundays excepted) after it shall have been presented to him, the same shall be a law, in like manner as if he had signed it, unless the Congress by their adjournment prevent its return, in which case it shall not be a law.

3. Every order, resolution, or vote to which the concurrence of the Senate and House of Representatives may be necessary (except on a question of adjournment) shall be presented to the President of the United States; and before the same shall take effect, shall be approved by him, or being disapproved by him, shall be repassed by two-thirds of the Senate and House of Representatives, according to the rules and limitations prescribed in the case of a bill.

Section 8—Powers of Congress.

The Congress shall have power

1. To lay and collect taxes, duties, imposts and excises, to pay the debts and provide for the common defense and general welfare of the United States; but all duties, imposts and excises shall be uniform throughout the United States;

2. To borrow money on the credit of the United States;

3. To regulate commerce with foreign nations, and among the several States, and with the Indian tribes;

4. To establish a uniform rule of naturalization, and uniform laws on the subject of bankruptcies throughout the United States;

5. To coin money, regulate the value thereof, and of foreign coin, and fix the standard of weights and measures;

6. To provide for the punishment of counterfeiting the securities and current coin of the United States;

7. To establish post-offices and post-roads;

8. To promote the progress of science and useful arts, by securing for limited times to authors and inventors the exclusive right to their respective writings and discoveries;

9. To constitute tribunals inferior to the Supreme Court;

10. To define and punish piracies and felonies committed on the high seas, and offenses against the law of nations;

11. To declare war, grant letters of marque and reprisal, and make rules concerning captures on land and water;

12. To raise and support armies, but no appropriation of money to that use shall be for a longer term than two years;

13. To provide and maintain a navy;

14. To make rules for the government and regulation of the land and naval forces;

15. To provide for calling forth the militia to execute the laws of the Union, suppress insurrections and repel invasions;

16. To provide for organizing, arming, and disciplining the militia, and for governing such part of them as may be employed in the service of the United States, reserving to the States respectively, the appointment of the officers, and the authority of training the militia according to the discipline prescribed by Congress;

17. To exercise exclusive legislation in all cases whatsoever, over such district (not exceeding ten miles square) as may, by cession of particular States, and the acceptance of Congress, become the seat of the Government of the United States, and to exercise like authority over all places purchased by the consent of the Legislature of the State in which the same shall be, for the erection of forts, magazines, arsenals, dockyards, and other needful buildings;—And

18. To make all laws which shall be necessary and proper for carrying into execution the foregoing powers, and all other powers vested by this Constitution in the Government of the United States, or in any department or officer thereof.

Section 9—Provision as to migration or importation of certain persons. Habeas corpus, bills of attainder, etc. Taxes, how apportioned. No export duty. No commercial preference. Money, how drawn from Treasury, etc. No titular nobility. Officers not to receive presents, etc.

1. The migration or importation of such persons as any of the States now existing shall think proper to admit, shall not be prohibited by the Congress prior to the year one thousand eight hundred and eight, but a tax or duty may be imposed on such importation, not exceeding ten dollars for each person.

2. The privilege of the writ of habeas corpus shall not be suspended, unless when in cases of rebellion or invasion the public safety may require it.

3. No bill of attainder or ex post facto law shall be passed.

4. No capitation, or other direct, tax shall be laid, unless in proportion to the census or enumeration herein before directed to be taken. *(Modified by Amendment XVI.)*

5. No tax or duty shall be laid on articles exported from any State.

6. No preference shall be given by any regulation of commerce or revenue to the ports of one State over those of another: nor shall vessels bound to, or from, one State, be obliged to enter, clear, or pay duties in another.

7. No money shall be drawn from the Treasury, but in consequence of appropriations made by law; and a regular statement and account of the receipts and expenditures of all public money shall be published from time to time.

8. No title of nobility shall be granted by the United States: and no person holding any office of profit or trust under them, shall, without the consent of the Congress, accept of any present, emolument, office, or title, of any kind whatever, from any king, prince, or foreign state.

Section 10—States prohibited from the exercise of certain powers.

1. No State shall enter into any treaty, alliance, or confederation; grant letters of marque and reprisal; coin money; emit bills of credit; make anything but gold and silver coin a tender in payment of debts; pass any bill of attainder, ex post facto law, or law impairing the obligation of contracts, or grant any title of nobility.

2. No State shall, without the consent of the Congress, lay any imposts or duties on imports or exports, except what may be absolutely necessary for executing its inspection laws: and the net produce of all duties and imposts, laid by any State on imports or exports, shall be for the use of the Treasury of the United States; and all such laws shall be subject to the revision and control of the Congress.

3. No State shall, without the consent of Congress, lay any duty of tonnage, keep troops, or ships of war in time of peace, enter into any agreement or compact with another State, or with a foreign power, or engage in war, unless actually invaded, or in such imminent danger as will not admit of delay.

ARTICLE II.

Section 1—President: his term of office. Electors of President; number and how appointed. Electors to vote on same day. Qualification of President. On whom his duties devolve in case of his removal, death, etc. President's compensation. His oath of office.

1. The Executive power shall be vested in a President of the United States of America. He shall hold his office during the term of four years, and together with the Vice President, chosen for the same term, be elected as follows

2. Each State shall appoint, in such manner as the Legis-

lature thereof may direct, a number of electors, equal to the whole number of Senators and Representatives to which the State may be entitled in the Congress: but no Senator or Representative, or person holding an office of trust or profit under the United States, shall be appointed an elector.

(The electors shall meet in their respective States, and vote by ballot for two persons, of whom one at least shall not be an inhabitant of the same State with themselves. And they shall make a list of all the persons voted for, and of the number of votes for each; which list they shall sign and certify, and transmit sealed to the seat of the Government of the United States, directed to the President of the Senate. The President of the Senate shall, in the presence of the Senate and House of Representatives, open all the certificates, and the votes shall then be counted. The person having the greatest number of votes shall be the President, if such number be a majority of the whole number of electors appointed; and if there be more than one who have such majority, and have an equal number of votes, then the House of Representatives shall immediately choose by ballot one of them for President; and if no person have a majority, then from the five highest on the list the said House shall in like manner choose the President. But in choosing the President, the votes shall be taken by States, the representation from each State having one vote; a quorum for this purpose shall consist of a member or members from two-thirds of the States, and a majority of all the States shall be necessary to a choice. In every case, after the choice of the President, the person having the greatest number of votes of the electors shall be the Vice President. But if there should remain two or more who have equal votes, the Senate shall choose from them by ballot the Vice President.)

(This clause was superseded by Amendment XII.)

3. The Congress may determine the time of choosing the electors, and the day on which they shall give their votes; which day shall be the same throughout the United States.

4. No person except a natural born citizen, or a citizen of the United States, at the time of the adoption of this Constitution, shall be eligible to the office of President; neither shall any person be eligible to that office who shall not have attained to the age of thirty-five years, and been fourteen years a resident within the United States.

(For qualification of the Vice President, see Amendment XII.)

5. In case of the removal of the President from office, or of his death, resignation, or inability to discharge the powers and duties of the said office, the same shall devolve on the Vice President, and the Congress may by law provide for the case of removal, death, resignation or inability, both of the President and Vice President, declaring what officer shall then act as President, and such officer shall act accordingly, until the disability be removed, or a President shall be elected.

(This clause has been modified by Amendments XX and XXV.)

6. The President shall, at stated times, receive for his services, a compensation, which shall neither be increased nor diminished during the period for which he shall have been elected, and he shall not receive within that period any other emolument from the United States, or any of them.

7. Before he enter on the execution of his office, he shall take the following oath or affirmation:

"I do solemnly swear (or affirm) that I will faithfully execute the office of President of the United States, and will to the best of my ability, preserve, protect and defend the Constitution of the United States."

Section 2—President to be Commander-in-Chief. He may require opinions of cabinet officers, etc., may pardon. Treaty-making power. Nomination of certain officers. When President may fill vacancies.

1. The President shall be Commander-in-Chief of the Army and Navy of the United States, and of the militia of the several States, when called into the actual service of the United States; he may require the opinion, in writing, of the principal officer in each of the executive departments, upon any subject relating to the duties of their respective offices, and he shall have power to grant reprieves and pardons for offenses against the United States, except in cases of impeachment.

2. He shall have power, by and with the advice and consent of the Senate, to make treaties, provided two-thirds of the Senators present concur; and he shall nominate, and by and with the advice and consent of the Senate, shall appoint ambassadors, other public ministers and consuls, judges of the Supreme Court, and all other officers of the United States, whose appointments are not herein otherwise provided for, and which shall be established by law: but the Congress may by law vest the appointment of such inferior officers, as they think proper, in the President alone, in the courts of law, or in the heads of departments.

3. The President shall have power to fill up all vacancies that may happen during the recess of the Senate, by granting commissions, which shall expire at the end of their next session.

Section 3—President shall communicate to Congress. He may convene and adjourn Congress, in case of disagreement, etc. Shall receive ambassadors, execute laws, and commission officers.

He shall from time to time give to the Congress information of the state of the Union, and recommend to their consideration such measures as he shall judge necessary and expedient; he may, on extraordinary occasions, convene both Houses, or either of them, and in case of disagreement between them, with respect to the time of adjournment, he may adjourn them to such time as he shall think proper; he shall receive ambassadors and other public ministers; he shall take care that the laws be faithfully executed, and shall commission all the officers of the United States.

Section 4—All civil offices forfeited for certain crimes.

The President, Vice President, and all civil officers of the United States, shall be removed from office on impeachment for, and conviction of, treason, bribery, or other high crimes and misdemeanors.

ARTICLE III.

Section 1—Judicial powers, Tenure. Compensation.

The judicial power of the United States, shall be vested in one Supreme Court, and in such inferior courts as the Congress may from time to time ordain and establish. The judges, both of the Supreme and inferior courts, shall hold their offices during good behavior, and shall at stated times, receive for their services, a compensation, which shall not be diminished during their continuance in office.

Section 2—Judicial power; to what cases it extends. Original jurisdiction of Supreme Court; appellate jurisdiction. Trial by jury, etc. Trial, where.

1. The judicial power shall extend to all cases, in law and equity, arising under this Constitution, the laws of the United States, and treaties made, or which shall be made, under their authority; to all cases affecting ambassadors, other public ministers and consuls; to all cases of admiralty and maritime jurisdiction; to controversies to which the United States shall be a party; to controversies between two or more States; between a State and citizens of another State; between citizens of different States, between citizens of the same State claiming lands under grants of different States, and between a State, or the citizens thereof, and foreign states, citizens or subjects.

(This section is modified by Amendment XI.)

2. In all cases affecting ambassadors, other public ministers and consuls, and those in which a State shall be party, the Supreme Court shall have original jurisdiction. In all the other cases before mentioned, the Supreme Court shall have appellate jurisdiction, both as to law and fact, with such exceptions, and under such regulations as the Congress shall make.

3. The trial of all crimes, except in cases of impeachment, shall be by jury; and such trial shall be held in the State where the said crimes shall have been committed; but when not committed within any State, the trial shall be at such place or places as the Congress may by law have directed.

Section 3—Treason Defined, Proof of, Punishment of.

1. Treason against the United States, shall consist only in levying war against them, or in adhering to their enemies,

giving them aid and comfort. No person shall be convicted of treason unless on the testimony of two witnesses to the same overt act, or on confession in open court.

2. The Congress shall have power to declare the punishment of treason, but no attainder of treason shall work corruption of blood, or forfeiture except during the life of the person attainted.

ARTICLE IV.

Section 1—Each State to give credit to the public acts, etc., of every other State.

Full faith and credit shall be given in each State to the public acts, records, and judicial proceedings of every other State. And the Congress may by general laws prescribe the manner in which such acts, records and proceedings shall be proved, and the effect thereof.

Section 2—Privileges of citizens of each State. Fugitives from justice to be delivered up. Persons held to service having escaped, to be delivered up.

1. The citizens of each State shall be entitled to all privileges and immunities of citizens in the several States.

2. A person charged in any State with treason, felony, or other crime, who shall flee from justice, and be found in another State, shall on demand of the Executive authority of the State from which he fled, be delivered up, to be removed to the State having jurisdiction of the crime.

(3. No person held to service or labor in one State, under the laws thereof, escaping into another, shall in consequence of any law or regulation therein, be discharged from such service or labor, but shall be delivered up on claim of the party to whom such service or labor may be due.) (This clause was superseded by Amendment XIII.)

Section 3—Admission of new States. Power of Congress over territory and other property.

1. New States may be admitted by the Congress into this Union; but no new State shall be formed or erected within the jurisdiction of any other State; nor any State be formed by the junction of two or more States, or parts of States, without the consent of the Legislatures of the States concerned as well as of the Congress.

2. The Congress shall have power to dispose of and make all needful rules and regulations respecting the territory or other property belonging to the United States; and nothing in this Constitution shall be so construed as to prejudice any claims of the United States, or of any particular State.

Section 4—Republican form of government guaranteed. Each state to be protected.

The United States shall guarantee to every State in this Union a Republican form of government, and shall protect each of them against invasion; and on application of the Legislature, or of the Executive (when the Legislature cannot be convened) against domestic violence.

ARTICLE V.

Constitution: how amended; proviso.

The Congress, whenever two-thirds of both Houses shall deem it necessary, shall propose amendments to this Constitution, or, on the application of the Legislatures of two-thirds of the several States, shall call a convention for proposing amendments, which, in either case, shall be valid to all intents and purposes, as part of this Constitution, when ratified by the Legislatures of three-fourths of the several States, or by conventions in three-fourths thereof, as the one or the other mode of ratification may be proposed by the Congress; provided that no amendment which may be made prior to the year one thousand eight hundred and eight shall in any manner affect the first and fourth clauses in the Ninth Section of the First Article; and that no State, without its consent, shall be deprived of its equal suffrage in the Senate.

ARTICLE VI.

Certain debts, etc., declared valid. Supremacy of Constitution, treaties, and laws of the United States. Oath to support Constitution, by whom taken. No religious test.

1. All debts contracted and engagements entered into, before the adoption of this Constitution, shall be as valid against the United States under this Constitution, as under the Confederation.

2. This Constitution, and the laws of the United States which shall be made in pursuance thereof; and all treaties made, or which shall be made, under the authority of the United States, shall be the supreme law of the land; and the judges in every State shall be bound thereby, any thing in the Constitution or laws of any State to the contrary notwithstanding.

3. The Senators and Representatives before mentioned, and the members of the several State Legislatures, and all executive and judicial officers, both of the United States and of the several States, shall be bound by oath or affirmation, to support this Constitution; but no religious test shall ever be required as a qualification to any office or public trust under the United States.

ARTICLE VII.

What ratification shall establish Constitution.

The ratification of the Conventions of nine States, shall be sufficient for the establishment of this Constitution between the States so ratifying the same.

Done in convention by the unanimous consent of the States present the Seventeenth day of September in the year of our Lord one thousand seven hundred and eighty seven, and of the independence of the United States of America the Twelfth. In witness whereof we have hereunto subscribed our names.

George Washington, President and deputy from Virginia.

New Hampshire—John Langdon, Nicholas Gilman.

Massachusetts—Nathaniel Gorham, Rufus King.

Connecticut—Wm. Saml. Johnson, Roger Sherman.

New York—Alexander Hamilton.

New Jersey—Wil. Livingston, David Brearley, Wm. Paterson, Jona: Dayton.

Pennsylvania—B. Franklin, Thomas Mifflin, Robt. Morris, Geo. Clymer, Thos. FitzSimons, Jared Ingersoll, James Wilson, Gouv. Morris.

Delaware—Geo: Read, Gunning Bedford Jun., John Dickinson, Richard Bassett, Jaco: Broom.

Maryland—James McHenry, Daniel of Saint Thomas' Jenifer, Danl. Carroll.

Virginia—John Blair, James Madison Jr.

North Carolina—Wm. Blount, Rich'd. Dobbs Spaight, Hugh Williamson.

South Carolina—J. Rutledge, Charles Cotesworth Pinckney, Charles Pinckney, Pierce Butler.

Georgia—William Few, Abr. Baldwin.

Attest: William Jackson, Secretary.

Ten Original Amendments: The Bill of Rights

In force Dec. 15, 1791

(The First Congress, at its first session in the City of New York, Sept. 25, 1789, submitted to the states 12 amendments to clarify certain individual and state rights not named in the Constitution. They are generally called the Bill of Rights.

(Influential in framing these amendments was the Declaration of Rights of Virginia, written by George Mason (1725-1792) in 1776. Mason, a Virginia delegate to the Constitutional Convention, did not sign the Constitution and opposed its ratification on the ground that it did not sufficiently oppose slavery or safeguard individual rights.

(In the preamble to the resolution offering the proposed amendments, Congress said: "The conventions of a number of the States having at the time of their adopting the Constitution, expressed a desire, in order to prevent misconstruction or abuse of its powers, that further declaratory and restrictive clauses should be added, and as extending the ground of public confidence in the government will best insure the beneficent ends of its institution, be it resolved," etc.

(Ten of these amendments now commonly known as one to 10 inclusive, but originally 3 to 12 inclusive, were ratified by the states as follows: New Jersey, Nov. 20, 1789; Maryland, Dec. 19, 1789; North Carolina, Dec. 22, 1789; South Carolina, Jan. 19, 1790; New Hampshire, Jan 25, 1790; Delaware, Jan 28, 1790; New York, Feb. 27, 1790; Pennsylvania, Mar. 10, 1790; Rhode

Island, June 7, 1790; Vermont, Nov 3, 1791; Virginia, Dec. 15, 1791; Massachusetts, Mar. 2, 1939; Georgia, Mar. 18, 1939; Connecticut, Apr. 19, 1939. These original 10 ratified amendments follow as Amendments I to X inclusive.

(Of the two original proposed amendments which were not ratified by the necessary number of states, the first related to apportionment of Representatives; the second, to compensation of members. See p. 451.)

AMENDMENT I.

Religious establishment prohibited. Freedom of speech, of the press, and right to petition.

Congress shall make no law respecting an establishment of religion, or prohibiting the free exercise thereof; or abridging the freedom of speech, or of the press; or the right of the people peaceably to assemble, and to petition the Government for a redress of grievances.

AMENDMENT II.

Right to keep and bear arms.

A well-regulated militia, being necessary to the security of a free State, the right of the people to keep and bear arms, shall not be infringed.

AMENDMENT III.

Conditions for quarters for soldiers.

No soldier shall, in time of peace be quartered in any house, without the consent of the owner, nor in time of war, but in a manner to be prescribed by law.

AMENDMENT IV.

Right of search and seizure regulated.

The right of the people to be secure in their persons, houses, papers, and effects, against unreasonable searches and seizures, shall not be violated, and no warrants shall issue, but upon probable cause, supported by oath or affirmation, and particularly describing the place to be searched, and the persons or things to be seized.

AMENDMENT V.

Provisions concerning prosecution. Trial and punishment—private property not to be taken for public use without compensation.

No person shall be held to answer for a capital, or otherwise infamous crime, unless on a presentment or indictment of a Grand Jury, except in cases arising in the land or naval forces, or in the militia, when in actual service in time of war or public danger; nor shall any person be subject for the same offense to be twice put in jeopardy of life or limb; nor shall be compelled in any criminal case to be a witness against himself, nor be deprived of life, liberty, or property, without due process of law; nor shall private property be taken for public use without just compensation.

AMENDMENT VI.

Right to speedy trial, witnesses, etc.

In all criminal prosecutions, the accused shall enjoy the right to a speedy and public trial, by an impartial jury of the State and district wherein the crime shall have been committed, which district shall have been previously ascertained by law, and to be informed of the nature and cause of the accusation; to be confronted with the witnesses against him; to have compulsory process for obtaining witnesses in his favor, and to have the assistance of counsel for his defense.

AMENDMENT VII.

Right of trial by jury.

In suits at common law, where the value in controversy shall exceed twenty dollars, the right of trial by jury shall be preserved, and no fact tried by a jury shall be otherwise reexamined in any court of the United States, than according to the rules of the common law.

AMENDMENT VIII.

Excessive bail or fines and cruel punishment prohibited.

Excessive bail shall not be required, nor excessive fines imposed, nor cruel and unusual punishments inflicted.

AMENDMENT IX.

Rule of construction of Constitution.

The enumeration in the Constitution, of certain rights, shall not be construed to deny or disparage others retained by the people.

AMENDMENT X.

Rights of States under Constitution.

The powers not delegated to the United States by the Constitution, nor prohibited by it to the States, are reserved to the States respectively, or to the people.

Amendments Since the Bill of Rights

AMENDMENT XI.

Judicial powers construed.

The judicial power of the United States shall not be construed to extend to any suit in law or equity, commenced or prosecuted against one of the United States by citizens of another State, or by citizens or subjects of any foreign state.

(This amendment was proposed to the Legislatures of the several States by the Third Congress on March 4, 1794, and was declared to have been ratified in a message from the President to Congress, dated Jan. 8, 1798.

(It was on Jan 5, 1798, that Secretary of State Pickering received from 12 of the States authenticated ratifications, and informed President John Adams of that fact.

(As a result of later research in the Department of State, it is now established that Amendment XI became part of the Constitution on Feb. 7, 1795, for on that date it had been ratified by 12 States as follows:

(1. New York, Mar. 27, 1794. 2. Rhode Island, Mar. 31, 1794. 3. Connecticut, May 8, 1794. 4. New Hampshire, June 16, 1794. 5. Massachusetts, June 26, 1794. 6. Vermont, between Oct 9, 1794, and Nov. 9, 1794. 7. Virginia, Nov. 18, 1794. 8. Georgia, Nov. 29, 1794. 9. Kentucky, Dec. 7, 1794. 10. Maryland, Dec. 26, 1794. 11. Delaware, Jan 23, 1795. 12. North Carolina, Feb. 7, 1795.

(On June 1, 1796, more than a year after Amendment XI had become a part of the Constitution (but before anyone was officially aware of this), Tennessee had been admitted as a State; but not until Oct. 16, 1797, was a certified copy of the resolution of Congress proposing the amendment sent to the Governor of Tennessee (John Sevier) by Secretary of State Pickering, whose office was then at Trenton, New Jersey, because of the epidemic of yellow fever at Philadelphia; it seems, however, that the Legislature of Tennessee took no action on Amendment XI, owing doubtless to the fact that public announcement of its adoption was made soon thereafter.

(Besides the necessary 12 States, one other, South Carolina, ratified Amendment XI, but this action was not taken until Dec. 4, 1797; the two remaining States, New Jersey and Pennsylvania, failed to ratify.)

AMENDMENT XII.

Manner of choosing President and Vice-President.

(Proposed by Congress Dec. 9, 1803; ratification completed June 15, 1804.)

The Electors shall meet in their respective States and vote by ballot for President and Vice-President, one of whom, at least, shall not be an inhabitant of the same State with themselves; they shall name in their ballots the person voted for as President, and in distinct ballots the person voted for as Vice-President, and they shall make distinct lists of all persons voted for as President, and of all persons voted for as Vice-President, and of the number of votes for each, which lists they shall sign and certify, and transmit sealed to the seat of the Government of the United States, directed to the President of the Senate; the President of the Senate shall, in the presence of the Senate and House of Representatives, open all the certificates and the votes shall then be counted;—The person having the greatest number of votes for President, shall be the President, if such number be a majority of the whole number of Electors appointed; and if no person have such majority, then from the persons having the highest numbers not exceeding three on the list of those voted for as President, the House of Representatives shall choose immediately, by ballot, the President. But in choosing the President, the votes shall be taken by States, the representation from each State having one vote; a quorum for this purpose shall consist of a member or members from two-thirds of the States, and a majority of all the States shall be necessary to a choice. *(And if the House of Representatives shall not choose a President whenever the right of choice shall devolve upon them, before the fourth day of March next following, then the Vice-President shall act as President, as in the case of the death or other constitutional disability of the President.) (The words in parentheses were superseded by Amendment XX, section 3.)* The person having the greatest number of votes as Vice-President, shall be the Vice-President, if such number be a majority of the whole number of Electors appointed, and if no person have a majority, then from the two highest numbers on the list, the Senate shall choose the Vice-President; a quorum for the purpose shall consist of two-thirds of the whole number of Senators, and a majority of the whole number shall be necessary to a choice. But no person constitutionally ineligible to the office of President shall be eligible to that of Vice-President of the United States.

THE RECONSTRUCTION AMENDMENTS

(Amendments XIII, XIV, and XV are commonly known as the Reconstruction Amendments, inasmuch as they followed the Civil War, and were drafted by Republicans who were bent on imposing their own policy of reconstruction on the South. Post-bellum legislatures there—Mississippi, South Carolina, Georgia, for example—had set up laws which, it was charged, were contrived to perpetuate Negro slavery under other names.)

AMENDMENT XIII.

Slavery abolished.

(Proposed by Congress Jan. 31, 1865; ratification completed Dec. 18, 1865. The amendment, when first proposed by a resolution in Congress, was passed by the Senate, 38 to 6, on Apr. 8, 1864, but was defeated in the House, 95 to 66 on June 15, 1864. On reconsideration by the House, on Jan. 31, 1865, the resolution passed, 119 to 56. It was approved by President Lincoln on Feb. 1, 1865, although the Supreme Court had decided in 1798 that the President has nothing to do with the proposing of amendments to the Constitution, or their adoption.)

1. Neither slavery nor involuntary servitude, except as a punishment for crime whereof the party shall have been duly convicted, shall exist within the United States or any place subject to their jurisdiction.

2. Congress shall have power to enforce this article by appropriate legislation.

AMENDMENT XIV.

Citizenship rights not to be abridged.

(The following amendment was proposed to the Legislatures of the several states by the 39th Congress, June 13, 1866, and was declared to have been ratified in a proclamation by the Secretary of State, July 28, 1868.

(The 14th amendment was adopted only by virtue of ratification subsequent to earlier rejections. Newly constituted legislatures in both North Carolina and South Carolina (respectively July 4 and 9, 1868), ratified the proposed amendment, although earlier legislatures had rejected the proposal. The Secretary of State issued a proclamation, which, though doubtful as to the effect of attempted withdrawals by Ohio and New Jersey, entertained no doubt as to the validity of the ratification by North and South Carolina. The following day (July 21, 1868), Congress passed a resolution which declared the 14th Amendment to be a part of the Constitution and directed the Secretary of State so to promulgate it. The Secretary waited, however, until the newly constituted Legislature of Georgia had ratified the amendment, subsequent to an earlier rejection, before the promulgation of the ratification of the new amendment.)

1. All persons born or naturalized in the United States, and subject to the jurisdiction thereof, are citizens of the United States and of the State wherein they reside. No State shall make or enforce any law which shall abridge the privileges or immunities of citizens of the United States; nor shall any State deprive any person of life, liberty, or property, without due process of law; nor deny to any person within its jurisdiction the equal protection of the laws.

2. Representatives shall be apportioned among the several States according to their respective numbers, counting the whole number of persons in each State, excluding Indians not taxed. But when the right to vote at any election for the choice of Electors for President and Vice-President of the United States, Representatives in Congress, the executive and judicial officers of a State, or the members of the Legislature thereof, is denied to any of the male inhabitants of such State, being twenty-one years of age, and, citizens of the United States, or in any way abridged, except for participation in rebellion, or other crime, the basis of representation therein shall be reduced in the proportion which the number of such male citizens shall bear to the whole number of male citizens twenty-one years of age in such State.

3. No person shall be a Senator or Representative in Congress, or Elector of President and Vice-President, or hold any office, civil or military, under the United States, or under any State, who, having previously taken an oath, as a member of Congress, or as an officer of the United States, or as a member of any State Legislature, or as an executive or judicial officer of any State, to support the Constitution of the United States, shall have engaged in insurrection or rebellion against the same, or given aid or comfort to the enemies thereof. But Congress may by a vote of two-thirds of each House, remove such disability.

4. The validity of the public debt of the United States, authorized by law, including debts incurred for payment of pensions and bounties for services in suppressing insurrection or rebellion, shall not be questioned. But neither the United States nor any State shall assume or pay any debt or obligation incurred in aid of insurrection or rebellion against the United States, or any claim for the loss or emancipation of any slave; but all such debts, obligations and claims, shall be held illegal and void.

5. The Congress shall have power to enforce, by appropriate legislation, the provisions of this article.

AMENDMENT XV.

Race no bar to voting rights.

(The following amendment was proposed to the legislatures of the several States by the 40th Congress, Feb. 26, 1869, and was declared to have been ratified in a proclamation by the Secretary of State, Mar. 30, 1870.)

1. The right of citizens of the United States to vote shall not be denied or abridged by the United States or by any State on account of race, color, or previous condition of servitude.

2. The Congress shall have power to enforce this article by appropriate legislation.

AMENDMENT XVI.

Income taxes authorized.

(Proposed by Congress July 12, 1909; ratification declared by the Secretary of State Feb. 25, 1913.)

The Congress shall have power to lay and collect taxes on incomes, from whatever source derived, without apportionment among the several States, and without regard to any census or enumeration.

AMENDMENT XVII.

United States Senators to be elected by direct popular vote.

(Proposed by Congress May 13, 1912; ratification declared by the Secretary of State May 31, 1913.)

1. The Senate of the United States shall be composed of two Senators from each State, elected by the people thereof, for six years; and each Senator shall have one vote. The electors in each State shall have the qualifications requisite for electors of the most numerous branch of the State Legislatures.

2. When vacancies happen in the representation of any State in the Senate, the executive authority of such State shall issue writs of election to fill such vacancies: Provided, That the Legislature of any State may empower the Executive thereof to make temporary appointments until the peo-

ple fill the vacancies by election as the Legislature may direct.

3. This amendment shall not be so construed as to affect the election or term of any Senator chosen before it becomes valid as part of the Constitution.

AMENDMENT XVIII.

Liquor prohibition amendment.

(Proposed by Congress Dec. 18, 1917; ratification completed Jan. 16, 1919. Repealed by Amendment XXI, effective Dec. 5, 1933.)

(1. After one year from the ratification of this article the manufacture, sale, or transportation of intoxicating liquors within, the importation thereof into, or the exportation thereof from the United States and all territory subject to the jurisdiction thereof for beverage purposes is hereby prohibited.

(2. The Congress and the several States shall have concurrent power to enforce this article by appropriate legislation.

(3. This article shall be inoperative unless it shall have been ratified as an amendment to the Constitution by the Legislatures of the several States, as provided in the Constitution, within seven years from the date of the submission hereof to the States by the Congress.)

(The total vote in the Senates of the various States was 1,310 for, 237 against—84.6% dry. In the lower houses of the States the vote was 3,782 for, 1,035 against—78.5% dry.

(The amendment ultimately was adopted by all the States except Connecticut and Rhode Island.)

AMENDMENT XIX.

Giving nationwide suffrage to women.

(Proposed by Congress June 4, 1919; ratification certified by Secretary of State Aug. 26, 1920.)

1. The right of citizens of the United States to vote shall not be denied or abridged by the United States or by any State on account of sex.

2. Congress shall have power to enforce this Article by appropriate legislation.

AMENDMENT XX.

Terms of President and Vice President to begin on Jan. 20; those of Senators, Representatives, Jan. 3.

(Proposed by Congress Mar. 2, 1932; ratification completed Jan. 23, 1933.)

1. The terms of the President and Vice President shall end at noon on the 20th day of January, and the terms of Senators and Representatives at noon on the 3rd day of January, of the years in which such terms would have ended if this article had not been ratified; and the terms of their successors shall then begin.

2. The Congress shall assemble at least once in every year, and such meeting shall begin at noon on the 3rd day of January, unless they shall by law appoint a different day.

3. If, at the time fixed for the beginning of the term of the President, the President elect shall have died, the Vice President elect shall become President. If a President shall not have been chosen before the time fixed for the beginning of his term, or if the President elect shall have failed to qualify, then the Vice President elect shall act as President until a President shall have qualified; and the Congress may by law provide for the case wherein neither a President elect nor a Vice President elect shall have qualified, declaring who shall then act as President, or the manner in which one who is to act shall be selected, and such person shall act accordingly until a President or Vice President shall have qualified.

4. The Congress may by law provide for the case of the death of any of the persons from whom the House of Representatives may choose a President whenever the right of choice shall have devolved upon them, and for the case of the death of any of the persons from whom the Senate may choose a Vice President whenever the right of choice shall have devolved upon them.

5. Sections 1 and 2 shall take effect on the 15th day of October following the ratification of this article (Oct., 1933).

6. This article shall be inoperative unless it shall have been ratified as an amendment to the Constitution by the Legislatures of three-fourths of the several States within seven years from the date of its submission.

AMENDMENT XXI.

Repeal of Amendment XVIII.

(Proposed by Congress Feb. 20, 1933; ratification completed Dec. 5, 1933.)

1. The eighteenth article of amendment to the Constitution of the United States is hereby repealed.

2. The transportation or importation into any State, Territory, or Possession of the United States for delivery or use therein of intoxicating liquors, in violation of the laws thereof, is hereby prohibited.

3. This article shall be inoperative unless it shall have been ratified as an amendment to the Constitution by conventions in the several States, as provided in the Constitution, within seven years from the date of the submission hereof to the States by the Congress.

AMENDMENT XXII.

Limiting Presidential terms of office.

(Proposed by Congress Mar. 24, 1947; ratification completed Feb. 27, 1951.)

1. No person shall be elected to the office of the President more than twice, and no person who has held the office of President, or acted as President, for more than two years of a term to which some other person was elected President shall be elected to the office of the President more than once. But this Article shall not apply to any person holding the office of President when this Article was proposed by the Congress, and shall not prevent any person who may be holding the office of President, or acting as President, during the term within which this Article becomes operative from holding the office of President or acting as President during the remainder of such term.

2. This article shall be inoperative unless it shall have been ratified as an amendment to the Constitution by the Legislatures of three-fourths of the several States within seven years from the date of its submission to the States by the Congress.

AMENDMENT XXIII.

Presidential vote for District of Columbia.

(Proposed by Congress June 16, 1960; ratification completed Mar. 29, 1961.)

1. The District constituting the seat of Government of the United States shall appoint in such manner as the Congress may direct:

A number of electors of President and Vice President equal to the whole number of Senators and Representatives in Congress to which the District would be entitled if it were a State, but in no event more than the least populous State; they shall be in addition to those appointed by the States, but they shall be considered, for the purposes of the election of President and Vice President, to be electors appointed by a State; and they shall meet in the District and perform such duties as provided by the twelfth article of amendment.

2. The Congress shall have power to enforce this article by appropriate legislation.

AMENDMENT XXIV.

Barring poll tax in federal elections.

(Proposed by Congress Aug. 27, 1962; ratification completed Jan. 23, 1964.)

1. The right of citizens of the United States to vote in any primary or other election for President or Vice President, for electors for President or Vice President, or for Senator or Representative in Congress, shall not be denied or abridged by the United States or any State by reason of failure to pay any poll tax or other tax.

2. The Congress shall have power to enforce this article by appropriate legislation.

AMENDMENT XXV.

Presidential disability and succession.

(Proposed by Congress July 6, 1965; ratification completed Feb. 10, 1967.)

1. In case of the removal of the President from office or of his death or resignation, the Vice President shall become President.

2. Whenever there is a vacancy in the office of the Vice President, the President shall nominate a Vice President who shall take office upon confirmation by a majority vote of both houses of Congress.

3. Whenever the President transmits to the President pro tempore of the Senate and the Speaker of the House of Representatives his written declaration that he is unable to discharge the powers and duties of his office, and until he transmits to them a written declaration to the contrary, such powers and duties shall be discharged by the Vice President as Acting President.

4. Whenever the Vice President and a majority of either the principal officers of the executive departments or of such other body as Congress may by law provide, transmit to the President pro tempore of the Senate and the Speaker of the House of Representatives their written declaration that the President is unable to discharge the powers and duties of his office, the Vice President shall immediately assume the powers and duties of the office as Acting President.

Thereafter, when the President transmits to the President pro tempore of the Senate and the Speaker of the House of Representatives his written declaration that no inability exists, he shall resume the powers and duties of his office unless the Vice President and a majority of either the principal officers of the executive department or of such other body as Congress may by law provide, transmit within four days to the President pro tempore of the Senate and the Speaker of the House of Representatives their written declaration that the President is unable to discharge the powers and duties of his office. Thereupon Congress shall decide the issue, assembling within forty-eight hours for that purpose if not in session. If the Congress, within twenty-one days after receipt of the latter written declaration, or, if Congress is not in session, within twenty-one days after Congress is required to assemble, determines by two-thirds vote of both houses that the President is unable to discharge the powers and duties of his office, the Vice President shall continue to discharge the same as Acting President; otherwise, the President shall resume the powers and duties of his office.

AMENDMENT XXVI.

Lowering voting age to 18 years.

(Proposed by Congress Mar. 23, 1971; ratification completed July 1, 1971.)

1. The right of citizens of the United States, who are 18 years of age or older, to vote shall not be denied or abridged by the United States or any state on account of age.

2. The Congress shall have the power to enforce this article by appropriate legislation.

PROPOSED AMENDMENT RELATING TO CONGRESSIONAL PAY

(Proposed by the first Congress Mar. 4, 1789 as one of the 12 amendments to the Constitution, the 10 that were accepted became the Bill of Rights; ratified as of April 1986 by 15 states: Maryland, North Carolina, South Carolina, Delaware, Vermont, Virginia 1789-1791; Ohio 1873; Wyoming 1978; Maine 1983; Colorado 1984; South Dakota, New Hampshire, Arizona, Tennessee, Oklahoma 1985; New Mexico, Indiana, Utah 1986.)

No law, varying the compensation for the services of the Senators and Representatives, shall take effect, until an election of Representatives shall have intervened.

Origin of the Constitution

200th Anniversary

The War of Independence was conducted by delegates from the original 13 states, called the Congress of the United States of America and generally known as the Continental Congress. In 1777 the Congress submitted to the legislatures of the states the Articles of Confederation and Perpetual Union, which were ratified by New Hampshire, Massachusetts, Rhode Island, Connecticut, New York, New Jersey, Pennsylvania, Delaware, Virginia, North Carolina, South Carolina, and Georgia, and finally, in 1781, by Maryland.

The first article of the instrument read: "The stile of this confederacy shall be the United States of America." This did not signify a sovereign nation, because the states delegated only those powers they could not handle individually, such as power to wage war, establish a uniform currency, make treaties with foreign nations and contract debts for general expenses (such as paying the army). Taxes for the payment of such debts were levied by the individual states. The president under the Articles signed himself "President of the United States in Congress assembled," but here the United States were considered in the plural, a cooperating group. Canada was invited to join the union on equal terms but did not act.

When the war was won it became evident that a stronger federal union was needed to protect the mutual interests of the states. The Congress left the initiative to the legislatures. Virginia in Jan. 1786 appointed commissioners to meet with representatives of other states, with the result that delegates from Virginia, Delaware, New York, New Jersey, and Pennsylvania met at Annapolis. Alexander Hamilton prepared for their call by asking delegates from all states to meet in Philadelphia in May 1787 "to render the Constitution of the Federal government adequate to the exigencies of the union." Congress endorsed the plan Feb. 21, 1787. Delegates were appointed by all states except Rhode Island.

The convention met May 14, 1787. George Washington was chosen president (presiding officer). The states certified 65 delegates, but 10 did not attend. The work was done by 55, not all of whom were present at all sessions. Of the 55 attending delegates, 16 failed to sign, and 39 actually signed Sept. 17, 1787, some with reservations. Some historians have said 74 delegates (9 more than the 65 actually certified) were named and 19 failed to attend. These 9 additional persons refused the appointment, were never delegates and never counted as absentees. Washington sent the Constitution to Congress with a covering letter and that body, Sept. 28, 1787, ordered it sent to the legislatures, "in order to be submitted to a convention of delegates chosen in each state by the people thereof."

The Constitution was ratified by votes of state conventions as follows: Delaware, Dec. 7, 1787, unanimous; Pennsylvania, Dec. 12, 1787, 43 to 23; New Jersey, Dec. 18, 1787, unanimous; Georgia, Jan 2, 1788, unanimous; Connecticut, Jan. 9, 1788, 128 to 40; Massachusetts, Feb. 6, 1788, 187 to 168; Maryland, Apr. 28, 1788, 63 to 11; South Carolina, May 23, 1788, 149 to 73; New Hampshire, June 21, 1788, 57 to 46; Virginia, June 25, 1788, 89 to 79; New York, July 26, 1788, 30 to 27. Nine states were needed to establish the operation of the Constitution "between the states so ratifying the same" and New Hampshire was the 9th state. The government did not declare the Constitution in effect until the first Wednesday in Mar. 1789 which was Mar. 4. After that North Carolina ratified it Nov. 21, 1789, 194 to 77; and Rhode Island, May 29, 1790, 34 to 32. Vermont in convention ratified it Jan. 10, 1791, and by act of Congress approved Feb. 18, 1791, was admitted into the Union as the 14th state, Mar. 4, 1791.

On Sept. 17, 1987, the nation began a four-year celebration of the 200th anniversary of the signing of the Constitution of the United States.

As of April 1987, 32 states have voted to issue convention calls to hold a second constitutional convention. Convention bills are pending before 11 more state legislatures, while bills to rescind previous calls are under consideration in four states. When the total reaches 34, the Constitution stipulates that a convention must be held. The convention drive began in the mid 1970s to bring about the consideration of an amendment requiring a balanced federal budget.

How the Declaration of Independence Was Adopted

On June 7, 1776, Richard Henry Lee, who had issued the first call for a congress of the colonies, introduced in the Continental Congress at Philadelphia a resolution declaring "that these United Colonies are, and of right ought to be, free and independent states, that they are absolved from all allegiance to the British Crown, and that all political connection between them and the state of Great Britain is, and ought to be, totally dissolved."

The resolution, seconded by John Adams on behalf of the Massachusetts delegation, came up again June 10 when a committee of 5, headed by Thomas Jefferson, was appointed to express the purpose of the resolution in a declaration of independence. The others on the committee were John Adams, Benjamin Franklin, Robert R. Livingston, and Roger Sherman.

Drafting the Declaration was assigned to Jefferson, who worked on a portable desk of his own construction in a room at Market and 7th Sts. The committee reported the result June 28, 1776. The members of the Congress suggested a number of changes, which Jefferson called "deplorable." They didn't approve Jefferson's arraignment of the British people and King George III for encouraging and fostering the slave trade, which Jefferson called "an execrable commerce." They made 86 changes, eliminating 480 words and leaving 1,337. In the final form capitalization was erratic. Jefferson had written that men were endowed with "inalienable" rights; in the final copy it came out as "unalienable" and has been thus ever since.

The Lee-Adams resolution of independence was adopted by 12 yeas July 2 — the actual date of the act of independence. The Declaration, which explains the act, was adopted July 4, in the evening.

After the Declaration was adopted, July 4, 1776, it was turned over to John Dunlap, printer, to be printed on broadsides. The original copy was lost and one of his broadsides was attached to a page in the journal of the Congress. It was read aloud July 8 in Philadelphia, Easton, Pa., and Trenton, N.J. On July 9 at 6 p.m. it was read by order of Gen. George Washington to the troops assembled on the Common in New York City (City Hall Park).

The Continental Congress of July 19, 1776, adopted the following resolution:

"Resolved, That the Declaration passed on the 4th, be fairly engrossed on parchment with the title and stile of 'The Unanimous Declaration of the thirteen United States of America' and that the same, when engrossed, be signed by every member of Congress."

Not all delegates who signed the engrossed Declaration were present on July 4. Robert Morris (Pa.), William Williams (Conn.) and Samuel Chase (Md.) signed on Aug. 2, Oliver Wolcott (Conn.), George Wythe (Va.), Richard Henry Lee (Va.) and Elbridge Gerry (Mass.) signed in August and September, Matthew Thornton (N. H.) joined the Congress Nov. 4 and signed later. Thomas McKean (Del.) rejoined Washington's Army before signing and said later that he signed in 1781.

Charles Carroll of Carrollton was appointed a delegate by Maryland on July 4, 1776, presented his credentials July 18, and signed the engrossed Declaration Aug. 2. Born Sept. 19, 1737, he was 95 years old and the last surviving signer when he died Nov. 14, 1832.

Two Pennsylvania delegates who did not support the Declaration on July 4 were replaced.

The 4 New York delegates did not have authority from their state to vote on July 4. On July 9 the New York state convention authorized its delegates to approve the Declaration and the Congress was so notified on July 15, 1776. The 4 signed the Declaration on Aug. 2.

The original engrossed Declaration is preserved in the National Archives Building in Washington.

The Liberty Bell: Its History and Significance

The Liberty Bell, in Independence Hall, Philadelphia, is an object of great reverence to Americans because of its association with the historic events of the War of Independence.

The original Province bell, ordered to commemorate the 50th anniversary of the Commonwealth of Pennsylvania, was cast by Thomas Lister, Whitechapel, London, and reached Philadelphia in Aug. 1752. It bore an inscription from Leviticus XXV, 10: "Proclaim liberty throughout all the land unto all the inhabitants thereof."

The bell was cracked by a stroke of its clapper in Sept. 1752 while it hung on a truss in the State House yard for testing. Pass & Stow, Philadelphia founders, recast the bell, adding 1 1/2 ounces of copper to a pound of the original metal to reduce brittleness. It was found that the bell contained too much copper, injuring its tone, so Pass & Stow recast it again, this time successfully.

In June 1753 the bell was hung in the wooden steeple of the State House, erected on top of the brick tower. In use while the Continental Congress was in session in the State House, it rang out in defiance of British tax and trade restrictions, and proclaimed the Boston Tea Party and the first public reading of the Declaration of Independence.

On Sept. 18, 1777, when the British Army was about to occupy Philadelphia, the bell was moved in a baggage train of the American Army to Allentown, Pa. where it was hidden in the Zion Reformed Church until June 27, 1778. It was moved back to Philadelphia after the British left.

In July 1781 the wooden steeple became insecure and had to be taken down. The bell was lowered into the brick section of the tower. Here it was hanging in July, 1835, when it cracked while tolling for the funeral of John Marshall, chief justice of the United States. Because of its association with the War of Independence it was not recast but remained mute in this location until 1846, the year of the Mexican War, when it was placed on exhibition in the Declaration Chamber of Independence Hall.

In 1876, when many thousands of Americans visited Philadelphia for the Centennial Exposition, it was placed in its old walnut frame in the tower hallway. In 1877 it was hung from the ceiling of the tower by a chain of 13 links. It was returned again to the Declaration Chamber and in 1896 taken back to the tower hall, where it occupied a glass case. In 1915 the case was removed so that the public might touch it. On Jan. 1, 1976, just after midnight to mark the opening of the Bicentennial Year, the bell was moved to a new glass and steel pavilion behind Independence Hall for easier viewing by the larger number of visitors expected during the year.

The measurements of the bell follow: circumference around the lip, 12 ft.; circumference around the crown, 7 ft. 6 in.; lip to the crown, 3 ft.; height over the crown, 2 ft. 3 in.; thickness at lip, 3 in.; thickness at crown, 1 1/4 in.; weight, 2080 lbs.; length of clapper, 3 ft. 2 in.; cost, £60 14s 5d.

Confederate States and Secession

The American Civil War, 1861-65, grew out of sectional disputes over the continued existence of slavery in the South and the contention of Southern legislators that the states retained many sovereign rights, including the right to secede from the Union.

The war was not fought by state against state but by one federal regime against another, the Confederate government in Richmond assuming control over the economic, political, and military life of the South, under protest from Georgia and South Carolina.

South Carolina voted an ordinance of secession from the Union, repealing its 1788 ratification of the U.S. Constitution on Dec. 20, 1860, to take effect Dec. 24. Other states seceded in 1861. Their votes in conventions were:

Mississippi, Jan. 9, 84-15; Florida, Jan. 10, 62-7; Alabama, Jan. 11, 61-39; Georgia, Jan. 19, 208-89; Louisiana, Jan. 26, 113-17; Texas, Feb. 1, 166-7, ratified by popular vote Feb. 23 (for 34,794, against 11,325); Virginia, Apr. 17, 88-55, ratified by popular vote May 23 (for 128,884; against 32,134); Arkansas, May 6, 69-1; Tennessee, May 7, ratified by popular vote June 8 (for 104,019, against 47,238); North Carolina, May 21.

Missouri Unionists stopped secession in conventions Feb. 28 and Mar. 9. The legislature condemned secession Mar. 7. Under the protection of Confederate troops, secessionist members of the legislature adopted a resolution of secession at Neosho, Oct. 31. The Confederate Congress seated the secessionists' representatives.

Kentucky did not secede and its government remained Unionist. In a part occupied by Confederate troops, Kentuckians approved secession and the Confederate Congress admitted their representatives.

The Maryland legislature voted against secession Apr. 27, 53-13. Delaware did not secede. Western Virginia held conventions at Wheeling, named a pro-Union governor June 11, 1861; admitted to Union as West Virginia June 20, 1863; its constitution provided for gradual abolition of slavery.

Confederate Government

Forty-two delegates from South Carolina, Georgia, Alabama, Mississippi, Louisiana, and Florida met in convention at Montgomery, Ala., Feb. 4, 1861. They adopted a provisional constitution of the Confederate States of America, and elected Jefferson Davis (Miss.) provisional president, and Alexander H. Stephens (Ga.) provisional vice president.

A permanent constitution was adopted Mar. 11; it abolished the African slave trade. The Congress moved to Richmond, Va. July 20. Davis was elected president in October, and was inaugurated Feb. 22, 1862.

The Congress adopted a flag, consisting of a red field with a white stripe, and a blue jack with a circle of white stars. Later the more popular flag was the red field with blue diagonal cross bars that held 13 white stars. The stars represented the 11 states actually in the Confederacy plus Kentucky and Missouri.

(See also Civil War, U.S., in Index)

Lincoln's Address at Gettysburg, 1863

Fourscore and seven years ago our fathers brought forth on this continent a new nation, conceived in liberty and dedicated to the proposition that all men are created equal.

Now we are engaged in a great civil war, testing whether that nation or any nation so conceived and so dedicated can long endure. We are met on a great battle field of that war. We have come to dedicate a portion of that field, as a final resting-place for those who here gave their lives that that nation might live. It is altogether fitting and proper that we should do this.

But, in a larger sense, we can not dedicate — we can not consecrate — we can not hallow — this ground. The brave men, living and dead, who struggled here, have consecrated it, far above our poor power to add or detract. The world will little note, nor long remember, what we say here, but it can never forget what they did here. It is for us the living, rather, to be dedicated here to the unfinished work which they who fought here have thus far so nobly advanced. It is rather for us to be here dedicated to the great task remaining before us — that from these honored dead we take increased devotion to that cause for which they gave the last full measure of devotion — that we here highly resolve that these dead shall not have died in vain — that this nation, under God, shall have a new birth of freedom — and that government of the people, by the people, for the people, shall not perish from the earth.

Origin of the United States National Motto

In God We Trust, designated as the U. S. National Motto by Congress in 1956, originated during the Civil War as an inscription for U. S. coins, although it was used by Francis Scott Key in a slightly different form when he wrote The Star Spangled Banner in 1814. On Nov. 13, 1861, when Union morale had been shaken by battlefield defeats, the Rev. M. R. Watkinson, of Ridleyville, Pa., wrote to Secy. of the Treasury Salmon P. Chase. "From my heart I have felt our national shame in disowning God as not the least of our present national disasters," the minister wrote, suggesting "recognition of the Almighty God in some form on our coins." Secy. Chase ordered designs prepared with the inscription *In God We Trust* and backed coinage legislation which authorized use of this slogan. It first appeared on some U. S. coins in 1864, disappeared and reappeared on various coins until 1955, when Congress ordered it placed on all paper money and all coins.

The National Anthem — The Star-Spangled Banner

The Star-Spangled Banner was ordered played by the military and naval services by President Woodrow Wilson in 1916. It was designated the National Anthem by Act of Congress, Mar. 3, 1931. It was written by Francis Scott Key, of Georgetown, D. C., during the bombardment of Fort McHenry, Baltimore, Md., Sept. 13-14, 1814. Key was a lawyer, a graduate of St. John's College, Annapolis, and a volunteer in a light artillery company. When a friend, Dr. Beanes, a physician of Upper Marlborough, Md., was taken aboard Admiral Cockburn's British squadron for interfering with ground troops, Key and J. S. Skinner, carrying a note from President Madison, went to the fleet under a flag of truce on a cartel ship to ask Beanes' release. Admiral Cockburn consented, but as the fleet was about to sail up the Patapsco to bombard Fort McHenry he detained them, first on H. M. S. Surprise, and then on a supply ship.

Key witnessed the bombardment from his own vessel. It began at 7 a.m., Sept. 13, 1814, and lasted, with intermissions, for 25 hours. The British fired over 1,500 shells, each weighing as much as 220 lbs. They were unable to approach closely because the Americans had sunk 22 vessels in the channel. Only four Americans were killed and 24 wounded. A British bomb-ship was disabled.

During the bombardment Key wrote a stanza on the back of an envelope. Next day at Indian Queen Inn, Baltimore, he wrote out the poem and gave it to his brother-in-law, Judge J. H. Nicholson. Nicholson suggested the tune, Anacreon in Heaven, and had the poem printed on broadsides, of which two survive. On Sept. 20 it appeared in the "Baltimore American." Later Key made 3 copies; one is in the Library of Congress and one in the Pennsylvania Historical Society.

The copy that Key wrote in his hotel Sept. 14, 1814, remained in the Nicholson family for 93 years. In 1907 it was sold to Henry Walters of Baltimore. In 1934 it was bought at auction in New York from the Walters estate by the Walters Art Gallery, Baltimore, for $26,400. The Walters Gallery in 1953 sold the manuscript to the Maryland Historical Society for the same price.

The flag that Key saw during the bombardment is preserved in the Smithsonian Institution, Washington. It is 30 by 42 ft., and has 15 alternate red and white stripes and 15 stars, for the original 13 states plus Kentucky and Vermont.

It was made by Mary Young Pickersgill. The Baltimore Flag House, a museum, occupies her premises, which were restored in 1953.

The Star-Spangled Banner

I

Oh, say can you see by the dawn's early light
What so proudly we hailed at the twilight's last gleaming?
Whose broad stripes and bright stars thru the perilous fight,
O'er the ramparts we watched were so gallantly streaming?
And the rocket's red glare, the bombs bursting in air,
Gave proof through the night that our flag was still there.
Oh, say does that star-spangled banner yet wave
O'er the land of the free and the home of the brave?

II

On the shore, dimly seen through the mists of the deep,
Where the foe's haughty host in dread silence reposes,
What is that which the breeze, o'er the towering steep,
As it fitfully blows, half conceals, half discloses?
Now it catches the gleam of the morning's first beam,
In full glory reflected now shines in the stream:
'Tis the star-spangled banner! Oh long may it wave
O'er the land of the free and the home of the brave!

III

And where is that band who so vauntingly swore
That the havoc of war and the battle's confusion,
A home and a country should leave us no more!
Their blood has washed out their foul footsteps' pollution.
No refuge could save the hireling and slave
From the terror of flight, or the gloom of the grave:
And the star-spangled banner in triumph doth wave
O'er the land of the free and the home of the brave!

IV

Oh! thus be it ever, when freemen shall stand
Between their loved home and the war's desolation!
Blest with victory and peace, may the heav'n rescued land
Praise the Power that hath made and preserved us a nation.
Then conquer we must, when our cause it is just,
And this be our motto: "In God is our trust."
And the star-spangled banner in triumph shall wave
O'er the land of the free and the home of the brave!

Statue of Liberty National Monument

Since 1886, the Statue of Liberty Enlightening the World has stood as a symbol of freedom in New York harbor. It also commemorates French-American friendship for it was given by the people of France, designed by Frederic Auguste Bartholdi (1834-1904). A $2.5 million building housing the American Museum of Immigration was opened by Pres. Nixon Sept. 26, 1972, at the base of the statue. It houses a permanent exhibition of photos, posters, and artifacts tracing the history of American immigration. The Monument is administered by the National Park Service.

Nearby Ellis Island, gateway to America for more than 12 million immigrants between 1892 and 1954, was proclaimed part of the National Monument in 1965 by Pres. Johnson.

Edouard de Laboulaye, French historian and admirer of American political institutions, suggested that the French present a monument to the United States, the latter to provide pedestal and site. Bartholdi visualized a colossal statue at the entrance of New York harbor, welcoming the peoples of the world with the torch of liberty.

On Washington's birthday, Feb. 22, 1877, Congress approved the use of a site on Bedloe's Island suggested by Bartholdi. This island of 12 acres had been owned in the 17th century by a Walloon named Isaac Bedloe. It was called Bedloe's until Aug. 3, 1956, when Pres. Eisenhower approved a resolution of Congress changing the name to Liberty Island.

The statue was finished May 21, 1884, and formally presented to U.S. Minister Morton July 4, 1884, by Ferdinand de Lesseps, head of the Franco-American Union, promoter of the Panama Canal, and builder of the Suez Canal.

On Aug. 5, 1884, the Americans laid the cornerstone for the pedestal. This was to be built on the foundations of Fort Wood, which had been erected by the Government in 1811. The American committee had raised $125,000, but this was found to be inadequate. Joseph Pulitzer, owner of the New York World, appealed on Mar. 16, 1885, for general donations. By Aug. 11, 1885, he had raised $100,000.

The statue arrived dismantled, in 214 packing cases, from Rouen, France, in June, 1885. The last rivet of the statue was driven Oct. 28, 1886, when Pres. Grover Cleveland dedicated the monument.

The statue weighs 450,000 lbs. or 225 tons. The copper sheeting weighs 200,000 lbs. There are 167 steps from the land level to the top of the pedestal, 168 steps inside the statue to the head, and 54 rungs on the ladder leading to the arm that holds the torch.

Two years of restoration work was completed before the statue's centennial celebration on July 4, 1986. Among other repairs, the multi-million dollar project included replacing the 1,600 wrought iron bands that hold its copper skin to its frame, replacing its torch, and installing an elevator.

A four-day extravaganza of concerts, tall ships, ethnic festivals, and fireworks celebrated the 100th anniversary. The festivities included Chief Justice Warren E. Burger's swearing-in of 5,000 new citizens on Liberty Island, while 20,000 others across the country were simultaneously sworn in through a satellite telecast.

The ceremonies were followed by others on Oct. 28, 1986, the statue's 100th birthday.

Dimensions of the Statue	Ft.	In.
Height from base to torch (45.3 meters)	151	1
Foundation of pedestal to torch (91.5 meters)	305	1
Heel to top of head	111	1
Length of hand	16	5
Index finger	8	0
Circumference at second joint	3	6
Size of finger nail	13x10 in.	
Head from chin to cranium	17	3
Head thickness from ear to ear	10	0
Distance across the eye	2	6
Length of nose	4	6
Right arm, length	42	0
Right arm, greatest thickness	12	0
Thickness of waist	35	0
Width of mouth	3	0
Tablet, length	23	7
Tablet, width	13	7
Tablet, thickness	2	0

Emma Lazarus' Famous Poem

A poem by Emma Lazarus is graven on a tablet within the pedestal on which the statue stands.

The New Colossus

Not like the brazen giant of Greek fame,
With conquering limbs astride from land to land;
Here at our sea-washed, sunset gates shall stand
A mighty woman with a torch, whose flame
Is the imprisoned lightning, and her name
Mother of Exiles. From her beacon-hand
Glows world-wide welcome; her mild eyes command
The air-bridged harbor that twin cities frame.
"Keep ancient lands, your storied pomp!" cries she
With silent lips. "Give me your tired, your poor,
Your huddled masses yearning to breathe free,
The wretched refuse of your teeming shore.
Send these, the homeless, tempest-tost to me,
I lift my lamp beside the golden door!"

Forms of Address for Persons of Rank and Public Office

In these examples John Smith is used as a representative American name. The salutation Dear Sir or Dear Madam is always permissible when addressing a person not known to the writer. Female equivalents should be substituted where appropriate.

President of the United States

Address: The President, The White House, Washington, DC 20500. Also, The President and Mrs. ___.

Salutation: Dear Sir or Mr. President or Dear Mr. President. More intimately: My dear Mr. President. Also: Dear Mr. President and Mrs. ___

The vice president takes the same forms.

Cabinet Officers

Address: Mr. John Smith, Secretary of State, Washington, D.C. or The Hon. John Smith. Similar addresses for other members of the cabinet. Also: Secretary and Mrs. John Smith.

Salutation: Dear Sir, or Dear Mr. Secretary. Also: Dear Mr. and Mrs. Smith.

The Bench

Address: The Hon. John Smith, Chief Justice of the United States. The Hon. John Smith, Associate Justice of the Supreme Court of the United States. The Hon. John Smith, Associate Judge, U.S. District Court.

Salutation: Dear Sir, or Dear Mr. Chief Justice. Dear Mr. Justice. Dear Judge Smith.

Members of Congress

Address: The Hon. John Smith, United States Senate, Washington, DC 20510, or Sen. John Smith, etc. Also The Hon. John Smith, House of Representatives, Washington, DC 20515, or Rep. John Smith, etc.

Salutation: Dear Mr. Senator or Dear Mr. Smith; for Representative, Dear Mr. Smith.

Officers of Armed Forces

Address: Careful attention should be given to the precise rank, thus: General of the Army John Smith, Fleet Admiral John Smith. The rules for Air Force are same as Army.

Salutation: Dear Sir, or Dear General. All general officers, whatever rank, are entitled to be addressed as generals. Likewise a lieutenant colonel is addressed as colonel and first and second lieutenants are addressed as lieutenant.

Warrant officers and flight officers are addressed as Mister. Chaplains are addressed as Chaplain. A Catholic chaplain may be addressed as Father. Cadets of the United States Military Academy and Air Force Academy are addressed as Cadet. Noncommissioned officers are addressed by their titles.

Ambassador, Governor, Mayor

Address: The Hon. John Smith, followed by his or her title. They can be addressed either at their embassy, or at the Department of State, Washington, D.C. An ambassador from a foreign nation may be addressed as His or Her Excellency. An American is not to be so addressed.

Salutation: Dear Mr. or Madam Ambassador. An ambassador from a foreign nation may be called Your Excellency.

Governors and mayors are often addressed as The Hon. Jane Smith, Governor of ______, or The Hon. John Smith, Mayor of ______; also Governor John Smith, State House, Albany, N.Y., or Mayor Jane Smith, City Hall, Erie, Pa.

The Clergy

Address: His Holiness, the Pope, or His Holiness Pope (name), State of Vatican City, Italy.

Salutation: Your Holiness or Most Holy Father.

Also: His Eminence, John, Cardinal Smith; salutation: Your Eminence. An archbishop or a bishop is addressed The Most Reverend, and the salutation is Your Excellency. A monsignor who is a papal chamberlain is The Very Reverend Monsignor and the salutation is Dear Sir or Very Reverend Monsignor; a monsignor who is a domestic prelate is The Right Reverend Monsignor and salutation is Right Reverend Monsignor. A priest is addressed Reverend John Smith. A brother of an order is addressed Brother —. A sister takes the same form.

A bishop of the Protestant Episcopal Church is The Right Reverend John Smith; salutation is Right Reverend Sir, or Dear Bishop Smith. If a clergyman is a doctor of divinity, he is addressed: The Reverend John Smith, D.D., and the salutation is Reverend Sir, or Dear Dr. Smith. When a clergyman does not have the degree the salutation is Dear Mr. Smith.

A bishop of the Methodist Church is addressed Bishop John Smith with titles following.

Royalty and Nobility

An emperor is to be addressed in a letter as Sir, or Your Imperial Majesty.

A king or queen is addressed as His Majesty (Name), King of (Name), or Her Majesty (Name), Queen of (Name), Salutation: Sir, or Madam, or May it please Your Majesty.

Princes and princesses and other persons of royal blood are addressed as His (or Her) Royal Highness, and saluted with May it please Your Royal Highness.

A duke or marquis is My Lord Duke (or Marquis), a duke is His (or Your) Grace.

The Mayflower Compact

The threat of James I to "harry them out of the land" sent a little band of religious dissenters from England to Holland in 1608. They were known as "Separatists" because they wished to cut all ties with the Established Church. In 1620, some of them, known now as the Pilgrims, joined with a larger group in England to set sail on the *Mayflower* for the New World. A joint stock company financed their venture.

In November, they sighted Cape Cod and decided to land an exploring party at Plymouth Harbor. However, a rebellious group picked up at Southhampton and London troubled the Pilgrim leaders, and to control their actions forty-one of the Pilgrims drew up the "Mayflower Compact," which was signed before going ashore. The voluntary agreement to govern themselves was America's first written constitution.

In the name of God, Amen. We, whose names are underwritten, the Loyal Subjects of our dread Sovereign Lord, King *James*, by the Grace of God, of *Great Britain, France and Ireland*, King, *Defender of the Faith*, etc.

Having undertaken for the Glory of God, and Advancement of the Christian Faith, and the Honour of our King and Country, a voyage to plant the first colony in the northern Parts of Virginia; do by these Presents, solemnly and mutually in the Presence of God and one of another, covenant and combine ouselves together into a civil Body Politick, for our better Ordering and Preservation, and Furtherance of the Ends aforesaid; And by Virtue hereof to enact, constitute, and frame, such just and equal Laws, Ordinances, Acts, Constitutions and Offices, from time to time, as shall be thought most meet and convenient for the General good of the Colony; unto which we promise all due Submission and Obedience.

In Witness whereof we have hereunto subscribed our names at *Cape Cod* the eleventh of *November*, in the Reign of our Sovereign Lord, King *James* of *England, France* and *Ireland*, the eighteenth, and of *Scotland* the fifty-fourth. *Anno Domini, 1620.*

The Great Seal of the U.S.

On July 4, 1776, the Continental Congress appointed a committee consisting of Benjamin Franklin, John Adams and Thomas Jefferson "to bring in a device for a seal of the United States of America." After many delays, a verbal description of a design by William Barton was finally approved by Congress on June 20, 1782. The seal shows an American bald eagle with a ribbon in its mouth bearing the device *E pluribus unum* (One out of many). In its talons are the arrows of war and an olive branch of peace. On the reverse side it shows an unfinished pyramid with an eye (the eye of Providence) above it.

The American's Creed

William Tyler Page, Clerk of the U.S. House of Representatives, wrote "The American's Creed" in 1917. It was accepted by the House on behalf of the American people on April 3, 1918.

"I believe in the United States of America as a government of the people, by the people, for the people; whose just powers are derived from the consent of the governed; a democracy in a republic; a sovereign Nation of many sovereign States; a perfect union, one and inseparable; established upon those principles of freedom, equality, justice, and humanity for which American patriots sacrificed their lives and fortunes.

"I therefore believe it is my duty to my country to love it, to support its Constitution, to obey its laws, to respect its flag, and to defend it against all enemies."

Code of Etiquette for Display and Use of the U.S. Flag

Although the Stars and Stripes originated in 1777, it was not until 146 years later that there was a serious attempt to establish a uniform code of etiquette for the U.S. flag. The War Department issued Feb. 15, 1923, a circular on the rules of flag usage. These were adopted almost in their entirety June 14, 1923, by a conference of 68 patriotic organizations in Washington. Finally, on June 22, 1942, a joint resolution of Congress, amended by Public Law 94-344 July 7, 1976, codified "existing rules and customs pertaining to the display and use of the flag. . ."

When to Display the Flag—The flag should be displayed on all days, especially on legal holidays and other special occasions, on official buildings when in use, in or near polling places on election days, and in or near schools when in session. A citizen may fly the flag at any time he wishes. It is customary to display the flag only from sunrise to sunset on buildings and on stationary flagstaffs in the open. However, it may be displayed at night on special occasions, preferably lighted. In Washington, the flag now flies over the White House both day and night. It flies over the Senate wing of the Capitol when the Senate is in session and over the House wing when that body is in session. It flies day and night over the east and west fronts of the Capitol, without floodlights at night but receiving light from the illuminated Capitol Dome. It flies 24 hours a day at several other places, including the Fort McHenry Nat'l Monument in Baltimore, where it inspired Francis Scott Key to write The Star Spangled Banner.

How to Fly the Flag—The flag should be hoisted briskly and lowered ceremoniously, and should never be allowed to touch the ground or the floor. When hung over a sidewalk from a rope extending from a building to a pole, the union should be away from the building. When hung over the center of a street it should have the union to the north in an east-west street and to the east in a north-south street. No other flag may be flown above or, if on the same level, to the right of the U.S. flag, except that at the United Nations Headquarters the UN flag may be placed above flags of all member nations and other national flags may be flown with equal prominence or honor with the flag of the U.S. At services by Navy chaplains at sea, the church pennant may be flown above the flag.

When two flags are placed against a wall with crossed staffs, the U.S. flag should be at right—its own right, and its staff should be in front of the staff of the other flag; when a number of flags are grouped and displayed from staffs, it should be at the center and highest point of the group.

Church and Platform Use—In an auditorium, the flag may be displayed flat, above and behind the speaker. When displayed from a staff in a church or public auditorium, the flag should hold the position of superior prominence, in advance of the audience, and in the position of honor at the clergyman's or speaker's right as he faces the audience. Any other flag so displayed should be placed on the left of the clergyman or speaker or to the right of the audience.

When the flag is displayed horizontally or vertically against a wall, the stars should be uppermost and at the observer's left.

How to Dispose of Worn Flags—The flag, when it is in such condition that it is no longer a fitting emblem for display, should be destroyed in a dignified way, preferably by burning in private.

When to Salute the Flag—All persons present should face the flag, stand at attention and salute on the following occasions: (1) When the flag is passing in a parade or in a review, (2) During the ceremony of hoisting or lowering, (3) When the National Anthem is played, and (4) During the Pledge of Allegiance. Those present in uniform should render the military salute. When not in uniform, men should remove the hat with the right hand holding it at the left shoulder, the hand being over the heart. Men without hats should salute in the same manner. Aliens should stand at attention. Women should salute by placing the right hand over the heart.

On Memorial Day, the flag should fly at half-staff until noon, then be raised to the peak.

As provided by Presidential proclamation the flag should fly at half-staff for 30 days from the day of death of a president or former president; for 10 days from the day of death of a vice president, chief justice or retired chief justice of the U.S., or speaker of the House of Representatives; from day of death until burial of an associate justice of the Supreme Court, cabinet member, former vice president, or Senate president pro tempore, majority or minority Senate leader, or majority or minority House leader; for a U.S. senator, representative, territorial delegate, or the resident commissioner of Puerto Rico, on day of death and the following day within the metropolitan area of the District of Columbia and from day of death until burial within the decedent's state, congressional district, territory or commonwealth; and for the death of the governor of a state, territory, or possession of the U.S., from day of death until burial within that state, territory, or possession.

When used to cover a casket, the flag should be placed so that the union is at the head and over the left shoulder. It should not be lowered into the grave nor touch the ground.

Prohibited Uses of the Flag—The flag should not be dipped to any person or thing. (An exception—customarily, ships salute by dipping their colors.) It should never be displayed with the union down save as a distress signal. It should never be carried flat or horizontally, but always aloft and free.

It should not be displayed on a float, motor car or boat except from a staff.

It should never be used as a covering for a ceiling, nor have placed upon it any word, design, or drawing. It should never be used as a receptacle for carrying anything. It should not be used to cover a statue or a monument.

The flag should never be used for advertising purposes, nor be embroidered on such articles as cushions or handkerchiefs, printed or otherwise impressed on boxes or used as a costume or athletic uniform. Advertising signs should not be fastened to its staff or halyard.

The flag should never be used as drapery of any sort, never festooned, drawn back, nor up, in folds, but always allowed to fall free. Bunting of blue, white and red always arranged with the blue above and the white in the middle, should be used for covering a speaker's desk, draping the front of a platform, and for decoration in general.

An Act of Congress approved Feb. 8, 1917, provided certain penalties for the desecration, mutilation or improper use of the flag within the District of Columbia. A 1968 federal law provided penalties of up to a year's imprisonment or a $1,000 fine or both, for publicly burning or otherwise desecrating any flag of the United States. In addition, many states have laws against flag desecration.

Pledge of Allegiance to the Flag

I pledge allegiance to the flag of the United States of America and to the republic for which it stands, one nation under God, indivisible, with liberty and justice for all.

This, the current official version of the Pledge of Allegiance, has developed from the original pledge, which was first published in the Sept. 8, 1892, issue of the Youth's Companion, a weekly magazine then published in Boston. The original pledge contained the phrase "my flag," which was changed more than 30 years later to "flag of the United States of America." An act of Congress in 1954 added the words "under God."

The authorship of the pledge had been in dispute for many years. The Youth's Companion stated in 1917 that the original draft was written by James B. Upham, an executive of the magazine who died in 1910. A leaflet circulated by the magazine later named Upham as the originator of the draft "afterwards condensed and perfected by him and his associates of the Companion force."

Francis Bellamy, a former member of the Youth's Companion editorial staff, publicly claimed authorship of the pledge in 1923. The United States Flag Assn., acting on the advice of a committee named to study the controversy, upheld in 1939 the claim of Bellamy, who had died 8 years earlier. The Library of Congress issued in 1957 a report attributing the authorship to Bellamy.

The Flag of the U.S.—The Stars and Stripes

The 50-star flag of the United States was raised for the first time officially at 12:01 a.m. on July 4, 1960, at Fort McHenry National Monument in Baltimore, Md. The 50th star had been added for Hawaii; a year earlier the 49th, for Alaska. Before that, no star had been added since 1912, when N.M. and Ariz. were admitted to the Union.

History of the Flag

The true history of the Stars and Stripes has become so cluttered by a volume of myth and tradition that the facts are difficult, and in some cases impossible, to establish. For example, it is not certain who designed the Stars and Stripes, who made the first such flag, or even whether it ever flew in any sea fight or land battle of the American Revolution.

One thing all agree on is that the Stars and Stripes originated as the result of a resolution offered by the Marine Committee of the Second Continental Congress at Philadelphia and adopted June 14, 1777. It read:

Resolved: that the flag of the United States be thirteen stripes, alternate red and white; that the union be thirteen stars, white in a blue field, representing a new constellation.

Congress gave no hint as to the designer of the flag, no instructions as to the arrangement of the stars, and no information on its appropriate uses. Historians have been unable to find the original flag law.

The resolution establishing the flag was not even published until Sept. 2, 1777. Despite repeated requests, Washington did not get the flags until 1783, after the Revolutionary War was over. And there is no certainty that they were the Stars and Stripes.

Early Flags

Although it was never officially adopted by the Continental Congress, many historians consider the first flag of the United States to have been the Grand Union (sometimes called Great Union) flag. This was a modification of the British Meteor flag, which had the red cross of St. George and the white cross of St. Andrew combined in the blue canton. For the Grand Union flag, 6 horizontal stripes were imposed on the red field, dividing it into 13 alternate red and white stripes. On Jan. 1, 1776, when the Continental Army came into formal existence, this flag was unfurled on Prospect Hill, Somerville, Mass. Washington wrote that "we hoisted the Union Flag in compliment to the United Colonies."

One of several flags about which controversy has raged for years is at Easton, Pa. Containing the devices of the national flag in reversed order, this has been in the public library at Easton for over 150 years. Some contend that this flag was actually the first Stars and Stripes, first displayed on July 8, 1776. This flag has 13 red and white stripes in the canton, 13 white stars centered in a blue field.

A flag was hastily improvised from garments by the defenders of Fort Schuyler at Rome, N.Y., Aug. 3-22, 1777. Historians believe it was the Grand Union Flag.

The Sons of Liberty had a flag of 9 red and white stripes, to signify 9 colonies, when they met in New York in 1765 to oppose the Stamp Tax. By 1775, the flag had grown to 13 red and white stripes, with a rattlesnake on it.

At Concord, Apr. 19, 1775, the minute men from Bedford, Mass., are said to have carried a flag having a silver arm with sword on a red field.

At Cambridge, Mass., the Sons of Liberty used a plain red flag with a green pine tree on it.

In June 1775, Washington went from Philadelphia to Boston to take command of the army, escorted to New York by the Philadelphia Light Horse Troop. It carried a yellow flag which had an elaborate coat of arms — the shield charged with 13 knots, the motto "For These We Strive" — and a canton of 13 blue and silver stripes.

In Feb., 1776, Col. Christopher Gadsden, member of the Continental Congress, gave the South Carolina Provincial Congress a flag "such as is to be used by the commander-in-chief of the American Navy." It had a yellow field, with a rattlesnake about to strike and the words "Don't Tread on Me."

At the battle of Bennington, Aug. 16, 1777, patriots used a flag of 7 white and 6 red stripes with a blue canton extending down 9 stripes and showing an arch of 11 white stars over the figure 76 and a star in each of the upper corners. The stars are seven-pointed. This flag is preserved in the Historical Museum at Bennington, Vt.

At the Battle of Cowpens, Jan. 17, 1781, the 3d Maryland Regt. is said to have carried a flag of 13 red and white stripes, with a blue canton containing 12 stars in a circle around one star.

Legends about the Flag

Who Designed the Flag? No one knows for a certainty. Francis Hopkinson, designer of a naval flag, declared he also had designed the flag and in 1781 asked Congress to reimburse him for his services. Congress did not do so. Dumas Malone of Columbia Univ. wrote: "This talented man . . . designed the American flag."

Who Called the Flag Old Glory? — The flag is said to have been named Old Glory by William Driver, a sea captain of Salem, Mass. One legend has it that when he raised the flag on his brig, the Charles Doggett, in 1824, he said: "I name thee Old Glory." But his daughter, who presented the flag to the Smithsonian Institution, said he named it at his 21st birthday celebration Mar. 17, 1824, when his mother presented the homemade flag to him.

The Betsy Ross Legend — The widely publicized legend that Mrs. Betsy Ross made the first Stars and Stripes in June 1776, at the request of a committee composed of George Washington, Robert Morris, and George Ross, an uncle, was first made public in 1870, by a grandson of Mrs. Ross. Historians have been unable to find a historical record of such a meeting or committee.

Adding New Stars

The flag of 1777 was used until 1795. Then, on the admission of Vermont and Kentucky to the Union, Congress passed and Pres. Washington signed an act that after May 1, 1795, the flag should have 15 stripes, alternate red and white, and 15 white stars on a blue field in the union.

When new states were admitted it became evident that the flag would become burdened with stripes. Congress thereupon ordered that after July 4, 1818, the flag should have 13 stripes, symbolizing the 13 original states; that the union have 20 stars, and that whenever a new state was admitted a new star should be added on the July 4 following admission. No law designates the permanent arrangement of the stars. However, since 1912 when a new state has been admitted, the new design has been announced by executive order. No star is specifically identified with any state.

HISTORY

Memorable Dates in U.S. History

1492

Christopher Columbus and crew sighted land **Oct. 12** in the present-day Bahamas.

1497

John Cabot explored northeast coast to Delaware.

1513

Juan Ponce de Leon explored Florida coast.

1524

Giovanni da Verrazano led French expedition along coast from Carolina north to Nova Scotia; entered New York harbor.

1539

Hernando de Soto landed in Florida **May 28**; crossed Mississippi River, **1541.**

1540

Francisco Vazquez de Coronado explored Southwest north of Rio Grande. Hernando de Alarcon reached Colorado River, Don Garcia Lopez de Cardenas reached Grand Canyon. Others explored California coast.

1565

St. Augustine, Fla. founded by Pedro Menendez. Razed by Francis Drake **1586.**

1579

Francis Drake claimed California for Britain. Metal plate, found **1936,** thought to be left by Drake, termed probable hoax **1979.**

1607

Capt. John Smith and 105 cavaliers in 3 ships landed on Virginia coast, started first permanent English settlement in New World at **Jamestown, May 13.**

1609

Henry Hudson, English explorer of Northwest Passage, employed by Dutch, sailed into New York harbor in **Sept.,** and up Hudson to Albany. The same year, **Samuel de Champlain** explored Lake Champlain just to the north.

Spaniards settled **Santa Fe, N.M.**

1619

House of Burgesses, first representative assembly in New World, elected **July 30** at Jamestown, Va.

First black laborers — indentured servants — in English N. American colonies, landed by Dutch at Jamestown in **Aug.** Chattel slavery legally recognized, **1650.**

1620

Plymouth Pilgrims, Puritan separatists from Church of England, some living in Holland, left Plymouth, England **Sept. 15** on Mayflower. Original destination Virginia, they reached Cape Cod **Nov. 19,** explored coast; 103 passengers landed **Dec. 21** (Dec. 11 Old Style) at Plymouth. Mayflower Compact was agreement to form a government and abide by its laws. Half of colony died during harsh winter.

1624

Dutch left 8 men from ship New Netherland on **Manhattan Island** in **May.** Rest sailed to Albany.

1626

Peter Minuit bought Manhattan for Dutch from Man-a-hat-a Indians **May 6** for trinkets valued at $24.

1634

Maryland founded as Catholic colony with religious tolerance.

1636

Harvard College founded **Oct. 28,** now oldest in U.S., Grammar school, compulsory education established at Boston.

Roger Williams founded Providence, R.I., **June,** as a democratically ruled colony with separation of church and state. Charter was granted, **1644.**

1654

First Jews arrived in New Amsterdam.

1660

British Parliament passed **Navigation Act,** regulating colonial commerce to suit English needs.

1664

Three hundred **British troops Sept. 8 seized New Netherland** from Dutch, who yield peacefully. Charles II granted province of New Netherland and city of New Amsterdam to brother, Duke of York; both renamed New York. The Dutch recaptured the colony **Aug. 9, 1673,** but ceded it to Britain **Nov. 10, 1674.**

1676

Nathaniel Bacon led planters against autocratic British Gov. Berkeley, burned Jamestown, Va. Bacon died, 23 followers executed.

Bloody **Indian** war in New England ended **Aug. 12.** King Philip, Wampanoag chief, and many Narragansett Indians killed.

1682

Robert Cavelier, Sieur de La Salle, claimed lower Mississippi River country for France, called it Louisiana **Apr. 9.** Had French outposts built in Illinois and Texas, **1684.** Killed during mutiny **Mar. 19, 1687.**

1683

William Penn signed treaty with Delaware Indians and made payment for Pennsylvania lands.

1692

Witchcraft delusion at Salem (now Danvers) **Mass.** inspired by preaching; 19 persons executed.

1696

Capt. William Kidd, American hired by British to fight pirates and take booty, becomes pirate. Arrested and sent to **England,** where he was hanged **1701.**

1699

French settlements made in Mississippi, Louisiana.

1704

Indians attacked Deerfield, Mass. **Feb. 28-29,** killed 40, carried off 100.

Boston News Letter, first regular newspaper, started by John Campbell, postmaster. (*Publick Occurences* was suppressed after one issue **1690.**)

1709

British-Colonial troops captured French fort, Port Royal, Nova Scotia, in **Queen Anne's War 1701-13. France yielded** Nova Scotia by treaty **1713.**

1712

Slaves revolted in New York **Apr. 6.** Six committed suicide, 21 were executed. Second rising, **1741;** 13 slaves hanged, 13 burned, 71 deported.

1716

First theater in colonies opened in **Williamsburg, Va.**

1728

Pennsylvania Gazette founded by Samuel Keimer in Philadelphia. Benjamin Franklin bought interest **1729.**

1732

Benjamin Franklin published first *Poor Richard's Almanac;* published annually to 1757.

1735

Freedom of the press recognized in New York by acquittal of John Peter Zenger, editor of *Weekly Journal,* on charge of libeling British Gov. Cosby by criticizing his conduct in office.

1740-41

Capt. Vitus Bering, Dane employed by Russians, reached Alaska.

1744

King George's War pitted British and colonials vs. French. Colonials captured Louisburg, Cape Breton Is. **June 17, 1745.** Returned to France **1748** by Treaty of Aix-la-Chapelle.

1752

Benjamin Franklin, flying kite in thunderstorm, proved

lightning is electricity **June 15;** invented lightning rod.

1754

French and Indian War (in Europe called 7 Years War, started 1756) began when French occupied Ft. Duquesne (Pittsburgh). British moved Acadian French from Nova Scotia to Louisiana **Oct. 1755.** British captured Quebec **Sept. 18, 1759** in battles in which French Gen. Montcalm and British Gen. Wolfe were killed. Peace signed **Feb. 10 1763.** French lost Canada and American Midwest. British tightened colonial administration in North America.

1764

Sugar Act placed duties on lumber, foodstuffs, molasses and rum in colonies.

1765

Stamp Act required revenue stamps to help defray cost of royal troops. Nine colonies, led by New York and Massachusetts at Stamp Act Congress in New York **Oct. 7-25, 1765,** adopted Declaration of Rights opposing taxation without representation in Parliament and trial without jury by admiralty courts. Stamp Act **repealed Mar. 17, 1766.**

1767

Townshend Acts levied taxes on glass, painter's lead, paper, and tea. In **1770** all duties except on tea were repealed.

1770

British troops fired **Mar. 5** into Boston mob, killed 5 including **Crispus Attucks,** a black man, reportedly leader of group; later called **Boston Massacre.**

1773

East India Co. tea ships turned back at Boston, New York, Philadelphia in **May.** Cargo ship burned at Annapolis **Oct. 14,** cargo thrown overboard at **Boston Tea Party Dec. 16.**

1774

"Intolerable Acts" of Parliament curtailed Massachusetts self-rule; barred use of Boston harbor till tea was paid for.

First Continental Congress held in Philadelphia **Sept. 5-Oct. 26; protested British measures,** called for civil disobedience.

Rhode Island abolished slavery.

1775

Patrick Henry addressed Virginia convention, **Mar. 23** said "Give me liberty or give me death."

Paul Revere and William Dawes on night of **Apr. 18** rode to alert patriots that British were on way to Concord to destroy arms. At Lexington, Mass. **Apr. 19** Minutemen lost 8 killed. On return from Concord British took 273 casualties.

Col. Ethan Allen (joined by Col. Benedict Arnold) captured Ft. **Ticonderoga, N.Y. May 10;** also Crown Point. Colonials headed for **Bunker Hill,** fortified Breed's Hill, Charlestown, Mass., repulsed British under Gen. William Howe twice before retreating **June 17;** British casualties 1,000; called Battle of Bunker Hill. Continental Congress **June 15** named **George Washington** commander-in-chief.

1776

France and Spain each agreed **May 2** to provide one million livres in arms to Americans.

In Continental Congress **June 7,** Richard Henry Lee (Va.) moved "that these united colonies are and of right ought to be free and independent states." Resolution adopted July 2. **Declaration of Independence** approved **July 4.**

Col. Moultrie's batteries at **Charleston, S.C.** repulsed British sea attack **June 28.**

Washington, with 10,000 men, lost **Battle of Long Island Aug. 27,** evacuated New York.

Nathan Hale executed as spy by British **Sept. 22.**

Brig. Gen. Arnold's **Lake Champlain** fleet was defeated at Valcour **Oct. 11,** but British returned to Canada. Howe failed to destroy Washington's army at **White Plains Oct. 28.** Hessians captured Ft. Washington, Manhattan, and 3,000 men **Nov. 16;** Ft. Lee, N.J. **Nov. 18.**

Washington in Pennsylvania, recrossed **Delaware River Dec. 25-26,** defeated 1,400 Hessians at Trenton, N.J. **Dec. 26.**

1777

Washington defeated Lord Cornwallis at **Princeton Jan. 3.** Continental Congress adopted Stars and Stripes. *See Flag article.*

Maj. Gen. John Burgoyne with 8,000 from Canada captured **Ft. Ticonderoga July 6.** Americans beat back Burgoyne at Bemis Heights **Oct. 7** and cut off British escape route. Burgoyne surrendered 5,000 men at **Saratoga N.Y. Oct. 17.**

Marquis de Lafayette, aged 20, made major general.

Articles of Confederation and Perpetual Union adopted by Continental Congress **Nov. 15**

France recognized independence of 13 colonies **Dec. 17.**

1778

France signed treaty of aid with U.S. **Feb. 6.** Sent fleet; British evacuated Philadelphia in consequence **June 18.**

1779

John Paul Jones on the *Bonhomme Richard* defeated *Serapis* in British North Sea waters **Sept. 23.**

1780

Charleston, S.C. fell to the British **May 12,** but a British force was defeated near **Kings Mountain, N.C. Oct. 7** by militiamen.

Benedict Arnold found to be a traitor **Sept. 23.** Arnold escaped, made brigadier general in British army.

1781

Bank of North America incorporated in Philadelphia **May 26.**

Cornwallis, sapped by patriot victories, retired to **Yorktown, Va.** Adm. De Grasse landed 3,000 French and stopped British fleet in Hampton Roads. Washington and Rochambeau joined forces, arrived near Williamsburg **Sept. 26.** When siege of Cornwallis began **Oct. 6,** British had 6,000, Americans 8,846, French 7,800. **Cornwallis surrendered Oct. 19.**

1782

New **British** cabinet agreed **in March** to **recognize U.S.** independence. Preliminary agreement signed in Paris **Nov. 30.**

1783

Massachusetts Supreme Court **outlawed slavery** in that state, noting the words in the state Bill of Rights "all men are born free and equal."

Britain, U.S. signed **peace treaty Sept. 3** (Congress ratified it **Jan. 14, 1784).**

Washington ordered army disbanded Nov. 3, bade farewell to his officers at **Fraunces Tavern,** N.Y. City **Dec. 4.**

Noah Webster published *American Spelling Book,* great bestseller.

1784

First successful daily newspaper, **Pennsylvania Packet & General Advertiser,** published **Sept. 21.**

1786

Delegates from 5 states at **Annapolis, Md. Sept. 11-14** asked Congress to call convention in Philadelphia to write practical constitution for the 13 states.

1787

Shays's Rebellion, of debt-ridden farmers in Massachusetts, failed **Jan. 25.**

Northwest Ordinance adopted **July 13** by Continental Congress. Determined government of Northwest Territory north of Ohio River, west of New York; 60,000 inhabitants could get statehood. Guaranteed freedom of religion, support for schools, no slavery.

Constitutional convention opened at Philadelphia **May 25** with George Washington presiding. Constitution adopted by delegates **Sept. 17;** ratification by 9th state, New Hampshire, **June 21, 1788,** meant adoption; declared in effect **Mar. 4, 1789.**

1789

George Washington chosen president by all electors voting (73 eligible, 69 voting, 4 absent); John Adams, vice president, 34 votes. **Feb. 4.** First Congress met at Federal Hall, N.Y. City; regular sessions began **Apr. 6.** Washington inaugurated there **Apr. 30.** Supreme Court created by Federal Judiciary Act **Sept. 24.**

1790

Congress met in Phila. **Dec. 6,** new temporary Capital.

1791

Bill of Rights went into effect **Dec. 15.**

1792

Gen. **"Mad" Anthony Wayne** made commander in Ohio-Indiana area, trained "American Legion"; established string of forts. Routed Indians at Fallen Timbers on Maumee River **Aug. 20, 1794,** checked British at Fort Miami, Ohio.

1793

Eli Whitney invented **cotton gin,** reviving southern slavery.

1794

Whiskey Rebellion, west Pennsylvania farmers protesting liquor tax of **1791,** was suppressed by 15,000 militiamen **Sept. 1794.** Alexander Hamilton used incident to establish authority of the new federal government in enforcing its laws.

1795

U.S. bought peace from **Algiers and Tunis** by paying $800,000, supplying a frigate and annual tribute of $25,000 **Nov. 28.**

Gen. Wayne signed peace with Indians at Fort Greenville.

Univ. of North Carolina became first operating state university.

1796

Washington's Farewell Address as president delivered **Sept. 19.** Gave strong warnings against permanent alliances with foreign powers, big public debt, large military establishment and devices of "small, artful, enterprising minority" to control or change government.

1797

U.S. frigate United States launched at Philadelphia **July 10**; Constellation at Baltimore **Sept. 7**; Constitution (Old Ironsides) at Boston **Sept. 20.**

1798

War with France threatened over French raids on U.S. shipping and rejection of U.S. diplomats. Congress voided all treaties with France, ordered Navy to capture French armed ships. Navy (45 ships) and 365 privateers captured 84 French ships. USS Constellation took French warship Insurgente **1799.** Napoleon stopped French raids after becoming First Consul.

1801

Tripoli declared war June 10 against U.S., which refused added tribute to commerce-raiding Arab corsairs. Land and naval campaigns forced Tripoli to conclude **peace June 4, 1805.**

1803

Supreme Court, in **Marbury v. Madison** case, for the first time overturned a U.S. law **Feb. 24.**

Napoleon, who had recovered Louisiana from Spain by secret treaty, sold all of **Louisiana,** stretching to Canadian border, to U.S., for $11,250,000 in bonds, plus $3,750,000 indemnities to American citizens with claims against France. U.S. took title **Dec. 20.** Purchases doubled U.S. area.

1804

Lewis and Clark expedition ordered by Pres. Jefferson to explore what is now northwest U.S. Started from St. Louis **May 14**; ended **Sept. 23, 1806.** Sacagawea, an Indian woman, served as guide.

Vice Pres. **Aaron Burr,** after long political rivalry, **shot Alexander Hamilton** in a duel **July 11** in Weehawken, N.J.; Hamilton died the next day.

1807

Robert Fulton made first practical steamboat trip; left N.Y. City **Aug. 17,** reached Albany, 150 mi., in 32 hrs.

1808

Slave importation outlawed. Some 250,000 slaves were illegally imported **1808-1860.**

1811

William Henry Harrison, governor of Indiana, defeated Indians under the Prophet, in battle of Tippecanoe **Nov. 7.**

Cumberland Road begun at Cumberland, Md.; became important route to West.

1812

War of 1812 had 3 main causes: Britain seized U.S. ships trading with France; Britain seized 4,000 naturalized U.S. sailors by **1810;** Britain armed Indians who raided western border. U.S. stopped trade with Europe **1807** and **1809.** Trade with Britain only was stopped, **1810.**

Unaware that Britain had raised the blockade 2 days before, **Congress declared war June 18** by a small majority. The West favored war, New England opposed it. The British were handicapped by war with France.

U.S. naval victories in **1812** included: USS Essex captured Alert **Aug. 13;** USS Constitution destroyed Guerriere **Aug. 19;** USS Wasp took Frolic **Oct. 18;** USS United States defeated Macedonian off Azores **Oct. 25;** Constitution beat Java **Dec. 29. British captured Detroit Aug. 16.**

1813

Oliver H. Perry defeated British fleet at Battle of Lake Erie, **Sept. 10.** U.S. victory at Battle of the Thames, Ont., **Oct. 5,** broke Indian allies of Britain, and made Detroit frontier safe for U.S. But Americans failed in Canadian invasion attempts. York (Toronto) and Buffalo were burned.

1814

British landed in Maryland in August, defeated U.S. force **Aug. 24, burned Capitol** and White House. Maryland militia stopped British advance **Sept. 12.** Bombardment of Ft. McHenry, Baltimore, for 25 hours, **Sept. 13-14,** by British fleet failed; Francis Scott Key wrote words to **Star Spangled Banner.**

U.S. won naval Battle of **Lake Champlain Sept. 11.** Peace treaty signed at Ghent **Dec. 24.**

1815

Some 5,300 British, unaware of peace treaty, attacked U.S. entrenchments near **New Orleans, Jan. 8.** British had over 2,000 casualties, Americans lost 71.

U.S. flotilla finally ended piracy by **Algiers, Tunis, Tripoli** by **Aug. 6.**

1816

Second Bank of the U.S. chartered.

1817

Rush-Bagot treaty signed **Apr. 28-29;** limited U.S., British armaments on the Great Lakes.

1819

Spain cedes **Florida** to U.S. **Feb. 22.**

American steamship Savannah made first part steam-powered, part sail-powered crossing of Atlantic, Savannah, Ga. to Liverpool, Eng., 29 days.

1820

Henry Clay's **Missouri Compromise** bill passed by Congress **May 3.** Slavery was allowed in Missouri, but not elsewhere west of the Mississippi River north of 36° 30′ latitude (the southern line of Missouri). Repealed **1854.**

1821

Emma Willard founded Troy Female Seminary, first U.S. women's college.

1823

Monroe Doctrine enunciated **Dec. 2,** opposing European intervention in the Americas.

1824

Pawtucket, R.I. **weavers strike** in first such action by women.

1825

Erie Canal opened; first boat left Buffalo **Oct. 26,** reached N.Y. City **Nov. 4.** Canal cost $7 million but cut travel time one-third, shipping costs nine-tenths; opened Great Lakes area, made N.Y. City chief Atlantic port.

John Stevens, of Hoboken, N.J., built and operated first experimental **steam locomotive** in U.S.

1828

South Carolina **Dec. 19** declared the right of state **nullification of federal laws,** opposing the "Tariff of Abominations."

Noah Webster published his *American Dictionary of the English Language.*

Baltimore & Ohio 1st U.S. passenger RR, was begun **July 4.**

1830

Mormon church organized by Joseph Smith in Fayette, N.Y. **Apr. 6.**

1831

Nat Turner, black slave in Virginia, led local slave rebellion, killed 57 whites in **Aug.** Troops called in, Turner captured, tried, and hanged.

1832

Black Hawk War (Ill.-Wis.) **Apr.-Sept.** pushed Sauk and Fox Indians west across Mississippi.

South Carolina convention passed **Ordinance of Nullification in Nov.** against permanent tariff, threatening to withdraw from the Union. Congress **Feb. 1833** passed a compromise tariff act, whereupon South Carolina repealed its act.

1833

Oberlin College, first in U.S. to adopt coeducation; refused to bar students on account of race, **1835.**

1835

Texas proclaimed right to secede from Mexico; Sam Houston put in command of Texas army, **Nov. 2-4.**

Gold discovered on **Cherokee land** in Georgia. Indians forced to cede lands **Dec. 20** and to cross Mississippi.

1836

Texans besieged in Alamo in San Antonio by Mexicans under Santa Anna **Feb. 23-Mar. 6;** entire garrison killed. Texas independence declared, **Mar. 2.** At San Jacinto **Apr. 21** Sam Houston and Texans defeated Mexicans.

Marcus Whitman, H.H. Spaulding and wives reached Fort Walla Walla on Columbia River, Oregon. **First white women to cross plains.**

Seminole Indians in Florida under Osceola began attacks **Nov. 1,** protesting forced removal. The unpopular 8-year war ended **Aug. 14, 1842;** Indians were sent to Oklahoma. War cost the U.S. 1,500 soldiers.

1841

First emigrant **wagon train for California,** 47 persons, left Independence, Mo. **May 1,** reached Cal. **Nov. 4.**

Brook Farm commune set up by New England transcendentalist intellectuals. Lasts to **1846.**

1842

Webster-Ashburton Treaty signed **Aug. 9,** fixing the U.S.-Canada border in Maine and Minnesota.

First use of **anesthetic** (sulphuric ether gas).

Settlement of Oregon begins via **Oregon Trail.**

1844

First message over first **telegraph line** sent **May 24** by inventor Samuel F.B. Morse from Washington to Baltimore: "What hath God wrought!"

1845

Texas Congress voted for annexation to U.S. **July 4.** U.S. Congress admits Texas to Union **Dec. 29.**

1846

Mexican War. Pres. James K. Polk ordered Gen. Zachary Taylor to seize disputed Texan land settled by Mexicans. After border clash, U.S. declared war **May 13;** Mexico **May 23.** Northern Whigs opposed war, southerners backed it.

Bear flag of Republic of California raised by American settlers at Sonoma **June 14.**

About 12,000 U.S. troops took Vera Cruz Mar. 27, 1847, Mexico City Sept. 14, 1847. By **treaty, Feb. 1848,** Mexico ceded claims to Texas, California, Arizona, New Mexico, Nevada, Utah, part of Colorado. U.S. assumed $3 million American claims and paid Mexico $15 million.

Treaty with Great Britain **June 15** set **boundary in Oregon** territory at 49th parallel (extension of existing line). Expansionists had used slogan "54° 40′ or fight."

Mormons, after violent clashes with settlers over polygamy, left Nauvoo, Ill. for West under Brigham Young, settled **July 1847 at Salt Lake City, Utah.**

Elias Howe invented **sewing machine.**

1847

First **adhesive U.S. postage stamps** on sale **July 1;** Benjamin Franklin 5¢, Washington 10¢.

Ralph Waldo Emerson published first book of poems; **Henry Wadsworth Longfellow** published *Evangeline.*

1848

Gold discovered Jan. 24 in California; 80,000 prospectors emigrate in **1849.**

Lucretia Mott and Elizabeth Cady Stanton lead **Seneca Falls, N.Y. Women's Rights Convention July 19-20.**

1850

Sen. Henry Clay's **Compromise of 1850** admitted California as 31st state **Sept. 9,** slavery forbidden; made Utah and New Mexico territories without decision on slavery; made Fugitive Slave Law more harsh; ended District of Columbia slave trade.

1851

Herman Melville's *Moby Dick,* **Nathaniel Hawthorne's** *House of the Seven Gables* published.

1852

Uncle Tom's Cabin, by **Harriet Beecher Stowe,** published.

1853

Commodore Matthew C. Perry, U.S.N., received by Lord of Toda, Japan **July 14; negotiated treaty to open Japan** to U.S. ships.

1854

Republican party formed at Ripon, Wis. **Feb. 28.** Opposed Kansas-Nebraska Act (became law **May 30**) which left issue of slavery to vote of settlers.

Henry David Thoreau published *Walden.*

1855

Walt Whitman published *Leaves of Grass.*

First railroad train crossed Mississippi on the river's first bridge, **Rock Island,** Ill.-Davenport, Ia. **Apr. 21.**

1856

Republican party's first nominee for president, **John C. Fremont,** defeated. Abraham Lincoln made 50 speeches for him.

Lawrence, Kan. sacked **May 21** by slavery party; abolitionist **John Brown** led anti-slavery men against Missourians at **Osawatomie, Kan. Aug. 30**

1857

Dred Scott decision by U.S. Supreme Court **Mar. 6** held, 6-3, that a slave did not become free when taken into a free state, Congress could not bar slavery from a territory, and blacks could not be citizens.

1858

First **Atlantic cable** completed by Cyrus W. Field **Aug. 5;** cable failed **Sept. 1.**

Lincoln-Douglas debates in Illinois **Aug. 21-Oct. 15.**

1859

First commercially productive **oil well,** drilled near Titusville, Pa., by Edwin L. Drake **Aug. 27.**

Abolitionist **John Brown** with 21 men seized U.S. Armory at **Harpers Ferry (then Va.) Oct. 16.** U.S. Marines captured raiders, killing several. Brown was hanged for treason by Virginia **Dec. 2.**

1860

New England shoe-workers, 20,000, strike, win higher wages.

Abraham Lincoln, Republican, elected president in 4-way race.

First **Pony Express** between Sacramento, Cal. and St. Joseph, Mo. started **Apr. 3;** service ended **Oct. 24, 1861** when first transcontinental telegraph line was completed.

1861

Seven southern states set up **Confederate States of America Feb. 8,** with Jefferson Davis as president. **Civil War** began as Confederates fired on **Ft. Sumter** in Charleston, S.C. **Apr. 12;** they captured it **Apr. 14.**

President **Lincoln called for 75,000 volunteers Apr. 15.** By **May,** 11 states had seceded. Lincoln blockaded southern ports **Apr. 19,** cutting off vital exports, aid.

Confederates repelled Union forces at first **Battle of Bull Run July 21.**

First **transcontinental telegraph** was put in operation.

1862

Homestead Act was approved **May 20;** it granted free

family farms to settlers.

Land Grant Act approved **July 7,** providing for public land sale to benefit agricultural education; eventually led to establishment of state university systems.

Union forces were victorious in western campaigns, took **New Orleans.** Battles in East were inconclusive.

1863

Lincoln issued **Emancipation Proclamation Jan. 1,** freeing "all slaves in areas still in rebellion."

The entire **Mississippi River** was in Union hands by **July 4.** Union forces won a major victory at **Gettysburg, Pa. July 1-July 4.** Lincoln read his **Gettysburg Address Nov. 19.**

Draft riots in N.Y. City killed about 1,000, including blacks who were hanged by mobs **July 13-16.** Rioters protested provision allowing money payment in place of service. Such payments were ended 1864.

1864

Gen. Sherman marched through Georgia, taking Atlanta **Sept. 1,** Savannah **Dec. 22.**

Sand Creek massacre of Cheyenne and Arapaho Indians **Nov. 29** in a raid by 900 cavalrymen who killed 150-500 men, women, and children; 9 soldiers died. The tribes were awaiting surrender terms when attacked.

1865

Robert E. Lee surrendered 27,800 Confederate troops to Grant at Appomattox Court House, Va. **Apr. 9.** J.E. Johnston surrendered 31,200 to Sherman at Durham Station, N.C. **Apr. 18.** Last rebel troops surrendered **May 26.**

President **Lincoln was shot Apr. 14** by John Wilkes Booth in Ford's Theater, Washington; died the following morning. Booth was reported dead **Apr. 26.** Four co-conspirators were hanged **July 7.**

Thirteenth Amendment, abolishing slavery, took effect **Dec. 18.**

1866

First post of the **Grand Army of the Republic** formed **Apr. 6;** was a major national political force for years. Last encampment, **Aug. 31, 1949,** attended by 6 of the 16 surviving veterans.

Ku Klux Klan formed secretly in South to terrorize blacks who voted. Disbanded **1869-71.** A second Klan was organized **1915.**

Congress took control of southern Reconstruction, backed freedmen's rights.

1867

Alaska sold to U.S. by Russia for $7.2 million **Mar. 30** through efforts of Sec. of State William H. Seward.

Horatio Alger published first book, *Ragged Dick.*

The **Grange** was organized **Dec 4,** to protect farmer interests.

1868

The World Almanac, a publication of the *New York World,* appeared for the first time.

Pres. **Andrew Johnson** tried to remove Edwin M. Stanton, secretary of war; was impeached by House **Feb. 24** for violation of Tenure of Office Act; acquitted by Senate **March-May.** Stanton resigned.

1869

Financial "**Black Friday**" in New York **Sept. 24;** caused by attempt to "corner" gold.

Transcontinental railroad completed; golden spike driven at Promontory, Utah **May 10** marking the junction of Central Pacific and Union Pacific.

Knights of Labor formed in Philadelphia. By **1886,** it had 700,000 members nationally.

Woman suffrage law passed in Territory of Wyoming **Dec. 10.**

1871

Great fire destroyed Chicago Oct. 8-11; loss est. at $196 million.

1872

Amnesty Act restored civil rights to citizens of the South **May 22** except for 500 Confederate leaders.

Congress founded first national park — **Yellowstone** in Wyoming.

1873

First U.S. **postal card** issued **May 1.**

Banks failed, panic began in **Sept.** Depression lasted 5 years.

"Boss" William Tweed of N.Y. City convicted of stealing public funds. He died in jail in **1878.**

Bellevue Hospital in N.Y. City started the first **school of nursing.**

1875

Congress passed **Civil Rights Act Mar. 1** giving equal rights to blacks in public accommodations and jury duty. Act invalidated in **1883** by Supreme Court.

First **Kentucky Derby** held **May 17** at Churchill Downs, Louisville, Ky.

1876

Samuel J. Tilden, Democrat, received majority of popular votes for president over **Rutherford B. Hayes,** Republican, but 22 electoral votes were in dispute; issue left to Congress. Hayes given presidency **in Feb., 1877** after Republicans agree to end Reconstruction of South.

Col. **George A. Custer** and 264 soldiers of the 7th Cavalry killed **June 25** in "last stand," Battle of the Little Big Horn, Mont., in Sioux Indian War.

Mark Twain published *Tom Sawyer.*

1877

Molly Maguires, Irish terrorist society in Scranton, Pa. mining areas, broken up by hanging of 11 leaders for murders of mine officials and police.

Pres. Hayes sent troops in violent national **railroad strike.**

1878

First commercial **telephone** exchange opened, New Haven, Conn. **Jan. 28.**

1879

F.W. Woolworth opened his first five-and-ten store in Utica, N.Y. **Feb. 22.**

Henry George published *Progress & Poverty,* advocating single tax on land.

1881

Pres. **James A. Garfield shot** in Washington, D.C. **July 2;** died **Sept. 19.**

Booker T. Washington founded Tuskegee Institute for blacks.

Helen Hunt Jackson published *A Century of Dishonor* about mistreatment of Indians.

1883

Pendleton Act, passed **Jan. 16,** reformed federal civil service.

Brooklyn Bridge opened **May 24.**

1886

Haymarket riot and bombing, evening of **May 4,** followed bitter labor battles for 8-hour day in Chicago; 7 police and 4 workers died, 66 wounded. Eight anarchists found guilty. Gov. John P. Altgeld denounced trial as unfair.

Geronimo, Apache Indian, finally surrendered **Sept. 4.**

American Federation of Labor (AFL) formed **Dec. 8** by 25 craft unions.

1888

Great blizzard in eastern U.S. **Mar. 11-14;** 400 deaths.

1889

Johnstown, Pa. flood May 31; 2,200 lives lost.

1890

First execution by **electrocution:** William Kemmler **Aug. 6** at Auburn Prison, Auburn, N.Y., for murder.

Battle of **Wounded Knee, S.D. Dec. 29,** the last major conflict between Indians and U.S. troops. About 200 Indian men, women, and children, and 29 soldiers were killed.

Castle Garden closed as N.Y. immigration depot; **Ellis Island** opened **Dec. 31, closed 1954.**

Sherman Antitrust Act begins federal effort to curb monopolies.

Jacob Riis published *How the Other Half Lives,* about city slums.

1892

Homestead, Pa., strike at Carnegie steel mills; 7 guards and 11 strikers and spectators shot to death **July 6;** setback for unions.

1893

Financial panic began, led to 4-year depression.

1894

Thomas A. Edison's **kinetoscope** (motion pictures) (invented 1887) given first public showing **Apr. 14.**

Jacob S. Coxey led 500 unemployed from the Midwest into Washington, D.C. **Apr. 29.** Coxey was arrested for trespassing on Capitol grounds.

1896

William Jennings Bryan delivered "Cross of Gold" into Washington, D.C. **Apr. 29.** Coxey was arrested for trespassing on Capitol grounds.

Supreme Court, in **Plessy v. Ferguson,** approved racial segregation under the "separate but equal" doctrine.

1898

U.S. **battleship Maine** blown up **Feb. 15** at Havana, 260 killed.

U.S. blockaded Cuba Apr. 22 in aid of independence forces. U.S. declared war on Spain, **Apr. 24,** destroyed Spanish fleet in Philippines **May 1,** took Guam **June 20.**

Puerto Rico taken by U.S. **July 25-Aug. 12.** Spain agreed **Dec. 10** to cede Philippines, Puerto Rico, and Guam, and approved independence for Cuba.

U.S. annexed independent republic of **Hawaii.**

1899

Filipino insurgents, unable to get recognition of independence from U.S., started guerrilla war **Feb. 4.** Crushed with capture **May 23, 1901** of leader, Emilio Aguinaldo.

U.S. declared **Open Door Policy** to make China an open international market and to preserve its integrity as a nation.

John Dewey published *School and Society,* backing progressive education.

1900

Carry Nation, Kansas anti-saloon agitator, began raiding with hatchet.

U.S. helped suppress **"Boxers"** in Peking

1901

Pres. **William McKinley was shot Sept. 6** by an anarchist, Leon Czolgosz; died **Sept. 14.**

1903

Treaty between U.S. and Colombia to have U.S. dig **Panama Canal** signed **Jan. 22,** rejected by Colombia. Panama declared independence with U.S. support **Nov. 3;** recognized by Pres. Theodore Roosevelt **Nov. 6.** U.S., Panama signed canal treaty **Nov. 18.**

Wisconsin set first **direct primary** voting system **May 23.**

First **automobile trip** across U.S. from San Francisco to New York **May 23-Aug. 1.**

First successful flight in heavier-than-air mechanically propelled airplane by **Orville Wright Dec. 17** near Kitty Hawk, N.C., 120 ft. in 12 seconds. Fourth flight same day by **Wilbur Wright,** 852 ft. in 59 seconds. Improved plane patented **May 22, 1906.**

Jack London published *Call of the Wild.*

Great Train Robbery, pioneering film, produced.

1904

Ida Tarbell published muckraking *History of Standard Oil.*

1905

First **Rotary Club** of businessmen founded in Chicago.

1906

San Francisco earthquake and fire **Apr. 18-19** left 503 dead, $350 million damages.

Pure Food and Drug Act and **Meat Inspection Act** both passed **June 30.**

1907

Financial panic and depression started **Mar. 13.**

First round-world cruise of U.S. **"Great White Fleet";** 16 battleships, 12,000 men.

1909

Adm. Robert E. Peary reached **North Pole Apr. 6** on 6th attempt, accompanied by Matthew Henson, a black man, and 4 Eskimos.

National Conference on the Negro convened **May 30,** leading to founding of the National Association for the Advancement of Colored People.

1910

Boy Scouts of America founded **Feb. 8.**

1911

Supreme Court dissolved **Standard Oil Co.**

First **transcontinental airplane flight** (with numerous stops) by C.P. Rodgers, New York to Pasadena, **Sept. 17-Nov. 5;** time in air 82 hrs., 4 min.

1912

Amer. Girl Guides founded **Mar. 12;** name changed in 1913 to **Girl Scouts.**

U.S. sent marines **Aug. 14** to **Nicaragua,** which was in default of loans to U.S. and Europe.

1913

N.Y. Armory Show brought modern art to U.S. **Feb. 17.**

U.S. blockaded Mexico in support of revolutionaries.

Charles Beard published his *Economic Interpretation of the Constitution.*

Federal Reserve System was authorized **Dec. 23,** in a major reform of U.S. banking and finance.

1914

Ford Motor Co. raised basic wage rates from $2.40 for 9-hr. day to $5 for 8-hr. day **Jan. 5.**

When U.S. sailors were arrested at Tampico **Apr. 9,** Atlantic fleet was sent to **Veracruz,** occupied city.

Pres. **Wilson** proclaimed **U.S. neutrality** in the European war **Aug. 4.**

The **Clayton Antitrust Act** was passed **Oct. 15,** strengthening federal anti-monopoly powers.

1915

First **telephone talk,** New York to San Francisco, **Jan. 25** by Alexander Graham Bell and Thomas A. Watson.

British ship **Lusitania** sunk **May 7** by German submarine, 128 American passengers lost (Germany had warned passengers in advance). As a result of U.S. campaign, Germany issued apology and promise of payments **Oct. 5.** Pres. Wilson asked for a military fund increase **Dec. 7.**

U.S. troops landed in **Haiti July 28.** Haiti became a virtual U.S. protectorate under **Sept. 16** treaty.

1916

Gen. **John J. Pershing entered Mexico** to pursue Francisco (Pancho) Villa, who had raided U.S. border areas. Forces withdrawn **Feb. 5, 1917.**

Rural Credits Act passed **July 17,** followed by Warehouse Act. **Aug. 11;** both provided financial aid to farmers.

Bomb exploded during **San Francisco** Preparedness Day parade **July 22,** killed 10. Thomas J. Mooney, labor organizer, and Warren K. Billings, shoe worker, were convicted; both pardoned in **1939.**

U.S. bought **Virgin Islands** from Denmark **Aug. 4.**

Jeanette Rankin, 1st U.S. Congresswoman (R-Montana) elected.

U.S. established military government in the **Dominican Republic Nov. 29.**

Trade and loans to **European Allies** soared during the year.

John Dewey published *Democracy and Education.*

Carl Sandburg published *Chicago Poems.*

1917

Germany, suffering from British blockade, declared almost unrestricted **submarine warfare Jan. 31.** U.S. cut diplomatic ties with Germany **Feb. 3,** and formally declared war **Apr. 6.**

Conscription law was passed **May 18.** First U.S. troops arrived in Europe **June 26.**

The 18th **(Prohibition)** Amendment to the Constitution was submitted to the states by Congress **Dec. 18.** On **Jan. 16, 1919,** the 36th state (Nevada) ratified it. Franklin D. Roosevelt, as 1932 presidential candidate, endorsed repeal; 21st Amendment repealed 18th; ratification completed **Dec. 5, 1933.**

1918

Over one million **American troops** were in Europe by **July.** War ended **Nov. 11.**

Influenza epidemic killed an estimated 20 million worldwide, 548,000 in U.S.

1919

First **transatlantic flight,** by U.S. Navy seaplane, left Rockaway, N.Y. **May 8,** stopped at Newfoundland, Azores, Lisbon **May 27.**

Boston police strike Sept. 9; National Guard breaks strike.

Sherwood Anderson published *Winesburg, Ohio.*

About 250 **alien radicals** were deported **Dec. 22.**

1920

In national **Red Scare,** some 2,700 Communists, anarchists, and other radicals were arrested **Jan.-May.**

Senate refused **Mar. 19** to ratify the **League of Nations Covenant.**

Nicola Sacco, 29, shoe factory employee and radical agitator, and **Bartolomeo Vanzetti,** 32, fish peddler and anarchist, accused of killing 2 men in Mass. payroll holdup **Apr. 15.** Found guilty **1921.** A 6-year worldwide campaign for release on grounds of want of conclusive evidence and prejudice failed. Both were executed **Aug. 23, 1927.** Vindicated July 19, 1977 by proclamation of Mass. Gov. Dukakis.

First regular licensed **radio broadcasting** begun **Aug. 20.**

19th Amendment ratified **Aug. 26,** giving women right to vote.

League of Women Voters founded.

Wall St., N.Y. City, **bomb** explosion killed 30, injured 100, did $2 million damage **Sept. 16.**

Sinclair Lewis' *Main Street,* **F. Scott Fitzgerald's** *This Side of Paradise* published.

1921

Congress sharply curbed **immigration,** set national quota system **May 19.**

Joint Congressional resolution declaring **peace with Germany, Austria, and Hungary** signed **July 2** by Pres. Harding; treaties were signed in **Aug.**

Limitation of Armaments Conference met in Washington **Nov. 12 to Feb. 6, 1922.** Major powers agreed to curtail naval construction, outlaw poison gas, restrict submarine attack on merchantmen, respect integrity of China.

Ku Klux Klan began revival with violence against blacks in North, South, and Midwest.

1922

Violence during **coal-mine strike** at Herrin, Ill., **June 22-23** cost 36 lives, 21 of them non-union miners.

Reader's Digest founded.

1923

First **sound-on-film motion picture,** "Phonofilm" was shown by Lee de Forest at Rivoli Theater, N.Y. City, beginning in **April.**

1924

Law approved by Congress **June 15** making all **Indians citizens.**

Nellie Tayloe Ross elected governor of Wyoming **Nov. 9** after death of her husband **Oct. 2;** installed **Jan. 5, 1925,** first woman governor. **Miriam (Ma) Ferguson** was elected governor of Texas **Nov. 9;** installed **Jan. 20, 1925.**

George Gershwin wrote *Rhapsody in Blue.*

1925

John T. Scopes found guilty of having taught evolution in Dayton, Tenn. high school, fined $100 and costs **July 24.**

1926

Dr. Robert H. Goddard demonstrated practicality of **rockets Mar. 16** at Auburn, Mass. with first liquid fuel rocket; rocket traveled 184 ft. in 2.5 secs.

Air Commerce Act passed, providing federal aid for airlines and airports.

1927

About 1,000 **marines landed in China Mar. 5** to protect property in civil war.

Capt. **Charles A. Lindbergh** left Roosevelt Field, N.Y. **May 20** alone in plane Spirit of St. Louis on first New York-Paris nonstop flight. Reached Le Bourget airfield **May 21,** 3,610 miles in 33 ½ hours.

The Jazz Singer, with **Al Jolson,** demonstrated part-talking pictures in N.Y. City **Oct. 6.**

Show Boat opened in New York **Dec. 27.**

O. E. Rolvaag published *Giants in the Earth.*

1929

"St. Valentine's Day massacre" in Chicago **Feb. 14;** gangsters killed 7 rivals.

Farm price stability aided by **Agricultural Marketing Act,** passed **June 15.**

Albert B. Fall, former sec. of the interior, was convicted of accepting a bribe of $100,000 in the leasing of the **Elk Hills (Teapot Dome)** naval oil reserve; sentenced **Nov. 1** to $100,000 fine and year in prison.

Stock Market crash Oct. 29 marked end of postwar prosperity as stock prices plummeted. Stock losses for 1929-31 estimated at $50 billion; worst American depression began.

Thomas Wolfe published *Look Homeward, Angel.* **William Faulkner** published *The Sound and the Fury.*

1930

London **Naval Reduction Treaty** signed by U.S., Britain, Italy, France, and Japan **Apr. 22;** in effect **Jan. 1, 1931;** expired **Dec. 31, 1936.**

Hawley-Smoot Tariff signed; rate hikes slash world trade.

1931

Empire State Building opened in N.Y. City **May 1.**

Pearl Buck published *The Good Earth.*

1932

Reconstruction Finance Corp. established **Jan. 22** to stimulate banking and business. Unemployment at 12 million.

Charles Lindbergh Jr. kidnaped Mar. 1, found dead **May 12.**

Bonus March on Washington **May 29** by World War I veterans demanding Congress pay their bonus in full.

1933

FDR named **Frances Perkins** U.S. Secy of Labor; 1st woman in U.S. Cabinet.

All banks in the U.S. were ordered closed by Pres. Roosevelt **Mar. 6.**

In the "100 days" special session, **Mar. 9—June 16,** Congress passed **New Deal** social and economic measures.

Gold standard dropped by U.S.; announced by Pres. Roosevelt **Apr. 19,** ratified by Congress **June 5.**

Prohibition ended in the U.S. as 36th state ratified 21st Amendment **Dec. 5.**

U.S. foreswore armed intervention in **Western Hemisphere** nations **Dec. 26.**

1934

U.S. troops pull out of **Haiti Aug. 6.**

1935

Comedian **Will Rogers** and aviator Wiley Post **killed Aug. 15** in Alaska plane crash.

Social Security Act passed by Congress **Aug. 14.**

Huey Long, Senator from Louisiana and national political leader, was **assassinated Sept. 8.**

Porgy and Bess, **George Gershwin** opera on American theme, opened **Oct. 10** in N.Y. City.

Committee for Industrial Organization (CIO) formed to expand industrial unionism **Nov. 9.**

1936

Boulder Dam completed.

Margaret Mitchell published *Gone With the Wind.*

1937

Amelia Earhart Putnam, aviator, and co-pilot Fred Noonan lost **July 2** near Howland Is. in the Pacific.

Pres. Roosevelt asked for 6 additional Supreme Court justices; **"packing" plan** defeated.

Auto, steel labor unions won first big contracts.

1938

Naval Expansion Act passed **May 17.**

National minimum wage enacted **June 28.**

Orson Welles radio dramatization of *War of the Worlds* caused nationwide scare **Oct. 30.**

1939

Pres. Roosevelt asked **defense budget hike Jan. 5, 12.**

N.Y. World's Fair opened **Apr. 30,** closed **Oct. 31;** reopened **May 11, 1940,** and finally closed **Oct. 21.**

Einstein alerts FDR to **A-bomb** opportunity in **Aug. 2** letter.

U.S. declares its neutrality in European war **Sept. 5.**

Roosevelt proclaimed a limited **national emergency Sept. 8,** an unlimited emergency **May 27, 1941.** Both ended by Pres. Truman **Apr. 28, 1952.**

John Steinbeck published *Grapes of Wrath.*

1940

U.S. okayed sale of **surplus war material** to Britain **June 3;** announced transfer of 50 overaged destroyers **Sept. 3.**

First **peacetime draft** approved **Sept. 14.**

Richard Wright published *Native Son.*

1941

The **Four Freedoms** termed essential by Pres. Roosevelt in speech to Congress **Jan. 6:** freedom of speech and religion, freedom from want and fear.

Lend-Lease Act signed **Mar. 11,** providing $7 billion in military credits for Britain. Lend-Lease for USSR approved in Nov.

U.S. occupied **Iceland July 7.**

The **Atlantic Charter,** 8-point declaration of principles, issued by Roosevelt and Winston Churchill **Aug. 14.**

Japan attacked **Pearl Harbor,** Hawaii, 7:55 a.m. **Dec. 7,** 19 ships sunk or damaged, 2,300 dead. U.S. declared war on Japan **Dec. 8,** on Germany and Italy **Dec. 11** after those countries declared war.

1942

Federal government forcibly moved 110,000 **Japanese-Americans** (including 75,000 U.S. citizens) from West Coast to detention camps. Exclusion lasted 3 years.

Battle of **Midway June 4-7** was Japan's first major defeat.

Marines landed on **Guadalcanal Aug. 7;** last Japanese not expelled until **Feb. 9, 1943.**

U.S., Britain invaded North Africa **Nov. 8.**

First **nuclear chain reaction** (fission of uranium isotope U-235) produced at Univ. of Chicago, under physicists Arthur Compton, Enrico Fermi, others **Dec. 2.**

1943

All war contractors barred from **racial discrimination May 27.**

Pres. Roosevelt signed **June 10** the pay-as-you-go income tax bill. Starting **July 1** wage and salary earners were subject to a **paycheck withholding** tax.

Race riot in Detroit June 21; 34 dead, 700 injured. Riot in Harlem section of N.Y. City; 6 killed.

U.S. troops invaded Italy **Sept. 9.**

Marines advanced in **Gilbert Is. in Nov.**

1944

U.S., Allied forces invaded Europe at **Normandy June 6.**

G.I. Bill of Rights signed **June 22,** providing veterans benefits.

U.S. forces landed on **Leyte,** Philippines **Oct. 20.**

1945

Yalta Conference met in the Crimea, USSR, **Feb. 3-11.** Roosevelt, Churchill, and Stalin agreed Russia would enter war against Japan.

Marines landed on **Iwo Jima Feb. 19;** U.S. forces invaded **Okinawa Apr. 1.**

Pres. Roosevelt, 63, died of cerebral hemorrhage in Warm Springs, Ga. **Apr. 12;** V.P. **Harry S. Truman** became pres.

Germany surrendered May 7.

First **atomic bomb,** produced at Los Alamos, N.M., exploded at Alamogordo, N.M. **July 16.** Bomb dropped on **Hiroshima Aug. 6,** on **Nagasaki Aug. 9.** Japan surrendered **Aug. 15.**

U.S. forces entered **Korea** south of 38th parallel to displace Japanese **Sept. 8.**

Gen. Douglas MacArthur took over supervision of Japan **Sept. 9.**

1946

Strike by 400,000 **mine workers** began **Apr. 1;** other industries followed.

Philippines given independence by U.S. **July 4.**

1947

Truman Doctrine: Pres. Truman asked Congress to aid Greece and Turkey to combat Communist terrorism **Mar. 12.** Approved **May 15.**

United Nations Security Council voted unanimously **Apr. 2** to place under **U.S. trusteeship** the Pacific islands formerly mandated to Japan.

Jackie Robinson on Brooklyn Dodgers **Apr. 11,** broke the color barrier in major league baseball.

Taft-Hartley Labor Act curbing strikes was vetoed by Truman **June 20;** Congress overrode the veto.

Proposals later known as the **Marshall Plan,** under which the U.S. would extend aid to European countries, were made by Sec. of State George C. Marshall **June 5.** Congress authorized some $12 billion in next 4 years.

1948

USSR began a land **blockade of Berlin's** Allied sectors **Apr. 1.** This blockade and Western counter-blockade were lifted **Sept. 30, 1949,** after British and U.S. planes had lifted 2,343,315 tons of food and coal into the city.

Organization of American States founded **Apr. 30.**

Alger Hiss, former State Dept. official, indicted Dec. 15 for perjury, after denying he had passed secret documents to Whittaker Chambers for transmission to a communist spy ring. His second trial ended in conviction **Jan. 21, 1950,** and a sentence of 5 years in prison.

Kinsey Report on Sexuality in the Human Male published.

1949

U.S. troops withdrawn from **Korea June 29.**

North Atlantic Treaty Organization (NATO) established **Aug. 24** by U.S., Canada, and 10 West European nations, agreeing that an armed attack against one or more of them would be considered an attack against all.

Mrs. I. Toguri D'Aquino (**Tokyo Rose** of Japanese wartime broadcasts) was sentenced **Oct. 7** to 10 years in prison for treason. Paroled **1956,** pardoned **1977.**

Eleven leaders of **U.S. Communist party** convicted **Oct. 14,** after 9-month trial in N.Y. City, of advocating violent overthrow of U.S. government. Ten defendants sentenced to 5 years in prison each and the 11th to 3 years. Supreme Court upheld the convictions **June 4, 1951.**

1950

U.S. **Jan 14** recalled all consular officials from **China** after the latter seized the American consulate general in Peking.

Masked bandits robbed **Brink's Inc.,** Boston express office, **Jan. 17** of $2.8 million, of which $1.2 million was in cash. Case solved **1956,** 8 sentenced to life.

Pres. Truman authorized production of **H-bomb Jan. 31.**

United Nations asked for troops to restore Korea peace **June 25.**

Truman ordered Air Force and Navy to Korea **June 27** after North Korea invaded South. Truman approved ground forces, air strikes against North **June 30.**

U.S. sent 35 military advisers to **South Vietnam June 27,** and agreed to provide military and economic aid to anti-Communist government.

Army seized all railroads Aug. 27 on Truman's order to prevent a general strike; roads returned to owners in 1952.

U.S. forces landed at Inchon Sept. 15; UN force took Pyongyang **Oct. 20,** reached China border **Nov. 20,** China sent troops across border **Nov. 26.**

Two members of a **Puerto Rican nationalist** movement tried to kill Pres. Truman **Nov. 1.** (see Assassinations)

U.S. **Dec. 8** banned shipments to **Communist China** and to Asiatic ports trading with it.

1951

Sen. **Estes Kefauver** led Senate investigation into organized crime. Preliminary report **Feb. 28** said gambling take was over $20 billion a year.

Julius Rosenberg, his wife, Ethel, and Morton Sobell, all U.S. citizens, were found guilty **Mar. 29** of conspiracy to commit wartime espionage. Rosenbergs sentenced to death, Sobell to 30 years. Rosenbergs **executed June 19, 1953.** Sobell released **Jan. 14, 1969.**

Gen. Douglas MacArthur was removed from his Korea command **Apr. 11** for unauthorized policy statements.

Korea cease-fire talks began in July; lasted 2 years. **Fighting ended July 27, 1953.**

Tariff concessions by the U.S. to the Soviet Union, Communist China, and all communist-dominated lands were suspended **Aug. 1.**

The U.S., **Australia,** and **New Zealand** signed a mutual security pact **Sept. 1.**

Transcontinental television inaugurated **Sept. 4** with Pres. Truman's address at the Japanese Peace Treaty Conference in San Francisco.

Japanese Peace Treaty signed in San Francisco **Sept. 8** by U.S., Japan, and 47 other nations.

J.D. Salinger published *Catcher in the Rye.*

1952

U.S. **seizure of nation's steel mills** was ordered by Pres. Truman **Apr. 8** to avert a strike. Ruled illegal by Supreme Court **June 2.**

Peace contract between West Germany, U.S., Great Britain, and France was signed **May 26.**

The last racial and ethnic barriers to naturalization were removed, **June 26-27,** with the passage of the **Immigration and Naturalization Act of 1952.**

First **hydrogen device** explosion **Nov. 1** at Eniwetok Atoll in Pacific.

1953

Pres. Eisenhower announced **May 8** that U.S. had given France $60 million for **Indochina War.** More aid was announced in **Sept.** In **1954** it was reported that three fourths of the war's costs were met by U.S.

1954

Nautilus, first atomic-powered submarine, was launched at Groton, Conn. **Jan. 21.**

Five members of Congress were wounded in the House **Mar. 1** by **4 Puerto Rican independence supporters** who fired at random from a spectators' gallery.

Sen. Joseph McCarthy led televised hearings **Apr. 22-June 17** into alleged Communist influence in the Army.

Racial segregation in public schools was unanimously ruled unconstitutional by the Supreme Court **May 17,** as a violation of the 14th Amendment clause guaranteeing equal protection of the laws.

Southeast Asia Treaty Organization **(SEATO)** formed by collective defense pact signed in Manila **Sept. 8** by the U.S., Britain, France, Australia, New Zealand, Philippines, Pakistan, and Thailand.

Condemnation of **Sen. Joseph R. McCarthy** (R., Wis.) voted by Senate, 67-22 **Dec. 2** for contempt of a Senate elections subcommittee, for abuse of its members, and for insults to the Senate during his Army investigation hearings.

1955

U.S. agreed **Feb. 12** to help train **South Vietnamese** army.

Supreme Court ordered **"all deliberate speed"** in integration of public schools **May 31.**

A **summit meeting** of leaders of U.S., Britain, France, and USSR took place **July 18-23** in Geneva, Switzerland.

Rosa Parks refused **Dec. 1** to give her seat to a white man on a bus in Montgomery, Ala. Bus segregation ordinance declared unconstitutional by a federal court following boycott and NAACP protest.

Merger of America's 2 largest labor organizations was effected **Dec. 5** under the name American Federation of Labor and Congress of Industrial Organizations. The merged **AFL-CIO** had a membership estimated at 15 million.

1956

Massive resistance to Supreme Court desegregation rulings was called for **Mar. 12** by 101 Southern congressmen.

Federal-Aid **Highway Act** signed **June 29,** inaugurating interstate highway system.

First transatlantic **telephone cable** went into operation **Sept. 25.**

1957

Congress approved first **civil rights bill** for blacks since Reconstruction **Apr. 29,** to protect voting rights.

National Guardsmen, called out by Arkansas Gov. Orval Faubus **Sept. 4,** barred 9 black students from entering previously all-white Central High School in **Little Rock.** Faubus complied **Sept. 21** with a federal court order to remove the National Guardsmen. The blacks entered school **Sept. 23** but were ordered to withdraw by local authorities because of fear of mob violence. Pres. Eisenhower sent federal troops **Sept. 24** to enforce the court's order.

Jack Kerouac published *On the Road.*

1958

First U.S. earth satellite to go into orbit, **Explorer I,** launched by Army **Jan. 31** at Cape Canaveral, Fla.; discovered Van Allen radiation belt.

Five thousand U.S. Marines sent to **Lebanon** to protect elected government from threatened overthrow **July-Oct.**

First domestic **jet airline** passenger service in U.S. opened by National Airlines **Dec. 10** between N.Y. and Miami.

1959

Alaska admitted as 49th state **Jan. 3; Hawaii** admitted **Aug. 21.**

St. Lawrence Seaway opened **Apr. 25.**

The George Washington, first U.S. ballistic-missile submarine, launched at Groton, Conn. **June 9.**

N.S. Savannah, world's first atomic-powered merchant ship, launched **July 21** at Camden, N.J.

Soviet Premier **Khrushchev** paid unprecedented visit to U.S. **Sept. 15-27,** made transcontinental tour.

1960

Sit-ins began **Feb. 1** when 4 black college students in Greensboro, N.C. refused to move from a Woolworth lunch counter when denied service. By **Sept. 1961** more than 70,000 students, whites and blacks, had participated in sit-ins.

U.S. launched first **weather satellite,** Tiros I, **Apr. 1.**

Congress approved a strong **voting rights act Apr. 21.**

A **U-2 reconnaisance plane** of the U.S. was shot down in the Soviet Union **May 1.** The incident led to cancellation of an imminent Paris summit conference.

Mobs attacked U.S. embassy in **Panama Sept. 17** in dispute over flying of U.S. and Panamanian flags.

U.S. announced **Dec. 15** it backed rightist group in **Laos,** which took power the next day.

1961

The U.S. severed diplomatic and consular relations with **Cuba Jan. 3,** after disputes over nationalizations of U.S. firms, U.S. military presence at Guantanamo base, etc.

Invasion of Cuba's **"Bay of Pigs" Apr. 17** by Cuban exiles trained, armed, and directed by the U.S., attempting to overthrow the regime of Premier Fidel Castro, was repulsed.

Commander Alan B. Shepard Jr. was rocketed from Cape Canaveral, Fla., 116.5 mi. above the earth in a Mercury capsule **May 5** in the first U.S. manned sub-orbital space flight.

1962

Lt. Col. John H. Glenn Jr. became the first American in orbit **Feb. 20** when he circled the earth 3 times in the Mercury capsule **Friendship 7.**

Pres. Kennedy said **Feb. 14** U.S. military advisers in Vietnam would fire if fired upon.

Supreme Court **Mar. 26** backed **one-man one-vote** apportionment of seats in state legislatures.

First U.S. **communications satellite** launched in **July.**

James Meredith became first black student at Univ. of Mississippi **Oct. 1** after 3,000 troops put down riots.

A Soviet **offensive missile buildup in Cuba** was revealed **Oct. 22** by Pres. Kennedy, who ordered a naval and air quarantine on shipment of offensive military equipment to the island. Kennedy and Soviet Premier Khrushchev reached agreement **Oct. 28** on a formula to end the crisis. Kennedy announced **Nov. 2** that Soviet missile bases in Cuba were being dismantled.

Rachel Carson's *Silent Spring* launched environmentalist movement.

1963

Supreme Court ruled **Mar. 18** that all **criminal defendants** must have counsel and that illegally acquired evidence was not admissible in state as well as federal courts.

Supreme Court ruled, 8-1, **June 17** that laws requiring **recitation of the Lord's Prayer** or Bible verses in public schools were unconstitutional.

A limited **nuclear test-ban treaty** was agreed upon **July 25** by the U.S., Soviet Union and Britain, barring all nuclear tests except underground.

Washington demonstration by 200,000 persons **Aug. 28** in support of **black demands** for equal rights. Highlight was speech in which Dr. Martin Luther King said: "I have a dream that this nation will rise up and live out the true meaning of its creed, 'We hold these truths to be self-evident: that all men are created equal.' "

South Vietnam Pres. **Ngo Dinh Diem assassinated Nov. 2;** U.S. had earlier withdrawn support.

Pres. John F. Kennedy was shot and fatally wounded by an assassin **Nov. 22** as he rode in a motorcade through downtown Dallas, Tex. Vice Pres. Lyndon B. Johnson was inaugurated president shortly after in Dallas. Lee Harvey Oswald was arrested and charged with the murder. Oswald was shot and fatally wounded **Nov. 24** by Jack Ruby, 52, a Dallas nightclub owner, who was convicted of murder **Mar. 14, 1964** and sentenced to death. Ruby died of natural causes **Jan. 3, 1967** while awaiting retrial.

U.S. troops in Vietnam totalled over 15,000 by year-end; aid to South Vietnam was over $500 million in **1963.**

1964

Panama suspended relations with U.S. **Jan. 9** after riots. U.S. offered **Dec. 18** to negotiate a new canal treaty.

Supreme Court ordered **Feb. 17** that **congressional districts** have equal populations.

U.S. reported **May 27** it was sending military planes to **Laos.**

Omnibus **civil rights bill** passed **June 29** banning discrimination in voting, jobs, public accommodations, etc.

Three **civil rights workers** were reported missing in Mississippi **June 22;** found buried **Aug. 4.** Twenty-one white men were arrested. On **Oct. 20, 1967,** an all-white federal jury convicted 7 of conspiracy in the slayings.

U.S. Congress **Aug. 7** passed **Tonkin Resolution,** authorizing presidential action in Vietnam, after North Vietnam boats reportedly attacked 2 U.S. destroyers **Aug. 2.**

Congress approved War on Poverty bill **Aug. 11.**

The **Warren Commission** released **Sept. 27** a report concluding that Lee Harvey Oswald was solely responsible for the Kennedy assassination.

1965

Pres. Johnson in **Feb.** ordered continuous **bombing of North Vietnam** below 20th parallel.

Some 14,000 U.S. troops sent to **Dominican Republic** during civil war **Apr. 28.** All troops withdrawn by next year.

New **Voting Rights Act** signed **Aug. 6.**

Los Angeles riot by blacks living in **Watts** area resulted in death of 35 persons and property damage est. at $200 million **Aug. 11-16.**

Water Quality Act passed **Sept. 21** to meet pollution, shortage problems.

National origins quota system of **immigration** abolished **Oct. 3.**

Electric power failure blacked out most of northeastern U.S., parts of 2 Canadian provinces the night of **Nov. 9-10.**

U.S. forces in **S. Vietnam** reached 184,300 by year-end.

1966

U.S. forces began firing into **Cambodia May 1.**

Bombing of Hanoi area of North Vietnam by U.S. planes began **June 29.** By **Dec. 31,** 385,300 U.S. troops were stationed in South Vietnam, plus 60,000 offshore and 33,000 in Thailand.

Medicare, government program to pay part of the medical expenses of citizens over 65, began **July 1.**

Edward Brooke (R, Mass.) elected **Nov. 8** as first black U.S. senator in 85 years.

1967

Black representative **Adam Clayton Powell** (D, N.Y.) was denied **Mar. 1** his seat in Congress because of charges he misused gvt. funds. Reelected in 1968, he was seated, but fined $25,000 and stripped of his 22 years' seniority.

Pres. Johnson and Soviet Premier Aleksei Kosygin met **June 23 and 25 at Glassboro State College** in N.J.; agreed not to let any crisis push them into war.

Black riots in **Newark, N.J. July 12-17** killed 26, injured 1,500; over 1,000 arrested. In Detroit, Mich., **July 23-30** at least 40 died; 2,000 injured, 5,000 left homeless by rioting, looting, burning in city's black ghetto. Quelled by 4,700 federal paratroopers and 8,000 National Guardsmen.

Thurgood Marshall sworn in **Oct. 2** as first black U.S. Supreme Court Justice. Carl B. Stokes (D, Cleveland) and Richard G. Hatcher (D, Gary, Ind.) were elected first black mayors of major U.S. cities **Nov. 7.**

By **December** 475,000 U.S. troops were in **South Vietnam,** all North Vietnam was subject to bombing. Protests against the war mounted in U.S. during year.

1968

USS Pueblo and 83-man crew seized in Sea of Japan **Jan. 23** by North Koreans; 82 men released **Dec. 22.**

"Tet offensive": Communist troops attacked Saigon, 30 province capitals **Jan. 30,** suffer heavy casualties.

Pres. Johnson **curbed bombing** of North Vietnam **Mar. 31.** Peace talks began in Paris **May 10.** All bombing of North halted **Oct. 31.**

Martin Luther King Jr., 39, assassinated Apr. 4 in Memphis, Tenn. James Earl Ray, an escaped convict, pleaded guilty to the slaying, was sentenced to 99 years.

Sen. Robert F. Kennedy (D, N.Y.) 42, **shot June 5** in Hotel Ambassador, Los Angeles, after celebrating presidential primary victories. Died **June 6.** Sirhan Bishara Sirhan, Jordanian, convicted of murder.

Rep. Shirley Chisholm (D., N.Y.) became the first black woman elected to Congress.

1969

Expanded four-party **Vietnam peace talks** began **Jan. 18.** U.S. force peaked at 543,400 in April. Withdrawal started **July 8.** Pres. Nixon set Vietnamization policy **Nov. 3.**

A car driven by **Sen. Edward M. Kennedy** (D, Mass.) plunged off a bridge into a tidal pool on Chappaquiddick Is., Martha's Vineyard, Mass. **July 18.** The body of Mary Jo Kopechne, a 28-year-old secretary, was found drowned in the car.

U.S. astronaut **Neil A. Armstrong,** 38, commander of the Apollo 11 mission, became the first man to **set foot on the moon July 20.** Air Force Col. Edwin E. Aldrin Jr. accompanied Armstrong.

Anti-Vietnam War **demonstrations reached peak** in U.S.; some 250,000 marched in Washington, D.C. **Nov. 15.**

Massacre of hundreds of civilians at **Mylai, South Vietnam** in 1968 incident was reported **Nov. 16.**

1970

United Mine Workers official **Joseph A. Yablonski,** his wife, and their daughter were found shot **Jan. 5** in their Clarksville, Pa. home. UMW chief W. A. (Tony) Boyle was later convicted of the killing.

A federal jury **Feb. 18** found the **"Chicago 7"** innocent of conspiring to incite riots during the 1968 Democratic National Convention. However, 5 were convicted of crossing state lines with intent to incite riots.

Millions of Americans participated in anti-pollution demonstrations **Apr. 22** to mark the first **Earth Day.**

U.S. and South Vietnamese forces crossed **Cambodian** borders **Apr. 30** to get at enemy bases. Four students were killed **May 4** at **Kent St.** Univ. in Ohio by National Guardsmen during a protest against the war.

Two **women generals,** the first in U.S. history, were named by Pres. Nixon **May 15.**

A **postal reform** measure was signed **Aug. 12,** creating an independent U.S. Postal Service, thus relinquishing governmental control of the U.S. mails after almost 2 centuries.

1971

Charles Manson, 36, and 3 of his followers were found guilty **Jan. 26** of first-degree murder in the 1969 slaying of actress Sharon Tate and 6 others.

U.S. air and artillery forces aided a 44-day incursion by South Vietnam forces into **Laos** starting **Feb. 8.**

A Constitutional Amendment lowering the **voting age to 18** in all elections was approved in the Senate by a vote of 94-0 **Mar. 10.** The proposed 26th Amendment got House approval by a 400-19 vote **Mar. 23.** Thirty-eighth state ratified **June 30.**

A court-martial jury Mar. 29, convicted **Lt. William L. Calley Jr.** of premeditated murder of 22 South Vietnamese at Mylai on **Mar. 16, 1968.** He was sentenced to life imprisonment **Mar. 31.** Sentence was reduced to 20 years **Aug. 20.**

Publication of classified **Pentagon papers** on the U.S. involvement in Vietnam was begun **June 13** by the New York Times. In a 6-3 vote, the U.S. Supreme Court **June 30** upheld the right of the Times and the Washington Post to publish the documents under the protection of the First Amendment.

U.S. bombers struck massively in North Vietnam for 5 days starting **Dec. 26,** in retaliation for alleged violations of agreements reached prior to the 1968 bombing halt. U.S. forces at year-end were down to 140,000.

1972

Pres. Nixon arrived in **Peking Feb. 21** for an 8-day visit to China, which he called a "journey for peace." The unprecedented visit ended with a joint communique pledging that both powers would work for "a normalization of relations."

By a vote of 84 to 8, the Senate approved **Mar. 22** a Constitutional Amendment banning **discrimination against women** because of their sex and sent the measure to the states for ratification.

North Vietnamese forces launched the biggest attacks in 4 years across the demilitarized zone **Mar. 30.** The U.S. responded **Apr. 15** by resumption of bombing of Hanoi and Haiphong after a 4-year lull.

Nixon announced **May 8** the mining of **North Vietnam ports.** Last U.S. combat troops left **Aug. 11.**

Alabama Gov. George C. Wallace, campaigning at a Laurel, Md. shopping center **May 15, was shot** and seriously wounded as he greeted a large crowd. Arthur H. Bremer, 21, was sentenced Aug. 4 to 63 years for shooting Wallace and 3 bystanders.

In the first visit of a U.S. president to Moscow, Nixon arrived **May 22** for a week of summit talks with Kremlin leaders which culminated in a landmark **strategic arms pact.**

Five men were arrested **June 17** for breaking into the offices of the Democratic National Committee in the **Watergate** office complex in Washington, D.C.

The White House announced **July 8** that the U.S. would sell to the USSR at least $750 million of **American wheat,** corn, and other grains over a period of 3 years.

1973

Five of seven defendants in the **Watergate** break-in trial pleaded guilty **Jan. 11 and 15,** and the other 2 were convicted **Jan. 30.**

The Supreme Court ruled 7-2, **Jan. 22,** that a state may not prevent a woman from having an **abortion** during the **first 6 months of pregnancy,** invalidating abortion laws in Texas and Georgia, and, by implication, overturning restrictive abortion laws in 44 other states.

Four-party **Vietnam peace pacts** were signed in Paris **Jan. 27,** and North Vietnam released some 590 U.S. prisoners by **Apr. 1.** Last U.S. troops left **Mar. 29.**

The **end of the military draft** was announced **Jan. 27.**

China and the U.S. agreed **Feb. 22** to set up permanent liaison offices in each other's country.

Top **Nixon aides** H.R. Haldeman, John D. Ehrlichman, and John W. Dean, and Attorney General Richard Kleindienst **resigned Apr. 30** amid charges of White House efforts to obstruct justice in the Watergate case.

The Senate Armed Services Committee **July 16** began a probe into allegations that the U.S. Air Force had made 3,500 secret **B-52 raids into Cambodia** in **1969** and **1970.**

John Dean, former Nixon counsel, told Senate hearings **June 25** that Nixon, his staff and campaign aides, and the Justice Department all had conspired to cover up Watergate facts. Nixon refused July 23 to release **tapes** of relevant White House conversations. Some tapes were turned over to the court **Nov. 26.**

The U.S. officially ceased bombing in **Cambodia** at midnight **Aug. 14** in accord with a June Congressional action.

Vice Pres. Spiro T. Agnew Oct. 10 resigned and pleaded "nolo contendere" (no contest) to charges of tax evasion on payments made to him by Maryland contractors when he was governor of that state. Gerald Rudolph Ford **Oct. 12** became first appointed vice president under the 25th Amendment; sworn in **Dec. 6.**

A total ban on **oil exports** to the U.S. was imposed by Arab oil-producing nations **Oct. 19-21** after the outbreak of an Arab-Israeli war. The ban was lifted **Mar. 18, 1974.**

Atty. Gen. Elliot Richardson resigned, and his deputy William D. Ruckelshaus and Watergate Special Prosecutor Archibald Cox were fired by Pres. Nixon **Oct. 20** when Cox threatened to secure a judicial ruling that Nixon was violating a court order to turn tapes over to Watergate case Judge John Sirica.

Leon Jaworski, conservative Texas Democrat, was named **Nov. 1** by the Nixon administration to be special prosecutor to succeed Archibald Cox.

Congress overrode **Nov. 7** Nixon's veto of the **war powers** bill which curbed the president's power to commit armed forces to hostilities abroad without Congressional approval.

1974

Impeachment hearings were opened **May 9** against Nixon by the House Judiciary Committee.

John D. Ehrlichman and 3 **White House "plumbers"** were found guilty **July 12** of conspiring to violate the civil rights of Dr. Lewis Fielding, formerly psychiatrist to Pentagon Papers leaker Daniel Ellsberg, by breaking into his Beverly Hills, Cal. office.

The U.S. Supreme Court ruled, 8-0, **July 24** that Nixon had to turn over **64 tapes** of White House conversations sought by Watergate Special Prosecutor Leon Jaworski.

The House Judiciary Committee, in televised hearings **July 24-30,** recommended 3 **articles of impeachment** against Nixon. The first, voted 27-11 **July 27,** charged Nixon with taking part in a criminal conspiracy to obstruct justice in the Watergate cover-up. The second, voted 28-10 **July 29,** charged he "repeatedly" failed to carry out his constitutional oath in a series of alleged abuses of power. The third, voted 27-17 **July 30,** accused him of unconstitutional defiance of committee subpoenas. The House of Representatives voted without debate **Aug. 20,** by 412-3, to accept the committee report, which included the recommended impeachment articles.

Nixon resigned Aug. 9. His support began eroding **Aug. 5** when he released 3 tapes, admitting he originated plans to have the FBI stop its probe of the Watergate break-in for political as well as national security reasons. **Vice President Gerald R. Ford** was sworn in as the 38th U.S. president on **Aug. 9.**

An **unconditional pardon** to ex-Pres. Nixon for all federal crimes that he "committed or may have committed" while president was issued by Pres. Gerald Ford **Sept. 8.**

1975

Found guilty of **Watergate** cover-up charges **Jan. 1** were ex-Atty. Gen. John N. Mitchell, ex-presidential advisers H.R. Haldeman and John D. Ehrlichman.

U.S. civilians were evacuated from **Saigon Apr. 29** as communist forces completed takeover of South Vietnam.

U.S. merchant ship **Mayaguez** and crew of 39 seized by Cambodian forces in Gulf of Siam **May 12.** In rescue operation, U.S. Marines attacked Tang Is., planes bombed air base; Cambodia surrendered ship and crew; U.S. losses were 15 killed in battle and 23 dead in a helicopter crash.

Congress voted $405 million for South **Vietnam refugees May 16;** 140,000 were flown to the U.S.

Illegal **CIA operations,** including records on 300,000 persons and groups, and infiltration of agents into black, anti-war and political movements, were described by a "blue-ribbon" panel headed by Vice Pres. Rockefeller **June 10.**

FBI agents captured **Patricia (Patty) Hearst,** kidnaped **Feb. 4, 1974,** in San Francisco **Sept. 18** with others. She was indicted for bank robbery; a San Francisco jury convicted her **Mar. 20, 1976.**

1976

Payments abroad of $22 million in bribes by Lockheed Aircraft Corp. to sell its planes were revealed **Feb. 4** by a Senate subcommittee. Lockheed admitted payments in Japan, Turkey, Italy, and Holland.

The U.S. celebrated its **Bicentennial July 4,** marking the 200th anniversary of its independence with festivals, parades, and N.Y. City's Operation Sail, a gathering of tall ships from around the world viewed by 6 million persons.

A mystery ailment **"legionnaire's disease"** killed 29 persons who attended an American Legion convention **July 21-24** in Philadelphia. The cause was found to be a bacterium, it was reported **June 18, 1977.**

The Viking II lander set down on **Mars'** Utopia Plains **Sept. 3,** following the successful landing by Viking I **July 20.**

1977

Pres. Jimmy Carter **Jan. 27** pardoned most Vietnam War **draft evaders,** who numbered some 10,000.

Convicted murderer **Gary Gilmore** was executed by a Utah firing squad **Jan. 17,** in the first exercise of capital punishment anywhere in the U.S. since **1967.** Gilmore had opposed all attempts to delay the execution.

Carter signed an act **Aug. 4** creating a new Cabinet-level **Energy Department.**

1978

Sen. Hubert H. Humphrey (D., Minn.), 66, lost a battle with cancer **Jan. 13,** after 32 years of public service, including 4 years as vice-president of the United States.

U.S. Senate voted **Apr. 18** to turn over the **Panama Canal** to Panama on Dec. 31, 1999, by a vote of 68-32, ending several months of heated debate; an earlier vote **(Mar. 16)** had given approval to a treaty guaranteeing the area's neutrality after the year 2000.

California voters **June 6** approved (by a 65% majority) the **Proposition 13** initiative to cut property taxes in the state by 57%, thus severely limiting government spending.

The U.S. Supreme Court **June 28** voted 5-4 not to allow a firm quota system in affirmative action plans; the Court did uphold programs that were more "flexible" in nature.

The **House Select Committee on Assassinations** opened hearings **Sept. 6** into assassinations of Pres. Kennedy and Martin Luther King Jr.; the committee recessed **Dec. 30** after concluding conspiracies likely in both cases, but with no further hard evidence for further prosecutions.

Congress passed the **Humphrey-Hawkins "full employment" Bill Oct. 15,** which set national goal of reducing unemployment to 4% by 1983, while reducing inflation to 3% in same period; Pres. Carter signed bill, **Oct. 27.**

1979

A major accident occurred, **Mar. 28,** at a nuclear reactor on **Three Mile Island** near Middletown, Pa. Radioactive gases escaped through the plant's venting system and a large hydrogen gas bubble formed in the top of the reactor containment vessel.

In the worst disaster in U.S. aviation history, an American Airlines **DC-10 jetliner** lost its left engine and crashed shortly after takeoff in Chicago, **May 25,** killing 275 people.

Pope John Paul II, Oct. 1-6, visited the U.S. and reaffirmed traditional Roman Catholic teachings.

The federal government announced, **Nov. 1,** a $1.5 billion loan-guarantee plan to aid the nation's 3d largest automaker, **Chrysler Corp.,** which had reported a loss of $460.6 million for the 3d quarter of 1979.

Some 90 people, including 63 Americans, were taken hostage, **Nov. 3,** at the **American embassy in Teheran,** Iran, by militant student followers of Ayatollah Khomeini who demanded the return of former Shah Mohammad Reza Pahlavi, who was undergoing medical treatment in New York City.

1980

Citing "an extremely serious threat to peace," Pres. Carter announced, **Jan. 4,** a series of **punitive measures against the USSR,** most notably an embargo on the sale of grain and high technology, in retaliation for the Soviet invasion of Afghanistan. At Carter's request, the **U.S. Olympic Committee** voted, **Apr. 12,** not to attend the Moscow Summer Olympics.

Eight Americans were killed and 5 wounded, **Apr. 24,** in an ill-fated attempt to **rescue the hostages** held by Iranian **militants** at the U.S. Embassy in Teheran.

In Washington, **Mt. St. Helens erupted, May 18,** in a violent blast estimated to be 500 times as powerful as the Hiroshima atomic bomb. The blast, followed by others on **May 25** and **June 12,** left 25 confirmed dead, at least 40 missing, and economic losses estimated at nearly $3 billion.

In a sweeping victory, **Nov. 4, Ronald Wilson Reagan** was elected 40th President of the United States, defeating incumbent Jimmy Carter. The stunning GOP victory extended to the U.S. Congress where Republicans gained control of the Senate and wrested 33 House seats from the Democrats.

Former Beatle **John Lennon** was shot and killed, **Dec. 8,** outside his apartment building in New York City, by Mark David Chapman, a former psychiatric patient.

1981

Minutes after the **inauguration of Pres. Ronald Reagan, Jan. 20,** the **52 Americans** who had been held **hostage** in **Iran** for 444 days were flown to freedom following an agreement in which the U.S. agreed to return to Iran $8 billion in frozen assets.

President Reagan was **shot in the chest** by John W. Hinckley, Jr., a would-be assassin, **Mar. 30,** in Washington, D.C., as he walked to his limousine following an address at the Washington Hilton.

The world's first reusable spacecraft, the **Space Shuttle Columbia,** was sent into space, **Apr. 12,** and completed its successful mission 2 days later.

Both houses of Congress passed, **July 29,** President Reagan's **tax-cut legislation.** The bill, the largest tax cut in the nation's history, was expected to reduce taxes by $37.6 billion in fiscal year 1982, and would save taxpayers $750 billion over the next 5 years.

Federal air traffic controllers, Aug. 3, began an **illegal nationwide strike** after their union rejected the government's final offer for a new contract. Most of the 13,000 striking controllers defied the back-to-work order, and were dismissed by President Reagan on **Aug. 5.**

In a 99-0 vote, the Senate confirmed, **Sept. 21,** the appointment of **Sandra Day O'Connor** as an **associate justice of the U.S. Supreme Court.** She was the first woman appointed to that body.

President Reagan ordered **sanctions against the new Polish military government, Dec. 23,** in response to the imposition of martial law in that country.

1982

The 13-year-old lawsuit against **AT&T** by the **Justice Dept.** was settled **Jan. 8.** AT&T agreed to give up the 22 Bell System companies but, in return, was allowed to expand into previously prohibited areas inc. data processing, telephone and computer equipment sales, and computer communication devices.

On **Mar. 2,** the Senate voted 57-37 for a bill that virtually eliminated busing for the purposes of racial integration.

On **June 12,** in **N.Y.'s Central Park,** hundreds of thousands demonstrated against **nuclear arms.**

The Equal Rights Amendment was defeated after a 10-year struggle for ratification.

The **elections** on **Nov. 2** resulted in gains for the Democrats—the margin in the new House was 269-166. In the Senate elections, Democrats won 20 out of 33 seats, but were still the minority, 54-46.

The **highest unemployment rate since 1940,** 10.4%, was reported on **Nov. 5.** The rate for Nov. reached 10.8%, with over 11 million unemployed.

Leonid Brezhnev, 75, general secretary of the central committee of the Communist Party and the **Soviet Union,** died of a heart attack on **Nov. 10.**

Lech Walesa, former leader of **Solidarity,** the Polish labor union, was freed **Nov. 13,** after 11 months of internment following the imposition of martial law and the outlawing of Solidarity. The Polish government declared Walesa "no longer a threat to internal security." Pres. Reagan lifted the **U.S. embargo on sales of oil and gas equipment to the Soviet Union.**

The **Space Shuttle Columbia** completed its first operational flight on **Nov. 16.**

A retired dentist, **Dr. Barney B. Clark,** 61, became the first recipient of a **permanent artificial heart** during a 7½ hour operation in Salt Lake City on **Dec. 2.** The heart was designed by **Dr. Robert Jarvik,** also on the surgical team.

On **Dec. 16, Anne M. Gorsuch,** administrator of the **Environmental Protection Agency,** became the first Cabinet level official to be cited for contempt by the House when she declined to submit certain documents requested by a House subcommittee.

1983

On **Mar. 14,** for the first time in its 23-year history, the **Organization of Petroleum Exporting Countries (OPEC)** agreed to cut the prices of its **crude oil.** The decision in London reflected falling worldwide demand for OPEC products.

On **Apr. 20, Pres. Reagan** signed a compromise, bipartisan bill designed to rescue the **Social Security System** from bankruptcy.

The National Commission on Excellence in Education issued its report on **Apr. 26.** The report labelled **U.S. elementary and secondary education** "mediocre," and recommended that: schools put more emphasis on English, math, social studies, and computer science; the school day be lengthened; teachers be rewarded for merit rather than seniority; and college admissions standards be raised.

In an 8-1 decision, **the U.S. Supreme Court held, May 24,** that the **Internal Revenue Service** could deny **tax exemptions to private schools** that practiced **racial discrimination.**

Sally Ride became the first American **woman** to travel in **space, June 18,** when the **space shuttle Challenger** was launched from Cape Canaveral, Fla.

The Soviet Union shot a **South Korean airliner** out of the sky on **Sept. 1,** killing all 269 people aboard. The attack occurred in Soviet air space, and the plane crashed into the Sea of Japan. The USSR charged that the plane, which carried 240 passengers and a crew of 29, had been on a **spying mission.** Most of the noncommunist world, led by **Pres. Reagan,** responded with condemnation.

The **Big 3 auto companies** reported, **Oct. 4,** that sales had increased 16.7 percent during the 1983 model year. It was the biggest gain from the previous year since 1978.

On **Oct. 23,** 241 **U.S. Marines and sailors,** members of the multinational **peacekeeping force** in **Lebanon,** were killed when a TNT-laden suicide **terrorist** blew up Marine headquarters at **Beirut** Intl. Airport. Almost simultaneously, a second truck bomb blew up a **French paratroop** barracks two miles away, killing more than 40.

U.S. Marines and Rangers and a small force from 6 **Caribbean** nations invaded the island of **Grenada** on **Oct. 25,** in response to a request from the **Organization of Eastern Caribbean States.** After a few days, Grenadian militia and Cuban "construction workers" were overcome, hundreds of U.S. citizens evacuated safely, and the hard-line Marxist regime deposed. The U.S. Congress applied the War Powers Resolution, requiring U.S. troops to leave Grenada by **Dec. 24.**

1984

In his **State of the Union address, Jan. 25,** Pres. Reagan called for budget cuts of $100 billion over 3 years, but opposed increased taxes.

Soviet leader **Yuri V. Andropov,** 69, **died in Moscow, Feb. 9,** after a long illness.

On **Feb. 26,** as the position of Pres. Amin Gemayel of Lebanon deteriorated and his army crumbled, Pres. Reagan **removed U.S. Marines from Beirut** and placed them on U.S. ships offshore.

The space shuttle *Challenger* was launched on its 4th trip into space, **Feb. 3.** On **Feb. 7,** Navy Capt. Bruce McCandless, followed by Army Lt. Colonel Robert Stewart, **became the first humans to fly free of a spacecraft.**

During **March,** the U.S. Senate rejected 2 Constitutional amendments that would have permitted **prayer in the public schools.**

The Central Intelligence Agency **(CIA) acknowledged** in April that it had participated in the **mining of Nicaraguan harbors.** This touched off a controversy in Congress, and the Senate, **Apr. 10,** adopted a nonbinding resolution condemning U.S. participation in the mining.

From **Apr. 26 to May 1, Pres. Reagan visited China** for the first time, holding a series of discussions with Chinese leaders.

On **May 7,** American **veterans of the Vietnam war** reached an **out-of-court settlement with 7 chemical companies** in their class-action suit relating to the herbicide **Agent Orange.**

A federal judge in Salt Lake City held, **May 10,** that the **U.S. government had been negligent** in its above-ground testing of **nuclear weapons** in Nevada from 1951 to 1962.

Jose Napoleon Duarte, the candidate of the Christian Democratic Party and a political moderate, was **elected president** of strife-torn **El Salvador, May 7.**

An **undamaged Mayan tomb** was discovered by archaeologists, **May 15.**

On **June 6,** former vice president **Walter Mondale claimed victory** in his struggle with Sen. Gary Hart for the **Democratic presidental nomination.** In a historic move, **July 12, Mondale chose a woman, Rep. Geraldine Ferraro (N.Y.)** to run with him as candidate for **vice president.**

A report written by Italian State Prosecutor Antonio Albano and made public in **June,** linked the **Bulgarian secret service to the plot to assassinate Pope John Paul II in 1981.**

Pres. Reagan, **Aug. 11,** signed a law prohibiting public high schools from barring students who wished to **assemble for religious or political activities outside of school hours.**

Pres. Ronald Reagan and Vice Pres. George Bush were renominated, Aug. 23, at the Republican National convention.

Indira Gandhi, the prime minister of India, was **slain by 2 of her own bodyguards in New Delhi, Oct. 31.** Her assassins were reportedly members of the Sikh religious minority, who had been in violent confrontation with the Gandhi government for months.

1985

On **Feb. 16,** Israeli troops completed their withdrawal from the Sidon area of Lebanon, in the first phase of a long-awaited 3-stage pullout.

Konstantin Chernenko, 73, president of the Soviet Union and general secretary of the Soviet Communist Party, died **Mar. 10.** He was succeeded by **Mikhail Gorbachev** as the **new party secretary.** The USSR's 4th leader in 3 years, Gorbachev, 54, was the youngest member of the Politburo.

The **war** between **Iran and Iraq** took a new turn in **mid-March** when planes from each side bombed civilian-occupied areas in each other's territory.

The controversial MX missile survived critical votes in the Senate and House. The **Senate,** on **Mar. 19** and **21,** voted to **authorize the missiles** and then to **appropriate $1.5 million** for the construction of 21 missiles. The **House** gave its endorsement **Mar. 26** and **28.**

E.F. Hutton, one of the nation's largest brokerage companies, **pleaded guilty, May 2,** to **2,000 federal charges** related to the manipulation of its checking accounts. The company agreed to pay $2 million in fines and to pay back up to $8 million to banks it had defrauded.

On **June 14, Shiite Muslim extremists seized** an **airplane** flying from Athens to Rome; 153 persons were aboard, including 104 Americans. One American was killed, more than 100 others freed, and 39 American men were kept hostage until their release on **June 30.**

The government of **South Africa** declared a **state of emergency** in July. The **U.S. Senate** had voted, **July 11,** to impose **economic sanctions** on South Africa in protest against its policy of apartheid. Violence, building for a year, had resulted in up to 500 deaths, almost all the victims black.

"Live Aid," a 17-hour rock concert broadcast **July 13** on radio and TV from London and Phila. to 152 countries, raised $70 million for the starving peoples of Africa.

On **Oct. 7, 5 hijackers seized an Italian cruise ship,** the ***Achille Lauro,*** in the open sea as it approached Port Said, Egypt. Some 400 persons were aboard, including about 340 crew. The hijackers, members of the Palestine Liberation Front, a faction broken from the PLO, demanded the release of 50 Palestinians held by Israel. On **Oct. 9,** Egypt said the hijackers had surrendered to a PLO representative and would be given safe conduct from Egypt. Italy then announced that Leon Klinghoffer, a 69-year-old, wheelchair-bound American, had been shot to death and thrown overboard. On **Oct. 10,** Egyptian Pres. Hosni Mubarek said the hijackers were in the hands of the PLO. However, they did not actually leave Egypt until that evening. The Reagan administration ordered the Egyptian plane intercepted in international air space, and Navy F-14 fighter jets forced the plane to land in Sicily.

In November, for the first time in 6 years, the leaders of the U.S. and the Soviet Union met at a **summit conference.** In Geneva, Switzerland, **Pres. Reagan** and **Mikhail Gorbachev,** the general secretary of the Soviet Communist Party, talked privately for 5 hours, **Nov. 19 and 20.** No substantive agreements were reached, but Pres. Reagan called the talks a "fresh start."

Arab gunmen seized an **Egyptian jetliner** en route from Athens to Cairo, **Nov. 23.** Of the 98 persons aboard, 60 were killed.

Congress passed a compromise **Gramm-Rudman bill, Dec. 11,** that was a last-ditch effort to end the huge federal deficit. Signed by Pres. Reagan **Dec. 12,** it was expected to require an initial $11.7 billion reduction in the fiscal 1986 budget deficit, then 4 reductions in equal amounts until a balanced budget was achieved in 1991.

Palestinian terrorists killed 20 civilians at airports in Rome and Vienna, Dec. 27. Both attacks were at ticket counters of El Al, Israel's national airline.

The **biggest corporate merger yet,** outside the oil industry, was announced **Dec. 11,** when General Electric Corp. agreed to buy RCA Corp. for $6.28 billion.

1986

On **Jan. 20,** for the 1st time, the U.S. officially observed **Martin Luther King Day.**

Moments after liftoff, **Jan. 28,** the **space shuttle *Challenger* exploded, killing 6 astronauts and Christa McAuliffe,** a **New Hampshire teacher.** Subsequent investigations found that NASA had abandoned "good judgment and common sense" regarding safety problems that caused the explosion.

The 20-year rule of Pres. **Ferdinand Marcos of the Philippines ended in Feb.,** when he fled into exile in Hawaii after a clumsy attempt by his supporters to steal the presidential election. He was succeeded by Corazon Aquino, the widow of opposition leader Benigno Aquino, who had been murdered in 1983 on his return from exile in the U.S.

Jean-Claude Duvalier, Haiti's "president for life" **fled into exile in France in Feb.,** ending 28 years of dictatorship by the Duvalier family.

Anatoly Shcharansky, a Soviet dissident imprisoned for 8 years, **was set free in Feb.**

U.S. warplanes struck targets in Tripoli and Benghazi, Libya, Apr. 14, in retaliation against the Libyan bombing of a West Berlin disco in which 2 died and 200 were injured, **Apr. 5,** On **Jan. 7,** Pres. Reagan had announced that the U.S. had aborted 26 "terrorist missions" in the past year, including 23 in the U.S. He had signed an executive order banning trade with and travel to Libya, and ordering all Americans in Libya to leave. A 2nd executive order, **Jan. 8,** had frozen all Libyan government assets in the U.S. and U.S. bank branches abroad.

Soviet authorities waited 3 days before reporting a **major accident at the Chernobyl nuclear power plant, Apr. 28.** The resultant cloud of radiation caused **23 deaths** and the evacuation of 40,000 people who lived near the plant in the Ukraine.

U.S. officials said, **June 12,** that **AIDS cases and deaths would increase tenfold in the next 5 years.** At that time, the government had recorded 21,517 cases and 11,713 deaths. An anti-viral drug, azidothymidine (AZT) was found to improve the health of a group of AIDS patients, but officials cautioned that this was not a cure.

Awareness of the mounting **abuse of illegal drugs** in the U.S., specifically **cocaine in the form of "crack,"** resulted in Congress's passing antidrug legislation, civic leaders' calling for more education, and the U.S.'s joining Bolivia in raids against cocaine processing hideouts.

A key provision of the **Gramm-Rudman "balanced budget" law was declared unconstitutional, July 7,** by the U.S. Supreme Court.

Apartheid in South Africa continued to cause unrest among the black majority. The U.S. (via a **Congressional override, in Sept., of Pres. Reagan's veto**) and other nations imposed **economic sanctions** in an attempt to pressure the Botha government to end the policy of racial separation.

The U.S. Senate confirmed, **Sept. 17,** Pres. Reagan's nomination of **William Rehnquist as chief justice** and **Antonin Scalia as associate justice of the Supreme Court.**

Several different **terrorist groups attacked** in **Sept.:** Bombers struck in **Paris,** killing 8 and injuring about 170; an airplane hijacking in **Karachi, Pakistan** left 21 people—including 2 Americans—fatally wounded and about 100 others injured; and 2 terrorists entered a synagogue in **Istanbul, Turkey** and opened fire on worshippers, killing 20 and wounding 3.

Congress passed, in late **Sept.,** the comprehensive **Tax Reform Law.** In effect in 1987, it drastically changed the tax brackets, deductions, corporate tax shelters, and generally simplified the system.

Pres. Reagan and **Soviet leader Mikhail Gorbachev** met for **arms talks in Iceland in Oct.,** but missed the chance for a comprehensive settlement when Gorbachev called for a limitation on the development of **"Star Wars,"**which Reagan refused to consider.

Historical Anniversaries

1963—25 Years Ago

Pres. John F. Kennedy was assassinated in a Dallas motorcade, Nov. 22. Vice-President Lyndon B. Johnson was sworn in as President. As millions watched on TV, alleged assassin Lee Harvey Oswald was shot to death by Dallas nightclub owner Jack Ruby.

Pres. Kennedy had asked Congress to enact far-reaching civil rights legislation, June 19.

On Jan. 1., Rev. Martin Luther King spoke at the Lincoln Memorial in Washington, commemorating the centennial of the Emancipation Proclamation.

NAACP leader Medger Evers was murdered, June 12, at his Jackson, Miss. home.

More than 200,000 people marched on Washington, Aug. 28, to demonstrate support for civil rights.

A "hot line" emergency communication link between Washington and Moscow was installed, Aug. 30, to reduce the risk of accidental war.

Valentina Tereshkova of the USSR became the first female astronaut.

Congress guaranteed women equal pay for equal work.

U.S. factory workers averaged more than $100 per week for the first time in history.

The first commercial nuclear reactor was installed by Jersey Central Power and Light.

The first artificial heart was used to take over the function of blood circulation during heart surgery by Houston surgeon Michael De Bakey.

Valium, a muscle relaxant and anti-convulsant, was introduced by Roche Laboratories.

Pope John XXIII died, June 2, after a 5-year papacy. He had called the Second Vatican Council to reassess the role of the Church in the modern world. Beginning in 1962, Vatican II would continue until 1965, passing 9 decrees that would liberalize the Church. Giovanni Battista Montini became the next Pope, Paul VI.

The Supreme Court held that reading the Lord's Prayer or verses from the Bible in U.S. public schools was unconstitutional.

Books: *The Feminine Mystique*, by Betty Friedan; *The Fire Next Time*, by James Baldwin; *Cat's Cradle*, by Kurt Vonnegut Jr.; *The Bell Jar*, by Sylvia Plath; *Raise High the Roof Beam, Carpenters and Seymour: An Introduction*, by J.D. Salinger; *The Centaur*, by John Updike; *The Spy Who Came in from the Cold*, by John Le Carré.

Painting: "Whaam! by Roy Lichtenstein; "Map," by Jasper Johns; "Red, Blue, Green," by Ellsworth Kelly.

Theater: "Barefoot in the Park," by Neil Simon, with Elizabeth Ashley, Robert Redford.

Movies: "Tom Jones;" Federico Fellini's "8½;" "Hud," with Paul Newman, Patricia Neal; "The Great Escape," with Steve McQueen; "Lilies of the Field," with Sidney Poitier.

Music: The Beatle's first U.S. hit—"I Want to Hold Your Hand."

Weight Watchers was formed; Kodak Instamatic cameras were introduced; Julia Child began teaching French cooking on Boston's educational TV station.

1938—50 Years Ago

Adolf Hitler annexed Austria. Britain and France agreed to the German acquisition of the Sudentenland, almost a third of Czechoslovakian land and citizens. British Prime Minister Neville Chamberlain remarked: "I believe it is peace in our time . . . peace with honor."

In Nov., in Germany, "Kristalnacht" took place: Nazis smashed Jewish shop windows, looted and burned Jewish homes, shops, and synagogues; took 20,000–30,000 Jews to concentration camps.

Anti-Jewish legislation was enacted in Italy.

Congress passed the Fair Labor Standards Act, the first national maximum on hours, minimum on wages. Working hours for the first year were limited to 44 per week, wages to a minimum of 25 cents per hour.

A Civil Aeronautics Authority was established to regulate the growing U.S. aviation industry.

Howard Hughes set a new round-the-world speed record, flying a twin-engine plane from California to California in 3 days, 19 hours, 14 minutes, 28 seconds.

The Food, Drug, and Cosmetic Act called for the listing of ingredients on labels.

The first tables showing reduced life expectancy for smokers were published by a Johns Hopkins Medical School professor.

The first high-definition color TV demonstration was made in London; the first true Xerox image was produced in New York. Fiberglass was perfected, Teflon discovered.

Superman appeared in Action comics.

Books: *Nausea*, by Jean-Paul Sartre; *Out of Africa*, by Isak Dinesen; *The 500 Hats of Bartholomew Cubbins*, by "Dr. Seuss."

Theater: "Our Town," by Thornton Wilder; "Helzapoppin'," with comics Ole Olsen and Chic Johnson; "Knickerbocker Holiday," with Walter Huston, music by Kurt Weill, book and lyrics by Maxwell Anderson.

Painting: "Cradling Wheat," by Thomas Hart Benton.

Movies: "The Adventures of Robin Hood," with Errol Flynn; "Test Pilot," with Clark Gable, Spencer Tracy, Myrna Loy; "Bringing Up Baby," with Katherine Hepburn, Cary Grant; "Jezebel," with Bette Davis, Henry Fonda; "Room Service," with the Marx Brothers; "Rebecca of Sunnybrook Farm," with Shirley Temple; "Snow White and the Seven Dwarfs," Walt Disney's first full-length animated cartoon.

Music: Benny Goodman and His Orchestra gave the first Carnegie Hall jazz concert, with guest performer Count Basie. Glenn Miller begain touring with his own band, after having played trombone for Tommy and Jimmy Dorsey, and Ray Noble. Woody Guthrie traveled the country singing pro-labor songs. Popular songs: "Two Sleepy People," "One O'Clock Jump," "Flat-Foot Floogie," "A-Tisket, A-Tasket."

Dance: The samba and the conga were introduced to U.S. dance floors. In ballet, "Billy the Kid," with music by Aaron Copland, choreography by Eugene Loring, opened at the Chicago Civic Opera House.

Sports: Don Budge won the tennis "Grand Slam"—the Australian, French, British, and U.S. singles championships, a feat never before accomplished and not duplicated for another 24 years.

1688—300 Years Ago

A "Glorious Revolution" ended nearly 3 years of Roman Catholic rule in England. William of Orange assumed the throne, James II escaped to France.

Lloyds of London began as a society to write marine insurance.

1588—400 Years Ago

An "invincible" Spanish armada of 132 vessels was defeated by the 32-ship English navy, opening the world to English trade and colonization.

1388–600 Years Ago

The first complete English translation of the Bible was completed.

AFGHANISTAN

ALBANIA

ALGERIA

ANGOLA

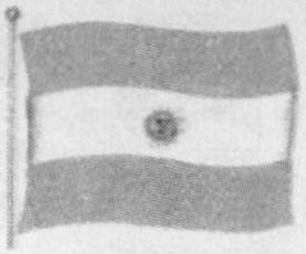
ARGENTINA

AUSTRALIA

AUSTRIA

BAHAMAS

BAHRAIN

BANGLADESH

BARBADOS

BELGIUM

BELIZE

BENIN

BHUTAN

BOLIVIA

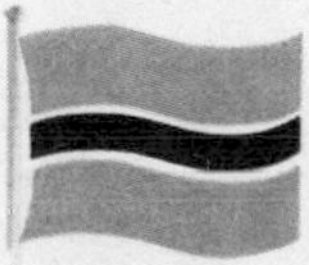
BOTSWANA

BRAZIL

BRUNEI

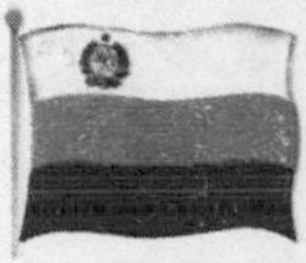
BULGARIA

BURKINA FASO

BURMA

BURUNDI

CAMBODIA
(Kampuchea)

CAMEROON

CANADA

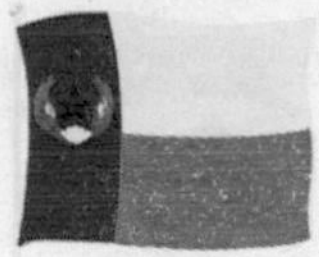
CAPE VERDE

CENTRAL AFRICAN
REPUBLIC

CHAD

CHILE

CHINA

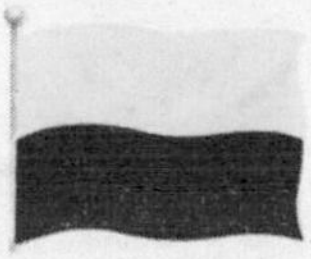
COLOMBIA

COMOROS

CONGO

COSTA RICA

CUBA

CYPRUS

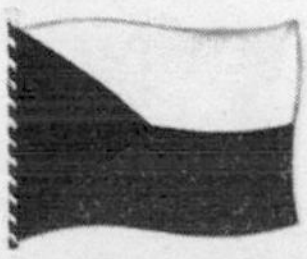
CZECHOSLOVAKIA

DENMARK

DJIBOUTI

DOMINICA

DOMINICAN REPUBLIC

ECUADOR

EGYPT

EL SALVADOR

EQUATORIAL GUINEA

ETHIOPIA

FIJI

FINLAND

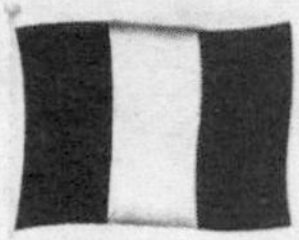
FRANCE

GABON

GAMBIA

GERMANY (EAST)

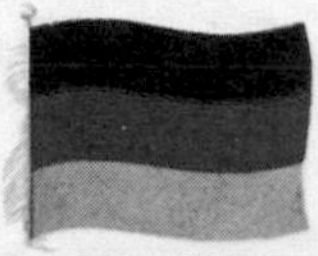
GERMANY (WEST)

GHANA

GREECE

GRENADA

GUATEMALA

GUINEA

GUINEA-BISSAU

GUYANA

HAITI

HONDURAS

HUNGARY

ICELAND

INDIA

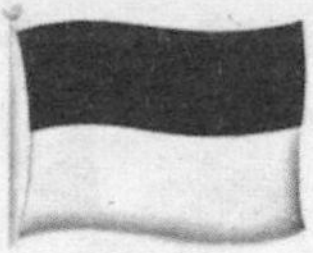
INDONESIA

IRAN

IRAQ

IRELAND

ISRAEL

ITALY

IVORY COAST

JAMAICA

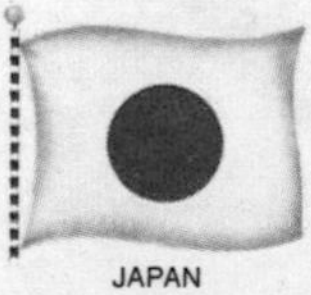
JAPAN

JORDAN

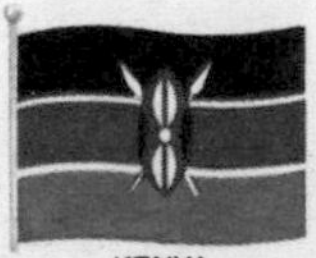
KENYA

KOREA (NORTH)

KOREA (SOUTH)

KUWAIT

LAOS

LEBANON

LESOTHO

LIBERIA

LIBYA

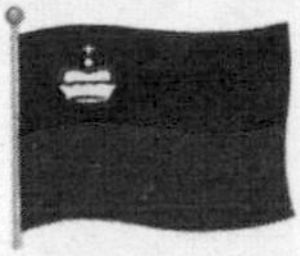
LIECHTENSTEIN

LUXEMBOURG

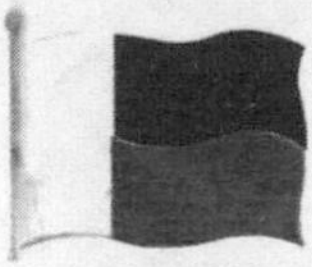
MADAGASCAR

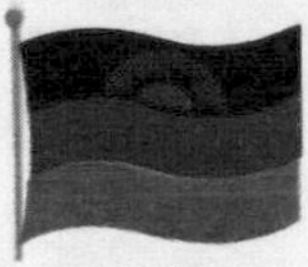
MALAWI

MALAYSIA

MALI

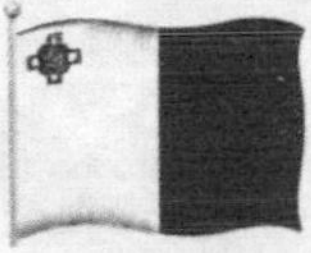
MALTA

MAURITANIA

MAURITIUS

MEXICO

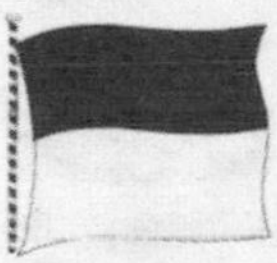
MONACO

MONGOLIA

MOROCCO

MOZAMBIQUE

NEPAL

NETHERLANDS

NEW ZEALAND

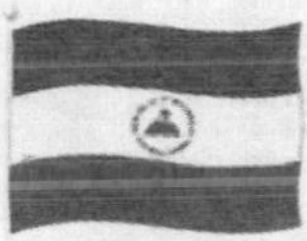
NICARAGUA

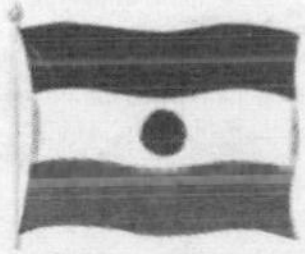
NIGER

NIGERIA

NORWAY

OMAN

PAKISTAN

PANAMA

PAPUA-NEW GUINEA

PARAGUAY

PERU

PHILIPPINES

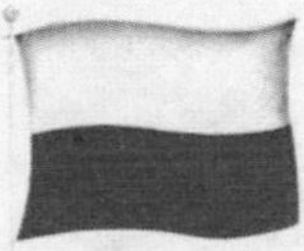
POLAND

PORTUGAL

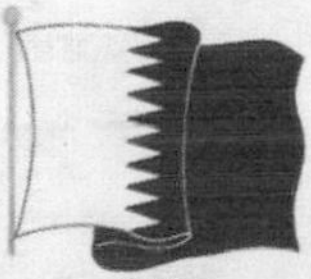
QATAR

ROMANIA

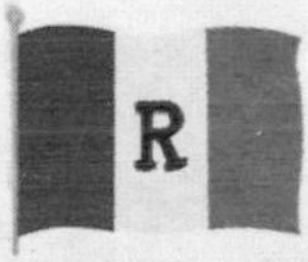

RWANDA

SAINT LUCIA

ST. VINCENT AND THE GRENADINES

F4

SAN MARINO

SAO TOME AND PRINCIPE

SAUDI ARABIA

SENEGAL

SIERRA LEONE

SINGAPORE

SOLOMON ISLANDS

SOMALIA

SOUTH AFRICA

SPAIN

SRI LANKA

SUDAN

SURINAME

SWAZILAND

SWEDEN

SWITZERLAND

SYRIA

TAIWAN

TANZANIA

THAILAND

TOGO

TRINIDAD AND TOBAGO

TUNISIA

TURKEY

UGANDA

UNION OF SOVIET SOCIALIST REPUBLICS

UNITED ARAB EMIRATES

UNITED KINGDOM

UNITED STATES

URUGUAY

VATICAN CITY

VENEZUELA

VIETNAM

WESTERN SAMOA

YEMEN

PEOPLE'S DEMOCRATIC REPUBLIC OF YEMEN

YUGOSLAVIA

ZAIRE

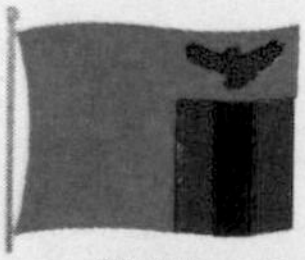
ZAMBIA

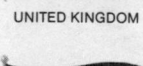

ZIMBABWE

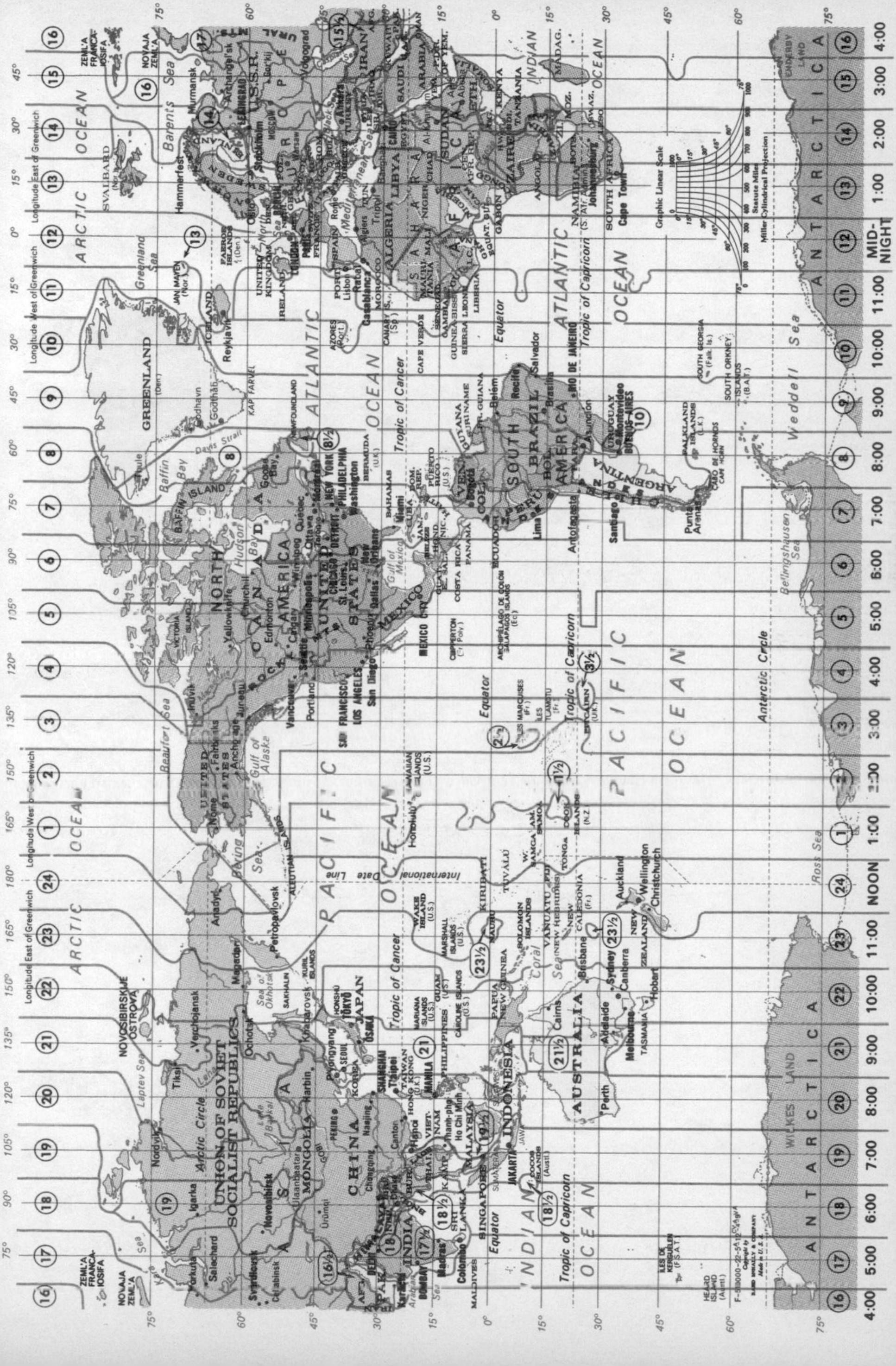
Longitude East of Greenwich
Longitude West of Greenwich
ARCTIC OCEAN
ATLANTIC OCEAN
PACIFIC OCEAN
INDIAN OCEAN
ANTARCTICA
International Date Line
Tropic of Cancer
Equator
Tropic of Capricorn
Arctic Circle
Antarctic Circle
4:00
5:00
6:00
7:00
8:00
9:00
10:00
11:00
NOON
1:00
2:00
3:00
4:00
5:00
6:00
7:00
8:00
9:00
10:00
11:00
MID-NIGHT
1:00
2:00
3:00
4:00

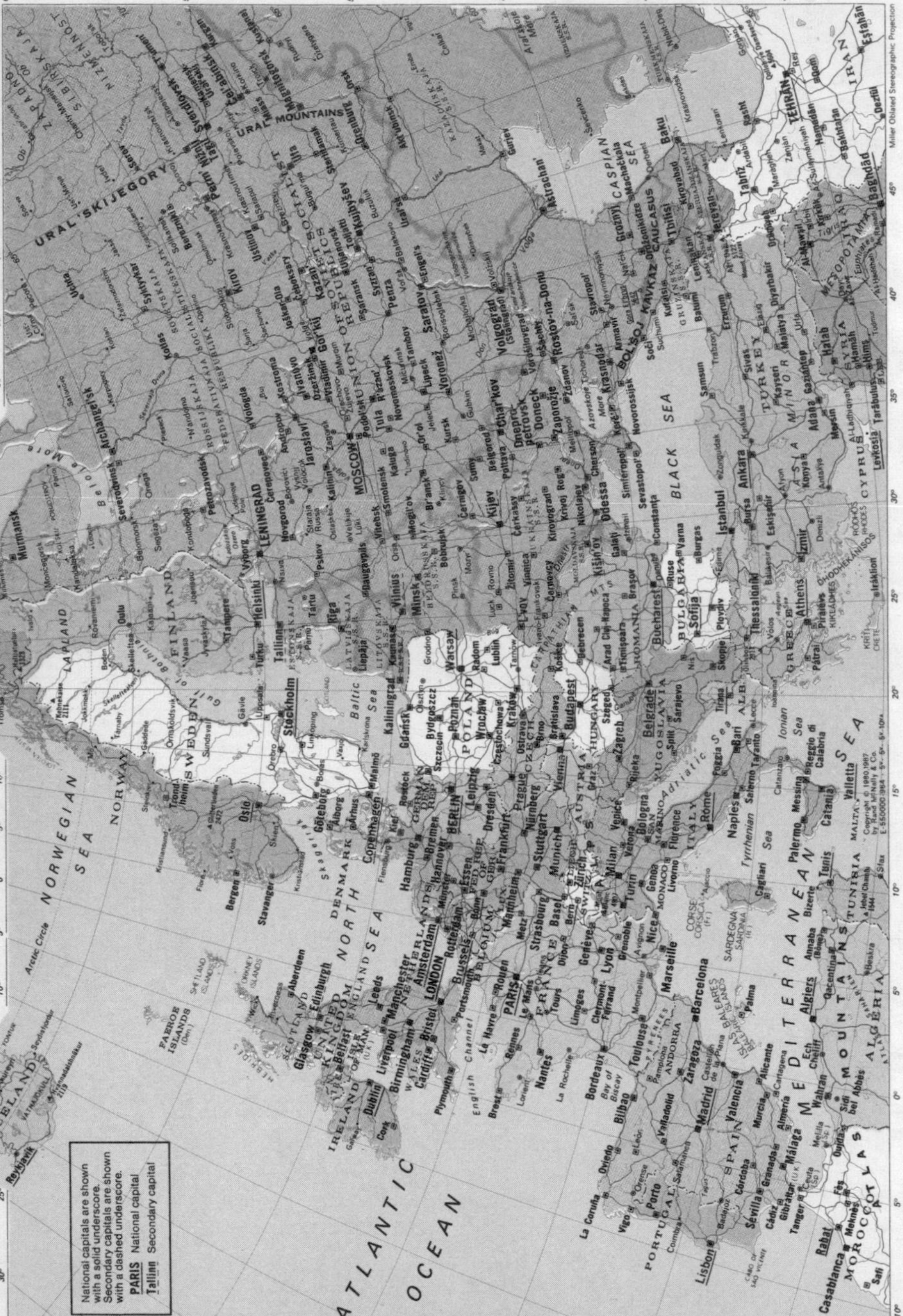
National capitals are shown with a solid underscore. Secondary capitals are shown with a dashed underscore.
PARIS National capital
Tallinn Secondary capital
ATLANTIC OCEAN
NORWEGIAN SEA
NORTH SEA
BLACK SEA
CASPIAN SEA
MEDITERRANEAN SEA
URAL MOUNTAINS
ICELAND
IRELAND
UNITED KINGDOM
FRANCE
SPAIN
PORTUGAL
NORWAY
SWEDEN
FINLAND
DENMARK
POLAND
HUNGARY
ROMANIA
BULGARIA
YUGOSLAVIA
ITALY
GREECE
TURKEY
CYPRUS
SYRIA
IRAN
MOROCCO
ALGERIA
TUNISIA
MOSCOW
LENINGRAD
LONDON
PARIS
BERLIN
Miller Oblated Stereographic Projection
Kilometres
Miles

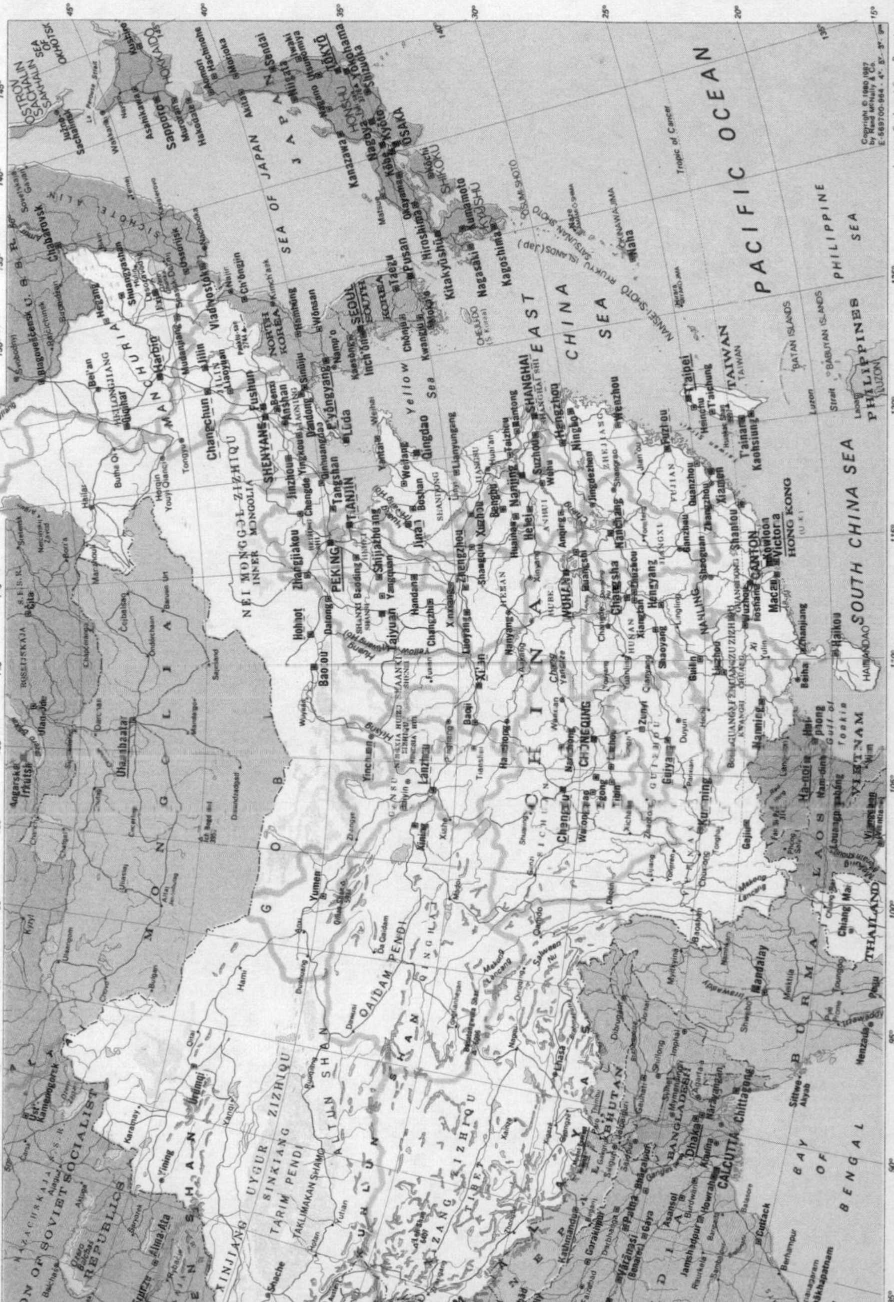
PACIFIC OCEAN
SEA OF JAPAN
EAST CHINA SEA
SOUTH CHINA SEA
PHILIPPINE SEA
BAY OF BENGAL
Yellow Sea
Tropic of Cancer
SEA OF OKHOTSK
UNION OF SOVIET SOCIALIST REPUBLICS
MONGOLIA
CHINA
MANCHURIA
NORTH KOREA
SOUTH KOREA
TAIWAN
PHILIPPINES
HONG KONG
VIETNAM
LAOS
THAILAND
BURMA
BANGLADESH
BHUTAN
NEPAL
INDIA
HOKKAIDO
HONSHU
SHIKOKU
KYUSHU
NEI MONGGOL ZIZHIQU
XINJIANG
UYGUR
SINKIANG
TARIM PENDI
TAKLIMAKAN SHAMO
XIZANG ZIZHIQU
QAIDAM PENDI
PEKING
SHANGHAI
TIANJIN
SHENYANG
WUHAN
CHONGQING
CANTON
SEOUL
TOKYO
OSAKA
CALCUTTA
Lanzhou
Xi'an
Chengdu
Kunming
Guiyang
Nanjing
Harbin
Changchun
Ulaanbaatar
Lhasa
Urumqi
Taipei
Victoria
Macau
Sapporo
Vladivostok
Hanoi
Dhaka
Chittagong
Kathmandu
Lambert Conformal Conic Projection
Kilometres 0 200 400 600 Km.
Miles 0 200 400 600 Mi.

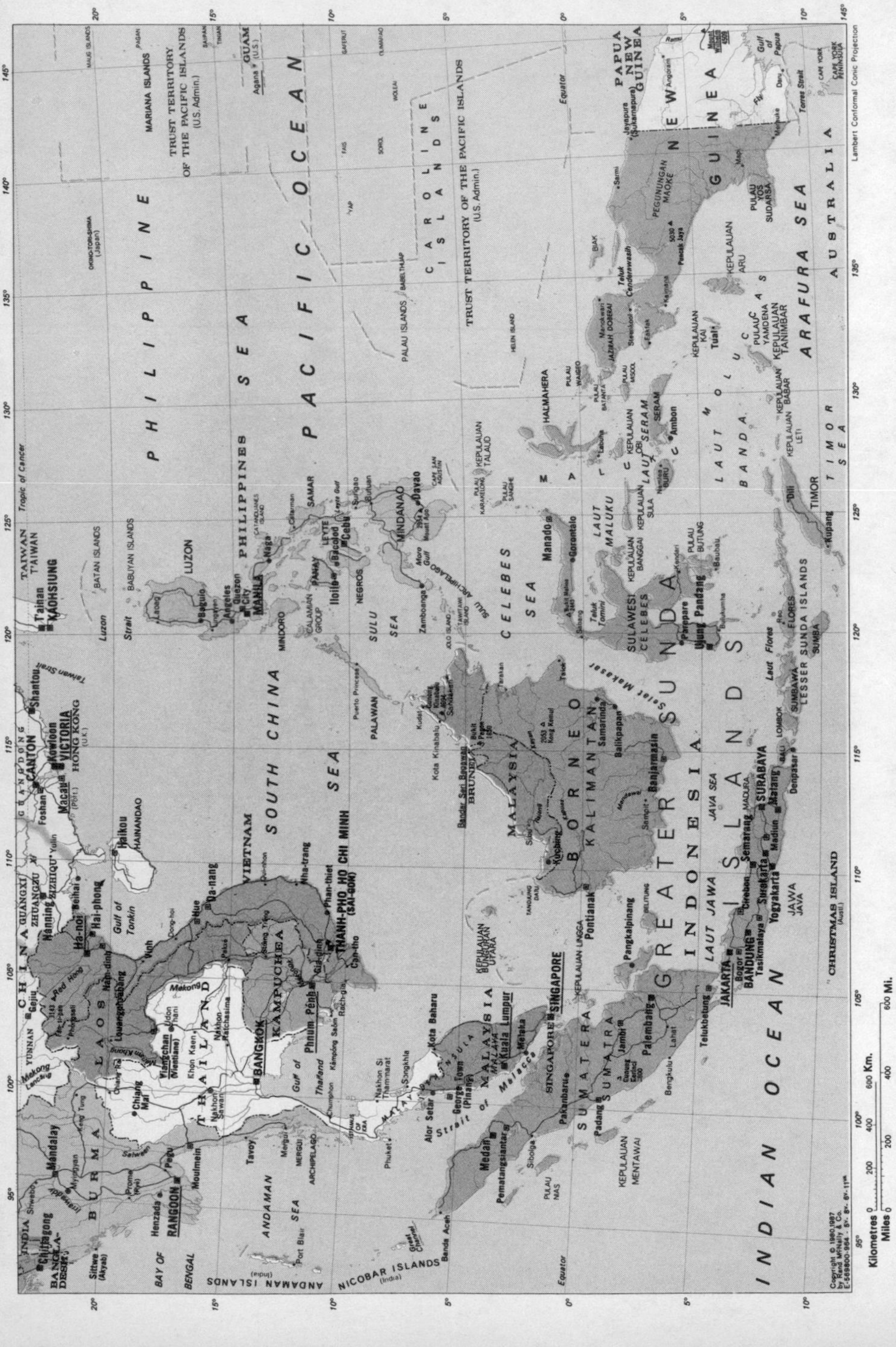
PHILIPPINE SEA
PACIFIC OCEAN
SOUTH CHINA SEA
INDIAN OCEAN
ANDAMAN SEA
BAY OF BENGAL
CELEBES SEA
SULU SEA
JAVA SEA
BANDA SEA
ARAFURA SEA
TIMOR SEA
Gulf of Thailand
Gulf of Tonkin
Strait of Malacca
Selat Makasar
CHINA
BURMA
LAOS
THAILAND
KAMPUCHEA
VIETNAM
MALAYSIA
SINGAPORE
BRUNEI
INDONESIA
PHILIPPINES
PAPUA NEW GUINEA
AUSTRALIA
BORNEO
KALIMANTAN
SUMATERA
SULAWESI CELEBES
NEW GUINEA
MINDANAO
LUZON
GREATER SUNDA ISLANDS
LESSER SUNDA ISLANDS
MOLUCCAS
CAROLINE ISLANDS
MARIANA ISLANDS
TRUST TERRITORY OF THE PACIFIC ISLANDS (U.S. Admin.)
GUAM (U.S.)
PALAU ISLANDS
ANDAMAN ISLANDS (India)
NICOBAR ISLANDS (India)
CHRISTMAS ISLAND (Austl.)
TAIWAN T'AIWAN
HONG KONG (U.K.)
HAINANDAO
BANGKOK
RANGOON
Mandalay
Ha-noi
Hai-phong
Da-nang
THANH-PHO HO CHI MINH (SAI-GON)
Phnum Penh
Viangchan (Vientiane)
Kuala Lumpur
JAKARTA
SURABAYA
MANILA
Cebu
Davao
Zamboanga
Ujung Pandang
Manado
Ambon
Dili
Kupang
Medan
Palembang
Padang
Pontianak
Banjarmasin
Balikpapan
Samarinda
Bandar Seri Begawan
Kota Kinabalu
George Town (Pinang)
Kota Baharu
Equator
Tropic of Cancer
Lambert Conformal Conic Projection
Kilometres
Miles
Copyright © 1980,1987 by Rand McNally & Co.

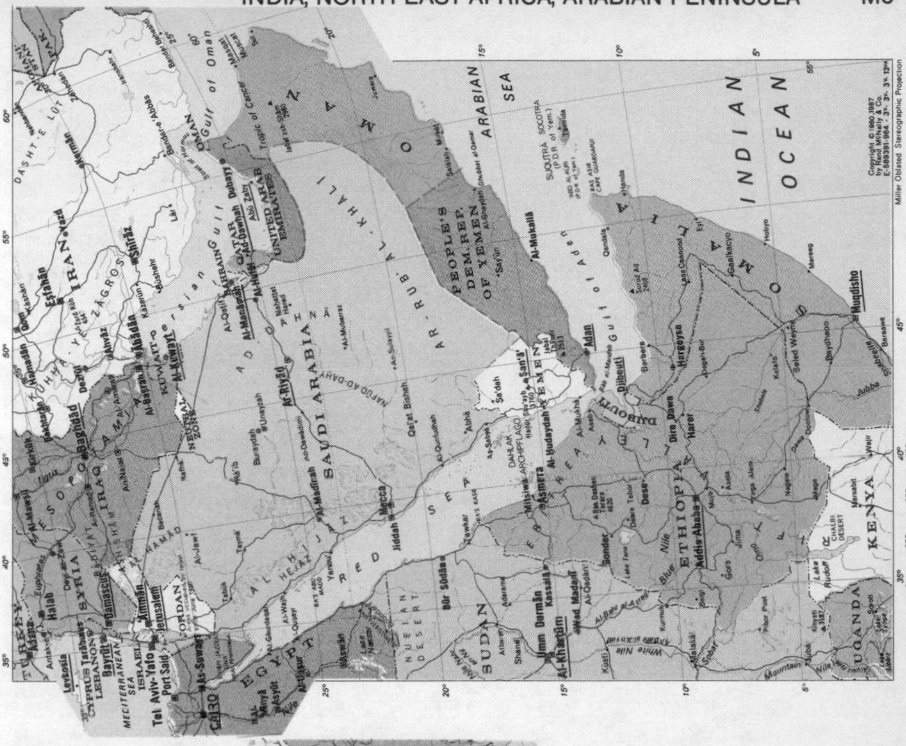
ARABIAN SEA
INDIAN OCEAN
RED SEA
SAUDI ARABIA
ETHIOPIA
EGYPT
SUDAN
Miller Oblated Stereographic Projection
Copyright © 1980,1987 by Rand McNally & Co.

ARABIAN SEA
INDIAN OCEAN
BAY OF BENGAL
The boundary between India and Pakistan through the disputed state of Jammu and Kashmir follows the "line of control" agreed upon by both countries in 1972.
Lambert Conformal Conic Projection
Copyright © 1980,1987 by Rand McNally & Co.

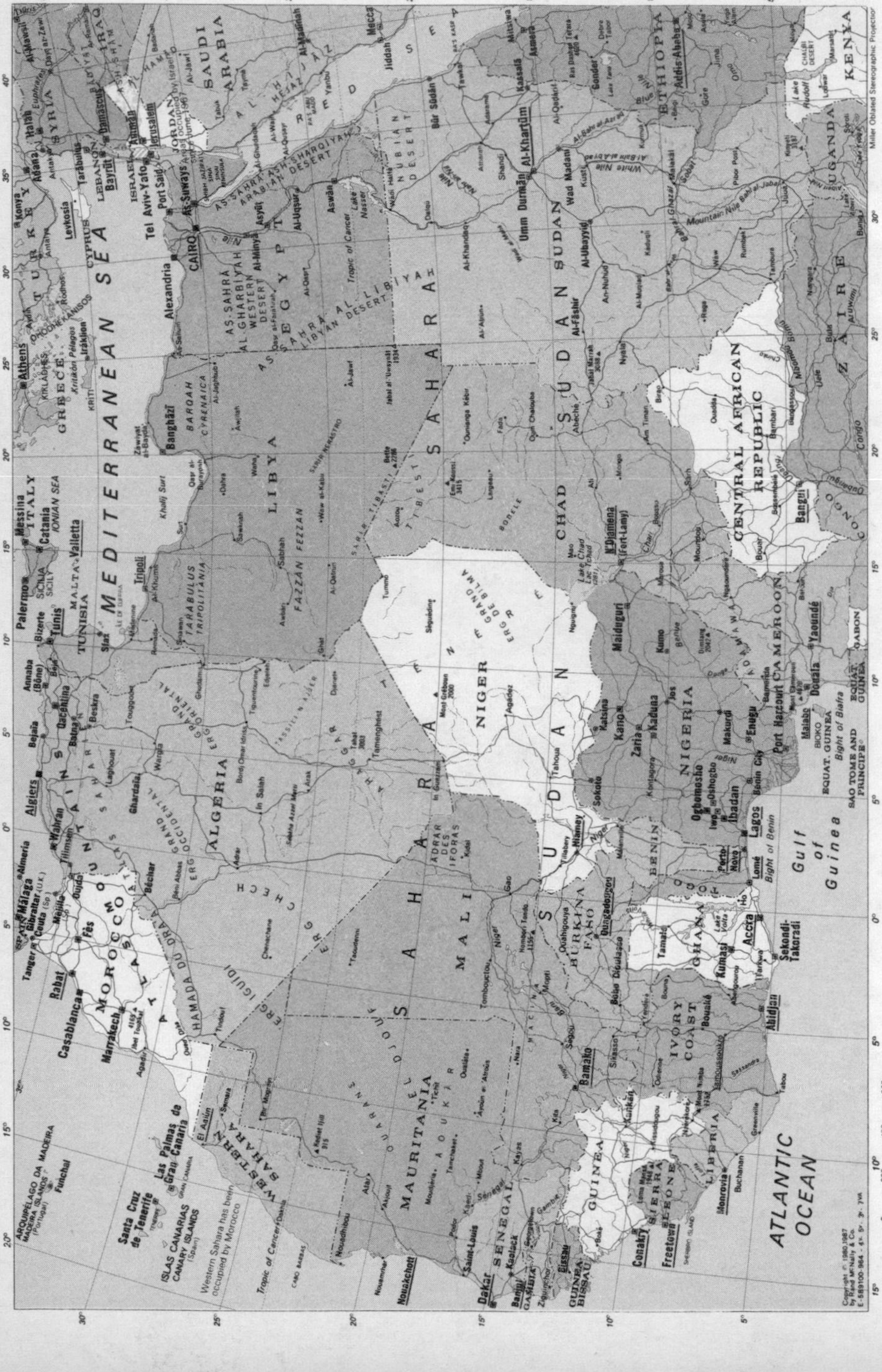
MEDITERRANEAN SEA
ATLANTIC OCEAN
Gulf of Guinea
Bight of Benin
Bight of Biafra
SAHARA
SUDAN
MOROCCO
ALGERIA
TUNISIA
LIBYA
EGYPT
MAURITANIA
MALI
NIGER
CHAD
SUDAN
ETHIOPIA
SENEGAL
GAMBIA
GUINEA-BISSAU
GUINEA
SIERRA LEONE
LIBERIA
IVORY COAST
GHANA
BURKINA FASO
BENIN
NIGERIA
CAMEROON
CENTRAL AFRICAN REPUBLIC
CONGO
ZAIRE
UGANDA
KENYA
SAUDI ARABIA
JORDAN
ISRAEL
LEBANON
SYRIA
IRAQ
TURKEY
CYPRUS
GREECE
ITALY
MALTA
WESTERN SAHARA
Western Sahara has been occupied by Morocco
ISLAS CANARIAS CANARY ISLANDS (Spain)
ARQUIPÉLAGO DA MADEIRA MADEIRA ISLANDS (Portugal)
Tropic of Cancer
CAIRO
Alexandria
Tripoli
Tunis
Algiers
Rabat
Casablanca
Marrakech
Dakar
Bamako
Niamey
Khartoum
Addis Ababa
Lagos
Accra
Abidjan
Monrovia
Freetown
Conakry
Nouakchott
Mecca
Jerusalem
Athens
Kilometres 0 200 400 600 Km.
Miles 0 200 400 Mi.
Miller Oblated Stereographic Projection
Copyright © 1980, 1987 by Rand McNally & Co.

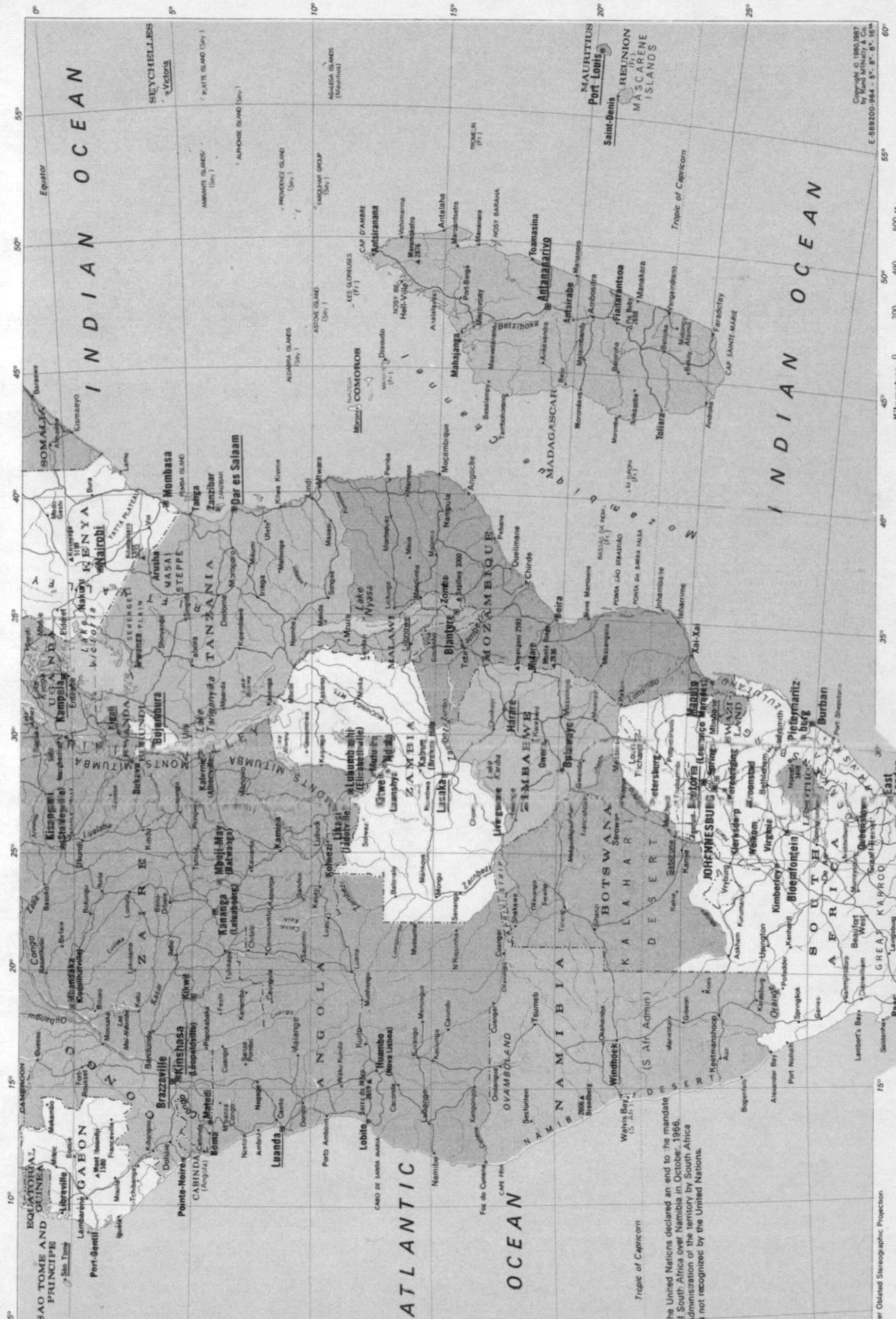
INDIAN OCEAN
ATLANTIC OCEAN
MADAGASCAR
ZAIRE
ANGOLA
NAMIBIA
BOTSWANA
ZAMBIA
ZIMBABWE
MOZAMBIQUE
TANZANIA
KENYA
SOUTH AFRICA
MALAWI
GABON
CONGO
COMOROS
SEYCHELLES
MAURITIUS
REUNION
SAO TOME AND PRINCIPE
EQUATORIAL GUINEA
Tropic of Capricorn
Equator
The United Nations declared an end to the mandate of South Africa over Namibia in October, 1966. Administration of the territory by South Africa is not recognized by the United Nations.
Miller Oblated Stereographic Projection
Kilometres
Miles

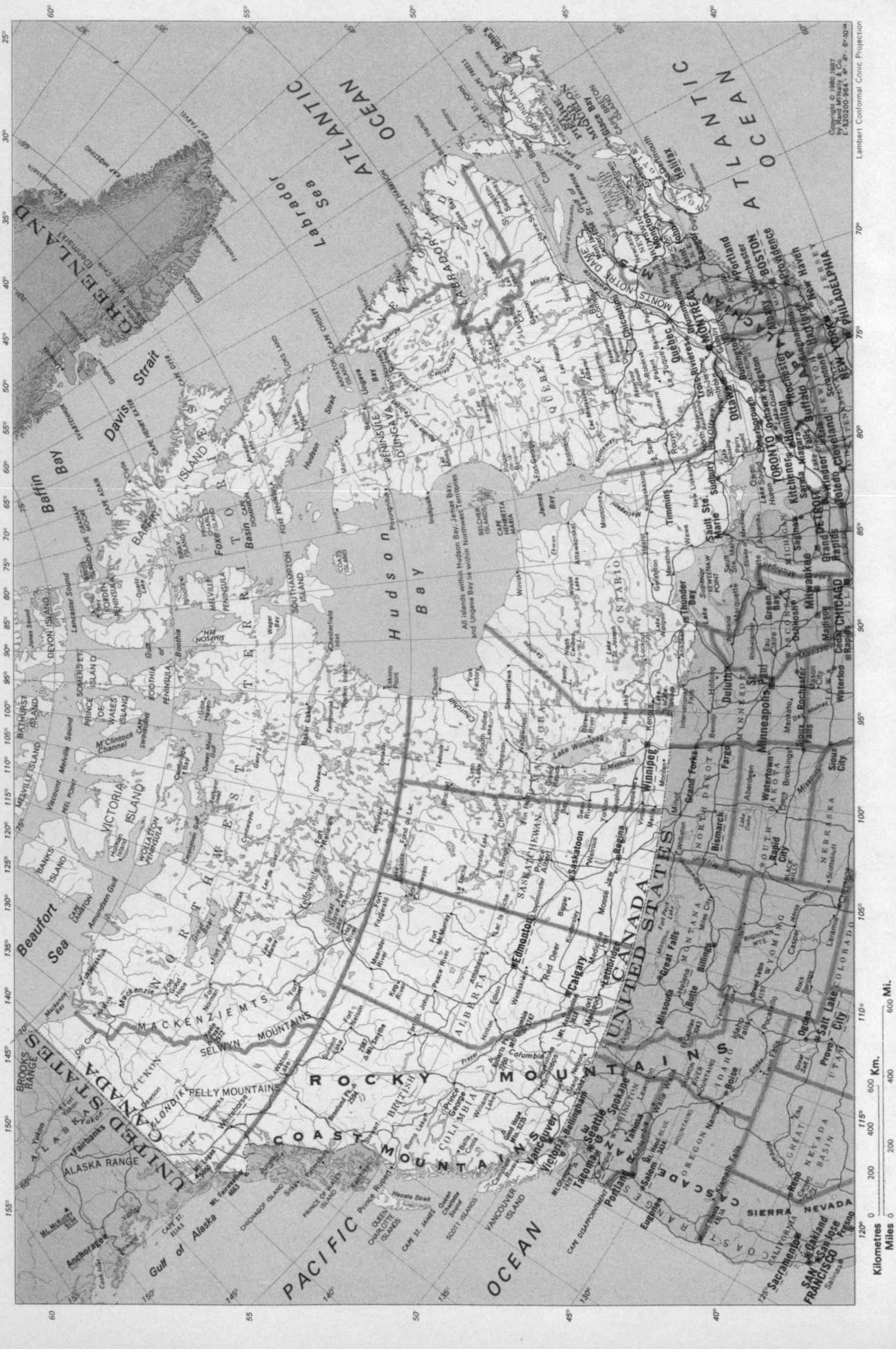
CANADA
UNITED STATES
Hudson Bay
PACIFIC OCEAN
ATLANTIC OCEAN
Labrador Sea
Baffin Bay
Davis Strait
Beaufort Sea
Gulf of Alaska
GREENLAND
ROCKY MOUNTAINS
COAST MOUNTAINS
SELWYN MOUNTAINS
MACKENZIE MTS
PELLY MOUNTAINS
ALASKA RANGE
Hudson Strait
James Bay
Foxe Basin
VICTORIA ISLAND
BAFFIN ISLAND
SOUTHAMPTON ISLAND
VANCOUVER ISLAND
All islands within Hudson Bay, James Bay, and Ungava Bay lie within Northwest Territories
Lambert Conformal Conic Projection
Kilometres
Miles

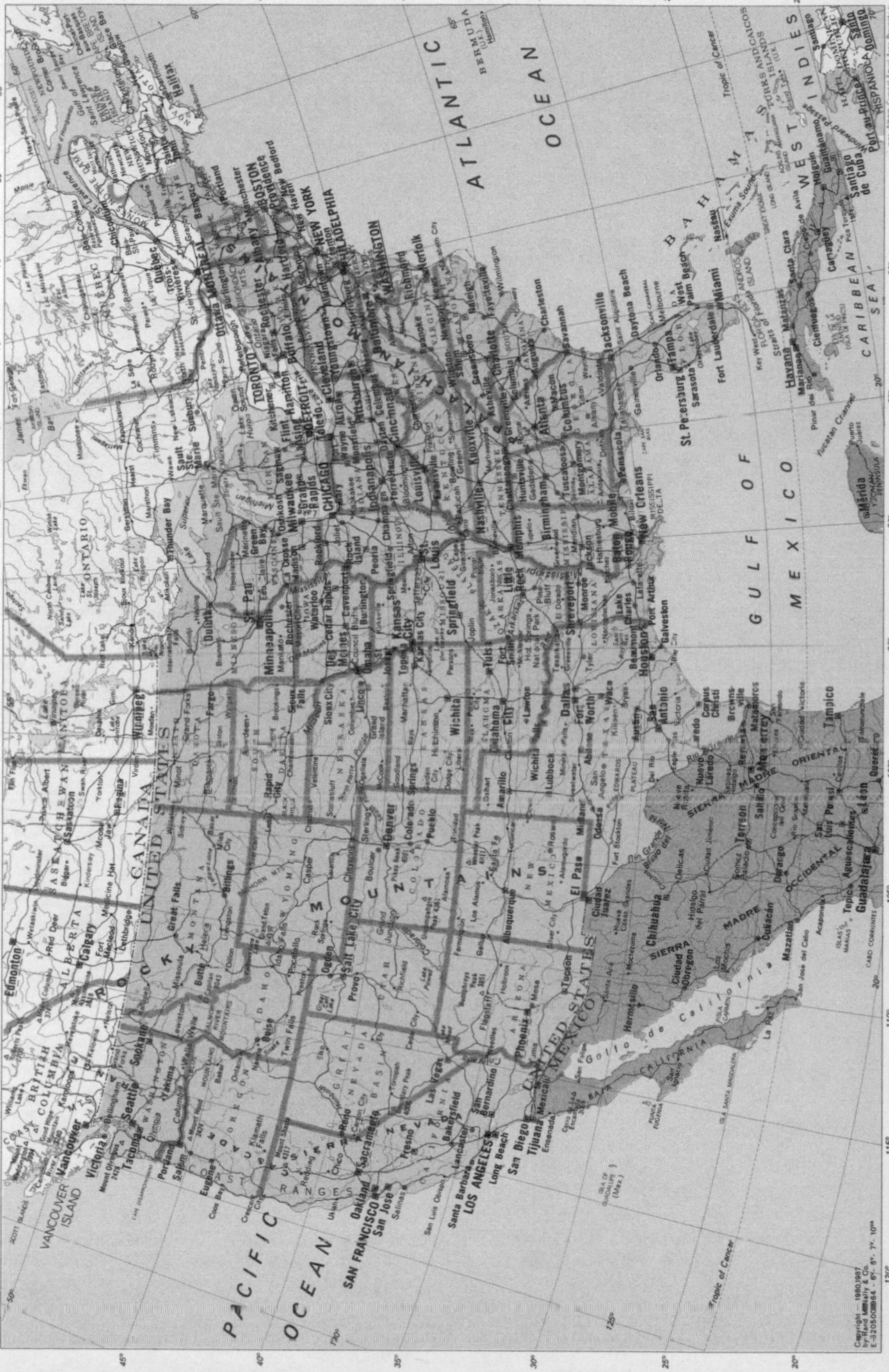
ATLANTIC OCEAN
PACIFIC OCEAN
GULF OF MEXICO
WEST INDIES
CARIBBEAN SEA
BAHAMAS
BERMUDA
UNITED STATES
CANADA
MEXICO
ONTARIO
QUEBEC
BRITISH COLUMBIA
ALBERTA
SASKATCHEWAN
MANITOBA
VANCOUVER ISLAND
Tropic of Cancer
WASHINGTON
NEW YORK
PHILADELPHIA
BOSTON
CHICAGO
DETROIT
TORONTO
MONTREAL
LOS ANGELES
SAN FRANCISCO
Seattle
Portland
Denver
Dallas
Houston
New Orleans
Miami
Atlanta
St. Louis
Minneapolis
Winnipeg
Calgary
Edmonton
Vancouver
Havana
Monterrey
Chihuahua
El Paso
Phoenix
Salt Lake City
Las Vegas
San Diego
Tijuana
Kilometres
Copyright 1980,1987 by Rand McNally & Co.
Albers Conical Equal-Area Projection

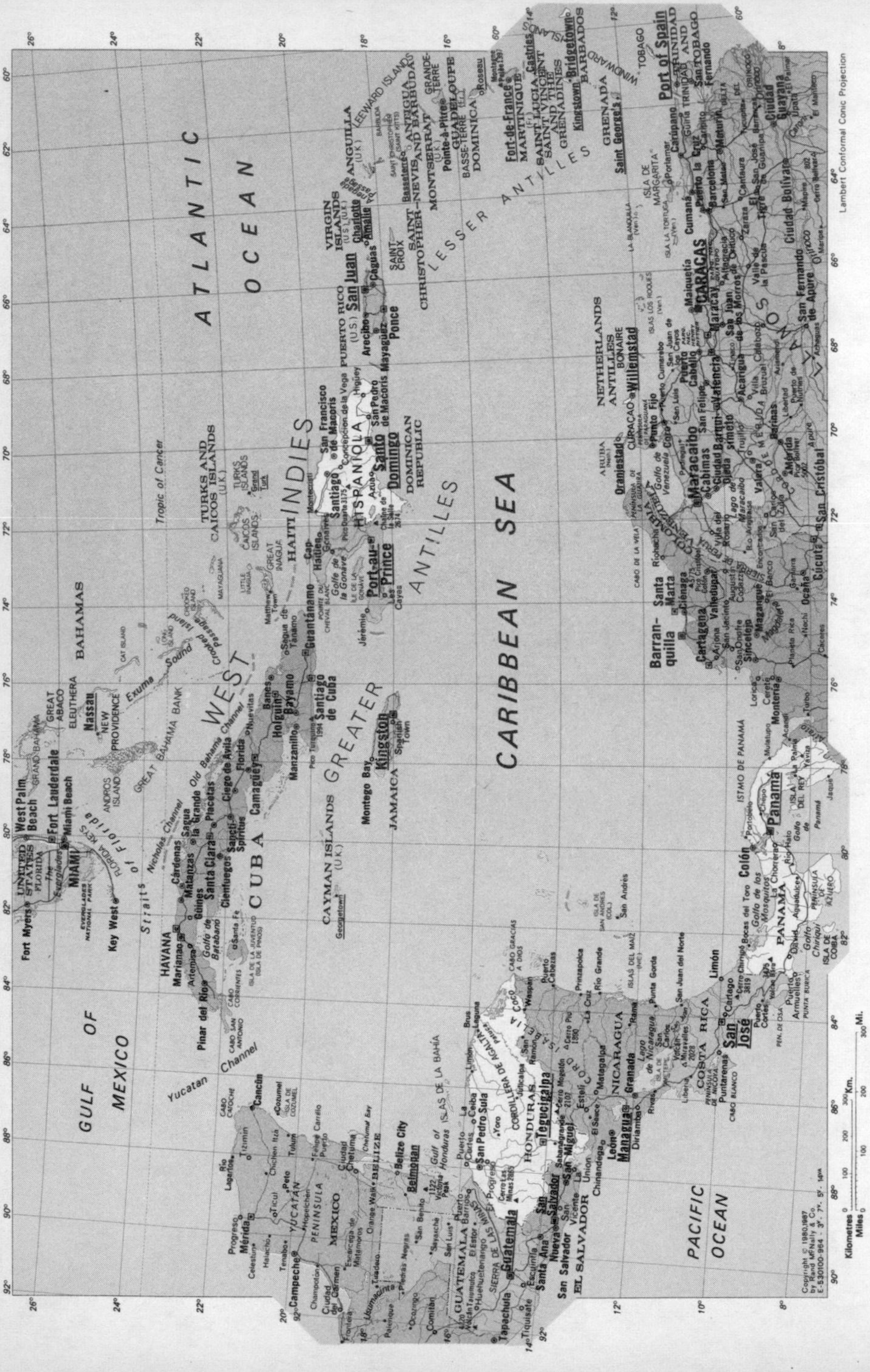
ATLANTIC
OCEAN
GULF OF MEXICO
CARIBBEAN SEA
PACIFIC OCEAN
WEST INDIES
GREATER ANTILLES
LESSER ANTILLES
BAHAMAS
TURKS AND CAICOS ISLANDS (U.K.)
CUBA
HAVANA
HAITI
HISPANIOLA
DOMINICAN REPUBLIC
Santo Domingo
Port-au-Prince
JAMAICA
Kingston
CAYMAN ISLANDS (U.K.)
PUERTO RICO (U.S.)
San Juan
VIRGIN ISLANDS
ANGUILLA
ANTIGUA AND BARBUDA
SAINT CHRISTOPHER-NEVIS
MONTSERRAT
GUADELOUPE
DOMINICA
MARTINIQUE
SAINT LUCIA
SAINT VINCENT AND THE GRENADINES
BARBADOS
GRENADA
TRINIDAD AND TOBAGO
Port of Spain
NETHERLANDS ANTILLES
ARUBA
CURAÇAO
BONAIRE
Willemstad
CARACAS
Maracaibo
Barranquilla
Cartagena
MEXICO
YUCATAN PENINSULA
BELIZE
Belmopan
GUATEMALA
Guatemala
HONDURAS
Tegucigalpa
EL SALVADOR
San Salvador
NICARAGUA
Managua
COSTA RICA
San José
PANAMA
Panamá
Colón
UNITED STATES
FLORIDA
MIAMI
Key West
Tropic of Cancer
Straits of Florida
Yucatan Channel
Lambert Conformal Conic Projection
Kilometres
Miles
Copyright © 1980, 1987 by Rand McNally & Co.

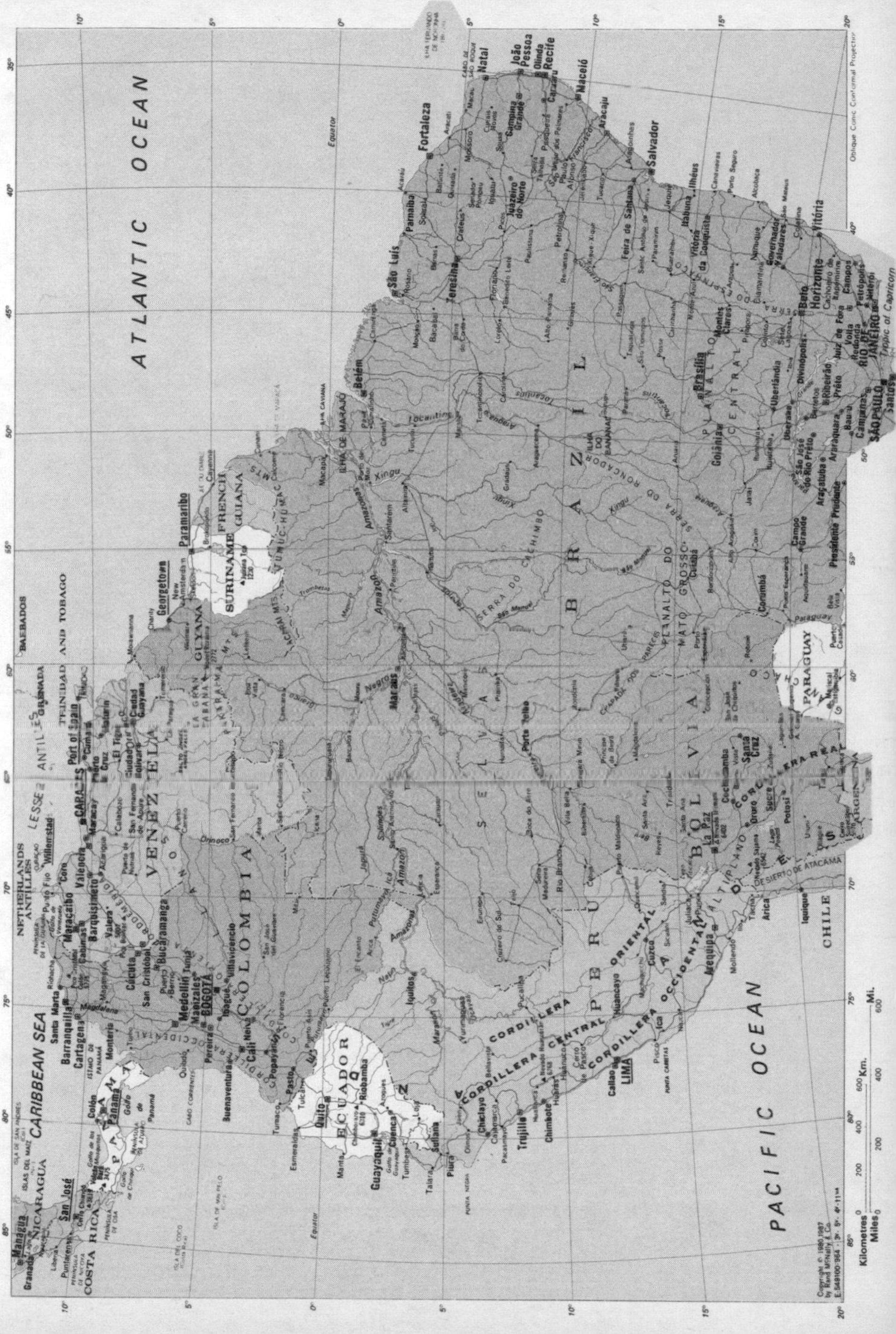
ATLANTIC OCEAN
PACIFIC OCEAN
CARIBBEAN SEA
BRAZIL
COLOMBIA
VENEZUELA
PERU
BOLIVIA
ECUADOR
PARAGUAY
CHILE
GUYANA
SURINAME
FRENCH GUIANA
PANAMA
COSTA RICA
NICARAGUA
NETHERLANDS ANTILLES
LESSER ANTILLES
TRINIDAD AND TOBAGO
BARBADOS
GRENADA
Equator
Tropic of Capricorn
CORDILLERA CENTRAL
CORDILLERA OCCIDENTAL
CORDILLERA ORIENTAL
CORDILLERA REAL
ALTIPLANO
DESIERTO DE ATACAMA
PLANALTO DO MATO GROSSO
PLANALTO CENTRAL
SERRA DO RONCADOR
SERRA DO CACHIMBO
SELVA
Amazon
Amazonas
Xingu
Tocantins
Negro
Orinoco
Paraguay
Solimões
Caracas
Bogotá
Quito
Lima
La Paz
Sucre
Brasília
Georgetown
Paramaribo
Cayenne
Port of Spain
Panamá
San José
Managua
Medellín
Cali
Barranquilla
Cartagena
Maracaibo
Valencia
Guayaquil
Cuenca
Manaus
Belém
Fortaleza
Recife
Natal
Salvador
Maceió
Aracaju
Teresina
São Luís
Belo Horizonte
Rio de Janeiro
São Paulo
Santos
Vitória
Goiânia
Cuiabá
Corumbá
Campo Grande
Porto Velho
Iquitos
Arequipa
Cuzco
Trujillo
Chiclayo
Piura
Arica
Iquique
Cochabamba
Santa Cruz
Oruro
Potosí
Huancayo
Callao
Oblique Conic Conformal Projection
Kilometres 0 200 400 600 Km.
Miles 0 200 400 600 Mi.
Copyright © 1980,1987 by Rand McNally & Co.

INDONESIA
Timor Sea
Kupang
MELVILLE ISLAND
Darwin
ARNHEM LAND
Katherine
Joseph Bonaparte Gulf
WESSEL ISLANDS
GROOTE EYLANDT
Gulf of Carpentaria
CAPE YORK PENINSULA
Torres Strait
PAPUA NEW GUINEA
GREAT BARRIER REEF
Coral Sea
Cooktown
Cairns
Townsville
Mackay
Rockhampton
Bundaberg
FRASER ISLAND
Maryborough
Brisbane
Ipswich
Toowoomba
Wyndham
KIMBERLEY PLATEAU
Broome
Port Hedland
DAMPIER ARCHIPELAGO
GREAT SANDY DESERT
NORTHERN TERRITORY
Tennant Creek
Mount Isa
Cloncurry
Hughenden
Winton
GREAT DIVIDING RANGE
QUEENSLAND
GREAT ARTESIAN BASIN
Alice Springs
MACDONNELL RANGES
SIMPSON DESERT
Lake Mackay (Dry Salt Lake)
Lake Disappointment (Dry Salt Lake)
WESTERN AUSTRALIA
GIBSON DESERT
Tropic of Capricorn
AUSTRALIA
Lake Carnegie (Dry)
GREAT VICTORIA DESERT
SOUTH AUSTRALIA
Lake Eyre North (Dry Salt Lake)
Lake Eyre South
Lake Torrens
Kalgoorlie
Perth
DARLING RANGE
Bunbury
Albany
Esperance
Geraldton
Great Australian Bight
Eucla
Port Augusta
Port Lincoln
Spencer Gulf
FLINDERS RANGES
Broken Hill
Adelaide
KANGAROO ISLAND
NEW SOUTH WALES
Dubbo
Newcastle
SYDNEY
Wollongong
Canberra
A.C.T.
Wagga Wagga
Albury
Bendigo
VICTORIA
Geelong
MELBOURNE
Mount Gambier
Tasman Sea
Bass Strait
KING ISLAND
FLINDERS ISLAND
TASMANIA
Launceston
Burnie
Hobart
INDIAN OCEAN
Copyright © 1980,1987 by Rand McNally & Co.
Kilometres 0 200 400 600 Km.
Statute Miles 0 200 400 600 Mi.
Lambert Conformal Conic Projection

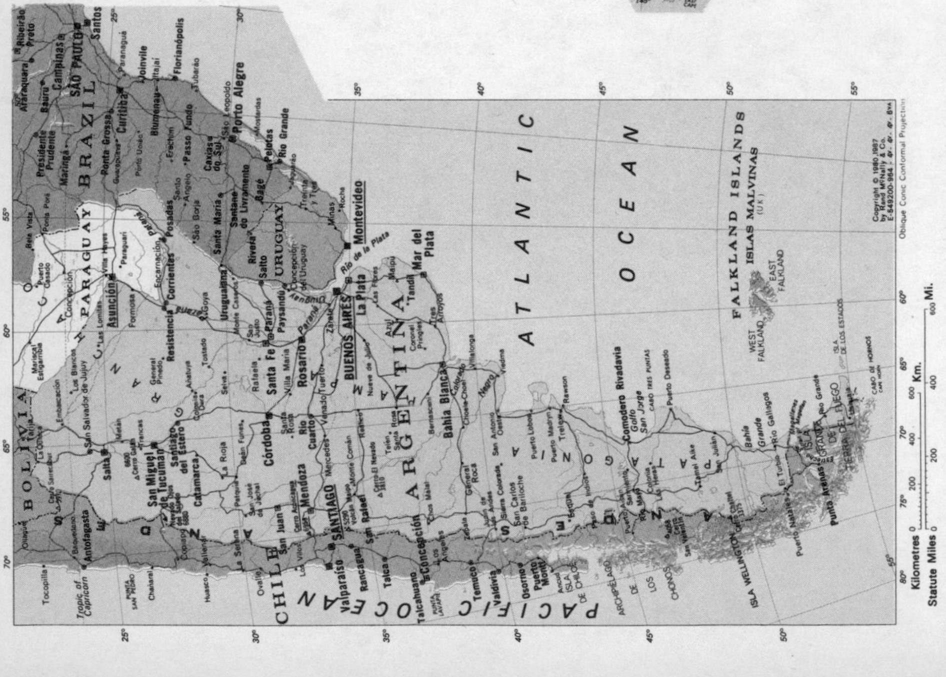
BOLIVIA
PARAGUAY
BRAZIL
SÃO PAULO
Santos
Campinas
Curitiba
Florianópolis
Porto Alegre
Pelotas
Rio Grande
URUGUAY
Montevideo
Río de la Plata
BUENOS AIRES
La Plata
Mar del Plata
Bahía Blanca
Asunción
Corrientes
Resistencia
Santa Fe
Rosario
Córdoba
San Miguel de Tucumán
Salta
Mendoza
San Juan
SANTIAGO
Valparaíso
Concepción
Antofagasta
Temuco
Valdivia
Osorno
Puerto Montt
ISLA CHILOÉ
ARCHIPIÉLAGO DE LOS CHONOS
ISLA WELLINGTON
Comodoro Rivadavia
Golfo San Jorge
Puerto Deseado
Río Gallegos
Punta Arenas
ISLA GRANDE DE TIERRA DEL FUEGO
FALKLAND ISLANDS
ISLAS MALVINAS
(U.K.)
WEST FALKLAND
EAST FALKLAND
CABO DE HORNOS
ARGENTINA
CHILE
ATLANTIC OCEAN
PACIFIC OCEAN
Tropic of Capricorn
Copyright © 1980,1987 by Rand McNally & Co.
Oblique Conic Conformal Projection
Kilometres 0 200 400 600 Km.
Statute Miles 0 200 400 600 Mi.

WORLD HISTORY

Prehistory: Our Ancestors Take Over

Homo sapiens. The precise origins of *homo sapiens,* the species to which all humans belong, are subject to broad speculation based on a small number of fossils, genetic and anatomical studies, and the geological record. But most scientists agree that we evolved from ape-like primate ancestors in a process that began millions of years ago.

Current theories say the first hominid (human-like primate) was *Ramapithecus,* who emerged 12 million years ago. Its remains have been found in Asia, Europe, and Africa. Further development was apparently limited to Africa, where 2 lines of hominids appeared some 5 or 6 million years ago. One was *Australopithecus,* a tool-maker and social animal, who lived from perhaps 4 to 3 million years ago, and then apparently became extinct.

The 2nd was a human line, *Homo habillus,* a large-brained specimen that walked upright and had a dextrous hand. *Homo habillus* lived in semi-permanent camps and had a food-gathering and sharing economy.

Homo erectus, our nearest ancestor, appeared in Africa perhaps 1.75 million years ago, and began spreading into Asia and Europe soon after. It had a fairly large brain and a skeletal structure similar to ours. *Homo erectus* learned to control fire, and probably had primitive language skills. The final brain development to *Homo sapiens* and then to our sub-species *Homo sapiens sapiens* occurred between 500,000 and 50,000 years ago, over a wide geographic area and in many different steps and recombinations. All humans of all races belong to this sub-species.

The spread of mankind into the remaining habitable continents probably took place during the last ice age up to 100,000 years ago: to the Americas across a land bridge from Asia, and to Australia across the Timor Straits.

Earliest cultures. A variety of cultural modes — in tool-making, diet, shelter, and possibly social arrangements and spiritual expression, arose as early mankind adapted to different geographic and climatic zones.

Three basic tool-making traditions are recognized by archeologists as arising and often coexisting from one million years ago to the near past: the *chopper tradition,* found largely in E. Asia, with crude chopping tools and simple flake tools; the *flake tradition,* found in Africa and W. Europe, with a variety of small cutting and flaking tools, and the *biface tradition,* found in all of Africa, W. and S. Europe, and S. Asia, producing pointed hand axes chipped on both faces. Later biface sites yield more refined axes and a variety of other tools, weapons, and ornaments using bone, antler, and wood as well as stone.

Only sketchy evidence remains for the different stages in man's increasing control over the environment. Traces of 400,000-year-old covered wood shelters have been found at Nice, France. Scraping tools at Neanderthal sites (200,000-30,000 BC in Europe, N. Africa, the Middle East and Central Asia) suggest the treatment of skins for clothing. Sites from all parts of the world show seasonal migration patterns and exploitation of a wide range of plant and animal food sources.

Painting and decoration, for which there is evidence at the Nice site, flourished along with stone and ivory sculpture after 30,000 years ago; 60 caves in France and 30 in Spain show remarkable examples of wall painting. Other examples have been found in Africa. Proto-religious rites are suggested by these works, and by evidence of ritual cannibalism by Peking Man, 500,000 BC, and of ritual burial with medicinal plants and flowers by Neanderthals at Shanidar in Iraq.

The Neolithic Revolution. Sometime after 10,000 BC, among widely separated human communities, a series of dramatic technological and social changes occurred that are summed up as the Neolithic Revolution. The cultivation of previously wild plants encouraged the growth of permanent settlements. Animals were domesticated as a work force and food source. The manufacture of pottery and cloth began. These techniques permitted a huge increase in world population and in human control over the earth.

No region can safely claim priority as the "inventor" of these techniques. Dispersed sites in Cen. and S. America, S.E. Europe, and the Middle East show roughly contemporaneous (10-8,000 BC) evidence of one or another "neolithic" trait. Dates near 6-3,000 BC have been given for E. and S. Asian, W. European, and sub-Saharan African neolithic remains. The variety of crops — field grains, rice, maize, and roots, and the varying mix of other traits suggest that the revolution occurred independently in all these regions.

History Begins: 4000 - 1000 BC

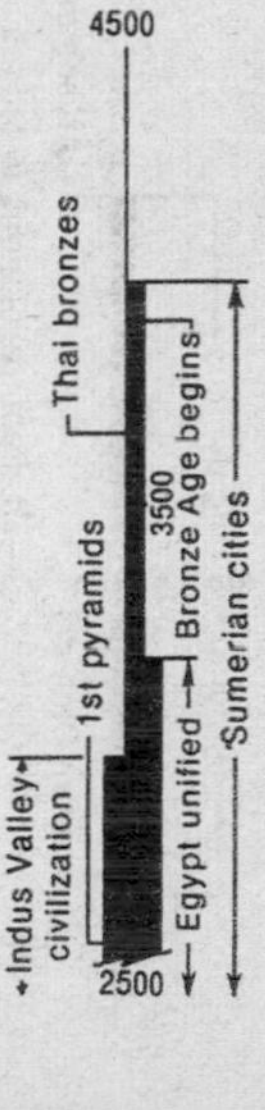

Near Eastern cradle. If history began with writing, the first chapter opened in Mesopotamia, the Tigris-Euphrates river valley. Clay tablets with pictographs were used by the Sumerians to keep records after 4000 BC. A **cuneiform** (wedge shaped) script evolved by 3000 BC as a full syllabic alphabet. Neighboring peoples adapted the script to their own language.

Sumerian life centered, from 4000 BC, on large cities (Eridu, Ur, Uruk, Nippur, Kish, Lagash) organized around temples and priestly bureaucracies, with the surrounding plains watered by vast irrigation works and worked with traction plows. Sailboats, wheeled vehicles, potters wheels, and kilns were used. Copper was smelted and tempered in Sumeria from c4000 BC and bronze was produced not long after. Ores, as well as precious stones and metals were obtained through long-distance ship and caravan trade. Iron was used from c2000 BC. Improved ironworking, developed partly by the **Hittites,** became widespread by 1200 BC.

Sumerian political primacy passed among cities and their kingly dynasties. Semitic-speaking peoples, with cultures derived from the Sumerian, founded a succession of dynasties that ruled in Mesopotamia and neighboring areas for most of 1800 years; among them the **Akkadians** (first under Sargon c2350 BC), the Amorites (whose laws, codified by **Hammurabi,** c1792-1750 BC, have Biblical parallels), and the Assyrians, with interludes of rule by the Hittites, Kassites, and Mitanni, all possibly Indo-Europeans. The political and cultural center of gravity shifted northwest with each successive empire.

Mesopotamian learning, maintained by scribes and preserved by successive rulers in vast libraries, was not abstract or theoretical. Algebraic and geometric problems could be solved on a practical basis in construction, commerce, or administration. Systematic lists of astronomical phenomena, plants, animals and stones were kept; medical texts listed ailments and their herbal cures.

The Sumerians worshipped anthropomorphic gods representing natural forces — Anu, god of heaven; Enlil (Ea), god of water. Epic poetry related these and other gods in a hierarchy. Sacrifices were made at **ziggurats** — huge stepped temples. Gods were thought to control all events, which could be foretold using oracular materials. This religious pattern persisted into the first millenium BC.

The Syria-Palestine area, site of some of the earliest urban remains (Jericho, 7000 BC), and of the recently uncovered **Ebla** civilization (fl. 2500 BC), experienced Egyptian cultural and political influence along with Mesopotamian. The **Phoenician** coast was an active commercial center. A phonetic alphabet was invented here before 1600 BC. It became the ancestor of all European, Middle Eastern, Indian, S.E.

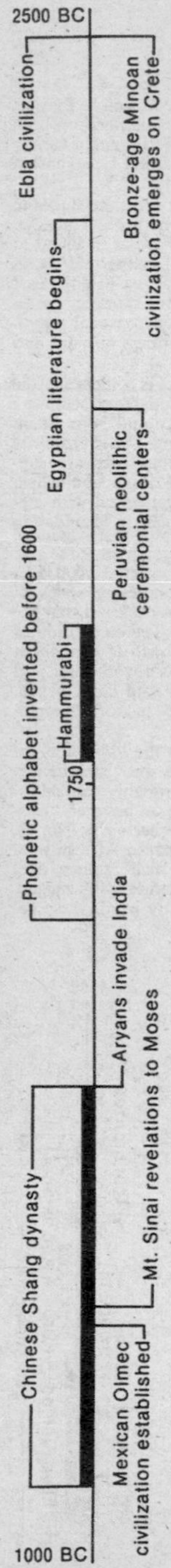

Asian, Ethiopian, and Korean alphabets.

Regional commerce and diplomacy were aided by the use of Akkadian as a *lingua franca*, later replaced by Aramaic.

Egypt. Agricultural villages along the Nile were united by 3300 BC into two kingdoms, Upper and Lower Egypt, unified under the Pharaoh Menes c3100 BC; Nubia to the south was added 2600 BC. A national bureaucracy supervised construction of canals and monuments (**pyramids** starting 2700 BC). Brilliant First Dynasty achievements in architecture, sculpture and painting, set the standards and forms for all subsequent Egyptian civilization and are still admired. **Hieroglyphic writing** appeared by 3400 BC, recording a sophisticated literature including romantic and philosophical modes after 2300 BC.

An ordered hierarchy of gods, including totemistic animal elements, was served by a powerful priesthood in Memphis. The pharaoh was identified with the falcon god Horus. Later trends were the belief in an afterlife, and the quasi-monotheistic reforms of **Akhenaton** (c1379-1362 BC).

After a period of conquest by Semitic Hyksos from Asia (c1700-1500 BC), the New Kingdom established an empire in Syria. Egypt became increasingly embroiled in Asiatic wars and diplomacy. Eventually it was conquered by Persia in 525 BC, and it faded away as an independent culture.

India. An urban civilization with a so-far-undeciphered writing system stretched across the Indus Valley and along the Arabian Sea c3000-1500 BC. Major sites are Harappa and **Mohenjo-Daro** in Pakistan, well-planned geometric cities with underground sewers and vast granaries. The entire region (600,000 sq. mi.) may have been ruled as a single state. Bronze was used, and arts and crafts were highly developed. Religious life apparently took the form of fertility cults.

Indus civilization was probably in decline when it was destroyed by **Aryan invaders** from the northwest, speaking an Indo-European language from which all the languages of Pakistan, north India and Bangladesh descend. Led by a warrior aristocracy whose legendary deeds are recorded in the **Rig Veda,** the Aryans spread east and south, bringing their pantheon of sky gods, elaborate priestly (Brahmin) ritual, and the beginnings of the caste system; local customs and beliefs were assimilated by the conquerors.

Europe. On Crete, the bronze-age **Minoan civilization** emerged c2500 BC. A prosperous economy and richly decorative art (e.g. at Knossos palace) was supported by seaborne commerce. Mycenae and other cities in Greece and Asia Minor (e.g. **Troy**) preserved elements of the culture to c1100 BC. Cretan Linear A script, c2000-1700 BC, is undeciphered; Linear B, c1300-1200 BC, records a Greek dialect.

Possible connection between Minoan-Mycenaean monumental stonework, and the great megalithic monuments and tombs of W. Europe, Iberia, and Malta (c4000-1500 BC) is unclear.

China. Proto-Chinese neolithic cultures had long covered northern and southeastern China when the first large political state was organized in the north by the **Shang dynasty** c1500 BC. Shang kings called themselves Sons of Heaven, and presided over a cult of human and animal sacrifice to ancestors and nature gods. The Chou dynasty, starting c1100 BC, expanded the area of the Son of Heaven's dominion, but feudal states exercised most temporal power.

A writing system with 2,000 different characters was already in use under the Shang, with **pictographs** later supplemented by phonetic characters. The system, with modifications, is still in use, despite changes in spoken Chinese.

Technical advances allowed urban specialists to create fine ceramic and jade products, and bronze casting after 1500 BC was the most advanced in the world.

Bronze artifacts have recently been discovered in northern Thailand dating to 3600 BC, hundreds of years before similar Middle Eastern finds.

Americas. Olmecs settled on the Gulf coast of Mexico, 1500 BC, and soon developed the first civilization in the Western Hemisphere. Temple cities and huge stone sculpture date to 1200 BC. A rudimentary calendar and writing system existed. Olmec religion, centering on a jaguar god, and art forms influenced all later Meso-American cultures.

Neolithic ceremonial centers were built on the Peruvian desert coast, c2000 BC.

Classical Era of Old World Civilizations

Greece. After a period of decline during the Dorian Greek invasions (1200-1000 BC), Greece and the Aegean area developed a unique civilization. Drawing upon Mycenaean traditions, Mesopotamian learning (weights and measures, lunisolar calendar, astronomy, musical scales), the Phoenician alphabet (modified for Greek), and Egyptian art, the revived **Greek city-states** saw a rich elaboration of intellectual life. Long-range commerce was aided by metal coinage (introduced by the Lydians in Asia Minor before 700 BC); colonies were founded around the Mediterranean and Black Sea shores (Cumae in Italy 760 BC, Massalia in France c600 BC).

Philosophy, starting with Ionian speculation on the nature of matter and the universe (Thales c634-546), and including mathematical speculation (Pythagoras c580-c500), culminated in Athens in the rationalist idealism of **Plato** (c428-347) and **Socrates** (c470-399); the latter was executed for alleged impiety. Aristotle (384-322) united all fields of study in his system. The arts were highly valued. Architecture culminated in the **Parthenon** in Athens (438, sculpture by Phidias); poetry and drama (Aeschylus 525-456) thrived. Male beauty and strength, a chief artistic theme, were enhanced at the gymnasium and the national games at Olympia.

Ruled by local tyrants or oligarchies, the Greeks were never politically united, but managed to resist inclusion in the Persian Empire (Darius defeated at Marathon 490 BC, Xerxes at Salamis, Plataea 479 BC). Local warfare was common; the **Peloponnesian Wars,** 431-404 BC, ended in Sparta's victory over Athens. Greek political power waned, but classical Greek cultural forms spread thoughout the ancient world from the Atlantic to India.

Hebrews. Nomadic Hebrew tribes entered Canaan before 1200 BC, settling among other Semitic peoples speaking the same language. They brought from the desert a **monotheistic faith** said to have been revealed to Abraham in Canaan c1800 BC and to Moses at Mt. Sinai c1250 BC, after the Hebrews' escape from bondage in Egypt. David (ruled 1000-961 BC) and Solomon (ruled 961-922 BC) united the Hebrews in a kingdom that briefly dominated the area. Phoenicians to the north established colonies

Paleontology: The History of Life

All dates are approximate, and are subject to change based on new fossil finds or new dating techniques; but the sequence of events is generally accepted. Dates are in years before the present.

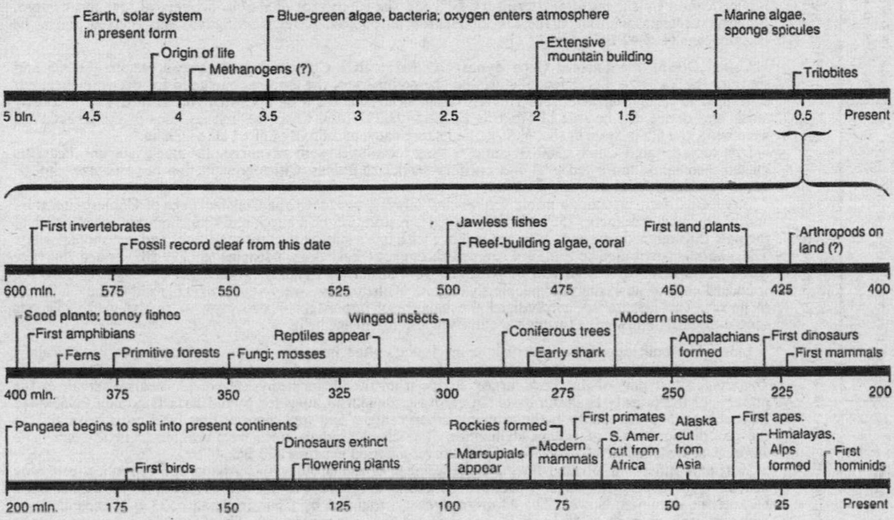

Ancient Near Eastern Civilizations 4000 B.C.-500 B.C.

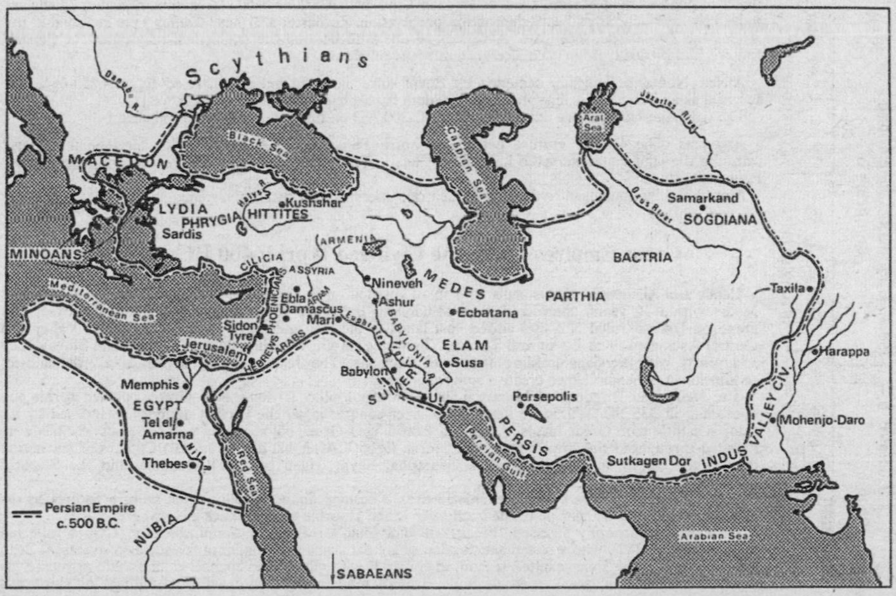

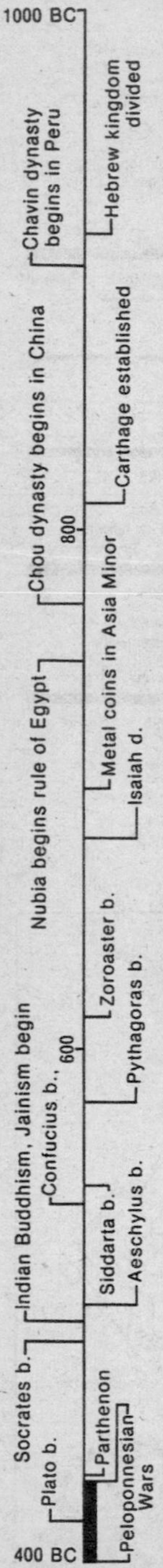

around the E. and W. Mediterranean (**Carthage** c814 BC) and sailed into the Atlantic.

A temple in Jerusalem became the national religious center, with sacrifices performed by a hereditary priesthood. Polytheistic influences, especially of the fertility cult of Baal, were opposed by **prophets** (Elijah, Amos, Isaiah).

Divided into **two kingdoms** after Solomon, the Hebrews were unable to resist the revived Assyrian empire, which conquered Israel, the northern kingdom in 722 BC. Judah, the southern kingdom, was conquered in 586 BC by the Babylonians under Nebuchadnezzar II. But with the fixing of most of the Biblical canon by the mid-fourth century BC, and the emergence of rabbis, arbiters of law and custom, Judaism successfully survived the loss of Hebrew autonomy. A Jewish kingdom was revived under the Hasmoneans (168-42 BC).

China. During the **Eastern Chou** dynasty (770-256 BC), Chinese culture spread east to the sea and south to the Yangtze. Large feudal states on the periphery of the empire contended for pre-eminence, but continued to recognize the Son of Heaven (king), who retained a purely ritual role enriched with courtly music and dance. In the Age of Warring States (403-221 BC), when the first sections of the **Great Wall** were built, the Ch'in state in the West gained supremacy, and finally united all of China.

Iron tools entered China c500 BC, and casting techniques were advanced, aiding agriculture. Peasants owned their land, and owed civil and military service to nobles. Cities grew in number and size, though barter remained the chief trade medium.

Intellectual ferment among noble scribes and officials produced the Classical Age of Chinese literature and philosophy. **Confucius** (551-479 BC) urged a restoration of a supposedly harmonious social order of the past through proper conduct in accordance with one's station and through filial and ceremonial piety. The *Analects*, attributed to him, are revered throughout East Asia. **Mencius** (d. 289 BC) added the view that the Mandate of Heaven can be removed from an unjust dynasty. The Legalists sought to curb the supposed natural wickedness of people through new institutions and harsh laws; they aided the Ch'in rise to power. The Naturalists emphasized the balance of opposites — yin, yang — in the world. **Taoists** sought mystical knowledge through meditation and disengagement.

India. The political and cultural center of India shifted from the Indus to the Ganges River Valley. Buddhism, Jainism, and mystical revisions of orthodox Vedism all developed around 500-300 BC. The *Upanishads*, last part of the *Veda*, urged escape from the illusory physical world. Vedism remained the preserve of the priestly Brahmin caste. In contrast, **Buddhism**, founded by Siddarta Gautama (c563-c483 BC), appealed to merchants in the growing urban centers, and took hold at first (and most lastingly) on the geographic fringes of Indian civilization. The classic Indian epics were composed in this era: The *Ramayana* around 300 BC, the *Mahabharata* over a period starting 400 BC.

Northern India was divided into a large number of monarchies and aristocratic republics, probably derived from tribal groupings, when the Magadha kingdom was formed in Bihar c542 BC. It soon became the dominant power. The **Maurya dynasty**, founded by Chandragupta c321 BC, expanded the kingdom, uniting most of N. India in a centralized bureaucratic empire. The third Mauryan king, **Asoka** (ruled c274-236) conquered most of the subcontinent: he converted to Buddhism, and inscribed its tenets on pillars throughout India. He downplayed the caste system and tried to end expensive sacrificial rites.

Before its final decline in India, Buddhism developed the popular worship of heavenly Bodhisatvas (enlightened beings), and produced a refined architecture (stupa—shrine—at Sanchi 100 AD) and sculpture (Gandhara reliefs 1-400 AD).

Persia. Aryan peoples (Persians, Medes) dominated the area of present Iran by the beginning of the first millenium BC. The prophet **Zoroaster** (born c628 BC) introduced a dualistic religion in which the forces of good (Ahura Mazda, Lord of Wisdom) and evil (Ahiram) battle for dominance; individuals are judged by their actions and earn damnation or salvation. Zoroaster's hymns (*Gathas*) are included in the *Avesta*, the Zoroastrian scriptures. A version of this faith became the established religion of the Persian Empire, and probably influenced later monotheistic religions.

Africa. Nubia, periodically occupied by Egypt since the third millenium, ruled Egypt c750-661, and survived as an independent Egyptianized kingdom (**Kush;** capital Meroe) for 1,000 years.

The Iron Age Nok culture flourished c500 BC-200 AD on the Benue Plateau of **Nigeria.**

Americas. The Chavin culture controlled north Peru from 900-200 BC. Its ceremonial centers, featuring the jaguar god, survived long after. Chavin architecture, ceramics, and textiles influenced other Peruvian cultures.

Mayan civilization began to develop in Central America in the 5th century BC.

Great Empires Unite the Civilized World: 400 BC - 400 AD

Persia and Alexander. Cyrus, ruler of a small kingdom in Persia from 559 BC, united the Persians and Medes within 10 years, conquered Asia Minor and Babylonia in another 10. His son Cambyses and grandson **Darius** (ruled 522-486) added vast lands to the east and north as far as the Indus Valley and Central Asia, as well as Egypt and Thrace. The whole empire was ruled by an international bureaucracy and army, with Persians holding the chief positions. The resources and styles of all the subject civilizations were exploited to create a rich syncretic art.

The Hellenized kingdom of Macedon, which under Phillip II dominated Greece, passed to his son **Alexander** in 336 BC. Within 13 years, Alexander conquered all the Persian dominions. Imbued by his tutor Aristotle with Greek ideals, Alexander encouraged Greek colonization, and Greek-style cities were founded throughout the empire (e.g. Alexandria, Egypt). After his death in 323 BC, wars of succession divided the empire into three parts — **Macedon,** Egypt (ruled by the **Ptolemies**), and the **Seleucid** Empire.

In the ensuing 300 years (the **Hellenistic Era**), a cosmopolitan Greek-oriented culture permeated the ancient world from W. Europe to the borders of India, absorbing native elites everywhere.

Hellenistic philosophy stressed the private individual's search for happiness. The Cynics followed Diogenes (c372-287), who stressed satisfaction of animal needs and contempt for social convention. Zeno (c335-c263) and the Stoics exalted reason, identified it with virtue, and counseled an ascetic disregard for misfortune. The Epicureans tried to build lives of moderate pleasure without political or emotional

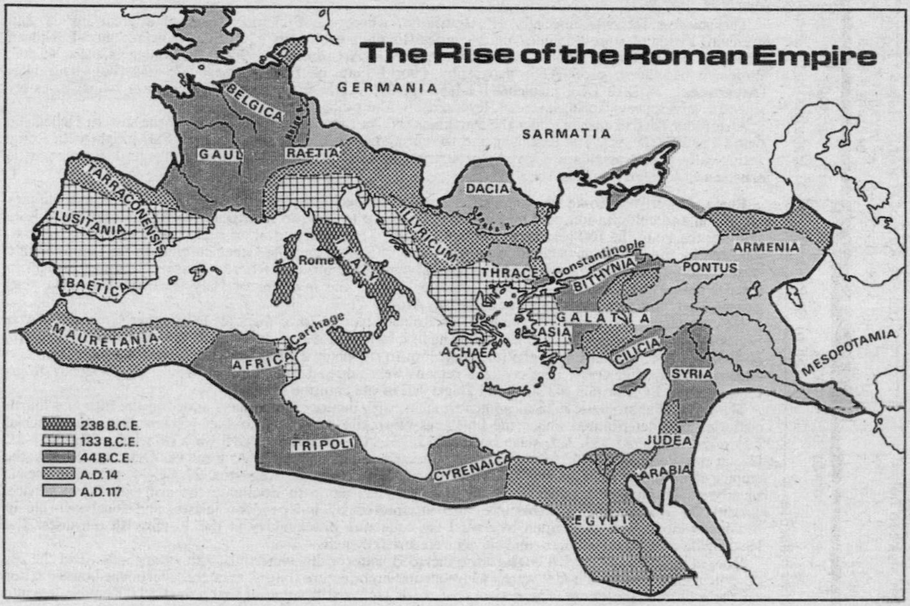
The Rise of the Roman Empire
GERMANIA
SARMATIA
BELGICA
GAUL
RAETIA
DACIA
TARRACONENSIS
LUSITANIA
ILLYRICUM
ITALY
Rome
BAETICA
THRACE
Constantinople
BITHYNIA
ARMENIA
PONTUS
GALATIA
ASIA
ACHAEA
MAURETANIA
Carthage
AFRICA
CILICIA
SYRIA
MESOPOTAMIA
JUDEA
ARABIA
TRIPOLI
CYRENAICA
EGYPT
238 B.C.E.
133 B.C.E.
44 B.C.E.
A.D. 14
A.D. 117

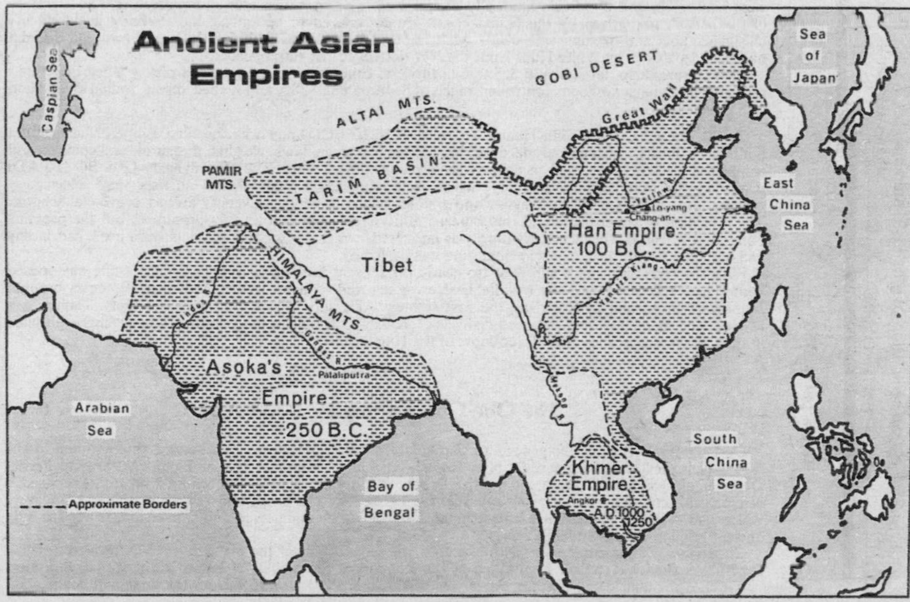
Ancient Asian Empires
Caspian Sea
GOBI DESERT
Great Wall
ALTAI MTS.
PAMIR MTS.
TARIM BASIN
Sea of Japan
East China Sea
Lo-yang
Chang-an
Han Empire 100 B.C.
Tibet
HIMALAYA MTS.
Asoka's Empire 250 B.C.
Pataliputra
Arabian Sea
South China Sea
Khmer Empire
Angkor
A.D. 1000
1250
Bay of Bengal
Approximate Borders

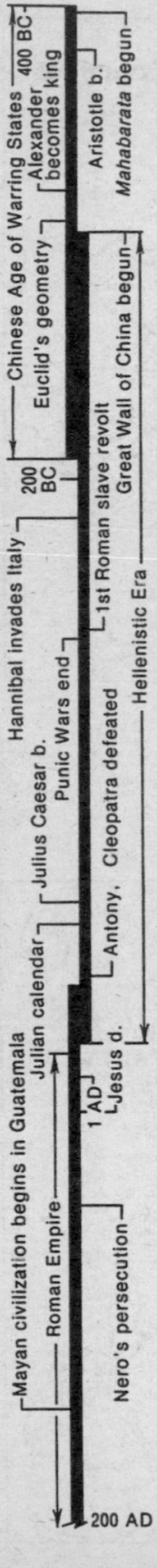

involvement. Hellenistic arts imitated life realistically, especially in sculpture and literature (comedies of Menander, 342-292).

The sciences thrived, especially at Alexandria, where the Ptolemies financed a great library and museum. Fields of study included mathematics (**Euclid's** geometry, c300 BC; Menelaus' non-Euclidean geometry, c100 AD); astronomy (heliocentric theory of Aristarchus, 310-230 BC; Julian calendar 45 BC; Ptolemy's *Almagest*, c150 AD); geography (world map of Eratosthenes, 276-194 BC); hydraulics (**Archimedes**, 287-212 BC); medicine (Galen, 130-200 AD), and chemistry. Inventors refined uses for siphons, valves, gears, springs, screws, levers, cams, and pulleys.

A restored Persian empire under the **Parthians** (N. Iranian tribesmen) controlled the eastern Hellenistic world 250 BC-229 AD. The Parthians and the succeeding Sassanian dynasty (229-651) fought with Rome periodically. The **Sassanians** revived Zoroastrianism as a state religion, and patronized a nationalistic artistic and scholarly renaissance.

Rome. The city of Rome was founded, according to legend, by Romulus in 753 BC. Through military expansion and colonization, and by granting citizenship to conquered tribes, the city annexed all of Italy south of the Po in the 100-year period before 268 BC. The Latin and other Italic tribes were annexed first, followed by the Etruscans (a civilized people north of Rome) and the Greek colonies in the south. With a large standing army and reserve forces of several hundred thousand, Rome was able to defeat Carthage in the 3 **Punic Wars**, 264-241, 218-201, 149-146 (despite the invasion of Italy by Hannibal, 218), thus gaining Sicily and territory in Spain and North Africa.

New provinces were added in the East, as Rome exploited local disputes to conquer Greece and Asia Minor in the 2d century BC, and Egypt in the first (after the defeat and suicide of **Antony and Cleopatra**, 30 BC). All the Mediterranean civilized world up to the disputed Parthian border was now Roman, and remained so for 500 years. Less civilized regions were added to the Empire: Gaul (conquered by Julius Caesar, 56-49 BC), Britain (43 AD) and Dacia NE of the Danube (117 AD).

The original aristocratic republican government, with democratic features added in the fifth and fourth centuries BC, deteriorated under the pressures of empire and class conflict (**Gracchus** brothers, social reformers, murdered 133, 121; slave revolts 135, 73). After a series of civil wars (Marius vs. Sulla 88-82, Caesar vs. Pompey 49-45, triumvirate vs. Caesar's assassins 44-43, Antony vs. Octavian 32-30), the empire came under the rule of a deified monarch (first emperor, **Augustus**, 27 BC-14 AD). Provincials (nearly all granted citizenship by Caracalla, 212 AD) came to dominate the army and civil service. Traditional Roman law, systematized and interpreted by independent jurists, and local self-rule in provincial cities were supplanted by a vast tax-collecting bureaucracy in the 3d and 4th centuries. The legal rights of women, children, and slaves were strengthened.

Roman innovations in **civil engineering** included water mills, windmills, and rotary mills, and the use of cement that hardened under water. Monumental architecture (baths, theaters, apartment houses) relied on the arch and the dome. The network of roads (some still standing) stretched 53,000 miles, passing through mountain tunnels as long as 3.5 miles. Aqueducts brought water to cities, underground sewers removed waste.

Roman art and literature were derivative of Greek models. Innovations were made in sculpture (naturalistic busts and equestrian statues), decorative wall painting (as at Pompeii), satire (Juvenal, 60-127), history (Tacitus 56-120), prose romance (Petronius, d. 66 AD). Violence and torture dominated mass public amusements, which were supported by the state.

India. The **Gupta** monarchs reunited N. India c320 AD. Their peaceful and prosperous reign saw a revival of Hindu religious thought and Brahmin power. The old Vedic traditions were combined with devotion to a plethora of indigenous deities (who were seen as manifestations of Vedic gods). **Caste lines** were reinforced, and Buddhism gradually disappeared. The art (often erotic), architecture, and literature of the period, patronized by the Gupta court, are considered to be among India's finest achievements (Kalidasa, poet and dramatist, fl. c400). Mathematical innovations included the use of zero and decimal numbers. Invasions by White Huns from the NW destroyed the empire c550.

Rich cultures also developed in S. India in this era. Emotional Tamil religious poetry aided the Hindu revival. The Pallava kingdom controlled much of S. India c350-880, and helped spread Indian civilization to S.E. Asia.

China. The Ch'in ruler Shih Huang Ti (ruled 221-210 BC), known as the First Emperor, centralized political authority in China, standardized the written language, laws, weights, measures, and coinage, and conducted a census, but tried to destroy most philosophical texts. The **Han dynasty** (206 BC-220 AD) instituted the Mandarin bureaucracy, which lasted for 2,000 years. Local officials were selected by examination in the Confucian classics and trained at the imperial university and at provincial schools. The invention of **paper** facilitated this bureaucratic system. Agriculture was promoted, but the peasants bore most of the tax burden. Irrigation was improved; water clocks and sundials were used; astronomy and mathematics thrived; landscape painting was perfected.

With the expansion south and west (to nearly the present borders of today's China), trade was opened with India, S.E. Asia, and the Middle East, over sea and caravan routes. Indian missionaries brought Mahayana Buddhism to China by the first century AD, and spawned a variety of sects. Taoism was revived, and merged with popular superstitions. Taoist and Buddhist monasteries and convents multiplied in the turbulent centuries after the collapse of the Han dynasty.

The One God Triumphs: 1-750 AD

Christianity. Religions indigenous to particular Middle Eastern nations became international in the first 3 centuries of the Roman Empire. Roman citizens worshipped **Isis** of Egypt, **Mithras** of Persia, **Demeter** of Greece, and the great mother **Cybele** of Phrygia. Their cults centered on mysteries (secret ceremonies) and the promise of an afterlife, symbolized by the death and rebirth of the god. Judaism, which had begun as the national cult of Judea, also spread by emigration and conversion. It was the only ancient religion west of India to survive.

Christians, who emerged as a distinct sect in the second half of the 1st century AD, revered **Jesus**, a Jewish preacher said to have been killed by the Romans at the request of Jewish authorities in Jerusalem c30 AD. They considered him the Savior (Messiah, or Christ) who rose from the dead and could grant eternal life to the faithful, despite their sinfulness. They believed he was an incarnation of the one god worshipped by the Jews, and that he would return soon to pass final judgment on the world. The missionary activities of such early leaders as **Paul of Tarsus** spread the faith, at first mostly among Jews or among quasi-Jews attracted by the Pauline rejection of such difficult Jewish laws as circumcision. Intermittent persecution, as in Rome under Nero in 64 AD, on grounds of suspected disloyalty, failed to disrupt the Christian communities. Each congregation, generally urban and of plebeian character, was tightly organized under a leader (bishop) elders (presbyters or priests), and assistants (deacons). Stories about Jesus (the Gospels) and the early church (Acts) were written down in the late first and early 2d centuries, and circulated along with letters of Paul. An authoritative canon of these writings was not fixed until the 4th century.

A school for priests was established at Alexandria in the second century. Its teachers (**Origen** c182-251) helped define Christian doctrine and promote the faith in Greek-style philosophical works. Pagan Neoplatonism was given Christian coloration in the works of Church Fathers such as Augustine (354-430). Christian hermits, often drawn from the lower classes, began to associate in monasteries, first in Egypt (St. Pachomius c290-345), then in other eastern lands, then in the West (**St. Benedict's rule,** 529). Popular devotion to saints, especially Mary, mother of Jesus, spread.

Under **Constantine** (ruled 306-337), Christianity became in effect the established religion of the Empire. Pagan temples were expropriated, state funds were used to build huge churches and support the hierarchy, and laws were adjusted in accordance with Christian notions. Pagan worship was banned by the end of the fourth century, and severe restrictions were placed on Judaism.

The newly established church was rocked by doctrinal disputes, often exacerbated by regional rivalries both within and outside the Empire. Chief heresies (as defined by church councils backed by imperial authority) were **Arianism,** which denied the divinity of Jesus; **Donatism,** which rejected the convergence of church and state and denied the validity of sacraments performed by sinful clergy; and the **Monophysite** position denying the dual nature of Christ.

Judaism. First century Judaism embraced several sects, including: the **Sadducees,** mostly drawn from the Temple priesthood, who were culturally Hellenized; the **Pharisees,** who upheld the full range of traditional customs and practices as of equal weight to literal scriptural law, and elaborated synagogue worship; and the **Essenes,** an ascetic, millenarian sect. Messianic fervor led to repeated, unsuccessful rebellions against Rome (66-70, 135). As a result, the Temple was destroyed, and the population decimated.

To avoid the dissolution of the faith, a program of codification of law was begun at the academy of Yavneh. The work continued for some 500 years in Palestine and Babylonia, ending in the final redaction of the **Talmud** (c600), a huge collection of legal and moral debates, rulings, liturgy, Biblical exegesis, and legendary materials.

Islam. The earliest Arab civilization emerged by the end of the 2d millenium BC in the watered highlands of Yemen. Seaborne and caravan trade in frankincense and myrrh connected the area with the Nile and Fertile Crescent. The Minaean, Sabean (Sheba), and Himyarite states successively held sway. By Mohammed's time (7th century AD), the region was a province of Sassanian Persia. In the North, the **Nabataean kingdom** at Petra and the kingdom of Palmyra were first Aramaicized and then Romanized, and finally absorbed like neighboring Judea into the Roman Empire. Nomads shared the central region with a few trading towns and oases. Wars between tribes and raids on settled communities were common, and were celebrated in a poetic tradition that by the 6th century helped establish a classic literary Arabic.

In 611 **Mohammed,** a wealthy 40-year-old Arab of Mecca, had a revelation from Allah, the one true god, calling on him to repudiate pagan idolatry. Drawing on elements of Judaism and Christianity, and eventually incorporating some Arab pagan traditions (such as reverence for the black stone at the kaaba shrine in Mecca), Mohammed's teachings, recorded in the Koran, forged a new religion, Islam (submission to Allah). Opposed by the leaders of Mecca, Mohammed made a *hejira* (migration) to Medina to the north in 622, the beginning of the Moslem lunar calendar. He and his followers defeated the Meccans in 624 in the first *jihad* (holy war), and by his death (632), nearly all the Arabian peninsula accepted his religious and secular leadership.

Under the first two **caliphs** (successors) Abu Bakr (632-34) and Oman (634-44), Moslem rule was confirmed over Arabia. Raiding parties into Byzantine and Persian border areas developed into campaigns of conquest against the two empires, which had been weakened by wars and by disaffection among subject peoples (including Coptic and Syriac Christians opposed to the Byzantine orthodox church). Syria, Palestine, Egypt, Iraq, and Persia all fell to the inspired Arab armies. The Arabs at first remained a distinct minority, using non-Moslems in the new administrative system, and tolerating Christians, Jews, and Zoroastrians as self-governing "Peoples of the Book," whose taxes supported the empire.

Disputes over the succession, and puritan reaction to the wealth and refinement that empire brought to the ruling strata, led to the growth of schismatic movements. The followers of Mohammed's son-in-law Ali (assassinated 661) and his descendants became the founders of the more mystical **Shi'ite** sect, still the largest non-orthodox Moslem sect. The Karijites, puritanical, militant, and egalitarian, persist as a minor sect to the present.

Under the **Ummayad** caliphs (661-750), the boundaries of Islam were extended across N. Africa and into Spain. Arab armies in the West were stopped at Tours in 732 by the Frank **Charles Martel.** Asia Minor, the Indus Valley, and Transoxiana were conquered in the East. The vast majority of the subject population gradually converted to Islam, encouraged by tax and career privileges. The Arab language supplanted the local tongues in the central and western areas, but Arab soldiers and rulers in the East eventually became assimilated to the indigenous languages.

New Peoples Enter History: 400-900

Barbarian invasions. Germanic tribes infiltrated S and E from their Baltic homeland during the 1st millenium BC, reaching S. Germany by 100 BC and the Black Sea by 214 AD. Organized into large federated tribes under elected kings, most resisted Roman domination and raided the empire in time of civil war (Goths took Dacia 214, raided Thrace 251-269). German troops and commanders came to dominate the Roman armies by the end of the 4th century. **Huns,** invaders from Asia, entered Europe 372, driving more Germans into the western empire. Emperor Valens allowed Visigoths to cross

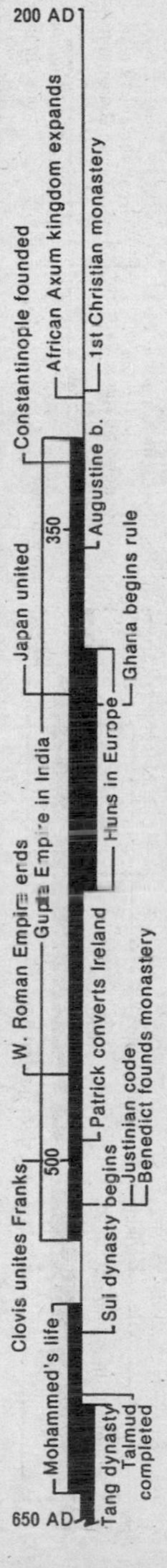

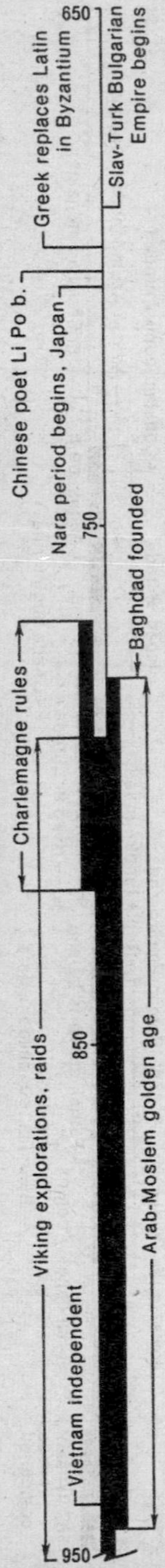

the Danube 376. Huns under Attila (d. 453) raided Gaul, Italy, Balkans. The western empire, weakened by overtaxation and social stagnation, was overrun in the 5th century. Gaul was effectively lost 406-7, Spain 409, Britain 410, Africa 429-39. Rome itself was sacked 410 by Visigoths under Alaric, 455 by Vandals. The last western emperor, Romulus Augustulus, was deposed 476 by the Germanic chief Odoacer.

Celts. Celtic cultures, which in pre-Roman times covered most of W. Europe, were confined almost entirely to the British Isles after the Germanic invasions. **St. Patrick** completed the conversion of Ireland (c457-92). A strong monastic tradition took hold. Irish monastic missionaries in Scotland, England, and the continent (Columba c521-597; Columban c543-615) helped restore Christianity after the Germanic invasions. The monasteries became renowned centers of classic and Christian learning, and presided over the recording of a Christianized Celtic mythology, elaborated by secular writers and bards. An intricate decorative art style developed, especially in book illumination (Lindisfarne Gospels, c700, Book of Kells, 8th century).

Successor states. The Visigoth kingdom in Spain (from 419) and much of France (to 507) saw a continuation of much Roman administration, language, and law (Breviary of Alaric 506), until its destruction by the Moslems, 711. The Vandal kingdom in Africa, from 429, was conquered by the Byzantines, 533. Italy was ruled in succession by an Ostrogothic kingdom under Byzantine suzerainty 489-554, direct Byzantine government, and the German Lombards (568-774). The latter divided the peninsula with the Byzantines and the papacy under the dynamic reformer Pope Gregory the Great (590-604) and his successors.

King Clovis (ruled 481-511) united the Franks on both sides of the Rhine, and after his conversion to orthodox Christianity, defeated the Arian Burgundians (after 500) and Visigoths (507) with the support of the native clergy and the papacy. Under the **Merovingian** kings a feudal system emerged: power was fragmented among hierarchies of military landowners. Social stratification, which in late Roman times had acquired legal, hereditary sanction, was reinforced. The Carolingians (747-987) expanded the kingdom and restored central power. **Charlemagne** (ruled 768-814) conquered nearly all the Germanic lands, including Lombard Italy, and was crowned Emperor by Pope Leo III in Rome in 800. A centuries-long decline in commerce and the arts was reversed under Charlemagne's patronage. He welcomed Jews to his kingdom, which became a center of Jewish learning (Rashi 1040-1105). He sponsored the "Carolingian Renaissance" of learning under the Anglo-Latin scholar Alcuin (c732-804), who reformed church liturgy.

Byzantine Empire. Under Diocletian (ruled 284-305) the empire had been divided into 2 parts to facilitate administration and defense. Constantine founded **Constantinople,** 330, (at old Byzantium) as a fully Christian city. Commerce and taxation financed a sumptuous, orientalized court, a class of hereditary bureaucratic families, and magnificent urban construction (Hagia Sophia, 532-37). The city's fortifications and naval innovations (Greek fire) repelled assaults by Goths, Huns, Slavs, Bulgars, Avars, Arabs, and Scandinavians. Greek replaced Latin as the official language by c700. Byzantine art, a solemn, sacral, and stylized variation of late classical styles (mosaics at S. Vitale, Ravenna, 526-48) was a starting point for medieval art in E. and W. Europe.

Justinian (ruled 527-65) reconquered parts of Spain, N. Africa, and Italy, codified Roman law (*codex Justinianus,* 529, was medieval Europe's chief legal text), closed the Platonic Academy at Athens and ordered all pagans to convert. Lombards in Italy, Arabs in Africa retook most of his conquests. The Isaurian dynasty from Anatolia (from 717) and the Macedonian dynasty (867-1054) restored military and commercial power. The Iconoclast controversy (726-843) over the permissibility of images, helped alienate the Eastern Church from the papacy.

Arab Empire. Baghdad, founded 762, became the seat of the **Abbasid** Caliphate (founded 750), while Ummayads continued to rule in Spain. A brilliant cosmopolitan civilization emerged, inaugurating an Arab-Moslem golden age. Arab lyric poetry revived; Greek, Syriac, Persian, and Sanskrit books were translated into Arabic, often by Syriac Christians and Jews, whose theology and Talmudic law, respectively, influenced Islam. The arts and music flourished at the court of **Harun al-Rashid** (786-809), celebrated in *The Arabian Nights.* The sciences, medicine, and mathematics were pursued at Baghdad, Cordova, and Cairo (founded 969). Science and Aristotelian philosophy culminated in the systems of Avicenna (980-1037), Averroes (1126-98), and Maimonides (1135-1204), a Jew; all influenced later Christian scholarship and theology. The Islamic ban on images encouraged a sinuous, geometric decorative tradition, applied to architecture and illumination. A gradual loss of Arab control in Persia (from 874) led to the capture of Baghdad by Persians, 945. By the next century, Spain and N. Africa were ruled by Berbers, while Turks prevailed in Asia Minor and the Levant. The loss of political power by the caliphs allowed for the growth of non-orthodox trends, especially the mystical **Sufi** tradition (theologian Ghazali, 1058-1111).

Africa. Immigrants from Saba in S. Arabia helped set up the **Axum** kingdom in Ethiopia in the 2d century (their language, Ge'ez, is preserved by the Ethiopian Church). In the 4th century, when the kingdom became Christianized, it defeated Kushite Meroe and expanded into Yemen. Axum was the center of a vast ivory trade; it controlled the Red Sea coast until c1100. Arab conquest in Egypt cut Axum's political and economic ties with Byzantium.

The Iron Age entered W. Africa by the end of the 1st millenium BC. **Ghana,** the first known sub-Saharan state, ruled in the upper Senegal-Niger region c400-1240, controlling the trade of gold from mines in the S to trans-Sahara caravan routes to the N. The **Bantu** peoples, probably of W. African origin, began to spread E and S perhaps 2000 years ago, displacing the Pygmies and Bushmen of central

Japan. The advanced Neolithic Yayoi period, when irrigation, rice farming, and iron and bronze casting techniques were introduced from China or Korea, persisted to c400 AD. The myriad Japanese states were then united by the **Yamato** clan, under an emperor who acted as the chief priest of the animistic **Shinto** cult. Japanese political and military intervention in Korea by the 6th century quickened a Chinese cultural invasion, bringing Buddhism, the Chinese language (which long remained a literary and governmental medium), Chinese ideographs and Buddhist styles in painting, sculpture, literature, and architecture (7th c. Horyu-ji temple at Nara). The Taika Reforms, 646, tried to centralize Japan according to Chinese bureaucratic and Buddhist philosophical values, but failed to curb traditional Japanese decentralization. A nativist reaction against the Buddhist **Nara period** (710-94) ushered in the

Heian period (794-1185) centered at the new capital, Kyoto. Japanese elegance and simplicity modified Chinese styles in architecture, scroll painting, and literature; the writing system was also simplified. The courtly novel *Tale of Genji* (1010-20) testifies to the enhanced role of women.

Southeast Asia. The historic peoples of southeast Asia began arriving some 2500 years ago from China and Tibet, displacing scattered aborigines. Their agriculture relied on rice and tubers (yams), which they may have introduced to Africa. Indian cultural influences were strongest; literacy and Hindu and Buddhist ideas followed the southern India-China trade route. From the southern tip of Indochina, the kingdom of **Funan** (1st-7th centuries) traded as far west as Persia. It was absorbed by Chenla, itself conquered by the **Khmer Empire** (600-1300). The Khmers, under Hindu god-kings (Suryavarman II, 1113-c1150), built the monumental Angkor Wat temple center for the royal phallic cult. The **Nam-Viet** kingdom in Annam, dominated by China and Chinese culture for 1,000 years, emerged in the 10th century, growing at the expense of the Khmers, who also lost ground in the NW to the new, highly-organized **Thai** kingdom. On Sumatra, the **Srivijaya** Empire at Palembang controlled vital sea lanes (7th to 10th centuries). A Buddhist dynasty, the Sailendras, ruled central **Java** (8th-9th centuries), building at Borobudur one of the largest stupas in the world.

China. The short-lived Sui dynasty (581-618) ushered in a period of commercial, artistic, and scientific achievement in China, continuing under the **T'ang** dynasty (618-906). Such inventions as the magnetic compass, gunpowder, the abacus, and printing were introduced or perfected. Medical innovations included cataract surgery. The state, from the cosmopolitan capital, Ch'ang-an, supervised foreign trade which exchanged Chinese silks, porcelains, and art works for spices, ivory, etc., over Central Asian caravan routes and sea routes reaching Africa. A golden age of poetry bequeathed tens of thousands of works to later generations (Tu Fu 712-70, Li Po 701-62). Landscape painting flourished. Commercial and industrial expansion continued under the **Northern Sung** dynasty (960-1126), facilitated by paper money and credit notes. But commerce never achieved respectability; government monopolies expropriated successful merchants. The population, long stable at 50 million, doubled in 200 years with the introduction of early-ripening rice and the double harvest. In art, native Chinese styles were revived.

Americas. An Indian empire stretched from the Valley of Mexico to Guatemala, 300-600, centering on the huge city **Teotihuacan** (founded 100 BC). To the S, in Guatemala, a high **Mayan** civilization developed, 150-900, around hundreds of rural ceremonial centers. The Mayans improved on Olmec writing and the calendar, and pursued astronomy and mathematics (using the idea of zero). In S. America, a widespread pre-Inca culture grew from **Tiahuanaco** near Lake Titicaca (Gateway of the Sun, c700).

Christian Europe Regroups and Expands: 900-1300

Scandinavians. Pagan Danish and Norse (**Viking**) adventurers, traders, and pirates raided the coasts of the British Isles (Dublin founded c831), France, and even the Mediterranean for over 200 years beginning in the late 8th century. Inland settlement in the W was limited to Great Britain (King Canute, 994-1035) and Normandy, settled under Rollo, 911, as a fief of France. Other Vikings reached Iceland (874), Greenland (c986), and probably N. America (Leif Eriksson c1000). Norse traders (**Varangians**) developed Russian river commerce from the 8th-11th centuries, and helped set up a state at Kiev in the late 9th century. Conversion to Christianity occurred during the 10th century, reaching Sweden 100 years later. Eleventh century Norman bands conquered S. Italy and Sicily. Duke **William of Normandy** conquered England, 1066, bringing continental feudalism and the French language, essential elements in later English civilization.

East Europe. Slavs inhabited areas of E. Central Europe in prehistoric times, and reached most of their present limits by c850. The first Slavic states were in the Balkans (Slav-Turk **Bulgarian Empire**, 680-1018) and Moravia (628). Missions of St. Cyril (whose Greek-based Cyrillic alphabet is still used by S. and E. Slavs) converted Moravia, 863. The Eastern Slavs, part-civilized under the overlordship of the Turkish-Jewish **Khazar** trading empire (7th-10th centuries), gravitated toward Constantinople by the 9th century. The **Kievan state** adopted Eastern Christianity under Prince Vladimir, 989. King Boleslav I (992-1025) began **Poland's** long history of eastern conquest. The Magyars (**Hungarians**) in Europe since 896, accepted Latin Christianity, 1001.

Germany. The German kingdom that emerged after the breakup of Charlemagne's Empire remained a confederation of largely autonomous states. The Saxon Otto I, king from 936, established the **Holy Roman Empire** of Germany and Italy in alliance with Pope John XII, who crowned him emperor, 962; he defeated the Magyars, 955. Imperial power was greatest under the **Hohenstaufens** (1138-1254), despite the growing opposition of the papacy, which ruled central Italy, and the Lombard League cities. Frederick II (1194-1250) improved administration, patronized the arts; after his death German influence was removed from Italy.

Christian Spain. From its northern mountain redoubts, Christian rule slowly migrated south through the 11th century, when Moslem unity collapsed. After the capture of **Toledo** (1085), the kingdoms of Portugal, Castile, and Aragon undertook repeated crusades of reconquest, finally completed in 1492. Elements of Islamic civilization persisted in recaptured areas, influencing all W. Europe.

Crusades. Pope Urban II called, 1095, for a crusade to restore Asia Minor to Byzantium and conquer the Holy Land from the Turks. Some 10 crusades (to 1291) succeeded only in founding 4 temporary Frankish states in the Levant. The 4th crusade sacked Constantinople, 1204. In Rhineland (1096), England (1290), France (1306), Jews were massacred or expelled, and wars were launched against Christian heretics (**Albigensian** crusade in France, 1229). Trade in eastern luxuries expanded, led by the Venetian naval empire.

Economy. The agricultural base of European life benefitted from improvements in **plow design** c1000, and by draining of lowlands and clearing of forests, leading to a rural population increase. Towns grew in N. Italy, Flanders, and N. Germany (Hanseatic League). Improvements in **loom design** permitted factory textile production. **Guilds** dominated urban trades from the 12th century. Banking (centered in Italy, 12th-15th century) facilitated long-distance trade.

The Church. The split between the Eastern and Western churches was formalized in 1054. W. and

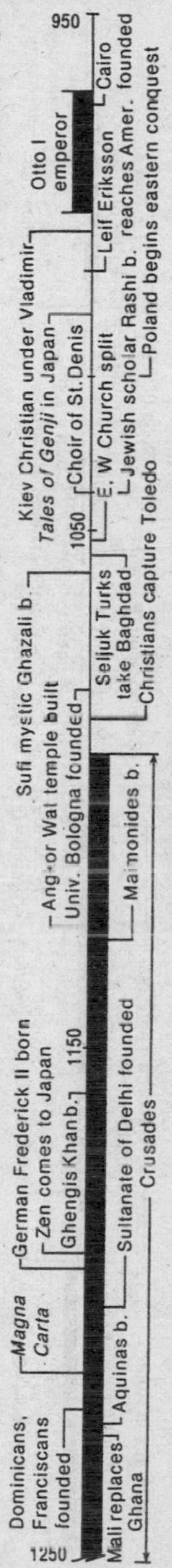

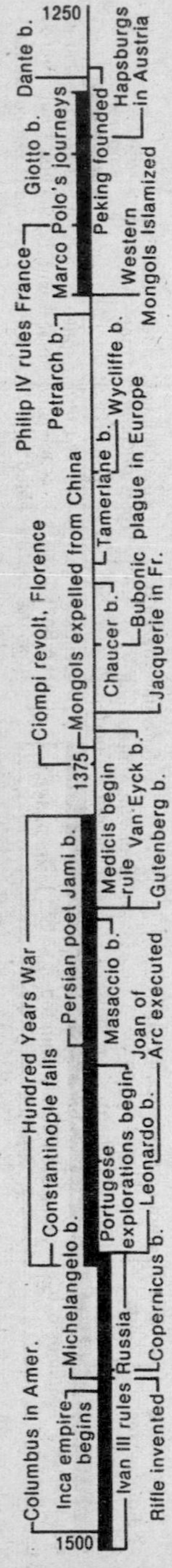

Central Europe was divided into 500 bishoprics under one united hierarchy, but conflicts between secular and church authorities were frequent (German **Investiture Controversy,** 1075-1122). Clerical power was first strengthened through the international monastic reform begun at Cluny, 910. Popular religious enthusiasm often expressed itself in heretical movements (Waldensians from 1173), but was channelled by the **Dominican** (1215) and **Franciscan** (1223) friars into the religious mainstream.

Arts. Romanesque architecture (11th-12th centuries) expanded on late Roman models, using the rounded arch and massed stone to support enlarged basilicas. Painting and sculpture followed Byzantine models. The literature of **chivalry** was exemplified by the epic (Chanson de Roland, c1100) and by courtly love poems of the troubadours of Provence and minnesingers of Germany. **Gothic architecture** emerged in France (choir of St. Denis, c1040) and spread as French cultural influence predominated in Europe. Rib vaulting and pointed arches were used to combine soaring heights with delicacy, and freed walls for display of stained glass. Exteriors were covered with painted relief sculpture and elaborate architectural detail.

Learning. Law, medicine, and philosophy were advanced at independent **universities** (Bologna, late 11th century), originally corporations of students and masters. Twelfth century translations of Greek classics, especially Aristotle, encouraged an analytic approach. Scholastic philosophy, from Anselm (1033-1109) to Aquinas (1225-74) attempted to reconcile reason and revelation.

Apogee of Central Asian Power; Islam Grows: 1250-1500

Turks. Turkic peoples, of Central Asian ancestry, were a military threat to the Byzantine and Persian Empires from the 6th century. After several waves of invasions, during which most of the Turks adopted Islam, the **Seljuk Turks** took Baghdad, 1055. They ruled Persia, Iraq, and, after 1071, Asia Minor, where massive numbers of Turks settled. The empire was divided in the 12th century into smaller states ruled by Seljuks, Kurds (**Saladin** c1137-93), and Mamelukes (a military caste of former Turk, Kurd, and Circassian slaves), which governed Egypt and the Middle East until the Ottoman era (c1290-1922).

Osman I (ruled c1290-1326) and succeeding sultans united Anatolian Turkish warriors in a militaristic state that waged holy war against Byzantium and Balkan Christians. Most of the Balkans had been subdued, and Anatolia united, when **Constantinople fell,** 1453. By the mid-16th century, Hungary, the Middle East, and North Africa had been conquered. The Turkish advance was stopped at Vienna, 1529, and at the naval battle of Lepanto, 1571, by Spain, Venice, and the papacy.

The Ottoman state was governed in accordance with orthodox Moslem law. Greek, Armenian, and Jewish communities were segregated, and ruled by religious leaders responsible for taxation; they dominated trade. State offices and most army ranks were filled by slaves through a system of child conscription among Christians.

India. Mahmud of Ghazni (971-1030) led repeated Turkish raids into N. India. Turkish power was consolidated in 1206 with the start of the **Sultanate at Delhi.** Centralization of state power under the early Delhi sultans went far beyond traditional Indian practice. Moslem rule of most of the subcontinent lasted until the British conquest some 600 years later.

Mongols. Genghis Khan (c1162-1227) first united the feuding Mongol tribes, and built their armies into an effective offensive force around a core of highly mobile cavalry. He and his immediate successors created the largest land empire in history; by 1279 it stretched from the east coast of Asia to the Danube, from the Siberian steppes to the Arabian Sea. East-West trade and contacts were facilitated (Marco Polo c1254-1324). The western Mongols were Islamized by 1295; successor states soon lost their Mongol character by assimilation. They were briefly reunited under the Turk Tamerlane (1336-1405).

Kublai Khan ruled China from his new capital Peking (founded 1264). Naval campaigns against Japan (1274, 1281) and Java (1293) were defeated, the latter by the Hindu-Buddhist maritime kingdom of Majapahit. The **Yuan** dynasty made use of Mongols and other foreigners (including Europeans) in official posts, and tolerated the return of Nestorian Christianity (suppressed 841-45) and the spread of Islam in the South and West. A native reaction expelled the Mongols, 1367-68.

Russia. The Kievan state in Russia, weakened by the decline of Byzantium and the rise of the Catholic Polish-Lithuanian state, was overrun by the Mongols, 1238-40. Only the northern trading republic of Novgorod remained independent. The grand dukes of Moscow emerged as leaders of a coalition of princes that eventually defeated the Mongols, by 1481. With the fall of Constantinople, the **Tsars** (Caesars) at Moscow (from Ivan III, ruled 1462-1505) set up an independent Russian Orthodox Church. Commerce failed to revive. The isolated Russian state remained agrarian, with the peasant class falling into serfdom.

Persia. A revival of Persian literature, using the Arab alphabet and literary forms, began in the 10th century (epic of Firdausi, 935-1020). An art revival, influenced by Chinese styles, began in the 12th. Persian cultural and political forms, and often the Persian language, were used for centuries by Turkish and Mongol elites from the Balkans to India. Persian mystics from Rumi (1207-73) to Jami (1414-92) promoted **Sufism** in their poetry.

Africa. Two Berber dynasties, imbued with Islamic militance, emerged from the Sahara to carve out empires from the Sahel to central Spain — the **Almoravids,** c1050-1140, and the fanatical **Almohads,** c1125-1269. The Ghanaian empire was replaced in the upper Niger by Mali, c1230-c1340, whose Moslem rulers imported Egyptians to help make **Timbuktu** a center of commerce (in gold, leather, slaves) and learning. The Songhay empire (to 1590) replaced Mali. To the S, forest kingdoms produced refined art works (Ife terra cotta, **Benin** bronzes). Other Moslem states in Nigeria (Hausas) and Chad originated in the 11th century, and continued in some form until the 19th century European conquest. Less developed Bantu kingdoms existed across central Africa.

Some 40 Moslem Arab-Persian trading colonies and city-states were established all along the E. African coast from the 10th century (Kilwa, Mogadishu). The interchange with Bantu peoples produced the **Swahili** language and culture. Gold, palm oil, and slaves were brought from the interior, stimulating the growth of the Monamatapa kingdom of the Zambezi (15th century). The Christian Ethiopian empire (from 13th century) continued the traditions of Axum.

Southeast Asia. Islam was introduced into Malaya and the Indonesian islands by Arab, Persian, and

Indian traders. Coastal Moslem cities and states (starting before 1300), enriched by trade, soon dominated the interior. Chief among these was the **Malacca** state, on the Malay peninsula, c1400-1511.

Arts and Statecraft Thrive in Europe: 1350-1600

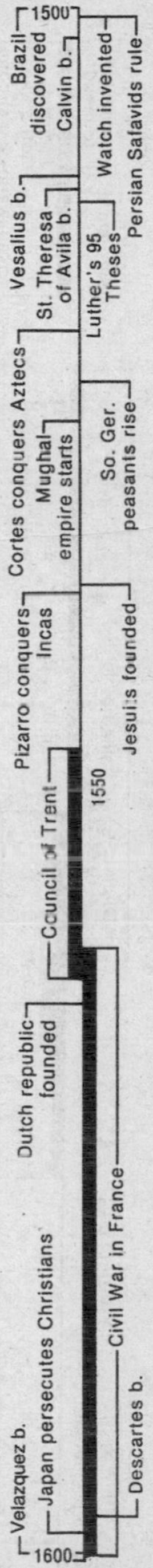

Italian Renaissance & humanism. Distinctive Italian achievements in the arts in the late Middle Ages (Dante, 1265-1321, Giotto, 1276-1337) led to the vigorous new styles of the Renaissance (14th-16th centuries). Patronized by the rulers of the quarreling petty states of Italy (Medicis in Florence and the papacy, c1400-1737), the plastic arts perfected realistic techniques, including **perspective** (Masaccio, 1401-28, Leonardo 1452-1519). Classical motifs were used in architecture and increased talent and expense were put into secular buildings. The Florentine dialect was refined as a national literary language (Petrarch, 1304-74). Greek refugees from the E strengthened the respect of humanist scholars for the classic sources (Bruni 1370-1444). Soon an international movement aided by the spread of **printing** (Gutenberg c1400-1468), **humanism** was optimistic about the power of human reason (Erasmus of Rotterdam, 1466-1536, Thomas More's *Utopia*, 1516) and valued individual effort in the arts and in politics (Machiavelli, 1469-1527).

France. The French monarchy, strengthened in its repeated struggles with powerful nobles (Burgundy, Flanders, Aquitaine) by alliances with the growing commercial towns, consolidated bureaucratic control under Philip IV (ruled 1285-1314) and extended French influence into Germany and Italy (popes at Avignon, France, 1309-1417). The **Hundred Years War,** 1338-1453, ended English dynastic claims in France (battles of Crécy, 1346, Poitiers, 1356; Joan of Arc executed, 1431). A French Renaissance, dating from royal invasions of Italy, 1494, 1499, was encouraged at the court of Francis I (ruled 1515-47), who centralized taxation and law. French vernacular literature consciously asserted its independence (La Pleiade, 1549).

England. The evolution of England's unique political institutions began with the Magna Carta, 1215, by which King John guaranteed the privileges of nobles and church against the monarchy and assured jury trial. After the Wars of the Roses (1455-85), the **Tudor dynasty** reasserted royal prerogatives (Henry VIII, ruled 1509-47), but the trend toward independent departments and ministerial government also continued. English trade (wool exports from c1340) was protected by the nation's growing maritime power (**Spanish Armada** destroyed, 1588).

English replaced French and Latin in the late 14th century in law and literature (Chaucer, 1340-1400) and English translation of the Bible began (Wycliffe, 1380s). Elizabeth I (ruled 1558-1603) presided over a confident flowering of poetry (Spenser, 1552-99), drama (**Shakespeare**, 1564-1616), and music.

German Empire. From among a welter of minor feudal states, church lands, and independent cities, the **Hapsburgs** assembled a far-flung territorial domain, based in Austria from 1276. The family held the title Holy Roman Emperor from 1452 to the Empire's dissolution in 1806, but failed to centralize its domains, leaving Germany disunited for centuries. Resistance to Turkish expansion brought Hungary under Austrian control from the 16th century. The Netherlands, Luxembourg, and Burgundy were added in 1477, curbing French expansion.

The Flemish painting tradition of naturalism, technical proficiency, and bourgeois subject matter began in the 15th century (Jan Van Eyck, 1366-1440), the earliest northern manifestation of the Renaissance. Durer (1471-1528) typified the merging of late Gothic and Italian trends in 16th century German art. Imposing civic architecture flourished in the prosperous commercial cities.

Spain. Despite the unification of Castile and Aragon in 1479, the 2 countries retained separate governments, and the nobility, especially in Aragon and Catalonia, retained many privileges. Spanish lands in Italy (Naples, Sicily) and the Netherlands entangled the country in European wars through the mid-17th century, while explorers, traders, and conquerors built up a Spanish empire in the Americas and the Philippines.

From the late 15th century, a **golden age** of literature and art produced works of social satire (plays of Lope de Vega, 1562-1635; Cervantes, 1547-1616), as well as spiritual intensity (El Greco, 1541-1614; Velazquez, 1599-1660).

Black Death. The bubonic plague reached Europe from the E in 1348, killing as much as half the population by 1350. Labor scarcity forced a rise in wages and brought greater freedom to the peasantry, making possible **peasant uprisings** (Jacquerie in France, 1358, Wat Tyler's rebellion in England, 1381). In the *ciompi* revolt, 1378, Florentine wage earners demanded a say in economic and political power.

Explorations. Organized European maritime exploration began, seeking to evade the Venice-Ottoman monopoly of eastern trade and to promote Christianity. Expeditions from Portugal beginning 1418 explored the west coast of Africa, until **Vasco da Gama** rounded the Cape of Good Hope in 1497 and reached India. A Portuguese trading empire was consolidated by the seizure of Goa, 1510, and Malacca, 1551. Japan was reached in 1542. Spanish voyages (**Columbus,** 1492-1504) uncovered a new world, which Spain hastened to subdue. Navigation schools in Spain and Portugal, the development of large sailing ships (carracks), and the invention of the rifle, c1475, aided European penetration.

Mughals and Safavids. East of the Ottoman empire, two Moslem dynasties ruled unchallenged in the 16th and 17th centuries. The Mughal empire in India, founded by Persianized Turkish invaders from the NW under Babur, dates from their 1526 conquest of Delhi. The dynasty ruled most of India for over 200 years, surviving nominally until 1857. **Akbar** (ruled 1556-1605) consolidated administration at his glorious court, where Urdu (Persian-influenced Hindi) developed. Trade relations with Europe increased. Under Shah Jahan (1629-58), a secularized art fusing Hindu and Moslem elements flourished in miniature painting and architecture (**Taj Mahal**). Sikhism, founded c1519, combined elements of both faiths. Suppression of Hindus and Shi'ite Moslems in S India in the late 17th century weakened the empire.

Fanatical devotion to the Shi'ite sect characterized the Safavids of Persia, 1502-1736, and led to hostilities with the Sunni Ottomans for over a century. The prosperity and strength of the empire are evidenced by the mosques at its capital, **Isfahan.** The dynasty enhanced Iranian national consciousness.

China. The Ming emperors, 1368-1644, the last native dynasty in China, wielded unprecedented personal power, while the Confucian bureaucracy began to suffer from inertia. European trade (Portugese

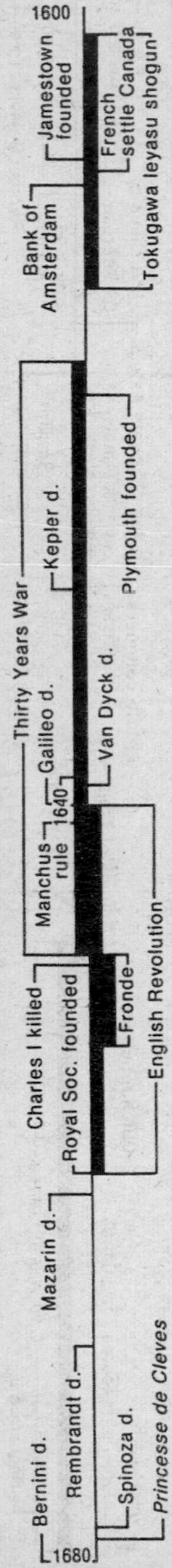

monopoly through **Macao** from 1557) was strictly controlled. Jesuit scholars and scientists (Matteo Ricci 1552-1610) introduced some Western science; their writings familiarized the West with China. Chinese technological inventiveness declined from this era, but the arts thrived, especially painting and ceramics.

Japan. After the decline of the first hereditary shogunate (chief generalship) at **Kamakura** (1185-1333), fragmentation of power accelerated, as did the consequent social mobility. Under Kamakura and the Ashikaga shogunate, 1338-1573, the daimyos (lords) and samurai (warriors) grew more powerful and promoted a martial ideology. Japanese pirates and traders plied the China coast. Popular Buddhist movements included the nationalist Nichiren sect (from c1250) and **Zen** (brought from China, 1191), which stressed meditation and a disciplined esthetic (tea ceremony, landscape gardening, judo, Noh drama).

Reformed Europe Expands Overseas: 1500-1700

Reformation begun. Theological debate and protests against real and perceived clerical corruption existed in the medieval Christian world, expressed by such dissenters as Wycliffe (c1320-84) and his followers, the Lollards, in England, and **Huss** (burned as a heretic, 1415) in Bohemia.

Luther (1483-1546) preached that only faith could lead to salvation, without the mediation of clergy or good works. He attacked the authority of the Pope, rejected priestly celibacy, and recommended individual study of the Bible (which he translated, c1525). His 95 Theses (1517) led to his excommunication (1520). **Calvin** (1509-64) said God's elect were predestined for salvation; good conduct and success were signs of election. Calvin in Geneva and Knox (1505-72) in Scotland erected theocratic states.

Henry VIII asserted English national authority and secular power by breaking away from the Catholic church, 1534. Monastic property was confiscated, and some Protestant doctrines given official sanction.

Religious wars. A century and a half of religious wars began with a South German peasant uprising, 1524, repressed with Luther's support. Radical sects—democratic, pacifist, milennarian—arose (Anabaptists ruled Muenster, 1534-35), and were suppressed violently. Civil war in France from 1562 between **Huguenots** (Protestant nobles and merchants) and Catholics ended with the 1598 Edict of Nantes tolerating Protestants (revoked 1685). Hapsburg attempts to restore Catholicism in Germany were resisted in 25 years of fighting; the 1555 Peace of Augsburg guarantee of religious independence to local princes and cities was confirmed only after the **Thirty Years War**, 1618-48, when much of Germany was devastated by local and foreign armies (Sweden, France).

A Catholic Reformation, or **counter-reformation,** met the Protestant challenge, clearly defining an official theology at the Council of Trent, 1545-63. The **Jesuit** order, founded 1534 by Loyola (1491-1556), helped reconvert large areas of Poland, Hungary, and S. Germany and sent missionaries to the New World, India, and China, while the Inquisition helped suppress heresy in Catholic countries. A revival of piety appeared in the devotional literature (Theresa of Avila, 1515-82) and the grandiose Baroque art (Bernini, 1598-1680) of Roman Catholic countries.

Scientific Revolution. The late nominalist thinkers (Ockham, c1300-49) of Paris and Oxford challenged Aristotelian orthodoxy, allowing for a freer scientific approach. But metaphysical values, such as the Neoplatonic faith in an orderly, mathematical cosmos, still motivated and directed subsequent inquiry. **Copernicus** (1473-1543) promoted the heliocentric theory, which was confirmed when Kepler (1571-1630) discovered the mathematical laws describing the orbits of the planets. The Christian-Aristotelian belief that heavens and earth were fundamentally different collapsed when **Galileo** (1564-1642) discovered moving sunspots, irregular moon topography, and moons around Jupiter. He and **Newton** (1642-1727) developed a mechanics that unified cosmic and earthly phenomena. To meet the needs of the new physics, Newton and Leibnitz (1646-1716) invented calculus, Descartes (1596-1650) invented analytic geometry.

An explosion of observational science included the discovery of blood circulation (Harvey, 1578-1657) and microscopic life (Leeuwenhoek, 1632-1723), and advances in anatomy (Vesalius, 1514-64, dissected corpses) and chemistry (Boyle, 1627-91). Scientific research institutes were founded: Florence, 1657, London (**Royal Society**), 1660, Paris, 1666. Inventions proliferated (Savery's steam engine, 1696).

Arts. Mannerist trends of the high Renaissance (**Michelangelo,** 1475-1564) exploited virtuosity, grace, novelty, and exotic subjects and poses. The notion of artistic genius was promoted, in contrast to the anonymous medieval artisan. Private connoisseurs entered the art market. These trends were elaborated in the 17th century **Baroque** era, on a grander scale. Dynamic movement in painting and sculpture was emphasized by sharp lighting effects, use of rich materials (colored marble, gilt), realistic details. Curved facades, broken lines, rich, deep-cut detail, and ceiling decoration characterized Baroque architecture, especially in Germany. Monarchs, princes, and prelates, usually Catholic, used Baroque art to enhance and embellish their authority, as in royal portraits by Velazquez (1599-1660) and Van Dyck (1599-1641).

National styles emerged. In France, a taste for rectilinear order and serenity (Poussin, 1594-1665), linked to the new rational philosophy, was expressed in classical forms. The influence of **classical values** in French literature (tragedies of Racine, 1639-99) gave rise to the "battle of the Ancients and Moderns." New forms included the essay (Montaigne, 1533-92) and novel (*Princesse de Cleves,* La Fayette, 1678).

Dutch painting of the 17th century was unique in its wide social distribution. The Flemish tradition of undemonstrative realism reached its peak in **Rembrandt** (1606-69) and Vermeer (1632-75).

Economy. European economic expansion was stimulated by the new trade with the East, New World gold and silver, and a doubling of population (50 mln. in 1450, 100 mln. in 1600). New business and financial techniques were developed and refined, such as joint-stock companies, insurance, and letters of credit and exchange. The Bank of Amsterdam, 1609, and the Bank of England, 1694, broke the old monopoly of private banking families. The rise of a business mentality was typified by the spread of clock towers in cities in the 14th century. By the mid-15th century, portable clocks were available; the first watch was invented in 1502.

By 1650, most governments had adopted the **mercantile system,** in which they sought to amass metallic wealth by protecting their merchants' foreign and colonial trade monopolies. The rise in prices and the new coin-based economy undermined the craft guild and feudal manorial systems. Expanding industries, such as clothweaving and mining, benefitted from technical advances. Coal replaced disappearing wood as the chief fuel; it was used to fuel new 16th century blast furnaces making cast iron.

New World. The **Aztecs** united much of the Mesoamerican culture area in a militarist empire by 1519, from their capital, Tenochtitlan (pop. 300,000), which was the center of a cult requiring enormous levels of ritual human sacrifice. Most of the civilized areas of S. America were ruled by the centralized **Inca Empire** (1476-1534), stretching 2,000 miles from Ecuador to N.W. Argentina. Lavish and sophisticated traditions in pottery, weaving, sculpture, and architecture were maintained in both regions.

These empires, beset by revolts, fell in 2 short campaigns to gold-seeking Spanish forces based in the Antilles and Panama. **Cortes** took Mexico, 1519-21; **Pizarro** Peru, 1531-35. From these centers, land and sea expeditions claimed most of N. and S. America for Spain. The Indian high cultures did not survive the impact of Christian missionaries and the new upper class of whites and mestizos. In turn, New World silver, and such Indian products as potatoes, tobacco, corn, peanuts, chocolate, and rubber exercised a major economic influence on Europe. While the Spanish administration intermittently concerned itself with the welfare of Indians, the population remained impoverished at most levels, despite the growth of a distinct South American civilization. European diseases reduced the native population.

Brazil, which the Portuguese discovered in 1500 and settled after 1530, and the Caribbean colonies of several European nations developed a plantation economy where sugar cane, tobacco, cotton, coffee, rice, indigo, and lumber were grown commercially by slaves. From the early 16th to the late 19th centuries, some 10 million Africans were transported to **slavery** in the New World.

Netherlands. The urban, Calvinist northern provinces of the Netherlands rebelled against Hapsburg Spain, 1568, and founded an oligarchic mercantile republic. Their strategic control of the Baltic grain market enabled them to exploit Mediterranean food shortages. Religious refugees — French and Belgian Protestants, Iberian Jews — added to the cosmopolitan commercial talent pool. After Spain absorbed Portugal in 1580, the Dutch seized Portuguese possessions and created a vast, though generally short-lived commercial empire in Brazil, the Antilles, Africa, India, Ceylon, Malacca, Indonesia, and Taiwan, and challenged or supplanted Portuguese traders in China and Japan.

England. Anglicanism became firmly established under Elizabeth I after a brief Catholic interlude under "Bloody Mary," 1553-58. But religious and political conflicts led to a rebellion by Parliament, 1642. Roundheads (Puritans) defeated Cavaliers (Royalists); Charles I was beheaded, 1649. The new **Commonwealth** was ruled as a military dictatorship by Cromwell, who also brutally crushed an Irish rebellion, 1649-51. Conflicts within the Puritan camp (democratic Levelers defeated 1649) aided the Stuart restoration, 1660, but Parliament was permanently strengthened and the peaceful **"Glorious Revolution"**, 1688, advanced political and religious liberties (writings of Locke, 1632-1704). British privateers (Drake, 1540-96) challenged Spanish control of the New World, and penetrated Asian trade routes (Madras taken, 1639). N. American colonies (Jamestown, 1607, Plymouth, 1620) provided an outlet for religious dissenters.

France. Emerging from the religious civil wars in 1628, France regained military and commercial great power status under the ministries of **Richelieu** (1624-42), Mazarin (1643-61), and Colbert (1662-83). Under Louis XIV (ruled 1643-1715) royal absolutism triumphed over nobles and local *parlements* (defeat of Fronde, 1648-53). Permanent colonies were founded in Canada (1608), the Caribbean (1626), and India (1674).

Sweden. Sweden seceded from the Scandinavian Union in 1523. The thinly-populated agrarian state (with copper, iron, and timber exports) was united by the Vasa kings, whose conquests by the mid-17th century made Sweden the dominant Baltic power. The empire collapsed in the Great Northern War (1700-21).

Poland. After the union with Lithuania in 1447, Poland ruled vast territories from the Baltic to the Black Sea, resisting German and Turkish incursions. Catholic nobles failed to gain the loyalty of the Orthodox Christian peasantry in the East; commerce and trades were practiced by German and Jewish immigrants. The bloody 1648-49 cossack uprising began the kingdom's dismemberment.

China. A new dynasty, the **Manchus,** invaded from the NE and seized power in 1644, and expanded Chinese control to its greatest extent in Central and Southeast Asia. Trade and diplomatic contact with Europe grew, carefully controlled by China. New crops (sweet potato, maize, peanut) allowed an economic and population growth (300 million pop. in 1800). Traditional arts and literature were pursued with increased sophistication (*Dream of the Red Chamber*, novel, mid-18th century).

Japan. Tokugawa Ieyasu, shogun from 1603, finally unified and pacified feudal Japan. Hereditary daimyos and samurai monopolized government office and the professions. An urban merchant class grew, literacy spread, and a cultural renaissance occurred (haiku of Basho, 1644-94). Fear of European domination led to persecution of Christian converts from 1597, and stringent isolation from outside contact from 1640.

Philosophy, Industry, and Revolution: 1700-1800

Science and Reason. Faith in human reason and science as the source of truth and a means to improve the physical and social environment, espoused since the Renaissance (Francis Bacon, 1561-1626), was bolstered by scientific discoveries in spite of theological opposition (**Galileo's forced retraction,** 1633). Descartes applied the logical method of mathematics to discover "self-evident" scientific and philosophical truths, while Newton emphasized induction from experimental observation.

The challenge of reason to traditional religious and political values and institutions began with **Spinoza** (1632-77), who interpreted the Bible historically and called for political and intellectual freedom.

French philosophes assumed leadership of the **"Enlightenment"** in the 18th century. Montesquieu (1689-1755) used British history to support his notions of limited government. Voltaire's (1694-1778) diaries and novels of exotic travel illustrated the intellectual trends toward secular ethics and relativism. Rousseau's (1712-1778) radical concepts of the **social contract** and of the inherent goodness of the common man gave impetus to anti-monarchical republicanism. The *Encyclopedia,* 1751-72, edited by Diderot and d'Alembert, designed as a monument to reason, was largely devoted to practical technology.

In England, ideals of political and religious liberty were connected with empiricist philosophy and science in the followers of Locke. But the extreme **empiricism of Hume** (1711-76) and Berkeley

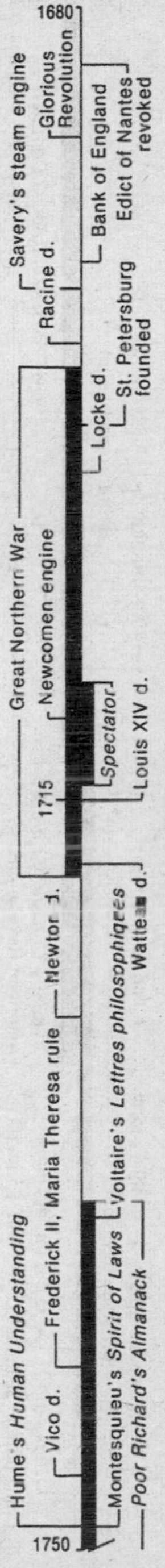

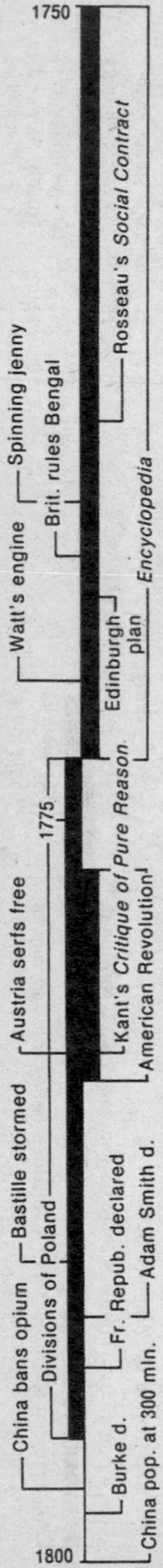

(1685-1753) posed limits to the identification of reason with absolute truth, as did the evolutionary approach to law and politics of Burke (1729-97) and the utilitarianism of Bentham (1748-1832). Adam Smith (1723-90) and other **physiocrats** called for a rationalization of economic activity by removing artificial barriers to a supposedly natural free exchange of goods.

Despite the political disunity and backwardness of most of Germany, German writers participated in the new philosophical trends popularized by Wolff (1679-1754). **Kant's** (1724-1804) **idealism**, unifying an empirical epistemology with *a priori* moral and logical concepts, directed German thought away from skepticism. Italian contributions included work on electricity by Galvani (1737-98) and Volta (1745-1827), the pioneer **historiography of Vico** (1668-1744), and writings on penal reform by Beccaria (1738-94). The American Franklin (1706-90) was celebrated in Europe for his varied achievements.

The growth of the **press** (*Spectator*, 1711-14) and the wide distribution of realistic but sentimental **novels** attested to the increase of a large bourgeois public.

Arts. Rococo art, characterized by extravagant decorative effects, asymmetries copied from organic models, and artificial pastoral subjects, was favored by the continental aristocracy for most of the century (Watteau, 1684-1721), and had musical analogies in the ornamentalized polyphony of late Baroque. The **Neoclassical** art after 1750, associated with the new scientific archeology, was more streamlined, and infused with the supposed moral and geometric rectitude of the Roman Republic (David, 1748-1825). In England, **town planning** on a grand scale began (Edinburgh, 1767).

Industrial Revolution in England. Agricultural improvements, such as the sowing drill (1701) and livestock breeding, were implemented on the large fields provided by enclosure of common lands by private owners. Profits from agriculture and from colonial and foreign trade (1800 volume, £ 54 million) were channelled through hundreds of banks and the **Stock Exchange** (founded 1773) into new industrial processes.

The Newcomen steam pump (1712) aided coal mining. Coal fueled the new efficient steam engines patented by Watt in 1769, and coke-smelting produced cheap, sturdy iron for machinery by the 1730s. The **flying shuttle** (1733) and **spinning jenny** (1764) were used in the large new cotton textile factories, where women and children were much of the work force. Goods were transported cheaply over **canals** (2,000 miles built 1760-1800).

American Revolution. The British colonies in N. America attracted a mass immigration of religious dissenters and poor people throughout the 17th and 18th centuries, coming from all parts of the British Isles, Germany, the Netherlands, and other countries. The population reached 3 million whites and blacks by the 1770s. The small native population was decimated by European diseases and wars with and between the various colonies. British attempts to control colonial trade, and to tax the colonists to pay for the costs of colonial administration and defense clashed with traditions of local self government, and eventually provoked the colonies to rebellion. (*See American Revolution in Index.*)

Central and East Europe. The monarchs of the three states that dominated eastern Europe — Austria, Prussia, and Russia — accepted the advice and legitimation of philosophes in creating more modern, centralized institutions in their kingdoms, enlarged by the division of Poland (1772-95).

Under **Frederick II** (ruled 1740-86) Prussia, with its efficient modern army, doubled in size. State monopolies and tariff protection fostered industry, and some legal reforms were introduced. Austria's heterogeneous realms were legally unified under **Maria Theresa** (ruled 1740-80) and **Joseph II** (1780-90). Reforms in education, law, and religion were enacted, and the Austrian serfs were freed (1781). With its defeat in the Seven Years' War in 1763, Austria lost Silesia and ceased its active role in Germany, but was compensated by expansion to the E and S (Hungary, Slavonia, 1699, Galicia, 1772).

Russia, whose borders continued to expand in all directions, adopted some Western bureaucratic and economic policies under **Peter I** (ruled 1682-1725) and Catherine II (ruled 1762-96). Trade and cultural contacts with the West multiplied from the new Baltic Sea capital, **St. Petersburg** (founded 1703).

French Revolution. The growing French middle class lacked political power, and resented aristocratic tax privileges, especially in light of liberal political ideals popularized by the American Revolution. Peasants lacked adequate land and were burdened with feudal obligations to nobles. Wars with Britain drained the treasury, finally forcing the king to call the **Estates-General** in 1789 (first time since 1614), in an atmosphere of food riots (poor crop in 1788).

Aristocratic resistance to absolutism was soon overshadowed by the reformist Third Estate (middle class), which proclaimed itself the **National Constituent Assembly** June 17 and took the "Tennis Court oath" on June 20 to secure a constitution. The storming of the **Bastille** July 14 by Parisian artisans was followed by looting and seizure of aristocratic property throughout France. Assembly reforms included abolition of class and regional privileges, a Declaration of Rights, suffrage by taxpayers (75% of males), and the **Civil Constitution of the Clergy** providing for election and loyalty oaths for priests. A republic was declared Sept. 22, 1792, in spite of royalist pressure from Austria and Prussia, which had declared war in April (joined by Britain the next year). Louis XVI was beheaded Jan. 21, 1793, Queen Marie Antoinette was beheaded Oct. 16, 1793.

Royalist uprisings in La Vendee and the S and military reverses led to a **reign of terror** in which tens of thousands of opponents of the Revolution and criminals were executed. Radical reforms in the **Convention** period (Sept. 1793-Oct. 1795) included the abolition of colonial slavery, economic measures to aid the poor, support of public education, and a short-lived de-Christianization.

Division among radicals (execution of Hebert, March 1794, Danton, April, and Robespierre, July) aided the ascendance of a moderate **Directory**, which consolidated military victories. **Napoleon Bonaparte** (1769-1821), a popular young general, exploited political divisions and participated in a coup Nov. 9, 1799, making himself first consul (dictator).

India. Sikh and Hindu rebels (Rajputs, Marathas) and Afghans destroyed the power of the Mughals during the 18th century. After France's defeat in the Seven Years War, 1763, Britain was the chief European trade power in India. Its control of inland **Bengal and Bihar** was recognized by the Mughal shah in 1765, who granted the **British East India Co.** (under Clive, 1727-74) the right to collect land revenue there. Despite objections from Parliament (1784 India Act) the company's involvement in local wars and politics led to repeated acquisitions of new territory. The company exported Indian textiles, sugar, and indigo.

World Population Growth 10,000 BC to 1982

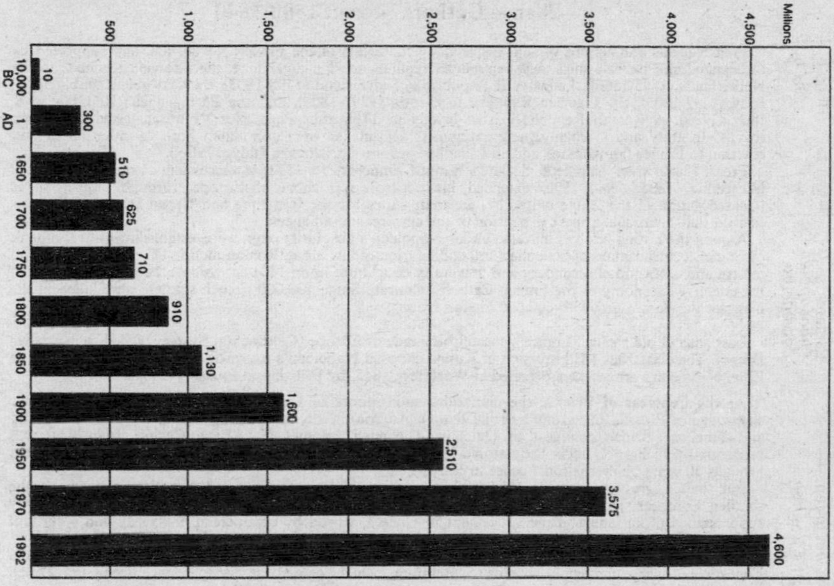

19th Century Railroad Growth in Selected Countries

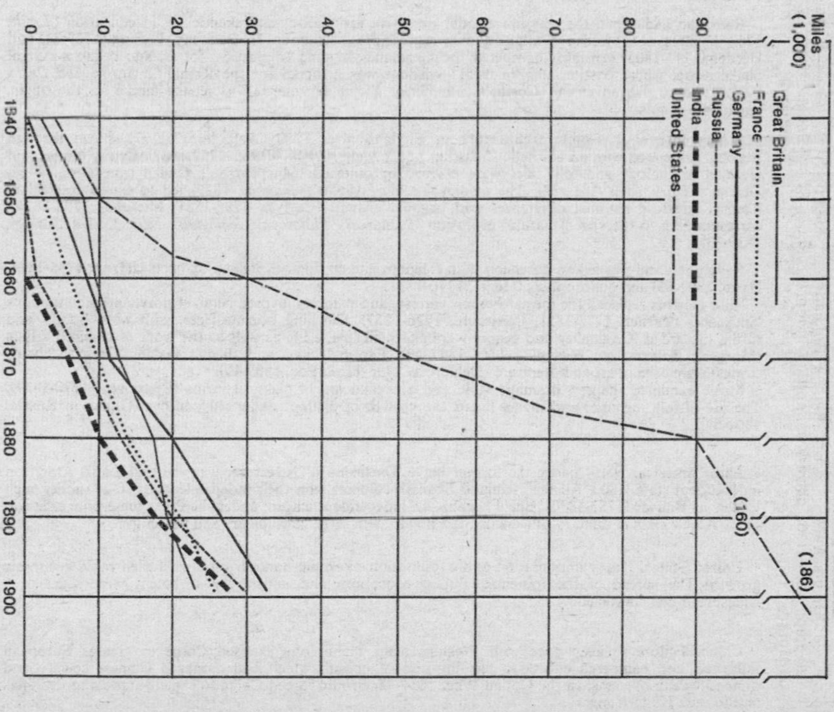

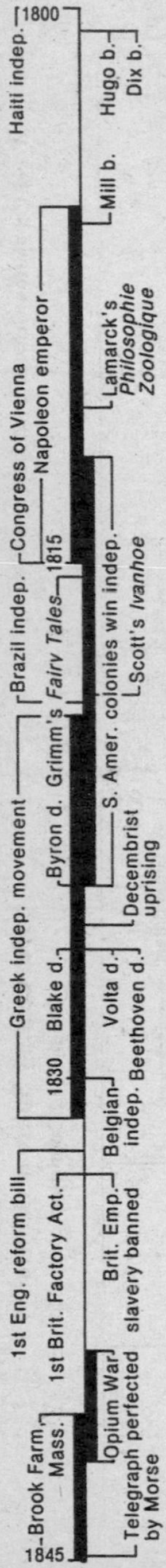

Change Gathers Steam: 1800-1840

French ideals and empire spread. Inspired by the ideals of the French Revolution, and supported by the expanding French armies, new republican regimes arose near France: the **Batavian** Republic in the Netherlands (1795-1806), the **Helvetic** Republic in Switzerland (1798-1803), the **Cisalpine** Republic in N. Italy (1797-1805), the **Ligurian** Republic in Genoa (1797-1805), and the **Parthenopean** Republic in S. Italy (1799). A Roman Republic existed briefly in 1798 after Pope Pius VI was arrested by French troops. In Italy and Germany, new nationalist sentiments were stimulated both in imitation of and reaction to France (anti-French and anti-Jacobin peasant uprisings in Italy, 1796-9).

From 1804, when Napoleon declared himself emperor, to 1812, a succession of military victories (Austerlitz, 1805, Jena, 1806) extended his control over most of Europe, through puppet states (**Confederation of the Rhine** united W. German states for the first time and **Grand Duchy of Warsaw** revived Polish national hopes), expansion of the empire, and alliances.

Among the lasting reforms initiated under Napoleon's absolutist reign were: establishment of the Bank of France, centralization of tax collection, codification of law along Roman models (*Code Napoleon*), and reform and extension of secondary and university education. In an 1801 concordat, the papacy recognized the effective autonomy of the French Catholic Church. Some 400,000 French soldiers were killed in the Napoleonic Wars, along with 600,000 foreign troops.

Last gasp of old regime. France's coastal blockade of Europe (**Continental System**) failed to neutralize Britain. The disastrous 1812 invasion of Russia exposed Napoleon's overextension. After an 1814 exile at Elba, Napoleon's armies were defeated at **Waterloo,** 1815, by British and Prussian troops.

At the **Congress of Vienna,** the monarchs and princes of Europe redrew their boundaries, to the advantage of Prussia (in Saxony and the Ruhr), Austria (in Illyria and Venetia), and Russia (in Poland and Finland). British conquest of Dutch and French colonies (S. Africa, Ceylon, Mauritius) was recognized, and France, under the restored Bourbons, retained its expanded 1792 borders. The settlement brought 50 years of international peace to Europe.

But the Congress was unable to check the advance of liberal ideals and of nationalism among the smaller European nations. The 1825 **Decembrist uprising** by liberal officers in Russia was easily suppressed. But an independence movement in **Greece,** stirred by commercial prosperity and a cultural revival, succeeded in expelling Ottoman rule by 1831, with the aid of Britain, France, and Russia.

A constitutional monarchy was secured in France by an **1830 revolution;** Louis Philippe became king. The revolutionary contagion spread to **Belgium,** which gained its independence from the Dutch monarchy, 1830; to **Poland,** whose rebellion was defeated by Russia, 1830-31; and to Germany.

Romanticism. A new style in intellectual and artistic life began to replace Neo-classicism and Rococo after the mid-18th century. By the early 19th, this style, Romanticism, had prevailed in the European world.

Rousseau had begun the reaction against excessive rationalism and skepticism; in education (*Emile,* 1762) he stressed subjective spontaneity over regularized instruction. In Germany, Lessing (1729-81) and Herder (1744-1803) favorably compared the German folk song to classical forms, and began a cult of Shakespeare, whose passion and "natural" wisdom was a model for the Romantic *Sturm und Drang* (storm and stress) movement. **Goethe's** *Sorrows of Young Werther* (1774) set the model for the tragic, passionate genius.

A new interest in **Gothic architecture** in England after 1760 (Walpole, 1717-97) spread through Europe, associated with an aesthetic Christian and mystic revival (Blake, 1757-1827). Celtic, Norse, and German mythology and folk tales were revived or imitated (Macpherson's Ossian translation, 1762, Grimm's *Fairy Tales,* 1812-22). The medieval revival (Scott's *Ivanhoe,* 1819) led to a new interest in history, stressing national differences and organic growth (Carlyle, 1795-1881; Michelet, 1798-1874), corresponding to theories of natural evolution (Lamarck's *Philosophie zoologique,* 1809, Lyell's *Geology,* 1830-33).

Revolution and war fed an obsession with freedom and conflict, expressed by poets (**Byron,** 1788-1824, **Hugo,** 1802-85) and philosophers (**Hegel,** 1770-1831).

Wild gardens replaced the formal French variety, and painters favored rural, stormy, and mountainous landscapes (**Turner,** 1775-1851; **Constable,** 1776-1837). Clothing became freer, with wigs, hoops, and ruffles discarded. Originality and genius were expected in the life as well as the work of inspired artists (Murger's *Scenes from Bohemian Life,* 1847-49). Exotic locales and themes (as in "Gothic" horror stories) were used in art and literature (Delacroix, 1798-1863, **Poe,** 1809-49).

Music exhibited the new dramatic style and a breakdown of classical forms (Beethoven, 1770-1827). The use of folk melodies and modes aided the growth of distinct national traditions (Glinka in Russia, 1804-57).

Latin America. Haiti, under the former slave **Toussaint L'Ouverture,** was the first Latin American independent state, 1800. All the mainland Spanish colonies won their independence 1810-24, under such leaders as **Bolivar** (1783-1830). Brazil became an independent empire under the Portuguese prince regent, 1822. A new class of military officers divided power with large landholders and the church.

United States. Heavy immigration and exploitation of ample natural resources fueled rapid economic growth. The spread of the franchise, public education, and antislavery sentiment were signs of a widespread democratic ethic.

China. Failure to keep pace with Western arms technology exposed China to greater European influence, and hampered efforts to bar imports of opium, which had damaged Chinese society and drained wealth overseas. In the **Opium War,** 1839-42, Britain forced China to expand trade opportunities and to cede Hong Kong.

Triumph of Progress: 1840-80

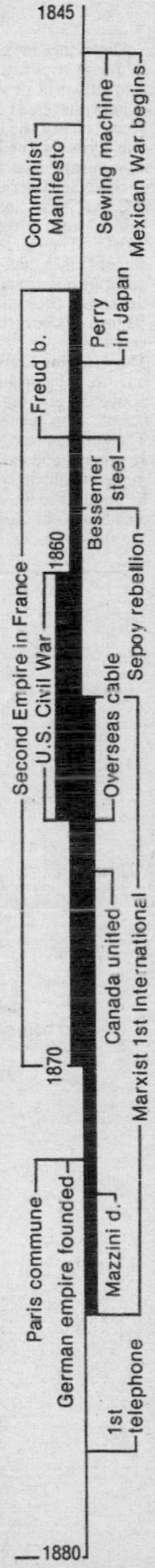

Idea of Progress. As a result of the cumulative scientific, economic, and political changes of the preceding eras, the idea took hold among literate people in the West that continuing growth and improvement was the usual state of human and natural life.

Darwin's statement of the **theory of evolution** and survival of the fittest (*Origin of Species*, 1859), defended by intellectuals and scientists against theological objections, was taken as confirmation that progress was the natural direction of life. The controversy helped define popular ideas of the dedicated scientist and ever-expanding human knowledge of and control over the world (Foucault's demonstration of earth's rotation, 1851, Pasteur's germ theory, 1861).

Liberals following Ricardo (1772-1823) in their faith that unrestrained competition would bring continuous economic expansion sought to adjust political life to the new social realities, and believed that unregulated competition of ideas would yield truth (Mill, 1806-73). In England, successive reform bills (1832, 1867, 1884) gave representation to the new industrial towns, and extended the franchise to the middle and lower classes and to Catholics, Dissenters, and Jews. On both sides of the Atlantic, reformists tried to improve conditions for the mentally ill (Dix, 1802-87), women (Anthony, 1820-1906), and prisoners. Slavery was barred in the British Empire, 1833; the United States, 1865; and Brazil, 1888.

Socialist theories based on ideas of human perfectibility or historical progress were widely disseminated. Utopian socialists like Saint-Simon (1760-1825) envisaged an orderly, just society directed by a technocratic elite. A model factory town, New Lanark, Scotland, was set up by utopian Robert Owen (1771-1858), and utopian communal experiments were tried in the U.S. (Brook Farm, Mass., 1841-7). Bakunin's (1814-76) anarchism represented the opposite utopian extreme of total freedom. Marx (1818-83) posited the inevitable triumph of socialism in the industrial countries through a historical process of class conflict.

Spread of industry. The technical processes and managerial innovations of the English industrial revolution spread to Europe (especially Germany) and the U.S., causing an explosion of industrial production, demand for raw materials, and competition for markets. Inventors, both trained and self-educated, provided the means for larger-scale production (Bessemer steel, 1856, sewing machine, 1846). Many inventions were shown at the 1851 London Great Exhibition at the Crystal Palace, whose theme was universal prosperity.

Local specialization and long-distance trade were aided by a revolution in transportation and communication. Railroads were first introduced in the 1820s in England and the U.S. Over 150,000 miles of track had been laid worldwide by 1880, with another 100,000 miles laid in the next decade. Steamships were improved (*Savannah* crossed Atlantic, 1819). The telegraph, perfected by 1844 (Morse), connected the Old and New Worlds by cable in 1866, and quickened the pace of international commerce and politics. The first commercial telephone exchange went into operation in the U.S. in 1878.

The new class of industrial workers, uprooted from their rural homes, lacked job security, and suffered from dangerous overcrowded conditions at work and at home. Many responded by organizing trade unions (legalized in England, 1824; France, 1884). The U.S. Knights of Labor had 700,000 members by 1886. The First International, 1864-76, tried to unite workers internationally around a Marxist program. The quasi-Socialist Paris Commune uprising, 1871, was violently suppressed. Factory Acts to reduce child labor and regulate conditions were passed (1833-50 in England). Social security measures were introduced by the Bismarck regime in Germany, 1883-89.

Revolutions of 1848. Among the causes of the continent-wide revolutions were an international collapse of credit and resulting unemployment, bad harvests in 1845-7, and a cholera epidemic. The new urban proletariat and expanding bourgeoisie demanded a greater political role. Republics were proclaimed in France, Rome, and Venice. Nationalist feelings reached fever pitch in the Hapsburg empire, as Hungary declared independence under Kossuth, a Slav Congress demanded equality, and Piedmont tried to drive Austria from Lombardy. A national liberal assembly at Frankfurt called for German unification.

But riots fueled bourgeois fears of socialism (Marx and Engels' 1848 *Communist Manifesto*) and peasants remained conservative. The old establishment — The Papacy, the Hapsburgs (using Croats and Romanians against Hungary), the Russian army — was able to rout the revolutionaries by 1849. The French Republic succumbed to a renewed monarchy by 1852 (Emperor Napoleon III).

Great nations unified. Using the "blood and iron" tactics of Bismarck from 1862, Prussia controlled N. Germany by 1867 (war with Denmark, 1864, Austria, 1866). After defeating France in 1870 (loss of Alsace-Lorraine), it won the allegiance of S. German states. A new **German Empire** was proclaimed, 1871. **Italy**, inspired by Mazzini (1805-72) and Garibaldi (1807-82), was unified by the reformed Piedmont kingdom through uprisings, plebiscites, and war.

The **U.S.**, its area expanded after the 1846-47 Mexican War, defeated a secession attempt by slave states, 1861-65. The Canadian provinces were united in an autonomous **Dominion of Canada**, 1867. Control in **India** was removed from the East India Co. and centralized under British administration after the 1857-58 Sepoy rebellion, laying the groundwork for the modern Indian State. Queen Victoria was named Empress of India, 1876.

Europe dominates Asia. The Ottoman Empire began to collapse in the face of Balkan nationalisms and European imperial incursions in N. Africa (Suez Canal, 1869). The Turks had lost control of most of both regions by 1882. Russia completed its expansion south by 1884 (despite the temporary setback of the Crimean War with Turkey, Britain, and France, 1853-56) taking Turkestan, all the Caucasus, and Chinese areas in the East and sponsoring Balkan Slavs against the Turks. A succession of reformist and reactionary regimes presided over a slow modernization (serfs freed, 1861). Persian independence suffered as Russia and British India competed for influence.

China was forced to sign a series of unequal treaties with European powers and Japan. Overpopulation and an inefficient dynasty brought misery and caused rebellions (Taiping, Moslems) leaving tens of millions dead. Japan was forced by the U.S. (Commodore Perry's visits, 1853-54) and Europe to end its isolation. The Meiji restoration, 1868, gave power to a Westernizing oligarchy. Intensified empire-building gave Burma to Britain, 1824-86, and Indo-China to France, 1862-95. Christian missionary activity followed imperial and trade expansion in Asia.

Respectability. The fine arts were expected to reflect and encourage the progress of morals and

The Seven Wonders of the World

These ancient works of art and architecture were considered awe-inspiring in splendor and/or size by the Greek and Roman world of the Alexandrian epoch and later. Classical writers disagreed as to which works made up the list of Wonders, but the following were usually included:

The Pyramids of Egypt: The only surviving Wonder, these monumental structures of masonry located on the west bank of the Nile River above Cairo were built from 3000 to 1800 B.C. as royal tombs. Three—Khufu, Khafra, and Menkaura—were often grouped as the first Wonder of the World. The largest, **The Great Pyramid of Khufu,** or Cheops, is a solid mass of limestone blocks covering 13 acres. It is estimated to contain 2.3 million blocks of stone, the stones themselves averaging 2½ tons and some weighing 30 tons. Its construction reputedly took 100,000 laborers 20 years.

The Hanging Gardens of Babylon: These gardens were laid out on a brick terrace about 400 feet square and 75 feet above the ground. To irrigate the trees, shrubs, and flowers, screws were turned to lift water from the Euphrates River. The gardens were probably built by King Nebuchandnezzar II around 600 B.C. **The Walls of Babylon,** long, thick, and made of colorfully glazed brick, were considered by some to be among the Seven Wonders.

The Statue of Zeus (Jupiter) at Olympia: This statue of the king of the gods showed him seated on a throne. His flesh was made of ivory, his robe and ornaments of gold. Reputedly 40 feet high, the statue was made by Phidias and was placed in the great temple of Zeus in the sacred grove of Olympia around 457 B.C.

The Colossus of Rhodes: A bronze statue of the sun god Helios, the Colossus was worked on for 12 years in the early 200's B.C. by the sculptor Chares. It was probably 120 feet high. A symbol of the city of Rhodes at its height, the statue stood on a promontory overlooking the harbor.

The Temple of Artemis (Diana) at Ephesus: This largest and most complex temple of ancient times was built around 550 B.C. and was made of marble except for its tile-covered wooden roof. It was begun in honor of a non-Hellenic goddess who later became identified with the Greek goddess of the same name. Ephesus was one of the greatest of the Ionian cities.

The Mausoleum at Halicarnassus: The source of our word "mausoleum," this marble tomb was built in what is now southeastern Turkey by Artemisia for her husband Mausolus, an official of the Persian Empire who died in 353 B.C. About 135 feet high, it was adorned with the works of 4 sculptors.

The Pharos (Lighthouse) of Alexandria: This sculpture was designed around 270 B.C., during the reign of King Ptolemy II, by the Greek architect Sostratos. Estimates of its height range from 200 to 600 feet.

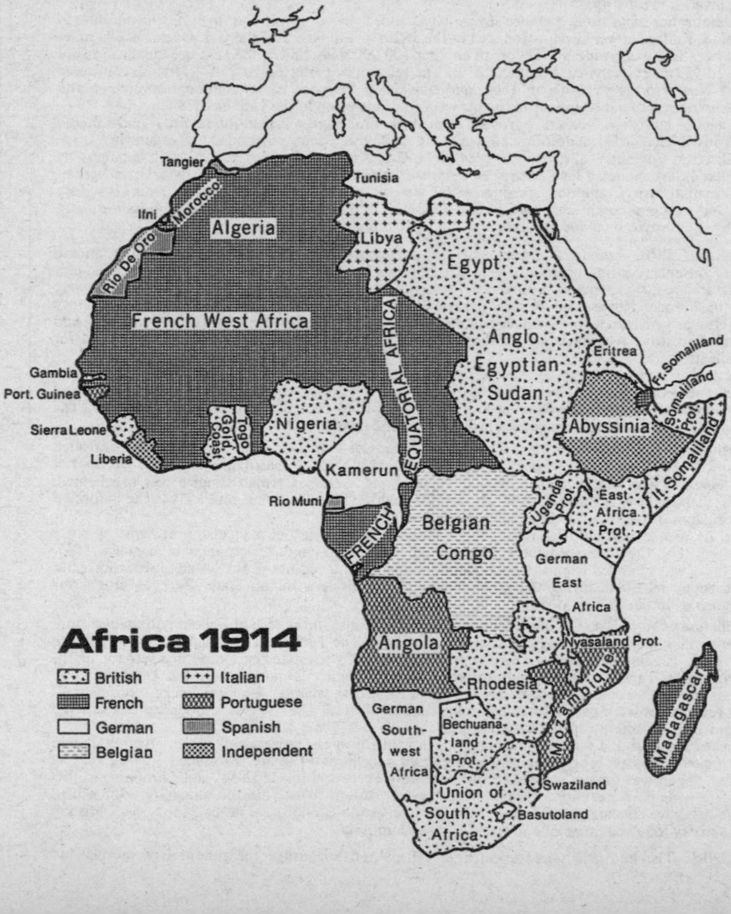

manners among the different classes. "Victorian" prudery, exaggerated delicacy, and familial piety were heralded by **Bowdler's** expurgated edition of Shakespeare (1818). Government-supported mass education inculcated a work ethic as a means to escape poverty (Horatio Alger, 1832-99).

The official **Beaux Arts** school in Paris set an international style of imposing public buildings (Paris Opera, 1861-74, Vienna Opera, 1861-69) and uplifting statues (Bartholdi's *Statue of Liberty,* 1885). Realist painting, influenced by photography (Daguerre, 1837), appealed to a new mass audience with social or historical narrative (Wilkie, 1785-1841, Poynter, 1836-1919) or with serious religious, moral, or social messages (pre-Raphaelites, Millet's Angelus, 1858) often drawn from ordinary life. The **Impressionists** (Pissarro, 1830-1903, Renoir, 1841-1919) rejected the central role of serious subject matter in favor of a colorful and sensual depiction of a moment, but their sunny, placid depictions of bourgeois scenes kept them within the respectable consensus.

Realistic **novelists** presented the full panorama of social classes and personalities, but retained sentimentality and moral judgment (Dickens, 1812-70, Eliot, 1819-80, Tolstoy, 1828-1910, Balzac, 1799-1850).

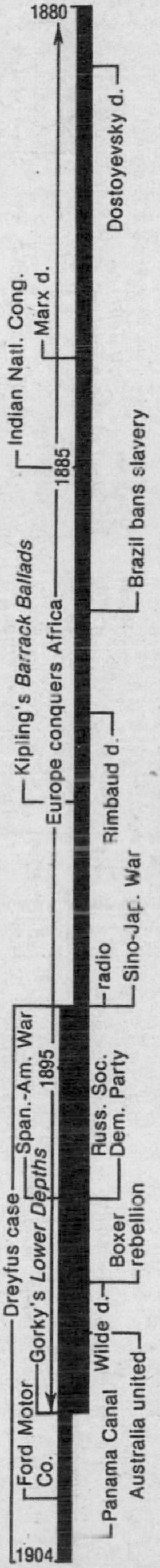

Veneer of Stability: 1880-1900

Imperialism triumphant. The vast African interior, visited by European explorers (Barth, 1821-65, Livingstone, 1813-73) was conquered by the European powers in rapid, competitive thrusts from their coastal bases after 1880, mostly for domestic political and international strategic reasons. W. African Moslem kingdoms (Fulani), Arab slave traders (Zanzibar), and Bantu military confederations (Zulu) were alike subdued. Only Christian Ethiopia (defeat of Italy, 1896) and Liberia resisted successfully. France (W. Africa) and Britain ("Cape to Cairo," Boer War, 1899-1902) were the major beneficiaries. The ideology of "the white man's burden" (Kipling, *Barrack Room Ballads,* 1892) or of a "civilizing mission" (France) justified the conquests.

West European foreign capital investments soared to nearly $40 billion by 1914, but most was in E. Europe (France, Germany) the Americas (Britain) and the white colonies. The foundation of the modern interdependent world economy was laid, with cartels dominating raw material trade.

An industrious world. Industrial and technological proficiency characterized the 2 new great powers — **Germany** and the **U.S.** Coal and iron deposits enabled Germany to reach second or third place status in iron, steel, and shipbuilding by the 1900s. German electrical and chemical industries were world leaders. The U.S. post-civil war boom (interrupted by "panics," 1884, 1893, 1896) was shaped by massive immigration from S. and E. Europe from 1880, government subsidy of railroads, and huge private monopolies (Standard Oil, 1870, U.S. Steel, 1901). The **Spanish-American War,** 1898 (Philippine rebellion, 1899-1901) and the Open Door policy in China (1899) made the U.S. a world power.

England led in **urbanization** (72% by 1890), with **London** the world capital of finance, insurance, and shipping. Electric subways (London, 1890), sewer systems (Paris, 1850s), parks, and bargain department stores helped improve living standards for most of the urban population of the industrial world.

Asians assimilate. Asian reaction to European economic, military, and religious incursions took the form of imitation of Western techniques and adoption of Western ideas of progress and freedom. The Chinese "self-strengthening" movement of the 1860s and 70s included rail, port, and arsenal improvements and metal and textile mills. Reformers like **K'ang Yu-wei** (1858-1927) won liberalizing reforms in 1898, right after the European and Japanese "scramble for concessions."

A universal education system in Japan and importation of foreign industrial, scientific, and military experts aided Japan's unprecedented rapid modernization after 1868, under the authoritarian Meiji regime. Japan's victory in the **Sino-Japanese War,** 1894-95, put Formosa and Korea in its power.

In **India,** the British alliance with the remaining princely states masked reform sentiment among the Westernized urban elite; higher education had been conducted largely in English for 50 years. The **Indian National Congress,** founded in 1885, demanded a larger government role for Indians.

"Fin-de-siecle" sophistication. **Naturalist** writers pushed realism to its extreme limits, adopting a quasi-scientific attitude and writing about formerly taboo subjects like sex, crime, extreme poverty, and corruption (Flaubert, 1821-80, Zola, 1840-1902, Hardy, 1840-1928). Unseen or repressed psychological motivations were explored in the clinical and theoretical works of **Freud** (1856-1939) and in the fiction of Dostoevsky (1821-81), James (1843-1916), Schnitzler (1862-1931) and others.

A contempt for bourgeois life or a desire to shock a complacent audience was shared by the French **symbolist** poets (Verlaine, 1844-96, Rimbaud, 1854-91), neo-pagan English writers (Swinburne, 1837-1909), continental dramatists (Ibsen, 1828-1906) and satirists (Wilde, 1854-1900). **Nietzsche** (1844-1900) was influential in his elitism and pessimism.

Post-impressionist art neglected long-cherished conventions of representation (Cezanne, 1839-1906) and showed a willingness to learn from primitive and non-European art (Gauguin, 1848-1903, Japanese prints).

Racism. Gobineau (1816-82) gave a pseudo-biological foundation to modern racist theories, which spread in the latter 19th century along with **Social Darwinism,** the belief that societies are and should be organized as a struggle for survival of the fittest. The Medieval period was interpreted as an era of natural Germanic rule (Chamberlain, 1855-1927) and notions of superiority were associated with German national aspirations (Treitschke, 1834-96). **Anti-Semitism,** with a new racist rationale, became a significant political force in Germany (Anti-Semitic Petition, 1880), Austria (Lueger, 1844-1910), and France (Dreyfus case, 1894-1906).

Last Respite: 1900-1909

Alliances. While the peace of Europe (and its dependencies) continued to hold (1907 **Hague Conference** extended the rules of war and international arbitration procedures), imperial rivalries, protectionist trade practices (in Germany and France), and the escalating arms race (British *Dreadnought* battleship launched, Germany widens Kiel canal, 1906) exacerbated minor disputes (German-French Moroccan "crises", 1905, 1911).

Security was sought through alliances: **Triple Alliance** (Germany, Austria-Hungary, Italy) renewed

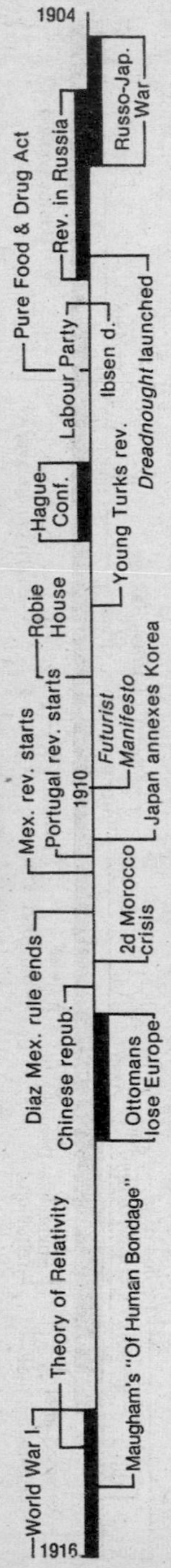

1902, 1907; Anglo-Japanese Alliance, 1902; Franco-Russian Alliance, 1899; **Entente Cordiale** (Britain, France) 1904; Anglo-Russian Treaty, 1907; German-Ottoman friendship.

Ottomans decline. The inefficient, corrupt Ottoman government was unable to resist further loss of territory. Nearly all European lands were lost in 1912 to Serbia, Greece, Montenegro, and Bulgaria. Italy took Libya and the Dodecanese islands the same year, and Britain took Kuwait, 1899, and the Sinai, 1906. The **Young Turk** revolution in 1908 forced the sultan to restore a constitution, introduced some social reform, industrialization, and secularization.

British Empire. British trade and cultural influence remained dominant in the empire, but constitutional reforms presaged its eventual dissolution: the colonies of **Australia** were united in 1901 under a self-governing commonwealth. **New Zealand** acquired dominion status in 1907. The old Boer republics joined Cape Colony and Natal in the self-governing **Union of South Africa** in 1910.

The 1909 Indian Councils Act enhanced the role of elected province legislatures in **India.** The Moslem League, founded 1906, sought separate communal representation.

East Asia. Japan exploited its growing industrial power to expand its empire. Victory in the 1904-05 war against Russia (naval battle of Tsushima, 1905) assured Japan's domination of **Korea** (annexed 1910) and Manchuria (took Port Arthur 1905).

In China, central authority began to crumble (empress died, 1908). Reforms (Confucian exam system ended 1905, modernization of the army, building of railroads) were inadequate and secret societies of reformers and nationalists, inspired by the Westernized **Sun Yat-sen** (1866-1925) fomented periodic uprisings in the south.

Siam, whose independence had been guaranteed by Britain and France in 1896, was split into spheres of influence by those countries in 1907.

Russia. The population of the Russian Empire approached 150 million in 1900. Reforms in education, law, and local institutions (*zemstvos*), and an industrial boom starting in the 1880s (oil, railroads) created the beginnings of a modern state, despite the autocratic tsarist regime. Liberals (1903 Union of Liberation), Socialists (Social Democrats founded 1898, Bolsheviks split off 1903), and populists (Social Revolutionaries founded 1901) were periodically repressed, and national minorities persecuted (anti-Jewish pogroms, 1903, 1905-6).

An industrial crisis after 1900 and harvest failures aggravated poverty in the urban proletariat, and the 1904-05 defeat by Japan (which checked Russia's Asian expansion) sparked the revolution of 1905-06. A **Duma** (parliament) was created, and an agricultural reform (under Stolypin, prime minister 1906-11) created a large class of landowning peasants (kulaks).

The world shrinks. Developments in transportation and communication and mass population movements helped create an awareness of an interdependent world. Early **automobiles** (Daimler, Benz, 1885) were experimental, or designed as luxuries. Assembly-line mass production (Ford Motor Co., 1903) made the invention practicable, and by 1910 nearly 500,000 motor vehicles were registered in the U.S. alone. **Heavier-than-air flights** began in 1903 in the U.S. (Wright brothers), preceded by glider, balloon, and model plane advances in several countries. Trade was advanced by improvements in **ship design** (gyrocompass, 1907), speed (Lusitania crossed Atlantic in 5 days, 1907), and reach (Panama Canal begun, 1904).

The first transatlantic **radio** telegraphic transmission occurred in 1901, 6 years after Marconi discovered radio. Radio transmission of human speech had been made in 1900. Telegraphic transmission of photos was achieved in 1904, lending immediacy to news reports. **Phonographs,** popularized by Caruso's recordings (starting 1902) made for quick international spread of musical styles (ragtime). **Motion pictures,** perfected in the 1890s (Dickson, Lumiere brothers), became a popular and artistic medium after 1900; newsreels appeared in 1909.

Emigration from crowded European centers soared in the decade: 9 million migrated to the U.S., and millions more went to Siberia, Canada, Argentina, Australia, South Africa, and Algeria. Some 70 million Europeans emigrated in the century before 1914. Several million Chinese, Indians, and Japanese migrated to Southeast Asia, where their urban skills often enabled them to take a predominant economic role.

Social reform. The social and economic problems of the poor were kept in the public eye by realist fiction writers (Dreiser's *Sister Carrie,* 1900; Gorky's *Lower Depths,* 1902; Sinclair's *Jungle,* 1906), journalists (U.S. **muckrakers** — Steffens, Tarbell) and artists (Ashcan school). Frequent labor strikes and occasional assassinations by anarchists or radicals (Austrian Empress, 1898; King Umberto I of Italy, 1900; U.S. Pres. McKinley, 1901; Russian Interior Minister Plehve, 1904; Portugal's King Carlos, 1908) added to social tension and fear of revolution.

But democratic reformism prevailed. In Germany, Bernstein's (1850-1932) **revisionist Marxism,** downgrading revolution, was accepted by the powerful Social Democrats and trade unions. The British Fabian Society (the Webbs, Shaw) and the Labour Party (founded 1906) worked for reforms such as social security and union rights (1906), while women's suffragists grew more militant. U.S. **progressives** fought big business (Pure Food and Drug Act, 1906). In France, the 10-hour work day (1904) and separation of church and state (1905) were reform victories, as was universal suffrage in Austria (1907).

Arts. An unprecedented period of experimentation, centered in France, produced several new **painting** styles: fauvism exploited bold color areas (Matisse, *Woman with Hat,* 1905); expressionism reflected powerful inner emotions (the Brücke group, 1905); cubism combined several views of an object on one flat surface (Picasso's *Demoiselles,* 1906-07); futurism tried to depict speed and motion (Italian Futurist Manifesto, 1910). **Architects** explored new uses of steel structures, with facades either neo-classical (Adler and Sullivan in U.S.); curvilinear Art Nouveau (Gaudi's Casa Mila, 1905-10); or functionally streamlined (Wright's Robie House, 1909).

Music and **Dance** shared the experimental spirit. Ruth St. Denis (1877-1968) and Isadora Duncan (1878-1927) pioneered modern dance, while Diaghilev in Paris revitalized classic ballet from 1909. Composers explored atonal music (Debussy, 1862-1918) and dissonance (Schönberg, 1874-1951), or revolutionized classical forms (Stravinsky, 1882-71), often showing jazz or folk music influences.

War and Revolution: 1910-1919

War threatens. Germany under Wilhelm II sought a political and imperial role consonant with its industrial strength, challenging Britain's world supremacy and threatening France, still resenting the loss of Alsace-Lorraine. Austria wanted to curb an expanded Serbia (after 1912) and the threat it posed to its own Slav lands. Russia feared Austrian and German political and economic aims in the Balkans and Turkey. An accelerated arms race resulted: the German standing army rose to over 2 million men by 1914. Russia and France had over a million each, Austria and the British Empire nearly a million each. Dozens of enormous battleships were built by the powers after 1906.

The **assassination of Austrian Archduke Ferdinand** by a Serbian, June 28, 1914, was the pretext for war. The system of alliances made the conflict Europe-wide; Germany's invasion of Belgium to outflank France forced Britain to enter the war. Patriotic fervor was nearly unanimous among all classes in most countries.

World War I. German forces were stopped in France in one month. The rival armies dug **trench networks.** Artillery and improved machine guns prevented either side from any lasting advance despite repeated assaults (600,000 dead at **Verdun**, Feb.-July 1916). Poison gas, used by Germany in 1915, proved ineffective. Over one million U.S. troops tipped the balance after mid-1917, forcing Germany to sue for peace.

In the East, the Russian armies were thrown back (battle of **Tannenberg,** Aug. 20, 1914) and the war grew unpopular. An allied attempt to relieve Russia through Turkey failed (**Gallipoli** 1916). The new Bolshevik regime signed the capitulatory Brest-Litovsk peace in March, 1918. Italy entered the war on the allied side, Apr. 1915, but was pushed back by Oct. 1917. A renewed offensive with Allied aid in Oct.-Nov. 1918 forced Austria to surrender.

The British Navy successfully blockaded Germany, which responded with submarine U-boat attacks; **unrestricted submarine warfare** against neutrals after Jan. 1917 helped bring the U.S. into the war. Other battlefields included Palestine and Mesopotamia, both of which Britain wrested from the Turks in 1917, and the African and Pacific colonies of Germany, most of which fell to Britain, France, Australia, Japan, and South Africa.

From 1916, the civilian population and economy of both sides were mobilized to an unprecedented degree. Over 10 million soldiers died (May 1917 French mutiny crushed). *For further details, see 1978 and earlier editions of The World Almanac.*

Settlement. At the **Versailles conference** (Jan.-June 1919) and in subsequent negotiations and local wars (Russian-Polish War 1920), the map of Europe was redrawn with a nod to U.S. Pres. Wilson's principle of self-determination. Austria and Hungary were separated and much of their land was given to Yugoslavia (formerly Serbia), Romania, Italy, and the newly independent Poland and Czechoslovakia. Germany lost territory in the West, North, and East, while Finland and the Baltic states were detached from Russia. Turkey lost nearly all its Arab lands to British-sponsored Arab states or to direct French and British rule.

A huge **reparations** burden and partial demilitarization were imposed on Germany. Wilson obtained approval for a League of Nations, but the U.S. Senate refused to allow the U.S. to join.

Russian revolution. Military defeats and high casualties caused a contagious lack of confidence in Tsar Nicholas, who was forced to abdicate, Mar. 1917. A liberal provisional government failed to end the war, and massive desertions, riots, and fighting between factions followed. A moderate socialist government under Kerensky was overthrown in a violent **coup by the Bolsheviks** in Petrograd under Lenin, who disbanded the elected Constituent Assembly, Nov. 1917.

The Bolsheviks brutally suppressed all opposition and ended the war with Germany, Mar. 1918. **Civil war** broke out in the summer between the Red Army, including the Bolsheviks and their supporters, and monarchists, anarchists, nationalities (Ukrainians, Georgians, Poles) and others. Small U.S., British, French and Japanese units also opposed the Bolsheviks, 1918-19 (Japan in Vladivostok to 1922). The civil war, anarchy, and pogroms devastated the country until the 1920 Red Army victory. The wartime total monopoly of political, economic, and police power by the Communist Party leadership was retained.

Other European revolutions. An unpopular monarchy in **Portugal** was overthrown in 1910. The new republic took severe anti-clerical measures, 1911.

After a century of Home Rule agitation, during which **Ireland** was devastated by famine (one million dead, 1846-47) and emigration, republican militants staged an unsuccessful uprising in Dublin, Easter 1916. The execution of the leaders and mass arrests by the British won popular support for the rebels. The Irish Free State, comprising all but the 6 northern counties, achieved dominion status in 1922.

In the aftermath of the world war, radical revolutions were attempted in Germany (**Spartacist** uprising Jan. 1919), **Hungary** (Kun regime 1919), and elsewhere. All were suppressed or failed for lack of support.

Chinese revolution. The Manchu Dynasty was overthrown and a republic proclaimed, Oct. 1911. First president Sun Yat-sen resigned in favor of strongman Yuan Shih-k'ai. Sun organized the parliamentarian **Kuomintang** party.

Students launched protests May 4, 1919 against League of Nations concessions in China to Japan. Nationalist, liberal, and socialist ideas and political groups spread. The **Communist Party** was founded 1921. A communist regime took power in Mongolia with Soviet support in 1921.

India restive. Indian objections to British rule erupted in nationalist riots as well as in the non-violent tactics of Gandhi (1869-1948). Nearly 400 unarmed demonstrators were shot at **Amritsar,** Apr. 1919. Britain approved limited self-rule that year.

Mexican revolution. Under the long Diaz dictatorship (1876-1911) the economy advanced, but Indian and mestizo lands were confiscated, and concessions to foreigners (mostly U.S.) damaged the middle class. A **revolution in 1910** led to civil wars and U.S. intervention (1914, 1916-17) Land reform and a more democratic constitution (1917) were achieved.

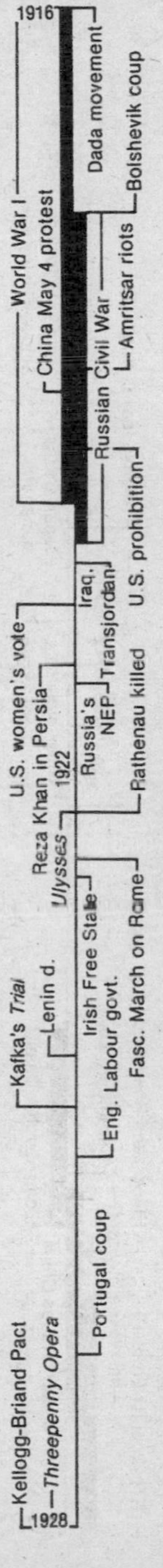

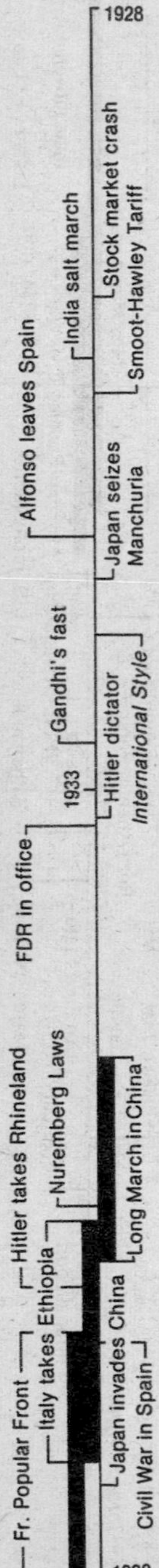

The Aftermath of War: 1920-29

U.S. Easy credit, technological ingenuity, and war-related industrial decline in Europe caused a long economic boom, in which ownership of the new products — autos, phones, radios — became democratized. Prosperity, an increase in women workers, women's suffrage (1920) and drastic change in fashion (flappers, mannish bob for women, clean-shaven men), created a wide perception of social change, despite prohibition of alcoholic beverages (1919-33). Union membership and strikes increased. Fear of radicals led to Palmer raids (1919-20) and Sacco/Vanzetti case (1921-27).

Europe sorts itself out. Germany's liberal **Weimar constitution** (1919) could not guarantee a stable government in the face of rightist violence (Rathenau assassinated 1922) and Communist refusal to cooperate with Socialists. Reparations and allied occupation of the Rhineland caused staggering inflation which destroyed middle class savings, but economic expansion resumed after mid-decade, aided by U.S. loans. A sophisticated, innovative culture developed in architecture and design (Bauhaus, 1919-28), film (Lang, *M*, 1931), painting (Grosz), music (Weill, *Threepenny Opera*, 1928), theater (Brecht, *A Man's a Man*, 1926), criticism (Benjamin), philosophy (Jung), and fashion. This culture was considered decadent and socially disruptive by rightists.

England elected its first labor governments (Jan. 1924, June 1929). A 10-day general strike in support of coal miners failed, May 1926. In **Italy**, strikes, political chaos and violence by small Fascist bands culminated in the Oct. 1922 Fascist March on Rome, which established Mussolini's dictatorship. Strikes were outlawed (1926), and Italian influence was pressed in the Balkans (Albania a protectorate 1926). A conservative dictatorship was also established in **Portugal** in a 1926 military coup.

Czechoslovakia, the only stable democracy to emerge from the war in Central or East Europe, faced opposition from Germans (in the Sudetenland), Ruthenians, and some Slovaks. As the industrial heartland of the old Hapsburg empire, it remained fairly prosperous. With French backing, it formed the Little Entente with Yugoslavia (1920) and **Romania** (1921) to block Austrian or Hungarian irredentism. **Hungary** remained dominated by the landholding classes and expansionist feeling. Croats and Slovenes in **Yugoslavia** demanded a federal state until King Alexander proclaimed a dictatorship (1929). Poland faced nationality problems as well (Germans, Ukrainians, Jews); Pilsudski ruled as dictator from 1926. The Baltic states were threatened by traditionally dominant ethnic Germans and by Soviet-supported communists.

An economic collapse and famine in **Russia**, 1921-22, claimed 5 million lives. The New Economic Policy (1921) allowed land ownership by peasants and some private commerce and industry. Stalin was absolute ruler within 4 years of Lenin's 1924 death. He inaugurated a brutal collectivization program 1929-32, and used foreign communist parties for Soviet state advantage.

Internationalism. Revulsion against World War I led to pacifist agitation, the Kellogg-Briand Pact renouncing aggressive war (1928), and **naval disarmament** pacts (Washington, 1922, London, 1930). But the League of Nations was able to arbitrate only minor disputes (Greece-Bulgaria, 1925).

Middle East. Mustafa Kemal (Ataturk) led **Turkish** nationalists in resisting Italian, French, and Greek military advances, 1919-23. The sultanate was abolished 1922, and elaborate reforms passed, including secularization of law and adoption of the Latin alphabet. Ethnic conflict led to persecution of **Armenians** (over 1 million dead in 1915, 1 million expelled), Greeks (forced Greek-Turk population exchange, 1923), and Kurds (1925 uprising).

With evacuation of the Turks from **Arab** lands, the puritanical Wahabi dynasty of eastern Arabia conquered present Saudi Arabia, 1919-25. British, French, and Arab dynastic and nationalist maneuvering resulted in the creation of two more Arab monarchies in 1921: Iraq and Transjordan (both under British control), and two French mandates: Syria and Lebanon. Jewish immigration into British-mandated **Palestine**, inspired by the Zionist movement, was resisted by Arabs, at times violently (1921, 1929 massacres).

Reza Khan ruled **Persia** after his 1921 coup (shah from 1925), centralized control, and created the trappings of a modern state.

China. The Kuomintang under **Chiang Kai-shek** (1887-1975) subdued the warlords by 1928. The Communists were brutally suppressed after their alliance with the Kuomintang was broken in 1927. Relative peace thereafter allowed for industrial and financial improvements, with some Russian, British, and U.S. cooperation.

Arts. Nearly all bounds of subject matter, style, and attitude were broken in the arts of the period. **Abstract** art first took inspiration from natural forms or narrative themes (Kandinsky from 1911), then worked free of any representational aims (Malevich's suprematism, 1915-19, Mondrian's geometric style from 1917). The **Dada** movement from 1916 mocked artistic pretension with absurd collages and constructions (Arp, Tzara, from 1916). Paradox, illusion, and psychological taboos were exploited by **surrealists** by the latter 1920s (Dali, Magritte). Architectural schools celebrated industrial values, whether vigorous abstract constructivism (Tatlin, *Monument to 3rd International*, 1919) or the machined, streamlined **Bauhaus** style, which was extended to many design fields (Helvetica type face).

Prose writers explored revolutionary narrative modes related to dreams (Kafka's *Trial*, 1925), internal monologue (Joyce's *Ulysses*, 1922), and word play (Stein's *Making of Americans*, 1925). Poets and novelists wrote of modern alienation (Eliot's *Waste Land*, 1922) and aimlessness (Lost Generation).

Sciences. Scientific specialization prevailed by the 20th century. Advances in knowledge and technological aptitude increased with the geometric increase in the number of practitioners. Physicists challenged common-sense views of causality, observation, and a mechanistic universe, putting science further beyond popular grasp (Einstein's general theory of relativity, 1915; Bohr's quantum mechanics, 1913; Heisenberg's uncertainty principle, 1927).

Rise of the Totalitarians: 1930-39

Depression. A worldwide financial panic and economic depression began with the Oct. 1929 U.S. stock market crash and the May 1931 failure of the Austrian Credit-Anstalt. A credit crunch caused international bankruptcies and **unemployment:** 12 million jobless by 1932 in the U.S., 5.6 million in Germany, 2.7 million in England. Governments responded with **tariff restrictions** (Smoot-Hawley Act 1930; Ottawa Imperial Conference, 1932) which dried up world trade. Government public works programs were vitiated by deflationary budget balancing.

Germany. Years of agitation by violent extremists was brought to a head by the Depression. Nazi leader **Hitler** was named chancellor by Pres. Hindenburg Jan. 1933, and given dictatorial power by the Reichstag in Mar. Opposition parties were disbanded, strikes banned, and all aspects of economic, cultural, and religious life brought under central government and Nazi party control and manipulated by sophisticated propaganda. Severe persecution of Jews began (**Nuremberg Laws** Sept. 1935). Many Jews, political opponents and others were sent to concentration camps (Dachau, 1933) where thousands died or were killed. Public works, renewed conscription (1935), arms production, and a 4-year plan (1936) ended unemployment.

Hitler's expansionism started with reincorporation of the Saar (1935), occupation of the **Rhineland** (Mar. 1936), and annexation of Austria (Mar. 1938). At **Munich,** Sept. 1938, an indecisive Britain and France sanctioned German dismemberment of Czechoslovakia.

Russia. Urbanization and education advanced. Rapid industrialization was achieved through successive **5-year-plans** starting 1928, using severe labor discipline and mass forced labor. Industry was financed by a decline in living standards and exploitation of agriculture, which was almost totally collectivized by the early 1930s (*kolkhoz,* collective farm; *sovkhoz,* state farm, often in newly-worked lands). Successive purges increased the role of professionals and management at the expense of workers. Millions perished in a series of man-made disasters: elimination of kulaks (peasant land-owners), 1929-34; severe famine, 1932-33; party purges (Great Purge, 1936-38); suppression of nationalities; and poor conditions in labor camps.

Spain. An industrial revolution during World War I created an urban proletariat, which was attracted to socialism and anarchism; Catalan nationalists challenged central authority. The 5 years after King Alfonso left Spain, Apr. 1931, were dominated by tension between intermittent leftist and anti-clerical governments and clericals, monarchists and other rightists. Anarchist and communist rebellions were crushed, but a July, 1936, extreme right rebellion led by Gen. Francisco Franco and aided by Nazi Germany and Fascist Italy succeeded, after a 3-year **civil war** (over 1 million dead in battles and atrocities). The war polarized international public opinion.

Italy. Despite propaganda for the ideal of the Corporate State, few domestic reforms were attempted. An entente with Hungary and Austria, Mar. 1934, a pact with Germany and Japan, Nov. 1937, and intervention by 50-75,000 troops in Spain, 1936-39, sealed Italy's identification with the fascist bloc (anti-Semitic laws after Mar. 1938). Ethiopia was conquered, 1935-37, and **Albania** annexed, Jan. 1939, in conscious imitation of ancient Rome.

East Europe. Repressive regimes fought for power against an active opposition (liberals, socialists, communists, peasants, Nazis). Minority groups and Jews were restricted within national boundaries that did not coincide with ethnic population patterns. In the destruction of **Czechoslovakia, Hungary** occupied southern Slovakia (Mar. 1938) and Ruthenia (Mar. 1939), and a pro-Nazi regime took power in the rest of Slovakia. Other boundary disputes (e.g. Poland-Lithuania, Yugoslavia-Bulgaria, Romania-Hungary) doomed attempts to build joint fronts against Germany or Russia. Economic depression was severe.

East Asia. After a period of liberalism in **Japan,** nativist militarists dominated the government with peasant support. Manchuria was seized, Sept. 1931-Feb. 1932, and a puppet state set up (Manchukuo). Adjacent Jehol (inner Mongolia) was occupied in 1933. China proper was invaded July 1937; large areas were conquered by Oct. 1938.

In **China** Communist forces left Kuomintang-besieged strongholds in the South in a Long March (1934-35) to the North. The Kuomintang-Communist civil war was suspended Jan. 1937 in the face of threatening Japan.

The democracies. The Roosevelt Administration, in office Mar. 1933, embarked on an extensive program of social reform and economic stimulation, including protection for labor unions (heavy industries organized), social security, public works, wages and hours laws, assistance to farmers. Isolationist sentiment (1937 Neutrality Act) prevented U.S. intervention in Europe, but military expenditures were increased in 1939.

French political instability and polarization prevented resolution of economic and international security questions. The **Popular Front** government under Blum (June 1936-Apr. 1938) passed social reforms (40-hour week) and raised arms spending. National coalition governments ruled Britain from Aug. 1931, brought some economic recovery, but failed to define a consistent foreign policy until Chamberlain's government (from May 1937), which practiced deliberate **appeasement** of Germany and Italy.

India. Twenty years of agitation for autonomy and then for independence (Gandhi's **salt march,** 1930) achieved some constitutional reform (extended provincial powers, 1935) despite Moslem-Hindu strife. Social issues assumed prominence with peasant uprisings (1921), strikes (1928), Gandhi's efforts for untouchables (1932 "fast unto death"), and social and agrarian reform by the provinces after 1937.

Arts. The streamlined, geometric design motifs of Art Deco (from 1925) prevailed through the 1930s. Abstract art flourished (Moore sculptures from 1931) alongside a new realism related to social and political concerns (**Socialist Realism** the official Soviet style from 1934; Mexican muralists Rivera, 1886-1957, and Orozco, 1883-1949), which was also expressed in fiction and poetry (Steinbeck's *Grapes of Wrath,* 1939; Sandburg's *The People, Yes,* 1936). Modern architecture (*International Style,* 1932) was unchallenged in its use of man-made materials (concrete, glass), lack of decoration, and monumentality (Rockefeller Center, 1929-40). U.S.-made films captured a world-wide audience with their larger-than-life fantasies (*Gone with the Wind,* 1939).

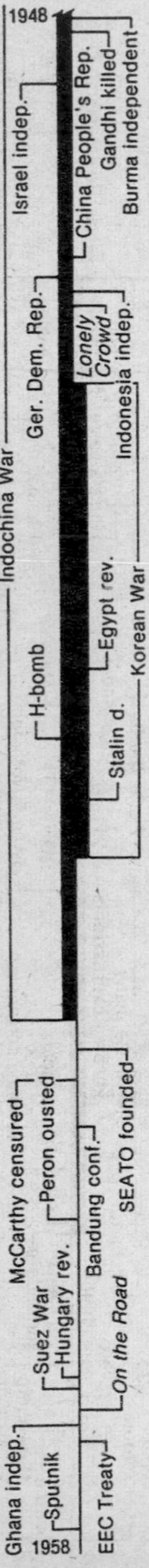

War, Hot and Cold: 1940-49

War in Europe. The Nazi-Soviet non-agression pact (Aug. '39) freed Germany to attack Poland (Sept.). Britain and France, who had guaranteed Polish independence, declared war on Germany. Russia seized East Poland (Sept.), attacked Finland (Nov.) and took the Baltic states (July '40). Mobile German forces staged **"blitzkrieg"** attacks Apr.-June, '40, conquering neutral Denmark, Norway, and the low countries and defeating France; 350,000 British and French troops were evacuated at **Dunkirk** (May). The Battle of Britain, June-Dec. '40, denied Germany air superiority, German-Italian campaigns won the Balkans by Apr. '41. Three million Axis troops **invaded Russia** June '41, marching through the Ukraine to the Caucasus, and through White Russia and the Baltic republics to Moscow and Leningrad.

Russian winter counterthrusts, '41-'42 and '42-'43 stopped the German advance (Stalingrad Sept. '42-Feb. '43). With British and U.S. Lend-Lease aid and sustaining great casualties, the Russians drove the Axis from all E. Europe and the Balkans in the next 2 years. Invasions of N. Africa (Nov. '42), Italy (Sept. '43), and Normandy (June '44) brought U.S., British, Free French and allied troops to Germany by spring '45. Germany surrendered May 7, 1945.

War in Asia-Pacific. Japan occupied Indochina Sept. '40, dominated Thailand Dec. '41, attacked Hawaii, the Philippines, Hong Kong, Malaya Dec. 7, 1941. Indonesia was attacked Jan. '42, Burma conquered Mar. 42. Battle of **Midway** (June '42) turned back the Japanese advance. "Island-hopping" battles (Guadalcanal Aug. '42-Jan. '43, **Leyte Gulf** Oct. '44, Iwo Jima Feb.-Mar. '45, Okinawa Apr. '45) and massive bombing raids on Japan from June '44 wore out Japanese defenses. Two U.S. atom bombs, dropped Aug. 6 and 9, forced Japan to surrender Aug. 14, 1945. *For further details, see 1978 and earlier editions of The World Almanac.*

Atrocities. The war brought 20th-century cruelty to its peak. Nazi murder camps (Auschwitz) systematically killed 6 million Jews. Gypsies, political opponents, sick and retarded people, and others deemed undesirable were murdered by the Nazis, as were vast numbers of Slavs, especially leaders.

Civilian deaths. German bombs killed 70,000 English civilians. Some 100,000 Chinese civilians were killed by Japanese forces in the capture of Nanking. Severe retaliation by the Soviet army, E. European partisans, Free French and others took a heavy toll. U.S. and British bombing of Germany killed hundreds of thousands, as did U.S. bombing of Japan (80-200,000 at Hiroshima alone). Some 45 million people lost their lives in the war.

Settlement. The United Nations charter was signed in San Francisco June 26, 1945 by 50 nations. The International Tribunal at Nuremberg convicted 22 German leaders for war crimes Sept. '46, 23 Japanese leaders were convicted Nov. '48. Postwar border changes included large gains in territory for the USSR, losses for Germany, a shift westward in Polish borders, and minor losses for Italy. Communist regimes, supported by Soviet troops, took power in most of E. Europe, including Soviet-occupied Germany (GDR proclaimed Oct. '49). Japan lost all overseas lands.

Recovery. Basic political and social changes were imposed on Japan and W. Germany by the western allies (Japan constitution Nov. '46, W. German basic law May '49). U.S. Marshall Plan aid ($12 billion '47-'51) spurred W. European economic recovery after a period of severe inflation and strikes in Europe and the U.S. The British Labour Party introduced a national health service and nationalized basic industries in 1946.

Cold War. Western fears of further Soviet advances (Cominform formed Oct. '47, Czechoslovakia coup, Feb. '48, Berlin blockade Apr.'48-Sept. '49) led to formation of NATO. Civil War in Greece and Soviet pressure on Turkey led to U.S. aid under the Truman Doctrine (Mar. '47). Other anti-communist security pacts were the Org. of American States (Apr. '48) and Southeast Asia Treaty Org. (Sept. '54). A new wave of Soviet purges and repression intensified in the last years of Stalin's rule, extending to E. Europe (Slansky trial in Czechoslovakia, 1951). Only Yugoslavia resisted Soviet control (expelled by Cominform, June '48; U.S. aid, June '49).

China, Korea. Communist forces emerged from World War II strengthened by the Soviet takeover of industrial Manchuria. In 4 years of fighting, the Kuomintang was driven from the mainland; the People's Republic was proclaimed Oct. 1, 1949. Korea was divided by Russian and U.S. occupation forces. Separate republics were proclaimed in the 2 zones Aug.-Sept. '48.

India. India and Pakistan became independent dominions Aug. 15, 1947. Millions of Hindu and Moslem refugees were created by the partition; riots, 1946-47, took hundreds of thousands of lives; Gandhi himself was assassinated Jan. '48. Burma became completely independent Jan. '48; Ceylon took dominion status in Feb.

Middle East. The UN approved partition of Palestine into Jewish and Arab states. Israel was proclaimed May 14, 1948. Arabs rejected partition, but failed to defeat Israel in war, May '48-July '49. Immigration from Europe and the Middle East swelled Israel's Jewish population. British and French forces left Lebanon and Syria, 1946. Transjordan occupied most of Arab Palestine.

Southeast Asia. Communists and others fought against restoration of French rule in Indochina from 1946; a non-communist government was recognized by France Mar. '49, but fighting continued. Both Indonesia and the Philippines became independent, the former in 1949 after 4 years of war with Netherlands, the latter in 1946. Philippine economic and military ties with the U.S. remained strong; a communist-led peasant rising was checked in '48.

Arts. New York became the center of the world art market; abstract expressionism was the chief mode (Pollock from '43, de Kooning from '47). Literature and philosophy explored existentialism (Camus' *Stranger*, 1942, Sartre's *Being and Nothingness*, 1943). Non-western attempts to revive or create regional styles (Senghor's Negritude, Mishima's novels) only confirmed the emergence of a universal culture. Radio and phonograph records spread American popular music (swing, bebop) around the world.

The American Decade: 1950-59

Polite decolonization. The peaceful decline of European political and military power in Asia and Africa accelerated in the 1950s. Nearly all of **N. Africa** was freed by 1956, but France fought a bitter war to retain Algeria, with its large European minority, until 1962. **Ghana**, independent 1957, led a parade of new black African nations (over 2 dozen by 1962) which altered the political character of the UN. Ethnic disputes often exploded in the new nations after decolonization (UN troops in Cyprus 1964; **Nigeria** civil war 1967-70). Leaders of the new states, mostly sharing socialist ideologies, tried to create an Afro-Asian bloc (Bandung Conf. 1955), but Western economic influence and U.S. political ties remained strong (Baghdad Pact, 1955).

Trade. World trade volume soared, in an atmosphere of monetary stability assured by international accords (**Bretton Woods** 1944). In Europe, economic integration advanced (**European Economic Community** 1957, European Free Trade Association 1960). Comecon (1949) coordinated the economies of Soviet-bloc countries.

U.S. Economic growth produced an abundance of consumer goods (9.3 million motor vehicles sold, 1955). Suburban housing tracts changed life patterns for middle and working classes (Levittown 1946-51). **Eisenhower's** landside election victories (1952, 1956) reflected consensus politics. Censure of McCarthy (Dec. '54) curbed the political abuse of anti-communism. A system of alliances and military bases bolstered U.S. influence on all continents. Trade and payments surpluses were balanced by overseas investments and foreign aid ($50 billion, 1950-59).

USSR. In the "thaw" after Stalin's death in 1953, relations with the West improved (evacuation of Vienna, Geneva summit conf., both 1955). Repression of scientific and cultural life eased, and many prisoners were freed or rehabilitated culminating in **de-Stalinization** (1956). Khrushchev's leadership aimed at consumer sector growth, but farm production lagged, despite the virgin lands program (from 1954). The 1956 Hungarian revolution, the 1960 U-2 spy plane episode, and other incidents renewed East-West tension and domestic curbs.

East Europe. Resentment of Russian domination and Stalinist repression combined with nationalist, economic and religious factors to produce periodic violence. East Berlin workers rioted in 1953, Polish workers rioted in Poznan, June 1956, and a broad-based revolution broke out in Hungary, Oct. 1956. All were suppressed by Soviet force or threats (at least 7,000 dead in Hungary). But Poland was allowed to restore private ownership of farms, and a degree of personal and economic freedom returned to Hungary. Yugoslavia experimented with worker self-management and a market economy.

Korea. The 1945 division of Korea left industry in the North, which was organized into a militant regime and armed by Russia. The South was politically disunited. Over 60,000 North Korean troops invaded the South June 25, 1950. The U.S., backed by the UN Security Council, sent troops. UN troops reached the Chinese border in Nov. Some 200,000 Chinese troops crossed the Yalu River and drove back UN forces. Cease-fire in July 1951 found the opposing forces near the original 38th parallel border. After 2 years of sporadic fighting, an armistice was signed July 27, 1953. U.S. troops remained in the South, and U.S. economic and military aid continued. The war stimulated rapid economic recovery in Japan. *For details, see 1978 and earlier editions of The World Almanac.*

China. Starting in 1952, industry, agriculture, and social institutions were forcibly collectivized. As many as several million people were executed as Kuomintang supporters or as class and political enemies. The Great Leap Forward, 1958-60, unsuccessfully tried to force the pace of development by substituting labor for investment.

Indochina. Ho's forces, aided by Russia and the new Chinese Communist government, fought French and pro-French Vietnamese forces to a standstill, and captured the strategic Dienbienphu camp in May, 1954. The Geneva Agreements divided Vietnam in half pending elections (never held), and recognized Laos and Cambodia as independent. The U.S. aided the anti-Communist Republic of Vietnam in the South.

Middle East. Arab revolutions placed leftist, militantly nationalist regimes in power in Egypt (1952) and Iraq (1958). But Arab unity attempts failed (United Arab Republic joined Egypt, Syria, Yemen 1958-61). Arab refusal to recognize Israel (Arab League economic blockade began Sept. 1951) led to a permanent state of war, with repeated incidents (Gaza, 1955). Israel occupied Sinai, Britain and France took the Suez Canal, Oct. 1956, but were replaced by the UN Emergency Force. The Mossadegh government in Iran nationalized the British-owned oil industry May 1951, but was overthrown in a U.S.-aided coup Aug. 1953.

Latin America. Dictator Juan Peron, in office 1946, enforced land reform, some nationalization, welfare state measures, and curbs on the Roman Catholic Church, but crushed opposition. A Sept. 1955 coup deposed Peron. The 1952 revolution in Bolivia brought land reform, nationalization of tin mines, and improvement in the status of Indians, who nevertheless remained poor. The Batista regime in Cuba was overthrown, Jan. 1959, by Fidel Castro, who imposed a communist dictatorship, aligned Cuba with Russia, improved education and health care. A U.S.-backed anti-Castro invasion (Bay of Pigs, Apr. 1961) was crushed. Self-government advanced in the British Caribbean.

Technology. Large outlays on research and development in the U.S. and USSR focussed on military applications (H-bomb in U.S. 1952, USSR 1953, Britain 1957, intercontinental missiles late 1950s). Soviet launching of the Sputnik satellite, Oct. 1957, spurred increases in U.S. science education funds (National Defense Education Act).

Literature and letters. Alienation from social and literary conventions reached an extreme in the theater of the absurd (Beckett's *Waiting for Godot* 1952), the "new novel" (Robbe-Grillet's *Voyeur* 1955), and avant-garde film (Antonioni's *L'Avventura* 1960). U.S. Beatniks (Kerouac's *On the Road* 1957) and others rejected the supposed conformism of Americans (Riesman's *Lonely Crowd* 1950).

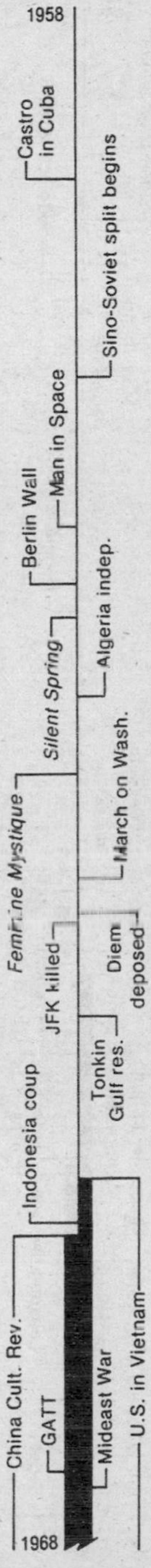

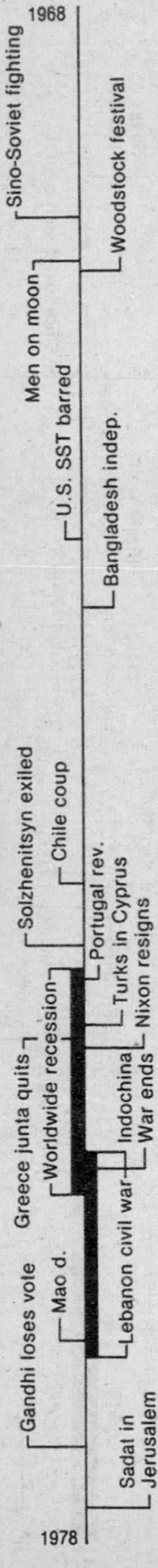

Rising Expectations: 1960-69

Economic boom. The longest sustained economic boom on record spanned almost the entire decade in the capitalist world; the closely-watched GNP figure doubled in the U.S. 1960-70, fueled by Vietnam War-related budget deficits. The **General Agreement on Tariffs and Trade,** 1967, stimulated West European prosperity, which spread to peripheral areas (Spain, Italy, E. Germany). Japan became a top economic power ($20 billion exports 1970). Foreign investment aided the industrialization of Brazil. Soviet 1965 economic reform attempts (decentralization, material incentives) were limited; but growth continued.

Reform and radicalization. A series of political and social reform movements took root in the U.S., later spreading to other countries with the help of ubiquitous U.S. film and television programs and heavy overseas travel (2.2 million U.S. passports issued 1970). Blacks agitated peaceably and with partial success against segregation and poverty (1963 March on Washington, 1964 **Civil Rights Act**); but some urban ghettos erupted in extensive riots (Watts, 1965; Detroit, 1967; King assassination, Apr. 4, 1968). New concern for the poor (Harrington's *Other America,* 1963) led to Pres. Johnson's **"Great Society"** programs (Medicare, Water Quality Act, Higher Education Act, all 1965). Concern with the **environment** surged (Carson's *Silent Spring,* 1962). **Feminism** revived as a cultural and political movement (Friedan's *Feminine Mystique,* 1963, National Organization for Women founded 1966) and a movement for homosexual rights emerged (Stonewall riot, in NYC, 1969).

Opposition to U.S. involvement in Vietnam, especially among university students (**Moratorium** protest Nov. '69) turned violent (Weatherman Chicago riots Oct. '69). New Left and Marxist theories became popular, and membership in radical groups swelled (Students for a Democratic Society, Black Panthers). Maoist groups, especially in Europe, called for total transformation of society. In France, students sparked a nationwide strike affecting 10 million workers May-June '68, but an electoral reaction barred revolutionary change.

Arts and styles. The boundary between fine and popular arts were blurred by Pop Art (Warhol) and rock musicals (Hair, 1968). Informality and exaggeration prevailed in fashion (beards, miniskirts). A non-political "counterculture" developed, rejecting traditional bourgeois life goals and personal habits, and use of marijuana and hallucinogens spread (Woodstock festival Aug. '69). Indian influence was felt in music (Beatles), religion (Ram Dass), and fashion.

Science. Achievements in space (men on moon July '69) and electronics (lasers, integrated circuits) encouraged a faith in scientific solutions to problems in agriculture ("green revolution"), medicine (heart transplants 1967) and other areas. The harmful effects of science, it was believed, could be controlled (1963 nuclear weapon test ban treaty, 1968 non-proliferation treaty).

China. Mao's revolutionary militance caused disputes with Russia under "revisionist" Khrushchev, starting 1960. The two powers exchanged fire in 1969 border disputes. China used force to capture areas disputed with India, 1962. The "Great Proletarian Cultural Revolution" tried to impose a utopian egalitarian program in China and spread revolution abroad; political struggle, often violent, convulsed China 1965-68.

Indochina. Communist-led guerrillas aided by N. Vietnam fought from 1960 against the S. Vietnam government of Ngo Dinh Diem (killed 1963). The U.S. military role increased after the 1964 Tonkin Gulf incident. U.S. forces peaked at 543,400, Apr. '69. Massive numbers of N. Viet troops also fought. Laotian and Cambodian neutrality were threatened by communist insurgencies, with N. Vietnamese aid, and U.S. intrigues. *For details, see 1978 and earlier editions of The World Almanac.*

Third World. A bloc of authoritarian leftist regimes among the newly independent nations emerged in political opposition to the U.S.-led Western alliance, and came to dominate the conference of nonaligned nations (Belgrade 1961, Cairo 1964, Lusaka 1970). Soviet political ties and military bases were established in Cuba, Egypt, Algeria, Guinea, and other countries, whose leaders were regarded as revolutionary heros by opposition groups in pro-Western or colonial countries. Some leaders were ousted in coups by pro-Western groups—Zaire's Lumumba (killed 1961), Ghana's Nkrumah (exiled 1966), and Indonesia's Sukarno (effectively ousted 1965 after a Communist coup failed).

Middle East. Arab-Israeli tension erupted into a brief war June 1967. Israel emerged as a major regional power. Military shipments before and after the war brought much of the Arab world into the Soviet political sphere. Most Arab states broke U.S. diplomatic ties, while Communist countries cut their ties to Israel. Intra-Arab disputes continued: Egypt and Saudi Arabia supported rival factions in a bloody Yemen civil war 1962-70; Lebanese troops fought Palestinian commandos in 1969.

East Europe. To stop the large-scale exodus of citizens, E. German authorities built a fortified wall across Berlin Aug. '61. Soviet sway in the Balkans was weakened by Albania's support of China (USSR broke ties Dec. '61) and Romania's assertion of industrial and foreign policy autonomy in 1964. Liberalization in Czechoslovakia, spring 1968, was crushed by troops of 5 Warsaw Pact countries. West German treaties with Russia and Poland, 1970, facilitated the transfer of German technology and confirmed post-war boundaries.

Disillusionment: 1970-79

U.S.: Caution and neoconservatism. A relatively sluggish economy, energy and resource shortages (natural gas crunch 1975, gasoline shortage 1979), and environmental problems contributed to a **"limits of growth"** philosophy that affected politics (Cal. Gov. Brown). Suspicion of science and technology killed or delayed major projects (supersonic transport dropped 1971, DNA recombination curbed 1976, Seabrook A-plant protests 1977-78) and was fed by the Three Mile Island nuclear reactor accident in Mar. '79.

Mistrust of big government weakened support for government reform plans among liberals. School busing and racial quotas were opposed (**Bakke decision** June '78); the Equal Rights Amendment for women languished; civil rights for homosexuals were opposed (Dade County referendum June '77).

U.S. defeat in **Indochina** (evacuation Apr. '75), revelations of Central Intelligence Agency misdeeds (Rockefeller Commission report June '75), and the **Watergate** scandals (Nixon quit Aug. '74) reduced faith in U.S. moral and material capacity to influence world affairs. Revelations of Soviet crimes (Solzhenitsyn's *Gulag Archipelago* from 1974) and Russian intervention in Africa aided a revival of anti-Communist sentiment.

Economy sluggish. The 1960s boom faltered in the 1970s; a severe recession in the U.S. and Europe 1974-75 followed a huge oil price hike Dec. '73. Monetary instability (U.S. cut ties to gold Aug. '71), the decline of the dollar, and **protectionist** moves by industrial countries (1977-78) threatened trade. Business investment and spending for research declined. Severe inflation plagued many countries (25% in Britain, 1975; 18% in U.S., 1979).

China picks up pieces. After the 1976 deaths of Mao and Chou, a power struggle for the leadership succession was won by pragmatists. A nationwide purge of orthodox Maoists was carried out, and the "**Gang of Four**", led by Mao's widow Chiang Ching, was arrested.

The new leaders freed over 100,000 political prisoners, and reduced public adulation of Mao. Political and trade ties were expanded with Japan, Europe, and the U.S. in the late 1970's, as relations worsened with Russia, Cuba, and Vietnam (4-week invasion by China in 1979). Ideological guidelines in industry, science, education, and the armed forces, which the ruling faction said had caused chaos and decline, were reversed (bonuses to workers, Dec. '77; exams for college entrance, Oct. '77). Severe restrictions on cultural expression were eased (Beethoven ban lifted Mar. '77).

Europe. European unity moves (EEC-EFTA trade accord 1972) faltered as economic problems appeared (Britain floated pound 1972; France floated franc 1974). Germany and Switzerland curbed guest workers from S. Europe. Greece and Turkey quarreled over Cyprus (Turks intervened 1974) and Aegean oil rights.

All of non-Communist Europe was under democratic rule after free elections were held in **Spain** June '76, 7 months after the death of Franco. The conservative, colonialist regime in **Portugal** was overthrown Apr. '74. In **Greece,** the 7-year-old military dictatorship yielded power in 1974. Northern Europe, though ruled mostly by Socialists (**Swedish** Socialists unseated 1976, after 44 years in power), turned conservative. The **British** Labour government imposed wage curbs 1975, and suspended nationalization schemes. Terrorism in **Germany** (1972 Munich Olympics killings) led to laws curbing some civil liberties. **French** "new philosophers" rejected leftist ideologies, and the shaky Socialist-Communist coalition lost a 1978 election bid.

Religion back in politics. The improvement in Moslem countries' political fortunes by the 1950s (with the exception of Central Asia under Soviet and Chinese rule), and the growth of Arab oil wealth, was followed by a resurgence of traditional piety. **Libyan** dictator Qaddafi mixed strict Islamic laws with socialism in his militant ideology and called for an eventual Moslem return to Spain and Sicily. The illegal Moslem Brotherhood in **Egypt** was accused of violence, while extreme Moslem groups bombed theaters, 1977, to protest secular values.

In **Turkey,** the National Salvation Party was the first Islamic group to share power (1974) since secularization in the 1920s. Religious authorities, such as Ayatollah Ruholla Khomeini, led the **Iranian** revolution and religiously motivated Moslems took part in the insurrection in Saudi Arabia that briefly seized the Grand Mosque in Mecca in 1979. Moslem puritan opposition to **Pakistan Pres.** Bhutto helped lead to his overthrow July '77. However, Moslem solidarity could not prevent Pakistan's eastern province (**Bangladesh**) from declaring independence, Dec. '71, after a bloody civil war.

Moslem and Hindu resentment against coerced sterilization in **India** helped defeat the Gandhi government, which was replaced Mar. '77 by a coalition including religious Hindu parties and led by devout Hindu Desai. Moslems in the southern **Philippines,** aided by Libya, conducted a long rebellion against central rule from 1973.

Evangelical Protestant groups grew in numbers and prosperity in the U.S. ("**born again**" Pres. Carter elected 1976), and the Catholic charismatic movement obtained respectability. A revival of interest in Orthodox Christianity occurred among **Russian** intellectuals (Solzhenitsyn). The secularist **Israeli** Labor party, after decades of rule, was ousted in 1977 by conservatives led by Begin, an observant Jew; religious militants founded settlements on the disputed West Bank, part of Biblically-promised Israel. U.S. Reform Judaism revived many previously discarded traditional practices.

The Buddhist Soka Gakkai movement launched the Komeito party in Japan, 1964, which became a major opposition party in 1972 and 1976 elections.

Old-fashioned religious wars raged intermittently in **N. Ireland** (Catholic vs. Protestant, 1969-   ) and **Lebanon** (Christian vs. Moslem, 1975-   ), while religious militancy complicated the Israel-Arab dispute (1973 Israel-Arab war. In spite of a **1979 peace treaty between Egypt and Israel** which looked forward to a resolution of the Palestinian issue, increased religious militancy on the West Bank made such a resolution seem unlikely.

Latin America. Repressive conservative regimes strengthened their hold on most of the continent, with the violent coup against the elected Allende government in **Chile,** Sept. '73, the 1976 military coup in **Argentina,** and coups against reformist regimes in **Bolivia,** 1971 and 1979, and **Peru,** 1976. In Central America, increasing liberal and leftist militancy led to the ouster of the Somoza regime of Nicaragua in 1979 and civil conflict in El Salvador.

Indochina. Communist victory in Vietnam, Cambodia, and Laos by May '75 did not bring peace. Attempts at radical social reorganization left over one million dead in Cambodia during 1975-78 and caused hundreds of thousands of ethnic Chinese and others to flee Vietnam ("boat people," 1979). The Vietnamese invasion of Cambodia swelled the refugee population and contributed to widespread starvation in that devastated country.

Russian expansion. Soviet influence, checked in some countries (troops ousted by Egypt 1972) was projected further afield, often with the use of Cuban troops (Angola 1975-   , Ethiopia 1977-   ), and aided by a growing navy, merchant fleet, and international banking ability. Detente with the West — 1972 Berlin pact, 1972 strategic arms pact (**SALT**) — gave way to a more antagonistic relationship in the late 1970s, exacerbated by the Soviet invasion of Afghanistan in 1979.

Africa. The last remaining European colonies were granted independence (**Spanish Sahara** 1976, **Djibouti** 1977) and, after 10 years of civil war and many negotiation sessions, a black government took over Zimbabwe (Rhodesia) in 1979; white domination remained in **S. Africa.** Great power involvement in local wars (Russia in **Angola, Ethiopia;** France in **Chad, Zaire, Mauritania**) and the use of tens of thousands of Cuban troops was denounced by some African leaders as neocolonialism. Ethnic or tribal clashes made Africa the chief world locus of sustained warfare in the late 1970s.

Arts. Traditional modes in painting, architecture, and music, pursued in relative obscurity for much of the 20th century, returned to popular and critical attention in the 1970s. The pictorial emphasis in neorealist and photorealist painting, the return of many architects to detail, decoration, and traditional natural materials, and the concern with ordered structure in musical composition were, ironically, novel experiences for artistic consumers after the exhaustion of experimental possibilities. However, these more conservative styles coexisted with modernist works in an atmosphere of variety and tolerance.

1980-1985

Rise of terrorism. Following the overthrow of the Shah, Iranian militants, with the support of Ayatollah Kohmeini, held 52 Americans hostage in Iran for 444 days, 1980-81; a TNT-laden suicide terrorist blew up Marine headquarters in Beirut, killing 241 Americans, while a truck bomb blew up a French paratroop barracks, killing 58, 1983; 1985 saw almost 700 terrorist attacks worldwide, including attacks in London, Paris, Rome, Vienna.

Assassinations included Egypt's Pres. Anwar el-Sadat by Moslem extremists (1981); India's Prime Minister Indira Gandhi by Sikh extremists (1984).

Anti-nuclear movement. Western Europe saw widespread anti-nuclear protests from the early 1980s. The U.S. nuclear freeze movement began in 1981; more than 500,000 people demonstrated in New York's Central Park (1982).

U.S.: Economic recession, recovery. Double-digit inflation, high unemployment, and a severe drop in industrial output strongly influenced Pres. Jimmy Carter's defeat and the election of former Calif. Gov. Ronald Reagan as U.S. President, 1980. With Reagan's supply-side economic program, interest rates and inflation decreased by 1983. The recovery was largely responsible for Reagan's landslide re-election, 1984, but that year the **deficit** was over $200 billion, and U.S. debt had doubled under Reagan to $2 trillion.

Technological advances, problems. From 1982-1985, 5 people were implanted with artificial hearts. Only 2 did not suffer strokes and other setbacks and these 2 died.

U.S.S.R. 1980-85 were troublesome years, with 3 consecutive heads of state dying in office (Brezhnev,'82; Andropov, '84; Chernenko,'85); a sluggish domestic economy, dissent dealt with harshly (Nobel Peace Prize winner Sakharov's exile to Gorky, 1980); emigration restricted for Jews, others. With the invasion of Afghanistan (Dec.'79), U.S. Pres. Carter embargoed grain sales, led a boycott of Moscow Olympics (1980); Pres. Reagan lifted the embargo (1981), but **mutual mistrust** and **recrimination** continued, climaxing with 1983 Soviet shooting down of an unarmed South Korean commercial airliner, killing 260, and U.S.-led worldwide condemnation. Soviets led most Eastern European nations in a boycott of Los Angeles Olympics (1984). In 1985, the economy improved slightly; Chernenko's successor, Mikhail Gorbachev, met with Pres. Reagan.

Poland. 17,000 Polish workers, embittered by food shortages, insufficient housing and public transport, went on strike (Aug.'80); they were joined by 120,000 other workers, and won the right to strike, to form independent trade unions, the release of political prisoners, and the end of government censorship. The unions formed a national body headed by Lech Walesa and by 1981, 1 million of 2.9 million Polish Communist Party members joined the 9.5-million-member **Solidarity.** But the union's call (Dec.'81) for a referendum on establishing a non-Communist government brought martial law, detention of Walesa; the U.S. imposed economic sanctions. In 1982, Parliament dissolved the unions, Walesa was released as a "private person, " martial law was ended. Walesa was awarded the Nobel Peace Prize. (Oct.'83).

The Middle East. This area remained the most militarily unstable in the world, with sharp divisions on economic, political, racial, and religious issues. In **Iran,** the revolution (1979-80) and violent political upheavals afterward, brought virtual civil war. A dispute with Iraq over the Shatt al-Arab waterway became open warfare, Sept.'80, with no end in sight in 1985.

Libya's support for international terrorism caused the U.S. to close their diplomatic mission in Washington (May '81). American jets shot down 2 Libyan warplanes off Libya after being fired on (Aug.'81). Pres. Reagan embargoed Libyan oil (Mar.'82). The U.S. accused **Muammar al-Qaddafi** of aiding terrorists in Dec.'85 Rome and Vienna airport attacks.

Israel affirmed all of Jerusalem as its capital (July'80); destroyed an Iraqi atomic reactor (1981); invaded Lebanon (1982), bringing the PLO to agree to withdraw peacefully. Christian militia killed more than 600 Palestinians at refugee camps in West Beirut (1982). Israeli withdrawal from **Lebanon** began in Feb.'85 and ended in June'85, as Lebanon continued to be torn with military and political conflict between rival factions.

Central America. In **Nicaragua,** the leftist Sandinista National Liberation Front, in power after the 1979 civil war, faced increasing problems because of Nicaragua's military aid to leftist guerrillas in El Salvador and the U.S. backing of antigovernment forces, or **"contras,"** based in Honduras and Costa Rica. The U.S. CIA admitted to directing the mining of Nicaraguan ports (1984). In 1985, the House rejected Pres. Reagan's request for military aid to the contras, but okayed $26 million in humanitarian aid. In **El Salvador,** a military coup (Oct.'79) failed to halt extreme right-wing violence and left-wing activity. Archbishop Oscar Romero was assassinated (Mar.'80), allegedly by rightists, and from Jan. to June, 1980 some 4,000 civilians reportedly were killed. U.S. support for the government was based on a declared commitment to land reform and human rights. From 1981, right-wing activity was increasingly directed not just against the left but against the junta, which received increasing U.S. military and economic aid. In 1984, the newly elected Pres. José Napoleón Duarte issued more humane codes of conduct to the Army, investigated alleged human rights abuses, and disbanded the military police's intelligence unit; the U.S. then approved $126 million in military aid.

Africa. 1980-85 marked the rapid decline of the economies of virtually all of Africa's 61 countries, due to accelerating desertification, the world economic recession, heavy indebtedness to overseas creditors, rapid population growth, and political instability. In 1981, 60 million Africans, almost one-fifth of the population, faced prolonged hunger. In 1983, a large part of the continent experienced one of the worst **droughts** ever, and by year's end, 150 million faced near-**famine;** 2 of 5 Africans in 24 countries were affected. In Nov.'85, the U.S. and many Western nations rushed assistance. Economic hardship fueled political unrest, influencing many political coups and attempted coups.

South Africa. Anti-apartheid sentiment gathered force. In 1981, the U.N. General Assembly voted against allowing South Africa to reoccupy the seat it was denied in 1974. In South Africa, anti-apartheid demonstrations grew, as did a violent response from the police. From 1983, **anti-apartheid protests** increased in the U.S. and Europe. South African white voters approved a constitution (Nov.'83) that for the first time gave "Coloureds" and Asians a limited voice, while still excluding Blacks—70% of the population. Bishop Desmond Tutu, a South African black, was awarded the Nobel Peace Price (Oct.'84). The South African government declared a state of emergency in July'85; Pres. Reagan imposed economic sanctions, Aug.'85; in Sept., 11 Western European nations imposed sanctions.

China. From 1980-85 the new leadership of the Chinese Communist Party, under Chairman Deng Xiaoping, pursued **far-reaching changes** in political and economic institutions and expanded China's commercial and technical ties to the industrialized world. A major effort was made to increase the role of market forces in stimulating urban economic development.

Japan. Relations with the U.S., Western Europe, and the Assn. of Southeast Asian Nations, 1980-85, were dominated by **trade imbalances** favoring Japan. Japanese automakers heeded U.S. criticism, agreeing to voluntary restraints (1984), but postponed negotiations over tariff reduction on imports. In 1984, Japan had achieved a record annual trade surplus, with U.S. exports of $60 billion. Pres. Reagan pressed for increased imports, and Japan reduced tariffs on 1,790 items.

In history's worst industrial accident, methyl isocyanate, a deadly gas, leaked from a Union Carbide plant at Bhopal, **India** (Dec.'84), killing more than 2,500.

Britain. In 1980, the British economy had its worst **recession** since the 1930s. A 13-week strike in the nationalized steel industry ended with a 15.5% wage rise. Prime Minister Margaret Thatcher trusted the British economy to the discipline of market forces, while unemployment continued to rise and black and white inner-city youths rioted (1981). The Natl. Union of Mineworkers year-long strike (1984-85) ended with the Natl. Coal Board's plan to close 20 "uneconomic" pits.

France elected its first socialist president, Francois Mitterand, in May '81; in Sept.'81 the government nationalized 5 major industries and most private banks. **Italy** elected its first socialist premier, Bettino Craxi, in June '83. **Greece** was reintegrated into the military wing of NATO in Oct.'80, and became the 10th full member of the European Community in Jan.'81.

HISTORICAL FIGURES

Ancient Greeks and Latins

Greeks

Aeschines, orator, 389-314BC.
Aeschylus, dramatist, 525-456BC.
Aesop, fableist, c620-c560BC.
Alcibiades, politician, 450-404BC.
Anacreon, poet, c582-c485BC.
Anaxagoras, philosopher, c500-428BC.
Anaximander, philosopher, 611-546BC.
Antiphon, speechwriter, c480-411BC.
Apollonius, mathematician, c265-170BC.
Archimedes, math. c287-212BC.
Aristophanes, dramatist, c448-380BC.
Aristotle, philosopher, 384-322BC.
Athenaeus, scholar, fl.c200.
Callicrates, architect, fl.5th cent.BC.
Callimachus, poet, c305-240BC.
Cratinus, comic dramatist, 520-421BC.
Democritus, philosopher, c460-370BC.
Demosthenes, orator, 384-322BC.
Diodorus, historian, fl.20BC.
Diogenes, philosopher, c372-c287BC.
Dionysius, historian, d.c7BC.
Empedocles, philosopher, c490-430BC.
Epicharmus, dramatist, c530-440BC.
Epictetus, philosopher, c55-c135.
Epicurus, philosopher, 341-270BC.
Eratosthenes, scientist, c276-194BC.
Euclid, mathematician, fl.c300BC.
Euripides, dramatist, c484-406BC.
Galen, physician, c129-199.
Heraclitus, philosopher, c535-c475BC.
Herodotus, historian, c484-420BC.
Hesiod, poet, 8th cent. BC.
Hippocrates, physician, c460-377BC.
Homer, poet, believed lived c850BC.
Isocrates, orator, 436-338BC.
Menander, dramatist, 342-292BC.
Phidias, sculptor, c500-435BC.
Pindar, poet, c518-c438BC.
Plato, philosopher, c428-c347BC.
Plutarch, biographer, c46-120.
Polybius, historian, c200-c118BC.
Praxiteles, sculptor, 400-330BC.
Pythagoras, phil., math., c580-c500BC.
Sappho, poet, c610-c580BC.
Simonides, poet, 556-c468BC.
Socrates, philosopher, c470-399BC.
Solon, statesman, 640-560BC.
Sophocles, dramatist, C496-406BC.
Strabo, geographer, c63BC-AD24.
Thales, philosopher, c634-c546BC.
Themistocles, politician, c524-c460BC.
Theocritus, poet, c310-250BC.
Theophrastus, phil. c372-c287BC.
Thucydides, historian, fl.5th cent.BC.
Timon, philosopher, c320-c230BC.
Xenophon, historian, c434-c355BC.
Zeno, philosopher, c495-c430BC.

Latins

Ammianus, historian, c330-395.
Apuleius, satirist, c124-c170.
Boethius, scholar, c480-524
Caesar, Julius, general, 100-44BC.
Catilina, politician, c108-62BC.
Carus, poet, c98-55BC.
Cato(Elder), statesman, 234-149BC.
Catullus, poet, c84-54BC.
Cicero, orator, 106-43BC.
Claudian, poet, c370-c404.
Ennius, poet, 239-170BC.
Gellius, author, c130-c165.
Horace, poet, 65-8BC.
Juvenal, satirist, c60-c127.
Livy, historian, 59BC-AD17.
Lucan, poet, 39-65.
Lucilius, poet, c180-c102BC.
Lucretius, poet, c99-c55BC.
Martial, epigrammatist, c38-c103.
Nepos, historian, c100-c25BC.
Ovid,poet, 43BC-AD17.
Persius, satirist, 34-62.
Plautus, dramatist, c254-c184BC
Pliny, scholar, 23-79.
Pliny(Younger), author, 62-113.
Quintilian, rhetorician, c35-c97.
Sallust, historian, 86-34BC.
Seneca, philosopher, 4BC-AD65.
Silius, poet, c25-101.
Statius, poet, c45-c96.
Suetonius, biographer, c69-c122.
Tacitus, historian, c56-c120.
Terence, dramatist, 185-c159BC.
Tibullus, poet, c55-c19BC.
Virgil, poet, 70-19BC.
Vitruvius, architect, fl.1st cent.BC.

Rulers of England and Great Britain

Name	England	Began	Died	Age	Rgd
	Saxons and Danes				
Egbert	King of Wessex, won allegiance of all English	829	839	—	10
Ethelwulf	Son, King of Wessex, Sussex, Kent, Essex	839	858	—	19
Ethelbald	Son of Ethelwulf, displaced father in Wessex	858	860	—	2
Ethelbert	2d son of Ethelwulf, united Kent and Wessex	860	866	—	6
Ethelred I	3d son, King of Wessex, fought Danes	866	871	—	5
Alfred	The Great, 4th son, defeated Danes, fortified London	871	899	52	28
Edward	The Elder, Alfred's son, united English, claimed Scotland	899	924	55	25
Athelstan	The Glorious, Edward's son, King of Mercia, Wessex	924	940	45	16
Edmund I	3d son of Edward, King of Wessex, Mercia	940	946	25	6
Edred	4th son of Edward	946	955	32	9
Edwy	The Fair, eldest son of Edmund, King of Wessex	955	959	18	3
Edgar	The Peaceful, 2d son of Edmund, ruled all English	959	975	32	17
Edward	The Martyr, eldest son of Edgar, murdered by stepmother	975	978	17	4
Ethelred II	The Unready, 2d son of Edgar, married Emma of Normandy	978	1016	48	37
Edmund II	Ironside, son of Ethelred II, King of London	1016	1016	27	0
Canute	The Dane, gave Wessex to Edmund, married Emma	1016	1035	40	19
Harold I	Harefoot, natural son of Canute	1035	1040	—	5
Hardecanute	Son of Canute by Emma, Danish King	1040	1042	24	2
Edward	The Confessor, son of Ethelred II (Canonized 1161)	1042	1066	62	24
Harold II	Edward's brother-in-law, last Saxon King	1066	1066	44	0
	House of Normandy				
William I	The Conqueror, defeated Harold at Hastings	1066	1087	60	21
William II	Rufus, 3d son of William I, killed by arrow	1087	1100	43	13
Henry I	Beauclerc, youngest son of William I	1100	1135	67	35
	House of Blois				
Stephen	Son of Adela, daughter of William I, and Count of Blois	1135	1154	50	19
	House of Plantagenet				
Henry II	Son of Geoffrey Plantagenet (Angevin) by Matilda, dau. of Henry I	1154	1189	56	35
Richard I	Coeur de Lion, son of Henry II, crusader	1189	1199	42	10
John	Lackland, son of Henry II, signed Magna Carta, 1215	1199	1216	50	17
Henry III	Son of John, acceded at 9, under regency until 1227	1216	1272	65	56
Edward I	Longshanks, son of Henry III	1272	1307	68	35
Edward II	Son of Edward I, deposed by Parliament, 1327	1307	1327	43	20
Edward III	Of Windsor, son of Edward II	1327	1377	65	50
Richard II	Grandson of Edw. III, minor until 1389, deposed 1399	1377	1400	33	22
	House of Lancaster				
Henry IV	Son of John of Gaunt, Duke of Lancaster, son of Edw. III	1399	1413	47	13
Henry V	Son of Henry IV, victor of Agincourt	1413	1422	34	9
Henry VI	Son of Henry V, deposed 1461, died in Tower	1422	1471	49	39

Name		Began	Died	Age	Rgd
	House of York				
Edward IV	Great-great-grandson of Edward III, son of Duke of York	1461	1483	41	22
Edward V	Son of Edward IV, murdered in Tower of London	1483	1483	13	0
Richard III	Crookback, bro. of Edward IV, fell at Bosworth Field	1483	1485	35	2
	House of Tudor				
Henry VII	Son of Edmund Tudor, Earl of Richmond, whose father had married the widow of Henry V; descended from Edward III through his mother, Margaret Beaufort via John of Gaunt. By marriage with dau. of Edward IV he united Lancaster and York	1485	1509	53	24
Henry VIII	Son of Henry VII by Elizabeth, dau. of Edward IV.	1509	1547	56	38
Edward VI	Son of Henry VIII, by Jane Seymour, his 3d queen. Ruled under regents. Was forced to name Lady Jane Grey his successor. Council of State proclaimed her queen July 10, 1553. Mary Tudor won Council, was proclaimed queen July 19, 1553. Mary had Lady Jane Grey beheaded for treason, Feb., 1554	1547	1553	16	6
Mary I	Daughter of Henry VIII, by Catherine of Aragon	1553	1558	43	5
Elizabeth I	Daughter of Henry VIII, by Anne Boleyn	1558	1603	69	44
	Great Britain				
	House of Stuart				
James I	James VI of Scotland, son of Mary, Queen of Scots. *First to call himself King of Great Britain. This became official with the Act of Union, 1707*	1603	1625	59	22
Charles I	Only surviving son of James I; beheaded Jan. 30, 1649	1625	1649	48	24
	Commonwealth, 1649-1660				
	Council of State, 1649; Protectorate, 1653				
The Cromwells	Oliver Cromwell, Lord Protector	1653	1658	59	—
	Richard Cromwell, son, Lord Protector, resigned May 25, 1659	1658	1712	86	—
	House of Stuart (Restored)				
Charles II	Eldest son of Charles I, died without issue	1660	1685	55	25
James II	2d son of Charles I. Deposed 1688. Interregnum Dec. 11, 1688, to Feb. 13, 1689	1685	1701	68	3
William III	Son of William, Prince of Orange, by Mary, dau. of Charles I	1689	1702	51	13
and Mary II	Eldest daughter of James II and wife of William III		1694	33	6
Anne	2d daughter of James II	1702	1714	49	12
	House of Hanover				
George I	Son of Elector of Hanover, by Sophia, grand-dau. of James I	1714	1727	67	13
George II	Only son of George I, married Caroline of Brandenburg	1727	1760	77	33
George III	Grandson of George II, married Charlotte of Mecklenburg	1760	1820	81	59
George IV	Eldest son of George III, Prince Regent, from Feb., 1811	1820	1830	67	10
William IV	3d son of George III, married Adelaide of Saxe-Meiningen	1830	1837	71	7
Victoria	Dau. of Edward, 4th son of George III; married (1840) Prince Albert of Saxe-Coburg and Gotha, who became Prince Consort	1837	1901	81	63
	House of Saxe-Coburg and Gotha				
Edward VII	Eldest son of Victoria, married Alexandra, Princess of Denmark	1901	1910	68	9
	House of Windsor				
	Name Adopted July 17, 1917				
George V	2d son of Edward VII, married Princess Mary of Teck	1910	1936	70	25
Edward VIII	Eldest son of George V; acceded Jan. 20, 1936, abdicated Dec. 11	1936	1972	77	1
George VI	2d son of George V; married Lady Elizabeth Bowes-Lyon	1936	1952	56	15
Elizabeth II	Elder daughter of George VI, acceded Feb. 6, 1952	1952	—	—	—

Rulers of Scotland

Kenneth I MacAlpin was the first Scot to rule both Scots and Picts, 846 AD.

Duncan I was the first general ruler, 1034. Macbeth seized the kingdom 1040, was slain by Duncan's son, Malcolm III MacDuncan (Canmore), 1057.

Malcolm married Margaret, Saxon princess who had fled from the Normans. Queen Margaret introduced English language and English monastic customs. She was canonized, 1250. Her son Edgar, 1097, moved the court to Edinburgh. His brothers Alexander I and David I succeeded. Malcolm IV, the Maiden, 1153, grandson of David I, was followed by his brother, William the Lion, 1165, whose son was Alexander II, 1214. The latter's son, Alexander III, 1249, defeated the Norse and regained the Hebrides. When he died, 1286, his granddaughter, Margaret, child of Eric of Norway and grandniece of Edward I of England, known as the Maid of Norway, was chosen ruler, but died 1290, aged 8.

John Baliol, 1292-1296. (Interregnum, 10 years).

Robert Bruce (The Bruce), 1306-1329, victor at Bannockburn, 1314.

David II, only son of Robert Bruce, ruled 1329-1371.

Robert II, 1371-1390, grandson of Robert Bruce, son of Walter, the Steward of Scotland, was called The Steward, first of the so-called Stuart line.

Robert III, son of Robert II, 1390-1406.

James I, son of Robert III, 1406-1437.

James II, son of James I, 1437-1460.

James III, eldest son of James II, 1460-1488.

James IV, eldest son of James III, 1488-1513.

James V, eldest son of James IV, 1513-1542.

Mary, daughter of James V, born 1542, became queen when one week old; was crowned 1543. Married, 1558, Francis, son of Henry II of France, who became king 1559, died 1560. Mary ruled Scots 1561 until abdication, 1567. She also married (2) Henry Stewart, Lord Darnley, and (3) James, Earl of Bothwell. Imprisoned by Elizabeth I, Mary was beheaded 1587.

James VI, 1566-1625, son of Mary and Lord Darnley, became King of England on death of Elizabeth in 1603. Although the thrones were thus united, the legislative union of Scotland and England was not effected until the Act of Union, May 1, 1707.

Rulers of France: Kings, Queens, Presidents

Caesar to Charlemagne

Julius Caesar subdued the Gauls, native tribes of Gaul (France) 57 to 52 BC. The Romans ruled 500 years. The Franks, a Teutonic tribe, reached the Somme from the East ca. 250 AD. By the 5th century the Merovingian Franks ousted the Romans. In 451 AD, with the help of Visigoths, Burgundians and others, they defeated Attila and the Huns at Chalons-sur-Marne.

Childeric I became leader of the Merovingians 458 AD. His son Clovis I (Chlodwig, Ludwig, Louis), crowned 481, founded the dynasty. After defeating the Alemanni (Germans) 496, he was baptized a Christian and made Paris his capital. His line ruled until Childeric III was deposed, 751.

The West Merovingians were called Neustrians, the eastern Austrasians. Pepin of Herstal (687-714) major domus, or head of the palace, of Austrasia, took over Neustria as dux (leader) of the Franks. Pepin's son, Charles, called Martel (the Hammer) defeated the Saracens at Tours-Poitiers, 732; was succeeded by his son, Pepin the Short, 741, who deposed Childeric III and ruled as king until 768.

His son, Charlemagne, or Charles the Great (742-814) became king of the Franks, 768, with his brother Carloman, who died 771. He ruled France, Germany, parts of Italy, Spain, Austria, and enforced Christianity. Crowned Emperor of the Romans by Pope Leo III in St. Peter's, Rome, Dec. 25, 800 AD. Succeeded by son, Louis I the Pious, 814. At death, 840, Louis left empire to sons, Lothair (Roman emperor), Pepin I (king of Aquitaine); Louis II (of Germany); Charles the Bald (France). They quarreled and by the peace of Verdun, 843, divided the empire.

AD Name, year of accession

The Carolingians

843 Charles I (the Bald), Roman Emperor, 875
877 Louis II (the Stammerer), son
879 Louis III (died 882) and Carloman, brothers
885 Charles II (the Fat), Roman Emperor, 881
888 Eudes (Odo) elected by nobles
898 Charles III (the Simple), son of Louis II, defeated by
922 Robert, brother of Eudes, killed in war
923 Rudolph (Raoul) Duke of Burgundy
936 Louis IV, son of Charles III
954 Lothair, son, aged 13, defeated by Capet
986 Louis V (the Sluggard), left no heirs

The Capets

987 Hugh Capet, son of Hugh the Great
996 Robert II (the Wise), his son
1031 Henry I, his son
1060 Philip I (the Fair), son
1108 Louis VI (the Fat), son
1137 Louis VII (the Younger), son
1180 Philip II (Augustus), son, crowned at Reims
1223 Louis VIII (the Lion), son
1226 Louis IX, son, crusader; Louis IX (1214-1270) reigned 44 years, arbitrated disputes with English King Henry III; led crusades, 1248 (captured in Egypt 1250) and 1270, when he died of plague in Tunis. Canonized 1297 as St. Louis.
1270 Philip III (the Hardy), son
1285 Philip IV (the Fair), son, king at 17
1314 Louis X (the Headstrong), son. His posthumous son, John I, lived only 7 days
1316 Philip V (the Tall), brother of Louis X
1322 Charles IV (the Fair), brother of Louis X

House of Valois

1328 Philip VI (of Valois), grandson of Philip III
1350 John II (the Good), his son, retired to England
1364 Charles V (the Wise), son
1380 Charles VI (the Beloved), son
1422 Charles VII (the Victorious), son. In 1429 Joan of Arc (Jeanne d'Arc) promised Charles to oust the English, who occupied northern France. Joan won at Orleans and Patay and had Charles crowned at Reims July 17, 1429. Joan was captured May 24, 1430, and executed May 30, 1431, at Rouen for heresy. Charles ordered her rehabilitation, effected 1455.
1461 Louis XI (the Cruel), son, civil reformer
1483 Charles VIII (the Affable), son
1498 Louis XII, great-grandson of Charles V
1515 Francis I, of Angouleme, nephew, son-in-law. Francis I (1494-1547) reigned 32 years, fought 4 big wars, was patron of the arts, aided Cellini, del Sarto, Leonardo da Vinci, Rabelais, embellished Fontainebleau.
1547 Henry II, son, killed at a joust in a tournament. He was the husband of Catherine de Medicis (1519-1589) and the lover of Diane de Poitiers (1499-1566). Catherine was born in Florence, daughter of Lorenzo de Medicis. By her marriage to Henry II she became the mother of Francis II, Charles IX, Henry III and Queen Margaret (Reine Margot) wife of Henry IV. She persuaded Charles IX to order the massacre of Huguenots on the Feast of St. Bartholomew, Aug. 24, 1572, the day her daughter was married to Henry of Navarre.
1559 Francis II, son. In 1548, Mary, Queen of Scots since infancy, was betrothed when 6 to Francis, aged 4. They were married 1558. Francis died 1560, aged 16; Mary ruled Scotland, abdicated 1567.
1560 Charles IX, brother
1574 Henry III, brother, assassinated

House of Bourbon

1589 Henry IV, of Navarre, assassinated. Henry IV made enemies when he gave tolerance to Protestants by Edict of Nantes, 1598. He was grandson of Queen Margaret of Navarre, literary patron. He married Margaret of Valois, daughter of Henry II and Catherine de Medicis; was divorced; in 1600 married Marie de Medicis, who became Regent of France, 1610-17 for her son, Louis XIII, but was exiled by Richelieu, 1631.
1610 Louis XIII (the Just), son. Louis XIII (1601-1643) married Anne of Austria. His ministers were Cardinals Richelieu and Mazarin.
1643 Louis XIV (The Grand Monarch), son. Louis XIV was king 72 years. He exhausted a prosperous country in wars for thrones and territory. By revoking the Edict of Nantes (1685) he caused the emigration of the Huguenots. He said: "I am the state."
1715 Louis XV, great-grandson. Louis XV married a Polish princess; lost Canada to the English. His favorites, Mme. Pompadour and Mme. Du Barry, influenced policies. Noted for saying "After me, the deluge".
1774 Louis XVI, grandson; married Marie Antoinette, daughter of Empress Maria Therese of Austria. King and queen beheaded by Revolution, 1793. Their son, called Louis XVII, died in prison, never ruled.

First Republic

1792 National Convention of the French Revolution
1795 Directory, under Barras and others
1799 Consulate, Napoleon Bonaparte, first consul. Elected consul for life, 1802.

First Empire

1804 Napoleon I, emperor. Josephine (de Beauharnais) empress, 1804-09; Marie Louise, empress, 1810-1814. Her son, Francois (1811-1832), titular King of Rome, later Duke de Reichstadt and "Napoleon II," never ruled. Napoleon abdicated 1814, died 1821.

Bourbons Restored

1814 Louis XVIII king; brother of Louis XVI.
1824 Charles X, brother; reactionary; deposed by the July Revolution, 1830.

House of Orleans

1830 Louis-Philippe, the "citizen king."

Second Republic

1848 Louis Napoleon Bonaparte, president, nephew of Napoleon I. He became:

Second Empire

1852 Napoleon III, emperor; Eugenie (de Montijo) empress. Lost Franco-Prussian war, deposed 1870. Son, Prince Imperial (1856-79), died in Zulu War. Eugenie died 1920.

Third Republic—Presidents

1871 Thiers, Louis Adolphe (1797-1877)
1873 MacMahon, Marshal Patrice M. de (1808-1893)
1879 Grevy, Paul J. (1807-1891)
1887 Sadi-Carnot, M. (1837-1894), assassinated
1894 Casimir-Perier, Jean P. P. (1847-1907)
1895 Faure, Francois Felix (1841-1899)
1899 Loubet, Emile (1838-1929)
1906 Fallieres, C. Armand (1841-1931)
1913 Poincare, Raymond (1860-1934)
1920 Deschanel, Paul (1856-1922)
1920 Millerand, Alexandre (1859-1943)
1924 Doumergue, Gaston (1863-1937)
1931 Doumer, Paul (1857-1932), assassinated
1932 Lebrun, Albert (1871-1950), resigned 1940
1940 **Vichy govt.** under German armistice: Henri Philippe Petain (1856-1951) Chief of State, 1940-1944.
Provisional govt. after liberation: Charles de Gaulle (1890-1970) Oct. 1944-Jan. 21, 1946; Felix Gouin (1884-1977) Jan. 23, 1946; Georges Bidault (1899-1983) June 24, 1946.

Fourth Republic—Presidents

1947 Auriol, Vincent (1884-1966)
1954 Coty, Rene (1882-1962)

Fifth Republic—Presidents

1959 de Gaulle, Charles Andre J. M. (1890-1970)
1969 Pompidou, Georges (1911-1974)
1974 Giscard d'Estaing, Valery (1926-)
1981 Mitterrand, Francois (1916-)

Rulers of Middle Europe; Rise and Fall of Dynasties

Carolingian Dynasty

Charles the Great, or Charlemagne, ruled France, Italy, and Middle Europe; established Ostmark (later Austria); crowned Roman emperor by pope in Rome, 800 AD; died 814.

Louis I (Ludwig) the Pious, son; crowned by Charlemagne 814, d. 840.

Louis II, the German, son; succeeded to East Francia (Germany) 843-876.

Charles the Fat, son; inherited East Francia and West Francia (France) 876, reunited empire, crowned emperor by pope, 881, deposed 887.

Arnulf, nephew, 887-899. Partition of empire.

Louis the Child, 899-911, last direct descendant of Charlemagne.

Conrad I, duke of Franconia, first elected German king, 911-918, founded House of Franconia.

Saxon Dynasty; First Reich

Henry I, the Fowler, duke of Saxony, 919-936.

Otto I, the Great, 936-973, son; crowned Holy Roman Emperor by pope, 962.

Otto II, 973-983, son; failed to oust Greeks and Arabs from Sicily.

Otto III, 983-1002, son; crowned emperor at 16.

Henry II, the Saint, duke of Bavaria, 1002-1024, great-grandson of Otto the Great.

House of Franconia

Conrad II, 1024-1039, elected king of Germany.

Henry III, the Black, 1039-1056, son; deposed 3 popes; annexed Burgundy.

Henry IV, 1056-1106, son; regency by his mother, Agnes of Poitou. Banned by Pope Gregory VII, he did penance at Canossa.

Henry V, 1106-1125, son; last of Salic House.

Lothair, duke of Saxony, 1125-1137. Crowned emperor in Rome, 1134.

House of Hohenstaufen

Conrad III, duke of Swabia, 1138-1152. In 2d Crusade.

Frederick I, Barbarossa, 1152-1190; Conrad's nephew.

Henry VI, 1190-1196, took lower Italy from Normans. Son became king of Sicily.

Philip of Swabia, 1197-1208, brother.

Otto IV, of House of Welf, 1198-1215; deposed.

Frederick II, 1215-1250, son of Henry VI; king of Sicily; crowned king of Jerusalem; in 5th Crusade.

Conrad IV, 1250-1254, son; lost lower Italy to Charles of Anjou.

Conradin (1252-1268) son, king of Jerusalem and Sicily, beheaded. Last Hohenstaufen.

interregnum, 1254-1273, Rise of the Electors.

Transition

Rudolph I of Hapsburg, 1273-1291, defeated King Ottocar II of Bohemia. Bequeathed duchy of Austria to eldest son, Albert.

Adolph of Nassau, 1292-1298, killed in war with Albert of Austria.

Albert I, king of Germany, 1298-1308, son of Rudolph.

Henry VII, of Luxemburg, 1308-1313, crowned emperor in Rome. Seized Bohemia, 1310.

Louis IV of Bavaria (Wittelsbach), 1314-1347. Also elected was Frederick of Austria, 1314-1330 (Hapsburg). Abolition of papal sanction for election of Holy Roman Emperor.

Charles IV, of Luxemburg, 1347-1378, grandson of Henry VII, German emperor and king of Bohemia, Lombardy, Burgundy; took Mark of Brandenburg.

Wenceslaus, 1378-1400, deposed.

Rupert, Duke of Palatine, 1400-1410.

Hungary

Stephen I, house of Arpad, 997-1038. Crowned king 1000; converted Magyars; canonized 1083. After several centuries of feuds Charles Robert of Anjou became Charles I, 1308-1342.

Louis I, the Great, son, 1342-1382; joint ruler of Poland with Casimir III, 1370. Defeated Turks.

Mary, daughter, 1382-1395, ruled with husband. Sigismund of Luxemburg, 1387-1437, also king of Bohemia. As bro. of Wenceslaus he succeeded Rupert as Holy Roman Emperor, 1410.

Albert II, 1438-1439, son-in-law of Sigismund; also Roman emperor. *(see under Hapsburg.)*

Ulaszlo I of Poland, 1440-1444.

Ladislaus V, posthumous son of Albert II, 1444-1457. John Hunyadi (Hunyadi Janos) governor (1446-1452), fought Turks, Czechs; died 1456.

Matthias I (Corvinus) son of Hunyadi, 1458-1490. Shared rule of Bohemia, captured Vienna, 1485, annexed Austria, Styria, Carinthia.

Ladislas II (king of Bohemia), 1490-1516.

Louis II, son, aged 10, 1516-1526. Wars with Suleiman, Turk. In 1527 Hungary was split between Ferdinand I, Archduke of Austria, bro.-in-law of Louis II, and John Zapolya of Transylvania. After Turkish invasion, 1547, Hungary was split between Ferdinand, Prince John Sigismund (Transylvania) and the Turks.

House of Hapsburg

Albert V of Austria, Hapsburg, crowned king of Hungary, Jan. 1438, Roman emperor, March, 1438, as Albert II; died 1439.

Frederick III, cousin, 1440-1493. Fought Turks.

Maximilian I, son, 1493-1519. Assumed title of Holy Roman Emperor (German), 1493.

Charles V, grandson, 1519-1556. King of Spain with mother co-regent; crowned Roman emperor at Aix, 1520. Confronted Luther at Worms; attempted church reform and religious conciliation; abdicated 1556.

Ferdinand I, king of Bohemia, 1526, of Hungary, 1527; disputed. German king, 1531. Crowned Roman emperor on abdication of brother Charles V, 1556.

Maximilian II, son, 1564-1576.

Rudolph II, son, 1576-1612.

Matthias, brother, 1612-1619, king of Bohemia and Hungary.

Ferdinand II of Styria, king of Bohemia, 1617, of Hungary, 1618, Roman emperor, 1619. Bohemian Protestants deposed him, elected Frederick V of Palatine, starting Thirty Years War.

Ferdinand III, son, king of Hungary, 1625, Bohemia, 1627, Roman emperor, 1637. Peace of Westphalia, 1648, ended war. Leopold I, 1658-1705; Joseph I, 1705-1711; Charles VI, 1711-1740.

Maria Theresa, daughter, 1740-1780, Archduchess of Austria, queen of Hungary; ousted pretender, Charles VII, crowned 1742; in 1745 obtained election of her husband Francis I as Roman emperor and co-regent (d. 1765). Fought Seven Years' War with Frederick II (the Great) of Prussia. Mother of Marie Antoinette, Queen of France.

Joseph II, son 1765-1790, Roman emperor, reformer; powers restricted by Empress Maria Theresa until her death, 1780. First partition of Poland. Leopold II, 1790-1792.

Francis II, son, 1792-1835. Fought Napoleon. Proclaimed first hereditary emperor of Austria, 1804. Forced to abdicate as Roman emperor, 1806; last use of title. Ferdinand I, son, 1835-1848, abdicated during revolution.

Austro-Hungarian Monarchy

Francis Joseph I, nephew, 1848-1916, emperor of Austria, king of Hungary. Dual monarchy of Austria-Hungary formed, 1867. After assassination of heir, Archduke Francis Ferdinand, June 28, 1914, Austrian diplomacy precipitated World War I.

Charles I, grand-nephew, 1916-1918, last emperor of Austria and king of Hungary. Abdicated Nov. 11-13, 1918, died 1922.

Rulers of Prussia

Nucleus of Prussia was the Mark of Brandenburg. First margrave was Albert the Bear (Albrecht), 1134-1170. First Hohenzollern margrave was Frederick, burgrave of Nuremberg, 1417-1440.

Frederick William, 1640-1688, the Great Elector. Son, Frederick III, 1688-1713, was crowned King Frederick of Prussia, 1701.

Frederick William I, son, 1713-1740.

Frederick II, the Great, son, 1740-1786, annexed Silesia part of Austria.

Frederick William II, nephew, 1786-1797.

Frederick William III, son, 1797-1840. Napoleonic wars.

Frederick William IV, son, 1840-1861. Uprising of 1848 and first parliament and constitution.

Second and Third Reich

William I, 1861-1888, brother. Annexation of Schleswig and Hanover; Franco-Prussian war, 1870-71, proclamation of German Reich, Jan. 18, 1871, at Versailles; William, German emperor (Deutscher Kaiser), Bismarck, chancellor.

Frederick III, son, 1888.

William II, son, 1888-1918. Led Germany in World War I, abdicated as German emperor and king of Prussia, Nov. 9, 1918. Died in exile in Netherlands June 4, 1941. Minor rulers of Bavaria, Saxony, Wurttemberg also abdicated.

Germany proclaimed a republic at Weimar, July 1, 1919. Presidents: Frederick Ebert, 1919-1925, Paul von Hindenburg-Beneckendorff, 1925, reelected 1932, d. Aug. 2, 1934. Adolf Hitler, chancellor, chosen successor as Leader-Chancellor (Fuehrer & Reichskanzler) of Third Reich. Annexed Austria, March, 1938. Precipitated World War II, 1939-1945. Committed suicide April 30, 1945.

Rulers of Poland

House of Piasts

Miesko I, 962?-992; Poland Christianized 966. Expansion under 3 Boleslavs: I, 992-1025, son, crowned king 1024; II, 1058-1079, great-grandson, exiled after killing bishop Stanislav who became chief patron saint of Poland: III, 1106-1138, nephew, divided Poland among 4 sons eldest suzerain.

1138-1306, feudal division. 1226 founding in Prussia of military order Teutonic Knights. 1226 invasion by Tartars/Mongols.

Vladislav I, 1306-1333, reunited most Polish territories, crowned king 1320. Casimir III the Great, 1333-1370, son, developed economic, cultural life, foreign policy.

House of Anjou

Louis I, 1370-1382, nephew/identical with Louis I of Hungary.

Jadwiga, 1384-1399, daughter, married 1386 Jagiello, Grand Duke of Lituania.

House of Jagelloneans

Vladislav II, 1386-1434, Christianized Lituania, founded personal union between Poland & Lituania. Defeated 1410 Teutonic Knights at Grunwald.

Vladislav III, 1434-1444, son, simultaneously king of Hungary. Fought Turks, killed 1444 in battle of Varna.

Casimir IV, 1446-1492, brother, competed with Hapsburgs, put son Vladislav on throne of Bohemia, later also of Hungary.

Sigismund I, 1506-1548, brother, patronized science & arts, his & son's reign "Golden Age."

Sigismund II, 1548-1572, son, established 1569 real union of Poland and Lituania (lasted until 1795).

Elective kings

Polish nobles proclaimed 1572 Poland a Republic headed by king to be elected by whole nobility.

Stephen Batory, 1576-1586, duke of Transylvania, married Ann, sister of Sigismund II August. Fought Russians.

Sigismund III Vasa, 1587-1632, nephew of Sigismund II. 1592-1598 also king of Sweden. His generals fought Russians, Turks.

Vladislav II Vasa, 1632-1648, son. Fought Russians.

John II Casimir Vasa, 1648-1668, brother. Fought Cossacks, Swedes, Russians, Turks, Tartars (the "Deluge"). Abdicated 1668.

John III Sobieski, 1674-1696. Won Vienna from Turks, 1683.

Stanislav II, 1764-1795, last king. Encouraged reforms; 1791 1st modern Constitution in Europe. 1772, 1793, 1795 Poland partitioned among Russia, Prussia, Austria. Unsuccessful insurrection against foreign invasion 1794 under Kosciuszko, Amer-Polish gen.

1795-1918 Poland under foreign rule

1807-1815 Grand Duchy of Warsaw created by Napoleon I, Frederick August of Saxony grand duke.

1815 Congress of Vienna proclaimed part of Poland "Kingdom" in personal union with Russia.

Polish uprisings: 1830 against Russia, 1846, 1848 against Austria, 1863 against Russia—all repressed.

1918-1939 Second Republic

1918-1922 Head of State Jozef Pilsudski. Presidents: Gabriel Narutowicz 1933, assassinated. Stanislav Wojsiechowski 1922-1926, had to abdicate after Pilsudski's coup d'état. Ignacy Moscieck, 1926-1939, ruled with Pilsudski as (until 1935) virtual dictator.

1939-1945 Poland under foreign occupation

Nazi aggression Sept. 1939. Polish govt.-in-exile, first in France, then in England. Vladislav Raczkiewicz pres., Gen. Vladislav Sikorski, then Stanislav Mikolajczyk, prime ministers. Polish Committee of Natl. Liberation proclaimed at Lublin July 1944, transformed into govt. Jan. 1, 1945.

Rulers of Denmark, Sweden, Norway

Denmark

Earliest rulers invaded Britain; King Canute, who ruled in London 1016-1035, was most famous. The Valdemars furnished kings until the 15th century. In 1282 the Danes won the first national assembly, Danehof, from King Erik V.

Most redoubtable medieval character was Margaret, daughter of Valdemar IV, born 1353, married at 10 to King Haakon VI of Norway. In 1376 she had her first infant son Olaf made king of Denmark. After his death, 1387, she was regent of Denmark and Norway. In 1388 Sweden accepted her as sovereign. In 1389 she made her grand-nephew, Duke Erik of Pomerania, titular king of Denmark, Sweden, and Norway, with herself as regent. In 1397 she effected the Union of Kalmar of the three kingdoms and had Erik VII crowned. In 1439 the three kingdoms deposed him and elected, 1440, Christopher of Bavaria king (Christopher III). On his death, 1448, the union broke up.

Succeeding rulers were unable to enforce their claims as rulers of Sweden until 1520, when Christian II conquered Sweden. He was thrown out 1522, and in 1523 Gustavus Vasa united Sweden. Denmark continued to dominate Norway until the Napoleonic wars, when Frederick VI, 1808-1839, joined the Napoleonic cause after Britain had destroyed the Danish fleet, 1807. In 1814 he was forced to cede Norway to Sweden and Helgoland to Britain, receiving Lauenburg. Successors Christian VIII, 1839; Frederick VII, 1848; Christian IX, 1863; Frederick VIII, 1906; Christian X, 1912; Frederick IX, 1947; Margrethe II, 1972.

Sweden

Early kings ruled at Uppsala, but did not dominate the country. Sverker, c1130-c1156, united the Swedes and Goths. In 1435 Sweden obtained the Riksdag, or parliament. After the Union of Kalmar, 1397, the Danes either ruled or harried the country until Christian II of Denmark conquered it anew, 1520. This led to a rising under Gustavus Vasa, who ruled Sweden 1523-1560, and established an independent kingdom. Charles IX, 1599-1611, crowned 1604, conquered Moscow. Gustavus II Adolphus, 1611-1632, was called the Lion of the North. Later rulers: Christina, 1632; Charles X, Gustavus 1654; Charles XI, 1660; Charles XII (invader of Russia and Poland, defeated at Poltava, June 28, 1709), 1697; Ulrika Eleanora, sister, elected queen 1718; Frederick I (of Hesse), her husband, 1720; Adolphus Frederick, 1751; Gustavus III, 1771; Gustavus IV Adolphus, 1792; Charles XIII, 1809. (Union with Norway began 1814.) Charles XIV John, 1818. He was Jean Bernadotte, Napoleon's Prince of Ponte Corvo, elected 1810 to succeed Charles XIII. He founded the present dynasty: Oscar I, 1844, Charles XV, 1859; Oscar II, 1872; Gustavus V, 1907; Gustav VI Adolf, 1950; Carl XVI Gustaf, 1973.

Norway

Overcoming many rivals, Harald Haarfager, 872-930, conquered Norway, Orkneys, and Shetlands; Olaf I, great-grandson, 995-1000, brought Christianity into Norway, Iceland, and Greenland. In 1035 Magnus the Good also became king of Denmark. Haakon V, 1299-1319, had married his daughter to Erik of Sweden. Their son, Magnus, became ruler of Norway and Sweden at 6. His son, Haakon VI, married Margaret of Denmark; their son Olaf IV became king of Norway and Denmark, followed by Margaret's regency and the Union of Kalmar, 1397.

In 1450 Norway became subservient to Denmark. Christian IV, 1588-1648, founded Christiania, now Oslo. After Napoleonic wars, when Denmark ceded Norway to Sweden, a strong nationalist movement forced recognition of Norway as an independent kingdom united with Sweden under the Swedish kings, 1814-1905. In 1905 the union was dissolved and Prince Carl of Denmark became Haakon VII. He died Sept. 21, 1957, aged 85; succeeded by son, Olav V, b. July 2, 1903.

Rulers of the Netherlands and Belgium

The Netherlands (Holland)

William Frederick, Prince of Orange, led a revolt against French rule, 1813, and was crowned King of the Netherlands, 1815. Belgium seceded Oct. 4, 1830, after a revolt, and formed a separate government. The change was ratified by the two kingdoms by treaty Apr. 19, 1839.

Succession: William II, son, 1840; William III, son, 1849; Wilhelmina, daughter of William III and his 2d wife Princess Emma of Waldeck, 1890; Wilhelmina abdicated, Sept. 4, 1948, in favor of daughter, Juliana. Juliana abdicated Apr. 30, 1980, in favor of daughter, Beatrix.

Belgium

A national congress elected Prince Leopold of Saxe-Coburg King; he took the throne July 21, 1831, as Leopold I. Succession: Leopold II, son 1865; Albert I, nephew of Leopold II, 1909; Leopold III, son of Albert, 1934; Prince Charles, Regent 1944; Leopold returned 1950, yielded powers to son Baudouin, Prince Royal, Aug. 6, 1950, abdicated July 16, 1951. Baudouin I took throne July 17, 1951.

For political history prior to 1830 see articles on the Netherlands and Belgium.

Roman Rulers

From Romulus to the end of the Empire in the West. Rulers of the Roman Empire in the East sat in Constantinople and for a brief period in Nicaea, until the capture of Constantinople by the Turks in 1453, when Byzantium was succeeded by the Ottoman Empire.

BC	Name
	The Kingdom
753	Romulus (Quirinus)
716	Numa Pompilius
673	Tullus Hostilius
640	Ancus Marcius
616	L. Tarquinius Priscus
578	Servius Tullius
534	L. Tarquinius Superbus
	The Republic
509	Consulate established
509	Quaestorship instituted
498	Dictatorship introduced
494	Plebeian Tribunate created
494	Plebeian Aedileship created
444	Consular Tribunate organized
435	Censorship instituted
366	Praetorship established
366	Curule Aedileship created
362	Military Tribunate elected
326	Proconsulate introduced
311	Naval Duumvirate elected
217	Dictatorship of Fabius Maximus
133	Tribunate of Tiberius Gracchus
123	Tribunate of Gaius Gracchus
82	Dictatorship of Sulla
60	First Triumvirate formed (Caesar, Pompeius, Crassus)
46	Dictatorship of Caesar
43	Second Triumvirate formed (Octavianus, Antonius, Lepidus)
	The Empire
27	Augustus (Gaius Julius Caesar Octavianus)
14	Tiberius I
37	Gaius Caesar (Caligula)
41	Claudius I
54	Nero
68	Galba
69	Galba; Otho, Vitellius
69	Vespasianus
79	Titus

AD	Name
81	Domitianus
96	Nerva
98	Trajanus
117	Hadrianus
138	Antoninus Pius
161	Marcus Aurelius and Lucius Verus
169	Marcus Aurelius (alone)
180	Commodus
193	Pertinax; Julianus I
193	Septimius Severus
211	Caracalla and Geta
212	Caracalla (alone)
217	Macrinus
218	Elagabalus (Heliogabalus)
222	Alexander Severus
235	Maximinus I (the Thracian)
238	Gordianus I and Gordianus II; Pupienus and Balbinus
238	Gordianus III
244	Philippus (the Arabian)
249	Decius
251	Gallus and Volusianus
253	Aemilianus
253	Valerianus and Gallienus
258	Gallienus (alone)
268	Claudius II (the Goth)
270	Quintillus
270	Aurelianus
275	Tacitus
276	Florianus
276	Probus
282	Carus
283	Carinus and Numerianus
284	Diocletianus
286	Diocletianus and Maximianus
305	Galerius and Constantius I
306	Galerius, Maximinus II, Severus I
307	Galerius, Maximinus II, Constantinus I, Licinius, Maxentius
311	Maximinus II, Constantinus I, Licinius, Maxentius
314	Maximinus II, Constantinus I, Licinius

AD	Name
314	Constantinus I and Licinius
324	Constantinus I (the Great)
337	Constantinus II, Constans I, Constantius II
340	Constantius II and Constans I
350	Constantius II
361	Julianus II (the Apostate)
363	Jovianus
	West (Rome) and East (Constantinople)
364	Valentinianus I (West) and Valens (East)
367	Valentinianus I with Gratianus (West) and Valens (East)
375	Gratianus with Valentinianus II (West) and Valens (East)
378	Gratianus with Valentinianus II (West) Theodosius I (East)
383	Valentinianus II (West) and Theodosius I (East)
394	Theodosius I (the Great)
395	Honorius (West) and Arcadius (East)
408	Honorius (West) and Theodosius II (East)
423	Valentinianus III (West) and Theodosius II (East)
450	Valentinianus III (West) and Marcianus (East)
455	Maximus (West), Avitus (West); Marcianus (East)
456	Avitus (West), Marcianus (East)
457	Majorianus (West), Leo I (East)
461	Severus II (West), Leo I (East)
467	Anthemius (West), Leo I (East)
472	Olybrius (West), Leo I (East)
473	Glycerius (West), Leo I (East)
474	Julius Nepos (West), Leo II (East)
475	Romulus Augustulus (West) and Zeno (East)
476	End of Empire in West; Odovacar, King, drops title of Emperor; murdered by King Theodoric of Ostrogoths 493 AD

Rulers of Modern Italy

After the fall of Napoleon in 1814, the Congress of Vienna, 1815, restored Italy as a political patchwork, comprising the Kingdom of Naples and Sicily, the Papal States, and smaller units. Piedmont and Genoa were awarded to Sardinia, ruled by King Victor Emmanuel I of Savoy.

United Italy emerged under the leadership of Camillo, Count di Cavour (1810-1861), Sardinian prime minister. Agitation was led by Giuseppe Mazzini (1805-1872) and Giuseppe Garibaldi (1807-1882), soldier. Victor Emmanuel I abdicated 1821. After a brief regency for a brother, Charles Albert was King 1831-1849, abdicating when defeated by the Austrians at Novara. Succeeded by Victor Emmanuel II, 1849-1861.

In 1859 France forced Austria to cede Lombardy to Sardinia, which gave rights to Savoy and Nice to France. In 1860 Garibaldi led 1,000 volunteers in a spectacular campaign, took Sicily and expelled the King of Naples. In 1860 the House of Savoy annexed Tuscany, Parma, Modena, Romagna, the Two Sicilies, the Marches, and Umbria. Victor Emmanuel assumed the title of King of Italy at Turin Mar. 17, 1861. In 1866 he allied with Prussia in the Austro-Prussian War, with Prussia's victory received Venetia. On Sept. 20, 1870, his troops under Gen. Raffaele Cadorna entered Rome and took over the Papal States, ending the temporal power of the Roman Catholic Church.

Succession: Umberto I; 1878, assassinated 1900; Victor Emmanuel III, 1900, abdicated 1946, died 1947; Umberto II, 1946, ruled a month. In 1921 Benito Mussolini (1883-1945) formed the Fascist party and became prime minister Oct. 31, 1922. He made the King Emperor of Ethiopia, 1937; entered World War II as ally of Hitler. He was deposed July 25, 1943.

At a plebiscite June 2, 1946, Italy voted for a republic; Premier Alcide de Gasperi became chief of state June 13, 1946. On June 28, 1946, the Constituent Assembly elected Enrico de Nicola, Liberal, provisional president. Successive presidents: Luigi Einaudi, elected May 11, 1948, Giovanni Gronchi, Apr. 29, 1955; Antonio Segni, May 6, 1962; Giuseppe Saragat, Dec. 28, 1964; Giovanni Leone, Dec. 29, 1971; Alessandro Pertini, July 9, 1978; Francesco Cossiga, July 9, 1985.

Rulers of Spain

From 8th to 11th centuries Spain was dominated by the Moors (Arabs and Berbers). The Christian reconquest established small competing kingdoms of the Asturias, Aragon, Castile, Catalonia, Leon, Navarre, and Valencia. In 1474 Isabella (Isabel), b. 1451, became Queen of Castile & Leon. Her husband, Ferdinand, b. 1452, inherited Aragon 1479, with Catalonia, Valencia, and the Balearic Islands, became Ferdinand V of Castile. By Isabella's request Pope Sixtus IV established the Inquisition, 1478. Last Moorish kingdom, Granada, fell 1492. Columbus opened New World of colonies, 1492. Isabella died 1504, succeeded by her daughter, Juana "the Mad," but Ferdinand ruled until his death 1516.

Charles I, b. 1500, son of Juana and grandson of Ferdinand and Isabella, and of Maximilian I of Hapsburg; succeeded later as Holy Roman Emperor, Charles V, 1520; abdicated 1556. Philip II, son, 1556-1598, inherited only Spanish throne; conquered Portugal, fought Turks, persecuted non-Catholics, sent Armada against England. Was briefly married to Mary I of England, 1554-1558. Succession: Philip III, 1598-1621; Philip IV, 1621-1665; Charles II, 1665-1700, left Spain to Philip of Anjou, grandson of Louis XIV, who as Philip V, 1700-1746, founded Bourbon dynasty. Ferdinand VI, 1746-1759; Charles III, 1759-1788; Charles IV, 1788-1808, abdicated.

Napoleon now dominated politics and made his brother Joseph King of Spain 1808, but the Spanish ousted him finally in 1813. Ferdinand VII, 1808, 1814-1833, lost American colonies; succeeded by daughter Isabella II, aged 3, with wife Maria Christina of Naples regent until 1843. Isabella deposed by revolution 1868. Elected king by the Cortes, Amadeo of Savoy, 1870; abdicated 1873. First republic, 1873-1874. Alphonso XII, son of Isabella, 1875-1885. His posthumous son was Alphonso XIII, with his mother, Queen Maria Christina regent; Spanish-American war, Spain lost Cuba, gave up Puerto Rico, Philippines, Sulu Is., Marianas. Alphonso took throne 1902, aged 16, married British Princess Victoria Eugenia of Battenberg. The dictatorship of Primo de Rivera, 1923-30, precipitated the revolution of 1931. Alphonso agreed to leave without formal abdication. The monarchy was abolished and the second republic established, with strong socialist backing. Presidents were Niceto Alcala Zamora, to 1936, when Manuel Azaña was chosen.

In July, 1936, the army in Morocco revolted against the government and General Francisco Franco led the troops into Spain. The revolution succeeded by Feb., 1939, when Azaña resigned. Franco became chief of state, with provisions that if he was incapacitated the Regency Council by two-thirds vote may propose a king to the Cortes, which must have a two-thirds majority to elect him.

Alphonso XIII died in Rome Feb. 28, 1941, aged 54. His property and citizenship had been restored.

A succession law restoring the monarchy was approved in a 1947 referendum. Prince Juan Carlos, son of the pretender to the throne, was designated by Franco and the Cortes in 1969 as the future king and chief of state. Upon Franco's death, Nov. 20, 1975, Juan Carlos was proclaimed king, Nov. 22, 1975.

Leaders in the South American Wars of Liberation

Simon Bolivar (1783-1830), Jose Francisco de San Martin (1778-1850), and Francisco Antonio Gabriel Miranda (1750-1816), are among the heroes of the early 19th century struggles of South American nations to free themselves from Spain. All three, and their contemporaries, operated in periods of intense factional strife, during which soldiers and civilians suffered.

Miranda, a Venezuelan, who had served with the French in the American Revolution and commanded parts of the French Revolutionary armies in the Netherlands, attempted to start a revolt in Venezuela in 1806 and failed. In 1810, with British and American backing, he returned and was briefly a dictator, until the British withdrew their support. In 1812 he was overcome by the royalists in Venezuela and taken prisoner, dying in a Spanish prison in 1816.

San Martin was born in Argentina and during 1789-1811 served in campaigns of the Spanish armies in Europe and Africa. He first joined the independence movement in Argentina in 1812 and then in 1817 invaded Chile with 4,000 men over the high mountain passes. Here he and General Bernardo O'Higgins (1778-1842) defeated the Spaniards at Chacabuco, 1817, and O'Higgins was named Liberator and became first director of Chile, 1817-1823. In 1821 San Martin occupied Lima and Callao, Peru, and became protector of Peru.

Bolivar, the greatest leader of South American liberation from Spain, was born in Venezuela, the son of an aristocratic family. His organizing and administrative abilities were superior and he foresaw many of the political difficulties of the future. He first served under Miranda in 1812 and in 1813 captured Caracas, where he was named Liberator. Forced out next year by civil strife, he led a campaign that captured Bogota in 1814. In 1817 he was again in control of Venezuela and was named dictator. He organized Nueva Granada with the help of General Francisco de Paula Santander (1792-1840). By joining Nueva Granada, Venezuela, and the present terrain of Panama and Ecuador, the republic of Colombia was formed with Bolivar president. After numerous setbacks he decisively defeated the Spaniards in the second battle of Carabobo, Venezuela, June 24, 1821.

In May, 1822, Gen. Antonio Jose de Sucre, Bolivar's trusted lieutenant, took Quito. Bolivar went to Guayaquil to confer with San Martin, who resigned as protector of Peru and withdrew from politics. With a new army of Colombians and Peruvians Bolivar defeated the Spaniards in a saber battle at Junín in 1824 and cleared Peru.

De Sucre organized Charcas (Upper Peru) as Republica Bolivar (now Bolivia) and acted as president in place of Bolivar, who wrote its constitution. De Sucre defeated the Spanish faction of Peru at Ayacucho, Dec. 19, 1824.

Continued civil strife finally caused the Colombian federation to break apart. Santander turned against Bolivar, but the latter defeated him and banished him. In 1828 Bolivar gave up the presidency he had held precariously for 14 years. He became ill from tuberculosis and died Dec. 17, 1830. He was honored as the great liberator and is buried in the national pantheon in Caracas.

Rulers of Russia; Premiers of the USSR

First ruler to consolidate Slavic tribes was Rurik, leader of the Russians who established himself at Novgorod, 862 A.D. He and his immediate successors had Scandinavian affiliations. They moved to Kiev after 972 AD and ruled as Dukes of Kiev. In 988 Vladimir was converted and adopted the Byzantine Greek Orthodox service, later modified by Slav influences. Important as organizer and lawgiver was Yaroslav, 1019-1054, whose daughters married kings of Norway, Hungary, and France. His grandson, Vladimir II (Monomakh), 1113-1125, was progenitor of several rulers, but in 1169 Andrew Bogolubski overthrew Kiev and began the line known as Grand Dukes of Vladimir.

Of the Grand Dukes of Vladimir, Alexander Nevsky, 1246-1263, had a son, Daniel, first to be called Duke of Muscovy (Moscow) who ruled 1294-1303. His successors became Grand Dukes of Muscovy. After Dmitri III Donskoi defeated the Tartars in 1380, they also became Grand Dukes of all Russia. Independence of the Tartars and considerable territorial expansion were achieved under Ivan III, 1462-1505.

Tsars of Muscovy—Ivan III was referred to in church ritual as Tsar. He married Sofia, niece of the last Byzantine emperor. His successor, Basil III, died in 1533 when Basil's son Ivan was only 3. He became Ivan IV, "the Terrible"; crowned 1547 as Tsar of all the Russias, ruled till 1584. Under the weak rule of his son, Feodor I, 1584-1598, Boris Godunov had control. The dynasty died, and after years of tribal strife and intervention by Polish and Swedish armies, the Russians united under 17-year-old Michael Romanov, distantly related to the first wife of Ivan IV. He ruled 1613-1645 and established the Romanov line. Fourth ruler after Michael was Peter I.

Tsars, or Emperors of Russia (Romanovs)—Peter I, 1682-1725, known as Peter the Great, took title of Emperor in 1721. His successors and dates of accession were: Catherine, his widow, 1725, Peter II, his grandson, 1727-1730; Anne, Duchess of Courland, 1730, daughter of Peter the Great's brother, Tsar Ivan V; Ivan VI, 1740-1741, great-grandson of Ivan V, child, kept in prison and murdered 1764; Elizabeth, daughter of Peter I, 1741; Peter III, grandson of Peter I, 1761, deposed 1762 for his consort, Catherine II, former princess of Anhalt Zerbst (Germany) who is known as Catherine the Great, 1762-1796; Paul I, her son, 1796, killed 1801; Alexander I, son of Paul, 1801-1825, defeated Napoleon; Nicholas I, his brother, 1825; Alexander II, son of Nicholas, 1855, assassinated 1881 by terrorists; Alexander III, son, 1881-1894.

Nicholas II, son, 1894-1917, last Tsar of Russia, was forced to abdicate by the Revolution that followed losses to Germany in WWI. The Tsar, the Empress, the Tsesarevich (Crown Prince) and the Tsar's 4 daughters were murdered by the Bolsheviks in Ekaterinburg, July 16, 1918.

Provisional Government—Prince Georgi Lvov and Alexander Kerensky, premiers, 1917.

Union of Soviet Socialist Republics

Bolshevik Revolution, Nov. 7, 1917, displaced Kerensky; council of People's Commissars formed, Lenin (Vladimir Ilyich Ulyanov), premier. Lenin died Jan. 21, 1924. Aleksei Rykov (executed 1938) and V. M. Molotov held the office, but actual ruler was Joseph Stalin (Joseph Vissarionovich Djugashvili), general secretary of the Central Committee of the Communist Party. Stalin became president of the Council of Ministers (premier) May 7, 1941, died Mar. 5, 1953. Succeeded by Georgi M. Malenkov, as head of the Council and premier and Nikita S. Khrushchev, first secretary of the Central Committee. Malenkov resigned Feb. 8, 1955, became deputy premier, was dropped July 3, 1957. Marshal Nikolai A. Bulganin became premier Feb. 8, 1955; was demoted and Khrushchev became premier Mar. 27 1958. Khrushchev was ousted Oct. 14-15, 1964, replaced by Leonid I. Brezhnev as first secretary of the party and by Aleksei N. Kosygin as premier. On June 16, 1977, Brezhnev took office as president. Brezhnev died Nov. 10, 1982; 2 days later the Central Committee unanimously elected former KGB head Yuri V. Andropov president. Andropov died Feb. 9, 1984; on Feb. 13, Konstantin U. Chernenko was chosen by Central Committee to succeed Andropov as its general secretary. Chernenko died Mar. 10, 1985. On Mar. 11, he was succeeded as general secretary by Mikhail Gorbachev.

Governments of China

(Until 221 BC and frequently thereafter, China was not a unified state. Where dynastic dates overlap, the rulers or events referred to appeared in different areas of China.)

Hsia	c1994BC	-	c1523BC
Shang	c1523	-	c1028
Western Chou	c1027	-	770
Eastern Chou	770	-	256
Warring States	403	-	222
Ch'in (first unified empire)	221	-	206
Han	202BC	-	220AD
Western Han (expanded Chinese state beyond the Yellow and Yangtze River valleys)	202BC	-	9AD
Hsin (Wang Mang, usurper)	9AD	-	23AD
Eastern Han (expanded Chinese state into Indo-China and Turkestan)	25	-	220
Three Kingdoms (Wei, Shu, Wu)	220	-	265
Chin (western)	265	-	317
(eastern)	317	-	420
Northern Dynasties (followed several short-lived governments by Turks, Mongols, etc.)	386	-	581
Southern Dynasties (capital: Nanking)	420	-	589
Sui (reunified China)	581	-	618
Tang (a golden age of Chinese culture; capital: Sian)	618	-	906
Five Dynasties (Yellow River basin)	902	-	960
Ten Kingdoms (southern China)	907	-	979
Liao (Khitan Mongols; capital: Peking)	947	-	1125
Sung	960	-	1279
Northern Sung (reunified central and southern China)	960	-	1126
Western Hsai (non-Chinese rulers in northwest)	990	-	1227
Chin (Tartars; drove Sung out of central China)	1115	-	1234
Yuan (Mongols; Kublai Khan made Peking his capital in 1267)	1271	-	1368
Ming (China reunified under Chinese rule; capital: Nanking, then Peking in 1420)	1368	-	1644
Ch'ing (Manchus, descendents of Tartars)	1644	-	1911
Republic (disunity; provincial rulers, warlords)	1912	-	1949
People's Republic of China (Nationalist China established on Taiwan)	1949	-	—

Prime Ministers of Canada

Canada is a constitutional monarchy with a parliamentary system of government. It is also a federal state. Canada's offical head of state is the King or Queen of England, represented by a resident Governor-General. However, in practice the nation is governed by the Prime Minister, leader of the party that commands the support of a majority of the House of Commons, dominant chamber of Canada's bicameral Parliament.

Name	Party	Term
Sir John A. MacDonald	Conservative	1867-1873 1878-1891
Alexander Mackenzie	Liberal	1873-1878
Sir John J. C. Abbott	Conservative	1891-1892
Sir John S. D. Thompson	Conservative	1892-1894
Sir Mackenzie Bowell	Conservative	1894-1896
Sir Charles Tupper	Conservative	1896
Sir Wilfrid Laurier	Liberal	1896-1911
Sir Robert L. Borden	Cons. Union.	1911-1920
Arthur Meighen	Cons. Union.	1920-1921
W.L. Mackenzie King	Liberal	1921-1926(1) 1926-1930 1935-1948
R. B. Bennett	Conservative	1930-1935
Louis St. Laurent	Liberal	1948-1957
John G. Diefenbaker	Prog. Cons.	1957-1963
Lester B. Pearson	Liberal	1963-1968
Pierre Elliott Trudeau	Liberal	1968-1979
Joe Clark	Prog. Cons.	1979-1980
Pierre Elliott Trudeau	Liberal	1980-1984
John Turner	Liberal	1984
Brian Mulroney	Prog. Cons.	1984-

(1) King's term was interrupted from June 26-Sept. 25, 1926, when Arthur Meighen again served as prime minister.

Chronological List of Popes

Source: Annuario Pontificio. Table lists year of accession of each Pope.

The Roman Catholic Church names the Apostle Peter as founder of the Church in Rome. He arrived there c. 42, was martyred there c. 67, and raised to sainthood.

The Pope's temporal title is: Sovereign of the State of Vatican City.

The Pope's spiritual titles are: Bishop of Rome, Vicar of Jesus Christ, Successor of St. Peter, Prince of the Apostles, Supreme Pontiff of the Universal Church, Patriarch of the West, Primate of Italy, Archbishop and Metropolitan of the Roman Province.

Anti-Popes are in *Italics.* Anti-Popes were illegitimate claimants of or pretenders to the papal throne.

Year	Name of Pope	Year	Name of Pope	Year	Name of Pope	Year	Name of Pope
See above.	St. Peter	615	St. Deusdedit	974	Benedict VII	1305	Clement V
67	St. Linus		or Adeodatus	983	John XIV	1316	John XXII
76	St. Anacletus	619	Boniface V	985	John XV	*1328*	*Nicholas V*
	or Cletus	625	Honorius I	996	Gregory V	1334	Benedict XII
88	St. Clement I	640	Severinus	*997*	*John XVI*	1342	Clement VI
97	St. Evaristus	640	John IV	999	Sylvester II	1352	Innocent VI
105	St. Alexander I	642	Theodore I	1003	John XVII	1362	Bl. Urban V
115	St. Sixtus I	649	St. Martin I, Martyr	1004	John XVIII	1370	Gregory XI
125	St. Telesphorus	654	St. Eugene I	1009	Sergius IV	1378	Urban VI
136	St. Hyginus	657	St. Vitalian	1012	Benedict VIII	*1378*	*Clement VII*
140	St. Pius I	672	Adeodatus II	*1012*	*Gregory*	1389	Boniface IX
155	St. Anicetus	676	Donus	1024	John XIX	*1394*	*Benedict XIII*
166	St. Soter	678	St. Agatho	1032	Benedict IX	1404	Innocent VII
175	St. Eleutherius	682	St. Leo II	1045	Sylvester III	1406	Gregory XII
189	St. Victor I	684	St. Benedict II	1045	Benedict IX	*1409*	*Alexander V*
199	St. Zephyrinus	685	John V	1045	Gregory VI	*1410*	*John XXIII*
217	St. Callistus I	686	Conon	1046	Clement II	1417	Martin V
217	*St. Hippolytus*	*687*	*Theodore*	1047	Benedict IX	1431	Eugene IV
222	St. Urban I	*687*	*Paschal*	1048	Damasus II	*1439*	*Felix V*
230	St. Pontian	687	St. Sergius I	1049	St. Leo IX	1447	Nicholas V
235	St. Anterus	701	John VI	1055	Victor II	1455	Callistus III
236	St. Fabian	705	John VII	1057	Stephen IX (X)	1458	Pius II
251	St. Cornelius	708	Sisinnius	*1058*	*Benedict X*	1464	Paul II
251	*Novatian*	708	Constantine	1059	Nicholas II	1471	Sixtus IV
253	St. Lucius I	715	St. Gregory II	1061	Alexander II	1484	Innocent VIII
254	St. Stephen I	731	St. Gregory III	*1061*	*Honorius II*	1492	Alexander VI
257	St. Sixtus II	741	St. Zachary	1073	St. Gregory VII	1503	Pius III
259	St. Dionysius	752	Stephen II (III)	*1080*	*Clement III*	1503	Julius II
269	St. Felix I	757	St. Paul I	1086	Bl. Victor III	1513	Leo X
275	St. Eutychian	*767*	*Constantine*	1088	Bl. Urban II	1522	Adrian VI
283	St. Caius	*768*	*Philip*	1099	Paschal II	1523	Clement VII
296	St. Marcellinus	768	Stephen III (IV)	*1100*	*Theodoric*	1534	Paul III
308	St. Marcellus I	772	Adrian I	*1102*	*Albert*	1550	Julius III
309	St. Eusebius	795	St. Leo III	*1105*	*Sylvester IV*	1555	Marcellus II
311	St. Melchiades	816	Stephen IV (V)	1118	Gelasius II	1555	Paul IV
314	St. Sylvester I	817	St. Paschal I	*1118*	*Gregory VIII*	1559	Pius IV
336	St. Marcus	824	Eugene II	1119	Callistus II	1566	St. Pius V
337	St. Julius I	827	Valentine	1124	Honorius II	1572	Gregory XIII
352	Liberius	827	Gregory IV	*1124*	*Celestine II*	1585	Sixtus V
355	*Felix II*	*844*	*John*	1130	Innocent II	1590	Urban VII
366	St. Damasus I	844	Sergius II	*1130*	*Anacletus II*	1590	Gregory XIV
366	*Ursinus*	847	St. Leo IV	*1138*	*Victor IV*	1591	Innocent IX
384	St. Siricius	855	Benedict III	1143	Celestine II	1592	Clement VIII
399	St. Anastasius I	*855*	*Anastasius*	1144	Lucius II	1605	Leo XI
401	St. Innocent I	858	St. Nicholas I	1145	Bl. Eugene III	1605	Paul V
417	St. Zosimus	867	Adrian II	1153	Anastasius IV	1621	Gregory XV
418	St. Boniface I	872	John VIII	1154	Adrian IV	1623	Urban VIII
418	*Eulalius*	882	Marinus I	1159	Alexander III	1644	Innocent X
422	St. Celestine I	884	St. Adrian III	*1159*	*Victor IV*	1655	Alexander VII
432	St. Sixtus III	885	Stephen V (VI)	*1164*	*Paschal III*	1667	Clement IX
440	St. Leo I	891	Formosus	*1168*	*Callistus III*	1670	Clement X
461	St. Hilary	896	Boniface VI	*1179*	*Innocent III*	1676	Bl. Innocent XI
468	St. Simplicius	896	Stephen VI (VII)	1181	Lucius III	1689	Alexander VIII
483	St. Felix III (II)	897	Romanus	1185	Urban III	1691	Innocent XII
492	St. Gelasius I	897	Theodore II	1187	Gregory VIII	1700	Clement XI
496	Anastasius II	898	John IX	1187	Clement III	1721	Innocent XIII
498	St. Symmachus	900	Benedict IV	1191	Celestine III	1724	Benedict XIII
498	*Lawrence*	903	Leo V	1198	Innocent III	1730	Clement XII
	(501-505)	*903*	*Christopher*	1216	Honorius III	1740	Benedict XIV
514	St. Hormisdas	904	Sergius III	1227	Gregory IX	1758	Clement XIII
523	St. John I, Martyr	911	Anastasius III	1241	Celestine IV	1769	Clement XIV
526	St. Felix IV (III)	913	Landus	1243	Innocent IV	1775	Pius VI
530	Boniface II	914	John X	1254	Alexander IV	1800	Pius VII
530	*Dioscorus*	928	Leo VI	1261	Urban IV	1823	Leo XII
533	John II	928	Stephen VII (VIII)	1265	Clement IV	1829	Pius VIII
535	St. Agapitus I	931	John XI	1271	Bl. Gregory X	1831	Gregory XVI
536	St. Silverius, Martyr	936	Leo VII	1276	Bl. Innocent V	1846	Pius IX
537	Vigilius	939	Stephen VIII (IX)	1276	Adrian V	1878	Leo XIII
556	Pelagius I	942	Marinus II	1276	John XXI	1903	St. Pius X
561	John III	946	Agapitus II	1277	Nicholas III	1914	Benedict XV
575	Benedict I	955	John XII	1281	Martin IV	1922	Pius XI
579	Pelagius II	963	Leo VIII	1285	Honorius IV	1939	Pius XII
590	St. Gregory I	964	Benedict V	1288	Nicholas IV	1958	John XXIII
604	Sabinian	965	John XIII	1294	St. Celestine V	1963	Paul VI
607	Boniface III	973	Benedict VI	1294	Boniface VIII	1978	John Paul I
608	St. Boniface IV	*974*	*Boniface VII*	1303	Bl. Benedict XI	1978	John Paul II

WORLD FACTS

Early Explorers of the Western Hemisphere

The first men to discover the New World or Western Hemisphere are believed to have walked across a "land bridge" from Siberia to Alaska, an isthmus since broken by the Bering Strait. From Alaska, these ancestors of the Indians spread through North, Central, and South America. Anthropologists have placed these crossings at between 18,000 and 14,000 B.C.; but evidence found in 1967 near Puebla, Mex., indicates mankind reached there as early as 35,000-40,000 years ago.

At first, these people were hunters using flint weapons and tools. In Mexico, about 7000-6000 B.C., they founded farming cultures, developing corn, squash, etc. Eventually, they created complex civilizations — Olmec, Toltec, Aztec, and Maya and, in South America, Inca. Carbon-14 tests show men lived about 8000 B.C. near what are now Front Royal, Va., Kanawha, W. Va., and Dutchess Quarry, N.Y. The Hopewell Culture, based on farming, flourished about 1000 B.C.; remains of it are seen today in large mounds in Ohio and other states.

Norsemen (Norwegian Vikings sailing out of Iceland and Greenland) are credited by most scholars with being the first Europeans to discover America, with at least 5 voyages around 1000 A.D. to areas they called Helluland, Markland, Vinland—possibly Labrador, Nova Scotia or Newfoundland, and New England.

Christopher Columbus, most famous of the explorers, was born at Genoa, Italy, but made his discoveries sailing for the Spanish rulers Ferdinand and Isabella. Dates of his voyages, places he discovered, and other information follow:

1492—First voyage. Left Palos, Spain, Aug. 3 with 88 men (est.). Discovered San Salvador (Guanahani or Watling Is., Bahamas) Oct. 12. Also Cuba, Hispaniola (Haiti-Dominican Republic); built Fort La Navidad on latter.

1493—Second voyage, first part, Sept. 25, with 17 ships, 1,500 men. Dominica (Lesser Antilles) Nov. 3; Guadeloupe, Montserrat, Antigua, San Martin, Santa Cruz, Puerto Rico, Virgin Islands. Settled Isabela on Hispaniola. **Second part** (Columbus having remained in Western Hemisphere), Jamaica, Isle of Pines, La Mona Is.

1498—Third voyage. Left Spain May 30, 1498, 6 ships. Discovered Trinidad. Saw South American continent Aug. 1, 1498, but called it Isla Sancta (Holy Island). Entered Gulf of Paria and landed, first time on continental soil. At mouth of Orinoco Aug. 14 he decided this was the mainland.

1502—Fourth voyage, 4 caravels, 150 men. St. Lucia, Guanaja off Honduras; Cape Gracias a Dios, Honduras; San Juan River, Costa Rica; Almirante, Portobelo, and Laguna de Chiriqui, Panama.

Year	Explorer	Nationality and employer	Discovery or exploration
1497	John Cabot	Italian-English	Newfoundland or Nova Scotia
1498	John and Sebastian Cabot	Italian-English	Labrador to Hatteras
1499	Alonso de Ojeda	Spanish	South American coast, Venezuela
1500, Feb.	Vicente y Pinzon	Spanish	South American coast, Amazon River
1500, Apr.	Pedro Alvarez Cabral	Portuguese	Brazil (for Portugal)
1500-02	Gaspar Corte-Real	Portuguese	Labrador
1501	Rodrigo de Bastidas	Spanish	Central America
1513	Vasco Nunez de Balboa	Spanish	Pacific Ocean
1513	Juan Ponce de Leon	Spanish	Florida
1515	Juan de Solis	Spanish	Rio de la Plata
1519	Alonso de Pineda	Spanish	Mouth of Mississippi River
1519	Hernando Cortes	Spanish	Mexico
1520	Ferdinand Magellan	Portuguese-Spanish	Straits of Magellan, Tierra del Fuego
1524	Giovanni da Verrazano	Italian-French	Atlantic coast-New York harbor
1532	Francisco Pizarro	Spanish	Peru
1534	Jacques Cartier	French	Canada, Gulf of St. Lawrence
1536	Pedro de Mendoza	Spanish	Buenos Aires
1536	A.N. Cabeza de Vaca	Spanish	Texas coast and interior
1539	Francisco de Ulloa	Spanish	California coast
1539-41	Hernando de Soto	Spanish	Mississippi River near Memphis
1539	Marcos de Niza	Italian-Spanish	Southwest (now U.S.)
1540	Francisco V. de Coronado	Spanish	Southwest (now U.S.)
1540	Hernando Alarcon	Spanish	Colorado River
1540	Garcia de L. Cardenas	Spanish	Grand Canyon of the Colorado
1541	Francisco de Orellana	Spanish	Amazon River
1542	Juan Rodriguez Cabrillo	Portuguese-Spanish	San Diego harbor
1565	Pedro Menendez de Aviles	Spanish	St. Augustine
1576	Martin Frobisher	Engish	Frobisher's Bay, Canada
1577-80	Francis Drake	English	California coast
1582	Antonio de Espejo	Spanish	Southwest (named New Mexico)
1584	Amadas & Barlow (for Raleigh)	English	Virginia
1585-87	Sir Walter Raleigh's men	English	Roanoke Is., N.C.
1595	Sir Walter Raleigh	English	Orinoco River
1603-09	Samuel de Champlain	French	Canadian interior, Lake Champlain
1607	Capt. John Smith	English	Atlantic coast
1609-10	Henry Hudson	English-Dutch	Hudson River, Hudson Bay
1634	Jean Nicolet	French	Lake Michigan; Wisconsin
1673	Jacques Marquette, Louis Jolliet	French	Mississippi S to Arkansas
1682	Sieur de La Salle	French	Mississippi S to Gulf of Mexico
1789	Alexander Mackenzie	Canadian	Canadian Northwest

Arctic Exploration

Early Explorers

1587 — John Davis (England). Davis Strait to Sanderson's Hope, 72° 12′ N.

1596 — Willem Barents and Jacob van Heemskerck (Holland). Discovered Bear Island, touched northwest tip of Spitsbergen, 79° 49′ N, rounded Novaya Zemlya, wintered at Ice Haven.

1607 — Henry Hudson (England). North along Greenland's east coast to Cape Hold-with-Hope, 73° 30′, then north of Spitsbergen to 80° 23′. Returning he discovered Hudson's Touches (Jan Mayen).

1616 — William Baffin and Robert Bylot (England). Baffin Bay to Smith Sound.

1728 — Vitus Bering (Russia). Proved Asia and America were separated by sailing through strait.

1733-40 — Great Northern Expedition (Russia). Surveyed Siberian Arctic coast.

1741 — Vitus Bering (Russia). Sighted Alaska from sea, named Mount St. Elias. His lieutenant, Chirikof, discovered coast.

1771 — Samuel Hearne (Hudson's Bay Co.). Overland from Prince of Wales Fort (Churchill) on Hudson Bay to mouth of Coppermine River.

1778 — James Cook (Britain). Through Bering Strait to Icy Cape, Alaska, and North Cape, Siberia.

1789 — Alexander Mackenzie (North West Co., Britain). Montreal to mouth of Mackenzie River.

1806 — William Scoresby (Britain). N. of Spitsbergen to 81° 30'.

1820-3 — Ferdinand von Wrangel (Russia). Completed a survey of Siberian Arctic coast. His exploration joined that of James Cook at North Cape, confirming separation of the continents.

1845 — Sir John Franklin (Britain) was one of many to seek the Northwest Passage—an ocean route connecting the Atlantic and Pacific via the Arctic. His 2 ships (the Erebus and Terror) were last seen entering Lancaster Sound July 26.

1888 — Fridtjof Nansen (Norway) crossed Greenland's icecap.

1893-96 — Nansen in Fram drifted from New Siberian Is. to Spitsbergen; tried polar dash in 1895, reached Franz Josef Land.

1896 — Salomon A. Andree (Sweden). In June, made first attempt to reach North Pole by balloon; failed and returned in August. On July 11, 1897, Andree and 2 others started in balloon from Danes, Is., Spitsbergen, to drift across pole to America, and disappeared. Over 33 years later, Aug. 6, 1930, their frozen bodies were found on White Is., 82° 57' N 29° 52' E.

1903-06 — Roald Amundsen (Norway) first sailed Northwest Passage.

Discovery of North Pole

Robert E. Peary explored Greenland's coast 1891-92, tried for North Pole 1893. In 1900 he reached northern limit of Greenland and 83° 50' N; in 1902 he reached 84° 06' N; in 1906 he went from Ellesmere Is. to 87° 06' N. He sailed in the *Roosevelt*, July, 1908, to winter off Cape Sheridan, Grant Land. The dash for the North Pole began Mar. 1 from Cape Columbia, Ellesmere Land. Peary reached the pole, 90° N, Apr. 6, 1909.

Peary had several supporting groups carrying supplies until the last group turned back at 87° 47' N. Peary, Matthew Henson, and 4 eskimos proceeded with dog teams and sleds. They crossed the pole several times, finally built an igloo at 90°, remained 36 hours. Started south Apr. 7 at 4 p.m. for Cape Columbia. Eskimos were Coqueeh, Ootah, Eginwah, and Seegloo.

1914 — Donald MacMillan (U.S.). Northwest, 200 miles, from Axel Heiberg Island to seek Peary's Crocker Land.

1915-17 — Vilhjalmur Stefansson (Canada) discovered Borden, Brock, Meighen, and Lougheed Islands.

1918-20 — Roald Amundsen sailed Northeast Passage.

1925 — Amundsen and Lincoln Ellsworth (U.S.) reached 87° 44' N in attempt to fly to North Pole from Spitsbergen.

1926 — Richard E. Byrd and Floyd Bennett (U.S.) first over North Pole by air, May 9.

1926 — Amundsen, Ellsworth, and Umberto Nobile (Italy) flew from Spitsbergen over North Pole May 12, to Teller, Alaska, in dirigible *Norge*.

1928 — Nobile crossed North Pole in airship May 24, crashed May 25. Amundsen lost while trying to effect rescue by plane.

North Pole Exploration Records

On Aug. 3, 1958, the *Nautilus*, under Comdr. William R. Anderson, became the first ship to cross the North Pole beneath the Arctic ice.

The nuclear-powered U.S. submarine *Seadragon*, Comdr. George P. Steele 2d, made the first east-west underwater transit through the Northwest Passage during August, 1960. It sailed from Portsmouth N.H., headed between Greenland and Labrador through Baffin Bay, then west through Lancaster Sound and McClure Strait to the Beaufort Sea. Traveling submerged for the most part, the submarine made 850 miles from Baffin Bay to the Beaufort Sea in 6 days.

On Aug. 16, 1977, the Soviet nuclear icebreaker *Arktika* reached the North Pole and became the first surface ship to break through the Arctic ice pack to the top of the world.

On April 30, 1978, Naomi Uemura, a Japanese explorer, became the first man to reach the North Pole alone by dog sled. During the 54-day, 600-mile trek over the frozen Arctic, Uemura survived attacks by a marauding polar bear.

In April, 1982, Sir Ranulph Fiennes and Charles Burton, British explorers, reached the North Pole and became the first to circle the earth from pole to pole. They had reached the South Pole 16 months earlier. The 52,000-mile trek took 3 years, involved 23 people, and cost an estimated $18 million. The expedition was also the first to travel down the Scott Glacier and the first to journey up the Yukon and through the Northwest Passage in a single season.

On May 2, 1986, 6 American and Canadian explorers reached the North Pole assisted only by dogs. They became the first to reach the Pole without mechanical assistance since Robert E. Peary planted a flag there in 1909. The explorers, Americans Will Steger, Paul Schurke, Anne Bancroft, and Geoff Carroll, and Canadians Brent Boddy and Richard Weber completed the 500-mile journey in 56 days.

Antarctic Exploration

Early History

Antarctica has been approached since 1773-75, when Capt. James Cook (Britain) reached 71° 10' S. Many sea and landmarks bear names of early explorers. Bellingshausen (Russia) discovered Peter I and Alexander I Islands, 1819-21. Nathaniel Palmer (U.S.) discovered Palmer Peninsula, 60° W, 1820, without realizing that this was a continent. James Weddell (Britain) found Weddell Sea, 74° 15' S, 1823.

First to announce existence of the continent of Antarctica was Charles Wilkes (U.S.), who followed the coast for 1,500 mi., 1840. Adelie Coast, 140° E, was found by Dumont d'Urville (France), 1840. Ross Ice Shelf was found by James Clark Ross (Britain), 1841-42.

1895 — Leonard Kristensen (Norway) landed a party on the coast of Victoria Land. They were the first ashore on the main continental mass. C.E. Borchgrevink, a member of that party, returned in 1899 with a British expedition, first to winter on Antarctica.

1902-04 — Robert F. Scott (Britain) discovered Edward VII Peninsula. He reached 82° 17' S, 146° 33' E from McMurdo Sound.

1908-09 — Ernest Shackleton (Britain) introduced the use of Manchurian ponies in Antarctic sledging. He reached 88° 23' S, discovering a route on to the plateau by way of the Beardmore Glacier and pioneering the way to the pole.

Discovery of South Pole

1911 — Roald Amundsen (Norway) with 4 men and dog teams reached the pole Dec. 14.

1912 — Capt. Scott reached the pole from Ross Island Jan. 18, with 4 companions. They found Amundsen's tent. None of Scott's party survived. They were found Nov. 12.

1928 — First man to use an airplane over Antarctica was Hubert Wilkins (Britain).

1929 — Richard E. Byrd (U.S.) established Little America on Bay of Whales. On 1,600-mi. airplane flight begun Nov. 28 he crossed South Pole Nov. 29 with 3 others.

1934-35 — Byrd led 2d expedition to Little America, explored 450,000 sq. mi., wintered alone at weather station, 80° 08' S.

1934-37 — John Rymill led British Graham Land expedition; discovered that Palmer Peninsula is part of Antarctic mainland.

1935 — Lincoln Ellsworth (U.S.) flew south along Palmer Peninsula's east coast, then crossed continent to Little America, making 4 landings on unprepared terrain in bad weather.

1939-41 — U.S. Antarctic Service built West Base on Ross Ice Shelf under Paul Siple, and East Base on Palmer Peninsula under Richard Black. U.S. Navy plane flights discovered about 150,000 sq. miles of new land.

1940 — Byrd charted most of coast between Ross Sea and Palmer Peninsula.

1946-47 — U.S. Navy undertook Operation High-jump under Byrd. Expedition included 13 ships and 4,000 men. Airplanes photomapped coastline and penetrated beyond pole.

1946-48 — Ronne Antarctic Research Expedition, Comdr. Finn Ronne, USNR, determined the Antarctic to be only one continent with no strait between Weddell Sea and Ross Sea; discovered 250,000 sq. miles of land by flights to 79° S Lat., and made 14,000 aerial photographs over 450,000 sq. miles of land. Mrs. Ronne and Mrs. H. Darlington were the first women to winter on Antarctica.

1955-57 — U.S. Navy's Operation Deep Freeze led by Adm. Byrd. Supporting U.S. scientific efforts for the International Geophysical Year, the operation was commanded by Rear Adm. George Dufek. It established 5 coastal stations fronting the Indian, Pacific, and Atlantic oceans and also 3 interior stations; explored more than 1,000,000 sq. miles in Wilkes Land.

1957-58 — During the International Geophysical year, July, 1957, through Dec. 1958, scientists from 12 countries conducted ambitious programs of Antarctic research. A network of some 60 stations on the continent and sub-Arctic islands studied oceanography, glaciology, meteorology, seismology, geomagnetism, the ionosphere, cosmic rays, aurora, and airglow.

Dr. V.E. Fuchs led a 12-man Trans-Antarctic Expedition on the first land crossing of Antarctica. Starting from the Weddell Sea, they reached Scott Station Mar. 2, 1958, after traveling 2,158 miles in 98 days.

1958 — A group of 5 U.S. scientists led by Edward C. Thiel, seismologist, moving by tractor from Ellsworth Station on Weddell Sea, identified a huge mountain range, 5,000 ft. above the ice sheet and 9,000 ft. above sea level. The range, originally seen by a Navy plane, was named the Dufek Massif, for Rear Adm. George Dufek.

1959 — Twelve nations — Argentina, Australia, Belgium, Chile, France, Japan, New Zealand, Norway, South Africa, the Soviet Union, the United Kingdom, and the U.S. — signed a treaty suspending any territorial claims for 30 years and reserving the continent for research.

1961-62 — Scientists discovered a trough, the Bentley Trench, running from Ross Ice Shelf, Pacific, into Marie Byrd Land, around the end of the Ellsworth Mtns., toward the Weddell Sea.

1962 — First nuclear power plant began operation at McMurdo Sound.

1963 — On Feb. 22 a U.S. plane made the longest nonstop flight ever made in the S. Pole area, covering 3,600 miles in 10 hours. The flight was from McMurdo Station south past the geographical S. Pole to Shackleton Mtns., southeast to the "Area of Inaccessibility" and back to McMurdo Station.

1964 — A British survey team was landed by helicopter on Cook Island, the first recorded visit since its discovery in 1775.

1964 — New Zealanders completed one of the last and most important surveys when they mapped the mountain area from Cape Adare west some 400 miles to Pennell Glacier.

Volcanoes

More than 75 per cent of the world's 850 active volcanoes lie within the "Ring of Fire," a zone running along the west coast of the Americas from Chile to Alaska and down the east coast of Asia from Siberia to New Zealand. Twenty per cent of these volcanoes are located in Indonesia. Other prominent groupings are located in Japan, the Aleutian Islands, and Central America. Almost all active regions are found at the boundaries of the large moving plates which comprise the earth's surface. The "Ring of Fire" marks the boundary between the plates underlying the Pacific Ocean and those underlying the surrounding continents. Other active regions, such as the Mediterranean Sea and Iceland, are located on plate boundaries.

Major Historical Eruptions

Approximately 7,000 years ago, Mazama, a 9,900-feet-high volcano in southern Oregon, erupted violently, ejecting ash and lava. The ash spread over the entire northwestern United States and as far away as Saskatchewan, Canada. During the eruption, the top of the mountain collapsed, leaving a caldera 6 miles across and about a half mile deep, which filled with rain water to form what is now called Crater Lake.

In 79 A.D., Vesuvio, or Vesuvius, a 4,190 feet volcano overlooking Naples Bay became active after several centuries of quiescence. On Aug. 24 of that year, a heated mud and ash flow swept down the mountain engulfing the cities of Pompeii, Herculaneum, and Stabiae with debris over 60 feet deep. About 10 percent of the population of the 3 towns was killed.

The largest eruptions in recent centuries have been in Indonesia. In 1883, an eruption similar to the Mazama eruption occurred on the island of Krakatau. On August 27, the 2,640-feet-high peak of the volcano collapsed to 1,000 feet below sea level, leaving only a small portion of the island standing above the sea. Ash from the eruption colored sunsets around the world for 2 years. A tsunami ("tidal wave") generated by the collapse killed 36,000 people in nearby Java and Sumatra and eventually reached England. A similar, but even more powerful, eruption had taken place 68 years earlier at Tambora volcano on the Indonesian island of Sumbawa.

Notable Active Volcanoes

Name, latest activity	Location	Feet
Africa		
Cameroon (1982)	Cameroon	13,354
Nyirangongo (1977)	Zaire	11,400
Nyamuragira (1986)	Zaire	10,028
Karthala (1977)	Comoro Is.	8,000
Piton de la Fournaise (1986)	Reunion Is.	5,981
Erta-Ale (1973)	Ethiopia	1,650
Antarctica		
Erebus (1987)	Ross Island	12,450
Big Ben (1960)	Heard Island	9,007
Deception Island (1970)	South Shetland Islands	1,890
Asia-Oceania		
Klyuchevskaya (1985)	USSR	15,584
Kerinci (1987)	Sumatra	12,467
Rindjani (1966)	Indonesia	12,224
Semeru (1987)	Java	12,060
Slamet (1967)	Java	11,247
Raung (1982)	Java	10,932
Shiveluch (1964)	USSR	10,771
Agung (1964)	Bali	10,308
On-Take (1980)	Japan	10,049
Mayon (1978)	Philippines	9,991
Merapi (1987)	Java	9,551
Bezymianny (1986)	USSR	9,514
Marapi (1982)	Sumatra	9,485
Ruapehu (1986)	New Zealand	9,175
Asama (1983)	Japan	8,300
Niigata Yakeyama (1983)	Japan	8,111
Yake Dake (1963)	Japan	8,064
Alaid (1972)	Kuril Is.	7,662
Ulawun (1986)	New Britain	7,532
Ngauruhoe (1975)	New Zealand	7,515
Chokai (1974)	Japan	7,300
Galunggung (1982)	Java	7,113
Amburombu (1969)	Indonesia	7,051
Azuma (1978)	Japan	6,700
Tangkuban Prahu (1967)	Java	6,637
Sangeang Api (1987)	Indonesia	6,351
Nasu (1977)	Japan	6,210
Tiatia (1973)	Kuril Islands	6,013
Manam (1987)	Papua New Guinea	6,000
Soputan (1984)	Indonesia	5,994
Siau (1976)	Indonesia	5,853
Kelud (1967)	Java	5,679
Batur (1968)	Bali	5,636
Ternate (1963)	Indonesia	5,627
Kirisima (1982)	Japan	5,577
Keli Mutu (1968)	Indonesia	5,460
Akita Komaga take (1970)	Japan	5,449
Gamkonora (1981)	Indonesia	5,364
Aso (1985)	Japan	5,223
Lewotobi Laki-Laki (1968)	Indonesia	5,217
Lokon-Empung (1987)	Indonesia	5,187
Bulusan (1983)	Philippines	5,115
Sarycheva (1976)	Kuril Islands	4,960
Me-akan (1966)	Japan	4,931
Karkar (1981)	Papua New Guinea	4,920
Karymsky (1985)	USSR	4,869
Lopevi (1982)	New Hebrides	4,755
Ambrym (1979)	New Hebrides	4,376
Awu (1968)	Indonesia	4,350
Sakurajima (1986)	Japan	3,668
Langila (1987)	New Britain	3,586
Dukono (1971)	Indonesia	3,566
Suwanosezima (1987)	Japan	2,640
O-Sima (1977)	Japan	2,550
Usu (1978)	Japan	2,400
Pagan (1985)	Mariana Is.	1,870
White Island (1987)	New Zealand	1,075
Taal (1977)	Philippines	984
Central America—Caribbean		
Acatenango (1972)	Guatemala	12,992
Fuego (1986)	Guatemala	12,582
Tacana (1986)	Guatemala	12,400
Santiaguito (Santa Maria) (1986)	Guatemala	12,362
Irazu (1967)	Costa Rica	11,260
Poas (1984)	Costa Rica	8,930
Pacaya (1986)	Guatemala	8,346
Izalco (1966)	El Salvador	7,749
San Miguel (1986)	El Salvador	6,994
Rincon de la Vieja (1987)	Costa Rica	6,234
El Viejo (San Cristobal) (1981)	Nicaragua	5,840
Ometepe (Concepcion) (1986)	Nicaragua	5,106

Name, latest activity	Location	Feet
Arenal (1987)	Costa Rica	5,092
Momotombo (1982)	Nicaragua	4,199
Soufriere (1979)	St. Vincent	4,048
Telica (1982)	Nicaragua	3,409
South America		
Lascar (1986)	Chile	19,652
Cotopaxi (1975)	Ecuador	19,347
Tupungatito (1980)	Chile	18,504
Sangay (1976)	Ecuador	17,159
Guagua Pichincha (1982)	Ecuador	15,696
Purace (1977)	Colombia	15,604
Llaima (1984)	Chile	10,239
Villarica (1984)	Chile	9,318
Hudson (1973)	Chile	8,580
Alcedo (1970)	Galapagos Is.	3,599
Ruiz (1987)	Colombia	...
Mid-Pacific		
Mauna Loa (1984)	Hawaii	13,680
Kilauea (1987)	Hawaii	4,077
Mid-Atlantic Ridge		
Beerenberg (1985)	Jan Mayen Is.	7,470
Hekla (1981)	Iceland	4,892
Leirhnukur (1975)	Iceland	2,145
Krafla (1984)	Iceland	2,145
Surtsey (1967)	Iceland	568
Europe		
Etna (1987)	Italy	11,053
Stromboli (1986)	Italy	3,038
North America		
Colima (1987)	Mexico	14,003
Redoubt (1966)	Alaska	10,197
Iliamna (1978)	Alaska	10,092
Mt. St. Helens (1986)	Washington	9,677
Shishaldin (1987)	Aleutian Is.	9,387
Veniaminof (1987)	Alaska	8,225
Pavlof (1987)	Aleutian Is.	8,215
El Chichon (1983)	Mexico	7,300
Makushin (1987)	Aleutian Is.	6,680
Pogromni (1964)	Alaska	6,568
Trident 1963)	Alaska	6,010
Great Sitkin (1974)	Aleutian Is.	5,710
Gareloi (1982)	Aleutian Is.	5,334
Korovin (1987)	Aleutian Is.	4,852
Akutan (1987)	Aleutian Is.	4,275
Kiska (1969)	Aleutian Is.	4,275
Augustine (1986)	Alaska	4,025
Okmok (1987)	Aleutian Is.	3,519
Seguam (1977)	Alaska	3,458

Notable Volcanic Eruptions

Date	Volcano	Deaths
79 A.D.	Mt. Vesuvius, Italy	16,000
1169	Mt. Etna, Sicily	15,000
1631	Mt. Vesuvius, Italy	4,000
1669	Mt. Etna, Sicily	20,000
1772	Mt. Papandayan, Java	3,000
1792	Mt. Unzen-Dake, Japan	10,400
1815	Tamboro, Java	12,000
Aug. 26-28, 1883	Krakatau, Indonesia	35,000
Apr. 8, 1902	Santa Maria, Guatemala	1,000
May 8, 1902	Mt. Pelée, Martinique	40,000
1911	Mt. Taal, Philippines	1,400
1919	Mt. Kelud, Java	5,000
Jan. 18-21, 1951	Mt. Lamington, New Guinea	3,000
Apr. 26, 1966	Mt. Kelud, Java	1,000
May 18, 1980	Mt. St. Helens, U.S.	60
Nov. 13, 1985	Nevado del Ruiz, Colombia	22,940
Aug. 24, 1986	NW Cameroon	1,700+

Record Oil Spills

Name, place	Date	Cause	Tons
Ixtoc I oil well, southern Gulf of Mexico	June 3, 1979	Blowout	600,000
Nowruz oil field, Persian Gulf	Feb., 1983	Blowout	600,000(est.)
Atlantic Empress & Aegean Captain, off Trinidad & Tobago	July 19, 1979	Collision	300,000
Castillo de Bellver, off Cape Town, South Africa	Aug. 6, 1983	Fire	250,000
Amoco Cadiz, near Portsall, France	March 16, 1978	Grounding	223,000
Torrey Canyon, off Land's End, England	March 18, 1967	Grounding	119,000
Sea Star, Gulf of Oman	Dec. 19, 1972	Collision	115,000
Urquiola, La Coruna, Spain	May 12, 1976	Grounding	100,000
Hawaiian Patriot, northern Pacific	Feb. 25, 1977	Fire	99,000
Othello, Tralhavet Bay, Sweden	March 20, 1970	Collision	60,000-100,000
Jacob Maersk, Porto do Leixoes, Portugal	Jan. 29, 1975	Grounding	84,000
Wafra, Cape Agulhas, South Africa	Feb. 27, 1971	Grounding	63,000
Epic Colacotroni, Caribbean	May, 1975	Grounding	57,000

Other Notable Oil Spills

Name, place	Date	Cause	Gallons
World Glory, off South Africa	June 13, 1968	Hull failure	13,524,000
Keo, off Massachusetts	Nov. 5, 1969	Hull failure	8,820,000
Storage tank, Sewaren, N.J.	Nov. 4, 1969	Tank rupture	8,400,000
Ekofisk oil field, North Sea	Apr. 22, 1977	Well blowout	8,200,000
Argo Merchant, Nantucket, Mass.	Dec. 15, 1976	Grounding	7,700,000
Pipeline, West Delta, La.	Oct. 15, 1967	Dragging anchor	6,720,000
Tanker off Japan	Nov. 30, 1971	Ship broke in half	6,258,000

Highest and Lowest Continental Altitudes

Source: National Geographic Society, Washington, D.C.

Continent	Highest point	Feet elevation	Lowest point	Feet below sea level
Asia	Mount Everest, Nepal-Tibet	**29,028**	Dead Sea, Israel-Jordan	1,312
South America	Mount Aconcagua, Argentina	**22,834**	Valdes Peninsula, Argentina	131
North America	Mount McKinley, Alaska	**20,320**	Death Valley, California	282
Africa	Kilimanjaro, Tanzania	**19,340**	Lake Assal, Djibouti	512
Europe	Mount El'brus, USSR	**18,510**	Caspian Sea, USSR	92
Antarctica	Vinson Massif	**16,864**	Unknown	...
Australia	Mount Kosciusko, New South Wales	**7,310**	Lake Eyre, South Australia	52

Mountains

Height of Mount Everest

Mt. Everest was considered to be 29,002 ft. tall when Edmund Hillary and Tenzing Norgay scaled it in 1953. This triangulation figure had been accepted since 1850. In 1954 the Surveyor General of the Republic of India set the height at 29,028 ft., plus or minus 10 ft. because of snow. The National Geographic Society accepts the new figure, but many mountaineering groups still use 29,002 ft.

In 1987, it was announced that new calculations based on U.S. satellite measurements indicate that the Himalayan peak K-2 may be the highest mountain in the world, a few feet higher than Mount Everest. According to the calculations, K-2 rises 29,064 feet above sea level and, with more refined survey work, may be found to be even higher. Scientists who conducted the survey were unwilling to conclude definitely that K-2 was the world's highest mountain until Mt. Everest could be remeasured using the same technique that had been used to measure K-2.

United States, Canada, Mexico

Name	Place	Feet
McKinley	Alas	20,320
Logan	Can	19,850
Citlaltepec (Orizaba)	Mexico	18,700
St. Elias	Alas-Can	18,008
Popocatepetl	Mexico	17,887
Foraker	Alas	17,400
Iztaccihuatl	Mexico	17,343
Lucania	Can	17,147
King	Can	16,971
Steele	Can	16,644
Bona	Alas	16,550
Blackburn	Alas	16,390
Kennedy	Alas	16,286
Sanford	Alas	16,237
South Buttress	Alas	15,885
Wood	Can	15,885
Vancouver	Alas-Can	15,700
Churchill	Alas	15,638
Fairweather	Alas-Can	15,300
Zinantecatl (Toluca)	Mexico	15,016
Hubbard	Alas-Can	15,015
Bear	Alas	14,831
Walsh	Can	14,780
East Buttress	Alas	14,730
Matlalcueyetl	Mexico	14,636
Hunter	Alas	14,573

Name	Place	Feet
Alverstone	Alas-Can	14,565
Browne Tower	Alas	14,530
Whitney	Cal	14,494
Elbert	Col	14,433
Massive	Col	14,421
Harvard	Col	14,420
Rainier	Wash	14,410
Williamson	Cal	14,375
Blanca Peak	Col	14,345
La Plata	Col	14,336
Uncompahgre	Col	14,309
Crestone	Col	14,294
Lincoln	Col	14,286
Grays Peak	Col	14,270
Antero	Col	14,269
Torreys	Col	14,267
Castle	Col	14,265
Quandary	Col	14,265
Evans	Col	14,264
Longs Peak	Col	14,256
McArthur	Can	14,253
Wilson	Col	14,246
White	Cal	14,246
North Palisade	Cal	14,242
Shavano	Col	14,229
Belford	Col	14,197

Name	Place	Feet
Princeton	Col	14,197
Crestone Needle	Col	14,197
Yale	Col	14,196
Bross	Col	14,172
Kit Carson	Col	14,165
Wrangell	Alas	14,163
Shasta	Cal	14,162
Sill	Cal	14,162
El Diente	Col	14,159
Maroon	Col	14,156
Tabeguache	Col	14,155
Oxford	Col	14,153
Sneffels	Col	14,150
Point Success	Wash	14,150
Democrat	Col	14,148
Capitol	Col	14,130
Liberty Cap	Wash	14,112
Pikes Peak	Col	14,110
Snowmass	Col	14,092
Windom	Col	14,087
Russell	Cal	14,086
Eolus	Col	14,084
Columbia	Col	14,073
Augusta	Alas-Can	14,070
Missouri	Col	14,067
Humboldt	Col	14,064

South America

Peak, Country	Feet
Aconcagua, Argentina	22,834
Ojos del Salado, Arg.-Chile	22,572
Bonete, Argentina	22,546
Tupungato, Argentina-Chile	22,310
Pissis, Argentina	22,241
Mercedario, Argentina	22,211
Huascaran, Peru	22,205
Llullaillaco, Argentina-Chile	22,057
El Libertador, Argentina	22,047
Cachi, Argentina	22,047
Yerupaja, Peru	21,709
Galan, Argentina	21,654
El Muerto, Argentina-Chile	21,457
Sajama, Bolivia	21,391
Nacimiento, Argentina	21,302
Illimani, Bolivia	21,201
Coropuna, Peru	21,083

Peak, Country	Feet
Laudo, Argentina	20,997
Ancohuma, Bolivia	20,958
Ausangate, Peru	20,945
Toro, Argentina-Chile	20,932
Illampu, Bolivia	20,873
Tres Cruces, Argentina-Chile	20,853
Huandoy, Peru	20,852
Parinacota, Bolivia-Chile	20,768
Tortolas, Argentina-Chile	20,745
Ampato, Peru	20,702
Condor, Argentina	20,669
Salcantay, Peru	20,574
Chimborazo, Ecuador	20,561
Huancarhuas, Peru	20,531
Famatina, Argentina	20,505
Pumasillo, Peru	20,492
Solo, Argentina	20,492

Peak, Country	Feet
Polleras, Argentina	20,456
Pular, Chile	20,423
Chani, Argentina	20,341
Aucanquilcha, Chile	20,295
Juncal, Argentina-Chile	20,276
Negro, Argentina	20,184
Quela, Argentina	20,128
Condoriri, Bolivia	20,095
Palermo, Argentina	20,079
Solimana, Peru	20,068
San Juan, Argentina-Chile	20,049
Sierra Nevada, Arg.-Chile	20,023
Antofalla, Argentina	20,013
Marmolejo, Argentina-Chile	20,013
Chachani, Peru	19,931
Licancabur, Argentina-Chile	19,425

The highest point in the West Indies is in the Dominican Republic, Pico Duarte (10,417 ft.)

Africa, Australia, and Oceania

Peak, country	Feet
Kilimanjaro, Tanzania	19,340
Kenya, Kenya	17,058
Margherita Pk., Uganda-Zaire	16,763
Jaja, New Guinea	16,500
Trikora, New Guinea	15,585
Mandala, New Guinea	15,420
Ras Dashan, Ethiopia	15,158

Peak, country	Feet
Meru, Tanzania	14,979
Wilhelm, Papua New Guinea	14,793
Karisimbi, Zaire-Rwanda	14,787
Elgon, Kenya-Uganda	14,178
Batu, Ethiopia	14,131
Guna, Ethiopia	13,881
Gughe, Ethiopia	13,780

Peak, country	Feet
Toubkal, Morocco	13,661
Kinabalu, Malaysia	13,455
Kerinci, Sumatra	12,467
Cook, New Zealand	12,349
Teide, Canary Islands	12,198
Semeru, Java	12,060
Kosciusko, Australia	7,310

Europe

Peak, country	Feet
Alps	
Mont Blanc, Fr. It.	15,771
Monte Rosa (highest peak of group), Switz.	15,203
Dom, Switz.	14,911

Peak, county	Feet
Liskamm, It., Switz.	14,852
Weisshorn, Switz.	14,780
Taschhorn, Switz.	14,733
Matterhorn, It., Switz.	14,690
Dent Blanche, Switz.	14,293

Peak, country	Feet
Nadelhorn, Switz.	14,196
Grand Combin, Switz.	14,154
Lenzpitze, Switz.	14,088
Finsteraarhorn, Switz.	14,022
Castor, Switz.	13,865

Peak, country	Feet
Zinalrothorn, Switz.	13,849
Hohberghorn, Switz.	13,842
Alphubel, Switz.	13,799
Rimpfischhorn, Switz.	13,776
Aletschorn, Switz.	13,763
Strahlhorn, Switz.	13,747
Dent D'Herens, Switz.	13,686
Breithorn, It., Switz.	13,665
Bishorn, Switz.	13,645
Jungfrau, Switz.	13,642
Ecrins, Fr.	13,461
Monch, Switz.	13,448
Pollux, Switz.	13,422
Schreckhorn, Switz.	13,379
Ober Gabelhorn, Switz.	13,330
Gran Paradiso, It.	13,323
Bernina, It., Switz.	13,284
Fiescherhorn, Switz.	13,283

Peak, county	Feet
Grunhorn, Switz.	13,266
Lauteraarhorn, Switz.	13,261
Durrenhorn, Switz.	13,238
Allalinhorn, Switz.	13,213
Weissmies, Switz.	13,199
Lagginhorn, Switz.	13,156
Zupo, Switz.	13,120
Fletschhorn, Switz.	13,110
Adlerhorn, Switz.	13,081
Gletscherhorn, Switz.	13,068
Schalihorn, Switz.	13,040
Scerscen, Switz.	13,028
Eiger, Switz.	13,025
Jagerhorn, Switz.	13,024
Rottalhorn, Switz.	13,022

Peak, country	Feet
Pyrenees	
Aneto, Sp.	11,168
Posets, Sp.	11,073
Perdido, Sp.	11,007
Vignemale, Fr., Sp.	10,820
Long, Sp.	10,479
Estats, Sp.	10,304
Montcalm, Sp.	10,105
Caucasus (Europe-Asia)	
El'brus, USSR	18,510
Shkara, USSR	17,064
Dykh Tau, USSR	17,054
Kashtan Tau, USSR	16,877
Dzhangi Tau, USSR	16,565
Kazbek, USSR	16,558

Asia

Peak	Country	Feet
K2 (Godwin Austen)	Kashmir	29,064
Everest	Nepal-Tibet	29,028
Kanchenjunga	India-Nepal	28,208
Lhotse I (Everest)	Nepal-Tibet	27,923
Makalu I	Nepal-Tibet	27,824
Lhotse II (Everest)	Nepal-Tibet	27,560
Dhaulagiri	Nepal	26,810
Manaslu I	Nepal	26,760
Cho Oyu	Nepal-Tibet	26,750
Nanga Parbat	Kashmir	26,660
Annapurna I	Nepal	26,504
Gasherbrum	Kashmir	26,470
Broad	Kashmir	26,400
Gosainthan	Tibet	26,287
Annapurna II	Nepal	26,041
Gyachung Kang	Nepal-Tibet	25,910
Disteghil Sar	Kashmir	25,868
Himalchuli	Nepal	25,801
Nuptse (Everest)	Nepal-Tibet	25,726
Masherbrum	Kashmir	25,660
Nanda Devi	India	25,645
Rakaposhi	Kashmir	25,550
Kamet	India-Tibet	25,447
Namcha Barwa	Tibet	25,445
Gurla Mandhata	Tibet	25,355
Ulugh Muz Tagh	Sinkiang-Tibet	25,340

Peak	Country	Feet
Kungur	Sinkiang	25,325
Tirich Mir	Pakistan	25,230
Makalu II	Nepal-Tibet	25,120
Minya Konka	China	24,900
Kula Gangri	Bhutan-Tibet	24,784
Changtzu (Everest)	Nepal-Tibet	24,780
Muz Tagh Ata	Sinkiang	24,757
Skyang Kangri	Kashmir	24,750
Communism Peak	USSR	24,590
Jongsang Peak	India-Nepal	24,472
Pobedy Peak	Sinkiang-USSR	24,406
Sia Kangri	Kashmir	24,350
Haramosh Peak	Pakistan	24,270
Istoro Nal	Pakistan	24,240
Tent Peak	India-Nepal	24,165
Chomo Lhari	Bhutan-Tibet	24,040
Chamlang	Nepal	24,012
Kabru	India-Nepal	24,002
Alung Gangri	Tibet	24,000
Baltoro Kangri	Kashmir	23,990
Mussu Shan	Sinkiang	23,890
Mana	India	23,860
Baruntse	Nepal	23,688
Nepal Peak	India-Nepal	23,500
Amne Machin	China	23,490
Gauri Sankar	Nepal-Tibet	23,440

Peak	Country	Feet
Badrinath	India	23,420
Nunkun	Kashmir	23,410
Lenina Peak	USSR	23,405
Pyramid	India-Nepal	23,400
Api	Nepal	23,399
Pauhunri	India-Tibet	23,385
Trisul	India	23,360
Kangto	India-Tibet	23,260
Nyenchhen Thanglha	Tibet	23,255
Trisuli	India	23,210
Pumori	Nepal-Tibet	23,190
Dunagiri	India	23,184
Lombo Kangra	Tibet	23,165
Saipal	Nepal	23,100
Macha Pucchare	Nepal	22,958
Numbar	Nepal	22,817
Kanjiroba	Nepal	22,580
Ama Dablam	Nepal	22,350
Cho Polu	Nepal	22,093
Lingtren	Nepal-Tibet	21,972
Khumbutse	Nepal-Tibet	21,785
Hlako Gangri	Tibet	21,266
Mt. Grosvenor	China	21,190
Thagchhab Gangri	Tibet	20,970
Damavand	Iran	18,606
Ararat	Turkey	16,804

Antarctica

Peak	Feet
Vinson Massif	16,864
Tyree	16,290
Shinn	15,750
Gardner	15,375
Epperly	15,100
Kirkpatrick	14,855
Elizabeth	14,698
Markham	14,290
Bell	14,117
Mackellar	14,098
Anderson	13,957
Bentley	13,934
Kaplan	13,878

Peak	Feet
Andrew Jackson	13,750
Sidley	13,720
Ostenso	13,710
Minto	13,668
Miller	13,650
Long Gables	13,620
Dickerson	13,517
Giovinetto	13,412
Wade	13,400
Fisher	13,386
Fridtjof Nansen	13,350
Wexler	13,202
Lister	13,200

Peak	Feet
Shear	13,100
Odishaw	13,008
Donaldson	12,894
Ray	12,808
Sellery	12,779
Waterman	12,730
Anne	12,703
Press	12,566
Falla	12,549
Rucker	12,520
Goldthwait	12,510
Morris	12,500
Erebus	12,450

Peak	Feet
Campbell	12,434
Don Pedro Christophersen	12,355
Lysaght	12,326
Huggins	12,247
Sabine	12,200
Astor	12,175
Mohl	12,172
Frankes	12,064
Jones	12,040
Gjelsvik	12,008
Coman	12,000

Ocean Areas and Average Depths

Four major bodies of water are recognized by geographers and mapmakers. They are: the Pacific, Atlantic, Indian, and Arctic oceans. The Atlantic and Pacific oceans are considered divided at the equator into the No. and So. Atlantic; the No. and So. Pacific. The Arctic Ocean is the name for waters north of the continental land masses in the region of the Arctic Circle.

	Sq. miles	Avg. depth in feet
Pacific Ocean	64,186,300	12,925
Atlantic Ocean	33,420,000	11,730
Indian Ocean	28,350,500	12,598
Arctic Ocean	5,105,700	3,407
South China Sea	1,148,500	4,802
Caribbean Sea	971,400	8,448
Mediterranean Sea	969,100	4,926
Bering Sea	873,000	4,893
Gulf of Mexico	582,100	5,297
Sea of Okhotsk	537,500	3,192
Sea of Japan	391,100	5,468

	Sq. miles	Avg. depth in feet
Hudson Bay	281,900	305
East China Sea	256,600	620
Andaman Sea	218,100	3,667
Black Sea	196,100	3,906
Red Sea	174,900	1,764
North Sea	164,900	308
Baltic Sea	147,500	180
Yellow Sea	113,500	121
Persian Gulf	88,800	328
Gulf of California	59,100	2,375

How Deep Is the Ocean?

Principal ocean depths. Source: Defense Mapping Agency Hydrographic/Topographic Center

Name of area	Location		Depth Meters	Fathoms	Feet
Pacific Ocean					
Mariana Trench	11°20'N	142°12'E	10,924	5,973	35,840
Tonga Trench	23°16'S	174°44'W	10,800	5,906	35,433
Philippine Trench	10°38'N	126°36'E	10,057	5,499	32,995
Kermadec Trench	31°53'S	177°21'W	10,047	5,494	32,963
Bonin Trench	24°30'N	143°24'E	9,994	5,464	32,788
Kuril Trench	44°15'N	150°34'E	9,750	5,331	31,988
Izu Trench	31°05'N	142°10'E	9,695	5,301	31,808
New Britain Trench	06°19'S	153°45'E	8,940	4,888	29,331
Yap Trench	08°33'N	138°02'E	8,527	4,663	27,976
Japan Trench	36°08'N	142°43'E	8,412	4,600	27,599
Peru-Chile Trench	23°18'S	71°14'W	8,064	4,409	26,457
Palau Trench	07°52'N	134°56'E	8,054	4,404	26,424
Aleutian Trench	50°51'N	177°11'E	7,679	4,199	25,194
New Hebrides Trench	20°36'S	168°37'E	7,570	4,139	24,836
North Ryukyu Trench	24°00'N	126°48'E	7,181	3,927	23,560
Mid. America Trench	14°02'N	93°39'W	6,662	3,643	21,857
Atlantic Ocean					
Puerto Rico Trench	19°55'N	65°27'W	8,605	4,705	28,232
So. Sandwich Trench	55°42'S	25°56'E	8,325	4,552	27,313
Romanche Gap	0°13'S	18°26'W	7,728	4,226	25,354
Cayman Trench	19°12'N	80°00'W	7,535	4,120	24,721
Brazil Basin	09°10'S	23°02'W	6,119	3,346	20,076
Indian Ocean					
Java Trench	10°19'S	109°58'E	7,125	3,896	23,376
Ob' Trench	09°45'S	67°18'E	6,874	3,759	22,553
Diamantina Trench	35°50'S	105°14'E	6,602	3,610	21,660
Vema Trench	09°08'S	67°15'E	6,402	3,501	21,004
Agulhas Basin	45°20'S	26°50'E	6,195	3,387	20,325
Arctic Ocean					
Eurasia Basin	82°23'N	19°31'E	5,450	2,980	17,881
Mediterranean Sea					
Ionian Basin	36°32'N	21°06'E	5,150	2,816	16,896

Principal World Rivers

Source: Geological Survey, U.S. Interior Department (length in miles)

River	Outflow	Lgth	River	Outflow	Lgth	River	Outflow	Lgth
Albany	James Bay	610	Indus	Arabian Sea	1,800	Red River of N.	Lake Winnipeg	545
Amazon	Atlantic Ocean	4,000	Irrawaddy	Bay of Bengal	1,337	Rhine	North Sea	820
Amu	Aral Sea	1,578	Japura	Amazon River	1,750	Rhone	Gulf of Lions	505
Amur	Tatar Strait	2,744	Jordan	Dead Sea	200	Rio de la Plata	Atlantic Ocean	150
Angara	Yenisey River	1,151	Kootenay	Columbia River	485	Rio Grande	Gulf of Mexico	1,760
Arkansas	Mississippi	1,459	Lena	Laptev Sea	2,734	Rio Roosevelt	Aripuana	400
Back	Arctic Ocean	605	Loire	Bay of Biscay	634	Saguenay	St. Lawrence R.	434
Brahmaputra	Bay of Bengal	1,800	Mackenzie	Arctic Ocean	2,635	St. John	Bay of Fundy	418
Bug, Southern	Dnieper River	532	Madeira	Amazon River	2,013	St. Lawrence	Gulf of St. Law.	800
Bug, Western	Wisla River	481	Magdalena	Caribbean Sea	956	Salween	Andaman Sea	1,500
Canadian	Arkansas River	906	Marne	Seine River	326	Sao Francisco	Atlantic Ocean	1,988
Chang Jiang	E. China Sea	3,964	Mekong	S. China Sea	2,600	Saskatchewan	Lake Winnipeg	1,205
Churchill, Man.	Hudson Bay	1,000	Meuse	North Sea	580	Seine	English Chan.	496
Churchill, Que.	Atlantic Ocean	532	Mississippi	Gulf of Mexico	2,348	Shannon	Atlantic Ocean	230
Colorado	Gulf of Calif.	1,450	Missouri	Mississippi	2,540	Snake	Columbia River	1,038
Columbia	Pacific Ocean	1,243	Murray-Darling	Indian Ocean	2,310	Sungari	Amur River	1,150
Congo	Atlantic Ocean	2,900	Negro	Amazon	1,400	Syr	Aral Sea	1,370
Danube	Black Sea	1,776	Nelson	Hudson Bay	1,410	Tajo, Tagus	Atlantic Ocean	626
Dnieper	Black Sea	1,420	Niger	Gulf of Guinea	2,590	Tennessee	Ohio River	652
Dniester	Black Sea	877	Nile	Mediterranean	4,160	Thames	North Sea	236
Don	Sea of Azov	1,224	Ob-Irtysh	Gulf of Ob	3,362	Tiber	Tyrrhenian Sea	252
Drava	Danube River	447	Oder	Baltic Sea	567	Tigris	Shatt al-Arab	1,180
Dvina, North	White Sea	824	Ohio	Mississippi	1,310	Tisza	Danube River	600
Dvina, West	Gulf of Riga	634	Orange	Atlantic Ocean	1,300	Tocantins	Para River	1,677
Ebro	Mediterranean	565	Orinoco	Atantic Ocean	1,600	Ural	Caspian Sea	1,575
Elbe	North Sea	724	Ottawa	St. Lawrence R.	790	Uruguay	Rio de la Plata	1,000
Euphrates	Shatt al-Arab	1,700	Paraguay	Parana River	1,584	Volga	Caspian Sea	2,194
Fraser	Str. of Georgia	850	Parana	Rio de la Plata	2,485	Weser	North Sea	454
Gambia	Atlantic Ocean	700	Peace	Slave River	1,210	Wisla	Bay of Danzig	675
Ganges	Bay of Bengal	1,560	Pilcomayo	Paraguay River	1,000	Yellow (See Huang)		
Garonne	Bay of Biscay	357	Po	Adriatic Sea	405	Yenisey	Kara Sea	2,543
Hsi	S. China Sea	1,200	Purus	Amazon River	2,100	Yukon	Bering Sea	1,979
Huang	Yellow Sea	2,903	Red	Mississippi	1,290	Zambezi	Indian Ocean	1,700

Major Rivers in North America

Source: U.S. Geological Survey

River	Source or Upper Limit of Length	Outflow	Miles
Alabama	Gilmer County, Ga.	Mobile River	729
Albany	Lake St. Joseph, Ont., Can.	James Bay	610
Allegheny	Potter County, Pa.	Ohio River	325
Altamaha-Ocmulgee	Junction of Yellow and South Rivers, Newton County, Ga.	Atlantic Ocean	392
Apalachicola-Chattahoochee	Towns County, Ga.	Gulf of Mexico, Fla.	524
Arkansas	Lake County, Col.	Mississippi River, Ark.	1,459
Assiniboine	Eastern Saskatchewan	Red River	450
Attawapiskat	Attawapiskat, Ont., Can.	James Bay	465
Big Black (Miss.)	Webster County, Miss.	Mississippi River	330
Black (N.W.T.)	Contwoyto Lake	Chantrey Inlet	600
Brazos	Junction of Salt and Double Mountain Forks, Stonewall County, Tex.	Gulf of Mexico	923
Canadian	Las Animas County, Col.	Arkansas River, Okla.	906
Cedar (Iowa)	Dodge County, Minn.	Iowa River, Ia.	329
Cheyenne	Junction of Antelope Creek and Dry Fork, Converse County, Wyo.	Missouri River	290
Churchill	Methy Lake	Hudson Bay	1,000
Cimarron	Colfax County, N.M.	Arkansas River, Okla.	600
Clark Fork-Pend Oreille	Silver Bow County, Mon.	Columbia River, B.C.	505
Colorado (Ariz.)	Rocky Mountain National Park, Col. (90 miles in Mexico)	Gulf of Cal., Mexico	1,450
Colorado (Texas)	West Texas	Matagorda Bay	862
Columbia	Columbia Lake, British Columbia	Pacific Ocean, bet. Ore. and Wash.	1,243
Columbia, Upper	Columbia Lake, British Columbia	To mouth of Snake River	890
Connecticut	Third Connecticut Lake, N.H.	L.I. Sound, Conn.	407
Coppermine (N.W.T.)	Lac de Gras	Coronation Gulf (Arctic Ocean)	525
Cumberland	Letcher County, Ky.	Ohio River	720
Delaware	Schoharie County, N.Y.	Liston Point, Delaware Bay	390
Fraser	Near Mount Robson (on Continental Divide)	Strait of Georgia	850
Gila	Catron County, N.M.	Colorado River, Ariz.	649
Green (Ut.-Wyo.)	Junction of Wells and Trail Creeks, Sublette County, Wyo.	Colorado River, Ut.	730
Hamilton (Lab.)	Lake Ashuanipi	Atlantic Ocean	532
Hudson	Henderson Lake, Essex County, N.Y.	Upper N.Y. Bay, N.Y.,-N.J.	306
Illinois	St. Joseph County, Ind.	Mississippi River	420
James (N.D.-S.D.)	Wells County, N.D.	Missouri River, S.D.	710
James (Va.)	Junction of Jackson and Cowpasture Rivers, Botetourt County, Va.	Hampton Roads	340
Kanawha-New	Junction of North and South Forks of New River, N.C.	Ohio River	352
Kentucky	Junction of North and Middle Forks, Lee County, Ky.	Ohio River	259
Klamath	Lake Ewauna, Klamath Falls, Ore.	Pacific Ocean	250
Koyukuk	Endicott Mountains, Alaska	Yukon River	470
Kuskokwim	Alaska Range	Kuskokwim Bay	724
Liard	Southern Yukon, Alaska	Mackenzie River	693
Little Missouri	Crook County, Wyo.	Missouri River	560
Mackenzie	Great Slave Lake	Arctic Ocean	2,635
Milk	Junction of North and South Forks, Alberta Province	Missouri River, Mon.	625
Minnesota	Big Stone Lake, Minn.	Mississippi River, St. Paul, Minn.	332
Mississippi	Lake Itasca, Minn.	Mouth of Southwest Pass	2,348
Mississippi, Upper	Lake Itasca, Minn.	To mouth of Missouri R.	1,171
Mississippi-Missouri-Red Rock	Source of Red Rock, Beaverhead Co., Mon.	Mouth of Southwest Pass	3,710
Missouri	Junction of Jefferson, Madison, and Gallatin Rivers, Madison County, Mon.	Mississippi River	2,315
Missouri-Red Rock	Source of Red Rock, Beaverhead Co., Mon.	Mississippi River	2,540
Mobile-Alabama-Coosa	Gilmer County, Ga.	Mobile Bay	774
Nelson (Manitoba)	Lake Winnipeg	Hudson Bay	410
Neosho	Morris County, Kan.	Arkansas River, Okla.	460
Niobrara	Niobrara County, Wyo.	Missouri River, Neb.	431
North Canadian	Union County, N.M.	Canadian River, Okla.	800
North Platte	Junction of Grizzly and Little Grizzly Creeks, Jackson County, Col.	Platte River, Neb.	618
Ohio	Junction of Allegheny and Monongahela Rivers, Pittsburgh, Pa.	Mississippi River, Ill.-Ky.	1,310
Ohio-Allegheny	Potter County, Pa.	Mississippi River	1,306
Osage	East-central Kansas	Missouri River, Mo.	500
Ottawa	Lake Capimitchigama	St. Lawrence	790
Ouachita	Polk County, Ark.	Red River, La.	605
Peace	Stikine Mountains, B.C.	Slave River	1,210
Pearl	Neshoba County, Miss.	Gulf of Mexico, Miss.-La.	411
Pecos	Mora County, N.M.	Rio Grande, Tex.	926
Pee Dee-Yadkin	Watauga County, N.C.	Winyah Bay, S.C.	435
Pend Oreille	Near Butte, Mon.	Columbia River	490
Platte	Junction of North and South Platte Rivers, Neb.	Missouri River, Neb.	310
Porcupine	Ogilvie Mountains, Alaska	Yukon River, Alaska	569
Potomac	Garrett County, Md.	Chesapeake Bay	383
Powder	Junction of South and Middle Forks, Wyo.	Yellowstone River, Mon.	375
Red (Okla.-Tex.-La.)	Curry County, N.M.	Mississippi River	1,290
Red River of the North	Junction of Otter Tail and Bois de Sioux Rivers, Wilkin County, Minn.	Lake Winnipeg, Manitoba	545

River	Source or Upper Limit of Length	Outflow	Miles
Republican	Junction of North Fork and Arikaree River, Neb.	Kansas River, Kan.	445
Rio Grande	San Juan County, Col.	Gulf of Mexico	1,760
Roanoke	Junction of North and South Forks, Montgomery County, Va.	Albemarle Sound, N.C.	380
Rock (Ill.-Wis.)	Dodge County, Wis.	Mississippi River, Ill.	300
Sabine	Junction of South and Caddo Forks, Hunt County, Tex.	Sabine Lake, Tex.-La.	380
Sacramento	Siskiyou County, Cal.	Suisun Bay	377
St. Francis	Iron County, Mo.	Mississippi River, Ark.	425
St. Lawrence	Lake Ontario	Gulf of St. Lawrence (Atlantic Ocean)	800
Salmon (Idaho)	Custer County, Ida.	Snake River, Ida.	420
San Joaquin	Junction of South and Middle Forks, Madera County, Cal.	Suisun Bay	350
San Juan	Silver Lake, Archuleta County, Col.	Colorado River, Ut.	360
Santee-Wateree-Catawba	McDowell County, N.C.	Atlantic Ocean, S.C.	538
Saskatchewan, North	Rocky Mountains	Lake Winnipeg	800
Saskatchewan, South	Rocky Mountains	Lake Winnipeg	865
Savannah	Junction of Seneca and Tugaloo Rivers, Anderson County, S.C.	Atlantic Ocean, Ga.-S.C.	314
Severn (Ontario)	Sandy Lake	Hudson Bay	610
Smoky Hill	Cheyenne County, Col.	Kansas River, Kan.	540
Snake	Teton County, Wyo.	Columbia River, Wash.	1,038
South Platte	Junction of South and Middle Forks, Park County, Col.	Platte River, Neb.	424
Susitna	Alaska Range	Cook Inlet	313
Susquehanna	Otsego Lake, Otsego County, N.Y.	Chesapeake Bay, Md.	444
Tallahatchie	Tippah County, Miss.	Yazoo River, Miss.	301
Tanana	Wrangell Mountains	Yukon River, Alaska	659
Tennessee	Junction of French Broad and Holston Rivers	Ohio River, Ky.	652
Tennessee-French Broad	Transylvania County, N.C.	Ohio River	883
Tombigbee	Prentiss County, Miss.	Mobile River, Ala.	525
Trinity	North of Dallas, Tex.	Galveston Bay, Tex.	360
Wabash	Darke County, Oh.	Ohio River, Ill.-Ind.	529
Washita	Hemphill County, Tex.	Red River, Okla.	500
White (Ark.-Mo.)	Madison County, Ark.	Mississippi River	720
Willamette	Douglas County, Ore.	Columbia River	309
Wind-Bighorn	Junction of Wind and Little Wind Rivers, Fremont Co., Wyo. (Source of Wind R. is Togwotee Pass, Teton Co., Wyo.)	Yellowstone R., Mon.	336
Wisconsin	LeVieux Desert, Vilas County, Wis.	Mississippi River	430
Yellowstone	Park County, Wyo.	Missouri River, N.D.	692
Yukon	Coast Mountains of British Columbia	Bering Sea, Alaska	1,979

Flows of Largest U.S. Rivers

Source: U.S. Geological Survey (average discharges for the period 1941-70). Ranked according to average discharge in cubic feet per second (cfs) at mouth.

Rank	River	Average discharge	Length[a] (miles)	Drainage area	Most distant source	Maximum discharge at gauging station farthest downstream	Date
1	Mississippi	[b]640,000	[c]3,710	[d]1,247,300	Beaverhead Co., Mont.	2,080,000	2-17-37
2	Columbia	262,000	1,243	258,000	Columbia Lake, B.C.	1,240,000	June 1894
3	Ohio	258,000	1,306	203,900	Potter Co., Pa.,	1,850,000	2-1-37
4	St. Lawrence	[e]243,000	—	[e]302,000	—	[f]350,000	July 1973
5	Yukon	[g]240,000	1,979	327,600	Coast Mountains, B.C.	1,030,000	6-22-64
6	[h]Atchafalaya	183,000	135	95,105	Curry Co., N. Mex.	—	—
7	Missouri	76,300	2,540	529,400	Beaverhead Co., Mont.	892,000	June 1844
8	Tennessee	[m]64,000	883	40,910	Bland Co., Va.	500,000	2-17-48
9	Red	[i]62,300	1,290	93,244	Curry Co., N. Mex.	233,000	4-17-45
10	Kuskokwim	62,000	724	48,000	Alaska Range, Alas.	392,000	6-5-64
11	Mobile	61,400	774	44,600	Gilmer Co., Ga.	—	—
12	Snake	50,000	1,038	109,000	Teton Co., Wyo.	409,000	June 1894
13	Arkansas	45,100	1,459	160,600	Lake Co., Col.	536,000	5-27-43
14	Copper	[j]43,000	286	24,400	Alaska Range, Alas.	380,000	8-8-81
15	Tanana	[k]41,000	659	44,500	Wrangell Mtn., Alas.	186,000	8-18-67
16	Susitna	[l]40,000	313	20,000	Alaska Range, Alas.	230,000	[t]7-29-80
17	Susquehanna	37,190	444	27,570	Otsego Co., N.Y.	1,080,000	6-23-72
18	Willamette	35,660	309	11,400	Douglas Co., Ore.	500,000	12-4-1861
19	Alabama	32,400	729	22,600	Gilmer Co., Ga.	267,000	3-7-61
20	White	32,100	720	28,000	Madison Co., Ark.	343,000	4-17-45
21	Wabash	30,400	529	33,150	Drake Co., Oh.	428,000	3-30-13
22	Pend Oreille	29,900	490	25,820	Near Butte, Mont.	200,000	June 1894
23	Tombigbee	27,300	525	20,100	Prentiss Co., Miss.	[s]343,000	4-18-79
24	Cumberland	[m]26,900	720	18,080	Letcher Co., Ky.	209,000	3-16-75
25	Stikine	[n]26,000	379	20,000	Stikine Range, B.C.	223,900	7-22-79
26	Sacramento	—	377	27,100	Siskiyou Co., Cal.	[o]322,000	12-25-64
27	Apalachicola	24,700	524	19,600	Towns Co., Ga.	293,000	3-20-29
28	Illinois	22,800	420	27,900	St. Joseph Co., Ind.	123,000	May 1943
29	Koyukuk	[p]22,000	470	32,400	Endicott Mtns., Alas.	266,000	6-6-64
30	Porcupine	[q]20,000	460	45,000	Ogilvie Mtns., Alas.	299,000	5-24-73

(a) Because river lengths and methods of measurement may change from time to time, the length figures given are subject to revision; (b) about 25 percent of flow occurs in the Atchafalaya River; (c) the length from mouth to source of the Mississippi River in Minnesota is 2,348 miles; (d) at Baptiste Collete Bayou, Louisiana; (e) at international boundary lat. 45°; (f) maximum monthly discharge; (g) period 1957-70; (h) continuation of Red River; (i) flow of Ouachita River added; (j) period 1956-69; (k) period 1962-69; (l) based on records of Chulitna, Talkeetna, and Yetna rivers; (m) period 1931-60; (n) period 1954-63; summer records only; (o) discharge of American River not included (p) period 1969-69; (q) period 1964-69; (r) at Liston Point on Delaware Bay; (s) near Coatopa, Ala. (t) also on 8-16-81.

Important Islands and Their Areas

Source: National Geographic Society, Washington, D.C.

Figure in parentheses shows rank among the world's 10 largest islands; some islands have not been surveyed accurately; in such cases estimated areas are shown.

Location-Ownership

Area in square miles

Arctic Ocean

Canadian

Axel Heiberg	16,671
Baffin (5)	195,928
Banks	27,038
Bathurst	6,194
Devon	21,331
Ellesmere (10)	75,767
Melville	16,274
Prince of Wales	12,872
Somerset	9,570
Southampton	15,913
Victoria (9)	83,896

USSR

Franz Josef Land	8,000
Novaya Zemlya (two is.)	35,000
Wrangel	2,800

Norwegian

Svalbard	23,940
Nordaustlandet	5,410
Spitsbergen	15,060

Atlantic Ocean

Anticosti, Canada	3,066
Ascension, UK	34
Azores, Portugal	888
Faial	67
Sao Miguel	291
Bahamas	5,353
Bermuda Is., UK	20
Block, Rhode Island	10
Canary Is., Spain	2,808
Fuerteventura	668
Gran Canaria	592
Tenerife	795
Cape Breton, Canada	3,981
Cape Verde Is.	1,750
Faeroe Is., Denmark	540
Falkland Is., UK	4,700
Fernando de Noronha Archipelago, Brazil	7
Greenland, Denmark (1)	840,000
Iceland	39,700
Long Island, N. Y.	1,396
Bioko Is. Equatorial Guinea	785
Madeira Is., Portugal	307
Marajo, Brazil	15,528
Martha's Vineyard, Mass.	91
Mount Desert, Me.	108
Nantucket, Mass.	46
Newfoundland, Canada	42,030
Prince Edward, Canada	2,184
St. Helena, UK	47
South Georgia, UK	1,450
Tierra del Fuego, Chile and Argentina	18,800
Tristan da Cunha, UK	40

British Isles

Great Britain, mainland (8)	84,200
Channel Islands	75
Guernsey	24
Jersey	45
Sark	2
Hebrides	2,744
Ireland	32,599
Irish Republic	27,136
Northern Ireland	5,463
Man	227
Orkney Is.	390
Scilly Is.	6
Shetland Is.	567
Skye	670
Wight	147

Baltic Sea

Aland Is., Finland	581
Bornholm, Denmark	227
Gotland, Sweden	1,164

Caribbean Sea

Antigua	108
Aruba, Netherlands	75
Barbados	166
Cuba	44,218
Isle of Youth	1,182
Curacao, Netherlands	171
Dominica	290
Guadeloupe, France	687
Hispaniola, Haiti and Dominican Republic	29,530
Jamaica	4,244
Martinique, France	425
Puerto Rico, U.S.	3,515
Tobago	116
Trinidad	1,864
Virgin Is., UK	59
Virgin Is., U.S.	132

Indian Ocean

Andaman Is., India	2,500
Madagascar (4)	226,658
Mauritius	720
Pemba, Tanzania	380
Reunion, France	969
Seychelles	171
Sri Lanka	25,332
Zanzibar, Tanzania	640

Persian Gulf

Bahrain	258

Mediterranean Sea

Balearic Is., Spain	1,936
Corfu, Greece	229
Corsica, France	3,369
Crete, Greece	3,186
Cyprus	3,572
Elba, Italy	86
Euboea, Greece	1,409
Malta	122
Rhodes, Greece	542
Sardinia, Italy	9,262
Sicily, Italy	9,822

Pacific Ocean

Aleutian Is., U.S.	6,821
Adak	289
Amchitka	121
Attu	388
Kanaga	135
Kiska	110
Tanaga	209
Umnak	675
Unalaska	1,064
Unimak	1,600
Canton, Kiribati*	4
Caroline Is., U.S. trust terr.	472
Christmas, Kiribati*	94
Diomede, Big, USSR	11
Diomede, Little, U.S.	2
Easter, Chile	69
Fiji	7,056
Vanua Levu	2,242
Viti Levu	4,109
Funafuti, Tuvalu*	2
Galapagos Is., Ecuador	3,043
Guadalcanal, UK	2,500
Guam	209
Hainan, China	13,000
Hawaiian Is., U.S.	6,450
Hawaii	4,037
Oahu	593
Hong Kong, UK	29
Japan	145,809
Hokkaido	30,144
Honshu (7)	87,805
Iwo Jima	8
Kyushu	14,114
Okinawa	459
Shikoku	7,049
Kodiak, U.S.	3,670
Marquesas Is., France	492
Marshall Is., U.S. trust terr.	70
Bikini*	2
Nauru	8
New Caledonia, France	6,530
New Guinea (2)	306,000
New Zealand	103,883
Chatham	372
North	44,035
South	58,305
Stewart	674
Northern Mariana Is.	184
Philippines	115,831
Leyte	2,787
Luzon	40,880
Mindanao	36,775
Mindoro	3,790
Negros	4,907
Palawan	4,554
Panay	4,446
Samar	5,050
Quemoy	56
Sakhalin, USSR	29,500
Samoa Is.	1,177
American Samoa	77
Tutulla	52
Samoa (Western)	1,133
Savaii	670
Upolu	429
Santa Catalina, U.S.	72
Tahiti, France	402
Taiwan	13,823
Tasmania, Australia	26,178
Tonga Is.	270
Vancouver, Canada	12,079
Vanuatu	5,700

East Indies

Bali, Indonesia	2,147
Borneo, Indonesia-Malaysia, UK (3)	280,100
Celebes, Indonesia	69,000
Java, Indonesia	48,900
Madura, Indonesia	2,113
Moluccas, Indonesia	28,766
New Britain, Papua New Guinea	14,093
New Ireland, Papua New Guinea	3,707
Sumatra, Indonesia (6)	165,000
Timor	11,570

*Atolls: Bikini (lagoon area, 230 sq. mi., land area 2 sq. mi.), U.S. Trust Territory of the Pacific Islands; Canton (lagoon 20 sq. mi., land 4 sq. mi.), Kiribati; Christmas (lagoon 140 sq. mi., land 94 sq. mi.), Kiribati; Funafuti (lagoon 84 sq. mi., land 2 sq. mi.), Tuvalu.

Australia, often called an island, is a continent. Its mainland area is 2,939,975 sq. mi.

Islands in minor waters; Manhattan (22 sq mi.) Staten (59 sq. mi.) and Governors (173 acres), all in New York Harbor, U.S.; Isle Royale (209 sq. mi.), Lake Superior, U.S.; Manitoulin (1,068 sq. mi.), Lake Huron, Canada; Pinang (110 sq. mi.), Strait of Malacca, Malaysia; Singapore (239 sq. mi.), Singapore Strait, Singapore.

Lakes of the World

Source: Geological Survey, U.S. Interior Department

A lake is a body of water surrounded by land. Although some lakes are called seas, they are lakes by definition. The Caspian Sea is bounded by the Soviet Union and Iran and is fed by eight rivers.

Name	Continent	Area sq. mi.	Length mi.	Depth feet	Elev. feet
Caspian Sea	Asia-Europe	143,244	760	3,363	−92
Superior	North America	31,700	350	1,330	600
Victoria	Africa	26,828	250	270	3,720
Aral Sea	Asia	24,904	280	220	174
Huron	North America	23,000	206	750	579
Michigan	North America	22,300	307	923	579
Tanganyika	Africa	12,700	420	4,823	2,534
Baykal	Asia	12,162	395	5,315	1,493
Great Bear	North America	12,096	192	1,463	512
Malawi	Africa	11,150	360	2,280	1,550
Great Slave	North America	11,031	298	2,015	513
Erie	North America	9,910	241	210	570
Winnipeg	North America	9,417	266	60	713
Ontario	North America	7,550	193	802	245
Balkhash	Asia	7,115	376	85	1,115
Ladoga	Europe	6,835	124	738	13
Chad	Africa	6,300	175	24	787
Maracaibo	South America	5,217	133	115	Sea level
Onega	Europe	3,710	145	328	108
Eyre	Australia	3,600	90	4	−52
Volta	Africa	3,276	250	....	....
Titicaca	South America	3,200	122	922	12,500
Nicaragua	North America	3,100	102	230	102
Athabasca	North America	3,064	208	407	700
Reindeer	North America	2,568	143	720	1,106
Turkana	Africa	2,473	154	240	1,230
Issyk Kul	Asia	2,355	115	2,303	5,279
Torrens	Australia	2,230	130	....	92
Vanern	Europe	2,156	91	328	144
Nettilling	North America	2,140	67	....	95
Winnipegosis	North America	2,075	141	38	830
Albert	Africa	2,075	100	168	2,030
Kariba	Africa	2,050	175	390	1,590
Nipigon	North America	1,872	72	540	1,050
Gairdner	Australia	1,840	90	....	112
Urmia	Asia	1,815	90	49	4,180
Manitoba	North America	1,799	140	12	813

The Great Lakes

Source: National Ocean Service, U.S. Commerce Department

The Great Lakes form the largest body of fresh water in the world and with their connecting waterways are the largest inland water transportation unit. Draining the great North Central basin of the U.S., they enable shipping to reach the Atlantic via their outlet, the St. Lawrence R., and also the Gulf of Mexico via the Illinois Waterway, from Lake Michigan to the Mississippi R. A third outlet connects with the Hudson R. and thence the Atlantic via the N. Y. State Barge Canal System. Traffic on the Illinois Waterway and the N.Y. State Barge Canal System is limited to recreational boating and small shipping vessels.

Only one of the lakes, Lake Michigan, is wholly in the United States; the others are shared with Canada. Ships carrying grain, lumber and iron ore move from the shores of Lake Superior to Whitefish Bay at the east end of the lake, thence through the Soo (Sault Ste. Marie) locks, through the St. Mary's River and into Lake Huron. To reach the steel mills at Gary, and Port of Indiana and South Chicago, Ill., ore ships move west from Lake Huron to Lake Michigan through the Straits of Mackinac.

Lake Huron discharges its waters into Lake Erie through a narrow waterway, the St. Clair R., Lake St. Clair (both included in the drainage basin figures) and the Detroit R. Lake St. Clair, a marshy basin, is 26 miles long and 24 miles wide at its maximum. A ship channel has been dredged through the lake.

Lake Superior is 600 feet above mean water level at Point-au-Pere, Quebec, on the International Great Lakes Datum (1955). From Duluth, Minn., to the eastern end of Lake Ontario is 1,156 mi.

	Superior	Michigan	Huron	Erie	Ontario
Length in miles	350	307	206	241	193
Breadth in miles	160	118	183	57	53
Deepest soundings in feet	1,330	923	750	210	802
Volume of water in cubic miles	2,900	1,180	850	116	393
Area (sq. miles) water surface—U.S.	20,600	22,300	9,100	4,980	3,560
Canada	11,100	.....	13,900	4,930	3,990
Area (sq. miles) entire drainage basin—U.S.	16,900	45,600	16,200	18,000	15,200
Canada	32,400	.....	35,500	4,720	12,100
Total Area (sq. miles) U.S. and Canada	**81,000**	**67,900**	**74,700**	**32,630**	**34,850**
Mean surface above mean water level at Point-au-Pere, Quebec, aver. level in feet (1900-1986)	600.61	578.33	578.33	570.49	244.73
Latitude, North	46° 25′	41° 37′	43° 00′	41° 23′	43° 11′
	49° 00′	46° 06′	46° 17′	42° 52′	44° 15′
Longitude, West	84° 22′	84° 45′	79° 43′	78° 51′	76° 03′
	92° 06′	88° 02′	84° 45′	83° 29′	79° 53′
National boundary line in miles	282.8	None	260.8	251.5	174.6
United States shore line (mainland only) miles	863	1,400	580	431	300

Large U.S. Lakes

Source: U.S. Geological Survey

Natural U.S. lakes (excluding the Great Lakes) with areas of 100 sq. mi.

Lake	State	Area (sq. mi.)	Lake	State	Area (sq. mi.)
Lake of the Woods	Minn., Canada	1,697	Flathead	Mon.	197
Great Salt[1]	Ut.	1,361[2]	Tahoe	Calif., Nev.	193
Iliamna	Alas.	1,000	Leech	Minn.	176
Okeechobee	Fla.	700	Pyramid[1]	Nev.	168[2]
Pontchartrain[1]	La.	625	Pend Oreille	Id.	148
Becharof	Alas.	458	Ugashik (upper and lower)	Alas.	147
Red Lake (upper and lower)	Minn.	451	Upper Klamath	Ore.	142
Champlain	N.Y., Vt., Canada	435	Utah	Ut.	140
St. Clair	Mich., Canada	432	Bear (including Mud Lake)	Id., Ut.	136
Salton Sea[1]	Calif.	374[2]	Yellowstone	Wy.	134
Rainy	Minn., Canada	360	Moosehead	Me.	117
Teshekpuk	Alas.	315	Tustumena	Alas.	117
Naknek	Alas.	242	Clark	Alas.	110
Winnebago	Wis.	215	Winnibigoshish	Minn.	109
Mille Lacs	Minn.	207	Dall	Alas.	100

(1) Salty. (2) Variable.

Famous Waterfalls

Source: National Geographic Society, Washington, D.C.

The earth has thousands of waterfalls, some of considerable magnitude. Their importance is determined not only by height but volume of flow, steadiness of flow, crest width, whether the water drops sheerly or over a sloping surface, and in one leap or a succession of leaps. A series of low falls flowing over a considerable distance is known as a cascade.

Sete Quedas or Guaira is the world's greatest waterfall when its mean annual flow (estimated at 470,000 cusecs, cubic feet per second) is combined with height. A greater volume of water passes over Boyoma Falls (Stanley Falls), though not one of its seven cataracts, spread over nearly 60 miles of the Congo River, exceeds 10 feet.

Estimated mean annual flow, in cusecs, of other major waterfalls are: Niagara, 212,200; Paulo Afonso, 100,000; Urubupunga, 97,000; Iguazu, 61,000; Patos-Maribondo, 53,000; Victoria, 35,400; and Kaieteur, 23,400.

Height = total drop in feet in one or more leaps. † = falls of more than one leap; * = falls that diminish greatly seasonally; ** = falls that reduce to a trickle or are dry for part of each year. If river names not shown, they are same as the falls. R. = river; L. = lake; (C) = cascade type.

Name and location	Ht.
Africa	
Angola	
Duque de Braganca, Lucala R.	344
Ruacana, Cuene R.	406
Ethiopia	
Dal Verme, Dorya R.	98
Fincha	508
Tisissat, Blue Nile R.	140
Lesotho	
*Maletsunyane	630
Zimbabwe-Zambia	
*Victoria, Zambezi R.	343
South Africa	
*Augrabies, Orange R.	480
Howick, Umgeni R.	364
† Tugela	2,014
Highest fall	597
Tanzania-Zambia	
*Kalambo	726
Uganda	
Kabalega (Murchison) Victoria Nile R.	130
Asia	
India—*Cauvery	330
*Gokak, Ghataprabha R.	170
*Jog (Gersoppa), Sharavathi R.	830
Japan	
*Kegon, Daiya R.	330
Laos	
Khon Cataracts, Mekong R. (C)	70
Australasia	
Australia	
New South Wales	
Wentworth	614
Highest fall	360
Wollomombi	1,100
Queensland	
Coomera	210
Tully	885
† Wallaman, Stony Cr.	1,137
Highest fall	937
New Zealand	
Bowen	540
Helena	890
Stirling	505
† Sutherland, Arthur R.	1,904
Highest fall	815
Europe	
Austria—† Gastein	492
Highest fall	280
† *Golling, Schwarzbach R.	250
† Krimml	1,312
France—*Gavarnie	1,385
Great Britain—Scotland	
Glomach	370
Wales	
Cain	150
Rhaiadr	240
Iceland—Detti	144
† Gull, Hvita R.	105
Italy—Frua, Toce R. (C)	470
Norway	
Mardalsfossen (Northern)	1,535
† Mardalsfossen (Southern)	2,149
† **Skjeggedal, Nybuai R.	1,378
**Skykje	984
Vetti, Morka-Koldedola R.	900
Voring, Bjoreio R.	597
Sweden	
† Handol	427
† Tannforsen, Are R.	120
Switzerland	
† Diesbach	394
Giessbach (C)	984
Handegg, Aare R.	150
Iffigen	120
Pissevache, Salanfe R.	213
† Reichenbach	656
Rhine	79
† Simmen	459
Staubbach	984
† Trummelbach	1,312
North America	
Canada	
Alberta	
Panther, Nigel Cr.	600
British Columbia	
† Della	1,443
† Takakkaw, Daly Glacier	1,200
Northwest Territories	
Virginia, S. Nahanni R.	294
Quebec	
Montmorency	274
Canada—United States	
Niagara: American	182
Horseshoe	173
United States	
California	
*Feather, Fall R.	640
Yosemite National Park	
*Bridalveil	620
*Illilouette	370
*Nevada, Merced R.	594
**Ribbon	1,612
**Silver Strand, Meadow Br.	1,170
*Vernal, Merced R.	317
† **Yosemite	2,425
Yosemite (upper)	1,430
Yosemite (lower)	320
Yosemite (middle) (C)	675
Colorado	
† Seven, South Cheyenne Cr.	300
Hawaii	
Akaka, Kolekole Str.	442
Idaho	
**Shoshone, Snake R.	212
Twin, Snake R.	120
Kentucky	
Cumberland	68
Maryland	
*Great, Potomac R. (C)	71
Minnesota	
**Minnehaha	53
New Jersey	
Passaic	70
New York	
*Taughannock	215

Name and location	Ht.
Oregon	
† Multnomah	620
Highest fall	542
Tennessee	
Fall Creek	256
Washington	
Mt. Rainier Natl. Park	
Narada, Paradise R.	168
Sluiskin, Paradise R.	300
Palouse	197
**Snoqualmie	268
Wisconsin	
*Big Manitou, Black R. (C)	165
Wyoming	
Yellowstone Natl. Pk. Tower	132
*Yellowstone (upper)	109
*Yellowstone (lower)	308

Name and location	Ht.
Mexico	
El Salto	218
**Juanacatlan, Santiago R.	72

South America

Name and location	Ht.
Argentina-Brazil	
Iguazu	230
Brazil	
Glass	1,325
Patos-Maribondo, Grande R.	115
Paulo Afonso, Sao Francisco R.	275
Urubupunga, Parana R.	40
Brazil-Paraguay	
Sete Quedas	
Parana R.	130

Name and location	Ht.
Colombia	
Catarata de Candelas,	
Cusiana R.	984
*Tequendama, Bogota R.	427
Ecuador	
*Agoyan, Pastaza R.	200
Guyana	
Kaieteur, Potaro R.	741
Great, Kamarang R.	1,600
† Marina, Ipobe R.	500
Highest fall	300
Venezuela—	
† *Angel	3,212
Highest fall	2,648
Cuquenan	2,000

Notable Deserts of the World

Arabian (Eastern), 70,000 sq. mi. in Egypt between the Nile river and Red Sea, extending southward into Sudan.

Atacama, 600 mi. long area rich in nitrate and copper deposits in N. Chile.

Chihuahuan, 140,000 sq. mi. in Tex., N.M., Ariz., and Mexico.

Death Valley, 3,300 sq. mi. in E. Cal. and SW Nev. Contains lowest point below sea level (282 ft.) in Western Hemisphere.

Gibson, 120,000 sq. mi. in the interior of W. Australia.

Gobi, 500,000 sq. mi. in Mongolia and China.

Great Sandy, 150,000 sq. mi. in W. Australia.

Great Victoria, 150,000 sq. mi. in W. and S. Australia.

Kalahari, 225,000 sq. mi. in southern Africa.

Kara-Kum, 120,000 sq. mi. in Turkmen SSR.

Kavir (Dasht-e Kavir), great salt waste in central Iran some 400 mi. long.

Kyzyl Kum, 100,000 sq. mi. in Kazakh and Uzbek SSRs.

Libyan, 450,000 sq. mi. in the Sahara extending from Lybia through SW Egypt into Sudan.

Lut (Dasht-e Lut), 20,000 sq. mi. in E. Iran.

Mojave, 15,000 sq. mi. in S. Cal.

Nafud (An Nafud), 40,000 sq. mi. near Jawf in Saudi Arabia.

Namib, long narrow area extending 800 miles along SW coast of Africa.

Nubian, 100,000 sq. mi. in the Sahara in NE Sudan.

Painted Desert, section of high plateau in N. Ariz. extending 150 mi.

Rub al Khali (Empty Quarter), 250,000 sq. mi. in the south Arabian Peninsula.

Sahara, 3,500,000 sq. mi. in N. Africa extending westward to the Atlantic. Largest desert in the world.

Simpson, 40,000 sq. mi. in central Australia.

Sonoran, 70,000 sq. mi. in SW Ariz. and SE Cal. extending into Mexico.

Syrian, 100,000 sq. mi. arid wasteland extending over much of N. Saudi Arabia, E. Jordan, S. Syria, and W. Iraq.

Taklimakan, 140,000 sq. mi. in Sinkiang Province, China.

Thar (Great Indian), 100,000 sq. mi. arid area extending 400 mi. along India-Pakistan border.

Area and Population of the World

Source: Rand McNally & Co.

Continent	Area (1,000 sq. mi.)	% of Earth	Population (est., thousands) 1650	1750	1850	1900	1950	1987	% World Total, 1987
North America	9,400	16.3	5,000	5,000	39,000	106,000	219,000	407,200	8.2
South America	6,900	11.9	8,000	7,000	20,000	38,000	111,000	276,700	5.6
Europe	3,800	6.6	100,000	140,000	265,000	400,000	530,000	680,100	13.7
Asia	17,300	29.9	335,000	476,000	754,000	932,000	1,418,000	2,985,300	60.0
Africa	11,700	20.2	100,000	95,000	95,000	118,000	199,000	600,600	12.1
Oceania, incl. Australia	3,300	5.7	2,000	2,000	2,000	6,000	13,000	25,100	0.5
Antarctica	5,400	9.3	Uninhabited						
World	**57,800**	—	**550,000**	**725,000**	**1,175,000**	**1,600,000**	**2,490,000**	**4,975,000**	—

World Population and Growth, by Continent and Region: 1960 to 1986

Source: U.S. Bureau of the Census

Continent and Region	Midyear Population (millions) 1960	1965	1970	1975	1980	1985	1986	Annual Rate of Growth (percent) 1960-1965	1965-1970	1970-1975	1975-1980	1980-1986
World total	**3,049**	**3,358**	**3,721**	**4,103**	**4,473**	**4,865**	**4,944**	**1.9**	**2.1**	**2.0**	**1.7**	**1.7**
More developed regions	945	1,002	1,049	1,096	1,136	1,173	1,180	1.2	.9	.9	.7	.6
Less developed regions	2,104	2,356	2,672	3,007	3,336	3,692	3,763	2.3	2.5	2.4	2.1	2.0
Percent of world	69	70	72	73	75	76	76	(x)	(x)	(x)	(x)	(x)
Africa[1]	293	330	375	427	491	566	583	2.4	2.5	2.6	2.8	2.8
Asia	1,685	1,871	2,112	2,364	2,593	2,831	2,877	2.1	2.4	2.3	1.8	1.7
East Asia	796	874	992	1,104	1,182	1,248	1,258	1.9	2.5	2.2	1.4	1.0
South Asia	889	998	1,120	1,260	1,411	1,583	1,619	2.3	2.3	2.3	2.3	2.3
Latin America[1]	218	250	286	324	364	410	419	2.8	2.7	2.5	2.3	2.3
Middle America[1]	51	60	70	81	93	106	109	3.1	3.1	3.0	2.7	2.6
Caribbean[1]	20	23	24	27	29	31	32	2.2	1.9	1.8	1.4	1.4
South America[1]	146	168	191	216	242	273	279	2.7	2.6	2.4	2.3	2.4
North America[2]	199	214	226	239	252	264	267	1.5	1.1	1.1	1.1	.9
Europe[2]	425	44	460	474	484	492	493	.9	.7	.6	.4	.3
Soviet Union[2]	214	231	243	254	266	278	280	1.5	1.0	.9	.9	.9
Oceania	16	17	19	21	23	24	25	2.1	2.1	1.9	1.3	1.4
Australia and New Zealand[2]	13	14	15	17	18	19	19	2.0	1.9	1.7	1.0	1.2

(x) Not applicable. (1) Less developed region. (2) More developed region.

DISASTERS

Some Notable Marine Disasters Since 1850

(Figures indicate estimated lives lost)

1854, Mar.—City of Glasgow; British steamer missing in North Atlantic; 480.

1854, Sept. 27—Arctic; U.S. (Collins Line) steamer sunk in collision with French steamer Vesta near Cape Race; 285-351.

1856, Jan. 23—Pacific; U.S. (Collins Line) steamer missing in North Atlantic; 186-286.

1858, Sept. 23—Austria; German steamer destroyed by fire in North Atlantic; 471.

1863, Apr. 27—Anglo-Saxon; British steamer wrecked at Cape Race; 238.

1865, Apr. 27—Sultana; a Mississippi River steamer blew up near Memphis, Tenn; 1,450.

1869, Oct. 27—Stonewall; steamer burned on Mississippi River below Cairo, Ill.; 200.

1870, Jan. 25—City of Boston; British (Inman Line) steamer vanished between New York and Liverpool; 177.

1870, Oct 19—Cambria; British steamer wrecked off northern Ireland; 196.

1872, Nov. 7—Mary Celeste; U.S. half-brig sailed from New York for Genoa; found abandoned in Atlantic 4 weeks later in mystery of sea; crew never heard from; loss of life unknown.

1873, Jan. 22—Northfleet; British steamer foundered off Dungeness, England; 300.

1873, Apr. 1—Atlantic; British (White Star) steamer wrecked off Nova Scotia; 585.

1873, Nov. 23—Ville du Havre; French steamer, sunk after collision with British sailing ship Loch Earn; 226.

1875, May 7—Schiller; German steamer wrecked off Scilly Isles; 312.

1875, Nov. 4—Pacific; U.S. steamer sunk after collision off Cape Flattery; 236.

1878, Sept. 3—Princess Alice; British steamer sank after collision in Thames River; 700.

1878, Dec. 18—Byzantin; French steamer sank after Dardanelles collision; 210.

1881, May 24—Victoria; steamer capsized in Thames River, Canada; 200.

1883, Jan. 19—Cimbria; German steamer sunk in collision with British steamer Sultan in North Sea; 389.

1887, Nov. 15—Wah Yeung; British steamer burned at sea; 400.

1890, Feb. 17—Duburg; British steamer wrecked, China Sea; 400.

1890, Sept. 19—Ertogrul; Turkish frigate foundered off Japan; 540.

1891, Mar. 17—Utopia; British steamer sank in collision with British ironclad Anson off Gibraltar; 562.

1895, Jan. 30—Elbe; German steamer sank in collision with British steamer Craithie in North Sea; 332.

1895, Mar. 11—Reina Regenta; Spanish cruiser foundered near Gibraltar; 400.

1898, Feb. 15—Maine; U.S. battleship blown up in Havana Harbor; 260.

1898, July 4—La Bourgogne; French steamer sunk in collision with British sailing ship Cromartyshire off Nova Scotia; 549.

1898, Nov. 26—Portland; U.S. steamer wrecked off Cape Cod; 157.

1904, June 15—General Slocum; excursion steamer burned in East River, New York City; 1,030.

1904, June 28—Norge; Danish steamer wrecked on Rockall Island, Scotland; 620.

1906, Aug. 4—Sirio; Italian steamer wrecked off Cape Palos, Spain; 350.

1908, Mar. 23—Matsu Maru; Japanese steamer sank in collision near Hakodate, Japan; 300.

1909, Aug. 1—Waratah; British steamer, Sydney to London, vanished; 300.

1910, Feb. 9—General Chanzy; French steamer wrecked off Minorca, Spain; 200.

1911, Sept. 25—Liberté; French battleship exploded at Toulon; 285.

1912, Mar. 5—Principe de Asturias; Spanish steamer wrecked off Spain; 500.

1912, Apr. 14-15—Titanic; British (White Star) steamer hit iceberg in North Atlantic; 1,503.

1912, Sept. 28—Kichemaru; Japanese steamer sank off Japanese coast; 1,000.

1914, May 29—Empress of Ireland; British (Canadian Pacific) steamer sunk in collision with Norwegian collier in St. Lawrence River; 1,014.

1915, May 7—Lusitania; British (Cunard Line) steamer torpedoed and sunk by German submarine off Ireland; 1,198.

1915, July 24—Eastland; excursion steamer capsized in Chicago River; 812.

1916, Feb. 26—Provence; French cruiser sank in Mediterranean; 3,100.

1916, Mar. 3—Principe de Asturias; Spanish steamer wrecked near Santos, Brazil; 558.

1916, Aug. 29—Hsin Yu; Chinese steamer sank off Chinese coast; 1,000.

1917, Dec. 6—Mont Blanc, Imo; French ammunition ship and Belgian steamer collided in Halifax Harbor; 1,600.

1918, Apr. 25—Kiang-Kwan Chinese steamer sank in collision off Hankow; 500.

1918, July 12—Kawachi; Japanese battleship blew up in Tokayama Bay; 500.

1918, Oct. 25—Princess Sophia; Canadian steamer sank off Alaskan coast; 398.

1919, Jan. 17—Chaonia; French steamer lost in Straits of Messina, Italy; 460.

1919, Sept. 9—Valbanera; Spanish steamer lost off Florida coast; 500.

1921, Mar. 18—Hong Kong; steamer wrecked in South China Sea; 1,000.

1922, Aug. 26—Niitaka; Japanese cruiser sank in storm off Kamchatka, USSR; 300.

1927, Oct. 25—Principessa Mafalda; Italian steamer blew up, sank off Porto Seguro, Brazil; 314.

1928, Nov. 12—Vestris; British steamer sank in gale off Virginia; 113.

1934, Sept. 8—Morro Castle; U.S. steamer, Havana to New York, burned off Asbury Park, N.J.; 134.

1939, May 23—Squalus; U.S. submarine sank off Portsmouth, N.H.; 26.

1939, June 1—Thetis; British submarine, sank in Liverpool Bay; 99.

1942, Feb. 18—Truxtun and Pollux; U.S. destroyer and cargo ship ran aground, sank off Newfoundland; 204.

1942, Oct. 2—Curacao; British cruiser sank after collision with liner Queen Mary; 338.

1944, Dec. 17-18—3 U.S. Third Fleet destroyers sank during typhoon in Philippine Sea; 790.

1947, Jan. 19—Himera; Greek steamer hit a mine off Athens; 392.

1947, Apr. 16—Grandcamp; French freighter exploded in Texas City, Tex., Harbor, starting fires; 510.

1948, Dec. 3—Kiangya; Chinese refugee ship wrecked in explosion S. of Shanghai; 1,100+.

1949, Sept. 17—Noronic; Canadian Great Lakes cruiser burned at Toronto dock; 130

1952, Apr. 26—Hobson and Wasp; U.S. destroyer and aircraft carrier collided in Atlantic; 176.

1953, Jan. 31—Princess Victoria; British ferry sank in storm off northern Irish coast; 134.

1954, Sept. 26—Toya Maru; Japanese ferry sank in Tsugaru Strait, Japan; 1,172.

1956, July 26—Andrea Doria and Stockholm; Italian liner and Swedish liner collided off Nantucket; 51.

1957, July 14—Eshghabad; Soviet ship ran aground in Caspian Sea; 270.

1961, July 8—Save; Portuguese ship ran aground off Mozambique; 259.

1962, Apr. 8—Dara; British liner exploded and sunk in Persian Gulf; 236.

1963, Apr. 10—Thresher; U.S. Navy atomic submarine sank in North Atlantic; 129.

1964, Feb. 10—Voyager, Melbourne; Australian destroyer sank after collision with Australian aircraft carrier Melbourne off New South Wales; 82.

1965, Nov. 13—Yarmouth Castle; Panamanian registered cruise ship burned and sank off Nassau; 90.

1967, July 29—Forrestal; U.S. aircraft carrier caught fire off N. Vietnam; 134.

1968, Jan. 25—Dakar; Israeli submarine vanished in Mediterranean Sea; 69.

1968, Jan. 27—Minerve; French submarine vanished in Mediterranean; 52.

1968, late May—Scorpion; U.S. nuclear submarine sank in Atlantic near Azores; 99 (located Oct. 31).

1969, June 2—Evans; U.S. destroyer cut in half by Australian carrier Melbourne, S. China Sea; 74.

1970, Mar. 4—Eurydice; French submarine sank in Mediterranean near Toulon; 57.

1970, Dec. 15—Namyong-Ho; South Korean ferry sank in Korea Strait; 308.

1974, May 1— Motor launch capsized off Bangladesh; 250.

1974, Sept. 26— Soviet destroyer burned and sank in Black Sea; 200+.

(continued)

1976, Oct. 20—George Prince and Frosta; ferryboat and Norwegian tanker collided on Mississippi R. at Luling, La.; 77.

1976, Dec. 25—Patria; Egyptian liner caught fire and sank in the Red Sea; c. 100.

1977, Jan. 11—Grand Zenith; Panamanian-registered tanker sank off Cape Cod, Mass.; 38.

1979, Aug. 14—23 yachts competing in Fastnet yacht race sunk or abandoned during storm in S. Irish Sea; 18.

1981, Jan. 27—Tamponas II; Indonesian passenger ship caught fire and sank in Java Sea; 580.

1981, May 26—Nimitz; U.S. Marine combat jet crashed on deck of U.S. aircraft carrier; 14.

1983, Feb. 12—Marine Electric; coal freighter sank during storm off Chincoteague, Va.; 33.

1983, May 25—10th of Ramadan; Nile steamer caught fire and sank in L. Nassar; 357.

1986, Aug. 31—Admiral Nakhimov; Soviet passenger ship and **Pyotr Vasev,** Soviet freighter, collided in the Black Sea; 398.

1987, Mar. 6—British ferry capsized off Zeebrugge, Belgium; 134.

Major Earthquakes

Magnitude of earthquakes (Mag.), distinct from deaths or damage caused, is measured on the Richter scale, on which each higher number represents a tenfold increase in energy measured in ground motion. Adopted in 1935, the scale has been applied in the following table to earthquakes as far back as reliable seismograms are available.

	Date	Place	Deaths	Mag.
526	May 20	Syria, Antioch	250,000	N.A.
856	....	Greece, Corinth	45,000	"
1057	....	China, Chihli	25,000	"
1268	....	Asia Minor, Cilicia	60,000	"
1290	Sept. 27	China, Chihli	100,000	"
1293	May 20	Japan, Kamakura	30,000	"
1531	Jan. 26	Portugal, Lisbon	30,000	"
1556	Jan. 24	China, Shaanxi	830,000	"
1667	Nov.	Caucasia, Shemaka	80,000	"
1693	Jan. 11	Italy, Catania	60,000	"
1730	Dec. 30	Japan, Hokkaido	137,000	"
1737	Oct. 11	India, Calcutta	300,000	"
1755	June 7	Northern Persia	40,000	"
1755	Nov. 1	Portugal, Lisbon	60,000	8.75*
1783	Feb. 4	Italy, Calabria	30,000	N.A.
1797	Feb. 4	Ecuador, Quito	41,000	N.A.
1811-12		New Madrid, Mo.	—	N.A.
1822	Sept. 5	Asia Minor, Aleppo	22,000	N.A.
1828	Dec. 28	Japan, Echigo	30,000	"
1868	Aug. 13-15	Peru and Ecuador	40,000	"
1875	May 16	Venezuela, Colombia	16,000	"
1896	June 15	Japan, sea wave	27,120	"
1906	Apr. 18-19	Cal., San Francisco	503	8.3
1906	Aug. 16	Chile, Valparaiso	20,000	8.6
1908	Dec. 28	Italy, Messina	83,000	7.5
1915	Jan. 13	Italy, Avezzano	29,980	7.5
1920	Dec. 16	China, Gansu	100,000	8.6
1923	Sept. 1	Japan, Yokohama	200,000	8.3
1927	May 22	China, Nan-Shan	200,000	8.3
1932	Dec. 26	China, Gansu	70,000	7.6
1933	Mar. 2	Japan	2,990	8.9
1934	Jan. 15	India, Bihar-Nepal	10,700	8.4
1935	May 31	India, Quetta	50,000	7.5
1939	Jan. 24	Chile, Chillan	28,000	8.3
1939	Dec. 26	Turkey, Erzincan	30,000	7.9
1946	Dec. 21	Japan, Honshu	2,000	8.4
1948	June 28	Japan, Fukui	5,131	7.3
1949	Aug. 5	Ecuador, Pelileo	6,000	6.8
1950	Aug. 15	India, Assam	1,530	8.7
1953	Mar. 18	NW Turkey	1,200	7.2
1956	June 10-17	N. Afghanistan	2,000	7.7
1957	July 2	Northern Iran	2,500	7.4
1957	Dec. 13	Western Iran	2,000	7.1
1960	Feb. 29	Morocco, Agadir	12,000	5.8
1960	May 21-30	Southern Chile	5,000	8.3
1962	Sept. 1	Northwestern Iran	12,230	7.1
1963	July 26	Yugoslavia, Skopje	1,100	6.0
1964	Mar. 27	Alaska	114	8.5
1966	Aug. 19	Eastern Turkey	2,520	6.9
1968	Aug. 31	Northeastern Iran	12,000	7.4
1970	Mar. 28	Western Turkey	1,086	7.4
1970	May 31	Northern Peru	66,794	7.7
1971	Feb. 9	Cal., San Fernando Valley	65	6.5
1972	Apr. 10	Southern Iran	5,057	6.9
1972	Dec. 23	Nicaragua	5,000	6.2
1974	Dec. 28	Pakistan (9 towns)	5,200	6.3
1975	Sept. 6	Turkey (Lice, etc.)	2,312	6.8
1976	Feb. 4	Guatemala	22,778	7.5
1976	May 6	Northeast Italy	946	6.5
1976	June 26	New Guinea, Irian Jaya	443	7.1
1976	July 28	China, Tangshan	242,000	8.2
1976	Aug. 17	Philippines, Mindanao	8,000	7.8
1976	Nov. 24	Eastern Turkey	4,000	7.9
1977	Mar. 4	Romania, Bucharest, etc.	1,541	7.5
1977	Aug. 19	Indonesia	200	8.0
1977	Nov. 23	Northwestern Argentina	100	8.2
1978	June 12	Japan, Sendai	21	7.5
1978	Sept. 16	Northeast Iran	25,000	7.7
1979	Sept. 12	Indonesia	100	8.1
1979	Dec. 12	Colombia, Ecuador	800	7.9
1980	Oct. 10	Northwestern Algeria	4,500	7.3
1980	Nov. 23	Southern Italy	4,800	7.2
1982	Dec. 13	North Yemen	2,800	6.0
1983	Mar. 31	Southern Colombia	250	5.5
1983	May 26	N. Honshu, Japan	81	7.7
1983	Oct. 30	Eastern Turkey	1,300	7.1
1985	Mar. 3	Chile	146	7.8
1985	Sept. 19, 21	Mexico City	4,200+	8.1
1987	Mar. 5-6	NE Ecuador	4,000+	7.3

(*) estimated from earthquake intensity. (N.A.) not available.

Some Recent Earthquakes

Source: Scientific Event Alert Network, Smithsonian Institution

Attached is a list of recent earthquakes. Magnitude of earthquakes is measured on the Richter scale, on which each higher number represents a tenfold increase in energy measured in ground motion.ND.10

Date	Place	Magnitude
Apr. 25, 1987	Philippines	6.3
Apr. 25	NW Sumatra, Indonesia	6.5
Apr. 22	Honshu, Japan	6.6
Apr. 7	Honshu, Japan	6.6
Mar. 18	Kyushu, Japan	6.7
Mar. 6	Ecuador/Colombia	6.9
Mar. 5	N. Chile	7.3
Mar. 2	New Zealand	6.6
Feb. 27	Aleutian Islands	6.7
Feb. 13	Molucca Sea, Indonesia	6.5
Feb. 8	Papua New Guinea	7.4
Nov. 14, 1986	Taiwan	7.8
Oct. 24	Santa Cruz Islands	6.7
Oct. 20	Kermadec Islands	8.2
Oct. 14	Papua New Guinea	6.6
Sept. 16	Northern Marianas	6.4
Sept. 12	Alaska	6.4
Sept. 11	Papua New Guinea	6.4
Aug. 30	Romania/USSR	6.9
Aug. 26	China/Tibet	6.0
Aug. 21	China/Tibet	6.5
Aug. 14	Molucca Sea	7.4
July 21	California/Nevada	6.2
July 9	Indonesia	6.5
July 8	Palm Springs, Cal.	6.0
June 24	Papua New Guinea	7.1
June 24	Honshu, Japan	6.6
June 11	Venezuela	6.2
May 26	Fiji	6.7
May 20	Taiwan	6.3
May 17	Aleutian Islands	6.6
May 7	Aleutian Islands	7.7

Some Notable Tornadoes In U.S. Since 1925

Date			Place	Deaths
1925	Mar.	18	Mo., Ill. Ind.	689
1927	Apr.	12	Rock Springs, Tex.	74
1927	May	9	Arkansas, Poplar Bluff, Mo.	92
1927	Sept.	29	St. Louis, Mo.	90
1930	May	6	Hill & Ellis Co., Tex.	41
1932	Mar.	21	Ala. (series of tornadoes)	268
1936	Apr.	5	Miss., Ga.	455
1936	Apr.	6	Gainesville, Ga.	203
1938	Sept.	29	Charleston, S.C.	32
1942	Mar.	16	Central to NE Miss.	75
1942	Apr.	27	Rogers & Mayes Co., Okla.	52
1944	June	23	Oh., Pa., W. Va., Md.	150
1945	Apr.	12	Okla.-Ark.	102
1947	Apr.	9	Tex., Okla. & Kan.	169
1948	Mar.	19	Bunker Hill & Gillespie, Ill.	33
1949	Jan.	3	La. & Ark.	58
1952	Mar.	21	Ark., Mo., Tenn. (series)	208
1953	May	11	Waco, Tex.	114
1953	June	8	Mich., Oh.	142
1953	June	9	Worcester and vicinity, Mass.	90
1953	Dec.	5	Vicksburg, Miss.	38
1955	May	25	Kan., Mo., Okla., Tex.	115
1957	May	20	Kan., Mo.	48
1958	June	4	Northwestern Wisconsin	30
1959	Feb.	10	St. Louis, Mo.	21
1960	May	5, 6	SE Oklahoma, Arkansas	30
1965	Apr.	11	Ind., Ill., Oh., Mich., Wis.	271
1966	Mar.	3	Jackson, Miss.	57
1966	Mar.	3	Mississippi, Alabama	61
1967	Apr.	21	Ill., Mich.	33
1968	May	15	Midwest	71
1969	Jan.	23	Mississippi	32
1971	Feb.	21	Mississippi delta	110
1973	May	26-27	South, Midwest (series)	47
1974	Apr.	3-4	Ala., Ga., Tenn., Ky., Oh.	350
1977	Apr.	4	Ala., Miss., Ga.	22
1979	Apr.	10	Tex., Okla.	60
1980	June	3	Grand Island, Neb. (series)	4
1982	Mar.	2-4	South, Midwest (series)	17
1982	May	29	So. Ill.	10
1983	May	18-22	Tex.	12
1984	Mar.	28	N. Carolina; S. Carolina	67
1984	Apr.	21-22	Mississippi	15
1984	Apr.	26	Series Okla to Minn.	17
1984	June	9	W. USSR	400
1985	May	31	N.Y., Pa., Oh., Ont. (series)	90
1987	May	22	Saragosa, Tex.	29

Hurricanes, Typhoons, Blizzards, Other Storms

Names of hurricanes and typhoons in italics—H.—hurricane; T.—typhoon

Date	Location	Deaths
1888 Mar. 11-14	Blizzard, Eastern U.S.	400
1900 Aug.-Sept.	H., Galveston, Tex.	6,000
1906 Sept. 21	H., La., Miss.	350
1906 Sept. 18	Typhoon, Hong Kong	10,000
1926 Sept. 11-22	H., Fla., Ala.	243
1926 Oct. 20	H., Cuba	600
1928 Sept. 6-20	H., So. Fla.	1,836
1930 Sept. 3	H., Dominican Rep.	2,000
1938 Sept. 21	H., Long, Island N.Y., New England	600
1940 Nov. 11-12	Blizzard, U.S. NE, Midwest	144
1942 Oct. 15-16	H., Bengal, India	40,000
1944 Sept. 9-16	H., N.C. to New Eng.	46
1952 Oct. 22	Typhoon, Philippines	6,300
1954 Aug. 30	H. *Carol*, Northeast U.S.	68
1954 Oct. 5-18	H. *Hazel*, Eastern, U.S., Haiti	347
1955 Aug. 12-13	H. *Connie*, Carolinas, Va., Md.	43
1955 Aug. 7-21	H. *Diane*, Eastern U.S.	400
1955 Sept. 19	H. *Hilda*, Mexico	200
1955 Sept. 22-28	H. *Janet*, Caribbean	500
1956 Feb. 1-29	Blizzard, Western Europe	1,000
1957 June 25-30	H. *Audrey*, Tex. to Ala.	390
1958 Feb. 15-16	Blizzard, NE U.S.	171
1959 Sept. 17-19	T. *Sarah*, Japan, S. Korea	2,000
1959 Sept. 26-27	T. *Vera*, Honshu, Japan	4,466
1960 Sept. 4-12	H. *Donna*, Caribbean, E. U.S.	148
1961 Sept. 11-14	H. *Carla*, Tex.	46
1961 Oct. 31	H. *Hattie*, Br. Honduras	400
1963 May 28-29	Windstorm, Bangladesh	22,000
1963 Oct. 4-8	H. *Flora*, Caribbean	6,000
1964 Oct. 4-7	H. *Hilda*, La., Miss., Ga.	38
1964 June 30	T. *Winnie*, N. Philippines	107
1964 Sept. 5	T. *Ruby*, Hong Kong and China	735
1965 May 11-12	Windstorm, Bangladesh	17,000
1965 June 1-2	Windstorm, Bangladesh	30,000
1965 Sept. 7-12	H. *Betsy*, Fla., Miss., La.	74
1965 Dec. 15	Windstorm, Bangladesh	10,000
1966 June 4-10	H. *Alma*, Honduras, SE U.S.	51
1966 Sept. 24-30	H. *Inez*, Carib., Fla., Mex.	293
1967 July 9	T. *Billie*, SW Japan	347
1967 Sept. 5-23	H. *Beulah*, Carib., Mex., Tex.	54
1967 Dec. 12-20	Blizzard, Southwest, U.S.	51
1968 Nov. 18-28	T. *Nina*, Philippines	63
1969 Aug. 17-18	H. *Camille*, Miss., La.	256
1970 July 30-Aug. 5	H. *Celia*, Cuba, Fla., Tex.	31
1970 Aug. 20-21	H. *Dorothy*, Martinique	42
1970 Sept. 15	T. *Georgia*, Philippines	300
1970 Oct. 14	T. *Sening*, Philippines	583
1970 Oct. 15	T. *Titang*, Philippines	526
1970 Nov. 13	Cyclone, Bangladesh	300,000
1971 Aug. 1	T. *Rose*, Hong Kong	130
1972 June 19-29	H. *Agnes*, Fla. to N.Y.	118
1972 Dec. 3	T. *Theresa*, Philippines	169
1973 June-Aug.	Monsoon rains in India	1,217
1974 June 11	Storm Dinah, Luzon Is., Philip.	71
1974 July 11	T. *Gilda*, Japan, S. Korea	108
1974 Sept. 19-20	H. *Fifi*, Honduras	2,000
1974 Dec. 25	Cyclone leveled Darwin, Aus.	50
1975 Sept. 13-27	H. *Eloise*, Caribbean, NE U.S.	71
1976 May 20	T. *Olga*, floods, Philippines	215
1977 July 25, 31	T. *Thelma*, T. *Vera*, Taiwan	39
1978 Oct. 27	T. *Rita*, Philippines	c. 400
1979 Aug. 30-Sept. 7	H. *David*, Caribbean, East. U.S.	1,100
1980 Aug. 4-11	H. *Allen*, Caribbean, Texas	272
1981 Nov. 25	T. *Irma*, Luzon Is., Philippines	176
1983 June	Monsoon rains in India	900
1983 Aug. 18	H. *Alicia*, southern Texas	17
1984 Sept. 2	T. *Ike*, southern Philippines	1,363
1985 May 25	Cyclone, Bangladesh	10,000
1985 Oct. 26-Nov. 6	H. *Juan*, SE U.S.	97

Floods, Tidal Waves

Date		Location	Deaths
1228	....	Holland	100,000
1642	....	China	300,000
1887	....	Huang He River, China	900,000
1889	May 31	Johnstown, Pa.	2,200
1900	Sept. 8	Galveston, Tex.	5,000
1903	June 15	Heppner, Ore.	325
1911	....	Chang Jiang River, China	100,000
1913	Mar. 25-27	Ohio, Indiana	732
1915	Aug. 17	Galveston, Tex.	275
1928	Mar. 13	Collapse of St. Francis Dam, Santa Paula, Cal.	450
1928	Sept. 13	Lake Okeechobee, Fla.	2,000
1931	Aug.	Huang He River, China	3,700,000
1937	Jan. 22	Ohio, Miss. Valleys	250
1939	....	Northern China	200,000

(*continued*)

Date		Location	Deaths
1946	Apr. 1	Hawaii, Alaska	159
1947	....	Honshu Island, Japan	1,900
1951	Aug.	Manchuria	1,800
1953	Jan. 31	Western Europe	2,000
1954	Aug. 17	Farahzad, Iran	2,000
1955	Oct. 7-12	India, Pakistan	1,700
1959	Nov. 1	Western Mexico	2,000
1959	Dec. 2	Frejus, France	412
1960	Oct. 10	Bangladesh	6,000
1960	Oct. 31	Bangladesh	4,000
1962	Feb. 17	German North Sea coast	343
1962	Sept. 27	Barcelona, Spain	445
1963	Oct. 9	Dam collapse, Vaiont, Italy	1,800
1966	Nov. 3-4	Florence, Venice, Italy	113
1967	Jan. 18-24	Eastern Brazil	894
1967	Mar. 19	Rio de Janeiro, Brazil	436
1967	Nov. 26	Lisbon, Portugal	464
1968	Aug. 7-14	Gujarat State, India	1,000
1968	Oct. 7	Northeastern India	780
1969	Jan. 18-26	So. Cal.	100
1969	Mar. 17	Mundau Valley, Alagoas, Brazil	218
1969	Aug. 20-22	Western Virginia	189
1969	Sept. 15	South Korea	250
1969	Oct. 1-8	Tunisia	500
1970	May 20	Central Romania	160
1970	July 22	Himalayas, India	500
1971	Feb. 26	Rio de Janeiro, Brazil	130
1972	Feb. 26	Buffalo Creek, W. Va.	118
1972	June 9	Rapid City, S.D.	236
1972	Aug. 7	Luzon Is., Philippines	454
1973	Aug. 19-31	Pakistan	1,500
1974	Mar. 29	Tubaro, Brazil	1,000
1974	Aug. 12	Monty-Long, Bangladesh	2,500
1976	June 5	Teton Dam collapse, Ida.	11
1976	July 31	Big Thompson Canyon, Col.	139
1976	Nov. 17	East Java, Indonesia	136
1977	July 19-20	Johnstown, Pa.	68
1978	June-Sept.	Northern India	1,200
1979	Jan.-Feb.	Brazil	204
1979	July 17	Lomblem Is., Indonesia	539
1979	Aug. 11	Morvi, India	5,000-15,000
1980	Feb. 13-22	So. Cal., Ariz.	26
1981	Apr.	Northern China	550
1981	July	Sichuan, Hubei Prov., China	1,300
1982	Jan. 23	Nr. Lima, Peru	600
1982	May 12	Guangdong, China	430
1982	June 6	So. Conn.	12
1982	Sept. 17-21	El Salvador, Guatemala	1,300+
1982	Dec. 2-9	Ill., Mo., Ark.	22
1983	Feb.-Mar.	Cal. coast	13
1983	Apr. 6-12	Ala., La., Miss., Tenn.	15
1984	May 27	Tulsa, Okla.	13
1984	Aug-Sept.	S. Korea	200+
1985	July 19	Northern Italy, dam burst	361

Fires

Date			Location	Deaths
1835	Dec.	16	New York City, 500 bldgs. destroyed	—
1845	May		Canton, China, theater	1,670
1871	Oct.	8	Chicago, $196 million loss	250
1871	Oct.	8	Peshtigo, Wis., forest fire	1,182
1872	Nov.	9	Boston, 800 bldgs. destroyed	—
1876	Dec.	5	Brooklyn (N.Y.), theater	295
1877	June	20	St. John, N. B., Canada	100
1881	Dec.	8	Ring Theater, Vienna	850
1887	May	25	Opera Comique, Paris	200
1887	Sept.	4	Exeter, England, theater	200
1894	Sept.	1	Minn., forest fire	413
1897	May	4	Paris, charity bazaar	150
1900	June	30	Hoboken, N. J., docks	326
1902	Sept.	20	Birmingham, Ala., church	115
1903	Dec.	30	Iroquois Theater, Chicago	602
1908	Jan.	13	Rhoads Theater, Boyertown, Pa.	170
1908	Mar.	4	Collinwood, Oh., school	176
1911	Mar.	25	Triangle factory, N. Y. City	145
1913	Oct.	14	Mid Glamorgan, Wales, colliery	439
1918	Apr.	13	Norman Okla., state hospital	38
1918	Oct.	12	Cloquet, Minn., forest fire	400
1919	June	20	Mayaguez Theater, San Juan	150
1923	May	17	Camden, S. C., school	76
1924	Dec.	24	Hobart, Okla., school	35
1929	May	15	Cleveland, Oh., clinic	125
1930	Apr.	21	Columbus, Oh., penitentiary	320
1931	July	24	Pittsburgh, Pa., home for aged	48
1934	Dec.	11	Hotel Kerns, Lansing, Mich.	34
1938	May	16	Atlanta, Ga., Terminal Hotel	35
1940	Apr.	23	Natchez, Miss., dance hall	198
1942	Nov.	28	Cocoanut Grove, Boston	491
1942			St. John's, Newfoundland, hostel	100
1943	Sept.	7	Gulf Hotel, Houston	55
1944	July	6	Ringling Circus, Hartford	168
1946	June	5	LaSalle Hotel, Chicago	61
1946	Dec.	7	Winecoff Hotel, Atlanta	119
1946	Dec.	12	New York, ice plant, tenement	37
1949	Apr.	5	Effingham, Ill., hospital	77
1950	Jan.	7	Davenport, Ia., Mercy Hospital	41
1953	Mar.	29	Largo, Fla., nursing home	35
1953	Apr.	16	Chicago, metalworking plant	35
1957	Feb.	17	Warrenton, Mo., home for aged	72
1958	Mar.	19	New York City, loft building	24
1958	Dec.	1	Chicago, parochial school	95
1958	Dec.	16	Bogota, Colombia, store	83
1959	June	23	Stalheim, Norway, resort hotel	34
1960	Mar.	12	Pusan, Korea, chemical plant	68
1960	July	14	Guatemala City, mental hospital	225
1960	Nov.	13	Amude, Syria, movie theater	152
1961	Jan.	6	Thomas Hotel, San Francisco	20
1961	Dec.	8	Hartford, Conn., hospital	16
1961	Dec.	17	Niteroi, Brazil, circus	323
1963	May	4	Diourbel, Senegal, theater	64
1963	Nov.	18	Surfside Hotel, Atlantic City, N.J.	25
1963	Nov.	23	Fitchville, Oh., rest home	63
1963	Dec.	29	Roosevelt Hotel, Jacksonville, Fla.	22
1964	May	8	Manila, apartment bldg	30
1964	Dec.	18	Fountaintown, Ind., nursing home	20
1965	Mar.	1	LaSalle, Canada, apartment	28
1966	Mar.	11	Numata, Japan, 2 ski resorts	31
1966	Aug.	13	Melbourne, Australia, hotel	29
1966	Sept.	12	Anchorage, Alaska, hotel	14
1966	Oct.	17	N. Y. City bldg. (firemen)	12
1966	Dec.	7	Erzurum, Turkey, barracks	68
1967	Feb.	7	Montgomery, Ala., restaurant	25
1967	May	22	Brussels, Belgium, store	322
1967	July	16	Jay, Fla., state prison	37
1968	Feb.	26	Shrewsbury, England, hospital	22
1968	May	11	Vijayawada, India, wedding hall	58
1968	Nov.	18	Glasgow, Scotland, factory	24
1969	Jan.	26	Victoria Hotel, Dunnville, Ont.	13
1969	Dec.	2	Notre Dame, Can., nursing home	54
1970	Jan.	9	Marietta, Oh., nursing home	27
1970	Mar.	20	Seattle, Wash., hotel	19
1970	Nov.	1	Grenoble, France, dance hall	145
1970	Dec.	20	Tucson, Arizona, hotel	28
1971	Mar.	6	Burghoezli, Switzerland, psychiatric clinic	28
1971	Apr.	20	Hotel, Bangkok, Thailand	24
1971	Oct.	19	Honesdale, Pa., nursing home	15
1971	Dec.	25	Hotel, Seoul, So. Korea	162
1972	May	13	Osaka, Japan, nightclub	116
1972	July	5	Sherborne, England, hospital	30
1973	Feb.	6	Paris, France, school	21
1973	Nov.	6	Fukui, Japan, train	28
1973	Nov.	29	Kumamoto, Japan, department store	107
1973	Dec.	2	Seoul, Korea, theater	50
1974	Feb.	1	Sao Paulo, Brazil, bank building	189
1974	June	30	Port Chester, N. Y., discotheque	24
1974	Nov.	3	Seoul, So. Korea, hotel discotheque	88
1975	Dec.	12	Mina, Saudi Arabia, tent city	138
1976	Oct.	24	Bronx, N.Y., social club	25
1977	Feb.	25	Moscow, Rossiya hotel	45
1977	May	28	Southgate, Ky., nightclub	164
1977	June	9	Abidjan, Ivory Coast, nightclub	41
1977	June	26	Columbia, Tenn., jail	42
1977	Nov.	14	Manila, PI, hotel	47
1978	Jan.	28	Kansas City, Coates House Hotel	16
1979	July	14	Saragossa, Spain, hotel	80
1979	Dec.	31	Chapais, Quebec, social club	42
1980	May	20	Kingston, Jamaica, nursing home	157
1980	Nov.	21	MGM Grand Hotel, Las Vegas	84
1980	Dec.	4	Stouffer Inn, Harrison, N.Y.	26
1981	Jan.	9	Keansburg, N.J., boarding home	30
1981	Feb.	10	Las Vegas Hilton	8
1981	Feb.	14	Dublin, Ireland, discotheque	44
1982	Sept.	4	Los Angeles, apartment house	24
1982	Nov.	8	Biloxi, Miss., county jail	29
1983	Feb.	13	Turin, Italy, movie theater	64

(continued)

Date			Location	Deaths
1983	Dec.	17	Madrid, Spain, discotheque	83
1984	May	11	Great Adventure Amusement Park, N.J.	8
1985	Apr.	21	Tabaco, Philippines, movie theater	44
1985	Apr.	26	Buenos Aires, Argentina hospital	79
1985	May	11	Bradford, England, soccer stadium	53
1986	Dec.	31	Puerto Rico, Dupont Plaza Hotel	96
1987	May		Northern China forest fire	200+

Explosions

Date			Location	Deaths
1910	Oct.	1	Los Angeles Times Bldg.	21
1913	Mar.	7	Dynamite, Baltimore harbor	55
1915	Sept.	27	Gasoline tank car, Ardmore, Okla.	47
1917	Apr.	10	Munitions plant, Eddystone, Pa.	133
1917	Dec.	6	Halifax Harbor, Canada	1,654
1918	May	18	Chemical plant, Oakdale, Pa.	193
1918	July	2	Explosives, Split Rock, N.Y.	50
1918	Oct.	4	Shell plant, Morgan Station, N.J.	64
1919	May	22	Food plant, Cedar Rapids, Ia.	44
1920	Sept.	16	Wall Street, New York, bomb	30
1924	Jan.	3	Food plant, Pekin, Ill.	42
1928	April	13	Dance hall, West Plains, Mo.	40
1937	Mar.	18	New London, Tex., school	413
1940	Sept.	11	Hercules Powder, Kenvil, N.J.	51
1942	June	5	Ordnance plant, Elwood, Ill.	49
1944	Apr.	14	Bombay, India, harbor	700
1944	July	17	Port Chicago, Cal., pier	322
1944	Oct.	21	Liquid gas tank, Cleveland	135
1947	Apr.	16	Texas City, Tex., pier	561
1948	July	28	Farben works, Ludwigshafen, Ger.	184
1950	May	19	Munitions barges, S. Amboy, N. J.	30
1956	Aug.	7	Dynamite trucks, Cali, Colombia	1,100
1958	Apr.	18	Sunken munitions ship, Okinawa	40
1958	May	22	Nike missiles, Leonardo, N.J.	10
1959	Apr.	10	World War II bomb, Philippines	38
1959	June	28	Rail tank cars, Meldrin, Ga.	25
1959	Aug.	7	Dynamite truck, Roseburg, Ore.	13
1959	Nov.	2	Jamuri Bazar, India, explosives	46
1959	Dec.	13	Dortmund, Ger., 2 apt. bldgs.	26
1960	Mar.	4	Belgian munitions ship, Havana	100
1960	Oct.	25	Gas, Windsor, Ont., store	11
1962	Jan.	16	Gas pipeline, Edson, Alberta, Canada	8
1962	Oct.	3	Telephone Co. office, N. Y. City	23
1963	Jan.	2	Packing plant, Terre Haute, Ind.	16
1963	Mar.	9	Dynamite plant, S. Africa	45
1963	Aug.	13	Explosives dump, Gauhiti, India	32
1963	Oct.	31	State Fair Coliseum, Indianapolis	73
1964	July	23	Bone, Algeria, harbor munitions	100
1965	Mar.	4	Gas pipeline, Natchitoches, La.	17
1965	Aug.	9	Missile silo, Searcy, Ark.	53
1965	Oct.	21	Bridge, Tila Bund, Pakistan	80
1965	Oct.	30	Cartagena, Colombia	48
1965	Nov.	24	Armory, Keokuk, Ia.	20
1966	Oct.	13	Chemical plant, La Salle, Que.	11
1967	Feb.	17	Chemical plant, Hawthorne, N.J.	11
1967	Dec.	25	Apartment bldg., Moscow	20
1968	Apr.	6	Sports store, Richmond, Ind.	43
1970	Apr.	8	Subway construction, Osaka, Japan	73
1971	June	24	Tunnel, Sylmar, Cal.	17
1971	June	28	School, fireworks, Pueblo, Mex.	13
1971	Oct.	21	Shopping center, Glasgow, Scot.	20
1973	Feb.	10	Liquified gas tank, Staten Is., N.Y.	40
1975	Dec.	27	Chasnala, India, mine	431
1976	Apr.	13	Lapua, Finland, munitions works	45
1977	Nov.	11	Freight train, Iri, S. Korea	57
1977	Dec.	22	Grain elevator, Westwego, La.	35
1978	Feb.	24	Derailed tank car, Waverly, Tenn.	12
1978	July	11	Propylene tank truck, Spanish coastal campsite	150
1980	Oct.	23	School, Ortuella, Spain	64
1981	Feb.	13	Sewer system, Louisville, Ky.	0
1982	Apr.	7	Tanker truck, tunnel, Oakland, Cal.	7
1982	Apr.	25	Antiques exhibition, Todi, Italy	33
1982	Nov.	2	Salang Tunnel, Afghanistan	1,000-3,000
1984	Feb.	25	Oil pipeline, Cubatao, Brazil	508
1984	June	21	Naval supply depot, Severomorsk, USSR	200+
1984	Nov.	19	Gas storage area, NE Mexico City	334
1984	Dec.	5	Coal mine, Taipei, Taiwan	94
1985	June	25	Fireworks factory, Hallett, Okla.	21

Notable Nuclear Accidents

Oct. 7, 1957 — A fire in the Windscale plutonium production reactor north of Liverpool, England spread radioactive material throughout the countryside. In 1983, the British government said that 39 people probably died of cancer as a result.

1957 — A chemical explosion in Kasli, USSR, in tanks containing nuclear waste, spread radioactive material and forced a major evacuation.

Jan. 3, 1961 — An experimental reactor at a federal installation near Idaho Falls, Id. killed three workers—the only deaths in U.S. reactor operations. The plant had high radiation levels but damage was contained.

Oct. 5, 1966 — A sodium cooling system malfunction caused a partial core meltdown at the Enrico Fermi demonstration breeder reactor near Detroit, Mich. Radiation was contained.

Jan. 21, 1969 — A coolant malfunction from an experimental underground reactor at Lucens Vad, Switzerland resulted in the release of a large amount of radiation into a cavern, which was then sealed.

Nov. 19, 1971 — The water-storage space at the Northern States Power Co.'s reactor in Monticello, Minn. filled to capacity and spilled over, dumping about 50,000 gallons of radioactive waste water into the Mississippi River. Some was taken into the St. Paul water system.

Mar. 22, 1975 — A technician checking for air leaks with a lighted candle caused a $100 million fire at the Brown's Ferry reactor in Decatur, Ala. The fire burned out electrical controls, lowering the cooling water to dangerous levels.

Mar. 28, 1979 — The worse commercial nuclear accident in the U.S. occured as equipment failures and human mistakes led to a loss of coolant, and partial core meltdown at the Three Mile Island reactor in Middletown, Pa.

Aug. 7, 1979 — Highly enriched uranium was released from a top-secret nuclear fuel plant near Erwin, Tenn. About 1,000 people were contaminated with up to 5 times as much radiation as would normally be received in a year.

Feb. 11, 1981 — Eight workers were contaminated when over 100,000 gallons of radioactive coolant leaked into the containment building of the TVA's Sequoyah 1 plant in Tennessee.

Apr. 25, 1981 — Some 100 workers were exposed to radioactive material during repairs of a nuclear plant at Tsuruga, Japan.

Jan. 25, 1982 — A steam-generator pipe broke at the Rochester Gas & Electric Co's Ginna plant near Rochester, N.Y. Small amounts of radioactive steam escaped into the air.

Jan. 6, 1986 — A cylinder of nuclear material burst after being improperly heated at a Kerr-McGee plant at Gore, Okla. One worker died and 100 were hospitalized.

Apr., 1986 — A serious accident at the Chernobyl nuclear plant about 60 miles from Kiev in the Soviet Union spewed clouds of radiation that spread over several European nations.

Some Notable Aircraft Disasters Since 1937

Date			Aircraft	Site of accident	Deaths
1937	May	6	German zeppelin Hindenburg	Burned at mooring, Lakehurst, N.J.	36
1944	Aug.	23	U.S. Air Force B-24	Hit school, Freckelton, England	76[1]
1945	July	28	U.S. Army B-25	Hit Empire State bldg., N.Y.C.	14[1]

(continued)

Date			Aircraft	Site of accident	Deaths
1947	May	30	Eastern Air Lines DC-4	Crashed near Port Deposit, Md.	53
1952	Dec.	20	U.S. Air Force C-124	Fell, burned, Moses Lake, Wash.	87
1953	Mar.	3	Canadian Pacific Comet Jet	Karachi, Pakistan	11[2]
1953	June	18	U.S. Air Force C-124	Crashed, burned near Tokyo	129
1955	Nov.	1	United Air Lines DC-6B	Exploded, crashed near Longmont, Col.	44[3]
1956	June	20	Venezuelan Super-Constellation	Crashed in Atlantic off Asbury Park, N.J.	74
1956	June	30	TWA Super-Const., United DC-7	Collided over Grand Canyon, Arizona	128
1960	Dec.	16	United DC-8 jet, TWA Super-Const.	Collided over N.Y. City	134[4]
1962	Mar.	4	Br. Caledonian Airlines DC-7C	Crashed near Douala, Cameroon.	111
1962	Mar.	16	Flying Tiger Super-Const.	Vanished in Western Pacific	107
1962	June	3	Air France Boeing 707 jet	Crashed on takeoff from Paris	130
1962	June	22	Air France Boeing 707 jet	Crashed in storm, Guadeloupe, W.I.	113
1963	June	3	Chartered Northw. Airlines DC-7	Crashed in Pacific off British Columbia	101
1963	Nov.	29	Trans-Canada Airlines DC-8F	Crashed after takeoff from Montreal	118
1965	May	20	Pakistani Boeing 720-B	Crashed at Cairo, Egypt, airport	121
1966	Jan.	24	Air India Boeing 707 jetliner	Crashed on Mont Blanc, France-Italy	117
1966	Feb.	4	All-Nippon Boeing 727	Plunged into Tokyo Bay	133
1966	Mar.	5	BOAC Boeing 707 jetliner	Crashed on Mount Fuji, Japan	124
1966	Dec.	24	U.S. military-chartered CL-44	Crashed into village in So. Vietnam	129[1]
1967	Apr.	20	Swiss Britannia turboprop	Crashed at Nicosia, Cyprus	126
1967	July	19	Piedmont Boeing 727, Cessna 310	Collided in air, Hendersonville, N.C.	82
1968	Apr.	20	S. African Airways Boeing 707	Crashed on takeoff, Windhoek, SW Africa	122
1968	May	3	Braniff International Electra	Crashed in storm near Dawson, Tex.	85
1969	Mar.	16	Venezuelan DC-9	Crashed after takeoff from Maracaibo, Venezuela	155[5]
1969	Mar.	20	United Arab Ilyushin-18	Crashed at Aswan airport, Egypt	87
1969	June	4	Mexican Boeing 727	Rammed into mountain near Monterrey, Mexico	79
1969	Dec.	8	Olympia Airways DC-6B	Crashed near Athens in storm	93
1970	Feb.	15	Dominican DC-9	Crashed into sea on takeoff from Santo Domingo	102
1970	July	3	British chartered jetliner	Crashed near Barcelona, Spain	112
1970	July	5	Air Canada DC-8	Crashed near Toronto International Airport	108
1970	Aug.	9	Peruvian turbojet	Crashed after takeoff from Cuzco, Peru	101[1]
1970	Nov.	14	Southern Airways DC-9	Crashed in mountains near Huntington, W. Va.	75[6]
1971	July	30	All-Nippon Boeing 727 and Japanese Air Force F-86	Collided over Morioka, Japan	162[7]
1971	Aug.	11	Soviet Aeroflot Tupolev-104	Crashed at Irkutsk airport, USSR	97
1971	Sept.	4	Alaska Airlines Boeing 727	Crashed into mountain near Juneau, Alaska	111
1972	Aug.	14	E. German Ilyushin-62	Crashed on take-off East Berlin	156
1972	Oct.	13	Aeroflot Ilyushin-62	E. German airline crashed near Moscow	176
1972	Dec.	3	Chartered Spanish airliner	Crashed on take-off, Canary Islands	155
1972	Dec.	29	Eastern Airlines Lockheed Tristar	Crashed on approach to Miami Int'l. Airport	101
1973	Jan.	22	Chartered Boeing 707	Burst into flames during landing, Kano Airport, Nigeria	176
1973	Apr.	10	British Vanguard turboprop	Crashed during snowstorm at Basel, Switzerland	104
1973	June	3	Soviet Supersonic TU-144	Exploded in air near Goussainville, France	14[8]
1973	July	11	Brazilian Boeing 707	Crashed on approach to Orly Airport, Paris	122
1973	July	31	Delta Airlines jetliner	Crashed, landing in fog at Logan Airport, Boston	89
1973	Dec.	23	French Caravelle jet	Crashed in Morocco	106
1974	Jan.	31	Pan American Boeing 707 jet	Crashed in Pago Pago, American Samoa	96
1974	Mar.	3	Turkish DC-10 jet	Crashed at Ermenonville near Paris	346
1974	Apr.	23	Pan American 707 jet	Crashed in Bali, Indonesia	107
1974	Sept.	8	TWA 707 jet	Crashed in Ionian Sea off Greece, after bomb explosion	80
1974	Dec.	1	TWA-727	Crashed in storm, Upperville, Va.	92
1974	Dec.	4	Dutch-chartered DC-8	Crashed in storm near Colombo, Sri Lanka	191
1975	Apr.	4	Air Force Galaxy C-58	Crashed near Saigon, So. Vietnam, after takeoff with load of orphans	172
1975	June	24	Eastern Airlines 727 jet	Crashed in storm, JFK Airport, N.Y. City	113
1975	Aug.	3	Chartered 707	Hit mountainside, Agadir, Morocco	168
1976	Sept.	10	British Airways Trident, Yugoslav DC-9	Collided near Zagreb, Yugoslavia	176
1976	Sept.	19	Turkish 727	Hit mountain, southern Turkey	155
1976	Oct.	6	Cuban DC-8	Crashed near Barbados after bomb explosion	73
1976	Oct.	12	Indian Caravelle jet	Crashed after takeoff, Bombay airport	95
1976	Oct.	13	Bolivian 707 cargo jet	Crashed in Santa Cruz, Bolivia	100[9]
1976	Dec.	28	Aeroflot TU-104	Crashed at Moscow's Sheremetyevo airport	72
1977	Jan.	13	Aeroflot TU-104	Exploded and crashed at Alma-Ata, Central Asia	90
1977	Mar.	27	KLM 747, Pan American 747	Collided on runway, Tenerife, Canary Islands	581
1977	Nov.	19	TAP Boeing 727	Crashed on Madeira	130
1977	Dec.	4	Malaysian Boeing 737	Hijacked, then exploded in mid-air over Straits of Johore	100
1977	Dec.	13	U.S. DC-3	Crashed after takeoff at Evansville, Ind.	29[10]
1978	Jan.	1	Air India 747	Exploded, crashed into sea off Bombay	213
1978	Mar.	16	Bulgarian TU-134	Crashed at Vratsa, Bulgaria	73
1978	Sept.	25	Boeing 727, Cessna 172	Collided in air, San Diego, Cal.	150
1978	Nov.	15	Chartered DC-8	Crashed near Colombo, Sri Lanka	183
1979	May	25	American Airlines DC-10	Crashed after takeoff at O'Hare Intl. Airport, Chicago	275[11]
1979	Aug.	17	Two Soviet Aeroflot jetliners	Collided over Ukraine	173
1979	Oct.	31	Western Airlines DC-10	Mexico City Airport	74
1979	Nov.	26	Pakistani Boeing 707	Crashed near Jidda, Saudi Arabia	156
1979	Nov.	28	New Zealand DC-10	Crashed into mountain in Antarctica	257
1980	Mar.	14	Polish Ilyushin 62	Crashed making emergency landing, Warsaw	87[12]
1980	Aug.	19	Saudi Arabian Tristar	Burned after emergency landing, Riyadh	301
1981	Dec.	1	Yugoslavian DC-9	Crashed into mountain in Corsica	174
1982	Jan.	13	Air Florida Boeing 737	Crashed into Potomac River after takeoff	78
1982	July	9	Pan-Am Boeing 727	Crashed after takeoff in Kenner, La.	153[13]
1982	Sept.	11	U.S. Army CH-47 Chinook helicopter	Crashed during air show in Mannheim, W. Germany	46
1983	Sept.	1	S. Korean Boeing 747	Shot down after violating Soviet airspace	269
1983	Nov.	27	Colombian Boeing 747	Crashed near Barajas Airport, Madrid	183
1985	Feb.	19	Spanish Boeing 727	Crashed into Mt. Oiz, Spain	148
1985	June	23	Air-India Boeing 747	Crashed into Atlantic Ocean S. of Ireland	329
1985	Aug.	2	Delta Air Lines jumbo jet	Crashed at Dallas-Ft. Worth Intl. Airport	133
1985	Aug.	12	Japan Air Lines Boeing 747	Crashed into Mt. Ogura, Japan	520[14]

(continued)

Date			Aircraft	Site of accident	Deaths
1985	Dec.	12	Arrow Air DC 8	Crashed after takeoff in Gander, Newfoundland	256[15]
1986	Mar.	31	Mexican Boeing 727	Crashed NW of Mexico City	166
1986	Aug.	31	Aeromexico DC-9	Collided with Piper PA-28 over Cerritos, Cal.	82[16]
1987	May	9	Ilyushin 62M	Crashed after takeoff at Warsaw, Poland	183

(1) Including those on the ground and in buildings. (2) First fatal crash of commercial jet plane. (3) Caused by bomb planted by John G. Graham in insurance plot to kill his mother, a passenger. (4) Including all 128 aboard the planes and 6 on ground. (5) Killed 84 on plane and 71 on ground. (6) Including 43 Marshall U. football players and coaches. (7) Airliner-fighter crash, pilot of fighter parachuted to safety, was arrested for negligence. (8) First supersonic plane crash killed 6 crewmen and 8 on the ground; there were no passengers. (9) Crew of 3 killed; 97, mostly children, killed on ground. (10) Including U. of Evansville basketball team. (11) Highest death toll in U.S. aviation history. (12) Including 22 members of U.S. boxing team. (13) Including 8 on ground. (14) Worst single-plane disaster. (15) Incl. 248 members of U.S. 101st Airborne Division. (16) Incl. 15 on the ground.

Major U.S. Railroad Wrecks

Date			Location	Deaths
1876	Dec.	29	Ashtabula, Oh.	92
1880	Aug.	11	Mays Landing, N. J.	40
1887	Aug.	10	Chatsworth, Ill.	81
1888	Oct.	10	Mud Run, Pa.	55
1896	July	30	Atlantic City, N. J.	60
1903	Dec.	23	Laurel Run, Pa.	53
1904	Aug.	7	Eden, Col.	96
1904	Sept.	24	New Market Tenn.	56
1906	Mar.	16	Florence, Col.	35
1906	Oct.	28	Atlantic City, N. J.	40
1906	Dec.	30	Washington, D. C.	53
1907	Jan.	2	Volland, Kan.	33
1907	Jan.	19	Fowler, Ind.	29
1907	Feb.	16	New York, N.Y.	22
1907	Feb.	23	Colton, Cal.	26
1907	July	20	Salem, Mich.	33
1910	Mar.	1	Wellington, Wash.	96
1910	Mar.	21	Green Mountain, Ia.	55
1911	Aug.	25	Manchester, N. Y.	29
1912	July	4	East Corning, N. Y.	39
1912	July	5	Ligonier, Pa.	23
1914	Aug.	5	Tipton Ford, Mo.	43
1914	Sept.	15	Lebanon, Mo.	28
1916	Mar.	29	Amherst, Oh.	27
1917	Sept.	28	Kellyville, Okla.	23
1917	Dec.	20	Shepherdsville, Ky.	46
1918	June	22	Ivanhoe, Ind.	68
1918	July	9	Nashville, Tenn.	101
1918	Nov.	1	Brooklyn, N. Y.	97
1919	Jan.	12	South Byron, N. Y.	22
1919	July	1	Dunkirk, N. Y.	12
1919	Dec.	20	Onawa, Maine	23
1921	Feb.	27	Porter, Ind.	37
1921	Dec.	5	Woodmont, Pa.	27
1922	Aug.	5	Sulphur Spring, Mo.	34
1922	Dec.	13	Humble, Tex.	22
1923	Sept.	27	Lockett, Wy.	31
1925	June	16	Hackettstown, N. J.	50
1925	Oct.	27	Victoria, Miss.	21
1926	Sept.	5	Waco, Col.	30
1928	Aug.	24	I.R.T. subway, Times Sq., N. Y.	18
1938	June	19	Saugus, Mont.	47
1939	Aug.	12	Harney, Nev.	24
1940	Apr.	19	Little Falls, N. Y.	31
1940	July	31	Cuyahoga Falls, Oh.	43
1943	Aug.	29	Wayland, N. Y.	27
1943	Sept.	6	Frankford Junction, Philadelphia, Pa.	79
1943	Dec.	16	Between Hennert and Buie, N. C.	72
1944	July	6	High Bluff, Tenn.	35
1944	Aug.	4	Near Stockton, Ga.	47
1944	Sept.	14	Dewey, Ind.	29
1944	Dec.	31	Bagley, Utah	50
1945	Aug.	9	Michigan, N. D.	34
1946	Apr.	25	Naperville, Ill.	45
1947	Feb.	18	Gallitzin, Pa.	24
1950	Feb.	17	Rockville Centre, N. Y.	31
1950	Sept.	11	Coshocton, Oh.	33
1950	Nov.	22	Richmond Hill, N. Y.	79
1951	Feb.	6	Woodbridge, N. J.	84
1951	Nov.	12	Wyuta, Wyo.	17
1951	Nov.	25	Woodstock, Ala.	17
1953	Mar.	27	Conneaut, Oh.	21
1956	Jan.	22	Los Angeles, Cal.	30
1956	Feb.	28	Swampscott, Mass.	13
1956	Sept.	5	Springer, N. M.	20
1957	June	11	Vroman, Col.	12
1958	Sept.	15	Elizabethport, N. J.	48
1960	Mar.	14	Bakersfield, Cal.	14
1960	July	28	Steelton, Pa.	19
1966	Dec.	28	Everett, Mass.	13
1971	June	10	Salem, Ill.	11
1972	Oct.	30	Chicago, Ill	45
1977	Feb.	4	Chicago, Ill., elevated train	11
1987	Jan.	4	Essex, Md.	16

World's worst train wreck occurred Dec. 12, 1917, Modane, France, passenger train derailed, 543 killed.

Principal U.S. Mine Disasters

Source: Bureau of Mines, U.S. Interior Department

Note: Prior to 1968, only disasters with losses of 60 or more lives are listed; since 1968, all disasters in which 5 or more people were killed are listed. Only fatalities to mining company employees are included. All bituminous-coal mines unless otherwise noted.

Date		Location	Deaths
1867	Apr. 3	Winterpock, Va.	69
1869[1]	Sept. 6	Plymouth, Pa.	110
1883	Feb. 16	Braidwood, Ill.	69
1884	Mar. 13	Pocahontas, Va.	112
1891	Jan. 27	Mount Pleasant, Pa.	109
1892	Jan. 7	Krebs, Okla.	100
1895	Mar. 20	Red Canyon, Wy.	60
1900	May 1	Scofield, Ut.	200
1902	May 19	Coal Creek, Tenn.	184
1902	July 10	Johnstown, Pa.	112
1903	June 30	Hanna, Wy.	169
1904	Jan. 25	Cheswick, Pa.	179
1905	Feb. 20	Virginia City, Ala.	112
1907	Jan. 29	Stuart W. Va.	84
1907	Dec. 6	Monongah, W. Va.	361
1907	Dec. 19	Jacobs Creek, Pa.	239
1908	Nov. 28	Marianna, Pa.	154
1909	Jan. 12	Switchback, W. Va.	67
1909	Nov. 13	Cherry, Ill.	259
1910	Jan. 31	Primero, Col.	75
1910	May 5	Palos, Ala.	90
1910	Nov. 8	Delagua, Col.	79
1911	Apr. 7	Throop, Pa.	72
1911	Apr. 8	Littleton, Ala.	128
1911	Dec. 9	Briceville, Tenn.	84
1912	Mar. 20	McCurtain, Okla.	73
1912	Mar. 26	Jed, W. Va.	83
1913	Apr. 23	Finleyville, Pa.	96
1913	Oct. 22	Dawson, N.M.	263
1914	Apr. 28	Eccles, W. Va.	181
1915	Mar. 2	Layland, W. Va.	112
1917	Apr. 27	Hastings, Col.	121
1917[2]	June 8	Butte, Mon.	163
1917	Aug. 4	Clay, Ky.	62
1919[1]	June 5	Wilkes-Barre, Pa.	92
1922	Nov. 6	Spangler, Pa.	77
1922	Nov. 22	Dolomite, Ala.	90
1923	Feb. 8	Dawson, N.M.	120
1923	Aug. 14	Kemmerer, Wy.	99
1924	Mar. 8	Castle Gate, Ut.	171
1924	Apr. 28	Benwood, W. Va.	119
1926	Jan. 13	Wilburton, Okla.	91
1926[2]	Nov. 3	Ishpeming, Mich.	51
1927	Apr. 30	Everettville, W. Va.	97
1928	May 19	Mather, Pa.	195

(continued)

Date		Location	Deaths	Date		Location	Deaths
1929	Dec. 17	McAlester, Okla.	61	1970	Dec. 30	Hyden, Ky.	38
1930	Nov. 5	Millfield, Oh.	79	1972[2]	May 2	Kellogg, Ida	91
1940	Jan. 10	Bartley, W. Va.	91	1976	Mar. 9, 11	Oven Fork, Ky.	26
1940	Mar. 16	St. Clairsville, Oh.	72	1977	Mar. 1	Tower City, Pa.	9
1940	July 15	Portage, Pa.	63	1981	Apr. 15	Redstone, Col.	15
1943	Feb. 27	Washoe, Mon.	74	1981	Dec. 7	Topmost, Ky.	8
1944	July 5	Belmont, Oh.	66	1981	Dec. 8	nr. Chattanooga, Tenn.	13
1947	Mar. 25	Centralia, Ill.	111	1982	Jan. 20	Floyd County, Ky.	7
1951	Dec. 21	West Frankfort, Ill.	119	1983	June 21	McClure, Va	7
1968[3]	Mar. 6	Calumet, La.	21	1984	Dec. 19	Huntington, Ut.	27
1968	Nov. 20	Farmington, W. Va.	78				

(1) Anthracite mine. (2) Metal mine. (3) Nonmetal mine.
World's worst mine disaster killed 1,549 workers in Honkeiko Colliery in Manchuria Apr. 25, 1942.

Historic Assassinations Since 1865

1865—Apr. 14. U. S. Pres. Abraham Lincoln, shot by John Wilkes Booth in Washington, D. C.; died Apr. 15.

1881—Mar. 13. Alexander II, of Russia—July 2. U. S. Pres. James A. Garfield, shot by Charles J. Guiteau, Washington D.C.; died Sept. 19.

1900—July 29. Umberto I, king of Italy.

1901—Sept. 6. U. S. Pres. William McKinley in Buffalo, N. Y., died Sept. 14. Leon Czolgosz executed for the crime Oct. 29.

1913—Feb. 23. Mexican Pres. Francisco I. Madero and Vice Pres. Jose Pino Suarez.—Mar. 18. George, king of Greece.

1914—June 28. Archduke Francis Ferdinand of Austria-Hungary and his wife in Sarajevo, Bosnia (later part of Yugoslavia), by Gavrilo Princip.

1916—Dec. 30. Grigori Rasputin, politically powerful Russian monk.

1918—July 12. Grand Duke Michael of Russia, at Perm.—July 16. Nicholas II, abdicated as czar of Russia; his wife, the Czarina Alexandra, their son, Czarevitch Alexis, and their daughters, Grand Duchesses Olga, Tatiana, Marie, Anastasia, and 4 members of their household were executed by Bolsheviks at Ekaterinburg.

1920—May 20. Mexican Pres. Gen. Venustiano Carranza in Tlaxcalantongo.

1922—Aug. 22. Michael Collins, Irish revolutionary.—Dec. 16. Polish President Gabriel Narutowicz in Warsaw by an anarchist.

1923—July 20. Gen. Francisco "Pancho" Villa, ex-rebel leader, in Parral, Mexico.

1928—July 17. Gen. Alvaro Obregon, president-elect of Mexico, in San Angel, Mexico.

1933—Feb. 15. In Miami, Fla. Joseph Zangara, anarchist, shot at Pres.-elect Franklin D. Roosevelt, but a woman seized his arm, and the bullet fatally wounded Mayor Anton J. Cermak, of Chicago, who died Mar. 6. Zangara was electrocuted on Mar. 20, 1933.

1934—July 25. In Vienna, Austrian Chancellor Engelbert Dollfuss by Nazis.

1935—Sept. 8. U. S. Sen. Huey P. Long, shot in Baton Rouge, La., by Dr. Carl Austin Weiss, who was slain by Long's bodyguards.

1940—Aug. 20. Leon Trotsky (Lev Bronstein), 63, exiled Russian war minister, near Mexico City. Killer identified as Ramon Mercador del Rio, a Spaniard, served 20 years in Mexican prison.

1948—Jan. 30. Mohandas K. Gandhi, 78, shot in New Delhi, India, by Nathuran Vinayak Godse.—Sept. 17. Count Folke Bernadotte, UN mediator for Palestine, ambushed in Jerusalem.

1951—July 20. King Abdullah ibn Hussein of Jordan.

1956—Sept. 21. Pres. Anastasio Somoza of Nicaragua, in Leon; died Sept. 29.

1957—July 26. Pres. Carlos Castillo Armas of Guatemala, in Guatemala City by one of his own guards.

1958—July 14. King Faisal of Iraq; his uncle, Crown Prince Abdul Illah, and July 15, Premier Nuri as-Said, by rebels in Baghdad.

1959—Sept. 25. Prime Minister Solomon Bandaranaike of Ceylon, by Buddhist monk in Colombo.

1961—Jan. 17. Ex-Premier Patrice Lumumba of the Congo, in Katanga Province—May 30. Dominican dictator Rafael Leonidas Trujillo Molina shot to death by assassins near Ciudad Trujillo.

1963—June 12. Medgar W. Evers, NAACP's Mississippi field secretary, in Jackson, Miss.—Nov. 2. Pres. Ngo Dinh Diem of the Republic of Vietnam and his brother, Ngo Dinh Nhu, in a military coup.—Nov. 22. U. S. Pres. John F. Kennedy fatally shot in Dallas, Tex.; accused Lee Harvey Oswald murdered by Jack Ruby while awaiting trial.

1965—Jan. 21. Iranian premier Hassan Ali Mansour fatally wounded by assassin in Teheran; 4 executed.—Feb. 21. Malcolm X, black nationalist, fatally shot in N. Y. City.

1966—Sept. 6. Prime Minister Hendrik F. Verwoerd of South Africa stabbed to death in parliament at Capetown.

1968—Apr. 4. Rev. Dr. Martin Luther King Jr. fatally shot in Memphis, Tenn. by James Earl Ray.—June 5. Sen. Robert F. Kennedy (D-N. Y.) fatally shot in Los Angeles; Sirhan Sirhan, resident alien, convicted of murder.

1971—Nov. 28. Jordan Prime Minister Wasfi Tal, in Cairo, by Palestinian guerrillas.

1973—Mar. 2. U. S. Ambassador Cleo A. Noel Jr., U. S. Charge d'Affaires George C. Moore and Belgian Charge d'Affaires Guy Eid killed by Palestinian guerrillas in Khartoum, Sudan.

1974—Aug. 15. Mrs. Park Chung Hee, wife of president of So. Korea, hit by bullet meant for her husband.—Aug. 19. U. S. Ambassador to Cyprus, Rodger P. Davies, killed by sniper's bullet in Nicosia.

1975—Feb. 11. Pres. Richard Ratsimandrava, of Madagascar, shot in Tananarive.—Mar. 25. King Faisal of Saudi Arabia shot by nephew Prince Musad Abdel Aziz, in royal palace, Riyadh.—Aug. 15. Bangladesh Pres. Sheik Mujibur Rahman killed in coup.

1976—Feb. 13. Nigerian head of state, Gen. Murtala Ramat Mohammed, slain by self-styled "young revolutionaries."

1977—Mar. 16. Kamal Jumblat, Lebanese Druse chieftain, was shot near Beirut.—Mar. 18. Congo Pres. Marien Ngouabi shot in Brazzaville.

1978—July 9. Former Iraqi Premier Abdul Razak Al-Naif shot in London.

1979—Feb. 14. U.S. Ambassador Adolph Dubs shot and killed by Afghan Moslem extremists in Kabul.—Mar. 30. British Tory MP Airey Neave killed when bomb in his car exploded. IRA claimed responsibility.—Aug. 27. Lord Mountbatten, WW2 hero, and 2 others were killed when a bomb exploded on his fishing boat off the coast of Co. Sligo, Ire. The IRA claimed responsibility.—Oct. 26. So. Korean President Park Chung Hee and 6 bodyguards fatally shot by Kim Jae Kyu, head of Korean CIA, and 5 aides in Seoul.

1980—Apr. 12. Liberian President William R. Tolbert slain in military coup.—Sept. 17. Former Nicaraguan President Anastasio Somoza Debayle and 2 others shot in Paraguay.

1981—Aug. 30. Iranian President Mohammed Ali Raji and Premier Mohammed Jad Bahonar killed by bomb in Teheran.—Oct. 6. Egyptian President Anwar El-Sadat fatally shot by a band of commandos while reviewing a military parade in Cairo.

1982—Sept. 14. Lebanese President-elect Bishir Gemayel killed by bomb in east Beirut.

1983—Apr. 10. PLO representative Dr. Issam Sartawi was fatally shot by an unknown gunman in Albufeira, Portugal. A PLO splinter group claimed responsibility.—Aug. 21. Philippine opposition political leader Benigno Aquino Jr. fatally shot by a gunman at Manila International Airport.—Oct. 9. Four S. Korea cabinet ministers and 15 others killed by bomb blast in Rangoon, Burma.

1984—Oct. 31. Indian Prime Minister Indira Gandhi shot and killed by 2 of her bodyguards, who were members of the minority Sikh sect, in New Delhi.

1986—Feb. 28. Swedish Premier Olof Palme shot and killed by a gunman in Stockholm.

Assassination Attempts

1910—Aug. 6. N. Y. City Mayor William J. Gaynor shot and seriously wounded by discharged city employee.

1912—Oct. 14. Former U. S. President Theodore Roosevelt shot and seriously wounded by demented man in Milwaukee, Wis.

1950—Nov. 1. In an attempt to assassinate President Truman, 2 members of a Puerto Rican nationalist movement—Griselio Torresola and Oscar Collazo—tried to shoot their way into Blair House. Torresola was killed, and a guard, Pvt. Leslie Coffelt was fatally shot. Collazo was convicted Mar. 7, 1951 for the murder of Coffelt.

1970—Nov. 27. Pope Paul VI unharmed by knife-wielding assailant who attempted to attack him in Manila airport.

1972—May 15. Alabama Gov. George Wallace shot in Laurel, Md. by Arthur Bremer; seriously crippled.

1972—Dec. 7. Mrs. Ferdinand E. Marcos, wife of the Philippine president, was stabbed and seriously injured in Pasay City, Philippines.

(continued)

1975—Sept. 5. Pres. Gerald R. Ford was unharmed when a Secret Service agent grabbed a pistol aimed at him by Lynette (Squeaky) Fromme, a Charles Manson follower, in Sacramento.

1975—Sept. 22. Pres. Gerald R. Ford escaped unharmed when Sara Jane Moore, a political activist, fired a revolver at him.

1980—Apr. 14. Indian Prime Minister Indira Gandhi was unharmed when a man threw a knife at her in New Delhi.

1980—May 29. Civil rights leader Vernon E. Jordan Jr. shot and wounded in Ft. Wayne, Ind.

1981—Jan. 16. Irish political activist Bernadette Devlin McAliskey and her husband were shot and seriously wounded by 3 members of a protestant paramilitary group in Co. Tyrone, Ire.

1981—Mar. 30. Pres. Ronald Reagan, Press Secy. James Brady, Secret Service agent Timothy J. McCarthy, and Washington, D.C. policeman Thomas Delahanty were shot and seriously wounded by John W. Hinckley Jr. in Washington, D.C.

1981—May 13. Pope John Paul II and 2 bystanders were shot and wounded by Mehmet Ali Agca, an escaped Turkish murderer, in St. Peter's Square, Rome.

1982—May 12. Pope John Paul II was unharmed when a man with a knife was overpowered by guards, in Fatima, Portugal.

1982—June 3. Israel's ambassador to Britain Shlomo Argov was shot and seriously wounded by Arab terrorists in London.

1986—Sept. 7. Chile President Gen. Augusto Pinochet Ugarte escaped unharmed when his motorcade was attacked by rebels using rockets, bazookas, grenades, and rifles.

Major Kidnapings

Edward A. Cudahy Jr., 16, in Omaha, Neb., **Dec. 18, 1900**. Returned Dec. 20 after $25,000 paid. Pat Crowe confessed.

Robert Franks, 13, in Chicago, **May 22, 1924**, by 2 youths, Richard Loeb and Nathan Leopold, who killed boy. Demand for $10,000 ignored. Loeb died in prison, Leopold paroled 1958.

Charles A. Lindbergh Jr., 20 mos. old, in Hopewell, N.J., **Mar. 1, 1932**; found dead May 12. Ransom of $50,000 was paid to man identified as Bruno Richard Hauptmann, 35, paroled German convict who entered U.S. illegally. Hauptmann was convicted after spectacular trial at Flemington, and electrocuted in Trenton, N.J. prison, Apr. 3, 1936.

William A. Hamm Jr., 39, in St. Paul, **June 15, 1933**. $100,000 paid. Alvin Karpis given life, paroled in 1969.

Charles F. Urschel, in Oklahoma City, **July 22, 1933**. Released July 31 after $200,000 paid. George (Machine Gun) Kelly and 5 others given life.

Brooke L. Hart, 22, in San Jose, Cal. Thomas Thurmond and John Holmes arrested after demanding $40,000 ransom. When Hart's body was found in San Francisco Bay, **Nov. 26, 1933**, a mob attacked the jail at San Jose and lynched the 2 kidnapers.

George Weyerhaeuser, 9, in Tacoma, Wash., **May 24, 1935**. Returned home June 1 after $200,000 paid. Kidnapers given 20 to 60 years.

Charles Mattson, 10, in Tacoma, Wash., **Dec. 27, 1936**. Found dead Jan. 11, 1937. Kidnaper asked $28,000, failed to contact.

Arthur Fried, in White Plains, N.Y., **Dec. 4, 1937**. Body not found. Two kidnapers executed.

Robert C. Greenlease, 6, taken from Kansas City, Mo. school **Sept. 28, 1953**, and held for $600,000. Body found Oct. 7. Mrs. Bonnie Brown Heady and Carl A. Hall pleaded guilty and were executed.

Peter Weinberger, 32 days old, Westbury, N.Y., **July 4, 1956**, for $2,000 ransom, not paid. Child found dead. Angelo John LaMarca, 31, convicted, executed.

Cynthia Ruotolo, 6 wks old, taken from carriage in front of Hamden, Conn. store Sept. 1, 1956. Body found in lake.

Lee Crary, 8 in Everett, Wash., **Sept. 22, 1957**, $10,000 ransom, not paid. He escaped after 3 days, led police to George E. Collins, who was convicted.

Eric Peugeot, 4, taken from playground at St. Cloud golf course, Paris, **Apr. 12, 1960**. Released unharmed 3 days later after payment of undisclosed sum. Two sentenced to prison.

Frank Sinatra Jr., 19, from hotel room in Lake Tahoe, Cal., **Dec. 8, 1963**. Released **Dec. 11** after his father paid $240,000 ransom. Three men sentenced to prison; most of ransom recovered.

Barbara Jane Mackle, 20, abducted **Dec. 17, 1968**, from Atlanta, Ga., motel, was found unharmed 3 days later, buried in a coffin-like wooden box 18 inches underground, after her father had paid $500,000 ransom; Gary Steven Krist sentenced to life, Ruth Eisenmann-Schier to 7 years; most of ransom recovered.

Anne Katherine Jenkins, 22, abducted **May 10, 1969**, from her Baltimore apartment, freed 3 days later after her father paid $10,000 ransom.

Mrs. Roy Fuchs, 35, and 3 children held hostage 2 hours, **May 14, 1969**, in Long Island, N. Y., released after her husband, a bank manager, paid kidnapers $129,000 in bank funds; 4 men arrested, ransom recovered.

C. Burke Elbrick, U.S. ambassador to Brazil, kidnaped by revolutionaries in Rio de Janeiro **Sept. 4, 1969**; released 3 days later after Brazil yielded to kidnaper's demands to publish manifesto and release 15 political prisoners.

Patrick Dolan, 18, found shot to death near Sao Paulo, Brazil, **Nov. 5, 1969**, after he was kidnaped and $12,500 paid.

Sean M. Holly, U.S. diplomat, in Guatemala **Mar. 6, 1970**; freed 2 days later upon release of 3 terrorists from prison.

Lt. Col. Donald J. Crowley, U.S. air attache, in Dominican Republic **Mar. 24, 1970**; released after government allowed 20 prisoners to leave the country.

Count Karl von Spreti, W. German ambassador to Guatemala, **Mar. 31, 1970**; slain after Guatemala refused demands for $700,000 and release of 22 prisoners.

Pedro Eugenio Aramburu, former Argentine president, by terrorists May 29, 1970; body found July 17.

Ehrenfried von Holleben, W. German ambassador to Brazil, by terrorists **June 11, 1970**; freed after release of 40 prisoners.

Daniel A. Mitrione, U.S. diplomat, **July 31, 1970**, by terrorists in Montevideo, Uruguay; body found Aug. 10 after government rejected demands for release of all political prisoners.

James R. Cross, British trade commissioner, **Oct. 5, 1970**, by French Canadian separatists in Quebec; freed Dec. 3 after 3 kidnapers and relatives flown to Cuba by government.

Pierre Laporte, Quebec Labor Minister, by separatists **Oct. 10, 1970**; body found Oct. 18.

Giovanni E. Bucher, Swiss ambassador **Dec. 7, 1970**, by revolutionaries in Rio de Janeiro; freed Jan. 16, 1971, after Brazil released 70 political prisoners.

Geoffrey Jackson, British ambassador, in Montevideo, **Jan. 8, 1971**, by Tupamaro terrorists. Held as ransom for release of imprisoned terrorists; released Sept. 9; prisoners escaped.

Ephraim Elrom, Israel consul general in Istanbul, **May 17, 1971**. Held as ransom for imprisoned terrorists; found dead May 23.

Mrs. Virginia Piper, 49 abducted **July 27, 1972**, from her home in suburban Minneapolis; found unharmed near Duluth 2 days later after her husband paid $1 million ransom to the kidnapers.

Victor E. Samuelson, Exxon executive, **Dec. 6, 1973**, in Campana, Argentina, by Marxist guerrillas, freed Apr. 29, 1974, after payment of record $14.2 million ransom.

J. Paul Getty 3d, 17, grandson of the U.S. oil mogul, released **Dec. 15, 1973**, in southern Italy after $2.8 million ransom paid.

Patricia (Patty) Hearst, 19, taken from her Berkeley, Cal., apartment **Feb. 4, 1974**. Symbionese Liberation Army demanded her father, Randolph A. Hearst, publisher, give millions to poor. She was identified by FBI as taking part in a San Francisco bank holdup, **Apr. 15**. FBI, **Sept. 18, 1975**, captured Patricia and others in San Francisco; they were indicted on various charges, Patricia for bank robbery. Convicted, **Mar. 20, 1976**. She was released from prison under executive clemency, **Feb. 1, 1979**. In 1978, William and Emily Harris were sentenced to 10 years to life for the Hearst kidnaping. Both were paroled in 1983.

J. Reginald Murphy, 40, an editor of *Atlanta* (Ga.) *Constitution*, kidnaped **Feb. 20, 1974**, freed **Feb. 22** after payment of $700,000 ransom by the newspaper. Police arrested William A. H. Williams, a contractor; most of the money was recovered.

J. Guadalupe Zuno Hernandez, 83, father-in-law of Mexican President Luis Echeverria Alvarez, seized by 4 terrorists **Aug. 28, 1974**; government refused to negotiate; he was released **Sept. 8**.

E. B. Reville, Hepzibah, Ga., banker, and wife Jean, kidnaped **Sept. 30, 1974**. Ransom of $30,000 paid. He was found alive; Mrs. Reville was found dead in car trunk **Oct. 2**.

Jack Teich, Kings Point, N.Y., steel executive, seized **Nov. 12, 1974**; released **Nov. 19** after payment of $750,000.

William F. Niehous, a U.S. businessman, was abducted from his suburban Caracas, Venezuela home, **Feb. 27, 1976**. He was rescued by police **June 29, 1979**, ending more than 3 years of captivity.

Hanns-Martin Schleyer, a West German industrialist, was kidnaped in Cologne, **Sept. 5, 1977** by armed terrorists. Schleyer was found dead, **Oct. 19**, in an abandoned car shortly after 3 jailed terrorist leaders of the Baader-Meinhof gang were found dead in their prison cells near Stuttgart, West Germany.

Aldo Moro, former Italian premier, kidnaped in Rome, **Mar. 16, 1978**, by left-wing terrorists. Five of his bodyguards killed during abduction. Moro's bullet-ridden body was found in a parked car, **May 9**, in Rome. Six members of the Red Brigades arrested, charged, June 5, with complicity in the kidnaping.

James L. Dozier, a U.S. Army general, kidnaped from his apartment in Verona, Italy, **Dec. 17, 1981**, by members of the Red Brigades terrorist organization. He was rescued, **Jan. 28, 1982**.

Enrique Camarena Salazar, and **Alfredo Zavala Avelar**, U.S. Drug Enforcement Agency employees were kidnaped in Guadalajara, Mexico, Feb. 7, 1985. Their bodies were found Mar. 6.

UNITED STATES POPULATION

Changing Population Patterns

By John G. Keane

Director, U.S. Bureau of the Census

On January 1, 1987, the estimated resident population of the United States was 242.2 million people, a 6.9 percent increase over the 1980 census count of 226.5 million.

California's San Francisco-Oakland-San Jose area grew by 441,000 from 1980 to 1985, to more than 5.8 million people, displacing Philadelphia as the fourth largest metropolitan area. The Dallas-Fort Worth metro area, with 3.5 million people, slipped past the Washington, D.C. area into ninth place, gaining on eighth-place Houston. Among the 37 metro areas having over one million in population, the Phoenix area led in 1980-85 growth with a 22.4 percent increase.

The South has been the only region to gain more residents than it lost through internal U.S. migration in this decade. Most of the influx in 1983-84 came from the Midwest, where loss of 624,000 people to the South marked the nation's largest flow of movers. The nation's 39.4 million total movers were about equal to the previous high of 38.8 million in 1964-65.

The nation's population center has continued to move west in Missouri since the 1980 census, to about 10 miles northwest of Potosi in west-central Washington County as of 1985. (The center is where the country would balance perfectly if it were a flat surface and every person on it had equal weight.)

The nation's **Hispanic population** in 1980-85 increased 16 percent to 16.9 million. Growing three times faster than the U.S. total, Hispanics may account for one-quarter of the nation's growth over the next 20 years. The Census Bureau's first-ever Hispanic projections show that their present 7 percet share of the population may rise to 19 percent by 2080. Even without migration for the next 100 years, the Hispanic population would continue growing at twice the national rate.

Disabled: A survey found more than 37 million Americans have a disability and that 13.5 million could not perform a basic physical activity or needed help to do so. Some 12.8 million had trouble seeing words in newsprint even with glasses, and 7.7 million had trouble hearing a normal conversation.

Education: Elementary and high school enrollment was significantly lower in 1984 than in 1980, while at college level it was higher. There were 27 million elementary school pupils, some 1.4 million less than in 1980 and 7.1 million below the 1970 peak. But nursery school and kindergarten children in 1985 chalked up the highest preprimary enrollment ever recorded, 2.5 million and 3.8 million, respectively.

Farms, Age, Households

The farm population, meanwhile, continued to fall, dropping 7 percent to 5.3 million in 1985. It was the first significant loss of the decade. About one of every 45 people, or 2.2 percent of the population, lived on farms. Their 1983 median income of $18,925 was only three-fourths that of nonfarm families.

The nation's median age on July 1, 1985 was estimated at 31.5 years compared with 30.0 in 1980. The aging trend should continue as more of the baby boom generation (1946-64) heads toward middle age. The 35 to 44 group grew the fastest, up 6.1 million or nearly 25 percent in 1980-85.

During those five years, the number of households grew faster than the total population, by a margin of 8.8 to 5.4 percent. This reflected a decline in average population per household from 2.76 to 2.69 persons. Households totaled 87.5 million in 1985, up 8.8 percent from 1980. Alaska, Nevada, and Arizona led the most rapid household growth. However, the annual growth rate of households is expected to decline over the next 15 years. The 37 percent gain from 1970 to 1985 is expected to fall to between 18 and 27 percent by the year 2000.

Income

Real median family income rose 1.3 percent in 1985, the third straight annual increase, while the poverty rate fell 0.4 percent to 14 percent. Median family income was $27,740, up 4.9 percent from 1984 before adjustment for a 3.6 percent rise in consumer prices. Per capita income was $11,010. The number of people below the poverty level fell slightly to 33.1 million.

A first-time report on household wealth and asset ownership found the median net worth of households to be $32,670 in 1984. Two-thirds of households reported homeownership with median home equity of $40,600. Householders 55 to 64 reported median wealth of $73,660 compared with $5,760 for those under 35 years and $55,180 for those aged 75 and over.

After taxes, household incomes averaged $21,560 in 1984, up 2.7 percent after adjustment for inflation. Households paid an average of $6,400 in the four types of taxes covered by the census study. The proportions of pre-tax income paid were 13 percent for federal income taxes, 5 percent for FICA payroll taxes (Social Security), 4 percent for state income taxes, and about 2 percent for property taxes.

Among the 26.1 million married couples having both partners as wage earners in 1983, nearly five million wives earned more than their husbands. The average earnings of married couples was $28,570, rising to $39,390 if both husband and wife worked full time.

Benefits

About 90 percent of U.S. households, 76.7 million, received at least one noncash benefit in 1984. That was up 972,000 in a year. About 17 percent of all households received means-tested noncash benefits; their median income was $8,420. About 8 percent received food stamps, while 21 percent of households with school-age children received free or reduced-price lunches. Of the 8.3 million households with Medicaid coverage, 29 percent had a householder 65 or older and 39 percent had a female householder with no husband present. About one of every three children in the nation lives in a household that received a means-tested benefit. There were 19.5 million children under age 18 in such households in the fourth quarter of 1984.

Women and Minority-Owned Businesses

Women owned nearly one-fourth of all businesses (excluding corporations) in 1982—some 2.9 million. Women-owned businesses had $98.3 billion in gross receipts, or one-tenth of all business receipts. California had the most distaff firms, nearly 400,000.

Hispanic-owned businesses generated $15 billion in sales and receipts. They accounted for 2.1 percent of the U.S. firms and 1.5 percent of revenues. Some 339,000 black-owned businesses accounted for $12.4 billion in receipts.

Just over a quarter-million businesses were owned by Asian Americans, American Indians, and other racial minorities excluding blacks. They had 1982 receipts of $17.9 billion. Chinese firms (52,839) accounted for one-third of all receipts. The Los Angeles-Long Beach metro area and California led the nation in the number of minority and women-owned businesses.

Household Characteristics

While not questioning the nature of the couples' relationships, the Census Bureau has found the annual rate of increase for unmarried couples slowing in the 1980s. The rate has averaged 5.6 percent since 1980, compared with 11.1 percent in the 1970s. Other findings: median age at first marriage in 1986 was 25.7 for men, 23.1 for women. About 21.2 million people lived alone. Families accounted for 72 percent of households in 1986 compared with 81 percent in 1970.

More new mothers are in the labor force. Some 48 percent who became mothers in the previous 11 months before a 1985 survey were back in the labor force, compared with 31 percent in 1976. About 12 percent of recent white mothers were unmarried compared with 55 percent of recent black mothers.

(continued)

Computers

The Census Bureau marked the 35th anniversary of the dawn of the computer age by dedicating a commemorative plaque at its Suitland, MD, headquarters. On June 14, 1951, the Bureau formally accepted UNIVAC I, the first general-purpose data processing computer, from its manufacturer. It was retired 12 years later and is now at the Smithsonian Institution.

U.S. manufacturers shipped some 3.9 million computers valued at $17.4 billion in 1985; they shipped another $18.2 billion worth of peripheral computer equipment. About 15 percent was exported. Nearly 74 percent of the digital computers shipped were priced at less than $2,500.

U.S. manufacturers shipped nearly 5,800 robots in 1985 valued at $317.7 million, down 13 percent from about 6,500 in 1984. Robot accessories and components totaled another $70 million.

Statistical Cooperation

In March 1986, Census Bureau and Commerce Department officials signed separate agreements with Mexico and Canada to cooperate more closely on statistical matters. The Bureau has similar agreements with other nations, including the People's Republic of China and Hungary. The Bureau has trained some four thousand statisticians from Third World countries over the last 40 years.

1990 Bicentennial Census

The Census Bureau is well along with plans to take the 21st decennial census in 1990. This count will mark the 200th anniversary of the first census in 1790 when George Washington was president and the young United States had just under 4 million residents.

Census workers in 1990 are expected to count about 250 million people and 106 million housing units.

In the spring of 1988, the Census Bureau will conduct three "dress rehearsal" censuses—in St. Louis, central Missouri, and eastern Washington—as a final check of its equipment, procedures, questionnaires, and statistical processing methods. Bureau workers also will prepare a nationwide mailing list of all residential addresses, since the 1990 count (as in 1970 and 1980) largely will be taken by the mail-out, mail-back technique.

More automation and computers will be used in the 1990 census, and processing of the returned questionnaires will be speeded up to hasten the release of final totals for people and housing. Even so, a "census army" of some 400,000 temporary employees will be hired between summer 1989 and summer 1990.

Further information about the 1990 census may be obtained from the 1990 Census Promotional Office, Bureau of the Census, Washington, D.C. 20233.

Estimated Population of American Colonies: 1630-1780

Source: U.S. Bureau of the Census (thousands)

Colony	1780	1770	1750	1740	1720	1700	1690	1670	1650	1630
Total	**2,780.4**	**2,148.1**	**1,170.8**	**905.6**	**466.2**	**250.9**	**210.4**	**111.9**	**50.4**	**4.6**
Maine (counties)	49.1	31.3	...	...	...	...	...	...	1.0	0.4
New Hampshire	87.8	62.4	27.5	23.3	9.4	5.0	4.2	1.8	1.3	0.5
Vermont	47.6	10.0	...	...	...	...	...	...	...	...
Plymouth and Massachusetts	268.6	235.3	188.0	151.6	91.0	55.9	56.9	35.3	15.6	0.9
Rhode Island	52.9	58.2	33.2	25.3	11.7	5.9	4.2	2.2	0.8	...
Connecticut	206.7	183.9	111.3	89.6	58.8	26.0	21.6	12.6	4.1	...
New York	210.5	162.9	76.7	63.7	36.9	19.1	13.9	5.8	4.1	0.4
New Jersey	139.6	117.4	71.4	51.4	29.8	14.0	8.0	1.0	...	...
Pennsylvania	327.3	240.1	119.7	85.6	31.0	18.0	11.4	...	...	...
Delaware	45.4	35.5	28.7	19.9	5.4	2.5	1.5	0.7	0.2	...
Maryland	245.5	202.6	141.1	116.1	66.1	29.6	24.0	13.2	4.5	...
Virginia	538.0	447.0	231.0	180.4	87.8	58.6	53.0	35.3	18.7	2.5
North Carolina	270.1	107.2	70.0	51.0	21.3	10.7	7.6	3.8	...	...
South Carolina	180.0	124.2	64.0	45.0	17.0	5.7	3.9	0.2	...	...
Georgia	56.1	23.4	5.2	2.0	...	...	...	...	...	...
Kentucky	45.0	15.7	...	...	...	...	...	...	...	...
Tennessee	10.0	1.0	...	...	...	...	...	...	...	...

Resident Population by Sex, Race, Residence, and Median Age: 1790 to 1986

Source: U.S. Bureau of the Census (thousands, except as indicated)

Date	Sex		Race				Residence		Median Age (years)		
				Black							
	Male	Female	White	Number	Percent	Other	Urban	Rural	All races	White	Black
Conterminous U.S.[1]											
1790 (Aug. 2)	NA	NA	3,172	757	19.3	NA	202	3,728	NA	NA	NA
1810 (Aug. 6)	NA	NA	5,862	1,378	19.0	NA	525	6,714	NA	16.0	NA
1820 (Aug. 7)	4,897	4,742	7,867	1,772	18.4	NA	693	8,945	16.7	16.5	17.2
1840 (June 1)	8,689	8,381	14,196	2,874	16.8	NA	1,845	15,224	17.8	17.9	17.3
1860 (June 1)	16,085	15,358	26,923	4,442	14.1	79	6,217	25,227	19.4	19.7	17.7
1870 (June 1)	19,494	19,065	33,589	4,880	12.7	89	9,902	28,656	20.2	20.4	18.5
1880 (June 1)	25,519	24,637	43,403	6,581	13.1	172	14,130	36,026	20.9	21.4	18.0
1890 (June 1)	32,237	30,711	55,101	7,489	11.9	358	22,106	40,841	22.0	22.5	17.8
1900 (June 1)	38,816	37,178	66,809	8,834	11.6	351	30,160	45,835	22.9	23.4	19.4
1920 (Jan. 1)	53,900	51,810	94,821	10,463	9.9	427	54,158	51,553	25.3	25.6	22.3
1930 (Apr. 1)	62,137	60,638	110,287	11,891	9.7	597	68,955	53,820	26.4	26.9	23.5
1940 (Apr. 1)	66,062	65,608	118,215	12,866	9.8	589	74,424	57,246	29.0	29.5	25.3
United States											
1950 (Apr. 1)	75,187	76,139	135,150	15,045	9.9	1,131	96,847	54,479	30.2	30.7	26.2
1960 (Apr. 1)	88,331	90,992	158,832	18,872	10.5	1,620	125,269	54,054	29.5	30.3	23.5
1970 (Apr. 1)[2]	98,926	104,309	178,098	22,581	11.1	2,557	149,325	53,887	28.0	28.9	22.4
1980 (Apr. 1)[3]	110,053	116,493	194,811	26,631	11.8	5,104	167,051	59,495	30.0	30.9	24.9
1985 (July 1, est)	116,161	122,579	202,765	28,878	14.2	7,097	NA	NA	31.5	32.4	26.6
1986 (July 1, est)	117,360	123,718	204,301	29,306	14.3	7,471	NA	NA	31.8	32.7	26.9

(NA) Not available. (1) Excludes Alaska and Hawaii. (2) The revised 1970 resident population count is 203,302,031, which incorporates changes due to errors found after tabulations were completed. The race and sex data shown here reflect the official 1970 census count while the residence data come from the tabulated count. (3) The race data shown for April 1, 1980 have been modified.

U.S. Population by Official

(Members of the Armed Forces overseas or

State	1790	1800	1810	1820	1830	1840	1850	1860	1870	1880
Ala. . .	....	1,250	9,046	127,901	309,527	590,756	771,623	964,201	996,992	1,262,505
Alas.. .	....	....	....	....	....	....	....	....	....	33,426
Ariz. . .	....	....	....	....	....	....	....	....	9,658	40,440
Ark. . .	....	....	1,062	14,273	30,388	97,574	209,897	435,450	484,471	802,525
Cal. . .	....	....	....	....	....	....	92,597	379,994	560,247	864,694
Col. . .	....	....	....	....	....	....	....	34,277	39,864	194,327
Conn. .	237,946	251,002	261,942	275,248	297,675	309,978	370,792	460,147	537,454	622,700
Del. . .	59,096	64,273	72,674	72,749	76,748	78,085	91,532	112,216	125,015	146,608
D.C. . .	....	8,144	15,471	23,336	30,261	33,745	51,687	75,080	131,700	177,624
Fla. . .	....	....	....	....	34,730	54,477	87,445	140,424	187,748	269,493
Ga.. . .	82,548	162,686	252,433	340,989	516,823	691,392	906,185	1,057,286	1,184,109	1,542,180
Ha.. . .	....	....	....	....	....	....	....	....	....	....
Ida. . .	....	....	....	....	....	....	....	....	14,999	32,610
Ill. . . .	....	....	12,282	55,211	157,445	476,183	851,470	1,711,951	2,539,891	3,077,871
Ind. . .	....	5,641	24,520	147,178	343,031	685,866	988,416	1,350,428	1,680,637	1,978,301
Ia. . . .	....	....	....	....	....	43,112	192,214	674,913	1,194,020	1,624,615
Kan. . .	....	....	....	....	....	....	....	107,206	364,399	996,096
Ky.. . .	73,677	220,955	406,511	564,317	687,917	779,828	982,405	1,155,684	1,321,011	1,648,690
La.. . .	....	....	76,556	153,407	215,739	352,411	517,762	708,002	726,915	939,946
Me. . .	96,540	151,719	228,705	298,335	399,455	501,793	583,169	628,279	626,915	648,936
Md. . .	319,728	341,548	380,546	407,350	447,040	470,019	583,034	687,049	780,894	934,943
Mass. .	378,787	422,845	472,040	523,287	610,408	737,699	994,514	1,231,066	1,457,351	1,783,085
Mich. .	....	....	4,762	8,896	31,639	212,267	397,654	749,113	1,184,059	1,636,937
Minn. .	....	....	....	....	....	....	6,077	172,023	439,706	780,773
Miss.. .	....	7,600	31,306	75,448	136,621	375,651	606,526	791,305	827,922	1,131,597
Mo. . .	....	....	19,783	66,586	140,455	383,702	682,044	1,182,012	1,721,295	2,168,380
Mon.. .	....	....	....	....	....	....	....	....	20,595	39,159
Neb.. .	....	....	....	....	....	....	....	28,841	122,993	452,402
Nev.. .	....	....	....	....	....	....	....	6,857	42,491	62,266
N.H. . .	141,885	183,858	214,460	244,161	269,328	284,574	317,976	326,073	318,300	346,991
N.J. . .	184,139	211,149	245,562	277,575	320,823	373,306	489,555	672,035	906,096	1,131,116
N.M.. .	....	....	....	....	....	....	61,547	93,516	91,874	119,565
N.Y. . .	340,120	589,051	959,049	1,372,812	1,918,608	2,428,921	3,097,394	3,880,735	4,382,759	5,082,871
N.C. . .	393,751	478,103	555,500	638,829	737,987	753,419	869,039	992,622	1,071,361	1,399,750
N.D. . .	....	....	....	....	....	....	....	....	*2,405	36,909
Oh. . .	....	45,365	230,760	581,434	937,903	1,519,467	1,980,329	2,339,511	2,665,260	3,198,062
Okla. .	....	....	....	....	....	....	....	....	....	....
Ore. . .	....	....	....	....	....	....	12,093	52,465	90,923	174,768
Pa.. . .	434,373	602,365	810,091	1,049,458	1,348,233	1,724,033	2,311,786	2,906,215	3,521,951	4,282,891
R.I.. . .	68,825	69,122	76,931	83,059	97,199	108,830	147,545	174,620	217,353	276,531
S.C. . .	249,073	345,591	415,115	502,741	581,185	594,398	668,507	703,708	705,606	995,577
S.D. . .	....	....	....	....	....	....	....	*4,837	*11,776	98,268
Tenn. .	35,691	105,602	261,727	422,823	681,904	829,210	1,002,717	1,109,801	1,258,520	1,542,359
Tex. . .	....	....	....	....	....	....	212,592	604,215	818,579	1,591,749
Ut. . . .	....	....	....	....	....	....	11,380	40,273	86,786	143,963
Vt. . . .	85,425	154,465	217,895	235,981	280,652	291,948	314,120	315,098	330,551	332,286
Va.. . .	691,737	807,557	877,683	938,261	1,044,054	1,025,227	1,119,348	1,219,630	1,225,163	1,512,565
Wash. .	....	....	....	....	....	....	1,201	11,594	23,955	75,116
W. Va..	55,873	78,592	105,469	136,808	176,924	224,537	302,313	376,688	442,014	618,457
Wis. . .	....	....	....	....	....	30,945	305,391	775,881	1,054,670	1,315,497
Wy. . .	....	....	....	....	....	....	....	....	9,118	20,789
U.S. . .	**3,929,214**	**5,308,483**	**7,239,881**	**9,638,453**	**12,860,702**	**17,063,353**[1]	**23,191,876**	**31,443,321**[1]	**38,558,371**	**50,189,209**

Note: Where possible, population shown is that of 1980 area of state.
*1860 figure is for Dakota Territory; 1870 figures are for parts of Dakota Territory. (1) U.S. total includes persons (5,318 in 1830 and 6,100 in 1840) on public ships in the service of the United States not credited to any region, division, or state.

Density of Population by States

(Per square mile, land area only)

State	1920	1960	1970	1980	State	1920	1960	1970	1980	State	1920	1960	1970	1980
Ala.. .	45.8	64.2	67.9	76.6	La. . .	39.6	72.2	81.0	94.5	Oh. . .	141.4	236.6	260.0	263.3
Alas.*	0.1	0.4	0.5	0.7	Me. . .	25.7	31.3	32.1	36.3	Okla. .	29.2	33.8	37.2	44.1
Ariz. .	2.9	11.5	15.6	23.9	Md. . .	145.8	313.5	396.6	428.7	Ore. .	8.2	18.4	21.7	27.4
Ark.. .	33.4	34.2	37.0	43.9	Mass.	479.2	657.3	727.0	733.3	Pa. . .	194.5	251.4	262.3	264.3
Cal.. .	22.0	100.4	127.6	151.4	Mich. .	63.8	137.7	156.2	162.6	R. I. .	566.4	819.3	902.5	897.8
Col.. .	9.1	16.9	21.3	27.9	Minn. .	29.5	43.1	48.0	51.2	S. C. .	55.2	78.7	85.7	103.4
Conn..	286.4	520.6	623.6	637.8	Miss. .	38.6	46.0	46.9	53.4	S. D. .	8.3	9.0	8.8	9.1
Del.. .	113.5	225.2	276.5	307.6	Mo. . .	49.5	62.6	67.8	71.3	Tenn..	56.1	86.2	94.9	111.6
D. C. .	7,292.9	12,523.9	12,401.8	10,132.3	Mon. .	3.8	4.6	4.8	5.4	Tex. .	17.8	36.4	42.7	54.3
Fla.. .	17.7	91.5	125.5	180.0	Neb. .	16.9	18.4	19.4	20.5	Ut. . .	5.5	10.8	12.9	17.8
Ga.. .	49.3	67.8	79.0	94.1	Nev. .	.7	2.6	4.4	7.3	Vt. . .	38.6	42.0	47.9	55.2
Ha.* .	39.9	98.5	119.6	150.1	N. H. .	49.1	67.2	81.7	102.4	Va. . .	57.4	99.6	116.9	134.7
Ida.. .	5.2	8.1	8.6	11.5	N. J. .	420.0	805.5	953.1	986.2	Wash.	20.3	42.8	51.2	62.1
Ill.. . .	115.7	180.4	199.4	205.3	N. M. .	2.9	7.8	8.4	10.7	W. Va.	60.9	77.2	72.5	80.8
Ind.. .	81.3	128.8	143.9	152.8	N. Y. .	217.9	350.6	381.3	370.6	Wis. .	47.6	72.6	81.1	86.5
Ia.. . .	43.2	49.2	50.5	52.1	N. C. .	52.5	93.2	104.1	120.4	Wy.. .	2.0	3.4	3.4	4.9
Kan.. .	21.6	26.6	27.5	28.9	N. D. .	9.2	9.1	8.9	9.4					
Ky. . .	60.1	76.2	81.2	92.3						**U.S. .**	***29.9**	**50.6**	**57.4**	**64.0**

*For purposes of comparison, Alaska and Hawaii included in above tabulation for 1920, even though not states then.

Census from 1790 to 1980

other U.S. nationals overseas are not included.

1890	1900	1910	1920	1930	1940	1950	1960	1970	1980[1]
1,513,401	1,828,697	2,138,093	2,348,174	2,646,248	2,832,961	3,061,743	3,266,740	3,444,354	3,894,025
32,052	63,592	64,356	55,036	59,278	72,524	128,643	226,167	302,583	401,851
88,243	122,931	204,354	334,162	435,573	499,261	749,587	1,302,161	1,775,399	2,716,598
1,128,211	1,311,564	1,574,449	1,752,204	1,854,482	1,949,387	1,909,511	1,786,272	1,923,322	2,286,357
1,213,398	1,485,053	2,377,549	3,426,861	5,677,251	6,907,387	10,586,223	15,717,204	19,971,069	23,667,764
413,249	539,700	799,024	939,629	1,035,791	1,123,296	1,325,089	1,753,947	2,209,596	2,889,735
746,258	908,420	1,114,756	1,380,631	1,606,903	1,709,242	2,007,280	2,535,234	3,032,217	3,107,564
168,493	184,735	202,322	223,003	238,380	266,505	318,085	446,292	548,104	594,338
230,392	278,718	331,069	437,571	486,869	663,091	802,178	763,956	756,668	638,432
391,422	528,542	752,619	968,470	1,468,211	1,897,414	2,771,305	4,951,560	6,791,418	[2]9,746,961
1,837,353	2,216,331	2,609,121	2,895,832	2,908,506	3,123,723	3,444,578	3,943,116	4,587,930	5,462,982
....	154,001	191,874	255,881	368,300	422,770	499,794	632,772	769,913	964,691
88,548	161,772	325,594	431,866	445,032	524,873	588,637	667,191	713,015	944,127
3,826,352	4,821,550	5,638,591	6,485,280	7,630,654	7,897,241	8,712,176	10,081,158	11,110,285	11,427,409
2,192,404	2,516,462	2,700,876	2,930,390	3,238,503	3,427,796	3,934,224	4,662,498	5,195,392	5,490,212
1,912,297	2,231,853	2,224,771	2,404,021	2,470,939	2,538,268	2,621,073	2,757,537	2,825,368	2,913,808
1,428,108	1,470,495	1,690,949	1,769,257	1,880,999	1,801,028	1,905,299	2,178,611	2,249,071	2,364,236
1,858,635	2,147,174	2,289,905	2,416,630	2,614,589	2,845,627	2,944,806	3,038,156	3,220,711	3,660,324
1,118,588	1,381,625	1,656,388	1,798,509	2,101,593	2,363,880	2,683,516	3,257,022	3,644,637	4,206,116
661,086	694,466	742,371	768,014	797,423	847,226	913,774	969,265	993,722	1,125,043
1,042,390	1,188,044	1,295,346	1,449,661	1,631,526	1,821,244	2,343,001	3,100,689	3,923,897	4,216,933
2,238,947	2,805,346	3,366,416	3,852,356	4,249,614	4,316,721	4,690,514	5,148,578	5,689,170	5,737,093
2,093,890	2,420,982	2,810,173	3,668,412	4,842,325	5,256,106	6,371,766	7,823,194	8,881,826	9,262,044
1,310,283	1,751,394	2,075,708	2,387,125	2,563,953	2,792,300	2,982,483	3,413,864	3,806,103	4,075,970
1,289,600	1,551,270	1,797,114	1,790,618	2,009,821	2,183,796	2,178,914	2,178,141	2,216,994	2,520,770
2,679,185	3,106,665	3,293,335	3,404,055	3,629,367	3,784,664	3,954,653	4,319,813	4,677,623	4,916,762
142,924	243,329	376,053	548,889	537,606	559,456	591,024	674,767	694,409	786,690
1,062,656	1,066,300	1,192,214	1,296,372	1,377,963	1,315,834	1,325,510	1,411,330	1,485,333	1,569,825
47,355	42,335	81,875	77,407	91,058	110,247	160,083	285,278	488,738	800,508
376,530	411,588	430,572	443,083	465,293	491,524	533,242	606,921	737,681	920,610
1,444,933	1,883,669	2,537,167	3,155,900	4,041,334	4,160,165	4,835,329	6,066,782	7,171,112	7,365,011
160,282	195,310	327,301	360,350	423,317	531,818	681,187	951,023	1,017,055	1,303,302
6,003,174	7,268,894	9,113,614	10,385,227	12,588,066	13,479,142	14,830,192	16,782,304	18,241,391	17,558,165
1,617,949	1,893,810	2,206,287	2,559,123	3,170,276	3,571,623	4,061,929	4,556,155	5,084,411	5,880,415
190,983	319,146	577,056	646,872	680,845	641,935	619,636	632,446	617,792	652,717
3,672,329	4,157,545	4,767,121	5,759,394	6,646,697	6,907,612	7,946,627	9,706,397	10,657,423	10,797,603
258,657	790,391	1,657,155	2,028,283	2,396,040	2,336,434	2,233,351	2,328,284	2,559,463	3,025,487
317,704	413,536	672,765	783,389	953,786	1,089,684	1,521,341	1,768,687	2,091,533	2,633,156
5,258,113	6,302,115	7,665,111	8,720,017	9,631,350	9,900,180	10,498,012	11,319,366	11,800,766	11,864,720
345,506	428,556	542,610	604,397	687,497	713,346	791,896	859,488	949,723	947,154
1,151,149	1,340,316	1,515,400	1,683,724	1,738,765	1,899,804	2,117,027	2,382,594	2,590,713	3,120,730
348,600	401,570	583,888	636,547	692,849	642,961	652,740	680,514	666,257	690,768
1,767,518	2,020,616	2,184,789	2,337,885	2,616,556	2,915,841	3,291,718	3,567,089	3,926,018	4,591,023
2,235,527	3,048,710	3,896,542	4,663,228	5,824,715	6,414,824	7,711,194	9,579,677	11,198,655	14,225,513
210,779	276,749	373,351	449,396	507,847	550,310	688,862	890,627	1,059,273	1,461,037
332,422	343,641	355,956	352,428	359,611	359,231	377,747	389,881	444,732	511,456
1,655,980	1,854,184	2,061,612	2,309,187	2,421,851	2,677,773	3,318,680	3,966,949	4,651,448	5,346,797
357,232	518,103	1,141,990	1,356,621	1,563,396	1,736,191	2,378,963	2,853,214	3,413,244	4,132,353
762,794	958,800	1,221,119	1,463,701	1,729,205	1,901,974	2,005,552	1,860,421	1,744,237	1,950,186
1,693,330	2,069,042	2,333,860	2,632,067	2,939,006	3,137,587	3,434,575	3,951,777	4,417,821	4,705,642
62,555	92,531	145,965	194,402	225,565	250,742	290,529	330,066	332,416	469,557
62,979,766	**76,212,168**	**92,228,496**	**106,021,537**	**123,202,624**	**132,164,569**	**151,325,798**	**179,323,175**	**203,302,031**	**226,542,580**

(1) Updated, April 1987. (2) According to 1986 estimates, Florida has passed Illinois in population.

U.S. Center of Population, 1790-1980

Center of Population is that point which may be considered as center of population gravity of the U.S. or that point upon which the U.S. would balance if it were a rigid plane without weight and the population distributed thereon with each individual being assumed to have equal weight and to exert an influence on a central point proportional to his distance from that point.

Year	N. Lat. °	'	"	W.Long. °	'	"	Approximate location
1790	39	16	30	76	11	12	23 miles east of Baltimore, Md.
1800	39	16	6	76	56	30	18 miles west of Baltimore, Md.
1810	39	11	30	77	37	12	40 miles northwest by west of Washington, D.C. (in Va.)
1820	39	5	42	78	33	0	16 miles east of Moorefield, W. Va.[1]
1830	38	57	54	79	16	54	19 miles west-southwest of Moorefield, W. Va.[1]
1840	39	2	0	80	18	0	16 miles south of Clarksburg, W. Va.[1]
1850	38	59	0	81	19	0	23 miles southeast of Parkersburg, W. Va.[1]
1860	39	0	24	82	48	48	20 miles south by east of Chillicothe, Oh.
1870	39	12	0	83	35	42	48 miles east by north of Cincinnati, Oh.
1880	39	4	8	84	39	40	8 miles west by south of Cincinnati, Oh. (in Ky.)
1890	39	11	56	85	32	53	20 miles east of Columbus, Ind.
1900	39	9	36	85	48	54	6 miles southeast of Columbus, Ind.
1910	39	10	12	86	32	20	In the city of Bloomington, Ind.
1920	39	10	21	86	43	15	8 miles south-southeast of Spencer, Owen County, Ind.
1930	39	3	45	87	8	6	3 miles northeast of Linton, Greene County, Ind.
1940	38	56	54	87	22	35	2 miles southeast by east of Carlisle, Sullivan County, Ind.
1950 (Inc. Alaska & Hawaii)	38	48	15	88	22	8	3 miles northeast of Louisville, Clay County, Ill.
1960	38	35	58	89	12	35	6 1/2 miles northwest of Centralia, Ill.
1970	38	27	47	89	42	22	5 miles east southeast of Mascoutah, St. Clair County, Ill.
1980	38	8	13	90	34	26	1/4 mile west of DeSoto, Mo

(1) West Virginia was set off from Virginia Dec. 31, 1862, and admitted as a state June 20, 1863.

Projections of the Total Population by Sex and Age: 1990 to 2000

Source: U.S. Bureau of the Census (thousands)

Sex and age	Lowest series[1] 1990	Lowest series[1] 1995	Lowest series[1] 2000	Middle series 1990	Middle series 1995	Middle series 2000	Highest series 1990	Highest series 1995	Highest series 2000
Total population	245,753	251,876	256,098	249,657	259,559	267,955	254,122	268,151	281,542
Male	119,620	122,608	124,671	121,518	126,368	130,491	123,698	130,577	137,163
Under 5 years old	8,964	8,288	7,647	9,827	9,529	9,022	10,550	10,653	10,508
5–17 years old	22,745	23,586	22,989	23,082	24,815	25,458	23,549	26,074	27,842
18–24 years old	13,016	11,904	12,314	13,127	12,072	12,530	13,283	12,325	12,881
25–44 years old	40,320	40,802	39,517	40,624	41,320	40,251	41,188	42,282	41,581
45–64 years old	22,072	24,885	28,949	22,221	25,192	29,468	22,377	25,518	30,074
65 years old and over	12,503	13,143	13,255	12,637	13,440	13,762	12,751	13,725	14,277
Female	126,133	129,268	131,427	128,139	133,191	137,464	130,424	137,574	144,379
Under 5 years old	8,551	7,906	7,295	9,371	9,086	8,604	10,065	10,161	10,022
5–17 years old	21,741	22,539	21,962	22,056	23,703	24,305	22,506	24,915	26,592
18–24 years old	12,532	11,443	11,843	12,667	11,630	12,071	12,854	11,908	12,445
25–44 years old	40,396	40,583	39,052	40,753	41,195	39,908	41,371	42,262	41,398
45–64 years old	24,063	26,813	30,909	24,231	27,130	31,418	24,390	27,435	31,953
65 years old and over	18,850	19,984	20,366	19,061	20,447	21,158	19,238	20,893	21,969

(1) For the series shown the following assumptions were made about fertility (ultimate lifetime births per woman), mortality (life expectancy in 2080), and immigration (yearly net immigration). Lowest series: 1.6 births per woman, 85.9 years, and 250,000 net immigration. Middle series: 1.9 births per woman, 81.0 years, and 450,000 net immigration. Highest series: 2.3 births per woman, 77.4 years, and 750,000 net immigration. Zero migration series: 1.9 births per woman and 81.0 years.

U.S. Area and Population: 1790 to 1980

Source: U.S. Bureau of the Census

Census date	Area (square miles) Gross	Land	Water	Population Number	Per sq. mile of land	Increase over preceding census Number	%
1980 (Apr. 1)	3,618,770	3,539,289	79,481	226,545,580	64.0	23,243,774	11.4
1970 (Apr. 1)	3,618,770	3,536,855	81,915	203,302,031	57.5	23,978,856	13.4
1960 (Apr. 1)	3,618,770	3,540,911	77,859	179,323,175	50.6	27,997,377	18.5
1950 (Apr. 1)	3,618,770	3,552,206	66,564	151,325,798	42.6	19,161,229	14.5
1940 (Apr. 1)	3,618,770	3,554,608	64,162	132,164,569	37.2	8,961,945	7.3
1930 (Apr. 1)	3,618,770	3,551,608	67,162	123,202,624	34.7	17,181,087	16.2
1920 (Jan. 1)	3,618,770	3,546,931	71,839	106,021,537	29.9	13,793,041	15.0
1910 (Apr. 15)	3,618,770	3,547,045	71,725	92,228,496	26.0	16,016,328	21.0
1900 (June 1)	3,618,770	3,547,314	71,456	76,212,168	21.5	13,232,402	21.0
1890 (June 1)	3,612,299	3,540,705	71,594	62,979,766	17.8	12,790,557	25.5
1880 (June 1)	3,612,299	3,540,705	71,594	50,189,209	14.2	11,630,838	30.2
1870 (June 1)	3,612,299	3,540,705	71,594	38,558,371	10.9	7,115,050	22.6
1860 (June 1)	3,021,295	2,969,640	51,655	31,443,321	10.6	8,251,445	35.6
1850 (June 1)	2,991,655	2,940,042	51,613	23,191,876	7.9	6,122,423	35.9
1840 (June 1)	1,792,552	1,749,462	43,090	17,069,453	9.8	4,203,433	32.7
1830 (June 1)	1,792,552	1,749,462	43,090	12,866,020	7.4	3,227,567	33.5
1820 (June 1)	1,792,552	1,749,462	43,090	9,638,453	5.5	2,398,572	33.1
1810 (Aug. 6)	1,722,685	1,681,828	40,857	7,239,881	4.3	1,931,398	36.4
1800 (Aug. 4)	891,364	864,746	26,618	5,308,483	6.1	1,379,269	35.1
1790 (Aug. 2)	891,364	864,746	26,618	3,929,214	4.5	—	—

NOTE: Percent changes are computed on basis of change in population since preceding census date, and period covered therefore is not always exactly 10 years.

Population density figures given for various years represent the area within the boundaries of the United States which was under the jurisdiction on date in question, including in some cases considerable areas not organized or settled and not covered by the census. In 1870, for example, Alaska was not covered by the census.

Revised figure of 39,818,449 for the 1870 population includes adjustments for undernumeration in the Southern states. On the basis of the revised figure, the population increased by 8,375,128, or 26.6 percent between 1860 and 1870, and by 10,370,760, or 26.1 percent between 1870 and 1880.

Congressional Apportionment

	1980	1970		1980	1970		1980	1970		1980	1970		1980	1970
Ala.	7	7	Ida.	2	2	Minn.	8	8	N. D.	1	1	Vt.	1	1
Alas.	1	1	Ill.	22	24	Miss.	5	5	Oh.	21	23	Va.	10	10
Ariz.	5	4	Ind.	10	11	Mo.	9	10	Okla.	6	6	Wash.	8	7
Ark.	4	4	Ia.	6	6	Mon.	2	2	Ore.	5	4	W. Va.	4	4
Cal.	45	43	Kan.	5	5	Neb.	3	3	Pa.	23	25	Wis.	9	9
Col.	6	5	Ky.	7	7	Nev.	2	1	R. I.	2	2	Wy.	1	1
Conn.	6	6	La.	8	8	N. H.	2	2	S. C.	6	6			
Del.	1	1	Me.	2	2	N. J.	14	15	S. D.	1	2	**Totals.**	**435**	**435**
Fla.	19	15	Md.	8	8	N. M.	3	2	Tenn.	9	8			
Ga.	10	10	Mass.	11	12	N. Y.	34	39	Tex.	27	24			
Ha.	2	2	Mich.	18	19	N. C.	11	11	Ut.	3	2			

The chief reason the Constitution provided for a census of the population every 10 years was to give a basis for apportionment of representatives among the states. This apportionment largely determines the number of electoral votes allotted to each state.

The number of representatives of each state in Congress is determined by the state's population, but each state is entitled to one representative regardless of population. A Congressional apportionment has been made after each decennial census except that of 1920.

Under provisions of a law that became effective Nov. 15, 1941, apportionment of representatives is made by the method of equal proportions. In the application of this method, the apportionment is made so that the average population per representative has the least possible variation between one state and any other. The first House of Representatives, in 1789, had 65 members, as provided by the Constitution. As the population grew, the number of representatives was increased but the total membership has been fixed at 435 since the apportionment based on the 1910 census.

Metropolitan Statistical Areas: 1980–1985

Source: U.S. Bureau of the Census
(MSAs over 281,000 listed by 1985 population)

By current standards, an area qualifies for recognition as a Metropolitan Statistical Area (MSA) in one of two ways: if there is a city of at least 50,000 population; or a Census Bureau-defined urbanized area of at least 50,000 with a total metropolitan population of at least 100,000 (75,000 in New England). In addition to the county containing the main city, an MSA also includes other counties having strong economic and social ties to the central county. If an area has more than one million population and meets certain other specified requirements, it now is termed a Consolidated Metropolitan Statistical Area (CMSA). MSAs are defined by the Office of Management and Budget as of June 30, 1986.

MSA	Population 1985 (estimate)	Population 1980	Percent Change 1980 to 1985
New York-Northern New Jersey-Long Island, NY-NJ-CT CMSA	17,931,100	17,539,532	2.2
Los Angeles-Anaheim-Riverside, CA CMSA	12,738,200	11,497,732	10.8
Chicago-Gary-Lake County, IL-IN-WI CMSA	8,085,200	7,937,307	1.9
San Francisco-Oakland-San Jose, CA CMSA	5,809,300	5,367,900	8.2
Philadelphia-Wilmington-Trenton, PA-NJ-DE-MD CMSA	5,776,500	5,680,509	1.7
Detroit-Ann Arbor, MI CMSA	4,581,200	4,752,764	−3.6
Boston-Lawrence-Salem, MA-NH CMSA	4,051,400	3,971,792	2.0
Houston-Galveston-Brazoria, TX CMSA	3,623,300	3,099,942	16.9
Dallas-Fort Worth, TX CMSA	3,511,600	2,930,539	19.8
Washington, DC-MD-VA	3,489,500	3,250,921	7.3
Miami-Fort Lauderdale, FL CMSA	2,878,300	2,643,868	8.9
Cleveland-Akron-Lorain, OH CMSA	2,776,400	2,834,062	2.0
Atlanta, GA	2,471,700	2,138,143	15.6
St. Louis, MO-IL	2,412,400	2,376,971	1.5
Pittsburgh-Beaver Valley, PA CMSA	2,337,400	2,423,311	−3.5
Minneapolis-St. Paul, MN-WI	2,262,400	2,137,133	5.9
Baltimore, MD	2,252,800	2,199,497	2.4
Seattle-Tacoma, WA CMSA	2,247,400	2,093,285	7.4
San Diego, CA	2,132,700	1,861,846	14.5
Tampa-St. Petersburg-Clearwater, FL	1,868,700	1,613,621	15.8
Phoenix, AZ	1,846,600	1,509,262	22.4
Denver-Boulder, CO	1,827,100	1,618,461	12.9
Cincinnati-Hamilton, OH-KY-IN CMSA	1,679,900	1,660,258	1.2
Milwaukee-Racine, WI CMSA	1,550,300	1,570,152	−1.3
Kansas City, MO-KS	1,493,900	1,433,464	4.2
Portland-Vancouver, OR-WA CMSA	1,353,800	1,297,977	4.3
New Orleans, LA	1,324,400	1,256,668	5.4
Norfolk-Virginia Beach-Newport News, VA	1,289,500	1,160,311	11.1
Columbus, OH	1,287,600	1,243,827	3.5
Sacramento, CA	1,258,200	1,099,814	14.4
San Antonio, TX	1,235,700	1,072,125	15.3
Indianapolis, IN	1,203,100	1,166,575	3.1
Buffalo-Niagara Falls, NY CMSA	1,187,900	1,242,826	−4.4
Providence-Pawtucket-Fall River, RI-MA CMSA	1,100,900	1,083,139	1.6
Charlotte-Gastonia-Rock Hill, NC-SC	1,049,000	971,447	8.0
Hartford-New Britain-Middletown, CT CMSA	1,035,000	1,013,508	2.1
Salt Lake City-Ogden, UT	1,024,800	910,222	12.6
Rochester, NY	982,300	971,230	1.1
Oklahoma City, OK	975,900	860,969	13.3
Louisville, KY-IN	964,300	956,486	0.8
Memphis, TN-AK-MS	944,700	913,472	3.4
Dayton-Springfield, OH	931,100	942,083	−1.2
Nashville, TN	909,700	850,505	7.0
Birmingham, AL	903,800	884,014	2.2
Greensboro-Winston-Salem-High Point, NC	892,500	851,444	4.8
Orlando, FL	866,400	699,906	23.8
Albany-Schenectady-Troy, NY	841,400	835,880	0.7
Jacksonville, FL	823,500	722,252	14.0
Honolulu, HI	814,600	762,565	6.8
Richmond-Petersburg, VA	800,700	761,311	5.2
Tulsa, OK	733,100	657,173	11.6
Scranton-Wilkes-Barre, PA	723,400	728,796	−0.7
West Palm Beach-Boca Raton-Delray Beach, FL	723,100	576,754	25.4
Austin, TX	695,500	536,688	29.6
Syracuse, NY	651,200	642,971	1.3
Allentown-Bethlehem, PA-NJ	650,000	635,481	2.3
Grand Rapids, MI	634,900	601,680	5.5
Raleigh-Durham, NC	632,000	560,774	12.7
Omaha, NE-IA	611,600	585,122	4.5
Toledo, OH	608,100	616,864	−1.4
Greenville-Spartanburg, SC	599,600	570,211	5.2
Knoxville, TN	592,700	565,970	4.7
Tucson, AZ	585,900	531,443	10.2
Fresno, CA	580,000	514,621	12.7
Harrisburg-Lebanon-Carlisle, PA	572,900	556,242	3.0
Las Vegas, NV	556,700	463,087	20.2
El Paso, TX	545,000	479,899	13.6
Baton Rouge, LA	544,000	494,151	10.1
Springfield, MA	517,100	515,259	0.4
Youngstown-Warren, OH	512,800	531,350	−3.5
New Haven-Meriden, CT	510,100	500,462	1.9
Little Rock-North Little Rock, AR	498,500	474,464	5.1
Charleston, SC	481,700	430,346	11.9
Bakersfield, CA	480,900	403,089	19.3
Mobile, AL	469,100	443,536	5.8
Albuquerque, NM	464,300	420,262	10.5
Johnson City-Kingsport-Bristol, TN-VA	442,700	433,638	2.1
Columbia, SC	439,400	409,955	7.2
Wichita, KS,	435,400	411,870	5.7
Flint, MI	433,900	450,449	−3.7
Chattanooga, TN-GA	425,600	426,540	−0.2
Lansing-East Lansing, MI	418,500	419,750	−0.3
Stockton, CA	418,300	347,342	20.4
Saginaw-Bay City-Midland, MI	407,400	421,518	−3.3
Worcester, MA	406,000	402,018	0.5
Canton, OH	401,200	404,421	−0.8
York, PA	380,700	381,255	0.0
Lancaster, PA	386,600	362,346	6.7
Jackson, MS	384,700	362,038	6.3
Beaumont-Port Arthur, TX	381,400	375,497	1.6
Augusta, GA-SC	380,500	345,923	10.0
Davenport-Rock Island-Moline, IA-IL	377,200	384,749	−2.0
Des Moines, IA	372,100	367,561	1.2
Lakeland-Winter Haven, FL	368,500	321,652	14.6
Colorado Springs, CO	365,900	309,424	18.3
Shreveport, LA	362,400	333,158	8.8
Corpus Christi, TX	358,800	326,228	10.0
Spokane, WA	356,300	341,835	4.2
McAllen-Edinburg-Mission, TX	352,200	283,323	24.3
Fort Wayne, IN	350,900	354,156	−0.9
Peoria, IL	347,700	365,864	−5.0
Melbourne-Titusville-Palm Bay, FL	345,700	272,959	26.6
Madison, WI	341,900	323,545	5.7
Santa Barbara-Santa Maria-Lompoc, CA	332,000	298,694	11.1
Huntington-Ashland, WVA-KY-OH	331,800	336,410	−1.4
Salinas-Seaside-Monterey, CA	329,900	290,444	13.6
Lexington-Fayette, KY	329,400	317,548	3.7
Pensacola, FL	328,500	289,782	13.4
Reading, PA	318,100	312,509	1.8
Utica-Rome, NY	317,700	320,180	−0.8
Daytona Beach, FL	310,600	258,762	20.0
Modesto, CA	305,800	265,900	15.0
Appleton-Oshkosh-Neenah, WI	303,700	291,369	4.2
Atlantic City, NJ	292,600	276,385	5.9
Montgomery, AL	288,700	272,687	5.9
Evansville, IN-KY	281,800	276,252	2.0
Visalia-Tulare-Porterville, CA	281,100	245,738	14.4

Population of U.S. Cities

Source: U.S. Bureau of the Census (100 most populated cities ranked by July 1, 1984 estimates)

Rank	City	1984	1980	1970	1960	1950	1900	1850
1	New York, N.Y.	7,164,742	7,071,639	7,895,563	7,781,984	7,891,957	3,437,202	696,115
2	Los Angeles, Cal.	3,096,721	2,966,850	2,811,801	2,479,015	1,970,358	102,479	1,610
3	Chicago, Ill.	2,992,472	3,005,072	3,369,357	3,550,404	3,620,962	1,698,575	29,963
4	Houston, Tex.	1,705,697	1,595,138	1,233,535	938,219	596,163	44,633	2,396
5	Philadelphia, Pa.	1,646,713	1,688,210	1,949,996	2,002,512	2,071,605	1,293,697	121,376
6	Detroit, Mich.	1,088,973	1,203,339	1,514,063	1,670,144	1,849,568	285,704	21,019
7	Dallas, Tex.	974,234	904,078	844,401	679,684	434,462	42,638	...
8	San Diego, Cal.	960,452	875,538	697,471	573,224	334,387	17,700	...
9	Phoenix, Ariz.	853,266	789,704	584,303	439,170	106,818	5,544	...
10	San Antonio, Tex.	842,779	785,880	654,153	587,718	408,442	53,321	3,488
11	Honolulu, Ha.	805,266	762,874	630,528	294,194	248,034	39,306	...
12	Baltimore, Md.	763,570	786,775	905,787	939,024	949,708	508,957	169,054
13	San Francisco, Cal.	712,753	678,974	715,674	740,316	775,357	342,782	34,776
14	Indianapolis, Ind.	710,280	700,807	736,856	476,258	427,173	169,164	8,091
15	San Jose, Cal.	686,178	629,442	459,913	204,196	95,280	21,500	...
16	Memphis, Tenn.	648,399	646,356	623,988	497,524	396,000	102,320	8,841
17	Washington, D.C.	622,823	638,333	756,668	763,956	802,178	278,718	40,001
18	Milwaukee, Wis.	620,811	636,212	717,372	741,324	637,392	285,315	20,061
19	Jacksonville, Fla.	577,971	540,920	504,265	201,030	204,517	28,429	1,045
20	Boston, Mass.	570,719	562,994	641,071	697,197	801,444	560,892	136,881
21	Columbus, Oh.	566,114	564,871	540,025	471,316	375,901	125,560	17,882
22	New Orleans, La.	559,101	557,515	593,471	627,525	570,445	287,104	116,375
23	Cleveland, Oh.	546,543	573,822	750,879	876,050	914,808	381,768	17,034
24	Denver, Col.	504,588	492,365	514,678	493,887	415,786	133,859	...
25	Seattle, Wash.	488,474	493,846	530,831	557,087	467,591	80,671	...
26	El Paso, Tex.	463,809	425,259	322,261	276,687	130,485	15,906	...
27	Nashville-Davidson, Tenn.	462,450	455,651	426,029	170,874	174,307	80,865	10,165
28	Oklahoma City, Okla.	443,172	403,213	368,164	324,253	243,504	10,037	...
29	Kansas City, Mo.	443,075	448,159	507,330	475,539	456,622	163,752	...
30	St. Louis, Mo.	429,296	453,085	622,236	750,026	856,796	575,238	77,860
31	Atlanta, Ga.	426,090	425,022	495,039	487,455	331,314	89,872	2,572
32	Fort Worth, Tex.	414,562	385,164	393,455	356,268	278,778	26,688	...
33	Pittsburgh, Pa.	402,583	423,938	520,089	604,332	676,806	321,616	46,601
34	Austin, Tex.	397,001	345,496	253,539	186,545	132,459	22,258	629
35	Long Beach, Cal.	378,752	361,334	358,879	344,168	250,767	2,252	...
36	Tulsa, Okla.	374,535	360,919	330,350	261,685	182,740	1,390	...
37	Miami, Fla.	372,634	346,865	334,859	291,688	249,276	1,681	...
38	Cincinnati, Oh.	370,481	385,457	453,514	502,550	503,998	325,902	115,435
39	Baton Rouge, La.	368,571	346,029	165,921	152,419	125,629	11,269	3,905
40	Portland, Ore.	365,861	366,383	379,967	372,676	373,628	90,426	...
41	Tucson, Ariz.	365,422	330,537	262,933	212,892	45,454	7,531	...
42	Minneapolis, Minn.	358,335	370,951	434,400	482,872	521,718	202,718	...
43	Oakland, Cal.	351,898	339,337	361,561	367,548	384,575	66,960	...
44	Albuquerque, N.M.	350,575	331,767	244,501	201,189	96,815	6,238	...
45	Toledo, Oh.	343,939	354,635	383,062	318,003	303,616	131,822	3,829
46	Buffalo, N.Y.	338,982	357,870	462,768	532,759	580,132	352,387	42,261
47	Omaha, Neb.	332,237	314,255	346,929	301,598	251,117	102,555	...
48	Charlotte, N.C.	330,838	314,447	241,420	201,564	134,042	18,091	1,065
49	Newark, N.J.	314,387	329,248	381,930	405,220	438,776	246,070	38,894
50	Virginia Beach, Va.	308,664	262,199	172,106	8,091	5,390	...	
51	Sacramento, Cal.	304,131	275,741	257,105	191,667	137,572	29,282	6,820
52	Louisville, Ky.	289,843	298,451	361,706	390,639	369,129	204,731	43,194
53	Wichita, Kan.	283,496	279,272	276,554	254,698	168,279	24,671	...
54	Birmingham, Ala.	279,813	284,413	300,910	340,887	326,037	38,415	...
55	Norfolk, Va.	279,683	266,979	307,951	304,869	213,513	46,624	14,326
56	Tampa, Fla.	275,479	271,523	277,714	274,970	124,681	15,839	...
57	Fresno, Cal.	267,377	218,202	165,655	133,929	91,669	12,470	...
58	St. Paul, Minn.	265,903	270,230	309,866	313,411	311,349	163,065	1,112
59	Corpus Christi, Tex.	258,067	231,999	204,525	167,690	108,287	4,703	...
60	Colorado Springs, Col.	247,739	215,150	135,517	70,194	45,472	21,085	...
61	Rochester, N.Y.	242,562	241,741	295,011	318,611	332,488	162,608	36,403
62	St. Petersburg, Fla.	241,294	238,647	216,159	181,298	96,738	1,575	...
63	Anaheim, Cal.	233,516	219,311	166,408	104,184	14,556	1,456	...
64	Akron, Oh.	226,877	237,177	275,425	290,351	274,605	42,728	3,266
65	Anchorage, Alas.	226,663	174,431	48,081	44,237	11,254	...	...
66	Santa Ana, Cal.	225,405	203,713	155,710	100,350	45,533	4,933	...
67	Jersey City, N.J.	223,004	223,532	260,350	276,101	299,017	206,433	6,856
68	Shreveport, La.	219,996	205,820	182,064	164,372	127,206	16,013	1,728
69	Richmond, Va.	219,056	219,214	249,332	219,958	230,310	85,050	27,570
70	Arlington, Tex.	213,832	160,113	90,229	44,775	7,692	1,079	...
71	Lexington-Fayette, Ky.	210,150	204,165	108,137	62,810	55,534	26,369	8,159
72	Jackson, Miss.	208,810	202,895	153,968	144,422	98,271	7,816	1,881
73	Mobile, Ala.	204,923	200,452	190,026	194,856	129,009	38,469	20,515
74	Aurora, Col.	194,772	158,588	74,974	48,548	11,421	202	...
75	Mesa, Ariz.	193,931	152,453	63,049	33,772	16,790	722	...
76	Yonkers, N.Y.	191,234	195,351	204,297	190,634	152,798	47,931	...
77	Des Moines, Ia.	190,832	191,003	201,404	208,982	177,965	62,139	...
78	Montgomery, Ala.	184,963	177,857	133,386	134,393	106,525	30,346	8,728
79	Las Vegas, Nev.	183,227	164,674	125,787	64,405	24,624	...	...
80	Grand Rapids, Mich.	183,000	181,843	197,649	177,313	176,515	87,565	2,686
81	Riverside, Cal.	182,245	170,876	140,089	84,332	46,764	7,973	...
82	Dayton, Oh.	181,159	203,371	243,023	262,332	243,872	85,333	10,977
83	Lincoln, Neb.	180,378	171,932	149,518	128,521	98,884	40,169	...
84	Huntington Beach, Cal.	179,335	170,505	115,960	11,492	5,237	...	...
85	Lubbock, Tex.	178,529	173,979	149,101	126,691	71,747		

(continued)

Rank	City	1984	1980	1970	1960	1950	1900	1850
86	Columbus, Ga.	174,824	169,441	155,028	116,779	79,611	17,614	9,621
87	Knoxville, Tenn.	173,972	175,030	174,587	111,827	124,769	32,637	2,076
88	Spokane, Wash.	173,349	171,300	170,516	181,608	161,721	36,848	...
89	Stockton, Cal.	171,659	149,779	109,963	86,321	70,853	17,506	...
90	Madison, Wis.	170,745	170,616	171,809	126,706	96,056	19,164	1,525
91	Little Rock, Ark.	170,140	158,461	132,483	107,813	102,213	38,307	2,167
92	Raleigh, NC	169,331	150,255	122,830	93,931	65,679	13,643	4,518
93	Fort Wayne, Ind.	165,416	172,196	178,269	161,776	133,607	45,115	4,282
94	Salt Lake City, Ut.	164,844	163,033	175,885	189,454	182,121	53,531	...
95	Chattanooga, Tenn.	164,400	169,565	119,923	130,009	131,041	30,154	...
96	Syracuse, N.Y.	164,219	170,105	197,297	216,038	220,583	108,374	22,271
97	Amarillo, Tex.	162,863	149,230	127,010	137,969	74,246	1,442	...
98	Kansas City, Kans.	160,468	161,087	168,213	121,901	129,553	51,418	...
99	Garland, Tex.	160,208	138,857	81,437	38,501	10,571	819	...
100	Worcester, Mass.	159,843	161,799	176,572	186,587	203,486	118,421	17,049

City Population by Race and Spanish Origin

Source: U.S. Bureau of the Census

This table presents a summary of the final 1980 census population estimates for cities over 250,000, classified by race and Spanish origin.

	Total	White	Black	Am. Indian Eskimos Aleut.	Asian & Pacific Islander	Race N.E.C.[1]	Spanish Origin[2]
Albuquerque, NM	331,767	275,758	7,691	7,163	3,755	37,400	112,030
Atlanta, GA	425,022	138,235	283,158	610	2,001	1,018	5,750
Austin, TX	345,544	263,618	42,108	1,516	4,127	34,175	64,945
Baltimore, MD	786,775	346,692	430,934	2,170	4,898	2,081	7,804
Birmingham, AL	284,413	124,767	158,200	220	933	293	2,054
Boston, MA	562,994	396,635	126,438	1,455	16,298	22,168	36,430
Buffalo, NY	357,870	253,507	95,622	2,084	1,335	5,322	8,926
Charlotte, NC	314,447	212,293	97,896	1,162	2,393	703	3,091
Chicago, IL	3,005,078	1,512,411	1,197,174	6,804	73,745	214,944	423,357
Cincinnati, OH	385,457	251,332	130,490	567	2,332	736	3,263
Cleveland, OH	573,822	309,299	251,084	1,282	3,372	8,785	17,896
Columbus, OH	564,866	431,966	124,689	1,024	5,410	1,777	5,300
Dallas, TX	904,074	558,443	265,105	3,878	9,163	67,485	110,511
Denver, CO	492,365	375,628	59,095	4,318	8,934	44,390	92,257
Detroit, MI	1,203,339	420,529	758,468	3,846	7,614	12,882	28,466
El Paso, TX	425,259	306,510	10,641	1,503	3,995	99,550	265,997
Fort Worth, TX	385,166	266,638	87,635	1,841	2,954	26,098	48,568
Honolulu, HI (County)	762,565	262,604	17,203	2,445	463,117	17,196	54,619
Houston, TX	1,595,167	981,563	439,604	3,945	35,448	134,607	280,691
Indianapolis, IN	700,719	540,496	152,590	1,356	4,539	1,738	6,430
Jacksonville, FL	540,920	394,661	137,150	1,950	5,485	1,674	9,879
Kansas City, MO	448,154	313,835	122,336	2,115	3,591	6,277	14,643
Long Beach, CA	361,334	272,272	40,400	3,501	22,025	23,043	50,460
Los Angeles, CA	2,966,850	1,842,050	504,301	19,296	206,536	394,667	815,305
Louisville, KY	298,455	212,052	84,254	408	1,327	414	2,049
Memphis, TN	646,356	334,363	307,573	680	2,864	876	5,730
Miami, FL	346,865	225,200	87,018	334	2,050	32,260	194,185
Milwaukee, WI	636,212	468,064	147,055	5,348	4,451	11,294	26,487
Minneapolis, MN	370,951	325,415	28,469	9,198	5,358	2,511	4,762
Nashville-Davidson, TN	455,663	345,766	105,869	743	2,418	867	3,257
New Orleans, LA	557,515	238,192	308,039	623	7,458	3,203	19,215
New York, NY	7,071,639	4,348,605	1,788,377	13,400	245,759	675,498	1,406,389
Newark, NJ	329,248	107,465	191,968	923	2,421	26,471	61,322
Norfolk, VA	266,979	163,052	93,977	822	7,075	2,053	5,792
Oakland, CA	339,337	131,127	159,351	2,754	28,053	18,052	32,133
Oklahoma City, OK	403,243	323,665	58,550	11,199	4,610	5,219	11,767
Omaha, NE	314,267	268,995	37,889	1,839	2,381	3,163	7,354
Philadelphia, PA	1,688,210	988,337	638,788	2,799	19,950	38,336	64,323
Phoenix, AZ	789,704	673,488	37,747	11,645	8,429	58,395	116,875
Pittsburgh, PA	423,938	318,287	101,549	584	2,818	700	3,370
Portland, OR	366,423	319,220	28,034	3,374	12,980	2,815	7,541
Sacramento, CA	275,741	187,992	36,842	3,506	24,558	22,843	38,905
St. Louis, MO	453,085	242,988	206,170	679	2,214	1,034	5,380
St. Paul, MN	270,230	245,795	13,018	2,558	5,345	3,514	7,553
San Antonio, TX	785,809	621,679	57,566	2,375	5,821	98,368	421,808
San Diego, CA	875,538	674,268	77,508	5,833	61,655	56,274	129,953
San Francisco, CA	678,974	402,131	86,190	3,566	149,269	37,818	84,194
San Jose, CA	629,442	470,458	28,792	5,801	53,205	71,186	140,318
Seattle, WA	493,846	396,275	46,565	6,821	38,936	5,249	12,744
Tampa, FL	271,523	202,507	63,578	607	1,894	2,937	35,781
Toledo, OH	354,635	284,104	61,855	989	2,005	5,682	10,984
Tucson, AZ	330,537	274,750	11,587	4,578	3,427	36,195	82,106
Tulsa, OK	360,919	298,926	42,845	13,816	2,962	2,370	6,291
Virginia Beach, VA	262,199	227,454	26,266	630	6,489	1,360	5,269
Washington, DC	638,333	174,705	448,370	1,014	6,883	7,361	17,777
Wichita, KS	279,272	236,549	30,263	2,942	4,525	4,993	9,455

(1) Not elsewhere classified.
(2) Persons of Spanish origin may be of any race.

Black and Hispanic Population by States

Source: U.S. Bureau of the Census (1980)

	Black	Hispanic
Ala.	996,335	33,299
Alas.	13,643	9,507
Ariz.	74,977	440,701
Ark.	373,768	17,904
Cal.	1,819,281	4,544,331
Col.	101,703	339,717
Conn.	217,433	124,499
Del.	95,845	9,661
D.C.	448,906	17,679
Fla.	1,342,688	858,158
Ga.	1,465,181	61,260
Ha.	17,364	71,263
Ida.	2,716	36,615
Ill.	1,675,398	635,602
Ind.	414,785	87,047
Ia.	41,700	25,536
Kan.	126,127	63,339
Ky.	259,477	27,406
La.	1,238,241	99,134
Me.	3,128	5,005
Md.	958,150	64,746
Mass.	221,279	141,043
Mich.	1,199,023	162,440
Minn.	53,344	32,123
Miss.	887,206	24,731
Mo.	514,276	51,653
Mon.	1,786	9,974
Neb.	48,390	28,025
Nev.	50,999	53,879
N.H.	3,990	5,587
N.J.	925,066	491,883
N.M.	24,020	477,222
N.Y.	2,402,006	1,659,300
N.C.	1,318,857	56,667
N.D.	2,568	3,902
Oh.	1,076,748	119,883
Okla.	204,674	57,419
Ore.	37,060	65,847
Pa.	1,046,810	153,961
R.I.	27,584	19,707
S.C.	948,623	33,426
S.D.	2,144	4,023
Tenn.	725,942	34,077
Tex.	1,710,175	2,985,824
Ut.	9,225	60,302
Vt.	1,135	3,304
Va.	1,008,668	79,868
Wash.	105,574	120,016
W.Va.	65,051	12,707
Wis.	182,592	62,972
Wy.	3,364	24,499
Total	**26,495,025**	**14,608,673**

Foreign-Born Population in Twelve Metropolitan Areas of the United States: 1980

Source: U.S. Bureau of the Census

Country of origin	New York City	Chicago	Los Angeles	Philadelphia	Houston	Detroit	Dallas	San Diego	Phoenix	San Antonio	San Francisco	Washington DC
Number of foreign-born persons	**1,946,800**	**744,930**	**1,664,793**	**242,658**	**220,861**	**282,766**	**124,697**	**235,593**	**82,536**	**76,944**	**509,352**	**249,994**
Percent of population foreign-born	**21.3**	**10.5**	**22.3**	**5.1**	**7.6**	**6.5**	**4.2**	**12.7**	**5.5**	**7.2**	**15.7**	**8.2**
Europe	**37.7**	**40.9**	**13.0**	**54.8**	**11.7**	**47.9**	**16.4**	**18.5**	**30.6**	**13.8**	**23.8**	**26.9**
Austria	1.6	1.2	0.4	1.6	0.3	1.2	0.4	0.4	0.9	0.3	0.6	0.8
Czechoslovakia	1.0	1.4	0.3	0.8	0.3	0.9	0.4	0.3	0.7	0.3	0.4	0.6
France	0.8	0.5	0.5	0.9	0.7	0.7	0.9	0.7	1.4	0.8	1.1	1.8
Germany	4.3	6.0	2.1	9.4	2.6	6.3	5.0	3.7	7.2	5.8	4.2	6.2
Greece	2.4	3.2	0.4	2.5	0.7	2.1	0.5	0.5	0.8	0.2	0.8	1.9
Hungary	1.3	0.9	0.7	1.6	0.3	1.6	0.4	0.4	1.2	0.2	0.5	0.7
Ireland	2.7	2.0	0.3	3.8	0.2	1.0	0.4	0.5	0.9	0.5	1.2	0.7
Italy	10.5	6.0	1.3	14.9	0.7	8.0	0.7	2.0	3.4	0.6	3.3	2.4
Netherlands	0.2	0.5	0.5	0.5	0.5	0.6	0.5	0.7	0.9	0.2	0.8	0.6
Poland	4.6	8.4	1.0	4.7	0.5	7.6	0.6	0.7	1.8	0.5	0.6	1.1
Portugal	0.5	0.1	0.2	0.9	0.1	*	*	0.8	0.1	0.1	1.4	0.6
Sweden	0.2	0.9	0.2	0.3	0.1	0.3	0.2	0.5	0.5	0.1	0.6	0.3
United Kingdom	2.5	2.5	2.8	7.8	3.2	8.1	4.6	4.7	6.4	3.0	4.1	5.2
England	1.6	1.6	1.9	4.6	2.2	4.4	3.4	3.2	4.3	2.3	2.8	3.6
Northern Ireland	0.1	0.1	0.1	0.5	*	0.2	0.1	0.1	0.1	0.1	0.1	0.1
Scotland	0.6	0.6	0.5	2.1	0.4	3.0	0.6	1.0	1.4	0.3	0.7	0.7
Wales	*	*	*	0.2	0.1	0.2	0.1	0.1	0.1	*	0.1	0.1
Yugoslavia	1.3	3.0	0.6	1.0	0.2	3.7	0.2	0.5	1.1	0.1	0.5	0.3
U.S.S.R.	**4.9**	**3.3**	**2.1**	**8.9**	**0.7**	**3.5**	**0.9**	**0.9**	**2.1**	**0.5**	**1.9**	**1.8**
Asia	**13.1**	**17.2**	**20.4**	**16.7**	**21.7**	**18.3**	**21.2**	**27.4**	**12.7**	**9.7**	**42.3**	**32.0**
China	3.3	1.2	2.0	1.4	2.1	0.9	1.5	1.0	1.6	0.6	11.0	2.8
India	1.4	2.9	0.6	2.8	3.5	2.2	2.4	0.4	0.8	0.6	1.3	3.6
Japan	0.9	0.8	2.0	0.9	1.1	0.6	1.5	2.8	1.5	1.7	2.7	1.6
Korea	1.2	2.3	3.0	3.4	1.4	1.1	2.0	0.9	1.6	1.1	1.8	5.9
Philippines	1.3	4.3	4.4	2.1	1.9	2.0	1.8	13.0	1.3	1.7	13.2	3.6
Vietnam	0.2	0.6	1.7	1.4	5.3	0.4	3.8	3.3	1.6	1.5	2.2	3.6
North and Central America	**27.4**	**28.7**	**54.8**	**9.5**	**51.0**	**23.1**	**48.5**	**44.9**	**44.6**	**69.4**	**21.9**	**17.4**
Canada	1.2	2.2	3.4	3.2	2.3	19.9	3.8	5.9	10.8	1.6	4.1	3.3
Mexico	0.4	21.6	41.9	0.6	42.4	1.7	40.0	36.9	31.9	64.9	11.0	0.9
West Indies	22.6	3.2	2.7	4.8	3.8	1.2	2.8	0.9	0.8	1.3	1.0	8.4
Cuba	2.8	1.9	2.1	1.2	2.0	0.3	2.0	0.3	0.3	0.7	0.6	2.0
Dominican Republic	6.6	0.1	0.1	0.3	0.1	0.1	0.1	0.1	0.1	0.1	*	0.5
Jamaica	5.1	0.6	0.2	1.7	0.5	0.4	0.2	0.2	0.1	0.2	0.2	2.8
South America	**8.8**	**2.5**	**3.5**	**2.5**	**3.9**	**1.0**	**2.4**	**1.7**	**1.9**	**1.0**	**2.5**	**9.6**
North Africa	**0.6**	**0.3**	**0.6**	**0.5**	**0.5**	**0.4**	**0.6**	**0.3**	**0.3**	**0.3**	**0.5**	**1.3**
Other Africa	**0.7**	**0.8**	**0.5**	**1.1**	**1.7**	**0.5**	**1.5**	**0.5**	**0.6**	**0.3**	**0.6**	**3.8**
All other countries	**0.2**	**0.2**	**0.5**	**0.3**	**0.3**	**0.2**	**0.5**	**1.0**	**0.6**	**0.3**	**1.6**	**0.8**
Country not reported	**6.5**	**6.2**	**4.7**	**5.6**	**8.5**	**5.0**	**7.9**	**4.8**	**6.6**	**4.8**	**4.9**	**6.4**

Note: * indicates amount less than 0.1 percent.

Immigration by Country of Last Residence 1820-1986

Source: U.S. Immigration and Naturalization Service (thousands)

Country	Total 1820-1986	Total 1961-1970	Total 1971-1980	1980[10]	1982[10]	1983[10]	1984	1985	1986	Percent 1820-1986	Percent 1961-1970	Percent 1971-1980
All countries*	**53,122**	**3,321.7**	**4,493.3**	**530.6**	**594.1**	**559.8**	**543.9**	**570.0**	**601.7**	**100.0**	**100.0**	**100.0**
Europe	**36,743**	**1,123.5**	**800.4**	**72.1**	**69.2**	**58.9**	**69.9**	**69.5**	**69.2**	**69.2**	**33.8**	**17.8**
Austria[1]	4,327	20.6	9.5	0.4	0.3	0.4	2.4	1.9	2.0	8.1	.6	0.2
Hungary		5.4	6.6	0.8	0.6	0.6	0.5	0.6	0.6		.2	0.1
Belgium	208	9.2	5.3	0.4	0.6	0.5	0.8	0.8	0.8	0.4	.3	0.1
Czechoslovakia	144	3.3	6.0	1.1	1.0	0.9	0.7	0.7	0.6	0.3	.1	0.1
Denmark	369	9.2	4.4	0.5	0.5	0.5	0.5	0.5	0.5	0.7	.3	0.1
Finland	36	4.2	2.9	0.4	0.3	0.3	0.2	0.2	0.3	0.1	.1	0.1
France	772	45.2	25.1	1.9	2.0	2.1	3.3	3.5	3.9	1.5	1.4	0.6
Germany[1]	7,041	190.8	74.4	6.6	6.7	7.2	9.4	10.2	9.9	13.3	5.7	1.7
Great Britain[2]	5,066	214.5	137.4	15.5	14.5	14.8	16.5	15.6	16.0	9.5	6.5	3.1
Greece	687	86.0	92.4	4.7	3.5	3.0	3.3	3.5	3.5	1.3	2.6	2.1
Ireland	4,699	33.0	11.5	1.0	0.9	1.1	1.1	1.3	1.8	8.8	1.0	0.3
Italy	5,338	214.1	129.4	5.5	3.6	3.2	6.3	6.4	5.7	10.0	6.4	2.9
Netherlands	369	30.6	10.5	1.2	1.1	1.2	1.3	1.2	1.3	0.7	.9	0.2
Norway[11]	859	15.5	3.9	0.4	0.3	0.4	0.4	0.4	0.4	1.6	.5	0.1
Poland[1]	562	53.5	37.2	4.7	5.9	6.4	7.2	7.4	6.5	1.1	1.6	0.8
Portugal	486	76.1	101.7	8.4	3.5	3.2	3.8	3.8	3.8	0.9	2.3	2.3
Spain	276	44.7	39.1	1.9	1.6	1.5	2.2	2.3	2.2	0.5	1.3	0.9
Sweden[11]	1,280	17.1	6.5	0.8	0.9	0.9	1.1	1.2	1.2	2.4	.5	0.1
Switzerland	355	18.5	8.2	0.7	0.6	0.7	0.8	1.0	0.9	0.7	.6	0.2
USSR[1,3]	3,422	2.5	39.0	10.5	15.5	5.2	3.3	1.5	1.0	6.4	.1	0.9
Yugoslavia	127	20.4	30.5	2.1	1.4	1.4	1.4	1.5	1.9	0.2	.6	0.7
Other Europe	332	9.1	18.9	2.6	3.9	3.4	3.4	4.0	4.4	0.6	.2	0.2
Asia	**4,893**	**427.6**	**1,588.2**	**236.1**	**313.3**	**277.7**	**247.8**	**255.2**	**258.5**	**9.2**	**12.9**	**35.2**
China[5]	737	34.8	124.3	27.7	37.0	42.5	29.1	33.1	16.5	1.4	1.0	2.8
Hong Kong	252	75.0	113.5	3.9	5.0	5.9	12.3	10.8	9.9	0.5	2.3	2.5
India	[5]347	27.2	164.1	22.6	21.7	25.5	23.6	24.5	24.8	0.7	.8	3.7
Iran	127	10.3	45.1	10.4	10.3	11.2	11.1	12.3	12.0	0.2	.3	1.0
Israel	[6]116	29.6	37.7	3.5	3.4	3.2	4.1	4.3	5.1	0.2	.9	0.8
Japan	[5]440	40.0	49.8	4.2	3.9	4.1	4.5	4.6	4.4	0.8	1.2	1.1
Jordan	61	11.7	27.5	3.3	2.9	2.7	2.2	2.7	2.8	0.1	.4	0.6
Korea	508	34.5	267.6	32.3	31.7	33.3	32.5	34.8	35.2	1.0	1.0	6.0
Lebanon	80	15.2	41.3	4.1	3.5	2.9	3.0	2.5	3.0	0.2	.6	0.9
Philippines	[5,6]705	98.4	355.0	42.3	45.1	41.5	47.0	53.1	61.5	1.4	3.0	7.9
Turkey	402	10.1	13.4	2.2	2.9	2.3	1.7	1.7	2.0	0.8	.3	0.3
Vietnam	[7]404	4.3	172.8	43.5	72.6	37.6	25.8	20.4	15.0	0.0	1.1	3.8
Other Asia	653	36.5	176.1	36.1	73.3	65.0	50.9	50.4	66.3	1.2	1.1	3.8
America	**10,784**	**1,716.4**	**1,982.5**	**204.5**	**193.5**	**204.6**	**208.1**	**225.5**	**254.1**	**20.3**	**51.7**	**44.3**
Argentina	[8]112	49.7	29.9	2.8	2.1	2.0	2.3	1.9	2.3	0.2	1.5	0.7
Brazil	[8]73	29.3	17.8	1.6	1.5	1.5	2.2	2.6	2.7	0.1	.9	0.4
Canada	4,220	413.3	169.9	13.6	10.8	11.4	15.7	16.4	16.1	7.9	12.4	3.8
Colombia	[8]230	72.0	77.3	11.3	8.6	9.7	10.9	11.8	11.2	0.4	2.2	1.7
Cuba	[9]634	208.5	264.9	15.1	8.2	9.0	5.7	17.1	30.8	1.2	6.3	5.9
Dominican Rep.	[9]382	93.3	148.1	17.2	17.5	22.1	23.2	23.9	26.2	0.7	2.8	3.3
Ecuador	[8]124	36.8	50.1	6.1	4.1	4.2	4.2	4.6	4.5	0.2	1.1	1.1
El Salvador	[8]109	15.0	34.4	6.1	7.1	8.6	8.8	10.1	10.9	0.2	.5	0.8
Guatemala	[8]71	15.9	25.9	3.8	3.6	4.1	4.0	4.4	5.3	0.1	.5	0.6
Haiti	[9]151	34.5	56.3	6.5	8.8	8.4	9.6	9.9	12.4	0.3	1.0	1.3
Honduras	[8]61	15.7	17.4	2.6	3.2	3.6	3.4	3.7	4.6	0.1	.5	0.4
Mexico	2,637	453.9	640.3	56.7	56.1	59.1	57.8	61.3	66.8	5.0	13.7	14.3
Panama	[8]74	19.4	23.5	3.6	3.3	2.5	3.2	3.2	3.1	0.1	.6	0.5
Peru	[8]82	19.1	29.2	4.0	4.2	4.4	4.3	4.1	4.8	0.2	.6	0.6
West Indies	1,124	133.9	271.8	34.5	32.9	33.8	29.9	28.5	29.2	2.1	4.0	6.1
Other America	702	106.1	125.7	19.0	21.5	20.2	22.9	22.0	23.2	1.3	3.1	2.8
Africa	**247**	**29.0**	**80.8**	**14.0**	**14.3**	**15.1**	**13.6**	**15.2**	**15.5**	**0.5**	**.9**	**1.8**
Australia and New Zealand	**136**	**19.6**	**23.8**	**2.2**	**2.0**	**1.9**	**2.3**	**2.5**	**2.4**	**0.3**	**.6**	**0.5**
Other Oceania	**25**	**5.6**	**17.6**	**1.7**	**1.8**	**1.6**	**1.9**	**2.1**	**1.9**	**0.1**	**.1**	**0.4**
Unknown or Not Reported	**294**	**—**	**—**	**—**	**—**	**—**	**0.3**	**—**	**0.1**	**0.6**	**—**	**—**

* Figures may not add to total due to rounding. (1) 1938-1945, Austria included with Germany; 1899-1919, Poland included with Austria-Hungary, Germany, and USSR. (2) Beginning 1952, includes data for United Kingdom not specified, formerly included with "Other Europe". (3) Europe and Asia. (4) Beginning 1957, includes Taiwan. (5) Prior to 1951, included with "Other Asia". (6) Prior to 1951, Philippines included with "All other". (7) Prior to 1953, data for Vietnam not available. (8) Prior to 1951, included with "Other America". (9) Prior to 1951, included with "West Indies". (10) Data on immigration by country of last residence for 1980–1983 are not available; data based on country of birth. (11) Norway and Sweden were combined from 1820-1868.

Poverty by Family Status, Sex, and Race

Source: U.S. Bureau of the Census, Current Population Reports
By thousands

	1985		1984		1983		1978	
	No.[1]	%[2]	No.[1]	%[2]	No.[1]	%[2]	No.[1]	%[2]
Total poor	**33,064**	**14.0**	**22,700**	**14.4**	**35,266**	**15.2**	**24,497**	**11.4**
In families	25,729	12.6	26,458	13.1	27,804	13.8	19,062	10.0
Head	7,223	11.4	7,277	11.6	7,641	12.3	5,280	9.1
Related children	12,483	20.1	12,929	21.0	13,326	21.7	9,722	15.7
Other relatives	6,032	7.7	6,251	8.0	6,837	8.8	4,509	5.7
Unrelated individuals	6,725	21.5	6,609	21.8	6,832	23.4	5,435	22.1
In female-head families	11,600	37.6	11,831	38.4	12,020	40.2	9,269	35.6
Head	3,474	34.0	3,498	34.5	3,557	36.0	2,654	31.4
Related children	6,716	53.6	6,772	54.0	6,709	55.4	5,687	50.6
Other relatives	1,410	17.3	1,562	19.1	1,755	22.1	928	14.6
Unrelated female individuals	4,226	24.8	4,035	24.4	4,213	26.2	3,611	26.0
In male-head families	14,129	8.2	14,627	8.5	15,784	9.2	9,793	5.9
Head	3,749	7.0	3,780	7.2	4,084	7.8	2,626	5.3
Related children	5,767	11.7	6,157	12.5	6,617	13.4	4,035	7.9
Other relatives	4,613	6.6	4,690	6.7	5,083	7.3	3,131	4.8
Unrelated male individuals	2,499	17.4	2,575	18.7	2,619	19.9	1,824	17.1
Total white poor	**22,860**	**11.4**	**22,955**	**11.5**	**23,074**	**12.1**	**16,259**	**8.7**
In families	17,125	9.9	17,299	10.1	18,269	10.1	12,050	7.3
Head	4,983	9.1	4,925	9.1	5,223	9.7	3,523	6.9
Female	1,950	27.4	1,878	27.1	1,920	28.3	1,391	23.5
Related children	7,838	15.6	8,086	16.1	8,456	16.9	5,674	11.0
Other relatives	4,304	6.4	4,289	6.4	4,590	6.8	2,852	4.5
Unrelated individuals	5,299	19.6	5,181	19.9	5,291	20.9	4,209	19.8
Total black poor	**8,926**	**31.3**	**9,490**	**33.8**	**9,885**	**35.7**	**7,625**	**30.6**
In families	7,504	30.5	8,104	33.2	8,381	34.7	6,493	29.5
Head	1,983	28.7	2,094	30.9	2,162	32.4	1,622	27.5
Female	1,452	50.5	1,533	51.7	1,545	53.8	1,208	50.6
Related children	4,057	43.1	4,320	46.2	4,258	46.3	3,781	41.2
Other relatives	1,464	17.7	1,691	20.5	1,961	23.7	1,094	15.7
Unrelated individuals	1,264	34.7	1,255	35.8	1,334	40.8	1,132	38.6

(1) Beginning in 1979, total includes members of unrelated subfamilies not shown separately. For earlier years, unrelated subfamily members are included in the "in family" category. (2) Percent of total population in that general category who fell below poverty level. For example, of all black female heads of households in 1978, 50.6% were poor.

Poverty Level by Family Size 1984, 1985

By thousands

	1985	1984
1 persons	$ 5,469	$ 5,278
Under 65 years	5,593	5,400
65 years and over	5,156	4,979
2 persons	6,998	6,762
Householder under 65 years	7,231	6,983
Householder 65 years and over	6,503	6,282
3 persons	$ 8,573	$ 8,277
4 persons	10,989	10,609
5 persons	13,007	12,566
6 persons	14,696	14,207
7 persons	16,656	16,096
8 persons	18,512	17,961
9 persons or more	22,083	21,247

Income Distribution by Population Fifths

Families, 1985	Top income of each fifth					Percent distribution of total income					
Race	Lowest	Second	Third	Fourth	Top 5%	Lowest fifth	Second fifth	Third fifth	Fourth fifth	Highest fifth	Top 5%
Total	$13,192	$22,275	$33,040	$48,000	$77,706	4.6	10.9	16.9	24.2	43.5	16.7
White	14,528	24,105	34,500	49,901	80,000	5.0	11.2	16.9	23.9	42.9	16.5
Black and other	7,400	14,500	23,560	37,100	59,980	3.6	9.1	15.7	25.1	46.4	17.1
Black	6,750	13,010	20,933	33,613	54,030	3.7	9.1	15.7	25.2	46.3	16.7
Region											
Northeast	$14,666	$25,001	$36,080	$51,130	$84,151	4.8	11.0	17.0	24.1	43.1	16.7
North Central	13,400	23,265	32,850	46,282	71,898	4.7	11.5	17.5	24.2	42.1	15.8
South	11,795	20,100	30,100	45,119	73,947	4.5	10.5	16.4	24.1	44.6	17.2
West	14,592	24,572	35,352	50,900	82,742	4.9	11.1	16.9	24.0	43.1	16.5

Persons Below Poverty Level, 1960-1985

Year	Number Below Poverty Level (mil.)				Percent Below Poverty Level				Average income cutoffs for non-farm family of 4[3] at poverty level
	All races[1]	White	Black	Spanish origin[2]	All races[1]	White	Black	Spanish origin[2]	
1960	39.9	28.3	NA	NA	22.2	17.8	NA	NA	$3,022
1965	33.2	22.5	NA	NA	17.3	13.3	NA	NA	3,223
1970	25.4	17.5	7.5	NA	12.6	9.9	33.5	NA	3,968
1975	25.9	17.8	7.5	3.0	12.3	9.7	31.3	26.9	5,500
1980[4]	29.3	19.7	8.6	3.5	13.0	10.2	32.5	25.7	8,414
1982[4]	34.4	23.5	9.7	4.3	15.0	12.0	35.6	29.9	9,862
1983[4]	35.3	23.9	9.8	4.2	15.2	12.1	35.7	28.4	10,178
1984[4]	33.7	22.9	9.5	4.8	14.4	11.5	33.8	28.4	10,609
1985[4]	33.1	22.9	8.9	5.2	14.0	11.4	31.3	29.0	10,989

NA = Not Available. (1) Includes other races not shown separately. (2) Persons of Spanish origin may be of any race. (3) Beginning in 1981, income cutoffs for nonfarm families are applied to both farm and nonfarm families. (4) Data based on revised poverty definition.

Aid to Families with Dependent Children

Source: Office of Research and Statistics, Social Security Administration

1986 State	Total Assistance Payments[1]	Average Monthly Caseload	Average Monthly Recipients	Average Monthly Children	Average Payment per Family	Average Payment per Person
Alabama	$68,313,096	50,091	145,993	102,348	$113.65	$38.99
Alaska	46,028,365	6,799	16,865	10,794	564.20	227.44
Arizona	78,550,151	26,048	74,363	52,105	251.30	88.03
Arkansas	48,384,642	22,553	66,609	46,859	178.79	60.53
California	3,573,555,115	564,645	1,644,162	1,097,997	527.40	181.12
Colorado	106,604,882	29,138	83,508	55,858	304.88	106.38
Connecticut	223,438,582	40,318	117,332	79,065	461.83	158.69
Delaware	24,719,340	8,218	21,947	14,743	250.65	93.86
Dist. of Col.	76,485,409	21,325	55,195	41,907	298.89	115.48
Florida	261,298,423	97,383	275,366	201,686	223.60	79.08
Georgia	222,832,541	83,902	237,932	165,883	221.32	78.04
Guam	3,996,159	1,600	5,830	4,155	208.20	57.12
Hawaii	73,314,671	15,177	47,008	30,494	402.54	129.97
Idaho	19,347,926	6,330	17,137	11,499	254.70	94.09
Illinois	885,778,603	241,349	736,880	493,964	305.84	100.17
Indiana	147,469,740	55,693	160,968	108,581	220.66	76.35
Iowa	169,693,564	40,804	127,112	79,546	346.57	111.25
Kansas	91,457,908	23,355	68,850	34,377	326.33	110.70
Kentucky	139,613,730	60,190	161,783	108,246	193.30	71.91
Lousiana	161,539,760	00,249	241,585	170,170	167.75	55.72
Maine	83,957,152	20,078	58,435	36,392	348.46	119.73
Maryland	249,697,762	69,541	191,950	124,249	299.22	108.40
Massachusetts	455,463,602	87,341	235,234	150,655	434.57	161.35
Michigan	1,247,808,948	220,191	672,678	430,649	472.25	154.58
Minnesota	322,312,406	53,756	160,093	100,849	499.65	167.77
Mississippi	73,956,601	53,334	159,804	114,874	115.56	38.57
Missouri	208,567,215	66,514	200,523	131,110	261.31	86.68
Montana	36,830,297	8,840	25,825	16,483	347.18	118.85
Nebraska	61,495,050	16,142	47,059	31,241	317.47	108.90
Nevada	15,663,594	5,471	15,883	10,762	238.59	82.18
New Hampshire	19,596,457	4,966	13,097	8,641	328.85	124.69
New Jersey	503,592,530	121,278	355,655	239,869	346.03	118.00
New Mexico	51,344,488	118,104	51,529	34,603	236.34	83.04
New York	2,098,575,562	368,361	1,099,520	718,202	474.76	159.05
North Carolina	183,127,989	66,864	174,967	118,865	228.23	87.22
North Dakota	19,895,304	4,843	13,427	8,897	342.34	123.48
Ohio	803,514,972	227,315	676,733	428,647	294.57	98.95
Oklahoma	100,201,837	30,223	87,860	60,918	276.29	95.04
Oregon	120,410,237	30,359	82,036	53,998	330.52	122.31
Pennsylvania	773,536,782	190,816	580,193	376,527	337.82	111.10
Puerto Rico	64,868,152	53,719	176,269	119,643	100.63	30.67
Rhode Island	78,819,337	16,035	44,439	28,720	409.61	147.80
South Carolina	103,153,952	46,116	130,272	90,808	186.40	65.99
South Dakota	19,485,200	6,161	17,346	12,018	263.55	93.61
Tennessee	[illegible]	59,080	161,635	109,392	140.90	51.50
Texas	280,511,165	136,333	413,455	291,335	171.46	56.54
Utah	54,482,867	13,384	39,788	25,598	339.23	114.11
Vermont	39,450,503	7,629	21,871	13,579	430.91	150.31
Virgin Islands	2,505,200	1,253	4,311	3,202	171.90	49.97
Virginia	178,822,935	58,500	153,393	102,748	254.74	97.15
Washington	363,552,617	70,687	197,611	125,735	428.59	153.31
West Virginia	109,001,393	36,514	115,144	69,692	248.76	78.89
Wisconsin	591,983,238	98,616	300,945	189,181	500.24	163.92
Wyoming	15,754,659	4,001	11,103	7,243	328.15	118.25
U.S. Total	**$15,854,338,285**	**3,747,531**	**10,996,505**	**7,295,601**	**$352.55**	**$120.15**

(1) Total assistance payments include basic, up, grant diversions and home repairs.

Welfare Recipients and Payments, 1955-1986

Category		1955, Dec.	1965, Dec.	1970, Dec.	1975, Dec.[1]	1980, Dec.	1985, Dec.	1986, Dec.
Old age:	Recipients	2,538,000	2,087,000	2,082,000	2,307,105	1,807,776	1,504,469	1,473,428
	Total amt.	$127,003,000	$131,674,000	$161,642,000	$209,777,000	$221,303,000	$247,133,000	$255,877,000
	Avg. amt.	$50.05	$63.10	$77.65	$90.93	$128.20	$164.26	$173.66
AFDC:	Recipients	2,192,000	4,396,000	9,659,000	11,389,000	11,101,556	10,900[2]	11,043[2]
	Total amt.	$51,472,000	$144,355,000	$485,877,000	$824,648,000	$1,105,777,000	$1,289.80[3]	$1,349.30[3]
	Avg. amt.	$23.50	$32.85	$50.30	$72.40	$99.61	$118.33	$122.19
Blind:	Recipients	104,000	85,100	81,000	74,489	78,401	82,220	83,115
	Total amt.	$5,803,000	$6,922,000	$8,446,000	$10,918,000	$16,381,000	$22,555,000	$23,877,000
	Avg. amt.	$55.55	$81.35	$104.35	$146.57	$213.23	$274.32	$287.27
Disabled:	Recipients	241,000	557,000	935,000	1,932,681	2,255,840	2,551,332	2,712,641
	Total amt.	$11,750,000	$37,035,000	$91,325,000	$272,800,000	$444,322,000	$665,774,000	$763,988,000
	Avg. amt.	$48.75	$66.50	$97.65	$141.15	$197.90	$260.95	$281.63

(1) Administration of the public assistance programs of Old-age Assistance, Aid to the Blind, and Aid to the Disabled was transferred to the Social Security Administration by Public Law 92-603 effective 1/1/74. (2) Thousands. (3) Millions.

U.S. Places of 5,000 or More Population—With ZIP and Area Codes

Source: U.S. Bureau of the Census; U.S. Postal Service; N.Y. Telephone Co.

The listings below show the official urban population of the United States. "Urban population" is defined as all persons living in (a) places of 5,000 inhabitants or more, incorporated as cities, villages, boroughs (except Alaska), and towns (except in New England, New York, New Jersey, Pennsylvania and Wisconsin), but excluding those persons living in the rural portions of extended cities; (b) unincorporated places of 5,000 inhabitants or more; and (c) other territory, incorporated or unincorporated, included in urbanized areas.

The non-urban portion of an extended city contains one or more areas, each at least 5 square miles in extent and with a population density of less than 100 persons per square mile. The area or areas constitute at least 25 percent of the legal city's land area of a total of 25 square miles or more.

In New England, New York, New Jersey, Pennsylvania, and Wisconsin, minor civil divisions called "towns" often include rural areas and one or more urban areas. Only the urban areas of these "towns" are included here, except in the case of New England where entire town populations, which may include some rural population, are shown; these towns are indicated by italics. Boroughs in Alaska may contain one or more urban areas which are included here. Population in Hawaii is counted by county subdivisions.

(u) means place is unincorporated.

The ZIP Code of each place appears before the name of that place, if it is obtainable. Telephone Area Code appears in parentheses after the name of the state or, if a state has more than one number, after the name of the place.

CAUTION—Where an asterisk (*) appears before the ZIP Code, ask your local postmaster for the correct ZIP Code for a specific address within the place listed.

Alabama (205)

ZIP code	Place	1980	1970
35007	Alabaster	7,079	2,642
35950	Albertville	12,039	9,963
35010	Alexander City	13,807	12,358
36420	Andalusia	10,415	10,092
36201	Anniston	29,135	31,533
35016	Arab	6,053	4,399
35611	Athens	14,558	14,360
36502	Atmore	8,789	8,293
35954	Attalla	7,737	7,510
36830	Auburn	28,471	22,767
36507	Bay Minette	7,455	6,727
35020	Bessemer	31,729	33,428
*35203	Birmingham	284,413	300,910
35957	Boaz	7,151	5,635
36426	Brewton	6,680	6,747
35020	Brighton	5,308	2,277
35215	Center Point(u)	23,317	15,675
36611	Chickasaw	7,402	8,447
35044	Childersburg	5,084	4,831
35045	Clanton	5,832	5,868
35055	Cullman	13,084	12,601
35601	Decatur	42,002	38,044
36732	Demopolis	7,678	7,651
36301	Dothan	48,750	36,733
36330	Enterprise	18,033	15,591
36027	Eufaula	12,097	9,102
35064	Fairfield	13,242	14,369
36532	Fairhope	7,286	5,720
35555	Fayette	5,287	4,568
35630	Florence	37,029	34,031
35214	Forestdale(u)	10,814	6,091
35967	Fort Payne	11,485	8,435
36360	Fort Rucker(u)	8,932	14,242
35068	Fultondale	6,217	5,163
*35901	Gadsden	47,565	53,928
35071	Gardendale	8,005	6,537
36037	Greenville	7,807	8,033
35976	Guntersville	7,041	6,491
35565	Haleyville	5,306	4,190
35640	Hartselle	8,858	7,355
35209	Homewood	21,271	21,245
35226	Hoover	18,996	688
35020	Hueytown	13,452	7,095
*35804	Huntsville	142,513	139,282
35210	Irondale	6,521	3,166
36545	Jackson	6,073	5,957
36265	Jacksonville	9,735	7,715
35501	Jasper	11,894	10,798
36863	Lanett	8,922	6,908
35094	Leeds	8,638	6,991
35228	Midfield	6,182	6,621
*36601	Mobile	200,452	190,026
36460	Monroeville	5,674	4,846
*36104	Montgomery	177,857	133,386
35223	Mountain Brook	17,400	19,474
35660	Muscle Shoals	8,911	6,907
35476	Northport	14,291	9,435
36801	Opelika	21,896	19,027
36467	Opp	7,204	6,493
36203	Oxford	8,939	4,361
36360	Ozark	13,188	13,555
35124	Pelham	6,759	931
35125	Pell City	6,616	5,602
36867	Phenix City	26,928	25,281
36272	Piedmont	5,544	5,063
35127	Pleasant Grove	7,102	5,090
36067	Prattville	18,647	13,116
36610	Prichard	39,541	41,578
35901	Rainbow City	6,299	3,099
35809	Redstone Arsenal(u)	5,728	....
36274	Roanoke	5,809	5,251
35653	Russellville	8,195	7,814
36201	Saks(u)	11,118	....
36571	Saraland	9,833	7,840
35768	Scottsboro	14,758	9,324
36701	Selma	26,684	27,379
36701	Selmont-West Selmont(u)	5,255	2,270
35660	Sheffield	11,903	13,115
35901	Southside	5,141	983
35150	Sylacauga	12,708	12,255
35160	Talladega	19,128	17,662
35217	Tarrant City	8,148	6,835
36582	Theodore(u)	6,392	....
36619	Tillman's Corner(u)	15,941	....
36081	Troy	13,124	11,482
35401	Tuscaloosa	75,143	65,773
35674	Tuscumbia	9,137	8,828
36083	Tuskegee	12,716	11,028
35216	Vestavia Hills	15,733	12,250
36201	West End-Cobb(u)	5,189	5,515

Alaska (907)

ZIP code	Place	1980	1970
*99502	Anchorage	174,431	48,081
99702	Eielson AFB(u)	5,232	6,149
99701	Fairbanks	22,645	14,771
99801	Juneau	19,528	6,050
99611	Kenai Peninsula borough	25,282	16,586
99901	Ketchikan	7,198	6,994
99835	Sitka	7,803	3,370

Arizona (602)

ZIP code	Place	1980	1970
85321	Ajo(u)	5,189	5,881
85220	Apache Junction	9,935	2,443
85323	Avondale	8,134	6,626
85603	Bisbee	7,154	8,328
86430	Bullhead City-Riviera(u)	10,364	....
85222	Casa Grande	14,971	10,536
85224	Chandler	29,673	13,763
85228	Coolidge	6,851	5,314
85707	Davis-Monthan AFB(u)	6,279	....
85607	Douglas	13,058	12,462
85205	Dreamland-VeldaRose(u)	5,969	....
85231	Eloy	6,240	5,381
86001	Flagstaff	34,641	26,117
85613	Fort Huachuca(u)	NA	6,659
85234	Gilbert	5,717	1,971
*85301	Glendale	96,988	36,228
85501	Globe	6,886	7,333
85614	Green Valley(u)	7,999	....
86025	Holbrook	5,785	4,759
86401	Kingman	9,257	7,312
86403	Lake Havasu City	15,737	4,111
85301	Luke(u)	NA	5,047
*85201	Mesa	152,404	63,049
85621	Nogales	15,683	8,946
86040	Page(u)	NA	1,439
85253	Paradise Valley	10,832	6,637
85345	Peoria	12,171	4,792
*85026	Phoenix	789,704	584,303
86301	Prescott	19,865	13,631
85546	Safford	7,010	5,493

ZIP code	Place	1980	1970
85631	San Manuel(u)	5,443	....
*85251	Scottsdale	88,622	67,823
85635	Sierra Vista	25,968	6,689
85350	Somerton	3,969	2,225
85713	South Tucson	6,554	6,220
85351	Sun City(u)	40,505	13,670
*85282	Tempe	106,919	63,550
86045	Tuba City(u)	5,045	....
*85726	Tucson	330,537	262,933
85364	West Yuma(u)	NA	5,552
86047	Winslow	7,921	8,066
85364	Yuma	42,481	29,007

Arkansas (501)

ZIP code	Place	1980	1970
71923	Arkadelphia	10,005	9,841
72501	Batesville	8,447	7,209
72015	Benton	17,437	16,499
72712	Bentonville	8,756	5,508
72315	Blytheville	24,314	24,752
71701	Camden	15,356	15,147
72830	Clarksville	5,237	4,616
72032	Conway	20,375	15,510
71635	Crossett	6,706	6,191
71639	Dumas	6,091	4,600
71730	El Dorado	26,685	25,283
72701	Fayetteville	36,604	30,729
71742	Fordyce	5,175	4,837
72335	Forrest City	13,803	12,521
72901	Fort Smith	71,384	62,802
72601	Harrison	9,567	7,239
72342	Helena	9,598	10,415
71801	Hope	10,290	8,830
71901	Hot Springs	35,166	35,631
72076	Jacksonville	27,589	19,832
72401	Jonesboro	31,530	27,050
*72201	Little Rock	150,159	132,483
71753	Magnolia	11,909	11,303
72104	Malvern	10,163	8,739
72360	Marianna	6,220	6,196
71654	McGehee	5,671	4,683
71953	Mena	5,154	4,530
71655	Monticello	8,259	5,085
72110	Morrilton	7,355	6,814
72653	Mountain Home	7,447	3,936
72112	Newport	8,339	7,725
*72114	North Little Rock	64,388	60,040
72370	Osceola	8,881	7,892
72450	Paragould	15,214	10,639
71601	Pine Bluff	56,576	57,389
72455	Pocahontas	5,995	4,544
72756	Rogers	17,429	11,050
72801	Russellville	14,518	11,750
72143	Searcy	13,612	9,040
72116	Sherwood	10,423	2,754
72761	Siloam Springs	7,940	6,009
72764	Springdale	23,458	16,783
72160	Stuttgart	10,941	10,477
75502	Texarkana	21,459	21,682
72472	Trumann	6,395	6,023
72956	Van Buren	12,020	8,373
71671	Warren	7,646	6,433
72390	West Helena	11,367	11,007
72301	West Memphis	28,138	26,070
72396	Wynne	7,927	6,696

California

ZIP code	Place	Area code	1980	1970
94501	Alameda	(415)	63,852	70,968
94507	Alamo(u)	(415)	8,505	14,050
94706	Albany	(415)	15,130	15,561
*91802	Alhambra	(818)	64,767	62,125
90249	Alondra Park(u)	(213)	12,096	12,193
92001	Alpine(u)	(619)	5,368	1,570
91001	Altadena(u)	(818)	40,510	42,415
95116	Alum Rock(u)	(408)	17,471	18,355
94590	American Canyon(u)	(707)	5,712	....
*92803	Anaheim	(714)	219,494	166,408
96007	Anderson	(916)	7,381	5,492
94509	Antioch	(415)	43,559	28,060
92307	Apple Valley(u)	(714)	14,305	6,702
95003	Aptos(u)	(408)	7,039	8,704
91006	Arcadia	(818)	45,993	45,138
95521	Arcata	(707)	12,849	8,985
95825	Arden-Arcade(u)	(916)	87,570	82,492
93420	Arroyo Grande	(805)	11,290	7,454
90701	Artesia	(213)	14,301	14,757
93203	Arvin	(805)	6,863	5,199
94577	Ashland(u)	(415)	13,893	14,810
93422	Atascadero	(805)	15,930	10,290
94025	Atherton	(415)	7,797	8,085
95301	Atwater	(209)	17,530	11,640
95603	Auburn	(916)	7,540	6,570
92505	August(u)	(714)	6,350	6,293
91746	Avocado Heights(u)	(818)	11,721	9,810
91702	Azusa	(818)	29,380	25,217
*93302	Bakersfield	(805)	105,611	69,515
91706	Baldwin Park	(818)	50,554	47,285
92220	Banning	(714)	14,020	12,034
92311	Barstow	(619)	17,690	17,442
93402	Baywood-Los Osos(u)	(805)	10,933	3,487
95903	Beale AFB East(u)	(916)	6,329	7,029
92223	Beaumont	(714)	6,818	5,484
90201	Bell	(213)	25,450	21,836
90706	Bellflower	(213)	53,441	52,334
90201	Bell Gardens	(213)	34,117	29,308
94002	Belmont	(415)	24,505	23,538
94510	Benicia	(707)	15,376	7,349
95005	Ben Lomond(u)	(408)	7,238	2,793
*94704	Berkeley	(415)	103,328	114,091
*90213	Beverly Hills	(213)	32,646	33,416
92314	Big Bear(u)	(714)	11,151	5,268
92316	Bloomington(u)	(714)	6,674	11,957
92225	Blythe	(619)	6,805	7,047
92002	Bonita(u)	(714)	6,257	....
95006	Boulder Creek(u)	(408)	5,662	1,806
92227	Brawley	(619)	14,946	13,746
92621	Brea	(714)	27,913	18,447
95605	Broderick-Bryte(u)	(916)	10,194	12,782
*90620	Buena Park	(714)	64,165	63,646
*91505	Burbank	(818)	84,625	88,871
94010	Burlingame	(415)	26,173	27,320
92231	Calexico	(714)	14,412	10,625
93725	Calwa(u)	(209)	6,640	5,191
93010	Camarillo	(805)	37,732	19,219
93010	Camarillo Heights(u)	(805)	6,341	5,892
95682	Cameron Park(u)	(916)	5,607	....
95008	Campbell	(408)	26,910	23,797
91351	Canyon Country(u)	(805)	15,728	
92055	Camp Pendleton South(u)	(714)	7,952	13,692
92624	Capistrano Beach(u)	(714)	6,168	4,149
95010	Capitola	(408)	9,095	5,080
92007	Cardiff-by-the-Sea(u)	(714)	10,054	5,724
92008	Carlsbad	(619)	35,490	14,944
95608	Carmichael(u)	(916)	43,108	37,625
93013	Carpinteria	(805)	10,835	6,982
90744	Carson	(213)	81,221	71,150
92077	Casa De Oro-Mt. Helix(u)	(714)	19,651	....
92010	Castle Park-Otay(u)	(714)	21,049	15,445
94546	Castro Valley(u)	(415)	44,011	44,760
95307	Ceres	(209)	13,281	6,029
90701	Cerritos	(213)	52,756	15,856
91724	Charter Oak(u)	(818)	6,840	....
94541	Cherryland(u)	(415)	9,425	9,969
92223	Cherry Valley(u)	(714)	5,012	3,165
95926	Chico	(916)	26,716	19,580
95926	Chico North(u)	(916)	11,739	6,656
95926	Chico West(u)	(916)	6,378	4,787
91710	Chino	(714)	40,165	20,411
93610	Chowchilla	(209)	5,122	4,349
*92010	Chula Vista	(619)	83,927	67,901
95610	Citrus(u)	(916)	12,450	....
95610	Citrus Heights(u)	(916)	85,911	21,700
91711	Claremont	(714)	31,028	24,776
93612	Clovis	(209)	33,021	13,856
92236	Coachella	(714)	9,129	8,353
93210	Coalinga	(209)	6,593	6,161
92324	Colton	(714)	27,419	20,016
90022	Commerce	(213)	10,509	10,635
*90220	Compton	(213)	81,350	78,547
*94520	Concord	(415)	103,763	85,164
93212	Corcoran	(209)	6,454	5,249
91720	Corona	(714)	37,791	27,519
92118	Coronado	(619)	18,790	20,020
94925	Corte Madera	(415)	8,074	8,464
*92626	Costa Mesa	(714)	82,291	72,660
	Country Club(u)	(209)	9,585	....
*91722	Covina	(818)	32,746	30,395
92325	Crestline(u)	(714)	6,715	....
90201	Cudahy	(213)	18,275	16,998
90230	Culver City	(213)	38,139	34,451
95014	Cupertino	(408)	34,297	17,895
90630	Cypress	(714)	40,738	31,569
*94017	Daly City	(415)	78,519	66,922
94526	Danville(u)	(415)	26,446	....
92629	Dana Point(u)	(714)	10,602	4,745
95616	Davis	(916)	36,640	23,488
90250	Del Aire(u)	(213)	8,487	11,930
93215	Delano	(805)	16,491	14,559
92014	Del Mar	(619)	5,017	3,956
92240	Desert Hot Springs	(619)	5,941	2,738
91765	Diamond Bar(u)	(714)	28,045	10,576
93618	Dinuba	(209)	9,907	7,917
95620	Dixon	(916)	7,541	4,432
*90241	Downey	(213)	82,602	88,573
91010	Duarte	(818)	16,766	14,981
94566	Dublin(u)	(415)	13,496	13,641
90220	East Compton(u)	(213)	6,435	5,853
92343	East Hemet(u)	(714)	14,712	8,598
90638	East La Mirada(u)	(213)	9,688	12,339
90022	East Los Angeles(u)	(213)	110,017	104,881
94303	East Palo Alto	(415)	18,191	18,727
93257	East Porterville(u)	(209)	5,218	4,042
92508	Edgemont(u)	(714)	5,215	....
93523	Edwards AFB(u)	(805)	8,554	10,331
*92020	El Cajon	(619)	73,892	52,273
92243	El Centro	(619)	23,996	19,272
94530	El Cerrito	(415)	22,731	25,190
95624	Elk Grove(u)	(916)	10,959	3,721

ZIP code	Place		1980	1970
*91734	El Monte	(818)	79,494	69,892
93446	El Paso de Robles	(213)	9,163	7,168
93030	El Rio(u)	(805)	5,674	6,173
90245	El Segundo	(213)	13,752	15,620
94803	El Sobrante(u)	(415)	10,535	....
92630	El Toro(u)	(714)	38,153	8,654
92709	El Toro Station(u)	(714)	7,632	6,970
92024	Encinitas(u)	(619)	10,796	5,375
*92025	Escondido	(619)	62,480	36,792
95501	Eureka	(707)	24,153	24,337
93221	Exeter	(209)	5,619	4,475
94930	Fairfax	(415)	7,391	7,661
94533	Fairfield	(707)	58,099	44,146
95628	Fair Oaks(u)	(916)	20,235	11,256
92028	Fallbrook(u)	(619)	14,041	6,945
93223	Farmersville	(209)	5,544	3,456
93015	Fillmore	(805)	9,602	6,285
90001	Florence-Graham(u)	(213)	48,662	42,900
95828	Florin(u)	(916)	16,523	9,646
95630	Folsom	(916)	11,003	5,810
92335	Fontana	(714)	36,804	20,673
95841	Foothill Farms(u)	(916)	13,700	....
95437	Fort Bragg	(707)	5,019	4,455
95540	Fortuna	(707)	7,591	4,203
94404	Foster City	(415)	23,287	9,522
92708	Fountain Valley	(714)	55,080	31,886
95019	Freedom(u)	(408)	6,416	5,563
*94536	Fremont	(415)	131,945	100,869
*93706	Fresno	(209)	217,491	165,655
*92631	Fullerton	(714)	102,246	85,987
95632	Galt	(209)	5,514	3,200
*90247	Gardena	(213)	45,165	41,021
95205	Garden Acres(u)	(213)	7,361	7,870
*92640	Garden Grove	(714)	123,351	121,155
92392	George AFB(u)	(714)	7,061	7,404
95020	Gilroy	(408)	21,641	12,684
92509	Glen Avon(u)	(714)	8,444	5,759
*91209	Glendale	(818)	139,060	132,664
91740	Glendora	(818)	38,500	32,143
92324	Grand Terrace	(714)	8,498	5,901
95945	Grass Valley	(916)	6,697	5,149
93308	Greenacres(u)	(805)	5,381	2,116
93433	Grover City	(805)	8,827	5,939
91745	Hacienda Heights	(818)	49,422	35,969
94019	Half Moon Bay	(415)	7,282	4,023
93230	Hanford	(209)	20,958	15,179
90716	Hawaiian Gardens	(213)	10,548	9,052
90250	Hawthorne	(213)	56,437	53,304
*94544	Hayward	(415)	93,585	93,058
95448	Healdsburg	(707)	7,217	5,438
92343	Hemet	(714)	22,531	12,252
94547	Hercules	(415)	5,963	252
90254	Hermosa Beach	(213)	18,070	17,412
92345	Hesperia(u)	(714)	13,540	4,592
92346	Highland(u)	(714)	10,908	12,669
94010	Hillsborough	(415)	10,372	8,753
95023	Hollister	(408)	11,488	7,663
91720	Home Gardens(u)	(714)	5,783	5,116
*92647	Huntington Beach	(714)	170,505	115,960
90255	Huntington Park	(213)	45,932	33,744
92032	Imperial Beach	(619)	22,689	20,244
92201	Indio	(619)	21,611	14,459
*90306	Inglewood	(213)	94,162	89,985
*92711	Irvine	(714)	62,134	7,381
94707	Kensington(u)	(415)	5,342	5,823
93930	King City	(408)	5,495	3,717
93631	Kingsburg	(209)	5,115	3,843
91011	La Canada-Flintridge	(818)	20,153	20,714
91214	La Crescenta-Montrose(u)	(818)	16,531	19,620
90045	Ladera Heights(u)	(213)	6,647	6,079
94549	Lafayette	(415)	20,837	20,484
*92651	Laguna Beach	(714)	17,858	14,550
92653	Laguna Hills(u)	(714)	33,600	13,676
92677	Laguna Niguel(u)	(714)	12,237	4,644
90631	La Habra	(213)	45,232	41,350
92352	Lake Arrowhead(u)	(714)	6,272	2,682
92040	Lakeside(u)	(714)	23,921	11,991
92330	Lake Elsinore	(714)	5,982	3,530
*90714	Lakewood	(213)	74,511	83,025
92041	La Mesa	(619)	50,342	39,178
90638	La Mirada	(213)	40,986	30,808
93241	Lamont(u)	(805)	9,616	7,007
93534	Lancaster	(805)	48,027	32,728
90624	La Palma	(213)	15,663	9,687
91747	La Puente	(818)	30,882	31,092
	La Riviera(u)	(916)	10,906	....
94939	Larkspur	(415)	11,064	10,487
91750	La Verne	(714)	23,508	12,965
90260	Lawndale	(213)	23,460	24,825
92045	Lemon Grove	(619)	20,780	19,794
93245	Lemoore	(209)	8,832	4,219
93245	Lemoore Station(u)	(209)	5,888	9,210
90304	Lennox(u)	(213)	18,445	16,121
92024	Leucadia(u)	(714)	9,478	....
95207	Lincoln Village(u)	(916)	7,067	6,112
95901	Linda(u)	(916)	10,225	7,112
93247	Lindsay	(209)	6,936	5,206
95062	Live Oak(u) (Santa Cruz)	(916)	11,482	6,443
94550	Livermore	(415)	48,349	37,703
95334	Livingston	(209)	5,326	2,588
95240	Lodi	(209)	35,221	28,691
92354	Loma Linda	(714)	10,694	7,651
90717	Lomita	(213)	17,191	19,784
93436	Lompoc	(805)	26,267	25,284
*90801	Long Beach	(213)	361,498	358,879
90720	Los Alamitos	(213)	11,529	11,346
94022	Los Altos	(415)	25,769	25,062
94022	Los Altos Hills	(415)	7,421	6,871
*90052	Los Angeles	(818)	2,968,528	2,811,801
93635	Los Banos	(209)	10,341	9,188
95030	Los Gatos	(408)	26,593	22,613
94903	Lucas Valley-Marinwood(u)	(415)	6,409	....
90262	Lynwood	(213)	48,289	43,354
93637	Madera	(209)	21,732	16,044
90266	Manhattan Beach	(213)	31,542	35,352
95336	Manteca	(209)	24,925	13,845
93933	Marina	(408)	20,647	8,343
90291	Marina Del Rey(u)	(213)	8,065	....
94553	Martinez	(415)	22,582	16,506
95901	Marysville	(916)	9,898	9,353
95655	Mather AFB(u)	(916)	5,245	7,027
91016	Mayflower Village(u)	(818)	5,017	....
90270	Maywood	(213)	21,810	16,996
93250	Mc Farland	(805)	5,151	4,177
95521	McKinleyville(u)	(707)	7,772	....
93023	Meiners Oaks-Mira Monte(u)	(805)	9,512	7,025
93640	Mendota	(209)	5,038	2,705
94025	Menlo Park	(415)	26,438	26,826
95340	Merced	(209)	36,423	22,670
94030	Millbrae	(415)	20,058	20,920
94941	Mill Valley	(415)	12,967	12,942
95035	Milpitas	(408)	37,820	26,561
91752	Mira Loma(u)	(714)	8,707	8,482
92675	Mission Viejo(u)	(714)	48,384	11,933
*95350	Modesto	(209)	106,963	61,712
91016	Monrovia	(818)	30,531	30,562
91763	Montclair	(714)	22,628	22,546
90640	Montebello	(213)	52,929	42,807
93940	Monterey	(408)	27,558	26,302
91754	Monterey Park	(818)	54,338	49,166
94556	Moraga	(415)	15,014	14,205
95037	Morgan Hill	(408)	17,060	5,579
93442	Morro Bay	(805)	9,064	7,109
*94042	Mountain View	(415)	58,655	54,132
92405	Muscoy(u)	(714)	6,188	7,091
94558	Napa	(707)	50,879	36,103
92050	National City	(619)	48,772	43,184
94560	Newark	(415)	32,126	27,153
91321	Newhall(u)	(805)	12,029	9,651
*92660	Newport Beach	(714)	63,475	49,582
93444	Nipomo(u)	(805)	5,247	3,642
91760	Norco	(714)	19,732	14,511
95603	North Auburn(u)	(916)	7,619	....
94025	North Fair Oaks(u)	(415)	10,294	9,740
95660	North Highlands(u)	(916)	37,825	31,854
90650	Norwalk	(213)	84,901	90,164
94947	Novato	(415)	43,916	31,006
95361	Oakdale	(209)	8,474	6,594
*94615	Oakland	(415)	339,337	361,561
92054	Oceanside	(619)	76,698	40,494
93308	Oildale(u)	(805)	23,382	20,879
93023	Ojai	(805)	6,816	5,591
95961	Olivehurst(u)	(916)	8,929	8,100
*91761	Ontario	(714)	88,820	64,118
95060	Opal Cliffs(u)	(408)	5,041	5,425
*92667	Orange	(714)	91,450	77,365
95662	Orangevale(u)	(916)	20,585	16,493
94563	Orinda (u)	(415)	16,825	6,790
95965	Oroville	(916)	8,683	7,536
93030	Oxnard	(805)	108,195	71,225
94044	Pacifica	(415)	36,866	36,020
93950	Pacific Grove	(408)	15,755	13,505
93550	Palmdale	(805)	12,277	8,511
92260	Palm Desert	(619)	11,801	6,171
92262	Palm Springs	(619)	32,359	20,936
94302	Palo Alto	(415)	55,225	56,040
90274	Palos Verdes Estates	(213)	14,376	13,631
95969	Paradise	(916)	22,571	14,539
90723	Paramount	(213)	36,407	34,734
95823	Parkway-Sacramento So.(u)	(916)	26,815	28,574
*91109	Pasadena	(818)	118,072	112,951
92370	Perris	(714)	6,740	4,228
94952	Petaluma	(707)	33,834	24,870
90660	Pico Rivera	(213)	53,387	54,170
94611	Piedmont	(415)	10,498	10,917
94564	Pinole	(415)	14,253	13,266
93449	Pismo Beach	(805)	5,364	4,043
94565	Pittsburg	(415)	33,465	21,423
92670	Placentia	(714)	35,041	21,948
95667	Placerville	(916)	6,739	5,416
94523	Pleasant Hill	(415)	25,547	24,610
94566	Pleasanton	(415)	35,160	18,328
91766	Pomona	(714)	92,742	87,384
93257	Porterville	(209)	19,707	12,602
93041	Port Hueneme	(805)	17,803	14,295
92064	Poway(u)	(619)	32,263	9,422
93534	Quartz Hill(u)	(213)	7,421	4,935
92065	Ramona(u)	(714)	8,173	3,554
95670	Rancho Cordova(u)	(916)	42,881	30,451
91730	Rancho Cucamonga	(714)	55,250	19,484

ZIP code	Place		1980	1970
92270	Rancho Mirage	(714)	6,281	2,767
90274	Rancho Palos Verdes	(213)	35,227	33,285
96080	Red Bluff	(916)	9,490	7,676
96001	Redding	(916)	42,103	16,659
92373	Redlands	(714)	43,619	36,355
*90277	Redondo Beach	(213)	57,102	57,451
*94064	Redwood City	(415)	54,965	55,686
93654	Reedley	(209)	11,071	8,131
92376	Rialto	(714)	37,862	28,370
*94802	Richmond	(415)	74,676	79,043
93555	Ridgecrest	(619)	15,929	7,629
95003	Rio Del Mar(u)	(408)	7,067	....
95673	Rio Linda(u)	(916)	7,359	7,524
95367	Riverbank	(209)	5,695	3,949
*92502	Riverside	(714)	170,591	140,089
95677	Rocklin	(916)	7,344	3,039
94572	Rodeo(u)	(415)	8,286	5,356
94928	Rohnert Park	(707)	22,965	6,133
90274	Rolling Hills Estates	(213)	9,412	6,735
95401	Roseland(u)	(707)	7,915	5,105
91770	Rosemead	(818)	42,604	40,972
95826	Rosemont(u)	(916)	18,888	....
95678	Roseville	(916)	24,347	18,221
90720	Rossmoor(u)	(213)	10,457	12,922
91745	Rowland Heights(u)	(818)	28,252	16,881
92509	Rubidoux(u)	(714)	16,763	13,969
*95813	Sacramento	(916)	275,741	257,105
93901	Salinas	(408)	80,479	58,896
94960	San Anselmo	(415)	12,067	13,031
*92403	San Bernardino	(714)	118,794	106,869
94066	San Bruno	(415)	35,417	36,254
...	San Buenaventura (*see Ventura*)	(805)		
94070	San Carlos	(415)	24,710	26,053
92672	San Clemente	(714)	27,325	17,063
*92109	San Diego	(619)	875,538	697,471
91773	San Dimas	(714)	24,014	15,692
*91340	San Fernando	(818)	17,731	16,571
*94101	San Francisco	(415)	678,974	715,674
91776	San Gabriel	(818)	30,072	29,336
93657	Sanger	(209)	12,558	10,088
92383	San Jacinto	(714)	7,098	4,385
*95101	San Jose	(408)	629,400	459,913
92375	San Juan Capistrano	(714)	18,959	3,781
94577	San Leandro	(415)	63,952	68,698
94580	San Lorenzo(u)	(415)	20,545	24,633
93401	San Luis Obispo	(805)	34,252	28,036
92069	San Marcos	(619)	17,479	3,896
91108	San Marino	(818)	13,307	14,177
*94402	San Mateo	(415)	77,640	78,991
94806	San Pablo	(415)	19,750	21,461
*94901	San Rafael	(415)	44,700	38,977
94583	San Ramon(u)	(415)	22,356	4,084
*92711	Santa Ana	(714)	204,023	155,710
*93102	Santa Barbara	(805)	74,542	70,215
*95050	Santa Clara	(408)	87,700	86,118
95060	Santa Cruz	(408)	41,483	32,076
90670	Santa Fe Springs	(213)	14,559	14,750
93454	Santa Maria	(805)	39,685	32,749
*90406	Santa Monica	(213)	88,314	88,289
93060	Santa Paula	(805)	20,658	18,001
*95402	Santa Rosa	(707)	83,205	50,006
92071	Santee(u)	(619)	47,080	21,107
95070	Saratoga	(408)	29,261	26,810
91350	Saugus-Bouquet Canyon(u)	(805)	16,283	....
94965	Sausalito	(415)	7,090	6,158
95066	Scotts Valley	(408)	6,891	3,621
90740	Seal Beach	(213)	25,975	24,441
93955	Seaside	(408)	36,567	36,883
95472	Sebastopol	(707)	5,500	3,993
93662	Selma	(209)	10,942	7,459
93263	Shafter	(805)	7,010	5,327
91024	Sierra Madre	(818)	10,837	12,140
90806	Signal Hill	(213)	5,734	5,588
93065	Simi Valley	(805)	77,500	59,832
92075	Solana Beach(u)	(714)	13,047	5,023
93960	Soledad	(408)	5,928	4,222
95476	Sonoma	(707)	6,054	4,259
95073	Soquel(u)	(408)	6,212	5,795
91733	South El Monte	(213)	16,623	13,443
90280	South Gate	(213)	66,784	56,909
92677	South Laguna(u)	(714)	6,013	2,566
95705	South Lake Tahoe	(916)	20,681	12,921
95350	South Modesto(u)	(209)	12,492	7,889
95965	South Oroville(u)	(916)	7,246	4,111
91030	South Pasadena	(818)	22,681	22,979
94080	South San Francisco	(415)	49,393	46,646
91770	South San Gabriel(u)	(213)	5,421	5,051
91744	South San Jose Hills(u)	(213)	16,049	12,386
90605	South Whittier(u)	(213)	43,815	46,641
95991	South Yuba(u)	(916)	7,530	5,352
*92077	Spring Valley(u)	(714)	40,191	29,742
94305	Stanford(u)	(415)	11,045	8,691
90680	Stanton	(714)	21,144	18,186
*95204	Stockton	(209)	148,283	109,963
94585	Suisun City	(707)	11,087	2,917
92381	Sun City(u)	(714)	8,460	5,519
92388	Sunnymead(u)	(714)	11,554	6,708
*94086	Sunnyvale	(408)	106,618	95,976
96130	Susanville	(916)	6,520	6,608
93268	Taft	(805)	5,316	4,285
94806	Tara Hills-Montalvin Manor(u)	(415)	9,471	....
94941	Tamalpais-Homestead Valley(u)	(415)	8,511	....
91780	Temple City	(818)	28,972	31,034
*91360	Thousand Oaks	(805)	77,797	35,873
94920	Tiburon	(415)	6,685	6,209
*90510	Torrance	(213)	131,497	134,968
95396	Tracy	(209)	18,428	14,724
93274	Tulare	(209)	22,530	16,235
95380	Turlock	(209)	26,291	13,992
92680	Tustin	(714)	32,248	22,313
92705	Tustin-Foothills(u)	(714)	26,174	26,699
92277	Twentynine Palms(u)	(619)	7,465	5,667
92278	Twentynine Palms Base(u)	(619)	7,079	5,647
95482	Ukiah	(707)	12,035	10,095
94587	Union City	(415)	39,406	14,724
91786	Upland	(714)	47,647	32,551
95688	Vacaville	(707)	43,367	21,690
91355	Valencia(u)	(805)	12,163	4,243
91744	Valinda(u)	(818)	18,700	18,837
94590	Vallejo	(707)	80,188	71,710
92343	Valle Vista(u)	(714)	5,474	....
93437	Vandenberg AFB(u)	(805)	8,136	13,193
93436	Vandenberg Village(u)	(805)	5,839	....
*93001	Ventura	(805)	73,774	57,964
92392	Victorville	(619)	14,220	10,845
90043	View Park-Windsor Hills(u)	(213)	12,101	12,268
92667	Villa Park	(714)	7,137	2,723
94553	Vine Hill-Pacheco(u)	(415)	6,129	....
93277	Visalia	(209)	49,729	27,130
92083	Vista	(619)	35,834	24,688
91789	Walnut	(714)	9,978	5,992
*94596	Walnut Creek	(415)	54,410	39,844
94596	Walnut Creek West(u)	(415)	5,893	8,330
90255	Walnut Park(u)	(213)	11,811	8,925
93280	Wasco	(805)	9,613	8,269
95076	Watsonville	(408)	23,662	14,719
90044	West Athens(u)	(213)	8,531	13,311
90502	West Carson(u)	(213)	17,997	15,501
90247	West Compton(u)	(213)	5,907	5,748
*91793	West Covina	(818)	80,292	68,034
90069	West Hollywood	(213)	35,754	34,622
92683	Westminster	(714)	71,133	60,076
95351	West Modesto(u)	(209)	NA	6,135
90047	Westmont(u)	(213)	27,916	29,310
94565	West Pittsburg(u)	(415)	8,773	5,969
91746	West Puente Valley(u)	(818)	20,445	20,733
95691	West Sacramento(u)	(916)	10,875	12,002
*90606	West Whittier-Los Nietos(u)	(213)	20,962	20,845
*90605	Whittier	(213)	68,558	72,863
90222	Willowbrook(u)	(213)	30,845	28,705
93286	Woodlake	(209)	5,375	3,371
95695	Woodland	(916)	30,235	20,677
94062	Woodside	(415)	5,291	4,734
92686	Yorba Linda	(714)	28,254	11,856
96097	Yreka City	(916)	5,916	5,394
95991	Yuba City	(916)	18,736	13,986
92399	Yucaipa(u)	(714)	23,345	19,284
92284	Yucca Valley(u)	(619)	8,294	3,893

Colorado (303)

ZIP code	Place	1980	1970
80840	Air Force Academy	8,655	....
81101	Alamosa	6,830	6,985
80401	Applewood(u)	12,040	8,214
*80001	Arvada	84,576	49,844
80010	Aurora	158,588	74,974
*80302	Boulder	76,685	66,870
80601	Brighton	12,773	8,309
80020	Broomfield	20,730	7,261
81212	Canon City	13,037	9,206
.....	Castlewood	16,413	....
80110	Cherry Hills Village	5,127	4,605
81220	Cimarron Hills	6,597	....
81520	Clifton	5,223	....
*80901	Colorado Springs	215,105	135,517
80120	Columbine	23,523	....
80022	Commerce City	16,234	17,407
81321	Cortez	7,095	6,032
81625	Craig	8,133	4,205
*80202	Denver	492,686	514,678
80022	Derby(u)	8,578	10,206
81301	Durango	11,649	10,333
80110	Englewood	30,021	33,695
80620	Evans	5,063	2,570
80439	Evergreen	6,376	2,321
80221	Federal Heights	7,846	1,502
80913	Fort Carson(u)	13,219	19,399
*80521	Fort Collins	64,632	43,337
80701	Fort Morgan	8,768	7,594
80017	Fountain	8,324	3,515
80401	Golden	12,237	9,817
81501	Grand Junction	27,956	20,170
80631	Greeley	53,006	38,902
80110	Greenwood Village	5,729	3,095
80501	Gunbarrel	5,172	....
81230	Gunnison	5,785	4,613

ZIP code	Place	1980	1970
.....	Ken Caryl	10,661	....
80026	Lafayette	8,985	3,498
81050	La Junta	8,338	8,205
80215	Lakewood	113,808	92,743
81052	Lamar	7,713	7,797
80120	Littleton	28,631	26,466
80120	Littleton Southeast(u)	33,029	22,899
80501	Longmont	42,942	23,209
80027	Louisville	5,593	2,409
80537	Loveland	30,215	16,220
81401	Montrose	8,722	6,496
80233	Northglenn	29,847	27,785
*81003	Pueblo	101,686	97,774
80911	Security-Widefield(u)	18,768	15,297
80110	Sheridan	5,377	4,787
80221	Sherrelwood(u)	17,629	18,868
80122	Southglenn	37,787	....
80477	Steamboat Springs	5,098	2,340
80751	Sterling	11,385	10,636
80906	Stratmoor	5,519	....
80229	Thornton	40,343	13,326
81082	Trinidad	9,663	9,901
80229	Welby(u)	9,668	6,875
80030	Westminster	50,211	19,512
80221	Westminster East(u)	6,002	7,576
80033	Wheat Ridge	30,293	29,778

Connecticut (203)

See Note on Page 544

ZIP code	Place	1980	1970
06401	Ansonia	19,039	21,160
06001	*Avon*	11,201	8,352
06037	*Berlin*	15,121	14,149
06801	*Bethel*	16,004	10,945
06002	*Bloomfield*	18,608	18,301
06405	*Branford*	23,363	20,444
*06602	Bridgeport	142,546	156,542
06010	Bristol	57,370	55,487
06804	*Brookfield*	12,872	9,688
06013	Burlington	5,660	4,070
06234	Brooklyn	5,691	4,965
06019	*Canton*	7,635	6,868
06410	*Cheshire*	21,788	19,051
06413	*Clinton*	11,195	10,267
06415	*Colchester*	7,761	6,603
06340	Conning Towers-Nautilus Park(u)	9,665	9,791
06238	*Coventry*	8,895	8,140
06416	*Cromwell*	10,265	7,400
06810	Danbury	60,470	50,781
06820	Darien	18,892	20,336
06418	Derby	12,346	12,599
06422	Durham	5,143	4,489
06423	East Haddam	5,621	4,676
06424	*East Hampton*	8,572	7,078
06108	*East Hartford*	52,563	57,583
06512	*East Haven*	25,028	25,120
06333	*East Lyme*	13,870	11,399
06425	Easton	5,962	4,885
06016	*East Windsor*	8,925	8,513
06029	*Ellington*	9,711	7,707
06082	*Enfield*	42,695	46,189
06426	Essex	5,078	4,911
06430	*Fairfield*	54,849	56,487
06032	*Farmington*	16,407	14,390
06033	*Glastonbury*	24,327	20,651
06035	*Granby*	7,956	6,150
06830	*Greenwich*	59,578	59,755
06351	*Griswold*	8,967	7,763
06340	*Groton*	41,062	38,244
06340	Groton Borough	10,086	8,933
06437	*Guilford*	17,375	12,033
06438	Haddam	6,383	4,934
06514	*Hamden*	51,071	49,357
*06101	Hartford	136,392	158,017
06082	Hazardville(u)	5,436	....
06248	Hebron	5,453	3,815
06037	Kensington(u)	7,502	....
06239	*Killingly*	14,519	13,573
06339	*Ledyard*	13,735	14,837
06759	*Litchfield*	7,605	7,399
06443	*Madison*	14,031	9,768
06040	*Manchester*	49,761	47,994
06250	*Mansfield*	20,634	19,994
06450	Meriden	57,118	55,959
06762	*Middlebury*	5,995	5,542
06457	Middletown	39,040	36,924
06460	Milford	50,898	50,858
06468	*Monroe*	14,010	12,047
06353	*Montville*	16,455	15,662
06770	Naugatuck	26,456	23,034
*06050	New Britain	73,840	83,441
06840	*New Canaan*	17,931	17,451
06810	*New Fairfield*	11,260	6,991
*06510	New Haven	126,089	137,707
06111	*Newington*	28,841	26,037
06320	New London	28,842	31,630
06776	*New Milford*	19,420	14,601
06470	*Newtown*	19,107	16,942
06471	*North Branford*	11,554	10,778
06473	*North Haven*	22,080	22,194
06856	Norwalk	77,767	79,288
06360	Norwich	38,074	41,739
06779	Oakville(u)	8,737	....
06371	Old Lyme	6,159	4,964
06475	*Old Saybrook*	9,287	8,468
06477	*Orange*	13,237	13,524
06483	Oxford	6,634	4,480
02891	Pawcatuck(u)	5,216	5,255
06374	*Plainfield*	12,774	11,957
06062	*Plainville*	16,401	16,733
06782	*Plymouth*	10,732	10,321
06480	*Portland*	8,383	8,812
06712	*Prospect*	6,807	6,543
06260	Putnam	6,855	6,918
.....	*Putnam*	8,580	8,598
06875	*Redding*	7,272	5,590
06877	Ridgefield Center(u)	6,066	5,878
.....	*Ridgefield*	20,120	18,188
06067	*Rocky Hill*	14,559	11,103
06483	*Seymour*	13,434	12,776
06484	Shelton	31,314	27,165
06082	Sherwood Manor(u)	6,303	....
06070	*Simsbury*	21,161	17,475
06071	Somers	8,473	6,893
06488	*Southbury*	14,156	7,852
06489	*Southington*	36,879	30,946
06074	*South Windsor*	17,198	15,553
06082	Southwood Acres(u)	9,779	....
06075	*Stafford*	9,268	8,680
*06904	Stamford	102,466	108,798
06378	*Stonington*	16,220	15,940
06268	Storrs(u)	11,394	10,691
06430	Stratfield-Brooklawn(u)	8,890	....
06497	*Stratford*	50,541	49,775
06078	*Suffield*	9,294	8,634
06786	Terryville(u)	5,234	....
06787	*Thomaston*	6,272	6,233
06277	*Thompson*	8,141	7,580
06084	*Tolland*	9,694	7,857
06790	Torrington	30,987	31,952
06611	*Trumbull*	32,989	31,394
06060	*Vernon*	27,974	27,237
06492	*Wallingford*	37,274	35,714
*06701	Waterbury	103,266	108,033
06385	*Waterford*	17,843	17,227
06795	*Watertown*	19,489	18,610
06498	Westbrook	5,216	3,820
06107	*West Hartford*	61,301	68,031
06516	West Haven	53,184	52,851
06880	*Weston*	8,284	7,417
06880	*Westport*	25,290	27,318
06109	*Wethersfield*	26,013	26,662
06226	Willimantic	14,652	14,402
06897	*Wilton*	15,351	13,572
06094	*Winchester*	10,841	11,106
06280	*Windham*	21,062	19,626
06095	*Windsor*	25,204	22,502
06096	*Windsor Locks*	12,190	15,080
06098	Winsted	8,092	8,954
06716	*Wolcott*	13,008	12,495
06525	*Woodbridge*	7,761	7,673
06798	*Woodbury*	6,942	5,869
06281	Woodstock	5,117	4,311

Delaware (302)

ZIP code	Place	1980	1970
19713	Brookside(u)	15,255	7,856
19703	Claymont(u)	10,022	6,584
19901	Dover	23,507	17,488
19802	Edgemoor(u)	7,397	....
19805	Elsmere	6,493	8,415
19963	Milford	5,366	5,314
*19711	Newark	25,247	21,298
19973	Seaford	5,256	5,537
19804	Stanton(u)	5,495	....
19803	Talleyville(u)	6,880	....
*19899	Wilmington	70,195	80,386
19720	Wilmington Manor —Chelsea—Leedom	9,233	10,134

District of Columbia (202)

ZIP code	Place	1980	1970
*20013	Washington	638,432	756,668

Florida

ZIP code	Place	Area code	1980	1970
*32701	Altamonte Springs	(305)	21,105	4,391
32703	Apopka	(305)	6,019	4,045
33821	Arcadia	(813)	6,002	5,658
32233	Atlantic Beach	(904)	7,847	6,132
33823	Auburndale	(813)	6,501	5,386
.....	Aventura(u)	(305)	10,162	....
33825	Avon Park	(813)	8,026	6,712
32807	Azalea Park(u)	(305)	8,304	7,367
33830	Bartow	(813)	14,780	12,891
.....	Bay Crest(u)	(813)	5,927	

ZIP code	Place		1980	1970
.....	Bayonet Point(u)	(813)	16,455	....
33542	Bay Pines(u)	(813)	5,757	....
33505	Bayshore Gardens(u)	(813)	14,945	9,255
33589	Beacon Square(u)	(813)	6,513	2,927
32073	Bellair-Meadowbrook Terrace(u)	(904)	12,144	....
33430	Belle Glade	(305)	16,535	15,949
32506	Belleview(u)	(904)	15,439	916
32661	Beverly Hills(u)	(904)	5,024	....
*33487	Boca Raton	(305)	49,447	28,506
33959	Bonita Springs(u)	(813)	5,435	1,932
*33435	Boynton Beach	(305)	35,624	18,115
*34206	Bradenton	(813)	30,228	21,040
33511	Brandon(u)	(813)	41,826	12,749
32525	Brent(u)	(904)	21,872	....
33314	Broadview Park(u)	(305)	6,022	6,049
33313	Broadview-Pompano Park(u)	(305)	5,256	....
*34601	Brooksville	(904)	5,582	4,060
33311	Browardale(u)	(305)	7,571	17,444
33142	Browns Village(u)	(305)	NA	23,442
33142	Brownsville(u)	(305)	18,058	....
33054	Bunche Park(u)	(305)	NA	5,773
32401	Callaway	(904)	7,154	3,240
32920	Cape Canaveral	(305)	5,733	4,258
33904	Cape Coral	(813)	32,103	11,470
33055	Carol City(u)	(305)	47,349	27,361
32707	Casselberry	(305)	15,037	9,438
33401	Century Village(u)	(305)	10,619	2,679
32324	Chattahoochee	(904)	5,332	7,944
*34615	Clearwater	(813)	85,450	52,074
32711	Clermont	(904)	5,461	3,661
33440	Clewiston	(813)	5,219	3,896
32922	Cocoa	(305)	16,096	16,110
32931	Cocoa Beach	(305)	10,926	9,952
32922	Cocoa West(u)	(305)	6,432	5,779
33066	Coconut Creek	(305)	6,288	1,359
33060	Collier City(u)	(305)	7135	....
33064	Collier Manor-Cresthaven(u)	(305)	7,045	7,202
33801	Combee Settlement(u)	(813)	5,400	4,963
32809	Conway(u)	(305)	23,940	8,642
33314	Cooper City	(305)	10,140	2,535
33134	Coral Gables	(305)	43,241	42,494
33065	Coral Springs	(305)	37,349	1,489
.....	Coral Terrace(u)	(305)	22,702	....
32536	Crestview	(904)	7,617	7,952
33803	Crystal Lake(u)	(813)	6,827	6,227
33157	Cutler(u)	(305)	15,593	....
33157	Cutler Ridge(u)	(305)	20,886	17,441
33880	Cypress Gardens(u)	(813)	8,043	3,757
.....	Cypress Lake(u)	(813)	8,721	....
33004	Dania	(305)	11,796	9,013
33314	Davie	(305)	20,515	5,859
*32015	Daytona Beach	(904)	54,176	45,327
33441	Deerfield Beach	(305)	39,193	16,662
32433	DeFuniak Springs	(904)	5,563	4,966
32720	De Land	(904)	15,354	11,641
*33444	Delray Beach	(305)	34,329	19,915
33617	Del Rio(u)	(813)	7,409	....
32725	Deltona(u)	(904)	15,710	4,868
*34698	Dunedin	(813)	30,203	17,639
33610	East Lake-Orient Park (u)	(813)	5,612	5,697
33940	East Naples(u)	(813)	12,127	6,152
32032	Edgewater	(904)	6,726	3,348
32542	Eglin AFB(u)	(904)	7,574	7,769
33614	Egypt Lake(u)	(813)	11,932	7,556
*34680	Elfers(u)	(813)	11,396	....
*34223	Englewood(u)	(813)	10,242	5,108
32504	Ensley(u)	(904)	14,422	....
32726	Eustis	(904)	9,453	6,722
32804	Fairview Shores(u)	(305)	10,174	....
32034	Fernandina Beach	(904)	7,224	6,955
32730	Fern Park(u)	(305)	8,890	....
32504	Ferry Pass(u)	(904)	16,910	....
33030	Florida City	(305)	6,174	5,133
32751	Forest City(u)	(305)	6,819	....
*33319	Fort Lauderdale	(305)	153,256	139,590
33841	Fort Meade	(813)	5,546	4,374
*33901	Fort Myers	(813)	36,638	27,351
33931	Fort Myers Beach(u)	(813)	5,753	4,305
*34950	Fort Pierce	(305)	33,802	29,721
33452	Fort Pierce NW(u)	(305)	5,929	3,269
32548	Fort Walton Beach	(904)	20,829	19,994
*32601	Gainesville	(904)	81,371	64,510
33801	Gibsonia(u)	(813)	5,011	....
32960	Gifford(u)	(305)	6,240	5,772
.....	Gladeview(u)	(305)	18,919	....
33143	Glenvar Heights(u)	(305)	13,216	....
33055	Golden Glades(u)	(305)	23,154	....
32733	Goldenrod(u)	(305)	13,681	....
32560	Gonzalez(u)	(904)	6,084	....
32603	Goulding(u)	(904)	5,352	....
33170	Goulds(u)	(305)	7,078	6,690
33463	Greenacres City	(305)	8,780	1,731
32561	Gulf Breeze	(904)	5,478	4,190
33581	Gulf Gate Estates(u)	(813)	9,248	5,874
33737	Gulfport	(813)	11,180	9,976
33844	Haines City	(813)	10,799	8,956
33009	Hallandale	(305)	36,517	23,849
*33010	Hialeah	(305)	145,254	102,452
33455	Hobe Sound(u)	(305)	6,822	2,029
32805	Holden Heights(u)	(305)	13,840	6,206
33590	Holiday(u)	(813)	18,392	....
32017	Holly Hill	(904)	9,953	8,191
*33022	Hollywood	(305)	117,188	106,873
33030	Homestead	(305)	20,668	13,674
33030	Homestead Base(u)	(305)	7,594	8,257
33568	Hudson(u)	(813)	5,799	2,278
33934	Immokalee(u)	(813)	11,038	3,764
32937	Indian Harbour Beach	(305)	5,967	5,371
33880	Inwood(u)	(813)	6,668	....
33162	Ives Estates(u)	(305)	12,623	....
*32201	Jacksonville	(904)	540,920	504,265
32250	Jacksonville Beach	(904)	15,462	12,779
33568	Jasmine Estates(u)	(813)	11,995	2,967
*34957	Jensen Beach(u)	(305)	6,639	....
33458	Jupiter	(305)	9,868	3,136
.....	Kendale Lakes(u)	(305)	32,769	....
33156	Kendall(u)	(305)	73,758	35,497
.....	Kendall Green(u)	(305)	6,768	....
33149	Key Biscayne(u)	(305)	6,313	....
33037	Key Largo(u)	(305)	7,447	2,866
33040	Key West	(305)	24,292	29,312
32303	Killearn(u)	(904)	8,700	....
.....	Kings Point(u)	(305)	8,724	....
32741	Kissimmee	(305)	15,487	7,119
33618	Lake Carroll(u)	(305)	13,012	5,577
32055	Lake City	(904)	9,257	10,575
*33802	Lakeland	(813)	47,406	42,803
33801	Lakeland Highlands(u)	(813)	10,426	....
.....	Lake Lorraine(u)	(904)	5,427	....
33054	Lake Lucerne(u)	(305)	9,762	....
33612	Lake Magdalene(u)	(813)	13,331	9,266
33403	Lake Park	(305)	6,909	6,993
....	Lakeside(u)	(904)	10,534	....
33853	Lake Wales	(813)	8,466	8,240
33460	Lake Worth	(305)	27,048	23,714
33460	Lantana	(305)	8,048	7,126
*34640	Largo	(813)	57,958	24,230
33313	Lauderdale Lakes	(305)	25,426	10,577
33313	Lauderhill	(305)	37,271	8,465
34272	Laurel(u)	(813)	6,368	....
33717	Lealman(u)	(813)	19,873	....
32748	Leesburg	(904)	13,191	11,869
*33936	Lehigh Acres(u)	(813)	9,604	4,394
33033	Leisure City(u)	(305)	17,905	....
33614	Leto(u)	(904)	9,003	8,458
33064	Lighthouse Point	(305)	11,488	9,071
.....	Lindgren Acres(u)	(305)	11,986	....
32060	Live Oak	(904)	6,732	6,830
32810	Lockhart(u)	(305)	10,571	5,809
34228	Longboat Key	(813)	8,221	2,850
*32750	Longwood	(305)	10,029	3,203
33549	Lutz(u)	(813)	5,555	....
32444	Lynn Haven	(904)	6,239	4,044
32751	Maitland	(305)	8,763	7,157
33550	Mango-Seffner(u)	(813)	6,493	....
33050	Marathon(u)	(305)	7,568	4,397
33063	Margate	(305)	35,900	8,867
[illegible]	Marianna	(904)	7,074	7,282
*32901	Melbourne	(305)	46,536	40,236
33314	Melrose Park(u)	(904)	5,725	6,111
33561	Memphis(u)	(813)	5,501	3,207
32952	Merritt Island(u)	(305)	30,708	29,233
*33152	Miami	(305)	346,681	334,859
33139	Miami Beach	(305)	96,298	87,072
33023	Miami Gardens—Utopia-Carver(u)	(305)	9,025	....
33014	Miami Lakes(u)	(305)	9,809	....
33153	Miami Shores	(305)	9,244	9,425
33166	Miami Springs	(305)	12,350	13,279
32570	Milton	(904)	7,206	5,360
32754	Mims(u)	(305)	7,583	8,309
33023	Miramar	(305)	32,813	23,997
32757	Mount Dora	(904)	5,883	4,646
32506	Myrtle Grove(u)	(904)	14,238	16,186
*33962	Naples	(813)	17,581	12,042
33940	Naples Park(u)	(813)	5,438	1,522
33032	Naranja-Princeton(u)	(305)	10,381	....
32233	Neptune Beach	(904)	5,248	4,281
*34652	New Port Richey	(813)	11,196	6,098
33552	New Port Richey East(u)	(813)	6,627	2,758
32069	New Smyrna Beach	(904)	13,557	10,580
32578	Niceville	(904)	8,543	4,155
33169	Norland(u)	(305)	19,471	....
33308	North Andrews Gardens(u)	(305)	8,967	7,082
33903	North Fort Myers(u)	(813)	22,808	8,798
33068	North Lauderdale	(305)	18,653	1,213
33161	North Miami	(305)	42,566	34,767
33160	North Miami Beach	(305)	36,481	30,544
33940	North Naples(u)	(813)	7,950	3,201
33408	North Palm Beach	(305)	11,344	9,035
33596	North Port	(813)	6,205	2,244
33169	Norwood(u)	(305)	NA	14,973
33308	Oakland Park	(305)	22,944	16,261
33860	Oak Ridge(u)	(813)	15,477	....
32670	Ocala	(904)	37,170	22,583
32548	Ocean City(u)	(904)	5,582	5,267
32761	Ocoee	(813)	7,803	3,937
33163	Ojus(u)	(305)	17,344	....
33165	Olympia Heights(u)	(305)	33,112	....

ZIP code	Place	Area code	1980	1970
33558	Oneco(u)	(813)	6,417	3,246
33054	Opa-Locka	(305)	14,460	11,902
33054	Opa-Locka North(u)	(305)	5,721	....
32073	Orange Park	(904)	8,766	5,019
*32820	Orlando	(305)	128,394	99,006
32811	Orlovista(u)	(305)	6,474	....
32074	Ormond Beach	(904)	21,438	14,063
32074	Ormond By-The-Sea(u)	(904)	7,665	6,002
32570	Pace(u)	(904)	5,006	1,776
33476	Pahokee	(305)	6,346	5,663
32077	Palatka	(904)	10,175	9,444
33505	Palma Sola(u)	(813)	5,297	1,745
32905	Palm Bay	(305)	18,560	7,176
33480	Palm Beach	(305)	9,729	9,086
33403	Palm Beach Gardens	(305)	14,407	6,102
33561	Palmetto	(813)	8,637	7,422
33157	Palmetto Estates(u)	(305)	11,116	....
*34683	Palm Harbor(u)	(813)	5,215	....
33619	Palm River-Clair Mel(u)	(813)	14,447	8,536
33460	Palm Springs	(305)	8,166	4,340
33012	Palm Springs North(u)	(305)	5,838	....
32401	Panama City	(904)	33,346	32,096
33866	Pembroke Park	(305)	5,326	2,949
33023	Pembroke Pines	(305)	35,776	15,496
32502	Pensacola	(904)	57,619	59,507
33157	Perrine(u)	(305)	16,129	10,257
32347	Perry	(904)	8,254	7,701
32809	Pine Castle(u)	(305)	9,992	....
32808	Pine Hills(u)	(305)	35,771	13,882
*34665	Pinellas Park	(813)	32,811	22,287
33168	Pinewood(u)	(305)	16,216	....
33566	Plant City	(813)	17,064	15,451
33314	Plantation	(813)	48,653	23,523
*33067	Pompano Beach	(305)	52,618	38,587
33064	Pompano Beach Highlands(u)	(305)	16,154	5,014
33950	Port Charlotte(u)	(813)	25,730	10,769
32019	Port Orange	(904)	18,756	3,781
33452	Port St. Lucie	(305)	14,690	330
*33950	Punta Gorda	(813)	6,797	3,879
32351	Quincy	(904)	8,591	8,334
33156	Richmond Heights(u)	(305)	8,577	6,663
33312	Riverland (u)	(305)	5,919	5,512
33404	Riviera Beach	(305)	26,596	21,401
33314	Rock Island(u)	(813)	5,022	....
32955	Rockledge	(305)	11,877	10,523
33570	Ruskin(u)	(813)	5,117	2,414
33572	Safety Harbor	(813)	6,461	3,103
32084	St. Augustine	(904)	11,985	12,352
32769	St. Cloud	(305)	7,840	5,041
*33702	St. Petersburg	(813)	238,647	216,159
33706	St. Petersburg Beach	(813)	9,354	8,024
33508	Samoset(u)	(813)	5,747	4,070
33432	Sandalfoot Cove(u)	(305)	5,299	....
32771	Sanford	(305)	23,176	17,393
*34263	Sarasota	(813)	48,868	40,237
33577	Sarasota Springs(u)	(813)	13,860	4,405
32937	Satellite Beach	(305)	9,163	6,558
.....	Scott Lake(u)	(305)	14,154	....
*33870	Sebring	(813)	8,736	7,223
33578	Siesta Key(u)	(813)	7,010	4,460
32809	Sky Lake(u)	(305)	6,692	....
32703	South Apopka(u)	(305)	5,687	2,293
33505	South Bradenton(u)	(813)	14,297	....
32021	South Daytona	(904)	9,608	4,979
33579	Southgate(u)	(813)	7,322	6,885
33143	South Miami	(305)	10,895	11,780
33157	South Miami Heights(u)	(305)	23,559	10,395
32937	South Patrick Shores(u)	(305)	9,816	10,313
33595	South Venice(u)	(813)	8,075	4,680
32401	Springfield	(904)	7,220	5,949
33526	Spring Hill(u)	(904)	6,468	....
32091	Starke	(904)	5,306	4,848
*34994	Stuart	(305)	9,467	4,820
33586	Sun City Center(u)	(813)	5,605	2,143
33160	Sunny Isles(u)	(305)	12,564	....
33304	Sunrise	(305)	39,681	7,403
33139	Sunset(u)	(305)	13,531	....
33144	Sweetwater	(305)	8,067	3,357
33614	Sweetwater Creek(u)	(813)	NA	19,453
*32303	Tallahassee	(904)	81,548	72,624
33313	Tamarac	(305)	29,142	5,193
33144	Tamiami(u)	(305)	17,607	....
*33625	Tampa	(813)	271,577	277,714
.....	Tanglewood(u)	(813)	8,229	....
*34689	Tarpon Springs	(813)	13,251	7,118
33617	Temple Terrace	(813)	11,097	7,347
33905	Tice(u)	(813)	6,645	7,254
32780	Titusville	(305)	31,910	30,515
32505	Town 'n' Country(u)	(904)	37,834	....
33740	Treasure Island	(813)	6,316	6,120
32807	Union Park(u)	(305)	19,175	2,595
33620	University (Hillsborough)(u)	(813)	24,514	10,039
32580	Valparaiso	(904)	6,142	6,504
*34285	Venice	(813)	12,153	6,648
33595	Venice Gardens(u)	(813)	6,568	....
32960	Vero Beach	(305)	16,176	11,908
32960	Vero Beach South(u)	(305)	12,636	7,330
33901	Villas(u)	(813)	8,724	....
32507	Warrington(u)	(904)	15,792	15,848
33314	Washington Park(u)	(305)	7,240	....
32703	Wekiva Springs(u)	(305)	13,386	....
33505	West Bradenton(u)	(813)	NA	6,162
33155	Westchester(u)	(305)	29,272	....
32446	West End(u)	(904)	NA	5,289
33138	West Little River(u)	(305)	32,492	....
32901	West Melbourne	(305)	5,078	3,050
33144	West Miami	(305)	6,076	5,494
*33404	West Palm Beach	(305)	62,530	57,375
32505	West Pensacola(u)	(904)	24,371	20,924
33168	Westview(u)	(305)	9,102	....
33880	West Winter Haven(u)	(813)	NA	7,716
33165	Westwood Lakes(u)	(305)	11,478	12,811
33305	Wilton Manors	(305)	12,742	10,948
33803	Winston(u)	(813)	9,315	4,505
*32787	Winter Garden	(305)	6,789	5,153
33880	Winter Haven	(813)	21,119	16,136
*32789	Winter Park	(305)	22,314	21,895
32708	Winter Springs	(305)	10,475	1,161
32548	Wright(u)	(904)	13,011	....
33599	Zephyrhills	(813)	5,742	3,369

Georgia

ZIP code	Place	Area code	1980	1970
31620	Adel	(912)	5,592	4,972
*31701	Albany	(912)	74,425	72,623
31709	Americus	(912)	16,120	16,091
*30601	Athens	(404)	42,549	44,342
*30304	Atlanta	(404)	425,022	495,039
*30901	Augusta	(404)	47,532	59,864
31717	Bainbridge	(912)	10,553	10,887
30032	Belvedere Park(u)	(404)	17,766	....
31723	Blakely	(912)	5,880	5,267
31520	Brunswick	(912)	17,605	19,585
30518	Buford	(404)	6,578	4,640
31728	Cairo	(912)	8,777	8,061
30701	Calhoun	(404)	5,335	4,748
31730	Camilla	(912)	5,414	4,987
30032	Candler-McAfee(u)	(404)	27,306	....
30117	Carrollton	(404)	14,078	13,520
30120	Cartersville	(404)	9,247	10,138
30125	Cedartown	(404)	8,619	9,253
30341	Chamblee	(404)	7,137	9,127
31014	Cochran	(912)	5,121	5,161
30337	College Park	(404)	24,632	18,203
*31902	Columbus	(404)	169,441	155,028
30027	Conley(u)	(404)	6,033	....
30207	Conyers	(404)	6,567	4,809
31015	Cordele	(912)	11,184	10,733
30209	Covington	(404)	10,586	10,267
30720	Dalton	(404)	20,581	18,872
31742	Dawson	(912)	5,699	5,383
*30030	Decatur	(404)	18,404	21,943
31520	Dock Junction(u)	(912)	6,189	6,009
30340	Doraville	(404)	7,414	9,157
31533	Douglas	(912)	10,980	10,195
30134	Douglasville	(404)	7,641	5,472
30333	Druid Hills(u)	(404)	12,700	....
31021	Dublin	(912)	16,083	15,143
30338	Dunwoody(u)	(404)	17,768	....
31023	Eastman	(912)	5,330	5,416
30344	East Point	(404)	37,486	39,315
30635	Elberton	(404)	5,686	6,438
30060	Fair Oaks(u)	(404)	8,486	....
30535	Fairview(u)	(404)	6,558	....
31750	Fitzgerald	(912)	10,187	8,187
30050	Forest Park	(404)	18,782	19,994
31905	Fort Benning South(u)	(404)	15,074	27,495
30905	Fort Gordon(u)	(404)	14,069	15,589
30741	Fort Oglethorpe	(404)	5,443	3,869
31313	Fort Stewart(u)	(912)	15,031	4,467
31030	Fort Valley	(912)	9,000	9,251
30501	Gainesville	(404)	15,280	15,459
31408	Garden City	(912)	6,895	5,790
30316	Gresham Park(u)	(404)	6,232	....
30223	Griffin	(404)	20,728	22,734
30354	Hapeville	(404)	6,166	9,567
31313	Hinesville	(912)	11,309	4,115
31545	Jesup	(912)	9,418	9,091
30144	Kennesaw	(404)	5,095	3,548
30728	La Fayette	(404)	6,517	6,044
30240	La Grange	(404)	24,204	23,301
30245	Lawrenceville	(404)	8,928	5,207
30057	Lithia Springs(u)	(404)	9,145	....
30059	Mableton(u)	(404)	25,111	....
*31201	Macon	(912)	116,860	122,423
30060	Marietta	(404)	30,821	27,216
30907	Martinez(u)	(404)	16,472	....
31034	Midway-Hardwick(u)	(912)	8,977	14,047
31061	Milledgeville	(912)	12,176	11,601
30655	Monroe	(404)	8,854	8,071
31768	Moultrie	(912)	15,105	14,400
30075	Mountain Park(u)	(404)	9,425	268
30263	Newnan	(404)	11,449	11,205
30319	North Atlanta(u)	(404)	30,521	....
30033	North Decatur(u)	(404)	11,830	....
30033	North Druid Hills(u)	(404)	12,438	....
30032	Panthersville(u)	(404)	11,366	....
30269	Peachtree City	(404)	6,429	793
31069	Perry	(912)	9,453	7,771
31643	Quitman	(912)	5,188	4,818

ZIP code	Place		1980	1970
*30274	Riverdale	(404)	7,121	2,521
30161	Rome	(404)	28,915	30,759
30075	Roswell	(404)	23,337	5,430
31522	St. Simons(u)	(912)	6,566	5,346
31082	Sandersville	(912)	6,137	5,546
30328	Sandy Springs(u)	(404)	46,877	....
*31401	Savannah	(912)	141,654	118,349
30079	Scottdale(u)	(404)	8,770	....
30080	Smyrna	(404)	20,312	19,157
30278	Snellville	(404)	8,514	1,990
30901	South Augusta(u)	(404)	51,072	....
30458	Statesboro	(912)	14,866	14,616
30401	Swainsboro	(912)	7,602	7,325
31791	Sylvester	(912)	5,860	4,226
30286	Thomaston	(404)	9,682	10,024
31792	Thomasville	(912)	18,463	18,155
30824	Thomson	(404)	7,001	6,503
31794	Tifton	(912)	13,749	12,179
30577	Toccoa	(404)	8,869	6,971
30084	Tucker(u)	(404)	25,399	....
31601	Valdosta	(912)	37,596	32,303
30474	Vidalia	(912)	10,393	9,507
31093	Warner Robins	(912)	39,893	33,491
31501	Waycross	(912)	19,371	18,996
30830	Waynesboro	(404)	5,760	5,530
30901	West Augusta(u)	(404)	24,242	....
31410	Wilmington Island(u)	(912)	7,546	3,284
30680	Winder	(404)	6,705	6,605

Hawaii (808)

See Note on Page 544

96706	Ewa	190,037	132,299
96720	Hilo	37,017	28,412
*96815	Honolulu	365,048	324,871
96732	Kahului	13,026	8,287
96749	Keaau-Mountain View	7,055	3,802
96752	Kekaha-Waimea	5,256	4,159
96753	Kihei	6,035	1,636
.....	Koolauloa	14,195	10,562
.....	Koolaupoko	109,373	92,219
96790	Kula	5,077	2,124
96761	Lahaina	10,284	5,524
96768	Makawao-Paia	10,361	5,788
.....	North Kona	13,748	4,832
96781	Papaikou-Wailea	5,261	5,503
.....	South Kona	5,914	4,004
96786	Wahiawa	41,562	37,329
96791	Waialua	9,849	9,171
96792	Waianae	32,810	24,077
96703	Wailua-Anahola	6,030	3,599
96793	Wailuku	10,674	9,084

Idaho (208)

83221	Blackfoot	10,065	8,716
*83708	Boise City	102,249	74,990
83318	Burley	8,761	8,279
83605	Caldwell	17,699	14,219
83201	Chubbuck	7,052	2,924
83814	Coeur D'Alene	19,913	16,228
83401	Idaho Falls	39,739	35,776
83338	Jerome	6,891	4,183
83501	Lewiston	27,986	26,068
83642	Meridian	6,658	2,616
83843	Moscow	16,513	14,146
83647	Mountain Home	7,540	6,451
83648	Mountain Home AFB(u)	6,403	6,038
83651	Nampa	25,112	20,768
83661	Payette	5,448	4,521
83201	Pocatello	46,340	40,036
83854	Post Falls	5,736	2,371
83440	Rexburg	11,559	8,272
83350	Rupert	5,476	4,563
83301	Twin Falls	26,209	21,914

Illinois

60101	Addison	(312)	29,826	24,482
60102	Algonquin	(312)	5,834	3,515
60658	Alsip	(312)	17,134	11,608
62002	Alton	(618)	34,171	39,700
62906	Anna	(618)	5,408	4,766
*60004	Arlington Heights	(312)	66,116	65,058
*60507	Aurora	(312)	81,293	74,389
60010	Barrington	(312)	9,029	8,581
60103	Bartlett	(312)	13,254	3,501
61607	Bartonville	(309)	6,110	7,221
60510	Batavia	(312)	12,574	9,060
62618	Beardstown	(217)	6,338	6,222
*62220	Belleville	(618)	42,150	41,223
60104	Bellwood	(312)	19,811	22,096
61008	Belvidere	(815)	15,176	14,061
60106	Bensenville	(312)	16,106	12,956
62812	Benton	(618)	7,778	6,833
60162	Berkeley	(312)	5,467	6,152
60402	Berwyn	(312)	46,849	52,502
62010	Bethalto	(618)	8,630	7,074
60108	Bloomingdale	(312)	12,656	2,974
61701	Bloomington	(309)	44,189	39,992
60406	Blue Island	(312)	21,855	22,629
60439	Bolingbrook	(312)	37,261	7,651
60538	Boulder Hill(u)	(312)	9,333	....
60914	Bourbonnais	(815)	13,280	5,909
60915	Bradley	(815)	11,015	9,881
60455	Bridgeview	(312)	14,155	12,506
60153	Broadview	(312)	8,618	9,623
60513	Brookfield	(312)	19,395	20,284
60090	Buffalo Grove	(312)	22,230	12,333
60459	Burbank	(312)	28,462	26,726
62206	Cahokia	(618)	18,904	20,649
62914	Cairo	(618)	5,931	6,277
60409	Calumet City	(312)	39,673	33,107
60643	Calumet Park	(312)	8,788	10,069
61520	Canton	(309)	14,626	14,217
62901	Carbondale	(618)	26,414	22,816
62626	Carlinville	(217)	5,439	5,675
62821	Carmi	(618)	6,107	6,033
60187	Carol Stream	(312)	15,472	4,434
60110	Carpentersville	(312)	23,272	24,059
60013	Cary	(312)	6,640	4,358
62801	Centralia	(618)	15,126	15,966
62206	Centreville	(618)	9,747	11,378
61820	Champaign	(217)	58,267	56,837
61920	Charleston	(217)	19,355	16,421
62629	Chatham	(217)	5,597	2,788
62233	Chester	(618)	8,027	5,310
*60607	Chicago	(312)	3,005,072	3,369,357
60411	Chicago Heights	(312)	37,026	40,900
60415	Chicago Ridge	(312)	13,473	9,187
61523	Chillicothe	(309)	6,176	6,052
60650	Cicero	(312)	61,232	67,058
60514	Clarendon Hills	(312)	6,857	6,750
61727	Clinton	(217)	8,014	7,581
62234	Collinsville	(618)	19,613	18,224
60477	Country Club Hills	(312)	14,676	6,920
60525	Countryside	(312)	6,242	2,864
60435	Crest Hill	(815)	9,252	7,460
60445	Crestwood	(312)	10,712	5,770
60417	Crete	(312)	5,417	4,656
61611	Creve Coeur	(309)	6,851	6,440
60014	Crystal Lake	(815)	18,590	14,541
61832	Danville	(217)	38,985	42,570
60559	Darien	(312)	14,968	7,789
*62521	Decatur	(217)	93,939	90,397
60015	Deerfield	(312)	17,432	18,876
60115	De Kalb	(815)	33,157	32,949
*60016	Des Plaines	(312)	53,568	57,239
61021	Dixon	(815)	15,710	18,147
60419	Dolton	(312)	24,766	25,990
60515	Downers Grove	(312)	42,691	32,544
62832	Du Quoin	(618)	6,594	6,691
62024	East Alton	(618)	7,096	7,309
60411	East Chicago Heights	(312)	5,347	5,000
61244	East Moline	(309)	20,907	20,832
61611	East Peoria	(309)	22,385	18,671
*62201	East St. Louis	(618)	55,200	70,169
62025	Edwardsville	(618)	12,460	11,070
62401	Effingham	(217)	11,270	9,458
62930	Eldorado	(618)	5,198	3,876
60120	Elgin	(312)	63,668	55,691
60007	Elk Grove Village	(312)	28,679	20,346
60126	Elmhurst	(312)	44,251	46,392
60635	Elmwood Park	(312)	24,016	26,160
*60204	Evanston	(312)	73,706	80,113
60642	Evergreen Park	(312)	22,260	25,921
62837	Fairfield	(618)	5,944	5,897
62208	Fairview Heights	(618)	12,414	10,050
62839	Flora	(618)	5,379	5,283
60422	Flossmoor	(312)	8,423	7,846
60130	Forest Park	(312)	15,177	15,472
60020	Fox Lake	(312)	6,831	4,511
60131	Franklin Park	(312)	17,507	20,348
61032	Freeport	(815)	26,406	27,736
60030	Gages Lake-Wildwood(u)	(312)	5,848	5,337
61401	Galesburg	(309)	35,305	36,290
61254	Geneseo	(309)	6,373	5,840
60134	Geneva	(312)	9,881	9,049
62034	Glen Carbon	(618)	5,197	1,897
60022	Glencoe	(312)	9,200	10,542
60137	Glendale Heights	(618)	23,251	11,406
60137	Glen Ellyn	(312)	23,691	21,909
60025	Glenview	(312)	30,842	24,880
60425	Glenwood	(312)	10,538	7,416
62040	Granite City	(618)	36,815	40,685
60030	Grayslake	(312)	5,260	4,907
62246	Greenville	(618)	5,271	4,631
60031	Gurnee	(312)	7,179	2,738
60103	Hanover Park	(312)	28,719	11,735
62946	Harrisburg	(618)	9,322	9,535
60033	Harvard	(815)	5,126	5,177
60426	Harvey	(312)	35,810	34,636
60656	Harwood Heights	(312)	8,228	9,060
60429	Hazel Crest	(312)	13,973	10,329
62948	Herrin	(618)	10,708	9,623
60457	Hickory Hills	(312)	13,778	13,176
62249	Highland	(618)	7,122	5,981

ZIP code	Place		1980	1970
60035	Highland Park	(312)	30,599	32,263
60040	Highwood	(312)	5,455	4,973
60162	Hillside	(312)	8,279	8,888
60521	Hinsdale	(312)	16,726	15,918
60172	Hoffman Estates	(312)	38,258	22,238
60456	Hometown	(312)	5,324	6,729
60430	Homewood	(312)	19,724	18,871
60942	Hoopeston	(217)	6,411	6,461
60143	Itasca	(312)	7,948	4,638
62650	Jacksonville	(217)	20,284	20,553
62052	Jerseyville	(618)	7,506	7,446
*60431	Joliet	(815)	77,956	78,827
60458	Justice	(312)	10,552	9,473
60901	Kankakee	(815)	29,633	30,944
61443	Kewanee	(309)	14,508	15,762
60525	La Grange	(312)	15,693	17,814
60525	La Grange Park	(312)	13,359	15,459
60045	Lake Forest	(312)	15,245	15,642
60102	Lake in the Hills	(312)	5,651	3,240
60047	Lake Zurich	(312)	8,225	4,082
60438	Lansing	(312)	29,039	25,805
61301	La Salle	(815)	10,347	10,736
62439	Lawrenceville	(618)	5,652	5,863
60439	Lemont	(312)	5,640	5,080
60048	Libertyville	(312)	16,520	11,684
62656	Lincoln	(217)	16,327	17,582
60645	Lincolnwood	(312)	11,921	12,929
60046	Lindenhurst	(312)	6,220	3,141
60532	Lisle	(312)	13,638	5,329
62056	Litchfield	(217)	7,204	7,190
60441	Lockport	(815)	9,192	9,861
60148	Lombard	(312)	36,879	34,043
61111	Loves Park	(815)	13,192	12,390
60534	Lyons	(312)	9,925	11,124
61455	Macomb	(309)	19,632	19,643
62060	Madison	(618)	5,301	7,042
62959	Marion	(618)	14,031	11,724
60426	Markham	(312)	15,172	15,987
60443	Matteson	(312)	10,223	4,741
61938	Mattoon	(217)	19,293	19,681
60153	Maywood	(312)	27,998	29,019
60050	McHenry	(815)	10,737	6,772
*60160	Melrose Park	(312)	20,735	22,716
61342	Mendota	(815)	7,134	6,902
62960	Metropolis	(618)	7,171	6,940
60445	Midlothian	(312)	14,274	14,422
61264	Milan	(309)	6,371	4,873
61265	Moline	(309)	46,407	46,237
61462	Monmouth	(309)	10,706	11,022
60450	Morris	(815)	8,833	8,194
61550	Morton	(309)	14,178	10,811
60053	Morton Grove	(312)	23,747	26,369
62863	Mount Carmel	(618)	8,908	8,096
60056	Mount Prospect	(312)	52,634	34,995
62864	Mount Vernon	(618)	16,995	16,270
60060	Mundelein	(312)	17,053	16,128
62966	Murphysboro	(618)	9,866	10,013
60540	Naperville	(312)	42,601	22,794
60451	New Lenox	(815)	5,792	2,855
60648	Niles	(312)	30,363	31,432
61761	Normal	(309)	35,672	26,396
60656	Norridge	(312)	16,483	17,113
60542	North Aurora	(312)	5,205	4,833
60062	Northbrook	(312)	30,735	25,422
60064	North Chicago	(312)	38,774	47,275
60164	Northlake	(312)	12,166	14,191
61111	North Park(u)	(815)	15,806	15,679
60546	North Riverside	(312)	6,764	8,097
60521	Oak Brook	(312)	6,676	4,164
60452	Oak Forest	(312)	25,040	19,271
*60454	Oak Lawn	(312)	60,590	60,305
*60301	Oak Park	(312)	54,887	62,511
62269	O'Fallon	(618)	12,173	7,268
62450	Olney	(618)	9,026	8,974
60462	Orland Park	(312)	23,045	6,391
61350	Ottawa	(815)	18,166	18,716
60067	Palatine	(312)	32,176	26,050
60463	Palos Heights	(312)	11,096	8,544
60465	Palos Hills	(312)	16,654	6,629
62557	Pana	(217)	6,040	6,326
61944	Paris	(217)	9,885	9,971
60466	Park Forest	(312)	26,222	30,638
60466	Park Forest South	(312)	6,245	1,748
60068	Park Ridge	(312)	38,704	42,614
61554	Pekin	(309)	33,967	31,375
*61601	Peoria	(309)	124,160	126,963
61614	Peoria Heights	(309)	7,453	7,943
61354	Peru	(815)	10,886	11,772
61764	Pontiac	(815)	11,227	10,595
61356	Princeton	(815)	7,342	6,959
60070	Prospect Heights	(312)	11,823	13,333
62301	Quincy	(217)	42,352	45,288
61866	Rantoul	(217)	20,161	25,562
60471	Richton Park	(312)	9,403	2,558
60627	Riverdale	(312)	13,233	15,806
60305	River Forest	(312)	12,392	13,402
60171	River Grove	(312)	10,368	11,465
60546	Riverside	(312)	9,236	10,357
60472	Robbins	(312)	8,119	9,641
62454	Robinson	(618)	7,285	7,178
61068	Rochelle	(815)	8,982	8,594
61071	Rock Falls	(815)	10,624	10,287
*61125	Rockford	(815)	139,712	147,370
61201	Rock Island	(309)	46,821	50,166
60008	Rolling Meadows	(312)	20,167	19,178
60441	Romeoville	(815)	15,519	12,888
60172	Roselle	(312)	17,034	6,207
62024	Rosewood Heights(u)	(618)	5,085	3,391
60073	Round Lake Beach	(312)	12,921	5,717
60174	St. Charles	(312)	17,492	12,945
62881	Salem	(618)	7,813	6,187
60548	Sandwich	(815)	5,365	5,056
60411	Sauk Village	(312)	10,906	7,479
60172	Schaumburg	(312)	53,355	18,531
60176	Schiller Park	(312)	11,458	12,712
62225	Scott AFB(u)	(618)	8,648	7,871
62565	Shelbyville	(217)	5,259	4,887
61282	Silvis	(309)	7,130	5,907
60076	Skokie	(312)	60,278	68,322
60177	South Elgin	(312)	5,970	4,289
60473	South Holland	(312)	24,977	23,931
*62703	Springfield	(217)	100,054	91,753
61362	Spring Valley	(815)	5,822	5,605
60475	Steger	(312)	9,269	8,104
61081	Sterling	(815)	16,273	16,113
60402	Stickney	(312)	5,893	6,601
60103	Streamwood	(312)	23,456	18,176
61364	Streator	(815)	14,795	15,600
60501	Summit	(312)	10,110	11,569
62221	Swansea	(618)	5,529	5,432
60178	Sycamore	(815)	9,219	7,843
62568	Taylorville	(217)	11,386	10,644
60477	Tinley Park	(312)	26,178	12,572
61801	Urbana	(217)	35,978	33,976
62471	Vandalia	(618)	5,338	5,160
60061	Vernon Hills	(312)	9,827	1,056
60181	Villa Park	(312)	23,155	25,891
60555	Warrenville	(312)	7,519	3,281
61571	Washington	(309)	10,364	6,790
62204	Washington Park	(618)	8,223	9,524
60970	Watseka	(815)	5,543	5,294
60084	Wauconda	(312)	5,688	5,460
60085	Waukegan	(312)	67,653	65,134
60153	Westchester	(312)	17,730	20,033
60185	West Chicago	(312)	12,550	9,988
60558	Western Springs	(312)	12,876	13,029
62896	West Frankfort	(618)	9,437	8,854
60559	Westmont	(312)	17,353	8,832
61604	West Peoria(u)	(309)	5,219	6,873
60187	Wheaton	(312)	43,043	31,138
60090	Wheeling	(312)	23,266	13,243
60091	Wilmette	(312)	28,221	32,134
60093	Winnetka	(312)	12,772	14,131
60096	Winthrop Harbor	(312)	5,427	4,794
60097	Wonder Lake(u)	(312)	5,917	4,806
60191	Wood Dale	(312)	11,251	8,831
60515	Woodridge	(312)	21,763	11,028
62095	Wood River	(618)	12,446	13,186
60098	Woodstock	(815)	11,725	10,226
60482	Worth	(312)	11,592	11,999
60099	Zion	(312)	17,865	17,268

Indiana

ZIP code	Place		1980	1970
46001	Alexandria	(317)	6,028	5,600
46011	Anderson	(317)	64,695	70,787
46703	Angola	(219)	5,486	5,117
46706	Auburn	(219)	8,122	7,388
47421	Bedford	(812)	14,410	13,087
46107	Beech Grove	(317)	13,196	13,559
47401	Bloomington	(812)	51,646	43,262
46714	Bluffton	(219)	8,705	8,297
47601	Boonville	(812)	6,300	5,736
47834	Brazil	(812)	7,852	8,163
46112	Brownsburg	(317)	6,242	5,751
46032	Carmel	(317)	18,272	6,691
46303	Cedar Lake	(219)	8,754	7,589
47111	Charlestown	(812)	5,596	5,933
46304	Chesterton	(219)	8,531	6,177
47130	Clarksville	(812)	15,164	13,298
47842	Clinton	(317)	5,267	5,340
46725	Columbia City	(219)	5,091	4,911
47201	Columbus	(812)	30,292	26,457
47331	Connersville	(317)	17,023	17,604
47933	Crawfordsville	(317)	13,325	13,842
46307	Crown Point	(219)	16,455	10,931
46733	Decatur	(219)	8,649	8,445
46514	Dunlap(u)	(219)	5,397	....
46311	Dyer	(219)	9,555	4,906
46312	East Chicago	(219)	39,786	46,982
46514	Elkhart	(219)	41,305	43,152
46036	Elwood	(317)	10,867	11,196
*47708	Evansville	(812)	130,496	138,764
*46802	Fort Wayne	(219)	172,391	178,269
46041	Frankfort	(317)	15,168	14,956
46131	Franklin	(317)	11,563	11,477
*46401	Gary	(219)	151,968	175,415
46933	Gas City	(317)	6,370	5,742
46526	Goshen	(219)	19,665	17,871
46135	Greencastle	(317)	8,403	8,852

ZIP code	Place		1980	1970
46140	Greenfield	(317)	11,299	9,986
47240	Greensburg	(812)	9,254	8,620
46142	Greenwood	(317)	19,327	11,869
46319	Griffith	(219)	17,026	18,168
*46320	Hammond	(219)	93,714	107,983
47348	Hartford City	(317)	7,622	8,207
46322	Highland	(219)	25,935	24,947
46342	Hobart	(219)	22,987	21,485
47542	Huntingburg	(812)	5,376	4,794
46750	Huntington	(219)	16,202	16,217
*46206	Indianapolis	(317)	700,807	736,856
47546	Jasper	(812)	9,097	8,641
47130	Jeffersonville	(812)	21,220	20,008
46755	Kendallville	(219)	7,299	6,838
46901	Kokomo	(317)	47,808	44,042
*47901	Lafayette	(317)	43,011	44,955
46405	Lake Station	(219)	15,087	9,858
46350	La Porte	(219)	21,796	22,140
46226	Lawrence	(317)	25,591	16,353
46052	Lebanon	(317)	11,456	9,766
47441	Linton	(812)	6,315	5,450
46947	Logansport	(219)	17,731	19,255
46356	Lowell	(219)	5,827	3,839
47250	Madison	(812)	12,472	13,081
46952	Marion	(317)	35,874	39,607
46151	Martinsville	(317)	11,311	9,723
46410	Merrillville	(219)	27,677	15,918
46360	Michigan City	(219)	36,850	39,369
46544	Mishawaka	(219)	40,224	36,060
47960	Monticello	(219)	5,162	4,869
46158	Mooresville	(317)	5,349	5,800
47620	Mount Vernon	(812)	7,656	6,770
*47302	Muncie	(317)	77,216	69,082
46321	Munster	(219)	20,671	16,514
47150	New Albany	(812)	37,103	38,402
47362	New Castle	(317)	20,056	21,215
46774	New Haven	(219)	6,714	5,346
46060	Noblesville	(317)	12,253	7,548
46962	North Manchester	(219)	5,998	5,791
47265	North Vernon	(812)	5,768	4,582
47130	Oak Park(u)	(812)	5,871	....
46970	Peru	(317)	13,764	14,139
46168	Plainfield	(317)	9,191	8,211
46563	Plymouth	(219)	7,693	7,661
46368	Portage	(219)	27,409	19,127
47371	Portland	(219)	7,074	7,115
47670	Princeton	(812)	8,976	7,431
47374	Richmond	(317)	41,349	43,999
46975	Rochester	(219)	5,050	4,631
46173	Rushville	(317)	6,113	6,686
47167	Salem	(812)	5,290	5,041
46375	Schererville	(219)	13,209	3,663
47170	Scottsburg	(812)	5,068	4,791
47274	Seymour	(812)	15,050	13,352
46176	Shelbyville	(317)	14,989	15,094
*46624	South Bend	(219)	109,727	125,580
46383	South Haven(u)	(219)	6,679	....
46224	Speedway	(317)	12,641	14,523
47586	Tell City	(812)	8,704	7,933
*47808	Terre Haute	(812)	61,125	70,335
46072	Tipton	(317)	5,004	5,313
46383	Valparaiso	(219)	22,247	20,020
47591	Vincennes	(812)	20,857	19,867
46992	Wabash	(219)	12,985	13,379
46580	Warsaw	(219)	10,647	7,506
47501	Washington	(812)	11,325	11,358
47906	West Lafayette	(317)	21,247	19,157
46394	Whiting	(219)	5,630	7,054
47394	Winchester	(317)	5,659	5,493

Iowa

ZIP code	Place		1980	1970
50511	Algona	(515)	6,289	6,032
50009	Altoona	(515)	5,764	2,883
50010	Ames	(515)	45,775	39,505
50021	Ankeny	(515)	15,429	9,151
50022	Atlantic	(712)	7,789	7,306
52722	Bettendorf	(319)	27,381	22,126
50036	Boone	(515)	12,602	12,468
52601	Burlington	(319)	29,529	32,366
51401	Carroll	(712)	9,705	8,716
50613	Cedar Falls	(319)	36,322	29,597
*52401	Cedar Rapids	(319)	110,243	110,642
52544	Centerville	(515)	6,558	6,531
50049	Chariton	(515)	5,116	5,009
50616	Charles City	(515)	8,778	9,268
51012	Cherokee	(712)	7,004	7,272
51632	Clarinda	(712)	5,458	5,420
50428	Clear Lake City	(515)	7,458	6,430
52732	Clinton	(319)	32,828	34,719
50053	Clive	(515)	5,906	3,005
52240	Coralville	(319)	7,687	6,130
51501	Council Bluffs	(712)	56,449	60,348
50801	Creston	(515)	8,429	8,234
*52802	Davenport	(319)	103,264	98,469
52101	Decorah	(319)	7,991	7,237
51442	Denison	(712)	6,675	6,218
*50318	Des Moines	(515)	191,003	201,404
52001	Dubuque	(319)	62,374	62,309
51334	Estherville	(712)	7,518	8,108
52556	Fairfield	(515)	9,428	8,715
50501	Fort Dodge	(515)	29,423	31,263
52627	Fort Madison	(319)	13,520	13,996
51534	Glenwood	(712)	5,280	4,421
50112	Grinnell	(515)	8,868	8,402
51537	Harlan	(712)	5,357	5,049
50644	Independence	(319)	6,392	5,910
50125	Indianola	(515)	10,843	8,852
52240	Iowa City	(319)	50,508	46,850
50126	Iowa Falls	(515)	6,174	6,454
52632	Keokuk	(319)	13,536	14,631
50138	Knoxville	(515)	8,143	7,755
51031	Le Mars	(712)	8,276	8,159
52060	Maquoketa	(319)	6,313	5,677
52302	Marion	(319)	19,474	18,028
50158	Marshalltown	(515)	26,938	26,219
50401	Mason City	(515)	30,144	30,379
52641	Mount Pleasant	(319)	7,322	7,007
52761	Muscatine	(319)	23,467	22,405
50201	Nevada	(515)	5,912	4,952
50208	Newton	(515)	15,292	15,619
50662	Oelwein	(319)	7,564	7,735
52577	Oskaloosa	(515)	10,629	11,224
52501	Ottumwa	(515)	27,381	29,610
50219	Pella	(515)	8,349	6,668
50220	Perry	(515)	7,053	6,906
51566	Red Oak	(712)	6,810	6,210
51201	Sheldon	(712)	5,003	4,535
51601	Shenandoah	(712)	6,274	5,968
*51101	Sioux City	(712)	82,003	85,925
51301	Spencer	(712)	11,726	10,278
50588	Storm Lake	(712)	8,814	8,591
50322	Urbandale	(515)	17,869	14,434
52349	Vinton	(319)	5,040	4,845
52353	Washington	(319)	6,584	6,317
*50701	Waterloo	(319)	75,985	75,533
50677	Waverly	(319)	8,444	7,205
50595	Webster City	(515)	8,572	8,488
50265	West Des Moines	(515)	21,894	16,441
50311	Windsor Heights	(515)	5,632	6,303

Kansas

ZIP code	Place		1980	1970
67410	Abilene	(913)	6,572	6,661
67005	Arkansas City	(316)	13,201	13,216
66002	Atchison	(913)	11,407	12,565
67010	Augusta	(316)	6,968	5,977
66012	Bonner Springs	(913)	6,266	3,884
66720	Chanute	(316)	10,506	10,341
67337	Coffeyville	(316)	15,185	15,116
67701	Colby	(913)	5,544	4,658
66901	Concordia	(913)	6,847	7,221
67037	Derby	(316)	9,786	7,947
67801	Dodge City	(316)	18,001	14,127
67042	El Dorado	(316)	11,551	12,308
66801	Emporia	(316)	25,287	23,327
66442	Fort Riley North(u)	(913)	16,086	12,469
66701	Fort Scott	(316)	[illegible]	8,067
67846	Garden City	(316)	18,256	14,790
67735	Goodland	(913)	5,708	5,510
67530	Great Bend	(316)	16,608	16,133
67601	Hays	(913)	16,301	15,396
67060	Haysville	(316)	8,006	6,531
67501	Hutchinson	(316)	40,284	36,885
67301	Independence	(316)	10,598	10,347
66749	Iola	(316)	6,938	6,493
66441	Junction City	(913)	19,305	19,018
*66110	Kansas City	(913)	161,148	168,213
66043	Lansing	(913)	5,307	3,797
66044	Lawrence	(913)	52,738	45,698
66048	Leavenworth	(913)	33,656	25,147
66206	Leawood	(913)	13,360	10,645
66215	Lenexa	(913)	18,639	5,549
67901	Liberal	(316)	14,911	13,862
67460	McPherson	(316)	11,753	10,851
66502	Manhattan	(913)	32,644	27,575
66203	Merriam	(913)	10,794	10,955
66222	Mission	(913)	8,643	8,125
67114	Newton	(316)	16,332	15,439
66061	Olathe	(913)	37,258	17,917
66067	Ottawa	(913)	11,016	11,036
66204	Overland Park	(913)	81,784	77,934
67357	Parsons	(316)	12,898	13,015
66762	Pittsburg	(316)	18,770	20,171
66208	Prairie Village	(913)	24,657	28,378
67124	Pratt	(316)	6,885	6,736
66203	Roeland Park	(913)	7,962	9,760
67665	Russell	(913)	5,427	5,371
67401	Salina	(913)	41,843	37,714
*66203	Shawnee	(913)	29,653	20,946
*66603	Topeka	(913)	118,690	125,011
67152	Wellington	(316)	8,212	8,072
*67202	Wichita	(316)	279,838	276,554
67156	Winfield	(316)	10,736	11,405

Kentucky

ZIP code	Place		1980	1970
41101	Ashland	(606)	27,064	29,245
40004	Bardstown	(502)	6,155	5,816

ZIP code	Place		1980	1970
41073	Bellevue	(606)	7,678	8,847
40403	Berea	(606)	8,226	6,956
42101	Bowling Green	(502)	40,450	36,705
40218	Buechel(u)	(502)	6,912	5,359
42718	Campbellsville	(502)	8,715	7,598
42330	Central City	(502)	5,250	5,450
40701	Corbin	(606)	8,075	7,474
*41011	Covington	(606)	49,585	52,535
41031	Cynthiana	(606)	5,881	6,356
40422	Danville	(606)	12,942	11,542
41074	Dayton	(606)	6,979	8,751
41017	Edgewood	(606)	7,243	4,139
42701	Elizabethtown	(502)	15,380	11,748
41018	Elsmere	(606)	7,203	5,161
41018	Erlanger	(606)	14,466	12,676
40118	Fairdale(u)	(502)	7,315	....
40291	Fern Creek(u)	(502)	16,866	....
41139	Flatwoods	(606)	8,354	7,380
41042	Florence	(606)	15,586	11,661
42223	Fort Campbell North(u)	(502)	17,211	13,616
40121	Fort Knox(u)	(502)	31,035	37,608
41017	Fort Mitchell	(606)	7,294	6,982
41075	Fort Thomas	(606)	16,012	16,338
40601	Frankfort	(502)	25,973	21,902
42134	Franklin	(502)	7,738	6,553
40324	Georgetown	(502)	10,972	8,629
42141	Glasgow	(502)	12,958	11,301
40330	Harrodsburg	(606)	7,265	6,741
41701	Hazard	(606)	5,429	5,459
42420	Henderson	(502)	24,834	22,976
40228	Highview(u)	(502)	13,286	....
40229	Hillview	(502)	5,196	....
42240	Hopkinsville	(502)	27,318	21,395
41051	Independence	(606)	7,998	1,715
40299	Jeffersontown	(502)	15,795	9,701
40342	Lawrenceburg	(502)	5,167	3,579
40033	Lebanon	(502)	6,590	5,528
*40511	Lexington-Fayette	(606)	204,165	108,137
*40201	Louisville	(502)	298,694	361,706
42431	Madisonville	(502)	16,979	15,332
42066	Mayfield	(502)	10,705	10,724
41056	Maysville	(606)	7,983	7,411
40965	Middlesborough	(606)	12,251	11,878
42633	Monticello	(606)	5,677	3,618
40351	Morehead	(606)	7,789	7,191
40353	Mount Sterling	(606)	5,820	5,083
42071	Murray	(502)	14,248	13,537
40218	Newburg(u)	(502)	24,612	....
*41071	Newport	(606)	21,587	25,998
40356	Nicholasville	(606)	10,400	5,829
40219	Okolona(u)	(502)	20,039	17,643
42301	Owensboro	(502)	54,450	50,329
42001	Paducah	(502)	29,315	31,627
40361	Paris	(606)	7,935	7,823
40258	Pleasure Ridge Park(u)	(502)	27,332	28,566
42445	Princeton	(502)	7,073	6,292
40160	Radcliff	(502)	14,656	8,426
40475	Richmond	(606)	21,705	16,861
42276	Russellville	(502)	7,520	6,456
40207	St. Matthews	(502)	13,519	13,152
40065	Shelbyville	(502)	5,308	4,182
40216	Shively	(502)	16,645	19,139
42501	Somerset	(606)	10,649	10,436
40272	Valley Station(u)	(502)	24,474	24,471
40383	Versailles	(606)	6,427	5,679
41101	Westwood(u)	(606)	5,973	777
40769	Williamsburg	(606)	5,560	3,687
40391	Winchester	(606)	15,216	13,402

Louisiana

ZIP code	Place		1980	1970
70510	Abbeville	(318)	12,391	10,996
71301	Alexandria	(318)	51,565	41,811
70032	Arabi(u)	(504)	10,248	....
70094	Avondale(u)	(504)	6,699	....
70714	Baker	(504)	12,865	8,281
71220	Bastrop	(318)	15,527	14,713
*70821	Baton Rouge	(504)	220,394	165,921
70360	Bayou Cane(u)	(504)	15,723	9,077
70380	Bayou Vista(u)	(504)	5,805	5,121
70037	Belle Chasse(u)	(504)	5,412	....
70427	Bogalusa	(504)	16,976	18,412
71010	Bossier City	(318)	49,969	43,769
70517	Breaux Bridge	(318)	5,922	4,942
....	Broadmoor(u)	(318)	7,051	....
71291	Brownsville-Bawcomville(u)	(318)	7,252	....
71322	Bunkie	(318)	5,364	5,395
70043	Chalmette(u)	(504)	33,847	....
71291	Claiborne(u)	(318)	6,278	....
70433	Covington	(504)	7,892	7,170
70526	Crowley	(318)	16,036	16,104
70345	Cut Off(u)	(504)	5,049	....
70726	Denham Springs	(504)	8,412	6,752
70634	De Ridder	(318)	10,337	8,030
70346	Donaldsonville	(504)	7,901	7,367
70072	Estelle(u)	(504)	12,724	....
70535	Eunice	(318)	12,479	11,390
70538	Franklin	(318)	9,584	9,325
70354	Galliano(u)	(504)	5,159	....
70737	Gonzales	(504)	7,287	4,512
70053	Gretna	(504)	20,615	24,875
70401	Hammond	(504)	15,226	12,487
70123	Harahan	(504)	11,384	13,037
70058	Harvey(u)	(504)	22,709	6,347
70360	Houma	(504)	32,602	30,922
70544	Jeanerette	(318)	6,511	6,322
70121	Jefferson(u)	(504)	15,550	16,489
70546	Jennings	(318)	12,401	11,783
71251	Jonesboro	(318)	5,061	5,072
70548	Kaplan	(318)	5,016	5,540
70062	Kenner	(504)	66,382	29,858
70445	Lacombe(u)	(504)	5,146	....
70501	Lafayette	(318)	80,584	68,908
70601	Lake Charles	(318)	75,051	77,998
71254	Lake Providence	(318)	6,361	6,183
70068	Laplace(u)	(504)	16,112	5,953
70373	Larose(u)	(504)	5,234	4,267
71446	Leesville	(318)	9,054	8,928
70123	Little Farms(u)	(504)	NA	15,713
70448	Mandeville	(504)	6,076	2,571
71052	Mansfield	(318)	6,485	6,432
71351	Marksville	(318)	5,113	4,519
70072	Marrero(u)	(504)	36,548	29,015
*70004	Metairie(u)	(504)	164,160	136,477
71055	Minden	(318)	15,074	13,996
71201	Monroe	(318)	57,597	56,374
70380	Morgan City	(504)	16,114	16,586
70601	Moss Bluff(u)	(318)	7,004	....
71457	Natchitoches	(318)	16,664	15,974
70560	New Iberia	(318)	32,766	30,147
*70113	New Orleans	(504)	557,927	593,471
71463	Oakdale	(318)	7,155	7,301
70570	Opelousas	(318)	18,903	20,387
71360	Pineville	(318)	12,034	8,951
70764	Plaquemine	(504)	7,521	7,739
70454	Ponchatoula	(504)	5,469	4,545
70767	Port Allen	(504)	6,114	5,728
70085	Poydras(u)	(504)	5,722	....
70601	Prien(u)	(318)	6,224	....
70394	Raceland(u)	(504)	6,302	4,880
70578	Rayne	(318)	9,066	9,510
70084	Reserve(u)	(504)	7,288	6,381
70123	River Ridge(u)	(504)	17,146	....
71270	Ruston	(318)	20,585	17,365
70582	St. Martinville	(318)	7,965	7,153
70807	Scotlandville(u)	(504)	15,113	22,599
*71102	Shreveport	(318)	205,820	182,064
70458	Slidell	(504)	26,718	16,101
71459	South Fort Polk(u)	(318)	12,498	15,600
71075	Springhill	(318)	6,516	6,496
70663	Sulphur	(318)	19,709	14,959
71282	Tallulah	(318)	11,341	9,643
71285	Terrytown(u)	(318)	23,548	13,382
70301	Thibodaux	(504)	15,810	15,028
70053	Timberlane(u)	(504)	11,579	....
71373	Vidalia	(318)	5,936	5,538
70586	Ville Platte	(318)	9,201	9,692
70092	Violet(u)	(504)	11,678	....
70094	Waggaman(u)	(504)	9,004	....
70669	Westlake	(318)	5,246	4,082
71291	West Monroe	(318)	14,993	14,868
70094	Westwego	(504)	12,663	11,402
71483	Winnfield	(318)	7,311	7,142
71295	Winnsboro	(318)	5,921	5,349
70791	Zachary	(504)	7,297	4,964

Maine (207)

See Note Page 544

ZIP code	Place	1980	1970
04210	Auburn	23,128	24,151
04330	Augusta	21,819	21,945
04401	Bangor	31,643	33,168
04530	Bath	10,246	9,679
04915	Belfast	6,243	5,957
04005	Biddeford	19,638	19,983
04412	Brewer	9,017	9,300
04011	Brunswick Center(u)	10,990	10,867
04011	*Brunswick*	17,366	16,195
04093	*Buxton*	5,775	3,135
04107	*Cape Elizabeth*	7,838	7,873
04736	Caribou	9,916	10,419
04021	*Cumberland*	5,284	4,096
04605	Ellsworth	5,179	4,603
04937	*Fairfield*	6,113	5,684
04105	*Falmouth*	6,853	6,291
04938	*Farmington*	6,730	5,657
04032	*Freeport*	5,863	4,781
04345	Gardiner	6,485	6,685
04038	*Gorham*	10,101	7,839
04444	*Hampden*	5,250	4,693
04730	Houlton Center(u)	5,730	6,760
04730	*Houlton*	6,766	8,111
04239	*Jay*	5,080	3,954
04043	*Kennebunk*	6,621	5,646
03904	Kittery Center(u)	5,465	7,363
03904	*Kittery*	9,314	11,028
04240	Lewiston	40,481	41,779

ZIP code	Place	1980	1970
04750	*Limestone*	8,719	10,360
04457	*Lincoln*	5,066	4,759
04250	*Lisbon*	8,769	6,544
04750	Loring(u)	6,572	7,881
04756	*Madawaska*	5,282	5,585
04462	Millinocket Center(u)	7,567	7,558
04462	*Millinocket*	7,567	7,742
04062	North Windham(u)	5,492	....
04963	*Oakland*	5,162	3,535
04064	Old Orchard Beach Ctr.(u)	6,023	5,273
04064	*Old Orchard Beach*	6,291	5,404
04468	Old Town	8,422	8,741
04473	Orono Center(u)	9,891	9,146
04473	*Orono*	10,578	9,989
*04101	Portland	61,572	65,116
04769	Presque Isle	11,172	11,452
04841	Rockland	7,919	8,505
04276	Rumford Compact(u)	6,256	6,198
04276	*Rumford*	8,240	9,363
04072	Saco	12,921	11,678
04073	Sanford Center(u)	10,268	10,457
04073	*Sanford*	18,020	15,812
04074	*Scarborough*	11,347	7,845
04976	Skowhegan Center(u)	6,517	6,571
04976	*Skowhegan*	8,098	7,601
04106	South Portland	22,712	23,267
04084	*Standish*	5,946	3,122
04086	*Topsham*	6,431	5,022
04901	Waterville	17,779	18,192
04090	*Wells*	8,211	4,448
04092	Westbrook	14,976	14,444
04082	*Windham*	11,282	6,593
04901	Winslow Center(u)	5,903	5,389
04901	*Winslow*	8,057	7,299
04364	*Winthrop*	5,889	4,335
04096	*Yarmouth*	6,585	4,854
03909	*York*	8,465	5,690

Maryland (301)

ZIP code	Place	1980	1970
21001	Aberdeen	11,533	7,403
21005	Aberdeen Proving Ground(u)	5,772	7,403
20783	Adelphi(u)	12,530	....
20331	Andrews AFB(u)	10,064	6,418
*21401	Annapolis	31,740	30,095
21227	Arbutus(u)	20,163	22,745
21012	Arnold(u)	12,285	....
20906	Aspen Hill(u)	47,455	16,887
*21233	Baltimore	786,741	905,787
21014	Bel Air	7,814	6,307
21050	Bel Air North(u)	5,043	....
21014	Bel Air South(u)	8,461	
20705	Beltsville(u)	12,760	8,912
*20815	Bethesda(u)	63,022	71,621
20710	Bladensburg	7,691	7,977
*20715	Bowie	33,695	35,028
21225	Brooklyn Park(u)	11,508	....
20818	Cabin John-Brookmont(u)	5,135	....
20619	California(u)	5,770	....
21613	Cambridge	11,703	11,595
20748	Camp Springs(u)	16,118	22,776
21401	Cape St. Clair(u)	6,022	....
20743	Carmody Hills-Pepper Mill(u)	5,571	6,245
21234	Carney(u)	21,488	....
21228	Catonsville(u)	33,208	54,812
20785	Cheverly	5,751	6,808
20815	Chevy Chase(u)	12,232	16,424
20783	Chillum(u)	32,775	35,656
20735	Clinton(u)	16,438	....
20904	Cloverly(u)	5,153	....
21030	Cockeysville(u)	17,013	....
20904	Colesville(u)	14,359	9,455
20740	College Park	23,614	26,156
*21044	Columbia(u)	52,518	8,815
20743	Coral Hills(u)	11,602	9,058
21114	Crofton(u)	12,009	4,478
21502	Cumberland	25,933	29,724
20747	District Heights	6,799	7,846
20785	Dodge Park(u)	5,275	....
21222	Dundalk(u)	71,293	85,377
21601	Easton	7,536	6,809
20737	East Riverdale(u)	14,117	....
21219	Edgemere(u)	9,078	10,352
21040	Edgewood	19,455	8,551
21921	Elkton	6,468	5,362
21043	Ellicott City(u)	21,784	9,435
21221	Essex(u)	39,614	38,193
20904	Fairland(u)	5,154	....
21047	Fallston(u)	5,572	....
21061	Ferndale(u)	14,314	9,929
20747	Forestville(u)	16,401	16,188
20755	Fort Meade(u)	14,083	16,699
21701	Frederick	27,557	23,641
.....	Friendly(u)	8,848	....
21532	Frostburg	7,715	7,327
*20877	Gaithersburg	26,424	8,344
20874	Germantown(u)	9,721	....
.....	Glassmanor(u)	7,751	....
21061	Glen Burnie(u)	37,263	38,608
20769	Glenn Dale(u)	5,106	....
20771	Goddard(u)	6,147	....
20770	Greenbelt	16,000	18,199
21122	Green Haven(u)	6,577	....
21740	Hagerstown	34,132	35,862
21740	Halfway(u)	8,659	6,106
21204	Hampton(u)	5,220	....
21078	Havre De Grace	8,763	9,791
20903	Hillandale(u)	9,686	....
20748	Hillcrest Heights	17,021	24,037
*20780	Hyattsville	12,709	14,998
21085	Joppatowne(u)	11,348	9,092
20785	Kentland(u)	8,596	9,649
20772	Kettering(u)	6,972	....
21122	Lake Shore(u)	10,181	....
20785	Landover(u)	5,374	5,597
20787	Langley Park(u)	14,038	11,564
20706	Lanham-Seabrook(u)	15,814	13,244
21227	Lansdowne-Baltimore Highlands(u)	16,759	17,770
20772	Largo(u)	5,557	....
*20707	Laurel	12,103	10,525
21502	La Vale-Narrows Park(u)	5,523	3,971
20653	Lexington Pk.(u)	10,361	9,136
21090	Linthicum(u)	7,457	9,775
21207	Lochearn(u)	26,908	....
21037	Londontowne(u)	6,052	3,864
21093	Lutherville-Timonium(u)	17,854	24,055
20748	Marlow Heights(u)	5,824	....
20707	Maryland City(u)	6,949	7,102
.....	Mays Chapel(u)	5,213	....
21220	Middle River(u)	26,756	19,935
.....	Milford Mill(u)	20,354	....
20879	Montgomery Village(u)	18,725	....
20822	Mount Rainier	7,361	8,180
21402	Naval Academy(u)	5,367	....
20784	New Carrollton	12,632	14,870
20815	North Bethesda(u)	22,671	....
20895	North Kensington(u)	9,039	....
20707	North Laurel(u)	6,093	....
21113	Odenton(u)	13,270	5,989
20832	Olney(u)	13,026	2,138
21206	Overlea(u)	12,965	13,124
21117	Owings Mills(u)	9,526	7,360
20745	Oxon Hill(u)	36,267	11,974
20785	Palmer Park(u)	7,986	8,172
21234	Parkville	35,159	33,589
21122	Pasadena(u)	7,439	....
21128	Perry Hall(u)	13,455	5,446
21208	Pikesville(u)	22,555	25,395
20854	Potomac(u)	40,402	....
21227	Pumphrey(u)	5,666	6,425
20878	Quince Orchard(u)	5,107	....
21133	Randallstown(u)	25,927	33,683
.....	Redland(u)	10,759	....
21136	Reisterstown(u)	19,385	12,568
21122	Riviera Beach(u)	8,812	7,464
*20850	Rockville	43,811	42,739
21237	Rosedale(u)	19,956	19,417
21221	Rossville(u)	8,646	....
20601	St. Charles(u)	13,921	....
21801	Salisbury	16,429	15,252
20743	Seat Pleasant	5,217	7,217
21207	Security(u)	29,453	....
21144	Severn(u)	20,147	....
21146	Severna Park	21,253	16,358
*20907	Silver Spring(u)	72,893	77,411
21061	South Gate(u)	24,185	9,356
20895	South Kensington(u)	9,344	10,289
20707	South Laurel(u)	18,034	13,345
20746	Suitland-Silver Hills(u)	32,164	30,355
20912	Takoma Park	16,231	18,507
.....	Tantallon(u)	9,945	....
20748	Temple Hills(u)	6,630	....
21204	Towson(u)	51,083	77,768
20601	Waldorf(u)	9,782	7,368
20743	Walker Mill(u)	10,651	7,103
21157	Westminster	8,808	7,207
20902	Wheaton Glenmont(u)	48,598	66,280
20903	White Oak(u)	13,700	19,769
20695	White Plains(u)	5,167	....
21207	Woodlawn(u)	5,306	....

Massachusetts

See Note on Page 544

ZIP code	Place	Area code	1980	1970
02351	*Abington*	(617)	13,517	12,334
01720	*Acton*	(617)	17,544	14,770
02743	*Acushnet*	(617)	8,704	7,767
01220	Adams Center(u)	(413)	6,857	11,256
.....	*Adams*	(413)	10,381	11,772
01001	*Agawam*	(413)	26,271	21,717
01913	Amesbury Center(u)	(617)	12,236	10,088
.....	*Amesbury*	(617)	13,971	11,388
01002	Amherst Center	(413)	17,773	17,926
.....	*Amherst*	(413)	33,229	26,331
01810	*Andover*	(617)	26,370	23,695
02174	*Arlington*	(617)	48,219	53,524
01721	*Ashland*	(617)	9,165	8,882

ZIP code	Place		1980	1970
01331	Athol Center(u)	(617)	8,708	9,723
.....	*Athol*	(617)	10,634	11,185
02703	Attleboro	(617)	34,196	32,907
01501	*Auburn*	(617)	14,845	15,347
02322	*Avon*	(617)	5,026	5,295
*01432	*Ayer*	(617)	6,993	8,325
02630	*Barnstable*	(617)	30,898	19,842
01730	*Bedford*	(617)	13,067	13,513
01007	*Belchertown*	(413)	8,339	5,936
02019	*Bellingham*	(617)	14,300	13,967
02178	*Belmont*	(617)	26,100	28,285
01915	Beverly	(617)	37,655	38,348
01821	*Billerica*	(617)	36,727	31,648
01504	*Blackstone*	(617)	6,570	6,566
*02109	Boston	(617)	562,994	641,071
02532	*Bourne*	(617)	13,874	12,636
01921	*Boxford*	(617)	5,374	4,032
02184	*Braintree*	(617)	36,337	35,050
02631	*Brewster*	(617)	5,226	1,790
02324	*Bridgewater*	(617)	17,202	12,911
*02403	Brockton	(617)	95,172	89,040
02146	*Brookline*	(617)	55,062	58,689
01803	*Burlington*	(617)	23,486	21,980
*02138	Cambridge	(617)	95,322	100,361
02021	*Canton*	(617)	18,182	17,100
02330	*Carver*	(617)	6,988	2,420
01507	*Charlton*	(617)	6,719	4,654
02633	*Chatham*	(617)	6,071	4,554
01824	*Chelmsford*	(617)	31,174	31,432
02150	Chelsea	(617)	25,431	30,625
*01021	Chicopee	(413)	55,112	66,676
01510	*Clinton*	(617)	12,771	13,383
01778	Cochituate(u)	(617)	6,126	....
02025	*Cohasset*	(617)	7,174	6,954
01742	*Concord*	(617)	16,293	16,148
01226	*Dalton*	(413)	6,797	7,505
01923	*Danvers*	(617)	24,100	26,151
02714	*Dartmouth*	(617)	23,966	18,800
02026	*Dedham*	(617)	25,298	26,938
02638	*Dennis*	(617)	12,360	6,454
02715	*Dighton*	(617)	5,352	4,667
01826	*Dracut*	(617)	21,249	18,214
01570	*Dudley*	(617)	8,717	8,087
02332	*Duxbury*	(617)	11,807	7,636
02333	*East Bridgewater*	(617)	9,945	8,347
02536	East Falmouth(u)	(617)	5,181	2,971
01027	*Easthampton*	(413)	15,580	13,012
01028	*East Longmeadow*	(413)	12,905	13,029
02334	*Easton*	(617)	16,623	12,157
02149	Everett	(617)	37,195	42,485
02719	*Fairhaven*	(617)	15,759	16,332
*02722	Fall River	(617)	92,574	96,898
*02540	Falmouth Center(u)	(617)	5,720	5,806
.....	*Falmouth*	(617)	23,640	15,942
01420	Fitchburg	(617)	39,580	43,343
01433	Fort Devens(u)	(617)	9,546	12,915
02035	*Foxborough*	(617)	14,148	14,218
01701	*Framingham*	(617)	65,113	64,048
02038	Franklin Center(u)	(617)	9,296	8,863
.....	*Franklin*	(617)	18,217	17,830
02702	*Freetown*	(617)	7,058	4,270
01440	Gardner	(617)	17,900	19,748
01833	*Georgetown*	(617)	5,687	5,290
01930	Gloucester	(617)	27,768	27,941
01519	*Grafton*	(617)	11,238	11,659
01033	*Granby*	(413)	5,380	5,473
01230	*Great Barrington*	(413)	7,405	7,537
01301	Greenfield Center(u)	(413)	14,198	14,642
.....	*Greenfield*	(413)	18,436	18,116
01450	*Groton*	(617)	6,154	5,109
01834	*Groveland*	(617)	5,040	5,382
02338	*Halifax*	(617)	5,513	3,537
01936	*Hamilton*	(617)	6,960	6,373
02339	*Hanover*	(617)	11,358	10,107
02341	*Hanson*	(617)	8,617	7,148
01451	*Harvard*	(617)	12,170	12,494
02645	*Harwich*	(617)	8,971	5,892
01830	Haverhill	(617)	46,865	46,120
02043	*Hingham*	(617)	20,339	18,845
02343	*Holbrook*	(617)	11,140	11,775
01520	*Holden*	(617)	13,336	12,564
01746	*Holliston*	(617)	12,622	12,069
01040	Holyoke	(413)	44,678	50,112
01748	*Hopkinton*	(617)	7,114	5,981
01749	Hudson Center(u)	(617)	14,156	14,283
.....	*Hudson*	(617)	16,408	16,084
02045	*Hull*	(617)	9,714	9,961
02601	Hyannis(u)	(617)	9,118	6,847
01938	Ipswich(u)	(617)	NA	5,022
.....	*Ipswich*	(617)	11,158	10,750
02364	*Kingston*	(617)	7,362	5,999
02346	*Lakeville*	(617)	5,931	4,376
01523	*Lancaster*	(617)	6,334	6,095
*01842	Lawrence	(617)	63,175	66,915
01238	*Lee*	(413)	6,247	6,426
01524	*Leicester*	(617)	9,446	9,140
01240	*Lenox*	(413)	6,523	5,804
01453	Leominster	(617)	34,508	32,939
02173	*Lexington*	(617)	29,479	31,886
01773	*Lincoln*	(617)	7,098	7,567
01460	*Littleton*	(617)	6,970	6,380
01106	*Longmeadow*	(413)	16,301	15,630
*01853	Lowell	(617)	92,418	94,239
01056	*Ludlow*	(413)	18,150	17,580
01462	*Lunenburg*	(617)	8,405	7,419
*01901	Lynn	(617)	78,471	90,294
01940	*Lynnfield*	(617)	11,267	10,826
02148	Malden	(617)	53,386	56,127
01944	*Manchester*	(617)	5,424	5,151
02048	*Mansfield*	(617)	13,453	9,939
01945	*Marblehead*	(617)	20,126	21,295
01752	Marlborough	(617)	30,617	27,936
02050	*Marshfield*	(617)	20,916	15,223
02739	*Mattapoisett*	(617)	5,597	4,500
01754	*Maynard*	(617)	9,590	9,710
02052	*Medfield*	(617)	10,220	9,821
02155	Medford	(617)	58,076	64,397
02053	*Medway*	(617)	8,447	7,938
02176	Melrose	(617)	30,055	33,180
01844	*Methuen*	(617)	36,701	35,456
02346	Middleborough Center(u)	(617)	7,012	6,259
.....	*Middleborough*	(617)	16,404	13,607
01757	Milford Center(u)	(617)	NA	13,740
.....	*Milford*	(617)	23,390	19,352
01527	*Millbury*	(617)	11,808	11,987
02054	*Millis*	(617)	6,908	5,686
02186	*Milton*	(617)	25,860	27,190
01057	*Monson*	(413)	7,315	7,355
01351	*Montague*	(413)	8,011	8,451
02554	*Nantucket*	(617)	5,087	3,774
01760	*Natick*	(617)	29,461	31,057
02192	*Needham*	(617)	27,901	29,748
*02741	New Bedford	(617)	98,478	101,777
01950	Newburyport	(617)	15,900	15,807
02158	Newton	(617)	83,622	91,263
02056	Norfolk	(617)	6,363	4,656
01247	North Adams	(413)	18,063	19,195
01002	North Amherst(u)	(413)	5,616	2,854
01060	Northampton	(413)	29,286	29,664
01845	*North Andover*	(617)	20,129	16,284
*02760	*North Attleborough*	(617)	21,095	18,665
01532	*Northborough*	(617)	10,568	9,218
01534	*Northbridge*	(617)	12,246	11,795
01864	*North Reading*	(617)	11,455	11,264
02060	North Scituate(u)	(617)	5,221	5,507
02766	*Norton*	(617)	12,690	9,487
02061	*Norwell*	(617)	9,182	7,796
02062	*Norwood*	(617)	29,711	30,815
01364	*Orange*	(617)	6,844	6,104
02653	*Orleans*	(617)	5,306	3,055
01253	Otis(u)	(413)	NA	5,596
01540	Oxford Center(u)	(617)	6,369	6,109
.....	*Oxford*	(617)	11,680	10,345
01069	*Palmer*	(413)	11,389	11,680
01960	Peabody	(617)	45,976	48,080
02359	*Pembroke*	(617)	13,487	11,193
01463	*Pepperell*	(617)	8,061	5,887
01866	Pinehurst(u)	(617)	6,588	....
01201	Pittsfield	(413)	51,974	57,020
02762	*Plainville*	(617)	5,857	4,953
*02360	Plymouth Center(u)	(617)	7,232	6,940
.....	*Plymouth*	(617)	35,913	18,606
02169	Quincy	(617)	84,743	87,966
02368	*Randolph*	(617)	28,218	27,035
02767	*Raynham*	(617)	9,085	6,705
01867	*Reading*	(617)	22,678	22,539
02769	*Rehoboth*	(617)	7,570	6,512
02151	Revere	(617)	42,423	43,159
02370	*Rockland*	(617)	15,695	15,674
01966	*Rockport*	(617)	6,345	5,636
01970	Salem	(617)	38,276	40,556
01950	*Salisbury*	(617)	5,973	4,179
02563	*Sandwich*	(617)	8,727	5,239
01906	*Saugus*	(617)	24,746	25,110
02066	*Scituate*	(617)	17,317	16,973
02771	*Seekonk*	(617)	12,269	11,116
02067	*Sharon*	(617)	13,601	12,367
01464	*Shirley*	(617)	5,124	4,909
01545	*Shrewsbury*	(617)	22,674	19,196
02725	*Somerset*	(617)	18,813	18,088
02143	Somerville	(617)	77,372	88,779
01772	*Southborough*	(617)	6,193	5,798
01550	Southbridge Center(u)	(617)	12,882	14,261
.....	*Southbridge*	(617)	16,665	17,057
01075	*South Hadley*	(413)	16,399	17,033
01077	*Southwick*	(413)	7,382	6,330
02664	South Yarmouth(u)	(617)	7,525	5,380
01562	Spencer Center	(617)	6,350	5,895
.....	*Spencer*	(617)	10,774	8,779
*01101	Springfield	(413)	152,319	163,905
01564	*Sterling*	(617)	5,440	4,247
02180	*Stoneham*	(617)	21,424	20,725
02072	*Stoughton*	(617)	26,710	23,459
01775	*Stow*	(617)	5,144	3,984
01566	*Sturbridge*	(617)	5,976	4,878
01776	*Sudbury*	(617)	14,027	13,506
01527	*Sutton*	(617)	5,855	4,590
01907	*Swampscott*	(617)	13,837	13,578
02777	*Swansea*	(617)	15,461	12,640
02780	Taunton	(617)	45,001	43,756

ZIP code	Place		1980	1970
01468	*Templeton*	(617)	6,070	5,863
01876	*Tewksbury*	(617)	24,635	22,755
01983	*Topsfield*	(617)	5,709	5,225
01469	*Townsend*	(617)	7,201	4,281
01376	Turners Falls(u)	(413)	NA	5,168
01879	*Tyngsborough*	(617)	5,683	4,204
01569	*Uxbridge*	(617)	8,374	8,253
01880	*Wakefield*	(617)	24,895	25,402
02081	*Walpole*	(617)	18,859	18,149
02154	Waltham	(617)	58,200	61,582
01082	Ware Center(u)	(413)	6,806	6,509
.....	*Ware*	(413)	8,953	8,187
02571	*Wareham*	(617)	18,457	11,492
02172	*Watertown*	(617)	34,384	39,307
01778	*Wayland*	(617)	12,170	13,461
01570	Webster Center(u)	(617)	11,175	12,432
.....	*Webster*	(617)	14,480	14,917
02181	*Wellesley*	(617)	27,209	28,051
01581	*Westborough*	(617)	13,619	12,594
01583	*West Boylston*	(617)	6,204	6,369
02379	*West Bridgewater*	(617)	6,359	6,070
01742	West Concord(u)	(617)	5,331	....
01085	Westfield	(413)	36,465	31,433
01886	*Westford*	(617)	13,434	10,368
01473	*Westminster*	(617)	5,139	4,273
02193	*Weston*	(617)	11,169	10,870
02790	*Westport*	(617)	13,763	9,791
01089	*West Springfield*	(413)	27,042	28,461
02090	*Westwood*	(617)	10,212	12,570
02188	*Weymouth*	(617)	55,601	54,610
01588	Whitinsville(u)	(617)	5,379	5,210
02382	*Whitman*	(617)	13,534	13,059
01095	*Wilbraham*	(413)	12,053	11,984
01267	*Williamstown*	(413)	8,741	8,454
01887	*Wilmington*	(617)	17,471	17,102
01475	*Winchendon*	(617)	7,019	6,635
01890	*Winchester*	(617)	20,701	22,269
02152	*Winthrop*	(617)	19,294	20,335
01801	Woburn	(617)	36,626	37,406
*01613	Worcester	(617)	161,799	176,572
02093	*Wrentham*	(617)	7,580	7,315
02675	*Yarmouth*	(617)	18,449	12,033
	Michigan			
49221	Adrian	(517)	21,276	20,382
49224	Albion	(517)	11,059	12,112
48101	Allen Park	(313)	34,196	40,747
48801	Alma	(517)	9,652	9,611
49707	Alpena	(517)	12,214	13,805
*48106	Ann Arbor	(313)	107,969	100,035
48063	Avon(u)	(313)	40,779	....
*49016	Battle Creek	(616)	35,724	38,931
48706	Bay City	(517)	41,593	49,449
48505	Beecher(u)	(313)	17,178	....
48809	Belding	(616)	5,634	5,121
49022	Benton Harbor	(616)	14,707	16,481
49022	Benton Heights(u)	(616)	6,787	....
48072	Berkley	(313)	18,637	21,879
48009	Beverly Hills	(313)	11,598	13,598
49307	Big Rapids	(616)	14,361	11,005
*48012	Birmingham	(313)	21,689	26,170
48013	Bloomfield(u)	(313)	42,876	....
49107	Buchanan	(616)	5,142	4,645
*48502	Burton	(313)	29,976	32,540
49601	Cadillac	(616)	10,199	9,990
48724	Carrollton(u)	(517)	7,482	7,300
48015	Center Line	(313)	9,293	10,379
48813	Charlotte	(517)	8,251	8,244
49721	Cheboygan	(616)	5,106	5,553
48017	Clawson	(313)	15,103	17,617
48043	Clinton(u)	(313)	72,400	1,677
49036	Coldwater	(517)	9,461	9,155
49321	Comstock Park(u)	(616)	5,506	5,766
49508	Cutlerville(u)	(616)	8,256	6,267
48423	Davison	(313)	6,087	5,259
*48120	Dearborn	(313)	90,660	104,199
48127	Dearborn Heights	(313)	67,706	80,069
*48233	Detroit	(313)	1,203,368	1,514,063
49047	Dowagiac	(616)	6,307	6,583
48021	East Detroit	(313)	38,280	45,920
49506	East Grand Rapids	(616)	10,914	12,565
48823	East Lansing	(517)	48,309	47,540
49001	Eastwood(u)	(517)	7,186	9,682
48229	Ecorse	(313)	14,447	17,515
49829	Escanaba	(906)	14,355	15,368
49022	Fair Plain(u)	(616)	8,289	3,680
48024	Farmington	(313)	11,022	10,329
48024	Farmington Hills	(313)	58,056	48,694
48430	Fenton	(313)	8,098	8,284
48220	Ferndale	(313)	26,227	30,850
48134	Flat Rock	(313)	6,853	5,643
*48502	Flint	(313)	159,611	193,317
48433	Flushing	(313)	8,624	7,190
48026	Fraser	(313)	14,560	11,868
48135	Garden City	(313)	35,640	41,864
48439	Grand Blanc	(313)	6,848	5,132
49417	Grand Haven	(616)	11,763	11,844
48837	Grand Ledge	(517)	6,920	6,032
*49501	Grand Rapids	(616)	181,843	197,649
49418	Grandville	(616)	12,412	10,764
48838	Greenville	(616)	8,019	7,493
48138	Grosse Ile(u)	(313)	9,320	8,306
48236	Grosse Pointe	(313)	5,901	6,637
48236	Grosse Pointe Farms	(313)	10,551	11,701
48236	Grosse Pointe Park	(313)	13,562	15,641
48236	Grosse Pointe Woods	(313)	18,886	21,878
48212	Hamtramck	(313)	21,300	26,783
49930	Hancock	(906)	5,122	4,820
48236	Harper Woods	(313)	16,361	20,186
48625	Harrison(u)	(517)	23,649	....
48840	Haslett(u)	(517)	7,025	....
49058	Hastings	(616)	6,418	6,501
48030	Hazel Park	(313)	20,914	23,784
48203	Highland Park	(313)	27,909	35,444
49242	Hillsdale	(517)	7,432	7,728
49423	Holland	(616)	26,281	26,479
48842	Holt(u)	(517)	10,097	6,980
49931	Houghton	(906)	7,512	6,067
48843	Howell	(517)	6,976	5,224
48070	Huntington Woods	(313)	6,937	8,536
48141	Inkster	(313)	35,190	38,595
48846	Ionia	(616)	5,920	6,361
49801	Iron Mountain	(906)	8,341	8,702
49938	Ironwood	(906)	7,741	8,711
49849	Ishpeming	(906)	7,538	8,245
*49201	Jackson	(517)	39,739	45,484
49428	Jenison(u)	(616)	16,330	11,266
*49001	Kalamazoo	(616)	79,722	85,555
49508	Kentwood	(616)	30,438	20,310
49801	Kingsford	(906)	5,290	5,276
49843	K.I. Sawyer(u)	(906)	7,345	8,224
49015	Lakeview(u)	(517)	13,345	11,391
48144	Lambertville(u)	(313)	6,341	5,711
*48924	Lansing	(517)	130,414	131,403
48446	Lapeer	(313)	6,225	6,314
48146	Lincoln Park	(313)	45,105	52,984
*48150	Livonia	(313)	104,814	110,109
49431	Ludington	(616)	8,937	9,021
48071	Madison Heights	(313)	35,375	38,599
49660	Manistee	(616)	7,665	7,723
49855	Marquette	(906)	23,288	21,967
49068	Marshall	(616)	7,201	7,253
48040	Marysville	(313)	7,345	5,610
48854	Mason	(517)	6,019	5,468
48122	Melvindale	(313)	12,322	13,862
49858	Menominee	(906)	10,099	10,748
49254	Michigan Center(u)	(517)	5,244	....
48640	Midland	(517)	37,269	35,176
48042	Milford	(313)	6,041	4,699
48161	Monroe	(313)	23,531	23,894
48043	Mount Clemens	(313)	18,991	20,476
48858	Mount Pleasant	(517)	23,746	20,524
*49440	Muskegon	(616)	40,823	44,631
49444	Muskegon Heights	(616)	14,611	17,304
49866	Negaunee	(906)	5,189	5,248
48047	New Baltimore	(313)	5,439	4,100
49120	Niles	(616)	13,115	12,988
.....	Northview(u)	....	11,662	....
48167	Northville	(313)	5,698	5,400
49441	Norton Shores	(616)	22,025	22,271
48050	Novi	(313)	22,525	9,668
48237	Oak Park	(313)	31,537	36,762
48864	Okemos(u)	(517)	8,882	7,770
48867	Owosso	(517)	16,455	17,179
49770	Petoskey	(616)	6,097	6,342
48170	Plymouth	(313)	9,986	11,758
*48053	Pontiac	(313)	76,715	85,279
49081	Portage	(616)	38,157	33,590
48060	Port Huron	(313)	33,981	35,794
48239	Redford(u)	(313)	58,441	....
48218	River Rouge	(313)	12,912	15,947
48192	Riverview	(313)	14,569	11,342
48063	Rochester	(313)	7,203	7,054
48174	Romulus	(313)	24,857	22,879
48066	Roseville	(313)	54,311	60,529
*48068	Royal Oak	(313)	70,893	86,238
*48605	Saginaw	(517)	77,508	91,849
*48083	St. Clair Shores	(313)	76,210	88,093
48879	St. Johns	(517)	7,376	6,672
49085	St. Joseph	(616)	9,622	11,042
48176	Saline	(313)	6,483	4,811
49793	Sault Ste. Marie	(906)	14,448	15,136
*48075	Southfield	(313)	75,568	69,285
48198	Southgate	(313)	32,058	33,909
49090	South Haven	(616)	5,943	6,471
48178	South Lyon	(313)	5,214	2,675
49015	Springfield	(616)	5,917	3,994
*48078	Sterling Heights	(313)	108,999	61,365
49091	Sturgis	(616)	9,468	9,295
48473	Swartz Creek	(313)	5,013	4,928
48180	Taylor	(313)	77,568	70,020
49286	Tecumseh	(517)	7,320	7,120
49093	Three Rivers	(616)	7,015	7,355
49684	Traverse City	(616)	15,516	18,048
48183	Trenton	(313)	22,762	24,127
48084	Troy	(313)	67,102	39,419
48087	Utica	(313)	5,282	3,504
49504	Walker	(616)	15,088	11,492

ZIP code	Place		1980	1970
*48089	Warren	(313)	161,134	179,260
48095	Waterford(u)	(313)	64,250	....
48184	Wayne	(313)	21,159	21,054
48033	West Bloomfield(u)	(313)	41,962	....
48185	Westland	(313)	84,603	86,749
49007	Westwood(u)	(616)	8,519	9,143
48019	White Lake-Seven Harbors(u)	(313)	7,557	....
48096	Wixom	(313)	6,705	2,010
48183	Woodhaven	(313)	10,902	3,566
48753	Wurtsmith(u)	(517)	5,166	6,932
*48192	Wyandotte	(313)	34,006	41,061
49509	Wyoming	(616)	59,616	56,560
48197	Ypsilanti	(313)	24,031	29,538

Minnesota

ZIP code	Place		1980	1970
56007	Albert Lea	(507)	19,190	19,418
56308	Alexandria	(612)	7,608	6,973
55303	Andover	(612)	9,387	....
55303	Anoka	(612)	15,634	13,298
55124	Apple Valley	(612)	21,818	8,502
55112	Arden Hills	(612)	8,012	5,149
55912	Austin	(507)	23,020	26,210
56601	Bemidji	(218)	10,949	11,490
55433	Blaine	(612)	28,558	20,573
55420	Bloomington	(612)	81,831	81,970
56401	Brainerd	(218)	11,489	11,667
55429	Brooklyn Center	(612)	31,230	35,173
55429	Brooklyn Park	(612)	43,332	26,230
55337	Burnsville	(612)	35,674	19,940
55316	Champlin	(612)	9,006	2,275
55317	Chanhassen	(612)	6,359	4,879
55318	Chaska	(612)	8,346	4,352
55719	Chisholm	(218)	5,930	5,913
55720	Cloquet	(218)	11,142	8,699
55421	Columbia Heights	(612)	20,029	23,997
55433	Coon Rapids	(612)	35,826	30,505
55016	Cottage Grove	(612)	18,994	13,419
56716	Crookston	(218)	8,628	8,312
55428	Crystal	(612)	25,543	30,925
56501	Detroit Lakes	(218)	7,106	5,797
*55806	Duluth	(218)	92,811	100,578
55121	Eagan	(612)	20,532	10,398
55005	East Bethel	(612)	6,626	2,586
56721	East Grand Forks	(218)	8,537	7,607
55343	Eden Prairie	(612)	16,263	6,938
55424	Edina	(612)	46,073	44,046
55330	Elk River	(612)	6,785	2,252
55734	Eveleth	(218)	5,042	4,721
56031	Fairmont	(507)	11,506	10,751
55113	Falcon Heights	(507)	5,291	5,530
55021	Faribault	(507)	16,241	16,595
56537	Fergus Falls	(218)	12,519	12,443
55421	Fridley	(612)	30,228	29,233
55427	Golden Valley	(612)	22,775	24,246
55744	Grand Rapids	(218)	7,934	7,247
55303	Ham Lake	(612)	7,832	3,327
55033	Hastings	(612)	12,827	12,195
55811	Hermantown	(218)	6,759	....
55746	Hibbing	(218)	21,193	16,104
55343	Hopkins	(612)	15,336	13,428
55350	Hutchinson	(612)	9,244	8,031
56649	International Falls	(218)	5,611	6,439
55075	Inver Grove Heights	(612)	17,171	12,148
55042	Lake Elmo	(612)	5,296	3,565
55044	Lakeville	(612)	14,790	7,556
55355	Litchfield	(612)	5,904	5,262
55110	Little Canada	(612)	7,102	3,481
56345	Little Falls	(612)	7,250	7,467
56001	Mankato	(507)	28,646	30,895
55369	Maple Grove	(612)	20,525	6,275
55109	Maplewood	(612)	26,990	25,186
56258	Marshall	(507)	11,161	9,886
55118	Mendota Heights	(612)	7,288	6,565
*55401	Minneapolis	(612)	370,951	434,400
55343	Minnetonka	(612)	38,683	35,776
56265	Montevideo	(612)	5,845	5,661
56560	Moorhead	(218)	29,998	29,687
56267	Morris	(612)	5,367	5,366
55364	Mound	(612)	9,280	7,572
55112	Mounds View	(612)	12,593	10,599
55112	New Brighton	(612)	23,269	19,507
54428	New Hope	(612)	23,087	23,180
56073	New Ulm	(507)	13,755	13,051
55057	Northfield	(507)	12,562	10,235
56001	North Mankato	(507)	9,145	7,347
55109	North St. Paul	(612)	11,921	11,950
55119	Oakdale	(612)	12,123	7,795
55323	Orono	(612)	6,845	6,787
55060	Owatonna	(507)	18,632	15,341
55427	Plymouth	(612)	31,615	18,077
55372	Prior Lake	(612)	7,284	1,114
55303	Ramsey	(612)	10,093	....
55066	Red Wing	(612)	13,736	10,441
56283	Redwood Falls	(507)	5,210	4,774
55423	Richfield	(612)	37,851	47,231
55422	Robbinsdale	(612)	14,422	16,845
55901	Rochester	(507)	57,906	53,766
55068	Rosemount	(612)	5,083	1,337
55113	Roseville	(612)	35,820	34,438
55418	St. Anthony	(612)	7,981	9,239
56301	St. Cloud	(612)	42,566	39,691
55426	St. Louis Park	(612)	42,931	48,883
*55101	St. Paul	(612)	270,230	309,866
56082	St. Peter	(507)	9,056	8,339
56379	Sauk Rapids	(612)	5,793	5,051
55379	Shakopee	(612)	9,941	6,876
55112	Shoreview	(612)	17,300	10,978
55075	South St. Paul	(612)	21,235	25,016
55432	Spring Lake Park	(612)	6,477	6,417
55082	Stillwater	(612)	12,290	10,191
56701	Thief River Falls	(218)	9,105	8,618
55110	Vadnais Heights	(612)	5,111	3,411
55792	Virginia	(218)	11,056	12,450
56093	Waseca	(507)	8,219	6,789
55118	West St. Paul	(612)	18,527	18,802
55110	White Bear Lake	(612)	22,538	23,313
56201	Willmar	(612)	15,895	12,869
55987	Winona	(507)	25,075	26,438
55119	Woodbury	(612)	10,297	6,184
56187	Worthington	(507)	10,243	9,916

Mississippi (601)

ZIP code	Place	1980	1970
39730	Aberdeen	7,184	6,507
38821	Amory	7,307	7,236
38606	Batesville	5,162	3,796
39520	Bay St. Louis	7,850	6,752
*39530	Biloxi	49,311	48,486
38829	Booneville	6,199	5,895
39042	Brandon	9,626	2,685
39601	Brookhaven	10,800	10,700
39046	Canton	11,116	10,503
38614	Clarksdale	21,137	21,673
38732	Cleveland	14,524	13,327
39056	Clinton	14,660	7,289
39429	Columbia	7,733	7,587
39701	Columbus	27,503	25,795
38834	Corinth	13,180	11,581
39532	D'Iberville(u)	13,369	7,288
39552	Escatawpa(u)	5,367	1,579
39074	Forest	5,229	4,085
39553	Gautier(u)	8,917	2,087
38701	Greenville	40,613	39,648
38930	Greenwood	20,115	22,400
38901	Grenada	11,508	9,944
39501	Gulfport	39,676	40,791
39401	Hattiesburg	40,829	38,277
38635	Holly Springs	7,285	5,728
38751	Indianola	8,050	8,947
*39205	Jackson	202,895	153,968
39090	Kosciusko	7,415	7,266
39440	Laurel	21,897	24,145
38756	Leland	6,667	6,000
39560	Long Beach	14,199	6,170
39339	Louisville	7,323	6,626
39648	McComb	12,331	11,851
39301	Meridian	46,577	45,083
39563	Moss Point	18,998	19,321
39120	Natchez	22,209	19,704
38652	New Albany	7,072	6,426
39501	North Gulfport(u)	6,660	6,996
39564	Ocean Springs	14,504	9,160
39567	Orange Grove(u)	13,476	....
38655	Oxford	9,882	8,519
39567	Pascagoula	29,318	27,264
39571	Pass Christian	5,014	2,979
39208	Pearl	18,602	9,623
39465	Petal	8,476	6,986
39350	Philadelphia	6,434	6,274
39466	Picayune	10,361	9,760
39157	Ridgeland	5,461	1,650
38668	Senatobia	5,013	4,247
38671	Southaven(u)	16,071	8,931
39759	Starkville	16,139	11,369
38801	Tupelo	23,905	20,471
39180	Vicksburg	25,434	25,478
39367	Waynesboro	5,349	4,368
39773	West Point	8,811	8,714
38967	Winona	6,177	5,521
39194	Yazoo City	12,092	11,688

Missouri

ZIP code	Place		1980	1970
63123	Affton(u)	(314)	23,181	24,264
63010	Arnold	(314)	19,141	17,381
65605	Aurora	(417)	6,437	5,359
63011	Ballwin	(314)	12,750	10,656
63137	Bellefontaine Neighbors	(314)	12,082	14,084
64012	Belton	(816)	12,708	12,270
63134	Berkeley	(314)	15,922	19,743
63031	Black Jack	(314)	5,293	4,145
64015	Blue Springs	(816)	25,936	6,779
65613	Bolivar	(417)	5,919	4,769
65233	Boonville	(816)	6,959	7,514
63114	Breckenridge Hills	(816)	5,666	7,011
63144	Brentwood	(314)	8,209	11,248
63044	Bridgeton	(314)	18,445	19,992

ZIP code	Place		1980	1970
64628	Brookfield	(816)	5,555	5,491
63701	Cape Girardeau	(314)	34,361	31,282
64836	Carthage	(417)	11,104	11,035
63830	Caruthersville	(314)	7,958	7,350
63834	Charleston	(314)	5,230	5,131
64601	Chillicothe	(816)	9,089	9,519
63105	Clayton	(314)	14,306	16,100
64735	Clinton	(816)	8,366	7,504
65201	Columbia	(314)	62,061	58,812
63128	Concord(u)	(314)	20,896	21,217
63126	Crestwood	(314)	12,815	15,123
63141	Creve Coeur	(314)	11,743	8,967
63136	Dellwood	(314)	6,200	7,137
63020	De Soto	(314)	5,993	5,984
63131	Des Peres	(314)	7,953	5,333
63841	Dexter	(314)	7,043	6,024
63011	Ellisville	(314)	6,233	4,681
64024	Excelsior Springs	(816)	10,424	9,411
63640	Farmington	(314)	8,270	6,590
63135	Ferguson	(314)	24,549	28,759
63028	Festus	(314)	7,574	7,530
*63033	Florissant	(314)	55,721	65,908
65473	Fort Leonard Wood(u)	(314)	21,262	33,799
65251	Fulton	(314)	11,046	12,248
64118	Gladstone	(816)	24,990	23,422
63122	Glendale	(314)	6,035	6,981
64030	Grandview	(816)	24,561	17,456
63401	Hannibal	(314)	18,811	18,609
64701	Harrisonville	(816)	6,372	5,052
*63042	Hazelwood	(314)	13,098	14,082
*64051	Independence	(816)	111,797	111,630
63755	Jackson	(314)	7,827	5,896
65101	Jefferson City	(314)	33,619	32,407
63136	Jennings	(314)	16,934	19,379
64801	Joplin	(417)	39,023	39,256
*64108	Kansas City	(816)	448,028	507,330
63857	Kennett	(314)	10,145	10,090
63501	Kirksville	(816)	17,167	15,560
63122	Kirkwood	(314)	27,739	31,679
63124	Ladue	(314)	9,369	10,306
65536	Lebanon	(417)	9,507	8,616
64063	Lee's Summit	(816)	28,741	16,230
63125	Lemay(u)	(314)	35,424	40,529
64067	Lexington	(816)	5,063	5,388
64068	Liberty	(816)	16,251	13,704
63552	Macon	(816)	5,680	5,301
63863	Malden	(314)	6,096	5,374
63011	Manchester	(314)	6,351	5,031
63143	Maplewood	(314)	10,960	12,785
65340	Marshall	(816)	12,781	12,051
63043	Maryland Heights(u)	(314)	5,676	8,805
64468	Maryville	(816)	9,558	9,970
65265	Mexico	(314)	12,276	11,807
65270	Moberly	(816)	13,418	12,988
65708	Monett	(417)	6,148	5,937
63026	Murphy(u)	(314)	8,121	....
64850	Neosho	(417)	9,493	7,517
64772	Nevada	(417)	9,044	9,736
63121	Normandy	(314)	5,174	6,236
63121	Northwoods	(314)	5,831	4,607
63366	O'Fallon	(314)	8,654	7,018
63124	Olivette	(314)	7,952	9,156
63114	Overland	(314)	19,620	24,819
63775	Perryville	(314)	7,343	5,149
63120	Pine Lawn	(314)	6,570	5,745
63901	Poplar Bluff	(314)	17,139	16,653
64133	Raytown	(816)	31,831	33,306
64085	Richmond	(816)	5,499	4,948
63117	Richmond Heights	(314)	11,516	13,802
63124	Rock Hill	(314)	5,702	6,815
65401	Rolla	(314)	13,303	13,571
63074	St. Ann	(314)	15,523	18,215
63301	St. Charles	(314)	37,379	31,834
63114	St. John	(314)	7,854	8,960
*64501	St. Joseph	(816)	76,691	72,748
*63155	St. Louis	(314)	452,801	622,236
63376	St. Peters	(314)	15,700	486
63126	Sappington(u)	(314)	11,388	10,603
65301	Sedalia	(816)	20,927	22,847
63119	Shrewsbury	(314)	5,077	5,896
63801	Sikeston	(314)	17,431	14,699
63138	Spanish Lake(u)	(314)	20,632	15,647
*65801	Springfield	(417)	133,116	120,096
63080	Sullivan	(314)	5,461	5,111
64683	Trenton	(816)	6,811	6,063
63084	Union	(314)	5,506	5,183
63130	University City	(314)	42,690	47,527
64093	Warrensburg	(816)	13,807	13,125
63090	Washington	(314)	9,251	8,499
64870	Webb City	(417)	7,309	6,923
63119	Webster Groves	(314)	23,097	27,457
65775	West Plains	(417)	7,741	6,893

Montana (406)

59711	Anaconda-Deer Lodge County	12,518	9,771
*59101	Billings	66,842	61,581
59101	Billings Heights(u)	8,480	....
59715	Bozeman	21,645	18,670
59701	Butte-Silver Bow	37,205	23,368
59330	Glendive	5,978	6,305
*59401	Great Falls	56,725	60,091
59501	Havre	10,891	10,558
59601	Helena	23,938	22,730
59901	Kalispell	10,689	10,526
59044	Laurel	5,481	4,454
59457	Lewistown	7,104	6,437
59047	Livingston	6,994	6,883
59402	Malmstrom AFB(u)	6,675	8,374
59301	Miles City	9,602	9,023
59801	Missoula	33,351	29,497
59801	Missoula South(u)	5,557	4,886
59801	Orchard Homes(u)	10,837	....
59270	Sidney	5,726	4,543

Nebraska

69301	Alliance	(308)	9,920	6,862
68310	Beatrice	(402)	12,891	12,389
68005	Bellevue	(402)	21,813	21,953
68008	Blair	(402)	6,418	6,106
69337	Chadron	(308)	5,933	5,921
68601	Columbus	(402)	17,328	15,471
68355	Falls City	(402)	5,374	5,444
68025	Fremont	(402)	23,979	22,962
69341	Gering	(308)	7,760	5,639
68801	Grand Island	(308)	33,180	32,358
68901	Hastings	(402)	23,045	23,580
68949	Holdrege	(308)	5,624	5,635
68847	Kearney	(308)	21,158	19,181
68128	La Vista	(402)	9,588	4,858
68850	Lexington	(308)	6,898	5,654
*68501	Lincoln	(402)	171,932	149,518
69001	McCook	(308)	8,404	8,285
68410	Nebraska City	(402)	7,127	7,441
68701	Norfolk	(402)	19,449	16,607
69101	North Platte	(308)	24,509	19,447
68113	Offutt AFB West(u)	(402)	8,787	8,445
69153	Ogallala	(308)	5,638	4,976
*68108	Omaha	(402)	313,939	346,929
68046	Papillion	(402)	6,399	5,606
68048	Plattsmouth	(402)	6,295	6,371
68127	Ralston	(402)	5,143	4,731
69361	Scottsbluff	(308)	14,156	14,507
68434	Seward	(402)	5,713	5,294
69162	Sidney	(308)	6,010	6,403
68776	South Sioux City	(402)	9,339	7,920
68787	Wayne	(402)	5,240	5,379
68467	York	(402)	7,723	6,778

Nevada (702)

89005	Boulder City	9,590	5,223
89701	Carson City	32,022	15,468
89112	East Las Vegas(u)	6,449	6,501
89801	Elko	8,758	7,621
89015	Henderson	24,363	16,395
89450	Incline Village-Crystal Bay(u)	6,225	....
*89114	Las Vegas	164,674	125,787
89110	Nellis AFB(u)	6,205	6,449
89030	North Las Vegas	42,739	46,067
89109	Paradise(u)	84,818	24,477
*89501	Reno	100,756	72,863
89431	Sparks	40,780	24,187
89110	Sunrise Manor(u)	44,155	9,684
89431	Sun Valley(u)	8,822	2,414
89109	Vegas Creek(u)	NA	8,970
89101	Winchester(u)	19,728	13,981

New Hampshire (603)

See note on page 544

03031	Amherst	8,243	4,605
03102	*Bedford*	9,481	5,859
03570	Berlin	13,084	15,256
03743	Claremont	14,557	14,221
03301	Concord	30,400	30,022
03818	Conway	7,158	4,865
03038	Derry Compact(u)	12,248	6,090
.....	*Derry*	18,875	11,712
03820	Dover	22,377	20,850
03824	Durham Compact(u)	8,448	7,221
.....	*Durham*	10,652	8,869
03833	Exeter Compact(u)	8,947	6,439
.....	*Exeter*	11,024	8,892
03235	Franklin	7,901	7,292
03045	*Goffstown*	11,315	9,284
03842	Hampton Compact(u)	6,779	5,407
.....	*Hampton*	10,493	8,011
03755	Hanover Compact(u)	6,861	6,147
.....	*Hanover*	9,119	8,494
03106	*Hooksett*	7,303	5,564
03061	*Hudson*	14,022	10,638
03431	Keene	21,449	20,467
03246	Laconia	15,575	14,888
03766	Lebanon	11,134	9,725

ZIP code	Place	1980	1970
03561	*Littleton*	5,558	5,290
03053	*Londonderry*	13,598	5,346
*03101	Manchester	90,936	87,754
03054	*Merrimack*	15,406	8,595
03055	*Milford*	8,685	6,622
03060	Nashua	67,865	55,820
03773	*Newport*	6,229	5,899
03076	*Pelham*	8,090	5,408
03865	Plaistow	5,609	4,712
03801	Portsmouth	26,254	25,717
03077	Raymond	5,453	3,003
03867	Rochester	21,560	17,938
03079	*Salem*	24,124	20,142
03874	*Seabrook*	5,917	3,053
03878	Somersworth	10,350	9,026
03087	Windham	5,664	3,008

New Jersey

ZIP code	Place	Area code	1980	1970
07747	Aberdeen(u)	(201)	17,235	....
08201	Absecon	(609)	6,859	6,094
07401	Allendale	(201)	5,901	6,240
07712	Asbury Park	(201)	17,015	16,533
*08401	Atlantic City	(609)	40,199	47,859
08106	Audubon	(609)	9,533	10,802
08007	Barrington	(609)	7,418	8,409
07002	Bayonne	(201)	65,047	72,743
08722	Beachwood	(201)	7,687	4,390
07109	Belleville	(201)	35,367	37,629
08031	Bellmawr	(609)	13,721	15,618
07719	Belmar	(201)	6,771	5,782
07621	Bergenfield	(201)	25,568	29,000
07922	Berkeley Hts. Twp.	(201)	12,549	13,078
08009	Berlin	(609)	5,786	4,997
07924	Bernardsville	(201)	6,715	6,652
08012	Blackwood(u)	(609)	5,219	....
07003	Bloomfield	(201)	47,792	52,029
07403	Bloomingdale	(201)	7,867	7,797
07603	Bogota	(201)	8,344	8,960
07005	Boonton	(201)	8,620	9,261
08805	Bound Brook	(201)	9,710	10,450
08723	Brick Twp	(201)	53,629	35,057
08302	Bridgeton	(609)	18,795	20,435
08203	Brigantine	(609)	8,318	6,741
08015	Browns Mills(u)	(609)	10,568	7,144
07828	Budd Lake	(201)	6,523	....
08016	Burlington	(609)	10,246	12,010
07405	Butler	(201)	7,616	7,051
07006	Caldwell	(201)	7,624	8,677
*08101	Camden	(609)	84,910	102,551
08701	Candlewood(u)	(201)	6,750	5,629
07072	Carlstadt	(201)	6,166	6,724
08069	Carney's Point	(609)	7,574	....
07008	Carteret	(201)	20,598	23,137
07009	Cedar Grove Twp.	(201)	12,600	15,582
07928	Chatham	(201)	8,537	9,566
*08002	Cherry Hill Twp.	(609)	68,785	64,395
08077	Cinnaminson Twp.	(609)	16,072	16,962
07066	Clark Twp.	(201)	16,699	18,829
08312	Clayton	(609)	6,013	5,193
08021	Clementon	(609)	5,764	4,492
07010	Cliffside Park	(201)	21,464	18,891
07721	Cliffwood-Cliffwood Beach(u)	(201)	NA	7,056
*07015	Clifton	(201)	74,388	82,437
07624	Closter	(201)	8,164	8,604
08108	Collingswood	(609)	15,838	17,422
07016	Cranford Twp.	(201)	24,573	27,391
07626	Cresskill	(201)	7,609	8,298
.....	Crestwood Village	(201)	7,965	....
08075	Delran Twp.	(609)	14,811	10,065
07834	Denville Twp.	(201)	14,380	14,045
08096	Deptford Twp.	(609)	23,473	24,232
07801	Dover	(201)	14,681	15,039
07628	Dumont	(201)	18,334	20,155
08812	Dunellen	(201)	6,593	7,072
08816	East Brunswick Twp.	(201)	37,711	34,166
07936	East Hanover	(201)	9,319	....
*07019	East Orange	(201)	77,878	75,471
07073	East Rutherford	(201)	7,849	8,536
08520	East Windsor Twp.	(609)	21,041	11,736
07724	Eatontown	(201)	12,703	14,619
08010	Edgewater Park	(609)	9,273	....
08817	Edison Twp.	(201)	70,193	67,120
*07201	Elizabeth	(201)	106,201	112,654
07407	Elmwood Park	(201)	18,377	20,511
07630	Emerson	(201)	7,793	8,428
*07631	Englewood	(201)	23,701	24,985
07632	Englewood Cliffs	(201)	5,698	5,938
08053	Evesham Twp.	(609)	21,659	13,477
08618	Ewing Twp.	(609)	34,842	32,831
07006	Fairfield	(201)	7,987	6,731
07701	Fair Haven	(201)	5,679	6,142
07410	Fair Lawn	(201)	32,229	38,040
07022	Fairview	(201)	10,519	10,698
07023	Fanwood	(201)	7,767	8,920
08518	Florence-Roebling(u)	(609)	7,677	7,551
07932	Florham Park	(201)	9,359	9,373
08640	Fort Dix(u)	(609)	14,297	26,290
07024	Fort Lee	(201)	32,449	30,631
07417	Franklin Lakes	(201)	8,769	7,550
07728	Freehold	(201)	10,020	10,545
07026	Garfield	(201)	26,803	30,797
08753	Gilford Park	(201)	6,528	4,007
08028	Glassboro	(609)	14,574	12,938
08029	Glendora	(609)	5,632	....
07028	Glen Ridge	(201)	7,855	8,518
07452	Glen Rock	(201)	11,497	13,011
08030	Gloucester City	(609)	13,121	14,707
.....	Gordon's Corner	(201)	6,320	....
07093	Guttenberg	(201)	7,340	5,754
*07602	Hackensack	(201)	36,039	36,008
07840	Hackettstown	(201)	8,850	9,472
08108	Haddon Twp.	(609)	15,875	18,192
08033	Haddonfield	(609)	12,337	13,118
08035	Haddon Heights	(609)	8,361	9,365
07508	Haledon	(201)	6,607	6,767
08037	Hammonton	(609)	12,298	11,464
07981	Hanover Twp.	(201)	11,846	10,700
07029	Harrison	(201)	12,242	11,811
07604	Hasbrouck Heights	(201)	12,166	13,651
07506	Hawthorne	(201)	18,200	19,173
07730	Hazlet Twp.	(201)	23,013	22,239
08904	Highland Park	(201)	13,396	14,385
07732	Highlands	(201)	5,187	3,916
07642	Hillsdale	(201)	10,495	11,768
07205	Hillside Twp.	(201)	21,440	21,636
07030	Hoboken	(201)	42,460	45,380
08753	Holiday City-Berkeley	(201)	9,019	....
07843	Hopatcong	(201)	15,531	9,052
08560	Hopewell Twp. (Mercer)	(609)	10,893	10,030
07111	Irvington	(201)	61,493	59,743
08527	Jackson Twp.	(201)	25,644	18,276
*07303	Jersey City	(201)	223,532	260,350
07734	Keansburg	(201)	10,613	9,720
07032	Kearny	(201)	35,735	37,585
08824	Kendall Park(u)	(201)	7,419	7,412
07033	Kenilworth	(201)	8,221	9,165
07735	Keyport	(201)	7,413	7,205
07405	Kinnelon	(201)	7,770	7,600
07034	Lake Hiawatha(u)	(201)	NA	11,389
07871	Lake Mohawk(u)	(201)	8,498	6,262
07054	Lake Parsippany(u)	(201)	NA	7,488
08701	Lakewood(u)	(201)	22,863	17,874
08879	Laurence Harbor(u)	(201)	6,737	6,715
07605	Leonia	(201)	8,027	8,847
07035	Lincoln Park	(201)	8,806	9,034
07036	Linden	(201)	37,836	41,409
08021	Lindenwold	(609)	18,196	12,199
08221	Linwood	(609)	6,144	6,159
07424	Little Falls Twp.	(201)	11,496	11,727
07643	Little Ferry	(201)	9,399	9,064
07739	Little Silver	(201)	5,548	6,010
07039	Livingston Twp.	(201)	28,040	30,127
07644	Lodi	(201)	23,956	25,163
07740	Long Branch	(201)	29,819	31,774
07071	Lyndhurst Twp.	(201)	20,326	22,729
07940	Madison	(201)	15,357	16,710
08859	Madison Park	(201)	7,447	....
07430	Mahwah Twp.	(201)	12,127	10,800
08736	Manasquan	(201)	5,354	4,971
08835	Manville	(201)	11,278	13,029
08052	Maple Shade Twp.	(609)	20,525	16,464
07040	Maplewood Twp.	(201)	22,950	24,932
08402	Margate City	(609)	9,179	10,576
07746	Marlboro Twp.	(201)	17,560	12,273
08053	Marlton(u)	(609)	9,411	10,180
07747	Matawan	(201)	8,837	9,136
07607	Maywood	(201)	9,895	11,087
08641	McGuire AFB(u)	(609)	7,853	10,933
08619	Mercerville-Hamilton Sq.(u)	(609)	25,446	24,465
08840	Metuchen	(201)	13,762	16,031
08846	Middlesex	(201)	13,480	15,038
07748	Middletown Twp.	(201)	61,615	54,623
07432	Midland park	(201)	7,381	8,159
07041	Milburn Twp.	(201)	19,543	21,089
08850	Milltown	(201)	7,136	6,470
08332	Millville	(609)	24,815	21,366
08094	Monroe Twp. (Gloucester)	(609)	21,639	14,071
*07042	Montclair	(201)	38,321	44,043
07645	Montvale	(201)	7,318	7,327
07045	Montville Twp.	(201)	14,290	11,846
08057	Moorestown-Lenola(u)	(609)	13,695	14,179
07950	Morris Plains	(201)	5,305	5,540
07960	Morristown	(201)	16,614	17,662
07092	Mountainside	(201)	7,118	7,520
08060	Mount Holly Twp.	(609)	10,818	12,713
07753	Neptune Twp.	(201)	28,366	27,863
07753	Neptune City	(201)	5,276	5,502
*07102	Newark	(201)	329,248	381,930
*08901	New Brunswick	(201)	41,442	41,885
08511	New Hanover	(201)	14,248	27,410
07646	New Milford	(201)	16,876	19,149
07974	New Providence	(201)	12,426	13,796
07860	Newton	(201)	7,748	7,297
07032	North Arlington	(201)	16,587	18,096
07047	North Bergen Twp.	(201)	47,019	47,751
08902	North Brunswick Twp.	(201)	22,220	16,691
07006	North Caldwell	(201)	5,832	6,733
08225	Northfield	(609)	7,795	8,646
07508	North Haledon	(201)	8,177	7,614

ZIP code	Place		1980	1970
07060	North Plainfield	(201)	19,108	21,796
07647	Northvale	(201)	5,046	5,177
07110	Nutley	(201)	28,998	31,913
07755	Oakhurst(u)	(201)	NA	5,558
07436	Oakland	(201)	13,443	14,420
08226	Ocean City	(609)	13,949	10,575
07757	Oceanport	(201)	5,888	7,503
08758	Ocean Twp	(609)	23,570	....
08857	Old Bridge	(201)	21,815	25,176
08857	Old Bridge Twp	(201)	51,515	48,715
07649	Oradell	(201)	8,658	8,903
*07050	Orange	(201)	31,136	32,566
07650	Palisades Park	(201)	13,732	13,351
08065	Palmyra	(609)	7,085	6,969
07652	Paramus	(201)	26,474	28,381
07656	Park Ridge	(201)	8,515	8,709
07054	Parsippany-Troy Hills	(201)	49,868	....
*07055	Passaic	(201)	52,463	55,124
*07510	Paterson	(201)	137,970	144,824
08066	Paulsboro	(609)	6,944	8,084
08110	Pennsauken Twp.	(609)	33,775	36,394
08069	Penns Grove	(609)	5,760	5,727
08070	Pennsville Center(u)	(609)	12,467	11,014
07440	Pequannock Twp.	(201)	13,776	14,350
*08861	Perth Amboy	(201)	38,951	38,798
08865	Phillipsburg	(201)	16,647	17,849
08021	Pine Hill	(201)	8,684	5,132
08854	Piscataway Twp.	(201)	42,223	36,418
08071	Pitman	(609)	9,744	10,257
*07061	Plainfield	(201)	45,555	46,862
08232	Pleasantville	(609)	13,435	14,007
08742	Point Pleasant	(201)	17,747	15,968
08742	Point Pleasant Beach	(201)	5,415	4,882
07442	Pompton Lakes	(201)	10,660	11,397
08540	Princeton	(609)	12,035	12,311
08540	Princeton North(u)	(609)	NA	5,488
07508	Prospect Park	(201)	5,142	5,176
*07065	Rahway	(201)	26,723	29,114
08057	Ramblewood(u)	(609)	6,475	5,556
07446	Ramsey	(201)	12,899	12,571
07869	Randolph Twp.	(201)	17,828	13,296
08869	Raritan	(201)	6,128	6,691
07701	Red Bank	(201)	12,031	12,847
07657	Ridgefield	(201)	10,294	11,308
07660	Ridgefield Park	(201)	12,738	13,990
*07451	Ridgewood	(201)	25,208	27,547
07456	Ringwood	(201)	12,625	10,393
07661	River Edge	(201)	11,111	12,850
08075	Riverside Twp.	(609)	7,941	8,591
07675	River Vale	(201)	9,489	....
07726	Robertsville	(201)	8,461	....
07662	Rochelle Park Twp.	(201)	5,603	6,380
07866	Rockaway	(201)	6,852	6,383
07068	Roseland	(201)	5,330	4,453
07203	Roselle	(201)	20,641	22,585
07204	Roselle Park	(201)	13,377	14,277
07760	Rumson	(201)	7,623	7,421
08078	Runnemede	(609)	9,461	10,475
*07070	Rutherford	(201)	19,068	20,802
07662	Saddle Brook Twp.	(201)	14,084	15,910
08079	Salem	(609)	6,959	7,648
08872	Sayreville	(201)	29,969	32,508
07076	Scotch Plains Twp.	(201)	20,774	22,279
07094	Secaucus	(201)	13,719	13,228
08753	Silverton	(201)	7,236	....
08083	Somerdale	(609)	5,900	6,510
08873	Somerset	(201)	21,731	....
08244	Somers Point	(609)	10,330	7,919
08876	Somerville	(201)	11,973	13,652
08879	South Amboy	(201)	8,322	9,338
07079	South Orange Vill. Twp.	(201)	15,864	....
07080	South Plainfield	(201)	20,521	21,142
08882	South River	(201)	14,361	15,428
07871	Sparta Twp.	(201)	13,333	10,819
08884	Spotswood	(201)	7,840	7,891
07081	Springfield Twp.	(201)	13,955	15,740
07762	Spring Lake Heights	(201)	5,424	4,602
08084	Stratford	(609)	8,005	9,801
07747	Strathmore(u)	(201)	NA	7,674
07876	Succasunna-Kenvil	(201)	10,931	....
07901	Summit	(201)	21,071	23,620
07666	Teaneck Twp.	(201)	39,007	42,355
07670	Tenafly	(201)	13,552	14,827
07724	Tinton Falls	(201)	7,740	8,395
*08753	Toms River(u)	(201)	7,465	7,303
07512	Totowa	(201)	11,448	11,580
*08608	Trenton	(609)	92,124	104,786
08520	Twin Rivers	(609)	7,742	....
07083	Union Twp.	(201)	50,184	53,077
07735	Union Beach	(201)	6,354	6,472
07087	Union City	(201)	55,593	57,305
07458	Upper Saddle River	(201)	7,958	7,949
08406	Ventnor City	(609)	11,704	10,385
07044	Verona	(201)	14,166	15,067
08251	Villas	(609)	5,909	3,155
08360	Vineland	(609)	53,753	47,399
07463	Waldwick	(201)	10,802	12,313
07057	Wallington	(201)	10,741	10,284
07465	Wanaque	(201)	10,025	8,636
07882	Washington	(201)	6,429	5,943
07675	Washington Twp. (Bergen)	(201)	9,550	10,577
07060	Watchung	(201)	5,290	4,750
07470	Wayne Twp.	(201)	46,474	49,141
07087	Weehawken Twp.	(201)	13,168	13,383
07006	West Caldwell	(201)	11,407	11,913
*07091	Westfield	(201)	30,447	33,720
07728	West Freehold	(201)	9,929	....
07764	West Long Branch	(201)	7,380	6,845
07480	West Milford Twp.	(201)	22,750	17,304
07093	West New York	(201)	39,194	40,627
07052	West Orange	(201)	39,510	43,715
07424	West Paterson	(201)	11,293	11,692
07675	Westwood	(201)	10,714	11,105
07885	Wharton	(201)	5,485	5,535
08610	White Horse	(609)	10,098	....
07886	White Meadow Lake(u)	(201)	8,429	8,499
08094	Williamstown	(609)	5,768	4,075
08046	Willingboro Twp.	(609)	39,912	43,386
08095	Winslow Twp.	(609)	20,034	11,202
07095	Woodbridge Twp.	(201)	90,074	98,944
08096	Woodbury	(609)	10,353	12,408
07675	Woodcliff Lake	(201)	5,644	5,506
07075	Wood-Ridge	(201)	7,929	8,311
07481	Wyckoff Twp.	(201)	15,500	16,039
08620	Yardville-Groveville	(609)	9,414	....
.....	Yorketown	(201)	5,330	....

New Mexico (505)

ZIP code	Place	1980	1970
88310	Alamogordo	24,024	23,035
*87101	Albuquerque	332,336	244,501
88210	Artesia	10,385	10,315
87410	Aztec	5,512	3,354
87002	Belen	5,617	4,823
88101	Cannon(u)	NA	5,461
88220	Carlsbad	25,496	21,297
88101	Clovis	31,194	28,495
88030	Deming	9,964	8,343
87532	Espanola	6,803	4,528
87401	Farmington	30,729	21,979
87301	Gallup	18,167	14,596
87020	Grants	11,451	8,768
88240	Hobbs	28,794	26,025
88330	Holloman AFB(u)	7,245	8,001
88001	Las Cruces	45,086	37,857
87701	Las Vegas	14,322	7,528
87544	Los Alamos(u)	11,039	11,310
88260	Lovington	9,727	8,915
87107	North Valley(u)	13,006	10,366
87114	Paradise Hills	5,096	....
88130	Portales	9,940	10,554
87740	Raton	8,225	6,962
87124	Rio Rancho Estates	9,985	....
88201	Roswell	39,676	33,908
87115	Sandia(u)	5,900	6,867
87501	Santa Fe	49,160	41,167
87420	Shiprock	7,237	....
88061	Silver City	9,887	8,557
87801	Socorro	7,576	5,849
87105	South Valley(u)	38,916	29,389
87901	Truth or Consequences	5,219	4,656
88401	Tucumcari	6,765	7,189
87544	White Rock	6,560	3,861
87327	Zuni Pueblo	5,551	3,958

New York

ZIP code	Place		1980	1970
*12207	Albany	(518)	101,727	115,781
11507	Albertson(u)	(516)	5,561	6,825
11701	Amityville	(516)	9,076	9,794
12010	Amsterdam	(518)	21,872	25,524
12603	Arlington(u)	(914)	11,305	11,203
13021	Auburn	(315)	32,548	34,599
*11702	Babylon	(516)	12,388	12,897
11510	Baldwin(u)	(516)	31,630	34,525
13027	Baldwinsville	(315)	6,446	6,298
14020	Batavia	(716)	16,703	17,338
14810	Bath	(607)	6,042	6,053
13088	Bayberry-Lynelle Meadows(u)	(315)	14,813	....
11705	Bayport(u)	(516)	9,282	8,232
11706	Bay Shore(u)	(516)	10,784	11,119
11709	Bayville	(516)	7,034	6,147
12508	Beacon	(914)	12,937	13,255
11710	Bellmore(u)	(516)	18,106	18,431
11714	Bethpage(u)	(516)	16,840	18,555
*13902	Binghamton	(607)	55,860	64,123
10913	Blauvelt(u)	(914)	NA	5,426
11716	Bohemia(u)	(516)	9,308	8,926
11717	Brentwood(u)	(516)	44,321	28,327
10510	Briarcliff Manor	(914)	7,115	6,521
14610	Brighton (u)	(716)	35,776	....
14420	Brockport	(716)	9,776	7,878
10708	Bronxville	(914)	6,267	6,674
*14240	Buffalo	(716)	357,870	462,768
14424	Canandaigua	(716)	10,419	10,488

ZIP code	Place		1980	1970
13617	Canton	(315)	7,055	6,398
11514	Carle Place(u)	(516)	5,470	6,326
11516	Cedarhurst	(516)	6,162	6,941
11720	Centereach(u)	(516)	30,136	9,427
11934	Center Moriches(u)	(516)	5,703	3,802
11721	Centerport(u)	(516)	6,576	....
11722	Central Islip(u)	(516)	19,734	36,391
14225	Cheektowaga(u)	(716)	92,145	....
12065	Clifton Park	(518)	23,989	14,867
12043	Cobleskill	(518)	5,272	4,368
12047	Cohoes	(518)	18,144	18,653
11724	Cold Spring Harbor(u)	(516)	5,336	5,509
12205	Colonie	(518)	8,869	8,701
11725	Commack(u)	(516)	34,719	24,138
10920	Congers(u)	(914)	7,123	5,928
11726	Copiague(u)	(516)	20,132	19,632
11727	Coram(u)	(516)	24,752	....
14830	Corning	(607)	12,953	15,792
13045	Cortland	(607)	20,138	19,621
10520	Croton-on-Hudson	(914)	6,889	7,523
11729	Deer Park(u)	(516)	30,394	32,274
12054	Delmar(u)	(518)	8,423	....
14043	Depew	(716)	19,819	22,158
13214	DeWitt(u)	(315)	9,024	10,032
11746	Dix Hills(u)	(516)	26,693	10,050
10522	Dobbs Ferry	(914)	10,053	10,353
14048	Dunkirk	(716)	15,310	16,855
14052	East Aurora	(716)	6,803	7,033
10709	Eastchester(u)	(914)	20,305	23,750
11735	East Farmingdale(u)	(516)	5,522	....
12302	East Glenville(u)	(518)	6,537	5,898
11746	East Half Hollow Hills(u)	(516)	NA	9,691
11576	East Hills	(516)	7,160	8,624
11730	East Islip(u)	(516)	13,852	6,861
11758	East Massapequa(u)	(516)	13,987	15,926
11554	East Meadow(u)	(516)	39,317	46,290
11743	East Neck(u)	(516)	NA	5,221
11731	East Northport(u)	(516)	20,187	12,392
11772	East Patchogue(u)	(516)	18,139	8,092
14445	East Rochester	(716)	7,596	8,347
11518	East Rockaway	(516)	10,917	11,795
13902	East Vestal(u)	(607)	NA	10,472
*14901	Elmira	(607)	35,327	39,945
11003	Elmont(u)	(516)	27,592	29,363
11731	Elwood(u)	(516)	11,847	15,031
13760	Endicott	(607)	14,457	16,556
13760	Endwell(u)	(607)	13,745	15,999
13219	Fairmount(u)	(315)	13,415	15,317
14450	Fairport	(716)	5,970	6,474
12601	Fairview(u)	(914)	5,852	8,517
11735	Farmingdale	(516)	7,946	9,297
11738	Farmingville(u)	(516)	13,398	....
*11001	Floral Park	(516)	16,805	18,466
11768	Fort Salonga(u)	(516)	9,550	....
11010	Franklin Square(u)	(516)	29,051	32,156
14063	Fredonia	(716)	11,126	10,326
11520	Freeport	(516)	38,272	40,374
13069	Fulton	(315)	13,312	14,003
11530	Garden City	(516)	22,927	25,373
11040	Garden City Park(u)	(516)	7,712	7,488
14624	Gates-North Gates(u)	(716)	15,244	....
14454	Geneseo	(716)	6,746	5,714
14456	Geneva	(315)	15,133	16,793
11542	Glen Cove	(516)	24,618	25,770
12801	Glens Falls	(518)	15,897	17,222
12801	Glens Falls North(u)	(518)	6,956	NA
12078	Gloversville	(518)	17,836	19,677
*11022	Great Neck	(516)	9,168	10,798
11020	Great Neck Plaza	(516)	5,604	6,043
14616	Greece(u)	(716)	16,177	....
11740	Greenlawn(u)	(516)	13,869	8,493
12083	Greenville(u)	(518)	8,706	....
11746	Half Hollow Hills(u)	(516)	NA	12,081
14075	Hamburg	(716)	10,582	10,215
11946	Hampton Bays(u)	(516)	7,256	1,862
14221	Harris Hill(u)	(716)	5,087	....
10528	Harrison	(914)	23,046	21,544
10530	Hartsdale(u)	(914)	10,216	12,226
10706	Hastings-on-Hudson	(914)	8,573	9,479
11787	Hauppauge(u)	(516)	20,960	13,957
10927	Haverstraw	(914)	8,800	8,198
10532	Hawthorne(u)	(914)	5,010	....
*11551	Hempstead	(516)	40,404	39,411
13350	Herkimer	(315)	8,383	8,960
11040	Herricks(u)	(516)	8,123	9,112
11557	Hewlett(u)	(516)	6,986	6,796
*11802	Hicksville(u)	(516)	43,245	49,820
10977	Hillcrest(u)	(914)	5,733	5,357
11741	Holbrook(u)	(516)	24,382	....
11742	Holtsville(u)	(516)	13,515	....
14843	Hornell	(607)	10,234	12,144
14845	Horseheads	(607)	7,348	7,989
12534	Hudson	(518)	7,986	8,940
12839	Hudson Falls	(518)	7,419	7,917
11743	Huntington(u)	(516)	21,727	12,601
11746	Huntington Station(u)	(516)	28,769	28,817
13357	Ilion	(315)	9,450	9,808
11696	Inwood(u)	(516)	8,228	8,433
14617	Irondequoit(u)	(716)	57,648	....
10533	Irvington	(914)	5,774	5,878
11751	Islip(u)	(516)	13,438	7,692
11752	Islip Terrace(u)	(516)	5,588	....
14850	Ithaca	(607)	28,732	26,226
14701	Jamestown	(716)	35,775	39,795
10535	Jefferson Valley-Yorktown(u)	(914)	13,380	9,008
11753	Jericho(u)	(516)	12,739	14,010
13790	Johnson City	(607)	17,126	18,025
12095	Johnstown	(518)	9,360	10,045
14217	Kenmore	(716)	18,474	20,980
11754	Kings Park(u)	(516)	16,131	5,555
11024	Kings Point	(516)	5,234	5,614
12401	Kingston	(914)	24,481	25,544
14218	Lackawanna	(716)	22,701	28,657
10512	Lake Carmel(u)	(914)	7,295	4,796
11755	Lake Grove	(516)	9,692	8,133
11779	Lake Ronkonkoma(u)	(516)	38,336	7,284
11552	Lakeview(u)	(516)	5,276	5,471
14086	Lancaster	(716)	13,056	13,365
10538	Larchmont	(914)	6,308	7,203
12110	Latham(u)	(518)	11,182	9,661
11559	Lawrence	(516)	6,175	6,566
11756	Levittown(u)	(516)	57,045	65,440
11757	Lindenhurst	(516)	26,919	28,359
13365	Little Falls	(315)	6,156	7,629
14094	Lockport	(716)	24,844	25,399
11791	Locust Grove(u)	(516)	9,670	11,626
11561	Long Beach	(516)	34,073	33,127
12211	Loudonville(u)	(518)	11,480	9,299
11563	Lynbrook	(516)	20,424	23,151
13208	Lyncourt(u)	(315)	5,129	....
10541	Mahopac(u)	(914)	7,681	5,265
12953	Malone	(518)	7,668	8,048
11565	Malverne	(516)	9,262	10,036
10543	Mamaroneck	(914)	17,616	18,909
11030	Manhasset(u)	(516)	8,485	8,541
13104	Manlius	(315)	5,241	4,295
11050	Manorhaven	(516)	5,384	5,488
11758	Massapequa(u)	(516)	24,454	26,821
11762	Massapequa Park	(516)	19,779	22,112
13662	Massena	(315)	12,851	14,042
11950	Mastic(u)	(516)	10,413	....
11951	Mastic Beach(u)	(516)	8,318	4,870
13211	Mattydale(u)	(315)	7,511	8,292
12118	Mechanicville	(518)	5,500	6,247
11763	Medford(u)	(516)	20,418	....
14103	Medina	(716)	6,392	6,415
11746	Melville(u)	(516)	8,139	6,641
11566	Merrick(u)	(516)	24,478	25,904
11953	Middle Island(u)	(516)	5,703	....
10940	Middletown	(914)	21,454	22,607
11764	Miller Place(u)	(516)	7,877	....
11501	Mineola	(516)	20,757	21,845
10950	Monroe	(914)	5,996	4,439
10952	Monsey(u)	(914)	12,380	8,797
12701	Monticello	(914)	6,306	5,991
10549	Mt. Kisco	(914)	8,025	8,172
11766	Mount Sinai(u)	(516)	6,591	....
*10551	Mount Vernon	(914)	66,713	72,788
12590	Myers Corner(u)	(914)	5,180	2,826
10954	Nanuet(u)	(914)	12,578	10,447
11767	Nesconset(u)	(516)	10,706	10,048
14513	Newark	(315)	10,017	11,644
12550	Newburgh	(914)	23,438	26,219
11590	New Cassel(u)	(516)	9,635	8,721
10956	New City(u)	(914)	35,859	27,344
11040	New Hyde Park	(516)	9,801	10,116
*10802	New Rochelle	(914)	70,794	75,385
*12550	New Windsor Center(u)	(914)	7,812	8,803
*10001	New York	(212)	7,071,639	7,895,563
*10451	Bronx	(212)	1,168,972	1,471,701
*11201	Brooklyn	(718)	2,230,936	2,602,102
*10001	Manhattan	(212)	1,428,285	1,539,233
*(Q)	Queens	(718)	1,891,325	1,987,174

(Q) There are 4 P.O.s for Queens: 11101 for L.I. City; 11690 Far Rockaway; 11351 Flushing; and 11431 Jamaica.

ZIP code	Place		1980	1970
*10314	Staten Island	(718)	352,121	295,443
14301	Niagara(u)	(716)	9,648	....
*14302	Niagara Falls	(716)	71,384	85,615
12309	Niskayuna(u)	(518)	5,223	6,186
11701	North Amityville(u)	(516)	13,140	11,936
11703	North Babylon(u)	(516)	19,019	39,526
11706	North Bay Shore(u)	(516)	35,020	....
11710	North Bellmore(u)	(516)	20,630	22,893
11713	North Bellport(u)	(516)	7,432	5,903
11752	North Great River(u)	(516)	11,416	12,080
11757	North Lindenhurst(u)	(516)	11,511	11,117
11758	North Massapequa(u)	(516)	21,385	23,123
11566	North Merrick(u)	(516)	12,848	13,650
11040	North New Hyde Park(u)	(516)	15,114	18,154
11772	North Patchogue(u)	(516)	7,126	5,232
11768	Northport	(516)	7,651	7,494
13212	North Syracuse	(315)	7,970	8,687
10591	North Tarrytown	(914)	7,994	8,334
14120	North Tonawanda	(716)	35,760	36,012
11580	North Valley Stream(u)	(516)	14,530	14,881
11793	North Wantagh(u)	(516)	12,677	15,053
13815	Norwich	(607)	8,082	8,843
10960	Nyack	(914)	6,428	6,659
11769	Oakdale(u)	(516)	8,090	7,334

ZIP code	Census Division		1980	1970
11572	Oceanside(u)	(516)	33,639	35,372
13669	Ogdensburg	(315)	12,375	14,554
11804	Old Bethpage(u)	(516)	6,215	7,084
14760	Olean	(716)	18,207	19,169
13421	Oneida	(315)	10,810	11,658
13820	Oneonta	(607)	14,933	16,030
12550	Orange Lake(u)	(914)	5,120	4,348
10562	Ossining	(914)	20,196	21,659
13126	Oswego	(315)	19,793	20,913
11771	Oyster Bay(u)	(516)	6,497	6,822
11772	Patchogue	(516)	11,291	11,582
10965	Pearl River(u)	(914)	15,893	17,146
10566	Peekskill	(914)	18,236	19,283
10803	Pelham	(914)	6,848	2,076
10803	Pelham Manor	(914)	6,130	6,673
14527	Penn Yan	(315)	5,242	5,293
13212	Pitcher Hill	(315)	6,063	....
11714	Plainedge(u)	(516)	9,629	10,759
11803	Plainview(u)	(516)	28,037	31,695
12901	Plattsburgh	(518)	21,057	18,715
12903	Plattsburgh AFB(u)	(518)	5,905	7,078
10570	Pleasantville	(914)	6,749	7,110
10573	Port Chester	(914)	23,565	25,803
11777	Port Jefferson	(516)	6,731	5,515
11776	Port Jefferson Station(u)	(516)	17,009	7,403
12771	Port Jervis	(914)	8,699	8,852
11050	Port Washington(u)	(516)	14,521	15,923
13676	Potsdam	(315)	10,635	10,303
*12601	Poughkeepsie	(914)	29,757	32,029
12603	Red Oaks Mill(u)	(914)	5,236	3,919
12144	Rensselaer	(518)	9,047	10,136
11961	Ridge(u)	(516)	8,977	....
11901	Riverhead(u)	(516)	6,339	7,585
11901	Riverside-Flanders(u)	(516)	5,400	....
*14603	Rochester	(716)	241,741	295,011
*11570	Rockville Centre	(516)	25,412	27,444
11778	Rocky Point(u)	(516)	7,012	....
12205	Roessleville(u)	(518)	11,685	5,476
13440	Rome	(315)	43,826	50,148
11575	Roosevelt(u)	(516)	14,109	15,008
11577	Roslyn Heights(u)	(516)	6,546	7,242
12303	Rotterdam(u)	(518)	22,933	25,214
10580	Rye	(914)	15,000	15,869
11780	St. James(u)	(516)	12,122	10,500
14779	Salamanca	(716)	6,890	7,877
12983	Saranac Lake	(518)	5,578	6,086
12866	Saratoga Springs	(518)	23,906	18,845
11782	Sayville(u)	(516)	12,013	11,680
10583	Scarsdale	(914)	17,650	19,229
*12301	Schenectady	(518)	67,072	77,958
10940	Scotchtown(u)	(914)	7,352	2,119
12302	Scotia	(518)	7,280	7,370
11579	Sea Cliff	(516)	5,304	5,890
11783	Seaford(u)	(516)	16,117	17,379
11784	Selden(u)	(516)	17,259	11,613
13148	Seneca Falls	(315)	7,466	7,794
11733	Setauket-East Setauket(u)	(516)	10,176	6,857
11967	Shirley(u)	(516)	18,072	6,280
11787	Smithtown(u)	(516)	30,906	....
13209	Solvay	(315)	7,140	8,280
11789	South Beach(u)	(516)	8,071	....
11735	South Farmingdale(u)	(516)	16,439	20,464
14850	South Hill(u)	(607)	5,276	....
11746	South Huntington(u)	(516)	14,854	9,115
14904	Southport(u)	(607)	8,329	8,685
11581	South Valley Stream(u)	(516)	5,462	6,595
11590	South Westbury(u)	(516)	9,732	10,978
10977	Spring Valley	(914)	20,537	18,112
11790	Stony Brook(u)	(516)	16,155	6,391
10980	Stony Point(u)	(914)	8,686	8,270
10901	Suffern	(914)	10,794	8,273
11791	Syosset(u)	(516)	9,818	10,084
*13201	Syracuse	(315)	170,105	197,297
10983	Tappan(u)	(914)	8,267	7,424
10591	Tarrytown	(914)	10,648	11,115
10594	Thornwood(u)	(914)	7,197	6,874
14150	Tonawanda	(716)	18,693	21,898
*12180	Troy	(518)	56,638	62,918
10707	Tuckahoe	(914)	6,076	6,236
11553	Uniondale(u)	(516)	20,016	22,077
*13503	Utica	(315)	75,632	91,373
10989	Valley Cottage(u)	(914)	8,214	6,007
*11580	Valley Stream	(516)	35,769	40,413
10901	Viola(u)	(914)	5,340	5,136
12586	Walden	(914)	5,659	5,277
11793	Wantagh(u)	(516)	19,817	21,783
12590	Wappingers Falls	(914)	5,110	5,607
13165	Waterloo	(315)	5,303	5,418
13601	Watertown	(315)	27,861	30,787
12189	Watervliet	(518)	11,354	12,404
14580	Webster	(716)	5,499	5,037
14895	Wellsville	(716)	5,769	5,815
11758	West Amityville(u)	(516)	6,623	6,424
11704	West Babylon(u)	(516)	41,699	12,893
11706	West Bay Shore(u)	(516)	5,118	....
11590	Westbury	(516)	13,871	15,362
14905	West Elmira(u)	(607)	5,485	5,901
12801	West Glens Falls(u)	(518)	5,331	3,363
10993	West Haverstraw	(914)	9,181	8,558
11552	West Hempstead(u)	(516)	18,536	20,375
11743	West Hills(u)	(516)	6,071	....
11795	West Islip(u)	(516)	29,533	17,374
12203	Westmere(u)	(518)	6,881	6,364
10994	West Nyack(u)	(914)	8,553	5,510
10996	West Point(u)	(914)	8,105	....
11796	West Sayville(u)	(516)	8,185	7,386
14224	West Seneca(u)	(716)	51,210	....
13219	Westvale(u)	(315)	6,169	7,253
*10602	White Plains	(914)	46,999	50,346
14221	Williamsville	(716)	6,017	6,878
11596	Williston Park	(516)	8,216	9,154
11797	Woodbury(u)	(516)	7,043	....
11598	Woodmere(u)	(516)	17,205	19,831
11798	Wyandach(u)	(516)	13,215	15,716
*10701	Yonkers	(914)	195,351	204,297
10598	Yorktown Heights(u)	(914)	7,696	6,805

North Carolina

ZIP code	Census Division		1980	1970
28001	Albemarle	(704)	15,110	11,126
27263	Archdale	(919)	5,326	4,874
27203	Asheboro	(919)	15,252	10,797
*28801	Asheville	(704)	54,022	57,820
28303	Bonnie Doone(u)	(919)	5,950	....
28607	Boone	(704)	10,191	8,754
28712	Brevard	(704)	5,323	5,243
27215	Burlington	(919)	37,266	35,930
28542	Camp Le Jeune(u)	(919)	30,764	34,549
27510	Carrboro	(919)	7,517	5,058
27511	Cary	(919)	21,612	7,640
27514	Chapel Hill	(919)	32,421	26,199
*28202	Charlotte	(704)	315,474	241,420
27012	Clemmons(u)	(919)	7,401	....
28328	Clinton	(919)	7,552	7,157
28025	Concord	(704)	16,942	18,464
28334	Dunn	(919)	8,962	8,302
*27701	Durham	(919)	101,149	95,438
28379	East Rockingham(u)	(919)	5,190	2,858
27288	Eden	(919)	15,672	15,871
27932	Edenton	(919)	5,264	4,956
27909	Elizabeth City	(919)	13,784	14,381
28728	Enka(u)	(704)	5,567	
*28302	Fayetteville	(919)	59,507	53,510
28043	Forest City	(704)	7,688	7,179
28307	Fort Bragg(u)	(919)	37,834	46,995
27529	Garner	(919)	9,556	4,923
28052	Gastonia	(704)	47,333	47,322
27530	Goldsboro	(919)	31,071	26,960
27253	Graham	(919)	8,415	8,172
*27420	Greensboro	(919)	155,642	144,076
27834	Greenville	(919)	35,740	29,063
28532	Havelock	(919)	17,710	3,012
27536	Henderson	(919)	13,522	13,896
28739	Hendersonville	(704)	6,862	6,443
28601	Hickory	(704)	20,757	20,569
*27260	High Point	(919)	63,479	63,229
28348	Hope Mills	(919)	5,412	1,866
28540	Jacksonville	(919)	18,237	16,289
28081	Kannapolis(u)	(704)	34,564	36,293
27284	Kernersville	(919)	5,875	4,815
27021	King(u)	(919)	8,757	1,033
.....	Kings Grant(u)	(919)	6,652	....
28086	Kings Mountain	(704)	9,080	8,465
28501	Kinston	(919)	25,234	23,020
28352	Laurinburg	(919)	11,480	8,859
28645	Lenoir	(704)	13,748	14,705
27292	Lexington	(704)	15,711	17,205
28358	Lumberton	(919)	18,340	16,961
28212	Mint Hill	(704)	9,830	....
28110	Monroe	(704)	12,639	11,282
28115	Mooresville	(704)	8,575	8,808
28655	Morganton	(704)	13,763	13,625
27030	Mount Airy	(919)	6,862	7,325
28560	New Bern	(919)	14,557	14,660
27604	New Hope (Wake)(u)	(919)	6,768	....
.....	New Hope (Wayne)(u)	(919)	6,685	....
28540	New River Station(u)	(919)	5,401	....
28658	Newton	(704)	7,624	7,857
28012	North Belmont(u)	(704)	10,762	10,672
27565	Oxford	(919)	7,709	7,178
.....	Piney Green-White Oak(u)	(919)	6,058	....
*27611	Raleigh	(919)	149,771	122,830
27320	Reidsville	(919)	12,492	13,636
27870	Roanoke Rapids	(919)	14,702	13,508
28379	Rockingham	(919)	8,300	5,852
27801	Rocky Mount	(919)	41,526	34,284
27573	Roxboro	(919)	7,532	5,370
28601	St. Stephens(u)	(704)	10,797	....
28144	Salisbury	(704)	22,677	22,515
27330	Sanford	(919)	14,773	11,716
28150	Shelby	(704)	15,310	16,328
27577	Smithfield	(919)	7,288	6,677
28387	Southern Pines	(919)	8,620	5,937
28390	Spring Lake	(919)	6,273	3,968
27045	Stanleyville(u)	(919)	5,039	2,362
28677	Statesville	(704)	18,622	20,007
28778	Swannanoa(u)	(704)	5,586	1,966
27886	Tarboro	(919)	8,741	9,425
27360	Thomasville	(919)	14,144	15,230

ZIP code	Place		1980	1970
27370	Trinity(u)	(919)	6,726	....
27889	Washington	(919)	8,418	8,961
28786	Waynesville	(704)	6,765	6,488
28025	West Concord(u)	(704)	5,859	5,347
28472	Whiteville	(919)	5,565	4,195
27892	Williamston	(919)	6,159	6,570
28401	Wilmington	(919)	44,000	46,169
27893	Wilson	(919)	34,424	29,347
*27102	Winston-Salem	(919)	131,885	133,683

North Dakota (701)

58501	Bismarck		44,485	34,703
58301	Devils Lake		7,442	7,078
58601	Dickinson		15,924	12,405
58102	Fargo		61,308	53,365
58237	Grafton		5,293	5,946
58201	Grand Forks		43,765	39,008
58201	Grand Forks AFB(u)		9,390	10,474
58401	Jamestown		16,280	15,385
58554	Mandan		15,513	11,093
58701	Minot		32,843	32,290
58701	Minot AFB(u)		9,880	12,077
58072	Valley City		7,774	7,843
58075	Wahpeton		9,064	7,076
58078	West Fargo		10,099	5,161
58801	Williston		13,336	11,280

Ohio

45810	Ada	(419)	5,669	5,309
*44309	Akron	(216)	237,177	275,425
44601	Alliance	(216)	24,315	26,547
44001	Amherst	(216)	10,638	9,902
44805	Ashland	(419)	20,326	19,872
44004	Ashtabula	(216)	23,449	24,313
45701	Athens	(614)	19,743	24,168
44202	Aurora	(216)	8,177	6,549
44515	Austintown(u)	(216)	33,636	29,393
44011	Avon	(216)	7,241	7,214
44012	Avon Lake	(216)	13,222	12,261
44203	Barberton	(216)	29,751	33,052
44140	Bay Village	(216)	17,846	18,163
44122	Beachwood	(216)	9,983	9,631
45385	Beavercreek	(513)	31,589	...
44146	Bedford	(216)	15,056	17,552
44146	Bedford Heights	(216)	13,214	13,063
43906	Bellaire	(614)	8,241	9,655
45305	Bellbrook	(513)	5,174	1,268
43311	Bellefontaine	(513)	11,888	11,255
44811	Bellevue	(419)	8,187	8,604
45714	Belpre	(614)	7,193	7,189
44017	Berea	(216)	19,567	22,465
43209	Bexley	(614)	13,405	14,888
43004	Blacklick Estates(u)	(614)	11,223	8,351
45242	Blue Ash	(513)	9,510	8,324
44512	Boardman(u)	(216)	39,161	30,852
43402	Bowling Green	(419)	25,728	14,656
44141	Brecksville	(216)	10,132	9,137
45231	Brentwood(u)	(513)	5,508	....
45211	Bridgetown(u)	(513)	11,460	13,352
44141	Broadview Heights	(216)	10,920	11,463
44144	Brooklyn	(216)	12,342	13,142
44142	Brook Park	(216)	26,195	30,774
44212	Brunswick	(216)	27,689	15,852
43506	Bryan	(419)	7,879	7,008
44820	Bucyrus	(419)	13,433	13,111
43725	Cambridge	(614)	13,573	13,656
44405	Campbell	(216)	11,619	12,577
44406	Canfield	(216)	5,535	4,997
*44711	Canton	(216)	93,077	110,053
45822	Celina	(419)	9,137	8,072
45459	Centerville	(513)	18,886	10,333
45211	Cheviot	(513)	9,888	11,135
45601	Chillicothe	(614)	23,420	24,842
*45234	Cincinnati	(513)	385,409	453,514
43113	Circleville	(614)	11,700	11,687
*44101	Cleveland	(216)	573,822	750,879
44118	Cleveland Heights	(216)	56,438	60,767
43410	Clyde	(419)	5,489	5,503
*43216	Columbus	(614)	565,032	540,025
44030	Conneaut	(216)	13,835	14,552
44410	Cortland	(216)	5,011	2,525
43812	Coshocton	(614)	13,405	13,747
45238	Covedale(u)	(513)	5,830	6,639
44827	Crestline	(419)	5,406	5,965
*44222	Cuyahoga Falls	(216)	43,710	49,815
*45401	Dayton	(513)	193,536	243,023
45236	Deer Park	(513)	6,745	7,415
43512	Defiance	(419)	16,810	16,281
43015	Delaware	(614)	18,780	15,008
45238	Delhi Hills(u)	(513)	27,647	....
45833	Delphos	(419)	7,314	7,608
44622	Dover	(216)	11,526	11,516
44112	East Cleveland	(216)	36,957	39,600
44094	Eastlake	(216)	22,104	19,690
43920	East Liverpool	(216)	16,687	20,020
44413	East Palestine	(216)	5,306	5,604
45320	Eaton	(513)	6,839	6,020
*44035	Elyria	(216)	57,504	53,427
45322	Englewood	(513)	11,329	7,885
44117	Euclid	(216)	59,999	71,552
45324	Fairborn	(513)	29,702	32,267
45014	Fairfield	(513)	30,777	14,680
44313	Fairlawn	(216)	6,100	6,102
44126	Fairview Park	(216)	19,311	21,699
45840	Findlay	(419)	35,594	35,800
45405	Forest Park	(513)	18,566	15,139
45426	Fort McKinley(u)	(513)	10,161	11,536
44830	Fostoria	(419)	15,743	16,037
45005	Franklin	(513)	10,711	10,075
43420	Fremont	(419)	17,834	18,490
43230	Gahanna	(614)	18,001	12,400
44833	Galion	(419)	12,391	13,123
45631	Gallipolis	(614)	5,576	7,490
44125	Garfield Heights	(216)	33,380	41,417
44041	Geneva	(216)	6,655	6,449
45327	Germantown	(513)	5,015	4,088
44420	Girard	(216)	12,517	14,119
43212	Grandview Heights	(614)	7,420	8,460
45123	Greenfield	(513)	5,150	4,780
45331	Greenville	(513)	12,999	12,380
45239	Groesbeck(u)	(513)	9,594	....
43123	Grove City	(614)	16,793	13,911
*45012	Hamilton	(513)	63,189	67,865
45030	Harrison	(513)	5,855	4,408
43055	Heath	(614)	6,969	6,768
44124	Highland Heights	(216)	5,739	5,926
43026	Hilliard	(614)	8,131	8,369
45133	Hillsboro	(513)	6,356	5,584
44484	Howland(u)	(216)	7,441	....
44425	Hubbard	(216)	9,245	8,583
45424	Huber Heights(u)	(513)	31,731	18,943
43081	Huber Ridge(u)	(614)	5,835	....
44839	Huron	(419)	7,123	6,896
44131	Independence	(216)	8,165	7,034
45638	Ironton	(614)	14,290	15,030
45640	Jackson	(614)	6,675	6,843
44240	Kent	(216)	26,164	28,183
43326	Kenton	(419)	8,605	8,315
45236	Kenwood(u)	(513)	9,928	15,789
45429	Kettering	(513)	61,186	71,864
44094	Kirtland	(216)	5,969	5,530
44107	Lakewood	(216)	61,963	70,173
43130	Lancaster	(614)	34,953	32,911
45036	Lebanon	(513)	9,636	7,934
*45802	Lima	(419)	47,827	53,734
45215	Lincoln Heights	(513)	5,259	6,099
43228	Lincoln Village(u)	(614)	10,548	11,215
43138	Logan	(614)	6,557	6,269
43140	London	(614)	6,958	6,481
*44052	Lorain	(216)	75,416	78,185
44641	Louisville	(216)	7,996	6,298
45140	Loveland	(513)	9,106	7,126
44124	Lyndhurst	(216)	18,092	19,749
44056	Macedonia	(216)	6,571	6,375
45243	Madeira	(513)	9,341	6,713
*44901	Mansfield	(419)	53,927	55,047
44137	Maple Heights	(216)	29,735	34,093
45750	Marietta	(614)	16,467	16,861
43302	Marion	(614)	37,040	38,646
43935	Martins Ferry	(614)	9,331	10,757
43040	Marysville	(513)	7,414	5,744
45040	Mason	(513)	8,692	5,677
44646	Massillon	(216)	30,557	32,539
43537	Maumee	(419)	15,747	15,937
44124	Mayfield Heights	(216)	21,550	22,139
44256	Medina	(216)	15,268	10,913
44060	Mentor	(216)	42,065	36,912
44060	Mentor-on-the-Lake	(216)	7,919	6,517
45342	Miamisburg	(513)	15,304	14,797
44130	Middleburg Heights	(216)	16,218	12,367
45042	Middletown	(513)	43,719	48,767
45042	Middletown South(u)	(513)	5,260	....
45150	Milford	(513)	5,232	4,828
45239	Monfort Heights(u)	(513)	9,745	....
45242	Montgomery	(513)	10,084	5,683
45439	Moraine	(513)	5,325	4,898
45231	Mount Healthy	(513)	7,562	7,446
43050	Mount Vernon	(614)	14,380	13,373
43545	Napoleon	(419)	8,614	7,791
43055	Newark	(614)	41,200	41,836
45344	New Carlisle	(513)	6,498	6,112
43764	New Lexington	(614)	5,179	4,921
44663	New Philadelphia	(216)	16,883	15,184
44446	Niles	(216)	23,088	21,581
45239	Northbrook(u)	(513)	8,357	....
44720	North Canton	(216)	14,228	15,228
45239	North College Hill	(513)	10,990	12,363
44057	North Madison(u)	(216)	8,741	6,882
44070	North Olmsted	(216)	36,486	34,861
45502	Northridge(u) (Clark)	(513)	5,559	12
45414	Northridge(u) (Montgomery)	(513)	9,720	10,084
44039	North Ridgeville	(216)	21,522	13,152
44133	North Royalton	(216)	17,671	12,807
.....	Northview(u)	(513)	9,973	....
43619	Northwood	(419)	5,495	4,222

ZIP code	Place		1980	1970
44203	Norton	(216)	12,242	12,308
44857	Norwalk	(419)	14,358	13,386
45212	Norwood	(513)	26,342	30,420
45873	Oakwood	(419)	9,372	10,095
44074	Oberlin	(216)	8,660	8,761
44138	Olmsted Falls	(216)	5,868	2,504
43616	Oregon	(419)	18,675	16,563
44667	Orrville	(216)	7,511	7,408
45431	Overlook-Page Manor(u)	(513)	14,825	19,719
45056	Oxford	(513)	17,655	15,868
44077	Painesville	(216)	16,391	16,536
45344	Park Layne(u)	(513)	5,372	....
44129	Parma	(216)	92,548	100,216
44130	Parma Heights	(216)	23,112	27,192
44124	Pepper Pike	(216)	6,177	5,382
44646	Perry Heights(u)	(216)	9,206	....
43551	Perrysburg	(419)	10,215	7,693
45356	Piqua	(513)	20,480	20,741
45069	Pisgah(u)	(513)	15,660	....
44319	Portage Lakes(u)	(216)	11,310	....
43452	Port Clinton	(419)	7,223	7,202
45662	Portsmouth	(614)	25,943	27,633
44266	Ravenna	(216)	11,987	11,780
45215	Reading	(513)	12,879	14,617
43068	Reynoldsburg	(614)	20,661	13,921
44143	Richmond Heights	(213)	10,095	9,220
44270	Rittman	(216)	6,063	6,308
44116	Rocky River	(216)	21,084	22,958
43460	Rossford	(419)	5,978	6,302
45217	St. Bernard	(513)	5,396	6,131
43950	St. Clairsville	(614)	5,452	4,754
45885	St. Marys	(419)	8,414	7,699
44460	Salem	(216)	12,869	14,186
44870	Sandusky	(419)	31,360	32,674
44870	Sandusky South(u)	(419)	6,548	8,501
44672	Sebring	(216)	5,078	4,954
44131	Seven Hills	(216)	13,650	12,700
44120	Shaker Heights	(216)	32,487	36,306
45241	Sharonville	(513)	10,108	11,393
44054	Sheffield Lake	(216)	10,484	8,734
44875	Shelby	(419)	9,703	9,847
45365	Sidney	(513)	17,657	16,332
45236	Silverton	(513)	6,172	6,588
44139	Solon	(216)	14,341	11,147
44121	South Euclid	(216)	25,713	29,579
45246	Springdale	(216)	10,111	8,127
*45501	Springfield	(513)	72,563	81,941
43952	Steubenville	(614)	26,400	30,771
44224	Stow	(216)	25,303	20,061
44240	Streetsboro	(216)	9,055	7,966
44136	Strongsville	(216)	28,577	15,182
44471	Struthers	(216)	13,624	15,343
43560	Sylvania	(419)	15,527	12,031
44278	Tallmadge	(216)	15,269	15,274
45243	The Village of Indian Hill	(513)	5,521	5,651
44883	Tiffin	(419)	19,549	21,596
45371	Tipp City	(513)	[illegible]	5,090
*43601	Toledo	(419)	354,635	383,062
43964	Toronto	(614)	6,934	7,705
45067	Trenton	(513)	6,401	5,278
45426	Trotwood	(513)	7,802	6,997
45373	Troy	(513)	19,086	17,186
44087	Twinsburg	(216)	7,632	6,432
44683	Uhrichsville	(614)	6,130	5,731
45322	Union	(513)	5,219	3,654
44118	University Heights	(216)	15,401	17,055
43221	Upper Arlington	(614)	35,648	38,727
43351	Upper Sandusky	(419)	5,967	5,645
43078	Urbana	(513)	10,762	11,237
45377	Vandalia	(513)	13,161	10,796
45891	Van Wert	(419)	11,035	11,320
44089	Vermilion	(216)	11,012	9,872
44281	Wadsworth	(216)	15,166	13,142
45895	Wapakoneta	(419)	8,402	7,324
*44481	Warren	(216)	56,629	63,494
44122	Warrensville Heights	(216)	16,565	18,925
43160	Washington	(614)	12,682	12,495
43567	Wauseon	(419)	6,173	4,932
45692	Wellston	(614)	6,016	5,410
43968	Wellsville	(216)	5,095	5,891
45449	West Carrollton	(513)	13,148	10,748
43081	Westerville	(614)	23,414	12,530
44145	Westlake	(216)	19,483	15,689
43213	Whitehall	(614)	21,299	25,263
45239	White Oak(u)	(513)	9,563	....
44092	Wickliffe	(216)	16,790	20,632
44890	Willard	(419)	5,674	5,510
44094	Willoughby	(216)	19,329	18,634
44094	Willoughby Hills	(216)	8,612	5,969
44094	Willowick	(216)	17,834	21,237
45177	Wilmington	(513)	10,431	10,051
45459	Woodbourne-Hyde Park(u)	(513)	8,826	....
44691	Wooster	(216)	19,289	18,703
43085	Worthington	(614)	15,016	15,326
45215	Wyoming	(513)	8,282	9,089
45385	Xenia	(513)	24,653	25,373
*44501	Youngstown	(216)	115,511	140,909
43701	Zanesville	(614)	28,655	33,045

Oklahoma

ZIP code	Place		1980	1970
74820	Ada	(405)	15,902	14,859
73521	Altus	(405)	23,101	23,302
73717	Alva	(405)	6,416	7,440
73005	Anadarko	(405)	6,378	6,682
73401	Ardmore	(405)	23,689	20,881
74003	Bartlesville	(918)	34,568	29,683
73008	Bethany	(405)	22,038	22,694
74008	Bixby	(918)	6,969	3,973
74631	Blackwell	(405)	8,400	8,645
74012	Broken Arrow	(918)	35,761	11,018
73018	Chickasha	(405)	15,828	14,194
73020	Choctaw	(405)	7,520	4,750
74017	Claremore	(918)	12,085	9,084
73601	Clinton	(405)	8,796	8,513
74023	Cushing	(918)	7,720	7,529
73115	Del City	(405)	28,523	27,133
73533	Duncan	(405)	22,517	19,718
74701	Durant	(405)	11,972	11,118
73034	Edmond	(405)	34,637	16,633
73644	Elk City	(405)	9,579	7,323
73036	El Reno	(405)	15,486	14,510
73701	Enid	(405)	50,363	44,986
73503	Fort Sill(u)	(405)	15,924	21,217
73542	Frederick	(405)	6,153	6,132
73044	Guthrie	(405)	10,312	9,575
73942	Guymon	(405)	8,492	7,674
74437	Henryetta	(918)	6,432	6,430
74848	Holdenville	(405)	5,469	5,181
74743	Hugo	(405)	7,172	6,585
74745	Idabel	(405)	7,622	5,946
74037	Jenks	(918)	5,876	2,685
73501	Lawton	(405)	80,054	74,470
73055	Marlow	(405)	5,017	3,995
74501	McAlester	(918)	17,255	18,802
74354	Miami	(918)	14,237	13,880
73110	Midwest City	(405)	49,559	48,212
73060	Moore	(405)	35,063	18,761
74401	Muskogee	(918)	40,011	37,331
73064	Mustang	(405)	7,406	2,637
73069	Norman	(405)	68,020	52,117
*73125	Oklahoma City	(405)	404,014	368,164
74447	Okmulgee	(918)	16,263	15,180
74055	Owasso	(918)	6,149	3,491
73075	Pauls Valley	(405)	5,664	5,769
73077	Perry	(405)	5,796	5,341
74601	Ponca City	(405)	26,238	25,940
74953	Poteau	(918)	7,089	5,500
74361	Pryor Creek	(918)	8,483	7,057
74955	Sallisaw	(918)	6,403	4,888
74063	Sand Springs	(918)	13,121	10,565
74066	Sapulpa	(918)	15,853	15,159
74868	Seminole	(405)	8,590	7,878
74801	Shawnee	(405)	26,506	25,075
74074	Stillwater	(405)	38,268	31,126
73086	Sulphur	(405)	5,516	5,158
74464	Tahlequah	(918)	9,708	9,254
74873	Tecumseh	(405)	5,123	4,451
73120	The Village	(405)	11,114	13,695
*74101	Tulsa	(918)	360,919	330,350
74156	Turley(u)	(918)	6,336	....
74301	Vinita	(918)	6,740	5,047
74467	Wagoner	(918)	6,191	4,959
73132	Warr Acres	(405)	9,940	9,887
73096	Weatherford	(405)	9,640	7,959
74884	Wewoka	(405)	5,472	5,284
73801	Woodward	(405)	13,781	9,563
73099	Yukon	(405)	17,112	8,411

Oregon (503)

ZIP code	Place	1980	1970
97321	Albany	26,511	18,181
97005	Aloha(u)	28,353	....
97601	Altamont(u)	19,805	15,746
97520	Ashland	14,943	12,342
97103	Astoria	9,998	10,244
97814	Baker	9,471	9,354
97005	Beaverton	31,926	18,577
97701	Bend	17,263	13,710
97013	Canby	7,659	3,813
97225	Cedar Hills(u)	9,619	....
.....	Centennial(u)	22,118	....
97502	Central Point	6,357	4,004
97420	Coos Bay	14,424	13,466
97330	Corvallis	40,960	35,056
97424	Cottage Grove	7,148	6,004
.....	Cully(u)	10,569	....
97338	Dallas	8,530	6,361
97266	Errol Heights(u)	10,487	....
*97401	Eugene	105,664	79,028
97116	Forest Grove	11,499	8,275
97301	Four Corners(u)	11,331	5,823
97223	Garden Home-Whitford(u)	6,926	....
97027	Gladstone	9,500	6,254
97526	Grants Pass	14,997	12,455
97030	Gresham	33,005	10,030
97303	Hayesville(u)	9,213	5,518
97230	Hazelwood(u)	25,541	....
97838	Hermiston	9,408	4,893

ZIP code	Place	1980	1970
97123	Hillsboro	27,664	14,675
97303	Keizer(u)	18,592	11,405
97601	Klamath Falls	16,661	15,775
97850	La Grande	11,354	9,645
97034	Lake Oswego	22,527	14,615
97355	Lebanon	10,413	6,636
97367	Lincoln City	5,469	4,198
97128	McMinnville	14,080	10,125
97501	Medford	39,603	28,973
97223	Metzger(u)	5,544	....
97862	Milton-Freewater	5,086	4,105
97222	Milwaukie	17,931	16,444
97361	Monmouth	5,594	5,237
97132	Newberg	10,394	6,507
97365	Newport	7,519	5,188
97459	North Bend	9,779	8,553
.....	North Springfield(u)	6,140	....
97268	Oak Grove(u)	11,640	....
97914	Ontario	8,814	6,523
97045	Oregon City	14,673	9,176
97220	Parkrose(u)	21,108	....
97801	Pendleton	14,521	13,197
*97208	Portland	368,148	379,967
97236	Powellhurst(u)	20,132	....
97754	Prineville	5,276	4,101
97225	Raleigh Hills(u)	6,517	....
97756	Redmond	6,452	3,721
97404	River Road(u)	10,370	....
97470	Roseburg	16,644	14,461
97051	St. Helens	7,064	6,212
*97301	Salem	89,233	68,725
97401	Santa Clara(u)	14,288	....
97138	Seaside	5,193	4,402
97381	Silverton	5,168	4,301
97477	Springfield	41,621	26,874
97386	Sweet Home	6,921	3,799
97058	The Dalles	10,820	10,423
97223	Tigard	14,799	6,499
97060	Troutdale	5,908	1,661
97062	Tualatin	7,483	750
97068	West Linn	11,358	7,091
97225	West Slope(u)	5,364	....
97501	White City(u)	5,445	....
97233	Wilkes-Rockwood(u)	23,216	....
97071	Woodburn	11,196	7,495

Pennsylvania

ZIP code	Place	Area code	1980	1970
19001	Abington Township(u)	(215)	59,084	63,625
15001	Aliquippa	(412)	17,094	22,277
*18101	Allentown	(215)	103,758	109,871
*16603	Altoona	(814)	57,078	63,115
19002	Ambler	(215)	6,628	7,800
15003	Ambridge	(412)	9,575	11,324
18403	Archbald	(717)	6,295	6,118
19003	Ardmore(u)	(215)	NA	5,131
15068	Arnold	(412)	6,853	8,174
19014	Aston Township(u)	(215)	14,530	13,704
15202	Avalon	(412)	6,240	7,010
15005	Baden	(412)	5,318	5,536
19004	Bala-Cynwyd(u)	(215)	NA	6,483
15234	Baldwin	(412)	24,714	26,729
18013	Bangor	(215)	5,006	5,425
15009	Beaver	(412)	5,441	6,100
15010	Beaver Falls	(412)	12,525	14,635
16823	Bellefonte	(814)	6,300	6,828
15202	Bellevue	(412)	10,128	11,586
19020	Bensalem Township(u)	(215)	52,399	33,038
18603	Berwick	(717)	12,189	12,274
15102	Bethel Park	(412)	34,755	34,758
*18016	Bethlehem	(215)	70,419	72,686
18447	Blakely	(717)	7,438	6,391
17815	Bloomsburg	(717)	11,717	11,652
15104	Braddock	(412)	5,634	8,795
16701	Bradford	(814)	11,211	12,672
15227	Brentwood	(412)	11,859	13,732
15017	Bridgeville	(412)	6,154	6,717
19007	Bristol	(215)	10,867	12,085
19007	Bristol Twp(u)	(215)	58,733	67,498
19015	Brookhaven	(215)	7,912	7,370
16001	Butler	(412)	17,026	18,691
15419	California	(412)	5,703	6,635
17011	Camp Hill	(717)	8,422	9,931
15317	Canonsburg	(412)	10,459	11,439
18407	Carbondale	(717)	11,255	12,478
17013	Carlisle	(717)	18,314	18,079
15106	Carnegie	(412)	10,099	10,864
15108	Carnot-Moon(u)	(412)	11,102	13,093
15234	Castle Shannon	(412)	10,164	12,036
18032	Catasauqua	(215)	7,944	5,702
17201	Chambersburg	(717)	16,174	17,315
15022	Charleroi	(412)	5,717	6,723
19012	Cheltenham Twp(u)	(215)	35,509	40,238
*19013	Chester	(215)	45,794	56,331
19013	Chester Twp(u)	(215)	5,687	5,708
15025	Clairton	(412)	12,188	15,051
16214	Clarion	(814)	6,198	6,095
18411	Clarks Summit	(717)	5,272	5,376
16830	Clearfield	(814)	7,580	8,176
19018	Clifton Heights	(215)	7,320	8,348
19320	Coatesville	(215)	10,698	12,331
19023	Collingdale	(215)	9,539	10,605
17512	Columbia	(717)	10,466	11,237
15425	Connellsville	(412)	10,319	11,643
19428	Conshohocken	(215)	8,591	10,195
15108	Coraopolis	(412)	7,308	8,435
16407	Corry	(814)	7,149	7,435
15205	Crafton	(412)	7,623	8,233
17821	Danville	(717)	5,239	6,176
19023	Darby	(215)	11,513	13,729
19036	Darby Twp(u)	(215)	12,264	.....
19333	Devon-Berwyn(u)	(215)	5,246	....
18519	Dickson City	(717)	6,699	7,698
15033	Donora	(412)	7,524	8,825
15216	Dormont	(412)	11,275	12,856
19335	Downingtown	(215)	7,650	7,437
18901	Doylestown	(215)	8,717	8,270
15801	Du Bois	(814)	9,290	10,112
18512	Dunmore	(717)	16,781	18,168
15110	Duquesne	(412)	10,094	11,410
18642	Duryea	(717)	5,415	5,264
19401	East Norriton(u)	(215)	12,711	....
18042	Easton	(215)	26,027	29,450
18301	East Stroudsburg	(717)	8,039	7,894
15005	Economy	(412)	9,538	7,176
16412	Edinboro	(814)	6,324	4,871
18704	Edwardsville	(717)	5,729	5,633
17022	Elizabethtown	(717)	8,233	8,072
16117	Ellwood City	(412)	9,998	10,857
18049	Emmaus	(215)	11,001	11,511
17522	Ephrata	(717)	11,095	9,662
*16501	Erie	(814)	119,123	129,265
18643	Exeter	(717)	5,493	4,670
19054	Falls Twp(u)	(215)	36,083	35,830
16121	Farrell	(412)	8,645	11,000
19032	Folcroft	(215)	8,231	9,610
15221	Forest Hills	(412)	8,198	9,561
18704	Forty Fort	(717)	5,590	6,114
15238	Fox Chapel	(412)	5,049	4,684
17931	Frackville	(717)	5,308	5,445
16323	Franklin	(814)	8,146	8,629
15143	Franklin Park	(412)	6,135	5,310
18052	Fullerton(u)	(215)	8,055	7,908
17325	Gettysburg	(717)	7,194	7,275
15045	Glassport	(412)	6,242	7,450
19036	Glenolden	(215)	7,633	8,697
15601	Greensburg	(412)	17,558	17,077
15220	Green Tree	(412)	5,722	6,441
16125	Greenville	(412)	7,730	8,704
16127	Grove City	(412)	8,162	8,312
17331	Hanover	(717)	14,890	15,623
*17105	Harrisburg	(717)	53,264	68,061
19040	Hatboro	(215)	7,579	8,880
19083	Haverford Twp(u)	(215)	52,349	55,132
18201	Hazleton	(717)	27,318	30,426
18055	Hellertown	(215)	6,025	6,615
17033	Hershey(u)	(717)	13,249	7,407
18042	Highland Park (Northampton)(u)	(215)	5,922	5,500
16648	Hollidaysburg	(814)	5,892	6,262
16001	Homeacre-Lyndora(u)	(412)	8,333	8,415
15120	Homestead	(412)	5,092	6,309
18431	Honesdale	(717)	5,128	5,224
19044	Horsham(u)	(215)	9,900	....
17036	Hummelstown	(717)	6,159	4,723
16652	Huntingdon	(814)	7,042	6,987
15701	Indiana	(412)	16,051	16,100
15644	Jeannette	(412)	13,106	15,209
15344	Jefferson	(412)	8,643	8,512
18229	Jim Thorpe	(717)	5,263	5,456
*15901	Johnstown	(814)	35,496	42,476
15108	Kennedy Twp(u)	(412)	7,159	6,859
18704	Kingston	(717)	15,681	18,325
16201	Kittanning	(412)	5,432	6,231
*17604	Lancaster	(717)	54,725	57,690
19446	Lansdale	(215)	16,526	18,451
19050	Lansdowne	(215)	11,891	14,090
15650	Latrobe	(412)	10,799	11,749
17042	Lebanon	(717)	25,711	28,572
18235	Lehighton	(215)	5,826	6,095
17837	Lewisburg	(717)	5,407	5,718
17044	Lewistown	(717)	9,830	11,098
17543	Lititz	(717)	7,590	7,072
17745	Lock Haven	(717)	9,617	11,427
15068	Lower Burrell	(412)	13,200	13,654
19003	Lower Merion Twp(u)	(215)	59,651	63,392
19006	Lower Moreland Twp(u)	(215)	12,472	11,746
19047	Lower Southampton Twp(u)	(215)	18,305	17,578
19008	Marple Twp(u)	(215)	23,642	25,040
15237	McCandless Twp(u)	(412)	26,250	22,404
*15134	McKeesport	(412)	31,012	37,977
15136	McKees Rocks	(412)	8,742	11,901
17948	Mahanoy City	(717)	6,167	7,257
17545	Manheim	(717)	5,015	5,434
16335	Meadville	(814)	15,544	16,573
17055	Mechanicsburg	(717)	9,487	9,385
*19063	Media	(215)	6,119	6,444
17057	Middletown (Dauphin)	(717)	10,122	9,080
18017	Middletown (Northampton)(u)	(215)	5,801	....

ZIP code	Place		1980	1970
.....	Middletown Twp (Delaware)(u)	(215)	12,463	12,878
17551	Millersville	(717)	7,668	6,396
17847	Milton	(717)	6,730	7,723
17954	Minersville	(717)	5,635	6,012
15061	Monaca	(412)	7,661	7,486
15062	Monessen	(412)	11,928	15,216
15063	Monongahela	(412)	5,950	7,113
15146	Monroeville	(412)	30,977	29,011
17754	Montoursville	(717)	5,403	5,985
18507	Moosic	(717)	6,068	4,646
19067	Morrisville	(215)	9,845	11,309
17851	Mount Carmel	(717)	8,190	9,317
17552	Mount Joy	(717)	5,680	5,041
15666	Mount Pleasant	(412)	5,354	5,895
15228	Mount Lebanon(u)	(412)	34,414	39,157
15120	Munhall	(412)	14,535	16,574
15668	Murrysville	(412)	16,036	12,661
18634	Nanticoke	(717)	13,044	14,638
18064	Nazareth	(215)	5,443	5,815
.....	Nether Providence Twp(u)	(215)	12,730	13,644
15066	New Brighton	(412)	7,364	7,637
*16101	New Castle	(412)	33,621	38,559
17070	New Cumberland	(717)	8,051	9,803
15068	New Kensington	(412)	17,660	20,312
*19401	Norristown	(215)	34,684	38,169
18067	Northampton	(215)	8,240	8,389
15104	North Braddock	(412)	8,711	10,838
15137	North Versailles(u)	(412)	13,294	....
16421	Northwest Harbor-Creek(u)	(814)	7,485	....
19074	Norwood	(215)	6,647	7,229
15139	Oakmont	(412)	7,039	7,550
16301	Oil City	(814)	13,881	15,033
18518	Old Forge	(717)	9,304	9,522
18447	Olyphant	(717)	5,204	5,422
18071	Palmerton	(215)	5,455	5,620
17078	Palmyra	(717)	7,228	7,615
19301	Paoli(u)	(215)	6,698	5,835
17331	Parkville(u)	(717)	5,009	5,120
15235	Penn Hills(u)	(412)	57,632	....
18944	Perkasie	(215)	5,241	5,451
*19104	Philadelphia	(215)	1,688,210	1,949,996
19460	Phoenixville	(215)	14,165	14,823
*15219	Pittsburgh	(412)	423,959	520,089
*18640	Pittston	(717)	9,930	11,113
18705	Plains(u)	(717)	5,455	6,606
15236	Pleasant Hills	(412)	9,604	10,409
15239	Plum	(412)	25,390	21,932
18651	Plymouth	(717)	7,605	9,536
19462	Plymouth Twp(u)	(215)	17,168	16,876
15133	Port Vue	(412)	5,316	5,862
19464	Pottstown	(215)	22,729	25,355
17901	Pottsville	(717)	18,106	19,715
19076	Prospect Park	(215)	6,593	7,250
15767	Punxsutawney	(814)	7,479	7,792
18951	Quakertown	(215)	8,867	7,276
19087	Radnor Twp(u)	(215)	[illegible]	[illegible]
*19603	Reading	(215)	78,686	87,643
17356	Red Lion	(717)	5,824	5,645
18954	Richboro(u)	(215)	5,141	....
15853	Ridgway	(814)	5,604	6,022
19078	Ridley Park	(215)	7,889	9,025
19033	Ridley Twp(u)	(215)	33,771	39,085
15237	Ross Twp(u)	(412)	35,102	32,892
15857	St. Marys	(814)	6,417	7,470
18840	Sayre	(717)	6,951	7,473
17972	Schuylkill Haven	(717)	5,977	6,125
15683	Scottdale	(412)	5,833	5,818
15106	Scott Twp(u)	(412)	20,413	21,856
*18503	Scranton	(717)	88,117	102,696
17870	Selinsgrove	(717)	5,227	5,116
15116	Shaler Twp(u)	(412)	33,712	33,360
17872	Shamokin	(717)	10,357	11,719
16146	Sharon	(412)	19,057	22,653
19079	Sharon Hill	(215)	6,221	7,464
16150	Sharpsville	(412)	6,375	6,126
17976	Shenandoah	(717)	7,589	8,287
19607	Shillington	(215)	5,601	6,249
17404	Shiloh(u)	(717)	5,315	....
17257	Shippensburg	(717)	5,261	6,536
15501	Somerset	(814)	6,474	6,269
18964	Souderton	(215)	6,657	6,366
17701	South Williamsport	(717)	6,581	7,153
19064	Springfield(u)	(215)	25,326	....
19118	Springfield Twp(u)	(215)	20,344	22,394
16801	State College	(814)	36,130	32,833
17113	Steelton	(717)	6,484	8,556
15136	Stowe Twp(u)	(412)	9,202	10,119
18360	Stroudsburg	(717)	5,148	5,451
16323	Sugar Creek	(717)	5,954	5,944
17801	Sunbury	(717)	12,292	13,025
19081	Swarthmore	(215)	5,950	6,156
17111	Swatara Twp(u)	(717)	18,796	17,178
15218	Swissvale	(412)	11,345	13,819
18704	Swoyersville	(717)	5,795	6,786
18252	Tamaqua	(717)	8,843	9,246
15084	Tarentum	(412)	6,419	7,379
18517	Taylor	(717)	7,246	6,977
16354	Titusville	(814)	6,884	7,331
19401	Trooper(u)	(215)	7,370	....
15145	Turtle Creek	(412)	6,959	8,308
16686	Tyrone	(814)	6,346	7,072
15401	Uniontown	(412)	14,510	16,282
19061	Upper Chichester Twp(u)	(215)	14,377	11,414
19082	Upper Darby(u)	(215)	84,054	95,910
19034	Upper Dublin Twp(u)	(215)	22,348	19,449
19406	Upper Merion Twp(u)	(215)	26,138	23,699
19090	Upper Moreland Twp(u)	(215)	25,874	24,866
19063	Upper Providence Twp(u)	(215)	9,477	9,234
15241	Upper St. Clair(u)	(412)	19,023	....
19006	Upper Southampton Twp(u)	(215)	15,806	13,936
15690	Vandergrift	(412)	6,823	7,889
18974	Warminster(u)	(215)	35,543	....
16365	Warren	(814)	12,146	12,998
15301	Washington	(412)	18,363	19,827
17268	Waynesboro	(717)	9,726	10,011
.....	Weigelstown(u)	(717)	5,213	....
*19380	West Chester	(215)	17,435	19,301
19380	West Goshen(u)	(215)	7,998	....
15122	West Mifflin	(412)	26,322	28,070
19401	West Norriton(u)	(215)	14,034	....
15905	Westmont	(814)	6,113	6,673
18643	West Pittston	(717)	5,980	7,074
15229	West View	(412)	7,648	8,312
18052	Whitehall	(215)	15,143	16,450
19428	Whitemarsh Twp(u)	(215)	15,101	15,886
15131	White Oak	(717)	9,480	9,304
*18701	Wilkes-Barre	(717)	51,551	58,856
15221	Wilkinsburg	(412)	23,669	26,780
15145	Wilkins Twp(u)	(412)	8,472	8,749
17701	Williamsport	(717)	33,401	37,918
15025	Wilson	(412)	7,564	8,406
15963	Windber	(814)	5,585	6,332
19610	Wyomissing	(215)	6,551	7,136
19050	Yeadon	(215)	11,727	12,136
*17405	York	(717)	44,619	50,335

Rhode Island (401)

See Note on Page 544

02806	*Barrington*	16,174	17,554
02809	*Bristol*	20,128	17,860
02830	*Burrillville*	13,164	10,087
02863	Central Falls	16,995	18,716
02816	*Coventry*	27,065	22,947
02910	Cranston	71,992	74,287
02864	*Cumberland*	27,069	26,605
02864	Cumberland Hill(u)	5,421	....
02818	*East Greenwich*	10,211	9,577
02914	East Providence	50,980	48,207
02814	*Glocester*	7,550	5,160
02828	Greenville(u)	7,576	....
02833	*Hopkinton*	6,406	5,392
02919	*Johnston*	24,907	22,037
02881	Kingston(u)	[illegible]	[illegible]
[illegible]	*Lincoln*	16,949	16,182
02840	*Middletown*	17,216	29,290
02882	*Narragansett*	12,088	7,138
02840	Newport	29,259	34,562
02843	Newport East(u)	11,030	10,285
02852	*North Kingstown*	21,938	29,793
02908	*North Providence*	29,188	24,337
02876	*North Smithfield*	9,972	9,349
*02860	Pawtucket	71,204	76,984
02871	*Portsmouth*	14,257	12,521
*02904	Providence	156,804	179,116
02857	*Scituate*	8,405	7,489
02917	*Smithfield*	16,886	13,468
02879	*South Kingstown*	20,414	16,913
02878	*Tiverton*	13,526	12,559
02864	Valley Falls(u)	10,892	....
*02880	Wakefield-Peacedale(u)	6,474	6,331
02885	*Warren*	10,640	10,523
*02887	Warwick	87,123	83,694
02891	*Westerly*	18,580	17,248
02891	Westerly Center(u)	14,093	13,654
02893	*West Warwick*	27,026	24,323
02895	Woonsocket	45,914	46,820

South Carolina (803)

29620	Abbeville	5,863	5,515
29801	Aiken	14,978	13,436
29621	Anderson	27,546	27,556
29407	Avondale-Moorland(u)	5,355	5,236
29812	Barnwell	5,572	4,439
29902	Beaufort	8,634	9,434
29627	Belton	5,312	5,257
29841	Belvedere(u)	6,859	....
29512	Bennettsville	8,774	7,468
29611	Berea(u)	13,164	7,186
.....	Brookdale(u)	6,123	....
29020	Camden	7,462	8,532
29209	Capitol View(u)	9,962	....
29033	Cayce	11,701	9,967
*29401	Charleston	69,779	66,945
29404	Charleston Base(u)	NA	6,238

ZIP code	Place	1980	1970
29408	Charleston Yard(u)	NA	13,565
29520	Cheraw	5,654	5,627
29706	Chester	6,820	7,045
29631	Clemson	8,118	6,690
29325	Clinton	8,596	8,138
*29201	Columbia	101,229	113,542
29526	Conway	10,240	8,151
29532	Darlington	7,989	6,990
29204	Dentsville(u)	13,579	....
29536	Dillon	7,042	6,391
29405	Dorchester Terrace-Brentwood(u)	7,862	....
29601	Dunean(u)	5,146	1,266
29640	Easley	14,264	11,175
29501	Florence	29,842	25,997
29206	Forest Acres	6,062	6,808
29340	Gaffney	13,453	13,131
29605	Gantt(u)	13,719	11,386
29440	Georgetown	10,144	10,449
29445	Goose Creek	17,811	3,825
*29602	Greenville	58,242	61,436
29203	Greenview(u)	5,515	....
29646	Greenwood	21,613	21,069
29651	Greer	10,525	10,642
29410	Hanahan	13,224	9,118
29550	Hartsville	7,631	8,017
29928	Hilton Head Island(u)	11,344	....
29621	Homeland Park(u)	6,720	....
29412	James Island(u)	24,124	....
29456	Ladson(u)	13,246	....
29560	Lake City	5,636	6,247
29720	Lancaster	9,703	9,186
29902	Laurel Bay(u)	5,238	....
29360	Laurens	10,587	10,298
29571	Marion	7,700	7,435
29662	Mauldin	8,143	3,797
29464	Mount Pleasant	14,464	6,879
29574	Mullins	6,068	6,006
29577	Myrtle Beach	18,758	9,035
29108	Newberry	9,866	9,218
29841	North Augusta	13,593	12,883
29406	North Charleston	62,504	21,211
.....	North Trenholm(u)	10,962	....
29565	Oak Grove(u)	7,092	....
29115	Orangeburg	14,933	13,252
29905	Parris Island(u)	7,752	8,868
29483	Pinehurst-Sheppard Park(u)	6,956	1,711
29730	Rock Hill	35,327	33,846
29407	St. Andrews (Charleston)(u)	9,908	9,202
29210	St. Andrews (Richland)(u)	20,245	....
29609	Sans Souci(u)	8,393	....
29678	Seneca	7,436	6,573
.....	Seven Oaks(u)	16,604	....
29152	Shaw AFB(u)	6,939	5,819
29681	Simpsonville	9,037	3,308
.....	South Sumter(u)	7,096	....
*29301	Spartanburg	43,826	44,546
29483	Summerville	6,492	3,839
29150	Sumter	24,921	24,555
29687	Taylors(u)	15,801	6,831
29379	Union	10,523	10,775
29205	Valencia Heights(u)	5,328	....
29607	Wade-Hampton(u)	20,180	17,152
29488	Walterboro	6,036	6,257
29405	Wando Woods(u)	5,266	....
29611	Welcome(u)	6,922	....
29169	West Columbia	10,409	7,838
29206	Woodfield(u)	9,588	....
29388	Woodruff	5,171	4,690
29745	York	6,412	5,081

South Dakota (605)

ZIP code	Place	1980	1970
57401	Aberdeen	25,851	26,476
57006	Brookings	14,951	13,717
57350	Huron	13,000	14,299
57042	Madison	6,210	6,315
57301	Mitchell	13,916	13,425
57501	Pierre	11,973	9,699
57701	Rapid City	46,492	43,836
*57101	Sioux Falls	81,343	72,488
57785	Sturgis	5,184	4,536
57069	Vermillion	9,582	9,128
57201	Watertown	15,649	13,388
57078	Yankton	12,011	11,919

Tennessee

ZIP code	Place	Area code	1980	1970
37701	Alcoa	(615)	6,870	7,739
37303	Athens	(615)	12,080	11,790
38134	Bartlett	(901)	17,170	1,150
37660	Bloomingdale(u)	(615)	12,088	3,120
38008	Bolivar	(901)	6,597	6,674
37027	Brentwood	(615)	9,431	4,099
37620	Bristol	(615)	23,986	20,064
38012	Brownsville	(901)	9,307	7,011
*37401	Chattanooga	(615)	169,728	119,923
37040	Clarksville	(615)	54,777	31,719
37311	Cleveland	(615)	26,415	21,446
37716	Clinton	(615)	5,245	4,794
38017	Collierville	(901)	7,839	3,651
37663	Colonial Heights(u)	(615)	6,744	3,027
38401	Columbia	(615)	26,571	21,471
37922	Concord (Knox)(u)	(615)	8,569	....
38501	Cookeville	(615)	20,350	14,403
38019	Covington	(901)	6,065	5,801
38555	Crossville	(615)	6,394	5,381
37321	Dayton	(615)	5,233	4,361
37055	Dickson	(615)	7,040	5,665
38024	Dyersburg	(901)	15,856	14,523
37801	Eagleton Village(u)	(615)	5,331	5,345
37412	East Ridge	(615)	21,236	21,799
37643	Elizabethton	(615)	12,431	12,269
37334	Fayetteville	(615)	7,559	7,691
37064	Franklin	(615)	12,407	9,497
37066	Gallatin	(615)	17,191	13,253
38138	Germantown	(901)	21,482	3,474
37072	Goodlettsville	(615)	8,327	6,168
37075	Greater Hendersonville(u)	(615)	25,029	11,996
37743	Greeneville	(615)	14,097	13,722
37918	Halls(u)	(615)	10,363	....
37748	Harriman	(615)	8,303	8,734
37341	Harrison(u)	(615)	6,206	....
37075	Hendersonville	(615)	26,561	412
38343	Humboldt	(901)	10,209	10,066
38301	Jackson	(901)	49,258	39,996
37760	Jefferson City	(615)	5,612	5,124
37601	Johnson City	(615)	39,753	33,770
*37662	Kingsport	(615)	32,027	31,938
*37901	Knoxville	(615)	175,045	174,587
37766	La Follette	(615)	8,176	6,902
37086	LaVergne	(615)	5,495	5,220
38464	Lawrenceburg	(615)	10,175	8,889
37087	Lebanon	(615)	11,872	12,492
37771	Lenoir City	(615)	5,180	5,324
37091	Lewisburg	(615)	8,760	7,207
38351	Lexington	(901)	5,934	5,024
37665	Lynn Garden(u)	(615)	7,213	....
38201	McKenzie	(901)	5,405	4,873
37110	McMinnville	(615)	10,683	10,662
37355	Manchester	(615)	7,250	6,208
38237	Martin	(901)	8,898	7,781
37801	Maryville	(615)	17,480	13,808
*38101	Memphis	(901)	646,174	623,988
37343	Middle Valley(u)	(615)	11,420	....
38358	Milan	(901)	8,083	7,313
38053	Millington	(901)	20,236	21,177
37814	Morristown	(615)	19,570	20,318
37130	Murfreesboro	(615)	32,845	26,360
*37202	Nashville-Davidson	(615)	455,651	**426,029
37821	Newport	(615)	7,580	7,328
37830	Oak Ridge	(615)	27,662	28,319
38242	Paris	(901)	10,728	9,892
37849	Powell(u)	(615)	7,220	....
38478	Pulaski	(615)	7,184	6,989
37415	Red Bank White Oak	(615)	13,129	12,715
38063	Ripley	(901)	6,366	4,794
37854	Rockwood	(615)	5,687	5,259
38372	Savannah	(901)	6,992	5,576
37160	Shelbyville	(615)	13,530	12,262
37377	Signal Mountain	(615)	5,818	4,839
37167	Smyrna	(615)	8,839	5,698
37379	Soddy-Daisy	(615)	8,388	7,569
37172	Springfield	(615)	10,814	9,720
37363	Summit (Hamilton)(u)	(615)	8,345	....
37388	Tullahoma	(615)	15,800	15,311
38261	Union City	(901)	10,436	11,925
37398	Winchester	(615)	5,821	5,256

***Comprises the Metropolitan Government of Nashville and Davidson County.*

Texas

ZIP code	Place	Area code	1980	1970
*79604	Abilene	(915)	98,315	89,653
75001	Addison	(214)	5,553	593
78516	Alamo	(512)	5,831	4,291
78209	Alamo Heights	(512)	6,252	6,933
77039	Aldine(u)	(713)	12,623	....
78332	Alice	(512)	20,961	20,121
75002	Allen	(214)	8,314	1,940
79830	Alpine	(915)	5,465	5,971
77511	Alvin	(713)	16,515	10,671
*79105	Amarillo	(806)	149,230	127,010
79714	Andrews	(915)	11,061	8,625
77515	Angleton	(409)	13,929	9,906
78336	Aransas Pass	(512)	7,173	5,813
*76010	Arlington	(817)	160,113	90,229
75751	Athens	(214)	10,197	9,582
75551	Atlanta	(214)	6,272	5,007
*78710	Austin	(512)	345,890	253,539
76020	Azle	(817)	5,822	4,493
75149	Balch Springs	(214)	13,746	10,464
77414	Bay City	(409)	17,837	13,445
77520	Baytown	(713)	56,923	43,980
*77704	Beaumont	(409)	118,102	117,548
76021	Bedford	(817)	20,821	10,049
78102	Beeville	(512)	14,574	13,506
77401	Bellaire	(713)	14,950	19,009

ZIP code	Place		1980	1970
76704	Bellmead	(817)	7,569	7,698
76513	Belton	(817)	10,660	8,696
76126	Benbrook	(817)	13,579	8,169
79720	Big Spring	(915)	24,804	28,735
75418	Bonham	(214)	7,338	7,698
79007	Borger	(806)	15,837	14,195
76230	Bowie	(817)	5,610	5,185
76825	Brady	(915)	5,969	5,557
76024	Breckenridge	(817)	6,921	5,944
77000	Brenham	(409)	10,966	8,922
77611	Bridge City	(713)	7,667	8,164
79316	Brownfield	(806)	10,387	9,647
78520	Brownsville	(512)	84,997	52,522
76801	Brownwood	(915)	19,203	17,368
77801	Bryan	(409)	44,337	33,719
76354	Burkburnett	(817)	10,668	9,230
76028	Burleson	(817)	11,734	7,713
76520	Cameron	(817)	5,721	5,546
79015	Canyon	(806)	10,724	8,333
78834	Carrizo Springs	(512)	6,886	5,374
75006	Carrollton	(214)	40,591	13,855
75633	Carthage	(214)	6,447	5,392
75104	Cedar Hill	(214)	6,849	2,610
75935	Center	(409)	5,827	4,989
....	Champions(u)	(713)	14,692	....
77530	Channelview(u)	(713)	17,471	....
79201	Childress	(817)	5,817	5,408
76031	Cleburne	(817)	19,218	16,015
77327	Cleveland	(713)	5,977	5,627
77015	Clover Leaf(u)	(713)	17,317	....
77531	Clute	(409)	9,577	6,023
76834	Coleman	(915)	5,960	5,608
77840	College Station	(409)	37,272	17,676
76034	Colleyville	(817)	6,700	3,342
79512	Colorado City	(915)	5,405	5,227
75428	Commerce	(214)	8,136	9,534
77301	Conroe	(409)	18,034	11,969
78109	Converse	(512)	5,150	1,383
76522	Copperas Cove	(817)	19,469	10,818
*78408	Corpus Christi	(512)	232,134	204,525
75110	Corsicana	(214)	21,712	19,972
75835	Crockett	(713)	7,405	6,616
76036	Crowley	(817)	5,852	2,662
78839	Crystal City	(512)	8,334	8,104
77954	Cuero	(512)	7,124	6,956
79022	Dalhart	(806)	6,854	5,705
*75260	Dallas	(214)	904,599	844,401
77536	Deer Park	(713)	22,648	12,773
78840	Del Rio	(512)	30,034	21,330
75020	Denison	(214)	23,884	24,923
76201	Denton	(817)	48,063	39,874
75115	De Soto	(214)	15,538	6,617
75941	Diboll	(713)	6,327	3,557
77539	Dickinson	(713)	7,505	10,776
79027	Dimmitt	(806)	5,019	4,327
78537	Donna	(512)	9,952	7,365
79029	Dumas	(806)	12,194	9,771
75116	Duncanville	(214)	27,781	14,105
78852	Eagle Pass	(512)	21,407	15,364
78539	Edinburg	(512)	24,075	17,163
77957	Edna	(512)	5,650	5,332
77437	El Campo	(409)	10,462	9,332
*79910	El Paso	(915)	425,259	322,261
78543	Elsa	(512)	5,061	4,400
75119	Ennis	(214)	12,110	11,046
76039	Euless	(817)	24,002	19,316
76140	Everman	(817)	5,387	4,570
78355	Falfurrias	(512)	6,103	6,355
75234	Farmers Branch	(214)	24,863	27,492
76119	Forest Hill	(817)	11,684	8,236
79906	Fort Bliss(u)	(915)	12,687	13,288
76544	Fort Hood(u)	(817)	31,250	32,597
79735	Fort Stockton	(915)	8,688	8,283
*76101	Fort Worth	(817)	385,164	393,455
78624	Fredericksburg	(512)	6,412	5,326
77541	Freeport	(409)	13,444	11,997
77546	Friendswood	(713)	10,719	5,675
76240	Gainesville	(817)	14,081	13,830
77547	Galena Park	(713)	9,879	10,479
77550	Galveston	(409)	61,902	61,809
*75040	Garland	(214)	138,857	81,437
76528	Gatesville	(817)	6,078	4,683
78626	Georgetown	(512)	9,468	6,395
75644	Gilmer	(214)	5,167	4,196
75647	Gladewater	(214)	6,548	5,574
78629	Gonzales	(512)	7,152	5,854
76046	Graham	(817)	9,055	7,477
75050	Grand Prairie	(214)	71,462	50,904
76051	Grapevine	(817)	11,801	7,049
75401	Greenville	(214)	22,161	22,043
77619	Groves	(713)	17,090	18,067
76117	Haltom City	(817)	29,014	28,127
76541	Harker Heights	(817)	7,345	4,216
78550	Harlingen	(512)	43,543	33,503
77859	Hearne	(713)	5,418	4,982
75652	Henderson	(214)	11,473	10,187
79045	Hereford	(806)	15,853	13,414
76643	Hewitt	(817)	5,247	569
75205	Highland Park	(214)	8,909	10,133
77562	Highlands	(713)	6,467	3,462
76645	Hillsboro	(817)	7,397	7,224
77563	Hitchcock	(713)	6,103	5,565
78861	Hondo	(512)	6,057	5,487
*77013	Houston	(713)	1,595,138	1,233,535
77338	Humble	(713)	6,729	3,272
77340	Huntsville	(409)	23,936	17,610
76053	Hurst	(817)	31,420	27,215
78362	Ingleside	(512)	5,436	3,763
76367	Iowa Park	(817)	6,184	5,796
*75061	Irving	(214)	[illegible]	[illegible]
77029	Jacinto City	(713)	8,953	9,563
75766	Jacksonville	(214)	12,264	9,734
75951	Jasper	(409)	6,959	6,251
77450	Katy	(713)	5,660	2,923
79745	Kermit	(915)	8,015	7,884
78028	Kerrville	(512)	15,276	12,672
75662	Kilgore	(214)	11,331	9,495
76541	Killeen	(817)	46,296	35,507
78363	Kingsville	(512)	28,808	28,915
.....	Kingwood	(713)	16,261	....
78219	Kirby	(512)	6,435	3,238
78236	Lackland AFB(u)	(512)	14,459	19,141
77566	Lake Jackson	(409)	19,102	13,376
77568	La Marque	(409)	15,372	16,131
79631	Lamesa	(806)	11,790	11,559
76550	Lampasas	(512)	6,165	5,922
75146	Lancaster	(214)	14,807	10,522
77571	La Porte	(713)	14,062	7,149
78040	Laredo	(512)	91,449	69,024
77573	League City	(713)	16,578	10,818
78238	Leon Valley	(512)	9,088	2,487
79336	Levelland	(806)	13,809	11,445
75067	Lewisville	(214)	24,273	9,264
77575	Liberty	(713)	7,945	5,591
79339	Littlefield	(806)	7,409	6,738
78233	Live Oak	(512)	8,183	2,779
78644	Lockhart	(512)	7,953	6,489
75601	Longview	(214)	62,762	45,547
*79408	Lubbock	(806)	173,873	149,101
75901	Lufkin	(409)	28,562	23,049
78648	Luling	(512)	5,039	4,719
78501	McAllen	(512)	67,042	37,636
75069	McKinney	(214)	16,249	15,193
76063	Mansfield	(817)	8,092	3,658
76661	Marlin	(817)	7,099	6,351
75670	Marshall	(214)	24,921	22,937
78368	Mathis	(512)	5,667	5,351
78570	Mercedes	(512)	11,851	9,355
75149	Mesquite	(214)	67,053	55,131
76667	Mexia	(817)	7,094	5,943
79701	Midland	(915)	70,525	59,463
76067	Mineral Wells	(817)	14,468	18,411
78572	Mission	(512)	22,653	13,043
77459	Missouri City	(713)	24,423	4,136
79756	Monahans	(915)	8,397	8,333
75455	Mount Pleasant	(214)	11,003	9,459
75961	Nacogdoches	(409)	27,149	22,544
77868	Navasota	(409)	5,971	5,111
77627	Nederland	(409)	16,855	16,810
78130	New Braunfels	(512)	22,402	17,859
76118	North Richland Hills	(817)	30,592	16,514
*79760	Odessa	(915)	90,027	78,380
77630	Orange	(409)	23,628	24,457
75801	Palestine	(214)	15,948	14,525
79065	Pampa	(806)	21,396	21,726
75460	Paris	(214)	25,498	23,441
*77501	Pasadena	(713)	112,560	89,957
77581	Pearland	(713)	13,248	6,444
78061	Pearsall	(512)	7,383	5,545
79772	Pecos	(915)	12,855	12,682
79070	Perryton	(806)	7,991	7,810
78577	Pharr	(512)	21,381	15,829
79072	Plainview	(806)	22,187	19,096
75074	Plano	(214)	72,331	17,872
78064	Pleasanton	(512)	6,346	5,407
77640	Port Arthur	(409)	61,195	57,371
78374	Portland	(512)	12,023	7,302
77979	Port Lavaca	(512)	10,911	10,491
77651	Port Neches	(713)	13,944	10,894
78580	Raymondville	(512)	9,493	7,987
75080	Richardson	(214)	72,496	48,405
76118	Richland Hills	(817)	7,977	8,865
77469	Richmond	(713)	9,692	5,777
78582	Rio Grande City(u)	(512)	8,930	5,676
77019	River Oaks	(817)	6,890	8,193
76701	Robinson	(817)	6,074	3,807
78380	Robstown	(512)	12,100	11,217
76567	Rockdale	(512)	5,611	4,655
75087	Rockwall	(214)	5,939	3,121
77471	Rosenberg	(713)	17,840	12,098
78664	Round Rock	(512)	12,740	2,811
75088	Rowlett	(214)	7,522	2,243
76179	Saginaw	(817)	5,736	2,382
76901	San Angelo	(915)	73,240	63,884
*78284	San Antonio	(512)	785,940	654,153
78586	San Benito	(512)	17,988	15,176
78384	San Diego	(512)	5,225	4,490
78589	San Juan	(512)	7,608	5,070
78666	San Marcos	(512)	23,420	18,860
77550	Santa Fe	(713)	5,413	...

ZIP code	Place		1980	1970
78154	Schertz	(512)	7,262	4,061
75159	Seagoville	(214)	7,304	4,390
78155	Seguin	(512)	17,854	15,934
79360	Seminole	(915)	6,080	5,007
75090	Sherman	(214)	30,413	29,061
77656	Silsbee	(713)	7,684	7,271
78387	Sinton	(512)	6,044	5,563
79364	Slaton	(806)	6,804	6,583
79549	Snyder	(915)	12,705	11,171
77587	South Houston	(713)	13,293	11,527
76401	Stephenville	(817)	11,881	9,277
77478	Sugar Land	(713)	8,826	3,318
75482	Sulphur Springs	(214)	12,804	10,642
79556	Sweetwater	(915)	12,242	12,020
76574	Taylor	(512)	10,619	9,616
76501	Temple	(817)	42,354	33,431
75160	Terrell	(214)	13,269	14,182
75501	Texarkana	(214)	31,271	30,497
77590	Texas City	(409)	41,201	38,908
75056	The Colony	(214)	11,586	...
77380	The Woodlands	(713)	8,443	....
79088	Tulia	(806)	5,033	5,294
75701	Tyler	(214)	70,508	57,770
78148	Universal City	(512)	10,720	7,613
76308	University Park	(214)	22,254	23,498
78801	Uvalde	(512)	14,178	10,764
76384	Vernon	(817)	12,695	11,454
77901	Victoria	(512)	50,695	41,349
77662	Vidor	(713)	11,834	9,738
*76701	Waco	(817)	101,261	95,326
76148	Watauga	(817)	10,284	3,778
75165	Waxahachie	(214)	14,624	13,452
76086	Weatherford	(817)	12,049	11,750
78596	Weslaco	(512)	19,331	15,313
77005	West University Place	(713)	12,010	13,317
77488	Wharton	(713)	9,033	7,881
76108	White Settlement	(817)	13,508	13,449
*76307	Wichita Falls	(817)	94,201	96,265
78239	Windcrest	(512)	5,332	3,371
76710	Woodway	(817)	7,091	4,819
77995	Yoakum	(512)	6,148	5,755

Utah (801)

ZIP code	Place	1980	1970
84003	American Fork	12,417	7,713
84118	Bennion(u)	9,632	....
84010	Bountiful	32,877	27,751
84302	Brigham City	15,596	14,007
84720	Cedar City	10,972	8,946
84014	Centerville	8,069	3,268
84015	Clearfield	17,982	13,316
84015	Clinton	5,777	1,768
84121	Cottonwood(u)	11,554	8,431
84121	Cottonwood Heights(u)	22,665	....
84020	Draper	5,530	...
84109	East Millcreek(u)	24,150	26,579
84106	Granite Park(u)	5,554	9,573
84117	Holladay(u)	22,189	23,014
84037	Kaysville	9,811	6,192
84118	Kearns(u)	21,353	17,247
84041	Layton	22,862	13,603
84043	Lehi	6,848	4,659
84321	Logan	26,844	22,333
84044	Magna(u)	13,138	5,509
84047	Midvale	10,144	7,840
84532	Moab	5,333	4,793
84117	Mount Olympus(u)	6,068	5,909
84107	Murray	25,750	21,206
84404	North Ogden	9,309	5,257
84054	North Salt Lake	5,548	2,143
*84401	Ogden	64,407	69,478
84057	Orem	52,399	25,729
84651	Payson	8,246	4,501
84062	Pleasant Grove	10,669	5,327
84501	Price	9,086	6,218
84601	Provo	74,111	53,131
84701	Richfield	5,482	4,471
84065	Riverton	7,032	2,820
84067	Roy	19,694	14,356
84770	St. George	11,350	7,097
*84101	Salt Lake City	163,034	175,885
84070	Sandy City	52,210	6,438
84121	South Cottonwood(u)	11,117	....
84065	South Jordan	7,492	2,942
84403	South Ogden	11,366	9,991
84115	South Salt Lake	10,413	7,810
84660	Spanish Fork	9,825	7,284
84663	Springville	12,101	8,790
84015	Sunset	5,733	6,268
84107	Taylorsville(u)	17,448	....
84074	Tooele	14,335	12,539
84047	Union-East Midvale(u)	9,663	....
84010	Val Verda(u)	6,422	....
84078	Vernal	6,600	3,908
84403	Washington Terrace	8,212	7,241
84084	West Jordan	27,325	4,221
84119	West Valley(u)	72,299	....
84070	White City(u)	7,180	6,402

Vermont (802)

See Note on Page 544

ZIP code	Place	1980	1970
05641	Barre	9,824	10,209
.....	*Barre*	7,090	6,509
05201	*Bennington*	15,815	14,586
.....	Bennington(u)	9,349	7,950
05301	Brattleboro Center(u)	8,596	9,055
.....	*Brattleboro*	11,886	12,239
05401	Burlington	37,712	38,633
05446	*Colchester*	12,629	8,776
05451	*Essex*	14,392	10,951
05452	Essex Junction	7,033	6,511
05753	*Middlebury*	7,574	6,532
05602	Montpelier	8,241	8,609
05701	Rutland	18,436	19,293
05478	St. Albans	7,308	8,082
05819	*St. Johnsbury*	7,938	8,409
05401	*South Burlington*	10,679	10,032
05156	Springfield Center(u)	5,603	5,632
.....	*Springfield*	10,190	10,063
05404	Winooski	6,318	7,309

Virginia

ZIP code	Place		1980	1970
*22313	Alexandria	(703)	103,217	110,927
22003	Annandale(u)	(703)	49,524	27,405
*22210	Arlington(u)	(703)	152,599	174,284
22041	Bailey's Crossroads(u)	(703)	12,564	7,295
24523	Bedford	(703)	5,991	6,011
22307	Belle Haven(u)	(703)	6,520	....
23234	Bellwood(u)	(804)	6,439	....
23234	Bensley(u)	(804)	5,299	....
24060	Blacksburg	(703)	30,638	9,384
24605	Bluefield	(703)	5,946	5,286
23235	Bon Air(u)	(804)	16,224	10,771
24201	Bristol	(703)	19,042	14,857
24416	Buena Vista	(703)	6,717	6,425
22015	Burke(u)	(703)	33,835	....
24018	Cave Spring(u)	(703)	21,682	....
22020	Centreville(u)	(703)	7,473	....
23227	Chamberlayne(u)	(804)	5,136	....
22021	Chantilly(u)	(703)	12,259	....
*22906	Charlottesville	(804)	45,010	38,880
*23320	Chesapeake	(804)	114,226	89,580
23831	Chester(u)	(804)	11,728	5,556
24073	Christiansburg	(703)	10,345	7,857
24422	Clifton Forge	(703)	5,046	5,501
24078	Collinsville(u)	(703)	7,517	6,015
23834	Colonial Heights	(804)	16,509	15,097
24426	Covington	(703)	9,063	10,060
22701	Culpeper	(703)	6,621	6,056
22191	Dale City(u)	(703)	33,127	13,857
24541	Danville	(804)	45,642	46,391
23228	Dumbarton(u)	(804)	8,149	....
22027	Dunn Loring(u)	(703)	6,077	....
23222	East Highland Park(u)	(804)	11,797	
22030	Fairfax	(703)	19,390	22,727
*22046	Falls Church	(703)	9,515	10,772
23901	Farmville	(804)	6,067	4,331
22060	Fort Belvoir(u)	(703)	7,726	14,591
22308	Fort Hunt(u)	(703)	14,294	10,415
23801	Fort Lee(u)	(804)	9,784	12,435
22310	Franconia(u)	(703)	8,476	....
23851	Franklin	(804)	7,308	6,880
22401	Fredericksburg	(703)	15,322	14,450
22630	Front Royal	(703)	11,126	8,211
24333	Galax	(703)	6,524	6,278
23060	Glen Allen(u)	(804)	6,202	....
23062	Gloucester Point(u)	(804)	5,841	....
22306	Groveton(u)	(703)	18,860	11,761
*23660	Hampton	(804)	122,617	120,779
22801	Harrisonburg	(703)	19,671	14,605
*22070	Herndon	(703)	11,449	4,301
23075	Highland Springs(u)	(804)	12,146	7,345
24019	Hollins(u)	(703)	12,187	....
23860	Hopewell	(804)	23,397	23,471
22303	Huntington(u)	(703)	5,813	5,559
22306	Hybla Valley(u)	(703)	15,533	
22043	Idylwood(u)	(703)	11,982	....
22042	Jefferson(u)	(804)	24,342	25,432
22041	Lake Barcroft(u)	(703)	8,725	11,605
22191	Lake Ridge(u)	(703)	11,072	....
23228	Lakeside(u)	(804)	12,289	11,137
23060	Laurel(u)	(804)	10,569	....
22075	Leesburg	(703)	8,357	4,821
24450	Lexington	(703)	7,292	7,597
22312	Lincolnia(u)	(703)	10,350	10,355
22079	Lorton(u)	(703)	5,813	....
*24505	Lynchburg	(804)	66,743	54,083
24572	Madison Heights(u)	(804)	14,146	....
22110	Manassas	(703)	15,438	9,164
22110	Manassas Park	(703)	6,524	6,844
22030	Mantua(u)	(703)	6,523	6,911
24354	Marion	(703)	7,287	8,158
24112	Martinsville	(703)	18,149	19,653
22101	McLean(u)	(703)	35,664	17,698
23111	Mechanicsville(u)	(804)	9,269	5,189
22116	Merrifield(u)	(703)	7,525	....

ZIP code	Place		1980	1970
23231	Montrose(u)	(804)	5,349	....
22121	Mount Vernon(u)	(703)	24,058	....
22122	Newington(u)	(703)	8,313	....
*23607	Newport News	(804)	144,903	138,177
*23501	Norfolk	(804)	266,979	307,951
22151	North Springfield(u)	(703)	9,538	8,631
22124	Oakton(u)	(703)	19,150	....
23803	Petersburg	(804)	41,055	36,103
22043	Pimmit Hills(u)	(703)	6,658	....
23662	Poquoson	(804)	8,726	5,441
*23705	Portsmouth	(804)	104,577	110,963
24301	Pulaski	(703)	10,106	10,279
22134	Quantico Station(u)	(703)	7,121	6,213
24141	Radford	(703)	13,225	11,596
22090	Reston(u)	(703)	36,407	5,723
24641	Richlands	(703)	5,796	4,843
*23232	Richmond	(804)	219,214	249,332
*24001	Roanoke	(703)	100,427	92,115
22310	Rose Hill(u)	(703)	11,926	14,492
24153	Salem	(703)	23,958	21,982
22044	Seven Corners(u)	(703)	6,058	5,590
24592	South Boston	(804)	7,093	6,889
*22150	Springfield	(703)	21,435	11,613
24401	Staunton	(703)	21,857	24,504
22170	Sterling Park(u)	(703)	16,080	8,321
23434	Suffolk	(804)	47,621	9,858
22170	Sugarland Run(u)	(703)	6,258	....
24502	Timberlake(u)	(804)	9,097	....
23229	Tuckahoe(u)	(804)	39,868	....
22101	Tysons Corner(u)	(703)	10,065	....
22180	Vienna	(703)	15,469	17,146
24179	Vinton	(703)	8,027	6,347
*23458	Virginia Beach	(804)	262,199	172,106
22980	Waynesboro	(703)	15,329	16,707
22110	West Gate(u)	(703)	7,119	....
22152	West Springfield(u)	(703)	25,012	14,143
23185	Williamsburg	(804)	9,870	9,069
22601	Winchester	(703)	20,217	14,643
24592	Wolf Trap(u)	(804)	9,875	....
22191	Woodbridge(u)	(703)	24,004	25,412
24382	Wytheville	(703)	7,135	6,069

Washington

ZIP code	Place		1980	1970
98520	Aberdeen	(206)	18,739	18,489
98036	Alderwood Manor(u)	(206)	16,524	....
98221	Anacortes	(206)	9,013	7,701
98002	Auburn	(206)	20,417	21,653
*98009	Bellevue	(206)	73,903	61,196
98225	Bellingham	(206)	45,794	39,375
98390	Bonney Lake	(206)	5,328	2,700
98011	Bothell	(206)	7,943	5,420
.....	Boulevard Park(u)	(206)	8,382	....
98310	Bremerton	(206)	36,208	35,307
98178	Bryn Mawr-Skyway(u)	(206)	11,754	....
98166	Burien(u)	(206)	23,189	....
98607	Camas	(206)	5,681	5,790
98055	Cascade-Fairwood(u)	(206)	16,939	....
98531	Centralia	(206)	10,009	10,054
98532	Chehalis	(206)	6,100	5,727
99004	Cheney	(509)	7,630	6,358
99403	Clarkston	(509)	6,903	6,312
99324	College Place	(509)	5,771	4,510
98188	Des Moines	(206)	7,378	3,951
99213	Dishman(u)	(509)	10,169	9,079
.....	Dumas Bay-Twin Lakes(u)	(206)	14,535	....
98004	Eastgate(u)	(206)	8,341	....
.....	East Renton Highlands(u)	(206)	12,033	....
98801	East Wenatchee Bench(u)	(509)	11,410	2,446
98020	Edmonds	(206)	27,526	23,684
98926	Ellensburg	(509)	11,752	13,568
98022	Enumclaw	(206)	5,427	4,703
98823	Ephrata	(509)	5,359	5,255
99210	Esperance(u)	(509)	11,120	....
*98201	Everett	(206)	54,413	53,622
99011	Fairchild AFB(u)	(509)	5,353	6,754
98201	Fairmont-Intercity(u)	(206)	6,997	....
98055	Fairwood(u)	(206)	5,337	....
98466	Fircrest	(206)	5,477	5,651
98433	Fort Lewis(u)	(206)	23,761	38,054
98930	Grandview	(509)	5,615	3,605
98660	Hazel Dell(u)	(206)	15,386	....
98550	Hoquiam	(206)	9,719	10,466
98011	Inglewood(u)	(206)	12,467	....
98027	Issaquah	(206)	5,536	4,313
98033	Juanita(u)	(206)	17,232	....
98626	Kelso	(206)	11,129	10,296
98028	Kenmore(u)	(206)	7,281	....
99336	Kennewick	(509)	34,397	15,212
98031	Kent	(206)	22,961	17,711
98033	Kingsgate(u)	(206)	12,652	....
98033	Kirkland	(206)	18,785	14,970
98503	Lacey	(206)	13,940	9,696
98155	Lake Forest North(u)	(206)	7,995	....
.....	Lakeland North(u)	(206)	11,451	....
.....	Lakeland South(u)	(206)	5,225	....
.....	Lake Stickney(u)	(206)	6,135	....
98499	Lakes District(u)	(206)	54,533	48,195
98632	Longview	(206)	31,052	28,373
98036	Lynnwood	(206)	21,937	17,381
.....	Martha Lake(u)	(206)	7,022	....
98270	Marysville	(206)	5,080	4,343
98438	McChord AFB(u)	(206)	5,746	6,515
98040	Mercer Island	(206)	21,522	19,047
98837	Moses Lake	(509)	10,629	10,310
98043	Mountlake Terrace	(206)	16,534	16,600
98273	Mount Vernon	(206)	13,009	8,804
98006	Newport Hills(u)	(206)	12,245	....
98155	North City-Ridgecrest(u)	(206)	13,551	....
.....	North Hill(u)	(206)	10,170	....
98270	North Marysville(u)	(206)	15,159	....
98277	Oak Harbor	(206)	12,271	9,167
*98501	Olympia	(206)	27,447	23,296
99214	Opportunity(u)	(509)	21,241	16,604
98662	Orchards(u)	(206)	8,828	....
98444	Parkland(u)	(206)	23,355	21,012
99301	Pasco	(509)	18,428	13,920
98362	Port Angeles	(206)	17,311	16,367
98368	Port Townsend	(206)	6,067	5,241
.....	Poverty Bay(u)	(206)	8,353	....
99163	Pullman	(509)	23,579	20,509
98371	Puyallup	(206)	18,251	14,742
98052	Redmond	(206)	23,318	11,020
98055	Renton	(206)	31,031	25,878
99352	Richland	(509)	33,578	26,290
98160	Richmond Beach-Innis Arden(u)	(206)	6,700	....
98113	Richmond Highlands(u)	(206)	24,463	....
98188	Riverton(u)	(206)	14,182	....
98033	Rose Hill(u)	(206)	7,616	....
*98109	Seattle	(206)	493,846	530,831
98284	Sedro Woolley	(206)	6,110	4,598
98584	Shelton	(206)	7,629	6,515
98155	Sheridan Beach(u)	(206)	6,873	....
98201	Silver Lake-Fircrest(u)		10,299	....
98290	Snohomish	(206)	5,294	5,174
98387	Spanaway(u)	(206)	8,868	5,768
*99210	Spokane	(509)	171,300	170,516
98944	Sunnyside	(509)	9,225	6,751
*98402	Tacoma	(206)	158,501	154,407
98501	Tanglewilde-Thompson Place(u)		5,910	3,423
98948	Toppenish	(509)	6,517	5,744
99268	Town and Country(u)	(509)	5,578	6,484
98502	Tumwater	(206)	6,705	5,373
98406	University Place(u)	(206)	20,381	13,230
.....	Valley Ridge(u)	(206)	17,961	....
*98660	Vancouver	(206)	42,834	41,859
99037	Veradale(u)	(509)	7,256	....
99362	Walla Walla	(509)	25,618	23,619
98801	Wenatchee	(509)	17,257	16,912
98003	West Federal Way(u)	(206)	16,872	....
99301	West Pasco(u)	(509)	6,210	....
98166	White Center-Shorewood(u)	(206)	19,362	....
*98901	Yakima	(509)	49,826	45,588
98198	Zenith Saltwater(u)	(206)	[illegible]	....

West Virginia (304)

ZIP code	Place	1980	1970
25801	Beckley	20,492	19,884
24701	Bluefield	16,060	15,921
26330	Bridgeport	6,604	4,777
26201	Buckhannon	6,820	7,261
*25301	Charleston	63,968	71,505
26301	Clarksburg	22,371	24,864
25064	Dunbar	9,285	9,151
26241	Elkins	8,536	8,287
26554	Fairmont	23,863	26,093
26354	Grafton	6,845	6,433
*25701	Huntington	63,684	74,315
26726	Keyser	6,569	6,586
25401	Martinsburg	13,063	14,626
26505	Morgantown	27,605	29,431
26041	Moundsville	12,419	13,560
26155	New Martinsville	7,109	6,528
25143	Nitro	8,074	8,019
25901	Oak Hill	7,120	4,738
26101	Parkersburg	39,946	44,208
25550	Point Pleasant	5,682	6,122
24740	Princeton	7,538	7,253
25177	St. Albans	12,402	14,356
25303	South Charleston	15,968	16,333
26105	Vienna	11,618	11,549
26062	Weirton	25,371	27,131
26452	Weston	6,250	7,323
26003	Wheeling	43,070	48,188
25661	Williamson	5,219	5,831

Wisconsin

ZIP code	Place		1980	1970
54301	Allouez(u)	(414)	14,882	13,753
54409	Antigo	(715)	8,653	9,005
54911	Appleton	(414)	58,913	56,377
54806	Ashland	(715)	9,115	9,615

ZIP code	Place		1980	1970
54304	Ashwaubenon	(414)	14,486	9,323
53913	Baraboo	(608)	8,081	7,931
53916	Beaver Dam	(414)	14,149	14,265
53511	Beloit	(608)	35,207	35,729
53511	Beloit North(u)	(608)	5,457	....
54923	Berlin	(414)	5,478	5,338
53005	Brookfield	(414)	34,035	31,761
53209	Brown Deer	(414)	12,921	12,582
53105	Burlington	(414)	8,385	7,479
53012	Cedarburg	(414)	9,005	7,697
54729	Chippewa Falls	(715)	11,845	12,351
53110	Cudahy	(414)	19,547	22,078
53115	Delavan	(414)	5,684	5,526
54115	De Pere	(414)	14,892	13,309
54701	Eau Claire	(715)	51,509	44,619
53122	Elm Grove	(414)	6,735	7,201
54935	Fond Du Lac	(414)	35,863	35,515
53538	Fort Atkinson	(414)	9,785	9,164
53217	Fox Point	(414)	7,649	7,939
53132	Franklin	(414)	16,871	12,247
53022	Germantown	(414)	10,729	6,974
53209	Glendale	(414)	13,882	13,426
53024	Grafton	(414)	8,381	5,998
*54305	Green Bay	(414)	87,899	87,809
53129	Greendale	(414)	16,928	15,089
53220	Greenfield	(414)	31,353	24,424
53130	Hales Corners	(414)	7,110	7,771
53027	Hartford	(414)	7,159	6,499
53029	Hartland	(414)	5,559	2,763
54303	Howard	(414)	8,240	4,911
54016	Hudson	(715)	5,434	5,049
53545	Janesville	(608)	51,071	46,426
53549	Jefferson	(414)	5,647	5,429
54130	Kaukauna	(414)	11,310	11,308
53140	Kenosha	(414)	77,685	78,805
54136	Kimberly	(414)	5,881	6,131
54601	La Crosse	(608)	48,347	50,286
53147	Lake Geneva	(414)	5,612	4,890
54140	Little Chute	(414)	7,907	5,522
*53701	Madison	(608)	170,616	171,809
54220	Manitowoc	(414)	32,547	33,430
54143	Marinette	(715)	11,965	12,696
54449	Marshfield	(715)	18,290	15,619
54952	Menasha	(414)	14,728	14,836
53051	Menomonee Falls	(414)	27,845	31,697
54751	Menomonie	(715)	12,769	11,112
53092	Mequon	(414)	16,193	12,150
54452	Merrill	(715)	9,578	9,502
53562	Middleton	(608)	11,851	8,246
*53203	Milwaukee	(414)	636,297	717,372
53716	Monona	(608)	8,809	10,420
53566	Monroe	(608)	10,027	8,654
53150	Muskego	(414)	15,277	11,573
54956	Neenah	(414)	23,272	22,902
53151	New Berlin	(414)	30,529	26,910
54961	New London	(414)	6,210	5,801
53154	Oak Creek	(414)	16,932	13,928
53066	Oconomowoc	(414)	9,909	8,741
54650	Onalaska	(608)	9,249	4,909
54901	Oshkosh	(414)	49,678	53,082
53818	Platteville	(608)	9,580	9,599
54467	Plover	(715)	5,310	...
53073	Plymouth	(414)	6,027	5,810
53901	Portage	(608)	7,896	7,821
53074	Port Washington	(414)	8,612	8,752
53821	Prairie du Chien	(608)	5,859	5,540
*53401	Racine	(414)	85,725	95,162
53959	Reedsburg	(608)	5,038	4,585
54501	Rhinelander	(715)	7,873	8,218
54868	Rice Lake	(715)	7,691	7,278
54971	Ripon	(414)	7,111	7,053
54022	River Falls	(715)	9,019	7,238
53207	St. Francis	(414)	10,095	10,489
54166	Shawano	(715)	7,013	6,488
53081	Sheboygan	(414)	48,085	48,484
53085	Sheboygan Falls	(414)	5,253	4,771
53211	Shorewood	(414)	14,327	15,576
53172	South Milwaukee	(414)	21,069	23,297
54656	Sparta	(608)	6,934	6,258
54481	Stevens Point	(715)	22,970	23,479
53589	Stoughton	(608)	7,589	6,096
54235	Sturgeon Bay	(414)	8,847	6,776
53590	Sun Prairie	(608)	12,931	9,935
54880	Superior	(715)	29,571	32,237
54660	Tomah	(608)	7,204	5,647
54241	Two Rivers	(414)	13,354	13,732
53094	Watertown	(414)	18,113	15,683
53186	Waukesha	(414)	50,365	39,695
53963	Waupun	(414)	8,132	7,946
54401	Wausau	(715)	32,426	32,806
54401	Wausau West Rib Mt.(u)	(715)	6,005	....
53213	Wauwatosa	(414)	51,308	58,676
53214	West Allis	(414)	63,982	71,649
53095	West Bend	(414)	21,484	16,555
54476	Weston(u)	(715)	8,775	3,375
53217	Whitefish Bay	(414)	14,930	17,402
53190	Whitewater	(414)	11,520	12,038
54494	Wisconsin Rapids	(715)	17,995	18,587

Wyoming (307)

82601	Casper	51,016	39,361
82001	Cheyenne	47,283	41,254
82414	Cody	6,599	5,161
82633	Douglas	6,030	2,677
82930	Evanston	6,265	4,462
82716	Gillette	12,134	7,194
82335	Green River	12,807	4,196
82520	Lander	9,126	7,125
82070	Laramie	24,410	23,143
82435	Powell	5,310	4,807
82301	Rawlins	11,547	7,855
82501	Riverton	9,562	7,995
82901	Rock Springs	19,458	11,657
82801	Sheridan	15,146	10,856
82240	Torrington	5,441	4,237
82201	Wheatland	5,816	2,498
82401	Worland	6,391	5,055

Census and Areas of Counties and States

Source: U.S. Bureau of the Census
With names of county seats or court houses

Population figures listed below are final counts in the 1980 census, conducted on Apr. 1, 1980, and updated in April 1987, for all counties and states. Figures are subject to change pending the outcome of various lawsuits dealing with the census counts.

Alabama

(67 counties, 50,708 sq. mi. land; pop., 3,894,025)

County	Pop.	County seat or court house	Land area sq. mi.
Autauga	32,259	Prattville	597
Baldwin	78,440	Bay Minette	1,589
Barbour	24,756	Clayton	884
Bibb	15,723	Centreville	625
Blount	36,459	Oneonta	643
Bullock	10,596	Union Springs	625
Butler	21,680	Greenville	779
Calhoun	116,936	Anniston	611
Chambers	39,191	Lafayette	596
Cherokee	18,760	Centre	553
Chilton	30,612	Clanton	695
Choctaw	16,839	Butler	909
Clarke	27,702	Grove Hill	1,230
Clay	13,703	Ashland	605
Cleburne	12,595	Heflin	561
Coffee	38,533	Elba	680
Colbert	54,519	Tuscumbia	589
Conecuh	15,884	Evergreen	854
Coosa	11,377	Rockford	657
Covington	36,850	Andalusia	1,038
Crenshaw	14,110	Luverne	611
Cullman	61,642	Cullman	738
Dale	47,821	Ozark	561
Dallas	53,981	Selma	975
De Kalb	53,658	Fort Payne	778
Elmore	43,390	Wetumpka	622
Escambia	38,392	Brewton	951
Etowah	103,057	Gadsden	542
Fayette	18,809	Fayette	630
Franklin	28,350	Russellville	643
Geneva	24,253	Geneva	578
Greene	11,021	Eutaw	631
Hale	15,604	Greensboro	661
Henry	15,302	Abbeville	557
Houston	74,632	Dothan	577
Jackson	51,407	Scottsboro	1,070
Jefferson	671,371	Birmingham	1,119
Lamar	16,453	Vernon	605
Lauderdale	80,504	Florence	661
Lawrence	30,170	Moulton	693
Lee	76,283	Opelika	609
Limestone	46,005	Athens	559
Lowndes	13,253	Hayneville	714
Macon	26,829	Tuskegee	614
Madison	196,966	Huntsville	806
Marengo	25,047	Linden	982
Marion	30,041	Hamilton	743
Marshall	65,622	Guntersville	567
Mobile	364,379	Mobile	1,238
Monroe	22,651	Monroeville	1,019
Montgomery	197,038	Montgomery	793
Morgan	90,231	Decatur	575
Perry	15,012	Marion	718
Pickens	21,481	Carrollton	890
Pike	28,050	Troy	672
Randolph	20,075	Wedowee	584

County	Pop.	County Seat or court house	Land area sq. mi.
Russell	47,356	Phenix City	634
St. Clair	41,205	Ashville & Pell City	646
Shelby	66,298	Columbiana	800
Sumter	16,908	Livingston	907
Talladega	73,826	Talladega	753
Tallapoosa	38,766	Dadeville	701
Tuscaloosa	137,473	Tuscaloosa	1,336
Walker	68,660	Jasper	804
Washington	16,821	Chatom	1,081
Wilcox	14,755	Camden	883
Winston	21,953	Double Springs	613

Alaska

(23 divisions, 569,600 sq. mi. land; pop., 401,851)

Census area	Pop.	Land area sq. mi.
Aleutian Islands	7,768	10,890
Anchorage Borough	173,017	1,732

Census division	Pop.	Land area sq. mi.
Bethel	10,999	36,104
Bristol Bay Borough	1,094	531
Dillingham	4,616	46,042
Fairbanks North Star Borough	53,983	7,404
Haines Borough	1,080	2,374
Juneau Borough	19,528	2,626
Kenai Peninsula Borough	25,282	16,056
Ketchikan Gateway Borough	11,316	1,242
Kobuk	4,831	31,593
Kodiak Island Borough	9,939	4,796
Matanuska-Susitna Borough	17,766	24,502
Nome	6,537	23,871
North Slope Borough	4,199	90,955
Prince of Wales-Outer Ketchikan	3,822	7,660
Sitka Borough	7,803	2,938
Skagway-Yakutat-Angoon	3,478	13,239
Southeast Fairbanks	5,770	24,169
Valdez-Cordova	8,348	39,229
Wade Hampton	4,665	17,816
Wrangell-Petersburg	6,167	5,965
Yukon-Koyukuk	7,873	159,099

Arizona

(15 counties, 113,417 sq. mi. land; pop. 2,716,598)

County	Pop.	County seat or court house	Land area sq. mi.
Apache	52,083	Saint Johns	11,211
Cochise	86,717	Bisbee	6,218
Coconino	74,947	Flagstaff	18,608
Gila	37,080	Globe	4,752
Graham	22,862	Safford	4,630
Greenlee	11,406	Clifton	1,837
La Paz	12,487	Parker	4,430
Maricopa	1,509,227	Phoenix	9,127
Mohave	55,693	Kingman	13,285
Navajo	67,709	Holbrook	9,955
Pima	531,263	Tucson	9,187
Pinal	90,918	Florence	5,343
Santa Cruz	20,459	Nogales	1,238
Yavapai	68,145	Prescott	8,123
Yuma	88,762	Yuma	9,994

Arkansas

(75 counties, 51,945 sq. mi. land; pop. 2,286,357)

County	Pop.	County seat or court house	Land area sq. mi.
Arkansas	24,175	DeWitt & Stuttgart	1,006
Ashley	26,538	Hamburg	934
Baxter	27,409	Mountain Home	546
Benton	78,115	Bentonville	843
Boone	26,067	Harrison	584
Bradley	13,803	Warren	654
Calhoun	6,079	Hampton	628
Carroll	16,203	Berryville and Eureka Sp.	634
Chicot	17,793	Lake Village	649
Clark	23,326	Arkadelphia	867
Clay	20,616	Corning; Piggott	641
Cleburne	16,909	Heber Springs	551
Cleveland	7,868	Rison	599
Columbia	26,644	Magnolia	767
Conway	19,505	Morrilton	558
Craighead	63,218	Jonesboro and Lake City	713
Crawford	36,892	Van Buren	594
Crittenden	49,097	Marion	599
Cross	20,434	Wynne	622
Dallas	10,515	Fordyce	668
Desha	19,760	Arkansas City	746
Drew	17,910	Monticello	831
Faulkner	46,192	Conway	645
Franklin	14,705	Charleston and Ozark	609
Fulton	9,975	Salem	616
Garland	69,916	Hot Spgs. Nat'l Pk.	657
Grant	13,008	Sheridan	633
Greene	30,744	Paragould	579
Hempstead	23,635	Hope	725
Hot Spring	26,819	Malvern	615
Howard	13,459	Nashville	574
Independence	30,147	Batesville	763
Izard	10,768	Melbourne	581
Jackson	21,646	Newport	633
Jefferson	90,718	Pine Bluff	882
Johnson	17,423	Clarksville	676
Lafayette	10,213	Lewisville	518
Lawrence	18,447	Walnut Ridge	589
Lee	15,539	Marianna	602
Lincoln	13,369	Star City	562
Little River	13,952	Ashdown	516
Logan	20,144	Booneville & Paris	717
Lonoke	34,518	Lonoke	783
Madison	11,373	Huntsville	837
Marion	11,334	Yellville	587
Miller	37,766	Texarkana	619
Mississippi	59,517	Blytheville and Osceola	896
Monroe	14,052	Clarendon	609
Montgomery	7,771	Mount Ida	774
Nevada	11,097	Prescott	620
Newton	7,756	Jasper	823
Ouachita	30,541	Camden	737
Perry	7,266	Perryville	550
Phillips	34,772	Helena	685
Pike	10,373	Murfreesboro	598
Poinsett	27,032	Harrisburg	762
Polk	17,007	Mena	860
Pope	38,964	Russellville	820
Prairie	10,140	Des Arc and De Valls Bluff	656
Pulaski	340,597	Little Rock	767
Randolph	16,834	Pocahontas	656
St. Francis	30,858	Forrest City	638
Saline	53,156	Benton	725
Scott	9,685	Waldron	896
Searcy	8,847	Marshall	668
Sebastian	94,930	Fort Smith; Greenwood	535
Sevier	14,060	De Queen	560
Sharp	14,007	Ash Flat	606
Stone	9,022	Mountain View	606
Union	49,988	El Dorado	1,053
Van Buren	13,357	Clinton	709
Washington	99,735	Fayetteville	951
White	50,835	Searcy	1,040
Woodruff	11,222	Augusta	592
Yell	17,026	Danville and Dardanelle	930

California

(58 counties, 156,361 sq. mi. land; pop. 23,667,764)

County	Pop.	County seat or court house	Land area sq. mi.
Alameda	1,105,379	Oakland	736
Alpine	1,097	Markleeville	738
Amador	19,314	Jackson	589
Butte	143,851	Oroville	1,646
Calaveras	20,710	San Andreas	1,021
Colusa	12,791	Colusa	1,152
Contra Costa	656,331	Martinez	730
Del Norte	18,217	Crescent City	1,007
El Dorado	85,812	Placerville	1,715
Fresno	515,010	Fresno	5,978
Glenn	21,350	Willows	1,319
Humboldt	108,525	Eureka	3,579
Imperial	92,110	El Centro	4,173
Inyo	17,895	Independence	10,223
Kern	403,089	Bakersfield	8,130
Kings	73,738	Hanford	1,392
Lake	36,366	Lakeport	1,262
Lassen	21,661	Susanville	4,553
Los Angeles	7,477,238	Los Angeles	4,070
Madera	63,116	Madera	2,145
Marin	222,592	San Rafael	523
Mariposa	11,108	Mariposa	1,456
Mendocino	66,738	Ukiah	3,512
Merced	134,558	Merced	1,944
Modoc	8,610	Alturas	4,064
Mono	8,577	Bridgeport	3,018
Monterey	290,444	Salinas	3,303
Napa	99,199	Napa	744
Nevada	51,645	Nevada City	960
Orange	1,932,921	Santa Ana	798
Placer	117,247	Auburn	1,416
Plumas	17,340	Quincy	2,573
Riverside	663,199	Riverside	7,214
Sacramento	783,381	Sacramento	971
San Benito	25,005	Hollister	1,388
San Bernardino	893,157	San Bernardino	20,064
San Diego	1,861,846	San Diego	4,212
San Francisco	678,974	San Francisco	46
San Joaquin	347,342	Stockton	1,415
San Luis Obispo	155,345	San Luis Obispo	3,308
San Mateo	588,164	Redwood City	447
Santa Barbara	298,660	Santa Barbara	2,748
Santa Clara	1,295,071	San Jose	1,293
Santa Cruz	188,141	Santa Cruz	446
Shasta	115,613	Redding	3,786
Sierra	3,073	Downieville	959
Siskiyou	39,732	Yreka	6,281
Solano	235,203	Fairfield	834
Sonoma	299,827	Santa Rosa	1,604
Stanislaus	265,902	Modesto	1,506
Sutter	52,246	Yuba City	602
Tehama	38,888	Red Bluff	2,953
Trinity	11,858	Weaverville	3,190

County	Pop.	County seat or court house	Land area sq. mi.
Tulare	245,751	Visalia	4,808
Tuolumne	33,920	Sonora	2,234
Ventura	529,899	Ventura	1,862
Yolo	113,374	Woodland	1,014
Yuba	49,733	Marysville	640

Colorado

(63 counties, 103,766 sq. mi. land; pop. 2,889,735)

Adams	245,944	Brighton	1,235
Alamosa	11,799	Alamosa	719
Arapahoe	293,300	Littleton	800
Archuleta	3,664	Pagosa Springs	1,353
Baca	5,419	Springfield	2,554
Bent	5,945	Las Animas	1,517
Boulder	189,625	Boulder	742
Chaffee	13,227	Salida	1,008
Cheyenne	2,153	Cheyenne Wells	1,783
Clear Creek	7,308	Georgetown	396
Conejos	7,794	Conejos	1,284
Costilla	3,071	San Luis	1,227
Crowley	2,988	Ordway	790
Custer	1,528	Westcliffe	740
Delta	21,225	Delta	1,141
Denver	492,686	Denver	111
Dolores	1,658	Dove Creek	1,064
Douglas	25,153	Castle Rock	841
Eagle	13,171	Eagle	1,690
Elbert	6,850	Kiowa	1,851
El Paso	309,424	Colorado Springs	2,129
Fremont	28,676	Canon City	1,538
Garfield	22,514	Glenwood Springs	2,952
Gilpin	2,441	Central City	149
Grand	7,475	Hot Sulphur Springs	1,854
Gunnison	10,689	Gunnison	3,238
Hinsdale	408	Lake City	1,115
Huerfano	6,440	Walsenburg	1,584
Jackson	1,863	Walden	1,614
Jefferson	371,741	Golden	768
Kiowa	1,936	Eads	1,758
Kit Carson	7,599	Burlington	2,160
Lake	8,830	Leadville	379
La Plata	27,195	Durango	1,692
Larimer	149,184	Fort Collins	2,604
Las Animas	14,897	Trinidad	4,771
Lincoln	4,663	Hugo	2,586
Logan	19,800	Sterling	1,818
Mesa	81,530	Grand Junction	3,309
Mineral	804	Creede	877
Moffat	13,133	Craig	4,732
Montezuma	16,510	Cortez	2,038
Montrose	24,352	Montrose	2,240
Morgan	22,513	Fort Morgan	1,276
Otero	22,567	LaJunta	1,247
Ouray	1,925	Ouray	542
Park	5,333	Fairplay	2,192
Phillips	4,542	Holyoke	688
Pitkin	10,338	Aspen	968
Prowers	13,070	Lamar	1,629
Pueblo	125,972	Pueblo	2,377
Rio Blanco	6,255	Meeker	3,222
Rio Grande	10,511	Del Norte	913
Routt	13,404	Steamboat Springs	2,367
Saguache	3,935	Saguache	3,167
San Juan	833	Silverton	388
San Miguel	3,192	Telluride	1,287
Sedgwick	3,266	Julesburg	540
Summit	8,848	Breckenridge	607
Teller	8,034	Cripple Creek	559
Washington	5,304	Akron	2,520
Weld	123,438	Greeley	3,990
Yuma	9,682	Wray	2,365

Connecticut

(8 counties, 4,862 sq. mi. land; pop. 3,107,564)

Fairfield	807,143	Bridgeport	632
Hartford	807,766	Hartford	739
Litchfield	156,769	Litchfield	921
Middlesex	129,017	Middletown	373
New Haven	761,325	New Haven	610
New London	238,409	Norwich	669
Tolland	114,823	Rockville	412
Windham	92,312	Putnam	515

Delaware

(3 counties, 1,982 sq. mi. land; pop. 594,338)

Kent	98,219	Dover	595
New Castle	399,002	Wilmington	396
Sussex	98,004	Georgetown	942

District of Columbia

(61 sq. mi. land; pop. 638,432)

Florida

(67 counties, 54,090 sq. mi. land; pop. 9,746,961)

Alachua	151,369	Gainesville	901
Baker	15,289	Macclenny	585
Bay	97,740	Panama City	758
Bradford	20,023	Starke	293
Brevard	272,959	Titusville	995
Broward	1,018,257	Fort Lauderdale	1,211
Calhoun	9,294	Blountstown	568
Charlotte	59,115	Punta Gorda	690
Citrus	54,703	Inverness	629
Clay	67,052	Green Cove Spgs.	592
Collier	85,791	Naples	1,994
Columbia	35,399	Lake City	796
Dade	1,625,509	Miami	1,955
De Soto	19,039	Arcadia	636
Dixie	7,751	Cross City	701
Duval	570,981	Jacksonville	776
Escambia	233,794	Pensacola	660
Flagler	10,913	Bunnell	491
Franklin	7,661	Apalachicola	545
Gadsden	41,674	Quincy	518
Gilchrist	5,767	Trenton	354
Glades	5,992	Moore Haven	763
Gulf	10,658	Port St. Joe	559
Hamilton	8,761	Jasper	517
Hardee	20,357	Wauchula	637
Hendry	18,599	La Belle	1,163
Hernando	44,469	Brooksville	477
Highlands	47,526	Sebring	1,029
Hillsborough	646,939	Tampa	1,053
Holmes	14,723	Bonifay	488
Indian River	59,896	Vero Beach	497
Jackson	39,154	Marianna	942
Jefferson	10,703	Monticello	609
Lafayette	4,035	Mayo	545
Lake	104,870	Tavares	954
Lee	205,266	Fort Myers	803
Leon	148,655	Tallahassee	676
Levy	19,870	Bronson	1,100
Liberty	4,260	Bristol	837
Madison	14,894	Madison	710
Manatee	148,445	Bradenton	747
Marion	122,488	Ocala	1,610
Martin	64,014	Stuart	555
Monroe	63,098	Key West	1,034
Nassau	32,894	Fernandina Beach	649
Okaloosa	109,920	Crestview	936
Okeechobee	20,264	Okeechobee	770
Orange	470,865	Orlando	910
Osceola	49,287	Kissimmee	1,350
Palm Beach	576,758	West Palm Beach	1,993
Pasco	193,661	Dade City	738
Pinellas	728,409	Clearwater	280
Polk	321,652	Bartow	1,823
Putnam	50,549	Palatka	733
St. Johns	51,303	Saint Augustine	617
St. Lucie	87,182	Fort Pierce	581
Santa Rosa	55,988	Milton	1,024
Sarasota	202,251	Sarasota	573
Seminole	179,752	Sanford	298
Sumter	24,272	Bushnell	561
Suwannee	22,287	Live Oak	690
Taylor	16,532	Perry	1,058
Union	10,166	Lake Butler	246
Volusia	258,762	De Land	1,113
Wakulla	10,887	Crawfordville	601
Walton	21,300	De Funiak Springs	1,066
Washington	14,509	Chipley	590

Georgia

(159 counties, 58,073 sq. mi. land; pop. 5,462,982)

Appling	15,565	Baxley	510
Atkinson	6,141	Pearson	344
Bacon	9,379	Alma	286
Baker	3,808	Newton	347
Baldwin	34,686	Milledgeville	257
Banks	8,702	Homer	234
Barrow	21,293	Winder	163
Bartow	40,760	Cartersville	456
Ben Hill	16,000	Fitzgerald	254
Berrien	13,525	Nashville	456
Bibb	151,085	Macon	253
Bleckley	10,767	Cochran	219
Brantley	8,701	Nahunta	445
Brooks	15,255	Quitman	491
Bryan	10,175	Pembroke	441
Bulloch	35,785	Statesboro	678
Burke	19,349	Waynesboro	833
Butts	13,665	Jackson	187
Calhoun	5,717	Morgan	284
Camden	13,371	Woodbine	649
Candler	7,518	Metter	248
Carroll	56,346	Carrollton	501
Catoosa	36,991	Ringgold	162
Charlton	7,343	Folkston	780
Chatham	202,226	Savannah	443
Chattahoochee	21,732	Cusseta	250
Chattooga	21,856	Summerville	313
Cherokee	51,699	Canton	424
Clarke	74,498	Athens	122
Clay	3,553	Fort Gaines	196
Clayton	150,357	Jonesboro	148
Clinch	6,660	Homerville	821
Cobb	297,694	Marietta	343
Coffee	26,894	Douglas	602
Colquitt	35,376	Moultrie	557

County	Pop.	County seat or court house	Land area sq. mi.
Columbia	40,118	Appling	290
Cook	13,490	Adel	233
Coweta	39,268	Newnan	444
Crawford	7,684	Knoxville	328
Crisp	19,489	Cordele	275
Dade	12,318	Trenton	176
Dawson	4,774	Dawsonville	210
Decatur	25,495	Bainbridge	586
De Kalb	483,024	Decatur	270
Dodge	16,955	Eastman	504
Dooly	10,826	Vienna	397
Dougherty	100,710	Albany	330
Douglas	54,573	Douglasville	203
Early	13,158	Blakely	516
Echols	2,297	Statenville	421
Effingham	18,327	Springfield	482
Elbert	18,758	Elberton	367
Emanuel	20,795	Swainsboro	688
Evans	8,428	Claxton	186
Fannin	14,748	Blue Ridge	384
Fayette	29,043	Fayetteville	199
Floyd	79,800	Rome	519
Forsyth	27,958	Cumming	226
Franklin	15,185	Carnesville	264
Fulton	589,904	Atlanta	534
Gilmer	11,110	Ellijay	427
Glascock	2,382	Gibson	144
Glynn	54,981	Brunswick	412
Gordon	30,070	Calhoun	055
Grady	19,845	Cairo	459
Greene	11,391	Greensboro	389
Gwinnett	166,808	Lawrenceville	435
Habersham	25,020	Clarkesville	278
Hall	75,649	Gainesville	379
Hancock	9,466	Sparta	470
Haralson	18,422	Buchanan	283
Harris	15,464	Hamilton	464
Hart	18,585	Hartwell	230
Heard	6,520	Franklin	292
Henry	36,300	McDonough	321
Houston	77,605	Perry	000
Irwin	8,988	Ocilla	362
Jackson	25,343	Jefferson	342
Jasper	7,550	Monticello	371
Jeff Davis	11,473	Hazlehurst	335
Jefferson	18,403	Louisville	529
Jenkins	8,841	Millen	353
Johnson	8,660	Wrightsville	306
Jones	16,579	Gray	394
Lamar	12,215	Barnesville	186
Lanier	5,654	Lakeland	194
Laurens	36,990	Dublin	816
Lee	11,684	Leesburg	358
Liberty	37,583	Hinesville	517
Lincoln	6,949	Lincolnton	196
Long	4,524	Ludowici	402
Lowndes	67,972	Valdosta	507
Lumpkin	10,762	Dahlonega	287
McDuffie	18,546	Thomson	256
McIntosh	8,046	Darien	425
Macon	14,003	Oglethorpe	404
Madison	17,747	Danielsville	285
Marion	5,297	Buena Vista	366
Meriwether	21,229	Greenville	506
Miller	7,038	Colquitt	284
Mitchell	21,114	Camilla	512
Monroe	14,610	Forsyth	397
Montgomery	7,011	Mount Vernon	244
Morgan	11,572	Madison	349
Murray	19,685	Chatsworth	345
Muscogee	170,108	Columbus	218
Newton	34,666	Covington	277
Oconee	12,427	Watkinsville	186
Oglethorpe	8,929	Lexington	442
Paulding	26,042	Dallas	312
Peach	19,151	Fort Valley	152
Pickens	11,652	Jasper	232
Pierce	11,897	Blackshear	344
Pike	8,937	Zebulon	219
Polk	32,382	Cedartown	311
Pulaski	8,950	Hawkinsville	249
Putnam	10,295	Eatonton	344
Quitman	2,357	Georgetown	146
Rabun	10,466	Clayton	370
Randolph	9,599	Cuthbert	431
Richmond	181,629	Augusta	326
Rockdale	36,570	Conyers	132
Schley	3,433	Ellaville	169
Screven	14,043	Sylvania	655
Seminole	9,057	Donalsonville	225
Spalding	47,899	Griffin	199
Stephens	21,761	Toccoa	177
Stewart	5,896	Lumpkin	452
Sumter	29,360	Americus	489
Talbot	6,536	Talbotton	395
Taliaferro	2,032	Crawfordville	196
Tattnall	18,134	Reidsville	484
Taylor	7,902	Butler	382
Telfair	11,445	MacRae	444
Terrell	12,017	Dawson	337
Thomas	38,098	Thomasville	551
Tift	32,862	Tifton	268
Toombs	22,592	Lyons	371
Towns	6,630	Hiawassee	165
Treutlen	6,087	Soperton	202
Troup	50,003	La Grange	414
Turner	9,510	Ashburn	289
Twiggs	9,354	Jeffersonville	362
Union	9,390	Blairsville	320
Upson	25,998	Thomaston	326
Walker	56,470	La Fayette	446
Walton	31,211	Monroe	330
Ware	37,180	Waycross	907
Warren	6,583	Warrenton	286
Washington	18,842	Sandersville	684
Wayne	20,750	Jesup	647
Webster	2,341	Preston	210
Wheeler	5,155	Alamo	299
White	10,120	Cleveland	242
Whitfield	65,775	Dalton	291
Wilcox	7,682	Abbeville	382
Wilkes	10,951	Washington	470
Wilkinson	10,368	Irwinton	451
Worth	18,064	Sylvester	575

Hawaii

(4 counties, 6,425 sq. mi. land; pop. 964,691)

Hawaii	92,053	Hilo	4,034
Honolulu	762,874	Honolulu	596
Kauai	39,082	Lihue	620
Maui*	70,991	Wailuku	1,175

*Includes population of Kalawao County (146).

Idaho

(44 counties, 82,677 sq. mi. land; pop. 944,127)

Ada	173,125	Boise	1,052
Adams	3,347	Council	1,362
Bannock	65,421	Pocatello	1,112
Bear Lake	6,031	Paris	990
Benewah	8,292	Saint Maries	784
Bingham	36,489	Blackfoot	2,096
Blaine	9,041	Hailey	2,634
Boise	2,999	Idaho City	1,901
Bonner	24,163	Sandpoint	1,726
Bonneville	65,080	Idaho Falls	1,840
Boundary	7,289	Bonners Ferry	1,268
Butte	3,342	Arco	2,236
Camas	818	Fairfield	1,071
Canyon	83,756	Caldwell	584
Caribou	8,695	Soda Springs	1,763
Cassia	19,427	Burley	2,560
Clark	798	Dubois	1,763
Clearwater	10,390	Orofino	2,236
Custer	3,385	Challis	4,927
Elmore	21,565	Mountain Home	3,071
Franklin	8,895	Preston	664
Fremont	10,813	Saint Anthony	1,852
Gem	11,972	Emmett	558
Gooding	11,874	Gooding	728
Idaho	14,760	Grangeville	8,497
Jefferson	15,304	Rigby	1,093
Jerome	14,840	Jerome	601
Kootenai	59,770	Coeur d'Alene	1,240
Latah	28,749	Moscow	1,077
Lemhi	7,460	Salmon	4,564
Lewis	4,118	Nezperce	478
Lincoln	3,436	Shoshone	1,205
Madison	19,480	Rexberg	468
Minidoka	19,718	Rupert	757
Nez Perce	33,220	Lewiston	845
Oneida	3,258	Malad City	1,200
Owyhee	8,272	Murphy	7,643
Payette	15,825	Payette	405
Power	6,844	American Falls	1,403
Shoshone	19,226	Wallace	2,641
Teton	2,897	Driggs	448
Twin Falls	52,927	Twin Falls	1,944
Valley	5,604	Cascade	3,670
Washington	8,803	Weiser	1,454

Illinois

(102 counties, 55,748 sq. mi. land; pop. 11,427,409)

Adams	71,622	Quincy	852
Alexander	12,264	Cairo	236
Bond	16,224	Greenville	377
Boone	28,630	Belvidere	282
Brown	5,411	Mount Sterling	306
Bureau	39,114	Princeton	869
Calhoun	5,867	Hardin	250
Carroll	18,779	Mount Carroll	444
Cass	15,084	Virginia	374
Champaign	168,392	Urbana	998
Christian	36,446	Taylorville	710
Clark	16,913	Marshall	506
Clay	15,283	Louisville	469
Clinton	32,617	Carlyle	472
Coles	52,992	Charleston	509

County	Pop.	County seat or court house	Land area sq. mi.
Cook	5,253,628	Chicago	958
Crawford	20,818	Robinson	446
Cumberland	11,062	Toledo	346
De Kalb	74,628	Sycamore	634
De Witt	18,108	Clinton	397
Douglas	19,774	Tuscola	417
Du Page	658,858	Wheaton	337
Edgar	21,725	Paris	623
Edwards	7,961	Albion	223
Effingham	30,944	Effingham	478
Fayette	22,167	Vandalia	709
Ford	15,265	Paxton	486
Franklin	43,201	Benton	414
Fulton	43,687	Lewiston	871
Gallatin	7,590	Shawneetown	325
Greene	16,661	Carrollton	543
Grundy	30,582	Morris	423
Hamilton	9,172	McLeansboro	436
Hancock	23,877	Carthage	796
Hardin	5,383	Elizabethtown	181
Henderson	9,114	Oquawka	373
Henry	57,968	Cambridge	824
Iroquois	32,976	Watseka	1,118
Jackson	61,649	Murphysboro	590
Jasper	11,318	Newton	496
Jefferson	36,558	Mount Vernon	570
Jersey	20,538	Jerseyville	373
Jo Daviess	23,520	Galena	603
Johnson	9,624	Vienna	346
Kane	278,405	Geneva	524
Kankakee	102,926	Kankakee	679
Kendall	37,202	Yorkville	322
Knox	61,607	Galesburg	720
Lake	440,388	Waukegan	454
La Salle	109,139	Ottawa	1,139
Lawrence	17,807	Lawrenceville	374
Lee	36,328	Dixon	725
Livingston	41,381	Pontiac	1,046
Logan	31,802	Lincoln	619
McDonough	37,236	Macomb	590
McHenry	147,724	Woodstock	606
McLean	119,149	Bloomington	1,185
Macon	131,375	Decatur	581
Macoupin	49,384	Carlinville	865
Madison	247,661	Edwardsville	728
Marion	43,523	Salem	573
Marshall	14,479	Lacon	388
Mason	19,492	Havana	536
Massac	14,990	Metropolis	241
Menard	11,700	Petersburg	315
Mercer	19,286	Aledo	559
Monroe	20,117	Waterloo	388
Montgomery	31,686	Hillsboro	705
Morgan	37,502	Jacksonville	568
Moultrie	14,546	Sullivan	325
Ogle	46,338	Oregon	759
Peoria	200,466	Peoria	621
Perry	21,714	Pinckneyville	443
Piatt	16,581	Monticello	439
Pike	18,896	Pittsfield	830
Pope	4,404	Golconda	374
Pulaski	8,840	Mound City	203
Putnam	6,085	Hennepin	160
Randolph	35,566	Chester	583
Richland	17,587	Olney	360
Rock Island	166,759	Rock Island	423
St. Clair	265,469	Belleville	672
Saline	27,360	Harrisburg	385
Sangamon	176,070	Springfield	866
Schuyler	8,365	Rushville	436
Scott	6,142	Winchester	251
Shelby	23,923	Shelbyville	747
Stark	7,389	Toulon	288
Stephenson	49,536	Freeport	564
Tazewell	132,078	Pekin	650
Union	16,851	Jonesboro	414
Vermilion	95,222	Danville	900
Wabash	13,713	Mt. Carmel	224
Warren	21,943	Monmouth	543
Washington	15,472	Nashville	563
Wayne	18,059	Fairfield	715
White	17,864	Carmi	497
Whiteside	65,970	Morrison	682
Will	324,460	Joliet	844
Williamson	56,538	Marion	427
Winnebago	250,884	Rockford	516
Woodford	33,320	Eureka	527

Indiana

(92 counties, 36,097 sq. mi. land; pop. 5,490,212)

County	Pop.	County seat or court house	Land area sq. mi.
Adams	29,619	Decatur	340
Allen	294,335	Fort Wayne	659
Bartholomew	65,088	Columbus	409
Benton	10,218	Fowler	407
Blackford	15,570	Hartford City	166
Boone	36,446	Lebanon	423
Brown	12,377	Nashville	312
Carroll	19,722	Delphi	372
Cass	40,936	Logansport	414
Clark	88,838	Jeffersonville	376
Clay	24,862	Brazil	360
Clinton	31,545	Frankfort	405
Crawford	9,820	English	307
Daviess	27,836	Washington	432
Dearborn	34,291	Lawrenceburg	307
Decatur	23,841	Greensburg	373
DeKalb	33,606	Auburn	364
Delaware	128,587	Muncie	392
Dubois	34,238	Jasper	429
Elkhart	137,330	Goshen	466
Fayette	28,272	Connersville	215
Floyd	61,205	New Albany	150
Fountain	19,033	Covington	398
Franklin	19,612	Brookville	385
Fulton	19,335	Rochester	369
Gibson	33,156	Princeton	490
Grant	80,934	Marion	415
Greene	30,416	Bloomfield	546
Hamilton	82,381	Noblesville	398
Hancock	43,939	Greenfield	307
Harrison	27,276	Corydon	486
Hendricks	69,804	Danville	409
Henry	53,336	New Castle	394
Howard	86,896	Kokomo	293
Huntington	35,596	Huntington	366
Jackson	36,523	Brownstown	513
Jasper	26,138	Rensselaer	561
Jay	23,239	Portland	384
Jefferson	30,419	Madison	363
Jennings	22,854	Vernon	378
Johnson	77,240	Franklin	321
Knox	41,838	Vincennes	520
Kosciusko	59,555	Warsaw	540
Lagrange	25,550	Lagrange	380
Lake	522,917	Crown Point	501
La Porte	108,632	La Porte	600
Lawrence	42,472	Bedford	452
Madison	139,336	Anderson	453
Marion	765,233	Indianapolis	396
Marshall	39,155	Plymouth	444
Martin	11,001	Shoals	339
Miami	39,820	Peru	369
Monroe	98,387	Bloomington	385
Montgomery	35,501	Crawfordsville	505
Morgan	51,999	Martinsville	409
Newton	14,844	Kentland	401
Noble	35,443	Albion	413
Ohio	5,114	Rising Sun	87
Orange	18,677	Paoli	408
Owen	15,840	Spencer	386
Parke	16,372	Rockville	444
Perry	19,346	Cannelton	382
Pike	13,465	Petersburg	341
Porter	119,816	Valparaiso	418
Posey	26,414	Mount Vernon	409
Pulaski	13,258	Winamac	435
Putnam	29,163	Greencastle	482
Randolph	29,997	Winchester	454
Ripley	24,398	Versailles	447
Rush	19,604	Rushville	408
St. Joseph	241,617	South Bend	459
Scott	20,422	Scottsburg	191
Shelby	39,887	Shelbyville	413
Spencer	19,361	Rockport	400
Starke	21,997	Knox	309
Steuben	24,694	Angola	308
Sullivan	21,107	Sullivan	452
Switzerland	7,153	Vevay	223
Tippecanoe	121,702	Lafayette	502
Tipton	16,819	Tipton	260
Union	6,860	Liberty	162
Vanderburgh	167,515	Evansville	236
Vermillion	18,229	Newport	260
Vigo	112,385	Terre Haute	405
Wabash	36,640	Wabash	398
Warren	8,976	Williamsport	366
Warrick	41,474	Boonville	391
Washington	21,932	Salem	516
Wayne	76,058	Richmond	404
Wells	25,401	Bluffton	370
White	23,867	Monticello	506
Whitley	26,215	Columbia City	336

Iowa

(99 counties; 55,941 sq. mi. land; pop. 2,913,808)

County	Pop.	County seat or court house	Land area sq. mi.
Adair	9,509	Greenfield	570
Adams	5,731	Corning	425
Allamakee	15,108	Waukon	633
Appanoose	15,511	Centerville	498
Audubon	8,559	Audubon	444
Benton	23,649	Vinton	718
Black Hawk	137,961	Waterloo	573
Boone	26,184	Boone	573
Bremer	24,820	Waverly	439
Buchanan	22,900	Independence	572
Buena Vista	20,774	Storm Lake	575
Butler	17,668	Allison	582
Calhoun	13,542	Rockwell City	571

County	Pop.	County seat or court house	Land area sq. mi.
Carroll	22,951	Carroll	570
Cass	16,932	Atlantic	565
Cedar	18,635	Tipton	582
Cerro Gordo	48,458	Mason City	569
Cherokee	16,238	Cherokee	577
Chickasaw	15,437	New Hampton	505
Clarke	8,612	Oscea	431
Clay	19,576	Spencer	569
Clayton	21,098	Elkader	779
Clinton	57,122	Clinton	695
Crawford	18,935	Denison	714
Dallas	29,513	Adel	591
Davis	9,104	Bloomfield	504
Decatur	9,794	Leon	535
Delaware	18,933	Manchester	578
Des Moines	46,203	Burlington	414
Dickinson	15,629	Spirit Lake	381
Dubuque	93,745	Dubuque	607
Emmet	13,336	Estherville	394
Fayette	25,488	West Union	731
Floyd	19,597	Charles City	501
Franklin	13,036	Hampton	583
Fremont	9,401	Sidney	515
Greene	12,119	Jefferson	571
Grundy	14,366	Grundy Center	501
Guthrie	11,983	Guthrie Center	590
Hamilton	17,862	Webster City	576
Hancock	13,833	Garner	571
Hardin	21,776	Eldora	569
Harrison	16,348	Logan	697
Henry	18,890	Mount Pleasant	436
Howard	11,114	Cresco	473
Humboldt	12,246	Dakota City	436
Ida	8,908	Ida Grove	432
Iowa	15,429	Marengo	587
Jackson	22,503	Maquokota	638
Jasper	36,425	Newton	731
Jefferson	16,316	Fairfield	440
Johnson	81,717	Iowa City	614
Jones	20,401	Anamosa	576
Keokuk	12,921	Sigourney	580
Kossuth	21,891	Algona	974
Lee	43,106	Fort Madison and Keokuk	522
Linn	160,775	Cedar Rapids	724
Louisa	12,055	Wapello	402
Lucas	10,313	Chariton	432
Lyon	12,896	Rock Rapids	588
Madison	12,597	Winterset	563
Mahaska	22,507	Oskaloosa	571
Marion	29,669	Knoxville	560
Marshall	41,652	Marshalltown	573
Mills	13,406	Glenwood	439
Mitchell	12,329	Osage	470
Monona	11,692	Onawa	697
Monroe	9,209	Albia	434
Montgomery	13,413	Red Oak	424
Muscatine	40,436	Muscatine	443
O'Brien	15,972	Primghar	574
Osceola	8,371	Sibley	399
Page	19,063	Clarinda	535
Palo Alto	12,721	Emmetsburg	562
Plymouth	24,743	Le Mars	864
Pocahontas	11,369	Pocahontas	577
Polk	303,170	Des Moines	582
Pottawattamie	86,500	Council Bluffs	953
Poweshiek	19,306	Montezuma	585
Ringgold	6,112	Mount Ayr	535
Sac	14,118	Sac City	576
Scott	160,022	Davenport	459
Shelby	15,043	Harlan	591
Sioux	30,813	Orange City	769
Story	72,326	Nevada	574
Tama	19,533	Toledo	721
Taylor	8,353	Bedford	537
Union	13,858	Creston	426
Van Buren	8,626	Keosauqua	484
Wapello	40,241	Ottumwa	434
Warren	34,878	Indianola	573
Washington	20,141	Washington	570
Wayne	8,199	Corydon	526
Webster	45,953	Fort Dodge	718
Winnebago	13,010	Forest City	401
Winneshiek	21,876	Decorah	690
Woodbury	100,884	Sioux City	873
Worth	9,075	Northwood	401
Wright	16,319	Clarion	579

Kansas

(105 counties, 81,787 sq. mi. land; pop. 2,364,236)

Allen	15,654	Iola	505
Anderson	8,749	Garnett	584
Atchison	18,397	Atchison	431
Barber	6,548	Medicine Lodge	1,136
Barton	31,343	Great Bend	895
Bourbon	15,969	Fort Scott	638
Brown	11,055	Hiawatha	572
Butler	44,782	El Dorado	1,443
Chase	3,309	Cottonwood Falls	777
Chautauqua	5,016	Sedan	644
Cherokee	22,304	Columbus	590
Cheyenne	3,678	Saint Francis	1,021
Clark	2,599	Ashland	975
Clay	9,802	Clay Center	632
Cloud	12,494	Concordia	718
Coffey	9,370	Burlington	615
Comanche	2,554	Coldwater	789
Cowley	36,824	Winfield	1,128
Crawford	37,916	Girard	595
Decatur	4,509	Oberlin	894
Dickinson	20,175	Abilene	852
Doniphan	9,268	Troy	388
Douglas	67,640	Lawrence	461
Edwards	4,271	Kinsley	620
Elk	3,918	Howard	650
Ellis	26,098	Hays	900
Ellsworth	6,640	Ellsworth	717
Finney	23,825	Garden City	1,302
Ford	24,315	Dodge City	1,099
Franklin	21,813	Ottawa	577
Geary	29,852	Junction City	377
Gove	3,726	Gove	1,072
Graham	3,995	Hill City	898
Grant	6,977	Ulysses	575
Gray	5,138	Cimarron	868
Greeley	1,845	Tribune	778
Greenwood	8,764	Eureka	1,135
Hamilton	2,514	Syracuse	998
Harper	7,778	Anthony	802
Harvey	30,531	Newton	540
Haskell	3,814	Sublette	578
Hodgeman	2,269	Jetmore	860
Jackson	11,644	Holton	658
Jefferson	15,207	Oskaloosa	535
Jewell	5,241	Mankato	910
Johnson	270,269	Olathe	478
Kearny	3,435	Lakin	868
Kingman	8,960	Kingman	865
Kiowa	4,046	Greensburg	723
Labette	25,682	Oswego	653
Lane	2,472	Dighton	717
Leavenworth	54,809	Leavenworth	463
Lincoln	4,145	Lincoln	720
Linn	8,204	Mound City	601
Logan	3,478	Oakley	1,073
Lyon	35,108	Emporia	844
McPherson	26,855	McPherson	900
Marion	13,522	Marion	944
Marshall	12,720	Marysville	878
Meade	4,788	Meade	979
Miami	21,618	Paola	590
Mitchell	8,117	Beloit	717
Montgomery	42,281	Independence	646
Morris	6,419	Council Grove	693
Morton	3,454	Elkhart	731
Nemaha	11,211	Seneca	719
Neosho	18,967	Erie	576
Ness	4,498	Ness City	1,074
Norton	6,689	Norton	873
Osage	15,319	Lyndon	695
Osborne	5,959	Osborne	882
Ottawa	5,971	Minneapolis	721
Pawnee	8,065	Larned	755
Phillips	7,406	Phillipsburg	887
Pottawatomie	14,782	Westmoreland	828
Pratt	10,275	Pratt	735
Rawlins	4,105	Atwood	1,069
Reno	64,983	Hutchinson	1,259
Republic	7,569	Belleville	719
Rice	11,900	Lyons	728
Riley	63,505	Manhattan	593
Rooks	7,006	Stockton	888
Rush	4,516	LaCrosse	718
Russell	8,868	Russell	869
Saline	48,905	Salina	721
Scott	5,782	Scott City	718
Sedgwick	367,088	Wichita	1,007
Seward	17,071	Liberal	640
Shawnee	154,916	Topeka	549
Sheridan	3,544	Hoxie	896
Sherman	7,759	Goodland	1,057
Smith	5,947	Smith Center	897
Stafford	5,539	Saint John	788
Stanton	2,339	Johnson	681
Stevens	4,736	Hugoton	727
Sumner	24,928	Wellington	1,183
Thomas	8,451	Colby	1,075
Trego	4,165	Wakeeney	890
Wabaunsee	6,867	Alma	797
Wallace	2,045	Sharon Springs	914
Washington	8,543	Washington	898
Wichita	3,041	Leoti	719
Wilson	12,128	Fredonia	575
Woodson	4,600	Yates Center	498
Wyandotte	172,335	Kansas City	149

Kentucky

(120 counties, 39,650 sq. mi. land; pop. 3,660,324)

Adair	15,233	Columbia	407

County	Pop.	County seat or court house	Land area sq. mi.
Allen	14,128	Scottsville	338
Anderson	12,567	Lawrenceburg	204
Ballard	8,798	Wickliffe	254
Barren	34,009	Glasgow	482
Bath	10,025	Owingsville	277
Bell	34,330	Pineville	361
Boone	45,842	Burlington	246
Bourbon	19,405	Paris	292
Boyd	55,513	Catlettsburg	160
Boyle	25,066	Danville	182
Bracken	7,738	Brooksville	203
Breathitt	17,004	Jackson	495
Breckinridge	16,861	Hardinsburg	565
Bullitt	43,346	Shepherdsville	300
Butler	11,064	Morgantown	431
Caldwell	13,473	Princeton	347
Calloway	30,031	Murray	386
Campbell	83,317	Alexandria	152
Carlisle	5,487	Bardwell	191
Carroll	9,270	Carrollton	130
Carter	25,060	Grayson	407
Casey	14,818	Liberty	445
Christian	66,878	Hopkinsville	722
Clark	28,322	Winchester	255
Clay	22,752	Manchester	471
Clinton	9,321	Albany	196
Crittenden	9,207	Marion	360
Cumberland	7,289	Burkesville	304
Daviess	85,949	Owensboro	463
Edmonson	9,962	Brownsville	302
Elliott	6,908	Sandy Hook	234
Estill	14,495	Irvine	256
Fayette	204,165	Lexington	285
Fleming	12,323	Flemingsburg	351
Floyd	48,764	Prestonsburg	393
Franklin	41,830	Frankfort	212
Fulton	8,971	Hickman	211
Gallatin	4,842	Warsaw	99
Garrard	10,853	Lancaster	232
Grant	13,308	Williamstown	259
Graves	34,049	Mayfield	557
Grayson	20,854	Leitchfield	493
Green	11,043	Greensburg	289
Greenup	39,132	Greenup	347
Hancock	7,742	Hawesville	189
Hardin	88,911	Elizabethtown	629
Harlan	41,889	Harlan	468
Harrison	15,166	Cynthiana	310
Hart	15,402	Munfordville	412
Henderson	40,849	Henderson	438
Henry	12,740	New Castle	291
Hickman	6,065	Clinton	245
Hopkins	46,174	Madisonville	552
Jackson	11,996	McKee	346
Jefferson	684,638	Louisville	386
Jessamine	26,065	Nicholasville	174
Johnson	24,432	Paintsville	264
Kenton	137,058	Independence	163
Knott	17,940	Hindman	352
Knox	30,239	Barbourville	388
Larue	11,983	Hodgenville	263
Laurel	38,982	London	434
Lawrence	14,121	Louisa	420
Lee	7,754	Beattyville	211
Leslie	14,882	Hyden	402
Letcher	30,687	Whitesburg	339
Lewis	14,545	Vanceburg	484
Lincoln	19,053	Stanford	337
Livingston	9,219	Smithland	312
Logan	24,138	Russellville	556
Lyon	6,490	Eddyville	209
McCracken	61,310	Paducah	251
McCreary	15,634	Whitley City	427
McLean	10,090	Calhoun	256
Madison	53,352	Richmond	443
Magoffin	13,515	Salyersville	310
Marion	17,910	Lebanon	347
Marshall	25,637	Benton	304
Martin	13,925	Inez	230
Mason	17,760	Maysville	241
Meade	22,854	Brandenburg	306
Menifee	5,117	Frenchburg	203
Mercer	19,011	Harrodsburg	250
Metcalfe	9,484	Edmonton	291
Monroe	12,353	Tompkinsville	331
Montgomery	20,046	Mount Sterling	199
Morgan	12,103	West Liberty	382
Muhlenberg	32,238	Greenville	478
Nelson	27,584	Bardstown	424
Nicholas	7,157	Carlisle	197
Ohio	21,765	Hartford	596
Oldham	28,094	La Grange	190
Owen	8,924	Owenton	354
Owsley	5,709	Booneville	198
Pendleton	10,989	Falmouth	281
Perry	33,763	Hazard	341
Pike	81,123	Pikeville	785
Powell	11,101	Stanton	180
Pulaski	45,803	Somerset	660
Robertson	2,270	Mount Olivet	100
Rockcastle	13,973	Mount Vernon	318
Rowan	19,049	Morehead	282
Russell	13,708	Jamestown	250
Scott	21,813	Georgetown	286
Shelby	23,328	Shelbyville	385
Simpson	14,673	Franklin	236
Spencer	5,929	Taylorsville	192
Taylor	21,178	Campbellsville	270
Todd	11,874	Elkton	377
Trigg	9,384	Cadiz	421
Trimble	6,253	Bedford	148
Union	17,821	Morganfield	341
Warren	71,828	Bowling Green	548
Washington	10,764	Springfield	301
Wayne	17,022	Monticello	446
Webster	14,832	Dixon	336
Whitley	33,396	Williamsburg	443
Wolfe	6,698	Campton	223
Woodford	17,778	Versailles	192

Louisiana

(64 parishes, 44,930 sq. mi. land; pop. 4,206,116)

Acadia	56,427	Crowley	657
Allen	21,408	Oberlin	765
Ascension	50,068	Donaldsville	296
Assumption	22,084	Napoleonville	342
Avoyelles	41,393	Marksville	846
Beauregard	29,692	De Ridder	1,163
Bienville	16,387	Arcadia	816
Bossier	80,721	Benton	845
Caddo	252,437	Shreveport	894
Calcasieu	167,048	Lake Charles	1,082
Caldwell	10,761	Columbia	541
Cameron	9,336	Cameron	1,417
Catahoula	12,287	Harrisonburg	732
Claiborne	17,095	Homer	765
Concordia	22,981	Vidalia	717
De Soto	25,664	Mansfield	880
East Baton Rouge	366,164	Baton Rouge	458
East Carroll	11,772	Lake Providence	426
East Feliciana	19,015	Clinton	455
Evangeline	33,343	Ville Platte	667
Franklin	24,141	Winnsboro	635
Grant	16,703	Colfax	653
Iberia	63,752	New Iberia	589
Iberville	32,159	Plaquemine	638
Jackson	17,321	Jonesboro	579
Jefferson	454,592	Gretna	348
Jefferson Davis	32,168	Jennings	655
Lafayette	150,017	Lafayette	270
Lafourche	82,483	Thibodaux	1,141
La Salle	17,004	Jena	638
Lincoln	39,763	Ruston	472
Livingston	58,655	Livingston	661
Madison	15,682	Tallulah	631
Morehouse	34,803	Bastrop	807
Natchitoches	39,863	Natchitoches	1,264
Orleans	557,927	New Orleans	199
Ouachita	139,241	Monroe	627
Plaquemines	26,049	Pointe a la Hache	1,035
Pointe Coupee	24,045	New Roads	566
Rapides	135,282	Alexandria	1,341
Red River	10,433	Coushatta	394
Richland	22,187	Rayville	563
Sabine	25,280	Many	855
St. Bernard	64,097	Chalmette	466
St. Charles	37,259	Hahnville	286
St. Helena	9,827	Greensburg	409
St. James	21,495	Convent	248
St. John The Baptist	31,924	Edgard	213
St. Landry	84,128	Opelousas	936
St. Martin	40,214	Saint Martinville	749
St. Mary	64,395	Franklin	613
St. Tammany	110,554	Covington	873
Tangipahoa	80,698	Amite	783
Tensas	8,525	Saint Joseph	623
Terrebonne	94,393	Houma	1,367
Union	21,167	Farmerville	884
Vermilion	48,458	Abbeville	1,205
Vernon	53,475	Leesville	1,332
Washington	44,207	Franklinton	676
Webster	43,631	Minden	602
West Baton Rouge	19,086	Port Allen	194
West Carroll	12,922	Oak Grove	360
West Feliciana	12,186	Saint Francisville	406
Winn	17,253	Winnfield	953

Maine

(16 counties, 30,920 sq. mi. land; pop. 1,125,043)

Androscoggin	99,509	Auburn	477
Aroostook	91,344	Houlton	6,721
Cumberland	215,789	Portland	876
Franklin	27,447	Farmington	1,699
Hancock	41,781	Ellsworth	1,537
Kennebec	109,889	Augusta	876
Knox	32,941	Rockland	370
Lincoln	25,691	Wiscasset	458
Oxford	49,043	South Paris	2,053

County	Pop.	County seat or court house	Land area sq. mi.
Penobscot	137,015	Bangor	3,430
Piscataquis	17,634	Dover-Foxcroft	3,986
Sagadahoc	28,795	Bath	257
Somerset	45,049	Skowhegan	3,930
Waldo	28,414	Belfast	730
Washington	34,963	Machias	2,586
York	139,739	Alfred	1,008

Maryland

(23 cos., 1 ind. city, 9,891 sq. mi. land; pop. 4,216,933)

County	Pop.	County seat or court house	Land area sq. mi.
Allegany	80,548	Cumberland	421
Anne Arundel	370,775	Annapolis	418
Baltimore	655,615	Towson	598
Calvert	34,638	Prince Frederick	213
Caroline	23,143	Denton	321
Carroll	96,356	Westminster	452
Cecil	60,430	Elkton	360
Charles	72,751	La Plata	452
Dorchester	30,623	Cambridge	593
Frederick	114,263	Frederick	663
Garrett	26,490	Oakland	657
Harford	145,930	Bel Air	448
Howard	118,572	Ellicott City	251
Kent	16,695	Chestertown	278
Montgomery	579,053	Rockville	495
Prince Georges	665,071	Upper Marlboro	487
Queen Annes	25,508	Centreville	372
St. Mary's	59,895	Leonardtown	373
Somerset	19,188	Princess Anne	338
Talbot	25,604	Easton	259
Washington	113,086	Hagerstown	455
Wicomico	64,540	Salisbury	379
Worcester	30,889	Snow Hill	475
Independent City			
Baltimore	786,775		80

Massachusetts

(14 counties; 7,826 sq. mi. land; pop. 5,737,093)

County	Pop.	County seat or court house	Land area sq. mi.
Barnstable	147,925	Barnstable	400
Berkshire	145,110	Pittsfield	929
Bristol	474,641	Taunton	557
Dukes	8,942	Edgartown	102
Essex	633,000	Salem	495
Franklin	64,317	Greenfield	702
Hampden	443,018	Springfield	618
Hampshire	138,813	Northampton	528
Middlesex	1,367,034	Cambridge	822
Nantucket	5,087	Nantucket	47
Norfolk	606,587	Dedham	400
Plymouth	405,437	Plymouth	655
Suffolk	650,142	Boston	57
Worcester	646,352	Worcester	1,513

Michigan

(83 counties; 56,817 sq. mi. land; pop. 9,262,044)

County	Pop.	County seat or court house	Land area sq. mi.
Alcona	9,740	Harrisville	679
Alger	9,225	Munising	912
Allegan	81,555	Allegan	832
Alpena	32,315	Alpena	567
Antrim	16,194	Bellaire	480
Arenac	14,706	Standish	367
Baraga	8,484	L'Anse	901
Barry	45,781	Hastings	560
Bay	119,881	Bay City	447
Benzie	11,205	Beulah	322
Berrien	171,276	Saint Joseph	576
Branch	40,188	Coldwater	508
Calhoun	141,579	Marshall	712
Cass	49,499	Cassopolis	496
Charlevoix	19,907	Charlevoix	421
Cheboygan	20,649	Cheboygan	720
Chippewa	29,029	Sault Sainte Marie	1,590
Clare	23,822	Harrison	570
Clinton	55,893	Saint Johns	573
Crawford	9,465	Grayling	559
Delta	38,947	Escanaba	1,173
Dickinson	25,341	Iron Mountain	770
Eaton	88,337	Charlotte	579
Emmet	22,992	Petoskey	468
Genesee	450,449	Flint	642
Gladwin	19,957	Gladwin	505
Gogebic	19,686	Bessemer	1,105
Grand Traverse	54,899	City	466
Gratiot	40,448	Ithaca	570
Hillsdale	42,071	Hillsdale	603
Houghton	37,872	Houghton	1,014
Huron	36,459	Bad Axe	830
Ingham	272,437	Mason	560
Ionia	51,815	Ionia	577
Iosco	28,349	Iawas City	546
Iron	13,635	Crystal Falls	1,163
Isabella	54,110	Mount Pleasant	577
Jackson	151,495	Jackson	705
Kalamazoo	212,378	Kalamazoo	562
Kalkaska	10,952	Kalkaska	563
Kent	444,506	Grand Rapids	862
Keweenaw	1,963	543 River	543
Lake	7,711	Baldwin	568
Lapeer	70,038	Lapeer	658
Leelanau	14,007	Leland	341
Lenawee	89,948	Adrian	753
Livingston	100,289	Howell	574
Luce	6,659	Newberry	904
Mackinac	10,178	Saint Ignace	1,025
Macomb	694,600	Mount Clemens	482
Manistee	23,019	Manistee	543
Marquette	74,101	Marquette	1,821
Mason	26,365	Ludington	494
Mecosta	36,961	Big Rapids	560
Menominee	26,201	Menominee	1,045
Midland	73,578	Midland	525
Missaukee	10,009	Lake City	565
Monroe	134,659	Monroe	557
Montcalm	47,555	Stanton	713
Montmorency	7,492	Atlanta	550
Muskegon	157,589	Muskegon	507
Newaygo	34,917	White Cloud	847
Oakland	1,011,793	Pontiac	875
Oceana	22,002	Hart	541
Ogemaw	16,436	West Branch	570
Ontonagon	9,861	Ontonagon	1,311
Osceola	18,928	Reed City	569
Oscoda	6,858	Mio	568
Otsego	14,993	Gaylord	516
Ottawa	157,174	Grand Haven	567
Presque Isle	14,267	Rogers City	656
Roscommon	16,374	Roscommon	528
Saginaw	228,059	Saginaw	815
St. Clair	138,802	Port Huron	734
St. Joseph	56,083	Centreville	503
Sanilac	40,789	Sandusky	964
Schoolcraft	8,575	Manistique	1,173
Shiawassee	71,140	Corunna	540
Tuscola	56,961	Caro	812
Van Buren	66,814	Paw Paw	611
Washtenaw	264,740	Ann Arbor	710
Wayne	2,337,843	Detroit	615
Wexford	25,102	Cadillac	566

Minnesota

(87 counties; 79,289 sq. mi. land; pop., 4,075,970)

County	Pop.	County seat or court house	Land area sq. mi.
Aitkin	13,404	Aitkin	1,834
Anoka	195,998	Anoka	430
Becker	29,336	Detroit Lakes	1,312
Beltrami	30,982	Bemidji	2,507
Benton	25,187	Foley	408
Big Stone	7,716	Ortonville	497
Blue Earth	52,314	Mankato	749
Brown	28,645	New Ulm	610
Carlton	29,936	Carlton	864
Carver	37,046	Chaska	351
Cass	21,050	Walker	2,033
Chippewa	14,941	Montevideo	584
Chisago	25,717	Center City	417
Clay	49,327	Moorhead	1,049
Clearwater	8,761	Bagley	999
Cook	4,092	Grand Marais	1,412
Cottonwood	14,854	Windom	640
Crow Wing	41,722	Brainerd	1,008
Dakota	194,111	Hastings	574
Dodge	14,773	Mantorville	439
Douglas	27,839	Alexandria	643
Faribault	19,714	Blue Earth	714
Fillmore	21,930	Preston	862
Freeborn	36,329	Albert Lea	705
Goodhue	38,749	Red Wind	763
Grant	7,171	Elbow Lake	547
Hennepin	941,411	Minneapolis	541
Houston	19,617	Caledonia	564
Hubbard	14,098	Park Rapids	936
Isanti	23,600	Cambridge	440
Itasca	43,006	Grand Rapids	2,661
Jackson	13,690	Jackson	699
Kanabec	12,161	Mora	527
Kandiyohi	36,763	Willmar	784
Kittson	6,672	Hallock	1,104
Koochiching	17,571	International Falls	3,108
Lac qui Parle	10,592	Madison	772
Lake	13,043	Two Harbors	2,053
Lake of the Woods	3,764	Baudette	1,296
Le Sueur	23,434	Le Center	446
Lincoln	8,207	Ivanhoe	538
Lyon	25,207	Marshall	714
McLeod	29,657	Glencoe	489
Mahnomen	5,535	Mahnomen	559
Marshall	13,027	Warren	1,760
Martin	24,687	Fairmont	706
Meeker	20,594	Litchfield	624
Mille Lacs	18,430	Milaca	578
Morrison	29,311	Falls	1,124
Mower	40,390	Austin	711
Murray	11,507	Slayton	702
Nicollet	26,929	Saint Peter	440
Nobles	21,840	Worthington	714
Norman	9,379	Ada	877
Olmsted	91,971	Rochester	655
Otter Tail	51,937	Fergus Falls	1,973

County	Pop.	County seat or court house	Land area sq. mi.
Pennington	15,258	Thief River Falls	618
Pine	19,871	Pine City	1,421
Pipestone	11,690	Pipestone	466
Polk	34,844	Crookston	1,982
Pope	11,657	Glenwood	668
Ramsey	459,784	Saint Paul	154
Red Lake	5,471	Red Lake Falls	433
Redwood	19,341	Redwood Falls	882
Renville	20,401	Olivia	984
Rice	46,087	Faribault	501
Rock	10,703	Luverne	483
Roseau	12,574	Roseau	1,677
St. Louis	222,229	Duluth	6,125
Scott	43,784	Shakopee	357
Sherburne	29,908	Elk River	435
Sibley	15,448	Gaylord	593
Stearns	108,161	Saint Cloud	1,338
Steele	30,328	Owatonna	431
Stevens	11,322	Morris	560
Swift	12,920	Benson	743
Todd	24,991	Long Prairie	941
Traverse	5,542	Wheaton	575
Wabasha	19,335	Wabasha	537
Wadena	14,192	Wadena	538
Waseca	18,448	Waseca	422
Washington	113,571	Stillwater	390
Watonwan	12,361	Saint James	435
Wilkin	8,382	Breckenridge	751
Winona	46,256	Winona	630
Wright	58,962	Buffalo	672
Yellow Medicine	13,653	Granite Falls	758

Mississippi

(82 counties, 47,296 sq. mi. land; pop. 2,520,770)

County	Pop.	County seat or court house	Land area sq. mi.
Adams	38,071	Natchez	456
Alcorn	33,036	Corinth	401
Amite	13,369	Liberty	732
Attala	19,865	Kosciusko	737
Benton	8,153	Ashland	407
Bolivar	45,965	Cleveland & Rosedale	892
Calhoun	15,664	Pittsboro	573
Carroll	9,776	Carrollton & Vaiden	634
Chickasaw	17,851	Houston & Okolona	503
Choctaw	8,996	Ackerman	420
Claiborne	12,279	Port Gibson	494
Clarke	16,945	Quitman	692
Clay	21,082	West Point	415
Coahoma	36,918	Clarksdale	559
Copiah	26,503	Hazlehurst	779
Covington	15,927	Collins	416
De Soto	53,930	Hernando	483
Forrest	66,018	Hattiesburg	469
Franklin	8,208	Meadville	566
George	15,297	Lucedale	483
Greene	9,827	Leakesville	718
Grenada	21,115	Grenada	421
Hancock	24,496	Bay Saint Louis	478
Harrison	157,665	Gulfport	581
Hinds	250,998	Jackson & Raymond	875
Holmes	22,970	Lexington	759
Humphreys	13,931	Belzoni	430
Issaquena	2,513	Mayersville	406
Itawamba	20,518	Fulton	540
Jackson	118,015	Pascagoula	731
Jasper	17,265	Bat Springs & Paulding	678
Jefferson	9,181	Fayette	523
Jefferson Davis	13,846	Prentiss	409
Jones	61,912	Ellisville & Laurel	696
Kemper	10,148	De Kalb	766
Lafayette	31,030	Oxford	669
Lamar	23,821	Purvis	499
Lauderdale	77,285	Meridian	705
Lawrence	12,518	Monticello	435
Leake	18,790	Carthage	584
Lee	57,061	Tupelo	451
Leflore	41,525	Greenwood	605
Lincoln	30,174	Brookhaven	587
Lowndes	57,304	Columbus	517
Madison	41,613	Canton	718
Marion	25,708	Columbia	548
Marshall	29,296	Holly Springs	709
Monroe	36,404	Aberdeen	772
Montgomery	13,366	Winona	408
Neshoba	23,789	Philadelphia	572
Newton	19,967	Decatur	580
Noxubee	13,212	Macon	698
Oktibbeha	36,018	Starkville	459
Panola	28,164	Batesville & Sardis	694
Pearl River	33,795	Poplarville	818
Perry	9,864	New Augusta	651
Pike	36,173	Magnolia	410
Pontotoc	20,918	Pontotoc	499
Prentiss	24,025	Booneville	418
Quitman	12,636	Marks	406
Rankin	69,427	Brandon	782
Scott	24,556	Forest	610
Sharkey	7,964	Rolling Fork	435
Simpson	23,441	Mendenhall	591
Smith	15,077	Raleigh	635
Stone	9,716	Wiggins	446
Sunflower	34,844	Indianola	706
Tallahatchie	17,157	Charleston & Sumner	651
Tate	20,119	Senatobia	406
Tippah	18,739	Ripley	458
Tishomingo	18,434	Iuka	434
Tunica	9,652	Tunica	460
Union	21,741	New Albany	416
Walthall	13,761	Tylertown	404
Warren	51,627	Vicksburg	596
Washington	72,344	Greenville	733
Wayne	19,135	Waynesboro	813
Webster	10,300	Walthall	424
Wilkinson	10,021	Woodville	678
Winston	19,474	Louisville	610
Yalobusha	13,183	Coffeeville & Water Valley	478
Yazoo	27,349	Yazoo City	933

Missouri

(114 cos., 1 ind. city, 68,995 sq. mi. land; pop. 4,916,762)

County	Pop.	County seat or court house	Land area sq. mi.
Adair	24,870	Kirksville	567
Andrew	13,980	Savannah	435
Atchison	8,605	Rockport	542
Audrain	26,458	Mexico	697
Barry	24,408	Cassville	773
Barton	11,292	Lamar	596
Bates	15,873	Butler	849
Benton	12,183	Warsaw	729
Bollinger	10,301	Marble Hill	621
Boone	100,376	Columbia	687
Buchanan	87,888	Saint Joseph	409
Butler	37,693	Poplar Buff	698
Caldwell	8,660	Kingston	430
Callaway	32,252	Fulton	842
Camden	19,963	Camdenton	641
Cape Girardeau	58,837	Jackson	577
Carroll	12,131	Carrollton	695
Carter	5,428	Van Buren	509
Cass	51,029	Harrisonville	701
Cedar	11,894	Stockton	470
Chariton	10,489	Keytesville	758
Christian	22,402	Ozark	564
Clark	8,493	Kahoka	507
Clay	136,488	Liberty	403
Clinton	15,916	Plattsburg	423
Cole	56,663	Jefferson City	392
Cooper	14,643	Boonville	567
Crawford	18,300	Steelville	744
Dade	7,383	Greenfield	491
Dallas	12,096	Buffalo	543
Daviess	8,905	Gallatin	568
De Kalb	8,222	Maysville	425
Dent	14,517	Salem	755
Douglas	11,594	Ava	814
Dunklin	36,320	Kennett	547
Franklin	71,233	Union	922
Gasconade	13,181	Hermann	521
Gentry	7,887	Albany	493
Greene	185,302	Springfield	677
Grundy	11,959	Trenton	437
Harrison	9,890	Bethany	725
Henry	19,672	Clinton	729
Hickory	6,367	Hermitage	379
Holt	6,882	Oregon	457
Howard	10,008	Fayette	465
Howell	28,807	West Plains	928
Iron	11,084	Ironton	552
Jackson	629,180	Independence	611
Jasper	86,958	Carthage	641
Jefferson	146,814	Hillsboro	661
Johnson	39,059	Warrensburg	834
Knox	5,508	Edina	507
Laclede	24,323	Lebanon	768
Lafayette	29,931	Lexington	632
Lawrence	28,973	Mount Vernon	613
Lewis	10,901	Monticello	509
Lincoln	22,193	Troy	627
Linn	15,495	Linneus	620
Livingston	15,739	Chillicothe	537
McDonald	14,917	Pineville	540
Macon	16,313	Macon	797
Madison	10,725	Fredericktown	497
Maries	7,551	Vienna	528
Marion	28,638	Palmyra	438
Mercer	4,685	Princeton	454
Miller	18,539	Tuscumbia	593
Mississippi	15,726	Charleston	410
Moniteau	12,068	California	417
Monroe	9,716	Paris	670
Montgomery	11,537	Montgomery City	540
Morgan	13,807	Versailles	594
New Madrid	22,945	New Madrid	658
Newton	40,555	Neosho	627
Nodaway	21,996	Maryville	875
Oregon	10,238	Alton	792
Osage	12,014	Linn	606
Ozark	7,961	Gainesville	731
Pemiscot	24,987	Caruthersville	517
Perry	16,784	Perryville	473

County	Pop.	County seat or court house	Land area sq. mi.
Pettis	36,378	Sedalia	686
Phelps	33,633	Rolla	674
Pike	17,568	Bowling Green	673
Platte	46,341	Platte City	421
Polk	18,822	Bolivar	636
Pulaski	42,011	Waynesville	550
Putnam	6,092	Unionville	520
Ralls	8,984	New London	482
Randolph	25,460	Huntsville	477
Ray	21,378	Richmond	568
Reynolds	7,230	Centerville	809
Ripley	12,458	Doniphan	631
St. Charles	143,455	St. Charles	558
St. Clair	8,622	Osceola	699
St. Francois	42,600	Farmington	451
St. Louis	974,180	Clayton	506
Ste. Genevieve	15,180	Ste. Genevieve	504
Saline	24,913	Marshall	755
Schuyler	4,979	Lancaster	309
Scotland	5,415	Memphis	438
Scott	39,647	Benton	423
Shannon	7,885	Eminence	1,004
Shelby	7,826	Shelbyville	501
Stoddard	29,009	Bloomfield	815
Stone	15,587	Galena	451
Sullivan	7,434	Milan	651
Taney	20,467	Forsyth	608
Texas	21,070	Houston	1,180
Vernon	19,806	Nevada	837
Warren	14,900	Warrenton	429
Washington	17,983	Potosi	762
Wayne	11,277	Greenville	762
Webster	20,414	Marshfield	594
Worth	3,008	Grant City	266
Wright	16,188	Hartville	682
Independent City			
St. Louis	453,085	.....	61

Montana

(56 counties, 145,587 sq. mi. land; pop., 786,690)

County	Pop.	County seat or court house	Land area sq. mi.
Beaverhead	8,186	Dillon	5,529
Big Horn	11,096	Hardin	4,983
Blaine	6,999	Chinook	4,257
Broadwater	3,267	Townsend	1,189
Carbon	8,000	Red Lodge	2,056
Carter	1,799	Ekalaka	3,342
Cascade	80,696	Great Falls	2,699
Chouteau	6,092	Fort Benton	3,987
Custer	13,109	Miles City	3,776
Daniels	2,835	Scobey	1,427
Dawson	11,805	Glendive	2,374
Deer Lodge	12,518	Anaconda	740
Fallon	3,763	Baker	1,620
Fergus	13,076	Lewistown	4,340
Flathead	51,966	Kalispell	[illegible]
Gallatin	[illegible]	Bozeman	2,510
Garfield	1,656	Jordan	4,491
Glacier	10,628	Cut Bank	2,994
Golden Valley	1,026	Ryegete	1,172
Granite	2,700	Phillipsburg	1,729
Hill	17,985	Havre	2,897
Jefferson	7,029	Boulder	1,657
Judith Basin	2,646	Stanford	1,871
Lake	19,056	Polson	1,445
Lewis & Clark	43,039	Helena	3,461
Liberty	2,329	Chester	1,426
Lincoln	17,752	Libby	3,616
McCone	2,702	Circle	2,626
Madison	5,448	Virginia City	3,590
Meagher	2,154	White Sulphur Springs	2,392
Mineral	3,675	Superior	1,216
Missoula	76,016	Missoula	2,582
Musselshell	4,428	Roundup	1,871
Park	12,869	Livingston	1,665
Petroleum	655	Winnett	1,652
Phillips	5,367	Malta	5,130
Pondera	6,731	Conrad	1,632
Powder River	2,520	Broadus	3,288
Powell	6,958	Deer Lodge	2,329
Prairie	1,836	Terry	1,732
Ravalli	22,493	Hamilton	2,384
Richland	12,243	Sidney	2,081
Roosevelt	10,467	Wolf Point	2,357
Rosebud	9,899	Forsyth	5,019
Sanders	8,675	Thompson Falls	2,749
Sheridan	5,414	Plentywood	1,681
Silver Bow	38,092	Butte	718
Stillwater	5,598	Columbus	1,793
Sweet Grass	3,216	Big Timber	1,903
Teton	6,491	Choteau	2,275
Toole	5,559	Shelby	1,931
Treasure	981	Hysham	975
Valley	10,250	Glasgow	4,936
Wheatland	2,359	Harlowton	1,419
Wibaux	1,476	Wibaux	888
Yellowstone	108,035	Billings	2,624

Nebraska

(93 counties, 76,483 sq. mi. land; pop., 1,569,825)

County	Pop.	County seat or court house	Land area sq. mi.
Adams	30,656	Hastings	564
Antelope	8,675	Neligh	859
Arthur	513	Arthur	711
Banner	918	Harrisburg	747
Blaine	867	Brewster	714
Boone	7,391	Albion	687
Box Butte	13,696	Alliance	1,077
Boyd	3,331	Butte	532
Brown	4,377	Ainsworth	1,214
Buffalo	34,797	Kearney	945
Burt	8,813	Tekamah	486
Butler	9,330	David City	584
Cass	20,297	Plattsmouth	557
Cedar	10,852	Hartington	740
Chase	4,758	Imperial	894
Cherry	6,758	Valentine	5,961
Cheyenne	10,057	Sidney	1,196
Clay	8,106	Clay Center	574
Colfax	9,890	Schuyler	410
Cuming	11,664	West Point	575
Custer	13,877	Broken Bow	2,571
Dakota	16,573	Dakota City	258
Dawes	9,609	Chadron	1,397
Dawson	22,162	Lexington	982
Deuel	2,462	Chappell	437
Dixon	7,137	Ponca	474
Dodge	35,847	Fremont	534
Douglas	397,884	Omaha	333
Dundy	2,861	Benkelman	920
Fillmore	7,920	Geneva	576
Franklin	4,377	Franklin	576
Frontier	3,647	Stockville	976
Furnas	6,486	Beaver City	721
Gage	24,456	Beatrice	858
Garden	2,802	Oshkosh	1,680
Garfield	2,363	Burwell	570
Gosper	2,140	Elwood	461
Grant	877	Hyannis	775
Greeley	3,462	Greeley	570
Hall	47,690	Grand Island	537
Hamilton	9,301	Aurora	543
Harlan	4,292	Alma	555
Hayes	1,356	Hayes Center	713
Hitchcock	4,079	Trenton	709
Holt	13,552	O'Neil	2,406
Hooker	990	Mullen	721
Howard	6,773	Saint Paul	564
Jefferson	9,817	Fairbury	575
Johnson	5,285	Tecumseh	377
Kearney	7,053	Minden	519
Keith	9,364	Ogallala	1,039
Keya Paha	1,301	Springview	769
Kimball	4,882	Kimball	952
Knox	11,457	Center	1,105
Lancaster	192,884	Lincoln	839
Lincoln	36,455	North Platte	[illegible]
Logan	983	Stapleton	571
Loup	859	Taylor	574
McPherson	593	Tryon	859
Madison	31,382	Madison	575
Merrick	8,945	Central City	478
Morrill	6,085	Bridgeport	1,405
Nance	4,740	Fullerton	439
Nemaha	8,367	Auburn	409
Nuckolls	6,726	Nelson	576
Otoe	15,183	Nebraska City	615
Pawnee	3,937	Pawnee City	433
Perkins	3,637	Grant	885
Phelps	9,769	Holdrege	540
Pierce	8,481	Pierce	575
Platte	28,852	Columbus	669
Polk	6,320	Osceola	437
Red Willow	12,615	McCook	718
Richardson	11,315	Falls City	553
Rock	2,383	Bassett	1,003
Saline	13,131	Wilber	575
Sarpy	86,015	Papillion	238
Saunders	18,716	Wahoo	753
Scotts Bluff	38,344	Gering	725
Seward	15,789	Seward	575
Sheridan	7,544	Rushville	2,453
Sherman	4,226	Loup City	564
Sioux	1,845	Harrison	2,070
Stanton	6,549	Stanton	431
Thayer	7,582	Hebron	575
Thomas	973	Thedford	713
Thurston	7,186	Pender	391
Valley	5,633	Ord	567
Washington	15,508	Blair	386
Wayne	9,858	Wayne	443
Webster	4,858	Red Cloud	575
Wheeler	1,060	Bartlett	575
York	14,798	York	576

Nevada

(16 cos., 1 ind. city, 109,889 sq. mi. land; pop., 800,508)

County	Pop.	County seat or court house	Land area sq. mi.
Churchill	13,917	Fallon	4,990
Clark	461,816	Las Vegas	7,881

County	Pop.	County seat or court house	Land area sq. mi.
Douglas	19,421	Minden	708
Elko	17,269	Elko	17,135
Esmeralda	777	Goldfield	3,587
Eureka	1,198	Eureka	4,175
Humboldt	9,449	Winnemucca	9,698
Lander	4,082	Austin	5,515
Lincoln	3,732	Pioche	10,635
Lyon	13,594	Yerington	2,007
Mineral	6,217	Hawthorne	3,744
Nye	9,048	Tonopah	18,155
Pershing	3,408	Lovelock	6,036
Storey	1,459	Virginia City	264
Washoe	193,623	Reno	6,317
White Pine	8,167	Ely	8.902
Independent City			
Carson City	32,022	Carson City	146

New Hampshire

(10 counties, 9,027 sq. mi. land; pop., 920,610)

Belknap	42,884	Laconia	404
Carroll	27,931	Ossipee	933
Cheshire	62,116	Keene	711
Coos	35,147	Lancaster	1,804
Grafton	65,806	Woodsville	1,719
Hillsborough	276,608	Nashua	876
Merrimack	98,302	Concord	936
Rockingham	190,345	Exeter	699
Strafford	85,408	Dover	370
Sullivan	36,063	Newport	540

New Jersey

(21 counties, 7,521 sq. mi. land; pop., 7,365,011)

Atlantic	194,119	Mays Landing	568
Bergen	845,385	Hackensack	237
Burlington	362,542	Mount Holly	808
Camden	471,650	Camden	223
Cape May	82,266	Cape May Court House	263
Cumberland	132,866	Bridgeton	498
Essex	851,304	Newark	127
Gloucester	199,917	Woodbury	327
Hudson	556,972	Jersey City	46
Hunterdon	87,361	Flemington	426
Mercer	307,863	Trenton	227
Middlesex	595,893	New Brunswick	316
Monmouth	503,173	Freehold	472
Morris	407,630	Morristown	470
Ocean	346,038	Toms River	641
Passaic	447,585	Paterson	187
Salem	64,676	Salem	338
Somerset	203,129	Somerville	305
Sussex	116,119	Newton	526
Union	504,094	Elizabeth	103
Warren	84,429	Belvidere	359

New Mexico

(33 counties, 121,412 sq. mi. land; pop., 1,303,302)

Bernalillo	420,261	Albuquerque	1,169
Catron	2,720	Reserve	6,929
Chaves	51,103	Roswell	6,066
Cibola	30,347	Grants	4,468
Colfax	13,706	Raton	3,762
Curry	42,019	Clovis	1,408
De Baca	2,454	Fort Sumner	2,323
Dona Ana	96,340	Las Cruces	3,819
Eddy	47,855	Carlsbad	4,184
Grant	26,204	Silver City	3,969
Guadalupe	4,496	Santa Rosa	3,032
Harding	1,090	Mosquero	2,122
Hidalgo	6,049	Lordsburg	3,445
Lea	55,634	Lovington	4,389
Lincoln	10,997	Carrizozo	4,832
Los Alamos	17,599	Los Alamos	109
Luna	15,585	Deming	2,965
McKinley	56,536	Gallup	5,442
Mora	4,205	Mora	1,930
Otero	44,665	Alamogordo	6,626
Quay	10,577	Tucumcari	2,874
Rio Arriba	29,282	Tierra Amarilla	5,856
Roosevelt	15,695	Portales	2,453
Sandoval	34,400	Bernalillo	3,707
San Juan	80,833	Aztec	5,521
San Miguel	22,751	Las Vegas	4,709
Santa Fe	75,519	Santa Fe	1,905
Sierra	8,454	Truth or Consequences	4,178
Socorro	12,969	Socorro	6,625
Taos	18,862	Taos	2,204
Torrance	7,491	Estancia	3,335
Union	4,725	Clayton	3,830
Valencia	60,853	Los Lunas	5,616

New York

(62 counties, 47,831 sq. mi. land; pop., 17,558,165)

Albany	285,909	Albany	524
Allegany	51,742	Belmont	1,032
Bronx	1,168,972	Bronx	42
Broome	213,648	Binghamton	712
Cattaraugus	85,697	Little Valley	1,306
Cayuga	79,894	Auburn	695
Chautauqua	146,925	Mayville	1,064
Chemung	97,656	Elmira	411
Chenango	49,344	Norwich	897
Clinton	80,750	Plattsburgh	1,043
Columbia	59,487	Hudson	638
Cortland	48,820	Cortland	500
Delaware	46,824	Delhi	1,440
Dutchess	245,055	Poughkeepsie	804
Erie	1,015,472	Buffalo	1,046
Essex	36,176	Elizabethtown	1,806
Franklin	44,929	Malone	1,642
Fulton	55,153	Johnstown	497
Genesee	59,400	Batavia	495
Greene	40,861	Catskill	648
Hamilton	5,034	Lake Pleasant	1,721
Herkimer	66,714	Herkimer	1,416
Jefferson	88,151	Watertown	1,273
Kings	2,231,028	Brooklyn	70
Lewis	25,035	Lowville	1,283
Livingston	57,006	Geneseo	633
Madison	65,150	Wampsville	656
Monroe	702,238	Rochester	663
Montgomery	53,439	Fonda	404
Nassau	1,321,582	Mineola	287
New York	1,428,285	New York	22
Niagara	227,354	Lockport	526
Oneida	253,466	Utica	1,219
Onondaga	463,920	Syracuse	784
Ontario	88,909	Canandaigua	644
Orange	259,603	Goshen	826
Orleans	38,496	Albion	391
Oswego	113,901	Oswego	954
Otsego	59,075	Cooperstown	1,004
Putnam	77,193	Carmel	231
Queens	1,891,325	Jamaica	109
Rensselaer	151,966	Troy	655
Richmond	352,029	Saint George	59
Rockland	259,530	New City	175
St. Lawrence	114,347	Canton	2,728
Saratoga	153,759	Ballston Spa	810
Schenectady	149,946	Schenectady	206
Schoharie	29,710	Schoharie	624
Schuyler	17,686	Watkins Glen	329
Seneca	33,733	Ovid & Waterloo	327
Steuben	99,217	Bath	1,396
Suffolk	1,284,231	Riverhead	911
Sullivan	65,155	Monticello	976
Tioga	49,812	Owego	519
Tompkins	87,085	Ithaca	477
Ulster	158,158	Kingston	1,131
Warren	54,854	Lake George	882
Washington	54,795	Hudson Falls	836
Wayne	84,581	Lyons	605
Westchester	866,599	White Plains	438
Wyoming	39,895	Warsaw	595
Yates	21,459	Penn Yan	339

North Carolina

(100 counties, 48,798 sq. mi. land; pop., 5,880,415)

Alamance	99,136	Graham	433
Alexander	24,999	Taylorsville	259
Alleghany	9,587	Sparta	235
Anson	25,562	Wadesboro	533
Ashe	22,325	Jefferson	426
Avery	14,409	Newland	247
Beaufort	40,266	Washington	826
Bertie	21,024	Windsor	701
Bladen	30,448	Elizabethtown	879
Brunswick	35,767	Southport	860
Buncombe	160,934	Asheville	659
Burke	72,504	Morganton	504
Cabarrus	85,895	Concord	364
Caldwell	67,746	Lenoir	471
Camden	5,829	Camden	240
Carteret	41,092	Beaufort	526
Caswell	20,705	Yanceyville	428
Catawba	105,208	Newton	396
Chatham	33,415	Pittsboro	708
Cherokee	18,933	Murphy	452
Chowan	12,558	Edenton	182
Clay	6,619	Hayesville	214
Cleveland	83,435	Shelby	468
Columbus	51,037	Whiteville	938
Craven	71,043	New Bern	701
Cumberland	247,160	Fayetteville	657
Currituck	11,089	Currituck	256
Dare	13,377	Manteo	391
Davidson	113,162	Lexington	548
Davie	24,599	Mocksville	267
Duplin	40,952	Kenansville	819
Durham	152,235	Durham	298
Edgecombe	55,988	Tarboro	506
Forsyth	243,704	Winston-Salem	412
Franklin	30,055	Louisburg	494
Gaston	162,568	Gastonia	357
Gates	8,875	Gatesville	338
Graham	7,217	Robbinsville	289
Granville	33,995	Oxford	534
Greene	16,117	Snow Hill	266

County	Pop.	County seat or court house	Land area sq. mi.
Guilford	317,154	Greensboro	651
Halifax	55,076	Halifax	724
Harnett	59,570	Lillington	601
Haywood	46,495	Waynesville	555
Henderson	58,580	Hendersonville	374
Hertford	23,368	Winton	356
Hoke	20,383	Raeford	391
Hyde	5,873	Swanquarter	624
Iredell	82,538	Statesville	574
Jackson	25,811	Sylva	491
Johnston	70,599	Smithfield	795
Jones	9,705	Trenton	470
Lee	36,718	Sanford	259
Lenoir	59,819	Kinston	402
Lincoln	42,372	Lincolnton	298
McDowell	35,135	Marion	437
Macon	20,178	Franklin	517
Madison	16,827	Marshall	451
Martin	25,948	Williamston	461
Mecklenburg	404,270	Charlotte	528
Mitchell	14,428	Bakersville	222
Montgomery	22,469	Troy	490
Moore	50,505	Carthage	701
Nash	67,153	Nashville	540
New Hanover	103,471	Wilmington	185
Northampton	22,195	Jackson	538
Onslow	112,784	Jacksonville	763
Orange	77,055	Hillsboro	400
Pamlico	10,398	Bayboro	341
Pasquotank	28,462	Elizabeth City	228
Pender	22,262	Burgaw	875
Perquimans	9,486	Hertford	246
Person	29,164	Roxboro	398
Pitt	83,651	Greenville	657
Polk	12,984	Columbus	238
Randolph	91,300	Asheboro	789
Richmond	45,481	Rockingham	477
Robeson	101,577	Lumberton	949
Rockingham	83,426	Wentworth	569
Rowan	99,186	Salisbury	519
Rutherford	53,787	Rutherfordton	568
Sampson	49,687	Clinton	947
Scotland	32,273	Laurinburg	319
Stanly	48,517	Albemarle	396
Stokes	33,086	Danbury	452
Surry	59,449	Dobson	539
Swain	10,283	Bryson City	526
Transylvania	23,417	Brevard	378
Tyrrell	3,975	Columbia	407
Union	70,436	Monroe	639
Vance	36,748	Henderson	249
Wake	301,429	Raleigh	854
Warren	16,232	Warrenton	427
Washington	14,801	Plymouth	332
Watauga	31,678	Boone	314
Wayne	97,054	Goldsboro	554
Wilkes	58,657	Wilkesboro	752
Wilson	63,132	Wilson	374
Yadkin	28,439	Yadkinville	336
Yancey	14,934	Burnsville	314

North Dakota

(53 counties, 69,273 sq. mi. land; pop., 652,717)

County	Pop.	County seat or court house	Land area sq. mi.
Adams	3,584	Hettinger	988
Barnes	13,960	Valley City	1,498
Benson	7,944	Minnewaukan	1,412
Billings	1,138	Medora	1,152
Bottineau	9,338	Bottineau	1,668
Bowman	4,229	Bowman	1,162
Burke	3,822	Bowbells	1,118
Burleigh	54,811	Bismarck	1,618
Cass	88,247	Fargo	1,767
Cavalier	7,636	Langdon	1,507
Dickey	7,207	Ellendale	1,139
Divide	3,494	Crosby	1,288
Dunn	4,627	Manning	1,993
Eddy	3,554	New Rockford	634
Emmons	5,877	Linton	1,499
Foster	4,611	Carrington	640
Golden Valley	2,391	Beach	1,003
Grand Forks	66,100	Grand Forks	1,440
Grant	4,274	Carson	1,660
Griggs	3,714	Cooperstown	708
Hettinger	4,275	Mott	1,133
Kidder	3,833	Steele	1,362
La Moure	6,473	La Moure	1,150
Logan	3,493	Napoleon	1,000
McHenry	7,858	Towner	1,887
McIntosh	4,800	Ashley	984
McKenzie	7,132	Watford City	2,754
McLean	12,288	Washburn	2,065
Mercer	9,378	Stanton	1,044
Morton	25,177	Mandan	1,921
Mountrail	7,679	Stanley	1,837
Nelson	5,233	Lakota	981
Oliver	2,495	Center	723
Pembina	10,399	Cavalier	1,120
Pierce	6,166	Rugby	1,037
Ramsey	13,048	Devils Lake	1,241
Ransom	6,698	Lisbon	862
Renville	3,608	Mohall	874
Richland	19,207	Wahpeton	1,436
Rolette	12,177	Rolla	914
Sargent	5,512	Forman	857
Sheridan	2,819	McClusky	989
Sioux	3,620	Fort Yates	1,099
Slope	1,157	Amidon	1,219
Stark	23,697	Dickinson	1,338
Steele	3,106	Finley	713
Stutsman	24,154	Jamestown	2,263
Towner	4,052	Cando	1,035
Traill	9,624	Hillsboro	861
Walsh	15,371	Grafton	1,290
Ward	58,392	Minot	2,041
Wells	6,979	Fessenden	1,288
Williams	22,237	Williston	2,074

Ohio

(88 counties, 40,975 sq. mi. land; pop., 10,797,603)

County	Pop.	County seat or court house	Land area sq. mi.
Adams	24,328	West Union	586
Allen	112,241	Lima	405
Ashland	46,178	Ashland	424
Ashtabula	104,215	Jefferson	703
Athens	56,399	Athens	508
Auglaize	42,554	Wapakoneta	398
Belmont	82,569	Saint Clairsville	537
Brown	31,920	Georgetown	493
Butler	258,787	Hamilton	470
Carroll	25,598	Carrollton	393
Champaign	33,649	Urbana	429
Clark	150,236	Springfield	398
Clermont	128,483	Batavia	456
Clinton	34,603	Wilmington	410
Columbiana	113,572	Lisbon	534
Coshocton	36,024	Coshocton	566
Crawford	50,075	Bucyrus	403
Cuyahoga	1,498,295	Cleveland	459
Darke	55,096	Greenville	600
Defiance	39,987	Defiance	414
Delaware	53,840	Delaware	443
Erie	79,655	Sandusky	264
Fairfield	93,678	Lancaster	506
Fayette	27,467	Washington C. H.	405
Franklin	869,126	Columbus	543
Fulton	37,751	Wauseon	407
Gallia	30,098	Gallipolis	471
Geauga	74,474	Chardon	408
Greene	129,769	Xenia	416
Guernsey	42,024	Cambridge	522
Hamilton	873,203	Cincinnati	412
Hancock	64,581	Findlay	532
Hardin	32,710	Kenton	471
Harrison	18,152	Cadiz	400
Henry	28,383	Napoleon	415
Highland	33,477	Hillsboro	553
Hocking	24,304	Logan	423
Holmes	29,416	Millersburg	424
Huron	54,608	Norwalk	494
Jackson	30,592	Jackson	420
Jefferson	91,564	Steubenville	410
Knox	46,309	Mount Vernon	529
Lake	212,801	Painesville	231
Lawrence	63,849	Ironton	457
Licking	120,981	Newark	686
Logan	39,155	Bellefontaine	458
Lorain	274,909	Elyria	495
Lucas	471,741	Toledo	341
Madison	33,004	London	467
Mahoning	289,487	Youngstown	417
Marion	67,974	Marion	403
Medina	113,150	Medina	422
Meigs	23,641	Pomeroy	432
Mercer	38,334	Celina	457
Miami	90,381	Troy	410
Monroe	17,382	Woodsfield	457
Montgomery	571,697	Dayton	458
Morgan	14,241	McConnelsville	420
Morrow	26,480	Mount Gilead	406
Muskingum	83,340	Zanesville	654
Noble	11,310	Caldwell	399
Ottawa	40,076	Port Clinton	253
Paulding	21,302	Paulding	419
Perry	31,032	New Lexington	412
Pickaway	43,662	Circleville	503
Pike	22,802	Waverly	443
Portage	135,856	Ravenna	493
Preble	38,223	Eaton	426
Putnam	32,991	Ottawa	484
Richland	131,205	Mansfield	497
Ross	65,004	Chillicothe	692
Sandusky	63,267	Fremont	409
Scioto	84,545	Portsmouth	613
Seneca	61,901	Tiffin	553
Shelby	43,089	Sidney	409
Stark	378,823	Canton	574
Summit	524,472	Akron	412
Trumbull	241,863	Warren	612
Tuscarawas	84,614	New Philadelphia	570

County	Pop.	County seat or court house	Land area sq. mi.
Union	29,536	Marysville	437
Van Wert	30,458	Van Wert	410
Vinton	11,584	McArthur	414
Warren	99,276	Lebanon	403
Washington	64,266	Marietta	640
Wayne	97,408	Wooster	557
Williams	36,369	Bryan	422
Wood	107,372	Bowling Green	619
Wyandot	22,651	Upper Sandusky	406

Oklahoma

(77 counties, 68,782 sq. mi. land; pop., 3,025,487)

County	Pop.	County seat or court house	Land area sq. mi.
Adair	18,575	Stillwell	577
Alfalfa	7,077	Cherokee	864
Atoka	12,748	Atoka	980
Beaver	6,806	Beaver	1,808
Beckham	19,243	Sayre	904
Blaine	13,443	Watonga	920
Bryan	30,535	Durant	902
Caddo	30,905	Anadarko	1,286
Canadian	56,452	El Reno	901
Carter	43,610	Ardmore	828
Cherokee	30,684	Tahlequah	748
Choctaw	17,203	Hugo	762
Cimarron	3,648	Boise City	1,842
Cleveland	133,173	Norman	529
Coal	6,041	Coalgate	520
Comanche	112,456	Lawton	1,076
Cotton	7,338	Walters	656
Craig	15,014	Vinita	763
Creek	59,210	Sapulpa	930
Custer	25,995	Arapaho	981
Delaware	23,946	Jay	720
Dewey	5,922	Taloga	1,007
Ellis	5,596	Arnett	1,232
Garfield	62,820	Enid	1,060
Garvin	27,856	Pauls Valley	813
Grady	39,490	Chickasha	1,106
Grant	6,518	Medford	1,004
Greer	6,877	Mangum	638
Harmon	4,519	Hollis	537
Harper	4,715	Buffalo	1,039
Haskell	11,010	Stigler	570
Hughes	14,338	Holdenville	806
Jackson	30,356	Altus	817
Jefferson	8,294	Waurika	769
Johnston	10,356	Tishomingo	639
Kay	49,852	Newkirk	921
Kingfisher	14,187	Kingfisher	906
Kiowa	12,711	Hobart	1,019
Latimer	9,840	Wilburton	728
Le Flore	40,698	Poteau	1,585
Lincoln	26,601	Chandler	964
Logan	26,881	Guthrie	748
Love	7,469	Marietta	519
McClain	20,291	Purcell	582
McCurtain	36,151	Idabel	1,826
McIntosh	15,495	Eufaula	599
Major	8,772	Fairview	958
Marshall	10,550	Madill	372
Mayes	32,261	Pryor	644
Murray	12,147	Sulphur	420
Muskogee	67,033	Muskogee	815
Noble	11,573	Perry	736
Nowata	11,486	Nowata	540
Okfuskee	11,125	Okemah	628
Oklahoma	568,933	Oklahoma City	708
Okmulgee	39,169	Okmulgee	698
Osage	39,327	Pawhuska	2,265
Ottawa	32,870	Miami	465
Pawnee	15,310	Pawnee	551
Payne	62,435	Stillwater	691
Pittsburg	40,524	McAlester	1,251
Pontotoc	32,598	Ada	717
Pottawatomie	55,239	Shawnee	783
Pushmataha	11,773	Antlers	1,417
Roger Mills	4,799	Cheyenne	1,146
Rogers	46,436	Claremore	683
Seminole	27,465	Wewoka	639
Sequoyah	30,749	Sallisaw	678
Stephens	43,419	Duncan	884
Texas	17,727	Guymon	2,040
Tillman	12,398	Frederick	904
Tulsa	470,593	Tulsa	572
Wagoner	41,801	Wagoner	559
Washington	48,113	Bartlesville	423
Washita	13,798	Cordell	1,006
Woods	10,923	Alva	1,291
Woodward	21,172	Woodward	1,242

Oregon

(36 counties, 96,184 sq. mi. land; pop., 2,633,156)

County	Pop.	County seat or court house	Land area sq. mi.
Baker	16,134	Baker	3,072
Benton	68,211	Corvallis	679
Clackamas	241,911	Oregon City	1,870
Clatsop	32,489	Astoria	805
Columbia	35,646	Saint Helens	651
Coos	64,047	Coquille	1,606
Crook	13,091	Prineville	2,984
Curry	16,992	Gold Beach	1,629
Deschutes	62,142	Bend	3,025
Douglas	93,748	Roseburg	5,044
Gilliam	2,057	Condon	1,213
Grant	8,210	Canyon City	4,525
Harney	8,314	Burns	10,174
Hood River	15,835	Hood River	521
Jackson	132,456	Medford	2,787
Jefferson	11,599	Madras	1,789
Josephine	58,820	Grants Pass	1,640
Klamath	59,117	Klamath Falls	5,954
Lake	7,532	Lakeview	8,251
Lane	275,226	Eugene	4,562
Lincoln	35,264	Newport	980
Linn	89,495	Albany	2,296
Malheur	26,896	Vale	9,861
Marion	204,692	Salem	1,184
Morrow	7,519	Heppner	2,044
Multnomah	562,647	Portland	431
Polk	45,203	Dallas	741
Sherman	2,172	Moro	827
Tillamook	21,164	Tillamook	1,101
Umatilla	58,861	Pendleton	3,218
Union	23,921	La Grande	2,035
Wallowa	7,273	Enterprise	3,150
Wasco	21,732	The Dalles	2,384
Washington	245,860	Hillsboro	725
Wheeler	1,513	Fossil	1,713
Yamhill	55,332	McMinnville	715

Pennsylvania

(67 counties, 44,966 sq. mi. land; pop., 11,864,720)

County	Pop.	County seat or court house	Land area sq. mi.
Adams	68,292	Gettysburg	521
Allegheny	1,450,195	Pittsburgh	727
Armstrong	77,768	Kittanning	646
Beaver	204,441	Beaver	436
Bedford	46,784	Bedford	1,017
Berks	312,509	Reading	861
Blair	136,621	Hollidaysburg	527
Bradford	62,919	Towanda	1,152
Bucks	479,180	Doylestown	610
Butler	147,912	Butler	789
Cambria	183,263	Ebensburg	691
Cameron	6,674	Emporium	398
Carbon	53,285	Jim Thorpe	384
Centre	112,760	Bellefonte	1,106
Chester	316,660	West Chester	758
Clarion	43,362	Clarion	607
Clearfield	83,578	Clearfield	1,149
Clinton	38,971	Lock Haven	891
Columbia	61,967	Bloomsburg	486
Crawford	88,869	Meadville	1,011
Cumberland	179,625	Carlisle	547
Dauphin	232,317	Harrisburg	528
Delaware	555,029	Media	184
Elk	38,338	Ridgeway	830
Erie	279,780	Erie	804
Fayette	160,395	Uniontown	794
Forest	5,072	Tionesta	428
Franklin	113,629	Chambersburg	774
Fulton	12,842	McConnellsburg	438
Greene	40,355	Waynesburg	577
Huntingdon	42,253	Huntingdon	877
Indiana	92,281	Indiana	829
Jefferson	48,303	Brookville	657
Juniata	19,188	Mifflintown	392
Lackawanna	227,908	Scranton	461
Lancaster	362,346	Lancaster	952
Lawrence	107,150	New Castle	363
Lebanon	109,829	Lebanon	363
Lehigh	273,582	Allentown	348
Luzerne	343,079	Wilkes-Barre	891
Lycoming	118,416	Williamsport	1,237
McKean	50,635	Smethport	979
Mercer	128,299	Mercer	672
Mifflin	46,908	Lewistown	413
Monroe	69,409	Stroudsburg	609
Montgomery	643,371	Norristown	486
Montour	16,675	Danville	131
Northampton	225,418	Easton	376
Northumberland	100,381	Sunbury	461
Perry	35,718	New Bloomfield	557
Philadelphia	1,688,210	Philadelphia	136
Pike	18,271	Milford	550
Potter	17,726	Coudersport	1,081
Schuylkill	160,630	Pottsville	782
Snyder	33,584	Middleburg	329
Somerset	81,243	Somerset	1,073
Sullivan	6,349	Laporte	451
Susquehanna	37,876	Montrose	826
Tioga	40,973	Wellsboro	1,131
Union	32,870	Lewisburg	317
Venango	64,444	Franklin	679
Warren	47,449	Warren	885
Washington	217,074	Washington	958
Wayne	35,237	Honesdale	731
Westmoreland	392,184	Greensburg	1,033
Wyoming	26,433	Tunkhannock	399
York	312,963	York	906

Rhode Island

(5 counties, 1,049 sq. mi. land; pop., 947,154)

County	Pop.	County seat or court house	Land area sq. mi.
Bristol	46,942	Bristol	26
Kent	154,163	East Greenwich	172
Newport	81,383	Newport	107
Providence	571,349	Providence	416
Washington	93,317	West Kingston	333

South Carolina

(46 counties, 30,225 sq. mi. land; pop., 3,120,730)

County	Pop.	County seat or court house	Land area sq. mi.
Abbeville	22,627	Abbeville	508
Aiken	105,630	Aiken	1,092
Allendale	10,700	Allendale	413
Anderson	133,235	Anderson	718
Bamberg	18,118	Bamberg	395
Barnwell	19,868	Barnwell	558
Beaufort	65,364	Beaufort	579
Berkeley	94,745	Moncks Corner	1,108
Calhoun	12,206	Saint Matthews	380
Charleston	276,573	Charleston	938
Cherokee	40,983	Gaffney	396
Chester	30,148	Chester	580
Chesterfield	38,161	Chesterfield	802
Clarendon	27,464	Manning	602
Colleton	31,676	Walterboro	1,052
Darlington	62,717	Darlington	563
Dillon	31,083	Dillon	406
Dorchester	59,028	Saint George	575
Edgefield	17,528	Edgefield	490
Fairfield	20,700	Winnsboro	685
Florence	110,163	Florence	804
Georgetown	42,461	Georgetown	822
Greenville	287,895	Greenville	795
Greenwood	55,860	Greenwood	451
Hampton	18,159	Hampton	561
Horry	101,419	Conway	1,143
Jasper	14,504	Ridgeland	655
Kershaw	39,015	Camden	723
Lancaster	53,361	Lancaster	552
Laurens	52,214	Laurens	712
Lee	18,929	Bishopville	411
Lexington	140,353	Lexington	707
McCormick	7,797	McCormick	350
Marion	34,179	Marion	493
Marlboro	31,634	Bennettsville	483
Newberry	31,111	Newberry	634
Oconee	48,611	Walhalla	629
Orangeburg	82,276	Orangeburg	1,111
Pickens	79,292	Pickens	499
Richland	269,600	Columbia	762
Saluda	16,136	Saluda	456
Spartanburg	203,023	Spartanburg	814
Sumter	88,243	Sumter	665
Union	30,764	Union	515
Williamsburg	38,226	Kingstree	934
York	106,720	York	[illegible]

South Dakota

(67 counties, 75,955 sq. mi. land; pop., 690,768)

County	Pop.	County seat or court house	Land area sq. mi.
Aurora	3,628	Plankinton	707
Beadle	19,195	Huron	1,259
Bennett	3,236	Martin	1,182
Bon Homme	8,059	Tyndall	552
Brookings	24,332	Brookings	795
Brown	36,962	Aberdeen	1,722
Brule	5,245	Chamberlain	815
Buffalo	1,795	Gannvalley	475
Butte	8,372	Belle Fourche	2,251
Campbell	2,243	Mound City	732
Charles Mix	9,680	Lake Andes	1,090
Clark	4,894	Clark	953
Clay	13,135	Vermillion	409
Codington	20,885	Watertown	694
Corson	5,196	McIntosh	2,467
Custer	6,000	Custer	1,559
Davison	17,820	Mitchell	436
Day	8,133	Webster	1,022
Deuel	5,289	Clear Lake	631
Dewey	5,366	Timber Lake	2,310
Douglas	4,181	Armour	434
Edmunds	5,159	Ipswich	1,149
Fall River	8,439	Hot Springs	1,740
Faulk	3,327	Faulkton	1,004
Grant	9,013	Milbank	681
Gregory	6,015	Burke	1,013
Haakon	2,794	Philip	1,822
Hamlin	5,261	Hayti	512
Hand	4,948	Miller	1,437
Hanson	3,415	Alexandria	433
Harding	1,700	Buffalo	2,678
Hughes	14,220	Pierre	757
Hutchinson	9,350	Olivet	816
Hyde	2,069	Highmore	860
Jackson	3,437	Kadoka	1,872
Jerauld	2,929	Wessington Spgs.	530
Jones	1,463	Murdo	971
Kingsbury	6,679	De Smet	824
Lake	10,724	Madison	560
Lawrence	18,339	Deadwood	800
Lincoln	13,942	Canton	578
Lyman	3,864	Kennebec	1,679
McCook	6,444	Salem	576
McPherson	4,027	Leola	1,148
Marshall	5,404	Britton	848
Meade	20,717	Sturgis	3,481
Mellette	2,249	White River	1,311
Miner	3,739	Howard	570
Minnehaha	109,435	Sioux Falls	810
Moody	6,692	Flandreau	520
Pennington	70,133	Rapid City	2,783
Perkins	4,700	Bison	2,884
Potter	3,674	Gettysburg	869
Roberts	10,911	Sisseton	1,102
Sanborn	3,213	Woonsocket	569
Shannon	11,323	(Attached to Fall River)	2,094
Spink	9,201	Redfield	1,505
Stanley	2,533	Fort Pierre	1,431
Sully	1,990	Onida	972
Todd	7,328	(Attached to Tripp)	1,388
Tripp	7,268	Winner	1,618
Turner	9,255	Parker	617
Union	10,938	Elk Point	453
Walworth	7,011	Selby	707
Washabaugh	—	(Attached to Jackson)	—
Yankton	18,952	Yankton	518
Ziebach	2,308	Dupree	1,969

Tennessee

(95 counties, 41,328 sq. mi. land; pop., 4,591,023)

County	Pop.	County seat or court house	Land area sq. mi.
Anderson	67,346	Clinton	339
Bedford	27,916	Shelbyville	475
Benton	14,901	Camden	392
Bledsoe	9,478	Pikeville	407
Blount	77,770	Maryville	558
Bradley	67,547	Cleveland	327
Campbell	34,841	Jacksboro	479
Cannon	10,234	Woodbury	266
Carroll	28,285	Huntingdon	600
Carter	50,205	Elizabethton	341
Cheatham	21,616	Ashland City	304
Chester	12,727	Henderson	289
Claiborne	24,595	Tazewell	432
Clay	7,676	Celina	227
Cocke	28,792	Newport	432
Coffee	38,311	Manchester	428
Crockett	14,941	Alamo	266
Cumberland	28,676	Crossville	682
Davidson	477,811	Nashville	501
Decatur	10,857	Decaturville	330
De Kalb	13,589	Smithville	291
Dickson	30,037	Charlotte	491
Dyer	34,663	Dyersburg	520
Fayette	25,305	Somerville	705
Fentress	14,826	Jamestown	498
Franklin	31,983	Winchester	543
Gibson	49,467	Trenton	602
Giles	[illegible]	Pulaski	610
Grainger	16,751	Rutledge	273
Greene	54,406	Greeneville	619
Grundy	13,787	Altamont	361
Hamblen	49,000	Morristown	156
Hamilton	287,643	Chattanooga	539
Hancock	6,887	Sneedville	223
Hardeman	23,873	Bolivar	670
Hardin	22,280	Savannah	578
Hawkins	43,751	Rogersville	486
Haywood	20,318	Brownsville	534
Henderson	21,390	Lexington	520
Henry	28,656	Paris	560
Hickman	15,151	Centerville	610
Houston	6,871	Erin	200
Humphreys	15,957	Waverly	528
Jackson	9,398	Gainesboro	308
Jefferson	31,284	Dandridge	265
Johnson	13,745	Mountain City	297
Knox	319,694	Knoxville	506
Lake	7,455	Tiptonville	169
Lauderdale	24,555	Ripley	474
Lawrence	34,110	Lawrenceburg	617
Lewis	9,700	Hohenwald	282
Lincoln	26,483	Fayetteville	571
Loudon	28,553	Loudon	235
McMinn	41,878	Athens	429
McNairy	22,525	Selmer	562
Macon	15,700	Lafayette	307
Madison	74,546	Jackson	558
Marion	24,416	Jasper	512
Marshall	19,698	Lewisburg	376
Maury	51,095	Columbia	616
Meigs	7,431	Decatur	189
Monroe	28,700	Madisonville	648
Montgomery	83,342	Clarksville	539
Moore	4,510	Lynchburg	129
Morgan	16,604	Wartburg	523
Obion	32,781	Union City	550
Overton	17,575	Livingston	433
Perry	6,111	Linden	412
Pickett	4,358	Byrdstown	159

County	Pop.	County seat or court house	Land area sq. mi.
Polk	13,602	Benton	438
Putnam	47,601	Cookeville	399
Rhea	24,235	Dayton	309
Roane	48,425	Kingston	357
Robertson	37,021	Springfield	476
Rutherford	84,058	Murfreesboro	606
Scott	19,259	Huntsville	528
Sequatchie	8,605	Dunlap	266
Sevier	41,418	Sevierville	590
Shelby	777,113	Memphis	772
Smith	14,935	Carthage	313
Stewart	8,665	Dover	454
Sullivan	143,968	Blountville	415
Sumner	85,790	Gallatin	529
Tipton	32,747	Covington	454
Trousdale	6,137	Hartsville	114
Unicoi	16,362	Erwin	186
Union	11,707	Maynardville	218
Van Buren	4,728	Spencer	273
Warren	32,653	McMinnville	431
Washington	88,755	Jonesboro	326
Wayne	13,946	Waynesboro	734
Weakley	32,896	Dresden	581
White	19,567	Sparta	373
Williamson	58,108	Franklin	584
Wilson	56,064	Lebanon	570

Texas

(254 counties, 262,134 sq. mi. land; pop., 14,225,513)

County	Pop.	County seat or court house	Land area sq. mi.
Anderson	38,381	Palestine	1,077
Andrews	13,323	Andrews	1,501
Angelina	64,172	Lufkin	807
Aransas	14,260	Rockport	280
Archer	7,266	Archer City	907
Armstrong	1,994	Claude	909
Atascosa	25,055	Jourdanton	1,218
Austin	17,726	Bellville	656
Bailey	8,168	Muleshoe	826
Bandera	7,084	Bandera	793
Bastrop	24,726	Bastrop	895
Baylor	4,919	Seymour	862
Bee	26,030	Beeville	880
Bell	157,820	Belton	1,055
Bexar	988,971	San Antonio	1,248
Blanco	4,681	Johnson City	714
Borden	859	Gail	900
Bosque	13,401	Meridian	989
Bowie	75,301	Boston	891
Brazoria	169,587	Angleton	1,407
Brazos	93,588	Bryan	589
Brewster	7,573	Alpine	6,169
Briscoe	2,579	Silverton	887
Brooks	8,428	Falfurrias	942
Brown	33,057	Brownwood	936
Burleson	12,313	Caldwell	669
Burnet	17,803	Burnet	994
Caldwell	23,637	Lockhart	546
Calhoun	19,574	Port Lavaca	540
Callahan	10,992	Baird	899
Cameron	209,680	Brownsville	906
Camp	9,275	Pittsburg	203
Carson	6,672	Panhandle	924
Cass	29,430	Linden	937
Castro	10,556	Dimmitt	899
Chambers	18,538	Anahuac	616
Cherokee	38,127	Rusk	1,052
Childress	6,950	Childress	707
Clay	9,582	Henrietta	1,086
Cochran	4,825	Morton	775
Coke	3,196	Robert Lee	908
Coleman	10,439	Coleman	1,277
Collin	144,490	McKinney	851
Collingsworth	4,648	Wellington	909
Colorado	18,823	Columbus	965
Comal	36,446	New Braunfels	555
Comanche	12,617	Comanche	930
Concho	2,915	Paint Rock	992
Cooke	27,656	Gainesville	893
Coryell	56,767	Gatesville	1,057
Cottle	2,947	Paducah	895
Crane	4,600	Crane	782
Crockett	4,608	Ozona	2,806
Crosby	8,859	Crosbyton	899
Culberson	3,315	Van Horn	3,815
Dallam	6,531	Dalhart	1,505
Dallas	1,556,419	Dallas	880
Dawson	16,184	Lamesa	903
Deaf Smith	21,165	Hereford	1,497
Delta	4,839	Cooper	278
Denton	143,126	Denton	911
Dewitt	18,903	Cuero	910
Dickens	3,539	Dickens	907
Dimmit	11,367	Carrizo Springs	1,307
Donley	4,075	Clarendon	929
Duval	12,517	San Diego	1,795
Eastland	19,480	Eastland	924
Ector	115,374	Odessa	903
Edwards	2,033	Rocksprings	2,121
Ellis	59,743	Waxahachie	939
El Paso	479,899	El Paso	1,014
Erath	22,560	Stephenville	1,080
Falls	17,946	Marlin	770
Fannin	24,285	Bonham	895
Fayette	18,832	La Grange	950
Fisher	5,891	Roby	897
Floyd	9,834	Floydada	992
Foard	2,158	Crowell	703
Fort Bend	130,962	Richmond	876
Franklin	6,893	Mount Vernon	294
Freestone	14,830	Fairfield	888
Frio	13,785	Pearsall	1,133
Gaines	13,150	Seminole	1,504
Galveston	195,738	Galveston	399
Garza	5,336	Post	895
Gillespie	13,532	Fredericksburg	1,061
Glasscock	1,304	Garden City	900
Goliad	5,193	Goliad	859
Gonzales	16,949	Gonzales	1,068
Gray	26,386	Pampa	921
Grayson	89,796	Sherman	934
Gregg	99,495	Longview	273
Grimes	13,580	Anderson	799
Guadalupe	46,708	Seguin	713
Hale	37,592	Plainview	1,005
Hall	5,594	Memphis	877
Hamilton	8,297	Hamilton	836
Hansford	6,209	Spearman	921
Hardeman	6,368	Quanah	688
Hardin	40,721	Kountze	898
Harris	2,409,544	Houston	1,734
Harrison	52,265	Marshall	908
Hartley	3,987	Channing	1,462
Haskell	7,725	Haskell	901
Hays	40,594	San Marcos	678
Hemphill	5,304	Canadian	903
Henderson	42,606	Athens	888
Hidalgo	283,323	Edinburg	1,569
Hill	25,024	Hillsboro	968
Hockley	23,230	Levelland	908
Hood	17,714	Granbury	425
Hopkins	25,247	Sulphur Springs	789
Houston	22,299	Crockett	1,234
Howard	33,142	Big Spring	901
Hudspeth	2,728	Sierra Blanca	4,567
Hunt	55,248	Greenville	840
Hutchinson	26,304	Stinnett	872
Irion	1,386	Mertzon	1,052
Jack	7,408	Jacksboro	920
Jackson	13,352	Edna	844
Jasper	30,781	Jasper	921
Jeff Davis	1,647	Fort Davis	2,257
Jefferson	248,652	Beaumont	937
Jim Hogg	5,168	Hebbronville	1,136
Jim Wells	36,498	Alice	867
Johnson	67,649	Cleburne	730
Jones	17,268	Anson	931
Karnes	13,593	Karnes City	753
Kaufman	39,038	Kaufman	788
Kendall	10,635	Boerne	663
Kenedy	543	Sarita	1,389
Kent	1,145	Jayton	878
Kerr	28,780	Kerrville	1,107
Kimble	4,063	Junction	1,250
King	425	Guthrie	914
Kinney	2,279	Brackettville	1,359
Kleberg	33,358	Kingsville	853
Knox	5,329	Benjamin	845
Lamar	42,156	Paris	919
Lamb	18,669	Littlefield	1,013
Lampasas	12,005	Lampasas	714
La Salle	5,514	Cotulla	1,517
Lavaca	19,004	Hallettsville	971
Lee	10,952	Giddings	631
Leon	9,594	Centerville	1,079
Liberty	47,088	Liberty	1,174
Limestone	20,224	Groesbeck	930
Lipscomb	3,766	Lipscomb	933
Live Oak	9,606	George West	1,057
Llano	10,144	Llano	939
Loving	91	Mentone	670
Lubbock	211,651	Lubbock	900
Lynn	8,605	Tahoka	888
McCulloch	8,735	Brady	1,071
McLennan	170,755	Waco	1,031
McMullen	789	Tilden	1,163
Madison	10,649	Madisonville	472
Marion	10,360	Jefferson	385
Martin	4,684	Staton	914
Mason	3,683	Mason	934
Matagorda	37,828	Bay City	1,127
Maverick	31,398	Eagle Pass	1,287
Medina	23,164	Hondo	1,331
Menard	2,346	Menard	902
Midland	82,636	Midland	902
Milam	22,732	Cameron	1,019
Mills	4,477	Goldthwaite	748
Mitchell	9,088	Colorado City	912
Montague	17,410	Montague	928
Montgomery	127,222	Conroe	1,047

County	Pop.	County seat or court house	Land area sq. mi.
Moore	16,575	Dumas	905
Morris	14,629	Daingerfield	256
Motley	1,950	Matador	959
Nacogdoches	46,786	Nacogdoches	939
Navarro	35,323	Corsicana	1,068
Newton	13,254	Newton	935
Nolan	17,359	Sweetwater	915
Nueces	268,215	Corpus Christi	847
Ochiltree	9,588	Perryton	919
Oldham	2,283	Vega	1,485
Orange	83,838	Orange	362
Palo Pinto	24,062	Palo Pinto	949
Panola	20,724	Carthage	812
Parker	44,609	Weatherford	902
Parmer	11,038	Farwell	885
Pecos	14,618	Fort Stockton	4,777
Polk	24,407	Livingston	1,061
Potter	98,637	Amarillo	902
Presidio	5,188	Marfa	3,857
Rains	4,839	Emory	243
Randall	75,062	Canyon	917
Reagan	4,135	Big Lake	1,173
Real	2,469	Leakey	697
Red River	16,101	Clarksville	1,054
Reeves	15,801	Pecos	2,626
Refugio	9,289	Refugio	771
Roberts	1,187	Miami	915
Robertson	14,653	Franklin	864
Rockwall	14,528	Rockwall	128
Runnels	11,872	Ballinger	1,056
Rusk	41,382	Henderson	932
Sabine	8,702	Hemphill	486
San Augustine	8,785	San Augustine	524
San Jacinto	11,434	Coldspring	572
San Patricio	58,013	Sinton	693
San Saba	5,841	San Saba	1,136
Schleicher	2,820	Eldorado	1,309
Scurry	18,192	Snyder	900
Shackelford	3,915	Albany	915
Shelby	23,084	Center	791
Sherman	3,174	Stratford	923
Smith	128,366	Tyler	932
Somervell	4,154	Glen Rose	188
Starr	27,266	Rio Grande City	1,226
Stephens	9,926	Breckenridge	894
Sterling	1,206	Sterling City	923
Stonewall	2,406	Aspermont	925
Sutton	5,130	Sonora	1,455
Swisher	9,723	Tulia	902
Tarrant	860,880	Fort Worth	868
Taylor	110,932	Abilene	917
Terrell	1,595	Sanderson	2,357
Terry	14,581	Brownfield	887
Throckmorton	2,053	Throckmorton	912
Titus	21,442	Mount Pleasant	412
Tom Green	84,784	San Angelo	1,515
Travis	419,335	Austin	989
Trinity	9,450	Groveton	692
Tyler	16,223	Woodville	922
Upshur	28,595	Gilmer	587
Upton	4,619	Rankin	1,243
Uvalde	22,441	Uvalde	1,564
Val Verde	35,910	Del Rio	3,150
Van Zandt	31,426	Canton	855
Victoria	68,807	Victoria	887
Walker	41,789	Huntsville	786
Waller	19,798	Hempstead	514
Ward	13,976	Monahans	836
Washington	21,998	Brenham	610
Webb	99,258	Laredo	3,362
Wharton	40,242	Wharton	1,086
Wheeler	7,137	Wheeler	904
Wichita	121,082	Wichita Falls	606
Wilbarger	15,931	Vernon	947
Willacy	17,495	Raymondville	589
Williamson	76,521	Georgetown	1,137
Wilson	16,756	Floresville	807
Winkler	9,944	Kermit	840
Wise	26,525	Decatur	902
Wood	24,697	Quitman	689
Yoakum	8,299	Plains	800
Young	19,001	Graham	919
Zapata	6,628	Zapata	999
Zavala	11,666	Crystal City	1,298

Utah

(29 counties, 82,096 sq. mi. land; pop. 1,461,037

Beaver	4,378	Beaver	2,586
Box Elder	33,222	Brigham City	5,614
Cache	57,176	Logan	1,171
Carbon	22,179	Price	1,479
Daggett	769	Manila	699
Davis	146,540	Farmington	299
Duchesne	12,565	Duchesne	3,233
Emery	11,451	Castle Dale	4,449
Garfield	3,673	Panguitch	5,148
Grand	8,241	Moab	3,689
Iron	17,349	Parowan	3,301
Juab	5,530	Nephi	3,396
Kane	4,024	Kanab	3,898
Millard	8,970	Fillmore	6,818
Morgan	4,917	Morgan	603
Piute	1,329	Junction	759
Rich	2,100	Randolph	1,034
Salt Lake	619,066	Salt Lake City	756
San Juan	12,253	Monticello	7,725
Sanpete	14,620	Manti	1,587
Sevier	14,727	Richfield	1,910
Summit	10,198	Coalville	1,865
Tooele	26,033	Tooele	6,919
Uintah	20,506	Vernal	4,479
Utah	218,106	Provo	2,018
Wasatch	8,523	Heber City	1,191
Washington	26,065	Saint George	2,422
Wayne	1,911	Loa	2,461
Weber	144,616	Ogden	566

Vermont

(14 counties, 9,267 sq. mi. land; pop. 511,456)

Addison	29,406	Middlebury	773
Bennington	33,345	Bennington	677
Caledonia	25,808	Saint Johnsbury	651
Chittenden	115,534	Burlington	540
Essex	6,313	Guildhall	666
Franklin	34,788	Saint Albans	649
Grand Isle	4,613	North Hero	89
Lamoille	16,767	Hyde Park	461
Orange	22,739	Chelsea	690
Orleans	23,440	Newport	697
Rutland	58,347	Rutland	932
Washington	52,393	Montpelier	690
Windham	36,933	Newfane	787
Windsor	51,030	Woodstock	972

Virginia

(95 cos., 41 ind. cities, 39,780 sq. mi. land; pop. 5,346,797)

Accomack	31,268	Accomac	476
Albemarle	50,689	Charlottesville	725
Alleghany	14,333	Covington	446
Amelia	8,405	Amelia, C.H.	357
Amherst	29,122	Amherst	479
Appomattox	11,971	Appomattox	336
Arlington	152,599	Arlington	26
Augusta	53,732	Staunton	989
Bath	5,860	Warm Springs	538
Bedford	34,927	Bedford	747
Bland	6,349	Bland	359
Botetourt	23,270	Fincastle	545
Brunswick	15,632	Lawrenceville	563
Buchanan	37,989	Grundy	504
Buckingham	11,751	Buckingham	583
Campbell	45,424	Rustburg	505
Caroline	17,904	Bowling Green	535
Carroll	27,270	Hillsville	478
Charles City	6,692	Charles City	181
Charlotte	12,266	Charlotte Courthouse	477
Chesterfield	141,372	Chesterfield	434
Clarke	9,965	Berryville	178
Craig	3,948	New Castle	330
Culpeper	22,620	Culpeper	382
Cumberland	7,881	Cumberland	300
Dickenson	19,806	Clintwood	331
Dinwiddie	22,602	Dinwiddie	507
Essex	8,864	Tappahannock	263
Fairfax	596,901	Fairfax	394
Fauquier	35,889	Warrenton	651
Floyd	11,563	Floyd	381
Fluvanna	10,244	Palmyra	290
Franklin	35,740	Rocky Mount	683
Frederick	34,150	Winchester	415
Giles	17,810	Pearisburg	362
Gloucester	20,107	Gloucester	225
Goochland	11,761	Goochland	281
Grayson	16,579	Independence	446
Greene	7,625	Stanardsville	157
Greensville	10,903	Emporia	300
Halifax	30,418	Halifax	816
Hanover	50,398	Hanover	467
Henrico	180,735	Richmond	238
Henry	57,654	Martinsville	382
Highland	2,937	Monterey	416
Isle of Wight	21,603	Isle of Wight	319
James City	22,763	Williamsburg	153
King and Queen	5,968	King and Queen	317
King George	10,543	King George	180
King William	9,327	King William	278
Lancaster	10,129	Lancaster	133
Lee	25,956	Jonesville	437
Loudoun	57,427	Leesburg	521
Louisa	17,825	Louisa	497
Lunenburg	12,124	Lunenburg	432
Madison	10,232	Madison	322
Mathews	7,995	Mathews	87
Mecklenburg	29,444	Boydton	616
Middlesex	7,719	Saluda	134
Montgomery	63,516	Christiansburg	390
Nelson	12,204	Lovingston	474
New Kent	8,781	New Kent	213

County	Pop.	County seat or court house	Land area sq. mi.
Northampton	14,625	Eastville	226
Northumberland	9,828	Heathsville	185
Nottoway	14,666	Nottoway	316
Orange	17,827	Orange	342
Page	19,401	Luray	313
Patrick	17,585	Stuart	481
Pittsylvania	66,147	Chatham	995
Powhatan	13,062	Powhatan	261
Prince Edward	16,456	Farmville	354
Prince George	25,733	Prince George	266
Prince William	144,703	Manassas	339
Pulaski	35,229	Pulaski	318
Rappahannock	6,093	Washington	267
Richmond	6,952	Warsaw	193
Roanoke	72,945	Salem	251
Rockbridge	17,911	Lexington	603
Rockingham	57,038	Harrisonburg	865
Russell	31,761	Lebanon	479
Scott	25,068	Gate City	535
Shenandoah	27,559	Woodstock	512
Smyth	33,345	Marion	452
Southampton	18,731	Courtland	603
Spotsylvania	34,435	Spotsylvania	404
Stafford	40,470	Stafford	271
Surry	6,046	Surry	281
Sussex	10,874	Sussex	491
Tazewell	50,511	Tazewell	520
Warren	21,200	Front Royal	217
Washington	46,487	Abingdon	562
Westmoreland	14,041	Montross	227
Wise	43,863	Wise	405
Wythe	25,522	Wytheville	465
York	35,463	Yorktown	113
Independent cities			
Alexandria	103,217		15
Bedford	5,991		7
Bristol	19,042		12
Buena Vista	6,717		3
Charlottesville	45,010		10
Chesapeake	114,226		340
Clifton Forge	5,046		3
Colonial Heights	16,509		8
Covington	9,063		4
Danville	45,642		17
Emporia	4,840		2
Fairfax	19,390		6
Falls Church	9,515		2
I,1 Franklin	7,308		4
Fredericksburg	15,322		6
Galax	6,524		8
Hampton	122,617		51
Harrisonburg	19,671		6
Hopewell	23,397		10
Lexington	7,292		2
Lynchburg	66,743		50
Manassas	15,438		8
Manassas Park	6,524		2
Martinsville	18,149		11
Newport News	144,903		65
Norfolk	266,979		53
Norton	4,757		7
Petersburg	41,055		23
Poquoson	8,726		17
Portsmouth	104,577		30
Radford	13,225		7
Richmond	219,214		60
Roanoke	100,427		43
Salem	23,958		14
South Boston	7,093		6
Staunton	21,857		9
Suffolk	47,621		409
Virginia Beach	262,199		256
Waynesboro	15,329		8
Williamsburg	9,870		5
Winchester	20,217		9

Washington

(39 counties, 66,570 sq. mi. land; pop., 4,132,353)

Adams	13,267	Ritzville	1,921
Asotin	16,823	Asotin	635
Benton	109,444	Prosser	1,715
Chelan	45,061	Wenatchee	2,916
Clallam	51,648	Port Angeles	1,753
Clark	192,227	Vancouver	627
Columbia	4,057	Dayton	865
Cowlitz	79,548	Kelso	1,140
Douglas	22,144	Waterville	1,817
Ferry	5,811	Republic	2,200
Franklin	35,025	Pasco	1,243
Garfield	2,468	Pomeroy	706
Grant	48,522	Ephrata	2,660
Grays Harbor	66,314	Montesano	1,918
Island	44,048	Coupeville	212
Jefferson	15,965	Port Townsend	1,805
King	1,269,898	Seattle	2,128
Kitsap	146,609	Port Orchard	393
Kittitas	24,877	Ellensburg	2,308
Klickitat	15,822	Goldendale	1,880
Lewis	55,279	Chehalis	2,409
Lincoln	9,604	Davenport	2,310
Mason	31,184	Shelton	961
Okanogan	30,663	Okanogan	5,281
Pacific	17,237	South Bend	908
Pend Oreille	8,580	Newport	1,400
Pierce	485,667	Tacoma	1,675
San Juan	7,838	Friday Harbor	179
Skagit	64,138	Mount Vernon	1,735
Skamania	7,919	Stevenson	1,672
Snohomish	337,016	Everett	2,098
Spokane	341,835	Spokane	1,762
Stevens	28,979	Colville	2,470
Thurston	124,264	Olympia	727
Wahkiakum	3,832	Cathlamet	261
Walla Walla	47,435	Walla Walla	1,261
Whatcom	106,701	Bellingham	2,125
Whitman	40,103	Colfax	2,151
Yakima	172,508	Yakima	4,287

West Virginia

(55 counties, 24,070 sq. mi. land; pop., 1,950,186)

Barbour	16,639	Philippi	343
Berkeley	46,775	Martinsburg	321
Boone	30,447	Madison	503
Braxton	13,894	Sutton	513
Brooke	31,117	Wellsburg	90
Cabell	106,835	Huntington	282
Calhoun	8,250	Grantsville	280
Clay	11,265	Clay	346
Doddridge	7,433	West Union	321
Fayette	57,863	Fayetteville	667
Gilmer	8,334	Glenville	340
Grant	10,210	Petersburg	480
Greenbrier	37,665	Lewisburg	1,025
Hampshire	14,867	Romney	644
Hancock	41,053	New Cumberland	84
Hardy	10,030	Moorefield	585
Harrison	77,710	Clarksburg	417
Jackson	25,794	Ripley	464
Jefferson	30,302	Charles Town	209
Kanawha	231,414	Charleston	901
Lewis	18,813	Weston	389
Lincoln	23,675	Hamlin	439
Logan	50,679	Logan	456
McDowell	49,899	Welch	535
Marion	65,789	Fairmont	312
Marshall	41,608	Moundsville	305
Mason	27,045	Point Pleasant	433
Mercer	73,870	Princeton	420
Mineral	27,234	Keyser	329
Mingo	37,336	Williamson	424
Monongalia	75,024	Morgantown	363
Monroe	12,873	Union	473
Morgan	10,711	Berkeley Springs	230
Nicholas	28,126	Summersville	650
Ohio	61,389	Wheeling	106
Pendleton	7,910	Franklin	698
Pleasants	8,236	St. Marys	131
Pocahontas	9,919	Marlinton	942
Preston	30,460	Kingwood	651
Putnam	38,181	Winfield	346
Raleigh	86,821	Beckley	608
Randolph	28,734	Elkins	1,040
Ritchie	11,442	Harrisville	454
Roane	15,952	Spencer	484
Summers	15,875	Hinton	353
Taylor	16,584	Grafton	174
Tucker	8,675	Parsons	421
Tyler	11,320	Middlebourne	258
Upshur	23,427	Buckhannon	355
Wayne	46,021	Wayne	508
Webster	12,245	Webster Springs	556
Wetzel	21,874	New Martinsville	359
Wirt	4,922	Elizabeth	235
Wood	93,627	Parkersburg	367
Wyoming	35,993	Pineville	502

Wisconsin

(72 counties, 54,464 sq. mi. land; pop., 4,705,642)

Adams	13,457	Friendship	648
Ashland	16,783	Ashland	1,048
Barron	38,730	Barron	865
Bayfield	13,822	Washburn	1,462
Brown	175,280	Green Bay	524
Buffalo	14,309	Alma	699
Burnett	12,340	Grantsburg	818
Calumet	30,867	Chilton	326
Chippewa	51,702	Chippewa Falls	1,017
Clark	32,910	Neillsville	1,218
Columbia	43,222	Portage	771
Crawford	16,556	Prairie du Chien	566
Dane	323,545	Madison	1,205
Dodge	74,747	Juneau	887
Door	25,029	Sturgeon Bay	492
Douglas	44,421	Superior	1,305
Dunn	34,314	Menomonie	853
Eau Claire	78,805	Eau Claire	638
Florence	4,172	Florence	486

County	Pop.	County seat or court house	Land area sq. mi.
Fond Du Lac	88,952	Fond du Lac	725
Forest	9,044	Crandon	1,011
Grant	51,736	Lancaster	1,144
Green	30,012	Monroe	583
Green Lake	18,370	Green Lake	357
Iowa	19,802	Dodgeville	760
Iron	6,730	Hurley	751
Jackson	16,831	Black River Falls	998
Jefferson	66,152	Jefferson	562
Juneau	21,037	Mauston	774
Kenosha	123,137	Kenosha	273
Kewaunee	19,539	Kewaunee	343
La Crosse	91,056	La Crosse	457
Lafayette	17,412	Darlington	634
Langlade	19,978	Antigo	873
Lincoln	26,311	Merrill	886
Manitowoc	82,918	Manitowoc	594
Marathon	111,270	Wausau	1,559
Marinette	39,314	Marinette	1,395
Marquette	11,672	Montello	455
Menominee	3,373	Keshena	359
Milwaukee	964,988	Milwaukee	241
Monroe	35,074	Sparta	904
Oconto	28,947	Oconto	1,002
Oneida	31,216	Rhinelander	1,130
Outagamie	128,730	Appleton	642
Ozaukee	66,981	Port Washington	235
Pepin	7,477	Durand	231
Pierce	31,149	Ellsworth	577
Polk	32,351	Balsam Lake	919
Portage	57,420	Stevens Point	810
Price	15,788	Phillips	1,256
Racine	173,132	Racine	335
Richland	17,476	Richland Center	585
Rock	139,420	Janesville	723
Rusk	15,589	Ladysmith	913
St. Croix	43,872	Hudson	723
Sauk	43,469	Baraboo	838
Sawyer	12,843	Hayward	1,255
Shawano	35,928	Shawano	897
Sheboygan	100,935	Sheboygan	515
Taylor	18,817	Medford	975
Trempealeau	26,158	Whitehall	736
Vernon	25,642	Viroqua	808
Vilas	16,535	Eagle River	867
Walworth	71,507	Elkhorn	556
Washburn	13,174	Shell Lake	815
Washington	84,848	West Bend	430
Waukesha	280,203	Waukesha	554
Waupaca	42,831	Waupaca	754
Waushara	18,526	Wautoma	628
Winnebago	131,772	Oshkosh	449
Wood	72,799	Wisconsin Rapids	801

Wyoming

(23 counties, 97,203 sq. mi. land; pop., 469,557)

Albany	29,062	Laramie	4,268
Big Horn	11,896	Basin	3,139
Campbell	24,367	Gillette	4,796
Carbon	21,896	Rawlins	7,877
Converse	14,069	Douglas	4,271
Crook	5,308	Sundance	2,855
Fremont	40,251	Lander	9,181
Goshen	12,040	Torrington	2,186
Hot Springs	5,710	Thermopolis	2,005
Johnson	6,700	Buffalo	4,166
Laramie	68,649	Cheyenne	2,684
Lincoln	12,177	Kemmerer	4,070
Natrona	71,856	Casper	5,347
Niobrara	2,924	Lusk	2,684
Park	21,639	Cody	6,936
Platte	11,975	Wheatland	2,023
Sheridan	25,048	Sheridan	2,532
Sublette	4,548	Pinedale	4,872
Sweetwater	41,723	Green River	10,352
Teton	9,355	Jackson	4,011
Uinta	13,021	Evanston	2,085
Washakie	9,496	Worland	2,243
Weston	7,106	Newcastle	2,402

Population of Outlying Areas

Source: U.S. Bureau of the Census

Population figures are final counts from the census conducted on Apr. 1, 1980.

Puerto Rico

ZIP code	Municipios	Pop.	Land area sq. mile
00601	Adjuntas	18,786	67
00602	Aguada	31,567	31
00603	Aguadilla	54,606	37
00607	Aguas Buenas	22,429	30
00609	Aibonito	22,167	31
00610	Anasco	23,274	40
00612	Arecibo	86,766	127
00615	Arroyo	17,014	15
00617	Barceloneta	18,942	24
00618	Barranquitas	21,639	34
00619	Bayamon	190,208	45
00623	Cabo Rojo	34,045	72
00625	Caguas	117,959	59
00627	Camuy	24,884	47
00629	Canovanas	31,880	33
00630	Carolina	165,954	48
00632	Catano	26,243	6
00633	Cayey	41,099	52
00635	Ceiba	14,944	27
00638	Ciales	16,211	67
00639	Cidra	28,365	36
00640	Coamo	30,822	78
00642	Comerio	18,212	29
00643	Corozal	28,221	43
00645	Culebra	1,265	13
00646	Dorado	25,511	24
00648	Fajardo	32,087	31
00650	Florida	7,232	10
00653	Guanica	18,799	37
00654	Guayama	40,183	65
00656	Guayanilla	21,050	42
00657	Guaynabo	80,742	27
00658	Gurabo	23,574	28
00659	Hatillo	28,958	42
00660	Hormigueros	14,030	11
00661	Humacao	46,134	45
00662	Isabela	37,435	56
00664	Jayuya	14,722	44
00665	Juana Diaz	43,505	61
00666	Juncos	25,397	27
00667	Lajas	21,236	60
00669	Lares	26,743	62
00670	Las Marias	8,747	46
00671	Las Piedras	22,412	34
00672	Loiza	20,867	21
00673	Luquillo	14,895	26
00701	Manati	36,562	46
00706	Maricao	6,737	37
00707	Maunabo	11,813	21
00708	Mayaguez	96,193	77
00716	Moca	29,185	50
00717	Morovis	21,142	39
00718	Naguabo	20,617	52
00719	Naranjito	23,633	28
00720	Orocovis	19,332	64
00723	Patillas	17,774	47
00724	Penuelas	19,116	45
00731	Ponce	189,046	117
00742	Quebradillas	19,728	23
00743	Rincon	11,788	14
00745	Rio Grande	34,283	62
00747	Sabana Grande	20,207	36
00751	Salinas	26,438	71
00753	San German	32,922	54
*00936	San Juan	434,849	47
00754	San Lorenzo	32,428	53
00755	San Sebastian	35,690	71
00757	Santa Isabel	19,854	35
00758	Toa Alta	31,910	28
00759	Toa Baja	78,246	24
00760	Trujillo Alto	51,389	21
00761	Utuado	34,505	115
00762	Vega Alta	28,696	28
00763	Vega Baja	47,115	48
00765	Vieques	7,662	53
00766	Villalba	20,734	37
00767	Yabucoa	31,425	55
00768	Yauco	37,742	69
Total		3,196,520	3,459

ZIP code	Area	Pop.	Land area sq. mile
	American Samoa		
96799	American Samoa	32,297	77
	Guam		
96910	Agana	896	1
	Agana Hts.	3,284	1
96915	Agat	3,999	10
	Asan	2,034	6
96913	Barrigada	7,756	9
	Chalan-Pago-Ordot	3,120	6
96912	Dededo	23,644	30
96916	Inarajan	2,059	19
	Mangilao	6,840	10
96916	Merizo	1,663	6
	Mongmong-Toto-Maite	5,245	2
	Piti	2,866	7
96915	Santa Rita	9,183	17
	Sinajana	2,485	1
	Talofofo	2,006	17
96911	Tamuning	13,580	6
	Umatac	732	6
	Yigo	10,359	35
96914	Yona	4,228	20
Total		105,979	209
	Virgin Islands		
	St. Croix	49,725	80
	St. John	2,472	20
	St. Thomas	44,372	32
00801	Charlotte Amalie	11,671	
00820	Christiansted	2,904	
00840	Frederiksted	1,046	
Total		96,569	132
	Trust Territory of Pacific Islands		
	Kosrae	NA	42
	Marshall Islands	NA	70
	Palau	NA	192
	Ponape	NA	176
	Truk	NA	49
	Yap	NA	46
Total		NA	533
	No. Mariana Islands	16,758	184

RELIGIOUS INFORMATION

Census of Religious Groups in the U.S.

Source: *1987 Yearbook of American and Canadian Churches*

The 1987 Yearbook of American and Canadian Churches reported a total of 142,926,363 members of religious groups in the U.S.—59.3 percent of the population; membership fell half a percent from the previous year.

Comparisons of membership statistics from group to group are not necessarily meaningful. Membership definitions vary—e.g., Roman Catholics count members from infancy, but some Protestant groups count only "adult" members, usually 13 years or older; some groups compile data carefully, but others estimate; not all groups report annually.

The number of churches appear in parentheses. Asterisk (*) indicates church declines to publish membership figures; (**) indicates figures date from 1977 or earlier.

Group	Members
Adventist churches:	
Advent Christian Ch. (368)	28,830
Primitive Advent Christian Ch. (10)	546
Seventh-day Adventists (4,009)	651,954
American Rescue Workers (20)	2,700
Anglican Orthodox Church (40)	6,000
Baha'i Faith (1,650)	100,000
Baptist churches:	
Amer. Baptist Assn. (1,641)	225,000
Amer. Baptist Chs. in U.S.A. (5,814)	1,559,683
Baptist General Conference (753)	132,546
Baptist Missionary Assn. of America (1,367)	227,720
Conservative Baptist Assn. of America (1,140)	225,000
Duck River (and Kindred) Assn. of Baptists (85)	**8,632
Free Will Baptists (2,548)	217,838
Gen. Assn. of Regular Baptist Chs. (1,571)	300,839
Natl. Baptist Convention of America (11,398)	**2,668,799
Natl. Baptist Convention, U.S.A. (26,000)	**5,500,000
Natl. Primitive Baptist Convention (606)	**250,000
No. Amer. Baptist Conference (258)	42,863
Seventh Day Baptist General Conference (60)	5,008
Southern Baptist Convention (36,898)	14,477,364
Brethren (German Baptists):	
Brethren Ch. (Ashland, Ohio) (122)	14,229
Christian Congregation (La Follette, IN) (1,441)	103,990
Fellowship of Grace Brethren (301)	41,733
Old German Baptist Brethren (52)	5,254
Brethren, River:	
Brethren in Christ Ch. (185)	16,783
Buddhist Churches of America (100)	100,000
Christadelphians (850)	**15,800
The Christian and Missionary Alliance (1,646)	227,846
Christian Catholic Church (4)	2,500
Christian Church (Disciples of Christ) (4,214)	1,116,326
Christian Churches and Churches of Christ (5,487)	1,051,469
Christian Methodist Episcopal Church (2,340)	718,922
Christian Nation Church U.S.A. (5)	226
Christian Union (114)	6,000
Churches of Christ (13,150)	1,604,000
Churches of Christ in Christian Union (260)	11,400
Churches of God:	
Chs. of God, General Conference (353)	34,870
Ch. of God (Anderson, Ind.) (2,291)	185,593
Ch. of God (Seventh Day), Denver, Col. (135)	5,830
Church of Christ, Scientist (3,000)	*
Church of God by Faith (105)	**4,500
Church of the Nazarene (4,989)	522,082
Conservative Congregational Christian Conference (163)	28,624
Eastern Orthodox churches:	
Albanian Orth. Diocese of America (10)	5,250
American Carpatho-Russian Orth. Greek Catholic Ch. (70)	**100,000
Antiochian Orth. Christian Archdiocese of No. Amer. (120)	280,000
Diocese of the Armenian Ch. of America (66)	**450,000
Bulgarian Eastern Orth. Ch. (13)	**86,000
Coptic Orthodox Ch. (28)	115,000
Greek Orth. Archdiocese of N. and S. America (535)	1,950,000
Orthodox Ch. in America (440)	1,000,000
Patriarchal Parishes of the Russian Orth. Ch. in the U.S.A. (38)	9,780
Romanian Orth. Episcopate of America (34)	60,000
Serbian Eastern Orth. Ch. (78)	97,123
Syrian Orth. Ch. of Antioch (Archdiocese of the U.S.A. and Canada) (22)	30,000
Ukrainian Orth. Ch. of America (Ecumenical Patriarchate) (28)	25,000
Ukrainian Orthodox Church in the U.S.A. (107)	**87,745
The Episcopal Church in the U.S.A. (7,274)	2,739,422
American Ethical Union (Ethical Culture Movement) (23)	3,500
Evangelical Church of North America (138)	12,591
Evangelical Congregational Church (158)	34,064
The Evangelical Covenant Church of America (566)	85,150
Evangelical Free Church of America (880)	95,722
Evangelical associations:	
Apostolic Christian Chs. of America (80)	16,916
Apostolic Christian Ch. (Nazarean) (48)	2,799
Christian Congregation (1,441)	103,990
Friends:	
Evangelical Friends Alliance (217)	24,095
Friends General Conference (505)	31,600
Friends United Meeting (536)	57,443
Grace Gospel Fellowship (52)	4,400
Independent Fundamental Churches of America (1,019)	120,446
Jehovah's Witnesses (8,220)	730,441
Jewish organizations:	
Union of Amer. Hebrew Congregations (Reform) (804)	1,300,000
Union of Orthodox Jewish Congregations of America (1,700)	1,000,000
United Synagogue of America (Conservative) (800)	1,250,000
Latter-day Saints:	
Ch. of Jesus Christ (Bickertonites) (53)	2,654
Ch. of Jesus Christ of Latter-day Saints (Mormon) (8,396)	3,860,000
Reorganized Ch. of Jesus Christ of Latter Day Saints (1,101)	192,082
Lutheran churches:	
American Lutheran Ch. (4,940)	2,332,316
Ch. of the Lutheran Brethren of America (108)	11,374
Ch. of the Lutheran Confession (67)	8,910
Assn. of Evangelical Lutheran Chs. (272)	110,934
Evangelical Lutheran Synod (116)	19,850
Assn. of Free Lutheran Congregations (156)	18,205
Latvian Evangelical Lutheran Church of America (59)	13,576
Lutheran Ch. in America (5,817)	2,898,202
Lutheran Ch.-Missouri Synod (5,876)	2,638,164
Protestant Conference (Lutheran) (9)	959
Wisconsin Evangelical Lutheran Synod (1,179)	415,389
Mennonite churches:	
Beachy Amish Mennonite Chs. (83)	5,862
Evangelical Mennonite Ch. (25)	3,813
General Conference of Mennonite Brethren Chs. (128)	16,942
The General Conference Mennonite Ch. (141)	16,942
Hutterian Brethren (77)	3,988
Mennonite Ch. (989)	91,167
Old Order Amish Ch. (598)	34,000
Old Order (Wisler) Mennonite Ch. (38)	9,731
Methodist churches:	
African Methodist Episcopal Ch. (6,200)	2,210,000
African Methodist Episcopal Zion Ch. (6,057)	1,202,229
Evangelical Methodist Ch. (126)	9,040
Free Methodist Ch. of North America (1,048)	72,223
Fundamental Methodist Ch. (14)	700
Primitive Methodist Ch., U.S.A. (87)	9,978
Reformed Methodist Union Episcopal Ch. (18)	3,800
Southern Methodist Ch. (150)	7,231
United Methodist Ch. (37,990)	9,266,853
Moravian churches:	
Moravian Ch. (Unitas Fratrum), Northern Province (100)	32,415

Group	Members
Moravian Ch. in America (Unitas Fratrum), Southern Province (56)	21,714
Unity of the Brethren (27)	3,006
Moslems	**2,000,000+**
New Apostolic Church of North America (457)	**33,068**
North American Old Roman Catholic Church (130)	**62,380**
Old Catholic churches:	
Christ Catholic Ch. (6)	1,269
Mariavite Old Cath. Ch. Province of North America (166)	357,927
No. Amer. Old Roman Cath. Ch. (Schweikert) (130)	62,380
Pentecostal churches:	
Apostolic Faith (Portland, Ore.) (45)	4,100
Assemblies of God (10,761)	2,082,878
Bible Church of Christ (6)	4,350
Bible Way Church of Our Lord Jesus Christ World Wide (350)	**30,000
Church of God (Cleveland, Tenn.) (5,346)	505,775
Church of God of Prophecy (2,051)	73,952
Congregational Holiness Ch. (174)	8,347
Gen. Council, Christian Ch. of No. Amer. (104)	13,500
Intl. Ch. of the Foursquare Gospel (1,185)	177,787
Open Bible Standard Chs. (290)	46,351
Pentecostal Assemblies of the World (550)	**4,500
Pentecostal Church of God (1,142)	89,508
United Pentecostal Ch. Intl. (3,408)	500,000
Pentecostal Free-Will Baptist Ch. (130)	10,700
Plymouth Brethren (1,150)	**98,000**
Polish Natl. Catholic Church of America (162)	****282,411**

Group	Members
Presbyterian churches:	
Associate Reformed Presbyterian Ch. (Gen. Synod) (172)	36,543
Cumberland Presbyterian Ch. (818)	98,037
Evangelical Presbyterian Ch. (100)	27,000
Orthodox Presbyterian Ch. (171)	18,502
Presbyterian Ch. in America (878)	177,917
Presbyterian Ch. (U.S.A.) (11,572)	3,092,151
Reformed Presbyterian Ch. of No. Amer. (71)	5,146
Reformed churches:	
Christian Reformed Ch. in N. America (650)	219,988
Hungarian Reformed Ch. in America (31)	11,000
Protestant Reformed Chs. in America (21)	4,544
Reformed Ch. in America (926)	342,275
Reformed Ch. in the U.S. (34)	3,778
The Roman Catholic Church (24,251)	**52,654,908**
The Salvation Army (1,088)	**427,825**
The Schwenkfelder Church (5)	**2,881**
Social Brethren (40)	****1,784**
Natl. Spiritualist Assn. of Churches (142)	**5,558**
Gen. Convention, The Swedenborgian Church (49)	**2,245**
Unitarian Universalist Assn. (948)	**171,838**
United Brethren:	
Ch. of the United Brethren in Christ (256)	26,869
United Christian Ch. (11)	421
United Church of Christ (6,408)	**1,683,777**
Universal Fellowship of Metropolitan Community Chs. (230)	**34,000**
Vedanta Society (13)	**1,500**
Volunteers of America (607)	**36,634**
The Wesleyan Church (1,714)	**109,541**

Religious Population of the U.S.

Source: *1987 Yearbook of American and Canadian Churches*

(Membership in thousands, except as indicated)

Religious Body	Membership 1960	1965	1970	1975	1980	1984	1985	Number of churches 1985
Total	114,449	124,682	131,045	131,013	134,817	142,172	142,926	345,861
Members as percent of population	64	64	63	61	59	59.5	59.3	
Buddhist Churches of America	20	92	100	60	60	70	100	100
Eastern Churches	2,699	3,172	3,850	3,696	3,823	4,052	4,026	1,660
Jews	5,367	5,600	5,870	6,115	5,920	5,817	5,835	3,416
Old Catholic, Polish National Catholic, and American Churches	590	484	848	846	924	1,025	1,024	428
The Roman Catholic Church	42,105	46,246	48,125	48,882	50,450	52,286	52,655	24,251
Protestants	63,669	69,088	71,173	71,043	73,479	78,702	79,096	314,713
Miscellaneous			449	372	161	1,902	1,911	1,124

Estimated Religious Population of the World

Source: The 1987 Encyclopaedia Britannica Book of the Year

Religionists	Africa	East Asia	Europe	Latin America	Northern America	Oceania	South Asia	U.S.S.R.	World	%
Christians	259,544,680	74,614,270	415,529,010	388,863,450	231,539,720	21,143,000	125,954,640	102,083,790	1,619,272,560	32.9
Roman Cath.	98,557,180	8,904,140	253,852,110	365,973,680	88,144,650	7,310,180	72,863,900	4,940,000	900,545,040	18.3
Protestants	69,087,120	28,871,510	79,973,650	13,417,650	96,293,800	7,449,790	23,049,300	8,409,000	326,551,820	6.6
Orthodox	24,129,950	74,190	35,351,060	421,240	5,948,530	506,130	3,201,260	88,720,290	158,352,650	3.2
Anglicans	21,496,950	326,770	33,076,370	1,191,100	7,760,000	5,463,380	286,990	500	69,602,060	1.4
Other	46,273,480	36,437,660	13,275,820	7,859,780	33,392,740	413,520	26,553,190	14,000	164,220,190	3.3
Muslims	237,067,660	24,143,740	9,042,340	625,180	2,675,720	93,520	535,079,210	31,494,020	840,221,390	17.1
Nonreligious	1,443,850	619,384,830	48,788,900	12,751,380	19,310,020	2,859,170	18,386,060	82,981,670	805,895,880	16.4
Hindus	1,395,390	9,740	585,540	636,340	764,200	284,080	644,218,360	1,300	647,894,950	13.2
Buddhists	13,850	155,159,650	209,600	496,980	193,440	16,880	150,975,920	349,710	307,416,030	6.2
Atheists	234,470	133,582,030	17,153,270	2,388,410	1,029,120	507,920	5,084,340	60,562,030	220,541,590	4.5
Chinese folk religionists	10,220	194,049,230	50,350	68,460	116,160	19,170	8,442,280	100	202,755,970	4.1
New Religionists	12,080	41,289,300	33,470	357,830	1,025,050	4,910	66,777,800	200	109,500,640	2.2
Tribal religionists	70,170,270	772,770	50	1,168,160	65,210	84,730	25,215,740	0	97,476,930	2.0
Jews	276,390	1,950	1,520,060	976,230	8,050,100	85,540	3,893,810	3,177,380	17,981,460	0.4
Sikhs	29,110	1,080	212,240	5,950	8,660	6,530	15,897,290	50	16,160,910	0.3
Shamanists	1,100	12,828,530	300	500	290	290	12,000	299,750	13,142,760	0.3
Confucians	550	5,635,590	990	500	1,020	290	1,500	200	5,640,640	0.1
Baha'is	1,319,350	44,200	67,090	543,460	300,110	56,540	2,228,260	4,900	4,563,910	0.1
Shintoists	50	3,423,960	390	990	710	590	200	100	3,426,990	0.1
Jains	49,980	430	9,870	1,980	2,040	980	3,304,650	20	3,369,950	0.1
World Pop.	**571,622,400**	**1,264,999,800**	**493,499,610**	**415,610,810**	**265,766,620**	**25,187,410**	**1,605,687,810**	**280,960,220**	**4,923,334,680**	**100.0**

Headquarters, Leaders of U.S. Religious Groups

See Associations and Societies section for religious organizations. (year organized in parentheses)

Adventist churches:

Advent Christian Church (1854) — Pres., Rev. Donald E. Wrigley; sec., Rev. Marshall Tidwell, 1002 Grove Ave. SW, Lenoir, NC 28645.

Primitive Advent Christian Church — Pres., Donald Young; sec.-treas., Hugh W. Good, 395 Frame Rd., Elkview, WV 25071.

Seventh-day Adventists (1863) — Pres., Neal C. Wilson; sec., G. Ralph Thompson, 6840 Eastern Ave. NW, Wash., DC 20012.

Baha'i Faith — Chpsn., Judge James E. Nelson; sec., Robert Henderson, 536 Sheridan Rd., Wilmette, IL 60091.

Baptist churches:

American Baptist Assn. (1905) — Pres., Ray O. Brooks; sec.-treas., D.S. Madden, P.O. Box 1050, Texarkana, AR-TX 75504.

American Baptist Churches in the U.S.A. (1907) — Pres., Rev. Walter B. Pulliam; gen. sec., Rev. Robert C. Campbell, Valley Forge, PA 19481.

Baptist General Conference (1879) — Gen. sec., Dr. Warren Magnuson, 2002 S. Arlington Heights Rd., Arlington Heights, IL 60005.

Baptist Missionary Assn. of America (formerly **North American Baptist Assn.**) (1950) — Pres., Rev. Ronald Morgan, rec. sec., Rev. Ralph Cottrell, Box 2866, Texarkana, AR 75501.

Conservative Baptist Assn. of America (1947) — Gen. Dir., Dr. Russell A. Shive, Box 66, Wheaton, IL 60189.

Free Will Baptists (1727) — Mod., Rev. Bobby Jackson; exec. sec., Dr. Melvin Worthington, Box 1088, Nashville, TN 37202.

General Assn. of General Baptists (1823) — Mod., Rev. Ralph Miller; clerk, Rev. Edwin Runyon, 801 Kendall, Poplar Bluff, MO 63901.

General Assn. of Regular Baptist Churches (1932) — Chpsn., Dr. John G. Balyo; sec., Dr. Ralph G. Colas, 1300 N. Meacham Rd., Schaumburg, IL 60173.

Natl. Baptist Convention, U.S.A. (1880) — Pres., Dr. T.J. Jemison; gen. sec., W. Franklyn Richardson, 52 S. 6th Ave., Mt. Vernon, NY 10550.

North American Baptist Conference (1865) — Mod., Rev. Ernie Radke; exec. dir., Dr. John Binder, 1 S. 210 Summit Ave., Oakbrook Terrace, IL 60181.

Southern Baptist Convention (1845) — Pres., Adrian P. Rogers; v.p., pub. rel., W.C. Fields, 901 Commerce, Nashville, TN 37203.

Brethren in Christ Church (1798) — Mod., Bishop Owen H. Alderfer; gen. sec., Dr. R. Donald Shafer, P.O. Box 245, Upland, CA 91785.

Brethren (German Baptists):

Brethren Church (Ashland, Oh.) (1882) — Mod., Dr. Warren K. Garner, 103 Damron Dr., N. Manchester, IN 49962; sec., Norma Waters, RR 1, Box 421, McGaheysville, VA 22840.

Church of the Brethren (1719) — Mod., James F. Meyer; gen. sec., Robert Neff, 1451 Dundee Ave., Elgin, IL 60120.

Buddhist Churches of America (1899) — Bishop, Rt. Rev. Seigen H. Yamaoka; exec. asst., Rev. Seikan Fukuma, 1710 Octavia St., San Francisco, CA 94109.

The Christian and Missionary Alliance (1887) — Pres., Louis L. King; sec., Elwood N. Nielsen, 350 N. Highland Ave., Nyack, NY 10960.

Christian Church (Disciples of Christ) (1809) — Gen. minister and pres., John O. Humbert, v.p. for communication, Carolyn W. Day, 222 S. Downey Ave., Box 1986, Indianapolis, IN 46206.

The Christian Congregation (1887) — Gen. supt., Rev. Ora Wilbert Eads, 804 W. Hemlock St., LaFollette, TN 37766.

Christian Methodist Episcopal Church (1870) — Exec. sec., Dr. W. Clyde Williams, 2805 Shoreland Dr., Atlanta, GA 30331. sec., Rev. Edgar L. Wade, P.O. Box 3403, Memphis, TN 38101.

Churches of Christ in Christian Union (1909) — Gen. supt., Rev. Robert Kline; gen. sec., Rev. Robert Barth, Box 30, Circleville, OH 43113.

Grace Brethren Church, Fellowship of (1882) — Mod., Rev. Tom Julien; sec., Rev. Kenneth Koontz, 855 Turnbull St., Delona, FL 32725.

Churches of God:

Churches of God, General Conference (1825) — Admin., Dr. Richard E. Wilkin; journalizing sec., Rev. Harry G. Cadamore, 157 Second St., W. Newton, PA 15089.

Church of God (Anderson, Ind.) (1880) — Chpsn., Samuel G. Hines; exec. sec., Paul A. Tanner, Box 2420, Anderson, IN 46018.

Church of Christ, Scientist (1879) — Pres., Mrs. Jean K. Weida; clk., Mrs. Virginia S. Harris, Christian Science Church Center, Boston, MA 02115.

Church of the Nazarene (1908) — Gen. sec., B. Edgar Johnson, 6401 The Paseo, Kansas City, MO 64131.

National Association of Congregational Christian Churches (1955) — Mod., Rev. John R. Elmore; exec. sec., J. Fred Rennebohm, Box 1620, Oak Creek, WI 53154.

Eastern Orthodox churches:

Antiochian Orthodox Christian Archdiocese of North America (formerly **Syrian Antiochian Orthodox Archdiocese**) (1894) — Primate, Metropolitan Archbishop Philip (Saliba); aux., Archbishop Michael (Shaheen), Bishop Antoun (Khouri), 358 Mountain Rd., Englewood, NJ 07631.

Diocese of the Armenian Church of America (1889) — Primate, Eastern Diocese, Archbishop Torkom Manoogian; sec., Dr. Arra Avakian, 6149 N. 9th, Fresno, CA 93710; Western Diocese, Primate, His Eminence Archbishop Vatche Housepian, 1201 N. Vine St., Hollywood, CA 90038.

Coptic Orthodox Ch. — Correspnt., Archpriest Fr. Gabriel Abdelsayed, 427 West Side Ave., Jersey City, NJ 07304.

Greek Orthodox Archdiocese of North and South America (1864) — Pres., Archbishop Iakovos; sec., Peter Kourides, 8-10 E. 79th St., N.Y., NY 10021.

Orthodox Church in America (formerly **Russian Orthodox Greek Catholic Church of North America**) (1792) — Primate, Metropolitan Theodosius; chancellor, V. Rev. Daniel Hubiak, P.O. Box 675, Syosset, NY 11791.

Romanian Orthodox Episcopate of America (1929) — Ruling bishop, Nathaniel (Popp); sec., Rev. Fr. Richard J. Grabowski, 3256 Warren Rd., Cleveland, OH 44111.

Serbian Orthodox Church for the U.S.A. and Canada — Bishops, Rt. Rev. Bishop Firmilian, Rt. Rev. Bishop Sava; Bishop Christopher; St. Sava Monastery, Box 519, Libertyville, IL 60048.

Syrian Orthodox Church of Antioch, Archdiocese of the U.S.A. and Canada (1957) — Primate, Archbishop MarAthanasius Y. Samuel; gen. sec., Very Rev. Chorepiscopus John Meno, 45 Fairmount Ave., Hackensack, NJ 07601.

Ukrainian Orthodox Church in America (Ecumenical Patriarchate) (1928) — Adm., Rt. Rev. Michael Pawlyskym; sec., Rt. Rev. Ivan Tkaczuk, 90-34 139th St., Jamaica, NY 11435.

Ukrainian Orthodox Church of the U.S.A. (1919) — Metropolitan, Most Rev. Mstyslav S. Skrypnyk, Box 495, South Bound Brook, NJ 08880.

The Episcopal Church (1789) — Presiding bishop and primate, Most Rev. Edmond L. Browning; sec., Rt. Rev. Herbert A. Donovan Jr., Box 6120, Little Rock, AR 72216.

The Evangelical Covenant Church (1885) — Pres., Dr. Paul E. Larsen; sec., Rev. Timothy C. Ek, 5101 N. Francisco Ave., Chicago, IL 60625.

Friends:

Evangelical Friends Alliance (1965) — Mid-America YM, Ron Johnson, 1201 30th St. NW, Canton, OH 44709.

Friends General Conference (1900) — Gen. sec., Meredith Walton, 1520B Race St., Phila., PA 19102.

Friends United Meeting (formerly **Five Years Meeting of Friends**) (1902) — Presiding clerk, Richard Whitehead, 101 Quaker Hill Dr., Richmond, IN 47374.

Independent Fundamental Churches of America (1930) — Pres., Dr. Leslie Madison, 10101 E. 147th St., Kansas City, MO 64149.

Federation of Islamic Assns. in U.S. and Canada — Pres., Dawud Assad, 300 E. 44th St., N.Y., NY 10017.

Jehovah's Witnesses (1879) — Pres., Frederick W. Franz, 25 Columbia Heights, Brooklyn, NY 11201.

Jewish congregations:

Union of American Hebrew Congregations (Reform) — Pres., Rabbi Alexander M. Schindler, 838 5th Ave., N.Y., NY 10021.

Union of Orthodox Jewish Congregations of America — Pres., Julius Berman, 45 W. 36th St., N.Y., NY 10018.

United Synagogue of America (Conservative) — Pres., Franklin D. Kreutzer, 155 5th Ave., N.Y., NY 10010.

Latter-day Saints:

The Church of Jesus Christ of Latter-day Saints (Mormon) (1830) — Pres., Ezra Taft Benson, 50 E. North Temple St., Salt Lake City, UT 84150.

Reorganized Church of Jesus Christ of Latter Day Saints (1830) — Pres., Wallace B. Smith; sec., W. Grant McMurray, The Auditorium, P.O. Box 1059, Independence, MO 64051.

Lutheran churches:

The American Lutheran Church (1961) — Pres., Dr. David W. Preus; gen. sec., Dr. Kathryn E. Baerwald, 422 S. 5th St., Minneapolis, MN 55415.

Church of the Lutheran Brethren of America (1900) — Pres., Rev. Robert M. Overgard Sr.; sec., Rev. Richard Vettrus, 707 Crestview Dr., W. Union, IA 52175.

Church of the Lutheran Confession (1961) — Pres., Rev. Daniel Fleischer; sec., Rev. Paul F. Nolting, 3956 Persimmon Dr., Apt. 104, Fairfax, VA 22013.

Assn. of Evangelical Lutheran Churches (1976) — Bishop, Dr. Will Herzfeld; exec. sec., Dr. Elwyn Ewald, 12015 Manchester Rd., St. Louis, MO 63131.

Evangelical Lutheran Synod (1853) — Pres., Rev. George Orvick; sec., Rev. Alf Merseth, 106 13th St. S., Northwood, IA 50459.

Assn. of Free Lutheran Congregations (1962) — Pres. Rev. Richard Snipstead; sec., Rev. Ronald Knutson, 402 W. 11th St., Canton, SD 57013.

Lutheran Church in America (1962) — Bishop, Rev. James R. Crumley Jr.; sec., Rev. Reuben T. Swanson, 231 Madison Ave., N.Y. NY 10016.

Lutheran Church — Missouri Synod (1847) — Pres., Dr. Ralph Bohlmann; sec., Dr. Walter L. Rosin, 1333 S. Kirkwood, St. Louis, MO 63122.

Wisconsin Evangelical Lutheran Synod (1850) — Pres., Rev. Carl H. Mischke; sec., Prof. David Worgull, 1201 W. Tulsa, Chandler, AZ 85224.

Mennonite churches:

The General Conference of Mennonite Brethren Churches (1860) — Chpsn., Herb Brandt; sec., Bill A. Wieber, 34118 Larch St., Abbotsford, BC V2S 2P5.

Mennonite Church (1690) — Mod., Ralph Lebold, 528 E. Madison St., Lombard, IL 60148.

Methodist churches:

African Methodist Episcopal Zion Church (1796) — Sr. Bishop, Henry W. Murph, gen. sec., Dr. Richard Allen Chappelle Sr., P.O. Box 183, St. Louis, MO 63166.

Evangelical Methodist Church (1946) — Gen. supt., Clyde Zehr; gen. sec., Rev. R.D. Driggers, 3000 W. Kellogg Dr., Wichita, KS 67213.

Free Methodist Church of North America (1860) — Bishops R.F. Andrews, D. Bastian, G.E. Bates, D.M. Foster, N. Nzeyimaha, C.E. Van Valin, gen. conf. sec., Melvin J. Spencer, 901 College Ave., Winona Lake, IN 46590.

The United Methodist Church (1968) — Pres. Counc. of Bishops, Bishop Earl G. Hunt Jr.; sec., Bishop Paul A. Duffey, 4010 Dupont Circle, Louisville, KY 40207.

Universal Fellowship of Metropolitan Community Churches — Mod., Rev. Elder Troy D. Perry; clerk, Rev. Elder Nancy L. Wilson, 5300 Santa Monica Blvd., Los Angeles, CA 90029.

Moravian Church (Unitas Fratrum) (1740) **Northern Province** — Pres., Dr. Gordon L. Sommers, 1021 Center St., P.O. Box 1245, Bethlehem, PA 18016. **Southern Province** — Pres., Rev. Graham H. Rights, 459 S. Church St., Winston Salem, NC 27108.

Old Catholic churches:

North American Old Roman Catholic Church (1915) — Archbishop, Most Rev. J.E. Schweikert, 4200 N. Kedvale Ave., Chicago, IL 60641.

Pentecostal churches:

Assemblies of God (1914) — Gen. supt., G. Raymond Carlson; gen. sec., Joseph R. Flower, 1445 Boonville Ave., Springfield, MO 65802.

Bible Way Church of Our Lord Jesus Christ World Wide (1927) — Presiding bishop, Smallwood E. Williams; gen. sec., Bishop Edward William, 5118 Clarendon Rd., Brooklyn, NY 11226.

Gen. Council, Christian Church of No. America (1948) — Gen. overseer; Rev. Guy BonGiovanni; gen. sec.-treas., Rev. Richard A. Tedesco, Box 141-A, RD #1, Rt. 18 & Rutledge Rd., Transfer, PA 16154.

The Church of God (1903) — Gen. overseer, Bishop Voy M. Bullen; gen. sec.-treas., Marie Powell, Box 13036, 1207 Willow Brook, Huntsville, AL 35802.

Church of God (Cleveland, Tenn.) (1886) — Gen. overseer, Raymond Crowley; gen. sec.-treas., John Nichols, Keith St. at 25th NW, Cleveland, TN 37311.

International Church of the Foursquare Gospel (1927) — Pres., Dr. Rolf K. McPherson; sec., Dr. Leland B. Edwards, 1100 Glendale Blvd., Los Angeles, CA 90026.

National Gay Pentecostal Alliance (1980) — Pres., Rev. Wm. H. Carey, P.O. Box 1391, Schenctady, NY 12301.

Open Bible Standard Churches (1919) — Gen. supt., Ray E. Smith; sec.-treas., Patrick L. Bowlin, 2020 Bell Ave., Des Moines, IA 50315.

Pentecostal Church of God (1919) — Gen. supt., Dr. Roy M. Chappell; gen. sec.-treas., Dr. Ronald R. Minor, 211 Main St., Joplin, MO 64801.

United Pentecostal Church International (1945) — Gen. supt., Rev. Nathaniel A. Urshan; gen. sec.-treas., Rev. C. M. Becton, 8855 Dunn Rd., Hazelwood, MO 63042.

Pentecostal Free Will Baptist Church (1959) — Gen. supt., Rev. Don Sauls; gen. sec., Rev. J.T. Hammond, Box 1568, Dunn, NC 28334.

Presbyterian churches:

Cumberland Presbyterian Church (1810) — Mod., James W. Knight; stated clerk, Roy E. Blakeburn, 1978 Union Ave., Memphis, TN 38104.

Evangelical Presbyterian Church (1981) — Mod., Roger Vonder Bruegge; stated clerk, Rev. L. Edward Davis, 26049 Five Mile Rd., Detroit, MI 48239.

The Orthodox Presbyterian Church (1936) — Mod., Rev. Robert B. Strimple; stated clerk, John P. Galbraith, 7401 Old York Rd., Phila., PA 19126.

Presbyterian Church in America (1973) — Mod., Rev. Frank M. Barker Jr.; stated clerk, Rev. Morton H. Smith, P.O. Box 1428, Decatur, GA 30031.

Presbyterian Church in the U.S.A. (1984) — Mod., Rev. Benjamin M. Weir; stated clerk, Rev. James E. Andrews, 475 Riverside Dr., N.Y. NY, 10115.

Reformed Presbyterian Church of No. America (1871) — Mod., Rev. John H. Tweed; clerk, Rev. Paul M. Martin, 1117 E. Devonshire, Phoenix, AZ 85014.

Reformed churches:

Christian Reformed Church in North America (1857) — Stated clerk, Rev. Leonard J. Hofman, 2850 Kalamazoo Ave., SE, Grand Rapids, MI 49560.

Reformed Church in America (1628) — Pres., James A. Neevel; gen. sec., Edwin G. Mulder, 475 Riverside Dr., N.Y., NY 10115.

Reformed Episcopal Church (1873) — Pres., Rev. Theophilus J. Herter; sec., Rev. Dale H. Crouthamel, 14 Culberson Rd., Basking Ridge, NJ 07920.

Roman Catholic Church — National Conference of Catholic Bishops. Pres., Archbishop John L. May; sec., Bishop Thomas C. Kelly, 1312 Massachusetts Ave. NW, Wash., DC 20005.

The Salvation Army (1880) — Natl. cmdr., Commissioner Andrew S. Miller; natl. chief sec., Col. Harold E. Shoults, 799 Bloomfield Ave., Verona, NJ 07044.

Sikh (1972) — Chief adm., Siri Singh Sahib, Harbhajan Singh Khalsa Yogiji; sec. gen., Mukhia Sardarni Sahiba, Sardarni Premka Kaur Khalsa, 1649 S. Robertson Blvd., Los Angeles, CA 90035.

Unitarian Universalist Assn. (1961) — Pres., Rev. William Schulz; sec., Dr. Donald W. Male, 25 Beacon St., Boston, MA 02108.

United Brethren in Christ (1789) — Chpsn., Bishop C. Ray Miller; 302 Lake St., Huntington, IN 46750.

United Church of Christ (1957) — Pres., Rev. Avery D. Post; sec., Rev. Carol Joyce Brun, 105 Madison Ave., N.Y., NY 10016.

Volunteers of America (1896) — Pres., Raymond C. Tremont; 3813 N. Causeway Blvd., Metairie, LA 70002.

The Wesleyan Church (1968) — Gen. supts., Drs. J. D. Abbott, O.D. Emery, R. W. McIntyre, Earle L. Wilson; gen. sec., Rev. Ronald R. Brannon, Box 2000, Marion, IN 46953.

Episcopal Church Calendar and Liturgical Colors

White—from Christmas Day through the First Sunday after Epiphany; Maundy Thursday (as an alternative to crimson at the Eucharist); from the Vigil of Easter to the Day of Pentecost (Whitsunday); Trinity Sunday; Feasts of the Lord (except Holy Cross Day); the Confession of St. Peter; the Conversion of St. Paul; St. Joseph; St. Mary Magdalene; St. Mary the Virgin; St. Michael and All Angels; All Saint's Day; St. John the Evangelist; memorials of other saints who were not martyred; Independence Day and Thanksgiving Day; weddings and funerals. **Red**.—the Day of Pentecost; Holy Cross Day; feasts of apostles and evangelists (except those listed above); feasts and memorials of martyrs (including Holy Innocents' Day). **Violet**—Advent and Lent. **Crimson** (dark red)—Holy Week. **Green**—the seasons after Epiphany and after Pentecost. **Black**—optional alternative for funerals. Alternative colors used in some churches: **Blue**—Advent; **Lenten White**—Ash Wednesday to Palm Sunday.

In the Episcopal Church the days of fasting are Ash Wednesday and Good Friday. Other days of special devotion (abstinence) are the 40 days of Lent and all Fridays of the year, except those in Christmas and Easter seasons and any Feasts of the Lord which occur on a Friday or during Lent. Ember Days (optional) are days of prayer for the Church's ministry. They fall on the Wednesday, Friday, and Saturday after the first Sunday in Lent, the Day of Pentecost, Holy Cross Day, and the Third Sunday of Advent. Rogation Days (also optional) are the three days before Ascension Day, and are days of prayer for God's blessing on the crops, on commerce and industry, and for the conservation of the earth's resources.

(continued)

Days, etc.	1987	1988	1989	1990	1991	1992
Golden Number	12	13	14	15	16	17
Sunday Letter	D	CB	A	G	F	ED
Sundays after Epiphany	8	6	5	8	5	8
Ash Wednesday	Mar. 4	Feb. 17	Feb. 8	Feb. 28	Feb. 13	Mar. 4
First Sunday in Lent	Mar. 8	Feb. 21	Feb. 12	Mar. 4	Feb. 17	Mar. 8
Passion/Palm Sunday	Apr. 12	Mar. 27	Mar. 19	Apr. 8	Mar. 24	Apr. 12
Good Friday	Apr. 17	Apr. 1	Mar. 24	Apr. 13	Mar. 29	Apr. 17
Easter Day	Apr. 19	Apr. 3	Mar. 26	Apr. 15	Mar. 31	Apr. 19
Ascension Day	May 28	May 12	May 4	May 24	May 9	May 28
The Day of Pentecost	June 7	May 22	May 14	June 3	May 19	June 7
Trinity Sunday	June 14	May 29	May 21	June 10	May 26	June 14
Numbered Proper of 2 Pentecost	#7	#5	#3	#6	#4	#7
First Sunday of Advent	Nov. 29	Nov. 27	Dec. 3	Dec. 2	Dec. 1	Nov. 29

Jewish Holy Days, Festivals, and Fasts

	1987 (5746-47)	1988 (5747-48)	1989 (5748-49)	1990 (5750-51)	1991 (5751-52)
Tu B'Shvat	Feb. 14 Sat	Feb. 3 Wed	Jan. 21 Sat	Feb. 10 Sat	Jan. 30 Wed
Ta'anis Esther (Fast of Esther)	Mar. 12 Thu*	Mar. 2 Wed	Mar. 20 Mon	Mar. 8 Thu*	Feb. 27 Wed
Purim	Mar. 15 Sun	Mar. 3 Thu	Mar. 21 Tue	Mar. 11 Sun	Feb. 28 Thu
Passover	April 14 Tue	April 2 Sat	April 20 Thu	April 10 Tue	Mar. 30 Sat
	April 21 Tue	April 9 Sat	April 27 Thu	April 17 Tue	April 6 Sat
Lag B'Omer	May 17 Sun	May 5 Thu	May 23 Tue	May 13 Sun	May 2 Thu
Shavuot	June 3 Wed	May 22 Sun	June 9 Fri	May 30 Wed	May 19 Sun
	June 4 Thu	May 28 Mon	June 10 Sat	May 31 Thu	May 20 Mon
Fast of the 17th Day of Tammuz	July 14 Tue	July 3 Sun	July 20 Thu	July 10 Tue	June 30 Sun*
Fast of the 9th Day of AV	Aug. 4 Tue	July 24 Sun	Aug. 10 Thu	July 31 Tue	July 21 Sun*
Rosh Hashanah	Sep. 24 Thu	Sep. 12 Mon	Sep. 30 Sat	Sep. 20 Thu	Sep. 9 Mon
	Sep. 25 Fri	Sep. 13 Tue	Oct. 1 Sun	Sep. 21 Fri	Sep. 10 Tue
Fast of Gedalya	Sep. 27 Sun*	Sep. 14 Wed	Oct. 2 Mon	Sep. 23 Sun*	Sep. 11 Wed
Yom Kippur	Oct. 3 Sat	Sep. 21 Wed	Oct. 9 Mon	Sep. 29 Sat	Sep. 18 Wed
Sukkot	Oct. 8 Thu	Sep. 26 Mon	Oct. 14 Sat	Oct. 4 Thu	Sep. 23 Mon
	Oct. 14 Wed	Oct. 2 Sun	Oct. 20 Fri	Oct. 10 Wed	Sep. 29 Sun
Shmini Atzeret	Oct. 15 Thu	Oct. 3 Mon	Oct. 21 Sat	Oct. 11 Thu	Sep. 30 Mon
	Oct. 16 Fri	Oct. 4 Tue	Oct. 22 Sun	Oct. 12 Fri	Oct. 1 Tue
Chanukah	Dec. 16 Wed	Dec. 4 Sun	Dec. 23 Sat	Dec. 12 Wed	Dec. 2 Mon
	Dec. 23 Wed	Dec. 11 Sun	Dec. 30 Sat	Dec. 19 Wed	Dec. 9 Mon
Fast of the 10th of Tevet	Dec. 31 Thu	Dec. 18 Sun	Jan. 7 Sun	Dec. 27 Thu	Dec. 17 Tue

The months of the Jewish year are: 1) Tishri; 2) Cheshvan (also Marcheshvan); 3) Kislev; 4) Tebet (also Tebeth); 5) Shebat (also Shebhat); 6) Adar; 6a) Adar Sheni (II) added in leap years; 7) Nisan; 8) Iyar; 9) Sivan; 10) Tammuz; 11) Av (also Abh); 12) Elul. All Jewish holy days, etc., begin at sunset on the day previous.

*Date changed to avoid Sabbath.

Greek Orthodox Church Calendar, 1988

Date		Holy Days
Jan.	1	Circumcision of Jesus Christ; feast day of St. Basil
Jan.	6	Epiphany: Baptism of Jesus Christ - Sanctification of the Waters
Jan.	7	Feast day of St. John the Baptist
Jan.	30	Feast day of the Three Hierarchs: St. Basil the Great, St. Gregory the Theologian, and St. John Chrysostom
Feb.	2	Presentation of Jesus Christ in the Temple
Feb.	22	Easter Lent begins
Feb.	28	Sunday of Orthodoxy (1st. Sunday of Lent)
Mar.	25	Annunciation of the Virgin Mary
Apr.	3	Palm Sunday
Apr. 3-Apr. 9		Holy Week
Apr.	8	Holy (Good) Friday: Burial of Jesus Christ
Apr.	10	Easter Sunday: Resurrection of Jesus Christ
*Apr.	23	Feast of St. George
May	19	Ascension of Jesus Christ
May	21	Feast day of Sts. Constantine and Helen
May	29	Sunday of Pentecost
June	4	Feast day of Sts. Peter and Paul
June	5	Feast day of the Twelve Apostles of Jesus Christ
Aug.	6	Transfiguration of Jesus Christ
Aug.	15	Dormition of the Virgin Mary
Aug.	29	Beheading of St. John the Baptist
Sept.	1	Beginning of the Church Year
Sept.	14	Adoration of the Holy Cross
Oct.	23	Feast day of St. James
Oct.	26	Feast day of St. Demetrios the Martyr
Nov.	15	Christmas Lent begins
Nov.	21	Presentation of the Virgin Mary
Nov.	30	Feast day of St. Andrew the Apostle
Dec.	6	Feast day of St. Nicholas, Bishop of Myra
Dec.	25	Christmas Day; Nativity of Jesus Christ

*Movable holy days dependent upon the date of Easter. (The feast day of St. George is normally celebrated Apr. 23. If this day arrives during Lent, it is then celebrated the day after Easter.) The Greek Orthodox Church celebrates holy days in accordance with the Gregorian Calendar. Some Eastern Orthodox Churches still adhere to the Julian Calendar and observe the holy days (with the exception of the Easter cycle) 13 days later.

Islamic (Moslem) Calendar 1987-1988

The Islamic Calendar is a lunar reckoning from the year of the *hegira,* 622 A.D., when Muhammed moved from Mecca to Medina. It runs in cycles of 30 years, of which the 2d, 5th, 7th, 10th, 13th, 16th, 18th, 21st, 24th, 26th, and 29th are leap years; 1407 is the 27th year, 1408 of the 27th year of the cycle. Common years have 354 days, leap years 355, the extra day being added to the last month, Zu'lhijjah. Except for this case, the 12 months beginning with Muharram have alternately 30 and 29 days.

Year	Name of month	Month begins
1408	Muharram (New Year)	Aug. 26, 1987
1408	Safar	Sept. 25, 1987
1408	Rabia I	Oct. 24, 1987
1408	Rabia II	Nov. 23, 1987
1408	Jumada I	Dec. 22, 1987
1408	Jumada II	Jan. 21, 1988
1408	Rajab	Feb. 19, 1988
1408	Shaban	Mar. 20, 1988
1408	Ramadan	Apr. 18, 1988
1408	Shawwai	May 18, 1988
1408	Zu'lkadah	June 16, 1988
1408	Zu'lhijjah	July 16, 1988
1409	Muharram (New Year)	Aug. 14, 1988
1409	Safar	Sept. 13, 1988
1409	Rabia I	Oct. 12, 1988
1409	Rabia II	Nov. 11, 1988
1409	Jumada I	Dec. 10, 1988

Ash Wednesday and Easter Sunday

Year	Ash Wed.	Easter Sunday	Year	Ash Wed.	Easter Sunday	Year	Ash Wed.	Easter Sunday	Year	Ash Wed.	Easter Sunday
1901	Feb. 20	Apr. 7	1951	Feb. 7	Mar. 25	2001	Feb. 28	Apr. 15	2051	Feb. 15	Apr. 2
1902	Feb. 12	Mar. 30	1952	Feb. 27	Apr. 13	2002	Feb. 13	Mar. 31	2052	Mar. 6	Apr. 21
1903	Feb. 25	Apr. 12	1953	Feb. 18	Apr. 5	2003	Mar. 5	Apr. 20	2053	Feb. 19	Apr. 6
1904	Feb. 17	Apr. 3	1954	Mar. 3	Apr. 18	2004	Feb. 25	Apr. 11	2054	Feb. 11	Mar. 29
1905	Mar. 8	Apr. 23	1955	Feb. 23	Apr. 10	2005	Feb. 9	Mar. 27	2055	Mar. 3	Apr. 18
1906	Feb. 28	Apr. 15	1956	Feb. 15	Apr. 1	2006	Mar. 1	Apr. 16	2056	Feb. 16	Apr. 2
1907	Feb. 13	Mar. 31	1957	Mar. 6	Apr. 21	2007	Feb. 21	Apr. 8	2057	Mar. 7	Apr. 22
1908	Mar. 4	Apr. 19	1958	Feb. 19	Apr. 6	2008	Feb. 6	Mar. 23	2058	Feb. 27	Apr. 14
1909	Feb. 24	Apr. 11	1959	Feb. 11	Mar. 29	2009	Feb. 25	Apr. 12	2059	Feb. 12	Mar. 30
1910	Feb. 9	Mar. 27	1960	Mar. 2	Apr. 17	2010	Feb. 17	Apr. 4	2060	Mar. 3	Apr. 18
1911	Mar. 1	Apr. 16	1961	Feb. 15	Apr. 2	2011	Mar. 9	Apr. 24	2061	Feb. 23	Apr. 10
1912	Feb. 21	Apr. 7	1962	Mar. 7	Apr. 22	2012	Feb. 22	Apr. 8	2062	Feb. 8	Mar. 26
1913	Feb. 5	Mar. 23	1963	Feb. 27	Apr. 14	2013	Feb. 13	Mar. 31	2063	Feb. 28	Apr. 15
1914	Feb. 25	Apr. 12	1964	Feb. 12	Mar. 29	2014	Mar. 5	Apr. 20	2064	Feb. 20	Apr. 6
1915	Feb. 17	Apr. 4	1965	Mar. 3	Apr. 18	2015	Feb. 18	Apr. 5	2065	Feb. 11	Mar. 29
1916	Mar. 8	Apr. 23	1966	Feb. 23	Apr. 10	2016	Feb. 10	Mar. 27	2066	Feb. 24	Apr. 11
1917	Feb. 21	Apr. 8	1967	Feb. 8	Mar. 26	2017	Mar. 1	Apr. 16	2067	Feb. 16	Apr. 3
1918	Feb. 13	Mar. 31	1968	Feb. 28	Apr. 14	2018	Feb. 14	Apr. 1	2068	Mar. 7	Apr. 22
1919	Mar. 5	Apr. 20	1969	Feb. 19	Apr. 6	2019	Mar. 6	Apr. 21	2069	Feb. 27	Apr. 14
1920	Feb. 18	Apr. 4	1970	Feb. 11	Mar. 29	2020	Feb. 26	Apr. 12	2070	Feb. 12	Mar. 30
1921	Feb. 9	Mar. 27	1971	Feb. 24	Apr. 11	2021	Feb. 17	Apr. 4	2071	Mar. 4	Apr. 19
1922	Mar. 1	Apr. 16	1972	Feb. 16	Apr. 2	2022	Mar. 2	Apr. 17	2072	Feb. 24	Apr. 10
1923	Feb. 14	Apr. 1	1973	Mar. 7	Apr. 22	2023	Feb. 22	Apr. 9	2073	Feb. 8	Mar. 26
1924	Mar. 5	Apr. 20	1974	Feb. 27	Apr. 14	2024	Feb. 14	Mar. 31	2074	Feb. 28	Apr. 15
1925	Feb. 25	Apr. 12	1975	Feb. 12	Mar. 30	2025	Mar. 5	Apr. 20	2075	Feb. 20	Apr. 7
1926	Feb. 17	Apr. 4	1976	Mar. 3	Apr. 18	2026	Feb. 18	Apr. 5	2076	Mar. 4	Apr. 19
1927	Mar. 2	Apr. 17	1977	Feb. 23	Apr. 10	2027	Feb. 10	Mar. 28	2077	Feb. 24	Apr. 11
1928	Feb. 22	Apr. 8	1978	Feb. 8	Mar. 26	2028	Mar. 1	Apr. 16	2078	Feb. 16	Apr. 3
1929	Feb. 13	Mar. 31	1979	Feb. 28	Apr. 15	2029	Feb. 14	Apr. 1	2079	Mar. 8	Apr. 23
1930	Mar. 5	Apr. 20	1980	Feb. 20	Apr. 6	2030	Mar. 6	Apr. 21	2080	Feb. 21	Apr. 7
1931	Feb. 18	Apr. 5	1981	Mar. 4	Apr. 19	2031	Feb. 26	Apr. 13	2081	Feb. 12	Mar. 30
1932	Feb. 10	Mar. 27	1982	Feb. 24	Apr. 11	2032	Feb. 11	Mar. 28	2082	Mar. 4	Apr. 19
1933	Mar. 1	Apr. 16	1983	Feb. 16	Apr. 3	2033	Mar. 2	Apr. 17	2083	Feb. 17	Apr. 4
1934	Feb. 14	Apr. 1	1984	Mar. 7	Apr. 22	2034	Feb. 22	Apr. 9	2084	Feb. 9	Mar. 26
1935	Mar. 6	Apr. 21	1985	Feb. 20	Apr. 7	2035	Feb. 7	Mar. 25	2085	Feb. 28	Apr. 15
1936	Feb. 26	Apr. 12	1986	Feb. 12	Mar. 30	2036	Feb. 27	Apr. 13	2086	Feb. 13	Mar. 31
1937	Feb. 10	Mar. 28	1987	Mar. 4	Apr. 19	2037	Feb. 18	Apr. 5	2087	Mar. 5	Apr. 20
1938	Mar. 2	Apr. 17	1988	Feb. 17	Apr. 3	2038	Mar. 10	Apr. 25	2088	Feb. 25	Apr. 11
1939	Feb. 22	Apr. 9	1989	Feb. 8	Mar. 26	2039	Feb. 23	Apr. 10	2089	Feb. 16	Apr. 3
1940	Feb. 7	Mar. 24	1990	Feb. 28	Apr. 15	2040	Feb. 15	Apr. 1	2090	Mar. 1	Apr. 16
1941	Feb. 26	Apr. 13	1991	Feb. 13	Mar. 31	2041	Mar. 6	Apr. 21	2091	Feb. 21	Apr. 8
1942	Feb. 18	Apr. 5	1992	Mar. 4	Apr. 19	2042	Feb. 19	Apr. 6	2092	Feb. 13	Mar. 30
1943	Mar. 10	Apr. 25	1993	Feb. 24	Apr. 11	2043	Feb. 11	Mar. 29	2093	Feb. 25	Apr. 12
1944	Feb. 23	Apr. 9	1994	Feb. 16	Apr. 3	2044	Mar. 2	Apr. 17	2094	Feb. 17	Apr. 4
1945	Feb. 14	Apr. 1	1995	Mar. 1	Apr. 16	2045	Feb. 22	Apr. 9	2095	Mar. 9	Apr. 24
1946	Mar. 6	Apr. 21	1996	Feb. 21	Apr. 7	2046	Feb. 7	Mar. 25	2096	Feb. 29	Apr. 15
1947	Feb. 19	Apr. 6	1997	Feb. 12	Mar. 30	2047	Feb. 27	Apr. 14	2097	Feb. 13	Mar. 31
1948	Feb. 11	Mar. 28	1998	Feb. 25	Apr. 12	2048	Feb. 19	Apr. 5	2098	Mar. 5	Apr. 20
1949	Mar. 2	Apr. 17	1999	Feb. 17	Apr. 4	2049	Mar. 3	Apr. 18	2099	Feb. 25	Apr. 12
1950	Feb. 22	Apr. 9	2000	Mar. 8	Apr. 23	2050	Feb. 23	Apr. 10	2100	Feb. 10	Mar. 28

Books of the Bible

Old Testament—Standard Versions

Genesis
Exodus
Leviticus
Numbers
Deuteronomy
Joshua
Judges
Ruth
I Samuel
II Samuel
I Kings
II Kings
I Chronicles
II Chronicles
Ezra
Nehemiah
Esther
Job
Psalms
Proverbs
Ecclesiastes
Song of Solomon
Isaiah
Jeremiah
Lamentations
Ezekiel
Daniel
Hosea
Joel
Amos
Obadiah
Jonah
Micah
Nahum
Habakkuk
Zephaniah
Haggai
Zechariah
Malachi

New Testament—Standard Versions

Matthew
Mark
Luke
John
Acts
Romans
Corinthians
Galatians
Ephesians
Phillippians
Colossians
Thessalonians
Timothy
Titus
Philemon
Hebrews
James
Peter
John
Jude
Revelation

Old Testament—Douay Version[1]

Genesis
Exodus
Leviticus
Numbers
Deuteronomy
Josue
Judges
Ruth
I Kings
II Kings
III Kings
IV Kings
I Paralipomenon
II Paralipomenon
I Esdras
II Esdras
Tobias
Judith
Esther
Job
Psalms
Proverbs
Ecclesiastes
Canticle of Canticles
Wisdom
Ecclesiasticus
Isaias
Jeremias
Lamentations
Baruch
Ezechiel
Daniel
Osee
Joel
Amos
Abdias
Jones
Micheas
Nahum
Habacuc
Sophonias
Aggeus
Zacharias
Malachias
I Machabees
II Machabees

(1) In the Douay Version, the books of the New Testament are the same as those of the Authorized (King James) Version, except that the Revelation of St. John is called the Apocalypse of St. John.

Major Christian Denominations:

Italics indicate that area which, generally speaking, most

Denomination	Origins	Organization	Authority	Special rites
Baptists	In radical Reformation objections to infant baptism, demands for church-state separation; John Smyth, English Separatist in 1609; Roger Williams, 1638, Providence, R.I.	Congregational, *i.e.*, each local church is autonomous.	Scripture; some Baptists, particularly in the South, interpret the Bible literally.	Baptism, after about age 12, by total immersion; Lord's Supper.
Church of Christ (Disciples)	Among evangelical Presbyterians in Ky. (1804) and Penn. (1809), in distress over Protestant factionalism and decline of fervor. Organized 1832.	Congregational.	"*Where the Scriptures speak, we speak; where the Scriptures are silent, we are silent.*"	Adult baptism, Lord's Supper (weekly).
Episcopalians	Henry VIII separated English Catholic Church from Rome, 1534, for political reasons. Protestant Episcopal Church in U.S. founded 1789.	*Bishops, in apostolic succession, are elected by diocesan representatives; part of Anglican Communion, symbolically headed by Archbishop of Canterbury.*	Scripture as interpreted by tradition, esp. *39 Articles* (1563); not dogmatic. Tri-annual convention of bishops, priests, and laymen.	Infant baptism, Holy Communion, others. Sacrament is symbolic, but has real spiritual effect.
Lutherans	Martin Luther in Wittenberg, Germany, 1517, objected to Catholic doctrine of salvation by merit and sale of indulgences; break complete by 1519.	Varies from congregational to episcopal; in U.S. a combination of regional synods and congregational polities is most common.	*Scripture, and tradition as spelled out in Augsburg Confession (1530) and other creeds. These confessions of faith are binding although interpretations vary.*	Infant baptism, Lord's Supper. Christ's true body and blood present "in, with, and under the bread and wine."
Methodists	Rev. John Wesley began movement, 1738, within Church of England. First U.S. denomination Baltimore, 1784.	Conference and superintendent system. *In United Methodist Church, general superintendents are bishops—not a priestly order, only an office—who are elected for life.*	Scripture as interpreted by tradition, reason, and experience.	Baptism of infants or adults, Lord's Supper commanded. Other rites, inc. marriage, ordination, solemnize personal commitments.
Mormons	In visions of the Angel Moroni by Joseph Smith, 1827, in New York, in which he received a new revelation on golden tablets: *The Book of Mormon.*	Theocratic; all male adults are in priesthood which culminates in Council of 12 Apostles and 1st Presidency (1st President, 2 counselors).	*The Bible, Book of Mormon and other revelations to Smith, and certain pronouncements of the 1st Presidency.*	Adult baptism, laying on of hands (which confers the gift of the Holy Spirit), Lord's Supper. Temple rites: baptism for the dead, marriage for eternity, others.
Orthodox	Original Christian proselytizing in 1st century; broke with Rome, 1054, after centuries of doctrinal disputes and diverging traditions.	Synods of bishops in autonomous, usually national, churches elect a patriarch, archbishop or metropolitan. These men, as a group, are the heads of the church.	Scripture, tradition, and the first 7 church councils up to Nicaea II in 787. Bishops in council have authority in doctrine and policy.	Seven sacraments: infant baptism and anointing, Eucharist (both bread and wine), ordination, penance, anointing of the sick, marriage.
Pentecostal	In Topeka, Kansas (1901), and Los Angeles (1906) in reaction to loss of evangelical fervor among Methodists and other denominations.	Originally a movement, not a formal organization, Pentecostalism now has a variety of organized forms and continues also as a movement.	Scripture, individual charismatic leaders, the teachings of the Holy Spirit.	*Spirit baptism, esp. as shown in "speaking in tongues"; healing and sometimes exorcism; adult baptism, Lord's Supper.*
Presbyterians	In Calvinist Reformation in 1500s; differed with Lutherans over sacraments, church government. John Knox founded Scotch Presbyterian church about 1560.	*Highly structured representational system of ministers and laypersons (presbyters) in local, regional and national bodies. (synods).*	Scripture.	Infant baptism, Lord's Supper; bread and wine symbolize Christ's spiritual presence.
Roman Catholics	Traditionally, by Jesus who named St. Peter the 1st Vicar; historically, in early Christian proselytizing and the conversion of imperial Rome in the 4th century.	Hierarchy with supreme power vested in Pope elected by cardinals. Councils of Bishops advise on matters of doctrine and policy.	*The Pope, when speaking for the whole church in matters of faith and morals, and tradition, which is partly recorded in scripture and expressed in church councils.*	Seven sacraments: baptism, contrition and penance, confirmation, Eucharist, marriage, ordination, and anointing of the sick (unction).
United Church of Christ	*By ecumenical union, 1957, of Congregationalists and Evangelical & Reformed, representing both Calvinist and Lutheran traditions.*	Congregational; a General Synod, representative of all congregations, sets general policy.	Scripture.	Infant baptism, Lord's Supper.

How Do They Differ?

distinguishes that denomination from any other.

Practice	Ethics	Doctrine	Other	Denomination
Worship style varies from staid to evangelistic. Extensive missionary activity.	Usually opposed to alcohol and tobacco; sometimes tends toward a perfectionist ethical standard.	*No creed; true church is of believers only, who are all equal.*	Since no authority can stand between the believer and God, the Baptists are strong supporters of church-state separation.	**Baptists**
Tries to avoid any rite or doctrine not explicitly part of the 1st century church. Some congregations may reject instrumental music.	Some tendency toward perfectionism; increasing interest in social action programs.	Simple New Testament faith; avoids any elaboration not firmly based on Scripture.	Highly tolerant in doctrinal and religious matters; strongly supportive of scholarly education.	**Church of Christ (Disciples)**
Formal, based on *Book of Common Prayer* (1549); services range from austerely simple to highly elaborate.	Tolerant; sometimes permissive; some social action programs.	*Apostles' Creed* is basic; otherwise, considerable variation ranges from rationalist and liberal to acceptance of most Roman Catholic dogma.	Strongly ecumenical, holding talks with all other branches of Christendom.	**Episcopalians**
Relatively simple formal liturgy with emphasis on the sermon.	Generally, conservative in personal and social ethics; doctrine of "2 kingdoms" (worldly and holy) supports conservatism in secular affairs.	Salvation by faith alone through grace. Lutheranism has made major contributions to Protestant theology.	Though still somewhat divided along ethnic lines (German, Swede, etc.), main divisions are between funamentalists and liberals.	**Lutherans**
Worship style varies widely by denomination, local church, geography.	Originally pietist and perfectionist; always strong social activist elements	No distinctive theological development; 25 Articles abriged from Church of England's 39 not binding.	In 1968, United Methodist Church joined pioneer English- and German-speaking groups. UMs leaders in ecumenical movement.	**Methodists**
Staid service with hymns, sermon. Secret temple ceremonies may be more elaborate. Strong missionary activity.	Temperance; strict tithing. Combine a strong work ethic with communal self-reliance.	God is a material being; he created the universe out of pre-existing matter; all persons can be saved and many will become divine. Most other beliefs are traditionally Christian.	Mormons regard mainline churches as apostate, corrupt. Reorganized Church (founded 1860) rejects most Mormon doctrine and practice except Book of Mormon.	**Mormons**
Elaborate liturgy, usually in the vernacular, though extremely traditional. The liturgy is the essence of Orthodoxy. Veneration of icons.	Tolerant; very little social action; divorce, remarriage permitted in some cases. Priests need not be celibate; bishops are.	Emphasis on Christ's resurrection, rather than crucifixion; the Holy Spirit proceeds from God the Father only.	Orthodox Church in America, orginally under Patriarch of Moscow, was granted autonomy in 1970. Greek Orthodox do not recognize this autonomy.	**Orthodox**
Loosely structured service with rousing hymns and sermons, culminating in spirit baptism.	Usually, emphasis on perfectionism with varying degrees of tolerance.	Simple traditional beliefs, usually Protestant, with emphasis on the immediate presence of God in the Holy Spirit	Once confined to lower-class "holy rollers," Pentecostalism now appears in mainline churches and has established middle-class congregations.	**Pentecostal**
A simple, sober service in which the sermon is central.	Traditionally, a tendency toward strictness with firm church- and self-discipline; otherwise tolerant.	Emphasizes the sovereignty and justice of God; no longer doctrinaire.	While traces of belief in predestination (that God has foreordained salvation for the "elect") remain, this idea is no longer a central element in Presbyterianism.	**Presbyterians**
Relatively elaborate ritual; wide variety of public and private rites, eg., rosary recitation, processions, novenas.	Theoretically very strict; tolerant in practice on most issues. Divorce and remarriage not accepted. Celibate clergy, except in Eastern rite.	Highly elaborated. Salvation by merit gained through faith. Unusual development of doctrines surrounding Mary. Dogmatic.	Roman Catholicism is presently in a period of relatively rapid change as a result of Vatican Councils I and II.	**Roman Catholics**
Usually simple services with emphasis on the sermon.	Tolerant; some social action emphasis.	Standard Protestant; *Statement of Faith* (1959) is not binding.	The 2 main churches in the 1957 union represented earlier unions with small groups of almost every Protestant denomination.	**United Church of Christ**

The Major World Religions

Buddhism

Founded: About 525 BC, reportedly near Benares, India.
Founder: Gautama Siddhartha (ca. 563-480), the Buddha, who achieved enlightenment through intense meditation.
Sacred Texts: The *Tripitaka*, a collection of the Buddha's teachings, rules of monastic life, and philosophical commentaries on the teachings; also a vast body of Buddhist teachings and commentaries, many of which are called *sutras*.
Organization: The basic institution is the *sangha* or monastic order through which the traditions are passed to each generation. Monastic life tends to be democratic and anti-authoritarian. Large lay organizations have developed in some sects.
Practice: Varies widely according to the sect and ranges from austere meditation to magical chanting and elaborate temple rites. Many practices, such as exorcism of devils, reflect pre-Buddhist beliefs.
Divisions: A wide variety of sects grouped into 3 primary branches: Therevada (sole survivor of the ancient Hinayana schools) which emphasizes the importance of pure thought and deed; Mahayana, which includes Zen and Soka-gakkai, ranges from philosophical schools to belief in the saving grace of higher beings or ritual practices, and to practical meditative disciplines; and Tantrism, an unusual combination of belief in ritual magic and sophisticated philosophy.
Location: Throughout Asia, from Ceylon to Japan. Zen and Soka-gakkai have several thousand adherents in the U.S.
Beliefs: Life is misery and decay, and there is no ultimate reality in it or behind it. The cycle of endless birth and rebirth continues because of desire and attachment to the unreal "self". Right meditation and deeds will end the cycle and achieve Nirvana, the Void, nothingness.

Hinduism

Founded: Ca. 1500 BC by Aryan invaders of India where their Vedic religion intermixed with the practices and beliefs of the natives.
Sacred texts: The *Veda*, including the *Upanishads*, a collection of rituals and mythological and philosophical commentaries; a vast number of epic stories about gods, heroes and saints, including the *Bhagavadgita*, a part of the *Mahabharata*, and the *Ramayana;* and a great variety of other literature.
Organization: None, strictly speaking. Generally, rituals should be performed or assisted by Brahmins, the priestly caste, but in practice simpler rituals can be performed by anyone. Brahmins are the final judges of ritual purity, the vital element in Hindu life. Temples and religious organizations are usually presided over by Brahmins.
Practice: A variety of private rituals, primarily passage rites (eg. initiation, marriage, death, etc.) and daily devotions, and a similar variety of public rites in temples. Of the latter, the *puja*, a ceremonial dinner for a god, is the most common.
Divisions: There is no concept of orthodoxy in Hinduism, which presents a bewildering variety of sects, most of them devoted to the worship of one of the many gods. The 3 major living traditions are those devoted to the gods Vishnu and Shiva and to the goddess Shakti; each of them divided into further sub-sects. Numerous folk beliefs and practices, often in amalgamation with the above groups, exist side-by-side with sophisticated philosophical schools and exotic cults.
Location: Confined to India, except for the missionary work of Vedanta, the Krishna Consciousness society, and individual *gurus* (teachers) in the West.
Beliefs: There is only one divine principle; the many gods are only aspects of that unity. Life in all its forms is an aspect of the divine, but it appears as a separation from the divine, a meaningless cycle of birth and rebirth (*samsara*) determined by the purity or impurity of past deeds (*karma*). To improve one's *karma* or escape *samsara* by pure acts, thought, and/or devotion is the aim of every Hindu.

Islam

Founded: 622 AD in Medina, Arabian peninsula.
Founder: Mohammed (ca. 570-632), the Prophet.
Sacred texts: *Koran*, the words of God. *Hadith*, collections of the sayings of the Prophet.
Organization: Theoretically the state and religious community are one, administered by a caliph. In practice, Islam is a loose collection of congregations united by a very conservative tradition. Islam is basically egalitarian and non-authoritarian.
Practice: Every Moslem has 5 duties: to make the profession of faith ("There is no god but Allah . . ."), pray 5 times a day, give a regular portion of his goods to charity, fast during the day in the month of Ramadan, and make at least one pilgrimage to Mecca if possible.
Divisions: The 2 major sects of Islam are the Sunni (orthodox) and the Shi'ah. The Shi'ah believe in 12 *imams*, perfect teachers, who still guide the faithful from Paradise. Shi'ah practice tends toward the ecstatic, while the Sunni is staid and simple. The Shi'ah sect affirms man's free will; the Sunni is deterministic. The mystic tradition in Islam is Sufism. A Sufi adept believes he has acquired a special inner knowledge direct from Allah.
Location: From the west coast of Africa to the Philipines across a broad band that includes Tanzania, southern USSR and western China, India, Malaysia and Indonesia. Islam claims over 2 million adherents in the U.S.
Beliefs: Strictly monotheistic. God is creator of the universe, omnipotent, just, and merciful. Man is God's highest creation, but limited and commits sins. He is misled by Satan, an evil spirit. God revealed the *Koran* to Mohammed to guide men to the truth. Those who repent and sincerely submit to God return to a state of sinlessness. In the end, the sinless go to Paradise, a place of physical and spiritual pleasure, and the wicked burn in Hell.

Judaism

Founded: About 1300 BCE.
Founder: Abrahm is regarded as the founding patriarch, but the Torah of Moses is the basic source of the teachings.
Sacred Texts: The five books of Moses constitute the written Torah. Special sanctity is also assigned other writings of the Hebrew Bible—the teachings of oral Torah are recorded in the Talmud, the Midrash, and various commentaries.
Organization: Originally theocratic, Judaism has evolved a congregational polity. The basic institution is the local synagogue, operated by the congregation and led by a rabbi of their choice. Chief Rabbis in France and Great Britain have authority only over those who accept it; in Israel, the 2 Chief Rabbis have civil authority in family law.
Practice: Among traditional practitioners, almost all areas of life are governed by strict religious discipline. Sabbath and holidays are marked by special observances, and attendance at public worship is regarded as especially important then. The chief annual observances are Passover, celebrating the liberation of the Israelites from Egypt and marked by the ritual Seder meal in the home, and the 10 days from Rosh Hashana (New Year) to Yom Kippur (Day of Atonement), a period of fasting and penitence.
Divisions: Judaism is an unbroken spectrum from ultra conservative to ultra liberal, largely reflecting different points of view regarding the binding character of the prohibitions and duties—particularly the dietary and Sabbath observations—prescribed in the daily life of the Jew.
Location: Almost worldwide, with concentrations in Israel and the U.S.
Beliefs: Strictly monotheistic. God is the creator and absolute ruler of the universe. Men are free to choose to rebel against God's rule. God established a particular relationship with the Hebrew people: by obeying a divine law God gave them they would be a special witness to God's mercy and justice. The emphasis in Judaism is on ethical behavior (and, among the traditional, careful ritual obedience) as the true worship of God.

Roman Catholic Hierarchy

Source: 1987 *Catholic Almanac*

Supreme Pontiff

At the head of the Roman Catholic Church is the Supreme Pontiff, Pope John Paul II, Karol Wojtyla, born at Wadowice (Krakow), Poland, May 18, 1920; ordained priest Nov. 1, 1946; promoted to Archbishop of Krakow Jan. 13, 1964; proclaimed Cardinal June 26, 1967; elected pope as successor of Pope John Paul I Oct. 16, 1978; solemn commencement as pope Oct. 22, 1978.

College of Cardinals

Members of the Sacred College of Cardinals are chosen by the Pope to be his chief assistants and advisors in the administration of the church. Among their duties is the election of the Pope when the Holy See becomes vacant. The title of cardinal is a high honor, but it does not represent any increase in the powers of holy orders.

In its present form, the College of Cardinals dates from the 12th century. The first cardinals, from about the 6th century, were deacons and priests of the leading churches of Rome, and bishops of neighboring diocese. The title of cardinal was limited to members of the college in 1567. The number of cardinals was set at 70 in 1586 by Pope Sixtus V. From 1959 Pope John XXIII began to increase the number. However, the number of cardinals eligible to participate in papal elections was limited to 120. There were lay cardinals until 1918, when the Code of Canon Law specified that all cardinals must be priests. Pope John XXIII in 1962 established that all cardinals must be bishops. The first age limits were set in 1971 by Pope Paul VI, who decreed that at age 80 cardinals must retire from curial departments and offices and from participation in papal elections. They continue as members of the college, with all rights and privileges.

An asterisk indicates cardinals ineligible to take part in papal elections.

Name	Office	Nationality	Born	Named
Alfrink, Bernard*	Archbishop emeritus of Utrecht	Dutch	1900	1960
Antonelli, Ferdinando*		Italian	1896	1973
Aponte Martinez, Luis	Archbishop of San Juan	American	1922	1973
Aramburu, Juan	Archbishop of Buenos Aires	Argentinian	1912	1976
Arinze, Francis A.	President of Secretariat for Non-Christians	Nigerian	1932	1985
Arns, Paulo	Archbishop of Sao Paulo	Brazilian	1921	1973
Bafile, Corrado*		Italian	1903	1976
Baggio, Sebastiano	Chamberlain of Holy Roman Church	Italian	1913	1969
Ballestrero, Anastasio	Archbishop of Turin	Italian	1913	1969
Baum, William	Prefect of Congregation for Catholic Education	American	1926	1976
Beras Rojas, Octavio	Archbishop emeritus of Santo Domingo	Dominican	1906	1976
Bernardin, Joseph	Archbishop of Chicago	American	1928	1983
Bertoli, Paolo		Italian	1908	1969
Biffi, Giacomo	Archbishop of Bologna	Italian	1928	1985
Brandao Vilela, Avelar	Archbishop of Sao Salvador de Bahia	Brazilian	1912	1973
Bueno y Monreal, Jose*	Archbishop emeritus of Seville	Spanish	1904	1958
Caprio, Giuseppe		Italian	1913	1969
Carberry, John*	Archbishop emeritus of St. Louis	American	1904	1969
Carpino, Francesco*		Italian	1905	1967
Carter, Gerald E.	Archbishop of Toronto	Canadian	1912	1979
Casaroli, Agostino	Secretary of State to His Holiness	Italian	1914	1979
Casoria, Giuseppe		Italian	1908	1983
Castillo Lara, Rosalio	President of Pontifical Commission for Authentic Interpretation of Code of Canon Law	Venezuelan	1922	1985
Cè, Marco	Patriarch of Venice	Italian	1925	1979
Ciappi, Mario Luigi	Pro-Theologian of Pontifical Household	Italian	1909	1977
Civardi, Ernesto		Italian	1906	1979
Colombo, Giovanni*	Archbishop emeritus of Milan	Italian	1902	1965
Cooray, Thomas B.*	Archbishop emeritus of Colombo, Sri Lanka	Sri Lankan	1901	1965
Cordeiro, Joseph	Archbishop of Karachi	Pakistani	1918	1973
Corripio Ahumada, Ernesto	Archbishop of Mexico City	Mexican	1919	1979
Dadaglio, Luigi	Deacon of St. Pius V Major Penitentiary	Italian	1914	1985
Danneels, Godfried	Archbishop of Mechelen-Brussels, Military Vicar of Belgium	Belgian	1933	1983
Darmojuwono, Justinus	Archbishop emeritus of Semarang	Indonesian	1914	1967
De Araujo Sales, Eugenio	Archbishop of St. Sebastian of Rio de Janeiro	Brazilian	1920	1969
Dearden, John	Archbishop emeritus of Detroit	American	1907	1969
Decourtray, Albert	Archbishop of Lyon	French	1923	1985
De Furstenberg, Maximilien*	Grand Master of Equestrian Order of Holy Sepulchre of Jerusalem	Algerian	1903	1965
De Lubac, Henri*	Deacon of St. Mary in Dominica	French	1896	1983
Deskur, Andrzej	Deacon of St. Cesario in Palatio	Polish	1924	1985
do Nascimento, Alexandre	Archbishop of Lubango	Angolan	1925	1983
Duval, Leon-Etienne	Archbishop of Algiers	French	1903	1965
Ekandem, Dominic	Bishop of Ikot Ekpene	Nigerian	1917	1976
Enrique y Tarancon, Vicente	Archbishop emeritus of Madrid	Spanish	1907	1969
Etchegaray, Roger	President of Pontifical Commission for Justice and Peace	French	1922	1979
Flahiff, George*	Archbishop emeritus of Winnipeg	Canadian	1905	1969
Freeman, James	Archbishop emeritus of Sydney	Australian	1907	1973
Fresno Larrain, Juan	Archbishop of Santiago	Chilean	1914	1985
Gagnon, Edouard	President of Pontifical Council for the Family	Canadian	1918	1985
Gantin, Bernardin	Pres. of Comm. for Latin America & Migration and Tourism	Benin	1922	1977
Garrone, Gabriel-Marie*		French	1901	1967
Glemp, Josef	Archbishop of Warsaw, Gniezno, Primate of Poland	Polish	1928	1983
Gonzalez Martin, Marcelo	Archbishop of Toledo	Spanish	1918	1973
Gouyon, Paul	Archbishop of Rennes	French	1910	1969
Gray, Gordon	Archbishop emeritus of St. Andrews and Edinburgh	Scottish	1910	1969
Guerri, Sergio		Italian	1905	1969
Gulbinowicz, Henryk	Archbishop of Wroclaw	Polish	1928	1985
Guyot, Jean*	Archbishop emeritus of Toulouse	French	1905	1973

Name	Office	Nationality	Born	Named
Hamer, Jean	Prefect of Congregation for Religious and Secular Institutes	Belgian	1916	1985
Hoeffner, Joseph	Archbishop of Cologne	German	1906	1969
Hume, George Basil	Archbishop of Westminster	English	1923	1976
Innocenti, Antonio	Dean of St. Marie in Aquiro	Italian	1915	1985
Jubany Arnau, Narciso	Archbishop of Barcelona	Spanish	1913	1973
Khoraiche, Anthony	Patriarch of Antioch for Maronites	Lebanese	1907	1983
Kim, Stephan Sou Hwan	Archbishop of Seoul	Korean	1922	1969
Kitbunchu, Michael	Archbishop of Bangkok	Thai	1929	1983
Koenig, Franz*	Archbishop of Vienna	Austrian	1905	1958
Krol, John	Archbishop of Philadelphia	American	1910	1967
Kuharic, Franjo	Archbishop of Zagreb	Croat	1919	1983
Landazuri Ricketts, Juan	Archbishop of Lima	Peruvian	1913	1962
Law, Bernard F.	Archbishop of Boston	American	1931	1985
Lebrun Moratinos, Jose	Archbishop of Caracas	Venezuelan	1919	1983
Leger, Paul*	Archbishop emeritus of Montreal	Canadian	1904	1953
Lékai, Laszlo	Archbishop of Esztergom	Hungarian	1910	1976
Lopez-Trujillo, Alfonso	Archbishop of Medellin	Colombian	1935	1983
Lorscheider, Aloisio	Archbishop of Fortaleza	Brazilian	1924	1976
Lourdusamy, D. Simon	Archbishop emeritus of Bangalore	Indian	1924	1985
Lubachivsky, Myroslav	Archbishop of Lwow, Major Archbishop of Ukrainians	Ukrainian	1914	1985
Lustiger, Jean-Marie	Archbishop of Paris	French	1926	1983
Macharski, Franciszek	Archbishop of Cracow	Polish	1927	1979
Malula, Joseph	Archbishop of Kinshasa	Congolese	1917	1969
Manning, Timothy	Archbishop emeritus of Los Angeles	American	1909	1973
Martini, Carlo Maria	Archbishop of Milan	Italian	1927	1983
Marty, Francois*	Archbishop emeritus of Paris	French	1904	1969
Maurer, Jose*	Archbishop emeritus of Sucre	Bolivian	1900	1967
Mayer, Paul Augustin	Pref. of Cong. for Sacraments and Divine Worship	German	1911	1985
McCann, Owen	Archbishop of Cape Town	S. African	1907	1965
Meisner, Joachim	Bishop of Berlin	German	1933	1983
Munoz Duque, Anibal	Archbishop emeritus of Bogota	Colombian	1908	1973
Munoz Vega, Pablo*	Archbishop emeritus of Quito	Ecuadorian	1903	1969
Nasalli Rocca di Corneliano, Mario*		Italian	1903	1969
Nsubuga, Emmanuel	Archbishop of Kampala	Ugandan	1914	1976
Obando Bravo, Miguel	Archbishop of Managua	Nicaraguan	1926	1985
O'Boyle, Patrick*	Archbishop emeritus of Washington, D.C.	American	1896	1967
O'Connor, John J	Archbishop of New York	American	1920	1985
Oddi, Silvio		Italian	1910	1969
O'Fiaich, Tomas	Archbishop of Armagh, Primate of all Ireland	Irish	1923	1979
Otunga, Maurice	Archbishop of Nairobi	Kenyan	1923	1973
Palazzini, Pietro	Prefect for Congregation for the Causes of Saints	Italian	1912	1973
Pappalardo, Salvatore	Archbishop of Palermo	Italian	1918	1973
Paupini, Giuseppe		Italian	1907	1969
Pavan, Pietro*	Deacon of St. Francis of Paola	Italian	1903	1985
Pellegrino, Michele*	Archbishop emeritus of Turin	Italian	1903	1967
Picachy, Lawrence	Archbishop of Calcutta	Indian	1916	1976
Piovanelli, Silvano	Archbishop of Florence	Italian	1924	1985
Pironio, Eduardo	President of the Pontifical Council for the Laity	Argentinian	1920	1976
Poletti, Ugo	Grand Chancellor of Laturan University	Italian	1914	1973
Poupard, Paul	President of Secretariat for Non-Believers	French	1930	1985
Primatesta, Raul Francisco	Archbishop of Cordoba	Argentinian	1919	1973
Ratzinger, Joseph	President of Biblical and Theological Commissions	German	1927	1977
Razafimahatra, Victor	Archbishop of Tananarive	Madagascan	1921	1976
Ribeiro, Antonio	Patriarch of Lisbon, Military Vicar	Portuguese	1928	1973
Righi-Lambertini, Egano	Deacon of St. John Bosco in Via Tuscolana	Italian	1906	1979
Rossi, Agnelo	Grand Chancellor of Pontifical Urban University	Brazilian	1913	1965
Rossi, Opilio	Pres. of Comm. for Sanctuaries of Pompeii and Loretto	Italian	1910	1976
Rubin, Wladyslaw	Prefect of Congregation for Oriental Churches	Polish	1917	1979
Rugambwa, Laurean	Archbishop of Dar-es-Salaam	Tanzanian	1912	1960
Sabattani, Aurelio	Prefect of Apostolic Signatura, Archpriest of St. Peter's	Italian	1912	1983
Salazar Lopez, Jose	Archbishop of Guadalajara	Mexican	1910	1973
Satowaki, Joseph A.*	Archbishop of Nagasaki	Japanese	1904	1979
Scherer, Alfred*	Archbishop emeritus of Porto Alegre, Brazil	Brazilian	1903	1969
Sensi, Giuseppe	Deacon of SS Biagio e Carlo	Italian	1907	1976
Sidarouss, Stephanos*	Coptic Patriarch of Alexandria	Egyptian	1904	1965
Silva Henriquez, Raul	Archbishop emeritus of Santiago de Chile	Chilean	1907	1962
Simonis, Adrianus	Archbishop of Utrecht	Dutch	1931	1985
Sin, Jaime	Archbishop of Manila	Filipino	1928	1976
Siri, Giuseppe*	Archbishop of Genoa	Italian	1906	1953
Suenens, Leo*	Archbishop emeritus of Mechelen-Brussels	Belgian	1904	1962
Suquia Goicoechea, Angel	Archbishop of Madrid	Spanish	1916	1985
Taofinu'u, Pio	Apostolic Administrator of Samoa	Samoan	1923	1973
Thiandoum, Hyacinthe	Archbishop of Dakar	Sengalese	1921	1976
Tomasek, Frantisek*	Archbishop of Prague	Czech	1899	1977
Tomko, Jozef	Pref. of the Cong. for the Evangelization of Peoples	Slovak-Italian	1924	1985
Trinh Van-Can, Joseph-Marie	Archbishop of Hanoi	Vietnamese	1921	1979
Tzadua, Paulos	Archbishop of Addis Ababa	Ethiopian	1921	1985
Ursi, Corrado	Archbishop of Naples	Italian	1908	1967
Vachon, Louis-Albert	Archbishop of Quebec	Canadian	1912	1985
Vaivods, Julijans*	Apostolic Administrator of Riga and Liepaja	Latvian	1905	1964
Vidal, Ricardo	Archbishop of Cebu	Filipino	1931	1985
Volk, Hermann*	Archbishop emeritus of Mainz	German	1903	1973
Wetter, Frederich	Archbishop of Munich and Freising	German	1928	1985
Willebrands, Johannes	President of Secretariat for Christian Unity	Dutch	1909	1969
Williams, Thomas Stafford	Archbishop of Wellington	New Zealander	1930	1983
Yago, Bernard	Archbishop of Abidjan, Ivory Coast	Ivorian	1916	1960
Zoungrana, Paul	Archbishop of Ougadougou	Burkina Fasan	1917	1965

STATES AND OTHER AREAS OF THE U.S.

Sources: Population: Commerce Dept., Bureau of the Census (July, 1986 provisional estimates, inc. armed forces personnel in each state but excluding such personnel stationed overseas); area: Bureau of the Census, Geography Division; forested land: Agriculture Dept., Forest Service; lumber production: Bureau of the Census, Industry Division; mineral production: Interior Dept., Bureau of Mines (preliminary); commercial fishing: Commerce Dept., Natl. Marine Fisheries Service; value of construction: McGraw-Hill Information Systems Co., F.W. Dodge Division; per capita income (estimate): Commerce Dept., Bureau of Economic Analysis; unemployment: Labor Dept., Bureau of Labor Statistics; finance: Federal Deposit Insurance Corp.; federal employees: Labor Dept., Office of Personnel Management; energy: Energy Dept., Energy Information Administration; education: Education Dept., National Education Assn. Other information from sources in individual states, usually Commerce Dept.

Alabama

Heart of Dixie, Camellia State

People. Population (1986): 4,053,000; **rank:** 22. **Pop. density:** 78.7 per sq. mi. **Urban** (1980): 60%. **Racial distrib.** (1980): 73.7% White; 26.3% Black; Hispanic 33,100. **Net change** (1980-86): +159,000; 4.1%.

Geography. Total area: 51,609 sq. mi.; **rank:** 29. **Land area:** 50,708 sq. mi. **Acres forested land:** 21,361,100. **Location:** in the east south central U.S., extending N-S from Tenn. to the Gulf of Mexico; east of the Mississippi River. **Climate:** long, hot summers; mild winters; generally abundant rainfall. **Topography:** coastal plains inc. Prairie Black Belt give way to hills, broken terrain; highest elevation, 2,407 ft. **Capital:** Montgomery.

Economy. Principal industries: pulp and paper, chemicals, electronics, apparel, textiles, primary metals, lumber and wood, food processing, fabricated metals, automotive tires. **Principal manufactured goods:** electronics, cast iron and plastic pipe, fabricated steel prods., ships, paper products, chemicals, steel, mobile homes, fabrics, poultry processing. **Agriculture: Chief crops:** peanuts, cotton, soybeans, hay, corn, wheat, potatoes, pecans, sweet potatoes, cottonseed. **Livestock** (1986): 1.85 mln. cattle; 380,000 hogs/pigs; 16.5 mln. poultry. **Timber/lumber** (1984): pine, hardwoods; 1.6 bln. bd. ft. **Minerals** (1986): $422.7 mln., mostly cement, clays, lime, sand & gravel, stone. **Commercial fishing** (1986): $64.0 mln. **Chief ports:** Mobile. **Value of construction** (1986): $3.0 bln. **Employment distribution** (1986): 24% manuf.; 22% trade; 18.7% serv. **Per capita income** (1986): $11,115. **Unemployment** (1986): 9.8%. **Tourism** (1986): tourists spent $3.6 bln.

Finance. Commercial bank deposits, per capita (1985): $5,141.

Federal government. No. federal civilian employees (Mar. 1986): 48,469. **Avg. salary:** $26,347. **Notable federal facilities:** George C. Marshall NASA Space Center, Huntsville; Maxwell AFB, Montgomery; Ft. Rucker, Ozark; Ft. McClellan, Anniston; Natl. Fertilizer Development Center, Muscle Shoals; U.S. Corps of Engineers, Mobile.

Energy. Electricity production (1986, mwh, by source): Hydroelectric: 5.2 mln. Mineral: 51.8 mln. Nuclear: 11.6 mln.

Education. Expenditure per pupil, public schools (1984-85): $2,325. **Avg. salary, public school teachers** (1987 est.): $23,500.

State data. Motto: We dare defend our rights. **Flower:** Camellia. **Bird:** Yellowhammer. **Tree:** Southern Pine. **Song:** Alabama. **Entered union** Dec. 14, 1819; rank, 22d. **State fair** at: Birmingham; early Oct.

History. First Europeans were Spanish explorers in the early 1500s. The French made the first permanent settlement, on Mobile Bay, 1701-02; later, English settled in the northern areas. France ceded the entire region to England at the end of the French and Indian War, 1763, but Spanish Florida claimed the Mobile Bay area until U. S. troops took it, 1813. Gen. Andrew Jackson broke the power of the Creek Indians, 1814, and they were removed to Oklahoma. The Confederate States were organized Feb. 4, 1861, at Montgomery, the first capital.

Tourist attractions. Jefferson Davis' "first White House" of the Confederacy; Ivy Green, Helen Keller's birthplace at Tuscumbia; statue of Vulcan in Birmingham; George Washington Carver Museum at Tuskegee Univ.; Alabama Space and Rocket Center at Huntsville; Alabama Shakespeare Festival in Montgomery; Gulf Shores beaches; Moundville State Monument in Moundville; Pike Pioneer Museum in Troy.

At Russell Cave National Monument, near Bridgeport: a detailed record of occupancy by humans from about 10,000 BC to 1650 AD.

Famous Alabamians include Hank Aaron, Tallulah Bankhead, Hugo L. Black, Paul "Bear" Bryant, George Washington Carver, Nat King Cole, William C. Handy, Helen Keller, Harper Lee, Joe Louis, John Hunt Morgan, Jesse Owens, George Wallace, Booker T. Washington, Hank Williams.

Alabama Business Council. 468 S. Perry St., P.O. Box 76, Montgomery, AL 36195.

Toll-free travel information. 1-800-392-8096; 1-800-ALABAMA out of state.

Alaska

Unofficial nickname: "The Last Frontier"

People. Population (1986): 534,000; **rank:** 48. **Pop. density:** 0.91 per sq. mi., **Urban** (1980): 64.3%. **Net change** (1980-86): +132,000; 32.8%.

Geography. Total area: 586,412 sq. mi.; **rank:** 1. **Land area:** 586,412 sq. mi. **Acres forested land:** 119,145,000. **Location:** NW corner of North America, bordered on east by Canada. **Climate:** SE, SW, and central regions, moist and mild; far north extremely dry. Extended summer days, winter nights, throughout. **Topography:** includes Pacific and Arctic mountain systems, central plateau, and Arctic slope. Mt. McKinley, 20,320 ft., is the highest point in North America. **Capital:** Juneau.

Economy. Principal industries: oil, gas, tourism, commercial fishing. **Principal manufactured goods:** fish products, lumber and pulp, furs. **Agriculture: Chief crops:** barley, hay, silage, potatoes, lettuce, milk, eggs. **Livestock:** 9,600 cattle; 3,200 hogs/pigs; 3,100 sheep; 78,000 poultry; 25,000 reindeer. **Timber/lumber:** spruce, yellow cedar, hemlock. **Minerals** (1986): $86.8 mln.; sand & gravel, crushed and broken stone, gold. **Commercial fishing** (1986): $752.4 mln. **Chief ports:** Anchorage, Dutch Harbor, Seward, Skagway, Juneau, Sitka, Valdez, Wrangell. **International airports at:** Anchorage, Fairbanks, Ketchikan, Juneau. **Value of construction** (1986): $1.2 bln. **Employment distribution:** 29.3% gvt.; 19.7% trade; 18.3% serv.; 8.7% transp. **Per capita income** (1986): $17,744. **Unemployment** (1986): 10.8%. **Tourism** (1983): out-of-state visitors spent $535 mln.

Finance. Commerical bank deposits, per capita (1985): $7,475.

Federal government. No. federal civilian employees (Mar. 1986): 11,190. **Avg. salary:** $30,480.

Energy. Electricity production (1986, mwh, by source): Hydroelectric: 803,000. Mineral: 3.4 mln.

Education. Expenditure per pupil, public schools (1984-85): $7,843. **Avg. salary, public school teachers** (1987 est.): $43,970.

State data. Motto: North to the future. **Flower:** Forget-me-not. **Bird:** Willow ptarmigan. **Tree:** Sitka spruce. **Song:** Alaska's Flag. **Entered union:** Jan. 3, 1959; rank, 49th. **State fair at:** Palmer; late Aug.—early Sept.

History. Vitus Bering, a Danish explorer working for Russia, was the first European to land in Alaska, 1741. Alexander Baranov, first governor of Russian America, set up headquarters at Archangel, near present Sitka, in 1799. Secretary of State William H. Seward in 1867 bought Alaska from Russia for $7.2 million, a bargain some called "Seward's Folly." In 1896 gold was discovered and the famed Gold Rush was on.

Tourist attractions: Glacier Bay National Park, Katmai National Park & Preserve, Denali National Park, one of North America's great wildlife sanctuaries, Pribilof Islands fur seal rookeries, restored St. Michael's Russian Orthodox Cathedral, Sitka.

Famous Alaskans include Carl Eielson, Ernest Gruening, Joe Juneau, Sydney Laurence, James Wickersham.

Tourist information. Alaska Division of Tourism, P.O. Box E, Juneau, AK 99811-0800.

Arizona

Grand Canyon State

People. Population (1986): 3,317,000; **rank:** 27. **Pop. density:** 28.1 per sq. mi. **Urban** (1980): 83.8% **Racial distrib. (1980):** 82.4% White; 2.7% Black; 14.8% Other (includes American Indians); Hispanic 440,915. **Net change** (1980-86): +601,000; 22.1%.

Geography. Total area: 113,909 sq. mi.; **rank:** 6. **Land area:** 113,417 sq. mi. **Acres forested land:** 18,493,900. **Location:** in the southwestern U.S. **Climate:** clear and dry in the southern regions and northern plateau; high central areas have heavy winter snows. **Topography:** Colorado plateau in the N, containing the Grand Canyon; Mexican Highlands running diagonally NW to SE; Sonoran Desert in the SW. **Capital:** Phoenix.

Economy: Principal industries: manufacturing, tourism, mining, agriculture. **Principal manufactured goods:** electronics, printing and publishing, foods, primary and fabricated metals, aircraft and missiles, apparel. **Agriculture: Chief crops:** cotton, sorghum, barley, corn, wheat, sugar beets, citrus fruits. **Livestock** (1986): 1.1 mln. cattle; 175,000 hogs/pigs; 278,000 sheep; 490,000 poultry. **Timber/lumber** (1985): pine, fir, spruce; 368 mln. bd. ft. **Minerals** (1986): $1.6 bln.; copper, molybdenum, gold, silver. **International airports at:** Phoenix, Tucson, Yuma. **Value of construction** (1986): $6.4 bln. **Employment distribution** (1986): 24.3% services; 24.2% trade; 16.9% gvt.; 13.7% manuf. **Per capita income** (1986): $13,220. **Unemployment** (1986): 6.9%. **Tourism** (1985): tourists spent $5.6 bln.

Finance. Commerical bank deposits, per capita (1985): $6,547.

Federal government: No. federal civilian employees (Mar. 1986): 26,132. **Avg. salary:** $24,541. **Notable federal facilities:** Williams, Luke, Davis-Monthan AF bases; Ft. Huachuca Army Base; Yuma Proving Grounds.

Energy. Electricity production (1986, mwh, by source): Hydroelectric: 14.5 mln.; Mineral: 26.8; Nuclear: 9.9.

Education. Expenditure per pupil, public schools (1984-85): $2,724. **Avg. salary, public school teachers** (1987 est.): $26,280.

State data. Motto: Ditat Deus (God enriches). **Flower:** Blossom of the Seguaro cactus. **Bird:** Cactus wren. **Tree:** Paloverde. **Song:** Arizona. **Entered union** Feb. 14, 1912; rank, 48th. **State fair** at: Phoenix; late Oct.–early Nov.

History. Marcos de Niza, a Franciscan, and Estevan, a black slave, explored the area, 1539. Eusebio Francisco Kino, Jesuit missionary, taught Indians Christianity and farming, 1690-1711, left a chain of missions. Spain ceded Arizona to Mexico, 1821. The U. S. took over at the end of the Mexican War, 1848. The area below the Gila River was obtained from Mexico in the Gadsden Purchase, 1854. Long Apache wars did not end until 1886, with Geronimo's surrender.

Tourist attractions. The Grand Canyon of the Colorado, an immense, vari-colored fissure 217 mi. long, 4 to 13 mi. wide at the brim, 4,000 to 5,500 ft. deep; the Painted Desert, extending for 30 mi. along U.S. 66; the Petrified Forest; Canyon Diablo, 225 ft. deep and 500 ft. wide; Meteor Crater, 4,150 ft. across, 570 ft. deep, made by a prehistoric meteor. Also, London Bridge at Lake Havasu City.

Famous Arizonans include Cochise, Geronimo, Barry Goldwater, Zane Grey, George W. P. Hunt, Helen Jacobs, Percival Lowell, William H. Pickering, Morris Udall, Stewart Udall, Frank Lloyd Wright.

Tourist information. Phoenix & Valley of the Sun Visitor and Convention Bureau, 1-602-254-6500.

Arkansas

Land of Opportunity

People. Population (1986): 2,372,000; **rank:** 33. **Pop. density:** 45.4 per sq. mi. **Urban** (1980): 51.5%. **Racial distrib.** (1980): 66.1% White; 16.3% Black; Hispanic 17,873. **Net change** (1980-86): +86,000; 3.8%.

Geography. Total area: 53,104 sq. mi.; **rank:** 27. **Land area:** 51,945 sq. mi. **Acres forested land:** 18,281,500. **Location:** in the west south-central U.S. **Climate:** long, hot summers, mild winters; generally abundant rainfall. **Topography:** eastern delta and prairie, southern lowland forests, and the northwestern highlands, which include the Ozark Plateaus. **Capital:** Little Rock.

Economy. Principal industries: manufacturing, agriculture, tourism. **Principal manufactured goods:** poultry products, forestry products, food products, home appliances, aluminum, electric motors, transformers, garments, bricks, fertilizer, petroleum products. **Agriculture: Chief crops:** soybeans, rice, cotton, hay, wheat, sorghum, tomatoes, strawberries, peaches. **Livestock** (1985): 1.8 mln. cattle; 436,000 hogs/pigs; 760 mln. poultry. **Timber/lumber** (1984): oak, hickory, gum, cypress, pine; 1.4 bln. bd. ft. **Minerals** (1986): $281.8 mln.; abrasives, bauxite, bromine, stone, sand & gravel. **Commercial fishing** (1984): $7.3 mln. **Chief ports:** Little Rock, Pine Bluff, Osceola, Helena, Fort Smith, Van Buren, Camden. **Value of construction** (1986): $1.5 bln. **Employment distribution** (1986): 21.6% manuf.; 18.8% trade; 14.9% serv.; 4.6% agric. **Per capita income** (1986): $10,773. **Unemployment** (1986): 8.7% **Tourism** (1985): travelers spent $1.9 bln.

Finance. Commerical bank deposits, per capita (1985): $6,331.

Federal government. No. federal civilian employees (Mar. 1986): 12,259. **Avg. salary:** $23,500. **Notable federal facilities:** Nat'l. Center for Toxicological Research, Jefferson; Pine Bluff Arsenal.

Energy. Electricity production (1986, mwh, by source): Hydroelectric: 2.8 mln.; Mineral: 23.5 mln.; Nuclear: 8.9 mln.

Education. Expenditure per pupil, public schools (1984-85): $2,353. **Avg. salary, public school teachers** (1987 est.): $19,951.

State data. Motto: Regnat Populus (The people rule). **Flower:** Apple Blossom. **Bird:** Mockingbird. **Tree:** Pine. **Song:** Arkansas. **Entered union:** June 15, 1836; rank, 25th. **State fair at:** Little Rock; late Sept.- early Oct.

History. First European explorers were de Soto, 1541, Jolliet, 1673; La Salle, 1682. First settlement was by the French under Henri de Tonty, 1686, at Arkansas Post. In 1762 the area was ceded by France to Spain, then back again in 1800, and was part of the Louisiana Purchase by the U.S. in 1803. Arkansas seceded from the Union in 1861, only after the Civil War began, and more than 10,000 Arkansans fought on the Union side.

Tourist attractions. Hot Springs National Park, water ranging from 95° to 147°F; Eureka Springs, resort since 1880s; Blanchard Caverns, near Mountain View, are among the nation's largest; Crater of Diamonds, near Murfreesboro, only U.S. diamond mine; Buffalo Natl. River; Mid-America Museum, Ozark Folk Center.

Famous Arkansans include Hattie Caraway, "Dizzy" Dean, Orval Faubus, James W. Fulbright, Douglas MacArthur, John L. McClellan, James S. McDonnel, Winthrop Rockefeller, Edward Durell Stone, Archibald Yell.

Chamber of Commerce. One Spring Bldg., Little Rock, AR 72201.

Toll-free travel information. 1-800-643-8383 out of state; 800-482-8999 in Arkansas.

California

Golden State

People. Population (1986): 26,981,000; **rank:** 1. **Pop. density:** 168.6 per sq. mi. **Urban** (1980): 91.3%. **Racial distrib.** (1980): 76.1% White; 7.6% Black; 16.1% Other (includes American Indians, Asian Americans, and Pacific Islanders); Hispanic 4,543,770. **Net change** (1980-1986): +3,313,000; 14.0%.

Geography. Total area 158,693 sq. mi.; **rank:** 3. **Land area:** 156,361 sq. mi. **Acres forested land:** 40,152,100. **Location:** on western coast of the U.S. **Climate:** moderate temperatures and rainfall along the coast; extremes in the interior. **Topography:** long mountainous coastline; central valley; Sierra Nevada on the east; desert basins of the southern interior; rugged mountains of the north. **Capital:** Sacramento.

Economy. Principal industries: agriculture, manufacturing, aerospace, construction. **Principal manufactured goods:** foods, primary and fabricated metals, machinery, electric and electronic equipment, transportation equipment. **Agriculture: Chief crops:** grapes, cotton, flowers, oranges, nursery products, hay, tomatoes, lettuce, strawberries, almonds. **Livestock** (1985): 1.9 mln. cattle; 1.8 mln. hogs/pigs; 1.5 mln. sheep; 209.8 mln. poultry. **Timber/ lumber** (1985): fir, pine, redwood, oak; 3.8 bln. bd. ft. **Minerals:** (1986): leading state in U.S. in nonfuel minerals, with value of $2.3 bln.; mostly cement, boron minerals, sand & gravel, crushed stone. **Commercial fishing** (1986): $139.2 mln. **Chief ports:** Long Beach, San Diego, Oakland, San Francisco, Sacramento, Stockton. **International airports at:** Los Angeles, San Francisco, San Jose. **Value of construction** (1986): $36.9 bln. **Employment distribution** (1986): 24.4% serv.; 24.1% trade; 18.2% manuf.; 16.3% gvt. **Per capita income** (1986): $16,778. **Unemployment** (1986): 6.7% **Tourism** (1986): $32.2 bln.

Finance. Commercial bank deposits, per capita (1985): $7,338.

Federal government. No. federal civilian employees (Mar. 1986): 212,769. **Avg. salary:** $25,818. **Notable federal facilities:** Vandenberg, Beale, Travis, McClellan AF bases, San Francisco Mint.

Energy. Electricity production (1986, mwh, by source): Hydroelectric: 41.7 mln.; Mineral: 41.1 mln.; Nuclear: 26.2 mln.

Education. Expenditure per pupil, public schools (1984-85): $3,256. **Avg. salary, public school teachers** (1987 est.): $31,170.

State Data. Motto: Eureka (I have found it). **Flower:** Golden poppy. **Bird:** California valley quail. **Tree:** California redwood. **Song:** I Love You, California. **Entered Union** Sept. 9, 1850; rank, 31st. **State fair** at: Sacramento; late Aug.—early Sept.

History. First European explorers were Cabrillo, 1542, and Drake, 1579. First settlement was the Spanish Alta California mission at San Diego, 1769, first in a string founded by Franciscan Father Junipero Serra. U. S. traders and settlers arrived in the 19th century and staged the abortive Bear Flag Revolt, 1846; the Mexican War began later in 1846 and U.S. forces occupied California; Mexico ceded the province to the U.S., 1848, the same year the Gold Rush began.

Tourist attractions. Scenic regions are Yosemite Valley; Lassen and Sequoia-Kings Canyon national parks; Lake Tahoe; the Mojave and Colorado deserts; San Francisco Bay; and Monterey Peninsula. Oldest living things on earth are believed to be a stand of Bristlecone pines in the Inyo National Forest, est. to be 4,600 years old. The world's tallest tree, the Howard Libbey redwood, 362 ft. with a girth of 44 ft., stands on Redwood Creek, Humboldt County.

Also, RMS Queen Mary, Spruce Goose, both Long Beach; Palomar Observatory; Disneyland; J. Paul Getty Museum, Malibu; Tournament of Roses and Rose Bowl.

Famous Californians include Luther Burbank, John C. Fremont, Bret Harte, Wm. R. Hearst, Jack London, Aimee Semple McPherson, John Muir, Richard M. Nixon, William Saroyan, Junipero Serra, Leland Stanford, John Steinbeck, Earl Warren.

Chamber of Commerce: 1027 10th, Sacramento, CA 95814.

Travel information. Dept. of Commerce, 1121 L St., Suite 600, Sacramento, CA 95814.

Colorado

Centennial State

People. Population (1986): 3,267,000; **rank:** 26. **Pop. density:** 31.1 per sq. mi. **Urban** (1980): 80.6%. **Racial distrib.** (1980): 88.9% White; 3.5% Black; Hispanic 339,300. **Net change** (1980-86): +377,500; 13.1%.

Geography. Total area: 104,247 sq. mi.; **rank:** 8. **Land area:** 103,766 sq. mi. **Acres forested land:** 22,271,000. **Location:** in west central U.S. **Climate:** low relative humidity, abundant sunshine, wide daily, seasonal temperatures ranges; alpine conditions in the high mountains. **Topography:** eastern dry high plains; hilly to mountainous central plateau; western Rocky Mountains of high ranges alternating with broad valleys and deep, narrow canyons. **Capital:** Denver.

Economy. Principal industries: manufacturing, government, tourism, agriculture, aerospace, electronics equipment. **Principal manufactured goods:** computer equipment, instruments, foods, machinery, aerospace products, rubber. **Agriculture: Chief crops:** corn, wheat, hay, sugar beets, barley, potatoes, apples, peaches, pears, dry edible beans, sorghum. **Livestock** (1987): 2.6 mln. cattle; 190,000 hogs/pigs; 690,000 sheep; 2.9 mln. poultry. **Timber/lumber** (1984): oak, ponderosa pine, Douglas fir; 168 mln. bd. ft. **Minerals** (1986): $424.9; construction sand & gravel, gold, crushed stone. **International airports at:** Denver. **Value of construction** (1986): $3.8 bln. **Employment distribution** (1986 est.): 24.9% trade; 23.2% serv.; 18.1% gvt.; 13.2% manuf. **Per capita income** (1986): $15,113. **Unemployment** (1986): 7.4%. **Tourism** (1986): $4.5 bln.

Finance. Commercial bank deposits, per capita (1985): $6,501.

Federal government. No. federal civilian employees (Mar. 1986): 35,557. **Avg. salary:** $26,599. **Notable federal facilities:** U.S. Air Force Academy; U.S. Mint; Ft. Carson, Lowry AFB; Solar Energy Research Institute; U.S. Rail Transport. Test Center; N. Amer. Aerospace Defense Command; Consolidated Space Operations Center; U.S. Documents Center.

Energy. Electricity production (1986, mwh, by source): Hydroelectric: 2.3 mln.; Mineral: 26.0 mln..

Education. Expenditures per pupil, public schools (1984-1985): $3,697. **Avg. salary, public school teachers** (1987 est.): $27,388.

State data. Motto: Nil Sine Numine (Nothing without Providence). **Flower:** Rocky Mountain columbine. **Bird:** Lark bunting. **Tree:** Colorado blue spruce. **Song:** Where the Columbines Grow. Entered union Aug. 1, 1876; rank 38th. **State fair** at: Pueblo; last week in Aug.

History. Early civilization centered around Mesa Verde 2,000 years ago. The U.S. acquired eastern Colorado in the Louisiana Purchase, 1803; Lt. Zebulon M. Pike explored the area, 1806, discovering the peak that bears his name. After the Mexican War, 1846-48, U.S. immigrants settled in the east, former Mexicans in the south.

Tourist attractions. 310 or more sunshine days per year; more than 1,000 peaks of 2 or more miles; Rocky

Mountain National Park; Garden of the Gods; Great Sand Dunes, Dinosaur, Black Canyon of the Gunnison, and Colorado national monuments; Pikes Peak and Mt. Evans highways; Mesa Verde National Park (Ancient Anasazi Indian cliff dwellings); 35 major ski areas; the Grand Mesa tableland comprises Grand Mesa Forest, 659,584 acres, with 200 lakes stocked with trout.

Famous Coloradans include Frederick Bonfils, Molly Brown, William N. Byers, M. Scott Carpenter, Jack Dempsey, Mamie Eisenhower, Douglas Fairbanks, Scott Hamilton, "Baby Doe" Tabor, Lowell Thomas, Byron R. White, Paul Whiteman.

Toll-free travel information. 1-800-433-2656.

Connecticut

Constitution State, Nutmeg State

People. Population (1986): 3,189,000; **rank:** 28. **Pop. density:** 652.8 per sq. mi. **Urban** (1980): 78.8% **Racial distrib.** (1980): 90.0% White; 6.9% Black; Hispanic 124,499. **Net change** (1980-86): +81,000; 2.6%.

Geography. Total area: 5,009 sq. mi.; **rank:** 48. **Land area:** 4,862 sq. mi. **Acres forested land:** 1,860,800. **Location:** New England state in the northeastern corner of the U.S. **Climate:** moderate; winters avg. slightly below freezing, warm, humid summers. **Topography:** western upland, the Berkshires, in the NW, highest elevations; narrow central lowland N-S; hilly eastern upland drained by rivers. **Capital:** Hartford.

Economy. Principal industries: manufacturing, retail trade, government, services. **Principal manufactured goods:** aircraft engines and parts, submarines, copper, helicopters, bearings, instruments, electrical equipment. **Agriculture: Chief crops:** tobacco, hay, apples, potatoes, nursery stock. **Livestock:** 110,000 cattle; 8,000 hogs/pigs; 9,200 sheep; 6.2 mln. poultry. **Timber/lumber:** oak, birch, beech, maple. **Minerals** (1986): $79 mln; crushed stone; construction sand & gravel. **Commercial fishing** (1986): $15.6 mln. **Chief ports:** New Haven, Bridgeport, New London. **International airports at:** Windsor Locks. **Value of construction** (1986): $4.0 bln. **Employment distribution:** 24.4% manuf.; 23% serv. **Per capita income** (1986): $19,208. **Unemployment** (1986): 3.8%. **Tourism** (1985): out-of-state visitors spent $2.5 bln.

Finance. Commercial bank deposits, per capita (1985): $6,536.

Federal Government. No. federal civilian employees (Mar. 1986): 9,392. **Avg. salary:** $26,914. **Notable federal facilities:** U.S. Coast Guard Academy; U.S. Navy Submarine Base.

Energy. Electricity production (1986, mwh, by source): Hydroelectric: 367,000; Mineral: 13.2 mln.; Nuclear: 18.7 mln.

Education. Expenditures per pupil, public schools (1984-85): $4,738. **Avg. salary, public school teachers** (1987 est.): $28,902.

State data. Motto: Qui Transtulit Sustinet (He who transplanted still sustains). **Flower:** Mountain laurel. **Bird:** American robin. **Tree:** White oak. **Song:** Yankee Doodle Dandy. **Fifth** of the 13 original states to ratify the Constitution, Jan. 9, 1788.

History. Adriaen Block, Dutch explorer, was the first European visitor, 1614. By 1634, settlers from Plymouth Bay started colonies along the Connecticut River and in 1637 defeated the Pequot Indians. In the Revolution, Connecticut men fought in most major campaigns and turned back British raids on Danbury and other towns, while Connecticut privateers captured British merchant ships.

Tourist attractions. Mark Twain House, Hartford; Yale University's Art Gallery, Peabody Museum, all in New Haven; Mystic Seaport; Mystic Marine Life Aquarium; P.T. Barnum Museum, Bridgeport; Gillette Castle, Hadlyme; U.S.S. Nautilus Memorial, Croton (1st nuclear-powered submarine).

Famous "Nutmeggers" include Ethan Allen, Phineas T. Barnum, Samuel Colt, Jonathan Edwards, Nathan Hale, Katharine Hepburn, Isaac Hull, J. Pierpont Morgan, Israel Putnam, Harriet Beecher Stowe, Mark Twain, Noah Webster, Eli Whitney.

Tourist information. State Dept. of Economic Development, 210 Washington St., Hartford, CT 06106.

Toll-free travel information. 1-800-243-1685 out of state; 800-842-7492 in Connecticut.

Delaware

First State, Diamond State

People. Population (1986): 633,000; **rank:** 47. **Pop. density:** 313.8 per sq. mi. **Urban** (1980): 70.6%. **Racial distrib.** (1980): 82.0% White; 16.1% Black; Hispanic 9,671. **Net change** (1980-86): +38,000; 6.5%.

Geography. Total area: 2,057 sq. mi.; **rank:** 49. **Land area:** 1,982 sq. mi. **Acres forested land:** 391,800. **Location:** occupies the Delmarva Peninsula on the Atlantic coastal plain. **Climate:** moderate. **Topography:** Piedmont plateau to the N, sloping to a near sea-level plain. **Capital:** Dover.

Economy. Principal industries: chemistry, agriculture, poultry, shellfish, tourism, auto assembly, food processing, transportation equipment. **Principal manufactured goods:** nylon, apparel, luggage, foods, autos, processed meats and vegetables, railroad and aircraft equipment. **Agriculture: Chief crops:** soybeans, potatoes, corn, mushrooms, lima beans, green peas, barley, cucumbers, snap beans, watermelons, apples. **Livestock** (1987): 31,000 cattle; 197.6 mln. poultry. **Timber/Lumber:** (1982) forest products $1.8 mln. **Minerals** (1986): $3.7 mln; construction sand & gravel, green sand marl. **Commercial fishing** (1986): $2.0 mln. **Chief ports:** Wilmington. **International airports at:** Philadelphia/Wilmington. **Value of construction** (1986): $662.9 mln. **Employment distribution** (1986): 77.4% non-manufacturing; 22.6% manuf. **Per capita income** (1986): $15,010. **Unemployment** (1986): 4.3%. **Tourism** (1984): out-of-state visitors spent $546 mln.

Finance. Commercial bank deposits, per capita (1985): $18,313.

Federal government. No. federal civilian employees (Mar. 1986): 3,010. **Avg. salary:** $24,585. **Notable federal facilities:** Dover Air Force Base, Federal Wildlife Refuge, Bombay Hook.

Energy. Electricity production (1986, mwh, by source): Mineral: 8.4 mln.

Education. Expenditure per pupil, public schools (1984-85): $4,184. **Avg. salary, public school teachers** (1987): $27,467.

State data. Motto: Liberty and independence. **Flower:** Peach blossom. **Bird:** Blue hen chicken. **Tree:** American holly. **Song:** Our Delaware. **First** of original 13 states to ratify the Constitution, Dec. 7, 1787. **State fair** at: Harrington; end of July.

History. The Dutch first settled in Delaware near present Lewes, 1631, but were wiped out by Indians. Swedes settled at present Wilmington, 1638; Dutch settled anew, 1651, near New Castle and seized the Swedish settlement, 1655, only to lose all Delaware and New Netherland to the British, 1664.

Tourist attractions. Ft. Christina Monument, the site of founding of New Sweden; John Dickinson "Penman of the Revolution" home, Dover; Henry Francis du Pont Winterthur Museum; Hagley Museum, Wilmington; Rehoboth Beach, "nation's summer capitol," Rehoboth; Dover Downs Intl. Speedway, Dover; Old Swedes (Trinity Parish) Church, erected 1698, is the oldest Protestant church in the U.S. still in use.

Famous Delawareans include Thomas F. Bayard, Henry Seidel Canby, E. I. du Pont, John P. Marquand, Howard Pyle, Caesar Rodney.

Chamber of Commerce. One Commerce Center, Wilmington, DE 19801.

Toll-free travel information. 1-800-441-8846.

Florida

Sunshine State

People. Population (1986): 11,675,000; **rank:** 5. **Pop. density:** 210 per sq. mi. **Urban** (1980): 84.3%. **Racial distrib.** (1980): 83.9% White; 13.7% Black; Hispanic 858,158. **Net change** (1980-86): +1,928,000; 19.8%.

Geography: Total area: 58,560 sq. mi.; **rank:** 22. **Land area:** 54,136 sq. mi. **Acres forested land:** 17,040,000. **Location:** peninsula jutting southward 500 mi. bet. the Atlantic and the Gulf of Mexico. **Climate:** subtropical N of Bradenton-Lake Okeechobee-Vero Beach line; tropical S of line. **Topography:** land is flat or rolling; highest point is 345 ft. in the NW. **Capital:** Tallahassee.

Economy. Principal industries: services, trade, gvt., manufacturing, tourism. **Principal manufactured goods:** electric & electronic equip., transp. equipment; food; printing & publishing; machinery. **Agriculture: Chief crops:** citrus fruits, vegetables, potatoes, melons, strawberries, sugar cane. **Livestock** (1985): 2.2 mln. cattle; 203,000 hogs/pigs; 7,360 sheep; 15.3 mln. poultry. **Timber/lumber** (1984): pine, cypress, cedar; 633 mln. bd. ft. **Minerals** (1986): $1.5 bln.; mostly cement, and phosphate rock, and crushed stone. **Commercial fishing** (1986): $154.5 mln. **Chief ports:** Pensacola, Tampa, Miami, Port Everglades, Jacksonville, St. Petersburg, Canaveral. **International airports at:** Miami, Tampa, Jacksonville, Orlando, Ft. Lauderdale, W. Palm Beach. **Value of construction** (1986): $17.6 bln. **Per capita income** (1986): $14,281. **Unemployment** (1986): 5.7% **Tourism** (1983): out-of-state visitors spent $20 bln.

Finance. Commercial bank deposits, per capita (1985): $6,455.

Federal government. No. federal civilian employees (Mar. 1986): 56,953. **Avg. salary:** $26,050. **Notable federal facilities:** John F. Kennedy Space Center, NASA-Kennedy Space Center's Spaceport USA; Eglin Air Force Base.

Energy. Electricity production (1986, mwh, by source): Hydroelectric: 212,000; Mineral: 86.2 mln.; Nuclear: 22.0 mln.

Education. Expenditure per pupil, public schools (1984-85): $3,238. **Avg. salary, public school teachers** (1987 est.): $23,785.

State data. Motto: In God we trust. **Flower:** Orange blossom. **Bird:** Mockingbird. **Tree:** Sabal palmetto palm. **Song:** Swanee River. **Entered union** Mar. 3, 1845; rank, 27th. **State fair** at: Tampa; early to mid-Feb.

History. First European to see Florida was Ponce de Leon, 1513. France established a colony, Fort Caroline, on the St. Johns River, 1564; Spain settled St. Augustine, 1565, and Spanish troops massacred most of the French. Britain's Francis Drake burned St. Augustine, 1586. Britain held the area briefly, 1763-83, returning it to Spain. After Andrew Jackson led a U.S. invasion, 1818, Spain ceded Florida to the U.S., 1819. The Seminole War, 1835-42, resulted in removal of most Indians to Oklahoma. Florida seceded from the Union, 1861, was readmitted, 1868.

Tourist attractions. Miami, with a variety of luxury hotels at Miami Beach; St. Augustine, oldest city in U.S.; Walt Disney World's Magic Kingdom and EPCOT; Spaceport U.S.A.

Everglades National Park, 3d largest of U.S. national parks, preserves the beauty of the vast Everglades swamp. Castillo de San Marcos, St. Augustine, is a national monument. Also, the Ringling Museum of Art, and the Ringling Museum of the Circus, both in Sarasota; Sea World, and Circus World, Orlando; Busch Gardens, Tampa.

Famous Floridians include Henry M. Flagler, James Weldon Johnson, MacKinlay Kantor, Henry B. Plant, Marjorie Kinnan Rawlings, Joseph W. Stilwell, Charles P. Summerall.

Tourist information. Florida Division of Tourism, Collins Bldg., Suite 509, Tallahassee, FL 32399-2000, 1-904-488-8230.

Georgia

Empire State of the South, Peach State

People. Population (1986): 5,975,000; **rank:** 11. **Pop. density:** 102.9 per sq. mi. **Urban** (1980): 62.4%. **Racial distrib.** (1980): 72.2% White; 26.8% Black; Hispanic 61,261. **Net** (1980-86): +641,000; +11.7%.

Geography. Total area: 58,876 sq. mi.; **rank:** 21. **Land area:** 58,073 sq. mi. **Acres forested land:** 25,256,100. **Location:** South Atlantic state. **Climate:** maritime tropical air masses dominate in summer; continental polar air masses in winter; east central area drier. **Topography:** most southerly of the Blue Ridge Mtns. cover NE and N central; central Piedmont extends to the fall line of rivers; coastal plain levels to the coast flatlands. **Capital:** Atlanta.

Economy. Principal industries: manufacturing, forestry, agriculture, chemicals. **Principal manufactured goods:** textiles, transportation equipment, foods, clothing, paper and wood products, chemical products, stone, glass & clay products. **Agriculture: Chief crops:** peanuts, corn, soybeans, tobacco, oats and wheat, cotton and cottonseed. **Livestock** (1983): 1.87 mln. cattle; 1.57 mln. hogs/pigs; 5,000 sheep; 68 mln. poultry. **Timber/lumber** (1984): pine, hardwood; 2.1 bln. bd. ft. **Minerals** (1986): $1.1 bln.; clays, crushed stone. **Commercial fishing** (1986): $24.5 mln. **Chief ports:** Savannah, Brunswick. **International airports at:** Atlanta. **Value of construction** (1986): $9.1 bln. **Employment distribution:** 32% trade; 25% mfg.; 20% gvt.; 23% serv. **Per capita income** (1986): $13,224. **Unemployment** (1986): 5.9% **Tourism** (1983): tourists spent $7.6 bln.

Finance. Commercial bank deposits, per capita (1985): $5,752.

Federal government. No. federal civilian employees (Mar. 1986): 67,093. **Avg. salary:** $24,908. **Notable federal facilities:** Dobbins AFB; Fts. Benning, Gordon, McPherson; Nat'l. Law Enforcement Training Ctr., Glynco, Warner Robins AFB.

Energy. Electricity production (1986, mwh, by source): Hydroelectric: 2.2 mln.; Mineral: 65.6 mln.; Nuclear: 10.1 mln.

Education. Expenditure per pupil, public schools (1984-85): $2,657. **Avg. salary, public school teachers** (1987 est.): $24,200.

State data. Motto: Wisdom, justice and moderation. **Flower:** Cherokee rose. **Bird:** Brown thrasher. **Tree:** Live oak. **Song:** Georgia On My Mind. **Fourth** of the 13 original states to ratify the Constitution, Jan. 2, 1788.

History. Gen. James Oglethorpe established the first settlements, 1733, for poor and religiously-persecuted Englishmen. Oglethorpe defeated a Spanish army from Florida at Bloody Marsh, 1742. In the Revolution, Georgians seized the Savannah armory, 1775, and sent the munitions to the Continental Army; they fought seesaw campaigns with Cornwallis' British troops, twice liberating Augusta and forcing final evacuation by the British from Savannah, 1782.

Tourist attractions. The Little White House in Warm Springs where Pres. Franklin D. Roosevelt died Apr. 12, 1945, 2,500-acre Callaway Gardens, Jekyll Island State Park, the restored 1850s farming community of Westville; Alpine Helen, tiny mountain town converted to Alpine Village. Dahlonega, site of America's first gold rush; Stone Mountain, and Six Flags Over Georgia, Air Force Museum, Robins AFB.

Okefenokee in the SE is one of the largest swamps in the U.S., a wetland wilderness and peat bog covering 660 sq. mi. A large part of it is a National Wildlife Refuge, a home for wild birds, alligators, bear, deer.

Famous Georgians include Hank Aaron, James Bowie, Erskine Caldwell, Jimmy Carter, Lucius D. Clay, Ty Cobb, John C. Fremont, Joel Chandler Harris, Martin Luther King Jr., Sidney Lanier, Margaret Mitchell, Jackie Robinson, Joseph Wheeler.

Chamber of Commerce. 235 International Blvd., Atlanta, GA 30303.

Hawaii

The Aloha State

People. Population (1986): 1,062,000; **rank:** 39. **Pop. density:** 164.0 per sq. mi. **Urban** (1980): 86.5%. **Racial distrib.** (1983): 24.5% Caucasian; 23.2% Japanese; 11.3% Filipino; 20% Hawaiian and part-Hawaiian. **Net change** (1980-86): +98,000; 10.1%.

Geography. Total area: 6,450 sq. mi.; **rank:** 47. **Land area:** 6,425 sq. mi. **Acres forested land:** 1,986,000. **Location:** Hawaiian Islands lie in the North Pacific, 2,397 mi. SW from San Francisco. **Climate:** temperate, mountain regions cooler; Waialeale, on Kauai, wettest spot in the U.S. (annual rainfall 451 in.) **Topography:** islands are tops of a chain of submerged volcanic mountains; active volcanoes: Mauna Loa, Kilauea. **Capital:** Honolulu.

Economy. Principal industries: tourism, defense and other government, sugar refining, pineapple and diversified agriculture, aquaculture, fishing, motion pictures, manufacturing. **Principal manufactured goods:** sugar, canned pineapple, clothing, foods, printing and publishing. **Agriculture: Chief crops:** sugar, pineapples, macadamia nuts, fruits, coffee, vegetables, melons, and floriculture. **Livestock** (1985): 209,000 cattle; 55,000 hogs/pigs; 1.2 mln. poultry. **Minerals** (1986): $68 mln.; mostly crushed stone & cement. **Commercial fishing** (1986): $20.1 mln. **Chief ports:** Honolulu, Nawiliwili, Barber's Point, Kahului, Hilo. **International airports at:** Honolulu. **Value of construction** (1986): $1.2 bln. **Employment distribution** (1985): 24.5% trade; 23.4% serv.; 19% gvt. **Per capita income** (1986): $14,691. **Unemployment** (1986): 4.8%. **Tourism** (1985): visitors spent $4.9 bln.

Finance. Commercial bank deposits, per capita (1985): $7,552.

Federal government. No. federal civilian employees (Mar. 1986): 23,262. **Avg. salary:** $27,387. **Notable federal facilities:** Pearl Harbor Naval Shipyard; Hickam AFB; Schofield Barracks.

Energy. Electricity production (1986, mwh, by source): Hydroelectric: 12,000; Mineral: 6.8 mln.

Education. Expenditure per pupil, public schools (1984-85): $3,465. **Avg. Salary, public school teachers** (1987 est.): $26,815.

State data. Motto: The life of the land is perpetuated in righteousness. **Flower:** Hibiscus. **Bird:** Hawaiian goose. **Tree:** Candlenut. **Song:** Hawaii Ponoi. **Entered union** Aug. 21, 1959; rank, 50th. **State fair** at: Honolulu; late May–mid-June.

History. Polynesians from islands 2,000 mi. to the south settled the Hawaiian Islands, probably about 700 A.D. First European visitor was British Capt. James Cook, 1778. Missionaries arrived, 1820, taught religion, reading and writing. King Kamehameha III and his chiefs created the first Constitution and a Legislature which set up a public school system. Sugar production began in 1835 and it became the dominant industry. In 1893, Queen Liliuokalani was deposed, followed, 1894, by a republic headed by Sanford B. Dole. Annexation by the U.S. came in 1898.

Tourist attractions. Natl. Memorial Cemetery of the Pacific, USS Arizona Memorial, Pearl Harbor; Hawaii Volcanoes, Haleakala National Parks; Polynesian Cultural Center, Diamond Head, Waikiki Beach, Nuuanu Pali, Oahu.

Famous Islanders include Bernice Pauahi Bishop, John A. Burns, Father Joseph Damien, Sanford B. Dole, Wallace R. Farrington, Hiram L. Fong, Daniel K. Inouye, Duke Kahanamoku, King Kamehameha the Great, Queen Kaahumanu, Queen Liliuokalani, Ellison Onizuka.

Chamber of Commerce. Dillingham Bldg., 735 Bishop St., Honolulu, HI 96813.

Idaho

Gem State

People. Population (1986): 1,003,000; **rank:** 41. **Pop. density:** 12.2 per sq. mi. **Urban** (1980): 54.0%. **Racial distrib.** (1980): 95.5% White; 0.3% Black; Hispanic 36,615. **Net change** (1980-86): +58,000; 6.2%.

Geography. Total area: 83,557 sq. mi.; **rank:** 13. **Land area:** 82,677 sq. mi. **Acres forested land:** 21,726,600. **Location:** Pacific Northwest-Mountain state bordering on British Columbia. **Climate:** tempered by Pacific westerly winds; drier, colder, continental clime in SE; altitude an important factor. **Topography:** Snake R. plains in the S; central region of mountains, canyons, gorges (Hells Canyon, 7,000 ft., deepest in N.A.); subalpine northern region. **Capital:** Boise.

Economy. Principal industries: agriculture, manufacturing, tourism, lumber, mining, electronics. **Principal manufactured goods:** processed foods, lumber and wood products, chemical products, primary metals, fabricated metal products, machinery, electronic components. **Agriculture: Chief crops:** potatoes, peas, sugar beets, alfalfa seed, wheat, hops, barley, plums and prunes, mint, onions, corn, cherries, apples, hay. **Livestock:** 1.89 mln. cattle; 120,000 hogs/pigs; 383,000 sheep; 1.27 mln. poultry. **Timber/lumber** (1984): yellow, white pine; Douglas fir; white spruce; 1.7 bln. bd. ft. **Minerals** (1986): $240 mln.; silver, gold, sand & gravel, crushed stone. **Chief ports:** Lewiston. **Value of construction** (1986) $659.5 mln. **Employment distribution:** 21% trade; 15% serv., 14% manuf.; 10% agric. **Per capita income** (1986): $11,432. **Unemployment** (1986): 8.7%. **Tourism** (1982): travellers spent $1.2 bln.

Finance. Commercial bank deposits, per capita (1985): $5,938.

Federal government. No. federal civilian employees (Mar. 1986): 6,879. **Avg. salary:** $26,074. **Notable federal facilities:** Ida. Nat'l. Engineering Lab, Idaho Falls; Nat'l. Reactor Testing Sta., Upper Snake River Plains.

Energy. Electricity production (1986, mwh, by source): Hydroelectric: 12.2 mln..

Education: Expenditure per pupil, public schools (1984-85): $2,401. **Avg. salary, public school teachers** (1987 est): $21,469.

State data. Motto: Esto Perpetua (It is perpetual). **Flower:** Syringa. **Bird:** Mountain bluebird. **Tree:** White pine. **Song:** Here We Have Idaho. **Entered union** July 3, 1890; rank, 43d. **State fair** at: Boise, late Aug.; and Blackfoot, early Sept.

History. Exploration of the Idaho area began with Lewis and Clark, 1805-06. Next came fur traders, setting up posts, 1809-34, and missionaries, establishing missions, 1830s-1850s. Mormons made their first permanent settlement at Franklin, 1860. Idaho's Gold Rush began that same year, and brought thousands of permanent settlers. Strangest of the Indian Wars was the 1,300-mi. trek in 1877 of Chief Joseph and the Nez Perce tribe, pursued by troops that caught them a few miles short of the Canadian border. In 1890, Idaho adopted a progressive Constitution and became a state.

Tourist attractions. Hells Canyon, deepest gorge in N.A.; Craters of the Moon; Sun Valley, year-round resort in the Sawtooth Mtns.; Crystal Falls Cave; Shoshone Falls; Lava Hot Springs; Lake Pend Oreille; Lake Coeur d'Alene; Sawtooth Natl. Recreation Area; River of No Return Wilderness Area.

Famous Idahoans include William E. Borah, Frank Church, Fred T. Dubois, Chief Joseph, Sacagawea.

Tourist information. Department of Commerce, Room 108, State House, Boise, ID 83720.

Illinois

The Prairie State

People. Population (1986): 11,553,000; **rank:** 6. **Pop. density:** 206.9 per sq. mi. **Urban** (1980): 83.3%. **Racial distrib.** (1980): 80.7% White; 14.6% Black; Hispanic 635,525. **Net change** (1980-86): 126,000; 1.1%.

Geography. Total area: 56,400 sq. mi.; **rank:** 24. **Land area:** 55,748 sq. mi. **Acres forested land:** 3,810,400. **Location:** east-north central state; western, southern, and eastern boundaries formed by Mississippi, Ohio, and Wabash Rivers, respectively. **Climate:** temperate; typically cold, snowy winters, hot summers. **Topography:** prairie and fertile plains throughout; open hills in the southern region. **Capital:** Springfield.

Economy. Principal industries: manufacturing, wholesale and retail trade, finance, insurance, foods, agriculture. **Principal manufactured goods:** machinery, electric and electronic equipment, primary and fabricated metals, chemical products, printing and publishing. **Agriculture: Chief crops:** corn, soybeans, wheat, oats, hay. **Livestock** (1986): 2.5 mln. cattle; 5.4 mln. hogs/pigs; 98,000 sheep; 3.6 mln. poultry. **Timber/lumber** (1984): oak, hickory, maple, cottonwood; 69 mln. bd. ft. **Minerals** (1986): $492.6 mln.; mostly crushed stone, cement, construction & industrial sand & gravel. **Commercial fishing** (1986): $2.1 mln. **Chief ports:** Chicago. **International airports at:** Chicago. **Value of construction** (1986): $9.0 bln. **Employment distribution** (1986): 24.5% trade; 23.09% serv.; 20.5% manuf. **Per capita income** (1986): $15,420. **Unemployment** (1986) 8.1%. **Tourism** (1986): out-of-state visitors spent $8.9 bln.

Finance. Commercial bank deposits, per capita (1985): $8,923.

Federal government. No. federal civilian employees (Mar. 1986): 53,763. **Avg. salary:** $26,256. **Notable federal facilities:** Fermi Nat'l. Accelerator Lab; Argonne Nat'l. Lab; Ft. Sheridan; Rock Island; Great Lakes, Rantoul.

Energy. Electricity production (1986, mwh, by source): Hydroelectric: 124,000; Mineral: 64.1 mln.; Nuclear: 42.6 mln.

Education. Expenditure per pupil, public schools (1984-85): $3,538. **Avg salary, public school teachers** (1987 est.): $28,430.

State data. Motto: State sovereignty—national union. **Flower:** Native violet. **Bird:** Cardinal. **Tree:** White oak. **Song:** Illinois. **Entered union** Dec. 3, 1818; rank, 21st. **State fair** at: Springfield; early Aug.

History. Fur traders were the first Europeans in Illinois, followed shortly, 1673, by Jolliet and Marquette, and, 1680, La Salle, who built a fort near present Peoria. First settlements were French, at Fort St. Louis on the Illinois River, 1692, and Kaskaskia, 1700. France ceded the area to Britain, 1763; Amer. Gen. George Rogers Clark, 1778, took Kaskaskia from the British without a shot. Defeat of Indian tribes in Black Hawk War, 1832, and railroads in 1850s, inspired imchange.

Tourist attractions: Chicago museums, parks; Lincoln shrines at Springfield, New Salem, Sangamon; Cahokia Mounds, E. St. Louis; Starved Rock State Park; Crab Orchard Wildlife Refuge; Mormon settlement at Nauvoo; Fts. Kaskaskia, Chartres, Massac (parks); Shawnee Natl. Forest, Southern Illinois.

Famous Illinoisans include Jane Addams, Saul Bellow, Jack Benny, Ray Bradbury, Gwendolyn Brooks, William Jennings Bryan, St. Francis Xavier Cabrini, Clarence Darrow, Stephen A. Douglas, James T. Farrell, Betty Friedan, Ulysses S. Grant, Ernest Hemingway, Abraham Lincoln, Edgar Lee Masters, Ronald Reagan, Carl Sandburg, Adlai Stevenson, Frank Lloyd Wright.

Tourist information. Illinois Dept. of Commerce and Community Affairs, 620 E. Adams St., Springfield, IL 62701

Toll-free travel information. 1-800-252-8987.

Indiana

Hoosier State

People. Population (1986): 5,504,000; **rank:** 14. **Pop. density:** 152.3 per sq. mi. **Urban** (1980): 64.2%. **Racial distrib.** (1980): 91.1 White; 7.5% Black; Hispanic 87,020. **Net change** (1980-86): +13,000; 0.2%.

Geography. Total area: 36,291 sq. mi.; **rank:** 38. **Land area:** 36,097 sq. mi. **Acres forested land:** 3,942,900. **Location:** east north-central state; Lake Michigan on northern border. **Climate:** 4 distinct seasons with a temperate climate. **Topography:** hilly southern region; fertile rolling plains of central region; flat, heavily glaciated north; dunes along Lake Michigan shore. **Capital:** Indianapolis.

Economy: Principal industries: manufacturing, wholesale and retail trade, agriculture, government, services. **Principal manufactured goods:** primary and fabricated metals, transportation equipment, electrical and electronic equipment, non-electrical machinery, plastics, chemical products, foods. **Agriculture: Chief crops** (1983): corn, soybeans, wheat, hay. **Livestock** (1986): 1.5 mln. cattle; 4.2 mln. hogs/pigs; 91,000 sheep; 28 mln. chickens. **Timber/lumber** (1984): oak, tulip, beech, sycamore; 358 mln. bd. ft. **Minerals** (1984): $293.0 mln.; mostly crushed stone, abrasives, cement, gypsum, lime, sand & gravel. **Commercial fishing** (1986): $896,000. **Chief ports:** Lake Michigan facility, east of Gary, Southwind Maritime Centre at Mt. Vernon. **International airports at:** Indianapolis. **Value of construction** (1986): $4.8 bln. **Employment distribution** (1986): 27.1% manuf.; 23.6% trade; 19.2% serv. **Per capita income** (1986): $12,944. **Unemployment** (1986): 6.7%. **Tourism** (1985): tourists spent $3 bln.

Finance. Commercial bank deposits, per capita (1985): $6,938.

Federal government. No. federal civilian employees (Mar. 1986): 25,095. **Avg. salary:** $24,492. **Notable federal facilities:** Naval Avionics Ctr.; Ft. Benjamin Harrison; Grissom AFB; Navy Weapons Support Ctr., Crane.

Energy. Electricity production (1986 mwh, by source): Hydroelectric: 506,000; Mineral: 76.8 mln.

Education. Expenditure per pupil, public schools (1984-85): $3,051. **Avg. salary, public school teachers** (1987 est.): $25,684.

State data. Motto: Crossroads of America. **Flower:** Peony. **Bird:** Cardinal. **Tree:** Tulip poplar. **Song:** On the Banks of the Wabash, Far Away. **Entered union** Dec. 11, 1816; rank, 19th. **State fair** at: Indianapolis; mid-Aug.

History: Pre-historic Indian Mound Builders of 1,000 years ago were the earliest known inhabitants. A French trading post was built, 1731-32, at Vincennes and La Salle visited the present South Bend area, 1679 and 1681. France ceded the area to Britain, 1763. During the Revolution, American Gen. George Rogers Clark captured Vincennes, 1778, and defeated British forces 1779; at war's end Britain ceded the area to the U.S. Miami Indians defeated U.S. troops twice, 1790, but were beaten, 1794, at Fallen Timbers by Gen. Anthony Wayne. At Tippecanoe, 1811, Gen. William H. Harrison defeated Tecumseh's Indian confederation.

Tourist attractions. Lincoln, George Rogers Clark memorials; Wyandotte Cave; Vincennes, Tippecanoe sites; Indiana Dunes; Hoosier Nat'l. Forest; Benjamin Harrison Home.

Famous "Hoosiers" include Ambrose Burnside, Hoagy Carmichael, Eugene V. Debs, Theodore Dreiser, Paul Dresser, Cole Porter, Gene Stratton Porter, Ernie Pyle, James Whitcomb Riley, Booth Tarkington, Lew Wallace, Wendell L. Willkie, Wilbur Wright.

Chamber of Commerce. One North Capital, Indianapolis, IN 46204.

Toll-free travel information. 1-800-2-WANDER.

Iowa

Hawkeye State

People. Population (1986): 2,851,000; **rank:** 29. **Pop. density:** 51.6 per sq. mi. **Urban** (1980): 58.6%. **Racial distrib.** (1980): 97.4% White; 1.4% Black; 0.5% Hispanic 15,852. **Net change** (1980-86): −63,000; −2.2%.

Geography. Total area: 56,290 sq. mi.; **rank:** 25. **Land area:** 55,941 sq. mi. **Acres forested land:** 1,561,300. **Location:** Midwest state bordered by Mississippi R. on the E and Missouri R. on the W. **Climate:** humid, continental. **Topography:** Watershed from NW to SE; soil especially rich and land level in the N central counties. **Capital:** Des Moines.

Economy. Principal industries: manufacturing, agriculture. **Principal manufactured goods:** tires, farm machinery, electronic products, appliances, office furniture, chemicals, fertilizers, auto accessories. **Agriculture: Chief crops:** silage and grain corn, soybeans, oats, hay. **Livestock** (1985): 1.8 mln. cattle; 22.8 mln. hogs/pigs; 341,000 sheep; 6.2 mln. poultry. **Timber/lumber** (1984): red cedar. **Minerals** (1986): $247.3 mln.; mostly crushed stone, cement, construction sand & gravel; 41 mln. bd. ft. **Value of construction** (1986): 1.3 bln. **Employment distribution** (1986): 25.7% trade; 22.1% serv; 18.7% manuf.; 19.3% gvt. **Per capita income** (1986): $13,222. **Unemployment** (1986): 7.0%. **Tourism** (1984): tourists spent $1.8 bln.

Finance. Commercial bank deposits, per capita (1985): $8,623.

Federal government. No. federal civilian employees (Mar. 1986): 7,833. **Avg. salary:** $24,853.

Energy. Electricity production (1986, mwh, by source): Hydroelectric: 952,000; Mineral: 20.1 mln.; Nuclear: 3.0 mln.

Education. Expenditure per pupil, public schools (1984-85): $3,439. **Avg. salary, public school teachers** (1987 est.): $22,603.

State data. Motto: Our liberties we prize and our rights we will maintain. **Flower:** Wild rose. **Bird:** Eastern goldfinch. **Tree:** Oak. **Rock:** Geode. **Entered union** Dec. 28, 1846; rank, 29th. **State fair** at: Des Moines; mid-to-late Aug.

History. A thousand years ago several groups of prehistoric Indian Mound Builders dwelt on Iowa's fertile plains. Marquette and Jolliet gave France its claim to the area, 1673. It became U.S. territory through the 1803 Louisiana Purchase. Indian tribes were moved into the area from states further east, but by mid-19th century were forced to move on to Kansas. Before and during the Civil War, Iowans strongly supported Abraham Lincoln and became traditional Republicans.

Tourist attractions. Herbert Hoover birthplace and library, West Branch; Effigy Mounds Nat'l. Monument, Marquette, a pre-historic Indian burial site; Amana colonies; Davenport Municipal Art Gallery's collection of Grant Wood's paintings and memorabilia; Living History farms, Des Moines; Adventureland, Altoona; Boone & Scenic Valley Railroad, Boone; Greyhound Parks in Dubuque, Council Bluffs & Waterloo.

Famous Iowans include James A. Van Allen, Marquis Childs, Buffalo Bill Cody, Mamie Dowd Eisenhower, George Gallup, Susan Glaspell, James Norman Hall, Harry Hansen, Herbert Hoover, Glenn Miller, Billy Sunday, Carl Van Vechten, Henry Wallace, John Wayne, Meredith Willson, Grant Wood.

Tourist information. Tourism/Film Office, Iowa Dept. of Economic Development, 200 E. Grand Ave. Des Moines, IA 50309.

Toll-free travel information. 1-800-345-IOWA.

Kansas

Sunflower State

People. Population (1986): 2,461,000; **rank:** 32. **Pop. density:** 30.0 per sq. mi. **Urban** (1980): 66.7%. **Racial distrib.** (1980): 91.7% White; 5.3% Black; Hispanic 63,333. **Net change** (1980-86): +97,000; 4.1%.

Geography. Total area: 82,264 sq. mi.; **rank:** 14. **Land area:** 81,787 sq. mi. **Acres forested land:** 1,344,400. **Location:** West North Central state, with Missouri R. on E. **Climate:** temperate but continental, with great extremes bet. summer and winter. **Topography:** hilly Osage Plains in the E; central region level prairie and hills; high plains in the W. **Capital:** Topeka.

Economy. Principal industries: agriculture, machinery, mining, aerospace. **Principal manufactured goods:** processed foods, aircraft, petroleum products, farm machinery. **Agriculture: Chief crops:** wheat, sorghum, corn, hay. **Livestock** (1985): 5.8 mln. cattle; 1.52 mln. hogs/pigs; 210,000 sheep; 2.52 mln. poultry. **Timber/lumber:** oak, walnut. **Minerals** (1986): $320.1 mln.; cement, salt, crushed stone. **Chief ports:** Kansas City. **International airports at:** Wichita. **Value of construction** (1986): $2.2 bln. **Employment distribution** (1986): 21.3% trade; 16.8% gvt.; 16.7% serv.; 15.2% manuf. **Per capita income** (1986): $14,379. **Unemployment** (1986): 5.4%. **Tourism** (1985): out-of-state visitors spent $1.9 bln.

Finance. Commercial bank deposits, per capita (1985): $8,430.

Federal government. No. federal civilian employees (Mar. 1986): 15,601. **Avg. salary:** $23,976. **Notable federal facilities:** McConnell AFB; Fts. Riley, Leavenworth.

Energy. Electricity production (1986, mwh, by source): Hydroelectric: 8,000; Mineral: 22.6 mln; Nuclear: 7.0 mln.

Education. Expenditure per pupil, public schools (1984-85): $3,560. **Avg. salary, public school teachers** (1987 est.): $23,550.

State data. Motto: Ad Astra per Aspera (To the stars through difficulties). **Flower:** Native sunflower. **Bird:** Western meadowlark. **Tree:** Cottonwood. **Song:** Home on the Range. **Entered union** Jan. 29, 1861; rank, 34th. **State fair** at: Hutchinson; 2d week of Sept.

History. Coronado marched through the Kansas area, 1541; French explorers came next. The U.S. took over in the Louisiana Purchase, 1803. In the pre-war North-South struggle over slavery, so much violence swept the area it was called Bleeding Kansas. Railroad construction after the war made Abilene and Dodge City terminals of large cattle drives from Texas.

Tourist attractions. Eisenhower Center and "Place of Meditation," Abilene; Agricultural Hall of Fame and National Ctr., Bonner Springs, displays farm equipment; Dodge City; Ft. Scott; Kansas Cosmosphere and Space Discovery Center, Hutchinson.

Famous Kansans include Thomas Hart Benton, John Brown, Walter P. Chrysler, John Steuart Curry, Amelia Earhart, Dwight D. Eisenhower, Ron Evans, Wild Bill Hickok, Cyrus Holliday, William Inge, Walter Johnson, Alf Landon, Carry Nation, Gordon Parks, Jim Ryun, William Allen White.

Tourist information. Kansas Dept. of Commerce, Travel and Tourism Div., 400 SW 8th St., 5th Fl., Topeka, KS 66603; 1-913-296-2009.

Kentucky

Bluegrass State

People. Population (1985): 3,728,000 **rank:** 23. **Pop. density:** 94.0 per sq. mi. **Urban** (1980): 50.9% **Racial Distrib.** (1980): 92.3% White; 7.1% Black; Hispanic (1980): 27,406. **Net change** (1980-86): +68,000; 1.9%.

Geography. Total area: 40,409 sq. mi.; **rank:** 37. **Land area:** 39,650 sq. mi. **Acres forested land:** 12,160,800. Location: east south central state, bordered on N by Illinois, Indiana, Ohio; on E by West Virginia and Virginia; in S by Tennessee; on W by Missouri. **Climate:** moderate, with plentiful rainfall. **Topography:** mountainous in E; rounded hills of the Knobs in the N; Bluegrass, heart of state; wooded rocky hillsides of the Pennyroyal; Western Coal Field; the fertile Purchase the SW. **Capital:** Frankfort.

Economy. Principal industries: manufacturing, coal mining, construction, agriculture. **Principal manufactured goods:** nonelectrical machinery, food products, electrical & electronic products, apparel, primary metals. **Agriculture: Chief crops:** tobacco, soybeans, corn, wheat. **Livestock** (1987): 2.5 mln. cattle; 880,000 hogs/pigs; 32,000 sheep; 1.8 mln. chickens; 1985 receipts for horse & mule sales, $520 mln. **Timber/lumber** (1984): hardwoods, pines; 272 mln. bd. ft. **Minerals** (1986): $259 mln.; crushed stone, ball clay, lime. **Chief ports:** Paducah, Louisville, Covington, Owensboro, Ashland, Henderson County, Lyon County, Hickman-Fulton County. **International airports at:** Covington. **Value of construction** (1986): $3.0 bln. **Employment distribution:** 23.8% trade; 20.4% manuf.; 19.7% serv.; 18.4% gvt. **Per capita income** (1986): $11,129. **Unemployment** (1986): 9.3%. **Tourism** (1985): tourists spent $3.2 bln.

Finance. Commercial bank deposits, per capita (1985): $6,410.

Federal government. No. federal civilian employees (Mar. 1986): 26,788. **Avg. salary:** $22,836. **Notable federal facilities:** U.S. Gold Bullion Depository, Fort Knox; Federal Correctional Institution, Lexington.

Energy. Electricity production (1986, mwh, by source): Hydroelectric: 2.7 mln.; Mineral: 64.2 mln.

Education. Expenditure per pupil, public schools (1984-85): $2,390. **Avg. salary, public school teachers** (1987 est.): $22,612.

State data. Motto: United we stand, divided we fall. **Flower:** Goldenrod. **Bird:** Cardinal. **Tree:** Kentucky coffee tree. **Song:** My Old Kentucky Home. **Entered union** June 1, 1792; rank, 15th. **State fair** at: Louisville.

History. Kentucky was the first area west of the Alleghenies settled by American pioneers; first permanent settlement, Harrodsburg, 1774. Daniel Boone blazed the Wilderness Trail through the Cumberland Gap and founded Fort Boonesborough, 1775. Indian attacks, spurred by the British, were unceasing until, during the Revolution, Gen. George Rogers Clark captured British forts in Indiana and Illinois, 1778. In 1792, after Virginia dropped its claims to the region, Kentucky became the 15th state.

Tourist attractions. Kentucky Derby and accompanying festivities, Louisville; Land Between the Lakes Nat'l. Recreation Area encompassing Kentucky Lake and Lake Barkley; Mammoth Cave with 300 mi. of explored passageways, 200-ft. high rooms, blind fish, and Echo River, 360 ft. below ground; Old Ft. Harrod State Park; Lincoln birthplace, Hodgenville; My Old Kentucky Home, Bardstown; Cumberland Gap Natl. Historical Park, Middlesboro; Kentucky Horse Park, Lexington.

Famous Kentuckians include Muhammad Ali, John James Audubon, Alben Barkley, Daniel Boone, Louis D. Brandeis, John C. Breckinridge, Kit Carson, Albert B. "Happy" Chandler, Cassius Marcellus Clay, Henry Clay, Jefferson Davis, John Fox Jr., John Marshall Harlan, Abraham Lincoln, Thomas Hunt Morgan, Elizabeth Madox Roberts, Col. Harland Sanders, Jesse Stuart, Adlai Stevenson, Zachary Taylor, Robert Penn Warren.

Chamber of Commerce. 452 Versailles Rd., P.O. Box 817, Frankfort, KY 40602.

Toll-free travel information. 1-800-225-TRIP in U.S., Ontario & Quebec, Canada.

Louisiana

Pelican State

People. Population (1986): 4,501,000; **rank:** 18. **Pop. density:** 99.7 per sq. mi. **Urban** (1980): 68.7%. **Racial distrib.** (1980): 69.2% White; 29.4% Black; Hispanic 99,105. **Net change** (1980-86): +295,000; 7.0%.

Geography. Total area: 48,523 sq. mi.; **rank:** 31. **Land area:** 44,930 sq. mi. **Acres forested land:** 14,558,100. **Location:** south central Gulf Coast state. **Climate:** subtropical, affected by continental weather patterns. **Topography:** lowlands of marshes and Mississippi R. flood plain; Red R. Valley lowlands; upland hills in the Florida Parishes; average elevation, 100 ft. **Capital:** Baton Rouge.

Economy. Principal industries: wholesale and retail trade, government, manufacturing, construction, transportation, mining. **Principal manufactured goods:** chemical products, foods, transportation equipment, electronic equipment, apparel, petroleum products. **Agriculture: Chief crops:** soybean, sugarcane, rice, corn, cotton, sweet potatoes, melons, pecans. **Livestock:** 1.3 mln. cattle; 240,000 hogs/pigs; 21,000 sheep; 3.2 mln. poultry. **Timber/lumber** (1984): pines, hardwoods, oak; 747 mln. bd. ft. **Minerals** (1986): Led U.S. in salt, 2nd in Frasch sulfur. Total nonfuel minerals $433.3 mln., mostly salt, sand & gravel, sulfur. **Commercial fishing** (1986): $321.5 mln. **Chief ports:** New Orleans, Baton Rouge, Lake Charles, S. Louisiana Port Commission at La Place. **International airports at:** New Orleans. **Value of construction** (1986): $3.1 bln. **Employment distribution** (1985): 23.8% trade; 21.5% gvt.; 21.3% serv.; 10.9% manuf. **Per capita income** (1986): $11,227. **Unemployment** (1986): 13.1%. **Tourism** (1985): out-of-state visitors spent $3.8 bln.

Finance. Commercial bank deposits, per capita (1985): $6,993.

Federal government. No. federal civilian employees (Mar. 1986): 20,405. **Avg. salary:** $24,283. **Notable federal facilities:** Barksdale, England, Ft. Polk military bases; Strategic Petroleum Reserve, New Orleans; Michoud Assembly Plant, New Orleans; U.S. Public Service Hospital, Carville.

Energy. Electricity production (1986, mwh, by source): Mineral: 42.0 mln; Nuclear: 10.6 mln.

Education. Expenditure per pupil, public schools (1984-85): $2,905. **Avg. salary, public school teachers** (1987 est.): $21,280.

State data. Motto: Union, justice and confidence. **Flower:** Magnolia. **Bird:** Eastern brown pelican. **Tree:** Cypress. **Song:** Give Me Louisiana. **Entered union** Apr. 30, 1812; rank, 18th. **State fair** at: Shreveport; Oct.

History. The area was first visited, 1530, by Cabeza de Vaca and Panfilo de Narvaez. The region was claimed for France by LaSalle, 1682. First permanent settlement was by French at Biloxi, now in Mississippi, 1699. France ceded the region to Spain, 1762, took it back, 1800, and sold it to the U.S., 1803, in the Louisiana Purchase. During the Revolution, Spanish Louisiana aided the Americans. Admitted to statehood, 1812, Louisiana was the scene of the Battle of New Orleans, 1815.

Louisiana Creoles are descendants of early French and/or Spanish settlers. About 4,000 Acadians, French settlers in Nova Scotia, Canada, were forcibly transported by the British to Louisiana in 1755 (an event commemorated in Longfellow's *Evangeline*) and settled near Bayou Teche; their descendants became known as Cajuns. Another group, the Islenos, were descendants of Canary Islanders brought to Louisiana by a Spanish governor in 1770. Traces of Spanish and French survive in local dialects.

Tourist attractions. Mardi Gras, French Quarter, Superdome, Dixieland jazz, all New Orleans; Battle of New Orleans site; Longfellow-Evangeline Memorial Park; Kent House Museum, Alexandria; Hodges Gardens, Natchitoches.

Famous Louisianans include Louis Armstrong, Pierre Beauregard, Judah P. Benjamin, Braxton Bragg, Grace King, Huey Long, Leonidas K. Polk, Henry Miller Shreve, Edward D. White Jr.

Tourist Information. State Dept. of Commerce, Culture, Recreation & Tourism, P.O. Box 94291, Baton Rouge, LA 70804-9291.

Toll-free travel information. 1-800-33-GUMBO.

Maine

Pine Tree State

People. Population (1986): 1,174,000; **rank:** 38. **Pop. density:** 37.6 per sq. mi. **Urban** (1980): 47.5% **Racial distrib.** (1980): 98.3% White; 0.3% Black; Hispanic: 5,005. **Net change** (1980-86): +49,000; 4.3%.

Geography. Total area: 33,215 sq. mi.; **rank:** 39. **Land area:** 30,920 sq. mi. **Acres forested land:** 17,718,300. **Location:** New England state at northeastern tip of U.S. **Climate:** Southern interior and coastal, influenced by air masses from the S and W; northern clime harsher, avg. +100 in. snow in winter. **Topography:** Appalachian Mtns. extend through state; western borders have rugged terrain; long sand beaches on southern coast; northern coast mainly rocky promontories, peninsulas, fjords. **Capital:** Augusta.

Economy. Principal industries: manufacturing, services, trade, government, agriculture, fisheries, forestry. **Principal manufactured goods:** paper and wood products, textiles, leather, processed foods. **Agriculture: Chief crops:** potatoes, apples, blueberries, sweet corn, peas, beans. **Livestock:** 148,000 cattle; 8,800 hogs/pigs; 17,000 sheep; 17.2 mln. poultry. **Timber/lumber** (1984): pine, spruce, fir; 918 mln. bd ft. **Minerals** (1986): $46 mln.; sand & gravel, crushed stone. **Commercial fishing** (1985): $108.7 mln. **Chief ports:** Searsport, Portland, Eastport. **International airports at:** Portland, Bangor. **Value of construction** (1986): $1.1 bln. **Employment distribution** (1985): 23.5% trade; 23.0% manuf.; 21.2% serv.; 18.6% gvt. **Per capita income** (1986): $12,709. **Unemployment** (1986): 5.3% **Tourism** (1986): $1.4 bln.

Finance. Commercial bank deposits, per capita (1985): $3,753.

Federal government. No. federal civilian employees (Mar. 1986): 12,830. **Avg. salary:** $24,236. **Notable federal facilities:** Kittery Naval Shipyard; Brunswick Naval Air Station; Loring Air Force Base.

Energy. Electricity production (1986, mwh, by source): Hydroelectric: 2.0 mln.; Mineral: 2.6 mln.; Nuclear: 6.2 mln.

Education. Expenditure per pupil, public schools (1984-85): $3,024. **Avg. salary, public school teachers** (1987 est.): $21,257.

State data. Motto: Dirigo (I direct). **Flower:** White pine cone and tassel. **Bird:** Chickadee. **Tree:** Eastern white pine. **Song:** State of Maine Song. **Entered union:** Mar. 15, 1820; rank, 23d.

History. Maine's rocky coast was explored by the Cabots, 1498-99. French settlers arrived, 1604, at the St. Croix River; English, 1607, on the Kennebec. In 1691, Maine was made part of Massachusetts. In the Revolution, a Maine regiment fought at Bunker Hill; a British fleet destroyed Falmouth (now Portland), 1775, but the British ship Margaretta was captured near Machiasport. In 1820, Maine broke off from Massachusetts, became a separate state.

Tourist attractions. Acadia Nat'l. Park, Bar Harbor, on Mt. Desert Is.; Bath Iron Works and Marine Museum; Boothbay (Harbor) Railway Museum; Portland Art Museum; Sugarloaf/USA Ski Area; Ogunquit, Portland, York.

Famous "Down Easters" include James G. Blaine, Cyrus H.K. Curtis, Hannibal Hamlin, Longfellow, Sir Hiram and Hudson Maxim, Edna St. Vincent Millay, Kate Douglas Wiggin, Ben Ames Williams.

Chamber of Commerce and Industry. 126 Sewall St., Augusta, ME 04330.

Toll-free travel information. 1-800-533-9595, winter only, out of state only; 1-207-289-2423 year round.

Maryland

Old Line State, Free State

People. Population (1986): 4,463,000; rank: 19 (tied with Washington). **Pop. density:** 444.0 per sq. mi. **Urban** (1980): 80.3% **Racial distrib.** (1980): 74.9% White; 22.7% Black; Hispanic 64,740. **Net change** (1980-86): 246,000; 5.8%.

Geography. Total area: 10,577 sq. mi.; **rank:** 42. **Land area:** 9,891 sq. mi. **Acres forested land:** 2,653,200. **Location:** Middle Atlantic state stretching from the Ocean to the Allegheny Mtns. **Climate:** continental in the west; humid subtropical in the east. **Topography:** Eastern Shore of coastal plain and Maryland Main of coastal plain, piedmont plateau, and the Blue Ridge, separated by the Chesapeake Bay. **Capital:** Annapolis.

Economy. Principal industries: manufacturing, tourism. **Principal manufactured goods:** electric and electronic equipment; food and kindred products; chemicals and allied products. **Agriculture: Chief crops** (1985): tobacco, corn, soybeans. **Livestock** (1985): 390,000 cattle; 215,000 hogs/pigs; 16,000 sheep; 4.6 mln. poultry. **Timber/lumber:** hardwoods. **Minerals** (1986): $294 mln.; crushed stone, sand & gravel, Portland cement. **Commercial fishing** (1986): $51.5 mln. **Chief ports:** Baltimore. **International airports at:** Baltimore. **Value of construction** (1986): 6.3 bln. **Employment distribution** (1986): 25.8% serv.; 25.4% trade; 20.1% gvt. **Per capita income** (1986): $16,588. **Unemployment** (1986): 4.5%. **Tourism** (1985): tourists spent $4.4 bln.

Finance. Commercial bank deposits, per capita (1985): $5,591.

Federal government. No. federal civilian employees (Mar. 1986): 105,836. **Avg. salary:** $29,143. **Notable federal facilities:** U.S. Naval Academy, Annapolis; Natl. Agric. Research Cen.; Ft. George C. Meade, Aberdeen Proving Ground; Goddard Space Flight Center.

Energy. Electricity production (1986, mwh, by source): Hydroelectric: 1.9 mln.; Mineral: 23.0 mln.; Nuclear: 12.8 mln.

Education. Expenditure per pupil, public schools (1984-85): $4,102. **Avg. salary, public school teachers** (1987 est.): $28,700.

State data. Motto. Fatti Maschii, Parole Femine (Manly deeds, womanly words). **Flower:** Black-eyed susan. **Bird:** Baltimore oriole. **Tree:** White oak. **Song:** Maryland, My Maryland. **Seventh** of the original 13 states to ratify Constitution, Apr. 28, 1788. **State fair** at: Timonium; late Aug.-early Sept.

History. Capt. John Smith first explored Maryland, 1608. William Claiborne set up a trading post on Kent Is. in Chesapeake Bay, 1631. Britain granted land to Cecilius Calvert, Lord Baltimore, 1632; his brother led 200 settlers to St. Marys River, 1634. The bravery of Maryland troops in the Revolution, as at the Battle of Long Island, won the state its nickname, The Old Line State. In the War of 1812, when a British fleet tried to take Fort McHenry, Marylander Francis Scott Key, 1814, wrote *The Star-Spangled Banner.*

Tourist Attractions. Racing events include the Preakness, at Pimlico track, Baltimore; the International at Laurel Race Course; the Maryland Million at Pimlico. Also Annapolis yacht races; Ocean City summer resort; restored Ft. McHenry, Baltimore, near which Francis Scott Key wrote *The Star-Spangled Banner;* Antietam Battlefield, 1862, near Hagerstown; South Mountain Battlefield, 1862; Edgar Allan Poe house, Baltimore; The State House, Annapolis, 1772, the oldest still in use in the U.S.; Montgomery & Prince George's County gateway to Washington, D.C.

Famous Marylanders include Benjamin Banneker, Francis Scott Key, H.L. Mencken, William Pinkney, Upton Sinclair, Roger B. Taney, Charles Willson Peale.

Chamber of Commerce. 60 West St., Suite 405, Annapolis, MD 21401.

Toll-free travel information. 1-800-331-1750.

Massachusetts

Bay State, Old Colony

People. Population (1986): 5,832,000; **rank:** 12. **Pop. density:** 743.9 per sq. mi. **Urban** (1980): 83.8% **Racial distrib.** (1980): 93.4% White; 3.8% Black; Hispanic 141,043. **Net change** (1980-86): +95,000; 1.7%.

Geography. Total area: 8,257 sq. mi.; **rank:** 45. **Land area:** 7,826 sq. mi. **Acres forested land:** 2,952,300. **Location:** New England state along Atlantic seaboard. **Climate:** temperate, with colder and drier clime in western region. **Topography:** jagged indented coast from Rhode Island around Cape Cod; flat land yields to stony upland pastures near central region and gentle hilly country in west; except in west, land is rocky, sandy, and not fertile. **Capital:** Boston.

Economy. Principal industries: manufacturing, services, trade, construction. **Principal manufactured goods** (1983): electronics, machinery, instruments, fabricated metals, printing and publishing. **Agriculture: Chief crops:** cranberries, greenhouse, nursery, vegetables. **Livestock** (1983): 120,000 cattle; 50,000 hogs/pigs; 8,000 sheep; 125,000 horses, ponies; 3.6 mln. poultry. **Timber/lumber** (1984): white pine, oak, other hard woods; 85 mln. bd. ft. **Minerals** (1986): $123 mln.; mostly sand & gravel, crushed stone, lime. **Commercial fishing** (1986): $243.5 mln. **Chief ports:** Boston, Fall River, New Bedford, Salem, Gloucester. **International airport at:** Boston. **Value of construction** (1986): $6.3 bln. **Employment distribution** (1983): 25.6% manuf.; 23.7% serv.; 22.3% trade. **Per capita income** (1986): $17,516. **Unemployment** (1986): 3.8%. **Tourism** (1983): out-of-state visitors spent $3.0 bln.

Finance. Commercial bank deposits, per capita (1985): $7,839.

Federal government. No. federal civilian employees (Mar. 1986): 31,932. **Avg. salary:** $25,296. **Notable federal facilities:** Ft. Devens; U.S. Customs House, John Fitzgerald Kennedy Federal Bldg., Boston; Q.M. Laboratory, Natick.

Energy. Electricity production (1986, mwh, by source): Hydroelectric: 330,000; Mineral: 31.7 mln.; Nuclear: 2.4 mln.

Education. Expenditure per pupil, public schools (1984-85): $4,026. **Avg. salary, public school teachers** (1987 est.): $28,410.

State data. Motto: Ense Petit Placidam Sub Libertate Quietem (By the sword we seek peace, but peace only under liberty). **Flower:** Mayflower. **Bird:** Chickadee. **Tree:** American elm. **Song:** All Hail to Massachusetts. **Sixth** of the original 13 states to ratify Constitution, Feb. 6, 1788.

History. The Pilgrims, seeking religious freedom, made their first settlement at Plymouth, 1620; the following year they gave thanks for their survival with the first Thanksgiving Day. Indian opposition reached a high point in King Philip's War, 1675-76, won by the colonists. Demonstrations against British restrictions set off the "Boston Massacre," 1770, and Boston "tea party," 1773. First bloodshed of the Revolution was at Lexington, 1775.

Tourist attractions. Cape Cod with Provincetown artists' colony; Freedom Trail; Berkshire Music Festival, Tanglewood; Boston "Pops" concerts; Museum of Fine Arts, Arnold Arboretum, all Boston; Jacob's Pillow Dance Festival, West Becket; historical Shaker Village, Old Sturbridge, Lexington, Concord, Salem, Plymouth Rock.

Famous "Bay Staters" include John Adams, John Quincy Adams, Samuel Adams, Louisa May Alcott, Horatio Alger, Clara Barton, Emily Dickinson, Emerson, Hancock, Hawthorne, Oliver W. Holmes, Winslow Homer, Elias Howe, John Fitzgerald Kennedy, Samuel F.B. Morse, Poe, Revere, Sargent, Thoreau, Whistler, Whittier.

Tourist information. Massachusetts Dept. of Commerce, 100 Cambridge St., Boston, MA 02202.

Toll-free travel information. 1-800-624-MASS.

Michigan

Great Lake State, Wolverine State

People. Population (1986): 9,145,000; **rank:** 8. **Pop. density:** 160.0 per sq. mi. **Urban** (1980): 70.7%. **Racial distrib.** (1980): 84.9% White; 12.9% Black; Hispanic 162,388. **Net change** (1980-86) −117,000; −1.3%.

Geography. Total area: 58,216 sq. mi.; **rank:** 23. **Land area.** 56,817 sq. mi. **Acres forested land.** 19,270,400. **Location:** east north central state bordering on 4 of the 5 Great Lakes, divided into an Upper and Lower Peninsula by the Straits of Mackinac, which link lakes Michigan and Huron. **Climate:** well-defined seasons tempered by the Great Lakes. **Topography:** low rolling hills give way to northern tableland of hilly belts in Lower Peninsula; Upper Peninsula is level in the east, with swampy areas; western region is higher and more rugged. **Capital:** Lansing.

Economy. Principal industries: manufacturing, mining, agriculture, food processing, tourism, fishing. **Principal manufactured goods:** automobiles, machine tools, chemicals, foods, primary metals and metal products, plastics, industrial robots, office furniture. **Agriculture: Chief crops:** corn, winter wheat, soybeans, dry beans, oats, hay, sugar beets, honey, asparagus, sweet corn, apples, cherries, grapes, peaches, blueberries, flowers. **Livestock** (1984): 1.5 mln. cattle; 1.2 mln. hogs/pigs; 100,000 sheep; 8.9 mln. poultry. **Timber/lumber:** maple, oak, aspen; 251 mln. bd. ft. **Minerals** (1985): $1.4 bln.; mostly cement, salt, crushed stone, sand & gravel. **Commercial fishing** (1986): $7.1 mln. **Chief ports:** Detroit, Saginaw River, Escanaba, Muskegon, Saulte Ste. Marie, Huron. **International airports at:** Detroit, Grand Rapids, Saginaw, Sault St. Marie. **Value of construction** (1986): $7.0 bln. **Employment distribution** (1986): 24.7% manuf.; 21.8% serv.; **Per capita income** (1986): $14,064. **Unemployment** (1986): 8.8%. **Tourism** (1984): out-of-state visitors spent $7.1 bln.

Finance. Commercial bank deposits, per capita (1985): $6,356.

Federal government. No. federal civilian employees (Mar. 1986): 27,335. **Avg. salary:** $25,831. **Notable federal facilities:** Isle Royal, Sleeping Bear Dunes national parks.

Energy. Electricity production (1986, mwh, by source): Hydroelectric: 604,000 mln; Mineral: 63.2 mln.; Nuclear: 12.3 mln.

Education. Expenditure per pupil, public schools (1984-85): $3,848. **Avg. salary, public school teachers** (1986): $31,500.

State data. Motto: Si Quaeris Peninsulam Amoenam Circumspice (If you seek a pleasant peninsula, look about you). **Flower:** Apple blossom. **Bird:** Robin. **Tree:** White pine. **Song:** Michigan, My Michigan. **Entered union** Jan. 26, 1837; rank, 26th. **State fair** at: Detroit, late Aug.-early Sept.; Upper Peninsula (Escanaba) mid-Aug.

History. French fur traders and missionaries visited the region, 1616, set up a mission at Sault Ste. Marie, 1641, and a settlement there, 1668. The whole region went to Britain, 1763. Anthony Wayne defeated their Indian allies at Fallen Timbers, Ohio, 1794. The British returned, 1812, seized Ft. Mackinac and Detroit. Oliver H. Perry's Lake Erie victory and William H. Harrison's troops, who carried the war to the Thames River in Canada, 1813, freed Michigan once more.

Tourist attractions. Henry Ford Museum, Greenfield Village, reconstruction of a typical 19th cent. American village, both in Dearborn; Michigan Space Ctr., Jackson; Tahquamenon *(Hiawatha)* Falls; DeZwaan windmill and Tulip Festival, Holland; "Soo Locks," St. Marys Falls Ship Canal, Sault Ste. Marie.

Famous Michiganians include Ralph Bunche, George Custer, Gerald R. Ford, Paul de Kruif, Thomas Dewey, Edna Ferber, Henry Ford, Edgar Guest, Robert Ingersoll, Will Kellogg, Ring Lardner, Elmore Leonard, Charles Lindbergh, Joe Louis, Pontiac, Stewart Edward White.

Chamber of Commerce: 200 N. Washington Sq., Suite 400, Lansing, MI 48933.

Minnesota

North Star State, Gopher State

People. Population (1986): 4,214,000; **rank:** 21. **Pop. density:** 52.9 per sq. mi. **Urban** (1980): 66.9%. **Racial distrib.** (1980): 96.5% White; 1.3% Black; Hispanic 32,124. **Net change** (1980-86): +138,000; 3.4%.

Geography. Total area: 84,068 sq. mi.; **rank:** 12. **Land area:** 79,289 sq. mi. **Acres forested land:** 16,709,200. **Location:** north central state bounded on the E by Wisconsin and Lake Superior, on the N by Canada, on the W by the Dakotas, and on the S by Iowa. **Climate:** northern part of state lies in the moist Great Lakes storm belt; the western border lies at the edge of the semi-arid Great Plains. **Topography:** central hill and lake region covering approx. half the state; to the NE, rocky ridges and deep lakes; to the NW, flat plain; to the S, rolling plains and deep river valleys. **Capital:** St. Paul.

Economy. Principal industries: agri business, forest products, mining, manufacturing, tourism. **Principal manufactured goods:** food processing, non-electrical machinery, chemicals, paper, electric and electronic equipment, printing and publishing, instruments, fabricated metal products. **Agriculture: Chief crops:** corn, soybeans, wheat, sugar beets, sunflowers, barley. **Livestock** (1986): 3.2 mln. cattle; 4.3 mln. hogs/pigs; 237,000 sheep; 12.8 mln. poultry. **Timber/lumber** (1984): needleleaves and hardwoods; 181 mln. bd. ft. **Minerals** (1986): 1.2 bln.; mostly iron ore, construction sand and gravel, crushed stone. **Commercial fishing:** $4.0 mln. **Chief ports:** Duluth, St. Paul, Minneapolis. **International airports at:** Minneapolis-St. Paul. **Value of construction** (1986): $4.9 bln. **Employment distribution** (1986): 24.9% trade; 23.7% serv.; 19.5% manuf.; 16.3% gvt. **Per capita income** (1986): $14,737. **Unemployment** (1986): 5.3%. **Tourism** (1985): out-of-state visitors spent $2.7 bln.

Finance. Commercial bank deposits, per capita (1985): $8,770.

Federal government. No. federal civilian employees (Mar. 1986): 13,491. **Avg. salary:** $26,205.

Energy. Electricity production (1986, mwh, by source): Hydroelectric: 936,000; Mineral: 16.4 mln.; Nuclear: 11.1 mln.

Education. Expenditure per pupil, public schools (1984-85): $3,674. **Avg. salary, public school teachers** (1987 est.): $29,140.

State data. Motto: L'Etoile du Nord (The star of the north). **Flower:** Pink and white lady's-slipper. **Bird:** Common loon. **Tree:** Red pine. **Song:** Hail! Minnesota. **Entered union** May 11, 1858; rank, 32d. **State fair** at: Saint Paul; late Aug. to early Sept.

History. Fur traders and missionaries from French Canada opened the region in the 17th century. Britain took the area east of the Mississippi, 1763. The U.S. took over that portion after the Revolution and in 1803 bought the western area as part of the Louisiana Purchase. The U.S. built present Ft. Snelling, 1820, bought lands from the Indians, 1837. Sioux Indians staged a bloody uprising, 1862, and were driven from the state.

Tourist attractions. Minnehaha Falls, Minneapolis, inspiration for Longfellow's *Hiawatha;* over 10,000 lakes; 64 state parks; 20 historical sites; Minneapolis Aquatennial; Ordway Theater, St. Paul; Guthrie Theater, Minneapolis; professional baseball, football, hockey. Voyageurs Nat'l. Park, a water wilderness along the Canadian border; Mayo Clinic, Rochester; St. Paul Winter Carnival.

Famous Minnesotans include F. Scott Fitzgerald, Cass Gilbert, Hubert Humphrey, Sister Elizabeth Kenny, Sinclair Lewis, Paul Manship, E. G. Marshall, William and Charles Mayo, Walter F. Mondale, Charles Schulz, Harold Stassen, Thorstein Veblen.

Tourist Information. Minnesota Office of Tourism, 375 Jackson St., 250 Skyway Level, St. Paul, MN 55101.

Toll-free travel information. 1-800-328-1461.

Mississippi

Magnolia State

People. Population (1986): 2,625,000; **rank:** 31. **Pop. density:** 55.2 per sq. mi. **Urban** (1980): 47.3%. **Racial distrib.** (1980): 64.1% White; 35.2% Black; Hispanic (1970): 8,182. **Net change** (1980-86): +104,000; 4.1%.

Geography. Total area: 47,716 sq. mi.; **rank:** 32. **Land area:** 47,296 sq. mi. **Acres forested land:** 16,715,600. **Location:** south central state bordered on the W by the Mississippi R. and on the S by the Gulf of Mexico. **Climate:** semi-tropical, with abundant rainfall, long growing season, and extreme temperatures unusual. **Topography:** low, fertile delta bet. the Yazoo and Mississippi rivers; loess bluffs stretching around delta border; sandy Gulf coastal terraces followed by piney woods and prairie; rugged, high sandy hills in extreme NE followed by black prairie belt. Pontotoc Ridge, and flatwoods into the north central highlands. **Capital:** Jackson.

Economy. Principal industries: manufacturing, food processing, seafood, government, wholesale and retail trade, agriculture. **Principal manufactured goods:** apparel, lumber and wood products, foods and kindred products, electrical machinery and equipment, transportation equip. **Agriculture: Chief crops:** cotton, soybeans, catfish, rice. **Livestock** (1984): 1.6 mln. cattle; 285,000 hogs/pigs; 4,500 sheep; 10.18 mln. poultry. **Timber/lumber** (1984): pine, oak, hardwoods; 1.8 bln. bd. ft. **Minerals** (1986): $104.6 mln., mostly sand & gravel, clays, crushed stone. **Commercial fishing** (1986): $45.6 mln. **Chief ports:** Pascagoula, Vicksburg, Gulfport, Natchez, Greenville. **Value of construction** (1986): $1.5 bln. **Employment distribution** (1986): 21.9% manuf.; 18.5% gvt.; 17.8% trade; 13.1% serv. **Per capita income** (1986): $9,552. **Unemployment** (1986): 11.7%. **Tourism** (1986): out-of-state visitors spent $1.3 bln.

Finance. Commercial bank deposits, per capita (1985): $5,502.

Federal government. No. federal civilian employees (Mar. 1986): 18,198. **Avg. salary:** $24,723. **Notable federal facilities:** Columbus, Keesler AF bases; Meridian Naval Air Station, NASA/NOAA International Earth Sciences Center.

Energy. Electricity production (1986, mwh, by source): Mineral 14.8 mln; Nuclear 4.1 mln.

Education. Expenditure per pupil, public schools (1984-85): $2,357. **Avg. salary, public school teachers** (1987 est.): $19,575.

State data. Motto: Virtute et Armis (By valor and arms). **Flower:** Magnolia. **Bird:** Mockingbird. **Tree:** Magnolia. **Song:** Go, Mississippi! **Entered union** Dec. 10, 1817; rank, 20th. **State fair** at: Jackson; Fall.

History. De Soto explored the area, 1540, discovered the Mississippi River, 1541. La Salle traced the river from Illinois to its mouth and claimed the entire valley for France, 1682. First settlement was the French Ft. Maurepas, near Ocean Springs, 1699. The area was ceded to Britain, 1763; American settlers followed. During the Revolution, Spain seized part of the area and refused to leave even after the U.S. acquired title at the end of the Revolution, finally moving out, 1798. Mississippi seceded 1861. Union forces captured Corinth and Vicksburg and destroyed Jackson and much of Meridian.

Tourist attractions. Vicksburg National Military Park and Cemetery, other Civil War sites; Natchez Trace; Indian mounds; estate pilgrimage at Natchez; Mardi Gras and blessing of the shrimp fleet, June, both in Biloxi.

Famous Mississippians include Dana Andrews, William Faulkner, L.Q.C. Lamar, Elvis Presley, Leontyne Price, Charlie Pride, Eudora Welty.

Chamber of Commerce. P.O. Box 1849, Jackson, MS 39205.

Toll-free travel information. 1-800-962-2346; 1-800-647-2290 out of state.

Missouri

Show Me State

People. Population (1986): 5,066,000; **rank:** 15. **Pop. density:** 72.9 per sq. mi. **Urban** (1980): 68.1%. **Racial distrib.** (1980): 88.3% White; 10.4% Black; Hispanic 51,667. **Net change** (1980-86): +149,000; 3.0%.

Geography. Total area: 69,686 sq. mi.; **rank:** 19. **Land area:** 68,995 sq. mi. **Acres forested land:** 12,876,000. **Location:** West North central state near the geographic center of the conterminous U.S.; bordered on the E by the Mississippi R., on the NW by the Missouri R. **Climate:** continental, susceptible to cold Canadian air, moist, warm Gulf air, and drier SW air. **Topography:** Rolling hills, open, fertile plains, and well-watered prairie N of the Missouri R.; south of the river land is rough and hilly with deep, narrow valleys; alluvial plain in the SE; low elevation in the west. **Capital:** Jefferson City.

Economy. Principal industries: agriculture, manufacturing, aerospace, tourism. **Principal manufactured goods:** transportation equipment, food and related products, electrical and electronic equipment, chemicals. **Agriculture: Chief crops:** soybeans, corn, wheat, cotton. **Livestock** (1986): 4.8 mln. cattle; 3 mln. hogs/pigs; 101,000 sheep; 7.7 mln. chickens, 12.5 mln. turkeys. **Timber/lumber** (1984): oak, hickory; 198 mln. bd. ft. **Minerals** (1986): $764.5 mln., mostly cement, lead, zinc. **Chief ports:** St. Louis, Kansas City. **International airports at:** St. Louis, Kansas City. **Value of construction** (1986): $4.3 bln. **Employment distribution** (1985): 24% trade; 22% serv.; 21.4% manuf.; 16.5% gvt. **Per capita income** (1986): $13,657. **Unemployment** (1986): 6.1%. **Tourism** (1986): total travelers spent $5 bln.

Finance. Commercial bank deposits, per capita (1985): $7,867.

Federal government: No. federal civilian employees (Mar. 1986): 45,537. **Avg. salary:** $24,951. **Notable federal facilities:** Federal Reserve banks, St. Louis, Kansas City; Ft. Leonard Wood, Rolla; Jefferson Barracks, St. Louis; Whiteman AFB, Knob Noster.

Energy. Electricity production (1986 mwh, by source): Hydroelectric: 2.1 mln.; Mineral: 45.0 mln; Nuclear: 7.2 mln.

Education. Expenditure per pupil, public schools (1984-85): $2,958. **Avg. salary, public school teachers** (1987 est.): $23,468.

State data. Motto: Salus Populi Suprema Lex Esto (The welfare of the people shall be the supreme law). **Flower:** Hawthorn. **Bird:** Bluebird. **Tree:** Dogwood. **Song:** Missouri Waltz. **Entered union** Aug. 10, 1821; rank, 24th. **State fair** at: Sedalia; 3d week in Aug.

History. DeSoto visited the area, 1541. French hunters and lead miners made the first settlement, c. 1735, at Ste. Genevieve. The U.S. acquired Missouri as part of the Louisiana Purchase, 1803. The fur trade and the Santa Fe Trail provided prosperity; St. Louis became the "jump-off" point for pioneers on their way West. Pro- and anti-slavery forces battled each other there during the Civil War.

Tourist attractions. Mark Twain Area, Hannibal; Pony Express Museum, St. Joseph; Harry S. Truman Library, Independence; Gateway Arch, St. Louis; Silver Dollar City, Branson Worlds of Fun, Kansas City; Lake of the Ozarks, Churchill Memorial, Fulton.

Famous Missourians include Thomas Hart Benton, George Caleb Bingham, Gen. Omar Bradley, George Washington Carver, Walter Cronkite, Dale Carnegie, Walt Disney, T.S. Eliot, Jesse James, Stan Musial, J. C. Penney, John J. Pershing, Joseph Pulitzer, Bess Truman, Harry S. Truman, Mark Twain, Tennessee Williams.

Chamber of Commerce: 400 E. High St., P.O. Box 149, Jefferson City, MO 65101.

Montana

Treasure State

People. Population (1986): 819,000; **rank:** 44. **Pop. density:** 5.67 per sq. mi. **Urban** (1980): 52.9%. **Racial distrib.** (1980): 94.0% White; 0.2% Black; 5.6% Other (includes American Indians); Hispanic 9,974. **Net change** (1980-86): +32,000; 4.1%.

Geography. Total area: 147,138 sq. mi.; **rank:** 4. **Land area:** 145,587 sq. mi. **Acres forested land:** 22,559,300. **Location:** Mountain state bounded on the E by the Dakotas, on the S by Wyoming, on the S/SW by Idaho, and on the N by Canada. **Climate:** colder, continental climate with low humidity. **Topography:** Rocky Mtns. in western third of the state; eastern two-thirds gently rolling northern Great Plains. **Capital:** Helena.

Economy. Principal industries: manufacturing, agriculture, mining, tourism. **Principal manufactured goods:** lumber and wood products, petroleum products, primary metals and minerals, farm machinery, processed foods. **Agriculture: Chief crops:** wheat, barley, sugar beets, hay, oats. **Livestock** (1986): 2.5 mln. cattle; 190,000 hogs/pigs; 423,000 sheep; 1.01 mln. poultry. **Timber/lumber** (1984): Douglas fir, pines, larch; 1.5 bln. bd. ft. **Minerals** (1986): $269 mln. mostly metallics. **International airports at:** Great Falls, Billings. **Value of construction** (1986): $487.9 mln. **Employment distribution** (1985): 23% trade; 22% serv.; 20% govt.; 10% agric; 7% manuf. **Per capita income** (1986): $11,904. **Unemployment** (1986): 8.1%. **Tourism** (1986): out-of-state visitors spent $475 mln.

Finance. Commercial bank deposits, per capita (1985): $7,430.

Federal government. No. federal civilian employees (Mar. 1986): 8,004. **Avg. salary:** $25,962. **Notable federal facilities:** Malmstrom AFB; Ft. Peck, Hungry Horse, Libby, Yellowtail dams.

Energy. Electricity production (1986, mwh, by source): Hydroelectric: 10.9 mln; Mineral: 11.5 mln.

Education. Expenditure per pupil, public schools (1984-85): $3,847. **Avg. salary, public school teachers** (1987 est.): $23,206.

State data. Motto: Oro y Plata (Gold and silver). **Flower:** Bitterroot. **Bird:** Western meadowlark. **Tree:** Ponderosa pine. **Song:** Montana. **Entered union** Nov. 8, 1889; rank, 41st. **State fair** at: Great Falls; late July to early Aug.

History. French explorers visited the region, 1742. The U.S. acquired the area partly through the Louisiana Purchase, 1803, and partly through the explorations of Lewis and Clark, 1805-06. Fur traders and missionaries established posts in the early 19th century. Indian uprisings reached their peak with the Battle of the Little Big Horn, 1876. The coming of the Northern Pacific Railway, 1883, brought population growth.

Tourist attractions. Glacier Natl. Park, on the Continental Divide, is a scenic and recreational wonderland, with 60 glaciers, 200 lakes, and many trout streams. Yellowstone Natl. Park, the largest & oldest national park, has 3 of 5 entrances in Montana, with 2,221,000 acres of scenic beauty, inc. geysers, mountains, canyons, streams, lakes, forests, waterfalls.

Also, Museum of the Plains Indian, Blackfeet Reservation near Browning; Custer Battlefield National Cemetery; Flathead Lake, in the NW, Lewis and Clark Cavern, Morrison Cave State Park, near Whitehall; 7 Indian reservations, covering over 5 million acres.

Famous Montanans include Gary Cooper, Marcus Daly, Chet Huntley, Will James, Myrna Loy, Mike Mansfield, Brent Musberger, Jeannette Rankin, Charles M. Russell, Lester Thurow.

Chamber of Commerce. 110 Neil Ave., P.O. Box 1730, Helena, MT 59624.

Toll-free travel information. 1-800-548-3390.

Nebraska

Cornhusker State

People. Population (1986): 1,598,000; **rank:** 36. **Pop. density:** 21.0 per sq. mi. **Urban** (1980): 62.9%. **Racial distrib.** (1980): 94.9% White; 3.1% Black; Hispanic 28,020. **Net change** (1980-86): +28,000; 1.8%.

Geography. Total area: 77,227 sq. mi.; **rank:** 15. **Land area:** 76,483 sq. mi. **Acres forested land:** 1,029,100. **Location:** West North Central state with the Missouri R. for a NE/E border. **Climate:** continental semi-arid. **Topography:** till plains of the central lowland in the eastern third rising to the Great Plains and hill country of the north central and NW. **Capital:** Lincoln.

Economy. Principal industries: agriculture, food processing, manufacturing. **Principal manufactured goods:** foods, machinery, electric and electronic equipment, primary and fabricated metal products, instruments & related prod. **Agriculture: Chief crops:** corn, soybeans, hay, sorghum, wheat, beans, oats, potatoes, sugar beets. **Livestock** (1986): 5.5 mln. cattle; 3.9 mln. hogs/pigs; 173,000 sheep; 4.0 mln. poultry. **Minerals** (1985): $101.9 mln.; mostly cement, crushed stone, sand & gravel. **Chief ports:** Omaha, Sioux City, Brownville, Blair, Plattsmouth, Nebraska City. **Value of construction** (1986): $1.0 bln. **Employment distribution** (1986): 22.4% serv.; 22.1% trade; 17.8% gvt.; 11.2% manuf.; 10% agric. **Per capita income** (1986): $13,777. **Unemployment** (1986): 5.0%. **Tourism** (1986): traveler expenditures $1.3 bln.

Finance. Commercial bank deposits, per capita (1985): $8,564.

Federal government. No. federal civilian employees (Mar. 1986): 8,861. **Avg. salary:** $25,078. **Notable federal facilities:** Strategic Air Command Base, Omaha.

Energy. Electricity production (1986, mwh, by source): Hydroelectric: 1.7 mln.; Mineral: 9.5 mln.; Nuclear: 7.7 mln.

Education. Expenditure per pupil, public schools (1984-85): $3,471. **Avg. salary, public school teachers** (1987 est.): $22,063.

State data. Motto: Equality before the law. **Flower:** Goldenrod. **Bird:** Western meadowlark. **Tree:** Cottonwood. **Song:** Beautiful Nebraska. **Entered union** Mar. 1, 1867; rank, 37th. **State fair** at: Lincoln; early to mid-Sept.

History. Spanish and French explorers and fur traders visited the area prior to the Louisiana Purchase, 1803. Lewis and Clark passed through, 1804-06. First permanent settlement was Bellevue, near Omaha, 1823. Many Civil War veterans settled under free land terms of the 1862 Homestead Act; struggles followed between homesteaders and ranchers.

Tourist attractions. Architecturally unique, 400' tall state capitol, Lincoln; Stuhr Museum of the Prairie Pioneer, Grand Island; Strategic Air Command Museum, Bellevue. Boys Town, founded by Fr. Flanagan, west of Omaha, is a self-contained community of under-privileged and homeless boys. Arbor Lodge State Park, Nebraska City, is a memorial to J. Sterling Morton, founder of Arbor Day. Buffalo Bill Ranch State Historical Park, North Platte, contains Cody's home and memorabilia of his Wild West Show.

Also, Pioneer Village, Minden; Oregon Trail landmarks, Scotts Bluff National Monument and Chimney Rock Historic Site, Ft. Robinson.

Famous Nebraskans include Fred Astaire, Charles W. and William Jennings Bryan, Johnny Carson, Willa Cather, William F. "Buffalo Bill" Cody, Michael and Edward A. Cudahy, Loren Eiseley, Rev. Edward J. Flanagan, Henry Fonda, Gerald R. Ford, Rollin Kirby, Harold Lloyd, Wright Morris, Gen. John J. Pershing, Mari Sandoz, Malcolm X, Roscoe Pound.

Chamber of Commerce. Suite 201, 1320 Lincoln Mall, Box 95128, Lincoln, NE 68509.

Toll-free travel information. 1-800-742-7595; 1-800-228-4307 out of state.

Nevada

Sagebrush State, Battle Born State, Silver State

People. Population (1986): 963,000; **rank:** 43. **Pop. density:** 8.5 per sq. mi. **Urban** (1980): 85.3%. **Racial distrib.** (1980): 87.5% White; 6.3% Black; Hispanic 53,786. **Net change** (1980-86): +163,000; 20.3%.

Geography. Total area: 110,540 sq. mi.; **rank:** 7. **Land area:** 109,889 sq. mi. **Acres forested land:** 7,683,300. **Location:** Mountain state bordered on N by Oregon and Idaho, on E by Utah and Arizona, on SE by Arizona, and on SW/W by California. **Climate:** semi-arid. **Topography:** rugged N-S mountain ranges; southern area is within the Mojave Desert; lowest elevation, Colorado R. Canyon, 470 ft. **Capital:** Carson City.

Economy. Principal industries: gaming, tourism, mining, manufacturing, government, agriculture, warehousing, trucking. **Principal manufactured goods:** gaming devices, electronics, chemicals, stone-clay-glass products. **Agriculture: Chief crops:** alfalfa, potatoes, hay, barley, wheat, cotton. **Livestock** (1986): 550,000 cattle; 14,000 hogs/pigs; 86,000 sheep; 17,000 poultry. **Timber/lumber:** piñon, juniper, other pines. **Minerals** (1986): $905 mln.; mostly gold, silver, construction sand & gravel. **International airports at** Las Vegas, Reno. **Value of construction** (1986): $2.0 bln. **Employment distribution** (1986): 44% serv.; 20% trade; 13% gvt. **Per capita income** (1986): $15,074. **Unemployment** (1986): 6.0%. **Tourism** (1984): out-of-state travelers spent $6.5 bln.

Finance. Commercial bank deposits, per capita (1985): $5,160.

Federal government. No. federal civilian employees (Mar. 1986): 6,314. **Avg. salary:** $27,002. **Notable federal facilities:** Nevada Test Site; Hawthorne Munitions Plant.

Energy. Electricity production (1986, mwh, by source): Hydroelectric: 4.6 mln.; Mineral: 15.3 mln.

Education. Expenditure per pupil, public schools (1984-85): $2,829. **Avg. salary, public school teachers** (1987 est.): $26,030.

State data. Motto: All for our country. **Flower:** Sagebrush. **Bird:** Mountain bluebird. **Tree:** Single-leaf pinon. **Song:** Home Means Nevada. **Entered union** Oct. 31, 1864; rank, 36th. **State fair** at Reno; early Sept.

History. Nevada was first explored by Spaniards in 1776. Hudson's Bay Co. trappers explored the north and central region, 1825; trader Jedediah Smith crossed the state, 1826 and 1827. The area was acquired by the U.S., in 1848, at the end of the Mexican War. First settlement, Mormon Station, now Genoa, was est. 1849. In the early 20th century, Nevada adopted progressive measures such as the initiative, referendum, recall, and woman suffrage.

Tourist attractions. Legalized casino gambling provided the impetus for the development of resort facilities at Lake Tahoe, Reno, Las Vegas, and elsewhere. Ghost towns, rodeos, mountain climbing, skiing, golfing, trout fishing, water sports and hunting important. Notable are Hoover Dam, Lake Mead Natl. Recreation Area, Lake Tahoe, Great Basin Natl. Park, Valley of Fire State Park & Virginia City. Annual events inc. Helldorado Days & Rodeo, Las Vegas; Reno Rodeo; Basque Festival, Elko; Nevada Day, Carson City.

Famous Nevadans include Walter Van Tilburg Clark, Sarah Winnemucca Hopkins, Paul Laxalt, John William MacKay, Pat McCarran, Dat So La Lee, Key Pittman, William Morris Stewart.

Tourist Information. Commission on Economic Development, Capitol Complex, Carson City, NV 89710.

Toll-free travel information. 1-800-237-0774.

New Hampshire

Granite State

People. Population (1986): 1,027,000; **rank:** 40. **Pop. density:** 110.6 per sq. mi. **Urban** (1980): 52.2%. **Racial distrib.** (1980): 98.8% White; 0.4% Black; Hispanic 5,587. **Net change** (1980-86): +106,000; 11.5%.

Geography. Total area: 9,304 sq. mi., **rank:** 44. **Land area:** 9,027 sq. mi. **Acres forested land:** 5,013,500. **Location:** New England state bounded on S by Massachusetts, on W by Vermont, on N/NW by Canada, on E by Maine and the Atlantic O. **Climate:** highly varied, due to its nearness to high mountains and ocean. **Topography:** low, rolling coast followed by countless hills and mountains rising out of a central plateau. **Capital:** Concord.

Economy. Principal industries: manufacturing, tourism, agriculture, trade, mining. **Principal manufactured goods:** machinery, electrical & electronic products, plastics, fabricated metal products, leather goods. **Agriculture: Chief crops:** dairy products, eggs, nursery and greenhouse products, hay, vegetables, fruit, maple syrup & sugar prods. **Livestock** (1982): 69,207 cattle; 6,343 hogs/pigs; 9,000 sheep; 693,765 poultry. **Timber/lumber** (1984): white pine, hemlock, oak, birch; 1.3 bln. bd. ft. **Minerals** (1986): $29 mln.; mostly sand & gravel. **Commercial fishing** (1986): $6.2 mln. **Chief ports:** Portsmouth, Hampton, Rye. **Value of construction** (1986): $1.6 bln. **Employment distribution** (1985): 31% manuf.; 28% trade; 24% serv; 15% gvt. **Per capita income** (1986): $15,922. **Unemployment** (1986): 2.8%. **Tourism** (1985): out-of-state visitors spent $1 bln.

Finance. Commercial bank deposits, per capita (1985): $5,686.

Federal government. No. federal civilian employees (Mar. 1986): 3,881. **Avg. salary:** $26,063. **Notable federal facilities:** Pease Air Base, Newington.

Energy. Electricity production (1986, mwh, by source): Hydroelectric: 1.1 mln.; Mineral: 5.0 mln.

Education: Expenditure per pupil, public schools (1984-85): $3,271. **Avg. salary, public school teachers** (1987 est.): $21,869.

State data. Motto: Live free or die. **Flower:** Purple lilac. **Bird:** Purple finch. **Tree:** White birch. **Song:** Old New Hampshire. **Ninth** of the original 13 states to ratify the Constitution, June 21, 1788.

History. First explorers to visit the New Hampshire area were England's Martin Pring, 1603, and Champlain, 1605. First settlement was Little Harbor, near Rye, 1623. Indian raids were halted, 1759, by Robert Rogers' Rangers. Before the Revolution, New Hampshire men seized a British fort at Portsmouth, 1774, and drove the royal governor out, 1775. Three regiments served in the Continental Army and scores of privateers raided British shipping.

Tourist attractions. Mt. Washington, highest peak in Northeast, hub of network of trails; Lake Winnipesaukee; White Mt. Natl. Forest; Crawford, Franconia, Pinkham notches in White Mt. region—Franconia famous for the Old Man of the Mountains, described by Hawthorne as the Great Stone Face; the Flume, a spectacular gorge; the aerial tramway on Cannon Mt; Strawbery Banke, Portsmouth; Shaker Village, Canterbury.

Famous New Hampshirites include Salmon P. Chase, Ralph Adams Cram, Mary Baker Eddy, Daniel Chester French, Robert Frost, Horace Greeley, Sarah Buell Hale, Franklin Pierce, Augustus Saint-Gaudens, Daniel Webster.

Tourist Information. Department of Resources and Economic Development, Office of Vacation Travel, P.O. Box 856, Concord, NH 03301.

Toll-free travel information. 1-800-258-3608 in northeast.

New Jersey

Garden State

People. Population (1986): 7,620,000; **rank:** 9. **Pop. density:** 1,005.5 per sq. mi. **Urban** (1980): 89.0%. **Racial distrib.** (1980): 83.2% White; 12.5% Black; Hispanic 491,867. **Net change** (1980-86): +225,000; 3.5%.

Geography. Total area: 7,836 sq. mi.; **rank:** 46. **Land area:** 7,521 sq. mi. **Acres forested land:** 1,928,400. **Location:** Middle Atlantic state bounded on the N and E by New York and the Atlantic O., on the S and W by Delaware and Pennsylvania. **Climate:** moderate, with marked difference bet. NW and SE extremities. **Topography:** Appalachian Valley in the NW also has highest elevation, High Pt., 1,801 ft.; Appalachian Highlands, flat-topped NE-SW mountain ranges; Piedmont Plateau, low plains broken by high ridges (Palisades) rising 400-500 ft.; Coastal Plain, covering three-fifths of state in SE, gradually rises from sea level to gentle slopes. **Capital:** Trenton.

Economy. Principal industries: trade, services, manufacturing. **Principal manufactured goods:** chemicals, electronic and electrical equipment, non-electrical machinery, fabricated metals. **Agriculture: Chief crops:** hay, corn, soybeans, tomatoes, blueberries, peaches, cranberries. **Livestock:** 95,000 cattle; 53,800 hogs/pigs; 11,900 sheep; 966,800 poultry. **Timber/lumber** (1984): pine, cedar, mixed hardwoods; 11 mln. bd. ft. **Minerals** (1986): $170 mln.; mostly crushed stone, sand & gravel. **Commercial fishing** (1986): $66.7 mln. **Chief ports:** Newark, Elizabeth, Hoboken, Camden. **International airports at:** Newark. **Value of construction** (1986): $8.7 bln. **Employment distribution** (1986): 23.9% trade; 23.8% serv.; 19.9% manuf.; 15.4% gvt. **Per capita income** (1986): $18,284. **Unemployment** (1986): 5.0%. **Tourism** (1986): tourists spent $11.4 bln.

Finance. Commercial bank deposits, per capita (1985): $6,612.

Federal government. No. federal civilian employees (Mar. 1986): 39,396. **Avg. salary:** $26,731. **Notable federal facilities:** McGuire AFB Fort Dix; Fort Monmouth; Picatinny Arsenal; Lakewood Naval Air Station, Lakehurst Naval Air Engineering Center.

Energy. Electricity production (1986, mwh, by source): Mineral: 19.2 mln.; Nuclear: 14.8 mln.

Education. Expenditure per pupil, public schools (1984-85): $4,504. **Avg. salary, public school teachers** (1987 est.): $28,927.

State Data. Motto: Liberty and prosperity. **Flower:** Purple violet. **Bird:** Eastern goldfinch. **Tree:** Red oak. **Third** of the original 13 states to ratify the Constitution, Dec. 18, 1787. **State fair:** usually Sept.

History. The Lenni Lenape (Delaware) Indians had mostly peaceful relations with European colonists who arrived after the explorers Verrazano, 1524, and Hudson, 1609. The Dutch were first; when the British took New Netherland, 1664, the area between the Delaware and Hudson Rivers was given to Lord John Berkeley and Sir George Carteret. New Jersey was the scene of nearly 100 battles, large and small, during the Revolution, including Trenton, 1776, Princeton, 1777, Monmouth, 1778.

Tourist attractions. 127 miles of beaches; Miss America Pageant and hotel-casinos, Atlantic City; Grover Cleveland birthplace, Caldwell. Cape May Historic District; Edison Labs, W. Orange; Great Adventure amusement park; Liberty State Park; Meadowlands Sports Complex; Pine Barrens wilderness area; Princeton University; numerous Revolutionary War historical sites.

Famous New Jerseyans include Count Basie, Aaron Burr, Grover Cleveland, James Fenimore Cooper, Stephen Crane, Thomas Edison, Albert Einstein, Alexander Hamilton, Joyce Kilmer, Gen. George McClellan, Thomas Paine, Molly Pitcher, Paul Robeson, Walter Schirra, Frank Sinatra, Bruce Springsteen, Walt Whitman, Woodrow Wilson.

Chamber of Commerce. 50 Commerce St., Newark, NJ 07102.

New Mexico

Land of Enchantment

People. Population (1986): 1,479,000; **rank:** 37. **Pop. density:** 11.9 per sq. mi. **Urban** (1980): 72.1%. **Racial distrib.** (1980): 75.1% White; 1.8% Black; 15.3% Other (includes American Indians); Hispanic 476,089. **Major ethnic groups:** Spanish, Indian, English. **Net change** (1980-86): +176,000; 13.5%.

Geography. Total area: 121,666 sq. mi.; **rank:** 5. **Land area:** 121,412 sq. mi. **Acres forested land:** 18,059,800. **Location:** southwestern state bounded by Colorado on the N, Oklahoma, Texas, and Mexico on the E and S, and Arizona on the W. **Climate:** dry, with temperatures rising or falling 5°F with every 1,000 ft. elevation. **Topography:** eastern third, Great Plains; central third Rocky Mtns. (85% of the state is over 4,000 ft. elevation); western third high plateau. **Capital:** Santa Fe.

Economy. Principal industries: extractive industries, tourism, agriculture. **Principal manufactured goods:** foods, electrical machinery, apparel, lumber, printing, transportation equipment. **Agriculture: Chief crops:** wheat, hay, sorghum, grain, onions, cotton, corn. **Livestock:** 1.72 mln. cattle; 72,000 hogs/pigs; 578,000 sheep; 1.21 mln. poultry. **Timber/lumber** (1984): Ponderosa pine, Douglas fir; 245 mln. bd. ft. **Minerals** (1986): $608.4 mln.; mostly potassium salts, sand & gravel. **International airports at:** Albuquerque. **Value of construction** (1986): $1.6 bln. **Employment distribution:** 23.0% serv.; 18.0% agric.; 10% manuf.; 8.9% gvt. **Per capita income** (1986): $11,037. **Unemployment** (1986): 9.2%. **Tourism** (1986): out-of-state visitors spent $2.1 bln.

Finance. Commercial bank deposits, per capita (1985): $5,580.

Federal government. No. federal civilian employees (Mar. 1986): 21,813. **Avg. salary:** $25,338. **Notable federal facilities:** Kirtland, Cannon, Holloman AF bases; Los Alamos Scientific Laboratory; White Sands Missile Range.

Energy. Electricity production (1986, mwh, by source): Hydroelectric: 166,000; Mineral: 23.4 mln.

Education. Expenditure per pupil, public schools (1984-85): $3,153. **Avg. salary, public school teachers** (1987 est.): $23,977.

State data. Motto: Crescit Eundo (It grows as it goes). **Flower:** Yucca. **Bird:** Roadrunner. **Tree:** Pinon. **Song:** O, Fair New Mexico, Asi Es Nuevo Mexico. **Entered union** Jan. 6, 1912; rank, 47th. **State fair** at: Albuquerque; mid-Sept.

History. Franciscan Marcos de Niza and a black slave Estevan explored the area, 1539, seeking gold. First settlements were at San Juan Pueblo, 1598, and Santa Fe, 1610. Settlers alternately traded and fought with the Apaches, Comanches, and Navajos. Trade on the Santa Fe Trail to Missouri started 1821. The Mexican War was declared May, 1846, Gen. Stephen Kearny took Santa Fe, August. In the 1870s, cattlemen staged the famed Lincoln County War in which Billy (the Kid) Bonney played a leading role. Pancho Villa raided Columbus, 1916.

Tourist Attractions. Carlsbad Caverns, a national park, has caverns on 3 levels and the largest natural cave "room" in the world, 1,500 by 300 ft., 300 ft. high; White Sands Natl. Monument, the largest gypsum deposit in the world.

Pueblo ruins from 100 AD, Chaco Canyon; Acoma, the "sky city," built atop a 357-ft. mesa; 19 Pueblo, 4 Navajo, and 2 Apache reservations. Also, ghost towns, dude ranches, skiing, hunting, and fishing.

Famous New Mexicans include Billy (the Kid) Bonney, Kit Carson, Peter Hurd, Archbishop Jean Baptiste Lamy, Bill Mauldin, Georgia O'Keeffe, Kim Stanley, Lew Wallace.

Tourist information. New Mexico Travel Division, Joseph M. Montoya Bldg., 1100 St. Francis Dr., Santa Fe, N.M. 87503.

Toll-free travel information. 1-800-545-2040.

New York

Empire State

People. Population (1986): 17,772,000; **rank:** 2. **Pop. density:** 371.8 per sq. mi. **Urban** (1980): 84.6%. **Racial distrib.** (1980): 79.5% White; 13.68% Black; Hispanic (1980): 1,659,245. **Net change** (1980-86): +214,000; 1.2%.

Geography. Total area: 49,576 sq. mi.; **rank:** 30. **Land area:** 47,831 sq. mi. **Acres forested land:** 17,218,400. **Location:** Middle Atlantic state, bordered by the New England states, Atlantic Ocean, New Jersey and Pennsylvania, Lakes Ontario and Erie, and Canada. **Climate:** variable; the SE region moderated by the ocean. **Topography:** highest and most rugged mountains in the NE Adirondack upland; St. Lawrence-Champlain lowlands extend from Lake Ontario NE along the Canadian border; Hudson-Mohawk lowland follows the flows of the rivers N and W, 10-30 mi. wide; Atlantic coastal plain in the SE; Appalachian Highlands, covering half the state westward from the Hudson Valley, include the Catskill Mtns., Finger Lakes; plateau of Erie-Ontario lowlands. **Capital:** Albany.

Economy. Principal industries: manufacturing, finance, communications, tourism, transportation, services. **Principal manufactured goods:** books and periodicals, clothing and apparel, pharmaceuticals, machinery, instruments, toys and sporting goods, electronic equipment, automotive and aircraft components. **Agriculture: Chief crops:** apples, cabbage, cauliflower, celery, cherries, grapes, corn, peas, snap beans, sweet corn. **Products:** milk, cheese, maple syrup, wine. **Livestock** (1985): 2.0 mln. cattle; 130,000 hogs/pigs; 55,000 sheep; 14.0 mln. poultry. **Timber/lumber** (1984): saw log production; 362 mln. bd. ft. **Minerals** (1986): $647 mln.; mostly crushed stone, cement, salt. **Commercial fishing** (1986): $45.5 mln. **Chief ports:** New York, Buffalo, Albany. **International airports at:** New York, Buffalo, Syracuse, Massena, Ogdensburg, Watertown, Niagara Falls, Newburgh, Sullivan county. **Value of construction** (1986): $12.0 bln. **Employment distribution:** 1.3% agric.; 21% manuf.; 33% serv.; 19% trade. **Per capita income** (1986): $17,118. **Unemployment** (1985): 6.3%. **Tourism** (1986): tourists spent $14.4 bln.

Finance. Commercial bank deposits, per captita (1985): $12,929.

Federal government. No. federal civilian employees (Mar. 1986): 69,675. **Avg. salary:** $25,134. **Notable federal facilities:** West Point Military Academy; Merchant Marine Academy; Ft. Drum; Griffiss, Plattsburgh AF bases; Watervliet Arsenal.

Energy. Electricity production (1986, mwh, by source): Hydroelectric: 29.5 mln.; Mineral: 59.7 mln.; Nuclear: 22.1 mln.

Education: Expenditure per pupil, public schools (1984-85): $5,492. **Avg. salary, public school teachers** (1987 est.): $32,620.

State data. Motto: Excelsior (Ever upward). **Flower:** Rose. **Bird:** Bluebird. **Tree:** Sugar maple. **Song:** I Love New York. **Eleventh** of the original 13 states to ratify the Constitution, July 26, 1788. **State fair** at: Syracuse, late Aug.-early Sept.

History. In 1609 Henry Hudson discovered the river that bears his name and Champlain explored the lake, far upstate, which was named for him. Dutch built posts near Albany 1614 and 1624; in 1626 they settled Manhattan. A British fleet seized New Netherland, 1664. Ninety-two of the 300 or more engagements of the Revolution were fought in New York, including the Battle of Bemis Heights-Saratoga, a turning point of the war.

Tourist attractions. New York City; Adirondack and Catskill mtns.; Finger Lakes, Great Lakes; Long Island beaches; Thousand Islands; Niagara Falls; Saratoga Springs racing and spas; Philipsburg Manor, Sunnyside, the restored home of Washington Irving, The Dutch Church of Sleepy Hollow, all in North Tarrytown; Corning Glass Center and Steuben factory, Corning; Fenimore House, National Baseball Hall of Fame and Museum, both in Cooperstown; Ft. Ticonderoga overlooking lakes

George and Champlain; Albany's Empire State Plaza, Lake Placid Olympic Village.

The Franklin D. Roosevelt National Historic Site, Hyde Park, includes the graves of Pres. and Mrs. Roosevelt, the family home since 1867, the Roosevelt Library. Sagamore Hill, Oyster Bay, the Theodore Roosevelt estate, includes his home.

Famous New Yorkers include Susan B. Anthony, Peter Cooper, George Eastman, Millard Fillmore, Julia Ward Howe, Charles Evans Hughes, Henry and William James, Herman Melville, Franklin Delano Roosevelt, Theodore Roosevelt, Alfred E. Smith, Elizabeth Cady Stanton, Martin Van Buren, Walt Whitman.

Tourist information: N.Y. State Dept. of Commerce, 1 Commerce Plaza, Albany, NY 12245.

Toll-free travel information. 1-800-CALLNYS, from the 48 contiguous states; 1-518-474-4116 from other areas and Canada.

North Carolina

Tar Heel State, Old North State

People. Population (1986): 6,331,000; **rank:** 10. **Pop. density:** 128.2 per sq. mi. **Urban** (1980): 42.9%. **Racial distrib.** (1980): 75.8% White; 22.4% Black; Hispanic (1980): 56,607. **Net change** (1980-86): +451,000; 7.7%.

Geography. Total area: 52,586 sq. mi.; **rank:** 28. **Land area:** 48,798 sq. mi. **Acres forested land:** 20,043,300. **Location:** South Atlantic state bounded by Virginia, South Carolina, Georgia, Tennessee, and the Atlantic O. **Climate:** sub-tropical in SE, medium-continental in mountain region; tempered by the Gulf Stream and the mountains in W. **Topography:** coastal plain and tidewater, two-fifths of state, extending to the fall line of the rivers; piedmont plateau, another two-fifths, 200 mi. wide of gentle to rugged hills; southern Appalachian Mtns. contains the Blue Ridge and Great Smoky mtns. **Capital:** Raleigh.

Economy. Principal industries: manufacturing, agriculture, tobacco, tourism. **Principal manufactured goods:** textiles, tobacco products, electrical/electronic equip., chemicals, furniture, food products, non-electrical machinery. **Agriculture: Chief crops:** tobacco, soybeans, corn, peanuts, small sweet potatoes, feed grains, vegetables, fruits. **Livestock** (1986): 1.2 mln. cattle; 2.7 mln. hogs/pigs; 22 mln. chickens. **Timber/lumber** (1984): yellow pine, oak, hickory, poplar, maple. 1.4 bln. bd. ft. **Minerals** (1986): Total $429.4 mln., mostly crushed stone, sand & gravel, feldspar. **Commercial fishing** (1986): $63.4 mln. **Chief ports:** Morehead City, Wilmington. **Value of construction** (1986): $6.9 bln. **Employment distribution** (1986): 30.5% manuf.; 22.2% trade; 16.6% serv.; 15.6% gvt. **Per capita income** (1986): $12,245. **Unemployment** (1986): 5.3%. **Tourism** (1985): out-of-state visitors spent $5+ bln.

Finance. Commercial bank deposits, per capita (1985): $5,218.

Federal government. No. federal civilian employees (Mar. 1986): 28,854. **Avg. salary:** $23,896. **Notable federal facilities:** Ft. Bragg; Camp LeJeune Marine Base; U.S. EPA Research and Development Labs, Cherry Point Marine Corps Air Station; Natl. Humanities Center; Natl. Inst. of Environmental Health Science; Natl. Center for Health Statistics Lab, Research Triangle Park.

Energy. Electricity production (1986, mwh, by source): Hydroelectric: 2.5 mln.; Mineral: 54.0 mln.; Nuclear: 20.3 mln.

Education. Expenditure per pupil, public schools (1984-85): $2,625. **Avg. salary, public school teachers** (1987 est.): $23,775.

State data. Motto: Esse Quam Videri (To be rather than to seem). **Flower:** Dogwood. **Bird:** Cardinal. **Tree:** Pine. **Song:** The Old North State. **Twelfth** of the original 13 states to ratify the Constitution, Nov. 21, 1789. **State fair** at: Raleigh; mid-Oct.

History. The first English colony in America was the first of 2 established by Sir Walter Raleigh on Roanoke Is., 1585 and 1587. The first group returned to England; the second, the "Lost Colony," disappeared without trace. Permanent settlers came from Virginia, c. 1660. Roused by British repressions, the colonists drove out the royal governor, 1775; the province's congress was the first to vote for independence; ten regiments were furnished to the Continental Army. Cornwallis' forces were defeated at Kings Mountain, 1780, and forced out after Guilford Courthouse, 1781.

Tourist attractions. Cape Hatteras and Cape Lookout national seashores; Great Smoky Mtns. (half in Tennessee); Guilford Courthouse and Moore's Creek parks, 66 Revolutionary battle sites; Bennett Place, NW of Durham, where Gen. Joseph Johnston surrendered the last Confederate army to Gen. Wm. Sherman; Ft. Raleigh, Roanoke Is., where Virginia Dare, first child of English parents in the New World, was born Aug. 18, 1587; Wright Brothers National Memorial, Kitty Hawk; N.C. Zoo, Asheboro.

Famous North Carolinians include Richard J. Gatling, Billy Graham, Andrew Jackson, Andrew Johnson, Wm. Rufus King, Dolley Madison, Edward R. Murrow, James K. Polk, Enos Slaughter, Moses Waddel, Thomas Wolfe.

Tourist information. Division of Travel & Tourism Development, P.O. Box 25249, Raleigh, NC 27611.

Toll-free travel information. 1-800-VISITNC.

North Dakota

Peace Garden State

People. Population (1986): 679,000; **rank:** 46. **Pop. density:** 9.9 per sq. mi. **Urban** (1980): 48.8%. **Racial distrib.** (1980): 95.8% White; 0.39% Black; Hispanic (1980): 3,903. **Net change** (1980-86): +26,000; 4.1%.

Geography. Total area: 70,665 sq. mi.; **rank:** 17. **Land area:** 69,273 sq. mi. **Acres forested land:** 421,800. **Location:** West North Central state, situated exactly in the middle of North America, bounded on the N by Canada, on the E by Minnesota, on the S by South Dakota, on the W by Montana. **Climate:** continental, with a wide range of temperature and moderate rainfall. **Topography:** Central Lowland in the E comprises the flat Red River Valley and the Rolling Drift Prairie; Missouri Plateau of the Great Plains on the W. **Capital:** Bismarck.

Economy. Principal industries: agriculture, mining, tourism, manufacturing. **Principal manufactured goods:** farm equipment, processed foods. **Agriculture: Chief crops:** spring wheat, durum, barley, rye, flaxseed, oats, potatoes, dried edible beans, honey, soybeans, sugarbeets, sunflowers, hay. **Livestock** (1986): 2.0 mln. cattle; 285,000 hogs/pigs; 180,000 sheep; 1.4 mln. poultry. **Minerals** (1986): $21.2 mln. mostly construction sand & gravel, lime. **International airports at:** Fargo, Grand Forks, Bismarck, Minot. **Value of construction** (1986): $482.8 mln. **Employment distribution:** 21.9% trade; 20.4% gvt.; 18.6% serv.; 17.2% agric. **Per capita income** (1986): $12,284. **Unemployment** (1986): 6.3%. **Tourism** (1986): out-of-state visitors spent $11.4 mln.

Finance. Commercial bank deposits, per capita (1985): $5,218.

Federal government. No. federal civilian employees (Mar. 1986): 5,154. **Avg. salary:** $24,325. **Notable federal facilities:** Strategic Air Command bases at Minot, Grand Forks; Northern Prairie Wildlife Research Center; Garrison Dam; Theodore Roosevelt Natl. Park; Grand Forks Energy Research Center; Ft. Union Natl. Historic Site.

Energy. Electricity production (1986, mwh, by source): Hydroelectric: 2.3 mln.; Mineral: 20.6 mln.

Education. Expenditure per pupil, public schools, (1984-85): $3,210. **Avg. salary, public school teachers** (1987 est.): $21,848.

State data. Motto: Liberty and union, now and forever, one and inseparable. **Flower:** Wild prairie rose. **Bird:** Western Meadowlark. **Tree:** American elm. **Song:** North Dakota Hymn. **Entered union** Nov. 2, 1889; rank, 39th. **State fair** at: Minot; 3d week in July.

History. Pierre La Verendrye was the first French fur trader in the area, 1738, followed later by the English. The U.S. acquired half the territory in the Louisiana Purchase,

1803. Lewis and Clark built Ft. Mandan, spent the winter of 1804-05 there. In 1818, American ownership of the other half was confirmed by agreement with Britain. First permanent settlement was at Pembina, 1812. Missouri River steamboats reached the area, 1832; the first railroad, 1873, bringing many homesteaders. The state was first to hold a presidential primary, 1912.

Tourist attractions. International Peace Garden, a 2,200-acre tract extending across the border into Manitoba, commemorates the friendly relations between the U.S. and Canada; 65,000-acre Theodore Roosevelt National Park, Badlands, contains the president's Elkhorn Ranch; Ft. Abraham Lincoln State Park and Museum, S of Mandan.

Famous North Dakotans include Maxwell Anderson, Angie Dickinson, John Bernard Flannagan; Louis L'Amour, Peggy Lee, Eric Sevareid, Vilhjalmur Stefansson, Lawrence Welk.

Chamber of Commerce. P.O. Box 2467, Fargo, ND 58108.

Toll-free travel information. 1-800-437-2077.

Ohio

Buckeye State

People. Population (1986): 10,752,000; **rank:** 7. **Pop. density:** 262.2 per sq. mi. **Urban** (1980): 73.3%. **Racial distrib.** (1980): 88.8% White; 9.9% Black; Hispanic (1980): 119,880. **Net change** (1980-86): −45,000; −0.4%.

Geography. Total area: 41,222 sq. mi.; **rank:** 35. **Land area:** 40,975 sq. mi. **Acres forested land:** 6,146,600. **Location:** East North Central state bounded on the N by Michigan and Lake Erie; on the E and S by Pennsylvania, West Virginia; and Kentucky; on the W by Indiana. **Climate:** temperate but variable; weather subject to much precipitation. **Topography:** generally rolling plain; Allegheny plateau in E; Lake [Erie] plains extend southward; central plains in the W. **Capital:** Columbus.

Economy. Principal industries: manufacturing, trade, services. **Principal manufactured goods:** transportation equipment, machinery, primary and fabricated metal products. **Agriculture: Chief crops:** corn, hay, winter wheat, oats, soybeans. **Livestock** (1985): 1.8 mln. cattle; 2.0 mln. hogs/pigs; 275,000 sheep; 22.0 mln. poultry. **Timber/lumber** (1984): oak, ash, maple, walnut, beech; 306 mln. bd. ft. **Minerals** (1986): $586 mln.; mostly crushed stone, sand & gravel, lime, clays, cement. **Commercial fishing** (1986): $734,000. **Chief ports:** Toledo, Conneaut, Cleveland, Ashtabula. **International airports at:** Cleveland, Cincinnati, Columbus, Dayton. **Value of construction** (1986): $8.4 bln. **Employment distribution** (1985): 25.6% manuf.; 24.2% trade; 21.8% serv.; 15.2% gvt. **Per capita income** (1986): $13,743. **Unemployment** (1986): 8.1%. **Tourism** (1982): travelers spent nearly $5.4 bln.

Finance. Commercial bank deposits, per capita (1985): $5,886.

Federal government. No. federal civilian employees (Mar. 1986): 54,600. **Avg. salary:** $27,312. **Notable federal facilities:** Wright Patterson AF base; Defense Construction Supply Center; Lewis Research Ctr.; Portsmouth Gaseous Diffusion Plant; Mound Laboratory.

Energy. Electricity production (1986, mwh, by source): Hydroelectric: 172,000; Mineral: 111.0 mln.

Education. Expenditure per pupil, public schools (1984-85): $3,257. **Avg. salary, public school teachers** (1987 est.): $26,317.

State data. Motto: With God, all things are possible. **Flower:** Scarlet carnation. **Bird:** Cardinal. **Tree:** Buckeye. **Song:** Beautiful Ohio. **Entered union** Mar. 1, 1803; rank, 17th. **State fair** at: Columbus; mid-Aug.

History. LaSalle visited the Ohio area, 1669. American fur-traders arrived, beginning 1685; the French and Indians sought to drive them out. During the Revolution, Virginians defeated the Indians, 1774, but hostilities were renewed, 1777. The region became U.S. territory after the Revolution. First organized settlement was at Marietta, 1788. Indian warfare ended with Anthony Wayne's victory at Fallen Timbers, 1794. In the War of 1812, Oliver H. Perry's victory on Lake Erie and William H. Harrison's invasion of Canada, 1813, ended British incursions.

Tourist attractions. Mound City Group National Monuments, a group of 24 prehistoric Indian burial mounds; Neil Armstrong Air and Space Museum, Wapakoneta; Air Force Museum, Dayton; Pro Football Hall of Fame, Canton; King's Island amusement park, King's Island; Cedar Point amusement park, Sandusky. birthplaces, homes, and memorials to Ohio's 8 U.S. presidents: Wm. Henry Harrison, Grant, Garfield, Hayes, McKinley, Harding, Taft, Benjamin Harrison; Lake Erie Islands, Sandusky; Amish Region, Tuscarawas/Holmes counties; German Village, Columbus; Sea World, Aurora; Jack Nicklaus Sports Center, Mason; Bob Evans Farm, Rio Grande.

Famous Ohioans include Sherwood Anderson, Neil Armstrong, George Bellows, Ambrose Bierce, Clarence Darrow, Paul Laurence Dunbar, Thomas Edison, Clark Gable, John Glenn, Bob Hope, Jack Nicklaus, Jesse Owens, Eddie Rickenbacker, John D. Rockefeller Sr. and Jr., Pete Rose, Gen. Wm. Sherman, Harriet Beecher Stowe, Charles Taft, Robert A. Taft, William H. Taft, James Thurber, Orville Wright.

Chamber of Commerce. 35 E. Gay St., Columbus, OH 43215.

Toll-free travel information. 1-800-BUCKEYE.

Oklahoma

Sooner State

People. Population (1986): 3,305,000; **rank:** 25. **Pop. density:** 48.0 per sq. mi. **Urban** (1980): 67.3%. **Racial distrib.** (1980): 85.8% White; 6.76% Black; 5.6% Amer. Ind. **Net change** (1980-86): +280,000; 9.2%.

Geography. Total area: 69,919 sq. mi.; **rank:** 18. **Land area:** 68,782 sq. mi. **Acres forested land:** 8,513,300. **Location:** West South Central state bounded on the N by Colorado and Kansas; on the E by Missouri and Arkansas; on the S and W by Texas and New Mexico. **Climate:** temperate; southern humid belt merging with colder northern continental; humid eastern and dry western zones. **Topography:** high plains predominate the W, hills and small mountains in the E; the east central region is dominated by the Arkansas R. Basin, and the Red R. Plains, in the S. **Capital:** Oklahoma City.

Economy. Principal industries: manufacturing, mineral and energy exploration and production, agriculture, printing & publishing. **Principal manufactured goods:** non-electrical machinery, oil field machinery and equipment, fabricated metal products. **Agriculture: Chief crops:** wheat, cotton, sorghum grain, peanuts, hay, soybeans, corn, barley, oats, rye, pecans. **Livestock** (1985): 5.2 mln. cattle; 200,000 hogs/pigs; 105,000 sheep; 4.6 mln. poultry. **Timber/lumber** (1984): pine, oaks, hickory; 234 mln. bd. ft. **Minerals** (1986): $258 mln.; mostly crushed stone, cement, sand & gravel, gypsum. **Chief ports:** Catoosa, Muskogee. **International airports at:** Oklahoma City, Tulsa. **Value of construction** (1986): $2.1 bln. **Employment distribution** (1984): 24.4% trade; 21.1% gvt.; 19.4% serv.; 14.4% manuf. **Per capita income** (1986): $12,368. **Unemployment** (1986): 8.2%. **Tourism** (1985): tourists spent $3.0 bln.

Finance. Commercial bank deposits, per capita (1985): $8,265.

Federal government. No. federal civilian employees (Mar. 1986): 39,980. **Avg. salary:** $24,129. **Notable federal facilities:** Federal Aviation Agency and Tinker AFB, both Oklahoma City; Ft. Sill, Lawton; Altus AFB, Altus; Vance AFB, Enid.

Energy. Electricity production (1986, mwh, by source): Hydroelectric: 2.8 mln.; Mineral: 38.1 mln.

Education. Expenditure per pupil, public schools (1984-85): $2,850. **Avg. salary, public school teachers** (1987 est.): $22,060.

State data. Motto: Labor Omnia Vincit (Labor conquers all things). **Flower:** Mistletoe. **Bird:** Scissortailed flycatcher. **Tree:** Redbud. **Song:** Oklahoma! **Entered union** Nov. 16, 1907; rank, 46th. **State fair** at: Oklahoma City; last week of Sept.

History. Part of the Louisiana Purchase, 1803, Oklahoma was known as Indian Territory (but was not given territorial government) after it became the home of the "Five Civilized Tribes"—Cherokee, Choctaw, Chickasaw, Creek, and Seminole—1828-1846. The land was also used by Comanche, Osage, and other Plains Indians. As white settlers pressed west, land was opened for homesteading by runs and lottery, the first run taking place Apr. 22, 1889. The most famous run was to the Cherokee Outlet, 1893.

Tourist attractions. Will Rogers Memorial, Claremore; National Cowboy Hall of Fame, Oklahoma City; restored Ft. Gibson Stockade, near Muskogee, the Army's largest outpost in Indian lands; Indian pow-wows; rodeos; fishing; hunting; Ouachita National Forest; Enterprise Square, museum devoted to American economic system.

Famous Oklahomans include Carl Albert, L. Gordon Cooper, Woody Guthrie, Gen. Patrick J. Hurley, Karl Jansky, Mickey Mantle, Carry Nation, Wiley Post, Oral Roberts, Will Rogers, Maria Tallchief, Jim Thorpe.

Chamber of Commerce. 4020 N. Lincoln Blvd., Oklahoma City, OK 73105.

Toll-free travel information. 1-800-652-6552.

Oregon

Beaver State

People. Population (1986): 2,698,000; **rank:** 30. **Pop. density:** 27.9 per sq. mi. **Urban** (1980): 67.9%. **Racial distrib.** (1980): 94.5% White; 1.4% Black; Hispanic (1980): 65,883. **Net change** (1980-86): +65,000; 2.5%.

Geography. Total area: 96,981 sq. mi., **rank:** 10. **Land area:** 96,184 sq. mi. **Acres forested land:** 29,810,000. **Location:** Pacific state, bounded on N by Washington; on E by Idaho; on S by Nevada and California; on W by the Pacific. **Climate:** coastal mild and humid climate; continental dryness and extreme temperatures in the interior. **Topography:** Coast Range of rugged mountains; fertile Willamette R. Valley to E and S; Cascade Mtn. Range of volcanic peaks E of the valley; plateau E of Cascades, remaining two-thirds of state. **Capital:** Salem.

Economy. Principal industries: manufacturing, agriculture, forestry, tourism, high technology. **Principal manufactured goods:** lumber & wood products, foods, machinery, fabricated metals, paper, printing & publishing, primary metals. **Agriculture: Chief crops:** hay, wheat, potatoes, pears, onions, barley, mint, strawberries, sweet corn, sweet cherries. **Livestock:** 1.6 mln. cattle; 99,000 hogs/pigs; 415,000 sheep; 20.6 mln. poultry. **Timber/lumber** (1984): Douglas fir, hemlock, ponderosa pine; 7.1 bln. bd. ft. **Minerals** (1986): $131 mln.; mostly crushed stone, sand & gravel. **Commercial fishing** (1986): $62.4 mln. **Chief ports:** Portland, Astoria, Newport, Coos Bay. **International airports at:** Portland. **Value of construction** (1986): $1.5 bln. **Employment distribution** (1985): 25.2% trade; 20.8% serv.; 19.4% manuf.; 19.2% gvt. **Per capita income** (1986): $13,217. **Unemployment** (1986): 8.5%. **Tourism** (1985): travel expenditures, $2.6 bln.

Finance: Commercial bank deposits, per capita (1985): $4,876.

Federal government. No. federal civilian employees (Mar. 1986): 17,978. **Avg. salary:** $26,931. **Notable federal facilities:** Bonneville Power Administration.

Energy: Electricity production (1986, mwh, by source): Hydroelectric: 40.9 mln.; Mineral: 592,000; Nuclear: 7.1 mln.

Education. Expenditure per pupil, public schools (1984-85): $3,889. **Avg. salary, public school teachers** (1987 est.): $26,800.

State data. Motto: The union. **Flower:** Oregon grape. **Bird:** Western meadowlark. **Tree:** Douglas fir. **Song:** Oregon, My Oregon. **Entered union** Feb. 14, 1859; rank, 33d. **State fair** at: Salem; late Aug. to early Sept.

History. American Capt. Robert Gray discovered and sailed into the Columbia River, 1792; Lewis and Clark, traveling overland, wintered at its mouth 1805-06; fur traders followed. Settlers arrived in the Willamette Valley, 1834. In 1843 the first large wave of settlers arrived via the Oregon Trail. Early in the 20th century, the "Oregon System," reforms which included the initiative, referendum, recall, direct primary, and woman suffrage, was adopted.

Tourist attractions. John Day Fossil Beds National Monument; Columbia River Gorge; Mt. Hood & Timberline Lodge; Crater Lake National Park; Oregon Dunes National Recreation Area; Ft. Clatsop National Memorial; Oregon Caves National Monument; Shakespearean Festival, Ashland; High Desert Museum, Bend. Also, skiing, fishing; Annual Albany Timber Carnival, Pendelton Round-Up, Portland Rose Festival.

Famous Oregonians include Ernest Bloch, Ernest Haycox, Chief Joseph, Edwin Markham, Tom McCall, Dr. John McLoughlin, Joaquin Miller, Linus Pauling, John Reed, Alberto Salazar, Mary Decker Slaney, William Simon U'Ren.

Tourist information: Economic Development Department, 595 Cottage St. NE, Salem, OR 97310.

Toll-free travel information. 1-800-233-3306; 1-800-547-7842 out of state.

Pennsylvania

Keystone State

People. Population (1986): 11,889,000; **rank:** 4. **Pop. density:** 264.7 per sq. mi. **Urban** (1980): 69.3%. **Racial distrib.** (1980): 89.7% White; 8.8% Black; Hispanic (1980): 154,004. **Net change** (1980-86): +24,000; 0.2%.

Geography. Total area: 45,333 sq. mi.; **rank:** 33. **Land area:** 44,966 sq. mi. **Acres forested land:** 16,825,900. **Location:** Middle Atlantic state, bordered on the E by the Delaware R., on the S by the Mason-Dixon Line; on the W by West Virginia and Ohio; on the N/NE by Lake Erie and New York. **Climate:** continental with wide fluctuations in seasonal temperatures. **Topography:** Allegheny Mtns. run SW to NE, with Piedmont and Coast Plain in the SE triangle; Allegheny Front a diagonal spine across the state's center; N and W rugged plateau falls to Lake Erie Lowland. **Capital:** Harrisburg.

Economy. Principal industries: steel, travel, health, apparel, machinery, food & agriculture. **Principal manufactured goods:** primary metals, foods, fabricated metal products, non-electrical machinery, electrical machinery. **Agriculture: Chief crops:** corn, hay, mushrooms, apples, potatoes, winter wheat, oats, vegetables, tobacco, grapes. **Livestock** (1985): 1.96 mln. cattle; 800,000 hogs/pigs; 88,000 sheep; 22.5 mln. poultry. **Timber/lumber** (1984): pine, oak, maple; 481 mln. bd. ft. **Minerals** (1986): $833 mln.; mostly cement, crushed stone, lime, sand & gravel. **Commercial fishing** (1986): $158,000. **Chief ports:** Philadelphia, Pittsburgh, Erie. **International airports at:** Philadelphia, Pittsburgh, Erie, Harrisburg. **Value of construction** (1986): $8.5 bln. **Employment distribution** (1986): 24.4% serv.; 23.9% trade; 23.3% manuf.; 14.9% gvt. **Per capita income** (1986): $13,944. **Unemployment** (1986): 6.8%. **Tourism** (1985): out-of-state visitors spent $8.9 bln.

Finance. Commercial bank deposits, per capita (1985): $7,826.

Federal government. No. federal civilian employees (Mar. 1986): 87,223. **Avg. salary:** $24,078. **Notable federal facilities:** Army War College, Carlisle; Ships Control Ctr., Mechanicsburg; New Cumberland Army Depot; Philadelphia Navy Yard, Philadelphia.

Energy. Electricity production (1986, mwh, by source): Hydroelectric: 1.5 mln. Mineral: 106.3 mln. Nuclear: 39.9 mln.

Education. Expenditure per pupil, public schools (1984-85): $4,237. **Avg. salary, public school teachers** (1987 est.): $27,429.

State data. Motto: Virtue, liberty and independence. **Flower:** Mountain laurel. **Bird:** Ruffed grouse. **Tree:** Hemlock. **Second** of the original 13 states to ratify the Constitution, Dec. 12, 1787. **State fair** at: Harrisburg; 2d week in Jan.

History. First settlers were Swedish, 1643, on Tinicum Is. In 1655 the Dutch seized the settlement but lost it to the British, 1664. The region was given by Charles II to William Penn, 1681, Philadelphia (brotherly love) was the capital of the colonies during most of the Revolution, and of the U.S., 1790-1800. Philadelphia was taken by the British, 1777; Washington's troops encamped at Valley Forge in the bitter winter of 1777-78. The Declaration of Independence, 1776, and the Constitution, 1787, were signed in Philadelphia.

Tourist attractions. Independence Hall & Natl. Historic Park, Franklin Institute Science Museum, Philadelphia Museum of Art, all in Philadelphia; Valley Forge Natl. Historic Park, Gettysburg Natl. Military Park; Pennsylvania Dutch Country; Hershey; Dusquesne Incline, Carnegie Institute, Heinz Hall, all in Pittsburgh; year 'round outdoor sports in Pocono Mtns., Pine Creek River Gorge, Alleghenies, Laurel Highlands & Presque Isle State Park.

Famous Pennsylvanians include Marian Anderson, Maxwell Anderson, James Buchanan, Andrew Carnegie, Stephen Foster, Benjamin Franklin, George C. Marshall, Andrew W. Mellon, Robert E. Peary, Mary Roberts Rinehart, Betsy Ross.

Chamber of Commerce. 222 N. 3d St., Harrisburg, PA 17101.

Toll-free travel information. 1-800-VISITPA.

Rhode Island

Little Rhody, Ocean State

People. Population (1986): 975,000; **rank:** 42. **Pop. density:** 922.8 per sq. mi. **Urban** (1980): 87.0% **Racial distrib.** (1980): 94.6% White; 2.9% Black; Hispanic (1980): 19,707. **Net change** (1980-86): +28,000; 2.9%.

Geography. Total area: 1,214 sq. mi.; **rank:** 50. **Land area:** 1,049 sq. mi. **Acres forested land:** 404,200. **Location:** New England state. **Climate:** invigorating and changeable. **Topography:** eastern lowlands of Narragansett Basin; western uplands of flat and rolling hills. **Capital:** Providence.

Economy. Principal industries: manufacturing, services. **Principal manufactured goods:** costume jewelry, machinery, textiles, electronics, silverware. **Agriculture: Chief crops:** potatoes, apples, corn. **Livestock:** 10,000 cattle; 8,700 hogs/pigs; 2,100 sheep; 260,000 poultry. **Timber/lumber:** oak, chestnut. **Minerals** (1986): $13 mln.; sand & gravel, crushed stone. **Commercial fishing** (1986): $75.1 mln. **Chief ports:** Providence, Newport, Tiverton. **Value of construction** (1986): $801.8 mln. **Employment distribution** (1986): 27.0% manuf.; 24.7% serv.; 22.4% trade. **Per capita income** (1986): $14,670. **Unemployment** (1986): 4.0%. **Tourism** (1983): out-of-state visitors spent $650 mln.

Finance. Commercial bank deposits, per capita (1985): $6,715.

Federal government. No. federal civilian employees (Mar. 1986): 6,052. **Avg. salary:** $26,249. **Notable federal facilities:** Naval War College; Naval Underwater Systems Center.

Energy. Electricity production (1986, mwh, by source): Mineral: 547,000.

Education. Expenditure per pupil, public schools (1984-85): $4,285. **Avg. salary, public school teachers** (1987 est.): $31,079.

State data. Motto: Hope. **Flower:** Violet. **Bird:** Rhode Island red. **Tree:** Red maple. **Song:** Rhode Island. **Thirteenth** of original 13 states to ratify the Constitution, May 29, 1790. **State fair** at: E. Greenwich; mid-Aug.

History. Rhode Island is distinguished for its battle for freedom of conscience and action, begun by Roger Williams, founder of Providence, who was exiled from Massachusetts Bay Colony in 1636, and Anne Hutchinson, exiled in 1638. Rhode Island gave protection to Quakers in 1657 and to Jews from Holland in 1658.

The colonists broke the power of the Narragansett Indians in the Great Swamp Fight, 1675, the decisive battle in King Philip's War. British trade restrictions angered the colonists and they burned the British revenue cutter Gaspee, 1772. The colony declared its independence May 4, 1776. Gen. John Sullivan and Lafayette won a partial victory, 1778, but failed to oust the British.

Tourist attractions. Newport mansions; summer resorts and water sports; various yachting races inc. Newport to Bermuda. Touro Synagogue, Newport, 1763; first Baptist Church in America, Providence, 1638; Gilbert Stuart birthplace, Saunderstown; Narragansett Indian Fall Festival.

Famous Rhode Islanders include Ambrose Burnside, George M. Cohan, Nelson Eddy, Jabez Gorham, Nathanael Greene, Christopher and Oliver La Farge, Matthew C. and Oliver Perry, Gilbert Stuart.

Chamber of Commerce. 91 Park St., Providence, RI 02908.

Toll-free travel information. 1-800-556-2484.

South Carolina

Palmetto State

People. Population (1986): 3,378,000. **rank:** 24. **Pop. density:** 110.8 per sq. mi. **Urban** (1980): 54.1%. **Racial distrib.** (1980): 68.8% White; 30.4% Black; Hispanic (1980): 33,414. **Net change** (1980-86): +255,000; 8.2%.

Geography. Total area: 31,055 sq. mi.; **rank:** 40. **Land area:** 30,203.37 sq. mi. **Acres forested land:** 12,249,400. **Location:** south Atlantic coast state, bordering North Carolina on the N; Georgia on the SW and W; the Atlantic O. on the E, SE and S. **Climate:** humid sub-tropical. **Topography:** Blue Ridge province in NW has highest peaks; piedmont lies between the mountains and the fall line; coastal plain covers two-thirds of the state. **Capital:** Columbia.

Economy: Principal industries: tourism, textiles, apparel, chemical, agriculture, manufacturing. **Principal manufactured goods:** textiles, chemicals and allied products, machinery & fabricated metal products, apparel and related products. **Agriculture: Chief crops:** tobacco, soybeans, corn, cotton, peaches, hay. **Livestock** (1985): 635,000 cattle; 440,000 hogs/pigs; 7.6 mln. poultry. **Timber/lumber** (1984): pine, oak; 1.2 bln. **Minerals** (1986): $296.5 mln.; mostly cement, crushed stone, clay, sand & gravel. **Commercial fishing** (1984): $25.1 mln. **Chief ports:** Charleston, Georgetown, Port Royal. **International airports at:** Charleston. **Value of construction** (1986): $3.2 bln. **Employment distribution** (1985): 28.1% manuf.; 18.9% gvt.; 16.2% serv. **Per capita income** (1986): $11,096. **Unemployment** (1986): 6.2%. **Tourism** (1982): out-of-state visitors spent $3 bln.

Finance. Commercial bank deposits, per capita (1985): $3,461.

Federal government: No. federal civilian employees (Mar. 1986): 25,640. **Avg. Salary:** $24,292. **Notable federal facilities:** Polaris Submarine Base; Barnwell Nuclear Power Plant; Ft. Jackson.

Energy. Electricity production (1986, mwh, by source): Hydroelectric: 1.9 mln.; Mineral: 19.8 mln.; Nuclear: 35.7 mln.

Education. Expenditure per pupil, public schools (1984-85): $2,591. **Avg. salary, public school teachers** (1987 est.): $23,039.

State data. Motto: Dum Spiro Spero (While I breathe, I hope). **Flower:** Carolina jessamine. **Bird:** Carolina wren. **Tree:** Palmetto. **Song:** Carolina. **Eighth** of the original 13 states to ratify the Constitution, May 23, 1788. **State fair** at: Columbia; mid-Oct.

History. The first English colonists settled, 1670, on the Ashley River, moved to the site of Charleston, 1680. The colonists seized the government, 1775, and the royal governor fled. The British took Charleston, 1780, but were defeated at Kings Mountain that year, and at Cowpens and Eutaw Springs, 1781. In the 1830s, South Carolinians, angered by federal protective tariffs, adopted the Nullification Doctrine, holding a state can void an act of Congress. The state was the first to secede and, in 1861, Confederate troops fired on and forced the surrender of U. S. troops at Ft. Sumter, in Charleston Harbor, launching the Civil War.

Tourist attractions. Restored historic Charleston harbor area and Charleston gardens: Middleton Place, Magnolia, Cypress; other gardens at Brookgreen, Edisto, Glencairn; state parks; coastal islands; shore resorts such as Myrtle Beach and Hilton Head Island; fishing and quail hunting; Ft. Sumter National Monument, in Charleston Harbor; Charleston Museum, est. 1773, is the oldest museum in the U.S.

Famous South Carolinians include James F. Byrnes, John C. Calhoun, DuBose Heyward, Ernest F. Hollings, Andrew Jackson, James Longstreet, Francis Marion, Ronald McNair, Charles Pinckney, John Rutledge, Thomas Sumter, Strom Thurmond.

Chamber of Commerce. 1301 Gervais St., Suite 520, Bankers Trust Tower, Columbia, SC 29201.

South Dakota

Coyote State, Sunshine State

People. Population (1986): 708,000; **rank:** 45. **Pop. density:** 9.3 per sq. mi. **Urban** (1980): 46.4%. **Racial distrib.** (1980): 92.6% White; 0.31% Black; 7.1% Other (includes American Indians); Hispanic (1980): 4,028. **Net change** (1980-86): +17,000; 2.5%.

Geography. Total area: 77,047 sq. mi.; **rank:** 16. **Land area:** 75,955 sq. mi. **Acres forested land:** 1,702,000. **Location:** West North Central state bounded on the N by North Dakota; on the E by Minnesota and Iowa; on the S by Nebraska; on the W by Wyoming and Montana. **Climate:** characterized by extremes of temperature, persistent winds, low precipitation and humidity. **Topography:** Prairie Plains in the E; rolling hills of the Great Plains in the W; the Black Hills, rising 3,500 ft. in the SW corner. **Capital:** Pierre.

Economy. Principal industries: agriculture, tourism, manufacturing. **Principal manufactured goods:** apparel, machinery, fabricated metals and stone, clay and glass products. **Agriculture: Chief crops:** wheat, corn, oats, hay, rye, barley, soybeans, flaxseed, sunflowers. **Livestock** (1987): 3.6 mln. cattle; 1.5 mln. hogs/ pigs; 605,000 sheep. **Timber/lumber** (1984): ponderosa pine; 132 mln. bd. ft. **Minerals** (1986): $235.8 mln.; mostly gold, cement. **Value of construction** (1986): $432.8 mln. **Employment distribution** (1985): 15.7% serv.; 13% agric.; 10% manuf. **Per capita income** (1986): $11,850. **Unemployment** (1986): 4.7%. **Tourism** (1986): travellers spent $520 mln.

Finance. Commercial bank deposits, per capita (1985): $11,468.

Federal government. No. federal civilian employees (Mar. 1986): 6,421. **Avg. salary:** $23,879. **Notable federal facilities:** Bureau of Indian Affairs, Ellsworth AFB, Corp of Engineers, Nat'l Park Service.

Energy. Electricity production (1986, mwh, by source): Hydroelectric: 5.7 mln.; Mineral: 2.1 mln.

Education: Expenditures per pupil, public schools (1984-85): $2,892. **Avg. salary, public school teachers** (1987 est.): $18,781.

State data. Motto: Under God, the people rule. **Flower:** Pasque flower. **Bird:** Ringnecked pheasant. **Tree:** Black Hills spruce. **Song:** Hail, South Dakota. **Entered union** Nov. 2, 1889; rank, 40th. **State fair** at: Huron; late Aug.-early Sept.

History. Les Verendryes explored the region, 1742-43. Lewis and Clark passed through the area, 1804 and 1806. First white American settlement was at Fort Pierre, 1817. Gold was discovered, 1874, on the Sioux Reservation; miners rushed in. The U.S. first tried to stop them, then relaxed its opposition. Custer's defeat by the Sioux followed; the Sioux relinquished the land, 1877 and the "great Dakota Boom" began, 1879. A new Indian uprising came in 1890, climaxed by the massacre of Indian families at Wounded Knee.

Tourist attractions. Black Hills; Mt. Rushmore, Needles Highway; Harney Peak, at 7,247 ft. the tallest peak between the Rockies and the Alps; Deadwood, an 1876 Gold Rush town; Custer State Park's buffalo and burro herds; Jewel Cave, the 4th largest cave in the world; Badlands Natl. Park's "moonscape"; "Great Lakes of So. Dakota"; Ft. Sisseton, restored 1864 army frontier post; Great Plains 200 & Museum; Corn Palace in Mitchell.

Famous South Dakotans include Catherine Bach, Tom Brokaw, "Calamity Jane," Crazy Horse, Myron Floren, Alvin H. Hansen, Cheryl Ladd, Dr. Ernest O. Lawrence, George McGovern, Billy Mills, Sacagawea, Sitting Bull, Laura Ingalls Wilder.

Tourist information. Industry & Commerce of So. Dakota, P.O. Box 190, Pierre, SD 57501.

Toll-free travel information. 1-800-843-8000.

Tennessee

Volunteer State

People. Population (1986): 4,803,000; **rank:** 16. **Pop. density:** 115.2 per sq. mi. **Urban** (1980): 60.4%. **Racial distrib.** (1980): 83.5% White; 15.8% Black; Hispanic (1980): 34,081. **Major ethnic groups:** German, English, Italian. **Net change** (1980-86): +212,000; 4.6%.

Geography. Total area: 42,244 sq. mi.; **rank:** 34. **Land area:** 41,328 sq. mi. **Acres forested land:** 13,160,500. **Location:** East South Central state bounded on the N by Kentucky and Virginia; on the E by North Carolina; on the S by Georgia, Alabama, and Mississippi; on the W by Arkansas and Missouri. **Climate:** humid continental to the N; humid sub-tropical to the S. **Topography:** rugged country in the E; the Great Smoky Mtns. of the Unakas; low ridges of the Appalachian Valley; the flat Cumberland Plateau; slightly rolling terrain and knobs of the Interior Low Plateau, the largest region; Eastern Gulf Coastal Plain to the W, is laced with meandering streams; Mississippi Alluvial Plain, a narrow strip of swamp and flood plain in the extreme W. **Capital:** Nashville.

Economy. Principal industries: trade, services, construction; transp., commun., public utilities; finance, ins., real estate. **Principal manufactured goods:** chemicals & allied prods.; food & kindred prods.; nonelectrical machinery; electric/electronic equip.; apparel; fabr. metal prods.; transp. equip.; rubber/misc. plastic prods.; paper & allied prods. **Agriculture: Chief crops:** soybeans, tobacco, wheat, cotton, corn. **Livestock** (1986): 2.5 mln. cattle; 950,000 hogs/pigs; 10,000 sheep; 3.3 mln. poultry. **Timber/lumber** (1984): red oak, white oak, yellow poplar, hickory; 400 mln. bd. ft. **Minerals** (1986): $480.1 mln.; mostly crushed stone, zinc. **Chief ports:** Memphis, Nashville, Chattanooga, Knoxville. **International airports at:** Memphis. **Value of construction** (1986): $4.5 bln. **Employment distribution** (1986): 25.5% manuf.; 23.3% trade; 19.9% serv.; 16.3% gvt. **Per capita income** (1986): $11,831. **Unemployment** (1986): 8.0%. **Tourism** (1984): out-of-state visitors spent $2.2 bln.

Finance. Commercial bank deposits, per capita (1985): $6,160.

Federal government. No. federal civilian employees (Mar. 1986): 43,823. **Avg. salary:** $26,157. **Notable federal facilities:** Tennessee Valley Authority; Oak Ridge Nat'l. Laboratories.

Energy: Electricity production (1986, mwh, by source): Hydroelectric: 5.4 mln.; Mineral: 51.2 mln.

Education. Expenditures per pupil, public schools (1984-85): $2,363. **Avg. salary, public school teachers** (1987 est.,): $22,720.

State data. Motto: Agriculture and commerce. **Flower:** Iris. **Bird:** Mockingbird. **Tree:** Tulip poplar. **Song:** The Tennessee Waltz. **Entered union** June 1, 1796; rank, 16th. **State fair** at: Nashville; mid-Sept.

History. Spanish explorers first visited the area, 1541. English traders crossed the Great Smokies from the east while France's Marquette and Jolliet sailed down the Mississippi on the west, 1673. First permanent settlement was by Virginians on the Watauga River, 1769. During the Revolution, the colonists helped win the Battle of Kings Mountain, N.C., 1780, and joined other eastern campaigns. The state seceded from the Union 1861, and saw many engagements of the Civil War, but 30,000 soldiers fought for the Union.

Tourist attractions. Natural wonders include Reelfoot Lake, the reservoir basin of the Mississippi R. formed by the 1811 earthquake; Lookout Mountain, Chattanooga; Fall Creek Falls, 256 ft. high; Great Smoky Mountains National Park.

Also, the Hermitage, 13 mi. E of Nashville, home of Andrew Jackson; the homes of presidents Polk and Andrew Johnson; the Parthenon, Nashville, a replica of the Parthenon of Athens; the Grand Old Opry, Nashville.

Famous Tennesseans include Davy Crockett, David Farragut, William C. Handy, Sam Houston, Cordell Hull, Grace Moore, Dinah Shore, Alvin York.

Tourist information. Dept. of Tourist Development, Rachel Jackson Bldg., Nashville, TN 37219.

Texas

Lone Star State

People. Population (1986): 16,682,000; **rank:** 3. **Pop. density:** 62.5 per sq. mi. **Urban** (1980): 79.6%. **Racial distrib.** (1980): 78.6% White; 12.0% Black; Hispanic (1980): 2,985,643. **Net change** (1980-86): +2,456,000; 17.3%.

Geography: Total area: 267,338 sq. mi.; **rank:** 2. **Land area:** 262,134 sq. mi.; **Acres forested land:** 23,279,300. **Location:** Southwestern state, bounded on the SE by the Gulf of Mexico; on the SW by Mexico, separated by the Rio Grande; surrounding states are Louisiana, Arkansas, Oklahoma, New Mexico. **Climate:** extremely varied; driest region is the Trans-Pecos; wettest is the NE. **Topography:** Gulf Coast Plain in the S and SE; North Central Plains slope upward with some hills; the Great Plains extend over the Panhandle, are broken by low mountains; the Trans-Pecos is the southern extension of the Rockies. **Capital:** Austin.

Economy. Principal industries: petroleum, manufacturing, construction. **Principal manufactured goods:** machinery, transportation equipment, foods, refined petroleum, apparel. **Agriculture: Chief crops:** cotton, grain sorghum, grains, vegetables, citrus and other fruits, pecans, peanuts. **Livestock** (1985): 14.1 mln. cattle; 415,000 hogs/pigs; 1.81 mln. sheep; 17.4 mln. poultry. **Timber/ lumber** (1984): pine, cypress; 837 mln. bd. ft. **Minerals** (1985): $1.9 bln.; mostly cement, stone, sand & gravel. **Commercial fishing** (1986): $246.1 mln. **Chief ports:** Houston, Galveston, Brownsville, Beaumont, Port Arthur, Corpus Christi. **Major international airports at:** Houston, Dallas/Ft. Worth, San Antonio. **Value of construction** (1986) $16.9 bln. **Employment distribution** (1986): 20.9% serv.; 19.1% trade; 17.0% gvt.; 14.6% manuf. **Per capita income** (1986): $13,523. **Unemployment** (1986): 8.9%. **Tourism** (1983): out-of-state visitors spent $13.7 bln.

Finance. Commercial bank deposits, per capita (1985): $9,529.

Federal government. No. federal civilian employees (Mar. 1986): 118,089. **Avg. salary:** $24,128. **Notable federal facilities:** Fort Hood (Killeen); Kelly AFB, and Ft. Sam Houston, both San Antonio.

Energy. Electricity production (1986, mwh, by source): Hydroelectric: 2.0 mln.; Mineral: 210.6 mln.

Education. Expenditures per pupil, public schools (1984-85): $3,043. **Avg. salary, public school teachers** (1987 est.): $25,308.

State data. Motto: Friendship. **Flower:** Bluebonnet. **Bird:** Mockingbird. **Tree:** Pecan. **Song:** Texas, Our Texas. **Entered union** Dec. 29, 1845; rank, 28th. **State fair** at: Dallas; mid-Oct.

History. Pineda sailed along the Texas coast, 1519; Cabeza de Vaca and Coronado visited the interior, 1541. Spaniards made the first settlement at Ysleta, near El Paso, 1682. Americans moved into the land early in the 19th century. Mexico, of which Texas was a part, won independence from Spain, 1821; Santa Anna became dictator, 1835. Texans rebelled; Santa Anna wiped out defenders of the Alamo, 1836. Sam Houston's Texans defeated Santa Anna at San Jacinto and independence was proclaimed the same year. In 1845, Texas was admitted to the Union.

Tourist attractions. Padre Island National Seashore; Big Bend, Guadalupe Mtns. national parks; The Alamo; Ft. Davis; Six Flags Amusement Park. Named for Pres. Lyndon B. Johnson are a state park, a natl. historic site marking his birthplace, boyhood home, and ranch, all near Johnson City, and a library in Austin.

Famous Texans include Stephen F. Austin, James Bowie, Carol Burnett, J. Frank Dobie, Dwight D. Eisenhower, Sam Houston, Howard Hughes, Lyndon B. Johnson, Mary Martin, Chester Nimitz, Katharine Ann Porter, Sam Rayburn.

Chamber of Commerce. One Capitol Square, eighth fl., Austin, TX 78701.

Utah

Beehive State

People. Population (1986): 1,665,000; **rank:** 35. **Pop. density:** 20.0 per sq. mi. **Urban** (1980): 84.4%. **Racial distrib.** (1980): 92.6% White; 4.1% Hispanic. **Net change** (1980-86): +204,000; 14.0%.

Geography. Total area: 84,916 sq. mi.; **rank:** 11. **Land area:** 82,096 sq. mi. **Acres forested land:** 15,557,400. **Location:** Middle Rocky Mountain state; its southeastern corner touches Colorado, New Mexico, and Arizona, and is the only spot in the U.S. where 4 states join. **Climate:** arid; ranging from warm desert in SW to alpine in NE. **Topography:** high Colorado plateau is cut by brilliantly-colored canyons of the SE; broad, flat, desert-like Great Basin of the W; the Great Salt Lake and Bonneville Salt Flats to the NW; Middle Rockies in the NE run E-W; valleys and plateaus of the Wasatch Front. **Capital:** Salt Lake City.

Economy. Principal industries: manufacturing, tourism, trade, services, mining, transportation, education. **Principal manufactured goods:** guided missiles and parts, electronic components, food products, fabricated metals, electrical and transportation equipment. **Agriculture: Chief crops:** wheat, hay, apples, barley, alfalfa seed, corn, potatoes, cherries, onions. **Livestock:** 850,000 cattle; 40,000 hogs/pigs; 650,000 sheep; 3.8 mln. poultry. **Timber/lumber:** aspen, spruce, pine. **Minerals** (1986): $285 mln.; construction sand & gravel, cement. **International airports at:** Salt Lake City. **Value of construction** (1986): $1.6 bln. **Employment distribution:** (1985) 24.0% trade; 22.3% govt., 21.7% serv.; 14.5% manuf. **Per capita income** (1986): $10,743. **Unemployment** (1986): 6.0%. **Tourism** (1985): travellers spent $1.9 bln.

Finance. Commercial bank deposits, per capita (1985): $5,016.

Federal government. No. federal civilian employees (Mar. 1986): 34,235. **Avg. salary:** $23,792. **Notable federal facilities:** Hill AFB; Tooele Army Depot, IRS Western Service Center.

Energy. Electricity production (1986, mwh, by source): Hydroelectric: 1.4 mln.; Mineral: 15.2 mln.

Education. Expenditures per pupil, public schools (1984-85): $2,820. **Avg. salary, public school teachers** (1987 est.): $23,374.

State data. Motto: Industry. **Flower:** Sego lily. **Bird:** Seagull. **Tree:** Blue spruce. **Song:** Utah, We Love Thee. **Entered union** Jan. 4, 1896; rank, 45th. **State fair** at: Salt Lake City; Sept.

History. Spanish Franciscans visited the area, 1776, the first white men to do so. American fur traders followed. Permanent settlement began with the arrival of the Mormons, 1847. They made the arid land bloom and created a prosperous economy, organized the State of Deseret, 1849, and asked admission to the Union. This was not achieved until 1896, after a long period of controversy over the Mormon Church's doctrine of polygamy, which it discontinued in 1890.

Tourist attractions. Temple Square, Mormon Church hdqtrs., Salt Lake City; Great Salt Lake; fishing streams, lakes and reservoirs, numerous winter sports; campgrounds. Natural wonders may be seen at Zion, Canyonlands, Bryce Canyon, Arches, and Capitol Reef national parks; Dinosaur, Rainbow Bridge, Timpanogas Cave, and Natural Bridges national monuments. Also Lake Powell and Flaming Gorge Reservoirs.

Famous Utahans include Maude Adams, Ezra Taft Benson, John Moses Browning, Mariner Eccles, Philo Farnsworth, James Fletcher, David M. Kennedy, J. Willard Marriott, Osmond Family, Merlin Olsen, Ivy Baker Priest, George Romney, Brigham Young, Loretta Young.

Tourist information. Utah Travel Council, Council Hall, Salt Lake City, UT 84114.

Vermont

Green Mountain State

People. Population (1986): 541,000; **rank:** 49. **Pop. density:** 57.7 per sq. mi. **Urban** (1980): 33.8%. **Racial distrib.** (1980): 99.0% White; 0.22% Black; Hispanic (1980): 3,304. **Net change** (1980-86): +29,000; 5.8%.

Geography. Total area: 9,609 sq. mi.; **rank:** 43. **Land area:** 9,267 sq. mi. **Acres forested land:** 4,511,700. **Location:** northern New England state. **Climate:** temperate, with considerable temperature extremes; heavy snowfall in mountains. **Topography:** Green Mtns. N-S backbone 20-36 mi. wide; avg. altitude 1,000 ft. **Capital:** Montpelier.

Economy. Principal industries: manufacturing, tourism, agriculture, mining, government. **Principal manufactured goods:** machine tools, furniture, scales, books, computer components, fishing rods. **Agriculture: Chief crops:** apples, maple syrup, silage corn, hay; also, dairy products. **Livestock** (1982): 355,000 cattle; 4,200 hogs/pigs; 12,698 sheep; 499,000 poultry. **Timber/lumber** (1984): pine, spruce, fir, hemlock; 94 mln. bd. ft. **Minerals** (1986): $53 mln.; mostly asbestos, dimension stone and talc. **International airports at:** Burlington. **Value of construction** (1986): $586.6 mln. **Employment distribution** (1986): 24% serv.; 22% trade; 21% manuf. **Per capita income** (1986): $12,846. **Unemployment** (1986): 4.7%. **Tourism** (1986): visitors spent $1.2 bln.

Finance. Commercial bank deposits, per capita (1985): $6,743.

Federal government. No. federal civilian employees (Mar. 1986): 2,258. **Avg. salary:** $24,998.

Energy. Electricity production (1986, mwh, by source): Hydroelectric: 974,000; Mineral: 32,000; Nuclear: 2.1 mln.

Education. Expenditures per pupil, public schools (1984-85): $3,651. **Avg. salary, public school teachers** (1987 est.): $21,835.

State data. Motto: Freedom and unity. **Flower:** Red clover. **Bird:** Hermit thrush. **Tree:** Sugar maple. **Song:** Hail, Vermont. **Entered union** Mar. 4, 1791; rank, 14th. **State fair** at: Rutland; early Sept.

History. Champlain explored the lake that bears his name, 1609. First American settlement was Ft. Dummer, 1724, near Brattleboro. Ethan Allen and the Green Mountain Boys captured Ft. Ticonderoga, 1775; John Stark defeated part of Burgoyne's forces near Bennington, 1777. In the War of 1812, Thomas MacDonough defeated a British fleet on Champlain off Plattsburgh, 1814.

Tourist attractions. Year-round outdoor sports, esp. hiking, camping and skiing; there are over 56 ski areas in the state. Popular are the Shelburne Museum; Rock of Ages Tourist Center, Graniteville; Vermont Marble Exhibit, Proctor; Bennington Battleground; Pres. Coolidge homestead, Plymouth; Maple Grove Maple Museum, St. Johnsbury.

Famous Vermonters include Ethan Allen, Chester A. Arthur, Calvin Coolidge, Adm. George Dewey, John Dewey, Stephen A. Douglas, Dorothy Canfield Fisher, James Fisk.

Tourist information. Vermont Travel Division, 134 State St., Montpelier, VT 05602.

Virginia

Old Dominion

People. Population (1986): 5,787,000; **rank:** 13. **Pop. density:** 143.4 per sq. mi. **Urban** (1980): 66.0% **Racial distrib.** (1980): 79.1% White; 18.9% Black; Hispanic (1980): 79,873. **Net change** (1980-86): +440,000; 8.2%.

Geography. Total area: 40,817 sq. mi.; **rank:** 36. **Land area:** 39,780 sq. mi. **Acres forested land:** 16,417,400. **Location:** South Atlantic state bounded by the Atlantic O. on the E and surrounded by North Carolina, Tennessee, Kentucky, West Virginia, and Maryland. **Climate:** mild and equable. **Topography:** mountain and valley region in the W, including the Blue Ridge Mtns.; rolling piedmont plateau; tidewater, or coastal plain, including the eastern shore. **Capital:** Richmond.

Economy. Principal industries: trade, services, government, manufacturing, tourism, agriculture. **Principal manufactured goods:** transportation equipment, textiles, electric & electronic equipment, food processing, chemicals. **Agriculture: Chief crops:** tobacco, soybeans, peanuts, corn. **Livestock** (1986): 1.84 mln. cattle; 400,000 hogs/pigs; 154,000 sheep; 4.82 mln. poultry. **Timber/lumber** (1984): pine and hardwoods; 851 mln. bd. ft. **Minerals** (1986): $382 mln.; mostly crushed stone, sand & gravel, lime. **Commercial fishing** (1986): $79.4 mln. **Chief ports:** Hampton Roads. **International airports at:** Norfolk, Dulles, Richmond, Newport News. **Value of construction** (1986): $8.6 bln. **Employment distribution** (1986): 23% trade.; 23% serv.; 20% gvt.; 17% manuf. **Per capita income** (1986): $15,374. **Unemployment** (1986): 5.0%. **Tourism** (1985): out-of-state visitors spent $3.6 bln.

Finance. Commerical bank deposits, per capita (1985): $6,901.

Federal government. No. federal civilian employees (Mar. 1986): 134,169. **Avg. salary:** $27,757. **Notable federal facilities:** Pentagon; Naval Sta., Norfolk; Naval Air Sta., Norfolk, Virginia Beach; Naval Shipyard, Portsmouth; Marine Corps Base, Quantico; Langley AFB; NASA at Langley.

Energy. Electricity production (1986, mwh, by source): Hydroelectric: 47,000; Mineral: 21.4 mln.; Nuclear: 21.2 mln.

Education. Expenditures per pupil, public schools (1984-85): $3,155. **Avg. salary, public school teachers** (1987 est.): $25,473.

State data. Motto: Sic Semper Tyrannis (Thus always to tyrants). **Flower:** Dogwood. **Bird:** Cardinal. **Tree:** Dogwood. **Song:** Carry Me Back to Old Virginia. **Tenth** of the original 13 states to ratify the Constitution, June 25, 1788. **State fair** at: Richmond; late Sept.-early Oct.

History. English settlers founded Jamestown, 1607. Virginians took over much of the government from royal Gov. Dunmore in 1775, forcing him to flee. Virginians under George Rogers Clark freed the Ohio-Indiana-Illinois area of British forces. Benedict Arnold burned Richmond and Petersburg for the British, 1781. That same year, Britain's Cornwallis was trapped at Yorktown and surrendered.

Tourist attractions. Colonial Williamsburg; Busch Gardens; Wolf Trap Farm, near Falls Church; Arlington National Cemetery; Mt. Vernon, home of George Washington; Jamestown Festival Park; Yorktown; Jefferson's Monticello, Charlottesville; Robert E. Lee's birthplace, Stratford Hall, and grave, at Lexington; Appomattox; Shenandoah National Park; Blue Ridge Parkway; Virginia Beach.

Famous Virginians include Richard E. Byrd, James B. Cabell, William Henry Harrison, Patrick Henry, Thomas Jefferson, Joseph E. Johnston, Robert E. Lee, Meriwether Lewis and William Clark, James Madison, James Monroe, John Marshall, Edgar Allan Poe, Walter Reed, Zachary Taylor, John Tyler, Booker T. Washington, George Washington, Woodrow Wilson.

Chamber of Commerce: 9th South Fifth St., Richmond, VA 23219.

Toll-free travel information. 1-800-VISITVA.

Washington

Evergreen State

People. Population (1986): 4,463,000; **rank:** 19. **Pop. density:** 66.2 per sq. mi. **Urban** (1980): 73.5%. **Racial distrib.** (1980): 91.4% White; 2.5% Black; Hispanic (1980): 119,986. **Net change** (1980-86): +330,000; 8.0%.

Geography. Total area: 68,192 sq. mi.; **rank:** 20. **Land area:** 66,570 sq. mi. **Acres forested land:** 23,181,000. **Location:** northwestern coastal state bordered by Canada on the N; Idaho on the E; Oregon on the S; and the Pacific O. on the W. **Climate:** mild, dominated by the Pacific O. and protected by the Rockies. **Topography:** Olympic Mtns. on NW peninsula; open land along coast to Columbia R.; flat terrain of Puget Sound Lowland; Cascade Mtns. region's high peaks to the E; Columbia Basin in central portion; highlands to the NE; mountains to the SE. **Capital:** Olympia.

Economy. Principal industries: aerospace, forest products, food products, petroleum refining, primary metals, agriculture. **Principal manufactured goods:** aircraft, pulp and paper, lumber and plywood, aluminum, processed fruits and vegetables. **Agriculture: Chief crops:** wheat, apples, hay, potatoes, barley, nursery/greenhouse products, hops, corn, pears. **Livestock** (1986): 1.5 mln. cattle; 51,000 hogs/pigs; 66,000 sheep; 6.13 mln. poultry. **Timber/lumber** (1984): Douglas fir, hemlock, cedar, pine; 4.0 bln. bd. ft. **Minerals** (1986): $254 mln.; mostly construction sand & gravel, cement, crushed stone. **Commercial fishing** (1986): $111.3 mln. **Chief ports:** Seattle, Tacoma, Vancouver, Kelso-Longview. **International airports at:** Seattle/Tacoma, Spokane, Boeing Field. **Value of construction** (1986): $4.9 bln. **Employment distribution** (1984): 24.6% trade; 20.1% serv.; 19.4% gvt.; 17.6% manuf. **Per capita income** (1986): $14,498. **Unemployment** (1986): 8.2%. **Tourism** (1985): $3.1 bln.

Finance. Commercial bank deposits, per capita (1985): $5,409.

Federal government. No. federal civilian employees (Mar. 1986): 48,143. **Avg. salary:** $26,588. **Notable federal facilities:** Bonneville Power Admin.; Ft. Lewis; McChord AFB; Hanford Nuclear Reservation; Bremerton Naval Shipyards.

Energy. Electricity production (1986, mwh, by source): Hydroelectric: 78.3 mln.; Mineral: 5.1 mln.; Nuclear: 8.4 mln.

Education. Expenditures per pupil, public schools (1984-85): $3,723. **Avg. salary, public school teachers** (1987 est.): $27,527.

State data. Motto. Alki (By and by). **Flower:** Western rhododendron. **Bird:** Willow goldfinch. **Tree:** Western hemlock. **Song:** Washington, My Home. **Entered union** Nov. 11, 1889; rank, 42d.

History. Spain's Bruno Hezeta sailed the coast, 1775. American Capt. Robert Gray sailed up the Columbia River, 1792. Canadian fur traders set up Spokane House, 1810; Americans under John Jacob Astor established a post at Fort Okanogan, 1811. Missionary Marcus Whitman settled near Walla Walla, 1836. Final agreement on the border of Washington and Canada was made with Britain, 1846, and gold was discovered in the state's northeast, 1855, bringing new settlers.

Tourist attractions. Mt. Rainier, Olympic and North Cascades National Parks; Mt. St. Helens; Pacific beaches; Puget Sound; wineries; Indian cultures; year-round outdoor sports; Seattle Waterfront, Seattle Center.

Famous Washingtonians include Bing Crosby, William O. Douglas, Henry M. Jackson, Mary McCarthy, Edward R. Murrow, Theodore Roethke, Marcus Whitman, Minoru Yamasaki.

Local Chambers of Commerce. P.O. Box 658, Olympia, WA 98507.

Toll-free travel information. 1-800-544-1800.

West Virginia

Mountain State

People. Population (1986): 1,919,000. **rank:** 34. **Pop. density:** 80.4 per sq. mi. **Urban** (1980): 36.2. **Racial distrib.** (1980): 96.1% White; 3.3% Black; Hispanic (1980): 12,707. **Net change** (1980-86): −31,000; −1.6%.

Geography. Total area: 24,181 sq. mi.; **rank:** 41. **Land area:** 24,070 sq. mi. **Acres forested land:** 11,668,600. **Location:** South Atlantic state bounded on the N by Ohio, Pennsylvania, Maryland; on the S and W by Virginia, Kentucky, Ohio; on the E by Maryland and Virginia. **Climate:** humid continental climate except for marine modification in the lower panhandle. **Topography:** ranging from hilly to mountainous; Allegheny Plateau in the W, covers two-thirds of the state; mountains here are the highest in the state, over 4,000 ft. **Capital:** Charleston.

Economy. Principal industries: mining, mineral and chemical production, primary metals and stone, clay, and glass prods., timber, tourism. **Principal manufactured goods:** machinery, plastic and hardwood prods., fabricated metals, basic organic and inorganic chemicals, aluminum, steel. **Agriculture: Chief crops:** apples, peaches, hay, tobacco, corn, wheat, oats, barley. **Chief products:** milk, eggs, honey. **Livestock** (1985): 520,000 cattle; 37,000 hogs/pigs; 78,000 sheep; 710,000 chickens. **Timber/ lumber** (1984): oak, yellow poplar, hickory, walnut, cherry; 285 mln. bd. ft. **Minerals** (1985): $111 mln. mostly crushed stone, sand & gravel, salt, cement, dimension stone. **Chief port:** Huntington. **Value of construction** (1986): $973.3 mln. **Employment distribution** (1986): 23% trade; 21.6% gvt.; 20.3% serv.; 15% manuf. **Per capita income** (1986): $10,530. **Unemployment** (1986): 11.8%. **Tourism** (1986): travel-related expenditures were $1.6 bln.

Finance. Commercial bank deposits, per capita (1985): $6,165.

Federal government. No. federal civilian employees (Mar. 1986): 9,558. **Avg. salary:** $24,977. **Notable federal facilities:** National Radio Astronomy Observatory, Green Bank; Bureau of Public Debt. Bldg., Parkersburg; Natl. Park, Harper's Ferry; Correctional Institution for Women, Alderson.

Energy. Electricity production (1986, mwh, by source): Hydroelectric: 361,000; Mineral: 77.2 mln.

Education. Expenditures per pupil, public schools (1984-85): $3,244. **Avg. salary, public school teachers** (1987 est.): $21,446.

State Data. Motto: Montani Semper Liberi (Mountaineers are always free) **Flower:** Big rhododendron. **Bird:** Cardinal. **Tree:** Sugar maple. **Songs:** The West Virginia Hills; This Is My West Virginia; West Virginia, My Home Sweet Home. **Entered union** June 20, 1863; rank, 35th. **State fair** at: Lewisburg (Fairlea), late Aug.

History. Early explorers included George Washington, 1753, and Daniel Boone. The area became part of Virginia and often objected to rule by the eastern part of the state. When Virginia seceded, 1861, the Wheeling Conventions repudiated the act and created a new state, Kanawha, subsequently changed to West Virginia. It was admitted to the Union as such, 1863.

Tourist attractions. Harpers Ferry National Historic Park has been restored to its condition in 1859, when John Brown seized the U.S. Armory.

Also Science and Cultural Center, Charleston; White Sulphur and Berkeley Springs mineral water spas; Monongahela Natl. Forest; state parks and forests; trout fishing; turkey, deer, and bear hunting; white water rafting; skiing; glass tours at Fentonglass in Williamstown, Viking Glass in New Martinsville, Blenk Glass in Milton; Sternwheel Regatta, Charleston; Mountain State Forest Festival.

Famous West Virginians include Newton D. Baker, Pearl Buck, John W. Davis, Thomas "Stonewall" Jackson, Don Knotts, Dwight Whitney Morrow, Michael Owens, Cyrus Vance, Col. Charles "Chuck" Yeager.

Tourist information. Dept. of Commerce, State Capitol, Charleston WV 25305.

Toll-free travel information. 1-800-CALLW.VA.

Wisconsin

Badger State

People. Population (1986): 4,785,000; **rank:** 17. **Pop. density:** 87.7 per sq. mi. **Urban** (1980): 64.2%. **Racial distrib.** (1980): 94.4% White; 3.8% Black; Hispanic (1980): 62,981. **Net change** (1980-86): +79,000; 1.7%.

Geography. Total area: 56,154 sq. mi.; **rank:** 26. **Land area:** 54,464 sq. mi. **Acres forested land:** 14,907,700. **Location:** North central state, bounded on the N by Lake Superior and Upper Michigan; on the E by Lake Michigan; on the S by Illinois; on the W by the St. Croix and Mississippi rivers. **Climate:** long, cold winters and short, warm summers tempered by the Great Lakes. **Topography:** narrow Lake Superior Lowland plain met by Northern Highland which slopes gently to the sandy crescent Central Plain; Western Upland in the SW; 3 broad parallel limestone ridges running N-S are separated by wide and shallow lowlands in the SE. **Capital:** Madison.

Economy. Principal industries: manufacturing, trade, services, government, transportation, communications, agriculture, tourism. **Principal manufactured goods:** machinery, foods, fabricated metals, transportation equipment, paper and wood products. **Agriculture: Chief crops:** corn, beans, beets, peas, hay, oats, cabbage, cranberries. **Chief products:** milk, butter, cheese. **Livestock** (1986): 4.3 mln. cattle, 1.9 mln. hogs/pigs; 75,000 sheep; 10.5 mln. poultry. **Timber/lumber** (1984): maple, birch, oak, evergreens; 372 mln. bd. ft. **Minerals** (1986): $138.6 mln.; mostly crushed stone, construction & industrial sand & gravel, lime. **Commercial fishing** (1986): $6.8 mln. **Chief ports:** Superior, Ashland, Milwaukee, Green Bay, Kewaunee, Pt. Washington, Manitowoc, Sheboygan, Marinette, Kenosha. **International airports at:** Milwaukee. **Value of construction** (1986): $3.2 bln. **Employment distribution** (1987): 25.3% manuf.; 23.4% trade; 21.7% serv.; 16.7% gvt. **Per capita income** (1986): $13,796. **Unemployment** (1986): 7.0%. **Tourism** (1982): out-of-state visitors spent $6.4 bln.

Finance. Commercial bank deposits, per capita (1985): $6,542.

Federal government. No. federal civilian employees (Mar. 1986): 12,029. **Avg. salary:** $24,515. **Notable federal facilities:** Ft. McCoy.

Energy. Electricity production (1986, mwh, by source): Hydroelectric: 2.2 mln.; Mineral: 29.3 mln.; Nuclear: 11.2 mln.

Education. Expenditures per pupil, public schools (1984-85): $3,816. **Avg. salary, public school teachers** (1987 est.): $28,206.

State data. Motto: Forward. **Flower:** Wood violet. **Bird:** Robin. **Tree:** Sugar maple. **Song:** On, Wisconsin! **Entered union** May 29, 1848; rank, 30th. **State fair** at: West Allis; mid-Aug.

History. Jean Nicolet was the first European to see the Wisconsin area, arriving in Green Bay, 1634; French missionaries and fur traders followed. The British took over, 1763. The U.S. won the land after the Revolution but the British were not ousted until after the War of 1812. Lead miners came next, then farmers. Railroads were started in 1851, serving growing wheat harvests and iron mines.

Tourist attractions. Old Wade House and Carriage Museum, Greenbush; Villa Louis, Prairie du Chien; Circus World Museum, Baraboo; Wisconsin Dells; Old World Wisconsin, Eagle; Door County peninsula; Chequamegon and Nicolet national forests; Lake Winnebago; numerous lakes for water sports, ice boating and fishing; skiing and hunting.

Famous Wisconsinites include Edna Ferber, King Camp Gillette, Harry Houdini, Robert LaFollette, Alfred Lunt, Spencer Tracy, Thorstein Veblen, Orson Welles, Thornton Wilder, Frank Lloyd Wright.

Tourist information. Wisconsin Dept. of Development, Division of Tourism, 123 W. Washington Ave., Madison, WI 53702.

Toll-free travel information. 1-800-372-2737.

Wyoming

Equality State

People. Population (1986) 507,000; **rank:** 50. **Pop. density:** 5.2 per sq. mi. **Urban** (1980): 62.7%. **Racial distrib.** (1980): 95.0% White; 0.71% Black; Hispanic (1980): 24,499. **Major ethnic groups:** German, English, Russian. **Net change** (1980-86): +38,000; 8.0%.

Geography. Total area: 97,914 sq. mi.; **rank:** 9. **Land area:** 97,203 sq. mi. **Acres forested land:** 9.8 mln. **Location:** Mountain state lying in the high western plateaus of the Great Plains. **Climate:** semi-desert conditions throughout; true desert in the Big Horn and Great Divide basins. **Topography:** the eastern Great Plains rise to the foothills of the Rocky Mtns.; the Continental Divide crosses the state from the NW to the SE. **Capital:** Cheyenne.

Economy. Principal industries: mineral extraction, tourism and recreation, agriculture. **Principal manufactured goods:** refined petroleum products, foods, wood products, stone, clay and glass products. **Agriculture: Chief crops:** wheat, beans, barley, oats, sugar beets, hay. **Livestock** (1986): 1.3 mln. cattle; 35,000 hogs/pigs; 775,000 sheep. **Timber/lumber** (1984): aspen, yellow pine; 182 mln. bd. ft. **Minerals** (1986): $614.8 mln.; mostly clays, cement, lime, sodium carbonate. **International airports at:** Casper. **Value of construction** (1986): $465.9 mln. **Employment distribution** (1984): 23% serv.; 11% mining; 20% trade. **Per capita income** (1986): $13,230. **Unemployment** (1986): 9.0%. **Tourism** (1985): out-of-state visitors spent $617 mln.

Finance. Commercial bank deposits, per capita (1985): $7,951.

Federal government. No. federal civilian employees (Mar. 1986): 4,729. **Avg. salary:** $25,560. **Notable federal facilities:** Warren AFB.

Energy. Electricity production (1986, mwh, by source): Hydroelectric: 1.1 mln.; Mineral: 29.0 mln.

Education. Expenditures per pupil, public schools (1984-85): $4,799. **Avg. salary, public school teachers** (1987 est.): $27,708.

State data. Motto: Equal Rights. **Flower:** Indian paintbrush. **Bird:** Meadowlark. **Tree:** Cottonwood. **Song:** Wyoming. **Entered union** July 10, 1890; rank, 44th. **State fair** at: Douglas; late Aug.

History. Francés Francois and Louis Verendrye were the first Europeans, 1743. John Colter, American, was first to traverse Yellowstone Park, 1807-08. Trappers and fur traders followed in the 1820s. Forts Laramie and Bridger became important stops on the pioneer trail to the West Coast. Indian wars followed massacres of army detachments in 1854 and 1866. Population grew after the Union Pacific crossed the state, 1869. Women won the vote, for the first time in the U.S., from the Territorial Legislature, 1869.

Tourist attractions. Yellowstone National Park, 3,472 sq. mi. in the NW corner of Wyoming and the adjoining edges of Montana and Idaho, the oldest U.S. national park, est. 1872, has some 10,000 geysers, hot springs, mud volcanoes, fossil forests, a volcanic glass (obsidian) mountain, the 1,000-ft.-deep canyon and 308-ft.-high waterfall of the Yellowstone River, and a wide variety of animals living free in their natural habitat.

Also, Grand Teton National Park, with mountains 13,000 ft. high; National Elk Refuge, covering 25,000 acres; Devils Tower, a columnar rock of igneous origin 1,280 ft. high; Fort Laramie and surrounding areas of pioneer trails; Buffalo Bill Museum, Cody; Cheyenne Frontier Days Celebration, last full week in July, the state's largest rodeo, and world's largest purse.

Famous Wyomingites include James Bridger, Buffalo Bill Cody, Nellie Tayloe Ross.

Tourist information. Travel Commission, Etchepare Circle, Cheyenne, WY 82002.

Toll-free travel information. 1-800-CALLWYO.

District of Columbia

Area: 67 sq. mi. **Population:** (1986): 626,000. **Motto:** Justitia omnibus, Justice for all. **Flower:** American beauty rose. **Tree:** Scarlet oak. **Bird:** Wood thrush. The city of Washington is coextensive with the District of Columbia.

The District of Columbia is the seat of the federal government of the United States. It lies on the west central edge of Maryland on the Potomac River, opposite Virginia. Its area was originally 100 sq. mi. taken from the sovereignty of Maryland and Virginia. Virginia's portion south of the Potomac was given back to that state in 1846.

The 23d Amendment, ratified in 1961, granted residents the right to vote for president and vice president for the first time and gave them 3 members in the Electoral College. The first such votes were cast in Nov. 1964.

Congress, which has legislative authority over the District under the Constitution, established in 1878 a government of 3 commissioners appointed by the president. The Reorganization Plan of 1967 substituted a single commissioner (also called mayor), assistant, and 9-member City Council. Funds were still appropriated by Congress; residents had no vote in local government, except to elect school board members.

In Sept. 1970, Congress approved legislation giving the District one delegate to the House of Representatives. The delegate could vote in committee but not on the House floor. The first was elected 1971.

In May 1974 voters approved a charter giving them the right to elect their own mayor and a 13-member city council; the first took office Jan. 2, 1975. The district won the right to levy its own taxes but Congress retained power to veto council actions, and approve the city's annual budget.

Proposals for a "federal town" for the deliberations of the Continental Congress were made in 1783, 4 years before the adoption of the Constitution that gave the Confederation a national government. Rivalry between northern and southern delegates over the site appeared in the First Congress, 1789. John Adams, presiding officer of the Senate, cast the deciding vote of that body for Germantown, Pa. In 1790 Congress compromised by making Philadelphia the temporary capital for 10 years. The Virginia members of the House wanted a capital on the eastern bank of the Potomac; they were defeated by the Northerners, while the Southerners defeated the Northern attempt to have the nation assume the war debts of the 13 original states, the Assumption Bill fathered by Alexander Hamilton. Hamilton and Jefferson arranged a compromise: the Virginia men voted for the Assumption Bill, and the Northerners conceded the capital to the Potomac. President Washington chose the site in Oct. 1790 and persuaded landowners to sell their holdings to the government at £25, then about $66, an acre. The capital was named Washington.

Washington appointed Pierre Charles L'Enfant, a French engineer who had come over with Lafayette, to plan the capital on an area not over 10 mi. square. The L'Enfant plan, for streets 100 to 110 feet wide and one avenue 400 feet wide and a mile long, seemed grandiose and foolhardy. But Washington endorsed it. When L'Enfant ordered a wealthy landowner to remove his new manor house because it obstructed a vista, and demolished it when the owner refused, Washington stepped in and dismissed the architect. The official map and design of the city was completed by Benjamin Banneker, a distinguished black architect and astronomer, and Andrew Ellicott.

On Sept. 18, 1793, Pres. Washington laid the cornerstone of the north wing of the Capitol. On June 3, 1800, Pres. John Adams moved to Washington and on June 10, Philadelphia ceased to be the temporary capital. The City of Washington was incorporated in 1802; the District of Columbia was created as a municipal corporation in 1871, embracing Washington, Georgetown, and Washington County.

Outlying U.S. Areas

Commonwealth of Puerto Rico

(Estado Libre Asociado de Puerto Rico)

People. Population (1985): 3,279,231. **Pop. density:** 955 per sq. mi. **Urban** (1980): 66.8%. **Racial distribution** (1980): 99.9% Hispanic. **Net migration** (1985): −27,691.

Geography. Total area: 3,435 sq. mi. **Land area:** 3,421 sq. mi. **Location:** island lying between the Atlantic to the N and the Caribbean to the S; it is easternmost of the West Indies group called the Greater Antilles, of which Cuba, Hispaniola, and Jamaica are the larger units. **Climate:** mild, with a mean temperature of 77°. **Topography:** mountainous throughout three-fourths of its rectangular area, surrounded by a broken coastal plain; highest peak is Cerro de Punta, 4,389 ft. **Capital:** San Juan.

Economy. Principal industries: manufacturing. **Principal manufactured goods:** pharmaceuticals; chemicals, machinery and metals, electric machinery and equipment, petroleum refining, food products, apparel. **Agriculture: Chief crops:** coffee; plantains; bananas; yams; taniers; pineapples; pidgeon peas; peppers; pumpkins; coriander; lettuce; tobacco. **Livestock** (1985): 579,810 cattle; 210,013 pigs; 7.4 mln. poultry. **Minerals** (1985): crushed stone, sand and gravel, lime; $122.2 mln., mostly marble. **Commercial fishing** (1984): $7.9 mln. **Chief ports/river shipping:** San Juan, Ponce, Mayaguez, Guayanillá, Guánica, Yabucoa, Aguirre. **Major airports at:** San Juan, Ponce, Mayaguez, Aguadilla. **Value of construction** (1983): $1.4 bln. **Employment distribution:** 24% gvt.; 18% manuf.; 19% trade; 20% serv. **Per capita income** (1985): $4,301. **Unemployment** (1985): 21%. **Tourism** (1985): Out-of-area visitors spent $710 mln.

Finance. No. banks (1985): 24; No. savings and loan assns. (1985): 13; Other: 4 retirement fund systems; over 100 credit unions; 268 credit and saving co-operatives.

Federal government. No. federal civilian employees (1985): 9,989. **Notable federal facilities:** U.S. Naval Station at Roosevelt Roads; U.S. Army Salinas Training Area and Ft. Allen; Sabana SECA Communications Center (U.S. Navy); Ft. Buchanan.

Energy Production (1985): Steam and gas: 11,938 mln. kwh; Other: 209 mln. kwh.

Education. No. schools (1985): 1,782 public, 818 private elem. and second.; 69 higher ed. **Avg. salary, public school teachers** (1985): $8,163.

Misc. Data. Motto. Joannes Est Nomen Eius (John is his name). **Flower:** Maga. **Bird:** Reinita. **Tree:** Ceiba. **Song:** La Borinqueña.

History: Puerto Rico (or Borinquen, after the original Arawak Indian name Boriquen), was discovered by Columbus, Nov. 19, 1493. Ponce de Leon conquered it for Spain, 1509, and established the first settlement at Caparra, across the bay from San Juan.

Sugar cane was introduced, 1515, and slaves were imported 3 years later. Gold mining petered out, 1570. Spaniards fought off a series of British and Dutch attacks; slavery was abolished, 1873. Under the treaty of Paris, Puerto Rico was ceded to the U.S. after the Spanish-American War, 1898.

General tourist attractions: Ponce Museum of Art; forts El Morro and San Cristobal; Old Walled City of San Juan; Arecibo Observatory; Cordillera Central and state parks; El Yunque Rain Forest; San Juan Cathedral; Porta Coeli Chapel and Museum of Religious Art, San Germán; Condado Convention Center; Casa Blanca, Ponce de León family home, Puerto Rican Family Museum of 16th and 17 centuries and the Fine Arts Center in San Juan.

Cultural facilities, festivals, etc.: Festival Casals classical music concerts, mid-June; Puerto Rico Symphony Orchestra at Music Conservatory; Botanical Garden and Museum of Anthropology, Art, and History at the University of Puerto Rico; Institute of Puerto Rican Culture, at the Dominican Convent.

The Commonwealth of Puerto Rico is a self-governing part of the U.S. with a primary Hispanic culture. Puerto Ricans are U.S. citizens and about 2.0 million now live on the mainland, although since 1974 there has also been a reverse migration flow.

The current commonwealth political status of Puerto Rico gives the island's citizens virtually the same control over their internal affairs as the fifty states of the U.S. However, they do not vote in national elections, although they do vote in national primary elections.

Puerto Rico is represented in Congress solely by a resident commissioner who has a voice but no vote, except in committees.

No federal income tax is collected from residents on income earned from local sources in Puerto Rico.

Puerto Rico's famous "Operation Bootstrap," begun in the late 1940s, succeeded in changing the island from "The Poorhouse of the Caribbean" to an area with the highest per capita income in Latin America. This pioneering program encouraged manufacturing and the development of the tourist trade by selective tax exemption, low-interest loans, and other incentives. Despite the marked success of Puerto Rico's development efforts over an extended period of time, per capita income in Puerto Rico is low in comparison to that of the U.S. In calendar year 1985, the transfer payments from the U.S. government to individuals and governments in Puerto Rico totalled $3.2 bln., or 22% of the Gross Domestic Product of $14.8 bln.

Famous Puerto Ricans include: José Celso Barbosa, Julia de Burgos, Pablo Casals, Orlando Cepeda, Roberto Clemente, José de Diego, José Feliciano, Luis A. Ferré, José Ferrer, Doña Felisa Rincón de Gautier, Commodore Diégo E. Hernández, Rafael Hernández (El Jibarito), Raúl Julia, Luis Muñoz Marín, René Marqués, Luis Palés Matos, Concha Meléndez, Rita Moreno, Adm. Horacio Rivero.

Chamber of Commerce: 100 Tetuán P.O Box. S-3789, San Juan, PR 00904; Ponce & South: El Señorial Bldg., Ponce, PR 00731.

Guam

Where America's Day Begins

People. Population (1985): 120,977. **Pop. density:** 572 per sq. mi. **Urban** (1980): 39.5%. **Major ethnic groups** (1980): Chamorro 41.0%, Filipino 21.2%. Native Guamanians, ethnically called Chamorros, are basically of Indonesian stock, with a mixture of Spanish and Filipino. In addition to the offical language, they speak the native Chamorro.

Geography. Total area: 209 sq. mi. land, 30 mi. long and 4 to 8.5 mi. wide. **Location:** largest and southernmost of the Mariana Islands in the West Pacific, 3,700 mi. W of Hawaii. **Climate:** tropical, with temperatures from 70° to 90°F; avg. annual rainfall, about 70 in. **Topography:** coral-line limestone plateau in the N; southern chain of low volcanic mountains sloping gently to the W, more steeply to coastal cliffs on the E; general elevation, 500 ft.; highest pt., Mt. Lamlam, 1,334 ft. **Capital:** Agana.

Economy. Principal industries: construction, light manufacturing, tourism, petroleum refining, banking. **Principal manufactured goods:** textiles, foods, petroleum products. **Agriculture: Chief crops:** cabbages, eggplants, cucumber, long beans, tomatoes, bananas, coconuts, watermelon, yams, canteloupe, papayas, maize, sweet potatoes. **Livestock** (1984): 2,000 cattle; 14,000 hogs/pigs. **Chief ports:** Apra Harbor. **International airports at:** Tamuning. **Value of construction** (1980): $80.60 mln. **Employment distribution** (1983): 50.5% gvt.; 17.7% trade; 13.3% serv.; **Per capita income** (1983): $6,070. **Unemployment** (1983): 9.6%. **Tourism** (1980): visitors' receipts $117.9 mln.

Finance. Notable industries: insurance, real estate, finance. **No. banks:** 13; **No. savings and loan assns.:** 2.

Federal government. No. federal employees (1980): 6,600. **Notable federal facilities:** Andersen AFB; other naval and air bases.

Education. No. public schools: 37 elementary; 19 secondary; 2 higher education. **Avg. salary, public school teachers** (1979): $12,684.

Misc. Data. Flower: Puti Tai Nobio (Bougainvillea). **Bird:** Toto (Fruit dove). **Tree:** Ifit (Intsiabijuga). **Song:** Stand Ye Guamanians.

History. Magellan arrived in the Marianas Mar. 6, 1521, and called them the Ladrones (thieves). They were colonized in 1668 by Spanish missionaries who renamed them the Mariana Islands in honor of Maria Anna, queen of Spain. When Spain ceded Guam to the U.S., it sold the other Marianas to Germany. Japan obtained a League of Nations mandate over the German islands in 1919; in Dec. 1941 it seized Guam; the island was retaken by the U.S. in July 1944.

Guam is a self-governing organized unincorporated U.S. territory. Under the jurisdiction of the Interior Department, it is administered under the Organic Act of 1950, which provides for a governor and a 21-member unicameral legislature, elected biennially by the residents who are American citizens but do not vote for president.

Beginning in Nov., 1970, Guamanians elected their own governor, previously appointed by the U.S. president. He took office in Jan. 1971. In 1972 a U.S. law gave Guam one delegate to the U.S. House of Representatives; the delegate may vote in committee but not on the House floor.

General tourist attractions. annual mid-Aug. Merizo Water Festival; Tarzan Falls; beaches; water sports, duty-free port shopping.

Virgin Islands

St. John, St. Croix, St. Thomas

People. Population (1984): 107,500. **Pop. density:** 814.47 per sq. mi. **Urban** (1980): 39%. **Racial distribution:** 15% White; 85% Black. **Major ethnic groups:** West Indian, French, Hispanic.

Geography. Total area: 133 sq. mi.; **Land area:** 132 sq. mi. **Location:** 3 larger and 50 smaller islands and cays in the S and W of the V.I. group (British V.I. colony to the N and E) which is situated 70 mi. E of Puerto Rico, located W of the Anegada Passage, a major channel connecting the Atlantic O. and the Caribbean Sea. **Climate:** subtropical; the sun tempered by gentle trade winds; humidity is low; average temperature, 78° F. **Topography:** St. Thomas is mainly a ridge of hills running E and W, and has little tillable land; St. Croix rises abruptly in the N but slopes to the S to flatlands and lagoons; St. John has steep, lofty hills and valleys with little level tillable land. **Capital:** Charlotte Amalie, St. Thomas.

Economy. Principal industries: tourism, rum, petroleum refining, watch industry, textiles, electronics. **Principal manufactured goods:** rum, textiles, pharmaceuticals, perfumes. **Gross Domestic Product** (1985): $1.036 bln. **Agriculture: Chief crops:** truck garden produce. **Minerals:** sand, gravel. **Chief ports:** Cruz Bay, St. John; Frederiksted and Christiansted, St. Croix; Charlotte Amalie, St. Thomas. **International airports on:** St. Thomas, St. Croix. **Value of construction** (1984): $93.9 mln. **Per capita income** (1984): $7,465. **Unemployment** (Dec. 1981): 7.0%. **Tourism** (1984): No. out-of-area visitors: 1.27 mln.; $377 mln. spent. **No. banks** (1985): 8.

Education (1985): **No. public schools:** 34 elem. and second.; 1 college. **Avg. starting salary, public school teachers:** $13,712.

Misc. data. Flower: Yellow elder or yellow trumpet, local designation Ginger Thomas. **Bird:** Yellow breast. **Song:** Virgin Islands March.

History. The islands were discovered by Columbus in 1493. Spanish forces, 1555, defeated the Caribes and claimed the territory; by 1596 the native population was annihilated. First permanent settlement in the U.S. territory, 1672, by the Danes; U.S. purchased the islands, 1917, for defense purposes.

The inhabitants have been citizens of the U.S. since 1927. Legislation originates in a unicameral house of 15 senators, elected for 2 years. The governor, formerly appointed by the U.S. president, was popularly elected for the first time in Nov. 1970. In 1972 a U.S. law gave the Virgin Islands one delegate to the U.S. House of Representatives; the delegate may vote in committee but not in the House.

General tourist attractions. Magens Bay, St. Thomas; duty-free shopping; Virgin Islands National Park, 14,488 acres on St. John of lush growth, beaches, Indian relics, and evidence of colonial Danes.

Tourist information. Dept. of Commerce, St. Thomas, P.O. Box 6400, St. Thomas, VI 00801; St. Croix, P.O. Box 4535, Christiansted, St. Croix 00820.

American Samoa

Capital: Pago Pago, Island of Tutuila. **Area:** 77 sq. mi. **Population:** (1985) 34,500. **Motto:** Samoa Muamua le Atua (In Samoa, God Is First). **Song:** Amerika Samoa. **Flower:** Paogo (Ula-fala). **Plant:** Ava.

Blessed with spectacular scenery and delightful South Seas climate, American Samoa is the most southerly of all lands under U. S. ownership. It is an unincorporated territory consisting of 6 small islands of the Samoan group: **Tutuila, Aunu'u, Manu'a Group (Ta'u, Olosega and Ofu),** and **Rose.** Also administered as part of American Samoa is **Swain's Island,** 210 mi. to the NW, acquired by the U.S. in 1925. The islands are 2,600 mi. SW of Honolulu.

American Samoa became U. S. territory by a treaty with the United Kingdom and Germany in 1899. The islands were ceded by local chiefs in 1900 and 1904.

Samoa (Western), comprising the larger islands of the Samoan group, was a New Zealand mandate and UN Trusteeship until it became an independent nation Jan. 1, 1962 *(see Index.)*

Tutuila and Annu'u have an area of 53 sq. mi. Ta'u has an area of 17 sq. mi., and the islets of Ofu and Olosega, 5 sq. mi. with a population of a few thousand. Swain's Island has nearly 2 sq. mi. and a population of about 100.

About 70% of the land is bush. Chief products and exports are fish products, copra, and handicrafts. Taro, bread-fruit, yams, coconuts, pineapples, oranges, and bananas are also produced.

Formerly under jurisdiction of the Navy, since July 1, 1951, it has been under the Interior Dept. On Jan. 3, 1978, the first popularly elected Samoan governor and lieutenant governor were inaugurated. Previously, the governor was appointed by the Secretary of the Interior. American Samoa has a bicameral legislature and elects its own member of Congress, who enjoys nearly all the privileges and powers as the members from the states.

The American Samoans are of Polynesian origin. They are nationals of the U.S.; there are approximately 20,000 in Hawaii and 65,000 in California and Washington.

Minor Caribbean Islands

Quita Sueño Bank, Roncador and Serrana, lie in the Caribbean between Nicaragua and Jamaica. They are uninhabited. U.S. claim to the islands was relinquished in a treaty with Colombia, which entered into force on Sept. 17, 1981.

Navassa lies between Jamaica and Haiti, covers about 2 sq. mi., is reserved by the U.S. for a lighthouse and is uninhabited.

Wake, Midway, Other Islands

Wake Island, and its sister islands, **Wilkes** and **Peale,** lie in the Pacific Ocean on the direct route from Hawaii to Hong Kong, about 2,300 mi. W of Hawaii and 1,290 mi. E of Guam. The group is 4.5 mi. long, 1.5 mi. wide, and totals less than 3 sq. mi.

The U.S. flag was hoisted over Wake Island, July 4, 1898, formal possession taken Jan. 17, 1899; Wake has been administered by the U.S. Air Force since 1972. Population (1983): 1,600.

The **Midway Islands,** acquired in 1867, consist of 2, **Sand** and **Eastern,** in the North Pacific 1,150 mi. NW of Hawaii, with area of about 2 sq. mi., administered by the Navy Dept. Population (1983): 2,200.

Johnston Atoll, SW of Hawaii, area 1 sq. mi., pop. 300 (1978), is operated by Nuclear Defense Agency, and **Kingman Reef,** S of Hawaii, is under Navy control.

Howland, Jarvis, and **Baker Islands,** 1500-1650 miles southwest of the Hawaiian group, uninhabited since World War II, are under the Interior Dept.

Palmyra is an atoll about 1,000 miles south of Hawaii, 4 sq. mi. Privately owned, it is under the Interior Dept.

Islands Under Trusteeship

The Trust Territory of the Pacific Islands was established in 1947, as the only strategic trusteeship of the 11 trusteeships established by the U.N. The territory has a heterogeneous population of about 140,000 people scattered among more than 2,100 islands and atolls in 3 major archipelagos: the Carolines, the Marshalls, and the Marianas. The entire geographic area is sometimes referred to as "Micronesia," meaning "little islands." The area of the Trust Territory covered some 3 million sq. miles of the Pacific Ocean, slightly larger than the continental U.S. However, its islands constituted a land area of only 715.8 sq. miles—half the size of Rhode Island. It formerly contained 4 political jurisdictions: The Commonwealth of the Northern Mariana Islands (CNMI), the Federated States of Micronesia (FSM), the Republic of the Marshall Islands (RMI), and the Republic of Palau (RP). As of Oct. 21, 1986, the RMI entered into free association with the U.S., as did the FSM effective Nov. 3, 1986. The CNMI became a commonwealth of the U.S., also effective Nov. 3. Only the RP remains under trusteeship.

Commonwealth of the Northern Mariana Islands

Located in the perpetually warm climes between Guam and the Tropic of Cancer, the 16 islands of the Northern Marianas form a 300-mile-long archipelago, comprising a total land area of 183.5 sq. miles. The native population, estimated at 20,000, is concentrated on the 3 largest of the 6 inhabited islands: **Saipan,** the seat of government and commerce (16,532), **Rota** (1,484), and **Tinian** (1,012).

The people of the Northern Marianas are predominantly of Chamorro cultural extraction, although numbers of Carolinians and immigrants from other areas of E. Asia and Micronesia have also settled in the islands. Pursuant to the Convenant Agreement, on Nov. 3, 1986, citizens were granted U.S. citizenship. English is among the several languages commonly spoken.

The Northern Mariana Islands has been self-governing since 1978, when both a constitution drafted and adopted by the people became effective, and a bicameral legislature with offices of governor and lieutenant governor was inaugurated. Commercial activity has increased steadily in the last few years, with 1,600 establishments operated in 1985, mostly in tourism, construction, and light industry. In 1986, more than 150,000 tourists visited, an increase of 10% over previous years. An agreement with the U.S. for 1986-1992 entitles the Northern Marianna Islands to $228 million for capital development, government operations and special programs.

Federated States of Micronesia

The Federated States of Micronesia extends across the 1,800-mile-long Caroline Island archipelago. The 4 states of the FSM are Pohnpei, Kosrae, Truk, and Yap. Each state consists of several islands, except for Kosrae, a single island. The capital of the FSM is Pohnpei. Populations are: Pohnpei, 26,000; Truk, 43,000; Kosrae, 6,000; Yap, 10,200. Pohnpei is 2,900 miles SW of Honolulu and 1,000 miles SE of Guam. The islands vary geologically from high, mountainous islands to low, coral atolls. The FSM lies between the equator and 9 degrees N and 138 degrees and 168 degrees E. Average year-round temperature is 80 degrees. Pohnpei gets the highest annual rainfall, averaging up to 250 inches.

The cultures of the FSM are very diverse. Several languages, each with dialects, are spoken throughout: Yapese, Ulithian, Woleaian, Ponapean, Nukuoran, Kapingamarangi, Trukese, and Kosraean. Each state has a constitution and government, headed by a governor. The status of free association recognizes that the FSM is a sovereign-self-governing state, with the U.S. responsible for defense and also extending agreed-upon amounts of economic and service assistance. Each of the state's constitutions recognizes a role for traditional leaders and customs.

Republic of the Marshall Islands

The Republic of the Marshall Islands consists of 2 island/atoll chains, the Ratak (sunrise) Chain, and the Ralik (sunset) Chain, totalling 31 atolls. Each atoll is a cluster of several small islands circling a lagoon. Total land area is 70 sq. miles. The capital is **Majuro,** 2,000 miles SW of Honolulu and 1,300 SE of Guam. Population is 35,000, 12,000 in Majuro. Average year-round temperature is 81 degrees.

Marshallese culture revolves around the complex clan system. Land is owned by each clan and passed down over the generations. In the late 1970's, the U.S. embarked upon an ambitious Capital Improvement Program, with a goal of building a major infrastructure (airport, dock, roads, water-power-sewer system) in Majuro. Funding was completed in 1985.

The Marshall Islands' Constitution includes both American and British concepts. The executive branch is the Nitijela (parliament) and is consulted by a Council of Iroij (local chiefs). The Nitijela elects the President from among its own members. The status of free association recognizes that the Marshall Islands is a sovereign, self-governing state, with the U.S. responsible for defense, and for extending agreed-upon amounts of economic and service assistance. A subsidiary agreement allows the U.S. continued use of Kwajalein Missile Range for 30 years. Another subsidiary agreement provides for settlement of all claims arising out of the nuclear testing programs conducted by the U.S. at Bikini and Enewetak Atolls from 1946 to 1958.

Republic of Palau

Palau consists of more than 200 islands in the Caroline chain, of which 8 are permanently inhabited. The Palau archipelago stretches over 400 miles. The capital of Palau, Koror, lies 4,450 miles SW of Honolulu and 720 miles S of Guam. Population of Palau is approximately 14,000, 8,100 in Koror. Average year-round temperature is 80 degrees, average annual rainfall 150 inches.

The High Commissioner of the Trust Territory is appointed by the Pres. of the U.S. Until 1979, the High Commissioner appointed a district administrator for Palau to oversee programs and administration there. In support of the evolving political status, the U.S. recognized the Constitution of Palau and the establishment of the Government of Palau. The Constitution became effective in 1980. The President and Vice President are elected by popular vote. A Council of Chiefs advises the President on matters concerning traditional law and custom. Palau has a bicameral national legislature composed of a House of Delegates and a Senate.

State Population by Age Group

Source: U.S. Bureau of the Census, 1985

	Percent Under 18 Yrs.	Percent 25-44 Yrs.	Percent 65 Yrs. and Over
Alabama	27.8	29.4	12.1
Alaska	32.6	37.4	3.2
Arizona	27.5	30.5	12.3
Arkansas	27.4	27.9	14.3
California	25.9	33.5	10.5
Colorado	26.7	35.8	8.8
Connecticut	23.8	30.6	13.0
Delaware	25.2	30.7	11.2
Florida	22.3	28.0	17.6
Georgia	27.7	31.7	9.9
Hawaii	27.5	32.7	9.4
Idaho	32.2	30.1	10.9
Illinois	26.9	30.5	11.9
Indiana	27.4	30.1	11.7
Iowa	26.8	29.0	14.3
Kansas	27.2	29.8	13.4
Kentucky	27.5	30.0	11.9
Louisiana	30.2	30.4	9.8
Maine	26.1	29.9	13.2
Maryland	25.0	32.5	10.4
Massachusetts	23.4	31.3	13.4
Michigan	27.3	30.7	11.2
Minnesota	27.2	30.9	12.5
Mississippi	30.2	27.7	11.9
Missouri	26.4	29.2	13.7
Montana	28.4	31.0	11.8
Nebraska	27.9	29.2	13.5
Nevada	23.5	35.6	9.9
New Hampshire	25.3	32.5	11.6
New Jersey	24.6	30.0	12.6
New Mexico	30.9	30.2	9.6
New York	24.6	30.2	12.7
North Carolina	25.4	31.2	11.3
North Dakota	28.8	29.7	12.7
Ohio	26.7	29.9	12.1
Oklahoma	28.0	30.0	12.3
Oregon	26.5	33.0	13.2
Pennsylvania	24.3	29.0	14.3
Rhode Island	23.3	30.0	14.4
South Carolina	27.6	31.1	10.2
South Dakota	29.1	27.6	13.7
Tennessee	25.9	30.8	12.1
Texas	29.3	32.1	9.4
Utah	37.3	29.4	7.9
Vermont	26.2	32.0	11.8
Virginia	25.3	32.7	10.3
Washington	26.8	33.6	11.4
West Virginia	26.7	28.4	13.3
Wisconsin	26.9	[illegible]	12.9
Wyoming	31.5	35.0	8.3

CITIES OF THE U.S.[1]

Sources: Bureau of the Census: population (1984 estimates); population growth (1970-1980); population over 65 and under 35 (1980). Geography Division, Bureau of the Census: population density (1980); area (1980). Bureau of Labor Statistics: employment (Jan. 1987). Bureau of Economic Analysis: per capita personal income (MSA, 1984).

Akron, Ohio

Population: 226,877; **Pop. density:** 4,312 per sq. mi.; **Pop. growth:** −13.9%; **Pop. over 65:** 13.5%; **Pop. under 35:** 57.1%. **Area:** 55 sq. mi. **Employment:** 96,188 employed, 10.7% unemployed; **Per capita income:** $12,801.

Transportation: Akron-Canton airport; major trucking industry; Conrail; metro transit system. **Communications:** 1 TV, and 7 radio stations; 2 public broadcast outlets. **Medical facilities:** 11 hospitals; specialized children's treatment center. **Educational facilities:** Univ. of Arkon and 12 others; 68 public schools. **Further information:** Akron Regional Development Board or Akron-Summit Convention and Visitors Bureau, both One Cascade Plaza, Akron, OH 44308.

Albuquerque, New Mexico

Population: 350,575; **Pop. density:** 3,492 per sq. mi.; **Pop. growth:** 35.7%; **Pop. over 65:** 8.4%; **Pop. under 35:** 61.6%. **Area:** 95 sq. mi. **Employment:** 195,569 employed, 6.4% unemployed; **Per capita income:** $12,305.

Transportation: 1 international airport; 2 railroads; 2 bus lines. **Communications:** 5 TV, 21 radio stations; 3 cable TV systems. **Medical facilities:** 9 major hospitals. **Educational facilities:** 2 universities. **Further information:** Convention & Visitors Bureau, 625 Silver S.W., Albuquerque, NM 87125.

Amarillo, Texas

Population: 162,863; **Pop. density:** 1,863 per sq. mi.; **Pop. growth:** 17.5%; **Pop. over 65:** 10.1%; **Pop. under 35:** 60.1%. **Area:** 80 sq. mi. **Employment:** 78,774 employed, 6.9% unemployed; **Per capita income:** $12,666.

Transportation: 2 railroads; 4 bus lines; city transit system; 1 airport with 6 airlines. **Communications:** 5 TV stations; 15 radio stations. **Medical facilities:** 9 hospitals; Amarillo Medical Ctr. **Educational facilities:** 47 public schools; Amarillo Jr. College. **Further information:** Chamber of Commerce, P.O. Box 9480, Amarillo, TX 79105.

Anaheim, California

Population: 233,516; **Pop. density:** 5,349 per sq. mi.; **Pop. growth:** 31.6%; **Pop. over 65:** 7.7%; **Pop. under 35:** 60.7%. **Area:** 41 sq. mi. **Employment:** 143,314 employed. 4.7% unemployed; **Per capita income:** $16,877.

Transportation: John Wayne, Fullerton, and Long Beach Municipal airports; 4 railroads; Greyhound buses. **Communications:** 12 TV channels, one CATV; 4 radio stations. **Medical facilities:** 6 general hospitals. **Educational facilities:** 3 colleges, 5 junior colleges; 62 elementary, 8 junior high, 8 high schools. **Further information:** Chamber of Commerce, 100 South Anaheim Blvd., Suite 300, Anaheim, CA 92805.

Anchorage, Alaska

Population: 226,663; **Pop. density:** 100 per sq. mi.; **Pop. growth:** 259.5%; **Pop. over 65:** 2.0%; **Pop. under 35:** 70.2%. **Area:** 1,732 sq. mi.. **Employment:** 103,209 employed, 8.3% unemployed; **Per capita income:** $19,188.

Transportation: Anchorage International Airport, 5 other airports. **Communications:** 5 TV, 11 radio stations. **Medical facilities:** 3 hospitals. **Educational facilities:** Univ. of Alaska, Anchorage Comm. College, Alaska Pacific Univ. **Further information:** Chamber of Commerce, 415 F St., Anchorage, AK 99501.

Arlington, Texas

Population: 213,822; **Pop. density:** 2,024 per sq. mi.; **Pop. growth:** 77.5%; **Pop. over 65:** 4.5%; **Pop. under 35:** 67.3%. **Area:** 79 sq. mi.; **Employment:** 111,930 employed, 6.5% unemployed; **Per capita income:** $14,138.

Transportation: Dallas/Ft. Worth airport is 20 minutes away; 12 railway lines; intracity transport system in planning stage. **Communications:** 9 TV stations; 39 radio stations. **Medical facilities:** almost 1,000 beds in hospital network. **Educational facilities:** 47 public schools; Univ. of Texas at Arlington. **Further information:** Chamber of Commerce, 316 W. Main St., Arlington, TX 76010.

Atlanta, Georgia

Population: 426,090; **Pop. density:** 3,244 per sq. mi.; **Pop. growth:** −14.1%; **Pop. over 65:** 11.5%; **Pop. under 35:** 60.7%. **Area:** 131 sq. mi.. **Employment:** 214,921 employed, 7.4% unemployed; **Per capita income:** $13,848.

Transportation: 1 international airport; 7 railroad lines, 2 systems; 2 bus terminals; rapid rail under construction; 6 legs of 3 interstate highways intersecting downtown interchange. **Communications:** 9 TV, 41 radio stations; 21 cable TV companies. **Medical facilities:** 60 hospitals; VA hospital; Natl. Centers for Disease Control; Natl. Cancer Center. **Educational facilities:** 30 colleges, universities, seminaries, junior colleges. **Further information:** Chamber of Commerce, 235 International Blvd., Atlanta, GA 30303.

Aurora, Colorado

Population: 194,772; **Pop. density:** 2,652 per sq. mi.; **Pop. growth:** 111.5%; **Pop. over 65:** 4.3%; **Pop. under 35:** 67.3%. **Area:** 60 sq. mi. **Employment:** 104,023 employed, 8.3% unemployed (1985); **Per capita income:** $15,783.

Transportation: 1 international airport; 4 railroads; 2 bus lines; city bus system. **Further information:** ECO Aurora, Inc., 1470 S. Havana, Ste. 708, Aurora, CO 80012.

Austin, Texas

Population: 397,001; **Pop. density:** 2,978 per sq. mi.; **Pop. growth:** 36.3%; **Pop. over 65:** 7.5%; **Pop. under 35:** 69%. **Area:** 116 sq. mi.. **Employment:** 266,005 employed, 7.0% unemployed; **Per capita income:** $13,483.

Transportation: 1 international airport; 4 railroads. **Communications:** 5 TV, 18 radio stations. **Medical facilities:** 15 hospitals. **Educational facilities:** 10 universities and colleges. **Further information:** Chamber of Commerce, P.O. Box 1967, Austin, TX 78767.

Baltimore, Maryland

Population: 763,570; **Pop. density:** 9,835 per sq. mi.; **Pop. growth:** −13.1%; **Pop. over 65:** 12.8%; **Pop. under 35%:** 56.9%. **Area:** 80 sq. mi.. **Employment:** 315,463 employed, 9.0% unemployed; **Per capita income:** $13,563.

Transportation: 1 major airport; 3 railroads, bus system; subway system: 1 underwater tunnel. **Communications:** 6 TV stations; 33 radio stations. **Medical facilities:** 29 hospitals; 2 major medical centers. **Educational facilities:** 189 public schools; over 30 universities and colleges; major public library system. **Further information:** Greater Baltimore Committee, Suite 900, Two Hopkins Plaza, Baltimore, MD 21202.

(1) Based on 1984 estimates, the 100 most populated cities.

Baton Rouge, Louisiana

Population: 368,571; **Pop. density:** 5,673 per sq. mi.; **Pop. growth:** 32.2%; **Pop. over 65:** 8.7%; **Pop. under 35:** 64.0%. **Area:** 61 sq. mi.. **Employment:** 103,571 employed, 10.8% unemployed; **Per capita income:** $11,851.

Transportation: 1 airport with 5 airlines; 3 bus lines; 4 railroad trunk lines; Port of Greater Baton Rouge is one of largest in U.S. **Communications:** 4 TV, 13 radio stations. **Medical facilities:** 7 hospitals. **Educational facilities:** 97 public schools; Louisiana St. Univ., center of 8-campus system; Southern Univ. **Further information:** Chamber of Commerce, P.O. Box 3217, Baton Rouge, LA 70821.

Birmingham, Alabama

Population: 279,813; **Pop. density:** 2,872 per sq. mi.; **Pop. growth:** −5.5%; **Pop. over 65%;** 13.9%; **Pop. under 35:** 57.5%. **Area:** 99 sq. mi.. **Employment:** 121,688 employed, 11.2% unemployed; **Per capita income:** $11,446.

Transportation: 1 airport; 5 major rail freight lines, Amtrak; 2 bus lines; 75 truck line terminals; 3 interstate highways. **Communications:** 3 TV, 16 radio stations; 1 educational TV, 1 educational radio station. **Medical facilities:** Univ. of Alabama in Birmingham Medical Center; VA hospital with organ transplant program; 15 other hospitals. **Educational facilities:** 1 university, 3 colleges, 2 junior colleges. **Further information:** Chamber of Commerce, 2027 First Ave. N., Birmingham, AL 35202.

Boston, Massachusetts

Population: 570,719; **Pop. density:** 11,979 per sq. mi.; **Pop. growth:** −12.2%; **Pop. over 65:** 12.7%; **Pop. under 35:** 60.4%. **Area:** 46 sq. mi.. **Employment:** 276,644 employed, 4.5% unemployed; **Per capita income:** $15,932.

Transportation: 1 major airport; 2 railroads; city rail and subway system; 2 underwater tunnels. **Communications:** 8 TV stations, 33 radio stations. **Medical facilities:** numerous hospitals; 8 major medical research centers. **Educational facilities:** 28 universities and colleges; major public library system. **Further information:** Chamber of Commerce, Federal Reserve Bank, 600 Atlantic Ave., 13th Fl., Boston, MA 02106.

Buffalo, New York

Population: 338,982; **Pop. density:** 8,520 per sq. mi.; **Pop. growth:** −22.7%; **Pop. over 65:** 15.0%; **Pop. under 35:** 55.3%. **Area:** 42 sq. mi.. **Employment:** 127,853 employed, 9.6% unemployed; **Per capita income:** $12,626.

Transportation: 1 international airport; 6 major railroads, metro rail system; direct highway & rail to all of Canada; water service to Great Lakes-St. Lawrence seaways system, overseas, and Atlantic seaboard. **Communications:** 5 TV, 23 AM & FM radio stations, 5 cable systems. **Medical facilities:** 21 hospitals. **Educational facilities:** 2 universities; 9 colleges, 78 public schools. **Further information:** Greater Buffalo Chamber of Commerce, 107 Delaware Ave., Buffalo, NY 14202.

Charlotte, North Carolina

Population: 330,838; **Pop. density:** 2,278 per sq. mi.; **Pop. growth:** 30.2%; **Pop. over 65:** 8.6%; **Pop. under 35:** 60.4%. **Area:** 138 sq. mi. **Employment:** 196,833 employed, 3.7% unemployed; **Per capita income:** $12,430.

Transportation: Charlotte/Douglas Airport; 2 major railway lines; 3 bus lines; 150 trucking firms. **Communications:** 6 TV, 12 radio stations. **Medical facilities:** 7 hospitals, 1 medical center. **Educational facilities:** 2 universities, 5 colleges. **Further information:** Chamber of Commerce, P.O. Box 32785, Charlotte, NC 28232.

Chattanooga, Tennessee

Population: 164,400; **Pop. density:** 1,370 per sq. mi.; **Pop. growth:** 41.4%; **Pop. over 65:** 12.7%; **Pop. under 35:** 57.3%. **Area:** 124 sq. mi. **Employment:** 73,640 employed, 6.9% unemployed; **Per capita income:** $10,783.

Transportation: Lovell Field airport, 4 airlines; 2 bus lines and local service; 2 railroads. **Communications:** 5 TV stations; cable TV; 22 radio stations. **Medical facilities:** 17 hospitals. **Educational facilities:** 53 public schools; 2 universities; 3 junior colleges, 4 colleges. **Further information:** Partners for Economic Progress, Civic Forum, 1001 Market St., Chattanooga, TN 37402.

Chicago, Illinois

Population: 2,992,472; **Pop. density:** 13,180 per sq. mi.; **Pop. growth:** −10.8%; **Pop. over 65:** 11.4%; **Pop. under 35:** 58.5%. **Area:** 228 sq. mi. **Employment:** 1,246,567 employed, 8.8% unemployed; **Per capita income:** $14,655.

Transportation: 3 airports; major railroad system; major trucking industry. **Communications:** 9 TV stations; 31 radio stations. **Medical facilities:** over 123 hospitals. **Educational facilities:** 95 institutions of higher learning; major public library system. **Further information:** Association of Commerce and Industry, 200 N. LaSalle St., Chicago, IL 60601.

Cincinnati, Ohio

Population: 370,481; **Pop. density:** 4,941 per sq. mi.; **Pop. growth:** −15.0%; **Pop. over 65:** 14.5%; **Pop. under 35:** 58.5%. **Area:** 78 sq. mi.. **Employment:** 174,092 employed, 9.0% unemployed; **Per capita income:** $12,905.

Transportation: 1 international airport; 3 railroads; 1 bus system. **Communications:** 6 TV, 5 cable TV systems; 24 radio stations. **Medical facilities:** 32 hospitals; Children's Hospital Medical Center; VA hospital. **Educational facilities:** 3 universities; 4 4-year colleges, 8 technical & 2-year colleges; major public library system. **Further information:** Chamber of Commerce, 120 W. 5th St., Cincinnati, OH 45202.

Cleveland, Ohio

Population: 546,543; **Pop. density:** 7,264 per sq. mi.; **Pop. growth:** −23.6%; **Pop. over 65:** 13.0%; **Pop. under 35:** 56.7%. **Area:** 79 sq. mi.. **Employment:** 214,004 employed, 11.0% unemployed; **Per capita income:** $14,216.

Transportation: Hopkin's Intl. airport; rail service; major port; rapid transit system. **Communications:** 7 TV stations; 20 radio stations. **Medical facilities:** numerous hospitals; major medical research center. **Educational facilities:** 23 universities and colleges; major public library system. **Further information:** Convention & Visitor's Bureau, 1301 E. 6th Street, Cleveland, OH 44114.

Colorado Springs, Colorado

Population: 247,739; **Pop. density:** 2,088 per sq. mi.; **Pop. growth:** 58.8%; **Pop. over 65:** 8.3%; **Pop. under 35:** 62.3%. **Area:** 103 sq. mi.. **Employment:** 125,312 employed, 9,5% unemployed (1985); **Per capita income:** $12,323.

Transportation: Municipal airport served by 9 air lines; Denver & Rio Grande, Santa Fe, Burlington railroads; Greyhound, Continental Trailways buses. **Communications:** 9 TV, 15 radio stations. **Medical facilities:** 9 hospitals, 1,418 beds. **Educational facilities:** Univ. of Colorado at Colo. Springs, U.S. Air Force Acad., Pikes Peak Comm. College. **Further information:** Chamber of Commerce, P.O. Drawer B, Colorado Springs, CO 80901.

Columbus, Georgia

Population: 174,824; **Pop. density:** 779 per sq. mi.; **Pop. growth:** 9.3%; **Pop. over 65:** 8.9%; **Pop. under 35:** 61.5%. **Area:** 218 sq. mi. **Employment:** 69,569 employed, 6.8% unemployed; **Per capita income:** $10,155.

Transportation: Metropolitan airport; metro bus system; 2 bus lines; 2 railroads. **Communications:** 5 TV stations, 11 radio stations. **Medical facilities:** 5 hospitals. **Educational facilities:** 53 public schools; 1 college. **Further information:** Chamber of Commerce, P.O. Box 1200, Columbus, GA 31902.

Columbus, Ohio

Population: 566,114; **Pop. density:** 3,121 per sq. mi.; **Pop. growth:** 4.6%; **Pop. over 65:** 8.9%; **Pop. under 35:** 64.4%. **Area:** 181 sq. mi.. **Employment:** 293,033 employed, 6.2% unemployed; **Per capita income:** $12,609.

Transportation: 2 airports; 3 railroads; 4 intercity bus lines; major highway system. **Communications:** 5 TV stations; 19 radio stations. **Medical facilities:** 22 hospitals. **Educational facilities:** 12 universities and colleges; major public library system. **Further information:** Chamber of Commerce, P.O. Box 1527, Columbus, OH 43216.

Corpus Christi, Texas

Population: 258,067; **Pop. density:** 2,230 per sq. mi.; **Pop. growth:** 13.4%; **Pop. over 65:** 8.2%; **Pop. under 35:** 63.2%. **Area:** 104 sq. mi.. **Employment:** 107,368 employed, 12.8% unemployed; **Per capita income:** $10,923.

Transportation: 5 airlines; 2 bus lines, metro bus system; 3 freight railroads. **Communications:** 6 TV stations; 17 radio stations. **Medical facilities:** 10 hospitals including a children's center. **Educational facilities:** 54 public schools; Del Mar Coll., Corpus Christi State Univ. **Further information:** Chamber of Commerce, PO Box 640, Corpus Christi, TX 78403.

Dallas, Texas

Population: 974,234; **Pop. density:** 2,715 per sq. mi.; **Pop. growth:** 7%; **Pop. over 65:** 9.5%; **Pop. under 35:** 61.1%. **Area:** 333 sq. mi.. **Employment:** 598,398 employed, 7.5% unemployed; **Per capita income:** $15,861.

Transportation: 1 international airport; 6 railroads; major transit system. **Communications:** 9 TV stations; 38 radio stations. **Medical facilities:** 42 hospitals; major medical center. **Educational facilities:** 37 universities and colleges; major public library system; 186 public schools. **Further information:** Chamber of Commerce, 1507 Pacific Ave., Dallas, TX 75201.

Dayton, Ohio

Population: 181,159; **Pop. density:** 4,236 per sq, mi.; **Pop, growth:** −16.3%; **Pop. over 65:** 11.8%; **Pop. under 35:** 59.8%. **Area:** 48 sq. mi. **Employment:** 78,856 employed, 9.4% unemployed; **Per capita income:** $12,624.

Transportation: 1 international airport; 9 airlines, 3 railroads; 4 bus lines; countywide Dayton Regional Transit Authority. **Communications:** 5 TV, 8 radio stations. **Medical facilities:** 14 hospitals including VA facility. **Educational facilities:** Univ. of Dayton, Wright St. Univ.. **Further information:** Chamber of Commerce, Suite 1980, Kettering Tower, Dayton Oh 45423.

Denver, Colorado

Population: 504,588; **Pop. density:** 4,435 per sq. mi.; **Pop. growth:** −4.3%; **Pop. over 65:** 12.6%; **Pop. under 35:** 58.9%. **Area:** 111 sq. mi.. **Employment:** 258,103 employed, 9.2% unemployed (1985); **Per capita income:** $15,783.

Transportation: 1 international airport; 5 major rail freight lines, Amtrak; 2 bus lines; 3 interstate highways intersect city. **Communications:** 7 TV, 35 radio stations. **Medical facilities:** 34 hospitals. **Educational facilities:** 2 universities; 3 colleges. **Further information:** Chamber of Commerce, 1301 Welton St., Denver, CO 80204.

Des Moines, Iowa

Population: 190,832; **Pop. density:** 2,890 per sq. mi.; **Pop. growth:** −5.2%; **Pop. over 65:** 12.5; **Pop. under 35:** 58.4%. **Area:** 66 sq. mi.. **Employment:** 105,179 employed, 6.3% unemployed; **Per capita income:** $13,869.

Transportation: 1 international airport; 3 bus lines; 4 railroads; metro bus system. **Communications:** 5 TV, 18 radio stations; CATV. **Medical facilities:** 8 hospitals with 2,700 beds. **Educational facilities:** Drake Univ.; 2 Bible colleges. **Further information:** Chamber of Commerce, 8th & High Sts., Des Moines, IA 50309.

Detroit, Michigan

Population: 1,088,973; **Pop. density:** 8,848 per sq. mi.; **Pop. growth:** −20.5%; **Pop. over 65:** 11.7%; **Pop. under 35:** 59.5%. **Area:** 136 sq. mi.. **Employment:** 416,999 employed, 10.1% unemployed (Dec. 1984); **Per capita income:** $13,943.

Transportation: 1 international airport; 10 railroads; major international port; public transit system. **Communications:** 9 TV stations, 37 radio stations. **Medical facilities:** 28 hospitals, major medical center. **Educational facilities:** 13 universities and colleges; major public library system. **Further information:** Chamber of Commerce, 150 Michigan Avenue, Detroit, MI 48226.

El Paso, Texas

Population: 463,809; **Pop. density:** 1,779 per sq. mi.. **Pop. growth:** 32.0%; **Pop. over 65:** 6.9%; **Pop. under 35:** 65%. **Area:** 239 sq. mi. **Employment:** 185,506 employed, 11.6% unemployed; **Per capita income:** $8,745.

Transportation: International airport; 5 major rail lines; 8 bus lines; 9 major highways; gateway to Mexico. **Communications:** 6 TV, 23 radio stations. **Medical facilities:** 16 hospitals; 1 medical school; 1 nursing school; 1 cancer treatment center. **Educational facilities:** 2 colleges and universities. **Further information:** Convention and Visitors Bureau, 5 Civic Center Plaza, El Paso, TX 79901.

Fort Wayne, Indiana

Population: 165,416; **Pop. density:** 3,274 per sq. mi.; **Pop. growth:** −3.4%; **Pop. over 65:** 11.9%; **Pop. under 35:** 60.5%. **Area:** 52 sq. mi. **Employment:** 86,077 employed, 6.6% unemployed; **Per capita income:** $12,190.

Transportation: 1 airport, 6 airlines; 3 railroads; 5 bus lines. **Communications:** 5 TV stations; 10 radio stations. **Medical facilities:** 3 major hospitals; Veteran's Admin. hospital. **Educational facilities:** 81 public schools; Indiana Univ.-Purdue Univ. **Further information:** Chamber of Commerce, 826 Ewing Street, Fort Wayne, IN 46802.

Fort Worth, Texas

Population: 414,562; **Pop. density:** 1,604 per sq. mi.; **Pop. growth:** −2.1%; **Pop. over 65:** 11.8%; **Pop. under 35:** 58.5%. **Area:** 240 sq. mi. **Employment:** 231,133 employed, 9.6% unemployed; **Per capita income:** $14,138.

Transportation: Dallas/Fort Worth airport; 8 major railroads, Amtrak; 41 motor carriers; local bus service; 2 transcontinental, 2 intrastate bus lines. **Communications:** 9 TV, 37 radio stations. **Medical facilities:** 35 hospitals; 2 children's hospitals; 4 government hospitals. **Educational facilities:** 8 colleges & universities. **Further information:** Chamber of Commerce, 700 Throckmorton, Fort Worth, TX 76102.

Fresno, California

Population: 267,377; **Pop. density:** 3,356 per sq. mi.; **Pop. growth:** 31.7%; **Pop. over 65:** 10.9%; **Pop. under 35:** 62.5%. **Area:** 65 sq. mi. **Employment:** 110,079 employed, 12.3% unemployed; **Per capita income:** $11,397.

Transportation: 7 airlines; Amtrak; freeways connect to all major areas in state; U.S. port of entry. **Communications:** one public, 6 commercial TV stations, 5 CATV services; 18 commercial, 2 public radio stations. **Medical facilities:** 6 general hospitals including a VA facility. **Educational facilities:** Cal. State-Fresno, Pacific Coll., Frenso City Coll. (oldest jr. coll. in Cal.). **Further information:** Chamber of Commerce, P.O. Box 1469, Fresno, CA 93721.

Garland, Texas

Population: 160,208; **Pop. density:** 2,493 per sq. mi.; **Pop. growth:** 70.5%; **Pop. over 65:** 4.1%; **Pop. under 35:** 33.7%. **Area:** 56 sq. mi. **Employment:** 94,320 employed, 5.0% unemployed; **Per capita income:** $15,272.

Transportation: 35 miles from Dallas/Ft. Worth airport; 2 railroads. **Communications:** 3 TV stations (from Dallas) plus 1 local station. **Medical facilities:** total of 333 hospital beds. **Educational facilities:** 48 public schools; 2 universities, 2 junior colleges. **Further information:** Chamber of Commerce, P.O. Box 460939, Garland, TX 75046.

Grand Rapids, Michigan

Population: 183,000; **Pop. density:** 4,190 per sq. mi.; **Pop. growth:** −8.0%; **Pop. over 65:** 13.4%; **Pop. under 35:** 60.5%. **Area:** 43.4 sq. mi. **Employment:** 88,207 employed, 8.3% unemployed (Dec. 1984); **Per capita income:** $12,385.

Transportation: 4 railroads; 1 international airport; 3 bus lines. **Communications:** 6 TV stations; 20 radio stations. **Medical facilities:** 12 hospitals. **Educational facilities:** 119 public schools; 8 colleges. **Further information:** Chamber of Commerce, 17 Fountain St., NW, Grand Rapids, MI 49503.

Honolulu Co., Hawaii

Population: 805,266 **Pop. density:** 1,280 per sq. mi.; **Pop. growth:** 20.9%; **Pop. over 65:** 7.4%; **Pop. under 35:** 62.4%. **Area:** 596 sq. mi.. **Employment:** 344,740 employed, 4.1% unemployed; **Per capita income:** $13,709.

Transportation: 1 major airport; large, active port for passengers and cargo. **Communications:** 5 TV stations; 23 radio stations. **Medical facilities:** 43 hospitals. **Educational facilities:** 230 public schools (state); 146 private schools (state); 1 university (9 campus centers); major public library system. **Further information:** Visitors Bureau, 2270 Kalakaua Avenue, Honolulu, HI 96815.

Houston, Texas

Population: 1,705,697; **Pop. density:** 2,869 per sq. mi.; **Pop. growth:** 29.3%; **Pop. over 65:** 6.9%; **Pop. under 35:** 64.4%. **Area:** 556 sq. mi.. **Employment:** 849,653 employed; 11.6% unemployed; **Per capita income:** $14,517.

Transportation: 2 commercial airports; 5 railroads; major bus transit system; major international port. **Communications:** 9 TV stations; 45 radio stations. **Medical facilities:** 59 hospitals; major medical center. **Educational facilities:** 27 universities and colleges; 7th largest U.S. public school system; major public library system. **Further information:** Chamber of Commerce, 1100 Milam, Houston, TX 77002.

Huntington Beach, California

Population: 179,335; **Pop. density:** 6,315 per sq. mi.; **Pop. growth:** 47%. **Area:** 27 sq. mi.. **Employment:** 113,450 employed, 4.0% unemployed; **Per capita income:** $16,877.

Transportation: 1 airport; 1 railroad; 2 bus lines. **Communications:** 1 TV station; cable TV. **Medical facilities:** 2 hospitals. **Educational facilities:** 45 public schools; 1 junior college. **Further information:** Chamber of Commerce, Seacliff Village, 2213 Main #32, Huntington Beach, CA 92648.

Indianapolis, Indiana

Population: 710,280; **Pop. density:** 1,991 per sq. mi.; **Pop. growth:** −4.9%; **Pop. over 65;** 10.3%; **Pop. under 35:** 59.4%. **Area:** 352 sq. mi.. **Employment:** 365,309 employed, 5.9% unemployed; **Per capita income:** $12,997.

Transportation: 1 international airport; 6 railroads; 3 interstate bus lines. **Communications:** 7 TV stations; 27 radio stations. **Medical facilities:** 17 hospitals; major medical center. **Educational facilities:** 6 universities and colleges; major public library system. **Further information:** Chamber of Commerce, 320 N. Meridian Street, Indianapolis, IN 46204.

Jackson, Mississippi

Population: 208,810; **Pop. density:** 1,914 per sq. mi.; **Pop. growth:** 31.8%; **Pop. over 65:** 9.9%; **Pop. under 35:** 59.3%. **Area:** 106.2 sq. mi.. **Employment:** 99,100 employed, 8.3% unemployed; **Per capita income:** $10,908.

Transportation: 6 airlines; 2 bus lines; Ill. Central Gulf railroad. **Communications:** 5 TV, 25 radio stations. **Medical facilities:** 12 hospitals including a VA facility. **Educational facilities:** Jackson St. Univ.; Belhaven, Millsaps, Mississippi, Tougaloo, and Wesley colleges. **Further information:** Chamber of Commerce, P.O. Box 22548, Jackson, MS 39225.

Jacksonville, Florida

Population: 577,971; **Pop. density:** 712 per sq. mi.; **Pop. growth:** 7.3%; **Pop. over 65:** 9.6%; **Pop. under 35:** 60.0%. **Area:** 760 sq. mi.. **Employment:** 292,248 employed, 5.2% unemployed; **Per capita income:** $12,168.

Transportation: 1 international airport; 3 railroads; 2 interstate bus lines. **Communications:** 6 TV stations; 21 radio stations. **Medical facilities:** 14 hospitals. **Educational facilities:** 5 universities and colleges; major public library system. **Further information:** Chamber of Commerce, 3 Independent Drive, P.O. Box 329, Jacksonville, FL 32201.

Jersey City, New Jersey

Population: 223,004; **Pop. density:** 16,934 per sq. mi.; **Pop. growth:** −14.1%; **Pop. over 65:** 11.8%; **Pop. under 35:** 57.6%. **Area:** 13.2 sq. mi. **Employment:** 90,084 employed, 8.0% unemployed; **Per capita income:** $12,147.

Transportation: bus and subway system. **Medical facilities:** 10 hospitals. **Educational facilities:** 3 colleges. **Further information:** Chamber of Commerce & Industry of Hudson County, 911 Bergen Ave., Jersey City, NJ 07303.

Kansas City, Kansas

Population: 160,468; **Pop. density:** 1,500 per sq. mi.; **Pop. growth:** −4.2%; **Pop. over 65:** 11.7%; **Pop. under 35:** 57.1%. **Area:** 107 sq. mi. **Employment:** 73,541 employed, 10.4% unemployed; **Per capita income:** $13,821.

Transportation: 1 airport, 11 airlines; 9 railroads; bus system. **Communications:** 4 TV stations; 32 radio stations. **Medical facilities:** 3 hospitals, medical center. **Educational facilities:** 50 public schools; 1 junior college, Univ. of Kansas Medical Ctr. **Further information:** Chamber of Commerce, P.O. Box 1310, Kansas City, KS 66117.

Kansas City, Missouri

Population: 443,075; **Pop. density:** 1,418 per sq. mi.; **Pop. growth:** −11.7%; **Pop. over 65:** 12.3%; **Pop. under 35:** 57.1%. **Area:** 316 sq. mi.. **Employment:** 231,621 employed, 6.4% unemployed; **Per capita income:** $13,821.

Transportation: 1 international airport; a major rail center; 191 trunk lines; several barge companies. **Communications:** 6 TV, 14 AM, 18 FM radio stations. **Medical facilities:** 41 hospitals; 18 clinics. **Educational facilities:** 13 colleges & universities. **Further information:** Chamber of Commerce, 600 Boatmen's Center, 920 Main St., Kansas City, MO 64105.

Knoxville, Tennessee

Population: 173,972; **Pop. density:** 2,273 per sq. mi.; **Pop. growth:** .25%; **Pop. over 65:** 13.8%; **Pop. under**

35: 57.8%. **Area:** 77 sq. mi.. **Employment:** 77,310 employed, 6.7% unemployed; **Per capita income:** $10,623.
Transportation: 13 airlines, 2 bus lines, 61 motor freight carriers; 2 railroads. **Communications:** 5 TV, 16 radio stations. **Medical facilities:** 8 hospitals. **Educational facilities:** 85 public schools; Univ. of Tennessee, Knoxville College. **Further information:** Chamber of Commerce, P.O. Box 2688, Knoxville, TN 37901.

Las Vegas, Nevada

Population: 183,227; **Pop. density:** 2,994 per sq. mi.; **Pop. growth:** 30.9%; **Pop. over 65:** 8.3%; **Pop. under 35:** 58.4%. **Area:** 55 sq. mi. **Employment:** 107,529 employed, 6.6% unemployed; **Per capita income:** $12,729.
Transportation: 1 international airport; 2 railroads; bus system. **Communcations:** 6 TV and 24 radio stations. **Medical facilities:** 8 hospitals. **Educational facilities:** 116 public schools; Clark Comm. College; Univ. of Nevada. **Further information:** Chamber of Commerce, 2301 E. Sahara Ave., Las Vegas, NV, 89104.

Lexington–Fayette, Kentucky

Population: 210,150; **Pop. density:** 719 per sq. mi.; **Pop. growth:** 88.8%; **Pop. over 65:** 8.6%; **Pop. under 35:** 63.3%. **Area:** 284 sq. mi.. **Employment:** 109,453 employed, 5.6% unemployed; **Per capita income:** $13,559.
Transportation: 8 airlines, 2 railroads; city buses. **Communications:** 5 TV stations, CATV; 9 radio stations. **Medical facilities:** 4 general, 5 specialized hospitals. **Educational facilities:** Univ. of Kentucky, Transylvania Univ., Lexington Baptist College. **Further information:** Chamber of Commerce, 330 East Main, Lexington, KY 40507.

Lincoln, Nebraska

Population: 180,378; **Pop. density:** 2,866 per sq. mi.; **Pop. growth:** 15.0%; **Pop. over 65:** 10.3%; **Pop. under 35:** 63.9%. **Area:** 60 sq. mi.. **Employment:** 99,239 employed, 3.7% unemployed; **Per capita income:** $12,617.
Transportation: 7 airlines serve Lincoln Municipal Airport; Greyhound, Trailways buses; Amtrak. **Communications:** 1 TV, 11 radio stations; CATV. **Medical facilities:** 4 hospitals including a VA facility. **Educational facilities:** 3 colleges; 6 business, professional, or technical schools. **Further information:** Chamber of Commerce, 1221 N St., Lincoln, NE 68508.

Little Rock, Arkansas

Population: 170,140; **Pop. density:** 1,996 per sq. mi.; **Pop. growth:** 19.6%; **Pop. over 65:** 11.0%; **Pop. under 35:** 60.8%. **Area:** 79 sq. mi. **Employment:** 84,160 employed, 6.7% unemployed; **Per capita income:** $11,812.
Transportation: 1 airport, 7 airlines; 3 railroads; 2 bus lines. **Communications:** 6 TV stations; 30 radio stations. **Medical facilities:** 15 hospitals; veterans' medical center. **Educational facilities:** 36 public schools; 7 colleges and universities; Univ. of Arkansas. **Further information:** Chamber of Commerce, One Spring St., Little Rock, AR 72201.

Long Beach, California

Population: 378,751; **Pop. density:** 7,256 per sq. mi.; **Pop. growth:** 0.7%; **Pop. over 65:** 14.0%; **Pop. under 35:** 56.6%. **Area:** 50 sq. mi.. **Employment:** 180,415 employed, 5.4% unemployed; **Per capita income:** $14,526.
Transportation: 1 airport; 3 railroads; major international port; 6 bus lines. **Communications:** 1 cable TV station; 2 AM, 6 FM radio stations. **Medical facilities:** 10 hospitals. **Educational facilities:** 78 public schools; 1 university; 1 college. **Further information:** Chamber of Commerce, 330 Golden Shore, Long Beach, CA 90802.

Los Angeles, California

Population: 3,096,721; **Pop. density:** 6,380 per sq. mi.; **Pop. growth:** +5.5%; **Pop. over 65:** 10.6%; **Pop. under 35:** 58.1%. **Area:** 465 sq. mi.. **Employment:** 1,545,614 employed, 6.3% unemployed; **Per capita income:** $14,526.
Transportation: 1 major airport; 4 railroads; major bus carrier service; major freeway system. **Communications:** 19 TV stations; 71 radio stations. **Medical facilities:** 822 hospitals and clinics; 409 nursing homes. **Educational facilities:** 11 universities and colleges; 1,642 public schools; 800 private schools; 61 public libraries. **Further information:** Chamber of Commerce, P.O. Box 3696, Terminal Annex, Los Angeles, CA 90051.

Louisville, Kentucky

Population: 289,843; **Pop. density:** 4,974 per sq. mi.; **Pop. growth:** −17.5%; **Pop. over 65:** 15.3%; **Pop. under 35:** 54.1%. **Area:** 60 sq. mi. **Employment:** 125,495 employed, 8.7% unemployed. **Per capita income:** $12,309.
Transportation: 2 municipal airports; 1 terminal, 6 trunk-line railroads; 3 bus lines; 125 inter-city truck lines; 5 barge lines. **Communications:** 4 TV, 20 radio stations, 2 educational, 1 cable. **Medical facilities:** 21 hospitals. **Educational facilities:** 10 colleges & universities, 9 business colleges & technical schools. **Further information:** Chamber of Commerce, One Riverfront Plaza, Louisville, KY 40202.

Lubbock, Texas

Population: 178,529; **Pop. density:** 1,933 per sq. mi.; **Pop. growth:** 16.7%; **Pop. over 65:** 7.8%; **Pop. under 35:** 66.9%. **Area:** 90 sq. mi. **Employment:** 86,837 employed, 7.0% unemployed; **Per capita income:** $11,584.
Transportation: Lubbock International Airport; 2 railroads, bus line. **Communications:** 5 TV, 18 radio stations. **Medical facilities:** 7 hospitals. **Educational facilities:** 51 public schools; Texas Tech Univ., South Plains College, Lubbock Christian College. **Further information:** Chamber of Commerce, P.O. Box 561, Lubbock, TX 79408.

Madison, Wisconsin

Population: 170,745; **Pop. density:** 3,165 per sq. mi.; **Pop. growth:** −.7%; **Pop. over 65:** 8.7%; **Pop. under 35:** 65.1%. **Area:** 60 sq. mi. **Employment:** 101,972 employed, 4.3% unemployed; **Per capita income:** $14,056.
Transportation: 1 airport, 9 airlines; 2 railroads; bus system. **Communications:** 4 TV stations; 19 radio stations. **Medical facilities:** 6 hospitals. **Educational facilities:** 41 public schools; 4 colleges and universities; Univ. of Wisconsin. **Further information:** Chamber of Commerce, P.O. Box 71, Madison, WI 53701.

Memphis, Tennessee

Population: 648,399; **Pop. density:** 2,448 per sq. mi.; **Pop. growth:** 3.6%; **Pop. over 65:** 10.4%; **Pop. under 35:** 60.5%. **Area:** 264 sq. mi.. **Employment:** 308,282 employed, 6.9% unemployed; **Per capita income:** $11,575.
Transportation: 1 major airport; 6 railroads; bus system. **Communications:** 6 TV stations; 26 radio stations. **Medical facilities:** 20 hospitals. **Educational facilities:** 10 universities and colleges; 149 public schools; 76 private schools. **Further information:** Chamber of Commerce, 555 Beale St., Box 224, Memphis TN 38101.

Mesa, Arizona

Population: 193,931; **Pop. density:** 2,242 per sq. mi.; **Pop. growth:** 141.8%; **Pop. over 65:** 11.2%; **Pop. under 35:** 62.4%. **Area:** 68 sq. mi. **Employment:** 92,494 employed, 6.3% unemployed; **Per capita income:** $13,199.

Transportation: Falcon Field Memorial and Sky Harbor Intl. airports; 2 railroads; trolley and bus lines. **Medical facilities:** 4 major hospitals. **Educational facilities:** 49 public schools; Mesa Community College; Ariz. State Univ. **Further information:** Convention and Visitor's Bureau, 120 N. Center, Mesa, AZ 85201.

Miami, Florida

Population: 372,634; **Pop. density:** 11,256 per sq. mi.; **Pop. growth:** 3.6%; **Pop. over 65:** 17.0%; **Pop. under 35:** 46.5%. **Area:** 34 sq. mi.. **Employment:** 178,508 employed; 8.0% unemployed; **Per capita income:** $13,249.

Transportation: 1 international airport; 2 passenger railroads, 1 all-freight; 2 bus lines; 65 truck lines. **Communications:** 6 commercial, 5 educational TV stations; 31 radio stations. **Medical facilities:** 41 hospitals, 39 nursing homes; VA Hospital. **Educational facilities:** 6 colleges & universities. **Further information:** Metro-Dade Department of Tourism, 234 W. Flagler St., Miami, FL 33130.

Milwaukee, Wisconsin

Population: 620,811; **Pop. density:** 6,627 per sq. mi.; **Pop. growth:** −11.3%; **Pop. over 65:** 12.5%; **Pop. under 35:** 59.8%. **Area:** 96 sq. mi.. **Employment:** 283,370 employed, 8.1% unemployed; **Per capita income:** $14,184.

Transportation: 1 international airport; 2 railroads; major port; 4 bus lines. **Communications:** 7 TV stations; 33 radio stations. **Medical facilities:** 29 hospitals; major medical center. **Educational facilities:** 12 universities and colleges; major public school and library system. **Further information:** Association of Commerce, 756 N. Milwaukee Street, Milwaukee, WI 53202.

Minneapolis, Minnesota

Population: 358,335; **Pop. density:** 6,744 per sq. mi.; **Pop. growth:** −14.6%; **Pop. over 65:** 15.4%; **Pop. under 35:** 59.4%. **Area:** 55 sq. mi.. **Employment:** 202,174 employed; 4.3% unemployed; **Per capita income:** $15,189.

Transportation: 1 international airport; 6 railroads; mass transit systems; 5 major barge lines. **Communications:** 6 TV, 39 radio stations. **Medical facilities:** 36 hospitals, including leading heart hospital at Univ. of Minnesota. **Educational facilities:** 48 public school districts; 13 colleges and universities. **Further information:** Chamber of Commerce, 15 S. 5th St., Minneapolis, MN 55402.

Mobile, Alabama

Population: 204,923; **Pop. density:** 1,630 per sq. mi.; **Pop. growth:** 5.5%; **Pop. over 65:** 11.1%; **Pop. under 35:** 59.3%. **Area:** 123 sq. mi.. **Employment:** 85,798 employed, 11.3% unemployed; **Per capita income:** $9,789.

Transportation: 4 railroads, 4 major airlines, 55 truck lines; leading river system. **Communications:** 5 TV, 12 radio stations; CATV. **Medical facilities:** 6 hospitals. **Educational facilities:** Univ. of South Alabama; Spring Hill, Mobile colleges. **Further information:** Chamber of Commerce, P.O. Box 2187, Mobile, AL 36652.

Montgomery, Alabama

Population: 184,963; **Pop. density:** 1,389 per sq. mi.; **Pop. growth:** 33.3%; **Pop. over 65:** 10.1%; **Pop. under 35:** 60.7%. **Area:** 128 sq. mi.. **Employment:** 82,107 employed, 7.8% unemployed; **Per capita income:** $11,283.

Transportation: 3 airlines, 5 railroads, 2 bus lines, city bus line; Interstate 65 and 85 intersect in city; Alabama River is navigable to Gulf of Mexico. **Communications:** 4 TV, 14 radio stations; CATV. **Medical facilities:** 5 general hospitals; VA and mental health facilities. **Educational facilities:** 5 colleges and universities. **Further information:** Chamber of Commerce, P.O. Box 79, Montgomery, AL 36192.

Nashville-Davidson, Tennessee

Population: 462,450; **Pop. density:** 949 per sq. mi.; **Pop. growth:** 7.0%; **Pop. over 65:** 11.0%; **Pop. under 35:** 58.7%. **Area:** 480 sq. mi.. **Employment:** 254,713 employed, 4.5% unemployed; **Per capita income:** $12,125.

Transportation: 1 airport, 9 airlines; 2 railroads; 3 bus lines. **Communications:** 7 TV, 30 radio stations. **Medical facilities:** 17 hospitals; 2 medical schools; VA Hospital, speech-hearing center. **Educational facilities:** 16 colleges & universities. **Further information:** Chamber of Commerce, 161 4th Ave., Nashville, TN 37219.

Newark, New Jersey

Population: 314,387; **Pop. density:** 13,718 per sq. mi.; **Pop. growth:** −13.8%; **Pop. over 65:** 8.8%; **Pop. under 35:** 61.6%. **Area:** 24 sq. mi.. **Employment:** 114,023 employed, 9.4% unemployed; **Per capita income:** $16,274.

Transportation: 1 international airport; 2 railroads; bus system; 2 subways. **Communications:** 3 TV, 5 radio stations. **Medical facilities:** 6 hospitals. **Educational facilities:** 5 universities and colleges; 71 public schools. **Further information:** Chamber of Commerce, 50 Park Pl., Newark, NJ 07102.

New Orleans, Louisiana

Population: 559,101; **Pop. density:** 2,802 per sq. mi.; **Pop. growth:** −6%; **Pop. over 65:** 11.7%; **Pop. under 35:** 60.1%. **Area:** 199 sq. mi.. **Employment:** 207,234 employed, 12.1% unemployed; **Per capita income:** $12,389.

Transportation: 2 airports; major railroad center; major international port. **Communications:** 2 TV stations; 28 radio stations. **Medical facilities:** numerous hospitals; major medical research center. **Educational facilities:** 13 universities and colleges; major public library system. **Further information:** Chamber of Commerce, 301 Camp Street, New Orleans, LA 70130.

New York City, New York

Population: 7,164,742; **Pop. density:** 23,494 per sq. mi.; **Pop. growth:** −10.4%; **Pop. over 65:** 13.5%; **Pop. under 35:** 53.7%. **Area:** 301 sq. mi.. **Employment:** 3,027,000 employed, 7.4% unemployed; **Per capita income:** $15,076.

Transportation: 2 airports; 4 heliports; 2 rail terminals; 40 bus carriers; major subway network; ferry system; 4 underwater tunnels. **Communications:** 17 TV stations, 117 radio stations. **Medical facilities:** 100 hospitals; 5 medical research centers. **Educational facilities:** 94 universities and colleges; 976 public schools, 914 private schools; 201 public libraries. **Further information:** Convention and Visitors Bureau, 2 Columbus Circle, New York, NY 10019.

Norfolk, Virginia

Population: 279,683; **Pop. density:** 5,037 per sq. mi.; **Pop. growth:** −13.3%; **Pop. over 65:** 9.2%; **Pop. under 35:** 68.6%. **Area:** 53 sq. mi.. **Employment:** 97,826 employed, 4.8% unemployed; **Per capita income:** $12,177.

Transportation: 1 international airport; 4 major railroad systems in area. **Communications:** 7 TV, 38 radio stations. **Medical facilities:** 11 hospitals, 1 medical school. **Educational facilities:** 53 public schools; 2 universities, 1 college. **Further information:** Hampton Roads Chamber of Commerce, 480 Bank St., Norfolk, VA 23510.

Oakland, California

Population: 351,898; **Pop. density:** 6,284 per sq. mi.; **Pop. growth:** −6.2%; **Pop. over 65:** 13.2%; **Pop. under 35:** 57%. **Area:** 54 sq. mi.. **Employment:** 166,668 employed, 8.7% unemployed; **Per capita income:** $16,365.

Transportation: 1 international airport; western terminus for 3 railroads; underground, underwater 75-mile subway. **Communications:** 1 TV, 3 radio stations. **Medical facilities:** 8 hospitals, including Children's Hospital Medical Center, VA hospital. **Educational facilities:** 94 public schools; 3 colleges and universities. **Further information:** Chamber of Commerce, 1939 Harrison St., Ste. 400, Oakland, CA 94612.

Oklahoma City, Oklahoma

Population: 443,172; **Pop. density:** 667 per sq. mi.; **Pop. growth:** 9.5%; **Pop. over 65:** 11.3%; **Pop. under 35:** 58.2%. **Area.** 604 sq. mi.. **Employment:** 218,365 employed, 6.7% unemployed; **Per capita income:** $13,201.

Transportation: 1 international airport; 3 railroads; public transit system; 5 major bus lines. **Communications:** 8 TV, 24 radio stations; cable TV. **Medical facilities:** 22 hospitals. **Educational facilities:** 87 public schools; 14 colleges and universities. **Further information:** Chamber of Commerce, One Santa Fe Plaza, Oklahoma City, OK 73102.

Omaha, Nebraska

Population: 332,237; **Pop. density:** 3,453 per sq. mi.; **Pop. growth:** −9.5%; **Pop. over 65:** 12.2%; **Pop. under 35:** 41.9%. **Area:** 91 sq. mi.. **Employment:** 160,024 employed, 6.5% unemployed; **Per capita income:** $13,156.

Transportation: 9 major airlines; major rail center, with 5 major railroads; intercity bus line. **Communications:** 6 TV, 17 radio stations. **Medical facilities:** 17 hospitals; 2 medical, 1 dental, 6 nursing schools; institute for cancer research. **Educational facilities:** 114 public schools; 3 universities, 6 colleges. **Further information:** Chamber of Commerce, 1301 Harney St., Omaha, NE 68102.

Philadelphia, Pennsylvania

Population: 1,646,713; **Pop. density:** 12,413 per sq. mi.; **Pop. growth:** −13.4%; **Pop. over 65:** 14.1%; **Pop. under 35:** 54.4%. **Area:** 136 sq. mi.. **Employment:** 670,397 employed, 6.2% unemployed; **Per capita income:** $13,746.

Transportation: 1 major airport; 3 railroads; biggest freshwater port in world; subway, el, rail commuter, bus, and streetcar system. **Communications:** 6 TV stations; 53 radio stations. **Medical facilities:** 124 hospitals. **Educational facilities:** 88 degree-granting institutions; major public library system. **Further information:** Office of City Representative, 1660 Municipal Services Bldg., Philadelphia, PA 19107.

Phoenix, Arizona

Population: 853,266; **Pop. density:** 2,438 per sq. mi.; **Pop. growth:** 35.1%; **Pop. over 65:** 9.3%; **Pop. under 35:** 60.4%. **Area:** 324 sq. mi.. **Employment:** 514,933 employed, 6.9% unemployed; **Per capita income:** $13,199.

Transportation: 1 major airport; 2 railroads; 2 transcontinental bus lines; public transit system. **Communications:** 9 TV stations; 34 radio stations. **Medical facilities:** 34 hospitals, 1 medical research center. **Educational facilities:** 8 universities and colleges; 6 community colleges; major public library system. **Further information:** Chamber of Commerce, 34 W. Monroe, Suite 900, Phoenix, AZ 85003.

Pittsburgh, Pennsylvania

Population: 402,583; **Pop. density:** 7,707 per sq. mi.; **Pop. growth:** −18%; **Pop. over 65:** 16.0%; **Pop. under 35:** 52.9%. **Area:** 55 sq. mi.. **Employment:** 156,263 employed, 7.2% unemployed; **Per capita income:** $12,680.

Transportation: 1 international airport; 20 railroads; 2 bus lines; trolley/subway system. **Communications:** 6 TV, 25 radio stations. **Medical facilities:** 32 hospitals; VA installation. **Educational facilities:** 86 public schools; 3 universities; 6 colleges. **Further information:** Chamber of Commerce, 3 Gateway Ctr., Pittsburgh, PA 15222.

Portland, Oregon

Population: 365,861; **Pop. density:** 3,557 per sq. mi.; **Pop. growth:** −3.6%; **Pop. over 65:** 10.9%; **Pop. under 35:** 58.9%. **Area:** 103 sq. mi.. **Employment:** 187,566 employed, 8.0% unemployed; **Per capita income:** $13,247.

Transportation: 1 international airport; 3 major rail freight lines, Amtrak; 2 bus lines; 27-mi. frontage freshwater port; mass transit system. **Communications:** 5 TV, 27 radio stations. **Medical facilities:** 32 hospitals; Oregon Health Sciences University Hospital; VA hospital. **Educational facilities:** 11 colleges and universities; 4 community colleges. **Further information:** Chamber of Commerce, 221 N.W. Second Ave., Portland, OR 97209.

Raleigh, North Carolina

Population: 169,331; **Pop. density:** 2,793 per sq. mi.; **Pop. growth:** 22.3%; **Pop. over 65:** 8.3%; **Pop. under 35:** 62.8%. **Area:** 54 sq. mi. **Employment:** 108,256 employed, 3.7% unemployed; **Per capita income:** $13,204.

Transportation: Raleigh-Durham airport, 15 airlines; 3 railroads; 1 bus line. **Communications:** 6 TV stations; 13 radio stations. **Medical facilities:** 11 hospitals. **Educational facilities:** 4 colleges and universities; 3 junior colleges; 78 public schools. **Further information:** Chamber of Commerce, 800 S. Salisbury St., P.O. Box 2978, Raleigh, NC 27602.

Richmond, Virginia

Population: 219,056; **Pop. density:** 3,650 per sq. mi.; **Pop. growth:** −12.1%; **Pop. over 65:** 14.1%; **Pop. under 35:** 56.9%. **Area:** 60 sq. mi.. **Employment:** 103,456 employed, 5.2% unemployed; **Per capita income:** $14,082.

Transportation: Richmond International airport; 4 railroads, 3 intercity bus lines; deepwater terminal accessible to ocean-going ships. **Communications:** 7 TV, 28 radio stations. **Medical facilities:** Medical Coll. of Virginia renowned for heart and kidney transplants; 19 other hospitals including VA facility. **Educational facilities:** 181 public schools; 9 colleges and universities. **Further information:** Chamber of Commerce, P.O. Box 12324, Richmond, VA 23241.

Riverside, California

Population: 182,245; **Pop. density:** 2,406 per sq. mi.; **Pop. growth:** 22.0%; **Pop. over 65:** 8.8%; **Pop. under 35:** 62.8%. **Area:** 71 sq. mi.. **Employment:** 102,853 employed, 6.8% unemployed; **Per capita income:** $12,336.

Communications: 11 TV, 13 radio stations. **Educational facilities:** Univ. of Cal.- Riverside, Cal. Baptist. **Further information:** Chamber of Commerce, 4261 Main St., Riverside, CA 92501.

Rochester, New York

Population: 242,562; **Pop. density:** 7,068 per sq. mi.; **Pop. growth:** −18.1%; **Pop. over 65:** 14.0%; **Pop. under 35:** 60.0%. **Area:** 34 sq. mi.. **Employment:** 107,332 employed, 7.2% unemployed; **Per capita income:** $13,874.

Transportation: Amtrak; Greyhound, Trailways, Blue Bird bus lines; Monroe Co. airport with 8 major airlines; Rochester Transit Service; Port of Rochester; some 75 motor freight firms. **Communications:** 5 TV, 18 radio stations. **Medical facilities:** 8 general hospitals including Strong Memorial. **Educational facilities:** 8 private and 2 public 4-year colleges; 3 community colleges. **Further information:** Chamber of Commerce, 55 St. Paul St., Rochester, NY 14604.

Sacramento, California

Population: 304,131; **Pop. density:** 2,872 per sq. mi.; **Pop. growth:** 10.7%; **Pop. over 65:** 9.6%; **Pop. under 35:** 59%. **Area:** 96 sq. mi.. **Employment:** 142,474 employed, 7.9% unemployed; **Per capita income:** $12,831.

Transportation: metropolitan airport; 2 mainline transcontinental rail carriers; bus and light rail system. **Communications:** 7 TV, 22 radio stations. **Medical facilities:** 15 hospitals. **Educational facilities:** 3 universities, 4 community colleges. **Further information:** Chamber of Commerce, 917 7th St., P.O. Box 1017, Sacramento, CA 95805.

St. Louis, Missouri

Population: 429,296; **Pop. density:** 7,427 per sq. mi.; **Pop. growth:** −27.2%; **Pop. over 65:** 17.6%; **Pop. under 35:** 54%. **Area:** 61 sq. mi.. **Employment:** 178,786 employed, 9.5% unemployed; **Per capita income:** $13,991.

Transportation: 1 international airport; 3d largest rail center in U.S.; 17 trunk line railroads; 2d largest inland port in U.S.; 14 bus lines; 350 motor freight lines, 14 barge lines. **Communications:** 6 TV, 35 radio stations. **Medical facilities:** 65 hospitals. **Educational facilities:** 5 universities, 26 colleges and seminaries. **Further information:** Regional Commerce and Growth Assoc., Ten Broadway, St. Louis, MO 63102.

St. Paul, Minnesota

Population: 265,903; **Pop. density:** 5,196 per sq. mi.; **Pop. growth:** −12.8%; **Pop. over 65:** 15.0%; **Pop. under 35:** 41.5%. **Area:** 52 sq. mi.. **Employment:** 139,511 employed, 5.1% unemployed; **Per capita income:** $15,189.

Transportation: 1 international airport; 5 major rail lines; 3 interstate bus lines; 10 barge lines. **Communications:** 5 TV, 36 radio stations. **Medical facilities:** 12 private hospitals; community hospital and research center. **Educational facilities:** 1 university; 5 colleges; 51 public schools. **Further information:** Chamber of Commerce, 600 N. Central Tower, 445 Minnesota St., St. Paul, MN 55101.

St. Petersburg, Florida

Population: 241,294; **Pop. density:** 4,186 per sq. mi.; **Pop. growth:** 10.4%; **Pop. over 65:** 25.8%; **Pop. under 35:** 43.7%. **Area:** 57 sq. mi.. **Employment:** 124,996 employed, 5.4% unemployed; **Per capita income:** $12,662.

Transportation: 1 international airport; bus system; 2 full-service ports. **Communications:** 9 TV, 49 radio stations. **Medical facilities:** 9 hospitals. **Educational facilities:** 106 public schools; 7 colleges. **Further information:** Chamber of Commerce, P.O. Box 1371, St. Petersburg, FL 33731.

Salt Lake City, Utah

Population: 164,844; **Pop. density:** 2,168 per sq. mi.; **Pop. growth:** −7.3%; **Pop. over 65:** 14.7%; **Pop. under 35:** 67.2%. **Area:** 75 sq. mi. **Employment:** 92,502 employed, 7.0% unemployed; **Per capita income:** $10,689.

Transportation: 1 international airport, 9 airlines; 3 railroads; mass transit system. **Communications:** 6 TV stations; 27 radio stations. **Medical facilities:** 13 hospitals; 5 emergency care centers. **Educational facilities:** 47 public schools (Salt Lake); Univ. of Utah, Salt Lake Community College. **Further information:** Chamber of Commerce, 175 E. 400 South, Ste. 600, Salt Lake City, UT 84111.

San Antonio, Texas

Population: 842,779; **Pop. density:** 2,988 per sq. mi.; **Pop. growth:** 20%; **Pop. over 65:** 9.5%; **Pop. under 35:** 62.1%. **Area:** 263 sq. mi.. **Employment:** 394,444 employed, 9.5% unemployed; **Per capita income:** $11,540.

Transportation: 1 major airport; 4 railroads; 5 bus lines. **Communications:** 6 TV, 28 radio stations. **Medical facilities:** 26 hospitals; major medical center. **Educational facilities:** 15 universities and colleges; major public library system. **Further information:** Chamber of Commerce, 602 E. Commerce, P.O. Box 1628, San Antonio, TX 78296.

San Diego, California

Population: 960,452; **Pop. density:** 2,736 per sq. mi.; **Pop. growth:** 25.5%; **Pop. over 65:** 9.7%; **Pop. under 35:** 62.1%. **Area:** 320 sq. mi.. **Employment:** 457,734 employed, 5.5% unemployed; **Per capita income:** $13,474.

Transportation: 1 major airport; 1 railroad; major freeway system; bus system. **Communications:** 7 TV, 27 radio stations. **Medical facilities:** 18 hospitals; 2 major medical research centers. **Educational facilities:** 8 universities and colleges; major public library system. **Further information:** Chamber of Commerce, 110 West "C," Suite 1600, San Diego, CA 92101.

San Francisco, California

Population: 712,753; **Pop. density:** 14,760 per sq. mi.; **Pop. growth:** −5.1%; **Pop. over 65:** 15.4%; **Pop. under 35:** 51.7%. **Area:** 46 sq. mi.. **Employment:** 373,373 employed, 5.8% unemployed; **Per capita income:** $19,592.

Transportation: 1 major airport; intra-city railway system; 2 railway transit systems; bus and railroad service; ferry system; 1 underwater tunnel. **Communications:** 7 TV stations; 27 radio stations. **Medical facilities:** 23 hospitals; 1 major medical center. **Educational facilities:** 4 universities and colleges; major public library system. **Further information:** Chamber of Commerce, 465 California Street, San Francisco, CA 94104.

San Jose, California

Population: 686,178; **Pop. density:** 3,984 per sq. mi.; **Pop. growth:** 36.9%; **Pop. over 65:** 6.2%; **Pop. under 35:** 64.7%. **Area:** 158 sq. mi.. **Employment:** 349,367 employed, 7.1% unemployed; **Per capita income:** $17,577.

Transportation: 1 international airport; 2 railroads; bus system. **Communications:** 4 TV stations; 14 radio stations. **Medical facilities:** 6 hospitals. **Educational facilities:** 3 universities and colleges; major public library system. **Further information:** Chamber of Commerce, One Paseo de San Antonio, San Jose, CA 95113.

Santa Ana, California

Population: 225,405; **Pop. density:** 7,544 per sq. mi.; **Pop. growth:** 30.8%; **Pop. over 65:** 7.4%; **Pop. under 35:** 66.9%. **Area:** 27 sq. mi.. **Employment:** 120,600 employed, 5.4% unemployed (county); **Per capita income:** $16,877.

Transportation: John Wayne airport; 5 major freeways including main Los Angeles-San Diego artery; Amtrak. **Communications:** $27 mln. installation of CATV system. **Medical facilities:** 4 hospitals with 561 beds. **Educational facilities:** 1 university, 1 community college. **Further information:** Chamber of Commerce, 600 W. Santa Ana Blvd., P.O. Box 205, Santa Ana, CA 92702.

Seattle, Washington

Population: 488,474; **Pop. density:** 5,879 per sq. mi.; **Pop. growth:** −7.0%; **Pop. over 65:** 15.4%; **Pop. under 35:** 54.9%. **Area:** 84 sq. mi.. **Employment:** 284,245 employed, 7.1% unemployed; **Per capita income:** $14,787.

Transportation: 1 international airport; 3 railroads; ferries serve Puget Sound, Alaska, Canada. **Communications:** 7 TV, 23 AM & 19 FM radio stations. **Medical facilities:** 27 hospitals. **Educational facilities:** 4 colleges; 11 community colleges. **Further information:** Chamber of Commerce, 215 Columbia St., Seattle, WA 98104.

Shreveport, Louisiana

Population: 219,996; **Pop. density:** 2,572 per sq. mi.; **Pop. growth:** 13%; **Pop. over 65:** 11.7%; **Pop. under 35:** 59.4%. **Area:** 80 sq. mi.. **Employment:** 89,241 employed, 13.9% unemployed; **Per capita income:** $11,627.

Transportation: 6 air lines service Shreveport Regional airport; 2 bus lines. **Communications:** 4 TV, 17 radio stations; CATV. **Medical facilities:** 11 hospitals with over 3,000 beds. **Educational facilities:** La. Tech., Northwestern St., and Grambling univs.; Centenary Coll., Bossier Parish Comm. College, Louisiana St. Univ. **Further information:** Chamber of Commerce, P.O. Box 20074, Shreveport, LA 71120.

Spokane, Washington

Population: 173,349; **Pop. density:** 3,313 per sq. mi.; **Pop. growth:** .5; **Pop. over 65:** 15.3%; **Pop. under 35:** 59.2%. **Area:** 52 sq. mi. **Employment:** 75,173 employed, 9.8% unemployed; **Per capita income:** $11,220.

Transportation: 1 international airport with 9 airlines; 2 railroads; bus system. **Communications:** 8 TV and 17 radio stations. **Medical facilities:** 6 major hospitals. **Educational facilities:** 8 colleges and universities; 14 public school districts, 11 high schools. **Further information:** Chamber of Commerce, W. 1020 Riverside Ave., P.O. Box 2147, Spokane, WA 99210.

Stockton, California

Population: 171,659; **Pop. density:** 3,744 per sq. mi.; **Pop. growth:** 36.2%; **Pop. over 65:** 11.0%; **Pop. under 35:** 58.0%. **Area:** 40 sq. mi. **Employment:** 67,850 employed, 13.3% unemployed; **Per capita income:** $11,392.

Transportation: 1 airport, 2 airlines; 7 railroads; 2 bus lines, city bus system. **Communications:** 5 TV stations. **Medical facilities:** 4 hospitals; regional burn center. **Educational facilities:** 45 public schools; 4 colleges and universities. **Further information:** Chamber of Commerce, 445 W. Weber Ave., Suite 220, Stockton, CA 95203.

Syracuse, New York

Population: 164,219; **Pop. density:** 7,147 per sq. mi.; **Pop. growth:** −13.8%; **Pop. over 65:** 14.6%; **Pop. under 35:** 58.9%. **Area:** 24 sq. mi. **Employment:** 76,727 employed, 7.3% unemployed; **Per capita income:** $12,497.

Transportation: 1 airport, 10 airlines; 5 bus lines; Amtrak, Conrail. **Communications:** 3 TV stations; 17 radio stations. **Medical facilities:** 7 hospitals. **Educational facilities:** 37 public schools; 5 colleges and universities; Syracuse Univ. **Further information:** Chamber of Commerce, 100 E. Onondaga St., Syracuse, NY 13202.

Tampa, Florida

Population: 275,479; **Pop. density:** 3,232 per sq. mi.; **Pop. growth:** −2.2%; **Pop. over 65:** 14.8%; **Pop. under 35:** 54%. **Area:** 84 sq. mi.. **Employment:** 160,445 employed, 6.5% unemployed; **Per capita income:** $12,662.

Transportation: 1 international airport; Port of Tampa, 140 steamship lines; 2 bus lines. **Communications:** 7 TV, 27 radio stations. **Medical facilities:** 19 hospitals. **Educational facilities:** 131 public schools; 4 colleges and universities. **Further information:** Chamber of Commerce, 801 E. Kennedy Blvd., P.O. Box 420, Tampa, FL 33601.

Toledo, Ohio

Population: 343,939; **Pop. density:** 4,221 per sq. mi.; **Pop. growth:** −7.4%; **Pop. over 65:** 12.5%; **Pop. under 35:** 58.5%. **Area:** 84 sq. mi.. **Employment:** 155,162 employed, 9.4% unemployed; **Per capita income:** $12,629.

Transportation: 10 major airlines; 9 railroads; 100 motor freight lines; 2 interstate bus lines. **Communications:** 5 TV, 17 radio stations; 4 cablevision company. **Medical facilities:** 9 major hospital complexes. **Educational facilities:** 7 colleges and universities. **Further information:** Office of Tourism and Conventions, 218 Huron, Toledo, OH 43604.

Tucson, Arizona

Population: 365,422; **Pop. density:** 3,338 per sq. mi.; **Pop. growth:** 25.7%; **Pop. over 65:** 11.7%; **Pop. under 35:** 60.7%. **Area:** 99 sq. mi.. **Employment:** 186,709 employed, 6.7% unemployed; **Per capita income:** $11,626.

Transportation: 1 international airport; 3 railroads; bus system. **Communications:** 7 TV, 23 radio stations. **Medical facilities:** 12 hospitals. **Educational facilities:** 1 university, 1 college; 157 public schools. **Further information:** Chamber of Commerce, P.O. Box 991, Tucson, AZ 85702.

Tulsa, Oklahoma

Population: 374,535; **Pop. density:** 1,940 per sq. mi.; **Pop. growth:** 9.3%; **Pop. over 65:** 10.8%; **Pop. under 35:** 58.1%. **Area:** 185.6 sq. mi.. **Employment:** 186,126 employed, 8.3% unemployed; **Per capita income:** $12,962.

Transportation: 1 international airport; 4 rail lines; 2 regional bus lines, 2 national bus lines. **Communications:** 7 TV, 21 radio stations. **Medical facilities:** 6 hospitals. **Educational facilities:** 89 public schools; 6 colleges and universities. **Further information:** Chamber of Commerce, 616 S. Boston Ave., Tulsa, OK 74119.

Virginia Beach, Virginia

Population: 308,664; **Pop. density:** 1,028 per sq. mi.; **Pop. growth:** 52.3%; **Pop. over 65:** 4.5%; **Pop. under 35:** 66.0%. **Area:** 255 sq. mi.. **Employment:** 138,442 employed, 3.6% unemployed; **Per capita income:** $12,177.

Transportation: 10 airlines serve Norfolk/Virginia Beach Airport; Greyhound, Trailways buses. **Communications:** 6 TV, 39 radio stations. **Medical facilities:** 2 hospitals. **Educational facilities:** 59 public schools; 1 university. **Further information:** Chamber of Commerce, 4512 Virginia Beach Blvd., Virginia Beach, VA 23462.

Washington, District of Columbia

Population: 622,823; **Pop. density:** 10,121 per sq. mi.; **Pop. growth:** −15.7%; **Pop. over 65:** 11.6%; **Pop. under 35:** 56.9%. **Area:** 63 sq. mi.. **Employment:** 300,623 employed, 8.0% unemployed; **Per capita income:** $17,724.

Transportation: 2 airports; rail transit system; extensive local bus service; long distance rail and bus service. **Communications:** 8 TV stations; 40 radio stations. **Medical facilities:** 43 hospitals; major medical research center. **Educational facilities:** 6 universities and colleges; 24 public libraries. **Further information:** Convention and Visitors Association, 1575 I Street NW, Suite 250, Washington, DC 20005.

Wichita, Kansas

Population: 283,496; **Pop. density:** 2,765 per sq. mi.; **Pop. growth:** 1.0%; **Pop. over 65:** 10.6%; **Pop. under 35:** 59.9%. **Area:** 101 sq. mi.. **Employment:** 144,571 employed, 7.0% unemployed; **Per capita income:** $14,173.

Transportation: 1 airport; 4 major rail freight lines; 2 bus lines. **Communications:** 5 TV stations; 16 radio stations. **Medical facilities:** 5 hospitals; speech & hearing rehabilitation center. **Educational facilities:** 101 public schools; Wichita St. Univ.; Butler County Comm. College. **Further information:** Chamber of Commerce, 350 W. Douglas, Wichita, KS 67202.

Worcester, Massachusetts

Population: 159,843; **Pop. density:** 4,326 per sq. mi.; **Pop. growth:** −8.4%; **Pop. over 65:** 16.3%; **Pop. under 35:** 54.6%. **Area:** 37 sq. mi. **Employment:** 76,148 employed, 4.4% unemployed; **Per capita income:** $12,640.

Transportation: 1 airport, 3 airlines; 4 railroads; 5 bus lines, city bus system. **Communications:** 1 local TV station; 10 radio stations. **Medical facilities:** 19 hospitals, including Univ. of Mass. Medical School and Teaching Hospital. **Educational facilities:** 193 public schools; 9 colleges and universities; 3 junior colleges. **Further information:** Chamber of Commerce, 350 Mechanics Tower, Worcester, MA 01608.

Yonkers, New York

Population: 191,234; **Pop. density:** 10,852 per sq. mi.; **Pop. growth:** −4%. **Pop. over 65:** 14.8%. **Area:** 18 sq. mi.. **Employment:** 101,630 employed, 4.2% unemployed; **Per capita income:** $15,076.

Transportation: intracity bus system; rail service. **Communications:** see New York City. **Medical facilities:** St. Joseph's Medical Center, St. John's Riverside Hospital, Yonkers General Hospital. **Educational facilities:** Elizabeth Seton, Mercy, Sarah Lawrence colleges. **Further information:** Chamber of Commerce, 480 N. Broadway, Yonkers, NY 10701.

Projected Job Growth in Metropolitan Areas: 1985-2000

Source: National Planning Association

Following are the top 30 metro area for employment growth:

City	Year 2000 job totals	1985-2000 increase
Los Angeles	5,306,000	1,032,000
Boston	3,056,800	754,700
Anaheim	1,849,900	701,500
San Jose	1,453,600	539,200
Phoenix	1,453,700	537,000
Washington	2,622,100	509,000
Houston	2,191,500	497,700
Chicago	3,627,700	493,500
Dallas	1,853,700	485,000
Atlanta	1,875,900	462,700
San Diego	1,438,200	422,400
Tampa	1,245,400	421,500
Philadelphia	2,700,000	406,100
New York	4,700,800	383,600
San Francisco	1,435,700	360,400
Denver	1,283,700	354,800

City	Year 2000 job Totals	1985-2000 increase
Minneapolis-St. Paul	1,652,800	352,000
Detroit	2,177,300	328,500
Nassau-Suffolk, NY	1,498,500	318,500
Orlando	773,700	308,600
Fort Lauderdale	796,400	299,400
Miami	1,198,400	284,100
Oakland	1,149,000	277,700
Seattle	1,202,500	268,400
Baltimore	1,445,800	249,000
Middlesex Cty., NJ	736,000	206,100
Riverside, CA	816,500	200,500
West Palm Beach	534,200	196,400
Newark	1,232,300	195,300
Hartford	844,800	190,200
United States	**140.1 mil.**	**26.1 mil**

Urban Revival

Los Angeles will grow to be the nation's most populous metropolitan area by the turn of the century. A study by the Bureau of Economic Analysis projects that the population in the Los Angeles metropolitan area will grow to 8,870,000 by the year 2000. New York, currently the largest metro area, is expected to have 8,433,000 at that time. The analysis projects growth of 13.5 percent in Los Angeles from 1983 to 2000, and 1.7 percent for New York.

The nation's five largest metropolitan areas in 2000 are expected to be Los Angeles, New York, Chicago, 6,131,000; Philadelphia, 4,914,000; and Boston, 4,301,000.

New figures contained in a draft verson of the Census Bureau's geographical mobility report for 1984, which measures permanent moves in the country in the previous 12 months, show that 2.6 million people moved from nonmetropolitan to metropolitan areas between March 1983 and March 1984, while 2.3 million moved the other way, resulting in a net loss to the rural areas of 351,000 people. In 1975, in contrast, the rural areas showed a net gain of 1.6 million.

Spending by Cities

A 1987 Census Bureau study said city governments averaged $781.34 in general revenue per resident and spent $720.13 per resident in the fiscal year 1985, the most recent period for which detailed figures were available.

Of the general revenue average, $537.06 came from such sources as taxes and fees, with the rest coming from the state and Federal governments.

The total revenues collected by the nation's cities in the period was $147.8 billion, up 9.9 percent from the previous fiscal year. Total spending was $140 billion, up 8.8 percent.

Cities' taxes raised $324.78 per resident, while $112.57 per resident came from fees and charges and $99.71 from miscellaneous sources. Aid from the state and federal governments amounted to $244.28 per resident.

The average city spends $85.71 annually per resident for police protection, the largest continuing item in city budgets. Among other major items were education, $77.93 per resident; general administration, $77.20; highways, $59.36; sewarage, $51.78; fire protection, $46.34; public welfare, $39.28; housing and community development, $34.76; hospitals, $34.17; parks and recreation, $34.03; and sanitation other than sewerage, $26.24.

Leading Convention Cities, 1986

Source: *Advertising Age*

City	Number of conventions[1]	Number of hotel rooms[2]
1. Dallas	2,090	37,601
2. Atlanta	1,470	35,000
3. New Orleans	1,000	26,000
4. New York	971	100,000[3]
5. San Antonio	954	16,000
6. Washington	857	47,000
7. Sacramento	856	2,500
8. St. Louis	782	20,000
9. Houston	727	36,000
10. Chicago	690	40,000

(1) Convention figures represent those held within city limits of city convention bureau designations. (2) Within 30-minute drive of downtown. (3) Within city.

Washington, Capital of the U.S.

Arlington National Cemetery

Arlington National Cemetery, on the former Custis estate in Virginia, is the site of the **Tomb of the Unknown Soldier** and the final resting place of John Fitzgerald Kennedy, president of the United States, who was buried there Nov. 25, 1963. A torch burns day and night over his grave. The remains of his brother Sen. Robert F. Kennedy (N.Y.) were interred on June 8, 1968, in an area adjacent. Many other famous Americans are also buried at Arlington, as well as 175,000 American soldiers from every major war.

Arlington House, The Robert E. Lee Memorial

On a hilltop above the cemetery, stands Arlington House, the Robert E. Lee Memorial, which from 1955 to 1972 was officially called the Custis-Lee Mansion.

U.S. Marine Corps War Memorial (Iwo Jima)

North of the National Cemetery, approximately 350 yards, stands the bronze statue of the raising of the United States flag on Mt. Suribachi during WWII, executed by Felix de Weldon from the photograph by Joe Rosenthal, and presented to the nation by members and friends of the U.S. Marine Corps.

Vietnam War Memorial

On November 13, 1982, a memorial was dedicated to the American soldiers killed or missing during the Vietnam War. It is located near the Lincoln Memorial and the Washingtom Monument.

The Capitol

The United States Capitol was originally designed by Dr. William Thornton, an amateur architect, who submitted a plan in the spring of 1793 that won him $500 and a city lot.

The south, or House wing, was completed in 1807 under the direction of Benjamin H. Latrobe.

The present Senate and House wings and the iron dome were designed and constructed by Thomas U. Walter, the 4th architect of the Capitol, between 1851-1863.

The present cast iron dome at its greatest exterior measures 135 ft. 5 in., and it is topped by the bronze Statue of Freedom that stands 19½ ft. and weighs 14,985 pounds. On its base are the words "E Pluribus Unum" (Out of Many One).

The Capitol is normally open from 9 a.m. to 4:30 p.m. Tours through the Capitol, including the House and Senate galleries, are conducted from 9 a.m. to 4 p.m. without charge.

Folger Shakespeare Library

The **Folger Shakespeare Library** on Capitol Hill, Washington, D. C., is a research institution devoted to the advancement of learning in the background of Anglo-American civilization in the 16th and 17th centuries, and in most aspects of the continental Renaissance. It has the largest collection of Shakespeareana in the world, with 79 copies of the First Folio.

Library of Congress

Established by and for Congress in 1800, the Library of Congress has extended its services over the years to other government agencies and other libraries, to scholars, and to the general public, and it now serves as the national library. It contains over 80 million items in 470 languages.

The library's exhibit halls are open to the public. Guided tours are given every hour from 9 a.m. through 4 p.m. Monday through Friday.

Thomas Jefferson Memorial

Dedicated in 1943, **The Thomas Jefferson Memorial** stands on the south shore of the Tidal Basin in West Potomac park. It is a circular stone structure, with Vermont marble on the exterior and Georgia white marble inside and combines architectural elements of the dome of the Pantheon in Rome and the rotunda designed by Jefferson for the University of Virginia.

The memorial is open daily from 8 a.m. to midnight. An elevator and curb ramps for the handicapped are in service.

Lincoln Memorial

The Lincoln Memorial in West Potomac Park, on the axis of the Capitol and the Washington Monument, consists of a large marble hall enclosing a heroic statue of Abraham Lincoln in meditation sitting on a large armchair. It was dedicated on Memorial Day, May 30, 1922. The Memorial was designed by Henry Bacon. The statue was made by Daniel Chester French and sculpted by the Piccirilli family. Murals and ornamentation on the bronze ceiling beams are by Jules Guerin.

The memorial is open daily from 8 a.m. to midnight. An elevator for the handicapped is in service.

John F. Kennedy Center

John F. Kennedy Center for the Performing Arts, designated by Congress as the National Cultural Center and the official memorial in Washington to President Kennedy, opened September 8, 1971. Tours are available daily between 10:00 a.m. and 1:00 p.m.

Mount Vernon

Mount Vernon on the south bank of the Potomac R., 16 miles below Washington, D. C., is part of a large tract of land in northern Virginia which was originally included in a royal grant made to Lord Culpepper, who in 1674 granted 5,000 acres to Nicholas Spencer and John Washington.

The present house is an enlargement of one apparently built on the site of an earlier one by John's grandson, Augustine Washington, who lived there 1735-1738. His son Lawrence came there in 1743, when he renamed the plantation Mount Vernon in honor of Admiral Vernon under whom he had served in the West Indies. Lawrence Washington died in 1752 and was succeeded as proprietor of Mount Vernon by his half-brother, George Washington.

National Arboretum

The National Arboretum, one of Washington's great showplaces, occupies 444 acres in the northeastern section of the city. The National Herb Garden and National Bonsai Collection are special attractions in the nation's only federally-supported gardens.

The Arboretum is open every day of the year except Christmas.

National Archives

The Declaration of Independence, the Constitution of the United States, and the Bill of Rights are on permanent display in the National Archives Exhibition Hall. They are sealed in glass-and-bronze cases. The National Archives also holds the permanently valuable federal records of the United States government.

National Gallery of Art

The National Gallery of Art, situated in an area bounded by Constitution Avenue and the Mall, between Third and Seventh Streets, was established by Joint Resolution of Congress Mar. 24, 1937, and opened Mar. 17, 1941.

Normally open daily from 10 a.m. to 5 p.m.; noon to 9 p.m. Sunday. Summer, 10 a.m. to 9 p.m., noon to 9 p.m. on Sunday.

The Pentagon

The Pentagon, headquarters of the Department of Defense, is one of the world's largest office buildings. Situated in Arlington, Va., it houses more than 23,000 employees in offices that occupy 3,707,745 square feet.

Tours are available Monday through Friday (excluding federal holidays), from 9 a.m. to 3:30 p.m.

Smithsonian Institution

The Smithsonian Institution is one of the world's great historical, scientific, educational, and cultural establishments. It is comprised of 13 museums and the National Zoo.

Washington Monument

The Washington Monument is a tapering shaft or obelisk of white marble, 555 ft., 5-⅛ inches in height and 55 ft., 1-½ inches square at base. Eight small windows, 2 on each side, are located at the 500-ft. level, where points of interest are indicated.

Open daily 9 a.m. to 5 p.m., 8 a.m. to 12 p.m. in summer.

The White House

The White House, the president's residence, stands on 18 acres on the south side of Pennsylvania Avenue, between the Treasury and the Executive Office Building.

The walls are of sandstone, quarried at Aquia Creek, Va. The exterior walls were painted, causing the building to be termed the "White House." On Aug. 24, 1814, during Madison's administration, the house was burned by the British. James Hoban rebuilt it by Oct. 1817.

The White House is normally open from 10 a.m. to 12 noon, Tuesday through Saturday, Jun. 1 through Labor Day, and 8 a.m. to noon. Only the public rooms on the ground floor and state floor may be visited.

Notable Tall Buildings in North American Cities

Height from sidewalk to roof, including penthouse and tower if enclosed as integral part of structure; actual number of stories beginning at street level. Asterisks (*) denote buildings still under construction Jan. 1988.

City	Hgt. ft.	Stories
Akron, Oh.		
First National Tower	330	28
National City Center	301	23
Albany, N.Y.		
Erastus Corning II Tower	589	44
State Office Building	388	34
Agency (4 bldgs.), So. Mall	310	23
Atlanta, Ga.		
*IBM Tower, 1179 W. Peachtree	813	50
Westin Peachtree Plaza	723	71
Georgia Pacific Tower	697	51
Southern Bell Telephone	677	47
First National Bank, 2 Peachtree	556	44
Marriott Marquis	554	52
*Concourse Tower, 1001 Hammond Dr.	534	34
Equitable Building, 100 Peachtree	453	34
101 Marietta Tower, 101 Marietta St.	446	36
Atlanta Center	443	35
Park Place, 2660 Peachtree	420	04
National Bank of Georgia	409	32
Peachtree Summit No. 1	406	31
North Avenue Tower, 310 North Ave.	403	26
Tower Place, 3361 Piedmont Road	401	29
Peachtree Place, 999 Peachtree	396	30
Richard B. Russell, Federal Bldg.	383	26
Atlanta Hilton Hotel	383	32
Peachtree Center, Harris Bldg.	382	31
AT&T Long Line Bldg.	380	...
Marquis One	378	30
Marquis Two, 275 Peachtree	378	30
Trust Company Bank	377	28
Coastal States Insurance	377	27
Peachtree Center Cain Building	376	30
Peachtree Center Building	374	31
One Georgia Center	371	29
The Campanile, 1145 Peachtree	367	25
*Resurgence Plaza	356	25
Georgia Power Tower, 333 Piedmont	349	24
Austin, Tex.		
One American Center	395	32
One Congress Plaza	391	30
Interfirst Bank	328	26
M Bank	313	21
State Capitol	309	...
Univ. of Texas Admin. Bldg.	307	29
Baltimore, Md.		
U.S. Fidelity & Guaranty Co.	529	40
Maryland National Bank Bldg.	509	34
6 St. Paul Place	493	37
World Trade Center Bldg.	395	32
Tremont Plaza Hotel	395	37
250 W. Pratt St.	360	26
Harbor Court	356	28
Blaustein Bldg.	342	30
Union Trust Tower	335	24
Central Savings Bank Bldg.	330	28
Charles Center South	330	26
Baton Rouge, La.		
State Capitol	460	34
American Bank Bldg.	315	24
Birmingham, Ala.		
South Trust Towers	454	34
First Natl. Southern Natural Bldg.	390	30
South Central Bell Hdqts. Bldg.	390	30
City Federal Bldg.	325	27
Boston, Mass.		
John Hancock Tower	790	60
Prudential Tower	750	52
Boston Co. Bldg., Court St.	605	41
Federal Reserve Bldg.	604	32
International Place, 100 Oliver St.	600	46
First National Bank of Boston	591	37
One Financial Center	590	46
Shawmut Bank Bldg.	520	38
Exchange Place, 53 State St.	510	39
Sixty State St.	509	38

City	Hgt. ft.	Stories
One Post Office Sq.	507	40
One Beacon St.	507	40
New England Merch. Bank Bldg.	500	40
U.S. Custom House	496	32
John Hancock Bldg.	495	26
State St. Bank Bldg.	477	34
One Hundred Summer St.	450	33
McCormack Bldg.	401	22
Keystone Custodian Funds	400	32
Saltonstall Office Bldg.	396	22
Devonshire, 250 Wash. St.	396	40
Harbor Towers (2 bldgs.)	396	40
Westin Hotel, Copley Place	395	36
John F. Kennedy Bldg.	387	24
Marriott Hotel, Copley Place	383	39
Longfellow Towers (2 bldgs.)	380	38
*75/101 Federal St.	365	31
Buffalo, N.Y.		
Marine Midland Center	529	40
City Hall	378	32
Rand Bldg., not incl. 40-ft. beacon	351	29
Main Place Tower	350	26
One M&T Plaza	317	21
Calgary, Alta.		
Petro-Canada Tower #2	689	52
Calgary Tower	626	...
First Canadian Centre	547	44
Scotia Centre	504	38
Nova Bldg., 801 7th Ave. SW	500	37
Petro-Canada Tower #1	469	33
Two Bow Valley Square	468	39
Fifth & Fifth Bldg.	460	35
Oxford Square North	463	34
Shell Tower	460	34
Oxford Square South	449	33
Four Bow Valley Square	441	37
Esso Plaza (twin towers)	435	34
Cascade 300	432	31
T.D. Square	421	33
Family Life Bldg.	410	33
Pan Canadian Bldg., 150 9th Ave. SW	410	28
Norcen Tower	408	33
Sun Oil Bldg.	397	34
Western Centre	385	40
Three Bow Valley Square	382	33
Sun Life Bldg. (twin towers)	374	28
Charlotte, N.C.		
One First Union Center	580	42
NCNB Plaza	503	40
Two First Union Center	433	32
Wachovia Center	420	32
Charlotte Plaza	388	27
Citizens Plaza	320	23
Southern National Center	300	22
Chicago, Ill.		
Sears Tower (world's tallest)	1,454	110
Amoco	1,136	80
John Hancock Center	1,127	100
Water Tower Place (a)	859	74
First Natl. Bank	852	60
Three First National Plaza	775	57
Olympia Centre	727	63
IBM Plaza	695	52
One Magnificent Mile	673	58
Daley Center	662	31
1,000 Lake Shore Plaza	648	55
Lake Point Tower	645	70
Board of Trade, incl. 81 ft. statue	605	44
Prudential Bldg., 130 E. Randolph	601	41
Antenna tower, 311 ft., makes total	912	...
Huron Apts.	599	56
Marina City Apts., 2 buildings	588	61
Mid Continental Plaza, 55 E. Monroe	580	50
Pittsfield, 55 E. Washington St.	557	38
Kemper Insurance Bldg.	555	45

City	Hgt. ft.	Stories
Newberry Plaza, State & Oak	553	56
One South Wacker Dr.	550	40
Harbor Point	550	54
LaSalle Natl. Bank, 135 S. LaSalle St.	535	44
One LaSalle Street	530	49
111 E. Chestnut St.	529	56
River Plaza, Rush & Hubbard	524	56
Pure Oil, 35 E. Wacker Drive	523	40
United Ins. Bldg., 1 E. Wacker Dr.	522	41
Lincoln Tower, 75 E. Wacker Dr.	519	42
Carbide & Carbon, 230 N. Mich.	503	37
Walton Colonnade	500	44
LaSalle-Wacker, 221 N. LaSalle St.	491	41
Amer. Nat'l. Bank, 33 N. LaSalle St.	479	40
Bankers, 105 W. Adams St.	476	41
Brunswick Bldg.	475	37
Continental Companies	475	45
American Furniture Mart	474	24
333 Wacker Dr.	472	36
Sheraton Hotel, 505 N. Mich. Ave.	471	42
Playboy Bldg., 919 N. Mich. Ave.	468	37
188 Randolph Tower	465	45
Tribune Tower, 435 N. Mich. Ave.	462	36
Chicago Marriott, Mich. & Ohio Sts.	460	45

(a) World's tallest reinforced concrete bldg.

Cincinnati, Oh.

City	Hgt. ft.	Stories
Carew Tower	568	49
Central Trust Tower	504	33
Dubois Tower, 5th & Walnut	423	32
Netherland Plaza	372	31
Central Trust Center	355	27
Atrium Two	350	30
First Natl. Bank Center	351	26
Clarion North Tower	350	33
Cinn. Commerce Center	346	29
Kroger Bldg.	320	25

Cleveland, Oh.

City	Hgt. ft.	Stories
Terminal Tower	708	52
Sohio Tower	650	46
Erieview Plaza Tower	529	40
One Cleveland Center	450	31
Justice Center, 1250 Ontario	420	26
Federal Bldg.	419	32
National City Complex	410	35
Cleveland Trust Tower No. 1	383	29
Eaton Center	360	28
Ohio-Bell Hqs.	360	22

Columbus, Oh.

City	Hgt. ft.	Stories
James A. Rhodes (State Office Tower)	624	41
LeVeque Tower, 50 W. Broad	555	47
Huntington Center, 41 S. High St.	512	37
*Gilmore-Riffe Bldg	503	32
One Nationwide Plaza	485	40
One Riverside Plaza	456	31
Borden Bldg., 180 E. Broad	438	34
One Columbus	366	26
Columbus Center, 100 E. Broad	357	24
Capitol Square	348	26
Ohio Bell Bldg., 150 E. Gay St.	346	26

Dallas, Tex.

City	Hgt. ft.	Stories
Interfirst Plaza, 901 Main St.	939	73
First International Bldg.	710	56
LTV Center	686	50
Arco Tower, 1601 Bryan St.	660	49
Thanksgiving Tower, 1600 Pacific Ave.	645	50
Two Dallas Centre	635	50
First National Bank	625	52
Republic Bank Tower	598	50
First City Center, 1700 Pacific Ave.	595	49
SW Bell Admin. Tower	580	37
One Lincoln Plaza	579	45
Olympia York, 1999 Bryan St.	562	37
Reunion Tower	560	50
Southland Life Tower	550	42
Diamond Shamrock, 717 N. Harwood St.	550	34
2001 Bryan St.	512	40
San Jacinto Tower	456	33
Republic Bank Bldg., not incl. 150-ft. ornamental tower	452	36
Wyndham Hotel	451	29
One Main Place	445	34
LTV Tower	434	31
Mercantile Natl. Bank Bldg., not incl. 115-ft. weather beacon	430	31
Mobil Bldg.	430	31
Mart Hotel	400	29
Fidelity Union Tower	400	33
One Dallas Centre	386	30
Southwestern Bell Toll Bldg.	372	22

Dayton, Oh.

City	Hgt. ft.	Stories
Kettering Tower, 2d & Main	405	30
Mead World Hqtrs, 10 W. 2d St.	365	28
Centre City Office Bldg, 40 S. Main St.	297	20

Denver, Col.

City	Hgt. ft.	Stories
Republic Plaza	714	56
Mountain Bell Center	706	54
United Bank of Denver	697	52
1999 Broadway	544	43
Arco Tower	527	41
Anaconda Tower	507	40
Tabor Center, #2	493	39
One Denver Place	467	35
Amoco Bldg., 17th Ave. & Broadway	450	36
17th Street Plaza	438	34
Brooks Towers, 1020 15th St.	420	42
Mellon Financial Center	415	32
Stellar Plaza	410	32
Tabor Center, #1	405	32
Energy Center 1	404	29
Colorado Nat'l. Bank, 17th & Curtis	389	26
First National Bank	385	28
Security National Bank	384	33
Centennial Plaza	374	31
Dominion Plaza	368	30
Lincoln Center	366	30
Denver Natl. Bank Plaza	363	29
Western Fed. Savings	357	27
Colorado State Bank	352	26

Des Moines, Ia.

City	Hgt. ft.	Stories
Ruan Center	457	36
Financial Center, 7th & Walnut	345	25
Marriott Hotel, 700 Grand Ave.	340	33
Plaza, 3d & Walnut	340	25
Hub Tower, 7th & Walnut	320	20

Detroit, Mich.

City	Hgt. ft.	Stories
Westin Hotel	720	71
Penobscot Bldg.	557	47
15000 Town Center Dr.	554	40
Guardian	485	40
Renaissance Center (4 bldgs.)	479	39
Book Tower	472	35
Prudential Town Center	448	32
13000 Town Center Dr.	443	32
Cadillac Tower	437	40
David Stott	436	38
Mich. Cons. Gas Co. Bldg.	430	32
Fisher	420	28
J. L. Hudson Bldg.	397	28
McNamara Federal Office Bldg.	393	27
American Center	374	27
Top of Troy Bldg.	374	27
Comerica Bldg., 211 N. Fort	370	28
Edison Plaza	365	25
Woodward Tower at the Park	358	34
Buhl, 535 Griswold	350	26
Ford Bldg.	346	25
Michigan Bell Telephone	340	19

Edmonton, Alta.

City	Hgt. ft.	Stories
Manulife Place, 10170-101 St.	479	39
Royal Trust Tower	476	30
AGT Tower, 10020-100 St.	441	34
CCB Tower, 10124-103 Ave.	410	34
Principal Plaza, 10303 Jasper Ave.	370	30
Scotia Place, 10060 Jasper Ave.	366	30
CN Tower, 1004-104 Ave.	365	26
Phipps McKinnon	359	21

Fort Wayne, Ind.

City	Hgt. ft.	Stories
One Summit Square, 911 S. Calhoun	442	27
Ft. Wayne Natl. Bank	339	26
Lincoln Bank Tower	312	23

Fort Worth, Tex.

City	Hgt. ft.	Stories
City Center Tower II	546	38
1st United Tower	536	40

City	Hgt. ft.	Stories
Continental Plaza	525	40
1st City Bank Tower	475	33
Texas American Bank	454	37
Texas Bldg.	380	30
Continental Life	307	24

Hamilton, Ont.

City	Hgt. ft.	Stories
Century Twenty One	418	43
Stelco Tower	339	25

Harrisburg, Pa.

City	Hgt. ft.	Stories
State Office Tower #2	334	21
333 Market St. (incl. tower)	327	19

Hartford, Conn.

City	Hgt. ft.	Stories
City Place	535	38
Travelers Ins. Co. Bldg.	527	34
Hartford Plaza	420	22
Hartford Natl. Bank & Trust	360	26
One Commercial Plaza	349	27
Bushnell Tower	349	27
One Financial Plaza, 755 Main	335	26

Honolulu, Hi.

City	Hgt. ft.	Stories
Ala Moana Americana Hotel	396	38
Pacific Tower	350	30
Franklin Towers	350	41
Honolulu Tower	350	40
Discovery Bay	350	42
Hyatt Regency Waikiki	350	39
Maile Court Hotel	350	43
Regency Tower, 2525 Date St.	350	42
Pearlridge Square	350	43
Yacht Harbor Towers	350	40
Canterbury Place	350	40
Royal Iolani	350	38
Island Colony	350	44
Century Center	350	41
Pacific Beach Hotel	350	43
Hawaiian Monarch Hotel	350	43
Waikiki Hobron	350	43
Honolulu Tower 2	350	40
Tapa Tower, 2005 Kalia Rd.	350	36
Executive Center, 1088 Bishop St.	350	41
1001 Bishop	350	28

Houston, Tex.

City	Hgt. ft.	Stories
Texas Commerce Tower	1,002	75
Allied Bank Plaza, 1000 Louisiana	985	71
Transco Tower	899	64
RepublicBank Center	780	56
Heritage Plaza, 1111 Bagby	762	53
InterFirst Plaza	744	55
1600 Smith St.	729	54
Gulf Tower, 1301 McKinney	725	52
One Shell Plaza (not incl. 285 ft. TV tower)	714	50
Four Allen Center	692	50
Capital Natl. Bank Plaza	685	50
One Houston Center	678	47
First City Tower	662	47
1100 Milam Bldg.	651	47
San Felipe Plaza	620	45
Exxon Bldg.	606	44
The America Tower	577	42
Marathon Oil Tower	572	41
Two Houston Center	570	40
Dresser Tower	550	40
1415 Louisiana Tower	550	44
Pennzoil, 700 Milam (2 bldgs.)	523	36
Two Allen Center	521	36
Entex Bldg.	518	35
Huntington	506	34
Tenneco Bldg.	502	33
Conoco Tower	465	32
One Allen Center	452	34
Summit Tower West	441	31
Coastal Tower	441	31
Four Leafs Towers (2 bldgs.)	439	40
Phoenix Tower	434	34
Gulf Bldg.	428	37
The Spires	426	41
Central Tower (4 Oaks Place)	420	30
First City Natl. Bank	410	32
Houston Lighting & Power	410	27
Niels Esperson Bldg.	409	31
Hyatt Regency Houston	401	34

Hull, Que.

City	Hgt. ft.	Stories
Les Terrasses De La Chaudiere	383	30
Place Du Portage, Phase 1	333	24

Indianapolis, Ind.

City	Hgt. ft.	Stories
American United Life Ins. Co.	533	38
Indiana Natl. Bank Tower	504	37
City-County Bldg.	377	26
Merchants Plaza/Hyatt Regency Hotel	328	26
Indiana Bell Telephone	320	20

Jacksonville, Fla.

City	Hgt. ft.	Stories
Independent Life & Acccident Ins. Co.	535	37
Gulf Life Ins. Co. Bldg.	432	28

Kansas City, Mo.

City	Hgt. ft.	Stories
One Kansas City Place	626	42
AT&T Town Pavilion	590	38
Hyatt Regency	504	40
Kansas City Power and Light Bldg.	476	32
City Hall	443	29
Federal Office Bldg.	413	35
Commerce Tower	402	32
City Center Sq.	402	30
Southwest Bell Telephone Bldg.	394	27
Pershing Road Associates	352	28

Las Vegas, Nev.

City	Hgt. ft.	Stories
Sundance Hotel	400	33
Landmark Hotel	356	31
Las Vegas Hilton	345	30

Lexington, Ky.

City	Hgt. ft.	Stories
Lexington Financial Center	410	30
Kincaid Tower	333	22

Little Rock, Ark.

City	Hgt. ft.	Stories
Capitol Towers	546	40
First Commercial Bank	454	30
Worthen Bank & Trust	375	24
First South Bldg.	365	25
Tower Bldg.	350	18
Union National Bank	331	21

Los Angeles, Cal.

City	Hgt. ft.	Stories
First Interstate Bank	858	62
Crocker Center, North	750	53
Security Pacific Natl. Bank	735	55
Atlantic Richfield Plaza (2 bldgs.)	699	52
Wells Fargo Bank	625	48
Crocker-Citizen Plaza	620	42
California Plaza	578	42
Century Plaza Towers (2 bldgs.)	571	44
Citycorp Plaza	534	42
Union Bank Square	516	41
MCA-Getty	506	36
Wilshire/Bixel	496	36
Fox Plaza, 2121 Ave. of Stars	492	36
Transpacific Center	459	32
City Hall	454	28
Equitable Life Bldg.	454	34
Transamerica Center	452	32
Mutual Benefit Life Ins. Bldg.	435	31
Broadway Plaza	414	33
1900 Ave. of Stars	398	27
1 Wilshire Bldg.	395	28
The Evian, 10490 Wilshire Blvd.	390	31
Bonaventure Hotel, 404 S. Figueroa	367	35
Beaudry Center	365	26
400 S. Hope St.	375	26
Home Savings Tower	368	25
Cal. Fed. Savings & Loan Bldg.	363	28
*Wilshire-Glendon	363	26
Century City Office Bldg.	363	26
Bunker Hill Towers	349	32
International Industries Plaza	347	24
Biltmore Office Bldg.	340	23
Century City Hotel	340	27

Louisville, Ky.

City	Hgt. ft.	Stories
First Natl. Bank	512	40
Citizen's Plaza	420	30
Humana Bldg.	350	27
Meindinger Tower	338	26
Brown & Williamson Tower	338	26
Galt House	325	25

Memphis, Tenn.

City	Hgt. ft.	Stories
100 N. Main Bldg.	430	37

City	Hgt. ft.	Stories
Commerce Square	396	31
Sterick Bldg.	365	31
Clark, 5100 Poplar	365	32
Morgan Keegan Tower, 50 Front St.	341	23
First Natl. Bank Bldg.	332	25
Hyatt Regency	329	28
Miami, Fla.		
Southeast Financial Center	764	55
Centrust Tower	562	35
Metro-Dade Administration Bldg.	510	30
Edward Ball Bldg.	484	35
One Biscayne Corp.	456	40
Amerifirst Bldg.	375	32
Hotel Inter-Continental Miami	366	35
Venitia, 1635 Bayshore Dr.	365	42
Dade County Court House	357	28
New World Center	340	30
Plaza Venetia	332	33
Concourse Tower	318	25
Milwaukee, Wis.		
First Wis. Center & Office Tower	625	42
*Milwaukee Center	422	28
411 Bldg.	385	30
City Hall	350	9
Hyatt Regency	320	22
Wisconsin Telephone Co.	317	19
Minneapolis, Minn.		
IDS Center	775	57
*Norwest	772	57
Multifoods Tower	668	52
Piper Jaffray Tower	579	42
Pillsbury Center, 200 S. 6th St.	561	42
*Opus, 150 S. 5th	503	36
Plaza VII, 45 S. 7th	475	36
Lincoln Centre, 333 S. 7th	454	32
Foshay Tower, not including 163-ft. antenna tower	447	32
Amfac Hotel	440	32
Northwestern Bell	416	26
Hennepin County Government Center	403	24
First Natl. Bank Bldg.	366	28
100 South Fifth	356	25
Municipal Building	355	14
100 Washington Square	340	22
Cedar-Riverside	337	39
Montreal, Que.		
Place Victoria	624	47
Place Ville Marie	616	42
Canadian Imperial Bank of Commerce	604	43
Le Complexe Desjardins		
La Tour du Sud	498	40
La Tour du L'Est	428	32
La Tour du Nord	355	27
La Tour Laurier	425	36
C.I.L. House	429	32
Chateau Champlain Hotel	420	38
Port Royal Apts.	400	33
Royal Bank Tower	397	22
Sun Life Bldg.	390	26
Banque Canadienne National	390	32
Place du Canada	372	33
Hydro Quebec	360	27
Nashville, Tenn.		
Third National Financial Center	490	30
American General Center	452	31
Landmark Center	409	30
James K. Polk State Office Bldg.	392	32
First American N.A. Bank	354	28
One Nashville Plaza	346	23
Hyatt Regency	300	28
Newark, N.J.		
Natl. Newark & Essex Bldg.	465	36
Raymond-Commerce	448	37
Park Plaza Bldg.	400	26
Prudential Plaza	370	24
Public Service Elec. & Gas	360	26
Prudential Ins. Co., 753 Broad St.	360	26
AT&T Bldg.	359	31
Gateway 1	355	28
American Insurance Company	326	21

City	Hgt. ft.	Stories
New Orleans, La.		
One Shell Square	697	51
Place St. Charles	645	53
Plaza Tower	531	45
Energy Centre	530	39
LL&E Tower, 901 Poydras	481	36
Sheraton Hotel	478	47
Marriott Hotel	450	42
Texaco Bldg.	442	33
Canal Place One	439	32
1010 Common	438	31
Int'l. Trade Mart Bldg.	407	33
225 Baronne St.	362	28
One Poydras Plaza	360	28
Hyatt-Regency Hotel, Poydras Plaza	360	25
Hibernia Bank Bldg.	355	23
1250 Poydras Plaza	341	24
1515 Poydras	340	27
New Orleans Hilton	340	27
American Bank Bldg.	330	23
New York, N.Y.		
World Trade Center (2 towers)	1,350	110
Empire State, 34th St. & 5th Ave.	1,250	102
TV tower, 164 ft., makes total	1,414	...
Chrysler, Lexington Ave. & 43d St.	1,046	77
American International Bldg., 70 Pine St.	950	67
40 Wall Tower	927	71
Citicorp Center	914	46
RCA Bldg., Rockefeller Center	850	70
1 Chase Manhattan Plaza	813	60
Pan Am Bldg., 200 Park Ave.	808	59
*Eichner Bldg.	799	70
Woolworth, 233 Broadway	792	60
1 Penn Plaza	764	57
Exxon, 1251 Ave. of Americas	750	54
Equitable Center Tower West	750	58
1 Liberty Plaza	743	50
Citibank	741	57
World Financial Center, Tower C	739	54
One Astor Plaza	730	54
Metropolitan Tower, 146 W. 57th St.	716	66
Union Carbide Bldg., 270 Park Ave.	707	52
General Motors Bldg.	705	50
Metropolitan Life, 1 Madison Ave.	700	50
500 5th Ave.	697	60
9 W. 57th St.	688	50
Chem. Bank, N.Y. Trust Bldg.	687	50
55 Water St.	687	53
Chanin, Lexington Ave. & 42d St.	680	56
Gulf & Western Bldg.	679	44
Marine Midland Bldg., 140 Bway.	677	52
McGraw Hill, 1221 Ave. of Am.	674	51
Lincoln, 60 E. 42d Street	673	53
1633 Broadway	670	48
Trump Tower, 725 5th Ave.	664	68
599 Lexington Ave.	653	47
Museum Tower Apts.	650	58
American Brands, 245 Park Ave.	648	47
A. T. & T. Tower, 570 Madison Ave.	648	37
World Financial Center Tower B	645	50
General Electric, 570 Lexington	640	50
Irving Trust, 1 Wall St.	640	50
345 Park Ave.	634	44
Grace Plaza, 1114 Ave. of Am.	630	50
1 New York Plaza	630	50
Home Insurance Co. Bldg.	630	44
N.Y. Telephone, 1095 Ave. of Am.	630	40
888 7th Ave.	628	42
1 Hammarskjold Plaza	628	50
Waldorf-Astoria, 301 Park Ave.	625	47
Burlington House, 1345 Ave. of Am.	625	50
Olympic Tower, 645 5th Ave.	620	51
10 E. 40th St.	620	48
101 Park Ave.	618	50
New York Life, 51 Madison Ave.	615	40
17 State St.	610	41
Penney Bldg., 1301 Ave. of Am.	609	46
IBM, 590 Madison Ave.	603	41
780 3rd Ave.	600	50
560 Lexington Ave.	600	22
Celanese Bldg., 1211 Ave. of Am.	592	45
U.S. Court House, 505 Pearl St.	590	37
Federal Bldg., Foley Square	587	41
Time & Life, 1271 Ave. of Am.	587	47
Cooper Bregstein Bldg., 1250 Bway.	580	40
1185 Ave. of Americas	580	42
Municipal, Park Row & Centre St.	580	34

City	Hgt. ft.	Stories
1 Madison Square Plaza	576	42
World Financial Center Tower A	575	42
Westvaco Bldg. 299 Park Ave.	574	42
Marriott Marquis Hotel	574	42
Socony Mobil Bldg., East 42d St.	572	45
Sperry Rand Bldg., 1290 Ave. of Am.	570	43
600 3d Ave.	570	42
Helmsley Bldg., 230 Park Ave.	565	35
1 Bankers Trust Plaza	565	40
Palace Hotel, Madison & 51st St.	563	51
30 Broad St.	562	48
Sherry-Netherland, 5th Ave. & 59th St.	560	40
Continental Can, 633 3d Ave.	557	39
Sperry & Hutchinson, 330 Madison	555	39
Galleria, 117 E. 57th St.	552	57
Interchem Bldg., 1133 Ave. of Am.	552	45
151 E. 44th St.	550	44
N.Y. Telephone, 323 Bway.	550	45
919 3d Ave.	550	47
Burroughs Bldg., 605 3d Ave.	550	44
Bankers Trust, 33 E. 48 St.	547	41
Transportation Bldg., 225 Bway.	546	45
Equitable, 120 Broadway	545	42
1 Brooklyn Bridge Plaza	540	42
Equitable Life, 1285 Ave. of Am.	540	42
Ritz Tower, Park Ave. & 57th St.	540	41
Bankers Trust, 6 Wall St.	540	30
1166 Ave. of Americas	540	44
1700 Broadway	533	41
Downtown Athletic Club, 19 West St.	530	45
Nelson Towers, 7th Ave. & 34th St.	525	45
767 3d Ave.	525	39
Hotel Pierre, 5th Ave. & 61st St.	525	44
House of Seagram, 375 Park Ave.	525	38
7 World Trade Center	525	44
Random House, 825 3d Ave.	522	40
3 Park Ave.	522	42
North American Plywood, 800 3d Ave.	520	41
Du Mont Bldg., 515 Madison Ave.	520	42
26 Broadway	520	31
Newsweek Bldg., 444 Madison Ave.	518	43
Sterling Drug Bldg., 90 Park Ave.	515	41
First National City Bank	515	41
Bank of New York, 48 Wall St.	513	32
Navarre, 512 7th Ave.	513	43
Williamsburgh Savings Bank, Bklyn.	512	42
ITT—American, 437 Madison Ave.	512	40
International, Rockefeller Center	512	41
1407 Broadway Realty Corp.	512	44
United Nations, 405 E. 42 St.	505	39

Oakland, Cal.

City	Hgt. ft.	Stories
Ordway Bldg., 2150 Valdez St.	404	28
Kaiser Bldg.	390	28
Lake Merritt Plaza	371	27
Raymond Kaiser Engineer Bldg.	336	25
Clorox Bldg.	330	24

Oklahoma City, Okla.

City	Hgt. ft.	Stories
Liberty Tower	500	36
First National Center	493	33
City National Bank & Trust Co.	440	32
First Oklahoma Tower	425	31
Kerr-McGee Center	393	30
Mid America Plaza	362	19
Citizens Plaza	321	21

Omaha, Neb.

City	Hgt. ft.	Stories
Woodmen Tower	469	30
Northwestern Bell Telephone Hdqrs.	334	16
Masonic Manor	320	22
First Natl. Center	320	22

Ottawa, Ont.

City	Hgt. ft.	Stories
Place de Ville, Tower C	368	29
R.H. Coats Bldg.	326	27

Philadelphia, Pa.

City	Hgt. ft.	Stories
*One Liberty Place	945	62
*Mellon Bank Center	880	56
*Blue Cross Tower	700	50
City Hall Tower, incl. 37-ft. statue of Wm. Penn	548	7
Commerce Sq., #1	530	41
*Bell Atlantic Tower	500	40
1818 Market St.	500	40
Provident Mutual Life	491	40
Fidelity Mutual Life Ins. Bldg.	490	38
Phila. Saving Fund Society	490	39
Central Penn Natl. Bank	490	36
Centre Square (2 towers)	490/416	38/32
Philadelphia National Bank	475	25
Two Mellon Plaza	450	30
One Reading Center	417	32
Fidelity Bank Bldg.	405	30
Industrial Valley Bank	400	32
One Logan Square	400	32
Lewis Tower, 15th & Locust	400	33
1500 Locust St.	390	44
Academy House, 1420 Locust St.	390	37
Philadelphia Electric Co.	384	29
2000 Market St. Bldg.	378	29
Penn Mutual Life	375	20
The Drake, 15th & Spruce	375	33
INA Annex, 1600 Arch St.	369	27
5 Penn Center	366	36
Medical Tower, 255 So. 17th.	364	33
State Bldg., 1400 Spring Garden	351	18
United Engineers, 17th & Ludlow	344	20
Land Title, Broad & Chestnut	344	22
Packard, 15th & Chestnut	340	25
Inquirer Building	340	18

Phoenix, Ariz.

City	Hgt. ft.	Stories
Valley National Bank	483	40
Arizona Bank Downtown	407	31
First Interstate Bank Plaza	372	27
United Bank Plaza	356	28
First Federal Savings Bldg.	341	26
Hyatt Regency	317	20

Pittsburgh, Pa.

City	Hgt. ft.	Stories
U.S. Steel Bldg.	841	64
One Mellon Bank Center	725	54
One PPG Place	635	40
One Oxford Centre	615	46
Gulf, 7th Ave. and Grant St.	582	44
University of Pittsburgh	535	42
Mellon Bank Bldg.	520	41
1 Oliver Plaza	511	39
Grant, Grant St. at 3rd Ave.	485	40
Koppers, 7th Ave. and Grant	475	34
Equibank Bldg.	445	34
Pittsburgh National Bldg.	424	30
Alcoa Bldg., 425 Sixth Ave.	410	30
Liberty Tower	358	29
Westinghouse Bldg.	355	23
Oliver, 535 Smithfield St.	347	25
Gateway Bldg. No. 3	344	24
Centre City Tower	341	26
Federal Bldg., 1000 Liberty Ave	340	23
Bell Telephone, 416 7th Ave.	339	21
Hilton Hotel	333	22
Frick, 437 Grant St.	330	20

Portland, Ore.

City	Hgt. ft.	Stories
First Interstate Tower	546	41
U.S. Bancorp Tower	536	39
Koin Tower Plaza	509	35
Standard Insurance Center	367	27
Pacwest Center	356	31

Providence, R.I.

City	Hgt. ft.	Stories
Fleet National Bank	420	26
Rhode Island Hospital Trust Tower	410	30
40 Westminster Bldg.	301	24

Richmond, Va.

City	Hgt. ft.	Stories
James Monroe Bldg.	450	29
City Hall (incl. penthouse)	425	17
United Virginia Bank Bldg.	400	24
Federal Reserve Bank	393	26
First & Merchants Natl. Bank.	333	25

Rochester, N.Y.

City	Hgt. ft.	Stories
Xerox Tower	443	30
Lincoln First Tower	390	26
Eastman Kodak Bldg.	360	19

St. Louis, Mo.

City	Hgt. ft.	Stories
Gateway Arch	630	...
Metropolitan Square Tower	591	40
S.W. Bell Telephone Bldg.	587	44
Mercantile Trust Bldg.	550	37
Centerre Bldg.	433	31
Laclede Gas. Bldg., 8th & Olive	400	30
S.W. Bell Telephone Bldg.	398	31
Civil Courts	387	13
Queeny Tower	321	24
Counsel Tower	320	30

City	Hgt. ft.	Stories
St. Paul, Minn.		
First Natl. Bank Bldg., incl. 100-ft. sign	517	32
Minn. World Trade Center	471	36
Galtier Plaza's Jackson Tower	440	46
Osborn Bldg., 320 Wabasha	368	20
Kellogg Square Apts.	366	32
Northwestern Bell Telephone (2 bldgs.)	340	16
American National Bank Bldg.	335	25
North Central Tower, 445 Minn.	328	27
Amhoist/Park Tower	324	26
Minn. Mutual Life Center	315	21
St. Paul Cathedral	307	...
Salt Lake City, Ut.		
L.D.S. Church Office Bldg.	420	30
Beneficial Life Tower	351	21
Amer. Towers (2 bldgs.)	324	27
San Antonio, Tex.		
Tower of the Americas	622	...
Tower Life	404	30
Interfirst Plaza	387	28
Nix Professional Bldg.	375	23
Natl. Bank of Commerce	310	24
Interfirst NW Finacial Center	302	20
San Diego, Cal.		
First Interstate Bank	398	24
California First Bank	388	27
First National Bank	379	27
The Meridan	371	27
Imperial Bank	355	24
Wells Fargo Bldg.	348	20
1010 Second	340	25
Great American	339	24
Central Federal	320	22
Union Bank	320	22
San Francisco, Cal.		
Transamerica Pyramid	853	48
Bank of America	778	52
101 California St.	600	48
5 Fremont Center	600	43
Embarcadero Center, No. 4	570	45
Security Pacific Bank	569	45
One Market Plaza, Spear St.	565	43
Wells Fargo Bldg.	561	43
Standard Oil, 575 Market St.	551	39
One Sansome-Citicorp	550	39
Shaklee Bldg., 444 Market	537	38
Aetna Life	529	38
First & Market Bldg.	529	38
Metropolitan Life	524	38
Crocker National Bank	500	38
Hilton Hotel	493	46
Pacific Gas & Electric	492	34
Union Bank	487	37
Pacific Insurance	476	34
Bechtel Bldg., Fremont St.	475	33
333 Market Bldg.	474	33
Hartford Bldg.	465	33
Mutual Benefit Life	438	32
Russ Bldg.	435	31
Pacific Telephone Bldg.	435	26
Pacific Gateway	416	30
Embarcadero Center, No. 3	412	31
Embarcadero Center, No. 2	412	31
595 Market Bldg.	410	31
101 Montgomery St.	405	28
Cal. State Automobile Assn.	399	29
Alcoa Bldg.	398	27
St. Francis Hotel	395	32
Shell Bldg.	386	29
Del Monte	378	28
Pacific 3-Apparel Mart	376	30
Meridien Hotel	374	34
Union Square Hyatt House Hotel	355	35
Seattle, Wash.		
Columbia Center	954	76
Seattle-1st Natl. Bank Bldg.	609	50
Space Needle	605	...
First Interstate Center	574	48
Seafirst 5th Ave. Plaza	543	42
Bank of Cal., 900 4th Ave.	536	42
Rainier Bank Tower, 4th & Univ.	514	42
Smith Tower	500	42
Federal Office Bldg.	487	37
Pacific Northwest Bell	466	33
One Union Square	456	38
1111 3d Ave. Bldg.	454	35
Washington Plaza Second Tower	448	44
Westin Bldg., 2001 6th Ave.	409	34
Washington Plaza	397	40
Financial Center	389	30
Daon Bldg., 840 Olive Way	381	19
Sheraton Seattle Hotel	371	34
Sixth & Pike Bldg.	365	29
Fourth & Blanchard Bldg.	360	24
Park Hilton Hotel	352	33
Tampa, Fla.		
Barnett Plaza	577	42
Tampa City Center	537	39
First Financial Tower	458	36
Toledo, Oh.		
Owens-Illinois Corp. Headquarters	411	32
Owens-Corning Fiberglas Tower	400	30
Ohio Citizens Bank Bldg.	368	27
Toledo Govt. Center	327	22
Toronto, Ont.		
CN Tower, World's tallest self-supporting structure	1,821	...
First Canadian Place	952	72
Scotia Plaza	886	68
Commerce Court West	784	57
Toronto-Dominion Tower (TD Centre)	758	56
Royal Trust Tower (TD Centre)	600	46
Royal Bank Plaza—South Tower	589	41
Manulife Centre	545	53
IBM Tower TD Centre	520	36
Two Bloor West	486	34
Exchange Tower	480	36
Commerce Court North	476	34
Simpson Tower	473	33
Cadillac-Fairview Bldg., 10 Queen St.	465	36
Palace Pier	452	46
Continental Bank Bldg.	450	35
Sheraton Centre	443	43
Hudson's Bay Centre	442	35
Leaside Towers (2 bldgs.)	423	44
Commercial Union Tower (TD Centre)	420	32
Maple Leaf Mills Tower	419	30
Plaza 2 Hotel	415	41
Sun Life Bldg., 150 King St.	410	28
Royal York Hotel	399	27
Tulsa, Okla.		
Bank of Oklahoma Tower	667	52
City of Faith Clinic Tower	648	60
Mid-Continent Tower	530	36
1st National Tower	516	41
4th Natl. Bank of Tulsa	412	33
320 South Boston Bldg.	400	24
Cities Service Bldg.	388	28
Univ. Club Tower	377	32
City of Faith Hospital	348	30
Philtower	343	24
Vancouver, B.C.		
Royal Bank Tower	460	37
Canada Trust Tower, 1055 Melville	454	35
Scotiabank Tower	451	36
Park Place	450	35
Bentall IV	443	34
T-D Bank Tower	432	30
Harbour Centre	428	32
200 Granville Square	403	30
Winston-Salem, N.C.		
Wachovia Bldg.	410	30
Reynolds Bldg.	315	21

Other Notable Tall Buildings

Cape Canaveral, Fla., Vehicle Assembly Bldg., 40 (552); Allentown, Pa., Power & Light Bldg., 23 (320); Amarillo, Tex., American Natl. Bank, 33 (374); Bethlehem, Pa., Martin Tower, 21 (332); Charleston, W. Va., Kanawha Valley Bldg., 20 (384); Frankfort, Ky., Capital Plaza Office Tower, 28 (338); Galveston, Tex., American National Ins., 20 (358); Knoxville, Tenn., United American Bank, 30 (400); Lansing, Mich., Michigan Natl. Tower, 25 (300, not including antenna tower); Lincoln, Neb., State Capitol (432); Mobile, Ala., First Natl. Bank, 33 (420); New Haven, Conn., Knights of Columbus Hqs. (319); Niagara Falls, Ont., Skylon, (520); Springfield, Mass., Valley Bank Tower, 29 (370); Tallahassee, Fla., State Capitol Tower, 22 (345).

Notable Bridges in North America

Source: State Highway Engineers; Canadian Civil Engineering — ASCE

Asterisk (*) designates railroad bridge. Span of a bridge is distance (in feet) between its supports.

Suspension

Year	Bridge	Location	Longest span
1964	Verrazano-Narrows	New York, N.Y.	4,260
1937	Golden Gate	San Fran. Bay, Cal.	4,200
1957	Mackinac	Sts. of Mackinac	3,800
1931	Geo. Washington	Hudson River, N.Y.-N.J.	3,500
1950	Tacoma Narrows	Washington	2,800
1936	[1]Transbay	San Fran. Bay, Cal.	2,310
1939	Bronx-Whitestone	East R., N.Y.C.	2,300
1970	Pierre Laporte	Quebec	2,190
1951	Del. Memorial	Wilmington, Del.	2,150
1968	Del. Mem. (new)	Wilmington, Del.	2,150
1957	Walt Whitman	Phila., Pa.	2,000
1929	Ambassador	Detroit-Canada	1,850
1961	Throgs Neck	Long Is. Sound	1,800
1926	Benjamin Franklin	Philadelphia	1,750
1924	Bear Mt., N.Y.	Hudson River	1,632
1952	[2]Wm.Preston Lane Mem.	Sandy Point, Md.	1,600
1903	Williamsburg	East R., N.Y.C.	1,600
1969	Newport	Narragansett Bay, R.I.	1,600
1883	Brooklyn	East R., N.Y.C.	1,595
1939	Lion's Gate	Burrard Inlet, B.C.	1,550
1930	Mid-Hudson, N.Y.	Poughkeepsie	1,500
1964	Vincent Thomas	Los Angeles Harbor	1,500
1909	Manhattan	East R., N.Y.C.	1,470
1936	Triboro	East R., N.Y.C.	1,380
1931	St. Johns	Portland, Ore.	1,207
1929	Mount Hope	Rhode Island	1,200
1960	Ogdensburg, N.Y.	St. Lawrence R.	1,150
1939	Deer Isle	Maine	1,080
1931	Maysville (Ky.)	Ohio River	1,060
1867	Cincinnati	Ohio River	1,057
1971	Dent	Clearwater Co., Ida.	1,050
1900	Miampimi	Mexico	1,030
1849	Wheeling, W. Va.	Ohio River	1,010

Cantilever

Year	Bridge	Location	Longest span
1917	Quebec	Quebec	1,800
1974	Commodore Barry	Chester, Pa.	1,644
1958	Mississippi R.	New Orleans, La.	1,575
1936	Transbay	San Fran. Bay	1,400
1968	Mississippi R.	Baton Rouge, La.	1,235
1955	Tappan Zee	Hudson River	1,212
1930	Longview, Wash.	Columbia River	1,200
1909	Queensboro	East R., N.Y.C.	1,182
1927	Carquinez Strait	California	1,100
1958	Parallel Span	"	1,100
1930	Jacques Cartier	Montreal, P.Q.	1,097
1868	Isaiah D. Hart	Jacksonville, Fla.	1,088
1957	[3]Richmond	San Fran. Bay, Cal.	1,070
1929	Grace Memorial	Charleston, S.C.	1,050
1963	Newburgh-Beacon	Hudson, R., N.Y.	1,000
1975	Caruthersville, Mo.	Mississippi R.	920
1977	Saint Marys	Saint Marys, W. Va.	900
1969	Silver Memorial	Pt. Pleasant, W. Va.	900
1987	Carl Perkins	Ohio River/So. Portsmouth, Ky.	900
1940	Natchez	Mississippi R.	875
1938	Blue Water	Pt. Huron, Mich.	871
1972	Vicksburg	Mississippi River	870
1954	Sunshine Skyway	St. Petersburg, Fla.	864
1972	N. Fork American R.	Auburn, Cal.	862
1940	*Baton Rouge	Mississippi R.	848
1899	*Cornwall	St. Lawrence R.	843
1940	Greenville	Mississippi R.	840
1961	Helena, Ark.	Mississippi R.	840
1963	Brent Spence	Covington, Ky.	831
1963	Cincinnati, Oh.	Ohio River	830
1963	Mississippi, R.	Donaldsonville, La.	825
1930	*Vicksburg	Mississippi R.	825
1929	Louisville	Ohio River	820
1961	Campbellton-Cross Point	New Brunswick-Quebec	815
1950	Maurice J. Tobin	Boston, Mass.	800
1935	Rip Van Winkle	Catskill, N.Y.	800
1938	Cairo	Ohio River, Ill.-Ky.	800
1932	Washington Mem.	Seattle, Wash.	800
1936	McCullough	Coos Bay, Ore.	793
1935	[4]Huey P Long	New Orleans	790
1916	*Memphis (Harahan)	Mississippi R.	790
1892	*Memphis	Mississippi R.	790
1949	Memphis-Arkansas	Mississippi R.	790
1904	*Mingo Jct., W. Va.	Ohio River	769
1910	*Beaver, Pa.	Ohio River	767
1966	[5]S.N. Pearman	Charleston, S.C.	760
1940	Owensboro	Ohio River	750
1911	Sewickley, Pa.	Ohio River	750
1928	Outerbridge, N.Y.-N.J.	Arthur Kill	750

Simple Truss

Year	Bridge	Location	Longest span
1977	Chester	Chester, W. Va.	746
1917	*Metropolis	Ohio River	720
1929	Irvin S. Cobb	Ohio River-Ill.-Ky.	716
1922	*Tanana River	Nenana, Alaska	700
1933	*Henderson	Ohio River-Ind.-Ky.	665
1967	I-77, Ohio River	Williamstown, W. Va.	650
1917	[4]MacArthur, Ill.-Mo.	St. Louis	647
1919	Louisville	Ohio River	644
1933	Atchafalaya	Morgan City, La.	608
1924	*Castleton	Hudson River	598
1889	*Cincinnati	Ohio River	542
1951	Allegheny River	Allegheny Co., Pa.	533
1914	Pittsburgh	Allegheny R.	531
1930	*Martinez	California	528
1967	Tanana River	Alaska	500

Steel Truss

Year	Bridge	Location	Longest span
1973	Atchafalaya R.	Krotz Springs, La.	780
1972	Atchafalaya R.	Simmesport, La.	720
1975	I-24	Tenn R., Ky.	720
1938	US-62, Ky.	Green River	700
1952	US-62, Ky.	Cumberland River	700
1940	Jamestown	Jamestown, R.I.	640
1940	Greenville	Mississippi R., Ark.	640
1949	Memphis	Mississippi R., Ark.	621
1978	Atchafalaya R.	Morgan City, La.	607
1938	US-22	Delaware River, N.J.	540
1955	Interstate	Columbia River, Ore.-Wash.	531
1910	[4]McKinley, St. Louis	Mississippi River	517
1972	Mississippi River	Muscatine, Ia.	512
1896	Newport	Ohio River, Ky.	511
1970	Lake Koocanusa	Lincoln Co., Mon.	500
1931	US-60	Cumberland R., Ky.	500
1958	Lake Oahe	Mobridge, S.D.	500
1958	Lake Oahe	Gettysburg, S.D.	500

Continuous Truss

Year	Bridge	Location	Longest span
1966	Columbia R. (Astoria)	Ore.-Wash.	1,232
1977	Francis Scott Key	Baltimore, Md.	1,200
1943	Dubuque, Ia.	Mississippi R.	845
1956	[6]Earl C. Clements	Ohio R., Ill-Ky.	825
1953	John E. Mathews	Jacksonville, Fla.	810
1940	Gov. Nice Mem.	Potomac River, Md.	800
1957	Kingston-Rhinecliff	Hudson R., N.Y.	800
1918	*Sciotoville	Ohio River	775
1984	13th St. Bridge, Ohio R.	Ashland, Ky.	740
1929	Madison-Milton	Ohio River	727
1966	[6]Matthew E. Welsh	Mauckport	707
1962	Champlain	Montreal, P.Q.	707
1975	Girard Point	Philadelphia, Pa.	700
1938	Port Arthur-Orange	Texas	680
1929	*Cincinnati	Ohio River	675
1928	Cape Girardeau, Mo.	Mississippi R.	672
1946	Chester, Ill.	Mississippi R.	670
1970	Gulfgate	Port Arthur, Tex.	664
1930	Quincy, Ill.	Mississippi R.	628
1959	US 181, over harbor	Corpus Christi, Tex.	620
1934	Bourne	Cape Cod Canal	616
1935	Sagamore	Cape Cod Canal	616
1965	Clarion River	Clarion Co., Pa.	612
1957	Blatnik	Duluth, Minn.	600
1965	Rio Grande Gorge	Taos, N.M.	600
1941	Columbia River	Kettle Falls, Wash.	600
1954	Columbia River	Umatilla, Ore.	600
1954	Columbia River	The Dalles, Ore.	576
1962	W. Br. Feather River	Oroville, Cal.	576
1936	Meredosia	Illinois River	567
1936	Mark Twain Mem.	Hannibal, Mo.	562
1957	Mackinac	Mackinac Straits, Mich.	560
1937	Homestead	Pittsburgh	553
1961	Ship Canal	Seattle, Wash.	552
1932	Pulaski Skyway	Passaic R., N.J.	550
1973	I-95, Thames River	New London, Conn.	540

Continuous Box and Plate Girder

Year	Bridge	Location	Longest span
1983	Mississippi R.	Luling, La.	1,222
1982	Houston Ship Chan	Texas	750
1967	San Mateo-Hayward No. 2	San Fran. Bay, Cal.	750
1977	Intracoastal Canal	Gibbstown, La.	750
1976	Intracoastal Canal	Forked Is., La.	750
1963	Gunnison River	Gunnison, Col.	720
1969	[7]San Diego-Coronado	San Diego Bay, Cal.	660
1973	Ship Channel (I-610)	Houston, Tex.	630
1981	Douglas	Juneau, Alaska	620
1976	Wax L. Outlet	Calumet, La.	618
1981	Glenn Jackson	Columbia R., Ore.-Wash.	600
1967	Poplar St.	St. Louis, Mo.	600
1982	Illinois R.	Perkin, Ill.	550
1982	I-440	Arkansas R.	540
1977	US-64, Tennessee R.	Savannah, Tenn.	525
1965	McDonald-Cartier	Ottawa, Ont.	520
1972	Sitka Harbor	Sitka, Alaska	450
1986	SR 76, Cumberland R.	Dover, Tenn.	440
1985	SR 20, Tennessee R.	Perryville, Tenn.	440
1970	I-204	Willamette R., Ore.	430
1974	I-430	Arkansas R.	430
1985	I-435	Missouri R., Ks.-Mo.	425
1984	US-36	Missouri R., Ks.-Mo.	425
1972	I-635, Kansas City	Missouri R., Kan.-Mo.	425
1985	FAU 3456, Tennessee R.	Chattanooga, Tenn.	420
1967	I-24, Tennessee R.	Marion Co., Tenn.	420
1978	Snake River	Clarkston, Wash.	420
1976	35th St. Bridge, Kanawha	Charleston, W. Va.	415
1986	SR 1, Tennessee R.	New Johnsonville, Tenn.	411
1979	Arkansas R.	Clarksville, Ark.	410
1975	Yukon River	Alaska	410
1973	Intracoastal Waterway	Corpus Christi, Tex.	400
1972	I-75, Tennessee River	Loudon Co., Tenn.	400
1941	Susquehanna	Susquehanna R., Md.	400

Continuous Plate

Year	Bridge	Location	Longest span
1971	W. Atchafalaya	Henderson, La.	573
1981	Illinois 23	Illinois R., Ill.	510
1968	Trinity R.	Dallas, Tex.	480
1978	San Joaquin R.	Antioch, Cal.	460
1975	I-129	Missouri R., Ia.	450
1967	Mississippi River	LaCrescent, Minn.	450
1966	I-480	Missouri R., Ia.-Neb.	425
1970	I-435	Missouri R., Mo.	425
1972	I-80	Missouri R., Ia.-Neb.	425
1971	St. Croix River	Hudson, Wisc.	390
1968	Lafayette St.	St. Paul, Minn.	362
1967	San Mateo Creek	Hillsborough, Cal.	360
1961	Whiskey Creek	Shasta Co., Cal.	350
1964	Lexington Ave.	St. Paul, Minn.	340

I-Beam Girder

Year	Bridge	Location	Longest span
1980	Shreveport Int.	Louisiana	438
1941	US-31E	Rolling Fork R., Ky.	340
1948	US-27	Licking River, Ky.	316
1947	US-31E	Green River, Ky.	316
1941	US-62	Rolling Fork, Ky.	240
1942	Licking River	Owingsville, Ky.	240
1954	Fuller Warren	Jacksonville, Fla.	224

Steel Arch

Year	Bridge	Location	Longest span
1977	New River Gorge	Fayetteville, W. Va.	1,700
1931	Bayonne, N.J.	Kill Van Kull	1,652
1973	Fremont	Portland, Ore.	1,255
1964	Port Mann	British Columbia	1,200
1916	*Hell Gate	East R., N.Y.C.	1,038
1959	Glen Canyon	Colorado River	1,028
1967	Trois-Rivieres	St. Lawrence R., P.Q.	1,100
1962	Lewiston-Queenston	Niagara River, Ont.	1,000
1976	Perrine	Twin Falls, Ida.	993
1941	Rainbow	Niagara Falls	984
1986	Moundsville Bridge, Ohio R.	Moundsville, W. Va.	912
1984	I-255	Mississippi R., Mo.	909
1972	[10]I-40, Mississippi R.	Memphis, Tenn.	900
1970	Lake Quinsigamond	Worcester, Mass.	849
1966	Charles Braga	Somerset, Mass.	840
1936	Henry Hudson	Harlem River, N.Y.C.	840
1967	Lincoln Trail	Ohio R., Ind.-Ky.	825
1978	I-57, Cairo, Ill.	Mississippi R.	821
1961	Sherman Minton	Louisville, Ky.	800
1936	French King	Conn. R. (Rt. 2, Mass.)	782
1978	I-470 Bridge, Ohio R.	Wheeling, W. Va.	780
1931	West End	Pittsburgh	778
1976	I-471, Ohio R.	Newport, Ky.	760

Concrete Arch

Year	Bridge	Location	Longest span
1971	Selah Creek (twin)	Selah, Wash.	549
1968	Cowlitz River	Mossyrock, Wash.	520
1931	Westinghouse	Pittsburgh	425
1923	Cappelen	Minneapolis	400
1930	Jack's Run	Pittsburgh	400
1973	Elwha River	Port Angeles, Wash.	380

Twin Concrete Trestle

Year	Bridge	Location	Longest span
1979	I-55/I-10	Manchae, La.	181,157
1969	L. Pontchartrain Cswy.	Mandeville, La.	126,720
1972	Atchafalaya Flwy.	Baton Rouge, La.	93,984
1963	[9]L. Pontchartrain	Slidell, La.	28,547

Concrete Slab Dam

Year	Bridge	Location	Longest span
1927	Conowingo Dam	Maryland	4,611
1952	SR-4, Roanoke R.	Mecklenberg Co., Va.	2,785
1936	Hoover Dam	Boulder City, Nev.	1,324

Drawbridges

Vertical Lift

Year	Bridge	Location	Longest span
1937	Marine Parkway	Jamaica Bay, N.Y.C.	590
1959	*Arthur Kill	N.Y.-N.J.	558
1935	*Cape Cod Canal	Massachusetts	544
1960	*Delair, N.J.	Delaware River	542
1931	Burlington, N.J.	Delaware R.	534
1968	Second Narrows	Vancouver, B.C.	493
1912	*A-S-B Fratt	Kansas City	428
1945	*Harry S. Truman	Kansas City	427
1955	Roosevelt Island	East River, N.Y.C.	418
1980	US-17, James R.	Isle of Wight, Co., Va.	415
1932	*M-K-T R.R.	Missouri R.	414
1969	Wilm'gtn Mem.	Wilmington, N.C.	408
1930	Aerial	Duluth, Minn.	386
1941	Main St.	Jacksonville, Fla.	386
1962	Burlington	Ontario	370
1941	Acosta	St. Johns R., Fla.	365
1922	*Cincinnati	Ohio River	365
1967	SR-156, James R.	Prince George Co., Va.	364
1964	Red R.	Alexandria, La.	360
1957	Industrial Canal	New Orleans, La.	360
1950	Red R.	Moncla, La.	360
1936	Tribo	Harlem River, N.Y.C.	344
1961	[4]Corpus Christi Harbor	Corpus Christi, Tex.	344
1939	U.S. 1&97, Passaic R.	Newark, N.J.	333
1929	Carlton	Bath-Woolwich, Me.	328
1930	*Martinez	California	328
1960	St. Andrews Bay	Panama City, Fla.	327
1929	*Penn-Lehigh	Newark Bay	322
1920	*Chattanooga	Tennessee R.	310

Bascule

Year	Bridge	Location	Longest span
1969	E. Pearl River	Slidell, La.	482
1955	Chehalis R.	Aberdeen, Wash.	340
1917	SR-8, Tennessee River	Chattanooga, Tenn.	306
1940	Lorain, Ohio	Black River	300
1968	Elizabeth River	Chesapeake, Va.	280
1913	Broadway	Portland, Ore.	278
1954	Fuller Warren	St. Johns R., Fla.	267
1958	Morrison	Portland, Ore.	262
1926	Burnside	Portland, Ore.	252
1977	Curtis Creek	Baltimore, Md.	251
1957	Craig Memorial	I-280, Toledo, Oh.	245

Swing Bridges

Year	Bridge	Location	Longest span
1926	[4]Fort Madison	Mississippi R.	525
1930	Rigolets Pass	New Orleans, La.	400
1950	Douglass Memorial	Wash. D.C.	386
1916	Keokuk Municipal	Mississippi R., Ia.	377
1945	Lord Delaware	Mattaponi River, Va.	252
1957	Eltham	Pamunkey River, Va.	237

Swing Span

Year	Bridge	Location	Longest span
1908	*Willamette R.	Portland, Ore.	521
1903	*East Omaha	Missouri R.	519
1952	US-17	York River, Va.	500
1897	*Duluth, Minn.	St. Louis Bay	486
1899	*C.M.&N.R.R.	Chicago	474
1914	*Coos Bay	Oregon	458

Floating Pontoon

Year	Bridge	Location	Longest span
1963	Evergreen Pt.	Seattle, Wash.	7,518
1940	Lacey V. Murrow	Seattle	6,561
1961	Hood Canal	Pt. Gamble, Wash.	6,471
1989	3rd Lake Washington Bridge	Seattle, Wash.	6,130

(1) The Transbay Bridge has 2 spans of 2,310 ft. each. (2) A second bridge in parallel was completed in 1973. (3) The Richmond Bridge has twin spans 1,070 ft. each. (4) Railroad and vehicular bridge. (5) Two spans each 760 ft. (6) Two spans each 707 ft. (7) Two spans each 660 ft. (8) Two spans each 825 ft. (9) Total length of bridge. (10) Two spans each 900 ft.

Notable International Bridges

Angostura, suspension type, span 2,336 feet, 1967 at Ciudad Bolivar, Venezuela. Total length, 5,507.

Bendorf Bridge on the Rhine River, 5 mi. n. of Coblenz, completed 1965, is a 3-span cement girder bridge, 3,378 ft. overall length, 101 ft. wide, with the main span 682 ft.

Bosporus Bridge linking Europe and Asia opened at Istanbul in 1973, at 3,524 ft. is the fifth longest suspension bridge in the world.

Gladesville Bridge at Sydney, Australia, has the longest concrete arch in the world (1,000 ft. span).

Humber Bridge, with a suspension span of 4,626 ft., the longest in the world, crosses the Humber estuary 5 miles west of the city of Kingston upon Hull, England. Unique in a large suspension bridge are the towers of reinforced concrete instead of steel.

Second Narrow's Bridge, Canada's longest railway lift span connecting Vancouver and North Vancouver over Burrard Inlet.

Oland Island Bridge in Sweden was completed in 1972. It is 19,882 feet long, Europe's longest.

Oosterscheldebrug, opened Dec. 15, 1965, is a 3.125-mile causeway for automobiles over a sea arm in Zeeland, the Netherlands. It completes a direct connection between Flushing and Rotterdam.

Rio-Niteroi, Guanabara Bay, Brazil, completed in 1972, is world's longest continuous box and plate girder bridge, 8 miles, 3,363 feet long, with a center span of 984 feet and a span on each side of 656 feet.

Tagus River Bridge near Lisbon, Portugal, has a 3,323-ft. main span. Opened Aug. 6, 1966, it was named Salazar Bridge for the former premier.

Zoo Bridge across the Rhine at Cologne, with steel box girders, has a main span of 850 ft.

Underwater Vehicular Tunnels in North America

(3,000 feet in length or more)

Name	Location	Waterway	Lgth. Ft.
Bart Trans-Bay Tubes (Rapid Transit)	San Francisco, Cal.	S.F. Bay	3.6 miles
Brooklyn-Battery	New York, N.Y.	East River	9,117
Holland Tunnel	New York, N.Y.	Hudson River	8,557
Lincoln Tunnel	New York, N.Y.	Hudson River	8,216
Thimble Shoal Channel	Newport News, Va.	Chesapeake Bay	8,187
Chesapeake Channel	Northampton Co., Va.	Chesapeake Bay	7,941
Baltimore Harbor Tunnel	Baltimore, Md.	Patapsco River	7,650
Hampton Roads	Newport News, Va.	Hampton Roads	7,479
Fort McHenry Tunnel	Baltimore, Md.	Baltimore Harbor	7,200
Queens Midtown	New York, N.Y.	East River	6,414
Sumner Tunnel	Boston, Mass.	Boston Harbor	5,650
Louis-Hippolyte Lafontaine Tunnel	Montreal, Que.	St. Lawrence River	5,280
Detroit-Windsor	Detroit, Mich.	Detroit River	5,135
Callahan Tunnel	Boston, Mass.	Boston Harbor	5,046
Midtown Tunnel	Norfolk, Va.	Elizabeth River	4,194
Baytown Tunnel	Baytown, Tex.	Houston Ship Channel	4,111
Posey Tube	Oakland, Cal.	Oakland Estuary	3,500
Downtown Tunnel	Norfolk, Va.	Elizabeth River	3,350
Webster St.	Alameda, Cal.	Oakland Estuary	3,350
Bankhead Tunnel	Mobile, Ala.	Mobile River	3,109
I-10 Twin Tunnel	Mobile, Ala.	Mobile River	3,000

Land Vehicular Tunnels in U.S.

(over 2,000 feet in length.)

Name	Location	Lgth. Ft.	Name	Location	Lgth. Ft.
E. Johnson Memorial	I-70, Col.	8,959	Fort Pitt	Pittsburgh, Pa	3,560
Eisenhower Memorial	I-70, Col.	8,941	Mall Tunnel	Dist. of Columbia	3,400
Allegheny (twin)	Penna. Turnpike	6,070	Caldecott	Oakland, Cal.	3,371
Liberty Tubes	Pittsburgh, Pa.	5,920	Cody No. 1	U.S. 14, 16, 20, Wyo.	3,224
Zion Natl. Park	Rte. 9, Utah.	5,766	Kalihi	Honolulu, Ha	2,780
East River Mt. (twin)	Interstate 77, W. Va.-Va.	5,412	Memorial	W. Va. Tpke. (I-77)	2,669
Tuscarora (twin)	Penna. Turnpike	5,326	Ft. Cronkhite	Sausalito, Cal.	2,690
Kittatinny (twin)	Penna. Turnpike	4,727	Cross-Town	178 St. N.Y.C.	2,414
Lehigh	Penna. Turnpike	4,379	F.D. Roosevelt Dr.	81-89 Sts. N.Y.C.	2,400
Blue Mountain (twin)	Penna. Turnpike	4,339	Dewey Sq.	Boston, Mass.	2,400
Wawona	Yosemite Natl. Park	4,233	Battery Park	N.Y.C.	2,300
Big Walker Mt.	Route I-77, Va.	4,229	Battery St.	Seattle, Wash.	2,140
Squirrel Hill	Pittsburgh, Pa.	4,225	Big Oak Flat	Yosemite Natl. Park	2,083

World's Longest Railway Tunnels

Source: Railway Directory & Year Book 1980. Tunnels over 5 miles in length.

Tunnel	Date	Miles	Operating railway	Country
Seikan	1985	33.5	Japanese National	Japan
Dai-shimizu	1979	14	Japanese National	Japan
Simplon No. 1 and 2	1906, 1922	12	Swiss Fed. & Italian St.	Switz.-Italy
Kanmon	1975	12	Japanese National	Japan
Apennine	1934	11	Italian State	Italy
Rokko	1972	10	Japanese National	Japan
Gotthard	1882	9	Swiss Federal	Switzerland
Lotschberg	1913	9	Bern-Lotschberg-Simplon	Switzerland
Hokuriku	1962	9	Japanese National	Japan
Mont Cenis (Frejus)	1871	8	Italian State	France-Italy
Shin-Shimizu	1961	8	Japanese National	Japan
Aki	1975	8	Japanese National	Japan
Cascade	1929	8	Burlington Northern	U.S.
Flathead	1970	8	Burlington Northern	U.S.
Keijo	1970	7	Japanese National	Japan
Lierasen	1973	7	Norwegian State	Norway
Santa Lucia	1977	6	Italian State	Italy
Arlberg	1884	6	Austrian Federal	Austria
Moffat	1928	6	Denver & Rio Grande Western	U.S.
Shimizu	1931	6	Japanese National	Japan

NATIONS OF THE WORLD

As of Mid-1987

The nations of the world are listed in alphabetical order. Initials in the following articles include UN (United Nations), OAS (Org. of American States), NATO (North Atlantic Treaty Org.), EC (European Communities or Common Market), OAU (Org. of African Unity), ILO (Intl. Labor Org.), FAO (Food & Agricultural Org.), WHO (World Health Org.), IMF (Intl. Monetary Fund), GATT (General Agreements on Tarriffs & Trade). **Sources:** U.S. Dept. of State; U.S. Census Bureau; International Monetary Fund; UN Statistical Yearbook; UN Demographic Yearbook; The Environmental Fund; International Iron and Steel Institute; The Statesman's Year-Book; Encyclopaedia Britannica. All embassy addresses are Wash., DC; area codes (202), unless otherwise noted. Literacy rates are usually based on the ability to read and write on a lower elementary school level. The concept of literacy is changing in the industrialized countries, where literacy is defined as the ability to read instructions necessary for a job or a license. By these standards, illiteracy may be more common than present rates suggest.

See special color section for maps and flags.

Afghanistan

Democratic Republic of Afghanistan

De Afghanistan Democrateek Jamhuriat

People: Population (1986 est.): 15,056,000. **Pop. density:** 67.1 per sq. mi. **Ethnic groups:** Pukhtun 40%; Tajiks 25%; Uzbek 9%; Hazara 9%. **Languages:** Pushtu, Dari Persian (spoken by Tajiks, Hazaras), Uzbek (Turkic). **Religions:** Sunni Moslem 80%, Shi'a Moslem 20%.

Geography: Area: 251,773 sq. mi., about the size of Texas. **Location:** Between Soviet Central Asia and the Indian subcontinent. **Neighbors:** Pakistan on E, S, Iran on W, USSR on N; the NE tip touches China. **Topography:** The country is landlocked and mountainous, much of it over 4,000 ft. above sea level. The Hindu Kush Mts. tower 16,000 ft. above Kabul and reach a height of 25,000 ft. to the E. Trade with Pakistan flows through the 35-mile long Khyber Pass. The climate is dry, with extreme temperatures, and large desert regions, though mountain rivers produce intermittent fertile valleys. **Capital:** Kabul. **Cities** (1985 est.): Kabul 2 mln.

Government: Type: People's republic. **Head of state, and President of the Revolutionary Council:** Pres. Haji Mohammad Chamkani b. 1947; in office: Nov. 24, 1986. **Head of Government:** Prime Min. Sultan Ali Keshtmand; in office: 1981. **Head of Communist Party:** Secy. Gen. Sayid Mohammad Najibullah; in office: May 4, 1986. **Local divisions:** 24 provinces, each under a governor. **Defense:** 3.0% of GNP (1984).

Economy: Industries: Textiles, carpets, cement. **Chief crops:** Cotton, wheat, fruits. **Minerals:** Copper, coal, zinc, iron. **Other resources:** Wool, hides, karacul pelts. **Arable land:** 13%. **Meat prod.** (1985): cattle: 3.7 mln.; sheep: 20 mln. **Electricity prod.** (1984): 1.3 bln. kwh. **Labor force:** cannot be estimated due to war.

Finance: Currency: Afghani (Mar. 1987: 50.60 = $1 US). **Gross national product** (1985): $3.3 bln. **Per capita income** (1978): $168. **Imports** (1984): $941 mln.; partners: USSR 57%, Jap. 21%, Iran 13%. **Exports** (1984): $681 mln.; partners: USSR 60%, Pak. 12%, UK 12%. **International reserves less gold** (Feb. 1987): $279.4 mln. **Gold:** 965,000 oz t.

Transport: Motor vehicles: in use (1982): 30,000 passenger cars, 35,000 comm. vehicles. **Civil aviation** (1982): 291 mln. passenger-km; 18.6 mln. net ton-km.

Communications: Television sets: 12,000 in use (1985); **Radios:** 135,000 in use (1985). **Telephones in use** (1985): 31,000. **Daily newspaper circ.** (1985): 5 per 1,000 pop.

Health: Life expectancy at birth (1985): 36.6 male; 37.3 female. **Births** (per 1,000 pop. 1985): 48.9. **Deaths** (per 1,000 pop. 1985): 27.3. **Natural increase** (1985): 2.1%. **Hospital beds:** 6,875. **Physicians:** 1,215 (1982).

Education (1986): **Literacy:** 10%. Over 85% of adults have no formal schooling.

Major International Organizations: UN (World Bank, IMF)
Embassy: 2341 Wyoming Ave. NW, 20008; 234-3770.

Afghanistan, occupying a favored invasion route since antiquity, has been variously known as Ariana or Bactria (in ancient times) and Khorasan (in the Middle Ages). Foreign empires alternated rule with local emirs and kings until the 18th century, when a unified kingdom was established. In 1973, a military coup ushered in a republic.

Pro-Soviet leftists took power in a bloody 1978 coup, and concluded an economic and military treaty with the USSR.

Late in Dec. 1979, the USSR began a massive military airlift into Kabul. The three-month old regime of Hafizullah Amin ended with a Soviet backed coup, Dec. 27th. He was replaced by Babrak Karmal, considered a more pro-Soviet leader. Soviet troops, estimated at between 60,000-100,000, fanned out over Afghanistan, fighting rebels. Fighting continued during 1987 as the Soviets found themselves engaged in a long, protracted guerrilla war.

Albania

Socialist Republic of Albania

Republika Popullore Socialiste e Shqipërisë

People: Population (1986 est.): 3,020,000. **Pop. density:** 267 per sq. mi. **Urban** (1984): 33%. **Ethnic groups:** Albanians (Gegs in N, Tosks in S) 96%, Greeks 2.5%. **Languages:** Albanian (Tosk is official dialect), Greek. **Religions:** officially atheist; (historically) mostly Moslems. All public worship and religious institutions were outlawed in 1967.

Geography: Area: 11,100 sq. mi., slightly larger than Maryland. **Location:** On SE coast of Adriatic Sea. **Neighbors:** Greece on S, Yugoslavia on N, E. **Topography:** Apart from a narrow coastal plain, Albania consists of hills and mountains covered with scrub forest, cut by small E-W rivers. **Capital:** Tirana. **Cities** (1986 est.): Tirana 272,000; Durres 127,000; Vlore 90,000.

Government: Type: Communist. **Head of state:** Pres. Ramiz Alia, in office: Nov. 22, 1982. **Head of government:** Premier Adil Carcani; in office: Jan. 18, 1982. **Head of Communist Party:** Ramiz Alia; b. Oct. 18, 1925; in office: Apr. 13, 1985. **Local divisions:** 26 districts. **Defense:** 10.9% of budget (1986).

Economy: Industries: Chem. fertilizers, textiles, electric cables. **Chief crops:** Grain, sugar beets, cotton, potatoes, tobacco, fruits. **Minerals:** Chromium, coal, oil. **Other resources:** Forests. **Arable land:** 26%. **Meat prod.** (1984): 600,000 cattle; 1.2 mln. sheep. **Electricity prod.** (1984): 3.8 bln. kwh. **Labor force:** 50% agric; 50% ind. & comm.

Finance: Currency: Lek (Nov. 1986: 6.99 = $1 US). **Gross national product** (1985 est.) $2.8 bln. **Per capita income** (1985): $900. **Imports** (1984): $320 mln.; partners: Czech., Yugoslavia, Rom. **Exports** (1984): $240 mln.; partners: Czech., Yugoslavia, N. Korea, Italy.

Transport: Motor vehicles: in use (1971): 3,500 passenger cars, 11,200 comm. vehicles. **Chief ports:** Durres, Vlone.

Communications: Television sets: 187,000 in use (1985). **Radios:** 210,000 in use (1985). **Daily newspaper circ.** (1985): 52 per 1,000 pop.

Health: Life expectancy at birth (1985): 70.4 yrs. **Births** (per 1,000 pop. 1985): 27.0. **Deaths** (per 1,000 pop. 1985): 6.0. **Natural increase** 2.0%. **Hospital beds** (per 1,000 pop. 1982): 70. **Physicians** (1982): 4,476 doctors & dentists. **Infant mortality** (per 1,000 live births 1982): 44.0.

Major International Organizations: UN (FAO, WHO).

Education (1986): **Literacy:** 75%. Free and compulsory ages 7-15.

Ancient Illyria was conquered by Romans, Slavs, and Turks (15th century); the latter Islamized the population. Independent Albania was proclaimed in 1912, republic was formed in 1920. Self-styled King Zog I ruled 1925-39, until Italy invaded.

Communist partisans took over in 1944, allied Albania with USSR, then broke with USSR in 1960 over de-Stalinization. Strong political alliance with China followed, leading to several billion dollars in aid, which was curtailed after 1974. China cut off aid in 1978 when Albania attacked its policies after the death of Chinese ruler Mao Tse-tung.

Large-scale purges of officials occurred during the 1970s. Enver Hoxha, the nation's ruler for 4 decades, died Apr. 11, 1985.

Algeria

Democratic and Popular Republic of Algeria

al-Jumhuriya al-Jazāiriya ad-Dimuqratiya ash-Shabiya

People: Population (1986 est.): 22,817,000. **Age distrib.** (%): 0–14: 46.4; 15–59: 47.6; 60+: 6.0. **Pop. density:** 24 per sq. mi. **Urban** (1984): 66%. **Ethnic groups:** Arabs 75%, Berbers 25%. **Languages:** Arabic (official), Berber (indigenous language), French. **Religions:** Sunni Moslem (state religion).

Geography: Area: 918,497 sq. mi., more than 3 times the size of Texas. **Location:** In NW Africa, from Mediterranean Sea into Sahara Desert. **Neighbors:** Morocco on W, Mauritania, Mali, Niger on S, Libya, Tunisia on E. **Topography:** The Tell, located on the coast, comprises fertile plains 50-100 miles wide, with a moderate climate and adequate rain. Two major chains of the Atlas Mts., running roughly E-W, and reaching 7,000 ft., enclose a dry plateau region. Below lies the Sahara, mostly desert with major mineral resources. **Capital:** Algiers (El Djazair). **Cities** (1984 est.): El Djazair 2,400,000; Wahran 633,000; Qacentina 384,000.

Government: Type: Republic. **Head of state:** Pres. Chadli Bendjedid; b. Apr. 14, 1929; in office: Feb. 9, 1979. **Head of government:** Premier Abdel Hamid Brahimi; in office: Jan. 22, 1984. **Local divisions:** 31 wilayaat (states). **Defense:** 2.0% of GDP (1984).

Economy: Industries: Oil, iron, steel, textiles, fertilizer, plastics. **Chief crops:** Grains, wine-grapes, potatoes, dates, tomatoes, oranges. **Minerals:** Mercury, iron, zinc, lead, copper. **Crude oil reserves** (1985): 7 bln. bbls. **Other resources:** Cork trees. **Arable land:** 17%; **Meat prod.** (1985): cattle: 1.7 mln. sheep: 13 mln. **Electricity prod.** (1984): 11.4 bln. kwh. **Crude steel prod.** (1984): 550,000 metric tons. **Labor force:** 30% agric.; 36% ind. and commerce; 19% government; 15% services.

Finance: Currency: Dinar (Mar. 1987: 4.66 = $1 US). **Gross national product** (1984): $51.7 bln. **Per capita income** (1984): $2,085. **Imports** (1985): $9.0 bln.; partners: France 18%, W. Ger. 18%, It. 11%, Japan 9%. **Exports** (1984): $12.9 bln.; partners: U.S. 51%, W. Ger. 14%, France 11%, It. 7%. **National budget** (1985): $23.2 bln. **International reserves less gold** (Mar. 1987): $1.5 bln. **Gold:** 5.58 mln. oz t. **Consumer prices** (change in 1985): 8.0%

Transport: Motor vehicles: in use (1983): 574,000 passenger cars, 360,000 comm. vehicles. **Chief ports:** El Djazair.

Communications: Television sets: 1.4 mln. in use (1985). **Radios:** 3.5 mln. in use (1985). **Telephones in use** (1983): 434,000. **Daily newspaper circ.** (1985): 22 per 1,000 pop.

Health: Life expectancy at birth (1984): 56.7 male; 58.9 female. **Births** (per 1,000 pop. 1985): 42.0. **Deaths** (per 1,000 pop. 1985): 10.0. **Natural increase** (1985); 3.2%. **Hospital beds** (1983): 41,188. **Physicians** (1983): 7,464. **Infant mortality** (per 1,000 live births 1985): 182

Education (1985): **Literacy:** 52%. **School:** Free and compulsory to age 13; Attendance: 86% primary, 31% secondary.

Major International Organizations: UN (FAO, IMF, WHO), OAU, Arab League, OPEC.

Embassy: 2118 Kalorama Rd. NW; 328-5300.

Earliest known inhabitants were ancestors of Berbers, followed by Phoenicians, Romans, Vandals, and, finally, Arabs. Turkey ruled 1518 to 1830, when France took control.

Large-scale European immigration and French cultural inroads did not prevent an Arab nationalist movement from launching guerilla war. Peace, and French withdrawal, was negotiated with French Pres. Charles de Gaulle. One million Europeans left.

Ahmed Ben Bella was the victor of infighting, and ruled 1962-65, when an army coup installed Col. Houari Boumedienne as leader.

In 1967, Algeria declared war with Israel, broke with U.S., and moved toward eventual military and political ties with the USSR. French oil interests were partly seized in 1971, but relations with the West have since improved.

The one-party Socialist regime faces endemic mass unemployment and poverty, despite land reform and industrialization attempts.

Andorra

Principality of Andorra

Principat d'Andorra

People: Population (1986 est.): 49,000. **Age distrib.** (%): 0–14: 27.0; 14–59: 60.5; 60+: 12.5. **Pop. density:** 255 per sq. mi. **Ethnic groups:** Spanish 55%, Andorran 27%, French 7%. **Languages:** Catalan (official), Spanish, French. **Religion:** Roman Catholic.

Geography: Area: 185 sq. mi., half the size of New York City. **Location:** In Pyrenees Mtns. **Neighbors:** Spain on S, France on N. **Topography:** High mountains and narrow valleys over the country. **Capital:** Andorra la Vella.

Government: Type: Co-principality. **Head of state:** Co-princes are the president of France and the Roman Catholic bishop of Urgel in Spain. **Local divisions:** 7 parishes.

Economy: Industries: Tourism, tobacco products. **Labor force:** 20% agric.; 80% ind. and commerce; services; government.

Finance: Currency: French franc, Spanish peseta.

Communications: Television sets: 4,000 in use (1984). **Radios:** 7,000 in use (1983). **Telephones in use** (1982): 17,719.

Health: Births (per 1,000 pop. 1985): 15.0. **Deaths** (per 1,000 pop. 1985): 4.0. **Natural increase** (1985): 1.0%.

Education (1987): **Literacy:** 100%. School compulsory to age 16.

The present political status, with joint sovereignty by France and the bishop of Urgel, dates from 1278.

Tourism, especially skiing, is the economic mainstay. A free port, allowing for an active trading center, draws some 10 million tourists annually. The ensuing economic prosperity accompanied by Andorra's virtual law-free status, has given rise to calls for reform.

Angola

People's Republic of Angola

República Popular de Angola

People: Population (1986 est.): 8,164,000. **Pop. density:** 18.3 per sq. mi. **Ethnic groups:** Ovimbundu 38%, Kimbundu 23%; Bakongo 13%, European 1%; Mesticos 2%. **Languages:** Portuguese (official), various Bantu languages. **Religions:** Roman Catholic 46%, Protestant 12%, animist 42%.

Geography: Area: 481,353 sq. mi., larger than Texas and California combined. **Location:** In SW Africa on Atlantic coast. **Neighbors:** Namibia (SW Africa) on S, Zambia on E, Zaire on N; Cabinda, an enclave separated from rest of country by short Atlantic coast of Zaire, borders Congo Republic. **Topography:** Most of Angola consists of a plateau elevated 3,000 to 5,000 feet above sea level, rising from a narrow coastal strip. There is also a temperate highland area in the west-central region, a desert in the S, and a tropical rain forest covering Cabinda. **Capital:** Luanda (1981 est.): 1.1 mln.

Government: Type: People's republic, one-party rule. **Head of state:** Pres. Jose Eduardo dos Santos b. Aug. 28, 1942; in office: Sept. 20, 1979. **Local divisions:** 18 provinces. **Defense:** 18% of GNP (1982).

Economy: Industries: Alcohol, cotton goods, fishmeal, paper, palm oil, footwear. **Chief crops:** Coffee, bananas. **Minerals:**

Iron, diamonds (over 2 mln. carats a year), copper, manganese, sulphur, phosphates, oil. **Crude oil reserves** (1985): 2.1 bln. bbls. **Arable land:** 3%. **Fish catch** (1984): 112,000 metric tons. **Electricity prod.** (1984): 1.7 bln.kwh. **Labor force:** 60% agric., 15% industry.

Finance: Currency: Kwanza (Nov. 1986: 29.92 = $1 US). **Gross domestic product** (1982): $7.6 bln. **Imports** (1984): $636 mln.; partners: Portugal 15%, Fra. 12%; USSR 8%. **Exports** (1984): $2.0 bln.; partners: Bahamas 15%, U.S. 49%.

Transport: Motor vehicles: in use (1984): 56,000 passenger cars, 29,000 comm. vehicles. **Chief ports:** Cabinda, Lobito, Luanda.

Communications: Radios: 230,000 in use (1985). **Telephones in use** (1982): 40,000. **Daily newspaper circ.** (1984): 13 per 1,000 pop.

Health: Life expectancy at birth (1984): 42.0 male; 44.0 female. **Births** (per 1,000 pop. 1985): 47.0. **Deaths** (per 1,000 pop. 1985): 20.0. **Natural increase** (1985): 2.7%. **Hospital beds** (1980): 20,000. **Physicians** (1980): 436. **Infant mortality** (per 1,000 live births 1985): 143.

Education (1980): **Literacy:** 28%.

Major International Organizations: UN (ILO, WHO), OAU.

From the early centuries AD to 1500, Bantu tribes penetrated most of the region. Portuguese came in 1583, allied with the Bakongo kingdom in the north, and developed the slave trade. Large-scale colonization did not begin until the 20th century, when 400,000 Portuguese immigrated.

A guerrilla war begun in 1961 lasted until 1974, when Portugal offered independence. Violence between the National Front, based in Zaire, the Soviet-backed Popular Movement, and the National Union, aided by the U.S. and S. Africa, killed thousands of blacks, drove most whites to emigrate, and completed economic ruin. Cuban troops and Soviet aid helped the Popular Movement win most of the country after independence Nov. 11, 1975.

S. African troops crossed the southern Angolan border June 7, 1981, killing more than 300 civilians and occupying several towns. The S. Africans withdrew in Sept.

Russian influence, backed by 25,000 Cubans, East Germans, and Portuguese communists, is strong in the Marxist regime.

Jonas Savimbi, leader of the National Union for Total Independence of Angola (UNITA), a rebel group fighting to overthrow the government, visited the U.S. in 1986 amid wide media exposure. He was favorably received by the Reagan administration and received some $15 million of covert military assistance; the aid was provided out of CIA funds.

Antigua and Barbuda

People: Population (1986 est.) 82,000. **Urban:** 34%. **Ethnic groups:** Mostly African. **Language:** English (official). **Religion:** Predominantly Church of England.

Geography: Area: 171 sq. mi. **Location:** Eastern Caribbean. **Neighbors:** approx. 30 mi. north of Guadeloupe. **Capital:** St. John's, (1983 est.) 27,000.

Government: Type: Constitutional monarchy with British-style parliament. **Head of State:** Queen Elizabeth II; represented by Sir Wilfred E. Jacobs. **Head of Government:** Prime Min. Vere Cornwall Bird; b. Dec. 7, 1910; in office Nov. 1, 1981.

Economy: Industries: manufacturing, tourists (195,000 in 1984). **Arable Land:** 18%.

Finance: Currency: East Caribbean dollar (Nov. 1986): 2.70 = $1 U.S. **Gross national product** (1984): $150 mln.

Health: Infant mortality (per 1,000 live births 1985): 31.5.

Education (1985): **Literacy:** 90%.

Major International Organizations: UN, Commonwealth of Nations.

Embassy: 2000 N St. NW; 296-6310.

Antigua was discovered by Columbus in 1493. The British colonized it in 1632.

The British associated state of Antigua achieved independence as Antigua and Barbuda on Nov. 1, 1981. The government maintains close relations with the U.S., United Kingdom, and Venezuela.

Argentina

Argentine Republic

República Argentina

People: Population (1986 est.): 31,186,000. **Age distrib.** (%): 0–14: 30.4; 15–59: 57.8; 60+: 11.8. **Pop. density:** 27.8 per sq. mi. **Urban** (1986): 80%. **Ethnic groups:** Europeans 98% (Spanish, Italian), Indians, Mestizos, Arabs. **Languages:** Spanish (official), English, Italian, German, French. **Religions:** Roman Catholic 92%.

Geography: Area: 1,065,189 sq. mi., 4 times the size of Texas, second largest in S. America. **Location:** Occupies most of southern S. America. **Neighbors:** Chile on W, Bolivia, Paraguay on N, Brazil, Uruguay on NE. **Topography:** The mountains in W: the Andean, Central, Misiones, and Southern. Aconcagua is the highest peak in the Western hemisphere, alt. 22,834 ft. E of the Andes are heavily wooded plains, called the Gran Chaco in the N, and the fertile, treeless Pampas in the central region. Patagonia, in the S, is bleak and arid. Rio de la Plata, 170 by 140 mi., is mostly fresh water, from 2,485-mi. Parana and 1,000-mi. Uruguay rivers. **Capital:** Buenos Aires. (The Senate has approved the moving of the capital to the Patagonia Region). **Cities** (1982 est.): Buenos Aires 2,908,000; Cordoba 969,000; Rosario 750,455; Mendoza 597,000; San Miguel de Tucuman 497,000.

Government: Type: Republic. **Head of state:** Pres. Raul Alfonsin; b. Mar. 3, 1926; in office: Dec. 10, 1983. **Local divisions:** 22 provinces, 1 natl. terr. and 1 federal dist., under military governors. **Defense:** 2.7% of GNP (1983).

Economy: Industries: Meat processing, flour milling, chemicals, textiles, machinery, autos. **Chief crops:** Grains, corn, grapes, linseed, sugar, tobacco, rice, soybeans, citrus fruits. **Minerals:** Oil, lead, zinc, iron, sulphur, silver, copper, gold, coal. **Crude oil reserves** (1985): 2.3 bln. bbls. **Arable land:** 13%. **Meat prod.** (1985): cattle: 54 mln.; sheep: 28 mln; pigs: 4 mln. **Fish catch** (1985): 405,000 metric tons. **Electricity prod.** (1984): 44.9 bln. kwh. **Crude steel prod.** (1984): 2.6 mln. metric tons. **Labor force:** 19% agric.; 36% ind. and comm.; 20% services.

Finance: Currency: Austral (June 1987: 1.56 = $1 US). **Gross domestic product** (1985): $65.4 bln. **Per capita income** (1978 est.): $2,331. **Imports** (1985): $3.8 bln.; partners: U.S. 21%, W. Ger. 10%, Braz. 14%, Jap. 10%. **Exports** (1985): $8.3 bln.; partners: USSR 21%, Neth. 9%, U.S. 9%, Chi. 6%. **Tourists** (1984): receipts: $602 mln. **National budget** (1982): $9.6 bln. revenues; $11.2 bln. expenditures. **International reserves less gold** (Jan. 1987): $2.1 bln. **Gold:** 4.37 mln. oz t. **Consumer prices** (change in 1986): 90.1%.

Transport: Railway traffic (1985): 10.7 bln. passenger-km; 9.5 bln. net ton-km. **Motor vehicles:** in use (1984): 3.6 mln. passenger cars, 1.3 mln. comm. vehicles. **Civil aviation:** (1985) 4.8 mln. passenger-km; 538 mln. net ton-km. **Chief ports:** Buenos Aires, Bahia Blanca, La Plata.

Communications: Television sets: 5.9 mln. in use (1984). **Radios:** 10 mln. in use (1984). **Telephones in use** (1983): 2.7 mln. **Daily newspaper circ.** (1982): 85 per 1,000 pop.

Health: Life expectancy at birth (1983): 66.8 male; 73.2 female. **Births** (per 1,000 pop. 1985): 24.0. **Deaths** (per 1,000 pop. 1985): 9.0 **Natural increase** (1985): 1.5%. **Hospital beds** (1980): 150,010. **Physicians** (1980): 79,000. **Infant mortality** (per 1,000 live births 1986): 34.1.

Education (1986): **Literacy:** 94%. School attendence 21.5% through secondary school.

Major International Organizations: UN (WHO, IMF, FAO), OAS.

Embassy: 1600 New Hampshire Ave. NW 20009; 939-6400.

Nomadic Indians roamed the Pampas when Spaniards arrived, 1515-1516, led by Juan Diaz de Solis. Nearly all the Indians were killed by the late 19th century. The colonists won independence, 1810-1819, and a long period of disorders ended in a strong centralized government.

Large-scale Italian, German, and Spanish immigration in the decades after 1880 spurred modernization, making Argentina the most prosperous, educated, and industrialized of the major Latin American nations. Social reforms were enacted in the 1920s, but military coups prevailed 1930-46, until the election of Gen. Juan Peron as president.

Peron, with his wife Eva Duarte effected labor reforms, but also suppressed speech and press freedoms, closed religious schools, and ran the country into debt. A 1955 coup exiled Peron, who was followed by a series of military and civilian regimes. Peron returned in 1973, and was once more elected president. He died 10 months later, succeeded by his wife, Isabel, who had been elected vice president, and who became the first woman head of state in the Western hemisphere.

A military junta ousted Mrs. Peron in 1976 amid charges of corruption. Under a continuing state of siege, the army battled guerrillas and leftists, killed 5,000 people, and jailed and tortured others. On Dec. 9, 1985, after a trial of 5 months and nearly 1,000 witnesses, 5 former junta members, including ex-presidents Jorge Videla and Gen. Roberto Eduardo Viola, were found guilty of murder and human rights abuses.

A severe worsening in economic conditions placed extreme pressure on the military government.

Argentine troops seized control of the British-held Falkland Islands on Apr. 2, 1982. Both countries had claimed sovereignty over the islands, located 250 miles off the Argentine coast, since 1833. The British dispatched a task force and declared a total air and sea blockade around the Falklands. Fighting began May 1; several hundred lost their lives as the result of the destruction of a British destroyer and the sinking of an Argentine cruiser.

British troops landed in force on East Falkland Island May 21. By June 2, the British had surrounded Stanley, the capital city and Argentine stronghold. The Argentine troops surrendered, June 14; Argentine President Leopoldo Galtieri resigned June 17.

Democratic rule returned to Argentina in 1983 as Raul Alfonsin's Radical Civic Union gained an absolute majority in the presidential electoral college and Congress. The nation was plagued by severe financial problems as inflation remained high; over 90% in 1986. Argentina reached agreement with foreign banks on a repayment schedule and interest rate adjustments on its foreign debt in 1987.

Australia

Commonwealth of Australia

People: Population (1986 est.): 15,763,000. **Age distrib.** (%): 0–14: 23.2; 15–59; 61.9; ; 59 +: 14.9. **Pop. density:** 5.4 per sq. mi. **Urban** (1984). 85%. **Ethnic groups:** European 96%, other Asian 2%, aborigines (including mixed) 1.5%. **Languages:** English, aboriginal languages. **Religions:** Anglican 36%, other Protestant 25%, Roman Catholic 33%.

Geography: Area: 2,966,200 sq. mi., almost as large as the continental U.S. **Location:** SE of Asia, Indian O. is W and S, Pacific O. (Coral, Tasman seas) is E; they meet N of Australia in Timor and Arafura seas: Tasmania lies 150 mi. S of Victoria state, across Bass Strait. **Neighbors:** Nearest are Indonesia, Papua New Guinea on N, Solomons, Fiji, and New Zealand on E. **Topography:** An island continent. The Great Dividing Range along the E coast has Mt. Kosciusko, 7,310 ft. The W plateau rises to 2,000 ft., with arid areas in the Great Sandy and Great Victoria deserts. The NW part of Western Australia and Northern Terr. are arid and hot. The NE has heavy rainfall and Cape York Peninsula has jungles. The Murray R. rises in New South Wales and flows 1,600 mi. to the Indian O. **Capital:** Canberra. **Cities** (1983 est.): Sydney 3,332,600; Melbourne 2,864,600; Brisbane 1,138,400; Adelaide 969,000; Perth 968,000.

Government: Type: Democratic, federal state system. **Head of state:** Queen Elizabeth II, represented by Gov.-Gen. Ninian Martin Stephen; in office: July 29, 1982. **Head of government:** Prime Min. Robert James Lee Hawke; b. Dec. 9, 1929; in office: Mar. 11, 1983. **Local divisions:** 6 states, 2 territories. **Defense:** 2.8% of GNP (1986).

Economy: Industries: Iron, steel, textiles, electrical equip., chemicals, autos, aircraft, ships, machinery. **Chief crops:** Wheat (a leading export), barley, oats, corn, hay, sugar, wine, fruit, vegetables. **Minerals:** Bauxite, coal, copper, iron, lead, nickel, silver, tin, tungsten, uranium, zinc. **Crude oil reserves** (1985): 1.4 bln. bbls. **Other resources:** Wool (30% of world output). **Arable land:** 9%. **Meat prod.** (1985); cattle: 23 mln.; sheep: 155.2 mln.; pigs: 2.5 mln. **Fish catch** (1985): 168,000 metric tons. **Electricity prod.** (1985): 118.9 bln. kwh. **Crude steel prod.** (1985): 6.3 mln. metric tons. **Labor force:** 6% agric.; 51% services; 22% govt.; 21% min. & manuf.

Finance: Currency: Dollar (Mar. 1987: 1.61 = $1 US). **Gross national product** (1984): $184 bln. **Per capita income** (1984): $10,282. **Imports** (1985): $25.9 bln; partners: U.S. 21%, Jap. 22%, UK 7%. **Exports** (1985): $22.7 bln.; partners: Jap. 27%, U.S. 11%, NZ 5%. **Tourists** (1984): $1.2 bln. receipts. **National budget** (1986): $49 bln. expenditures. **International reserves less gold** (Mar. 1987): $6.5 bln. **Gold:** 7.93 mln. oz t. **Consumer prices** (change in 1986): 9.1%.

Transport: Railway traffic (1984): 39.2 bln. net ton-km. **Motor vehicles:** in use (1985): 8.2 mln. passenger cars, 1 mln. comm. vehicles; manuf. (1982): 368,000 passenger cars; 37,000 comm. vehicles. **Civil aviation** (1985): 24.3 mln. passenger-km.; 1.8 bln. freight ton-km. **Chief ports:** Sydney, Melbourne, Newcastle, Port Kembla, Fremantle, Geelong.

Communications: Television sets: 6.5 mln. (1985). **Radios:** 20 mln. (1985). **Telephones in use** (1985): 8.7 mln. **Daily newspaper circ.** (1982): 426 per 1,000 pop.

Health: Life expectancy at birth (1985): 72.6 male; 79.1 female. **Births** (per 1,000 pop. 1986): 15.7. **Deaths** (per 1,000 pop. 1986): 7.4. **Natural increase** (1986): .8%. **Hospital beds** (1984): 91,054. **Physicians** (1982): 27,500. **Infant mortality** (per 1,000 live births 1986): 9.6.

Education (1986): **Literacy:** 100%. **School:** compulsory to age 15; attendance 94%.

Major International Organizations: UN and all its specialized agencies, OECD, Commonwealth of Nations.

Embassy: 1601 Massachusetts Ave NW 20036; 797-3000.

Capt. James Cook explored the E coast in 1770, when the continent was inhabited by a variety of different tribes. Within decades, Britain had claimed the entire continent, which became a penal colony until immigration increased in the 1850s. The commonwealth was proclaimed Jan. 1, 1901. Northern Terr. was granted limited self-rule July 1, 1978. Their capitals and 1984 pop.:

	Area (sq. mi.)	Population
New South Wales, Sydney	309,418	5,405,100
Victoria, Melbourne	87,854	4,075,900
Queensland, Brisbane	666,699	2,505,100
South Aust., Adelaide	379,824	1,353,000
Western Aust., Perth	974,843	1,382,600
Tasmania, Hobart	26,178	407,000
Aust. Capital Terr., Canberra	926	245,600
Northern Terr., Darwin	519,633	138,900

Australia's racially discriminatory immigration policies were abandoned in 1973, after 3 million Europeans (half British) had entered since 1945. The 50,000 aborigines and 150,000 part-aborigines are mostly detribalized, but there are several preserves in the Northern Territory. They remain economically disadvantaged.

Australia's agricultural success makes it among the top exporters of beef, lamb, wool, and wheat. Major mineral deposits have been developed as well, largely for exports. Industrialization has been completed. The economy suffered in 1986 because of large balance of payments deficits.

Australia harbors many plant and animal species not found elsewhere, including the kangaroo, koala bear, platypus, dingo (wild dog), Tasmanian devil (racoon-like marsupial), wombat (bear-like marsupial), and barking and frilled lizards.

Australian External Territories

Norfolk Is., area 13½ sq. mi., pop. (1985) 1,800, was taken over, 1914. The soil is very fertile, suitable for citrus fruits, bananas, and coffee. Many of the inhabitants are descendants of the Bounty mutineers, moved to Norfolk 1856 from Pitcairn Is. Australia offered the island limited home rule, 1978.

Coral Sea Is. Territory, 1 sq. mi., is administered from Norfolk Is.

Territory of Ashmore and Cartier Is., area 2 sq. mi., in the Indian O. came under Australian authority 1934 and are administered as part of Northern Territory. **Heard** and **McDonald Is.** are administered by the Dept. of Science.

Cocos (Keeling) Is., 27 small coral islands in the Indian O. 1,750 mi. NW of Australia. Pop. (1981) 569, area: 5½ sq. mi. The residents voted to become part of Australia, Apr. 1984.

Christmas Is., 52 sq. mi., pop. 3,000 (1983), 230 mi. S of Java, was transferred by Britain in 1958. It has phosphate deposits.

Australian Antarctic Territory was claimed by Australia in 1933, including 2,472,000 sq. mi. of territory S of 60th parallel S Lat. and between 160th-45th meridians E Long.

Austria

Republic of Austria

Republik Österreich

People: Population (1986 est.): 7,546,000. **Age distrib.** (%): 0–14: 18.6; 15–59: 61.6; 60+: 19.8. **Pop. density:** 233 per sq. mi. **Urban** (1981): 55.1%. **Ethnic groups:** German 98%, Slovene, Croatian. **Languages:** German 95%, Slovene. **Religions:** Roman Catholic 85%.

Geography: Area: 32,374 sq. mi., slightly smaller than Maine. **Location:** In S Central Europe. **Neighbors:** Switzerland, Liechtenstein on W, W. Germany, Czechoslovakia on N, Hungary on E, Yugoslavia, Italy on S. **Topography:** Austria is primarily mountainous, with the Alps and foothills covering the western and southern provinces. The eastern provinces and Vienna are located in the Danube River Basin. **Capital:** Vienna. **Cities** (1981 cen.): Vienna 1,504,200.

Government: Type: Parliamentary democracy. **Head of state:** Pres. Kurt Waldheim; b. Dec. 21, 1918; in office: June 8, 1986. **Head of government:** Chancellor Franz Vranitzky; b. Oct. 4, 1937; in office: June 16, 1986. **Local divisions:** 9 lander (states), each with a legislature. **Defense:** 1.2% of GNP (1984).

Economy: Industries: Steel, machinery, autos, electrical and optical equip., glassware, sport goods, paper, textiles, chemicals, cement. **Chief crops:** Grains, potatoes, beets, grapes. **Minerals:** Iron ore, oil, magnesite, aluminum, coal, lignite, copper. **Crude oil reserves** (1985): 116 mln. bbls. **Other resources:** Forests, hydro power. **Arable land:** 18.3%. **Meat prod.** (1985): Cattle: 2.6 mln.; pigs: 3.9 mln. **Electricity prod.** (1984): 42.3 bln. kwh. **Crude steel prod.** (1985): 4.6 mln. metric tons. **Labor force:** 13.8% agric.; 60% ind. & comm.; 25.5% service.

Finance: Currency: Schilling (Mar. 1987: 12.68 = $1 US). **Gross national product** (1984): $68.8 bln. **Per capita income** (1980): $8,280. **Imports** (1986): $26.8 bln.; partners: W. Ger. 41%, It. 9%, Switz. 5%. **Exports** (1986): $22.5 bln.; partners: W. Ger. 29%, It. 9%, Switz. 7%. **Tourists** (1984): receipts: $5.0 bln. **National budget** (1984): $20.3 bln. expenditures. **International reserves less gold** (Mar. 1987): $6.4 bln. **Gold:** 21.14 mln. oz t. **Consumer prices** (change in 1985): 11.7%.

Transport: Railway traffic (1984): 7.0 bln. passenger-km; 11.2 bln. net ton-km. **Motor vehicles:** in use (1984): 2.4 mln. passenger cars, 232,000 comm. **Civil aviation** (1984): 1.4 bln. passenger-km; 23.4 mln. freight ton-km.

Communications: Television sets: 2.4 mln. (1984). **Radios:** 2.6 mln. (1984). **Telephones in use** (1984): 2.6 mln. **Daily newspaper circ.** (1983): 312 per 1,000 pop.

Health: Life expectancy at birth (1981): 69.3 male; 76.4 female. **Births** (per 1,000 pop. 1985): 12. **Deaths** (per 1,000 pop. 1985): 13.0. **Natural increase** (1985): –.1%. **Hospital beds** (1985): 84,125. **Physicians** (1985): 21,513. **Infant mortality** (per 1,000 live births 1985): 11.

Education (1983): Literacy: 98%. School years compulsory 9; attendance 95%.

Major International Organizations: UN and all of its specialized agencies, EFTA, OECD.

Embassy: 2343 Massachusetts Ave. NW 20008; 483-4474.

Rome conquered Austrian lands from Celtic tribes around 15 BC. In 788 the territory was incorporated into Charlemagne's empire. By 1300, the House of Hapsburg had gained control; they added vast territories in all parts of Europe to their realm in the next few hundred years.

Austrian dominance of Germany was undermined in the 18th century and ended by Prussia by 1866. But the Congress of Vienna, 1815, confirmed Austrian control of a large empire in southeast Europe consisting of Germans, Hungarians, Slavs, Italians, and others.

The dual Austro-Hungarian monarchy was established in 1867, giving autonomy to Hungary and almost 50 years of peace.

World War I, started after the June 28, 1914 assassination of Archduke Franz Ferdinand, the Hapsburg heir, by a Serbian nationalist, destroyed the empire. By 1918 Austria was reduced to a small republic, with the borders it has today.

Nazi Germany invaded Austria Mar. 13, 1938. The republic was reestablished in 1945, under Allied occupation. Full independence and neutrality were restored in 1955.

Austria produces most of its food, as well as an array of industrial products. A large part of Austria's economy is controlled by state enterprises. Socialists have shared or alternated power with the conservative People's Party.

Economic agreements with the Common Market give Austria access to a free-trade area encompassing most of West Europe.

The presidential campaign of former UN Secretary General Kurt Waldheim drew worldwide attention in 1986 amid allegations that he had World War II links to the Nazis.

The Bahamas

The Commonwealth of the Bahamas

People: Population (1986 est.): 235,000. **Age distrib.** (%): 0–14: 38.0; 15–59: 56.3; 60+: 5.7. **Pop. density:** 43 per sq. mi. **Urban** (1985): 75%. **Ethnic groups:** Black 85%, White (British, Canadian, U.S.) 15%. **Languages:** English. **Religions:** Baptist 29%, Anglican 23%, Roman Catholic 22%.

Geography: Area: 5,380 sq. mi., about the size of Connecticut. **Location:** In Atlantic O., E of Florida. **Neighbors:** Nearest are U.S. on W, Cuba on S. **Topography:** Nearly 700 islands (30 inhabited) and over 2,000 islets in the western Atlantic extend 760 mi. NW to SE. **Capital:** Nassau. **Cities:** (1985 est.) New Providence 135,437; Freeport 16,000.

Government: Type: Independent commonwealth. **Head of state:** Queen Elizabeth II, represented by Gov.-Gen. Gerald C. Cash; b. May 28, 1917, in office: Sept. 29, 1979. **Head of government:** Prime Min. Lynden Oscar Pindling; b. Mar. 22, 1930; in office: Jan. 16, 1967. **Local divisions:** 18 districts.

Economy: Industries: Tourism (70% of GNP), rum, drugs. **Chief crops:** Fruits, vegetables. **Minerals:** Salt. **Other resources:** Lobsters. **Arable land:** 2%. **Electricity prod.** (1984): 870 mln. kwh. **Labor force:** 6% agric.; 25% tourism, 30% government.

Finance: Currency: Dollar (June 1987: 1 = $1 US). **Gross national product** (1984): $960 mln. **Per capita income** (1982): $5,756. **Imports** (1986): $1.6 bln.; partners: U.S. 74%, EC 30%. **Exports** (1986): $825 mln. (not incl. oil); partners: U.S. 41%, U.K. 7%. **Tourists** (1985): $865 mln. **National budget** (1985): $383 mln. expenditures. **International reserves less gold** (Mar. 1987): $252 mln. **Consumer prices** (change in 1986): 5.4%.

Transport: Motor vehicles: in use (1984): 88,000 passenger cars, 5,600 comm. vehicles. **Chief ports:** Nassau, Freeport.

Communications: Radios: 116,000 in use (1985). **Television sets** (1985): 51,000. **Telephones in use** (1983): 67,000. **Daily newspaper circ.** (1984): 133 per 1,000 pop.

Health: Life expectancy at birth (1985): 64.0 male; 70 female. **Births** (per 1,000 pop. 1985): 24.0. **Deaths** (per 1,000 pop. 1985): 6.0. **Natural increase** (1985): 1.8%. **Infant mortality** (per 1,000 live births 1985): 20.2.

Education (1985): Literacy: 93%; School compulsory through age 14.

Major International Organizations: UN (World Bank, IMF, WHO), OAS.

Embassy: 600 New Hampshire Ave. NW 20037; 338-3940.

Christopher Columbus first set foot in the New World on San Salvador (Watling I.) in 1492, when Arawak Indians inhabited the islands. British settlement began in 1647; the islands became a British colony in 1783. Internal self-government was granted in 1964; full independence within the Commonwealth was attained July 10, 1973.

International banking and investment management has be-ome a major industry alongside tourism, despite controversy ver financial irregularities.

Bahrain

State of Bahrain

Dawlat al-Bahrayn

People: Population (1986 est.): 442,000. **Age distrib.** (%): -14: 32.0; 15–59: 64.4; 60+: 3.6. **Pop. density:** 1,778 per sq. ni. **Urban** (1984): 79%. **Ethnic groups:** Arabs 73%, Iranians %, Indians, Pakistanis 5%. **Languages:** Arabic (official), Per-ian. **Religions:** Sunni Moslem 40%, Shi'ah Moslem 60%.

Geography: Area: 258 sq. mi., smaller than New York City. **ocation:** In Persian Gulf. **Neighbors:** Nearest are Saudi Arabia n W. Qatar on E. **Topography:** Bahrain Island, and several ad-acent, smaller islands, are flat, hot and humid, with little rain. **apital:** Manama. **Cities** (1981 cen.): Manama 121,986.

Government: Type: Traditional emirate. **Head of state:** Amir a bin Sulman al-Khalifa; b. July 3, 1933; in office: Nov. 2, 1961. **ead of government:** Prime Min. Kahlifa ibn Sulman al-Khalifa; . 1935; in office: Jan. 19, 1970. **Local divisions:** 6 towns and ities. **Defense:** 4.0% of GNP (1983).

Economy: Industries: Oil products, aluminum smelting, ship-ing. **Chief crops:** Fruits, vegetables. **Minerals:** Oil, gas. **Crude il reserves** (1985): 173 mln. bbls. **Arable land:** 5%. **Electric-y prod.** (1984): 2.0 bln. kwh. **Labor force:** 5% agric.; 85% ind. nd commerce; 5% services; 3% gov.

Finance: Currency: Dinar (Mar. 1987: 0.38 = $1 US). **Gross ational product** (1984): $4.2 bln. **Per capita income** (1980 st.): $6,315. **Imports** (1984): $3.5 bln.; partners: Sau. Ar. 60%, K 6%, U.S. 9%. **Exports** (1985): $2.8 bln.; partners: UAE 8%, Jap. 12%, Sing. 10%, U.S. 6%. **National Budget** (1982): .3 bln. expenditures. **International reserves less gold** (Mar. 987): $1.4 bln. **Gold:** 150,000 oz t. **Consumer prices** (change 1985): −2.5%.

Transport: Motor vehicles: in use (1983): 65,000 passenger ars, 21,000 comm. vehicles. **Chief ports:** Sitra.

Communications: Television sets: 170,000 in use (1985). **adios:** 142,000 in use (1985). **Telephones in use** (1983): 7,000.

Health: Births (per 1,000 pop. 1985): 30. **Deaths** (per 1,000 op. 1985): 7.0. **Natural increase** (1985): 3.5. Medical services re free; there are 49 govt. hospitals and health centers.

Education (1984): **Literacy:** 74%.

Major International Organizations: UN (GATT, IMF, WHO), rab League.

Embassy: 3502 International Dr. NW 20008; 342-0741.

Long ruled by the Khalifa family, Bahrain was a British protec-orate from 1861 to 1971, when it regained independence.

Pearls, shrimp, fruits, and vegetables were the mainstays of e economy until oil was discovered in 1932. By the 1970s, oil eserves were depleted; international banking thrived.

Bahrain took part in the 1973-74 Arab oil embargo against the .S. and other nations. The government bought controlling inter-st in the oil industry in 1975.

Saudi Arabia has built a $1 billion, 15-mile causeway linking ahrain with the Arab mainland.

Bangladesh

People's Republic of Bangladesh

Gama Prajātantrī Bangladesh

People: Population (1986 est.): 104,204,000. **Age distrib.** %): 0-14: 44.3; 15-59: 50.4; 60+: 5.3. **Pop. density:** 1,843 per q. mi. **Urban** (1985): 20%. **Ethnic groups:** Bengali 98%, Bihari, ibesmen. **Languages:** Bengali (official), English. **Religions:** loslem 86%, Hindu 12%.

Geography: Area: 55,598 sq. mi. slightly smaller than Wis-onsin. **Location:** In S Asia, on N bend of Bay of Bengal. **Neigh-ors:** India nearly surrounds country on W, N, E; Burma on SE. **opography:** The country is mostly a low plain cut by the Gan-es and Brahmaputra rivers and their delta. The land is alluvial nd marshy along the coast, with hills only in the extreme SE nd NE. A tropical monsoon climate prevails, among the rainiest in the world. **Capital:** Dhaka. **Cities** (1984 est.): Dhaka (met.) 3.5 mln.; Chittagong (met.) 1.4 mln.; Khulna (met.) 623,000.

Government: Type: Martial law. **Head of state:** Pres. Hossain Mohammad Ershad, b. Feb. 1, 1930, in office: Dec. 11, 1983. **Head of Government:** Prime Min. Mizanur Rahman Chowdhury, in office: July 9, 1986. **Local divisions:** 20 districts. **Defense:** 1.4% of GNP (1984).

Economy: Industries: Cement, jute, textiles, fertilizers, petroleum products. **Chief crops:** Jute (most of world output), rice. **Minerals:** Natural gas, offshore oil, coal. **Fish catch** (1984): 728,000 metric tons. **Electricity prod.** (1984): 4.2 bln. kwh. **Labor force:** 74% agric.

Finance: Currency: Taka (Mar. 1987: 30.8 = $1 US). **Gross national product** (1985): $15.0 bln. **Per capita income** (1986) $113. **Imports** (1983): $2.4 bln.; partners: Jap. 13%, U.S. 8%. **Exports** (1983): $782 mln.; partners: U.S. 10%, Sing. 11%; Pak 5%. **International reserves less gold** (Mar. 1987): $750.4 mln. **Gold:** 54,000 oz t. **Consumer prices** (change in 1986): 11.0%.

Transport: Railway traffic (1984): 6.2 bln. passenger-km; 724 mln. net ton-km. **Motor vehicles:** in use (1981): 35,000 passenger cars, 21,000 comm. vehicles. **Chief ports:** Chittagong, Khulna.

Communications: Radios: 775,000 (1985). **Television sets:** 300,000 (1985). **Telephones in use** (1984): 143,000. **Daily newspaper circ.** (1984) 6 per 1,000 pop.

Health: Life expectancy at birth (1985): 49.2 male; 48.2 female. **Births** (per 1,000 pop. 1985): 44.8. **Deaths** (per 1,000 pop. 1985): 17.5. **Natural increase** (1985): 2.7%. **Hospital beds** (1984): 21,370. **Physicians** (1984): 12,306. **Infant mortality** (per 1,000 live births 1985): 140.

Education (1984): **Literacy:** 25%. **Attendance:** 65% primary school; 25% secondary school.

Major International Organizations: UN (GATT, IMF, WHO).

Embassy: 2201 Wisconsin Ave. NW 20007; 342-8372.

Moslem invaders conquered the formerly Hindu area in the 12th century. British rule lasted from the 18th century to 1947, when East Bengal became part of Pakistan.

Charging West Pakistani domination, the Awami League, based in the East, won National Assembly control in 1971. Assembly sessions were postponed; riots broke out. Pakistani troops attacked Mar. 25; Bangladesh independence was proclaimed the next day. In the ensuing civil war, one million died and 10 million fled to India.

War between India and Pakistan broke out Dec. 3, 1971. Pakistan surrendered in the East Dec. 15. Sheik Mujibur Rahman became prime minister. The country moved into the Indian and Soviet orbits, in response to U.S. support of Pakistan, and much of the economy was nationalized.

In 1974, the government took emergency powers to curb widespread violence; Mujibur was assassinated and a series of coups followed.

Chronic destitution among the densely crowded population has been worsened by the decline of jute as a major world commodity.

On May 30, 1981, Pres. Ziaur Rahman was shot and killed in an unsuccessful coup attempt by army rivals. Vice President Abdus Sattar assumed the presidency but was ousted in a coup led by army chief of staff Gen. H.M. Ershad, Mar. 1982. Bangladesh remains one of the world's poorest countries.

Barbados

People: Population (1986 est.): 253,000 **Age distrib.** (%): 0–14: 27.3%; 15–59: 59.8; 60+: 12.9. **Pop. density:** 1,524 per sq. mi. **Urban** (1985): 42%. **Ethnic groups:** African 80%, mixed 16%, Caucasian 4%. **Languages:** English. **Religions:** Anglican 70%, Methodist 9%, Roman Catholic 4%.

Geography: Area: 166 sq. mi. **Location:** In Atlantic, farthest E of W. Indies. **Neighbors:** Nearest are Trinidad, Grenada on SW. **Topography:** The island lies alone in the Atlantic almost completely surrounded by coral reefs. Highest point is Mt. Hillaby, 1,115 ft. **Capital:** Bridgetown. **Cities** (1982 est.): Bridgetown 7,600.

Government: Type: Independent sovereign state within the Commonwealth. **Head of state:** Queen Elizabeth II, represented by Gov.-Gen. Hugh Springer. **Head of government:** Prime Min. Erskine Sandiford; in office: June 2, 1987. **Local divisions:** 11 parishes and Bridgetown.

Economy: Industries: Rum, molasses, tourism. **Chief crops:** Sugar, corn. **Minerals:** Lime. **Other resources:** Fish. **Arable land:** 76%. **Electricity prod.** (1984): 361.0 mln. kwh. **Labor force:** 6.9% agric.; 12.7% ind. and comm.; 80.9% services and government.

Finance: Currency: Dollar (June 1987: 2.01 = $1 US). **Gross national product** (1984): $1 bln. **Per capita income** (1982): $3,040. **Imports** (1984): $650 mln.; partners: U.S. 47%, UK 7%, Trin./Tob. 8%. **Exports** (1984): $300 mln.; partners: U.S. 27%, UK 9%, Trin./Tob. 9%. **Tourists** (1984): 367,000. **National budget** (1985): $330 mln. **International reserves less gold** (Mar. 1986): $156.7 mln. **Consumer prices** (change in 1986): 1.3%.

Transport: Motor vehicles: in use (1984): 31,000 passenger cars; 5,454 comm. vehicles. **Chief ports:** Bridgetown.

Communications: Television sets: 60,000 in use (1985). **Radios:** 192,000 in use (1984). **Telephones in use** (1984): 81,000. **Daily newspaper circ.** (1984): 159 per 1,000 pop.

Health: Life expectancy at birth (1984): 70.8. **Births** (per 1,000 pop. 1985): 19.0. **Deaths** (per 1,000 pop. 1985): 7.0. **Natural increase** (1985): 1.2%. **Hospital beds** (1983): 2,110. **Physicians** (1983): 213. **Infant mortality** (per 1,000 live births 1985): 14.

Education (1984): **Literacy:** 99%. **Years compulsory:** 9.

Major International Organizations: UN (FAO, GATT, ILO, IMF, WHO), OAS.

Embassy: 2144 Wyoming Ave. NW 20008; 387-7374.

Barbados was probably named by Portuguese sailors in reference to bearded fig trees. An English ship visited in 1605, and British settlers arrived on the uninhabited island in 1627. Slaves worked the sugar plantations, but were freed in 1834.

Self-rule came gradually, with full independence proclaimed Nov. 30, 1966. British traditions have remained.

Belgium

Kingdom of Belgium

Koninkrijk België (Dutch)
Royaume de Belgique (French)

People: Population (1986 est.): 9,868,000. **Age distrib.** (%): 0–14: 20.0; 15–59: 61.4; 60+: 18.6 **Pop. density:** 837 per sq. mi. **Urban** (1980): 73%. **Ethnic groups:** Flemings 58%, Walloons 41%. **Languages:** Flemish (Dutch) 57%, French 33%, legally bilingual 10%, German 1%. **Religions:** Roman Catholic 96%.

Geography: Area: 11,779 sq. mi., slightly larger than Maryland. **Location:** In NW Europe, on N. Sea. **Neighbors:** France on W, S, Luxembourg on SE, W. Germany on E, Netherlands on N. **Topography:** Mostly flat, the country is trisected by the Scheldt and Meuse, major commercial rivers. The land becomes hilly and forested in the SE (Ardennes) region. **Capital:** Brussels. **Cities** (1985 est.): Brussels (met.) 980,196; Antwerp (met.) 486,000; Ghent 234,000; Charleroi 211,000; Liege 202,000.

Government: Type: Parliamentary democracy under a constitutional monarch. **Head of state:** King Baudouin; b. Sept. 7, 1930; in office: July 17, 1951. **Head of government:** Premier Wilfried Martens; b. Apr. 19, 1936; in office: Dec. 17, 1981. **Local divisions:** 9 provinces; 589 communes. **Defense:** 3.3% of GNP (1984).

Economy: Industries: Steel, glassware, diamond cutting, textiles, chemicals. **Chief crops:** Grains, barley, potatoes, sugar beets. **Minerals:** Coal, coke. **Other resources:** Forests. **Arable land** (incl. Lux.): 26.5%. **Meat prod.** (1985): cattle: 3.1 mln; pigs: 5.5 mln. **Fish catch** (1984): 49,000 metric tons. **Electricity prod.** (1984): 54.6 bln. kwh. **Crude steel prod.** (1985): 10.8 mln. metric tons. **Labor force:** 3% agric.; 33% ind. & comm.; 36% services & transportation; 21% public service.

Finance: Currency: Franc (Mar. 1987: 37.39 = $1 US). **Gross national product** (1984): $77 bln. **Per capita income** (1984): $7,803. *Note:* the following trade and tourist data includes Luxembourg. **Imports** (1986): $68.5 bln.; partners: W. Ger. 21%, Neth. 18%, France 14%, UK 7%, U.S. 7%. **Exports** (1986): $68.8 bln.; partners: W. Ger. 21%, France 18%, Neth. 14%, UK 10%. **Tourists** (1984): receipts: $1.7 bln. **National budget** (1984): $31.20 bln. **International reserves less gold** (Mar. 1987): $6.1 bln. **Gold:** 34.11 mln. oz t. **Consumer prices** (change in 1986): 1.3%.

Transport: Railway traffic (1984): 6.4 bln. passenger-km; 7.8 bln. net ton-km. **Motor vehicles:** in use (1984): 3.3 mln. passenger cars, 310,000 comm. vehicles. **Civil aviation** (1985): 5.6 bln. passenger-km; 583 mln. freight ton-km. **Chief ports:** Antwerp, Zeebrugge, Ghent.

Communications: Television sets: 2.9 mln. licensed (1984). **Radios:** 4.6 mln. licensed (1984); **Telephones in use** (1984): 3.9 mln. **Daily newspaper circ.** (1985): 272 per 1,000 pop.

Health: Life expectancy at birth (1985): 70.1 male; 76.7 female. **Births** (per 1,000 pop. 1985): 12.0. **Deaths** (per 1,000 pop. 1985): 12.0. **Natural increase** (1985) .0%. **Hospital beds** (1983): 92,138. **Physicians:** 28,828. **Infant mortality** (per 1,000 live births 1985): 10.

Education (1985): Literacy: 98%. School compulsory to age 16.

Major International Organizations: UN and all of its specialized agencies, NATO, EC, OECD.

Embassy: 3330 Garfield St. NW 20008; 333-6900

Belgium derives its name from the Belgae, the first recorded inhabitants, probably Celts. The land was conquered by Julius Caesar, and was ruled for 1800 years by conquerors, including Rome, the Franks, Burgundy, Spain, Austria, and France. After 1815, Belgium was made a part of the Netherlands, but it became an independent constitutional monarchy in 1830.

Belgian neutrality was violated by Germany in both world wars. King Leopold III surrendered to Germany, May 28, 1940. After the war, he was forced by political pressure to abdicate in favor of his son, King Baudouin.

The Flemings of northern Belgium speak Dutch while French is the language of the Walloons in the south. The language difference has been a perennial source of controversy. Antagonism between the 2 groups has continued.

Belgium lives by its foreign trade; about 50% of its entire production is sold abroad.

Belize

People: Population (1986 est.): 168,400. **Age distrib.** (%): 0–14: 45.3; 15–59: 47.6; 60+: 7.1. **Pop. density:** 19.3 per sq. mi. **Ethnic groups:** African, Mestizo, Amerindian, Creole. **Languages:** English (official), Spanish, native Creole dialects. **Religions:** Roman Catholic 66%, Methodist 13%, Anglican 13%.

Geography: Area: 8,867 sq. mi. **Location:** eastern coast of Central America. **Neighbors:** Mexico on N., Guatemala on W. and S. **Capital:** Belmopan. **Cities:** (1984 est.): Belize City 40,000.

Government: Type: Parliamentary. **Head of State:** Gov. Gen. Minita Gordon. **Head of government:** Prime Min. Manual Esquivel; b. 1940; in office: Dec. 17, 1984. **Local divisions:** 6 districts.

Economy: Sugar is the main export.

Finance: Currency: Belize dollar (Mar. 1987) 2 = $1 U.S. **Gross domestic product** (1983): 176 mln. **Per capita income** (1984): $1,000. **Imports** (1984) $130 mln.; partners: U.S. 43%, UK 8%. **Exports:** (1984): 73 mln.; partners: U.S. 57%, UK 20%. **National Budget** (1986): $106 mln. expenditures.

Health: life expectancy (1981) 60 yrs. **Births** (per 1,000 pop. 1985): 38.0. **Deaths** (per 1,000 pop. 1985): 7.0. **Hospital beds** (1984): 584; **Physicians** (1984): 78. (1983). **Infant mortality** (per 1,000 live births, 1985): 54.

Education: (1985) **Literacy:** 80%.; **Years compulsory:** 9; attendance 55%.

Major International Organizations: UN (IMF, World Bank), Commonwealth of Nations.

Embassy: 1575 i St. NW 20005; 289-1416.

Belize (formerly called British Honduras), Great Britain's last colony on the American mainland, achieved independence on Sept. 21, 1981. Guatemala claims territorial sovereignty over the country and has refused to recognize Belize's independence. British troops in Belize guarantee security.

Benin

People's Republic of Benin

République Populaire du Benin

People: Population (1986 est.): 4,141,000. **Age distrib.** (%): 0–14: 46.5; 15–59: 49.0; 60+: 4.5. **Pop. density:** 94.9 per sq. mi. **Urban** (1984): 20%. **Ethnic groups:** Fons, Adjas, Baribas, Yorubas. **Languages:** French (official), local dialects. **Religions:** Mainly animist with Christian, Muslim minorities.

Geography: Area: 43,483 sq. mi., slightly smaller than Pennsylvania. **Location:** In W Africa on Gulf of Guinea. **Neighbors:** Togo on W, Burkina Faso, Niger on N, Nigeria on E. **Topography:** most of Benin is flat and covered with dense vegetation. The coast is hot, humid, and rainy. **Capital:** Porto-Novo. **Cities** (1984 est.): Cotonou 330,000.

Government: Type: Marxist-Leninist. **Head of state:** Pres. Ahmed Kerekou; b. Sept. 2, 1933; in office: Oct. 27, 1972. **Local divisions:** 6 provinces, 84 districts. **Defense:** 2.6% of GNP (1983).

Economy: Chief crops: Palm products, peanuts, cotton, kapok, coffee, tobacco. **Minerals:** Oil. **Arable land:** 16%. **Fish catch** (1983): 21,000 metric tons. **Electricity prod.** (1984): 160 mln. kwh. **Labor force:** 60% agric; 30% serv. & comm.

Finance: Currency: CFA franc (Mar. 1987: 300 = $1 US). **Gross national product** (1984): $1.1 bln. **Per capita income** (1983): $290. **Imports** (1982): $590 mln.; partners: Fr. 27%, UK 13%, W. Ger. 6%, Neth. 6%. **Exports** (1982): $304 mln.; partners: Neth. 28%, Jap. 27%, Fr. 24%. **International reserves less gold** (Feb. 1987): $5.4 mln.

Transport: Railway traffic (1984): 187.6 mln. passenger-km; 176 mln. net ton-km. **Chief ports:** Cotonou.

Communications: Radios: 290,000 in use (1984). **Televisions:** 17,000 (1984). **Daily newspaper circ.** (1985): 3 per 1,000 pop.

Health: Life expectancy at birth (1984): 46.9 yrs. **Births** (per 1,000 pop. 1985): 47. **Deaths** (per 1,000 pop. 1985): 16. **Natural increase** (1985): 3.1%. **Hospital beds** (1982): 4,902. **Physicians** (1982): 204. **Infant mortality** (per 1,000 live births 1985): 143.

Education (1984): **Literacy:** 11%. Years compulsory 6; attendance 43%.

Major International Organizations: UN (GATT, IMF, WHO), OAU.

Embassy: 2737 Cathedral Ave. NW 20008; 232-6656.

The Kingdom of Abomey, rising to power in wars with neighboring kingdoms in the 17th century, came under French domination in the late 19th century, and was incorporated into French West Africa by 1904.

Under the name Dahomey, the country became independent Aug. 1, 1960. The name was changed to Benin in 1975. In the fifth coup since independence Col. Ahmed Kerekou took power in 1972; two years later he declared a socialist state with a "Marxist-Leninist" philosophy. The economy relies on the development of agriculturally-based industries.

Bhutan

Kingdom of Bhutan

Druk-Yul

People: Population (1986 est.): 1,446,000. **Age distrib.** (%): 0–14: 40.0; 15–59: 54.5; over 60: 5.5 **Pop. density:** 79 per sq. mi. **Ethnic groups:** Bhote (Tibetan) 60%. Nepalese 25%, Lepcha (indigenous), Indians. **Languages:** Dzongkha (official), Nepali. **Religions:** Buddhist 75%, Hindu 25%, Moslem 5%.

Geography: Area: 18,147 sq. mi., the size of Vermont and New Hampshire combined. **Location:** In eastern Himalayan Mts. **Neighbors:** India on W (Sikkim) and S, China on N. **Topography:** Bhutan is comprised of very high mountains in the N, fertile valleys in the center, and thick forests in the Duar Plain in the S. **Capital:** Thimphu. **City** (1985 est.): Thimphu 20,000.

Government: Type: Monarchy. **Head of state:** King Jigme Singye Wangchuk; b. Nov. 11, 1955; in office: July 21, 1972. **Local divisions:** 18 districts.

Economy: Industries: Handicrafts. **Chief crops:** Rice, corn, wheat. **Other resources:** Timber. **Arable land:** 2%. **Labor force:** 95% agric.

Finance: Currency: Ngultrum (Nov. 1986: 12.78 = 1 US) (Indian Rupee also used). **Gross national product** (1984): $135 mln. **Per capita income** (1983): $120. **Imports** (1983): $58 mln.; partners India 99%. **Exports** (1983): $16.7 mln.; partners India 99%.

Communications: Radios: 12,500 licensed (1986). **Telephones in use** (1982): 14,000.

Health: Life expectancy at birth (1985): 46.6 male; 45.1 female. **Births** (per 1,000 pop. 1985): 38. **Deaths** (per 1,000 pop. 1985): 17. **Natural increase** (1985): 2.1%. **Hospital beds** (1983): 831. **Physicians** (1983): 65. **Infant mortality** (per 1,000 live births 1985): 122.

Education (1985): **Literacy:** 10%. School attendance: 20%.

Major International Organizations: UN (IMF, World Bank).

The region came under Tibetan rule in the 16th century. British influence grew in the 19th century. A monarchy, set up in 1907, became a British protectorate by a 1910 treaty. The country became independent in 1949, with India guiding foreign relations and supplying aid.

Links to India have been strengthened by airline service and a road network. Most of the population engages in subsistence agriculture.

Bolivia

Republic of Bolivia

República de Bolivia

People: Population (1986 est.): 6,200,000. **Age distrib.** (%): 0–14: 43; 15–59: 51.8; 60+: 5.2. **Pop. density:** 15 per sq. mi. **Ethnic groups:** Quechua 30%, Aymara 25%, mixed 30%, European 14%. **Languages:** Spanish (official), Quechua, Aymara. **Religions:** Roman Catholic 95%.

Geography: Area: 424,165 sq. mi., the size of Texas and California combined. **Location:** In central Andes Mtns. **Neighbors:** Peru, Chile on W, Argentina, Paraguay on S, Brazil on E and N. **Topography:** The great central plateau, at an altitude of 12,000 ft., over 500 mi. long, lies between two great cordilleras having 3 of the highest peaks in S. America. Lake Titicaca, on Peruvian border, is highest lake in world on which steamboats ply (12,506 ft.). The E central region has semitropical forests; the llanos, or Amazon-Chaco lowlands are in E. **Capitals:** Sucre, (legal), La Paz (de facto). **Cities** (1986 est.): La Paz 955,000; Santa Cruz 419,000; Cochabamba 304,000.

Government: Type: Republic. **Head of state:** Pres. Victor Paz Estenssoro, b. Oct. 2, 1907; in office: Aug. 6, 1985. **Local divisions:** 9 departments, 94 provinces.

Economy: Industry: Textiles, food processing, chemicals, plastics. **Chief crops:** Potatoes, sugar, coffee, barley, cocoa, rice, corn, bananas, citrus. **Minerals:** Antimony, tin, tungsten, silver, zinc, oil, gas, iron. **Crude oil reserves** (1985): 157 mln. bbls. **Other resources:** rubber, cinchona bark. **Arable land:** 27%. **Electricity prod.** (1984): 1.6 bln. kwh. **Labor force:** 47% agric., 19% ind. & comm, 34% serv. & govt.

Finance: Currency: Peso (Mar. 1987: 2,000 = $1 US). **Gross domestic product** (1985): $4.0 bln. **Per capita income** (1985): $536. **Imports** (1985): $552 mln.; partners: U.S. 28%, Jap. 7.3%, Arg. 14%, Braz. 14%. **Exports** (1985): $663 mln.; partners: U.S. 20%. **National budget** (1980): $3.8 bln. revenues; $4.7 bln. expenditures. **International reserves less gold** (Mar. 1987): $234 mln. **Gold:** 894,000 oz t. **Consumer prices** (change in 1985): +11,743%.

Transport: Railway traffic (1985): 771 mln. passenger-km; 590 mln. net ton-miles. **Motor vehicles:** in use (1983): 40,000 passenger cars, 36,000 comm. vehicles. **Civil aviation** (1985): 779 mln. passenger-km.; 98.1 mln. freight ton-km.

Communications: Television sets: 386,000 (1984). **Radios:** 480,000 in use (1984). **Telephones in use** (1983): 204,000. **Daily newspaper circ.** (1984): 40 per 1,000 pop.

Health: Life expectancy at birth (1985): 48.6 male; 53.0 female. **Births** (per 1,000 pop. 1985): 42.0. **Deaths** (per 1,000 pop. 1985): 15. **Natural increase** (1985): 2.9%. **Hospital beds**

(per 100,000 pop. 1977): 228. **Physicians** (per 100,000 pop. 1977): 38. **Infant mortality** (per 1,000 live births 1986): 123.

Education (1986): **Literacy:** 75%. **Years compulsory:** ages 7-14; attendance 82%.

Major International Organizations: UN (IMF, FAO, WHO), OAS.

Embassy: 3014 Massachusetts Ave. NW 20008; 483-4410.

The Incas conquered the region from earlier Indian inhabitants in the 13th century. Spanish rule began in the 1530s, and lasted until Aug. 6, 1825. The country is named after Simon Bolivar, independence fighter.

In a series of wars, Bolivia lost its Pacific coast to Chile, the oilbearing Chaco to Paraguay, and rubber-growing areas to Brazil, 1879-1935.

Economic unrest, especially among the militant mine workers, has contributed to continuing political instability. A reformist government under Victor Paz Estenssoro, 1951-64, nationalized tin mines and attempted to improve conditions for the Indian majority, but was overthrown by a military junta. A series of coups and countercoups continued through 1981, until the military junta elected Gen. Villa as president.

In July 1982, the military junta assumed power amid a growing economic crisis and foreign debt difficulties. The junta resigned in October and allowed the Congress, elected democratically in 1980, to take power.

Bolivia has instituted strict fiscal and monetary restraints to control inflation which is the highest in the world.

In 1986, U.S. troops and helicopters assisted Bolivia in its fight against cocaine trafficking.

Botswana

Republic of Botswana

People: Population (1986 est.): 1,104,000. **Age distrib.** (%): 0–14: 46.1; 15–59: 43.1; 60+: 7.4. **Pop. density:** 5 per sq. mi. **Urban** (1984): 17%. **Ethnic groups:** Batswana, others. **Languages:** English (official), Setswana (national). **Religions:** indigenous beliefs (majority), Christian 15%.

Geography: Area: 231,804 sq. mi., slightly smaller than Texas. **Location:** In southern Africa. **Neighbors:** Namibia (S.W. Africa) on N and W, S. Africa on S, Zimbabwe on NE; Botswana claims border with Zambia on N. **Topography:** The Kalahari Desert, supporting nomadic Bushmen and wildlife, spreads over SW; there are swamplands and farming areas in N, and rolling plains in E where livestock are grazed. **Capital:** Gaborone. **Cities** (1985): Gaborone 79,000.

Government: Type: Republic, parliamentary democracy. **Head of state:** Pres. Quett Masire; b. 1925; in office: July 13, 1980. **Local divisions:** 10 district councils and 4 town councils. **Defense:** 1.8% of national budget (1985).

Economy: Industries: Tourism. **Chief crops:** Corn, sorghum, peanuts. **Minerals:** Copper, coal, nickel, diamonds. **Other resources:** Big game. **Arable land:** 2%. **Electricity prod.** (1985): 621 mln. kwh. **Labor force:** 70% agric.

Finance: Currency: Pula (Mar. 1987: 0.40 = $1 US). **Gross national product** (1984): $940 mln. **Imports** (1984): $411 mln.; partners: S. Africa 88%. **Exports** (1984): $469 mln.; partners: Europe 67%, U.S. 17%, S. Africa 7%. **National budget** (1985): $241 mln. **International reserves less gold** (Mar. 1987): $1.2 bln. **Consumer prices** (change in 1986): 10.0%

Transport: Railway traffic (1984): 1.0 bln. net ton km. **Motor vehicles:** in use (1983): 11,000 passenger cars, 20,500 comm. vehicles.

Communications: Radios: 77,000 in use (1985). **Daily newspaper circ.** (1985): 22 per 1,000 pop.

Health: Life expectancy at birth (1981): 52.7 male; 59.3 female. **Births** (annual per 1,000 pop. 1985): 45. **Deaths** (per 1,000 pop. 1985): 12. **Natural increase** (1985): 3.3%. **Hospital beds** (1981): 2,067. **Physicians** (1981): 113. **Infant mortality** (per 1,000 live births 1985): 63.

Education (1985): **Literacy:** 35% (in English).

Major International Organizations: UN (GATT, IMF, WHO), OAU, Commonwealth of Nations.

Embassy: 4301 Connecticut Ave. NW 20008; 244-4990.

First inhabited by bushmen, then by Bantus, the region became the British protectorate of Bechuanaland in 1886, halting encroachment by Boers and Germans from the south and southwest. The country became fully independent Sept. 30, 1966, changing its name to Botswana.

Cattle-raising and mining (diamonds, copper, nickel) have contributed to the country's economic growth.

Brazil

Federative Republic of Brazil

República Federativa do Brasil

People: Population (1986 est.): 143,277,000. **Age distrib.** (%): 0–14: 36.4; 15–59: 57.0; 60+: 6.6. **Pop. density:** 43 per sq. mi. **Urban** (1985): 72%. **Ethnic groups:** Portuguese, Africans, and mulattoes make up the vast majority; Italians, Germans, Japanese, Indians, Jews, Arabs. **Languages:** Portuguese (official), English. **Religions:** Roman Catholic 89%.

Geography: Area: 3,286,470 sq. mi., larger than contiguous 48 U.S. states; largest country in S. America. **Location:** Occupies eastern half of S. America. **Neighbors:** French Guiana, Suriname, Guyana, Venezuela on N, Colombia, Peru, Bolivia, Paraguay, Argentina on W, Uruguay on S. **Topography:** Brazil's Atlantic coastline stretches 4,603 miles. In N is the heavily-wooded Amazon basin covering half the country. Its network of rivers navigable for 15,814 mi. The Amazon itself flows 2,093 miles in Brazil, all navigable. The NE region is semiarid scrubland, heavily settled and poor. The S central region, favored by climate and resources, has almost half of the population, produces 75% of farm goods and 80% of industrial output. The narrow coastal belt includes most of the major cities. Almost the entire country has a tropical or semitropical climate. **Capital:** Brasilia. **Cities** (1980 cen.): Sao Paulo 7 mln.; Rio de Janeiro 5 mln.; Belo Horizonte 1.4 mln.; Recife 1.1 mln.; Salvador 1.4 mln.; Porto Alegre 1.1 mln.

Government: Type: Federal republic. **Head of state:** Pres. Jose Sarney; b. Apr. 30, 1930; in office: Apr. 22, 1985. **Local divisions:** 23 states, with individual constitutions and elected governments; 3 territories, federal district. **Defense:** 0.7% of GNP (1985).

Economy: Industries: Steel, autos, chemicals, ships, appliances, petrochemicals, machinery. **Chief crops:** Coffee (largest grower), cotton, soybeans, sugar, cocoa, rice, corn, fruits. **Minerals:** Chromium, iron, manganese, tin, quartz crystals, beryl, sheet mica, columbium, titanium, diamonds, thorium, gold, nickel, gem stones, coal, tin, tungsten, bauxite, oil. **Crude oil reserves** (1985): 2 bln. bbls. **Arable land:** 17%. **Meat prod.** (1985): cattle: 133 mln.; pigs: 30.5 mln.; sheep: 19 mln. **Fish catch** (1984): 946,000 metric tons. **Electricity prod.** (1984): 175.7 bln. kwh. **Crude steel prod.** (1985): 20.4 mln. metric tons. **Labor force:** 40% services, 35% agric.; 25% ind.

Finance: Currency: Cruzeiro (May 1987: 30.99 = $1 US). **Gross domestic product** (1984): $218 bln. **Per capita income** (1978): $1,523. **Imports** (1985): $13.2 bln.; partners: U.S. 16%, Jap. 6%. **Exports** (1985): $25.6 bln.; partners: U.S. 28%, W. Ger. 5%, Neth. 6%, Japan 6%. **Tourists** (1984): receipts: $1.5 bln. **National budget** (1979): $18.91 bln. revenues; $18.83 bln. expenditures. **International reserves less gold** (Jan. 1986): $5.8 bln. **Gold:** 2.2 mln. oz t. **Consumer prices** (change in 1986): 81%.

Transport: Railway traffic (1984): 15.4 bln. passenger-km; 92 bln. net ton-km. **Motor vehicles:** in use (1984): 10 mln. passenger cars, 1.1 mln. **Civil aviation** (1985): 18.2 bln. passenger-km; 907 mln. freight ton-km: **Chief ports:** Santos, Rio de Janeiro, Vitoria, Salvador, Rio Grande, Recife.

Communications: Television sets: 30 mln. in use (1985). **Radios:** 53 mln. in use (1985). **Telephones in use** (1984): 10.8 mln. **Daily newspaper circ.** (1983): 44 per 1,000 pop.

Health: Life expectancy at birth (1985): 60.9 male; 66.0 female. **Births** (per 1,000 pop. 1985): 30.6. **Deaths** (per 1,000 pop. 1985): 8.4. **Natural increase** (1985): 2.2%. **Hospital beds** (1982): 530,000. **Physicians** (per 100,000 pop. 1980): 68.1. **Infant mortality** (per 1,000 live births 1985): 64.

Education (1985): **Literacy:** 76%.

Major International Organizations: UN and all of its specialized agencies, OAS.

Embassy: 3006 Massachusetts Ave. NW 20008; 745-2700.

Pedro Alvares Cabral, a Portuguese navigator, is generally credited as the first European to reach Brazil, in 1500. The country was thinly settled by various Indian tribes. Only a few have survived to the present, mostly in the Amazon basin.

In the next centuries, Portuguese colonists gradually pushed inland, bringing along large numbers of African slaves. Slavery was not abolished until 1888.

The King of Portugal, fleeing before Napoleon's army, moved the seat of government to Brazil in 1808. Brazil thereupon became a kingdom under Dom Joao VI. After his return to Portugal, his son Pedro proclaimed the independence of Brazil, Sept. 7, 1822, and was acclaimed emperor. The second emperor, Dom Pedro II, was deposed in 1889, and a republic proclaimed, called the United States of Brazil. In 1967 the country was renamed the Federative Republic of Brazil.

A military junta took control in 1930; dictatorial power was assumed by Getulio Vargas, who alternated with military coups until finally forced out by the military in 1954. A democratic regime prevailed 1956-64, during which time the capital was moved from Rio de Janeiro to Brasilia in the interior.

The next 5 presidents were all military leaders. Censorship was imposed, and much of the opposition was suppressed amid charges of torture. In 1974 elections, the official opposition party made gains in the chamber of deputies; some relaxation of censorship occurred.

Since 1930, successive governments have pursued industrial and agricultural growth and the development of interior areas. Exploiting vast mineral resources, fertile soil in several regions, and a huge labor force, Brazil became the leading industrial power of Latin America by the 1970s, while agricultural output soared. Democratic elections were held in 1985 as the nation returned to civilian rule.

However, income maldistribution, inflation and government land policies have all led to severe economic recession. Foreign debt is among the largest in the world. Brazil announced, Feb. 1987, that it was unilaterally suspending payment of interest on debt to foreign commercial banks.

Brunei

Negara Brunei Darussalam

People: Population (1986 est.): 240,000. **Pop. Density:** 104 per sq. mi. **Ethnic groups:** Malay 65%, Chinese 20%. **Language:** Malay (official), English. **Religion:** Moslem 64%, Buddhist 14%, Christian 10%.

Geography: Area: 2,226 sq. mi. **Location:** on the north coast of the island of Borneo; it is surrounded on its landward side by the Malaysian state of Sarawak. **Capital:** Bandar Seri Begawan. **Cities** (1982 est.): Bandar Seri Begawan 51,000.

Government: Type: Independent sultanate. **Head of Government:** Sultan Sir Muda Hassanal Bolkiah Mu'izzadin Waddaulah; in office: Jan. 1, 1984.

Economy: Industries: petroleum (about 90% of revenue is derived from oil exports). **Chief crops:** rice, bananas, cassava.

Finance: Currency: Brunei dollar (Dec. 1986: 2.17 = $1). **Gross domestic product** (1983): $3.8 bln. **Per capita income** (1984): $20,000.

Communications: Television sets: 45,000 (1985). **Radios:** 70,000 (1985). **Telephones:** 32,000 (1985).

Education (1984): **Literacy:** 80%.

Heath: Infant Mortality (per 1,000 live births 1985): 12.1.

The Sultanate of Brunei was a powerful state in the early 16th century with authority over all of the island of Borneo as well as parts of the Sulu Islands and the Philippines. In 1888, a treaty was signed which placed the state under the protection of Great Britain.

Brunei became a fully sovereign and independent state on Jan. 1, 1984.

The Sultan of Brunei donated $10 million to the Nicaraguan contras in 1987.

Bulgaria

People's Republic of Bulgaria

Narodna Republika Bulgaria

People: Population (1986 est.): 8,990,000. **Age distrib.** (%): 0–14: 22.2; 15–59: 60.2; 60+: 17.6. **Pop. density:** 209 per sq. mi. **Urban** (1984): 65%. **Ethnic groups:** Bulgarians 85%, Turks 8.5%. **Languages:** Bulgarian, Turkish, Greek. **Religions:** Orthodox 85%, Moslem 13%.

Geography: Area: 44,365 sq. mi., about the size of Ohio. **Location:** In eastern Balkan Peninsula on Black Sea. **Neighbors:** Romania on N, Yugoslavia on W, Greece, Turkey on S. **Topography:** The Stara Planina (Balkan) Mts. stretch E-W across the center of the country, with the Danubian plain on N, the Rhodope Mts. on SW, and Thracian Plain on SE. **Capital:** Sofia. **Cities** (1986 est.): Sofia 1,114,759; Plovdiv 377,637; Varna 297,090.

Government: Type: Communist. **Head of state:** Pres. Todor Zhivkov; b. Sept. 7, 1911; in office: July 7, 1971. **Head of government:** Premier Georgy Atanasov; in office: Mar. 21, 1986. **Head of Communist Party:** First Sec. Todor Zhivkov; b. 1911; in office: Jan. 1954. **Local divisions:** 27 provinces, one city. **Defense:** 8.1% of GNP (1983).

Economy: Industries: Chemicals, machinery, metals, textiles, fur, leather goods, vehicles, wine, processed food. **Chief crops:** Grains, fruit, corn, potatoes, tobacco. **Minerals:** Lead, bauxite, coal, oil, zinc. **Arable land:** 38%. **Meat prod.** (1985): cattle: 1.7 mln.; pigs: 3.9 mln.; sheep: 9.7 mln. **Fish catch** (1982): 115,000 metric tons. **Electricity prod.** (1984): 44.6 bln. kwh. **Crude steel prod.** (1985): 2.8 mln. metric tons. **Labor force:** 22% agric.; 43% ind. & comm.

Finance: Currency: Lev (Dec. 1986: .93 = $1 US). **Gross National Product** (1985): $25 bln. **Per capita income** (1985): $2,806. **Imports** (1985): $14.0 bln.; partners: USSR 54%, E. Ger. 6%, W. Ger. 5%. **Exports** (1985): $13.7 bln.; partners: USSR 48%, E. Ger. 6%. **Tourists** (1984): revenues $286 mln. **National budget** (1983): $16.7 bln. expenditures.

Transport: Railway traffic (1984): 8.2 bln. passenger-km; 18 bln. net ton-km. **Motor vehicles:** in use (1983) 937,000 passenger cars, 519,000 commercial. **Chief ports:** Burgas, Varna.

Communications: Television sets: 1.6 mln. licensed (1985). **Radios:** 2.1 mln. licensed (1985). **Telephones in use** (1985): 1.0 mln. **Daily newspaper circ.** (1984): 249 per 1,000 pop.

Health: Life expectancy at birth (1984): 68 male; 74 female. **Births** (per 1,000 pop. 1985): 13.0. **Deaths** (per 1,000 pop. 1985): 12.0. **Hospital beds** (1985): 82,300. **Physicians:** 24,000. **Infant mortality** (per 1,000 live births 1986): 16.1

Education (1986). **Literacy:** 98%. **Years compulsory:** ages 7-16.

Major International Organizations: UN, Warsaw Pact.

Embassy: 1621-22d St. NW 20008; 387-7970.

Bulgaria was settled by Slavs in the 6th century. Turkic Bulgars arrived in the 7th century, merged with the Slavs, became Christians by the 9th century, and set up powerful empires in the 10th and 12th centuries. The Ottomans prevailed in 1396 and remained for 500 years.

A revolt in 1876 led to an independent kingdom in 1908. Bulgaria expanded after the first Balkan War but lost its Aegean coastline in World War I, when it sided with Germany. Bulgaria joined the Axis in World War II, but withdrew in 1944. Communists took power with Soviet aid; the monarchy was abolished Sept. 8, 1946.

Burkina Faso

People: Population (1986 est.): 7,084,000. **Pop. density:** 76 per sq. mi. **Ethnic groups:** Voltaic groups (Mossi, Bobo), Mande. **Languages:** French (official), More, Sudanic tribal languages. **Religions:** animist 65%, Moslems 25%, Christian 10%.

Geography: Area: 105,869 sq. mi., the size of Colorado. **Location:** In W. Africa, S of the Sahara. **Neighbors:** Mali on NW, Niger on NE, Benin, Togo, Ghana, Côte d' Ivoire on S. **Topography:** Landlocked Burkina Faso is in the savannah region of W. Africa. The N is arid, hot, and thinly populated. **Capital:** Ouagadougou. **Cities** (1986): Ouagadougou 366,000; Bobo-Dioulasso 202,000.

Government: Type: Military. **Head of state:** Pres. Thomas Sankara; b. 1948; in office: Aug. 4, 1983. **Local divisions:** 30 provinces. **Defense:** 2.8% of GNP (1983).

Economy: Chief crops: Millet, sorghum, rice, peanuts, grain. **Minerals:** Manganese, gold, limestone. **Arable land:** 10%. **Electricity prod.** (1984): 121 mln. kwh. **Labor force:** 83% agric.; 12% industry.

Finance: Currency: CFA franc (Mar. 1987: 300 = $1 US). **Gross domestic product** (1983): $1.2 bln. **Per capita income**

(1983): $150. **Imports** (1983): $279 mln.; partners: EC, Ivory Coast. **Exports** (1983): $55 mln.; partners: Ivory Coast, EC, China. **International reserves less gold** (Jan. 1987): $263.9 mln. **Gold:** 11,000 oz t. **Consumer prices** (change in 1985): 6.9%.

Transport: Motor vehicles: in use (1983): 21,000 passenger cars, 6,600 comm. vehicles.

Communications: Television sets: 18,000 in use (1985). **Radios:** 116,000 in use (1985). **Telephones in use** (1981): 10,000. **Daily newspaper circ.** (1984): 2 per 1,000 pop.

Health: Life expectancy at birth (1984): 42 yrs. **Births** (per 1,000 pop. 1985): 48. **Deaths** (per 1,000 pop. 1985): 22. **Natural increase** (1985): 2.6%. **Hospital beds** (1980): 4,587. **Physicians** (1984): 118. **Infant mortality** (per 1,000 live births 1985): 176.

Education (1986): **Literacy:** 8%. Only 8% attend school.

Major International Organizations: UN and many of its specialized agencies, OAU.

Embassy: 2340 Massachusetts Ave. NW 20008; 332-5577.

The Mossi tribe entered the area in the 11th to 13th centuries. Their kingdoms ruled until defeated by the Mali and Songhai empires.

French control came by 1896, but Upper Volta (name changed to Burkina Faso on Aug. 4, 1984), was not finally established as a separate territory until 1947. Full independence came Aug. 5, 1960, and a pro-French government was elected. A 1982 coup established the current regime.

Several hundred thousand farm workers migrate each year to Ivory Coast and Ghana. Droughts brought famine in the 1970s. Burkina Faso is heavily dependent on foreign aid.

Burma

Socialist Republic of the Union of Burma

Pyidaungsu Socialist Thammada Myanma Naingngandaw

People: Population (1986 est.): 37,641,000. **Age distrib.** (%): 0–14: 41.2; 15–59: 52.8; 60+: 6.0. **Pop. density:** 147 per sq. mi. **Ethnic groups:** Burmans (related to Tibetans) 68%; Karen 7%, Shan 9%, Rakhine 4%. **Languages:** Burmese (official). **Religions:** Buddhist 85%; animists, Christians.

Geography: Area: 261,789 sq. mi., nearly as large as Texas. **Location:** Between S. and S.E. Asia, on Bay of Bengal. **Neighbors:** Bangladesh, India on W, China, Laos, Thailand on E. **Topography:** Mountains surround Burma on W, N, and E, and dense forests cover much of the nation. N-S rivers provide habitable valleys and communications, especially the Irrawaddy, navigable for 900 miles. The country has a tropical monsoon climate. **Capital:** Rangoon. **Cities** (1983 est.): Rangoon 2,458,712; Mandalay 458,000; Karbe ('73 cen.): 253,600; Moulmein 188,000.

Government: Type: Socialist republic. **Head of state:** Pres. U San Yu in office: Nov. 9, 1981. **Head of government:** Prime Min. U. Maung Maung Kha; b. Nov. 2, 1917; in office: Mar. 29, 1977. **Local divisions:** 7 states and 7 divisions. **Defense:** 4.2% of GNP (1985).

Economy: Chief crops: Rice, sugarcane, peanuts, beans. **Minerals:** Oil, lead, silver, tin, tungsten, precious stones. **Crude oil reserves** (1985): 733 mln. bbls. **Other resources:** Rubber, teakwood. **Arable land:** 15%. **Meat prod.** (1985): cattle: 9.9 mln.; pigs: 3.1 mln. **Fish catch** (1984): 585,000 metric tons. **Electricity prod.** (1984): 1.7 bln. kwh. **Labor force:** 66% agric; 12% ind.

Finance: Currency: Kyat (Mar. 1987: 6.68 = $1 US). **Gross national product** (1985): $6.5 bln. **Per capita income** (1985): $179. **Imports** (1985): $648 mln.; partners: Jap. 34%, U.S. 12%, UK 9%, W. Ger. 9%. **Exports** (1985): $399 mln.; partners: Switz. 12%, Sing. 10%. **National budget** (1986): $4.3 bln. **International reserves less gold** (Mar. 1987): $24.4 mln. **Gold:** 251,000 oz t. **Consumer prices** (change in 1986): 9.2%.

Transport: Railway traffic (1984): 2.9 bln. passenger-km; 445 mln. net ton-km. **Motor vehicles:** in use (1980): 43,000 passenger cars, 44,000 comm. vehicles. **Civil aviation** (1984): 224 mln. passenger-km.; 1.7 mln. net ton-km. **Chief ports:** Rangoon, Sittwe, Bassein, Moulmein, Tavoy.

Communications: Television sets: 35,000 (1985), **Radios:** 725,000 in use (1985). **Telephones in use** (1984): 53,000. **Daily newspaper circ.** (1985): 14 per 1,000 pop.

Health: Life expectancy at birth (1985): 53.4 male; 56.7 female. **Births** (per 1,000 pop. 1985): 37.9. **Deaths** (per 1,000 pop. 1985): 12.7. **Natural increase** (1985): 2.5%. **Hospital beds** (1984): 25,919. **Physicians** (1984): 8,931. **Infant mortality** (per 1,000 live births 1986): 96.

Education (1986): **Literacy:** 66%. **Years compulsory:** 4; **Attendance:** 84%.

Major International Organizations: UN (World Bank, IMF, GATT).

Embassy: 2300 S St. NW 20008; 332-9044.

The Burmese arrived from Tibet before the 9th century, displacing earlier cultures, and a Buddhist monarchy was established by the 11th. Burma was conquered by the Mongol dynasty of China in 1272, then ruled by Shans as a Chinese tributary, until the 16th century.

Britain subjugated Burma in 3 wars, 1824-84, and ruled the country as part of India until 1937, when it became self-governing. Independence outside the Commonwealth was achieved Jan. 4, 1948.

Gen. Ne Win dominated politics from the 1960s to 1986 when he abdicated power. He led a Revolutionary Council set up in 1962, which drove Indians from the civil service and Chinese from commerce. Socialization of the economy was advanced, isolation from foreign countries enforced. Lagging production and export have begun to turn around, due to government incentives in the agriculture and petroleum sectors and receptivity to foreign investment in the economy.

Burundi

Republic of Burundi

Republika y'Uburundi

People: Population (1986 est.): 4,807,000. **Age distrib.** (%): 0–14: 44.3; 15–59: 49.6; 60+: 6.1. **Pop. density:** 481 per sq. mi. **Urban** (1985): 2.5%. **Ethnic groups:** Hutu 85%, Tutsi 14%, Twa (pygmy) 1%. **Languages:** French, Rundi (both official). **Religions:** Roman Catholic 62%, traditional African 32%.

Geography: Area: 10,759 sq. mi., the size of Maryland. **Location:** In central Africa. **Neighbors:** Rwanda on N, Zaire on W, Tanzania on E. **Topography:** Much of the country is grassy highland, with mountains reaching 8,900 ft. The southernmost source of the White Nile is located in Burundi. Lake Tanganyika is the second deepest lake in the world. **Capital:** Bujumbura. **Cities** (1986 est.): Bujumbura 272,000.

Government: Type: Republic. **Head of state and head of government:** Pres. Jean Baptiste Bagaza; b. Aug. 29, 1946; in office: Nov. 9, 1976 (govt: Oct. 1978). **Local divisions:** 15 provinces, 114 communes. **Defense** (1983): 3.2% of GNP.

Economy: Chief crops: Coffee (90% of exports), cotton, tea. **Minerals:** Nickel. **Arable land:** 50%. **Fish catch** (1984): 12,000 metric tons. **Electricity prod.** (1984): 20 mln. kwh. **Labor force:** 93% agric.

Finance: Currency: Franc (Apr. 1987: 125.2 = $1 US). **Gross national product** (1984): $1.0 bln. **Per capita income** (1984) $273. **Imports** (1984): $183 mln.; partners: Iran 14%, Belg.-Lux. 16%, Jap. 8%. **Exports** (1984): $99 mln; partners: U.S. 32%, Belg. 10%. **National budget** (1984): $160 mln. expenditures. **International reserves less gold** (Mar. 1987): $74.5 mln. **Gold:** 17,000 oz t. **Consumer prices** (change in 1986): 1.9%.

Transport: Motor vehicles: in use (1984): 7,500 passenger cars, 6,000 comm. vehicles.

Communications: Radios: 160,000 in use (1984). **Telephones in use** (1982): 5,601.

Health: Life expectancy at birth (1985): 42.4 male; 45.6 female. **Births** (per 1,000 pop. 1985): 47.6. **Deaths** (per 1,000 pop. 1985): 20.9. **Natural increase** (1985): 2.6%. **Hospital beds** (1983): 2,893. **Physicians** (1983): 216. **Infant mortality** (per 1,000 live births 1985): 137.

Education (1985): **Literacy:** 30%.

Major International Organizations: UN (GATT, IMF, WHO), OAU.

Embassy: 2233 Wisconsin Ave. NW 20007; 342-2574.

The pygmy Twa were the first inhabitants, followed by Bantu Hutus, who were conquered in the 16th century by the tall Tutsi (Watusi), probably from Ethiopia. Under German control in 1899, the area fell to Belgium in 1916, which exercised successively a League of Nations mandate and UN trusteeship over Ruanda-Urundi (now 2 countries).

Independence came in 1962, and the monarchy was overthrown in 1966. An unsuccessful Hutu rebellion in 1972-73 left 10,000 Tutsi and 150,000 Hutu dead. Over 100,000 Hutu fled to Tanzania and Zaire. The present regime is pledged to ethnic reconciliation, but Burundi remains one of the poorest and most densely populated countries in Africa.

Cambodia (Kampuchea)

Cambodian People's Republic

People: Population (1986 est.): 6,388,000. **Pop. density:** 108 per sq. mi. **Ethnic groups:** Khmers 93%, Vietnamese 4%, Chinese 3%. **Languages:** Khmer (official), French. **Religions:** Theravada Buddhism, animism.

Geography: Area: 69,898 sq. mi., the size of Missouri. **Location:** In Indochina Peninsula. **Neighbors:** Thailand on W, N, Laos on NE, Vietnam on E. **Topography:** The central area, formed by the Mekong R. basin and Tonle Sap lake, is level. Hills and mountains are in SE, a long escarpment separates the country from Thailand on NW. 75% of the area is forested. **Capital:** Phnom Penh. **Cities** (1984 est.): Phnom Penh 200,000.

Government: Type: No single authority controls the whole country. Vietnamese-installed government controls Phnom Penh. **Head of State:** Pres., People's Revolutionary Party Heng Samrin; in office: Jan. 7, 1979. **Head of Government:** Premier Hun Sen; in office: Jan. 14, 1985. **Local divisions:** 18 provinces.

Economy: Industries: Textiles, cement. **Chief crops:** Rice, sugar. **Minerals:** Iron, copper, manganese, gold. **Other resources:** Forests, rubber, kapok. **Meat prod.** (1980): beef: 17,000 metric tons; pork: 26,000 metric tons. **Fish catch** (1984): 63,000 metric tons. **Electricity prod.** (1984): 140.00 mln. kwh.

Finance: Currency: Riel (Jan. 1986: 4 = $1 US). **Per capita income** (1984): $100. **Imports** (1981): $103 mln. **Exports** (1981): $43 mln.

Transport: Railway traffic (1981): 54 mln. passenger-miles; 6.8 mln. net ton-miles. **Motor vehicles:** in use (1981): 700 passenger cars, (1981) 700 trucks. **Chief ports:** Kompong Som.

Communications: Television sets: 52,000 in use (1985). **Radios:** 200,000 in use (1985). **Telephones in use** (1981): 7,000.

Health: Life expectancy at birth (1985): 44.5 male; 47.4 female. **Births** (per 1,000 pop. 1985): 39. **Deaths** (per 1,000 pop. 1985): 18. **Natural increase** (1985): 2.1. **Infant Mortality** (per 1,000 live births 1985): 145.

Education (1980): **Literacy:** 48%.

Major International Organizations: UN.

Early kingdoms dating from that of Funan in the 1st century AD culminated in the great Khmer empire which flourished from the 9th century to the 13th, encompassing present-day Thailand, Cambodia, Laos, and southern Vietnam. The peripheral areas were lost to invading Siamese and Vietnamese, and France established a protectorate in 1863. Independence came in 1953.

Prince Norodom Sihanouk, king 1941-1955 and head of state from 1960, tried to maintain neutrality. Relations with the U.S. were broken in 1965, after South Vietnam planes attacked Vietcong forces within Cambodia. Relations were restored in 1969, after Sihanouk charged Viet communists with arming Cambodian insurgents.

In 1970, pro-U.S. premier Lon Nol seized power, demanding removal of 40,000 North Viet troops; the monarchy was abolished. Sihanouk formed a government-in-exile in Peking, and open war began between the government and Khmer Rouge. The U.S. provided heavy military and economic aid.

Khmer Rouge forces captured Phnom Penh April 17, 1975. Over 100,000 people had died in 5 years of fighting. The new government evacuated all cities and towns, and shuffled the rural population, sending virtually the entire population to clear jungle, forest, and scrub, which covered half the country. Over one million people were killed in executions and enforced hardships.

Severe border fighting broke out with Vietnam in 1978; developed into a full-fledged Vietnamese invasion. The Vietnamese-backed Kampuchean National United Front for National Salvation, a Cambodian rebel movement, announced, Jan. 8, 1979, the formation of a government one day after the Vietnamese capture of Phnom Pehn. Thousands of refugees flowed into Thailand. Widespread starvation was reported; by Sept., when the UN confirmed diplomatic recognition to the ousted Pol Pot government, international food assistance was allowed to aid the famine-stricken country.

On Jan. 10, 1983, Vietnam launched an offensive against rebel forces in the west. They overran a refugee camp, Jan. 31, driving 30,000 residents into Thailand. In March, Vietnam launched a major offensive against camps on the Cambodian-Thailand border, engaged Khmer Rouge guerrillas, and crossed the border instigating clashes with Thai troops. By Feb. 1985, Vietnamese forces had overrun all major Khmer Rouge bases.

Cameroon

United Republic of Cameroon

People: Population (1986 est.): 10,008,000. **Age distrib.** (%): 0–14: 44.6; 15–59: 49.8; 60+: 5.6. **Pop. density:** 55 per sq. mi. **Urban** (1985): 31%. **Ethnic groups:** Some 200 tribes; largest are Bamileke 30%, Fulani 7%. **Languages:** English, French (both official), Bantu, Sudanic. **Religions:** Roman Catholic 35%, animist 25%, Moslem 22%, Protestant 18%.

Geography: Area: 185,568 sq. mi., somewhat larger than California. **Location:** Between W and central Africa. **Neighbors:** Nigeria on NW, Chad, Central African Republic on E, Congo, Gabon, Equatorial Guinea on S. **Topography:** A low coastal plain with rain forests is in S; plateaus in center lead to forested mountains in W, including Mt. Cameroon, 13,000 ft.; grasslands in N lead to marshes around Lake Chad. **Capital:** Yaounde. **Cities** (1985 est.): Douala 852,000; Yaounde 583,000.

Government: Type: Independent republic. **Head of state:** Pres. Paul Biya; b. Feb. 13, 1933; in office: Nov. 6, 1982. **Local divisions:** 10 provinces. **Defense:** 15% of budget (1985).

Economy: Industries: Aluminum processing, palm products. **Chief crops:** Cocoa, coffee, peanuts, tea, bananas, cotton, tobacco. **Crude oil reserves** (1985): 531 mln. bbls. **Other resources:** Timber, rubber. **Arable land:** 14%. **Fish catch** (1984): 75,000 metric tons. **Electricity prod.** (1984): 2.2 bln. kwh. **Labor force:** 74% agric., 13% ind. and commerce.

Finance: Currency: CFA franc (Mar. 1987: 300 = $1 US). **Gross national product** (1984): $7.3 bln. **Per capita income** (1984): $802. **Imports** (1984): 1.1 bln.; partners: Fr. 47%, U.S. 8%. **Exports** (1983): $1.5 mln.; partners: Fr. 27%, U.S. 26%, It. 5%. **National budget** (1985): $1.4 bln. **International reserves less gold** (Jan. 1987): $59 mln. **Gold:** 30,000 oz t. **Consumer prices** (change in 1985): 1.3%.

Transport: Railway traffic (1985): 492 mln. passenger-km; 869 mln. net ton-km. **Motor vehicles:** in use (1985): 72,000 passenger cars, 41,000 comm. vehicles. **Chief ports:** Douala.

Communications: Radios: 790,000 in use (1985). **Telephones in use** (1981): 26,000. **Daily newspaper circ.** (1984): 3 per 1,000 pop.

Health: Life expectancy at birth (1983): 43.2 male; 45.6 female. **Births** (per 1,000 pop. 1985): 44. **Deaths** (per 1,000 pop. 1985): 17. **Natural increase** (1985): 2.8%. **Hospital beds** (1981): 24,541. **Physicians** (1982): 604. **Infant mortality** (per 1,000 live births 1985): 113.

Education (1985): **Literacy:** 65%. About 70% attend school.

Major International Organizations: UN, OAU, EC (Associate).

Embassy: 2349 Massachusetts Ave. NW 20008; 265-8790.

Portuguese sailors were the first Europeans to reach Cameroon, in the 15th century. The European and American slave trade was very active in the area. German control lasted from 1884 to 1916, when France and Britain divided the territory, later receiving League of Nations mandates and UN trusteeships. French Cameroon became independent Jan. 1, 1960; one part of British Cameroon joined Nigeria in 1961, the other part joined Cameroon. Stability has allowed for development of roads, railways, agriculture, and petroleum production. Some 3,000 died in

1986 as a result of clouds of toxic gas of volcanic origin emanating from Lake Nyos.

Canada

People: Population (1986 est.): 25,625,000. **Age distrib.** (%): 0–14: 21.5; 15–59: 63.7; 60+: 14.8. **Pop. density:** 7 per sq. mi. **Urban** (1985): 75.9%. **Ethnic groups:** English 40%; French 27%. other European 23%. **Language:** English, French (both official). **Religion:** Roman Catholic 46%, Protestant 41%.

Geography: Area: 3,851,790 sq. mi., the 2d largest country in land size, Canada stretches 3,223 miles from east to west and extends southward from the North Pole to the U.S. border. Its seacoast includes 36,356 miles of mainland and 115,133 miles of islands, including the Arctic islands almost from Greenland to near the Alaskan border. Climate, while generally temperate, varies from freezing winter cold to blistering summer heat. **Capitol:** Ottawa. **Cities** (met. 1985 est.): Montreal 2,878,000; Toronto 3,202,400; Vancouver 1,348,000; Ottawa-Hull 769,000; Winnipeg 612,000; Edmonton 683,000, Calgary 625,000, Quebec 593,000.

Government: Type: Confederation with parliamentary democracy. **Head of state:** Queen Elizabeth II, represented by Gov.-Gen. Jeanne Sauve; in office: May 14, 1985. **Head of government:** Prime Min. Brian Mulroney; born: Mar. 20, 1939; in office: Sept. 4, 1984. **Local divisions:** 10 provinces, 2 territories. **Defense:** 2% of GNP (1986).

Economy: Minerals: Nickel, zinc, copper, gold, lead, molybdenum, potash, silver. **Crude oil reserves** (1985): 6.5 bln. bbls. **Meat prod.** (1985): cattle: 10.5 mln.; pigs: 11.2 mln.; sheep: 783,000. **Fish catch** (1985): 1.0 mln. metric tons. **Electricity prod.** (1985): 446 bln. kwh. **Crude steel prod.** (1985): 14.6 mln. metric tons. **Labor force:** 3% agric.; 52% ind. & comm., 28% services.

Finance: Currency: Dollar (June 1987: 1.33 = $1 US). **Gross national product** (1986): $367 bln. **Per capita income** (1984 est.) $13,000. **Imports** (1986): $85.6 bln.; partners: U.S. 72%, EC 8%, Jap. 5%. **Exports** (1986): $89.6 bln.; partners: U.S. 78%, EC 9%, Jap. 5%. **Tourists** (1984): receipts: $2.8 bln. **National budget** (1984-85): Can $98 bln. expenditures. **International reserves less gold** (Mar. 1987): $6.8 bln. **Gold:** 19.4 mln. oz t. **Consumer prices** (change in 1986): 4.2%.

Transport: Railway traffic (1984): 2.0 bln. passenger-km; 244 bln. net ton-km. **Motor vehicles:** in use (1983): 10.7 mln. passenger cars, 3.3 mln. comm. vehicles; manuf. (1984): 1 mln. passenger cars; 808,000 comm. vehicles. **Civil aviation** (1985): 73.2 bln. passenger-km: 4.7 bln. net ton-km.

Communications: Television sets: 14.6 mln. in use (1985). **Radios:** 28 mln. in use (1985). **Telephones in use** (1984): 16.4 mln. **Daily newspaper circ.** (1984): 217 per 1,000 pop.

Health: Life expectancy at birth (1987): 69 male; 76 female. **Births** (per 1,000 pop. 1985): 15.0. **Deaths** (per 1,000 pop. 1985): 7.0. **Natural increase** (1985): .8%. **Hospital beds** (1982): 180,000. **Physicians** (1982): 45,000. **Infant mortality** (per 1,000 live births 1985): 8.

Education (1987): **Literacy:** 99%.

Major International Organizations: UN and all of its specialized agencies, NATO, OECD, Commonwealth of Nations.

Embassy: 1746 Massachusetts Ave. NW 20036; 785-1400.

French explorer Jacques Cartier, who discovered the Gulf of St. Lawrence in 1534, is generally regarded as the founder of Canada. But English seaman John Cabot sighted Newfoundland 37 years earlier, in 1497, and Vikings are believed to have reached the Atlantic coast centuries before either explorer.

Canadian settlement was pioneered by the French who established Quebec City (1608) and Montreal (1642) and declared New France a colony in 1663.

Britain, as part of its American expansion, acquired Acadia (later Nova Scotia) in 1717 and, through military victory over French forces in Canada (an extension of a European conflict between the 2 powers), captured Quebec (1759) and obtained control of the rest of New France in 1763. The French, through the Quebec Act of 1774, retained the rights to their own language, religion, and civil law.

The British presence in Canada increased during the American Revolution when many colonials, proudly calling themselves United Empire Loyalists, moved north to Canada.

Fur traders and explorers led Canadians westward across the continent. Sir Alexander Mackenzie reached the Pacific in 1793 and scrawled on a rock by the ocean, "from Canada by land."

In Upper and Lower Canada (later called Ontario and Quebec) and in the Maritimes, legislative assemblies appeared in the 18th century and reformers called for responsible government. But the War of 1812 intervened. The war, a conflict between Great Britain and the United States fought mainly in Upper Canada, ended in a stalemate in 1814.

In 1837 political agitation for more democratic government culminated in rebellions in Upper and Lower Canada. Britain sent Lord Durham to investigate and, in a famous report (1839), he recommended union of the 2 parts into one colony called Canada. The union lasted until Confederation, July 1, 1867, when proclamation of the British North America (BNA) Act launched the Dominion of Canada, consisting of Ontario, Quebec, and the former colonies of Nova Scotia and New Brunswick.

Since 1840 the Canadian colonies had held the right to internal self-government. The BNA act, which became the country's written constitution, established a federal system of government on the model of a British parliament and cabinet structure under the crown. Canada was proclaimed a self-governing Dominion within the British Empire in 1931.

In 1982 Canada severed its last formal legislative link with Britain by obtaining the right to amend its constitution (the British North America Act of 1867).

The Meech Lake Agreement was signed June 3, 1987. The historic accord, subject to ratification by Parliament and the provincial legislatures, assured constitutional protection for Quebec's efforts to preserve its French language and culture.

Canadian Provinces

	Sq. mi.	Population, 1985 est.
Alberta	255,290	2,337,500
British Columbia	365,950	2,883,000
Manitoba	250,950	1,065,000
New Brunswick	28,360	717,200
Newfoundland	156,650	578,900
Nova Scotia	21,420	878,300
Ontario	412,580	9,023,900
Prince Edward Island	2,184	126,800
Quebec	594,860	6,562,200
Saskatchewan	251,870	1,016,400
Territories		
Northwest Territories	1,322,900	50,500
Yukon	186,660	22,800

Cape Verde

Republic of Cape Verde

Republica de Cabo Verde

People: Population (1986 est.): 318,000. **Age distrib.** (%): 0–14: 46.9; 15–59: 44.9; 60+: 7.9. **Pop. density:** 219 per sq. mi. **Urban** (1980): 26.2%. **Ethnic groups:** Creole (mulatto) 71%, African 28%, European 1%. **Languages:** Portuguese (official), Crioulo. **Religions:** 80% Roman Catholic.

Geography: Area: 1,557 sq. mi., a bit larger than Rhode Island. **Location:** In Atlantic O., off western tip of Africa. **Neighbors:** Nearest are Mauritania, Senegal. **Topography:** Cape Verde Islands are 15 in number, volcanic in origin (active crater on Fogo). The landscape is eroded and stark, with vegetation mostly in interior valleys. **Capital:** Praia. **Cities** (1986 est.): Mindelo 40,000; Praia 50,000.

Government: Type: Republic. **Head of state:** Pres. Aristide Pereira; b. Nov. 17, 1923; in office: July 5, 1975. **Head of government:** Prime Min. Pedro Pires, b. Apr. 29, 1934; in office: July 5, 1975. **Local divisions:** 14 administrative districts.

Economy: Chief crops: Bananas, coffee, sugarcane, corn, beans. **Minerals:** Salt. **Other resources:** Fish. **Arable land:** 10%. **Electricity prod.** (1985): 12 mln. kwh.

Finance: Currency: Escudo (Dec. 1986: 89.27 = $1 US). **Gross national product** (1984): $121 mln. **Per capita income** (1984): $350. **Imports** (1981): $104 mln.; partners: Port. 58%, Neth. 5%. **Exports** (1981): $6 mln.; partners: Port. 63%, Ang. 14%, UK 5%, Zaire 5%.

Transport: Motor vehicles: in use (1981): 4,000 passenger cars, 1,343 comm. vehicles. **Chief ports:** Mindelo, Praia.

Communications: Radios: 47,000 licensed (1985). **Telephones in use** (1981): 1,739.

Health: Life expectancy at birth (1985): 60.3 male, 64.0 female. **Births** (per 1,000 pop. 1985): 36. **Deaths** (per 1,000 pop. 1985): 10. **Natural increase** (1985): 2.5%. **Hospital beds** (1980): 632. **Physicians** (1980): 51. **Infant mortality** (per 1,000 live births 1985): 89.

Education (1986): **Literacy:** 37%.

Major International Organizations: UN (GATT, IMF, WHO), OAU.

Embassy: 3415 Massachusetts Ave. NW 20007; 965-6820.

The uninhabited Cape Verdes were discovered by the Portuguese in 1456 or 1460. The first Portuguese colonists landed in 1462; African slaves were brought soon after, and most Cape Verdeans descend from both groups. Cape Verde independence came July 5, 1975. The islands have suffered from repeated extreme droughts and famines. Emphasis is placed on the development of agriculture and on fishing.

Central African Republic

Republique Centrafricaine

People: Population (1986 est.): 2,744,000. **Pop. density:** 11 per sq. mi. **Ethnic groups:** Banda 27%, Baya 34%, Mandja 21%, Sara 10%. **Languages:** French (official), local dialects. **Religions:** Protestant 25%, Roman Catholic 25%, traditional 24%.

Geography: Area: 240,534 sq. mi., slightly smaller than Texas. **Location:** In central Africa. **Neighbors:** Chad on N, Cameroon on W, Congo, Zaire on S, Sudan on E. **Topography:** Mostly rolling plateau, average altitude 2,000 ft., with rivers draining S to the Congo and N to Lake Chad. Open, well-watered savanna covers most of the area, with an arid area in NE, and tropical rainforest in SW. **Capital:** Bangui. **Cities** (1985 est.): Bangui (met.) 473,000.

Government: Type: Republic. **Head of state:** Gen. Andre Kolingba; in office: Sept. 1, 1981. **Local divisions:** 16 prefectures. **Defense:** 2% of GNP (1983).

Economy: Industries: Textiles, light manuf. **Chief crops:** Cotton, coffee, peanuts, corn, sorghum. **Minerals:** Diamonds (chief export), uranium, iron, copper. **Other resources:** Timber. **Arable land:** 15%. **Electricity prod.** (1984): 73 mln. kwh. **Labor force:** 86% agric.

Finance: Currency: CFA franc (Mar. 1987: 300 = $1 US). **Gross national product** (1984): $680 mln. **Per capita income** (1982): $310. **Imports** (1981): $145 mln.; partners: Fr. 58%. **Exports** (1981): $118 mln.; partners: Fr. 52%, Bel.-Lux. 14%. **International reserves less gold** (Jan. 1987): $64.3 mln. **Gold:** 11,000 oz t. **Consumer prices** (change in 1985): 8.9%.

Transport: Motor vehicles: in use (1984): 43,000 passenger cars, 3,861 comm. vehicles.

Communications: Radios: 135,000 in use (1982).

Health: Life expectancy at birth (1983): 44 years. **Births** (per 1,000 pop. 1985): 47. **Deaths** (per 1,000 pop. 1985): 19%. **Natural increase** (1985): 2.8%. **Hospital beds** (1980): 3,605. **Physicians** (1980): 108. **Infant mortality** (per 1,000 live births 1985): 134.

Education (1983): **Literacy:** 20%. **Attendance:** primary school 64%; secondary school 11%.

Major International Organizations: UN (GATT, IMF, WHO), OAU.

Embassy: 1618 22d St. NW 20008; 483-7800.

Various Bantu tribes migrated through the region for centuries before French control was asserted in the late 19th century, when the region was named Ubangi-Shari. Complete independence was attained Aug. 13, 1960.

All political parties were dissolved in 1960, and the country became a center for Chinese political influence in Africa. Relations with China were severed after 1965. Elizabeth Domitien, premier 1975-76, was the first woman to hold that post in an African country. Pres. Jean-Bedel Bokassa, who seized power in a 1965 military coup, proclaimed himself constitutional emperor of the renamed Central African Empire Dec. 1976.

Emp. Bokassa's rule was characterized by virtually unchecked ruthless and cruel authority, and human rights violations. Bokassa was ousted in a bloodless coup aided by the French government, Sept. 20, 1979, and replaced by his cousin David Dacko, former president from 1960 to 1965. In 1981, the political situation deteriorated amid strikes and economic crisis. Gen. Kolingba replaced Dacko as head of state in a bloodless coup.

Chad

Republic of Chad

République du Tchad

People: Population (1986 est.): 5,231,000. **Age distrib. (%):** 0–14: 42.5; 15–59: 51.7; 60+: 5.8. **Pop. density:** 10 per sq. mi. **Urban** (1983): 20%. **Ethnic groups:** Sudanese Arab 30%, Sudanic tribes 25%, Nilotic, Saharan tribes. **Languages:** French (official), Arabic, others. **Religions:** Moslems 44%, animist 23%, Christian 33%.

Geography: Area: 495,755 sq. mi., four-fifths the size of Alaska. **Location:** In central N. Africa. **Neighbors:** Libya on N, Niger, Nigeria, Cameroon on W, Central African Republic on S, Sudan on E. **Topography:** Southern wooded savanna, steppe, and desert, part of the Sahara, in the N. Southern rivers flow N to Lake Chad, surrounded by marshland. **Capital:** N'Djamena. **Cities** (1985 est.): N'Djamena 511,000.

Government: Type: Republic. **Head of state:** Pres. Hissen Habre; b. 1942; in office: June 19, 1982. **Local divisions:** 14 prefectures with appointed governors. **Defense:** 2.4% of GNP (1983).

Economy: Chief crops: Cotton. **Minerals:** Uranium. **Arable land:** 7%. **Fish catch** (1984): 110,000 metric tons. **Electricity prod.** (1984): 65 mln. kwh. **Labor force:** 81% agric.

Finance: Currency: CFA franc (Mar. 1987: 300 = $1 US). **Gross national product** (1984): $360 mln. **Per capita income** (1984): $88. **Imports** (1984): $114 mln.; partners: Fr. 47%. **Exports** (1984): $113 mln.; partners Fra. EDEAC countries. **Tourist receipts** (1981): $2 mln. **International reserves less gold** (Jan. 1987): $15.9 mln. **Gold:** 11,000 oz t.

Transport: Motor vehicles: in use (1982): 7,000 passenger cars, 5,000 comm. vehicles.

Communications: Radios: 75,000 in use (1984). **Telephones in use** (1981): 1,000.

Health: Life expectancy at birth (1984): 43.0 male; 45.0 female. **Births** (per 1,000 pop. 1985): 51. **Deaths** (per 1,000 pop. 1985): 28. **Natural increase** (1985): 2.3%. **Hospital beds** (1980): 3.500. **Physicians** (1980): 94. **Infant mortality** (per 1,000 live births 1985): 140.

Education (1980): **Literacy:** 17%.

Major International Organizations: UN, (GATT, IMF, WHO), OAU, EEC.

Embassy: 2002 R St. NW 20009; 462-4009.

Chad was the site of paleolithic and neolithic cultures before the Sahara Desert formed. A succession of kingdoms and Arab slave traders dominated Chad until France took control around 1900. Independence came Aug. 11, 1960.

Northern Moslem rebels, have fought animist and Christian southern government and French troops from 1966, despite numerous cease-fires and peace pacts.

Libyan troops entered the country at the request of the Chad government, December 1980. On Jan. 6, 1981 Libya and Chad announced their intention to unite. France together with several African nations condemned the agreement as a menace to African security. The Libyan troops were withdrawn from Chad in November 1981.

Rebel forces, led by Hissen Habre, captured the capital and forced Pres. Oueddei to flee the country in June 1982.

In 1983, France sent some 3,000 troops to Chad to assist Habre in opposing Libyan-backed rebels. France and Libya agreed to a simultaneous withdrawal of troops from Chad in September 1984 but Libyan forces remained in the north until Mar. 1987 when Chad forces drove them from their last major stronghold. Libyan troops abandoned almost $1 billion of military equipment during their retreat.

Chile

Republic of Chile

República de Chile

People: Population (1986 est.): 12,261,000. **Age distrib.** (%): 0–14: 31.4; 15–59: 60.4; 60+: 8.2. **Pop. density:** 43 per sq. mi. **Urban** (1983): 82%. **Ethnic groups:** Mestizo 66%, Spanish 25%, Indian 5%. **Languages:** Spanish. **Religions:** Roman Catholic 79%, Protestant 6%.

Geography: Area: 292,257 sq. mi., larger than Texas. **Location:** Occupies western coast of southern S. America. **Neighbors:** Peru on N, Bolivia on NE, Argentina on E. **Topography:** Andes Mtns. are on E border including some of the world's highest peaks; on W is 2,650-mile Pacific Coast. Width varies between 100 and 250 miles. In N is Atacama Desert, in center are agricultural regions, in S are forests and grazing lands. **Capital:** Santiago. **Cities** (1985 metro est.) Santiago 4,271,500.

Government: Type: Military. **Head of state:** Pres. Augusto Pinochet Ugarte; b. Nov. 25, 1915; in office: Sept. 11, 1973. **Local divisions:** 12 regions and Santiago region. **Defense:** 6.5% of GNP (1982).

Economy: Industries: Steel, textiles, wood products. **Chief crops:** Grain, onions, beans, potatoes, peas, fruits, grapes. **Minerals:** Copper (27% world resources), molybdenum, nitrates, iodine (half world output), iron, coal, oil, gas, gold, cobalt, zinc, manganese, borate, mica, mercury, salt, sulphur, marble, onyx. **Crude oil reserves** (1985): 224 mln. bbls. **Other resources:** Water, forests. **Arable land:** 7%. **Meat prod.** (1985): cattle: 3.5 mln.; pigs: 1.1 mln. **Fish catch** (1984): 3.9 mln. metric tons. **Electricity prod.** (1984): 13.3 bln. kwh. **Crude steel prod.** (1984): 684,000 metric tons. **Labor force:** 9% agric.; 33% ind & comm., 31% serv.

Finance: Currency: Peso (May 1987: 213 = $1 US). **Gross national product** (1984): $20.3 bln. **Per capita income** (1979): $1,950. **Imports** (1985): $2.7 bln.; partners: U.S. 26%, Braz. 7%. **Exports** (1985): $3.7 bln.; partners: W. Ger. 10%, Jap. 11%, U.S. 26%. **Tourists** (1984): $104 mln. receipts. **National budget** (1982): $9.4 bln. **International reserves less gold** (Mar. 1987): $2.2 bln. **Gold:** 1.53 mln. oz. t. **Consumer prices** (change in 1986): 19.5%

Transport: Railway traffic (1985): 1.5 bln. passenger-km; 2.3 bln. net ton-km. **Motor vehicles:** in use (1984): 622,000 passenger cars, 240,000 comm. vehicles. **Civil aviation** (1984): 1.5 bln. passenger-km; 112 mln. net ton-km. **Chief ports:** Valparaiso, Arica, Antofagasta.

Communications: Television sets: 2.6 mln. in use (1984). **Radios:** 17 mln. in use (1984). **Telephones in use** (1983): 608,000.

Health: Life expectancy at birth (1983): 63.8 male; 70.4 female. **Births** (per 1,000 pop. 1985): 24. **Deaths** (per 1,000 pop. 1985): 6. **Natural increase** (1985): 1.8%. **Hospital beds** (1982): 39,000. **Physicians** (1981): 10,877. **Infant mortality** (per 1,000 live births 1985): 22.

Education (1983): **Literacy:** 90%. Compulsory ages 6-14.

Major International Organizations: UN and all of its specialized agencies, OAS.

Embassy: 1732 Massachusetts Ave. NW 20036; 785-1746.

Northern Chile was under Inca rule before the Spanish conquest, 1536-40. The southern Araucanian Indians resisted until the late 19th century. Independence was gained 1810-18, under Jose de San Martin and Bernardo O'Higgins; the latter, as supreme director 1817-23, sought social and economic reforms until deposed. Chile defeated Peru and Bolivia in 1836-39 and 1879-84, gaining mineral-rich northern land.

Eduardo Frei Montalva came into office in 1964, instituting social programs and gradual nationalization of foreign-owned mining companies. In 1970, Salvador Allende Gossens, a Marxist, became president with a third of the national vote.

The Allende government furthered nationalizations, and improved conditions for the poor. But illegal and violent actions by extremist supporters of the government, the regime's failure to attain majority support, and poorly planned socialist economic programs led to political and financial chaos.

A military junta seized power Sept. 11, 1973, and said Allende killed himself. The junta named a mostly military cabinet, and announced plans to "exterminate Marxism."

Repression has continued during the 1980s with no sign of any political liberalization.

Tierra del Fuego is the largest (18,800 sq. mi.) island in the archipelago of the same name at the southern tip of South America, an area of majestic mountains, tortuous channels, and high winds. It was discovered 1520 by Magellan and named the Land of Fire because of its many Indian bonfires. Part of the island is in Chile, part in Argentina. Punta Arenas, on a mainland peninsula, is a center of sheep-raising and the world's southernmost city (pop. 67,600); Puerto Williams, pop. 949, is the southernmost settlement.

China

People's Republic of China

Zhonghua Renmin Gonghe Guo

People: Population (1986 est.): 1,045,537,000. **Pop. density:** 284 per sq. mi. **Urban** (1984): 32%. **Ethnic groups:** Han Chinese 94%, Mongol, Korean, Manchu, others. **Languages:** Mandarin Chinese (official), Shanghai, Canton, Fukien, Hakka dialects; Tibetan, Vigus (Turkic). **Religions:** officially atheist; Confucianism, Buddhism, Taoism, are traditional.

Geography: Area: 3,705,390 sq. mi., slightly larger than the U.S. **Location:** Occupies most of the habitable mainland of E. Asia. **Neighbors:** Mongolia on N, USSR on NE and NW, Afghanistan, Pakistan on W, India, Nepal, Bhutan, Burma, Laos, Vietnam on S, N. Korea on NE. **Topography:** Two-thirds of the vast territory is mountainous or desert, and only one-tenth is cultivated. Rolling topography rises to high elevations in the N in the Daxinganlingshanmai separating Manchuria and Mongolia; the Tienshan in Xinjiang; the Himalayan and Kunlunshanmai in the SW and in Tibet. Length is 1,860 mi. from N to S, width E to W is more than 2,000 mi. The eastern half of China is one of the best-watered lands in the world. Three great river systems, the Changjiang, the Huanghe, and the Xijiang provide water for vast farmlands. **Capital:** Peking. **Cities** (1981 est.): Shanghai 12,000,000; Peking 8,500,000; Tianjin 7,200,000; Canton 5,200,000; Shenyang 4,800,000; Wuhan 4,400,000; Chendu 4,000,000.

Government: Type: People's republic. **Head of state:** Pres. Li Xiannian; in office: June 18, 1983. **Effective head of government & party secy.:** Premier Zhao Ziyang; b. 1919; in office: Sept. 1980. **Local divisions:** 21 provinces, 5 autonomous regions, and 3 cities. **Defense:** 8.5% of GNP (1982).

Economy: Industries: Iron and steel, plastics, agriculture implements, trucks. **Chief crops:** Grain, rice, cotton, tea. **Minerals:** Tungsten, antimony, coal, iron, lead, manganese, mercury, molybdenum, phosphates, potash, tin. **Crude oil reserves** (1985): 19.5 bln. bbls. **Other resources:** Silk. **Arable land:** 11%. **Meat prod.** (1985): cattle: 66.9 mln.; pigs: 328 mln.; sheep: 94.2 mln. **Fish catch** (1984): 6.1 mln. metric tons. **Electricity prod.** (1984): 376 bln. kwh. **Crude steel prod.** (1985): 46.7 mln. metric tons. **Labor force:** 74% agric.; 15% ind. & comm.

Finance: Currency: Yuan (Mar. 1987): 3.72 = $1 US). **Gross national product** (1984): $318 bln. **Per capita income** (1980): $566. **Imports** (1985): $45.5 bln.; partners: Jap. 31%, U.S. 14%, Hong Kong 11%. **Exports** (1985): $27.3 bln.; partners: Hong Kong 26%, Jap. 20%, U.S. 9%. **Tourism** (1984): $1.1 bln. receipts. **National budget** (1987): $66.1 bln. **International reserves less gold** (Feb. 1987): 11.4 bln. **Gold:** 12.7 mln. oz t. **Consumer prices** (change in 1984): 2.7%.

Transport: Railway traffic (1985): 812 bln. net ton-km. **Motor vehicles:** in use (1982): 265,000 passenger cars, 1.7 mln. comm. vehicles. **Civil aviation** (1985): 11.7 bln. passenger km, 420 mln. net ton-km. **Chief ports:** Shanghai, Tianjin, Luda.

Communications: Television sets: 69 mln. in use. (1986). **Radios:** 15 mln. in use (1984). **Telephones** (1986): 2.7 mln.; **Daily newspaper circ.** (1984): 22 per 1,000 pop.

Health: Life expectancy at birth (1985): 65.5 male; 69.4 female. **Births** (per 1,000 pop. 1985): 16. **Deaths** (per 1,000 pop. 1985): 8. **Natural increase** (1985): 0.8%. **Infant Mortality** (per 1,000 live births 1985): 50. **Hospital beds** (1982): 2.2 mln. **Physicians** (1984): 1.5 mln.

Education (1984): **Literacy:** 75%. Years compulsory 5; first grade enrollment 93%.
Major International Organizations: UN (IMF, FAO, WHO).
Embassy: 2300 Conn. Ave. NW 20008; 328-2520.

History. Remains of various man-like creatures who lived as early as several hundred thousand years ago have been found in many parts of China. Neolithic agricultural settlements dotted the Huanghe basin from about 5,000 BC. Their language, religion, and art were the sources of later Chinese civilization.

Bronze metallurgy reached a peak and Chinese pictographic writing, similar to today's, was in use in the more developed culture of the Shang Dynasty (c. 1500 BC-c. 1000 BC) which ruled much of North China.

A succession of dynasties and interdynastic warring kingdoms ruled China for the next 3,000 years. They expanded Chinese political and cultural domination to the south and west, and developed a brilliant technologically and culturally advanced society. Rule by foreigners (Mongols in the Yuan Dynasty, 1271-1368, and Manchus in the Ch'ing Dynasty, 1644-1911) did not alter the underlying culture.

A period of relative stagnation left China vulnerable to internal and external pressures in the 19th century. Rebellions left tens of millions dead, and Russia, Japan, Britain, and other powers exercised political and economic control in large parts of the country. China became a republic Jan. 1, 1912, following the Wuchang Uprising inspired by Dr. Sun Yat-sen.

For a period of 50 years, 1894-1945, China was involved in conflicts with Japan. In 1895, China ceded Korea, Taiwan, and other areas. On Sept. 18, 1931, Japan seized the Northeastern Provinces (Manchuria) and set up a puppet state called Manchukuo. The border province of Jehol was cut off as a buffer state in 1933. Japan invaded China proper July 7, 1937. After its defeat in World War II, Japan gave up all seized land.

Following World War II, internal disturbances arose involving the Kuomintang, communists, and other factions. China came under domination of communist armies, 1949-1950. The Kuomintang government moved to Taiwan, 90 mi. off the mainland, Dec. 8, 1949.

The People's Republic of China was proclaimed in Peking Sept. 21, 1949, by the Chinese People's Political Consultative Conference under Mao Tse-tung.

China and the USSR signed a 30-year treaty of "friendship, alliance and mutual assistance," Feb. 15, 1950.

The U.S. refused recognition of the new regime. On Nov. 26, 1950, the People's Republic sent armies into Korea against U.S. troops and forced a stalemate.

By the 1960s, relations with the USSR deteriorated, with disagreements on borders, ideology and leadership of world communism. The USSR cancelled aid accords, and China, with Albania, launched anti-Soviet propaganda drives. High level talks have been held with the USSR to seek improved trade and cultural contracts; little progress was reported.

On Oct. 25, 1971, the UN General Assembly ousted the Taiwan government from the UN and seated the People's Republic in its place. The U.S. had supported the mainland's admission but opposed Taiwan's expulsion.

U.S. Pres. Nixon visited China Feb. 21-28, 1972, on invitation from Premier Chou En-lai, ending years of antipathy between the 2 nations. China and the U.S. opened liaison offices in each other's capitals, May-June 1973. The U.S., Dec. 15, 1978, formally recognized the People's Republic of China as the sole legal government of China; diplomatic relations between the 2 nations were established, Jan. 1, 1979.

In a continuing "reassessment" of the policies of Mao Zedong, Mao's widow, Jiang Quing, and other Gang of Four members were convicted of "committing crimes during the 'Cultural Revolution,'" Jan. 25, 1981.

Internal developments. After an initial period of consolidation, 1949-52, industry, agriculture, and social and economic institutions were forcibly molded according to Maoist ideals. However, frequent drastic changes in policy and violent factionalism interfered with economic development.

In 1957, Mao Tse-tung admitted an estimated 800,000 people had been executed 1949-54; opponents claimed much higher figures.

The Great Leap Forward, 1958-60, tried to force the pace of economic development through intensive labor on huge new rural communes, and through emphasis on ideological purity and enthusiasm. The program caused resistance and was largely abandoned. Serious food shortages developed, and the government was forced to buy grain from the West.

The Great Proletarian Cultural Revolution, 1965, was an attempt to oppose pragmatism and bureaucratic power and instruct a new generation in revolutionary principles. Massive purges took place. A program of forcibly relocating millions of urban teenagers into the countryside was launched.

By 1968 the movement had run its course; many purged officials returned to office in subsequent years, and reforms in education and industry that had placed ideology above expertise were gradually weakened.

In the mid-1970s, factional and ideological fighting increased, and emerged into the open after the 1976 deaths of Mao and Premier Chou En-lai. Mao's widow and 3 other leading leftists were purged and placed under arrest, after reportedly trying to seize power. Their opponents said the "gang of four" had used severe repression and mass torture, had sparked local fighting and had disrupted production. The new ruling group modified Maoist policies in education, culture, and industry, and sought better ties with non-communist countries.

Relations with Vietnam deteriorated in 1978 as China charged persecution of ethnic Chinese. In retaliation for Vietnam's invasion of Cambodia, China attacked 4 Vietnamese border provinces Feb. 17, 1979; heavy border fighting ensued.

Sweeping reforms of the central bureaucracy were announced March 1982. By the mid 1980's, China had enacted far-reaching economic reforms highlighed by the departure from rigid central planning.

Manchuria. Home of the Manchus, rulers of China 1644-1911, Manchuria has accommodated millions of Chinese settlers in the 20th century. Under Japanese rule 1931-45, the area became industrialized. China no longer uses the name Manchuria for the region, which is divided into the 3 NE provinces of Heilongjiang, Jilin, and Liaoning.

Guandong is the southernmost part of Manchuria. Russia in 1898 forced China to lease it Guandong, and built Port Arthur (Lushun) and the port of Dairen (Luda). Japan seized Port Arthur in 1905. It was turned over to the USSR by the 1945 Yalta agreement, but finally returned to China in 1950.

Inner Mongolia was organized by the People's Republic in 1947. Its boundaries have undergone frequent changes, reaching its greatest extent (and restored in 1979) in 1956, with an area of 540,000 sq. mi., allegedly in order to dilute the minority Mongol population. Chinese settlers outnumber the Mongols more than 10 to 1. Pop. (1983 est.): 19.5 mln. Capital: Hohhot.

Xinjiang Uygur Autonomous Region, in Central Asia, is 633,802 sq. mi., pop. (1983 est.): 13 mln. (75% Uygurs, a Turkic Moslem group, with a heavy Chinese increase in recent years). Capital: Urumqi. It is China's richest region in strategic minerals. Some Uygurs have fled to the USSR, claiming national oppression.

Tibet, 470,000 sq. mi., is a thinly populated region of high plateaus and massive mountains, the Himalayas on the S, the Kunluns on the N. High passes connect with India and Nepal; roads lead into China proper. Capital: Lhasa. Average altitude is 15,000 ft. Jiachan, 15,870 ft., is believed to be the highest inhabited town on earth. Agriculture is primitive. Pop. (1985 est.): 1.9 mln. (of whom 500,000 are Chinese). Another 4 million Tibetans form the majority of the population of vast adjacent areas that have long been incorporated into China.

China ruled all of Tibet from the 18th century, but independence came in 1911. China reasserted control in 1951, and a communist government was installed in 1953, revising the theocratic Lamaist Buddhist rule. Serfdom was abolished, but all land remained collectivized.

A Tibetan uprising within China in 1956 spread to Tibet in 1959. The rebellion was crushed with Chinese troops, and Buddhism was almost totally suppressed. The Dalai Lama and 100,000 Tibetans fled to India.

Colombia

Republic of Colombia

República de Colombia

People: Population (1986 est.): 29,956,000. **Age distrib.** (%): 0–14: 35.5; 15–59: 47.1; 60+: 7.4. **Pop. density:** 64 per sq. mi. **Urban** (1983): 65.4%. **Ethnic groups:** Mestizo 60%, Caucasian 20%, Negro 5%, Indian 7%. **Languages:** Spanish. **Religions:** Roman Catholic 97%.

Geography: Area: 439,735 sq. mi., about the size of Texas, Arkansas, and New Mexico combined. **Location:** At the NW corner of S. America. **Neighbors:** Panama on NW, Ecuador, Peru on S, Brazil, Venezuela on E. **Topography:** Three ranges of Andes, the Western, Central, and Eastern Cordilleras, run through the country from N to S. The eastern range consists mostly of high table lands, densely populated. The Magdalena R. rises in Andes, flows N to Carribean, through a rich alluvial plain. Sparsely-settled plains in E are drained by Orinoco and Amazon systems. **Capital:** Bogota. **Cities** (1985 cen.): Bogota 3,967,000; Medellin 1,664,000; Cali 1,450,000; Barranquilla 924,000.

Government: Type: Republic. **Head of state:** Pres. Virgilio Barco Vargas; b. Sept. 17, 1921; in office: Aug. 7, 1986. **Local divisions:** 23 departments, 8 national territories, and special district of Bogota. **Defense:** 2.1% of GNP (1985).

Economy: Industries: Textiles, processed goods, hides, steel, cement, chemicals. **Chief crops:** Coffee (50% of exports), rice, tobacco, cotton, sugar, bananas. **Minerals:** Oil, gas, emeralds (90% world output), gold, copper, lead, coal, iron, nickel, salt. **Crude oil reserves** (1985): 1.2 bln. bbls. **Other resources:** Rubber, balsam, dye-woods, copaiba, hydro power. **Arable land:** 5%. **Meat prod.** (1985): cattle: 20.5 mln.; pigs: 2.4 mln.; sheep: 2.7 mln. **Fish catch** (1985): 78,000 metric tons. **Electricity prod.** (1984): 27.8 bln. kwh. **Crude steel prod.** (1982): 215,000 metric tons. **Labor force:** 26% agric.; 21% ind.; 53% services.

Finance: Currency: Peso (May 1987: 235 = $1 US). **Gross national product** (1985): $32.0 bln. **Per capita income** (1981): $1,112. **Imports** (1986): $3.8 bln.; partners: U.S. 34%, EEC 14%, Jap. 8%. **Exports** (1986): $5.1 bln.; partners: U.S. 28%, EEC 38%. **Tourists** (1984): $205 mln. receipts. **National budget** (1985): $2.4 bln. **International reserves less gold** (Mar. 1987): $2.6 bln. **Gold** 1.3 mln. oz t. **Consumer prices** (change in 1985): 18.9.

Transport: Railway traffic (1985): 228 mln. passenger-km; 780 mln. net ton-km. **Motor vehicles:** in use (1982): 476,000 passenger cars, 312,000. **Civil aviation** (1985): 3.9 bln. passenger-km; 205 mln. net ton-km. **Chief ports:** Buena Ventura, Santa Marta, Barranquilla, Cartagena.

Communications: Television sets: 1.8 mln. in use (1984). **Radios:** 3.2 mln. in use (1984). **Telephones in use** (1984): 2.5 mln. **Daily newspaper circ.** (1984): 44 per 1,000 pop.

Health: Life expectancy at birth (1985): 61.4 male; 66 female. **Births** (per 1,000 pop. 1985): 31. **Deaths** (per 1,000 pop. 1985): 7.7. **Natural increase** (1985): 2.3%. **Hospital beds** (1982): 28,880. **Physicians** (1983): 21,778. **Infant mortality** (per 1,000 live births 1985): 62%.

Education (1986): **Literacy:** 80%. Only 28% finish primary school.

Major International Organizations: UN (World Bank, GATT), OAS.

Embassy: 2118 Leroy Pl. NW, 20008; 387-8338.

Spain subdued the local Indian kingdoms (Funza, Tunja) by the 1530s, and ruled Colombia and neighboring areas as New Granada for 300 years. Independence was won by 1819. Venezuela and Ecuador broke away in 1829-30, and Panama withdrew in 1903.

One of the few functioning Latin American democracies, Colombia is nevertheless plagued by rural and urban violence, though scaled down from "La Violencia" of 1948-58, which claimed 200,000 lives. Attempts at land and social reform, and progress in industrialization have not yet succeeded in reducing massive social problems aggravated by a very high birth rate.

Comoros

Federal Islamic Republic of the Comoros

Jumhurīyat al-Qumur al-Itthādīyah al-Islāmīyah

People: Population (1986 est.): 420,000. **Pop. density:** 588 per sq. mi. **Ethnic groups:** Arabs, Africans, East Indians. **Languages:** Shaafi Islam, (a Swahili dialect), French (official), Malagasy. **Religions:** Islam (official), Roman Catholic.

Geography: Area: 838 sq. mi., half the size of Delaware. **Location:** 3 islands (Grande Comore, Anjouan, and Moheli) in the Mozambique Channel between NW Madagascar and SE Africa. **Neighbors:** Nearest are Mozambique on W, Madagascar on E. **Topography:** The islands are of volcanic origin, with an active volcano on Grand Comoro. **Capital:** Moroni. **Cities** (1985 est.): Moroni (met.) 26,000.

Government: Type: Republic. **Head of state:** Pres. Ahmed Abdallah Abderemane; b. 1919; in office: May 23, 1978. **Head of govt.:** Prime Min. Ali Mroudjae; in office: Feb. 8, 1982. **Local divisions:** each of the 3 main islands is a prefecture.

Economy: Industries: Perfume. **Chief crops:** Vanilla, copra, perfume plants, fruits. **Arable land:** 42%. **Electricity prod.** (1984): 10 mln. kwh. **Labor force:** 87% agric.

Finance: Currency: CFA franc (Dec 1986: 332 = $1 US). **Gross national product** (1983): $106 mln. **Per capita income** (1982): $339. **Imports** (1979): $24 mln.; partners: Fr. 51%, Madag. 6%, Pak. 13%, Ken. 5%. **Exports** (1979): $15 mln.; partners: Fr. 43%, U.S. 6%.

Transport: Chief ports: Dzaoudzi.

Communications: Radios: 40,000 in use (1984). **Telephones in use** (1981): 3,000.

Health: Life expectancy at birth (1984): 46.4 male; 49.7 female. **Births** (per 1,000 pop. 1985): 44. **Deaths** (per 1,000 pop. 1985): 15. **Natural increase** (1985): 2.9%. **Infant mortality** (per 1,000 live births 1985): 92.3.

Education: (1985): **Literacy:** 15%; less than 20% attend secondary school.

Major International Organizations: UN (IMF, World Bank); OAU.

The islands were controlled by Moslem sultans until the French acquired them 1841-1909. A 1974 referendum favored independence, with only the Christian island of Mayotte preferring association with France. The French National Assembly decided to allow each of the islands to decide its own fate. The Comoro Chamber of Deputies declared independence July 6, 1975. In a referendum in 1976, Mayotte voted to remain French. A leftist regime that seized power in 1975 was deposed in a pro-French 1978 coup.

Congo

People's Republic of the Congo

République Populaire du Congo

People: Population (1986 est.): 1,853,000. **Pop. density:** 15 per sq. mi. **Ethnic groups:** Bakongo 45%, Bateke 20%, others. **Languages:** French (official), Bantu dialects. **Religions:** Christians 50% (two-thirds Roman Catholic), animists 47%, Muslim 2%.

Geography: Area: 132,046 sq. mi., slightly smaller than Montana. **Location:** In western central Africa. **Neighbors:** Gabon, Cameroon on W, Central African Republic on N, Zaire on E, Angola (Cabinda) on SW. **Topography:** Much of the Congo is covered by thick forests. A coastal plain leads to the fertile Niari Valley. The center is a plateau; the Congo R. basin consists of flood plains in the lower and savanna in the upper portion. **Capital:** Brazzaville. **Cities** (1984 est.): Brazzaville (met.) 595,000; Pointe-Noire 297,000; Loubomo 35,000.

Government: Type: People's republic. **Head of state:** Pres. Denis Sassou-Nguesso; b. 1943; in office: Feb. 8, 1979. **Head of government:** Prime Min. Ange Edouard Poungui; in office: Aug. 12, 1984. **Local divisions:** 9 regions and capital district. **Defense:** 4.7% of GNP (1982).

Economy: Chief crops: Palm oil and kernels, cocoa, coffee, tobacco. **Minerals:** Oil, potash, natural gas, load, copper, zinc. **Crude oil reserves** (1985): 798 mln. bbls. **Arable land:** 2%. **Fish catch** (1983): 31,000 metric tons. **Electricity prod.** (1984): 237 mln. kwh. **Labor force:** 90% agric.

Finance: Currency: CFA franc (Mar. 1987: 300 = $1 US). **Gross national product** (1984 est.): $2.0 bln. **Per capita income** (1978): $500. **Imports** (1982): $610 mln.; partners: Fr. 63%. **Exports** (1982): $810 mln.; partners: U.S. 50%, Ital. 21%. **Tourist receipts** (1982): $13 mln. **International reserves less gold** (Jan. 1987): $6.8 mln. **Gold:** 11,000 oz t. **Consumer prices** (change in 1986): 4.0%.

Transport: Railway traffic (1983): 381 mln. passenger-km; 437 mln. net ton-km. **Motor vehicles:** in use (1982): 41,000 passenger cars, 79,000 comm. vehicles. **Chief ports:** Pointe-Noire, Brazzaville.

Communications: Television sets: 5,000 in use (1985). **Radios:** 99,000 in use (1985). **Telephones in use** (1982): 9,000.

Health: Life expectancy at birth (1986): 44.9 male; 48.1 female. **Births** (per 1,000 pop. 1985): 44.5. **Deaths** (per 1,000 pop. 1985): 17.1. **Natural increase** (1985): 2.7%. **Hospital beds** (1978): 6,876. **Physicians** (1980): 278. **Infant mortality** (per 1,000 live births 1985): 110.

Education (1980): **Literacy:** 80%. Years compulsory 10; attendance 80%.

Major International Organizations: UN (GATT, IMF, WHO), OAU.

Embassy: 4891 Colorado Ave. NW 20011; 726-5500.

The Loango Kingdom flourished in the 15th century, as did the Anzico Kingdom of the Batekes; by the late 17th century they had become weakened. France established control by 1885. Independence came Aug. 15, 1960.

After a 1963 coup sparked by trade unions, the country adopted a Marxist-Leninist stance, with the USSR and China vying for influence. Tribal divisions remain strong. France remains a dominant trade partner and source of technical assistance, and French-owned private enterprise retained a major economic role. However, the government of Pres. Sassou-Nguesso favored a strengthening of relations with the USSR, a socialist constitution was adopted, 1979.

Costa Rica

Republic of Costa Rica

República de Costa Rica

People: Population (1986 est.): 2,714,000. **Age distrib.** (%): 0–14: 35; 15–49: 51.8; 50+: 13.2. **Pop. density:** 135 per sq. mi. **Urban** (1982): 43%. **Ethnic groups:** Spanish (with Mestizo minority). **Language:** Spanish (official). **Religions:** Roman Catholicism prevails.

Geography: Area: 19,575 sq. mi., smaller than W. Virginia. **Location:** In central America. **Neighbors:** Nicaragua on N, Panama on S. **Topography:** Lowlands by the Caribbean are tropical. The interior plateau, with an altitude of about 4,000 ft., is temperate. **Capital:** San Jose. **Cities** (1984 est.): San Jose 241,000, Limon 52,000.

Government: Type: Democratic republic. **Head of state:** Pres. Oscar Arias Sanchez; b. 1942; in office May 8, 1986. **Local divisions:** 7 provinces and 80 cantons.

Economy: Industries: Fiberglass, aluminum, textiles, fertilizers, roofing, cement. **Chief crops:** Coffee (chief export), bananas, sugar, cocoa, cotton, hemp. **Minerals:** Gold, salt, sulphur, iron. **Other resources:** Fish, forests. **Arable land:** 12%. **Fish catch** (1983): 15,000 metric tons. **Electricity prod.** (1983): 2.7 bln. kwh. **Labor force:** 33% agric.; 40% ind. & comm.; 25% service and government.

Finance: Currency: Colone (Mar. 1987: 60.1 = $1 US). **Gross national product** (1985): $3.7 bln. **Per capita income** (1985): $1,352. **Imports** (1985): $1.0 bln.; partners: U.S. 40%, CACM 10%, Jap. 10%. **Exports** (1985): $928 mln.; partners: U.S. 53%, W. Ger. 9%. **Tourists** (1984): receipts: $130 mln. **National budget** (1985): $603 mln. expenditures. **International reserves less gold** (Mar. 1987): $512 mln. **Gold:** 72,000 oz t. **Consumer prices** (change in 1986): 11.8%.

Transport: Motor vehicles: in use (1984): 106,000 passenger cars, 69,000 comm. vehicles. **Civil aviation** (1984): 540 mln. passenger-km; 24 mln. net ton-km. **Chief ports:** Limon, Puntarenas, Golfito.

Communications: Television sets: 450,000 in use (1984). **Radios:** 190,000 in use (1984). **Telephones in use** (1983): 281,000. **Daily newspaper circ.** (1985): 71 per 1,000 pop.

Health: Life expectancy at birth (1986): 67.5 male; 71.9 female. **Births** (per 1,000 pop. 1985): 31. **Deaths** (per 1,000 pop. 1985): 4. **Natural increase** (1985): 2.7%. **Hospital beds** (1980): 7,570. **Physicians** (1979): 1,506. **Infant mortality** (per 1,000 live births 1986): 15.2.

Education (1986): **Literacy:** 90%. Years compulsory 6; attendance 99%.

Major International Organizations: UN (FAO, ILO, IMF, WHO), OAS.

Embassy: 1825 Connecticut Ave. NW, 20008; 234-2945.

Guaymi Indians inhabited the area when Spaniards arrived, 1502. Independence came in 1821. Costa Rica seceded from the Central American Federation in 1838. Since the civil war of 1948-49, there has been little violent social conflict, and free political institutions have been preserved.

Costa Rica, though still a largely agricultural country, has achieved a relatively high standard of living and social services, and land ownership is widespread.

Côte d'Ivoire

Ivory Coast

République de la Côte d'Ivoire

People: Population (1986 est.): 10,500,000. **Age distrib.** (%): 0–14: 45.1; 15–59: 50.2; 60+: 4.7. **Pop. density:** 85 per sq. mi. **Urban** (1985): 42%. **Ethnic groups:** Baule 23%, Bete 18%, Senufo 15%, Malinke 11%, over 60 tribes. **Languages:** French (official), tribal languages. **Religions:** Moslems 15%, Christians 12%, indigenous 63%.

Geography: Area: 124,503 sq. mi., slightly larger than New Mexico. **Location:** On S. coast of W. Africa. **Neighbors:** Liberia, Guinea on W, Mali, Burkina Faso on N, Ghana on E. **Topography:** Forests cover the W half of the country, and range from a coastal strip to halfway to the N on the E. A sparse inland plain leads to low mountains in NW. **Capital:** Abidjan. **Cities** (1981 est.): Abidjan 1,686,100 (met.)

Government: Type: Republic. **Head of state:** Pres. Felix Houphouet-Boigny; b. Oct. 18, 1905; in office: Aug. 7, 1960. **Local divisions:** 34 departments.

Economy: Chief crops: Coffee, cocoa. **Minerals:** Diamonds, manganese. **Other resources:** Timber, rubber. **Arable land:** 12%. **Meat prod.** (1984): goats: 1.4 mln.; sheep: 1.4 mln.; cattle: 760,000. **Fish catch** (1983): 83,000 metric tons. **Electricity prod.** (1984): 1.9 bln. kwh. **Labor force:** 75% agric.; 25% ind. and commerce.

Finance: Currency: CFA franc (Mar. 1987: 300 = $1 US). **Gross national product** (1984): $6.0 bln. **Per capita income** (1984): $1,100. **Imports** (1985): $1.7 bln.; partners: Fr. 31%, Venez. 8%, Jap. 5%, U.S. 5%. **Exports** (1985): $2.9 bln.; partners: Fr. 19%, Neth. 13%, U.S. 11%, It. 8%. **Tourists** (1984): $72 mln receipts; **International reserves less gold** (Jan. 1987): $19.7 mln. **Gold:** 45,000 oz t. **Consumer prices** (change in 1986): 5.5%.

Transport: Railway traffic (1984): 857 mln. passenger-km; 530 mln. net ton-km. **Motor vehicles:** in use (1984): 182,000 passenger cars, 52,000 comm. vehicles. **Chief ports:** Abidjan, Sassandra.

Communications: Television sets: 340,000 in use (1984). **Radios:** 900,000 in use (1984). **Telephones in use** (1981): 88,000. **Daily newspaper circ.** (1984): 8 per 1,000 pop.

Health: Life expectancy at birth (1983): 46.9 male; 50.2 female. **Births** (per 1,000 pop. 1985): 48.0. **Deaths** (per 1,000 pop. 1985): 12.0. **Natural increase** (1985): 3.6%. **Hospital beds** (1978): 9,962. **Physicians** (1978): 429. **Infant mortality** (per 1,000 live births 1985): 93.

Education (1985): **Literacy:** 41%. **Years compulsory:** none; attendance 75%.

Major International Organizations: UN and all of its specialized agencies, OAU.

Embassy: 2424 Massachusetts Ave. NW 20008; 483-2400.

A French protectorate from 1842, Côte D'Ivoire became independent in 1960. It is the most prosperous of tropical African nations, due to diversification of agriculture for export, close ties to France, and encouragement of foreign investment. About 20% of the population are workers from neighboring countries. Côte D'Ivoire, which officially changed its name from Ivory Coast in Oct. 1985, is a leader of the pro-Western bloc in Africa.

Cuba

Republic of Cuba

República de Cuba

People: Population (1986 est.): 10,221,000. **Age distrib.** (%): 0–29: 55.9; 30–59: 32.8; 60+: 11.3. **Pop. density:** 238 per sq. mi. **Urban** (1986): 70%. **Ethnic groups:** Spanish, African.

Languages: Spanish. **Religions:** Roman Catholic 42%, none 49%.

Geography: Area: 44,218 sq. mi., nearly as large as Pennsylvania. **Location:** Westernmost of West Indies. **Neighbors:** Bahamas, U.S., on N, Mexico on W, Jamaica on S, Haiti on E. **Topography:** The coastline is about 2,500 miles. The N coast is steep and rocky, the S coast low and marshy. Low hills and fertile valleys cover more than half the country. Sierra Maestra, in the E is the highest of 3 mountain ranges. **Capital:** Havana. **Cities** (1985 est.): Havana 1,992,000; Santiago de Cuba 356,000; Camaguey 287,000.

Government: Type: Communist state. **Head of state:** Pres. Fidel Castro Ruz; b. Aug. 13, 1926; in office: Dec. 3, 1976 (formerly Prime Min. since Feb. 16, 1959). **Local divisions:** 14 provinces, 169 municipal assemblies. **Defense:** 8% of GNP (1983).

Economy: Industries: Texiles, wood products, cement, chemicals, cigars. **Chief crops:** Sugar (75% of exports), tobacco, coffee, pineapples, bananas, citrus fruit, coconuts. **Minerals:** Cobalt, nickel, iron, copper, manganese, salt. **Other resources:** Forests. **Arable land:** 29%. **Meat prod.** (1985): cattle: 6.5 mln.; pigs: 2.4 mln.; sheep: 382,000. **Fish catch** (1985): 221,000 metric tons. **Electricity prod.** (1984): 12.3 bln. kwh. **Crude steel prod.** (1984): 412,000 metric tons. **Labor force:** 25% agric.; 47% ind. & comm.; 28% services & govt.

Finance: Currency: Peso (Dec. 1986: 0.80 = $1 US). **Disposable national income** (1983): $15.8 bln. **Per capita income** (1983): $1,590. **Imports** (1983): $7.2 bln.; partners: USSR 67%. **Exports** (1983): $6.5 bln.; partners: USSR 74%.

Transport: Railway traffic (1985): 2.3 bln. passenger-km; 2.8 bln. net ton-km. **Motor vehicles:** in use (1982): 182,000 passenger cars, 152,000 comm. vehicles. **Civil aviation** (1985): 2.4 bln. passenger-km.; 33 mln. net ton-km. **Chief ports:** Havana, Matanzas, Cienfuegos, Santiago de Cuba.

Communications: Television sets: 1.5 mln. in use (1985). **Radios:** 2.1 mln. in use (1985). **Telephones in use** (1984): 430,000. **Daily newspaper circ.** (1984): 129 per 1,000 pop.

Health: Life expectancy at birth: (1980): 71.0 male; 74.0 female. **Births** (per 1,000 pop. 1985): 18. **Deaths** (per 1,000 pop. 1985): 6. **Natural increase** (1985): 1.2%. **Hospital beds** (1985): 53,000. **Physicians** (1985): 20,490. **Infant mortality** (per 1,000 live births 1985): 21.

Education (1985): **Literacy:** 96%. 92% of those between ages 6–14 attend school.

Major International Organizations: UN (GATT, WHO).

Some 50,000 Indians lived in Cuba when it was discovered by Columbus in 1492. Its name derives from the Indian Cubanacan. Except for British occupation of Havana, 1762-63, Cuba remained Spanish until 1898. A slave-based sugar plantation economy developed from the 18th century, aided by early mechanization of milling. Sugar remains the chief product and chief export despite government attempts to diversify.

A ten-year uprising ended in 1878 with guarantees of rights by Spain, which Spain failed to carry out. A full-scale movement under Jose Marti began Feb. 24, 1895.

The U.S. declared war on Spain in April, 1898, after the sinking of the U.S.S. Maine in Havana harbor, and defeated it in the short Spanish-American War. Spain gave up all claims to Cuba. U.S. troops withdrew in 1902, but under 1903 and 1934 agreements, the U.S. leases a site at Guantanamo Bay in the SE as a naval base. U.S. and other foreign investments acquired a dominant role in the economy. In 1952, former president Fulgencio Batista seized control and established a dictatorship, which grew increasingly harsh and corrupt. Former student leader Fidel Castro assembled a rebel band in 1956; guerrilla fighting intensified in 1958. Batista fled Jan. 1, 1959, and in the resulting political vacuum Castro took power, becoming premier Feb. 16.

The government began a program of sweeping economic and social changes, without restoring promised liberties. Opponents were imprisoned and some were executed. Some 700,000 Cubans emigrated in the years after the Castro takeover, mostly to the U.S.

Cattle and tobacco lands were nationalized, while a system of cooperatives was instituted. By the end of 1960 all banks and industrial companies had been nationalized, including over $1 billion worth of U.S.-owned properties, mostly without compensation.

Poor sugar crops resulted in collectivization of farms, stringent labor controls, and rationing, despite continued aid from the USSR and other communist countries.

The U.S. imposed an export embargo in 1962, severely damaging the economy. In 1961, some 1,400 Cubans, trained and backed by the U.S. Central Intelligence Agency, unsuccessfully tried to invade and overthrow the regime.

In the fall of 1962, the U.S. learned that the USSR had brought nuclear missiles to Cuba. After an Oct. 22 warning from Pres. Kennedy, the missiles were removed.

In 1977, Cuba and the U.S. signed agreements to exchange diplomats, without restoring full ties, and to regulate offshore fishing. In 1978, and again in 1980, the U.S. agreed to accept political prisoners released by Cuba some of whom, it was later discovered, were criminals and mental patients .

In 1975-78, Cuba sent troops to aid one faction in the Angola Civil War. Cuban troops or advisers are stationed in several African countries. This presence, along with Cuba's involvement in Central America and the Caribbean, has contributed to poor relations with the U.S.

In 1983, 24 Cubans died and over 700 were captured, later repatriated, as a result of the U.S. led invasion of Grenada.

Cyprus

Republic of Cyprus

Kypriaki Dimokratia (Greek)
Kibris Cumhuriyeti (Turkish)

People: Population (1986 est.): 673,000. **Age distrib.** (%): 0–14: 25.0; 15–59: 61.0; 60+: 14.0. **Pop. density:** 189 per sq. mi. **Urban** (1982): 53%. **Ethnic groups:** Greeks 80%, Turks 18.7%, Armenians, Maronites. **Languages:** Greek, Turkish (both official), English. **Religions:** Orthodox 77%, Moslems 18%.

Geography: Area: 3,572 sq. mi., smaller than Connecticut. **Location:** In eastern Mediterranean Sea, off Turkish coast. **Neighbors:** Nearest are Turkey on N, Syria, Lebanon on E. **Topography:** Two mountain ranges run E-W, separated by a wide, fertile plain. **Capital:** Nicosia. **Cities** (1984 est.): Nicosia 124,300.

Government: Type: Republic. **Head of state:** Pres. Spyros Kyprianou; b. Oct. 28, 1932; in office: Aug. 3, 1977. **Local divisions:** 6 districts. **Defense:** over 6% of govt. budget. Greek: regulars 10,000; Turkish: 4,500 (1984).

Economy: Industries: Wine, clothing, construction, chemicals. **Chief crops:** Grains, grapes, carobs, citrus fruits, potatoes, olives. **Minerals:** Copper, pyrites, asbetos, gypsum, umber. **Arable land:** 47%. **Meat prod.** (1980): pork: 15,000 metric tons; lamb: 10,000 metric tons. **Electricity prod.** (1984): 1.2 mln. kwh. **Labor force:** 21% agric.; 20% ind., 18% comm., 19% serv.

Finance: Currency: Pound (Mar. 1987: 0.52 = $1 US). **GNP** (1984): $2.3 bln. **Per capita income** (1983): $3,986. **Imports** (1983): $1.21 bln.; partners: UK 13%, Itl. 12%. **Exports** (1983): $495 mln.; partners: UK 17%, Sau. Ar. 7%. **Tourists** (1984): receipts: $270 mln. **National budget** (1984): $540 mln. revenues; $737 mln. expenditures. **International reserves less gold** (Mar. 1987): $736 mln. **Gold:** 459,000 oz. t. **Consumer prices** (change in 1986): 1.2%.

Transport: Motor vehicles: in use (1984): 113,000 passenger cars, 43,000 comm. vehicles. **Civil aviation** (1984): 1.1 bln. passenger-km; 26 mln. net ton-km. **Chief ports:** Famagusta, Limassol.

Communications: Television sets: 158,000 (1985). **Radios:** 300,000 (1985). **Telephones in use** (1983): 164,000. **Daily newspaper circ.** (1985): 91 per 1,000 pop.

Health: Life expectancy at birth (1984): 72.3 male; 76.0 female. **Births** (per 1,000 pop. 1985): 21. **Deaths** (per 1,000 pop. 1985): 8. **Natural increase** (1985): 1.3%. **Hospital beds** (1983): 5,375. **Physicians** (1983): 635. **Infant mortality** (per 1,000 live births 1985): 12.

Education (1984): **Literacy:** 99%. **Years compulsory:** 9; attendance 99%.

Major International Organizations: UN (GATT, IMF, WHO), Commonwealth of Nations, EC (Assoc.).

Embassy: 2211 R St. NW, 20008; 462-5772.

Agitation for enosis (union) with Greece increased after World War II, with the Turkish minority opposed, and broke into violence in 1955-56. In 1959, Britain, Greece, Turkey, and Cypriot leaders approved a plan for an independent republic, with constitutional guarantees for the Turkish minority and permanent division of offices on an ethnic basis. Greek and Turkish Communal Chambers dealt with religion, education, and other matters.

Archbishop Makarios, formerly the leader of the enosis movement, was elected president, and full independence became final Aug. 16, 1960. Makarios was re-elected in 1968 and 1973.

Further communal strife led the United Nations to send a peace-keeping force in 1964; its mandate has been repeatedly renewed.

The Cypriot National Guard, led by officers from the army of Greece, seized the government July 15, 1974, and named Nikos Sampson, an advocate of union with Greece, president. Makarios fled the country. On July 20, Turkey invaded the island; Greece mobilized its forces but did not intervene. A cease-fire was arranged July 22. On the 23d, Sampson turned over the presidency to Glafkos Clerides (on the same day, Greece's military junta resigned). A peace conference collapsed Aug. 14; fighting resumed. By Aug. 16 Turkish forces had occupied the NE 40% of the island, despite the presence of UN peace forces. Makarios resumed the presidency in Dec., until his death, 1977.

Turkish Cypriots voted overwhelmingly, June 8, 1975, to form a separate Turkish Cypriot federated state. A president and assembly were elected in 1976. Some 200,000 Greeks have been expelled from the Turkish-controlled area, replaced by thousands of Turks, some from the mainland.

A unilateral declaration of independence was announced by Turkish-Cypriot leader Rauf Denktash, Nov. 15, 1983. The new state, which was not recognized by other nations, was named the Turkish Rep. of Northern Cyprus.

Czechoslovakia

Czechoslovak Socialist Republic

Československá Socialistická Republika

People: Population (1986 est.): 15,542,000. **Age distrib.** (%): 0–14: 24.2; 15–59: 59.3; 60+: 16.3. **Pop. density:** 314 per sq. mi. **Urban** (1983): 73%. **Ethnic groups:** Czechs 63%, Slovaks 31%, Hungarians 4%, Germans, Poles, Ukrainians. **Languages:** Czech, Slovak (both official). **Religions:** Roman Catholic 65%.

Geography: Area: 49,365 sq. mi., the size of New York. **Location:** In E central Europe. **Neighbors:** Poland, E. Germany on N, W. Germany on W. Austria, Hungary on S, USSR on E. **Topography:** Bohemia, in W, is a plateau surrounded by mountains; Moravia is hilly, Slovakia, in E, has mountains (Carpathians) in N, fertile Danube plain in S. Vltava (Moldau) and Labe (Elbe) rivers flow N from Bohemia to G. **Capital:** Prague. **Cities** (1985 est.): Prague 1.1 mln., Brno 385,000; Bratislava 417,000; Ostrava 327,000.

Government: Type: Communist. **Head of state:** Pres. Gustav Husak; b. Jan 10, 1913; in office: May 29, 1975; **Head of government:** Prime Min. Lubomir Strougal; b. Oct. 19, 1924; in office: Jan. 28, 1970. **Head of Communist Party:** First Sec. Gustav Husak; in office: Apr. 17, 1969. **Local divisions:** Czech and Slovak republics each have an assembly. **Defense:** 5.9% of GNP (1983).

Economy: Industries: Machinery, oil products, iron and steel, glass, chemicals, motor vehicles, cement. **Chief crops:** Wheat, sugar beets, potatoes, rye, corn, barley. **Minerals:** Mercury, coal, iron. Jachymor has Europe's greatest pitchblende (for uranium and radium) deposits. **Arable land:** 40%. **Meat prod.** (1985): cattle: 5 mln.; pigs: 6.6 mln.; sheep: 1 mln. **Electricity prod.** (1985): 80.6 bln. kwh. **Crude steel prod.** (1985): 15.0 mln. metric tons. **Labor force:** 12% agric.; 66% ind., comm.; 18% service, govt.

Finance: Currency: Koruna (Jan. 1987: 5.75 = $1 US). **Gross national product** (1984): $83.9 bln. **Per capita income** (1980): $5,800. **Imports** (1982): $15.6 bln.; partners: USSR 46%, E. Ger. 10%, Pol. 6%, W. Ger. 5%. **Exports** (1982): $15.7 bln.; partners: USSR 41%, E. Ger. 9%, Pol. 7%, Hung. 5%.

Transport: Railway traffic (1984): 18.8 bln. passenger-km; 68 bln. net ton-km. **Motor vehicles:** in use (1984): 2.6 mln. passenger cars, 412,000 comm. **Civil aviation** (1984): 1.2 bln. passenger-km; 52.3 mln. net ton-km.

Communications: Television sets: 4.3 mln. (1985). **Radios:** 4.2 mln. (1985). **Telephones in use** (1985): 3.4 mln. **Daily newspaper circ.** (1984): 284 per 1,000 pop.

Health: Life expectancy at birth (1985): 67.2 male; 74.4 female. **Births** (per 1,000 pop. 1985): 15. **Deaths** (per 1,000 pop. 1985): 12. **Natural increase** (1985): .3%. **Hospital beds** (1985): 121,000; **Physicians** (1985): 46,492. **Infant mortality** (per 1,000 live births 1985): 15.6.

Education (1981): **Literacy:** 99%. **Pop. 5–19:** in school: 60%, teachers per 1,000: 30.

Major International Organizations: UN (GATT, WHO), Warsaw Pact.

Embassy: 3900 Linnean Ave. NW 20008; 263-6315.

Bohemia, Moravia and Slovakia were part of the Great Moravian Empire in the 9th century. Later, Slovakia was overrun by Magyars, while Bohemia and Moravia became part of the Holy Roman Empire. Under the kings of Bohemia, Prague in the 14th century was the cultural center of Central Europe. Bohemia and Hungary became part of Austria-Hungary.

In 1914-1918 Thomas G. Masaryk and Eduard Benes formed a provisional government with the support of Slovak leaders including Milan Stefanik. They proclaimed the Republic of Czechoslovakia Oct. 30, 1918.

By 1938 Nazi Germany had worked up disaffection among German-speaking citizens in Sudetenland and demanded its cession. Prime Min. Neville Chamberlain of Britain, with the acquiescence of France, signed with Hitler at Munich, Sept. 30, 1938, an agreement to the cession, with a guarantee of peace by Hitler and Mussolini. Germany occupied Sudetenland Oct. 1-2.

Hitler on Mar. 15, 1939, dissolved Czechoslovakia, made protectorates of Bohemia and Moravia, and supported the autonomy of Slovakia, which was proclaimed independent Mar. 14, 1939.

Soviet troops with some Czechoslovak contingents entered eastern Czechoslovakia in 1944 and reached Prague in May 1945; Benes returned as president. In May 1946 elections, the Communist Party won 38% of the votes, and Benes accepted Klement Gottwald, a communist, as prime minister.

In February, 1948, the communists seized power in advance of scheduled elections. In May 1948 a new constitution was approved. Benes refused to sign it. On May 30 the voters were offered a one-slate ballot and the communists won full control. Benes resigned June 7 and Gottwald became president. A harsh Stalinist period followed, with complete and violent suppression of all opposition.

In Jan. 1968 a liberalization movement spread explosively through Czechoslovakia. Antonin Novotny, long the Stalinist boss of the nation, was deposed as party leader and succeeded by Alexander Dubcek, a Slovak, who declared he intended to make communism democratic. On Mar. 22 Novotny resigned as president and was succeeded by Gen. Ludvik Svoboda. On Apr. 6, Premier Joseph Lenart resigned and was succeeded by Oldrich Cernik, whose new cabinet was pledged to carry out democratization and economic reforms.

In July 1968 the USSR and 4 Warsaw Pact nations demanded an end to liberalization. On Aug. 20, the Russian, Polish, East German, Hungarian, and Bulgarian armies invaded Czechoslovakia.

Despite demonstrations and riots by students and workers, press censorship was imposed, liberal leaders were ousted from office and promises of loyalty to Soviet policies were made by some old-line Communist Party leaders.

On Apr. 17, 1969, Dubcek resigned as leader of the Communist Party and was succeeded by Gustav Husak. In Jan. 1970, Premier Cernik was ousted. Censorship was tightened and the Communist Party expelled a third of its members. In 1972, more than 40 liberals were jailed on subversion charges. In 1973, amnesty was offered to some of the 40,000 who fled the country after the 1968 invasion, but repressive policies continue to remain in force.

More than 700 leading Czechoslovak intellectuals and former party leaders signed a human rights manifesto in 1977, called Charter 77, prompting a renewed crackdown by the regime.

Czechoslovakia has long been an industrial and technological leader of the eastern European countries, though its relative standing has declined in recent years because of the government's rejection of economic reforms.

Denmark

Kingdom of Denmark

Kongeriget Danmark

People: Population (1986 est.): 5,097,000. **Age distrib.** (%): 0–14: 18.3 15–59: 61.4; 60+: 20.3. **Pop. density:** 307 per sq. mi. **Urban** (1985): 84%. **Ethnic groups:** Almost all Scandinavian. **Languages:** Danish. **Religions:** Evangelical Lutheran 97%.

Geography: Area: 16,633 sq. mi., the size of Massachusetts and New Hampshire combined. **Location:** In northern Europe, separating the North and Baltic seas. **Neighbors:** W. Germany on S., Norway on NW, Sweden on NE. **Topography:** Denmark consists of the Jutland Peninsula and about 500 islands, 100 inhabited. The land is flat or gently rolling, and is almost all in productive use. **Capital:** Copenhagen. **Cities** (1985): Copenhagen 633,412; Arhus 252,071.

Government: Type: Constitutional monarchy. **Head of state:** Queen Margrethe II; b. Apr. 16, 1940; in office: Jan. 14, 1972. **Head of government:** Prime Min. Poul Schluter; b. 1929; in office: Sept. 10, 1982. **Local divisions:** 14 counties and one city (Copenhagen). **Defense:** 2.1% of GNP (1985).

Economy: Industries: Machinery, textiles, furniture, electronics. **Chief crops:** Dairy products. **Crude oil reserves** (1985): 533 mln. bbls. **Arable land:** 62%. **Meat prod.** (1985): cattle: 2.5 mln.; pigs: 9.4 mln. **Fish catch** (1985): 1.6 mln. metric tons. **Electricity prod.** (1984): 22.1 bln. kwh. **Crude steel prod.** (1982): 560,000 metric tons. **Labor force:** 8.2% agric.; 46% ind. & comm.; 13% serv.

Finance: Currency: Krone (May 1987: 6.68 = $1 US). **Gross national product** (1985): $57.9 bln. **Per capita income** (1985): $11,312. **Imports** (1986): $22.8 bln.; partners: W. Ger. 20%, Swed. 12%, UK 9%, Neth. 5%. **Exports** (1986): $21.2 bln.; partners: W. Ger. 19%, UK 11%, Swed. 13%, U.S. 8%. **Tourists** (1984): $1.3 bln. receipts. **National budget** (1980): $23 bln. expenditures. **International reserves less gold** (Mar. 1987): $6.5 bln. **Gold:** 1.62 mln. oz t. **Consumer prices** (change in 1986): 3.7%.

Transport: Railway traffic (1984): 4.3 bln. passenger-km; 1.6 bln. net ton-km. **Motor vehicles:** in use (1984): 1.4 mln. passenger cars, 251,000 comm. vehicles. **Civil aviation** (1985): 3.1 bln. passenger-km; 127 mln. net ton-km. **Chief ports:** Copenhagen, Alborg, Arhus, Odense.

Communications: Television sets: 1.9 mln. licensed (1984). **Radios:** 2 mln. licensed (1984). **Telephones in use** (1983): 3.4 mln. **Daily newspaper circ.** (1984): 359 per 1,000 pop.

Health: Life expectancy at birth (1986): 71.5 male; 77.5 female. **Births** (per 1,000 pop. 1985): 10.1. **Deaths** (per 1,000 pop. 1985): 12.0. **Hospital beds** (1985): 36,000. **Physicians** (1984): 12,806. **Infant mortality** (per 1,000 live births 1985): 7.8.

Education (1986): **Literacy:** 99%. Years compulsory 9; attendance 100%.

Major International Organizations: UN and all of its specialized agencies, OECD, EC.

Embassy: 3200 Whitehaven St. NW 20008; 234-4300.

The origin of Copenhagen dates back to ancient times, when the fishing and trading place named Havn (port) grew up on a cluster of islets, but Bishop Absalon (1128-1201) is regarded as the actual founder of the city.

Danes formed a large component of the Viking raiders in the early Middle Ages. The Danish kingdom was a major north European power until the 17th century, when it lost its land in southern Sweden. Norway was separated in 1815, and Schleswig-Holstein in 1864. Northern Schleswig was returned in 1920.

There was severe labor strife in 1985.

The **Faeroe Islands** in the N. Atlantic, about 300 mi. NE of the Shetlands, and 850 mi. from Denmark proper, 18 inhabited, have an area of 540 sq. mi. and pop. (1985) of 45,000. They are self-governing in most matters.

Greenland

(Kalaallit Nunaat)

Greenland, a huge island between the N. Atlantic and the Polar Sea, is separated from the North American continent by Davis Strait and Baffin Bay. Its total area is 840,000 sq. mi., 84% of which is ice-capped. Most of the island is a lofty plateau 9,000 to 10,000 ft. in altitude. The average thickness of the cap is 1,000 ft. The population (1985 est.) is 53,000. Under the 1953 Danish constitution the colony became an integral part of the realm with representatives in the Folketing. The Danish parliament, 1978, approved home rule for Greenland, effective May 1, 1979. Accepting home rule the islanders elected a socialist-dominated legislature, Apr. 4th. With home rule, Greenlandic place names came into official use. The technically-correct name for Greenland is now Kalaallit Nunaat; its capital is Nuuk, rather than Gothab. Fish is the principal export.

Djibouti

Republic of Djibouti

Jumhouriyya Djibouti

People: Population (1986 est.): 304,000. **Pop. density:** 49 per sq. mi. **Ethnic groups:** Issa (Somali) 47%; Afar 37%; European 8%; Arab 6%. **Languages:** French, Arabic (both official); Somali, Saho-Afar, Arabic. **Religions:** Sunni Moslem 94%.

Geography: Area: 8,494 sq. mi., about the size of New Hampshire. **Location:** On E coast of Africa, separated from Arabian Peninsula by the strategically vital strait of Bab el-Mandeb. **Neighbors:** Ethiopia on N (Eritrea) and W, Somalia on S. **Topography:** The territory, divided into a low coastal plain, mountains behind, and an interior plateau, is arid, sandy, and desolate. The climate is generally hot and dry. **Capital:** Djibouti. **Cities** (1982): Djibouti (met.) 200,000.

Government: Type: Republic. **Head of state:** Pres. Hassan Gouled Aptidon b. 1916; in office: June 24, 1977; **Head of government:** Prem. Barkat Gourad Hamadou; in office: Sept. 30, 1978. **Local divisions:** 5 cercles (districts).

Economy: Minerals: Salt. **Electricity prod.** (1985): 164 mln. kwh.

Finance: Currency Franc (Jan. 1987: 177=$1 US). **Gross national product:** (1984): $307 mln. **Per capita income** (1982): $400. **Imports** (1979): $140 mln.; partners: Fr. 47%, Jap. 8%, UK 8%. **Exports** (1979): $20 mln.; partners: Fr. 87%.

Transport: Motor vehicles: in use (1985): 12,000 passenger cars, 950 commercial vehicles. **Chief ports:** Djibouti.

Communications: Television sets: 11,000 in use (1985). **Radios:** 30,000 in use (1985). **Telephones in use** (1984): 6,400.

Health: Life expectancy at birth (1985): 50 years. **Births** (per 1,000 pop. 1985): 49.2. **Deaths** (per 1,000 pop. 1985): 18.3. **Natural increase** (1985): 3.0%. **Infant mortality** (per 1,000 live births 1985): 132.

Education (1985): **Literacy:** 17%.

Major International Organizations: UN, OAU, Arab League.

Embassy: 866 United Nations Plaza, New York, NY 10017; (212) 753-3163.

France gained control of the territory in stages between 1862 and 1900.

Ethiopia and Somalia have renounced their claims to the area, but each has accused the other of trying to gain control. There were clashes between Afars (ethnically related to Ethiopians) and Issas (related to Somalis) in 1976. Immigrants from both countries continued to enter the country up to independence, which came June 27, 1977.

Unemployment is high and there are few natural resources. French aid is the mainstay of the economy and some 5,000 French troops are present.

Dominica

Commonwealth of Dominica

People: Population (1986 est.): 74,000. **Pop. density:** 255 per sq. mi. **Ethnic groups:** nearly all African or mulatto, Caribs. **Languages:** English (official), French patois. **Religions:** mainly Roman Catholic.

Geography: Area: 290 sq. mi., about one-fourth the size of Rhode Island. **Location:** In Eastern Caribbean, most northerly Windward Is. **Neighbors:** Guadeloupe to N, Martinique to S. **Topography:** Mountainous, a central ridge running from N to S, terminating in cliffs; volcanic in origin, with numerous thermal springs; rich deep topsoil on leeward side, red tropical clay on windward coast. **Capital** (1983 est.) Roseau 18,000.

Government: Head of state: Pres. Clarence Augustus Seignoret; in office: 1984. **Head of government:** Prime Min. Mary Eugenia Charles; b. 1919; in office: July 21, 1980. **Local divisions:** 25 village councils and 2 town councils.

Economy: Industries: Agriculture, tourism. **Chief crops:** Bananas, citrus fruits, coconuts. **Minerals:** Pumice. **Other resources:** Forests. **Arable land:** 23%. **Electricity prod.** (1984): 20 mln. kwh.

Finance: Currency: East Caribbean dollar (May 1987: 2.70 = $1 US). **Gross national product** (1984): $80 mln. **Imports** (1984): $47 mln.; partners: UK 12%, U.S. 27%, Can. 7%. **Exports** (1984): $22 mln.; partners: UK 47%. **Tourists** (1984): 23,826. **Consumer prices** (change in 1985): 2.1%.

Transport: Chief ports: Roseau.

Communications: Telephones in use (1983): 4,000.

Health: Life expectancy at birth (1982): 66.5 male; 72.8 female. **Births** (per 1,000 pop. 1985): 19. **Deaths** (per 1,000 pop. 1985): 6. **Natural increase** (1985). 1.3%. **Hospital beds** (1983): 237. **Physicians** (1983): 26. **Infant mortality** (per 1,000 live births 1985): 20.

Education: Literacy: 80%.

Major International Organizations: UN, OAS.

A British colony since 1805, Dominica was granted self government in 1967. Independence was achieved Nov. 3, 1978.

Hurricane David struck, Aug. 30, 1979, devastating the island and destroying the banana plantations, Dominica's economic mainstay. Coups were attempted in 1980 and 1981.

Dominica took a leading role in the instigation of the 1983 invasion of Grenada.

Dominican Republic

República Dominicana

People: Population (1986 est.): 6,785,000. **Age distrib.** (%): 0–14: 40.7; 15–59: 54.6; 60+: 4.7. **Pop. density:** 341 per sq. mi. **Urban** (1985): 56%. **Ethnic groups:** Caucasian 15%, múlatto 75%, black 10%. **Languages:** Spanish. **Religions:** Roman Catholic 93%.

Geography: Area: 18,816 sq. mi., the size of Vermont and New Hampshire combined. **Location:** In West Indies, sharing I. of Hispaniola with Haiti. **Neighbors:** Haiti on W. **Topography:** The Cordillera Central range crosses the center of the country, rising to over 10,000 ft., highest in the Caribbean. The Cibao valley to the N is major agricultural area. **Capital:** Santo Domingo. **Cities** (1983 est.): Santo Domingo 1,400,000; Santiago de Los Caballeros 285,000.

Government: Type: Representative democracy. **Head of state:** Pres. Joaquin Balaguer; in office: Aug. 16, 1986. **Local divisions:** 26 provinces and Santo Domingo. **Defense:** 1.5% of GDP. (1983).

Economy: Industries: Sugar refining, cement, textiles, pharmaceuticals. **Chief crops:** sugar, cocoa, coffee, tobacco, rice. **Minerals:** Nickel, gold, silver, bauxite. **Other resources:** Timber. **Arable land:** 30%. **Meat prod.** (1984): cattle: 1.9 mln. **Electricity prod.** (1984): 4.0 bln. kwh. **Labor force:** 47% agric.; 23% manuf.

Finance: Currency: Peso (Mar. 1987: 3.34 = $1 US). **Gross national product** (1984): $6.0 bln. **Per capita income** (1980): $1,221. **Imports** (1985): $1.4 bln.; partners: U.S. 35%, Venez. 21%, Mex. 11%. **Exports** (1985): $735 mln.; partners: U.S. 64%, Swit. 5%, Neth. 4%. **Tourists** (1984): $277 mln. receipts. **National budget** (1983): $1.1 bln. revenues; $1.1 bln. expenditures. **International reserves less gold** (Mar. 1987): $379 mln. **Gold:** 18,000 oz t. **Consumer prices** (change in 1985): 37.0%

Transport: Motor vehicles: in use (1983): 94,000 passenger cars, 55,000 comm. vehicles. **Chief ports:** Santo Domingo, San Pedro de Macoris, Puerto Plata.

Communications: Television sets: 392,000 in use (1985). **Radios:** 227,000 in use (1985). **Telephones in use** (1983): 175,054. **Daily newspaper circ.** (1985): 33 per 1,000 pop.

Health: Life expectancy at birth (1985): 60.7 male; 64.6 female. **Births** (per 1,000 pop. 1985): 34. **Deaths** (per 1,000 pop. 1985): 9. **Natural increase** (1985): 2.5%. **Hospital beds** (1980): 8,953. **Physicians** (1980): 2,142. **Infant mortality** (per 1,000 live births 1985): 74.

Education (1985): **Literacy:** 77%. Years compulsory 8; attendance 60%.

Major International Organizations: UN (World Bank, IMF, GATT), OAS.

Embassy: 1715-22d St. NW 20008; 332-6280.

Carib and Arawak Indians inhabited the island of Hispaniola when Columbus landed in 1492. The city of Santo Domingo, founded 1496, is the oldest settlement by Europeans in the hemisphere and has the supposed ashes of Columbus in an elaborate tomb in its ancient cathedral.

The western third of the island was ceded to France in 1697. Santo Domingo itself was ceded to France in 1795. Haitian leader Toussaint L'Ouverture seized it, 1801. Spain returned intermittently 1803-21, as several native republics came and went. Haiti ruled again, 1822-44, and Spanish occupation occurred 1861-63.

The country was occupied by U.S. Marines from 1916 to 1924, when a constitutionally elected government was installed.

In 1930, Gen. Rafael Leonidas Trujillo Molina was elected president. Trujillo ruled brutally until his assassination in 1961. Pres. Joaquin Balaguer, appointed by Trujillo in 1960, resigned under pressure in 1962. Juan Bosch, elected president in the first free elections in 38 years, was overthrown in 1963.

On April 24, 1965, a revolt was launched by followers of Bosch and others, including a few communists. Four days later U.S. Marines intervened against the pro-Bosch forces. Token units were later sent by 5 So. American countries as a peacekeeping force.

A provisional government supervised a June 1966 election, in which Balaguer defeated Bosch by a 3-2 margin; there were some charges of election fraud. The Inter-American Peace Force completed its departure Sept. 20, 1966.

Continued depressed world prices have affected the main export commodity, sugar.

Ecuador

Republic of Ecuador

República del Ecuador

People: Population (1986 est.): 9,647,000. **Age distrib.** (%): 0–14: 44.5; 15–59: 49.6; 60+: 6.0. **Pop. density:** 92 per sq. mi. **Urban** (1986): 52% **Ethnic groups:** Indians 25%, Mestizo 55%, Spanish 10%, African 10%. **Languages:** Spanish (official), Quechuan, Jivaroan. **Religions:** Predominantly Roman Catholic.

Geography: Area: 109,483 sq. mi., the size of Colorado. **Location:** In NW S. America, on Pacific coast, astride Equator. **Neighbors:** Colombia to N, Peru to E and S. **Topography:** Two ranges of Andes run N and S, splitting the country into 3 zones: hot, humid lowlands on the coast; temperate highlands between the ranges, and rainy, tropical lowlands to the E. **Capital:** Quito. **Cities** (1986 est.): Guayaquil 1,500,000; Quito 1,200,000.

Government: Type: Republic. **Head of state:** Pres. Leon Febres-Cordero; b. Mar. 9, 1931; in office: Aug. 10, 1984. **Local divisions:** 20 provinces. **Defense:** 1.6% of GNP (1983).

Economy: Industries: Food processing, wood prods., textiles. **Chief crops:** Bananas (largest exporter), coffee, rice, sugar, corn. **Minerals:** Oil, copper, iron, lead, silver, sulphur. **Crude oil reserves** (1985): 831 mln. bbls. **Other resources:** Rubber, bark. **Arable land:** 9%. **Meat prod.** (1984): cattle: 3.3 mln.; pigs: 4.2 mln.; sheep: 2.3 mln. **Fish catch** (1984): 159,000 metric tons. **Electricity prod.** (1984): 4.8 bln. kwh. **Labor force:** 34% agric., 12% ind., 35% services.

Finance: Currency: Sucre (May 1987: 173 = $1 US). **Gross national product** (1985): $12.1 bln. **Per capita income** (1985):

$1,299. **Imports** (1986): $1.8 bln.; partners: U.S. 32%, EC 16%, Jap. 13%. **Exports** (1986): $2.1 bln.; partners: U.S. 64%. **National budget** (1986): $1.2 bln. **International reserves less gold** (Mar. 1987): $547 mln. **Gold:** 414,000 oz t. **Consumer prices** (change in 1986): 23.0%.

Transport: Railway traffic (1985) 63 mln. passenger-km; 32 mln. net ton-km. **Motor vehicles:** in use (1984): 248,000 passenger cars, 32,000 comm. vehicles. **Civil aviation** (1982): 862 mln. passenger-km; 39.4 mln. net ton-km. **Chief ports:** Guayaquil, Manta, Esmeraldas, Puerto Bolivar.

Communications: Television sets: 600,000 in use (1985). **Radios:** 1.9 mln. in use (1985). **Telephones in use** (1984): 295,000. **Daily newspaper circ.** (1985): 57 per 1,000 pop.

Health: Life expectancy at birth (1981): 59.8 male, 63.6 female. **Births** (per 1,000 pop. 1985): 36.0. **Deaths** (per 1,000 pop. 1985): 8.0. **Natural increase** (1985): 2.9%. **Hospital beds** (1984): 15,455. **Physicians** (1984): 11,000. **Infant mortality** (per 1,000 live births 1985): 63.

Education (1986): Literacy: 90%. Attendance through 6th grade—76% urban, 33% rural.

Major International Organizations: UN (IMF, WHO), OAS, OPEC.

Embassy: 2535 15th St. NW 20009; 234-7200.

Spain conquered the region, which was the northern Inca empire, in 1633. Liberation forces defeated the Spanish May 24, 1822, near Quito. Ecuador became part of the Great Colombia Republic but seceded, May 13, 1830.

Ecuador had been ruled by civilian and military dictatorships since 1968. A peaceful transfer of power from the military junta to the democratic civilian government took place, 1979.

Since 1972, the economy has revolved around its petroleum exports, which have declined since 1982 causing severe economic problems. Ecuador suspended interest payments for 1987 on its estimated $8.2 billion foreign debt following a Mar. 5-6 earthquake which left 20,000 homeless, and destroyed a stretch of the country's main oil pipeline.

Ecuador and Peru have long disputed their Amazon Valley boundary.

The **Galapagos Islands,** 600 mi. to the W, are the home of huge tortoises and other unusual animals.

Egypt

Arab Republic of Egypt

Jumhūrīyah Misr al-Arabiya

People: Population (1986 est.): 50,525,000. **Pop. density:** 124 per sq. mi. **Urban** (1985): 48.8%. **Ethnic groups:** Egyptian, Bedouin, Nubian. **Languages:** Arabic, English. **Religions:** 90% Sunni Moslem.

Geography: Area: 386,650 sq. mi, the size of Texas, Oklahoma, and Arkansas combined. **Location:** NE corner of Africa. **Neighbors:** Libya on W, Sudan on S, Israel on E. **Topography:** Almost entirely desolate and barren, with hills and mountains in E and along Nile. The Nile Valley, where most of the people live, stretches 550 miles. **Capital:** Cairo. **Cities** (1985 est.): Cairo 6,205,000; Alexandria 2,821,000; al-Jizah 1,608,000.

Government: Type: Republic. **Head of state:** Pres. Hosni Mubarak; b. 1929; in office: Oct. 14, 1981. **Head of Government:** Atef Sedki in office: Nov. 10, 1986. **Local divisions:** 26 governorates. **Defense:** 8.3% of GNP (1983).

Economy: Industries: Textiles, chemicals, petrochemicals, cement. **Chief crops:** Cotton (one of largest producers), rice, beans, fruits, grains, vegetables, sugar, corn. **Minerals:** Oil, phosphates, gypsum, iron, manganese, limestone. **Crude oil reserves** (1985): 4 bln. bbls. **Arable land:** 4%. **Meat prod.** (1984): cattle: 1.8 mln.; sheep: 1.4 mln. **Fish catch** (1983): 140,000 metric tons. **Electricity prod.** (1984): 22.8 bln. kwh. **Crude steel prod.** (1981 est.): 900,000 metric tons. **Labor force:** 50% agric.; 26% services.

Finance: Currency: Pound (May 1987: 2.17 = $1 US). **Gross national product** (1984): $33 bln. **Per capita income** (1983): $686. **Imports** (1985): $9.9 bln.; partners: U.S. 19%, W. Ger. 10%, It. 8%, France 8%. **Exports** (1985): $3.7 bln.; partners: It. 22%, Isr. 14%. **Tourists** (1984): 1.5 mln. visitors; $233 mln. receipts. **International reserves less gold** (Jan. 1987): $837 mln. **Gold:** 2.43 mln. oz t. **Consumer prices** (change in 1986): 22.6%.

Transport: Railway traffic (1984): 24.1 bln. passenger-km; 2.5 bln. net ton-km. **Motor vehicles:** in use (1983): 597,000 passenger cars, 227,000 comm. vehicles. **Civil aviation** (1984): 4.8 bln. passenger-km, 88 mln. freight ton-km. **Chief ports:** Alexandria, Port Said, Suez.

Communications: Television sets: 3.8 mln. in use (1985). **Radios:** 12 mln. in use (1985). **Telephones in use** (1982): 522,000. **Daily newspaper circ.** (1985): 99 per 1,000 pop.

Health: Life expectancy at birth (1985): 55.9 male; 58.4 female. **Births** (per 1,000 pop. 1985): 40. **Deaths** (per 1,000 pop. 1985): 11. **Natural increase** (1985): 2.9%. **Hospital beds** (1984): 85,350. **Physicians** (1984): 73,300. **Infant mortality** (per 1,000 live births 1985): 103.

Education (1985): **Literacy:** 44%. Compulsory ages 6-12.

Major International Organizations: UN (IMF, World Bank, GATT), OAU, Islamic Conference Org.

Embassy: 2310 Decatur Pl. NW 20008; 232-5400.

Archeological records of ancient Egyptian civilization date back to 4000 BC. A unified kingdom arose around 3200 BC, and extended its way south into Nubia and north as far as Syria. A high culture of rulers and priests was built on an economic base of serfdom, fertile soil, and annual flooding of the Nile banks.

Imperial decline facilitated conquest by Asian invaders (Hyksos, Assyrians). The last native dynasty fell in 341 BC to the Persians, who were in turn replaced by Greeks (Alexander and the Ptolemies), Romans, Byzantines, and Arabs, who introduced Islam and the Arabic language. The ancient Egyptian language is preserved only in the liturgy of the Coptic Christians.

Egypt was ruled as part of larger Islamic empires for several centuries. The Mamluks, a military caste of Caucasian origin, ruled Egypt from 1250 until defeat by the Ottoman Turks in 1517. Under Turkish sultans the khedive as hereditary viceroy had wide authority. Britain intervened in 1882 and took control of administration, though nominal allegiance to the Ottoman Empire continued until 1914.

The country was a British protectorate from 1914 to 1922. A 1936 treaty strengthened Egyptian autonomy, but Britain retained bases in Egypt and a condominium over the Sudan. Britain fought German and Italian armies from Egypt, 1940-42, but Egypt did not declare war against Germany until 1945. In 1951 Egypt abrogated the 1936 treaty. The Sudan became independent in 1956.

The uprising of July 23, 1952, led by the Society of Free Officers, named Maj. Gen. Mohammed Naguib commander in chief and forced King Farouk to abdicate. When the republic was proclaimed June 18, 1953, Naguib became its first president and premier. Lt. Col. Gamal Abdel Nasser removed Naguib and became premier in 1954. In 1956, he was voted president. Nasser died in 1970 and was replaced by Vice Pres. Anwar Sadat.

A series of decrees in July, 1961, nationalized about 90% of industry. Economic liberalization was begun, 1974, with more emphasis on private domestic and foreign investment.

The Aswan High Dam, completed 1971, provides irrigation for more than a million acres of land. Artesian wells, drilled in the Western Desert, reclaimed 43,000 acres, 1960-66.

When the state of Israel was proclaimed in 1948, Egypt joined other Arab nations invading Israel and was defeated.

After terrorist raids across its border, Israel invaded Egypt's Sinai Peninsula, Oct. 29, 1956. Egypt rejected a cease-fire demand by Britain and France; on Oct. 31 the 2 nations dropped bombs and on Nov. 5-6 landed forces. Egypt and Israel accepted a UN cease-fire; fighting ended Nov. 7.

A UN Emergency Force guarded the 117-mile long border between Egypt and Israel until May 19, 1967, when it was withdrawn at Nasser's demand. Egyptian troops entered the Gaza Strip and the heights of Sharm el Sheikh and 3 days later closed the Strait of Tiran to all Israeli shipping. Full-scale war broke out June 5 and before it ended under a UN cease-fire June 10, Israel had captured Gaza and the Sinai Peninsula, controlled the east bank of the Suez Canal and reopened the gulf.

Sporadic fighting with Israel broke out late in 1968 and continued almost daily, 1969-70. Military and economic aid was received from the USSR. Israel and Egypt agreed, Aug. 7, 1970, to a cease-fire and peace negotiations proposed by the U.S. Negotiations failed to achieve results, but the cease-fire continued.

In July 1972 Sadat ordered most of the 20,000 Soviet military advisers and personnel to leave Egypt.

In a surprise attack Oct. 6, 1973, Egyptian forces crossed the Suez Canal into the Sinai. (At the same time, Syrian forces attacked Israelis on the Golan Heights.) Egypt was supplied by a

USSR military airlift; the U.S. responded with an airlift to Israel. Israel counter-attacked, crossed the canal, surrounded Suez City. A UN cease-fire took effect Oct. 24.

A disengagement agreement was signed Jan. 18, 1974. Under it, Israeli forces withdrew from the canal's W bank; limited numbers of Egyptian forces occupied a strip along the E bank. A second accord was signed in 1975, with Israel yielding Sinai oil fields. Pres. Sadat's surprise visit to Jerusalem, Nov. 1977, opened the prospect of peace with Israel, but worsened relations with Libya (border clashes, July 1977). On Mar. 26, 1979, Egypt and Israel signed a formal peace treaty, ending 30 years of war, and establishing diplomatic relations. Israel returned control of the Sinai to Egypt in April 1982.

Tension between Moslem fundamentalists and Christians in 1981 caused street riots and culminated in a nationwide security crackdown in Sept. Pres Sadat was assassinated on Oct. 6.

Relations with the U.S. were strained in 1985 because of the U.S. interception of an Egyptian airliner carrying the hijackers of the *Achille Lauro*.

The Suez Canal, 103 mi. long, links the Mediterranean and Red seas. It was built by a French corporation 1859-69, but Britain obtained controlling interest in 1875. The last British troops were removed June 13, 1956. On July 26, Egypt nationalized the canal. French and British stockholders eventually received some compensation.

Egypt had barred Israeli ships and cargoes destined for Israel since 1948, and closed the canal to all shipping after the 1967 Arab-Israeli War. The canal was reopened in 1975; Egypt agreed to allow passage to Israeli cargo in third party ships.

El Salvador

Republic of El Salvador

República de El Salvador

People: Population (1986 est.): 5,105,000. **Age distrib.** (%): 0–14: 45.3; 15–59: 51; 60+: 4.7. **Pop. density:** 672 per sq. mi. **Urban** (1982): 39.2%. **Ethnic groups:** Mestizos 89%, Indians 10%, Caucasians 1%. **Languages:** Spanish, Nahuatl (among some Indians). **Religions:** Roman Catholicism prevails.

Geography: Area: 8,260 sq. mi., the size of Massachusetts. **Location:** In Central America. **Neighbors:** Guatemala on W, Honduras on N. **Topography:** A hot Pacific coastal plain in the south rises to a cooler plateau and valley region, densely populated. The N is mountainous, including many volcanoes. **Capital:** San Salvador. **Cities** (1984 est.): San Salvador 455,000.

Government: Type: Republic. **Head of state:** Pres., Jose Napoleon Duarte; b. Nov. 23, 1926; in office: June 1, 1984. **Local divisions:** 14 departments. **Defense:** 4.3% of GNP (1983).

Economy: Industries: Food and beverages, textiles, petroleum products. **Chief crops:** Coffee, cotton, corn, sugar. **Other resources:** Rubber, forests. **Arable land:** 35%. **Meat prod.** (1984): cattle: 937,000; pigs: 379,000. **Electricity prod.** (1984): 1.6 bln. kwh. **Labor force:** 50% agric.; 22% ind.; 27% services.

Finance: Currency: Colon (Mar. 1987: 5.00 = $1 US). **Gross national product** (1984): $4.3 bln. **Per capita income** (1984): $854. **Imports** (1985): $961 mln.; partners: U.S. 35%, CACM 22%. **Exports** (1985): $676 mln.; partners: U.S. 35%, CACM 23%. **National budget** (1984): $944 mln. expenditures. **International reserves less gold** (Mar. 1987): $137 mln. **Gold:** 469,000 oz t. **Consumer prices** (change in 1986): 31.9%.

Transport: Railway traffic (1984): 4.6 mln. passenger-km; 25 mln. net ton-km. **Motor vehicles:** in use (1984): 128,000 passenger cars, 19,000 comm. vehicles. **Chief ports:** La Union, Acajutla.

Communications: Television sets: 350,000 in use (1985). **Radios:** 1 mln. in use (1985). **Telephones in use** (1982): 86,000. **Daily newspaper circ.** (1982): 71 per 1,000 pop.

Health: Life expectancy at birth (1985): 62.6 male; 66.3 female. **Births** (per 1,000 pop. 1985): 34. **Deaths** (per 1,000 pop. 1985): 10. **Natural increase** (1985): 2.4%. **Hospital beds** (1980): 7,668. **Physicians** (1981): 1,793. **Infant mortality** (per 1,000 live births 1985): 71.

Education (1985): **Literacy:** 62% (urban areas); 40% (rural areas). Years compulsory 6; attendance 82%.

Major International Organizations: UN (IMF, WHO, ILO), OAS, CACM.

Embassy: 2308 California St. NW 20008; 265-3480.

El Salvador became independent of Spain in 1821, and of the Central American Federation in 1839.

A fight with Honduras in 1969 over the presence of 300,000 Salvadorean workers left 2,000 dead. Clashes were renewed 1970 and 1974.

A military coup overthrew the Romero government, 1979, but the ruling military-civilian junta failed to quell the civil war which has resulted in some 50,000 deaths. Some 10,000 leftists insurgents, armed by Cuba and Nicaragua, control about 25% of the country, mostly in the east. Extreme right-wing death squads organized to eliminate suspected leftists were blamed for over 1,000 deaths in 1983. The Reagan administration has staunchly supported the government with military aid.

Voters turned out in large numbers in the May 1984 presidential election. Christian Democrat Jose Napoleon Duarte, a moderate, was victorious with 54% of the vote.

Leftist guerrillas have continued their offensive in 1987.

Equatorial Guinea

Republic of Equatorial Guinea

República de Guinea Ecuatorial

People: Population (1986 est.): 359,000. **Age distrib.** (%): 0–14: 35.2; 15–59: 57.1; 60+: 7.7. **Pop. density:** 30 per sq. mi. **Ethnic groups:** Fangs 80%, Bubi 15%. **Languages:** Spanish (official), Fang, English. **Religions:** Roman Catholics 83%, Protestants, others.

Geography: Area: 10,832 sq. mi., the size of Maryland. **Location:** Bioko Is. off W. Africa coast in Gulf of Guinea, and Rio Muni, mainland enclave. **Neighbors:** Gabon on S, Cameroon on E, N. **Topography:** Bioko Is. consists of 2 volcanic mountains and a connecting valley. Rio Muni, with over 90% of the area, has a coastal plain and low hills beyond. **Capital:** Malabo. **Cities** (1986 est.): Malabo 34,980.

Government: Type: Unitary Republic. **Head of state:** Pres., Supreme Military Council Teodoro Obiang Nguema Mbasogo; b. June 5, 1942; in office: Oct. 10, 1979. **Local divisions:** 2 provinces.

Economy: Chief crops: Cocoa, coffee, bananas, sweet potatoes. **Other resources:** Timber. **Arable land:** 8%. **Electricity prod.** (1983): 15 mln. kwh. **Labor force:** agric. 50%; public sector 40%.

Finance: Currency: Ekuele (Jan. 1987: 332 = $1 US). **Gross national product** (1985): $95 mln. **Per capita income** (1985): $250. **Imports** (1985): $34 mln.; partners: Spain 54%, China 17%. **Exports** (1985): $24 mln.; partners: Sp. 40%, Neth. 28%, W. Ger. 23%.

Transport: Chief ports: Malabo, Bata.

Communications: Radios: 90,000 in use (1984).

Health: Life expectancy at birth (1984): 44.4 male; 47.6 female. **Births** (per 1,000 pop. 1985): 42.2. **Deaths** (per 1,000 pop. 1985): 17.6. **Natural increase** (1985): 2.4% **Hospital beds** (1982): 3,200. **Infant mortality** (per 1,000 live births 1986): 142.

Education (1986): **Literacy:** 55%. About 65% attend primary school.

Major International Organizations: UN (IMF, World Bank), OAU.

Embassy: 801 2d Ave., New York, NY 10017; (212) 599-1523.

Fernando Po (now Bioko) Island was discovered by Portugal in the late 15th century and ceded to Spain in 1778. Independence came Oct. 12, 1968. Riots occurred in 1969 over disputes between the island and the more backward Rio Muni province on the mainland. Masie Nguema Biyogo, himself from the mainland, became president for life in 1972.

Masie's 11-year reign was one of the most brutal in Africa, resulting in a bankrupted nation. Most of the nation's 7,000 Europeans emigrated. In 1976, 45,000 Nigerian workers were evacuated amid charges of a reign of terror. Masie was ousted in a military coup, Aug., 1979.

Ethiopia

People's Republic of Ethiopia

Hebretasebawit Etyopia

People: Population (1986 est.): 43,882,000. **Age distrib.** (%): 0–14: 46.6; 15–59: 47.2; 60+: 6.2. **Pop. density:** 94 per sq. mi. **Urban** (1985): 11%. **Ethnic groups:** Oromo 40%, Amhara 25%, Tigre 12%, Sidama 9%. **Languages:** Amharic (official), Tigre (Semitic languages); Galla (Hamitic), Arabic, others. **Religions:** Orthodox Christian 40%, Moslem 40%.

Geography: Area: 471,776 sq. mi., four-fifths the size of Alaska. **Location:** In E. Africa. **Neighbors:** Sudan on W, Kenya on S. Somalia, Djibouti on E. **Topography:** A high central plateau, between 6,000 and 10,000 ft. high, rises to higher mountains near the Great Rift Valley, cutting in from the SW. The Blue Nile and other rivers cross the plateau, which descends to plains on both W and SE. **Capital:** Addis Ababa. **Cities** (1984 est.): Addis Ababa 1,412,000.

Government: Type: Provisional military govt. **Head of state and head of gov't.:** Chmn. of Provisional Military Administrative Council Mengistu Haile Mariam; b. 1937; in office: Feb. 11, 1977. **Local divisions:** 14 administrative regions. **Defense:** 9.8% of GDP (1982).

Economy: Industries: Food processing, cement, textiles. **Chief crops:** Coffee (61% export earnings), grains. **Minerals:** Platinum, gold, copper, potash. **Arible Land:** 13%. **Meat prod.** (1985): cattle: 26.3 mln.; sheep: 23.5 mln. **Electricity prod.** (1984): 740 mln. kwh. **Labor force:** 86% agric.

Finance: Currency: Birr (Mar. 1987: 2.07 = $1 US). **Gross national product** (1984): $4.7 bln. **Per capita income** (1984): $141. **Imports** (1985): $993 mln.; partners: USSR 22%, U.S. 15%, Italy 10%, Jap. 6%, W.Ger, 10%. **Exports** (1985): $333 mln.; partners: U.S. 20%, W. Ger. 18%, Italy 7%. **National budget** (1984): $1.7 bln. revenues; $1.8 bln. expenditures. **International reserves less gold** (Mar. 1987): $238.2 mln. **Gold:** 209,000 oz t. **Consumer prices** (change in 1986): −9.8%.

Transport: Railway traffic (1985): 307 mln. passenger-km; 108 mln. net ton-km. **Motor vehicles:** in use (1984): 41,300 passenger cars, 11,800 comm. vehicles. **Civil aviation** (1983): 762 mln. passenger-km; 27.1 mln. net ton-km. **Chief ports:** Masewa, Aseb.

Communications: Television sets: 45,000 in use (1985). **Radios:** 2 mln. in use (1985). **Telephones in use** (1983): 100,000. **Daily newspaper circ.** (1984): 1 per 1,000 pop.

Health: Life expectancy at birth (1985): 41.3 male; 44.5 female. **Births** (per 1,000 pop. 1985): 49.2. **Deaths** (per 1,000 pop. 1985): 21.5. **Natural increase** (1985): 4.7%. **Hospital beds** (1982): 10,993. **Physicians** (1982): 504. **Infant mortality** (per 1,000 live births 1985): 168.

Education (1985): **Literacy:** 18%.

Major International Organizations: UN (IMF, WHO), OAU.

Embassy: 2134 Kalorama Rd. NW 20008; 234-2281.

Ethiopian culture was influenced by Egypt and Greece. The ancient monarchy was invaded by Italy in 1880, but maintained its independence until another Italian invasion in 1936. British forces freed the country in 1941.

The last emperor, Haile Selassie I, established a parliament and judiciary system in 1931, but barred all political parties.

A series of droughts since 1972 have killed hundreds of thousands. An army mutiny, strikes, and student demonstrations led to the dethronement of Selassie in 1974. The ruling junta pledged to form a one-party socialist state, and instituted a successful land reform; opposition was violently suppressed. The influence of the Coptic Church, embraced in 330 AD, was curbed, and the monarchy was abolished in 1975.

The regime, torn by bloody coups, faced uprisings by tribal and political groups in part aided by Sudan and Somalia. Ties with the U.S., once a major arms and aid source, deteriorated, while cooperation accords were signed with the USSR in 1977. In 1978, Soviet advisors and Cuban troops helped defeat Somali rebels & Somalia forces.

A world-wide relief effort began in 1984, as an extended drought caused millions to face starvation and death.

Fiji

Dominion of Fiji

People: Population (1986 est.): 715,000. **Age distrib.** (%): 0–14: 36.6; 15–59: 57.8; 60+: 5.6. **Pop. density:** 101 per sq. mi. **Urban** (1983): 45%. **Ethnic groups:** Indian 50%, Fijian (Melanesian-Polynesian) 45%, Europeans 2%. **Languages:** English (official), Fijian, Hindustani. **Religions:** Christian 49%, Hindu 40%.

Geography: Area: 7,056 sq. mi., the size of Massachusetts. **Location:** In western S. Pacific O. **Neighbors:** Nearest are Solomons on NW, Tonga on E. **Topography:** 322 islands (106 inhabited), many mountainous, with tropical forests and large fertile areas. Viti Levu, the largest island, has over half the total land area. **Capital:** Suva. **Cities** (1985 est.): Suva 71,000.

Government: Type: Parliamentary democracy. **Head of state:** Queen Elizabeth II, represented by Gov. Gen. Penaia Ganilau; in office: 1984. **Head of government:** Prime Min. Kamisese Mara; b. May 13, 1920; in office: Oct. 10, 1970. **Local divisions:** 4 divisions.

Economy: Industries: Sugar refining, light industry, tourism. **Chief crops:** Sugar, bananas, ginger. **Minerals:** Gold. **Other resources:** Timber. **Arable land:** 12%. **Electricity prod.** (1984): 369 mln. kwh. **Labor force:** 44% agric.

Finance: Currency: Dollar (Mar. 1987: 1.08 = $1 US). **Gross national product** (1984): $1.2 bln. **Per capita income** (1984): $1,086. **Imports** (1984): $487 mln.; partners: Austral. 34%, Jap. 16%, N.Z. 16%. **Exports** (1984): $279 mln.; partners: UK 42%, Aust. 18%. **Tourists** (1984): 235,000; receipts $161 mln. **National budget** (1984): $378 mln. expenditures. **International reserves less gold** (Mar. 1987): $156 mln. **Gold:** 11,000 oz t. **Consumer prices** (change in 1985): 4.4%.

Transport: Motor vehicles: in use (1983): 27,000 passenger cars, 19,700 comm. vehicles. **Civil aviation** (1985): 527 mln. passenger-km; 135 mln. net ton-km. **Chief ports:** Suva, Lautoka.

Communications: Radios: 400,000 in use (1985). **Telephones in use** (1983): 46,252. **Daily newspaper circ.** (1985): 76 per 1,000 pop.

Health: Life expectancy at birth (1985): 70.2 male; 74.1 female. **Births** (per 1,000 pop. 1985): 31. **Deaths** (per 1,000 pop. 1985): 7. **Natural increase** (1985): 2.4%. **Hospital beds** (1984): 1,736. **Physicians** (1984): 329. **Infant mortality** (per 1,000 live births 1985): 29.

Education (1985): **Literacy:** 80%. 95% attend school.

Major International Organizations: UN (IMF, WHO), Commonwealth of Nations.

Embassy: 2233 Wisconsin Ave. NW 20007; 337-8320.

A British colony since 1874, Fiji became an independent parliamentary democracy Oct. 10, 1970.

Cultural differences between the majority Indian community, descendants of contract laborers brought to the islands in the 19th century, and the less modernized native Fijians, who by law own 83% of the land in communal villages, have led to political polarization.

The discovery of copper on Viti Levu along with increased sugar production bode well for the economy.

In 1987, a military coup ousted the government; order was restored May 21 when a compromise was reached granting Lt. Col. Sitiveni Rabuka, the coup's leader, increased power.

Finland

Republic of Finland

Sudmen Tasavalta

People: Population (1986 est.): 4,931,000. **Age distrib.** (%): 0–14: 19.5; 15–59: 63.2; 60+: 17.3. **Pop. density:** 41 per sq. mi. **Urban** (1983): 59.9%. **Ethnic groups:** Finns 94%, Swedes, Lapps. **Languages:** Finnish, Swedish (both official). **Religions:** Lutheran 90%.

Geography: Area: 130,119 sq. mi., slightly smaller than Montana. **Location:** In northern Europe. **Neighbors:** Norway on N, Sweden on W, USSR on E. **Topography:** South and central Finland are mostly flat areas with low hills and many lakes. The N has mountainous areas, 3,000-4,000 ft. **Capital:** Helsinki. **Cities** (1985 est.). Helsinki 484,263; Tampere 168,150; Turku 162,282.

Government: Type: Constitutional republic. **Head of state:** Pres. Mauno Koivisto; b. Nov. 25, 1923; in office: Jan. 27, 1982. **Head of government:** Prime Min. Harri Holkeri; in office: Apr. 30, 1987. **Local divisions:** 12 laanit (provinces). **Defense:** 1.5% of GNP (1985).

Economy: Industries: Machinery, metal, shipbuilding, textiles, clothing. **Chief crops:** Grains, potatoes, dairy prods. **Minerals:** Copper, iron, zinc. **Other resources:** Forests (40% of exports). **Arable land:** 8%. **Meat prod.** (1980): beef: 115,000 metric tons; pork: 176,000 metric tons. **Fish catch** (1983): 119,000 metric tons. **Electricity prod.** (1984): 43.3 bln. kwh. **Crude steel prod.** (1985): 2.5 mln. metric tons. **Labor force:** 11% agric.; 46% ind. & comm.; 28% services.

Finance: Currency: Markkaa (May 1987: 4.32 = $1 US). **Gross national product** (1985): $54.0 bln. **Per capita income** (1985): $11,007. **Imports** (1986): $15.3 bln.; partners: USSR 21%, Swed. 12%, W. Ger. 14%, UK 7%. **Exports** (1986): $16.3 bln.; partners: USSR 21%, Swed. 13%, UK 11%, W. Ger. 9%. **Tourists** (1984): $489 mln. receipts. **National budget** (1985): $18.6 bln. expenditures. **International reserves less gold** (Mar. 1987): $3.4 bln. **Gold** 1.9 mln. oz t. **Consumer prices** (change in 1986): 3.6%.

Transport: Railway traffic (1985): 3.2 bln. passenger-km; 8.0 bln. net ton-km. **Motor vehicles:** in use (1984): 1.4 mln. passenger cars, 182,000 comm. vehicles; **Civil aviation** (1985): 2.9 bln. passenger-km; 84.3 mln. freight ton-km. **Chief ports:** Helsinki, Turku.

Communications: Television sets: 1.7 mln. licensed (1985). **Radios:** 2.5 mln. licensed (1983). **Telephones in use** (1984): 2.8 mln. **Daily newspaper circ.** (1984): 533 per 1,000 pop.

Health: Life expectancy at birth (1986): 70.4 male; 78.8 female. **Births** (per 1,000 pop. 1985): 12.7. **Deaths** (per 1,000 pop. 1985): 9.5. **Natural increase** (1985): .03%. **Hospital beds** (1984): 61,103. **Physicians** (1984): 9,979. **Infant mortality** (per 1,000 live births 1985): 6.0.

Education (1986): **Literacy:** 99%. Years compulsory 9; attendance 99%.

Major International Organizations: UN (IMF, GATT), EFTA, OECD.

Embassy: 3216 New Mexico Ave. NW 20016; 363-2430.

The early Finns probably migrated from the Ural area at about the beginning of the Christian era. Swedish settlers brought the country into Sweden, 1154 to 1809, when Finland became an autonomous grand duchy of the Russian Empire. Russian exactions created a strong national spirit; on Dec. 6, 1917, Finland declared its independence and in 1919 became a republic. On Nov. 30, 1939, the Soviet Union invaded, and the Finns were forced to cede 16,173 sq. mi., including the Karelian Isthmus, Viipuri, and an area on Lake Ladoga. After World War II, in which Finland tried to recover its lost territory, further cessions were exacted. In 1948, Finland signed a treaty of mutual assistance with the USSR. In 1956 Russia returned Porkkala, which had been ceded as a military base.

Finland is an integral member of the Nordic group of five countries and maintains good relations with the Soviet Union.

Aland, constituting an autonomous department, is a group of small islands, 572 sq. mi., in the Gulf of Bothnia, 25 mi. from Sweden, 15 mi. from Finland. Mariehamn is the principal port.

France

French Republic

République Francaise

People: Population (1986 est.): 55,239,000. **Age distrib.** (%): 0–14: 20.0; 15–60: 62.3; 60+: 17.7. **Pop. density:** 263 per sq. mi. **Urban** (1985): 77.2%. **Ethnic groups:** A mixture of various European and Mediterranean groups. **Languages:** French; minorities speak Breton, Alsatian German, Flemish, Italian, Basque, Catalan. **Religions:** Mostly Roman Catholic.

Geography: Area: 220,668 sq. mi., four-fifths the size of Texas. **Location:** In western Europe, between Atlantic O. and Mediterranean Sea. **Neighbors:** Spain on S, Italy, Switzerland, W. Germany on E, Luxembourg, Belgium on N. **Topography:** A wide plain covers more than half of the country, in N and W, drained to W by Seine, Loire, Garonne rivers. The Massif Central is a mountainous plateau in center. In E are Alps (Mt. Blanc is tallest in W. Europe, 15,771 ft.), the lower Jura range, and the forested Vosges. The Rhone flows from Lake Geneva to Mediterranean. Pyrenees are in SW, on border with Spain. **Capital:** Paris. **Cities** (1982 cen.): Paris 2,188,918; Marseille 878,689; Lyon 418,476; Toulouse 354,289; Nice 338,486; Nantes 247,227; Strasbourg 252,264; Bordeaux 211,197.

Government: Type: Republic. **Head of state:** Pres. François Mitterrand; b. Oct. 26, 1916; in office: May 21, 1981. **Head of government:** Prime Min. Jacques Chirac; b. Nov. 29, 1932; in office: Mar. 20, 1986. **Local divisions:** 22 administrative regions containing 95 departments. **Defense:** 18% of govt. budget. (1985).

Economy: Industries: Steel, chemicals, autos, textiles, wine, perfume, aircraft, ships, electronic equipment. **Chief crops:** Grains, corn, rice, fruits, vegetables. France is largest food producer, exporter, in W. Eur. **Minerals:** Bauxite, iron, coal. **Crude oil reserves** (1985): 221 mln. bbls. **Other resources:** Forests. **Arable land:** 34%. **Meat prod.** (1985): cattle: 22.8 mln.; pigs: 10.9 mln.; sheep: 10.7 mln. **Fish catch** (1984): 784,000 metric tons. **Electricity prod.** (1984): 333 bln. kwh. **Crude steel prod.** (1985): 18.8 mln. metric tons. **Labor force:** 9% agric.; 45% ind. & comm.; 46% services.

Finance: Currency: Franc (May 1987: 5.95 = $1 US). **Gross national product** (1985). $563 bln. **Per capita income** (1985): $10,260. **Imports** (1986): $129.4 bln.; partners: W. Ger. 17%, It. 10%, Belg. 8%, U.S. 8%. **Exports** (1986): $124.9 bln.; partners: W. Ger. 14%, It. 11%, Belg. 8%, UK 7%. **Tourists** (1983) receipts: $7.2 bln. **National budget** (1984): $119 bln. expenditures. **International reserves less gold** (Feb. 1987): $31.8 bln. **Gold:** 81.85 mln. oz t. **Consumer prices** (change in 1986): 2.5%.

Transport: Railway traffic (1985): 60.7 bln. passenger-km; 58.4 bln. net ton-km. **Motor vehicles:** in use (1985): 20.8 mln. passenger cars, 3.3 mln. comm. vehicles; manuf. (1982): 3 mln. passenger cars; 466,000 comm. vehicles. **Civil aviation** (1984): 38.4 bln. passenger-km; 2.0 bln net ton-km. **Chief ports:** Marseille, LeHavre, Nantes, Bordeaux, Rouen.

Communications: Television sets: 17.6 mln. in use (1985). **Radios:** 20 mln. in use (1983). **Telephones in use** (1982): 18 mln. **Daily newspaper circ.** (1985): 244 per 1,000 pop.

Health: Life expectancy at birth (1982): 70.2 male; 78.5 female. **Births** (per 1,000 pop. 1985): 14. **Deaths** (per 1,000 pop. 1985): . 10. **Natural increase** (1985): .4%. **Hospital beds** (1983): 496,896. **Physicians** (1983): 114,000. **Infant mortality** (per 1,000 live births 1986): 8.2.

Education (1986): **Literacy:** 99%. Years compulsory 10; 17.7% of natl. budget.

Major International Organizations: UN and most of its specialized agencies, OECD, EC, NATO.

Embassy: 4101 Reservoir Rd. NW 20007; 944-6000.

Celtic Gaul was conquered by Julius Caesar 58-51 BC; Romans ruled for 500 years. Under Charlemagne, Frankish rule extended over much of Europe. After his death France emerged as one of the successor kingdoms.

The monarchy was overthrown by the French Revolution (1789-93) and succeeded by the First Republic; followed by the First Empire under Napoleon (1804-15), a monarchy (1814-48), the Second Republic (1848-52), the Second Empire (1852-70), the Third Republic (1871-1946), the Fourth Republic (1946-58), and the Fifth Republic (1958 to present).

France suffered severe losses in manpower and wealth in the first World War, 1914-18, when it was invaded by Germany. By the Treaty of Versailles, France exacted return of Alsace and Lorraine, French provinces seized by Germany in 1871. Germany invaded France again in May, 1940, and signed an armistice with a government based in Vichy. After France was liberated by the Allies Sept. 1944, Gen. Charles de Gaulle became head of the provisional government, serving until 1946.

De Gaulle again became premier in 1958, during a crisis over Algeria, and obtained voter approval for a new constitution, ushering in the Fifth Republic. Using strong executive powers, he promoted French economic and technological advances in the context of the European Economic Community, and guarded French foreign policy independence.

France had withdrawn from Indochina in 1954, and from Morocco and Tunisia in 1956. Most of its remaining African territories were freed 1958-62, but France retained strong economic and political ties.

In 1966, France withdrew all its troops from the integrated military command of NATO, though 60,000 remained stationed in

Germany. France continued to attend political meetings of NATO.

In May 1968 rebellious students in Paris and other centers rioted, battled police, and were joined by workers who launched nationwide strikes. The government awarded pay increases to the strikers May 26. In elections to the Assembly in June, de Gaulle's backers won a landslide victory. Nevertheless, he resigned from office in April, 1969, after losing a nationwide referendum on constitutional reform. De Gaulle's policies were largely continued after his death in 1970.

On May 10, 1981, France elected François Mitterrand, a Socialist candidate, president in a stunning victory over Valéry Giscard d'Estaing. In September, the government nationalized 5 major industries and most private banks.

France has supported Chad in its war with Libya. On Oct. 23, 58 members of the French peacekeeping force in Lebanon were killed in a suicide terrorist attack.

Agents of France's external security service were responsible for the July 10, 1985 sinking of the *Rainbow Warrior,* flagship of the Greenpeace environmental movement, in the port of Auckland, New Zealand.

The island of **Corsica,** in the Mediterranean W of Italy and N of Sardinia, is an official region of France comprising 2 departments. Area: 3,369 sq. mi.; pop. (1975 cen.): 289,842. The capital is Ajaccio, birthplace of Napoleon.

Overseas Departments

French Guiana is on the NE coast of South America with Suriname on the W and Brazil on the E and S. Its area is 32,252 sq. mi.; pop. (1986): 85,700. Guiana sends one senator and one deputy to the French Parliament. Guiana is administered by a prefect and has a Council General of 16 elected members; capital is Cayenne.

The famous penal colony, Devil's Island, was phased out between 1938 and 1951.

Immense forests of rich timber cover 90% of the land. Placer gold mining is the most important industry. Exports are shrimp, timber, and machinery.

Guadeloupe, in the West Indies' Leeward Islands, consists of 2 large islands, Basse-Terre and Grande-Terre, separated by the Salt River, plus Marie Galante and the Saintes group to the S and, to the N, Desirade, St. Barthelemy, and over half of St. Martin (the Netherlands portion is St. Maarten). A French possession since 1635, the department is represented in the French Parliament by 2 senators and 3 deputies; administration consists of a prefect (governor) and an elected General Council.

Area of the islands is 687 sq. mi.; pop. (1985 est.) 330,000, mainly descendants of slaves; capital is Basse-Terre on Basse-Terre Is. The land is fertile; sugar, rum, and bananas are exported; tourism is an important industry.

Martinique, one of the Windward Islands, in the West Indies, has been a possession since 1635, and a department since March, 1946. It is represented in the French Parliament by 2 senators and 3 deputies. The island was the birthplace of Napoleon's Empress Josephine.

It has an area of 425 sq. mi.; pop. (1986 est.) 328,000, mostly descendants of slaves. The capital is Fort-de-France. It is a popular tourist stop. The chief exports are rum, bananas, and petroleum products.

Mayotte, formerly part of Comoros, voted in 1976 to become an overseas department of France. An island NW of Madagascar, area is 144 sq. mi., pop. (1986 est.) 70,000.

Reunion is a volcanic island in the Indian O. about 420 mi. E of Madagascar, and has belonged to France since 1665. Area, 969 sq. mi.; pop. (1985 est.) 543,000, 30% of French extraction. Capital: Saint-Denis. The chief export is sugar. It elects 3 deputies, 2 senators to the French Parliament.

St. Pierre and Miquelon, formerly an Overseas Territory, made the transition to department status in 1976. It consists of 2 groups of rocky islands near the SW coast of Newfoundland, inhabited by fishermen. The exports are chiefly fish products. The St. Pierre group has an area of 10 sq. mi.; Miquelon, 83 sq. mi. Total pop. (1982 cen.), 6,041. The capital is St. Pierre. A deputy and a senator are elected to the French Parliament.

Overseas Territories

French Polynesia Overseas Territory, comprises 130 islands widely scattered among 5 archipelagos in the South Pacific; administered by a governor. Territorial Assembly and a Council with headquarters at Papeete, Tahiti, one of the **Society Islands** (which include the **Windward** and **Leeward** islands). A deputy and a senator are elected to the French Parliament.

Other groups are the **Marquesas Islands,** the **Tuamotu Archipelago,** including the **Gambier Islands,** and the **Austral Islands.**

Total area of the islands administered from Tahiti is 1,544 sq. mi.; pop. (1986 est.), 180,000, more than half on Tahiti. Tahiti is picturesque and mountainous with a productive coastline bearing coconut, banana and orange trees, sugar cane and vanilla.

Tahiti was visited by Capt. James Cook in 1769 and by Capt. Bligh in the Bounty, 1788-89. Its beauty impressed Herman Melville, Paul Gauguin, and Charles Darwin.

French Southern and Antarctic Lands Overseas Territory, comprises **Adelie Land,** on Antarctica, and 4 island groups in the Indian O. Adelie, discovered 1840, has a research station, a coastline of 185 mi. and tapers 1,240 mi. inland to the South Pole. The U.S. does not recognize national claims in Antarctica. There are 2 huge glaciers, Ninnis, 22 mi. wide, 99 mi. long, and Mentz, 11 mi. wide, 140 mi. long. The Indian O. groups are:

Kerguelen Archipelago, discovered 1772, one large and 300 small islands. The chief is 87 mi. long, 74 mi. wide, and has Mt. Ross, 6,429 ft. tall. Principal research station is Port-aux-Francais. Seals often weigh 2 tons; there are blue whales, coal, peat, semi-precious stones. **Crozet Archipelago,** discovered 1772, covers 195 sq. mi. Eastern Island rises to 6,560 ft. **Saint Paul,** in southern Indian O., has warm springs with earth at places heating to 120° to 390° F. **Amsterdam** is nearby; both produce cod and rock lobster.

New Caledonia and its dependencies, an overseas territory, are a group of islands in the Pacific O. about 1,115 mi. E of Australia and approx. the same distance NW of New Zealand. Dependencies are the **Loyalty Islands,** the **Isle of Pines, Huon Islands** and the **Chesterfield Islands.**

New Caledonia, the largest, has 6,530 sq. mi. Total area of the territory is 8,548 sq. mi.; population (1985 est.) 149,000. The group was acquired by France in 1853.

The territory is administered by a governor and government council. There is a popularly elected Territorial Assembly. A deputy and a senator are elected to the French Parliament. Capital: Noumea.

Mining is the chief industry. New Caledonia is one of the world's largest nickel producers. Other minerals found are chrome, iron, cobalt, manganese, silver, gold, lead, and copper. Agricultural products include coffee, copra, cotton, manioc (cassava), corn, tobacco, bananas and pineapples.

A referendum on New Caledonian independence is scheduled for 1987.

Wallis and Futuna Islands, 2 archipelagos raised to status of overseas territory July 29, 1961, are in the SW Pacific S of the Equator between Fiji and Samoa. The islands have a total area of 106 sq. mi. and population (1982 cen.) of 11,943. **Alofi,** attached to Futuna, is uninhabited. Capital: Mata-Utu. Chief products are copra, yams, taro roots, bananas. A senator and a deputy are elected to the French Parliament.

Gabon

Gabonese Republic

République Gabonaise

People: Population (1986 est.): 1,017,000. **Pop. density:** 11 per sq. mi. **Urban** (1980): 35%. **Ethnic groups:** Fangs 25%, Bapounon 10%, others. **Languages:** French (official), Bantu dialects. **Religions:** Tribal beliefs, Christian minority.

Geography: Area: 103,346 sq. mi., the size of Colorado. **Location:** On Atlantic coast of central Africa. **Neighbors:** Equatorial Guinea, Cameroon on N, Congo on E, S. **Topography:** Heavily forested, the country consists of coastal lowlands plateaus in N, E, and S, mountains in N, SE, and center. The Ogooue R. system covers most of Gabon. **Capital:** Libreville. **Cities** (1983 est.): Libreville 180,000.

Government: Type: Republic. **Head of state:** Pres. Omar Bongo; b. Dec. 30, 1935; in office: Dec. 2, 1967. **Head of government:** Prime Min. Leon Mebiame, b. Sept. 1, 1934; in office: Apr. 16, 1975. **Local divisions:** 9 provinces, 37 prefectures. **Defense:** 2.7% of GNP (1982).

Economy: Industries: Oil products. **Chief crops:** Cocoa, coffee, rice, peanuts, palm products, cassava, bananas. **Minerals:**

Manganese, uranium, oil, iron, gas. **Crude oil reserves** (1985): 623 mln. bbls. **Other resources:** Timber. **Arable land:** 2%. **Electricity prod.** (1984): 792 mln. kwh. **Labor force:** 65% agric.; 30% ind. & comm.

Finance: Currency: CFA franc (Mar. 1987: 300 = $1 US). **Gross national product** (1984) $2.8 bln. **Per capita income** (1983): $2,613. **Imports** (1985): $949 mln.; partners: Fr. 51%, U.S. 14%. **Exports** (1985): $1.9 bln.; partners: Fr. 26%, U.S. 25%. **Tourists receipts** (1984): $4 mln. **National budget** (1983): $466 mln. **International reserves less gold** (Jan. 1987): $126.3 mln. **Gold:** 13,000 oz t. **Consumer prices** (change in 1985): 7.3%.

Transport: Motor vehicles: in use (1983): 16,000 passenger cars, 10,000 comm. vehicles. **Civil aviation** (1983): 430 mln. passenger-km. **Chief ports** Port-Gentil, Owendo, Mayumba.

Communications: Television sets: 21,000 licensed (1985). **Radios:** 100,000 licensed (1985). **Telephones in use** (1984): 11,600.

Health: Life expectancy at birth (1985): 48.0 male; 51.4 female. **Births** (per 1,000 pop. 1985): 33.7. **Deaths** (per 1,000 pop. 1985): 19.9. **Natural increase** (1985): 1.3%. **Hospital beds** (1985): 4,617. **Physicians** (1985): 265. **Infant mortality** (per 1,000 live births 1985): 162.

Education (1985): **Literacy:** 65%. Compulsory to age 16; attendance: 84% primary, 14% secondary.

Major International Organizations: UN (World Bank), OAU, OPEC.

Embassy: 2034 20th St NW 20009; 797-1000.

France established control over the region in the second half of the 19th century. Gabon became independent Aug. 17, 1960. It is one of the most prosperous black African countries, thanks to abundant natural resources, foreign private investment, and government development programs.

The Gambia

Republic of The Gambia

People: Population (1986 est.): 774,000. **Age distrib.** (%): 0–14: 45.9; 15–59: 54.4; 60+: 3.8. **Pop. density:** 172 per sq. mi. **Urban** (1983): 21%. **Ethnic groups:** Mandinka 36%, Fula 17%, Wolof 14%, others. **Languages:** English (official), Mandinka, Wolof. **Religions:** Moslems 95%.

Geography: Area: 4,361 sq. mi., smaller than Connecticut. **Location:** On Atlantic coast near western tip of Africa. **Neighbors:** Surrounded on 3 sides by Senegal. **Topography:** A narrow strip of land on each side of the lower Gambia. **Capital:** Banjul. **Cities** (1986 est.): Banjul 40,000.

Government: Type: Republic. **Head of state:** Pres. Dawda Kairaba Jawara; b. May 16, 1924; in office: Apr. 24, 1970 (prime min. from June 12, 1962). **Local divisions:** 5 divisions and Banjul.

Economy: Industries: Tourism. **Chief crops:** Peanuts (main export), rice. **Arable land:** 28%. **Fish catch** (1983): 9,500 metric tons. **Electricity prod.** (1984): 42 mln. kwh. **Labor force:** 75% agric.; 18% ind. & comm.

Finance: Currency: Dalasi (Mar. 1987: 1.00 = $1.34 US). **Gross national product** (1985): $179 mln. **Per capita income** (1985): $255. **Imports** (1985): $104 mln.; partners: UK 21%, China 11%. **Exports** (1985): $32 mln.; partners: EEC 40%. **Tourists** (1985): 65,000. **National budget** (1985): $57 mln. expenditures. **International reserves less gold** (Mar. 1987): $15.2 mln. **Consumer prices** (change in 1986): 56.6%.

Transport: Motor vehicles: in use (1983): 6,500 passenger cars, 1,500 comm. vehicles. **Chief ports:** Banjul.

Communications: Radios: 105,000 in use (1985). **Telephones in use** (1980): 3,500.

Health: Life expectancy at birth (1985): 40.9 male; 44.1 female. **Births** (per 1,000 pop. 1985): 47.5. **Deaths** (per 1,000 pop. 1985): 21.7. **Natural increase** (1985): 2.5%. **Hospital beds** (1980): 635. **Physicians** (1980): 65. **Infant mortality** (per 100,000 live births 1986): 217.

Education (1986): **Literacy:** 12%.

Major International Organizations: UN (GATT, IMF, WHO), OAU.

Embassy: 19 E. 42 St., New York, NY 10017.

The tribes of Gambia were at one time associated with the West African empires of Ghana, Mali, and Songhay. The area became Britain's first African possession in 1588.

Independence came Feb. 18, 1965; republic status within the Commonwealth was achieved in 1970. Gambia is one of the only functioning democracies in Africa. The country suffered from severe famine in 1977-78.

Gambia has a treaty with Senegal to form a confederation of the 2 countries under the name of Senegambia. However, each country will retain its sovereignty.

Germany

Now comprises 2 nations: Federal Republic of Germany (West Germany), German Democratic Republic (East Germany).

Germany, prior to World War II, was a central European nation composed of numerous states which had a common language and traditions and which had been united in one country since 1871; since World War II it has been split in 2 parts.

History and government. Germanic tribes were defeated by Julius Caesar, 55 and 53 BC, but Roman expansion N of the Rhine was stopped in 9 AD. Charlemagne, ruler of the Franks, consolidated Saxon, Bavarian, Rhenish, Frankish, and other lands; after him the eastern part became the German Empire. The Thirty Years' War, 1618-1648, split Germany into small principalities and kingdoms. After Napoleon, Austria contended with Prussia for dominance, but lost the Seven Weeks' War to Prussia, 1866. Otto von Bismarck, Prussian chancellor, formed the North German Confederation, 1867.

In 1870 Bismarck maneuvered Napoleon III into declaring war. After the quick defeat of France, Bismarck formed the **German Empire** and on Jan. 18, 1871, in Versailles, proclaimed King Wilhelm I of Prussia German emperor (Deutscher kaiser).

The German Empire reached its peak before World War I in 1914, with 208,780 sq. mi., plus a colonial empire. After that war Germany ceded Alsace-Lorraine to France; West Prussia and Posen (Poznan) province to Poland; part of Schleswig to Denmark; lost all of its colonies and the ports of Memel and Danzig.

Republic of Germany, 1919-1933, adopted the Weimar constitution; met reparation payments and elected Friedrich Ebert and Gen. Paul von Hindenburg presidents.

Third Reich, 1933-1945, Adolf Hitler led the National Socialist German Workers' (Nazi) party after World War I. In 1923 he attempted to unseat the Bavarian government and was imprisoned. Pres. von Hindenburg named Hitler chancellor Jan. 30, 1933; on Aug. 3, 1934, the day after Hindenburg's death, the cabinet joined the offices of president and chancellor and made Hitler fuehrer (leader). Hitler abolished freedom of speech and assembly, and began a long series of persecutions climaxed by the murder of millions of Jews and opponents.

Hitler repudiated the Versailles treaty and reparations agreements. He remilitarized the Rhineland 1936 and annexed Austria (Anschluss, 1938). At Munich he made an agreement with Neville Chamberlain, British prime minister, which permitted Hitler to annex part of Czechoslovakia. He signed a non-aggression treaty with the USSR, 1939. He declared war on Poland Sept. 1, 1939, precipitating World War II.

With total defeat near, Hitler committed suicide in Berlin Apr. 1945. The victorious Allies voided all acts and annexations of Hitler's Reich.

Postwar changes. The zones of occupation administered by the Allied Powers and later relinquished gave the USSR Saxony, Saxony-Anhalt, Thuringia, and Mecklenburg, and the former Prussian provinces of Saxony and Brandenburg.

The territory E of the Oder-Neisse line within 1937 boundaries comprising the provinces of Silesia, Pomerania, and the southern part of East Prussia, totaling about 41,220 sq. mi., was taken by Poland. Northern East Prussia was taken by the USSR.

The Western Allies ended the state of war with Germany in 1951. The USSR did so in 1955.

There was also created the area of Greater Berlin, within but not part of the Soviet zone, administered by the 4 occupying powers under the Allied Command. In 1948 the USSR withdrew, established its single command in East Berlin, and cut off supplies. The Allies utilized a gigantic airlift to bring food to West

Berlin, 1948-1949. In Aug. 1961 the East Germans built a wall dividing Berlin, after over 3 million E. Germans had emigrated.

East Germany

German Democratic Republic

Deutsche Demokratische Republik

People: Population (1986 est.): 16,692,000. **Age distrib.** (%): 0–14: 19.3; 15–59: 61.3; 60+: 19.4. **Pop. density:** 397 per sq. mi. **Urban** (1984): 76.6%. **Ethnic groups:** German 99%. **Languages:** German. **Religions:** traditionally 80% Protestant.

Geography: Area: 41,768 sq. mi., the size of Virginia. **Location:** In E. Central Europe. **Neighbors:** W. Germany on W, Czechoslovakia on S, Poland on E. **Topography:** E. Germany lies mostly on the North German plains, with lakes in N, Harz Mtns., Elbe Valley, and sandy soil of Bradenburg in center, and highlands in S. **Capital:** East Berlin. **Cities** (1985 est.): East Berlin 1,196,000; Leipzig 555,000; Dresden 520,000.

Government: Type: Communist. **Head of state:** Chmn. Erich Honecker; b. Aug. 25, 1912; in office: Oct. 29, 1976. **Head of government:** Prime Min. Willi Stoph; b. July 9, 1914; in office: Oct. 29, 1976. **Head of Communist Party:** Sec.-Gen. Erich Honecker; in office: May 3, 1971. **Local divisions:** 14 districts. **Defense:** 6.4% of GNP (1983).

Economy: Industries: Steel, chemicals, electrical prods., textiles, machinery. **Chief crops:** Grains, potatoes, sugarbeets. **Minerals:** Potash, lignite, uranium, coal. **Arable land:** 47%. **Meat prod.** (1985): cattle: 5.8 mln.; pigs: 12.9 mln.; sheep: 2.5 mln. **Fish catch** (1984): 265,000 metric tons. **Electricity prod.** (1984): 110 bln. kwh. **Crude steel prod.** (1985): 7.8 mln metric tons. **Labor force:** 10% agric.; 42.5% ind. & construction.

Finance: Currency: Mark (Jan. 1987: 2.03 = $1 US). **Gross national product:** (1984): $93 bln. **Per capita income** (1984): $8,000. **Imports:** (1983): $22.4 bln.; partners: USSR, E. Europe. **Exports** (1983): $24 bln.; partners: USSR, E. Europe. **Tourists** (1983): 933,000. **National budget** (1984): $78 bln.

Transport: Railway traffic (1984): 22.9 bln. passenger-km; 56 bln. net ton-km. **Motor vehicles:** in use (1984): 3.1 mln. passenger cars, 272,000 comm. vehicles; manuf. (1982): 183,000 passenger cars; 39,000 comm. vehicles. **Civil aviation** (1984): 2.4 bln. passenger-km; 75 mln. freight ton-km. **Chief ports:** Rostack, Wismar, Stralsund.

Communications: Television sets: 6.0 mln. licensed (1985). **Radios:** 6.6 mln. licensed (1985). **Telephones in use** (1985): 3.5 mln. **Daily newspaper circ.** (1984): 537 per 1,000 pop.

Health: Life expectancy at birth (1984): 68.8 male; 74.7 female. **Births** (per 1,000 pop. 1985): 14.0. **Deaths** (per 1,000 pop. 1985): 13.0. **Natural increase** (1985): 0.0%. **Hospital beds** (1985): 170,000. **Physicians** (1985): 37,000. **Infant mortality** (per 1,000 live births 1985): 13.1.

Education (1985): **Literacy:** 99%. **Years compulsory:** through 10th grade.

Major International Organizations: UN (IMF, GATT), Warsaw Pact.

Embassy: 1717 Massachusetts Ave. NW 20036; 232-3134.

The German Democratic Republic was proclaimed in the Soviet sector of Berlin Oct. 7, 1949. It was proclaimed fully sovereign in 1954, but Soviet troops remain on grounds of security and the 4-power Potsdam agreement.

Coincident with the entrance of W. Germany into the European Defense community in 1952, the East German government decreed a prohibited zone 3 miles deep along its 600-mile border with W. Germany and cut Berlin's telephone system in two. Berlin was further divided by erection of a fortified wall in 1961, but the exodus of refugees to the West continued, though on a smaller scale.

E. Germany suffered severe economic problems until the mid-1960s. A "new economic system" was introduced, easing the former central planning controls and allowing factories to make profits provided they were reinvested in operations or redistributed to workers as bonuses. By the early 1970s, the economy was highly industrialized. In May 1972 the few remaining private firms were ordered sold to the government. The nation was credited with the highest standard of living among communist countries. But growth slowed in the late 1970s, due to shortages of natural resources and labor, and a huge debt to lenders in the West.

West Germany

Federal Republic of Germany

Bundesrepublik Deutschland

People: Population (1986 est.): 60,734,000. **Age distrib.** (%): 0–14: 15.3; 15–59: 64.4; 60+: 20.3. **Pop. density:** 635 per sq. mi. **Ethnic groups:** German 93%. **Languages:** German. **Religions:** Protestant 44%, Roman Catholic 45%.

Geography: Area: 95,975 sq. mi. (incl. W. Berlin), the size of Wyoming. **Location:** In central Europe. **Neighbors:** Denmark on N, Netherlands, Belgium, Luxembourg, France on W, Switzerland, Austria on S, Czechoslovakia, E. Germany on E. **Topography:** West Germany is flat in N, hilly in center and W, and mountainous in Bavaria. Chief rivers are Elbe, Weser, Ems, Rhine, and Main, all flowing toward North Sea, and Danube, flowing toward Black Sea. **Capital:** Bonn. **Cities** (1985 est.): Berlin 1.8 mln.; Hamburg 1.5 mln.; Munich 1.2 mln.; Cologne 919,000; Essen 622,000; Frankfurt 598,000; Dortmund 575,000; Dusseldorf 593,000; Stuttgart 561,000.

Government: Type: Federal republic. **Head of state:** Pres. Richard von Weizsacker; b. Apr. 15, 1920; in office: May 23, 1984. **Head of government:** Chan. Helmut Kohl; b. Apr. 3, 1930; in office: Oct. 1, 1982. **Local divisions:** West Berlin and 10 laender (states) with substantial powers: Schleswig-Holstein, Hamburg, Lower Saxony, Bremen, North Rhine-Westphalia, Hessen, Rhineland-Palatinate, Baden-Wurttemberg, Bavaria, Saarland. **Defense:** 5% of GNP (1985).

Economy: Industries: Steel, ships, autos, machinery, coal, cement, chemicals. **Chief crops:** Grains, potatoes, sugar beets. **Minerals:** Coal, mercury, potash, lignite, iron, zinc, lead, copper, salt, oil. **Crude oil reserves** (1985): 289 mln. bbls. **Arable land:** 30%. **Meat prod.** (1985): cattle: 15.6 mln.; pigs: 24.3 mln.; sheep: 1.2 mln. **Fish catch** (1984): 305,000 metric tons. **Electricity prod.** (1984): 394 bln. kwh. **Crude steel prod.** (1985): 40.5 mln. metric tons. **Labor force:** 6% agric.; 42% ind. & comm.; 42% service.

Finance: Currency: Mark (May 1987: 1.78 = $1 US). **Gross national product** (1984): $678 bln. **Per capita income** (1985): $9,450. **Imports** (1986): $191.0 bln.; partners: Neth. 12%, Fr. 11%, It. 8%, Belg. 7%. **Exports** (1986): $243.3 bln.; partners: Fr. 14%, Neth. 8%, Belg. 7%, It. 8%. **Tourists** (1984): receipts $4.0 bln. **National budget** (1985): $81.3 bln. **International reserves less gold** (Mar. 1987): $60.4 bln. **Gold:** 95.18 mln. oz t. **Consumer prices** (change in 1986): −0.2%.

Transport: Railway traffic (1985): 42 bln. passenger-km; 62 bln. net ton-km. **Motor vehicles:** in use (1985): 25 mln. passenger cars, 1.3 mln. comm. vehicles; manuf. (1982): 3.7 mln. passenger cars; 286,000 comm. vehicles. **Civil aviation** (1985): 24.4 bln. passenger-km; 2.4 bln. freight ton-km. **Chief ports:** Hamburg, Bremen, Lubeck.

Communications: Television sets: 22.1 mln. in use (1985). **Radios:** 25 mln. in use (1985). **Telephones in use** (1983): 30.1 mln. **Daily newspaper circ.** (1985): 447 per 1,000 pop.

Health: Life expectancy at birth (1985): 67.2 male; 73.4 female. **Births** (per 1,000 pop. 1985): 10. **Deaths** (per 1,000 pop. 1985): 12. **Natural increase** (1985): −.2%. **Hospital beds** (1984): 682,747. **Physicians** (1985): 153,000. **Infant mortality** (per 1,000 live births 1985): 9.

Education (1985): **Literacy:** 99%. **Years compulsory:** 10; attendance 100%.

Major International Organizations: UN and all of its specialized agencies, EC, OECD, NATO.

Embassy: 4645 Reservoir Rd. NW 20007; 298-4000.

The Federal Republic of Germany was proclaimed May 23, 1949, in Bonn, after a constitution had been drawn up by a consultative assembly formed by representatives of the 11 laender (states) in the French, British, and American zones. Later reorganized into 9 units, the laender numbered 10 with the addition of the Saar, 1957. Berlin also was granted land (state) status, but the 1945 occupation agreements placed restrictions on it.

The occupying powers, the U.S., Britain, and France, restored the civil status, Sept. 21, 1949. The U. S. resumed diplomatic relations July 2, 1951. The powers lifted controls and the republic became fully independent May 5, 1955.

Dr. Konrad Adenauer, Christian Democrat, was made chancellor Sept. 15, 1949, re-elected 1953, 1957, 1961. Willy Brandt, heading a coalition of Social Democrats and Free Democrats, became chancellor Oct. 21, 1969.

In 1970 Brandt signed friendship treaties with the USSR and Poland. In 1971, the U.S., Britain, France, and the USSR signed an agreement on Western access to West Berlin. In 1972 the Bundestag approved the USSR and Polish treaties and East and West Germany signed their first formal treaty, implementing the agreement easing access to West Berlin. In 1973 a West Germany-Czechoslovakia pact normalized relations and nullified the 1938 "Munich Agreement."

In May 1974 Brandt resigned, saying he took full responsibility for "negligence" for allowing an East German spy to become a member of his staff.

West Germany has experienced economic growth since the 1950s. The country leads Europe in provisions for worker participation in the management of industry.

The NATO decision to deploy medium-range nuclear missiles in Western Europe sparked a demonstration by some 400,000 protesters in 1983. Chancellor Kohl continued to support the U.S. "Star Wars" antimissile program.

Helgoland, an island of 130 acres in the North Sea, was taken from Denmark by a British Naval Force in 1807 and later ceded to Germany to become a part of Schleswig-Holstein province in return for rights in East Africa. The heavily fortified island was surrendered to UK, May 23, 1945, demilitarized in 1947, and returned to W. Germany, Mar 1, 1952. It is a free port.

Ghana

Republic of Ghana

People: Population (1986 est.): 13,552,000. **Age distrib.** (%): 0–14: 46.6; 15-59: 48.9; 60+: 4.5. **Pop. density:** 142 per sq. mi. **Urban** (1981): 36.6%. **Ethnic groups:** Akan 44%, Moshi-Dagomba 16%, Ewe 13%, Ga 8%, others. **Languages:** English (official), 50 tribal languages. **Religions:** Christian 43%, traditional beliefs 45%.

Geography: Area: 92,098 sq. mi., slightly smaller than Oregon. **Location:** On southern coast of W. Africa. **Neighbors:** Ivory Coast on W, Burkina Faso on N, Togo on E. **Topography:** Most of Ghana consists of low fertile plains and scrubland, cut by rivers and by the artificial Lake Volta. **Capital:** Accra. **Cities** (1984 est.): Accra 859,000.

Government: Type: Authoritarian. **Head of government:** Pres. Jerry Rawlings; b. 1947; in office: Dec. 31, 1981. **Local divisions:** 10 regions.

Economy: Industries: Aluminum, light industry. **Chief crops:** Cocoa (70% of exports), coffee. **Minerals:** Gold, manganese, industrial diamonds, bauxite. **Crude oil reserves:** (1980): 7 mln. bbls. **Other resources:** Timber, rubber. **Arable land:** 12%. **Fish catch** (1984): 228,000 metric tons. **Electricity prod.** (1984): 1.8 bln. kwh. **Labor force:** 60% agric.; 10% ind.

Finance: Currency: Cedi (Mar. 1987: 12.00 = $1 US). **Gross national product** (1984): $4.7 bln. **Per capita income** (1980): $420. **Imports** (1985): $731 mln.; partners: UK 18%, W. Ger. 12%, Nigeria 12%. **Exports** (1985): $617 mln.; partners: UK 16%, U.S. 16%, Neth. 9%, W. Ger. 9%. **International reserves less gold** (Mar. 1987): 631 mln. **Gold:** 314,000 oz t. **Consumer prices** (change in 1986): 24.6%.

Transport: Railway traffic (1984): 157 mln. passenger-km; 43 mln. net ton-km. **Motor vehicles:** in use (1983): 52,000 passenger cars, 24,000 comm. vehicles. **Civil aviation** (1982): 291 mln. passenger-km; 4.8 mln. freight ton-km. **Chief ports:** Tema, Takoradi.

Communications: Television sets: 140,000 in use (1985). **Radios:** 2.5 mln. in use (1985). **Telephones in use** (1982): 70,653.

Health: Life expectancy at birth (1985): 50.3 male; 53.7 female. **Births** (per 1,000 pop. 1985): 47.0. **Deaths** (per 1,000 pop. 1985): 14.6. **Natural increase** (1985): 3.2%. **Physicians** (1982): 1,435. **Infant mortality** (per 1,000 live births 1985): 98.

Education (1983): **Literacy:** 30%.

Major International Organizations: UN and all of its specialized agencies, OAU.

Embassy: 2460 16th St. NW 20009; 462-0761.

Named for an African empire along the Niger River, 400-1240 AD, Ghana was ruled by Britain for 113 years as the Gold Coast. The UN in 1956 approved merger with the British Togoland trust territory. Independence came March 6, 1957. Republic status within the Commonwealth was attained in 1960.

Pres. Kwame Nkrumah built hospitals and schools, promoted development projects like the Volta R. hydroelectric and aluminum plants, but ran the country into debt, jailed opponents, and was accused of corruption. A 1964 referendum gave Nkrumah dictatorial powers and set up a one-party socialist state.

Nkrumah was overthrown in 1966 by a police-army coup, which expelled Chinese and East German teachers and technicians. Elections were held in 1969, but 4 further coups occurred in 1972, 1978, 1979, and 1981. The 1979 and 1981 coups were led by Flight Lieut. Jerry Rawlings.

Greece

Hellenic Republic

Elliniki Dimokratia

People: Population (1986 est.): 9,954,000. **Age distrib.** (%): 0–14: 21.3; 15-59: 60.9; 60+: 17.8. **Pop. density:** 196 per sq. mi. **Urban** (1981): 58.1%. **Ethnic groups:** Greeks 98.5%. **Languages:** Greek, others. **Religions:** Greek Orthodox 97%.

Geography: Area: 51,146 sq. mi., the size of Alabama. **Location:** Occupies southern end of Balkan Peninsula in SE Europe. **Neighbors:** Albania, Yugoslavia, Bulgaria on N, Turkey on E. **Topography:** About 75% of Greece is non-arable, with mountains in all areas. Pindus Mts. run through the country N to S. The heavily indented coastline is 9,385 mi. long. Of over 2,000 islands, only 169 are inhabited, among them Crete, Rhodes, Milos, Kerkira (Corfu), Chios, Lesbos, Samos, Euboea, Delos, Mykonos. **Capital:** Athens. **Cities** (1981 est.): Athens (met.) 3,016,457; Thessaloniki (met.) 800,000; Patras 120,000.

Government: Type: Presidential parliamentary republic. **Head of state:** Pres. Christos Sartzetakis; in office: Mar. 30, 1985. **Head of government:** Prime Min. Andreas Papandreou; b. Feb. 5, 1919, in office: Oct. 21, 1981. **Local divisions:** 51 prefectures. **Defense:** 5% of GDP (1985).

Economy: Industries: Textiles, chemicals, metals, wine, food processng, cement. **Chief crops:** Grains, corn, rice, cotton, tobacco, olives, citrus fruits, raisins, figs. **Minerals:** Bauxite, lignite, oil, manganese. **Crude oil reserves** (1985): 35 mln. bbls. **Arable land:** 30%. **Meat prod.** (1983): beef: 90,000 metric tons; pork: 155,000 metric tons; lamb: 120,000 metric tons. **Fish catch** (1984): 100,000 metric tons. **Electricity prod.** (1985): 26.2 bln. kwh. **Crude steel prod.** (1984): 580,000 metric tons. **Labor force:** 28% agric.; 29% ind., 42% service.

Finance: Currency: Drachma (May 1987: 132.40 = $1 US). **Gross national product** (1984): $32.4 bln. **Per capita income** (1984): $3,260. **Imports** (1985): $10.1 bln.; partners: W. Ger. 16%, It. 9%, Fr. 7%. **Exports** (1985): $4.5 bln.; partners: W. Ger. 19%, It. 12%, Fr. 9%, U.S. 8%. **Tourists** (1984): $1.1 bln. receipts. **National budget** (1985): $13.2 bln. **International reserves less gold** (Mar. 1987): $1.7 bln. **Gold:** 3.3 mln. oz t. **Consumer prices** (change in 1986): 23.0%.

Transport: Railway traffic (1985): 1.5 bln. passenger-km; 732 mln. net ton-km. **Motor vehicles:** in use (1985): 1.1 mln. passenger cars, 589,000 comm. vehicles. **Civil aviation** (1984): 6.1 bln. passenger-km; 78.1 mln. freight ton-km. **Chief ports:** Piraeus, Thessaloniki, Patrai.

Communications: Television sets: 1.7 mln. in use (1984). **Radios:** 4 mln. in use (1984). **Telephones in use** (1983): 3.1 mln. **Daily newspaper circ.** (1982): 88 per 1,000 pop.

Health: Life expectancy at birth (1985): 72 male; 75 female. **Births** (per 1,000 pop. 1985): 12. **Deaths** (per 1,000 pop. 1985): 9. **Natural increase** (1985): .3%. **Hospital beds** (1984): 57,081. **Physicians** (1984): 27,607. **Infant mortality** (per 1,000 live births 1985): 13.8.

Education (1985): **Literacy:** men 96%, women 89%. **Years compulsory:** 9.

Major International Organizations: UN (GATT, IMF, WHO, ILO), EC, NATO, OECD.

Embassy: 2221 Massachusetts Ave. NW 20008; 667-3168.

The achievements of ancient Greece in art, architecture, science, mathematics, philosophy, drama, literature, and democracy became legacies for succeeding ages. Greece reached the height of its glory and power, particularly in the Athenian city-state, in the 5th century BC.

Greece fell under Roman rule in the 2d and 1st centuries BC. In the 4th century AD it became part of the Byzantine Empire and, after the fall of Constantinople to the Turks in 1453, part of the Ottoman Empire.

Greece won its war of independence from Turkey 1821-1829, and became a kingdom. A republic was established 1924; the monarchy was restored, 1935, and George II, King of the Hellenes, resumed the throne. In Oct., 1940, Greece rejected an ultimatum from Italy. Nazi support resulted in its defeat and occupation by Germans, Italians, and Bulgarians. By the end of 1944 the invaders withdrew. Communist resistance forces were defeated by Royalist and British troops. A plebiscite recalled King George II. He died Apr. 1, 1947, was succeeded by his brother, Paul I.

Communists waged guerrilla war 1947-49 against the government but were defeated with the aid of the U.S.

A period of reconstruction and rapid development followed, mainly with conservative governments under Premier Constantine Karamanlis. The Center Union led by George Papandreou won elections in 1963 and 1964. King Constantine, who acceded in 1964, forced Papandreou to resign. A period of political maneuvers ended in the military takeover of April 21, 1967, by Col. George Papadopoulos. King Constantine tried to reverse the consolidation of the harsh dictatorship Dec. 13, 1967, but failed and fled to Italy. Papadopoulos was ousted Nov. 25, 1973.

Greek army officers serving in the National Guard of Cyprus staged a coup on the island July 15, 1974. Turkey invaded Cyprus a week later, precipitating the collapse of the Greek junta, which was implicated in the Cyprus coup.

The military turned the government over to Karamanlis, who named a civilian cabinet, freed political prisoners, and sought to solve the Cyprus crisis. In Nov. 1974 elections his party won a large parliamentary majority, reduced by socialist gains in 1977. A Dec. 1974 referendum resulted in the proclamation of a republic.

Greece was reintegrated into the military wing of NATO in October 1980, and it became the 10th full member of the European Community on Jan. 1, 1981.

The 1981 victory of the Panhellenic Socialist Movement (Pasok) of Andreas Papandreou has brought about substantial changes in the internal and external policies that Greece has pursued for the past 5 decades. Relations with the U.S. have been strained since 1985. Greece has been victimized by several incidents of international terrorism.

Grenada

State of Grenada

People: Population (1986 est.): 86,000. **Pop. density:** 649 per sq. mi. **Ethnic groups:** Mostly African descent. **Languages:** English (official), French-African patois. **Religions:** Roman Catholic 64%, Anglican 22%.

Geography: Area: 133 sq. mi., twice the size of Washington, D.C. **Location:** 90 mi. N. of Venezuela. **Topography:** Main island is mountainous; country includes Carriacon and Petit Martinique islands. **Capital:** St. George's. **Cities** (1980 est.): St. George's 7,500.

Government: Head of state: Queen Elizabeth II, represented by Gov.-Gen. Paul Scoon, b. July 4, 1935; in office: Sept. 30, 1978. **Head of government:** Prime Minister: Herbert Blaize; b. Feb. 26, 1918; in office: Dec. 4, 1984. **Local divisions:** 6 parishes and one dependency.

Economy: Industries: Rum. **Chief crops:** Nutmegs, bananas, cocoa, mace. **Arable land:** 41%. **Electricity prod.** (1985): 25.00 mln. kwh. **Labor force:** 23% agric.; 24% ind.

Finance: Currency: East Caribbean dollar (Apr. 1987: 2.70 = $1 US). **Gross domestic product** (1983): $116 mln. **Per capita income** (1977): $500. **Imports** (1983): $64 mln.; partners: UK 19%, Trin./Tob. 25%. U.S. 17%. **Exports** (1983): $18 mln.; partners: UK 25%, CARICOM countries 38%. **Tourists** (1985): $23 mln. receipts. **National budget** (1985): $92.4 mln. **International reserves less gold** (Jan. 1987): $18.6 mln.

Transport: Motor vehicles: in use (1981): 4,700 passenger cars, 1,000 comm. vehicles. **Chief ports:** Saint George's.

Communications: Radios: 50,000 in use (1985). **Telephones in use** (1985): 5,000.

Health: Life expectancy at birth (1985): 68.5 male; 72.5 female. **Births** (per 1,000 pop. 1985): 27. **Deaths** (per 1,000 pop. 1985): 7. **Natural increase** (1985): 2.0%. **Infant mortality** (per 1,000 live births 1985): 16.7.

Education (1985): **Literacy:** 85%; **Years compulsory:** 6.

Major International Organizations: UN (IMF, WHO), OAS.

Embassy: 1701 New Hampshire Ave. NW 20009; 265-2561.

Columbus sighted the island 1498. First European settlers were French, 1650. The island was held alternately by France and England until final British occupation, 1784. Grenada became fully independent Feb. 7, 1974 during a general strike. It is the smallest independent nation in the Western Hemisphere. The U.S. has criticized the government for following Soviet and Cuban policies.

On Oct. 14, 1983, a military coup ousted Prime Minister Maurice Bishop, who was put under house arrest, later freed by supporters, rearrested, and, finally, on Oct. 19, executed. U.S. forces, with a token force from 6 area nations, invaded Grenada, Oct. 25. Resistance from the Grenadian army and Cuban advisors was quickly overcome as most of the population welcomed the invading forces as liberators. U.S. troops left Grenada in June 1985.

Guatemala

Republic of Guatemala

República de Guatemala

People: Population (1986 est.): 8,600,000. **Age distrib.** (%): 0–14: 45.9; 15–59: 49.4; 60+: 4.7. **Pop. density:** 194 per sq. mi. **Urban** (1981): 34.3%. **Ethnic groups:** Maya 55%, Mestizos 42%. **Languages:** Spanish, Indian dialects. **Religions:** Roman Catholics over 88%; Mayan religion practiced.

Geography: Area: 42,042 sq. mi., the size of Tennessee. **Location:** In Central America. **Neighbors:** Mexico N, W; El Salvador on S, Honduras, Belize on E. **Topography:** The central highland and mountain areas are bordered by the narrow Pacific coast and the lowlands and fertile river valleys on the Caribbean. There are numerous volcanoes in S, more than half a dozen over 11,000 ft. **Capital:** Guatemala City. **Cities** (1986 est.): Guatemala City 1,800,000.

Government: Type: Constitutional. **Head of state:** Pres. Marco Vinicio Cerezo Arevalo; b. Dec. 26, 1942; in office: Jan. 14, 1986. **Local divisions:** Guatemala City and 22 departments. **Defense:** 2.2% of GNP (1986).

Economy: Industries: Prepared foods, tires, textiles. **Chief crops:** Coffee (one third of exports), sugar, bananas, cotton, corn. **Minerals:** Oil, nickel. **Crude oil reserves** (1985): 500 mln. bbls. **Other resources:** Rare woods, fish, chicle. **Arable land:** 16%. **Electricity prod.** (1984): 1.6 bln. kwh. **Labor force:** 50% agric.; 27% ind. & comm., 12% services.

Finance: Currency: Quetzal (Apr. 1987: 1.00 = $1 US). **Gross national product** (1985): $8.9 bln. **Per capita income** (1985): $1,000. **Imports** (1985): $1.1 bln.; partners: U.S. 37%, CACM 8%. **Exports** (1985): $1.1 bln.; partners: U.S. 34%, CACM 20%. **National budget** (1986): $2.4 bln. **International reserves less gold** (Mar. 1987): $404 mln. **Gold:** 523,000 oz t. **Consumer prices** (change in 1986): 36.9%.

Transport: Railway traffic. Motor vehicles: in use (1983): 188,000 passenger cars, 58,000 comm. vehicles. **Civil aviation** (1985) 143 mln. passenger-km; 21 mln. freight ton-km. **Chief ports:** Puerto Barrios, San Jose.

Communications: Television sets: 207,000 in use (1985). **Radios:** 325,000 in use (1985). **Telephones in use** (1983): 161,000. **Daily newspaper circ.** (1983): 30 per 1,000 pop.

Health: Life expectancy at birth (1986): 55 yrs. **Births** (per 1,000 pop. 1985): 42. **Deaths** (per 1,000 pop. 1985): 10. **Natural increase** (1985): 3.2% **Health:** There are about 1,250 doctors, 60 hospitals, and 100 dispensaries. **Infant mortality** (per 1,000 live births 1985): 67.

Education (1987): **Literacy:** 48%. **Years compulsory:** 6; **Attendance:** 35%.

Major International Organizations: UN (IMF, World Bank), OAS.

Embassy: 2220 R St. NW 20008; 745-4952.

The old Mayan Indian empire flourished in what is today Guatemala for over 1,000 years before the Spanish.

Guatemala was a Spanish colony 1524-1821; briefly a part of Mexico and then of the U.S. of Central America, the republic was established in 1839.

Since 1945 when a liberal government was elected to replace the long-term dictatorship of Jorge Ubico, the country has seen a swing toward socialism, an armed revolt, renewed attempts at social reform, a military coup, and, in 1986, civilian rule. The Guerrilla Army of the Poor, an insurgent group founded 1975, led a military offensive by attacking army posts and succeeded in incorporating segments of the large Indian population in its struggle against the government.

Dissident army officers seized power, Mar. 23, 1982, denouncing the Mar. 7 Presidential election as fraudulent and pledging to restore "authentic democracy" to the nation. Political violence has caused some 200,000 Guatemalans to seek refuge in Mexico. A second military coup occurred Oct. 8, 1983. The nation returned to civilian rule in 1986.

Guinea

Republic of Guinea

République de Guinée

People: Population (1986 est.): 5,734,000. **Pop. density:** 59 per sq. mi. **Ethnic groups:** Foulah 40%, Malinké 25%, Soussous 10%, 15 other tribes. **Languages:** French (official), tribal languages. **Religions:** Moslem 85%, Christian 10%.

Geography: Area: 94,964 sq. mi., slightly smaller than Oregon. **Location:** On Atlantic coast of W. Africa. **Neighbors:** Guinea-Bissau, Senegal, Mali on N, Côte d'Ivoire on E, Liberia on S. **Topography:** A narrow coastal belt leads to the mountainous middle region, the source of the Gambia, Senegal, and Niger rivers. Upper Guinea, farther inland, is a cooler upland. The SE is forested. **Capital:** Conakry. **Cities** (1983 est.): Conakry 656,000; Labe 273,000; N'Zerekore 250,000; Kankan 278,000.

Government: Type: Republic under Military Committee For National Recovery. **Head of state:** Pres. Brig. Gen. Lansana Conte; b. 1944; in office: Apr. 5, 1984. **Local divisions:** 33 districts. **Defense:** 5.1% of GNP (1981).

Economy: Chief crops: Bananas, pineapples, rice, corn, palm nuts, coffee, honey. **Minerals:** Bauxite, iron, diamonds. **Arable land:** 6%. **Electricity prod.** (1984) 499 mln. kwh. **Labor force:** 82% agric., 11% ind. & comm.

Finance: Currency: Franc (Jan. 1987: 340 = $1 US). **Gross national product** (1984): $1.9 bln. **Per capita income** (1984): $305. **Imports** (1983): $350 mln.; partners: Fr. 36% USSR 11%, U.S. 6% It. 6%. **Exports** (1983): $465 mln.; partners: U.S. 18%, Fr. 13%, W. Ger. 12%, USSR 12%. **National budget** (1982): 140 mln.

Transport: Motor vehicles: in use (1982): 10,000 passenger cars, 10,000 comm. vehicles. **Chief ports:** Conakry.

Communications: Radios: 100,000 in use (1985). **Daily newspaper circ.** (1982): 2 per 1,000 pop.

Health: Life expectancy at birth (1985): 38.7 male; 41.8 female. **Births** (per 1,000 pop. 1985): 46.8. **Deaths** (per 1,000 pop. 1985): 23.5. **Natural increase** (1985): 2.3%. **Physicians** (1980): 301. **Infant mortality** (per 1,000 live births 1985): 159.

Education (1983): **Literacy:** 48%. **Years compulsory:** 8; attendance: 34% primary, 15% secondary.

Major International Organizations: UN and most specialized agencies, OAU.

Embassy: 2112 Leroy Pl. NW 20008; 483-9420.

Part of the ancient West African empires, Guinea fell under French control 1849-98. Under Sekou Toure, it opted for full independence in 1958, and France withdrew all aid.

Toure turned to communist nations for support, and set up a militant one-party state. Western firms, as well as the Soviet government, have invested in Guinea's vast bauxite mines.

Thousands of opponents were jailed in the 1970s, in the aftermath of an unsuccessful Portuguese invasion. Many were tortured and killed.

The military took control of the government in a bloodless coup after the March 1984 death of Toure.

Guinea-Bissau

Republic of Guinea-Bissau

Republica da Guiné-Bissau

People: Population (1986 est.): 858,000. **Pop. density:** 63 per sq. mi. **Ethnic groups:** Balanta 30%, Fula 20%, Manjaca 14%, Mandinga 13%. **Languages:** Portuguese (official), Criolo, tribal languages. **Religion:** Traditional 65%, Moslem 30%, Christian 4%.

Geography: Area: 13,948 sq. mi. **Location:** On Atlantic coast of W. Africa. **Neighbors:** Senegal on N, Guinea on E, S. **Topography:** A swampy coastal plain covers most of the country; to the east is a low savanna region. **Capital:** Bissau. **Cities** (1979): Bissau 109,500.

Government: Type: Republic. **Head of government:** Gen. Joao Bernardo Vieira; b. 1939; in office: Nov. 14,1980. **Local divisions:** 8 regions. **Defense:** 8.4% of GNP (1983).

Economy: Chief crops: Peanuts, cotton, rice. **Minerals:** Bauxite. **Arable land:** 10%. **Electricity prod.** (1984): 14 mln. kwh. **Labor force:** 90% agric.

Finance: Currency: Peso (Jan. 1987: 170 = $1 US). **Gross national product** (1984): $190 mln. **Per capita income** (1983): $165. **Imports** (1982): $61 mln.; partners: Port. 32%, It. 11%, Fr. 7%. **Exports** (1982): $13 mln.; partners: Port. 65%.

Communications: Radios: 26,000 receivers (1985). **Daily newspaper circ.** (1984): 7 per 1,000 pop.

Health: Life expectancy at birth (1985): 42 years. **Births** (per 1,000 pop. 1985): 39. **Deaths** (per 1,000 pop. 1985): 20. **Natural increase** (1985): 1.9%. **Infant mortality** (per 1,000 live births 1985): 137.

Education (1985): Literacy 15%. **Years compulsory:** 4.

Major International Organizations: UN, OAU.

Embassy: 211 E 43d St., New York, NY 10017; (212) 661-3977.

Portuguese mariners explored the area in the mid-15th century; the slave trade flourished in the 17th and 18th centuries, and colonization began in the 19th.

Beginning in the 1960s, an independence movement waged a guerrilla war and formed a government in the interior that achieved international support. Full independence came Sept. 10, 1974, after the Portuguese regime was overthrown.

The November 1980 coup gave Joao Bernardo Vieira absolute power.

Guyana

Cooperative Republic of Guyana

People: Population (1986 est.): 771,000. **Age distrib.** (%): 0–14: 43.7; 5–59: 50.7; 60+: 5.6. **Pop. density:** 9.3 per sq. mi. **Urban** (1983): 28%. **Ethnic groups:** East Indians 51%, African and mixed 43%. **Languages:** English (official), Amerindian dialects. **Religions:** Christians 57%, Hindus 34%, Moslems 9%.

Geography: Area: 83,000 sq. mi., the size of Idaho. **Location:** On N coast of S. America. **Neighbors:** Venezuela on W, Brazil on S, Suriname on E. **Topography:** Dense tropical forests cover much of the land, although a flat coastal area up to 40 mi. wide, where 90% of the population lives, provides rich alluvial soil for agriculture. A grassy savanna divides the 2 zones. **Capital:** Georgetown. **Cities** (1985 est.): Georgetown 170,000.

Government: Type: Republic within the Commonwealth of Nations. **Head of state:** President Hugh Desmond Hoyte; b. Mar. 9, 1929; in office: Aug. 6, 1985. **Head of Government:** Prime Min. Hamilton Green; in office: Aug. 6, 1985. **Local divisions:** 10 regions. **Defense:** 9% of GDP (1985).

Economy: Industries: Cigarettes, rum, clothing, furniture, drugs. **Chief crops:** Sugar, rice, citrus and other fruits. **Minerals:** Bauxite, diamonds. **Other resources:** Timber, shrimp. **Arable land:** 2%. **Electricity prod.** (1984): 390 bln. kwh. **Labor force:** 33% agric.; 45% ind. & comm.; 22% services.

Finance: Currency: Dollar (Mar. 1987: 10.00 = $1 US). **Gross national product** (1984): $470 mln. **Per capita income**

(1983): $457. **Imports** (1983): $243 mln.; partners: U.S. 28%, Trin-Tob. 24%, UK 20%. **Exports** (1983): $193 mln.; partners: UK 28%, U.S. 18%, Trin-Tob. 7%. **National budget** (1984): $441 mln. **International reserves less gold** (Feb. 1987): $1.8 mln. **Consumer prices** (change in 1984): 25.2%.

Transport: Motor vehicles: in use (1984): 20,000 passenger cars, 4,600 comm. vehicles. **Chief ports:** Georgetown.

Communications: Radios: 320,000 in use (1985). **Telephones in use** (1982): 28,000. **Daily newspaper circ.** (1985): 99 per 1,000 pop.

Health: Life expectancy at birth (1985): 70 years. **Births** (per 1,000 pop. 1985): 28.0. **Deaths** (per 1,000 pop. 1985): 7.0. **Natural increase** (1985): 2.1% **Health** (1982): 270 doctors, 29 hospitals, 149 health centers. **Infant mortality** (per 1,000 live births 1985): 32.

Education (1985): **Literacy:** 86%. **Years compulsory:** ages 5-14.

Major International Organizations: UN (GATT, ILO, IMF, World Bank), CARICOM, Commonwealth of Nations.

Embassy: 2490 Tracy Pl. NW 20008; 265-6900.

Guyana became a Dutch possession in the 17th century, but sovereignty passed to Britain in 1815. Indentured servants from India soon outnumbered African slaves. Ethnic tension has affected political life.

Guyana became independent May 26, 1966. A Venezuelan claim to the western half of Guyana was suspended in 1970 but renewed in 1982. The Suriname border is also disputed. The government has nationalized most of the economy which has remained severely depressed.

The Port Kaituma ambush of U.S. Rep. Leo J. Ryan and others investigating mistreatment of American followers of the Rev. Jim Jones' People's Temple cult, triggered a mass suicide-execution of 911 cultists in the Guyana jungle, Nov. 18, 1978.

Haiti

Republic of Haiti

Républiqe d'Haiti

People: Population (1986 est.): 5,870,000. **Age distrib.** (%): 4–14: 41.5; 15–59: 51.8; 60+: 6.7. **Pop. density:** 513 per sq. mi. **Urban** (1984): 20.7%. **Ethnic groups:** African descent 95%. **Languages:** French, Creole (both official). **Religions:** Roman Catholics 80%, Protestants 10%; Voodoo widely practiced.

Geography: Area: 10,714 sq. mi., the size of Maryland. **Location:** In West Indies, occupies western third of I. of Hispaniola. **Neighbors:** Dominican Republic on E, Cuba on W. **Topography:** About two-thirds of Haiti is mountainous. Much of the rest is semiarid. Coastal areas are warm and moist. **Capital:** Port-au-Prince. **Cities** (1986 est.): Port-au-Prince 557,000.

Government: Type: Provisional. **Head of state:** Gen. Henri Namphy; b. Nov. 2, 1932; in office: Feb. 7, 1986. **Local divisions:** 9 departments. **Defense:** 1.4% of GNP (1983).

Economy: Industries: Sugar refining, textiles. **Chief crops:** Coffee, sugar, bananas, cocoa, tobacco, rice. **Minerals:** Bauxite, copper, gold, silver, metric tons. **Other resources:** Timber. **Arable land:** 32%. **Meat prod.** (1980): beef: 24,000 metric tons; pork: 33,000 metric tons; lamb: 6,000 metric tons. **Electricity prod.** (1984): 335 mln. kwh. **Labor force:** 75% agric.; 18% ind. & comm.; 7% services.

Finance: Currency: Gourde (Apr. 1987: 5.00 = $1 US). **Gross national product** (1985): $2.0 bln. **Per capita income** (1983): $300. **Imports** (1986): $340 mln.; partners: U.S. 60%. **Exports** (1986): $200 mln.; partners: U.S. 75%. **Tourists** (1984): receipts $91 mln. **National budget** (1987): $258 mln. expenditures. **International reserves less gold** (Mar. 1987): $25 mln. **Gold:** 18,000 oz t. **Consumer prices** (change in 1985): 10.6%.

Transport: Motor vehicles: in use (1983): 34,000 passenger cars, 4,000 comm. vehicles. **Chief ports:** Port-au-Prince, Les Cayes.

Communications: Television sets: 75,000 in use (1985). **Radios:** 120,000 in use (1985). **Telephones in use** (1983): 38,000 **Daily newspaper circ.** (1985): 4 per 1,000 pop.

Health: Life expectancy at birth (1985): 51.2 male; 54.4 female. **Births** (per 1,000 pop. 1985): 35.6. **Deaths** (per 1,000 pop. 1985): 13.0. **Natural increase** (1985): 2.2%. **Hospital beds** (1980): 3,964. **Physicians** (1982): 270. **Infant mortality rate** (per 1,000 live births, 1985): 107.

Education (1987): **Literacy:** 23%. **Years compulsory:** 6; attendance 20%.

Major International Organizations: UN and some of its specialized agencies, OAS.

Embassy: 2311 Massachusetts Ave. NW 20008; 332-4090.

Haiti, visited by Columbus, 1492, and a French colony from 1677, attained its independence, 1804, following the rebellion led by former slave Toussaint L'Ouverture. Following a period of political violence, the U.S. occupied the country 1915-34.

Dr. Francois Duvalier was voted president in 1957; in 1964 he was named president for life. Upon his death in 1971, he was succeeded by his son, Jean-Claude. Drought in 1975-77 brought famine, and Hurricane Allen in 1980 destroyed most of the rice, bean, and coffee crops.

Haiti is the poorest nation in the Western hemisphere; unemployment was estimated at 50% in 1987.

Following several weeks of unrest, President Jean Claude Duvalier fled Haiti aboard a U.S. Air Force jet Feb. 7, 1986, ending the 28-year dictatorship by the Duvalier family. A military-civilian council assumed control.

In 1987, voters approved a new constitution.

Honduras

Republic of Honduras

Republica de Honduras

People: Population (1986 est.): 4,648,000. **Age distrib.** (%): 0–14: 48.1; 15–59: 47.5; 60+: 4.5. **Pop. density:** 91 per sq. mi. **Urban** (1985): 38.0%. **Ethnic groups:** Mestizo 90%, Europeans, Negroes, Indians. **Languages:** Spanish, Indian dialects. **Religions:** Roman Catholics, small Protestant minority.

Geography: Area: 43,277 sq. mi., slightly larger than Tennessee. **Location:** In Central America. **Neighbors:** Guatemala on W, El Salvador, Nicaragua on S. **Topography:** The Caribbean coast is 500 mi. long. Pacific coast, on Gulf of Fonseca, is 40 mi. long. Honduras is mountainous, with wide fertile valleys and rich forests. **Capital:** Tegucigalpa. **Cities** (1985 est.) Tegucigalpa 571,000; San Pedro Sula 372,000.

Government: Type: Democratic constitutional republic. **Head of State:** Pres. Jose Azcona Hoyo; b. 1927; in office: Jan. 27, 1986. **Local divisions:** 18 departments. **Defense:** 7% of govt. budget (1986).

Economy: Industries: Clothing, textiles, cement, wood prods, cigars. **Chief crops:** Bananas (chief export), coffee, corn, beans. **Minerals:** Gold, silver, copper, lead, zinc, iron, antimony, coal. **Other resources:** Timber. **Arable land:** 16%. **Meat prod.** (1984): cattle: 2.4 mln. **Electricity prod.** (1984): 1.1 bln. kwh. **Labor force:** 62% agric.; 20% services; 9% manuf.

Finance: Currency: Lempira (Apr. 1987): 2.00 = $1 US). **Gross national product** (1985): $3.3 bln. **Per capita income** (1985): $815. **Imports** (1985): $1.5 bln.; partners: U.S. 41%, Jap. 7%, Guat. 6%. **Exports** (1985): $958 mln.; partners: U.S. 52%, W. Ger. 8%, Jap. 5%. **Tourists** (1983): $23 mln. receipts. **National budget** (1984): $805 mln. revenues; $1.3 bln. expenditures. **International reserves less gold** (Mar. 1987): $125.8 mln. **Gold:** 16,000 oz t. **Consumer prices** (change in 1986): 3.4%.

Transport: Motor vehicles: in use (1985) 66,000 passenger cars, 18,000 comm. vehicles. **Civil aviation** (1983): 348 mln. passenger-km; 2.3 mln. freight ton-km. **Chief ports:** Puerto Cortes, La Ceiba.

Communications: Television sets: 136,000 in use (1984). **Radios:** 1.5 mln. in use (1983). **Telephones in use** (1983): 37,000. **Daily newspaper circ.** (1984): 58 per 1,000 pop.

Health: Life expectancy at birth (1984): 58.7 yrs. **Births** (per 1,000 pop. 1985): 41. **Deaths** (per 1,000 pop. 1985): 8. **Natural increase** (1985): 3.3%. **Hospital beds** (1985): 5,220. **Physicians** (1985): 1,900. **Infant mortality** (per 1,000 live births 1985): 73.

Education (1987): **Literacy:** 56%. **Years compulsory:** 6; attendance 70%.

Major International Organizations: UN, (IMF, WHO, ILO), OAS.

Embassy: 4301 Connecticut Ave. NW 20008; 966-7700.

Mayan civilization flourished in Honduras in the 1st millenium AD. Columbus arrived in 1502. Honduras became independent after freeing itself from Spain, 1821 and from the Fed. of Central America, 1838.

Gen. Oswaldo Lopez Arellano, president for most of the period 1963-75 by virtue of one election and 2 coups, was ousted by the army in 1975 over charges of pervasive bribery by United Brands Co. of the U.S.

The government has resumed land distribution, raised minimum wages, and started a literacy campaign. An elected civilian government took power in 1982, the country's first in 10 years.

The U.S. has provided military aid and advisors to help withstand pressures from Nicaragua and help block arms shipments from Nicaragua to rebel forces in El Salvador. The U.S. has contriibuted over $100 mln. in economic and military aid. Additional funds were given in Mar. 1986 following border skirmishes and incursions by Nicaraguan troops.

Hungary

Hungarian People's Republic

Magyar Népköztáraság

People: Population (1986 est.): 10,624,000. **Age distrib.** (%): 0–14: 21.4; 15–59: 60.4; 60+: 18.2. **Pop. density:** 296 per sq. mi. **Urban** (1984): 56%. **Ethnic groups:** Magyar 92%, German 2.5%, Gypsy 3%. **Languages:** Hungarian (Magyar). **Religions:** Roman Catholics 67%, Protestant 25%.

Geography: Area: 35,919 sq. mi., slightly smaller than Indiana. **Location:** In East Central Europe. **Neighbors:** Czechoslovakia on N, Austria on W, Yugoslavia on S, Romania, USSR on E. **Topography:** The Danube R. forms the Czech border in the NW, then swings S to bisect the country. The eastern half of Hungary is mainly a great fertile plain, the Alfold; the W and N are hilly. **Capital:** Budapest. **Cities** (1986 est.): Budapest 2,080,000; Miskolc 211,000; Debrecen 212,000.

Government: Type: Communist unitary state. **Head of state:** Pres. Karoly Nemeth; in office: June 25, 1987. **Head of government:** Prem. Karoly Grosz; in office: June 25, 1987. **Head of Hungary Socialist Workers Party:** Janos Kadar; b. May 26, 1912; in office: Oct. 25, 1956. **Local divisions:** 19 counties, 5 cities with county status. **Defense:** 4.3% of GNP (1983).

Economy: Industries: Iron and steel, machinery, pharmaceuticals, vehicles, communications equip., milling, distilling. **Chief crops:** Grains, vegetables, fruits, grapes. **Minerals:** Bauxite, natural gas. **Arable land:** 57%. **Meat prod.** (1985): cattle: 1.7 mln., pigs: 8.2 mln.; sheep: 2.4 mln. **Electricity prod.** (1984): 26.2 bln. kwh. **Crude steel prod.** (1985): 3.6 mln. metric tons. **Labor force:** 20% agric.; 42% ind. & comm.; 32% services.

Finance: Currency: Forint (Mar. 1987: 47 = $1 US). **Gross national product** (1983): $18.6 bln. **Per capita income** (1982): $4,180. **Imports** (1986): $9.5 bln.; partners: USSR 29%, W. Ger. 11%, E. Ger. 7%, Czech. 5%. **Exports** (1986): $9.1 bln.; partners: USSR 34%, E. Ger. 6%, W. Ger. 7%, Czech. 6%. **National budget** (1983): $13.4 bln. **Tourists** (1985): $506 mln. receipts. **Consumer prices** (change in 1985): 7.0%.

Transport: Railway traffic (1985): 11.2 bln. passenger-km; 22.3 bln. net ton-km. **Motor vehicles:** in use (1986): 1.4 mln. passenger cars, 157,000 comm. vehicles. **Civil aviation** (1985): 1.3 bln. Passenger-km; 21.8 mln. net freight-km.

Communications: Television sets: 2.9 mln. licensed (1985). **Radios:** 5.5 mln. licensed (1985). **Telephones in use** (1985): 1.4 mln. **Daily newspaper circ.** (1984): 281 per 1,000 pop.

Health: Life expectancy at birth (1984): 65.6 male; 73.7 female. **Births** (per 1,000 pop. 1985): 12. **Deaths** (per 1,000 pop. 1985): 14. **Natural increase** (1985): 0%. **Hospital beds** (1985): 102,000. **Physicians** (1985): 34,000. **Infant mortality** (per 1,000 live births 1985): 20.2

Education (1985): **Literacy:** 98%. **Years compulsory:** to age 16; attendance 99%.

Major International Organizations: UN (IMF, World Bank, GATT), Warsaw Pact.

Embassy: 3910 Shoemaker St. NW 20008; 362-6730.

Earliest settlers, chiefly Slav and Germanic, were overrun by Magyars from the east. Stephen I (997-1038) was made king by Pope Sylvester II in 1000 AD. The country suffered repeated Turkish invasions in the 15th-17th centuries. After the defeats of the Turks, 1686-1697, Austria dominated, but Hungary obtained concessions until it regained internal independence in 1867, with the emperor of Austria as king of Hungary in a dual monarchy with a single diplomatic service. Defeated with the Central Powers in 1918, Hungary lost Transylvania to Romania, Croatia and Bacska to Yugoslavia, Slovakia and Carpatho-Ruthenia to Czechoslovakia, all of which had large Hungarian minorities. A republic under Michael Karolyi and a bolshevist revolt under Bela Kun were followed by a vote for a monarchy in 1920 with Admiral Nicholas Horthy as regent.

Hungary joined Germany in World War II, and was allowed to annex most of its lost territories. Russian troops captured the country, 1944-1945. By terms of an armistice with the Allied powers Hungary agreed to give up territory acquired by the 1938 dismemberment of Czechoslovakia and to return to its borders of 1937.

A republic was declared Feb. 1, 1946; Zoltan Tildy was elected president. In 1947 the communists forced Tildy out. Premier Imre Nagy, in office since mid-1953, was ousted for his moderate policy of favoring agriculture and consumer production, April 18, 1955.

In 1956, popular demands for the ousting of Erno Gero, Communist Party secretary, and for formation of a government by Nagy, resulted in the latter's appointment Oct. 23; demonstrations against communist rule developed into open revolt. Gero called in Soviet forces. On Nov. 4 Soviet forces launched a massive attack against Budapest with 200,000 troops, 2,500 tanks and armored cars.

About 200,000 persons fled the country. In the spring of 1963 the regime freed many anti-communists and captives from the revolution in a sweeping amnesty. Nagy was executed by the Russians. In Mar. 1987, some 2,000 marched in Budapest calling for democracy.

Soviet troops are stationed in Hungary. Hungarian troops participated in the 1968 Warsaw Pact invasion of Czechoslovakia.

Major economic reforms were launched early in 1968, switching from a central planning system to one in which market forces and profit control much of production. Productivity and living standards have improved. Hungary leads the communist states in comparative tolerance for cultural freedoms and small private enterprise.

Iceland

Republic of Iceland

Lýoveldio Island

People: Population (1986 est.): 244,000. **Age distrib.** (%): 0–14: 26.7; 15–59: 59.5; 60+: 13.8. **Pop. density:** 6 per sq. mi. **Urban** (1986): 85% **Ethnic groups:** Homogeneous, descendants of Norwegians, Celts. **Language:** Icelandic. **Religion:** Evangelical Lutheran 97%.

Geography: Area: 39,769 sq. mi., the size of Virginia. **Location:** At N end of Atlantic O. **Neighbors:** Nearest is Greenland. **Topography:** Iceland is of recent volcanic origin. Three-quarters of the surface is wasteland: glaciers, lakes, a lava desert. There are geysers and hot springs, and the climate is moderated by the Gulf Stream. **Capital:** Reykjavik. **Cities** (1986 est.): Reykjavik 89,000.

Government: Type: Constitutional republic. **Head of state:** Pres. Vigdis Finnbogadottir; b. Apr. 15, 1930; in office: Aug. 1, 1980. **Head of government:** Prime Min. Steingrimur Hermannsson; b. June 22, 1928; in office: May 26, 1983. **Local divisions:** 20 syslur.

Economy: Industries: Fish products (some 80% of exports), aluminum. **Chief crops:** Potatoes, turnips, hay. **Arable land:** 0.5%. **Meat prod.** (1985): lamb: 14,000 metric tons. **Fish catch** (1985): 839,000 metric tons. **Electricity prod.** (1984): 3.9 bln. kwh. **Labor force:** 7% agric.; 49% ind. & comm.; 30% services & govt; fisheries 14%.

Finance: Currency: Kronur (Mar. 1987: 38.9 = $1 US). **Gross national product** (1985): $2.5 bln. **Per capita income** (1984): $10,216. **Imports** (1984): $842 mln.; partners: USSR 8%, W. Ger. 12%, UK 9%, Den. 10%. **Exports** (1984): $744 mln.; partners: U.S. 28%, UK 19%. **Tourists** (1984): receipts: $76 mln. **National budget** (1984): $500 mln. expenditures. **International reserves less gold** (Mar. 1987): $287 mln. **Gold:** 49,000 oz t. **Consumer prices** (change in 1986): 22.2%.

Transport: Motor vehicles: in use (1986): 100,000 passenger cars, 12,000 comm. vehicles. **Civil aviation** (1985): 2.3 bln. passenger-km ; 22.4 mln. freight ton-km . **Chief ports:** Reykjavik.

Communications: Television sets: 70,000 in use (1985). **Radios:** 70,000 licensed (1985). **Telephones in use** (1985): 97,245. **Daily newspaper circ.** (1982): 557 per 1,000 pop.

Health: Life expectancy at birth (1985): 73.5 male; 79.5 female. **Births** (per 1,000 pop. 1985): 18. **Deaths** (per 1,000 pop. 1985): 7. **Natural increase** (1985): 1.1%. **Hospital beds** (1983): 2,678. **Physicians** (1983): 545. **Infant mortality** per (1,000 live births 1985): 6.2.

Education (1986): **Literacy:** 99%. **Years compulsory:** 8; **Attendance:** 99%.

Major International Organizations: UN (GATT), NATO, OECD.

Embassy: 2022 Connecticut Ave. NW 20008; 235-6653.

Iceland was an independent republic from 930 to 1262, when it joined with Norway. Its language has maintained its purity for 1,000 years. Danish rule lasted from 1380-1918; the last ties with the Danish crown were severed in 1941. The Althing, or assembly, is the world's oldest surviving parliament.

U.S. president Ronald Reagan and Soviet leader Mikhail Gorbachev held a summit meeting in Reykjavik on Oct. 11-12, 1986.

India

Republic of India

Bharat

People: Population (1986 est.): 783,940,000. **Age distrib.** (%): 0–14: 40.8; 15–59: 53.9; 60+: 5.3. **Pop. density:** 612 per sq. mi. **Urban** (1981): 21.5%. **Ethnic groups:** Indo-Aryan groups 72%, Dravidians 25%, Mongoloids 3%. **Languages:** 16 languages, including Hindi (official) and English (associate official). **Religions:** Hindu 83%, Moslem 11%, Christian 3%, Sikh 2%.

Geography: Area: 1,266,595 sq. mi., one third the size of the U.S. **Location:** Occupies most of the Indian subcontinent in S. Asia. **Neighbors:** Pakistan on W, China, Nepal, Bhutan on N, Burma, Bangladesh on E. **Topography:** The Himalaya Mts., highest in world, stretch across India's northern borders. Below, the Ganges Plain is wide, fertile, and among the most densely populated regions of the world. The area below includes the Deccan Peninsula. Close to one quarter the area is forested. The climate varies from tropical heat in S to near-Arctic cold in N. Rajasthan Desert is in NW; NE Assam Hills get 400 in. of rain a year. **Capital:** New Delhi. **Cities** (1981 cen.): Calcutta 9.1 mln.; Bombay (met.) 8.2 mln.; Delhi 5.2 mln.; Madras 4.3 mln.; Bangalore 2.9 mln.; Hyderabad 1.5 mln.; Ahmedabad 2.5 mln.; Kanpur 1.7 mln.; Pune 1.7 mln.; Nagpur 1.3 mln.

Government: Type: Federal Republic. **Head of state:** Pres. Ramaswamy Venkataraman; b. Dec. 4, 1910; in office: July 16, 1987. **Head of government:** Prime Min. Rajiv Gandhi, b. Aug. 20, 1944; in office: Oct. 31, 1984. **Local divisions:** 25 states, 7 union territories. **Defense:** 3.9% of GNP (1984).

Economy: Industries: Textiles, steel, processed foods, cement, machinery, chemicals, fertilizers, consumer appliances, autos. **Chief crops:** Rice, grains, coffee, sugar cane, spices, tea, cashews, cotton, copra, coir, juta, linseed. **Minerals:** Chromium, coal, iron, manganese, mica salt, bauxite, gypsum, oil. **Crude oil reserves** (1985): 3.7 bln. bbls. **Other resources:** Rubber, timber. **Arable land:** 57%. **Meat prod.** (1985): cattle: 185 mln.; pigs: 9 mln.; sheep: 54.4 mln. **Fish catch** (1984): 2.8 mln. metric tons. **Electricity prod.** (1984): 165 bln. kwh. **Crude steel prod.** (1985): 11 mln. metric tons. **Labor force:** 70% agric.; 19% ind. & comm.

Finance: Currency: Rupee (May 1987: 12.6 = $1 US). **Gross national product** (1983): $190 bln. **Per capita income** (1977): $150. **Imports** (1985): $14.8 bln.; partners: U.S. 12%, USSR 8%, W. Ger. 6%, Iran 11%. **Exports** (1985): $8.0 bln.; partners: U.S. 11%, USSR 18%, UK 6%, Jap. 9%. **Tourists** (1983): receipts: $820 mln. **National budget** (1987): $48 bln. expenditures. **International reserves less gold** (Jan. 1987): $6.3 bln. **Gold:** 10.4 mln. oz. t. **Consumer prices** (change in 1986): 8.7%.

Transport: Railway traffic (1985): 240 bln. passenger-km; 196 bln. net ton-km. **Motor vehicles:** in use (1985): 1.5 bln. passenger cars, 952,000 comm. **Civil aviation:** (1985): 14.8 bln. passenger-km; 522 mln. freight ton-km. **Chief ports:** Calcutta, Bombay, Madras, Cochin, Vishakhapatnam.

Communications: Television sets: 2.2 mln. (1985). **Radios:** 25 mln. (1985). **Telephones in use** (1984): 3.2 mln. **Daily newspaper circ.** (1985): 16 per. 1,000 pop.

Health: Life expectancy at birth (1981): 52 male; 50 female. **Births** (per 1,000 pop. 1985): 33. **Deaths** (per 1,000 pop. 1985): 12. **Natural increase** (1985): 2.1%. **Hospital beds** (1984): 599,000. **Physicians** (1984): 284,000. **Infant mortality** (per 1,000 live births 1985): 101.

Education (1981): **Literacy:** 36%.

Major International Organizations: UN (IMF, World Bank).

Embassy: 2107 Massachusetts Ave. NW 20008; 939-7000.

India has one of the oldest civilizations in the world. Excavations trace the Indus Valley civilization back for at least 5,000 years. Paintings in the mountain caves of Ajanta, richly carved temples, the Taj Mahal in Agra, and the Kutab Minar in Delhi are among relics of the past.

Aryan tribes, speaking Sanskrit, invaded from the NW around 1500 BC, and merged with the earlier inhabitants to create classical Indian civilization.

Asoka ruled most of the Indian subcontinent in the 3d century BC, and established Buddhism. But Hinduism revived and eventually predominated. During the Gupta kingdom, 4th-6th century AD, science, literature, and the arts enjoyed a "golden age."

Arab invaders established a Moslem foothold in the W in the 8th century, and Turkish Moslems gained control of North India by 1200. The Mogul emperors ruled 1526-1857.

Vasco de Gama established Portuguese trading posts 1498-1503. The Dutch followed. The British East India Co. sent Capt. William Hawkins, 1609, to get concessions from the Mogul emperor for spices and textiles. Operating as the East India Co. the British gained control of most of India. The British parliament assumed political direction; under Lord Bentinck, 1828-35, rule by rajahs was curbed. After the Sepoy troops mutinied, 1857-58, the British supported the native rulers.

Nationalism grew rapidly after World War I. The Indian National Congress and the Moslem League demanded constitutional reform. A leader emerged in Mohandas K. Gandhi (called Mahatma, or Great Soul), born Oct. 2, 1869, assassinated Jan. 30, 1948. He began advocating self-rule, non-violence, removal of untouchability in 1919. In 1930 he launched "civil disobedience," including boycott of British goods and rejection of taxes without representation.

In 1935 Britain gave India a constitution providing a bicameral federal congress. Mohammed Ali Jinnah, head of the Moslem League, sought creation of a Moslem nation, Pakistan.

The British government partitioned British India into the dominions of India and Pakistan. Aug. 15, 1947, was designated Indian Independence Day. India became a self-governing member of the Commonwealth and a member of the UN. It became a democratic republic, Jan. 26, 1950.

More than 12 million Hindu & Moslem refugees crossed the India-Pakistan borders in a mass transferral of some of the 2 peoples during 1947; about 200,000 were killed in communal fighting.

After Pakistan troops began attacks on Bengali separatists in East Pakistan, Mar. 25, 1971, some 10 million refugees fled into India. On Aug. 9, India and the USSR signed a 20-year friendship pact while U.S.-India relations soured. India and Pakistan went to war Dec. 3, 1971, on both the East and West fronts. Pakistan troops in the east surrendered Dec. 16; Pakistan agreed to a cease-fire in the west Dec. 17.

India and Pakistan signed a pact agreeing to withdraw troops from their borders and seek peaceful solutions, July 3, 1972. In Aug. 1973 India agreed to release 93,000 Pakistanis held prisoner since 1971; the return was completed in Apr. 1974. The 2 countries resumed full relations in 1976.

In 2 days of carnage, the Bengali population of the village of Mandai, Tripura State, 700 people, were massacred in a raid by indigenous tribal residents of the area, June 8-9, 1980. A similar year-long campaign against Bengali immigrants had been going on in Assam State.

Prime Min. Mrs. Indira Gandhi, named Jan. 19, 1966, was the 2d successor to Jawaharlal Nehru, India's prime minister from 1947 to his death, May 27, 1964.

Long the dominant power in India's politics, the Congress Party lost some of its near monopoly by 1967. The party split into New and Old Congress parties in 1969. Mrs. Gandhi's New Congress party won control of the House.

Threatened with adverse court rulings in a voting law case, an opposition protest campaign and strikes, Gandhi invoked emergency provisions of the constitution June, 1975. Thousands of opponents were arrested and press censorship imposed. Measures to control prices, protect small farmers, and improve productivity were adopted.

The emergency, especially enforcement of coercive birth control measures in some areas, and the prominent extra-constitutional role of Indira Gandhi's son Sanjay, was widely resented. Opposition parties, united in the Janata coalition, scored massive victories in federal and state parliamentary elections in 1977, turning the New Congress Party from power.

Indira Gandhi became prime minister for the second time, Jan. 14, 1980. Gandhi was assassinated by Sikh extremists Oct. 31, 1984. Widespread rioting followed causing over 1,000 deaths. Rajiv, her son, replaced her as prime minister.

On Dec. 3, 1984, methyl isocyanate, a deadly gas, escaped from a tank owned by the Union Carbide Corp. at Bhopal and killed over 2,500, in history's worst industrial accident.

Extremist Sikhs ignited several violent clashes in the northern state of Punjab in 1986 and 1987. The government's May 1987 decision to bring the state of Punjab under the rule of the central government sparked increased violence.

Sikkim, bordered by Tibet, Bhutan and Nepal, formerly British protected, became a protectorate of India in 1950. Area, 2,740 sq. mi.; pop. 1981 cen. 315,000; capital, Gangtok. In Sept. 1974 India's parliament voted to make Sikkim an associate Indian state, absorbing it into India. The monarchy was abolished in an April, 1975, referendum.

Kashmir, a predominantly Moslem region in the northwest, has been in dispute between India and Pakistan since 1947. A cease-fire was negotiated by the UN Jan. 1, 1949; it gave Pakistan control of one-third of the area, in the west and northwest, and India the remaining two-thirds, the Indian state of Jammu and Kashmir, which enjoys internal autonomy. Repeated clashes broke out along the line.

There were also clashes in April 1965 along the Assam-East Pakistan border and in the **Rann** (swamp) **of Kutch** area along the West Pakistan-Gujarat border near the Arabian Sea. An international arbitration commission on Feb. 19, 1968, awarded 90% of the Rann to India, 10% to Pakistan.

France, 1952-54, peacefully yielded to India its 5 colonies, former French India, comprising Pondicherry, Karikal, Mahe, Yanaon (which became Pondicherry Union Territory, area 185 sq. mi., pop. 1981, 604,136) and Chandernagor (which was incorporated into the state of West Bengal).

Goa, 1,429 sq. mi., pop., 1981, 1 mln., which had been ruled by Portugal since 1505 AD, was taken by India by military action Dec. 18, 1961, together with 2 other Portuguese enclaves, **Daman and Diu,** located near Bombay. They became states of India in 1987.

Indonesia

Republic of Indonesia

Republik Indonesia

People: Population (1986 est.): 176,764,000. **Age distrib.** (%): 0–14: 39.2; 15–59: 56.5; 60+: 5.3. **Pop. density:** 227 per sq. mi. **Urban** (1980): 22.3%. **Ethnic groups:** Malay, Chinese, Irianese. **Languages:** Bahasa Indonesian (Malay) (official), Javanese, other Austronesian languages. **Religions:** Muslims 90%.

Geography: Area: 735,268 sq. mi. **Location:** Archipelago SE of Asia along the Equator. **Neighbors:** Malaysia on N, Papua New Guinea on E. **Topography:** Indonesia comprises 13,500 islands, including Java (one of the most densely populated areas in the world with 1,500 persons to the sq. mi.), Sumatra, Kalimantan (most of Borneo), Sulawesi (Celebes), and West Irian (Irian Jaya, the W. half of New Guinea). Also: Bangka, Billiton, Madura, Bali, Timor. The mountains and plateaus on the major islands have a cooler climate than the tropical lowlands. **Capital:** Jakarta. **Cities** (1984 est.): Jakarta 7,585,000; Surabaja 2,271,000; Bandung 1,613,000; Medan 1,506,000.

Government: Type: Independent Republic. **Head of state:** Pres. Suharto; b. June 8, 1921; in office: Mar. 6, 1967. **Local divisions:** 27 provinces, 281 regencies. **Defense:** 2.8% of GNP (1983).

Economy: Industries: Food processing, textiles, light industry. **Chief crops:** Rice, coffee, sugar. **Minerals:** Nickel, tin, oil, bauxite, copper, natural gas. **Crude oil reserves** (1985): 9.1 bln. bbls. **Other resources:** Rubber. **Arable land:** 11%. **Meat prod.** (1985): cattle: 6.9 mln.; pigs: 4.3 mln.; sheep: 5.1 mln. **Fish catch** (1985): 2.2 mln. metric tons. **Electricity prod.** (1984): 21.3 bln. kwh. **Crude steel prod.** (1981): 375,000 metric tons. **Labor force:** 66% agric.; 23% ind. & comm.; 10% services.

Finance: Currency: Rupiah (May 1987: 1,637 = $1 US). **Gross national product** (1984): $78.8 bln. **Per capita income** (1982): $560. **Imports** (1985): $10.2 bln.; partners: Jap. 25%, U.S. 17%, Sing. 8%. **Exports** (1985): $18.5 bln.; partners: Jap. 47%, U.S. 20%, Sing. 10%. **Tourists** (1984): $519 mln. receipts. **National budget** (1986): $13.8 bln. **International reserves less gold** (Feb. 1987): $3.8 bln. **Gold:** 3.10 mln. oz t. **Consumer prices** (change in 1986): 5.8%.

Transport: Railway traffic (1985): 6.3 bln. passenger-km; 1.1 bln. net ton-km. **Motor vehicles:** in use (1985): 958,000 passenger cars, 1 mln. comm. **Civil aviation** (1984): 9.4 bln. passenger-km; 169 mln. freight ton-km. **Chief ports:** Jakarta, Surabaja, Medan, Palembang, Semarang.

Communications: Television sets: 4.9 mln. in use (1985). **Radios:** 32 mln. in use (1985). **Telephones in use** (1984): 795,000.

Health: Life expectancy at birth (1985): male: 51.2; female 53.9 years. **Births** (per 1,000 pop. 1985): 30.7. **Deaths** (per 1,000 pop. 1985): 13.0. **Natural increase** (1985) 1.7%. **Hospital beds** (1984): 103,500. **Physicians** (1983): 10,262. **Infant mortality** (per 1,000 live births 1985): 90.3.

Education (1984): **Literacy:** 72%. 86% attend primary school; 15% secondary school.

Major International Organizations: UN and all of its specialized agencies, ASEAN, OPEC.

Embassy: 2020 Massachusetts Ave. NW 20036; 393-1745.

Hindu and Buddhist civilization from India reached the peoples of Indonesia nearly 2,000 years ago, taking root especially in Java. Islam spread along the maritime trade routes in the 15th century, and became predominant by the 16th century. The Dutch replaced the Portuguese as the most important European trade power in the area in the 17th century. They secured territorial control over Java by 1750. The outer islands were not finally subdued until the early 20th century, when the full area of present-day Indonesia was united under one rule for the first time.

Following Japanese occupation, 1942-45, nationalists led by Sukarno and Hatta proclaimed a republic. The Netherlands ceded sovereignty Dec. 27, 1949, after 4 years of fighting. West Irian, on New Guinea, remained under Dutch control.

After the Dutch in 1957 rejected proposals for new negotiations over West Irian, Indonesia stepped up the seizure of Dutch property. A U.S. mediator's plan was adopted in 1962. In 1963 the UN turned the area over to Indonesia, which promised a plebiscite. In 1969, voting by tribal chiefs favored staying with Indonesia, despite an uprising and widespread opposition.

Sukarno suspended Parliament in 1960, and was named president for life in 1963. Russian-armed Indonesian troops staged raids in 1964 and 1965 into Malaysia, whose formation Sukarno had opposed.

Indonesia's popular, pro-Peking Communist Party tried to seize control in 1965; the army smashed the coup, later intimated that Sukarno had played a role in it. In parts of Java, communists seized several districts before being defeated; over 300,000 communists were executed.

Gen. Suharto, head of the army, was named president in 1968, reelected 1973 and 1978. A coalition of his supporters won a strong majority in House elections in 1971. Moslem opposition parties made gains in 1977 elections but lost ground in the 1982 elections. The military retains a predominant political role.

In 1966 Indonesia and Malaysia signed an agreement ending hostility. After ties with Peking were cut in 1967, there were riots against the economically important ethnic Chinese minority. Riots against Chinese and Japanese also occurred in 1974. Indonesia and China agreed to begin bilateral trade talks in 1985.

The former Portuguese Timor became Indonesia's 27th province in 1976 during a local civil war.

Oil export earnings, and political stability have made Indonesia's economy stable.

Iran

Islamic Republic of Iran

Jomhori-e-Islami-e-Irân

People: Population (1986 est.): 46,604,000. **Age distrib.** (%): 0–14: 44.4; 15–59: 50.3; 60+: 5.2. **Pop. density:** 72 per sq. mi. **Urban** (1980): 50%. **Ethnic groups:** Persian 63%, Turkomans & Baluchis 19%, Kurds 3%, Arabs 4%. **Languages:** Persian, Turk, Kurdish, Arabic, English, French. **Religions:** Shi'a Moslems 93%.

Geography: Area: 636,293 sq. mi. **Location:** Between the Middle East and S. Asia. **Neighbors:** Turkey, Iraq on W, USSR of N (Armenia, Azerbaijan, Turkmenistan), Afghanistan, Pakistan on E. **Topography:** Interior highlands and plains are surrounded by high mountains, up to 18,000 ft. Large salt deserts cover much of the area, but there are many oases and forest areas. Most of the population inhabits the N and NW. **Capital:** Teheran. **Cities** (1985 est.): Teheran 5,751,000; Isfahan 1,121,000; Mashhad 1,103,000; Shiraz 834,000.

Government: Type: Islamic republic. **Religious head (Faghi):** Ayatollah Ruhollah Khomeini, b. 1901. **Head of state:** Pres. Sayyed Ali Khamenei. **Head of government:** Prime Minister Mir Hussein Moussavi; b. 1937; in office: Oct. 29, 1981. **Local divisions:** 23 provinces, 9 governates. **Defense:** 5% of GNP (1983).

Economy: Industries: Steel, petrochemicals, cement, auto assembly, sugar refining, carpets. **Chief crops:** Grains, rice, fruits, sugar beets, cotton, grapes. **Minerals:** Chromium, oil, gas, copper, iron, lead, manganese, zinc, barite, sulphur, coal, emeralds, turquoise. **Crude oil reserves** (1985): 37.00 bln. bbls. **Other resources:** Gums, wool, silk, caviar. **Arable land:** 9%. **Meat prod.** (1985): cattle: 8.3 mln.; sheep: 34.5 mln. **Electricity prod.** (1984): 37.1 bln. kwh. **Crude steel prod.** (1985) 1.2 mln. metric tons. **Labor force:** 40% agric.; 33% ind. & comm; 27% services.

Finance: Currency: Rial (Mar. 1987: 71.7 = $1 US). **Gross national product** (1984): $162 bln. **Per capita income** (1977): $2,160. **Imports** (1985): $11.6 bln.; partners: W. Ger. 16%, Jap. 13%, UK 6%. **Exports** (1985): $13.1 bln.; partners: Jap. 16%, It. 10%. **National budget** (1983): $33.3 bln. expenditures. **Consumer prices** (change in 1985) 4.4%.

Transport: Motor vehicles: in use (1981): 1.5 mln. passenger cars, 313,000 comm. vehicles. **Chief ports:** Bandar Abbas.

Communications: Television sets: 2.1 mln. in use (1985). **Radios:** 10 mln. in use (1985). **Telephones in use** (1983): 2.1 mln. **Daily newspaper circ.** (1984): 22 per 1,000 pop.

Health: Life expectancy at birth (1985): 58.0 male; 58.3 female. **Births** (per 1,000 pop. 1985): 43. **Deaths** (per 1,000 pop. 1985): 12. **Natural increase** (1985): 3.1%. **Hospital beds** (1983): 67,734. **Physicians** (1983): 15,945. **Infant mortality** (per 1,000 live births 1985): 112.

Education (1980): **Literacy:** 48%.

Major International Organizations: UN (IMF, WHO), OPEC.

Iran was once called Persia. The Iranians, who supplanted an earlier agricultural civilization, came from the E during the 2d millenium BC; they were an Indo-European group related to the Aryans of India.

In 549 BC Cyrus the Great united the Medes and Persians in the Persian Empire, conquered Babylonia in 538 BC, restored Jerusalem to the Jews. Alexander the Great conquered Persia in 333 BC, but Persians regained their independence in the next century under the Parthians, themselves succeeded by Sassanian Persians in 226 AD. Arabs brought Islam to Persia in the 7th century, replacing the indigenous Zoroastrian faith. After Persian political and cultural autonomy was reasserted in the 9th century, the arts and sciences flourished for several centuries.

Turks and Mongols ruled Persia in turn from the 11th century to 1502, when a native dynasty reasserted full independence. The British and Russian empires vied for influence in the 19th century, and Afghanistan was severed from Iran by Britain in 1857.

The previous dynasty was founded by Reza Khan, a military leader, in 1925. He abdicated as shah in 1941, and was succeeded by his son, Mohammad Reza Pahlavi.

Parliament, under Premier Mohammed Mossadegh, nationalized the oil industry in 1951, leading to a British blockade. Mossadegh was overthrown in 1953; the shah assumed control. Under his rule, Iran underwent economic and social change but political opposition was not tolerated.

Conservative Moslem protests led to 1978 violence. Martial law in 12 cities was declared Sept. 8. A military government was appointed Nov. 6 to deal with striking oil workers. Prime Min. Shahpur Bakhtiar was designated by the shah to head a regency council in his absence. The shah left Iran Jan. 16, 1979.

Exiled religious leader Ayatollah Ruhollah Khomeini named a provisional government council in preparation for his return to Iran, Jan. 31. Clashes between Khomeini's supporters and government troops culminated in a rout of Iran's elite Imperial Guard Feb. 11, leading to the fall of Bakhtiar's government.

The Iranian revolution was marked by revolts among the ethnic minorities and by a continuing struggle between the clerical forces and westernized intellectuals and liberals. The Islamic Constitution established final authority to be vested in a Faghi, the Ayatollah Khomeini.

Iranian militants seized the U.S. embassy, Nov. 4, 1979, and took hostages including 62 Americans. The militants vowed to stay in the embassy until the deposed shah was returned to Iran. Despite international condemnations and U.S. efforts, including an abortive Apr., 1980, rescue attempt, the crisis continued. The U.S. broke diplomatic relations with Iran, Apr. 7th. The shah died in Egypt, July 27th. The hostage drama finally ended Jan. 21, 1981 when an accord, involving the release of frozen Iranian assets, was reached.

The ruling Islamic Party, increasingly dissatisfied with President Abolhassan Bani-Sadr, declared him unfit for office. In the weeks following Bani-Sadr's dismissal, June 22, 1981, a new wave of executions began. The political upheavals have brought Iran to almost total isolation from other countries.

A dispute over the Shatt al-Arab waterway that divides the two countries brought Iran and Iraq, Sept. 22, 1980, into open warfare. Iraqi planes attacked Iranian air fields including Teheran airport. Iranian planes bombed Iraqi bases. Iraqi troops occupied Iranian territory including the port city of Khorramshahr in October. Iranian troops recaptured the city and drove Iraqi troops back across the border, May 1982. Iraq, and later Iran, attacked several oil tankers in the Persian Gulf during 1984. Saudi Arabian war planes shot down 2 Iranian jets, June 5, which they felt were threatening Saudi shipping.

Iran and Iraw continued to fight to a standstill in 1987.

In Nov. 1986, senior U.S. officials secretly visited Iran and exchanged arms for Iran's help in obtaining the release of U.S. hostages held by terrorists in Lebanon. (*See Chronology.*)

Iraq

Republic of Iraq

al Jumhouriya al 'Iraqia

People: Population (1986 est.): 16,019,000. **Age distrib.** (%): 0–14: 45.7; 15–59: 49.0; 60+: 5.3. **Pop. density:** 94 per sq. mi. **Urban** (1982): 68.0%. **Ethnic groups:** Arabs, 75% Kurds, 15% Turks. **Languages:** Arabic (official), Kurdish, others. **Religions:** Moslems 95% (Shiites 55%, Sunnis 40%), Christians 5%.

Geography: Area: 167,924 sq. mi., larger than California. **Location:** In the Middle East, occupying most of historic Mesopotamia. **Neighbors:** Jordan, Syria on W, Turkey on N, Iran on E, Kuwait, Saudi Arabia on S. **Topography:** Mostly an alluvial plain, including the Tigris and Euphrates rivers, descending from mountains in N to desert in SW. Persian Gulf region is marshland. **Capital:** Baghdad. **Cities** (1985 est.): Baghdad (met.) 3,400,000.

Government: Type: Ruling council. **Head of state:** Pres. Saddam Hussein At-Takriti, b. 1935 in office: July 16, 1979. **Local divisions:** 18 provinces. **Defense:** 47% of GNP (1983).

Economy: Industries: Textiles, petrochemicals, oil refining, cement. **Chief crops:** Grains, rice, dates, cotton. **Minerals:** Oil, gas. **Crude oil reserves** (1985): 38 bln. bbls. **Other resources:**

Wool, hides. **Arable land:** 13%. **Meat prod.** (1984): cattle: 3 mln.; sheep 8.3 mln. **Electricity prod.** (1987): 14.5 bln. kwh. **Labor force:** 50% agric.

Finance: Currency: Dinar (Mar. 1987: 0.30 = $1 US). **Gross national product** (1981): $31 bln. **Per capita income** (1981): $2,410. **Imports** (1985): $10.5 bln.; partners: W. Ger. 16%, Jap. 14%, Fr. 7%. **Exports** (1984): $11.7 bln.; partners: It. 13%, Tur. 11%, Braz. 22%, Jap. 6%. **Consumer prices** (change in 1984): 25%

Transport: Railway traffic (1983): 54 mln. passenger-km; 1.1 bln. net ton-km. **Motor vehicles:** in use (1982): 229,000 passenger cars, 118,700 comm. vehicles. **Civil aviation** (1982): 1.7 bln. passenger-km; 54.7 mln. freight ton-km. **Chief ports:** Basra.

Communications: Television sets: 634,000 in use (1985). **Radios:** 2.2 mln. in use (1985). **Telephones in use** (1983): 624,000. **Daily newspaper circ.** (1985): 21 per 1,000 pop.

Health: Life expectancy at birth (1985): 55.9 male; 59.1 female. **Births** (per 1,000 pop. 1985): 45.1. **Deaths** (per 1,000 pop. 1985): 11.5. **Natural increase** (1985): 3.3%. **Hospital beds** (1982): 24,772. **Physicians** (1982): 7,634. **Infant mortality** (per 1,000 live births 1985): 80.

Major International Organizations: UN (IMF, WHO, ILO), Arab League, OPEC.

Education (1984): **Literacy:** 70%. Compulsory to age 10.

The Tigris-Euphrates valley, formerly called Mesopotamia, was the site of one of the earliest civilizations in the world. The Sumerian city-states of 3,000 BC originated the culture later developed by the Semitic Akkadians, Babylonians, and Assyrians.

Mesopotamia ceased to be a separate entity after the conquests of the Persians, Greeks, and Arabs. The latter founded Baghdad, from where the caliph ruled a vast empire in the 8th and 9th centuries. Mongol and Turkish conquests led to a decline in population, the economy, cultural life, and the irrigation system.

Britain secured a League of Nations mandate over Iraq after World War I. Independence under a king came in 1932. A leftist, pan-Arab revolution established a republic in 1958, which oriented foreign policy toward the USSR. Most industry has been nationalized, and large land holdings broken up.

A local faction of the international Baath Arab Socialist party has ruled by decree since 1968. Russia and Iraq signed an aid pact in 1972, and arms were sent along with several thousand advisers. The 1978 execution of 21 communists and a shift of trade to the West signalled a more neutral policy, straining relations with the USSR. In the 1973 Arab-Israeli war Iraq sent forces to aid Syria. Within a month of assuming power, Saddam Hussein instituted a bloody purge in the wake of a reported coup attempt against the new regime.

Years of battling with the Kurdish minority resulted in total defeat for the Kurds in 1975, when Iran withdrew support. Kurdish rebels continued their war, 1979; fighting led to Iraqi bombing of Kurdish villages in Iran, causing relations with Iran to deteriorate.

After skirmishing intermittently for 10 months over the sovereignty of the disputed Shatt al-Arab waterway that divides the two countries, Iraq and Iran, Sept. 22, 1980, entered into open warfare when Iraqi fighter-bombers attacked 10 Iranian airfields, including Teheran airport, and Iranian planes retaliated with strikes on 2 Iraqi bases. In the following days, there was heavy ground fighting around Abadan and the adjacent port of Khorramshahr as Iraq pressed its attack on Iran's oil-rich province of Khuzistan. In May 1982, Iraqi troops were driven back across the border. A fierce border war continued through 1985 with both sides suffering heavy casualties.

Israeli airplanes destroyed a nuclear reactor near Baghdad on June 7, 1981, claiming that it could be used to produce nuclear weapons.

Iraq and Iran expanded their war to the Persian Gulf in Apr. 1984. Several attacks on oil tankers were reported. An Iraqi warplane launched a missile attack on the U.S.S. *Stark*, a U.S. Navy frigate on patrol in the Persian Gulf, May 17, 1987; 37 U.S. sailors died. Iraq apologized for the attack claiming it was inadvertent. (*See Chronology.*)

The bloody war with Iran continued to be fought to a standstill in 1987; Iraq's superiority in equipment was matched by Iran's three-to-one advantage in population.

Ireland

People: Population (1986 est.): 3,624,000. **Age distrib. (%):** 0–14: 30.5; 15–59: 54.5; 60+:15.0. **Pop. density:** 133 per sq. mi. **Urban** (1985): 57%. **Ethnic groups:** Celtic, English minority. **Languages:** English predominates, Irish (Gaelic) spoken by minority. **Religions:** Roman Catholic 94%, Anglican 4%.

Geography: Area: 27,137 sq. mi. slightly larger than W. Va. **Location:** In the Atlantic O. just W of Great Britain. **Neighbors:** United Kingdom (Northern Ireland). **Topography:** Ireland consists of a central plateau surrounded by isolated groups of hills and mountains. The coastline is heavily indented by the Atlantic O. **Capital:** Dublin. **Cities** (1985 est.): Dublin 502,000; Cork (met.) 133,000.

Government: Type: Parliamentary republic. **Head of State:** Pres. Patrick J. Hillery; b. May 2, 1923; in office: Dec. 3, 1976. **Head of government:** Prime Min. Charles Haughey; in office: Mar. 10, 1987. **Local divisions:** 26 counties. **Defense:** 2% of GNP (1985).

Economy: Industries: Food processing, auto assembly, metals, textiles, chemicals, brewing, electrical and non-electrical machinery, tourism. **Chief crops:** Potatoes, grain, sugar beets, fruits, vegetables. **Minerals:** Zinc, lead, silver, gas. **Arable land:** 17%. **Meat prod.** (1985): cattle: 5.7 mln.; pigs: 994,000; sheep: 2.7 mln. **Fish catch** (1983): 203,000 metric tons. **Electricity prod.** (1984): 11.5 bln. kwh. **Crude steel prod.** (1981): 32,000 metric tons. **Labor force:** 16% agric.; 29% ind.; 31% services.

Finance: Currency: Pound (May 1987: 0.66 = $1 US). **Gross national product** (1986): $21.3 bln. **Per capita income** (1986): $6,000. **Imports** (1986): $11.6 bln.; partners: UK 48%, U.S. 13%, W. Ger. 8%, Fr. 5%. **Exports** (1986): $12.6 bln.; partners: UK 39%, Fr. 9%, W. Ger. 9%, U.S. 7%. **Tourists** (1984); receipts: $461 mln. **National budget** (1984): $6.2 bln. expenditures. **International reserves less gold** (Feb. 1987): $3.5 bln. **Gold:** 359,000 oz. t. **Consumer prices** (change in 1986): 3.8%.

Transport: Railway traffic (1984): 816 mln. passenger-km; 552 mln. net ton-km. **Motor vehicles:** in use (1984): 711,000 passenger cars, 88,000 comm. vehicles. **Civil aviation:** (1985): 2.4 bln. passenger-km; 85 mln. freight ton-km. **Chief ports:** Dublin, Cork.

Communications: Television sets: 851,000 receivers (1985). **Radios:** 2 mln. receivers (1985). **Telephones in use** (1984): 640,000. **Daily newspaper circ.** (1983): 266 per 1,000 pop.

Health: Life expectancy at birth (1986): 70.1 male; 75.6 female. **Births** (per 1,000 pop. 1986): 19. **Deaths** (per 1,000 pop. 1985): 9. **Natural increase** (1985): .1%. **Hospital beds** (1980): 33,028. **Physicians** (1984): 4,250 **Infant mortality** (per 1,000 live births 1986): 10.5

Education (1986): **Literacy:** 99%. **Years compulsory:** 9; attendance 91%.

Major International Organizations: UN (GATT, IMF, World Bank), EC, OECD.

Embassy: 2234 Massachusetts Ave. NW 20008; 462-3939.

Celtic tribes invaded the islands about the 4th century BC; their Gaelic culture and literature flourished and spread to Scotland and elsewhere in the 5th century AD, the same century in which St. Patrick converted the Irish to Christianity. Invasions by Norsemen began in the 8th century, ended with defeat of the Danes by the Irish King Brian Boru in 1014. English invasions started in the 12th century; for over 700 years the Anglo-Irish struggle continued with bitter rebellions and savage repressions.

The Easter Monday Rebellion (1916) failed but was followed by guerrilla warfare and harsh reprisals by British troops, the "Black and Tans." The Dail Eireann, or Irish parliament, reaffirmed independence in Jan. 1919. The British offered dominion status to Ulster (6 counties) and southern Ireland (26 counties) Dec. 1921. The constitution of the Irish Free State, a British dominion, was adopted Dec. 11, 1922. Northern Ireland remained part of the United Kingdom.

A new constitution adopted by plebiscite came into operation Dec. 29, 1937. It declared the name of the state Eire in the Irish language (Ireland in the English) and declared it a sovereign democratic state.

On Dec. 21, 1948, an Irish law declared the country a republic rather than a dominion and withdrew it from the Commonwealth. The British Parliament recognized both actions, 1949, but reasserted its claim to incorporate the 6 northeastern counties in the United Kingdom. This claim has not been recognized by Ireland. *(See United Kingdom — Northern Ireland.)*

Irish governments have favored peaceful unification of all Ireland. Ireland cooperated with England against terrorist groups.

Ireland has suffered economic hardship in the 1980's; unemployment reached 18% in 1987.

Israel

State of Israel

Medinat Israel

People: Population (1986 est.): 4,208,000. **Age distrib.** (%): 0–14: 32.6; 15–59: 55.0; 60+: 12.4. **Pop. density:** 548 per sq. mi. **Urban** (1983): 86%. **Ethnic groups:** Jewish 83%, Arab 16% **Languages:** Hebrew and Arabic (official), Yiddish, various European and West Asian languages. **Religions:** Jewish 83%, Moslem 13%

Geography: Area: 7,847 sq. mi. about the size of New Jersey. **Location:** On eastern end of Mediterranean Sea. **Neighbors:** Lebanon on N, Syria, Jordan on E, Egypt on W. **Topography:** The Mediterranean coastal plain is fertile and well-watered. In the center is the Judean Plateau. A triangular-shaped semi-desert region, the Negev, extends from south of Beersheba to an apex at the head of the Gulf of Aqaba. The eastern border drops sharply into the Jordan Rift Valley, including Lake Tiberias (Sea of Galilee) and the Dead Sea, which is 1,296 ft. below sea level, lowest point on the earth's surface. **Capital:** Jerusalem. Most countries maintain their embassy in Tel Aviv. **Cities** (1983 est.): Jerusalem 431,000; Tel Aviv-Yafo 330,000; Haifa 227,000.

Government: Type: Parliamentary democracy. **Head of state:** Pres. Chaim Herzog; b. Sept. 17, 1918; in office: May 5, 1983. **Head of government:** Prime Min. Yitzhak Shamir; b. 1915; in office: Oct. 20, 1986. **Local divisions:** 6 administrative districts. **Defense:** 24.4% of GNP (1984).

Economy: Industries: Diamond cutting, textiles, electronics, machinery, plastics, tires, drugs, aircraft, munitions, wine. **Chief crops:** Citrus fruit, grains, olives, cotton, vegetables. **Minerals:** Potash, limestone, copper, phosphates, magnesium, manganese, salt, sulphur. **Crude oil reserves** (1980): 1.0 mln. bbls. **Arable land:** 21%. **Meat prod.** (1980): beef: 21,000 metric tons; pork: 13,000 metric tons. **Fish catch** (1984): 22,000 metric tons. **Electricity prod.** (1984): 14.9 bln. kwh. **Crude steel prod.** (1981): 114,000 metric tons. **Labor force:** 6% agric.; 23% ind., 30% public services.

Finance: Currency: Shekel (May 1987: 1.58 = $1 US). **GNP** (1984): $21 bln. **Per capita income** (1983): $5,609. **Imports** (1985): $8.3 bln.; partners: U.S. 21%, W. Ger. 11%, UK 9%. **Exports** (1985): $6.2 bln.; partners: U.S. 34%, W. Ger. 5%, UK 7%. **Tourists** (1985): receipts $1.1 bln. **National budget** (1985): $23 bln. expenditures. **International reserves less gold** (Jan. 1987): $5.7 bln. **Gold:** 1.01 mln. oz t. **Consumer prices** (change in 1986): 48.1%.

Transport: Railway traffic (1986): 205 mln. passenger-km; 942 mln. net ton-km. **Motor vehicles:** in use (1984): 599,000 passenger cars, 125,000 comm. vehicles. **Civil aviation** (1985): 542 mln. passenger-km; 49 mln. freight ton-km. **Chief ports:** Haifa, Ashdod, Eilat.

Communications: Television sets: 606,000 in use (1985). **Radios:** 400,000 (1985). **Telephones in use** (1984): 1.4 mln. **Daily newspaper circ.** (1985): 196 per 1,000 pop.

Health: Life expectancy at birth (1984) Jewish pop. only 72.1 male; 75.7 female. **Births** (per 1,000 pop. 1985): 23.2. **Deaths** (per 1,000 pop. 1985): 7%. **Natural increase** (1985): 1.6%. **Hospital beds** (1983): 26,402. **Physicians** (1983): 9,000. **Infant mortality** (per 1,000 live births 1985): 13.

Education (1984): **Literacy:** 88% (Jewish), 48% (Arab).

Major International Organizations: UN (GATT).

Embassy: 3541 International Dr. NW 20008; 364-5500.

Occupying the SW corner of the ancient Fertile Crescent, Israel contains some of the oldest known evidence of agriculture and of primitive town life. A more advanced civilization emerged in the 3d millenium BC. The Hebrews probably arrived early in the 2d millenium BC. Under King David and his successors (c.1000 BC-597 BC), Judaism was developed and secured. After conquest by Babylonians, Persians, and Greeks, an independent Jewish kingdom was revived, 168 BC, but Rome took effective control in the next century, suppressed Jewish revolts in 70 AD and 135 AD, and renamed Judea Palestine, after the earlier coastal inhabitants, the Philistines.

Arab invaders conquered Palestine in 636. The Arabic language and Islam prevailed within a few centuries, but a Jewish minority remained. The land was ruled from the 11th century as a part of non-Arab empires by Seljuks, Mamluks, and Ottomans (with a crusader interval, 1098-1291).

After 4 centuries of Ottoman rule, during which the population declined to a low of 350,000 (1785), the land was taken in 1917 by Britain, which in the Balfour Declaration that year pledged to support a Jewish national homeland there, as foreseen by the Zionists. In 1920 a British Palestine Mandate was recognized; in 1922 the land east of the Jordan was detached.

Jewish immigration, begun in the late 19th century, swelled in the 1930s with refugees from the Nazis; heavy Arab immigration from Syria and Lebanon also occurred. Arab opposition to Jewish immigration turned violent in 1920, 1921, 1929, and 1936. The UN General Assembly voted in 1947 to partition Palestine into an Arab and a Jewish state. Britain withdrew in May 1948.

Israel was declared an independent state May 14, 1948; the Arabs rejected partition. Egypt, Jordan, Syria, Lebanon, Iraq, and Saudi Arabia invaded, but failed to destroy the Jewish state, which gained territory. Separate armistices with the Arab nations were signed in 1949; Jordan occupied the West Bank, Egypt occupied Gaza, but neither granted Palestinian autonomy. No peace settlement was obtained, and the Arab nations continued policies of economic boycott, blockade in the Suez Canal, and support of guerrillas. Several hundred thousand Arabs left the area of Jewish control; an equal number of Jews left the Arab countries for Israel 1949-53.

After persistent terrorist raids, Israel invaded Egypt's Sinai, Oct. 29, 1956, aided briefly by British and French forces. A UN cease-fire was arranged Nov. 6.

An uneasy truce between Israel and the Arab countries, supervised by a UN Emergency Force, prevailed until May 19, 1967, when the UN force withdrew at the demand of Egypt's Pres. Nasser. Egyptian forces reoccupied the Gaza Strip and closed the Gulf of Aqaba to Israeli shipping. In a 6-day war that started June 5, the Israelis took the Gaza Strip, occupied the Sinai Peninsula to the Suez Canal, and captured Old Jerusalem, Syria's Golan Heights, and Jordan's West Bank. The fighting was halted June 10 by UN-arranged cease-fire agreements.

Egypt and Syria attacked Israel, Oct. 6, 1973 (Yom Kippur, most solemn day on the Jewish calendar). Egypt and Syria were supplied by massive USSR military airlifts; the U.S. responded with an airlift to Israel. Israel counter-attacked, driving the Syrians back, and crossed the Suez Canal.

A cease fire took effect Oct. 24; a UN peace-keeping force went to the area. A disengagement agreement was signed Jan. 18, 1974. Israel withdrew from the canal's W bank. A second withdrawal was completed in 1976; Israel returned the Sinai to Egypt in 1982.

Israel and Syria agreed to disengage June 1; Israel completed withdrawing from its salient (and a small part of the land taken in the 1967 war) June 25.

In the wake of the war, Golda Meir, long Israel's premier, resigned; severe inflation gripped the nation. Palestinian guerrillas staged massacres, killing scores of civilians 1974-75. Israel aided Christian forces in the 1975-76 Lebanese civil war.

Israeli forces raided Entebbe, Uganda, July 3, 1976, and rescued 103 hostages seized by Arab and German terrorists.

In 1977, the conservative opposition, led by Menachem Begin, was voted into office for the first time. Egypt's Pres. Sadat visited Jerusalem Nov. 1977 and on Mar. 26, 1979. Egypt and Israel signed a formal peace treaty, ending 30 years of war, and establishing diplomatic relations.

Israel invaded S. Lebanon, March 1978, following a Lebanon-based terrorist attack in Israel. Israel withdrew in favor of a 6,000-man UN force, but continued to aid Christian militiamen.

A 5-day occupation of Israeli forces in southern Lebanon took place April 1980, in retaliation to the Palestinian raid on a kibbutz earlier that month. Violence on the Israeli-occupied West Bank rose in 1982 when Israel announced plans to build new Jewish settlements.

Israel affirmed the entire city of Jerusalem as its capital, July, 1980, encompassing the annexed Arab East Jerusalem.

Israel shot down, Apr. 28, 1981, two Syrian helicopters Israel claimed were attacking Lebanese Christian militia forces in the Beirut-Zahle area of Lebanon. Syria responded by installing Soviet-built surface-to-air missiles in Lebanon. Both the U.S. and Israel were unable to persuade Syria to withdraw the missles, and Israel threatened to destroy them.

On June 7, 1981, Israeli jets destroyed an Iraqi atomic reactor near Baghdad that, Israel claimed, would have enabled Iraq to manufacture nuclear weapons.

In a close election, June 30, 1981, Prime Min. Menachem Begin was able to assemble a narrow coalition, he survived a no confidence motion in the Knesset by one vote, May 1982. He retired Oct. 1983.

Israeli jets bombed Palestine Liberation Organization (PLO) strongholds in Lebanon April, May 1982. In reaction to the wounding of the Israeli ambassador to Great Britain, Israeli forces in a coordinated land, sea, and air attack invaded Lebanon, June 6, to destroy PLO strongholds in that country. Israeli and Syrian forces engaged in the Bekka Valley, June 9, but quickly agreed to a truce. Israeli forces encircled Beirut June 14. Following massive Israeli bombing of West Beirut, the PLO agreed to evacuate the city.

Israeli troops entered West Beirut after newly-elected Lebanese president Bashir Gemayel was assassinated on Sept. 14. Israel received widespread condemnation when Lebanese Christian forces, Sept. 16, entered 2 West Beirut refugee camps and slaughtered hundreds of Palestinian refugees. Israeli troops withdrew from Lebanon in June 1986.

Italy

Italian Republic

Repubblica Italiana

People: Population (1986 est.): 57,226,000. **Age distrib.** (%): 0–14: 19.9; 15–59: 61.3; 60+: 18.8. **Pop. density:** 492 per sq. mi. **Urban** (1985): 71%. **Ethnic groups:** Italians, small minorities of Germans, Slovenes, Albanians, French, Ladins, Greeks. **Languages:** Italian. **Religions:** Predominantly Roman Catholic.

Geography: Area: 116,303 sq. mi., about the size of Florida and Georgia combined. **Location:** In S Europe, jutting into Mediterranean S. **Neighbors:** France on W, Switzerland, Austria on N, Yugoslavia on E. **Topography:** Occupies a long boot-shaped peninsula, extending SE from the Alps into the Mediterranean, with the islands of Sicily and Sardinia offshore. The alluvial Po Valley drains most of N. The rest of the country is rugged and mountainous, except for intermittent coastal plains, like the Campajna, S of Rome. Appenine Mts. run down through center of peninsula. **Capital:** Rome. **Cities** (1985 est.): Rome 2.8 mln.; Milan 1.5 mln.; Naples 1.2 mln.; Turin 1.0 mln.

Government: Type: Republic. **Head of state:** Pres. Francesco Cossiga; b. July 26, 1929; in office: July 9, 1985; **Head of government:** Prime Min. Giovanni Goria; b. July 30, 1943; in office: July 28, 1987. **Local divisions:** 20 regions with some autonomy, 94 provinces. **Defense:** 2.5% of GNP (1986).

Economy: Industries: Steel, machinery, autos, textiles, shoes, machine tools, chemicals. **Chief crops:** Grapes, olives, citrus fruits, vegetables, wheat, rice. **Minerals:** Mercury, potash, gas, marble, sulphur, coal. **Crude oil reserves** (1985): 598 mln. bbls. **Arable land:** 41%. **Meat prod.** (1985): cattle: 8.9 mln.; pigs: 9.1 mln.; sheep: 9.6 mln. **Fish catch** (1984): 428,000 metric tons. **Electricity prod.** (1984): 188 bln. kwh. **Crude steel prod.** (1984): 23.7 mln. metric tons. **Labor force:** 10% agric.; 30% ind. and comm.; 60% services and govt.

Finance: Currency: Lira (June 1987: 1,291 = $1 US). **Gross national product** (1986): $368 bln. **Per capita income** (1986): $6,447. **Imports** (1986): $99.9 bln.; partners: W. Ger. 16%, Fr. 12%, U.S. 7%. **Exports** (1986): $97.8 bln.; partners: W. Ger. 16%, Fr. 15%, U.S. 7%, UK 6%. **Tourists** (1984): receipts $8.5 bln. **National budget** (1983): $173 bln. expenditures. **International reserves less gold** (Apr. 1987): $25 bln. **Gold:** 66.67 mln. oz t. **Consumer prices** (change in 1986): 5.9%.

Transport: Railway traffic (1985): 24.3 bln. passenger-km; 18.1 bln. net ton-km. **Motor vehicles:** in use (1984): 20.4 mln. passenger cars, 1.7 mln. comm. **Civil aviation** (1985): 14.5 bln. passenger-km; 780 mln. freight ton-km. **Chief ports:** Genoa, Venice, Trieste, Taranto, Naples, La Spezia.

Communications: Television sets: 13.9 mln. in use (1985). **Radios:** 14 mln. in use (1984). **Telephones in use** (1983): 21.6 mln. **Daily newspaper circ.** (1985): 109 per 1,000 pop.

Health: Life expectancy at birth (1983): 73.0 male; 79.1 female. **Births** (per 1,000 pop. 1985): 10.0. **Deaths** (per 1,000 pop. 1985): 10.0. **Natural increase** (1985): .0%. **Hospital beds** (1983): 500,828. **Physicians** (1981): 97,003. **Infant mortality** (per 1,000 live births 1985): 12.

Education (1985): **Literacy:** 97%. **Years compulsory:** 8.

Major International Organizations: UN and all of its specialized agencies, NATO, OECD, EC.

Embassy: 1601 Fuller St. NW 20009; 328-5500.

Rome emerged as the major power in Italy after 500 BC, dominating the more civilized Etruscans to the N and Greeks to the S. Under the Empire, which lasted until the 5th century AD, Rome ruled most of Western Europe, the Balkans, the Near East, and North Africa.

After the Germanic invasions, lasting several centuries, a high civilization arose in the city-states of the N, culminating in the Renaissance. But German, French, Spanish, and Austrian intervention prevented the unification of the country. In 1859 Lombardy came under the crown of King Victor Emmanuel II of Sardinia. By plebiscite in 1860, Parma, Modena, Romagna, and Tuscany joined, followed by Sicily and Naples, and by the Marches and Umbria. The first Italian parliament declared Victor Emmanuel king of Italy Mar. 17, 1861. Mantua and Venetia were added in 1866 as an outcome of the Austro-Prussian war. The Papal States were taken by Italian troops Sept. 20, 1870, on the withdrawal of the French garrison. The states were annexed to the kingdom by plebiscite. Italy recognized the State of Vatican City as independent Feb. 11, 1929.

Fascism appeared in Italy Mar. 23, 1919, led by Benito Mussolini, who took over the government at the invitation of the king Oct. 28, 1922. Mussolini acquired dictatorial powers. He made war on Ethiopia and proclaimed Victor Emmanuel III emperor, defied the sanctions of the League of Nations, joined the Berlin-Tokyo axis, sent troops to fight for Franco against the Republic of Spain and joined Germany in World War II.

After Fascism was overthrown in 1943, Italy declared war on Germany and Japan and contributed to the Allied victory. It surrendered conquered lands and lost its colonies. Mussolini was killed by partisans Apr. 28, 1945.

Victor Emmanuel III abdicated May 9, 1946, his son Humbert II was king until June 10, when Italy became a republic after a referendum, June 2-3.

Reorganization of the Fascist party is forbidden. The cabinet normally represents a coalition of the Christian Democrats, largest of Italy's many parties, and one or 2 other parties.

The Vatican agreed in 1976 to revise its 1929 concordat with the state, depriving Roman Catholicism of its status as state religion. In 1974 Italians voted by a 3-to-2 margin to retain a 3-year-old law permitting divorce, which was opposed by the church.

Italy has enjoyed an extraordinary growth in industry and living standards since World War II, in part due to membership in the Common Market. Italy joined the European Monetary System, 1980. A wave of left-wing political violence began in the late 1970s with kidnappings and assassinations and continued through the 1980s. Christian Dem. leader and former Prime Min. Moro was murdered May 1978 by Red Brigade terrorists.

U.S. Brig. Gen. James Dozier, a senior NATO officer, was kidnapped by terrorists in 1981, but was later rescued by Italian police.

The Cabinet of Prime Min. Arnaldo Forlani resigned, May 26, 1981, in the wake of revelations that numerous high-ranking officials were members of an illegally secret Masonic lodge. The June 1983 elections saw Bettino Craxi chosen the nation's first Socialist premier. Craxi's government faced a severe crisis as the result of a chain of events sparked by the Oct. 17, 1985 hijacking of the Italian cruise ship *Achille Lauro* and the subsequent U.S. downing on Italian soil of an Egyptian aircraft carrying the 4 hijackers and Abul Abbas, a PLO leader suspected of planning the hijacking. Craxi's release of Abbas and refusal to turn the 4 hijackers over to the U.S. caused an internal crisis that almost saw his government fall. Craxi ended the longest tenure of an Italian leader since World War II by resigning Mar. 1987.

Italy has accepted U.S. cruise missiles. Some 2,000 troops were contributed to the Lebanese peace-keeping force.

Sicily, 9,926 sq. mi., pop. (1985) 5,051,000, is an island 180 by 120 mi., seat of a region that embraces the island of **Pantel-**

leria, 32 sq. mi., and the **Lipari** group, 44 sq. mi., 63 14,000, including 2 active volcanoes: **Vulcano,** 1,637 ft. and **Stromboli,** 3,038 ft. From prehistoric times Sicily has been settled by various peoples; a Greek state had its capital at Syracuse. Rome took Sicily from Carthage 215 BC. **Mt. Etna,** 11,053 ft. active volcano, is tallest peak.

Sardinia, 9,301 sq. mi., pop. (1985) 1,628,000, lies in the Mediterranean, 115 mi. W of Italy and 7-½ mi. S of Corsica. It is 160 mi. long, 68 mi. wide, and mountainous, with mining of coal, zinc, lead, copper. In 1720 Sardinia was added to the possessions of the Dukes of Savoy in Piedmont and Savoy to form the Kingdom of Sardinia. Giuseppe Garibaldi is buried on the nearby isle of Caprera. **Elba,** 86 sq. mi., lies 6 mi. W of Tuscany. Napoleon I lived in exile on Elba 1814-1815.

Trieste. An agreement, signed Oct. 5, 1954, by Italy and Yugoslavia, confirmed, Nov. 10, 1975, gave Italy provisional administration over the northern section and the seaport of Trieste, and Yugoslavia the part of Istrian peninsula it has occupied.

Jamaica

People: Population (1986 est.): 2,288,000. **Age distrib.** (%): 0–14: 36.7; 15–59: 52.8; 60+: 8.5. **Pop. density:** 553 per sq. mi. **Urban** (1982): 46%. **Ethnic groups:** African 76%, mixed 15%, Chinese, Caucasians, East Indians. **Languages:** English, Jamaican Creole. **Religions:** Protestant 70%.

Geography: Area: 4,232 sq. mi., slightly smaller than Connecticut. **Location:** In West Indies. **Neighbors:** Nearest are Cuba on N, Haiti on E. **Topography:** The country is four-fifths covered by mountains. **Capital:** Kingston. **Cities** (1984 est.): St. Andrews 393,000, Kingston 100,000.

Government: Type: Constitutional monarchy. **Head of state:** Queen Elizabeth II, represented by Gov.-Gen. Florizel A. Glasspole; b. Sept. 25, 1909; in office: Mar. 2, 1973. **Head of government:** Prime Min. Edward Seaga; b. May 28, 1930; in office: Oct., 1980. **Local divisions:** 12 parishes; Kingston and St. Andrew corporate area. **Defense:** 1.1% of GDP (1986).

Economy: Industries: Rum, molasses, cement, paper, tourism. **Chief crops:** Sugar cane, coffee, bananas, coconuts, citrus fruits. **Minerals:** Bauxite, limestone, gypsum. **Arable land:** 24%. **Meat prod.** (1984): cattle: 318,000; goats: 420,000. **Electricity prod.** (1984): 2.4 bln. kwh. **Labor force:** 35% agric.; 19% services; 13% manuf.

Finance: Currency: Dollar (Apr. 1987: 5.48 = $1 US). **Gross national product** (1984): $2.4 bln. **Per capita income** (1981): $1,340. **Imports** (1986): $964 mln.; partners: U.S. 44%, Venez. 11%, Neth. Ant. 10%, UK 17%. **Exports** (1986): $596 mln.; partners: U.S. 33%, UK 17%, Can. 16%. **Tourists** (1985): 394,000; receipts: $399 mln. **National budget** (1986): $584 mln. **International reserves less gold** (Feb. 1987): $117 mln. **Consumer prices** (change in 1986): 15.1%.

Transport: Railway traffic (1984): 49 mln. passenger-km; 129 mln. net ton-km. **Motor vehicles:** in use (1983): 40,000 passenger cars, 20,000 comm. vehicles. **Civil aviation** (1985): 1.4 bln. passenger km.; 19.4 mln. freight ton-km. **Chief ports:** Kingston, Montego Bay.

Communications: Television sets: 215,000 in use (1985). **Radios:** 860,000 in use (1985). **Telephones in use** (1984): 136,000. **Daily newspaper circ.** (1985): 36 per 1,000 pop.

Health: Life expectancy at birth (1984): 65 years. **Births** (per 1,000 pop. 1985): 26. **Deaths** (per 1,000 pop. 1985): 6. **Natural increase** (1985): 2.0%. **Hospital beds** (1984): 6,066. **Physicians** (1985): 319. **Infant mortality** (per 1,000 live births 1986): 28.0.

Education (1987): **Literacy:** 73%. Compulsory to age 14.

Major International Organizations: UN (World Bank, GATT), OAS.

Embassy: 1850 K St. NW 20006; 452-0660.

Jamaica was visited by Columbus, 1494, and ruled by Spain (under whom Arawak Indians died out) until seized by Britain, 1655. Jamaica won independence Aug. 6, 1962.

In 1974 Jamaica sought an increase in taxes paid by U.S. and Canadian companies which mine bauxite on the island. The socialist government acquired 50% ownership of the companies' Jamaican interests in 1976, and was reelected that year. Rudimentary welfare state measures were passed, but unemployment increased. Relations with the U.S. improved greatly in the 1980s following the election of Edward Seaga. Jamaica has broken diplomatic relations with Cuba.

In 1982, Reagan became the first U.S. President to visit Jamaica and voiced strong support for the free-enterprise policies of the Seaga government. Jamaica took part in the October 1983 invasion of Grenada.

Japan

Nippon

People: Population (1986 est.): 121,402,000. **Age distrib.** (%): 0–14: 21.1; 15–59: 63.8; 60+: 15.1. **Pop. density:** 833 per sq. mi. **Urban** (1980): 76.2%. **Language:** Japanese. **Ethnic groups:** Japanese 99.4%, Korean 0.5%. **Religions:** Buddhism, Shintoism shared by large majority.

Geography: Area: 145,856 sq. mi., slightly smaller than California. **Location:** Archipelago off E. coast of Asia. **Neighbors:** USSR on N, S. Korea on W. **Topography:** Japan consists of 4 main islands: Honshu ("mainland"), 87,805 sq. mi.; Hokkaido, 30,144 sq. mi.; Kyushu, 14,114 sq. mi.; and Shikoku, 7,049 sq. mi. The coast, deeply indented, measures 16,654 mi. The northern islands are a continuation of the Sakhalin Mts. The Kunlun range of China continues into southern islands, the ranges meeting in the Japanese Alps. In a vast transverse fissure crossing Honshu E-W rises a group of volcanoes, mostly extinct or inactive, including 12,388 ft. Fuji-San (Fujiyama) near Tokyo. **Capital:** Tokyo. **Cities** (1986 est.): Tokyo 8.4 mln.; Osaka 2.6 mln.; Yokohama 3.0 mln.; Nagoya 2.1 mln.; Kyoto 1.4 mln.; Kobe 1.4 mln.; Sapporo 1.5 mln.; Kitakyushu 1 mln.; Kawasaki 1 mln; Fukuoka 1.1 mln.

Government: Type: Parliamentary democracy. **Head of state:** Emp. Hirohito; b. Apr. 29, 1901; in office: Dec. 25, 1926. **Head of government:** Prime Min. Yasuhiro Nakasone; b. May 27, 1918; in office: Nov. 26, 1982. **Local divisions:** 47 prefectures. **Defense:** Less than 1% of GNP (1984).

Economy: Industries: Electrical & electronic equip., autos, machinery, chemicals. **Chief crops:** Rice, grains, vegetables, fruits. **Minerals:** negligible. **Crude oil reserves** (1985): 26 mln. bbls. **Arable land:** 13%. **Meat prod.** (1985): cattle: 4.6 mln.; pigs: 10.3 mln. **Fish catch** (1985): 12.1 mln. metric tons. **Electricity prod.** (1985): 603 bln. kwh. **Crude steel prod.** (1985): 105.2 mln. metric tons. **Labor force:** 9% agric.; 34% manuf; 48% services.

Finance: Currency: Yen (May 1987: 140.05 = $1 US). **Gross national product** (1985): $1.3 trl. **Per capita income** (1984): $10,266. **Imports** (1986): $127 bln.; partners: U.S. 20%, Middle East 26%, SE Asia 22%, EC 6%. **Exports** (1986): $210 bln.; partners: U.S. 37%, EC 12%, SE Asia 23%. **Tourists** (1984): $416 mln. receipts. **National budget** (1987): $382 bln. expenditures. **International reserves less gold** (Mar. 1987): $58 bln. **Gold:** 24.60 mln. oz. t. **Consumer prices** (change in 1986): 0.6%.

Transport: Railway traffic (1984): 330 bln. passenger-km; 22.1 bln. net ton-km. **Motor vehicles:** in use (1986): 27.8 mln. passenger cars, 17.3 mln. **Civil aviation** (1985): 65.5 bln. passenger-km; 3.0 bln. freight ton-km. **Chief ports:** Yokohama, Tokyo, Kobe, Osaka, Nagoya, Chiba, Kawasaki, Hakodate.

Communications: Television sets: 30.2 mln. in use (1985). **Radios:** 94 mln. in use (1985). **Telephones in use** (1984): 66.6 mln. **Daily newspaper circ.** (1985): 569 per 1,000 pop.

Health: Life expectancy at birth (1984): 74.5 male; 80.2 female. **Births** (per 1,000 pop. 1985): 12. **Deaths** (per 1,000 pop. 1985): 6. **Natural increase** (1985): .06%. **Hospital beds** (1984): 1.4 mln. **Physicians** (1984): 181,000. **Infant mortality** (per 1,000 live births 1985): 6.0.

Education (1985): **Literacy:** 99%. Most attend school for 12 years.

Major International Organizations: UN (IMF, GATT, ILO), OECD.

Embassy: 2520 Massachusetts Ave. NW 20008; 939-6700.

According to Japanese legend, the empire was founded by Emperor Jimmu, 660 BC, but earliest records of a unified Japan date from 1,000 years later. Chinese influence was strong in the formation of Japanese civilization. Buddhism was introduced before the 6th century.

A feudal system, with locally powerful noble families and their samurai warrior retainers, dominated from 1192. Central power was held by successive families of shoguns (military dictators), 1192-1867, until recovered by the Emperor Meiji, 1868. The Portuguese and Dutch had minor trade with Japan in the 16th and

17th centuries; U.S. Commodore Matthew C. Perry opened it to U.S. trade in a treaty ratified 1854. Japan fought China, 1894-95, gaining Taiwan. After war with Russia, 1904-05, Russia ceded S half of Sakhalin and gave concessions in China. Japan annexed Korea 1910. In World War I Japan ousted Germany from Shantung, took over German Pacific islands. Japan took Manchuria 1931, started war with China 1932. Japan launched war against the U.S. by attack on Pearl Harbor Dec. 7, 1941. Japan surrendered Aug. 14, 1945.

In a new constitution adopted May 3, 1947, Japan renounced the right to wage war; the emperor gave up claims to divinity; the Diet became the sole law-making authority.

The U.S. and 48 other non-communist nations signed a peace treaty and the U.S. a bilateral defense agreement with Japan, in San Francisco Sept. 8, 1951, restoring Japan's sovereignty as of April 28, 1952. Japan signed separate treaties with China, 1952; India, 1952; a declaration with USSR ending a technical state of war, 1956. In Dec. 1965 Japan and South Korea agreed to resume diplomatic relations.

On June 26, 1968, the U.S. returned to Japanese control the Bonin Is., the Volcano Is. (including Iwo Jima) and Marcus Is. On May 15, 1972, Okinawa, the other Ryukyu Is. and the Daito Is. were returned to Japan by the U.S.; it was agreed the U.S. would continue to maintain military bases on Okinawa. Japan and the USSR have failed to resolve disputed claims of sovereignty over 4 of the Kurile Is. and over offshore fishing rights.

In 1972, Japan and China resumed diplomatic relations.

Industrialization was begun in the late 19th century. After World War II, Japan emerged as one of the most powerful economies in the world, and as a leader in technology.

The U.S. and EC member nations have criticized Japan for its restrictive policy on imports which has given Japan a substantial trade surplus.

Japan hosted an economic summit of the 7 major industrial democracies May 4-6, 1986; the 7 nations issued an antiterrorism declaration and established a framework for greater economic policy coordination.

In Apr. 1987, the U.S. imposed 100% tariffs on Japanese electronics imports in retaliation for what the U.S. considered various unfair trade practices.

Jordan

Hashemite Kingdom of Jordan

al Mamlaka al Urduniya al Hashemiyah

Population (1986 est.): 2,756,000. **Age distrib.** (%): 0–14: 48.1; 15–59: 46.9; 60+: 4.0. **Pop. density:** 80 per sq. mi. **Urban** (1985): 60%. **Ethnic groups:** Arabs, small minorities of Circassians, Armenians, Kurds. **Languages:** Arabic (official), English. **Religions:** Sunni Moslems 93.6%, Christians 5%.

Geography: Area: 37,737 sq. mi., slightly larger than Indiana. **Location:** In W Asia. **Neighbors:** Israel on W, Saudi Arabia on S, Iraq on E, Syria on N. **Topography:** About 88% of Jordan is arid. Fertile areas are in W. Only port is on short Aqaba Gulf coast. Country shares Dead Sea (1,296 ft. below sea level) with Israel. **Capital:** Amman. **Cities** (1985 est.): Amman 800,000; az-Zarqa 274,000; Irbid 144,000.

Government: Type: Constitutional monarchy. **Head of state:** King Hussein I; b. Nov. 14, 1935; in office: Aug. 11, 1952. **Head of government:** Prime Min. Zaid Rifai; b. 1937; in office: Apr. 4, 1985. **Local divisions:** 8 governorates. **Defense:** 12% of GNP (1985).

Economy: Industries: Textiles, cement, food processing. **Chief crops:** Grains, olives, vegetables, fruits. **Minerals:** Phosphate, potash. **Arable land:** 11%. **Electricity prod.** (1984): 2.2 bln. kwh. **Labor force:** 20% agric. 20% manuf. & mining.

Finance: Currency: Dinar (Mar. 1987: 0.33 = $1 US). **Gross national product** (1984): $4.2 bln. **Imports** (1985): $2.7 bln.; partners: Saudi Ar. 19%, U.S. 11%, Jap. 8%. **Exports** (1985): $789 mln.; partners: Saudi Ar. 12%, Ind. 13%, Iraq. 26%. **Tourists** (1984): receipts: $516 mln. **National budget** (1985): $2.2 bln. revenues; $1.68 bln. expenditures. **International reserves less gold** (Mar. 1987): $250 mln. **Gold:** 1.06 mln oz t. **Consumer prices** (change in 1985): 3.0%.

Transport: Motor vehicles: in use (1982): 118,900 passenger cars, 43,600 comm. vehicles. **Civil aviation** (1984): 3.6 bln. passenger-km; 139 mln. freight ton-km. **Chief ports:** Aqaba.

Communications: Television sets: 181,000 in use (1985). **Radios:** 550,000 in use (1985). **Telephones in use** (1983): 86,000. **Daily newspaper circ.** (1985): 68 per 1,000 pop.

Health: Life expectancy at birth (1985): 60.3 male; 64.2 female. **Births** (per 1,000 pop. 1985): 45.3. **Deaths** (per 1,000 pop. 1985): 9.1. **Natural increase** (1985): 3.6%. **Hospital beds** (1984): 3,578. **Physicians** (1984): 2,310. **Infant mortality** (per 1,000 live births 1985): 51.

Education (1980): **Literacy:** 31%.

Major International Organizations: UN (WHO, IMF), Arab League.

Embassy: 3405 International Dr. NW 20008; 966-2664.

From ancient times to 1922 the lands to the E of the Jordan were culturally and politically united with the lands to the W. Arabs conquered the area in the 7th century; the Ottomans took control in the 16th. Britain's 1920 Palestine Mandate covered both sides of the Jordan. In 1921, Abdullah, son of the ruler of Hejaz in Arabia, was installed by Britain as emir of an autonomous Transjordan, covering two-thirds of Palestine. An independent kingdom was proclaimed, 1946.

During the 1948 Arab-Israeli war the West Bank and old city of Jerusalem were added to the kingdom, which changed its name to Jordan. All these territories were lost to Israel in the 1967 war, which swelled the number of Arab refugees on the East Bank. A 1974 Arab summit conference designated the Palestine Liberation Organization as the sole representative of Arabs on the West Bank. Jordan accepted the move, and was granted an annual subsidy by Arab oil states. The U.S. has also provided substantial economic and military support.

King Hussein actively promoted rejection of the Egyptian-Israeli peace treaty; Jordan was the first Arab country to sever diplomatic relations with Egypt, Mar. 1979; relations were restored, Sept., 1984.

Kenya

Republic of Kenya

Jamhuri ya Kenya

People: Population (1986 est.): 21,044,000. **Age distrib.** (%): 0–14: 52.3; 15–59: 43.2; 60+: 4.5. **Pop. density:** 96 per sq. mi. **Urban** (1985): 16%. **Ethnic groups:** Kikuyu 21%, Luo 13%, Luhya 14%, Kalenjin 11%, Kamba 11%, others, including 280,000 Asians, Arabs, Europeans. **Languages:** Swahili (official), English. **Religions:** Protestants 38%, Roman Catholics 28%, Moslems 6%, others.

Geography: Area: 224,960 sq. mi., slightly smaller than Texas. **Location:** On Indian O. coast of E. Africa. **Neighbors:** Uganda on W, Tanzania on S, Somalia on E, Ethopia, Sudan on N. **Topography:** The northern three-fifths of Kenya is arid. To the S, a low coastal area and a plateau varying from 3,000 to 10,000 ft. The Great Rift Valley enters the country N-S, flanked by high mountains. **Capital:** Nairobi. **Cities** (1985): Nairobi (met.) 1.1 mln.; Mombasa (met.) 425,000.

Government: Type: Republic. **Head of state:** Pres. Daniel arap Moi, b. Sept., 1924; in office: Aug. 22, 1978. **Local divisions:** Nairobi and 7 provinces. **Defense:** 4.8% of GDP (1985).

Economy: Industries: Tourism, light industry. **Chief crops:** Coffee, corn, tea, cereals, cotton, sisal. **Minerals:** Gold, limestone, diatomite, salt, barytes, magnesite, felspar, sapphires, fluospar, garnets. **Other resources:** Timber, hides. **Arable land:** 4%. **Meat prod.** (1985): cattle: 12.5 mln. **Fish catch** (1984): 78,000 metric tons. **Electricity prod.** (1984): 1.9 bln. kwh. **Labor force:** 21% agric.; 21% ind. and commerce; 13% services; 47% public sector.

Finance: Currency: Shilling (Mar. 1987: 16.04 = $1 US). **Gross national product** (1984): $5.7 bln. **Per capita income** (1983): $309. **Imports** (1986): $1.6 bln.; partners: UK 14%, W. Ger. 8%, Jap. 8, Saudi Ar. 7%. **Exports** (1986): $1.2 bln.; partners: W. Ger. 11%, UK 18%, Ugan. 9%. **Tourists** (1984): receipts: $673 mln. **National budget** (1985): $2 bln. **International reserves less gold** (Mar. 1987): $442 mln. **Gold:** 80,000 oz t. **Consumer prices** (change in 1986): 4.0%.

Transport: Motor vehicles: in use (1983): 115,000 passenger cars, 90,000 comm. vehicles **Civil Aviation** (1984): 1.0 bln. passenger-km; 123 mln. freight ton-km. **Chief ports:** Mombasa.

Communications: Television sets: 100,000 in use (1985). **Radios:** 1.6 mln. in use (1985). **Telephones in use** (1983): 216,000. **Daily newspaper circ.** (1984): 16 per 1,000 pop.

Health: Life expectancy at birth (1983): 56.3 male; 60.0 female. **Births** (per 1,000 pop. 1985): 55.1. **Deaths** (per 1,000 pop. 1985): 14.0. **Natural increase** (1985): 4.1%. **Hospital beds** (1984): 30,886. **Physicians** (1984): 2,591. **Infant mortality** (per 1,000 live births 1985): 83.

Education (1985): **Literacy:** 50%. 83% attend primary school.

Major International Organizations: UN and all of its specialized agencies, OAU, Commonwealth of Nations.

Embassy: 2249 R St. NW 20008; 387-6101.

Arab colonies exported spices and slaves from the Kenya coast as early as the 8th century. Britain obtained control in the 19th century. Kenya won independence Dec. 12, 1963, 4 years after the end of the violent Mau Mau uprising.

Kenya has shown steady growth in industry and agriculture under a modified private enterprise system, and has had a relatively free political life. But stability was shaken in 1974-5, with opposition charges of corruption and oppression.

In 1968 ties with Somalia were restored after 4 years of skirmishes. Tanzania closed its Kenya border in 1977 in a dispute over the collapse of the East African Community.

Kenya has close ties to the West.

Kiribati

Republic of Kiribati

People: Population (1986 est.): 63,000. **Pop. density:** 234 per sq. mi. **Ethnic groups:** nearly all Micronesian, some Polynesians. **Languages:** Gilbertese and English (official). **Religions:** evenly divided between Protestant and Roman Catholic.

Geography: Area: 266 sq. mi., slightly smaller than New York City. **Location:** 33 Micronesian islands (the Gilbert, Line, and Phoenix groups) in the mid-Pacific scattered in a 2-mln. sq. mi. chain around the point where the International Date Line cuts the Equator. **Neighbors:** Nearest are Nauru to SW, Tuvalu and Tokelau Is. to S. **Topography:** except Banaba (Ocean) I., all are low-lying, with soil of coral sand and rock fragments, subject to erratic rainfall. **Capital** (1980): Tarawa 22,148.

Government: Head of state and of government: Pres. Ieremia Tabai, b. Dec. 16, 1950; in office: July 12, 1979.

Economy: Industries: Copra. **Chief crops:** Coconuts, breadfruit, pandanus, bananas, paw paw. **Other resources:** Fish. **Electricity prod.** (1983): 6 mln. kwh.

Finance: Currency: Australian dollar. **Gross national product** (1983): $30 mln. **Imports** (1981): $13.0 mln.; partners: Austral. 42%, NZ 7%, Jap. 13%. **Exports** (1981): $1.5 mln.; partners: S. Kor. 40%; Neth. 36%. **National budget** (1982): $11 mln. expenditures.

Transport: Chief port: Tarawa.

Communications: Radios: 10,000 in use (1985). **Telephones in use** (1984): 1,400.

Health: Hospital beds (1981): 307; **Physicians:** 16.

Education: Literacy (1982): 90%.

A British protectorate since 1892, the Gilbert and Ellice Islands colony was completed with the inclusion of the Phoenix Islands, 1937. Self-rule was granted 1971; the Ellice Islands separated from the colony 1975 and became independent Tuvalu, 1978. Kiribati (pronounced *Kiribass)* independence was attained July 12, 1979. Under a Treaty of Friendship the U.S. relinquished its claims to several of the Line and Phoenix islands, including Christmas, Canton, and Enderbury.

Tarawa Atoll was the scene of some of the bloodiest fighting in the Pacific during WW II.

North Korea

Democratic People's Republic of Korea

Chosun Minchu-chui Inmin Konghwa-guk

People: Population (1986 est.): 20,543,000. **Pop. density:** 434 per sq. mi. **Urban** (1985): 62%. **Ethnic groups:** Korean. **Languages:** Korean. **Religions:** activities discouraged, traditionally Buddhism, Confucianism, Chondokyo.

Geography: Area: 46,540 sq. mi., slightly smaller than Mississippi. **Location:** In northern E. Asia. **Neighbors:** China, USSR on N, S. Korea on S. **Topography:** Mountains and hills cover nearly all the country, with narrow valleys and small plains in between. The N and the E coast are the most rugged areas. **Capital:** Pyongyang. **Cities** (1981 est.): Pyongyang 1,283,000.

Government: Type: Communist state. **Head of state:** Pres. Kim Il-Sung; b. Apr. 15, 1912; in office: Dec. 28, 1972. **Head of government:** Premier Li Gunmo; in office: Dec. 29, 1986. **Head of Communist Party:** Gen. Sec. Kim Il-Sung; in office: 1945. **Local divisions:** 9 provinces, 4 municipalities. **Defense** (1984): 23.3% of GNP.

Economy: Industries: Textiles, petrochemicals, cement. **Chief crops:** Corn, potatoes, fruits, vegetables, rice. **Minerals:** Coal, lead tungsten, zinc, graphite, magnesite, iron, copper, gold, phosphate, salt, fluorspar. **Arable land:** 19%. **Meat prod.** (1984): cattle: 1.0 mln; pigs: 2.7 mln. **Fish catch** (1984): 1.6 mln. metric tons. **Crude steel prod.** (1985) 8.4 mln. metric tons. **Electricity prod.** (1983): 41 bln. kwh. **Labor force:** 48% agric.

Finance: Currency: Won (Jan. 1987): 0.94 = $1 US). **Gross national product** (1984 est.): $23 bln. **Imports** (1984): $1.3 bln.; partners: China 17%, USSR 22%, Jap. 18%. **Exports** (1984): $1.3 bln.; partners: USSR 26% China 17%, Saudi Ar. 9%, Jap. 9%.

Communications: Television sets: 1 mln. in use (1984). **Radios:** 4.1 mln. in use (1984).

Transport: Chief ports: Chonglin, Hamhung, Nampo.

Health: Life expectancy at birth (1984): 65 male; 72 female. **Births** (per 1,000 pop. 1985): 30. **Deaths** (per 1,000 pop. 1985): 7. **Natural increase** (1985): 2.3%. **Hospital beds** (1982): 244,000. **Physicians** (1982): 45,000. **Infant mortality** (per 1,000 live births, 1985): 30.

Education (1986): **Literacy:** 99%. **Years compulsory:** 11.

The Democratic People's Republic of Korea was founded May 1, 1948, in the zone occupied by Russian troops after World War II. Its armies tried to conquer the south, 1950. After 3 years of fighting with Chinese and U.S. intervention, a cease-fire was proclaimed.

Industry, begun by the Japanese during their 1910-45 occupation, and nationalized in the 1940s, had grown substantially, using N. Korea's abundant mineral and hydroelectric resources.

Two N. Korean Army officers were sentenced to death by Burmese authorities after they confessed to the October 9, 1983 bombing which killed 17, including 4 S. Korean cabinet ministers, in Rangoon.

South Korea

Republic of Korea

Taehan Min'guk

People: Population (1986 est.): 43,284,000. **Age distrib.** (%): 0–14: 30.6; 15–59: 52.7; 60+: 6.7. **Pop. density:** 1,094 per sq. mi. **Urban** (1985): 65%. **Ethnic groups:** Korean. **Languages:** Korean. **Religions:** Buddhism, Confucianism, Christian.

Geography: Area: 38,025 sq. mi., slightly larger than Indiana. **Location:** In Northern E. Asia. **Neighbors:** N. Korea on N. **Topography:** The country is mountainous, with a rugged east coast. The western and southern coasts are deeply indented, with many islands and harbors. **Capital:** Seoul. **Cities** (1984 est.): Seoul 9,501,413; Pusan 3,495,289; Taegu 2,012,039.

Government: Type: Republic, with power centralized in a strong executive. **Head of state:** Pres. Chun Doo Hwan; b. Jan. 18, 1931; in office: Dec. 1979. **Head of government:** Prime Min. Lho Shin Yong; in office: Feb. 18, 1985. **Local divisions:** 9 provinces and Seoul, Pusan, Inchon, and Taegu. **Defense:** 5.5% of GNP (1986).

Economy: Industries: Electronics, ships, textiles, clothing, motor vehicles. **Chief crops:** Rice, barley, vegetables. **Minerals:** Tungsten, coal, graphite. **Arable land:** 22%. **Meat prod.** (1984): cattle: 2.2 mln.; pigs: 3.6 mln. **Fish catch:** (1983): 2.7 mln. metric tons. **Electricity prod.** (1985): 58.0 bln. kwh. **Crude steel prod.** (1985): 13.5 mln. metric tons. **Labor force:** 30% agric.; 22% manuf. & mining; 47% services.

Finance: Currency: Won (Mar. 1987: 846 = $1 US). **Gross national product** (1986): $90.6 bln. **Per capita income** (1986): $2,100. **Imports** (1986): $31.5 bln.; partners: Jap. 24%, U.S. 25%, Saudi Ar. 8%. **Exports** (1986): $34.7 bln.; partners: U.S.

31%, Jap. 12%. **Tourists** (1985): receipts: $673 mln. **National budget** (1985): 17.4 bln. expenditures. **International reserves less gold** (Mar. 1987): $3.5 bln. **Gold:** 317,000 oz t. **Consumer prices** (change in 1986): 2.3%.

Transport: Railway traffic (1986): 21.6 bln. passenger-km; 11.6 bln. net ton-km. **Motor vehicles:** in use (1985): 465,000 passenger cars, 556,000 comm. vehicles. **Civil aviation** (1985): 10.2 bln. passenger-km; 2.0 bln. freight ton-km. **Chief ports:** Pusan, Inchon.

Communications: Television sets: 8.1 mln. in use (1984), 5.8 mln. manuf. (1979). **Radios:** 10.2 mln. in use (1984). **Telephones in use** (1984): 5.9 mln. **Daily newspaper circ.** (1985): 171 per 1,000 pop.

Health: Life expectancy at birth (1985): 64.9 male; 76.3 female. **Births** (per 1,000 pop. 1985): 23.5. Deaths (per 1,000 pop. 1985): 7. **Natural increase** (1985): 1.6%. **Hospital beds** (1984): 68,700. **Physicians** (1984): 28,015. **Infant mortality** (per 1,000 live births 1985): 30.

Education (1987): **Literacy:** 92%. **Attendance:** High school 90%, college 14%.

Embassy: 2320 Massachusetts Ave. NW 20008; 939-5600.

Korea, once called the Hermit Kingdom, has a recorded history since the 1st century BC. It was united in a kingdom under the Silla Dynasty, 668 AD. It was at times associated with the Chinese empire; the treaty that concluded the Sino-Japanese war of 1894-95 recognized Korea's complete independence. In 1910 Japan forcibly annexed Korea as Chosun.

At the Potsdam conference, July, 1945, the 38th parallel was designated as the line dividing the Soviet and the American occupation. Russian troops entered Korea Aug. 10, 1945, U.S. troops entered Sept. 8, 1945. The Soviet military organized socialists and communists and blocked efforts to let the Koreans unite their country. *(See Index for Korean War.)*

The South Koreans formed the Republic of Korea in May 1948 with Seoul as the capital. Dr. Syngman Rhee was chosen president but a movement spearheaded by college students forced his resignation Apr. 26, 1960.

In an army coup May 16, 1961, Gen. Park Chung Hee became chairman of the ruling junta. He was elected president, 1963; a 1972 referendum allowed him to be reelected for 6 year terms unlimited times. Park was assassinated by the chief of the Korean CIA, Oct. 26, 1979. The calm of the new government was halted by the rise of Gen. Chun Doo Hwan, head of the military intelligence, who reinstated martial law, and reverted South Korea to the police state it was under Park.

North Korean raids across the border tapered off in 1971, but incidents occurred in 1973 and 1974. In July 1972 South and North Korea agreed on a common goal of reunifying the 2 nations by peaceful means. But there had been no sign of a thaw in relations between the two regimes until 1985 when they agreed to discuss economic issues.

A Korean Air Lines passenger airliner was shot down by a Soviet jet fighter, Sept. 1, 1983, after it strayed into Soviet airspace; all 269 people aboard died.

On June 10, 1987, middle class office workers, shopkeepers, and business executives joined students in antigovernment protests in Seoul. They were protesting President Chun's decision to choose his successor and not allow the next president to be chosen by direct vote of the people. Following weeks of rioting and violence, Chun, July 1, agreed to permit election of the next president by direct popular vote and other constitutional reforms.

South Korea will host the 1988 Olympic Games.

Kuwait

State of Kuwait

Dowlat al-Kuwait

People: Population (1986 est.): 1,771,000. **Age distrib.** (%): 0–14: 40.2; 15–59: 57.6; 60+: 2.3. **Pop. density:** 260 per sq. mi. **Ethnic groups:** Arabs 84%, Iranians, Indians, Pakistanis. **Languages:** Arabic, others. **Religions:** Sunni Moslem 78%.

Geography: Area: 6,880 sq. mi., slightly smaller than New Jersey. **Location:** In Middle East, at N end of Persian Gulf. **Neighbors:** Iraq on N, Saudi Arabia on S. **Topography:** The country is flat, very dry, and extremely hot. **Capital:** Kuwait. **Cities** (1980 cen.): Hawalli 152,300; Kuwait City 60,400.

Government: Type: Constitutional monarchy. **Head of state:** Emir Shaikh Jabir al-Ahmad al-Jabir as-Sabah; b. 1928; in office: Jan. 1, 1978. **Head of government:** Prime Min. Shaikh Saad Abdulla as-Salim as-Sabah; in office: Feb. 8, 1978. **Local divisions:** 4 governorates. **Defense:** 4% of GNP (1983).

Economy: Industries: Oil products. **Minerals:** Oil, gas. **Crude oil reserves** (1985): 82 bln. bbls. **Cultivated land:** 1%. **Electricity prod.** (1984): 13.8 bln. kwh. **Labor force:** social services 45%; construction 20%.

Finance: Currency: Dinar (May 1987: 0.27 = $1 US). **Gross national product** (1984): $22 bln. **Per capita income** (1975): $11,431. **Imports** (1985): $6.6 bln.; partners: Jap. 21%, Fra. 10%, U.S. 9%. **Exports** (1985): $12.2 bln.; partners: Jap. 13%, It. 10%. **National budget** (1984): $15.2 bln. revenues; $10.7 bln. expenditures. **International reserves less gold** (Mar. 1987): $5.2 bln. **Gold:** 2.53 mln. oz t. **Consumer prices** (change in (1985): 1.5%.

Transport: Motor vehicles: in use (1985): 411,000 passenger cars, 200,000 comm. vehicles. **Civil aviation** (1984): 3.7 bln. passenger-km; 177 mln. freight ton-km. **Chief ports:** Mina al-Ahmadi.

Communications: Television sets: 600,000 in use (1985). **Radios:** 710,000 in use (1984). **Telephones in use** (1984): 419,000. **Daily newspaper circ.** (1985): 267 per 1,000 pop.

Health: Life expectancy at birth (1985): 68.0 male; 72.9 female. **Births** (per 1,000 pop. 1985): 40.9. **Deaths** (per 1,000 pop. 1985): 4.1. **Natural increase** (1985): 3.6%. **Hospital beds** (1984): 5,523 plus 232 clinics and health centers. **Physicians** (1984): 2,983. **Infant mortality** (per 1,000 live births 1985): 26.1.

Education (1985): **Literacy:** 71%. **Years compulsory:** 8.

Major International Organizations: UN (World Bank, IMF, GATT), Arab League, OPEC.

Embassy: 2940 Tilden St. NW 20008; 966-0702.

Kuwait is ruled by the Al-Sabah dynasty, founded 1759. Britain ran foreign relations and defense from 1899 until independence in 1961. The majority of the population is non-Kuwaiti, with many Palestinians, and cannot vote.

Oil, first exported in 1946, is the fiscal mainstay, providing most of Kuwait's income. Oil pays for free medical care, education, and social security. There are no taxes, except customs duties.

Kuwaiti oil tankers have come under frequent attack by Iran because of Kuwait's support of Iraq in the Iran-Iraq War. In July 1987, U.S. Navy warships began escorting Kuwaiti tankers in the Persian Gulf. (*See Chronology*).

Laos

Lao People's Democratic Republic

Sathalanalat Paxathipatai Paxaxōn Lao

People: Population (1986 est.): 3,679,000. **Pop. density:** 40 per sq. mi. **Urban** (1985): 15%. **Ethnic groups:** Lao 48%, Mon-Khmer tribes 25%, Thai 14%, Meo and Yao 13%, others. **Languages:** Lao (official), French. **Religions:** Buddhists 58%, tribal 34%.

Geography: Area: 91,428 sq. mi., slightly larger than Utah. **Location:** In Indochina Peninsula in SE Asia. **Neighbors:** Burma, China on N, Vietnam on E, Cambodia on S, Thailand on W. **Topography:** Landlocked, dominated by jungle. High mountains along the eastern border are the source of the E-W rivers slicing across the country to the Mekong R., which defines most of the western border. **Capital:** Vientiane. **Cities** (1984 est.); Vientiane 120,000.

Government: Type: Communist. **Head of state:** Pres. Phoumi Vongvichit in office: Oct. 31, 1986. **Head of government:** Prime Min. Kaysone Phomvihan; b. Dec. 13, 1920; in office: Dec. 2, 1975. **Local divisions:** 17 provinces. **Armed forces: Defense:** 9% of GNP (1981).

Economy: Industries: Wood products. **Chief crops:** Rice, corn, tobacco, cotton, opium, citrus fruits, coffee. **Minerals:** Tin. **Other resources:** Forests. **Arable land:** 4%. **Meat prod.** (1985): pigs: 1.5 mln. **Fish catch** (1984): 20,000 metric tons. **Electricity prod.** (1984): 990 mln. kwh. **Labor force:** 76% agric.; 6% ind.

Finance: Currency: New kip (Jan. 1987): 35 = $1 US). **Gross national product** (1985): $1.8 bln. **Per capita income**

(1985 est.): $500. **Imports** (1985): $163 mln.; partners: Thai. 39%, Jap. 11%, Sing. 14%. **Exports** (1985): $48 mln.; partners: Chi. 43%, U.S. 17%, Thai. 8%.

Transport: Motor vehicles: in use (1982): 15,100 passenger cars, 3,000 comm. vehicles. **Civil Aviation** (1982): 8 mln. passenger km; 100,000 net ton-km.

Communications: Radios: 225,000 in use (1984).

Health: Life expectancy at birth (1985): 49.4 male; 52.4 female. **Births** (per 1,000 pop. 1985): 39.5. **Deaths** (per 1,000 pop. 1985): 14.8. **Natural increase** (1985): 2.4%. **Hospital beds** (1983): 9,495. **Physicians** (1983): 1,654. **Infant mortality** (per 1,000 live births, 1986): 126.

Education: (1986): **Literacy:** 41%.

Major International Organizations: UN (FAO, IMF, WHO).

Embassy: 2222 S St. NW 20008; 332-6416.

Laos became a French protectorate in 1893, but regained independence as a constitutional monarchy July 19, 1949.

Conflicts among neutralist, communist and conservative factions created a chaotic political situation. Armed conflict increased after 1960.

The 3 factions formed a coalition government in June 1962, with neutralist Prince Souvanna Phouma as premier. A 14-nation conference in Geneva signed agreements, 1962, guaranteeing neutrality and independence. By 1964 the Pathet Lao had withdrawn from the coalition, and, with aid from N. Vietnamese troops, renewed sporadic attacks. U.S. planes bombed the Ho Chi Minh trail, supply line from N. Vietnam to communist forces in Laos and S. Vietnam. An estimated 2.75 million tons of bombs were dropped on Laos during the fighting.

In 1970 the U.S. stepped up air support and military aid. After Pathet Lao military gains, Souvanna Phouma in May 1975 ordered government troops to cease fighting; the Pathet Lao took control. A Lao People's Democratic Republic was proclaimed Dec. 3, 1975; it is strongly influenced by Vietnam.

Lebanon

Republic of Lebanon

al-Jumhouriya al-Lubnaniya

People: Population (1986 est.): 2,674,000. **Age distrib.** (%): 0–14: 35.6; 15–59: 56.4; 60+: 8.0. **Pop. density:** 685 per sq. mi. **Urban** (1985): 83%. **Ethnic groups:** Lebanese 82%, Armenians 5%, Palestinian 9%. **Languages:** Arabic (official), French, Armenian. **Religions:** Predominately Moslem 60%; Maronite Christian 25%; Greek Orthodox 7%; Druze 7%.

Geography: Area: 4,015 sq. mi., smaller than Connecticut. **Location:** On Eastern end of Mediterranean Sea. **Neighbors:** Syria on E. Israel on S. **Topography:** There is a narrow coastal strip, and 2 mountain ranges running N-S enclosing the fertile Beqaa Valley. The Litani R. runs S through the valley, turning W to empty into the Mediterranean. **Capital:** Beirut. **Cities** (1985 est.): Beirut 1,500,000; Tripoli 500,000.

Government: Type: Parliamentary republic. **Head of state:** Pres. Amin Gemayel; in office: Sept. 23, 1982; **Head of government:** Prime Min. Selim al-Hoss in office: June 1, 1987. **Local divisions:** 6 provinces. **Defense:** 18% of govt. budget (1984).

Economy: Industries: Trade, food products, textiles, cement, oil products. **Chief crops:** Fruits, olives, tobacco, grapes, vegetables, grains. **Minerals:** Iron. **Arable land:** 29%. **Meat prod.** (1984): goats: 440,000; sheep: 130,000. **Electricity prod.** (1984): 1.3 bln. kwh. **Labor force:** 17% agric.; 75% ind., comm., services.

Finance: Currency: Pound (Mar. 1987: 109 = $1 US). **Gross national product** (1983): $3.0 bln. **Per capita income** (1983): $1,150. **Imports** (1985): $2.2 bln.; partners: It. 15%, Fr. 10%, U.S. 9%, Saudi Ar. 6%. **Exports** (1985): $482 mln.; partners: Saudi Ar. 33%, Syria 8%, Jor. 6%, Kuw. 8%. **National budget** (1983): $1.8 bln. **International reserves less gold** (Mar. 1987): $579 mln. **Gold:** 9.22 mln. oz t.

Transport: Railway traffic (1982): 5.3 mln. passenger-km; 42 mln. net ton-km. **Motor vehicles:** in use (1982): 460,000 passenger cars, 21,000 comm. vehicles. **Civil aviation** (1984): 830 mln. passenger-km; 19 mln. freight ton-km. **Chief ports:** Beirut, Tripoli, Sidon.

Communications: Television sets: 451,000 in use (1985). **Radios:** 1.5 mln. in use (1984). **Telephones:** in use (1978): 231,000. **Daily newspaper circ.** (1985): 228 per 1,000 pop.

Health: Life expectancy at birth (1985): 65.0 male; 68.9 female. **Births** (per 1,000 pop. 1985): 30. **Deaths** (per 1,000 pop. 1985): 8. **Natural increase** (1985): 2.2%. **Hospital beds** (1982): 11,400. **Physicians** (1982): 3,000. **Infant mortality** (per 1,000 live births 1985): 42.

Education: (1984): **Literacy:** 75%. **Years compulsory:** 5; attendance 93%.

Major International Organizations: UN (IMF, ILO, WHO).

Embassy: 2560 28th St. NW 20008; 939-6300.

Formed from 5 former Turkish Empire districts, Lebanon became an independent state Sept. 1, 1920, administered under French mandate 1920-41. French troops withdrew in 1946.

Under the 1943 National Covenant, all public positions were divided among the various religious communities, with Christians in the majority. By the 1970s, Moslems became the majority, and demanded a larger political and economic role.

U.S. Marines intervened, May-Oct. 1958, during a Syrian-aided revolt. Lebanon's efforts to restrain Palestinian commandos caused armed clashes in 1969. Continued raids against Israeli civilians, 1970-75, brought Israeli attacks against guerrilla camps and villages. Israeli troops occupied S. Lebanon, March 1978, and again in Apr. 1980.

An estimated 60,000 were killed and billions of dollars in damage inflicted in a 1975-76 civil war. Palestinian units and leftist Moslems fought against the Maronite militia, the Phalange, and other Christians. Several Arab countries provided political and arms support to the various factions, while Israel aided Christian forces. Up to 15,000 Syrian troops intervened in 1976, and fought Palestinian groups. Arab League troops from several nations tried to impose a cease-fire.

Clashes between Syrian troops and Christian forces erupted, Apr. 1, 1981, near Zahle, Lebanon, bringing to an end the cease-fire that had been in place. By Apr. 22, fighting had broken out not only between Syrians and Christians, but also between two Moslem factions. Israeli commandos attacked Palestinian positions at Tyre and Tulin. In July, Israeli air raids on Beirut killed or wounded some 800 persons. A cease-fire between Israel and the Palestinians was concluded July 24, but hostilities continued.

Israeli forces invaded Lebanon June 6, 1982, in a coordinated land, sea, and air attack aimed at crushing strongholds of the Palestine Liberation Organization (PLO). Israeli and Syrian forces engaged in the Bekka Valley. By June 14, Israeli troops had encircled Beirut. On Aug. 21, the PLO evacuated West Beirut following massive Israeli bombings of the city. The withdrawal was supervised by U.S., French, and Italian troops. Israeli troops withdrew from Lebanon in June 1985.

Israeli troops entered West Beirut following the Sept. 14 assassination of newly-elected Lebanese Pres. Bashir Gemayel. On Sept. 16, Lebanese Christian troops entered 2 refugee camps and massacred hundreds of Palestinian refugees.

In 1983, terrorist bombings became a way of life in Beirut as some 50 people were killed in an explosion at the U.S. Embassy, Apr. 18; 241 U.S. servicemen and 58 French soldiers died in separate Moslem suicide attacks, Oct. 23.

PLO leader Yasir Arafat and PLO dissidents backed by Syria fought a 6-week battle in Tripoli until negotiations allowed Arafat and some 4,000 followers to evacuate the city.

On Apr. 26, 1984, pro-Syrian Rashid Karami was appointed premier. The appointment failed to end virtual civil war in Beirut between Christian forces, and Druse and Shiite Moslem militias. There was heavy fighting between Shiite militiamen and Palestinian guerrillas in May 1985. In June, Beirut Airport was the scene of a hostage crisis where Shiite terrorists held U.S. citizens for 17 days.

Kidnapping of foreign nationals by Islamic militants has become common in the 1980s. U.S., British, French, and Soviet citizens have been victims.

Premier Karami was assassinated June 1, 1987, when a bomb exploded aboard a helicopter in which he was traveling.

Lesotho

Kingdom of Lesotho

People: Population (1986 est.): 1,552,000. **Age distrib.** (%): 0–14: 42.3; 15–59: 52.2; 60+: 5.7. **Pop. density:** 135 per sq. mi. **Ethnic groups:** Sotho 99%. **Languages:** English, Sesotho (official). **Religions:** Roman Catholic 43%, Protestant 49%.

Geography: Area: 11,716 sq. mi., slightly larger than Maryland. **Location:** In Southern Africa. **Neighbors:** Completely surrounded by Republic of South Africa. **Topography:** Landlocked and mountainous, with altitudes ranging from 5,000 to 11,000 ft. **Capital:** Maseru. **Cities** (1984 est.): Maseru 80,250.

Government: Type: Constitutional monarchy. **Head of state:** King Moshoeshoe II, b. May 2, 1938; in office: Mar. 12, 1960. **Head of government:** Gen. Justin Lekhanya; b. Apr. 7, 1938; in office: Jan. 20, 1986. **Local divisions:** 10 districts. **Defense:** 4.5% of govt. budget (1982).

Economy: Industries: Diamond polishing, food processing. **Chief crops:** Corn, grains, peas, beans. **Other resources:** Wool, mohair. **Arable land:** 10%. **Electricity prod.** (1985): 1 mln. kwh. **Labor force:** 36% agric.; 5% ind. and comm., 53% services.

Finance: Currency: Maloti (Mar. 1987: 2.00 = $1 US). **Gross national product** (1984): $790 mln. **Per capita income** (1984): $520. **Imports** (1982): $396 mln.; partners: Mostly So. Afr. **Exports** (1982): $50 mln.; partners: Mostly So. Afr. **National budget** (1983): $153.5 mln.

Transport: Motor vehicles: in use (1982): 5,000 passenger cars, 11,000 comm. vehicles.

Communications: Radios: 43,000 in use (1985). **Daily newspaper circ.** (1985): 28 per 1,000 pop.

Health: Life expectancy at birth (1983): 51.5 yrs. **Births** (per 1,000 pop. 1985): 41.7. **Deaths** (per 1,000 pop. 1985): 16.4. **Natural increase** (1985): 2.5%. **Hospital beds** (1982): 2,300. **Physicians** (1982): 114. **Infant mortality** (per 1,000 live births 1985): 98.

Education (1984): **Literacy:** 65%.

Major International Organizations: UN (IMF, UNESCO, WHO), OAU.

Embassy: 1601 Connecticut Ave. NW 20009; 462-4190.

Lesotho (once called Basutoland) became a British protectorate in 1868 when Chief Moshesh sought protection against the Boers. Independence came Oct. 4, 1966. Elections were suspended in 1970. Over 50% of Lesotho's GNP is provided by citizens working in S. Africa. Livestock raising is the chief industry; diamonds are the chief export.

So. Africa imposed a blockade, Jan. 1, 1986, because of Lesotho's giving sanctuary to rebel groups fighting to overthrow the So. African Government. The blockade sparked a Jan. 20 military coup, and was lifted, Jan. 25, when the new leaders agreed to expel the rebels.

Liberia

Republic of Liberia

People: Population (1986 est.): 2,307,000. **Age distrib.** (%): 0–14: 46.8; 15–59: 48.3; 60+: 4.9. **Pop. density:** 60 per sq. mi. **Urban** (1985): 39.5%. **Ethnic groups:** Americo-Liberians 5%, 16 tribes 95% **Languages:** English (official), tribal dialects. **Religions:** Moslem 15%, Christian 10%, traditional beliefs 65%.

Geography: Area: 38,250 sq. mi., slightly smaller than Pennsylvania. **Location:** On SW coast of W. Africa. **Neighbors:** Sierra Leone on W, Guinea on N, Côte d'Ivoire on E. **Topography:** Marshy Atlantic coastline rises to low mountains and plateaus in the forested interior; 6 major rivers flow in parallel courses to the ocean. **Capital:** Monrovia. **Cities** (1984 est.): Monrovia 306,000.

Government: Type: Military. **Head of state:** Pres. Samuel K. Doe; in office: Apr. 12, 1980. **Local divisions:** 10 counties and 5 territories. **Defense:** 2.8% of GDP (1983).

Economy: Industries: Food processing and other light industry. **Chief crops:** Rice, cassava, coffee, cocoa, sugar. **Minerals:** Iron, diamonds, gold. **Other resources:** Rubber, timber. **Arable land:** 4%. **Fish catch** (1984): 13,500 metric tons. **Electricity prod.** (1984): 897 mln. kwh. **Labor force:** 70.5% agric.

Finance: Currency: Dollar (May 1987: 1.00 = $1 US). **Gross national product** (1983): $900 mln. **Per capita income** (1982): $400. **Imports** (1983): $411 mln.; partners: U.S. 27%, W. Ger. 10%, Jap. 6%, Neth. 7%. **Exports** (1983): $427 mln.; partners: W. Ger. 31%, U.S. 17%, It. 14%, Fr. 9%. **National budget** (1984): $387 mln. **International reserves less gold** (Feb. 1987): $710,000. **Consumer prices** (change in 1985): −0.6%.

Transport: Motor vehicles: in use (1983): 12,000 passenger cars, 7,000 comm. vehicles. **Chief ports:** Monrovia, Buchanan.

Communications: Television sets: 35,000 in use (1985). **Radios:** 330,000 in use (1985): **Telephones in use** (1983): 8,500. **Daily newspaper circ.** (1985): 12 per 1,000 pop.

Health: Life expectancy at birth (1984): 54 yrs.; **Births** (per 1,000 pop. 1985): 48.7. **Deaths** (per 1,000 pop. 1985): 17.2. **Natural increase** (1985): 3.1%. **Hospital beds** (1981): 3,000. **Physicians** (1981): 236. **Infant mortality** (per 1,000 live births 1985): 127.

Education (1985): **Literacy:** 35%. **School attendance:** primary 50%, secondary 20%.

Major International Organizations: UN and most specialized agencies, OAU.

Embassy: 5201 16th St. NW 20011; 723-9437.

Liberia was founded in 1822 by U.S. black freedmen who settled at Monrovia with the aid of colonization societies. It became a republic July 26, 1847, with a constitution modeled on that of the U.S. Descendants of freedmen dominated politics.

Charging rampant corruption, an Army Redemption Council of enlisted men staged a bloody predawn coup, April 12, 1980, in which Pres. Tolbert was killed and replaced as head of state by Sgt. Samuel Doe. Doe was chosen president in a disputed election, and survived a subsequent coup, in 1985.

Libya

Socialist People's Libyan Arab Jamahiriya

al-Jamahiriyah al-Arabiya al-Libya al-Shabiya al-Ishtirakiya

People: Population: (1986 est.): 3,876,000. **Age distrib.** (%): 0–14: 51.4; 15–59: 42.6; 60+: 5.9. **Pop. density:** 6 per sq. mi. **Urban** (1985): 64% **Ethnic groups:** Arab-Berber 80%. **Languages:** Arabic. **Religions:** Sunni Moslem 97%.

Geography: Area: 679,359 sq. mi., larger than Alaska. **Location:** On Mediterranean coast of N. Africa. **Neighbors:** Tunisia, Algeria on W, Niger, Chad on S, Sudan, Egypt on E. **Topography:** Desert and semidesert regions cover 92% of the land, with low mountains in N, higher mountains in S, and a narrow coastal zone. **Capital:** Tripoli. **Cities** (1982 est.): Tripoli 820,000.

Government. Type: Islamic Arabic Socialist "Mass-State." **Head of state:** Col. Muammar al-Qaddafi; b. Sept. 1942; in office: Sept. 1969. **Head of government:** Premier Muhammad az-Zaruq Rajab; in office: Feb. 16, 1984. **Local divisions:** 10 regions. **Defense:** 17.5% of GNP (1983).

Economy: Industries: Carpets, textiles, petroleum. **Chief crops:** Dates, olives, citrus and other fruits, grapes, wheat. **Minerals:** Gypsum, oil, gas. **Crude oil reserves** (1985): 22 bln. bbls. **Arable land:** 2%. **Meat prod.** (1985): sheep: 4.8 mln.; goats: 1.5 mln. **Electricity prod.** (1983): 7.1 bln. kwh. **Labor force:** 18% agric.; 31% ind.; 27% services; 24% govt.

Finance: Currency: Dinar (Feb. 1987: 0.30 = $1 US). **Gross domestic product** (1984): $25 bln. **Per capita income** (1984): $7,000. **Imports** (1985): $5.4 bln.; partners: It. 30%, W. Ger. 11%, Fr. 6%, Jap. 8%. **Exports** (1985): $10.9 bln.; partners: U.S. 27%, It. 24%, W. Ger. 10%, Sp. 7%. **International reserves less gold** (Mar. 1987): $5.9 bln. **Gold:** 3.6 mln. oz t.

Transport: Motor vehicles: in use (1982): 415,000 passenger cars, 334,000 comm. vehicles. **Chief ports:** Tripoli, Benghazi.

Communications: Television sets: 175,000 licensed (1985). **Radios:** 165,000 (1985). **Daily newspaper circ.** (1985): 10 per 1,000 pop.

Health: Life expectancy at birth (1985): 56.1 male; 59.4 female. **Births** (per 1,000 pop. 1985): 46. **Deaths** (per 1,000 pop. 1985): 11.2. **Natural increase** (1985): 3.4%. **Hospital beds** (1982): 16,051. **Physicians** (1982): 5,200. **Infant mortality** (per 1,000 live births 1985): 84.

Education (1985): Literacy: 60%. **Years compulsory:** 7; **Attendance:** 90%.

Major International Organizations: UN, Arab League, OAU, OPEC.

First settled by Berbers, Libya was ruled by Carthage, Rome, and Vandals, the Ottomans, Italy from 1912, and Britain and France after WW II. It became an independent constitutional monarchy Jan. 2, 1952. In 1969 a junta lead by Col. Muammar al-Qaddafi seized power.

In the mid-1970s, Libya helped arm violent revolutionary groups in Egypt and Sudan, and had aided terrorists of various nationalities. The USSR sold Libya advanced arms, and established close political ties.

Libya and Egypt fought several air and land battles along their border in July, 1977. Chad charged Libya with military occupation of its uranium-rich northern region in 1977. Libya's 1979 offensive into the Aouzou Strip was repulsed by Chadian forces. Libyan forces withdrew from Chad, Nov. 1981 but returned. Libyan troops were driven from their last major stronghold by Chad forces in 1987, leaving over $1 billion in military equipment behind.

Widespread nationalization, arrests, imposition of currency regulations, wholesale conscription of civil servants into the army, and the fall in crude oil prices have hurt the economy.

On May 6, 1981, the U.S., citing "a wide range of Libyan provocations and misconduct," closed the Libyan mission in Wash. In August, 2 Libyan jets were shot down by U.S. Navy planes taking part in naval exercises in the Gulf of Sidra which Libya claims as its territory. Great Britain severed diplomatic relations with Libya April 22, 1984, following the death of a British policewoman and the wounding of 10 Libyan-exile demonstrators by machine-gun fire from within the Libyan embassy in London.

The U.S. has accused Libya of masterminding numerous international terrorist actions, including the Dec. 1985 attacks on the Rome and Vienna airports.

On Jan. 7, 1986, the U.S. imposed economic sanctions against Libya, ordered all Americans to leave that country and froze all Libyan assets in the U.S. The U.S. commenced flight operations over the Gulf of Sidra, Jan. 27, and a U.S. Navy task force began conducting exercises in the Gulf, Mar. 23. When Libya fired antiaircraft missiles at American warplanes, the U.S. responded by sinking 2 Libyan ships and bombing a missile installation in Libya. The U.S. withdrew from the Gulf, Mar. 27.

The U.S. accused Libyan leader Qaddafi of having ordered the April 5 bombing of a West Berlin discotheque which killed 2, including a U.S. serviceman. After failing to get their European allies to join them in imposing economic sanctions against Libya, the U.S. sent warplanes to attack terrorist-related targets in Tripoli and Benghazi, Libya, Apr. 14.

At the economic summit of the 7 major industrial democracies in Tokyo, May 4–6, a joint statement was issued which condemned terrorism and singled out Libya as a target for action.

Liechtenstein

Principality of Liechtenstein

Fürstentum Liechtenstein

People: Population (1986 est.): 28,000. **Age distrib.** (%): 0–14: 20.4; 15–59: 66.1; 60+: 11.5. **Pop. density:** 432 per sq. mi. **Ethnic groups:** Alemannic 95%, Italian 5%. **Languages:** German (official), Alemannic dialect. **Religions:** Roman Catholic 86%, Protestant 8%.

Geography: Area: 62 sq. mi., the size of Washington, D.C. **Location:** In the Alps. **Neighbors:** Switzerland on W, Austria on E. **Topography:** The Rhine Valley occupies one-third of the country, the Alps cover the rest. **Capital:** Vaduz. **Cities** (1985 cen.): Vaduz 4,872.

Government: Type: Hereditary constitutional monarchy. **Head of state:** Prince Franz Josef II; b. Aug. 16, 1906; in office: Mar. 30, 1938. **Head of government:** Hans Brunhart; b. Mar. 28, 1945; in office: Apr. 26, 1978. **Local divisions:** 2 districts, 11 communities.

Economy: Industries: Machines, instruments, chemicals, furniture, ceramics. **Arable land:** 25%. **Labor force:** 54% industry, trade and building; 41% services; 4% agric., fishing, forestry.

Finance: Currency: Swiss Franc. **Tourists** (1984): 83,589.

Communications: Radios: 8,700 in use (1985). **Telephones in use** (1984): 83,859. **Daily newspaper circ.** (1984): 542 per 1,000 pop.

Health: Births (per 1,000 pop. 1985): 14. **Deaths** (per 1,000 pop. 1985): 7. **Natural increase** (1985): .7%. **Infant mortality** (per 1,000 live births 1985): 6.3.

Education (1986): **Literacy:** 100%. **Years compulsory** 9; attendance 100%.

Liechtenstein became sovereign in 1866. Austria administered Liechtenstein's ports up to 1920; Switzerland has administered its postal services since 1921. Liechtenstein is united with Switzerland by a customs and monetary union. Taxes are low; many international corporations have headquarters there. Foreign workers comprise a third of the population.

The 1986 general elections were the first in which women were allowed to vote.

Luxembourg

Grand Duchy of Luxembourg

Grand-Duché de Luxembourg

People: Population: (1986 est.): 367,000. **Age distrib.** (%): 0–14: 19.0; 15–59: 63.5; 60+: 17.6. **Pop. density:** 367 per sq. mi. **Urban** (1985): 81%. **Ethnic groups:** Mixture of French and Germans predominate. **Languages:** French, German, Luxembourgian. **Religions:** Roman Catholic 94%.

Geography: Area: 998 sq. mi., smaller than Rhode Island. **Location:** In W. Europe. **Neighbors:** Belgium on W, France on S, W. Germany on E. **Topography:** Heavy forests (Ardennes) cover N, S is a low, open plateau. **Capital:** Luxembourg. **Cities** (1985 est.): Luxembourg 76,000.

Government: Type: Constitutional monarchy. **Head of state:** Grand Duke Jean; b. Jan. 5, 1921; in office: Nov. 12, 1964. **Head of government:** Prime Min. Jacques Santer; in office: July 21, 1984. **Local divisions:** 3 districts, 12 cantons. **Defense:** 0.7% of GNP (1984).

Economy: Industries: Steel, chemicals, beer, tires, tobacco, metal products, cement. **Chief crops:** Corn, wine. **Minerals:** Iron. **Arable land:** 21%. **Electricity prod.** (1984): 905 mln. kwh. **Crude steel prod.** (1984): 3.9 mln. metric tons. **Labor force:** 1% agric.; 42% ind. & comm.; 45% services.

Finance: Currency: Franc (Mar. 1987: 37.39 = $1 US). **Gross national product** (1984): $4.9 bln. **Per capita income** (1981): $10,444. **Note:** trade and tourist data included in Belgian statistics. **Consumer prices** (change in 1986): 0.3%.

Transport: Railway traffic (1985): 288 mln. passenger-km; 648 mln. net ton-km. **Motor vehicles:** in use (1985): 151,000 passenger cars, 13,000 comm. vehicles.

Communications: Television sets: 91,000 in use (1985). **Radios:** 227,000 in use (1985). **Telephones in use** (1984): 147,000. **Daily newspaper circ.** (1983): 365 per 1,000 pop.

Health: Life expectancy at birth (1984): 66.9 male; 73.5 female. **Births** (per 1,000 pop. 1985): 11. **Deaths** (per 1,000 pop. 1985): 11. **Hospital beds** (1984): 4,688. **Physicians** (1984): 637. **Infant mortality** (per 1,000 live births 1985): 10.

Education (1983): **Literacy:** 100%. **Years compulsory** 9; attendance 100%.

Major International Organizations: UN, OECD, EC, NATO.

Embassy: 2200 Massachusetts Ave. NW 20008; 265-4171.

Luxembourg, founded about 963, was ruled by Burgundy, Spain, Austria, and France from 1448 to 1815. It left the Germanic Confederation in 1866. Overrun by Germany in 2 world wars, Luxembourg ended its neutrality in 1948, when a customs union with Belgium and Netherlands was adopted.

Madagascar

Democratic Republic of Madagascar

Repoblika Demokratika Malagasy

People: Population (1986 est.): 10,227,000. **Pop. density:** 45 per sq. mi. **Urban** (1985): 21.8%. **Ethnic groups:** 18 Malayan-Indonesian tribes (Merina 26%), with Arab and African presence. **Languages:** Malagasy (national), French. **Religions:** animists 47%, Christian 51%, Muslim 2%.

Geography: Area: 226,657 sq. mi., slightly smaller than Texas. **Location:** In the Indian O., off the SE coast of Africa. **Neighbors:** Comoro Is., Mozambique (across Mozambique Channel). **Topography:** Humid coastal strip in the E, fertile valleys in the mountainous center plateau region, and a wider coastal strip on the W. **Capital:** Antananarivo. **Cities** (1985 est.): Antananarivo 650,000.

Government: Type: Republic. **Head of state:** Pres. Didier Ratsiraka; b. Nov. 4, 1936; in office: June 15, 1975. **Head of government:** Prime Min. Desire Rakotoarijaona, b. June 19, 1934; in office: Aug. 4, 1977. **Local divisions:** 6 provinces. **Defense:** 10.2% of govt. budget (1984).

Economy: Industries: Light industry. **Chief crops:** Coffee (over 50% of exports), cloves, vanilla, rice, sugar, sisal, tobacco, peanuts. **Minerals:** Chromium, graphite. **Arable land:** 5%. **Meat prod.** (1985): cattle: 10.8 mln.; pigs: 1.2 mln. **Fish catch** (1983): 48,000 metric tons. **Electricity prod.** (1984): 420 mln. kwh. **Labor force:** 88% agric.

Finance: Currency: Franc (Mar. 1987: 790 = $1 US). **Gross national product** (1984): $2.6 bln. **Per capita income** (1984): $270. **Imports** (1982): $487 mln.; partners: Fr. 36%, W. Ger. 4%. **Exports** (1982): $325 mln.; partners: Fr. 41%, U.S. 14%. **National budget** (1984): $660 mln. **International reserves less gold** (June 1986): $102 mln. **Consumer prices** (change in 1985): 10.6%.

Transport: Railway traffic (1984): 205 mln. passenger-km; 222 mln. net ton-km. **Motor vehicles:** in use (1982): 55,000 passenger cars, 50,000 comm. vehicles. **Civil aviation:** (1983): 384 mln. passenger-km; 20 mln. freight ton-km. **Chief ports:** Tamatave, Diego-Suarez, Majunga, Tulear.

Communications: Television sets: 70,000 in use (1985). **Radios:** 900,000 in use (1985). **Telephones in use** (1983): 37,000.

Health: Life expectancy at birth (1984): 46 years. **Births** (per 1,000 pop. 1985): 45. **Deaths** (per 1,000 pop. 1985): 17. **Natural increase** (1985): 2.8%. **Hospital beds** (1982): 20,800. **Physicians** (1982): 940. **Infant mortality** (per 1,000 live births 1985): 101.

Education (1984): **Literacy:** 53%. **Years compulsory:** 5; attendance 83%.

Major International Organizations: UN (GATT, WHO, IMF), OAU.

Embassy: 2374 Massachusetts Ave. NW 20008; 265-5525.

Madagascar was settled 2,000 years ago by Malayan-Indonesian people, whose descendants still predominate. A unified kingdom ruled the 18th and 19th centuries. The island became a French protectorate, 1885, and a colony 1896. Independence came June 26, 1960.

Discontent with inflation and French domination led to a coup in 1972. The new regime nationalized French-owned financial interests, closed French bases and a U.S. space tracking station, and obtained Chinese aid. The government conducted a program of arrests, expulsion of foreigners, and repression of strikes, 1979.

Malawi

Republic of Malawi

People: Population (1986 est.): 7,292,000. **Age distrib.** (%): 0–14: 47.6; 15–59: 48.2; 60+: 4.2. **Pop. density:** 200 per sq. mi. **Urban** (1980): 9.6%. **Ethnic groups:** Chewa, 90%, Nyanja, Lomwe, other Bantu tribes. **Languages:** English, Chichewa (both official). **Religions:** Christian 75%, Moslem 20%.

Geography: Area: 45,747 sq. mi., the size of Pennsylvania. **Location:** In SE Africa. **Neighbors:** Zambia on W, Mozambique on SE, Tanzania on N. **Topography:** Malawi stretches 560 mi. N-S along Lake Malawi (Lake Nyasa), most of which belongs to Malawi. High plateaus and mountains line the Rift Valley the length of the nation. **Capital:** Lilongwe. **Cities** (1985 est.): Blantyre 355,000; Lilongwe 186,000.

Government: Type: Republic. **Head of state:** Pres. Hastings Kamuzu Banda, b. May 14, 1906; in office: July 6, 1966. **Local divisions:** 24 administrative districts. **Defense:** 8% of govt. budget (1983).

Economy: Industries: Textiles, sugar, farm implements. **Chief crops:** Tea, tobacco, sugar, coffee. **Other resources:** Rubber. **Arable land:** 34%. **Fish catch** (1984): 58 metric tons. **Electricity prod.** (1984): 467 mln. kwh. **Labor force:** 51% agric.; 18% ind. and comm.; 20% govt.; 17% services.

Finance: Currency: Kwacha (Mar. 1987: 2.26 = $1 US). **Gross national product** (1984): $1.1 bln. **Imports** (1984): $287 mln.; partners: So. Afr. 38%, UK 13%, Jap. 6%. **Exports** (1984): $302 mln.; partners: UK 27%, S. Afr. 8%., W. Ger. 7%. **National budget** (1983): $386.4 mln. **International reserves less gold** (Mar. 1987): $20.9 mln. **Gold:** 13,000 oz t. **Consumer prices** (change in 1986): 17.5%.

Transport: Railway traffic (1984): 72 mln. passenger-km; 120 mln. net ton-km. **Motor vehicles:** in use (1981): 14,100 passenger cars, 13,600 comm. vehicles. **Civil aviation** (1984) 72 mln. passenger-km; 1.2 freight ton-km.

Communications: Radios: 1 mln. in use (1985). **Telephones in use** (1981): 15,130. **Daily newspaper circ.** (1985): 5 per 1,000 pop.

Health: Life expectancy at birth (1981): 42.7 male; 45.4 female. **Births** (per 1,000 pop. 1985): 54.0. **Deaths** (per 1,000 pop. 1985): 21.0. **Natural increase** (1985): 3.3%. **Hospital beds** (1984): 6,596. **Infant mortality** (per 1,000 live births 1985): 170.

Education (1985): **Literacy:** 25%. About 45% attend school.

Major International Organizations: UN (World Bank, IMF), OAU, Commonwealth of Nations.

Embassy: 1400 20th St. NW 20036; 296-5530.

Bantus came in the 16th century, Arab slavers in the 19th. The area became the British protectorate Nyasaland, in 1891. It became independent July 6, 1964, and a republic in 1966. It has a pro-West foreign policy and cooperates economically with S. Africa.

Malaysia

People: Population (1986 est.): 15,820,000. **Age distrib.** (%): 0–14: 41.5; 15–59: 53.0; 60+: 5.4. **Pop. density:** 126 per sq. mi. **Urban** (1980): 34.2%. **Ethnic groups:** Malays 59%, Chinese 32%, Indian 12%. **Languages:** Malay (official), English, Chinese, Indian languages. **Religions:** Moslem, Hindu, Buddhist, Confucian, Taoist, local religions.

Geography: Area: 127,316 sq. mi., slightly larger than New Mexico. **Location:** On the SE tip of Asia, plus the N. coast of the island of Borneo. **Neighbors:** Thailand on N, Indonesia on S. **Topography:** Most of W. Malaysia is covered by tropical jungle, including the central mountain range that runs N-S through the peninsula. The western coast is marshy, the eastern, sandy. E. Malaysia has a wide, swampy coastal plain, with interior jungles and mountains. **Capital:** Kuala Lumpur. **Cities** (1986 est.): Kuala Lumpur 1 mln.

Government: Type: Federal parliamentary democracy with a constitutional monarch. **Head of state:** Paramount Ruler Mahmood Iskander; b. 1932; in office: Apr. 26, 1984. **Head of government:** Prime Min. Datuk Seri Mahathir bin Mohamad; b. Dec. 20, 1925; in office: July 16, 1981. **Local divisions:** 13 states and capital. **Defense:** 3.7% of GNP (1984).

Economy: Industries: Rubber goods, steel, electronics. **Chief crops:** Palm oil, copra, rice, pepper. **Minerals:** Tin (35% world output), iron. **Crude oil reserves** (1985): 2.9 bln. bbls. **Other resources:** Rubber (35% world output). **Arable land:** 13%. **Meat prod.** (1984): pigs: 2.1 mln. **Fish catch** (1983): 713,000 metric tons. **Electricity prod.** (1984): 13.7 bln. kwh. **Labor force:** 21% agric.; 18% manuf.; 14% tourism & trade.

Finance: Currency: Ringgit (Mar. 1987: 2.50 = $1 US). **Gross national product** (1984): $29.8 bln. **Imports** (1985): $12.3 bln.; partners: Jap. 25%, U.S. 18%, Sing. 14%. **Exports** (1985): $15.4 bln.; partners: Jap. 20%, U.S. 12% Sing. 25%, Neth. 6%. **National budget** (1985): $12.2 bln. **International reserves less gold** (Mar. 1987): $6.4 bln. **Gold:** 2.34 mln. oz t. **Consumer prices** (change in 1986): 0.7%.

Transport: Railway traffic (incl. Singapore) (1983): 1.5 bln. passenger-km; 1.1 bln. net ton-km. **Motor vehicles:** in use (1983): 1.1 mln. passenger cars, 266,000 comm. vehicles. **Civil aviation:** (1984): 5.9 bln. passenger-km; 200 mln. metric ton-km. **Chief ports:** George Town, Kelang, Melaka, Kuching.

Communications: Television sets: 1.6 mln. in use (1985). **Radios:** 2 mln. in use (1985). **Telephones in use** (1983): 976,000. **Daily newspaper circ.** (1985): 133 per 1,000 pop.

Health: Life expectancy at birth (1983): 68.2 male; 72.9 female. **Births** (per 1,000 pop. 1985): 29. **Deaths** (per 1,000 pop. 1985): 7. **Natural increase** (1985): 2.2%. **Hospital beds** (1983): 34,538. **Physicians** (1983): 4,234. **Infant mortality** (per 1,000 live births 1986): 25.0.

Education (1986): **Literacy:** 80%; 96% attend primary school, 48% attend secondary.

Major International Organizations: UN (World Bank, IMF, GATT), ASEAN.
Embassy: 2401 Massachusetts Ave. NW 20008; 328-2700.

European traders appeared in the 16th century; Britain established control in 1867. Malaysia was created Sept. 16, 1963. It included Malaya (which had become independent in 1957 after the suppression of Communist rebels), plus the formerly-British Singapore, Sabah (N Borneo), and Sarawak (NW Borneo). Singapore was separated in 1965, in order to end tensions between Chinese, the majority in Singapore, and Malays in control of the Malaysian government. Chinese have charged economic and political discrimination.

A monarch is elected by a council of hereditary rulers of the Malayan states every 5 years.

Abundant natural resources have assured prosperity, and foreign investment has aided industrialization.

Maldives

Republic of Maldives

Divehi Jumhuriya

People: Population (1986 est.): 179,000. **Age distrib.** (%): 0–14: 44.9; 15–59: 51.3; 60+: 3.8. **Pop. density:** 1,554 per sq. mi. **Urban** (1978): 20.7%. **Ethnic groups:** Sinhalese, Dravidian, Arab mixture. **Languages:** Divehi (Sinhalese dialect). **Religions:** Sunni Moslem.

Geography: Area: 115 sq. mi., twice the size of Washington, D.C. **Location:** In the Indian O. SW of India. **Neighbors:** Nearest is India on N. **Topography:** 19 atolls with 1,087 islands, about 200 inhabited. None of the islands are over 5 sq. mi. in area, and all are nearly flat. **Capital:** Male. **Cities** (1985 est.): Male 46,334.

Government: Type: Republic. **Head of state:** Pres. Maumoon Abdul Gayoom; b. Dec. 29, 1939; in office: Nov. 11, 1978. **Local divisions:** 19 atolls, each with an elected committee and a government-appointed chief.

Economy: Industries: Fish processing, tourism. **Chief crops:** Coconuts, fruit, millet. **Other resources:** Shells. **Fish catch** 1984): 38,000 metric tons. **Electricity prod.** (1984): 11 mln. kwh. **Labor force:** 80% fishing, agriculture, & manufacturing.

Finance: Currency: Rufiyaa (Jan. 1987: 9.69 = $1 US). **Gross national product** (1984): $76 mln. **Per capita income** (1985): $470. **Imports** (1984): $51.5 mln.; partners: Sing., Jap., Sri Lan. **Exports** (1984): $17.6 mln.; partners: Jap., Europe. **Tourists** (1985): 50,000.

Transport: Chief ports: Male Atoll.

Communications: Radios: 17,000 in use (1984). **Telephones in use** (1984): 3,000.

Health: Life expectancy at birth (1984): 46.5 yrs. **Births** (per 1,000 pop. 1985): 45. **Deaths** (per 1,000 pop. 1985): 14. **Infant morality** (per 1,000 live births 1985): 81.

Education (1987): **Literacy:** 82%. (claimed by govt.). Only 6% of those aged 11-15 attend school.

Major International Organizations: UN.

The islands had been a British protectorate since 1887. The country became independent July 26, 1965. Long a sultanate, the Maldives became a republic in 1968. Natural resources and tourism are being developed; however, it remains one of the world's poorest countries.

Mali

Republic of Mali

République du Mali

People: Population (1986 est.): 7,898,000. **Age distrib.** (%): 0–14: 46.0; 15–59: 49.4; 60+: 4.6. **Pop. density:** 17 per sq. mi. **Urban** (1985): 20.8%. **Ethnic groups:** Mande (Bambara, Malinke, Sarakolle) 50%, Peul 17%, Voltaic 12%, Songhai 6%, Tuareg, Moors. **Languages:** French (official), Bambara. **Religions:** Moslem 90%.

Geography: Area: 478,764 sq. mi., about the size of Texas and California combined. **Location:** In the interior of W. Africa. **Neighbors:** Mauritania, Senegal on W, Guinea, Côte d'Ivoire, Burkina Faso on S, Niger on E, Algeria on N. **Topography:** A landlocked grassy plain in the upper basins of the Senegal and Niger rivers, extending N into the Sahara. **Capital:** Bamako. **Cities** (1986 est.): Bamako (met.) 800,000.

Government: Type: Republic. **Head of state:** Pres. Moussa Traore; b. Sept. 25, 1936; in office: Dec. 6, 1968. **Head of Government:** Mamadou Dembele; in office: June 6, 1986. **Local divisions:** 7 regions and a capital district. **Defense:** 3% of GDP (1986).

Economy: Chief crops: Millet, rice, peanuts, cotton. **Other resources:** Bauxite, iron, gold. **Arable land:** 2%. **Meat prod.** (1984): lamb: 43,000 metric tons. **Fish catch** (1984): 33,000 metric tons. **Electricity prod.** (1984): 161 mln. kwh. **Labor force:** 73% agric.; 12% ind. & comm.; 16% services.

Finance: Currency: Franc (Mar. 1987: 300 = $1 US). **Gross national product** (1984): $1.1 bln. **Per capita income** (1984): $190. **Imports** (1983): $254 mln.; partners: Fr. 22%, Ivory Coast 25%. **Exports** (1983): $166 mln.; partners: Belg.-Lux. 25%, Fr. 15%. **Tourists** (1984): $13 mln. receipts. **International reserves less gold** (Feb. 1987): $15.4 mln. **Gold:** 19,000 oz t.

Transport: Railway traffic (1985): 172 mln. passenger-km; 241 mln. net ton-km. **Motor vehicles:** in use (1982): 20,000 passenger cars, 5,000 comm. vehicles.

Communications: Radios: 110,000 in use (1985). **Telephones in use** (1984): 9,500.

Health: Life expectancy at birth (1985): 40.4 male; 43.6 female. **Births** (per 1,000 pop. 1985): 50.2. **Deaths** (per 1,000 pop. 1985): 22.4. **Natural increase** (1985): 2.7%. **Hospital beds** (1980): 3,200. **Physicians** (1980): 337. **Infant mortality** (per 1,000 live births 1985): 173.

Education (1984): **Literacy:** 10%. **Attendance:** 28% under 15 attend school.

Major International Organizations: UN and all of its specialized agencies, OAU, EC.

Embassy: 2130 R St. NW 20008; 332-2250.

Until the 15th century the area was part of the great Mali Empire. Timbuktu was a center of Islamic study. French rule was secured, 1898. The Sudanese Rep. and Senegal became independent as the Mali Federation June 20, 1960, but Senegal withdrew, and the Sudanese Rep. was renamed Mali.

Mali signed economic agreements with France and, in 1963, with Senegal. In 1968, a coup ended the socialist regime. Famine struck in 1973-74, killing as many as 100,000 people. Drought conditions returned in the 1980s.

Mali and Burkina Faso fought a border war in Dec. 1985.

Malta

Repubblika Ta' Malta

People: Population (1986 est.): 354,000. **Age distrib.** (%): 0–14: 24.2; 15–59: 62.5; 60+: 13.3. **Pop. density:** 2,755 per sq. mi. **Ethnic groups:** Italian, Arab, French. **Languages:** Maltese, English both official. **Religions:** Mainly Roman Catholic.

Geography: Area: 122 sq. mi., twice the size of Washington, D.C. **Location:** In center of Mediterranean Sea. **Neighbors:** Nearest is Italy on N. **Topography:** Island of Malta is 95 sq. mi.; other islands in the group: Gozo, 26 sq. mi., Comino, 1 sq. mi. The coastline is heavily indented. Low hills cover the interior. **Capital:** Valletta. **Cities** (1984 est.): Valletta 14,000; Sliema 20,000.

Government: Type: Republic. **Head of state:** Pres. Agatha Barbara; in office: Feb. 16, 1982. **Head of government:** Prime Min. Eddie Fenech Adami; in office: May 9, 1987.

Economy: Industries: Textiles, tourism. **Chief crops:** Potatoes, onions, beans. **Arable land:** 44%. **Electricity prod.** (1984): 722 mln. kwh. **Labor force:** 35% ind. & comm.; 30% services; 22% gov.

Finance: Currency: Pound (Mar. 1987: 1.00 = $2.88 US). **Gross national product** (1984): $1.2 bln. **Per capita income** (1984): $3,660. **Imports** (1983): $316 mln.; partners: UK 18%, It. 23%, W. Ger. 14%, U.S. 7%. **Exports** (1983): $156 mln.; partners: W. Ger. 31%, UK 20%, Libya 8%. **Tourists** (1984): receipts: $130 mln. **National budget** (1984): $483. **International reserves less gold** (Mar. 1987): 1 bln. **Gold:** 466,000 oz t. **Consumer prices** (change in 1986): 2.0% .

Transport: Motor vehicles: in use (1984): 77,000 passenger cars, 17,000 comm. vehicles. **Civil aviation** (1985): 1.2 bln. passenger-km; 4.8 mln. freight ton-km. **Chief ports:** Valletta.

Communications: Television sets: 90,000 licensed (1983). **Radios:** 150,000 in use (1985). **Telephones in use** (1985): 115,000.

Health: Life expectancy at birth (1984): 70.7 male; 75.2 female. **Births** (per 1,000 pop. 1985): 16. **Deaths** (per 1,000 pop. 1985): 8. **Natural increase** (1985): .8%. **Hospital beds** (1980): 3,431. **Physicians** (1982): 413. **Infant mortality** (per 1,000 live births 1985): 13.4.

Education (1985): **Literacy:** 90%. **Compulsory:** until age 16.

Major International Organizations: UN (GATT, WHO, IMF), Commonwealth of Nations.

Embassy: 2017 Connecticut Ave. NW 20008; 462-3611.

Malta was ruled by Phoenicians, Romans, Arabs, Normans, the Knights of Malta, France, and Britain (since 1814). It became independent Sept. 21, 1964. Malta became a republic in 1974. The withdrawal of the last of its sailors, Apr. 1, 1979, ended 179 years of British military presence on the island.

With Malta's approval, Egyptian commandos stormed a hijacked EgyptAir passenger plane at Valletta airport Nov. 23, 1985; 57 died in the battle.

Malta is democratic but nonaligned.

Mauritania

Islamic Republic of Mauritania

République Islamique de Mauritanie

People: Population (1986 est.): 1,691,000. **Age distrib.** (%): 0–14: 46.4; 15–59: 49.0; 60+: 4.6. **Pop. density:** 4.2 per sq. mi. **Urban** (1983): 25%. **Ethnic groups:** Arab-Berber 80%, Negroes 20%. **Languages:** French (official), Hassanya Arabic (national), Toucouleur, Fula, Sarakole, Wolof. **Religion:** Predominately Moslems.

Geography: Area: 397,954 sq. mi., the size of Texas and California combined. **Location:** In W. Africa. **Neighbors:** Morocco on N, Algeria, Mali on E, Senegal on S. **Topography:** The fertile Senegal R. valley in the S gives way to a wide central region of sandy plains and scrub trees. The N is arid and extends into the Sahara. **Capital:** Nouakchott. **Cities** (1981 est.): Nouakchott 250,000; Nouadhibou 22,000; Kaedi 21,000.

Government: Type: Military republic. **Head of Government:** President & Premier Maaouya Ould Sidi Ahmed Taya; in office: Apr. 25, 1981. **Local divisions:** 8 regions, one district. **Defense:** 5.8% of GNP (1983).

Economy: Chief crops: Dates, grain. **Minerals:** Iron, ore, gypsum. **Meat prod.** (1984): sheep: 5.2 mln.; goats: 3.2 mln.; cattle: 1.3 mln. **Fish catch** (1985): 60,000 metric tons. **Electricity prod.** (1984): 114 mln. kwh. **Labor force:** 47% agric., 14% ind. & comm., 29% services.

Finance: Currency: Ouguiya (Mar. 1987: 72.25 = $1 US). **Gross national product** (1984): $614 mln. **Per capita income** (1984): $466. **Imports** (1984): $382 mln.; partners: Fr. 29%, Sp. 9%. **Exports** (1984): $286 mln.; partners: Fr. 21%, It. 26%, Jap. 20%. **International reserves less gold** (Feb. 1987): $48.2 mln. **Gold:** 12,000 oz t. **Consumer prices** (change in 1984): 7%.

Transport: Motor vehicles: in use (1981): 11,000 passenger cars, 8,000 comm. vehicles. **Chief ports:** Nouakchott, Nouadhibou.

Communications: Radios: 95,000 in use (1985).

Health: Life expectancy at birth (1985): 45 years. **Births** (per 1,000 pop. 1985): 47.0. **Deaths** (per 1,000 pop. 1985): 27. **Natural increase** (1985): 2.0%. **Hospital beds** (1980): 561. **Physicians** (1980): 103. **Infant mortality** (per 1,000 live births 1985): 138.

Education (1985): **Literacy:** 17%. **Attendance:** 36% in primary school, 4% in secondary school.

Major International Organizations: UN (GATT, IMF, WHO), OAU, Arab League.

Embassy: 2129 Leroy Pl. NW 20008; 232-5700.

Mauritania became independent Nov. 28, 1960. It annexed the south of former Spanish Sahara in 1976. Saharan guerrillas stepped up attacks in 1977; 8,000 Moroccan troops and French bomber raids aided the government. Mauritania signed a peace treaty with the Polsario Front, 1980, resumed diplomatic relations with Algeria while breaking a defense treaty with Morocco, and renounced sovereignty over its share of former Spanish Sahara. Morocco annexed the territory.

Famine has struck repeatedly during the last decade.

Mauritius

People: Population (1986 est.): 1,020,900. **Age distrib.** (%): 0–14: 36.3; 15–59: 57.2; 60+: 6.4. **Pop. density:** 1,308 per sq. mi. **Urban** (1984): 41%. **Ethnic groups:** Indo-Mauritians 68%, Creoles 27%, others. **Languages:** English (official), French, Creole. **Religions:** Hindu 51%, Christian 30%, Moslem 16%.

Geography: Area: 790 sq. mi., about the size of Rhode Island. **Location:** In the Indian O., 500 mi. E of Madagascar. **Neighbors:** Nearest is Madagascar on W. **Topography:** A volcanic island nearly surrounded by coral reefs. A central plateau is encircled by mountain peaks. **Capital:** Port Louis. **Cities** (1986 est.): Port Louis 155,000.

Government: Type: Parliamentary democracy under a constitutional monarch. **Head of state:** Queen Elizabeth II, represented by Gov.-Gen. Sir Veerasamy Ringadoo; in office: Jan. 17, 1986. **Head of government:** Prime Min. Aneerood Jugnauth; in office: June 12, 1982. **Local divisions:** 9 administrative divisions.

Economy: Industries: Tourism. **Chief crops:** Sugar cane, tea. **Arable land:** 58%. **Electricity prod.** (1984): 378 mln. kwh. **Labor force:** 27% agric. & fishing; 22% ind. and commerce; 29% govt. services.

Finance: Currency: Rupee (Mar. 1987: 12.61 = $1 US). **Gross national product** (1984): $957 mln. **Per capita income** (1982): $1,240. **Imports** (1985): $529 mln.; partners: UK 9%, Fr. 12%, So. Afr. 9%. **Exports** (1985): $434 mln.; partners: UK 50%, Fr. 22%, U.S. 8%. **Tourists** (1984): $44 mln. receipts. **National budget** (1985): $310 mln. **International reserves less gold** (Feb. 1987): $199 mln. **Gold:** 38,000 oz t. **Consumer prices** (change in 1986): 1.9%.

Transport: Motor vehicles: in use (1984): 26,000 passenger cars, 17,000 comm. vehicles. **Chief ports:** Port Louis.

Communications: Television sets: 98,000 in use (1984). **Radios:** 129,000 in use (1984). **Telephones in use** (1983): 47,000. **Daily newspaper circ.** (1985): 75 per 1,000 pop.

Health: Life expectancy at birth (1982): 69 years. **Births** (per 1,000 pop. 1985): 20. **Deaths** (per 1,000 pop. 1985): 6. **Natural increase** (1985): 1.4%. **Hospital beds** (1985): 2,811. **Physicians** (1984): 690. **Infant mortality** (per 1,000 live births 1986): 28.

Education (1986): **Literacy:** 79%. **Attendance:** most children attend school.

Major International Organizations: UN and all of its specialized agencies, OAU, Commonwealth of Nations.

Embassy: 4301 Connecticut Ave. NW 20008; 244-1491.

Mauritius was uninhabited when settled in 1638 by the Dutch, who introduced sugar cane. France took over in 1721, bringing African slaves. Britain ruled from 1810 to Mar. 12, 1968, bringing Indian workers for the sugar plantations.

The economy has suffered in the 1980s because of low world sugar prices.

Mexico

United Mexican States

Estados Unidos Mexicanos

People: Population (1986 est.): 81,709,000. **Age distrib.** (%): 0–14: 42.9; 15–59: 52.3; 60+: 5.9. **Pop. density:** 106 per sq. mi. **Urban** (1985): 70%. **Ethnic groups:** Mestizo 55%, American Indian 29%, Caucasian 10%. **Languages:** Spanish. **Religions:** Roman Catholics 97%.

Geography: Area: 761,604 sq. mi., three times the size of Texas. **Location:** In southern N. America. **Neighbors:** U.S. on N, Guatemala, Belize on S. **Topography:** The Sierra Madre Occidental Mts. run NW-SE near the west coast; the Sierra Madre Oriental Mts., run near the Gulf of Mexico. They join S of Mexico City. Between the 2 ranges lies the dry central plateau, 5,000 to 8,000 ft. alt., rising toward the S, with temperate vegetation. Coastal lowlands are tropical. About 45% of land is arid. **Capital:** Mexico City. **Cities** (1980 est.): Mexico City (metro) 15 mln.; Guadalajara (metro) 2.4 mln.; Monterrey (metro) 2 mln.

Government: Type: Federal republic. **Head of state:** Pres. Miguel de la Madrid Hurtado; b. Dec. 12, 1934; in office: Dec. 1, 1982. **Local divisions:** Federal district and 31 states. **Defense:** 0.3% of GNP (1984).

Economy: Industries: Steel, chemicals, electric goods, textiles, rubber, petroleum handicrafts, tourism. **Chief crops:** Cotton, coffee, sugar cane, vegetables, corn. **Minerals:** Silver, lead, zinc, gold, oil, natural gas. **Crude oil reserves** (1985): 50 bln. bbls. **Arable land:** 13%. **Meat prod.** (1985): cattle: 31.1 mln.; pigs: 19 mln.; sheep: 6.5 mln. **Fish catch** (1984): 1.1 mln. metric tons. **Electricity prod.** (1984): 87.0 bln. kwh. **Crude steel prod.** (1985): 7.2 mln. metric tons. **Labor force:** 41% agric.; 18% manuf.

Finance: Currency: Peso (May 1987: 1,231 = $1 US). **Gross national product** (1984): $158 bln. **Per capita income** (1984): $2,082. **Imports** (1985): $13.9 bln.; partners: U.S. 62%, Jap. 5%, W. Ger. 5%. **Exports** (1985): $21.8 bln.; partners: U.S. 58% Spa. 7%. **Tourists** (1985): receipts: $1.7 bln. **National budget** (1981): $93.3 bln. revenues; $93.3 bln. expenditures. **International reserves less gold** (Jan. 1987): $5.6 bln. **Gold:** 2.5 mln. oz t. **Consumer prices** (change in 1986): 86.2%.

Transport: Railway traffic (1985): 5.9 bln. passenger-km; 45.4 bln. net ton-km. **Motor vehicles:** in use (1982): 5.2 mln. passenger cars, 1.8 mln. comm. **Civil aviation** (1985): 17.8 bln. passenger-km; 173 mln. freight ton-km. **Chief ports:** Veracruz, Tampico, Mazatlan, Coatzacoalcos.

Communications: Television sets: 7.7 mln. in use (1985). **Radios:** 22 mln. in use (1985). **Telephones in use** (1983): 5.8 mln. **Daily newspaper circ.** (1982): 130 per 1,000 pop.

Health: Life expectancy at birth (1985): 63.9 male; 68.2 female. **Births** (per 1,000 pop. 1985): 32. **Deaths** (per 1,000 pop. 1985): 6. **Natural increase** (1985): 2.6%. **Hospital beds** (1984): 72,000. **Physicians** (1980): 53,053. **Infant mortality** (per 1,000 live births 1985): 42.

Education (1983): **Literacy:** 74%. **Years compulsory:** 10.

Major International Organizations: UN (IMF, WHO, ILO), OAS.

Embassy: 2829 16th St. NW 20009; 234-6000.

Mexico was the site of advanced Indian civilizations. The Mayas, an agricultural people, moved up from Yucatan, built immense stone pyramids, invented a calendar. The Toltecs were overcome by the Aztecs, who founded Tenochtitlan 1325 AD, now Mexico City. Hernando Cortes, Spanish conquistador, destroyed the Aztec empire, 1519-1521.

After 3 centuries of Spanish rule the people rose, under Fr. Miguel Hidalgo y Costilla, 1810, Fr. Morelos y Payon, 1812, and Gen. Agustin Iturbide, who made independence effective Sept. 27, 1821, but made himself emperor as Agustin I. A republic was declared in 1823.

Mexican territory extended into the present American Southwest and California until Texas revolted and established a republic in 1836; the Mexican legislature refused recognition but was unable to enforce its authority there. After numerous clashes, the U.S.-Mexican War, 1846-48, resulted in the loss by Mexico of the lands north of the Rio Grande.

French arms supported an Austrian archduke on the throne of Mexico as Maximilian I, 1864-67, but pressure from the U.S. forced France to withdraw. A dictatorial rule by Porfirio Diaz, president 1877-80, 1884-1911, led to fighting by rival forces until the new constitution of Feb. 5, 1917 provided social reform. Since then Mexico has developed large-scale programs of social security, labor protection, and school improvement. A constitutional provision requires management to share profits with labor.

The Institutional Revolutionary Party has been dominant in politics since 1929. Radical opposition, including some guerrilla activity, has been contained by strong measures.

The presidency of Luis Echeverria, 1970-76, was marked by a more leftist foreign policy and domestic rhetoric. Some land redistribution begun in 1976 was reversed under the succeeding administration.

Some gains in agriculture, industry, and social services have been achieved. The land is rich, but the rugged topography and lack of sufficient rainfall are major obstacles. Crops and farm prices are controlled, as are export and import. Economic prospects brightened with the discovery of vast oil reserves, perhaps the world's greatest. But much of the work force is jobless or underemployed.

Inflation and the drop in world oil prices has caused economic problems in the 1980s. The peso was devalued and private banks were nationalized to restore financial stability.

President de la Madrid has urged the U.S. to avoid the use of force to solve differences in Central America. Mexico has friendly relations with Cuba and Nicaragua.

Many thousands died when a disastrous earthquake struck Mexico City, Sept. 19, 1985.

The U.S. has been critical of Mexico for its failure to combat the production of illegal drugs.

Monaco

Principality of Monaco

People: Population (1986 est.): 28,000. **Age distrib.** (%): 0–14: 12.7; 15–59: 56.3 60+: 30.7. **Pop. density:** 28,072 per sq. mi. **Ethnic groups:** French 47%, Italian 16%, Monegasque 16%. **Languages:** French (official). **Religions:** Predominantely Roman Catholic.

Geography: Area: 0.6 sq. mi. **Location:** On the NW Mediterranean coast. **Neighbors:** France to W, N, E. **Topography:** Monaco-Ville sits atop a high promontory, the rest of the principality rises from the port up the hillside. **Capital:** Monaco-Ville (1985 est.): 1,700.

Government: Type: Constitutional monarchy. **Head of state:** Prince Rainier III; b. May 31, 1923; in office: May 9, 1949. **Head of government:** Min. of State Jean Ausseil; in office: Sept 1985.

Economy: Industries: Tourism, gambling, chemicals, precision instruments, plastics.

Finance: Currency: French franc or Monégasque franc.

Transport: Chief ports: La Condamine.

Communications: Television sets: 17,000 in use (1984). **Telephones in use** (1984): 18,000. **Daily newspaper circ.** (1977): 11,000; 420 per 1,000 pop.

Health: Births (per 1,000 pop. 1985): 7. **Deaths** (per 1,000 pop. 1985): 10. **Natural increase** (1985): –.3%. **Infant mortality** (per 1,000 live births 1970): 9.3.

Education: (1985): **Literacy:** 99%. **Years compulsory:** 10; attendance 99%.

An independent principality for over 300 years, Monaco has belonged to the House of Grimaldi since 1297 except during the French Revolution. It was placed under the protectorate of Sardinia in 1815, and under that of France, 1861. The Prince of Monaco was an absolute ruler until a 1911 constitution.

Monaco's fame as a tourist resort is widespread. It is noted for its mild climate and magnificent scenery. The area has been extended by land reclamation.

Mongolia

Mongolian People's Republic

Bügd Nayramdakh Mongol Ard Uls

People: Population (1986 est.): 1,942,000. **Pop. density:** 3 per sq. mi. **Urban** (1985): 52%. **Ethnic groups:** Khalkha Mongols 75%, other Mongols 8%, Kazakhs 5%. **Languages:** Khalkha Mongolian (official, written in Cyrillic letters since 1941), Russian, Chinese. **Religions:** Lama Buddhism prevailed, has been curbed.

Geography: Area: 604,247 sq. mi., more than twice the size of Texas. **Location:** In E Central Asia. **Neighbors:** USSR on N, China on S. **Topography:** Mostly a high plateau with mountains, salt lakes, and vast grasslands. Arid lands in the S are part of the Gobi Desert. **Capital:** Ulaanbaatar. **Cities** (1985 est.): Ulaanbaatar 488,000, Darhan 69,000.

Government: Type: Communist state. **Head of state:** Chmn. Zhambyn Batmunkh; b. May 10, 1926; in office: Aug. 23, 1984. **Head of government:** Premier Dumaagiyn Sodnom; in office: Aug. 23, 1984. **Local divisions:** 18 provinces, 3 autonomous municipalities. **Defense:** 11.5% of GNP (1984).

Economy: Industries: Food processing, textiles, chemicals, cement. **Chief crops:** Grain. **Minerals:** Coal, tungsten, copper, molybdenum, gold, tin. **Arable land:** 1%. **Meat prod.** (1983): beef: 70,000 metric tons; lamb: 129,000 metric tons. **Electricity prod.** (1984): 1.8 bln. kwh. **Labor force:** 52% agric.; 10% manuf.

Finance: Currency: Tugrik (Jan. 1987: 3.35 = $1 US). **Gross national product** (1984): $1.8 bln. **Per capita income** (1984): $1,000. **Imports** (1984): $750 mln.; partners: USSR 91%. **Exports** (1984): $520 mln.; partners: USSR 80%.

Transport: Railway traffic (1984): 386 mln. passenger-km; 4.4 bln. net ton-km.

Communications: Television sets: 78,000 in use (1985). **Radios:** 170,000 in use (1985). **Telephones in use** (1985): 46,000. **Daily newspaper circ.** (1985): 91 per 1,000 pop.

Health: Life expectancy at birth (1985): 62.9 male; 66.8 female. **Births** (per 1,000 pop. 1985): 35. **Deaths** (per 1,000 pop. 1985): 10. **Natural increase** (1985): 2.5%. **Hospital beds** (1985): 20,400. **Physicians** (1985): 4,234. **Infant mortality** (per 1,000 live births 1985): 46.

Major International Organizations: UN (ILO, WHO).

Education (1983): **Literacy:** 89%. **Years compulsory:** 7 in major population centers.

One of the world's oldest countries, Mongolia reached the zenith of its power in the 13th century when Genghis Khan and his successors conquered all of China and extended their influence as far W as Hungary and Poland. In later centuries, the empire dissolved and Mongolia came under the suzerainty of China.

With the advent of the 1911 Chinese revolution, Mongolia, with Russian backing, declared its independence. A Mongolian Communist regime was established July 11, 1921.

Mongolia has been changed from a nomadic culture to one of settled agriculture and growing industries with aid from the USSR and East European nations.

Mongolia has sided with the Russians in the Sino-Soviet dispute. A Mongolian-Soviet mutual assistance pact was signed Jan. 15, 1966, and some 60,000 Soviet troops are based in the country.

Morocco

Kingdom of Morocco

al-Mamlaka al-Maghrebia

People: Population (1986 est.): 23,667,000. **Age distrib.** (%): 0–14: 46.4; 15–59: 49.2; 60+: 4.2. **Pop. density:** 126 per sq. mi. **Urban** (1985): 43%. **Ethnic groups:** Arab-Berber 99%. **Languages:** Arabic (official), with Berber, French, Spanish minorities. **Religions:** Sunni Moslems 99%.

Geography: Area: 172,413 sq. mi., larger than California. **Location:** on NW coast of Africa. **Neighbors:** W. Sahara on S, Algeria on E. **Topography:** Consists of 5 natural regions: mountain ranges (Riff in the N, Middle Atlas, Upper Atlas, and Anti-Atlas); rich plains in the W; alluvial plains in SW; well-cultivated plateaus in the center; a pre-Sahara arid zone extending from SE. **Capital:** Rabat. **Cities** (1984): Casablanca 2,600,000; Rabat 550,000, Fes 852,000.

Government: Type: Constitutional monarchy. **Head of state:** King Hassan II; b. July 9, 1929; in office: Mar. 3, 1961. **Head of government:** Prime Min. Azzedine Laraki; in office: Sept. 30, 1986. **Local divisions:** 6 prefectures, 35 provinces. **Defense:** 8.2% of GNP (1983).

Economy: Industries: Carpets, clothing, leather goods, tourism. **Chief crops:** Grain, fruits, dates, grapes. **Minerals:** Antimony, cobalt, manganese, phosphates, lead, oil, coal. **Crude oil reserves** (1980): 100 mln. bbls. **Arable land:** 18%. **Meat prod.** (1984): cattle: 3.3 mln.; sheep; 12 mln.; goats: 4.5 mln. **Fish catch** (1984): 439,000 metric tons. **Electricity prod.** (1984): 6.4 bln. kwh. **Labor force:** 50% agric., 26% services.

Finance: Currency: Dirham (Mar. 1987: 8.40 = $1 US). **Gross national product** (1984): $14.3 bln. **Per capita income** (1984): $630. **Imports** (1985): $3.8 bln.; partners: Fr. 25%, Sp. 7%, Saudi Ar. 15%. **Exports** (1985): $2.1 bln.; partners: Fr. 22%, W. Ger. 7%, Sp. 7%, It. 5%. **Tourists** (1984): $440 mln. receipts. **National budget** (1985): $6.8 bln. expenditures. **International reserves less gold** (Mar. 1987): $196 mln. **Gold:** 704,000 oz t. **Consumer prices** (change in 1986): 8.7%.

Transport: Railway traffic (1984): 1.4 bln. passenger-km; 4.1 bln. net ton-km. **Motor vehicles:** in use (1983): 470,000 passenger cars, 232,000 comm. vehicles. **Civil aviation** (1985): 2.1 bln. passenger-km; 38.7 mln. freight ton-km. **Chief ports:** Tangier, Casablanca, Kenitra.

Communications: Television sets: 1 mln. in use (1985). **Radios:** 2.5 mln. in use (1985). **Telephones in use** (1983): 265,000. **Daily newspaper circ.** (1985): 12 per 1,000 pop.

Health: Life expectancy at birth (1985): 56.1 male; 59.4 female. **Births** (per 1,000 pop. 1985): 44.1. **Deaths** (per 1,000 pop. 1985): 11.7. **Natural increase** (1985): 3.2%. **Hospital beds** (1984): 26,538. **Physicians** (1984): 2,957. **Infant mortality** (per 1,000 live births 1985): 93.

Education (1980): **Literacy:** 70%.

Major International Organizations: UN (ILO, IMF, WHO), OAU, Arab League.

Embassy: 1601 21st St. NW 20009; 462-7979.

Berbers were the original inhabitants, followed by Carthaginians and Romans. Arabs conquered in 683. In the 11th and 12th centuries, a Berber empire ruled all NW Africa and most of Spain from Morocco.

Part of Morocco came under Spanish rule in the 19th century; France controlled the rest in the early 20th. Tribal uprisings lasted from 1911 to 1933. The country became independent Mar. 2, 1956. Tangier, an internationalized seaport, was turned over to Morocco, 1956. Ifni, a Spanish enclave, was ceded in 1969.

Morocco annexed over 70,000 sq. mi. of phosphate-rich land Apr. 14, 1976, two-thirds of former Spanish Sahara, with the remainder annexed by Mauritania. Spain had withdrawn in February. Polisario, a guerrilla movement, proclaimed the region independent Feb. 27, and launched attacks with Algerian support. Morocco accepted U.S. military and economic aid. When Mauritania signed a treaty with the Polisario Front, and gave up its portion of the former Spanish Sahara, Morocco occupied the area, 1980. Morocco accused Algeria of instigating Polisario attacks.

After years of bitter fighting, Morocco controls the main urban areas, but the Polisario Front's guerrillas move freely in the vast, sparsely populated deserts.

Mozambique

People's Republic of Mozambique

República Popular de Mocambique

People: Population (1986 est.): 14,022,000. **Age distrib.** (%): 0–14: 45.3; 15–59: 50.6; 60+: 4.1. **Pop. density:** 46 per sq. mi. **Ethnic groups:** Bantu tribes. **Languages:** Portuguese (official), Bantu languages predominate. **Religions:** Traditional beliefs 50%, Christian 30%, Moslem 10%.

Geography: Area: 309,494 sq. mi., larger than California. **Location:** On SE coast of Africa. **Neighbors:** Tanzania on N, Malawi, Zambia, Zimbabwe on W, South Africa, Swaziland on S. **Topography:** Coastal lowlands comprise nearly half the country with plateaus rising in steps to the mountains along the western border. **Capital:** Maputo. **Cities:** (1982 est.): Maputo 785,000.

Government: Type: Socialist one-party state. **Head of state:** Pres. Joaquim Chissano; b. Oct. 22, 1939; in office: Oct. 19, 1986. **Head of Goverment:** Mario De Graca Machungo; in office: July 17, 1986. **Local divisions:** 10 provinces. **Defense:** 30% of govt. budget (1983).

Economy: Industries: Cement, alcohol, textiles. **Chief crops:** Cashews, cotton, sugar, copra, tea. **Minerals:** Coal, bauxite. **Arable land:** 4%. **Meat prod.** (1980): beef: 36,000 metric tons; pork: 8,000 metric tons. **Fish catch** (1984): 42,000 metric tons. **Electricity prod.** (1984): 9.6 bln. kwh. **Labor force:** 85% agric., 9% ind. & comm., 2% services.

Finance: Currency: Metical (Jan. 1987: 40 = $1 US). **Gross domestic product** (1983): $2.7 bln. **Per capita income** (1983): $220. **Imports** (1983): $636 mln.; partners: So. Afr. 20%, W. Ger. 15%, Port. 10%. **Exports** (1983): $132 mln.; partners: U.S. 27%, Port. 16%, UK 7%, So. Afr. 7%. **National budget** (1983): $640 mln.

Transport: Railway traffic (1985): 225 mln. passenger-km; 289 mln. net ton-km. **Motor vehicles:** in use (1981): 49,000 passenger cars, 24,700 comm. vehicles. **Chief ports:** Maputo, Beira, Nacala, Quelimane.

Communications: Television sets: 6,500 in use (1985). **Radios:** 450,000 licensed (1985). **Telephones in use** (1982): 56,000. **Daily newspaper circ.** (1984): 3 per 1,000 pop.

Health: Life expectancy at birth (1985): 47 years. **Births** (per 1,000 pop. 1985): 44.6. **Deaths** (per 1,000 pop. 1985): 17.2. **Natural increase** (1985): 2.7%. **Hospital beds** (1985): 12,427. **Physicians** (1985): 317. **Infant mortality** (per 1,000 live births 1985): 158.

Education (1985): **Literacy:** 14%.

Major International Organization: UN (IMF, World Bank), OAU.

The first Portuguese post on the Mozambique coast was established in 1505, on the trade route to the East. Mozambique became independent June 25, 1975, after a ten-year war against Portuguese colonial domination. The 1974 revolution in

Portugal paved the way for the orderly transfer of power to Frelimo (Front for the Liberation of Mozambique). Frelimo took over local administration Sept. 20, 1974, over the opposition, in part violent, of some blacks and whites. The new government, led by Maoist Pres. Samora Machel, promised a gradual transition to a communist system. Private schools were closed, rural collective farms organized, and private homes nationalized. Economic problems included the emigration of most of the country's 160,000 whites, a politically untenable economic dependence on white-ruled South Africa, and a large external debt.

In the 1980s, severe drought caused famine and heavy loss of life.

Nauru

Republic of Nauru

Naoero

People: Population (1986): 8,000. **Pop density:** 974 per sq. mi. **Ethnic groups:** Nauruans 57%, Pacific Islanders 26%, Chinese 8%, European 8%. **Languages:** Nauruan (official), English. **Religions:** Predominately Christian.

Geography: Area: 8 sq. mi. **Location:** In Western Pacific O. just S of Equator. **Neighbors:** Nearest are Solomon Is. **Topography:** Mostly a plateau bearing high grade phosphate deposits, surrounded by a coral cliff and a sandy shore in concentric rings. **Capital:** Yaren.

Government: Type: Republic. **Head of state:** Pres. Hammer DeRoburt, b. Sept. 25, 1922; in office: May 11, 1978. **Local divisions:** 14 districts.

Economy: Phosphate mining. **Electricity prod.** (1983): 27.00 mln. kwh.

Finance: Currency: Australian dollar. **Gross national product** (1981): $155 mln. **Per capita income** (1981): $21,400. **Imports** (1979): $11 mln. **Exports** (1979): $75 mln. **National budget** (1979): $46 mln. revenues; $38 mln. expenditures.

Communications: Radios: 4,000 in use (1985). **Telephones in use** (1980): 1,500.

Health: Births (per 1,000 pop. 1985): 21. **Deaths** (per 1,000 pop. 1985): 5. **Natural increase** (1985): 1.6%. **Infant mortality** (per 1,000 live births 1985): 26.

Education: Literacy 99%; Compulsory ages 6-16.

The island was discovered in 1798 by the British but was formally annexed to the German Empire in 1886. After World War I, Nauru became a League of Nations mandate administered by Australia. During World War II the Japanese occupied the island and shipped 1,200 Nauruans to the fortress island of Truk as slave laborers.

In 1947 Nauru was made a UN trust territory, administered by Australia. Nauru became an independent republic Jan. 31, 1968.

Phosphate exports provide one of the world's highest per capita revenues for the Nauru people. The deposits are expected to be nearly exhausted by 1990.

Nepal

Kingdom of Nepal

Sri Nepala Sarkar

People: Population (1986 est.): 17,422,000. **Age distrib.** (%): 0–14: 40.5; 15–59: 53.9; 60+: 5.6. **Pop. density:** 296 per sq. mi. **Urban** (1981): 6.4%. **Ethnic groups:** The many tribes are descendants of Indian, Tibetan, and Central Asian migrants. **Languages:** Nepali (official) (an Indic language), 12 others. **Religions:** Hindus 90%, Buddhists 7%.

Geography: Area: 56,136 sq. mi., the size of North Carolina. **Location:** Astride the Himalaya Mts. **Neighbors:** China on N, India on S. **Topography:** The Himalayas stretch across the N, the hill country with its fertile valleys extends across the center, while the southern border region is part of the flat, subtropical Ganges Plain. **Capital:** Kathmandu. **Cities** (1982 est.): Kathmandu 125,000, Pokhara, Biratnagar, Birganj.

Government: Type: Constitutional monarchy. **Head of state:** King Birendra Bir Bikram Shah Dev; b. Dec. 28, 1945; in office: Jan. 31, 1972. **Head of government:** Prime Min. Marich Man Singh Shrestha; in office: July 15, 1986. **Local divisions:** 14 zones; 75 districts. **Defense:** 1.3% of GNP (1984).

Economy: Industries: Sugar, jute mills, tourism. **Chief crops:** Jute, rice, grain. **Minerals:** Quartz. **Other resources:** Forests. **Arable land:** 17%. **Meat prod.** (1986): cattle: 7 mln. **Electricity prod.** (1984): 350 mln. kwh. **Labor force:** 93% agric.

Finance: Currency: Rupee (Mar. 1987: 21.00 = $1 US). **Gross national product** (1984): $2.6 bln. **Per capita income** (1984): $160. **Imports** (1981): $369 mln.; partners: India 47%, Jap. 25%. **Exports** (1981): $134 mln.; partners: India 68%. **Tourists** (1984): receipts: $32 mln. **National budget** (1985): $150 mln. **International reserves less gold** (Mar. 1987): $85 mln. **Gold:** 151,000 oz t. **Consumer prices** (change in 1986): 19.0%.

Communications: Radios: 310,000 in use (1984). **Telephones in use** (1984): 23,000. **Daily newspaper circ.** (1983): 5 per 1,000 pop.

Health: Life expectancy at birth (1984): 47.2 male; 45.7 female. **Births** (per 1,000 pop. 1985): 42. **Deaths** (per 1,000 pop. 1985): 17. **Natural increase** (1985): 2.5%. **Hospital beds** (1984): 3,048. **Physicians** (1984): 571. **Infant mortality** (per 1,000 live births 1985): 313.

Education (1981): **Literacy:** 23%. **Years compulsory:** 3; Attendance: 71% primary, 14% secondary.

Major International Organizations: UN (IMF).

Embassy: 2131 Leroy Pl. NW 20008; 667-4550.

Nepal was originally a group of petty principalities, the inhabitants of one of which, the Gurkhas, became dominant about 1769. In 1951 King Tribhubana Bir Bikram, member of the Shah family, ended the system of rule by hereditary premiers of the Ranas family, who had kept the kings virtual prisoners, and established a cabinet system of government.

Virtually closed to the outside world for centuries, Nepal is now linked to India and Pakistan by roads and air service and to Tibet by road. Polygamy, child marriage, and the caste system were officially abolished in 1963.

Netherlands

Kingdom of the Netherlands

Konindrijk der Nederlanden

People: Population (1986 est.) 14,536,000. **Age distrib. (%):** 0–14: 19.7; 15–60: 63.6; 60+: 16.7. **Pop. density:** 1,112 per sq. mi. **Urban** (1983): 88.3%. **Ethnic groups:** Dutch 97%. **Languages:** Dutch. **Religions:** Roman Catholic 36%, Dutch Reformed 19.3%.

Geography: Area: 15,770 sq. mi., the size of Mass., Conn., and R.I. combined. **Location:** In NW Europe on North Sea. **Topography:** The land is flat, an average alt. of 37 ft. above sea level, with much land below sea level reclaimed and protected by 1,500 miles of dikes. Since 1927 the government has been draining the IJsselmeer, formerly the Zuider Zee. By 1972, 410,000 of a planned 550,000 acres had been drained and reclaimed. **Capital:** Amsterdam. **Cities** (1986): Amsterdam 679,000; Rotterdam 571,100; Hague 443,500.

Government: Type: Parliamentary democracy under a constitutional monarch. **Head of state:** Queen Beatrix; b. Jan. 31, 1938; in office: Apr. 30, 1980. **Head of government:** Prime Min. Ruud Lubbers; in office: Nov. 4, 1982. **Seat of govt.:** The Hague. **Local divisions:** 11 provinces. **Defense:** 3.2% of GNP (1984).

Economy: Industries: Metals, machinery, chemicals, oil refinery, diamond cutting, electronics, tourism. **Chief crops:** Grains, potatoes, sugar beets, vegetables, fruits, flowers. **Minerals:** Natural gas, oil. **Crude oil reserves** (1985): 170 mln. bbls. **Arable land:** 26%. **Meat prod.** (1985): cattle: 5 mln.; pigs: 12.9 mln. **Fish catch** (1984): 503,000 metric tons. **Electricity prod.** (1984): 62.7 bln. kwh. **Crude steel prod.** (1985): 5.5 mln. metric tons. **Labor force:** 6% agric.; 36% ind. and commerce, 34% services, 15% govt.

Finance: Currency: Guilder (May 1987: 2.00 = $1 US). **Gross national product** (1984): $122.4 bln. **Per capita income** (1984): $9,420. **Imports** (1986): $75.5 bln.; partners: W. Ger. 22%, Belg. 11%, U.S. 9%, U.K. 9%. **Exports** (1986): $80.5 bln.; partners : W. Ger. 30%, Belg. 14%, Fr. 10%, UK 9%. **Tourists** (1984): 2.8 mln.; receipts: $1.4 bln. **National budget** (1984): $66 bln. expenditures. **International reserves less gold** (Mar. 1987): $12.1 bln. **Gold:** 43.94 mln. oz t. **Consumer prices** (change in 1986): 0.2%.

Transport: Railway traffic (1984): 8.9 bln. passenger-km; 2.7 bln. net ton-km. **Motor vehicles:** in use (1984): 4.8 mln. passenger cars, 357,000 comm. vehicles. **Civil aviation** (1985): 18.2 bln. passenger-km; 1.2 bln. freight ton-km. **Chief ports:** Rotterdam, Amsterdam, IJmuiden.

Communications: Television sets: 4.4 mln. licensed (1985). **Radios:** 4.7 mln. licensed (1985). **Telephones in use** (1983): 8 mln. **Daily newspaper circ.** (1984): 312 per 1,000 pop.

Health: Life expectancy at birth (1984): 72 male; 78 female. **Births** (per 1,000 pop. 1985): 12. **Deaths** (per 1,000 pop. 1985): 8. **Natural increase** (1985): .4%. **Hospital beds** (1985): 68,943. **Physicians** (1985): 31,185. **Infant mortality** (per 1,000 live births 1985): 8.

Education (1985): **Literacy:** 99%. **Years compulsory:** 10; attendance: 100%.

Major International Organizations: UN and all of its specialized agencies, NATO, EC.

Embassy: 4200 Linnean Ave. NW 20008; 244-5300.

Julius Caesar conquered the region in 55 BC, when it was inhabited by Celtic and Germanic tribes.

After the empire of Charlemagne fell apart, the Netherlands (Holland, Belgium, Flanders) split among counts, dukes and bishops, passed to Burgundy and thence to Charles V of Spain. His son, Philip II, tried to check the Dutch drive toward political freedom and Protestantism (1568-1573). William the Silent, prince of Orange, led a confederation of the northern provinces, called Estates, in the Union of Utrecht, 1579. The Estates retained individual sovereignty, but were represented jointly in the States-General, a body that had control of foreign affairs and defense. In 1581 they repudiated allegiance to Spain. The rise of the Dutch republic to naval, economic, and artistic eminence came in the 17th century.

The United Dutch Republic ended 1795 when the French formed the Batavian Republic. Napoleon made his brother Louis king of Holland, 1806; Louis abdicated 1810 when Napoleon annexed Holland. In 1813 the French were expelled. In 1815 the Congress of Vienna formed a kingdom of the Netherlands, including Belgium, under William I. In 1830, the Belgians seceded and formed a separate kingdom.

The constitution, promulgated 1814, and subsequently revised, assures a hereditary constitutional monarchy.

The Netherlands maintained its neutrality in World War I, but was invaded and brutally occupied by Germany from 1940 to 1945. After the war, neutrality was abandoned, and the country joined NATO, the Western European Union, the Benelux Union, and, in 1957, became a charter member of the Common Market.

In 1949, after several years of fighting, the Netherlands granted independence to Indonesia, where it had ruled since the 17th century. In 1963, West New Guinea was turned over to Indonesia, after five years of controversy and seizure of Dutch property in Indonesia.

The independence of former Dutch colonies has instigated mass emigrations to the Netherlands, adding to problems of unemployment.

Though the Netherlands has been heavily industrialized, its productive small farms export large quantities of pork and dairy foods.

The Netherlands has agreed to allow NATO to deploy 48 cruise missiles on their soil by 1988.

Rotterdam, located along the principal mouth of the Rhine, handles the most cargo of any ocean port in the world. Canals, of which there are 3,478 miles, are important in transportation.

Netherlands Antilles

The **Netherlands Antilles,** constitutionally on a level of equality with the Netherlands homeland within the kingdom, consist of 2 groups of islands in the West Indies. **Curacao, Aruba,** and **Bonaire** are near the South American coast; **St. Eustatius, Saba,** and the southern part of **St. Maarten** are SE of Puerto Rico. Northern two-thirds of St. Maarten belong to French Guadeloupe; the French call the island St. Martin. Total area of the 2 groups is 385 sq. mi., including: Aruba 75, Bonaire 111, Curacao 171, St. Eustatius 11, Saba 5, St. Maarten (Dutch part) 13.

Aruba became independent on Jan. 1, 1986; it is an autonomous member of The Netherlands, the same status as the Netherland Antilles.

Total pop. (est. 1985) was 244,000. Willemstad, on Curacao, is the capital. Chief products are corn, pulse, salt and phosphate; principal industry is the refining of crude oil from Venezuela. Tourism is an important industry, as are electronics and shipbuilding.

New Zealand

People: Population: (1986 est.): 3,305,000. **Age distrib.** (%): 0–14: 23.3, 15–59: 61.1; 60+: 15.6 **Pop. density:** 32 per sq. mi. **Urban** (1984): 83.0%. **Ethnic groups:** European (mostly British) 87%, Polynesian (mostly Maori) 9%. **Languages:** English (official), Maori. **Religions:** Anglican 29%, Presbyterian 18%, Roman Catholic 15%, others.

Geography: Area: 103,736 sq. mi., the size of Colorado. **Location:** In SW Pacific O. **Neighbors:** Nearest are Australia on W, Fiji, Tonga on N. **Topography:** Each of the 2 main islands (North and South Is.) is mainly hilly and mountainous. The east coasts consist of fertile plains, especially the broad Canterbury Plains on South Is. A volcanic plateau is in center of North Is. South Is. has glaciers and 15 peaks over 10,000 ft. **Capital:** Wellington. **Cities** (1985 met. est.): Auckland 894,000; Christchurch 323,000; Wellington 342,000.

Government: Type: Parliamentary. **Head of state:** Queen Elizabeth II, represented by Gov.-Gen. Paul Reeves. **Head of government:** Prime Min. David Lange; b. Aug. 4, 1942; elected: July 14, 1984. **Local divisions:** 96 counties, 132 boroughs, 3 towns, 4 districts. **Defense:** 1.9% of GNP (1985).

Economy: Industries: Food processing, textiles, machinery, fish, forest prods. **Chief crops:** Grain. **Minerals:** Oil, gas, iron, coal **Crude oil reserves** (1985): 187 mln. bbls. **Other resources:** Wool, timber. **Arable land:** 2%. **Meat prod.** (1985): cattle: 8.4 mln.; sheep: 67.2 mln. **Fish catch** (1984): 141,000 metric tons. **Electricity prod.** (1985): 26.7 bln. kwh. **Crude steel prod.** (1981): 221,000 metric tons. **Labor force:** 11% agric. & mining; 40% ind. and commerce, 47% services and gov.

Finance: Currency: Dollar (May 1987: 1.71 = $1 US). **Gross national product** (1986): $23.2 bln. **Per capita income** (1986): $7,282. **Imports** (1986): $6.0 bln.; partners: Austral. 18%, U.S. 16%, Jap. 20%. **Exports** (1986): $5.9 bln.; partners: UK 14%, U.S. 13%, Jap. 13%, Austral. 15%. **Tourists** (1984): receipts $309 mln. **National budget** (1985): $7.4 bln. **International reserves less gold** (Feb. 1987): $5.9 bln. **Gold:** 22,000 oz t. **Consumer prices** (change in 1986): 10.4%.

Transport: Railway traffic (1984): 458 mln. passenger-km; 3.1 bln. net ton-km. **Motor vehicles:** in use (1985): 1.5 min. passenger cars; 308,000 comm. vehicles. **Civil aviation:** (1985): 7.8 bln. passenger-km; 1.0 bln. freight ton-km. **Chief ports:** Auckland, Wellington, Lyttleton, Tauranga.

Communications: Television sets: 959,000 in use (1985). **Radios:** 2.7 mln. in use (1984). **Telephones in use** (1985): 2.1 mln. **Daily newspaper circ.** (1985): 323 per 1,000 pop.

Health: Life expectancy at birth (1985): 71.0 male; 76.8 female. **Births** (per 1,000 pop. 1985): 16.2. **Deaths** (per 1,000 pop. 1985): 7.6. **Natural increase** (1985): .8%. **Hospital beds** (1984): 24,891. **Physicians** (1984): 7,750. **Infant mortality** (per 1,000 live births 1985): 10.

Education (1987): **Literacy:** 99%. Compulsory ages 6-15; attendance: 100%.

Major International Organizations: UN (GATT, World Bank, IMF), Commonwealth of Nations, OECD.

Embassy: 37 Observatory Cir. NW 20008; 328-4800.

The Maoris, a Polynesian group from the eastern Pacific, reached New Zealand before and during the 14th century. The first European to sight New Zealand was Dutch navigator Abel Janszoon Tasman, but Maoris refused to allow him to land. British Capt. James Cook explored the coasts, 1769-1770.

British sovereignty was proclaimed in 1840, with organized settlement beginning in the same year. Representative institutions were granted in 1853. Maori Wars ended in 1870 with British victory. The colony became a dominion in 1907, and is an independent member of the Commonwealth.

New Zealand fought on the side of the Allies in both world wars, and signed the ANZUS Treaty of Mutual Security with the U.S. and Australia in 1951. New Zealand's refusal to allow U.S. ships with nuclear weapons to use their port facilities caused a strain on the ANZUS alliance in 1985. New Zealand joined with Australia and Britain in a pact to defend Singapore and Malaysia; New Zealand units are stationed in those 2 countries.

In July 1985, the *Rainbow Warrior*, flagship of the Greenpeace organization, was bombed and sunk in Auckland harbour by French secret service agents.

The ANZUS defense alliance ended in 1986 because of differences with the U.S. over the refusal of New Zealand port entry to ships that might be carrying nuclear weapons; defense commitments with the 3d ANZUS partner, Australia, remained.

A labor tradition in politics dates back to the 19th century. Private ownership is basic to the economy, but state ownership or regulation affects many industries. Transportation, broadcasting, mining, and forestry are largely state-owned.

The native Maoris number about 250,000. Four of 92 members of the House of Representatives are elected directly by the Maori people.

New Zealand comprises **North Island,** 44,035 sq. mi.; **South Island,** 58,304 sq. mi.; **Stewart Island,** 674 sq. mi.; **Chatham Islands,** 372 sq. mi.

In 1965, the **Cook Islands** (pop. 1983 est., 16,900; area 93 sq. mi.) became self-governing although New Zealand retains responsibility for defense and foreign affairs. **Niue** attained the same status in 1974; it lies 400 mi. to W (pop. 1981 est., 3,400; area 100 sq. mi.). **Tokelau Is.,** (pop. 1981 est., 1,600; area 4 sq. mi.) are 300 mi. N of Samoa.

Ross Dependency, administered by New Zealand since 1923, comprises 160,000 sq. mi. of Antarctic territory.

Nicaragua

Republic of Nicaragua

Republica de Nicaragua

People: Population (1986 est.): 3,342,000. **Age distrib.** (%): 0–14: 48.1; 15–59: 46.7; 60+: 4.1. **Pop. density:** 73 per sq. mi. **Urban** (1983): 55.3%. **Ethnic groups:** Mestizo 69%, Caucasian 17%, black 9%, Indian 5%. **Languages:** Spanish, English (on Caribbean coast). **Religion:** Roman Catholic 85%.

Geography: Area: 50,193 sq. mi., about the size of Iowa. **Location:** In Central America. **Neighbors:** Honduras on N, Costa Rica on S. **Topography:** Both Atlantic and Pacific coasts are over 200 mi. long. The Cordillera Mtns., with many volcanic peaks, runs NW-SE through the middle of the country. Between this and a volcanic range to the E lie Lakes Managua and Nicaragua. **Capital:** Managua. **Cities** (1986): Managua 1 mln.

Government: Type: Republic. **Head of Government:** Daniel Ortega Saavedra; in office Jan. 10, 1985. **Local divisions:** 16 departments, 137 municipalities, one national district. **Defense:** 10.2% of GNP (1983).

Economy: Industries: Oil refining, food processing, chemicals, textiles. **Chief crops:** Bananas, cotton, fruit, yucca, coffee, sugar, corn, beans, cocoa, rice, sesame, tobacco, wheat. **Minerals:** Gold, silver, copper, tungsten. **Other resources:** Forests, shrimp. **Arable land:** 25%. **Meat prod.** (1980): beef: 69,000 metric tons; pork: 11,000 metric tons. **Fish catch:** (1984): 4,500 metric tons. **Electricity prod.** (1983): 1.1 bln. kwh. **Labor force:** 41% agric.; 13% ind.; 46% services.

Finance: Currency: Cordoba (Apr. 1987: 70.00 = $1 US). **Gross national product** (1985): $2.8 bln. **Per capita income** (1985): $868. **Imports** (1985): $843 mln.; partners Comecon, CACM, EC. **Exports** (1985): $260 mln.; partners EC, Japan, Comecon. **National budget** (1984): $1.4 bln. expenditures. **International reserves less gold** (June 1983): $233 mln. **Gold:** 18,000 oz t. **Consumer prices** (change in 1985): 219%.

Transport: Railway traffic (1984): 20.2 mln. passenger-miles; 13 mln. net ton-miles. **Motor vehicles;** in use (1982): 25,000 passenger cars, 7,900 comm. vehicles. **Civil aviation** (1982): 20 mln. passenger-km; 14 mln. freight ton-km. **Chief ports:** Corinto, Puerto Somoza, San Juan del Sur.

Communications: Television sets: 160,000 in use (1985). **Radios:** 200,000 in use (1985). **Telephones in use** (1984): 51,000. **Daily newspaper circ.** (1985): 46 per 1,000 pop.

Health: Life expectancy at birth (1982): 56 male; 60 female. **Births** (per 1,000 pop. 1985): 44. **Deaths** (per 1,000 pop. 1985): 9. **Natural increase** (1985): 3.5%. **Hospital beds** (1984): 5,045. **Physicians** (1984): 2,172. **Infant mortality** (per 1,000 live births 1986): 37.0.

Education (1986): **Literacy:** 66%. **Years compulsory:** 11 years or 16 years old.

Major International Organizations: UN and all of its specialized agencies, OAS.

Embassy: 1627 New Hampshire Ave. NW 20009; 387-4371.

Nicaragua, inhabited by various Indian tribes, was conquered by Spain in 1552. After gaining independence from Spain, 1821, Nicaragua was united for a short period with Mexico, then with the United Provinces of Central America, finally becoming an independent republic, 1838.

U.S. Marines occupied the country at times in the early 20th century, the last time from 1926 to 1933.

Gen. Anastasio Somoza-Debayle was elected president 1967. He resigned 1972, but was elected president again in 1974. Martial law was imposed in Dec. 1974, after officials were kidnapped by the Marxist Sandinista guerrillas. The country's Roman Catholic bishops charged in 1977 that the government had mistreated civilians in its anti-guerrilla campaign. Violent opposition spread to nearly all classes, 1978; a nationwide strike called against the government Aug. 25 touched off a state of civil war at Matagalpa.

Months of simmering civil war erupted when Sandinist guerrillas invaded Nicaragua May 29, 1979, touching off a 7-week-offensive that culminated in the resignation and exile of Somoza, July 17.

Relations with the U.S. have been strained due to Nicaragua's military aid to leftist guerrillas in El Salvador and the U.S. backing anti-Sandinista contra guerrilla groups. Nicaragua accused the U.S. CIA of directing the mining of its ports, Apr. 6, 1984. It asked the International Court of Justice in The Hague to order the U.S. to halt the mining and cease aiding attacks on its territory. The Court ruled, May 10, that the U.S. should immediately halt any actions to blockade or mine Nicaragua's ports.

In 1983, Nicaragua accused the U.S. of aiding anti-Sandinista contras who were invading from Honduras. The charge sparked a debate in the U.S. Congress over funds for covert aid to the contras. In 1985, the U.S. House rejected Pres. Reagan's request for military aid to the contras; but in June voted to provide $27 mln. in humanitarian aid.

In June 1986, the House approved $100 mln. in aid for the contras fighting to overthrow the Nicaraguan government. It was the first time that the House had granted overt military aid to the contras and represented a major foreign policy victory for Pres. Reagan. The diversion of funds to the contras from the proceeds of a secret arms sale to Iran caused a major scandal in the U.S. The plan, masterminded by the administration's national security advisor and his deputy, took place at a time when military aid to the contras was forbidden by law. (*See Chronology*).

Niger

Republic of Niger

République du Niger

People: Population (1986 est.): 6,715,000. **Age distrib.** (%): 0–14: 46.7; 15–59: 48.5; 60+: 4.8. **Pop. density:** 14 per sq. mi. **Urban** (1985): 16.2%. **Ethnic groups:** Hausa 56%, Djerma 22%, Fulani 8%, Tuareg 8%. **Languages:** French (official), Hausa, Djerma. **Religions:** Sunni Moslem 97%.

Geography: Area: 489,189 sq. mi., almost 3 times the size of California. **Location:** In the interior of N. Africa. **Neighbors:** Libya, Algeria on N, Mali, Burkina Faso on W, Benin, Nigeria on S, Chad on E. **Topography:** Mostly arid desert and mountains. A narrow savanna in the S and the Niger R. basin in the SW contain most of the population. **Capital:** Niamey. **Cities** (1984 est.): Niamey 300,000.

Government: Type: Republic. **Head of state:** Pres. Seyni Kountche; b. 1931; in office: Apr. 15, 1974. **Head of government:** Premier Hamid Algabid; in office: Nov. 11, 1983. **Local divisions:** 7 departments. **Defense:** 0.7% of GNP (1984).

Economy: Chief crops: Peanuts, cotton. **Minerals:** Uranium. **Arable land:** 3%. **Meat prod.** (1980): beef: 37,000 metric tons; lamb: 33,000 metric tons. **Electricity prod.** (1983): 252 mln. kwh. **Labor force:** 90% agric.

Finance: Currency: CFA franc (Mar. 1987: 300 = $1 US). **Gross domestic product** (1984): $1.1 bln. **Per capita income** (1984) : $200. **Imports** (1982): $270 mln.; partners: Fr. 36%, Nig. 13%. **Exports** (1982): $178 mln.; partners: Fr. 36%, Nig. 17%. **National budget** (1983): $232 mln. **International reserves less gold** (Jan. 1987): $230 mln. **Gold:** 11,000 oz t. **Consumer prices** (change in 1986): −3.2%.

Transport: Motor vehicles: in use (1984): 23,000 passenger cars, 9,500 comm. vehicles.

Communications: Radios: 160,000 in use (1985). **Telephones in use** (1981): 10,000. **Daily newspaper cir.** (1985): 1 per 1,000 pop.

Health: Life expectancy at birth (1984): 43 years. **Births** (per 1,000 pop. 1985): 51.0. **Deaths** (per 1,000 pop. 1985): 22.9. **Natural increase** (1985): 2.8%. **Health** (1982): 2 hospitals, 36 medical centers. **Infant mortality** (per 1,000 live births 1985): 135.

Education (1984): **Literacy:** 8%. **Years compulsory:** 6; attendance: 15%.

Major International Organizations: UN (GATT, IMF, WHO, FAO), OAU.

Embassy: 2204 R St. NW 20008; 483-4224.

Niger was part of ancient and medieval African empires. European explorers reached the area in the late 18th century. The French colony of Niger was established 1900-22, after the defeat of Tuareg fighters, who had invaded the area from the N a century before. The country became independent Aug. 3, 1960. The next year it signed a bilateral agreement with France retaining close economic and cultural ties, which have continued. Hamani Diori, Niger's first president, was ousted in a 1974 coup. Drought and famine struck in 1973-74, and again in 1975.

Nigeria

Federal Republic of Nigeria

People: Population (1986 est.): 105,448,000. **Pop. density:** 275 per sq. mi. **Urban** (1985): 23%. **Ethnic groups:** Hausa 21%, Yoruba 20%, Ibo 17%, Fulani 9%, others. **Languages:** English (official), Hausa, Yoruba, Ibo. **Religions:** Moslems 47% (in N), Christians 34% (in S), others.

Geography: Area: 356,667 sq. mi., more than twice the size of California. **Location:** On the S coast of W. Africa. **Neighbors:** Benin on W, Niger on N, Chad, Cameroon on E. **Topography:** 4 E-W regions divide Nigeria: a coastal mangrove swamp 10-60 mi. wide, a tropical rain forest 50-100 mi. wide, a plateau of savanna and open woodland, and semidesert in the N. **Capital:** Lagos. **Cities:** (1983 est.): Lagos 1,097,000; Ibadan 1,060,000.

Government: Type: Military. **Head of state:** Gen. Ibrahim Babangida; b. Aug. 17, 1941; in office: Aug. 30, 1985. **Local divisions:** 19 states plus federal capital territory. **Defense:** 9.3% of govt. budget (1984).

Economy: Industries: Crude oil (95% of export), food processing, assembly of vehicles and other equipment. **Chief crops:** Cocoa (main export crop), tobacco, palm products, peanuts, cotton, soybeans. **Minerals:** Oil, gas, coal, iron, limestone, columbium, tin. **Crude oil reserves** (1985): 16.8 bln. bbls. **Other resources:** Timber, rubber, hides. **Arable land:** 34%. **Meat prod.** (1985): cattle: 12.1 mln.; pigs: 1.3 mln.; sheep: 13.1 mln. **Fish catch** (1984): 515,000 metric tons. **Electricity prod.** (1984): 8.8 bln. kwh. **Labor force:** 60% agric., 19% ind., comm. and serv.

Finance: Currency: Naira (Feb. 1987: 35 = $1 US). **Gross national product** (1984): $74 bln. **Per capita income** (1984): $790. **Imports** (1985): $8.8 bln.; partners: U.S., EC. **Exports** (1985): $12.5 bln.; partners: U.S., EC. **Tourist receipts** (1984): $102 mln. **National budget** (1984): $13.4 bln. **International reserves less gold** (Jan. 1987): $1.7 bln. **Gold:** 687,000 oz t. **Consumer prices** (change in 1985): 5.5%.

Transport: Motor vehicles: in use (1981): 262,000 passenger cars, 90,000 comm. vehicles. **Civil aviation** (1983): 2.4 bln. passenger-km; 29.8 mln. freight ton-km. **Chief ports:** Port Harcourt, Lagos, Warri, Calabar.

Communications: Television sets: 500,000 licensed (1985). **Radios:** 6 mln. licensed (1985). **Telephones in use** (1983): 708,000. **Daily newspaper circ.** (1984): 15 per 1,000 pop.

Health: Life expectancy at birth (1983): 48.3 male; 51.7 female. **Births** (per 1,000 pop. 1985): 46. **Deaths** (per 1,000 pop. 1985): 18. **Natural increase** (1985): 2.8%. **Hospital beds** (1980): 74,901. **Physicians** (1980): 8,037. **Infant mortality** (per 1,000 live births 1985): 127.

Education (1985): **Literacy:** 42%. **Primary school attendance:** 42%.

Major International Organizations: UN (GATT, IMO, WHO), OPEC, OAU, Commonwealth of Nations.

Embassy: 2201 M St. NW 20037; 822-1500.

Early cultures in Nigeria date back to at least 700 BC. From the 12th to the 14th centuries, more advanced cultures developed in the Yoruba area, at Ife, and in the north, where Moslem influence prevailed.

Portuguese and British slavers appeared from the 15th-16th centuries. Britain seized Lagos, 1861, during an anti-slave trade campaign, and gradually extended control inland until 1900. Nigeria became independent Oct. 1, 1960, and a republic Oct. 1, 1963.

On May 30, 1967, the Eastern Region seceded, proclaiming itself the Republic of Biafra, plunging the country into civil war. Casualties in the war were est. at over 1 million, including many "Biafrans" (mostly Ibos) who died of starvation despite international efforts to provide relief. The secessionists, after steadily losing ground, capitulated Jan. 12, 1970. Within a few years, the Ibos were reintegrated into national life, but mistrust among the regions persists.

Oil revenues have made possible a massive economic development program, largely using private enterprise, but agriculture has lagged. Oil revenues continued to decline in 1987.

After 13 years of military rule, the nation experienced a peaceful return to civilian government, Oct., 1979.

Military rule returned to Nigeria, Dec. 31, 1983 as a coup ousted the democratically-elected government. The government has promised a return to democracy by 1990. Violence erupted between Christians and Moslems in March 1987; 15 died and numerous churches and mosques were torched.

Norway

Kingdom of Norway

Kongeriket Norge

People: Population (1986 est.): 4,165,000. **Age distrib.** (%): 0–14: 20.2; 15–59: 58.6; 60+: 21.2. **Pop. density:** 33 per sq. mi. **Urban** (1985): 80%. **Ethnic groups:** Germanic (Nordic, Alpine, Baltic), minority Lapps. **Languages:** Norwegian (official), Lappish. **Religions:** Evangelical Lutheran 94%.

Geography: Area: 125,181 sq. mi., slightly larger than New Mexico. **Location:** Occupies the W part of Scandinavian peninsula in NW Europe (extends farther north than any European land). **Neighbors:** Sweden, Finland, USSR on E. **Topography:** A highly indented coast is lined with tens of thousands of islands. Mountains and plateaus cover most of the country, which is only 25% forested. **Capital:** Oslo. **Cities** (1986): Oslo 447,000; Bergen 207,000.

Government: Type: Hereditary constitutional monarchy. **Head of state:** King Olav V, b. July 2, 1903; in office: Sept. 21, 1957. **Head of government:** Prime Min. Gro Harlem Brundtland; b. April. 20, 1939; in office: May, 2, 1986. **Local divisions:** Oslo, Svalbard and 18 fylker (counties). **Defense:** 2.8% of GNP (1984).

Economy: Industries: Paper, shipbuilding, engineering, metals, chemicals, food processing oil, gas. **Chief crops:** Grains, potatoes, fruits. **Minerals:** Oil, copper, pyrites, nickel, iron, zinc, lead. **Crude oil reserves** (1985): 10.8 bln. bbls. **Other resources:** Timber. **Cultivated land:** 3%. **Meat prod.** (1984): beef: 74,000 metric tons; pork: 83,000 metric tons; lamb: 25,000 metric tons. **Fish catch** (1984): 2.4 mln. metric tons. **Electricity prod.** (1984): 106.6 bln. kwh. **Crude steel prod.** (1985): 850,000 metric tons. **Labor force:** 7% agric.; 47% ind., banking, comm.; 18% services, 26% govt.

Finance: Currency: Kroner (May 1987: 6.60 = $1 US). **Gross national product** (1984): $57 bln. **Per capita income** (1984): $13,790. **Imports** (1986): $20.3 bln.; partners: Swed. 17%, W. Ger. 16%, UK 10%, U.S. 9%. **Exports** (1986): $18.2 bln.; partners: UK 37%, W. Ger. 17%, Swed. 9%. **Tourists** (1985): receipts: $583 mln. **National budget** (1986): $32.5 bln. expenditures. **International reserves less gold** (Mar. 1987): $13.1 bln. **Gold:** 1.18 mln. oz t. **Consumer prices** (change in 1986): 7.2%.

Transport: Railway traffic (1985): 2.2 bln. passenger-km; 2.6 bln. net ton-km. **Motor vehicles:** in use (1985): 1.4 mln. passenger cars, 214,000 comm. vehicles. **Civil aviation:** (1984): 3.7 bln. passenger-km; 133 mln. net ton-km. **Chief ports:** Bergen, Stavanger, Oslo, Tonsberg.

Communications: Television sets: 1.3 mln. licensed (1985). **Radios:** 1.5 mln. in use (1984) **Telephones in use** (1985): 2.5 mln. **Daily newspaper circ.** (1984): 454 per 1,000 pop.

Health: Life expectancy at birth (1986): 72.7 male; 79.5 female. **Births** (per 1,000 pop. 1985): 12.2. **Deaths** (per 1,000 pop. 1985): 10. **Natural increase** (1985): .2%. **Hospital beds** (1983): 18,729. **Physicians** (1983): 9,722. **Infant mortality** (per 1,000 live births 1985): 8.

Education (1987): **Literacy:** 100%. **Years Compulsory:** 9.

Major International Organizations: UN and all of its specialized agencies, NATO, OECD.

Embassy: 2720 34th St. NW 20008; 333-6000.

The first supreme ruler of Norway was Harald the Fairhaired who came to power in 872 AD. Between 800 and 1000, Norway's Vikings raided and occupied widely dispersed parts of Europe.

The country was united with Denmark 1381-1814, and with Sweden, 1814-1905. In 1905, the country became independent with Prince Charles of Denmark as king.

Norway remained neutral during World War I. Germany attacked Norway Apr. 9, 1940, and held it until liberation May 8, 1945. The country abandoned its neutrality after the war, and joined the NATO alliance. Norway rejected membership in the Common Market in a 1972 referendum.

Abundant hydroelectric resources provided the base for Norway's industrialization, producing one of the highest living standards in the world.

Norway's merchant marine is one of the world's largest.

Norway and the Soviet Union have disputed their territorial waters boundary in the Barents Sea, north of the 2 countries' common border.

Petroleum output from oil and mineral deposits under the continental shelf has raised state revenues.

Svalbard is a group of mountainous islands in the Arctic O., c. 23,957 sq. mi., pop. varying seasonally from 1,500 to 3,600. The largest, Spitsbergen (formerly called West Spitsbergen), 15,060 sq. mi., seat of governor, is about 370 mi. N of Norway. By a treaty signed in Paris, 1920, major European powers recognized the sovereignty of Norway, which incorporated it in 1925. Both Norway and the USSR mine rich coal deposits. Mt. Newton (Spitsbergen) is 5,633 ft. tall.

Oman

Sultanate of Oman

Saltanat 'Uman

People: Population (1986 est.): 1,271,000. **Pop. density:** 10 per sq. mi. **Urban** (1985): 8.8%. **Ethnic groups:** Arab 88%, Baluchi 4%, Persian 3%, Indian 2%, African 2%. **Languages:** Arabic (official), English, Urdu, others. **Religions:** Ibadhi Moslem 75%, Sunni Moslem.

Geography: Area: 82,030 sq. mi., about the size of New Mexico. **Location:** On SE coast of Arabian peninsula. **Neighbors:** United Arab Emirates, Saudi Arabia, South Yemen on W. **Topography:** Oman has a narrow coastal plain up to 10 mi. wide, a range of barren mountains reaching 9,900 ft., and a wide, stony, mostly waterless plateau, avg. alt. 1,000 ft. Also the tip of the Ruus-al-Jebal peninsula controls access to the Persian Gulf. **Capital:** Muscat. **Cities** (1982 est.): Muscat 85,000.

Government: Type: Absolute monarchy. **Head of state:** Sultan Qabus bin Said; b. Nov. 18, 1942; in office: July 23, 1970. **Local divisions:** 1 province, numerous districts. **Defense:** 25% of GNP (1985).

Economy: Chief crops: Dates, fruits vegetables, wheat, bananas. **Minerals:** Oil (95% of exports). **Crude oil reserves** (1985): 4.5 bln. bbls. **Fish catch** (1983): 108,000 metric tons. **Electricity prod.** (1983): 1.3 bln. kwh. **Labor force:** 80% agric. & fishing.

Finance: Currency: Rial Omani (Mar. 1987: .38 = $1 US). **Gross national product** (1984): $8.8 bln. **Imports** (1984): $3 bln.; partners: Jap. 21%, UAE 17%, UK 14%. **Exports** (1984): $5 bln.; partners: Jap. 58%, Europe 30%. **National budget** (1985): $4.4 bln. revenues; $5.4 bln. expenditures. **International reserves less gold** (Mar. 1987): $987 mln. **Gold:** 289,000 oz t.

Transport: Chief ports: Matrah, Muscat.

Communications: Television sets: 46,000 in use (1984). **Radios:** 800,000 in use (1984). **Telephones in use** (1982): 19,000.

Health: Life expectancy at birth (1986): 48 yrs. 15 hospitals, 21 health centers, 74 clinics.

Education (1986): **Literacy:** 20%. **Attendance:** 60% primary, 10% secondary.

Major International Organizations: UN (World Bank, IMF), Arab League.

Embassy: 2342 Massachusetts Ave. NW 20008; 387-1980.

A long history of rule by other lands, including Portugal in the 16th century, ended with the ouster of the Persians in 1744. By the early 19th century, Muscat and Oman was one of the most important countries in the region, controlling much of the Persian and Pakistan coasts, and ruling far-away Zanzibar, which was separated in 1861 under British mediation.

British influence was confirmed in a 1951 treaty, and Britain helped suppress an uprising by traditionally rebellious interior tribes against control by Muscat in the 1950s. Enclaves on the Pakistan coast were sold to that country in 1958.

On July 23, 1970, Sultan Said bin Taimur was overthrown by his son. The new sultan changed the nation's name to Sultanate of Oman. He launched a domestic development program, and battled leftist rebels in the southern Dhofar area to their defeat, Dec. 1975.

Oil has been the major source of income. Oman has close political ties to the U.S. and established diplomatic relations with the USSR in 1985.

Pakistan

Islamic Republic of Pakistan

People: Population (1986 est.): 101,855,000. **Pop. density:** 334 per sq. mi. **Urban** (1985): 30%. **Ethnic groups:** Punjabi 66%, Sindhi 13%, Pushtun (Iranian) 8.5%, Urdu 7.6%, Baluchi 2.5%, others. **Languages:** Urdu, English are both official. **Religions:** Moslem 97%.

Geography: Area: 310,403 sq. mi., larger than Texas. **Location:** In W part of South Asia. **Neighbors:** Iran on W, Afghanistan, China on N, India on E. **Topography:** The Indus R. rises in the Hindu Kush and Himalaya mtns. in the N (highest is K2, or Godwin Austen, 28,250 ft., 2d highest in world), then flows over 1,000 mi. through fertile valley and empties into Arabian Sea. Thar Desert, Eastern Plains flank Indus Valley. **Capital:** Islamabad. **Cities** (1981 cen.): Karachi 5.1 mln.; Lahore 2.9 mln.; Faisalabad 1 mln.; Hyderabad 795,000; Rawalpindi 928,000.

Government: Type: Parliamentary democracy in a federal setting. **Head of government:** Pres. Mohammad Zia ul-Haq; b. 1924; in office: July 5, 1977. **Head of state:** Muhammad Khan Junejo; in office: Mar. 24, 1985. **Local divisions:** Federal capital, 4 provinces, tribal areas. **Defense:** 5.4% of GNP (1983).

Economy: Industries: Textiles, food processing, chemicals, tobacco, **Chief crops:** Rice, wheat. **Minerals:** Natural gas, iron ore. **Crude oil reserves** (1985): 102 mln. bbls. **Other resources:** Wool. **Arable land:** 26%. **Meat prod.** (1985): cattle: 16.7 mln.; sheep: 25.8 mln. **Fish catch** (1984): 343,000 metric tons. **Electricity prod.** (1984): 20.7 bln. kwh. **Labor force:** 53% agric.; 13% ind.

Finance: Currency: Rupee (Mar. 1987: 17.3 = $1 US). **Gross national product** (1984): $35 bln. **Per capita income** (1984): $360. **Imports** (1986): $5.3 bln.; partners: Sau. Ar. 15%, Jap. 12%, U.S. 9%, Kuwait 10%. **Exports** (1986): $3.3 bln.; partners: China 6%, Jap. 8%, U.S. 7%. **National budget** (1984): $7.2 bln. **International reserves less gold** (Mar. 1987): $724 mln. **Gold:** 1.93 mln. oz t. **Consumer prices** (change in 1986): 3.7%.

Transport: Railway traffic (1985): 178 bln. passenger-km; 7.2 bln. net ton-km. **Motor vehicles:** in use (1984): 211,000 passenger cars, 66,000 comm. vehicles. **Civil aviation** (1985): 68 bln. passenger-km; 291 mln. freight ton-km. **Chief ports:** Karachi.

Communications: Television sets: 1 mln. in use (1985). **Radios:** 5.2 mln. in use (1984). **Telephones in use** (1985): 533,000. **Daily newspaper circ.** (1984): 22 per 1,000 pop.

Health: Life expectancy at birth (1985): 52.0 male; 50.2 female. **Births** (per 1,000 pop. 1985): 44. **Deaths** (per 1,000 pop. 1985): 15. **Natural increase** 1985): 2.6%. **Hospital beds** (1985): 53,603. **Physicians** (1985): 38,322. **Infant mortality** (per 1,000 live births 1985): 125.

Education (1985): **Literacy:** 26%.

Major International Organizations: UN (GATT, ILO, IMF, WHO).

Embassy: 2315 Massachusetts Ave. NW 20008; 939-6200.

Present-day Pakistan shares the 5,000-year history of the India-Pakistan sub-continent. At present day Harappa and Mohenjo Daro, the Indus Valley Civilization, with large cities and elaborate irrigation systems, flourished c. 4,000-2,500 BC.

Aryan invaders from the NW conquered the region around 1,500 BC, forging a Hindu civilization that dominated Pakistan as well as India for 2,000 years.

Beginning with the Persians in the 6th century BC, and continuing with Alexander the Great and with the Sassanians, successive nations to the west ruled or influenced Pakistan, eventually separating the area from the Indian cultural sphere.

The first Arab invasion, 712 AD, introduced Islam. Under the Mogul empire (1526-1857), Moslems ruled most of India, yielding to British encroachment and resurgent Hindus.

After World War I the Moslems of British India began agitation for minority rights in elections. Mohammad Ali Jinnah (1876-1948) was the principal architect of Pakistan. A leader of the Moslem League from 1916, he worked for dominion status for India; from 1940 he advocated a separate Moslem state.

When the British withdrew Aug. 14, 1947, the Islamic majority areas of India acquired self-government as Pakistan, with dominion status in the Commonwealth. Pakistan was divided into 2 sections, West Pakistan and East Pakistan. The 2 areas were nearly 1,000 mi. apart on opposite sides of India.

Pakistan became a republic in 1956. Pakistan had a National Assembly (legislature) with equal membership from East and West Pakistan, and 2 Provincial Assemblies. In Oct. 1958, Gen. Mohammad Ayub Khan took power in a coup. He was elected president in 1960, reelected in 1965.

As a member of the Central Treaty Organization, Pakistan had been aligned with the West. Following clashes between India and China in 1962, Pakistan made commercial and aid agreements with China.

Ayub resigned Mar. 25, 1969, after several months of violent rioting and unrest, most of it in East Pakistan, which demanded autonomy. The government was turned over to Gen. Agha Mohammad Yahya Khan and martial law was declared.

The Awami League, which sought regional autonomy for East Pakistan, won a majority in Dec. 1970 elections to a National Assembly which was to write a new constitution. In March, 1971 Yahya postponed the Assembly. Rioting and strikes broke out in the East.

On Mar. 25, 1971, government troops launched attacks in the East. The Easterners, aided by India, proclaimed the independent nation of Bangladesh. In months of widespread fighting, countless thousands were killed. Some 10 million Easterners fled into India.

Full scale war between India and Pakistan had spread to both the East and West fronts by December 3. Pakistan troops in the East surrendered Dec. 16; Pakistan agreed to a cease-fire in the West Dec. 17. On July 3, 1972, Pakistan and India signed a pact agreeing to withdraw troops from their borders and seek peaceful solutions to all problems. Diplomatic relations were resumed in 1976.

Zulfikar Ali Bhutto, leader of the Pakistan People's Party, which had won the most West Pakistan votes in the Dec. 1970 elections, became president Dec. 20.

Bhutto was overthrown in a military coup July, 1977. Convicted of complicity in a 1974 political murder, Bhutto was executed Apr.4, 1979. Benazir Bhutto, his daughter, returned to Pakistan from exile in Europe in 1986. Her efforts to relaunch the Pakistan People's Party sparked violence and antigovernment riots.

There are some 2 million Afghan refugees now in Pakistan.

Panama

Republic of Panama

República de Panamá

People: Population (1986 est.): 2,227,000. **Age distrib.** (%): 0–14: 38.7; 15–59: 55.8; 60+: 5.5. **Pop. density:** 75 per sq. mi. **Urban** (1980): 49.3%. **Ethnic groups:** Mestizo 70%, West Indian 14%, Caucasian 10%, Indian 6%. **Languages:** Spanish (official), English. **Religions:** Roman Catholic 93%, Protestant.

Geography: Area: 29,208 sq. mi., slightly larger than West Virginia. **Location:** In Central America. **Neighbors:** Costa Rica on W., Colombia on E. **Topography:** 2 mountain ranges run the length of the isthmus. Tropical rain forests cover the Caribbean coast and eastern Panama. **Capital:** Panama. **Cities** (1986 est.): Panama 434,000.

Government: Type: Constitutional democracy, centralized republic. **Head of state and head of government:** Pres. Eric Arturo Delvalle; b. Feb. 2, 1937; in office: Sept. 28, 1985. **Local divisions:** 9 provinces, 1 territory. **Defense:** 2% of GNP (1985).

Economy: Industries: Oil refining, international banking. **Chief crops:** Bananas, pineapples, cocoa, corn, coconuts, sugar. **Minerals:** Copper. **Other resources:** Forests (mahogany), shrimp. **Arable land:** 8%. **Meat prod.** (1980): beef: 52,000 metric tons; pork: 7,000 metric tons. **Fish catch** (1984): 166,000 metric tons. **Electricity prod.** (1984): 2.3 bln. kwh. **Labor force:** 28% agric., 29.4% ind. and commerce, 30% services.

Finance: Currency: Balboa (Apr. 1987: 1.00 = $1 US). **Gross national product** (1984): $4.2 bln. **Per capita income** (1984): $1,970. **Imports** (1983): $1.2 bln.; partners: U.S. 31%, Saudi Ar. 8%. **Exports** (1983): $303 mln.; partners: U.S. 53%, W. Ger. 5%. **Tourists** (1984): $186 mln. receipts. **National budget** (1985): $2.7 bln. **International reserves less gold** (Jan. 1987): $134 mln. **Consumer prices** (change in 1985): 1.0%.

Transport: Motor vehicles: in use (1984): 104,000 passenger cars, 35,000 comm. vehicles. **Civil aviation** (1985): 551 mln. passenger-km; 55 mln. net ton-km. **Chief ports:** Balboa, Cristobal.

Communications: Television sets: 400,000 in use (1985). **Radios:** 295,000 in use (1985). **Telephones in use** (1984): 213,000. **Daily newspaper circ.** (1984): 62 per 1,000 pop.

Health: Life expectancy at birth (1985): 69.2 male; 72.9 female. **Births** (per 1,000 pop. 1985): 26. **Deaths** (per 1,000 pop. 1985): 5. **Natural increase** (1985): 2.1%. **Hospital beds** (1984): 7,669. **Physicians** (1984): 2,438. **Infant mortality** (per 1,000 live births 1985): 25.

Education (1985): **Literacy:** 87%. **Primary school attendance:** almost 100%.

Major International Organizations: UN (IMF, IMO, World Bank), OAS.

Embassy: 2862 McGill Terrace NW 20008; 483-1407.

The coast of Panama was sighted by Rodrigo de Bastidas, sailing with Columbus for Spain in 1501, and was visited by Columbus in 1502. Vasco Nunez de Balboa crossed the isthmus and "discovered" the Pacific O. Sept. 13, 1513. Spanish colonies were ravaged by Francis Drake, 1572-95, and Henry Morgan, 1668-71. Morgan destroyed the old city of Panama which had been founded in 1519. Freed from Spain, Panama joined Colombia in 1821.

Panama declared its independence from Colombia Nov. 3, 1903, with U.S. recognition. U.S. naval forces deterred action by Colombia. On Nov. 18, 1903, Panama granted use, occupation and control of the Canal Zone to the U.S. by treaty, ratified Feb. 26, 1904.

New treaties were proposed in 1967 and 1974. In 1978, a new treaty provided for a gradual takeover by Panama of the canal, and withdrawal of U.S. troops, to be completed by 1999. U.S. payments were substantially increased in the interim. The permanent neutrality of the canal was also guaranteed.

Due to easy Panama ship regulations and strictures in the U.S., merchant tonnage registered in Panama since World War II ranks high in size. Similarly easy financial regulations have made Panama a center for international banking.

Papua New Guinea

People: Population (1986 est.): 3,395,000. **Age distrib.** (%): 0–14: 43.8; 15–59: 50.3; 60+: 11.4. **Pop. density:** 19 per sq. mi. **Urban** (1980): 13.1%. **Ethnic groups:** Papuans (in S and interior), Melanesian (N,E), pygmies, minorities of Chinese, Australians, Polynesians. **Languages:** English (official), Melanesian Pidgin, Police Motu, numerous local languages. **Religions:** Protestant 63%, Roman Catholic 31%, local religions.

Geography: Area: 176,280 sq. mi., slightly larger than California. **Location:** Occupies eastern half of island of New Guinea. **Neighbors:** Indonesia (West Irian) on W, Australia on S. **Topography:** Thickly forested mtns. cover much of the center of the country, with lowlands along the coasts. Included are some of the nearby islands of Bismarck and Solomon groups, including Admiralty Is., New Ireland, New Britain, and Bougainville. **Capital:** Port Moresby. **Cities** (1984 est.): Port Moresby 144,000.

Government: Type: Parliamentary democracy. **Head of state:** Queen Elizabeth II, represented by Gov. Gen. Sir Kingsford Dibela; in office: Mar. 1, 1983. **Head of government:** Prime Min. Paias Wingti; in office: Nov. 21, 1985. **Local divisions:** National capital and 19 provinces with elected legislatures. **Defense:** approx. 1.3% of GDP (1984).

Economy: Chief crops: Coffee, coconuts, cocoa. **Minerals:** Gold, copper, silver, gas. **Arable land:** 1%. **Meat prod.** (1984): pigs: 1.4 mln. **Electricity prod.** (1984): 1.4 bln. kwh. **Labor force:** 75% agric., 8% ind. and commerce, 2% services.

Finance: Currency: Kina (Mar. 1987: .97 = $1 US). **Gross national product** (1984): $2.4 bln. **Per capita income** (1984): $760. **Imports** (1984): $866 mln.; partners: Austral. 34%, Jap. 14%, Sing. 12%. **Exports** (1984): $802 mln.; partners: Jap. 29%, W. Ger. 21%, Austral. 8%. **National budget** (1986): $976 mln. **International reserves less gold** (June 1986): $589 mln. **Gold:** 63,000 oz t. **Consumer prices** (change in 1985): 3.7%.

Transport: Motor vehicles: in use (1984): 22,000 passenger cars, 39,000 comm. vehicles. **Chief ports:** Port Moresby, Lae.

Communications: Radios: 230,000 in use (1985). **Telephones in use** (1984): 51,000. **Daily newspaper circ.** (1985) 8 per 1,000 pop.

Health: Life expectancy at birth (1984): 49 yrs. **Births** (per 1,000 pop. 1985): 43. **Deaths** (per 1,000 pop. 1985): 12. **Natural increase** (1985): 3.1%. **Hospital beds** (1984): 14,661. **Physicians** (1984): 280. **Infant mortality** (per 1,000 live births 1985): 91.

Education (1986): **Literacy:** 32%. **Attendance:** 65% primary school; 13% secondary school.

Major International Organizations: UN (GATT), Commonwealth of Nations.

Embassy: 1330 Connecticut Ave., NW 20036.

Human remains have been found in the interior of New Guinea dating back at least 10,000 years and possibly much earlier. Successive waves of peoples probably entered the country from Asia through Indonesia. Europeans visited in the 15th century, but land claims did not begin until the 19th century, when the Dutch took control of the western half of the island.

The southern half of eastern New Guinea was first claimed by Britain in 1884, and transferred to Australia in 1905. The northern half was claimed by Germany in 1884, but captured in World War I by Australia, which was granted a League of Nations mandate and then a UN trusteeship over the area. The 2 territories were administered jointly after 1949, given self-government Dec. 1, 1973, and became independent Sept. 16, 1975.

The indigenous population consists of a huge number of tribes, many living in almost complete isolation with mutually unintelligible languages.

Paraguay

Republic of Paraguay

República del Paraguay

People: Population (1986 est.): 4,119,000. **Age distrib.** (%): 0–14: 41.0; 15–59: 52.0; 60+: 7.0. **Pop. density:** 21 per sq. mi. **Urban** (1985): 43%. **Ethnic groups:** Mestizos 95%, small Caucasian, Indian, black minorities. **Languages:** Spanish (official), Guarani (used by 90%). **Religions:** Roman Catholic (official) 97%.

Geography: Area: 157,047 sq. mi., the size of California. **Location:** One of the 2 landlocked countries of S. America. **Neighbors:** Bolivia on N, Argentina on S, Brazil on E. **Topography:** Paraguay R. bisects the country. To E are fertile plains, wooded slopes, grasslands. To W is the Chaco plain, with marshes and scrub trees. Extreme W is arid. **Capital:** Asunción. **Cities** (1985 cen.): Asunción 477,000.

Government: Type: Constitutional republic with powerful executive branch. **Head of state:** Pres. Alfredo Stroessner; b. Nov. 3, 1912; in office: Aug. 15, 1954. **Local divisions:** 19 departments. **Defense:** 14.4% of govt. budget (1984).

Economy: Industries: Food processing, wood products, textiles, cement. **Chief crops:** Corn, wheat, cotton, beans, peanuts, tobacco, citrus fruits, yerba mate. **Minerals:** Iron, manganese, limestone. **Other resources:** Forests. **Arable land:** 2%. **Meat prod.** (1984): cattle: 6.7 mln.; pigs: 1.1 mln. **Electricity prod.** (1984): 2.9 bln. kwh. **Labor force:** 44% agric., 34% ind. and commerce, 18% services.

Finance: Currency: Guarani (Mar. 1987 240.00 = $1 US). **Gross national product** (1984): $4.1 bln. **Per capita income** (1984): $1,260. **Imports** (1984): $513 mln.; partners: Braz. 32%, Arg. 15%, U.S. 8%. **Exports** (1984): $334 mln.; partners: Arg. 12%, W. Ger. 13%, Braz. 16%. **Tourists** (1984): $96 mln. receipts. **National budget** (1984): $300 mln. **International reserves less gold** (Mar. 1987): $416 mln. **Gold:** 35,000 oz t. **Consumer prices** (change in 1985): 25.2%.

Transport: Railway traffic (1980): 22 mln. passenger-km; 34 mln. net ton-km. **Motor vehicles:** in use (1984): 90,000 passenger cars, 35,000 comm. vehicles. **Civil aviation** (1982): 479 mln. passenger-km; 2.9 mln. net ton-km. **Chief ports:** Asuncion.

Communications: Television sets: 82,000 in use (1984). **Radios:** 200,000 in use (1984). **Telephones in use** (1984): 83,000. **Daily newspaper circ.** (1985): 60 per 100,000 pop.

Health: Life expectancy at birth (1984): 63 yrs. **Births** (per 1,000 pop. 1985): 36.0. **Deaths** (per 1,000 pop. 1985): 7.2. **Natural increase** (1985): 2.8%. **Hospital beds** (1982): 3,345. **Physicians** (1982): 2,201. **Infant mortality** (per 1,000 live births 1985): 52.

Education (1984): **Literacy:** 83%. **Years compulsory:** 7; **Attendance:** 83%.

Major International Organizations: UN (IMF, WHO, ILO), OAS.

Embassy: 2400 Massachusetts Ave. NW 20008; 483-6960.

The Guarani Indians were settled farmers speaking a common language before the arrival of Europeans.

Visited by Sebastian Cabot in 1527 and settled as a Spanish possession in 1535, Paraguay gained its independence from Spain in 1811. It lost much of its territory to Brazil, Uruguay, and Argentina in the War of the Triple Alliance, 1865-1870. Large areas were won from Bolivia in the Chaco War, 1932-35.

Gen. Alfredo Stroessner has ruled since 1954. Suppression of the opposition and decimation of small Indian groups has been charged by international rights groups.

Peru

Republic of Peru

República del Peru

People: Population (1986 est.): 20,207,000. **Age distrib.** (%): 0–14: 40.5; 15–59: 46.0; 60+: 5.5. **Pop. density:** 40 per sq. mi. **Urban** (1985): 70%. **Ethnic groups:** Indians 45%, Mestizos 37%, Caucasians 15%, blacks, Asians. **Languages:** Spanish, Quechua both official, Aymara; 30% speak no Spanish. **Religions:** Roman Catholics over 90%.

Geography: Area: 496,222 sq. mi., five-sixths the size of Alaska. **Location:** On the Pacific coast of S. America. **Neighbors:** Ecuador, Colombia on N, Brazil, Bolivia on E, Chile on S. **Topography:** An arid coastal strip, 10 to 100 mi. wide, supports much of the population thanks to widespread irrigation. The Andes cover 27% of land area. The uplands are well-watered, as are the eastern slopes reaching the Amazon basin, which covers half the country with its forests and jungles. **Capital:** Lima. **Cities** (1984 est.): Lima 4,169,000; Arequipa 531,000; Callao 515,000.

Government: Type: Constitutional republic. **Head of state:** Pres. Alan Garcia Perez; b. May 23, 1949; in office: July 28, 1985. **Head of government:** Prime Min. Luis Alva Castro; in office: July 28, 1985. **Local divisions:** 24 departments, 1 province. **Defense:** 7.8% of GDP (1984).

Economy: Industries: Fish meal, steel, cement. **Chief crops:** Cotton, sugar, coffee, corn. **Minerals:** Copper, lead, molybdenum, silver, zinc, iron, oil. **Crude oil reserves** (1985): 670 mln. bbls. **Other resources:** Wool, sardines. **Arable land:** 3%. **Meat prod.** (1985): cattle: 3.8 mln.; pigs: 2.1 mln.; sheep: 13.5 mln. **Fish catch** (1985): 3.1 mln. metric tons. **Electricity prod.** (1984): 12.7 bln. kwh. **Labor force:** 40% agric.; 19% ind. and mining; 41% govt. and other services.

Finance: Currency: Intl (Mar. 1987: 15.18 = $1 US). **Gross national product** (1984): $17.9 bln. **Per capita income** (1984): $940. **Imports** (1985): $1.8 bln.; partners: U.S. 33%, W. Ger. 7%. **Exports** (1985). $2.9 bln.; partners: U.S. 33%, Jap. 10%,

Tourists (1984): $292 mln. receipts. **National budget** (1984): $4.3 bln. **International reserves less gold** (Mar. 1987): $1.3 bln. **Gold:** 1.8 mln. oz t. **Consumer prices** (change in 1986): 77.9%.

Transport: Railway traffic (1983): 563 mln. passenger-km; 839 mln. net ton-km. **Motor vehicles:** in use (1982): 359,000 passenger cars, 196,000 comm. vehicles. **Civil aviation** (1985): 1.6 bln. passenger-km; 182 mln. net ton-km. **Chief ports:** Callao, Chimbate, Mollendo.

Communications: Television sets: 1.3 mln. in use (1985). **Radios:** 2.2 mln. in use (1985). **Telephones in use** (1983): 519,000. **Daily newspaper circ.** (1985): 57 per 1,000 pop.

Health: Life expectancy at birth (1985): 58.3 male; 62.2 female. **Births** (per 1,000 pop. 1985): 36. **Deaths** (per 1,000 pop. 1985): 10. **Natural increase** (1985): 2.5%. **Hospital beds** (1982): 29,991. **Physicians** (1982): 14,751. **Infant mortality** (per 1,000 live births 1985): 82.

Education (1978): **Literacy:** 72%. **Years compulsory:** 10.

Major International Organizations: UN and all of its specialized agencies, OAS.

Embassy: 1700 Massachusetts Ave. NW 20036; 833-9860.

The powerful Inca empire had its seat at Cuzco in the Andes covering most of Peru, Bolivia, and Ecuador, as well as parts of Colombia, Chile, and Argentina. Building on the achievements of 800 years of Andean civilization, the Incas had a high level of skill in architecture, engineering, textiles, and social organization.

A civil war had weakened the empire when Francisco Pizarro, Spanish conquistador, began raiding Peru for its wealth, 1532. In 1533 he had the seized ruling Inca, Atahualpa, fill a room with gold as a ransom, then executed him and enslaved the natives.

Lima was the seat of Spanish viceroys until the Argentine liberator, Jose de San Martin, captured it in 1821; Spain was defeated by Simon Bolivar and Antonio J. de Sucre; recognized Peruvian independence, 1824. Chile defeated Peru and Bolivia, 1879-84, and took Tarapaca, Tacna, and Arica; returned Tacna, 1929.

On Oct. 3, 1968, a military coup ousted Pres. Fernando Belaunde Terry. In 1968-74, the military government put through sweeping agrarian changes, and nationalized oil, mining, fishmeal, and banking industries.

Food shortages, escalating foreign debt, and strikes led to another coup, Aug. 29, 1976, and to a slowdown of socialist programs.

After 12 years of military rule, Peru returned to democratic leadership under former Pres. Fernando Belaunde Terry, July 1980. The new government encouraged the return of private enterprise to stimulate the inflation-ridden economy.

Fighting again erupted, Jan. 28, 1981, in the ongoing border dispute between Peru and Ecuador. The border was reopened in April. There were strikes by police, oil workers, and other labor unions in 1987. Terrorist activity, mostly by Maoist groups, continued in 1987.

Philippines

Republic of the Philippines

People: Population (1986 est.): 58,091,000. **Age distrib.** (%): 0–14: 42.9; 15–59: 52.5; 60+: 4.6. **Pop. density:** 483 per sq. mi. **Urban** (1980): 36%. **Ethnic groups:** Malays the large majority, Chinese, Americans, Spanish are minorities. **Languages:** Pilipino (based on Tagalog), English both official; numerous others spoken. **Religions:** Roman Catholics 83%, Protestants 9%, Moslems 5%.

Geography: Area: 115,831 sq. mi., slightly larger than Nevada. **Location:** An archipelago off the SE coast of Asia. **Neighbors:** Nearest are Malaysia, Indonesia on S, Taiwan on N. **Topography:** The country consists of some 7,100 islands stretching 1,100 mi. N-S. About 95% of area and population are on 11 largest islands, which are mountainous, except for the heavily indented coastlines and for the central plain on Luzon. **Capital:** Quezon City (Manila is de facto capital). **Cities** (1981 est.): Manila 1.6 mln.; Quezon City 1.1 mln.; Davao 611,311.

Government: Type: Republic. **Head of state:** Pres. Corazon C. Aquino; b. 1932; in office: Feb. 25, 1986. **Local divisions:** 12 regions, 74 provinces, 60 cities. **Defense:** 1.9% of GNP (1983).

Economy: Industries: Food processing, textiles, clothing, drugs, wood prods., appliances. **Chief crops:** Sugar, rice, corn, pineapple, coconut. **Minerals:** Cobalt, copper, gold, nickel, silver, iron, petroleum. **Crude oil reserves** (1985): 31 mln. bbls. **Other resources:** Forests (42% of area). **Arable land:** 34%. **Meat prod.** (1985): cattle: 1.7 mln.; pigs: 7.2 mln. **Fish catch** (1984): 1.8 mln. metric tons. **Electricity prod.** (1984): 18.9 bln. kwh. **Labor force:** 52% agric., 16% ind. and comm., 13% services.

Finance: Currency: Peso (May 1987: 19.80 = $1 US). **Gross national product** (1985): $32.6 bln. **Per capita income** (1985): $598. **Imports** (1985): $5.4 bln.; partners: U.S. 22%, Jap. 16%, Saudi Ar. 10%. **Exports** (1985): $4.5 bln.; partners: U.S. 35%, Jap. 20%. **Tourists** (1984): $350 mln. receipts. **National budget** (1984): $3 bln. expenditures. **International reserves less gold** (Mar. 1987): $1.6 bln. **Gold:** 2.4 mln. oz t. **Consumer prices** (change in 1986): 0.8%.

Transport: Railway traffic (1985): 144 mln. passenger-km; 12 mln. net ton-km. **Motor vehicles:** in use (1984): 894,000 passenger cars, 128,800 comm. vehicles. **Civil aviation** (1985): 7.8 bln. passenger-km; 966 mln. freight ton-km. **Chief ports:** Cebu, Manila, Iloilo, Davao.

Communications: Television sets: 2.7 mln. in use (1985). **Radios:** 3.5 mln. in use (1985). **Telephones in use** (1983): 658,000. **Daily newspaper circ.** (1985): 44 per 1,000 pop.

Health: Life expectancy at birth (1986): 61.6 male; 65.2 female. **Births** (per 1,000 pop. 1985): 31. **Deaths** (per 1,000 pop. 1985): 7. **Natural increase** (1985): 2.4%. **Hospital beds** (1983): 76,653. **Physicians** (1982): 46,579. **Infant mortality** (per 1,000 live births 1985): 52.5.

Education (1986): **Literacy:** 88%. **Attendance:** 95% in elementary, 57% secondary.

Major International Organizations: UN (World Bank, IMF, GATT), ASEAN.

Embassy: 1617 Massachusetts Ave. NW 20036; 483-1414

The Malay peoples of the Philippine islands, whose ancestors probably migrated from Southeast Asia, were mostly hunters, fishers, and unsettled cultivators when first visited by Europeans.

The archipelago was visited by Magellan, 1521. The Spanish founded Manila, 1571. The islands, named for King Philip II of Spain, were ceded by Spain to the U.S. for $20 million, 1898, following the Spanish-American War. U.S. troops suppressed a guerrilla uprising in a brutal 6-year war, 1899-1905.

Japan attacked the Philippines Dec. 8, 1941 (Far Eastern time). Japan occupied the islands during WW II.

On July 4, 1946, independence was proclaimed in accordance with an act passed by the U.S. Congress in 1934. A republic was established.

A rebellion by Communist-led Huk guerrillas was put down by 1954, But urban and rural political violence periodically reappears.

The Philippines and the U.S. have treaties for U.S. military and naval bases and a mutual defense treaty. Riots by radical youth groups and terrorism by leftist guerrillas and outlaws, increased from 1970. On Sept. 21, 1972, President Marcos declared martial law. Ruling by decree, he ordered some land reform and stabilized prices. But opposition was suppressed, and a high population growth rate aggravated poverty and unemployment. Political corruption was believed to be widespread. On Jan. 17, 1973, Marcos proclaimed a new constitution with himself as president. His wife received wide powers in 1978 to supervise planning and development.

Government troops battled Moslem (Moro) secessionists, 1973-76, in southern Mindanao. Fighting resumed, 1977, after a Libyan-mediated agreement on autonomy was rejected by the region's mainly Christian voters.

Martial law was lifted Jan. 17, 1981. Marcos turned over legislative power to the National Assembly, released political prisoners, and said he would no longer rule by decree. He was re-elected to a new 6-year term as president.

The assassination of prominent opposition leader Benigno S. Aquino Jr, Aug. 21, 1983, sparked demonstrations calling for the resignation of Marcos. An independent commission appointed by Marcos concluded that a military conspiracy was responsible for Aquino's death. The May 1984 elections saw Marcos retain his majority in the National Assembly although opponents made a strong showing in key areas like Manila.

A bitter presidential election campaign ended Feb. 7, 1986 as elections were held amid allegations of widespread fraud. On Feb. 16, Marcos was declared the victor over Corazon Aquino, widow of slain opposition leader Benigno Aquino. Aquino declared herself president and announced a nonviolent "active resistance" to overthrow the Marcos government; the 2 held separate inaugurals on Feb. 25.

On Feb. 22, 2 leading military allies of Marcos quit their posts to protest the rigged elections. Marcos, Feb. 24, declared a state of emergency as his military and religious support continued to erode. That same day U.S. President Ronald Reagan urged Marcos to resign. Marcos ended his 20-year tenure as president Feb. 26 as he fled the country. Aquino was recognized immediately as president by the U.S. and other nations.

In 1987, Aquino announced the start of land reforms. Candidates endorsed by Aquino won large majorities in legislative elections held in May, attesting to her popularity. She was plagued, however, by a weak economy, widespread poverty, communist insurgents, and lukewarm support from the military.

The archipelago has a coastline of 10,850 mi. Manila Bay, with an area of 770 sq. mi., and a circumference of 120 mi., is the finest harbor in the Far East.

All natural resources of the Philippines belong to the state; their exploitation is limited to citizens of the Philippines or corporations of which 60% of the capital is owned by citizens.

Poland

Polish People's Republic

Polska Rzeczpospolita Ludowa

People: Population (1986 est.): 37,546,000. **Age distrib.** (%): 0–14: 25.4; 15–59: 60.8; 60+: 13.8. **Pop. density:** 310 per sq. mi. **Urban** (1984): 59.5%. **Ethnic groups:** Polish 98%, Germans, Ukrainians, Byelorussians. **Language:** Polish. **Religions:** Roman Catholic 95%.

Geography: Area: 120,727 sq. mi. **Location:** On the Baltic Sea in E Central Europe. **Neighbors:** E. Germany on W, Czechoslovakia on S, USSR (Lithuania, Byelorussia, Ukraine) on E. **Topography:** Mostly lowlands forming part of the Northern European Plain. The Carpathian Mts. along the southern border rise to 8,200 ft. **Capital:** Warsaw. **Cities** (1986 est.): Warsaw 1.6 mln., Lodz 848,000, Cracow 740,000, Wroclaw 627,000, Poznan 563,000.

Government: Type: Communist. **Head of state:** Gen. Wojciech Jaruzelski; in office: Oct. 18, 1981. **Head of government:** Premier Zbigniew Messner. **Local divisions:** 49 provinces. **Defense:** 5.8% of GNP (1983).

Economy: Industries: Shipbuilding, chemicals, metals, autos, food processing. **Chief crops:** Grains, potatoes, sugar beets, tobacco, flax. **Minerals:** Coal, copper, zinc, silver, zinc, sulphur, natural gas. **Arable land:** 49%. **Meat prod.** (1985): cattle: 10.9 mln.; pigs: 18.9 mln.; sheep: 5 mln. **Fish catch** (1984): 671,000 metric tons. **Electricity prod.** (1984): 134 bln. kwh. **Crude steel prod.** (1985): 15.8 mln. metric tons. **Labor force:** 30% agric.; 41% ind. & comm.; 11% services.

Finance: Currency: Zloty (Jan. 1986: 199 = $1 US). **Gross national product** (1984): $110 bln. **Per capita income** (1984): $2,750. **Imports** (1986): $5.4 bln.; partners: USSR 38%, E. Ger. 7% W. Ger. 7% Czech. 5%. **Exports** (1986): $6.5 bln.; partners: USSR 30%, E. Ger. 6%, Czech. 6%, W. Ger. 10%. **National budget** (1984): $23.3 bln. **Tourists** (1983): $85 mln. receipts. **Consumer prices** (change in 1985): 14%.

Transport: Railway traffic (1984): 59 bln. passenger-km; 124 bln. net ton-km. **Motor vehicles:** in use (1985): 3.1 mln. passenger cars, 733,000 comm. vehicles. **Civil aviation** (1985): 2.8 bln. passenger-km; 256 mln. freight ton-km. **Chief ports:** Gdansk, Gdynia, Szczecin.

Communications: Television sets: 8.8 mln. licensed (1985). **Radios:** 9.2 mln. licensed (1985). **Telephones in use** (1985): 4.0 mln. **Daily newspaper circ.** (1983): 217 per 1,000 pop.

Health: Life expectancy at birth (1982): 67.2 male; 75.2 female. **Births** (per 1,000 pop. 1985): 19. **Deaths** (per 1,000 pop. 1985): 10. **Natural increase** (1985): .9%. **Hospital beds** (1985): 242,000. **Physicians** (1985): 71,000. **Infant mortality** (per 1,000 live births 1985): 18.

Education (1985): **Literacy:** 98%. **Years compulsory:** 8; attendance 97%.

Major International Organizations: UN (GATT, WHO), Warsaw Pact.

Embassy: 2640 16th St. NW 20009; 234-3800.

Slavic tribes in the area were converted to Latin Christianity in the 10th century. Poland was a great power from the 14th to the 17th centuries. In 3 partitions (1772, 1793, 1795) it was apportioned among Prussia, Russia, and Austria. Overrun by the Austro-German armies in World War I, its independence, self-declared on Nov.11, 1918, was recognized by the Treaty of Versailles, June 28, 1919. Large territories to the east were taken in a war with Russia, 1921.

Nazi Germany and the USSR invaded Poland Sept. 1-27, 1939, and divided the country. During the war, some 6 million Polish citizens were killed by the Nazis, half of them Jews. With Germany's defeat, a Polish government-in-exile in London was recognized by the U.S., but the USSR pressed the claims of a rival group. The election of 1947 was completely dominated by the Communists.

In compensation for 69,860 sq. mi. ceded to the USSR, 1945, Poland received approx. 40,000 sq. mi. of German territory E of the Oder-Neisse line comprising Silesia, Pomerania, West Prussia, and part of East Prussia.

In 12 years of rule by Stalinists, large estates were abolished, industries nationalized, schools secularized, and Roman Catholic prelates jailed. Farm production fell off. Harsh working conditions caused a riot in Poznan June 28-29, 1956.

A new Politburo, committed to development of a more independent Polish Communism, was named Oct. 1956, with Wladyslaw Gomulka as first secretary of the Communist Party. Collectivization of farms was ended and many collectives were abolished.

In Dec. 1970 workers in port cities rioted because of price rises and new incentive wage rules. On Dec. 20 Gomulka resigned as party leader; he was succeeded by Edward Gierek; the incentive rules were dropped, price rises were revoked.

Poland was the first communist state to get most-favored nation trade terms from the U.S.

A law promulgated Feb. 13, 1953, required government consent to high Roman Catholic church appointments. In 1956 Gomulka agreed to permit religious liberty and religious publications, provided the church kept out of politics. In 1961 religious studies in public schools were halted. Government relations with the Church improved in the 1970s. The number of priests and churches was greater in 1971 than in 1939.

After 2 months of labor turmoil had crippled the country, the Polish government, Aug. 30, 1980, met the demands of striking workers at the Lenin Shipyard, Gdańsk. Among the 21 concessions granted were the right to form independent trade unions and the right to strike — unprecedented political developments in the Soviet bloc. By 1981, 9.5 mln. workers had joined the independent trade union (Solidarity). Farmers won official recognition for their independent trade union in May. Solidarity leaders proposed, Dec. 12, a nationwide referendum on establishing a non-Communist government if the government failed to agree to a series of demands which included access to the mass media and free and democratic elections to local councils in the provinces.

Spurred by the fear of Soviet intervention, the government, Dec. 13, imposed martial law. Public gatherings, demonstrations, and strikes were banned and an internal and external blackout was imposed. Solidarity leaders called for a nationwide strike, but there were only scattered work stoppages. Lech Walesa and other Solidarity leaders were arrested. The U.S. imposed economic sanctions which were lifted when martial law was suspended December 1982.

In 1983 there were demonstrations outside the Lenin Shipyards in March, and antigovernment protests in some 20 cities in May. Pope John Paul II visited his homeland in June.

Portugal

Republic of Portugal

República Portuguesa

People: Population (1986 est.): 10,095,000. **Age distrib.** (%): 0–14: 23.8; 15–59: 59.4; 60+: 16.8. **Pop. density:** 287 per sq. mi. **Urban**(1983): 30%. **Ethnic groups:** Homogeneous Mediterranean stock with small African minority. **Languages:** Portuguese. **Religions:** Roman Catholics 97%.

Geography: Area: 35,553 sq. mi., slightly smaller than Indiana. **Location:** At SW extreme of Europe. **Neighbors:** Spain on N, E. **Topography:** Portugal N of Tajus R, which bisects the country NE-SW, is mountainous, cool and rainy. To the S there are drier, rolling plains, and a warm climate. **Capital:** Lisbon. **Cities** (1981 est.): Lisbon 812,400.

Government: Type: Parliamentary democracy. **Head of state:** Pres. Mario Soares; b. Dec. 7, 1924; in office: Mar. 9, 1986. **Head of government:** Prime Min. Anibal Cavaco Silva; in office: Nov. 6, 1985. **Local divisions:** 18 districts, 2 autonomous regions, one dependency. **Defense:** 3.2% of GNP (1985).

Economy: Industries: Textiles, footwear, cork, chemicals, fish canning, wine, paper. **Chief crops:** Grains, potatoes, rice, grapes, olives, fruits. **Minerals:** Tungsten, uranium, iron. **Other resources:** Forests (world leader in cork production). **Arable land:** 39%. **Meat prod.** (1984): beef: 102,000 metric tons; pork: 180,000 metric tons; lamb: 25,000 metric tons. **Fish catch** (1983): 243,000 metric tons. **Electricity prod.** (1984): 19.0 bln. kwh. **Crude steel prod.** (1982): 362,000 metric tons. **Labor force:** 24% agric.; 31% ind. and comm.; 44% services and govt.

Finance: Currency: Escudo (May 1987: 137.85 = $1 US). **Gross national product** (1984): $19.4 bln. **Per capita income** (1984): $1,930. **Imports** (1986): $9.4 bln.; partners: W. Ger. 12%, U.S. 11%, UK 8%, Fr. 9%. **Exports** (1986): $7.2 bln.; partners: UK 15%, W. Ger. 13%, Fr. 13%, U.S. 6%. **Tourists** (1984): $949 mln. receipts. **National budget** (1985): $6.2 bln expenditures. **International reserves less gold** (Jan. 1987): $1.5 bln. **Gold:** 20.1 mln. oz t. **Consumer prices** (change in 1986): 11%.

Transport: Railway traffic (1985): 5.7 bln. passenger-km; 1.3 bln. net ton-km. **Motor vehicles:** in use (1984): 1.6 mln. passenger cars, 103,000 comm. vehicles. **Civil aviation** (1984): 4.2 bln. passenger-km; 116 mln. freight ton-km. **Chief ports:** Lisbon, Setubal, Leixoes.

Communications: Television sets: 1.5 mln. in use (1984). **Radios:** 2.1 mln. in use (1984). **Telephones in use** (1983): 1.5 mln. **Daily newspaper circ.** (1985): 58 per 1,000 pop.

Health: Life expectancy at birth (1985): 67.6 male; 74.1 female. **Births** (per 1,000 pop. 1985): 14. **Deaths** (per 1,000 pop. 1985): 9. **Natural increase** (1985): .4%. **Hospital beds** (1985): 53,566. **Physicians** (1984): 24,095. **Infant mortality** (per 1,000 live births 1985): 18.

Education (1985): **Literacy:** 80%. **Years compulsory:** 6; attendance 60%.

Major International Organizations: UN (GATT, IMF, WHO), NATO, EFTA, OECD.

Embassy: 2125 Kalorama Rd. NW 20008; 328-8610.

Portugal, an independent state since the 12th century, was a kingdom until a revolution in 1910 drove out King Manoel II and a republic was proclaimed.

From 1932 a strong, repressive government was headed by Premier Antonio de Oliveira Salazar. Illness forced his retirement in Sept. 1968; he was succeeded by Marcello Caetano.

On Apr. 25, 1974, the government was seized by a military junta led by Gen. Antonio de Spinola, who was named president.

The new government reached agreements providing independence for Guinea-Bissau, Mozambique, Cape Verde Islands, Angola, and Sao Tome and Principe. Spinola resigned Sept. 30, 1974, in face of increasing pressure from leftist officers. Despite a 64% victory for democratic parties in April 1975, the Soviet-supported Communist party increased its influence. Banks, insurance companies, and other industries were nationalized. A countercoup in November halted this trend. After years of turmoil the economy and political life were in disarray, despite aid from the U.S. and West European countries.

Azores Islands, in the Atlantic, 740 mi. W. of Portugal, have an area of 888 sq. mi. and a pop. (1975) of 292,000. A 1951 agreement gave the U.S. rights to use defense facilities in the Azores. The **Madeira Islands,** 350 mi. off the NW coast of Africa, have an area of 307 sq. mi. and a pop. (1976) of 270,000. Both groups were offered partial autonomy in 1976.

Macau, area of 6 sq. mi., is an enclave, a peninsula and 2 small islands, at the mouth of the Canton R. in China. Portugal granted broad autonomy in 1976. In 1987, Portugal and China agreed that Macau would revert to China in 1999. Macao, like Hong Kong, was guaranteed 50 years of noninterference in its way of life and capitalist system. Pop. (1986 est.): 433,000.

Qatar

State of Qatar

Dawlet al-Qatar

People: Population (1986 est.): 305,000. **Pop. density:** 71 per sq. mi. **Ethnic groups:** Arabs 40%, Pakistani 18%, Indian 18%, Iranian 10%, others. **Languages:** Arabic (official), English. **Religions:** Moslems 95%.

Geography: Area: 4,247 sq. mi., smaller than Connecticut. **Location:** Occupies peninsula on W coast of Persian Gulf. **Neighbors:** Saudi Arabia on W, United Arab Emirates on S. **Topography:** Mostly a flat desert, with some limestone ridges, vegetation of any kind is scarce. **Capital:** Doha. **Cities** (1985 est.): Doha 190,000.

Government: Type: Traditional emirate. **Head of state and head of government:** Khalifah ibn Hamad ath-Thani; b. 1932; in office: Feb. 22, 1972 (amir), 1970 (prime min.) **Defense:** 13.1% of GNP (1983).

Economy: Crude oil reserves (1985): 4.5 mln. bbls. **Arable land:** 2.9%. **Electricity prod.** (1984): 3.4 bln. kwh. **Labor force:** 10% agric., 70% ind., services and commerce.

Finance: Currency: Riyal (Mar. 1987: 3.64 = $1 US). **Gross national product** (1984): $6.0 bln. **Per capita income** (1984): $20,690. **Imports** (1982): $1.9 bln.; partners: Jap. 20%, UK 16%, U.S. 11%. **Exports** (1982): $4.5 bln.; partners: Jap. 52%, Fr. 10%. **National budget** (1983): $3.7 bln. expenditures.

Transport: Chief ports: Doha, Musayid.

Communications: Radios: 120,000 in use (1985). **Telephones in use** (1984): 105,000.

Health: Life expectancy at birth (1985): 68.2 male; 73.2 female. **Hospital beds** (1983): 891. **Physicians** (1984): 891.

Education (1985): **Literacy:** 60%. **Compulsory:** ages 6-16; attendance: 98%.

Major International Organizations: UN (FAO, GATT, IMF, World Bank), Arab League, OPEC.

Embassy: 600 New Hampshire Ave. NW 20037; 338-0111.

Qatar was under Bahrain's control until the Ottoman Turks took power, 1872 to 1915. In a treaty signed 1916, Qatar gave Great Britain responsibility for its defense and foreign relations. After Britain announced it would remove its military forces from the Persian Gulf area by the end of 1971, Qatar sought a federation with other British protected states in the area; this failed and Qatar declared itself independent, Sept. 1 1971.

Oil revenues give Qatar a per capita income among the highest in the world, but lack of skilled labor hampers development plans.

Romania

Socialist Republic of Romania

Republica Socialistă România

People: Population (1986 est.): 22,830,000. **Age distrib.** (%): 0–14: 25.4; 15–59; 60.5; 60+: 14.2. **Pop. density:** 248 per sq. mi. **Urban** (1985): 50%. **Ethnic groups:** Romanians 88.1%, Hungarians 7.9%, Germans 1.6%. **Languages:** Romanian, Hungarian, German. **Religions:** Orthodox 80%, Roman Catholics 6%.

Geography: Area: 91,699 sq. mi., slightly smaller than New York and Pennsylvania combined. **Location:** In SE Europe on the Black Sea. **Neighbors:** USSR on E (Moldavia) and N (Ukraine), Hungary, Yugoslavia on W, Bulgaria on S. **Topography:** The Carpathian Mts. encase the north-central Transylvanian plateau. There are wide plains S and E of the mountains, through which flow the lower reaches of the rivers of the Danube system. **Capital:** Bucharest. **Cities** (1984 est.): Bucharest 1,961,000, Brasov 331,000, Timisoara 303,000, Constanta 315,000.

Government: Type: Communist. **Head of state:** Pres. Nicolae Ceausescu; b. Jan. 26, 1918; in office; Dec. 9, 1967. **Head of government:** Prime Min. Constantin Dascalescu; in office; May 21, 1982. **Head of Communist Party:** Pres. Nicolae Ceausescu; in office: Mar. 23, 1965. **Local divisions:** Bucharest and 40 counties. **Defense:** 4.7% of GNP (1983).

Economy: Industries: Steel, metals, machinery, oil products, chemicals, textiles, shoes, tourism. **Chief crops:** Corn, wheat, oilseeds, potatoes. **Minerals:** Oil, gas, coal. **Other resources:** Timber. **Arable land:** 45%. **Meat prod.** (1985): cattle: 6.8 mln.; pigs: 12.6 mln.; sheep: 18.7 mln. **Fish catch** (1984): 251,000 metric tons. **Electricity prod.** (1984): 71.6 bln. kwh. **Crude steel prod.** (1985): 13.7 mln. metric tons. **Labor force:** 28% agric.; 44% ind. and commerce.

Finance: Currency: Leu (Mar. 1987: 14.66 = $1 US). **Gross national product** (1984): $45 bln. **Per capita income** (1984): $2,020. **Imports** (1984): $8.1 bln.; partners: USSR 18%, W. Ger. 6%, U.S. 8%, Iran 7%. **Exports** (1984): $10.7 bln.; partners: USSR 18%, W. Ger. 7%. **Tourists** (1984): $230 mln. receipts. **National budget** (1982): $142 mln. expenditures. **International reserves less gold** (Dec. 1986): $506 mln. **Gold:** 3.3 mln. oz t.

Transport: Railway traffic (1984): 28.7 bln. passenger-km; 75.1 bln. net ton-km. **Motor vehicles:** in use (1980): 250,000 passenger cars; 130,000 comm. vehicles. **Civil aviation** (1984): 2.6 bln. passenger-km; 80 mln. freight ton-km. **Chief ports:** Constanta, Galati, Braila.

Communications: Television sets: 3.9 mln. licensed (1985). **Radios:** 3.3 mln. in use (1985). **Telephones in use** (1984): 1.8 mln. **Daily newspaper circ.** (1985): 187 per 1,000 pop.

Health: Life expectancy at birth (1984): 67.0 male; 72.6 female. **Births** (per 1,000 pop. 1985): 15. **Deaths** (per 1,000 pop. 1984): 10. **Natural increase** (1985): 0.5%. **Hospital beds** (1984): 211,800. **Physicians** (1984): 46,300. **Infant mortality** (per 1,000 live births 1985): 22.

Education (1983): **Literacy:** 98%. **Years compulsory:** 10; attendance 98%.

Major International Organizations: UN (World Bank, IMF, GATT), Warsaw Pact.

Embassy: 1607 23d St. NW 20008; 232-4747.

Romania's earliest known people merged with invading Proto-Thracians, preceding by centuries the Dacians. The Dacian kingdom was occupied by Rome, 106 AD-271 AD; people and language were Romanized. The principalities of Wallachia and Moldavia, dominated by Turkey, were united in 1859, became Romania in 1861. In 1877 Romania proclaimed independence from Turkey, became an independent state by the Treaty of Berlin, 1878, a kingdom, 1881, under Carol I. In 1886 Romania became a constitutional monarchy with a bicameral legislature.

Romania helped Russia in its war with Turkey, 1877-78. After World War I it acquired Bessarabia, Bukovina, Transylvania, and Banat. In 1940 it ceded Bessarabia and Northern Bukovina to the USSR, part of southern Dobrudja to Bulgaria, and Transylvania to Hungary.

In 1941, Romanian premier Marshal Ion Antonescu led his country in support of Germany against the USSR. In 1944 Antonescu was overthrown by King Michael and Romania joined the Allies.

With occupation by Soviet troops the communist-headed National Democratic Front displaced the National Peasant party. A People's Republic was proclaimed, Dec. 30, 1947; Michael was forced to abdicate. Land owners were dispossessed; most banks, factories and transportation units were nationalized.

On Aug. 22, 1965, a new constitution proclaimed Romania a Socialist, rather than a People's Republic. Since 1959, USSR troops have not been permitted to enter Romania.

Internal policies remain oppressive. Ethnic Hungarians have protested cultural and job discrimination.

Romania has become industrialized, but lags in consumer goods and in personal freedoms. All industry is state owned, and state farms and cooperatives own over 90% of arable land.

A major earthquake struck Bucharest in March, 1977, killing over 1,300 people and causing extensive damage to housing and industry.

Rwanda

Republic of Rwanda

Republika y'u Rwanda

People: Population (1986 est.): 6,489,000. **Age distrib.** (%): 0–14: 48.7; 15–59: 47.1; 60+: 4.2. **Pop. density:** 662 per sq. mi. **Urban** (1985): 5.1%. **Ethnic groups:** Hutu 90%, Tutsi 9%, Twa (pygmies) 1%. **Languages:** French, Kinyarwandu (both official), Swahili. **Religions:** Christian 68%, traditional 23%, Moslem 9%.

Geography: Area: 10,169 sq. mi., the size of Maryland. **Location:** In E central Africa. **Neighbors:** Uganda on N, Zaire on W, Burundi on S, Tanzania on E. **Topography:** Grassy uplands and hills cover most of the country, with a chain of volcanoes in the NW. The source of the Nile R. has been located in the headwaters of the Kagera (Akagera) R., SW of Kigali. **Capital:** Kigali. **Cities** (1983 est.): Kigali 150,000.

Government: Type: Republic. **Head of state:** Pres. Juvenal Habyarimana; b. Mar. 8, 1937; in office: July 5, 1973. **Local divisions:** 10 prefectures, 143 communes. **Defense:** 1.4% of GNP (1983).

Economy: Chief crops: Coffee, tea. **Minerals:** Tin, gold, wolframite. **Arable land:** 48%. **Electricity prod.** (1984): 135 mln. kwh. **Labor force:** 93% agric.

Finance: Currency: Franc (Apr. 1987: 79 = $1 US). **Gross national product** (1984): $1.7 bln. **Per capita income** (1984): $270. **Imports** (1984): $204 mln.; partners: Ken. 21%, Belg. 16%, Jap. 12%, W. Ger. 9%. **Exports** (1984): $147 mln.; partners: Belg.-Lux. 17%, Ugan. 12%. **National budget** (1984): $185 mln. revenues; $208 mln. expenditures. **International reserves less gold** (Mar. 1987): $164 mln. **Consumer prices** (change in 1985): 1.7%.

Transport: Motor vehicles: in use (1984): 9,000 passenger cars, 5,000 comm. vehicles.

Communications: Radios: 175,000 in use (1984). **Telephones in use** (1984): 6,000.

Health: Life expectancy at birth (1985): 48 years. **Births** (per 1,000 pop. 1985): 54.0. **Deaths** (per 1,000 pop. 1985): 16.0. **Natural increase** (1985): 3.8%. **Hospital beds** (1983): 9,000. **Physicians** (1983): 258. **Infant mortality** (per 1,000 live births 1985): 124.

Education (1985): **Literacy:** 37%. **Years compulsory:** 8; **attendance:** 70%.

Major International Organizations: UN (GATT, IMF, WHO), OAU.

Embassy: 1714 New Hampshire Ave. NW 20009; 232-2882.

For centuries, the Tutsi (an extremely tall people) dominated the Hutus (90% of the population). A civil war broke out in 1959 and Tutsi power was ended. A referendum in 1961 abolished the monarchic system.

Rwanda, which had been part of the Belgian UN trusteeship of Rwanda-Urundi, became independent July 1, 1962. The government was overthrown in a 1973 military coup. Rwanda is one of the most densely populated countries in Africa. All available arable land is being used, and is being subject to erosion. The government has carried out economic and social improvement programs, using foreign aid and volunteer labor on public works projects.

St. Christopher (St. Kitts) and Nevis

St. Christopher Nevis

People: Population (1986 est.): 40,000. **Ethnic groups:** black 95%. **Language:** English. **Religion:** Protestant 76%.

Geography: Area: 101 sq. mi. in the northern part of the Leeward group of the Lesser Antilles in the eastern Caribbean Sea. **Capitol:** Basseterre. **Cities:** (1982 est.): 18,500.

Government: Head of State: Queen Elizabeth represented by Sir Clement Arrindell. **Head of Government:** Prime Minister Kennedy A. Simmonds; b. Apr. 12, 1936; in office: Sept. 19, 1983.

Economy: Sugar is the principal industry.

Finance: Currency: E. Caribbean Dollar (Mar. 1987): 2.70 = $1 U.S. **Gross national product** (1984): $60 mln. **Tourists** (1985): 40,000.

Communications: 3,259 telephones (1983).

Health: Infant mortality (per 1,000 live births, 1985): 39.

Education: Literacy (1984): 90%; school compulsory ages 5-14.

St. Christopher (known by the natives as Liamuiga) and Nevis were discovered and named by Columbus in 1493. They were settled by Britain in 1623, but ownership was disputed with France until 1713. They were part of the Leeward Islands Federation, 1871-1956, and the Federation of the W. Indies, 1958-62. The colony achieved self-government as an Associated State of the UK in 1967, and became fully independent Sept. 19, 1983. Nevis, the smaller of the islands, has the right of secession.

Saint Lucia

People: Population (1986 est.): 123,000. **Age distrib.** (%): 0-20: 49.6; 21-64: 42.7; 65+: 7.7. **Pop. density:** 585 per sq. mi. **Ethnic groups:** Predominantly African descent. **Languages:** English (official), French patois. **Religions:** Roman Catholic 90%.

Geography: Area: 238 sq. mi., about one-fifth the size of Rhode Island. **Location:** In Eastern Caribbean, 2d largest of the Windward Is. **Neighbors:** Martinique to N, St. Vincent to SW. **Topography:** Mountainous, volcanic in origin; Soufriere, a volcanic crater, in the S. Wooded mountains run N-S to Mt. Gimie, 3,145 ft., with streams through fertile valleys. **Capital:** Castries. **City:** Castries (1984 est.): 45,000.

Government: Type: Parliamentary democracy. **Head of state:** Queen Elizabeth II, represented by Gov.-Gen. Sir Allen Lewis; **Head of government:** Prime Min. John Compton; in office: May 3, 1982. **Local divisions:** 16 parishes and Castries.

Economy: Industries: Agriculture, tourism, manufacturing. **Chief crops:** Bananas, coconuts, cocoa, citrus fruits. **Other resources:** Forests. **Arable land:** 50%. **Electricity prod.** (1984): 65.8 mln. kwh. **Labor force:** 36% agric., 20% ind. & commerce, 18% services.

Finance: Currency: East Caribbean dollar (Mar. 1987: 2.70 = $1 US). **Gross national product** (1984): $150 mln. **Per capita income** (1984): $1,120. **Imports** (1982): $118 mln.; partners: U.S. 36%, UK 12%, Trin./Tob. 11%. **Exports** (1982): $41 mln.; partners: U.S. 28%, UK 25%. **Tourists** (1984): receipts: $42 mln.

Transport: Motor vehicles: in use (1984): 7,000 passenger cars, 2,000 comm. vehicles. **Chief ports:** Castries, Vieux Fort.

Communications: Television sets: 5,000 in use (1985). **Radios:** 92,000 in use (1985). **Telephones in use** (1983). 9,500.

Health: Life expectancy at birth (1985): 68.6 male; 75.5 female. **Births** (per 1,000 pop. 1985): 30. **Deaths** (per 1,000 pop. 1985): 6. **Natural increase** (1985): 2.4%. **Hospital beds** (1984): 522. **Infant mortality** (per 1,000 live births 1985): 20.

Education: Literacy (1984) 78%; **Years compulsory:** ages 5-15; **Attendance:** 80%.

Major International Organizations: UN (IMF, ILO), CARICOM, OAS.

St. Lucia was ceded to Britain by France at the Treaty of Paris, 1814. Self government was granted with the West Indies Act, 1967. Independence was attained Feb. 22, 1979.

Saint Vincent and the Grenadines

People: Population (1986 est.): 103,000. **Pop. density:** 738 per sq. mi. **Ethnic groups:** Mainly of African descent. **Languages:** English. **Religions:** Methodists, Anglicans, Roman Catholics.

Geography: Area: 150 sq. mi., about twice the size of Washington, D.C. **Location:** In the eastern Caribbean, St. Vincent (133 sq. mi.) and the northern islets of the Grenadines form a part of the Windward chain. **Neighbors:** St. Lucia to N, Barbados to E, Grenada to S. **Topography:** St. Vincent is volcanic, with a ridge of thickly-wooded mountains running its length; Soufriere, rising in the N, erupted in Apr. 1979. **Capital:** Kingstown. **Cities** (1985 est.): Kingstown 18,378

Government: Head of state: Queen Elizabeth II, represented by Gov.-Gen. Joseph Lambert Eustace; in office: Feb. 28, 1985. **Head of government:** James Mitchell; in office: July 30, 1984.

Economy: Industries: Agriculture, tourism. **Chief crops:** Bananas (62% of exports), arrowroot, coconuts. **Arable land:** 50%. **Electricity prod.** (1984): 34 mln. kwh. **Labor force:** 30% agric.

Finance: Currency: East Caribbean dollar (Mar. 1987: 2.70 = $1 US). **Gross national product** (1984): $100 mln. **Per capita income** (1984): $920. **Imports** (1981): $60 mln.; partners: UK 17%, Trin./Tob. 14%, U.S. 32%. **Exports** (1981): $12 mln.; partners: UK 45%, Trin./Tob. 23%. **Tourists** (1984): $29 mln. receipts. **National budget** (1982): $19 mln. revenues; $20.3 mln. expenditures.

Transport: Motor vehicles: in use (1984): 4,400 passenger cars, 2,000 comm. vehicles. **Chief port:** Kingstown.

Communications: Telephones in use (1983): 6,000.

Health: Life expectancy at birth (1985): 67.5 male; 71.4 female. **Births** (per 1,000 pop. 1985): 30. **Deaths** (per 1,000 pop. 1985): 7. **Natural increase** (1985): 2.3%. **Infant mortality** (per 1,000 live births 1985): 40.

Education (1984): **Literacy:** 85%.

Columbus landed on St. Vincent on Jan. 22, 1498 (St. Vincent's Day). Britain and France both laid claim to the island in the 17th and 18th centuries; the Treaty of Versailles, 1783, finally ceded it to Britain. Associated State status was granted 1969; independence was attained Oct. 27, 1979.

The entire economic life of St. Vincent is dependent upon agriculture and tourism.

San Marino

Most Serene Republic of San Marino

Serenissima Repubblica di San Marino

People: Population (1986 est.): 23,000. **Age distrib.** (%): 0-14: 19.0; 15-59: 63.7; 60+: 17.3. **Pop. density:** 956 per sq. mi. **Urban** (1985): 90.5%. **Ethnic groups:** Sanmarinese 88%, Italian 11%. **Languages:** Italian. **Religions:** Roman Catholics predominate.

Geography: Area: 24 sq. mi. **Location:** In N central Italy near Adriatic coast. **Neighbors:** Completely surrounded by Italy. **Topography:** The country lies on the slopes of Mt. Titano. **Capital:** San Marino. **City** (1985 est.): San Marino 4,000.

Government: Type: Independent republic. **Head of state:** Two co-regents appt. every 6 months. **Local divisions:** 11 districts, 9 sectors.

Economy: Industries: Postage stamps, tourism, woolen goods, paper, cement, ceramics. **Arable land:** 17%.

Finance: Currency: Italian lira. **Tourists** (1985): 2.8 mln; $56 mln. receipts.

Communications: Television sets: 5,000 licensed (1981). **Radios:** 6,000 licensed (1976). **Telephones in use** (1983): 9,000. **Daily newspaper circ.** (1983): 60 per 1,000 pop.

Births (per 1,000 pop. 1985): 11. **Deaths** (per 1,000 pop. 1985): 7.2. **Natural increase** (1985): 0.4%. **Infant mortality** (per 1,000 live births 1985): 9.6.

Education (1985): **Literacy:** 98%. **Years compulsory:** 8. **Attendance:** 93%.

San Marino claims to be the oldest state in Europe and to have been founded in the 4th century. A communist-led coalition ruled 1947-57; a similar coalition took power in 1978. It has had a treaty of friendship with Italy since 1862.

Sao Tome and Principe

Democratic Republic of Sao Tome and Principe

República Democrática de Sao Tome e Principe

People: Population (1986 est.): 108,000. **Pop. density:** 284 per sq. mi. **Ethnic groups:** Portuguese-African mixture, African minority (Angola, Mozambique immigrants). **Languages:** Portuguese. **Religions:** Christian 80%.

Geography: Area: 372 sq. mi., slightly larger than New York City. **Location:** In the Gulf of Guinea about 125 miles off W Central Africa. **Neighbors:** Gabon, Equatorial Guinea on E. **Topography:** Sao Tome and Principe islands, part of an extinct volcano chain, are both covered by lush forests and croplands. **Capital:** Sao Tome. **Cities** (1984 est.): Sao Tome 35,000.

Government: Type: Republic. **Head of state and head of government:** Pres. Manuel Pinto da Costa, b. 1910; in office: July 12, 1975. **Local divisions:** 7 counties.

Economy: Chief crops: Cocoa (82% of exports), coconut products, cinchona. **Arable land:** 38%. **Electricity prod.** (1984): 15 mln. kwh.

Finance: Currency: Dobra (Nov. 1986): 37 = $1 US). **Gross national product** (1984): $34 mln. **Per capita income** (1984): $330. **Imports** (1981): $20 mln.; partners: Port. 61%, Angola 13%. **Exports** (1981): $8 mln.; partners: Neth. 52%, Port. 33%, W. Ger. 8%.

Transport: Motor vehicles: in use (1979): 1,300 passenger cars, 1,900 comm. vehicles. **Chief ports:** Sao Tome, Santo Antonio.

Communications: Radios: 26,000 in use (1985).

Health: Births (per 1,000 pop. 1985): 28. **Deaths** (per 1,000 pop. 1985): 7. **Natural increase** (1985): 2.1%. **Hospital beds** (1978): 665. **Physicians** (1978): 43. **Infant mortality** (per 1,000 live births 1985): 65.

Education (1985): **Literacy:** 50%.

Major International Organizations: UN, OAU.

Embassy: 801 2d Ave., New York, NY 10017; 212-697-4211.

The islands were uninhabited when discovered in 1471 by the Portuguese, who brought the first settlers — convicts and exiled Jews. Sugar planting was replaced by the slave trade as the chief economic activity until coffee and cocoa were introduced in the 19th century.

Portugal agreed, 1974, to turn the colony over to the Gabon-based Movement for the Liberation of Sao Tome and Principe, which proclaimed as first president its East German-trained leader Manuel Pinto da Costa. Independence came July 12, 1975.

Agriculture and fishing are the mainstays of the economy.

Saudi Arabia

Kingdom of Saudi Arabia

al-Mamlaka al-'Arabiya as-Sa'udiya

People: Population (1986 est.): 11,519,000. **Pop. density:** 13 per sq. mi. **Urban** (1985): 73%. **Ethnic groups:** Arab tribes, immigrants from other Arab and Moslem countries. **Languages:** Arabic. **Religions:** Moslem 99%.

Geography: Area: 839,996 sq. mi., one-third the size of the U.S. **Location:** Occupies most of Arabian Peninsula in Middle East. **Neighbors:** Kuwait, Iraq, Jordan on N, Yemen, South Yemen, Oman on S, United Arab Emirates, Qatar on E. **Topography:** The highlands on W, up to 9,000 ft., slope as an arid, barren desert to the Persian Gulf. **Capital:** Riyadh. **Cities** (1986 est.): Riyadh 1,380,000; Jidda 1,210,000; Mecca 463,000.

Government: Type: Monarchy with council of ministers. **Head of state and head of government:** King Fahd; b. 1922; in office: June 13, 1982. **Local divisions:** 14 provinces. **Defense:** 29.6% of govt. budget (1983).

Economy: Industries: Oil products. **Chief crops:** Dates, wheat, barley, fruit. **Minerals:** Oil, gas, gold, copper, iron. **Crude oil reserves** (1985): 167 bln. bbls. **Arable land:** 2%. **Meat prod.** (1984): sheep: 3.6 mln.; goats: 2.3 mln. **Electricity prod.** (1985): 42 bln. kwh. **Labor force:** 14% agric.; 11% ind; 53% serv., comm., & govt.; 20% construction.

Finance: Currency: Riyal (May 1987: 3.74 = $1 US). **Gross national product** (1986): $98.1 bln. **Per capita income** (1979): $11,500. **Imports** (1985): $24 bln.; partners: US 18%, Jap. 18%, W. Ger. 17%. **Exports** (1985): $30.2 bln.; partners: US 13%, Jap., 17%, Fr. 10%. **Tourist receipts** (1981): $1.5 bln. **International reserves less gold** (Mar. 1987): $20.2 bln. **Gold:** 4.59 mln. oz t. **Consumer prices** (change in 1986): −3.0%.

Transport: Railway traffic (1983): 82 mln. passenger-km; 973 mln. net ton-km. **Motor vehicles:** in use (1983): 1.8 mln. passenger cars, 1.7 mln. comm. vehicles. **Civil aviation** (1985): 15.4 bln. passenger-km. 482 mln. net ton-km. **Chief ports:** Jidda, Ad-Dammam, Ras Tannurah.

Communications: Television sets: 3.7 mln. in use (1985). **Radios:** 2.8 mln. in use (1985). **Telephones in use** (1985): 927,000. **Daily newspaper circ.** (1985): 56 per 1,000 pop.

Health: Life expectancy at birth (1986): 60 years. **Births** (per 1,000 pop. 1985): 43.7. **Deaths** (per 1,000 pop. 1985): 12.6. **Natural increase** (1985): 3.1%. **Hospital beds** (1985): 20,463. **Physicians** (1985): 8,243. **Infant mortality** (per 1,000 live births 1985): 100.

Education (1986): **Literacy:** 50% (men).

Major International Organizations: UN (IMF, WHO, FAO), Arab League, OPEC.

Embassy: 601 New Hampshire Ave. NW 20037; 342-3800.

Arabia was united for the first time by Mohammed, in the early 7th century. His successors conquered the entire Near East and North Africa, bringing Islam and the Arabic language. But Arabia itself soon returned to its former status.

Nejd, long an independent state and center of the Wahhabi sect, fell under Turkish rule in the 18th century, but in 1913 Ibn Saud, founder of the Saudi dynasty, overthrew the Turks and captured the Turkish province of Hasa; took the Hejaz in 1925 and by 1926, most of Asir. The discovery of oil in the 1930s transformed the new country.

Crown Prince Khalid was proclaimed king on Mar. 25, 1975, after the assassination of King Faisal. Fahd became king on June 13, 1982 following Khalid's death. There is no constitution and no parliament. The king exercises authority together with a Council of Ministers. The Islamic religious code is the law of the land. Alcohol and public entertainments are restricted, and women have an inferior legal status.

Saudi units fought against Israel in the 1948 and 1973 Arab-Israeli wars. Many billions of dollars of advanced arms have been purchased from Britain, France, and the U.S., including jet fighters, missiles, and, in 1981, 5 airborne warning and control system (AWACS) aircraft from the U.S., despite strong opposition from Israel. Beginning with the 1967 Arab-Israeli war, Saudi Arabia provided large annual financial gifts to Egypt; aid was later extended to Syria, Jordan, and Palestinian guerrilla groups, as well as to other Moslem countries. The country has aided anti-radical forces in Yemen and Oman.

Faisal played a leading role in the 1973-74 Arab oil embargo against the U.S. and other nations in an attempt to force them to adopt an anti-Israel policy. Saudi Arabia joined most other Arab states, 1979, in condemning Egypt's peace treaty with Israel.

Between 1973 and 1976, Saudi Arabia acquired full ownership of Aramco (Arabian American Oil Co.). In the 1980s, Saudi Arabia's moderate position on crude oil prices has often prevailed at OPEC meetings.

The Hejaz contains the holy cities of Islam — Medina where the Mosque of the Prophet enshrines the tomb of Mohammed, who died in the city June 7, 632, and Mecca, his birthplace. More than 600,000 Moslems from 60 nations pilgrimage to Mecca annually. The regime faced its first serious opposition when Moslem fundamentalists seized the Grand Mosque in Mecca, Nov. 20, 1979.

Two Saudi oil tankers were attacked May 1984, as Iran and Iraq began air attacks against shipping in the Persian Gulf. On May 29, the U.S., citing grave concern over the growing escalation of the Iran-Iraq war in the Persian Gulf, authorized the sale of 400 Stinger antiaircraft missiles. In 1986, U.S. President Reagan vetoed a congressional resolution that would have blocked sale of advanced U.S. missiles to the Saudis.

In Aug. 1987, Iranians making a pilgrimage to Mecca clashed with Saudi police (See Chronology).

Senegal

Republic of Senegal

République du Sénégal

People: Population (1986 est.): 6,980,000. **Age distrib.** (%): 0–14: 45; 15–59: 50.2; 60+: 4.8. **Pop. density:** 89 per sq. mi. **Urban** (1986): 30%. **Ethnic groups:** Wolof 36%, Serer 17%, Peulh 17%, Diola 9%, Mandingo 9%. **Languages:** French (official), tribal languages. **Religions:** Moslems 75%, Christians 5%.

Geography: Area: 75,750 sq. mi., the size of South Dakota. **Location:** At western extreme of Africa. **Neighbors:** Mauritania on N, Mali on E, Guinea, Guinea-Bissau on S, Gambia surrounded on three sides. **Topography:** Low rolling plains cover most of Senegal, rising somewhat in the SE. Swamp and jungles are in SW. **Capital:** Dakar. **Cities** (1984): Dakar 671,000; Thies 126,889; Kaolack 115,679.

Government: Type: Republic. **Head of state:** Pres. Abdou Diouf; b. Sept. 7, 1935; in office: Jan. 1, 1981. **Local divisions:** 10 regions. **Defense:** 2.3% of GNP (1983).

Economy: Industries: Food processing, fishing. **Chief crops:** Peanuts are chief export; millet, rice. **Minerals:** Phosphates. **Arable land:** 27%. **Meat prod.** (1984): cattle: 2.2 mln.; sheep: 2.1 mln.; goats: 1 mln. **Fish catch** (1984): 212,000 metric tons. **Electricity prod.** (1984): 684 mln. kwh. **Labor force:** 70% agric.

Finance: Currency: CFA franc (Mar. 1987: 300 = $1 US). **Gross national product** (1984): $2.4 bln. **Per capita income** (1984): $380. **Imports** (1982): $713 mln.; partners Fr. 37%, U.S. 6%. **Exports** (1982): $476 mln.; partners Fr. 25%, UK 6%. **Tourists** (1983): $63 mln. receipts. **International reserves less gold** (Jan. 1987): $12.2 mln. **Gold:** 29,000 oz t. **Consumer prices** (change in 1986): 6.4%.

Transport: Railway traffic (1984): 133 mln. passenger-km; 309 mln. net ton-km. **Motor vehicles:** in use (1980): 50,000 passenger cars, 27,000 comm. vehicles. **Chief ports:** Dakar, Saint-Louis.

Communications: Television sets: 52,000 in use (1985). **Radios:** 350,000 in use (1985). **Telephones in use** (1982): 56,000. **Daily newspaper circ.** (1984): 4 per 1,000 pop.

Health: Life expectancy at birth (1984): 45.0 male, 48.0 female. **Births** (per 1,000 pop. 1985): 47.9. **Deaths** (per 1,000 pop. 1985): 21.1. **Natural increase** (1985): 2.6%. **Hospital beds** (1982): 6,200. **Physicians** (1982): 470. **Infant mortality** (per 1,000 live births 1985): 102.

Education (1984): **Literacy:** 10%. **Attendance:** 53% primary, 11% secondary.

Major International Organizations: UN and all of its specialized agencies, OAU.

Embassy: 2112 Wyoming Ave. NW 20008; 234-0540.

Portuguese settlers arrived in the 15th century, but French control grew from the 17th century. The last independent Moslem state was subdued in 1893. Dakar became the capital of French West Africa.

Independence as part, along with the Sudanese Rep., of the Mali Federation, came June 20, 1960. Senegal withdrew Aug. 20 that year. French political and economic influence is strong.

A long drought brought famine, 1972-73, and again in 1978.

Senegal is recognized as the most democratic of the French-speaking West African nations.

Senegal, Dec. 17, 1981, signed an agreement with The Gambia for confederation of the 2 countries under the name of Senegambia. The confederation began Feb. 1, 1982. The 2 nations retained their individual sovereignty but adopted joint defense and monetary policies.

Seychelles

Republic of Seychelles

People: Population (1986 est.): 67,000. **Age distrib.** (%): 0–14: 36.3; 15–64; 57.3; 65+: 6.4. **Pop. density:** 377 per sq. mi. **Urban** (1977): 37.1% **Ethnic groups:** Creoles (mixture of Asians, Africans, and French) predominate. **Languages:** English and French (both official), Creole. **Religions:** Roman Catholic 90%.

Geography: Area: 171 sq. mi. **Location:** In the Indian O. 700 miles NE of Madagascar. **Neighbors:** Nearest are Madagascar on SW, Somalia on NW. **Topography:** A group of 86 islands, about half of them composed of coral, the other half granite, the latter predominantly mountainous. **Capital:** Victoria. **Cities** (1986): Victoria 23,000.

Government: Type: Single party republic. **Head of state:** Pres. France-Albert Rene, b. Nov. 16, 1935; in office: June 5, 1977. **Defense:** 11.7% of govt. budget (1983).

Economy: Industries: Food processing. **Chief crops:** Coconut products, cinnamon, vanilla, patchouli. **Other resources:** Guano, shark fins, tortoise shells, fish. **Electricity prod.** (1984): 56.5 mln. kwh. **Labor force:** 18.5% agric.; 19.4% ind. & comm.; 13.5% serv.; 49% govt.

Finance: Currency: Rupee (Mar. 1987: 5.62 = $1 US). **Gross national product** (1985): $140 mln. **Per capita income** (1985): $2,100. **Imports** (1984): $70.9 mln.; partners: UK 15%, So. Afr. 8%, Bah. 17%. **Exports** (1984): $4.3 mln.; partners: Pak. 38%; Jap. 26%. **National Budget** (1985): $65 mln. **Tourists** (1984): $39 mln. receipts. **International reserves less gold** (Mar. 1987): $9.9 mln. **Consumer prices** (change in 1986): 0.3%.

Transport: Motor vehicles: in use (1984): 3,500 passenger cars, 1,000 comm. vehicles. **Port:** Victoria.

Communications: Radios: 16,000 in use (1985). **Telephones in use** (1981): 7,105. **Daily newspaper circ.** (1984): 52 per 1,000 pop.

Health: Life expectancy at birth (1986): 66 years. **Births** (per 1,000 pop. 1985): 25. **Deaths** (per 1,000 pop. 1985): 7. **Natural increase** (1985): 1.8%. **Hospital beds** (1984): 359. **Physicians** (1984): 34. **Infant mortality** (per 1,000 live births 1986): 15.

Education (1986): **Literacy:** 80%. **Years compulsory** 9; attendance 95%.

Major International Organizations: UN, OAU, Commonwealth of Nations.

The islands were occupied by France in 1768, and seized by Britain in 1794. Ruled as part of Mauritius from 1814, the Seychelles became a separate colony in 1903. The ruling party had opposed independence as impractical, but pressure from the OAU and the UN became irresistible, and independence was declared June 29, 1976. The first president was ousted in a coup a year later by a socialist leader.

A new constitution, announced Mar. 1979, turned the country into a one-party state.

Sierra Leone

Republic of Sierra Leone

People: Population (1986 est.): 3,987,000. **Age distrib.** (%): 0–14: 40.9; 15–59: 53.6; 60+: 5.5. **Pop. density:** 134 per sq. mi. **Ethnic groups:** Temne 30%, Mende 29%, others. **Languages:** English (official), tribal languages. **Religions:** animist 30%, Moslem 60%.

Geography: Area: 27,925 sq. mi., slightly smaller than South Carolina. **Location:** On W coast of W. Africa. **Neighbors:** Guinea on N, E, Liberia on S. **Topography:** The heavily-indented, 210-mi. coastline has mangrove swamps. Behind are wooded hills, rising to a plateau and mountains in the E. **Capital:** Freetown. **Cities** (1985 est.): Freetown 469,000; Bo, Kenema, Makeni.

Government: Type: Republic. **Head of state and head of government:** Pres. Gen. Joseph Saidu Momoh; b. Jan. 26, 1937; in office: Nov. 28, 1985. **Local divisions:** 12 districts and one region including Freetown.

Economy: Industries: Mining, tourism. **Chief crops:** Cocoa, coffee, palm kernels, rice, ginger. **Minerals:** Diamonds, bauxite. **Arable land:** 25%. **Fish catch** (1984): 52,000 metric tons. **Electricity prod.** (1984): 112 mln. kwh. **Labor force:** 75% agric.; 15% ind. & serv.

Finance: Currency: Leone (Mar. 1987: 4.00 = $1 US). **Gross national product** (1985): $445. **Per capita income** (1984): $320. **Imports** (1985): $135 mln.; partners: UK 22%, Fr. 11%. **Exports** (1985): $111 mln.; partners: Neth. 31%; UK 15%, U.S. 9%. **National budget** (1981): $185 mln. revenues; $161 mln. expenditures. **International reserves less gold** (Mar. 1987): $13.7 mln. **Consumer prices** (change in 1985): 76.6%.

Transport: Motor Vehicles: in use (1984): 19,000 passenger cars, 36,000 comm. vehicles. **Chief ports:** Freetown, Bonthe.

Communications: Television sets: 21,000 in use (1984). **Radios:** 100,000 in use (1984). **Telephones in use** (1981): 220,000. **Daily newspaper circ.** (1984): 3 per 1,000 pop.

Health: Life expectancy at birth (1986): 46 yrs. **Births** (per 1,000 pop. 1985): 45.3. **Deaths** (per 1,000 pop. 1985): 17.4. **Natural increase** (1985): 2.7%. **Hospital beds** (1984): 4,754. **Physicians** (1984): 197. **Infant mortality** (per 1,000 live births 1985): 195.

Education (1986): **Literacy:** 15%.

Major International Organizations: UN (GATT, IMF, WHO), Commonwealth of Nations, OAU.

Embassy: 1701 19th St. NW 20009; 939-9261.

Freetown was founded in 1787 by the British government as a haven for freed slaves. Their descendants, known as Creoles, number more than 60,000.

Successive steps toward independence followed the 1951 constitution. Full independence arrived Apr. 27, 1961. Sierra Leone became a republic Apr. 19, 1971. A one-party state approved by referendum 1978, brought political stability, but the economy has been plagued by inflation, corruption, and dependence upon the International Monetary Fund and creditors.

Singapore

Republic of Singapore

People: Population (1986 est.): 2,584,000. **Age distrib.** (%): 0–14: 24.4; 15–59: 67.8; 60+: 7.8. **Pop. density:** 10,824 per sq. mi. **Ethnic groups:** Chinese 77%, Malays 15%, Indians 6%. **Languages:** Chinese, Malay, Tamil, English all official. **Religions:** Buddhism, Taoism, Islam, Hinduism, Christianity.

Geography: Area: 224 sq. mi., smaller than New York City. **Location:** Off tip of Malayan Peninsula in S.E. Asia. **Neighbors:** Nearest are Malaysia on N, Indonesia on S. **Topography:** Singapore is a flat, formerly swampy island. The nation includes 40 nearby islets. **Capital:** Singapore. **Cities** (1978 est.): Singapore 2,334,400.

Government: Type: Parliamentary democracy. **Head of state:** Pres. Wee Kim Wee; in office: Sept. 3, 1985. **Head of government:** Prime Min. Lee Kuan Yew; b. Sept. 16, 1923; in office: June 5, 1959. **Defense:** 6% of GNP (1985).

Economy: Industries: Shipbuilding, oil refining, electronics, banking, textiles, food, rubber, lumber processing, tourism. **Meat prod.** (1984): pigs: 1.3 mln. **Fish catch** (1984): 25,000 metric tons. **Electricity prod.** (1984): 9.4 bln. kwh. **Crude steel prod.** (1981): 350,000 metric tons. **Labor force:** 1% agric.; 58% ind. & comm.; 35% services.

Finance: Currency: Dollar (May 1987: 2.11 = $1 US). **Gross national product** (1985): $16.0 bln. **Per capita income** (1985): $6,200. **Imports** (1986): $25.5 bln.; partners: Jap. 18%, Malay. 13%, U.S. 13%, Sau. Ar. 9%. **Exports** (1986): $22.5 bln., partners: U.S. 20%, Malay. 16%, Jap. 11%, HK 6%. **Tourists** (1984): $2.0 bln. receipts. **National budget** (1986): $10 bln. expenditures. **Consumer prices** (change in 1986): −1.4%.

Transport: Motor vehicles: in use (1985): 236,000 passenger cars, 120,000 comm. vehicles. **Civil aviation:** (1985) 21.7 bln. passenger-km; 1 bln. freight ton-km.

Communications: Television sets: 373,000 (1985). **Radios:** 111,000 licensed (1984). **Telephones in use** (1984): 972,000. **Daily newspaper circ.** (1984): 249 per 1,000 pop.

Health: Life expectancy at birth (1985): 69.7 male; 75.2 female. **Births** (per 1,000 pop. 1985): 16. **Deaths** (per 1,000 pop. 1985): 5. **Natural increase** (1985): 1%. **Hospital beds** (1985): 9,866. **Physicians** (1985): 2,631. **Infant mortality** (per 1,000 live births 1985): 8.9

Education (1987): **Literacy:** 85%. **Years compulsory:** none; attendance 85%.

Major International Organizations: UN (GATT, IMF, WHO), ASEAN.

Embassy: 1824 R St. NW 20009; 667-7555.

Founded in 1819 by Sir Thomas Stamford Raffles, Singapore was a British colony until 1959 when it became autonomous within the Commonwealth. On Sept. 16, 1963, it joined with Malaya, Sarawak and Sabah to form the Federation of Malaysia.

Tensions between Malayans, dominant in the federation, and ethnic Chinese, dominant in Singapore, led to an agreement under which Singapore became a separate nation, Aug. 9, 1965.

Singapore is one of the world's largest ports. Standards in health, education, and housing are high. International banking has grown.

Solomon Islands

People: Population (1986 est.): 283,000. **Age distrib.** (%): 0–14: 49; 15–59: 45.5; 60+: 5.5. **Pop. density:** 26 per sq. mi. **Urban** (1985): 9%. **Ethnic groups:** Melanesian 93%, Polynesian 4%. **Languages:** English (official), Pidgin, local languages. **Religions:** Anglican 34%, Roman Catholic 19%, Evangelical 24%, traditional religions.

Geography: Area: 10,640 sq. mi., slightly larger than Maryland. **Location:** Melanesian archipelago in the western Pacific O. **Neighbors:** Nearest is Papua New Guinea on W. **Topography:** 10 large volcanic and rugged islands and 4 groups of smaller ones. **Capital:** Honiara. **Cities:** (1981): Honiara 19,200.

Government: Type: Parliamentary democracy within the Commonwealth of Nations. **Head of state:** Queen Elizabeth II, represented by Gov.-Gen. Baddeley Devesi; b. Oct. 16, 1941; in office: July 7, 1978. **Head of government:** Prime Min. Ezekial Alebua; in office: Dec. 1, 1986. **Local divisions:** 7 provinces and Honiara.

Economy: Industries: Fish canning. **Chief crops:** Coconuts, rice, bananas, yams. **Other resources:** Forests, marine shell. **Arable land:** 2%. **Fish catch** (1984): 35,000 metric tons. **Electricity prod.** (1984): 28.0 mln. kwh. **Labor force:** 32% agric., 32% services, 18% ind. & comm.

Finance: Currency: Dollar (Mar. 1987: 1.98 = $1 US). **Gross national product** (1983): $160 mln. **Per capita income** (1982): $628. **Imports** (1982): $57 mln.; partners: Austral. 34%, Jap. 14%, Sing. 18%. **Exports** (1982): $56 mln.; partners: Jap. 59%, UK 14%, Neth. 15%.

Communications: Radios: 35,000 in use (1985). **Telephones in use** (1985): 4,000.

Health: Life expectancy at birth: 54 years. **Births:** (per 1,000 pop. 1985): 47. **Deaths** (per 1,000 pop. 1985): 10. **Natural increase** (1985): 3.7%. **Infant mortality** (per 1,000 live births 1985): 46.

Education (1980): **Literacy:** 13%. **Primary school** 73%. **Secondary school:** 13%.

Major International Organizations: UN, Commonwealth of Nations.

The Solomon Islands were sighted in 1568 by an expedition from Peru. Britain established a protectorate in the 1890s over most of the group, inhabited by Melanesians. The islands saw major World War II battles. Self-government came Jan. 2, 1976, and independence was formally attained July 7, 1978.

Somalia

Somali Democratic Republic

Jamhuriyadda Dimugradiga Somaliya

People: Population (1986 est.): 7,825,000. **Pop. density:** 25 per sq. mi. **Ethnic groups:** mainly Hamitic, others. **Languages:** Somali, Arabic (both official). **Religions:** Sunni Moslems 99%.

Geography: Area: 246,300 sq. mi., slightly smaller than Texas. **Location:** Occupies the eastern horn of Africa. **Neighbors:** Djibouti, Ethiopia, Kenya on W. **Topography:** The coastline extends for 1,700 mi. Hills cover the N; the center and S are flat. **Capital:** Mogadishu. **Cities** (1986 est.): Mogadishu 700,000.

Government: Type: Independent republic. **Head of state:** Pres. Mohammed Siad Barrah; b. 1919; in office: Oct. 21, 1969. **Local divisions:** 15 regions. **Defense:** 29% of govt. expenditures (1983).

Economy: Chief crops: Incense, sugar, bananas, sorghum, corn, gum. **Minerals:** Iron, tin, gypsum, bauxite, uranium. **Arable land:** 2%. **Meat prod.** (1980): beef: 45,000 metric tons; lamb: 66,000 metric tons. **Fish catch** (1983): 15,000 metric tons. **Electricity prod.** (1984): 75 mln. kwh. **Labor force:** 82% agric.

Finance: Currency: Shilling (Mar. 1987: 90.50 = $1 US). **Gross national product** (1985): $1.8 bln. **Per capita income** (1985): $300. **Imports** (1985): $470 mln.; partners: It. 35%, UK 8%, U.S. 9%. **Exports** (1985): $110 mln.; partners: Saudi Ar. 66%, It. 12%. **International reserves less gold** (Nov. 1986): $12.8 mln. **Gold:** 19,000 oz t. **Consumer prices** (change in 1986): 35.8%.

Transport: Motor vehicles: in use (1981): 17,200 passenger cars, 9,500 comm. vehicles. **Chief ports:** Mogadishu, Berbera.

Communications: Radios: 100,000 in use (1985).

Health: Life expectancy at birth (1985): 43.9 yrs. **Births** (per 1,000 pop. 1985): 47. **Deaths** (per 1,000 pop. 1985): 17. **Natural increase** (1985): 3.0%. **Hospital beds** (1978): 5,232. **Physicians** (1981): 292. **Infant mortality** (per 1,000 live births 1985): 163.

Education (1986): Literacy: 40%. 50% attend primary school, 7% attend secondary school.

Major International Organizations: UN, OAU, Arab League.

Embassy: 600 New Hampshire Ave. NW 20037; 342-1575.

Arab trading posts developed into sultanates. The Italian Protectorate of Somalia, acquired from 1885 to 1927, extended along the Indian O. from the Gulf of Aden to the Juba R. The UN in 1949 approved eventual creation of Somalia as a sovereign state and in 1950 Italy took over the trusteeship held by Great Britain since World War II.

British Somaliland was formed in the 19th century in the NW. Britain gave it independence June 26, 1960; on July 1 it joined with the former Italian part to create the independent Somali Republic.

On Oct. 21, 1969, a Supreme Revolutionary Council seized power in a bloodless coup, named a Council of Secretaries of State, and abolished the Assembly. In May, 1970, several foreign companies were nationalized.

A severe drought in 1975 killed tens of thousands, and spurred efforts to resettle nomads on collective farms.

Somalia has laid claim to Ogaden, the huge eastern region of Ethiopia, peopled mostly by Somalis. Ethiopia battled Somali rebels and accused Somalia of sending troops and heavy arms in 1977. Russian forces were expelled in 1977 in retaliation for Soviet support of Ethiopia. Some 11,000 Cuban troops with Soviet arms defeated Somali army troops and ethnic Somali rebels in Ethiopia, 1978. As many as 1.5 mln. refugees entered Somalia. Guerrilla fighting in Ogaden has continued, although the Somali government no longer officially supports the Ogaden secessionists.

South Africa

Republic of South Africa

Republiek van Suid-Afrika

People: Population (1986 est.): 33,241,000. **Age distrib.** (%): 0–14: 41.5; 15–59: 54.5; 60+: 3.8. **Pop. density:** 65 per sq. mi. **Urban** (1985): 55%. **Ethnic groups:** black 68%, white 18%, coloured 10%, Asian 3%. **Religions:** Mainly Christian. **Languages:** Afrikaans, English (both official), Bantu languages predominate.

Geography: Area: 472,359 sq. mi., about twice the size of Texas. **Location:** At the southern extreme of Africa. **Neighbors:** Namibia (SW Africa), Botswana, Zimbabwe on N, Mozambique, Swaziland on E; surrounds Lesotho. **Topography:** The large interior plateau reaches close to the country's 2,700-mi. coastline. There are few major rivers or lakes; rainfall is sparse in W, more plentiful in E. **Capitals:** Cape Town (legislative), Pretoria (administrative), and Bloemfontein (judicial). **Cities** (1983 met.): Durban 714,000; Cape Town 1,567,000; Johannesburg 600,000; Pretoria 712,000.

Government: Type: Tricameral parliament with one chamber each for whites, coloureds, and Asians. **Head of State:** State President Pieter Willem Botha; b. Jan. 12, 1916; in office: Sept. 28, 1978. **Local divisions:** 4 provinces, 10 "homelands" for black Africans. **Defense:** 15% of govt. budget (1985).

Economy: Industries: Steel, tires, motors, textiles, plastics. **Chief crops:** Corn, wool, dairy products, grain, tobacco, sugar, fruit, peanuts, grapes. **Minerals:** Gold (largest producer), chromium, antimony, coal, iron, manganese, nickel, phosphates, tin, uranium, gem diamonds, platinum, copper, vanadium. **Other resources:** Wool. **Arable land:** 12%. **Meat prod.** (1985): cattle: 12.7 mln.; pigs: 1.4 mln.; sheep: 30.3 mln. **Fish catch** (1983): 599,000 metric tons. **Electricity prod.** (1985): 140 bln. kwh. **Crude steel prod.** (1985): 8.5 mln. metric tons. **Labor force:** 30% agric.; 29% ind. and commerce; 34% serv.; 7% mining.

Finance: Currency: Rand (May 1987: 1.98 = $1 US). **Gross national product** (1985): $112 bln. **Per capita income** (1985): $4,000. **Imports** (1986): $12.9 bln.; partners: W. Ger. 15%, U.S. 19%, Jap. 13%. **Exports** (1986): $18.4 bln.; partners: U.S. 9%, Jap. 9%. **Tourism** (1982): $630 mln. receipts. **National budget** (1984): $20.7 bln. **International reserves less gold** (Mar. 1987): $1 bln. **Gold:** 5.5 mln. oz t. **Consumer prices** (change in 1986): 18.6%.

Transport: Railway traffic (1985): 91.8 bln. net ton-km. **Motor vehicles:** in use (1984): 2.8 mln. passenger cars, 1.2 mln. comm. vehicles. **Civil aviation:** (1985): 8.7 bln. passenger-km: 397 mln. freight ton-km. **Chief ports:** Durban, Cape Town, East London, Port Elizabeth.

Communications: Television sets (1985): 2.1 mln.; **Radios:** 10 mln. in use (1985). **Telephones in use** (1984): 3.4 mln. **Daily newspaper circ.** (1985): 46 per 1,000 pop.

Health: Life expectancy at birth (1982): White: 70 years; Asians: 65 years; Africans: 59 years. **Births** (per 1,000 pop. 1985): 33. **Deaths** (per 1,000 pop. 1985): 10. **Natural increase** (1985): 2.3%. **Health** (1983): 18,003 medical practitioners, 4,379 specialists, 3,140 interns. **Infant mortality** (per 1,000 live births 1982): Africans 94, Asians 25.3, whites 14.9.

Education (1984): **Literacy:** 93% (whites), 69% (Asians), 62% (coloureds), 32% (Africans).

Major International Organizations: UN (GATT).

Embassy: 3051 Massachusetts Ave. NW 20008; 232-4400.

Bushmen and Hottentots were the original inhabitants. Bantus, including Zulu, Xhosa, Swazi, and Sotho, had occupied the area from Transvaal to south of Transkei before the 17th century.

The Cape of Good Hope area was settled by Dutch, beginning in the 17th century. Britain seized the Cape in 1806. Many Dutch trekked north and founded 2 republics, the Transvaal and the Orange Free State. Diamonds were discovered, 1867, and gold, 1886. The Dutch (Boers) resented encroachments by the British and others; the Anglo-Boer War followed, 1899-1902. Britain won and, effective May 31, 1910, created the Union of South Africa, incorporating the British colonies of the Cape and Natal, the Transvaal and the Orange Free State. After a referendum, the Union became the Republic of South Africa, May 31, 1961, and withdrew from the Commonwealth.

With the election victory of Daniel Malan's National party in 1948, the policy of separate development of the races, or apartheid, already existing unofficially, became official. This called for separate development, separate residential areas, and ultimate political independence for the whites, Bantus, Asians, and Coloreds. In 1959 the government passed acts providing the eventual creation of several Bantu nations or Bantustans on 13% of the country's land area, though most black leaders have opposed the plan.

Under apartheid, blacks are severely restricted to certain occupations, and are paid far lower wages than are whites for similar work. Only whites may vote or run for public office, and militant white opposition has been curbed. There is an advisory Indian Council, partly elected, partly appointed. In 1969, a Colored People's Representative Council was created. Some liberalization measures were allowed in the 1980s.

At least 600 persons, mostly Bantus, were killed in 1976 riots protesting apartheid. Black protests continued through 1985 as violence broke out in several black townships. Police reaction to the protests caused several hundred deaths. A new constitution was approved by referendum, Nov. 1983, which extended the parliamentary franchise to the Coloured and Asian minorities. Laws banning interracial sex and marriage were repealed in 1985.

In 1963, the Transkei, an area in the SE, became the first of these partially self-governing territories or "Homelands." Transkei became independent on Oct. 26, 1976, Bophuthatswana on Dec. 6, 1977, and Venda on Sept. 13, 1979; none received international recognition.

In 1981, So. Africa launched military operations in Angola and Mozambique to combat terrorists groups; So. African troops attacked the South West African People's Organization (SWAPO) guerrillas in Angola, March, 1982. South Africa and Mozambique signed a non-agression pact in 1984.

A car bomb exploded outside air force headquarters in Pretoria, May 20, 1983, killing or injuring hundreds of people. The African National Congress (ANC), a black nationalist group, claimed responsibility. In the U.S., there were nationwide antiapartheid protests in 1985; pressure was building in the U.S. Congress for economic sanctions against S. Africa unless racial reforms were enacted.

In 1986, Nobel Peace Prize winner Bishop Desmond Tutu called for Western nations to apply sanctions against S. Africa to force an end to apartheid. President Botha announced in Apr. the end to the nation's system of racial pass laws and offered blacks an advisory role in government.

On May 19, S. Africa attacked 3 neighboring countries—Zimbabwe, Botswana, Zambia—to strike at guerrilla strongholds of the African National Congress. The raids drew international condemnation.

A nationwide state of emergency was declared June 12, giving almost unlimited power to the security forces. Millions of blacks, June 16, staged a strike to mark the 10th anniversary of the Soweto uprising. On Apr. 22, 1987, a 6-week-old walkout by railway workers erupted into violence after the dismissal of 16,000 strikers. As confrontation between blacks and government increased, there was widespread support in Western nations for a complete trade embargo on S. Africa. Rev. Leon H. Sullivan, author of the antidiscrimination code of conduct for U.S. companies operating in So. Africa, called for a complete corporate withdrawal from So. Africa in 1987.

Bophuthatswana: Population (1986 est.): 1,564,000. **Area:** 15,444 sq. mi., 6 discontinuous geographic units. **Capital:** Mmabatho. **Head of state:** Pres. Kgosi Lucas Manyane Mangope, b. Dec. 27, 1923; in office: Dec. 6, 1977.

Ciskei: Population (1986 est.): 798,000. **Area:** 2,080 sq. mi. **Capitol:** Bisho. **Head of State:** Pres. Lennox Sebe.

Transkei: Population (1986 est.): 2,755,000. **Area:** 16,816 sq. mi., 3 discontinuous geographic units. **Capital:** Umtata (1978 est.): 30,000. **Head of state:** Pres. Nyangelizwe Vulindlela Ndamase; in office: Feb. 20, 1986. **Head of government:** Prime Min. George Matanzima; in office: Feb. 20, 1979.

Venda: Population (1986 est.): 448,000. **Area:** 2,390 sq. mi., 2 discontinuous geographic units. **Capital:** Thohoyandou. **Head of state:** Patrick Mphephu; in office: Sept. 13, 1979.

Namibia (South-West Africa)

South-West Africa is a sparsely populated land twice the size of California. Made a German protectorate in 1884, it was surrendered to South Africa in 1915 and was administered by that country under a League of Nations mandate. S. Africa refused to accept UN authority under the trusteeship system.

Other African nations charged S. Africa imposed apartheid, built military bases, and exploited S-W Africa. The UN General Assembly, May 1968, created an 11-nation council to take over administration of S-W Africa and lead it to independence. The council charged that S. Africa had blocked its efforts to visit S-W Africa.

In 1968 the UN General Assembly gave the area the name Namibia. In Jan. 1970 the UN Security Council condemned S. Africa for "illegal" control of the area. In an advisory opinion, June 1971, the International Court of Justice declared S. Africa was occupying the area illegally.

In a 1977 referendum, white voters backed a plan for a multiracial interim government to lead to independence. The Marxist South-West Africa People's Organization (SWAPO) rejected the plan, and launched a guerrilla war. Both S. Africa and Namibian rebels agreed to a UN plan for independence by the end of 1978. S. Africa rejected the plan, Sept. 20, 1978, and held elections, without UN supervision, for Namibia's constituent assembly, Dec., that were ignored by the major black opposition parties.

The UN peace plan, proposed 1980, called for a cease-fire and a demilitarized zone 31 miles deep on each side of S-W Africa's borders with Angola and Zambia that would be patrolled by UN peacekeeping forces against guerrilla actions. Impartial elections would follow. In 1982, So. African and SWAPO agreed in principle on a cease-fire and the holding of UN-supervised elections. So. Africa, however, insisted on the withdrawal of Cuban forces from Angola as a precondition to Namibian independence. On Jan. 18, 1983, South Africa dissolved the Namibian National Assembly and resumed direct control of the territory.

Most of Namibia is a plateau, 3,600 ft. high, with plains in the N, Kalahari Desert to the E, Orange R. on the S, Atlantic O. on the W. Area is 320,827 sq. mi.; pop. (1986 est.) 1,203,000; capital, Windhoek.

Products include cattle, sheep, diamonds, copper, lead, zinc, fish. People include Namas (Hottentots), Ovambos (Bantus), Bushmen, and others.

Walvis Bay, the only deepwater port in the country, was turned over to South African administration in 1922. S. Africa said in 1978 it would discuss sovereignty only after Namibian independence.

Spain

España

People: Population (1986 est.): 39,074,000 **Age distrib.** (%): 0–14: 24.6; 15–59: 59.5; 60+: 15.9. **Pop. density:** 199 per sq. mi. **Ethnic groups:** Spanish (Castilian, Valencian, Andalusian, Asturian) 72.8%, Catalan 16.4%, Galician 8.2%, Basque 2.3%. **Languages:** Spanish (official), Catalan, Galician, Basque. **Religions:** Roman Catholic.

Geography: Area: 194,896 sq. mi., the size of Arizona and Utah combined. **Location:** In SW Europe. **Neighbors:** Portugal on W. France on N. **Topography:** The interior is a high, arid plateau broken by mountain ranges and river valleys. The NW is heavily watered, the south has lowlands and a Mediterranean climate. **Capital:** Madrid. **Cities** (1985 est.): Madrid 3,217,000; Barcelona 1,756,000; Valencia 763,000; Seville 673,000.

Government: Type: Constitutional monarchy. **Head of state:** King Juan Carlos I de Borbon y Borbon, b. Jan. 5, 1938; in office: Nov. 22, 1975. **Head of government:** Prime Min. Felipe Gonzalez Marquez; in office: Dec. 2, 1982. **Local divisions:** 50 provinces, 2 territories, 3 islands. **Defense:** 2.4% of GNP (1984).

Economy: Industries: Machinery, steel, textiles, shoes, autos, ships. **Chief crops:** Grains, olives, grapes, citrus fruits, vegetables, olives. **Minerals:** Mercury, potash, uranium, lead, iron, copper, zinc, coal. **Crude oil reserves** (1985): 74 mln. bbls. **Other resources:** Forests (cork). **Arable land:** 41%. **Meat prod.** (1985): cattle: 4.9 mln.; pigs: 11.9 mln.; sheep: 17.3 mln. **Fish catch** (1984): 1.2 mln. tons. **Electricity prod.** (1984): 115.4 bln. kwh. **Crude steel prod.** (1985): 14.2 mln. metric tons. **Labor force:** 17% agric.; 34% ind. and comm.; 49% serv.

Finance: Currency: Peseta (May 1987: 124.40 = $1 US). **Gross national product** (1984): $160.4 bln. **Per capita income** (1984): $4,490. **Imports** (1986): $35.0 bln.; partners: U.S. 11%, EC 33%. **Exports** (1986): $27.1 bln.; partners: EC 49%, U.S. 10%. **Tourists** (1984): $7.7 bln. receipts. **National budget** (1985): $25.8 bln. revenues; $35.5 bln. expenditures. **International reserves less gold** (Jan. 1987): $15.4 bln. **Gold:** 14.83 mln. oz t. **Consumer prices** (change in 1986): 8.8%.

Transport: Railway traffic (1985): 15 bln. passenger-km; 11.6 bln. net ton-km. **Motor vehicles:** in use (1984): 8.8 mln. passenger cars, 1.5 mln. comm. **Civil aviation:** (1984): 16.3 bln. passenger-km; 517 mln. freight ton-km. **Chief ports:** Barcelona, Bilbao, Valencia, Cartagena, Gijon.

Communications: Television sets: 9.9 mln. in use (1985). **Radios:** 10.8 mln. in use (1985). **Telephones in use** (1984): 13.8 mln. **Daily newspaper circ.** (1983): 89 per 1,000 pop.

Health: Life expectancy at birth (1985): 71.3 male; 77.5 female. **Births** (per 1,000 pop. 1985): 11. **Deaths** (per 1,000 pop. 1985): 8. **Natural increase** (1985): .3%. **Hospital beds** (1983): 201,035. **Physicians** (1984): 121,362. **Infant mortality** (per 1,000 live births 1985): 9.

Education (1985): Literacy: 97%. **School compulsory:** to age 14.

Major International Organizations: UN and all of its specialized agencies, NATO, OECD, EC.

Embassy: 2700 15th St. NW 20009; 265-0190.

Spain was settled by Iberians, Basques, and Celts, partly overrun by Carthaginians, conquered by Rome c.200 BC. The Visigoths, in power by the 5th century AD, adopted Christianity but by 711 AD lost to the Islamic invasion from Africa. Christian reconquest from the N led to a Spanish nationalism. In 1469 the kingdoms of Aragon and Castile were united by the marriage of Ferdinand II and Isabella I, and the last Moorish power was broken by the fall of the kingdom of Granada, 1492. Spain became a bulwark of Roman Catholicism.

Spain obtained a colonial empire with the discovery of America by Columbus, 1492, the conquest of Mexico by Cortes, and Peru by Pizarro. It also controlled the Netherlands and parts of Italy and Germany. Spain lost its American colonies in the early 19th century. It lost Cuba, the Philippines, and Puerto Rico during the Spanish-American War, 1898.

Primo de Rivera became dictator in 1923. King Alfonso XIII revoked the dictatorship, 1930, but was forced to leave the country 1931. A republic was proclaimed which disestablished the church, curtailed its privileges, and secularized education. A conservative reaction occurred 1933 but was followed by a Popular Front (1936-1939) composed of socialists, communists, republicans, and anarchists.

Army officers under Francisco Franco revolted against the government, 1936. In a destructive 3-year war, in which some one million died, Franco received massive help and troops from Italy and Germany, while the USSR, France, and Mexico supported the republic. War ended Mar. 28, 1939. Franco was named caudillo, leader of the nation. Spain was neutral in World War II but its relations with fascist countries caused its exclusion from the UN until 1955.

In July 1969, Franco and the Cortes designated Prince Juan Carlos as the future king and chief of state. After Franco's death, Nov. 20, 1975, Juan Carlos was sworn in as king. He presided over the formal dissolution of the institutions of the Franco regime. In free elections June 1977, moderates and democratic socialists emerged as the largest parties.

In an unsuccessful attempt at a military coup, Feb. 23, 1981, rightist Civil Guards seized the lower house of Parliament and took most of the country's leaders hostage. The plot collapsed the next day when the army remained loyal to King Juan Carlos.

Catalonia and the Basque country were granted autonomy, Jan. 1980, following overwhelming approval in home-rule referendums. Basque extremists, however, have continued their campaign for independence.

The **Balearic Islands** in the western Mediterranean, 1,935 sq. mi., are a province of Spain; they include **Majorca** (Mallorca), with the capital, Palma; **Minorca, Cabrera, Ibiza** and **Formentera.** The **Canary Islands,** 2,807 sq. mi., in the Atlantic W of Morocco, form 2 provinces, including the islands of **Tenerife, Palma, Gomera, Hierro, Grand Canary, Fuerteventura,** and **Lanzarote** with Las Palmas and Santa Cruz thriving ports. **Ceuta** and **Melilla,** small enclaves on Morocco's Mediterranean coast, are part of Metropolitan Spain.

Spain has sought the return of Gibraltar, in British hands since 1704.

Sri Lanka

Democratic Socialist Republic of Sri Lanka

Sri Lanka Prajathanthrika Samajavadi Janarajaya

People: Population (1986 est.): 16,638,000. **Age distrib.** (%): 0–14: 35.3; 15–59: 58.1; 60+: 6.6. **Pop. density:** 634 per sq. mi. **Urban** (1985): 21.5%. **Ethnic groups:** Sinhalese 75%, Tamils 18%, Moors 7%. **Languages:** Sinhala (official), Tamil, English. **Religions:** Buddhists 69%, Hindus 15%, Christians 7%, Muslims 7%.

Geography: Area: 25,332 sq. mi. about the size of W. Va. **Location:** In Indian O. off SE coast of India. **Neighbors:** India on NW. **Topography:** The coastal area and the northern half are flat; the S-central area is hilly and mountainous. **Capital:** Colombo. **Cities** (1983): Colombo 1,262,000.

Government: Type: Republic. **Head of state:** Pres. Junius Richard Jayawardene; b. Sept. 17, 1906; in office: Feb. 4, 1978. **Head of government:** Prime Minister Ranasinghe Premadasa, b. June 23, 1924, in office: Feb. 6, 1978. **Local divisions:** 25 districts. **Defense:** 2.5% of GNP (1984).

Economy: Industries: Plywood, paper, milling, chemicals, textiles. **Chief crops:** Tea, coconuts, rice. **Minerals:** Graphite, limestone, gems, phosphate. **Other resources:** Forests, rubber. **Arable land:** 34%. **Meat prod.** (1980): beef: 18,000 metric tons. **Fish catch** (1984): 221,000 metric tons. **Electricity prod.** (1983): 2.1 bln. kwh. **Labor force:** 46% agric.; 29% ind. and comm.; 19% serv.

Finance: Currency: Rupee (Mar. 1987: 28.78 = $1 US). **Gross national product** (1984): $5.3 bln. **Per capita income** (1984): $340. **Imports** (1986): $1.9 bln.; partners: Jap. 15%, Saudi Ar. 12%, UK 7%. **Exports** (1986): $1.2 bln.; partners: U.S. 14%, UK 7%. **Tourists** (1984): $105 mln. receipts. **National budget** (1984): $1.5 bln. revenues; $1.8 bln. expenditures. **International reserves less gold** (Mar. 1987): $362 mln. **Gold:** 63,000 oz t. **Consumer prices** (change in 1986): 8.0%

Transport: Railway traffic (1985): 2.1 bln. passenger-km; 247 mln. net ton-km. **Motor vehicles:** in use (1984): 141,000 passenger cars, 125,000 comm. vehicles. **Civil aviation** (1985): 2.5 bln. passenger-km; 47 mln. freight ton-km. **Chief ports:** Colombo, Trincomalee, Galle.

Communications: Radios: 3 mln. in use (1985). **Telephones in use** (1982): 109,900.

Health: Life expectancy at birth (1985): 67.6 male; 70.9 female. **Births** (per 1,000 pop. 1985): 27. **Deaths** (per 1,000 pop. 1985): 6. **Natural increase** (1985): 2.1%. **Hospital beds** (1984): 44,919. **Physicians** (1984): 1,951. **Infant mortality** (per 1,000 live births 1985): 28.

Education (1985): **Literacy:** 87%. **Years compulsory:** To age 12; attendance 84%.

Major International Organizations: UN (World Bank, IMF), Commonwealth of Nations.

Embassy: 2148 Wyoming Ave. NW 20008; 483-4025.

The island was known to the ancient world as Taprobane (Greek for copper-colored) and later as Serendip (from Arabic). Colonists from northern India subdued the indigenous Veddahs about 543 BC; their descendants, the Buddhist Sinhalese, still form most of the population. Hindu descendants of Tamil immigrants from southern India account for one-fifth of the population. Parts were occupied by the Portuguese in 1505 and by the Dutch in 1658. The British seized the island in 1796. As Ceylon it became an independent member of the Commonwealth in 1948. On May 22, 1972, Ceylon became the Republic of Sri Lanka.

Prime Min. W. R. D. Bandaranaike was assassinated Sept. 25, 1959. In new elections, the Freedom Party was victorious under Mrs. Sirimavo Bandaranaike, widow of the former prime minister. In Apr., 1962, the government expropriated British and U.S. oil companies. In Mar. 1965 elections, the conservative United National Party won; the new government agreed to pay compensation for the seized oil companies.

After May 1970 elections, Mrs. Bandaranaike became prime minister again. In 1971 the nation suffered economic problems and terrorist activities by ultra-leftists, thousands of whom were executed. Massive land reform and nationalization of foreign-owned plantations was undertaken in the mid-1970s. Mrs. Bandaranaike was ousted in 1977 elections by the United Nationals. A presidential form of government was installed in 1978 to restore stability.

Tension between the Sinhalese and Tamil separatists has often erupted into violence. In 1987, hundreds died in an attack by Tamil rebels Apr. 17. Sri Lanka forces retaliated in June with attacks on the rebel-held Jaffna peninsula.

Sudan

Republic of Sudan

Jamhuryat as-Sudan

People: Population (1986 est.): 22,932,000. **Pop. density:** 25 per sq. mi. **Urban** (1983): 35%. **Ethnic groups:** North: Arabs, Nubians; South; Nilotic; Sudanic, Negro tribes. **Languages:** Arabic (official), various tribal languages. **Religions:** Muslims 73%, animist 18%, Christians 9%.

Geography: Area: 966,757 sq. mi., the largest country in Africa, over one-fourth the size of the U.S. **Location:** At the E end of Sahara desert zone. **Neighbors:** Egypt on N, Libya, Chad, Central African Republic on W, Zaire, Uganda, Kenya on S, Ethiopia on E. **Topography:** The N consists of the Libyan Desert in the W, and the mountainous Nubia desert in E, with narrow Nile valley between. The center contains large, fertile, rainy areas with fields, pasture, and forest. The S has rich soil, heavy rain. **Capital:** Khartoum. **Cities** (1983 est.): Khartoum 476,000; Omdurman 526,000; North Khartoum 341,000; Port Sudan 206,000.

Government: Type: Republic. **Head of government:** Pres. Sadiq al Mahdi; b. 1936; in office: May 6, 1986. **Local divisions:** 8 regions. **Defense:** 1.7% of GNP (1983).

Economy: Industries: Textiles, food processing. **Chief crops:** Gum arabic (principal world source), durra (sorghum), cotton (main export), sesame, peanuts, rice, coffee, sugar cane, tobacco, wheat, dates. **Minerals:** Chrome, gold, copper, white mica, vermiculite, asbestos. **Other resources:** Mahogany. **Arable land:** 5%. **Meat prod.** (1983): beef: 239,000 metric tons; lamb: 137,000 metric tons. **Electricity prod.** (1984): 1 bln. kwh. **Labor force:** 78% agric.; 9% ind., comm.

Finance: Currency: Pound (Mar. 1987: 2.30 = $1 US). **Gross national product** (1984): $7.3 bln. **Per capita income** (1982 est.): $361. **Imports** (1985): $771 mln.; partners: UK 13%, W. Ger. 8%, Saudi Ar. 11%. **Exports** (1985): $374 mln.; partners: China 6%, It. 9%, Saudi Ar. 21%. **National budget** (1985): $1.5 bln. expenditures. **International reserves less gold** (Mar. 1987): $49.4 mln.

Transport: Railway traffic (1982): 1.1 bln. net ton-km. **Motor vehicles:** in use (1982): 150,000 passenger cars, 22,000 comm. vehicles. **Civil aviation:** (1982): 657 mln. passenger-km; 6.3 mln. freight ton-km. **Chief ports:** Port Sudan.

Communications: Television sets: 125,000 in use (1985). **Radios:** 1.3 mln. (1985). **Telephones in use** (1983): 68,000. **Daily newspaper circ.** (1985): 6 per 1,000 pop.

Health: Life expectancy at birth (1985): 48.0 male; 50.0 female. **Births** (per 1,000 pop. 1985): 45.3. **Deaths** (per 1,000 pop. 1985): 16.6. **Natural increase** (1985): 2.8%. **Hospital beds** (1985): 17,328. **Physicians** (1983): 2,169. **Infant mortality** (per 1,000 live births 1985): 118.

Education (1985): **Literacy:** 20%. **Years compulsory:** 9; attendance 50%.

Major International Organizations: UN (IMF, WHO, FAO), Arab League, OAU.

Embassy: 2210 Massachusetts Ave. NW 20008; 338-8565.

Northern Sudan, ancient Nubia, was settled by Egyptians in antiquity, and was converted to Coptic Christianity in the 6th century. Arab conquests brought Islam in the 15th century.

In the 1820s Egypt took over the Sudan, defeating the last of earlier empires, including the Fung. In the 1880s a revolution was led by Mohammed Ahmed who called himself the Mahdi (leader of the faithful) and his followers, the dervishes.

In 1898 an Anglo-Egyptian force crushed the Mahdi's successors. In 1951 the Egyptian Parliament abrogated its 1899 and 1936 treaties with Great Britain, and amended its constitution, to provide for a separate Sudanese constitution.

Sudan voted for complete independence as a parliamentary government effective Jan. 1, 1956. Gen. Ibrahim Abboud took power 1958, but resigned under pressure, 1964.

In 1969, in a second military coup, a Revolutionary Council took power, but a civilian premier and cabinet were appointed; the government announced it would create a socialist state. The northern 12 provinces are predominantly Arab-Moslem and have been dominant in the central government. The 3 southern provinces are Negro and predominantly pagan. A 1972 peace agreement gave the South regional autonomy.

The government nationalized a number of businesses in May 1970.

Sudan charged Libya with aiding an unsuccessful coup in Sudan in 1976. Sudan claimed that Libyan planes bombed several border towns, Sept. 1981, and the city of Omdurman, 1984.

Economic problems plagued the nation in the 1980s, aggravated by a hugh influx of refugees from neighboring countries. After 16 years in power, Pres. Nimeiry was overthrown in a bloodless military coup, Apr. 6, 1985. The Sudan held its first democratic parliamentary elections in 18 years in 1986.

Suriname

Republic of Suriname

People: Population (1986 est.): 381,000. **Pop. density:** 6.2 per sq. mi. **Ethnic groups** Hindustanis 37%, Creole 31%, Javanese 15%. **Languages:** Dutch (official), Sranan (Creole), English, others. **Religions:** Muslim, Hindu, Christian.

Geography: Area: 63,037 sq. mi., slightly larger than Georgia. **Location:** On N shore of S. America. **Neighbors:** Guyana on W, Brazil on S, French Guiana on E. **Topography:** A flat Atlantic coast, where dikes permit agriculture. Inland is a forest belt; to the S, largely unexplored hills cover 75% of the country. **Capital:** Paramaribo. **Cities** (1984): Paramaribo 180,000.

Government: Type: Military-civilian executive. **Head of Military Council:** Col. Desire Bouterse; in office: Feb. 5, 1982. **Head of government:** Pretaapnarian Radhakishun; in office: July 17, 1986. **Local divisions:** 9 districts.

Economy: Industries: Aluminum. **Chief crops:** Rice, sugar, fruits. **Minerals:** Bauxite. **Other resources:** Forests, shrimp. **Arable land:** 1%. **Electricity prod.** (1984): 1.2 bln. kwh. **Labor force:** 29% agric.; 15% ind. and commerce; 42% govt.

Finance: Currency: Guilder (Mar. 1987: 1.78 = $1 US). **Gross national product** (1984): $1.3 bln. **Per capita income** (1981): $2,600. **Imports** (1982): $449 mln.; partners: U.S. 31%, Neth. 19%, Trin./Tob. 15%, Jap. 7%. **Exports** (1982): $366 mln.; partners: U.S. 36%, Neth. 17%, Nor. 13%. **Tourists** (1983): receipts: $4 mln. **National budget** (1983): $454. **International reserves less gold** (Mar. 1987): $19.4 mln. **Gold:** 54,000 oz t. **Consumer prices** (change in 1984): 3.7%.

Transport: Motor vehicles: in use (1983): 31,000 passenger cars, 12,000 comm. vehicles. **Chief ports:** Paramaribo, Nieuw-Nickerie.

Communications: Television sets: 44,000 in use (1985). **Radios:** 187,000 in use (1985). **Telephones in use** (1982): 27,495. **Daily newspaper circ.** (1984): 80 per 1,000 pop.

Health: Life expectancy at birth (1985): 67.0 male; 71.9 female. **Births** (per 1,000 pop. 1985): 26. **Deaths** (per 1,000 pop. 1985): 8. **Natural increase** (1985): 2.1%. **Infant mortality** (per 1,000 live births 1985): 21.

Education (1984): Literacy: 65%; compulsory ages 6–12.

Major International Organizations: UN (WHO, ILO, FAO, World Bank, IMF), OAS.

Embassy: 2600 Virginia Ave. NW 20037; 338-6980.

The Netherlands acquired Suriname in 1667 from Britain, in exchange for New Netherlands (New York). The 1954 Dutch constitution raised the colony to a level of equality with the Netherlands and the Netherlands Antilles. In the 1970s the Dutch government pressured for Suriname independence, which came Nov. 25, 1975, despite objections from East Indians. Some 40% of the population (mostly East Indians) emigrated to the Netherlands in the months before independence.

The National Military Council took over control of the government, Feb. 1982.

Swaziland

Kingdom of Swaziland

People: Population (1986 est.): 692,000. **Age distrib.** (%): 0–14: 46.1; 15–59: 48.9; 60+: 5.0. **Pop. density:** 100 per sq. mi. **Urban** (1980): 8.9%. **Ethnic groups:** Swazi 90%, Zulu 2.3%, European 2.1%, other African, non-African groups. **Languages:** siSwati, English, (both official). **Religions:** Christians 77%, animist 23%.

Geography: Area: 6,704 sq. mi., slightly smaller than New Jersey. **Location:** In southern Africa, near Indian O. coast. **Neighbors:** South Africa on N, W, S, Mozambique on E. **Topography:** The country descends from W-E in broad belts, becoming more arid in the lowveld region, then rising to a plateau in the E. **Capital:** Mbabane. **Cities** (1985 est.): Mbabane 45,000.

Government: Type: Monarchy. **Head of state:** King Mswati 3d; as of: Apr. 25, 1986. **Head of government:** Prime Min. Sotsha Dlamini; in office: Oct. 6, 1986. **Local divisions:** 4 districts, 2 municipalities, 40 regions.

Economy: Industries: Wood pulp. **Chief crops:** Sugar, corn, cotton, rice, pineapples, sugar, citrus fruits. **Minerals:** Asbestos, iron, coal. **Other resources:** Forests. **Arable land:** 19%. **Electricity prod.** (1981): 310 mln. kwh. **Labor force:** 53% agric.; 9% ind. and commerce; 9% serv.

Finance: Currency: Lilangeni (Mar. 1987: 2.00 = $1 US). **Gross national product** (1984): $590 mln. **Per capita income** (1983 est.): $790. **Imports** (1983): $516 mln.; partners: So. Afr., 96%. **Exports** (1983): $286 mln.; partners: UK 33%, So. Afr. 20%. **National budget** (1986): $120 mln. **International reserves less gold** (Feb. 1987): $96.9 mln. **Consumer prices** (change in 1986): 11.8%.

Transport: Motor vehicles: in use (1983): 17,000 passenger cars, 8,000 comm. vehicles.

Communications: Radios: 85,000 in use (1985). **Telephones in use** (1983): 8,000. **Daily newspaper circ.** (1984): 34 per 1,000 pop.

Health: Life expectancy at birth (1983): 46.8 male; 50.0 female. **Births** (per 1,000 pop. 1985): 47.5. **Deaths** (per 1,000 pop. 1985): 17.2. **Natural increase** (1985): 3.0%. **Hospital beds** (1984): 1,608. **Physicians** (1984): 80. **Infant mortality rate** (per 1,000 live births 1985): 156.

Education (1985): **Literacy:** 65%. Almost all attend primary school.

Major International Organizations: UN (IMF, WHO, FAO), OAU, Commonwealth of Nations.

Embassy: 4301 Connecticut Ave. NW 20008; 362-6683.

The royal house of Swaziland traces back 400 years, and is one of Africa's last ruling dynasties. The Swazis, a Bantu people, were driven to Swaziland from lands to the N by the Zulus in 1820. Their autonomy was later guaranteed by Britain and Transvaal, with Britain assuming control after 1903. Independence came Sept. 6, 1968. In 1973 the king repealed the constitution and assumed full powers.

Under the constitution political parties are forbidden; parliament's role in government is limited to debate and advice.

Sweden

Kingdom of Sweden

Konungariket Sverige

People: Population (1986 est.): 8,357,000. **Age distrib.** (%): 0–14: 18.2; 15–59: 58.8; 60+: 23.0. **Pop. density:** 52 per sq. mi. **Urban** (1985): 85%. **Ethnic groups:** Swedish 91%, Finnish 3%, Lapps, European immigrants. **Languages:** Swedish, Finnish. **Religions:** Lutheran (official) 95%.

Geography: Area: 173,731 sq. mi., larger than California. **Location:** On Scandinavian Peninsula in N. Europe. **Neighbors:** Norway on W, Denmark on S (across Kattegat), Finland on E. **Topography:** Mountains along NW border cover 25% of Sweden, flat or rolling terrain covers the central and southern areas, which includes several large lakes. **Capital:** Stockholm. **Cities** (1985 est.): Stockholm 653,000; Goteborg 424,000; Malmo 229,000.

Government: Type: Constitutional monarchy. **Head of state:** King Carl XVI Gustaf; b. Apr. 30, 1946; in office: Sept. 19, 1973. **Head of government:** Prime Min. Ingvar Carlsson; b. Nov. 9, 1934; in office: Mar. 1, 1986. **Local divisions:** 24 lan (counties), 284 municipalities. **Defense:** 2.2% of GNP (1984).

Economy: Industries: Steel, machinery, instruments, autos, shipbuilding, shipping, paper. **Chief crops:** Grains, potatoes, sugar beets. **Minerals:** Zinc, iron, lead, copper, gold, silver. **Other resources:** Forests (half the country); yield one fourth exports. **Arable land:** 7%. **Meat prod.** (1985): cattle: 1.7 mln.; pigs: 2.4 mln. **Fish catch** (1984): 258,000 metric tons. **Electricity prod.** (1984): 119.5 bln. kwh. **Crude steel prod.** (1985): 4.8 mln. metric tons. **Labor force:** 5% agric.; 30% ind; 21% comm. & finance; 44% services.

Finance: Currency: Krona (May 1987: 6.22 = $1 US). **Gross national product** (1985): $100 bln. **Per capita income** (1985): $11,989. **Imports** (1986): $32.6 bln.; partners: W. Ger. 17%, UK 13%, U.S. 9%, Fin. 7%. **Exports** (1986): $37.2 bln.; partners: UK 10%, W. Ger. 10%, Nor. 11%. **Tourists** (1984): $1.1 bln. receipts. **National budget** (1986): $42.9 bln. expenditures. **International reserves less gold** (Mar. 1987): $7.9 bln. **Gold:** 6.06 mln. oz t. **Consumer prices** (change in 1986): 4.2%.

Transport: Railway traffic (1984): 6.6 bln. passenger-km; 17.7 bln. net ton-km. **Motor vehicles:** in use (1985): 3.0 mln. passenger cars, 223,000 comm. vehicles. **Civil aviation** (1985): 5.0 bln. passenger-km; 191 mln. freight ton-km. **Chief ports:** Goteborg, Stockholm, Malmo.

Communications: Television sets: 3.2 mln. licensed (1984). **Radios:** 3.3 mln. (1984). **Telephones in use** (1984): 7.4 mln. **Daily newspaper circ.** (1984): 574 per 1,000 pop.

Health: Life expectancy at birth (1984): 73.1 male; 79.1 female. **Births** (per 1,000 pop. 1985): 11. **Deaths** (per 1,000 pop. 1985): 11. **Natural increase** (1985): 0%. **Hospital beds** (1983): 116,688. **Physicians** (1983): 19,300. **Infant mortality** (per 1,000 live births (1986): 3.3.

Education (1987): **Literacy:** 99%. **Years compulsory:** 9; attendance 100%.

Major International Organizations: UN and all of its specialized agencies, EFTA, OECD.

Embassy: 600 New Hampshire Ave. NW 20037; 944-5600.

The Swedes have lived in present-day Sweden for at least 5,000 years, longer than nearly any other European people. Gothic tribes from Sweden played a major role in the disintegration of the Roman Empire. Other Swedes helped create the first Russian state in the 9th century.

The Swedes were Christianized from the 11th century, and a strong centralized monarchy developed. A parliament, the Riksdag, was first called in 1435, the earliest parliament on the European continent, with all classes of society represented.

Swedish independence from rule by Danish kings (dating from 1397) was secured by Gustavus I in a revolt, 1521-23; he built up the government and military and established the Lutheran Church. In the 17th century Sweden was a major European power, gaining most of the Baltic seacoast, but its international position subsequently declined.

The Napoleonic wars, in which Sweden acquired Norway (it became independent 1905), were the last in which Sweden participated. Armed neutrality was maintained in both world wars.

Over 4 decades of Social Democratic rule was ended in 1976 parliamentary elections but the party was returned to power in the 1982 elections. Although 90% of the economy is in private hands, the government holds a large interest in water power production and the railroads are operated by a public agency.

Consumer cooperatives are in extensive operation and also are important in agriculture and housing. Per capita GNP is among the highest in the world.

A labor crisis of strikes locking out more than 800,000 workers, May 1980, brought the country to an industrial standstill.

A Soviet submarine went aground inside Swedish territorial waters near the Karlskrona Naval Base, Oct. 27, 1981. Sweden claimed the submarine was armed with nuclear weapons and the incident a "flagrant violation" of Swedish neutrality. The submarine was towed back to international waters Nov. 6. Sweden charged that the USSR has repeatedly violated its territorial waters and airspace.

Premier Olof Palme was shot and killed on a Stockholm street Feb. 28, 1986.

Switzerland

Swiss Confederation

People: Population (1986 est.): 6,466,000. **Age distrib.** (%): 0–14: 17.8; 15–59: 63.2; 60+: 19.0. **Pop. density:** 411 per sq. mi. **Urban** (1985): 60.4%. **Ethnic groups:** Mixed European stock. **Languages:** German 65%, French 18%, Italian 12%, Romansh 1%. (all official). **Religions:** Roman Catholic 49%, Protestant 48%.

Geography: Area: 15,941 sq. mi., as large as Mass., Conn., and R.I., combined. **Location:** In the Alps Mts. in Central Europe. **Neighbors:** France on W, Italy on S, Austria on E, W. Germany on N. **Topography:** The Alps cover 60% of the land area, the Jura, near France, 10%. Running between, from NE to SW, are midlands, 30%. **Capital:** Bern. **Cities** (1986): Zurich 351,000; Basel 174,200; Geneva 159,000.

Government: Type: Federal state. **Head of government:** Pres. Pierre Aubert; in office: Jan. 1, 1986. **Local divisions:** 20 full cantons, 6 half cantons. **Defense:** 2.2% of GNP (1984).

Economy: Industries: Machinery, machine tools, steel, instruments, watches, textiles, foodstuffs (cheese, chocolate), chemicals, drugs, banking, tourism. **Chief crops:** Grains, potatoes, sugar beets, vegetables, tobacco. **Minerals:** Salt. **Other resources:** Hydro power potential. **Arable land:** 10%. **Meat prod.** (1985): cattle: 1.9 mln.; pigs: 1.9 mln. **Electricity prod.** (1984): 49.1 bln. kwh. **Crude steel prod.** (1985): 990,000 metric tons. **Labor force:** 39% ind. and commerce, 7% agric., 50% serv.

Finance: Currency: Franc (May 1987: 1.46 = $1 US). **Gross national product** (1984): $93.7 bln. **Per capita income** (1984): $14,408. **Imports** (1986): $41.0 bln.; partners: W. Ger. 30%, Fr. 11%, It. 10%, U.K. 5%. **Exports** (1986): $37.4 bln.; partners: W. Ger. 18%, Fr. 9%, It. 8%, U.S. 8%. **Tourists** (1984); receipts: $3.1 bln. **National budget** (1984): $10.1 bln. **International reserves less gold** (Mar. 1987): $20.7 bln. **Gold:** 83.28 mln. oz t. **Consumer prices** (change in 1986): 0.8%.

Transport: Railway traffic (1984): 8.9 bln. passenger-km; 6.8 bln. net ton-km. **Motor vehicles:** in use (1984): 2.5 mln. passenger cars, 201,000 comm. vehicles. **Civil aviation:** (1984): 12.0 bln. passenger-km; 680 mln. freight ton-km.

Communications: Television sets: 2.1 mln. (1985). **Radios:** 2.4 mln. (1985). **Telephones in use** (1983): 4.9 mln. **Daily newspaper circ.** (1985): 491 per 1,000 pop.

Health: Life expectancy at birth (1985): 70.3 male; 76.2 female. **Births** (per 1,000 pop. 1985): 11. **Deaths** (per 1,000 pop. 1985): 9. **Natural increase** (1985): .2%. **Hospital beds** (1984): 66,192. **Physicians** (1984): 14,712. **Infant mortality** (per 1,000 live births 1985): 9.

Education (1985): **Literacy:** 99%. **Years compulsory:** 9; attendance 100%.

Major International Organizations: Many UN specialized agencies (though not a member).

Embassy: 2900 Cathedral Ave. NW 20008; 745-7900.

Switzerland, the Roman province of Helvetia, is a federation of 23 cantons (20 full cantons and 6 half cantons), 3 of which in 1291 created a defensive league and later were joined by other districts. Voters in the French-speaking part of Canton Bern voted for self-government, 1978; Canton Jura was created Jan. 1, 1979.

In 1648 the Swiss Confederation obtained its independence from the Holy Roman Empire. The cantons were joined under a federal constitution in 1848, with large powers of local control retained by each canton.

Switzerland has maintained an armed neutrality since 1815, and has not been involved in a foreign war since 1515. Switzerland is a member of several UN agencies and of the European Free Trade Assoc. and has ties with the EC. It is also the seat of many UN and other international agencies.

Switzerland is a leading world banking center; stability of the currency brings funds from many quarters. Some 20% of all workers are foreign residents.

Syria

Syrian Arab Republic

al-jamhouriya al Arabia as-Souriya

People: Population (1986 est.): 10,931,000. **Age distrib.** (%): 0–14: 49.3; 15–59: 44.2; 60+: 6.5. **Pop. density:** 148 per sq. mi. **Urban** (1986): 49%. **Ethnic groups:** Arabs 90%, Kurds, Armenians, Turks, Circassians, Assyrians. **Languages:** Arabic (official), Kurdish, Armenian, French, English. **Religions:** Sunni Moslem 70%, Christian 13%.

Geography: Area: 71,498 sq. mi., the size of North Dakota. **Location:** At eastern end of Mediterranean Sea. **Neighbors:** Lebanon, Israel on W, Jordan on S, Iraq on E, Turkey on N. **Topography:** Syria has a short Mediterranean coastline, then stretches E and S with fertile lowlands and plains, alternating with mountains and large desert areas. **Capital:** Damascus. **Cities** (1986 est.): Damascus 2,083,000; Aleppo 1,857,000; Homs 490,000.

Government: Type: Socialist. **Head of state:** Pres. Hafez al-Assad; b. Mar. 1930; in office: Feb. 22, 1971. **Head of government:** Prime Min. Abdul Rauf al-Kassem; in office: Jan. 16, 1980. **Local divisions:** Damascus and 13 provinces. **Defense:** 13% of GNP (1983).

Economy: Industries: Oil products, textiles, cement, tobacco, glassware, sugar, brassware. **Chief crops:** Cotton, grain, olives, fruits, vegetables. **Minerals:** Oil, phosphate, gypsum. **Crude oil reserves** (1985): 1.3 bln. bbls. **Other resources:** Wool. **Arable land:** 48%. **Meat prod.** (1983): beef: 26,000 metric tons; lamb: 99,000 metric tons. **Electricity prod.** (1984): 6.7 bln. kwh. **Labor force:** 32% agric.; 29% ind. & comm.; 39% services.

Finance: Currency: Pound (Mar. 1987: 3.92 = $1 US). **Gross national product** (1984): $13.9 bln. **Imports** (1984): $3.0 bln.; partners: Iran, It., W. Ger., Fr. **Exports** (1984): $1.3 bln.; partners: It. 20%, Rom. 28%. **Tourists** (1984): receipts: $130 mln. **Consumer prices** (change in 1986): −3.0%.

Transport: Railway traffic (1984): 757 mln. passenger-km; 966 mln. net ton-km. **Motor vehicles:** in use (1984): 114,000 passenger cars, 85,000 comm. vehicles **Civil aviation** (1985): 942 mln. passenger-km; 15.6 mln. net ton-km. **Chief ports:** Latakia, Tartus.

Communications: Television sets: 400,000 in use (1985). **Radios:** 1.8 mln. in use (1985). **Telephones in use** (1984): 474,000. **Daily newspaper circ.** (1984): 17 per 1,000 pop.

Health: Life expectancy at birth (1980): 64.9 male; 67.6 female. **Births** (per 1,000 pop. 1985): 45. **Deaths** (per 1,000 1985): 7. **Natural increase** (1985): 3.8%. **Hospital beds** (1984): 11,595. **Physicians** (1984): 5,543. **Infant mortality** (per 1,000 live births 1985): 57.

Education (1986): **Literacy:** 78% males. **Years compulsory:** 6; attendance: 94%.

Major International Organizations: UN (IMF, WHO, FAO), Arab League.

Embassy: 2215 Wyoming Ave. NW 20008; 232-6313.

Syria contains some of the most ancient remains of civilization. It was the center of the Seleucid empire, but later became absorbed in the Roman and Arab empires. Ottoman rule prevailed for 4 centuries, until the end of World War I.

The state of Syria was formed from former Turkish districts, made a separate entity by the Treaty of Sevres 1920 and divided into the states of Syria and Greater Lebanon. Both were administered under a French League of Nations mandate 1920-1941.

Syria was proclaimed a republic by the occupying French Sept. 16, 1941, and exercised full independence effective Jan. 1, 1944. Syria joined in the Arab invasion of Israel in 1948.

Syria joined with Egypt in Feb. 1958 in the United Arab Republic but seceded Sept. 30, 1961. The Socialist Baath party and military leaders seized power in Mar. 1963. The Baath, a pan-Arab organization, became the only legal party. The government has been dominated by members of the minority Alawite sect.

In the Arab-Israeli war of June 1967, Israel seized and occupied the Golan Heights area inside Syria, from which Israeli settlements had for years been shelled by Syria.

Syria aided Palestinian guerrillas fighting Jordanian forces in Sept. 1970 and, after a renewal of that fighting in July 1971, broke off relations with Jordan. But by 1975 the 2 countries had entered a military coordination pact.

On Oct. 6, 1973, Syria joined Egypt in an attack on Israel. Arab oil states agreed in 1974 to give Syria $1 billion a year to aid anti-Israel moves. Military supplies used or lost in the 1973 war were replaced by the USSR in 1974. Some 30,000 Syrian troops entered Lebanon in 1976 to mediate in a civil war, and fought Palestinian guerrillas and, later, fought Christian militiamen. Syrian troops again battled Christian forces in Lebanon, Apr. 1981, ending a ceasefire that had been in place.

Following the June 6, 1982 Israeli invasion of Lebanon, Israeli planes destroyed 17 Syrian antiaircraft missile batteries in the Bekka Valley, June 9. Some 25 Syrian planes were downed during the engagement. Syrian and Israeli troops exchanged fire in central Lebanon. Israel and Syria agreed to a cease fire June 11. In 1983, Syria backed the PLO rebels who ousted Yasir Arafat's forces from Tripoli.

In Feb. 1982, an uprising by antigovernment Moslem brotherhood militants brought heavy fighting and caused some 5,000 deaths.

Syria has taken a radical stance in Arab and Middle Eastern affairs. It has led opposition to Arab-Israeli peace intitiatives, maintained close ties to Libya and the USSR, and supports Iran in the Gulf war.

Syria's alleged role in promoting acts of international terrorism led to the breaking of diplomatic relations with Great Britain and the implementation of limited sanctions by the European Communities in 1986.

Taiwan

Republic of China

Chung-hua Min-kuo

People: Population (1986 est.): 19,601,000. **Pop. density:** 1,396 per sq. mi. **Ethnic groups:** Han Chinese (14% from mainland), aborigines (of Indonesian origin) 2%. **Languages:** Mandarin Chinese (official), Taiwan, Hakka dialects. **Religions:** Buddhism, Taoism, Confucianism prevail.

Geography: Area: 13,885 sq. mi., about the size of W. Virginia. **Location:** Off SE coast of China, between E. and S. China Seas. **Neighbors:** Nearest is China. **Topography:** A mountain range forms the backbone of the island; the eastern half is very steep and craggy, the western slope is flat, fertile, and well-cultivated. **Capital:** Taipei. **Cities** (1986): Taipei (met.) 2,534,000; Kaohsiung 1,309,000; Taichung 682,000; Tainan 642,000.

Government: Type: One-party system. **Head of state:** Chiang Ching-kuo; b. Mar. 18, 1910; in office: May 20, 1978. **Head of government:** Prime Min. Yu Kuo-hwa; in office: May 20, 1984. **Local divisions:** Taiwan province, Taipei and Kaohsiung municipalities. **Defense:** 9% of GNP (1984).

Economy: Industries: Textiles, clothing, electronics, processed foods, chemicals, plastics. **Chief crops:** Rice, bananas, pineapples, sugarcane, sweet potatoes, peanuts. **Minerals:** Coal, limestone, marble. **Crude oil reserves** (1985): 11 mln. bbls. **Cultivated land:** 25%. **Meat prod.** (1984): pigs: 5.8 mln. **Fish catch** (1984): 1.0 mln. metric tons. **Electricity prod.** (1984): 49.2 bln. kwh. **Crude steel prod.** (1985): 5.0 mln. metric tons. **Labor force:** 20% agric.; 41% ind. & comm.; 32% services.

Finance: Currency: New Taiwan dollar (Jan. 1986: 36.71 = $1 US). **Gross national product** (1984): $56.6 bln. **Per capita income** (1984): $3,000. **Imports** (1984): $21.9 bln.; partners: U.S. 23%, Jap. 27%, Kuw. 6%, Saudi Ar. 10%. **Exports** (1984): $30.4 bln.; partners: U.S. 45%, Jap. 10%, Hong Kong 6%. **Tour-**

ists (1984): $1 bln. receipts. **National budget** (1985): $10.3 bln. **Consumer prices** (change in 1984): 1.6%.

Transport: Motor vehicles: in use (1985): 915,000 passenger cars, 429,000 commercial vehicles. **Civil Aviation** (1985): 11 bln. passenger-km; 1.8 mln. net ton-km. **Chief ports:** Kaohsiung, Keelung, Hualien, Taichung.

Communications: Television sets: 6 mln. in use (1985). **Radios:** 13 mln. in use (1985). **Telephones in use** (1985): 4.2 mln. **Daily newspaper circ.** (1984): 259 per 1,000 pop.

Health: Life expectancy at birth (1984): 70.5 male; 75.5 female. **Births** (per 1,000 pop. 1985): 19. **Deaths** (per 1,000 pop. 1985): 5. **Natural increase** (1985): 1.4%. **Physicians** (1984): 15,182. **Hospital beds** (1984): 62,467. **Infant mortality** (per 1,000 live births 1985): 20.

Education (1984): **Literacy:** 91%. Years compulsory 9; attendance 99%.

Large-scale Chinese immigration began in the 17th century. The island came under mainland control after an interval of Dutch rule, 1620-62. Taiwan (also called Formosa) was ruled by Japan 1895-1945. Two million Kuomintang supporters fled to Taiwan in 1949. Both the Taipei and Peking governments consider Taiwan an integral part of China. Taiwan has rejected Pekings efforts at reunification.

The U.S. upon its recognition of the People's Republic of China, Dec. 15, 1978, severed diplomatic ties with Taiwan. It maintains the unofficial American Institute in Taiwan, while Taiwan has established the Coordination Council for North American Affairs in Washington, D.C.

Land reform, government planning, U.S. aid and investment, and free universal education have brought huge advances in industry, agriculture, and mass living standards.

The Penghu (Pescadores), 50 sq. mi., pop. 120,000, lie between Taiwan and the mainland. **Quemoy** and **Matsu**, pop. (1980) 61,000 lie just off the mainland.

Tanzania

United Republic of Tanzania

Jamhuri ya Mwungano wa Tanzania

People: Population (1986 est.) 22,415,000. **Pop. density:** 63 per sq. mi. **Urban** (1984): 20%. **Ethnic groups:** African. **Languages:** Swahili, English are official. **Religions:** Moslems 35%, Christians 30%, traditional beliefs 35%.

Geography: Area: 364,886 sq. mi., more than twice the size of California. **Location:** On coast of E. Africa. **Neighbors:** Kenya, Uganda on N, Rwanda, Burundi, Zaire on W, Zambia, Malawi, Mozambique on S. **Topography:** Hot, arid central plateau, surrounded by the lake region in the W, temperate highlands in N and S, the coastal plains. Mt. Kilimanjaro, 19,340 ft., is highest in Africa. **Capital:** Dar-es-Salaam. **Cities** (1986): Dar-es-Salaam 1.4 mln.

Government: Type: Republic. **Head of state:** Pres. Ali Hassan Mwinyi; b. May 8, 1925; in office: Nov. 5, 1985. **Head of government:** Prime Min. Joseph Warioba. **Local divisions:** 25 regions (20 on mainland). **Defense:** 3.4% of GNP (1985).

Economy: Industries: Food processing, clothing. **Chief crops:** Sisal, cotton, coffee, tea, tobacco. **Minerals:** Diamonds, gold, nickel. **Other resources:** Hides. **Arable land:** 15%. **Meat prod.** (1980): beef: 139,000 metric tons; lamb: 34,000 metric tons. **Fish catch** (1983): 272,000 metric tons. **Electricity prod.** (1985): 870 mln. kwh. **Labor force:** 85% agric., 15% ind., comm. & govt.

Finance: Currency: Shilling (Mar. 1987: 57.1 = $1 US). **Gross national product** (1984): $4.1 bln. **Per capita income** (1984): $200. **Imports** (1985): $1.0 bln.; partners: UK 14%, Jap. 12%, W. Ger. 10%. **Exports** (1985): $255 mln.; partners: W. Ger. 15%, UK 13%. **Tourists** (1984): $13 mln. receipts. **National budget** (1983): $870 mln. expenditures. **International reserves less gold** (Jan. 1987): $51.5 mln. **Consumer prices** (change in 1985): 33.3%.

Transport: Motor vehicles: in use (1984): 84,000 passenger and comm. vehicles. **Chief ports:** Dar-es-Salaam, Mtwara, Tanga.

Communications: Radios: 2 mln. in use (1985). **Telephones in use** (1983): 99,000. **Daily newspaper circ.** (1984): 5 per 1,000 pop.

Health: Life expectancy at birth (1986): 52 yrs. **Births** (per 1,000 pop. 1985): 49. **Deaths** (per 1,000 pop. 1985): 16.0. **Natural increase** (1985): 3.4%. **Hospital beds** (1984): 22,800. **Physicians** (1984): 1,065. **Infant mortality** (per 1,000 live births 1986): 110.

Education (1985): **Literacy:** 80%. **Attendance:** 87% attend primary school.

Major International Organizations: UN and all of its specialized agencies, OAU, Commonwealth of Nations.

Embassy: 2139 R. St. NW 20008; 939-6125.

The Republic of Tanganyika in E. Africa and the island Republic of Zanzibar, off the coast of Tanganyika, joined into a single nation, the United Republic of Tanzania, Apr. 26, 1964. Zanzibar retains internal self-government.

Tanganyika. Arab colonization and slaving began in the 8th century AD; Portuguese sailors explored the coast by about 1500. Other Europeans followed.

In 1885 Germany established German East Africa of which Tanganyika formed the bulk. It became a League of Nations mandate and, after 1946, a UN trust territory, both under Britain. It became independent Dec. 9, 1961, and a republic within the Commonwealth a year later.

In 1967 the government set on a socialist course; it nationalized all banks and many industries. The government also ordered that Swahili, not English, be used in all official business. Nine million people have been moved into cooperative villages.

Tanzanian forces drove Idi Amin from Uganda, Mar., 1979.

Zanzibar, the Isle of Cloves, lies 23 mi. off the coast of Tanganyika; its area is 640 sq. mi. The island of **Pemba,** 25 mi. to the NE, area 380 sq. mi., is included in the administration. The total population (1985 est.) is 571,000.

Chief industry is the production of cloves and clove oil of which Zanzibar and Pemba produce the bulk of the world's supply.

Zanzibar was for centuries the center for Arab slave-traders. Portugal ruled for 2 centuries until ousted by Arabs around 1700. Zanzibar became a British Protectorate in 1890; independence came Dec. 10, 1963. Revolutionary forces overthrew the Sultan Jan. 12, 1964. The new government ousted Western diplomats and newsmen, slaughtered thousands of Arabs, and nationalized farms. Union with Tanganyika followed, 1964. The ruling parties of Tanganyika and Zanzibar were united in 1977, as political tension eased.

Thailand

Kingdom of Thailand

Muang Thai or Prathet Thai

People: Population (1986 est.): 52,438,000. **Age distrib.** (%): 0–14: 38.5; 15–59: 54.9; 60+: 6.6. **Pop. density:** 265 per sq. mi. **Urban** (1984): 17%. **Ethnic groups:** Thais 75%, Chinese 14%, others 11%. **Languages:** Thai, regional dialects. **Religions:** Buddhists 95%, Moslems 4%.

Geography: Area: 198,456 sq. mi., about the size of Texas. **Location:** On Indochinese and Malayan Peninsulas in S.E. Asia. **Neighbors:** Burma on W. Laos on N, Cambodia on E, Malaysia on S. **Topography:** A plateau dominates the NE third of Thailand, dropping to the fertile alluvial valley of the Chao Phraya R. in the center. Forested mountains are in N, with narrow fertile valleys. The southern peninsula region is covered by rain forests. **Capital:** Bangkok. **Cities** (1980 est.): Bangkok (met.): 4.7 mln.

Government: Type: Constitutional monarchy. **Head of state:** King Bhumibol Adulyadej; b. Dec. 5, 1927; in office: June 9, 1946. **Head of government:** Prime Min. Prem Tinsulanonda; b. 1920; in office: Mar. 3, 1980. **Local divisions:** 73 provinces. **Defense:** 4.2% of GNP (1985).

Economy: Industries: Textiles, mining, wood products. **Chief crops:** Rice (a major export), corn tapioca, sugarcane. **Minerals:** Antimony, tin (among largest producers), tungsten, iron, gas. **Other resources:** Forests (teak is exported), rubber. **Arable land:** 24%. **Meat prod.** (1985): cattle: 4.8 mln.; pigs: 4.2 mln. **Fish catch** (1983): 2.2 mln. metric tons. **Electricity prod.** (1984): 22.0 bln. kwh. **Crude steel prod.** (1981): 450,000 metric tons. **Labor force:** 73% agric.; 11% ind. & comm.; 10% serv.; 6% govt.

Finance: Currency: Baht (Mar. 1987: 25.7 = $1 US). **Gross national product** (1985): $42 bln. **Per capita income** (1985): $828. **Imports** (1986): $9.1 bln.; partners: Jap. 24%, U.S. 13%, Saudi Ar. 13%. **Exports** (1986): $8.7 bln.; partners: Jap. 14%,

U.S. 13%, Sing. 14%. **Tourists** (1984): $1.1 mln. receipts. **National budget** (1985): $7.9 bln. **International reserves less gold** (Mar. 1987): $3.2 bln. **Gold:** 2.48 mln. oz t. **Consumer prices** (change in 1986): 1.8%.

Transport: Railway traffic (1984): 9.6 bln. passenger-km; 2.6 bln. net ton-km. **Motor vehicles:** in use (1983): 411,000 passenger cars, 789,000 comm. vehicles. **Civil aviation** (1983): 9.0 bln. passenger-km; 328 mln. freight ton-km. **Chief ports:** Bangkok, Sattahip.

Communication: Television sets: 3 mln. in use (1985). **Radios:** 7.7 mln. in use (1985). **Telephones in use** (1983): 623,000. **Daily newspaper circ.** (1985): 50 per 1,000 pop.

Health: Life expectancy at birth (1985): 61.0 male; 66.9 female. **Births** (per 1,000 pop. 1985): 25. **Deaths** (per 1,000 pop. 1985): 8. **Natural increase** (1985): 1.7%. **Hospital beds** (1983): 88,504. **Physicians** (1983): 7,902. **Infant mortality** (per 1,000 live births 1985): 51.

Education (1985): **Literacy:** 86%. **Years compulsory:** 7; attendance 83%.

Major International Organizations: UN (GATT, World Bank).
Embassy: 2300 Kalorama Rd. NW 20008; 667-1446.

Thais began migrating from southern China in the 11th century. Thailand is the only country in SE Asia never taken over by a European power, thanks to King Mongkut and his son King Chulalongkorn who ruled from 1851 to 1910, modernized the country, and signed trade treaties with both Britain and France. A bloodless revolution in 1932 limited the monarchy.

Japan occupied the country in 1941. After the war, Thailand followed a pro-West foreign policy.

The military took over the government in a bloody 1976 coup. Kriangsak Chomanan, prime minister resigned, Feb. 1980, under opposition over soaring inflation, oil price increases, labor unrest and growing crime.

Vietnamese troops have crossed the border and been repulsed by Thai forces in the 1980s.

Togo

Republic of Togo

République Togolaise

People: Population (1986 est.): 3,118,000. **Age distrib.** (%): 0-14: 49.8; 15-59: 44.6; 60+:5.6.**Pop. density:** 140 per sq. mi. **Urban** (1981): 15.2%. **Ethnic groups:** Ewe 35%, Mina 6%, Kabye 22%. **Languages:** French (official), others. **Religions:** Traditional 58%, Christian 22%, Moslem 20%.

Geography: Area: 21,622 sq. mi., slightly smaller than West Virginia. **Location:** On S coast of W. Africa. **Neighbors:** Ghana on W, Burkina Faso on N, Benin on E. **Topography:** A range of hills running SW-NE splits Togo into 2 savanna plains regions. **Capital:** Lomé. **Cities** (1985 est.): Lomé 300,000.

Government: Type: Republic. **Head of state:** Pres. Gnassingbe Eyadema; b. Dec. 26, 1937; in office: Apr. 14, 1967. **Local divisions:** 21 prefectures.

Economy: Industries: Textiles, shoes. **Chief crops:** Coffee, cocoa, yams, manioc, millet, rice. **Minerals:** Phosphates. **Arable land:** 26%. **Electricity prod.** (1984): 84 mln. kwh. **Labor force:** 67% agric.; 15% industry.

Finance: Currency: CFA franc (Mar. 1987: 300 = $1 US). **Gross national product** (1985): $696 mln. **Per capita income** (1985): $240. **Imports** (1985): $262 mln.; partners: Fr., U.K., W. Ger. **Exports** (1985): $242 mln.; partners: Neth., Fr., W. Ger. **International reserves less gold** (Jan. 1987): $342.5 mln. **Gold:** 13,000 oz t. **Consumer prices** (change in 1985): −1.8%.

Transport: Railway traffic (1981): 84.5 mln. passenger-km; 37.7 mln. net ton-km. **Motor vehicles:** in use (1984): 36,000 passenger cars, 17,000 comm. vehicles. **Chief ports:** Lome.

Communications: Radios: 250,000 in use (1985). **Telephones in use** (1983): 11,000. **Daily newspaper circ.** (1985): 3 per 1,000 pop.

Health: Life expectancy at birth (1984): 47 yrs. **Births** (per 1,000 pop. 1985): 48. **Deaths** (per 1,000 pop. 1985): 17. **Natural increase** (1985): 3.1%. **Hospital beds** (1982): 3,655. **Physicians** (1980): 132. **Infant mortality** (per 1,000 live births 1985): 107.

Education (1985): **Literacy:** 45% (males).

Major International Organizations: UN (GATT, IMF), OAU.
Embassy: 2208 Massachusetts Ave. NW 20008; 234-4212.

The Ewe arrived in southern Togo several centuries ago. The country later became a major source of slaves. Germany took control in 1884. France and Britain administered Togoland as UN trusteeships. The French sector became the republic of Togo Apr. 27, 1960.

The population is divided between Bantus in the S and Hamitic tribes in the N. Togo has actively promoted regional integration, as a means of stimulating the economy.

Tonga

Kingdom of Tonga

Pule ‘anga Tonga

People: Population (1986 est.): 104,000. **Age distrib.** (%): 0–14: 44.4; 15–59; 50.5; 60+:5.1. **Pop. density:** 353 per sq. mi. **Ethnic groups:** Tongans 98%, other Polynesian, European. **Languages:** Tongan, English. **Religions:** Free Wesleyan 47%, Roman Catholics 14%, Free Church of Tonga 14%, Mormons 9%, Church of Tonga 9%.

Geography: Area: 270 sq. mi., smaller than New York City. **Location:** In western S. Pacific O. **Neighbors:** Nearest is Fiji, on W, New Zealand, on S. **Topography:** Tonga comprises 169 volcanic and coral islands, 45 inhabited. **Capital:** Nuku'alofa. **Cities** (1984): Nuku'alofa (met.) 22,000.

Government: Type: Constitutional monarchy. **Head of state:** King Taufa'ahau Tupou IV; b. July 4, 1918; in office: Dec. 16, 1965. **Head of government:** Prime Min. Fatafehi Tu'ipelehake; b. Jan. 7, 1922; in office: Dec. 16, 1965. **Local divisions:** 3 island districts.

Economy: Industries: Tourism. **Chief crops:** Coconut products, bananas are exported. **Other resources:** Fish. **Arable land:** 77%. **Electricity prod.** (1984): 12 mln. kwh. **Labor force:** 51% agric, 22% services.

Finance: Currency: Pa'anga (Jan. 1987: 1.59 = $1 US). **Gross national product** (1983): $80 mln. **Per capita income** (1976): $430. **Imports** (1982): $39 mln.; partners: N Z 37%, Austral. 23%, Jap. 6%, Fiji 7%. **Exports** (1982): $4 mln.; partners: Aust. 45%, N Z 38%.

Transport: Motor vehicles: in use (1983): 443 passenger cars, 1,300 comm. vehicles. **Chief ports:** Nuku'alofa.

Communications: Radios: 65,000 in use (1985). **Telephones in use** (1983): 3,485.

Health: Births (per 1,000 pop. 1985): 28. **Deaths** (per 1,000 pop. 1985): 8. **Natural increase** (1985): 2.0%. **Infant mortality** (per 1,000 live births 1985): 45.

Education (1985): **Literacy:** 93%. **Years compulsory:** 8. **Attendance:** 77%.

The islands were first visited by the Dutch in the early 17th century. A series of civil wars ended in 1845 with establishment of the Tupou dynasty. In 1900 Tonga became a British protectorate. On June 4, 1970, Tonga became independent and a member of the Commonwealth.

Trinidad and Tobago

Republic of Trinidad and Tobago

People: Population (1986 est.): 1,204,000. **Age distrib.** (%): 0–14: 32.9; 15–59: 58.7; 60+: 8.4. **Pop. density:** 607 per sq. mi. **Ethnic groups:** Africans 40%, East Indians 40%, mixed 14%. **Languages:** English (official). **Religions:** Roman Catholic 33%, Protestant 14%, Hindu 24%, Moslem 6%.

Geography: Area: 1,980 sq. mi., the size of Delaware. **Location:** Off eastern coast of Venezuela. **Neighbors:** Nearest is Venezuela on SW. **Topography:** Three low mountain ranges cross Trinidad E-W, with a well-watered plain between N and Central Ranges. Parts of E and W coasts are swamps. Tobago, 116 sq. mi., lies 20 mi. NE. **Capital:** Port-of-Spain. **Cities** (1984 est.): Port-of-Spain (met.) 300,000; San Fernando 50,000.

Government: Type: Parliamentary democracy. **Head of state:** Pres. Ellis E. I. Clarke; b. Dec. 28, 1917; in office: July 31, 1976. **Head of government:** Prime Min. A.N.R. Robinson; in office: Dec. 18, 1986. **Local divisions:** 7 counties, Tobago, 4 cities.

Economy: Industries: Oil products, rum, cement, tourism. **Chief crops:** Sugar, cocoa, coffee, citrus fruits, bananas. **Miner-**

als: Asphalt, oil. **Crude oil reserves** (1985): 538 mln. bbls. **Arable land:** 30%. **Electricity prod.** (1984): 2.6 bln. kwh. **Labor force:** 7% agric., 60% construction, mining, commerce, 22% services.

Finance: Currency: Dollar (Mar. 1987: 3.60 = $1 US). **Gross national product** (1984): $8.3 bln. **Per capita income** (1982): $6,800. **Imports** (1985): $1.5 bln.; partners: U.S. 37%, UK 11%. **Exports** (1985): $2.2 bln.; partners: U.S. 62%. **National budget** (1980): $1.7 bln. expenditures. **International reserves less gold** (Mar. 1987): $355.3 mln. **Gold:** 54,000 oz t. **Consumer prices** (change in 1985): 7.6%.

Transport: Motor vehicles: in use (1984): 210,000 passenger cars, 60,000 comm. vehicles. **Civil aviation:** (1985): 2.0 bln. passenger-km; 9.9 mln. freight ton-km. **Chief ports:** Port-of-Spain.

Communications: Television sets: 300,000 in use (1985). **Radios:** 350,000 licensed (1985). **Telephones in use** (1983): 86,000. **Daily newspaper circ.** (1985): 151 per 1,000 pop.

Health: Life expectancy at birth (1985): 67.8 male; 72.6 female. **Births** (per 1,000 pop. 1985): 27. **Deaths** (per 1,000 pop. 1985): 7. **Natural increase** (1985): 2.0%. **Hospital beds** (1982): 4,321. **Physicians** (1982): 786. **Infant mortality** (per 1,000 pop. 1985): 21.

Education (1984): **Literacy:** 96%. **Years compulsory:** 8.

Major International Organizations: UN (GATT, IMF, WHO), Commonwealth of Nations, OAS.

Embassy: 1708 Massachusetts Ave. NW 20036; 467-6490.

Columbus sighted Trinidad in 1498. A British possession since 1802, Trinidad and Tobago won independence Aug. 31, 1962. It became a republic in 1976. The People's National Movement party has held control of the government since 1956.

The nation is one of the most prosperous in the Caribbean. Oil production has increased with offshore finds. Middle Eastern oil is refined and exported, mostly to the U.S.

Tunisia

Republic of Tunisia

al Jumhuriyah at-Tunisiyah

People: Population (1986 est.): 7,424,000. **Age distrib.** (%) 0–14: 39.6 15–59: 53.7; 60+: 6.7. **Pop. density:** 122 per sq. mi. **Ethnic groups:** Arab 90%. **Languages:** Arabic (official), French. **Religions:** Moslem 99%.

Geography: Area: 63,170 sq. mi., about the size of Missouri. **Location:** On N coast of Africa. **Neighbors:** Algeria on W, Libya on E. **Topography:** The N is wooded and fertile. The central coastal plains are given to grazing and orchards. The S is arid, approaching Sahara Desert. **Capital:** Tunis. **Cities** (1984 est.) Tunis 1,000,000, Sfax 475,000.

Government: Type: Republic. **Head of state:** Pres. Habib Bourguiba; b. Aug. 3, 1903; in office: July 25, 1957. **Head of government:** Prime Min. Rachid Sfar; b. 1926; in office: July 8, 1986. **Local divisions:** 21 governorates. **Defense:** 2.9% of GNP (1983).

Economy: Industries: Food processing, textiles, oil products, construction materials, tourism. **Chief crops:** Grains, dates, olives, citrus fruits, figs, vegetables, grapes. **Minerals:** Phosphates, iron, oil, lead, zinc. **Crude oil reserves** (1985): 1.8 bln. bbls. **Arable land:** 30%. **Meat prod.** (1984): sheep: 5.2 mln.; goats: 1 mln. **Fish catch** (1984): 74,000 metric tons. **Electricity prod.** (1984): 3.7 bln. kwh. **Crude steel prod.** (1982): 106,000 metric tons. **Labor force:** 35% agric.; 22% industry; 11% serv.

Finance: Currency: Dinar (Mar. 1987: .82 = $1 US). **Gross national product** (1985): $8.3 bln. **Per capita income** (1986) $1,163. **Imports** (1986): $2.8 bln.; partners: Fr. 26%, It. 12%. **Exports** (1986): $1.0 bln.; partners: It. 17%, Fr. 26%, W. Ger. 10%, U.S. 19%. **Tourists** (1984): $463 mln. receipts. **National budget** (1986): $3.3 bln. expenditures. **International reserves less gold** (Mar. 1987): $101.6 mln. **Gold:** 187,000 oz t. **Consumer prices** (change in 1986): 5.8%.

Transport: Railway traffic (1985): 744 mln. passenger-km; 1.7 bln. net ton-km. **Motor vehicles:** in use (1982): 141,000 passenger cars, 141,000 comm. vehicles; **Civil aviation:** (1984): 1.5 bln. passenger-km; 18.3 mln. freight ton-km. **Chief ports:** Tunis, Sfax, Bizerte.

Communications: Television sets: 275,000 in use (1985). Radios: 1.1 mln. in use (1985). **Telephones in use** (1983): 218,000. **Daily newspaper circ.** (1985): 35 per 1,000 pop.

Health: Life expectancy at birth (1985): 60.1 male; 61.1 female. **Births** (per 1,000 pop. 1985): 30. **Deaths** (per 1,000 pop. 1985): 6. **Natural increase** (1985): 2.4%. **Hospital beds** (1982): 14,071. **Physicians** (1982): 1,732. **Infant mortality** (per 1,000 pop. live births 1985): 53.

Education (1985): **Literacy:** 46%. **Years compulsory:** 8; attendance 85%.

Major International Organizations: UN, Arab League, OAU.

Embassy: 1515 Massachusetts Ave. NW 20005; 862-1850.

Site of ancient Carthage, and a former Barbary state under the suzerainty of Turkey, Tunisia became a protectorate of France under a treaty signed May 12, 1881. The nation became independent Mar. 20, 1956, and ended the monarchy the following year. Habib Bourguiba has headed the country since independence.

Although Tunisia is a member of the Arab League, Bourguiba in the 1960s urged negotiations to end Arab-Israeli disputes and was denounced by other members.

Tunisia survived a Libyan-engineered raid against the southern mining center of Gafsa, Jan. 1980. Some 1,000 rioters were arrested in 1984 following an announced 125% increase in the price of bread.

Turkey

Republic of Turkey

Turkiye Cumhuriyeti

People: Population (1986 est.): 51,819,000. **Age distrib.** (%): 0–14: 38.5; 15–59: 54.9; 60+: 6.6. **Pop. density:** 171 per sq. mi. **Urban** (1987): 55%. **Ethnic groups:** Turks 85%, Kurds 12%. **Languages:** Turkish (official), Kurdish, Arabic. **Religions:** Moslem 98%, Christians, Jews.

Geography: Area: 301,381 sq. mi., twice the size of California. **Location:** Occupies Asia Minor, between Mediterranean and Black Seas. **Neighbors:** Bulgaria, Greece on W, USSR (Georgia, Armenia) on N, Iran on E, Iraq, Syria on S. **Topography:** Central Turkey has wide plateaus, with hot, dry summers and cold winters. High mountains ring the interior on all but W, with more than 20 peaks over 10,000 ft. Rolling plains are in W; mild, fertile coastal plains are in S, W. **Capital:** Ankara. **Cities** (1985 est.): Istanbul 5,494,000; Ankara 2,251,000, Izmir 1,489,000; Adana 776,000.

Government: Type: Republic. **Head of state:** Pres. Kenan Evren; b. 1918; in office: Oct. 27, 1980. **Head of government:** Prime Min. Turgut Ozal; b. 1927; in office: Dec. 13, 1983. **Local divisions:** 67 provinces, with appointed governors. **Defense:** 4.9% of GNP (1983).

Economy: Industries: Iron, steel, machinery, metal prods., cars, processed foods. **Chief crops:** Tobacco, cereals, cotton, barley, corn, fruits, potatoes, sugar beets. **Minerals:** Antimony, chromium, mercury, borate, copper, coal. **Crude oil reserves** (1985): 312 mln. bbls. **Other resources:** Wool, silk, forests. **Arable land:** 34%. **Meat prod.** (1985): cattle: 17.4 mln.; sheep: 40.4 mln. **Fish catch** (1985): 567,000 metric tons. **Electricity prod.** (1984): 30.6 bln. kwh. **Crude steel prod.** (1985): 4.9 mln. metric tons. **Labor force:** 59% agric.; 12% ind. and comm.; 28% serv.

Finance: Currency: Lira (Mar. 1987: 777 = $1 US). **Gross national product** (1984): $57 bln. **Per capita income** (1984): $1,000 **Imports** (1985): $11.3 bln.; partners: W. Ger. 13%, U.S. 12%. **Exports** (1985): $7.9 bln.; partners: W. Ger. 17%, UK 10%. **Tourists** (1984): 548 mln. receipts. **National budget** (1984): $8.7 bln. expenditures. **International reserves less gold** (Feb. 1987): $1.5 bln. **Gold:** 3.8 mln. oz t. **Consumer prices** (change in 1985): 43.1%.

Transport: Railway traffic (1985): 6.8 bln. passenger-km; 7.7 bln. net ton-km. **Motor vehicles:** in use (1985): 983,000 passenger cars, 553,000 comm. vehicles. **Civil aviation** (1984): 2.3 bln. passenger-km; 26 mln. freight ton-km. **Chief ports:** Istanbul, Izmir, Mersin, Samsun.

Communications: Television sets: 5 mln. in use (1985). **Radios:** 4.3 mln. licensed (1985). **Telephones in use** (1983): 2.6 mln.

Health: Life expectancy at birth (1985): 57 years. **Births** (per 1,000 pop. 1985): 33.6. **Deaths** (per 1,000 pop. 1985): 9.3. **Natural increase** (1985): 2.4%. **Hospital beds** (1983): 99,396. **Physicians** (1983): 32,265. **Infant mortality** (per 1,000 live births 1985): 90.

Education (1985): **Literacy:** 70%. **Years compulsory:** 8; attendance 95%.

Major International Organizations: UN (GATT, WHO, IMF), NATO, OECD.

Embassy: 1606 23d St. NW 20008; 667-6400.

Ancient inhabitants of Turkey were among the worlds first agriculturalists. Such civilizations as the Hittite, Phrygian, and Lydian flourished in Asiatic Turkey (Asia Minor), as did much of Greek civilization. After the fall of Rome in the 5th century, Constantinople was the capital of the Byzantine Empire for 1,000 years. It fell in 1453 to Ottoman Turks, who ruled a vast empire for over 400 years.

Just before World War I, Turkey, or the Ottoman Empire, ruled what is now Syria, Lebanon, Iraq, Jordan, Israel, Saudi Arabia, Yemen, and islands in the Aegean Sea.

Turkey joined Germany and Austria in World War I and its defeat resulted in loss of much territory and fall of the sultanate. A republic was declared Oct. 29, 1923. The Caliphate (spiritual leadership of Islam) was renounced 1924.

Long embroiled with Greece over Cyprus, off Turkey's south coast, Turkey invaded the island July 20, 1974, after Greek officers seized the Cypriot government as a step toward unification with Greece. Turkey sought a new government for Cyprus, with Greek Cypriot and Turkish Cypriot zones. In reaction to Turkey's moves, the U.S. cut off military aid in 1975. Turkey, in turn, suspended the use of most U.S. bases. Aid was restored in 1978. There was a military takeover, Sept. 12, 1980.

Religious and ethnic tensions and active left and right extremists have caused endemic violence. Martial law, imposed in 1978, was lifted in 1984. The military formally transferred power to an elected parliament in 1983.

Tuvalu

People: Population (1986 est.): 8,580. **Pop. density:** 886 per sq. mi. **Ethnic group:** Polynesian. **Languages:** Tuvaluan, English. **Religions:** mainly Protestant.

Geography: Area: 10 sq. mi., less than one-half the size of Manhattan. **Location:** 9 islands forming a NW-SE chain 360 mi. long in the SW Pacific O. **Neighbors:** Nearest are Samoa on SE, Fiji on S. **Topography:** The islands are all low-lying atolls, nowhere rising more than 15 ft. above sea level, composed of coral reefs. **Capital:** Funafuti (pop. 1985): 2,800.

Government: Head of state: Queen Elizabeth II, represented by Gov.-Gen. Tupua Leupena; in office: Mar. 1, 1986. **Head of government:** Prime Min. Tomasi Puapua; in office: Sept. 8, 1981. **Local divisions:** 8 island councils on the permanently inhabited islands.

Economy: Industries: Copra. **Chief crops:** Coconuts. **Labor force:** Approx. 1,500 Tuvaluans work overseas in the Gilberts' phosphate industry, or as overseas seamen.

Finance: Currency: Australian dollar.

Transport: Chief port: Funafuti.

Health: (including former Gilbert Is.) **Life expectancy at birth** (1979): 57 male; 60 female. **Births** (per 1,000 pop. 1985): 27. **Deaths** (per 1,000 pop. 1985): 11. **Natural increase** (1985): 1.6%. **Infant mortality** (per 1,000 live births 1985) : 35.

Education: Literacy (1979): 96%.

The Ellice Islands separated from the British Gilbert and Ellice Islands colony, 1975, and became independent Tuvalu Oct. 1, 1978.

Britain and New Zealand provide extensive economic aid.

Uganda

Republic of Uganda

People: Population (1986 est.): 15,158,000. **Age distrib.** (%): 0–14: 48.5; 15–59: 47.3; 60+: 4.2. **Pop. density:** 183 per sq. mi. **Urban** (1980): 8.1%. **Ethnic groups:** Bantu, Nilotic, Nilo-Hamitic, Sudanic tribes. **Languages:** English (official), Luganda, Swahili. **Religions:** Christians 63%, Moslems 6%, traditional beliefs.

Geography: Area: 93,354 sq. mi., slightly smaller than Oregon. **Location:** In E. Central Africa. **Neighbors:** Sudan on N, Zaire on W, Rwanda, Tanzania on S, Kenya on E. **Topography:** Most of Uganda is a high plateau 3,000-6,000 ft. high, with high Ruwenzori range in W (Mt. Margherita 16,750 ft.), volcanoes in SW, NE is arid, W and SW rainy. Lakes Victoria, Edward, Albert form much of borders. **Capital:** Kampala. **Cities** (1985): Kampala 331,000.

Government: Type: Military. **Head of state:** Pres. Yoweri Kaguta Museveni; b. 1944; in office: Jan. 29, 1986. **Head of government:** Prime Min. Samson Kisekka; in office: Jan. 3, 1986. **Local divisions:** 10 provinces, 34 districts. **Defense:** 1% of GNP (1983).

Economy: Chief Crops: Coffee, cotton, tea, corn, bananas, sugar. **Minerals:** Copper, cobalt. **Arable land:** 29%. **Meat prod.** (1984): cattle: 5.2 mln.; goats: 2.5 mln.; sheep: 1.3 mln. **Fish catch** (1983): 172,000 metric tons. **Electricity prod.** (1984): 655 mln. kwh. **Labor force:** 90% agric.

Finance: Currency: Shilling (Mar. 1987: 1,400 = $1 US). **Gross national product** (1984): $6.2 bln. **Per capita income** (1976): $240. **Imports** (1983): $509 mln.; partners: OPEC countries, EC. **Exports** (1982): $380 mln.; partners: EC. **National budget** (1981): $641 mln. revenues; $871 mln. expenditures.

Transport: Motor vehicles: in use (1982): 10,000 passenger cars, 11,000 comm. vehicles.

Communications: Television sets: 76,000 in use (1985). **Radios:** 280,000 in use (1985). **Telephones in use** (1983): 55,000. **Daily newspaper circ.** (1984): 2 per 1,000 pop.

Health: Life expectancy at birth (1985): 49.0 male; 53.0 female. **Births** (per 1,000 pop. 1985): 48.0. **Deaths** (per 1,000 pop. 1985): 17. **Natural increase** (1985): 3.1%. **Hospital beds** (1983): 19,650. **Physicians** (1983): 655. **Infant mortality** (per 1,000 live births 1985): 113.

Education (1980): **Literacy:** 52%. About 50% attend primary school.

Major International Organizations: UN (GATT, WHO, IMF), OAU, Commonwealth of Nations.

Embassy: 5909 16th St. NW 20011; 726-7100.

Britain obtained a protectorate over Uganda in 1894. The country became independent Oct. 9, 1962, and a republic within the Commonwealth a year later. In 1967, the traditional kingdoms, including the powerful Buganda state, were abolished and the central government strengthened.

Gen. Idi Amin seized power from Prime Min. Milton Obote in 1971. As many as 300,000 of his opponents were reported killed in subsequent years. Amin was named president for life in 1976.

In 1972 Amin expelled nearly all of Uganda's 45,000 Asians. In 1973 the U.S. withdrew all diplomatic personnel.

A June 1977 Commonwealth conference condemned the Amin government for its "disregard for the sanctity of human life."

Amid worsening economic and domestic crises, Uganda's troops exchanged invasion attacks with long-standing foe Tanzania, 1978 to 1979. Tanzanian forces, coupled with Ugandan exiles and rebels, ended the dictatorial rule of Amin, Apr. 11, 1979.

The U.S. reopened its embassy, reinstated economic aid, and ended its trade embargo in 1979.

Union of Soviet Socialist Republics

Soyuz Sovetskykh Sotsialisticheskikh Respublic

People: Population (1986 est.): 279,904,000. **Age distrib.** (%): 0–19: 24.8; 20-59: 62.1; 60+: 13.0. **Pop. density:** 32 per sq. mi. **Urban** (1984): 64%. **Ethnic groups:** Russians 52% Ukrainians 16%, Uzbeks 5%, Byelorussians 4%, many others. **Languages:** Slavic (Russian, Ukrainian, Byelorussian, Polish), Altaic (Turkish, etc.), other Indo-European, Uralian, Caucasian. **Religions:** Russian Orthodox, Moslems, Protestants, Jews, Buddhists.

Geography: Area: 8,649,496 sq. mi., the largest country in the world, nearly 2½ times the size of the U.S. **Location:** Stretches from E. Europe across N Asia to the Pacific O. **Neighbors:** Finland, Poland, Czechoslovakia, Hungary, Norway, Romania on W, Turkey, Iran, Afghanistan, China, Mongolia, N. Korea on S. **Topography:** Covering one-sixth of the earth's land area, the USSR contains every type of climate except the distinctly tropical, and has a varied topography.

The European portion is a low plain, grassy in S, wooded in N with Ural Mtns. on the E. Caucasus Mts. on the S. Urals stretch N-S for 2,500 mi. The Asiatic portion is also a vast plain, with mountains on the S and in the E; tundra covers extreme N, with forest belt below; plains, marshes are in W, desert in SW.

Capital: Moscow. **Cities** (1985 est.): Moscow 8.6 mln.; Leningrad 4.8 mln.; Kiev 2.4 mln.; Tashkent 1.9 mln.; Kharkov 1.5 mln.; Baku 1.6 mln.; Gorky 1.3 mln.; Novosibirsk 1.3 mln.; Minsk 1.4 mln.; Kuibyshev 1.2 mln.; Sverdlovsk 1.2 mln.

Government: Type: Federal Union controlled by the Communist Party. **Head of state:** Pres. Andrei Gromyko; b. July 18, 1909; in office: July 27, 1985. **Head of government:** Premier Nikolai I. Ryzhkov; b. 1929; in office: Sept. 27, 1985. **Head of Communist Party:** Mikhail Sergeyvich Gorbachev; b. Mar. 2, 1931; in office: Mar. 11, 1985. **Local divisions:** 15 union republics, within which are 20 autonomous republics, 6 krays (territories), 120 oblasts (regions), 8 autonomous oblasts. **Defense:** 12-15% of GNP (1985).

Economy: Industries: Steel, machinery, machine tools, vehicles, chemicals, cement, textiles, appliances, paper. **Chief crops:** Grain, cotton, sugar beets, potatoes, vegetables, sunflowers. **Minerals:** Iron, manganese, mercury, potash, antimony, bauxite, cobalt, chromium, copper, coal, gold, lead, molybdenum, nickel, phosphates, silver, tin, tungsten, zinc, oil (59%), potassium salts. **Crude oil reserves** (1985): 81 bln. bbls. **Other resources:** Forests (25% of world reserves). **Arable land:** 11%. **Meat prod.** (1980): beef: 6.7 mln. metric tons; pork; 5.0 mln. metric tons; lamb: 853,000 metric tons. **Fish catch** (1984): 9.9 mln. metric tons. **Electricity prod.** (1985): 1.5 bln. kwh. **Crude steel prod.** (1985): 154 mln. metric tons. **Labor force:** 19% agric.; 29% industry, 26% services.

Finance: Currency: Ruble (Nov. 1986: 1.00 = $1.48 US). **Gross national product** (1984): $2.0 trl. **Per capita income** (1976): $2,600. **Imports** (1983): $80.4 bln.; partners: E. Ger. 10%, Pol. 7%, Czech. 8%, Bulg. 8%. **Exports** (1983): $91.7 bln.; partners: E. Ger. 10%, Pol. 8%, Bulg. 8%, Czech. 8%. **National budget** (1982): $350 bln. **Tourists** (1984): 7.2 mln.

Transport: Railway traffic (1985): 364 bln. passenger-km; 3.6 bln. net ton-km. **Motor vehicles:** in use (1980): 9.2 mln. passenger cars, 7.9 mln. comm. vehicles; manuf. (1982): 1.3 mln. passenger cars; 874,000 comm. vehicles. **Civil aviation** (1985): 188 bln. passenger-km; 3 bln. freight ton km. **Chief ports:** Leningrad, Odessa, Murmansk, Kaliningrad, Archangelsk, Riga, Vladivostok.

Communications: Television sets: 80 mln. in use (1985). **Radios:** 81 mln. in use (1985). **Telephones in use** (1985): 29.5 mln. **Daily newspaper circ.** (1984): 726 per 1,000 pop.

Health: Life expectancy at birth (1982): 62.0 male; 73.0 female. **Births** (per 1,000 pop. 1985): 19. **Deaths** (per 1,000 pop. 1985): 11. **Natural increase** (1985): .8%. **Hospital beds** (1986): 3.6 mln. **Physicians** (1986): 1.1 mln. **Infant mortality** (per 1,000 live births 1985): 31.

Education (1985): **Literacy:** 99%. Most receive 11 years of schooling.

Major International Organizations: UN (ILO, UNESCO, WHO), Warsaw Pact.

Embassy: 1125 16th St. NW 20036; 628-8548.

The USSR is nominally a federation consisting of 15 union republics, the largest being the Russian Soviet Federated Socialist Republic. Important positions in the republics are filled by centrally chosen appointees, often ethnic Russians.

Beginning in 1939 the USSR by means of military action and negotiation overran contiguous territory and independent republics, including all or part of Lithuania, Latvia, Estonia, Poland, Czechoslovakia, Romania, Germany, Finland, Tannu Tuva, and Japan. The union republics are:

Republic	Area sq. mi.	Pop. (1985 est.)
Russian SFSR	6,592,800	143,090,000
Ukrainian SSR	233,100	50,840,000
Uzbek SSR	172,700	17,974,000
Kazakh SSR	1,049,200	15,842,000
Byelorussian SSR	80,200	9,942,000
Azerbaijan SSR	33,436	6,614,000
Georgian SSR	26,911	5,201,000
Tadzhik SSR	54,019	4,499,000
Moldavian SSR	13,012	4,111,000
Kirghiz SSR	76,642	3,967,000
Lithuanian SSR	26,173	3,590,000
Armenian SSR	11,306	3,317,000
Turkmen SSR	188,417	3,189,000
Latvian SSR	24,695	2,604,000
Estonian SSR	17,413	1,530,000

The **Russian Soviet Federated Socialist Republic** contains over 50% of the population of the USSR and includes 76% of its territory. It extends from the old Estonian, Latvian, and Finnish borders and the Byelorussian and Ukrainian lines on the W, to the shores of the Pacific, and from the Arctic on the N to the Black and Caspian seas and the borders of Kazakh SSR, Mongolia, and Manchuria on the S. Siberia encompasses a large part of the RSFSR area. Capital: Moscow.

Parts of eastern and western Siberia have been transformed by steel mills, huge dams, oil and gas industries, electric railroads, and highways.

The **Ukraine,** the most densely populated of the republics, borders on the Black Sea, with Poland, Czechoslovakia, Hungary, and Romania on the W and SW. Capital: Kiev.

The Ukraine contains the arable black soil belt, the chief wheat-producing section of the Soviet Union. Sugar beets, potatoes, and livestock are important.

The Donets Basin has large deposits of coal, iron and other metals. There are chemical and machine industries and salt mines.

Byelorussia (White Russia). Capital: Minsk. Chief industries include machinery, tools, appliances, tractors, clocks, cameras, steel, cement, textiles, paper, leather, glass. Main crops are grain, flax, potatoes, sugar beets.

Azerbaijan boasts near Baku, the capital, important oil fields. Its natural wealth includes deposits of iron ore, cobalt, etc. A high-yield winter wheat is grown, as are fruits. It produces iron, steel, cement, fertilizers, synthetic rubber, electrical and chemical equipment. It borders on Iran and Turkey.

Georgia, in the western part of Transcaucasia, contains the largest manganese mines in the world. There are rich timber resources and coal mines. Basic industries are food, textiles, iron, steel. Grain, tea, tobacco, fruits, grapes are grown. Capital: Tbilisi (Tiflis). Despite massive party and government purges since 1972, illegal private enterprise and Georgian nationalist feelings persist; attempts to repress them have led to violence.

Armenia is mountainous, sub-tropical, extensively irrigated. Copper, zinc, aluminum, molybdenum, and marble are mined. Instrument making is important. Capital: Erevan.

Uzbekistan, most important economically of the Central Asia republics, produces 67% of USSR cotton, 50% of rice, 33% of silk, 34% of astrakhan, 85% of hemp. Industries include iron, steel, cars, tractors, TV and radio sets, textiles, food. Mineral wealth includes coal, sulphur, copper, and oil. Capital: Tashkent.

Turkmenistan in Central Asia, produces cotton, maize, carpets, chemicals. Minerals: oil, coal, sulphur, barite, lime, salt, gypsum. The Kara Kum desert occupies 80% of the area. Capital: Ashkhabad.

Tadzhikistan borders on China and Afghanistan. Over half the population are Tadzhiks, mostly Moslems, speaking an Iranian dialect. Chief occupations are farming and cattle breeding. Cotton, grain, rice, and a variety of fruits are grown. Heavy industry, based on rich mineral deposits, coal and hydroelectric power, has replaced handicrafts. Capital: Dushanbe.

Kazakhstan extends from the lower reaches of the Volga in Europe to the Altai Mtns. on the Chinese border. It has vast deposits of coal, oil, iron, tin, copper, lead, zinc, etc. Fish for its canning industry are caught in Lake Balkhash and the Caspian and Aral seas. The capital is Alma-Ata. About 50% of the population is Russian or Ukrainian, working in the virgin-grain lands opened up after 1954, and in the growing industries. Capital: Alma-Ata.

Kirghizia is the eastern part of Soviet Central Asia, on the frontier of Xinjiang, China. The people breed cattle and horses and grow tobacco, cotton, rice, sugar beets. Industries include machine and instrument making, chemicals. Capital: Frunze.

Moldavia, in the SW part of the USSR, is a fertile black earth plain bordering Romania and includes Bessarabia. It is an agricultural region that grows grains, fruits, vegetables, and tobacco. Textiles, wine, food and electrical equipment industries have been developed. Capital: Kishinev. The region was taken from Romania in 1940; the people speak Romanian.

Lithuania, on the Baltic, produces cattle, hogs, electric motors, and appliances. The capital is Vilnius (Vilna). **Latvia** on the Baltic and the Gulf of Riga, has timber and peat resources est. at 3 bln. tons. In addition to agricultural products it produces rubber goods, dyes, fertilizers, glassware, telephone apparatus, TV and radio sets, railroad cars. Capital: Riga.

Estonia, also on the Baltic, has textiles, shipbuilding, timber, roadmaking and mining equipment industries and a shale oil refining industry. Capital: Tallinn. The 3 Baltic states were provinces of imperial Russia before World War I, were independent nations between World Wars I and II, but were conquered by

Russia in 1940. The U.S. has never formally recognized the takeover.

Economy. Almost all legal economic enterprises are state-owned. A huge illegal black market plays an important role in distribution; illegal private production and service firms are periodically exposed.

The USSR is incalculably rich in natural resources; distant Siberian reserves are being exploited with Japanese assistance. Its heavy industry is 2d only to the U.S. It leads the world in oil and steel production. Consumer industries have lagged comparatively. Agricultural output has expanded, but in poor crop years the USSR has been forced to make huge grain purchases from the West. Shortages and rationing of basic food products periodically occur.

Industrial growth has dropped, due to short falls in oil, coal, and steel industries, as well as poor grain harvests since 1979.

History. Slavic tribes began migrating into Russia from the W in the 5th century AD. The first Russian state, founded by Scandinavian chieftains, was established in the 9th century, centering in Novgorod and Kiev.

In the 13th century the Mongols overran the country. It recovered under the grand dukes and princes of Muscovy, or Moscow, and by 1480 freed itself from the Mongols. Ivan the Terrible was the first to be formally proclaimed Tsar (1547). Peter the Great (1682-1725), extended the domain and in 1721, founded the Russian Empire.

Western ideas and the beginnings of modernization spread through the huge Russian empire in the 19th and early 20th centuries. But political evolution failed to keep pace.

Military reverses in the 1905 war with Japan and in World War I led to the breakdown of the Tsarist regime. The 1917 Revolution began in March with a series of sporadic strikes for higher wages by factory workers. A provisional democratic government under Prince Georgi Lvov was established but was quickly followed in May by the second provisional government, led by Alexander Kerensky. The Kerensky government and the freely-elected Constituent Assembly were overthrown in a communist coup led by Vladimir Ilyich Lenin Nov. 7.

Lenin's death Jan. 21, 1924, resulted in an internal power struggle from which Joseph Stalin eventually emerged the absolute ruler of Russia. Stalin secured his position at first by exiling opponents, but from the 1930s to 1953, he resorted to a series of "purge" trials, mass executions, and mass exiles to work camps. These measures resulted in millions of deaths, according to most estimates.

Germany and the USSR signed a non-aggression pact Aug. 1939; Germany launched a massive invasion of the Soviet Union, June 1941. Notable heroic episode was the "900 days" siege of Leningrad, lasting to Jan. 1944, and causing a million deaths; the city was never taken. Russian winter counterthrusts, 1941 to '42 and 1942 to '43, stopped the German advance. Turning point was the failure of German troops to take and hold Stalingrad, Sept. 1942 to Feb. 1943. With British and U.S. Lend-Lease aid and sustaining great casualties, the Russians drove the German forces from eastern Europe and the Balkans in the next 2 years.

After Stalin died, Mar. 5, 1953, Nikita Khrushchev was elected first secretary of the Central Committee. In 1956 he condemned Stalin. "De-Stalinization" of the country on all levels was effected after Stalin's body was removed from the Lenin-Stalin tomb in Moscow.

Under Khrushchev the open antagonism of Poles and Hungarians toward domination by Moscow was brutally suppressed in 1956. He advocated peaceful co-existence with the capitalist countries, but continued arming the USSR with nuclear weapons. He aided the Cuban revolution under Fidel Castro but withdrew Soviet missiles from Cuba during confrontation by U.S. Pres. Kennedy, Sept.-Oct. 1962.

Khrushchev was suddenly deposed, Oct. 1964, and replaced as party first secretary by Leonid I. Brezhnev, and as premier by Aleksei N. Kosygin.

In Aug. 1968 Russian, Polish, East German, Hungarian, and Bulgarian military forces invaded Czechoslovakia to put a curb on liberalization policies of the Czech government.

The USSR in 1971 continued heavy arms shipments to Egypt. In July 1972 Egypt ordered most of the 20,000 Soviet military personnel in that country to leave. When Egypt and Syria attacked Israel in Oct. 1973, the USSR launched huge arms airlifts to the 2 Arab nations. In 1974, the Soviet replenished the arms used or lost by the Syrians in the 1973 war, and continued some shipments to Egypt.

Massive Soviet military aid to North Vietnam in the late 1960s and early 1970s helped assure communist victories throughout Indo-China. Soviet arms aid and advisers were sent to several African countries in the 1970s, including Algeria, Angola, Somalia, and Ethiopia.

In 1972, the U.S. and USSR reached temporary agreements to freeze intercontinental missiles at their current levels, to limit defensive missiles to 200 each and to cooperate on health, environment, space, trade, and science.

More than 130,000 Jews and over 40,000 ethnic Germans were allowed to emigrate from the USSR in the 1970s, following pressure from the West. Many leading figures in the arts also left the country.

There were serious food shortages reported in the early 1980s and a new agricultural program, covering 1982-90, was announced amid Soviet fears of becoming dependent on foreign, especially U.S., grain imports. The Afghan invasion continued to go badly in 1987 with no end in sight.

The USSR drew international condemnation on Sept. 1, 1983 when it shot down a Korean 747 commercial airliner, killing 269. The airliner had strayed off course. The Soviets have been unable to prevent U.S. Pershing II and cruise missiles from being deployed in Western Europe. The Soviets led the Eastern bloc boycott of the 1984 Los Angeles Olympics.

Soviet leader Gorbachev held summit meetings with U.S. Pres. Reagan in 1985 and 1986.

In 1987, Gorbachev initiated a program of reforms, including expanded freedoms and the democratization of the political process, and increased openness (*glasnost*). The reforms were opposed by most Eastern bloc countries and many old-line communists in the USSR.

The Soviets received worldwide criticism for their secrecy regarding the Apr. 25, 1986 accident at the Chernobyl nuclear plant.

Government. The Communist Party leadership dominates all areas of national life. A Politburo of 14 full members and 8 candidate members makes all major political, economic, and foreign policy decisions. Party membership in 1978 was reported to be over 16,000,000.

United Arab Emirates

Ittihād al-Imarat al-Arabiyah

People: Population (1986 est.): 1,326,000. **Pop. density:** 44 per sq. mi. **Ethnic groups:** Arab, Iranian, Pakistani, Indian. **Languages:** Arabic (official), Farsi, English, Hindi, Urdu. **Religions:** Moslems 90%, Christian, Hindu.

Geography: Area: 32,000 sq. mi., the size of Maine. **Location:** On the S shore of the Persian Gulf. **Neighbors:** Qatar on N, Saudi Ar. on W, S, Oman on E. **Topography:** A barren, flat coastal plain gives way to uninhabited sand dunes on the S. Hajar Mtns. are on E. **Capital:** Abu Dhabi. **Cities** (1984 est.): Abu Dhabi 537,000; Dubai 278,000.

Government: Type: Federation of emirates. **Head of state:** Pres. Zaid ibn Sultan an-Nahayan b. 1923; in office: Dec. 2, 1971. **Head of government:** Prime Min. Rashid ibn Said al-Maktum; in office: June 25, 1979. **Local divisions:** 7 autonomous emirates: Abu Dhabi, Ajman, Dubai, Fujaira, Ras al-Khaimah, Sharjah, Umm al-Qaiwain. **Defense:** 7.9% of GNP (1983).

Economy: Chief crops: Vegetables, dates, limes. **Minerals:** Oil. **Crude oil reserves** (1985): 36 bln. bbls. **Arable land:** 1%. **Electricity prod.** (1984): 6.6 bln. kwh. **Labor force:** 6% agric.; 67% ind. and commerce; 14% serv.; 13% gvt.

Finance: Currency: Dirham (Apr. 1987: 3.67 = $1 US). **Gross national product** (1984): $28 bln. **Per capita income** (1983 est.) $23,000. **Imports** (1983): $8.3 bln.; partners: Jap. 18%, UK 11%, W. Ger. 6%. **Exports** (1983): $15.4 bln.; partners: Jap. 36%, U.S. 7%, Fr. 10%. **International reserves less gold** (Feb. 1987): $3.8 bln. **Gold:** 817,000 oz t.

Transport: Chief ports: Dubai, Abu Dhabi.

Communications: Radios: 240,000 in use (1985). **Telephones in use** (1983): 319,000.

Health: Life Expectancy at Birth (1985): 61.6 male, 65.6 female. **Hospital beds** (1984): 4,853. **Physicians** (1984): 1,840.

Education (1985): **Literacy:** 56%. **Years Compulsory:** ages 6-12.

Major International Organizations: UN (World Bank, IMF, ILO), Arab League, OPEC.

Embassy: 600 New Hampshire Ave. NW 20037; 338-6500.

The 7 "Trucial Sheikdoms" gave Britain control of defense and foreign relations in the 19th century. They merged to become an independent state Dec. 2, 1971.

The Abu Dhabi Petroleum Co. was fully nationalized in 1975. Oil revenues have given the UAE one of the highest per capita GNPs in the world. International banking has grown in recent years.

United Kingdom of Great Britain and Northern Ireland

People: Population (1986 est.): 56,458,000. **Age distrib.** (%): 0–14: 19.0; 15–59: 60.3; 60+: 20.7. **Pop. density:** 601 per sq. mi. **Urban** (1985): 92.5%. **Ethnic groups:** English 81.5%, Scottish 9.6%, Irish 2.4%, Welsh 1.9%, Ulster 1.8%; West Indian, Indian, Pakistani over 2%; others. **Languages:** English, Welsh spoken in western Wales; Gaelic. **Religions:** Church of England, Roman Catholic.

Geography: Area: 94,226 sq. mi., slightly smaller than Oregon. **Location:** Off the NW coast of Europe, across English Channel, Strait of Dover, and North Sea. **Neighbors:** Ireland to W, France to SE. **Topography:** England is mostly rolling land, rising to Uplands of southern Scotland; Lowlands are in center of Scotland, granite Highlands are in N. Coast is heavily indented, especially on W. British Isles have milder climate than N Europe, due to the Gulf Stream, and ample rainfall. Severn, 220 mi., and Thames, 215 mi., are longest rivers. **Capital:** London. **Cities** (1984 est.): London 6,756,000; Birmingham 1,012,800; Glasgow 751,000; Leeds 714,000; Sheffield 542,000; Liverpool 502,000; Manchester 457,000; Edinburgh 440,000; Bradford 463,000; Bristol 399,000.

Government: Type: Constitutional monarchy. **Head of state:** Queen Elizabeth II; b. Apr. 21, 1926; in office: Feb. 6, 1952. **Head of government:** Prime Min. Margaret Thatcher; b. Oct. 13, 1925; in office: May 4, 1979. **Local divisions:** England and Wales: 47 non-metro counties, 6 metro counties, Greater London; Scotland: 9 regions, 3 island areas; N. Ireland: 26 districts. **Defense:** 5.1% of GDP (1985).

Economy: Industries: Steel, metals, vehicles, shipbuilding, shipping, banking, insurance, textiles, chemicals, electronics, aircraft, machinery, distilling. **Chief crops:** Grains, sugar beets, fruits, vegetables. **Minerals:** Coal, tin, oil, gas, limestone, iron, salt, clay, chalk, gypsum, lead, silica. **Crude oil reserves** (1985): 5.8 bln. bbls. **Arable land:** 30%. **Meat prod.** (1985): cattle: 12.6 mln.; pigs: 7.9 mln.; sheep: 25.5 mln. **Fish catch** (1984): 714,000 metric tons. **Electricity prod.** (1984): 280 bln. kwh. **Crude steel prod.** (1985): 15.7 mln. metric tons. **Labor force:** 1.7% agric.; 26% manuf. & eng., 64% services.

Finance: Currency: Pound (June 1987: .59 = $1 US). **Gross national product** (1985): $453 bln. **Per capita income** (1979): $7,216. **Imports** (1986): $126.1 bln.; partners: W. Ger. 13%, U.S. 12%, Fr. 7%, Neth. 8%. **Exports** (1986): $106.9 bln.; partners: U.S. 13%, W. Ger. 10%, Fr. 8%, Neth. 8%. **Tourists** (1984): receipts: $5.5 bln.; **National budget** (1985): $172 bln. expenditures. **International reserves less gold** (Mar. 1987): $21.5 bln. **Gold:** 19.01 mln. oz t. **Consumer prices** (change in 1986): 3.5%.

Transport: Railway traffic (1985): 30.2 bln. passenger-km; 12.7 bln. net ton-km. **Motor vehicles:** in use (1984): 18 mln. passenger cars, 2.3 mln. comm. vehicles. **Civil aviation** (1985): 51.6 bln. passenger-km: 1.5 bln. freight ton-km. **Chief ports:** London, Liverpool, Glasgow, Southampton, Cardiff, Belfast.

Communications: Television sets: 18.7 mln. licensed (1985). **Radios:** 18 mln. licensed (1985). **Telephones in use** (1984): 29 mln. **Daily newspaper circ.** (1984): 538 per 1,000 pop.

Health: Life expectancy at birth: (1983): 70.2 male; 76.2 female. **Births:** (per 1,000 pop. 1985): 13. **Deaths:** (per 1,000 pop. 1985): 12. **Natural increase:** (1985): .01%. **Hospital beds** (1984): 430,915. **Physicians** (1984): 83,690. **Infant mortality:** (per 1,000 live births 1985): 10.

Education (1987): **Literacy:** 99%. **Years compulsory:** 12; attendance 99%.

Major International Organizations: UN all of and its specialized agencies, NATO, EC, OECD.

Embassy: 3100 Massachusetts Ave. NW 20008; 462-1340.

The United Kingdom of Great Britain and Northern Ireland comprises England, Wales, Scotland, and Northern Ireland.

Queen and Royal Family. The ruling sovereign is Elizabeth II of the House of Windsor, born Apr. 21, 1926, elder daughter of King George VI. She succeeded to the throne Feb. 6, 1952, and was crowned June 2, 1953. She was married Nov. 20, 1947, to Lt. Philip Mountbatten, born June 10, 1921, former Prince of Greece. He was created Duke of Edinburgh, Earl of Merioneth, and Baron Greenwich, and given the style H.R.H., Nov. 19, 1947; he was given the title Prince of the United Kingdom and Northern Ireland Feb. 22, 1957. Prince Charles Philip Arthur George, born Nov. 14, 1948, is the Prince of Wales and heir apparent. His son, William Philip Arthur Louis, born June 21, 1982, is second in line to the throne.

Parliament is the legislative governing body for the United Kingdom, with certain powers over dependent units. It consists of 2 houses: The **House of Lords** includes 763 hereditary and 314 life peers and peeresses, certain judges, 2 archbishops and 24 bishops of the Church of England. Total membership is over 1,000. The **House of Commons** has 635 members, who are elected by direct ballot and divided as follows: England 516; Wales 36; Scotland 71; Northern Ireland 12.

Resources and Industries. Great Britain's major occupations are manufacturing and trade. Metals and metal-using industries contribute more than 50% of the exports. Of about 60 million acres of land in England, Wales and Scotland, 46 million are farmed, of which 17 million are arable, the rest pastures.

Large oil and gas fields have been found in the North Sea. Commercial oil production began in 1975. There are large deposits of coal.

The railroads, nationalized since 1948, have been reduced in total length, with a basic network, Dec. 1978, of 11,123 mi. The merchant marine totaled 126,000 gross registered tons in 1982.

A year-long coal strike costing some $3 bln. ended March 1985. The issue of the closing of uneconomic mines was unresolved.

Britain imports all of its cotton, rubber, sulphur, 80% of its wool, half of its food and iron ore, also certain amounts of paper, tobacco, chemicals. Manufactured goods made from these basic materials have been exported since the industrial age began. Main exports are machinery, chemicals, woolen and synthetic textiles, clothing, autos and trucks, iron and steel, locomotives, ships, jet aircraft, farm machinery, drugs, radio, TV, radar and navigation equipment, scientific instruments, arms, whisky.

Religion and Education. The Church of England is Protestant Episcopal. The queen is its temporal head, with rights of appointments to archbishoprics, bishoprics, and other offices. There are 2 provinces, Canterbury and York, each headed by an archbishop. About 48% of the population is baptized into the Church, less than 10% is confirmed. Most famous church is Westminster Abbey (1050-1760), site of coronations, tombs of Elizabeth I, Mary of Scots, kings, poets, and of the Unknown Warrior.

The most celebrated British universities are Oxford and Cambridge, each dating to the 13th century. There are about 40 other universities.

History. Britain was part of the continent of Europe until about 6,000 BC, but migration of peoples across the English Channel continued long afterward. Celts arrived 2,500 to 3,000 years ago. Their language survives in Welsh, Cornish, and Gaelic enclaves.

England was added to the Roman Empire in 43 AD. After the withdrawal of Roman legions in 410, waves of Jutes, Angles, and Saxons arrived from German lands. They contended with Danish raiders for control from the 8th through 11th centuries.

The last successful invasion was by French speaking Normans in 1066, who united the country with their dominions in France.

Opposition by nobles to royal authority forced King John to sign the Magna Carta in 1215, a guarantee of rights and the rule of law. In the ensuing decades, the foundations of the parliamentary system were laid.

English dynastic claims to large parts of France led to the Hundred Years War, 1338-1453, and the defeat of England. A long civil war, the War of the Roses, lasted 1455-85, and ended with the establishment of the powerful Tudor monarchy. A distinct English civilization flourished. The economy prospered over long periods of domestic peace unmatched in continental Europe. Religious independence was secured when the Church of England was separated from the authority of the Pope in 1534.

Under Queen Elizabeth I, England became a major naval power, leading to the founding of colonies in the new world and the expansion of trade with Europe and the Orient. Scotland was united with England when James VI of Scotland was crowned James I of England in 1603.

A struggle between Parliament and the Stuart kings led to a bloody civil war, 1642-49, and the establishment of a republic under the Puritan Oliver Cromwell. The monarchy was restored in 1660, but the "Glorious Revolution" of 1688 confirmed the sovereignty of Parliament: a Bill of Rights was granted 1689.

In the 18th century, parliamentary rule was strengthened. Technological and entrepreneurial innovations led to the Industrial Revolution. The 13 North American colonies were lost, but replaced by growing empires in Canada and India. Britain's role in the defeat of Napoleon, 1815, strengthened its position as the leading world power.

The extension of the franchise in 1832 and 1867, the formation of trade unions, and the development of universal public education were among the drastic social changes which accompanied the spread of industrialization and urbanization in the 19th century. Large parts of Africa and Asia were added to the empire during the reign of Queen Victoria, 1837-1901.

Though victorious in World War I, Britain suffered huge casualties and economic dislocation. Ireland became independent in 1921, and independence movements became active in India and other colonies.

The country suffered major bombing damage in World War II, but held out against Germany singlehandedly for a year after the fall of France in 1940.

Industrial growth continued in the postwar period, but Britain lost its leadership position to other powers. Labor governments passed socialist programs nationalizing some basic industries and expanding social security. The Thatcher government has however, tried to increase the role of private enterprise. In 1987, Margaret Thatcher became the first British leader in 160 years to be elected to a 3d consecutive term as prime minister.

Britain broke diplomatic relations with Libya, Apr. 22, 1984, 5 days after a policewoman was killed and 10 Libyan exile demonstrators wounded by machine-gun fire from within the Libyan embassy in London. The embassy occupants, including the killer, left Britain, Apr. 27.

Wales

The Principality of Wales in western Britain has an area of 8,016 sq. mi. and a population (1985 est.) of 2,811,000. Cardiff is the capital, pop. (1981 est.) 273,856.

England and Wales are administered as a unit. Less than 20% of the population of Wales speak both English and Welsh; about 32,000 speak Welsh solely. A 1979 referendum rejected, 4-1, the creation of an elected Welsh Assembly.

Early Anglo-Saxon invaders drove Celtic peoples into the mountains of Wales, terming them Waelise (Welsh, or foreign). There they developed a distinct nationality. Members of the ruling house of Gwynedd in the 13th century fought England but were crushed, 1283. Edward of Caernarvon, son of Edward I of England, was created Prince of Wales, 1301.

Scotland

Scotland, a kingdom now united with England and Wales in Great Britain, occupies the northern 37% of the main British island, and the Hebrides, Orkney, Shetland and smaller islands. Length, 275 mi., breadth approx. 150 mi., area, 30,405 sq. mi., population (1985 est.) 5,136,000.

The Lowlands, a belt of land approximately 60 mi. wide from the Firth of Clyde to the Firth of Forth, divide the farming region of the Southern Uplands from the granite Highlands of the North, contain 75% of the population and most of the industry. The Highlands, famous for hunting and fishing, have been opened to industry by many hydroelectric power stations.

Edinburgh, pop. (1983 est.) 440,000, is the capital. Glasgow, pop. (1983 est.) 751,000, is Britain's greatest industrial center. It is a shipbuilding complex on the Clyde and an ocean port. Aberdeen, pop. (1981 cen.) 190,200, NE of Edinburgh, is a major port, center of granite industry, fish processing, and North Sea oil exploitation. Dundee, pop. (1981 cen.) 174,746, NE of Edinburgh, is an industrial and fish processing center. About 90,000 persons speak Gaelic as well as English.

History. Scotland was called Caledonia by the Romans who battled early Pict and Celtic tribes and occupied southern areas from the 1st to the 4th centuries. Missionaries from Britain introduced Christianity in the 4th century; St. Columba, an Irish monk, converted most of Scotland in the 6th century.

The Kingdom of Scotland was founded in 1018. William Wallace and Robert Bruce both defeated English armies 1297 and 1314, respectively.

In 1603 James VI of Scotland, son of Mary, Queen of Scots, succeeded to the throne of England as James I, and effected the Union of the Crowns. In 1707 Scotland received representation in the British Parliament, resulting from the union of former separate Parliaments. Its executive in the British cabinet is the Secretary of State for Scotland. The growing Scottish National Party urges independence. A 1979 referendum on the creation of an elected Scotland Assembly was defeated.

There are 8 universities. Memorials of Robert Burns, Sir Walter Scott, John Knox, Mary, Queen of Scots draw many tourists, as do the beauties of the Trossachs, Loch Katrine, Loch Lomond and abbey ruins.

Industries. Engineering products are the most important industry, with growing emphasis on office machinery, autos, electronics and other consumer goods. Oil has been discovered offshore in the North Sea, stimulating on-shore support industries.

Scotland produces fine woolens, worsteds, tweeds, silks, fine linens and jute. It is known for its special breeds of cattle and sheep. Fisheries have large hauls of herring, cod, whiting. Whisky is the biggest export.

The Hebrides are a group of c. 500 islands, 100 inhabited, off the W coast. The Inner Hebrides include **Skye, Mull,** and **Iona,** the last famous for the arrival of St. Columba, 563 AD. The Outer Hebrides include **Lewis** and **Harris.** Industries include sheep raising and weaving. The **Orkney Islands,** c. 90, are to the NE. The capital is Kirkwall, on Pomona Is. Fish curing, sheep raising and weaving are occupations. NE of the Orkneys are the 200 **Shetland Islands,** 24 inhabited, home of Shetland pony. The Orkneys and Shetlands have become centers for the North Sea oil industry.

Northern Ireland

Six of the 9 counties of Ulster, the NE corner of Ireland, constitute Northern Ireland, with the parliamentary boroughs of Belfast and Londonderry. Area 5,463 sq. mi., 1985 est. pop. 1,568,000, capital and chief industrial center, Belfast, (1981 cen.) 297,862.

Industries. Shipbuilding, including large tankers, has long been an important industry, centered in Belfast, the largest port. Linen manufacture is also important, along with apparel, rope, and twine. Growing diversification has added engineering products, synthetic fibers, and electronics. They are large numbers of cattle, hogs, and sheep, potatoes, poultry, and dairy foods are also produced.

Government. An act of the British Parliament, 1920, divided Northern from Southern Ireland, each with a parliament and government. When Ireland became a dominion, 1921, and later a republic, Northern Ireland chose to remain a part of the United Kingdom. It elects 12 members to the British House of Commons.

During 1968-69, large demonstrations were conducted by Roman Catholics who charged they were discriminated against in voting rights, housing, and employment. The Catholics, a minority comprising about a third of the population, demanded abolition of property qualifications for voting in local elections. Violence and terrorism intensified, involving branches of the Irish Republican Army (outlawed in the Irish Republic), Protestant groups, police, and up to 15,000 British troops.

A succession of Northern Ireland prime ministers pressed reform programs but failed to satisfy extremists on both sides. Over 2,000 were killed in over 15 years of bombings and shootings through 1986, many in England itself. Britain suspended the Northern Ireland parliament Mar. 30, 1972, and imposed direct British rule. A coalition government was formed in 1973 when moderates won election to a new one-house Assembly. But a Protestant general strike overthrew the government in 1974 and direct rule was resumed.

The turmoil and agony of Northern Ireland was dramatized in 1981 by the deaths of 10 imprisoned Irish nationalist hunger strikers in Maze Prison near Belfast. The inmates had starved themselves to death in an attempt to achieve status as political prisoners, but the British government refused to yield to their demands. In 1985, the Hillsborough agreement gave the Rep. of

Ireland a voice in the governing of Northern Ireland; the accord was strongly opposed by Ulster loyalists.

Education and Religion. Northern Ireland is 2/3 Protestant, 1/3 Roman Catholic. Education is compulsory through age 15. There are 2 universities and 24 technical colleges.

Channel Islands

The Channel Islands, area 75 sq. mi., cen. pop. 1980 130,000, off the NW coast of France, the only parts of the one-time Dukedom of Normandy belonging to England, are **Jersey, Guernsey** and the dependencies of Guernsey — **Alderney, Brechou, Great Sark, Little Sark, Herm, Jethou and Lihou.** Jersey and Guernsey have separate legal existences and lieutenant governors named by the Crown. The islands were the only British soil occupied by German troops in World War II.

Isle of Man

The Isle of Man, area 227 sq. mi., 1982 est. pop. 61,000, is in the Irish Sea, 20 mi. from Scotland, 30 mi. from Cumberland. It is rich in lead and iron. The island has its own laws and a lieutenant governor appointed by the Crown. The Tynwald (legislature) consists of the Legislative Council, partly elected, and House of Keys, elected. Capital: Douglas. Farming, tourism (413,000 visitors in 1982), fishing (kippers, scallops) are chief occupations. Man is famous for the Manx tailless cat.

Gibraltar

Gibraltar, a dependency on the southern coast of Spain, guards the entrance to the Mediterranean. The Rock has been in British possession since 1704. The Rock is 2.75 mi. long, 3/4 of a mi. wide and 1,396 ft. in height; a narrow isthmus connects it with the mainland. Est. pop. 1982, 30,000.

In 1966 Spain called on Britain to give "substantial sovereignty" of Gibraltar to Spain and imposed a partial blockade. In 1967, residents voted for remaining under Britain. A new constitution, May 30, 1969, gave an elected House of Assembly more control in domestic affairs. A UN General Assembly resolution requested Britain to end Gibraltar's colonial status by Oct. 1, 1969. No settlement has been reached.

British West Indies

Swinging in a vast arc from the coast of Venezuela NE, then N and NW toward Puerto Rico are the Leeward Islands, forming a coral and volcanic barrier sheltering the Caribbean from the open Atlantic. Many of the islands are self-governing British possessions. Universal suffrage was instituted 1951-54, ministerial systems were set up 1956-1960.

The **Leeward Islands,** are **Montserrat** (1980 pop. 11,600, area 32 sq. mi., capital Plymouth), and **St. Kitts (St. Christopher)-Nevis,** 2 islands which became independent in 1983. Nearby are the small **British Virgin Islands.**

Anguilla gained its independence from St. Kitts Dec. 19, 1980. A 1976 constitution provides for an autonomous elected government. Area 35 sq. mi., pop. (1982 est.) 7,000.

The three **Cayman Islands,** a dependency, lie S of Cuba, NW of Jamaica. Pop. 18,000 (1981), most of it on Grand Cayman. It is a free port; in the 1970s Grand Cayman became a tax-free refuge for foreign funds and branches of many Western banks were opened there. Total area 102 sq. mi., capital Georgetown.

The **Turks and Caicos Islands,** at the SE end of the Bahama Islands, are a separate possession. There are about 30 islands, only 6 inhabited, 1980 pop. est. 7,000, area 193 sq. mi., capital Grand Turk. Salt, crayfish and conch shells are the main exports.

Bermuda

Bermuda is a British dependency governed by a royal governor and an assembly, dating from 1620, the oldest legislative body among British dependencies. Capital is Hamilton.

It is a group of 360 small islands of coral formation, 20 inhabited, comprising 20.6 sq. mi. in the western Atlantic, 580 mi. E of North Carolina. Pop., 1986 est., was 57,400 (about 61% of African descent). Density is high.

The U.S. has air and naval bases under long-term lease, and a NASA tracking facility.

Bermuda boasts many resort hotels, serving 417,000 tourists in 1984. The government raises most revenue from import duties. Exports: petroleum products, drugs.

South Atlantic

Falkland Islands and Dependencies, a British dependency, lies 300 mi. E of the Strait of Magellan at the southern end of South America.

The Falklands or Islas Malvinas include about 200 islands, area 4,700 sq. mi., pop. (1980 est.) 1,800. Sheep-grazing is the main industry; wool is the principal export. There are indications of large oil and gas deposits. The islands are also claimed by Argentina though 97% of inhabitants are of British origin. Argentina invaded the islands Apr. 2, 1982. The British responded by sending a task force to the area, landing their main force on the Falklands, May 21, and forcing an Argentine surrender at Port Stanley, June 14. **South Georgia,** area 1,450 sq. mi., and the uninhabited **South Sandwich Is.** are dependencies of the Falklands.

British Antarctic Territory, south of 60° S lat., was made a separate colony in 1962 and comprises mainly the **South Shetland Islands,** the **South Orkneys** and **Graham's Land.** A chain of meteorological stations is maintained.

St. Helena, an island 1,200 mi. off the W coast of Africa and 1,800 E of South America, has 47 sq. mi. and est. pop., 1981 of 5,300. Flax, lace and rope making are the chief industries. After Napoleon Bonaparte was defeated at Waterloo the Allies exiled him to St. Helena, where he lived from Oct. 16, 1815, to his death, May 5, 1821. Capital is Jamestown.

Tristan da Cunha is the principal of a group of islands of volcanic origin, total area 40 sq. mi., half way between the Cape of Good Hope and South America. A volcanic peak 6,760 ft. high erupted in 1961. The 262 inhabitants were removed to England, but most returned in 1963. The islands are dependencies of St. Helena.

Ascension is an island of volcanic origin, 34 sq. mi. in area, 700 mi. NW of St. Helena, through which it is administered. It is a communications relay center for Britain, and has a U.S. satellite tracking center. Est. pop., 1976, was 1,179, half of them communications workers. The island is noted for sea turtles.

Asia and Indian Ocean

Hong Kong is a Crown Colony at the mouth of the Canton R. in China, 90 mi. S of Canton. Its nucleus is Hong Kong Is., 35½ sq. mi., acquired from China 1841, on which is located Victoria, the capital. Opposite is Kowloon Peninsula, 3 sq. mi. and Stonecutters Is., ¼ sq. mi., added, 1860. An additional 355 sq. mi. known as the New Territories, a mainland area and islands, were leased from China, 1898, for 99 years. Britain and China, Dec. 19, 1985, signed an agreement under which Hong Kong would be allowed to keep its capitalist system for 50 years after 1997, the year that the 99-year lease will expire. Total area of the colony is 409 sq. mi., with a population, 1983 est., of 5,287,000 including fewer than 20,000 British. From 1949 to 1962 Hong Kong absorbed more than a million refugees from the mainland.

Hong Kong harbor was long an important British naval station and one of the world's great trans-shipment ports.

Principal industries are textiles and apparel (25% of exports); also tourism, 2.5 mln. visitors, $1.5 bln. expenditures (1981), shipbuilding, iron and steel, fishing, cement, and small manufactures.

Spinning mills, among the best in the world, and low wages compete with textiles elsewhere and have resulted in the protective measures in some countries. Hong Kong also has a booming electronics industry.

British Indian Ocean Territory was formed Nov. 1965, embracing islands formerly dependencies of Mauritius or Seychelles: the Chagos Archipelago (including Diego Garcia), Aldabra, Farquhar and Des Roches. The latter 3 were transferred to Seychelles, which became independent in 1976. Area 22 sq mi. No civilian population remains.

Pacific Ocean

Pitcairn Island is in the Pacific, halfway between South America and Australia. The island was discovered in 1767 by Carteret but was not inhabited until 23 years later when the mutineers of the Bounty landed there. The area is 18 sq. mi. and pop. 1983, was 61. It is a British colony and is administered by a British Representative in New Zealand and a local Council. The uninhabited islands of **Henderson, Ducie** and **Oeno** are in the Pitcairn group.

United States of America

People: Population (1986 est.): 240,856,000. **Age distrib.**(%): 0–14: 21.7; 15–59: 61.8; 60+: 16.5. **Pop. density:** 66 per sq. mi. **Urban** (1980): 79.2%.

Defense: 6.4% of GNP (1984).

Economy: Minerals: Coal, copper, lead, molybdenum, phosphates, uranium, bauxite, gold, iron, mercury, nickel, potash, silver, tungsten, zinc. **Crude oil reserves** (1985): 27 bln. bbls. **Arable land:** 21%. **Meat prod.** (1985): cattle: 105.4 mln.; pigs: 52.2 mln.; sheep: 9.9 mln. **Fish catch** (1985): 2.8 mln. metric tons. **Electricity prod.** (1985): 2,469 bln. kwh. **Crude steel prod.** (1985): 79.3 mln. metric tons.

Finance: Gross national product (1985): $3,855 bln. **Per capita income** (1985): $13,451. **Imports** (1986): $387.0 bln.; partners: Can. 19%, Jap. 20%, Mex. 6%. **Exports** (1986): $217.3 bln.; partners: Can. 22%, Jap. 10%, Mex. 6%, UK 5%. **Tourists** (1985): receipts $11 bln. **International reserves less gold** (Mar. 1987): $37.7 bln. **Gold:** 262.5 mln. oz t. **Consumer prices** (change in 1986): 1.9%.

Transport: Railway traffic (1985): 15.5 bln. passenger-km; 1.3 bln. net ton-km. **Motor vehicles:** in use (1985): 130 mln. passenger cars, 39 mln. comm. vehicles. **Civil aviation** (1985): 478 bln. passenger-km; 11.5 bln. freight ton-km.

Communications: Television sets: 145 mln. in use (1985). **Radios:** 480 mln. in use (1985). **Telephones in use** (1984): 134 mln. **Daily newspaper circ.** (1984): 267 per 1,000 pop.

Health: Life expectancy at birth (1986): 71.5 male; 78.5 female. **Births** (per 1,000 pop. 1985): 15.5. **Deaths** (per 1,000 pop. 1985): 8.7. **Natural increase** (1986): .6%. **Hospital beds** (1985): 1.3 mln. **Physicians** (1985): 527,900. **Infant mortality** (per 1,000 live births 1986): 10.4.

Major International Organizations: UN (GATT, IMF, WHO, FAO), OAS, NATO, OECD.

Education (1987): **Literacy:** 99%.

Uruguay

Oriental Republic of Uruguay

República Oriental del Uruguay

People: Population (1986 est.): 2,947,000. **Age distrib.** (%): 0–14: 26.9; 15–59: 57.7; 60+: 15.4. **Pop. density:** 45 per sq. mi. **Urban** (1983): 83.0%. **Ethnic groups:** Caucasians (Iberians, Italians) 89%, mestizos 10%, mulatto and black. **Languages:** Spanish. **Religions:** 66% Roman Catholic.

Geography: Area: 68,037 sq. mi., the size of Washington State. **Location:** In southern S. America, on the Atlantic O. **Neighbors:** Argentina on W, Brazil on N. **Topography:** Uruguay is composed of rolling, grassy plains and hills, well-watered by rivers flowing W to Uruguay R. **Capital:** Montevideo. **Cities** (1983 est.): Montevideo 1,255,600.

Government: Type: Republic. **Head of state:** Pres. Julio Maria Sanguinetti; b. Jan. 6, 1936; in office: Mar. 1, 1985. **Local divisions:** 19 departments. **Defense:** 3.3% of GNP (1983).

Economy: Industries: Meat-packing, metals, textiles, wine, cement, oil products. **Chief crops:** Corn, wheat, citrus fruits, rice, oats, linseed. **Arable land:** 12%. **Meat prod.** (1984): beef: 355,000 metric tons; pork: 18,000 metric tons; lamb: 41,000 metric tons. **Fish catch** (1984): 134,000 metric tons. **Electricity prod.** (1984): 3.6 bln. kwh. **Labor force** 16% agric.; 31% ind. and commerce; 12% serv.; 19% govt.

Finance: Currency: New Peso (Mar. 1987: 201 = $1 US). **Gross national product** (1984): $5.9 bln. **Per capita income** (1985): $1,665. **Imports** (1986): $820 mln.; partners: Nig. 17%, Braz. 12%, Arg. 10%, U.S. 8%. **Exports** (1986): $1.0 bln.; partners: Braz. 14%, U.S. 7%, W. Ger. 9%, Arg. 11%. **Tourists** (1984): $107 mln. receipts. **National budget** (1983): $1.3 bln. expeditures. **International reserves less gold** (Jan. 1987): $501 mln. **Gold:** 2.60 mln. oz t. **Consumer prices** (change in 1986): 76.4%.

Transport: Railway traffic (1984): 330 mln. passenger-km; 273 mln. net ton-km. **Motor vehicles:** in use (1981): 281,000 passenger cars, 43,000 comm. vehicles. **Civil aviation** (1985): 240 mln. passenger-km; 36 mln. freight ton-km. **Chief ports:** Montevideo.

Communications: Television sets: 500,000 in use (1985). **Radios:** 1.7 mln. in use (1985). **Telephones in use** (1983): 307,000. **Daily newspaper circ.** (1985): 185 per 1,000 pop.

Health: Life expectancy at birth (1983): 67.1 male; 73.7 female. **Births** (per 1,000 pop. 1985): 18. **Deaths** (per 1,000 pop. 1985): 10. **Natural increase** (1985): .8%. **Hospital beds** (1983): 23,400. **Physicians:** (1984): 5,756. **Infant mortality** (per 1,000 live births 1985): 26.

Education (1984): **Literacy:** 96%.

Major International Organizations: UN (GATT, IMF, WHO), OAS.

Embassy: 1919 F St. NW 20006; 331-1313.

Spanish settlers did not begin replacing the indigenous Charrua Indians until 1624. Portuguese from Brazil arrived later, but Uruguay was attached to the Spanish Viceroyalty of Rio de la Plata in the 18th century. Rebels fought against Spain beginning in 1810. An independent republic was declared Aug. 25, 1825.

Liberal governments adopted socialist measures as far back as 1911. The state owns the power, telephone, railroad, cement, oil-refining and other industries. Social welfare programs are among the most advanced in the world.

Uruguay's standard of living was one of the highest in South America, and political and labor conditions among the freest. Economic stagnation, inflation, plus floods, drought in 1967 and a general strike in 1968 brought attempts by the government to strengthen the economy through a series of devaluations of the peso and wage and price controls. But inflation continued in the 1980s and the country was forced to ask international creditors to restructure $2.7 billion in debt in 1983.

Tupamaros, leftist guerrillas drawn from the upper classes, increased terrorist actions in 1970. Violence continued and in Feb. 1973 Pres. Juan Maria Bordaberry agreed to military control of his administration. In June he abolished Congress and set up a Council of State in its place. By 1974 the military had apparently defeated the Tupamaros, using severe repressive measures. Bordaberry was removed by the military in a 1976 coup. Civilian government was restored to the country in 1985.

Vanuatu

Republic of Vanuatu

Ripablik Blong Vanuatu

People: Population (1986 est.): 136,000. **Population density:** 23 per sq. mi. **Ethnic groups:** Mainly Melanesian, some European, Polynesian, Micronesian. **Languages:** Bislama (national), French and English both official. **Religions:** Presbyterian 40%, Anglican 14%, Roman Catholic 16%, animist 15%.

Geography: Area: 5,700 sq. mi. **Location:** SW Pacific, 1,200 mi NE of Brisbane, Australia. **Topography:** dense forest with narrow coastal strips of cultivated land. **Capital:** Vila. **Cities:** Vila (1981): 9,000.

Government: Type: Republic. **Head of state:** Pres. George Sokomanu; in office: July 30, 1980. **Head of gov't:** Prime Min. Rev. Walter Lini; in office: July 30, 1980.

Economy: Industries: Fish-freezing, meat canneries, tourism. **Chief crops:** Copra (38% of export), cocoa, coffee. **Minerals:** Manganese. **Other resources:** Forests, cattle. **Fish catch** (1984): 2.4 metric tons.

Finance: Currency: Australian dollar and Vanuatu franc (Mar. 1987: 110 vatu = $1 US). **Imports** (1982): $66 mln.; partners: Aus. 36%, Fr. 8%, Japan 13%. **Exports** (1982): $22 mln.; partners: Neth. 48%, Jap. 17%, Fr. 12%, Belg.-Lux. 14%.

Health: Life expectancy at birth (1984): 56.2 male, 53.7 female. **Infant mortality** (per 1,000 live births 1985): 78.

Education: Education not compulsory, but 85-90% of children of primary school age attend primary schools.

The Anglo-French condominium of the New Hebrides, administered jointly by France and Great Britain since 1906, became the independent Republic of Vanuatu on July 30, 1980.

Vatican City

State of the Vatican City

People: Population (1986 est.): 1,000. **Ethnic groups:** Italians, Swiss. **Languages:** Italian, Latin.

Geography: Area: 108.7 acres. **Location:** In Rome, Italy. **Neighbors:** Completely surrounded by Italy.

Currency: Lira.

Apostolic Nunciature in U.S.: 3339 Massachusetts Ave. NW 20008; 333-7121.

The popes for many centuries, with brief interruptions, held temporal sovereignty over mid-Italy (the so-called Papal States), comprising an area of some 16,000 sq. mi., with a population in the 19th century of more than 3 million. This territory was incorporated in the new Kingdom of Italy, the sovereignty of the pope being confined to the palaces of the Vatican and the Lateran in Rome and the villa of Castel Gandolfo, by an Italian law, May 13, 1871. This law also guaranteed to the pope and his successors a yearly indemnity of over $620,000. The allowance, however, remained unclaimed.

A Treaty of Conciliation, a concordat and a financial convention were signed Feb. 11, 1929, by Cardinal Gasparri and Premier Mussolini. The documents established the independent state of Vatican City, and gave the Catholic religion special status in Italy. The treaty (Lateran Agreement) was made part of the Constitution of Italy (Article 7) in 1947. Italy and the Vatican reached preliminary agreement in 1976 on revisions of the concordat, that would eliminate Roman Catholicism as the state religion and end required religious education in Italian schools.

Vatican City includes St. Peter's, the Vatican Palace and Museum covering over 13 acres, the Vatican gardens, and neighboring buildings between Viale Vaticano and the Church. Thirteen buildings in Rome, outside the boundaries, enjoy extraterritorial rights; these buildings house congregations or officers necessary for the administration of the Holy See.

The legal system is based on the code of canon law, the apostolic constitutions and the laws especially promulgated for the Vatican City by the pope. The Secretariat of State represents the Holy See in its diplomatic relations. By the Treaty of Conciliation the pope is pledged to a perpetual neutrality unless his mediation is specifically requested. This, however, does not prevent the defense of the Church whenever it is persecuted.

The present sovereign of the State of Vatican City is the Supreme Pontiff John Paul II, Karol Wojtyla, born in Wadowice, Poland, May 18, 1920, elected Oct. 16, 1978 (the first non-Italian to be elected Pope in 456 years).

The U.S. restored formal relations in 1984 after the U.S. Congress repealed an 1867 ban on diplomatic relations with the Vatican.

Venezuela

Republic of Venezuela

Republica de Venezuela

People: Population (1986 est.): 17,791,000. **Age distrib.** (%): 0–14: 42.8; 15–59: 52.4; 60+: 4.8. **Pop. density:** 50 per sq. mi. **Urban** (1985): 85%. **Ethnic groups:** Mestizo 69%, white (Spanish, Portuguese, Italian) 20%, Negro 9%, Indian 2%. **Languages:** Spanish (official), Indian languages 2%. **Religions:** Roman Catholic 96%.

Geography: Area: 352,143 sq. mi., more than twice the size of California. **Location:** On the Caribbean coast of S. America. **Neighbors:** Colombia on W, Brazil on S, Guyana on E. **Topography:** Flat coastal plain and Orinoco Delta are bordered by Andes Mtns. and hills. Plains, called llanos, extend between mountains and Orinoco. Guyana Highlands and plains are S of Orinoco, which stretches 1,600 mi. and drains 80% of Venezuela. **Capital:** Caracas. **Cities** (1987 est.): Caracas 3,247,000; Maracaibo 1,295,000; Barquisimeto 718,000; Valencia 1,135,000.

Government: Type: Federal republic. **Head of state:** Pres. Jaime Lusinchi; b. 1924; in office: Feb. 2, 1984. **Local divisions:** 20 states, 2 federal territories, federal district, federal dependency. **Defense:** 1.3% of GNP (1983).

Economy: Industries: Steel, oil products, textiles, containers, paper, shoes. **Chief crops:** Coffee, rice, fruits, sugar. **Minerals:** Oil (5th largest producer), iron (extensive reserves and production), gold. **Crude oil reserves** (1985): 28 bln. bbls. **Arable land:** 4%. **Meat prod.** (1985): cattle: 12.3 mln.; pigs: 2.8 mln. **Fish catch** (1983): 226,000 metric tons. **Electricity prod.** (1984): 44.3 bln. kwh. **Crude steel prod.** (1985): 3.0 mln. metric tons. **Labor force:** 15% agric.; 35% ind. and commerce; 26% services.

Finance: Currency: Bolivar (Apr. 1987: 27.75 = $1 US). **Gross national product** (1985): $50 bln. **Per capita income** (1985): $2,629. **Imports** (1985): $8.1 bln.; partners: U.S. 48%, W. Ger. 6%, Jap. 8%. **Exports** (1985): $12.2 bln.; partners: U.S. 25%, Neth Ant. 21%, Can. 9%. **Tourists** (1984): $343 mln. receipts. **National budget** (1986): $13.1 bln. expenditures. **International reserves less gold** (Mar. 1987): $6.1 bln. **Gold:** 11.46 mln. oz t. **Consumer prices** (change in 1986): 11.5%.

Transport: Railway traffic (1982): 19 mln. passenger-km; 29 mln. net ton-km. **Motor vehicles:** in use (1985): 1.5 mln. passenger cars, 763,000 comm. vehicles. **Civil aviation** (1985): 2.4 bln. passenger-km; 215 mln. freight ton-km. **Chief ports:** Maracaibo, La Guaira, Puerto Cabello.

Communications: Television sets: 2 mln. in use (1984). **Radios:** 5.2 mln. in use (1984). **Telephones in use** (1983): 1.0 mln. **Daily newspaper circ.** (1982): 120 per 1,000 pop.

Health: Life expectancy at birth (1985): 65 male; 70.6 female. **Births** (per 1,000 pop. 1985): 32. **Deaths** (per 1,000 pop. 1985): 6. **Natural increase** (1985): 2.6%. **Hospital beds** (1978): 41,366. **Physicians** (1978): 14,771. **Infant mortality** (per 1,000 live births 1985): 37.

Education (1987): **Literacy:** 88%. **Years compulsory:** 8; attendance 82%.

Major International Organizations: UN (IMF, WHO, FAO), OAS, OPEC.

Embassy: 2445 Massachusetts Ave. NW 20008; 797-3800.

Columbus first set foot on the South American continent on the peninsula of Paria, Aug. 1498. Alonso de Ojeda, 1499, found Lake Maracaibo, called the land Venezuela, or Little Venice, because natives had houses on stilts. Venezuela was under Spanish domination until 1821. The republic was formed after secession from the Colombian Federation in 1830.

Military strongmen ruled Venezuela for most of the 20th century. They promoted the oil industry; some social reforms were implemented. Since 1959, the country has enjoyed progressive, democratically-elected governments.

Venezuela helped found the Organization of Petroleum Exporting States (OPEC). The government, Jan. 1, 1976, nationalized the oil industry with compensation. Development has begun of the Orinoco tar belt, believed to contain the world's largest oil reserves. Oil accounts for much of total export earnings and the economy suffered a severe cash crisis in the 1980s as the result of falling oil revenues.

There were anti-government demonstrations in Apr. 1987.

Vietnam

Socialist Republic of Vietnam

Cong Hoa Xa Hoi Chu Nghia Viet Nam

People: Population (1986 est.): 61,994,000. **Pop. density:** 478 per sq. mi. **Urban** (1984): 19%. **Ethnic groups:** Vietnamese 84%, Chinese 2%, remainder Muong, Thai, Meo, Khmer, Man, Cham. **Languages:** Vietnamese (official), French, English. **Religions:** Buddhists, Confucians, and Taoists most numerous, Roman Catholics, animists, Muslims, Protestants.

Geography: Area: 128,401 sq. mi., the size of New Mexico. **Location:** On the E coast of the Indochinese Peninsula in SE Asia. **Neighbors:** China on N, Laos, Cambodia on W. **Topography:** Vietnam is long and narrow, with a 1,400-mi. coast. About 24% of country is readily arable, including the densely settled Red R. valley in the N, narrow coastal plains in center, and the wide, often marshy Mekong R. Delta in the S. The rest consists of semi-arid plateaus and barren mountains, with some stretches of tropical rain forest. **Capital:** Hanoi. **Cities** (1981): Ho Chi Minh City 3.5 mln.; Hanoi 2 mln.

Government: Type: Communist people's republic. **Head of state:** Pres. Vo Chi Cong; in office: June 18, 1987. **Head of government:** Prime Min. Pham Hung; in office: June 18, 1987. **Head of Communist Party:** Nguyen Van Linh; in office: Dec. 18, 1986. **Local divisions:** 39 provinces. **Defense:** 50% of govt. budget (1982 est.)

Economy: Industries: Food processing, textiles, cement, chemical fertilizers, steel. **Chief crops:** Rice, rubber, fruits and vegetables, corn, manioc, sugarcane. **Minerals:** Phosphates, coal, iron, manganese, bauxite, apatite, chromate. **Other resources:** Forests. **Arable land:** 23%. **Meat prod.** (1985): cattle: 5 mln.; pigs: 11.7 mln.; sheep & goats: 262,000. **Fish catch** (1984): 765,000 metric tons. **Electricity prod.** (1984): 4.8 bln. kwh. **Labor force:** 70% agric.; 8% ind. and commerce.

Finance: Currency: Dong (Nov. 1986: 11.76 = $1 US). **Gross national product** (1983): $9.8 bln. **Per capita income**

(1987): $180. **Imports** (1984): $1.3 bln.; partners: USSR 23%, Jap. 21%. **Exports** (1984): $620 mln.; partners: Hong Kong 31%; USSR 10%, Jap. 18%.

Transport: Motor vehicles: in use (1976): 100,000 passenger cars, 200,000 comm. vehicles. **Chief ports:** Ho Chi Minh City, Haiphong, Da Nang.

Communications: Television sets (1984) 2.2 mln. **Radios:** 6 mln. in use (1984). **Daily newspaper circ.** (1984): 8 per 1,000 pop.

Health: Life expectancy at birth (1985): 57.7 male; 62.1 female. **Births** (per 1,000 pop. 1985): 34.3. **Deaths** (per 1,000 pop. 1985): 8.8. **Natural increase** (1985): 2.5%. **Hospital beds** (1985): 208,000. **Physicians** (1985): 17,100. **Infant mortality** (per 1,000 live births 1985): 59.

Education (1978): **Literacy:** 78%.

Major International Organizations: UN (IMF, WHO).

Vietnam's recorded history began in Tonkin before the Christian era. Settled by Viets from central China, Vietnam was held by China, 111 BC-939 AD, and was a vassal state during subsequent periods. Vietnam defeated the armies of Kublai Khan, 1288. Conquest by France began in 1858 and ended in 1884 with the protectorates of Tonkin and Annam in the N. and the colony of Cochin-China in the S.

In 1940 Vietnam was occupied by Japan; nationalist aims gathered force. A number of groups formed the Vietminh (Independence) League, headed by Ho Chi Minh, communist guerrilla leader. In Aug. 1945 the Vietminh forced out Bao Dai, former emperor of Annam, head of a Japan-sponsored regime. France, seeking to reestablish colonial control, battled communist and nationalist forces, 1946-1954, and was finally defeated at Dienbienphu, May 8, 1954. Meanwhile, on July 1, 1949, Bao Dai had formed a State of Vietnam, with himself as chief of state, with French approval. China backed Ho Chi Minh.

A cease-fire accord signed in Geneva July 21, 1954, divided Vietnam along the Ben Hai R. It provided for a buffer zone, withdrawal of French troops from the North and elections to determine the country's future. Under the agreement the communists gained control of territory north of the 17th parallel, 22 provinces with area of 62,000 sq. mi. and 13 million pop., with its capital at Hanoi and Ho Chi Minh as president. South Vietnam came to comprise the 39 southern provinces with approx. area of 65,000 sq. mi. and pop. of 12 million. Some 900,000 North Vietnamese fled to South Vietnam. Neither South Vietnam nor the U.S. signed the agreement.

On Oct. 26, 1955, Ngo Dinh Diem, premier of the interim government of South Vietnam, proclaimed the Republic of Vietnam and became its first president.

The Democratic Republic of Vietnam, established in the North, adopted a constitution Dec. 31, 1959, based on communist principles and calling for reunification of all Vietnam. North Vietnam sought to take over South Vietnam beginning in 1954. Fighting persisted from 1956, with the communist Vietcong, aided by North Vietnam, pressing war in the South and South Vietnam receiving U.S. aid. Northern aid to Vietcong guerrillas was intensified in 1959, and large-scale troop infiltration began in 1964, with Soviet and Chinese arms assistance. Large Northern forces were stationed in border areas of Laos and Cambodia.

A serious political conflict arose in the South in 1963 when Buddhists denounced authoritarianism and brutality. This paved the way for a military coup Nov. 1-2, 1963, which overthrew Diem. Several military coups followed. In elections Sept. 3, 1967, Chief of State Nguyen Van Thieu was chosen president.

In 1964, the U.S. began air strikes against North Vietnam. Beginning in 1965, the raids were stepped up and U.S. troops became combatants. U.S. troop strength in Vietnam, which reached a high of 543,400 in Apr. 1969, was ordered reduced by President Nixon in a series of withdrawals, beginning in June 1969. U.S. bombings were resumed in 1972-73.

A ceasefire agreement was signed in Paris Jan. 27, 1973 by the U.S., North and South Vietnam, and the Vietcong. It was never implemented. U.S. aid was curbed in 1974 by the U.S. Congress. Heavy fighting continued for two years throughout Indochina.

North Vietnamese forces launched attacks against remaining government outposts in the Central Highlands in the first months of 1975. Government retreats turned into a rout, and the Saigon regime surrendered April 30. A Provisional Revolutionary Government assumed control, aided by officials and technicians from Hanoi, and first steps were taken to transform society along communist lines. All businesses and farms were collectivized.

The U.S. accepted over 165,000 Vietnamese refugees, while scores of thousands more sought refuge in other countries.

The war's toll included — Combat deaths: U.S. 47,752; South Vietnam over 200,000; other allied forces 5,225. Civilian casualties were over a million. Displaced war refugees in South Vietnam totaled over 6.5 million.

After the fighting ended, 8 Northern divisions remained stationed in the South. Over 1 million urban residents and 260,000 Montagnards were resettled in the countryside by 1978.

The first National Assembly of both parts of the country met and the country was officially reunited July 2, 1976. The Northern capital, flag, anthem, emblem, and currency were applied to the new state. Nearly all major government posts went to officials of the former Northern government.

Heavy fighting with Cambodia took place, 1977-80, amid mutual charges of aggression and atrocities against civilians. Increasing numbers of Vietnamese civilians, ethnic Chinese, escaped the country, via the sea, or the overland route across Cambodia. Vietnam launched an offensive against Cambodian refugee strongholds along the Thai-Cambodian border in 1985; they also engaged Thai troops.

Relations with China soured as 140,000 ethnic Chinese left Vietnam charging discrimination; China cut off economic aid. Reacting to Vietnam's invasion of Cambodia, China attacked 4 Vietnamese border provinces, Feb., 1979, instigating heavy fighting.

Vietnam announced a package of reforms aimed at reducing central control of the economy in 1987.

Western Samoa

Independent State of Western Samoa

Malotuto'atasi o Samoa i Sisifo

People: Population (1986 est.): 165,000. **Age distrib. (%):** 0–14: 50.4; 15–59: 45.4; 60+: 4.3. **Pop. density:** 146 per sq. mi. **Urban** (1981): 21.2%. **Ethnic groups:** Samoan (Polynesian) 88%, Euronesian (mixed) 10%, European, other Pacific Islanders. **Languages:** Samoan, English both official. **Religions:** Protestants 70%, Roman Catholics 20%.

Geography: Area: 1,133 sq. mi., the size of Rhode Island. **Location:** In the S. Pacific O. **Neighbors:** Nearest are Fiji on W, Tonga on S. **Topography:** Main islands, Savai'i (670 sq. mi.) and Upolu (429 sq. mi.), both ruggedly mountainous, and small islands Manono and Apolima. **Capital:** Apia. **Cities** (1983 est.): Apia 35,000.

Government: Type: Parliamentary democracy. **Head of state:** King Malietoa Tanumafili II; b. Jan. 4, 1913; in office: Jan. 1, 1962. **Head of government:** Prime Min. Va'ai Kolone; in office: Jan. 1986. **Local divisions:** 24 districts.

Economy: Chief crops: Cocoa, copra, bananas. **Other resources:** Hardwoods, fish. **Arable land:** 43%. **Electricity prod.** (1984): 33.7 mln. kwh. **Labor force:** 67% agric.

Finance: Currency: Tala (Mar. 1987: 2.16 = $1 US). **Gross national product** (1980): $128 mln. **Per capita income** (1978): $400. **Imports** (1982): $38 mln.; partners: NZ 32% Austral. 20%, Jap. 13%, U.S. 4%. **Exports** (1982): $9 mln.; partners: NZ 18%, Aust. 9%, US. 61%. **International reserves less gold** (Mar. 1987): $26.4 mln. **Consumer prices** (change in 1986): 5.7%.

Transport: Motor vehicles: in use (1984): 2,000 passenger cars, 2,400 comm. vehicles. **Chief ports:** Apia, Asau.

Communications: Radios: 70,000 in use (1985). **Telephones in use** (1984): 6,000.

Health: Life expectancy at birth (1985): 62.2 male; 65.5 female. **Births** (per 1,000 pop. 1985): 38. **Deaths** (per 1,000 pop. 1985): 8. **Natural increase** (1985): 3.0%. **Hospital beds** (1982): 735. **Physicians** (1981): 63. **Infant mortality** (per 1,000 live births 1985): 28.

Education (1983): **Literacy:** 90%. 95% attend elementary school.

Major International Organizations: UN (IMF, World Bank), Commonwealth of Nations.

Western Samoa was a German colony, 1899 to 1914, when New Zealand landed troops and took over. It became a New Zealand mandate under the League of Nations and, in 1945, a New Zealand UN Trusteeship.

An elected local government took office in Oct. 1959 and the country became fully independent Jan. 1, 1962.

North Yemen

Yemen Arab Republic

al-Jumhuriyat al-Arabiyah al-Yamaniyah

People: Population (1986 est.): 6,339,000. **Pop. density:** 134 per sq. mi. **Ethnic groups:** Arabs, some Negroids. **Languages:** Arabic. **Religions:** Sunni Moslems 50%, Shiite Moslems 50%.

Geography: Area: 75,290 sq. mi., slightly smaller than South Dakota. **Location:** On the southern Red Sea coast of the Arabian Peninsula. **Neighbors:** Saudi Arabia on NE, South Yemen on S. **Topography:** A sandy coastal strip leads to well-watered fertile mountains in interior. **Capital:** Sanaa. **Cities** (1986 est.): Sanaa 427,000.

Government: Type: Republic. **Head of state:** Pres. Ali Abdullah Saleh, b. 1942; in office: July 17, 1978. **Head of government:** Prime Min. Abdul Aziz Abdel Ghani; in office: Nov. 13, 1983. **Local divisions:** 10 governorates. **Defense:** 17.8% of GNP (1984).

Economy: Industries: Textiles, cement. **Chief crops:** Wheat, sorghum, gat, fruits, coffee, cotton. **Minerals:** Salt. **Crude oil reserves** (1978): 370 mln. bbls. **Arable land:** 14%. **Meat prod.** (1984): beef: 14,000 metric tons; lamb: 47,000 metric tons. **Fish catch** (1984): 12,000 metric tons. **Electricity prod.** (1984): 295 mln. kwh. **Labor force:** 74% agric.; 17% ind. and commerce; 9% serv.

Finance: Currency: Rial (Apr. 1987: 8.99 = $1 US). **Gross national product** (1984): $3.9 bln. **Per capita income** (1977-78): $475. **Imports** (1985): $2.9 bln.; partners: Saudi Ar. 20%, Fr. 8%, Jap. 16%. **Exports** (1985): $30 mln.; partners: S. Yemen 23%, Saudi Ar. 8%, Pak. 19%. **National budget** (1984): 1.5 bln. **International reserves less gold** (Mar. 1987): $499 mln. **Consumer prices** (change in 1984): 12.8%.

Transport: Chief ports: Al-Hudaydah, Al-Mukha.

Communications: Television sets: (1985): 28,000. **Radios:** 110,000 in use (1985). **Telephones in use** (1981): 90,350.

Health: Life expectancy at birth (1985): 42.7 male; 44.8 female. **Births** (per 1,000 pop. 1985): 53. **Deaths** (per 1,000 pop. 1985): 19. **Natural increase** (1985): 3.4%. **Hospital beds** (1983): 4,000. **Infant mortality** (per 1,000 live births 1985): 137.

Education (1985): **Literacy:** 20%. **Primary school attendance:** 29%.

Major International Organizations: UN (IMF, WHO), Arab League.

Embassy: 600 New Hampshire Ave. NW 20037; 965-4760.

Yemen's territory once was part of the ancient kindgom of Sheba, or Saba, a prosperous link in trade between Africa and India. A Biblical reference speaks of its gold, spices and precious stones as gifts borne by the Queen of Sheba to King Solomon.

Yemen became independent in 1918, after years of Ottoman Turkish rule, but remained politically and economically backward. Imam Ahmed ruled 1948-1962. The king was reported assassinated Sept. 26, 1962, and a revolutionary group headed by Brig. Gen. Abdullah al-Salal declared the country to be the Yemen Arab Republic.

The Imam Ahmed's heir, the Imam Mohamad al-Badr, fled to the mountains where tribesmen joined royalist forces; internal warfare between them and the republican forces continued. Egypt sent troops and Saudi Arabia military aid to the royalists. About 150,000 people died in the fighting.

There was a bloodless coup Nov. 5, 1967.

In April 1970 hostilities ended with an agreement between Yemen and Saudi Arabia and appointment of several royalists to the Yemen government. There were border skirmishes with forces of South Yemen in 1972-73.

On June 13, 1974, an army group, led by Col. Ibrahim al-Hamidi, seized the government. Hamidi pursued close Saudi and U.S. ties; he was assassinated in 1977.

The People's Democratic Republic of Yemen went to war with Yemen on Feb. 24, 1979. Swift Arab mediation led to a cease-fire and a mutual withdrawal of forces, Mar. 19. An Arab League-sponsored agreement between North and South Yemen on unification of the 2 countries was signed Mar. 29th.

The remittances from 400,000 Yemenis living in Arab oil countries provide most of foreign earnings.

South Yemen

People's Democratic Republic of Yemen

Jumhuriyat al-Yaman ad-Dimuqratiyah ash-Sha'biyan

People: Population (1986 est.): 2,275,000. **Age distrib.** (%): 0–14: 48.1; 15–59: 45.6; 60+: 5.3. **Pop. density:** 18 per sq. mi. **Urban** (1973): 33.3%. **Ethnic groups:** Arabs, 75%, Indians 11%, Somalis 8%, others. **Languages:** Arabic. **Religions:** Sunni Moslem 91%, Christians 4%, Hindus 3.5%.

Geography: Area: 128,559 sq. mi., the size of Nevada. **Location:** On the southern coast of the Arabian Peninsula. **Neighbors:** Yemen on W, Saudi Arabia on N, Oman on E. **Topography:** The entire country is very hot and very dry. A sandy coast rises to mountains which give way to desert sands. **Capital:** Aden. **Cities** (1981 est.): Aden 365,000.

Government: Type: Republic. **Head of state:** Chairman, Council of Ministers and President: Haidar Abu Bakr al-Attas; in office: Nov. 6, 1986. **Head of Government:** Prime Min. Yasin Said Numan; in office: Feb. 8, 1986. **Local divisions:** 6 governorates. **Defense:** 17.4% of GNP (1983).

Economy: Industries: Transshipment. **Chief crops:** Cotton (main export), grains. **Meat prod.** (1984): sheep: 1 mln.; goats: 1.3 mln. **Fish catch** (1983): 74,000 metric tons. **Electricity prod.** (1983) 280 mln. kwh. **Labor force:** 43.8% agric.; 28% ind. and commerce; 28% serv.

Finance: Currency: Dinar (Mar. 1987: 1.00 = $2.89 US). **Gross national product** (1984): $1 bln. **Per capita income** (1977): $310. **Imports** (1983) $756 mln.; partners: UAE 28%, Kuw. 9%, Jap. 6%. **Exports** (1983): $30 mln.; partners: It. 11%, UAE 22%. **International reserves less gold** (Jan. 1986): $197 mln. **Gold:** 42,000 oz t. **Consumer prices** (change in 1983): 11%.

Transport: Motor vehicles: in use (1980): 12,200 passenger cars, 15,300 comm. vehicles. **Chief ports:** Aden.

Communications: Television sets: 39,000 in use (1985). **Radios:** 150,000 in use (1985). **Daily newspaper circ.** (1985): 10 per 1,000 pop.

Health: Life expectancy at birth (1985): 45.3 male; 47.7 female. **Births** (per 1,000 pop. 1985): 47.6. **Deaths** (per 1,000 pop. 1985): 18.9. **Natural increase** (1985): 2.8%. **Hospital beds** (1984): 3,805. **Physicians** (1984): 406. **Infant mortality rate** (per 1,000 live births in 1985): 131.

Major International Organizations: UN (IMF, WHO), Arab League.

Education (1980): **Literacy:** 39%. About 90% attend primary school.

Aden, mentioned in the Bible, has been a port for trade in incense, spice and silk between the East and West for 2,000 years. British rule began in 1839. Aden provided Britain with a controlling position at the southern entrance to the Red Sea.

A war for independence began in 1963. The National Liberation Front (NLF) and the Egypt-supported Front for the Liberation of Occupied South Yemen, waged a guerrilla war against the British and local dynastic rulers. The 2 groups vied with each other for control. The NLF won out. Independence came Nov. 30, 1967. In 1969, the left wing of the NLF seized power and inaugurated a thorough nationalization of the economy and regimentation of daily life.

The new government broke off relations with the U.S. and nationalized some foreign firms.

In 1972-73 there were border skirmishes with forces of the Yemen Arab Republic. South Yemen aided leftist guerrillas in neighboring Oman. Relations with Saudi Arabia later improved. S. Yemen troops fought in Ethiopia against Eritrean rebels in 1978.

Pres. Salem Robaye Ali, who had tried to improve relations with Yemen, Saudi Arabia, Oman, and the U.S., was executed after a bloody coup June 1978. N. Yemen, Egypt, and Saudi Arabia froze ties with S. Yemen in July.

South Yemen went to war with North Yemen on Feb. 24, 1979. Swift Arab mediation led to a cease-fire and a mutual withdrawal of forces, Mar. 19th. An Arab League-sponsored agreement between North and South Yemen on unification of the 2 countries was signed Mar. 29th.

The government was overthrown in a bloody coup on Jan. 13, 1986, which escalated into civil war. Some 10,000 were killed and 12,000 fled the country before order was restored.

The Port of Aden is the country's most valuable resource.

Socotra, the largest island in the Arabian Sea, Kamaran, an island in the Red Sea near the coast of North Yemen, and Perim, an island in the strait between the Gulf of Aden and the Red Sea, are controlled by South Yemen.

Yugoslavia

Socialist Federal Republic of Yugoslavia

Socijalistička Federativna Republika Jugoslavija

People: Population (1986 est.): 23,284,000. **Age distrib.** (%): 0–14: 23.5; 15-59: 63.7; 60+: 12.8. **Pop. density:** 234 per sq. mi. **Urban** (1978): 46.5%. **Ethnic groups:** Serbs 36%, Croats 20%, Bosnian Moslems 9%, Slovenes 8%, Macedonians 6%, Albanians 8%. **Languages:** Serbo-Croatian, Macedonian, Slovenian (all official), Albanian. **Religions:** Orthodox 41%, Roman Catholic 32%, Moslem 12%.

Geography: Area: 98,766 sq. mi., the size of Wyoming. **Location:** On the Adriatic coast of the Balkan Peninsula in SE Europe. **Neighbors:** Italy on W, Austria, Hungary on N, Romania, Bulgaria on E, Greece, Albania on S. **Topography:** The Dinaric Alps run parallel to the Adriatic coast, which is lined by offshore islands. Plains stretch across N and E river basins. S and NW are mountainous. **Capital:** Belgrade. **Cities** (1980 est.): Belgrade 1,300,000; Zagreb 700,000; Skopje 440,000; Sarajevo 400,000; Ljubljana 300,000.

Government: Type: Federal republic. **Head of state:** Pres. Sinan Hasani; in office: May 15, 1986. **Head of government:** Prime Min. Branko Mikulic; in office: May 15, 1985. **Head of Communist Party:** Milanko Renovica; in office: June 28, 1986. **Local divisions:** 6 republics, 2 autonomous provinces. **Defense:** 3.7% of GNP (1983).

Economy: Industries: Steel, wood products, cement, textiles, tourism. **Chief crops:** Corn, grains, tobacco, sugar beets. **Minerals:** Antimony, bauxite, lead, mercury, coal, iron, copper, chrome, zinc, salt. **Crude oil reserves** (1985): 273 mln. bbls. **Arable land:** 33%. **Meat prod.** (1985): cattle: 5 mln.; pigs: 7.8 mln.; sheep: 7.6 mln. **Fish catch:** (1983): 79,000 metric tons. **Electricity prod.** (1984): 71.5 bln. kwh. **Crude steel prod.** (1985): 4.4 mln. metric tons. **Labor force:** 30% agric.; 70% ind.

Finance: Currency: Dinar (Mar. 1987: 507 = $1 US). **Gross national product** (1984): $46.3 bln. **Per capita income:** $3,109. **Imports** (1985): $12.2 bln.; partners: W. Ger. 15%, USSR 19%, It. 8%, U.S. 6%. **Exports** (1985): $10.7 bln.; partners: USSR 27%, It. 9%, W. Ger. 8%, Czech. 7%. **Tourists** (1984): $1 bln. receipts. **National budget** (1983): $7.6 bln. expenditures. **International reserves less gold** (Mar. 1987): $1.2 bln. **Gold:** 1.86 mln. oz t. **Consumer prices** change in 1985): 74.4%.

Transport: Railway traffic (1985): 11.9 bln. passenger-km; 28.7 bln. net ton-km. **Motor vehicles:** in use (1985): 2.8 mln. passenger cars, 264,000 comm. vehicles. **Civil aviation** (1985): 6.3 bln. passenger-km; 92.5 mln. freight ton-km. **Chief ports:** Rijeka, Split, Dubrovnik.

Communications: Television sets: 4.0 mln. in use (1983). **Radios:** 4.6 mln. licensed (1985). **Telephones in use** (1984): 3.0 mln. **Daily newspaper circ.** (1984): 104 per 1,000 pop.

Health: Life expectancy at birth (1983): 68 male; 73 female. **Births** (per 1,000 pop. 1985): 16. **Deaths** (per 1,000 pop. 1985): 9. **Natural increase** (1985): .7%. **Hospital beds** (1984): 138,786. **Physicians** (1984): 44,715. **Infant mortality** (per 1,000 live births 1985): 30.

Education (1985): **Literacy:** 90%. Almost all attend primary school.

Major International Organizations: UN (IMF, World Bank, GATT).

Embassy: 2410 California St. NW 20008; 462-6566.

Serbia, which had since 1389 been a vassal principality of Turkey, was established as an independent kingdom by the Treaty of Berlin, 1878. Montenegro, independent since 1389, also obtained international recognition in 1878. After the Balkan wars Serbia's boundaries were enlarged by the annexation of Old Serbia and Macedonia, 1913.

When the Austro-Hungarian empire collapsed after World War I, the Kingdom of the Serbs, Croats, and Slovenes was formed from the former provinces of Croatia, Dalmatia, Bosnia, Herzegovina, Slovenia, Voyvodina and the independent state of Montenegro. The name was later changed to Yugoslavia.

Nazi Germany invaded in 1941. Many Yugoslav partisan troops continued to operate. Among these were the Chetniks led by Draja Mikhailovich, who fought other partisans led by Josip Broz, known as Marshal Tito. Tito, backed by the USSR and Britain from 1943, was in control by the time the Germans had been driven from Yugoslavia in 1945. Mikhailovich was executed July 17, 1946, by the Tito regime.

A constituent assembly proclaimed Yugoslavia a republic Nov. 29, 1945. It became a federated republic Jan. 31, 1946, and Marshal Tito, a communist, became head of the government.

The Stalin policy of dictating to all communist nations was rejected by Tito. He accepted economic aid and military equipment from the U.S. and received aid in foreign trade also from France and Great Britain. Tito also supported the liberal government of Czechoslovakia in 1968 before the Russian invasion.

A separatist movement among Croatians, 2d to the Serbs in numbers, brought arrests and a change of leaders in the Croatian Republic in Jan. 1972. Violence by extreme Croatian nationalists and fears of Soviet political intervention have led to restrictions on political and intellectual dissent, which had previously been freer than in most East European countries. Serbians, Montenegrins, and Macedonians use Cyrillic, Croatians and Slovenians use Latin letters. Croatia and Slovenia have been the most prosperous republics.

Most industry is socialized and private enterprise is restricted to small-scale production. Since 1952 workers are guaranteed a basic wage and a share in cooperative profits. Management of industrial enterprises is handled by workers' councils. Farmland is 85% privately owned but farms are restricted to 25 acres.

Beginning in 1965, reforms designed to decentralize the administration of economic development and to force industries to produce more efficiently in competition with foreign producers were introduced.

Yugoslavia has developed considerable trade with Western Europe. Money earned by Yugoslavs working temporarily in Western Europe helps pay for imports.

Pres. Tito died May 4, 1980; with his death, the post as head of the Collective Presidency and also that as head of the League of Communists became a rotating system of succession among the members representing each republic and autonomous province.

Zaire

Republic of Zaire

République du Zaïre

People: Population (1986 est.): 31,333,000. **Pop. density:** 34 per sq. mi. **Urban** (1985): 44.2%. **Ethnic groups:** Bantu tribes 80%, over 200 other tribes. **Languages:** French (official), Bantu dialects. **Religions:** Christian 70%, Moslem 10%.

Geography: Area: 905,563 sq. mi., one-fourth the size of the U.S. **Location:** In central Africa. **Neighbors:** Congo on W, Central African Republic, Sudan on N, Uganda, Rwanda, Burundi, Tanzania on E, Zambia, Angola on S. **Topography:** Zaire includes the bulk of the Zaire (Congo) R. Basin. The vast central region is a low-lying plateau covered by rain forest. Mountainous terraces in the W, savannas in the S and SE, grasslands toward the N, and the high Ruwenzori Mtns. on the E surround the central region. A short strip of territory borders the Atlantic O. The Zaire R. is 2,718 mi. long. **Capital:** Kinshasa. **Cities** (1985 est.): Kinshasa 3,000,000; Kananga 601,239.

Government: Type: Republic with strong presidential authority. **Head of state:** Pres. Mobutu Sese Seko; b. Oct. 14, 1930; in office: Nov. 25, 1965. **Local divisions:** 9 regions, Kinshasa. **Defense:** 1.5% of GNP (1983).

Economy: Chief crops: Coffee, rice, sugar cane, bananas, plantains, manioc, mangoes, tea, cocoa, palm oil. **Minerals:** Cobalt (60% of world reserves), copper, cadmium, gold, silver, tin, germanium, zinc, iron, manganese, uranium, radium. **Crude oil reserves** (1985): 125 mln. bbls. **Other resources:** Forests, rubber, ivory. **Arable land:** 50%. **Meat prod.** (1984): pork: 28,000 metric tons; lamb: 9,000 metric tons. **Fish catch** (1983): 102,000 metric tons. **Electricity prod.** (1984): 4.5 bln. kwh. **Labor force:** 75% agric..

Finance: Currency: Zaire (Mar. 1987: 97.04 = $1 US). **Gross national product** (1984): $4.2 bln. **Per capita income** (1975): $127. **Imports** (1986): $872 mln.; partners: Belg. 22%, U.S. 10%, W. Ger. 10%, Fra. 13%. **Exports** (1986): $1.0 bln.; partners: Belg.-Lux. 31%, U.S. 36%. **International reserves less gold** (Mar. 1987): $146 mln. **Gold:** 472,000 oz t. **Consumer prices** (change in 1986): 40.7%.

Transport: Railway traffic (1985): 291 mln. passenger-km; 1.9 bln. net ton-km. **Motor vehicles:** in use (1982): 89,000 passenger cars, 16,000 comm. vehicles. **Civil aviation** (1985): 355 mln. passenger-km. 30.5 mln. freight ton-km. **Chief ports:** Matadi, Boma.

Communications: Television sets: 13,000 in use (1985). **Radios:** 500,000 mln. in use (1985). **Telephones in use** (1983): 27,000. **Daily newspaper circ.** (1984): 1 per 1,000 pop.

Health: Life expectancy at birth (1985): 48.3 male; 51.7 female. **Births** (per 1,000 pop. 1985): 45.2. **Deaths** (per 1,000 pop. 1985): 15.8. **Natural increase** (1985): 2.9%. **Hospital beds** (1982): 74,000. **Physicians** (1982): 2,000. **Infant mortality** (per 1,000 live births 1985): 106.

Education (1985): **Literacy:** males 78%, females 44%.

Major International Organizations: UN and all of its specialized agencies, OAU.

Embassy: 1800 New Hampshire Ave. NW 20008; 234-7690.

The earliest inhabitants of Zaire may have been the pygmies, followed by Bantus from the E and Nilotic tribes from the N. The large Bantu Bakongo kingdom ruled much of Zaire and Angola when Portuguese explorers visited in the 15th century.

Leopold II, king of the Belgians, formed an international group to exploit the Congo in 1876. In 1877 Henry M. Stanley explored the Congo and in 1878 the king's group sent him back to organize the region and win over the native chiefs. The Conference of Berlin, 1884-85, organized the Congo Free State with Leopold as king and chief owner. Exploitation of native laborers on the rubber plantations caused international criticism and led to granting of a colonial charter, 1908.

Belgian and Congolese leaders agreed Jan. 27, 1960, that the Congo would become independent June 30. In the first general elections, May 31, the National Congolese movement of Patrice Lumumba won 35 of 137 seats in the National Assembly. He was appointed premier June 21, and formed a coalition cabinet.

Widespread violence caused Europeans and others to flee. The UN Security Council Aug. 9, 1960, called on Belgium to withdraw its troops and sent a UN contingent. President Kasavubu removed Lumumba as premier. Lumumba fought for control backed by Ghana, Guinea and India; he was murdered in 1961.

The last UN troops left the Congo June 30, 1964, and Moise Tshombe became president.

On Sept. 7, 1964, leftist rebels set up a "People's Republic" in Stanleyville. Tshombe hired foreign mercenaries and sought to rebuild the Congolese Army. In Nov. and Dec. 1964 rebels slew scores of white hostages and thousands of Congolese; Belgian paratroops, dropped from U.S. transport planes, rescued hundreds. By July 1965 the rebels had lost their effectiveness.

In 1965 Gen. Joseph D. Mobutu was named president. He later changed his name to Mobutu Sese Seko. The country changed its name to Republic of Zaire on Oct. 27, 1971; in 1972 Zairians with Christian names were ordered to change them to African names.

In 1969-74, political stability under Mobutu was reflected in improved economic conditions. In 1974 most foreign-owned businesses were ordered sold to Zaire citizens, but in 1977 the government asked the original owners to return.

In 1977, a force of Zairians invaded Shaba province (Katanga) from Angola. Zaire repelled the attack, with the aid of Egyptian pilots and Moroccan troops flown in by France. But many European mining experts failed to return after a 2d unsuccessful invasion from Angola in May 1978.

Serious economic difficulties, amid charges of corruption by government officials, have plagued Zaire in the 1980s.

Zambia

Republic of Zambia

People: Population (1986 est.): 7,054,000. **Age distrib.** (%): 0–14: 48.2; 15–59: 47.8; 60+: 4.0. **Pop. density:** 24 per sq. mi. **Urban** (1984): 40%. **Ethnic groups:** Mostly Bantu tribes. **Languages:** English (official), Bantu dialects. **Religions:** Predominantly animists, Roman Catholics 21%, Protestant, Hindu, Muslim minorities.

Geography: Area: 290,586 sq. mi., larger than Texas. **Location:** In southern central Africa. **Neighbors:** Zaire on N, Tanzania, Malawi, Mozambique on E, Zimbabwe, Namibia on S, Angola on W. **Topography:** Zambia is mostly high plateau country covered with thick forests, and drained by several important rivers, including the Zambezi. **Capital:** Lusaka. **Cities** (1984 est.): Lusaka 538,000; Kitwe 314,794; Ndola 282,439.

Government: Type: Republic. **Head of state:** Pres. Kenneth David Kaunda; b. Apr. 28, 1924; in office: Oct. 24, 1964. **Head of government:** Prime Min. Kebby Musokotwane; in office: Apr. 24, 1985. **Local divisions:** 9 provinces. **Defense:** 20% of GDP (1984 est).

Economy: Chief crops: Corn, tobacco, peanuts, cotton, sugar. **Minerals:** Cobalt, copper, zinc, gold, lead, vanadium, manganese, coal. **Other resources:** Rubber, ivory. **Arable land:** 7%. **Meat prod.** (1980): beef: 24,000 metric tons; pork: 7,000 metric tons. **Fish catch** (1983): 67,000 metric tons. **Electricity prod.** (1984): 10.0 bln. kwh. **Labor force:** 60% agric.; 40% ind. and commerce.

Finance: Currency: Kwacha (Mar. 1987: 9.00 = $1 US). **Gross national product** (1984): $2.6 bln. **Per capita income** (1982): $570. **Imports** (1985): $654 mln.; partners: UK 26%, Saudi Ar. 18%, W. Ger. 18%, U.S. 9%. **Exports** (1985): $1.5 bln.; partners: Jap. 19%, Fr. 15%, UK 13%, U.S. 10%, W. Ger. 9%. **National budget** (1982): $510 mln. revenues; $750 mln. expenditures. **International reserves less gold** (Jan. 1987): $70.3 mln. **Gold:** 3,000 oz t. **Consumer prices** (change in 1985): 37.4%.

Transport: Motor vehicles: in use (1982): 105,000 passenger cars, 97,000 comm. vehicles. **Civil aviation** (1984): 552 mln. passenger-km.

Communications: Television sets: 100,000 in use (1985). **Radios:** 200,000 in use (1985). **Telephones in use** (1982): 32,000. **Daily newspaper circ.** (1984): 16 per 1,000 pop.

Health: Life expectancy at birth (1984): 47 yrs. **Births** (per 1,000 pop. 1985): 47.4. **Deaths** (per 1,000 pop. 1985): 15.4. **Natural increase** (1985): 3.2%. **Hospital beds** (1982): 21,257. **Physicians** (1982): 839. **Infant mortality** (per 1,000 live births 1985): 107.

Education (1984): **Literacy:** 54%. **Attendance:** less than 50% in grades 1–7.

Major International Organizations: UN (GATT, IMF, WHO), OAU, Commonwealth of Nations.

Embassy: 2419 Massachusetts Ave. NW 20008; 265-9717.

As Northern Rhodesia, the country was under the administration of the South Africa Company, 1889 until 1924, when the office of governor was established, and, subsequently, a legislature. The country became an independent republic within the Commonwealth Oct. 24, 1964.

After the white government of Rhodesia declared its independence from Britain Nov. 11, 1965, relations between Zambia and Rhodesia became strained and use of their jointly owned railroad was disputed.

Britain gave Zambia an extra $12 million aid in 1966 after imposing an oil embargo on Rhodesia, and Zambia set up a temporary airlift to carry copper out from its mines and gasoline in. In Aug. 1968 a 1,058-mi. pipeline was completed, bringing oil from Tanzania. In 1973 a truck road to carry copper to Tanzania's port of Dar es Salaam was completed with U.S. aid. A railroad, built with Chinese aid across Tanzania, reached the Zambian border in 1974.

As part of a program of government participation in major industries, a government corporation in 1970 took over 51% of the ownership of 2 foreign-owned copper mining companies. Privately-held land and other enterprises were nationalized in 1975, as were all newspapers. In the 1980s, decline in copper prices has hurt the economy and severe drought has caused famine.

Zimbabwe

People: Population (1986 est.): 8,984,000. **Age distrib.** (%): 0–14: 50.9; 15–59: 46.2; 60+: 2.9. **Pop. density:** 58 per sq. mi. **Urban** (1985): 25%. **Ethnic groups:** Shona 80%, Ndebele 19%. **Languages:** English (official), Shona, Sindebele. **Religions:** Predominantly traditional tribal beliefs, Christian minority.

Geography: Area: 150,803 sq. mi., slightly larger than Montana. **Location:** In southern Africa. **Neighbors:** Zambia on N,

Botswana on W, S. Africa on S, Mozambique on E. **Topography:** Rhodesia is high plateau country, rising to mountains on eastern border, sloping down on the other borders. **Capital:** Harare. **Cities** (1983 est.): Harare (met.) 681,000; Bulawayo (met.) 429,000.

Government: Type: Parliamentary democracy. **Head of state:** Pres. Rev. Cannan Banana, b. Mar. 5, 1936; in office: Apr. 18, 1980. **Head of government:** Prime Min. Robert G. Mugabe; b. Apr. 14, 1928; in office: Apr. 18, 1980. **Local divisions:** 8 provinces. **Defense:** 15.3% of govt. budget (1983).

Economy: Industries: Clothing, chemicals, light industries. **Chief crops:** Tobacco, sugar, cotton, corn, wheat. **Minerals:** Chromium, gold, nickel, asbestos, copper, iron, coal. **Arable land:** 7%. **Meat prod.** (1984): cattle: 5.5 mln.; goats: 1.1 mln. **Electricity prod.** (1984): 4.5 bln. kwh. **Crude steel prod.** (1981): 691,000 metric tons. **Labor force:** 35% agric.; 30% ind. and commerce; 20% serv.; 15% gvt.

Finance: Currency: Dollar (Mar. 1987: 1.00 = $.61 US). **Gross domestic product** (1984): $6 bln. **Per capita income** (1983): $640. **Imports** (1984): $891 mln.; partners: UK 10%, So. Afr. 27%, U.S. 7%, W. Ger. 7%. **Exports** (1984): $1.1 bln.; partners: UK 7%, So. Afr. 22%, W. Ger. 8%. **Consumer prices** (change in 1986): 14.3%.

Transport: Railway traffic (1984): 6.4 bln. net ton-km. **Motor vehicles:** in use (1984): 248,000 passenger cars, 27,000 comm. vehicles.

Communications: Television sets: 120,000 in use (1985). **Radios:** 375,000 in use (1985). **Telephones in use** (1983): 242,252. **Daily newspaper circ.** (1985): 23 per 1,000 pop.

Health: Life expectancy at birth (1983): 53.0 male; 60.0 female. **Births** (per 1,000 pop. 1985): 53.0. **Deaths** (per 1,000 pop. 1985): 13. **Natural increase** (1985): 4.0%. **Health** (1983): 161 hospitals, 438 rural clinics. **Infant mortality** (per 1,000 live births 1985): 77.

Education (1985): **Literacy:** 50%. **Attendance:** 90% primary, 15% secondary for Africans; higher for whites, Asians.

Major International Organizations: UN (IMF, World Bank), OAU, Commonwealth of Nations.

Embassy: 2852 McGill Terrace NW 20008; 332-7100.

Britain took over the area as Southern Rhodesia in 1923 from the British South Africa Co. (which, under Cecil Rhodes, had conquered the area by 1897) and granted internal self-government. Under a 1961 constitution, voting was restricted to maintain whites in power. On Nov. 11, 1965, Prime Min. Ian D. Smith announced his country's unilateral declaration of independence. Britain termed the act illegal, and demanded Rhodesia broaden voting rights to provide for eventual rule by the majority Africans.

Urged by Britain, the UN imposed sanctions, including embargoes on oil shipments to Rhodesia. Some oil and gasoline reached Rhodesia, however, from South Africa and Mozambique, before the latter became independent in 1975. In May 1968, the UN Security Council ordered a trade embargo.

A new constitution came into effect, Mar. 2, 1970, providing for a republic with a president and prime minister. The election law effectively prevented full black representation through income tax requirements.

A proposed British-Rhodesian settlement was dropped in May 1972 when a British commission reported most Rhodesian blacks opposed it. Intermittent negotiations between the government and various black nationalist groups failed to prevent increasing skirmishes. By mid-1978, over 6,000 soldiers and civilians had been killed. Rhodesian troops battled guerrillas within Mozambique and Zambia. An "internal settlement" signed Mar. 1978 in which Smith and 3 popular black leaders share control until transfer of power to the black majority was rejected by guerrilla leaders.

In the country's first universal-franchise election, Apr. 21, 1979, Bishop Abel Muzorewa's United African National Council gained a bare majority control of the black-dominated parliament. Britain, 1979, began efforts to normalize its relationship with Zimbabwe. A British cease-fire was accepted by all parties, Dec. 5th. Independence was finally achieved Apr. 18, 1980.

Population Projections, by Region and for Selected Countries: 1990 to 2025

Source: Population Division of the United Nations

(in millions)

Region and Country	1990	1995	2000	2025
World, total	**5,248.5**	**5,679.3**	**6,127.1**	**8,177.1**
More developed[1]	1,208.8	1,242.8	1,275.7	1,396.7
Less developed[1]	4,039.7	4,436.4	4,851.5	6,780.4
Africa	**645.3**	**753.2**	**877.4**	**1,642.9**
Eastern Africa[2]	189.7	224.7	266.2	531.4
Burundi	5.3	6.1	7.0	11.0
Ethiopia	42.7	50.1	58.4	112.0
Kenya	25.4	31.4	38.5	82.9
Madagascar	11.6	13.4	15.6	29.7
Malawi	8.3	9.8	11.7	23.2
Mozambique	16.2	18.8	21.8	39.7
Rwanda	7.3	8.8	10.6	22.2
Somalia	5.9	6.2	7.1	13.2
Uganda	18.8	22.5	26.8	52.3
Tanzania	27.0	32.5	39.1	83.8
Zambia	7.9	9.4	11.2	23.8
Zimbabwe	10.5	12.6	15.1	32.7
Middle Africa[2]	71.9	83.0	96.1	183.5
Angola	10.0	11.5	13.2	24.5
Cameroon	11.1	12.6	14.4	25.2
Cen. African Rep.	2.9	3.3	3.7	6.7
Chad	5.7	6.4	7.3	13.1
Zaire	38.4	44.8	52.4	104.4
Northern Africa[2]	143.8	164.3	185.7	295.0
Algeria	26.0	30.5	35.2	57.3
Egypt	52.7	58.9	65.2	97.4
Libya	4.3	5.2	6.1	11.1
Morocco	27.6	31.9	36.3	59.9
Sudan	24.9	28.7	32.9	55.4
Tunisia	8.1	8.9	9.7	13.6
Southern Africa[2]	42.3	48.1	54.5	90.7
South Africa	36.8	41.6	46.9	76.3
Western Africa[2]	197.6	233.1	275.0	542.4
Benin	4.7	5.4	6.4	12.2
Burkina Faso[3]	8.0	9.1	10.5	19.5
Côte d'Ivoire[4]	11.5	13.4	15.6	28.1
Ghana	15.9	18.7	21.9	37.7
Guinea	6.1	7.0	7.9	13.9
Mali	9.3	10.7	12.4	21.4

Region and Country	1990	1995	2000	2025
Niger	7.1	8.3	9.8	18.9
Nigeria	113.3	135.5	161.9	338.1
Senegal	7.5	8.7	10.0	18.9
Togo	3.4	3.9	4.6	9.0
Latin America	**453.2**	**501.3**	**550.0**	**786.6**
Caribbean[2]	34.6	37.7	40.8	57.7
Cuba	10.5	11.2	11.7	13.6
Dominican Rep.	7.0	7.7	8.4	12.2
Haiti	7.5	8.6	9.9	18.3
Middle America[2]	119.7	134.4	149.6	222.6
El Salvador	6.5	7.5	8.7	15.0
Guatemala	9.7	11.1	12.7	21.7
Honduras	5.1	6.0	7.0	13.3
Mexico	89.0	99.2	109.2	154.1
Nicaragua	3.9	4.5	5.3	9.2
Temperate South America[2]	49.1	52.3	55.5	70.1
Argentina	32.9	35.1	37.2	47.4
Chile	13.1	14.0	14.9	18.8
Uruguay	3.1	3.2	3.4	3.9
Tropical South America[2]	249.8	276.9	304.1	436.3
Bolivia	7.3	8.4	9.7	18.3
Brazil	150.4	165.1	179.5	245.8
Colombia	31.8	34.9	38.0	51.7
Ecuador	10.9	12.7	14.6	25.7
Paraguay	4.2	4.8	5.4	8.6
Peru	22.3	25.1	28.0	41.0
Venezuela	21.3	24.2	27.2	42.8
Northern America[2]	**275.2**	**286.8**	**297.7**	**347.3**
Canada	27.1	28.3	29.4	34.4
United States	248.0	258.3	268.1	312.7
East Asia[2]	**1,317.2**	**1,390.4**	**1,470.0**	**1,696.1**
China: Mainland	1,119.6	1,184.2	1,255.7	1,460.1
Hong Kong	6.1	6.6	6.9	7.9
Japan	122.7	125.1	127.7	127.6
Korea, Dem. People's Rep. of	22.4	24.9	27.3	37.6
Korea, Rep. of	43.8	46.8	49.5	58.6

Region and Country	1990	1995	2000	2025
South Asia.	**1,740.2**	**1,909.4**	**2,073.7**	**2,770.6**
Eastern So. Asia[2]	440.4	460.8	519.7	684.7
Burma	44.5	49.8	55.2	82.2
Indonesia	178.4	191.9	204.5	255.3
Kampuchea	8.4	9.2	9.9	12.5
Laos	5.0	5.6	6.2	9.2
Malaysia	17.3	19.1	20.6	26.9
Philippines	61.4	68.3	74.8	102.3
Singapore	2.7	2.9	3.0	3.2
Thailand	56.2	61.1	66.1	86.3
Vietnam	65.4	71.7	78.1	105.1
Middle So. Asia[2]	1,169.9	1,279.9	1,385.7	1,815.9
Afghanistan	19.3	21.7	24.2	35.9
Bangladesh	115.2	130.3	145.8	219.4
India	831.9	899.1	961.5	1,188.5
Iran	51.8	58.7	65.5	96.2
Nepal	18.5	20.7	23.0	33.9
Pakistan	113.3	128.0	142.6	212.8
Sri Lanka	18.0	19.5	20.8	26.2
Western So. Asia[2]	129.9	148.7	168.3	270.0
Iraq	18.5	21.6	24.9	42.7
Israel	4.7	5.0	5.4	7.0
Jordan	4.3	5.2	6.4	13.4
Lebanon	3.0	3.3	3.6	5.2
Saudi Arabia	13.5	16.1	18.9	33.5
Syria	12.8	15.3	18.1	32.3
Turkey	56.0	62.4	68.5	99.3
Yemen Arab Rep.	7.5	8.6	9.9	16.5
Europe (excl. Soviet Union)	**499.5**	**506.5**	**513.1**	**526.9**
Eastern Europe	115.7	118.2	121.0	131.2
Bulgaria	9.4	9.6	9.7	10.2
Czechoslovakia	16.0	16.3	16.8	18.8
German Dem. Rep.	16.6	16.5	16.6	16.1
Hungary	10.8	10.8	10.9	10.9
Poland	39.0	40.2	41.4	45.9
Romania	23.9	24.8	25.6	29.2
Northern Europe[2]	82.6	83.0	83.4	83.6
Denmark	5.2	5.1	5.1	4.8
Finland	4.9	5.0	5.0	4.8
Ireland	3.8	4.0	4.2	5.2
Norway	4.2	4.2	4.2	4.3
Sweden	8.2	8.2	8.1	7.5
United Kingdom	55.8	56.0	56.2	56.4
Southern Europe[2]	146.4	150.0	153.1	162.8
Albania	3.4	3.8	4.1	5.8
Greece	10.2	10.5	10.7	11.8
Italy	57.4	57.9	58.2	56.9
Portugal	10.4	10.7	11.0	11.9
Spain	40.5	42.0	43.4	49.2
Yugoslavia	23.9	24.6	25.2	26.6
Western Europe[2]	154.8	155.3	155.6	149.3
Austria	7.5	7.5	7.5	7.3
Belgium	9.9	9.9	9.9	9.8
France	55.4	56.3	57.1	58.5
Germany, Fed. Rep. of	60.7	60.3	59.8	53.8
Netherlands	14.7	14.9	15.0	14.6
Switzerland	6.2	6.0	5.9	4.9
Soviet Union	**291.3**	**303.1**	**314.8**	**367.1**
Oceania[2]	**26.7**	**28.5**	**30.4**	**39.5**
Australia	16.7	17.7	18.7	23.5
New Zealand	3.4	3.6	3.7	4.2
Papua New Guinea	4.2	4.8	5.3	8.2

(1) Regions. (2) Includes countries not shown separately. (3) Formerly Upper Volta. (4) Ivory Coast.

Population of World's Largest Cities

Source: U.S. Bureau of the Census

The table below represents one attempt at comparing the world's largest cities. The cities are defined as population clusters of continuous built-up areas with a population density of a least 5,000 persons per square mile. The boundary of the city was determined by examining detailed maps of each city in conjunction with the most recent official population statistics. Exclaves of areas exceeding the minimum population density were added to the city if the intervening gap was less than one mile. To the extent practical, nonresidential areas such as parks, airports, industrial complexes and water were excluded from the area reported for each city, thus making the population density reflective of the concentrations in the residential portions of the city. By using a consistent definition for the city, it is possible to make comparisons of the cities on the basis of total population, area, and population density.

Political and administrative boundaries were disregarded in determining the population of the city. Berlin includes both East and West Berlin, as well as population from East Germany. Detroit includes Windsor, Canada.

The population of each city was projected based on the proportion each city was of its country total at the time of the last 2 censuses and projected country populations. The areal expansion of the city was not projected, hence density figures are valid only for 1985. Figures in the table below may differ from city population figures elsewhere in the World Almanac because of different methods of determining population.

City, Country	1985 (thousands)	2000 (thousands projected)	Area (sq. mi.)	Density (pop per sq. mi.)
Tokyo-Yokahama, Japan	25,434	29,971	1,089	23,356
Mexico City, Mexico	16,901	27,872	522	32,377
Sao Paolo, Brazil	14,911	25,354	451	33,062
New York, U.S.	14,598	14,648	1,274	11,458
Seoul, South Korea	13,665	21,976	342	39,956
Osaka-Kobe-Kyoto, Japan	13,562	14,333	495	27,397
Buenos Aires, Argentina	10,750	12,911	535	20,093
Calcutta, India	10,462	14,088	209	50,057
Bombay, India	10,137	15,357	95	10,670
Rio de Janeiro, Brazil	10,116	14,169	260	38,907
Moscow, USSR	9,873	11,121	379	26,050
Los Angeles, U.S.	9,638	10,714	1,110	8,682
London, U.K.	9,442	8,574	874	10,803
Paris, France	8,633	8,803	432	19,983
Cairo, Egypt	8,595	12,512	104	82,644
Manila, Philippines	8,485	12,846	188	45,132
Jakarta, Indonesia	8,122	12,804	76	10,686
Essen, W. Germany	7,604	7,239	704	10,801
Teheran, Iran	7,354	14,251	112	65,660
Delhi, India	6,993	11,849	138	50,673
Shanghai, China	6,698	7,540	78	85,871
Chicago, U.S.	6,511	6,568	762	8,544
Karachi, Pakistan	6,351	11,299	190	33,426
Lagos, Nigeria	6,054	12,528	56	10,810
Beijing, China	5,608	5,993	151	37,139
Taipei, Taiwan	5,550	8,516	138	40,217
Lima, Peru	5,447	9,241	120	45,392
Hong Kong	5,415	5,956	20	270,750
Istanbul, Turkey	5,389	8,875	165	32,661
Bangkok, Thailand	4,998	7,587	102	49,000
Madras, India	4,983	7,384	115	43,330
Bogota, Colombia	4,711	7,935	79	59,633
Santiago, Chile	4,700	6,294	128	36,719
Milan, Italy	4,635	4,839	344	13,474
Tianjin, China	4,622	5,298	49	94,327
Leningrad, USSR	4,569	4,738	139	32,871
Nagoya, Japan	4,452	5,303	307	14,502
Manchester, U.K.	4,151	3,827	357	11,627
Madrid, Spain	4,137	5,104	66	62,682
Shenyang, China	4,086	4,684	39	104,769
Philadelphia, U.S.	4,025	3,979	471	8,546
Pusan, S. Korea	3,996	6,700	54	74,000
Barcelona, Spain	3,842	4,834	87	44,161
San Francisco, U.S.	3,790	4,214	428	8,855
Bangalore, India	3,685	6,764	50	73,700
Lahore, Pakistan	3,603	5,864	57	63,211
Sydney, Australia	3,396	3,708	338	10,047
Baghdad, Iraq	3,371	5,237	97	34,753
Dhaka, Bangladesh	3,283	6,492	32	102,594
Athens, Greece	3,252	3,866	116	28,034
Ho Chi Minh City, Vietnam	3,250	4,481	31	104,839
Guangzhou, China	3,248	3,652	79	41,114
Detroit, U.S.	3,133	2,735	468	6,694
Miami, U.S.	3,123	3,894	448	6,971
Belo Horizonte, Brazil	3,059	5,125	79	38,722
Wuhan, China	3,048	3,495	65	46,892
Ahmadabad, India	3,037	4,837	32	94,906
Greater Berlin, Germany	3,033	3,006	274	11,069
Hyderabad, India	3,022	4,765	88	34,341
Caracas, Venezuela	2,993	3,435	54	55,426
Toronto, Canada	2,972	3,296	154	19,299

(continued)

City, Country	1985 (thousands)	2000 (thousands projected)	Area (sq. mi.)	Density (pop per sq. mi.)
Surabaya, Indonesia	2,962	3,632	43	68,884
Rome, Italy	2,944	3,129	69	42,667
Naples, Italy	2,862	3,134	62	46,161
Melbourne, Australia	2,852	2,968	327	8,722
Montreal, Canada	2,827	3,071	164	17,238
Kinshasa, Zaire	2,794	5,646	57	49,018
Guadalajara, Mexico	2,746	4,451	78	35,205
Alexandria, Egypt	2,660	3,304	35	76,000
Rangoon, Burma	2,558	3,332	47	54,426
Singapore, Singapore	2,556	2,913	78	32,769
Porto Allegre, Brazil	2,536	4,109	231	10,978
Harbin, China	2,518	2,887	30	83,933
Casablanca, Morocco	2,495	3,795	35	71,286
Kiev, USSR	2,489	3,237	62	40,145
Dallas, U.S.	2,486	3,257	419	5,933
Boston, U.S.	2,470	2,485	303	8,152
Washington, U.S.	2,456	2,707	357	6,880
Monterrey, Mexico	2,351	3,974	77	30,532
Ankara, Turkey	2,338	3,777	55	42,509
Budapest, Hungary	2,297	2,335	138	16,645
Chengdu, China	2,260	2,591	25	90,400
Birmingham, U.K.	2,211	2,078	223	9,915
Houston, U.S.	2,104	2,651	310	6,787
Bucharest, Romania	2,095	2,271	52	40,288

The World's Refugees in 1986

The following information is from the *World Refugee Survey 1986*, a publication of the U.S. Committee for Refugees, a nonprofit corp. The refugees in this table include only those who are in need of protection and/or assistance, and do not include refugees who have resettled.

In some areas, the United States and Western Europe for example, there are large numbers of undocumented aliens and asylum seekers. These individuals are not included although many might be considered refugees. There is, however, no reliable way to document their number.

Country of Asylum	From	Number
Total Africa		**3,112,950**
Algeria	Mostly Western Sahara	167,000[1]
Angola	Namibia, Zaire, S. Africa	92,200
Benin	Chad	4,000
Botswana	Zimbabwe	5,050
Burkina Faso	various	180
Burundi	Rwanda, Zaire	61,000[1]
Cameroon	Chad	15,000
Central African Rep.	Chad	15,000
Congo	various	1,200
Côte d'Ivoire	Ghana, SE Asia	600
Djibouti	Ethiopia	17,000
Egypt	Palestinians, others	7,350
Ethiopia	Sudan	110,000
Ghana	Chad	140
Kenya	Ethiopia, Rwanda, Uganda	8,500
Lesotho	South Africa	2,500[1]
Liberia	various	100
Malawi	Mozambique	70,000
Morocco	various	800
Mozambique	S. Africa	400
Namibia	Angola	40,000
Nigeria	Chad, others	7,300
Rwanda	Burundi	19,000[1]
Senegal	Guinea Bissau	5,000
Sierra Leone	Namibia	180
Somalia	Ethiopia	550,000[1]
S. Africa	Mozambique	175,000[1]
Sudan	Ethiopia, Uganda, Chad	914,000[1]
Swaziland	South Africa, Mozambique	11,800
Tanzania	Burundi, Zaire, S. Africa	200,000
Togo	Ghana	1,700
Uganda	Rwanda, Zaire, Sudan	120,400[1]
Zaire	Angola, Uganda, Rwanda	333,000
Zambia	Angola, Mozambique, Zaire	141,000
Zimbabwe	Mozambique	66,500
Total East Asia/Pacific		**573,775**
Burma	China, Malaysia	1,050
China	Vietnam	11,500[1]
Hong Kong	Vietnam	8,500
Indonesia	Vietnam	4,400
Japan	Vietnam	800
Korea	Vietnam	200
Macau	Vietnam	600
Malaysia	Philippines, Vietnam	97,900[1]
Papua New Guinea	Indonesia	10,050[1]
Philippines	Vietnam, Cambodia, Laos	12,900
Singapore	Vietnam	125
Thailand	Burma, Laos, Cambodia	405,300
Vietnam	Cambodia	20,000
Total Europe		**70,640**
Austria	Eastern Europe	20,000
Greece	Middle East, E. Europe	3,640
Italy	various	15,000
Spain	various	9,300
Sweden	various	8,250
Switzerland	various	12,200
Yugoslavia	Eastern Europe	2,250
Total Latin America/Caribbean		**323,090**
Argentina	Latin America	12,000[1]
Belize	El Salvador, Guatemala	9,000
Bolivia	Guatemala	220
Brazil	Europe, other	450
Chile	Europe	500
Colombia	Europe	410
Costa Rica	El Salvador, Nicaragua	30,900
Cuba	various	2,000
Dominican Rep.	Haiti	5,500[1]
Ecuador	various	800
El Salvador	Europe	200
French Guiana	Suriname	6,000
Guatemala	El Salvador, Nicaragua	12,000[1]
Honduras	El Salvador, Nicaragua	62,450[1]
Mexico	El Salvador, Guatemala	175,000[1]
Nicaragua	El Salvador, Guatemala	3,300
Panama	El Salvador, others	1,000
Peru	various	700
Uruguay	various	160
Venezuela	Latin America	500
Total Middle East/South Asia		**7,617,400**
India	Afghanistan, Tibet, Sri Lanka	227,000
Iran	Afghanistan, Iraq	2,330,000[1]
Iraq	Iran	75,000[1]
Pakistan	Afghanistan, Iran	2,802,500[1]
Turkey	various	1,900
Yemen, North	S. Yemen	30,000
Palestinians		
Gaza Strip		435,000
Jordan		823,000
Lebanon		277,000
Syria		251,000
West Bank		365,000
Total Refugees		**11,698,000**

(1) Significant variance among sources in number reported.

Principal Sources of Refugees

Afghanistan	4,715,000
Palestinians	2,149,850
Ethiopia	1,299,850
Iraq	430,000
Angola	376,000
Mozambique	348,800
Cambodia	308,200
Burundi	189,000
Rwanda	188,900
Uganda	185,900
El Salvador	180,200
Western Sahara	165,000
Sri Lanka	125,000
Chad	122,000
Sudan	111,000
Laos	90,700
China	85,800
Iran	78,800
Namibia	78,000
Vietnam	51,925
Guatemala	51,620
Nicaragua	50,000

Major International Organizations

Association of Southeast Asian Nations (ASEAN), was formed in 1967 to promote political and economic cooperation among the non-communist states of the region. Members in 1987 are Brunei, Indonesia, Malaysia, Philippines, Singapore, Thailand. Annual ministerial meetings set policy; a central Secretariat in Jakarta and 9 permanent committees work in trade, transportation, communications, agriculture, science, finance, and culture.

Commonwealth of Nations originally called the British Commonwealth of Nations, is an association of nations and dependencies loosely joined by a common interest based on having been parts of the old British Empire. The British monarch is the symbolic head of the Commonwealth.

There are 48 self-governing independent nations in the Commonwealth, plus various colonies and protectorates. As of May 1987, the members were the United Kingdom of Great Britain and Northern Ireland and 17 other nations recognizing the British monarch, represented by a governor-general, as their head of state: Antigua and Barbuda, Australia, Bahamas, Barbados, Belize, Canada, Fiji, Grenada, Jamaica, Mauritius, New Zealand, Papua New Guinea, St. Kitts-Nevis, St. Lucia, St. Vincent and the Grenadines, Solomon Islands, and Tuvalu (a special member); and 30 countries with their own heads of state: Bangladesh, Botswana, Brunei, Cyprus, Dominica, The Gambia, Ghana, Guyana, India, Kenya, Kiribati, Lesotho, Malawi, Malaysia, The Maldives, Malta, Nauru (a special member), Nigeria, Samoa, Seychelles, Sierra Leone, Singapore, Sri Lanka, Swaziland, Tanzania, Tonga, Trinidad and Tobago, Uganda, Vanuatu, Zambia, and Zimbabwe. In addition various Caribbean dependencies take part in certain Commonwealth activities.

The Commonwealth facilitates consultation among member states through meetings of prime ministers and finance ministers, and through a permanent Secretariat. Members consult on economic, scientific, educational, financial, legal, and military matters, and try to coordinate policies.

European Communities (EC, the Common Market) is the collective designation of three organizations with common membership: the European Economic Community (Common Market), the European Coal and Steel Community, and the European Atomic Energy Community. The 12 full members are: Belgium, Denmark, France, West Germany, Greece, Ireland, Italy, Luxembourg, Netherlands, Portugal, Spain, United Kingdom. Some 60 nations in Africa, the Caribbean, and the Pacific are affiliated under the Lomé Convention.

A merger of the 3 communities executives went into effect July 1, 1967, though the component organizations date back to 1951 and 1958. A Council of Ministers, a Commission, a European Parliament, and a Court of Justice comprise the permanent structure. The communities aim to integrate their economies, coordinate social developments, and bring about political union of the democratic states of Europe.

European Free Trade Association (EFTA), consisting of Austria, Iceland, Norway, Portugal, Sweden, Switzerland and associated member Finland, was created Jan. 4, 1960, to gradually reduce customs duties and quantitative restrictions between members on industrial products. By Dec. 31, 1966, all tariffs and quotas had been eliminated. The association entered into free trade agreements with the EC, Jan. 1, 1973. Trade barriers were removed July 1, 1976.

League of Arab States (The Arab League) was created Mar. 22, 1945, by Egypt, Iraq, Jordan, Lebanon, Saudi Arabia, Syria, and Yemen. Joining later were Algeria, Bahrain, Djibouti, Kuwait, Libya, Mauritania, Morocco, Oman, Qatar, Somalia, Sudan, Tunisia, United Arab Emirates and South Yemen. The Palestine Liberation Org. has been admitted as a full member. The League fosters cultural, economic, and communication ties and mediates disputes among the Arab states; it represents Arab states in certain international negotiations, and coordinates a military, economic, and diplomatic offensive against Israel. As a result of Egypt signing a peace treaty with Israel, the League, Mar. 1979, suspended Egypt's membership and transferred the League's headquarters from Cairo to Tunis.

North Atlantic Treaty Org. (NATO) was created by treaty (signed Apr. 4, 1949; in effect Aug. 24, 1949) among Belgium, Canada, Denmark, France, Iceland, Italy, Luxembourg, Netherlands, Norway, Portugal, United Kingdom, and the U.S. Greece, Turkey, West Germany, and Spain have joined since. The members agreed to settle disputes by peaceful means; to develop their individual and collective capacity to resist armed attack; to regard an attack on one as an attack on all, and to take necessary action to repel an attack under Article 51 of the United Nations Charter.

The NATO structure consists of a Council and a Military Committee of 3 commands (Allied Command Europe, Allied Command Atlantic, Allied Command Channel) and the Canada-U.S. Regional Planning Group.

Following announcement in 1966 of nearly total French withdrawal from the military affairs of NATO, organization hq. moved, 1967, from Paris to Brussels. In August, 1974, Greece announced a total withdrawal of armed forces from NATO, in response to Turkish intervention in Cyprus. Greece rejoined NATO's military wing, Oct. 20, 1980.

Organization of African Unity (OAU), formed May 25, 1963, by 32 African countries (50 in 1987) to coordinate cultural, political, scientific and economic policies; to end colonialism in Africa; and to promote a common defense of members' independence. It holds annual conferences of heads of state. Hq. is in Addis Ababa, Ethiopia.

Organization of American States (OAS) was formed in Bogota, Colombia, in 1948. Hq. is in Washington, D.C. It has a Permanent Council, Inter-American Economic and Social Council, and Inter-American Council for Education, Science and Culture, a Juridical Committee and a Commission on Human Rights. The Permanent Council can call meetings of foreign ministers to deal with urgent security matters. A General Assembly meets annually. A secretary general and assistant are elected for 5-year terms. There are 32 members, each with one vote in the various organizations: Antigua, Argentina, Bahamas, Barbados, Bolivia, Brazil, Chile, Colombia, Costa Rica, Cuba, Dominica, Dominican Republic, Ecuador, El Salvador, Grenada, Guatemala, Haiti, Honduras, Jamaica, Mexico, Nicaragua, Panama, Paraguay, Peru, St. Kitts-Nevis, St. Lucia, St. Vincent, Suriname, Trinidad & Tobago, U.S., Uruguay, Venezuela. In 1962, the OAS excluded Cuba from OAS activities but not from membership.

Organization for Economic Cooperation and Development (OECD) was established Sept. 30, 1961 to promote economic and social welfare in member countries, and to stimulate and harmonize efforts on behalf of developing nations. Nearly all the industrialized "free market" countries belong, with Yugoslavia as an associate member. OECD collects and disseminates economic and environmental information. Members in 1987 were: Australia, Austria, Belgium, Canada, Denmark, Finland, France, West Germany, Greece, Iceland, Ireland, Italy, Japan, Luxembourg, Netherlands, New Zealand, Norway, Portugal, Spain, Sweden, Switzerland, Turkey, United Kingdom, United States, Yugoslavia (special member). Hq. is in Paris.

Organization of Petroleum Exporting Countries (OPEC) was created Nov. 14, 1960 at Venezuelan initiative. The group attempts to set world oil prices by controlling oil production. It is also involved in advancing members' interests in trade and development dealings with industrialized oil-consuming nations. Members in 1987 were Algeria, Ecuador, Gabon, Indonesia, Iran, Iraq, Kuwait, Libya, Nigeria, Qatar, Saudi Arabia, United Arab Emirates, Venezuela.

Warsaw Pact was created May 14, 1955, as a mutual defense alliance. Members in 1987 were Bulgaria, Czechoslovakia, East Germany, Hungary, Poland, Romania, and the USSR. Hq. is in Moscow. It provides for a unified military command; if one member is attacked, the others will aid it with all necessary steps including armed force.

Ambassadors and Envoys

As of mid-1987.

The address of U.S. embassies abroad is the appropriate foreign capital. The U.S. does not have diplomatic relations with the following countries: Albania,[1] Angola,[2] Cambodia,[3] Taiwan,[4] Cuba,[5] Iran,[6] Libya,[6] Vietnam,[3] S. Yemen.[3], N. Korea, Mongolia. There were informal relations with Bhutan and Vanuatu.

Countries	Envoys from United States	Envoys to United States
Afghanistan	James M. Ealum, Chargé	Rohullah Erfaqi, Chargé
Algeria	L. Craig Johnstone, Amb.	Mohamed Sahnoun, Amb.
Antigua & Barbuda	Paul A. Russo, Amb.	Edmund H. Lake, Amb.
Argentina	Theodore E. Gildred Amb.	Enrique J.A. Candioti, Amb.
Australia	Lawrence W. Lane Jr., Amb.	F. Rawdon Dalrymple, Amb.
Austria	Ronald S. Lauder, Amb.	Thomas Klestil, Amb.
Bahamas	Carol Boyd Hallett, Amb.	Margaret E. McDonald, Amb.
Bahrain	Sam H. Zakhem, Amb.	Ghazi M. Algosaibi, Amb.
Bangladesh	Willard De Pree, Amb.	A.Z.M. Obaidullah Khan, Amb.
Barbados	Paul A. Russo, Amb.	Peter D. Laurie, Amb.
Belgium	Geoffrey Swaebe, Amb.	Herman Dehennin, Amb.
Belize	Keith Guthrie, Chargé	Edward A. Laing, Amb.
Benin	Walter E. Stadtler, Amb.	Guy L. Hazoume, Amb.
Bolivia	Edward M. Rowell, Amb.	Fernando Illanes, Amb.
Botswana	Natale H. Bellocchi, Amb.	Serara T. Ketlogetswe, Amb.
Brazil	Harry Shlaudeman, Amb.	Marcilio M. Moreira, Amb.
Brunei	Barrington King, Amb.	Pengiran Haji Idriss, Amb.
Bulgaria	Melvin Levitsky, Amb.	Stoyan I. Zhulev, Amb.
Burkina Faso	David H. Shinn, Amb.	*Vacant*
Burma	Daniel A. O'Donohue, Amb.	U. Myo Aung, Amb.
Burundi	James Daniel Phillips, Amb.	Edouard Kadigiri, Amb.
Cameroon	Myles R. Frechette, Amb.	Paul Pondi, Amb.
Canada	Thomas M. T. Niles, Amb.	Allan Gotlieb, Amb.
Cape Verde	Vernon D. Penner Jr., Amb.	Jose Luis Fernandes Lopes, Amb.
Central African Rep.	David C. Fields, Amb.	Christian Lingama-Toleque, Amb.
Chad	John Blane, Amb.	Mahamat Ali Adoum, Amb.
Chile	Harry G. Barnes Jr., Amb.	Hernan F. Errazuriz, Amb.
China	Winston Lord, Amb.	Han Xu, Amb.
Colombia	Charles A. Gillespie Jr., Amb.	Ximena Andrade de Casalino, Amb.
Comoros	Patricia G. Lynch, Amb.	Ali Mlahaili, Amb.
Congo	Alan Shurtleff, Amb.	Stanislas Batchi, Amb.
Costa Rica	Lewis A. Tambs, Amb.	Guido Fernandez, Amb.
Côte d'Ivoire	Dennis Kux, Amb.	Charles Gomis, Amb.
Cyprus	Richard W. Boehm, Amb.	Andrew J. Jacovides, Amb.
Czechoslovakia	Julian M. Niemczyk, Amb.	Mirolsav Houstecky, Amb.
Denmark	Terence A. Todman, Amb	Eigil Jorgensen, Amb.
Djibouti	John P. Ferriter, Amb.	Salah Hadji Farah Dirir, Amb.
Dominica	Paul A. Russo, Amb.	McDonald P. Benjamin, Amb.
Dominican Republic	Lowell C. Kilday, Amb.	Eduardo Leon, Amb.
Ecuador	Fernando E. Rondon, Amb.	Mario Ribadeniera, Amb.
Egypt	Frank G. Wisner, Amb.	El Sayed A. R. El Reedy, Amb.
El Salvador	Edwin G. Corr, Amb.	Ernesto Rivas-Gallont, Amb.
Equatorial Guinea	Francis S. Ruddy, Amb.	Florencio Maye Ela, Amb.
Estonia[7]		Ernst Jaakson, Consul General
Ethiopia	James R. Cheek, Chargé	Girma Amare, Chargé
Fiji	C. Edward Dillery, Amb.	Abdul H. Yusuf, Chargé
Finland	Rockwell A. Schnabel, Amb.	Paavo Rantanen, Amb.
France	Joe M. Rodgers, Amb.	Emmanuel de Margerie, Amb.
Gabon	Larry C. Williamson, Amb.	Jean Robert Odzaga, Amb.
Gambia, The	Herbert E. Horowitz, Amb.	*Vacant*
Germany, East	Francis J. Meehan, Amb.	Gerhard Herder, Amb.
Germany, West	Richard Burt, Amb.	Guenther van Well, Amb.
Ghana	Arlene Rendor, Chargé	Eric K. Otoo, Amb.
Greece	Robert V. Keeley, Amb.	George D. Papaulias, Amb.
Grenada	John C. Leary, Chargé	Albert O. Xavier, Amb.
Guatemala	Alberto M. Piedra, Amb.	Oscar Padilla-Vidaurre, Amb.
Guinea	William C. Mithoefer Jr., Chargé	Tolo Beavogui, Amb.
Guinea-Bissau	John D. Blacken, Amb.	Alfredo Lopes Cabral, Amb.
Guyana	Clint A. Lauderdale, Amb.	Cedric H. Grant, Amb.
Haiti	Brunson McKinley, Amb.	Pierre D. Sam, Amb.
Honduras	Everett E. Briggs, Amb.	Juan Agurcia Ewing, Amb.
Hungary	Marcus H. Palmer, Amb.	Vencel Hazi, Amb.
Iceland	L. Nicholas Ruwe, Amb.	Ingvi S. Ingvarsson, Amb.
India	John G. Dean, Amb.	P. K. Kaul, Amb.
Indonesia	Paul Wolfowitz, Amb.	Soesilo Soedarman, Amb.
Iraq	David G. Newton, Amb.	Nizar Hamdoon, Amb.
Ireland	Margaret M. Heckler, Amb.	Padraic N. McKernan, Amb.
Israel	Thomas P. Pickering, Amb.	Meir Rosenne, Amb.
Italy	Maxwell M. Rabb, Amb.	Rinaldo Petrignani, Amb.
Jamaica	Michael G. Sotirhos, Amb.	Keith Johnson, Amb.
Japan	Michael J. Mansfield, Amb.	Nobuo Matsunaga, Amb.
Jordan	Paul H. Boeker, Amb.	Mohamed Kamel, Amb.
Kenya	Elinor G. Constable, Amb.	Sospeter O. Mageto, Amb.
Kiribati	C. Edward Dillery, Amb.	Atanradi Baiteke, Amb.
Korea, South	James R. Lilley, Amb.	Kyung-Won Kim, Amb.
Kuwait	Anthony C. Quainton, Amb.	Shaikh S. N. Al-Sabah, Amb.
Laos	Harriet Isom, Amb.	Bounkeut Sangsomsak, Chargé
Latvia[7]		Anatol Dinbergs, Chargé
Lebanon	John H. Kelly, Amb.	Adballah Bouhabib, Amb.
Lesotho	S. L. Abbott, Amb.	W. T. van Tonder, Amb.
Liberia	Keith L. Wauchope, Chargé	Eugenia A. Wordsworth-Stevenson, Amb.

Countries	Envoys from United States	Envoys to United States
Lithuania[7]		Stasys A. Backis, Chargé
Luxembourg	Jean B. Gerard, Amb.	Andre Philippe, Amb.
Madagascar	Patricia G. Lynch, Amb.	Leon M. Rajaobelina, Amb.
Malawi	Dennis C. Jett, Chargé	Timon S. Mangwazu, Amb.
Malaysia	Thomas P. Shoesmith, Amb.	Albert S. Talalla, Amb.
Mali	Robert M. Pringle, Amb.	Lassana Keita, Amb.
Malta	Gary L. Matthews, Amb.	Alfred Falzon, Amb.
Mauritania	Robert L. Pugh, Amb.	Abdellah Ould Daddah, Amb.
Mauritius	Robert D. Palmer, Amb.	Chitmansing Jesseramsing, Amb.
Mexico	Charles J. Pilliod Jr., Amb.	J. Espinosa de los Reyes, Amb.
Morocco	Thomas A. Nassif, Amb.	M'hamed Bargach, Amb.
Mozambique	Melissa F. Wells, Amb.	Valeriano Ferrao, Amb.
Nauru	Laurence W. Lane Jr., Amb.	T.W. Star, Amb.
Nepal	Leon J. Weil, Amb.	Bishwa Pradhan, Amb.
Netherlands	John S.R. Shad, Amb.	Richard H. Fein, Amb.
New Zealand	Paul M. Cleveland, Amb.	Wallace E. Rowling, Amb.
Nicaragua	*Vacant*	Carlos Tunnermann, Amb.
Niger	Richard W. Bogosian, Amb.	Joseph Diatta, Amb.
Nigeria	Princeton N. Lyman, Amb.	Ignatius C. Olisemeka, Amb.
Norway	Robert D. Stuart, Amb.	Kjell Eliassen, Amb.
Oman	C. Cranwell Montgomery, Amb.	Ali Salim Bader Al-Hanai, Amb.
Pakistan	John T. McCarthy, Chargé	Jamsheed K. A. Marker, Amb.
Panama	Arthur H. Davis Amb.	Dominador K. Bazan, Amb.
Papua New Guinea	Everett E. Bierman, Amb.	Longas Solomon, Chargé
Paraguay	Clyde D. Taylor, Amb.	Marcos Martinez Mendieta, Amb.
Peru	Alexander F. Watson, Amb.	Cesar G. Atala, Amb.
Philippines	Nicholas Platt, Amb.	Emmanuel Pelaez, Amb.
Poland	John R. Davis Jr., Chargé	Zdzislaw Ludwiczak, Chargé
Portugal	Alan H. Flanigan, Chargé	Joao Eduardo M. Periera Bastos, Amb.
Qatar	Joseph Ghougassian, Amb.	Rashid Saud Al-Solaiti, Chargé
Romania	Roger Kirk, Amb.	Nicolae Gavrilescu, Amb.
Rwanda	John E. Upston, Amb.	Simon Insonere, Amb.
St. Christopher & Nevis	Paul A. Russo	William Herbert
St. Lucia	Paul A. Russo	Joseph E. Edmunds, Amb.
St. Vincent and The Grenadines	Paul A. Russo	*Vacant*
Samoa, Western	*Vacant*	Maiava I. Toma, Amb.
Sao Tome and Principe	Lary C. Williamson, Amb.	Joaquim R. Branco, Amb.
Saudi Arabia	Walter L. Cutler, Amb.	Bandar Bin Sultan, Amb.
Senegal	Lannon Walker, Amb.	Falilou Kane, Amb.
Seychelles	Irvin Hicks, Amb.	Giovinella Gonthier, Amb.
Sierra Leone	Cynthia S. Perry, Amb.	Sahr Matturi, Amb.
Singapore	J. Stapleton Roy, Amb.	Tommy T. B. Koh, Amb.
Solomon Islands	Paul F. Gardner, Amb.	Francis Saemala, Amb.
Somalia	David R. Rawson, Chargé	Abdullahi Ahmed Addou, Amb.
South Africa	Edward J. Perkins, Amb.	J.H.A. Beukes, Amb.
Spain	Reginald Bartholomew, Amb.	Juan Jose Arboli, Amb.
Sri Lanka	James Spain, Amb.	W. Susanta de Alwis, Amb.
Sudan	G. Norman Anderson, Amb.	Salah Ahmed, Amb.
Suriname	Robert E. Barbour, Amb.	Arnolt T. Halfhide, Amb.
Swaziland	Harvey F. Nelson Jr., Amb.	Peter H. Mtetwa, Amb.
Sweden	Gregory J. Newell, Amb.	Wilhelm Wachtmeister, Amb.
Switzerland	Faith R. Whittlesey, Amb.	Klaus Jacobi, Amb.
Syria	William L. Eagleton Jr., Amb.	Bushra Kanafani, Amb.
Tanzania	Donald K. Petterson, Amb.	Asterius M. Hyera, Amb.
Thailand	William A. Brown, Amb.	Arsa Sarasin, Amb.
Togo	David A. Korn, Amb.	Ellom-Kodjo Schuppius, Amb.
Tonga	C. Edward Dillery, Amb.	*Vacant*
Trinidad and Tobago	Sheldon J. Krys, Amb.	James O'Neil-Lewis, Amb.
Tunisia	Peter Sebastian, Amb.	Habib B. Yahia, Amb.
Turkey	Robert Strausz-Hupe, Amb.	Sukru Elekdag, Amb.
Tuvalu	C. Edward Dillery, Amb.	Ionatana Ionatana, Amb.
Uganda	Robert G. Houdek, Amb.	Elizabeth Bagaaya-Nyabongo, Amb.
USSR	Arthur A. Hartman, Amb.	Yuri Dubinin, Amb.
United Arab Emirates	David L. Mack Jr., Amb.	A.S. Al-Mokarrab, Amb.
United Kingdom	Charles S. Price 2d, Amb.	Antony Acland, Amb.
Uruguay	Malcolm R. Wilkey, Amb.	Hector Luisi, Amb.
Vatican	Frank Shakespeare, Amb.	Pio Laghi, Pro-Nuncio
Venezuela	Otto J. Reich, Amb.	Valentin Hernandez, Amb.
Yemen Arab Rep.	William A. Rugh, Amb.	Mohsin A. Alaini, Amb.
Yugoslavia	John D. Scanlon, Amb.	Mico Rakic, Amb.
Zaire	Brandon H. Grove Jr., Amb.	Nguz a Karl-i-Bond, Amb.
Zambia	Paul J. Hare, Amb.	Nalumino Mundia, Amb.
Zimbabwe	James W. Rawlings, Amb.	Edmund R. M. Garwe, Amb.

Ambassadors at Large: Daniel J. Terra, Richard T. Kennedy, Paul H. Nitze, Jonathan Moore, E. Paul Bremer.

Special Missions

U.S. Mission to North Atlantic Treaty Organization, Brussels—David M. Abshire
U.S. Mission to the European Communities, Brussels—J. William Middendorf 2d
U.S. Mission to the United Nations, New York—Vernon Walters
U.S. Mission to the European Office of the UN, Geneva—vacant
U.S. Mission to the Organization for Economic Cooperation and Development, Paris—Edward J. Streator
U.S. Mission to the Organization of American States, Washington—Richard T. McCormick, Amb.
U.S. Mission to International Civic Aviation Organization, Montreal—Edmond P. Stohr

(1) Relations severed in 1939. (2) Post closed in 1975. (3) U.S. embassy closed in 1975. (4) U.S. severed relations in 1978; unofficial relations are maintained. (5) Relations severed in 1961; limited ties restored in 1977. (6) U.S. severed relations on Apr. 7, 1980. (7) U.S. does not officially recognize 1940 annexation by USSR. (8) Embassy closed, May 2, 1980. U.S. closed the Libyan mission, May 6, 1981.

United Nations

The 41st regular session of the United Nations General Assembly opened in September, 1987. *See Chronology for developments at UN sessions during 1987.*

UN headquarters are in New York, N.Y., between First Ave. and Roosevelt Drive and E. 42d St. and E. 48th St. The General Assembly Bldg., Secretariat, Conference and Library bldgs. are interconnected. A new UN office building-hotel was opened in New York in 1976.

A European office at Geneva includes Secretariat and agency staff members. Other offices of UN bodies and related organizations are scattered throughout the world.

The UN has a post office originating its own stamps.

Proposals to establish an organization of nations for maintenance of world peace led to the United Nations Conference on International Organization at San Francisco, Apr. 25-June 26, 1945, where the charter of the United Nations was drawn up. It was signed June 26 by 50 nations, and by Poland, one of the original 51, on Oct. 15, 1945. The charter came into effect Oct. 24, 1945, upon ratification by the permanent members of the Security Council and a majority of other signatories.

Roster of the United Nations

(As of mid-1987)

The 159 members of the United Nations, with the years in which they became members.

Member	Year
Afghanistan	1946
Albania	1955
Algeria	1962
Angola	1976
Antigua and Barbuda	1981
Argentina	1945
Australia	1945
Austria	1955
Bahamas	1973
Bahrain	1971
Bangladesh	1974
Barbados	1966
Belgium	1945
Belize	1981
Benin	1960
Bhutan	1971
Bolivia	1945
Botswana	1966
Brazil	1945
Brunei	1984
Bulgaria	1955
Burkina Faso	1960
Burma	1948
Burundi	1962
Byelorussia	1945
Cambodia (Kampuchea)	1955
Cameroon	1960
Canada	1945
Cape Verde	1975
Central Afr. Rep.	1960
Chad	1960
Chile	1945
China[4]	1945
Colombia	1945
Comoros	1975
Congo	1960
Costa Rica	1945
Côte d'Ivoire	1960
Cuba	1945
Cyprus	1960
Czechoslovakia	1945
Denmark	1945
Djibouti	1977
Dominica	1978
Dominican Rep.	1945
Ecuador	1945
Egypt[2]	1945
El Salvador	1945
Equatorial Guinea	1968
Ethiopia	1945
Fiji	1970
Finland	1955
France	1945
Gabon	1960
Gambia	1965
Germany, East	1973
Germany, West	1973
Ghana	1957
Greece	1945
Grenada	1974
Guatemala	1945
Guinea	1958
Guinea-Bissau	1974
Guyana	1966
Haiti	1945
Honduras	1945
Hungary	1955
Iceland	1946
India	1945
Indonesia[6]	1950
Iran	1945
Iraq	1945
Ireland	1955
Israel	1949
Italy	1955
Jamaica	1962
Japan	1956
Jordan	1955
Kenya	1963
Kuwait	1963
Laos	1955
Lebanon	1945
Lesotho	1966
Liberia	1945
Libya	1955
Luxembourg	1945
Madagascar (Malagasy)	1960
Malawi	1964
Malaysia[1]	1957
Maldives	1965
Mali	1960
Malta	1964
Mauritania	1961
Mauritius	1968
Mexico	1945
Mongolia	1961
Morocco	1956
Mozambique	1975
Nepal	1955
Netherlands	1945
New Zealand	1945
Nicaragua	1945
Niger	1960
Nigeria	1960
Norway	1945
Oman	1971
Pakistan	1947
Panama	1945
Papua New Guinea	1975
Paraguay	1945
Peru	1945
Philippines	1945
Poland	1945
Portugal	1955
Qatar	1971
Romania	1955
Rwanda	1962
Saint Christopher & Nevis	1983
Saint Lucia	1979
Saint Vincent and the Grenadines	1980
Samoa (Western)	1976
Sao Tome e Principe	1975
Saudi Arabia	1945
Senegal	1960
Seychelles	1976
Sierra Leone	1961
Singapore[1]	1965
Solomon Islands	1978
Somalia	1960
South Africa[5]	1945
Spain	1955
Sri Lanka	1955
Sudan	1956
Suriname	1975
Swaziland	1968
Sweden	1946
Syria[2]	1945
Tanzania[3]	1961
Thailand	1946
Togo	1960
Trinidad & Tobago	1962
Tunisia	1956
Turkey	1945
Uganda	1962
Ukraine	1945
USSR	1945
United Arab Emirates	1971
United Kingdom	1945
United States	1945
Uruguay	1945
Vanuatu	1981
Venezuela	1945
Vietnam	1977
Yemen	1947
Yemen, South	1967
Yugoslavia	1945
Zaire	1960
Zambia	1964
Zimbabwe	1980

(1) Malaya joined the UN in 1957. In 1963, its name was changed to Malaysia following the accession of Singapore, Sabah, and Sarawak. Singapore became an independent UN member in 1965. (2) Egypt and Syria were original members of the UN. In 1958, the United Arab Republic was established by a union of Egypt and Syria and continued as a single member of the UN. In 1961, Syria resumed its separate membership. (3) Tanganyika was a member of the United Nations from 1961 and Zanzibar was a member from 1963. Following the ratification in 1964 of Articles of Union between Tanganyika and Zanzibar, the United Republic of Tanganyika and Zanzibar continued as a single member of the United Nations, later changing its name to United Republic of Tanzania. (4) The General Assembly voted in 1971 to expel the Chinese government on Taiwan and admit the Peking government in its place. (5) The General Assembly rejected the credentials of the South African delegates in 1974, and suspended the country from the Assembly. (6) Indonesia withdrew from the UN in 1965 and rejoined in 1966.

Organization

The text of the UN Charter, and further information, may be obtained from the Office of Public Information, United Nations, New York, NY 10017.

General Assembly. The General Assembly is composed of representatives of all the member nations. Each nation is entitled to one vote.

The General Assembly meets in regular annual sessions and in special session when necessary. Special sessions are convoked by the Secretary General at the request of the Security Council or of a majority of the members of the UN.

On important questions a two-thirds majority of members present and voting is required; on other questions a simple majority is sufficient.

The General Assembly must approve the budget and apportion expenses among members. A member in arrears will have no vote if the amount of arrears equals or exceeds the amount of the contributions due for the preceeding two full years.

Security Council. The Security Council consists of 15 members, 5 with permanent seats. The remaining 10 are elected for 2-year terms by the General Assembly; they are not eligible for immediate reelection.

Permanent members of the Council: China, France, USSR, United Kingdom, United States.

Non-permanent members are Bulgaria, Congo, Ghana, Venezuela, and United Arab Emirates (until Dec. 31, 1987); Argentina, W. Germany, Italy, Japan, and Zambia (until Dec. 31, 1988).

The Security Council has the primary responsiblity within the UN for maintaining international peace and security. The Council may investigate any dispute that threatens international peace and security.

Any member of the UN at UN headquarters may participate in its discussions and a nation not a member of UN may appear if it is a party to a dispute.

Decisions on procedural questions are made by an affirmative vote of 9 members. On all other matters the affirmative vote of 9 members must include the concurring votes of all permanent members; it is this clause which gives rise to the so-called "veto." A party to a dispute must refrain from voting.

The Security Council directs the various truce supervisory forces deployed throughout the world.

Economic and Social Council. The Economic and Social Council consists of 54 members elected by the General Assembly for 3-year terms of office. The council is responsible under the General Assembly for carrying out the functions of the United Nations with regard to international economic, social, cultural, educational, health and related matters. The council meets usually twice a year.

Trusteeship Council. The administration of trust territories is under UN supervision. The only remaining trust territory is the Pacific Islands, administered by the U.S.

Secretariat. The Secretary General is the chief administrative officer of the UN. He may bring to the attention of the Security Council any matter that threatens international peace. He reports to the General Assembly.

Javier Perez de Cuellar (Peru), secretary general, was elected to a 5-year term beginning Jan. 1, 1982.

The U.S. usually contributes 25% of the regular budget, the Soviet Union 11.33%, Japan 8.66%, W. Germany 7.74%, and France, China, and Britain about 5% each.

International Court of Justice (World Court). The International Court of Justice is the principal judicial organ of the United Nations. All members are *ipso facto* parties to the statute of the Court, as are three nonmembers — Liechtenstein, San Marino, and Switzerland. Other states may become parties to the Court's statute.

The jurisdiction of the Court comprises cases which the parties submit to it and matters especially provided for in the charter or in treaties. The Court gives advisory opinions and renders judgments. Its decisions are only binding between the parties concerned and in respect to a particular dispute. If any party to a case fails to heed a judgment, the other party may have recourse to the Security Council.

The 15 judges are elected for 9-year terms by the General Assembly and the Security Council. Retiring judges are eligible for re-election. The Court remains permanently in session, except during vacations. All questions are decided by majority. The Court sits in The Hague, Netherlands.

Judges: 9-year term in office ending 1994: Ni Vhengyo, China. Jens Evensen, Norway. Manfred Lachs, Poland. Taslim Olawala Elias, Nigeria. **9-year term in office ending 1991:** Nagendra Singh, India. Jose Maria Ruda, Argentina. Robert Y. Jennings, United Kingdom. Guy Ladreit de Lacharriere, France. Keba Mbaye, Senegal. **9-year term in office ending 1988:** Robert Ago, Italy. Stephen M. Schwebel, U.S. Mohammed Bedjaoui, Algeria. Platon D. Morozov, USSR. Jose Sette Camara, Brazil.

United Nations Secretaries General

Year	Secretary, Nation	Year	Secretary, Nation	Year	Secretary, Nation
1946	Trygve Lie, Norway	1961	U Thant, Burma	1982	Javier Perez de Cuellar, Peru
1953	Dag Hammarskjold, Sweden	1972	Kurt Waldheim, Austria		

U.S. Representatives to the United Nations

The U.S. Representative to the United Nations is the Chief of the U.S. Mission to the United Nations in New York and holds the rank and status of Ambassador Extraordinary and Plenipotentiary.

Year	Representative	Year	Representative	Year	Representative
1946	Edward R. Stettinius Jr.	1965	Arthur J. Goldberg	1975	Daniel P. Moynihan
1946	Herschel V. Johnson (act.)	1968	George W. Ball	1976	William W. Scranton
1947	Warren R. Austin	1968	James Russell Wiggins	1977	Andrew Young
1953	Henry Cabot Lodge Jr.	1969	Charles W. Yost	1979	Donald McHenry
1960	James J. Wadsworth	1971	George Bush	1981	Jeane J. Kirkpatrick
1961	Adlai E. Stevenson	1973	John A. Scali	1985	Vernon A. Walters

Specialized and Related Agencies

These agencies are autonomous, with their own memberships and organs which have a functional relationship or working agreement with the UN (headquarters.)

Food & Agriculture Org. (FAO) aims to increase production from farms, forests, and fisheries; improve distribution, marketing, and nutrition; better conditions for rural people. (Viale delle Terme di Caracalla, 00100 Rome, Italy.)

General Agreement on Tariffs and Trade (GATT) is the only treaty setting rules for world trade. Provides a forum for settling trade disputes and negotiating trade liberalization. (Centre William Rappard, 154 rue de Lausanne, 1211 Geneva 21, Switzerland.)

International Atomic Energy Agency (IAEA) aims to promote the safe, peaceful uses of atomic energy. (Vienna International Centre, PO Box 100, A-1400, Vienna, Austria.)

(*continued*)

International Bank for Reconstruction and Development (IBRD) (World Bank) provides loans and technical assistance for economic development projects in developing member countries; encourages cofinancing for projects from other public and private sources. **International Development Association (IDA),** an affiliate of the Bank, provides funds for development projects on concessionary terms to the poorer developing member countries. (both 1818 H St., NW, Washington, DC 20433.) **International Finance Corporation (IFC)** an affiliate of the Bank, promotes the growth of the private sector in developing member countries; encourages the development of local capital markets; stimulates the international flow of private capital. (1818 H St., NW, Washington, DC 20433.)

International Civil Aviation Org. (ICAO) promotes international civil aviation standards and regulations. (1000 Sherbrooke St. W., Montreal, Quebec, Canada H3A 2R2.)

International Fund for Agricultural Development (IFAD) aims to mobilize funds for agricultural and rural projects in developing countries. (107 Via del Serafico, Rome, Italy.)

International Labor Org. (ILO) aims to promote employment; improve labor conditions and living standards. (4 route de Morillons, CH-1211, Geneva 22, Switzerland.)

International Maritime Org. (IMO) aims to promote cooperation on technical matters affecting international shipping. (4 Albert Embankment, London, SE1 7SR, England.)

International Monetary Fund (IMF) aims to promote international monetary co-operation and currency stabilization; expansion of international trade. (700 19th St., NW, Washington, DC, 20431.)

International Telecommunication Union (ITU) sets up international regulations of radio, telegraph, telephone and space radio-communications. Allocates radio frequencies. (Place des Nations, 1211 Geneva 20, Switzerland.)

United Nations Educational, Scientific, & Cultural Org. (UNESCO) aims to promote collaboration among nations through education, science, and culture. The U.S. withdrew from this organization in 1985 because of UNESCO's anti-Western bias. (9 Place de Fontenoy, 75700 Paris, France.)

United Nations Children's Fund (UNICEF) provides aid and development assistance to children and mothers in developing countries. (1 UN Plaza, New York, NY 10017.)

Universal Postal Union (UPU) aims to perfect postal services and promote international collaboration. (Weltpoststrasse 4, 3000 Berne, 15 Switzerland.)

World Health Org. (WHO) aims to aid the attainment of the highest possible level of health. (20 Ave. Appia, 1211 Geneva, Switzerland.)

World Intellectual Property Organization (WIPO) seeks to protect, through international cooperation, literary, industrial, scientific, and artistic works. (34, Chemin des Colom Bettes, 1211 Geneva, Switzerland.)

World Meteorological Org. (WMO) aims to co-ordinate and improve world meteorological work. (Case Postale 5, CH-1211, Geneva, Switzerland.)

U.S. Outvoted in the United Nations in 1986

A report to Congress on voting practices in the United Nations issued by the United States Mission showed that most of the world voted against the United States during the regular session of the 41st United Nations General Assembly, which began in the fall of 1986. The report shows the percentage of votes each country cast in agreement with the U.S. Countries that abstained or did not take part in votes were counted as if they voted against the U.S.

Africa

Malawi	36.8	Botswana	17.5	Zambia	13.8
Cote d'Ivoire	32.2	Tunisia	17.4	Uganda	13.6
Zaire	30.3	Rwanda	17.4	Mali	13.1
Liberia	30.1	Egypt	17.3	Zimbabwe	13.0
Chad	29.0	Kenya	17.2	Tanzania	12.4
Mauritius	27.4	Comoros	17.1	Congo	12.3
Morocco	24.5	Sierra Leone	17.1	Burkina Faso	11.8
Equatorial Guinea	23.4	Mauritania	16.0	Ethiopia	11.8
Swaziland	21.7	Guinea-Bissau	16.2	Gambia	11.1
Togo	21.7	Ghana	16.1	Seychelles	10.6
Cameroon	20.9	Cape Verde	16.0	Madagascar	10.0
Central African Rep.	19.7	Djibouti	15.8	Benin	9.8
Gabon	19.4	Sudan	15.7	Algeria	7.4
Senegal	18.4	Somalia	15.3	Mozambique	7.2
Sao Tome & Principe	18.2	Guinea	14.9	Angola	6.8
Niger	18.2	Burundi	14.2	Libya	6.2
Lesotho	17.6	Nigeria	14.1		

Asia and the Pacific

Israel	89.9	Solomon Islands	16.5	Kuwait	12.9
Japan	68.8	Pakistan	16.4	Qatar	12.3
Australia	63.7	Lebanon	16.1	Maldives	11.3
New Zealand	57.9	Saudi Arabia	16.0	Mongolia	10.3
Western Samoa	36.5	Malaysia	15.8	India	10.1
Fiji	35.5	China	15.7	Iran	9.5
Cambodia	25.6	Oman	15.4	Afghanistan	8.9
Thailand	23.5	Sri Lanka	14.5	Iraq	8.8
Singapore	20.9	United Arab Emirates	14.5	Yemen, South	8.0
Papua New Guinea	20.8	Bhutan	14.4	Syria	7.9
Philippines	19.0	Vanuatu	14.2	Yemen, North	7.5
Bangladesh	18.6	Cyprus	13.8	Laos	6.4
Brunei	17.0	Bahrain	13.6	Vietnam	6.4
Burma	16.8	Jordan	13.3		
Nepal	16.7	Indonesia	13.2		

The Americas

Canada	72.0	Guatemala	32.2	Brazil	18.5
Dominica	70.8	Antigua & Barbuda	29.5	Peru	18.4
El Salvador	43.7	Ecuador	28.7	Bolivia	18.3
Costa Rica	42.4	Belize	28.3	Mexico	17.6
Saint Kitts & Nevis	38.4	Paraguay	26.5	Suriname	17.1
Chile	38.3	Jamaica	24.4	Argentina	16.4
Saint Vincent & Grenadines	36.5	Bahamas	23.1	Trinidad & Tobago	16.2
Honduras	36.4	Panama	22.5	Guyana	13.1
Dominican Rep.	35.7	Uruguay	21.7	Nicaragua	9.3
Saint Lucia	35.4	Barbados	21.4	Cuba	6.8
Grenada	35.1	Haiti	19.7		
Colombia	32.4	Venezuela	19.0		

Western Europe

United Kingdom	88.2	Portugal	74.3	Sweden	47.3
W. Germany	87.3	Iceland	66.0	Finland	46.3
Luxembourg	79.2	Denmark	62.0	Greece	42.7
Belgium	78.9	Norway	58.1	Turkey	37.1
France	78.3	Spain	57.8	Malta	22.7
Italy	77.3	Ireland	55.1		
Netherlands	74.5	Austria	48.1		

Eastern Europe

Romania	16.3	Byelorussian SSR	12.6	Poland	12.0
Yugoslavia	13.1	Czechoslovakia	12.6	USSR	12.0
Hungary	12.8	E. Germany	12.6	Albania	6.3
Bulgaria	12.7	Ukranian SSR	12.6		

U.S. Immigration Law

Source: Immigration and Naturalization Service, U.S. Justice Department

The Immigration and Nationality Act, as amended, provides for the numerical limitation of most immigration. Not subject to any numerical limitations are immigrants classified as immediate relatives who are spouses or children of U.S. citizens, or parents of citizens who are 21 years of age or older; returning residents; certain former U.S. citizens; ministers of religion; and certain long-term U.S. government employees.

The Refugee Act of 1980 (P.L. 96-212) became effective on April 1, 1980. Congress stated that the objectives of the Refugee Act are to provide a permanent and systematic procedure for the admission of refugees who are of special humanitarian concern to the U.S. and to provide uniform provisions for the effective settlement and absorption of those refugees. The number of refugees who may be admitted is determined by the President, after consultation with the Committees on the Judiciary of the Senate and of the House of Representatives.

Numerical Limitation of Immigrants

Immigration to the U.S. is numerically limited to 270,000 per year. Within this quota there is an annual limitation of 20,000 for each country. The colonies and dependencies of foreign states are limited to 600 (5,000 in 1988) per year, chargeable to the country limitation of the mother country.

Visa Categories

Of those immigrants subject to numerical limitations, applicants for immigration are classified as either preference or nonpreference. The preference visa categories are based on certain relationships to persons in the U.S., i.e., unmarried sons and daughters over 21 of U.S. citizens, spouses and unmarried sons and daughters of resident aliens, married sons and daughters of U.S. citizens, brothers and sisters of U.S. citizens 21 or over (first, 2d, 4th, and 5th preference, respectively); members of the professions or persons of exceptional ability in the sciences and arts whose services are sought by U.S. employers (3d preference); and skilled and unskilled workers in short supply (6th preference). Spouses and children of preference applicants are entitled to the same preference if accompanying or following to join such persons.

Preference status is based upon approved petitions, filed with the Immigration and Naturalization Service, by the appropriate relative or employer (or in the 3d preference by the alien himself).

Other immigrants not within one of the above-mentioned preference groups may qualify as nonpreference applicants and receive only those visa numbers not needed by preference applicants. The nonpreference category has not been available since 1978 due to 6 preferences using the allocation.

Labor Certification

The Act of October 3, 1965, established controls to protect the U.S. labor market from an influx of skilled and unskilled foreign labor. Prior to the issuance of a visa, the potential 3d, 6th, and nonpreference immigrant must obtain the Secretary of Labor's certification, establishing that there are not sufficient workers in the U.S. at the alien's destination who are able, willing, and qualified to perform the job; and that the employment of the alien will not adversely affect the wages and working conditions of workers in the U.S. similarly employed; or that there is satisfactory evidence that the provisions of that section do not apply to the alien's case.

The Immigration Reform and Control Act of 1986

The Immigration Reform and Control Act, PL 99-603, was signed into law on November 6, 1986. The legislation contains 3 major segments—legalization, employer sanctions, and temporary agricultural worker provisions. The legalization segment of the law provides a method for legalizing the status of many of the aliens who have been in the U.S. unlawfully since before January 1, 1982. Legalization is a 2-tiered program which provides for temporary resident status for qualified applicants. After 18 months residence in the U.S., temporary residents are eligible to apply to adjust to permanent resident status.

The employer sanctions section of the legislation, for the first time, imposes civil and criminal penalties on employers who knowingly hire, recruit, or refer aliens who are not authorized to work in the U.S. The civil fines range from $250 to $10,000 per alien. Criminal penalties are possible for habitual violators. Employer sanction provisions were to begin in May 1987 but were delayed by Congress until Sept. 1 when a 12-month education period will begin.

The temporary agricultural worker provisions of the act expand the existing temporary worker (H2) program. The law divides H2 workers into two categories: temporary workers for agricultural labor or services, and all other temporary H2 workers. The changes made by the law affect only the agricultural area and are effective as of June 1, 1987. A grower wishing to hire H2 workers must file a petition with the Department of Labor. The Department will grant the petition provided there are insufficient workers who are able, willing, qualified, and available where and when needed to perform the labor, and there will be no adverse effect on the wages and working conditions of workers similarly employed in the U.S.

In addition to these major provisions, there are many other provisions of the act, including anti-discrimination provisions as well as increasing the numerical limitation for colonies of foreign states from 600 to 5,000 immigrant visas a year. Qualified aliens who are in the category Cuban/Haitian Entrant (Status Pending) are eligible to adjust to permanent resident status. The act also provides an additional 5,000 nonpreference visa numbers to be made available in fiscal years 1987 and 1988 to natives of countries which were adversely effected by the changes in the preference system created by the 1965 Immigration and Nationality Act amendments.

As of mid-July 1987, about 305,000 aliens have sought legal status under the new immigration law.

U.S. Aid to Foreign Nations

Source: Bureau of Economic Analysis, U.S. Commerce Department

Figures are in millions of dollars. (*Less than $500,000.) Data include military supplies and services furnished under the Foreign Assistance Act and direct Defense Department appropriations, and include credits extended to private entities.

Net grants and credits take into account all known returns to the U.S., including reverse grants, returns of grants, and payments of principal. A minus sign (–) indicates that the total of these returns is greater than the total of grants or credits. Nations with net grant or credit under $2 mln. not incl.

Other assistance represents the transfer of U.S. farm products in exchange for foreign currencies, less the government's disbursements of the currencies as grants, credits, or for purchases.

Amounts do not include investments in the following: Asian Development Bank, $110 mln.; Inter-American Development Bank, $351 mln.; International Development Assn., $658 mln.; International Bank for Reconstruction and Development, $241 mln.; African Development Bank, $15 mln.; African Development Fund, $53 mln; International Finance Corp., $28 mln.; Special Facility for Sub-Saharan Africa, $24 mln.

	Total	Net grants	Net credits	Net other
Calendar Year 1986				
Total	**13,419**	**12,031**	**1,367**	**21**
Western Europe	**–7**	**405**	**–415**	**2**
Austria	–9	(*)	–9	—
Belgium-Luxembourg	–9	—	–9	—
Denmark	–7	—	–7	—
Finland	–47	(*)	–47	(*)
France	–26	(*)	–26	—
Italy	–107	12	–119	—
Norway	–16	—	–16	—
Portugal	178	171	7	—
Spain	67	14	52	1
Sweden	–6	—	–6	—
United Kingdom	–202	—	–202	—
Yugoslavia	21	(*)	21	(*)
Fund for Ireland	50	50	—	—
Other & unspecified	–153	158	–5	—
Eastern Europe	**1,168**	**15**	**1,151**	**2**
Hungary	6	—	6	—
Poland	1,267	15	1,250	2
Romania	–26	—	–26	—
USSR	–66	—	–66	—
Near East & South Asia	**7,931**	**7,140**	**775**	**15**
Afghanistan	–3	2	–5	—
Bangladesh	178	117	60	—
Cyprus	21	22	–1	(*)
Egypt	2,730	2,395	331	3
Greece	72	2	70	(*)
India	36	115	–79	1
Iraq	–5	—	–5	—
Israel	4,030	3,704	265	1
Jordan	7	29	–22	(*)
Lebanon	–12	11	–24	—
Nepal	20	20	(*)	(*)
Oman	12	4	8	—
Pakistan	350	206	136	9
Sri Lanka	66	17	48	2
Turkey	298	311	–13	(*)
Yemen, North	39	33	5	(*)
Other & unspecified	88	88	—	—
East Asia & Pacific	**–64**	**696**	**–759**	**(*)**
Australia	–117	—	–117	—
Burma	7	9	–2	—
China	–8	—	–8	—
Hong Kong	–11	(*)	–11	—
Indonesia	13	32	–19	(*)
Japan	–88	–1	–87	—
Korea, South	–146	1	–147	—
Malaysia	–15	1	–16	—
New Zealand	–10	—	–10	—
Philippines	449	373	76	(*)
Singapore	–183	(*)	–184	—
Taiwan	262	(*)	262	(*)
Thailand	62	35	27	—
Trust Terr. Pacific	218	218	—	—
Other & unspecified	20	19	1	—
Africa	**1,291**	**1,116**	**175**	**(*)**
Algeria	–128	(*)	–128	—
Angola	27	7	20	—
Benin	3	3	(*)	—
Botswana	20	19	1	—
Burkina Faso	29	29	—	(*)
Burundi	5	5	—	(*)
Cameroon	11	18	–8	—

	Total	Net grants	Net credits	Net other
Cape Verde	9	9	—	—
Cen. African Rep.	3	3	(*)	—
Chad	25	25	—	—
Djibouti	6	6	—	—
Ethiopia	88	94	–5	(*)
Gabon	6	2	4	—
Gambia	9	9	—	—
Ghana	13	13	(*)	(*)
Guinea	14	9	6	–1
Guinea-Bissau	3	3	—	—
Ivory Coast	5	1	4	(*)
Kenya	39	40	–1	(*)
Lesotho	23	23	—	—
Liberia	52	41	11	—
Madagascar	21	11	9	(*)
Malawi	11	14	–3	—
Mali	45	45	(*)	(*)
Mauritania	19	20	–1	—
Mauritius	4	5	–1	—
Morocco	175	70	105	(*)
Mozambique	33	19	14	—
Niger	39	38	1	—
Rwanda	25	24	(*)	—
Senegal	45	40	5	—
Seychelles	4	4	—	—
Sierra Leone	12	5	7	—
Somalia	112	92	20	—
Sudan	164	120	44	(*)
Swaziland	9	9	(*)	—
Tanzania	10	8	1	—
Togo	10	10	(*)	—
Tunisia	3	45	–42	1
Uganda	4	4	–1	—
Zaire	104	35	69	(*)
Zambia	77	30	47	—
Zimbabwe	22	27	–5	—
Other & unspecified	75	75	(*)	—
Western Hemisphere	**1,756**	**1,310**	**444**	**2**
Antigua & Barbuda	5	1	4	—
Argentina	69	(*)	69	—
Belize	14	7	7	—
Bolivia	110	67	42	(*)
Brazil	–19	14	–33	(*)
Canada	–61	—	–61	—
Chile	57	7	49	1
Colombia	63	9	54	(*)
Costa Rica	139	92	48	–1
Dominican Republic	238	17	221	(*)
Ecuador	67	41	25	—
El Salvador	376	310	66	(*)
Grenada	11	11	(*)	—
Guatemala	88	52	36	(*)
Haiti	87	77	10	—
Honduras	224	205	19	(*)
Jamaica	121	66	54	1
Mexico	–52	56	–108	—
Panama	24	21	4	—
Peru	92	62	30	—
St. Vincnet	4	1	2	—
Trinidad-Tobago	–32	(*)	–32	—
Uruguay	11	14	–3	—
Venezuela	–31	(*)	–31	—
Other & unspecified	150	174	–24	—
Intl. orgs. & unspecified	**1,345**	**1,349**	**–4**	**—**

POSTAL INFORMATION

U.S. Postal Service

The Postal Reorganization Act, creating a government-owned postal service under the executive branch and replacing the old Post Office Department, was signed into law by President Nixon on Aug. 12, 1970. The service officially came into being on July 1, 1971.

The new U.S. Postal Service is governed by an 11-man Board of Governors. Nine members are appointed to 9-year terms by the president with Senate approval. These 9, in turn, choose a postmaster general, who is no longer a member of the president's cabinet. The board and the new postmaster general choose the 11th member, who serves as deputy postmaster general. An independent Postal Rate Commission of 5 members, appointed by the president, recommends postal rates to the governors for their approval.

As of July 4, 1987, there were 29,319 post offices throughout the U.S. and possessions.

U.S. Domestic Rates

In effect from Feb. 17, 1985.

Domestic includes the U.S., territories and possessions, APO and FPO.

First Class

Letters written, and matter sealed against inspection, 22¢ for 1st oz. or fraction, 17¢ for each additional oz. or fraction.

U.S. Postal cards; single 14¢; double 28¢; private postcards, same.

First class includes written matter, namely letters, postal cards, postcards (private mailing cards) and all other matter wholly or partly in writing, whether sealed or unsealed, except manuscripts for books, periodical articles and music, manuscript copy accompanying proofsheets or corrected proofsheets of the same and the writing authorized by law on matter of other classes. Also matter sealed or closed against inspection, bills and statements of accounts.

Greeting Cards

May be sent first class or single piece third class.

Express Mail

Express Mail Service is available for any mailable article up to 70 pounds, and guarantees delivery between major U.S. cities or your money back. Articles received by the acceptance time authorized by the postmaster at a postal facility offering Express Mail will be delivered by 3 p.m. the next day or, if you prefer, your shipment can be picked up as early as 10 a.m. the next business day. Rates include insurance, Shipment Receipt, and Record of Delivery at the destination post office.

Consult Postmaster for other Express Mail Services and rates. (The Postal Service will refund, upon application to originating office, the postage for any Express Mail shipments not meeting the service standard except for those delayed by strike or work stoppage.)

Second Class

Single copy mailings by general public 22¢ for first ounce, 39¢ for over 1 to 2 ozs., 56¢ for over 2 to 3 ozs., 73¢ for over 3 to 4 ozs., 88¢ for 4–5 ozs. and 10¢ for each additional ounce up to 16 ozs.

Third Class

Third class (limit up to but not including 16 ounces): Mailable matter not in 1st and 2d classes.

Single mailing: Greeting cards (sealed or unsealed), small parcels, printed matter, booklets and catalogs, 22¢ the first ounce, 39¢ for over 1 to 2 ozs., 56¢ for over 2 to 3 ozs., 73¢ for over 3 to 4 ozs., 88¢ for over 4 to 6 ozs., 98¢ for over 6 to 8 ozs., $1.08 for over 8 to 10 ozs., $1.18 for over 10 to 12 ozs., $1.28 for over 12 to 14 ozs., $1.38 for over 14 but less than 16 ozs.

Bulk material: books, catalogs of 24 pages or more, seeds, cuttings, bulbs, roots, scions, and plants. 38¢ per pound, 12.5¢ minimum per piece.

Other matter: newsletters, shopper's guides, advertising circulars, 45¢ per pound, 10.9¢ minimum per piece. Separate rates for some nonprofit organizations. Bulk mailing fee, $40 per calendar year. Apply to postmaster for permit. One-time fee for permit imprint, $50.

Parcel Post—Fourth Class

Fourth class or parcel post (16 ounces and over): merchandise, printed matter, etc., may be sealed, subject to inspection.

Priority Mail

First class mail of more than 12 ounces can be sent "Priority Mail (Heavy Pieces)" service. The most expeditious handling and transportation available will be used for fastest delivery.

On parcels weighing less than 15 lbs. and measuring more than 84 inches, but not more than 100 inches in length and girth combined, the minimum postal charge shall be the zone charge applicable to a 15-pound parcel.

Forwarding Addresses

The mailer, in order to obtain a forwarding address, must endorse the envelope or cover "Address Correction Requested." The destination post office then will determine whether a forwarding address has been left on file and provide it for a fee of 30¢.

Priority Mail

Packages weighing up to 70 pounds and exceeding 100 inches in length and girth combined, including written and other material of the first class, whether sealed or unsealed, fractions of a pound being charged as a full pound, except in the 1 to 5 pound weight category where half-pound weight increments apply.

Rates according to zone apply between the U.S. and Puerto Rico and Virgin Islands.

Parcels weighing less than 15 pounds, measuring over 84 inches but not exceeding 100 inches in length and girth combined are chargeable with a minimum rate equal to that for a 15 pound parcel for the zone to which addressed.

Zones	To 2	3	4	5	Zones	To 2	3	4	5
1, 2, 3.	$2.40	$2.74	3.18	$3.61	6.	2.40	3.74	4.53	5.27
4.	2.40	3.16	3.75	4.32	7.	2.40	3.96	4.92	5.81
5.	2.40	3.45	4.13	4.86	8.	2.40	4.32	5.33	6.37

*Consult postmaster for parcels over 5 lbs.

Special Handling

Third and fourth class parcels will be handled and delivered as expeditiously as practicable (but not special delivery) upon payment, in addition to the regular postage: up to 10 lbs., $1.10; over 10 lbs., $1.30. Such parcels must be endorsed, Special Handling.

Special Delivery

First class mail up to 2 lbs. $2.95, over 2 lbs. and up to 10 lbs., $3.15; over 10 lbs. $4.00. All other classes up to 2 lbs. $3.10, over 2 and up to 10 lbs., $3.60, over 10 lbs. $4.50.

Bound Printed Matter Rates

(Fourth class single piece zone rate)

Weight lbs.	Local	Zones 1&2	3	4	5	6	7	8
1.5	$0.55	$0.77	$0.81	$0.89	$1.00	$1.11	$1.26	$1.38
2	0.58	0.81	0.87	0.97	1.12	1.27	1.46	1.62
2.5	0.60	0.85	0.92	1.05	1.23	1.42	1.67	1.86
3	0.63	0.89	0.98	1.12	1.35	1.58	1.87	2.10
3.5	0.65	0.93	1.03	1.20	1.47	1.73	2.07	2.34
4	0.68	0.97	1.09	1.28	1.58	1.89	2.28	2.59
4.5	0.70	1.01	1.14	1.36	1.70	2.04	2.48	2.83
5	0.73	1.06	1.20	1.44	1.82	2.20	2.69	3.07
6	0.77	1.14	1.30	1.60	2.05	2.50	3.09	3.55
7	0.82	1.22	1.41	1.76	2.28	2.81	3.50	4.04
8	0.87	1.30	1.52	1.91	2.51	3.12	3.91	4.52
9	0.92	1.38	1.63	2.07	2.75	3.43	4.31	5.01
10	0.97	1.46	1.74	2.23	2.98	3.74	4.72	5.49

Domestic Mail Special Services

Registry — Only matter prepaid with postage at First-class postage rates may be registered. Stamps or meter stamps must be attached. The face of the article must be at least 5" long, 3½" high. The mailer is required to declare the value of mail presented for registration.

Registered Mail

	Insured	Uninsured
$0.00 to $100.	$3.60	$3.55
$100.01 to $500	3.90	3.80
$500.01 to $1,000 . . .	4.25	4.15
$1,000.01 to $2,000 . .	4.60	4.40
$2,000.01 to $3,000 . .	4.95	4.65
$3,000.01 to $4,000 . .	5.30	4.90
$4,000.01 to $5,000 . .	5.65	5.15
$5,000.01 to $6,000 . .	6.00	5.40
$6,000.01 to $7,000 . .	6.35	5.65
$7,000.01 to $8,000 . .	6.70	5.90
$8,000.01 to $9,000 . .	7.05	6.15
$9,000.01 to $10,000 .	7.40	6.40

Consult postmaster for registry rates above $10,000.

C.O.D.: Unregistered — is applicable to 3d and 4th class matter and sealed domestic mail of any class bearing postage at the 1st class rate. Such mail must be based on bona fide orders or be in conformity with agreements between senders and addressees. **Registered** — for details consult postmaster.

Insurance — is applicable to 3d and 4th class matter. Matter for sale addressed to prospective purchasers who have not ordered it or authorized its sending will not be insured.

Insured Mail

$0.01 to $25.	$1.50
25.01 to 50	1.80
50.01 to 100.	2.10
100.01 to 200	2.40
200.01 to 300	3.00
300.01 to 400	3.70
400.01 to 500	4.70

Liability for insured mail is limited to $400.

Certified mail — service is available for any matter having no intrinsic value on which 1st class or air mail postage is paid. Receipt is furnished at time of mailing and evidence of delivery obtained. The fee is 75¢ ($1.25 restricted delivery) in addition to postage. Return receipt, restricted delivery, and special delivery are available upon payment of additional fees. No indemnity.

Special Fourth Class Rate

(limit 70 lbs.)

First pound or fraction, 69¢ (47¢ if 500 pieces or more of special rate matter are presorted to 5 digit ZIP code or 60¢ if 500 pieces or more are presorted to Bulk Mail Cntrs.); each additional pound or fraction through 7 pounds, 25¢; each additional pound, 15¢. Only the following specific articles: Books of at least 8 printed pages consisting wholly of reading matter or scholarly bibliography, or reading matter with incidental blank spaces for notations and containing no advertising matter other than incidental announcements of books; 16-millimeter or narrower width films in final form and catalogs of such films of 24 pages or more (at least 22 of which are printed) except films and film catalogs sent to or from commercial theaters; printed music in bound or sheet form; printed objective test materials; sound recordings, playscripts, and manuscripts for books, periodicals, and music; printed educational reference charts; loose-leaf pages and binders therefor consisting of medical information for distribution to doctors, hospitals, medical schools, and medical students. Package must be marked "Special 4th Class Rate" stating item contained.

Library Rate (limit 70 lbs.)

First pound 54¢, each additional pound through 7 pounds, 19¢; each additional pound, 10¢. Books when loaned or exchanged between schools, colleges, public libraries, and certain non-profit organizations; books, printed music, bound academic theses, periodicals, sound recordings, other library materials, museum materials (specimens, collections), scientific or mathematical kits, instruments or other devices; also catalogs, guides or scripts for some of these materials. Must be marked "Library Rate".

Postal Union Mail Special Services

Registration — available to practically all countries. Fee $3.60. The maximum indemnity payable — generally only in case of complete loss (of both contents and wrapper) — is $20.40. To Canada only the fee is $3.60 providing indemnity for loss up to $100, $3.90 for loss up to $200.

Parcel Post Rate Schedule

(Inter BMC/ASF Zip Codes Only, Machinable Parcels, No Discount, No Surcharge)

Single Piece Zone Rates Not Exceeding (pounds)	Zones 1 and 2	3	4	5	6	7	8
2	1.41	1.51	1.66	1.89	2.13	2.25	2.30
3	1.49	1.65	1.87	2.21	2.58	2.99	3.87
4	1.57	1.78	2.08	2.54	3.03	3.57	4.74
5	1.65	1.92	2.29	2.86	3.47	4.16	5.62
6	1.74	2.05	2.50	3.18	3.92	4.74	6.49
7	1.82	2.19	2.71	3.51	4.37	5.32	7.36
8	1.90	2.32	2.92	3.83	4.82	5.91	8.25
9	1.99	2.46	3.13	4.15	5.26	6.49	9.12
10	2.07	2.59	3.34	4.48	5.71	7.07	10.00
11	2.13	2.70	3.49	4.71	6.03	7.49	10.62
12	2.20	2.79	3.65	4.94	6.34	7.89	11.23
13	2.26	2.89	3.79	5.15	6.63	8.27	11.78
14	2.32	2.98	3.92	5.35	6.90	8.62	12.30
15	2.37	3.06	4.04	5.54	7.15	8.94	12.79
16	2.42	3.14	4.16	5.71	7.39	9.25	13.24
17	2.48	3.22	4.27	5.88	7.61	9.54	13.67
18	2.52	3.29	4.38	6.03	7.83	9.81	14.08
19	2.57	3.36	4.48	6.18	8.03	10.07	14.46
20	2.62	3.43	4.58	6.33	8.22	10.32	14.83
21	2.67	3.49	4.67	6.47	8.41	10.56	15.18
22	2.71	3.56	4.76	6.60	8.59	10.79	15.51
23	2.75	3.62	4.85	6.73	8.76	11.01	15.83
24	2.80	3.68	4.94	6.85	8.92	11.22	16.14
25	2.84	3.74	5.02	6.97	9.08	11.42	16.43

Return receipt — showing to whom and date delivr'd, 70¢.

Special delivery — Available to most countries. Consult post office. Fees: for post cards, letter mail, and airmail "other articles," \$2.95 up to 2 pounds; over 2 to 10 pounds, \$3.15; over 10 pounds, \$4.00. For surface "other articles," \$3.10, \$3.60, and \$4.50, respectively.

Marking — an article intended for special delivery service must have affixed to the cover near the name of the country of destination "EXPRESS" (special delivery) label, obtainable at the post office, or it may be marked on the cover boldly in red "EXPRESS" (special delivery).

Special handling — entitles AO surface packages to priority handling between mailing point and U.S. point of dispatch. Fees: \$1.10 for packages to 10 pounds, and \$1.60 for packages over 10 pounds.

Airmail — there is daily air service to practically all countries.

Prepayment of replies from other countries — a mailer who wishes to prepay a reply by letter from another country may do so by sending his correspondent one or more international reply coupons, which may be purchased at United States post offices. One coupon should be accepted in any country in exchange for stamps to prepay a surface letter of the first unit of weight to the U.S.

Post Office-Authorized 2-Letter State Abbreviations

The abbreviations below are approved by the U.S. Postal Service for use in addresses only. They do not replace the traditional abbreviations in other contexts. The official list follows, including the District of Columbia, Guam, Puerto Rico, the Canal Zone, and the Virgin Islands (all capital letters are used):

Alabama	AL	Hawaii	HI	Missouri	MO	Puerto Rico	PR
Alaska	AK	Idaho	ID	Montana	MT	Rhode Island	RI
American Samoa	AS	Illinois	IL	Nebraska	NE	South Carolina	SC
Arizona	AZ	Indiana	IN	Nevada	NV	South Dakota	SD
Arkansas	AR	Iowa	IA	New Hampshire	NH	Tennessee	TN
California	CA	Kansas	KS	New Jersey	NJ	Texas	TX
Canal Zone	CZ	Kentucky	KY	New Mexico	NM	Trust Territories	TT
Colorado	CO	Louisiana	LA	New York	NY	Utah	UT
Connecticut	CT	Maine	ME	North Carolina	NC	Vermont	VT
Delaware	DE	Maryland	MD	North Dakota	ND	Virginia	VA
Dist. of Col.	DC	Massachusetts	MA	Northern Mariana Is.	CM	Virgin Islands	VI
Florida	FL	Michigan	MI	Ohio	OH	Washington	WA
Georgia	GA	Minnesota	MN	Oklahoma	OK	West Virginia	WV
Guam	GU	Mississippi	MS	Oregon	OR	Wisconsin	WI
				Pennsylvania	PA	Wyoming	WY

Also approved for use in addressing mail are the following abbreviations:

Alley	Aly	Court	Ct	Grove	Grv	Rural	R
Arcade	Arc	Courts	Cts	Heights	Hts	Square	Sq
Avenue	Ave	Crescent	Cres	Highway	Hwy	Street	St
Boulevard	Blvd	Drive	Dr	Lane	Ln	Terrace	Ter
Branch	Br	Expressway	Expy	Manor	Mnr	Trail	Trl
Bypass	Byp	Extended	Ext	Place	Pl	Turnpike	Tpke
Causeway	Cswy	Extension	Ext	Plaza	Plz	Viaduct	Via
Center	Ctr	Freeway	Fwy	Point	Pt	Vista	Vis
Circle	Cir	Gardens	Gdns	Road	Rd		

Size Standards for Domestic Mail

Minimum Size

Pieces which do not meet the following requirements are prohibited from the mails:

a. All pieces must be at least .007 of an inch thick, and

b. All pieces (except keys and identification devices) which are ¼ inch or less thick must be:

(1) Rectangular in shape,

(2) At least 3½ inches high, and

(3) At least 5 inches long.

Note: Pieces greater than ¼ inch thick can be mailed even if they measure less than 3½ by 5 inches.

Nonstandard Mail

All First-Class Mail weighing one ounce or less and all single-piece rate Third-Class mail weighing one ounce or less is nonstandard (and subject to a 9¢ surcharge in addition to the applicable postage and fees) if:

1. Any of the following dimensions are exceeded:
   Length—11½ inches,
   Height—6⅛ inches,
   Thickness—¼ inch, or
2. The piece has a height to length (aspect) ratio which does not fall between 1 to 1.3 and 1 to 2.5 inclusive. (The aspect ratio is found by dividing the length by the height. If the answer is between 1.3 and 2.5 inclusive, the piece has a standard aspect ratio.)

Envelopes Available at Post Offices

Kind	Size	Denomination	Item No.	Less than 500 each	500	1,000
Regular	6¾	22 cents	631	\$0.27	115.90	231.80
	10	22 cents	131	.27	117.40	234.80
Window	6¾	22 cents	632		116.50	233.00
	10	22 cents	132		118.00	236.00
Precanceled.	6¾	6.0 cents.	666		35.90	71.80
(Regular)	10	6.0 cents.	166		37.40	74.80
Precanceled.	6¾	6.0 cents.	667		36.50	73.00
(Window)	10	6.0 cents.	167		38.00	76.00

Postal Receipts at Large Cities

Fiscal year	Boston	Chicago	L.A.	New York	Phila.	St. Louis	Wash., D.C.
1975	\$136,453,079	\$365,378,795	\$193,229,077	\$453,905,277	\$134,571,376	\$85,591,774	\$115,489,343
1980	224,428,760	528,233,991	271,136,828	666,377,778	221,161,624	127,427,555	187,334,312
1981	256,524,082	551,988,015	301,159,594	741,286,845	235,116,018	142,548,957	201,191,995
1982	292,971,572	597,246,568	338,798,409	848,507,590	265,242,959	160,596,946	215,772,861
1983	294,932,399	589,476,264	330,734,928	856,569,717	273,210,529	165,000,437	212,117,368
1984	314,230,399	598,141,605	338,760,060	907,426,500	295,917,848	177,041,331	225,378,646
1985	339,550,469	563,693,370	358,859,412	938,829,064	300,811,081	194,786,119	236,131,464
1986	378,861,842	579,432,633	381,254,469	960,987,314	330,671,509	211,134,497	253,607,563

Other cities for fiscal year 1986: Dallas, \$371,214,113; Atlanta, \$351,164,868; Houston, \$289,085,323; Minneapolis, \$241,114,124; San Francisco, \$229,070,583; Denver, \$189,736,088; Baltimore, \$199,824,127; Hartford, \$203,842,832; Cleveland, \$190,819,160; Pittsburgh, \$175,291,412.

Air Mail, Parcel Post International Rates

Aerogrammes — 36¢ each to all countries.
Air mail postcards (single) - 33¢ to all countries except Canada and Mexico (14¢)

Country	First 4 oz.	Air parcel post rates: Each add'l. 4 oz. or fraction up to first 5 lbs.	Each add'l. ½ lb. or fraction of ½ lb.
Afghanistan	$7.05	1.35	2.50
Albania	6.00	1.10	2.00
Algeria	7.05	1.35	2.50
Andorra	4.95	.90	1.50
Angola	8.10	1.60	3.00
Argentina	7.05	1.35	2.50
Ascension	No Air Service		
Australia	7.05	1.35	2.50
Austria	4.95	.90	1.50
Azores	6.00	1.10	2.00
Bahamas	3.90	.65	1.00
Bahrain	7.05	1.35	2.50
Bangladesh	8.10	1.60	3.00
Barbados	4.95	.90	1.50
Belgium	7.05	1.35	2.50
Belize	3.90	.65	1.00
Benin	7.05	1.35	2.50
Bermuda	3.90	.65	1.00
Bhutan	8.10	1.60	3.00
Bolivia	4.95	.90	1.50
Botswana	8.10	1.60	3.00
Brazil	7.05	1.35	2.50
Brunei	7.05	1.35	2.50
Bulgaria	7.05	1.35	2.50
Burkina Faso	6.00	1.10	2.00
Burma	7.05	1.35	2.50
Burundi	8.10	1.60	3.00
Cameroon	7.05	1.35	2.50
Canada[1]	Separate rate schedule		
Cape Verde	7.05	1.35	2.50
Cayman Islands	3.90	.65	1.00
Central African Rep.	8.10	1.60	3.00
Chad	7.05	1.35	2.50
Chile	7.05	1.35	2.50
China (People's Republic of)	7.05	1.35	2.50
Colombia	4.95	.90	1.50
Comoros	8.10	1.60	3.00
Congo	7.05	1.35	2.50
Corsica	8.10	1.60	3.00
Costa Rica	3.90	.65	1.00
Cuba	No Parcel Post Service		
Cyprus	7.05	1.35	2.50
Czechoslovakia	6.00	1.10	2.00
Denmark	6.00	1.10	2.00
Djibouti	8.10	1.60	3.00
Dominica	3.90	.65	1.00
Dominican Republic	3.90	.65	1.00
East Timor	No Parcel Post Service		
Ecuador	4.95	.90	1.50
Egypt	6.00	1.10	2.00
El Salvador	3.90	.65	1.00
Equatorial Guinea	7.05	1.35	2.50
Estonia	8.10	1.60	3.00
Ethiopia	7.05	1.35	2.50
Faeroe Islands	6.00	1.10	2.00
Falkland Islands	7.05	1.35	2.50
Fiji	4.95	.90	1.50
Finland	7.05	1.35	2.50
France (Including Monaco)	7.05	1.35	2.50
French Guiana	6.00	1.10	2.00
French Polynesia	7.05	1.35	2.50
Gabon	7.05	1.35	2.50
Gambia	4.95	.90	1.50
German Democratic Republic (East Germany)	6.00	1.10	2.00
Germany, Federal Rep. of (West Germany)	6.00	1.10	2.00
Ghana	7.05	1.35	2.50
Gibraltar	7.05	1.35	2.50
Great Britain	6.00	1.10	2.00
Greece	6.00	1.10	2.00
Greenland	7.05	1.35	2.50
Grenada	4.95	.90	1.50
Guadeloupe	3.90	.65	1.00
Guatemala	3.90	.65	1.00
Guinea	4.95	.90	1.50
Guinea-Bissau	4.95	.90	1.50
Guyana	4.95	.90	1.50
Haiti	3.90	.65	1.00
Honduras	4.95	.90	1.50
Hong Kong	6.00	1.10	2.00
Hungary	6.00	1.10	2.00
Iceland	7.05	1.35	2.50
India	7.05	1.35	2.50
Indonesia	8.10	1.60	3.00
Iran	7.05	1.35	2.50
Iraq	7.05	1.35	2.50
Ireland (Eire)	6.00	1.10	2.00
Israel	6.00	1.10	2.00
Italy	6.00	1.10	2.00
Ivory Coast	7.05	1.35	2.50
Jamaica	3.90	.65	1.00
Japan	8.10	1.60	3.00
Jordan	6.00	1.10	2.00
Kampuchea	No Parcel Post Service		
Kenya	7.05	1.35	2.50
Kiribati	4.95	.90	1.50
Korea, Democratic People's Rep. (North)	No Parcel Post Service		
Korea, Rep. of (South)	6.00	1.10	2.00
Kuwait	6.00	1.10	2.00
Lao	8.10	1.60	3.00
Latvia	8.10	1.60	3.00
Lebanon	6.00	1.10	2.00
Leeward Islands	3.90	.65	1.00
Lesotho	8.10	1.60	3.00
Liberia	6.00	1.10	2.00
Libya	6.00	1.10	2.00
Lithuania	8.10	1.60	3.00
Luxembourg	4.95	.90	1.50
Macao	6.00	1.10	2.00
Madagascar	8.10	1.60	3.00
Madeira Islands	4.95	.90	1.50
Malawi	7.05	1.35	2.50
Malaysia	7.05	1.35	2.50
Maldives	8.10	1.60	3.00
Mali	6.00	1.10	2.00
Malta	6.00	1.10	2.00
Martinique	3.90	.65	1.00
Mauritania	7.05	1.35	2.50
Mauritius	8.10	1.60	3.00
Mexico	3.90	.65	1.00
Mongolia	No Parcel Post Service		
Morocco	6.00	1.10	2.00
Mozambique	8.10	1.60	3.00
Nauru	6.00	1.10	2.00
Nepal	7.05	1.35	2.50
Netherlands	6.00	1.10	2.00
Netherlands Antilles	3.90	.65	1.00
New Caledonia	7.05	1.35	2.50
New Zealand	7.05	1.35	2.50
Nicaragua	4.95	.90	1.50
Niger	7.05	1.35	2.50
Nigeria	6.00	1.10	2.00
Norway	7.05	1.35	2.50
Oman	7.05	1.35	2.50
Pakistan	7.05	1.35	2.50
Panama	3.90	.65	1.00
Papua New Guinea	7.05	1.35	2.50
Paraguay	6.00	1.10	2.00
Peru	4.95	.90	1.50
Philippines	7.05	1.35	2.50
Pitcairn Islands	4.95	.90	1.50
Poland	6.00	1.10	2.00
Portugal	6.00	1.10	2.00
Qatar	6.00	1.10	2.00
Reunion	8.10	1.60	3.00
Romania	6.00	1.10	2.00
Rwanda	7.05	1.35	2.50
St. Helena	6.00	1.10	2.00
St. Lucia	3.90	.65	1.00
St. Pierre & Miquelon	3.90	.65	1.00
St. Thomas & Principe	7.05	1.35	2.50

Country	First 4 oz.	Air parcel post rates: Each add'l. 4 oz. or fraction up to first 5 lbs.	Each add'l. ½ lb. or fraction of ½ lb.
St. Vincent & The Grenadines	3.90	.65	1.00
Santa Cruz Islands	6.00	1.10	2.00
Saudi Arabia	7.05	1.35	2.50
Senegal	7.05	1.35	2.50
Seychelles	8.10	1.60	3.00
Sierre Leone	7.05	1.35	2.50
Singapore	7.05	1.35	2.50
Solomon Islands	6.00	1.10	2.00
Somalia (Southern Region)	7.05	1.35	2.50
Somalia (Northern Region)	7.05	1.35	2.50
South Africa	7.05	1.35	2.50
Spain	6.00	1.10	2.00
Sri Lanka	7.05	1.35	2.50
Sudan	7.05	1.35	2.50
Suriname	4.95	.90	1.50
Swaziland	7.05	1.35	2.50
Sweden	7.05	1.35	2.50
Switzerland	4.95	.90	1.50
Syria	6.00	1.10	2.00
Taiwan	6.00	1.10	2.00
Tanzania	8.10	1.60	3.00
Thailand	7.05	1.35	2.50

Country	First 4 oz.	Air parcel post rates: Each add'l. 4 oz. or fraction up to first 5 lbs.	Each add'l. ½ lb. or fraction of ½ lb.
Togo	7.05	1.35	2.50
Tonga	4.95	.90	1.50
Trinidad & Tobago	4.95	.90	1.50
Tristan da Cunha	8.10	1.60	3.00
Tunisia	6.00	1.10	2.00
Turkey	6.00	1.10	2.00
Turks & Caicos Islands	3.90	.65	1.00
Tuvalu (Ellice Islands)	4.95	.90	1.50
Uganda	7.05	1.35	2.50
USSR[2]	8.10	1.60	3.00
United Arab Emirates	7.05	1.35	2.50
Uruguay	4.95	.90	1.50
Vanuatu	4.95	.90	1.50
Vatican City State	6.00	1.10	2.00
Venezuela	4.95	.90	1.50
Vietnam[1]	No Parcel Post Service		
Western Samoa	4.95	.90	1.50
Yemen Arab Republic	7.05	1.35	2.50
Yemen, Peoples Democratic Republic of	7.05	1.35	2.50
Yugoslavia	6.00	1.10	2.00
Zaire	7.05	1.35	2.50
Zambia	8.10	1.60	3.00
Zimbabwe	8.10	1.60	3.00

Weight limits. minimum 1 lb., maximum 66 lbs.; up to 1½ lbs., $3.38; each add'l 8 oz. or fraction, up to first 5 lbs., 54¢; each add'l 8 oz. or fraction, $1.08.

(1) Restrictions apply; consult post office. (2) To facilitate distribution and delivery, include "Union of Soviet Socialist Republics" or "USSR" as part of the address.

Miscellaneous International Rates

Letters and Letter Pkgs (Surface)

Weight steps: Over Lbs.	Over Ozs.	Through Lbs.	Through Ozs.	Canada and Mexico	All other countries
0	0	0	1	$.22	$.37
0	1	0	2	.40	.57
0	2	0	3	.58	.77
0	3	0	4	.76	.97
0	4	0	5	.94	1.17
0	5	0	6	1.12	1.37
0	6	0	7	1.30	1.57
0	7	0	8	1.48	1.77
0	8	0	9	1.66	3.40
0	9	0	10	1.84	3.40
0	10	0	11	2.02	3.40
0	11	0	12	2.20	3.40
0	12	1	0	2.84	3.40
1	0	1	8	3.38	4.08
1	8	2	0	3.92	5.92
2	0	2	8	4.40	6.84
2	8	3	0	5.00	7.76
3	0	3	8	5.54	8.68
3	8	4	0	6.08	9.60

Maximum limit: 66 pounds to Canada, 4 pounds to Mexico and all other countries.

Letters and Letter Pkgs (Air)

Canada and Mexico: Refer to rates listed under Letter and Letter Pkgs. (Surface). Mail paid at this rate receives First-Class service in the United States and air service in Canada and Mexico.

Colombia, Venezuela, Central America, the Caribbean Islands, Bahamas, Bermuda, St. Pierre & Miquelon; also from Amer. Samoa to Western Samoa and from Guam to Philippines: 39 cents per half ounce up to and including 2 ounces; 33 cents each additional half ounce up to and including 32 ounces; 33 cents per additional ounce over 32 ounces.

All Other Countries: 44 cents per half ounce up to and including 2 ounces; 39 cents each additional half ounce up to and including 32 ounces; 39 cents per additional ounce over 32 ounces.

Parcel Post (Surface)

Canada: $3.35 for over 1 lb. and up to 2 lbs.; $1.05 each add'l lb.

Mexico, Central America, The Caribbean Islands, Bahamas, Bermuda, St. Pierre and Miquelon: $3.70 for the first 2 pounds and $1.20 each additional pound or fraction.

All Other Countries: $3.90 for the first 2 pounds and $1.30 for each additional pound or fraction.

For Parcel Post air rates, see tables, pages 752-753.

Postcards

Surface rates to Canada and Mexico, 14¢; to all other countries, 25¢. By air, Canada and Mexico, 14¢; to all other countries, 33¢. Maximum size permitted, 6 x 4¼ in.; minimum, 5½ x 3½.

International Parcel Post

For rates see pages 752-753.

General dimensional limits — greatest length, 3½ feet; greatest length and girth combined, 6 feet.

Prohibited articles. Before sending goods abroad the mailer should consult the post office that they will not be confiscated or returned because their importation is prohibited or restricted by the country of address.

Packing. Parcels for transmission overseas should be even more carefully packed than those intended for delivery within the continental U.S. Containers should be used which will be strong enough to protect the contents from the weight of other mail, from pressure and friction, climatic changes, and repeated handlings.

Sealing. Registered or insured parcels must be sealed. To some countries the sealing of ordinary (unregistered and uninsured) parcels is optional, and to others compulsory. Consult post office.

Customs declarations and other forms. At least one customs declaration is required for parcel post packages (surface or air) mailed to another country. In addition, to some countries, a dispatch note is required. The forms may be obtained at post offices.

ASSOCIATIONS AND SOCIETIES

Source: World Almanac questionnaire

Arranged according to key words in titles. Founding year of organization in parentheses; last figure after ZIP code indicates membership.

ATV Owners Assn., Natl. (1972), P.O. Box 1272, Bensalem, PA 19020; 1,712.

Aaron Burr Assn. (1946), 2064 Faculty Dr., Winston-Salem, NC 27106; 400.

Abortion Federation, Natl. (1977), 900 Pennsylvania Ave. SE, Washington, DC 20003; 270 institutions.

Abortion Rights Action League, Natl. (1968), 1424 K St. NW, Wash., DC 20005; 150,000.

Accountants, Amer. Institute of Certified Public (1887), 1211 Ave. of the Americas, N.Y., NY 10036; 250,000.

Accountants, Natl. Assn. of (1919), 10 Paragon Dr., Box 433, Montvale, NJ 07645; 90,000.

Accountants, Natl. Soc. of for Cooperatives (1936), 6320 Augusta Dr., Springfield, VA 22150; 2,079.

Accountants, Natl. Society of Public (1945), 1010 N. Fairfax St., Alexandria, VA 22314.

Acoustical Society of America (1929), 500 Sunnyside Blvd., Woodbury, NY 11797; 6,000.

Actors' Equity Assn. (1913), 165 W. 46 St., N.Y., NY 10036.

Actors' Fund of America (1882), 1501 Broadway, N.Y., NY 10036; 3,500.

Actuaries, American Academy of (1965), 1720 I St. NW, Wash., DC 20006; 6,400.

Actuaries, Society of (1949), 500 Park Blvd., Itasca, IL 60143; 10,000.

Adirondack Mountain Club (1922), 174 Glen St., Glens Falls, NY 12801; 12,000.

Advertisers, Assn. of Natl. (1910), 155 E. 44th St., 33d fl., N.Y., NY 10017; 450 cos.

Advertising Agencies, Amer. Assn. of (1917), 666 Third Ave., N.Y., NY 10017; 600 agencies.

Aeronautic Assn. of USA, Inc., Natl. (1922), 1400 Eye St. NW, #550, Wash., DC 20005; 5,000.

Aeronautics and Astronautics, Amer. Institute of (1963), 1633 Broadway, N.Y., NY 10019; 38,000.

Aerospace Industries Assn. of America (1919), 1725 De Sales St. NW, Wash., DC 20036; 48 cos.

Aerospace Medical Assn. (1923), Washington Natl. Airport, Wash., DC 20001; 4,000.

Afro-American Life and History, Assn. for the Study of (1915), 1401 14th St. NW, Wash., DC 20005; 1,800.

Aging Assn., Amer. (1970), Univ. of Nebraska Medical Center, 42d & Dewey Ave., Omaha, NE 68105; 500.

Agnostics, Soc. of Evangelical (1975), Box 515, Auberry, CA 93602.

Agricultural Chemicals Assn., Natl. (1933), 1155 15th St. NW, Wash., DC 20005; 125 cos.

Agricultural Economics Assn., Amer. (1910), Dept. of Economics, Iowa State Univ., Ames, IA 50011; 4,500.

Agricultural History Society (1919), 1301 New York Ave. NW, Wash., DC 20250; 1,400.

Agronomy, Amer. Society of (1907), 677 S. Segoe Rd., Madison, WI 53711; 13,000.

Aircraft Owners and Pilots Assn. (1939), 421 Aviation Way, Frederick, MD 21701; 260,000.

Air Force Assn. (1946), 1501 Lee Hwy., Arlington, VA 22209-1198; 235,000.

Air Force Sergeants Assn. (1961), P.O. Box 31050, Temple Hills, MD 20748.

Air Line Employees Assn. (1951), 5600 S. Central Ave., Chicago, IL 60638; 9,000.

Air Line Pilots Assn. (1931), 1625 Massachusetts Ave. NW, Wash., DC 20036; 33,000.

Air Pollution Control Assn. (1907), P.O. Box 2861, Pittsburgh, PA 15230; 8,500.

Air Transport Assn. of America (1936), 1709 New York Ave. NW, Wash., DC 20006; 27 airlines.

Alcohol Problems, Amer. Council on (1895), 2908 Patricia Dr., Des Moines, IA 50322.

Alcoholics Anonymous (1935), 468 Park Ave. So., N.Y., NY 10016; 1 mln.+.

Alcoholism, Natl. Council on (1944), 12 W. 21st St., N.Y., NY 10010; 184 affiliates.

All-Terrain Vehicle Owners Assn., Natl. (1972), P.O. Box 1272, Bensalem, PA 19020; 2,514.

Allergy and Immunology, Amer. Academy of (1943), 611 E. Wells St., Milwaukee, WI 53202; 3,500.

Alpine Club, Amer. (1902), 113 E. 90th St., N.Y., NY 10028.

Altrusa Intl. (1917), 8 S. Michigan Ave., Chicago, IL 60603.

Alzheimer's Disease and Related Disorders Assn. (1980), 70 E. Lake St., Chicago, IL 60601-5997; 140 chapters.

Amer. Feder. of Labor & Congress of Industrial Organizations (AFL-CIO) (1955, by merging **Amer. Feder. of Labor** estab. 1881 and **Congress of Industrial Organizations** estab. 1935), 815 16th St. NW, Wash., DC 20006; 15,000,000.

Amer. Indian Affairs, Assn. on (1923), 95 Madison Ave., N.Y., NY, 10016; 10,500.

American Legion, The (1919), 700 N. Pennsylvania St., Indianapolis, IN 46204; 2.6 mln. **American Legion Auxiliary** (1921), 777 N. Meridian St., Indianapolis, IN 46204; 950,000.

Amer. States, Organization of (1890), 17th & Constitution Ave. NW, Wash., DC 20006; 32 countries.

Amer. Veterans of World War II, Korea & Vietnam (AMVETS), (1944), 4647 Forbes Blvd., Lanham, MD 20706; 200,000. **AMVETS Auxiliary** (1946), 4647 Forbes Blvd., Lanham, MD 20706; 28,000.

Amideast (Amer. Mideast Educational & Training Services) (1951), 1100 17th St. NW, Suite 300, Wash., DC 20036.

Amnesty Intl. USA (1961), 322 Eighth Ave., N.Y., NY 10001.

Amputation Foundation, Natl. (1919), 12-45 150th St., Whitestone, NY 11357; 1,200.

Anderson, Inc., Historical (1973), P.O. Box 268, Anderson, TX 77830; 250.

Andersonville, Natl. Soc. of (1975), P.O. Box 65, Andersonville, GA 31711; 155.

Animal Protection Institute of America (1968), 6130 Freeport Blvd., Sacramento, CA 95822; 180,000.

Animal Welfare Institute (1951), P.O. Box 3650, Wash., DC 20007; 8,653.

Animals, Amer. Society for Prevention of Cruelty to (ASPCA) (1866), 441 E. 92d St., N.Y., NY 10128; 45,000.

Animals, Friends of (1957), One Pine St., Neptune, NJ 07753; 125,000.

Animals, The Fund for (1967), 200 W. 57th St., N.Y., NY 10019; 175,000.

Antelopes, Grand United Order of (1925), 162 Fourth Ave., E. Orange, NJ 01017; 499.

Anthropological Assn., Amer. (1902), 1703 New Hampshire Ave. NW, Wash., DC 20009; 10,200.

Antiquarian Society, Amer. (1812), 185 Salisbury St., Worcester, MA 01609; 468.

Anti-Vivisection Society, Amer. (1883), Suite 204, Noble Plaza, 801 Old York Rd., Jenkintown, PA 19046; 10,000+.

Appalachian Mountain Club (1876), 5 Joy St., Boston, MA 02108; 33,000.

Appalachian Trail Conference (1937), Washington & Jackson Sts., Harpers Ferry, WV 25425; 18,000.

Appraisers, Amer. Society of (1936), P.O. Box 17265, Wash., DC 20041; 5,000+.

Arab Americans, Natl. Assn. of (1972), 2033 M St. NW, Wash., DC 20036.

Arbitration Assn., Amer. (1926), 140 W. 51st St., N.Y., NY 10020; 5,300.

Arboriculture, Intl. Society of (1924), 5 Lincoln Sq., Urbana, IL 61801; 4,500.

Archaeological Institute of America (1879), P.O. Box 1901, Kenmore Station, Boston, MA 02215; 10,000.

Archaeology, Institute of Nautical (1976), P.O. Drawer AU, College Station, TX 77840; 1,000

Archery, Assn., Natl. (1879), 1750 E. Boulder St., Colorado Springs, CO 80909; 3,000.

Architects, Amer. Institute of (1857), 1735 New York Ave. NW, Wash., DC 20006; 51,000.

Architectural Historians, Society of (1940), 1232 Pine Street, Phila., PA 19107-5944; 3,800.

Armed Forces Communications and Electronics Assn. (1946), 5641 Burke Centre Pkwy., Burke, VA 22015; 29,000+.

Army, Assn. of the United States (1950), 2425 Wilson Blvd., Arlington, VA 22201; 163,000.

Arts, Amer. Council for the (1960), 1285 Avenue of the Americas, N.Y., NY 10019; 3,000.

Arts, Amer. Federation of (1909), 41 E. 65th St., N.Y., NY 10021; 1,100.

Arts, Associated Councils of the (1969), 570 Seventh Ave., N.Y., NY 10018; 2,000.

Arts and Letters, Amer. Academy and Institute of (1898), 633 W. 155th St., N.Y., NY 10032; 246.

Arts and Letters, Natl. Society of (1944), 9915 Litzsinger Rd., St. Louis, MO 63124; 1,600.
Arts & Psychology, Assn. for the (1976), P.O. Box 160371, Sacramento, CA 95816.
Arts & Sciences, Amer. Academy of (1780), Norton's Woods, 136 Irving St., Cambridge, MA 02138; 2,800.
Assistance League, Natl. (1949), 5627 Fernwood Ave., Los Angeles, CA 90038; 16,650.
Astrologers, Amer. Federation of (1938), 6535 S. Rural Rd., Tempe, AZ 85283; 4,500.
Astronautical Society, Amer. (1953), 6212-B Old Keene Mill Ct., Springfield, VA 22152; 1,500.
Astronomical Society, Amer. (1899), 2000 Florida Ave., NW, Suite 300, Wash., DC 20009; 4,300.
Atheist Assn. (1925), Box 2832, San Diego, CA 92112.
Atheists, Amer. (1963), P.O. Box 2117, Austin, TX 78768.
Athletic Associations, Natl. Federation of State H. S. (1920), 11724 Plaza Circle, Box 20626, Kansas City, MO 64195.
Athletic Assn., Natl. Scholastic (1985), 6991 Simson St., Oakland, CA 94605-2226.
Athletic Union of the U.S., Amateur (1888), 3400 W. 86th St., Box 68207, Indianapolis, IN 46268.
Athletics Congress/USA, The (1979), 200 S. Capital Ave., Suite 140, Indianapolis, IN 46225; 250,000.
Auctioneers Assn., Natl. (1949), 8880 Ballentine, Overland Park, KS 66214; 6,000.
Audubon Society, Natl. (1905), 950 Third Ave., N.Y., NY 10022; 400,000.
Authors and Composers, Amer. Guild of (1931), 40 W. 57th St., N.Y., NY 10019; 3,000.
Authors League of America (1912), 234 W. 44th St., N.Y., NY 10036; 14,500.
Autism, Natl. Society for Children and Adults with, (1965), 1234 Massachusetts Ave. NW, Wash., DC 20005; 7,000.
Autograph Collectors Club, Universal (1965), P.O. Box 467, Rockville Centre, NY 11571-0467; 2,850.
Automobile Assn., Amer. (1902), 8111 Gatehouse Rd., Falls Church, VA 22047; 27 million+.
Automobile Club, Natl. (1924), One Market Plaza, San Francisco, CA 94105; 316,000.
Automobile Club of America, Antique (1935), 501 W. Governor Rd., Hershey, PA 17033; 50,000.
Automobile Dealers Assn., Natl. (1917), 8400 Westpark Dr., McLean, VA 22102; 19,500.
Automobile License Plate Collectors' Assn. (1954), P.O. Box 712, Weston, W. VA 26452; 2,000.
Automotive Booster Clubs Intl. (1921), 501 W. Algonquin Rd., Arlington Heights, IL 60005; 2,918.
Automotive Hall of Fame (1939), P.O. Box 1727, Midland, MI 48641-1727; 2,400.
Avon Collectors, Inc., Natl. Assn. of (1971), P.O. Box 398, New Lenox, IL 60451; 15,000.

B-24 Liberator Club, Intl. (1968), P.O. Box 841, San Diego, CA 92112; 15,000.
Backpackers' Assn., Intl. (1973), P.O. Box 85, Lincoln Center, ME 04458; 22,861.
Badminton Assn., U.S. (1936), 501 W. Sixth Street, Papillion, NE 68046; 1,730.
Bald-Headed Men of America (1973), P.O. Box 1466, Morehead Pl., Morehead City, N.C. 28557-1466; 15,000–18,000.
Ball Players of Amer., Assn. of Professional (1924), 12062 Valley View St., #211, Garden Grove, CA 92645; 10,000.
Bankers Assn., Amer. (1875), 1120 Connecticut Ave. NW, Wash., DC 20036.
Bankers Assn. of America, Independent (1930), 1625 Massachusetts Ave. NW, Suite 202, Wash. DC 20036; 7,000 banks.
Banks, Natl. Assn. of Mutual Savings (1920), 200 Park Ave., N.Y., NY 10166; 435 banks.
Bar Assn., Amer. (1878), 1155 E. 60th St., Chicago, IL 60637; 300,000.
Bar Assn., Federal (1920), 1815 H St. NW, Wash., DC 20006; 15,000.
Barbershop Quartet Singing in Amer., Soc. for Preservation & Encouragement of (1938), 6315 Third Ave., Kenosha, WI 53140-5199; 38,000.
Baseball Congress, Amer. Amateur (1935), 215 E. Green, Marshall, WI 49033; 1,419 teams.
Baseball Congress, Natl. (1931), 338 S. Sycamore, P.O. Box 1420, Wichita, KS 67213.
Baseball Players of America, Assn. of Pro. (1924), 12062 Valley View St., Garden Grove, CA 92645.
Baseball Research, Society for Amer. (1971), P.O. Box 1010, Cooperstown, NY 13326; 6,300+.
Basketball Assn., Natl. (1946), 645 5th Ave., N.Y., NY 10022.
Battleship Assn., Amer. (1963), P.O. Box 11247, San Diego, CA 92111; 1,310.
Beer Can Collectors of America (1970), 747 Merus Ct., Fenton, MO 63026; 5,000.
Bertrand Russell Soc., The (1974), 3802 N. Kenneth Ave., Chicago, IL 60641; 300.
Beta Gamma Sigma (1913), 605 Old Ballas, Suite 200, St. Louis, MO 63141; 240,000.
Beta Sigma Phi (1931), P.O. Box 8500, Kansas City, MO 64114; 250,000.
Bible Society, Amer. (1816), 1865 Broadway, N.Y., NY 10023; 580,000.
Biblical Literature, Society of (1880), P.O. Box 1608, Decatur, GA 30031-1608; 6,000.
Bibliographical Society of America (1904), P.O. Box 397, Grand Central Sta., N.Y., NY 10163; 1,300.
Big Brothers/Big Sisters of America (1903), 230 No. 13th St., Philadelphia, PA 19107; 80,000.
Biological Chemists, Amer. Society of (1906), 9650 Rockville Pike, Bethesda, MD 20814; 6,302.
Birding Assn., Amer. (1969), 618 Lavaca, Austin, TX 78701.
Blind, Amer. Council of the (1961) 1010 Vermont Ave. NW, Suite 1100, Wash., DC 20005; 18,000.
Blind, Amer. Foundation for the (1921), 15 W. 16th St., N.Y., NY 10011.
Blind, Natl. Federation of the (1940), 1629 K St., NW, Wash., DC 20006; 50,000.
Blindness, Natl. Society to Prevent (1908), 79 Madison Ave., N.Y., NY 10016.
Blindness, Research to Prevent (1960), 598 Madison Ave., N.Y., NY 10022; 3,300.
Blizzard Club, January 12th, 1888, (1940), 1201 Lincoln Mall, #611, Lincoln, NE 68508; 35.
Blue Cross Assn. (1948), 676 St. Clair, Chicago, IL 60611.
Blue Shield Plans, Natl. Assn. of (1946), 676 St. Clair, Chicago, IL 60611; 69 plans.
Blueberry Council, No. Amer. (1965), P.O. Box 166, Marmora, NJ 08223; 35 organizations.
Bluebird Society, No. Amer. (1978), 2 Countryside, Silver Spring, MD 20906; 5,000.
B'nai B'rith Intl. (1843), 1640 Rhode Island Ave. NW, Wash., DC 20036; 500,000.
Boat Assn., Amer. Power (1903), 17640 E. Nine Mile Rd., E. Detroit, MI 48021; 5,000.
Boat Club, Chris Craft Antique (1973), 217 S. Adams St., Tallahassee, FL 32301; 1,125.
Boat Owners Assn. of the U.S. (1966), 880 S. Pickett St., Alexandria, VA 22304; 200,000.
Bodybuilders Assn., Amer. (1981), 6991 Simson St., Oakland, CA 94605-2226; 854.
Bookplate Collectors and Designers, Amer. Soc. of (1922), 605 N. Stoneman Ave. #F, Alhambra, CA 91801; 200.
Booksellers Assn., Amer. (1900), 122 E. 42d St., N.Y., NY 10168; 5,557.
Botanical Gardens & Arboreta, Amer. Assn. of (1940), P.O. Box 206, Swarthmore, PA 19081; 1,100+.
Bottle Clubs, Federation of Historical (1969), 5001 Queen Ave. N., Minneapolis, MN 55430; 120 clubs.
Bowling Congress, Amer. (1895), 5301 S. 76th St., Greendale, WI 53129; 3.6 mln.
Boys' Brigades of America, United (1893), P.O. Box 8406, Baltimore, MD 21234; 150.
Boys' Clubs of America (1906), 771 First Ave., N.Y., NY 10017; 1.2 mln.
Boy Scouts of America (1910), 1325 Walnut Hill Lane, Irving, TX 75038-3096; 5.2 mln.
Bread for the World (1975), 802 Rhode Island Ave. NE, Washington, DC 20018; 50,000.
Bridge, Tunnel and Turnpike Assn., Intl. (1932), 2120 L St., Suite 305, Wash., DC 20037.
Brith Sholom (1905), 3939 Conshohocken Ave., Philadelphia, PA 19131; 6,000.
Broadcasters, Natl. Assn. of (1922), 1771 N St. NW, Wash., DC 20036; 5,700+ radio & TV stations.
Burroughs Bibliophiles, The (1960), 454 Elaine Dr., Pittsburgh, PA 15236; 186.
Bus Assn., Amer. (1926), 1025 Connecticut Ave. NW, Wash., DC 20036; 700.
Business Bureaus, Council of Better (1970), 1515 Wilson Blvd., Arlington, VA 22209.
Business Clubs, Natl. Assn. of Amer. (1922), 3315 No. Main St., High Point, NC 27260; 7,059.
Business Communication Assn., Amer. (1935), Univ. of Illinois, English Bldg., 608 S. Wright St., Urbana, IL 61801; 1,750.
Business Communicators, Intl. Assn. of (1970), 870 Market St., Suite 940, San Francisco, CA 94102; 12,000.
Business Education Assn., Natl. (1946), 1906 Association Dr., Reston, VA 22091; 18,000.
Business Real Estate & Law Assn., Amer. (1923), Dept. of Legal Studies, Univ. of Georgia, Athens, GA 30602; 1,050+.

Business-Professional Advertising Assn. (1922), 205 E. 42d St., N.Y., NY 10017; 4,500.
Button Society, Natl. (1939), 2733 Juno Pl., Akron, OH 44313; 2,200+.
Byron Society, The (1971 England, 1973 in U.S.), 259 New Jersey Ave., Collingswood, NJ 08108; 300.

CARE (Cooperative For American Relief Everywhere) (1946), 660 First Ave., N.Y., NY 10016.
CB Radio Patrol of Amer., Federation of Police (1966), 1100 NE 125th St., N. Miami, FL 33161; 68,000.
CORE (Congress of Racial Equality) (1942), 1457 Flatbush Ave., Brooklyn, NY 11210; 110,000.
Campers & Hikers Assn., Natl. (1954), 4804 Transit Rd., Bld. 2, Depew, NY 14043; 26,000 families.
Camp Fire (1910), 4601 Madison Ave., Kansas City, MO 64112; 400,000.
Campers & Hikers Assn., Inc. (1954), 7172 Transit Rd., Buffalo, NY 14221; 30,000.
Camping Assn., Amer. (1910), Bradford Woods, Martinsville, IN 46151; 5,400.
Cancer Council, United (1959), 650 E. Carmel Dr., Suite 340, Carmel, IN 46032; 50 agencies.
Cancer Society, Amer. (1913), 90 Park Ave., N.Y., NY 10017; 257.
Canoe Assn., U.S. (1968), 1152 W Meinecke Apt. 3, Milwaukee, WI 53266-1251; 1,500.
Carillonneurs in North America, Guild of (1936), 3718 Settle Rd., Cincinnati, OH 45227; 483.
Carnegie Hero Fund Commission (1904), 606 Oliver Bldg., Pittsburgh, PA 15222.
Cartoonists Society, Natl. (1946), 9 Ebony Ct., Brooklyn, NY 11229; 450.
Cat Fanciers' Assn. (1906), 1309 Allaire Ave., Ocean, NJ 07712; 570 member clubs.
Catholic Bishops, Natl. Conference of/U.S. Cath. Conference (1966), 1312 Massachusetts Ave. NW, Wash., DC 20005.
Catholic Charities, USA (1910), 1319 F St. NW, Wash., DC 20004; 4,000.
Catholic Church Extension Society of the U.S.A. (1905), 35 E. Wacker Dr., Chicago, IL 60601.
Catholic Daughters of the Americas (1903), 10 W. 71st St., N.Y., NY 10023; 158,000.
Catholic Educational Assn., Natl. (1908), 1077-30th St. NW, Suite 100, Wash, DC 20007; 15,000.
Catholic Historical Soc., Amer. (1884), 263 S. Fourth St., Philadelphia, PA 19106; 950.
Catholic Library Assn. (1921), 461 W. Lancaster Ave., Haverford, PA 19041; 1,518.
Catholic Press Assn. of U.S. and Canada (1911), 119 N. Park Ave., Rockville Centre, NY 11570; 548.
Catholic Rural Life Conference, Natl. (1923), 4625 NW Beaver Dr., Des Moines, IA 50310; 3,000.
Catholic War Veterans of the U.S.A. (1935), 419 North Lee Street, Alexandria, VA 22314; 35,000.
Cemetery Assn., Amer. (1887), 5201 Leesburg Pike, Falls Church, VA 22041; 2,300.
Ceramic Society, Amer. (1899), 65 Ceramic Dr., Columbus, OH 43214; 9,594.
Cerebral Palsy Assns., United (1949), 66 E. 34th St., N.Y., NY 10016.
Chamber of Commerce of the U.S.A. (1912), 1615 H St. NW, Wash., DC 20062; 200,000.
Chamber Music Players, Amateur (1947), 545 Eighth Ave., N.Y., NY 10018; 4,000.
Chaplain's Assn., Intl. (1962), U.S. Box 4266, Norton Air Force Base, CA 92409; 500.
Chaplains Assn. of the U.S.A., Military (1925), 6216 Baltimore Ave., P.O. Box 645, Riverdale, MD 20737; 1,567.
Checker Federation, Amer., (1948), 3475 Belmont Ave., Baton Rouge, LA 70808; 1,025.
Chemical Manufacturers Assn. (1872), 2501 M St. NW, Wash., DC 20037; 170 companies.
Chemical Society, Amer. (1876), 1155 16th St. NW, Wash., DC 20036; 135,000.
Chemistry, Amer. Assn. for Clinical (1948), 1725 K St. NW, Wash., DC 20006; 6,247.
Chemists, Amer. Institute of (1923), 7315 Wisconsin Ave., Bethesda, Md. 20814; 7,000
Chemists, Amer. Soc. of Biological (1906), 9650 Rockville Pike, Bethesda, MD 20814; 5,891.
Chemists, Amer. Society of Brewing (1934), 3340 Pilot Knob Rd., St. Paul MN 55121; 870.
Chemists, Amer. Assn. of Cereal (1915), 3340 Pilot Knob Rd., St. Paul, MN 55121; 3,300+.
Chess Federation, U.S. (1939), 186 Rte. 9W, New Windsor, NY 12550; 57,000.
Chess League of Amer., Correspondence (1897), Box 416, Warrenville, IL 60555; 1,300.
Child Welfare League of America (1920), 67 Irving Pl., N.Y., NY 10003; 350 agencies.
Childbirth Without Pain Education Assn. (1959), 20134 Snowden, Detroit, MI 48235; 3,000.
Childhood Education Intl., Assn. for (1892), 11141 Georgia Ave., Suite 200, Wheaton, MD 20902; 12,000.
Children of the Amer. Revolution, Natl. Society (1895), 1776 D St. NW, Wash., DC 20006; 12,000+.
Children's Aid Society (1853), 105 E. 22d St., N.Y., NY 10010; 1,207.
Children's Book Council (1945), 67 Irving Pl., N.Y., NY 10003; 65 publishing houses.
Chiropractic Assn., Amer. (1930), 1916 Wilson Blvd., Arlington, VA 22201; 20,000.
Chiropractors Assn., Intl. (1926), 1901 L St. NW, Wash., DC 20036; 6,000.
Christian Endeavor, Intl. Society of (1881), 1221 E. Broad St., Columbus, OH 43216.
Christian Laity Counseling Board (1970), 5901 Plainfield Dr., Charlotte, NC 28215; 38 mln.
Christians and Jews, Natl. Conference of (1928), 71 Fifth Ave., N.Y., NY 10003; 100,000.
Church Business Administration, Natl. Assn. of (1956), Suite 324, 7001 Grapevine Hwy., Ft. Worth, TX 76180; 1,200.
Church Federation, Ecumenical (1982), 13014-270, N. Dalemabry, Tampa, FL 33618-2808.
Churches, U.S. Conference for the World Council of (1948), 475 Riverside Dr., N.Y., NY 10115; 27 churches.
Church Women United (1945), 475 Riverside Dr., N.Y., NY 10027.
Cincinnati, Society of the (1783), 2118 Massachusetts Ave. NW, Wash., DC 20008; 3,225.
Circulation Managers Assn., Intl. (1889), 11600 Sunrise Valley Dr., Reston, VA 22091; 1,536.
Circus Fans Assn. of America (1926), 4 Center Dr., Camp Hill, PA 17011; 2,550.
Cities, Natl. League of (1924), 1301 Pennsylvania Ave. NW, Wash., DC 20004; 15,000 cities.
Citizens Band Radio Patrol (1977), 1100 NE 125th St., N. Miami, FL 33161; 35,000.
City Management Assn., Intl. (1914), 1120 G St. NW, Wash., DC 20005; 7,240.
Civil Air Patrol, (1941), Maxwell AFB, AL 36112; 66,000.
Civil Engineers, Amer. Society of (1852), 345 E. 47th St., N.Y., NY 10017; 88,000.
Civil Liberties Union, Amer. (1920), 132 W. 43rd St., N.Y. NY 10036; 250,000.
Civil War Round Table of New York (1951), 820 Carleton Rd., Westfield, NJ 07090; 150.
Civitan Internatl. (1921), P.O. Box 2102, Birmingham, AL 35201; 185,000.
Classical League, Amer. (1919), Miami Univ., Oxford, OH 45056; 3,500.
Clergy, Academy of Parish (1968), 12604 Britton Dr., Cleveland, OH 44120; 401.
Clinical Pastoral Education, Assn. for (1967), 1549 Clairmont Rd., Decatur, GA 30033; 3,900.
Clinical Pathologists, Amer. Society of (1922), 2100 W. Harrison St., Chicago, IL 60612; 34,000.
Coal Association, Natl. (1917), 1130 17th St. NW, Wash., DC 20036; 100+ companies.
College Athletic Assn., Natl. Junior (1949), P.O. Box 7305, Colorado Springs, CO 80933-7305; 570 schools.
College Athletic Conference, Eastern (1938), 1311 Craigville Beach Rd., P.O. Box 3, Centerville, MA 02632.
College Board, The (1900), 45 Columbus Ave., N.Y., NY 10023; 2,550 institutions.
College Music Society (1958), 1444 Fifteenth St., Boulder, CO 80302; 6,000.
College Physical Education Assn. for Men, Natl. (1897), 108 Cooke Hall, Univ. of Minnesota, Minneapolis, MN 55455.
College Placement Council (1956), 62 Highland Ave., Bethlehem, PA 18017; 2,500.
Colleges, Amer. Assn. of Community and Jr. (1920), One Dupont Circle, Wash., DC 20036; 1,280 institutions.
Colleges, Assn. of Amer. (1915), 1818 R St. NW, Wash., DC 20009; 584 institutions.
Colleges and Universities, Assn. of Intl. (1973), I301 S. Noland Rd., Independence, MO 64055; 11,000+.
Collegiate Athletic Assn., Natl. (1906), 6299 Nall, Mission, KS 66202; 983.
Collegiate Body-Building Assn., Natl. (1983), 6991 Simson St., Oakland, CA 94605; 683.
Collegiate Schools of Business, Amer. Assembly of (1916), 605 Old Ballas Rd., St. Louis, MO 63141; 800 schools.

Colonial Dames of Amer. (1890), 421 E. 61 St., N.Y., NY 10021; 2,000.
Colonial Dames XVII Century, Natl. Society (1915), 1300 New Hampshire Ave. NW, Wash., DC 20036; 14,000.
Colonial Wars, General Society of (1893), 840 Woodbine Ave., Glendale, OH 45246; 4,450.
Commercial Collectors Assn., Amer. (1969), 4040 W. 70th St., Minneapolis, MN 55435; 3,159.
Commercial Law League of America (1895), 222 W. Adams St., Chicago, IL 60606; 5,200.
Commercial Travelers of America, Order of United (1888), 632 N. Park St., Columbus, OH 43215; 186,000.
Common Cause (1970), 2030 M St. NW, Wash., DC 20036.
Communication, Intl. Training In (1938), 2519 Woodland Dr., Anaheim, CA 92801; 21,000.
Community Cultural Center Assoc., Amer. (1978), 19 Foothills Dr., Pompton Plains, NJ 07444.
Composers/USA, Natl. Assn. of (1932), P.O. Box 49652, Barrington Sta., Los Angeles, CA 90049; 500.
Composers, Authors & Publishers, Amer. Society of (ASCAP) (1914), One Lincoln Plaza, N.Y., NY 10023; 24,000.
Computing Machinery, Assn. for (1947), 11 W. 42nd St., N.Y., NY 10036; 55,000.
Concrete Institute, Amer. (1904), 22400 W. Seven Mile Rd., Detroit, MI 48219; 18,000.
Conscientious Objection, Central Committee for (1948), 2208 South St., Phila., PA 19146.
Conservation Corps Alumni, Natl. Assn. of Civilian (1977), 7245 Arlington Blvd., Falls Church, VA 22042; 12,300.
Conservation Engineers, Assn. of (1961), Missouri Dept. of Conservation, P.O. Box 180, Jefferson City, MO 65076.
Constantian Society, The (1970), 123 Orr Rd., Pittsburgh, PA 15241; 450.
Construction Industry Manufacturers Assn. (1911), 111 E. Wisconsin Ave., Milwaukee, WI 53202; 200 companies.
Construction Specifications Institute (1948), 601 Madison St., Alexandria, VA 22314.
Consumer Credit Assn., Intl. (1912), 243 N. Lindbergh, St. Louis, MO 63141; 20,000.
Consumer Federation of America (1968), 1314 14th St. NW, Wash., DC 20005; 200+.
Consumer Interests, Amer. Council on (1953), 240 Stanley Hall, Univ. of Missouri, Columbia, MO 65211; 2,000.
Consumer Protection Institute (1970), 5901 Plainfield Dr., Charlotte, NC 28215.
Consumers League, Natl. (1899), 815 15th St. NW, Suite 516, Wash., DC 20005; 5,000.
Consumers Union of the U.S. (1936), 256 Washington St., Mount Vernon, NY 10553; 291,000.
Contraception, Assn. for Voluntary Surgical (1943), 122 E. 42nd St., New York, NY 10168; 3,500.
Contract Bridge League, Amer. (1937), 2200 Democrat Rd., Memphis, TN 38116; 180,000.
Contract Management Assn., Natl. (1959), 6728 Old McLean Village Dr., McLean, VA 22101; 20,176.
Contractors of Amer., General (1918), 1957 E St. NW, Wash., DC 20036; 30,000.
Cooperative Business Assn., Natl. (1916), 1401 New York Ave. NW, #1100, Wash., DC 20005.
Cooperative League of the U.S.A. (1916), 1401 New York Ave. NW, #1100, Wash., DC 20005; 176 co-ops.
Correctional Assn., Amer. (1870), 4321 Hartwick Rd., Suite L-208, College Park, MD 20740; 22,000.
Correctional Officers, Amer. Assn. of (1979), P.O. Box 7051, Marquette, MI 49855.
Costmetology Assn., Natl. (1921), 3510 Olive St., St. Louis, MO 63103; 50,000.
Cosmopolitan Intl. (1914), P.O. Box 4588, Overland Park, KS 66204.
Cotton Council of America, Natl. (1938), 1918 North Parkway, Memphis, TN 38112; 299 delegates.
Counseling and Development, Amer. Assn. for (1952), 5999 Stevenson Ave., Alexandria, VA 22304; 56,000.
Counselors and Family Therapists, Natl. Academy of (1972), 225 Jericho Turnpike, Suite 4, Floral Park, NY 11001; 800.
Country Music Assn. (1958), P.O. Box 22299, Nashville, TN 37202; 8,000+.
Creative Children and Adults, Natl. Assn. for (1974), 8080 Springvalley Dr., Cincinnati, OH 45236; 1,500.
Credit Assn., International (1912), 243 N. Lindberg, St. Louis, MO 63141; 14,767.
Credit Management, Nat. Assn. of (1896), 520 Eighth Ave., N.Y., NY 10018; 43,000.
Credit Union Natl. Assn. (1934), P.O.Box 431, 5710 Mineral Point Rd., Madison, WI 53701; 52 leagues.
Crime and Delinquency, Natl. Council on (1907), 77 Maiden Lane, 4th fl., San Francisco, CA 94606; 3,000.
Criminal Investigators Assn., Intl. (1970), P.O. Box 15350, Chevy Chase, MD 20815; 300.
Criminology, Amer. Society of (1941), 1314 Kinnear Rd., Columbus, OH 43212; 1,800.
Crop Science Society of America (1955), 677 S. Segoe Rd., Madison, WI 53711; 5,800.
Cross-Examination Debate Assn. (1971), California State Univ.-Northridge, Northridge, CA 91330.
Cryptogram Assn., Amer. (1929) 4 Hawthorne Dr., Cherry Hill, NJ 08003; 1,100.
Customs Brokers & Forwarders Assn. of Amer. (1897), 5 World Trade Center, Suite 9273, N.Y., NY 10048; 520.
Cyprus, Sovereign Order of (1192, 1964 in U.S.), 853 Seventh Ave., N.Y., NY 10019; 464.

Dairy Council, Natl. (1915), 6300 N. River Rd., Rosemont, IL 60018.
Dairy and Food Industries Supply Assn. (1917), 6245 Executive Blvd., Rockville, MD 20852; 650.
Dairylea Cooperative (1919), 831 James St., Syracuse, NY13203; 4,000.
Daughters of the American Revolution, Natl. Society, (1890), 1776 D St. NW, Wash., DC 20006; 210,000.
Daughters of the Confederacy, United (1894), 328 N. Blvd., Richmond, VA 23220; 28,000.
Daughters of 1812, Natl. Society, U.S. (1892), 1461 Rhode Island Ave. NW, Wash., DC 20005; 4,700.
Daughters of Union Veterans of the Civil War (1885), 503 S. Walnut St., Springfield, IL 62704; 5,000.
Deaf, Alexander Graham Bell Assn. for the (1890), 3417 Volta Pl. NW, Wash., DC 20024; 6,000.
Deaf, Natl. Assn. of the (1880), 814 Thayer Ave., Silver Spring, MD 20910; 18,000.
Defense Preparedness Assn., Amer. (1919), 1700 N. Moore St., Arlington, VA 22209; 45,000.
Delta Kappa Gamma Society Intl. (1929), P.O. Box 1589, Austin, TX 78767; 164,000.
Deltiologists of America (1960), 10 Felton Ave., Ridley Park, PA 19078; 450.
DeMolay, Intl. Council, Order of (1919), 10200 N. Executive Hills Blvd., Kansas City, MO 64153; 70,000.
Dental Assn., Amer. (1859), 211 E. Chicago Ave., Chicago, IL 60611; 145,872.
Descendants of the Colonial Clergy, Society of the (1933), 30 Leewood Rd., Wellesley, MA 02181; 1,400.
Descendants of the Signers of the Declaration of Independence (1907), 1300 Locust St., Phila., PA 19107; 937.
Descendants of Washington's Army at Valley Forge, Society of (1976), P.O. Box 915, Valley Forge, PA 19482-0915.
Desert Protective Council (1954), 85-159 Ave. 66, Thermal, CA 92274; 400.
Diabetes Assn., Amer. (1940), 1660 Duke St., Alexandria, VA 22314; 225,000.
Dialect Society, Amer. (1889), MacMurray College, Jacksonville, IL 62650; 575.
Dietetic Assn., Amer. (1917), 430 N. Michigan Ave., Chicago, IL 60611; 55,000.
Ding-A-Ling Club, Natl. (1971), 3930-D Montclair Rd., Birmingham, AL 35213; 2,055.
Direct Marketing Assn. (1917), 6 E. 43d St., N.Y., NY 10017.
Directors Guild of America (1936), 7950 Sunset Blvd., Los Angeles, CA 90046; 7,800.
Disability Examiners, Natl. Assn. of (1964), P.O. Box 44237, Indianapolis, IN 46244; 1,800.
Disabled Amer. Veterans (1920), 3725 Alexandria Pike, Cold Spring, KY 41076; 850,000.
Disc Sports, U.S. (1983), 462 Main, W. Hampton Beach, NY 11978; 2,200.
Discount Club, Neighborhood (1985), 11015 Cumpston St., N. Hollywood, CA 91601; 8,500.
Dogs on Stamps Study Unit, Amer. Topical Assn. (1979), 75 Maple Ave., Newark, NJ 07112; 250.
Dowsers, Amer. Society of (1961), P.O. Box 24, Danville, VT 05828; 3,500.
Dozenal Soc. of America (1944), Math Dept., Nassau Community College, Garden City, NY 11530; 144.
Dracula Society, Count (1962), 334 W. 54th St., Los Angeles, CA 90037; 1,000.
Drug, Chemical and Allied Trades Assn. (1890), 42-40 Bell Blvd., Suite 604, Bayside, NY 11361; 500+ companies.
Ducks Unlimited (1937), One Waterfowl Way at Gilmer Rd., Long Grove, IL 60014; 600,000.
Dulcimer Assn., Southern Appalachian (1973), Rt. 10, Box 198, Jasper, AL 35501; 82.

Dutch Settlers Soc. of Albany (1924), Box 163, R.D. 2, Troy, NY 12182; 277.

Eagles, Fraternal Order of (1898), 12660 West Capitol Dr., Brookfield, WI 53055; 1.1 mln.
Earth, Friends of the (1969), 530 7th St. SE, Washington, DC 20003; 20,000.
Easter Seal Society, Natl. (1919), 2023 W. Ogden Ave., Chicago, IL 60612.
Eastern Star, Order of the (1876), 1618 New Hampshire Ave. NW, Wash., DC 20009.
Economic Assn., Amer. (1885), 1313 21st Ave. So., Nashville, TN 37212; 19,500.
Economic Development, Committee for (1942), 1700 K St., NW, Suite 700, Washington, DC 20006; 365.
Edison Electric Institute (1933), 1111 19th St. NW, Wash., DC 20036; 185 companies.
Education, Amer. Assn. for Adult and Continuing (1982), 1201 16th St. NW, Suite 230, Wash., DC 20036; 3,500.
Education, Amer. Council on (1918), One Dupont Circle NW, #800, Wash., DC 20036; 1,600 schools.
Education, Amer. Soc. for Engineering (1893), 11 Dupont Circle NW, Suite 200, Washington, DC 20036; 9,500.
Education, Council for Advancement & Support of (1974), 11 Dupont Circle NW, Wash., DC 20036; 2,500 schools.
Education, Council for Basic (1956), 725 15th St. NW, Wash., DC 20005; 10,000.
Education, Institute of Intl. (1919), 809 United Nations Plaza, N.Y., NY 10017.
Education, Natl. Committee for Citizens in (1973), 10840 Little Patuxent Pwky., Suite 301, Columbia, MD 21044.
Education, Natl. Society for the Study of (1902), 5835 Kimbark Ave., Chicago, IL 60637; 4,500.
Education, Society for the Advancement of (1939), 1860 Broadway, N.Y., NY 10023; 3,000.
Education Assn., Natl. (1857), 1201 16th St. NW, Wash., DC 20036; 1.7 mln.
Education Society, Comparative and Intl. (1956), Univ. of S. California, Univ. Park, Los Angeles, CA 90089; 2,500.
Education of Young Children, Natl. Assn. for the (1926), 1834 Connecticut Ave. NW, Wash., DC 20009; 54,000+.
Educational Exchange, Council on Intl. (1947), 205 E. 42d St., N.Y., NY 10017; 179 organizations.
Educational Research Assn., Amer. (1916), 1230 17th St. NW, Wash., DC 20036; 14,000+.
8th Air Force Historical Society (1975), P.O. Box 3556, Hollywood, FL 33083.
Electrical and Electronics Engineers, Institute of (1884), 345 E. 47th St., N.Y., NY 10017; 234,875.
Electrical Manufacturers Assn., Natl. (1926), 2101 L St. NW, Wash., DC 20037; 560 companies.
Electrochemical Society (1902), 10 S. Main St., Pennington, NJ 08534; 6,300.
Electronic Industries Assn. (1924), 2001 Eye St. NW, Wash., DC 20006; 1,000 companies.
Electronics, Sales & Service Dealers Assn., Natl. (1963), 2708 W. Berry, Ft. Worth, TX 76109; 2,284.
Electronics Technicians, Intl. Society of Certified (1970), 2708 W. Berry, Ft. Worth, TX 76109; 1,300.
Electroplaters' and Surface Finishers' Society, Amer. (1909), 12644 Research Pkway, Orlando, FL 32826; 9,000.
Elks of the U.S.A., Benevolent and Protective Order of (1868), 2750 N. Lake View Ave., Chicago, IL 60614; 1.6 mln.
Energy Research Institute, Clean (1974), P.O. Box 248294, Coral Gables, FL, 33124.
Energy, Intl. Assn. for Hydrogen (1974), P.O. Box 24866, Coral Gables, FL 33124; 1,500.
Engine and Boat Manufacturers, Natl. Assn. of (1904), 401 N. Michigan Ave., Chicago, IL 60611.
Engineering, Natl. Academy of (1964), 2101 Constitution Ave. NW, Wash., DC 20418; 1,272.
Engineering, Soc. for the Advancement of Material & Process (1944), P.O. Box 2459, Covina, CA 91722; 8,000.
Engineering Societies, Amer. Assn. of (1979), 345 E. 47th St., N.Y., NY 10017; 38 societies.
Engineering Society of N. America, Illuminating (1907), 345 E. 47th St., N.Y., NY 10017; 8,773.
Engineering Trustees, United (1904), 345 E. 47th St., N.Y., NY 10017.
Engineers, Amer. Inst. of Chemical (1908), 345 E. 47th St., N.Y., N.Y. 10017; 56,000.
Engineers, Amer. Institute of Mining, Metallurgical and Petroleum (1871), 345 E. 47th St., N.Y., NY 10017.
Engineers, Amer. Soc. of Agricultural (1907), 2950 Niles Rd., St. Joseph, MI 49085; 11,000+.
Engineers, Amer. Soc. of Civil (1852), 345 E. 47th St., N.Y., NY 10017; 100,000.
Engineers, Amer. Society of Lubrication (1944), 838 Busse Hwy., Park Ridge, IL 60068; 3,800.
Engineers, Amer. Soc. of Naval (1888), 1452 Duke St., Alexandria, VA 22314; 8,100.
Engineers, Amer. Soc. of Plumbing (1964), 3617 Thousand Oaks Blvd., #210, Westlake Vlge, CA 91362-3625; 4,500.
Engineers, Amer. Soc. of Safety (1911), 850 Busse Hwy., Park Ridge, IL 60068; 20,000.
Enginners, Assn. of Conservation (1961), Missouri Conservation Dept., P.O. Box 180, Jefferson City, MO 65102; 200.
Engineers, Assn. of Energy (1977), 4025 Pleasantdale Rd., Suite 420, Atlanta, GA 30340; 6,200.
Engineers, Inst. of Industrial (1948), 25 Technology Park, Atlanta, GA 30092; 43,000.
Engineers, Inst. of Transportation (1930), Suite 410, 525 School St. NW, Wash., DC 20024, 7,700.
Engineers, Natl. Society of Professional (1934), 1420 King St., Alexandria, VA 22314; 75,000.
Engineers, Soc. of Fire Protection (1951), 60 Batterymarch St., Boston, MA 02110; 3,100.
Engineers, Soc. of Logistics (1966), 125 W Park Loop, Suite 201, Huntsville, AL 35806-1745; 9,500.
Engineers, Soc. of Manufacturing (1932), One SME Drive, P.O. Box 930, Dearborn, MI 48121; 80,000.
Engineers, Society of Mining (1871), 8307 Shaffer Pkwy., Littleton, CO 80127; 22,159.
Engineers, Society of Plastics (1942), 14 Fairfield Dr., Brookfield Ctr., CT 06805; 25,500.
English Assn., College (1939), English Dept., Nazareth College, 4245 East Ave., Rochester, NY 14610; 1,640.
English-Speaking Union of the U.S. (1920), 16 E. 69th St., N.Y., NY 10021; 27,000.
Entomological Society of America (1889), 4603 Calvert Rd., College Park, MD 20740; 9,100.
Epigraphic Society, Inc., The (1974), 6625 Bamburgh Dr., San Diego, CA 92117; 900.
Esperanto League for North America (1952), P.O. Box 1129, El Cerrito, CA 94530; 750.
Evangelism Crusades, Intl. (1959), 14617 Victory Blvd., Van Nuys, CA 91411; 3,000.
Exchange Club, Natl. (1911), 3050 Central Ave., Toledo, OH 43606; 44,000.
Executive Management Services Corp. (1971), 99 W. Hawthorne Ave., Valley Stream, NY 11580.
Experiment in Internatl. Living (1932), Kipling Rd., Brattleboro, VT 05301; 64,000.

Fairs & Expositions, Intl. Assn. of (1919), P.O. Box 985, Springfield, MO 65801; 1,500.
Family Life, Natl. Alliance for, Inc. (1973), Ste. 4, 225 Jericho Tpk., Floral Park, NY 11001; 499.
Family Relations, Natl. Council on (1938), 1910 W. Country Rd. B, Suite 147, St. Paul, MN 55113; 3,400.
Family Service Assn. of America (1911), 11700 W. Lake Park Dr., Park Pl, Milwaukee, WI 53224; 300 family service agencies.
Farm Bureau Federation, Amer. (1919), 225 Touhy Ave., Park Ridge, IL 60068; 3.3 mln.
Farmer Cooperatives, Natl. Council of (1929), 1800 Massachusetts Ave. NW, Wash., DC 20036; 121 co-ops.
Farmers of America, Future (1928), 5632 Mt. Vernon Memorial Hwy., Alexandria, VA 22309; 460,000.
Farmers Educational and Co-Operative Union of America (1902), 10065 E. Harvard Ave., Denver, CO 80251; 275,000.
Fat Americans, Natl. Assn. to Aid (NAAFA) (1969), P.O. Box 43, Bellerose, NY 11426; 1,500.
Federal Employees, Natl. Federation of (1917), 1016 16th St. NW, Wash., DC 20036; 150,000.
Federal Employees Veterans Assn. (1953), P.O. Box 183, Merion Sta., PA 19066; 896.
Feminists for Life of America (1972), 811 E. 47th St., Kansas City, MO 64110; 2,000.
Fencers League of America, Amateur (1893), 601 Curtis St., Albany, CA 94706; 8,000.
Film Library Assn., Educational (1943), 45 John St., Suite 301, N.Y., NY 10038; 1,600.
Financial Analysts Federation (1945), 1633 Broadway, N.Y., NY 10019; 15,137.
Financial Executives Institute (1931), 10 Madison Ave., P.O. Box 1938, Morristown, NJ 07960, 13,000.
Financiers, Intl. Soc. of (1979), P.O. Box 18508, Asheville, NC 28814-0508; 500+.
Fire Chiefs, Intl. Assn. of (1873), 1329 18th St. NW, Wash., DC 20036; 7,000.
Fire Marshals Assn. of No. America (1906), Capital Gallery, Suite #1290, 1110 Vermont Ave., NW, Wash., DC 20005; 1,165.

Fire Protection Assn., Natl. (1896), Batterymarch Park, Quincy MA 02269; 38,000.

Fish Assn., Intl. Game (1939), 3000 E. Las Olas Blvd., Ft. Lauderdale, FL 33316; 25,000.

Fisheries Institute, Natl. (1945), 2000 M St., Washington, DC 20036; 1,250.

Fishes, Soc. for the Protection of Old (1967), School of Fisheries, Univ. of Washington, Seattle, WA 98195; 250.

Fishing Institute, Sport (1949), 1010 Massachusetts Ave. NW, Suite 100, Wash., DC 20006; 15,000.

Fishing Tackle Manufacturers Assn., Amer. (1933), 2625 Clearbrook Dr., Arlington Heights, IL 60005; 550 organizations.

Fluid Power Society (1957), 3333 N. Mayfair Rd., Milwaukee, WI 53222; 1,600.

Food Brokers Assn., Natl. (1904), 1010 Massachusetts Ave. NW, Wash., DC 20001; 2,400 companies.

Food Institute, Amer. Frozen (1942), 1764 Old Meadow Ln., Suite 350, McLean, VA 22102; 500 firms.

Food Processing Machinery and Supplies Assn. (1885), 200 Dangerfield Rd., Alexandria, VA 22314; 545.

Food Society, Living (1983), 5227 Corteen Pl., N. Hollywood, CA 91607; 1,200.

Footwear Industries Assn., Amer. (1871), 3700 Market St., Philadelphia, PA 19104; 180.

Foreign Policy Assn. (1918), 205 Lexington Ave., N.Y., NY 10016.

Foreign Relations, Council on (1921), 58 E. 68th St., N.Y., NY 10021; 2,391.

Foreign Student Affairs, Natl. Assn. for (1948), 1860 19th St. NW, Wash., DC 20009; 5,500.

Foreign Study, Amer. Institute for (1964), 102 Greenwich Ave., Greenwich, CT 06830; 300,000.

Foreign Trade Council, Inc., Natl. (1914), 100 E. 42d St., N.Y., NY 10017; 550+ companies.

Forensic Sciences, Amer. Academy of (1948), 225 S. Academy Blvd., Colorado Springs, CO 80910; 2,500.

Forest Institute, Amer. (1932), 1619 Massachusetts Ave. NW, Wash., DC 20036; 60 companies.

Forest Products Assn., Natl. (1902), 1619 Massachusetts Ave. NW, Wash., DC 20036; 2,500 companies.

Forest Products Research Society (1947), 2801 Marshall Ct., Madison, WI 53705; 3,600.

Foresters, Society of Amer. (1900), 5400 Grosvenor La., Bethesda, MD 20814; 21,000

Forestry Assn., Amer. (1875), 1319 18th St. NW, Wash., DC 20036; 40,000.

Fortean Organization, Intl. (1965), P.O. Box 367, Arlington, VA 22210; 600.

Foundrymen's Society, Amer. (1896), Golf & Wolf Rds., Des Plaines, IL 60016; 13,600.

4-H Clubs (1901-1905), Extension Service, U.S. Dept of Agriculture, Wash., DC 20250; 5.8 mln.

Franklin D. Roosevelt Philatelic Society (1963), 154 Laguna Ct., St. Augustine Shores, FL 32086; 696.

Frederick A. Cook Society, The (1977), Sullivan County Historical Society, Harleyville, NY 14747; 90.

Freedom, Young Americans for (1960), Box 1002, Woodland Rd. Sterling, VA 22170; 80,000.

Freedoms Foundation at Valley Forge (1969), Valley Forge, PA 19481.

Friedreich's Ataxia Group in America (1969), P.O. Box 11116, Oakland, CA 94611; 2,100.

French Institute (1911), 22 E. 60th St., N.Y., NY 10022.

Friendship and Good Will (1978), 1100 W. Elm St., Shelby, NC 28151-0756.

Frisbee Assn., Intl. (1967), 900 E. El Monte, San Gabriel, CA 91776; 110,000.

Funeral and Memorial Societies, Continental Assn. of (1963), 2001 S. St. NW, Suite 530, Washington, DC 20009.

GASP (Group Against Smokers' Pollution) (1971), P.O. Box 632, College Park, MD 20740; 200 chapters.

Gamblers Anonymous (1957), 1543 W. Olympic, Suite 533, Los Angeles, CA 90017; 12,000.

Garden Club of Amer. (1913), 598 Madison Ave., N.Y., NY 10022; 15,000.

Garden Clubs, Natl. Council of State (1929), 4401 Magnolia Ave., St. Louis, MO 63110; 308,623.

Garden Clubs of America, Men's (1932), 5560 Merle Hay Rd., Johnston, IA 50131; 9,500.

Gas Appliance Manufacturers Assn. (1935), 1901 N. Ft. Myer Dr., Arlington, VA 22209; 240 companies.

Gas Assn., Amer. (1918), 1515 Wilson Blvd., Arlington, VA 22209; 300 cos.

Gay Academic Union (1973), P.O. Box 82123, San Diego, CA 92138; 1,100.

Gay and Lesbian Task Force, Natl. (1973), 1517 U St. NW, Washington, DC 20009; 10,000.

Genealogical Society, Natl. (1903), 4527 17th St. N., Arlington, VA 22207-2363; 7,000.

Genetic Assn., Amer. (1913), 818 18th St. NW, Wash., DC 20006; 1,583.

Geographers, Assn. of Amer. (1904), 1710 16th St. NW, Wash., DC 20009; 5,800.

Geographic Education, Natl. Council for (1915), Western Illinois Univ., Macomb, IL 61455; 3,000.

Geographic Society, Natl. (1888), 1145 17 St. NW, Wash., DC 20036.

Geographical Society, Amer. (1851), 156 Fifth Ave., Suite 600, N.Y., NY 10010; 1,200.

Geolinguistics, Amer. Society of (1965), University of Rhode Island, Kingston, RI 02892; 60.

Geological Institute, Amer. (1948), 4220 King St., Alexandria, VA 22302; 18 societies.

Geological Society of America (1888), 3300 Penrose Pl., P.O. Box 9140, Boulder, CO 80301; 13,386.

Geologists, Assn. of Engineering (1957), 3479 Rainbow Dr., Palo Alto, CA 94306; 3,500.

Geologists, Amer. Assn. of Petroleum (1917), 1444 S. Boulder, Tulsa, OK 74119; 42,900.

Geophysicists, Society of Exploration (1930), P.O. Box 702740, 8801 S. Yale, Tulsa OK 74170-2740; 16,766.

George S. Patton, Jr. Historical Society (1970), 11307 Vela Dr., San Diego, CA 92126.

Geriatrics Society, Amer. (1942), 770 Lexington Ave., Suite 400, N.Y., NY 10021; 5,300.

Gideons Intl. (1899), 2900 Lebanon Rd., Nashville, TN 37214; 86,195.

Gifted Children, Amer. Assn. for (1946), 15 Gramercy Park, N.Y., NY 10003.

Gifted Children, Natl. Assn. for (1954), 5100 N. Edgewood Dr., St. Paul, MN 55112; 5,000.

Girls Clubs of America (1945), 205 Lexington Ave., N.Y., NY 10016; 250,000.

Girl Scouts of the U.S.A. (1912), 830 Third Ave., N.Y., NY 10022; 2.9 mln.

Gladiolus Council, No. Amer. (1945), 9338 Manzanita Dr., Sun City, AZ 85373; 1,400.

Goat Assn., American Dairy (1904), 209 W. Main St., Spindale, NC 28160; 14,500.

Gold Star Mothers, Amer. (1929), 2128 Leroy Pl. NW, Wash., DC 20008; 5,000.

Golf Association, U.S. (1894), Golf House, Far Hills, NJ 07931; 5,400 clubs.

Goose Island Bird & Girl Watching Society (1960), 301 Arthur Ave., Park Ridge, IL 60068; 919.

Gospel Music Assn. (1964), 38 Music Square W., Nashville, TN 37203; 3,000.

Governing Boards, Assn. of (1922), 1 Dupont Circle, Ste. 400, Washington, DC 20036; 1,600.

Government Finance Officers Assn. (1906), 180 N. Michigan Ave., Suite 800, Chicago, IL 60601; 11,000.

Gov't. Funding of Soc. Serv., Greater Wash. Organizations for (1981), 6612 Virginia View Ct. NW, Wash., DC 20816.

Graduate Schools in the U.S., Council of (1961), One Dupont Circle NW, Wash., DC 20036; 365 institutions.

Grandmother Clubs of America, Natl. Federation of (1938), 203 N. Wabash Ave., Chicago, IL 60601; 14,000.

Grange, Natl. (1867), 1616 H St. NW, Wash., DC 20006.

Graphic Artists, Society of Amer. (1915), 32 Union Sq., East, N.Y., NY 10003; 255.

Graphic Arts, Amer. Institute of (1914), 1059 Third Ave., N.Y., NY 10021; 2,200.

Gray Panthers (1970), 311 S. Juniper St., Suite 601, Phila., PA 19107; 80,000.

Greek-Amer. War Veterans in America, Natl. Legion of (1938), 739 W. 186th St., N.Y., NY 10033; 11.

Green Mountain Club, The (1910), 43 State St., Box 889, Montpelier, VT 05602; 4,200.

Grocers, Natl. Assn. of (1893), 1825 Samuel Morse Dr., Reston, VA 22090.

Grocery Manufacturers of America (1908), 1010 Wisconsin Ave., Wash., DC 20007; 140 companies.

Guide Dog Foundation for the Blind (1946), 371 Jericho Tpke., Smithtown, NY 11787; 2,500.

Gyro Intl. (1912), 1096 Mentor Ave., Painesville, OH 44077.

HIAS (Hebrew Immigrant Aid Society) (1881), 200 Park Ave. S, N.Y., NY 10003; 5,000.

Hadassah, the Women's Zionist Organization of America (1912), 50 W. 58th St., N.Y., NY 10019; 385,000.

Hairdressers and Cosmetologists Assn., Natl. (1921), 3510 Olive St., St. Louis, MO 63103; 50,406.

Handball Assn., U.S. (1951), 930 N. Benton Ave., Tucson, AZ 85711; 10,000.

Handgun, Intl. Metallic Silhouette Assn. (1976), Box 1609, 1409 Benton, Idaho Falls, ID 83401; 45,672.
Handicapped, Federation of the (1935), 211 W. 14th St., N.Y., NY 10011; 650.
Handicapped, Natl. Assn. of the Physically (1958), 76 Elm St., London, OH 43140; 775.
Hang Gliding Assn., U.S. (1971), P.O. Box 66306, Los Angeles, CA 90066; 6,000.
Health Council, Natl. (1920), 622 Third Ave., 34 fl., N.Y., NY 10017.
Health Insurance Institute (1956), 1850 K St. NW, Wash., DC; 325 companies.
Health, Physical Education, Recreation and Dance, Amer. Alliance for (1885), 1900 Association Dr., Reston, VA 22091.
Hearing Aid Society, Natl. (1951), 20361 Middlebelt Rd., Livonia, MI 48152; 2,500.
Hearing and Speech Action, Natl. Assn. for (1910), 10801 Rockville Pike, Rockville, MD 20852; 3,500.
Heart Assn., Amer. (1924), 7320 Greenville Ave., Dallas TX 75231; 144,000.
Hearts, Mended (1955), 7320 Greenville Ave., Dallas TX 75231; 15,000+.
Heating, Refrigerating & Air Conditioning Engineers, Amer. Soc. of (1894), 1791 Tullie Circle NE, Atlanta, GA 30329.
Helicopter Assn. Intl. (1948), 1619 Duke St., Alexandria, VA 22314; 1,100.
Helicopter Society, Amer. (1943), 217 N. Washington St., Alexandria VA 22314; 8,000+.
Hemispheric Affairs, Council on (1975), 1612 20th St. NW, Wash., DC 20009; 1,450.
High School Assns., Natl. Federation of State (1920), 11724 Plaza Circle, Kansas City, MO 64195; 51.
High School Band Inst., Natl. (1985), 519 N. Halifax Ave., Daytona Beach, FL 32018.
High Twelve Internatl. (1921), 11155-B2 South Towne Square, St. Louis, MO 63123; 28,200.
Historians, Organization of Amer. (1907), 112 N. Bryan St., Bloomington, IN 47401; 8,000 individuals.
Historical Assn., Amer. (1884), 400 A St. SE, Wash., DC 20003; 13,000.
Historic Preservation, Natl. Trust for (1949), 1785 Massachusetts Ave. NW, Wash., DC 20036; 140,000.
Hockey Assn. of the U.S., Amateur (1937), 2997 Broadmoor Valley Rd., Colorado Springs, CO 80906; 250,000.
Holy Cross of Jerusalem, Order of (1965), 853 Seventh Ave., N.Y., NY 10019; 2,019.
Home Builders, Natl. Assn. of (1942), 15th & M Sts. NW, Wash., DC 20005; 104,000+ firms.
Home Economics Assn., Amer. (1909), 2010 Massachusetts Ave. NW, Wash., DC 20020; 30,000.
Homemakers of America, Future (1945), 1910 Association Dr., Reston, VA 22091.
Homemakers Council, Natl. Extension (1936), Box 389, Hollis, NY 03049; 471,418.
Horatio Alger Soc. (1961), 4907 Allison Dr., Lansing, MI 48910; 300.
Horse Council, American (1969), 1700 K St., NW, #300, Washington, DC 20006; 2,000.
Horse Protection Assn., Amer. (1966), 1038 31st St. NW, Wash., DC 20007; 15,000.
Horse Show Assn. of America Ltd., Natl. (1883), 680 5th Ave., #1602, N.Y., NY 10019.
Horse Shows Assn., Amer. (1917), 220 E. 42 St., N.Y., NY 10017-5806; 45,000.
Hospital Association, Amer. (1899), 840 N. Lake Shore Dr., Chicago, IL 60611; 40,000.
Hospital Public Relations, Amer. Society for (1964), 840 N. Lake Shore Dr., Chicago, IL 60611; 3,000.
Hotel & Motel Assn., Amer. (1910), 888 Seventh Ave., N.Y., NY 10106; 10,000.
Hot Rod Assn., Natl. (1951), 10639 Riverside Dr., N. Hollywood, CA 91602; 40,000.
Human Rights and Social Justice, Americans for (1977), P.O. Box 6258, Ft. Worth, TX 76115.
Humane Society of the U.S. (1954), 2100 L St. NW, Wash., DC 20037; 500,000.
Humanics, American (1948), 4601 Madison Ave., Kansas City, MO 64112; 2,000.
Hydrogen Energy, Intl. Assn. for (1975), P.O. Box 248266, Coral Gables, FL 33124; 2,653.

Idaho, U.S.S.(BB-42) Assn. (1957), P.O. Box 11247, San Diego, CA 92111; 1,000.
Identification, Intl. Assn. for (1915), 2516 Otis Drive, Alameda, CA 94501-6370; 2,500.
Illustrators, Society of (1901), 128 E. 63 St., N.Y., NY 10021; 950.
Indian Rights Assn. (1882), 1505 Race St., Phila., PA 19102.
Industrial Democracy, League for (1905), 181 Hudson St., N.Y., NY 10013; 1,500.
Industrial Designers Society of America (1965), 1142-E Walker Rd., Great Falls, VA 22066; 1,900.
Industrial Engineers, Amer. Institute of (1948), 25 Technology Park, Norcross, GA 30092; 35,000.
Industrial Health Foundation (1935), 34 Penn Circle West, Pittsburgh, PA 15206; 170 companies.
Industrial Security, Amer. Soc. for (1955), 1655 N. Ft. Myer Dr., Suite 1200, Arlington, VA 22209; 20,000.
Information, Freedom of, Center (1958), P.O. Box 858, Columbia, MO 65205.
Information and Image Management, Assn. for (1943), 1100 Wayne Ave., Silver Spring, MD 20910; 8,900.
Information Industry Assn. (1969), 555 New Jersey Ave. NW, Suite 800, Wash., DC 20001; 460 companies.
Information Managers, Associated (1981), 1776 E. Jefferson St., Rockville, MD 20852; 600.
Insurance Assn., Amer. (1964), 1025 Connecticut Ave. NW, Wash., DC 20036; 171 companies.
Insurance Seminars, Intl. (1964), P.O. Box J, University, AL 35486; 5,000.
Intelligence Officers, Assn. of Former (1975), 6723 Whittier Ave., Suite 303A, McLean, VA 22101; 3,500.
Intercollegiate Athletics, Natl. Assn. of (1940), 1221 Baltimore Ave., Kansas City, MO 64105; 485 schools.
Interior Designers, Amer. Society of (1975), 1430 Broadway, N.Y., NY 10018; 23,000.
International Interculture Programs, AFS (1947), 313 E. 43rd St., N.Y., NY 10017; 100,000.
Inventors, Amer. Assn. of (1975), 6562 E. Curtis Rd., Bridgeport, MI 48722; 3,961.
Investors, Natl. Assn. of (1951), 1515 E. Eleven Mile Rd., Royal Oak, MI 48067; 120,000.
Investment Clubs, Natl. Assn. of (1951), 1515 E. Eleven Mile Rd., Royal Oak, MI 48067; 65,000.
Irish-American Cultural Inst. (1962), 683 Osceola Ave., St. Paul, MN 55105; 79,700.
Iron Castings Society (1897), 455 State St., Des Plaines, IL 60016; 200 firms.
Iron and Steel Engineers, Assn. of (1907), Three Gateway Center, Suite 2350, Pittsburgh, PA 15222; 11,856.
Iron and Steel Institute, Amer. (1908), 1000 16th St. NW, Wash., DC 20036; 1,300.
Italian Historical Society of America (1949), 111 Columbia Heights, Bklyn., NY 11201.
Italy-America Chamber of Commerce (1887), 350 Fifth Ave., N.Y., NY 10118; 650.
Izaak Walton League of America, The (1922), 1701 N. Ft. Suite 1100, Myer Dr., Arlington, VA 22209; 50,000.

JAPOS Study Group (1974), 154 Laguna Ct., St. Augustine Shores, FL 32086-7031; 180+.
Jamestowne Society (1936), P.O. Box 14523, Richmond, VA 23221; 2,430.
Jane Austen Society of N. Amer. (1979), P.O. Box 252, Wayne, PA 19087; 2,000.
Japanese Amer. Citizens League (1929), 1765 Sutter St., San Francisco, CA 94115; 26,000.
Jaycees, U.S. (1920), 4 W. 21st St., Tulsa, OK 74114.
Jewish Appeal, United (1939), 99 Park Avenue, N.Y., NY 10016.
Jewish Center Workers, Assn. of (1918), 15 E. 26th St., N.Y., NY 10009; 1,000.
Jewish Committee, Amer. (1906), 165 E. 56th St., N.Y., NY 10022; 50,000.
Jewish Congress, Amer. (1918), 15 E. 84th St., N.Y., NY 10028; 50,000.
Jewish Federations, Council of (1932), 575 Lexington Ave., N.Y., NY 10022; 200 agencies.
Jewish Historical Society, Amer. (1892), 2 Thornton Rd., Waltham, MA 02154; 3,550.
Jewish War Veterans of the U.S.A. (1896), 1811 R St. NW, Wash., DC 20009; 100,000.
Jewish Welfare Bd. Natl. (1917), 15 E. 26th St., N.Y., NY 10010.
Jewish Women, Natl. Council of (1893), 15 E. 26th St., N.Y., NY 10010; 100,000.
Job's Daughters, Internatl. Order of (1921), 2515 St. Mary's Ave., Omaha, NE 68105; 38,000.
Jockey Club (1894), 380 Madison Ave., N.Y., NY 10017; 90.
John Birch Society (1958), 395 Concord Ave., Belmont, MA 02178; 50,000.

Joseph Diseases Foundation, Intl. (1977), P.O. Box 2550, Livermore, CA 94550; 3,800.
Journalists, Society of Professional (Sigma Delta Chi) (1909), 53 W. Jackson Blvd., Suite 731, Chicago, IL 60604.
Journalists and Authors, Amer. Society of (1948), 1501 Broadway, Suite 1907, N.Y., NY 10036; 777.
Judaism, Amer. Council for (1943), 298 Fifth Ave., N.Y., NY 10001; 20,000.
Judicature Society, Amer. (1913), 25 E. Washington, Chicago, IL 60602; 30,000.
Juggler's Assn., Intl. (1947), P.O. Box 29, Kenmore, NY 14217; 3,000.
Junior Achievement (1919), 550 Summer St., Stamford, CT 06901; 300,000.
Junior Auxiliaries, Natl. Assn. of (1941), 255 S. Poplar, Greenville, MS 38702-1873; 7,500+.
Junior Colleges, Amer. Assn. of Community and (1920), One Dupont Circle NW, Wash., DC 20036; 900.
Junior Leagues, Assn. of (1921), 825 Third Ave., N.Y., NY 10022; 140,000+.

Kennel Club, Amer. (1884), 51 Madison Ave., N.Y., NY 10010; 438 clubs.
Kiwanis Intl. (1915), 3636 Woodview, Indianapolis, IN 46268.
Knights of Columbus (1882), One Columbus Plaza, New Haven, CT 06507; 1.4 mln.
Knights Templar U.S.A., Grand Encampment (1816), 14 E. Jackson Blvd., Suite 1700, Chicago, IL 60604; 315,000.
Krishna Consciousness, Intl. Soc. for (1966), 3764 Watseka Ave., Los Angeles, CA 90034; 2 mln.

Labor, Amer. Federation of and Congress of Industrial Organizations (1955), 815 16th St. NW, Wash., DC 20006.
La Leche League Intl. (1956), 9616 Minneapolis, Franklin Park, IL 60131; 50,000.
Lambs, The (1874), 3 W. 51st St., N.Y., NY 10019; 400.
Landscape Architects, Amer. Society of (1899), 1733 Connecticut Ave., NW, Wash., DC 20009; 7,000.
Law, Amer. Society of Intl. (1906), 2223 Massachusetts Ave. NW, Wash., DC 20008; 4,500.
Law Enforcement Officers Assn., Amer. (1966), 1000 Connecticut Ave. NW, Suite 9, Wash., DC 20036; 50,000.
Law Libraries, Amer. Assn. of (1904), 53 W. Jackson Blvd., Chicago, IL 60604; 3,600.
Law and Social Policy, Center for (1969), 1751 N St. NW, Wash., DC 20036.
Learned Societies, Amer. Council of (1919), 228 E. 45th St., N.Y., NY 10017; 45 societies.
Lefthanders, League of (1975), P.O. Box 89, New Milford, NJ 07646; 500.
Lefthanders Intl. (1975), P.O. Box 8249, N. Topeka, Topeka, KS 66608; 23,000.
Legal Administrators, Assn. of (1971), 104 Wilmot, Suite 205, Deerfield, IL 60015-5195; 5,300.
Legion of Valor of the U.S.A. (1890), 92 Oak Leaf Lane, Chapel Hill, NC 27514-9440; 677.
Leif Ericson Society (1962), Box 301, Chicago, IL 60690-0301; 1,200.
Leprosy Missions, Amer. (1906), One Broadway, Elmwood Park, NJ 07407.
Lesbian & Gay Academic Union (1979), P.O. Box 82123, San Diego, CA 92138; 3,500.
Leukemia Society of America (1949), 733 Third Ave., N.Y., NY 10017.
Lewis Carroll Society of N. America (1974), 617 Rockford Rd., Silver Spring, MD 20902; 300.
Liberty Lobby (1955), 300 Independence Ave. SE, Wash., DC 20003; 23,871.
Libraries Assn., Special (1909), 1700 18th St., NW, Wash., DC 20009; 12,500.
Library Assn., Amer. (1876), 50 E. Huron St., Chicago, IL 60611; 40,000.
Library Assn., Medical (1898), 919 N. Michigan Ave., Chicago, IL 60611; 5,100.
Life, Americans United for (1971), 343 S. Dearborn, Chicago, IL 60604.
Life Insurance, Amer. Council of (1976), 1001 Pennsylvania Ave., NW, Wash., DC 20004; 620 firms.
Life Office Management Assn. (1924), 5770 Powers Ferry Rd., Atlanta, GA 30327; 700+companies.
Life Underwriters, Amer. Soc. of Certified (1929), 270 Bryn Mawr Ave., Byrn Mawr, PA 19010; 28,000.
Life Underwriters, Natl. Assn. of (1890), 1922 F St. NW, Wash., DC 20006; 135,000.
Lighter-Than-Air Society (1952), 1800 Triplett Blvd., Akron, OH 44306; 1,200.
Lions Clubs, Intl. Assn. of (1917), 300 22d St., Oak Brook, IL 60570; 1,340,605.
Litchfield Institute, The (1984), Box 1000, South St., Litchfield, CT 06759; 32.
Literacy Volunteers of America (1962), 5795 Widewaters Parkway, Syracuse, NY 13214.
Little League Baseball (1939), P.O. Box 3485, Williamsport, PA 17701; 16,144 leagues.
Little People of America (1957), Box 633, San Bruno, CA 94066; 4,000.
London Club (1975), P.O. Box 4527, Topeka, KS 66604.
Longwave Club of America (1974), 45 Wildflower Rd., Levittown, PA 19057; 536.
Lung Assn., Amer. (1904), 1740 Broadway, N.Y., NY 10019.
Lutheran Education Assn. (1942), 7400 Augusta St., River Forest, IL 60305; 3,750.

Magazine Publishers Assn. (1919), 575 Lexington Ave., N.Y., NY 10022; 250 publishers.
Magicians, Intl. Brotherhood of (1926), 28 N. Main St., Kenton, OH 43326; 10,500.
Magicians, Society of Amer. (1902), 325 Maple St., Lynn, MA 01904; 5,300.
Male Nurse Assn., Natl. (1971), Rush Univ., 1725 W. Harrison St., Chicago, IL 60612; 1,400.
Management Assn., Amer. (1923), 135 W. 50th St., N.Y., NY 10020; 75,000.
Management Consultants, Institute of (1968), 19 W. 44th St., N.Y., NY 10036; 1,500.
Management Consulting Firms, Assn. of (1929), 230 Park Ave., N.Y., NY 10169; 60 firms.
Manufacturers, Natl. Assn. of (1897), 1776 F St. NW, Wash., DC 20006; 13,000 companies.
Manufacturers' Agents Natl. Assn. (1947), 23016 Mill Creek Rd., Laguna Hills, CA 92653; 10,000.
March of Dimes Birth Defects Foundation (1938), 1275 Mamaroneck Ave., White Plains, NY 10605.
Marijuana Laws, Natl. Organization for the Reform of (NORML) (1970), 2001 S St., #640, Wash., DC 20009; 10,000.
Marine Corps League (1923), 956 N. Monroe St., P.O. Box 11100, Arlington, VA 22201; 29,000.
Marine Manufacturers Assn., Natl. (1904), 401 N. Michigan Ave., Chicago, IL 60611; 1,200 companies.
Marine Technology Society (1963), 2000 Florida Ave. NW, #500, Wash., DC 20009; 3,500.
Marketing Assn., Amer. (1937), 250 S. Wacker Dr., Chicago, IL 60606; 50,000.
Mary Stuart Society (1982), 6 St. John's Pl., N.Y., NY 10014.
Masonic Relief Assn. of U.S. and Canada (1885), 32613 Seidel Dr., Burlington, WS 53105; 14,700.
Masonic Service Assn. of the U.S. (1919), 8120 Fenton St., Silver Spring, MD 20910; 43 Grand Lodges.
Masons, Ancient and Accepted Scottish Rite, Southern Jurisdiction, Supreme Council (1801), 1733 16th St. NW, Wash., DC 20009; 625,000.
Masons, Supreme Council 33°, Ancient and Accepted Scottish Rite, Northern Masonic Jurisdiction (1813), 33 Marrett Rd., Lexington, MA 02173; 456,580.
Masons, Royal Arch, General Grand Chapter (1797), 1084 New Circle Rd. NE, Lexington, KY 40505; 318,293.
Mathematical Assn. of America (1915), 1225 Connecticut Ave. NW, Wash., DC 20036; 18,500.
Mathematical Society, Amer. (1888), P.O. Box 6248, Providence, RI 02940; 22,000.
Mathematical Statistics, Institute of (1935), 3401 Investment Blvd., #7, Hayward, CA 94545; 3,200.
Mathematics, Society for Industrial and Applied (1952), 117 S. 17th St., Phila., PA 19103-5052; 5,500.
Mayflower Descendants, General Society of (1897), 4 Winslow St., Plymouth, MA 02361; 22,000.
Mayors, U.S. Conference of (1933), 1620 Eye St. NW, Wash., DC 20006; over 30,000.
Mechanical Engineers, Amer. Society of (1880), 345 E. 47th St., N.Y., NY 10017; 114,922.
Mechanics, Amer. Academy of (1969), Dept. of Civil Engineering, Northwestern Univ., Evanston, IL 60201; 1,200.
Mechanics, State Council of VA Jr. Order of Amer. (1853), 170 Railway Rd., Grafton, VA; 1,200.
Medical Assn., Amer. (1847), 535 N. Dearborn St., Chicago, IL 60610; 258,000.
Medical Assn., Natl. (1895), 1012 Tenth St. NW, Wash., DC 20001; 13,500.
Medical Record Assn., Amer. (1928), 875 N. Michigan Ave., Chicago, IL 60611; 25,000.
Medieval Academy of America (1926), 1430 Massachusetts Ave., Cambridge, MA 02138; 3,600.

Medical Technologists, Amer. College of (1942), 5608 Lane, Raytown, MO 64133; 368.
Mensa, Amer. (1960), 2626 E. 14th St., Brooklyn, NY 11235.
Mental Health Assn., Natl. (1909), 1021 Prince St., Alexandria, VA 22314; 1 mln.
Mental Health Program Directors, Natl. Assn. of State (1963), 1101 King St., Suite 160, Alexandria, VA 22314; 55.
Mentally Ill, The Natl. Alliance for the (1979), 1901 N. Ft. Myer Dr., Suite 500, Arlington, VA 22209; 60,000.
Merchant Marine Library Assn., Amer. (1921), One World Trade Center, Suite 1365, N.Y., NY 10048.
Merchant Marine Veterans, Amer. (1984), 905 Cape Coral Pkwy., Cape Coral, FL 33904; 884.
Merchant Marine Veterans of WWII, U.S. (1944), 1712 Harbor Way, Seal Beach, CA 90740; 6,000.
Merchants Assn., Natl. Retail (1911), 100 W. 31st St., N.Y., NY 10001; 45,000.
Metal Finishers, Natl. Assn. of (1955), 111 E. Wacker Dr., Chicago, IL 60601; 1,100.
Metallurgy Institute, Amer. Powder (1958), 105 College Rd. East, Princeton, NJ 08540; 2,300.
Metal Powder Industries Federation, (1946), 105 College Rd. East, Princeton, NJ 08540; 275 cos.
Metals, Amer. Society for (1913), Metals Park, OH 44073.
Meteorological Society, Amer. (1919), 45 Beacon St., Boston, MA 02108; 10,000.
Metric Assn., U.S. (1916), 10245 Andasol Ave., Northridge, CA 91325; 2,500.
Microbiology, Amer. Society for (1899), 1913 Eye St. NW, Wash. DC 20006; 32,000.
Micrographics Assn., Natl. (1942), 926 Philadelphia Ave., Silver Spring, MD 20910; 9,000.
Mideast Educational and Training Services, America-, (1951), 1100 17th Street, NW, Wash., DC 20036.
Military Order of the Loyal Legion of the U.S.A. (1865), 1805 Pine St., Phila., PA 19103; 1,200.
Military Order of the Purple Heart of the USA (1932), 5413-B Backlick Rd., Springfield, VA 22151; 18,000.
Military Order of the World Wars (1920), 435 N. Lee St., Alexandria, VA 22314; 17,000.
Mining and Metallurgical Society of America (1908), 275 Madison Ave., N.Y., NY 10016; 295.
Ministerial Assn., Amer. (1929), 2210 Wilshire Blvd., Suite 582, Santa Monica, CA 90403; 2,500.
Model Railroad Assn., Natl. (1935), 4121 Cromwell Rd., Chattanooga, TN 37421; 25,000.
Modern Language Assn. of America (1883), 10 Astor Pl., N.Y., NY 10003; 25,000.
Modern Language Teachers Assns., Natl. Federation of (1916), Gannon Univ., Erie, PA 16541.
Moose, Loyal Order of (1888), Mooseheart, IL 60539.
Mothers, American (1933), 301 Park Ave., N.Y., NY 10022.
Mothers-in-Law Club Intl. (1970), 420 Adelberg Ln., Cedarhurst, NY 11516; 5,000.
Mothers of Twins Clubs, Natl. Organization of (1960), 12404 Princess Jeanne NE, Albuquerque, NM 87112; 10,000.
Motion Picture Arts & Sciences, Academy of (1927), 8949 Wilshire Blvd., Beverly Hills, CA 90211; 4,768.
Motion Pictures, Natl. Board of Review of (1909), P.O. Box 589, Lenox Hill Sta., N.Y., NY 10021.
Motion Picture & Television Engineers, Society of (1916), 595 West Hartsdale Ave., White Plains, NY 10607; 9,100.
Motor Vehicle Administrators, Amer. Assn. of (1933), 1201 Connecticut Ave. NW, Wash., DC 20036; 1,000.
Motor Vehicle Manufacturers Assn. (1900), 300 New Center Building, Detroit, MI 48202; 11 companies.
Motorcyclist Assn., Amer. (1924), 33 Collegeview, Westerville, OH 43081; 134,000.
Multiple Sclerosis Society, Natl. (1946), 205 E. 42d St., N.Y., NY 10017; 485,000.
Municipal Finance Officers Assn. (1906), 180 N. Michigan Ave., Suite 800, Chicago, IL 60601.
Municipal League, Natl. (1894), 55 W. 44th St., N.Y., NY 10036; 3,000.
Muscular Dystrophy Assn. (1950), 810 Seventh Ave., N.Y., NY 10019; 2 mln. volunteers.
Museums, Amer. Assn. of (1906), 1055 Thomas Jefferson St. NW, Wash., DC 20007; 8,780.
Music Center, Amer. (1939), 250 W. 54th St., Suite 300, N.Y., NY 10019; 2,000.
Music Council, Natl. (1940), 570 Seventh Ave., N.Y., NY 10018; 50+ organizations.
Music Educators Natl. Conference (1907), 1902 Association Dr., Reston, VA 22090; 54,069.
Musicians, Amer. Federation of (1896), 1500 Broadway, N.Y., NY 10036; 330,000.
Musicological Society, Amer. (1934), 201 S. 34th St., Phila., PA 19104, 3,500.
Music Publishers' Assn., Natl. (1917), 205 E. 42nd St., N.Y., NY 10017; 350.
Music Scholarship Assn., Amer. (1956), 1826 Carew Tower, Cincinnati, OH 45202; 2,500.
Music Teachers Natl. Assn. (1876), 2113 Carew Tower, Cincinnati, OH 45202; 23,000.
Muzzle Loading Rifle Assn., Natl. (1933), P.O. Box 67, Friendship, IN 47021; 25,800.

NAACP (Natl. Assn. for the Advancement of Colored People) (1909), 4805 Mt. Hope Drive, Baltimore, MD 21215; 450,000.
Na'amat USA, Women's Labor Zionist Organization (1925), 200 Madison Ave., N.Y., NY 10016; 50,000.
Narcolepsy and Cataplexy Foundation of Amer. (1975), 1410 York Ave., Suite 2D, N.Y. NY 10021; 3,991.
Narcolepsy Assoc., Amer. (1975), 335 Quarry Rd., Belmont, CA 94002; 3,500.
National Guard Assn. of the U.S. (1878), One Massachusetts Ave. NW, Wash., DC 20001; 54,000.
Naturalists, Assn. of Interpretive (1961), 6700 Needwood Rd., Derwood, MD 20855; 1,100.
Nature Conservancy (1951), 1800 N. Kent St., Arlington, VA 22209; 300,000.
Navajo Code Talkers Assn. (1971), Box 1182, Window Rock, AZ 86515; 475.
Naval Architects & Marine Engineers, Society of (1893), One World Trade Center, Suite 1369, N.Y., NY 10048; 12,900.
Naval Engineers, Amer. Society of (1888), 1452 Duke St., Alexandria, VA 22203; 8,000.
Naval Institute, U.S. (1873), U.S. Naval Academy, Annapolis, MD 21402; 100,000.
Naval Reserve Assn. (1954), 1619 King St., Alexandria, VA 22314; 23,000.
Navigation, Institute of (1945), 815 15th St. NW, Suite 832, Wash., DC 20005; 2,500.
Navy Club of the U.S.A. Auxiliary (1941), 418 W. Pontiac St., Ft. Wayne, IN 46807; 1,000.
Navy League of the U.S. (1902); 2300 Wilson Blvd., Arlington, VA 22201; 57,070.
Needlework Guild of America (1885), 1007B St. Road, Southhampton, PA 18966; 150,000.
Negro College Fund, United (1944), 500 E. 62d St., N.Y., NY 10021; 42 institutions.
Neurofibromatosis Foundation, Natl. (1978), 141 Fifth Ave., N.Y., NY 10010; 22,000.
Newspaper Editors, Amer. Society of (1922), P.O. Box 17004, Washington, DC 20041; 897.
Newspaper Promotion Assn., Intl. (1930), 11600 Sunrise Valley Dr., Reston, VA 22091; 1,300.
Newspaper Publishers Assn., Amer. (1887), 11600 Sunrise Valley Dr., Reston, VA 22091; 1,400 newspapers.
Ninety-Nines (Intl. Organization of Women Pilots) (1929), P.O. Box 59965; Will Rogers Airport, Oklahoma City, OK 73159; 6,500.
Nobel Anniversary Committee, Amer. (1942), 1 Morningside Dr. No., Westport, CT 06880.
Non-Commissioned Officers Assn. (1960), 10635 IH 35 No., San Antonio, TX 78233; 165,000.
Northern Cross Society (1983), Northern Cross Ranch, P.O. Box 4527, Topeka, KS 66604; 300+.
Notaries, Amer. Society of (1965), 918 16th St. NW, Wash., DC 20006; 24,231.
Nuclear Society, Amer. (1954), 555 N. Kensington Ave., La Grange Park, IL 60525; 14,000.
Numismatic Assn., Amer. (1891), 818 N. Cascade Ave., Colorado Springs, CO 80903; 35,000.
Numismatic Society, Amer. (1858), Broadway at 155th St., N.Y., NY 10032; 2,169.
Nurses' Assn., Amer. (1896), 2420 Pershing Rd., Kansas City, MO 64108.
Nursing, Amer. Assembly of Men in (1971), Rush Univ., 600 S. Paulina, #474-H, Chicago, IL 60612; 280.
Nursing, Natl. League for (1952), 10 Columbus Circle, N.Y., NY 10019; 18,000.
Nutrition, Amer. Institute of (1928), 9650 Rockville Pike, Bethesda, MD 20814; 2,323.

ORT Federation, Amer. (Org. for Rehabilitation through Training) (1925), 817 Broadway, N.Y., NY 10014; 20,000.
Odd Fellows, Sovereign Grand Lodge Independent Order of (1819), 422 N. Trade St., Winston Salem, NC 27101.
Old Crows, Assn. of (1964), 2300 9th St. S., Arlington, VA 22204; 18,000.
Olympic Committee, U.S. (1921), 1750 E. Boulder St., Colorado Springs, CO 80909; 60 organizations.

Optical Society of America (1916), 1816 Jefferson Pl. NW, Wash., DC 20036; 9,800.

Optimist Intl. (1919), 4494 Lindell Blvd., St. Louis, MO 63108.

Optometric Assn., Amer. (1898), 243 N. Lindbergh Blvd., St. Louis, MO 63141; 25,729.

Oral and Maxillofacial Surgeons, Amer. Assn. of (1918), 211 E. Chicago Ave., Ste. 930, Chicago, IL 60611; 5,132.

Organists, Amer. Guild of (1896), 815 Second Ave., Suite 318, N.Y., NY 10017; 22,000.

Oriental Society, Amer. (1842), 329 Sterling Memorial Library, Yale Sta., New Haven, CT 06520; 1,350.

Ornithologists' Union, Amer. (1883), c/o National Museum of Natural History, Smithsonian, Wash., DC 20560; 4,500.

Ortho Missions (1934), 14526 Haynes St., #4, Van Nuys CA 91411; 1,600.

Osteopathic Assn., Amer. (1887), 212 E. Ohio St., Chicago, IL 60611; 23,292.

Ostomy Assn., United (1962), 2001 W. Beverly Blvd., Los Angeles, CA 90057; 48,880.

Outlaw and Lawman History, Natl. Assn. for (1974), Univ. of Wyoming, Box 3334, Laramie, WY 82071; 470.

Overeaters Anonymous (1960), P.O. Box 92870, Los Angeles, CA 90009; 120,000.

Over-the-Counter Cos., Natl. Assn. of (1973), 1735 K St. NW, Washington, DC 20006; 500+.

PTA (Natl. Congress of Parents and Teachers), Natl. (1897), 700 N. Rush St., Chicago, IL 60611; 5.8 mln.

Paleontological Research Institution (1932), 1259 Trumansburg Rd., Ithaca, NY 14850; 700+.

Paper Converters Assn. (1934), 1133 15th St. NW, Wash., DC 20005.

Paper Industry, Technical Assn. of the Pulp and (1916), P.O. Box 105113, Atlanta, GA 30348; 24,000.

Paper Institute, Amer. (1964), 260 Madison Ave., N.Y., NY 10016; 166 companies.

Parasitologists, Amer. Society of (1924), 1041 New Hampshire St., Box 368, Lawrence, KS 66044; 1,400.

Parents Without Partners (1958), 7910 Woodmont Ave. NW, Wash., DC 20814; 210,000.

Parkinson's Disease Foundation (1957), 650 W. 168th St., N.Y., NY 10032; 40,000.

Parliamentarians, Amer. Institute of (1958), 124 W. Washington Blvd. Ft. Wayne, IN 46802; 1,400.

Parliamentarians, Natl. Assn. of (1930), 6301 James A. Reed Rd., Suite 114, Kansas City, MO 64133; 195.

Parliamentary Law, Intl. Organization of Professionals in (1977), 3611 Victoria Ave., Los Angeles, CA 90016; 300.

Pasta Assn., Natl. (1904), 1901 N. Ft. Myer Dr., Suite 1000, Arlington, VA 22209; 100 member companies.

Pathologists, Amer. Assn. of (1976), 9650 Rockville Pike, Bethesda, MD 20814; 2,400.

Patriotism, Natl. Committee for Responsible (1967), P.O. Box 665, Grand Central Sta., N.Y., NY 10163; 150.

Pearl Harbor History Associates (1983), P.O. Box 205, Sperryville, VA 22740-0205; 300+.

PEN Amer. Center (1922), 568 Broadway, N.Y., NY 10012.

PEN Women, Natl. League of Amer. (1897), 1300 17th St. NW, Wash., DC 20036; 6,000.

Pen Friends, Intl. (1967), P.O. Box 20924, Grantville Station, San Diego, CA 92120; 140,000.

Pennsylvania Society of New York (1899), 80 N. Main St., Sellersville, PA 18960; 1,900.

Pension Actuaries, Amer. Society of (1966), 1413 K St. NW, Wash., DC 20005; 2,200.

P.E.O (Philanthropic Educational Organization) Sisterhood (1869), 3700 Grand Ave., Des Moines, IA 50312; 235,000.

Personnel Administration, Amer. Society for (1948), 606 N. Washington St., Alexandria, VA 22314; 33,000.

Petroleum Equipment Inst. (1951), 3739 E. 31st St., Tulsa, OK 74135; 1,200 member companies.

Petroleum Institute, Amer. (1919), 1220 L St. NW, Wash., DC 20005; 5,000.

Petroleum Landmen, Amer. Assn. of (1955), 777 Main St., Suite 1470, Fort Worth, TX 76102; 11,200.

Pharmaceutical Assn., Amer. (1852), 2215 Constitution Ave. NW, Wash., DC 20037; 50,000.

Philatelic Pages & Panels, Amer. Soc. for (1984), 1138 Princeton Dr., Richardson, TX 75081-3615; 576.

Philatelic Society, Amer. (1886), P.O. Box 8000, State College, PA 16803; 55,000+.

Philaticians, Society of (1972), 154 Laguna Ct., St. Augustine Shores, FL 32086; 400+.

Philological Assn., Amer. (1869), 617 Hamilton Hall, Columbia Univ., N.Y., NY 10027; 2,500+.

Philosophical Assn., Amer. (1901), Univ. of Delaware, Newark, DE 19716; 7,000.

Philosophical Enquiry, Intl. Society for (1974), 304 Lexington Blvd., Carmel, IN 46032; 443.

Philosophical Society, Amer. (1743), 104 S. 5th St., Phila., PA 19106; 650.

Photogrammetry and Remote Sensing, Amer. Society of (1934), 210 Little Falls St., Falls Church, VA 22046; 8,000.

Photographers of America, Professional (1880), 1090 Executive Way, Des Plaines, IL 60018; 14,000.

Photographic Society of Amer. (1934), 2005 Walnut St., Phila. PA 19103; 14,000.

Physical Therapy Assn., Amer. (1921), 1111 N. Fairfax St., Alexandria, VA 22314; 44,000.

Physicians, Amer. Academy of Family (1947), 1740 W. 92nd St., Kansas City, MO 64114; 57,000.

Physics, Amer. Inst. of (1931), 335 E. 45th St., N.Y., NY 10017; 10 member societies.

Physiological Society, Amer. (1887), 9650 Rockville Pike, Bethesda, MD 20814.

Phytopathological Soc., The Amer. (1908), 3340 Pilot Knob Rd., St. Paul, MN 55121; 4,300+.

Pilgrim Society (1820), 75 Court St., Plymouth, MA 02360.

Pilgrims of the U.S. (1903), 80 Broadway, N.Y., NY 10005.

Pilot Club Intl. (1921), 244 College St., Macon, GA 31213.

Planetary Society (1980), 65 N. Catalina, Pasadena, CA 91106; 105,000.

Planned Parenthood Federation of America (1916), 810 Seventh Ave., N.Y., NY 10019; 187 affiliates.

Planning Assn., Amer. (1917), 1976 Massachusetts Ave. NW, Wash., DC 20036; 21,000.

Plastic Modelers Society, Intl. (1965), 1615 Calvert, Lincoln, NE 68502; 6,000.

Plastics Industry, Society of (1937), 355 Lexington Ave., N.Y., NY 10017; 1,200 companies.

Platform Assn., Intl. (1831), Box 250, Winnetka, IL 60093; 5,000.

Podiatric Medical Assn., Amer. (1912), 20 Chevy Chase Circle NW, Wash., DC 20015; 8,416.

Poetry Day Committee, Natl. (1947), 1110 N. Venetian Dr., Miami, FL 33139; 17,500.

Poetry Society of America (1910), 15 Gramercy Park, N.Y., NY 10003; 1,800.

Poets, Academy of Amer. (1934), 177 E. 87th St., N.Y., NY 10128; 3,000+.

Polar Society, Amer. (1934), 98-20 62d Dr., Apt. 7H, Rego Park, NY 11374; 2,143.

Police, Internatl. Assn. of Chiefs of (1893), 13 Firstfield Rd., Gaithersburg, MD 20878; 14,000.

Police Officers Assn., Natl. (1987), 1316 Gardiner St., Louisville, KY 40213; 11,000.

Polish Army Veterans Assn. of America (1921), 19 Irving Pl., N.Y., NY 10003; 9,762.

Polish Cultural Society of America (1940), P.O. Box 31, Wall Street P.O., N.Y., NY 10005; 112,400.

Polish Legion of American Veterans (1921), 3024 N. Laramie Ave., Chicago, IL 60641; 15,000.

Political Items Collectors, Amer. (1945), P.O. Box 340339, San Antonio, TX 78234; 1,800.

Political Science, Academy of (1880), 2852 Broadway, N.Y., NY 10025; 11,000.

Political Science Assn., Amer. (1903), 1527 New Hampshire Ave. NW, Wash., DC 20036; 9,800.

Political & Social Science, Amer. Academy of (1889), 3937 Chestnut St., Phila., PA 19104; 4,673.

Pollution Control, Internatl. Assn. for (1970), 444 N. Capital St. NW, Wash. DC 20001; 500.

Polo Assn., U.S. (1890), 120 N. Mill St., Lexington, KY, 40507; 2,400.

Population Assn. of America (1931), 806 15th St. NW, Wash., DC 20005; 2,800.

Portuguese Continental Union of the U.S.A. (1925), 899 Boylston St., Boston, MA 02115; 9,280.

Postmasters of the U.S., Natl. Assn. of (1898), 4212 King St., Arlington, VA 22302; 41,204.

Postmasters of the U.S., Natl. League of (1904), 1023 N. Royal St., Alexandria, VA 22314-1569; 22,000.

Poultry Science Assn. (1908), 309 W. Clark, Champaign, IL 61820; 1,900.

Power Boat Assn., Amer. (1903), 17640 E. Nine Mile Rd., E. Detroit, MI 48021; 8,000.

Precancel Collectors, Natl. Assn. of (1950), 5121 Park Blvd., Wildwood, NJ 08260; 7,025.

Press, Associated (1848), 50 Rockefeller Plaza, N.Y., NY 10020; 1,365 newspapers & 3,600 broadcast stations.

Press Club, Natl. (1908), 529 14th St. NW, Wash., DC 20045.

Press Intl., United (1907), 1400 I St. NW, Wash. DC 20005.

Press and Radio Club (1948), P.O. Box 7023, Montgomery, AL 36107; 726.

Press Women, Natl. Federation of (1937), 1105 Main St., Box 99, Blue Springs, MD 64015; 5,000.
Printing Industries of America (1887), 1730 N. Lynn St., Arlington, VA 22209; 12,000 companies.
Prisoners of War, Amer. Ex- (1942), 3201 E. Pioneer Pkwy. #40, Arlington, TX 76010; 27,000.
Procrastinators' Club of America (1956), 1111 Broad-Locust Bldg., Phila., PA 19102; 4,900.
Propeller Club of the U.S. (1927), 1030 15th St. NW, Suite 430, Wash., DC 20005; 14,000.
Psychiatric Assn., Amer. (1844), 1400 K St. NW, Wash., DC 20005; 32,000.
Psychical Research, Amer. Society for (1885), 5 W. 73d St., N.Y., NY 10023; 2,000.
Psychoanalytic Assn., Amer. (1911), 309 E. 49th St., N.Y., NY 10017; 2,800.
Psychological Assn., Amer. (1892), 1200 17th St. NW, Wash., DC 20036; 60,000.
Psychological Assn. for Psychoanalysis, Natl. (1948), 150 W. 13th St., N.Y., NY 10011; 295.
Psychological Minorities, Society for the Aid of (1953), 42-25 Hampton St., Elmhurst, NY 11373; 624.
Psychotherapy Assn., Amer. Group (1942), 25 E. 21st St., N.Y., NY 10010; 3,000.
Public Health Assn., Amer. (1972), 1015 15th St. NW, Wash., DC 20005; 30,000.
Public Relations Soc. of Amer. (1947), 845 Third Ave., N.Y., NY 10022; 14,000.
Publishers, Assn. of Amer. (1970), One Park Ave., N.Y., NY 10016; 330 publishing houses.
Puppeteers of Amer. (1937), 5 Cricklewood Path, Pasadena, CA 91107; 2,000.

Quality Control, Amer. Society for (1946), 230 W. Wells St., Milwaukee, WI 53203; 50,000.
Quota Internatl. (1919), 1828 L St. NW, Suite 908, Wash., DC 20036.

Rabbinical Alliance of America (1944), 156 5th Ave., N.Y., NY 10010; 502.
Rabbinical Assembly (1900), 3080 Broadway, N.Y., NY 10027; 1,170.
Rabbis, Central Conference of Amer. (1889), 21 E. 40th St., N.Y., NY 10016; 1,500.
Radio, The Natl. Assn. of Business and Educational (1965), 1501 Duke St., Suite 200, Alexandria, VA 22314; 5,600.
Radio Union, Intl. Amateur (1925), P.O. Box AAA, Newington, CT 06111; 124 societies.
Radio and TV Society, Intl. (1939), 420 Lexington Ave., N.Y., NY 10170; 2,000.
Radio Relay League, Amer. (1914), 225 Main St., Newington, CT 06111; 139,494.
Railroad Passengers, Natl. Assn. of (1967), 236 Massachusetts Ave. NE, Suite 603, Wash., DC 20002; 12,659.
Railroads, Assn. of Amer. (1934), 1920 L St. NW, Wash., DC 20036; 450.
Railway Historical Society, Natl. (1935), P.O. Box 58153, Phila., PA 19102; 13,500.
Railway Progress Institute (1908), 700 N. Fairfax St., Alexandria, VA 22314; 140 companies.
Range Management, Society for (1946), 2760 W. 5th Ave., Denver, CO 80204; 5,500.
Rape, Feminist Alliance Against (1974), P.O. Box 21033, Wash., DC 20009.
Reading Assn., Intl. (1956), P.O. Box 8139, 800 Barksdale Rd., Newark, DE 19714; 64,917.
Real Estate Appraisers, Natl. Assn. of (1967), 853 Broadway, N.Y., NY 10003; 1,000.
Real Estate Institute, Intl. (1975), 8715 Via De Commercio, Scottsdale, AZ 85258; 5,200.
Real Estate Investment Trusts, Natl. Assn. of (1960), 1101 17th St. NW, Wash., DC 20036; 370 associates.
Rebekah Assemblies, Intl. Assn. of (1916), P.O. Box 153, Minneapolis, KS 67467; 294,142.
Reconciliation, Fellowship of (1914), 523 N. Broadway, Nyack, NY 10960; 33,000.
Records Managers & Administrators, Assn. of (1955), 4200 Somerset Dr., Suite 215, Prairie Village, KS 66208; 9,000.
Recreation and Park Assn., Natl. (1965), 3101 Park Ctr. Dr., 12th Fl., Alexandria, VA 22302.
Red Cross, Amer. Natl. (1881), 17th & D Sts. NW, Wash., DC 20006.
Red Men, Improved Order of (1765), 1525 West Avenue, Waco, TX, 76707; 40,000.
Redwoods League, Save-the- (1918), 114 Sansome St., Rm. 605, San Francisco, CA 94104; 50,000.
Reed Organ Society, Inc. (1981), The Musical Museum, Deansboro, NY 13328; 640.
Regional Plan Assn. (1929), 1040 Ave. of the Americas, N.Y., NY 10018; 1,200.
Rehabilitation Assn., Natl. (1925), 633 S. Washington St., Alexandria, VA 22314; 18,000.
Religion, Amer. Academy of (1909), 501 Hall of Languages, Syracuse Univ., Syracuse, NY 13244; 4,600.
Religion, Freedom from, Foundation (1978), P.O. Box 750, Madison, WI 53701; 2,000.
Remodeling Industry, Natl. Assn. of the (1956), 1901 N. Moore St., Suite 808, Arlington, VA 22209.
Renaissance Society of America (1954), 1161 Amsterdam Ave., N.Y., NY 10027; 3,000.
Reserve Officers Assn. of the U.S. (1922), One Constitution Ave., NE, Wash., DC 20002; 125,000.
Restaurant Assn., Natl. (1919), 311 First St. NW, Wash., DC 20001; 24,034.
Retarded Citizens of the U.S., Assn. for (1950), 2501 Ave. J, Arlington, TX 76006; 160,000.
Retired Credit Union People, Natl. Assn. for (1978), 5910 Mineral Pt. Rd., Madison, WI 53701; 92,000.
Retired Federal Employees, Natl. Assn. of (1921), 1533 New Hampshire Ave. NW, Wash., DC 20036; 490,000.
Retired Officers Assn. (1929), 201 N. Washington St., Alexandria, VA 22314; 353,000.
Retired Persons, Amer. Assn. of (1958), 1909 K St. NW, Wash., DC 20049; 18 mln.
Retired Teachers Assn., Natl. (1947), 1909 K St. NW, Wash., DC 20049; 540,000.
Retreads (of World War I & II) (1947), 40-07 154th St., Flushing, NY 11354; 1,000.
Revolver Assn., U.S. (1900), 96 W. Union St., Ashland, MA 01721; 1,350.
Reye's Syndrome Foundation, Natl. (1974), 426 N. Lewis, Bryan, OH 43506; 10,000.
Richard III Society (1969), P.O. Box 13787, New Orleans, LA 70185; 700.
Rifle Assn., Natl. (1871), 1600 Rhode Island Ave. NW, Wash., DC 20036; 3 mln.
Road & Transportation Builders' Assn., Amer. (1902), 525 School St. SW, Wash., DC 20024; 4,500.
Rodeo Cowboys Assn., Professional (1936), 101 Pro Rodeo Dr., Colorado Springs, CO 80919; 7,867.
Roller Skating, U.S. Amateur Confederation of (1971), 7700 A St., Lincoln, NE 68510; 40,000.
Roller Skating Rink Operators Assn. (1937), 7700 A St., Lincoln, NE 68510; 1,500 rinks.
Rose Society, Amer. (1899), P.O. Box 30,000, Shreveport, LA 71130; 19,060.
Rotary Intl. (1905), 1600 Ridge Ave., Evanston, IL 60201.
Running and Fitness Assn., Amer. (1968), 2001 S St. NW, Suite 540, Wash, DC 20009; 25,000.
Ruritan Natl. (1928), Ruritan Natl. Rd., Dublin, VA 24141.

Safety and Fairness Everywhere, Natl. Assn. Taunting (1980), P.O. Box 5743WA, Montecito, CA 93150; 9,800.
Safety Council, Natl. (1913), 444 N. Michigan Ave., Chicago, IL 60611; 12,000.
Sailors, Tin Can (1976), Battleship Cove, Fall River, MA 02726; 7,000.
St. Andrew the Apostle, The Soc. of (1983), Route 3, Sylvester, WV 25193; 450.
St. Dennis of Zante, Sovereign Greek Order of (1096; 1953 in U.S.), 739 W. 186th St., N.Y., NY 10033; 91.
St. George the Martyr, Knightly Assn. of (1980), State Route #3, Sylvester, WV 25193; 10,000.
St. Paul, Natl. Guild of (1937), 601 Hill 'n Dale, Lexington, KY 40503; 13,652.
Salespersons, Natl. Assn. of Professional (1970), P.O. Box 76461, Atlanta, GA 30358; 35,000.
Salt Institute (1914), 206 N. Washington St., Alexandria, VA; 35.
Samuel Butler Society (1978), Chaplain Library, Williams College, P.O. Box 426, Williamstown, MA 01267; 100.
Sane Nuclear Policy, Committee for a (1957), 711 G St. SE, Wash., DC 20003; 130,000.
Savings Institutions, Natl. Council of (1983), 11101 15th St. NW, Wash., DC 20005.
Savings & Loan League, Natl. (1943), 1101 15th St. NW, Wash., DC 20005; 300 associations.
School Administrators, Amer. Assn. of (1876), 1801 N. Moore St., Arlington, VA 22209; 17,561.
School Boards Assn., Natl. (1940), 1680 Duke St., Alexandria, VA 22314.
School Counselor Assn., Amer. (1953), 5999 Stevenson Ave., Alexandria, VA 22304; 10,830.
Schools of Art, Natl. Assn. of (also: School of Art and Design, School of Dance, Music, and Theater) (1944), 11250 Roger Bacon Dr., #5, Reston, VA 22090.

Schools & Colleges, Amer. Council on (1927), 13014 Dale Mabry Hwy., Ste. 270-B, Tampa, FL 33180-2808; 137.
Science, Amer. Assn. for the Advancement of (1848), 1333 H St. NW, Wash., DC 20005; 132,000.
Science Fiction Society, World (1939), P.O. Box 1270, Kendall Sq. Sta., Cambridge, MA 02142; 5,000.
Science Service (1921), 1719 N St. NW, Wash., DC 20036.
Science Teachers Assn., Natl. (1946), 1742 Connecticut Ave. NW, Wash., DC 20009; 41,000.
Science Writers, Natl. Assn. of (1934), P.O. Box 294, Greenlawn, NY 11740; 1,298.
Sciences, Natl. Academy of (1863), 2101 Constitution Ave. NW, Wash., DC 20418; 1,415.
Scientists, Federation of Amer. (1945), 307 Massachusetts Ave. NE, Wash., DC 20002; 5,000.
Scientists of America Foundation, Young (1979), P.O. Box 9066, Phoenix, AZ 85068; 250 chapters.
Screen Actors Guild (1933), 7065 Hollywood Blvd. Hollywood, CA 90028; 67,000.
Sculpture Soc., Natl. (1893), 15 E. 26th St., N.Y., NY 10010.
Seamen's Service, United (1942), One World Trade Ctr., Suite 1365, N.Y., NY 10048.
2d Air Division Assn. (1947), 1 Jeffrey's Neck Rd., Ipswich, MA 01938; 6,000.
Secondary School Principals, Natl. Assn. of (1916), 1904 Association Dr., Reston, VA 22091; 37,000.
Secretaries, Natl. Assn. of Legal (1950), 2250 E73, #550, Tulsa, OK 74136-6805; 17,000.
Secularists of America, United (1947), 1301 E. Ventura Blvd. #36, Oxnard, CA 93030.
Securities Industry Assn. (1972), 120 Broadway, N.Y., NY 10271; 500 firms.
Semantics, Institute of General (1938), Office of the Director, 3029 Eastern Ave., Baltimore, MD 21224; 500.
Separation of Church & State, Americans United for (1947), 8120 Fenton St., Silver Spring, MD 20910; 53,000.
Sertoma Internatl. (1912), 1912 E. Meyer Blvd., Kansas City, MO 64132; 35,000.
Sex Information & Education Council of the U.S. (SIECUS) (1964), New York University, 32 Washington Place, N.Y., NY 10003; 3,000.
Shakespeare Assn. of America (1972), Box 6328, Vanderbilt Sta. B, Nashville, TN 37235; 850.
Sheet Metal & Air Conditioning Contractor's Natl. Assn., The (1943), 8224 Old Courthouse Rd., Vienna, VA 22180; 2,500.
Shipbuilders Council of America (1921), 1110 Vermont Ave. NW, Wash., DC 20005; 60 organizations.
Ships in Bottles Assn. of Amer. (1983), P.O. Box 550, Coronado, CA 92118; 300.
Shoe Retailers Assn., Natl. (1913), 1414 Ave. of the Americas, N.Y., NY 10016; 4,000.
Shore & Beach Preservation Assn., Amer. (1926), 3000 Citrus Circle, Suite 230, Walnut Creek, CA 94598; 1,000.
Shrine, Ancient Arabic Order of the Nobles of the Mystic (1872), 2900 Rocky Pt. Dr., Tampa, FL 33607; 1,000,000.
Shut-Ins, Natl. Society for (1970), P.O. Box 1392, Reading, PA 19603; 90.
Sierra Club (1892), 730 Polk St., San Francisco, CA 94109; 400,000.
Signalmen, Society of (1971), P.O. Box 11247, San Diego, CA 92111; 5,100.
Silurians, Soc. of the (1924), 45 John St., N.Y., NY 10038.
Skating Union of the U.S., Amateur (1928), 1033 Shady Lane, Glen Ellyn, IL 60137; 2,500.
Skeet Shooting Assn., Natl. (1946), P.O. Box 680007, San Antonio, TX 78268; 15,800.
Ski Assn., U.S. (1904), 1750 E. Boulder St., Colorado Springs, CO 80909; 23,244.
Small Business, Amer. Federation of (1938), 407 S. Dearborn St., Chicago, IL 60605; 25,000.
Small Business Assn., Natl. (1937), 1155 15th St., Wash., DC 20005; 50,000.
Smoking & Health, Natl. Clearinghouse for (1965), Center for Disease Control, 1600 Clifton Road NE, Atlanta, GA 30333.
Soaring Society of America (1932), P.O. Box 66071, Los Angeles, CA 90066-0071; 16,000.
Soccer Federation, U.S. (1913), Viscount Hotel, 40 JFK Intl. Airport, Jamaica, NY 11430; 700,000.
Social Biology, Society for the Study of (1926), Medical Dept., Brookhaven Natl. Laboratory, Upton, NY 11973; 415.
Social Sciences, Natl. Institute of (1899), c/o Mr. J. Sinclair Armstrong, 30 Rockefeller Plaza, Suite 4528, N.Y., NY 10112-0119; 800.
Social Work Education, Council on (1952), 1744 R St. NW, Wash. DC 20009; 3,500.
Social Workers, Natl. Assn. of (1955), 7981 Eastern Ave., Silver Spring, MD 20910; 98,000+.
Socialists of America, Democratic (1982), 15 Dutch St., Suite 500, N.Y., NY 10038; 6,000.
Sociological Assn., Amer. (1905), 1722 N St. NW, Wash., DC 20036; 12,000.
Softball Assn. of America, Amateur (1933), 2801 N.E. 50th St., Oklahoma City, OK 73111; 4 mln+.
Softball League, Cinderella (1958), P.O. Box 1411, Corning, NY 14830.
Soft Drink Assn., Natl. (1919), 1101 16th St. NW, Wash., DC 20036; 1,400.
Soil Conservation Society of America (1945), 7515 N.E. Ankeny Rd., Ankeny, IA 50021; 12,000.
Soil Science Society of America (1936), 677 S. Segoe Rd., Madison, WI 53711; 6,500.
Sojourners, Natl. (1919), 8301 E. Boulevard Dr., Alexandria, VA 22308; 9,349.
Soldier's, Sailor's and Airmen's Club (1919), 283 Lexington Ave., N.Y., NY 10016; 2,054.
Songwriters Guild, The (1931), 276 Fifth Ave., N.Y., NY 10001; 5,000.
Sons of the Amer. Legion (1932), Box 1055, Indianapolis, IN 46206; 59,577.
Sons of the American Revolution, Natl. Society of (1889), 1000 S. 4th, Louisville, KY 40203; 24,000.
Sons of Confederate Veterans (1896), Southern Station, Box 5164, Hattiesburg, MS 39406; 9,000.
Sons of the Desert (1965), P.O. Box 8341, Universal City, CA 91608; 3,500.
Sons of Italy in America, Supreme Lodge Order (1905), 219 E. St., NE, Wash. DC 20002; 100,000.
Sons of Norway (1895), 1455 W. Lake St., Minneapolis, MN 55408; 105,000.
Sons of Poland, Assn. of the (1903), 591 Summit Ave., Rm. 702, Jersey City, NJ 07306; 10,000.
Sons of St. Patrick, Society of the Friendly (1784), 80 Wall St., N.Y., NY 10005; 1,350.
Sons of Sherman's March to the Sea (1966), 1725 Farmers Ave., Tempe, AZ 85281; 626.
Sons of Union Veterans of the Civil War (1881), P.O. Box 24, Gettysburg, PA 17325; 3,500.
Soroptimist Intl. of the Americas (1921), 1616 Walnut St., Phila., PA 19103; 40,000.
Southern Christian Leadership Conference (1957), 334 Auburn Ave. NE, Atlanta, GA 30303; 1 mln.
Space Education Assoc., U.S. (1973), 746 Turnpike Rd., Elizabethtown, PA 17022; 1,000.
Speech Communication Assn. (1914), 5105 Backlick Rd., Annandale, VA 22003; 6,078.
Speech-Language-Hearing Assn., Amer. (1925), 10801 Rockville Pike, Rockville, MD 20852; 50,000.
Speleological Society, Natl. (1941), 2813 Cave Ave., Huntsville, AL 35810; 7,000.
Spiritual Awareness, Assn. for (1984), P.O. Box 224, Clarence, MO 63437.
Sports Car Club of America (1944), 6750 S. Emporia, Englewood, CO 80112; 24,000.
Sports Club, Indoor (1930), 1145 Highland St., Napoleon, OH 43545.
Standards Institute, Amer. Natl. (1918), 1430 Broadway, N.Y., NY 10018; 1,000.
State Communities Aid Assn. (1872), 151 Chestnut St., Albany, NY 12210; 95.
State Governments, Council of (1933), P.O. Box 11910, Iron Works Pike, Lexington, KY 40578; 50 states.
State & Local History, Amer. Assn. for (1940), 172 Second Ave. N., Nashville, TN 37201; 7,700.
Statistical Assn., Amer. (1839), 806 15th St. NW, Wash., DC 20005; 15,000.
Steamship Historical Society of America (1935), 414 Pelton Ave., Staten Island, NY 10310; 3,358.
Steel Construction, Amer. Institute of (1921), 400 N. Michigan Ave., Chicago, IL 60611; 400.
Stock Car Auto Racing, Natl. Assn. for (NASCAR) (1948), 1801 Speedway Blvd., Daytona Beach, FL 32015; 17,000.
Stock Exchange, Amer. (1911), 86 Trinity Pl., N.Y., NY 10006; 871.
Stock Exchange, N.Y. (1792), 11 Wall St., N.Y., NY 10005.
Stock Exchange, Phila. (1790), 1900 Market St., Phila., PA 19103; 505.
Structural Stability Research Council (1944), Fritz Engineering Laboratory No. 13, Lehigh Univ., Bethlehem, PA 18015.
Student Assn., U.S. (1947), 1012 14th St. NW, Suite 403, Wash., DC 20005.
Student Councils, Natl. Assn. of (1931), 1904 Association Dr., Reston, VA 22091; 200,000.
Stuttering Project, Natl. (1977), 1269 7th Ave., San Francisco, CA 94122; 2,500.
Sudden Infant Death Syndrome Foundation, Inc., Natl. (1962), 8200 Professional Pl., Landover, MA 20785.
Sugar Brokers Assn., Natl. (1903), 1 World Trade Center, N.Y., NY 10047; 100.

Sunbathing Assn., Amer. (1932), 1703 N. Main St., Kissimmee, FL 32743-3396; 30,000.
Sunday League (1933), 279 Highland Ave., Newark, NJ 07104; 25,000.
Surgeons, Amer. College of (1913), 55 E. Erie St., Chicago IL 60611; 47,636.
Surgeons, Intl. College of (1935), 1516 N. Lake Shore Dr., Chicago IL 60610; 15,000.
Surgeons of the U.S., Assn. of Military (1903), 10605 Concord St., #306, Kensington, MD 20895; 15,000.
Surveying & Mapping, Amer. Congress on (1941), 210 Little Falls, Falls Church, VA 22046; 10,500.
Symphony Orchestra League, Amer. (1942), 633 E St. NW, Wash., DC 20004.
Systems Management, Assn. for (1947), 24587 Bagley Rd., Cleveland, OH 44138; 9,000.

Table Tennis Assn., U.S. (1933), Olympic Complex, 1750 E. Boulder, Colorado Springs, CO 80909; 5,000.
Tailhook Assn., The (1956), Bldg. M-244, NAS, Miramar, P.O. Box 409, Borita, CA 92002; 10,251.
Tall Buildings and Urban Habitat, Council on (1969), Bldg. 13, Lehigh Univ., Bethlehem, PA 18015; 2,300.
Tattoo Club of America (1976), 822 Ave. of the Americas, N.Y., NY 10001; 10,000.
Tax Accountants, Natl. Assn. of Enrolled Federal (1960), 6108 N. Harding Ave., Chicago, IL 60659.
Tax Administrators, Federation of (1937), 444 N. Capitol St. NW, Wash., DC 20001; 50 agencies.
Tax Assn., Natl.–Tax Institute of America (1907), 21 E. State St., Columbus, OH 43215; 1,900.
Tax Foundation, Inc. (1937), 1 Thomas Circle NW, Suite 500, Wash., DC 20005; 850 corporations.
Tax Free America (1986), 11015 Cumpston St., N. Hollywood, CA 91601; 38,000.
Taxpayers Union, Natl. (1969), 713 Maryland Ave., NE, Washington, DC 20002; 150,000.
Tea Assn. of the U.S.A. (1899), 230 Park Ave., N.Y., NY 10169; 179.
Teachers, Amer. String Assn. (1954), UGA Sta. Box 2066, Athens, GA 30612; 6,000+.
Teachers of English, Natl. Council of (1911), 1111 Kenyon Rd., Urbana, IL 61801; 100,000.
Teachers of English to Speakers of Other Languages (1966), 1118 22nd St. NW, Suite 205, Wash., DC 20037.
Teachers of French, Amer. Assn. of (1927), 57 E. Armory Ave., Champaign, IL 61820; 11,000.
Teachers of German, American Assn. of (1928), 523 Building, Suite 201, Route 38, Cherry Hill, NJ 08034; 6,800.
Teachers of Mathematics, Natl. Council of (1920), 1906 Association Dr., Reston, VA 22091; 64,000.
Teachers of Singing, Natl. Assn. of (1944), 2800 Univ. Blvd. N, J.U. Sta., Jacksonville, FL 32211; 4,600.
Teachers of Spanish & Portuguese, Amer. Assn. of (1917), P.O. Box 6349, Lee Hall 218, Mississippi State Univ., Mississippi State, MS 39762-6349; 12,500.
Telephone Pioneers of Amer. (1911), 22 Cortland, St., 25th fl., N.Y., NY 10007; 640,534.
Television Arts & Sciences, Natl. Academy of (1947), 110 W. 57th St., N.Y., NY 10019.
Television Bureau of Advertising (1954), 485 Lexington Ave., N.Y., NY 10017.
Television & Radio Artists, Amer. Federation of (1937), 1350 Ave. of the Americas, N.Y., NY 10019; 66,000.
Telluride Assn. (1910), 217 West Ave., Ithaca, NY 14850.
Tennis Assn., U.S. (1881), 1212 Ave. of Americas, N.Y., NY 10036.
Terraplane Club, Hudson-Essex (1959), 100 E. Cross St., Ypsilanti, MI 48197; 2,500.
Tesla Memorial Soc., Inc. (1979), 453 Martin Rd., Lackawanna, NY 14218; 2,300.
Testing & Materials, Amer. Society for (1898), 1916 Race St., Phila., PA 19103; 30,000.
Texas State Genealogical Society (1960), 2507 Tannehill, Houston, TX 77008-3052; 700.
Textile Assn., Northern (1854), 230 Congress St., Boston, MA 02110; 300.
Textile Manufacturers Institute, Amer. (1949), 1101 Connecticut Ave. NW, Suite 300, Wash., DC 20036.
Theatre Organ Society, Amer. (1955), P.O. Box 3043, Olivenhain, CA 92024.
Theodore Roosevelt Assn. (1919), P.O. Box 720, Oyster Bay, NY 11771; 1,225.
Theological Library Assn., Amer. (1947), 5600 S. Woodlawn Ave., Chicago, IL 60637; 502.
Theological Schools, Assn. of (1936), P.O. Box 130, Vandalia, OH 45377.
Theosophical Society (1875), P.O. Box 270, 1926 N. Main St., Wheaton, IL 60187; 5,000.
Thoreau Society (1941), 156 Belknap St., Concord, MA 01742; 2,000.
Thoroughbred Racing Assns. of No. America (1942), 3000 Marcus Ave., Lake Success, NY 11042; 49 racetracks.
Titanic Historical Society (1963), P.O. Box 53, Indian Orchard, MA 01151; 2,500.
Toastmasters Intl. (1924), 2200 N. Grand Ave., Santa Ana,, CA 92711; 125,000.
Topical Assn., Amer. (1949), P.O. Box 630, Johnstown, PA 15907; 7,000.
Torch Clubs, Internatl. Assn. of (1924), 435 N. Michigan Ave., #1717, Chicago, IL 60611; 3,500.
Toy Manufacturers of America (1916), 200 Fifth Ave., N.Y., NY 10010; 250.
Trade Relations Council of the U.S. (1885), 1001 Connecticut Ave. NW, Wash., DC 20036; 50 companies.
Traffic and Transportation, Amer. Society of (1946), 1816 Norris Pl. #4, Louisville, KY 40205; 2,400.
Trail Association, North Country (1980), 2780 Mundy Ave., White Cloud, MI 49349; 200.
Transit Assn., Amer. Public (1974), 1225 Connecticut Ave. NW, Wash., DC 20036; 825.
Translators Assn., Amer. (1959), 109 Croton Ave., Ossining, NY 10562; 2,500+.
Transportation and Logistics, Inc., Amer. Society of (1946), P.O. Box 33095, Louisville, KY 40232; 1,900.
Trapshooting Assn., Amateur (1900), 601 W. National Rd. Vandalia, OH 45377; 90,000+.
Travel Agents, Amer. Society of (1931), 4400 MacArthur Blvd. NW, Wash., DC 20007; 22,000.
Travel Industry Assn. of America (1941), 1899 L St. NW, Wash., DC 20036; 1,700.
Travelers Protective Assn. of America (1890), 3755 Lindell Blvd., St. Louis, MO 63108; 194,326.
Trilateral Commission (1973), 345 E. 46th, N.Y., NY 10017.
Triple Nine Society (1979), 2119 College St., Cedar Falls, IA 50613; 650.
Trucking Assn., Amer. (1933), 2200 Mill Rd., Alexandria, VA 22314.
True Sisters, United Order (1846), 212 Fifth Ave., N.Y., NY 10010; 8,600.
Tuberous Sclerosis Assn. of Amer. (1970), P.O. Box 44, Rockland, MA 02370; 2,500.

UFOs, Natl. Investigation Committee on (1967), 14617 Victory Blvd., Suite 4, Van Nuys, CA 91411; 2,000.
UNICEF, U.S. Committee for (1947), 331 E. 38th St., N.Y., NY 10016.
USO (United Service Organizations) (1941), 601 Indiana Ave., NW, Wash., DC 20004.
USS (BB-42) Assn. Idaho, P.O. Box 11247, San Diego, CA 92111.
Underwriters, Amer. Soc. of Chartered Life (1927), 270 Bryn Mawr Ave., Bryn Mawr, PA 19010; 30,000.
Underwriters, Soc. of Chartered Property and Casualty (1944), Kahler Hall, 720 Providence Rd., Malvern, PA 19355.
Uniformed Services, Natl. Assn. for (1968), 5535 Hempstead Way, Springfield, VA 22151; 40,000.
United Nations Assn. of the U.S.A. (1923, as League of Nations Assn.) 300 E. 42d St., N.Y., NY 10017; 31,500.
U.S., Amer. Assn. for the Study of in World Affairs (1948), 3813 Annandale Rd., Annandale, VA 22003; 1,500.
United Way of America (1918), 801 N. Fairfax St., Alexandria, VA 22309; 1,200.
Universities, Assn. of Amer. (1900), One Dupont Circle NW, Wash., DC 20036; 53 institutions.
Universities & Colleges, Assn. of Governing Bds. of (1921), One Dupont Circle NW, Wash., DC 20036; 26,000.
University Extension Assn., Natl. (1915), One Dupont Circle, Suite 360, NW, Wash., DC 20036; 1,200.
University Foundation, Intl. (1973), 1301 S. Noland Rd., Independence, MO 64055; 10,500+.
University Professors, Amer. Assn. of (1915), 1012 14th St. NW, Wash., DC 20035; 70,000.
University Professors for Academic Order (1970), 635 SW 4th St., Corvallis, OR 97333; 500.
University Women, Amer. Assn. of (1881), 2401 Virginia Ave. NW, Wash., DC 20037; 193,000.
Urban Coalition, Natl. (1967), 1120 G St. NW, Suite 900, Wash., DC 20005; 42 affiliates.
Urban League, Natl. (1910), 500 E. 62d St., N.Y., NY 10020.
Utility Commissioners, Natl. Assn. of Regulatory (1889), P.O. Box 684, Wash., DC 20044; 374.

Valley Forge, Society of the Descendants of Washington's Army at (1976) P.O. Box 915, Valley Forge, PA 19481; 500+.

Vampire Research Center (1972), P.O. Box 252, Elmhurst, NY 11373; 150.
Variety Clubs Intl. (1928), 1560 Bdway., Suite 1209, N.Y., NY 10036.
VASA Order of America (1896), 65 Bryant Rd., Cranston, R.I. 02910; 32,000.
Ventriloquists, No. Amer. Assn. of (1944), 800 W. Littleton Blvd., Box 420, Littleton, CO 80160; 1,825.
Veterans Assn., Blinded (1945), 1726 M St. NW, Suite 800, Wash., DC 20036; 6,200.
Veterans Assn., China-Burma-India (1947), 750 N. Lincoln Memorial Dr., Milwaukee, WI 53201; 3,221+.
Veterans Committee, Amer. (1944), 1735 De Sales St. NW, Suite 402, Wash., DC 20817; 25,000.
Veterans of Foreign Wars of the U.S. (1899) & Ladies Auxiliary (1914), 406 W. 34th St., Kansas City, MO 64111.
Veterans of World War I (1958), 941 N. Capitol St. NE, Room 1201-C, Wash., DC 20421; 196,489.
Veterans of WWII, Submarine, (1955), 6523 San Joaquin St., Sacramento, CA 95820; 7,300.
Veterinary Medical Assn., Amer. (1863), 930 N. Meacham Rd., Schaumburg, IL 60196; 36,636.
Victorian Society in America (1966), 219 S. Sixth St., Phila., PA 19106; 4,088.
Vocational Assn., Amer. (1925), 2020 N. 14th St., Arlington, VA 22201; 56,000.
Volleyball Assn., U.S. (1928), 1750 E. Boulder, Colorado Springs, CO 80909; 35,000.

Walking Assn. (1976), P.O. Box 37228, Tucson, AZ 85740.
Walking Club Intl., Singles (1984), 4370 Fairlawn Dr., La Canada, CA 91011; 300.
Walking Society Amer. (1980), Viana House, Box 2174, Palm Beach, FL 33480; 117,672.
War Mothers, Amer. (1917), 2615 Woodley Pl. NW, Wash., DC 20008; 6,000.
Warrant and Warrant Officers' Assn., Chief, U.S. Coast Guard (1929), c/o Fort McNair Yacht Basin, 200 V Street, SW, Wash., DC 20024.
Washington, DC Area Trucking Assn. (1933), 2200 Mill Rd., Alexandria, VA 22314; 110 companies.
Watch & Clock Collectors, Natl. Assn. of (1943), 514 Poplar St., Columbia, PA 17512; 30,844.
Watercolor Soc., American (1866), 47 Fifth Ave., N.Y., NY 10003.
Water Pollution Control Admin., Assn. of State and Interstate (1962), 444 N. Capital St. NW, #330, Wash., DC 20001; 58.
Water Pollution Control Federation (1928), 2626 Pennsylvania Ave. NW, Wash., DC 20037; 30,000.
Water Resources Assn., Amer. (1964), 5410 Grosvenor Ln., Suite 220, Bethesda, MD 20814; 2,950.
Water Ski Assn., Amer. (1939), P.O. Box 191, Winter Haven, FL 33882; 20,000.
Water Well Assn., Natl. (1948), 6375 Riverside Drive, Dublin, OH 43017; 12,000.
Water Works Assn., Amer. (1881), 6666 W. Quincy Ave., Denver, CO 80235; 36,500.
Watts Family Assn. (1969), 12401 Burton St., N. Hollywood, CA 91605; 12 branches.
Weather Modification Assn. (1950), P.O. Box 8116, Fresno, CA 93747; 200.
Welding Society, Amer. (1919), 550 N.W. LeJeune Rd., Miami, FL 33126; 32,000.
Wheelchair Athletic Assn., Natl. (1956), 2107 Templeton Gap, Colorado Springs, CO 80907; 2,100.
Widows, Society of Military (1968), 5535 Hemstead Way, Springfield, VA 22151; 2,000.
Wilderness Society (1935), 1400 Eye St. NW, Wash., DC 20005; 130,000.
Wild Horse Organized Assistance (WHOA!) (1971), 140 Greenstone Dr., Reno, NV 89512; 10,000.
Wildlife, Defenders of (1925), 1244 19th St. NW, Wash., DC 20036; 80,000.
Wildlife Federation, Natl. (1936), 1412 16th St. NW, Wash., DC 20036; 4.2 mln.
Wildlife Foundation, No. Amer. (1911), 1266 W. Northwest Hwy., Suite 806, Palantine, IL 60067; 535.
Wildlife Fund, World (1961), 1255 23rd St. NW, Wash., DC 20037; 230,000.
Wildlife Management Institute (1911), 1101-14th St., Suite 725, NW, Wash., DC 20005.
William Penn Assn. (1886), 709 Brighton Rd., Pittsburgh, PA 15233; 90,000.
Wilsonian Club (1920), 1331 Parkside Dr., Riverside, CA 92506; 150.
Wireless Pioneers, Society of (1968), 3366—15 Mendocino Ave., Santa Rosa, CA 95402; 5,744.
Wizard of Oz Club, Intl. (1957), 220 North 11th St., Escanaba, MI 49829; 2,400.
Women, Natl. Assn. of Bank (1920), 500 No. Michigan Ave., Suite 1400, Chicago, IL 60611; 30,000.
Women, Natl. Organization for (NOW) (1966), 1401 New York Ave. NW, Wash., DC 20005; 150,000.
Women Artists, Natl. Assn. of (1889), 41 Union Sq., N.Y., NY 10003; 700.
Women Engineers, Society of (1950), 345 E. 47th St., N.Y., NY 10017; 14,000.
Women in Communications (1909), 3724 Executive Center Dr., #165, Austin, TX 78731; 10,000.
Women in Radio and TV, Inc. (1951), 1321 Connecticut Ave. NW, Washington, DC 20036; 3,000.
Women Geographers, Society of (1925), 1619 New Hampshire Ave. NW, Wash., DC 20009; 500.
Women Marines Assn. (1960), 1907-A Ruhland Ave., Redondo Beach, CA 90278; 3,000.
Women Strike for Peace (1961), 145 S. 13th St., Rm. 706, Phila., PA 19107; 8,000.
Women of the U.S., Natl. Council of (1888), 777 U.N. Plaza, N.Y., NY 10017; 28 organizations.
Women Voters of the U.S., League of (1920), 1730 M St. NW, Wash., DC 20036; 120,000.
Women World War Veterans (1919), 237 Madison Ave., N.Y., NY 10016; 85,000.
Women's Army Corps Veterans Assn. (1946), 1409 E. Euclid Ave., Arlington Heights, IL 60004; 2,400.
Women's Assn., Amer. Business (1949), 9100 Ward Pkwy., P.O. Box 8728, Kansas City, MO 64114; 112,000.
Women's Christian Temperance Union, Natl. (1874), 1730 Chicago Ave., Evanston, IL 60201; 200,000.
Women's Clubs, General Federation of (1890), 1734 N St. NW., Wash. DC, 20036.
Women's Clubs, Natl. Federation of Business & Professional (1919), 2012 Massachusetts Ave. NW, Wash., DC 20036.
Women's Educational & Industrial Union (1877), 356 Boylston St., Boston, MA 02116; 3,000.
Women's Intl. League for Peace & Freedom (1915), 1213 Race St., Phila., PA 19107; 15,000.
Women's Legal Defense Fund (1971), 2000 P St. NW, Suite 400, Washington, DC 20036; 1,600.
Women's Overseas Service League (1921), P.O. Box 39058, Friendship Sta., Wash., DC 20016; 1,500.
Woodmen of America, Modern (1883), Mississippi River at 17th St., Rock Island, IL 61201; 384,294.
Woodmen of the World (1890), 1700 Farnam St., Omaha, NE 68102; 900,000.
Wool Growers Assn., Natl. (1865), 1301 Pa. Ave., NW, Rm. 300, Wash., DC. 20004; 24 state assns.
Workmen's Circle (1900), 45 E. 33d St., N.Y., NY 10016.
World Future Society (1966), 4916 St. Elmo Ave., Bethesda, MD 20814; 25,000.
World Health, Amer. Assn. for (1953), 2001 S St., NW, Suite 530, Washington, DC 20009; 500.
World Peace, International Assn. of Educators for (1969), P.O. Box 3282, Mastin Lake Station, Huntsville, AL 35810-0282; 18,500.
Writers Guild of America, West (1933), 8955 Beverly Blvd., Los Angeles, CA 90048; 6,000.

Yeoman F. Natl. (1936), 223 El Camino Real, Vallejo, CA 94590; 800.
Young Americans for Freedom (1960), Woodland Rd., Sterling, VA 22170; 55,000.
Young Men's Christian Assns. of the U.S.A., (1851), 101 N. Wacker Dr., Chicago, IL 60606; 13 mln.
YM-YMHAs of Greater New York, Associated (1957), 130 E. 59th St., N.Y., NY 10020; 55,100.
Young Women's Christian Assn. of the U.S.A. (1906), 726 Broadway, N.Y., NY 10003; 1.6 mln.
Young Engineers & Scientists of America Foundation, Inc. (1959), P.O. Box 9066, Phoenix, AZ 85020.
Youth Hostels, American (1934), P.O. Box 37613, Wash., DC 20013; 100,000.

Zero Population Growth (1968), 1601 Connecticut Ave. NW, Wash., DC 20009; 15,000.
Ziegfeld Club (1936), 593 Park Ave., N.Y., NY 10021; 303.
Zionist Organization of America (1897), 4 E. 34th St., N.Y., NY 10016; 140,000.
Zonta Intl. (1919), 35 E. Wacker Dr., Chicago, IL 60601.
Zoological Parks & Aquariums, Amer. Assn. of (1924), Oglebay Park, Wheeling, WV 26003; 4,500.
Zoologists, Amer. Society of (1890), Box 2739, California Lutheran College, Thousand Oaks, CA 91360; 4,300.

HEALTH

Ethics on Care of the Terminally Ill

The Joint Commission on Accreditation of Hospitals announced, on June 4, 1987, that hospitals would be required to have formal policies specifying when doctors and nurses could refrain from trying to resuscitate terminally ill patients. The Commission said that the policy must be developed in consultation with the medical staff and the nursing staff, adopted by the medical staff and then approved by the hospital's governing body. The policy must define the roles of physicians, nursing personnel, and members of the patient's family in any decision to withhold resuscitation. It must also include "provisions designed to assure that a patient's rights are respected." The new standard would take effect in January, 1988. The Commission proposed a similar requirement for nursing homes; this was under review by experts in long-term care.

In March 1986, the American Medical Association announced that it would be ethical for doctors to withhold "all means of life prolonging medical treatment," including food and water, from patients in irreversible comas even if death was not imminent. The withholding of such therapy should occur only when a patient's coma "is beyond doubt irreversible and there are adequate safeguards to confirm the accuracy of the diagnosis," the association's judicial council said. The opinion could affect at least 10,000 Americans who are in irreversible comas.

While the opinion of the 271,000-member association does not constitute a hard and fast rule for doctors, it opens the way for them to withdraw life prolonging treatment with less fear of being taken to court, and to use the opinion as a defense if they are challenged. The A.M.A. said that stopping therapy is a decision that each physician and each patient's family and legal guardians would address on a case by case basis.

The A.M.A. opinion also said: "Life prolonging medical treatment includes medication and artificially or technologically supplied respiration, nutrition or hydration. In treating a terminally ill or irreversibly comatose patient, the physician should determine whether the benefits of treatment outweigh its burdens. At all times, the dignity of the patient should be maintained."

Many states have tried to clear the issue of treating the comatose who are terminally ill by acting to define brain death. In at least 37 states, legislatures or courts have worked out a definition modeled along the lines of a recommendation previously released by the A.M.A. that said a person is brain dead when he has suffered "irreversible cessation of the functions of the entire brain, including the brain stem."

Immunization Schedule for Children*

Source: American Academy of Pediatrics

Age	Type of Vaccination	Disease Immunized Against
2 months	D-T-P	Diphtheria, Tetanus (Lockjaw), Pertussis (Whooping Cough)
	Oral Polio Vaccine	Polio Myelitis
4 months	D-T-P	
	Oral Polio Vaccine	
6 months	D-T-P	
15 months	Measles Vaccine	Measles
	Rubella Vaccine[1]	German Measles
	Mumps Vaccine[1] (Or a single injection combined vaccine for all three diseases may be given at 15 months.)	Mumps
18 months (2)	D-T-P Booster	
	Oral Polio Booster	
School Entry	D-T-P Booster	
	Oral Polio Booster	

(1) Rubella or mumps vaccine alone may be given as early as 12 months. (2) The national Center for Disease Control advises immunization of children 24 months and older against Haemolphilus influenza type B, which causes the most common and serious form of meningitis in children under 5 and can also cause pneumonia, bronchitis, tonsilitis and ear infections.

*The American College of Physicians recommends that adolescents and adults consult with their physicians about further vaccinations. Those without natural infection or proper immunization against childhood diseases like measles, mumps, rubella, and poliomyelitis may be at increased risk for such disease and their complications as adults; in addition, tetanus and diphtheria should be boosted periodically; and various ages, occupations, lifestyles, environmental risks, and diseases may call for adult immunization.

Heart and Blood Vessel Disease

Warning Signs

Source: American Heart Association, Dallas

Of Heart Attack

- Uncomfortable pressure, fullness, squeezing or pain in the center of the chest lasting two minutes or longer
- Pain may radiate to the shoulder, arm, neck or jaw
- Sweating may accompany pain or discomfort
- Nausea and vomiting may also occur
- Shortness of breath, dizziness, or fainting may accompany other signs

The American Heart Association advises immediate action at the onset of these symptoms. The Association points out that more than half of heart attack victims die before they reach the hospital and that the average victim waits 2 hours before seeking help.

Of Stroke

- Sudden temporary weakness or numbness of face or limbs on one side of the body
- Temporary loss of speech, or trouble speaking or understanding speech
- Temporary dimness or loss of vision, particularly in one eye
- Unexplained dizziness, unsteadiness, or sudden falls

Major Risk Factors

Blood pressure—High blood pressure increases the risk of stroke, heart attack, kidney failure and congestive heart failure.

Cholesterol—More than 50% of adult Americans have cholesterol levels of 200 milligrams per deciliter of blood, a level at which the risk of coronary heart disease begins to rise sharply.

Cigarettes—Cigarette smokers have more than twice the risk of heart atttacks than non-smokers. Young smokers have a higher risk for early death due to stroke.

Cardiovascular Disease Statistical Summary

Prevalence — 64,890,000 Americans have one or more forms of heart and blood vessel disease.
- hypertension — 59,130,000.
- coronary heart disease — 4,870,000
- rheumatic heart disease — 2,150,000.
- stroke — 1,990,000.

Mortality — 991,300 in 1985 (47.6% of all deaths).
- nearly one-fifth of all persons killed by CVD are under age 65.

Congenital or inborn heart defects — 35 recognizable types of defects.
- about 25,000 babies are born every year with heart defects.
- post-natal mortality from heart defects was estimated at more than 6,000 in 1985.

Heart attack — caused 548,000 deaths in 1985.
- 4,810,000 alive today have history of heart attack and/or angina pectoris.
- 300,000+ a year die of heart attack before they reach hospital.
- As many as 1,500,000 Americans will have a heart attack this year and about 540,000 of them will die.

Stroke — killed 152,700 in 1985; afflicts 1,990,000.

CCU — most of the over 6,000 general hospitals in U.S. have coronary care capability.

Hypertension (high blood pressure) — 59,130,000 Americans age 6 and above—nearly one in 3 adults.
- easily detected and usually controllable, but only a minority have it under adequate control.

Rheumatic heart disease — 100,000 children; 2,050,000 adults.
- killed about 6,200 in 1985.

Note: 1985 mortality data are estimates based on 1985 provisional data as published by the National Center for Health Statistics.

Estimated Cost of Cardiovascular Disease, 1988

According to the Health Care Financing Review, the estimated total expenditures on cardiovascular disease in 1988 will be $83.7 billion. These costs break down in the following manner: hospital and nursing home services, $53.7 billion; lost output due to disability, $14.6 billion; physician and nursing services, $11.3 billion; and medications, $4.1 billion.

Cancer Prevention

Source: American Cancer Society, 1987

PRIMARY PREVENTION: steps that might be taken to avoid those factors that might lead to the development of cancer.

Smoking — Cigarette smoking is responsible for 85% of lung cancer cases among men, 75% among women—about 83% overall. Smoking accounts for about 30% of all cancer deaths. Those who smoke two or more packs of cigarettes a day have lung cancer mortality rates 15-25 times greater than non-smokers.

Nutrition — Risk for colon, breast and uterine cancers increases for obese people. High-fat diet may be a factor in the development of certain cancers such as breast, colon and prostate. High-fiber foods may help reduce risk of colon cancer. Foods rich in vitamins A and C may help lower risk for cancers of larynx, esophagus and lung. Eating cruciferous vegetables such as cabbage, broccoli, brussels sprouts, kohlrabi and cauliflower, may help protect against certain cancers. Salt-cured, smoked and nitrite-cured foods have been linked to esophageal and stomach cancer. The heavy use of alcohol, especially when accompanied by cigarette smoking or chewing tobacco, increases risk of cancers of the mouth, larynx, throat, esophagus, and liver.

Sunlight — Almost all of the more than 500,000 cases of non-melanoma skin cancer developed each year in the U.S. are considered to be sun-related. Such exposure is a major factor in the development of melanoma, and the incidence increases for those living near the equator.

Alcohol — Oral cancer and cancers of the larynx, throat, esophagus, and liver occur more frequently among heavy drinkers of alcohol.

Smokeless Tobacco — Increased risk factor for cancers of the mouth, larynx, throat, and esophagus.

Estrogen — For mature women, certain risks associated with estrogen treatment to control menopausal symptoms, including an increased risk of endometrial cancer. However, estrogen can be given safely under careful physician control.

Radiation — Excessive exposure to radiation can increase cancer risk. Most medical X rays are adjusted to deliver the lowest dose possible without sacrificing image quality.

Occupational hazards — Exposure to a number of industrial agents (nickel, chromate, asbestos, vinyl chloride, etc.) increases risk. Risk factor greatly increased when combined with smoking.

SECONDARY PREVENTION: steps to be taken to diagnose a cancer or precursor as early as possible after it has developed.

Colorectal tests — The ACS recommends 3 tests for the early detection of colon and rectum cancer in people without symptoms: The digital rectal examination performed by a physician during an office visit, every year after the age of 40; the stool blood test every year after 50; and the proctosigmoidoscopy examination every 3 to 5 years after the age of 50 following 2 annual exams with negative results.

Pap test — For the average risk person, a Pap test is recommended annually until 2 consecutive satisfactory tests are negative, and then once every 3 years. The Pap test is highly effective in detecting cancer of the uterine cervix, but is less effective in detecting endometrial cancer.

Breast cancer detection — The ACS recommends the monthly practice of breast self-examination by women 20 years and older. Physical examination of the breast should be done every 3 years from ages 20-40 and then every year. The ACS recommends a mammogram every year for asymptomatic women age 50 and over, and a baseline mammogram between ages 35-39. Women 40-49 should have mammography every 1-2 years.

Estimated New Cancer Cases and Deaths By Sex for Selected Cities, 1987*

Source: American Cancer Society

	Estimated New Cases			Estimated Deaths		
	Total	Male	Female	Total	Male	Female
All Sites	**965,000[1]**	**485,000[1]**	**480,000[1]**	**483,000**	**259,000**	**224,000**
Oral	29,800	20,200	9,600	9,400	6,350	3,050
Colon-Rectum	145,000	70,000	75,000	60,000	29,100	30,900
Lung	150,000	99,000	51,000	136,000	92,000	44,000
Skin	25,800[2]	13,600[2]	12,200[2]	7,800[3]	4,800	3,000
Breast	130,900[4]	900[4]	130,000[4]	41,300	300	41,000
Uterus	12,800[4]	—	12,800[4]	6,800	—	6,800

*Note: The estimates of new cancer cases are offered as a rough guide and should not be regarded as definitive. (1) Carcinoma in situ and non-melanoma skin cancers are not included in totals. Carcinoma in situ of the uterine cervix accounts for more than 45,000 new cases annually, and carcinoma in situ of the female breast accounts for more than 5,000 new cases annually. Non-melanoma skin cancer accounts for more than 400,000 new cases annually. (2) Melanoma only. (3) Melanoma 5,800; other skin 2,000. (4) Invasive cancer of the cervix and uteri, only.

Cancer's 7 Warning Signals*

Source: American Cancer Society

1. A change in bowel or bladder habits.
2. A sore that does not heal.
3. Unusual bleeding or discharge.
4. Thickening or lump in breast or elsewhere.
5. Indigestion or difficulty in swallowing.
6. Obvious change in wart or mole.
7. Nagging cough or hoarseness.

*If you have a warning signal, see your doctor.

Basic First Aid

First aid experts stress that knowing what to do for an injured person until a doctor or trained person gets to an accident scene can save a life, especially in cases of stoppage of breath, severe bleeding, and shock.

People with special medical problems, such as diabetes, cardiovascular disease, epilepsy, or allergy, are also urged to wear some sort of emblem identifying it, as a safeguard against use of medication that might be injurious or fatal in an emergency. Emblems may be obtained from Medic Alert Foundation, Turlock, CA 95380.

Most accidents occur in homes. National Safety Council figures show that home accidents annually far outstrip those in other locations, such as in autos, at work, or in public places.

In all cases, get medical assistance as soon as possible.

Animal bite — Wound should be washed with soap under running water and animal should be caught alive for rabies test.

Asphyxiation — Start mouth-to-mouth resuscitation immediately after getting patient to fresh air.

Bleeding — Elevate the wound above the heart if possible. Press hard on wound with sterile compress until bleeding stops. Send for doctor if it is severe.

Burn — If mild, with skin unbroken and no blisters, plunge into ice water until pain subsides. Apply a dry dressing if necessary. Send for physician if burn is severe. Apply sterile compresses and keep patient quiet and comfortably warm until doctor's arrival. Do not try to clean burn, or to break blisters.

Chemical in eye — With patient lying down, pour cupsful of water immediately into corner of eye, letting it run to other side to remove chemicals thoroughly. Cover with sterile compress. Get medical attention immediately .

Choking — Do not use back slaps to dislodge obstruction. (See **Abdominal Thrust**)

Convulsions — Place person on back on bed or rug so he can't hurt himself. Loosen clothing. Turn head to side. Do not place a blunt object between the victim's teeth. If convulsions do not stop, get medical attention immediately.

Cut (minor) — Apply mild antiseptic and sterile compress after washing with soap under warm running water.

Drowning — (See Mouth-to-Mouth Resuscitation) Artificial breathing must be started at once, before victim is out of the water, if possible. If the victim's stomach is bloated with water, put victim on stomach, place hands under stomach, and lift. If no pulse is felt, begin cardiopulmonary resuscitation. This should only be done by those professionally trained. If necessary, treat for shock. (See **Shock**)

Electric shock — If possible, turn off power. Don't touch victim until contact is broken; pull him from contact with electrical source using rope, wooden pole, or loop of dry cloth. Start mouth-to-mouth resuscitation if breathing has stopped.

Foreign body in eye — Touch object with moistened corner of handkerchief if it can be seen. If it cannot be seen or does not come out after a few attempts, take patient to doctor. Do not rub eye.

Fainting — If victim feels faint, lower head to knees. Lay him down with head turned to side if he becomes unconscious. Loosen clothing and open windows. Keep patient lying quietly for at least 15 minutes after he regains consciousness. Call doctor if faint lasts for more than a few minutes.

Fall — Send for physician if patient has continued pain. Cover wound with sterile dressing and stop any severe bleeding. Do not move patient unless absolutely necessary — as in case of fire — if broken bone is suspected. Keep patient warm and comfortable.

Loss of Limb — If a limb is severed, it is important to properly protect the limb so that it can possibly be reattached to the victim. After the victim is cared for, the limb should be placed in a clean plastic bag, garbage can or other suitable container. Pack ice around the limb on the OUTSIDE of the bag to keep the limb cold. Call ahead to the hospital to alert them of the situation.

Poisoning — Call doctor. Use antidote listed on label if container is found. Call local Poison Control Center if possible. Except for lye, other caustics, and petroleum products, induce vomiting unless victim is unconscious. Give milk if poison or antidote is unknown.

Shock (injury-related) — Keep the victim lying down; if uncertain as to his injuries, keep the victim flat on his back. Maintain the victim's normal body temperature; if the weather is cold or damp, place blankets or extra clothing over and under the victim; if weather is hot, provide shade.

Snakebite — Immediately get victim to a hospital. If there is mild swelling or pain, apply a consticting band 2 to 4 inches above the bite.

Sting from insect — If possible, remove stinger and apply solution of ammonia and water, or paste of baking soda. Call physician immediately if body swells or patient collapses.

(continued)

Unconsciousness — Send for doctor and place person on his back. Start resuscitation if he stops breathing. Never give food or liquids to an unconscious person.

Abdominal Thrust

The American Red Cross and the American Heart Association both agree that the recommended first aid for choking victims is the abdominal thrust, also known as the Heimlich maneuver, after its creator, Dr. Henry Heimlich. Slaps on the back are no longer advised and may even prove detrimental in an attempt to assist a choking victim.

- Get behind the victim and wrap your arms around him above his waist.
- Make a fist with one hand and place it, with the thumb knuckle pressing inward, just below the point of the "v" of the rib cage.
- Grasp the wrist with the other hand and give one or more upward thrusts or hugs.
- Start mouth-to-mouth resuscitation if breathing stops.

Mouth-to-Mouth Resuscitation

Stressing that your breath can save a life, the American Red Cross gives the following directions for mouth-to-mouth resuscitation if the victim is not breathing:

- Determine consciousness by tapping the victim on the shoulder and asking loudly, "Are you okay?"
- Tilt the victim's head back so that his chin is pointing upward. Do not press on the soft tissue under the chin, as this might obstruct the airway. If you suspect that an accident victim might have neck or back injuries, open the airway by placing the tips of your index and middle fingers on the corners of the victim's jaw to lift it forward without tilting the head.
- Place your cheek and ear close to the victim's mouth and nose. Look at the victim's chest to see if it rises and falls. Listen and feel for air to be exhaled for about 5 seconds.
- If there is no breathing, pinch the victim's nostrils shut with the thumb and index finger of your hand that is pressing on the victim's forehead. Another way to prevent leakage of air when the lungs are inflated is to press your cheek against the victim's nose.
- Blow air into victim's mouth by taking a deep breath and then sealing your mouth tightly around the victim's mouth. Initially, give two, quick (approx. 1.5 seconds each), full breaths without allowing the lungs to deflate completely between each breath.
- Watch the victim's chest to see if it rises.
- Stop blowing when the victim's chest is expanded. Raise your mouth; turn your head to the side and listen for exhalation.
- Watch the chest to see if it falls.
- Repeat the blowing cycle until the victim starts breathing.

  Note: Infants (up to one year) and children (1 to 8 years) should be administered mouth-to-mouth resuscitation as described above, except for the following:
- Do not tilt the head as far back as an adult's head.
- Both the mouth and nose of the infant should be sealed by the mouth.
- Give breaths to a child once every four seconds.
- Blow into the infant's mouth and nose once every three seconds with less pressure and volume than for a child.

Stress: How Much Can Affect Your Health?

Source: Reprinted with permission from the *Journal of Psychosomatic Research*, Vol. 11, pp. 213-218, T.H. Holmes, M.D., R.H. Rahe, M.D.; The Social Readjustment Rating Scale © 1967, Pergamon Press, Ltd.

Change, both good and bad, can create stress and stress, if sufficiently severe, can lead to illness. Drs. Thomas Holmes and Richard Rahe, psychiatrists at the University of Washington in Seattle, have developed the Social Readjustment Rating Scale. In their study, they gave a point value to stressful events. The psychiatrists discovered that in 79 percent of the persons studied, major illness followed the accumulation of stress-related changes totaling over 300 points in one year.

The Social Readjustment Rating Scale

Life Event	Value
Death of Spouse	100
Divorce	73
Marital separation from mate	65
Detention in jail or other institution	63
Death of a close family member	63
Major personal injury or illness	53
Marriage	50
Being fired at work	47
Marital reconciliation with mate	45
Retirement from work	45
Major change in the health or behavior of a family member	44
Pregnancy	40
Sexual difficulties	39
Gaining a new family member (e.g., through birth, adoption, moving in, etc.)	39
Major business readjustment (e.g., merger, reorganization, bankruptcy, etc.)	39
Major change in financial state (e.g., a lot worse off or a lot better off than usual)	38
Death of a close friend	37
Changing to a different line of work	36
Major change in the number of arguments with spouse (e.g., either a lot more or a lot less than usual regarding child-rearing, personal habits, etc.)	35
Taking out a mortgage or loan for a major purchase (e.g. for a home, business, etc.)	31
Foreclosure on a mortgage or loan	30
Major change in responsibilities at work (e.g., promotion, demotion, lateral transfer)	29
Son or daughter leaving home (e.g., marriage, attending college, etc.)	29
In-law troubles	29
Outstanding personal achievement	28
Wife beginning or ceasing work outside the home	26
Beginning or ceasing formal schooling	26
Major change in living conditions (e.g., building a new home, remodeling, deterioration of home or neighborhood)	25
Revision of personal habits (dress, manners, association, etc.)	24
Troubles with the boss	23
Major change in working hours or conditions	20
Change in residence	20
Changing to a new school	20
Major change in usual type and/or amount of recreation	19
Major change in church activities (e.g., a lot more or a lot less than usual)	19
Major change in social activities (e.g., clubs, dancing, movies, visiting, etc.)	18
Taking out a mortgage or loan for a lesser purchase (e.g., for a car, TV, freezer, etc.)	17
Major change in sleeping habits (a lot more or a lot less sleep, or change in part of day when asleep)	16
Major change in number of family get-togethers (e.g., a lot more or a lot less than usual)	15
Major change in eating habits (a lot more or a lot less food intake, or very different meal hours or surroundings)	15
Vacation	13
Christmas	12
Minor violations of the law (e.g., traffic tickets, jaywalking, disturbing the peace, etc.)	11

Effects of Commonly Abused Drugs

Source: National Institute on Drug Abuse

Tobacco

Effects and dangers: Nicotine, the active ingredient in tobacco, acts as a stimulant on the heart and nervous system. When tobacco smoke is inhaled the immediate effects on the body are a faster heart beat and elevated blood pressure. These effects, however, are quickly dissipated. Tar (in the smoke) contains many carcinogens. These compounds, many of which are in polluted air but are found in vastly greater quantities in cigarette smoke, have been identified as major causes of cancer and respiratory difficulties. Even relatively young smokers can have shortness of breath, nagging cough, or develop cardiovascular and respiratory difficulties. A third principal component of cigarette smoke, carbon monoxide, is also a cause of some of the more serious health effects of smoking. Carbon monoxide can reduce the blood's ability to carry oxygen to body tissues and can promote the development of arteriosclerosis (hardening of the arteries). Long-term effects of smoking cigarettes are emphysema, chronic bronchitis, heart disease, lung cancer, and cancer in other parts of the body.

Risks during pregnancy: Women who smoke during pregnancy are more likely to have babies that weigh less, and more frequently lose their babies through stillbirth or death soon after birth.

Alcohol

Effects: Like sedatives, it is a central nervous system depressant. In small doses, it has a tranquilizing effect on most people, although it appears to stimulate others. Alcohol first acts on those parts of the brain which affect self-control and other learned behaviors; lowered self-control often leads to the aggressive behavior associated with some people who drink.

Dangers: In large doses, alcohol can dull sensation and impair muscular coordination, memory, and judgment. Taken in larger quantities over a long period time, alcohol can damage the liver and heart and can cause permanent brain damage. A large dose of alcohol, which can be as little as a pint or less of whiskey consumed at once, can interfere with the part of the brain that controls breathing. The respiratory failure which results can bring death. Delirium tremens, the most extreme manifestation of alcohol withdrawal, can also cause death. On the average, heavy drinkers shorten their life span by about 10 years.

Risks during pregnancy: Women who drink heavily during pregnancy (more than 3 ounces of alcohol per day or about 2 mixed drinks) run a higher risk than other women of delivering babies with physical, mental and behavioral abnormalities.

Dependence: Repeated drinking produces tolerance to the drug's effects and dependence. The drinker's body then needs alcohol to function. Once dependent, drinkers experience withdrawal symptoms when they stop drinking.

Marijuana ("grass", "pot", "weed")

What is it?: A common plant (*Cannabis sativa*), its chief psychoactive ingredient is delta-9-tetrahydrocannabinol, or THC. The amount of THC in the marijuana cigarette (joint) primarily determines its psychoactive potential.

Effects: Most users experience an increase in heart rate, reddening of the eyes, and dryness in the mouth and throat. Studies indicate the drug temporarily impairs short-term memory, alters sense of time, and reduces the ability to perform tasks requiring concentration, swift reactions, and coordination. Many feel that their hearing, vision, and skin sensitivity are enhanced by the drug, but these reports have not been objectively confirmed by research. Feelings of euphoria, relaxation, altered sense of body image, and bouts of exaggerated laughter are also commonly reported.

Dangers: Scientists believe marijuana can be particularly harmful to lungs because users typically inhale the filtered smoke deeply and hold it in their lungs for prolonged periods of time. Marijuana smoke has been found to have more cancer-causing agents than are found in cigarette smoke (see above). Because marijuana use increases heart rate as much as 50% and brings on chest pain in people who have a poor blood supply to the heart (and more rapidly than tobacco smoke does), doctors believe people with heart conditions or who are at high risk for heart ailments, should not use marijuana. Findings also suggest that regular use may reduce fertility in women and that men with marginal fertility or endocrine functioning should avoid marijuana use and that it is especially harmful during adolescence, a period of rapid physical and sexual development.

Risks during pregnancy: Research is limited, but scientists believe marijuana which crosses the placential barrier, may have a toxic effect on embryos and fetuses.

Dependence: Tolerance to marijuana, the need to take more and more of the drug over time to get the original effect, has been proven in humans and animals. Physical dependence has been demonstrated in research subjects who ingested an amount equal to smoking 10 to 20 joints a day. When the drug was discontinued, subjects experienced withdrawal symptoms—irritability, sleep disturbances, loss of appetite and weight, sweating, and stomach upset.

Bad reactions: Most commonly reported immediate adverse reaction to marijuana use is the "acute panic anxiety reaction," usually described as an exaggeration of normal marijuana effects in which intense fears of losing control accompany severe anxiety. The symptoms often disappear in a few hours when the acute drug effects have worn off.

Hallucinogens ("psychodelics")

What are they?: Drugs which affect perception, sensation, thinking, self-awareness, and emotion.

(1) **LSD (lysergic acid diethylamide)**, a synthetic, is converted from lysergic acid which comes from fungus (ergot).

Effects: Vary greatly according to dosage, personality of the user, and conditions under which the drug is used. Basically, it causes changes in sensation. Vision alters; users describe changes in depth perception and in the meaning of the perceived object. Illusions and hallucinations often occur. Physical reactions range from minor changes such as dilated pupils, a rise in temperature and heartbeat, or a slight increase in blood pressure, to tremors. High doses can greatly alter the state of consciousness. Heavy use of the drug may produce flashbacks, recurrences of some features of a previous LSD experience days or months after the last dose.

Dangers: After taking LSD, a person loses control over normal thought processes. Although many perceptions are pleasant, others may cause panic or may make a person believe that he or she cannot be harmed. Longer-term harmful reactions include anxiety and depression, or "breaks from reality" which may last from a few days to months. Heavy users sometimes develop signs of organic brain damage, such as impaired memory and attention span, mental confusion, and difficulty with abstract thinking. It is not known yet whether such mental changes are permanent.

(2) **Mescaline:** Comes from peyote cactus and its effects are similar to those of LSD.

Phencyclidine (PCP or "angel dust")

What is it?: A drug that was developed as a surgical anesthetic for humans in the late 1950s. Because of its unpleasant and unusual side effects, PCP was soon restricted to its only current legal use as a veterinary anesthetic and tranquilizer.

Effects: Vary according to dosage. Low doses may provide the usual releasing effects of many psychoactive drugs. A floaty euphoria is described, sometimes associated with a feeling of numbness (part of the drug's anesthetic effects). Increased doses produce an excited, confused intoxification, which may include muscle rigidity, loss of concentration and memory, visual disturbances, delirium, feelings of isolation, convulsions, speech impairment, violent behavior, fear of death, and changes in the user's perceptions of their bodies.

Dangers: PCP intoxication can produce violent and bizarre behavior even in people not otherwise prone to such behavior. Violent actions may be directed at themselves or others and often account for serious injuries and death. More people die from accidents caused by the erratic behavior produced by the drug than from the drug's direct effect on the body. A temporary, schizophrenic-like psychosis, which can last for days or weeks, has also occurred in users of moderate or higher doses.

(*continued*)

Stimulants ("Uppers")

What are they?: A class of drugs which stimulate the central nervous system and produce an increase in alertness and activity.

(1) **Amphetamines** promote a feeling of alertness and increase in speech and general physical activity. Under medical supervision, the drugs are taken to control appetite.

Effects and dangers: Even small, infrequent doses can produce toxic effects in some people. Restlessness, anxiety, mood swings, panic, circulatory and cardiac disturbances, paranoid thoughts, hallucinations, convulsions, and coma have all been reported. Heavy, frequent doses can produce brain damage which results in speed disturbances and difficulty in turning thoughts into words. Death can result from injected amphetamine overdose. Long-term users often have acne resembling a measles rash; trouble with teeth, gums and nails, and dry lifeless hair. As heavy users who inject amphetamines accumulate larger amounts of the drug in their bodies, the resulting toxicity can produce amphetamine psychosis. People in this extremely suspicious, paranoid state, frequently exhibit bizarre, sometimes violent behavior.

Dependence: People with a history of sustained low-dose use quite often become dependent and feel they need the drug to get by.

(2) **Cocaine** is a stimulant extracted from the leaves of the coca plant. It is available in many forms, the most available of which is cocaine hydrochloride. Cocaine hydrochloride is often used medically as a local anesthetic, but is also sold illegally on the street in large pieces called rocks. Street cocaine is a white, crystal-like powder that is most commonly inhaled or snorted, though some users ingest, inject, or smoke a form of the drug called freebase or crack.

Freebase and crack are formed by chemically converting street cocaine to a purified substance that is more suitable for smoking. Smoking freebase or crack produces a shorter, but more intense high than other ways of using the drug. It is the most direct and rapid means of getting the drug to the brain, and because larger amounts are reaching the brain more quickly, the effects of the drug are more intense and the dangers associated with its use are greater.

Effects: The drug's usual effects are dilated pupils and increased blood pressure, heart rate, breathing rate, and body temperature. Even small doses may elicit feelings of euphoria; illusions of increased mental and physical strength and sensory awareness; and a decrease in hunger, pain, and the perceived need for sleep. Large doses significantly magnify these effects, sometimes causing irrational behavior and confusion.

Dangers: Paranoia is not an uncommon response to heavy doses. Psychosis may be triggered in users prone to mental instability. Repeated inhalation often results in nostril and nasal membrane irritation. Some regular users have reported feelings of restlessness, irritability, and anxiety. Others have experienced hallucinations of touch, sight, taste, or smell. When people stop using cocaine after taking it for a long time, they frequently become depressed. They tend to fight off this depression by taking more cocaine, just as in the up/down amphetamine cycle.

Cocaine is toxic. Although few people realize it, overdose deaths, though rare, have occurred as a result of injecting, ingesting and even snorting cocaine. The deaths are a result of seizures followed by respiratory arrest and coma, or sometimes by cardiac arrest. Other dangers associated with cocaine include the risk of infection, such as hepatitis, resulting from the use of unsterile needles and the risk of fire or explosion resulting from the use of volatile substances necessary for freebase preparation.

Dependence: Cocaine is not a narcotic; no evidence suggests that it produces a physical dependence. However, cocaine is psychologically a very dangerous, dependence-producing drug. Smoking freebase or crack increases this risk of dependence.

(3) **Caffeine** may be the world's most popular drug. It is primarily consumed in coffee and tea, but is also found in cocoa, cola and other soft drinks, as well as in many over-the-counter medicines.

Effects: Two to four cups of coffee increase heart rate, body temperature, urine production, and gastric juice secretion. Caffeine can also raise sugar levels and cause tremors, loss of coordination, decreased appetite, and postponement of fatigue. It can interfere with the depth of sleep and the amount of dream sleep by causing more rapid eye movement (REM) sleep at first, but less than average over an entire night. Extremely high doses may cause diarrhea, sleeplessness, trembling, severe headache, and nervousness.

Dependence: A form of physical dependence may result with regular consumption. In such cases, withdrawal symptoms may occur if caffeine use is stopped or interrupted. These symptoms include headache, irritability, and fatigue. Tolerance may develop with the use of six to eight cups or more a day. A regular user of caffeine who has developed a tolerance may also develop a craving for the drug's effects.

Dangers: Poisonous doses of caffeine have occurred occasionally and have resulted in convulsions, breathing failure, and even death. However, it is almost impossible to die from drinking too much coffee or tea. The deaths that have been reported have resulted from the misuse of tablets containing caffeine.

Sedatives (Tranquilizers, sleeping pills)

What are they?: Drugs which depress the central nervous system, more appropriately called sedative-hypnotics because they include drugs which calm the nerves (the sedation effect) and produce sleep (the hypnotic effect). Of drugs in this class, barbiturates ("barbs", "downers," "reds") have the highest rate of abuse and misuse. The most commonly abused barbiturates include pentobarbital (Nembutal), secobarbital (Seconal), and amobarbital (Amytal). These all have legitimate use as sedatives or sleeping aids. Among the most commonly abused nonbarbiturate drugs are glutethimide (Doriden), meprobamate (Miltown), methyprylon (Noludar), ethchlorvynol (Placidyl), and methaqualone (Sopor, Quaalude). These are prescribed to help people sleep. Benzodiazepines, especially diazepam (Valium), prescribed to relieve anxiety, are commonly abused, and their rate of abuse and misuse is increasing.

Dangers: These can kill. Barbiturate overdose is implicated in nearly one-third of all reported drug-induced deaths. Accidental deaths may occur when a user takes an unintended larger or repeated dose of sedatives because of confusion or impairment in judgment caused by initial intake of the drug. With lesser, but still large doses, users can go into coma. Moderately large doses often produce an intoxicated stupor. Users' speech is often slurred, memory vague, and judgment impaired. Taken along with alcohol, the combination can be fatal. Tranquilizers act somewhat differently from other sedatives and are considered less hazardous. But even by themselves, or in combination with other drugs (especially alcohol and other sedatives) they can be quite dangerous.

Dependence: Potential for dependence is greatest with barbiturates, but all sedatives, tranquilizers, can be addictive. Barbiturate withdrawal is often more severe than heroin withdrawal.

Narcotics

What they are?: Drugs that relieve pain and often induce sleep. The opiates, which are narcotics, include opium and drugs derived from opium, such as morphine, codeine, and heroin. Narcotics also include certain synthetic chemicals that have a morphine-like action, such as methadone.

Which are abused?: Heroin ("junk," "smack") accounts for 90% of narcotic abuse in the U.S. Sometimes medicinal narcotics are also abused, including paregoric containing codeine, and methadone, meperidine, and morphine.

Dependence: Anyone can become heroin dependent if he or she takes the drug regularly. Although environmental stress and problems of coping have often been considered as factors that lead to heroin addiction, physicians or psychologists do not agree that some people just have an "addictive personality" and are prone to dependence. All we know for certain is that continued use of heroin causes dependence.

Dangers: Physical dangers depend on the specific drug, its source, and the way it is used. Most medical problems are caused by the uncertain dosage level, use of unsterile needles and other paraphernalia, contamination of the drug, or combination of a narcotic with other drugs, rather than by the effects of the heroin (or another narcotic) itself. The life expectancy of a heroin addict who injects the drug intravenously is significantly lower than that of one who does not. An overdose can result in death. If, for example, an addict obtains pure heroin and is not tolerant of the dose, he or she

(continued)

may die minutes after injecting it. Infections from unsterile needles, solutions, syringes, cause many diseases. Serum hepatitis is common. Skin abscesses, inflammation of the veins and congestion of the lungs also occur.

Withdrawal: When a heroin-dependent person stops taking the drug, withdrawal begins within 4-6 hours after the last injection. Full-blown withdrawal symptoms—which include shaking, sweating, vomiting, a running nose and eyes, muscle aches, chills, abdominal pains, and diarrhea—begin some 12-16 hours after the last injection. The intensity of symptoms depends on the degree of dependence.

Drug Usage: America's High School Students

Source: National Institute on Drug Abuse/Univ. of Michigan Inst. for Social Research

Results are based on large, representative sample surveys of nearly 130 graduating classes enrolled in public and private high schools across the United States.

	Percent ever used										
	Class of 1975	Class of 1976	Class of 1978	Class of 1979	Class of 1980	Class of 1981	Class of 1983	Class of 1984	Class of 1985	Class of 1986	'85-'86 change
Marijuana/Hashish	47.3	52.8	59.2	60.4	60.3	59.5	57.0	54.9	54.2	50.9	−3.3ss
Inhalants	NA	10.3	12.0	12.7	11.9	12.3	13.6	14.4	15.4	15.9	+0.5
Inhalants Adjusted[1]	NA	NA	NA	18.7	17.6	17.4	18.8	19.0	18.1	20.1	+2.0s
Amyl & Butyl Nitrites	NA	NA	NA	11.1	11.1	10.1	8.4	8.1	7.9	8.6	+0.7
Hallucinogens	16.3	15.1	14.3	14.1	13.3	13.3	11.9	10.7	10.3	9.7	−0.6
Hallucinogens Adjusted[2]	NA	NA	NA	18.6	15.7	15.7	14.7	13.3	12.1	11.9	−0.2
LSD	11.3	11.0	9.7	9.5	9.3	9.8	8.9	8.0	7.5	7.2	−0.3
PCP	NA	NA	NA	12.8	9.6	7.8	5.6	5.0	4.9	4.8	−0.1
Cocaine	9.0	9.7	12.9	15.4	15.7	16.5	16.2	16.1	17.3	16.9[5]	−0.4
Heroin	2.2	1.8	1.6	1.1	1.1	1.1	1.2	1.3	1.2	1.1	−0.1
Other opiates[3]	9.0	9.6	9.9	10.1	9.8	10.1	9.4	9.7	10.2	9.0	−1.2s
Stimulants[3]	22.3	22.6	22.9	24.2	26.4	32.2	35.4	NA	NA	NA	NA
Stimulants Adjusted[3,4]	NA	NA	NA	NA	NA	NA	26.9	27.9	26.2	23.4	−2.8ss
Sedatives[3]	18.2	17.7	16.0	14.6	14.9	16.0	14.4	13.3	11.8	10.4	−1.4s
Barbiturates[3]	16.9	16.2	13.7	11.8	11.0	11.3	9.9	9.9	9.2	8.4	−0.8
Methaqualone[3]	8.1	7.8	7.9	8.3	9.5	10.6	10.1	8.3	6.7	5.2	−1.5ss
Tranquilizers[3]	17.0	16.8	17.0	16.3	15.2	14.7	13.3	12.4	11.9	10.9	−1.0
Alcohol	90.4	91.9	93.1	93.0	93.2	92.6	92.6	92.6	92.2	91.3	−0.9
Cigarettes	73.6	75.4	75.3	74.0	71.0	71.0	70.6	69.7	68.8	67.6	−1.2

NA=Not available. Level of significance between the two most recent classes: s=.05, ss=.01.
(1) Adjusted for underreporting of amyl and butyl nitrites. (2) Adjusted for underreporting of PCP. (3) Only drug use which was not under a doctor's orders. (4) Adjusted for overreporting of the non-prescription stimulants. (5) In 1986, 12.6 percent of those who used cocaine used it in powder form, while 4.1 percent used the "crack" form.

A Patient's Bill of Rights

Source: American Hospital Association, © copyright 1972.

Often, as a hospital patient, you feel you have little control over your circumstances. You do, however, have some important rights. They have been enumerated by the American Hospital Association.

1. The patient has the right to considerate and respectful care.
2. The patient has the right to obtain from his physician complete current information concerning his diagnosis, treatment, and prognosis in terms the patient can be reasonably expected to understand. When it is not medically advisable to give such information to the patient, the information should be made available to an appropriate person in his behalf. He has the right to know, by name, the physician responsible for coordinating his care.
3. The patient has the right to receive from his physician information necessary to give informed consent prior to the start of any procedure and/or treatment. Except in emergencies, such information for informed consent should include but not necessarily be limited to the specific procedure and/or treatment, the medically significant risks involved, and the probable duration of incapacitation. Where medically significant alternatives for care or treatment exist, or when the patient requests information concerning medical alternatives, the patient has the right to such information. The patient also has the right to know the name of the person responsible for the procedures and/or treatment.
4. The patient has the right to refuse treatment to the extent permitted by law and to be informed of the medical consequences of his action.
5. The patient has the right to every consideration of his privacy concerning his own medical care program. Case discussion, consultation, examination, and treatment are confidential and should be conducted discreetly. Those not directly involved in his care must have the permission of the patient to be present.
6. The patient has the right to expect that all communications and records pertaining to his care should be treated as confidential.
7. The patient has the right to expect that within its capacity a hospital must make reasonable response to the request of a patient for services. The hospital must provide evaluation, service, and/or referral as indicated by the urgency of the case. When medically permissable, a patient may be transferred to another facility only after he has received complete information and explanation concerning the need for and alternatives to such a transfer. The institution to which the patient is to be transferred must first have accepted the patient for transfer.
8. The patient has the right to obtain information as to any relationship of his hospital to other health care and education institutions insofar as this care is concerned. The patient has the right to obtain information as to the existence of any professional relationships among individuals, by name, who are treating him.
9. The patient has the right to be advised if the hospital proposes to engage in or perform human experimentation affecting his care or treatment. The patient has the right to refuse to participate in such research projects.
10. The patient has the right to expect reasonable continuity of care. He has the right to know in advance what appointment times and physicians are available and where. The patient has the right to expect that the hospital will provide a mechanism whereby he is informed by his physician of the patient's continuing health care requirements following discharge.
11. The patient has the right to examine and receive an explanation of his bill, regardless of the source of payment.
12. The patient has the right to know what hospital rules and regulations apply to his conduct as a patient.

Food and Nutrition

Food contains proteins, carbohydrates, fats, water, vitamins and minerals. Nutrition is the way your body takes in and uses these ingredients to maintain proper functioning.

According to the U.S. Dept. of Agriculture's Economic Research Service, Americans are eating more vegetables than ever before, especially fresh vegetables. In 1970, the consumption of vegetables averaged 147.2 lbs. per person; in 1985, 190.9 lbs.—a 30% increase. The 1970 total included: fresh vegetables, 71.3 lbs.; canned, 64.7; and freezing, 11.2. By 1985, the breakdown was: fresh, 91.1 lbs.; canned, 82.2; and freezing, 17.6.

Protein

Proteins are composed of amino acids and are indispensable in the diet. They build, maintain, and repair the body. Best sources: eggs, milk, fish, meat, poultry, soybeans, nuts. High quality proteins such as eggs, meat, or fish supply all 8 amino acids needed in the diet. Low quality proteins such as nuts and grain do not.

Fats

Fats provide energy by furnishing calories to the body, and by carrying vitamins A, D, E, and K. They are the most concentrated source of energy in the diet. Best sources: butter, margarine, salad oils, nuts, cream, egg yolks, most cheeses, lard, meat.

Carbohydrates

Carbohydrates provide energy for body function and activity by supplying immediate calories. The carbohydrate group includes sugars, starches, fiber, and starchy vegetables. Best sources: grains, legumes, nuts, potatoes, fruits.

Water

Water dissolves and transports other nutrients throughout the body, aiding the processes of digestion, absorption, circulation, and excretion. It also helps regulate body temperature. We get water from all foods.

Vitamins

Vitamin A—promotes good eyesight and helps keep the skin and mucous membranes resistant to infection. Best sources: liver, carrots, sweet potatoes, kale, collard greens, turnips, fortified milk.

Vitamin B1 (thiamine)—prevents beriberi. Essential to carbohydrate metabolism and health of nervous system.

Vitamin B2 (riboflavin)—protects skin, mouth, eye, eyelids, and mucous membranes. Essential to protein and energy metabolism. Best sources: liver, milk, meat, poultry, broccoli, mushrooms.

Vitamin B6 (pyridoxine)—important in the regulation of the central nervous system and in protein metabolism. Best sources: whole grains, meats, nuts, brewers' yeast.

Vitamin B12 (cobalamin)—needed to form red blood cells. Best sources: liver, meat, fish, eggs, soybeans.

Niacin—maintains the health of skin, tongue, and digestive system. Best sources: poultry, peanuts, fish, organ meats, enriched flour and bread.

Other B vitamins—biotin, choline, folic acid (folacin), inositol, PABA (para-aminobenzoic acid), and pantothenic acid.

Vitamin C (ascorbic acid)—maintains collagen, a protein necessary for the formation of skin, ligaments, and bones. It helps heal wounds and mend fractures, and aids in resisting some types of virus and bacterial infections. Best sources: citrus fruits and juices, turnips, broccoli, Brussels sprouts, potatoes and sweet potatoes, tomatoes, cabbage.

Vitamin D—important for bone development. Best sources: sunlight, fortified milk and milk products, fish-liver oils, egg yolks, organ meats.

Vitamin E (tocopherol)—helps protect red blood cells. Best sources: vegetable oils, wheat germ, whole grains, eggs, peanuts, organ meats, margarine, green leafy vegetables.

Vitamin K—necessary for formation of prothrombin, which helps blood to clot. Also made by intestinal bacteria. Best dietary sources: green leafy vegetables, tomatoes.

Minerals

Calcium—the most abundant mineral in the body, works with phosphorus in building and maintaining bones and teeth. Best sources: milk and milk products, cheese, and blackstrap molasses.

Phosphorus—the 2d most abundant mineral, performs more functions than any other mineral, and plays a part in nearly every chemical reaction in the body. Best source: whole grains, cheese, milk.

Iron—Necessary for the formation of myoglobin, which transports oxygen to muscle tissue, and hemoglobin, which transports oxygen in the blood. Best sources: organ meats, beans, green leafy vegetables, and shellfish.

Other minerals—chromium, cobalt, copper, fluorine, iodine, magnesium, manganese, molybdenum, potassium, selenium, sodium, sulfur, and zinc.

Recommended Daily Dietary Allowances

Source: Food and Nutrition Board, National Academy of Sciences—National Research Council; 1980

The Food and Nutrition Bd. did not issue 1985 revisions of recommended daily dietary allowances, due to "scientific differences of opinion." The allowances are amounts of nutrients recommended as adequate for maintenance of good nutrition in almost all healthy persons in the U.S. Diets should be based on a variety of common foods in order to provide other nutrients for which human requirements have been less well-defined.

				Fat soluble Vitamins			Water soluble Vitamins							Minerals					
	Age (years)	Weight (lbs.)	Protein (grams)	Vitamin A[1]	Vitamin D[2]	Vitamin E[3]	Vitamin C (mg.)	Thiamin (mg.)	Riboflavin (mg.)	Niacin (mg.)[4]	Vitamin B_6 (mg.)	Folacin (micrograms)	Vitamin B_{12} (micrograms)	Calcium (mg.)	Phosphorus (mg.)	Magnesium (mg.)	Iron (mg.)	Zinc (mg.)	Iodine (micrograms)
Infants. . .	to 6 mos.	13	kg × 2.2	420	10	3	35	0.3	0.4	6	0.3	30	0.5	360	240	50	10	3	40
	to 1 yr.	20	kg × 2.0	400	10	4	35	0.5	0.6	8	0.6	45	1.5	540	360	70	15	5	50
Children. .	1-3	29	23	400	10	5	45	0.7	0.8	9	0.9	100	2.0	800	800	150	15	10	70
	4-6	44	30	500	10	6	45	0.9	1.0	11	1.3	200	2.5	800	800	200	10	10	90
	7-10	62	34	700	10	7	45	1.2	1.4	16	1.6	300	3.0	800	800	250	10	10	120
Males . . .	11-14	99	45	1000	10	8	50	1.4	1.6	18	1.8	400	3.0	1200	1200	350	18	15	150
	15-18	145	56	1000	10	10	60	1.4	1.7	18	2.0	400	3.0	1200	1200	400	18	15	150
	19-22	154	56	1000	7.5	10	60	1.5	1.7	19	2.2	400	3.0	800	800	350	10	15	150
	23-50	154	56	1000	5	10	60	1.4	1.6	18	2.2	400	3.0	800	800	350	10	15	150
	51+	154	56	1000	5	10	60	1.2	1.4	16	2.2	400	3.0	800	800	350	10	15	150
Females .	11-14	101	46	800	10	8	50	1.1	1.3	15	1.8	400	3.0	1200	1200	300	18	15	150
	15-18	120	46	800	10	8	60	1.1	1.3	14	2.0	400	3.0	1200	1200	300	18	15	150
	19-22	120	44	800	7.5	8	60	1.1	1.3	14	2.0	400	3.0	800	800	300	18	15	150
	23-50	120	44	800	5	8	60	1.0	1.2	13	2.0	400	3.0	800	800	300	18	15	150
	51+	120	44	800	5	8	60	1.0	1.2	13	2.0	400	3.0	800	800	300	10	15	150
Pregnant			+30	+200	+5	+2	+20	+0.4	+0.3	+2	+0.6	+400	+1.0	+400	+400	+150	[5]	+5	+25
Lactating			+20	+400	+5	+3	+40	+0.5	+0.5	+5	+0.5	+100	+1.0	+400	+400	+150	[5]	+10	+50

(1) Retinol equivalents. (2) Micrograms of cholecalciferol. (3) Milligrams alpha-tocopherol equivalents. (4) Niacin equivalents. (5) The use of 30-60 milligrams of supplemental iron is recommended.

Nutritive Value of Food (Calories, Proteins, etc.)

Source: Home and Garden Bulletin No. 72; available from Supt. of Documents, U. S. Government Printing Office, Washington, DC 20402

Food	Measure	Grams	Food Energy (calories)	Protein (grams)	Fat (grams)	Saturated fats (grams)	Carbohydrate (grams)	Calcium (milligrams)	Iron (milligrams)	Vitamin A (I.U.)	Thiamin (milligrams)	Riboflavin (milligrams)
Dairy products												
Cheese, cheddar	1 oz.	28	115	7	9	6.1	T	204	.2	300	.01	.11
Cheese, cottage, small curd	1 cup	210	220	26	9	6.0	6	126	.3	340	.04	.34
Cheese, cream	1 oz.	28	100	2	10	6.2	1	23	.3	400	T	.06
Cheese, Swiss	1 oz.	28	105	8	8	5.0	1	272	T	240	.01	.10
Cheese, pasteurized process spread, American	1 oz.	28	82	5	6	3.8	2	159	.1	220	.01	.12
Half-and-Half	1 tbsp.	15	20	T	2	1.1	1	16	T	20	.01	.02
Cream, sour	1 tbsp.	15	25	T	3	1.6	1	14	T	90	T	.02
Milk, whole	1 cup	244	150	8	8	5.1	11	291	.1	310	.09	.40
Milk, nonfat (skim)	1 cup	244	85	8	T	.3	12	302	.1	500	.09	.37
Buttermilk	1 cup	245	100	8	2	1.3	12	285	.1	80	.08	.38
Milkshake, chocolate	10.6 oz.	300	355	9	8	5.0	63	396	.9	260	.14	.67
Ice Cream, hardened	1 cup	133	270	5	14	8.9	32	176	.1	540	.05	.33
Sherbet	1 cup	193	270	2	4	2.4	59	103	.3	190	.03	.09
Yogurt, fruit-flavored	8 oz.	227	230	10	3	1.8	42	343	.2	120	.08	.40
Eggs												
Fried in butter	1	46	85	5	6	2.4	1	26	.9	290	.03	.13
Hard-cooked	1	50	80	6	6	1.7	1	28	1.0	260	.04	.14
Scrambled in butter (milk added)	1	64	95	6	7	2.8	1	47	.9	310	.04	.16
Fats & oils												
Butter	1 tbsp.	14	100	T	12	7.2	T	3	T	430	T	T
Margarine	1 tbsp.	14	100	T	12	2.1	T	3	T	470	T	T
Salad dressing, blue cheese	1 tbsp.	15	75	1	8	1.6	1	12	T	30	T	.02
Salad dressing, French	1 tbsp.	16	65	T	6	1.1	3	2	1	-	-	-
Salad dressing, Italian	1 tbsp.	15	85	T	9	1.6	1	2	T	T	T	T
Mayonnaise	1 tbsp.	14	100	T	11	2.0	T	3	.1	40	T	.01
Meat, poultry, fish												
Bluefish, baked with butter or margarine	3 oz.	85	135	22	4	-	0	25	0.6	40	.09	.08
Clams, raw, meat only	3 oz.	85	65	11	1	-	2	59	5.2	90	.08	.15
Crabmeat, white or king, canned	1 cup	135	135	24	3	.6	1	61	1.1	-	.11	.11
Fish sticks, breaded, cooked, frozen	1 oz.	28	50	5	3	-	2	3	.1	0	.01	.02
Salmon, pink, canned	3 oz.	85	120	17	5	.9	0	167	.7	60	.03	.16
Sardines, Atlantic, canned in oil	3 oz.	85	175	20	9	3.0	0	372	2.5	190	.02	.17
Shrimp, French fried	3 oz.	85	190	17	9	2.3	9	61	1.7	-	.03	.07
Tuna, canned in oil	3 oz.	85	170	24	7	1.7	0	7	1.6	70	.04	.10
Bacon, broiled or fried crisp	2 slices	15	85	4	8	2.5	T	2	.5	0	.08	.05
Ground beef, broiled, 10% fat	3 oz.	85	185	23	10	4.0	0	10	3.0	20	.08	.20
Roast beef, relatively lean	3 oz.	85	165	25	7	2.8	0	11	3.2	10	.06	.19
Beef steak, lean and fat	3 oz.	85	330	20	27	11.3	0	9	2.5	50	.05	.15
Beef & vegetable stew	1 cup	245	220	16	11	4.9	15	29	2.9	2,400	.15	.17
Lamb, chop, lean and fat	3.1 oz.	89	360	18	32	14.8	0	8	1.0	-	.11	.19
Liver, beef	3 oz.	85	195	22	9	2.5	5	9	7.5	45,390	.22	3.56
Ham, light cure, lean and fat	3 oz.	85	245	18	19	6.8	0	8	2.2	0	.40	.15
Pork, chop, lean and fat	2.7 oz	78	305	19	25	8.9	0	9	2.7	0	.75	.22
Bologna	1 slice	28	85	3	8	3.0	T	2	.5	-	.05	.06
Frankfurter, cooked	1	56	170	7	15	5.6	1	3	.8	-	.08	.11
Sausage, pork link, cooked	1 link	13	60	2	6	2.1	T	1	.3	0	.10	.04
Veal, cutlet, braised or boiled	3 oz.	85	185	23	9	4.0	0	9	2.7	-	.06	.21
Chicken, drumstick, fried, bones removed	1.3 oz.	38	90	12	4	1.1	T	6	.9	50	.03	.15
Chicken, half broiler, broiled, bones removed	6.2 oz.	176	240	42	7	2.2	0	16	3.0	160	.09	.34
Chicken a la king	1 cup	245	470	27	34	12.7	12	127	2.5	1,130	.10	.42
Chicken potpie, baked, 1/3 of 9 in. diam. pie	1 piece	232	545	23	31	11.3	42	70	3.0	3,090	.34	.31
Fruits & products												
Apple, raw, 2-3/4 in. diam.	1	138	80	T	1	-	20	10	.4	120	.04	.03
Applejuice	1 cup	248	120	T	T	-	30	15	1.5	-	.02	.05
Applesauce, canned, sweetened	1 cup	255	230	1	T	-	61	10	1.3	100	.05	.03
Apricots, raw	3	107	55	1	T	-	14	18	.5	2,890	.03	.04
Banana, raw	1	119	100	1	T	-	26	10	.8	230	.06	.07
Cherries, sweet, raw	10	68	45	1	T	-	12	15	.3	70	.03	.04
Fruit cocktail, canned, in heavy syrup	1 cup	255	195	1	T	-	50	23	1.0	360	.05	.03
Grapefruit, raw, medium, white	1/2	241	45	1	T	-	12	19	.5	10	.05	.02
Grapes, Thompson seedless	10	50	35	T	T	-	9	6	.2	50	.03	.02
Lemonade, frozen, diluted	1 cup	248	105	T	T	-	28	2	.1	10	.01	.02
Cantaloupe, 5-in. diam.	1/2	477	80	2	T	-	20	38	1.1	9,240	.11	.08
Orange, 2-5/8 in. diam.	1	131	65	1	T	-	16	54	.5	260	.13	.05
Orange juice, frozen, diluted	1 cup	249	120	2	T	-	29	25	.2	540	.23	.03
Peach, raw, 2-1/2 in. diam.	1	100	40	1	T	-	10	9	.5	1,330	.02	.05
Peaches, canned in syrup	1 cup	256	200	1	T	-	51	10	.8	1.100	.03	.05
Pear, raw, Bartlett, 2-1/2 in. diam.	1	164	100	1	1	-	25	13	.5	30	.03	.07
Pineapple, heavy syrup pack, crushed, chunks	1 cup	255	190	1	T	-	49	28	.8	130	.20	.05
Raisins, seedless	1 cup	145	420	4	T	-	112	90	5.1	30	.16	.12
Strawberries, whole	1 cup	149	55	1	1	-	13	31	1.5	90	.04	.10
Watermelon, 4 by 8 in. wedge	1 wedge	926	110	2	1	-	27	30	2.1	2,510	.13	.13
Grain products												
Bagel, egg	1	55	165	6	2	.5	28	9	1.2	30	.14	.10
Biscuit, 2 in. diam., from home recipe	1	28	105	2	5	1.2	13	34	.4	T	.08	.08
Bread, raisin	1 slice	25	65	2	1	.2	13	18	.6	T	.09	.06
Bread, white, enriched, soft-crumb	1 slice	25	70	2	1	.2	13	21	.6	T	.10	.06
Bread, whole wheat, soft-crumb	1 slice	28	65	3	1	.1	14	24	.8	T	.09	.03
Oatmeal or rolled oats	1 cup	240	130	5	2	.4	23	22	1.4	0	.19	.05
Bran flakes (40% bran), added sugar, salt, iron, vitamins	1 cup	35	105	4	1	-	28	19	12.4	1,650	.41	.49
Corn flakes, added sugar, salt, iron, vitamins	1 cup	25	95	2	T	-	21	*	0.6	1,180	.29	.35
Rice, puffed, added iron, thiamin, niacin	1 cup	15	60	1	T	-	13	3	.3	0	.07	.01

(continued)

Food	Measure	Grams	Food Energy (calories)	Protein (grams)	Fat (grams)	Saturated fats (grams)	Carbohydrate (grams)	Calcium (milligrams)	Iron (milligrams)	Vitamin A (I.U.)	Thiamin (milligrams)	Riboflavin (milligrams)
Wheat, shredded, plain, 1 biscuit or 1/2 cup	1 serving	25	90	2	1	-	20	11	.9	0	.06	.03
Cake, angel food, 1/12 of cake	1	53	135	3	T	-	32	50	.2	0	.03	.08
Coffeecake, 1/6 cake	1	72	230	5	7	2.0	38	44	1.2	120	.14	.15
Cupcake, 2-1/2 in. diam., with chocolate icing	1	36	130	2	5	2.0	21	47	.4	60	.05	.06
Boston cream pie with custard filling, 1/12 of cake	1	69	210	3	6	1.9	34	46	.7	140	.09	.11
Fruitcake, dark, 1/30 of loaf	1	15	55	1	2	.5	9	11	.4	20	.02	.02
Cake, pound, 1/17 of loaf	1	33	160	2	10	2.5	16	6	.5	80	.05	.06
Brownies, with nuts, from commercial recipe	1	20	85	1	4	.9	13	9	.4	20	.03	.02
Cookies, chocolate chip, from home recipe	4	40	205	2	12	3.5	24	14	.8	40	.06	.06
Vanilla wafers	10	40	185	2	6	-	30	16	.6	50	.10	.09
Crackers, graham	2	14	55	1	1	.3	10	6	.5	0	.02	.08
Crackers, saltines	4	11	50	1	1	.3	8	2	.5	0	.05	.05
Danish pastry, round piece	1	65	275	5	15	4.7	30	33	1.2	200	.18	.19
Doughnut, cake type	1	25	100	1	5	1.2	13	10	.4	20	.05	.05
Macaroni and cheese, from home recipe	1 cup	200	430	17	22	8.9	40	362	1.8	860	.20	.40
Muffin, corn	1	40	125	3	4	1.2	19	42	.7	120	.10	.10
Noodles, enriched, cooked	1 cup	160	200	7	2	-	37	16	1.4	110	.22	.13
Pancake, plain, from home recipe	1	27	60	2	2	.5	9	27	.4	30	.06	.07
Pie, apple, 1/7 of pie	1	135	345	3	15	3.9	51	11	.9	40	.15	.11
Pie, banana cream, 1/7 of pie	1	130	285	6	12	3.8	40	86	1.0	330	.11	.22
Pie, cherry, 1/7 of pie	1	135	350	4	15	4.0	52	19	.9	590	.16	.12
Pie, lemon meringue, 1/7 of pie	1	120	305	4	12	3.7	45	17	1.0	200	.09	.12
Pie, pecan, 1/7 of pie	1	118	495	6	27	4.0	61	55	3.7	190	.26	.14
Pie, pumpkin, 1/7 of pie	1	130	275	5	15	5.4	32	66	1.0	3,210	.11	.18
Pizza, cheese, 1/8 of 12 in. diam. pie	1	60	145	6	4	1.7	22	86	1.1	230	.16	.18
Popcorn, popped, plain	1 cup	6	25	1	T	T	5	1	.2	-	-	.01
Pretzels, stick	10	3	10	T	T	-	2	1	T	0	.01	.01
Rice, white, enriched, instant, cooked	1 cup	165	180	4	T	T	40	5	1.3	0	.21	**
Rolls, enriched, brown & serve	1	26	85	2	2	.4	14	20	.5	T	.10	.06
Rolls, frankfurter & hamburger	1	40	120	3	2	.5	21	30	.8	T	.16	.10
Spaghetti with meat balls & tomato sauce, from home recipe	1 cup	248	330	19	12	3.3	39	124	3.7	1,590	.25	.30
Legumes, nuts, seeds												
Beans, Great Northern, cooked	1 cup	180	210	14	1	-	38	90	4.9	0	.25	.13
Peanuts, roasted in oil, salted	1 cup	144	840	37	72	13.7	27	107	3.0	-	.46	.19
Peanut butter	1 tbsp.	16	95	4	8	1.5	3	9	.3	-	.02	.02
Sunflower seeds	1 cup	145	810	35	69	8.2	29	174	10.3	70	2.84	.33
Sugars & sweets												
Candy, caramels	1 oz.	28	115	1	3	1.6	22	42	.4	T	.01	.05
Candy, milk chocolate	1 oz.	28	145	2	9	5.5	16	65	.3	80	.02	.10
Fudge, chocolate	1 oz.	28	115	1	3	1.3	21	22	.3	T	.01	.03
Candy, hard	1 oz.	28	110	0	T	-	28	6	.5	0	0	0
Honey	1 tbsp.	21	65	T	0	0	17	1	.1	0	T	.01
Jams & Preserves	1 tbsp.	20	55	T	T	-	14	4	.2	T	T	.01
Sugar, white, granulated	1 tbsp.	12	45	0	0	0	12	0	T	0	0	0
Vegetables												
Asparagus, canned, spears	4 spears	80	15	2	T	-	3	15	1.5	640	.05	.08
Beans, lima, thick-seeded	1 cup	170	170	10	T	-	32	34	2.9	390	.12	.09
Beans, green, from frozen, cuts	1 cup	135	35	2	T	-	8	54	.9	700	.09	.12
Beets, canned, diced or sliced	1 cup	170	65	2	T	-	15	32	1.2	30	.02	.05
Broccoli, cooked	1 stalk	180	45	6	1	-	8	158	1.4	4,500	.16	.36
Cabbage, raw, coarsely shredded or sliced	1 cup	70	15	1	T	-	4	34	.3	90	.04	.04
Carrots, raw, 7-1/2 by 1-1/8 in.	1	72	30	1	T	-	7	27	.5	7,930	.04	.04
Cauliflower, raw	1 cup	115	31	3	T	-	6	29	1.3	70	.13	.12
Celery, raw	1 stalk	40	5	T	T	-	2	16	.1	110	.01	.01
Collards, cooked	1 cup	190	65	7	1	-	10	357	1.5	14,820	.21	.38
Corn, sweet, cooked	1 ear	140	70	2	1	-	16	2	.5	310	.09	.08
Corn, cream style	1 cup	256	210	5	2	-	51	8	1.5	840	.08	.13
Cucumber, with peel	6-8 slices	28	5	T	T	-	1	7	.3	70	.01	.01
Lettuce, Iceberg, chopped	1 cup	55	5	T	T	-	2	11	.3	180	.03	.03
Mushrooms, raw	1 cup	70	20	2	T	-	3	4	.6	T	.07	.32
Onions, raw, chopped	1 cup	170	65	3	T	-	15	46	.9	T	.05	.07
Peas, frozen, cooked	1 cup	160	110	8	T	-	19	30	3.0	960	.43	.14
Potatoes, baked, peeled	1	156	145	4	T	-	33	14	1.1	T	.15	.07
Potatoes, frozen, French fried	10	50	110	2	4	1.1	17	5	.9	T	.07	.01
Potatoes, mashed, milk added	1 cup	210	135	4	2	.7	27	50	.8	40	.17	.11
Potato chips	10	20	115	1	8	2.1	10	8	.4	T	.04	.01
Potato salad	1 cup	250	250	7	7	2.0	41	80	1.5	350	.20	.18
Sauerkraut, canned	1 cup	235	40	2	T	-	9	85	1.2	120	.07	.09
Spinach, chopped, from frozen	1 cup	205	45	6	1	-	8	232	4.3	16,200	.14	.31
Squash, summer, cooked	1 cup	210	30	2	T	-	7	53	.8	820	.11	.17
Sweet potatoes, baked in skin, peeled	1	114	160	2	1	-	37	46	1.0	9,230	.10	.08
Tomatoes, raw	1	135	25	1	T	-	6	16	.6	1,110	.07	.05
Tomato catsup	1 tbsp.	15	15	T	T	-	4	3	.1	210	.01	.01
Tomato juice	1 cup	243	45	2	T	-	10	17	2.2	1,940	.12	.07
Miscellaneous												
Beer	12 fl. oz.	360	150	1	0	0	14	18	T	-	.01	.11
Gin, rum, vodka, whisky, 86 proof	1-1/2 fl. oz.	42	105	-	-	0	T	-	-	-	-	-
Wine, table	3-1/2 fl. oz.	102	85	T	0	0	4	9	.4	-	T	.01
Cola-type beverage	12 fl. oz.	369	145	0	0	0	37	-	-	0	0	0
Ginger ale	12 fl. oz	366	115	0	0	0	29	-	-	0	0	0
Gelatin dessert	1 cup	240	140	4	0	0	34	-	-	-	-	-
Mustard, prepared	1 tsp.	5	5	T	T	-	T	4	.1	-	-	-
Olives, pickled, green	4 medium	16	15	T	2	.2	T	8	.2	40	-	-
Pickles, dill, whole	1	65	5	T	T	-	1	17	.7	70	T	.01
Popsicle, 3 fl. oz.	1	95	70	0	0	0	18	0	T	0	0	0
Soup, cream of chicken, prepared with milk	1 cup	245	180	7	10	4.2	15	172	.5	610	.05	.27
Soup, cream of mushroom, prepared with milk	1 cup	245	215	7	14	5.4	16	191	.5	250	.05	.34
Soup, tomato, prepared with water	1 cup	245	90	2	3	.5	16	15	.7	1,000	.05	.05

T — Indicates trace * — Varies by brand

CONSUMER INFORMATION

Consumer Information Catalog

Source: Consumer Information Center, U.S. General Services Administration

The *Consumer Information Catalog* is a free listing of more than 200 of the best federal consumer publications. They range from booklets on financial planning to planning a diet, from learning about federal benefits to getting an education, from fixing a car to dealing effectively with consumer problems. It also lists many resources that will help you get a passport or a birth certificate, find government documents or national parks, learn your rights and stand up for them. Many of these booklets are free.

The *Consumer Information Catalog* is published quarterly by the Consumer Information Center of the U.S. General Services Administration, so you will be able to send for the most current booklets. For your free copy of the *Consumer Information Catalog*, send your name and address to: Consumer Information Catalog, Pueblo, CO 81009. Educators, libraries, and other non-profit groups who are able to distribute 25 or more copies of the *Consumer Information Catalog* on a quarterly basis should write to the same address for an application to be placed on the mailing list. Costs prevent the Consumer Information Center from maintaining a mailing list for individuals.

The booklets listed below are available free from the *Consumer Information Catalog* as of Oct. 1, 1987. Quantities of some may be limited. There is a $1 fee for handling. To order, please send your name and address, the item numbers of the booklets you want, and the $1 fee to: S. James, Consumer Information Center, Pueblo, CO 81009.

Free Publications

Children

Handbook on Child Support Enforcement. The basic steps to follow if you need child support enforcement services; tips on solving enforcement problems; and how to find help locally. 40 pp. (1985) **505R.**

Plain Talk about Adolescence. For parents and teenagers, suggestions on how to improve communication in the family. 2 pp. (1981) **506R.**

Plain Talk about Raising Children. Suggestions and advice from experienced parents. 4 pp. (1979) **508R.**

Plain Talk about When Your Child Starts School. Suggestions for helping your child during the first days of school. 2 pp. (1985) **509R.**

Education

International Youth Exchange: Advisory List of International Educational Travel and Exchange Programs, 1986-87. Guidelines for evaluating programs; descriptions of 34 for-profit and non-profit organizations' exchange programs. 75 pp. (1986) **501R.**

Schools Without Drugs. Guide for parents, schools, students, and communities on how to fight drug use by children. Describes extent of the problem, effects of various drugs, and signs of use. Includes legal considerations and an extensive list of resources. 78 pp. (1986) **502R.**

Federal Benefits

Student Guide—Five Financial Aid Programs. Important information about five grant and loan programs for colleges, vocational, and technical school students. 52 pp. (1987) **503R.**

What You Should Know About Medicare. An overview of health benefits available to people over 64 and some severely disabled younger persons. 20 pp. (1987) **511R.**

Nutrition

Diet and the Elderly. Discusses the specific nutrient needs of the elderly and possible dangers of food and drug interaction. 4 pp. (1985) **516R.**

Diet, Nutrition, and Cancer Prevention: The Good News. An estimated one-third of all cancer deaths may be related to what we eat. This booklet will help you select, prepare and serve healthier food. Includes lists of high-fiber and low-fat foods. 11 pp. (1987) **517R.**

Nutrition and Your Health: Dietary Guidelines for Americans. Seven dietary guidelines to help you stay healthy, based on the latest nutrition research. Includes charts on desirable body weights and caloric expenditures for various exercises. 23 pp. (1985) **519R.**

Some Facts and Myths about Vitamins. What vitamins are and are not, and which foods are the best sources. 4 pp. (1982) **522R.**

Purchase, Preparation & Food Storage

Do Yourself a Flavor. Tips for cooking with herbs and spices; includes chart on herb blends, saltless seasonings, and herbs that go well with different meats. 4 pp. (1984) **525R.**

The Safe Food Book: Your Kitchen Guide. Common causes and symptoms of food poisoning; what you can do to reduce the risks with specific instructions for handling meat and poultry, home canning, what to do when the freezer fails, and more. 32 pp. (1985) **526R.**

Health

Back Pain. Common causes and treatments of this all-too-common problem. 3 pp. (1983) **545R.**

Breast Exams: What You Should Know. Eighty percent of breast lumps are not cancer: how to check for lumps, how doctors examine them, what types of treatment are available. 14 pp. (1981) **546R.**

Clearing the Air: A Guide to Quitting Smoking. No-nonsense tips on kicking the habit. 32 pp. (1984) **548R.**

Facing Surgery: Why Not Get a Second Opinion? Answers this and other questions of the prospective patient. Includes toll-free number for locating specialists. 5 pp. (1979) **555R.**

Money Management

A Comprehensive Guide to Life Insurance. Comprehensive guide to different types of policies, costs, and coverage; includes a glossary of commonly used terms. 21 pp. (1986) **592R.**

Investment Swindles: How They Work and How to Avoid Them. How to spot investment fraud and protect yourself. Includes examples of common schemes used to entice investors. 20 pp. (1987) **610R.**

Investors' Bill of Rights. Trips to help you make an informed decision on investment risks and costs. 6 pp. (1987) **611R.**

Mental Health

Plain Talk about Stress. What stress is and how to deal with it. 2 pp. (1985) **564R.**

Travel

Access Travel. Design features, facilities, and services for the handicapped at 519 airport terminals in 62 countries. 39 pp. (1985) **584R.**

Federal Recreation Passport Program. How to get reduced admission fees to national parks, wildlife refuges, and other federal recreation areas; free admission and other savings for handicapped and senior citizens. 9 pp. (1987) **572R.**

Miscellaneous

How to Choose and Use a Lawyer. Discusses fees, advertising, referrals, other legal resources, and how to resolve disputes with lawyers. 6 pp. (1986) **586R.**

Mail Order Rights. What to do about cancelled orders, unordered merchandise, unsatisfactory delays, and payment disputes. 4 pp. (1985) **577R.**

Lista de Publicaciones Federales en Espanol para el Consumidor. Lists 74 free federal consumer publications available in Spanish. 4 pp. (1986) **579R.**

U.S. Government Books. A catalog featuring more than 700 government publications and posters for sale by the Superintendent of Documents. 56 pp. (1987) **602R.**

How to Get the Most for Your Money

Source: *Consumer's Resource Handbook.* For further information, free single copies of this publication may be obtained by writing to *Handbook,* Consumer Information Center, Pueblo, Colorado 81009.

Before Making a Purchase:

(1) Analyze what you need and what features are important to you.

(2) Compare brands. Use word-of-mouth recommendations and formal product comparison reports. Check with your local library for magazines and other publicatons containing consumer information.

(3) Compare stores. Look for a store with a good reputation and take advantage of sales.

(4) Check for any additional charges, such as delivery and service costs.

(5) Compare warranties.

(6) Read terms of contracts carefully.

(7) Check the return or exchange policy.

After Your Purchase:

(1) Follow proper use and care instructions for products.

(2) Read and understand the warranty provisions. Keep in mind that you may have additional warranty rights in your state. Check with your state or local consumer office to find out.

(3) If trouble develops, report the problem as soon as possible. Do not try to fix the product yourself as this may void the warranty.

(4) Keep a record of efforts to have your problem remedied. This record should include names of people you speak to, times, dates, and other relevant information.

(5) Send for the *Consumer's Resource Handbook* (see *Source,* above) to find out where and how to get your problem resolved.

(6) Clearly state your problem and the solution you want.

(7) Include all relevant details, along with copies of documents (proof of purchase).

(8) Briefly describe what you have done to resolve the problem.

(9) Allow each person you contact a reasonable period of time to resolve your problem before contacting another source for assistance.

Handling Your Own Complaint:

(1) Identify your problem and what you believe would be a fair settlement. Do you want your money back? Would you like the product repaired? Will an exchange do?

(2) Gather documentation regarding your complaint. Sales receipts, repair orders, warranties, cancelled checks, or contracts will back up your complaint and help the company solve your problem.

(3) Go back to where you made the purchase. Contact the person who sold you the item or performed the service. Calmly and accurately explain the problem and what action you would like taken. If that person is not helpful, ask for the supervisor or manager and repeat your complaint. A large percentage of consumer problems are resolved at this level. Chances are yours will be too.

(4) Don't give up if you are not satisfied with the response. If the company operates nationally or the product is a national brand, write a letter to the person responsible for consumer complaints at the company's headquarters. A listing of many of these companies can be found in the World Almanac's Business Directory on pages 781–787. If the company doesn't have a consumer office, direct your letter to the president of the company.

How to Write a Complaint Letter:

(1) If you have already contacted the person who sold you the product or service or the company is out of town, you will need to write a letter to pursue your complaint.

(2) If you need the president's name and the address of the company, first check in your phone directory to see if the company has a local office. If it does, call and ask for the name and address of the company's president. If there is no local listing, check *Standard & Poor's Register of Corporations, Directors and Executives.* It lists over 37,000 American business firms and can be found in most libraries.

(3) If you don't have the name of the manufacturer of the product, check your local library for the *Thomas Register.* It lists the manufacturers of thousands of products.

Basic Tips on Letter Writing:

(1) Include your name, address, and home and work phone numbers.

(2) Type your letter if possible. If it is handwritten, make sure it is neat and easy to read.

(3) Make your letter brief and to the point. Include all important facts about your purchase, including the date and place where you made the purchase, and any information you can give about the product or service such as serial or model numbers or specific type of service.

(4) State exactly what you want done about the problem and how long you are willing to wait to get it resolved. Be reasonable.

(5) Include all documents regarding your problems. Be sure to send COPIES, not originals.

(6) Avoid writing an angry, sarcastic, or threatening letter. The person reading your letter probably was not responsible for your problem, but may be very helpful in resolving it.

(7) Keep a copy of the letter for your records.

How to Obtain Birth, Marriage, Death Records

The United States government has published a series of inexpensive booklets entitled: Where to Write for Birth & Death Records; Where to Write for Marriage Records; Where to Write for Divorce Records; Where to Write for Birth and Death Records of U. S. Citizens Who were Born or Died Outside of the U. S.; Birth Certifications for Alien Children Adopted by U. S. Citizens; You May Save Time Proving Your Age and Other Birth Facts. They tell where to write to get a certified copy of an original vital record. Supt. of Documents, Government Printing Office, Washington, DC 20402.

Airline Complaints

There were almost as many complaints about unsatisfactory airline service in the month of June 1987, as there were for the first 6 months of 1986. The U.S. Transportation Department reported that over the first 6 months of 1987, it received 15,621 complaints from air travelers, nearly two and a half times as many as in the same period of 1986. According to the department, about 60 percent of the complaints involved flight delays, cancellations, or lost baggage.

Some airlines attribute the increase in complaints to publicity about the complaint-reporting system rather than to a decline in service. But critics of the airlines blame the decline in service to the 1978 congressional legislation which began the process of deregulating the airline industry and resulted in the fierce competition in which service became secondary to lower ticket prices.

Continental Airlines had the most complaints per 100,000 passengers, followed by Northwest and Eastern airlines; Aloha and Air California airlines had the fewest. The Transportation Department points out that their figures are only a fraction of air traveler complaints, since travelers are encouraged to first complain directly to the airlines.

Who Owns What: Familiar Consumer Products

The following is a list of familiar consumer products and their parent companies. If you wish to register a complaint beyond the local level, the address of the parent company can be found on pages 781-787.

Admiral appliances: Maytag
Ajax cleanser: Colgate-Palmolive
Allstate Insurance Co.: Sears, Roebuck
Anacin: American Home Products
Aqua Velva: RJR Nabisco
Arrid anti-perspirant: Carter-Wallace
Ban anti-perspirant: Bristol-Myers
Bayer aspirin: Sterling Drug
Beech Aircraft: Raytheon
Benson & Hedges cigarettes; Philip Morris
Betty Crocker products: General Mills
Big Boy restaurants: Marriott
Bolla wines: Brown-Forman
Budweiser beer: Anheuser-Busch
Bufferin: Bristol-Myers
Burger King restaurants: Pillsbury
Business Week magazine: McGraw-Hill
Buster Brown shoes: Brown Group
Cabbage Patch Kids dolls: Coleco
Cap'n Crunch cereal: Quaker Oats
Carrier air conditioners: United Technologies
Celeste Pizza: Quaker Oats
Chap Stick: A.H. Robins
Charmin toilet tissues: Procter & Gamble
Chef Boy-ar-dee products: American Home Products
Cheerios cereal: General Mills
Chicken of the Sea tuna: Ralston Purina
Clairol hair products: Bristol-Myers
Clorets mints: Warner-Lambert
Colt 45 malt liquor: Heileman Brewing
Columbia Pictures: Coca Cola
Continental Airlines: Texas Air.
Copenhagen snuff: UST
Cover Girl cosmetics: Noxell
Cracker Jack: Borden
Crest toothpaste: Procter & Gamble
Crisco shortening: Procter & Gamble
Dash detergent: Procter & Gamble
Dean Witter financial services: Sears, Roebuck
Del Monte foods: RJR Nabisco
Doritos chips: PepsiCo
Drano: Bristol-Meyers
Dristan: American Home Products
Duncan Hines cookies: Procter & Gamble
Duracell batteries: Kraft
Eastern Airlines: Texas Air
Easy-Off oven cleaner: American Home Products
Efferdent dental cleanser: Warner-Lambert
Ethan Allen furniture: Interco
Eveready batteries: Ralston Purina
Excedrin: Bristol-Myers
Fab detergent: Colgate-Palmolive
Family Circle magazine: New York Times
Fisher Price toys: Quaker Oats
Flagg Bros. shoe stores: Genesco
Foamy shaving cream: Gillette
Folger coffee: Procter & Gamble
Formula 409 spray cleaner: Clorox
Franco-American foods: Campbell Soup
Friendly Ice Cream restaurants: Hershey Foods
Frito-Lay snacks: PepsiCo
Gatorade: Quaker Oats
Geritol: RJR Nabisco
Gleem toothpaste: Procter & Gamble
Green Giant vegetables: Pillsbury
Haagen-Dazs ice cream: Pillsbury
Handy Wipes: Colgate-Palmolive
Hanes hosiery: Sara Lee
Harrah's resorts, casinos: Holiday Corp.
Head and Shoulders shampoo: Procter & Gamble
Hellman's mayonnaise: CPC International
Hertz car rental: Allegis
Hi-C fruit drinks: Coca Cola
Hostess baked goods: Ralston Purina
Ivory soap products: Procter & Gamble
Jack Daniel bourbon: Brown-Forman
Jell-o: Philip Morris
Jim Beam whiskey: American Brands
Katharine Gibbs schools: Macmillan
Ken-L-Ration pet foods: Quaker Oats
Kinney shoe stores: Woolworth
Knorr soups: CPC International
La Menu frozen dinners: Campbell Soup
Lee jeans: VF Corp.
Lenox china: Brown-Forman
Lerner stores: The Limited
Lestoil: Noxell
Life Savers candy: RJR Nabisco
Lipton tea: Unilever
Log Cabin syrup: Philip Morris
Lucite paints: Clorox
Lysol cleanser: Sterling Drug
Maalox: Rorer Group
Magnavox products: North American Philips
Marlboro cigarettes: Philip Morris
Mazola oil: CPC International
Michelob beer: Anheuser-Busch
Midas automotive centers: IC Industries
Miller beer: Philip Morris
Milton Bradley games: Hasbro
Minute Rice: Philip Morris
NBC Broadcasting: General Electric
Newsweek magazine: Washington Post
9-Lives cat food: H.J. Heinz
Norelco products: North American Philips
North American Van Lines: Norfolk Southern
Noxzema skin products: Noxell
Ore-Ida frozen foods: H.J. Heinz
Oreo cookies: RJR Nabisco
Oscar Mayer meats: Philip Morris
Pall Mall cigarettes: American Brands
Pampers: Procter & Gamble
Paper Mate pens: Gillette
Paramount Pictures: Gulf & Western
Paul Masson wines: Seagram
People magazine: Time
Pepto-Bismol: Procter & Gamble
Pepperidge Farm products: Campbell Soup
Pizza Hut restaurants: PepsiCo
Playskool toys: Hasbro
Prego spaghetti sauce: Campbell Soup
Prell shampoo: Procter & Gamble
Q-Tips: Unilever
Radio Shack retail outlets: Tandy
Ramblin root beer: Coca Cola
Red Devil paints: Insilco
Red Lobster Inns: General Mills
Right Guard deodorant: Gillette
Rise shave lathers: Carter-Wallace
Ritz crackers: RJR Nabisco
Robitussin cough syrup: A. H. Robins
Ronzoni pasta: Philip Morris
Roy Rogers restaurants: Marriott
Sea World Amusement Park: Harcourt Brace Jovanovich
Sealy bedding: Ohio Mattress
San Giorgio pasta: Hershey
Sergeant's pet care products: A.H. Robins
7-Eleven stores: Southland

Simon & Schuster publishing: Gulf & Western
Soft and Dri deodorant: Gillette
Sports Illustrated magazine: Time
Sprite soda: Coca-Cola
Steak and Ale restaurants: Pillsbury
Sugartwin: Alberto Culver
Sunkist soft drink: General Cinema
Sunshine Biscuits: American Brands
Taco Bell restaurants: PepsiCo
Tagamet: Smithkline Beckman
Thom McAn shoe stores: Melville
Tide detergent: Procter & Gamble
Tiparillo's: Culbro
Tropicana hotels & casinos: Ramada Inns
Tylenol: Johnson & Johnson
Ultra Brite toothpaste: Colgate-Palmolive
United Airlines: Allegis
V-8 vegetable juice: Campbell Soup
Vanity Fair apparel: VF Corp.
Virginia Slims cigarettes: Philip Morris
Walden Book stores: K mart
Wall Street Journal: Dow Jones
Weight Watchers: H.J. Heinz
Westin Hotels: Allegis
Wheaties cereal: General Mills
White Owl cigars: Culbro
White Rain shampoo: Gillette
Wizard air freshener: American Home Products
Wyler's drink mixes: Borden

Business Directory

Listed below are major U.S. corporations, and major foreign corporations, **whose operations—products and services—directly concern the American consumer.** At the end of each listing is a **representative sample** of some of the company's products.

Company. . .Address. . .Phone Number. . .Chief executive officer. . .Business.

AMR Corp. . .PO Box 619616, Dallas/Ft. Worth Airport, TX 75261. . .(214) 355-1234. . .R.C. Crandell. . .Air transportation (American Airlines).

Abbott Laboratories. . . Abbott Park, No. Chicago, IL 60064. . .(312) 937-6100. . .R.A. Schoellhorn. . .health care prods.

Aetna Life & Casualty Co. . .151 Farmington Ave., Hartford, CT 06156 . . .(203) 273-0123. . .James T. Lynn. . .insurance, financial services.

H.F. Ahmanson & Co. . .3731 Wilshire Blvd., Los Angeles, CA 90010. . .(213) 487-4277. . .R.H. Deihl. . .operates largest S&L assn. in U.S. (Home Savings of America).

Alberto-Culver Co. . .2525 Armitage Ave., Melrose Park, IL 60160. . .(312) 450-3000. . .Leonard H. Lavin. . .hair care preparations, feminine hygiene products, household and grocery items.

Albertson's Inc. . .250 Parkchester Blvd., Boise, ID 83726. . .(208) 385-6200. . .W.E. McCain . . .supermarkets

Alcan Aluminium Ltd. . .P.O. Box 6077 Montreal, Que., Canada H3C 3A7. . .(514) 848-8050. . .D.M. Culver. . . aluminum producer.

Alexander & Alexander Services. . .1211 Ave. of the Amer., New York, NY 10036. . .(212) 840-8500. . .T.H. Irvin. . .insurance & financial services.

Allegis Corp. . .1200 Algonquin Rd., Elk Grove Township, IL 60007. . .(312) 956-2400. . .R.J. Ferris. . .Air transportation (United Airlines), car rental (Hertz), hotels (Westin).

Allied-Signal Inc. . . Box 2245R, Morristown, NJ 07960 (201) 455-2000. . .Edward L. Hennessy Jr.. . .aerospace, engineered materials, automotive prods.

Alltel Corp. . .100 Executive Pkwy., Hudson, OH 44236. . .(216) 650-7000. . .J.T. Ford. . .telephone service in Midwest, South, and Eastern U.S.

Aluminum Co. of America. . .1501 Alcoa Bldg., Pittsburgh, PA 15219. . .(412) 553-4545. . .P.H. O'Neill. . .mining, refining, & processing of aluminum.

Amerada Hess Corp. . .1185 Ave. of the Americas, N.Y., NY 10036. . .(212) 997-8500. . .L. Hess. . .integrated petroleum co.

American Brands, Inc. . .1700 E. Putnam Ave., Old Greenwich, CT. . .(203) 698-5000. . .E.H. Whittemore. . .tobacco (Pall Mall, Lucky Strike cigarettes, Half and Half, Paleden pipe tobacco), whiskey (Jim Beam), snack foods (Sunshine Biscuits), golf & leisure prods, food, financial services, toiletries.

American Cyanamid Co. . . One Cyanamid Plaza, Wayne, NJ 07470. . .(201) 831-2000. . .G.J. Sella, Jr.. . .medical, agricultural, chemical, and consumer prods.

American Express Co. . . American Express Tower, N.Y., NY 10285 (212) 640-2000. . .J.D. Robinson 3d . . . travelers checks, credit card services, insurance, investment services (Shearson Lehman Bros.).

American Greetings Corp. . .10500 American Rd., Cleveland, OH 44144. . .(216) 252-7300. . .Irving I. Stone. . .greeting cards.

American Hoist & Derrick Co. . .1800 Amhoist Tower, 345 St. Peter St., St. Paul, MN 55102. . .(612) 293-4567. . .R.H. Nassau. . .heavy equip.

American Home Products Corp. . .685 3d Ave., N.Y., NY 10017. . .(212) 986-1000. . .J.R. Stafford. . .prescription drugs, household prods. (Woolite, Easy-Off oven cleaner; Black Flag, Wizard air fresheners), food (Chef Boy-ar-dee), drugs (Anacin, Dristan).

American Medical International Inc. . .414 N. Camdon Dr., Beverly Hills, CA 90210. . .(213) 278-6200. . .W.L. Weisman. . .hospital management.

American Stores Co. . .5201 Amelia Earhart Dr., Salt Lake City, UT 84127. . .(801) 539-0112. . .L.S. Skaggs. . .retail food markets, dept. & drug stores.

American Telephone & Telegraph Co. . .550 Madison Ave. N.Y., NY 10022. . .(212) 605-5500. . .J.E. Olson. . .communications.

Ames Department Stores, Inc. . .2418 Main St., Rocky Hill, CT 06067. . .(203) 563-8234. . .H. Gilman. . .self-service discount stores.

Amoco Corp. . .200 E. Randolph Dr., Chicago, IL 60601. . .(312) 856-6111. . .R.M. Morrow. . .oil and gas exploration, production, and marketing.

Anheuser-Busch, Inc. . . One Busch Place, St. Louis, MO 63118. . .(314) 577-2000. . .A.A. Busch 3d. . .brewing (Budweiser, Michelob, Bud Light, Natural Light).

Armstrong World Industries. . .W. Liberty St., Lancaster, PA 17604. . .(717) 397-0611. . .J.L. Jones. . .interior furnishings.

Arvin Industries, Inc. . .1531 13th St., Columbus, IN 47201. . .(812) 379-3000. . .J.K. Baker. . .auto exhaust systems, electric heaters, stereos.

Ashland Oil, Inc. . .1401 Westchester Ave., Ashland, KY 41114. . .(606) 329-3333. . .J.R. Hall. . .petroleum refiner, chemicals.

Atlantic Richfield Co. . .515 S. Flower St., Los Angeles, CA 90071 . . . (213) 486-3511 . . . L.M. Cook. . .petroleum, chemicals, other natural resources.

Avery International Corp. . .150 N. Orange Grove Blvd., Pasadena, CA 91103. . .(213) 304-2000. . .Charles D. Miller. . .self-adhesive labels.

Avon Products, Inc. . .9 West 57th St., N.Y., NY 10019. . .(212) 546-6015. . .Hicks B. Waldron. . .cosmetics, fragrances, toiletries, jewelry, health care.

Bally Manufacturing Corp. . .8700 W. Bryn Mawr Ave., Chicago, IL 60631. . .(312) 399-1300. . .R.E. Mullane. . .coin-operated amusement and gaming equip., hotel-casino operator.

Bausch & Lomb. . . One Lincoln First Square, Rochester, NY 14601. . .(716) 338-6000. . .D.E. Gill. . .manuf. of vision care products, accessories.

Baxter Travenol Labs Inc. . . One Baxter Pky., Deerfield, IL. 60015. . .(312) 948-2000. . .Vernon R. Loucks, Jr.. . .medical care prods & services.

Bell Atlantic Corp. . .1600 Market St., Philadelphia, PA 19103. . .(215) 963-6000. . .T.E. Bolger. . .telephone service in mid-Atlantic region.

Bell & Howell Co. . .5512 Old Orchard Rd., Skokie, IL 60077. . .(312) 470-7100. . .D.N. Frey. . .audio-visual instruments, business equip., educational & training equip., publishing.

BellSouth Corp. . .675 W. Peachtree NE, Atlanta, GA 30367. . .(404) 420-8600. . .J.L. Clendenin. . .telephone service in the South.

Best Products Co. . . Box 26303, Richmond, VA 23260. . .(804) 261-2000. . .R. Huntley. . .catalog/showroom merchandiser.

Bethlehem Steel Corp. . .8th & Eaton Ave., Bethlehem, PA 18016. . .(215) 694-2424. . .W.F. Williams. . .steel & steel prods.

Bic Corporation...Wiley Street, Milford, CT 06401...(203) 783-2000...Bruno Bich...writing instruments, disposable lighters, and shavers.
Black & Decker Mfg. Co....701 E. Joppa Rd., Towson, MD 21204...(301) 583-3900...N.D. Archibald...manuf. power tools.
H & R Block, Inc....4410 Main St., Kansas City, MO 64111...(816) 753-6900...Henry W. Bloch...tax preparation.
Boeing Company...7755 E. Marginal Way So., Seattle, WA 98108...(206) 655-2121...T.A. Wilson...aircraft manuf.
Boise Cascade Corp....One Jefferson Square, Boise, ID 83728...(208) 384-6161...J.B. Fery...timber, paper, wood prod.
Borden, Inc....277 Park Ave., N.Y., NY 10172...(212) 573-4000...R.J. Ventres...food, cheese and cheese products, snacks (Cracker Jack), beverages.
Bristol-Myers Co....345 Park Ave., N.Y., NY 10154...(212) 546-4000...Richard L. Gelb...toiletries (Ban anti-perspirant), hair items (Clairol), drugs (Bufferin, Excedrin), household prods.(Drano), infant formula (Enfamil).
Brown-Forman Inc....850 Dixie Hwy., Louisville, KY 40210...(502) 585-1100...W.L.L. Brown, Jr....distilled spirits (Jack Daniel), wines (Bolla, Cella), champagne (Korbel), cognac (Martell), liquor (Southern Comfort), Lenox china and crystal.
Brown Group, Inc....8400 Maryland Ave., St. Louis, MO 63166...(314) 854-4000...B.A. Brightwater, Jr....manuf. and wholesaler of women's and children's shoes (Buster Brown, Regal Shoes).
Brunswick Corp....One Brunswick Plaza, Skokie, IL 60077...(312) 470-4700...J.F. Reichert...marine, recreation prods, bowling centers & equip., fishing equip.
Burlington Coat Factory Warehouse Corp....Route 130 North, Burlington, NJ 08016...(609) 386-3314...M.G. Milstein...discount apparel stores.
Burlington Industries, Inc....3330 W. Friendly Ave., Greensboro, NC 27410...(919) 379-2000...F.S. Greenberg...largest U.S. textile mfg.
Burlington Northern Inc....999 3d Ave., Seattle, WA 98104...(206) 467-3838...R.M. Bressler...rail transportation, natural resources.
CBS Inc....51 W. 52d St., N.Y., NY 10019...(212) 975-6075...L.A. Tisch...broadcasting, video cassettes, recorded music, leisure prods.
CPC International, Inc....International Plaza, Englewood Cliffs, NJ 07632...(201) 894-4000...J.R. Eiszner...branded food items (Hellman's, Best Foods, Mazola, Skippy, Knorr Soups), corn wet milling prods.
Caesar's World, Inc....1801 Century Park East, Los Angeles, CA 90067...(213) 552-2711...H. Gluck...hotels & casinos.
Campbell Soup Co....Campbell Pl., Camden, NJ 08103...(609) 342-4800...R. G. McGovern...canned soups, spaghetti (Franco-American), vegetable juice (V-8), pork and beans, pet foods, restaurants, confections, Le Menu frozen dinners, Prego spaghetti sauce, Mrs. Pauls frozen fish, Pepperidge Farm breads.
Capital Cities/ABC Inc....24 E. 51st Street, New York, NY 10022...(212) 421-9595...T.S. Murphy...operates television and radio stations, newspapers.
Carter Hawley Hale Stores, Inc....550 S. Flower St., Los Angeles, CA 90071...(213) 620-0150...P.M. Hawley...dept. stores (Bergdorf Goodman, Neiman-Marcus), specialty stores.
Carter-Wallace, Inc....767 5th Ave., New York, NY 10153...(212) 758-4500...H.H. Hoyt, Jr....personal care items, anti-perspirant (Arrid), shave lathers (Rise), laxative (Carter's Pills), pet products.
Castle & Cooke, Inc....10900 Wilshire Blvd., Los Angeles, CA 90024...(213) 842-1500...D.H. Murdock... food processing, Dole.
Caterpillar Inc....100 N.E. Adams St., Peoria, IL 61629...(309) 675-1000...G.A. Schaefer...heavy duty earth-moving equip.
Champion International Corp....1 Champion Plaza, Stamford, CT 06921...(203) 358-7000...A.C. Sigler...forest prods.
Champion Spark Plug Co....900 Upton Ave., Toledo, OH 43661...(419) 535-2567...R.A. Stranahan, Jr....ignition devices.
Chase Manhattan Corp....1 Chase Manhattan Plaza, New York, NY 10081...(212) 552-2222...W.C. Butcher...Bank holding co.
Chevron Corp....225 Bush St., San Francisco, CA 94104...(415) 894-7700...G.M. Keller...integrated oil co.
Chrysler Corp....1200 Chrysler Dr., Detroit, MI 48203...(313) 956-5203...Lee Iacocca...cars, trucks.
Church's Fried Chicken, Inc....355A Spencer Lane, San Antonio, TX 78284...(512) 735-9392...J.D. Bamberger...fried chicken restaurants.
Circle K Corp....1601 N 7th St., Phoenix, AZ 85072...(602) 253-9600...R.M. Reade...convenience store chain.
Circuit City Stores, Inc....2040 Thalbro St., Richmond, VA 23230...(804) 257-4292...R.L. Sharp...retailer of electronic equip., consumer appliances.
Citicorp...399 Park Ave., N.Y., NY 10043...(212) 559-1000...J.S. Reed...largest U.S. commercial bank.
Clorox Co....1221 Broadway, Oakland, CA 94612...(415) 271-7000...C.R. Weaver...retail consumer prods (Formula 409, Twice As Fresh, Lucite paints, Kingsford charcoal briquets, Hidden Valley Ranch salad dressing).
Coachman Industries Inc....601 E. Beardsley Ave., Elkhart, IN 46515...(219) 262-0123...T.H. Corson...manuf. recreational vehicles.
Coca-Cola Co....One Coca-Cola Plaza, Atlanta, GA 30313...(404) 676-2121...R.C. Goizueta...soft drink (Coca Cola, Sprite, Ramblin root beer), syrups, citrus and fruit juices (Minute Maid, Hi-C), films (Columbia Pictures).
Coleco Industries, Inc....999 Quaker Lane S., Hartford, CT 06110...(203) 725-6000...A.C. Greenberg...consumer electronics, games, toys (Cabbage Patch Kids).
Coleman Co., Inc....250 N. St. Francis Ave., Wichita, KS 67202...(316) 261-3485...S. Coleman...outdoor recreation prods., heating & air conditioning equip.
Colgate-Palmolive Co....300 Park Ave., N.Y., NY 10022...(212) 310-2000...R. Mark...soaps (Palmolive, Irish Spring), detergents (Fab, Ajax, Fresh Start), tooth paste (Colgate, Ultra Brite), household prods. (Handy Wipes, Curad bandages), restaurants (Ranch House, Lum's).
Commodore International Ltd....P.O. Box N-10256, Nassau, Bahamas...(215) 431-9100...I. Gould...microcomputer systems, semiconductors component, consumer electronics, office equipment.
Control Data Corp....8100 34th Ave. South, Minneapolis, MN 55420...(612) 853-8100...R.M. Price...computer systems & services.
Adolph Coors Co....East of Town, Golden, CO 80401...(303) 279-6565...W. K. Coors...brewery.
Corning Glass Works...Houghton Park, Corning, NY 14831...(607) 974-9000...J.R. Houghton...glass mfg.
Crane Co....737 3d Ave., N.Y., NY 10017...(212) 415-7300...R.S. Evans...fluid & pollution controls, aircraft and aerospace, building prods.
A.T. Cross Co....One Albion Rd., Lincoln, RI 02865...(401) 333-1200...B.R. Boss...writing instruments.
Culbro Corp....387 Park Avenue South, New York, NY 10016...(212) 561-8700...E. M. Cullman...cigars (Corina, Robert Burns, White Owl, Tiparillo's), snack foods.
Dana Corp....4500 Dorr St., Toledo, OH 43697...(419) 535-4500...Gerald B. Mitchell...truck and auto parts supplies.
Data General Corp....4400 Computer Dr., Westboro, MA 01580...(617) 366-8911...E. D. deCastro...computer manuf.
Dayton-Hudson Corp....777 Nicollet Mall, Minneapolis, MN 55402...(612) 370-6948...K.A. Macke...department, specialty, stores, Mervyn's, Target.
Deere & Company...John Deere Rd., Moline, IL 61265...(309) 752-8000...Robert A. Hanson...farm, industrial, and outdoor power equip.
Delta Air Lines, Inc....Hartsfield Atlanta Intl. Airport, Atlanta, GA 30320...(404) 765-2600...David C. Garrett, Jr....air transportation.
Diebold, Inc....Canton, OH 44711...(216) 489-4000...R. Mahoney...equip. for financial insts.
Digital Equipment Corp....146 Main St., Maynard, MA 01754...(617) 897-5111...Kenneth H. Olsen...computer manuf.
Walt Disney Productions...500 S. Buena Vista St., Burbank, CA 91521...(213) 840-1000...M.D. Eisner...motion pictures, CATV, amusement parks, Disneyland, Walt Disney World, Epcot Center.
Donnelly & Sons Co....2223 Martin Luther King Drive, Chicago, IL 60616...(312) 326-8000...J.B. Schwemm...largest commercial printer.
Dow Chemical Co....2030 Dow Center, Midland, MI 48674...(517) 636-1000...P.F. Oreffice...chemicals, plastics, metals, consumer prods.
Dow Jones & Co....World Financial Center, New York, NY 10281...(212) 416-2000...W. H. Phillips...financial news service, publishing (Wall Street Journal, Barron's, Ottaway Newspapers).

Dresser Industries, Inc....1501 Elm Street, Dallas, TX 75201...(214) 740-6000...J.J. Murphy...supplier of technology and services to energy related industries.

Dun & Bradstreet Corp....299 Park Ave., New York, NY 10171...(212) 593-6800...C.W. Moritz...business information and computer services, publishing, broadcasting.

E.I. du Pont de Nemours & Co....1007 Market St., Wilmington, DE 19898...(302) 774-1000...R.E. Heckert...chemicals, petroleum, consumer prods., coal.

Eastman Kodak Co....343 State St., Rochester, NY 14650...(716) 724-4000...C.H. Chandler...photographic prods, chemicals.

Eaton Corp....Eaton Center, Cleveland, OH 44114...(216) 523-5000...J.R. Stover...manuf. of electronic, electrical prods., vehicle components.

Emerson Electric Co....8000 W. Florissant Ave., St. Louis, MO 63136...(314) 553-2000...C.F. Knight...electrical/electronics products & systems

Emery Air Freight Corp....Old Danbury Rd., Wilton, CT 06897...(203) 762-8601...John C. Emery, Jr....air freight forwarder.

Ethyl Corp....330 S. 4th St., Richmond, VA 23217...(804) 788-5000...Floyd D. Gottwald, Jr....petroleum and industrial chemicals, plastics, aluminum.

Exxon Corp....1251 Ave. of the Americas, N.Y., NY 10020...(212) 398-3093...C.C. Garvin Jr....world's largest oil co.

Family Dollars Stores, Inc....10401 Old Monroe Rd., Charlotte, NC 28212...(704)847-6961...L.E. Levine...discount variety stores.

Federal Express Corp....2990 Airways Blvd., Memphis, TN 38116...(901) 369-3600...F.W. Smith...small package delivery service.

Federated Department Stores, Inc....7 W. 7th St., Cincinnati, OH 45202...(513) 579-7000...H. Goldfeder...dept. stores, Abraham & Straus, Bloomingdale's, Filene's, Foley's, Lazarus, Rich's, Children's Place.

Fieldcrest Cannon, Inc....326 East Stadium Dr., Eden, NC 27288...(919) 623-2123...F.X. Larkin...household textile prods., rugs (Karastan, Laurelcrest).

Firestone Tire & Rubber Co....1200 Firestone Pkwy., Akron, OH 44317...(216) 379-7000...J.J. Nevin...tires, rubber and metal prods.

Fleetwood Enterprises, Inc....3125 Myers St., Riverside, CA 92523...(714) 351-3500...John C. Crean...mobile homes, recreational vehicles.

Fluor Corp....3333 Michelson Dr., Irvine, CA 92730...(714) 975-2000...D.S. Tappan Jr....engineering and construction.

Ford Motor Co....The American Rd., Dearborn, MI 48121...(313) 845-8540...D.E. Peterson...motor vehicles, Ford Tractor, Lincoln-Mercury.

Fort Howard Paper Co....1919 S. Broadway, Green Bay, WI 54307...(414) 435-8821...P.J. Schierl...disposable paper prods.

GAF Corp....1361 Alps Road, Wayne, NJ 07470...(201) 628-3000...S.J. Heyman...chemicals, bldg. materials, radio broadcasting.

GTE Corp....One Stamford Forum, Stamford, CT 06904...(203) 965-2000...Theodore F. Brophy...communications prods. (U.S. Sprint), electronics.

Gannett Co., Inc....P.O. Box 7858, Washington, DC 20044...(703) 284-6000...A.H. Neuharth...newspaper publishing (USA Today), TV stations, outdoor advertising.

Gencorp....One General St., Akron, OH 44329...(216) 798-3000...J.L. Heckel...tires, rubber prods.

General Cinema Corp....27 Boylston St., Chestnut Hill, MA 02167...(617) 232-8200...R. A. Smith...movie exhibitor, soft drinks (Sunkist).

General Dynamics Corp....Pierre Laclede Ctr., St. Louis, MO 63105...(314) 889-8200...S.C. Pace...military and commercial aircraft, tactical missiles.

General Electric Co....3135 Easton Ave., Fairfield, CT 06431...(203) 373-2210...J. F. Welch, Jr....electrical, electronic equip, finance (Kidder, Peabody & Co.), radio, television (NBC).

General Instrument Corp....767 5th Ave., New York, NY 10153...(212) 207-6230...F. G. Hickey...race track betting systems, CATV, semiconductors, electronic equip.

General Mills, Inc....9200 Wayzatta Blvd., Minneapolis, MN 55440...(612) 540-2311...H.B. Atwater Jr....foods, toys, restaurants, fashion and specialty retailing, Total, Bisquick, Wheaties, Cheerios, Hamberger Helper, Betty Crocker, Red Lobster Inns).

General Motors Corp....Gen. Motors Bldg., Detroit, MI 48202...(313) 556-5000...R. B. Smith...world's largest auto manuf.

Genesco Inc....Genesco Park, Nashville, TN 37202...(615) 367-7000...W.S. Wire 2d...footwear and men's clothing, Hardy, Cover Girl, Jarman, Flagg Bros., Johnston & Murphy.

Genuine Parts Co....2999 Circle 75 Pkwy, Atlanta, GA 30339...(404) 953-1700...W. Looney...distributes auto replacement parts (NAPA).

Georgia-Pacific Corp....133 Peachtree St., NE, Atlanta, GA 30303...(404) 521-4720...T.M. Hahn, Jr....building prods., pulp, paper, chemicals.

Gerber Products Co....445 State St., Fremont, MI 49412...(616) 928-2000...W.L. McKinley...baby foods, clothing, nursery accessories.

Gillette Co....Prudential Tower Bldg., Boston, MA 02199...(617) 421-7000...Colman M. Mockler, Jr....razors, pens (Paper Mate; Flair), toiletries (Right Guard, Dri, Soft deodorants, Foamy shaving cream, Earth Born shampoo), hair products (Toni, Adorn, White Rain).

Golden Nugget, Inc....129 Freemont St., Las Vegas, NV 89101...(702) 385-7111...Steve Wynn...operates casino-hotels.

B.F. Goodrich Company...500 S. Main St., Akron, OH 44318...(216) 374-2632...John D. Ong...rubber, chemical, plastic prods.

Goodyear Tire & Rubber Co....1144 E. Market St., Akron, OH 44316...(216) 796-2121...R.E. Mercer...tires, rubber prods.

Gordon Jewelry Corp....820 Fannin St., Houston TX 77002...(713) 222-8080...D.P. Gordon...largest jewelry retailer.

Gould Inc....10 Gould Center, Rolling Meadows, IL 60008...(312) 640-4000...W.T. Ylvisaker...electronic and industrial prods.

W.R. Grace & Co....Grace Plaza, 1114 Ave. of the Americas, N.Y., NY 10036...(212) 819-5500...J. Peter Grace...chemicals, natural resources, consumer prods. and services, restaurants, Channel Home Centers.

Great Atlantic & Pacific Tea Co....2 Paragon Dr., Montvale, NJ 07645...(201) 573-9700...James Wood...retail food stores.

Greyhound Corp....Greyhound Tower, Phoenix, AZ 85077...(602) 248-4000...John W. Teets...bus manuf., soap (Dial), food, financial services.

Grumman Corp....1111 Stewart, Bethpage, NY 11714...(516) 575-0574...John C. Bierwirth...aerospace, truck bodies, electronics.

Gulf + Western, Inc....One Gulf + Western Plaza, N.Y., NY 10023...(212) 373-8000...M.S. Davis...financial services, consumer and food products, home furnishings, entertainment (Paramount Pictures, Madison Square Garden), publishing (Simon & Schuster).

Hannaford Bros. Co....145 Pleasant Hill Rd., Scarborough, ME 04074...(207) 883-2911...J.L. Moody Jr....operates supermarkets, drug stores.

Harcourt Brace Jovanovich, Inc....Orlando, FL 32887...(305) 345-2000...W. Jovanovich...textbook publisher, entertainment (Sea World), insurance.

Hartmarx...101 N. Wacker Dr., Chicago, IL 60606...(312) 372-6300...H.A. Weinberg...apparel manufacturer and retailer (Hickey-Freeman).

Hasbro Inc....1027 Newport Ave., P.O. Box 1059, Pawtucket, R.I. 02862...(401) 727-5000...S.D. Hassenfeld...toy manuf. & marketer (Milton Bradley, Playskool).

Heileman (G.) Brewing Co....100 Harborview Plaza, La Crosse, WI 54601...(608) 785-1000...R. G. Cleary...brewery (Schmidt, Blatz, Colt 45 Malt Liquor).

H.J. Heinz Co....P.O. Box 57, Pittsburgh, PA 15230...(412) 546-5700...Anthony J.F. O'Reilly...foods (Star-Kist, Ore-Ida, '57 Varieties), 9-Lives cat food, Weight Watchers.

Helene Curtis Industries, Inc....325 N. Wells St., Chicago, IL 60610...(312) 292-2224...R.J. Gidwitz...hair care prods. (Finesse, Sauve).

Hershey Foods Corp....100 Mansion Rd., Hershey, PA 17033...(717) 534-4000...R.A. Zimmerman...chocolate & confectionery prods., pasta (San Giorgio), restaurants (Friendly Ice Cream).

Hewlett-Packard Co....3000 Hanover Street, Palo Alto, CA 94304...(415) 856-1501...John A. Young...electronic instruments.

Hillenbrand Industries, Inc.... Highway 46, Batesville, IN 47006...(812) 934-7000...D.A. Hillenbrand...manuf. burial caskets, electronically operated hospital beds.

Holiday Corp....1023 Cherry Rd., Memphis, TN 38117...(901) 362-4001...M.D. Rose...hotels, (Holiday Inn, Hampton Inn Hotels, Embassy Suite Hotels), motels, casinos (Harrah's).

Home Depot, Inc....6300 Powers Ferry Rd., Atlanta, GA 30339...(404) 433-8211...Bernard Marcus...retailer of building materials & home improvement prods.

Honda Motor Co., LTD...1270 Ave. of the Americas, N.Y., NY 10020...(212) 765-3804...Tadashi Kume...manuf. autos, motorcycles.

Honeywell, Inc.... Honeywell Plaza, Minneapolis, MN 55408...(612) 870-5200...E.W. Spencer...industrial systems & controls, aerospace guidance systems, information systems.

Geo. A. Hormel & Co....501 16th Ave. N.E., Austin, MN 55912...(507) 437-5611...R.L. Knowlton...meat packaging, pork and beef prods (Spam, Light & Lean, Dinty Moore, Mary Kitchen).

Houghton-Mifflin Co.... One Beacon St., Boston, MA 02108...(617) 725-5000...H.T. Miller...book publishing.

Household International Inc....2700 Sanders Rd., Prospect Heights, IL 60070...(312) 564-5000...D.C. Clark...financial and insurance services, merchandising, manufacturing.

Huffy Corp....7701 Byers Rd., Miamisburg, OH 45342...(513) 866-6251...H.A. Shaw 3d...bicycle manuf.

Humana, Inc....P.O. Box 1438, Louisville, KY 40201...(502) 561-2000...D. A. Jones...operates hospitals, provides health care plans.

IC Industries, Inc... One Illinois Ctr., 111 E. Wacker Dr., Chicago, IL 60601...(312) 565-3000...William B. Johnson... diversified prods. and services, railroads, consumer products, food, auto prods (Midas).

ITT Corp....320 Park Ave., N.Y., NY 10022...(212) 752-6000...R.V. Araskog...manuf., installs communciation and electronic equip., auto equip., insurance, financial services, hotels, educational services.

Imperial Oil Ltd....111 St. Clair Ave. W., Toronto, Ont., Canada...(416) 968-4111...A.R. Haynes...Canada's largest oil co.

Insilco Corp....1000 Research Pkwy., Meriden, CT 06450...(203) 634-2000...D.J. Harper...diversified manufacturer, Red Devil Paints and Chemicals, Rolodex, Taylor Publishing, Dual-Lite.

Interco Inc....P.O. Box 8777, St. Louis, MO 63102...(314) 231-1100...H. Saligman...apparel, footwear mfg., specialty apparel shops, home furnishings (Ethan Allen).

International Business Machines Corp.... Old Orchard Rd., Armonk, NY 10504...(914) 765-1900...J.F. Akers...information-handling systems, equip., and services.

International Paper Co....77 W. 45th St., New York, NY 10036...(212) 536-6000...J.A. Georges...paper, wood prods.

Johnson & Johnson... One Johnson & Johnson Plaza, Brunswick, NJ 08933...(201) 524-0400...James E. Burke...surgical dressings, pharmaceuticals (Tylenol), health and baby prods.

Jostens, Inc....5501 Norman Center Dr., Minneapolis, MN 55437...(612) 830-3300...H. W. Lurton...school rings, yearbooks.

K mart Corp....3300 W. Big Beaver Rd., Troy, MI 48084...(313) 643-1000...B. M. Fauber...largest U.S. chain of discount stores, book stores (Walden Book), cafeterias (Furr's, Bishop Buffets), drug stores (Pay Less Drug Stores).

Kaisertech Ltd....300 Lakeside Dr., Oakland, CA 94643...(415) 271-3300...A.E. Clore... aluminum, chemicals.

Kaufman and Broad, Inc....11601 Wilshire Blvd., Los Angeles, CA 90025...(213) 312-5000...Eli Broad...home builder.

Kellogg Co.... One Kellogg Sq., Battle Creek, MI 49016...(616) 961-2000...William E. LaMothe...ready to eat cereals & other food prods., Mrs. Smith's Pie Co., Salada Foods.

Kidde, Inc.... Park 80 West-Plaza Two, Box 5555, Saddle Brook, NJ 07662...(201) 368-9000...Fred R. Sullivan...mfgr. safety, security, protection, industrial, commercial, consumer and recreation prods. and services.

Kimberly-Clark Corp....P.O. Box 619100, Dallas, TX 75261...(214) 830-1200...Darwin E. Smith...paper and lumber prods., consumer prods. (Kleenex, Huggies).

Knight-Ridder, Inc.... One Herold Plaza, Miami, FL 33132...(305) 376-3800...A.H. Chapman, Jr....newspaper publishing, TV broadcasting, book publishing, information services.

Kraft, Inc.... Kraft Court, Glenville, IL 60025...(312) 998-2000...J.R. Richman...food prods. (salad dressing, mayonnaise, cheese prods.); Duracell batteries.

Kroger Co....1014 Vine St., Cincinnati, OH 45201...(513) 762-4000...Lyle Everingham...grocery chain, drugstores (SupeRx).

Eli Lilly & Company... Lilly Corp. Center, Indianapolis, IN 46285...(317) 261-2000...Richard D. Wood...mfg. human health and agricultural products.

The Limited, Inc.... Two Limited Pkwy., Columbus, OH 43216...(614) 475-4000...L.H. Wexner...women's apparel stores, Lane Bryant, Lerner, Victoria's Secret.

Litton Industries, Inc....360 N. Crescent Dr., Beverly Hills, CA 90210...(213) 859-5000...F.W. O'Green...industrial systems & services, advanced electronic systems, electronic & electrical prods., marine engineering.

Lockheed Corp....4500 Park Granada Blvd., Calabasas, CA 91399...(818) 847-6121...L.O. Kitchen...commercial and military aircraft, missiles.

Loews Corp....666 5th Ave., N.Y., NY 10103...(212) 841-1000...Laurence A. Tisch...tobacco prods., motion picture theaters, hotels, real estate, insurance.

Long's Drug Stores Corp....141 North Civic Dr., Walnut Creek, CA 94596...(415) 937-1170...R.M. Long...drug store chain.

Lowe's Cos., Inc.... Hway 268 East, N. Wilkesboro, NC 28656...(919) 651-4000...L.G. Herring...retailer of building materials & related prods.

Luby's Cafeterias, Inc....211 Northeast Loop 410, San Antonio, TX 78265...(512) 654-9000...J.B. Lahourcade...operates cafeterias in SW U.S.

Lucky Stores, Inc....6300 Clark Ave., Dublin, CA 94568...(415) 833-6000...J.M. Lillie...supermarkets, food centers.

MCA Inc....100 Universal City Plaza, Universal City, CA 91608...(818) 777-1000...Lew R. Wasserman...motion pictures, television, music publishing, mail order, novelty, and gift merchandise.

Macmillan, Inc....866 3d Ave., New York, NY 10022...(212) 702-2000...E. P. Evans...book printing and publishing, education (Berlitz, Katharine Gibbs).

Manor Care, Inc....10750 Columbia Pike, Silver Spring, MD 20901...(301) 681-9400...S. Bainum...operates nursing centers.

Marriott Corp.... Marriott Dr., Wash., DC 20058...(301) 897-9000...J. Willard Marriott, Jr....restaurants (Roy Rogers, Big Boy), hotels (Howard Johnson), food services, theme parks.

Martin Marietta Corp....6801 Rockledge Dr., Bethesda, MD 20817...(301) 897-6000...T.G. Pownall...electronics, aerospace.

Mattel, Inc....5150 Rosecrans Ave., Hawthorne, CA 90250...(213) 978-5150...J.W. Amerman...toy & hobby prods (Barbie doll, Masters of the Universe).

May Department Stores Co....611 Olive Street, St. Louis, MO 63101...(314) 342-6300...D.C. Farrell...department stores (O'Neils, Hecht's, Famous Barr, G. Fox, and May Cohens), discount chain (Caldor).

Maytag Corp.... One Dependability Sq., Newton, IA 50208...(515) 792-7000...Daniel J. Krumm...manuf. home laundry equip, appliances (Magic Chef prods).

McCormick & Co., Inc....11350 McCormick Rd., Hunt Valley, MD 21031...(301) 667-7301...C.P. McCormick...world's leading manuf. of seasoning & flavoring prods.

McDonald's Corp.... McDonald's Plaza, Oak Brook, IL 60521...(312) 887-3200...M.R. Quinlan...fast service restaurants.

McDonnell Douglas Corp....P.O. Box 516, St. Louis, MO 63166...(314) 232-0232...Sanford N. McDonnell...commercial & military aircraft, space systems & missiles.

McGraw-Hill, Inc....1221 Ave. of the Americas, New York, NY 10020...(212) 512-2000...J.L. Dionne...book, magazine publishing (Business Week), information & financial services (Standard and Poor's), TV stations.

Mead Corporation...Courthouse Plaza Northeast, Dayton, OH 45463...(513) 222-6323...B.R. Roberts...printing and writing paper, paperboard, packaging, shipping containers, pulp and lumber.
Media General, Inc....333 E. Grace St., Richmond, VA 23219...(804) 649-6000...J.S. Evans...broadcasting, newspaper publishing.
Medtronic, Inc....3055 Hway 8, Minneapolis, MN 55440...(612) 574-4000...W.R. Wallin...heart pacemakers and support systems.
Melville Corp....3000 Westchester Ave., Harrison, NY 10528...(914) 253-8000...S.P. Goldstein...shoe stores (Thom McAn), apparel (Marshalls, Chess King), drug stores.
Merck & Co., Inc....P.O. Box 2000, Rahway, NJ 07065...(201) 574-4000...P. Roy Vagelos...human & animal health care prods.
Merrill Lynch & Co., Inc....One Liberty Plaza, N.Y., NY 10080...(212) 637-7455...W.A Schreyer...securities broker, financial services, real estate.
Minnesota Mining & Manuf. Co....3M Center, St. Paul, MN 55144...(612) 733-1100...A.F. Jacobson...abrasives, adhesives, building services & chemicals, electrical, health care, photographic, printing, recording materials.
Mobil Corp....150 E. 42d St., N.Y., NY 10017...(212) 883-4242...A.E. Murray...international oil co., chemicals, dept. stores (Montgomery Ward).
Mohasco Corp....57 Lyon St., Amsterdam, NY 12010...(518) 841-2211...H. J. Broner...interior furnishings.
Monsanto Company...800 N. Lindbergh Blvd., St. Louis, MO 63167...(314) 694-1000...R. J. Mahoney...chemicals, electronics, agricultural prods., consumer prods. (NutraSweet).
Morton Thiokol, Inc....110 N. Wacker Dr., Chicago, IL 60606...(312) 807-2000...Charles S. Locke...salt (Morton), household cleaning prods. (Fantastik, Spray 'n Wash), specialty chemicals, aerospace.
Motorola, Inc....1303 E. Algonquin Rd., Schaumburg, IL 60196...(312) 397-5000...W.J. Weisz...electronic equipment and components.
Murray Ohio Manuf. Co....219 Franklin Rd., Brentwood, TN 37027...(615) 373-6500...J.L. Duncan...bicycles, power lawnmowers.
NCR Corp....1700 S. Patterson Blvd., Dayton, OH 45479...(513) 445-5000...Charles E. Exley, Jr....business information processing systems.
National Distillers & Chemical Corp....99 Park Ave., N.Y., NY 10016...(212) 551-0436...J.H. Stookey...petrochemicals, liquid petroleum gases.
National Medical Enterprises, Inc....11620 Wilshire Blvd, Los Angeles, CA 90025...(213) 479-5526...R.K. Eamer...operates hospitals.
National Semiconductor Corp....2900 Semiconductor Dr., Santa Clara, CA 95051...(408) 721-5000...Charles E. Sporck...manuf. of semiconductors.
Navistar Intl. Corp....401 N. Michigan Ave, Chicago, IL 60611...(312) 836-2000...J.C. Cotting...manuf. heavy duty trucks, parts.
New York Times Co....229 W. 43rd St., N.Y., NY 10036...(212) 556-1091...A. O. Sulzberger...newspapers, radio, CATV stations, magazines (Family Circle, Golf Digest).
Norfolk Southern Corp....One Commercial Place, Norfolk, VA 23510...(804) 629-2600...A.B. McKinnon...operates Norfolk & Southern railways, freight carrier (North American Van Lines).
North American Philips Corp....100 E. 42d St., N.Y., NY 10017...(212) 697-3600...C. Bruynes...consumer prods., electrical, electronic prods., professional equip, Magnavox, Norelco.
Northrop Corp....1840 Century Park E., Los Angeles, CA 90067...(213) 553-6262...Thomas V. Jones...aircraft, electronics, communications.
Noxell Corp....11050 York Rd., Hunt Valley, MD 21030...(301) 628-7300...G. L. Bunting, Jr....toiletry, household, consumer prods. (Noxzema, Lestoil, Clarion, Cover Girl).
Nynex Corp....335 Madison Ave., N.Y., NY 10017...(212) 370-7400...D.C. Staley...telephone co. in northeast U.S.
Occidental Petroleum Corp....10889 Wilshire Blvd., Los Angeles, CA 90024...(213) 879-1700...Dr. Armand Hammer...oil, gas, chemicals, coal.
Ogden Corp....277 Park Ave., New York NY 10172...(212) 754-4000...R. E. Ablon...transportation, foods, metals.
Ohio Mattress Co....1501 Bond Court Bldg., Cleveland OH 44114...(216) 522-1310...E.M. Wuliger...bedding manuf. (Sealy, Sterns & Foster).
Olin Corp....120 Long Ridge Rd., Stamford, CT 06904...(203) 356-2000...J.W. Johnstone Jr....chemicals, metals, sporting and defense ammunition.
Olsten Corp....One Merrick Ave., Westbury, NY 11590...(516) 832-8200...W. Olsten...provides temporary workers.
Outboard Marine Corp....100 Sea Horse Dr., Waukegan, IL 60085...(312) 689-6200...C.D. Strang...outboard motors, mowers (Lawn Boy).
Owens-Corning Fiberglas Corp....Fiberglas Tower, Toledo, OH 43659...(419) 248-8000...W.W. Boeschenstein...glass fiber and related prods.
Oxford Industries, Inc....222 Piedmont Ave., N.E., Atlanta, GA 30308...(404) 659-2424...J.H. Lanier...men's and women's apparel products.
Pan Am Corp....Pan Am Bldg., 200 Park Ave., N.Y., NY 10166...(212) 880-1234...C. Edward Acker...air transportation.
J.C. Penney Co....1301 Ave. of the Americas, N.Y., NY 10019...(212) 957-4321...W. R. Howell, chmn...dept. stores, catalog sales, drug stores, insurance.
Pennzoil Co....P.O. Box 2967, Houston, TX 77252...(713) 546-4000...J.H. Liedtke...Integrated oil and gas co.
Pep Boys—Manny, Moe & Jack...3111 W. Allegheny Ave., Philadelphia, Pa. 19132...(215) 229-9000...B. Strauss... automotive parts and accessories, retail stores, household items, hardware, bicycles.
PepsiCo, Inc....Anderson Hill Rd., Purchase, NY 10577...(914) 253-2000...D.W. Calloway...soft drinks, (Pepsi-Cola, Slice), snack foods (Frito-Lay, Doritos) restaurants (Pizza Hut, Kentucky Fried Chicken, Taco Bell).
Perry Drug Stores, Inc....5400 Perry Dr., Pontiac, MI 48056...J.A. Robinson...drug stores, auto parts stores.
Petrie Stores Corp....70 Enterprise Ave., Seacaucus, NJ 07094...(201) 866-3600...M.J. Petrie...operates chain of women's specialty stores.
Pfizer Inc....235 E. 42d St., N.Y., NY 10017...(212) 573-2323...E.T. Pratt, Jr....pharmaceutical, hospital, agricultural, chemical prods.
Philip Morris Cos., Inc....120 Park Ave., N.Y., NY 10017...(212) 880-5000...H. Maxwell...cigarettes (Marlboro, Benson & Hedges, Merit, Virginia Slims), beer (Miller High Life, Lite, Lowenbrau brands), packaged foods (Jell-o, Ronzoni pasta, Entenmann baked goods).
Phillips-Van Heusen Corp....1290 Ave. of the Americas, New York, NY 10104...(212) 541-5200...L. S. Phillips...manuf. apparel for men & women; operates retail stores.
Pillsbury Co....200 S. 6th St., Minneapolis, MN 55402...(612) 330-4966...J.M. Stafford...canned & frozen vegetables (Green Giant), bakery, flour mixes, ice cream (Haagen Dazs), restaurants (Burger King, Godfather's Pizza, Steak and Ale).
Pitney Bowes, Inc....Walter H. Wheeler Dr., Stamford, CT 06904...(203) 356-5000...G. B. Harvey...postage meters, mail handling equip., office equipment.
Playboy Enterprises, Inc....919 N. Michigan Ave., Chicago, IL 60691...(312) 751-8000...Hugh Hefner...magazine publishing, CATV.
Polaroid Corp....549 Technology Sq., Cambridge, MA 02139...(617) 577-2000...I.M. Booth...photographic equip., supplies and optical goods.
Primerica, Corp....American Lane, Greenwich, CT 06836...(203) 552-2000...G. Tsai...financial services (Smith Barney), retailing (Fingerhut, Musicland, Durham's).
Procter & Gamble Co....One Procter & Gamble Plaza, Cincinnati, OH 45202...(513) 983-1100...J. G. Smale...soap & detergent (Ivory, Dash, Tide, Spic and Span), shortenings (Crisco), toiletries (Crest and Gleem toothpastes, Prell, and Head and Shoulders shampoos), pharmaceuticals (Pepto-Bismol), Pampers disposable diapers, Folger coffee, Charmin toilet tissues, Bounty towels.
Purolator Courier Corp....131 Morristown Road, Basking Ridge, NJ 07920...(201) 953-6400...C.H. Hardesty Jr....auto equip., courier and guard services, package express delivery service.
Quaker Oats Co....Merchandise Mart Plaza, Chicago, IL 60654...(312) 222-7111...William D. Smithburg...foods, cereal (Life, Cap'n Crunch, Puffed Wheat, Puffed Rice), foods (Aunt Jemima, Celeste pizza, Van Camp's pork and beans, Gatorade), pet foods (Ken-L-Ration, Gaines, Puss 'Boots), Fisher Price toys, Magic Pan restaurants.

Quaker State Corp....255 Elm St., Oil City, PA 16301...(814) 676-7676...Q.E. Wood...refining, marketing petroleum prods., filters, mining & marketing coal.

Ralston Purina Co.... Checkerboard Sq., St. Louis, MO 63164...(314) 982-1000...W. R. Stritz...pet and livestock food, consumer prods. (Chex cereal, Chicken of the Sea tuna, Wonder bread, Drake, Hostess baked goods, Everready batteries.)
Ramada Inns, Inc....3838 E. Van Buren, Phoenix, AZ 85008...(602) 273-4000...Richard Snell...hotel operation, casinos (Tropicana).
Raytheon Company...141 Spring St., Lexington, MA 02173...(617) 862-6600...Thomas L. Phillips...electronics, aviation, appliances...Amana Refrigeration, Beech Aircraft.
Reebok Intl. Ltd....150 Royall St., Canton, MA 02021...(617) 821-2800...P.B. Fireman...athletic & casual footwear.
Reynolds Metals Co....6601 W. Broad St., Richmond, VA 23261...(804) 281-2000...W.O. Bourke...aluminum prods.
RJR Nabisco, Inc....1100 Reynolds Blvd., Winston-Salem, NC 27102...(919) 773-2000...F.R. Johnson...crude oil, petroleum, transportation, tobacco (Camels, More), food, candy, gum, and beverage prods (Del Monte and Nabisco brands, Canada Dry), toiletries (Aqua Velva), pharmaceutical prods (Geritol).
Rite Aid Corp.... Shiremanstown, PA 17011...(717) 761-2633...A. Grass...discount drug stores.
A.H. Robins Co., Inc....1407 Cummings Dr., Richmond, VA 23261...(804) 257-2000...E.C. Robins, Jr...health care, consumer prods. (Chap Stick, Quencher, Robitussin cough syrups), Sergeant's pet care prods.
Rockwell Intl. Corp....P.O. Box 57, Pittsburgh, PA 15219...(412) 565-2000...R. Anderson...aerospace, electronic, automotive prods.
Rorer Group Inc....500 Virginia Dr., Ft. Washington, PA 19034...(215) 628-6000...R.E. Cawthorn...pharmaceuticals (Maalox, Ascriptin).
Rubbermaid Inc....1147 Akron Rd., Wooster, OH 44691...(216) 264-6464...S. C. Gault...rubber and plastic consumer prods.
Russell Corp....P.O. Box 272, Alexander City, AL 35010...(205) 234-4251...E.C. Gwaltney...leisure apparel, athletic uniforms.
Ryder System, Inc....3600 NW 82d Ave., Miami, FL 33166...(305) 593-3726...M. A. Burns...truck leasing service.

Santa Fe Southern Pacific Corp.,...224 S. Michigan Ave., Chicago, IL 60604...(312) 786-6000...Robert Krebs...railroad, real estate, construction, natural resources.
Sara Lee Corp....3 First National Plaza, Chicago, IL 60602...(312) 726-2600...J.H. Bryan, Jr...baked goods, fresh and processed meats, fresh and frozen fruits and vegetables and other packaged foods, beverages, tobacco products, hosiery, intimate apparel and knitwear, Electrolux, Fuller Brush, Hanes, Gant, Kiwi, Shasta.
Schering-Plough Corp.... One Giralda Farms, Madison, NJ 07940...(201) 822-7000...R. P. Luciano...pharmaceuticals, consumer prods, radio stations.
Schlumberger Ltd....277 Park Ave., New York, NY 10172...(212) 350-9400...E. Baird...oilfield services, electronics, measurement and control devices.
Scott Paper Co.... Scott Plaza, Phila., PA 19113...(215) 521-5000...P. E. Lippincott...sanitary paper prods.
Seagram Co. Ltd....1430 Peel St., Montreal, Que., Canada H3A 1S9...(514) 849-5271...E.M. Bronfman...distilled spirits & wine (Crown Royal, Chivas Regal, Calvert, Wolfschmidt Vodka, Paul Masson, Christian Brothers, Gold Seal, Myer's Jamaica Rum).
Sears, Roebuck & Co.... Sears Tower, Chicago, IL 60684...(312) 875-2500...E.A. Brennan...merchandising, insurance (Allstate), financial services (Dean Witter), real estate (Coldwell Banker).
Shaw Industries, Inc....616 E. Walnut Ave., Dalton, GA 30722...(404) 278-3812...R.E. Shaw...manuf. tufted carpeting (Magee, Philadelphia).
Sherwin-Williams Co....101 Prospect Ave. N.W., Cleveland, OH 44115...(216) 566-2000...John G. Breen...world's largest paint producer (Dutch Boy, Kem-Tone).
Singer Co....8 Stanford Forum, Stanford, CT 06904...(203) 356-4200...J.B. Flavin...manuf. of aerospace electronic prods.
Skyline Corp....2520 By-Pass Rd., Elkhart, IN 46515...(219) 294-6521...Arthur J. Decio...mfg. housing and recreational vehicles.
Smithkline Beckman Corp.... One Franklin Plaza, Phila., PA 19101...(215) 751-4000...H. Wendt...pharmaceuticals (Tagamet, Dyazide), animal health prods., diagnostic instruments.
Smucker (J.M.) Co.... Strawberry Lane, Orville, OH 44667...(216) 682-0015...P. H. Smucker...preserves, jams, jellies, toppings.
Snap-on Tools Corp....2801 80th St., Kenosha, WI 53141...(414) 656-5200...W. B. Rayburn...manuf. mechanic's tools, equip.
Sony Corp.... Tokyo, Japan...A. Morita...manuf. televisions, radios, tape recorders, audio equip., video tape recorders.
Southland Corp....2828 N. Haskell Ave., Dallas, TX 75221...(214) 828-7011...J.P. Thompson...convenience stores (7-Eleven, Gristede's), auto parts stores.
Southwest Airlines Co....P.O. Box 37611, Love Field, Dallas, TX 75235...(214) 353-6100...H.D. Kelleher...air transportation.
Southwestern Bell Corp.... One Bell Center, St. Louis, MO 63101...(314) 247-9800...Z.E. Barnes...telephone communications.
Squibb Corp....P.O. Box 4000, Princeton, NJ 08540...(609) 921-4000...Richard M. Furlaud...drugs (Capoten, Capozide), confectionery, household prods, Charles of the Ritz.
Staley Continental, Inc....1701 Golf Rd., Rolling Meadow, IL 60008...(312) 981-1696...Donald E. Nordlund...corn and soybean processing, consumer prods.
Stanley Works...1000 Stanley Drive, P.O. Box 7000, New Britain CT 06050...(203) 225-5111...R.A. Ayers...hand tools, hardware, door opening equipment.
Sterling Drug Inc....90 Park Ave., N.Y., NY 10016...(212) 907-2000...J.M. Pietruski...pharmaceuticals, cosmetics & toiletries, household, proprietary prods., chemicals (Bayer Aspirin, Panadol, Lysol, Dorothy Gray).
J.P. Stevens & Co....1185 Ave. of the Americas, N.Y., NY 10036...(212) 930-2000...W. Stevens...fabrics, carpets, other textile home furnishings.
Stop & Shop Companies, Inc....P.O. Box 369, Boston, MA 02101...(617) 770-8000...A.J. Goldberg...supermarkets, discount department stores (Bradlees and Medi Mart), The Charles B. Perkins Co. (which operates tobacco shops, Hallmark Card and Gift Shops, and Perkins/Hallmark).
Stride Rite Corp....5 Cambridge Center, Cambridge, MA 02142...(617) 491-8800...A. Hiatt...manuf. & retailer children's footwear.
Sun Company, Inc....100 Matsonford Rd., Radnor, PA 19087...(215) 293-6000...R.P. Hauptfuhrer...petroleum.
Supermarkets General Corp....200 Milk St., Carteret, NJ 07008...(201) 499-3000...L. Lieberman...supermarkets (Pathmark), Rickel Home Centers.

Taft Broadcasting Co....1718 Young St., Cincinnati, OH 45210...(513) 721-1414...C.S. Mechem Jr......radio, TV broadcasting, TV cartoons (Hanna-Barbera), amusement parks.
Talley Industries, Inc....2702 N. 6th St., Phoenix, AZ 85008...(602) 957-7711...W.H. Mallender...clocks (West Clox, Seth Thomas), technical prods., apparel.
Tambrands Inc.... One Marcus Ave., Lake Success, NY 11042...(516) 358-8300...E. H. Shutt Jr...menstrual tampons (Tampax, Maxithins).
Tandy Corp....1800 One Tandy Center, Fort Worth, TX 76102...(817) 390-3700...J.V. Roach...consumer electronics retailing & mfg, Radio Shack.
Teledyne, Inc....1901 Ave. of the Stars, Los Angeles, CA 90067...(213) 277-3311...H. E. Singleton...electronics, aerospace prods., industrial prods., insurance, finance.
Tenneco, Inc....P.O. Box 2511, Houston, TX 77252...(713) 757-2131...J. L. Ketelsen...oil, natural gas pipelines, manuf.
Texaco Inc....2000 Westchester Ave., White Plains, NY 10650...(914) 253-4000...J.W. Kinnear...petroleum and petroleum prods.
Texas Air Corp....333 Clay St., Houston, TX 77002...(713) 658-9588...F.A. Lorenzo...air transportation (Continental, Eastern airlines).
Texas Instruments Inc....P.O. Box 225474, Dallas, TX 75265...(214) 995-2011...J.R. Junkins...electrical & electronics prods.

Textron Inc....40 Westminster St., Providence, RI 02903...(401) 421-2800...B.F. Dolan...aerospace, consumer, industrial, metal prods, consumer finance, insurance, management services.

Tidewater Inc....1440 Canal St., New Orleans, LA 70112...(504) 568-1010...J.P. Laborde...marine equip. and services for oil industry.

Time Inc.... Time & Life Bldg., New York, NY 10020...(212) 586-1212...J.R. Munro...magazine publisher (Time, Sports Illustrated, Fortune, Money, People), CATV (Home Box Office), publishing.

Tonka Corp....6000 Clearwater Dr., Minnetonka, MN 55343...(612) 936-3300...S.G. Shank...toy manuf.

Tootsie Roll Industries, Inc.,...7401 S. Cicero Ave., Chicago, IL 60629...(312) 838-3400...M.J. Gordon...candy (Tootsie Roll, Mason Dots, Mason Crows, Bonomo Turkish Taffy).

The Toro Company...811 Lyndale Ave. South, Bloomington, MN 55420...(612) 887-5900...S.F. Keating...lawn and turf maintenance, snow removal equipment.

Toys "R" Us...395 W. Passaic St., Rochelle Park, NJ 07662...(201) 845-5033...Charles Lazarus...toy retailer, clothing stores (Kids "R" Us).

Transamerica Corp....600 Montgomery St., San Francisco, CA 94111...(415) 983-4400...J.R. Harvey...insurance, financial, business services (Occidental Life Ins.).

Travelers Corp.... One Tower Sq., Hartford, CT 06183...(203) 277-0111...E. H. Budd...insurance.

Tribune Co....435 N. Michigan Ave., Chicago, IL 60611...(312) 222-3883...S.R. Cook...newpaper publishing, broadcasting, entertainment (Chicago Cubs baseball team).

Trinity Industries, Inc....2525 Stemmons Freeway, P.O. Box 10587, Dallas, TX 75207...(214) 631-4420...W.R. Wallace...manufactures variety of metal products.

TRW Inc....1900 Richmond Rd., Cleveland, OH 44124...(216) 291-7000...R.F. Mettler...car and truck operations, electronics, and space systems.

TW Services, Inc....605 3d Ave., New York, NY 10158...(212) 972-4700...L.E. Smart...food service, restaurants, nursing homes.

USAIR Group, Inc....1911 Jefferson Hwy., Arlington, VA 22002...(703) 892-7000...E.I. Colodny...air carrier of passengers, property, and mail.

UST Inc....100 W. Putnam Ave., Greenwich, CT 06830...(203) 661-1100...L.F. Bantle...smokeless tobacco (Copenhagen, Skoal, Happy Days), pipes, pipe tobacco.

USX Corp....600 Grant St., Pittsburgh, PA 15230...D.M. Roderick...steel manuf., oil & gas.

Unilever, N.V.... Burgemeester's Jacobplein 1, Rotterdam, The Netherlands...H.F. van der Hoven...soap, detergent, margarine, frozen food, toothpaste, tea, dried soups, ice cream (Lever Brothers, Lipton, Pond's Vaseline Intensive Care, Q-Tips, Cutex).

Union Carbide Corp.... Old Ridgebury Rd., Danbury, CT 06817...(203) 794-2000...R.D. Kennedy...chemicals, batteries (Eveready).

Union Pacific Corp....345 Park Ave., N.Y., NY 10154...(212) 418-7800...W.S. Cook...railroad, natural resources.

Unisys Corp.... Burroughs Place, Detroit, MI 48232...(313) 972-7000...W. Michael Blumenthal...business equip., data processing prods.

Uniroyal, Inc.... Middlebury, CT 06749...(203) 573-2000...Joseph P. Flannery...tires, chemical, plastic prods.

U.S. Home Corp....1800 W. Loop South, Houston, TX 77252...(713) 877-2311...G.H. Matters...leading homebuilder in U.S.

U.S. Leasing Int'l, Inc....733 Front Street, San Francisco, CA 94111...(415) 627-9000...D.E. Mundell...equipment leasing (autos, test instruments, office products, computer peripherals, health-care equipment).

United States Shoe Corp.... One Eastwood Dr., Cincinnati, OH 45227...(513) 527-7000...P. G. Barach...apparel, retailer (Casual Corner, J. Riggins), shoes (Red Cross, Joyce).

United Technologies Corp.... United Technologies Bldg., Hartford, CT 06101...(203) 728-7000...R.F. Daniell...aerospace, industrial prods. & services, Carrier Corp., Otis Elevator; Pratt & Whitney, Sikorsky Aircraft.

Univar, Corp....1600 Norton Building, Seattle, WA 98104...(206) 447-5911...J.W. Bernard...industrial and agricultural chemicals, laboratory and graphic arts products distributor, home furnishing supplies and fabrics distributors.

Universal Foods Corp....433 East Michigan St., Milwaukee, WI 53202...(414) 271-6755...J.L. Murray...yeast products, cheese products, dehydrated seasonings, food colors and flavors, imported gourmet foods.

Upjohn Co....7000 Portage Rd., Kalamazoo, MI 49001...(616) 323-4000...T. Cooper...pharmaceuticals (Motrin, Nuprin, Xanax, Halcion, Cleocin), chemicals, agricultural and health care prods.

VF Corp....1047 No. Park Rd., Wyomissing, PA 19610...(215) 378-1151...L.R. Pugh...apparel, Vanity Fair, Lee jeans, Bassett-Walker.

Vulcan Materials Co.... One Metroplex Dr., Birmingham, AL 35209...(205) 877-3000...H.A. Sklenar...construction materials, chemicals, metals.

Wal-Mart Stores Inc....702 W. 8th St., Bentonville, AR 72716...(501) 273-4000...S.M. Walton...discount dept. stores.

Walgreen Co....200 Wilmot Rd., Deerfield, IL 60015...(312) 940-2500...Charles R. Walgreen 3d...retail drug chain, restaurants (Wags).

Wang Laboratories, Inc.... One Industrial Ave., Lowell, MA 01851...A. Wang...word processors.

Warner Communications Inc....75 Rockefeller Plaza, N.Y., NY 10019...(212) 484-8000...Steven J. Ross...filmed entertainment, records & music publishing (Atlantic Records), book publishing (Atlantic Records, CATV system, consumer prods.

Warner-Lambert Co....201 Tabor Rd., Morris Plains, NJ 07950...(201) 540-2000...J.D. Williams...health care prods. (Benadryl), consumer prods. (Efferdent dental cleanser, Hall cough tablets, Schick razors, Clorets breath mints).

Washington Post Co....1150 15th St., N.W., Washington, DC 20071...(202) 223-6000...Katharine Graham...newspapers, magazines (Newsweek), TV stations.

Weis Markets, Inc....1000 South Second Street, Sunbury, PA 17801...(717) 286-4571...S. Weis...operates supermarkets, distributes frozen foods and grocery items.

Wells Fargo & Co....420 Montgomery St., San Francisco, CA 94163...(415) 396-0123...P. Hazen...banking.

Wendy's Intl., Inc....4288 W. Dublin-Granville, Dublin, OH 43017...(614) 764-3100...R. L. Barney...quick service restaurants.

West Point-Pepperell, Inc.... West Point, GA 31833...(404) 645-4000...J.L. Lanier, Jr...apparel, households and industrial textiles.

Westinghouse Electric Corp.... Westinghouse Bldg., Gateway Center, Pittsburgh, PA 15222...(412) 244-2000...D. D. Danforth...manuf. electrical, mechanical equip., radio and television stations.

Westvaco Corp....299 Park Avenue, New York, NY 10171...(212) 688-5000...D.L. Luke III...manufactures paper for graphic reproduction, communications, and packaging (largest producer of envelopes in the world).

Weyerhaeuser Co.... Tacoma, WA 98477...(206) 924-2345...George H. Weyerhaeuser...manuf., distribution of forest prods.

Whirlpool Corp.... Administrative Center, Benton Harbor, MI 49022...(616) 926-5000...D.R. Whitwam...major home appliances.

Willamette Industries, Inc....3800 1st Interstate Tower, Portland, OR 97201...(503) 227-5581...William Swindells Jr.... building materials and paper prods.

Winn-Dixie Stores, Inc....5050 Edgewood Ct., Jacksonville, FL 32203...(904) 783-5000...A.D. Davis...retail grocery chain.

Winnebago Industries, Inc....P.O. Box 152, Forest City, IA 50436...(515) 582-3535...G.W. Gilbert...manuf. of motor homes, recreation vehicles.

F.W. Woolworth Co....233 Broadway, N.Y., NY 10279...(212) 553-2000...H.E. Sells...variety stores, shoe stores (Kinney), men's clothing (Richman Brothers), children's apparel (Little Folk shop), athletic footwear (Foot Locker).

Wm. Wrigley, Jr. Co....410 N. Michigan Ave., Chicago, IL 60611...(312) 644-2121...William Wrigley...chewing gum.

Xerox Corp.... Stamford, CT 06904...(203) 329-8700...D. T. Kearns...equip. for reproduction, reduction, and transmission of printed information.

Zayre Corp....770 Cochituate Rd., Framingham, Mass. 01701...(617) 620-5000...M. Segall...discount department stores, off-price specialty shops (Zayre, Hit or Miss, T.J. Maxx).

Zenith Electronics Corp....1000 Milwaukee Ave., Glenview, IL 60025...(312) 391-7000...Jerry K. Pearlman...consumer electronic prods.

Interest Laws and Consumer Finance Loan Rates

Source: Revised by Christian T. Jones. Editor, Consumer Finance Law Bulletin, San Diego, Ca.

All states have laws regulating interest rates. These laws fix a legal or conventional rate which applies when there is no contract for interest. They also fix a general maximum contract rate, but there are so many exceptions that the general contract maximum actually applies only to exceptional cases. Also, federal law has preempted state limits on first home mortgages, subject to each state's right to reinstate its own law, and given depository institutions parity with other state lenders.

Legal rate of interest. The legal or conventional rate of interest applies to money obligations when no interest rate is contracted for and also to judgments. The rate is usually somewhat below the general interest rate.

General maximum contract rates. General interest laws in most states set the maximum rate between 8% and 16% per year. The general maximum is fixed by the state constitution at 5% over the Federal Reserve Discount rate in Arkansas. Loans to corporations are frequently exempted or subject to a higher maximum. In recent years, it has also been common to provide special rates for home mortgage loans and variable usury rates that are indexed to market rates.

Specific enabling acts. In many states special statutes permit industrial loan companies, second mortgage lenders, and banks to charge 1.5% a month or more. Laws regulating revolving loans, charge accounts and credit cards generally limit charges between 1.5% and 2% per month plus annual fees for credit cards. Rates for installment sales contracts in most states are somewhat higher. Credit unions may generally charge 1% to 1.5% a month. Pawnbrokers' rates vary widely. Savings and loan associations, and loans insured by federal agencies, are also specially regulated. A number of states allow regulated lenders to charge any rate agreed to with the customer either for all credit or over a certain dollar amount.

Consumer finance loan statutes. Most consumer finance loan statutes are based on early models drafted by the Russell Sage Foundation (1916-42) to provide small loans to wage earners under license and other protective regulations. Since 1969 the model has frequently been the Uniform Consumer Credit Code which applies to credit sales and loans for consumer purposes. In general, licensed lenders may charge 3% a month and reduced rates for additional amounts. An add-on of 17% ($17 per $100) per year yields about 2.5% per month if paid in equal monthly installments. Discount rates produce higher yields than add-on rates of the same amount. In the table below, unless otherwise stated, monthly and annual rates are based on reducing principal balances, annual add-on rates are based on the original principal for the full term, and two or more rates apply to different portions of balance or original principal.

States with consumer finance loan laws and the rates of charge as of Oct. 1, 1987:

Maximum monthly rates computed on unpaid balances, unless otherwise stated.

Ala.. . . Annual add-on: 15% to $750, 10% to $2,000 (min. 1.5% on unpaid balances), plus 2% fee (max. $20). Higher rates for loans up to $749. Over $2,000, any agreed rate.

Alas. . . 3% to $850, 2% to $10,000. Over $10,000, any agreed rate.

Ariz. . . To $1,000: 3%. Over $1,000: 3% to $500, 2% to $10,000. Over $10,000, any agreed rate.

Cal.. . . 2.5% to $225, 2% to $900, 1.5% to $1,650, 1% to $5,000 (1.6% min.). Over $2,500, any agreed rate. 5% fee (max. $50) to $2,500

Colo.. . 36% per year to $630, 21% to $2,100, 15% to $25,000 (21% min.).

Conn. . Annual Add-on: 17% to $600, 11% to $5,000; 11% over $1,800 to $5,000 for certain secured loans. Any agreed rate for second mortgages.

Del.. . . Any agreed rate.

D.C. . . 24% per year.

Fla.. . . 30% per year to $500, 24% to $1,000, 18% to $5,000; 18% per year on any amount over $5,000.

Ga.. . . 10% per year discount to 18 months, add-on to 36½ months; 8% fee to $600, 4% on excess plus $2 per month. Over $3,000, any agreed rate.

Ha.. . . 3.5% to $100, 2.5% to $300; 2% on entire balance over $300 or discount rates.

Ida.. . . Any agreed rate.

Ill.. . . . Any agreed rate.

Ind.. . . 36% per year to $780, 21% to $2,600, 15% to $25,000 (21% min.).

Ia. . . . 3% to $1,000, 2% to $2,800, 1.5% to $10,000; or equivalent flat rate. Over $10,000: 21% per year.

Kan. . . 36% per year to $600, 21% to $2,000, 14.45% to $25,000, 3% for real estate loans.

Ky.. . . 3% to $1,000, 2% to $3,000. Over $3,000, 2%.

La.. . . 36% per year to $1,400, 27% to $4,000, 24% to $7,000, 21% over $7,000, plus $25 fee.

Me.. . . 30% per year to $700, 21% to $2,000, 15% to $25,000 (18% min.).

Md.. . . 2.75% to $1,000, 2% to $2,000. Over $2,000, 2%.

Mass. . 23% per year plus $20 fee to $6,000; 18% over $6,000.

Mich.. . 31% per year to $500, 13% to $3,000 (18% min.); 18% for second mortgages.

Minn.. . 33% per year to $420, 19% over $420 (21.75% min.).

Miss.. . 36% per year to $1,000, 33% to $2,500, 24% to $5,000, 14% over $5,000. Over $25,000, 18%. 2% fee (max. $50).

Mo.. . . 2.218% to $1,200, 1.67% over $1,200, plus 5% fee (max. $15); 1.67% plus 2% for second mortgages.

Mont.. . Any agreed rate.

Neb. . . 24% per year to $1,000. 21% over, plus fee of 7% to $2,000 and 5% over (max. $500).

Nev. . . Any agreed rate.

N.H. . . 2% to $600, 1.5% to $1,500; Any agreed rate over $1,500 or for second mortgages.

N.J.. . . 30% per year to $5,000 or for second mortgages.

N.M. . . Any agreed rate.

N.Y. . . Any agreed rate.

N.C. . . 3% to $1,000, 1.5% to $7,500; 1.5% on entire amount to $10,000. 1.5% or variable plus 2% fee for second mortgages.

N.D. . . 2.5% to $250, 2% to $500, 1.75% to $750, 1.5% to $1,000; any agreed rate over $1,000.

Ohio . . 28% per year to $1,000, 22% to $3,000; 25% on entire amount over $3,000; plus fee.

Okla.. . 30% per annum to $690, 21% to $2,300, 15% to $45,000. (21% min.). Special rates to $100.

Ore. . . Any agreed rate.

Pa.. . . 9.5% per year discount to 48 months, 6% for remaining time plus 2% fee (max. $100); or 2% on unpaid balances; 1.85% for second mortgages over $5,000.

P.R. . . 24% per year.

R.I.. . . 3% to $300, 2.5% for loans between $300 and $800; 2% for larger loans to $5,000. 1.75% over $5,000.

S.C. . . Any agreed and posted rate.

S.D. . . Any agreed rate.

Tenn.. . Over $100, 24% per year or discount rates plus fees.

Texas . Annual add-on: 18% to $930, 8% to $7,750 or formula rate (max. 24% per year on unpaid balances.)

Utah . . Any agreed rate.

Vt. . . . 2% to $1,000, 1% to $3,000 (min. 1.5%); 1.5% for second mortgages.

Va.. . . 3% to $600, 2.25% to $1,800, 1.5% to $2,800; or annual add-on of 21% to $600, 17% to $1,800, 13% to $2,800; 2% fee. Any agreed rate over $2,800 for second mortgages, plus 2% fee.

Wash. . 2.5% to $500, 1.5% to $1,000, 1% to $2,500. Over $2,500, 25% per year or discount rates.

W.Va. . 36% per year to $500, 24% to $1,500, 18% to $2,000. Over $2,000, 27% per year to $2,000, 25% to $10,000, 18% on remainder.

Wis. . . Any agreed rate, to 10/31/87; therafter 23% per year to $3,000, 21% over $3,000.

Wyo.. . 36% per year to $1,000, 21% to $25,000. No limit over $25,000.

Shopping for Credit: Ask the Right Questions

Source: New York State Banking Department

Under federal law, all institutions that extend or arrange for the extension of consumer credit must give the borrower meaningful information about the cost of each loan. The cost must be expressed as the dollar amount of the interest or finance charge, and as the annual percentage rate computed on the amount financed.

To be sure the loan or credit agreement you are considering suits both your budget and your individual needs, shop around. Ask questions to compare and evaluate a lender's rate and services. For instance:

1. What is the annual percentage rate?
2. What is the total cost of the loan in dollars?
3. How long do you have to pay off the loan?
4. What are the number, amounts, and due dates of payments?
5. What is the cost of deferring or extending the time period of the loan?
6. What is the cost of late charges for overdue payments?
7. If you pay the loan off early, are there any prepayment penalties?
8. Does the loan have to be secured? If so, what collateral is required?
9. What is the cost of credit life or other insurance that is being offered or may be required?
10. Are there any other charges you may have to pay?

Fair Credit: What You Should Know

Source: Federal Trade Commission

Federal legislation has made it easier for you to be treated fairly in credit-related areas:

Billing. Don't let the anonymous computer get you down. The Fair Credit Billing Act states that, if you find an error in the amount of $50 or more in your credit card statement or department store revolving charge statement and you write to the company about it (on a separate sheet of paper, not the bill), the company must acknowledge your letter within 30 days and must resolve the dispute within 90 days.

Equal Credit. The Equal Credit Opportunity Act (ECOA) bans any discrimination according to sex or marital status in the granting of credit. Discrimination is also prohibited on the basis of age, race, color, religion, national origin, or receipt of public assistance payments.

However, the creditor may ask questions relating to these areas if they have bearing on your credit worthiness. The creditor does have the right to determine whether you are willing and able to repay your debts. For instance, the creditor can ask you if you are "married," "unmarried," or "separated" if, and only if, (1) you are applying jointly with your spouse; (2) your spouse will be an authorized user of the account; (3) you live in a community property state or you list assets located in a community property state. Similarly, a creditor may ask about alimony, child support, and separate maintenance if, and only if, you are depending on these as sources to establish your ability to repay your debts. In this case, the creditor may ask whether there is a court order that requires the payments or may inquire about the length of time and regularity of the payments, as well as your ex-spouse's credit history.

The ECOA also requires that if you are turned down for credit, the creditor must tell you the reason you were turned down.

Mail-Order Merchandise. By law, you have the right to receive merchandise ordered through the mail within 30 days, unless another deadline has been specified. Promises such as "one week" or "4 to 6 weeks" must be met. If either the seller's or the FTC's deadline is missed, you have the right to cancel and have all your money returned. If you run into a problem with late or non-delivery, contact the Federal Trade Commission for help.

Managing Credit: How Much Debt is Safe?

Source: Citibank

It is extremely important for consumers to keep close track of their individual use of credit and debt.

Before you make any new purchases that involve moving income from the optional spending part of your budget to your fixed budget as a loan to be repaid, you must be sure that you have those extra dollars and that you can do without them each month.

How Much Average Debt is Safe?

Once you've decided to apply for credit, you face the most-asked question about consumer debt: how much is safe?

There is no simple answer that applies to each consumer's situation. Most experts, today, avoid general rules of thumb.

Don't be misled by the percents of gross income that lenders may use to decide how much institutional risk they run in any specific application for a loan. The lending institution can use only gross income and loan-commitment averages to estimate its own average risk, and cannot know how any individual consumer will actually repay. Only you can gauge that, based on your own habits, values, and needs.

How do you determine what you can handle? To help decide, you must know at a given time how many dollars you have for optional spending, and then how many of those dollars you can move into fixed repayments.

Here's one technique for determining how many optional dollars you have:

1. Write down your annual take-home income after deductions (for taxes, etc.) and divide by 12 to get your monthly take-home income.
2. From the monthly figure, subtract all your current monthly fixed expenses—those to which you are currently committed or must cover over the next year. Include your gasoline and car costs, other transportation, heating, utilities, food, rent, or mortgage (but no other loan repayments), real estate taxes, insurance, etc.
3. Next, total your monthly nonmortgage loan repayments and subtract them from the previous amount.

The total figure you're left with is your monthly optional spending amount. Now you must consider how comfortably you're managing with this amount. Consider that amount less the new monthly repayment. Can you still manage on the remaining amount, or should you wait until your take-home income goes up or your present debt loan goes down?

Are You Headed for Financial Trouble?

Although there is no dependable formula for determining your individual debt ratio, there are certain clear warning signals that you may have reached or have already passed it.

(continued)

Consider the following signals and, if several of them describe your financial situation, it may be time to look for help.

1. Your checkbook balance is getting lower and lower each month.
2. You don't seem to be able to make it from month to month without writing overdrafts on your checking account.
3. You pay only the minimum due or even less on your charge accounts each month.
4. You have borrowed on your life insurance and see little possibility of paying it back soon.
5. Your savings account is slowly disappearing or has completely disappeared, and you're not able to put any of your regular income into savings.
6. You manage to get through each month by depending on undependable extra income like overtime or odd jobs.
7. You find yourself depending on credit cards for day-to-day living expenses and using cash advances to pay off other debts.
8. You are behind on one or more of your installment payments.
9. You don't really know how much money you owe.
10. You are receiving overdue notices or phone calls from creditors.
11. Family disputes over money are growing.
12. You occasionally juggle paying bills, paying one creditor while giving excuses to another.
13. You've had to ask creditors for extensions on due dates.
14. You've taken out loans to pay debts, or taken out a debt consolidation loan.
15. You are at or near the limit on the credit lines allowed on your credit cards.
16. When you use credit, you try to get it for the longest time period and the lowest payments without considering how much more this will cost you in interest.
17. You must borrow money to pay bills you can anticipate, like quarterly property taxes.
18. Although you regularly pay all of your debts, you are forced to continue living on credit and, as a result, your debt loan never really shrinks or is even increasing.

What can you do if you find yourself in financial trouble? The first step is to drastically cut your optional spending. Put yourself and your family on a crash tight-cash program until you can stabilize your financial situation. Also, you may need to turn some assets into cash and apply it to your debts.

If these attempts fail, get in touch with your creditors. Candidly, explain your situation. Some of them may agree to a longer repayment schedule to insure that they get their money back and that they will keep you as a customer. You may pay more in interest, but you'll have a better credit record.

If you're still in trouble, you probably need good financial counseling.

How to Check Your Credit File

Any individual can investigate the contents of his or her credit file by directly contacting one or more of the approximately 2,000 credit bureaus, or consumer credit clearinghouses, in the United States. The nearest ones can be found by calling a local Better Business Bureau or by looking in the telephone Yellow Pages under "Credit Rating or Reporting Agencies."

Although the Fair Credit Reporting Act requires that a bureau give a person no more than an oral or written credit history review, many bureaus will go beyond the technical requirements of the law and furnish the same computer-generated compilation of facts that they give the banks, retailers and other companies that subscribe to their service. An individual who has been denied credit on the basis of negative information from a credit bureau can obtain this review without charge within 30 days of the denial. Otherwise, the fee typically ranges from $8 to $12 for such a credit check.

After inspecting this record of past credit behavior, a consumer can question any item believed to be inaccurate, misleading or vague. The credit bureau must then investigate and remove any item that cannot be substantiated.

When a bureau affirms, rather than removes, a questionable item, an individual can present a 100-word explanation that must be placed in his or her file. And whenever an adverse item is deleted from the file or an explantory statement is added to one, a consumer may request that the credit bureau inform every credit grantor who received a report within the last six months.

Credit Card Rates

(As of Aug., 1987)

(Prepared by Christian T. Jones, San Diego, CA)

Nearly all states have special laws dealing with rates charged for credit cards issued by state banks and other financial institutions. Although some state laws apply only to banks, under Federal parity law, the same charges can be made by other financial institutions. A national bank can charge the highest rates allowed for revolving credit extended by any other creditor in the state where the bank is located and such rates may also be charged to residents of any other state.

Ala.	21-18% @ $750; no limit over $2,000; $15 annual fee.
Alas.	18-10.5% @ $1,000; 3% cash advance fee (max. $12).
Ariz.	No limit.
Ark.	5% over FRB discount rate (max. 17%).
Cal.	No limit.
Colo.	21%.
Conn.	15%; $10 annual fee.
D.C.	24%.
Del.	No limit.
Fla.	18%.
Ga.	No limit on rate or fee.
Ha.	18%.
Ida.	No limit.
Ill.	No limit; $20 annual fee.
Ind.	36-21-15%, @ $780, $2,600; or 21%.
Ia.	No limit.
Kan.	18-14.45% @ $1,000.
Ky.	21%; $20 annual fee.
La.	18%; 4% cash advance and $12 annual fee.
Me.	18%.
Md.	24%; 2% fee.
Mass.	23% to $6,000; no limit over $6,000; $20 annual fee.
Mich.	18%; no limit on annual fee.
Minn.	18%; $50 annual fee.
Miss.	21%; or 18% plus $12 annual fee.
Mo.	22-10% @ $1,000.
Mont.	No limit.
Neb.	No limit; $20 annual fee or no limit for premium card.
Nev.	No limit.
N.H.	No limit.
N.J.	30%; $15 annual fee or $50 over $5,000.
N.M.	No limit.
N.Y.	No limit on rate or annual fee to 6/30/93.
N.C.	18%; $20 annual fee.
N.D.	No limit.
Oh.	25% to 1/1/89.
Okla.	30-21-15% @ $690, $2,300; or 21%.
Ore.	No limit.
Pa.	12% loans; 15% purchases; $15 annual fee.
P.R.	17% loans; 26% purchases.
R.I.	18%.
S.C.	No limit.
S.D.	No limit.
Tenn.	24%.
Tex.	18%.
Utah	No limit.
Vt.	18%; no limit on annual fee.
Va.	No limit.
Wash.	12% or 4% over U.S. T-bill rate.
W.Va.	18%.
Wis.	No limit to 10/31/87; thereafter 18%.
Wyo.	36-21% @ $25,000; no limit over $25,000.

Options for Savers

	Minimum Deposit	Maturity	Comments
Passbook savings	None	None	Competitive interest rate; money can be withdrawn at any time.
Time deposits	$2,500*	Varies	Savings earn market yields; checking privileges; penalty for early withdrawal.
Money-market fund accounts	$1,000*	None	Money-market rate paid on savings; withdrawals and transfers allowed.
Certificates of deposit	Varies	Varies	Savings earn market yields; penalty for early withdrawal; no check writing.
Long-term certificates	Varies	2½ years +	Savings locked up for long time; savers can shop around for best yields. Interest compounded.
Individual Retirement Accts.	Varies	Varies	Interest income is deferred from federal income taxes until money is withdrawn; $2,000 maximum individual contribution.
Money-market mutual funds	$100-$1,000	None	Market yields paid on funds that can be withdrawn at any time; checks can be written; no federal deposit insurance.
Bond funds	Varies	None	Shares can be easily resold but lose value if interest rates rise.
Tax-exempt bond funds	Varies	None	Interest income is exempt from federal taxes; shares lose value if interest rates rise.
Stock funds	Varies	None	Small investors can diversify their holdings; shares lose value if stock prices fall.
Treasury bills	$10,000	6 months	Market yields and safety; easily sold; not subject to state and local income taxes.
U.S. savings bonds	$25	5 years	Safe; long term.
Corporate bonds	$1,000	10-30 years	Market yields plus liquidity; investment will lose value if interest rates rise.
Common stocks	—	None	Potential for dividends, long-term capital gains; risk of capital loss.
Zero-coupon bonds	$1,000 is usual minimum	6 months to 10 years +	Yields fixed for term of investment; backed by U.S. securities and sold at a deep discount; no interest is received until notes mature and are redeemed at face value.

*None if account is an IRA or Keogh Plan.

Year-End Assets and Liabilities of Individuals in the U.S.[1]

Source: Federal Reserve System

(billions of dollars)

	1960	1965	1970	1975	1980	1984	1985	1986
Total financial assets	**1007.6**	**1504.7**	**1971.7**	**2610.7**	**4654.5**	**6877.8**	**8013.0**	**8946.2**
Checkable deposits & currency	91.5	107.3	137.2	187.1	293.3	401.4	446.5	545.5
Time & savings deposits	164.0	288.4	426.3	764.1	1275.3	1884.3	2024.3	2129.1
Money market fund shares	—	—	—	3.7	74.4	209.7	207.5	228.3
Securities	512.1	766.9	928.3	914.6	1608.9	2285.9	2922.3	3358.5
U.S. savings bonds	45.6	49.7	52.1	67.4	72.5	74.5	79.8	93.3
Other U.S. Treasury securities	25.9	26.3	32.8	51.1	133.1	358.2	347.9	283.0
U.S. Govt. agency securities	2.3	3.7	20.9	12.2	52.8	99.0	162.2	221.0
Tax-exempt obligations	30.8	36.4	46.0	68.1	88.3	190.2	249.6	260.7
Corporate & foreign bonds	10.0	9.5	36.2	65.9	56.2	38.5	52.4	71.7
Open-market paper	2.0	5.6	11.7	8.9	39.3	34.6	82.4	78.5
Mutual fund shares	17.0	35.2	46.8	43.0	63.7	162.5	283.0	487.6
Other corporate equities	378.4	600.4	681.8	598.0	1103.0	1328.2	1665.0	1862.8
Private life insurance res.	78.8	98.9	123.3	158.5	207.4	236.1	246.5	256.7
Private insured pension res.	18.9	27.3	41.0	72.3	172.0	331.6	400.0	468.8
Private noninsured pen. res.	38.1	73.6	110.4	212.6	467.4	659.1	757.4	826.3
Govt. insurance & pen. res.	40.2	60.8	95.2	154.7	283.6	496.5	591.0	682.8
Miscellaneous financial assets	63.1	81.5	109.9	143.1	272.2	373.4	417.3	450.2
Total liabilities	**280.4**	**444.8**	**650.0**	**1090.8**	**2046.4**	**2973.7**	**3358.5**	**3735.6**
Mtg. debt on nonfarm homes	137.4	214.4	290.2	469.7	943.3	1303.4	1450.0	1644.5
Other mortgage debt[2]	35.7	65.3	119.4	247.8	422.4	647.3	731.9	831.8
Consumer credit	65.0	103.1	143.1	219.6	375.9	569.9	666.5	723.0
Security credit	5.4	9.1	10.4	12.1	27.2	34.6	51.3	59.9
Policy loans	5.7	8.3	17.0	25.5	42.6	55.6	55.5	55.3
Other debt[2]	31.2	44.6	69.9	116.1	235.0	362.9	403.4	421.1

(1) Combined statement for households, farm business, and nonfarm noncorporate business. (2) Includes corporate farms.

Life Insurance: Facts You Need to Know

Source: American Council of Life Insurance

For many people, one of the most important purchases they can make—and one they need to be well-informed about—is life insurance.

Most insurance companies are currently simplifying their life insurance plans in order that consumers might have a better idea of what they're really buying. In addition to making policies easier to read and understand, the companies are developing new premium payment methods to lower the financial burden of insurance purchase. Sixty two percent of all life insurance is bought by people between the ages of 20–39, and 36% by people 40 years and over and 2% by people under the age of 20. The average premium per policy is $346 and such innovations as monthly payment plans (instead of annual or semi-annual, lump sum payments) are becoming common.

(continued)

There are 2 basic types of life insurance policies: (1) term insurance and (2) whole life insurance. All other kinds of life insurance are variations of these 2 types. *Term insurance* is protection that insures for a specified and finite period of time. It pays a benefit only if you die during the period covered by the policy. *Whole life insurance* (often referred to as straight or permanent life) is protection that can be kept in force as long as you live. Whole life insurance builds "cash value," which increases over the years on a tax-deferred basis. The other variations on term and whole life insurance are: Universal life, Excess Interest Whole life, Variable life, and Adjustable life.

Life Insurance as an Investment?

There's a good deal of controversy about the value of insurance as an investment. Whole life policies, with their fixed premiums and cash value that grows over the course of the years (that can be collected when you decide to terminate the policy or borrowed against up to the current value of the policy), are considered by many to be an effective way to protect a family financially and invest wisely. Term insurance, on the other hand, is a much less expensive type of insurance, and achieves much the same purpose as whole life (of course, only during the "term" of its existence). But there is no cash surrender value or borrowing privilege.

Since both current protection and a good future investment are necessary, the consumer must carefully weigh the advantages of life insurance before making a purchase.

How to Read a Life Insurance Policy

All life insurance policies, regardless of type, can be divided into 3 parts:

1. **Summary**—This is the basic agreement of the policy. It includes the name of the insured, the face amount of the policy, the beneficiary's name, and premium amount, as well as the type of policy, any riders (additions to the policy you might have bought), and whether or not the cost of the insurance has been figured on a guaranteed basis or a participating basis.
2. **Details**—Approximately 10 clauses giving the specifics of the policy's operation, such as due date of premium, value of the policy when you surrender it for either cash or a loan, the amount paid at the time of your death, and options for how your beneficiary can receive that money are included.
3. **Application**—This is a two-fold section that gives personal information about you and lets you make some decisions about how the policy will work. Among typical items covered are what happens in the event of your suicide, whether you engage in dangerous sports or occupations, what your rights are under the policy, etc.

As with any legal document, it is important to read and understand what you are purchasing. If you need further information, a good source is the American Council of Life Insurance, 1001 Pennsylvania Ave., N.W., Washington, DC 20004.

Home Buyer's Glossary

Amortization: The gradual repayment of a mortgage over time, usually according to a predetermined schedule.

Appraisal: An opinion or estimate of the value of property, usually made by lenders before they will determine how much of a mortgage they will extend.

Assumable mortgage: The purchaser takes ownership of real estate encumbered by an existing mortgage and assumes responsibility as the guarantor for the unpaid balance of the mortgage.

Balloon payment: The final payment on a loan, usually substantially larger than previous payments, which repays the loan in full.

Binder: A preliminary and temporary agreement between the seller and the buyer, generally agreeing to the price of a house before a formal contract.

Broker: Usually, a licensed agent of, and paid by, the seller to serve as an intermediary in real estate transactions.

Closing: The day of judgment, when after writing numerous checks to cover various fees, the title passes to the buyer.

Commission: The fee paid by a seller to a broker for the sale of the house. Fee is negotiable.

Condominium: A form of ownership, not a kind of development, in which the owner gets title to a housing unit and an interest in the common areas.

Cooperative apartment: A type of ownership in which buyers get shares in the cooperative corporation that owns the building. Those shares give the buyer a proprietary lease on an apartment in that building.

Deed: A written document that conveys title in the property.

Equity: The value of property minus the mortgage and other liens against it.

Escrow: Money paid monthly to the lender, along with the mortgage payment, for use in paying taxes and sometimes insurance. The lender keeps the funds separately and pays bills when due.

Freddie Mac: The Federal Home Loan Mortgage Corp., a major secondary mortgage market agency that buys mortgages from lenders, allowing them to make new loans with the proceeds.

FHA: The Federal Housing Administration, a division of the Department of Housing and Urban Development that insures, but does not make, mortgages.

Fannie Mae: Federal National Mortgage Association, the largest secondary mortgage agency.

Ginnie Mae: Government National Mortgage Association, a government-owned secondary market agency that buys FHA-insured loans from lenders.

Indexing: Adjusting the interest rate on a loan in accordance with the movements of an index or economic indicator, i.e., the U.S. Treasury bill rate or the consumer price index.

Interest: Money paid for the use of money. There are two kinds of interest. Simple interest is interest that is earned and paid. Compound interest is the accumulated interest that is added to the principal amount.

Lien: A right to property obtained as collateral to a loan or debt. A mortgage is a lien.

Mortgage: A written pledge of property as collateral for a loan.

Origination Fee: A fee paid by a borrower for the cost of evaluating and documenting a loan.

Points: Additional payments made by a borrower to a lender; a point equals 1 percent of the loan.

Prepayment penalty: An extra fee charged for paying off a mortgage before it is due.

Principal: The total amount of a mortgage debt. The amount upon which the interest is computed.

Title: Evidence of a person's ownership of a piece of property.

100 Million Housing Units

According to the U.S. Bureau of the Census, there are 100 million housing units in the nation (as of March 1987). While the bureau made no effort to locate the particular house or apartment that is the 100 millionth, it said that it probably is a single-family home in the South, since two-thirds of new housing are one-unit structures, and half of those built since 1980 have been in the South. In 1940, the first time the Census Bureau made such a count, they found 37.3 million dwelling units.

Owners occupy 57.3 percent of the dwellings, a drop from the 1980 peak of 64.4 percent. The average household is 2.67 people, and they have more than two rooms apiece in their homes. It was found that 2.4 percent of housing units lack complete private plumbing, compared to 45 percent in 1940.

The estimated value of all 100 million housing units in the United States is $5 trillion.

Mortgages: Alternatives to the Long-term Fixed-rate Loan

Source: Federal Home Loan Bank Board

At one time the only type mortgage generally available in most parts of the U.S. was the long-term fixed-rate mortgage which had identical monthly payments and a term of 25 to 30 years. Lately, new mortgage forms have been developed, which have more flexible payment schedules and/or adjustable interest rates. These mortgages are described below.

Graduated-Payment Mortgage:
The graduated-payment mortgage (GPM) has a fixed interest rate, but the payments start out at a lower level than on a fixed-rate mortgage. The payments on a GPM increase at a known rate during the early years of the loan. On the most popular GPM plan, the payments increase at 7½ percent each year for the first 5 years of the loan. Payments on a GPM ultimately rise to a level higher than on a comparable fixed-payment mortgage.

Because the payments on a GPM start out at a low level, they may be insufficient to pay all the interest owed. That portion of the monthly interest in excess of the monthly payment is added to the loan balance. The outstanding balance on most GPM's actually increases for the first several years. This addition to the loan balance is called negative amortization.

A GPM is advantageous for a first-time homeowner who cannot, at the outset, handle the payments of a conventional loan, but hopes to be able to when his income rises.

Pledged-Account Mortgage:
The pledged-account mortgage (PAM) is a special type of GPM. On most GPM plans the low initial payments are insufficient to pay all the interest owed. On a PAM, that portion of the interest due that is not covered by the monthly payment is deducted from a savings account pledged by the borrower. A part of the borrower's down payment is used to establish the savings account which is then pledged over to the lender. Some, but not all graduated payment mortgages have the pledged account feature.

Adjustable-Rate Mortgages:
Adjustable-rate mortgages are the newest and most complex of the new mortgage forms. The common feature of adjustable-rate mortgages is that the interest rate is not fixed and will vary according to some interest rate index that is selected at the time the loan is originated. Lenders are not required to increase the interest rate on the mortgage as the index increases, but they are required to lower the interest rate if the index decreases. Adjustable-rate mortgage contracts may contain limitations on the minimum and maximum size of an interest rate change.

Depending upon a particular lender's adjustable-rate mortgage plan, a change in the interest rate may result in a change in the monthly payment, the term of the loan, the outstanding balance of the loan, or some combination of these. Some lenders offer plans in which the interest rate can change every 3 or 6 months, but the payment changes every 3 years. Under such a plan an increase in the interest rate may mean that the monthly payment is insufficient to pay all the interest due that month. When this happens the unpaid interest will be added to the loan balance. Negative amortization can occur on adjustable-rate mortgages if payments are adjusted less frequently than the interest rate.

Graduated-Payment Adjustable-Rate Mortgage:
The graduated-payment adjustable-rate mortgage (GPARM) combines the scheduled payment increase feature of the GPM with an adjustable interest rate. All of the variations involve a deferral of some of the interest owed during the early years of the loan. Some plans have payments rising by a set amount each year for the first several years; other plans fix the low payments for the first 3 or 5 years. There are a limitless number of possible GPARM variations.

Wraparound Mortgages:
The wraparound mortgage is a technique by which a homebuyer can assume a low interest rate mortgage from the seller. Suppose a buyer needs a $50,000 mortgage and the previous owner has an assumable mortgage with a relatively low interest rate and a remaining balance of $30,000. The buyer might obtain a wraparound mortage for $50,000. The payments to the wraparound lender must be large enough to continue to make payments on the assumed mortgage and to amortize the additional $20,000 loan. The advantage to the buyer is that the "blended" interest rate is lower than the new mortgage rates and the payments to the wraparound lender are lower than the payments on a new $50,000 mortgage at current interest rates.

Shared-Appreciation Mortgage:
A shared-appreciation mortgage (SAM) is a mortgage loan in which the borrower agrees to share the appreciation, or increase in value, of the property with the lender in return for an interest rate lower than that on a standard mortgage. SAMs have a contingent interest feature; a portion of the total interest due is contingent upon the appreciation of the property. At either the sale or transfer of the property, or the refinancing or maturity of the loan, the borrower must pay the lender a share of the appreciation of the property securing the loan. Payments on SAMs are based on a long amortization schedule, but the loan may become due at the end of 5 to 10 years.

The borrower and the lender jointly determine the size of the interest rate discount, the term of the loan, and the share of the appreciation due to the lender. The amount of appreciation is unknown at the time of origination, hence the total interest due and the effective interest rate are also uncertain. Although SAMs have a relatively low initial payment, the household's mortgage payment could increase very significantly if the lender's share of the appreciation and remaining principal balance had to be refinanced at market rate. At the current time, SAMs are offered by relatively few lenders.

Reverse Mortgages:
Reverse mortgages, often called reverse-annuity mortgages, are not financing techniques but rather a means by which elderly homeowners may convert some of their accumulated housing equity into a monthly stream of cash payments. Reverse mortgages may be structured as single-distribution or periodic distribution plans, and in some cases a single-premium annuity is purchased with the distribution. Reverse mortgages can provide significant monthly cash payments to single people over age 75.

Interest Rates
Interest rates on mortgage loans dropped to their lowest level in almost 9 years in March 1987, according to a report by the Federal Home Loan Bank Board. Lenders were offering, on average, 9.48 percent for fixed-rate mortgages, down from 11.36 percent a year earlier.

Adjustable-rate loans, with limits on rate changes, dropped to 8.43 percent from 10.05 percent a year earlier.

Mortgage Payment Tables

Source: *The Mortgage Money Guide*, Federal Trade Commission

8% Annual Percent Rate

Monthly Payments (Principal and Interest)*

Amount Financed	10 Years	15 Years	20 Years	25 Years	30 Years
$ 25,000	303.32	238.91	209.11	192.95	183.44
30,000	363.98	286.70	250.93	231.54	220.13
35,000	424.65	334.48	292.75	270.14	256.82
40,000	485.31	382.26	334.58	308.73	293.51
45,000	545.97	430.04	376.40	347.32	330.19
50,000	606.64	477.83	418.22	385.91	366.88
60,000	727.97	573.39	501.86	463.09	440.26
70,000	849.29	668.96	585.51	540.27	513.64
80,000	970.62	764.52	669.15	617.45	587.01
90,000	1091.95	860.09	752.80	694.63	660.39
100,000	1213.28	955.65	836.44	771.82	733.76

9% Annual Percent Rate

Monthly Payments (Principal and Interest)*

Amount Financed	10 Years	15 Years	20 Years	25 Years	30 Years
$ 25,000	316.69	253.57	224.93	209.80	201.16
30,000	380.03	304.28	269.92	251.76	241.39
35,000	443.36	354.99	314.90	293.72	281.62
40,000	506.70	405.71	359.89	335.68	321.85
45,000	570.04	456.42	404.88	377.64	362.08
50,000	633.38	507.13	449.86	419.60	402.31
60,000	760.05	608.56	539.84	503.52	482.77
70,000	886.73	709.99	629.81	587.44	563.24
80,000	1013.41	811.41	719.78	671.36	643.70
90,000	1140.08	912.84	809.75	755.28	724.16
100,000	1266.76	1014.27	899.73	839.20	804.62

10% Annual Percentage Rate

Monthly Payments (Principal and Interest)*

Amount Financed	10 Years	15 Years	20 Years	25 Years	30 Years
$ 25,000	330.38	268.65	241.26	227.18	219.39
30,000	396.45	322.38	289.51	272.61	263.27
35,000	462.53	376.11	337.76	318.05	307.15
40,000	528.60	429.84	386.01	363.48	351.03
45,000	594.68	483.57	434.26	408.92	394.91
50,000	660.75	537.30	482.51	454.35	438.79
60,000	792.90	644.76	579.01	545.22	526.54
70,000	925.06	752.22	675.52	636.09	614.30
80,000	1057.20	859.68	772.02	726.96	702.06
90,000	1189.36	967.14	868.52	817.83	789.81
100,000	1321.51	1074.61	965.02	908.70	877.57

11% Annual Percentage Rate

Monthly Payments (Principal and Interest)*

Amount Financed	10 Years	15 Years	20 Years	25 Years	30 Years
$ 25,000	344.38	284.15	258.05	245.03	238.08
30,000	413.25	340.98	309.66	294.03	285.70
35,000	482.13	397.81	361.27	343.04	333.31
40,000	551.00	454.64	412.88	392.05	380.93
45,000	619.88	511.47	464.48	441.05	428.55
50,000	688.75	568.30	516.09	490.06	476.16
60,000	826.50	681.96	619.31	588.07	571.39
70,000	964.25	795.62	722.53	686.08	666.63
80,000	1102.00	909.28	825.75	784.09	761.86
90,000	1239.75	1022.94	928.97	882.10	857.09
100,000	1377.50	1136.60	1032.19	980.11	952.32

*For loans that fully pay off the debt over the loan term.

12% Annual Percentage Rate

Monthly Payments (Principal and Interest)*

Amount Financed	10 Years	15 Years	20 Years	25 Years	30 Years
$ 25,000	358.68	300.05	275.28	263.31	257.16
30,000	430.42	360.06	330.33	315.97	308.59
35,000	502.15	420.06	385.39	368.63	360.02
40,000	573.89	480.07	440.44	421.29	411.45
45,000	645.62	540.08	495.49	473.96	462.88
50,000	717.36	600.09	550.55	526.62	514.31
60,000	860.83	720.11	660.66	631.93	617.17
70,000	1004.30	840.12	770.77	737.26	720.03
80,000	1147.77	960.14	880.87	842.58	822.90
90,000	1291.24	1080.15	990.98	947.90	925.75
100,000	1434.71	1200.17	1101.09	1053.23	1028.62

13% Annual Percentage Rate

Monthly Payments (Principal and Interest)*

Amount Financed	10 Years	15 Years	20 Years	25 Years	30 Years
$ 25,000	373.28	316.32	292.90	281.96	276.55
30,000	447.94	379.58	351.48	338.36	331.86
35,000	522.59	442.84	410.06	394.75	387.17
40,000	597.25	506.10	468.64	451.14	442.48
45,000	671.90	569.36	527.21	507.53	497.79
50,000	746.56	632.63	585.79	563.92	553.10
60,000	895.87	759.15	702.95	676.71	663.72
70,000	1045.18	885.67	820.11	789.49	774.34
80,000	1194.49	1012.20	937.27	902.27	884.96
90,000	1343.80	1138.72	1054.42	1015.05	995.58
100,000	1493.11	1265.25	1171.58	1127.84	1106.20

14% Annual Percentage Rate

Monthly Payments (Principal and Interest)*

Amount Financed	10 Years	15 Years	20 Years	25 Years	30 Years
$ 25,000	388.17	332.94	310.89	300.95	296.22
30,000	465.80	399.53	373.06	361.13	355.47
35,000	543.44	466.11	435.24	421.32	414.71
40,000	621.07	532.70	497.41	481.51	473.95
45,000	698.70	599.29	559.59	541.70	533.20
50,000	776.34	665.88	621.77	601.89	592.44
60,000	931.60	799.05	746.12	722.26	710.93
70,000	1086.87	932.22	870.47	842.64	829.42
80,000	1242.14	1065.40	994.82	963.01	947.90
90,000	1397.40	1198.57	1119.17	1083.38	1066.38
100,000	1552.67	1331.75	1243.53	1203.77	1184.88

15% Annual Percentage Rate

Monthly Payments (Principal and Interest)*

Amount Financed	10 Years	15 Years	20 Years	25 Years	30 Years
$ 25,000	403.34	349.90	329.90	320.21	316.12
30,000	484.01	419.88	395.04	384.25	379.34
35,000	564.68	489.86	460.88	448.30	442.56
40,000	645.34	559.84	526.72	512.34	505.78
45,000	726.11	629.82	592.56	576.38	569.00
50,000	806.68	699.80	658.40	640.42	632.23
60,000	968.01	839.76	790.08	768.50	758.67
70,000	1129.35	979.72	921.76	896.59	885.12
80,000	1290.68	1119.67	1053.44	1024.67	1011.56
90,000	1452.63	1259.63	1185.11	1152.75	1138.00
100,000	1613.35	1399.59	1316.79	1280.84	1264.45

Condominiums and Cooperatives

Source: U.S. Dept. of Housing and Urban Development

The condominium and the cooperative are legal forms that permit multiple ownership of a multi-family building or complex. In the United States, each form is defined by the states, so that details of laws governing condominium and cooperative formation and operation vary from place to place.

Condominium: a housing unit in a multi-family building or complex owned by an individual, who also owns a partial interest in the common areas of the building or complex.

Cooperative: a nonprofit housing corporation in which individual households own shares entitling them to live in a particular unit in a multi-family building or complex and to use the common areas and facilities of the building or complex.

Median Price of Single-Family Homes

Source: National Association of Realtors

The medial sale price for existing single-family homes rose 7.4 percent in the first quarter of 1987 from the same period in 1986.

City[1]	Median price first quarter 1986	1987	Pct. chng.
Akron, Oh.	$51,100	$54,700	+7.0%
Albany, N.Y.	67,500	80,100	+18.7%
Albuquerque, N.M.	77,600	83,100	+7.1%
Orange Co., Cal.	138,000	156,000	+13.1%
Baltimore, Md.	71,600	81,000	+13.1%
Baton Rouge, La.	73,600	68,300	−7.2%
Birmingham, Ala.	67,100	67,500	+0.6%
Boston, Mass.	145,600	170,000	+16.8%
Buffalo, N.Y.	49,700	55,600	+11.9%
Chicago, Ill.	82,000	85,700	+4.5%
Cincinnati, Oh.	62,100	63,800	+2.7%
Columbus, Oh.	62,600	66,900	+6.9%
Dallas/Ft. Worth, Tex.	93,400	93,200	−0.2%
Denver, Col.	84,600	89,900	+6.3%
Des Moines, Ia.	52,700	55,900	+6.1%
Detroit, Mich.	54,000	64,300	+19.1%
El Paso, Tex.	57,200	58,000	+1.4%
Ft. Lauderdale, Fla.	72,600	76,600	+5.5%
Grand Rapids, Mich.	48,900	51,700	+5.7%
Hartford, Conn.	106,400	136,600	+28.4%
Houston, Tex.	70,400	64,700	−8.1%
Indianapolis, Ind.	55,700	61,600	+10.6%
Jacksonville, Fla.	58,900	62,700	+6.5%
Kansas City, Mo.	65,700	74,200	+12.9%
Las Vegas, Nev.	74,600	76,100	+2.0%
Los Angeles, Cal.	120,400	130,100	+8.1%
Louisville, Ky.	48,100	52,100	+8.3%

City[1]	Median price First quarter 1986	1987	Pct. chng.
Memphis, Tenn.	66,300	70,600	+6.5%
Miami/Hialeah, Fla.	78,500	75,300	−4.1%
Milwaukee, Wis.	67,600	67,800	+0.3%
Minneapolis, Minn.	76,300	80,400	+5.4%
Nashville, Tenn.	68,400	73,100	+6.9%
New York, N.Y.	147,200	169,400	+15.1%
Oklahoma City, Okla.	62,800	62,400	−0.6%
Omaha, Neb.	58,600	57,800	−1.4%
Orlando, Fla.	70,300	73,600	+4.7%
Philadelphia, Pa.	72,200	79,800	+10.5%
Phoenix, Ariz.	76,200	78,400	+2.9%
Portland, Ore.	59,900	62,700	+4.7%
Providence, R.I.	71,900	101,300	+40.9%
Rochester, N.Y.	66,300	69,500	+4.8%
St. Louis, Mo.	67,500	71,900	+6.5%
Salt Lake City, Ut.	66,400	68,100	+2.6%
San Antonio, Tex.	67,000	67,600	+0.9%
San Diego, Cal.	110,000	121,100	+10.1%
Syracuse, N.Y.	59,600	65,200	+9.4%
Tampa, Fla.	56,800	59,800	+5.3%
Toledo, Oh.	52,100	53,700	+3.1%
Tulsa, Okla.	66,400	64,100	−3.5%
Washington, D.C.	101,100	107,700	+6.5%
W. Palm Beach, Fla.	86,000	96,900	+12.7%
U.S. average	**78,100**	**83,900**	**+7.4%**

(1) All areas are metropolitan statistical areas as defined by the U.S. Office of Management and Budget. They include the named central city and surrounding suburban areas.

U.S. Passport, Visa, and Health Requirements

Source: Passport Services, U.S. State Department as of May, 1987

Passports are issued by the U.S. Department of State to citizens and nationals of the United States for the purpose of documenting them for foreign travel and identifying them as Americans.

How to Obtain a Passport

Applicants who have never been issued a passport in their own names, must execute an application in person before (1) a passport agent; (2) a clerk of any federal court or state court of record or a judge or clerk of any probate court accepting applications; (3) a postal employee designated by the postmaster at a post office which has been selected to accept passport applications; or (4) a U.S. diplomatic or consular officer abroad. Since 1981, all persons are required to obtain individual passports in their own name. Neither spouses nor children may be included in each other's passports. An applicant who is 13 years of age or older is required to appear in person before the clerk or agent executing the application. A parent or legal guardian may execute the application for children under 13.

A passport previously issued to the applicant, or one in which he was included, will be accepted as proof of U.S. citizenship. If the applicant has no prior passport and was born in the United States a certified copy of their birth certificate shall be presented to the agent accepting the passport application. To be acceptable, the certificate must show the given name and surname, the date and place of birth, and that the birth record was filed shortly after birth. A delayed birth certificate (a record filed more than one year after the date of birth) is acceptable provided that it shows that the report of birth was supported by acceptable secondary evidence of birth.

If such primary evidence is not obtainable, a notice from the registrar shall be submitted stating that no birth record exists. The notice shall be accompanied by the best obtainable secondary evidence such as a baptismal certificate, or a hospital birth record.

A naturalized citizen with no previous passport should present a naturalization certificate. A person born abroad claiming U.S. citizenship through either a native-born or naturalized citizen parent must submit a certificate of citizenship issued by the Immigration and Naturalization Service; or a Consular Report of Birth or Certification of Birth issued by the Dept. of State. If one of the above documents has not been obtained, evidence of citizenship of the parent(s) through whom citizenship is claimed and evidence which would establish the parent/child relationship must be submitted. Additionally, if citizenship is derived through birth to citizen parent(s), the following documents will be required: parents' marriage certificate plus an affidavit from parent(s) showing periods and places of residence or physical presence in the U.S. and abroad, specifying periods spent abroad in the employment of the U.S. government, including the armed forces, or with certain international organizations. If citizenship is derived through naturalization of parents, evidence of admission to the U.S. for permanent residence also will be required.

Persons who have been issued a passport in their own names within the last 12 years may obtain new passports by filling out, signing and mailing a passport-by-mail application together with their previous passport, 2 recent identical photographs and $35.00 to the nearest passport agency. Those persons applying for a passport for the first time, or whose prior passport was issued before their 16th birthday, must execute a passport application in person.

Contract Employees — Persons traveling because of a contract with the U.S. Government must submit with their application: letters from their employer stating position, destination and purpose of travel, armed forces contract number, and expiration date of contract when pertinent.

Photographs and Fees

Photographs — Submit 2 identical photographs which are sufficiently recent (normally not more than 6 months old) to be a good likeness of and satisfactorily identify the applicant. Photographs should be 2 × 2 inches in size. The image size measured from the bottom of the chin to the top of the head (including hair) should be not less than one inch nor

(continued)

more than 1 3/8 inches. Photographs should be portrait-type prints. They must be clear, front view, full face, with a plain light (white or off-white) background. Photographs which depict the applicant as relaxed and smiling are encouraged.

Fees — The passport fee is $20.00 for passports issued to persons under 18 years of age. These passports are valid for 5 years from the date of issue. The passport fee is $35.00 for passports issued to persons 18 and older. These passports are valid for 10 years from the date of issuance except where limited by the Secretary of State to a shorter period. A fee of $7.00 shall be charged for the execution of the application. No acceptance fee is payable when using DSP-82, "Application For Passport By Mail." Applicants eligible to use this form pay the $35.00 passport fee.

The loss or theft of a valid passport is a serious matter and should be reported in writing immediately to Passport Services, Dept. of State, Wash., D.C. 20524, or to the nearest Passport Agency or the nearest consular office of the U.S. when abroad.

Foreign Regulations

A visa, usually rubber stamped in a passport by a representative of the country to be visited, indicates that the bearer of the passport is permitted to enter that country for a certain purpose and length of time. Visa information can be obtained by writing directly to foreign consular officials.

Aliens — An alien leaving the U.S. must request a passport from the embassy of the country of their nationality, must have a permit from his local Collector of Internal Revenue, and if they wish to return, should request a re-entry permit from the Immigration and Naturalization Service if it is required.

Customs Exemptions and Advice to Travelers

Source: U.S. Customs Service

U.S. residents returning after a stay abroad of at least 48 hours are usually granted customs exemptions of $400 each. The duty-free articles must accompany the traveler at the time of his return, be for personal or household use, have been acquired as an incident of his trip, and be properly declared to Customs. Not more than one liter of alcoholic beverages may be included in the $400 exemption.

If a U.S. resident arrives directly or indirectly from American Samoa, Guam, or the U.S. Virgin Islands, the purchase may be valued up to $800 fair retail value, but not more than $400 of the exemption may be applied to the value of articles acquired elsewhere than in such insular possessions, and 5 liters of alcoholic beverages may be included in the exemption, but not more than 1 liter of such beverages may have been acquired elsewhere than in the designated islands.

The exemption for alcoholic beverages is accorded only when the returning resident has attained 21 years of age at the time of his arrival. One hundred cigars and 200 cigarettes may be included in either exemption. Cuban cigars may be included if obtained in Cuba and all articles acquired there do not exceed $100 in retail value.

The $400 or $800 exemption may be granted only if the exemption, or any part of it, has not been used within the preceding 30-day period and the stay abroad was for at least 48 hours. The 48-hour absence requirement does not apply if you return from Mexico or the U.S. Virgin Islands.

Gifts costing no more than $50 fair retail value or $100 from American Samoa, Guam, or the Virgin Islands, may be mailed duty-free.

Most items—including alcoholic beverages, cigars, cigarettes and perfume—made in designated Caribbean and Central American countries may enter the U.S. duty-free under the Caribbean Basin Economic Recovery Act. Countries currently designated for such duty-free treatment are: Aruba, Antigua and Barbuda, Bahamas, Barbados, Belize, British Virgin Islands, Costa Rica, Dominica, Dominican Republic, El Salvador, Grenada, Guatemala, Haiti, Honduras, Jamaica, Montserrat, Netherlands Antilles, Panama, Saint Christopher-Nevis, Saint Lucia, Saint Vincent and the Grenadines, and Trinidad and Tobago. Exceptions are: most textiles (incl. clothing), footwear, handbags, luggage, flat goods, work gloves and leather wearing apparel, and certain watches and watch parts. Alcoholic beverages and perfumes, remain subject to IRS tax.

Naturalization: How to Become an American Citizen

Source: The Federal Statutes

A person who desires to be naturalized as a citizen of the United States may obtain the necessary application form as well as detailed information from the nearest office of the Immigration and Naturalization Service or from the clerk of a court handling naturalization cases.

An applicant must be at least 18 years old. He must have been a lawful resident of the United States continuously for 5 years. For husbands and wives of U.S. citizens the period is 3 years in most instances. Special provisions apply to certain veterans of the Armed Forces.

An applicant must have been physically present in this country for at least half of the required 5 years' residence.

Every applicant for naturalization must:

(1) demonstrate an understanding of the English language, including an ability to read, write, and speak words in ordinary usage in the English language (persons physically unable to do so, and persons who, on the date of their examinations, are over 50 years of age and have been lawful permanent residents of the United States for 20 years or more are exempt).

(2) have been a person of good moral character, attached to the principles of the Constitution, and well disposed to the good order and happiness of the United States for five years just before filing the petition or for whatever other period of residence is required in his case and continue to be such a person until admitted to citizenship; and

(3) demonstrate a knowledge and understanding of the fundamentals of the history, and the principles and form of government, of the U.S.

When the applicant files his petition he pays the court clerk $50. At the preliminary hearing he may be represented by a lawyer or social service agency. There is a 30-day wait. If action is favorable, there is a final hearing before a judge, who administers the following oath of allegiance:

I hereby declare, on oath, that I absolutely and entirely renounce and abjure all allegiance and fidelity to any foreign prince, potentate, state or sovereignty, to whom or which I have heretofore been a subject or citizen; that I will support and defend the Constitution and laws of the United States of America against all enemies, foreign and domestic; that I will bear true faith and allegiance to the same; that I will bear arms on behalf of the United States when required by the law; that I will perform noncombatant service in the armed forces of the United States when required by the law; that I will perform work of national importance under civilian direction when required by the law; and that I take this obligation freely without any mental reservation or purpose of evasion; so help me God.

Marriage Laws

Source: Compiled from individual states.

Revised by Gary N. Skoloff, lecturer on Matrimonial Law, Institute for Continuing Legal Education, Newark, N.J.; as of Mar. 18, 1987.

State	Age with parental consent		Age without consent		Physical exam & blood test for male and female			
	Male	Female	Male	Female	Maximum period between exam and license	Scope of medical exam	Waiting period Before license	Waiting period After licence
Alabama*	14a	14a	18	18	30 da.	b	—	s
Alaska	16c, z	16c, z	18	18	30 da.	b	3 da., w	—
Arizona	16c, z	16c, z	18	18	30 da.	—	—	—
Arkansas	17c	16c	18	18	—	—	v	—
California	aa	aa	18	18	30 da.	bb	—	h
Colorado*	16z	16z	18	18	30 da.	bb	—	s
Connecticut	16z	16z	18	18	35 da., w	b	4 da., w	ttt
Delaware	18c	16c	18	18	—	—	—	e, s
Florida	16a, c	16a, c	18	18	60 da.	b	3 da.	s
Georgia*	16c, f	16c, f	16	16	30 da.	b	3 da., g	—
Hawaii	16d	16d	18	18	—	b	3 da., w	—
Idaho*	16z	16z	18	18	—	bb	—	—
Illinois	16c	16c	18	18	15 da.	b, n	—	ee
Indiana	17c	17c	18	18	60 da.	bb, n	72 hrs.	t
Iowa*	aa	aa	18	18	20 da.	b	3 da.	tt
Kansas*[y]	18z	18z	18	18	30 da.	b	3 da., w	—
Kentucky	18a, c	18a, c	18	18	—	—	3 da.	—
Louisiana	18d	16d	18	18	10 da.	b	—	72 hrs., w
Maine	16d	16d	18	18	60 da.	—	3 da., v, w	f
Maryland	16c	16c	18	18	—	—	48 hrs., w	ff
Massachusetts	18d	18d	18	18	33 da.	bb	3 da., v	t
Michigan	16c	16c	18	18	30 da.	b	3 da.	—
Minnesota	16z	16z	18	18	—	—	5 da., w	—
Mississippi	17d	15d	18	18	30 da.	b	3 da., w	—
Missouri	15d	15d	18	18	—	—	3 da., w	—
Montana*[yy]	15d	15d	18	18	20 da.	bb	3 da.	ff, 3 da., w
Nebraska[yy]	18c	16c	18	18	30 da.	bb	2 da.	—
Nevada	16z	16z	18	18	—	—	—	—
New Hampshire	14k	13k	18	18	30 da.	b, l	5 da., v	h
New Jersey	16z, c	16z, c	18	18	30 da.	b	72 hrs., w	s
New Mexico[y]	16c	16c	18	18	30 da.	b	—	—
New York	16j	14j	18	18	30 da.	nn	10 da.	24 hrs., w, t
North Carolina	16c	16c	18	18	00 da.	m	—	—
North Dakota	16	16	18	18	—	b	—	—
Ohio*	18c, z	16c, z	18	18	30 da.	b	5 da.	t
Oklahoma*	16c	16c	18	18	30 da.	b	p	—
Oregon	17	17	18	18	—	—	3 da., w	t
Pennsylvania*	16d	16d	18	18	30 da.	b	3 da., w	t
Puerto Rico[y]	18d	16d	21	21	—	b	—	—
Rhode Island*	18d	16d	21	21	40 da., w	bb	—	—
South Carolina*	16c	14c	18	18	—	—	1 da.	—
South Dakota	16c	16c	18	18	—	—	—	tt
Tennesee	16d	16d	18	18	30 da.	—	3 da., cc	s
Texas*[y]	14j	14j	18	18	21 da.	b	—	s
Utah	14	14	18x	18x	30 da.	b	—	s
Vermont	16z	16z	18	18	30 da.	b	—	3 da., w
Virginia	16a, c	16a, c	18	18	30 da.	b	—	t
Washington	17d	17d	18	18	—	—	3 da.	t
West Virginia	18c	16c	18	18	30 da.	b	3 da., w	—
Wisconsin	16	16	18	18	20 da.	b	5 da., w	s
Wyoming	16d	16d	18	18	30 da.	b	—	—
Dist. of Columbia*	16a	16a	18	18	30 da., w	b	3 da., w	—

*Indicates 1987 common-law marriage recognized; in many states, such marriages are only recognized if entered into many years before. (a) Parental consent not required if minor was previously married. (aa) No age limits. (b) Veneral diseases. (bb) Veneral diseases and Rubella (for female). In Colorado, Rubella for female under 45 and Rh type. (c) Younger parties may obtain license in case of pregnancy or birth of child. (cc) Unless parties are over 18 years of age. (d) Younger parties may obtain license in special circumstances. (e) Residents before expiration of 24-hour waiting period; non-residents formerly residents, before expiration of 96-hour waiting period; others 96 hours. (ee) License effective 1 day after issuance, unless court orders otherwise, valid for 60 days only. (f) If parties are under 16 years of age, proof of age and the consent of parents in person is required. If a parent is ill, an affidavit by the incapacitated parent and a physician's affidavit to that effect required. (ff) License valid for 180 days only. (g) Unless parties are 18 years of age or more, or female is pregnant, or applicants are the parents of a living child born out of wedlock. (h) License valid for 90 days only. (j) Parental consent and permission of judge required. (k) Below age of consent parties need parental consent and permission of judge. (l) With each certificate issued to couples, a list of family planning agencies and services available to them is provided. (m) Mental incompetence, infectious tuberculosis, venereal diseases and Rubella (certain counties only). (n) Venereal diseases; test for sickle cell anemia given at request of examining physician. (nn) Tests for sickle cell anemia may be required for certain applicants. Marriage prohibited unless it is established that procreation is not possible. (p) If one or both parties are below the age for marriage without parental consent (3 day waiting period). (s) License valid for 30 days only. (t) License valid for 60 days only. (tt) License valid for 20 days only. (ttt) License valid for 65 days. (v) Parties must file notice of intention to marry with local clerk. (w) Waiting period may be avoided. (x) Authorizes counties to provide for premarital counseling as a requisite to issuance of license to persons under 19 and persons previously divorced. (y) Marriages by proxy are valid. (yy) Proxy marriages are valid under certain conditions. (z) Younger parties may marry with parental consent and/or permission of judge. In Connecticut, judicial approval.

Divorce Laws

Adapted from a revision by Gary N. Skoloff of the N.J. Bar, lecturer on Matrimonial Law for the Institute for Continuing Legal Education, Newark, N.J.; as of Mar. 18, 1987. Important: almost all states also have other laws, as well as qualifications of the laws shown below and proposed divorce-reform laws pending. It would be wise to consult a lawyer in conjunction with the use of this chart.

Some grounds for absolute divorce

	Residence	Adultery	Cruelty	Desertion	Alcoholism	Impotency	Non-support	Insanity	Pregnancy at marriage	Bigamy	Separation	Felony conviction or imprisonment	Drug addiction	Fraud force, duress
AL	6 mos.*	Yes	Yes	1 yr.	Yes	No	2 yrs.	5 yrs.	Yes	A	1-2 yrs.*	*	Yes	A
AK	*	Yes	Yes	1 yr.	1 yr.	A	No	18 mos.	No	A	No	Yes	Yes	A
AZ	90 da.	No	No	No	No	No	No	No	No	No	No	No	No	A
AR	60 da.	Yes	Yes	1 yr.	1 yr.	A	Yes	3 yrs.	No	Yes	3 yrs.	Yes	A	A
CA	6 mos.	No	No	No	No	No	No	Yes	No	No	No	No	No	A
CO	90 da.	No	No	No	No	No	No	No	No	A	No	No	No	A
CT	1 yr.*	Yes	Yes	1 yr.	Yes	A	1 yr.	5 yrs.	Yes*	A	18 mos.*	*	No	Yes
DE	6 mos.	No	Yes	No	No	A	No	A	No	A	6 mos.	No	A	A
FL	6 mos.	No	No	No	No	A	No	No	No	No	No	No	No	No
GA	6 mos.	Yes	Yes	1 yr.	Yes	Yes	No	Yes	Yes	A	No	*	Yes	Yes
HI	6 mos.*	No	No	No	No	No	No	A	Yes	A	2 yrs.*	2 yrs.*	No	A
ID	6 wks.	Yes	Yes	1 yr.	1 yr.	A	1 yr.	3 yrs.	Yes	A	5 yrs.	Yes	No	A
IL	90 da.	Yes	Yes	1 yr.	2 yrs.	Yes	No	No	Yes	Yes	2 yrs.*	Yes	2 yrs.	No
IN	6 mos.*	No	No	No	No	A	No	2 yrs.	Yes	A	No	Yes	No	A
IA	1 yr.*	No	No	No	No	A	No	A	Yes	A	No	No	No	No
KS	60 da.	No	No	No	No	No	Yes	2 yrs.	A	A	No	No	No	A
KY	180 da.	No	No	No	No	A	No	No	No	No	No	No	No	A
LA	1 yr.*	Yes	No	No	No	No	No	No	No	A	1 yr.	*	No	No
ME	6 mos.*	Yes	Yes	3 yrs.	Yes	Yes	Yes	7 yrs.	No	No	No	No	Yes	No
MD	none*	Yes	No	1 yr.*	No	No	Yes	3 yrs.	No	A	1 yr.*	*	No	No
MA	none*	Yes	Yes	1 yr.	Yes	Yes	Yes	No	No	A	No	No	Yes	A
MI	180 da.*	No	No	No	No	No	No	No	No	A	No	No	No	No
MN	180 da.	No	No	No	No	No	No	No	No	No	No	No	No	A
MS	6 mos.	Yes	Yes	1 yr.	Yes	Yes	No	3 yrs.	Yes	Yes	No	No	Yes	A
MO	90 da.	No	No	No	No	A	No	A	No	A	1-2 yrs.	No	No	A
MT	90 da.	No	No	No	No	A	No	No	No	A	180 da.	No	No	A
NE	1 yr.*	No	No	No	No	A	No	No	No	A	No	No	No	A
NV	6 wks.	No	No	No	No	No	No	2 yrs.	No	A	1 yr.	No	No	A
NH	none*	Yes	Yes	2 yrs.	2 yrs.	Yes	2 yrs.	No	No	No	2 yrs.	*	No	No
NJ	1 yr.*	Yes	Yes	1 yr.	1 yr.	A	No	2 yrs.	No	A	18 mos.	18 mos.	1 yr.	A
NM	6 mos.	Yes	Yes	Yes*	No	No	No	No	No	No	No	No	No	No
NY	1 yr.*	Yes	Yes	1 yr.	No	No	No	No	No	A	No	Yes	No	No
NC	6 mos.	No	No	No	No	A	No	3 yrs.	No	A	1 yr.	No	No	No
ND	6 mos.	Yes	Yes	1 yr.	1 yr.	A	1 yr.	5 yrs.	No	A	No	Yes	1 yr.	A
OH	6 mos.	Yes	Yes	1 yr.	Yes	Yes	Yes	4 yrs.	No	Yes	1 yr.	Yes	No	A
OK	6 mos.	Yes	Yes	1 yr.	Yes	Yes	Yes	5 yrs.	Yes	No	No	Yes	No	Yes
OR	6 mos.*	No	No	No	No	No	No	No	No	No	No	No	No	A
PA	6 mos.	Yes	Yes	1 yr.	No	No	No	3 yrs.	No	Yes	3 yrs.*	Yes	No	No
RI	1yr.	Yes	Yes	5 yrs.*	Yes	Yes	1 yr.	No	No	Yes	3 yrs.	No	1 yr.	No
SC	1 yr.*	Yes	physical only	1 yr.	Yes	No	No	No	No	No	1 yr.	No	Yes	No*
SD	none*	Yes	Yes	1 yr.	1 yr.	A	1 yr.	A/5 yrs.	No	A	No	Yes	No	A*
TN	6 mos.	Yes	Yes	1 yr.	Yes	Yes	Yes	No	Yes	Yes	No	Yes	Yes	A
TX	6 mos.*	Yes	Yes	1 yr.	*	A	No	3 yrs.	No	A	3 yrs.	Yes	No	No
UT	3 mos.	Yes	Yes	1 yr.	Yes	Yes	Yes	Yes	No	A	3 yrs.*	Yes	Yes	A
VT	6 mos.*	Yes	No	Yes*	No	No	Yes	5 yrs.	No	A	6 mos.	Yes	No	A
VA	6 mos.*	Yes	Yes	1 yr.	No	A	No	No	A	A	1 yr.*	Yes	No	No
WA	bona fide res.	No	No	No	No	No	No	No	No	No	90 da.*	No	No	No
WV	1 yr.	Yes	Yes	6 mos.	Yes	A	A	3 yrs.	A	A	1 yr.	Yes	Yes	No
WI	6 mos.	No	No	No	No	No	No	No	No	A	1 yr.	No	No	A
WY	2 mos.*	No	No	No	No	No	No	2 yrs.	No	A	No	No	No	No
DC	6 mos.	No	No	No	No	A	No	A	No	A	6 mos.-1 yr.	No	No	A

(*) indicates qualification-check local statutes; (A) indicates grounds for annulment.

Wedding Anniversaries

The traditional names for wedding anniversaries go back many years in social usage. As such names as wooden, crystal, silver, and golden were applied it was considered proper to present the married pair with gifts made of these products or of something related. The list of traditional gifts, with a few allowable revisions in parentheses, is presented below, followed by modern gifts in **bold face.**

1st-Paper, **clocks**
2d-Cotton, **china**
3d-Leather, **crystal & glass**
4th-Linen (silk), **electrical appliances**
5th-Wood, **silverware**
6th-Iron, **wood**
7th-Wool (copper), **desk sets**
8th-Bronze, **linens & lace**
9th-Pottery (china), **leather**
10th-Tin (aluminum), **diamond jewelry**
11th-Steel, **fashion jewelry, accessories**
12th-Silk, **pearls or colored gems**
13th-Lace, **textiles & furs**
14th-Ivory, **gold jewelry**
15th-Crystal, **watches**
20th-China, **platinum**
25th-Silver, **sterling silver jubliee**
30th-Pearl, **diamond**
35th-Coral (jade), **jade**
40th-Ruby, **ruby**
45th-Sapphire, **sapphire**
50th-Gold, **gold**
55th-Emerald, **emerald**
60th-Diamond, **diamond**

Birthstones

Source: Jewelry Industry Council

Month	Ancient	Modern
January	Garnet	Garnet
February	Amethyst	Amethyst
March	Jasper	Bloodstone or Aquamarine
April	Sapphire	Diamond
May	Agate	Emerald
June	Emerald	Pearl, Moonstone, or Alexandrite
July	Onyx	Ruby
August	Carnelian	Sardonyx or Peridot
September	Chrysolite	Sapphire
October	Aquamarine	Opal or Tourmaline
November	Topaz	Topaz
December	Ruby	Turquoise or Zircon

Copyright Law of The United States

Source: Copyright Office, Library of Congress

Original works of authorship in any tangible medium of expression are entitled to protection under the copyright law (Title 17 of the United States Code). The law came into effect on January 1, 1978 (Public Law 94-553, 90 Stat. 2541); it superseded the Copyright Act of 1909, as amended. Before the 1976 Act, there had been only three general revisions of the original copyright law of 1790, namely those of 1831, 1870, and 1909.

Categories of Works

Copyright protection under the new law extends to original works of authorship fixed in any tangible medium of expression, now known or later developed, from which they can be perceived, reproduced, or otherwise communicated, either directly or with the aid of a machine or device. Works of authorship include books, periodicals, computer programs and other literary works, musical compositions with accompanying lyrics, dramas and dramatico-musical compositions, pantomimes and choreographic works, motion pictures and other audiovisual works, pictorial, graphic, and sculptural works, and sound recordings.

The owner of a copyright is given the exclusive right to reproduce the copyrighted work in copies or phonorecords and distribute them to the public by sale, rental, lease, or lending. The owner of a copyright also enjoys the exclusive right to make derivative works based upon the copyrighted work, to perform the work publicly if it be a literary, musical, dramatic, or choreographic work, a pantomime, motion picture, or other audiovisual work, and in the case of literary, musical, dramatic, and choreographic works, pantomimes, and pictorial, graphic, or sculptural works, including the individual images of a motion picture or other audiovisual work, to display the copyrighted work publicly. All of these rights are subject to certain specified exceptions, including the so-called judicial doctrine of "fair use," which is included in the law for the first time.

The act also provides special provisions permitting compulsory licensing for the recording and distribution of phonorecords of nondramatic musical compositions, noncommercial transmissions by public broadcasters of published nondramatic, musical, pictorial, sculptural, and graphic works, performances of copyrighted nondramatic music by means of jukeboxes, and the secondary transmission of copyrighted works on cable television systems.

Single National System

The law establishes a single national system of statutory protection for all copyrightable works fixed in tangible form, whether published or unpublished. Before Jan. 1, 1978 unpublished works were entitled to protection under the common law of the various states while published works came under the Federal statute.

Registration of a claim to copyright in any work, whether published or unpublished, may be made voluntarily at any time during the copyright term by the owner of the copyright or of any exclusive right in the work. Registration is not a condition of copyright protection, but is a prerequisite to an infringement suit. Subject to certain exceptions, the remedies of statutory damages and attorney's fees are not available for those infringements occurring before registration. Even if registration is not made, copies or phonorecords of works published in the U.S. with notice of copyright are required to be deposited for the collections of the Library of Congress. This deposit requirement is not a condition of protection, but does render the copyright owner subject to penalties for failure to deposit after a demand by the Register of Copyrights.

Duration of Copyright

For works created on or after Jan. 1, 1978, copyright subsists from their creation for a term consisting of the life of the author and 50 years after the author's death. For works made for hire, and for anonymous and pseudonymous works (unless the author's identity is revealed in Copyright Office records), the term is 100 years from creation or 75 years from first publication, whichever is shorter.

The law retains for works that were under statutory protection on January 1, 1978, the 28 year term of copyright from first publication (or from registration in some cases), renewable by certain persons for a second term of protection of 47 years. Copyrights in their first 28-year term on Jan. 1, 1978, have to be renewed in order to be protected for the full maximum term of 75 years. Copyrights in their second term on Jan. 1, 1978 were automatically extended to last for a total term of 75 years.

For works that had been created before the law came into effect but had neither been published nor registered for copyright before Jan. 1, 1978, the term of copyright is generally computed in the same way as for new works: the life-plus-50 or 75/100-year terms will apply. However, all works in this category are guaranteed at least 25 years of statutory protection. The law specifies that copyright in a work of this kind will not expire before Dec. 31, 2002, and if the work is published before that date the term is extended by another 25 years, through the end of the year 2027.

Notice of Copyright

Under the 1909 copyright law the copyright notice was the most important requirement for obtaining copyright protection for a published work. For published works, all copies had to bear the prescribed notice from the time of first publication. If a work was published before Jan. 1, 1978 without the required notice, copyright protection was lost permanently and cannot be regained.

The present copyright law requires a notice on copies or phonorecords of sound recordings that are distributed to the public. Errors and omissions, however, do not immediately result in forfeiture of the copyright and can be corrected within prescribed time limits. Innocent infringers misled by an omission or error in the notice generally are shielded from liability.

The notice of copyright required on all visually perceptible copies published in the U.S. or elsewhere under the 1976 Act consists of the symbol © (the letter C in a circle), the word "Copyright," or the abbreviation "Copr.," and the year of first publication, and the name of the owner of copyright in the work. Example: © 1987 JOHN DOE

The notice must be affixed in such manner and location as to give reasonable notice of the claim of copyright.

The notice of copyright prescribed for all published phonorecords of sound recordings consists of the symbol ℗ (the letter P in a circle), the year of first publication of the sound recording, and the name of the owner of copyright in the

(continued)

sound recording, placed on the surface of the phonorecord, or on the phonorecord label or container in such manner and location as to give reasonable notice of the claim of copyright. Example: ℗ 1987 DOE RECORDS, INC.

International Protection

The U.S. has copyright relations with more than 70 countries, under which works of American authors are protected in those countries, and the works of their authors are protected in the U.S. The basic feature of this protection is "national treatment," under which the alien author is treated by a country in the same manner that it treats its own authors. Relations exist by virtue of bilateral agreements or through the Buenos Aires Convention or the Universal Copyright Convention, which became effective Sept. 16, 1955.

Works published on or after Jan. 1, 1978, are subject to protection under the copyright statute if, on the date of first publication, one or more of the authors is a national or domiciliary of the U.S., or is a national, domiciliary, or sovereign authority of a foreign nation that is a party to a copyright treaty to which the United States is also a party, or is a stateless person, regardless of domicile, or if the work is first published either in the U.S. or in a foreign nation that, on the date of first publication is a party to the Universal Copyright Convention. All unpublished works are protected here regardless of the citizenship or domicile of the author.

A U.S. author may obtain copyright protection in all countries that are members of the Universal Copyright Convention (UCC). In member countries, where no formalities are required, the works of U.S. authors are protected automatically. Member countries whose laws impose formalities protect U.S. works if all published copies bear a convention notice which consists of the symbol ©, together with the name of the copyright owner and the year date of publication. Example: © JOHN DOE 1987.

Further information and application forms may be obtained free of charge by writing to the Information Section LM-455, Copyright Office, The Library of Congress, Washington, D.C. 20559.

Copyright registration application forms may be ordered on a 24-hour basis by calling (202) 287-9100.

Tips on Cutting Energy Costs in Your Home

Source: Con Edison Conservation Services, New York City

Heating

In many homes, in areas where temperatures drop during the winter, more energy is used for heating than anything else. Installing the right amount of insulation, storm windows and doors, caulking and weatherstripping pays off. Also consider the following advice:

- Make sure the thermostat and heating system are in good working order. An annual checkup is recommended.
- If your heating system has air filters, make sure they are clean.
- Set the thermostat no higher than 68 degrees. When no one is home, or when everyone is sleeping, the setting should be turned down to 60 degrees or lower. An automatic setback thermostat can raise and lower your home's temperature at times you specify.
- Close off and do not heat unused areas.
- Cover all air conditioner units.
- If you do not have conventional storm windows or doors, use kits to make plastic storm windows.
- Special glass fireplace doors help keep a room's heat from being drawn up the chimney when the fire is burning low. Close the damper when a fireplace is not in use.
- Use the sun's heat by opening blinds and draperies on sunny days.
- Keep radiators and warm air outlets clean. Do not block them with furniture or draperies.

Water Heater

In many homes, the water heater ranks second only to the heating system in total energy consumption.

- Put an insulation blanket on your water heater; when you go on vacation turn it to a minimum setting.
- If you have a dishwasher, set the water heater thermostat no higher than 140 degrees. If not, or if you have a separate water heater for baths, a setting as low as 110 degrees may be sufficient.
- Run the dishwasher and clothes washer only when you have a full load. Use warm or cold water cycles for laundry when you can.
- Take showers instead of tub baths. About half as much hot water is used for a shower.
- Install a water-saver shower head.
- Install aerators or restrictors on all your sink faucets.
- Do not leave the hot water running when rinsing dishes or shaving. Plug and partially fill the basin, or fill a pan with water.
- Use the right size water heater for your needs. An oversized unit wastes energy heating unneeded water. An undersized unit will not deliver all the hot water you want when you need it.
- When shopping for a water heater, look for the yellow-and-black federal EnergyGuide label to learn the estimated yearly energy cost of a unit.

Air Conditioning

- Clean or replace the filter in an air conditioner at the beginning of the cooling season. Then check it once a month and clean or change the filter if necessary. A dirty filter blocks the flow of air.
- Adjust the temperature control setting to provide a room temperature no lower than 78 degrees. Use a good wall thermometer to tell which setting will provide the desired temperature.
- Close windows and doors when the air conditioner is running.
- When the outside temperature is 78 degrees or cooler, turn off the air conditioner and open windows to cool your home.
- Always keep your air conditioner turned off when you are away from home or not using the areas that it cools. An air conditioner timer can be set to turn on just before family members arrive home.
- Close draperies and shades to block out the sun's heat.
- When shopping for a new room air conditioner, look for the yellow-and-black federal EnergyGuide label to learn the Energy Efficiency Rating (EER) and the estimated yearly operating cost. The higher the EER, the less electricity will be used for a cooling job.
- Read the manufacturer's instructions; follow closely.
- If you have a central air conditioning system, run your hands along the ducts while it is operating to check for air leaks. Repair leaks with duct tape. Make sure the duct system is properly insulated.
- On many days, a window fan can cool an apartment as effectively as an air conditioner, and it is less costly.

Refrigerators and Freezers

The refrigerator operates 24 hours a day, every day, so it is one of the biggest users of energy in the home all year.

- Keep the condenser coils clean. The coils are on the back or at the bottom of the refrigerator. Carefully wipe, vacuum or brush the coils to remove dust and dirt at least once a year.
- Examine door gaskets and hinges regularly for air leaks. The doors should fit tightly. To check, place a piece of paper between the door and the cabinet. Close the door with normal force, then try to pull the paper straight out. There should be a slight resistance. Test all around the door, including the hinge side. If there are any places where the paper slides out easily, you need to adjust the hinges or replace the gasket, or both.
- Pause before opening your refrigerator door. Think of everything you will need before you open the door so you do not have to go back several times. When you open the door, close it quickly to keep the cool air in.
- Adjust the temperature-setting dial of the refrigerator as the manufacturer recommends. Use a thermometer to check the temperature (38 to 40 degrees is usually recommended for the refrigerator; zero degrees for the freezer). Settings that are too cold waste electricity.
- If you have a manual-defrost refrigerator, do not allow the ice to build up more than 1/4 inch thick.
- Keep your refrigerator well-stocked but allow room for air to circulate around the food.
- The freezer, on the other hand, should be packed full. If necessary, fill empty spaces with bags of ice cubes or fill milk cartons with water and freeze.
- When you are going to be away from home for a week or more, turn off and unplug the refrigerator, empty and clean it, and prop the door open.
- If you are buying a new refrigerator, look for one with a humid-dry ("power-saver") switch. This switch is used to turn off "anti-sweat" heaters in the doors to save electricity when the heaters are not needed.
- When shopping for a new refrigerator or freezer, eliminate those too large for your needs; look for the federal EnergyGuide label to help you select an efficient unit.

Cooking

- Cook as many dishes in the oven at one time as you can instead of cooking each separately. If recipes call for slightly different temperatures, say 325, 350, and 375 degrees, pick the middle temperature of 350 to cook all 3 dishes and remove each dish as it's done.
- Don't preheat the oven unnecessarily. Usually, any food that takes more than an hour of cooking can be started in a cold oven.
- Turn off your oven or range just before the cooking is done. The heat that is left will usually finish the cooking.
- Whenever you peek into an oven by opening a door, the temperature drops about 25 degrees. So open the oven door as little as possible.
- Use tight-fitting covers on pots and pans to retain heat and cook foods more quickly.
- Use the lowest possible heat setting to cook foods on top of the range.
- Match the pot to the size of the surface unit. Putting a small pot on a large surface unit wastes energy without cooking the food any faster.
- Adjust the flame on a gas burner so that it does not extend beyond the base of the pot. Using too high a flame wastes energy, and can be dangerous.
- On gas ranges, the flame should burn in a firm, blue cone. If not, get a service representative to check it.

Lighting

- Get all family members in the habit of turning off lights when they leave a room, even if they will be gone only for a short time.
- During the day, try to get along with as few lights as possible. Let the daylight do the work. White or lightcolored walls make a room seem brighter.
- Use bulbs of lower wattage.
- When possible, use one large bulb rather than several smaller ones. One 100-watt incandescent bulb, for example, produces more light than three 40-watt. However, never use bulbs of a higher wattage than a fixture is designed to take.
- Use three-way bulbs wherever possible.
- Buy energy-saving incandescent bulbs to replace standard bulbs with slightly higher wattage. There's a ten percent energy cost saving.
- Modern solid-state dimmer controls let you save energy by reducing your lighting level and wattage. Many are easy to install.
- Use plug-in timers to turn lights on and off automatically.
- Consider changing to fluorescent lighting, especially in kitchens, bathrooms, and work areas. Fluorescent tubes give more light at lower energy cost than incandescent bulbs with the same wattage.
- For outdoor lighting, replace standard incandescent floodlights with the new energy-saving halogen type.

Measuring Energy

Source: Energy Information Administration, U.S. Energy Dept.

The following tables of equivalents contain those figures commonly used to compare different types of energy sources and their various measurements.

Btu — a British thermal unit — the amount of heat required to raise one pound of water one degree Fahrenheit. Equivalent to 1,055 joules or about 252 gram calories. A therm is usually 100,000 Btu but is sometimes used to refer to other units.

Calorie — The amount of heat required to raise one gram of water one degree Centigrade; abbreviated cal.; equivalent to about .003968 Btu. More common is the kilogram calorie, also called a kilocalorie and abbreviated Cal. or Kcal; equivalent to about 3.97 Btu. (One Kcal is equivalent to one food calorie.)

Btu Values of Energy Sources

(These are conventional or average values, not precise equivalents.)

Coal (per 2,000 lb. ton of U.S. production):

Anthracite	= 22.9 × 10^6 Btu
Bituminous coal and lignite	= 22.6 × 10^6

Average heating value of coal used to generate electricity in 1979 was 21.4 x 10^6 Btu per metric ton.

Natural Gas:

Dry (per cubic foot)	= 1,028 Btu
Liquefied Natural Gas (Methane) (per barrel)	= 3.0 × 10^6

Electricity — 1 kwh	= 3,412 Btu

Petroleum (per barrel):

Crude oil	= 5.80 × 10^6 Btu
Residual fuel oil	= 6.29 × 10^6
Distillate fuel oil	= 5.83 × 10^6
Gasoline (including aviation gas)	= 5.25 × 10^6

(continued)

Jet fuel (kerosene) = 5.67×10^6
Jet fuel (naphtha) = 5.36×10^6
Kerosene = 5.67×10^6

Nuclear — (per kilowatt hour) = 10,769

The Btu and calorie, being small amounts of energy, are usually expressed as follows when large numbers are involved.

1×10^3 Btu = 1,000
1×10^6 = 1,000,000
1×10^9 = 1,000,000,000
1×10^{12} = 1 trillion
1×10^{15} = 1 quadrillion
1×10^{18} = 1 quintillion or 1 Q unit
One Q unit = 44.3 billion short tons of coal
= 172.4 billion tons of oil
= 980 trillion cubic feet of natural gas

Other Conversion Factors

Electricity — 1 kwh = 0.3 pounds of coal
= 0.025 gallon of crude oil
= 3.3 cubic feet of natural gas

Natural gas — 1 tcf (trillion cubic feet) = 45×10^6 short tons of bituminous and lignite coal produced
= 176×10^6 barrels of crude oil

Coal — 1 mstce (million short tons of coal equivalent) = 3.9×10^6 barrels of crude oil
= 1.7×10^6 short tons of crude oil
= 22.1×10^9 cubic feet of natural gas

Oil — 1 million short tons (6.65×10^6 barrels) = 4×10^9 kwh of electricity (when used to generate power)
= 12×10^9 kwh uncoverted
= 1.7×10^6 short tons of coal
= 37×10^9 cubic feet of natural gas

Approximate Conversion Factors for Oils

To convert	Barrels to metric tons	Metric tons to barrels	Barrels/ day to tons/ year	Tons/year to barrels/ day
	Multiply by:			
Crude oil[1] . .	.136	7.33	49.8	.0201
Gasoline . .	.118	8.45	43.2	.0232
Kerosene . .	.128	7.80	46.8	.0214
Diesel fuel .	.133	7.50	48.7	.0205
Fuel oil . . .	.149	6.70	54.5	.0184

(1) Based on world average gravity (excluding natural gas liquids).

Fuel Economy in 1988 Autos; Comparative Miles per Gallon

Source:U.S. Envirnomental Protection Agency

Top Overall

Model	City	Hwy.	Annual fuel cost	Engine size/# Cyl.	Trans.	size[1]
Chevrolet Sprint Metro	54	58	$268	1.0L/3	M5	MC
Honda Civic CRX HF	50	56	288	1.5L/4	M5	2-S
Honda Civic CRX HF	45	53	312	1.5L/4	M5	2-S
Pontiac Firefly	44	49	326	1.0L/3	M5	subC
Suzuki Forsa	44	49	326	1.0L/3	M5	subC
Chevrolet Sprint	44	49	384	1.0L/3	M5	subC
Ford Festiva	39	43	366	1.3L/4	M5	subC
Daihatsu Motor Co. Charade	38	42	384	1.0L/3	M5	subC
Ford Festiva	38	40	384	1.3L/4	M4	subC
Pontiac Firefly	38	40	384	1.0L/3	A3	subC
Suzuki Forsa	38	40	384	1.0L/3	A3	subC
Chevrolet Sprint	38	40	384	1.0L/3	A3	subC

(1) MC = minicompact, 2-S = two-seater, subC = subcompact.

Lowest Overall

Model	City	Hwy.	Annual fuel cost	Engine size/# Cyl.	Trans.	size[1]
Lamborghini East Countach	6	10	$2,156	5.2L/12	M5	2-S
Rolls-Royce Bentley Continental	9	11	1,500	6.8L/8	A3	subC
Rolls-Royce Bentley Eight/Mulsan	9	11	1,500	6.8L/8	A3	M-S
Rolls-Royce Corniche II	9	11	1,500	6.8L/8	A3	subC
Rolls-Royce Silver Spirit/Spur	9	11	1,500	6.8L/8	A3	M-S
Rolls-Royce Silver Spur Limousine	9	11	1,500	6.8L/8	A3	L
Ferrari Testarossa	10	15	1,364	4.9L/12	M5	2-S
BMW 5-Series	10	19	1,327	3.5L/6	M5	C
BMW 6-Series	10	19	1,327	3.5L/6	M5	subC
Mercedes-Benz 560 SEL	13	16	1,232	5.6L/8	A4	M-S
Mercedes-Benz 560 SEC	13	16	1,232	5.6L/8	A4	C

(1) 2-S = two-seater, subC = subcompact, M-S = mid-size, L = large, C = compact.

Highest and Lowest in Each Size

Size Class	Highest: Model	City	Hwy.	Annual Fuel Cost	Lowest: Model	City	Hwy.	Annual Fuel Cost
Two Seater	Honda Civic CRX HF	50	56	$288	Lamborghini East	6	10	$2,156
Minicompact . . .	Chevrolet Sprint Metro	54	58	268	Ferrari 3.2 Mondial Cabriolet	13	18	1,000
Subcompact . . .	Pontiac Firefly	44	49	326	Rolls Royce Bentley . . . . Continental/Corniche II	9	11	1,500
	Suzuki Forsa	44	49	326				
	Chevrolet Sprint	44	49	326				
Compact	Ford Escort	33	42	405	BMW-5 Series.	10	19	1,327
Mid Size.	Dodge Lancer	25	34	536	Rolls Royce Bentley . . . . Eight/Bentley Mulsan/ Silver Spirit/Silver Spur	9	10	1,500
Large	Eagle Premier	24	32	555	Rolls Royce Silver Spur . . Limousine	9	11	1,500
Small Wagons . .	Ford Escort Wagon	33	42	405	Volkswagen Quantum . . . Syncro Wagon	17	21	789

SOCIAL SECURITY

Social Security Programs

Source: Social Security Administration, U.S. Department of Health and Human Services

Old-Age, Survivors, and Disability Insurance; Medicare; Supplemental Security Income

New Legislation

On November 10, 1986, President Reagan signed into law the "Employment Opportunities for Disabled Americans Act of 1986" (P.L. 99-643). The most important change that this law made was to make permanent what had been an experimental provision scheduled to expire June 30, 1987, for special cash benefits and Medicaid coverage for individuals receiving benefits under the supplemental security income program who work despite severe impairments.

On October 21, 1986, the President signed into law the "Omnibus Budget Reconciliation Act of 1986." This law included a provision permanently eliminating the cost-of-living adjustment (COLA) "trigger" with the result that Social Security beneficiaries will now receive benefit increases when the Consumer Price Index rises, even if the rise is less than 3 percent (the amount of the trigger). See discussion below.

Social Security Benefits

Social Security benefits are based on a worker's primary insurance amount (PIA), which is related by law to the average indexed monthly earnings (AIME) on which social security contributions have been paid. The full PIA is payable to a retired worker who becomes entitled to benefits at age 65 and to an entitled disabled worker at any age. Spouses and children of retired or disabled workers and survivors of deceased workers receive set proportions of the PIA subject to a family maximum amount. The PIA is calculated by applying varying percentages to succeeding parts of the AIME. The formula is adjusted annually to reflect changes in average annual wages in the economy.

Automatic increases in Social Security benefits are initiated whenever the Consumer Price Index (CPI) of the Bureau of Labor Statistics for the third calendar quarter of a year increases relative to the CPI for the base quarter, which is either the third calendar quarter of the preceding year or the quarter in which an increase legislated by Congress becomes effective. The size of the benefit increase is determined by the actual percentage rise of the CPI between the quarters measured. However, if the balance in the combined OASDI trust funds falls below a specified level, the automatic benefit increase will be based on the lesser of the increase in the CPI or the increase in average wages. If one or more benefit increases are based on the increase in average wages, a "catch up" benefit increase will be made in a subsequent year when the combined trust fund balance reaches a higher specified level.

Average monthly benefits payable to all retired workers was $491.00 in May 1987. The average amount for disabled workers in that month was $488.00.

Amount of Work Required

To qualify for benefits, the worker must have worked in covered employment long enough to become insured. Just how long depends on when the worker reaches age 62 or, if earlier, when he or she dies or becomes disabled.

A person is fully insured if he or she has one quarter of coverage for every year after 1950 (or year age 21 is reached, if later) up to but not including the year in which the worker reaches age 62, dies, or becomes disabled. In 1987, a person earns one quarter of coverage for each $460 of annual earnings in covered employment, up to a maximum of 4 quarters per year.

The law permits special monthly payments under the Social Security program to certain very old persons who are not eligible for regular social security benefits since they had little or no opportunity to earn social security work credits during their working lifetime.

To get disability benefits, in addition to being fully insured, the worker must also have credit for 20 quarters of coverage out of the 40 calendar quarters before he or she becomes disabled. A disabled blind worker need meet only the fully insured requirement. Persons disabled before age 31 can qualify with a briefer period of coverage. Certain survivor benefits are payable if the deceased worker had 6 quarters of coverage in the 13 quarters preceding death.

Work credit for fully insured status for benefits

Born after 1929; die, become disabled, or reach age 62 in	Years needed
1980	7¼
1981	7½
1982	7¾
1983	8
1984	8¼
1985	8½
1986	8¾
1987	9

Contribution and benefit base

Calendar year	Base
1978	$17,700
1979	22,900
1980	25,900
1981	29,700
1982	32,400
1983	35,700
1984	37,800
1985	39,600
1986	42,000
1987	43,800

Tax-rate schedule
[Percent of covered earnings]

Year	Total	OASDI	HI
	Employees and employers, each		
1979-80	6.13	5.08	1.05
1981	6.65	5.35	1.30
1982-83	6.70	5.40	1.30
1984	7.00	5.70	1.30
1985	7.05	5.70	1.35
1986-87	7.15	5.70	1.45
1988-89	7.51	6.06	1.45
1990 and after	7.65	6.20	1.45
	Self-employed		
1979-80	8.10	7.05	1.05
1981	9.30	8.00	1.30
1982-83	9.35	8.05	1.30
1984	14.00	11.40	2.60
1985	14.10	11.40	2.70
1986-87	14.30	11.40	2.90
1988-89	15.02	12.12	2.90
1990 and after	15.30	12.40	2.90

What Aged Workers Get

When a person has enough work in covered employment and reaches retirement age (currently 65 for full benefit, 62 for reduced benefit), he or she may retire and get monthly old-age benefits. The age at which unreduced benefits are payable will be increased gradually from 65 to 67 over a 21-year period beginning with workers age 62 in the year 2000; (reduced benefits will still be available as early as age 62 but with a larger reduction at age 62.) If a person aged 65 or older continues to work and has earnings of more than $8,160 in 1987, $1 in benefits will be withheld for every $2 above $8,160. The annual exempt amount for people under age 65 is $6,000 in 1987. The annual exempt amount is raised automatically as the general earnings level rises. The eligible worker who is 70 receives the full benefit regardless of earnings. Beginning in 1990, benefits for persons who reach the normal retirement age will be reduced $1 for each $3 of excess earnings.

For workers who reach age 65 after 1981, the worker's benefit will be raised by 3% for each year for which the worker between 65 and 70 (72 before 1984) did not receive benefits because of earnings from work or because the worker had not applied for benefits. The delayed retirement credit is 1 percent a year for workers reaching age 65 before

1982. The delayed retirement credit will gradually rise from the current 3% per year to 8% per year from 1990 through 2008.

Effective December 1986, the special benefit for persons aged 72 or over who do not meet the regular coverage requirements is $140.30 a month. Like the monthly benefits, these payments are subject to cost-of-living increases. The special payment is not made to persons on the public assistance or supplemental security income rolls.

Workers retiring before age 65 have their benefits permanently reduced by 5/9 of 1% for each month they receive benefits before age 65. Thus, workers entitled to benefits in the month they reach age 62 receive 80% of the PIA, while a worker retiring at age 65 receives a benefit equal to 100% of the PIA. The nearer to age 65 the worker is when he or she begins collecting a benefit, the larger the benefit will be.

Benefits for Worker's Spouse

The spouse of a worker who is getting Social Security retirement or disability payments may become entitled to a spouse's insurance benefit when he or she reaches 65 of one-half of the worker's PIA. Reduced spouse's benefits are available at age 62 (25/36 of 1% reduction for each month of entitlement before age 65). Benefits are also payable to the divorced spouse of an insured worker if he or she was married to the worker for at least 10 years.

Benefits for Children of Retired or Disabled Workers

If a retired or disabled worker has a child under 18 the child will get a benefit that is half of the worker's unreduced benefit, and so will the worker's spouse, even if he or she is under 62 if he or she is caring for an entitled child of the worker who is under 16 or who became disabled before age 22. Total benefits paid on a worker's earnings record are subject to a maximum and if the total that would be paid to a family exceeds that maximum, the individual dependents' benefits are adjusted downward. (Total benefits paid to the family of a worker who retired in January 1987 at age 65 and who always had the maximum amount of earnings creditable under Social Security can be no higher than $1,380.60.)

When entitled children reach 18, their benefits will generally stop, except that a child disabled before 22 may get a benefit as long as his or her disability meets the definition in the law. Additionally, benefits will be paid to a child until age 19 if the child is in full-time attendance at an elementary or secondary school.

Benefits may also be paid to a grandchild or step-grandchild of a worker or of his or her spouse, in special circumstances.

OASDI	May 1987	May 1986	May 1985
Monthly beneficiaries, total (in thousands)	37,942	37,344	36,686
Aged 65 and over, total	27,386	26,805	26,227
Retired workers	20,591	20,105	19,619
Survivors and dependents	6,744	6,671	6,572
Special age-72 beneficiaries	22	28	36
Under age 65, total	10,556	10,539	10,458
Retired workers	2,555	2,509	2,458
Disabled workers	2,749	2,688	2,621
Survivors and dependents	5,252	5,342	5,379
Total monthly benefits (in millions)	$16,706	$16,057	$15,164

What Disabled Workers Get

If a worker becomes so severely disabled that he or she is unable to work, he or she may be eligible to receive a monthly disability benefit. Benefits continue until it is determined that the individual is no longer disabled. Each beneficiary's eligibility is reviewed periodically. If the individual is still disabled when he or she reaches 65, the disability benefit becomes a retired-worker benefit.

Benefits generally like those provided for dependents of retired-worker beneficiaries may be paid to dependents of disabled beneficiaries.

Survivor Benefits

If an insured worker should die, one or more types of benefits may be payable to survivors, again subject to a maximum family benefit as described above.

1. If claiming benefits at 65, the surviving spouse will receive a benefit that is 100% of the deceased worker's PIA. The surviving spouse may choose to get the benefit as early as age 60, but the benefit is then reduced by 19/40 of 1% for each month it is paid before age 65. However, for those aged 62 and over whose spouses claimed their benefits before 65, the benefit is the reduced amount the worker would be getting if alive but not less than 82 1/2% of the worker's PIA.

Disabled widows and widowers may under certain circumstances qualify for benefits after attaining age 50 at the rate of 71.5% of the deceased worker's PIA. The widow or widower must have become totally disabled before or within 7 years after the spouse's death, the last month in which he or she received mother's or father's insurance benefits, or the last month he or she previously received surviving spouse's benefits

2. A benefit for each child until the child reaches 18. The monthly benefit of each child of a worker who has died is three-quarters of the amount the worker would have received if he or she had lived and drawn full retirement benefits. A child with a disability that began before age 22 may receive benefits. Also, a child may receive benefits until age 19 if he or she is in full-time attendance at an elementary or secondary school.

3. A mother's or father's benefit for the widow(er), if children of the worker under 16 are in his or her care. The benefit is 75% of the PIA and he or she draws it until the youngest child reaches 16, at which time payments stop even if the child's benefit continues. They may start again when he or she is 60 (50 if disabled) unless he or she is married. If he or she marries and the marriage is ended, he or she regains benefit rights (A marriage after age 60, 50 if disabled, is deemed not to have occurred for benefit purposes.). If he or she has a disabled child beneficiary aged 16 or over in care, benefits also continue. This benefit may also be paid to the divorced spouse, if the marriage lasted for at least 10 years.

4. Dependent parents may be eligible for benefits, if they have been receiving at least half their support from the worker before his or her death, have reached age 62, and (except in certain circumstances) have not remarried since the worker's death. Each parent gets 75% of the worker's PIA; if only one parent survives the benefit is 82 1/2%.

5. A lump sum cash payment of $255. Payment is made only when there is a spouse who was living with the worker or a spouse or child eligible for immediate monthly survivor benefits.

Self-Employed

A self-employed person who has net earnings of $400 or more in a year must report such earnings for social security tax purposes. The person reports net returns from the business. Income from real estate, savings, dividends, loans, pensions or insurance policies may not be included unless they are part of the business.

A self-employed person gets a quarter of coverage for each $460 (for 1987), up to a maximum of 4 quarters of coverage. The nonfarm self-employed person must make estimated payments of his or her social security taxes, on a quarterly basis, for 1987, if combined estimated income tax and social security tax amount to at least $500.

The nonfarm self-employed have the option of reporting their earnings as ⅔ of their gross income from self-employment but not more than $1,600 a year and not less than their actual net earnings. This option can be used only if actual net earnings from self-employment income is less than $1,600 and may be used only 5 times. Also, the self-employed person must have actual net earnings of $400 or more in 2 of the 3 taxable years immediately preceding the year in which he or she uses the option.

When a person has both taxable wages and earnings from self-employment, the wages are credited for Social Security purposes first; only as much of the self-employment income as will bring total earnings up to the current taxable maximum is subject to the self-employment tax.

Farm Owners and Workers

Self-employed farmers whose gross annual earnings from

farming are $2,400 or less may report ⅔ of their gross earnings instead of net earnings for social security purposes. Farmers whose gross income is over $2,400 and whose net earnings are less than $1,600 can report $1,600. Cash or crop shares received from a tenant or share farmer count if the owner participated materially in production or management. The self-employed farmer pays contributions at the same rate as other self-employed persons.

Agricultural employees. Earnings from farm work count toward benefits (1) if the employer pays $150 or more in cash during the year; or (2) if the employee works on 20 or more days for cash pay figured on a time basis. Under these rules a person gets credit for one calendar quarter for each $460 in cash pay in 1987 up to four quarters.

Foreign farm workers admitted to the United States on a temporary basis are not covered.

Household Workers

Anyone working as maid, cook, laundress, nursemaid, baby-sitter, chauffeur, gardener and at other household tasks in the house of another is covered by Social Security if he or she is paid $50 or more in cash in a calendar quarter by any one employer. Room and board do not count, but carfare counts if paid in cash. The job does not have to be regular or fulltime. The employee should get a Social Security card at the social security office and show it to the employer.

The employer deducts the amount of the employee's social security tax from the worker's pay, adds an identical amount as the employer's social security tax and sends the total amount to the federal government, with the employee's social security number.

Medicare

Under Medicare, protection against the costs of hospital care is provided for Social Security and Railroad Retirement beneficiaries aged 65 and over and, for persons entitled for 24 months to receive a social security disability benefit, certain persons (and their dependents) with end-stage renal disease, and, on a voluntary basis with payment of a special premium, persons aged 65 and over not otherwise eligible for hospital benefits; all those eligible for hospital benefits may enroll for medical benefits and pay a monthly premium and so may persons aged 65 and over who are not eligible for hospital benefits.

Persons eligible for both hospital and medical insurance may choose to have their covered services provided through a Health Maintenance Organization.

Hospital insurance.—In 1987, nearly $55 billion was withdrawn from the hospital insurance trust fund for hospital and related benefits.

The hospital insurance program pays the cost of covered services for hospital and posthospital care as follows:

- Up to 90 days of hospital care during a benefit period (spell of illness) starting the first day that care as a bed-patient is received in a hospital or skilled-nursing facility and ending when the individual has not been a bed-patient for 60 consecutive days. For the first 60 days, the hospital insurance pays for all but the first $520 of expenses; for the 61st day to 90th day, the program pays all but $130 a day for covered services. In addition, each person has a 60-day lifetime reserve that can be used after the 90 days of hospital care in a benefit period are exhausted, and all but $260 a day of expenses during the reserve days are paid. Once used, the reserve days are not replaced. (Payment for care in a mental hospital is limited to 190 days.)
- Up to 100 days' care in a skilled-nursing facility (skilled-nursing home) in each benefit period. Hospital insurance pays for all covered services for the first 20 days and all but $65 daily for the next 80 days. At least 3 days' hospital stay must precede these services.
- Visits by nurses or other health workers (not doctors) from a home health agency in the 365 days after release from a hospital or extended-care facility.

Medical insurance. Aged persons can receive benefits under this supplementary program only if they sign up for them and agree to a monthly premium ($17.90 in 1987). The Federal Government pays the rest of the cost.

In 1987, about $25 billion was paid out for medical insurance benefits. As of September 1987, about 33 million persons were enrolled — 3 million of them disabled persons under age 65.

The medical insurance program pays 80% of the reasonable charges (after the first $75 in each calendar year) for the following services:

- Physicians' and surgeons' services, whether in the doctor's office, a clinic, or hospital or at home (but physician's charges for X-ray or clinical laboratory services for hospital bed-patients are paid in full and without meeting the deductible).
- Other medical and health services, such as diagnostic tests, surgical dressings and splints, and rental or purchase of medical equipment. Services of a physical therapist in independent practice, furnished in his office or the patient's home. A hospital or extended-care facility may provide covered outpatient physical therapy services under the medical insurance program to its patients who have exhausted their hospital insurance coverage.
- Physical therapy services furnished under the supervision of a practicing hospital, clinic, skilled nursing facility, or agency.
- Certain services by podiatrists.
- All outpatient services of a participating hospital (including diagnostic tests).
- Outpatient speech pathology services, under the same requirements as physical therapy.
- Services of licensed chiropractors who meet uniform standards, but only for treatment by means of manual manipulation of the spine and treatment of subluxation of the spine demonstrated by X-ray.
- Supplies related to colostomies are considered prosthetic devices and payable under the program.
- Home health services even without a hospital stay are paid up to 100% when medically necessary.

To get medical insurance protection, persons approaching age 65 may enroll in the 7-month period that includes 3 months before the 65th birthday, the month of the birthday, and 3 months after the birthday, but if they wish coverage to begin in the month they reach 65 they must enroll in the 3 months before their birthday. Persons not enrolling within their first enrollment period may enroll later, during the first 3 months of each year but their premium is 10% higher for each 12-month period elapsed since they first could have enrolled.

The monthly premium is deducted from the cash benefit for persons receiving Social Security, Railroad Retirement, or Civil Service retirement benefits. Income from the medical premiums and the federal matching payments are put in a Supplementary Medical Insurance Trust Fund, from which benefits and administrative expenses are paid.

Medicare card. Persons qualifying for hospital insurance under Social Security receive a health insurance card similar to cards now used by Blue Cross and other health agencies. The card indicates whether the individual has taken out medical insurance protection. It is to be shown to the hospital, skilled-nursing facility, home health agency, doctor, or whoever provides the covered services.

Payments are made only in the 50 states, Puerto Rico, the Virgin Islands, Guam, and American Samoa, except that hospital services may be provided in border areas immediately outside the U.S. if comparable services are not accessible in the U.S. for a beneficiary who becomes ill or is injured in the U.S.

Social Security Financing

Social Security is paid for by a tax on earnings (for 1987, up to $43,800; the taxable earnings base is now subject to automatic adjustment to reflect increases in average wages). The employed worker and his or her employer share the tax equally. (Cash tips count as covered wages if they amount to $20 or more in a month from one place of employment. The worker reports them to the employer, who includes them in the Social Security tax reports. The worker pays contributions on the full amount of the tips and the employer pays Social Security taxes on an amount that, when added to the employee's wages, equals the minimum wage).

Employers remit amounts withheld from employee wages for Social Security and income taxes to the Internal Revenue Service; employer Social Security taxes are also payable at the same time. (Self-employed workers pay their Social Security taxes along with their regular income tax forms). The Social Security taxes (along with revenues arising from partial taxation of the Social Security benefits of certain high-income people) are transferred to the Social Security Trust Funds (Federal Old-Age and Survivors Insurance Trust Fund, the Federal Disability Insurance Trust Fund, and the Federal Hospital Insurance Trust Fund); they can be used only to pay benefits, the cost of rehabilitation services, and administrative expenses.

Supplemental Security Income

On Jan. 1, 1974, the Supplemental Security Income (SSI) program established by the 1972 Social Security Act amendments replaced the former federal grants to states for aid to the needy aged, blind, and disabled in the 50 states and the District of Columbia. The program provides both for federal payments based on uniform national standards and eligibility requirements and for state supplementary payments varying from state to state. The Social Security Administration administers the federal payments financed from general funds of the Treasury—and the state supplements as well, if the state elects to have its supplementary program federally administered. The states may supplement the federal payment for all recipients and must supplement it for persons otherwise adversely affected by the transition from the former public assistance programs. In April 1987, the number of persons receiving federal payments and federally administered state payments was 4,302,772 and the amount of these payments was $1.08 billion.

The maximum monthly federal SSI payment for an individual with no other countable income, living in his own household, was $340.00 in 1987. For a couple it was $510.00.

Minimum and maximum monthly retired-worker benefits payable to individuals who retired at age 65[1]

Year of attainment of age 65[2]	Minimum benefit: Payable at the time of retirement	Minimum benefit: Payable effective December 1986	Maximum benefit: Payable at the time of retirement, Men[3]	Maximum benefit: Payable at the time of retirement, Women	Maximum benefit: Payable effective December 1986, Men[3]	Maximum benefit: Payable effective December 1986, Women
1965 . . .	$44.00	$204.50	$131.70	$135.90	$546.50	$563.90
1970 . . .	64.00	204.50	189.80	196.40	605.60	627.00
1980 . . .	133.90	204.50	572.00	...	873.50	...
1985 . . .	(4)	(4)	717.20	...	749.00	...
1986 . . .	(4)	(4)	760.10	...	769.90	...

(1) Assumes retirement at beginning of year. (2) The final benefit amount payable after SMI premium or any other deductions is rounded to next lower $1 (if not already a multiple of $1). (3) Benefit for both men and women are shown in men's columns except where women's benefit appears separately. (4) Minimum eliminated for workers who reach age 62 after 1981.

Examples of monthly cash benefit awards for selected beneficiary families with first entitlement in 1987, effective January 1987

Beneficiary Family	Career Earnings Level: Low Earnings ($6,968 in 1987)	Average Earnings ($18,456 in 1987)[1]	Maximum Earnings ($43,800 in 1987)
Primary Insurance amount (worker retiring at 65)	$391.10	$593.80	$789.20
Maximum family benefit (worker retiring at 65)	612.80	1,079.90	1,380.60
Disability maximum family benefit (worker disabled at 55)	625.80	943.00	1,253.70
Disabled worker: (worker disabled at 55)			
Worker alone	417.00	628.00	835.00
Worker, spouse, and 1 child	625.80	943.00	1,253.70
Retired worker claiming benefits at age 62:			
Worker alone[2]	333.00	502.00	662.00
Worker with spouse claiming benefits at—			
Age 65 or over	541.00	816.00	1,075.00
Age 62[2]	489.00	737.00	972.00
Widow or widower claiming benefits at—			
Age 65 or over[3]	391.00	593.00	789.00
Age 60	279.00	424.00	564.00
Disabled widow or widower claiming benefits at age 50-59[4]	279.00	424.00	564.00
1 surviving child	293.00	445.00	591.00
Widow or widower age 65 or over and 1 child	612.80	1,038.00	1,380.00
Widowed mother or father and 1 child	586.00	890.00	1,182.00
Widowed mother or father and 2 children	612.80	1,079.90	1,380.60

[1]Estimate. [2]Assumes maximum reduction. [3]A widow(er)'s benefit amount is limited to the amount the spouse would have been receiving if still living but not less than 82.5 percent of the PIA. [4]Effective January 1984, disabled widow(er)s claiming benefit at ages 50-59 will receive benefit equal to 71.5 percent of the PIA (based on 1983 Social Security Amendment provision).

Estimated Workers Under Social Insurance Programs

(In millions)

Employment and Coverage Status	1960	1965	1970	1975	1977	1980	1981	1982	1983	1984	1985
Total labor force[1]	**73.1**	**78.5**	**86.2**	**94.9**	**100.6**	**106.9**	**108.4**	**112.7**	**113.5**	**115.7**	**117.5**
Paid civilian population	64.6	71.6	77.6	84.8	92.0	97.0	96.9	98.4	102.2	105.5	107.7
Wage and salary workers	55.3	63.6	70.8	77.6	84.3	88.4	88.5	89.5	93.0	96.4	98.5
Self-employed	9.3	8.0	6.9	7.2	7.7	8.6	8.4	8.9	9.2	9.1	9.2
Unpaid family workers	1.4	1.1	.8	.7	.7	.6	.5	.5	.6	.5	.4
Unemployed	4.5	2.9	2.6	7.2	5.9	7.2	8.8	11.6	9.0	8.0	7.7
Armed Forces	2.5	2.8	3.4	2.2	2.1	2.1	2.2	2.2	1.7	1.7	1.7
Civilian population covered by:											
Public retirement programs	**60.9**	**68.4**	**75.3**	**82.2**	**88.8**	**93.5**	**93.6**	**94.8**	**99.5**	**104.2**	**106.3**
OASDHI[2]	55.4	62.7	69.2	75.7	82.1	86.5	86.6	87.9	92.7	97.5	99.7
Unemployment insurance	**43.7**	**50.3**	**55.8**	**69.7**	**75.8**	**87.2**	**89.9**	**87.9**	**91.3**	**95.4**	**NA**
Workers compensation	**44.6**	**52.3**	**59.0**	**68.6**	**74.2**	**79.4**	**79.8**	**77.8**	**80.9**	**84.5**	**NA**
Temporary disability insurance	**11.3**	**13.0**	**14.6**	**15.7**	**16.7**	**18.4**	**18.4**	**18.1**	**18.7**	**19.3**	**NA**

(1) Data from U.S. Bureau of Labor Statistics and based on U.S. Bureau of the Census' Current Population Survey. (2) OASDHI = Old-age, survivors, disability, and health insurance. Excludes members of Armed Forces and railroad employees. NA = not available.

Social Security Trust Funds

Old-Age and Survivors Insurance Trust Fund, 1940-86

[in millions]

Calendar year	Receipts: Total	Net contrib. inc., reimbursements from gen'l rev.	Net interest received	Cash benefit payments, rehabilitation services	Transfers to Railroad Retirement acct.	Administrative expenses	Total assets at end of year	Expenditures: Total
1940	$368	$325	$43	$35	...	$26	$2,031	$62
1950	2,928	2,667	257	961	...	61	13,721	1,022
1960	11,382	10,866	516	10,677	$318	203	20,324	11,198
1970	32,220	30,256	1,515	28,798	579	471	32,454	29,848
1980	105,841	103,456	1,845	105,083	1,442	1,154	22,823	107,678
1981	125,361	122,627	2,060	123,803	1,585	1,307	21,490	129,695
1982	125,198	123,673	845	138,806	1,793	1,519	22,088	142,119
1983	150,584	138,337	6,706	149,221	2,251	1,528	19,628	152,999
1984	169,328	164,122	2,266	157,841	2,404	1,638	27,117	161,883
1985	184,239	176,958	1,871	167,248	2,310	1,592	35,842	171,150
1986	197,393	190,741	3,069	176,813	2,585	1,601	39,081	181,000

Disability Insurance Trust Fund, 1960-86

Calendar year	Total	Net contrib. inc., reimbursements from gen'l rev.	Net interest received	Cash benefit payments, rehabilitation services	Transfers to Railroad Retirement acct.	Administrative expenses	Total assets at end of year	Total
1960		$1,010	$53	$568	$ −5	$36	$2,289	
1970		4,481	277	3,085	10	164	5,614	
1980		13,255	485	15,515	−12	368	3,629	
1981		16,738	172	17,192	29	436	3,040	
1982		21,995	540	17,376	26	590	2,691	
1983		17,991	1,569	17,524	28	625	5,195	
1984		15,945	1,174	17,898	22	626	3,959	
1985		17,191	870	18,827	43	608	6,321	
1986		18,399	803	19,853	68	600	7,780	

Hospital Insurance Trust Fund, 1967-86

[In millions]

Fiscal Year[1]	Income: Payroll taxes	Transfers from railroad retirement account	Reimbursement for uninsured persons	Premiums from voluntary enrollees	Payments for military wage credits	Interest on investments and other income[2]	Total income	Disbursements: Benefits payments[3]	Administrative expense[4]	Total disbursements	Trust Fund: Net increase fund	Fund at end of year
1967	$ 2,689	$ 16	$327	—	$ 11	$ 46	$ 3,089	$ 2,508	$ 89	$ 2,597	$492	$1,343
1970	4,785	16	617	—	11	137	5,614	4,804	149	4,953	661	2,677
1975	11,291	132	481	6	48	609	12,568	10,353	259	10,612	1,956	9,870
1980	23,244	244	697	17	141	1,072	25,415	23,700	497	24,288	1,127	14,490
1981	30,425	276	659	21	141	1,341	32,863	28,907	353	29,260	3,603	18,093
1982	34,390	351	808	25	207	1,829	37,611	34,343	521	34,864	2,747	20,840
1983	36,387	358	878	26	3,663[5]	2,629	43,940	38,102	522	38,624	−7,121	13,719
1984	41,364	351	752	35	250	2,812	46,560	41,476	633	42,108	3,455	17,174
1985	46,490	371	766	38	86	3,182	50,933	47,841	813	48,654	4,103	21,277
1986	53,020	364	566	40	−714	3,167	56,442	49,018	667	49,685	17,370	38,648

(1) For 1967 through 1976, fiscal years cover the interval from July 1 through June 30; fiscal years 1977-84 cover the interval from October 1 through September 30. (2) Other income includes recoveries of amounts reimbursed from the trust fund which are not obligations of the trust fund and other miscellaneous income. (3) Includes costs of Peer Review Organizations (beginning with the implementation of the Prospective Payment System on October 1, 1983). (4) Includes costs of experiments and demonstration projects. (5) Includes the lump sum general revenue transfer of −$805 million as provided for by Section 151 of P.L. 98-21.
NOTE: Totals do not necessarily equal the sum of rounded components.

Supplementary Medical Insurance Trust Fund, 1967-1986

[In millions]

Fiscal year[1]	Income: Premium from participants	Government contributions[2]	Interest and other income[3]	Total income	Disbursements: Benefit payments	Administrative expenses	Total disbursements	Balance in fund at end of year[4]
1967	$ 647	$ 623	$ 15	$1,285	$ 664	$ 135[5]	$ 799	$ 486
1970	936	928	12	1,876	1,979	217	2,196	57
1975	1,887	2,330	105	4,322	3,765	405	4,170	1,424
1976	1,951	2,939	104	4,994	4,672	528	5,200	1,219
1977	2,193	5,053	137	7,383	5,867	475	6,342	2,279
1978	2,431	6,386	228	9,045	6,852	504	7,356	3,968
1979	2,635	6,841	363	9,839	8,259	555	8,814	4,994
1980	2,928	6,932	415	10,275	10,144	593	10,737	4,532
1981	3,320	8,747	372	12,439	12,345	883	13,228	3,743
1982	3,831	13,323	473	17,627	14,806	754	15,560	5,810
1983	4,227	14,238	682	19,147	17,487	824	18,311	6,646
1984	4,907	16,811	807	22,525	19,473	899	20,372	8,799
1985	5,524	17,898	1,155	24,577	21,808	922	22,730	10,646
1986	5,699	18,076	1,228	25,004	25,169	1,049	26,217	9,432

(1) For 1967 through 1976, fiscal years cover the interval from July 1 through June 30; fiscal year 1977-86 cover the interval from October 1 through September 30. (2) The payments shown as being from the general fund of the Treasury include certain interest-adjustment items. (3) Other income includes recoveries of amounts reimbursed from the trust fund which are not obligations of the trust fund and other miscellaneous income. (4) The financial status of the program depends on both the total net assets and the liabilities of the program. (5) Administrative expenses shown include those paid in fiscal years 1966 and 1967.

VITAL STATISTICS

Source: National Center for Health Statistics, U.S. Department of Health and Human Services

Births

According to provisional statistics for the first quarter of 1987, there were 903,000 live births, 2 percent fewer than the number reported for the same 3-month period in 1986 (917,000). The birth rate was 15.1 and the fertility rate was 63.4. These rates were respectively, 2 and 3 percent lower than the rates for the Jan.-March 1986 period when the birth rate was 15.5 and the fertility rate was 65.0.

During the 12 months ending with March 1987, there were an estimated 3,717,000 live births, 1 percent below the number reported for the comparable period ending a year earlier (3,770,000). The birth rate was 15.4, 3 percent below the rate for the 12 months ending with March 1986 (15.8). The fertility rate was 64.6, also 3 percent lower than the rate for the same period a year earlier (66.3).

Natural Increase

The rate of natural increase for the first quarter of 1987 was 5.8 persons per 1,000 population, 3 percent below the rate for the first 3 months of 1986 (6.0). This decline was due to the decline in the birth rate.

Marriages

The total number of marriages for the first quarter of 1987 was 446,000. The marriage rate was 7.5 per 1,000 population, 3 percent above the rate for the first quarter of 1986 (7.3). Marriage rates for the first quarter of the year typically are lower than rates for the rest of the year.

During the 12 months ending with March 1987, an estimated 2,414,000 couples married, less than 1 percent below the number who married during the previous 12-month period. The marriage rate for the 12 months ending with March 1987 was 10.0 per 1,000 population, 1 percent below the rate for the previous 12-month period.

Divorces

A total of 274,000 couples divorced during the first quarter of 1987. The divorce rate was 4.6 per 1,000 population, the same as the rate for the first quarter of 1986.

During the 12 months ending with March 1987, an estimated 1,160,000 couples divorced. The divorce rate was 4.8 per 1,000 population, 2 percent below the figure for the comparable period a year earlier.

Deaths

According to provisional statistics, there were 554,000 deaths during the first quarter of 1987, 2 percent less than estimated for the first quarter of 1986 (564,000). The death rate was 9.3 per 1,000 population, 2 percent lower than the Jan.-March 1986 rate. Among the 554,000 deaths for the first quarter of 1987, were 9,600 deaths at ages under 1 year, yielding an infant mortality rate of 10.6 per 1,000 live births.

The death rate for the 12 months ending with March 1987 (8.6 deaths per 1,000 population) was 1 percent lower than the rate of 8.7 for the comparable 12-month period a year earlier. The infant mortality rate for this 12-month-period was 10.3 per 1,000 live births, 2 percent lower than the rate of 10.5 for the 12 months ending with March 1986.

Provisional Statistics
12 months ending with March

	Number		Rate*	
	1986	1987	1986	1987
Live births	3,770,000	3,717,000	15.8	15.4
Deaths	2,085,000	2,089,000	8.7	8.6
Natural increase.	1,685,000	1,628,000	7.1	6.8
Marriages	2,425,000	2,414,000	10.1	10.0
Divorces	1,184,000	1,160,000	5.0	4.8
Infant deaths. . .	39,400	38,300	10.5	10.3
Population base (in millions)			241.6	238.9

*Per 1,000 population
Note: Rates are based on the 1980 Census of Population.

Annual Report for the Year 1986 (Provisional Statistics)

The provisional totals show fewer live births, marriages, and divorces in 1986 than in 1985, and the same death rate per 1,000 population.

Births

During 1986 an estimated 3,731,000 babies were born in the United States, slightly fewer than in 1985 (3,749,000). The decline marks the first reduction in total births since 1983. The birth rate was 15.5 per 1,000 total population, 1 percent below the rate for 1985. The fertility rate was 64.9 live births per 1,000 women aged 15-44 years, 2 percent lower than the rate for 1985, and the lowest birth rate ever observed in the U.S.

The number of births declined because the 1-percent increase in the number of women in the childbearing ages (15-44 years) was not enough to compensate for the 2-percent decline in the fertility rate.

As a result of natural increase—the number of births over deaths—an estimated 1,632,000 persons were added to the population in 1986. The rate of increase was 6.8 per 1,000 population, the same as in 1985.

Deaths

The provisional count of deaths in the United States during 1986 totaled 2,099,000, about 15,000 more than in 1985 and the largest number ever reported for the nation. Despite the large number of deaths, the death rate remained unchanged from that of 1985, because the number of deaths between the two years increased at about the same rate as the population.

About 38,600 of the deaths in 1986 were to infants under 1 year of age. The infant mortality rate was 10.4 per 1,000 live births, as compared with 10.6 for 1985, 2 percent lower than in 1984.

Marriages and Divorces

The number of marriages declined from 2,425,000 in 1985 to 2,400,000 in 1986, a decrease of 1 percent. The marriage rate was 10.0 per 1,000 population. This rate was 2 percent below the 10.2 rate for 1985. The 1986 rate was the lowest since 1977.

According to provisional data, 1,159,000 couples were divorced during 1986, 2 percent less than in 1985. The divorce rate fell from 5.0 per 1,000 in 1985 to 4.8 in 1986, the lowest since 1975.

Births and Deaths in the U.S.

Refers only to events occurring within the U.S., including Alaska and Hawaii beginning in 1960. Excludes fetal deaths. Rates per 1,000 population enumerated as of April 1 for 1960, and 1970; estimated as of July 1 for all other years. (p) provisional. (NA) not available. Beginning 1970 excludes births and deaths occurring to nonresidents of the U.S.

	Births		Deaths	
Year	Total number	Rate	Total number	Rate
1955.	4,097,000	25.0	1,528,717	9.3
1960.	4,257,850	23.7	1,711,982	9.5
1965.	3,760,358	19.4	1,828,136	9.4
1970.	3,731,386	18.4	1,921,031	9.5
1975.	3,144,198	14.6	1,892,879	8.8
1980.	3,612,258	15.9	1,986,000	8.7
1985.	3,749,000	15.7	2,084,000	8.7
1986.	3,731,000	15.5	2,099,000	8.7

Births and Deaths by States and Regions

Source: National Center for Health Statistics, U.S. Department of Health and Human Services

	Births 1986p January-December	Births 1985 January-December	Deaths 1986p January-December	Deaths 1985 January-December
New England	**170,440**	**173,127**	**115,900**	**117,601**
Maine	16,022	16,211	10,983	11,351
New Hampshire	16,361	15,724	8,387	8,311
Vermont	7,529	7,925	4,840	4,800
Massachusetts	79,998	82,872	54,393	54,935
Rhode Island	13,935	13,517	9,915	9,829
Connecticut	40,595	36,878	27,382	28,375
Middle Atlantic	**528,069**	**521,643**	**365,159**	**365,307**
New York	264,844	256,049	172,857	171,089
New Jersey	102,785	103,308	67,609	69,966
Pennsylvania	160,440	162,286	124,693	124,252
East North Central	**618,696**	**626,650**	**371,994**	**364,866**
Ohio	158,277	160,898	99,947	98,371
Indiana	79,630	80,774	50,175	48,430
Illinois	172,321	177,803	100,536	99,381
Michigan	136,198	134,090	79,157	77,191
Wisconsin	72,270	73,085	42,179	41,493
West North Central	**265,986**	**275,155**	**164,394**	**165,110**
Minnesota	64,819	66,270	35,136	34,797
Iowa	38,794	42,084	26,617	27,051
Missouri	76,224	77,186	53,844	54,109
North Dakota	11,900	12,717	5,685	5,979
South Dakota	11,714	12,253	6,658	6,610
Nebraska	24,433	25,688	14,812	14,934
Kansas	38,102	38,957	21,642	21,630
South Atlantic	**606,735**	**601,687**	**373,524**	**362,837**
Delaware	9,768	9,843	5,688	5,491
Maryland	61,953	60,019	36,595	35,928
District of Columbia	20,541	20,368	8,158	8,403
Virginia	83,184	84,209	44,521	45,701
West Virginia	24,195	25,589	19,834	19,672
North Carolina	90,597	89,859	54,871	53,377
South Carolina	49,604	49,300	27,339	25,780
Georgia	98,786	99,792	50,241	47,712
Florida	167,255	163,560	124,852	122,198
East South Central	**221,525**	**223,449**	**142,825**	**141,136**
Kentucky	51,682	51,710	34,419	34,299
Tennessee	71,890	70,547	47,436	45,525
Alabama	56,417	58,807	37,335	37,322
Mississippi	41,536	42,385	23,635	23,990
West South Central	**474,837**	**483,106**	**210,959**	**210,703**
Arkansas	34,063	35,079	23,896	24,067
Louisiana	77,953	81,136	36,614	37,121
Oklahoma	48,061	51,910	28,787	29,195
Texas	314,760	314,981	121,662	120,320
Mountain	**229,868**	**236,406**	**91,829**	**89,167**
Montana	12,372	13,236	6,609	6,626
Idaho	16,329	17,492	7,017	6,877
Wyoming	8,011	8,838	3,049	3,087
Colorado	55,724	55,319	21,318	20,636
New Mexico	23,952	28,904	10,354	9,552
Arizona	60,890	58,829	26,413	25,344
Utah	37,368	38,431	9,317	9,348
Nevada	15,222	15,357	7,752	7,697
Pacific	**600,906**	**618,184**	**262,179**	**269,668**
Washington	68,754	76,205	32,899	35,579
Oregon	40,356	40,448	23,418	24,030
California	461,162	470,733	197,538	201,901
Alaska	12,371	12,570	2,175	2,054
Hawaii	18,228	18,263	6,104	6,149
Puerto Rico	NA	61,128	NA	21,838

p = provisional

Marriages and Divorces by States and Regions

Source: National Center for Health Statistics, U.S. Department of Health and Human Services

	Marriages January-December 1986p	Marriages 1985	Divorces³ January-December 1986p	Divorces³ 1985
New England	**104,415**	**114,857**	**45,469**	**47,310**
Maine	12,082	11,257	5,573	6,243
New Hampshire	11,708	11,159	4,737	4,941
Vermont	5,607	5,622	2,377	2,282
Massachusetts	40,717	51,648	19,958	19,794
Rhode Island	8,044	7,963	3,672	3,589
Connecticut	26,257	27,208	9,152	10,470
Middle Atlantic	**323,374**	**315,466**	**128,004**	**137,410**
New York	174,467	164,864	59,542	68,310
New Jersey	60,740	61,915	28,397	29,295
Pennsylvania	88,167	88,887	40,065	39,805
East North Central	**359,461**	**365,658**	**154,231²**	**156,254²**
Ohio	96,994	94,176	53,358	53,208
Indiana	50,514	52,688	NA	NA
Illinois	95,797	97,909	46,511	48,431
Michigan	77,770	80,813	37,654	37,735
Wisconsin	38,386	40,072	16,708	16,880
West North Central	**155,803**	**157,251**	**73,704**	**73,882**
Minnesota	34,964	34,458	13,893	13,750
Iowa	23,350	24,720	10,206	10,578
Missouri	50,270	49,014	25,889	25,393
North Dakota	5,164	5,467	2,264	2,300
South Dakota	7,447	7,836	2,585	2,567
Nebraska	12,027	12,185	6,233	6,465
Kansas	22,578	23,571	12,634	12,829
South Atlantic	**442,498**	**443,595**	**211,093**	**210,757**
Delaware	5,473	5,345	3,082	2,981
Maryland	45,985	47,069	15,520	16,202
District of Columbia	5,040	5,125	2,829	2,384
Virginia	66,670	66,836	24,220	24,974
West Virginia	13,783	14,649	9,821	9,990
North Carolina	60,204	60,575	31,650	30,270
South Carolina	54,126	52,776	13,454	13,628
Georgia	71,952	73,541	32,637	33,042
Florida	129,014	127,930	77,562	77,592
East South Central	**176,682**	**172,440**	**87,945**	**86,301**
Kentucky	47,147	46,949	19,288	18,774
Tennessee	58,877	54,942	29,172	30,210
Alabama	46,539	45,816	25,315	25,137
Mississippi	24,119	24,733	14,170	12,180
West South Central	**306,097**	**319,824**	**141,141²**	**143,733²**
Arkansas	31,162	30,496	16,563	16,171
Louisiana	36,663	39,666	NA	NA
Oklahoma	33,366	35,896	24,678	26,360
Texas	204,906	213,766	99,900	101,202
Mountain	**122,149¹**	**233,304**	**87,470**	**85,753**
Montana	6,785	7,179	4,341	4,261
Idaho	10,524	12,542	6,023	6,223
Wyoming	5,348	5,355	3,553	3,799
Colorado	32,454	33,938	19,308	19,172
New Mexico	14,142	14,585	8,867	9,027
Arizona	38,021	35,706	23,399	21,204
Utah	16,869	17,077	8,480	8,580
Nevada	NA	106,922	13,499	13,487
Pacific	**306,591**	**314,542**	**50,038²**	**177,649**
Washington	43,782	44,514	26,108	25,563
Oregon	21,638	22,414	15,490	15,848
California	218,959	226,113	NA	127,406
Alaska	5,924	6,182	3,836	3,996
Hawaii	15,319	16,288	4,836	4,604
Puerto Rico	NA	27,555	NA	NA

p = provisional (1) Excludes figures for Nevada; (2) Excludes figures for state shown below as not available; (3) Divorces are by state of occurrence, not by state of residence. NA = not available.

Marriages, Divorces, and Rates in the U.S.

Source: National Center for Health Statistics; U.S. Department of Health and Human Services

Data refer only to events occurring within the United States, including Alaska and Hawaii beginning with 1960. Rates per 1,000 population.

Year	Marriages¹ No.	Marriages¹ Rate	Divorces² No.	Divorces² Rate
1895	620,000	8.9	40,387	0.6
1900	709,000	9.3	55,751	0.7
1905	842,000	10.0	67,976	0.8
1910	948,166	10.3	83,045	0.9
1915	1,007,595	10.0	104,298	1.0
1920	1,274,476	12.0	170,505	1.6
1925	1,188,334	10.3	175,449	1.5
1930	1,126,856	9.2	195,961	1.6
1935	1,327,000	10.4	218,000	1.7
1940	1,595,879	12.1	264,000	2.0
1945	1,612,992	12.2	485,000	³3.5
1950	1,667,231	11.1	385,144	2.6
1955	1,531,000	9.3	377,000	2.3
1960	1,523,000	8.5	393,000	2.2
1965	1,800,000	9.3	479,000	2.5
1970	2,158,802	10.6	708,000	3.5
1975	2,152,662	10.0	1,036,000	4.8
1980	2,413,000	10.6	1,182,000	5.2
1985	2,425,000	10.2	1,187,000	5.0
1986	2,400,000	10.0	1,159,000	4.8

(1) Includes estimates and marriage licenses for some states for all years. (2) Includes reported annulments. (3) Divorce rates for 1945 based on population including armed forces overseas.

Estimated Death Rates for Selected Causes, 1985-86

Source: National Center for Health Statistics, U.S. Department of Health and Human Services

Cause of death (est.)	Rate* 1985	Rate* 1986
All causes	**873.7**	**872.2**
Viral hepatitis	0.4	0.5
Tuberculosis, all forms	0.7	0.7
Septicemia	7.0	7.1
Syphilis and its sequelae	0.0	0.0
All other infective and para1itic diseases		
Malignant neoplasms, including neoplasms of lymphatic and hematopoietic tissues	192.6	193.4
Diabetes mellitus	15.8	15.1
Meningitis	0.5	0.5
Major cardiovascular diseases	408.3	400.2
Diseases of heart	322.6	317.2
Rheumatic fever and rheumatic heart disease	2.6	2.7
Hypertensive heart disease	8.6	8.3
Ischemic heart disease	224.9	216.5
Acute myocardial infarction	114.4	108.4
All other forms of heart disease	81.7	81.3
Hypertension	3.0	3.1
Cerebrovascular diseases	64.1	61.6
Artherosclerosis	9.9	9.2
Other diseases of arteries, arterioles, and capillaries	8.7	9.1

Cause of death (est.)	Rate* 1985	Rate* 1986
Acute bronchitis and bronchiolitis	0.2	0.2
Influenza and pneumonia	27.8	28.8
Influenza	0.9	0.9
Pneumonia	26.9	27.9
Chronic obstructive pulmonary diseases	31.2	31.4
Chronic and unspecified bronchitis	1.5	1.4
Emphysema	6.0	6.1
Asthma	1.6	1.6
Ulcer of stomach and duodenum	2.8	2.5
Hernia and intestinal obstruction	2.1	2.2
Cirrhosis of liver	11.3	10.9
Cholelithiasis, cholecystitis, and cholangitis	1.2	1.2
Nephritis, nephrosis and nephrotic syn.	9.4	9.0
Infections of kidney	0.8	0.8
Hyperplasia of prostate	0.2	0.3
Congenital anomalies	5.6	5.1
Certain causes of mortality in early infancy	7.9	7.5
Symptoms and ill-defined conditions	17.5	18.2
All other diseases	62.2	64.3
Accidents	38.5	39.5
Motor vehicle accidents	18.6	19.6
Suicide	11.5	12.8
Homicide	8.2	8.9
All other external causes	1.1	1.1

*Per 100,000 population; based on a 10% sampling of all death certificates for an 11-month (Jan.-Nov.) period.

Principal Types of Accidental Deaths

Source: National Safety Council

Year	Motor vehicle	Falls	Fires, Burns	Drown-ing	Fire-arms	Injestion of Food, Object	Poison by gas	Other poisons
1965	49,163	19,984	7,347	5,485	2,344	1,973	1,526	2,110
1970	54,633	16,926	6,718	6,391	2,406	2,877	1,620	3,679
1975	45,853	14,896	6,071	6,640	2,380	3,106	1,577	4,694
1980	52,600	12,300	5,500	7,000	1,800	3,249	1,500	2,800
1981	50,800	11,700	4,900	6,000	1,900	3,200	1,700	2,600
1982	46,000	11,600	5,000	6,200	1,900	3,200	1,400	3,000
1984	46,200	11,800	5,100	5,600	1,700	3,100	1,300	4,000
1985	45,600	11,300	4,900	5,700	1,600	3,200	1,200	3,800
1986	47,900	11,000	4,800	5,600	1,800	3,600	900	4,000
Death rates per 100,000 population								
1965	25.4	10.3	3.8	2.8	1.2	1.1	0.8	1.1
1970	26.9	8.3	3.3	3.1	1.2	1.4	0.8	1.8
1975	21.5	7.0	2.8	3.1	1.1	1.1	0.7	2.2
1980	23.2	5.4	2.4	3.1	0.8	1.4	0.7	1.2
1981	22.2	5.1	2.1	2.6	0.8	1.4	0.8	1.1
1982	19.9	5.0	2.2	2.7	0.8	1.4	0.6	1.3
1984	19.5	5.0	2.2	2.4	0.7	1.3	0.5	1.7
1985	19.1	4.7	2.1	2.4	0.7	1.3	0.5	1.6
1986	19.9	4.6	2.0	2.3	0.7	1.5	0.4	1.7

U.S. Civil Aviation Accidents

Source: National Safety Council

	Accidents			Accident Rates			
				Per 100,000 Aircraft-Hours		Per million Aircraft-Miles	
1986	Total	Fatal	Deaths[1]	Total	Fatal	Total	Fatal
Large airlines	22	1	3	0.246	0.011	0.006	0.0003
Commuter airlines	14	2	4	0.82	0.12	0.05	0.01
On-demand air taxis	118	31	64	4.27	1.12	—	—
General aviation	2,568	466	958	8.46	1.53	—	—

(1) Includes passengers, crew members and others.

Transportation Accident Passenger Death Rates, 1985

Source: National Safety Council

Kind of transportation	Passenger miles (billions)	Passenger deaths	Rate per 100,000,000 pass. miles	1984-1985 aver. death rate
Passenger automobiles and taxis[1]	2,466.6	22,974	0.93	0.96
Buses	116.8	47	0.04	—
Intercity buses	24.0	12	0.05	0.03
Railroad passenger trains	11.4	3	0.03	0.06
Scheduled air transport planes (domestic)	277.8	201	0.07	0.03

(1) Drivers of passenger automobiles are considered passengers.

Motor Vehicle Traffic Deaths by State

Source: National Safety Council

Place of accidents	Number 1985	Number 1986	Mileage Rate[b] 1985	Mileage Rate[b] 1986
Total U.S.[a]	45,600	47,900	2.6	2.6
Alabama	889	1,080	2.5	2.9
Alaska	120	98	3.1	2.5
Arizona	893	1,002	4.1	4.5
Arkansas	534	601	3.1	3.4
California	4,933	5,223	2.3	2.4
Colorado	579	603	2.2	2.2
Connecticut	449	455	2.0	1.9
Delaware	105	138	2.0	2.7
Dist. of Col.	61	45	1.9	1.4
Florida	2,870	2,875	3.3	3.1
Georgia	1,362	1,540	2.6	3.1
Hawaii	126	117	1.9	1.7
Idaho	255	258	3.3	3.5
Illinois	1,552	1,616	2.2	2.3
Indiana	980	1,038	2.4	2.6
Iowa	473	440	2.3	2.3
Kansas	486	500	2.5	2.6
Kentucky	715	808	2.5	2.7
Louisiana	933	844	2.8	2.6
Maine	206	208	2.2	2.1
Maryland	740	790	2.2	2.3
Massachusetts	742	752	1.9	1.8
Michigan	1,569	1,624	2.3	2.3
Minnesota	610	572	1.9	1.8
Mississippi	665	768	3.5	4.0
Missouri	948	1,135	2.4	2.7

Place of accidents	Number 1984	Number 1985	Mileage Rate[b] 1984	Mileage Rate[b] 1985
Montana	223	222	3.0	2.9
Nebraska	237	290	2.0	2.3
Nevada	259	233	3.4	3.0
New Hampshire	190	172	2.5	2.1
New Jersey	964	1,040	1.8	1.8
New Mexico	535	498	4.0	3.7
New York	1,995	2,114	2.2	2.2
North Carolina	1,482	1,640	3.0	3.1
North Dakota	90	100	1.7	1.9
Ohio	1,644	1,673	2.2	2.1
Oklahoma	750	710	2.4	2.4
Oregon	558	619	2.6	2.8
Pennsylvania	1,809	1,928	2.4	2.6
Rhode Island	106	114	1.8	1.9
South Carolina	949	1,058	3.5	3.7
South Dakota	130	134	2.1	2.0
Tennessee	1,111	1,232	3.4	3.0
Texas	3,682	3,568	2.6	2.4
Utah	303	311	2.5	2.4
Vermont	115	109	2.5	2.2
Virginia	980	1,118	2.0	2.2
Washington	759	714	2.2	2.0
West Virginia	420	437	3.3	3.4
Wisconsin	757	757	2.1	2.0
Wyoming	152	168	2.8	3.1

(a) Includes both traffic and nontraffic motor-vehicle deaths. (b) The mileage death rate is deaths per 100,000,000 vehicle miles. 1986 mileage death rates are National Safety Council estimates.

Accidental Deaths and Injuries by Severity of Injury

Source: National Safety Council

In 1986 accidental deaths were estimated to number 94,000, an increase of 1,500 or 2 percent more than the 1985 total. This was the fifth year since 1962 that accidental deaths were estimated to number less than 100,000. The death rate per 100,000 population was 39.0, up 1 percent from 1985, the lowest rate on record.

1986 Severity of injury	Total*	Motor vehicle	Work	Home	Public[1]
Deaths*	94,000	47,900	10,700	20,500	19,000
Disabling injuries*	8,900,000	1,800,000	1,800,000	3,100,000	2,400,000
Permanent impairments	330,000	140,000	60,000	80,000	60,000
Temporary total disabilities	8,600,000	1,700,000	1,700,000	3,000,000	2,400,000
Certain Costs of Accidental Deaths or Injuries, 1986 ($ billions)					
Total*	$118.0	$57.8	$34.8	$16.0	$11.3
Wage loss	32.0	16.9	6.8	4.8	4.9
Medical expense	20.5	4.4	5.2	6.7	4.7
Insurance administration	21.2	15.3	4.4	0.8	0.7

*Duplication between motor vehicle, work, and home are eliminated in the total column. (1) Excludes motor vehicle and work accidents in public places.

Home Accident Deaths

Source: National Safety Council

Year	Total home	Falls	Fires, burns[2]	Suffo., ingesting object	Suffo., mechanical	Poison (solid, liquid)	Poison by gas	Firearms	Other
1950	29,000	14,800	5,000	(1)	1,600	1,300	1,250	950	4,100
1955	28,500	14,100	5,400	(1)	1,250	1,150	900	1,100	4,600
1960	28,000	12,300	6,350	1,850	1,500	1,350	900	1,200	2,550
1965	28,500	11,700	6,100	1,300*	1,200	1,700	1,100	1,300	4,100
1970	27,000	9,700	5,600	1,800	1,100	3,000	1,100	1,400	3,300
1975	25,000	8,000	5,000	1,800	800	3,700	1,000	1,300	3,400
1980	22,800	7,100	4,800	2,000	500	2,500	700	1,100	4,100[3]
1984	21,200	6,400	4,100	2,300	600	3,000	700	900	3,200
1985	21,000	6,100	4,000	2,400	500	2,800	600	1,000	3,600
1986	20,500	5,700	3,900	2,400	500	3,200	500	900	3,400

*Data for this year and subsequent years not comparable with previous years due to classification changes. (1) Included in Other. (2) Includes deaths resulting from conflagration, regardless of nature of injury. (3) Includes about 1,000 excessive deaths due to summer heat wave.

Pedalcycle Accidents

Source: National Safety Council

Year	Pedalcycles (millions)	Deaths	Death Rate[a]	Percent of Deaths by Age 0-14	15-24	25 & over
1940	7.8	750	9.59	48	39	13
1950	13.8	440	3.18	82	9	9
1960	28.2	460	1.63	78	9	13
1970	56.5	780	1.38	66	15	19
1980	100.0	1,200	1.20	35	36	29
1984	106.1	1,000	1.04	39	27	34
1985	108.0	1,100	1.02	34	30	36
1986	111.0	1,200	1.08	32	33	35

(a) Deaths per 100,000 pedalcycles.

Accidental Deaths by Month and Type, 1984 and 1986

Source: National Safety Council

Month	1986 totals	1984 totals	Motor vehicle	Falls	Drowning†	Fires, burns*	Ingest. of food, object	Firearms	Poison (solid, liquid)	Poison by gas
			1984 details by type							
All months	94,000	92,911	46,263	11,937	5,388	5,010	3,541	1,668	3,808	1,103
January	6,950	7,027	3,011	1,046	170	708	317	139	309	166
February	6,350	6,596	2,921	943	230	589	298	111	288	125
March	7,650	7,302	3,485	992	260	532	325	131	296	135
April	7,250	7,035	3,373	977	374	393	281	117	310	91
May	8,300	7,859	3,966	978	610	369	265	123	318	58
June	8,500	8,435	4,244	957	920	298	245	127	321	59
July	9,150	8,803	4,437	984	990	247	267	125	349	38
August	8,800	8,447	4,386	964	780	213	304	110	340	44
September	7,600	7,925	4,277	994	430	299	266	131	313	44
October	7,950	7,886	4,260	1,028	254	316	310	169	306	79
November	7,650	7,610	3,919	1,018	200	482	314	212	328	127
December	7,850	7,986	3,984	1,056	170	564	349	173	330	137
Average	7,830	7,743	3,855	995	449	418	295	139	317	92

† Partly estimated; includes drowning in water transport accidents. * Includes deaths resulting from conflagration regardless of nature of injury.

Accidental Deaths by Age, Sex, and Type, 1984

Age and Sex	1984 totals	Motor-vehicle	Falls	Drowning	Fires, burns	Ingest. of food, object	Firearms	Poison (solid, liquid)	Poison by gas	% Male all types
All ages	92,911	16,263	11,937	5,388	5,010	3,541	1,668	3,808	1,103	69
Under 5	3,652	1,138	114	638	742	271	34	64	34	60
5 to 14	4,198	2,263	68	532	466	45	253	23	33	69
15 to 24	19,801	14,738	399	1,353	443	97	515	498	191	77
25 to 44	25,498	15,036	963	1,549	980	293	514	2,111	405	79
45 to 64	15,273	6,954	1,624	763	946	648	222	627	258	71
65 to 74	8,424	3,020	1,702	281	624	643	86	243	79	62
75 & over	16,065	3,114	7,067	272	809	1,544	44	242	103	47
Male	64,053	32,949	6,210	4,420	3,141	1,994	1,461	2,595	825	
Female	28,858	13,314	5,727	968	1,869	1,547	207	1,213	278	
Percent male	69	71	52	82	63	56	88	68	75	

Ownership of Life Insurance in the U.S. and Assets of U.S. Life Insurance Companies

Source: American Council of Life Insurance

Legal Reserve Life Insurance Companies (millions of dollars)

Year	Purchases of life insurance: Ordinary	Group	Industrial	Total	Insurance in force: Ordinary	Group	Industrial	Credit	Total	Assets
1940	6,689	691	3,350	10,730	79,346	14,938	20,866	380	115,530	30,802
1950	17,326	6,068	5,402	28,796	149,116	47,793	33,415	3,844	234,168	64,020
1960	52,883	14,645	6,880	74,408	341,881	175,903	39,563	29,101	586,448	119,576
1965	83,485	51,385*	7,296	142,166*	499,638	308,078	39,818	53,020	900,554	158,884
1970	122,820	63,690*	6,612	193,122*	734,730	551,357	38,644	77,392	1,402,123	207,254
1975	188,003	95,190*	6,729	289,922*	1,083,421	904,695	39,423	112,032	2,139,571	289,304
1980	385,575	183,418	3,609	572,602	1,760,474	1,579,355	35,994	165,215	3,541,038	479,210
1981	481,895	346,702*	2,517	831,114*	1,978,080	1,888,612	34,547	162,356	4,063,595	525,803
1982	585,444	250,532	1,898	837,874	2,216,388	2,066,361	32,766	161,144	4,476,659	588,163
1983	753,444	271,609	1,388	1,026,441	2,544,275	2,219,573	31,354	170,659	4,965,861	654,948
1984	820,315	293,521	943	1,114,779	2,887,574	2,392,558	30,104	189,951	5,499,987	722,979
1985	910,944	319,503	722	1,231,169	3,247,289	2,561,595	28,250	215,973	6,053,107	825,901
1986	933,592	374,741*	418	1,308,751*	3,658,203	2,801,049	27,168	233,859	6,720,279	937,551

*Includes Servicemen's Group Life Insurance $27.8 billion in 1965, $17.1 billion in 1970, $1.7 billion in 1975, $45.6 billion in 1981, and $51.0 in 1986, as well as $84.4 billion of Federal Employees' Group Life Insurance in 1981 and $10.8 billion in 1986.

Births to Unmarried Women, 1985

Source: National Center for Health Statistics

Childbearing by unmarried women increased substantially between 1984 and 1985, the number of births up 8%, the birth rate up 6%, and the ratio of births to unmarried women up 5%, the greatest single year increases since 1980.

Age of mother	Number: All races	White	All other: Total	Black	Rate per 1,000 unmarried women in specified group: All races	White	All other: Total	Black	Ratio per 1,000 live births: All races	White	All other: Total	Black
All ages	828,174	432,969	395,205	365,527	32.8(1)	21.8(1)	73.2(1)	78.8(1)	220.2	144.7	513.8	601.0
Under 15	9,386	3,380	6,006	5,783	—	—	—	—	918.4	824.2	981.5	986.9
15–19	270,922	142,131	128,791	120,378	31.6	20.5	79.4	88.8	579.5	445.9	865.8	896.5
15	20,930	9,563	11,367	10,779					837.1	720.3	969.4	979.8
16	39,630	20,342	19,288	18,188	22.5	14.2	59.1	67.0	741.1	615.5	944.5	961.7
17	58,371	31,436	26,935	25,169					653.6	526.4	910.0	935.8
18	72,934	39,021	33,913	31,495	46.6	30.9	109.9	121.1	562.9	433.8	856.1	889.7
19	79,057	41,769	37,288	34,747					464.7	340.3	386.7	826.1
20–24	300,365	156,568	143,797	133,360	46.8	30.9	105.7	116.1	263.2	175.1	581.9	643.2
25–29	152,024	78,834	73,190	67,300	39.8	27.3	77.9	81.4	126.5	79.1	358.6	441.9
30–34	67,315	35,871	31,444	28,305	25.0	17.5	48.8	48.8	96.7	61.8	271.2	362.3
35–39	24,038	13,714	10,324	9,027	11.6	8.6	21.4	21.3	112.2	79.0	253.9	344.3
40 and over	4,124	2,471	1,653	1,374	2.5(2)	1.9(2)	4.7(2)	4.5(2)	139.8	107.2	256.0	336.6

(1) Rates computed by relating total births to unmarried mothers, regardless of age of mother, to unmarried women aged 15–44.
(2) Rates computed by relating births to unmarried mothers aged 40 and over to unmarried women aged 40–44.

Families, 1960-1985

Source: U.S. Bureau of the Census
(in thousands)

	All Families Number	Married Couple Number	Male Householder[1] Number	Female Householder[1] Number	Black Families Number
1960	45,111	39,329	1,275	4,507	4,242[2]
1965	47,956	41,749	1,181	5,026	4,767[2]
1970	51,586	44,755	1,239	5,591	4,887
1975	55,712	46,971	1,499	7,242	5,498
1979	57,804	47,692	1,655	8,458	5,906
1980	59,550	49,112	1,733	8,705	6,184
1981	60,309	49,294	1,933	9,082	6,317
1982	61,019	49,630	1,986	9,403	6,413
1983	61,393	49,908	2,016	9,469	6,530
1984	61,997	50,090	2,030	9,878	6,675

	Number	%	Number	%	Number	%	Number	%	Number	%
1985, total	**62,706**	**100.0**	**50,350**	**100.0**	**2,228**	**100.0**	**10,129**	**100.0**	**6,778**	**100.0**
White	54,400	86.8	45,643	90.7	1,816	81.5	6,941	68.5	(x)	(x)
Black	6,778	10.8	3,469	6.9	344	15.4	2,964	29.3	6,778	100.0
Spanish origin[3]	3,939	6.3	2,824	5.6	210	9.4	905	8.9	(x)	(x)
Size of family:										
2 persons	25,349	40.4	19,220	38.2	1,382	62.0	4,747	46.9	2,261	33.4
3 persons	14,804	23.6	11,346	22.5	520	23.3	2,938	29.0	1,730	25.5
4 persons	13,259	21.1	11,666	23.2	210	9.4	1,383	13.7	1,358	20.0
5 persons	5,894	9.4	5,218	10.4	66	3.0	600	6.0	762	11.2
6 persons	2,175	3.5	1,888	3.7	24	1.1	263	2.6	366	5.4
7 or more persons	1,225	2.0	1,012	2.0	26	1.2	188	1.9	300	4.4
Median size	3.23	(x)	3.28	(x)	2.77	(x)	3.05	(x)	3.60	(x)
Own children under age 18:										
None	31,594	50.4	26,140	51.9	1,331	59.7	4,123	40.7	2,887	42.6
1	13,108	20.9	9,640	19.1	584	26.2	2,885	28.5	1,579	23.3
2	11,645	18.6	9,456	18.8	213	9.6	1,977	19.5	1,330	19.6
3	4,486	7.2	3,635	7.2	80	3.6	771	7.6	612	9.0
4 or more	1,873	3.0	1,480	2.9	20	.9	373	3.7	370	5.5
Own children under age 6:										
None	48,505	77.4	38,635	76.7	1,952	87.6	7,918	78.2	4,993	73.7
1	9,677	15.4	7,827	15.5	220	9.9	1,629	16.1	1,279	18.9
2	3,884	6.2	3,359	6.7	47	2.1	477	4.7	416	6.1
3 or more	641	1.0	528	1.0	9	.4	104	1.0	90	1.3

(x) = Not applicable; (1) No spouse present; (2) Black and other races; (3) Persons of Spanish origin may be of any race.

Marital Status of the Population, By Sex and Age, 1985

Source: U.S. Bureau of the Census

	Number of Persons (1,000)					Percent Distribution				
Sex and Age	Total	Single	Married	Widowed	Divorced	Total	Single	Married	Widowed	Divorced
Male	**81,452**	**20,543**	**53,536**	**2,109**	**5,264**	**100.0**	**25.2**	**65.7**	**2.6**	**6.5**
18-19 years	3,640	3,534	106	—	—	100.0	97.1	2.9	—	—
20-24 years	10,055	7,605	2,310	9	138	100.0	75.6	23.0	—	1.4
25-29 years	10,420	4,037	5,751	3	629	100.0	38.7	55.2	—	6.0
30-34 years	9,764	2,027	6,804	7	926	100.0	20.8	69.7	.1	9.5
35-44 years	15,333	1,444	12,254	54	1,581	100.0	9.4	79.9	.4	10.3
45-54 years	10,848	682	9,096	131	939	100.0	6.3	83.8	1.2	8.7
55-64 years	10,377	633	8,711	388	644	100.0	6.1	83.9	3.7	6.2
65-74 years	7,259	380	5,899	672	307	100.0	5.2	81.3	9.3	4.2
75 years old and over	3,755	200	2,604	851	100	100.0	5.3	69.3	22.7	2.7
Female	**89,917**	**16,377**	**54,354**	**11,372**	**7,814**	**100.0**	**18.2**	**60.4**	**12.6**	**8.7**
18-19 years	3,738	3,240	468	2	28	100.0	86.7	12.5	.1	.7
20-24 years	10,411	6,091	3,953	20	347	100.0	58.5	38.0	.2	3.3
25-29 years	10,686	2,824	6,963	57	843	100.0	26.4	65.2	.5	7.9
30-34 years	9,987	1,351	7,299	104	1,234	100.0	13.5	73.1	1.0	12.4
35-44 years	15,966	1,091	12,312	323	2,242	100.0	6.8	77.1	2.0	14.0
45-54 years	11,550	529	8,812	809	1,401	100.0	4.6	76.3	7.0	12.1
55-64 years	11,774	440	8,240	2,047	1,047	100.0	3.7	70.0	17.4	8.9
65-74 years	9,317	412	4,764	3,622	519	100.0	4.4	51.1	38.9	5.6
75 years old and over	6,487	400	1,543	4,390	154	100.0	6.2	23.8	67.7	2.4

Never-Married Persons as Percent of Population, 1960-1985

Source: U.S. Bureau of the Census

	Male					Female				
Age	1960	1970	1980	1984	1985	1960	1970	1980	1984	1985
Total	**17.3**	**18.9**	**23.8**	**25.5**	**25.2**	**11.9**	**13.7**	**17.1**	**18.4**	**18.2**
18 years	94.6	95.1	97.4	98.2	98.5	75.6	82.0	88.0	91.4	90.7
19 years	87.1	89.9	90.9	95.3	95.8	59.7	68.8	77.6	82.9	82.7
20-24 years	53.1	54.7	68.8	74.8	75.6	28.4	35.8	50.2	56.9	58.5
25-29 years	20.8	19.1	33.1	37.8	38.7	10.5	10.5	20.9	25.9	26.4
30-34 years	11.9	9.4	15.9	20.9	20.8	6.9	6.2	9.5	13.3	13.5
35-39 years	8.8	7.2	7.8	11.6	10.1	6.1	5.4	6.2	7.5	8.1
40-44 years	7.3	6.3	7.1	6.9	8.6	6.1	4.9	4.8	5.4	5.3
45-54 years	7.4	7.5	6.1	6.2	6.3	7.0	4.9	4.7	4.6	4.6
55-64 years	8.0	7.8	5.3	5.4	6.1	8.0	6.8	4.5	4.2	3.7
65 years old and over	7.7	7.5	4.9	5.0	5.3	8.5	7.7	5.9	5.6	5.1

Persons Living Alone, By Sex and Age, 1960-1985

Source: U.S. Bureau of the Census

Sex and age	Number of Persons (1,000)					Percent Distribution				
	1960	1970	1975	1980	1985	1960	1970	1975	1980	1985
Both sexes	7,064	10,851	13,939	18,296	20,602	100.0	100.0	100.0	100.0	100.0
14-24 years	234	556	1,111	1,726	1,324	3.3	5.1	8.0	9.4	6.4
25-44 years	1,212	1,604	2,744	4,729	6,228	17.2	14.8	19.7	25.8	30.2
45-64 years	2,720	3,622	4,076	4,514	4,939	38.5	33.4	29.2	24.7	24.0
65 years old and over	2,898	5,071	6,008	7,328	8,112	41.0	46.7	43.1	40.1	39.4
Male	**2,628**	**3,532**	**4,918**	**6,966**	**7,922**	**37.2**	**32.5**	**35.3**	**38.1**	**38.5**
14-24 years	124	274	610	947	750	1.8	2.5	4.4	5.2	3.6
25-44 years	686	933	1,689	2,920	3,713	9.7	8.6	12.1	16.0	18.0
45-64 years	965	1,152	1,329	1,613	1,845	13.7	10.6	9.5	8.8	9.0
65 years old and over	853	1,174	1,290	1,486	1,614	12.1	10.8	9.3	8.1	7.8
Female	**4,436**	**7,319**	**9.021**	**11,330**	**12,680**	**62.8**	**67.5**	**64.7**	**61.9**	**61.5**
14-24 years	110	282	501	779	573	1.6	2.6	3.6	4.3	2.8
25-44 years	526	671	1,055	1,809	2,514	7.4	6.2	7.6	9.9	12.2
45-64 years	1,755	2,470	2,747	2,901	3,095	24.8	22.8	19.7	15.9	15.0
65 years old and over	2,045	2,897	4,718	5,842	6,498	28.9	35.9	33.8	31.9	31.5

Unmarried Couples

Source: U.S. Bureau of the Census

(thousands)

Presence of Children and Age of householders	1970	1980	1984	1985
Unmarried couples	**523**	**1,589**	**1,988**	**1,983**
No children under 15 yr	327	1,159	1,373	1,380
Some children under 15 yr.	196	431	614	603
Under 25 yr. old	55	411	432	425

Presence of Children and Age of Householder	1970	1980	1984	1985
25-44 yr. old	103	837	1,208	1,203
45-64 yr. old	186	221	234	239
65 yr. old or over	178	119	114	116

Women, Age 18-44, Who Gave Birth in 1985

Source: U.S. Bureau of the Census

	Total 18-44 Years Old			18-29 Years Old			30-44 Years Old		
		Women who have had a child in the last year			Women who have had a child in the last year			Women who have had a child in the last year	
	Number of women (1,000)	Total births per 1,000 women	First births per 1,000 women	Number of women (1,000)	Total births per 1,000 women	First births per 1,000 women	Number of women (1,000)	Total births per 1,000 women	First births per 1,000 women
Total[1]	**50,951**	**68.6**	**27.1**	**24,788**	**101.4**	**47.1**	**26,163**	**37.6**	**8.0**
White	42,782	66.9	27.2	20,581	99.9	47.6	22,202	36.4	8.3
Black	6,523	76.4	27.1	3,433	110.8	47.1	3,090	38.1	4.9
Spanish origin[2]	3,816	107.3	33.1	2,023	153.6	55.6	1,793	55.2	7.8
Married, spouse present	29,118	92.0	34.8	10,634	169.4	76.8	18,484	47.5	10.6
Married, spouse absent[3]	2,216	86.8	24.8	982	164.6	55.4	1,234	24.9	.5
Widowed or divorced	5,199	27.5	7.7	1,312	81.0	28.1	3,888	9.5	.9
Single	14,417	33.4	18.8	11,860	37.4	21.9	2,557	15.1	4.1
Labor force status: In labor force	36,075	46.9	21.6	17,685	68.1	36.7	18,390	26.5	7.1
Employed	33,034	43.5	19.9	15,772	62.0	33.9	17,262	26.6	7.1
Unemployed	3,041	83.5	40.0	1,913	118.3	59.5	1,128	24.5	7.1
Not in labor force	14,876	121.4	40.2	7,103	184.2	73.0	7,773	63.9	10.2
Family income: Under $10,000	8,726	93.6	34.0	5,184	132.9	53.5	3,542	36.0	5.5
$10,000-$14,999	5,858	76.9	30.5	3,291	110.3	52.3	2,567	34.1	2.7
$15,000-$19,999	5,702	69.6	29.8	2,973	108.1	55.3	2,730	27.7	2.1
$20,000-$24,999	5,457	67.5	22.1	2,629	97.5	39.9	2,828	39.6	5.5
$25,000-$29,999	4,703	70.0	28.9	2,185	110.8	53.1	2,518	34.6	7.8
$30,000-$34,999	4,606	83.0	31.6	2,014	118.8	54.1	2,592	55.2	14.1
$35,000 and over	13,801	46.0	20.3	5,584	59.6	34.1	8,217	36.7	11.0
Years of school completed: Not a high school graduate	7,877	98.2	28.3	4,028	155.7	52.5	3,850	38.0	3.0
High school, 4 years	22,117	68.3	29.2	10,972	109.6	53.9	11,145	27.6	5.0
College, 1-3 years	11,594	57.6	24.7	6,134	75.7	39.8	5,460	37.2	7.6
College, 4 years	6,238	61.3	22.7	2,885	61.6	31.2	3,354	61.0	15.5
College, 5 or more years	3,124	52.3	26.0	768	53.3	40.6	2,355	52.0	21.3

(1) Includes women of other races and women with family income not reported, not shown separately. (2) Persons of Spanish origin may be of any race. (3) Includes separated women.

Households, By Number of Persons, 1960-1985

Source: U.S. Bureau of the Census

The average number of people per household in the U.S. declined in 1986 to 2.67, th least ever recorded. The number declined from 2.69 in 1985, 2.76 in 1980, and 3.14 in 1970.

Size of Household	1960	1965	1970	1975	1977	1978	1980	1981	1982	1983	1984	1985
Total (million) . .	**52.6**	**57.3**	**63.4**	**71.1**	**74.1**	**76.0**	**80.8**	**82.4**	**83.5**	**83.9**	**85.4**	**86.8**
1 person	6.9	8.6	10.9	13.9	15.5	16.7	18.3	18.9	19.4	19.3	20.0	20.6
Male	2.3	2.9	3.5	4.9	5.6	6.4	7.0	7.3	7.5	7.5	7.5	7.9
Female	4.6	5.7	7.3	9.0	9.9	10.4	11.3	11.7	11.9	11.8	12.4	12.7
2 persons	14.6	16.1	18.3	21.8	22.8	23.3	25.3	25.8	26.5	26.4	26.9	27.4
3 persons	9.9	10.2	10.9	12.4	12.8	13.0	14.1	14.6	14.6	14.8	15.1	15.5
4 persons	9.3	9.2	10.0	11.1	11.6	12.0	12.7	12.8	12.9	13.3	13.6	13.6
5 persons	6.1	6.3	6.5	6.4	6.3	6.4	6.1	6.1	6.1	6.1	6.1	6.1
6 persons	3.0	3.3	3.5	3.1	2.9	2.7	2.5	2.5	2.5	2.5	2.4	2.3
7 persons or more .	2.9	3.5	3.2	2.5	2.3	1.9	1.8	1.6	1.6	1.6	1.4	1.3
Percent of total:												
1 person.	13.1	15.0	17.1	19.6	20.9	22.0	22.7	23.0	23.2	22.9	23.4	23.7
2 persons	27.8	28.1	28.9	30.6	30.7	30.7	31.4	31.3	31.7	31.5	31.5	31.6
3 persons	18.9	17.9	17.3	17.4	17.3	17.2	17.5	17.7	17.5	17.6	17.7	17.8
4 persons	17.6	16.1	15.8	15.6	15.7	15.7	15.7	15.5	15.4	15.9	15.9	15.7
5 persons	11.5	11.0	10.3	9.0	8.5	8.4	7.5	7.4	7.3	7.3	7.1	7.0
6 persons	5.7	5.8	5.6	4.3	3.9	3.6	3.1	3.1	3.0	2.9	2.8	2.6
7 persons or more	5.4	6.1	5.0	3.5	3.1	2.5	2.2	2.0	1.9	1.9	1.6	1.5

Households, By Selected Characteristics of Householder, 1970-1985

Source: U.S. Bureau of the Census

Characteristic	1970	1973	1974	1975	1976	1977	1978	1980	1981	1982	1983	1984	1985
Total (million) . .	**63.4**	**68.3**	**69.9**	**71.1**	**72.9**	**74.1**	**76.0**	**80.8**	**82.4**	**83.5**	**83.9**	**85.4**	**86.8**
Percent Distribution													
Male	78.9	77.4	77.1	76.4	75.8	75.4	74.6	71.8	71.2	70.6	70.6	69.5	69.2
Female.	21.1	22.6	22.9	23.6	24.2	24.6	25.4	28.2	28.8	29.4	29.4	30.5	30.8
White.	89.5	88.8	88.7	88.5	88.4	88.1	88.0	87.6	87.3	17.2	87.2	87.1	86.8
Black.	9.8	10.0	10.1	10.2	10.3	10.5	10.5	10.6	10.7	10.7	10.6	10.8	10.9
Age of householder													
14–24 years . . .	6.8	8.0	8.4	8.2	8.1	8.1	8.2	8.1[1]	7.8[1]	7.3[1]	6.8[1]	6.5[1]	6.3[1]
25–34 years . . .	18.5	19.9	20.5	21.0	21.3	21.8	22.1	22.9	23.3	23.1	22.8	23.2	23.1
35–44 years . . .	18.6	17.2	16.8	16.7	16.8	16.8	17.1	17.3	17.6	18.3	19.1	19.4	20.1
45–54 years . . .	19.5	18.8	18.5	18.2	17.6	17.4	16.6	15.7	15.4	15.0	14.7	14.6	14.6
55–64 years . . .	17.1	16.4	16.0	15.9	16.0	15.9	16.0	15.5	15.4	15.5	15.6	15.4	15.1
65 years and over	19.5	19.7	19.9	20.1	20.3	20.0	20.0	20.5	20.5	20.7	21.1	21.0	20.9

(1) 15 to 24 years old.

Total Related and Unrelated Adoptions, U.S., 1982

Source: *Adoption Factbook*,

Total adoptions	**141,861**
Total related adoptions	91,141
Total unrelated adoptions by public agencies	19,428
Total unrelated adoptions by private agencies	14,549
Total unrelated adoptions by private individuals	16,743
Total unrelated adoptions of healthy infants	17,602*
Total unrelated adoptions of children from other countries	5,707
Total unrelated adoptions of children with special needs	14,005
Total adoptions of children by foster parents	9,591

*NCFA estimates that this may be an undercount and the true figure may be 24,602.

Total Adoptions of Unrelated Children From Other Countries to the U.S.

Source: Compiled from data purchased by the National Committee For Adoption from the Statistical Analysis Branch, U.S. Immigration and Naturalization Service.

Age, sex and country of origin of adoptee	Number	Percent distribution
1975	5,633	100.0
1980	5,139	100.0
1981	4,868	100.0
1982	5,749	100.0
1983	7,127	100.0
1984, total[1]	**8,327**	**100.0**
Under 1 year old	5,062	60.8
1-4 years old.	1,935	23.2
5-9 years old.	792	9.5
10 years old or over.	538	6.5
Male	3,380	40.6
Female	4,947	59.4
Korea, Rep. of	5,157	61.9
Colombia	595	7.1
India.	468	5.6
Philippines	408	4.9
El Salvador.	364	4.4

(1) Includes other countries, not shown separately.

Hospitals, 1960-1984

Source: American Hospital Association, *Hospital Statistics*, 1985 © 1984

	1960	1970	1975	1980	1981	1982	1983	1984
Number								
All hospitals	6,876	7,123	7,156	6,965	6,933	6,915	6,888	6,872
With 100 beds or more	2,903	3,488	3,691	3,755	3,804	3,807	3,812	3,808
Non-Federal	6,441	6,715	6,774	6,606	6,585	6,569	6,546	6,531
Short-term general and special	5,407	5,859	5,979	5,904	5,879	5,863	5,843	5,814
Nongovernmental nonprofit	3,291	3,386	3,364	3,339	3,356	3,354	3,363	3,366
For profit	856	769	775	730	729	748	757	786
State and local government	1,260	1,704	1,840	1,835	1,794	1,761	1,723	1,662
Long-term general and special	308	236	215	157	146	138	131	131
Psychiatric	488	519	544	534	549	558	564	579
Tuberculosis	238	101	36	11	11	10	8	7
Federal	435	408	382	359	348	346	342	341
Beds (1,000)								
All hospitals	1,658	1,616	1,466	1,365	1,362	1,360	1,350	1,339
Rate per 1,000 population[1]	9.3	7.9	6.8	6.0	5.9	5.9	5.8	5.7
Beds per hospital	241	227	205	196	196	197	196	195
Non-Federal	1,481	1,455	1,334	1,248	1,246	1,246	1,237	1,226
Short-term general and special	639	848	947	992	1,007	1,015	1,021	1,020
Rate per 1,000 population[1]	3.6	4.2	4.4	4.4	4.4	4.4	4.4	4.3
Nongovernmental nonprofit	446	592	659	693	706	712	718	717
For profit	37	53	73	87	88	91	94	100
State and local government	156	204	215	212	213	212	209	203
Long-term general and special	67	60	51	39	35	34	30	30
Psychiatric	722	527	330	215	202	195	185	175
Tuberculosis	52	20	6	2	2	1	1	1
Federal	177	161	132	117	116	114	113	112
Occupancy rate[2]								
All hospitals	84.6	80.3	76.7	77.7	77.9	77.4	76.1	72.5
Non-Federal	NA	NA	76.3	77.4	77.8	77.2	75.7	71.9
Short-term general and special	74.7	78.0	74.8	75.4	75.9	75.2	73.4	68.9
Nongovernmental nonprofit	76.6	80.1	77.4	78.2	78.5	77.8	75.8	71.4
For profit	65.4	72.2	65.9	65.2	66.4	65.5	63.1	57.0
State and local government	71.6	73.2	69.7	70.7	71.2	70.7	70.0	65.9
Long-term general and special	86.9	82.0	82.1	85.9	86.2	87.9	86.5	88.7
Psychiatric	93.1	84.8	80.3	85.2	85.9	86.1	86.5	86.3
Tuberculosis	75.4	61.8	57.7	67.0	66.5	62.3	67.5	63.4
Federal	87.2	79.6	80.7	80.1	79.0	79.4	80.5	79.0
Personnel per 100 patients[3]								
All hospitals	114	196	269	329	345	376	361	374
Non-Federal	113	198	272	333	348	380	365	379
Short-term general and special	226	292	339	385	398	434	414	430
Nongovernmental nonprofit	232	292	336	385	399	438	417	434
For profit	196	256	288	334	348	374	358	375
State and local government	215	298	365	401	411	443	422	438
Long-term general and special	95	140	162	170	200	200	202	203
Psychiatric	35	68	110	150	158	167	165	172
Tuberculosis	99	146	216	290	287	334	351	342
Federal	120	169	240	297	310	335	314	327

(NA) Not available. (1) Based on Bureau of the Census estimated resident population as of July 1; (2) Ratio of average daily census to every 100 beds; (3) Includes full-time equivalents of part-time personnel.

U.S. Health Expenditures

Source: Health Care Financing Administration, U.S. Department of Health and Human Services

Type of expenditure	1965	1970	1980	1985	1986	Projected 1987	Projected 1990	Projected 2000
				Amount in billions				
Total	$41.9	$75.0	$248.1	$422.6	$458.2	$496.6	$647.3	$1,529.3
Health services and supplies	38.4	69.6	236.2	407.2	442.0	479.3	626.5	1,493.8
Personal health care	35.9	65.4	219.7	371.3	404.0	438.9	573.5	1,398.1
Hospital care	14.0	28.0	101.6	167.2	179.6	192.6	250.4	621.0
Physician services	8.5	14.3	46.8	82.8	92.0	101.4	132.6	319.6
Dentist services	2.8	4.7	15.4	27.1	29.6	32.4	41.8	89.6
Other professional services	1.0	1.6	5.7	12.4	14.1	16.2	22.9	60.4
Drugs and medical sundries	5.2	8.0	18.8	28.7	30.6	32.8	42.1	102.6
Eyeglasses and appliances	1.2	1.9	5.1	7.5	8.2	8.8	11.2	24.7
Nursing home care	2.1	4.7	20.4	35.0	38.1	41.6	54.5	129.0
Other personal health care	1.1	2.1	5.9	10.8	11.9	13.1	18.0	51.2
Program administration and net cost of private health insurance	1.7	2.8	9.2	23.6	24.5	25.9	34.6	57.7
Government public health activities	0.8	1.4	7.3	12.3	13.4	14.4	18.5	38.0
Research and construction of medical facilities	3.5	5.4	11.9	15.4	16.3	17.3	20.7	35.5
Noncommercial research[1]	1.5	2.0	5.4	7.4	8.2	9.0	11.5	20.2
Construction	2.0	3.4	6.5	8.1	8.0	8.3	9.3	15.3

(1) Research and development expenditures of drug companies and other manufacturers and providers of medical equipment and supplies are excluded from "research expenditures," but included in the expenditure class in which the product falls.

Persons with Selected Chronic Conditions, 1983

Source: National Center for Health Statistics

Chronic condition	Persons with condition (1,000)	Rate per 1,000 persons: Total	Male	Female	Under 18 yrs.	18–44 yrs.	45–64 yrs.	65 yrs. and over
Heart conditions	18,978	82.8	79.3	86.0	19.4	37.1	143.3	303.0
High blood pressure (Hypertension)	27,813	121.3	104.1	137.4	1.9[1]	62.1	263.6	387.9
Varicose veins of lower extremities	6,838	29.8	11.6	46.8	.2[1]	22.1	55.1	87.1
Hemorrhoids	10,924	47.6	46.1	49.1	1.0[1]	57.5	76.5	74.2
Chronic bronchitis	10,864	47.4	42.0	52.4	59.3	37.9	44.7	58.3
Asthma	8,787	38.3	34.5	41.9	45.2	36.1	34.6	36.4
Chronic sinusitis	30,767	134.2	119.0	148.4	49.5	162.8	182.4	149.6
Hay fever, allergic rhinitis without asthma	19,771	86.2	83.7	88.6	55.4	109.7	91.9	63.1
Dermatitis, including eczema	9,108	39.7	29.6	49.2	37.4	40.8	43.9	34.0
Diseases of sebaceous glands[2]	6,192	27.0	25.9	28.1	28.5	38.2	12.9	5.8
Arthritis	30,115	131.3	94.9	165.3	2.2[1]	53.6	284.8	471.6
Diabetes	5,613	24.5	21.3	27.5	1.8[1]	9.0	58.2	79.5
Migraine	7,258	31.6	15.8	46.5	6.4	47.0	42.5	16.9
Diseases of urinary system	7,061	30.8	14.4	46.1	9.4	29.8	43.1	65.3
Visual impairments	8,081	35.2	42.7	28.2	10.3	29.5	49.7	92.1
Hearing impairments	20,698	90.3	107.1	74.5	18.8	49.8	148.4	314.8
Deformities or orthopedic impairments	22,152	96.0	93.8	99.2	27.0	105.9	136.8	161.6

(1) Figure does not meet standards of reliability or precision. (2) Acne and sebaceous skin cyst.

Mental Health Facilities

Source: National Institute of Mental Health

	Unit	Total	Mental Hospitals: State and county	Private[1]	General hospitals[2]	Veterans Administration[3]	Community mental health centers[4]	Psychiatric outpatient clinics[5]
Number of facilities:								
1970	Number	3,005	310	411	797	115	196	1,109
1976	Number	3,480	303	513	870	126	517	1,078
1980	Number	3,727	280	552	923	136	691	1,053
1982	Number	4,302	277	550	1,531[6]	129	(6)	1,473[6]
1984	Number	4,622	277	542	1,531	139	(6)	792[6,7]
Inpatient beds:								
1970	1,000	524.9	413.1	29.4	22.4	50.7	8.1	(x)
1976	1,000	339.0	222.2	34.1	28.7	35.9	17.0	(x)
1980	1,000	274.7	158.5	37.4	29.4	33.8	16.3	(x)
1982	1,000	247.3	140.1	37.5	36.5[6]	24.6	(6)	(x)
1984	1,000	243.0	128.6	37.1	36.5	23.5	(6)	(x)
Per 100,000 population								
1970	Rate	263.6	207.4	14.8	11.2	25.5	4.1	(x)
1980	Rate	124.3	70.2	16.8	13.7	15.7	7.3	(x)
1982	Rate	108.1	61.2	16.4	16.0[6]	10.8	(6)	(x)
1984	Rate	104.9	55.4	16.0	16.0	10.1	(6)	(x)
Inpatients:								
1975	1,000	284.2	193.4	27.9	18.9	31.9	10.8	(x)
1981	1,000	214.1	125.2	31.9	28.7[6]	21.0	(6)	(x)
1983	1,000	220.7	116.8	31.9	28.7	20.2	(6)	(x)
Per 1,000,000 population								
1975	Rate	134.4	91.5	13.2	8.9	15.1	5.1	(x)
1981	Rate	93.5	54.7	13.9	12.6[6]	9.2	(6)	(x)
1983	Rate	95.2	50.3	13.7	12.6	8.7	(6)	(x)
Total expenditures								
1975	Mil. dol.	6,564	3,185	746	621	699	776	422
1979	Mil. dol.	8,764	3,757	1,179	723	848	481	589[6]
1981	Mil. dol.	(NA)	4,493	1,643	2,033[6]	(NA)	(6)	1,554
1983	Mil. dol.	14,289	5,491	2,285	2,033	1,316	(6)	430[6,7]
Constant (1969) dollars:								
1975	Mil. dol.	4,414	2,142	501	418	470	522	283
1981	Mil. dol.	(NA)	1,763	645	797[6]	(NA)	(6)	610[6]
1983	Mil. dol.	4,687	1,743	725	797	418	(6)	136[6,7]
Constant (1969) dollars per capita								
1975	Dollars	20.88	10.13	2.37	1.98	2.22	2.47	1.34
1981	Dollars	(NA)	7.74	2.83	3.50[6]	(NA)	(6)	2.68[6]
1983	Dollars	20.24	7.50	3.12	3.50	1.80	(6)	.59[6,7]

NA = Not available. X = Not applicable.

(1) Includes residential treatment centers for emotionally disturbed children. (2) Non-Federal hospitals with separate psychiatric services. (3) Includes Veterans Administration (VA) neuropsychiatric hospitals, VA general hospitals with separate psychiatric settings and VA freestanding psychiatric outpatient clinics. (4) Federally funded. (5) Freestanding. (6) Due to the shift in funding of the community mental health center (CMHC) program from categorical to block grants, the category CMHC was dropped in 1981. Organizations previously classified as federally funded CMHCs were reclassified as multiservice mental health organizations, freestanding psychiatric outpatient clincis, or psychiatric units of non-Federal general hospitals. (7) As of 1983, a number of freestanding psychiatric outpatient clinics were reclassified as multiservice mental health organizations.

Procedures in Short-Stay Hospitals, 1975-1984

Source: National Center for Health Statistics

Sex and Type of Procedure[1]	Number of Procedures (1,000) 1975	1980	1982	1983	1984	Rate per 1,000 Population 1975	1980	1982	1983	1984
Both Sexes										
Surgical procedures, total[2,3]	20,040	24,494	25,825	26,220	25,590	93.7	108.6	112.3	112.9	109.2
Male										
Surgical procedures, total[2]	7,379	8,505	9,062	9,268	9,164	71.4	78.1	81.7	82.6	81.0
Repair of inguinal hernia	484	483	489	456	411	4.7	4.4	4.4	4.1	3.6
Cardiac catherization	125	228	309	326	372	1.2	2.1	2.8	2.9	3.3
Prostatectomy	266	335	358	357	361	2.6	3.1	3.2	3.2	3.2
Reduction of fracture[4]	348	325	340	313	330	3.4	3.0	3.1	2.8	2.9
Diagnostic and other non-surgical procedures[5]	(NA)	3,386	4,269	4,725	5,195	(NA)	31.1	38.5	42.1	45.9
CAT scan[6]	(NA)	152	289	431	530	(NA)	1.4	2.6	3.8	4.7
Cystoscopy	(NA)	543	532	515	513	(NA)	5.0	4.8	4.6	4.5
Female										
Surgical procedures, total[2,3]	12,661	15,989	16,763	16,953	16,426	114.6	137.1	141.0	141.1	135.5
Procedures to assist delivery	(NA)	2,391	2,459	2,405	2,362	(NA)	20.5	20.7	20.0	19.5
Cesarean section	328	619	730	808	813	3.0	5.3	6.1	6.7	6.7
Hysterectomy	725	649	650	672	664	6.6	5.6	5.5	5.6	5.5
Oophorectomy and salpingo-oophorectomy	471	483	500	512	498	4.3	4.1	4.2	4.3	4.1
Diagnostic and other non-surgical procedures[5]	(NA)	3,532	4,539	4,994	5,370	(NA)	30.3	38.2	41.6	44.3
CAT scan[6]	(NA)	154	311	440	561	(NA)	1.3	2.6	3.7	4.6
Diagnostic ultrasound	(NA)	204	357	431	519	(NA)	1.7	3.0	3.6	4.3

NA=Not available.

(1) Excludes newborn infants and discharges from Federal hospitals; before 1979, a maximum of 3 operations were coded per discharge, after 1979, a maximum of 4. (2) Includes other types of surgical procedures not shown separately. (3) Figures for 1975 should be compared with caution to those for 1980–1984 because data prior to 1979 exclude the following obstetrical procedures: Episiotomy, artificial rupture of membrane, internal version and outlet, and low forceps delivery. (4) Excluding skull, nose, and jaw. (5) Includes other non-surgical procedures not shown separately. (6) Computerized axial tomography. (7) Using contrast material.

Legal Abortions in the U.S.

Source: Centers for Disease Control, U.S. Department of Health and Human Services

Legal abortions, according to selected characteristics of the patient.

	1974	1976	1978	1980	1981	1982	1983
Number	763,476	988,267	1,157,776	1,297,606	1,300,760	1,303,980	1,268,987
Age Characteristic				Percent distribution			
Under 20 years	32.7	32.1	30.0	29.2	28.0	27.1	27.1
20-24 years	31.8	33.3	35.0	35.5	35.3	35.1	34.7
25 years and over	35.6	34.6	34.9	35.3	36.7	37.8	38.2
Marital status							
Married	27.4	24.6	26.4	23.1	22.1	20.0	21.4
Unmarried	72.6	75.4	73.6	76.9	77.9	78.0	78.6
Number of living children							
0	47.8	47.7	56.6	58.4	58.3	57.8	57.1
1	19.6	20.7	19.2	19.5	19.7	20.3	20.7
2	14.8	15.4	14.1	13.7	13.7	13.9	14.2
3	8.7	8.3	5.9	5.3	5.3	5.2	5.2
4	4.5	4.1	4.2*	3.2	3.0	2.9	2.8
5 or more*	4.5	3.7	—	—	—	—	—
Period of gestation							
Under 8 weeks	42.6	47.0	53.2	51.7	51.2	50.6	49.7
9-10 weeks	28.7	28.0	26.9	26.2	26.8	26.7	26.8
11-12 weeks	15.4	14.4	12.3	12.2	12.1	12.4	12.8
13-15 weeks	5.5	4.5	4.0	5.2	5.2	5.3	5.8
16-20 weeks	6.5	5.1	3.7	3.9	3.7	3.9	3.9
21 weeks and over	1.2	0.9	0.9	0.9	1.0	1.1	1.0

*Beginning with 1978, 4 or more.

Suicides, by Method and by Sex

Source: National Center for Health Statistics

Suicide is the leading cause of premature death for Americans each year after accidents, cancer and heart disease, according to the Centers for Disease Control. In 1984, 29,286 Americans committed suicide. The average age was 43, the highest rate was among white men, followed by men of minority groups excluding blacks, then black males and white females. Firearms were involved in 57 percent of the 1984 suicides.

Method	Male 1960	1970	1975	1980	1983	Female 1960	1970	1975	1980	1983
Total	14,539	16,629	19,622	20,505	21,786	4,502	6,851	7,441	6,364	6,509
Firearms[1]	7,879	9,704	12,185	12,937	13,959	1,138	2,068	2,688	2,459	2,641
Percent of total	54.2	58.4	62.1	63.1	64.1	25.3	30.2	36.1	38.6	40.6
Poisoning[2]	2,631	3,299	3,297	2,997	3,148	1,699	3,285	3,129	2,456	2,469
Hanging and strangulation[3]	2,576	2,422	2,815	2,997	3,222	790	831	846	694	709
Other[4]	1,453	1,204	1,325	1,574	1,457	875	667	778	755	690

(1) Includes explosives through 1975. (2) Includes solids, liquids, and gases. (3) Includes suffocation. (4) Beginning 1979 includes explosives.

Physicians, By Age, Sex, and State

Source: American Medical Association, Dec. 31, 1985

	Total Physicians[1]		Under 35 yrs.		35–44 yrs.		45–54 yrs.		55–64 yrs.	
	Male	Female	Male	Female	Male	Female	Male	Female	Male	Female
Total Physicians	**471,991**	**80,725**	**107,357**	**34,265**	**130,148**	**24,604**	**89,786**	**9,906**	**72,859**	**6,128**
Alabama	5,691	644	1,446	314	1,585	206	1,037	54	895	48
Alaska	713	132	130	40	295	61	178	16	82	13
Arizona	6,471	852	1,259	385	1,710	255	1,255	88	973	61
Arkansas	3,333	365	787	181	933	93	648	39	496	31
California	61,855	10,234	11,311	3,797	17,876	3,381	12,128	1,269	10,376	835
Colorado	6,382	965	1,397	463	2,007	307	1,249	80	918	65
Connecticut	8,268	1,457	1,980	670	2,162	395	1,542	171	1,314	102
Delaware	1,082	217	210	76	249	70	249	37	203	21
Dist. of Col.	3,260	897	757	409	836	234	679	121	506	75
Florida	24,772	2,762	4,071	902	6,393	822	4,713	411	3,754	303
Georgia	9,550	1,301	2,266	609	2,743	391	1,987	140	1,473	93
Hawaii	2,357	386	512	142	711	114	424	45	343	46
Idaho	1,287	95	174	40	425	29	280	10	187	5
Illinois	20,786	4,717	5,321	1,981	5,692	1,564	3,848	581	2,953	313
Indiana	7,666	1,001	1,680	453	2,026	286	1,424	105	1,335	75
Iowa	3,957	463	957	242	1,080	119	684	45	655	33
Kansas	3,965	581	906	253	1,075	190	762	60	597	41
Kentucky	5,351	783	1,202	364	1,566	225	1,066	103	823	56
Louisiana	7,471	1,070	2,044	506	2,108	308	1,352	126	1,090	83
Maine	2,037	265	304	107	595	74	371	28	355	24
Maryland	13,147	2,906	3,408	1,246	0,951	976	2,543	361	1,736	181
Massachusetts	16,112	3,581	4,183	1,734	4,578	1,092	2,893	343	1,959	201
Michigan	14,750	2,706	3,717	1,147	3,874	891	2,832	363	2,423	175
Minnesota	8,187	1,330	2,183	711	2,308	372	1,474	117	1,209	67
Mississippi	3,189	362	739	160	845	101	639	50	539	23
Missouri	8,606	1,405	2,329	705	2,292	413	1,612	144	1,282	87
Montana	1,255	82	137	27	411	31	277	8	236	11
Nebraska	2,540	275	608	155	693	74	455	25	412	13
Nevada	1,543	136	236	41	500	54	343	20	260	12
New Hampshire	1,886	231	336	80	570	61	354	36	261	22
New Jersey	15,238	3,379	3,139	1,053	4,166	1,240	3,085	603	2,476	293
New Mexico	2,415	407	475	145	783	167	435	33	347	27
New York	46,462	11,030	11,780	4,375	11,355	3,187	8,576	1,604	6,970	935
North Carolina	10,363	1,447	2,641	766	2,841	355	1,866	119	1,599	99
North Dakota	1,102	88	242	46	339	22	245	11	173	6
Ohio	18,567	3,271	4,591	1,450	4,678	961	3,381	429	3,174	236
Oklahoma	4,511	598	1,070	295	1,243	152	919	68	682	46
Oregon	5,236	687	762	282	1,694	229	1,123	72	816	53
Pennsylvania	23,666	4,519	6,092	2,017	6,058	1,312	4,154	513	3,581	335
Rhode Island	2,097	381	456	183	533	102	397	41	354	27
South Carolina	5,106	531	1,247	285	1,471	131	878	52	770	35
South Dakota	1,011	78	232	42	294	19	176	9	158	4
Tennessee	8,259	993	2,128	500	2,341	279	1,488	101	1,239	64
Texas	26,335	3,903	6,445	1,879	7,587	1,198	5,065	343	4,061	275
Utah	2,850	280	634	146	936	77	495	22	436	15
Vermont	1,259	212	292	88	309	57	192	26	172	13
Virginia	10,885	1,871	2,632	869	3,059	537	2,077	215	1,683	134
Washington	9,018	1,301	1,612	566	2,887	432	1,748	116	1,358	101
West Virginia	2,984	433	649	164	901	151	601	69	411	25
Wisconsin	8,045	1,106	1,841	562	2,234	293	1,589	106	1,341	80
Wyoming	696	55	144	20	212	24	145	3	103	7

(1) Includes those 65 years and over, those living in U.S. possessions, APO's and FPO's, and those with addresses unknown, not shown separately.

Physicians by Age, Sex, and Selected Specialty

Source: American Medical Association, Dec. 31, 1985.

	Total Male	Total Female	Under 35 yrs.		35–44 yrs.		45–54 yrs.		55–64 yrs.	
			Male	Female	Male	Female	Male	Female	Male	Female
Total Physicians[1]	**471,991**	**80,725**	**107,357**	**34,265**	**130,148**	**24,604**	**89,786**	**9,906**	**72,859**	**6,128**
Anesthesiology	18,311	3,710	4,954	1,203	5,390	1,258	3,817	752	3,114	392
Cardiovascular Dis.	12,626	598	2,499	217	4,605	237	2,869	81	1,679	45
Dermatology	5,500	1,082	862	480	1,952	375	1,311	128	778	65
Diagnostic Radiology	11,106	1,781	3,962	1,017	4,270	571	1,808	127	782	51
Emergency Medicine	9,935	1,348	2,911	625	4,468	510	1,235	139	930	59
Family Practice	34,364	5,657	12,186	3,445	10,283	1,477	4,622	419	4,981	214
Gastroenterology	5,648	269	1,254	112	2,501	123	1,192	24	460	7
General Practice	24,691	2,339	929	290	2,679	665	4,715	512	7,895	477
General Surgery	36,182	1,987	10,535	1,399	8,402	419	7,139	95	6,268	50
Internal Medicine	75,701	14,716	26,614	8,500	22,469	4,188	11,948	1,197	9,156	575
Neurology	6,717	1,059	1,655	444	2,670	390	1,473	152	672	58
Obstetrics/Gynecology	25,270	5,597	4,887	2,977	7,286	1,573	6,073	571	4,714	312
Ophthalmology	13,761	1,120	2,707	536	4,179	342	3,394	126	1,919	71
Orthopedic Surgery	16,873	293	4,242	183	5,204	76	4,118	13	2,228	15
Otolaryngology	6,980	287	1,382	148	2,118	101	1,932	22	863	11
Pathology-Anat./Clin.	12,239	3,217	2,290	1,117	3,334	1,158	3,306	564	2,464	296
Pediatrics	23,244	12,373	6,413	5,692	7,342	4,102	4,534	1,472	3,383	780
Psychiatry	25,716	6,539	3,987	2,003	7,095	2,076	6,398	1,198	5,458	827
Radiology	8,077	680	387	116	1,807	296	2,845	163	2,158	80
Urological Surgery	8,738	98	1,525	60	2,743	29	2,358	6	1,394	2

(1) Includes specialties with fewer than 1,500 practitioners, unspecified specialties, physicians not classified, inactive, or with addresses unknown, not shown separately.

U.S. Crime Rate Up 5.2% in 1986

Source: 1986 Uniform Crime Reports, FBI

The crime rate rose 5.2 percent in 1986, according to the FBI's Uniform Crime Reports. There were increases in all major categories of crime, with violent crime up 11.0 percent and property crime up 4.6 percent.

Overall, the number of crimes committed nationwide rose to 13.2 million in 1986. The South had the greatest rise; there, the crime rate went up by 8.6 percent. The South averaged 11 murders per 100,000 people; the West, 9 per 100,000; and both the Northeast and the Midwest, 7 per 100,000.

The rate of murders was up 8.9 percent; rape, 2.2 percent; robbery, 8.0 percent; aggravated assault, 14.3 percent; burlary, 4.5 percent; larceny, 3.8 percent; and auto theft, 9.9 percent.

The FBI urged caution in interpreting the figures.

Crime Rates by Region, Geographic Division, and State

Source: 1986 Uniform Crime Reports, FBI

(Per 100,000)

Area	Total	Violent Crime[1]	Property crime[2]	Murder	Rape	Robbery	Aggravated Assault	Burglary	Larceny-theft	Motor vehicle theft
United States Total	**5,479.9**	**617.3**	**4,862.6**	**8.6**	**37.5**	**225.1**	**346.1**	**1,344.6**	**3,010.3**	**507.8**
Northeast	**4,731.9**	**629.3**	**4,102.6**	**6.8**	**28.3**	**298.2**	**296.0**	**1,042.7**	**2,472.7**	**587.2**
New England	**4,503.4**	**418.4**	**4,085.0**	**3.5**	**25.2**	**150.9**	**238.8**	**1,064.5**	**2,398.4**	**622.1**
Connecticut	4,828.8	425.8	4,403.0	4.6	23.8	192.2	205.1	1,197.6	2,758.3	447.1
Maine	3,461.2	147.0	3,314.2	2.0	14.8	27.9	102.3	803.5	2,346.5	164.2
Massachusetts	4,723.3	556.9	4,166.5	3.6	29.7	192.7	330.9	1,070.9	2,189.1	906.5
New Hampshire	3,330.1	139.5	3,190.6	2.2	21.5	23.6	92.2	755.0	2,207.9	227.7
Rhode Island	4,902.5	335.5	4,567.0	3.5	21.4	118.7	191.9	1,293.9	2,568.3	704.7
Vermont	3,976.9	149.2	3,827.7	2.0	21.8	22.2	103.1	949.2	2,697.4	181.1
Middle Atlantic	**4,810.0**	**701.3**	**4,108.6**	**8.0**	**29.3**	**348.5**	**315.6**	**1,035.3**	**2,498.1**	**575.3**
New Jersey	5,241.3	572.5	4,668.8	5.2	33.2	268.7	265.4	1,070.8	2,822.5	775.5
New York	5,767.7	985.9	4,781.8	10.7	30.5	514.1	430.6	1,221.1	2,923.5	637.2
Pennsylvania	3,101.8	358.6	2,743.3	5.5	25.1	152.1	175.8	734.8	1,654.1	354.4
Midwest	**4,832.5**	**510.8**	**4,321.7**	**6.6**	**35.4**	**178.6**	**290.2**	**1,081.8**	**2,791.8**	**448.1**
East North Central	**5,058.3**	**576.2**	**4,482.1**	**7.5**	**39.4**	**212.9**	**316.4**	**1,118.5**	**2,845.3**	**518.3**
Illinois	5,546.1	800.0	4,746.0	8.9	32.4	325.3	433.5	1,179.8	2,937.9	628.3
Indiana	3,854.8	307.7	3,547.1	6.0	25.9	90.0	185.9	886.7	2,332.9	327.5
Michigan	6,491.5	803.9	5,687.6	11.3	67.4	301.3	423.9	1,509.5	3,377.7	800.4
Ohio	4,358.7	420.9	3,937.8	5.5	38.6	142.1	234.7	987.8	2,574.2	375.7
Wisconsin	4,096.8	257.9	3,838.9	3.1	20.1	72.8	161.9	782.9	2,802.2	253.8
West North Central	**4,296.2**	**355.6**	**3,940.6**	**4.6**	**26.1**	**97.0**	**227.9**	**994.8**	**2,664.6**	**281.2**
Iowa	4,150.7	235.1	3,915.6	1.8	12.5	42.0	178.8	956.0	2,801.3	158.3
Kansas	4,822.6	368.8	4,453.8	4.4	32.9	79.6	251.9	1,187.7	3,008.1	258.0
Minnesota	4,362.2	284.6	4,077.6	2.5	31.8	102.0	148.3	1,004.2	2,785.3	288.1
Missouri	4,654.0	578.6	4,075.5	9.2	29.2	170.2	370.0	1,136.1	2,500.5	438.9
Nebraska	3,855.7	262.6	3,593.1	3.1	24.6	51.1	183.7	748.2	2,677.3	167.6
North Dakota	2,605.4	51.3	2,554.2	1.0	11.6	6.9	31.7	385.1	2,049.2	119.9
South Dakota	2,716.0	124.7	2,591.2	4.0	17.7	16.2	86.9	553.5	1,939.0	98.7
South	**5,709.5**	**621.8**	**5,087.7**	**10.6**	**40.6**	**199.5**	**371.2**	**1,522.5**	**3,107.4**	**457.8**
South Atlantic	**5,724.1**	**684.2**	**5,039.9**	**9.8**	**40.1**	**221.8**	**412.4**	**1,473.5**	**3,158.9**	**407.5**
Delaware	4,831.6	427.0	4,404.6	4.9	56.9	124.2	241.1	1,042.3	3,090.4	271.9
District of Columbia	8,339.3	1,505.2	6,834.0	31.0	52.4	754.0	667.9	1,727.6	4,131.2	975.2
Florida	8,228.4	1,036.5	7,191.9	11.7	52.7	366.8	605.3	2,221.3	4,372.6	598.1
Georgia	5,455.4	587.6	4,867.8	11.2	43.9	213.9	318.6	1,453.1	2,984.5	430.3
Maryland	5,601.8	833.0	4,768.8	9.0	43.6	304.0	476.4	1,245.6	2,977.9	545.2
North Carolina	4,331.8	475.9	3,856.0	8.1	26.4	87.7	353.6	1,225.0	2,422.7	208.3
South Carolina	5,137.4	674.6	4,462.8	8.6	41.3	99.5	525.2	1,340.3	2,845.8	276.6
Virginia	3,859.8	306.0	3,553.8	7.1	26.5	105.7	166.7	812.5	2,521.8	219.5
West Virginia	2,316.7	164.5	2,152.2	5.9	18.9	41.0	98.6	625.3	1,357.7	169.2
East South Central	**3,910.0**	**448.4**	**3,461.6**	**9.6**	**32.5**	**126.7**	**279.6**	**1,115.1**	**2,030.4**	**316.1**
Alabama	4,288.4	558.0	3,730.3	10.1	28.4	111.6	407.9	1,159.0	2,304.4	267.0
Kentucky	3,092.2	334.4	2,757.8	6.7	23.1	82.5	222.2	824.2	1,740.4	193.2
Mississippi	3,345.1	274.1	3,070.9	11.2	25.8	64.6	172.4	1,075.9	1,845.0	150.1
Tennessee	4,534.2	539.6	3,994.6	10.4	47.0	207.7	274.5	1,325.2	2,125.8	543.6
West South Central	**6,705.8**	**624.9**	**6,081.0**	**12.3**	**45.8**	**206.6**	**360.2**	**1,827.9**	**3,638.6**	**614.6**
Arkansas	3,924.7	394.8	3,529.9	8.1	28.9	79.7	278.2	1,029.9	2,305.1	194.9
Louisiana	6,078.0	758.2	5,319.8	12.8	40.1	223.8	481.6	1,460.8	3,417.4	441.6
Oklahoma	6,014.1	436.4	5,577.7	8.1	36.4	106.5	285.4	1,786.8	3,141.7	649.2
Texas	7,408.1	658.9	6,749.2	13.5	51.6	239.9	353.9	2,048.6	3,986.5	714.1
West	**6,644.2**	**726.8**	**5,917.4**	**9.2**	**44.3**	**250.6**	**422.7**	**1,670.9**	**3,662.4**	**584.0**
Mountain	**6,323.1**	**507.2**	**5,815.9**	**7.4**	**38.4**	**126.6**	**334.8**	**1,539.6**	**3,910.8**	**365.5**
Arizona	7,321.4	658.3	6,663.1	9.3	43.0	169.2	436.8	1,907.7	4,336.6	418.8
Colorado	7,031.9	523.6	6,508.3	7.0	42.3	144.8	329.4	1,791.6	4,230.8	486.0
Idaho	4,207.0	222.5	3,984.4	3.2	20.0	21.3	178.0	1,003.5	2,799.7	181.3
Montana	4,478.9	157.4	4,321.5	2.9	17.3	19.5	117.6	792.6	3,314.0	214.9
Nevada	6,289.7	718.9	5,570.8	12.6	64.9	286.9	354.5	1,603.9	3,489.2	477.7
New Mexico	6,625.9	725.6	5,900.3	11.5	46.9	129.5	537.7	1,844.7	3,712.4	343.3
Utah	5,478.4	266.7	5,211.7	3.2	25.3	58.6	179.6	914.9	4,073.6	223.2
Wyoming	4,357.2	293.1	4,064.1	5.3	21.9	22.5	243.4	817.4	3,078.1	168.6

Area	Total	Violent Crime[1]	Property crime[2]	Murder	Rape	Robbery	Aggravated Assault	Burglary	Larceny-theft	Motor vehicle theft
Pacific	**6,761.4**	**806.9**	**5,954.5**	**9.9**	**46.4**	**295.8**	**454.8**	**1,718.8**	**3,572.0**	**663.7**
Alaska	6,245.9	570.4	5,675.5	8.6	72.7	88.0	401.1	1,161.8	3,909.9	603.7
California	6,762.8	920.5	5,842.3	11.3	44.9	342.9	521.5	1,696.4	3,383.9	762.0
Hawaii	5,671.4	245.2	5,426.2	4.8	31.0	106.3	103.1	1,338.8	3,759.1	328.2
Oregon	7,080.7	549.7	6,531.0	6.6	51.1	205.9	286.1	1,966.7	4,162.8	401.5
Washington	6,879.7	437.0	6,442.6	5.0	53.4	135.1	243.5	1,861.5	4,266.6	314.5
Puerto Rico	**3,490.4**	**762.4**	**2,728.0**	**17.9**	**12.9**	**485.2**	**246.4**	**1,144.4**	**954.1**	**629.6**

(1) Violent crimes are murder, rape, robbery and aggravated assault; (2) Property crimes are burglary, larceny-theft, and motor vehicle theft.

Federal Bureau of Investigation

The Federal Bureau of Investigation (FBI) is the principal investigative arm of the U.S. Department of Justice, and is located at 10th Street and Pennsylvania Avenue, Northwest, Washington, D.C. 20535. It investigates all violations of Federal law except those specifically assigned to some other agency by legislative action. The FBI's jurisdiction includes a wide range of responsibilities in the criminal, civil, and security fields. Priority has been assigned to five areas—organized crime; drug program; foreign counterintelligence; terrorism; and white-collar crime. On Jan. 28, 1982, the Attorney General assigned concurrent jurisdiction for the enforcement of the Controlled Substances Act to the FBI and the Drug Enforcement Administration (DEA).

The FBI also offers cooperative services to duly authorized law enforcement agencies; these services include fingerprint identification, laboratory examination, police training, and the National Crime Information Center.

The FBI has 59 field offices in the principal cities of the country. (Consult telephone directories for locations and phone numbers.)

An applicant for the position of Special Agent of the FBI must be a citizen of the U.S., at least 23 and under 35 years old, and a graduate of an accredited law school or of an accredited college or university with a major in accounting. In addition, applicants with a four-year degree from an accredited college or university with a major in other academic areas may qualify with three additional years of full-time work experience. Specialized need areas include languages, science, and financial analysis. Those appointed to the Special Agent position must complete an initial training period of 13 weeks at the FBI Academy, Quantico, Virginia.

Index of U.S. Crime, 1986

Source: Federal Bureau of Investigation

Offense	Number 1986	% Change over 1985	1977
Murder	20,610	8.6	7.8
Forcible Rape	90,430	3.2	42.4
Robbery	542,780	9.0	31.5
Aggravated Assault	834,320	15.4	56.1
Burglary	3,241,400	5.5	5.5
Larceny-theft	7,257,200	4.8	22.9
Motor Vehicle theft	1,224,100	11.0	25.2

Law Enforcement Officers

Source: 1986 Uniform Crime Reports, FBI

The U.S. law enforcement community employed an average of 2.1 full-time officers for every 1,000 inhabitants as of October 31, 1986. Considering full-time civilians, the overall law enforcement employee rate was 2.8 per 1,000 inhabitants. A total of 12,132 city, county, and state police agencies reported employing 475,853 officers and 153,892 civilians, collectively offering law enforcement service to a population of more than 225 million.

City law enforcement employee averages in 1986 ranged from 2.1 per 1,000 inhabitants in those with populations from 10,000 to 99,999 to 3.5 for those with populations of 250,000 or more. Rural and suburban counties averaged full-time law enforcement employee rates of 3.4 and 3.0 per 1,000 population, respectively.

Regionally, the highest law enforcement employee rate was in the Northeast, with 2.9, followed by the South with 2.8, the Midwest with 2.5, and the West with 2.4.

Nationally, males comprised 93 percent of all sworn employees. Civilians made up 24 percent of the total U.S. law enforcement employee force.

Sixty-six law enforcement officers were feloniously slain in the line of duty during 1986, 6 fewer than in 1985.

Murder Weapons, 1981-1986

Source: 1986 Uniform Crime Reports, FBI

Weapon	1981	1982	1983	1984	1985	1986
Total	**20,053**	**19,485**	**18,673**	**16,689**	**17,545**	**19,257**
Total Firearms	12,523	11,721	10,895	9,819	10,296	11,381
Handguns	9,193	8,474	8,193	7,277	7,548	8,460
Rifles	968	1,017	831	763	810	788
Shotguns	1,528	1,377	1,243	1,154	1,188	1,296
Other guns	82	38	19	18	24	22
Firearms-not stated	752	815	609	607	726	815
Cutting or stabbing instruments	3,886	4,065	4,075	3,540	3,694	3,957
Blunt objects (clubs, hammers, etc.)	1,038	957	1,062	973	972	1,099
Personal weapons (hands, fists, feet, etc.)[1]	1,132	1,298	1,280	1,090	1,180	1,310
Poison	12	19	20	6	7	14
Explosives	16	12	5	8	11	16
Fire	258	279	216	192	243	230
Narcotics	20	16	17	19	31	23
Drowning	51	52	40	44	43	49
Strangulation	337	359	376	317	311	341
Asphyxiation	150	108	123	111	115	160
Other weapons or weapons not stated	630	599	564	570	642	677

(1) Pushing is included in personal weapons.

Percent of Households Touched by Crime, 1977-1986

Source: Bureau of Justice Statistics

	1977	1978	1979	1980	1981	1982	1983	1984	1985	1986
Any crime	**31.3%**	**31.3%**	**31.3%**	**30.0%**	**30.0%**	**29.3%**	**27.4%**	**26.0%**	**25.0%**	**24.7%**
Violent crime	5.7	5.7	5.9	5.5	5.9	5.6	5.1	5.0	4.8	4.7
Rape	.2	.2	.2	.2	.2	.2	.1	.2	.1	.1
Robbery	1.2	1.1	1 2	1.2	1.3	1.4	1.1	1.0	.9	.9
Assault	4.7	4.6	4.8	4.4	4.7	4.5	4.2	4.1	4.0	3.8
Personal theft	16.3	16.2	15.4	14.2	13.9	13.9	13.0	12.3	11.5	11.2
Household theft	10.2	9.9	10.8	10.4	10.2	9.6	8.9	8.5	8.1	8.0
Burglary	7.2	7.2	7.1	7.0	7.4	6.9	6.1	5.5	5.3	5.3
Motor vehicle theft	1.5	1.7	1.6	1.6	1.6	1.6	1.4	1.4	1.4	1.4
Households touched by crime (in millions)	23.741	24.277	24.730	24.222	24.863	24.989	23.621	22.806	22.191	22.201
Households in U.S. (in millions)	75.904	77.578	78.964	80.622	82.797	85.178	86.146	87.791	88.852	90.014

Note: Detail does not add to total because of overlap in thousands touched by various crimes.

Juvenile Arrests, 1986

Source: 1986 Uniform Crime Reports, FBI

Offense charged	Total all ages	Number of persons arrested			Percent of total all ages		
		Under 15	Under 18	Under 21	Under 15	Under 18	Under 21
TOTAL	**10,392,177**	**536,609**	**1,747,675**	**3,216,752**	**5.2**	**16.8**	**31.0**
Murder and nonnegligent manslaughter	16,066	156	1,396	3,717	1.0	8.7	23.1
Forcible rape	31,128	1,514	4,798	8,634	4.9	15.4	27.7
Robbery	124,245	6,615	27,987	51,168	5.3	22.5	41.2
Aggravated assault	293,952	10,816	37,528	71,758	3.7	12.8	24.4
Burglary	375,544	47,080	134,823	206,908	12.5	35.9	55.1
Larceny-theft	1,182,099	156,033	378,283	549,190	13.2	32.0	46.5
Motor vehicle theft	128,514	11,961	50,319	74,788	9.3	39.2	58.2
Arson	15,523	3,837	6,271	7,959	24.7	40.4	51.3
Violent crime	**465,391**	**19,101**	**71,709**	**135,277**	**4.1**	**15.4**	**29.1**
Property crime	**1,701,680**	**218,911**	**569,696**	**838,845**	**12.9**	**33.5**	**49.3**
Crime Index total[1]	**2,167,071**	**238,012**	**641,405**	**974,122**	**11.0**	**29.6**	**45.0**
Other assaults	593,902	30,411	85,905	153,596	5.1	14.5	25.9
Forgery and counterfeiting	76,546	1,101	7,234	19,341	1.4	9.5	25.3
Fraud	284,790	6,722	17,727	42,141	2.4	6.2	14.8
Embezzlement	10,500	52	696	2,268	.5	6.6	21.6
Stolen property; buying, receiving, possessing	114,105	7,613	28,739	51,054	6.7	25.2	44.7
Vandalism	223,231	45,247	95,479	129,034	20.3	42.8	57.8
Weapons; carrying, possessing, etc.	160,204	6,394	25,170	49,876	4.0	15.7	31.1
Prostitution and commercialized vice	96,882	247	2,192	14,804	.3	2.3	15.3
Sex offenses (except forcible rape and prostitution)	83,934	6,110	13,753	21,625	7.3	16.4	25.8
Drug abuse violations	691,882	9,374	68,351	177,864	1.4	9.9	25.7
Gambling	25,839	105	610	1,859	.4	2.4	7.2
Offenses against family and children	47,327	1,255	2,521	6,403	2.7	5.3	13.5
Driving under the influence	1,458,531	456	22,749	156,143	(2)	1.6	10.7
Liquor laws	490,436	10,163	132,335	310,193	2.1	27.0	63.2
Drunkenness	777,866	3,283	26,589	96,341	.4	3.4	12.4
Disorderly conduct	564,882	22,517	82,986	173,800	4.0	14.7	30.8
Vagrancy	32,992	539	2,550	7,100	1.6	7.7	21.5
All other offenses (except traffic)	2,272,589	70,918	276,876	614,253	3.1	12.2	27.0
Suspicion	7,455	846	2,595	3,722	11.3	34.8	49.9
Curfew and loitering law violations	72,627	19,260	72,627	72,627	26.5	100.0	100.0
Runaways	138,586	55,984	138,586	138,586	40.4	100.0	100.0

(1) Includes arson; (2) Less than one-tenth of 1 percent.

Drug Arrests and Seizures

Source: Drug Enforcement Administration

Fiscal Year

	1983	1984	1985	1986
People arrested in Federal drug cases	12,997	13,126	15,695	18,746
Kilograms or marijuana and hashish seized	1,029,825	1,399,925	740,270	824,367
Kilograms of cocaine seized	7,399	11,742	17,613	26,872

	1983	1984	1985	1986
Kilograms of heroin seized	302	346	446	356
Dosage units of stimulants, depressants and hallucinogens seized	19,785,000	13,777,000	25,868,000	45,528,000

State and Federal Prison Population; Death Penalty

Prison population as of Jan. 1987; death penalty as of Jan. 1986.

Source: Bureau of Justice Statistics, U.S. Justice Department

At years end 1986, there were a record 546,659 prisoners under the jurisdiction of federal and state correctional authorities. From 1980 to 1986, the prison population increased by 217,000—66 percent.

The increase of more than 43,,000 in the nation's prisons from Dec. 31, 1985 to Dec. 31, 1986 was the second-largest absolute increase recorded in the 60-year history of the National Prisoner Statistics program.

	Total 1986p	Sentenced to more than a yearp	Sentenced per 100,000 population	Death penalty: Under sentence of death	Death penalty: Executions	Death penalty: Death penalty
Total	**546,659**	**523,922**	**216**	**1,519**	**18**	**—**
Federal institutions	**44,408**	**36,531**	**15**	**0**	**0**	**Yes**
State institutions	**502,251**	**487,391**	**201**	**1,591**	**18**	**37**
Northeast	**82,388**	**79,071**	**158**	**73**	**0**	**—**
Connecticut	6,905	4,043	135	0	0	Yes
Maine	1,316	1,165	99	0	0	No
Massachusetts	5,678	5,678	97	0	0	No
New Hampshire	782	782	76	0	0	Yes
New Jersey	12,020	12,020	157	17	0	Yes
New York	38,449	38,449	216	0	0	No
Pennsylvania	15,201	15,165	128	56	0	Yes
Rhode Island	1,361	1,010	103	0	0	No
Vermont	676	476	88	0	0	Yes
Midwest	**103,101**	**102,689**	**173**	**221**	**1**	**—**
Illinois	19,456	19,456	168	83	0	Yes
Indiana	10,175	9,963	181	34	1	Yes
Iowa	2,777	2,777	98	0	0	No
Kansas	5,425	5,425	220	0	0	No
Michigan	20,742	20,742	227	0	0	No
Minnesota	2,462	2,462	58	0	0	No
Missouri	10,485	10,485	206	36	0	Yes
Nebraska	1,953	1,863	116	12	0	Yes
North Dakota	421	361	53	0	0	No
Ohio	22,463	22,463	209	56	0	Yes
South Dakota	1,045	1,014	143	0	0	Yes
Wisconsin	5,697	5,678	119	0	0	No
South	**215,713**	**208,374**	**249**	**1,001**	**16**	**—**
Alabama	11,710	11,504	283	79	0	Yes
Arkansas	4,701	4,701	198	28	0	Yes
Delaware	2,828	2,026	324	4	0	Yes
District of Columbia	6,746	4,786	753	0	0	No
Florida	32,228	32,219	272	226	3	Yes
Georgia	17,363	16,291	265	107	3	Yes
Kentucky	6,322	6,322	169	25	0	Yes
Louisiana	14,580	14,580	322	39	1	Yes
Maryland	13,326	12,559	280	17	0	Yes
Mississippi	6,747	6,565	249	41	0	Yes
North Carolina	17,762	16,460	258	56	0	Yes
Oklahoma	9,596	9,596	288	68	0	Yes
South Carolina	11,676	11,022	324	42	0	Yes
Tennessee	7,182	7,182	149	46	0	Yes
Texas	38,534	38,534	228	206	6	Yes
Virginia	12,930	12,546	215	27	2	Yes
West Virginia	1,482	1,482	77	0	0	No
West	**101,049**	**97,257**	**198**	**296**	**1**	**—**
Alaska	2,460	1,666	306	0	0	No
Arizona	9,434	9,038	268	56	0	Yes
California	59,484	57,725	212	170	0	Yes
Colorado	3,673	3,673	111	1	0	Yes
Hawaii	2,180	1,521	142	0	0	No
Idaho	1,451	1,451	144	14	0	Yes
Montana	1,111	1,111	135	5	0	Yes
Nevada	4,505	4,505	462	31	1	Yes
New Mexico	2,701	2,545	170	5	0	Yes
Oregon	4,737	4,737	175	0	0	Yes
Utah	1,845	1,817	108	6	0	Yes
Washington	6,603	6,603	147	5	0	Yes
Wyoming	865	865	170	3	0	Yes

Women in Prison, 1986

Source: Bureau of Justice Statistics

Jurisdiction	Number women inmates	Percent of all inmates	Percent change in women inmates 1985-86
U.S., total	**26,610**	**4.9%**	**15.1%**
Federal	**2,833**	**6.4**	**17.8**
State	**23,777**	**4.7**	**14.8**
States with at least 500 women inmates:			
California	3,564	6.0%	22.6%
Texas	1,758	4.6	10.3
Florida	1,630	5.1	25.0
New York	1,326	3.4	25.6
Ohio	1,213	5.4	5.2

Jurisdiction	Number of women inmates	Percent of all inmates	Percent change in women inmates 1985-86
Michigan	1,018	4.9	25.1
Georgia	947	5.5	13.7
North Carolina	827	4.7	10.7
Illinois	764	3.9	13.5
Oklahoma	679	7.1	33.9
Louisiana	637	4.4	4.4
Alabama	616	5.3	9.6
South Carolina	601	5.1	20.0
Pennsylvania	591	3.9	18.2

Crime in the U.S., 1977-1986

Source: F.B.I., Crime in the United States

Population[1]	Crime Index total[2]	Violent crime[3]	Property crime[4]	Murder and non-negligent man-slaughter	Forcible rape	Robbery	Burglary	Larceny theft
Number of offenses:								
1977-216,332,000. . .	10,984,500	1,029,580	9,955,000	19,120	63,500	412,610	3,071,500	5,905,700
1978-218,059,000. . .	11,209,000	1,085,550	10,123,400	19,560	67,610	426,930	3,128,300	5,991,000
1979-220,099,000. . .	12,249,500	1,208,030	11,041,500	21,460	76,390	480,700	3,327,700	6,601,000
1980-225,349,264. . .	13,408,300	1,344,520	12,063,700	23,040	82,990	565,840	3,795,200	7,136,900
1981-229,146,000. . .	13,423,800	1,361,820	12,061,900	22,520	82,500	592,910	3,779,700	7,194,400
1982-231,534,000. . .	12,974,400	1,322,390	11,652,000	21,010	78,770	553,130	3,447,100	7,142,500
1983-233,981,000. . .	12,108,600	1,258,090	10,850,500	19,310	78,920	506,570	3,129,900	6,712,800
1984-236,158,000. . .	11,881,800	1,273,280	10,608,500	18,690	84,230	485,010	2,984,400	6,591,900
1985-238,740,000. . .	12,430,400	1,327,770	11,102,600	18,980	87,670	497,870	3,073,300	6,926,400
1986-241,077,000. . .	13,210,800	1,488,140	11,722,700	20,610	90,430	542,780	3,241,400	7,257,200
Percent change; number of offenses:								
1986/1985.	+6.3	+12.1	+5.6	+8.6	+3.2	+9.0	+5.5	+4.8
1986/1982.	+1.8	+12.5	+.6	−1.9	+14.8	−1.9	−6.0	+1.6
1986/1977.	+20.3	+44.5	+17.8	+7.8	+42.4	+31.5	+5.5	+22.9
Rate per 100,000 inhabitants:								
1977	5,077.6	475.9	4,601.7	8.8	29.4	190.7	1,419.8	2,729.9
1978	5,140.3	497.8	4,642.5	9.0	31.0	195.8	1,434.6	2,747.4
1979	5,565.5	548.9	5,016.6	9.7	34.7	218.4	1,511.9	2,999.1
1980	5,950.0	596.6	5,353.3	10.2	36.8	251.1	1,684.1	3,167.0
1981	5,858.2	594.3	5,263.9	9.8	36.0	258.7	1,649.5	3,139.7
1982	5,603.6	571.1	5,032.5	9.1	34.0	238.9	1,488.8	3,084.8
1983	5,175.0	537.7	4,637.4	8.3	33.7	216.5	1,337.7	2,868.9
1984	5,031.3	539.2	4,492.1	7.9	35.7	205.4	1,263.7	2,791.3
1985	5,206.7	556.2	4,650.5	7.9	36.7	208.5	1,287.3	2,901.2
1986	5,479.9	617.3	4,862.6	8.6	37.5	225.1	1,344.6	3,010.3
Percent change; rate per 100,000 inhabitants:								
1986/1985.	+5.2	+11.0	+4.6	+8.9	+2.2	+8.0	+4.5	+3.8
1986/1982.	−2.2	+8.1	−3.4	−5.5	+10.3	−5.8	−9.7	−2.4
1986/1977.	+7.9	+29.7	+5.7	−2.3	+27.6	+18.0	−5.3	+10.3

(1) Populations are Bureau of the Census provisional estimates as of July 1, except April 1, 1980, preliminary census counts, and are subject to change. (2) Because of rounding, the offenses may not add to totals. (3) Violent crimes are offenses of murder, forcible rape, robbery, and aggravated assault. Property crimes are offenses of burglary, larceny-theft, and motor vehicle theft. Data are not included for the property crime of arson. (4) All rates were calculated on the offenses before rounding.

U.S. Fires

Source: National Fire Protection Association

Fires attended by the public fire service (1985 estimates)

Civilian Fire Deaths and Injuries

	Deaths	Percent of all civilian deaths	Injuries	Percent of all civilian injuries
Residential (total)	5,025	81.2	19,825	69.8
One-and Two-Family Dwellings[1]	4,020	65.0	15,250	53.7
Apartment	865	14.0	3,925	13.8
Hotels and Motels	85	1.3	375	1.3
Other Residential. . . .	55	0.9	275	1.0
Non Residential Structures[2]	240	3.9	3,525	12.4
Highway Vehicles	770	12.5	3,250	11.4
Other Vehicles[3]	55	0.9	350	1.2
All Other[4]	95	1.5	1,475	5.2
Total	**6,185**		**28,425**	

Structure Fires by Property Use

	No. of fires	Property loss (thousands)
Public assembly	23,500	$462,000
Educational.	13,500	114,000
Institutional	22,500	17,000
Residential	622,000	3,774,000
One-/2-family dwellings[5]. .	501,500	3,217,000
Apartments	104,500	476,000
Hotels, motels.	7,500	56,000
Other residential	8,500	25,000
Stores and offices.	49,000	654,000
Industry, utility, defense[6] . . .	36,500	572,000
Storage in structures[6].	51,500	683,000
Special structures.	41,000	161,000
Total	**859,500**	**$6,437,000**

(1) Includes mobile homes. (2) Includes public assembly, educational, institutional, stores and offices, industry, utility, storage, and special structure properties. (3) Includes trains, boats, ships, aircraft, farm vehicles and construction vehicles. (4) Includes properties outside with value, brush, rubbish, and other.

Fire Fighters: Deaths and Injuries

Source: National Fire Protection Association

Year	Line of Duty Deaths	Line of Duty Injuries
1977	156	112,540
1978	169	101,100
1979	122	95,780
1980	137	98,070
1981	133	103,340
1982	122	98,150
1983	111	103,150
1984	118	102,300
1985	123	100,900

% of Deaths by Cause	
Stress	42.9
Struck by object	20.2
Falls	10.1
Caught or trapped	16.0
Exposure to smoke	2.5
Exposure to chemicals	.8
Structural collapse	6.7

% of Deaths by Nature of Injury	
Internal trauma	26.1
Heart attack	40.3
Burns and smoke inhalation	17.6
Crushing	5.9
Electrocution	1.7
Drowning	2.5
Stroke (C.V.A.)	1.7
Cerebral hemorrhage	.8
Aneurysm	1.7

% of Fire Ground Injuries by Cause	
Exposure to fire products	23.8
Fell, slipped	20.9
Stepped on, contact with object	14.8
Overexertion	14.0
Struck by object	10.8
Extreme weather	2.8
Caught, trapped	1.3
Exposure to chemicals	4.0
Other	7.6

% of Fire Ground Injuries by Nature of Injury	
Strain, sprain	27.0
Wound, cut, bruise	22.7
Smoke or gas inhalation	15.7
Eye irritation	7.5
Burns	10.1
Dislocation, fracture	2.5
Heat exhaustion	5.9
Other	8.6

Years of Life Expected at Birth

Source: National Center for Health Statistics

Year	Total: Total	Total: Male	Total: Female	White: Total	White: Male	White: Female	Black and Other: Total	Black and Other: Male	Black and Other: Female
1920*	54.1	53.6	54.6	54.9	54.4	55.6	45.3	45.5	45.2
1930	59.7	58.1	61.6	61.4	59.7	63.5	48.1	47.3	49.2
1940	62.9	60.8	65.2	64.2	62.1	66.6	53.1	51.5	54.9
1950	68.2	65.6	71.1	69.1	66.5	72.2	60.8	59.1	62.9
1955	69.6	66.7	72.8	70.5	67.4	73.7	63.7	61.4	66.1
1960	69.7	66.6	73.1	70.6	67.4	74.1	63.6	61.1	66.3
1965	70.2	66.8	73.7	71.0	67.6	74.7	64.1	61.1	67.4
1970	70.8	67.1	74.7	71.7	68.0	75.6	65.3	61.3	69.4
1971	71.1	67.4	75.0	72.0	68.3	75.8	65.6	61.6	69.8
1972	71.2	67.4	75.1	72.0	68.3	75.9	65.7	61.5	70.1
1973	71.4	67.6	75.3	72.2	68.5	76.1	66.1	62.0	70.3
1974	72.0	68.2	75.9	72.8	69.0	76.7	67.1	62.9	71.3
1975	72.6	68.8	76.6	73.4	69.5	77.3	68.0	63.7	72.4
1976	72.9	69.1	76.8	73.6	69.9	77.5	68.4	64.2	72.7
1977	73.3	69.5	77.2	74.0	70.2	77.9	68.9	64.7	73.2
1978	73.5	69.6	77.3	74.1	70.4	78.0	69.3	65.0	73.5
1979	73.9	70.0	77.8	74.6	70.8	78.4	69.8	65.4	74.1
1980	73.7	70.0	77.5	74.4	70.7	78.1	69.5	65.3	73.6
1981	74.2	70.4	77.8	74.8	71.1	78.4	70.3	66.1	74.4
1982	74.5	70.9	78.1	75.1	71.5	78.7	71.0	66.8	75.0
1983	74.6	71.0	78.1	75.2	71.7	78.7	71.1	67.2	74.3
1984p	74.7	71.1	78.3	75.3	71.8	78.8	71.3	67.3	75.2
1985p	74.7	71.2	78.2	75.3	71.8	78.7	71.2	67.2	75.2

p = preliminary * Data prior to 1940 for death-registration states only.

Average Height and Weight for Children

Source: *Physicians Handbook*, 1983.

Boys: Age Years	Height ft	Height in	Height cm	Weight lb	Weight kg	Girls: Age Years	Height ft	Height in	Height cm	Weight lb	Weight kg
(Birth)	1	8	50.8	7½	3.4	(Birth)	1	8	50.8	7½	3.4
½	2	2	66.0	17	7.7	½	2	2	66.0	16	7.2
1	2	5	73.0	21	9.5	1	2	5	73.6	20	9.1
2	2	9	83.8	26	11.8	2	2	9	83.8	25	11.3
3	3	0	91.4	31	14.0	3	3	0	91.4	30	13.6
4	3	3	99.0	34	15.4	4	3	3	99.0	33	15.0
5	3	6	106.6	39	17.7	5	3	5	104.1	38	17.2
6	3	9	114.2	46	20.9	6	3	8	111.7	45	20.4
7	3	11	119.3	51	23.1	7	3	11	119.3	49	22.2
8	4	2	127.0	57	25.9	8	4	2	127.0	56	25.4
9	4	4	132.0	63	28.6	9	4	4	132.0	62	28.1
10	4	6	137.1	69	31.3	10	4	6	137.1	69	31.3
11	4	8	142.2	77	34.9	11	4	8	142.2	77	34.9
12	4	10	147.3	83	37.7	12	4	10	147.3	86	39.0
13	5	0	152.4	92	41.7	13	5	0	152.4	98	45.5
14	5	2	157.5	107	48.5	14	5	2	157.5	107	48.5

This table gives a general picture of American children at specific ages. When used as a standard, the individual variation in children's growth should not be overlooked. In most cases the height-weight relationship is probably a more valid index of weight status than a weight-for-age assessment.

Average Weight of Americans by Height and Age

Source: Society of Actuaries; from the *1979 Build and Blood Pressure Study*

The figures represent weights in ordinary indoor clothing and shoes, and heights with shoes.

Men: Height	20-24	25-29	30-39	40-49	50-59	60-69	Women: Height	20-24	25-29	30-39	40-49	50-59	60-69
5'2"	130	134	138	140	141	140	4'10"	105	110	113	118	121	123
5'3"	136	140	143	144	145	144	4'11"	110	112	115	121	125	127
5'4"	139	143	147	149	150	149	5'0"	112	114	118	123	127	130
5'5"	143	147	151	154	155	153	5'1"	116	119	121	127	131	133
5'6"	148	152	156	158	159	158	5'2"	120	121	124	129	133	136
5'7"	153	156	160	163	164	163	5'3"	124	125	128	133	137	140
5'8"	157	161	165	167	168	167	5'4"	127	128	131	136	141	143
5'9"	163	166	170	172	173	172	5'5"	130	132	134	139	144	147
5'10"	167	171	174	176	177	176	5'6"	133	134	137	143	147	150
5'11"	171	175	179	181	182	181	5'7"	137	138	141	147	152	155
6'0"	176	181	184	186	187	186	5'8"	141	142	145	150	156	158
6'1"	182	186	190	192	193	191	5'9"	146	148	150	155	159	161
6'2"	187	191	195	197	198	196	5'10"	149	150	153	158	162	163
6'3"	193	197	201	202	204	200	5'11"	155	156	159	162	166	167
6'4"	198	202	206	208	209	207	6'0"	157	159	164	168	171	172

SPORTS IN 1987

Olympic Games Records

The modern Olympic Games, first held in Athens, Greece, in 1896, were the result of efforts by Baron Pierre de Coubertin, a French educator, to promote interest in education and culture, also to foster better international understanding through the universal medium of youth's love of athletics.

His source of inspiration for the Olympic Games was the ancient Greek Olympic Games, most notable of the four Panhellenic celebrations. The games were combined patriotic, religious, and athletic festivals held every four years. The first such recorded festival was that held in 776 B.C., the date from which the Greeks began to keep their calendar by "Olympiads," or four-year spans between the games.

The first Olympiad is said to have consisted merely of a 200-yard foot race near the small city of Olympia, but the games gained in scope and became demonstrations of national pride. Only Greek citizens — amateurs — were permitted to participate. Winners received laurel, wild olive, and palm wreaths and were accorded many special privileges. Under the Roman emperors, the games deteriorated into professional carnivals and circuses. Emperor Theodosius banned them in 394 A.D.

Baron de Coubertin enlisted 9 nations to send athletes to the first modern Olympics in 1896; now more than 100 nations compete. Winter Olympic Games were started in 1924.

Sites and Unofficial Winners of Games

1896 Athens (U.S.)
1900 Paris (U.S.)
1904 St. Louis (U.S.)
1906 Athens (U.S.)*
1908 London (U.S.)
1912 Stockholm (U.S.)
1920 Antwerp (U.S.)
1924 Paris (U.S.)
1928 Amsterdam (U.S.)
1932 Los Angeles (U.S.)
1936 Berlin (Germany)
1948 London (U.S.)
1952 Helsinki (U.S.)
1956 Melbourne (USSR)
1960 Rome (USSR)
1964 Tokyo (U.S.)
1968 Mexico City (U.S.)
1972 Munich (USSR)
1976 Montreal (USSR)
1980 Moscow (USSR)
1984 Los Angeles (U.S.)
1988 Seoul, S. Korea (scheduled)

*Games not recognized by International Olympic Committee. Games 6 (1916), 12 (1940), and 13 (1944) were not celebrated. The 1980 games were boycotted by 62 nations, including the U.S. The 1984 games were boycotted by the USSR and most eastern bloc nations. East and West Germany began competing separately in 1968.

Olympic Games Champions, 1896—1984

(*Indicates Olympic Records)

Track and Field — Men

100-Meter Run

1896	Thomas Burke, United States	12s
1900	Francis W. Jarvis, United States	10.8s
1904	Archie Hahn, United States	11s
1908	Reginald Walker, South Africa	10.8s
1912	Ralph Craig, United States	10.8s
1920	Charles Paddock, United States	10.8s
1924	Harold Abrahams, Great Britain	10.6s
1928	Percy Williams, Canada	10.8s
1932	Eddie Tolan, United States	10.3s
1936	Jesse Owens, United States	10.3s
1948	Harrison Dillard, United States	10.3s
1952	Lindy Remigino, United States	10.4s
1956	Bobby Morrow, United States	10.5s
1960	Armin Hary, Germany	10.2s
1964	Bob Hayes, United States	10.0s
1968	Jim Hines, United States	9.9s*
1972	Valeri Borzov, USSR	10.14s
1976	Hasely Crawford, Trinidad	10.06s
1980	Allan Wells, Great Britain	10.25s
1984	Carl Lewis, United States	9.99s

200-Meter Run

1900	Walter Tewksbury, United States	22.2s
1904	Archie Hahn, United States	21.6s
1908	Robert Kerr, Canada	22.4s
1912	Ralph Craig, United States	21.7s
1920	Allan Woodring, United States	22s
1924	Jackson Scholz, United States	21.6s
1928	Percy Williams, Canada	21.8s
1932	Eddie Tolan, United States	21.2s
1936	Jesse Owens, United States	20.7s
1948	Mel Patton, United States	21.1s
1952	Andrew Stanfield, United States	20.7s
1956	Bobby Morrow, United States	20.6s
1960	Livio Berruti, Italy	20.5s
1964	Henry Carr, United States	20.3s
1968	Tommie Smith, United States	19.83s
1972	Valeri Borzov, USSR	20.00s
1976	Donald Quarrie, Jamaica	20.23s
1980	Pietro Mennea, Italy	20.19s
1984	Carl Lewis, United States	19.80s*

400-Meter Run

1896	Thomas Burke, United States	54.2s
1900	Maxey Long, United States	49.4s
1904	Harry Hillman, United States	49.2s
1908	Wyndham Halswelle, Great Britain, walkover	50s
1912	Charles Reidpath, United States	48.2s
1920	Bevil Rudd, South Africa	49.6s
1924	Eric Liddell, Great Britain	47.6s
1928	Ray Barbuti, United States	47.8s
1932	William Carr, United States	46.2s
1936	Archie Williams, United States	46.5s
1948	Arthur Wint, Jamaica, B W I	46.2s
1952	George Rhoden, Jamaica, B W I	45.9s
1956	Charles Jenkins, United States	46.7s
1960	Otis Davis, United States	44.9s
1964	Michael Larrabee, United States	45.1s
1968	Lee Evans, United States	43.8s*
1972	Vincent Matthews, United States	44.66s
1976	Alberto Juantorena, Cuba	44.26s
1980	Viktor Markin, USSR	44.60s
1984	Alonzo Babers, United States	44.27s

800-Meter Run

1896	Edwin Flack, Great Britain	2m. 11s
1900	Alfred Tysoe, Great Britain	2m. 1.4s
1904	James Lightbody, United States	1m. 56s
1908	Mel Sheppard, United States	1m. 52.8s
1912	James Meredith, United States	1m. 51.9s
1920	Albert Hill, Great Britain	1m. 53.4s
1924	Douglas Lowe, Great Britain	1m. 52.4s
1928	Douglas Lowe, Great Britain	1m. 51.8s
1932	Thomas Hampson, Great Britain	1m. 49.8s
1936	John Woodruff, United States	1m. 52.9s
1948	Mal Whitfield, United States	1m. 49.2s
1952	Mal Whitfield, United States	1m. 49.2s
1956	Thomas Courtney, United States	1m. 47.7s
1960	Peter Snell, New Zealand	1m. 46.3s
1964	Peter Snell, New Zealand	1m. 45.1s
1968	Ralph Doubell, Australia	1m. 44.3s
1972	Dave Wottle, United States	1m. 45.9s
1976	Alberto Juantorena, Cuba	1m. 43.50s
1980	Steve Ovett, Great Britain	1m. 45.40s
1984	Joaquim Cruz, Brazil	1m. 43.00*

1,500-Meter Run

1896	Edwin Flack, Great Britain	4m. 33.2s
1900	Charles Bennett, Great Britain	4m. 6s
1904	James Lightbody, United States	4m. 5.4s
1908	Mel Sheppard, United States	4m. 3.4s
1912	Arnold Jackson, Great Britain	3m. 56.8s
1920	Albert Hill, Great Britain	4m. 1.8s
1924	Paavo Nurmi, Finland	3m. 53.6s

1928	Harry Larva, Finland	3m. 53.2s
1932	Luigi Beccali, Italy	3m. 51.2s
1936	Jack Lovelock, New Zealand	3m. 47.8s
1948	Henri Eriksson, Sweden	3m. 49.8s
1952	Joseph Barthel, Luxemburg	3m. 45.2s
1956	Ron Delany, Ireland	3m. 41.2s
1960	Herb Elliott, Australia	3m. 35.6s
1964	Peter Snell, New Zealand	3m. 38.1s
1968	Kipchoge Keino, Kenya	3m. 34.9s
1972	Pekka Vasala, Finland	3m. 36.3s
1976	John Walker, New Zealand	3m. 39.17s
1980	Sebastian Coe, Great Britain	3m. 38.4s
1984	Sebastian Coe, Great Britain	3m. 32.53*

3,000-Meter Steeplechase

1920	Percy Hodge, Great Britain	10m. 0.4s
1924	Willie Ritola, Finland	9m. 33.6s
1928	Toivo Loukola, Finland	9m. 21.8s
1932	Volmari Iso-Hollo, Finland	10m. 33.4s
	(About 3,450 mtrs. extra lap by error)	
1936	Volmari Iso-Hollo, Finland	9m. 3.8s
1948	Thure Sjoestrand, Sweden	9m. 4.6s
1952	Horace Ashenfelter, United States	8m. 45.4s
1956	Chris Brasher, Great Britain	8m. 41.2s
1960	Zdzislaw Krzyszkowiak, Poland	8m. 34.2s
1964	Gaston Roelants, Belgium	8m. 30.8s
1968	Amos Biwott, Kenya	8m. 51s
1972	Kipchoge Keino, Kenya	8m. 23.6s
1976	Anders Garderud, Sweden	8m. 08.2s*
1980	Bronislaw Malinowski, Poland	8m. 09.7s
1984	Julius Korir, Kenya	8m. 11.8s

5,000-Meter Run

1912	Hannes Kolehmainen, Finland	14m. 36.6s
1920	Joseph Guillemot, France	14m. 55.6s
1924	Paavo Nurmi, Finland	14m. 31.2s
1928	Willie Ritola, Finland	14m. 38s
1932	Lauri Lehtinen, Finland	14m. 30s
1936	Gunnar Hockert, Finland	14m. 22.2s
1948	Gaston Reiff, Belgium	14m. 17.6s
1952	Emil Zatopek, Czechoslovakia	14m. 6.6s
1956	Vladimir Kuts, USSR	13m. 39.6s
1960	Murray Halberg, New Zealand	13m. 43.4s
1964	Bob Schul, United States	13m. 48.8s
1968	Mohamed Gammoudi, Tunisia	14m. 05.0s
1972	Lasse Viren, Finland	13m. 26.4s
1976	Lasse Viren, Finland	13m. 24.76s
1980	Miruts Yifter, Ethiopia	13m. 21.0s
1984	Said Aouita, Morocco	13m. 05.59s*

10,000-Meter Run

1912	Hannes Kolehmainen, Finland	31m. 20.8s
1920	Paavo Nurmi, Finland	31m. 45.8s
1924	Willie Ritola, Finland	30m. 23.2s
1928	Paavo Nurmi, Finland	30m. 18.8s
1932	Janusz Kusocinski, Poland	30m. 11.4s
1936	Ilmari Salminen, Finland	30m. 15.4s
1948	Emil Zatopek, Czechoslovakia	29m. 59.6s
1952	Emil Zatopek, Czechoslovakia	29m. 17.0s
1956	Vladimir Kuts, USSR	28m. 45.6s
1960	Pytor Bolotnikov, USSR	28m. 32.2s
1964	Billy Mills, United States	28m. 24.4s
1968	Naftali Temu, Kenya	29m. 27.4s
1972	Lasse Viren, Finland	27m. 38.4s*
1976	Lasse Viren, Finland	27m. 40.38s
1980	Miruts Yifter, Ethiopia	27m. 42.7s
1984	Alberto Cova, Italy	27m. 47.54

Marathon

1896	Spiridon Loues, Greece	2h. 58m. 50s
1900	Michel Teato, France	2h. 59m. 45s
1904	Thomas Hicks, United States	3h. 28m. 53s
1908	John J. Hayes, United States	2h. 55m. 18.4s
1912	Kenneth McArthur, South Africa	2h. 36m. 54.8s
1920	Hannes Kolehmainen, Finland	2h. 32m. 35.8s
1924	Albin Stenroos, Finland	2h. 41m. 22.6s
1928	A.B. El Ouafi, France	2h. 32m. 57s
1932	Juan Zabala, Argentina	2h. 31m. 36s
1936	Kitei Son, Japan	2h. 29m. 19.2s
1948	Delfo Cabrera, Argentina	2h. 34m. 51.6s
1952	Emil Zatopek, Czechoslovakia	2h. 23m. 03.2s
1956	Alain Mimoun, France	2h. 25m.
1960	Abebe Bikila, Ethiopia	2h. 15m. 16.2s
1964	Abebe Bikila, Ethiopia	2h. 12m. 11.2s
1968	Mamo Wolde, Ethiopia	2h. 20m. 26.4s
1972	Frank Shorter, United States	2h. 12m. 19.8s
1976	Waldemar Cierpinski, E. Germany	2h. 09m. 55s
1980	Waldemar Cierpinski, E. Germany	2h. 11m. 03s
1984	Carlos Lopes, Portugal	2h. 09m. 21 s*

10,000-Meter Cross-Country

1920	Paavo Nurmi, Finland	27m. 15s*
1924	Paavo Nurmi, Finland	32m. 54.8s

20-Kilometer Walk

1956	Leonid Spirine, USSR	1h. 31m. 27.4s
1960	Vladimir Golubnichy, USSR	1h. 34m. 7.2s
1964	Kenneth Mathews, Great Britain	1h. 29m. 34.0s
1968	Vladimir Golubnichy, USSR	1h. 35m. 58.4s
1972	Peter Frenkel, E. Germany	1h. 26m. 42.4s
1976	Daniel Bautista, Mexico	1h. 24m. 40.6s
1980	Maurizio Damilano, Italy	1h. 23m. 35.5s
1984	Ernesto Canto, Mexico	1h. 23m. 13.2s*

50-Kilometer Walk

1932	Thomas W. Green, Great Britain	4h. 50m. 10s
1936	Harold Whitlock, Great Britain	4h. 30m. 41.4s
1948	John Ljunggren, Sweden	4h. 41m. 52s
1952	Giuseppe Dordoni, Italy	4h. 28m. 07.8s
1956	Norman Read, New Zealand	4h. 30m. 42.8s
1960	Donald Thompson, Great Britain	4h. 25m. 30s
1964	Abdon Pamich, Italy	4h. 11m. 11.4s
1968	Christoph Hohne, E. Germany	4h. 20m. 13.6s
1972	Born Kannenberg, W. Germany	3h. 56m. 11.6s
1980	Hartwig Gauter, E. Germany	3h. 49m. 24.0s
1984	Raul Gonzalez, Mexico	3h. 47m. 26.05*

110-Meter Hurdles

1896	Thomas Curtis, United States	17.6s
1900	Alvin Kraenzlein, United States	15.4s
1904	Frederick Schule, United States	16s
1908	Forrest Smithson, United States	15s
1912	Frederick Kelly, United States	15.1s
1920	Earl Thomson, Canada	14.8s
1924	Daniel Kinsey, United States	15s
1928	Sydney Atkinson, South Africa	14.8s
1932	George Saling, United States	14.6s
1936	Forrest Towns, United States	14.2s
1948	William Porter, United States	13.9s
1952	Harrison Dillard, United States	13.7s
1956	Lee Calhoun, United States	13.5s
1960	Lee Calhoun, United States	13.8s
1964	Hayes Jones, United States	13.6s
1968	Willie Davenport, United States	13.3s
1972	Rod Milburn, United States	13.24s
1976	Guy Drut, France	13.30s
1980	Thomas Munkelt, E. Germany	13. 39s
1984	Roger Kingdom, United States	13.20s*

400-Meter Hurdles

1900	J.W.B. Tewksbury, United States	57.6s
1904	Harry Hillman, United States	53s
1908	Charles Bacon, United States	55s
1920	Frank Loomis, United States	54s
1924	F. Morgan Taylor, United States	52.6s
1928	Lord Burghley, Great Britain	53.4s
1932	Robert Tisdall, Ireland	51.8s
1936	Glenn Hardin, United States	52.4s
1948	Roy Cochran, United States	51.1s
1952	Charles Moore, United States	50.8s
1956	Glenn Davis, United States	50.1s
1960	Glenn Davis, United States	49.3s
1964	Rex Cawley, United States	49.6s
1968	Dave Hemery, Great Britain	48.1s
1972	John Akii-Bua, Uganda	47.82s
1976	Edwin Moses, United States	47.64s*
1980	Volker Beck, E. Germany	48.70s
1984	Edwin Moses, United States	47.75s

High Jump

1896	Ellery Clark, United States	5ft. 11 1-4 in.
1900	Irving Baxter, United States	6ft. 2 4-5 in.
1904	Samuel Jones, United States	5ft. 11 in.
1908	Harry Porter, United States	6ft. 3 in.
1912	Alma Richards, United States	6ft. 4 in.
1920	Richard Landon, United States	6ft. 4 1-4 in.
1924	Harold Osborn, United States	6ft. 6 in.
1928	Robert W. King, United States	6ft. 4 3-8 in.
1932	Duncan McNaughton, Canada	6ft. 5 5-8 in.
1936	Cornelius Johnson, United States	6ft. 7 15-16 in.
1948	John L. Winter, Australia	6ft. 6 in.
1952	Walter Davis, United States	6ft. 8.32 in.
1956	Charles Dumas, United States	6ft. 11 1-4 in.
1960	Robert Shavlakadze, USSR	7ft. 1 in.

1964	Valery Brumel, USSR	7ft. 1 3-4 in.
1968	Dick Fosbury, United States	7ft. 4 1-4 in.
1972	Yuri Tarmak, USSR	7ft. 3 3-4 in.
1976	Jacek Wszola, Poland	7ft. 4 1-2 in.
1980	Gerd Wessig, E. Germany	7ft. 8 3-4 in.*
1984	Dietmar Mogenburg, W. Germany	7 ft. 8 1-2 in.

Long Jump

1896	Ellery Clark, United States	20ft. 9 3-4 in.
1900	Alvin Kraenzlein, United States	23ft. 6 7-8 in.
1904	Myer Prinstein, United States	24ft. 1 in.
1908	Frank Irons, United States	24ft. 6 1-2 in.
1912	Albert Gutterson, United States	24ft. 11 1-4 in.
1920	William Petterssen, Sweden	23ft. 5 1-2 in.
1924	DeHart Hubbard, United States	24ft. 5 1-8 in.
1928	Edward B. Hamm, United States	25ft. 4 3-4 in.
1932	Edward Gordon, United States	25ft. 3-4 in.
1936	Jesse Owens, United States	26ft. 5 5-16 in.
1948	William Steele, United States	25ft. 8 in.
1952	Jerome Biffle, United States	24ft. 10 in.
1956	Gregory Bell, United States	25ft. 8 1-4 in.
1960	Ralph Boston, United States	26ft. 7 3-4 in.
1964	Lynn Davies, Great Britain	26ft. 5 3-4 in.
1968	Bob Beamon, United States	29ft. 2 1-2 in.*
1972	Randy Williams, United States	27ft. 1-2 in.
1976	Arnie Robinson, United States	27ft. 4 1-2 in.
1980	Lutz Dombrowski, E. Germany	28ft. 1-4 in.
1984	Carl Lewis, United States	28ft. 1-4 in.

400-Meter Relay

1912	Great Britain	42.4s
1920	United States	42.2s
1924	United States	41s
1928	United States	41s
1932	United States	40s
1936	United States	39.8s
1948	United States	40.6s
1952	United States	40.1s
1956	United States	39.5s
1960	Germany (U.S. disqualified)	39.5s
1964	United States	39.0s
1968	United States	38.2s
1972	United States	38.19s
1976	United States	38.33s
1980	USSR	38.26s
1984	United States	37.83s*

1,600-Meter Relay

1908	United States	3m. 27.2s
1912	United States	3m. 16.6s
1920	Great Britain	3m. 22.2s
1924	United States	3m. 16s
1928	United States	3m. 14.2s
1932	United States	3m. 8.2s
1936	Great Britain	3m. 9s
1948	United States	3m. 10.4s
1952	Jamaica, B.W.I.	3m. 03.9s
1956	United States	3m. 04.8s
1960	United States	3m. 02.2s
1964	United States	3m. 00.7s
1968	United States	2m. 56.1s*
1972	Kenya	2m. 59.8s
1976	United States	2m. 59.52s
1980	USSR	3m. 01.1s
1984	United States	2m.57.91 s

Pole Vault

1896	William Hoyt, United States	10ft. 9 3-4 in.
1900	Irving Baxter, United States	10ft. 9 7-8 in.
1904	Charles Dvorak, United States	11ft. 6 in.
1908	A. C. Gilbert, United States Edward Cook Jr., United States	12ft. 2 in.
1912	Harry Babcock, United States	12ft. 11 1-2 in.
1920	Frank Foss, United States	13ft. 5 in.
1924	Lee Barnes, United States	12ft. 11 1-2 in.
1928	Sabin W. Carr, United States	13ft. 9 3-8 in.
1932	William Miller, United States	14ft. 1 7-8 in.
1936	Earle Meadows, United States	14ft. 3 1-4 in.
1948	Guinn Smith, United States	14ft. 1 1-4 in.
1952	Robert Richards, United States	14ft. 11 1-8 in.
1956	Robert Richards, United States	14ft. 11 1-2 in.
1960	Don Bragg, United States	15ft. 5 1-8 in.
1964	Fred Hansen, United States	16ft. 8 3-4 in.
1968	Bob Seagren, United States	17ft. 8 1-2 in.
1972	Wolfgang Nordwig, E. Germany	18ft. 1-2 in.
1976	Tadeusz Slusarski, Poland	18ft. 1-2 in.
1980	Wladyslaw Kozakiewicz, Poland	18ft. 11 1-2 in.*
1984	Pierre Quinon, France	18ft. 10 1-4 in.

Hammer Throw

1900	John Flanagan, United States	167ft. 4 in.
1904	John Flanagan, United States	168ft. 1 in.
1908	John Flanagan, United States	170ft. 4 1-4 in.
1912	Matt McGrath, United States	179ft. 7 1-8 in.
1920	Pat Ryan, United States	173ft. 5 5-8 in.
1924	Fred Tootell, United States	174ft. 10 1-8 in.
1928	Patrick O'Callaghan, Ireland	168ft. 7 1-2 in.
1932	Patrick O'Callaghan, Ireland	176ft. 11 1-8 in.
1936	Karl Hein, Germany	185ft. 4 in.
1948	Imre Nemeth, Hungary	183ft. 11 1-2 in.
1952	Jozsef Csermak, Hungary	197ft. 11 9-16 in.
1956	Harold Connolly, United States	207ft. 3 1-2 in.
1960	Vasily Rudenkov, USSR	220ft. 1 5-8 in.
1964	Romuald Klim, USSR	228ft. 9 1-2 in.
1968	Gyula Zsivotsky, Hungary	240ft. 8 in.
1972	Anatoli Bondarchuk, USSR	248ft. 8 in.
1976	Yuri Syedykh, USSR	254ft. 4 in.
1980	Yuri Syedykh, USSR	268ft. 4 1-2 in.*
1984	Juha Tiainen, Finland	256ft. 2 in.

Discus Throw

1896	Robert Garrett, United States	95ft. 7 1-2 in.
1900	Rudolf Bauer, Hungary	118ft. 2.9-10 in.
1904	Martin Sheridan, United States	128ft. 10 1-2 in.
1908	Martin Sheridan, United States	134ft. 2 in.
1912	Armas Taipale, Finland	148ft. 4 in.
	Both hands—Armas Taipale, Finland	271ft. 10 1-4 in.
1920	Elmer Niklander, Finland	146ft. 7 1-4 in.
1924	Clarence Houser, United States	151ft. 5 1-8 in.
1928	Clarence Houser, United States	155ft. 3 in.
1932	John Anderson, United States	162ft. 4 7-8 in.
1936	Ken Carpenter, United States	165ft. 7 3-8 in.
1948	Adolfo Consolini, Italy	173ft. 2 in.
1952	Sim Iness, United States	180ft. 6.85 in.
1956	Al Oerter, United States	184ft. 10 1-2 in.
1960	Al Oerter, United States	194ft. 2 in.
1964	Al Oerter, United States	200ft. 1 1-2 in.
1968	Al Oerter, United States	212ft. 6 1-2 in.
1972	Ludvik Danek, Czechoslovakia	211ft. 3 in.
1976	Mac Wilkins, United States	221ft. 5.4 in.*
1980	Viktor Rashchupkin, USSR	218ft. 8 in.
1984	Rolf Dannenberg, W. Germany	218ft. 6 in.

Triple Jump

1896	James Connolly, United States	45ft.
1900	Myer Prinstein, United States	47ft. 4 1-4 in.
1904	Myer Prinstein, United States	47 ft.
1908	Timothy Aheame, Great Britain	48ft. 11 1-4 in.
1912	Gustaf Lindblom, Sweden	48ft. 5 1-8 in.
1920	Vilho Tuulos, Finland	47ft. 6 7-8 in.
1924	Archie Winter, Australia	50ft. 11 1-4 in.
1928	Mikio Oda, Japan	49ft. 11 in.
1932	Chuhei Nambu, Japan	51ft. 7 in.
1936	Naoto Tajima, Japan	52ft. 5 7-8 in.
1948	Arne Ahman, Sweden	50ft. 6 1-4 in.
1952	Adhemar de Silva, Brazil	53ft. 2 9-16 in.
1956	Adhemar de Silva, Brazil	53ft. 7 1-2 in.
1960	Jozef Schmidt, Poland	55ft. 1 3-4 in.
1964	Jozef Schmidt, Poland	55ft. 3 1-4 in.
1968	Viktor Saneev, USSR	57ft. 3-4 in.*
1972	Viktor Saneev, USSR	56ft. 11 in.
1976	Viktor Saneev, USSR	56ft. 8 3-4 in.
1980	Jaak Uudmae, USSR	56ft. 11 1-8 in.
1984	Al Joyner, United States	56ft. 7 1-2 in.

16-lb. Shot Put

1896	Robert Garrett, United States	36ft. 9 3-4 in.
1900	Robert Sheldon, United States	46ft. 3 1-8 in.
1904	Ralph Rose, United States	48ft. 7 in.
1908	Ralph Rose, United States	46ft. 7 1-2 in.
1912	Pat McDonald, United States	50ft. 4 in.
	Both hands—Ralph Rose, United States	90ft. 5 1-2 in.
1920	Ville Porhola, Finland	48ft. 7 1-8 in.
1924	Clarence Houser, United States	49ft. 2 1-2 in.
1928	John Kuck, United States	52ft. 3-4 in.
1932	Leo Sexton, United States	52ft. 6 3-16 in.
1936	Hans Woellke, Germany	53ft. 1 3-4 in.
1948	Wilbur Thompson, United States	56ft. 2 in.
1952	Parry O'Brien, United States	57ft. 1 7-16 in.
1956	Parry O'Brien, United States	60ft. 11 in.
1960	William Nieder, United States	64ft. 6 3-4 in.
1964	Dallas Long, United States	66ft. 8 1-4 in.
1968	Randy Matson, United States	67ft. 4 3-4 in.
1972	Wladyslaw Komar, Poland	69ft. 6 in.
1976	Udo Beyer, E. Germany	69ft. 3-4 in.
1980	Vladimir Kiselyov, USSR	70ft. 1-2 in.*
1984	Alessandro Andrei, Italy	69ft. 9 in.

Javelin

1908	Erik Lemming, Sweden	178ft. 7 1-2 in.
	Held in middle—Erik Lemming, Sweden	179ft. 10 1-2 in.
1912	Erik Lemming, Sweden	198ft. 11 1-4 in.
	Both hands, Julius Saaristo, Finland	358ft. 11 7-8 in.
1920	Jonni Myrra, Finland	215ft. 9 3-4 in.
1924	Jonni Myrra, Finland	206ft. 6 3-4 in.
1928	Eric Lundquist, Sweden	218ft. 6 1-8 in.
1932	Matti Jarvinen, Finland	238ft. 7 in.
1936	Gerhard Stoeck, Germany	235ft. 8 5-16 in.
1948	Kaj Rautavaara, Finland	228ft. 10 1-2 in.
1952	Cy Young, United States	242ft. 0.79 in.
1956	Egil Danielsen, Norway	281ft. 2 1-4 in.
1960	Viktor Tsibulenko, USSR	277ft. 8 3-8 in.
1964	Pauli Nevala, Finland	271ft. 2 1-2 in.
1968	Janis Lusis, USSR	295ft. 7 1-4 in.
1972	Klaus Wolfermann, W. Germany	296ft. 10 in.
1976	Miklos Nemeth, Hungary	310ft. 4 in.*
1980	Dainis Kula, USSR	299ft. 2 3-8 in.
1984	Arto Haerkoenen, Finland	284ft. 8 in.

Decathlon

1912	Hugo Wieslander, Sweden	7,724.49 pts.(a)
1920	Helge Lovland, Norway	6,804.35 pts.
1924	Harold Osborn, United States	7,710.77 pts.
1928	Paavo Yrjola, Finland	8,053.29 pts.
1932	James Bausch, United States	8,462.23 pts.
1936	Glenn Morris, United States	7,900 pts.
1948	Robert Mathias, United States	7,139 pts.
1952	Robert Mathias, United States	7,887 pts.
1956	Milton Campbell, United States	7,937 pts.
1960	Rafer Johnson, United States	8,392 pts.
1964	Willi Holdorf, Germany	7,887 pts.
1968	Bill Toomey, United States	8,193 pts.
1972	Nikola Avilov, USSR	8,454 pts.
1976	Bruce Jenner, United States	8,618 pts.
1980	Daley Thompson, Great Britain	8,495 pts.
1984	Daley Thompson, Great Britain	8,646 pts.*(b)

Former point systems used prior to 1964.

(a) Jim Thorpe of the U.S. won the 1912 Decathlon with 8,413 pts. but was disqualified and had to return his medals because he had played professional baseball prior to the Olympic games. The medals were restored posthumously in 1982. (b) Scoring change effective Apr., 1985.

Track and Field—Women

100-Meter Run

1928	Elizabeth Robinson, United States	12.2s
1932	Stella Walsh, Poland	11.9s
1936	Helen Stephens, United States	11.5s
1948	Francina Blankers-Koen, Netherlands	11.9s
1952	Marjorie Jackson, Australia	11.5s
1956	Betty Cuthbert, Australia	11.5s
1960	Wilma Rudolph, United States	11.0s
1964	Wyomia Tyus, United States	11.4s
1968	Wyomia Tyus, United States	11.0s
1972	Renate Stecher, E. Germany	11.07s
1976	Annegret Richter, W. Germany	11.08s
1980	Ludmila Kondratyeva, USSR	11.6s
1984	Evelyn Ashford, United States	10.97s*

200-Meter Run

1948	Francina Blankers-Koen, Netherlands	24.4s
1952	Marjorie Jackson, Australia	23.7s
1956	Betty Cuthbert, Australia	23.4s
1960	Wilma Rudolph, United States	24.0s
1964	Edith McGuire, United States	23.0s
1968	Irena Szewinska, Poland	22.5s
1972	Renate Stecher, E. Germany	22.40s
1976	Barbel Eckert, E. Germany	22.37s
1980	Barbel Wockel, E. Germany	22.03
1984	Valerie Brisco-Hooks, United States	21.81s*

400-Meter Run

1964	Betty Cuthbert, Australia	52s
1968	Colette Besson, France	52s
1972	Monika Zehrt, E. Germany	51.08s
1976	Irena Szewinska, Poland	49.29s
1980	Marita Koch, E. Germany	48.88s
1984	Valerie Brisco-Hooks, United States	48.83s*

800-Meter Run

1928	Lina Radke, Germany	2m. 16.8s
1960	Ludmila Shevcova, USSR	2m. 4.3s
1964	Ann Packer, Great Britain	2m. 1.1s
1968	Madeline Manning, United States	2m. 0.9s
1972	Hildegard Flack, W. Germany	1m. 58.6s
1976	Tatyana Kazankina, USSR	1m. 54.94s
1980	Nadezhda Olizayrenko, USSR	1m. 53.5s*
1984	Doina Melinte, Romania	1m. 57.6s

1,500-Meter Run

1972	Ludmila Bragina, USSR	4m. 01.4s
1976	Tatyana Kazankina, USSR	4m. 05.48s
1980	Tatyana Kazankina, USSR	3m. 56.6s*
1984	Gabriella Dorio, Italy	4m. 03.26s

3,000-Meter Run

1984	Maricica Puica, Romania	8:35.96*

400-Meter Relay

1928	Canada	48.4s
1932	United States	47.0s
1936	United States	46.9s
1948	Netherlands	47.5s
1952	United States	45.9s
1956	Australia	44.5s
1960	United States	44.5s
1964	Poland	43.6s
1968	United States	42.8s
1972	West Germany	42.81s
1976	East Germany	42.55s
1980	East Germany	41.60s*
1984	United States	41.65s

1,600-Meter Relay

1972	East Germany	3m. 23s
1976	East Germany	3m. 19.23s
1980	USSR	3m. 20.02s
1984	United States	3m. 18.29s*

80-Meter Hurdles

1932	Mildred Didrikson, United States	11.7s
1936	Trebisonda Villa, Italy	11.7s
1948	Francina Blankers-Koen, Netherlands	11.2s
1952	Shirley Strickland de la Hunty, Australia	10.9s
1956	Shirley Strickland de la Hunty, Australia	10.7s
1960	Irina Press, USSR	10.8s
1964	Karen Balzer, Germany	10.5s
1968	Maureen Caird, Australia	10.3s*

100-Meter Hurdles

1972	Annelie Ehrhardt, E. Germany	12.59s
1976	Johanna Schaller, E. Germany	12.77s
1980	Vera Komisova, USSR	12.56s*
1984	Benita Brown-Fitzgerald, United States	12.84s

400-Meter Hurdles

1984	Nawal el Moutawakii, Morocco	54.61s*

Heptathlon

1984	Glynis Nunn, Australia	6,390 pts.*

High Jump

1928	Ethel Catherwood, Canada	5ft. 3 in.
1932	Jean Shiley, United States	5ft. 5 1-4 in.
1936	Ibolya Csak, Hungary	5ft. 3 in.
1948	Alice Coachman, United States	5ft. 6 1-8 in.
1952	Esther Brand, South Africa	5ft. 5 3-4 in.
1956	Mildred L. McDaniel, United States	5ft. 9 1-4 in.
1960	Iolanda Balas, Romania	6ft. 3-4 in.
1964	Iolanda Balas, Romania	6ft. 2 3-4 in.
1968	Miloslava Reskova, Czechoslovakia	5ft. 11 3-4 in.
1972	Ulrike Meyfarth, W. Germany	6ft. 3 1-4 in.
1976	Rosemarie Ackermann, E. Germany	6ft. 3 3-4 in.
1980	Sara Simeoni, Italy	6ft. 5 1-2 in.
1984	Ulrike Meyfarth, W. Germany	6ft. 7 1-2 in.*

Discus Throw

1928	Helena Konopacka, Poland	129ft. 11 7-8 in.
1932	Lillian Copeland, United States	133ft. 2 in.
1936	Gisela Mauermayer, Germany	156ft. 3 3-16 in.
1948	Micheline Ostermeyer, France	137ft. 6 1-2 in.
1952	Nina Romaschkova, USSR	168ft. 8 1-2 in.
1956	Olga Fikotova, Czechoslovakia	176ft. 1 1-2 in.
1960	Nina Ponomareva, USSR	180ft. 8 1-4 in.
1964	Tamara Press, USSR	187ft. 10 1-2 in.
1968	Lia Manoliu, Romania	191ft. 2 1-2 in.
1972	Faina Melnik, USSR	218ft. 7 in.
1976	Evelin Schlaak, E. Germany	226ft. 4 1-2 in.
1980	Evelin Jahl, E. Germany	229ft. 6 1-4 in.*
1984	Ria Stalman, Netherlands	214ft. 5 in.

Javelin Throw

1932	Mildred Didrikson, United States	143ft. 4 in.

1936	Tilly Fleischer, Germany	148ft. 2 3-4 in.
1948	Herma Bauma, Austria	149ft. 6 in.
1952	Dana Zatopkova, Czechoslovakia	165ft. 7 in.
1956	Inessa Janzeme, USSR	176ft. 8 in.
1960	Elvira Ozolina, USSR	183ft. 8 in.
1964	Mihaela Penes, Romania	198ft. 7 1-2 in.
1968	Angela Nemeth, Hungary	198ft. 1-2 in.
1972	Ruth Fuchs, E. Germany	209ft. 7 in.
1976	Ruth Fuchs, E. Germany	216ft. 4 in.
1980	Maria Colon, Cuba	224ft. 5 in.
1984	Tessa Sanderson, Great Britain	228ft. 2 in.*

Shot Put (8lb., 13oz.)

1948	Micheline Ostermeyer, France	45ft. 1 1-2 in.
1952	Galina Zybina, USSR	50ft. 1 1-2 in.
1956	Tamara Tishkyevich, USSR	54ft. 5 in.
1960	Tamara Press, USSR	56ft. 9 7-8 in.
1964	Tamara Press, USSR	59ft. 6 1-4 in.
1968	Margitta Gummel, E. Germany	64ft. 4 in.
1972	Nadezhda Chizova, USSR	69ft.
1976	Ivanka Christova, Bulgaria	69ft. 5 in.
1980	Ilona Slupianek, E. Germany	73ft. 6 1-4 in. *
1984	Claudia Losch, W. Germany	67ft. 2 1-4 in.

Long Jump

1948	Olga Gyarmati, Hungary	18ft. 8 1-4 in.
1952	Yvette Williams, New Zealand	20ft. 5 3-4 in.
1956	Elzbieta Krzeskinska, Poland	20ft. 9 3-4 in.
1960	Vyera Krepkina, USSR	20ft. 10 3-4 in.
1964	Mary Rand, Great Britain	22ft. 2 1-4 in.
1968	Viorica Viscopoleanu, Romania	22ft. 4 1-2 in.
1972	Heidemarie Rosendahl, W. Germany	22ft. 3 in.
1976	Angela Voigt, E. Germany	22ft. 2 1-2 in.
1980	Tatyana Kolpakova, USSR	23ft. 2 in.*
1984	Anisoara Stanciu, Romania	22ft. 10 in.

Pentathlon

1964	Irina Press, USSR	5,246 pts.
1968	Ingrid Becker, W. Germany	5,098 pts.
1972	Mary Peters, England	4,801 pts.
1976	Sigrun Siegl, E. Germany	4,745 pts.
1980	Nadyezhda Tkachenko, USSR	5,083pts.*

Former point system, 1964–1968

Marathon

1984	Joan Benoit, United States	2h. 24m. 52s*

Swimming—Men

100-Meter Freestyle

1896	Alfred Hajos, Hungary	1:22.2
1904	Zoltan de Halmay, Hungary (100 yards)	1:02.8
1908	Charles Daniels, U.S.	1:05.6
1912	Duke P. Kahanamoku, U.S.	1:03.4
1920	Duke P. Kahanamoku, U.S.	1:01.4
1924	John Weissmuller, U.S.	59.0
1928	John Weissmuller, U.S.	58.6
1932	Yasuji Miyazaki, Japan	58.2
1936	Ferenc Csik, Hungary	57.6
1948	Wally Ris, U.S.	57.3
1952	Clark Scholes, U.S.	57.4
1956	Jon Henricks, Australia	55.4
1960	John Devitt, Australia	55.2
1964	Don Schollander, U.S.	53.4
1968	Mike Wenden, Australia	52.2
1972	Mark Spitz, U.S.	51.22
1976	Jim Montgomery, U.S.	49.99
1980	Jorg Woithe, E. Germany	50.40
1984	Rowdy Gaines, U.S.	49.80*

200-Meter Freestyle

1968	Mike Wenden, Australia	1:55.2
1972	Mark Spitz, U.S.	1:52.78
1976	Bruce Furniss, U.S.	1:50.29
1980	Sergei Kopliakov, USSR	1:49.81
1984	Michael Gross, W. Germany	1:47.44*

400-Meter Freestyle

1904	C. M. Daniels, U.S. (440 yards)	6:16.2
1908	Henry Taylor, Great Britain	5:36.8
1912	George Hodgson, Canada	5:24.4
1920	Norman Ross, U.S.	5:26.8
1924	John Weissmuller, U.S.	5:04.2
1928	Albert Zorilla, Argentina	5:01.6
1932	Clarence Crabbe, U.S.	4:48.4
1936	Jack Medica, U.S.	4:44.5
1948	William Smith, U.S.	4:41.0
1952	Jean Boiteux, France	4:30.7
1956	Murray Rose, Australia	4:27.3
1960	Murray Rose, Australia	4:18.3
1964	Don Schollander, U.S.	4:12.2
1968	Mike Burton, U.S.	4:09.0
1972	Brad Cooper, Australia	4:00.27
1976	Brian Goodell, U.S.	3:51.93
1980	Vladimir Salnikov, USSR	3:51.31
1984	George DiCarlo, U.S.	3:51.23*

1,500-Meter Freestyle

1908	Henry Taylor, Great Britain	22:48.4
1912	George Hodgson, Canada	22:00.0
1920	Norman Ross, U.S.	22:23.2
1924	Andrew Charlton, Australia	20:06.6
1928	Arne Borg, Sweden	19:51.8
1932	Kusuo Kitamura, Japan	19:12.4
1936	Noboru Terada, Japan	19:13.7
1948	James McLane, U.S.	19:18.5
1952	Ford Konno, U.S.	18:30.0
1956	Murray Rose, Australia	17:58.9
1960	Jon Konrads, Australia	17:19.6
1964	Robert Windle, Australia	17:01.7
1968	Mike Burton, U.S.	16:38.9
1972	Mike Burton, U.S.	15:52.58
1976	Brian Goodell, U.S.	15:02.40
1980	Vladimir Salnikov, USSR	14:58.27*
1984	Michael O'Brien, U.S.	15:05.20

400-Meter Medley Relay

1960	United States	4:05.4
1964	United States	3:58.4
1968	United States	3:54.9
1972	United States	3:48.16
1976	United States	3:42.22
1980	Australia	3:45.70
1984	United States	3:39.30*

400-Meter Freestyle Relay

1964	United States	3:33.2
1968	United States	3:31.7
1972	United States	3:26.42
1984	United States	3:19.03*

800-Meter Freestyle Relay

1908	Great Britain	10:55.6
1912	Australia	10:11.6
1920	United States	10:04.4
1924	United States	9:53.4
1928	United States	9:36.2
1932	Japan	8:58.4
1936	Japan	8:51.5
1948	United States	8:46.0
1952	United States	8:31.1
1956	Australia	8:23.6
1960	United States	8:10.2
1964	United States	7:52.1
1968	United States	7:52.3
1972	United States	7:35.78
1976	United States	7:23.22
1980	USSR	7:23.50
1984	United States	7:15.69*

100-Meter Backstroke

1904	Walter Brack, Germany (100 yds.)	1:16.8
1908	Arno Bieberstein, Germany	1:24.6
1912	Harry Hebner, U.S.	1:21.2
1920	Warren Kealoha, U.S.	1:15.2
1924	Warren Kealoha, U.S.	1:13.2
1928	George Kojac, U.S.	1:08.2
1932	Masaji Kiyokawa, Japan	1:08.6
1936	Adolph Kiefer, U.S.	1:05.9
1948	Allen Stack, U.S.	1:06.4
1952	Yoshi Oyakawa, U.S.	1:05.4
1956	David Thiele, Australia	1:02.2
1960	David Thiele, Australia	1:01.9
1968	Roland Matthes, E. Germany	58.7
1972	Roland Matthes, E. Germany	56.58
1976	John Naber, U.S.	55.49*
1980	Bengt Baron, Sweden	56.53
1984	Rick Carey, U.S.	55.79

200-Meter Backstroke

1964	Jed Graef, U.S.	2:10.3
1968	Roland Matthes, E. Germany	2:09.6
1972	Roland Matthes, E. Germany	2:02.82
1976	John Naber, U.S.	1:59.19*
1980	Sandor Wladar, Hungary	2:01.93
1984	Rick Carey, U.S.	2:00.23

100-Meter Breaststroke

1968	Don McKenzie, U.S.	1:07.7
1972	Nobutaka Taguchi, Japan	1:04.94
1976	John Hencken, U.S.	1:03.11
1980	Duncan Goodhew, Great Britain	1:03.34
1984	Steve Lundquist, U.S.	1:01.65*

200-Meter Breaststroke

1908	Frederick Holman, Great Britain	3:09.2
1912	Walter Bathe, Germany	3:01.8
1920	Haken Malmroth, Sweden	3:04.4
1924	Robert Skelton, U.S.	2:56.6
1928	Yoshiyuki Tsuruta, Japan	2:48.8
1932	Yoshiyuki Tsuruta, Japan	2:45.4
1936	Tetsuo Hamuro, Japan	2:42.5
1948	Joseph Verdeur, U.S.	2:39.3
1952	John Davies, Australia	2:34.4
1956	Masura Furukawa, Japan	2:34.7
1960	William Mulliken, U.S.	2:37.4
1964	Ian O'Brien, Australia	2:27.8
1968	Felipe Munoz, Mexico	2:28.7
1972	John Hencken, U.S.	2:21.55
1976	David Wilkie, Great Britain	2:15.11
1980	Robertas Zulpa, USSR	2:15.85
1984	Victor Davis, Canada	2:13.34*

100-Meter Butterfly

1968	Doug Russell, U.S.	55.9
1972	Mark Spitz, U.S.	54.27
1976	Matt Vogel, U.S.	54.35
1980	Par Arvidsson, Sweden	54.92
1984	Michael Gross, W. Germany	53.08*

200-Meter Butterfly

1956	William Yorzyk, U.S.	2:19.3
1960	Michael Troy, U.S.	2:12.8
1964	Kevin J. Berry, Australia	2:06.6
1968	Carl Robie, U.S.	2:08.7
1972	Mark Spitz, U.S.	2:00.70
1976	Mike Bruner, U.S.	1:59.23
1980	Sergei Fesenko, USSR	1:59.76
1984	Jon Sieben, Australia	1:57.04*

200-Meter Individual Medley

1968	Charles Hickcox, U.S.	2:12.0
1972	Gunnar Larsson, Sweden	2:07.17*
1984	Alex Baumann, Canada	2:10.42

400-Meter Individual Medley

1964	Dick Roth, U.S.	4:45.4
1968	Charles Hickcox, U.S.	4:48.4
1972	Gunnar Larsson, Sweden	4:31.98
1976	Rod Strachan, U.S.	4:23.68
1980	Aleksandr Sidorenko, USSR	4:22.89
1984	Alex Baumann, Canada	4:17.41*

Springboard Diving

	Springboard Diving	Points
1908	Albert Zurner, Germany	85.5
1912	Paul Guenther, Germany	79.23
1920	Louis Kuehn, U.S.	675.00
1924	Albert White, U.S.	696.40
1928	Pete Desjardins, U.S.	185.04
1932	Michael Galitzen, U.S.	161.38
1936	Richard Degener, U.S.	161.57
1948	Bruce Harlan, U.S.	163.64
1952	David Browning, U.S.	205.29
1956	Robert Clotworthy, U.S.	159.56
1960	Gary Tobian, U.S.	170.00
1964	Kenneth Sitzberger, U.S.	159.90
1968	Bernie Wrightson, U.S.	170.15
1972	Vladimir Vasin, USSR	594.09
1976	Phil Boggs, U.S.	619.52
1980	Aleksandr Portnov, USSR	905.02
1984	Greg Louganis, U.S.	754.41

Platform Diving

	Platform Diving	Points
1904	Dr. G.E. Sheldon, U.S.	12.75
1908	Hjalmar Johansson, Sweden	83.75
1912	Erik Adlerz, Sweden	73.94
1920	Clarence Pinkston, U.S.	100.67
1924	Albert White, U.S.	487.30
1928	Pete Desjardins, U.S.	98.74
1932	Harold Smith, U.S.	124.80
1936	Marshall Wayne, U.S.	113.58
1948	Sammy Lee, U.S.	130.05
1952	Sammy Lee, U.S.	156.28
1956	Joaquin Capilla, Mexico	152.44
1960	Robert Webster, U.S.	165.56
1964	Robert Webster, U.S.	148.58
1968	Klaus Dibiasi, Italy	164.18
1972	Klaus Dibiasi, Italy	504.12
1976	Klaus Dibiasi, Italy	600.51
1980	Falk Hoffmann, E. Germany	835.65
1984	Greg Louganis, U.S.	710.91

Swimming—Women

100-Meter Freestyle

1912	Fanny Durack, Australia	1:22.2
1920	Ethelda Bleibtrey, U.S.	1:13.6
1924	Ethel Lackie, U.S.	1:12.4
1928	Albina Osipowich, U.S.	1:11.0
1932	Helene Madison, U.S.	1:06.8
1936	Hendrika Mastenbroek, Holland	1:05.9
1948	Greta Anderson, Denmark	1:06.3
1952	Katalin Szoke, Hungary	1:06.3
1956	Dawn Fraser, Australia	1:02.0
1960	Dawn Fraser, Australia	1:01.2
1964	Dawn Fraser, Australia	59.5
1968	Jan Henne, U.S.	1:00.0
1972	Sandra Neilson, U.S.	58.59
1976	Kornelia Ender, E. Germany	55.65
1980	Barbara Krause, E. Germany	54.79*
1984	(tie) Carrie Steinseifer, U.S.	55.92
	Nancy Hogshead, U.S.	55.92

200-Meter Freestyle

1968	Debbie Meyer, U.S.	2:10.5
1972	Shane Gould, Australia	2:03.56
1976	Kornelia Ender, E. Germany	1:59.26
1980	Barbara Krause, E. Germany	1:58.33*
1984	Mary Wayte, U.S.	1:59.23

400-Meter Freestyle

1924	Martha Norelius, U.S.	6:02.2
1928	Martha Norelius, U.S.	5:42.8
1932	Helene Madison, U.S.	5:28.5
1936	Hendrika Mastenbroek, Netherlands	5:26.4
1948	Ann Curtis, U.S.	5:17.8
1952	Valerie Gyenge, Hungary	5:12.1
1956	Lorraine Crapp, Australia	4:54.6
1960	Susan Chris von Saltza, U.S.	4:50.6
1964	Virginia Duenkel, U.S.	4:43.3
1968	Debbie Meyer, U.S.	4:31.8
1972	Shane Gould, Australia	4:19.04
1976	Petra Thuemer E. Germany	4:09.89
1980	Ines Diers, E. Germany	4:08.76
1984	Tiffany Cohen, U.S.	4:07.10*

800-Meter Freestyle

1968	Debbie Meyer, U.S.	9:24.0
1972	Keena Rothhammer, U.S.	8:53.68
1976	Petra Thuemer, E. Germany	8:37.14
1980	Michelle Ford, Australia	8:28.90
1984	Tiffany Cohen, U.S.	8:24.95*

100-Meter Backstroke

1924	Sybil Bauer, U.S.	1:23.3
1928	Marie Braun, Netherlands	1:22.0
1932	Eleanor Holm, U.S.	1:19.4
1936	Dina Senff, Netherlands	1:18.9
1948	Karen Harup, Denmark	1:14.4
1952	Joan Harrison, South Africa	1:14.3
1956	Judy Grinham, Great Britain	1:12.9
1960	Lynn Burke, U.S.	1:09.3
1964	Cathy Ferguson, U.S.	1:07.7
1968	Kaye Hall, U.S.	1:06.2
1972	Melissa Belote, U.S.	1:05.78
1976	Ulrike Richter, E. Germany	1:01.83
1980	Rica Reinisch, E. Germany	1:00.86*
1984	Theresa Andrews, U.S.	1:02.55

200-Meter Backstroke

1968	Pokey Watson, U.S.	2:24.8
1972	Melissa Belote, U.S.	2:19.19
1976	Ulrike Richter, E. Germany	2:13.43
1980	Rica Reinisch, E. Germany	2:11.77*
1984	Jolanda De Rover, Netherlands	2:13.38

100-Meter Breaststroke

1968	Djurdjica Bjedov, Yugoslavia	1:15.8
1972	Cathy Carr, U.S.	1:13.58
1976	Hannelore Anke, E. Germany	1:11:16
1980	Ute Geweniger, E. Germany	1:10.22
1984	Petra Van Staveren, Netherlands	1:09.88*

200-Meter Breaststroke

1924	Lucy Morton, Great Britain	3:32.2
1928	Hilde Schrader, Germany	3:12.6
1932	Clare Dennis, Australia	3:06.3
1936	Hideko Maehata, Japan	3:03.6
1948	Nelly Van Vliet, Netherlands	2:57.2
1952	Eva Szekely, Hungary	2:51.7
1956	Ursula Happe, Germany	2:53.1
1960	Anita Lonsbrough, Great Britain	2:49.5
1964	Galina Prozumenschikova, USSR	2:46.4
1968	Sharon Wichman, U.S.	2:44.4
1972	Beverly Whitfield, Australia	2:41.71
1976	Marina Koshevaia, USSR	2:33.35
1980	Lina Kachushite, USSR	2:29.54*
1984	Anne Ottenbrite, Canada	2:30.38

200-Meter Individual Medley

1968	Claudia Kolb, U.S.	2:24.7
1972	Shane Gould, Australia	2:23.07
1984	Tracy Caulkins, U.S.	2:12.64*

400-Meter Individual Medley

1964	Donna de Varona, U.S.	5:18.7
1968	Claudia Kolb, U.S.	5:08.5
1972	Gail Neall, Australia	5:02.97
1976	Ulrike Tauber, E. Germany	4:42.77
1980	Petra Schneider, E. Germany	4:36.29*
1984	Tracy Caulkins, U.S.	4:39.24

100-Meter Butterfly

1956	Shelley Mann, U.S.	1:11.0
1960	Carolyn Schuler, U.S.	1:09.5
1964	Sharon Stouder, U.S.	1:04.7
1968	Lynn McClements, Australia	1:05.5
1972	Mayumi Aoki, Japan	1:03.34
1976	Kornelia Ender, E. Germany	1:00.13
1980	Caren Metschuck, E. Germany	1:00.42
1984	Mary T. Meagher, U.S.	59.26*

200-Meter Butterfly

1968	Ada Kok, Netherlands	2:24.7
1972	Karen Moe, U.S.	2:15.57
1976	Andrea Pollack, E. Germany	2:11.41
1980	Ines Geissler, E. Germany	2:10.44
1984	Mary T. Meagher, U.S.	2:06.90*

400-Meter Medley Relay

1960	United States	4:41.1
1960	United States	4:33.9
1968	United States	4:28.3
1972	United States	4:20.75
1976	East Germany	4:07.95
1980	East Germany	4:06.67*
1984	United States	4:08.34

400-Meter Freestyle Relay

1912	Great Britain	5:52.8
1920	United States	5:11.6
1924	United States	4:58.8
1928	United States	4:47.6
1932	United States	4:38.0
1936	Netherlands	4:36.0
1948	United States	4:29.2
1952	Hungary	4:24.4
1956	Australia	4:17.1
1960	United States	4:08.9
1964	United States	4:03.8
1968	United States	4:02.5
1972	United States	3:55.19
1976	United States	3:44.82
1980	East Germany	3:42.71*
1984	United States	3:43.43

Springboard Diving

		Points
1920	Aileen Riggin, U.S.	539.90
1924	Elizabeth Becker, U.S.	474.50
1928	Helen Meany, U.S.	78.62
1932	Georgia Coleman U.S.	87.52
1936	Marjorie Gestring, U.S.	89.27
1948	Victoria M. Draves, U.S.	108.74
1952	Patricia McCormick, U.S.	147.30
1956	Patricia McCormick, U.S.	142.36
1960	Ingrid Kramer, Germany	155.81
1964	Ingrid Engel-Kramer, Germany	145.00
1968	Sue Gossick, U.S.	150.77
1972	Micki King, U.S.	450.03
1976	Jenni Chandler, U.S.	506.19
1980	Irina Kalinina, USSR	725.91
1984	Sylvie Bernier, Canada	530.70

Platform Diving

		Points
1912	Greta Johansson, Sweden	39.90
1920	Stefani Fryland-Clausen, Denmark	34.60
1924	Caroline Smith, U.S.	166.00
1928	Elizabeth B. Pinkston, U.S.	31.60
1932	Dorothy Poynton, U.S.	40.26
1936	Dorothy Poynton Hill, U.S.	33.93
1948	Victoria M. Draves, U.S.	68.87
1952	Patricia McCormick, U.S.	79.37
1956	Patricia McCormick, U.S.	84.85
1960	Ingrid Kramer, Germany	91.28
1964	Lesley Bush, U.S.	99.80
1968	Milena Duchkova, Czech.	109.59
1972	Ulrika Knape, Sweden	390.00
1976	Elena Vaytsekhouskaya, USSR	406.59
1980	Martina Jaschke, E. Germany	596.25
1984	Zhou Jihong, China	435.51

Other Summer Olympics Gold Medalists in 1984

Archery

Men—Darrell Pace, U.S.
Women—Hyang-Soun Seo, S. Korea.

Basketball

Men—1. U.S.; 2. Spain; 3. Yugoslavia.
Women—1. U.S.; 2. S. Korea; 3. China.

Boxing

106 lbs.—Paul Gonzales, U.S.
112 lbs.—Steve McCrory, U.S.
119 lbs.—Maurizio Stecca, Italy.
126 lbs.—Meldrick Taylor, U.S.
132 lbs.—Pernell Whitaker, U.S.
139 lbs.—Jerry Page, U.S.
147 lbs.—Mark Breland, U.S.
157 lbs.—Frank Tate, U.S.
165 lbs.—Joun-Sup Shin, S. Korea.
178 lbs.—Anton Josipovic, Yugoslavia.
201 lbs.—Henry Tillman, U.S.
Over 201 lbs.—Tyrell Biggs, U.S.

Canoeing—Men

500m One-Man Canoe—Larry Cain, Canada.
500m Two-Man Canoe—Yugoslavia.
500m One-Man Kayak—Ian Ferguson, New Zealand.
500m Two-Man Kayak—New Zealand.
1,000m One-Man Kayak—Alan Thompson, New Zealand.
1,000m Two-Man Kayak—Canada.
1,000m Four-Man Kayak—New Zealand.
1,000m One-Man Canoe—Ulrich Eiche, W. Germany.
1,000m Two-Man Canoe—Romania.

Canoeing—Women

500m One-Woman Kayak—Agneta Andersson, Sweden.
500m Two-Woman Kayak—Sweden.
500m Four-Woman Kayak—Romania.

Cycling

4,000 Individual Pursuit—Steve Hegg, U.S.
Individual Road Race—Alexi Grewal, U.S.
1,000m Time Trials—Fredy Schmidtke, W. Germany.

4,000m Team Pursuit—Australia.
Sprint—Mark Gorski, U.S.
Points Race—Roger Ilegems, Belgium.
100km Road Team Trials—Italy.
Women's Individual Road Race—Connie Carpenter, U.S.

Diving

Men's Springboard—Greg Louganis, U.S.
Men's Platform—Greg Louganis, U.S.
Women's Springboard—Sylvie Bernier, Canada.
Women's Platform—Zhou Jihong, China.

Equestrian

Individual 3-Day Event—Mark Todd, New Zealand.
Team 3-Day Event—U.S.
Team Jumping—U.S.
Team Dressage—W. Germany.
Individual Dressage—Reiner Klimke, W. Germany.
Individual Jumping—Jose Fargis, U.S.

Fencing—Men

Individual Epee—Phillippe Boisse, France.
Individual Foil—Mauro Numa, Italy.
Individual Sabre—Jean Francois Lamour, France.
Team Foil—Italy.
Team Epee—W. Germany.
Team Sabre—Italy.

Fencing—Women

Individual Foil—Luan Jujie, China.
Team Foil—W. Germany.

Field Hockey

Men—1. Pakistan; 2. W. Germany; 3. Great Britain.
Women—1. Netherlands; 2. W. Germany; 3. U.S.

Gymnastics—Men

All Around—Koji Gushiken, Japan.
Team—U.S.
Floor Exercise—Li Ning, China.
Horizontal Bar—Shinji Morisue, Japan.
Parallel Bars—Bart Conner, U.S.
Pommel Horse—Li Ning, China & Peter Vidmar, U.S. (tie).
Rings—Koji Gushiken, Japan & Li Ning, China (tie).
Vault—Lou Yung, China.

Gymnastics—Women

Floor Exercise—Ecaterina Szabo, Romania.
Balance Beam—Simona Pauca & Ecaterina Szabo, both Romania (tie).
Vault—Ecaterina Szabo, Romania.
Uneven Parallel Bars—Ma Yanhonjg, China & Julianne McNamara, U.S. (tie).
All-Around—Mary Lou Retton, U.S.
Team—Romania.
Rhythmic—Lori Fung, Canada.

Team Handball

Men—1. Yugoslavia; 2. W. Germany; 3. Romania.
Women—1. Yugoslavia; 2. S. Korea; 3. China.

Judo

Lightweight—Byeong-Keun Ahn, S. Korea.
Extra Lightweight—Shinji Hosokawa, Japan.
Half Lightweight—Yoshiyuki Matsuoka, Japan.
Half Middleweight—Frank Wieneke, W. Germany.
Middleweight—Peter Seisenbacher, Austria.
Half Heavyweight—Hyong-Zoo Ha, S. Korea.
Heavyweight—Hitoshi Saito, Japan.
Open—Yasuhiro Yamashita, Japan.

Modern Pentathlon

Individual—Daniele Masala, Italy.
Team—1. Italy; 2. U.S.; 3. France.

Rowing

Single Sculls—Pertti Karppinen, Finland.
Double Sculls—U.S.
Quadruple Sculls—W. Germany.
Pair Oars With Coxswain—Italy.
Pair Oars Without Coxswain—Romania.
Four Oars With Coxswain—Great Britain.
Four Oars Without Coxswain—New Zealand.
Eight Oars With Coxswain—Canada.

Rowing—Women

Single Sculls—Valarie Racila, Romania.
Double Sculls—Romania.
Quadruple Sculls with Coxswain—Romania.
Pair Oars Without Coxswain—Romania.
Four Oars Without Coxswain—Romania.
Eight Oars—U.S.

Shooting—Men

Air Rifle—Philippe Heberle, France.
Clay Target Trap—Luciano Giovanetti, Italy.
English Small Bore Rifle—Ed Etzel, U.S.
Free Pistol—Xu Haifeng, China.
Rapid-Fire Pistol—Takeo Kamachi, Japan
Running Game Targets—Li Yuwei, China.
Small Bore Rifle, 3 Positions—Malcolm Cooper, Great Britain.
Clay Target Skeet—Matthew Dryke, U.S.

Shooting—Women

Air Rifle—Pat Spurgin, U.S.
Small Bore Rifle, 3 Positions—Wu Xiaoxuan, China.
Sport Pistol—Linda Thom, Canada.

Soccer

Championship—1. France; 2. Brazil; 3. Yugoslavia.

Synchronized Swimming

Solo—Tracie Ruiz, U.S.
Duet—1. U.S.; 2. Canada; 3. Japan.

Volleyball

Men—1. U.S.; 2. Brazil; 3. Italy.
Women—1. China; 2. U.S.; 3. Japan.

Water Polo

Championship—1. Yugoslavia; 2. U.S.; 3. W. Germany.

Weight Lifting

Bantamweight—Wu Shude, China.
Flyweight—Zeng Guoqiang, China.
Featherweights—Chen Weiquiang, China.
Lightweights—Yao Jingyuang, China.
Middleweights—Karl-Heinz Radschinsky, W. Germany.
Light Heavyweights—Petre Becheru, Romania.
Middle Heavyweights—Niku Vlad, Romania.
100 Kilograms—Rolf Milser, W. Germany.
110 Kilograms—Norberto Oberburger, Italy.
Super Heavyweights—Dinko Lukim, Australia.

Wrestling—Freestyle

106 Pounds—Robert Weaver, U.S.
115 Pounds—Saban Trstena, Yugoslavia.
126 Pounds—Hideaki Tomiyama, Japan.
137 Pounds—Randy Lewis, U.S.
150 Pounds—In Tak Yoo, S. Korea.
163 Pounds—Dave Schultz, U.S.
181 Pounds—Mark Schultz, U.S.
198 Pounds—Ed Banach, U.S.
220 Pounds—Lou Banach, U.S.
Over 220 Pounds—Bruce Baumgartner, U.S.

Wrestling—Greco-Roman

106 Pounds—Vicenzo Maenza, Italy.
115 Pounds—Atsuji Miyahara, Japan.
126 Pounds—Pasquale Passarelli, W. Germany.
137 Pounds—Weon Kee Kim, S. Korea.
150 Pounds—Vlado Lisjak, Yugoslavia.
163 Pounds—Jouko Salomaki, Finland.

181 Pounds—Ion Draica, Romania.
198 Pounds—Steven Fraser, U.S.
202 Pounds—Vasile Andrei, Romania.
Over 202 Pounds—Jeff Blatnick, U.S.

Yachting

Windglider Class—Stephen Van Den Berg, Netherlands.
Soling Class—1. U.S.; 2. Brazil; 3. Canada.
Flying Dutchman Class—1. U.S.; 2. Canada; 3. Great Britain.
Star Class—1. U.S.; 2. W. Germany; 3. Italy.
Finn Class—1. Russell Coutts, New Zealand.
Tornado Class—1. New Zealand; 2. U.S.; 3. Australia.
470 Class—1. Spain; 2. U.S.; 3. France.

23d Summer Olympics

Los Angeles, Cal., July 29-Aug. 12, 1984

Final Medal Standings

(nations in alphabetical order)

	Gold	Silver	Bronze	Total
Algeria	0	0	2	2
Australia	4	8	12	24
Austria	1	1	1	3
Belgium	1	1	2	4
Brazil	1	5	2	8
Cameroon	0	0	1	1
Canada	10	18	16	44
China	15	8	9	32
Columbia	0	1	0	1
Denmark	0	3	3	6
Dom. Republic	0	0	1	1
Egypt	0	1	0	1
Finland	4	3	6	13
France	5	7	15	27
Germany, West	17	19	23	59
Great Britain	5	10	22	37
Greece	0	1	1	2
Iceland	0	0	1	1
Ireland	0	1	0	1
Italy	14	6	12	32
Ivory Coast	0	1	0	1
Jamaica	0	1	2	3
Japan	10	8	14	32
Kenya	1	0	1	2
Korea, South	6	6	7	19
Mexico	2	3	1	6
Morocco	2	0	0	2
Netherlands	5	2	6	13
New Zealand	8	1	2	11
Nigeria	0	1	1	2
Norway	0	1	2	3
Pakistan	1	0	0	1
Peru	0	1	0	1
Portugal	1	0	2	3
Puerto Rico	0	1	1	2
Romania	20	16	17	53
Spain	1	2	2	5
Sweden	2	11	6	19
Switzerland	0	4	4	8
Syria	0	1	0	1
Taipei	0	0	1	1
Thailand	0	1	0	1
Turkey	0	0	3	3
United States	83	61	30	174
Venezuela	0	0	3	3
Yugoslavia	7	4	7	18
Zambia	0	0	1	1

Duplicate medals awarded in some events

Olympic Information

Symbol: Five rings or circles, linked together to represent the sporting friendship of all peoples. The rings also symbolize the 5 continents—Europe, Asia, Africa, Australia, and America. Each ring is a different color—blue, yellow, black, green, and red.

Flag: The symbol of the 5 rings on a plain white background.

Motto: "Citius, Altius, Fortius." Latin meaning "faster, higher, braver," or the modern interpretation "swifter, higher, stronger". The motto was coined by Father Didon, a French educator, in 1895.

Creed: "The most important thing in the Olympic Games is not to win but to take part, just as the most important thing in life is not the triumph but the struggle. The essential thing is not to have conquered but to have fought well."

Oath: An athlete of the host country recites the following at the opening ceremony. "In the name of all competitors I promise that we will take part in these Olympic Games, respecting and abiding by the rules which govern them, in the true spirit of sportsmanship for the glory of sport and the honor of our teams." Both the oath and the creed were composed by Pierre de Coubertin, the founder of the modern Games.

Flame: Symbolizes the continuity between the ancient and modern Games. The modern version of the flame was adopted in 1936. The torch used to kindle the flame is first lit by the sun's rays at Olympia, Greece, and then carried to the site of the Games by relays of runners. Ships and planes are used when necessary.

Winter Olympic Games Champions, 1924-1984

Sites and Unofficial Winners of Games

1924 Chamonix, France (Norway)
1928 St. Moritz, Switzerland (Norway)
1932 Lake Placid, N.Y. (U.S.)
1936 Garmisch-Partenkirchen (Norway)
1948 St. Moritz (Sweden)
1952 Oslo, Norway (Norway)
1956 Cortina d'Ampezzo, Italy (USSR)
1960 Squaw Valley, Cal. (USSR)
1964 Innsbruck, Austria (USSR)
1968 Grenoble, France (Norway)
1972 Sapporo, Japan (USSR)
1976 Innsbruck, Austria (USSR)
1980 Lake Placid, N.Y. (E. Germany)
1984 Sarajevo, Yugoslavia (USSR)
1988 Calgary, Alberta (scheduled)

Biathlon

10 Kilometers	Time
1980 Frank Ulrich, E. Germany	32:10.69
1984 Eirik Kvalfoss, Norway	30:53.8

20 Kilometers	Time
1960 Klas Lestander, Sweden	1:33:21.6
1964 Vladimir Melanin, USSR	1:20:26.8
1968 Magnar Solberg, Norway	1:13:45.9
1972 Magnar Solberg, Norway	1:15:55.50
1976 Nikolai Kruglov, USSR	1:14:12.26
1980 Anatoly Alabyev, USSR	1:08:16.31
1984 Peter Angerer, W. Germany	1:11:52.7

	40-Kilometer Relay	Time
1968	USSR, Norway, Sweden	2:13:02
1972	USSR, Finland, E. Germany	1:51:44
1976	USSR, Finland, E. Germany	1:57:55.64
1980	USSR, E. Germany, W. Germany (30 km.)	1:34:03.27
1984	USSR, Norway, W. Germany	1:38:51.70

Bobsledding

4-Man Bob

	(Driver in parentheses)	Time
1924	Switzerland (Edward Scherrer)	5:45.54
1928	United States (William Fiske) (5-man)	3:20.50
1932	United States (William Fiske)	7:53.68
1936	Switzerland (Pierre Musy)	5:19.85
1948	United States (Edward Rimkus)	5:20.10
1952	Germany (Andreas Ostler)	5:07.84
1956	Switzerland (Frank Kapus)	5:10.44
1964	Canada (Victor Emery)	4:14.46
1968	Italy (Eugenio Monti) (2 races)	2:17.39
1972	Switzerland (Jean Wicki)	4:43.07
1976	E. Germany (Mainhard Nehmer)	3:40.43
1980	E. Germany (Mainhard Nehmer)	3:59.92
1984	E. Germany (Wolfgang Hoppe)	3:20.22

	2-Man Bob	Time
1932	United States (Hubert Stevens)	8:14.74
1936	United States (Ivan Brown)	5:29.29
1948	Switzerland (F. Endrich)	5:29.20
1952	Germany (Andreas Ostler)	5:24.54
1956	Italy (Dalla Costa)	5:30.14
1964	Great Britain (Antony Nash)	4:21.90
1968	Italy (Eugenio Monti)	4:41.54
1972	W. Germany (Wolfgang Zimmerer)	4:47.07
1976	E. Germany (Meinhard Nehmer)	3:40.43
1980	Switzerland (Erich Schaerer)	4:09.36
1984	E.Germany (Wolfgang Hoppe)	3:25.56

Figure Skating

Men's Singles

1908 Ulrich Sachow, Sweden
1920 Gillis Grafstrom, Sweden
1924 Gillis Grafstrom, Sweden
1928 Gillis Grafstrom, Sweden
1932 Karl Schaefer, Austria
1936 Karl Schaefer, Austria
1948 Richard Button, U.S.
1952 Richard Button, U.S.
1956 Hayes Alan Jenkins, U.S.
1960 David W. Jenkins, U.S.
1964 Manfred Schnelldorfer, Germany
1968 Wolfgang Schwartz, Austria
1972 Ondrej Nepela, Czechoslovakia
1976 John Curry, Great Britain
1980 Robin Cousins, Great Britain
1984 Scott Hamilton, U.S.

Women's Singles

1908 Madge Syers, Great Britain
1920 Magda Julin-Mauroy, Sweden
1924 Helma von Szabo-Planck, Austria
1928 Sonja Henie, Norway
1932 Sonja Henie, Norway
1936 Sonja Henie, Norway
1948 Barbara Ann Scott, Canada
1952 Jeanette Altwegg, Great Britain
1956 Tenley Albright, U.S.
1960 Carol Heiss, U.S.
1964 Sjoukje Dijkstra, Netherlands
1968 Peggy Fleming, U.S.
1972 Beatrix Schuba, Austria
1976 Dorothy Hamill, U.S.
1980 Anett Poetzsch, E. Germany
1984 Katarina Witt, E. Germany

Pairs

1908 Anna Hubler & Heinrich Burger, Germany
1920 Ludovika & Walter Jakobsson, Finland
1924 Helene Engelman & Alfred Berger, Austria
1928 Andree Joly & Pierre Brunet, France
1932 Andree Joly & Pierre Brunet, France
1936 Maxie Herber & Ernest Baier, Germany
1948 Micheline Lannoy & Pierre Baugniet, Belgium
1952 Ria and Paul Falk, Germany
1956 Elisabeth Schwarz & Kurt Oppelt, Austria
1960 Barbara Wagner & Robert Paul, Canada
1964 Ludmila Beloussova & Oleg Protopopov, USSR
1968 Ludmila Beloussova & Oleg Protopopov, USSR
1972 Irina Rodnina & Alexei Ulanov, USSR
1976 Irina Rodnina & Aleksandr Zaitzev, USSR
1980 Irina Rodnina & Aleksandr Zaitzev, USSR
1984 Elena Valova & Oleg Vassiliev, USSR

Ice Dancing

1976 Ludmila Pakhomova & Aleksandr Gorschkov, USSR
1980 Natalya Linichuk & Gennadi Karponosov, USSR
1984 Jayne Torvill & Christopher Dean, Great Britain

Ice Hockey

1920 Canada, U.S., Czechoslovakia
1924 Canada, U.S., Great Britain
1928 Canada, Sweden, Switzerland
1932 Canada, U.S., Germany
1936 Great Britain, Canada, U.S.
1948 Canada, Czechoslovakia, Switzerland
1952 Canada, U.S., Sweden
1956 USSR, U.S., Canada
1960 U.S., Canada, USSR
1964 USSR, Sweden, Czechoslovakia
1968 USSR, Czechoslovakia, Canada
1972 USSR, U.S., Czechoslovakia,
1976 USSR, Czechoslovakia, W. Germany
1980 U.S., USSR, Sweden
1984 USSR, Czechoslovakia, Sweden

Luge

	Men's Singles	Time
1964	Thomas Keohler, Germany	3:26.77
1968	Manfred Schmid, Austria	2:52.48
1972	Wolfgang Scheidel, E. Germany	3:27.58
1976	Detlef Guenther, E. Germany	3:27.688
1980	Bernhard Glass, E. Germany	2:54.796
1984	Paul Hildgartner, Italy	3:04.258

	Men's Doubles	Time
1964	Austria	1:41.62
1968	E. Germany	1:35.85
1972	Italy, E. Germany (tie)	1:28.35
1976	E. Germany	1:25.604
1980	E. Germany	1:19.331
1984	W. Germany	1:23.620

	Women's Singles	Time
1964	Ortun Enderlein, Germany	3:24.67
1968	Erica Lechner, Italy	2:28.66
1972	Anna M. Muller, E. Germany	2:59.18
1976	Margit Schumann, E. Germany	2:50.621
1980	Vera Zozulya, USSR	2:36.537
1984	Steffi Martin, E. Germany	2:46.570

Alpine Skiing

	Men's Downhill	Time
1948	Henri Oreiller, France	2:55.0
1952	Zeno Colo, Italy	2:30.8
1956	Anton Sailer, Austria	2:52.2
1960	Jean Vuarnet, France	2:06.0
1964	Egon Zimmermann, Austria	2:18.16
1968	Jean Claude Killy, France	1:59.85
1972	Bernhard Russi, Switzerland	1:51.43
1976	Franz Klammer, Austria	1:45.73
1980	Leonhard Stock, Austria	1:45.50
1984	Bill Johnson, U.S.	1:45:59

	Men's Giant Slalom	Time
1952	Stein Eriksen, Norway	2:25.0
1956	Anton Sailer, Austria	3:00.1
1960	Roger Staub, Switzerland	1:48.3
1964	Francois Bonlieu, France	1:46.71

1968	Jean Claude Killy, France	3:29.28
1972	Gustavo Thoeni, Italy	3:09.62
1976	Heini Hemmi, Switzerland	3:26.97
1980	Ingemar Stenmark, Sweden	2:40.74
1984	Max Julen, Switzerland	2:41.18

	Men's Slalom	Time
1948	Edi Reinalter, Switzerland	2:10.3
1952	Othmar Schneider, Austria	2:00.0
1956	Anton Sailer, Austria	194.7 pts.
1960	Ernst Hinterseer, Austria	2:08.9
1964	Josef Stiegler, Austria	2:11.13
1968	Jean Claude Killy, France	1:39.73
1972	Francesco Fernandez Ochoa, Spain	1:49.27
1976	Piero Gros, Italy	2:03.29
1980	Ingemar Stenmark, Sweden	1:44.26
1984	Phil Mahre, U.S.	1:39.41

	Women's Downhill	Time
1948	Heidi Schlunegger, Switzerland	2:28.3
1952	Trude Jochum-Beiser, Austria	1:47.1
1956	Madeline Berthod, Switzerland	1:40.7
1960	Heidi Biebl, Germany	1:37.6
1964	Christi Haas, Austria	1:55.39
1968	Olga Pall, Austria	1:40.87
1972	Marie Therese Nadig, Switzerland	1:36.68
1976	Rosi Mittermaier, W. Germany	1:46.16
1980	Annemarie Proell Moser, Austria	1:37.52
1984	Michela Figini, Switzerland	1:13.36

	Women's Giant Slalom	Time
1952	Andrea Mead Lawrence, U.S.	2:06.8
1956	Ossi Reichert, Germany	1:56.5
1960	Yvonne Ruegg, Switzerland	1:39.9
1964	Marielle Goitschel, France	1:52.24
1968	Nancy Greene, Canada	1:51.97
1972	Marie Therese Nadig, Switzerland	1:29.90
1976	Kathy Kreiner, Canada	1:29.13
1980	Hanni Wenzel, Liechtenstein (2 runs)	2:41.66
1984	Debbie Armstrong, U.S.	2:20.98

	Women's Slalom	Time
1948	Gretchen Fraser, U.S.	1:57.2
1952	Andrea Mead Lawrence, U.S.	2:10.6
1956	Renee Colliard, Switzerland	112.3 pts.
1960	Anne Heggtveigt, Canada	1:49.6
1964	Christine Goitschel, France	1:29.86
1968	Marielle Goitschel, France	1:25.86
1972	Barbara Cochran, U.S.	1:31.24
1976	Rosi Mittermaier, W. Germany	1:30.54
1980	Hanni Wenzel, Liechtenstein	1:25.09
1984	Paoletta Magoni, Italy	1:36.47

Nordic Skiing

Men's Cross-Country Events

	15 kilometers (9.3 miles)	Time
1924	Thorleif Haug, Norway	1:14:31
1928	Johan Grottumsbraaten, Norway	1:37:01
1932	Sven Utterstrom, Sweden	1:23:07
1936	Erik-August Larsson, Sweden	1:14:38
1948	Martin Lundstrom, Sweden	1:13:50
1952	Hallgeir Brenden, Norway	1:01:34
1956	Hallgeir Brenden, Norway	49:39.0
1960	Haakon Brusveen, Norway	51:55.0
1964	Eero Maentyranta, Finland	50:54.1
1968	Harald Groenningen, Norway	47:54.2
1972	Sven-Ake Lundback, Sweden	45:28.24
1976	Nikolai Bajukov, USSR	43:58.47
1980	Thomas Wassberg, Sweden	41:57.63
1984	Gunde Svan, Sweden	41:25.6

(Note: approx. 18-km. course 1924-1952)

	30 kilometers (18.6 miles)	Time
1956	Veikko Hakulinen, Finland	1:44:06.0
1960	Sixten Jernberg, Sweden	1:51:03.9
1964	Eero Maentyranta, Finland	1:30:50.7
1968	Franco Nones, Italy	1:35:39.2
1972	Vyacheslav Vedenin, USSR	1:36:31.15
1976	Sergei Savaliev, USSR	1:30:29.38
1980	Nikolai Zimyatov, USSR	1:27:02.80
1984	Nikolai Zimyatov, USSR	1:28:56.3

	50 kilometers (31.2 miles)	Time
1924	Thorleif Haug, Norway	3:44:32.0
1928	Per Erik Hedlund, Sweden	4:52:03.0
1932	Veli Saarinen, Finland	4:28:00.0
1936	Elis Viklund, Sweden	3:30:11.0
1948	Nils Karlsson, Sweden	3:47:48.0
1952	Veikko Hakulinen, Finland	3:33:33.0
1956	Sixten Jernberg, Sweden	2:50:27.0
1960	Kalevi Hamalainen, Finland	2:59:06.3
1964	Sixten Jernberg, Sweden	2:43:52.6
1968	Ole Ellefsaeter, Norway	2:28:45.8
1972	Paal Tyldum, Norway	2:43:14.75
1976	Ivar Formo, Norway	2:37:30.05
1980	Nikolai Zimyatov, USSR	2:27:24.60
1984	Thomas Wassberg, Sweden	2:15:55.8

	40-km. Cross-Country Relay	Time
1936	Finland, Norway, Sweden	2:41:33.0
1948	Sweden, Finland, Norway	2:32:08.0
1952	Finland, Norway, Sweden	2:20:16.0
1956	USSR, Finland, Sweden	2:15:30.0
1960	Finland, Norway, USSR	2:18:45.6
1964	Sweden, Finland, USSR	2:18:34.6
1968	Norway, Sweden, Finland	2:08:33.5
1972	USSR, Norway, Switzerland	2:04:47.94
1976	Finland, Norway, USSR	2:07:59.72
1980	USSR, Norway, Finland	1:57:03.46
1984	Sweden, USSR, Finland	1:55:06.30

	Combined Cross-Country & Jumping	Points
1924	Thorleif Haug, Norway	453.800
1928	Johan Grottumsbraaten, Norway	427.800
1932	Johan Grottumsbraaten, Norway	446.200
1936	Oddbjorn Hagen, Norway	430.300
1948	Heikki Hasu, Finland	448.800
1952	Simon Slattvik, Norway	451.621
1956	Sverre Stenersen, Norway	455.000
1960	Georg Thoma, Germany	457.952
1964	Tormod Knutsen, Norway	469.280
1968	Franz Keller, W. Germany	449.040
1972	Ulrich Wehling, E. Germany	413.340
1976	Ulrich Wehling, E. Germany	423.390
1980	Ulrich Wehling, E. Germany	432.200
1984	Tom Sandberg, Norway	422.595

	Ski Jumping (90 meters)	Points
1924	Jacob Thams, Norway	227.5
1928	Alfred Andersen, Norway	230.5
1932	Birger Ruud, Norway	228.0
1936	Birger Ruud, Norway	232.0
1948	Petter Hugsted, Norway	228.1
1952	Anders Bergmann, Norway	226.0
1956	Antti Hyvarinen, Finland	227.0
1960	Helmut Recknagel, Germany	227.2
1964	Toralf Engan, Norway	230.7
1968	Vladimir Beloussov, USSR	231.3
1972	Wojiech Fortuna, Poland	219.9
1976	Karl Schnabl, Austria	234.8
1980	Jouko Tormanen, Finland	231.5
1984	Matti Nykaenen, Finland	231.2

	Ski Jumping (70 meters)	Points
1964	Veikko Kankkonen, Finland	229.9
1968	Jiri Raska, Czechoslovakia	216.5
1972	Yukio Kasaya, Japan	244.2
1976	Hans Aschenbach, E. Germany	252.0
1980	Anton Innauer, Austria	266.3
1984	Jens Weissflog, E. Germany	215.2

Women's Events

	5 kilometers (approx. 3.1 miles)	Time
1964	Claudia Boyarskikh, USSR	17:50.5
1968	Toini Gustafsson, Sweden	16:45.2
1972	Galina Koulacova, USSR	17:00.50
1976	Helena Takalo, Finland	15:48.69
1980	Raisa Smetanina, USSR	15:06.92
1984	Marja-Liisa Haemaelainen, Finland	17:04.0

	10 kilometers	Time
1952	Lydia Wideman, Finland	41:40.0
1956	Lyubov Kosyreva, USSR	38:11.0
1960	Maria Gusakova, USSR	39:46.6
1964	Claudia Boyarskikh, USSR	40:24.3
1968	Toini Gustafsson, Sweden	36:46.5
1972	Galina Koulacova, USSR	34:17.82
1976	Raisa Smetanina, USSR	30:13.41
1980	Barbara Petzold, E. Germany	30:31.54
1984	Marja-Liisa Haemaelainen, Finland	31:44.2

20 kilometers		Time
1984	Marja-Liisa Haemaelainen, Finland	1:01:45.0

20-km. Cross-Country Relay		Time
1956	Finland, USSR, Sweden (15 km.)	1:09:01.0
1960	Sweden, USSR, Finland (15 km.)	1:04:21.4
1964	USSR, Sweden, Finland (15 km.)	59:20.2
1968	Norway, Sweden, USSR (15 km.)	57:30.0
1972	USSR, Finland, Norway (15 km.)	48:46.1
1976	USSR, Finland, E. Germany	1:07:49.75
1980	E. Germany, USSR, Norway	1:02:11.10
1984	Norway, Czechoslovakia, Finland	1:06:49.70

Speed Skating

Men's 500 meters		Time
1924	Charles Jewtraw, U.S.	0:44.0
1928	Thunberg, Finland & Evensen, Norway (tie)	0:43.4
1932	John A. Shea, U.S.	0:43.4
1936	Ivar Ballangrud, Norway	0:43.4
1948	Finn Helgesen, Norway	0:43.1
1952	Kenneth Henry, U.S.	0:43.2
1956	Evgeniy Grishin, USSR	0:40.2
1960	Evgeniy Grishin, USSR	0:40.2
1964	Terry McDermott, U.S.	0:40.1
1968	Erhard Keller, W. Germany	0:40.3
1972	Erhard Keller, W. Germany	0:39.44
1976	Evgeny Kulikov, USSR	0:39.17
1980	Eric Heiden, U.S.	0:38.03
1984	Sergei Fokichov, USSR	0:38.19

Men's 1,000 meters		Time
1976	Peter Mueller, U.S.	1:19.32
1980	Eric Heiden, U.S.	1:15.18
1984	Gaetan Boucher, Canada	1:15.80

Men's 1,500 meters		Time
1924	Clas Thunberg, Finland	2:20.8
1928	Clas Thunberg, Finland	2:21.1
1932	John A. Shea, U.S.	2:57.2
1936	Charles Mathiesen, Norway	2:19.2
1948	Sverre Farstad, Norway	2:17.6
1952	Hjalmar Andersen, Norway	2:20.4
1956	Grishin, & Mikhailov, both USSR (tie)	2:08.6
1960	Aas, Norway & Grishin, USSR (tie)	2:10.4
1964	Ants Anston, USSR	2:10.3
1968	Cornetis Verkerk, Netherlands	2:03.4
1972	Ard Schenk, Netherlands	2:02.96
1976	Jan Egil Storholt, Norway	1:59.38
1980	Eric Heiden, U.S.	1:55.44
1984	Gaetan Boucher, Canada	1:58.36

Men's 5,000 meters		Time
1924	Clas Thunberg, Finland	8:39.0
1928	Ivar Ballangrud, Norway	8:50.5
1932	Irving Jaffee, U.S.	9:40.8
1936	Ivar Ballangrud, Norway	8:19.6
1948	Reidar Liaklev, Norway	8:29.4
1952	Hjalmar Andersen, Norway	8:10.6
1956	Boris Shilkov, USSR	7:48.7
1960	Viktor Kosichkin, USSR	7:51.3
1964	Knut Johannesen, Norway	7:38.4
1968	F. Anton Maier, Norway	7:22.4
1972	Ard Schenk, Netherlands	7:23.61
1976	Sten Stensen, Norway	7:24.48
1980	Eric Heiden, U.S.	7:02.29
1984	Sven Tomas Gustafson, Sweden	7:12:28

Men's 10,000 meters		Time
1924	Julius Skutnabb, Finland	18:04.8
1928	Event not held, thawing of ice	
1932	Irving Jaffee, U.S.	19:13.6
1936	Ivar Ballangrud, Norway	17:24.3
1948	Ake Seyffarth, Sweden	17:26.3
1952	Hjalmar Andersen, Norway	16:45.8
1956	Sigvard Ericsson, Sweden	16:35.9
1960	Knut Johannesen, Norway	15:46.6
1964	Jonny Nilsson, Sweden	15:50.1
1968	Jonny Hoeglin, Sweden	15:23.6
1972	Ard Schenk, Netherlands	15:01.3
1976	Piet Kleine, Netherlands	14:50.59
1980	Eric Heiden, U.S.	14:28.13
1984	Igor Malkov, USSR	14.39.90

Women's 500 meters		Time
1960	Helga Haase, Germany	0:45.9
1964	Lydia Skoblikova, USSR	0:45.0
1968	Ludmila Titova, USSR	0:46.1
1972	Anne Henning, U.S.	0:43.44
1976	Sheila Young, U.S.	0:42.76
1980	Karin Enke, E. Germany	0:41.78
1984	Christa Rothenburger, E. Germany	0:41.02

Women's 1,000 meters		Time
1960	Klara Guseva, USSR	1:34.1
1964	Lydia Skoblikova, USSR	1:33.2
1968	Caroline Geijssen, Netherlands	1:32.6
1972	Monika Pflug, W. Germany	1:31.40
1976	Tatiana Averina, USSR	1:28.43
1980	Natalya Petruseva, USSR	1:24.10
1984	Karin Enke, E. Germany	1:21.61

Women's 1,500 meters		Time
1960	Lydia Skoblikova, USSR	2:52.2
1964	Lydia Skoblikova, USSR	2:22.6
1968	Kaija Mustonen, Finland	2:22.4
1972	Dianne Holum, U.S.	2:20.85
1976	Galina Stepanskaya, USSR	2:16.58
1980	Anne Borckink, Netherlands	2:10.95
1984	Karin Enke, E. Germany	2:03.42

Women's 3,000 meters		Time
1960	Lydia Skoblikova, USSR	5:14.3
1964	Lydia Skoblikova, USSR	5:14.9
1968	Johanna Schut, Netherlands	4:56.2
1972	Stien Baas-Kaiser, Netherlands	4:52.14
1976	Tatiana Averina, USSR	4:45.19
1980	Bjoerg Eva Jensen, Norway	4:32.13
1984	Andrea Schoene, E. Germany	4:24.79

Winter Olympic Medal Winners in 1984

Sarajevo, Yugoslavia, Feb. 7-18, 1984

	Gold	Silver	Bronze	Total
Austria	0	0	1	1
Canada	2	1	1	4
Czechoslovakia	0	2	4	6
Finland	4	3	6	13
France	0	1	2	3
Germany, East	9	9	6	24
Germany, West	2	1	1	4
Great Britain	1	0	0	1
Italy	2	0	0	2
Japan	0	1	0	1
Liechtenstein	0	0	2	2
Norway	3	2	4	9
Sweden	4	2	2	8
Switzerland	2	2	1	5
USSR	6	10	9	25
United States	4	4	0	8
Yugoslavia	0	1	0	1

IGFA Freshwater & Saltwater All-Tackle World Records

Source: International Game Fish Association. Records confirmed to June, 1987

Saltwater Fish

Species	Weight	Where caught	Date	Angler
Albacore	88 lbs. 2 oz.	Pt. Mogan, Canary Islands	Nov. 19, 1977	Siegfried Dickemann
Amberjack, greater	155 lbs. 10 oz.	Bermuda	June 24, 1981	Joseph Dawson
Amberjack, Pacific	104 lbs.	Baja, Mexico	July 4, 1984	Richard Cresswell
Barracuda, great	83 lbs.	Lagos, Nigeria	Jan. 13, 1952	K.J.W. Hackett
Barracuda, Mexican	15 lbs. 4 oz.	Zihuatanejo, Mexico	Oct. 7, 1984	Tony Pena
Barracuda, slender	17 lbs. 4 oz.	Sitra Channel, Bahrain	Nov. 21, 1985	Roger Cranswick
Bass, barred sand	8 lbs. 4 oz.	Dana Pt., Cal.	Mar. 14, 1981	Richard Marsell
Bass, black sea	9 lbs. 8 oz.	Virginia Beach, Va.	Jan. 9, 1987	Joe Mizelle Jr.
Bass, European	20 lbs. 11 oz.	Stes Maries de la Mer, France	May 6, 1986	Jean Baptiste Bayle
Bass, giant sea	563 lbs. 8 oz.	Anacaba Island, Cal.	Aug. 20, 1968	James D. McAdam Jr.
Bass, striped	78 lbs. 8 oz.	Atlantic City, N.J.	Sept. 21, 1982	Albert McReynolds
Blackjack	20 lbs. 15 oz.	Cocos Is., Costa Rica	Feb. 15, 1985	Carlos M. Barrantes
Bluefish	31 lbs. 12 oz.	Hatteras Inlet, N.C.	Jan. 30, 1972	James M. Hussey
Bonefish	19 lbs.	Zululand, S. Africa	May 26, 1962	Brian W. Batchelor
Bonito, Atlantic	18 lbs. 14 oz.	Fayal I., Azores	July 8, 1953	D. G. Higgs
Bonito, Pacific	23 lbs. 8 oz.	Victoria, Mahe Seychelles	Feb. 19, 1975	Anne Cochain
Cabezon	9 lbs. 11 oz.	Barkley Sound, B.C., Canada	Aug. 16, 1983	Doug Olander
Cobia	135 lbs. 9 oz.	Shark Bay, Australia	July 9, 1985	Peter W. Goulding
Cod, Atlantic	98 lbs. 12 oz.	Isle of Shoals, N.H.	June 8, 1969	Alphonse Bielevich
Cod, Pacific	30 lbs.	Andrew Bay, Alaska	June 7, 1984	Donald Vaughn
Conger	102 lbs. 8 oz.	Devon, England	July 18, 1983	Raymond E. Street
Dolphin	87 lbs.	Papagallo Gulf, Costa Rica	Sept. 25, 1976	Manual Salazar
Drum, black	113 lbs. 1 oz.	Lewes, Del.	Sept. 15, 1975	Gerald Townsend
Drum, red	94 lbs. 2 oz.	Avon, N.C.	Nov. 7, 1984	David Deuel
Eel, African mottled	36 lbs. 1 oz.	Durban, So. Africa	June 10, 1984	Ferdie van Nooten
Eel, American	4 lb. 7 oz.	Lake Ronkonkoma, N.Y.	Nov. 15, 1986	William C. Cummings
Flounder, southern	20 lb. 9 oz.	Nassau Sound, Fla.	Dec. 23, 1983	Larenza Mungin
Flounder, summer	22 lbs. 7 oz.	Montauk, N.Y.	Sept. 15, 1975	Charles Nappi
Grouper, Warsaw	436 lbs. 12 oz.	Gulf of Mexico, Destin, Fla.	Dec. 22, 1985	Steve Haeusler
Halibut, Atlantic	250 lbs.	Gloucester, Mass.	July 3, 1981	Louis Sirard
Halibut, California	45 lbs.	Santa Cruz Is., Cal.	June 19, 1982	Jack Meserve
Halibut, Pacific	350 lbs.	Homer, Alaska	June 30, 1982	Vern S. Foster
Jack, crevalle	54 lbs. 7oz.	Pt. Michel, Gabon	Jan. 15, 1982	Thomas Gibson Jr.
Jack, horse-eye	24 lbs. 8 oz.	Miami, Fla.	Dec. 20, 1982	Tito Schnau
Jack, Pacific crevalle	23 lbs. 14 oz.	Las Arenes, Baja, Cal., Mex.	June 11, 1985	Ken Mayer
Jewfish	680 lbs.	Fernandina Beach, Fla.	May 20, 1961	Lynn Joyner
Kawakawa	29 lbs.	New South Wales, Australia	Dec. 17, 1986	Ronald Nakamura
Lingcod	61 lbs.	San Juan Is., Wash.	July 30, 1986	Tom Nelson
Mackerel, cero	17 lbs. 2 oz.	Islamorada, Fla.	Apr. 5, 1986	G. Michael Mills
Mackerel, king	90 lbs.	Key West, Fla.	Feb. 16, 1976	Norton Thornton
Mackeral, Spanish	12 lbs.	Ft. Pierce, Fla.	Nov. 17, 1984	John Colligar
Marlin, Atlantic blue	1,282 lbs.	St. Thomas, Virgin Islands	Aug. 6, 1977	Larry Martin
Marlin, black	1,560 lbs.	Cabo Blanco, Peru	Aug. 4, 1953	A. C. Glassell Jr.
Marlin, Pacific blue	1,376 lbs.	Kaaiwa Pt., Hawaii	May. 31, 1982	J.W. deBeaubien
Marlin, striped	494 lbs.	Tutukaka, New Zealand	Jan. 16, 1986	Bill Boniface
Marlin, white	181 lbs. 14 oz.	Vitoria, Brazil	Dec. 8, 1979	Evandro Luiz Caser
Permit	51 lbs. 8 oz.	Lake Worth, Fla.	Apr. 28, 1978	William M. Kenney
Pollack	26 lbs. 7 oz.	Devon, England	Dec. 30, 1984	Robert Perry
Pollock	46 lbs. 7 oz.	Brielle, N.J.	May 26, 1975	John Tomes Holton
Pompano, African	49 lbs.	Stuart, Fla.	Feb. 4, 1977	Lawrence Hofman
Roosterfish	114 lbs.	La Paz, Mexico	June 1, 1960	Abe Sackheim
Runner, blue	6 lbs. 4 oz.	Hilton Head, S.C.	June 12, 1986	Glen S. Long
Runner, rainbow	33 lbs. 10 oz.	Clarion Is., Mexico	Mar. 14, 1976	Ralph A. Mikkelsen
Sailfish, Atlantic	128 lbs. 1 oz.	Luanda, Angola	Mar. 27, 1974	Harm Steyn
Sailfish, Pacific	221 lbs.	Santa Cruz Is., Ecuador	Feb. 12, 1947	C. W. Stewart
Seabass, white	83 lbs. 12 oz.	San Felipe, Mexico	Mar. 31, 1953	L.C. Baumgardner
Seatrout, spotted	16 lbs.	Mason's Beach, Va.	May 28, 1977	William Katko
Shark, blue	437 lbs.	Catherine Bay, N.S.W. Australia	Oct. 2, 1976	Peter Hyde
Shark, Greenland	952 lbs. 6 oz.	Trondheim, Norway	May 19, 1984	Eirik Nielsen
Shark, hammerhead	991 lbs.	Sarasota, Fla.	May 30, 1982	Allen Ogle
Shark, man-eater or white	2,664 lbs.	Ceduna, Australia	Apr. 21, 1959	Alfred Dean
Shark, mako	1,080 lbs.	Montauk, N.Y.	Aug. 26, 1979	James Melanson
Shark, porbeagle	465 lbs.	Cornwall, England	July 23, 1976	Jorge Potier
Shark, thresher	802 lbs.	Tutukaka, New Zealand	Feb. 8, 1981	Dianne North
Shark, tiger	1,780 lbs.	Cherry Grove, S.C.	June 14, 1964	Walter Maxwell
Skipjack, black	20 lbs. 5 oz.	Baja, Mexico	Oct. 14, 1983	Roger Torriero
Snapper, cubera	121 lbs. 8 oz.	Cameron, La.	July 5, 1982	Mike Hebert
Snook	53 lbs. 10 oz.	Costa Rica	Oct. 18, 1978	Gilbert Ponzi
Spearfish	90 lbs. 13 oz.	Madeira Island, Portugal	June 2, 1980	Joseph Larkin
Swordfish	1,182 lbs.	Iquique, Chile	May 7, 1953	L. Marron
Tanguigue	99 lbs.	Natal, So. Africa	Mar. 14, 1982	Michael J. Wilkinson
Tarpon	283 lbs.	Lake Maracaibo, Venezuela	Mar. 19, 1956	M. Salazar
Tautog	21 lbs. 8 oz.	Wachapreagee, Va.	Aug. 4, 1984	Tommy Wood
Tope	72 lbs. 12 oz.	Parengarenga Harbor, New Zealand	Dec. 19, 1986	Melanie Feldman
Trevally, bigeye	15 lbs.	Isla Coiba, Panama	Jan. 18, 1984	Sally Timms
Trevally, giant	137 lbs. 9 oz.	McKenzie St. Park, Hawaii	July 13, 1983	Roy Gushiken
Tuna, Atlantic bigeye	375 lbs. 8 oz.	Ocean City, Md.	Aug. 26, 1977	Cecil Browne
Tuna, blackfin	42 lbs.	Bermuda	June 2, 1978	Alan J. Card
Tuna, bluefin	1,496 lbs.	Aulds Cove, Nova Scotia	Oct. 26, 1979	Ken Fraser
Tuna, longtail	79 lbs. 2 oz.	Montague Is., N.S.W., Australia	Apr. 12, 1982	Tim Simpson

Species	Weight	Where caught	Date	Angler
Tuna, Pacific bigeye	435 lbs.	Cabo Blanco, Peru	Apr. 17, 1957	Dr. Russel Lee
Tuna, skipjack	41 lbs. 12 oz.	Mauritius	Mar. 13, 1982	Bruno de Ravel
Tuna, southern bluefin	348 lbs. 5 oz.	Whakatane, New Zealand	Jan. 16, 1981	Rex Wood
Tuna, yellowfin	388 lbs. 12 oz.	San Benedicto Island, Mexico	Apr. 1, 1977	Curt Wiesenhutter
Tunny, little	27 lbs.	Key Largo, Fla.	Apr. 20, 1976	William E. Allison
Wahoo	149 lbs.	Cay Cay, Bahamas	June 15, 1962	John Pirovano
Weakfish	19 lbs. 2 oz.	Jones Beach Inlet, N.Y.	Oct. 11, 1984	Dennis Rooney
Yellowtail, California	71 lbs. 15 oz.	Alijos Rocks, Mexico	June 24, 1979	Michael Carpenter
Yellowtail, southern	114 lbs. 10 oz.	Tauranga, New Zealand	Feb. 5, 1984	Mike Godfrey

Freshwater Fish

Species	Weight	Where caught	Date	Angler
Barramundi	59 lbs. 12 oz.	Pt. Stuart, Australia	Apr. 7, 1983	Andrew Davern
Bass, largemouth	22 lbs. 4 oz.	Montgomery Lake, Ga.	June 2, 1932	George W. Perry
Bass, peacock	26 lbs. 8 oz.	Matevini R., Colombia	Jan. 26, 1982	Rod Neubert
Bass, redeye	8 lbs. 3 oz.	Flint River, Ga.	Oct. 23, 1977	David A. Hubbard
Bass rock	3 lbs.	York River, Ont.	Aug. 1, 1974	Peter Gulgin
Bass, sand	11 lb. 4 oz.	Imperial Beach, Cal.	Aug. 16, 1986	Dale Barrington
Bass, smallmouth	11 lbs. 15 oz.	Dale Hollow Lake, Ky.	July 9, 1955	David L. Hayes
Bass, spotted	9 lbs.	Lake Perris, Cal.	Feb. 5, 1984	Jeffrey Mathews
Bass, Suwannee	3 lbs. 14 oz.	Suwannee River, Fla.	Mar. 2, 1985	Ronnie Everett
Bass, white	5 lbs. 14 oz.	Kerr Lake, N.C.	Mar. 15, 1986	Jim King
Bass, whiterock	22 lbs. 6 oz.	New Savannah Dam, Ga.	July 20, 1986	Jerry L. Adams
Bass, yellow	2 lbs. 4 oz.	Lake Monroe, Ind.	Mar. 27, 1977	Donald L. Stalker
Bluegill	4 lbs. 12 oz.	Ketona Lake, Ala.	Apr. 9, 1950	T.S. Hudson
Bowfin	21 lbs. 8 oz.	Florence, S.C.	Jan. 29, 1980	Robert Harmon
Buffalo, bigmouth	70 lbs. 5 oz.	Bastrop, La.	Apr. 21, 1980	Delbert Sisk
Buffalo, black	55 lbs. 8 oz.	Cherokee L., Tenn.	May 3, 1984	Edward McLain
Buffalo, smallmouth	68 lbs. 8 oz.	L. Hamilton, Ark.	May 16, 1984	Jerry Dolezal
Bullhead, brown	5 lbs. 8 oz.	Veal Pond, Ga.	May 22, 1975	Jimmy Andrews
Bullhead, yellow	4 lbs. 4 oz.	Mormon Lake, Ariz.	May 11, 1984	Emily Williams
Burbot	18 lbs. 4 oz.	Pickford, Mich.	Jan. 31, 1980	Thomas Courtemanche
Carp	57 lbs. 13 oz.	Potomac R., Wash., D.C.	June 19, 1983	David Nikolow
Catfish, blue	97 lbs.	Missouri River, S.D.	Sept. 16, 1959	E.B. Elliott
Catfish, channel	58 lbs.	Santee-Cooper Res., S.C.	July 7, 1964	W.B. Whaley
Catfish, flathead	98 lbs.	Lewisville, Tex.	June 2, 1986	William Stephens
Catfish, white	17 lbs. 7 oz.	Success L., Tulare, Cal.	Nov. 15, 1981	Chuck Idell
Char, Arctic	32 lbs. 9 oz.	Tree River, Canada	July 30, 1981	Jeffrey Ward
Crappie, white	5 lbs. 3 oz.	Enid Dam, Miss.	July 31, 1957	Fred L. Bright
Dolly Varden	8 lbs. 1 oz.	Nakwasina R., Alaska	July 14, 1985	Loyal Johnson
Dorado	51 lbs. 5 oz.	Corrientes, Argentina	Sept. 27, 1984	Armando Giudice
Drum, freshwater	54 lbs. 8 oz.	Nickajack Lake, Tenn.	Apr. 20, 1972	Benny E. Hull
Gar, alligator	279 lbs.	Rio Grande River, Tex.	Dec. 2, 1951	Bill Valverde
Gar, Florida	21 lbs. 3 oz.	Boca Raton, Fla.	June 3, 1981	Jeff Sabol
Gar, longnose	50 lbs. 5 oz.	Trinity River, Tex.	July 30, 1954	Townsend Miller
Gar, shortnose	4 lbs. 9 oz.	Mississippi R., Minn.	July 22, 1984	Matthew Ocel
Gar, spotted	8 lbs. 4 oz.	Cataco Creek, Ala.	Aug. 29, 1985	April Kilpatrick
Grayling, Arctic	5 lbs. 15 oz.	Katseyedie River, N.W.T.	Aug. 16, 1967	Jeanne P. Branson
Inconnu	53 lbs.	Pah R., Alaska	Aug. 20, 1986	Lawrence Hudnall
Kokanee	6 lbs. 9 oz.	Priest Lake, Ida.	June 9, 1975	Jerry Verge
Muskellunge	69 lbs. 15 oz.	St. Lawrence River, N.Y.	Sept. 22, 1957	Arthur Lawton
Muskellunge, tiger	51 lbs. 3 oz.	Lac Vieux-Desert, Wis., Mich.	July 16, 1919	John Knobla
Perch, white	4 lbs. 12 oz.	Messalonskee Lake, Me.	June 4, 1949	Mrs. Earl Small
Perch, yellow	4 lbs. 3 oz.	Bordentown, N.J.	May, 1865	Dr. C.C. Abbot
Pickerel, chain	9 lbs. 6 oz.	Homerville, Ga.	Feb. 17, 1961	Baxley McQuaig Jr.
Pike, northern	46 lbs. 2 oz.	Sacandaga Reservoir, N.Y.	Sept. 15, 1940	Peter Dubuc
Redhorse, shorthead	9 lbs. 3 oz.	Salmon R., Pulaski, N.Y.	May 11, 1985	Jason Wilson
Redhorse, silver	11 lbs. 7 oz.	Plum Creek, Wis.	May 29, 1985	Neal Long
Salmon, Atlantic	79 lbs. 2 oz.	Tana River, Norway	1928	Henrik Henriksen
Salmon, chinook	97 lbs. 4 oz.	Kenai R., Alas.	May 17, 1985	Les Anderson
Salmon, chum	32 lbs.	Behm Canal, Alas.	June 7, 1985	Fredrick Thynes
Salmon, coho	31 lbs.	Cowichan Bay, B.C.	Oct. 11, 1947	Mrs. Lee Hallberg
Salmon, pink	12 lbs. 9 oz.	Morse, Kenai rivers, Alas.	Aug. 17, 1974	Steven A. Lee
Salmon, sockeye	12 lbs. 8 oz.	Situk R., Alaska	June 23, 1983	Mike Boswell
Sauger	8 lbs. 12 oz.	Lake Sakakawea, N.D.	Oct. 6, 1971	Mike Fischer
Shad, American	11 lbs. 4 oz.	Connecticut R., Mass.	May 19, 1986	Bob Thibodo
Sturgeon	468 lbs.	Benicia, Cal.	July 9, 1983	Joey Pallotta 3d
Sunfish, green	2 lbs. 2 oz.	Stockton Lake, Mo.	June 18, 1971	Paul M. Dilley
Sunfish, redbreast	1 lb. 12 oz.	Suwannee R., Fla.	May 29, 1984	Alvin Buchanan
Sunfish, redear	4 lbs. 13 oz.	Marianna, Fla.	Mar. 13, 1986	Joey Floyd
Tigerfish	71 lbs. 10 oz.	Zaire R., Kinshasa, Zaire	July 28, 1985	Raymond Houtmans
Tilapia	4 lbs. 5 oz.	Mittry L., Ariz.	Sept. 17, 1984	John B. Adkins
Trout, Apache	1 lb. 8 oz.	Apache Res., Ariz.	Oct. 19, 1984	Burton Leed
Trout, brook	14 lbs. 8 oz.	Nipigon River, Ont.	July 1916	Dr. W.J. Cook
Trout, brown	35 lbs. 15 oz.	Nahuel Huapi, Argentina	Dec. 16, 1952	Eugenio Cavaglia
Trout, bull	32 lbs.	L. Pend Oreille, Ida.	Oct. 27, 1949	N.L. Higgins
Trout, cutthroat	41 lbs.	Pyramid Lake, Nev.	Dec. 1925	J. Skimmerhorn
Trout, golden	11 lbs.	Cook's Lake, Wyo.	Aug. 5, 1948	Charles S. Reed
Trout, lake	65 lbs.	Great Bear Lake, N.W.T.	Aug. 8, 1970	Larry Daunis
Trout, rainbow	42 lbs. 2 oz.	Bell Island, Alas.	June 22, 1970	David Robert White
Trout, tiger	20 lbs. 13 oz.	Lake Michigan, Wis.	Aug. 12, 1978	Pete Friedland
Walleye	25 lbs.	Old Hickory Lake, Tenn.	Aug. 1, 1960	Mabry Harper
Warmouth	2 lbs. 7 oz.	Yellow R., Holt, Fla.	Oct. 19, 1985	Tony D. Dempsey
Whitefish, lake	14 lbs. 6 oz.	Meaford, Ont.	May 21, 1984	Dennis Laycock
Whitefish, mountain	5 lbs. 2 oz.	Columbia R., Wash.	Nov. 30, 1983	Steven Becken
Whitefish, river	11 lbs. 2 oz.	Nymoua, Sweden	Dec. 9, 1984	Jorgen Larsson
Whitefish, round	6 lbs.	Putahow R., Manitoba	June 14, 1984	Allen Ristori
Zander	22 lbs. 2 oz.	Trosa, Sweden	June 12, 1986	Harry Lee Tennison

National Hockey League, 1986-87

Final Standings

Wales Conference

Adams Division

	W	L	T	Pts	GF	GA
Hartford	43	30	7	93	287	270
Montreal	41	29	10	92	277	241
Boston	39	34	7	85	301	276
Quebec	31	39	10	72	267	276
Buffalo	28	44	8	64	280	308

Patrick Division

	W	L	T	Pts	GF	GA
Philadelphia	46	26	8	100	310	245
Washington	38	32	10	86	285	278
N.Y. Islanders	35	33	12	82	279	281
N.Y. Rangers	34	38	8	76	307	323
Pittsburgh	30	38	12	72	297	290
New Jersey	29	45	6	64	293	368

Campbell Conference

Norris Division

	W	L	T	Pts	GF	GA
St. Louis	32	33	15	79	281	293
Detroit	34	36	10	78	260	274
Chicago	29	37	14	72	290	310
Toronto	32	42	6	70	286	319
Minnesota	30	40	10	70	296	314

Smythe Division

	W	L	T	Pts	GF	GA
Edmonton	50	24	6	106	372	284
Calgary	46	31	3	95	318	289
Winnipeg	40	32	8	88	279	271
Los Angeles	31	41	8	70	318	341
Vancouver	29	43	8	66	282	314

Stanley Cup Playoff Results

Wales Conference

Montreal defeated Boston 4-0.
Philadelphia defeated N.Y. Rangers 4-2.
Quebec defeated Hartford 4-2.
N.Y. Islanders defeated Washington 4-3.
Montreal defeated Quebec 4-3.
Philadelphia defeated N.Y. Islanders 4-3.
Philadelphia defeated Montreal 4-2.

Campbell Conference

Edmonton defeated Los Angeles 4-1.
Winnipeg defeated Calgary 4-2.
Detroit defeated Chicago 4-0.
Toronto defeated St. Louis 4-2.
Edmonton defeated Winnipeg 4-0.
Detroit defeated Toronto 4-3.
Edmonton defeated Detroit 4-1.

Finals

Edmonton defeated Philadelphia 4-3.

Stanley Cup Champions Since 1928

Year	Champion	Coach	Final opponent
1928	N.Y. Rangers	Lester Patrick	Montreal
1929	Boston	Cy Denneny	N.Y. Rangers
1930	Montreal	Cecil Hart	Boston
1931	Montreal	Cecil Hart	Chicago
1932	Toronto	Dick Irvin	N.Y. Rangers
1933	New York	Lester Patrick	Toronto
1934	Chicago	Tommy Gorman	Detroit
1935	Montreal Maroons	Tommy Gorman	Toronto
1936	Detroit	Jack Adams	Toronto
1937	Detroit	Jack Adams	N.Y. Rangers
1938	Chicago	Bill Stewart	Toronto
1939	Boston	Art Ross	Toronto
1940	N.Y. Rangers	Frank Boucher	Toronto
1941	Boston	Cooney Weiland	Detroit
1942	Toronto	Hap Day	Detroit
1943	Detroit	Jack Adams	Boston
1944	Montreal	Dick Irvin	Chicago
1945	Toronto	Hap Day	Detroit
1946	Montreal	Dick Irvin	Boston
1947	Toronto	Hap Day	Montreal
1948	Toronto	Hap Day	Detroit
1949	Toronto	Hap Day	Detroit
1950	Detroit	Tommy Ivan	N.Y. Rangers
1951	Toronto	Joe Primeau	Montreal
1952	Detroit	Tommy Ivan	Montreal
1953	Montreal	Dick Irvin	Boston
1954	Detroit	Tommy Ivan	Montreal
1955	Detroit	Jimmy Skinner	Montreal
1956	Montreal	Toe Blake	Detroit
1957	Montreal	Toe Blake	Boston
1958	Montreal	Toe Blake	Boston
1959	Montreal	Toe Blake	Toronto
1960	Montreal	Toe Blake	Toronto
1961	Chicago	Rudy Pilous	Detroit
1962	Toronto	Punch Imlach	Chicago
1963	Toronto	Punch Imlach	Detroit
1964	Toronto	Punch Imlach	Detroit
1965	Montreal	Toe Blake	Chicago
1966	Montreal	Toe Blake	Detroit
1967	Toronto	Punch Imlach	Montreal
1968	Montreal	Toe Blake	St. Louis
1969	Montreal	Claude Ruel	St. Louis
1970	Boston	Harry Sinden	St. Louis
1971	Montreal	Al MacNeil	Chicago
1972	Boston	Tom Johnson	N.Y. Rangers
1973	Montreal	Scotty Bowman	Chicago
1974	Philadelphia	Fred Shero	Boston
1975	Philadelphia	Fred Shero	Buffalo
1976	Montreal	Scotty Bowman	Philadelphia
1977	Montreal	Scotty Bowman	Boston
1978	Montreal	Scotty Bowman	Boston
1979	Montreal	Scotty Bowman	N.Y. Rangers
1980	N.Y. Islanders	Al Arbour	Philadelphia
1981	N.Y. Islanders	Al Arbour	Minnesota
1982	N.Y. Islanders	Al Arbour	Vancouver
1983	N.Y. Islanders	Al Arbour	Edmonton
1984	Edmonton	Glen Sather	N.Y. Islanders
1985	Edmonton	Glen Sather	Philadelphia
1986	Montreal	Jean Perron	Calgary
1987	Edmonton	Glen Sather	Philadelphia

Conn Smythe Trophy (MVP in Playoffs)

1965 Jean Beliveau, Montreal
1966 Roger Crozier, Detroit
1967 Dave Keon, Toronto
1968 Glenn Hall, St. Louis
1969 Serge Savard, Montreal
1970 Bobby Orr, Boston
1971 Ken Dryden, Montreal
1972 Bobby Orr, Boston
1973 Yvan Cournoyer, Montreal
1974 Bernie Parent, Philadelphia
1975 Bernie Parent, Philadelphia
1976 Reg Leach, Philadelphia
1977 Guy Lafleur, Montreal
1978 Larry Robinson, Montreal
1979 Bob Gainey, Montreal
1980 Bryan Trottier, N.Y. Islanders
1981 Butch Goring, N.Y. Islanders
1982 Mike Bossy, N.Y. Islanders
1983 Billy Smith, N.Y. Islanders
1984 Mark Messier, Edmonton
1985 Wayne Gretzky, Edmonton
1986 Patrick Roy, Montreal
1987 Ron Hextall, Philadelphia

Individual Leaders

Points

Gretzky, Edmonton, 183; Kurri, Edmonton, 108; Lemieux, Pittsburgh, 107; Messier, Edmonton, 107; Gilmour, St. Louis, 105.

Goals

Gretzky, Edmonton, 62; Kerr, Philadelphia, 58; Kurri, Edmonton, 54; Lemieux, Pittsburgh, 54; Ciccarelli, Minnesota, 52.

Assists

Gretzky, Edmonton, 121; Bourque, Boston, 72; Messier, Edmonton, 70; Trottier, N.Y. Islanders, 64; Francis, Hartford, 63; Gilmour, St. Louis, 63.

Power-play goals

Kerr, Philadelphia, 26; Ciccarelli, Minnesota, 22; LaFontaine, N.Y. Islanders, 19; Lemieux, Pittsburgh, 19.

Shorthanded goals

Gretzky, Edmonton, 7; Courtnall, Toronto, 6; Gartner, Washington, 6; Skriko, Vancouver, 6.

Game-winning goals

Mullen, Calgary, 12; Gartner, Washington, 10; Kerr, Philadelphia, 10; Kurri, Edmonton, 10.

Shooting percentage

(minimum 80 shots)

Ferraro, Hartford, 28.1; Tikkanen, Edmonton, 27.0; Kurri, Edmonton, 25.6; McCarthy, Boston, 24.8; Verbeek, New Jersey, 24.5.

Goaltending Leaders

(minimum 25 games)

Goals-against average

Hayward, Montreal, 2.81; Roy, Montreal, 2.93; Hextall, Philadelphia, 3.00; Berthiaume, Winnipeg, 3.17; Hanlon, Detroit, 3.18.

Wins

Hextall, Philadelphia, 37; Liut, Hartford, 31; Vernon, Calgary, 30; Moog, Edmonton, 28; Chevrier, New Jersey, 24.

Save percentage

Hextall, Philadelphia, .902; Sauve, Chicago, .894; Hanlon, Detroit, .893; Hayward, Montreal, .893; Ranford, Boston, .891.

Shutouts

Liut, Hartford, 4; Ranford, Boston, 3; Barrasso, Buffalo, 2; Lemelin, Calgary, 2; Bester, Toronto, 2.

Individual Scoring

(40 or more games played)

Boston Bruins

	GP	G	A	Pts	+/–	PIM
Ray Bourque	78	23	72	95	44	36
Cam Neely	75	36	36	72	23	143
Charlie Simmer	80	29	40	69	20	59
Rick Middleton	76	31	37	68	7	6
Tom McCarthy	68	30	29	59	10	31
Keith Crowder	58	22	30	52	20	100
Steve Kasper	79	20	30	50	4–	51
Ken Linseman	64	15	34	49	15	126
Thomas Gradin	64	12	31	43	4	18
Geoff Courtnall	65	13	23	36	4–	117
Reed Larson	66	12	24	36	9	95
Greg Johnston	76	12	15	27	7–	79
Mike Milbury	68	6	16	22	22	96
Nevin Markwart	64	10	9	19	6–	225
Dwight Foster	47	4	12	16	1	37
Allen Pedersen	79	1	11	12	15–	71
Jay Miller	55	1	4	5	11–	208
Mats Thelin	59	1	3	4	8–	69

Calgary Flames

	GP	G	A	Pts	+/–	PIM
Joe Mullen	79	47	40	87	18	14
Al MacInnis	79	20	56	76	20	97
Paul Reinhart	76	15	54	69	7	22
Mike Bullard	71	30	36	66	9	51
Carey Wilson	80	20	38	58	2–	42
John Tonelli	78	20	31	51	2–	72
Joel Otto	68	19	31	50	8	185
Jim Peplinski	80	18	32	50	10	185
Gary Suter	68	9	40	49	10–	70
Hakan Loob	68	18	26	44	13–	26
Jamie Macoun	79	7	33	40	33	111
Steve Bozek	71	17	18	35	3	22
Brian Bradely	40	10	18	28	6	16
Colin Patterson	68	13	14	27	7	41
Lanny McDonald	58	14	12	26	3–	54
Tim Hunter	73	6	15	21	1–	357
Neil Sheehy	54	4	6	10	11	151
Nick Fotiu	42	5	3	8	3–	145

Buffalo Sabres

	GP	G	A	Pts	+/–	PIM
Dave Andreychuk	77	25	48	73	2	46
Phil Housley	78	21	46	67	2–	57
Christian Ruuttu	76	22	43	65	9	62
Mike Foligno	75	30	29	59	13	176
John Tucker	54	17	34	51	3–	21
Adam Creighton	56	18	22	40	4	26
Doug Smith	62	16	24	40	20–	106
Mike Ramsey	80	8	31	39	1	109
Wilf Paiement	56	20	17	37	2	108
Mark Napier	77	13	18	31	2–	2
Paul Cyr	73	11	16	27	16–	122
Clark Gillies	61	10	17	27	0	81
Scott Arniel	63	11	14	25	1–	59
Tom Kurvers	56	6	17	23	9–	24
Lindy Ruff	50	6	14	20	12–	74
Jim Korn	51	4	10	14	3–	158
Shawn Anderson	41	2	11	13	0	23
Joe Reekie	56	1	8	9	6	82
Lee Fogolin	44	1	5	6	4–	25

Chicago Black Hawks

	GP	G	A	Pts	+/–	PIM
Denis Savard	70	40	50	90	15	108
Steve Larmer	80	28	56	84	20	22
Troy Murray	77	28	43	71	14	59
Wayne Presley	80	32	29	61	18–	114
Al Secord	77	29	29	58	20–	196
Ed Olczyk	79	16	35	51	4–	119
Curt Fraser	75	25	25	50	5	182
Doug Wilson	69	16	32	48	15	36
Bob Murray	79	6	38	44	9–	80
Bill Watson	51	13	19	32	19	6
Gary Nylund	80	7	20	27	9–	190
Keith Brown	73	4	23	27	5	86
Mark Lavarre	58	8	15	23	11	33
Dave Donnelly	71	6	12	18	7–	81
Rich Preston	73	8	9	17	8–	19
Steve Ludzik	52	5	12	17	3–	34
Darryl Sutter	44	8	6	14	3–	16
Marc Bergevin	66	4	10	14	4	66
Jack O'Callahan	48	1	13	14	10	59
Dave Manson	63	1	8	9	2–	146

Detroit Red Wings

	GP	G	A	Pts	+/−	PIM
Steve Yzerman	80	31	59	90	1−	43
Brent Ashton	81	40	35	75	15−	39
Gerard Gallant	80	38	34	72	5−	216
Darren Veitch	77	13	45	58	14	52
Petr Klima	77	30	23	53	9−	42
Shawn Burr	80	22	25	47	2	107
Adam Oates	76	15	32	47	0	21
Mel Bridgman	64	10	33	43	7−	99
Dave Barr	69	15	17	32	7	68
Mike O'Connell	77	5	26	31	25−	70
Lee Norwood	57	6	21	27	23−	163
Tim Higgins	77	12	14	26	2−	124
Bob Probert	63	13	11	24	6−	221
Joey Kocur	77	9	9	18	10−	276
Harold Snepsts	54	1	13	14	7	129
Ric Seiling	74	3	8	11	4−	49
Mark Kumpel	45	1	9	10	10−	16
Gilbert Delorme	43	4	3	7	2−	47
Dave Lewis	58	2	5	7	12	66
Rick Zombo	44	1	4	5	6−	59
Steve Chiasson	45	1	4	5	7−	73

Edmonton Oilers

	GP	G	A	Pts	+/−	PIM
Wayne Gretzky	79	62	121	183	70	28
Jari Kurri	79	54	54	108	35	41
Mark Messier	77	37	70	107	21	73
Esa Tikkanen	76	34	44	78	44	120
Glenn Anderson	80	35	38	73	27	65
Paul Coffey	59	17	50	67	12	49
Kent Nilsson	61	18	45	63	12	16
Mike Krushelnyski	80	16	35	51	26	67
Craig MacTavish	79	20	19	39	9	55
Kevin Lowe	77	8	29	37	41	94
Moe Lemay	62	10	19	29	0	164
Craig Muni	79	7	22	29	45	85
Kevin McClelland	72	12	13	25	4−	238
Randy Gregg	52	8	16	24	36	42
Steve Smith	62	7	15	22	11	165
Charlie Huddy	58	4	15	19	27	35
Dave Hunter	77	6	9	15	1	75
Normand Lacombe	40	4	7	11	10−	10
Jeff Beukeboom	44	3	8	11	7	124
Marty McSorley	41	2	4	6	4−	159

Hartford Whalers

	GP	G	A	Pts	+/−	PIM
Ron Francis	75	30	63	93	10	45
Kevin Dineen	78	40	39	79	7	110
John Anderson	76	31	44	75	11	19
Ray Ferraro	80	27	32	59	9−	42
Dean Evason	80	22	37	59	5	67
Paul Lawless	60	22	32	54	24	14
Stewart Gavin	79	20	21	41	10	28
Dave Babych	66	8	33	41	18−	44
Sylvain Turgeon	41	23	13	36	3−	45
Ulf Samuelsson	78	2	31	33	28	162
Dave Tippett	80	9	22	31	0	42
Dana Murzyn	74	9	19	28	17	95
Doug Jarvis	80	9	13	22	0	20
Paul MacDermid	72	7	11	18	3	202
Mike McEwen	48	8	8	16	9−	32
Randy Ladouceur	70	5	9	14	2	121
Dave Semenko	56	4	8	12	7−	87
Scot Kleinendorst	66	3	9	12	4	130
Sylvain Cote	67	2	8	10	11	20
Pat Hughes	45	1	5	6	7−	28

Los Angeles Kings

	GP	G	A	Pts	+/−	PIM
Luc Robitaille	79	45	39	84	18−	28
Bernie Nicholls	80	33	48	81	16−	101
Jimmy Carson	80	37	42	79	5−	22
Dave Taylor	67	18	44	62	0	84
Jim Fox	76	19	42	61	10−	48
Bryan Erickson	68	20	30	50	12−	26
Steve Duchesne	75	13	25	38	8	74
Grant Ledyard	67	14	23	37	40−	93
Jay Wells	77	7	29	36	19−	155
Morris Lukowich	60	14	21	35	0	64
Dave Williams	76	16	18	34	1−	358
Sean McKenna	69	14	19	33	11	10

	GP	G	A	Pts	+/−	PIM
Mark Hardy	73	3	27	30	16	120
Bob Carpenter	60	9	18	27	27−	47
Bob Bourne	78	13	9	22	13−	35
Phil Sykes	58	6	15	21	10	133
Dean Kennedy	66	6	14	20	9	91
Tom Laidlaw	74	1	13	14	17−	69
Joe Paterson	45	2	1	3	15−	158

Minnesota North Stars

	GP	G	A	Pts	+/−	PIM
Dino Ciccarelli	80	52	51	103	10	92
Brian Maclellan	76	32	31	63	12−	69
Craig Hartsburg	73	11	50	61	2−	93
Dirk Graham	76	25	29	54	2−	142
Brian Bellows	65	26	27	53	13−	34
Neal Broten	46	18	35	53	12	35
Dennis Maruk	67	16	30	46	5	50
Keith Acton	78	16	29	45	15−	56
Brian Lawton	66	21	23	44	20	86
Ron Wilson	65	12	29	41	9−	36
Bob Brooke	80	13	23	36	9−	98
Brad Maxwell	56	3	18	21	7−	65
Paul Boutilier	62	7	13	20	1−	92
Larry DePalma	56	9	6	15	7−	219
Gordie Roberts	67	3	10	13	7−	68
Bob Rouse	72	2	10	12	6	179
Willi Plett	67	6	5	11	1	263
Frantisek Musil	72	2	9	11	0	148
Steve Payne	48	4	6	10	12−	19
Jari Gronstrand	47	1	6	7	4	27
Chris Pryor	50	1	3	4	6−	49

Montreal Canadiens

	GP	G	A	Pts	+/−	PIM
Mats Naslund	79	25	55	80	3−	16
Bobby Smith	80	28	47	75	6	72
Claude Lemieux	76	27	26	53	0	156
Larry Robinson	70	13	37	50	24	44
Ryan Walter	76	23	23	46	6−	34
Guy Carbonneau	79	18	27	45	9	68
Gaston Gingras	66	11	34	45	2−	21
Chris Chelios	71	11	33	44	5−	124
Stephane Richer	57	20	19	39	11	80
Mike McPhee	79	18	21	39	7	58
Sergio Momesso	59	14	17	31	0	96
Brian Skrudland	79	11	17	28	18	107
Shayne Corson	55	12	11	23	10	144
Petr Svoboda	70	5	17	22	14	63
Kjell Dahlin	41	12	8	20	3−	0
Chris Nilan	44	4	16	20	2	266
David Maley	48	6	12	18	1−	55
Bob Gainey	47	8	8	16	0	19
Craig Ludwig	75	4	12	16	3	105
Rick Green	72	1	9	10	1−	10
Mike Lalor	57	0	10	10	5	47
John Kordic	44	5	3	8	7−	151

New Jersey Devils

	GP	G	A	Pts	+/−	PIM
Aaron Broten	80	26	53	79	5	36
Kirk Muller	79	26	50	76	7−	75
John MacLean	80	31	36	67	23−	120
Pat Verbeek	74	35	24	59	23−	120
Doug Sulliman	78	27	26	53	17−	14
Mark Johnson	68	25	26	51	21−	22
Greg Adams	72	20	27	47	16−	19
Claude Loiselle	75	16	24	40	7−	137
Bruce Driver	74	6	28	34	26−	36
Joe Cirella	65	9	22	31	20−	111
Andy Brickley	51	11	12	23	15−	8
Peter McNab	46	8	12	20	14−	8
Uli Hiemer	40	6	14	20	6−	45
Anders Carlsson	48	2	18	20	11−	14
Perry Anderson	57	10	9	19	13−	105
Randy Velischek	64	2	16	18	12−	54
Jan Ludvig	47	7	9	16	5−	98
Ken Daneyko	79	2	12	14	13−	183
Craig Wolanin	68	4	6	10	31−	109
Steve Richmond	44	1	17	8	12−	143

New York Islanders

	GP	G	A	Pts	+/–	PIM
Bryan Trottier	80	23	64	87	2	50
Mike Bossy	63	38	37	75	8–	33
Pat LaFontaine	80	38	32	70	10–	70
Brent Sutter	69	27	36	63	23	73
Mikko Makela	80	24	33	57	3	24
Patrick Flatley	63	16	35	51	17	81
Denis Potvin	58	12	30	42	6–	70
Duane Sutter	80	14	17	31	1	169
Tomas Jonsson	47	6	25	31	8–	36
Rich Kromm	70	12	17	29	2	20
Ken Leiter	74	9	20	29	1	30
Brad Lauer	61	7	14	21	0	65
Steve Konroyd	72	5	16	21	5–	70
Alan Kerr	72	7	10	17	10–	175
Bob Bassen	77	7	10	17	17–	89
Gord Dineen	71	4	10	14	8–	110
Greg Gilbert	51	6	7	13	12–	26
Ken Morrow	64	3	8	11	7	32
Ari Haanpaa	41	6	4	10	8	17
Brian Curran	68	0	10	10	3	356

New York Rangers

	GP	G	A	Pts	+/–	PIM
Walt Poddubny	75	40	47	87	16	49
Marcel Dionno	01	28	56	84	16–	60
Tomas Sandstrom	64	40	34	74	8	60
Kelly Kisio	70	24	40	64	5–	73
Pierre Larouche	73	28	35	63	7–	12
Don Maloney	72	19	38	57	7	117
James Patrick	78	10	45	55	13	62
Tony McKegney	75	31	20	51	1	72
Ron Greschner	61	6	34	40	6–	62
Ron Duguay	74	14	25	39	16–	39
Willie Huber	66	8	22	30	13–	70
Jan Erixon	68	8	18	26	3	24
Curt Giles	72	2	20	22	5	54
Jeff Jackson	64	13	8	21	14–	79
Larry Melnyk	73	3	12	15	13–	182
Terry Carkner	52	2	13	15	1–	120
Lucien DeBlois	40	3	8	11	7–	27
Pat Price	60	0	8	8	15–	130
Stu Kulak	54	4	2	6	9–	78

Philadelphia Flyers

	GP	G	A	Pts	+/–	PIM
Tim Kerr	75	58	37	95	38	57
Peter Zezel	71	33	39	72	21	71
Dave Poulin	75	25	45	70	47	53
Brian Propp	53	31	36	67	30	45
Mark Howe	69	15	43	58	57	37
Per-Erik Eklund	72	14	41	55	2–	2
Murray Craven	77	19	30	49	1	38
Rick Tocchet	69	21	26	47	16	286
Doug Crossman	78	9	31	40	18	29
Brad McCrimmon	71	10	29	39	45	52
Scott Mellanby	71	11	21	32	8	94
Derrick Smith	71	11	21	32	4–	34
Ilkka Sinisalo	42	10	21	31	14	8
Lindsay Carson	71	11	15	26	2–	141
J.J. Daigneault	77	6	16	22	12	56
Kjell Samuelsson	76	3	12	15	11–	136
Brad Marsh	77	2	9	11	9	124
Dave Brown	62	7	3	10	7–	274
Ed Hospodar	45	2	2	4	8–	136

Pittsburgh Penguins

	GP	G	A	Pts	+/–	PIM
Mario Lemieux	63	54	53	107	13	57
Dan Quinn	80	31	49	80	8	54
Randy Cunneyworth	79	26	27	53	14	142
Craig Simpson	72	26	25	51	11	57
Terry Ruskowski	70	14	37	51	8	147
Doug Bodger	76	11	38	49	6	52
Moe Mantha	62	9	31	40	6–	44
John Chabot	72	14	22	36	7–	8
Bob Errey	72	16	18	34	5–	46
Jim Johnson	80	5	25	30	6–	116
Dan Frawley	78	14	14	28	10–	218
Dave Hannan	58	10	15	25	2–	56
Willy Lindstrom	60	10	13	23	9	6
Ville Siren	69	5	17	22	8	50
Warren Young	50	8	13	21	5–	103
Rod Buskas	68	3	15	18	2	123
Randy Hillier	55	4	8	12	12	97

Quebec Nordiques

	GP	G	A	Pts	+/–	PIM
Michel Goulet	75	49	47	96	12–	61
Peter Stastny	64	24	52	76	21–	43
John Ogrodnick	71	23	44	67	8–	10
Anton Stastny	77	27	35	62	3	8
Paul Gillis	76	13	26	39	5–	267
Dale Hunter	46	10	29	39	4	135
Risto Siltanen	66	10	29	39	2–	32
Alain Cote	80	12	24	36	4–	38
Mike Eagles	73	13	19	32	15–	55
Jeff Brown	44	7	22	29	11	16
Jason LaFreniere	56	13	15	28	3–	8
Robert Picard	78	8	20	28	17–	71
Doug Shedden	49	6	14	20	2–	14
David Shaw	75	0	19	19	35–	69
Basil McRae	69	11	7	18	2–	342
Bill Derlago	48	6	11	17	7–	18
Normand Rochefort	70	6	9	15	2	46
Mike Hough	56	6	8	14	8–	79
Randy Moller	71	5	9	14	11–	144

St. Louis Blues

	GP	G	A	Pts	+/–	PIM
Doug Gilmour	80	42	63	105	2–	58
Bernie Federko	64	20	52	72	25–	32
Mark Hunter	74	36	33	69	19–	169
Greg Paslawski	76	29	35	64	1	27
Brian Benning	78	13	36	49	2	110
Gino Cavallini	80	18	26	44	4	54
Rick Meagher	80	18	21	39	9–	54
Rob Ramage	59	11	28	39	12–	106
Ron Flockhart	60	16	19	35	9–	12
Doug Wickenheiser	80	13	15	28	22–	37
Ric Nattress	73	6	22	28	34–	24
Cliff Ronning	42	11	14	25	1–	6
Mark Reeds	68	9	16	25	20–	16
Tim Bothwell	76	6	16	22	19–	46
Jocelyn Lemieux	53	10	8	18	1	94
Herb Raglan	62	6	10	16	6	159
Bruce Bell	45	3	13	16	3	18
Doug Evans	53	3	13	16	2	91
Charlie Bourgeois	66	2	12	14	16	164
Jim Pavese	69	2	9	11	21–	129

Toronto Maple Leafs

	GP	G	A	Pts	+/–	PIM
Russ Courtnall	79	29	44	73	20–	90
Rick Vaive	73	32	34	66	12	61
Steve Thomas	78	35	27	62	3–	114
Wendel Clark	80	37	23	60	23–	271
Gary Leeman	80	21	31	52	26–	66
Tom Fergus	57	21	28	49	1	57
Mark Osborne	74	22	25	47	16–	113
Vincent Damphousse	80	21	25	46	6–	26
Peter Ihnacak	58	12	27	39	5	16
Todd Gill	61	4	27	31	3–	92
Al Iafrate	80	9	21	30	18–	55
Rick Lanz	61	3	25	28	9–	42
Mike Allison	71	7	16	23	1	66
Borje Salming	56	4	16	20	17	42
Greg Terrion	67	7	8	15	5–	6
Brad Smith	47	5	7	12	15	174
Chris Kotsopoulos	43	2	10	12	8	75
Bob McGill	56	1	4	5	2–	103
Terry Johnson	48	0	1	1	5–	104

Vancouver Canucks

	GP	G	A	Pts	+/–	PIM
Tony Tanti	77	41	38	79	5	84
Barry Pederson	79	24	52	76	13–	50
Petri Skriko	76	33	41	74	4–	44
Patrik Sundstrom	72	29	42	71	9	40
Doug Lidster	80	12	51	63	35–	40
Stan Smyl	66	20	23	43	20–	84
Rich Sutter	74	20	22	42	17–	113
Steve Tambellini	72	16	20	36	22–	14
Jim Sandlak	78	15	21	36	4–	66
Raimo Summanen	58	14	11	25	2–	15
Michel Petit	69	12	13	25	5–	131
Dan Hodgson	43	9	13	22	9–	25
Brent Peterson	69	7	15	22	14–	77
Garth Butcher	70	5	15	20	12–	207
Dave Lowry	70	8	10	18	23–	176

(continued)

	GP	G	A	Pts	+/–	PIM
Dave Richter	78	2	15	17	2–	172
David Bruce	50	9	7	16	2	109
Jim Benning	59	2	11	13	9	44
Robin Bartel	40	0	1	1	2	14

	GP	G	A	Pts	+/–	PIM
Dave Jensen	46	8	8	16	10–	12
John Blum	66	2	8	10	1	133
Greg Smith	45	0	9	9	6–	31
John Barrett	55	2	2	4	16–	43

Washington Capitols

	GP	G	A	Pts	+/–	PIM
Larry Murphy	80	23	58	81	25	39
Mike Gartner	78	41	32	73	1	61
Mike Ridley	78	31	39	70	11–	40
Scott Stevens	77	10	51	61	13	285
Craig Laughlin	80	22	30	52	3–	67
Gaetan Duchesne	74	17	35	52	18	53
Dave Christian	76	23	27	50	5–	8
Bob Gould	78	23	27	50	18	74
Greg Adams	67	14	30	44	9	184
Michal Pivonka	73	18	25	43	19–	41
Kelly Miller	77	16	26	42	5	48
Alan Haworth	50	25	16	41	3	43
Garry Galley	48	6	21	27	6–	67
Rod Langway	78	2	25	27	11	53
Kevin Hatcher	78	8	16	24	29–	144
Lou Franceschetti	75	12	9	21	9–	127

Winnipeg Jets

	GP	G	A	Pts	+/–	PIM
Dale Hawerchuk	80	47	53	100	3	54
Paul MacLean	72	32	42	74	12	75
Brian Mullen	69	19	32	51	2–	20
Thomas Steen	75	17	33	50	7	59
Gilles Hamel	79	27	21	48	3	24
Dave Ellett	78	13	31	44	19	53
Mario Marois	79	4	40	44	1–	106
Doug Smail	78	25	18	43	18	36
Randy Carlyle	71	16	26	42	6–	93
Laurie Boschman	80	17	24	41	17–	152
Ray Neufeld	80	18	18	36	13–	105
Fredrick Olausson	72	7	29	36	3–	24
Andrew McBain	71	11	21	32	6	106
Tim Watters	63	3	13	16	5	119
Ron Wilson	80	3	13	16	10	13
Jim Kyte	72	5	5	10	4	162
Brad Berry	52	2	8	10	6	60

NHL Trophy Winners

Ross Trophy
Leading scorer

1987	Wayne Gretzky, Edmonton
1986	Wayne Gretzky, Edmonton
1985	Wayne Gretzky, Edmonton
1984	Wayne Gretzky, Edmonton
1983	Wayne Gretzky, Edmonton
1982	Wayne Gretzky, Edmonton
1981	Wayne Gretzky, Edmonton
1980	Marcel Dionne, Los Angeles
1979	Bryan Trottier, N.Y. Islanders
1978	Guy Lafleur, Montreal
1977	Guy Lafleur, Montreal
1976	Guy Lafleur, Montreal
1975	Bobby Orr, Boston
1974	Phil Esposito, Boston
1973	Phil Esposito, Boston
1972	Phil Esposito, Boston
1971	Phil Esposito, Boston
1970	Bobby Orr, Boston
1969	Phil Esposito, Boston
1968	Stan Mikita, Chicago

Norris Trophy
Best defenseman

1987	Ray Bourque, Boston
1986	Paul Coffey, Edmonton
1985	Paul Coffey, Edmonton
1984	Rod Langway, Washington
1983	Rod Langway, Washington
1982	Doug Wilson, Chicago
1981	Randy Carlyle, Pittsburgh
1980	Larry Robinson, Montreal
1979	Denis Potvin, N.Y. Islanders
1978	Denis Potvin, N.Y. Islanders
1977	Larry Robinson, Montreal
1976	Denis Potvin, N.Y. Islanders
1975	Bobby Orr, Boston
1974	Bobby Orr, Boston
1973	Bobby Orr, Boston
1972	Bobby Orr, Boston
1971	Bobby Orr, Boston
1970	Bobby Orr, Boston
1969	Bobby Orr, Boston
1968	Bobby Orr, Boston

Calder Trophy
Best rookie

1987	Luc Robitaille, Los Angeles
1986	Gary Suter, Calgary
1985	Mario Lemieux, Pittsburgh
1984	Tom Barrasso, Buffalo
1983	Steve Larmer, Chicago
1982	Dale Hawerchuk, Winnipeg
1981	Peter Stastny, Quebec
1980	Ray Bourque, Boston
1979	Bob Smith, Minnesota
1978	Mike Bossy, N.Y. Islanders
1977	Willi Plett, Atlanta
1976	Bryan Trottier N.Y. Islanders
1975	Eric Vail, Atlanta
1974	Denis Potvin, N.Y. Islanders
1973	Steve Vickers, N.Y. Rangers
1972	Ken Dryden, Montreal
1971	Gil Perreault, Buffalo
1970	Tony Esposito, Chicago
1969	Danny Grant, Minnesota
1968	Derek Sanderson, Boston

Hart Trophy
MVP

1987	Wayne Gretzky, Edmonton
1986	Wayne Gretzky, Edmonton
1985	Wayne Gretzky, Edmonton
1984	Wayne Gretzky, Edmonton
1983	Wayne Gretzky, Edmonton
1982	Wayne Gretzky, Edmonton
1981	Wayne Gretzky, Edmonton
1980	Wayne Gretzky, Edmonton
1979	Bryan Trottier, N.Y. Islanders
1978	Guy Lafleur, Montreal
1977	Guy Lafleur, Montreal
1976	Bobby Clarke, Philadelphia
1975	Bobby Clarke, Philadelphia
1974	Phil Esposito, Boston
1973	Bobby Clarke, Philadelphia
1972	Bobby Orr, Boston
1971	Bobby Orr, Boston
1970	Bobby Orr, Boston
1969	Phil Esposito, Boston
1968	Stan Mikita, Chicago

Vezina Trophy
Leading goalie[1]

1987	Ron Hextall, Philadelphia
1986	John Vanbiesbrouck, N.Y. Rangers
1985	Pelle Lindbergh, Philadelphia
1984	Tom Barrasso, Buffalo
1983	Pete Peeters, Boston
1982	Billy Smith, N.Y. Islanders
1981	Sevigny, Herron, Larocque, Montreal
1980	Edwards, Sauve, Buffalo
1979	Dryden, Larocque, Montreal
1978	Dryden, Larocque, Montreal
1977	Dryden, Larocque, Montreal
1976	Ken Dryden, Montreal
1975	Bernie Parent, Philadelphia
1974	Tony Esposito, Chicago Bernie Parent, Philadelphia
1973	Ken Dryden, Montreal
1972	Esposito, Smith, Chicago
1971	Giacomin, Villemure, N.Y. Rangers
1970	Tony Esposito, Chicago

Lady Byng Trophy
Sportsmanship

1987	Joe Mullen, Calgary
1986	Mike Bossy, N.Y. Islanders
1985	Jari Kurri, Edmonton
1984	Mike Bossy, N.Y. Islanders
1983	Mike Bossy, N.Y. Islanders
1982	Rick Middleton, Boston
1981	Rick Kehoe, Pittsburgh
1980	Wayne Gretzky, Edmonton
1979	Bob MacMillan, Atlanta
1978	Butch Goring, Los Angeles
1977	Marcel Dionne, Los Angeles
1976	Jean Ratelle, Boston
1975	Marcel Dionne, Detroit
1974	John Bucyk, Boston
1973	Gilbert Perreault, Buffalo
1972	Jean Ratelle, N.Y. Rangers
1971	John Bucyk, Boston
1970	Phil Goyette, St. Louis
1969	Alex Delvecchio, Detroit
1968	Stan Mikita, Chicago

Frank Selke Trophy (best defensive forward)—1978-81, Bob Gainey, Montreal; 1982, Steve Kasper, Boston; 1983, Bobby Clarke, Philadelphia; 1984, Doug Jarvis, Washington; 1985, Craig Ramsey, Buffalo; 1986, Troy Murray, Chicago; 1987, Dave Poulin, Philadelphia.

(1) Most valuable goalie beginning in 1982.

NHL All Star Team, 1987

First team	Position	Second team
Ron Hextall, Philadelphia	Goalie	Mike Liut, Hartford
Mark Howe, Philadelphia	Defense	Al MacInnis, Boston
Ray Bourque, Boston	Defense	Larry Murphy, Washington
Wayne Gretzky, Edmonton	Center	Mario Lemieux, Pittsburgh
Jari Kurri, Edmonton	Right Wing	Tim Kerr, Philadelphia
Michel Goulet, Quebec	Left Wing	Luc Robitaille, Los Angeles

All-time NHL Scoring Leaders

At end of 1986-87 season. *Active player.

	Games	G	A	Pts
Gordie Howe	1,767	801	1,049	1,850
Marcel Dionne*	1,244	693	990	1,683
Phil Esposito	1,282	717	873	1,590
Wayne Gretzky*	632	543	977	1,520
Stan Mikita	1,394	541	926	1,467
John Bucyk	1,540	556	813	1,369
Gil Perreault	1,191	512	814	1,326
Alex Delvecchio	1,549	456	825	1,281
Jean Ratelle	1,281	491	776	1,267
Guy Lafleur	961	518	728	1,246
Norm Ullman	1,410	490	739	1,229
Jean Beliveau	1,215	507	712	1,219
Bobby Clarke	1,144	358	852	1,210
Bobby Hull	1,063	610	560	1,170

NCAA Hockey Champions

1948	Michigan
1949	Boston College
1950	Colorado College
1951	Michigan
1952	Michigan
1953	Michigan
1954	RPI
1955	Michigan
1956	Michigan
1957	Colorado College
1958	Denver
1959	North Dakota
1960	Denver
1961	Denver
1962	Michigan Tech
1963	North Dakota
1964	Michigan
1965	Michigan Tech
1966	Michigan State
1967	Cornell
1968	Denver
1969	Denver
1970	Cornell
1971	Boston Univ.
1972	Boston Univ
1973	Wisconsin
1974	Minnesota
1975	Michigan Tech
1976	Minnesota
1977	Wisconsin
1978	Boston Univ.
1979	Minnesota
1980	North Dakota
1981	Wisconsin
1982	North Dakota
1983	Wisconsin
1984	Bowling Green
1985	RPI
1986	Michican State
1987	North Dakota

THOROUGHBRED RACING

Triple Crown Winners, Jockeys, and Trainers

(Kentucky Derby, Preakness, and Belmont Stakes)

Year	Horse	Jockey	Trainer
1919	Sir Barton	J. Loftus	H. G. Bedwell
1930	Gallant Fox	E. Sande	J. Fitzsimmons
1935	Omaha	W. Sanders	J. Fitzsimmons
1937	War Admiral	C. Kurtsinger	G. Conway
1941	Whirlaway	E. Arcaro	D.A. Jones
1943	Count Fleet	J. Longden	G.D. Cameron
1946	Assault	Mehrtens	M. Hirsch
1948	Citation	E. Arcaro	H.A. Jones
1973	Secretariat	R. Turcotte	L. Laurin
1977	Seattle Slew	J. Cruguet	W.H. Turner Jr.
1978	Affirmed	S. Cauthen	L.S. Barrera

Annual Leading Money-Winning Horses

Year	Horse	Dollars
1948	Citation	709,470
1949	Ponder	321,825
1950	Noor	346,940
1951	Counterpoint	250,525
1952	Crafty Admiral	277,255
1953	Native Dancer	513,425
1954	Determine	328,700
1955	Nashua	752,550
1956	Needles	440,850
1957	Round Table	600,383
1958	Round Table	662,780
1959	Sword Dancer	537,004
1960	Bally Ache	455,045
1961	Carry Back	565,349
1962	Never Bend	402,969
1963	Candy Spots	604,481
1964	Gun Bow	580,100
1965	Buckpasser	568,096
1966	Buckpasser	669,078
1967	Damascus	817,941
1968	Forward Pass	546,674
1969	Arts and Letters	555,604
1970	Personality	444,049
1971	Riva Ridge	503,263
1972	Droll Roll	471,633
1973	Secretariat	860,404
1974	Chris Evert	551,063
1975	Foolish Pleasure	716,278
1976	Forego	491,701
1977	Seattle Slew	641,370
1978	Affirmed	901,541
1979	Spectacular Bid	1,279,334
1980	Temperence Hill	1,130,452
1981	John Henry	1,148,800
1982	Perrault	1,197,400
1983	All Along	2,138,963
1984	Slew O'Gold	2,627,944
1985	Spend a Buck	3,552,704
1986	Snow Chief	1,875,200

Annual Leading Jockey—Money Won

Year	Jockey	Dollars
1957	Bill Hartack	3,060,501
1958	Willie Shoemaker	2,961,693
1959	Willie Shoemaker	2,843,133
1960	Willie Shoemaker	2,123,961
1961	Willie Shoemaker	2,690,819
1962	Willie Shoemaker	2,916,844
1963	Willie Shoemaker	2,526,925
1964	Willie Shoemaker	2,649,553
1965	Braulio Baeza	2,582,702
1966	Braulio Baeza	2,951,022
1967	Braulio Baeza	3,088,888
1968	Braulio Baeza	2,835,108
1969	Jorge Velasquez	2,542,315
1970	Laffit Pincay Jr.	2,626,526
1971	Laffit Pincay Jr.	3,784,377
1972	Laffit Pincay Jr.	3,225,827
1973	Laffit Pincay Jr.	4,093,492
1974	Laffit Pincay Jr.	4,251,060
1975	Braulio Baeza	3,695,198
1976	Angel Cordero Jr.	4,709,500
1977	Steve Cauthen	6,151,750
1978	Darrel McHargue	6,029,885
1979	Laffit Pincay Jr.	8,193,535
1980	Chris McCarron	7,663,300
1981	Chris McCarron	8,397,604
1982	Angel Cordero Jr.	9,483,590
1983	Angel Cordero Jr.	10,116,697
1984	Chris McCarron	12,045,813
1985	Laffit Pincay Jr.	13,353,299
1986	Jose Santos	11,329,297

Eclipse Awards in 1986

Sponsored by the Thoroughbred Racing Assn., Daily Racing Form, and the National Turf Writers Assn.

Horse of the Year—Lady's Secret
Best 2-year-old colt—Capote
Best 2-year-old filly—Brave Raj
Best 3-year-old colt—Snow Chief
Best 3-year-old filly—Tiffany Lass
Best colt, horse, or gelding (4-year-olds & up)—Turkoman
Best filly or mare (4-year-olds & up)—Lady's Secret
Best male turf horse—Manila
Best turf filly or mare—Estrapade
Best sprinter—Smile
Best steeplechase horse—Flatterer
Best trainer—D. Wayne Lucas
Best jockey—Pat Day
Best apprentice jockey—Allen Stacy
Best owner—Eugene V. Klein
Best breeder—Paul Mellon

Kentucky Derby

Churchill Downs, Louisville, Ky.; inaugurated 1875; distance 1-1/4 miles; 1-1/2 miles until 1896. 3-year olds. Times—seconds in fifths.

Year	Winner	Jockey	Trainer	Wt.	Second	Winner's share	Time
1913	Donerail	R. Goose	T. P. Hayes	117	Ten Point	$5,475	2:04.4
1914	Old Rosebud	J. McCabe	F. D. Weir	114	Hodge	9,125	2:03.2
1915	Regret*	J. Notter	J. Rowe Sr.	112	Pebbles	11,450	2:05.2
1916	George Smith	J. Loftus	H. Hughes	117	Star Hawk	16,600	2:04.3
1917	Omar Khayyam	C. Borel	C. T. Patterson	117	Ticket	9,750	2:04.
1918	Exterminator	W. Knapp	H. McDaniel	114	Escoba	14,700	2:10.4
1919	Sir Barton	J. Loftus	H. G. Bedwell	112	Billy Kelly	20,825	2:09.4
1920	Paul Jones	T. Rice	W. Garth	126	Upset	30,375	2:09.
1921	Behave Yourself	C. Thompson	H. J. Thompson	126	Black Servant	38,450	2:04.1
1922	Morvich	A. Johnson	F. Burlew	126	Bet Mosie	46,775	2:04.3
1923	Zev	E. Sande	D. J. Leary	126	Martingale	53,600	2:05.2
1924	Black Gold	J. D. Mooney	H. Webb	126	Chilhowee	52,775	2:05.1
1925	Flying Ebony	E. Sande	W. B. Duke	126	Captain Hal	52,950	2:07.3
1926	Bubbling Over	A. Johnson	H. J. Thompson	126	Bagenbaggage	50,075	2:03.4
1927	Whiskery	L. McAtee	F. Hopkins	126	Osmand	51,000	2:06.
1928	Reigh Count	C. Lang	B. S. Michell	126	Misstep	55,375	2:10.2
1929	Clyde Van Dusen	L. McAtee	C. Van Dusen	126	Naishapur	53,950	2:10.4
1930	Gallant Fox	E. Sande	J. Fitzsimmons	126	Gallant Knight	50,725	2:07.3
1931	Twenty Grand	C. Kurtsinger	J. Rowe Jr.	126	Sweep All	48,725	2:01.4
1932	Burgoo King	E. James	H. J. Thompson	126	Economic	52,350	2:05.1
1933	Brokers Tip	D. Meade	H. J. Thompson	126	Head Play	48,925	2:06.4
1934	Cavalcade	M. Garner	R. A. Smith	126	Discovery	28,175	2:04.
1935	Omaha	W. Saunders	J. Fitzsimmons	126	Roman Soldier	39,525	2:05.
1936	Bold Venture	I. Hanford	M. Hirsch	126	Brevity	37,725	2:03.3
1937	War Admiral	C. Kurtsinger	G. Conway	126	Pompoon	52,050	2:03.1
1938	Lawrin	E. Arcaro	B. A. Jones	126	Dauber	47,050	2:04.4
1939	Johnstown	J. Stout	J. Fitzsimmons	126	Challedon	46,350	2:03.2
1940	Gallahadion	C. Bierman	R. Waldron	126	Bimelech	60,150	2:05.
1941	Whirlaway	E. Arcaro	B. A. Jones	126	Staretor	61,275	2:01.2
1942	Shut Out	W. D. Wright	J. M. Gaver	126	Alsab	64,225	2:04.2
1943	Count Fleet	J. Longden	G. D. Cameron	126	Blue Swords	60,275	2:04.
1944	Pensive	C. McCreary	B. A. Jones	126	Broadcloth	64,675	2:04.1
1945	Hoop, Jr.	E. Arcaro	I. H. Parke	126	Pot o'Luck	64,850	2:07.
1946	Assault	W. Mehrtens	M. Hirsch	126	Spy Song	96,400	2:06.3
1947	Jet Pilot	E. Guerin	T. Smith	126	Phalanx	92,160	2:06.3
1948	Citation	E. Arcaro	B. A. Jones	126	Coaltown	83,400	2:05.2
1949	Ponder	S. Brooks	B. A. Jones	126	Capot	91,600	2:04.1
1950	Middleground	W. Boland	M. Hirsch	126	Hill Prince	92,650	2:01.3
1951	Count Turf	C. McCreary	S. Rutchick	126	Royal Mustang	98,050	2:02.3
1952	Hill Gail	E. Arcaro	B. A. Jones	126	Sub Fleet	96,300	2:01.3
1953	Dark Star	H. Moreno	E. Hayward	126	Native Dancer	90,050	2:02.
1954	Determine	R. York	W. Molter	126	Hasty Road	102,050	2:03.
1955	Swaps	W. Shoemaker	M. A. Tenney	126	Nashua	108,400	2:01.4
1956	Needles	D. Erb	H. L. Fontaine	126	Fabius	123,450	2:03.2
1957	Iron Liege	W. Hartack	H. A. Jones	126	Gallant Man	107,950	2:02.1
1958	Tim Tam	I. Valenzuela	H. A. Jones	126	Lincoln Road	116,400	2:05.
1959	Tomy Lee	W. Shoemaker	F. Childs	126	Sword Dancer	119,650	2:02.1
1960	Venetian Way	W. Hartack	V. Sovinski	126	Bally Ache	114,850	2:02.2
1961	Carry Back	J. Sellers	J. A. Price	126	Crozier	120,500	2:04.
1962	Decidedly	W. Hartack	H. Luro	126	Roman Line	119,650	2:00.2
1963	Chateaugay	B. Baeza	J. Conway	126	Never Bend	108,900	2:01.4
1964	Northern Dancer	W. Hartack	H. Luro	126	Hill Rise	114,300	2:00.
1965	Lucky Debonair	W. Shoemaker	F. Catrone	126	Dapper Dan	112,000	2:01.1
1966	Kauai King	D. Brumfield	H. Forrest	126	Advocator	120,500	2:02.
1967	Proud Clarion	R. Ussery	L. Gentry	126	Barbs Delight	119,700	2:00.3
1968	Dancer's Image (a)	R. Ussery	H. Forrest	126	Forward Pass	122,600	2:02.1
1969	Majestic Prince	W. Hartack	J. Longden	126	Arts and Letters	113,200	2:01.4
1970	Dust Commander	M. Manganello	D. Combs	126	My Dad George	127,800	2:03.2
1971	Canonero II	G. Avila	J. Arias	126	Jim French	145,500	2:03.1
1972	Riva Ridge	R. Turcotte	L. Laurin	126	No Le Hace	140,300	2:01.4
1973	Secretariat	R. Turcotte	L. Laurin	126	Sham	155,050	1:59.2
1974	Cannonade	A. Cordero	W. Stephens	126	Hudson County	274,000	2:04.
1975	Foolish Pleasure	J. Vasquez	L. Jolley	126	Avatar	209,611	2:02.
1976	Bold Forbes	A. Cordero	L. Barrera	126	Honest Pleasure	165,200	2:01.3
1977	Seattle Slew	J. Cruguet	W. H. Turner Jr.	126	Run Dusty Run	214,700	2:02.1
1978	Affirmed	S. Cauthen	L. Barrera	126	Alydar	186,900	2:01.1
1979	Spectacular Bid	R. Franklin	G. Delp	126	General Assembly	228,650	2:02.2
1980	Genuine Risk*	J. Vasquez	L. Jolley	121	Rumbo	250,550	2:02
1981	Pleasant Colony	J. Velasquez	J. Campo	126	Woodchopper	317,200	2:02
1982	Gato del Sol	E. Delahoussaye	E. Gregson	126	Laser Light	428,850	2:02.2
1983	Sunny's Halo	E. Delahoussaye	D. Cross	126	Desert Wine	426,000	2:02.1
1984	Swale	L. Pincay	W. Stephens	126	Coax Me Chad	537,000	2:02.2
1985	Spend a Buck	A. Cordero	C. Gambolati	126	Stephan's Odyssey	406,800	2:00.1
1986	Ferdinand	W. Shoemaker	C. Whittingham	126	Bold Arrangement	609,400	2:02.4
1987	Alysheba	C. McCarron	J. Van Berg	126	Bet Twice	618,600	2:03.2

(a) Dancer's Image was disqualified from purse money after tests disclosed that he had run with a pain-killing drug, phenylbutazone, in his system. All wagers were paid on Dancer's Image. Forward Pass was awarded first place money.

The Kentucky Derby has been won five times by two jockeys, Eddie Arcaro, 1938, 1941, 1945, 1948 and 1952; and Bill Hartack, 1957, 1960, 1962, 1964 and 1969; four times by Willie Shoemaker, 1955, 1959, 1965, and 1986; and three times by each of three jockeys, Isaac Murphy, 1884, 1890, and 1891; Earle Sande, 1923, 1925 and 1930, and Angel Cordero in 1974, 1976 and 1985. *Regret and Genuine Risk are the only fillies to win the Derby.

Preakness

Pimlico, Baltimore, Md.; inaugurated 1873; 1 3-16 miles, 3 yr. olds. Time—seconds in fifths.

Year	Winner	Jockey	Trainer	Second	Winner's share	Time
1949	Capot	T. Atkinson	J.M. Gaver	Palestinian	$79,985	1:56
1950	Hill Prince	E. Arcaro	J.H. Hayes	Middleground	56,115	1:59.1
1951	Bold	E. Arcaro	P.M. Burch	Counterpoint	83,110	1:56.2
1952	Blue Man	C. McCreary	W.C. Stephens	Jampol	86,135	1:57.2
1953	Native Dancer	E. Guerin	W.C. Winfrey	Jamie K.	65,200	1:57.4
1954	Hasty Road	J. Adams	H. Trotsek	Correlation	91,600	1:57.2
1955	Nashua	E. Arcaro	J. Fitzsimmons	Saratoga	67,550	1:54.3
1956	Fabius	W. Hartack	H.A. Jones	Needles	84,250	1:58.2
1957	Bold Ruler	E. Arcaro	J. Fitzsimmons	Iron Liege	65,250	1:56.1
1958	Tim Tam	I. Valenzuela	H.A. Jones	Lincoln Road	97,900	1:57.1
1959	Royal Orbit	W. Harmatz	R. Cornell	Sword Dancer	136,200	1:57
1960	Bally Ache	R. Ussery	H.J. Pitt	Victoria Park	121,000	1:57.3
1961	Carry Back	J. Sellers	J.A. Price	Globemaster	126,200	1:57.3
1962	Greek Money	J.L. Rotz	V.W. Raines	Ridan	135,800	1:56.1
1963	Candy Spots	W. Shoemaker	M.A. Tenney	Chateaugay	127,500	1:56.1
1964	Northern Dancer	W. Hartack	H. Luro	The Scoundrel	124,200	1:56.4
1965	Tom Rolfe	R. Turcotte	F.Y. Whiteley Jr.	Dapper Dan	128,100	1:56.1
1966	Kauai King	D. Brumfield	H. Forrest	Stupendous	129,000	1:55.2
1967	Damascus	W. Shoemaker	F.Y. Whiteley Jr.	In Reality	141,500	1:55.1
1968	Forward Pass	I. Valenzuela	H. Forrest	Out of the Way	142,700	1:56.4
1969	Majestic Prince	W. Hartack	J. Longden	Arts and Letters	129,500	1:55.3
1970	Personality	E. Belmonte	J.W. Jacobs	My Dad George	151,300	1:56.1
1971	Canonero II	G. Avila	J. Arias	Eastern Fleet	137,400	1:54
1972	Bee Bee Bee	E. Nelson	D.W. Carroll	No Le Hace	135,300	1:55.3
1973	Secretariat	R. Turcotte	L. Laurin	Sham	129,900	1:54.2
1974	Little Current	M. Rivera	L. Rondinello	Neopolitan Way	156,000	1:54.3
1975	Master Derby	D. McHargue	W.E. Adams	Foolish Pleasure	158,100	1:56.2
1976	Elocutionist	J. Lively	P.T. Adwell	Play The Red	129,700	1:55
1977	Seattle Slew	J. Cruguet	W.H. Turner Jr.	Iron Constitution	138,600	1:54.2
1978	Affirmed	S. Cauthen	L. Barrera	Alydar	136,200	1:54.2
1979	Spectacular Bid	R. Franklin	G. Delp	Golden Act	165,300	1:54.1
1980	Codex	A. Cordero	D.W. Lucas	Genuine Risk	180,600	1:54.1
1981	Pleasant Colony	J. Velasquez	J. Campo	Bold Ego	270,800	1:54.3
1982	Aloma's Ruler	J. Kaenel	J. Lenzini	Linkage	209,990	1:55.2
1983	Deputed Testamony	D. Miller	J.W. Boniface	Desert Wine	251,200	1:55.2
1984	Gate Dancer	A. Cordero	J. Van Berg	Play On	243,600	1:53.3
1985	Tank's Prospect	P. Day	D.W. Lucas	Chief's Crown	423,200	1:53.2
1986	Snow Chief	A. Solis	M.F. Stute	Ferdinand	411,900	1:54.4
1987	Alysheba	C. McCarron	J. Van Berg	Bet Twice	421,100	1:55.4

Belmont Stakes

Elmont, N.Y.; inaugurated 1867; 1 ½ miles, 3 year olds. Time—seconds in fifths.

Year	Winner	Jockey	Trainer	Second	Winner's share	Time
1949	Capot	T. Atkinson	J.M. Gaver	Ponder	$60,900	2:30.1
1950	Middleground	W. Boland	M. Hirsch	Lights Up	61,350	2:28.3
1951	Counterpoint	D. Gorman	S. Veitch	125 Battlefield	82,000	2:29
1952	One Count	E. Arcaro	O. White	Blue Man	82,400	2:30.1
1953	Native Dancer	E. Guerin	W.C. Winfrey	Jamie K.	82,500	2:28.3
1954	High Gun	E. Guerin	M. Hirsch	Fisherman	89,000	2:30.4
1955	Nashua	E. Arcaro	J. Fitzsimmons	Blazing Count	83,700	2:29
1956	Needles	D. Erb	H. Fontaine	Career Boy	83,600	2:29.4
1957	Gallant Man	W. Shoemaker	J. Nerud	Inside Tract	77,300	2:26.3
1958	Cavan	P. Anderson	T.J. Barry	Tim Tam	73,440	2:30.1
1959	Sword Dancer	W. Shoemaker	J.E. Burch	Bagdad	93,525	2:28.2
1960	Celtic Ash	W. Hartack	T.J. Barry	Venetian Way	96,785	2:29.3
1961	Sherluck	B. Baeza	H. Young	Globemaster	104,900	2:29.1
1962	Jaipur	W. Shoemaker	W.F. Mulholland	Admiral's Voyage	109,550	2:28.4
1963	Chateaugay	B. Baeza	J.P. Conway	Candy Spots	101,700	2:30.1
1964	Quadrangle	M. Ycaza	J.E. Burch	Roman Brother	110,850	2:28.2
1965	Hail to All	J. Sellers	E. Yowell	Tom Rolfe	104,150	2:28.2
1966	Amberoid	W. Boland	L. Laurin	Buffle	117,700	2:29.3
1967	Damascus	W. Shoemaker	F.Y. Whiteley Jr.	Cool Reception	104,950	2:28.4
1968	Stage Door Johnny	H. Gustines	J.M. Gaver	Forward Pass	117,700	2:27.1
1969	Arts and Letters	B. Baeza	J.E. Burch	Majestic Prince	104,050	2:28.4
1970	High Echelon	J.L. Rotz	J.W. Jacobs	Needles N Pens	115,000	2:34
1971	Pass Catcher	W. Blum	E. Yowell	Jim French	97,710	2:30.2
1972	Riva Ridge	R. Turcotte	L. Laurin	Ruritania	93,950	2:28
1973	Secretariat	R. Turcotte	L. Laurin	Twice A Prince	90,120	2:24
1974	Little Current	M. Rivera	L. Rondinello	Jolly Johu	101,970	2:29.1
1975	Avatar	W. Shoemaker	A.T. Doyle	Foolish Pleasure	116,160	2:28.1
1976	Bold Forbes	A. Cordero	Laz Barrera	McKenzie Bridge	116,850	2:29
1977	Seattle Slew	J. Cruguet	W.H. Turner Jr.	Run Dusty Run	109,080	2:29.3
1978	Affirmed	S. Cauthen	Laz Barrera	Alydar	110,580	2:26.4
1979	Coastal	R. Hernandez	D.A. Whiteley	Golden Act	161,400	2:28.3
1980	Temperence Hill	E. Maple	J. Cantey	Genuine Risk	176,220	2:29.4
1981	Summing	G. Martens	Luis Barrera	Highland Blade	170,580	2:29
1982	Conquistador Cielo	L. Pincay	W. Stephens	Gato Del Sol	159,720	2:28.1
1983	Caveat	L. Pincay	W. Stephens	Slew o'Gold	215,100	2:27.4
1984	Swale	L. Pincay	W. Stephens	Pine Circle	310,020	2:27.1
1985	Creme Fraiche	E. Maple	W. Stephens	Stephan's Odyssey	307,740	2:27
1986	Danzig Connection	C. McCarron	W. Stephens	John's Treasure	338,640	2:29.4
1987	Bet Twice	C. Perret	W.A. Croll Jr.	Cryptoclearance	329,160*	2:28.1

*Not incl. $1 million Triple Crown point system bonus.

COLLEGE BASKETBALL

Final Regular Season Conference Standings, 1986–87

Atlantic Coast

	Conference W	Conference L	All Games W	All Games L
North Carolina	14	0	29	3
Clemson	10	4	25	5
Duke	9	5	22	8
Virginia	8	6	21	9
Georgia Tech	7	7	16	12
North Carolina St.	6	8	20	14
Wake Forest	2	12	14	15
Maryland	0	14	9	17

Tournament Champion—North Carolina St.

Atlantic 10

	Conference W	Conference L	All Games W	All Games L
Temple	17	1	31	3
West Virginia	15	3	23	7
Rhode Island	12	6	20	9
Penn St.	9	9	15	12
St. Joseph's	9	9	16	13
Duquesne	7	11	12	17
Massachusetts	7	11	11	16
George Washington	6	12	10	19
Rutgers	5	13	8	20
St. Bonaventure	3	15	5	23

Tournament Champion—Temple.

Big East

	Conference W	Conference L	All Games W	All Games L
Georgetown	12	4	26	4
Pittsburgh	12	4	24	7
Syracuse	12	4	26	6
Providence	10	6	21	8
St. John's	10	6	20	8
Villanova	6	10	15	15
Soton Hall	4	12	15	13
Boston College	3	13	11	18
Connecticut	3	13	9	19

Tournament Champion—Georgetown.

Big Eight

	Conference W	Conference L	All Games W	All Games L
Missouri	11	3	24	9
Kansas	9	5	23	10
Oklahoma	9	5	22	9
Kansas St.	8	6	19	10
Nebraska	7	7	17	11
Iowa St.	5	9	13	15
Oklahoma St.	4	10	8	20
Colorado	3	11	9	19

Tournament Champion—Missouri.

Big Sky

	Conference W	Conference L	All Games W	All Games L
Montana St.	12	2	21	7
Boise St.	10	4	21	7
Montana	8	6	18	11
Nevada-Reno	7	7	15	15
Idaho	5	9	16	14
Idaho St.	5	9	15	15
N. Arizona	5	9	11	17
Weber St.	4	10	7	22

Tournament Champion—Idaho St.

Big South

	Conference W	Conference L	All Games W	All Games L
Baptist, S.C.	12	2	21	9
Campbell	10	4	17	13
N.C.-Asheville	5	3	15	11
Radford	7	7	17	14
Winthrop	4	4	8	20
Coast Carolina	4	4	12	16
Armstrong St.	2	6	6	22
Augusta	3	11	8	19

Tournament Champion—Baptist.

Big Ten

	Conference W	Conference L	All Games W	All Games L
Indiana	15	3	24	4
Purdue	15	3	24	4
Iowa	14	4	27	4
Illinois	13	5	23	7
Michigan	10	8	19	11
Ohio St.	9	9	19	12
Michigan St.	6	12	11	17
Wisconsin	4	14	14	17
Minnesota	2	16	9	19
Northwestern	2	16	7	21

Colonial

	Conference W	Conference L	All Games W	All Games L
Navy	13	1	26	5
N.C.-Wilmington	9	5	18	12
Richmond	8	6	15	14
James Madison	8	6	20	9
George Mason	7	7	15	13
American	5	9	13	14
East Carolina	4	10	12	16
William & Mary	2	12	5	22

Tournament Champion—Navy.

East Coast

	Conference W	Conference L	All Games W	All Games L
Bucknell	11	3	22	8
Lafayette	10	4	16	13
Rider	8	6	12	16
Lehigh	8	6	15	14
Drexel	7	7	14	14
Towson St.	5	9	14	16
Hofstra	4	10	9	19
Delaware	3	11	12	16

Tournament Champion—Bucknell.

ECAC Metro

	Conference W	Conference L	All Games W	All Games L
Marist	15	1	20	9
FDU-Teaneck	11	5	19	10
Loyola (Md.)	10	6	15	14
Wagner	8	8	16	13
Robert Morris	7	9	13	14
St. Francis (Pa.)	7	9	11	16
Long Island U.	5	11	13	14
St. Francis (NY)	5	11	11	16
Monmouth	4	12	8	19

Tournament Champion—Marist.

ECAC North

	Conference W	Conference L	All Games W	All Games L
Northeastern	17	1	27	6
Niagara	14	4	20	9
Boston U.	12	6	18	12
Canisius	12	6	16	12
Siena	12	6	16	12
Hartford	8	10	14	14
Maine	6	12	10	18
Vermont	3	15	5	23
New Hampshire	3	15	4	24
Colgate	3	15	4	23

Tournament Champion—Northeastern.

Gulf Star

	Conference W	Conference L	All Games W	All Games L
Stephen F. Austin	10	0	21	7
Sam Houston St.	6	4	16	12
SW Texas St.	5	5	13	15
NW Louisiana	4	6	15	13
SE Louisiana	4	6	10	21
Nicholls St.	1	9	9	18

Ivy League

	Conference W	Conference L	All Games W	All Games L
Pennsylvania	10	4	13	13
Princeton	9	5	16	9
Cornell	9	5	15	11
Dartmouth	7	7	15	11
Yale	7	7	14	12
Columbia	6	8	12	14
Harvard	4	10	9	17
Brown	4	10	9	18

Metro AC

	Conference W	Conference L	All Games W	All Games L
Louisville	9	3	18	14
Memphis St.	8	4	26	8
Florida St.	6	6	18	10
Southern Miss	6	6	18	11
Virginia Tech	5	7	10	18
South Carolina	5	7	15	14
Cincinnati	3	9	12	16

Tournament Champion—Memphis St.

Metro Atlantic

	Conference W	Conference L	All Games W	All Games L
St. Peter's	11	3	21	7
LaSalle	10	4	16	12
Iona	8	6	16	14
Army	8	6	14	15
Holy Cross	6	8	9	19
Fordham	6	8	14	16
Fairfield	5	9	15	15
Manhattan	2	12	6	21

Tournament Champion—Fairfield.

Mid-American

	Conference W	Conference L	All Games W	All Games L
Central Mich.	14	2	22	7
Kent St.	11	5	19	10
Bowling Green	10	6	15	14
E. Michigan	8	8	14	15
Miami (Ohio)	7	9	14	14
Ohio U.	7	9	14	14
W. Michigan	7	9	12	16
Toledo	4	12	11	17
Ball St.	4	12	9	18

Tournament Champion—Central Mich.

Mid-Continent

	Conference W	Conference L	All Games W	All Games L
SW Missouri St.	13	1	27	5
Cleveland St.	10	4	24	7
Ill.-Chicago	9	5	17	15
Wis.-Green Bay	8	6	15	14
N. Iowa	7	7	13	15
Valparaiso	4	10	12	16
E. Illinois	3	11	9	19
W. Illinois	2	12	12	16

Tournament Champion—SW Missouri St.

Mid-Eastern

	Conference W	Conference L	All Games W	All Games L
Howard	13	1	25	5
No. Carolina A&T	12	2	24	5
S. Carolina St.	9	5	14	15
Coppin St.	7	6	8	19
Bethune-Cookman	6	8	10	19
Morgan St.	5	9	8	19
Delaware St.	3	11	4	24
Maryland-E. Shore	0	13	2	25
Flordia A&M	—	—	12	16

Tournament Champion—No. Carolina A&T

Midwestern

	Conference W	Conference L	All Games W	All Games L
Evansville	8	4	16	12
Loyola (Ill.)	8	4	16	13
Xavier (Ohio)	7	5	18	12
St. Louis	7	5	24	9
Oral Roberts	5	7	11	17
Butler	5	7	12	16
Detroit	2	10	7	21

Tournament Champion—Xavier.

Missouri Valley

	Conference W	Conference L	All Games W	All Games L
Tulsa	11	3	22	7
Bradley	10	4	17	12
Wichita St.	9	5	22	10
Illinois St.	7	7	17	12
Drake	6	8	17	14
So. Illinois	5	9	12	17
Indiana St.	4	10	9	20
Creighton	4	10	9	19

Tournament Champion—Wichita St.

Ohio Valley

	Conference W	Conference L	All Games W	All Games L
Middle Tennessee	11	3	22	6
Akron	9	5	21	8
E. Kentucky	9	5	19	11
Austin Peay	8	6	19	11
Morehead St.	8	6	14	14
Murray St.	6	8	13	15
Youngstown St.	4	10	11	17
Tennessee Tech	1	13	7	20

Tournament Champion—Austin Peay.

Pacific Coast

	Conference W	Conference L	All Games W	All Games L
UNLV	18	0	33	1
Cal-Santa Barb	10	8	16	13
San Jose St.	10	8	16	14
Fullerton St.	9	9	17	12
Cal-Irvine	9	9	14	14
New Mexico St.	9	9	15	15
Utah St.	8	10	15	16
Long Beach St.	7	11	12	19
Pacific	6	12	10	17
Fresno St.	4	14	9	20

Tournament Champion—UNLV.

Pacific-10	Conference W	Conference L	All Games W	All Games L
UCLA	14	4	23	6
Arizona	13	5	18	11
Oregon St.	10	8	18	10
California	10	8	18	14
Washington	10	8	18	13
Stanford	9	9	15	13
Oregon	8	10	16	14
Arizona St.	6	12	11	17
Washington St.	6	12	10	18
USC	4	14	9	19

Tournament Champion—UCLA.

Southern	Conference W	Conference L	All Games W	All Games L
Marshall	15	1	25	5
Tenn.-Chattanooga	14	2	21	7
Davidson	12	4	20	10
Furman	10	6	17	12
Citadel	6	10	13	15
VMI	5	11	11	17
W. Carolina	4	12	10	19
Appalachian St.	3	13	7	21
E. Tenn. St.	3	13	7	21

Tournament Champion—Marshall.

Southland	Conference W	Conference L	All Games W	All Games L
Louisiana Tech	9	1	22	7
McNeese St.	5	5	14	14
Arkansas St.	5	5	21	12
Lamar	4	6	14	15
N. Texas St.	4	6	11	17
NE Louisiana	3	7	13	15

Tournament Champion—Louisiana Tech.

Southeastern	Conference W	Conference L	All Games W	All Games L
Alabama	16	2	26	4
Florida	12	6	21	10
Georgia	10	8	18	11
Kentucky	10	8	18	10
Auburn	9	9	17	12
Mississippi	8	10	15	13
Louisiana St.	8	10	21	14
Vanderbilt	7	11	16	15
Tennessee	7	11	14	15
Mississippi St.	3	15	7	21

Tournament Champion—Alabama.

Southwest	Conference W	Conference L	All Games W	All Games L
TCU	14	2	23	6
Baylor	10	6	18	12
Houston	9	7	18	11
Texas Tech	9	7	15	14
Arkansas	8	8	18	13
Texas	7	9	14	17
SMU	7	9	16	13
Texas A&M	6	10	17	13
Rice	2	14	8	19

Tournament Champion—Texas A&M.

Southwestern	Conference W	Conference L	All Games W	All Games L
Grambling	11	3	16	14
Southern U.	9	5	19	11
Miss. Valley	9	5	13	15
Jackson St.	8	6	15	14
Alabama St.	7	7	14	14
Texas Southern	7	7	11	18
Alcorn St.	3	11	5	23
Prairie View	2	12	6	22

Tournament Champion—Southern U.

Sun Belt	Conference W	Conference L	All Games W	All Games L
W. Kentucky	12	2	28	8
Jacksonville	11	3	19	10
Alabama-Birmingham	10	4	21	10
VCU	7	7	17	14
N.C.-Charlotte	6	8	18	14
South Alabama	6	8	14	14
South Florida	3	11	8	20
Old Dominion	1	13	6	22

Tournament Champion—Ala.-Birmingham.

Trans America	Conference W	Conference L	All Games W	All Games L
Ark.-Little Rock	16	2	23	9
Houston-Baptist	13	5	18	11
Stetson	13	5	18	13
Georgia Southern	12	6	20	10
Hardin-Simm.	9	9	13	15
Texas-S.A.	7	11	13	15
Mercer	7	11	12	18
Georgia St.	7	11	11	17
Centenary	5	13	10	17
Samford	1	17	4	22

Tournament Champion—Ga. Southern.

West Coast	Conference W	Conference L	All Games W	All Games L
San Diego	13	1	24	5
Gonzaga	9	5	18	10
St. Mary's	7	7	17	13
San Francisco	6	8	16	12
Santa Clara	6	8	18	13
Portland	6	8	14	14
Pepperdine	5	9	12	18
Loyola (Cal.)	4	10	12	16

Tournament Champion—Santa Clara.

Western Athletic	Conference W	Conference L	All Games W	All Games L
Texas-El Paso	13	3	24	6
Brigham Young	12	4	21	10
New Mexico	11	5	25	9
Wyoming	11	5	22	9
Utah	9	7	17	12
Colorado St.	7	9	13	16
Air Force	5	11	12	15
San Diego St.	2	14	5	25
Hawaii	2	14	7	21

Tournament Champion—Wyoming.

Independents	W	L
DePaul	26	2
New Orleans	25	3
Notre Dame	22	7
Marquette	16	12
Pan American	16	12
Tennessee St.	15	12
Miami (Fla.)	15	16
Dayton	13	15
Central Florida	12	15
Maryland-Balt. County	11	16
Chicago St.	11	17
SW Louisiana	11	17
U.S. International	11	17
Utica	10	16
Brooklyn	10	18
Texas-Arlington	10	18
N. Illinois	9	19
Central Conn.	8	21
E. Washington	5	23

NCAA Basketball Championships in 1987

East

First round—North Carolina 113, Penn 82; Michigan 97, Navy 82; Notre Dame 84, Middle Tennessee 71; TCU 76, Marshall 60; Florida 82, North Carolina St. 70; Purdue 104, Northeastern 95; W. Kentucky 64, West Virginia 62; Syracuse 79, Georgia Southern 73.

Second round—North Carolina 109, Michigan 97; Notre Dame 58, TCU 57; Florida 85, Purdue 66; Syracuse 104, W. Kentucky 86.

Regionals—North Carolina 74, Notre Dame 68; Syracuse 87, Florida 81.

Championship—Syracuse 79, North Carolina 75.

Southeast

First round—Georgetown 75, Bucknell 53; Ohio St. 91, Kentucky 77; Kansas 66, Houston 55; SW Missouri 65, Clemson 60; Providence 90, Alabama-Birmingham 68; Austin Peay 68, Illinois 67; New Orleans 83, BYU 79; Alabama 88, North Carolina A&T 71.

Second round—Georgetown 82, Ohio St. 79; Kansas 67, SW Missouri 63; Providence 90, Austin Peay 87; Alabama 101, New Orleans 76.

Regionals—Georgetown 70, Kansas 57; Providence 103, Alabama 82.

Championship—Providence 88, Georgetown 73.

Midwest

First round—Indiana 92, Fairfield 58; Auburn 62, San Diego 61; Duke 58, Texas A&M 51; Xavier, Oh. 70, Missouri 69; St. John's 57, Wichita St. 55; DePaul 76, Louisiana Tech 62; LSU 85, Georgia Tech 79; Temple 75, Southern 56.

Second round—Indiana 107, Auburn 90; Duke 65, Xavier, Oh. 60; DePaul 83, St. John's 75; LSU 72, Temple 62.

Regionals—Indiana 88, Duke 82; LSU 63, DePaul 58.

Championship—Indiana 77, LSU 76.

West

First round—UNLV 95, Idaho St. 70; Kansas St. 82, Georgia 79; Wyoming 64, Virginia 60; UCLA 92, Central Michigan 73; Oklahoma 74, Tulsa 69; Pittsburgh 93, Marist 68; UTEP 93, Arizona 91; Iowa 99, Santa Clara 76.

Second round—UNLV 80, Kansas St. 61; Wyoming 78, UCLA 68; Oklahoma 96, Pittsburgh 93; Iowa 84, UTEP 82.

Regionals—UNLV 92, Wyoming 78; Iowa 93, Oklahoma 91.

Championship—UNLV 84, Iowa 81.

National Semifinals

Syracuse 77, Providence 63; Indiana 97, UNLV 93.

Championship

Indiana 74, Syracuse 73.

World Almanac All-America Team in 1987

First team	Position	Second team
David Robinson, Navy, senior	Center	Chris Welp, Washington, senior
Armon Gilliam, UNLV, senior	Forward	Danny Manning, Kansas, junior
Reggie Williams, Georgetown, senior	Forward	Jerome Lane, Pittsburgh, sophmore
Kenny Smith, North Carolina, senior	Guard	Dennis Hopson, Ohio St., senior
Steve Alford, Indiana, senior	Guard	Reggie Miller, UCLA, senior

NCAA Division I Champions

Year	Champion	Coach	Final opponent	Score	MVP	Site
1939	Oregon	Howard Hobson	Ohio St.	46-33	None	Evanston, Ill.
1940	Indiana	Branch McCracken	Kansas	60-42	Marvin Huffman, Indiana	Kansas City, Mo.
1941	Wisconsin	Harold Foster	Washington St.	39-34	John Kotz, Wisconsin	Kansas City, Mo.
1942	Stanford	Everett Dean	Dartmouth	53-38	Howard Dallmar, Stanford	Kansas City, Mo.
1943	Wyoming	Everett Shelton	Georgetown	46-34	Ken Sailors, Wyoming	New York, N.Y.
1944	Utah	Vadal Peterson	Dartmouth	42-40(1)	Arnold Ferrin, Utah	New York, N.Y.
1945	Oklahoma St.(2)	Henry Iba	NYU	49-45	Bob Kurland, Oklahoma St.	New York, N.Y.
1946	Oklahoma St.(2)	Henry Iba	North Carolina	43-40	Bob Kurland, Oklahoma St.	New York, N.Y.
1947	Holy Cross	Alvin Julian	Oklahoma	58-47	George Kaftan, Holy Cross	New York, N.Y.
1948	Kentucky	Adolph Rupp	Baylor	58-42	Alex Groza, Kentucky	New York, N.Y.
1949	Kentucky	Adolph Rupp	Oklahoma St.	46-36	Alex Groza, Kentucky	Seattle, Wash.
1950	CCNY	Nat Holman	Bradley	71-68	Irwin Dambrot, CCNY	New York, N.Y.
1951	Kentucky	Adolph Rupp	Kansas St.	68-58	None	Minneapolis, Minn.
1952	Kansas	Forrest Allen	St. John's	80-63	Clyde Lovellette, Kansas	Seattle, Wash.
1953	Indiana	Branch McCracken	Kansas	69-68	B.H. Born, Kansas	Kansas City, Mo.
1954	La Salle	Kenneth Loeffler	Bradley	92-76	Tom Gola, La Salle	Kansas City, Mo.
1955	San Francisco	Phil Woolpert	LaSalle	77-63	Bill Russell, San Francisco	Kansas City, Mo.
1956	San Francisco	Phil Woolpert	Iowa	83-71	Hal Lear, Temple	Evanston, Ill.
1957	N. Carolina	Frank McGuire	Kansas	54-53(1)	Wilt Chamberlain, Kansas	Kansas City, Mo.
1958	Kentucky	Adolph Rupp	Seattle	84-72	Elgin Baylor, Seattle	Louisville, Ky.
1959	California	Pete Newell	W. Virginia	71-70	Jerry West, W. Virginia	Louisville, Ky.
1960	Ohio St.	Fred Taylor	California	75-55	Jerry Lucas, Ohio St.	San Francisco, Cal.
1961	Cincinnati	Edwin Jucker	Ohio St.	70-65(1)	Jerry Lucas, Ohio St.	Kansas City, Mo.
1962	Cincinnati	Edwin Jucker	Ohio St.	71-59	Paul Hogue, Cincinnati	Louisville, Ky.
1963	Loyola (Ill.)	George Ireland	Cincinnati	60-58(1)	Art Heyman, Duke	Louisville, Ky.
1964	UCLA	John Wooden	Duke	98-83	Walt Hazzard, UCLA	Kansas City, Mo.
1965	UCLA	John Wooden	Michigan	91-80	Bill Bradley, Princeton	Portland, Ore.
1966	Texas-El Paso(3)	Don Haskins	Kentucky	72-65	Jerry Chambers, Utah	College Park, Md.
1967	UCLA	John Wooden	Dayton	79-64	Lew Alcindor, UCLA	Louisville, Ky.
1968	UCLA	John Wooden	N. Carolina	78-55	Lew Alcindor, UCLA	Los Angeles, Cal.
1969	UCLA	John Wooden	Purdue	92-72	Lew Alcindor, UCLA	Louisville, Ky.
1970	UCLA	John Wooden	Jacksonville	80-69	Sidney Wicks, UCLA	College Park, Md.
1971	UCLA	John Wooden	Villanova*	68-62	Howard Porter, Villanova*	Houston, Tex.
1972	UCLA	John Wooden	Florida St.	81-76	Bill Walton, UCLA	Los Angeles, Cal.
1973	UCLA	John Wooden	Memphis St.	87-66	Bill Walton, UCLA	St. Louis, Mo.
1974	N. Carolina St.	Norm Sloan	Marquette	76-64	David Thompson, N.C. St.	Greensboro, N.C.
1975	UCLA	John Wooden	Kentucky	92-85	Richard Washington, UCLA	San Diego, Cal.
1976	Indiana	Bob Knight	Michigan	86-68	Kent Benson, Indiana	Philadelphia, Pa.
1977	Marquette	Al McGuire	N. Carolina	67-59	Butch Lee, Marquette	Atlanta, Ga.
1978	Kentucky	Joe Hall	Duke	94-88	Jack Givens, Kentucky	St. Louis, Mo.
1979	Michigan St.	Jud Heathcote	Indiana St.	75-64	Magic Johnson, Michigan St.	Salt Lake City, Ut.
1980	Louisville	Denny Crum	UCLA*	59-54	Darrell Griffith, Louisville	Indianapolis, Ind.
1981	Indiana	Bob Knight	N. Carolina	63-50	Isiah Thomas, Indiana	Philadelphia, Pa.
1982	N. Carolina	Dean Smith	Georgetown	63-62	James Worthy, No. Carolina	New Orleans, La.
1983	N. Carolina St.	Jim Valvano	Houston	54-52	Akeem Olajuwon, Houston	Albuquerque, N.M.
1984	Georgetown	John Thompson	Houston	84-75	Patrick Ewing, Georgetown	Seattle, Wash.
1985	Villanova	Rollie Massimino	Georgetown	66-64	Ed Pinckney, Villanova	Lexington, Ky.
1986	Louisville	Denny Crum	Duke	72-69	Pervis Ellison, Louisville	Dallas, Tex.
1987	Indiana	Bob Knight	Syracuse	74-73	Keith Smart, Indiana	New Orleans, La.

*Declared ineligible subsequent to the tournament. (1) Overtime. (2) Known as Oklahoma A&M at that time. (3) Known as Texas Western at that time.

NCAA Division I Career Scoring Leaders

Player, team	Seasons	G	FG	FT	Pts.	Avg.
Pete Maravich, Louisiana State	1968-70	83	1387	893	3667	44.2
Austin Carr, Notre Dame	1969-71	74	1017	526	2560	34.6
Oscar Robertson, Cincinnati	1958-60	88	1052	869	2973	33.8
Calvin Murphy, Niagara	1968-70	77	947	654	2548	33.1
Dwight Lamar, SW Louisiana	1972-73	57	768	326	1862	32.7
Frank Selvy, Furman	1952-54	78	922	694	2538	32.5
Rick Mount, Purdue	1968-70	72	910	503	2323	32.3
Darrell Floyd, Furman	1954-56	71	868	545	2281	32.1
Nick Werkman, Seton Hall	1962-64	71	812	649	2273	32.0
Willie Humes, Idaho State	1970-71	48	565	380	1510	31.5
William Averitt, Pepperdine	1972-73	49	615	311	1541	31.4
Elgin Baylor, Col. Idaho, Seattle	55, 57-58	80	956	588	2500	31.3
Elvin Hayes, Houston	1966-68	93	1215	454	2884	31.0
Freeman Williams, Portland State	1975-1978	106	1369	511	3249	30.7
Larry Bird, Indiana State	1977-79	94	1154	542	2850	30.3

John R. Wooden Award

Awarded annually to the nation's outstanding college basketball playing student-athlete by a poll of sports writers and broadcasters.

1977 Marques Johnson, UCLA
1978 Phil Ford, North Carolina
1979 Larry Bird, Indiana State
1980 Darrell Griffith, Louisville
1981 Danny Ainge, Brigham Young
1982 Ralph Sampson, Virginia
1983 Ralph Sampson, Virginia
1984 Michael Jordan, North Carolina
1985 Chris Mullin, St. John's
1986 Walter Berry, St. John's
1987 David Robinson, Navy

National Invitation Tournament Champions

Year	Champion	Year	Champion	Year	Champion	Year	Champion
1938	Temple	1951	Brigham Young	1964	Bradley	1976	Kentucky
1939	Long Island Univ.	1952	LaSalle	1965	St. John's	1977	St. Bonaventure
1940	Colorado	1953	Seton Hall	1966	Brigham Young	1978	Texas
1941	Long Island Univ.	1954	Holy Cross	1967	Southern Illinois	1979	Indiana
1942	West Virginia	1955	Duquesne	1968	Dayton	1980	Virginia
1943	St. John's	1956	Louisville	1969	Temple	1981	Tulsa
1944	St. John's	1957	Bradley	1970	Marquette	1982	Bradley
1945	De Paul	1958	Xavier (Ohio)	1971	North Carolina	1983	Fresno State
1946	Kentucky	1959	St. John's	1972	Maryland	1984	Michigan
1947	Utah	1960	Bradley	1973	Virginia Tech	1985	UCLA
1948	St. Louis	1961	Providence	1974	Purdue	1986	Ohio State
1949	San Francisco	1962	Dayton	1975	Princeton	1987	Southern Mississippi
1950	CCNY	1963	Providence				

NCAA Division II Champions

Year	Champion	Year	Champion	Year	Champion	Year	Champion
1966	Kentucky Wesleyan	1972	Roanoke	1978	Cheyney State	1983	Wright State
1967	Winston-Salem	1973	Kentucky Wesleyan	1979	North Alabama	1984	Central Missouri St.
1968	Kentucky Wesleyan	1974	Morgan State	1980	Virginia Union	1985	Jacksonville St.
1969	Kentucky Wesleyan	1975	Old Dominion	1981	Florida Southern	1986	Sacred Heart (Conn.)
1970	Philadelphia Textile	1976	Puget Sound	1982	Univ. of D.C.	1987	Kentucky Wesleyan
1971	Evansville	1977	Tennessee-Chattanooga				

NCAA Division I Women's Champions

Year	Champion	Coach	Final opponent	Year	Champion	Coach	Final opponent
1982	Louisiana Tech	Sonja Hogg	Cheyney	1985	Old Dominion	Marianne Stanley	Georgia
1983	USC	Linda Sharp	Louisiana Tech	1986	Texas	Jody Conradt	USC
1984	USC	Linda Sharp	Tennessee	1987	Tennessee	Pat Head Summitt	Louisiana Tech

NCAA Division I Basketball Statistical Trends

Averages and percentages are for both teams, per game.

Year	Games	FG Made	FG Att.	Pct.	FT Made	FT Att.	Pct.	PF	Pts.
1948	3945	40.6	138.7	29.3	25.3	42.2	59.8	36.9	106.5
1950	3659	43.2	136.8	31.6	28.7	46.5	61.8	39.0	115.1
1952	4009	47.5	140.6*	33.7	31.6	50.6	62.0	44.9*	126.6
1953	3754	48.0	138.1	34.7	42.1	65.8*	64.0	42.5	138.1
1955	3829	51.1	138.6	36.9	43.1*	64.7	66.5	37.9	145.3
1956	4008	52.1	139.0	37.5	42.3	63.3	66.8	37.7	146.5
1958	4153	51.6	134.2	38.4	33.6	50.5	66.4	36.4	136.8
1960	4295	52.6	132.3	39.8	34.7	51.5	67.4	36.7	139.9
1961	4238	53.3	131.1	40.7	34.7	50.9	68.2	36.4	141.3
1963	4180	53.2	127.6	41.7	32.6	47.8	68.2	36.4	139.0
1965	4520	58.3	135.4	43.1	34.7	50.3	69.0	38.5	151.4
1967	4602	57.7	131.9	43.8	34.4	49.8	69.0	38.3	149.8
1969	4883	58.2	132.8	43.8	34.8	50.8	68.4	37.9	151.2
1971	5232	60.2	135.6	44.4	35.0	51.3	68.1	38.5	155.4*
1973	5582	62.3*	139.2	44.8	26.2	38.3	68.4	38.4	150.9
1975	6147	62.9	136.7	46.0	27.4	39.7	69.0	40.3	153.1
1977	6676	60.7	129.8	46.7	28.4	41.0	69.4	40.2	149.7
1979	7131	59.2	124.1	47.7	29.5	42.2	69.7*	41.1	147.9
1981	7407	55.6	115.9	48.0	29.0	42.0	68.9	40.2	140.2
1982	7646	53.3	111.2	47.9	28.5	41.6	68.6	38.7	135.1
1983	7957	54.3	114.0	47.7	29.0	42.3	68.5	39.7	138.7
1984	8029	53.4	111.1	48.1*	29.5	42.8	68.9	39.9	136.3
1985	8269	54.5	113.9	47.9	29.3	42.5	68.9	39.3	138.3
1986	8360*	54.7	114.6	47.7	29.4	42.5	69.1	39.1	138.7

*All-time high.

American Basketball Association Champions, 1968-1976

	Regular season		Playoffs	
Year	Eastern division	Western division	Winner	Runner-up
1968	Pittsburgh	New Orleans	Pittsburgh	New Orleans
1969	Indiana	Oakland	Oakland	Indiana
1970	Indiana	Denver	Indiana	Los Angeles
1971	Virginia	Indiana	Utah	Kentucky
1972	Kentucky	Utah	Indiana	New York
1973	Carolina	Utah	Indiana	Kentucky
1974	New York	Utah	New York	Utah
1975	Kentucky	Denver	Kentucky	Indiana
1976	Denver		New York	Denver

NATIONAL BASKETBALL ASSOCIATION, 1986-87

Final Standings

Eastern Conference

Atlantic Division

Club	W	L	Pct	GB
Boston	59	23	.720	...
Philadelphia	45	37	.549	14
Washington	42	40	.512	17
New Jersey	24	58	.293	35
New York	24	58	.293	35

Central Division

Club	W	L	Pct	GB
Atlanta	57	25	.695	...
Detroit	52	30	.634	5
Milwaukee	50	32	.610	7
Indiana	41	41	.500	16
Chicago	40	42	.488	17
Cleveland	31	51	.378	26

Western Conference

Midwest Division

Club	W	L	Pct	GB
Dallas	55	27	.671	...
Utah	44	38	.537	11
Houston	42	40	.512	13
Denver	37	45	.451	18
Sacramento	29	53	.354	26
San Antonio	28	54	.341	27

Pacific Division

Club	W	L	Pct	GB
L.A. Lakers	65	17	.793	...
Portland	49	33	.598	16
Golden State	42	40	.512	23
Seattle	39	43	.476	26
Phoenix	36	46	.439	29
L.A. Clippers	12	70	.146	53

NBA Playoff Results

Eastern Division

Boston defeated Chicago 3 games to 0.
Detroit defeated Washington 3 games to 0.
Milwaukee defeated Philadelphia 3 games to 2.
Atlanta defeated Indiana 3 games to 1.
Detroit defeated Atlanta 4 games to 1.
Boston defeated Milwaukee 4 games to 3.
Boston defeated Detroit 4 games to 3.

Western Division

L.A. Lakers defeated Denver 3 games to 0.
Denver defeated Dallas 3 games to 1.
Houston defeated Portland 3 games to 1.
Golden State defeated Utah 3 games to 2.
L.A. Lakers defeated Golden State 4 games to 1.
Seattle defeated Houston 4 games to 2.
L.A. Lakers defeated Seattle 4 games to 0.

Championship

L.A. Lakers defeated Boston 4 games to 2.

NBA Champions 1947-1987

Year	Regular season: Eastern Conference	Western Conference	Playoffs: Winner	Runner-up
1947	Washington	Chicago	Philadelphia	Chicago
1948	Philadelphia	St. Louis	Baltimore	Philadelphia
1949	Washington	Rochester	Minneapolis	Washington
1950	Syracuse	Minneapolis	Minneapolis	Syracuse
1951	Philadelphia	Minneapolis	Rochester	New York
1952	Syracuse	Rochester	Minneapolis	New York
1953	New York	Minneapolis	Minneapolis	New York
1954	New York	Minneapolis	Minneapolis	Syracuse
1955	Syracuse	Ft. Wayne	Syracuse	Ft. Wayne
1956	Philadelphia	Ft. Wayne	Philadelphia	Ft. Wayne
1957	Boston	St. Louis	Boston	St. Louis
1958	Boston	St. Louis	St. Louis	Boston
1959	Boston	St. Louis	Boston	Minneapolis
1960	Boston	St. Louis	Boston	St. Louis
1961	Boston	St. Louis	Boston	St. Louis
1962	Boston	Los Angeles	Boston	Los Angeles
1963	Boston	Los Angeles	Boston	Los Angeles
1964	Boston	San Francisco	Boston	San Francisco
1965	Boston	Los Angeles	Boston	Los Angeles
1966	Philadelphia	Los Angeles	Boston	Los Angeles
1967	Philadelphia	San Francisco	Philadelphia	San Francisco
1968	Philadelphia	St. Louis	Boston	Los Angeles
1969	Baltimore	Los Angeles	Boston	Los Angeles
1970	New York	Atlanta	New York	Los Angeles

Year	Atlantic	Central	Midwest	Pacific	Winner	Runner-up
1971	New York	Baltimore	Milwaukee	Los Angeles	Milwaukee	Baltimore
1972	Boston	Baltimore	Milwaukee	Los Angeles	Los Angeles	New York
1973	Boston	Baltimore	Milwaukee	Los Angeles	New York	Los Angeles
1974	Boston	Capital	Milwaukee	Los Angeles	Boston	Milwaukee
1975	Boston	Washington	Chicago	Golden State	Golden State	Washington
1976	Boston	Cleveland	Milwaukee	Golden State	Boston	Phoenix
1977	Philadelphia	Houston	Denver	Los Angeles	Portland	Philadelphia
1978	Philadelphia	San Antonio	Denver	Portland	Washington	Seattle
1979	Washington	San Antonio	Kansas City	Seattle	Seattle	Washington
1980	Boston	Atlanta	Milwaukee	Los Angeles	Los Angeles	Philadelphia
1981	Boston	Milwaukee	San Antonio	Phoenix	Boston	Houston
1982	Boston	Milwaukee	San Antonio	Los Angeles	Los Angeles	Philadelphia
1983	Philadelphia	Milwaukee	San Antonio	Los Angeles	Philadelphia	Los Angeles
1984	Boston	Milwaukee	Utah	Los Angeles	Boston	Los Angeles
1985	Boston	Milwaukee	Denver	L.A. Lakers	L.A. Lakers	Boston
1986	Boston	Milwaukee	Houston	L.A. Lakers	Boston	Houston
1987	Boston	Atlanta	Dallas	L.A. Lakers	L.A. Lakers	Boston

Statistical Leaders, 1986-1987

Individual Scoring

(Minimum: 70 games played or 1400 points)

	G	Pts	Avg
Jordan, Chicago	82	3041	37.1
Wilkins, Atlanta	79	2294	29.0
English, Denver	82	2345	28.6
Bird, Boston	74	2076	28.1
Vandeweghe, Portland	79	2122	26.9
McHale, Boston	77	2008	26.1
Aguirre, Dallas	80	2056	25.7
Ellis, Seattle	82	2041	24.9
M. Malone, Washington	73	1760	24.1
Johnson, L.A. Lakers	80	1909	23.9
Davis, Phoenix	79	1867	23.6
Olajuwon, Houston	75	1755	23.4
Chambers, Seattle	82	1909	23.3
McDaniel, Seattle	82	1890	23.0
Barkley, Philadelphia	68	1564	23.0
Harper, Cleveland	82	1874	22.9
Nance, Phoenix	69	1552	22.5
J. Malone, Washington	80	1758	22.0
Drexler, Portland	82	1782	21.7
Malone, Utah	82	1779	21.7

Field Goal Percentage

(Minimum: 300 field goals)

	FG	FGA	Pct
McHale, Boston	790	1307	.604
Gilmore, San Antonio	346	580	.597
Barkley, Philadelphia	557	937	.594
Donaldson, Dallas	311	531	.586
Abdul-Jabbar, L.A. Lakers	560	993	.564
B. Williams, New Jersey	521	936	.557
Parish, Boston	588	1057	.556
Johnson, Portland	494	889	.556
McCray, Houston	432	783	.552
Nance, Phoenix	585	1062	.551

Free Throw Percentage

(Minimum: 125 made)

	FT	FTA	Pct
Bird, Boston	414	455	.910
Ainge, Boston	148	165	.897
Laimbeer, Detroit	245	274	.894
Scott, L.A. Lakers	224	251	.892
Hodges, Milwaukee	131	147	.891
Long, Indiana	219	246	.890
Vandeweghe, Portland	467	527	.886
J. Malone, Washington	376	425	.885
Blackman Dallas	419	474	.884
Pierce, Milwaukee	387	440	.880

3-Pt. Field Goal Leaders

(Minimum: 25 made)

	FG	FGA	Pct
Vandeweghe, Portland	39	81	.481
Schrempf, Dallas	33	69	.478
Ainge, Boston	83	192	.443
Scott, L.A. Lakers	65	149	.436

Assists Per Game

(Minimum: 70 games or 400 assists)

	G	No	Avg
Johnson, L.A. Lakers	80	977	12.2
Floyd, Golden State	82	848	10.3
Thomas, Detroit	81	813	10.0
Rivers, Atlanta	82	823	10.0
Porter, Portland	80	715	8.9
Theus, Sacramento	79	692	8.8
McMillan, Seattle	71	583	8.2
Stockton, Utah	82	670	8.2
Lever, Denver	82	654	8.0
Cheeks, Philadelphia	68	538	7.9

Rebounds

(Minimum: 70 games or 800 rebounds)

	G	Tot	Avg
Barkley, Philadelphia	68	994	14.6
Oakley, Chicago	82	1074	13.1
B. Williams, New Jersey	82	1023	12.5
Donaldson, Dallas	82	973	11.9
Laimbeer, Detroit	82	955	11.6
Cage, L.A. Clippers	80	922	11.5
L. Smith, Golden State	80	917	11.5
Olajuwon, Houston	75	858	11.4
M. Malone, Washington	73	824	11.3
Parish, Boston	80	851	10.6

Steals Per Game

(Minimum: 70 games or 125 steals)

	G	No	Avg
Robertson, San Antonio	81	260	3.21
Jordan, Chicago	82	236	2.88
Cheeks, Philadelphia	68	180	2.65
Harper, Cleveland	82	209	2.55
Drexler, Portland	82	204	2.49
Lever, Denver	82	201	2.45
Harper, Dallas	77	167	2.17
Stockton, Utah	82	177	2.16
Rivers, Atlanta	82	171	2.09
Porter, Portland	80	159	1.99

Blocked Shots Per Game

(Minimum: 70 games or 100 blocked shots)

	G	No	Avg
Eaton, Utah	79	321	4.06
Bol, Washington	82	302	3.68
Olajuwon, Houston	75	254	3.39
Benjamin, L.A. Clippers	72	187	2.60
Lister, Seattle	75	180	2.40
Ewing, New York	63	147	2.33
McHale, Boston	77	172	2.23
Nance, Phoenix	69	148	2.14
Hinson, Philadelphia	76	161	2.12
C. Jones, Washington	79	165	2.09

1987 NBA Player Draft

The following are the first round picks of the National Basketball Assn.

San Antonio—David Robinson, Navy
Phoenix—Armon Gilliam, UNLV
New Jersey—Dennis Hopson, Ohio St.
L.A. Clippers—Reggie Williams, Georgetown
Seattle—Scottie Pippen, Central Arkansas
Sacramento—Kenny Smith, North Carolina
Cleveland—Kevin Johnson, California
Chicago—Olden Polynice, Virginia
Seattle—Derrick McKey, Alabama
Chicago—Horace Grant, Clemson
Indiana—Reggie Miller, UCLA
Washington—Tyrone Bogues, Wake Forest
L.A. Clippers—Joe Wolf, North Carolina
Golden State—Tellis Frank, W. Kentucky
Utah—Jose Ortiz, Oregon St.
Philadelphia—Chris Welp, Washington
Portland—Ronnie Murphy, Jacksonville
New York—Mark Jackson, St. John's
L.A. Clippers—Ken Norman, Illinois
Dallas—Jim Farmer, Alabama
Atlanta—Dallas Comegys, DePaul
Boston—Reggie Lewis, Northeastern
San Antonio—Greg Anderson, Houston

All-Time NBA Statistical Leaders

(at the start of the 1986-87 season unless otherwise noted)

Scoring Average
(400 games or 10,000 Points Minimum)

	G	Pts.	Avg
Wilt Chamberlain	1,045	31,419	30.1
Elgin Baylor	846	23,149	27.4
Jerry West	932	25,192	27.0
Bob Pettit	792	20,880	26.4
George Gervin	791	20,708	26.2
*Kareem Abdul Jabbar	1,406	36,474	25.9
Oscar Robertson	1,040	26,710	25.7
*Adrian Dantley	758	19,678	25.0
*Larry Bird	635	15,508	24.4
Pete Maravich	658	15,948	24.2

Field Goal Percentage
(2,000 FGM Minimum)

	FTA	FTM	Pct.
Artis Gillmore	8,809	5,287	.600
Darryl Dawkins	6,019	3,446	.573
James Worthy	3,814	2,181	.572
Larry Nance	4,427	2,513	.568
Jeff Ruland	3,657	2,061	.564
Kareem Abdul-Jabbar	25,752	14,484	.562
Bill Cartwright	4,646	2,585	.556
Kevin McHale	5,529	3,056	.553
Bobby Jones	6,199	3,412	.550
Buck Williams	4,764	2,621	.550

Free Throw Percentage
(1,200 FTM Minimum)

	FTA	FTM	Pct.
Rick Barry	4,243	3,818	.900
Calvin Murphy	3,864	3,445	.892
Bill Sharman	3,357	3,143	.884
*Larry Bird	2,454	2,819	.878
Mike Newlin	3,456	3,005	.870
*Kiki Vandeweghe	2,642	2,296	.868
Fred Brown	2,211	1,896	.858
Larry Siegfried	1,945	1,662	.854
James Silas	1,690	1,440	.852
Flynn Robinson	1,881	1,597	.849

Points

	Pts.
*Kareem Abdul-Jabbar	36,474
Wilt Chamberlain	31,419
Elvin Hayes	27,313
Oscar Robertson	26,710
John Havlicek	26,395
Jerry West	25,192
Elgin Baylor	23,149
Hal Greer	21,586
Walt Bellamy	20,941
Bob Pettit	20,880

Games Played

*Kareem Abdul-Jabbar	1,406
Elvin Hayes	1,303
John Havlicek	1,270
Paul Silas	1,254
Hal Greer	1,122
Len Wilkens	1,077
Dolph Schayes	1,059
Johnny Green	1,057
Don Nelson	1,053
Leroy Ellis	1,048

Assists

Oscar Robertson	9,887
Len Wilkens	7,211
Bob Cousy	6,955
Guy Rodgers	6,917
Nate Archibald	6,476
Jerry West	6,238
John Havlicek	6,114
Norm Nixon	6,047
Dave Bing	5,397
Kevin Porter	5,314

Field Goals Made

*Kareem Abdul-Jabbar	15,044
Wilt Chamberlain	12,681
Elvin Hayes	10,976
John Havlicek	10,513
Oscar Robertson	9,508
Jerry West	9,016
Elgin Baylor	8,693
Hal Greer	8,504
George Gervin	8,045
Walt Bellamy	7,914

Rebounds

Wilt Chamberlain	23,924
Bill Russell	21,620
*Kareem Abdul-Jabbar	16,479
Elvin Hayes	16,279
Nate Thurmond	14,464
Walt Bellamy	14,241
Wes Unseld	13,769
Jerry Lucas	12,942
Bob Pettit	12,849
Paul Silas	12,357

*Includes 1986-87 season.

NBA Scoring Leaders

Year	Scoring champion	Pts	Avg
1947	Joe Fulks, Philadelphia	1,389	23.2
1948	Max Zaslofsky, Chicago	1,007	21.0
1949	George Mikan, Minneapolis	1,698	28.3
1950	George Mikan, Minneapolis	1,865	27.4
1951	George Mikan, Minneapolis	1,932	28.4
1952	Paul Arizin, Philadelphia	1,674	25.4
1953	Neil Johnston, Philadelphia	1,564	22.3
1954	Neil Johnston, Philadelphia	1,759	24.4
1955	Neil Johnston, Philadelphia	1,631	22.7
1956	Bob Pettit, St. Louis	1,849	25.7
1957	Paul Arizin, Philadelphia	1,817	25.6
1958	George Yardley, Detroit	2,001	27.8
1959	Bob Pettit, St. Louis	2,105	29.2
1960	Wilt Chamberlain, Philadelphia	2,707	37.9
1961	Wilt Chamberlain, Philadelphia	3,033	38.4
1962	Wilt Chamberlain, Philadelphia	4,029	50.4
1963	Wilt Chamberlain, San Francisco	3,586	44.8
1964	Wilt Chamberlain, San Francisco	2,948	36.5
1965	Wilt Chamberlain, San Fran., Phila.	2,534	34.7
1966	Wilt Chamberlain, Philadelphia	2,649	33.5
1967	Rick Barry, San Francisco	2,775	35.6
1968	Dave Bing, Detroit	2,142	27.1
1969	Elvin Hayes, San Diego	2,327	28.4
1970	Jerry West, Los Angeles	2,309	31.2
1971	Lew Alcindor, Milwaukee	2,596	31.7
1972	Kareem Abdul-Jabbar (Alcindor), Milwaukee	2,822	34.8
1973	Nate Archibald, Kansas City-Omaha	2,719	34.0
1974	Bob McAdoo, Buffalo	2,261	30.6
1975	Bob McAdoo, Buffalo	2,831	34.5
1976	Bob McAdoo, Buffalo	2,427	31.1
1977	Pete Maravich, New Orleans	2,273	31.1
1978	George Gervin, San Antonio	2,232	27.2
1979	George Gervin, San Antonio	2,365	29.6
1980	George Gervin, San Antonio	2,585	33.1
1981	Adrian Dantley, Utah	2,452	30.7
1982	George Gervin, San Antonio	2,551	32.3
1983	Alex English, Denver	2,326	28.4
1984	Adrian Dantley, Utah	2,418	30.6
1985	Bernard King, New York	1,809	32.9
1986	Dominique Wilkins, Atlanta	2,366	30.3
1987	Michael Jordan, Chicago	3,041	37.1

NBA Rookie of the Year

Year	Player
1953	Don Meineke, Ft. Wayne
1954	Ray Felix, Baltimore
1955	Bob Pettit, Milwaukee
1956	Maurice Stokes, Rochester
1957	Tom Heinsohn, Boston
1958	Woody Sauldsberry, Philadelphia
1959	Elgin Baylor, Minneapolis
1960	Wilt Chamberlain, Philadelphia
1961	Oscar Robertson, Cincinnati
1962	Walt Bellamy, Chicago
1963	Terry Dischinger, Chicago
1964	Jerry Lucas, Cincinnati
1965	Willis Reed, New York
1966	Rick Barry, San Francisco
1967	Dave Bing, Detroit
1968	Earl Monroe, Baltimore
1969	Wes Unseld, Baltimore
1970	Lew Alcindor, Milwaukee
1971	Dave Cowens, Boston; Geoff Petrie, Portland (tie)
1972	Sidney Wicks, Portland
1973	Bob McAdoo, Buffalo
1974	Ernie DiGregorio, Buffalo
1975	Keith Wilkes, Golden State
1976	Alvan Adams, Phoenix
1977	Adrian Dantley, Buffalo
1978	Walter Davis, Phoenix
1979	Phil Ford, Kansas City
1980	Larry Bird, Boston
1981	Darrell Griffith, Utah
1982	Buck Williams, New Jersey
1983	Terry Cummings, San Diego
1984	Ralph Sampson, Houston
1985	Michael Jordan, Chicago
1986	Patrick Ewing, New York
1987	Chuck Person, Indiana

Individual Statistics, 1986-1987

(Over 500 Minutes Played)

Atlanta Hawks

	Min	FG%	FT%	RBs	Ast	Pts	Avg
Wilkins	2969	.463	.818	494	261	2294	29.0
Willis	2626	.536	.709	849	62	1304	16.1
Rivers	2590	.451	.828	299	823	1053	12.8
Wittman	2049	.503	.787	124	211	900	12.7
McGee	1420	.459	.584	159	149	788	10.4
Levingston	1848	.506	.731	533	40	657	8.0
Webb	532	.438	.762	60	167	223	6.8
Battle	804	.457	.738	60	124	381	6.0
Koncak	1684	.480	.654	493	31	463	5.6
Rollins	1764	.546	.724	488	22	405	5.4
Carr	695	.506	.709	156	34	342	5.3

Boston Celtics

	Min	FG%	FT%	RBs	Ast	Pts	Avg
Bird	3005	.525	.910	682	566	2076	28.1
McHale	3060	.604	.836	763	198	2008	26.1
Parish	2995	.556	.735	851	173	1403	17.5
Ainge	2499	.486	.897	242	400	1053	14.8
Johnson	2933	.444	.833	261	594	1062	13.4
Sichting	1566	.508	.881	91	187	448	5.7
Roberts	1079	.515	.810	190	62	402	5.5
Daye	724	.500	.523	124	75	236	3.9
Kite	745	.427	.382	169	27	123	1.7

Chicago Bulls

	Min	FG%	FT%	RBs	Ast	Pts	Avg
Jordan	3281	.482	.857	430	377	3041	37.1
Oakley	2980	.445	.686	1074	296	1192	14.5
Paxson	2689	.487	.809	139	467	930	11.3
Banks	1822	.539	.767	308	170	610	6.7
Threatt	1446	.448	.798	108	259	580	8.5
Sellers	1751	.455	.728	373	102	680	8.5
Corzine	2287	.475	.736	540	209	683	8.3
Cureton	1105	.467	.534	227	70	297	6.9
Brown	818	.527	.639	214	24	258	4.2
Turner	936	.444	.742	115	102	248	3.5
Poquette	604	.508	.800	101	35	164	2.8
Waiters	534	.430	.556	87	22	85	1.9

Cleveland Cavaliers

	Min	FG%	FT%	RBs	Ast	Pts	Avg
Harper	3064	.455	.684	392	394	1874	22.9
Daugherty	2695	.538	.696	647	304	1253	15.7
Williams	2714	.485	.745	629	154	1168	14.6
Hubbard	2083	.531	.596	388	136	804	11.8
Bagley	2182	.426	.831	252	379	768	10.7
Price	1217	.400	.833	117	202	464	6.9
West	1333	.543	.514	339	41	507	6.6
Corbin	1170	.409	.734	215	97	404	6.4
Ehlo	890	.414	.707	161	92	273	6.2
Lee	870	.455	.713	251	69	412	6.1
Turpin	801	.462	.714	190	33	393	6.1
Newman	630	.411	.868	70	27	293	5.0

Dallas Mavericks

	Min	FG%	FT%	RBs	Ast	Pts	Avg
Aguirre	2663	.495	.770	427	254	2056	25.7
Blackman	2758	.495	.884	278	266	1676	21.0
Harper	2556	.501	.684	199	609	1230	16.0
Perkins	2687	.482	.828	616	146	1186	14.8
Donaldson	3028	.586	.812	973	63	889	10.8
Schrempf	1711	.472	.742	303	161	756	9.3
Tarpley	1405	.467	.676	533	52	561	7.5
Davis	1582	.456	.860	114	373	577	7.0
Wood	657	.390	.784	94	34	358	6.6
Wennington	560	.424	.750	129	24	157	2.7

Denver Nuggets

	Min	FG%	FT%	RBs	Ast	Pts	Avg
English	3085	.503	.844	344	422	2345	28.6
Lever	3054	.469	.782	729	654	1552	18.9
Hanzlic	1990	.412	.786	256	280	952	13.0
Walker	2020	.482	.745	327	282	988	12.2
Evans	1567	.458	.780	128	185	817	10.1
Rasmussen	1421	.470	.782	465	60	705	9.5
Schayes	1556	.519	.779	380	85	649	8.5
Cooper	1561	.448	.725	473	68	549	8.0
Alarie	1110	.490	.663	214	74	503	7.9
Dunn	1932	.428	.655	265	147	272	3.4

Detroit Pistons

	Min	FG%	FT%	RBs	Ast	Pts	Avg
Dantley	2736	.534	.812	332	162	1742	21.5
Thomas	3013	.463	.768	319	813	1671	20.6
Johnson	2166	.462	.786	257	300	1228	15.7
Laimbeer	2854	.501	.894	955	151	1263	15.4
Dumars	2439	.493	.748	167	352	931	11.8
Green	1792	.472	.672	653	62	631	7.9
Rodman	1155	.545	.587	332	56	500	6.5
Mahorn	1278	.447	.821	375	38	384	6.1
Nimphius	1088	.470	.675	187	25	391	5.9
Salley	1463	.562	.614	296	54	431	5.3

Golden State Warriors

	Min	FG%	FT%	RBs	Ast	Pts	Avg
Carroll	2724	.472	.787	589	214	1720	21.2
Floyd	3064	.488	.860	268	848	1541	18.8
Short	950	.479	.856	137	86	621	18.3
Mullin	2377	.514	.825	181	261	1242	15.1
Teagle	1650	.458	.778	175	105	922	11.2
L. Smith	2374	.546	.574	917	95	707	8.8
Higgins	1497	.519	.833	237	96	631	8.6
Ballard	1579	.440	.747	340	108	579	7.1
McDonald	1284	.456	.632	183	84	353	5.6
Whitehead	937	.450	.690	262	24	373	5.1
Moss	698	.440	.710	95	90	232	3.6

Houston Rockets

	Min	FG%	FT%	RBs	Ast	Pts	Avg
Olajuwon	2760	.508	.702	858	220	1755	23.4
Sampson	1326	.489	.624	372	120	672	15.6
McCray	3136	.552	.779	578	434	1170	14.4
Reid	2594	.417	.768	289	323	1029	13.7
Lloyd	688	.532	.756	48	90	396	12.4
Petersen	2403	.511	.727	557	127	924	11.3
Wiggins	788	.437	.754	133	76	355	11.1
Maxwell	1968	.530	.775	435	197	809	10.0
Harris	1174	.419	.854	170	100	613	8.3
Leavell	1175	.411	.840	61	224	412	7.8
Minniefield	1600	.452	.689	140	348	509	6.9
Johnson	520	.468	.690	88	40	228	3.8

Indiana Pacers

	Min	FG%	FT%	RBs	Ast	Pts	Avg
Person	2956	.468	.747	677	295	1541	18.8
Long	2265	.419	.890	217	258	1218	15.2
Williams	2526	.480	.740	543	174	1101	14.9
Tisdale	2159	.513	.709	475	117	1174	14.5
Stipanovich	2761	.503	.837	670	180	1072	13.2
Fleming	2549	.509	.788	334	473	980	12.0
Richardson	1396	.467	.797	143	241	501	6.4
Anderson	721	.473	.787	151	54	363	5.8
Macy	1250	.481	.829	113	197	376	4.9
Russell	511	.388	.730	55	129	157	3.3

Los Angeles Clippers

	Min	FG%	FT%	RBs	Ast	Pts	Avg
Woodson	2126	.437	.828	162	196	1262	17.1
Cage	2922	.521	.730	922	131	1255	15.7
Drew	1566	.432	.837	103	326	741	12.4
Benjamin	2230	.449	.715	586	135	828	11.5
Valentine	1759	.410	.815	150	447	726	11.2
Dailey	924	.407	.768	83	79	520	10.6
White	1545	.480	.653	194	79	624	9.2
Fields	883	.452	.777	148	61	394	8.2
Gordon	1130	.406	.737	126	139	526	7.5
Cureton	1973	.476	.539	452	122	568	7.3
Kempton	936	.471	.693	194	53	289	4.4

Los Angeles Lakers

	Min	FG%	FT%	RBs	Ast	Pts	Avg
Johnson	2904	.522	.848	504	977	1909	23.9
Worthy	2819	.539	.751	466	226	1594	19.4
Abdul-Jabbar	2441	.564	.714	523	203	1366	17.5
Scott	2729	.489	.892	286	281	1397	17.0

(continued)

	Min	FG%	FT%	RBs	Ast	Pts	Avg
M. Thompson	1890	.450	.737	412	115	938	11.4
Green	2240	.538	.780	615	84	852	10.8
Cooper	2253	.438	.851	254	373	859	10.5
Rambis	1514	.521	.764	453	63	446	5.7
B. Thompson	762	.544	.649	171	60	332	5.6
Matthews	532	.476	.806	47	100	208	4.2

Milwaukee Bucks

	Min	FG%	FT%	RBs	Ast	Pts	Avg
Cummings	2770	.511	.662	700	229	1707	20.8
Pierce	2505	.534	.880	266	144	1540	19.5
Lucas	1358	.457	.787	125	290	753	17.5
Pressey	2057	.477	.738	296	441	846	13.9
Sikma	2536	.463	.847	822	203	1045	12.7
Moncrief	992	.488	.840	127	121	460	11.8
Hodges	2147	.462	.891	140	240	846	10.8
Breuer	1467	.485	.584	350	47	600	7.9
Reynolds	963	.393	.641	173	106	404	7.0
Bradley	900	.357	.810	102	66	212	3.1
Mokeski	626	.403	.719	138	22	150	2.4

New Jersey Nets

	Min	FG%	FT%	RBs	Ast	Pts	Avg
Woolridge	2638	.521	.777	367	261	1551	20.7
B. Williams	2976	.557	.731	1023	129	1472	18.0
Gminski	2272	.457	.846	630	99	1179	16.4
Brown	2339	.442	.738	219	259	873	11.3
R. Williams	800	.452	.817	75	185	318	9.9
King	1291	.426	.810	214	103	582	9.5
Washington	1600	.478	.784	129	301	616	8.6
Bailey	542	.469	.725	137	20	282	8.3
Wood	1733	.373	.799	120	370	557	7.3
McKenna	942	.454	.754	77	93	401	7.2
Coleman	1029	.581	.727	288	37	452	6.6
Turner	1003	.465	.731	197	60	378	5.0

New York Knickerbockers

	Min	FG%	FT%	RBs	Ast	Pts	Avg
Ewing	2206	.503	.713	555	104	1356	21.5
G. Wilkins	2758	.486	.701	294	354	1527	19.1
Cartwright	1989	.531	.790	445	96	1016	17.5
Tucker	1691	.470	.762	135	166	795	11.4
Henderson	2045	.442	.826	175	471	805	10.9
Walker	1719	.491	.757	338	75	710	10.4
Cummings	1056	.450	.718	312	38	423	8.6
Sparrow	1951	.446	.798	115	432	608	7.6
Orr	1440	.427	.727	232	110	458	7.0
Oldham	776	.408	.544	179	19	173	3.9
McNealy	972	.492	.650	227	46	228	3.9

Philadelphia 76ers

	Min	FG%	FT%	RBs	Ast	Pts	Avg
Barkley	2740	.594	.761	994	331	1564	23.0
Erving	1918	.471	.813	264	191	1005	16.8
Cheeks	2624	.527	.777	215	538	1061	15.6
Robinson	1586	.464	.755	307	89	815	14.8
Hinson	2489	.478	.758	488	60	1059	13.9
McCormick	2817	.545	.719	611	114	1033	12.8
Toney	1058	.451	.796	85	188	549	10.6
Wingate	1612	.430	.741	156	155	680	8.8
Colter	1322	.426	.766	108	210	424	6.1
Vranes	817	.428	.467	146	30	140	2.4

Phoenix Suns

	Min	FG%	FT%	RBs	Ast	Pts	Avg
Davis	2646	.514	.862	244	364	1867	23.6
Nance	2569	.551	.773	599	233	1552	22.5
Humphries	2579	.477	.769	260	632	923	11.3
Adams	1690	.503	.788	338	223	756	11.1
Sanders	1655	.494	.781	271	126	859	10.5
Pinckney	2250	.584	.739	580	116	837	10.5
Bedford	979	.397	.581	246	57	334	6.7
Addison	711	.441	.797	106	45	359	5.8
Gondrezick	836	.450	.701	110	81	349	5.5
Hornacek	1561	.454	.777	184	361	424	5.3
Gattison	1104	.476	.632	270	36	404	5.2
Vanos	640	.411	.644	180	43	168	2.9

Portland Trail Blazers

	Min	FG%	FT%	RBs	Ast	Pts	Avg
Vandeweghe	3029	.523	.886	251	220	2122	26.9
Drexler	3114	.502	.760	518	566	1782	21.7
Johnson	2345	.556	.698	566	155	1330	16.8
Porter	2714	.488	.838	337	715	1045	13.1
Kersey	2088	.509	.720	496	194	1009	12.3
Paxson	1798	.460	.806	139	237	874	12.1
Carr	1443	.504	.746	499	83	528	10.8
Duckworth	875	.476	.687	223	29	352	5.4
Jones	1578	.496	.782	455	64	319	4.1

Sacramento Kings

	Min	FG%	FT%	RBs	Ast	Pts	Avg
Theus	2872	.472	.867	266	692	1600	20.3
Thorpe	2956	.540	.761	819	201	1547	18.9
Johnson	2457	.463	.829	353	251	1516	18.7
Smith	1658	.447	.781	182	204	863	16.6
Thompson	2166	.481	.737	687	122	912	11.1
Tyler	1930	.495	.721	328	73	760	9.3
Kleine	1658	.471	.786	483	71	622	7.9
Steppe	665	.477	.830	61	81	266	7.8
Pressley	913	.423	.729	176	120	310	4.6
Wilson	789	.443	.796	81	207	210	4.0
Olberding	1002	.418	.885	185	91	254	3.3

San Antonio Spurs

	Min	FG%	FT%	RBs	Ast	Pts	Avg
Robertson	2697	.466	.753	424	421	1435	17.7
Berry	1586	.531	.649	309	105	1001	15.9
Mitchell	922	.435	.821	103	38	509	12.7
Thompson	1210	.436	.735	276	87	605	12.3
Greenwood	2587	.513	.785	783	237	916	11.6
Gilmore	2405	.597	.680	579	150	934	11.4
Sundvold	1765	.486	.833	98	315	850	11.2
Dawkins	1682	.437	.801	169	290	835	10.3
Corbin	732	.428	.731	119	80	275	8.9
Moore	1234	.442	.800	100	250	474	8.6
Krystkowiak	1004	.456	.743	239	85	451	6.6
Jones	858	.413	.769	104	73	323	5.0
Nealy	980	.438	.739	284	83	223	3.7

Seattle SuperSonics

	Min	FG%	FT%	RBs	Ast	Pts	Avg
Ellis	3073	.516	.787	447	238	2041	24.9
Chambers	3018	.456	.849	545	245	1909	23.3
McDaniel	3031	.509	.696	705	207	1890	23.0
Lister	2288	.504	.675	705	110	871	11.6
E. Johnson	508	.457	.764	46	115	217	9.0
Lucas	1120	.451	.802	307	65	500	7.9
McMillan	1972	.475	.617	331	583	373	5.3
Williams	703	.446	.833	83	66	319	4.9
Young	1482	.458	.831	113	353	352	4.8
C. Johnson	1051	.494	.636	277	21	246	3.2
Schoene	579	.374	.630	117	27	173	2.7

Utah Jazz

	Min	FG%	FT%	RBs	Ast	Pts	Avg
Malone	2857	.512	.598	855	158	1779	21.7
Griffith	1843	.446	.703	227	129	1142	15.0
Bailey	2155	.447	.805	432	102	1116	13.8
Tripucka	1865	.469	.872	242	243	798	10.1
Hansen	1453	.453	.760	203	102	696	9.7
Green	2090	.467	.827	163	541	781	9.6
Stockton	1858	.499	.782	151	670	648	7.9
Eaton	2505	.400	.657	697	105	608	7.7
Scurry	753	.498	.701	198	57	344	5.0
Curry	636	.426	.789	78	58	325	4.9
Benson	895	.443	.810	231	39	329	4.5
Iavaroni	845	.465	.672	173	36	278	3.6

Washington Bullets

	Min	FG%	FT%	RBs	Ast	Pts	Avg
M. Malone	2488	.454	.824	824	120	1760	24.1
J. Malone	2763	.457	.885	218	298	1758	22.0
Vincent	1386	.447	.769	210	85	678	13.3
Catledge	2149	.495	.594	560	56	1025	13.1
Williams	1773	.454	.646	366	191	718	9.2
Whatley	1816	.478	.764	194	392	618	8.5
Cook	1420	.426	.796	145	151	614	7.5
Adams	1303	.407	.847	123	244	453	7.2
Roundfield	669	.409	.792	170	39	238	6.6
C. Jones	1609	.474	.632	356	80	284	3.6
Bol	1552	.446	.672	362	11	251	3.1

NBA Most Valuable Player

1956	Bob Pettit, St. Louis
1957	Bob Cousy, Boston
1958	Bill Russell, Boston
1959	Bob Pettit, St. Louis
1960	Wilt Chamberlain, Philadelphia
1961	Bill Russell, Boston
1962	Bill Russell, Boston
1963	Bill Russell, Boston
1964	Oscar Robertson, Cincinnati
1965	Bill Russell, Boston
1966	Wilt Chamberlain, Philadelphia
1967	Wilt Chamberlain, Philadelphia
1968	Wilt Chamberlain, Philadelphia
1969	Wes Unseld, Baltimore
1970	Willis Reed, New York
1971	Lew Alcindor, Milwaukee
1972	Kareem Abdul-Jabbar (Alcindor), Milwaukee
1973	Dave Cowens, Boston
1974	Kareem Abdul-Jabbar, Milwaukee
1975	Bob McAdoo, Buffalo
1976	Kareem Abdul-Jabbar, Los Angeles
1977	Kareem Abdul-Jabbar, Los Angeles
1978	Bill Walton, Portland
1979	Moses Malone, Houston
1980	Kareem Abdul-Jabbar, Los Angeles
1981	Julius Erving, Philadelphia
1982	Moses Malone, Houston
1983	Moses Malone, Philadelphia
1984	Larry Bird, Boston
1985	Larry Bird, Boston
1986	Larry Bird, Boston
1987	Magic Johnson, L.A. Lakers

MVP in Playoffs

1969	Jerry West, Los Angeles
1970	Willis Reed, New York
1971	Lew Alcindor, Milwaukee
1972	Wilt Chamberlain, Los Angeles
1973	Willis Reed, New York
1974	John Havlicek, Boston
1975	Rick Barry, Golden State
1976	Jo Jo White, Boston
1977	Bill Walton, Portland
1978	Wes Unseld, Washington
1979	Dennis Johnson, Seattle
1980	Magic Johnson, Los Angeles
1981	Cedric Maxwell, Boston
1982	Magic Johnson, Los Angeles
1983	Moses Malone, Philadelphia
1984	Larry Bird, Boston
1985	Kareem Abdul-Jabbar, L.A. Lakers
1986	Larry Bird, Boston
1987	Magic Johnson, L.A. Lakers

NBA All League Team in 1987

First team	Position	Second team
Larry Bird, Boston	Forward	Charles Barkley, Philadelphia
Kevin McHale, Boston	Forward	Dominique Wilkins, Atlanta
Akeem Olajuwon, Houston	Center	Moses Malone, Washington
Magic Johnson, L.A. Lakers	Guard	Islah Thomas, Detroit
Michael Jordan, Chicago	Guard	Lafayette Lever, Denver

NBA All-Defensive Team in 1987

First team	Position	Second team
Michael Cooper, L.A. Lakers	Forward	Paul Pressey, Milwaukee
Kevin McHale, Boston	Forward	Rodney McCray, Houston
Akeem Olajuwon, Houston	Center	Mark Eaton, Utah
Alvin Robertson, San Antonio	Guard	Derek Harper, Dallas
Dennis Johnson, Boston	Guard	Maurice Cheeks, Philadelphia

Individuals in The Basketball Hall of Fame

Springfield, Mass.

Players
Arizin, Paul
Barry, Rick
Baylor, Elgin
Beckman, John
Borgmann, Bennie
Bradley, Bill
Brennan, Joseph
Barlow, Thomas
Cervi, Al
Chamberlain, Wilt
Cooper, Charles
Cousy, Bob
Cunningham, Billy
Davies, Bob
DeBernardi, Forrest
DeBusschere, Dave
Dehnert, Dutch
Endacott, Paul
Foster, Bud
Frazier, Walt
Friedman, Max
Fulks, Joe
Gale, Lauren
Gola, Tom
Greer, Hal
Gruenig, Ace
Hagan, Cliff
Hanson, Victor
Havlicek, John
Heinsohn, Tom
Holman, Nat
Houbregs, Bob
Hyatt, Chuck
Johnson, William
Jones, Sam
Krause, Moose
Kurland, Bob
Lapchick, Joe
Lucas, Jerry
Luisetti, Hank
Maravich, Pete
Martin, Slater
McCracken, Branch
McCracken, Jack
Macauley, Ed
Mikan, George
Murphy, Stretch
Page, Pat
Pettit, Bob
Phillip, Andy
Pollard, Jim
Ramsey, Frank
Reed, Willis
Robertson, Oscar
Roosma, John S.
Russell, Honey
Russell, Bill
Schayes, Adolph
Schmidt, Ernest
Schommer, John
Sedran, Barney
Sharman, Bill
Steinmetz, Christian
Thompson, Cat
Thurmond, Nate
Twyman, Jack
Vandivier, Fuzzy
Wachter, Edward
Wanzer, Bobby
West, Jerry
Wooden, John

Coaches
Auerbach, Red
Barry, Sam
Blood, Ernest
Cann, Howard
Carlson, Dr. H. C.
Carnevale, Ben
Case, Everett
Dean, Everett
Diddle, Edgar
Drake, Bruce
Gaines, Clarence
Gardner, Jack
Gill, Slats
Hickey, Edgar
Hobson, Howard
Holzman, Red
Iba, Hank
Julian, Alvin
Keaney, Frank
Keogan, George
Lambert, Ward
Litwack, Harry
Loeffler, Kenneth
Lonborg, Dutch
McCutchan, Arad
McGuire, Frank
McLendon, John
Meyer, Ray
Meanwell, Dr. W.E.
Newell, Pete
Rupp, Adolph
Sachs, Leonard
Shelton, Everett
Smith, Dean
Taylor, Fred
Teague, Bertha
Wade, Margaret
Watts, Stan
Wooden, John

Referees
Enright, James
Hepbron, George
Hoyt, George
Kennedy, Matthew
Leith, Lloyd
Mihalik, Red
Nucatola, John
Quigley, Ernest
Shirley, J. Dallas
Tobey, David
Walsh, David

Contributors
Abbott, Senda B.
Allen, Phog
Bee, Clair
Brown, Walter
Bunn, John
Douglas, Bob
Duer, Al O.
Fagan, Cliff
Fisher, Harry
Gottlieb, Edward
Gulick, Dr. L. H.
Harrison, Lester
Hepp, Dr. Ferenc
Hickox, Edward
Hinkle, Tony
Irish, Ned
Jones, R. W.
Kennedy, Walter
Liston, Emil
Mokray, Bill
Morgan, Ralph
Morgenweck, Frank
Naismith, Dr. James
O'Brien, John
Olsen, Harold
Podoloff, Maurice
Porter, H. V.
Reis, William
Ripley, Elmer
St. John, Lynn
Saperstein, Abe
Schabinger, Arthur
Stagg, Amos Alonzo
Steitz, Edward
Taylor, Chuck
Tower, Oswald
Trester, Arthur
Wells, Clifford
Wilke, Lou

Professional Sports Directory

Baseball

Commissioner's Office
350 Park Ave.
New York, NY 10022

National League

National League Office
350 Park Ave.
New York, NY 10022

Atlanta Braves
PO Box 4064
Atlanta, GA 30302

Chicago Cubs
Wrigley Field
Chicago, IL 60613

Cincinnati Reds
100 Riverfront Stadium
Cincinnati, OH 45202

Houston Astros
Astrodome
Houston, TX 77001

Los Angeles Dodgers
Dodger Stadium
Los Angeles, CA 90012

Montreal Expos
PO Box 500, Station M
Montreal, Que. H1V 3P2

New York Mets
Shea Stadium
Flushing, NY 11368

Philadelphia Phillies
PO Box 7575
Philadelphia, PA 19101

Pittsburgh Pirates
Three Rivers Stadium
Pittsburgh, PA 15212

St. Louis Cardinals
Busch Stadium
St. Louis, MO 63102

San Diego Padres
PO Box 2000
San Diego, CA 92120

San Francisco Giants
Candlestick Park
San Francisco, CA 94124

American League

American League Office
350 Park Ave.
New York, NY 10022

Baltimore Orioles
Memorial Stadium
Baltimore, MD 21218

Boston Red Sox
4 Yawkey Way
Boston, MA 02215

California Angels
Anaheim Stadium
Anaheim, CA 92806

Chicago White Sox
324 W. 35th St.
Chicago, IL 60616

Cleveland Indians
Cleveland Stadium
Cleveland, OH 44114

Detroit Tigers
Tiger Stadium
Detroit, MI 48216

Kansas City Royals
1 Royal Way
Kansas City, MO 64129

Milwaukee Brewers
Milwaukee County Stadium
Milwaukee, WI 53214

Minnesota Twins
501 Chicago Ave. South
Minneapolis, MN 55415

New York Yankees
Yankee Stadium
Bronx, NY 10451

Oakland A's
Oakland Coliseum
Oakland, CA 94621

Seattle Mariners
P.O. Box 4100
Seattle, WA 98104

Texas Rangers
1250 Copeland Rd.
Arlington, TX 76010

Toronto Blue Jays
Box 7777
Adelaide St. PO
Toronto, Ont. M5C 2K7

National Football League

League Office
410 Park Avenue
Now York, NY 10022

Atlanta Falcons
Suwanee Road
Suwanee, GA 30174

Buffalo Bills
1 Bills Drive
Orchard Park, NY 14127

Chicago Bears
250 N. Washington
Lake Forest, IL 60045

Cincinnati Bengals
200 Riverfront Stadium
Cincinnati, OH 45202

Cleveland Browns
Cleveland Stadium
Cleveland, OH 44114

Dallas Cowboys
One Cowboys Pkwy.
Irving, TX 75063

Denver Broncos
5700 Logan St.
Denver, CO 80216

Detroit Lions
1200 Featherstone Rd.
Pontiac, MI 48057

Green Bay Packers
1265 Lombardi Ave.
Green Bay, WI 54307

Houston Oilers
P.O. Box 1516
Houston, TX 77001

Indianapolis Colts
P.O. Box 24100
Indianapolis, IN 46224

Kansas City Chiefs
1 Arrowhead Drive
Kansas City, MO 64129

Los Angeles Raiders
332 Center St.
El Segundo, CA 90245

Los Angeles Rams
2327 W. Lincoln Ave.
Anaheim, CA 92801

Miami Dolphins
4770 Biscayne Blvd.
Miami, FL 33137

Minnesota Vikings
9520 Viking Dr.
Eden Prairie, MN 55344

New England Patriots
Sullivan Stadium
Foxboro, MA 02035

New Orleans Saints
1500 Poydras St.
New Orleans, LA 70112

New York Giants
Giants Stadium
E. Rutherford, NJ 07073

New York Jets
598 Madison Ave.
New York, NY 10022

Philadelphia Eagles
Veterans Stadium
Philadelphia, PA 19148

Pittsburgh Steelers
Three Rivers Stadium
Pittsburgh, PA 15212

St. Louis Cardinals
Busch Stadium
St. Louis, MO 63188

San Diego Chargers
P.O. Box 20666
San Diego, CA 92120

San Francisco 49ers
711 Nevada St.
Redwood City, CA 94061

Seattle Seahawks
11220 NE 53d St.
Kirkland, WA 98033

Tampa Bay Buccaneers
1 Buccaneer Place
Tampa, FL 33607

Washington Redskins
PO Box 17247
Dulles Intl. Airport
Washington, DC 20041

National Basketball Association

League Office
645 5th Ave.
New York, NY 10022

Atlanta Hawks
100 Techwood Drive NW
Atlanta, GA 30303

Boston Celtics
Boston Garden
Boston, MA 02114

Chicago Bulls
980 North Michigan Ave.
Chicago, IL 60611

Cleveland Cavaliers
2923 Statesboro Rd.
Richfield, OH 44286

Dallas Mavericks
777 Sports St.
Dallas, TX 75207

Denver Nuggets
1635 Clay St.
Denver, CO 80204

Detroit Pistons
1200 Featherstone
Pontiac, MI 48057

Golden State Warriors
Oakland Coliseum
Oakland, CA 94621

Houston Rockets
The Summit
Houston, TX 77046

Indiana Pacers
2 W. Washington St.
Indianapolis, IN 46204

Los Angeles Clippers
3939 Figueroa
Los Angeles, CA 90037

Los Angeles Lakers
PO Box 10
Inglewood, CA 90306

Milwaukee Bucks
901 North 4th St.
Milwaukee, WI 53203

New Jersey Nets
Meadowlands Arena
E. Rutherford, NJ 07073

New York Knickerbockers
4 Pennsylvania Plaza
New York, NY 10001

Philadelphia 76ers
PO Box 25040
Philadelphia, PA 19147

Phoenix Suns
2910 N. Central
Phoenix, AZ 85012

Portland Trail Blazers
700 NE Multnomah St.
Portland, OR 97232

Sacramento Kings
1515 Sports Dr.
Sacramento, CA 95834

San Antonio Spurs
P.O. Box 530
San Antonio, TX 78292

Seattle SuperSonics
190 Queen Ann Ave. N.
Seattle, WA 98109

Utah Jazz
5 Triad Center
Salt Lake City, UT 84180

Washington Bullets
Capital Centre
Landover, MD 20785

National Hockey League

League Headquarters
Sun Life Bldg.
Montreal, Quebec H3B 2W2

Boston Bruins
150 Causeway St.
Boston, MA 02114

Buffalo Sabres
Memorial Auditorium
Buffalo, NY 14202

Calgary Flames
P.O. Box 1540
Calgary, Alta. T2P 3B9

Chicago Black Hawks
1800 W. Madison St.
Chicago, IL 60612

Detroit Red Wings
600 Civic Center Drive
Detroit, MI 48226

Edmonton Oilers
Northlands Coliseum
Edmonton, Alta. T5B 4M9

Hartford Whalers
One Civic Center Plaza
Hartford, CT 06103

Los Angeles Kings
PO Box 10
Inglewood, CA 90306

Minnesota North Stars
7901 Cedar Ave. S.
Bloomington, MN 55420

Montreal Canadiens
2313 St. Catherine St., West
Montreal, Quebec H3H 1N2

New Jersey Devils
Meadowlands Arena
E. Rutherford, NJ 07073

New York Islanders
Nassau Coliseum
Uniondale, NY 11553

New York Rangers
4 Pennsylvania Plaza
New York, NY 10001

Philadelphia Flyers
Pattison Place
Philadelphia, PA 19148

Pittsburgh Penguins
Civic Arena
Pittsburgh, PA 15219

Quebec Nordiques
2205 Ave. du Colisee
Quebec, Que. G1L 4W7

St. Louis Blues
5700 Oakland Ave.
St. Louis, MO 63110

Toronto Maple Leafs
60 Carlton St.
Toronto, Ont. M5B 1L1

Vancouver Canucks
100 North Renfrew St.
Vancouver, B.C. V5K 3N7

Washington Capitals
Capital Centre
Landover, MD 20785

Winnipeg Jets
15-1430 Maroons Road
Winnipeg, Man. R3G 0L5

Bowling

Leading PBA Averages in 1986

(400 or more games in PBA tournaments)

Name	Games	Average	Name	Games	Average	Name	Games	Average
John Gant	751	214.378	Brian Voss	959	212.733	Ron Palombi Jr.	803	212.103
Dave Husted	1,046	213.917	Marshall Holman	856	212.521	Mats Karlsson	711	212.091
Walter Ray Williams Jr.	998	213.837	Marc McDowell	580	212.333	Pete Weber	881	212.044
David Ozio	849	213.086	Mark Roth	722	212.925	Mark Baker	759	211.779
Amleto Monacelli	851	212.806	Dave Ferraro	701	212.185	Mike Aulby	689	211.562

PBA Leading Money Winners

Total winnings are from PBA, ABC Masters, and BPAA All-Star tournaments only, and do not include numerous other tournaments or earnings from special television shows and matches.

Year	Bowler	Dollars	Year	Bowler	Dollars	Year	Bowler	Dollars
1960	Don Carter	22,525	1969	Billy Hardwick	64,160	1978	Mark Roth	134,500
1961	Dick Weber	26,280	1970	Mike McGrath	52,049	1979	Mark Roth	124,517
1962	Don Carter	49,972	1971	Johnny Petraglia	85,065	1980	Wayne Webb	116,700
1963	Dick Weber	46,333	1972	Don Johnson	56,648	1981	Earl Anthony	164,735
1964	Bob Strampe	33,592	1973	Don McCune	69,000	1982	Earl Anthony	134,760
1965	Dick Weber	47,674	1974	Earl Anthony	99,585	1983	Earl Anthony	135,605
1966	Wayne Zahn	54,720	1975	Earl Anthony	107,585	1984	Mark Roth	158,712
1967	Dave Davis	54,165	1976	Earl Anthony	110,833	1985	Mike Aulby	201,200
1968	Jim Stefanich	67,377	1977	Mark Roth	105,583	1986	Walter Ray Williams Jr.	145,550

Leading PBA Averages by Year

Year	Bowler	Average	Year	Bowler	Average	Year	Bowler	Average
1962	Don Carter	212.844	1971	Don Johnson	213.977	1980	Earl Anthony	218.535
1963	Billy Hardwick	210.346	1972	Don Johnson	215.290	1981	Mark Roth	216.699
1964	Ray Bluth	210.512	1973	Earl Anthony	215.799	1982	Marshall Holman	212.844
1965	Dick Weber	211.895	1974	Earl Anthony	219.394	1983	Earl Anthony	216.645
1966	Wayne Zahn	208.663	1975	Earl Anthony	219.060	1984	Marshall Holman	213.911
1967	Wayne Zahn	212.342	1976	Mark Roth	215.970	1985	Mark Baker	213.718
1968	Jim Stefanich	211.895	1977	Mark Roth	218.174	1986	John Gant	214.378
1969	Bill Hardwick	212.957	1978	Mark Roth	219.834			
1970	Nelson Burton Jr.	214.908	1979	Mark Roth	221.662			

Firestone Tournament of Champions

This is professional bowling's richest tournament and has been held each year since its inception in 1965, in Akron, Oh., the home of the Professional Bowlers Association.

Year	Winner	Year	Winner	Year	Winner	Year	Winner
1965	Billy Hardwick	1971	Johnny Petraglia	1977	Mike Berlin	1983	Joe Berardi
1966	Wayne Zahn	1972	Mike Durbin	1978	Earl Anthony	1984	Mike Durbin
1967	Jim Stefanich	1973	Jim Godman	1979	George Pappas	1985	Mark Williams
1968	Dave Davis	1974	Earl Anthony	1980	Wayne Webb	1986	Marshall Holman
1969	Jim Godman	1975	Dave Davis	1981	Steve Cook	1987	Pete Weber
1970	Don Johnson	1976	Marshall Holman	1982	Mike Durbin		

PBA Hall of Fame

Performance
Bill Allen
Glenn Allison
Earl Anthony
Ray Bluth
Nelson Burton Jr.
Don Carter
Dave Davis
Mike Durbin
Buzz Fazio
Jim Godman
Johnny Guenther
Billy Hardwick
Don Johnson
Larry Laub
George Pappas
Johnny Petraglia
Dick Ritger
Mark Roth
Carmen Salvino
Bob Strampe
Harry Smith
Dave Soutar
Jim Stefanich
Dick Weber
Billy Welu
Wayne Zahn

Meritorious service
Eddie Elias
Frank Esposito
Dick Evans
Raymond Firestone
E. A. "Bud" Fisher
Lou Frantz
Harry Golden
Ted Hoffman Jr.
Joe Joseph
Steve Nagy
Chuck Pezzano
Joe Richards
Chris Schenkel
Lorraine Stilzlein

American Bowling Congress Championships in 1987

84th Tournament, Niagara Falls, N.Y.

Regular Division

Individual—Terry Taylor, Nashville, Tenn., 749.
All Events—Ryan Shafer, Elmira, N.Y., 2,044.
Doubles—Ray Betchkal & Dennis Schlichting, Racine, Wis., 1,380.
Team—Sound Track, Salamanca, N.Y., 3,197.

Booster Division

Team—DeFazio's Stadium Grill #2, Niagara Falls, N.Y. 2,794.

Masters Bowling Tournament Champions

Year	Winner	Year	Winner	Year	Winner
1977	Earl Anthony, Tacoma, Wash.	1981	Randy Lightfoot, St. Charles, Mo.	1985	Steve Wunderlich, St. Louis, Mo.
1978	Frank Ellenburg, Mesa, Ariz.	1982	Joe Berardi, Brooklyn, N.Y.	1986	Mark Fahy, Chicago, Ill.
1979	Doug Myers, El Toro, Cal.	1983	Mike Lastowski, Havre de Grace, Md.	1987	Rick Steelsmith, Wichita, Kan.
1980	Neil Burton, St. Louis, Mo.	1984	Earl Anthony, Dublin, Cal.		

All-Time Records for League and Tournament Play

Type of record	Holder of record	Year	Score	Competition
High team total	Budweiser Beer, St. Louis	1958	3,858	League
High team game	Concept III, Philadelphia, Pa.	1987	1,374	League
High doubles total	Bob Perry & Mike Foti, Lodi, N.J.	1986	1,639	Tournament
High doubles game	John Cotta and Steve Larson, Manteca, Cal.	1981	600	Tournament
High individual total	Albert Brandt, Lockport, N.Y.	1939	886	League
High all events score	Paul Andrews, East Moline, Ill.	1981	2,415	Tournament

Bowlers with 15 or More Sanctioned 300 Games

Elvin Mesger, Sullivan, Mo.	27
John Wilcox Jr., Shavertown, Pa.	25
Ron Woolet, Louisville, Ky.	24
Teata Semiz, Fairfield, N.J.	21
Tony Torrice, Wolcott, Conn.	21
Mark Stibora, Cleveland, Oh.	20
Dave Soutar, Kansas City, Mo.	19
Mitch Jabczenski, Detroit, Mich.	18
Dick Weber, St. Louis, Mo.	18
George Billick, Old Forge, Pa.	17
Steve Carson, Oklahoma City, Okla	17
Dave Williams, Sebastopal, Cal.	17
Len Holmquist, Wilmington, Del.	15
Dave Davis, Tinton Falls, N.J.	15
Ronnie Graham, Louisville, Ky.	15
Don Johnson, Las Vegas, Nev.	15

Women's International Bowling Congress Champions in 1987

Individual—Regi Jonak, St. Peters, Mo., 728.
All Events—Leanne Barrette, Oklahoma City, Okla., 1,972.
Doubles—Laura Grant, Norwalk, Conn. & Robin Romeo, Van Nuys, Cal., 1,328.
Team—Tool Warehouse, Hollywood, Fla., 3,003.

Most Sanctioned 300 Games

Jeanne Maiden, Solon, Oh.	11
Betty Morris, Stockton, Cal.	8
Donna Adamek, Duarte, Cal.	7
Tish Johnson, Downey, Cal.	6
Toni Gillard, Beverly, Oh.	6
Vicki Fischel, Westminster, Col.	6
Alayne Blomenberg, Cranston, R.I.	5
Pam Buckner, Reno, Nev.	5
Cindy Coburn, Tonawanda, N.Y.	5
Regi Jonak, St. Peters, Mo.	5
Ann Marie Pike, Cypress, Cal.	5
Carol Norman, Ardmore, Okla.	5
Voli Brandt, Lee's Summit, Mo.	4
Beverly Ortner, Tucson, Ariz.	4
Judith Seckel, Florissant, Mo.	4
Debbie Timberlake, Blue Springs, Mo.	4
Linda Kelly, Union, Oh.	4
Rose Kotnik, Brook Park, Oh.	4
Robin Romeo, Van Nuys, Cal.	4

World Swimming Records

As of Sept., 1987

Men's Records

Freestyle

Distance	Time	Holder	Country	Where made	Date
50 Meters	0:22.32	Tom Jager	U.S.	Brisbane	Aug. 13, 1987
100 Meters	0:48.74	Matt Biondi	U.S.	Orlando, Fla.	June 24, 1986
200 Meters	1:47.44	Michael Gross	W. Germany	Munich	July 30, 1984
400 Meters	3:47.80	Michael Gross	W. Germany	W. Germany	June 27, 1985
800 Meters	7:50.64	Vladimir Salnikov	USSR	Moscow	July 4, 1986
1,500 Meters	14:54.76	Vladimir Salnikov	USSR	Moscow	Feb. 22, 1983

Breaststroke

Distance	Time	Holder	Country	Where made	Date
100 Meters	1:01.65	Steve Lundquist	U.S.	Los Angeles	July 9, 1984
200 Meters	2:13.34	Victor Davis	Canada	Los Angeles	Aug. 2, 1984

Butterfly

Distance	Time	Holder	Country	Where made	Date
100 Meters	0:52.84	Pablo Morales	U.S.	Orlando, Fla.	June 23, 1986
200 Meters	1:56.24	Michael Gross	W. Germany	Bonn, W. Germany	June 24, 1986

Backstroke

Distance	Time	Holder	Country	Where made	Date
100 Meters	0:55.19	Rick Carey	U.S.	Caracas	Aug. 21, 1983
200 Meters	1:58.14	Igor Polianskiy	USSR	Erfurt, E. Germany	Mar. 3, 1985

Individual Medley

Distance	Time	Holder	Country	Where made	Date
200 Meters	2:00.56	Tamas Darnyi	Hungary	Strasbourg, France	Aug., 1987
400 Meters	4:12.42	Tamas Darnyi	Hungary	Strasbourg, France	Aug., 1987

Freestyle Relays

Distance	Time	Holder	Country	Where made	Date
400 M. (4×100)	3:17.08	McCadam, Heath, Wallace, Biondi	U.S.	Tokyo	Aug. 17, 1985
800 M. (4×200)	7:13.10	Sitt, Henkel, Fahrner, Gross	W. Germany	Strasbourg, France	Aug., 1987

Medley Relays

Distance	Time	Holder	Country	Where made	Date
400 M. (4×100)	3:38.28	Carey, Moffet, Morales, Biondi	U.S.	Tokyo	Aug. 18, 1985

Women's Records

Freestyle

Distance	Time	Holder	Country	Where made	Date
50 Meters	0:25.28	Tamara Costache	Romania	Madrid	Aug., 1986
100 Meters	0:54.73	Kristin Otto	E. Germany	Madrid	Aug., 1986
200 Meters	1:57.75	Kristin Otto	E. Germany	Magdeburg, E. Ger.	May 23, 1984
400 Meters	4:06.28	Tracey Wickham	Australia	W. Berlin	Aug. 24, 1978
800 Meters	8:19.53	Anke Mohring	E. Germany	Strasbourg, France	Aug., 1987
1,500 Meters	16:00.73	Janet Evans	U.S.	Clovis, Cal.	July, 1987

Breaststroke

Distance	Time	Holder	Country	Where made	Date
100 Meters	1:07.91	Silke Hoerner	E. Germany	Strasbourg, France	Aug., 1987
200 Meters	2:27.40	Silke Hoerner	E. Germany	Madrid	Aug., 1986

Butterfly

Distance	Time	Holder	Country	Where made	Date
100 Meters	0:57.93	Mary T. Meagher	U.S.	Brown Deer, Wis.	Aug. 16, 1981
200 Meters	2:05.96	Mary T. Meagher	U.S.	Brown Deer, Wis.	Aug. 13, 1981

Backstroke

Distance	Time	Holder	Country	Where made	Date
100 Meters	1:00.59	Ina Kleber	E. Germany	Moscow	Aug. 24, 1984
200 Meters	2:08.60	Betsy Mitchell	U.S.	Orlando, Fla.	June 27, 1986

Individual Medley

Distance	Time	Holder	Country	Where made	Date
200 Meters	2:10.60	Petra Schneider	E. Germany	Gainesville, Fla.	Aug. 1, 1982
400 Meters	4:36.10	Petra Schneider	E. Germany	Ecuador	Aug. 1, 1982

Freestyle Relays

Distance	Time	Holder	Country	Where made	Date
400 M. (4×100)	3:40.57	(Otto, Stellmach, Friedrich, Schulze)	E. Germany	Madrid	Aug., 1986
800 M. (4×200)	7:55:47	Stellmach, Strauss, Mohring, Friedrich)	E. Germany	Strasbourg, France	Aug., 1987

Medley Relays

Distance	Time	Holder	Country	Where made	Date
400 M. (4×100)	4:03.69	National Team (Kleber, Gerasch, Geissler, Meineke)	E. Germany	Moscow	Aug. 24, 1984

U.S. Diving Championships in 1987

Men

One Meter—Doug Shaffer.
Three Meter—Greg Louganis.
Platform—Greg Louganis.

Women

One Meter—Megan Neyer.
Three Meter—Kelly McCormick.
Platform—Mary Ellen Clark.

U.S. Long Course Swimming Champions in 1987

Clovis, Cal., July 28-30, 1987

Men

50-Meter Freestyle—Matt Biondi. Time—0:22.33.
100-Meter Freestyle—Matt Biondi. Time—0:49.34.
200-Meter Freestyle—Richard Oppel. Time—1:48.88.
400-Meter Freestyle—Matt Cetlinksi. Time—3:49.69.
800-Meter Freestyle—Sean Killion. Time—7:52.45.
1,500-Meter Freestyle—Daniel Jorgenson. Time—15:17.04.
100-Meter Backstroke—Jay Mortenson. Time—0:56.58.
200-Meter Backstroke—Scott Johnson. Time—2:01.58.
100-Meter Breaststroke—Richard Schroeder. Time—1:03.40.
200-Meter Breaststroke—Steve Bentley. Time—2:15.30.
100-Meter Butterfly—Pablo Morales. Time—0:53.74.
200-Meter Butterfly—Melvin Stewart. Time—1:58.13.
200-Meter Individual Medley—Dave Wharton. Time—2:02.76.
400-Meter Individual Medley—Dave Wharton. Time—4:17.81.
400-Meter Freestyle Relay—San Jose Aquatics. Time—3:24.19.
800-Meter Freestyle Relay—San Jose Aquatics. Time—7:26.53.

Women

50-Meter Freestyle—Lisa Dorman. Time—0:25.94.
100-Meter Freestyle—Dora Torres. Time—0:56.14.
200-Meter Freestyle—Francie O'Leary. Time—2:01.27.
400-Meter Freestyle—Janet Evans. Time—4:08.89.
800-Meter Freestyle—Janet Evans. Time—8:22.44.
1,500-Meter Freestyle—Janet Evans. Time—16:00.73.
100-Meter Backstroke—Betsy Mitchell. Time—1:02.38.
200-Meter Backstroke—Andrea Hayes. Time—2:12.37.
100-Meter Breaststroke—Susan Johnson. Time—1:11.40.
200-Meter Breaststroke—Amy Shaw. Time—2:29.78.
100-Meter Butterfly—Loury LaDonnis. Time—1:00.99.
200-Meter Butterfly—Melanie Buddemeyer. Time—2:12.27.
200-Meter Individual Medley—Kay Arris. Time—2:17.52.
400-Meter Individual Medley—Janet Evans. Time—4:41.74.
400-Meter Freestyle Relay—Concord-Pleasant Hill, Cal. Time—3:44.98.
800-Meter Freestyle Relay—Pine Crest, Ft. Lauderdale, Fla. Time—8:11.19.

The America's Cup

The United States yacht *Stars & Stripes* defeated the Australian yacht *Kookaburra III* 4-0 in the best-of-seven series of races in seas off Fremantle, Australia to recapture the America's Cup on Feb. 4, 1987. Dennis Connor, skipper of the *Stars & Stripes,* avenged his 1983 loss of the America's Cup to Australia; the only defeat for the United States in America's Cup competition. The Cup resides at the San Diego Yacht Club, which sponsored the U.S. entry.

Competition for the America's Cup grew out of the first contest to establish a world yachting championship, one of the carnival features of the London Exposition of 1851. The race, open to all classes of yachts from all over the world, covered a 60-mile course around the Isle of Wight; the prize was a cup worth about $500, donated by the Royal Yacht Squadron of England, known as the "America's Cup" because it was first won by the United States yacht *America.* Successive efforts of British and Australian yachtsmen had failed to win the famous trophy until 1983 when the Australian yacht *Australia II* defeated the U.S. entry *Liberty.*

Winners of the America's Cup

1851	America
1870	Magic defeated Cambria, England, (1-0)
1871	Columbia (first three races) and Sappho (last two races) defeated Livonia, England, (4-1)
1876	Madeline defeated Countess of Dufferin, Canada, (2-0)
1881	Mischief defeated Atalanta, Canada, (2-0)
1885	Puritan defeated Genesta, England, (2-0)
1886	Mayflower defeated Galatea, England, (2-0)
1887	Volunteer defeated Thistle, Scotland, (2-0)
1893	Vigilant defeated Valkyrie II, England, (3-0)
1895	Defender defeated Valkyrie III, England, (3-0)
1899	Columbia defeated Shamrock, England, (3-0)
1901	Columbia defeated Shamrock II, England, (3-0)
1903	Reliance defeated Shamrock III, England, (3-0)
1920	Resolute defeated Shamrock IV, England, (3-2)
1930	Enterprise defeated Shamrock V, England, (4-0)
1934	Rainbow defeated Endeavour, England, (4-2)
1937	Ranger defeated Endeavour II, England, (4-0)
1958	Columbia defeated Sceptre, England, (4-0)
1962	Weatherly defeated Gretel, Australia, (4-1)
1964	Constellation defeated Sovereign, England, (4-0)
1967	Intrepid defeated Dame Pattie, Australia, (4-0)
1970	Intrepid defeated Gretel II, Australia, (4-1)
1974	Courageous defeated Southern Cross, Australia, (4-0)
1977	Courageous defeated Australia, Australia, (4-0)
1980	Freedom defeated Australia, Australia, (4-1)
1983	Australia II, Australia defeated Liberty, (4-3)
1987	Stars & Stripes defeated Kookaburra III, Australia, (4-0)

Pro Rodeo Championship Standings in 1986

Event	Winner	Money won
All Around	Lewis Feild, Elk Ridge, Ut.	$166,042
Saddle Bronc	Bud Munroe, Valley Mills, Tex.	100,932
Bareback	Lewis Feild, Elk Ridge, Ut.	114,675
Bull Riding	Tuff Hederman, Gainesville, Tex.	137,061
Calf Roping	Chris Lybbert, Argyle, Tex.	88,877
Steer Wrestling	Steve Duhon, Opelousas, La.	114,535
Steer Roping	Jim Davis, Bandera, Tex.	33,377
Team Roping	Jake Barnes, Bloomfield, N.M. & Clay O'Brien Cooper, Gilbert, Ariz.	89,498
Women's Barrel Racing	Charmayne James, Clayton, N.M.	151,969

Pro Rodeo Cowboy All Around Champions

Year	Winner	Money won
1966	Larry Mahan, Brooks, Ore.	$40,358
1967	Larry Mahan, Brooks, Ore.	51,996
1968	Larry Mahan, Salem, Ore.	49,129
1969	Larry Mahan, Brooks, Ore.	57,726
1970	Larry Mahan, Brooks, Ore.	41,493
1971	Phil Lyne, George West, Tex.	49,245
1972	Phil Lyne, George West, Tex.	60,852
1973	Larry Mahan, Dallas, Tex.	64,447
1974	Tom Ferguson, Miami, Okla.	66,929
1975	Leo Camarillo, Oakdale, Cal.	50,300
	Tom Ferguson, Miami, Okla.	50,300
1976	Tom Ferguson, Miami, Okla.	$87,908
1977	Tom Ferguson, Miami, Okla.	76,730
1978	Tom Ferguson, Miami, Okla.	103,734
1979	Tom Ferguson, Miami, Okla.	96,272
1980	Paul Tierney, Rapid City, S.D.	105,568
1981	Jimmie Cooper, Monument, N.M.	105,862
1982	Chris Lybbert, Coyote, Cal.	123,709
1983	Roy Cooper, Durant, Okla.	153,391
1984	Dee Pickett, Caldwell, Ida.	122,618
1985	Lewis Feild, Elk Ridge, Ut.	130,347
1986	Lewis Feild, Elk Ridge, Ut.	166,042

Figure Skating Champions

U.S. Champions			World Champions	
Men	**Women**	**Year**	**Men**	**Women**
Richard Button	Tenley Albright	**1952**	Richard Button, U.S.	Jacqueline du Bief, France
Hayes Jenkins	Tenley Albright	**1953**	Hayes Jenkins, U.S.	Tenley Albright, U.S.
Hayes Jenkins	Tenley Albright	**1954**	Hayes Jenkins, U.S.	Gundi Busch, W. Germany
Hayes Jenkins	Tenley Albright	**1955**	Hayes Jenkins, U.S.	Tenley Albright, U.S.
Hayes Jenkins	Tenley Albright	**1956**	Hayes Jenkins, U.S.	Carol Heiss, U.S.
Dave Jenkins	Carol Heiss	**1957**	Dave Jenkins, U.S.	Carol Heiss, U.S.
Dave Jenkins	Carol Heiss	**1958**	Dave Jenkins, U.S.	Carol Heiss, U.S.
Dave Jenkins	Carol Heiss	**1959**	Dave Jenkins, U.S.	Carol Heiss, U.S.
Dave Jenkins	Carol Heiss	**1960**	Alain Giletti, France	Carol Heiss, U.S.
Bradley Lord	Laurence Owen	**1961**	none	none
Monty Hoyt	Barbara Roles Pursley	**1962**	Don Jackson, Canada	Sjoukje Dijkstra, Neth.
Tommy Litz	Lorraine Hanlon	**1963**	Don McPherson, Canada	Sjoukje Dijkstra, Neth.
Scott Allen	Peggy Fleming	**1964**	Manfred Schnelldorfer, W. Germany	Sjoukje Dijkstra, Neth.
Gary Visconti	Peggy Fleming	**1965**	Alain Calmat, France	Petra Burka, Canada
Scott Allen	Peggy Fleming	**1966**	Emmerich Danzer, Austria	Peggy Fleming, U.S.
Gary Visconti	Peggy Fleming	**1967**	Emmerich Danzer, Austria	Peggy Fleming, U.S.
Tim Wood	Peggy Fleming	**1968**	Emmerich Danzer, Austria	Peggy Fleming, U.S.
Tim Wood	Janet Lynn	**1969**	Tim Wood, U.S.	Gabriele Seyfert, E. Germany
Tim Wood	Janet Lynn	**1970**	Tim Wood, U.S.	Gabriele Seyfert, E. Germany
John Misha Petkevich	Janet Lynn	**1971**	Ondrej Nepela, Czech.	Beatrix Schuba, Austria
Ken Shelley	Janet Lynn	**1972**	Ondrej Nepela, Czech.	Beatrix Schuba, Austria
Gordon McKellen Jr.	Janet Lynn	**1973**	Ondrej Nepela, Czech.	Karen Magnussen, Canada
Gordon McKellen Jr.	Dorothy Hamill	**1974**	Jan Hoffmann, E. Germany	Christine Errath, E. Germany
Gordon McKellen Jr.	Dorothy Hamill	**1975**	Sergei Volkov, USSR	Dianne de Leeuw, Neth.-U.S.
Terry Kubicka	Dorothy Hamill	**1976**	John Curry, Gt. Britain	Dorothy Hamill, U.S.
Charles Tickner	Linda Fratianne	**1977**	Vladimir Kovalev, USSR	Linda Fratianne, U.S.
Charles Tickner	Linda Fratianne	**1978**	Charles Tickner, U.S.	Anett Potzsch, E. Germany
Charles Tickner	Linda Fratianne	**1979**	Vladimir Kovalev, USSR	Linda Fratianne, U.S.
Charles Tickner	Linda Fratianne	**1980**	Jan Hoffmann, E. Germany	Anett Potzsch, E. Germany
Scott Hamilton	Elaine Zayak	**1981**	Scott Hamilton, U.S.	Denise Biellmann, Switzerland
Scott Hamilton	Rosalynn Sumners	**1982**	Scott Hamilton, U.S.	Elaine Zayak, U.S.
Scott Hamilton	Rosalynn Sumners	**1983**	Scott Hamilton, U.S.	Rosalynn Sumners, U.S.
Scott Hamilton	Rosalynn Sumners	**1984**	Scott Hamilton, U.S.	Katarina Witt, E. Germany
Brian Boitano	Tiffany Chin	**1985**	Aleksandr Fadeev, USSR	Katarina Witt, E. Germany
Brian Boitano	Debi Thomas	**1986**	Brian Boitano, U.S.	Debi Thomas, U.S.
Brian Boitano	Jill Trenary	**1987**	Brian Orser, Canada	Katarina Witt, E. Germany

U.S. Pairs and Dancing Champions in 1986

Jill Watson and Peter Oppegard won the 1987 U.S. pairs figure skating championship in Tacoma, Wash. Suzy Semanick and Scott Gregory triumphed in ice dancing.

Curling Champions

Source: North American Curling News

World Champions

Year	Country, skip	Year	Country, skip	Year	Country, skip
1970	Canada, Don Duguid	1976	United States, Bruce Roberts	1982	Canada, Al Hackner
1971	Canada, Don Duguid	1977	Sweden, Ragnar Kamp	1983	Canada, Ed Werenich
1972	Canada, Crest Melesnuk	1978	United States, Bob Nichols	1984	Norway, Eigil Ramsfjell
1973	Sweden, Kjell Oscarius	1979	Norway, Kristian Soerum	1985	Canada, Al Hackner
1974	United States, Bud Somerville	1980	Canada, Rich Folk	1986	Canada, Ed Luckowich
1975	Switzerland, Otto Danieli	1981	Switzerland, Jurg Tanner	1987	Canada, Russ Howard

U.S. Men's Champions

Year	State, skip	Year	State, skip	Year	State, skip
1970	North Dakota, Art Tallackson	1976	Minnesota, Bruce Roberts	1982	Wisconsin, Steve Brown
1971	North Dakota, Dale Dalziel	1977	Minnesota, Bruce Roberts	1983	Colorado, Don Cooper
1972	North Dakota, Bob LaBonte	1978	Wisconsin, Bob Nichols	1984	Minnesota, Bruce Roberts
1973	Massachusetts, Barry Blanchard	1979	Minnesota, Scotty Baird	1985	Illinois, Tim Wright
1974	Wisconsin, Bud Somerville	1980	Minnesota, Paul Pustover	1986	Wisconsin, Steve Brown
1975	Washington, Ed Risling	1981	Wisconsin, Somerville-Nichols	1987	Washington, Jim Vukich

U.S. Ladies Champions

Year	State, skip	Year	State, skip	Year	State, skip
1978	Wisconsin, Sandy Robarge	1982	Illinois, Ruth Schwenker	1986	Minnesota, Gerri Tilden
1979	Washington, Nancy Langley	1983	Washington, Nancy Langley	1987	Washington, Sharon Good
1980	Washington, Sharon Kozai	1984	Minnesota, Amy Hatten		
1981	Washington, Nancy Langley	1985	Alaska, Bev Birklid		

Major Indoor Soccer League in 1987

The Dallas Sidekicks defeated the Tacoma Stars 4-3 in the 7th and final game of the championship series to win the 1987 Major Indoor Soccer League championship. Mark Karpun scored the winning goal at 9:23 of the overtime period.

James E. Sullivan Memorial Trophy Winners

The James E. Sullivan Memorial Trophy, named after the former president of the AAU and inaugurated in 1930, is awarded annually by the AAU to the athlete who "by his or her performance, example and influence as an amateur, has done the most during the year to advance the cause of sportmanship."

Year	Winner	Sport	Year	Winner	Sport	Year	Winner	Sport
1930	Bobby Jones	Golf	1950	Fred Wilt	Track	1969	Bill Toomey	Track
1931	Barney Berlinger	Track	1951	Rev. Robert Richards	Track	1970	John Kinsella	Swimming
1932	Jim Bausch	Track	1952	Horace Ashenfelter	Track	1971	Mark Spitz	Swimming
1933	Glenn Cunningham	Track	1953	Dr. Sammy Lee	Diving	1972	Frank Shorter	Track
1934	Bill Bonthron	Track	1954	Mal Whitfield	Track	1973	Bill Walton	Basketball
1935	Lawson Little	Golf	1955	Harrison Dillard	Track	1974	Rick Wohlhuter	Track
1936	Glenn Morris	Track	1956	Patricia McCormick	Diving	1975	Tim Shaw	Swimming
1937	Don Budge	Tennis	1957	Bobby Joe Morrow	Track	1976	Bruce Jenner	Track
1938	Don Lash	Track	1958	Glenn Davis	Track	1977	John Naber	Swimming
1939	Joe Burk	Rowing	1959	Parry O'Brien	Track	1978	Tracy Caulkins	Swimming
1940	Greg Rice	Track	1960	Rafer Johnson	Track	1979	Kurt Thomas	Gymnastics
1941	Leslie MacMitchell	Track	1961	Wilma Rudolph Ward	Track	1980	Eric Heiden	Speed Skating
1942	Cornelius Warmerdam	Track	1962	James Beatty	Track	1981	Carl Lewis	Track
1943	Gilbert Dodds	Track	1963	John Pennel	Track	1982	Mary Decker	Track
1944	Ann Curtis	Swimming	1964	Don Schollander	Swimming	1983	Edwin Moses	Track
1945	Doc Blanchard	Football	1965	Bill Bradley	Basketball	1984	Greg Louganis	Diving
1946	Arnold Tucker	Football	1966	Jim Ryun	Track	1985	Joan Benoit Samuelson	Marathon
1947	John Kelly Jr.	Rowing	1967	Randy Matson	Track	1986	Jackie Joyner-Kersee	Track
1948	Robert Mathias	Track	1968	Debbie Meyer	Swimming			
1949	Dick Button	Skating						

Westminster Kennel Club

Year	Best-in-show	Breed	Owner
1975	Ch. Sir Lancelot of Barvan	Old English sheepdog	Mr. & Mrs. Ronald Vanword
1976	Ch. Jo-Ni's Red Baron of Crofton	Lakeland terrier	Virginia Dickson
1977	Ch. Dersade Bobby's Girl	Sealyham	Dorothy Wymer
1978	Ch. Cede Higgens	Yorkshire terrier	Barbara & Charles Switzer
1979	Ch. Oak Tree's Irishtocrat	Irish water spaniel	Anne E. Snelling
1980	Ch. Sierra Cinnar	Siberian husky	Kathleen Kanzler
1981	Ch. Dhandy Favorite Woodchuck	Pug	Robert Houslohner
1982	Ch. St. Aubrey Dragonora of Elsdon	Pekingese	Anne Snelling
1983	Ch. Kabik's The Challenger	Afghan	Chris & Marguerite Terrell
1984	Ch. Seaward's Blackbeard	Newfoundland	Elinor Ayers
1985	Ch. Braeburn's Close Encounter	Scottish terrier	Sonnie Novick
1986	Ch. Marjetta National Acclaim	Pointer	Mrs. Alan Robson & Michael Zollo
1987	Ch. Covy Tucker Hill's Manhattan	German shepherd	Shirley Braunstein & Jane Firestone

Lacrosse Champions in 1987

U.S. Club Lacrosse Association Championship—Baltimore, Md., June 13: Long Island-Hofstra LC 14, Maryland LC 12.

NCAA Division I Championship—Piscataway, N.J., May 25: Johns Hopkins 11, Cornell 10.

NCAA Division III Championship—Geneva, N.Y., May 16: Hobart 9, Ohio Wesleyan 5.

All-Star College Game—Baltimore, Md., June 12: North 17, South 16.

National Junior College Championship—Troy, N.Y., May 9: SUNY-Farmingdale 11, Herkimer (N.Y.) CC 4.

NCAA Women's Lacrosse Championship—College Park, Md., May 16: Penn State 7, Temple 6.

USILA Division I All America Team

Attack: Tom Carmean, Massachusetts; Brian Wood, Johns Hopkins; Tim Goldstein, Cornell.
Midfield: Bob Cummings, Cornell; Steve Mitchell, Johns Hopkins; Tom Worstell, Maryland; Todd Curry, Syracuse.
Defense: Brian Jackson, Maryland; Dave Pietramala, Johns Hopkins; Tom Haus, North Carolina.
Goal: Jim Beardmore, Maryland.
Coach of the Year: Richie Moran, Cornell.
Note: 4 midfielders selected for the 3 midfield positions.

USILA Division III All America Team

Attack: Robert Alvino, Ohio Wesleyan; Tom Gravante, Hobart; Ray Gilliam, Hobart.
Midfield: Michael Guy, Hobart; Charles Blanchard, Ohio Wesleyan; Toby Boucher, Ohio Wesleyan.
Defense: Dave Hilliard, Washington College; Devin Arkison, Hobart; Jim Kimmel, Rochester Tech.
Goal: Dan O'Neil, Ohio Wesleyan.
Coach of the Year: Mike Pressler, Ohio Wesleyan.

NCAA Divisions I Champions

1971	Cornell	1976	Cornell	1980	Johns Hopkins	1984	Johns Hopkins
1972	Virginia	1977	Cornell	1981	North Carolina	1985	Johns Hopkins
1973	Maryland	1978	Johns Hopkins	1982	North Carolina	1986	North Carolina
1974	Johns Hopkins	1979	Johns Hopkins	1983	Syracuse	1987	Johns Hopkins
1975	Maryland						

National Football League

Final 1986 Standings

National Conference

Eastern Division

	W	L	T	Pct	Pts	Opp
N.Y. Giants	14	2	0	.875	371	236
Washington	12	4	0	.750	368	296
Dallas	7	9	0	.438	346	337
Philadelphia	5	10	1	.344	256	312
St. Louis	4	11	1	.281	218	351

Central Division

	W	L	T	Pct	Pts	Opp
Chicago	14	2	0	.875	352	187
Minnesota	9	7	0	.563	398	273
Detroit	5	11	0	.313	277	326
Green Bay	4	12	0	.250	254	418
Tampa Bay	2	14	0	.125	239	473

Western Division

	W	L	T	Pct	Pts	Opp
San Francisco	10	5	1	.656	374	247
L.A. Rams	10	6	0	.625	309	267
Atlanta	7	8	1	.469	280	280
New Orleans	7	9	0	.438	288	287

American Conference

Eastern Division

	W	L	T	Pct	Pts	Opp
New England	11	5	0	.688	412	307
N.Y. Jets	10	6	0	.625	364	386
Miami	8	8	0	.500	430	405
Buffalo	4	12	0	.250	287	348
Indianapolis	3	13	0	.188	229	400

Central Division

	W	L	T	Pct	Pts	Opp
Cleveland	12	4	0	.750	391	310
Cincinnati	10	6	0	.625	409	394
Pittsburgh	6	10	0	.375	307	336
Houston	5	11	0	.313	274	329

Western Division

	W	L	T	Pct	Pts	Opp
Denver	11	5	0	.688	378	327
Kansas City	10	6	0	.625	358	326
Seattle	10	6	0	.625	366	293
L.A. Raiders	8	8	0	.500	323	346
San Diego	4	12	0	.250	335	396

NFC playoffs—Washington 19, L.A. Rams 7; N.Y. Giants 49, San Francisco 3; Washington 27, Chicago 13; N.Y. Giants 17, Washington 0.

AFC playoffs—N.Y. Jets 35, Kansas City 15; Denver 22, New England 17; Cleveland 23, N.Y. Jets 20; Denver 23, Cleveland 20.

Giants Defeat Broncos in Super Bowl

The New York Giants won their first Super Bowl championship by defeating the Denver Broncos 39-20 at the Rose Bowl in Pasadena, Cal. It was the Giants' first NFL championship since they defeated the Chicago Bears for the 1956 title. The Giants' quarterback Phil Simms was chosen the game's most valuable player.

Score by Quarters

Denver	10	0	0	10—20
New York	7	2	17	13—39

Scoring

Denver—Karlis 48 yd. field goal
New York—Mowatt 6 yd. pass from Simms (Allegre kick)
Denver—Elway 4 yd. run (Karlis kick)
New York—Safety, Elway tackled by Martin
New York—Bavaro 13 yd. pass from Simms (Allegre kick)
New York—Allegre 21 yd. field goal
New York—Morris 1 yd. run (Allegre kick)
New York—McConkey 6 yd. pass from Simms (Allegre kick)
Denver—Karlis 28 yd. field goal
New York—Anderson 2 yd. run
Denver—V. Johnson 47 yd. pass from Elway (Karlis kick)

Individual Statistics

Rushing — Denver, Elway 6-27, Willhite 4-19, Sewell 3-4, Lang 2-2, Winder 4-0. New York, Morris 20-67, Simms 3-25, Rouson 3-22, Galbreath 4-17, Carthon 3-4, Anderson 2-1, Rutledge 3-0.

Passing — Denver, Elway 22-37-1-304, Kubiak 4-4-0-48. New York, Simms 22-25-0-268.

Receiving — Denver, V. Johnson 5-121, Willhite 5-39, Winder 4-34, Jackson 3-51, Watson 2-54, Sampson 2-20, Mobley 2-17, Sewell 2-12, Lang 1-4. New York, Bavaro 4-51, Morris 4-20, Carthon 4-13, Robinson 3-62, Manuel 3-43, McConkey 2-50, Rouson 1-23, Mowatt 1-6.

Team Statistics

	Denver	New York
First downs	23	24
Total net yards	372	399
Rushing yards	52	136
Passing yards	320	263
Completed-attempts	26-41	22-25
Punts, avg.	2-41	3-46
Penalties-yards	4-28	6-48
Fumbles-lost	2-0	0-0
Time of possession	25:21	34:39

Super Bowl

Year	Winner	Loser	Site
1967	Green Bay Packers, 35	Kansas City Chiefs, 10	Los Angeles Coliseum
1968	Green Bay Packers, 33	Oakland Raiders, 14	Orange Bowl, Miami
1969	New York Jets, 16	Baltimore Colts, 7	Orange Bowl, Miami
1970	Kansas City Chiefs, 23	Minnesota Vikings, 7	Tulane Stadium, New Orleans
1971	Baltimore Colts, 16	Dallas Cowboys, 13	Orange Bowl, Miami
1972	Dallas Cowboys, 24	Miami Dolphins, 3	Tulane Stadium, New Orleans
1973	Miami Dolphins, 14	Washington Redskins, 7	Los Angeles Coliseum
1974	Miami Dolphins, 24	Minnesota Vikings, 7	Rice Stadium, Houston
1975	Pittsburgh Steelers, 16	Minnesota Vikings, 6	Tulane Stadium, New Orleans
1976	Pittsburgh Steelers, 21	Dallas Cowboys, 17	Orange Bowl, Miami
1977	Oakland Raiders, 32	Minnesota Vikings, 14	Rose Bowl, Pasadena
1978	Dallas Cowboys, 27	Denver Broncos, 10	Superdome, New Orleans
1979	Pittsburgh Steelers, 35	Dallas Cowboys, 31	Orange Bowl, Miami
1980	Pittsburgh Steelers, 31	Los Angeles Rams, 19	Rose Bowl, Pasadena
1981	Oakland Raiders, 27	Philadelphia Eagles, 10	Superdome, New Orleans
1982	San Francisco 49ers, 26	Cincinnati Bengals, 21	Silverdome, Pontiac, Mich.
1983	Washington Redskins, 27	Miami Dolphins, 17	Rose Bowl, Pasadena
1984	Los Angeles Raiders, 38	Washington Redskins, 9	Tampa Stadium
1985	San Francisco 49ers, 38	Miami Dolphins, 16	Stanford Stadium, Palo Alto, Cal.
1986	Chicago Bears, 46	New England Patriots, 10	Superdome, New Orleans
1987	New York Giants, 39	Denver Broncos, 20	Rose Bowl, Pasadena

Super Bowl MVPs

1967 Bart Starr, Green Bay
1968 Bart Starr, Green Bay
1969 Joe Namath, N.Y. Jets
1970 Len Dawson, Kansas City
1971 Chuck Howley, Dallas
1972 Roger Staubach, Dallas
1973 Jake Scott, Miami
1974 Larry Csonka, Miami
1975 Franco Harris, Pittsburgh
1976 Lynn Swann, Pittsburgh
1977 Fred Biletnikoff, Oakland
1978 Randy White, Harvey Martin, Dallas
1979 Terry Bradshaw, Pittsburgh
1980 Terry Bradshaw, Pittsburgh
1981 Jim Plunkett, Oakland
1982 Joe Montana, San Francisco
1983 John Riggins, Washington
1984 Marcus Allen, L.A. Raiders
1985 Joe Montana, San Francisco
1986 Richard Dent, Chicago
1986 Phil Simms, N.Y. Giants

National Football League Champions

Year	East Winner (W.L.T.)	West Winner (W.L.T.)	Playoff
1933	New York Giants (11-3-0)	Chicago Bears (10-2-1)	Chicago Bears 23, New York 21
1934	New York Giants (8-5-0)	Chicago Bears (13-0-0)	New York 30, Chicago Bears 13
1935	New York Giants (9-3-0)	Detroit Lions (7-3-2)	Detroit 26, New York 7
1936	Boston Redskins (7-5-0)	Green Bay Packers (10-1-1)	Green Bay 21, Boston 6
1937	Washington Redskins (8-3-0)	Chicago Bears (9-1-1)	Washington 28, Chicago Bears 21
1938	New York Giants (8-2-1)	Green Bay Packers (8-3-0)	New York 23, Green Bay 17
1939	New York Giants (9-1-1)	Green Bay Packers (9-2-0)	Green Bay 27, New York 0
1940	Washington Redskins (9-2-0)	Chicago Bears (8-3-0)	Chicago Bears 73, Washington 0
1941	New York Giants (8-3-0)	Chicago Bears (10-1-1)(a)	Chicago Bears 37, New York 9
1942	Wash. Redskins (10-1-1)	Chicago Bears (11-0-0)	Washington 14, Chicago Bears 6
1943	Wash. Redskins (6-3-1)(a)	Chicago Bears (8-1-1)	Chicago Bears, 41, Washington 21
1944	New York Giants (8-1-1)	Green Bay Packers (8-2-0)	Green Bay 14, New York 7
1945	Wash. Redskins (8-2-0)	Cleveland Rams (9-1-0)	Cleveland 15, Washington 14
1946	New York Giants (7-3-1)	Chicago Bears (8-2-1)	Chicago Bears 24, New York 14
1947	Philadelphia Eagles (8-4-0)(a)	Chicago Cardinals (9-3-0)	Chicago Cardinals 28, Philadelphia 21
1948	Philadelphia Eagles (9-2-1)	Chicago Cardinals (11-1-0)	Philadelphia 7, Chicago Cardinals 0
1949	Philadelphia Eagles (11-1-0)	Los Angeles Rams (8-2-2)	Philadelphia 14, Los Angeles 0
1950	Cleveland Browns (10-2-0)(a)	Los Angeles Rams (9-3-0)(a)	Cleveland 30, Los Angeles 28
1951	Cleveland Browns (11-1-0)	Los Angeles Rams (8-4-0)	Los Angeles 24, Cleveland 17
1952	Cleveland Browns (8-4-0)	Detroit Lions (9-3-0)(a)	Detroit 17, Cleveland 7
1953	Cleveland Browns (11-1-0)	Detroit Lions (10-2-0)	Detroit 17, Cleveland 16
1954	Cleveland Browns (9-3-0)	Detroit Lions (9-2-1)	Cleveland 56, Detroit 10
1955	Cleveland Browns (9-2-1)	Los Angeles Rams (8-3-1)	Cleveland 38, Los Angeles 14
1956	New York Giants (8-3-1)	Chicago Bears (9-2-1)	New York 47, Chicago Bears 7
1957	Cleveland Browns (9-2-1)	Detroit Lions (8-4-0)(a)	Detroit 59, Cleveland 14
1958	New York Giants (9-3-0)(a)	Baltimore Colts (9-3-0)	Baltimore 23, New York 17(b)
1959	New York Giants (10-2-0)	Baltimore Colts (9-3-0)	Baltimore 31, New York 16
1960	Philadelphia Eagles (10-2-0)	Green Bay Packers (8-4-0)	Philadelphia 17, Green Bay 13
1961	New York Giants (10-3-1)	Green Bay Packers (11-3-0)	Green Bay 37, New York 0
1962	New York Giants (12-2-0)	Green Bay Packers (13-1-0)	Green Bay 16, New York 7
1963	New York Giants (11-3-0)	Chicago Bears (11-1-2)	Chicago 14, New York 10
1964	Cleveland Browns (10-3-1)	Baltimore Colts (12-2-0)	Cleveland 27, Baltimore 0
1965	Cleveland Browns (11-3-0)	Green Bay Packers (10-3-1)(a)	Green Bay 23, Cleveland 12
1966	Dallas Cowboys (10-3-1)	Green Bay Packers (12-2-0)	Green Bay 34, Dallas 27

(a) Won divisional playoff. (b) Won at 8:15 sudden death overtime period.

Year	Conference	Division	Winner (W-L-T)	Playoff
1967	East	Century	Cleveland (9-5-0)	Dallas 52, Cleveland 14
		Capitol	Dallas (9-5-0)	
	West	Central	Green Bay (9-4-1)	Green Bay 28, Los Angeles 7
		Coastal	Los Angeles (11-1-2)(a)	Green Bay 21, Dallas 17
1968	East	Century	Cleveland (10-4-0)	Cleveland 31, Dallas 20
		Capitol	Dallas (12-2-0)	
	West	Central	Minnesota (8-6-0)	Baltimore 24, Minnesota 14
		Coastal	Baltimore (13-1-0)	Baltimore 34, Cleveland 0
1969	East	Century	Cleveland (10-3-1)	Cleveland 38, Dallas 14
		Capitol	Dallas (11-2-1)	
	West	Central	Minnesota (12-2-0)	Minnesota 23, Los Angeles 20
		Coastal	Los Angeles (11-3-0)	Minnesota 27, Cleveland 7
1970	American	Eastern	Baltimore (11-2-1)	Baltimore 17, Cincinnati 0
		Central	Cincinnati (8-6-0)	Oakland 21, Miami 14
		Western	Oakland (8-4-2)	Baltimore 27, Oakland 17
	National	Eastern	Dallas (10-4-0)	Dallas 5, Detroit 0
		Central	Minnesota (12-2-0)	San Francisco 17, Minnesota 14
		Western	San Francisco (10-3-1)	Dallas 17, San Francisco 10
1971	American	Eastern	Miami (10-3-1)	Miami 27, Kansas City 24
		Central	Cleveland (9-5-0)	Baltimore 20, Cleveland 3
		Western	Kansas City (10-3-1)	Miami 21, Baltimore 0
	National	Eastern	Dallas (11-3-0)	Dallas 20, Minnesota 12
		Central	Minnesota (11-3-0)	San Francisco 24, Washington 20
		Western	San Francisco (9-5-0)	Dallas 14, San Francisco 3
1972	American	Eastern	Miami (14-0-0)	Miami 20, Cleveland 14
		Central	Pittsburgh (11-3-0)	Pittsburgh 13, Oakland 7
		Western	Oakland (10-3-1)	Miami 21, Pittsburgh 17
	National	Eastern	Washington (11-3-0)	Washington 16, Green Bay 3
		Central	Green Bay (10-4-0)	Dallas 30, San Francisco 28
		Western	San Francisco (8-5-1)	Washington 26, Dallas 3

(continued)

Year	Conference	Division	Winner (W-L-T)	Playoff
1973	American	Eastern	Miami (12-2-0)	Miami 34, Cincinnati 16
		Central	Cincinnati (10-4-0)	Oakland 33, Pittsburgh 14
		Western	Oakland (9-4-1)	Miami 27, Oakland 10
	National	Eastern	Dallas (10-4-0)	Dallas 27, Los Angeles 16
		Central	Minnesota (12-2-0)	Minnesota 27, Washington 20
		Western	Los Angeles (12-2-0)	Minnesota 27, Dallas 10
1974	American	Eastern	Miami (11-3-0)	Oakland 28, Miami 26
		Central	Pittsburgh (10-3-1)	Pittsburgh 32, Buffalo 14
		Western	Oakland (12-2-0)	Pittsburgh 24, Oakland 13
	National	Eastern	St. Louis (10-4-0)	Minnesota 30, St. Louis 14
		Central	Minnesota (10-4-0)	Los Angeles 19, Washington 10
		Western	Los Angeles (10-4-0)	Minnesota 14, Los Angeles 10
1975	American	Eastern	Baltimore (10-4-0)	Pittsburgh 28, Baltimore 10
		Central	Pittsburgh (12-2-0)	Oakland 31, Cincinnati 28
		Western	Oakland (11-3-0)	Pittsburgh 16, Oakland 10
	National	Eastern	St. Louis (11-3-0)	Dallas 17, Minnesota 14
		Central	Minnesota (12-2-0)	Los Angeles 35, St. Louis 23
		Western	Los Angeles (12-2-0)	Dallas 37, Los Angeles 7
1976	American	Eastern	Baltimore (11-3-0)	Pittsburgh 40, Baltimore 14
		Central	Pittsburgh (10-4-0)	Oakland 24, New England 21
		Western	Oakland (13-1-0)	Oakland 24, Pittsburgh 7
	National	Eastern	Dallas (11-3-0)	Minnesota 35, Washington 20
		Central	Minnesota (11-2-1)	Los Angeles 14, Dallas 12
		Western	Los Angeles (10-3-1)	Minnesota 24, Los Angeles 13
1977	American	Eastern	Baltimore (10-4-0)	Oakland 37, Baltimore 31
		Central	Pittsburgh (9-5-0)	Denver 34, Pittsburgh 21
		Western	Denver (12-2-0)	Dallas 37, Chicago 7
	National	Eastern	Dallas (12-2-0)	Minnesota 14, Los Angeles 7
		Central	Minnesota (9-5-0)	Denver 20, Oakland 17
		Western	Los Angeles (10-4-0)	Dallas 23, Minnesota 6
1978	American	Eastern	New England (11-5-0)	Pittsburgh 33, Denver 10
		Central	Pittsburgh (14-2-0)	Houston 31, New England 14
		Western	Denver (10-6-0)	Pittsburgh 34, Houston 5
	National	Eastern	Dallas (12-4-0)	Dallas 27, Atlanta 20
		Central	Minnesota (8-7-1)	Los Angeles 34, Minnesota 10
		Western	Los Angeles (12-4-0)	Dallas 28, Los Angeles 0
1979	American	Eastern	Miami (10-6-0)	Houston 17, San Diego 14
		Central	Pittsburgh (12-4-0)	Pittsburgh 34, Miami 14
		Western	San Diego (12-4-0)	Pittsburgh 27, Houston 13
	National	Eastern	Dallas (11-5-0)	Tampa Bay 24, Philadelphia 17
		Central	Tampa Bay (10-6-0)	Los Angeles 21, Dallas 19
		Western	Los Angeles (9-7-0)	Los Angeles 9, Tampa Bay 0
1980	American	Eastern	Buffalo (11-5-0)	San Diego 20, Buffalo 14
		Central	Cleveland (11-5-0)	Oakland 14, Cleveland 12
		Western	San Diego (11-5-0)	Oakland 34, San Diego 27
	National	Eastern	Philadelphia (12-4-0)	Philadelphia 31, Minnesota 16
		Central	Minnesota (9-7-0)	Dallas 30, Atlanta 27
		Western	Atlanta (12-4-0)	Philadelphia 20, Dallas 7
1981	American	Eastern	Miami (11-4-1)	San Diego 41, Miami 38
		Central	Cincinnati (12-4-0)	Cincinnati 28, Buffalo 21
		Western	San Diego (10-6-0)	Cincinnati 27, San Diego 7
	National	Eastern	Dallas (12-4-0)	Dallas 38, Tampa Bay 0
		Central	Tampa Bay (9-7-0)	San Francisco 38, N.Y. Giants 24
		Western	San Francisco (13-3-0)	San Francisco 28, Dallas 27
1982(1)	American		L.A. Raiders (8-1-0)	
	National		Washington (8-1-0)	

AFC playoffs—Miami 28, New England 13; L.A. Raiders 27, Cleveland 10; N.Y. Jets 44, Cincinnati 17; San Diego 31, Pittsburgh 28; N.Y. Jets 17, L.A. Raiders 14; Miami 34, San Diego 13; Miami 14, N.Y. Jets 0. **NFC playoffs**—Washington 31, Detroit 7; Green Bay 41, St. Louis 16; Dallas 30, Tampa Bay 17; Minnesota 30, Atlanta 24; Washington 21, Minnesota 7; Dallas 37, Green Bay 26; Washington 31, Dallas 17.

Year	Conference	Division	Winner (W-L-T)	Playoff
1983	American	Eastern	Miami (12-4-0)	Seattle 27, Miami 20
		Central	Pittsburgh (10-6-0)	L.A. Raiders 38, Pittsburgh 10
		Western	L.A. Raiders (12-4-0)	L.A. Raiders 30, Seattle 14
	National	Eastern	Washington (14-2-0)	Washington 51, L.A. Rams 7
		Central	Detroit (9-7-0)	San Francisco 24, Detroit 23
		Western	San Francisico (10-6-0)	Washington 24, San Francisco 21
1984	American	Eastern	Miami (14-2-0)	Miami 31, Seattle 10
		Central	Pittsburgh (9-7-0)	Pittsburgh 24, Denver 17
		Western	Denver (13-3-0)	Miami 45, Pittsburgh 28
	National	Eastern	Washington (11-5-0)	Chicago 23, Washington 19
		Central	Chicago (10-6-0)	San Francisco 21, N.Y. Giants 10
		Western	San Francisco (15-1-0)	San Francisco 23, Chicago 0
1985	American	Eastern	Miami (12-4-0)	New England 27, L.A. Raiders 20
		Central	Cleveland (8-8-0)	Miami 24, Cleveland 21
		Western	L.A. Raiders (12-4-0)	New England 31, Miami 14
	National	Eastern	Dallas (10-6-0)	Chicago 21, N.Y. Giants 0
		Central	Chicago (15-1-0)	L.A. Rams 20, Dallas 0
		Western	L.A. Rams (11-5-0)	Chicago 24, L.A. Rams 0
1986	American	Eastern	New England (11-5-0)	Denver 22, New England 17
		Central	Cleveland (12-4-0)	Cleveland 23, N.Y. Jets 20
		Western	Denver (11-5-0)	Denver 23, Cleveland 20
	National	Eastern	N.Y. Giants (14-2-0)	N.Y. Giants 49, San Francisco 3
		Central	Chicago (14-2-0)	Washington 27, Chicago 13
		Western	San Francisco (10-5-1)	N.Y. Giants 17, Washington 0

(1) Strike-shortened season

1986 NFL Individual Leaders

National Football Conference

Passing

	Att	Comp	Pct Comp	Yards	Avg Gain	TD	Pct TD	Int	Rating Points
Kramer, Minnesota	372	208	55.9	3000	8.06	24	6.5	10	92.6
Montana, San Francisco	307	191	62.2	2236	7.28	8	2.6	9	80.7
Hipple, Detroit	305	192	63.0	1919	6.29	9	3.0	11	75.6
Simms, N.Y. Giants	468	259	55.3	3487	7.45	21	4.5	22	74.6
Lomax, St. Louis	421	240	57.0	2583	6.14	13	3.1	12	73.6
Schroeder, Washington	541	276	51.0	4109	7.60	22	4.1	22	72.9
Archer, Atlanta	294	150	51.0	2007	6.83	10	3.4	9	71.6
Jaworski, Philadelphia	245	128	52.2	1405	5.73	8	3.3	6	70.2
Pelluer, Dallas	378	215	56.9	2727	7.21	8	2.1	17	67.9
Wright, Green Bay	492	263	53.5	3247	6.60	17	3.5	23	66.2
D. Wilson, New Orleans	342	189	55.3	2353	6.88	10	2.9	17	65.8
Young, Tampa Bay	363	195	53.7	2282	6.29	8	2.2	13	65.5

Rushing

	Att	Yds	Avg	TD
Dickerson, LA Rams	404	1821	4.5	11
Morris, N.Y. Giants	341	1516	4.4	14
Mayes, New Orleans	286	1353	4.7	8
Payton, Chicago	321	1333	4.2	8
Riggs, Atlanta	343	1327	3.9	9
Rogers, Washington	303	1203	4.0	18
Jones, Detroit	252	903	3.6	8
Craig, San Francisco	204	830	4.1	7
Mitchell, St. Louis	174	800	4.6	5
D. Nelson, Minnesota	191	793	4.2	4

Pass Receiving

	No	Yds	Avg	TD
Rice, San Francisco	86	1570	18.3	15
Craig, San Francisco	81	624	7.7	0
J. Smith, St. Louis	80	1014	12.7	6
Walker, Dallas	76	837	11.0	2
Clark, Washington	74	1265	17.1	7
Monk, Washington	73	1068	14.6	4
Bavaro, N.Y. Giants	66	1001	15.2	4
Lofton, Green Bay	64	840	13.1	4
C. Brown, Atlanta	63	918	14.6	4
Clark, San Francisco	61	794	13.0	2

Scoring-Touchdowns

	TD	Rush	Pass	Pts
Rogers, Washington	18	18	0	108
Rice, San Francisco	16	1	15	96
Morris, N.Y. Giants	15	14	1	90
Walker, Dallas	14	12	2	84
Dickerson, L.A. Rams	11	11	0	66
Payton, Chicago	11	8	3	66
Jones, Detroit	9	8	1	54
Quick, Philadelphia	9	0	9	54
Riggs, Atlanta	9	9	0	54
Mayes, New Orleans	8	8	0	48

Scoring-Kicking

	XP	XPA	FG	FGA	Pts
Butler, Chicago	36	37	28	41	120
Wersching, San Francisco	41	42	25	35	116
C. Nelson, Minnesota	44	47	22	28	110
Andersen, New Orleans	30	30	26	30	108
Allegre, N.Y. Giants	33	33	24	32	105
Septien, Dallas	43	43	15	21	88
McFadden, Philadelphia	26	27	20	31	86
Lansford, L.A. Rams	34	35	17	24	85
Murray, Detroit	31	32	18	25	85
Del Greco, Green Bay	29	29	17	27	80

Punt Returns

	No	Yds	Avg	TD
Sikahema, St. Louis	43	522	12.1	2
Griffin, San Francisco	38	377	9.9	1
Mandley, Detroit	43	420	9.8	1
Jenkins, Washington	28	270	9.6	0
Stanley, Green Bay	33	316	9.6	1
Martin, New Orleans	24	227	9.5	0
Barnes, Chicago	57	482	8.5	0
Sutton, L.A. Rams	28	234	8.4	0
McConkey, N.Y. Giants	32	253	7.9	0
Bess, Minnesota	23	162	7.0	0

Punters

	No	Yds	Avg
Landeta, N.Y. Giants	79	3539	37.1
Donnelly, Atlanta	78	3421	35.0
Cox, Washington	75	3271	36.4
Hansen, New Orleans	81	3456	36.6
Teltschik, Philadelphia	108	4493	33.6
Runager, San Francisco	83	3450	34.3
Coleman, Minnesota	67	2774	34.9
Buford, Chicago	69	2850	36.9
Saxon, Dallas	86	3498	34.4
Garcia, Tampa Bay	77	3089	32.7

Interceptions

	No	Yds	TD
Lott, San Francisco	10	134	1
Waymer, New Orleans	9	48	0
Lee, Green Bay	9	33	0
Gray, L.A. Rams	8	101	0
Holt, Minnesota	8	54	0
Richardson, Chicago	7	69	0

Kickoff Returns

	No	Yds	Avg	TD
Gentry, Chicago	20	576	28.8	1
Gray, New Orleans	31	866	27.9	1
Sikahema, St. Louis	37	847	22.9	0
Bess, Minnesota	31	705	22.7	0
Brown, L.A. Rams	36	794	22.1	0
Stamps, Atlanta	24	514	21.4	0

Sacks

	No.
Taylor, N.Y. Giants	20.5
Manley, Washington	18.5
White, Philadelphia	18.0
Jeffcoat, Dallas	14.0
Haley, San Francisco	12.0
Marshall, N.Y. Giants	12.0
Dent, Chicago	11.5
Stover, San Francisco	11.0

American Football Conference

Passing

	Att	Comp	Pct comp	Yards	Avg gain	TD	Pct TD	Int	Rating Points
Marino, Miami	623	378	60.7	4746	7.62	44	7.1	23	92.5
Krieg, Seattle	375	225	60.0	2921	7.79	21	5.6	11	91.0
Eason, New England	448	276	61.6	3328	7.43	19	4.2	10	89.2
Esiason, Cincinatti	469	273	58.2	3959	8.44	24	5.1	17	87.7
O'Brien, N.Y. Jets	482	300	62.2	3690	7.66	25	5.2	20	85.8
Kosar, Cleveland	531	310	58.4	3854	7.26	17	3.2	10	83.8
Kelly, Buffalo	480	285	59.4	3593	7.49	22	4.6	17	83.3
Plunkett, L.A. Raiders	252	133	52.8	1986	7.88	14	5.6	9	82.5
Elway, Denver	504	280	55.6	3485	6.91	19	3.8	13	79.0
Fouts, San Diego	430	252	58.6	3031	7.05	16	3.7	22	71.4
Kenney, Kansas City	308	161	52.3	1922	6.24	13	4.2	11	70.8
Wilson, L.A Raiders	240	129	53.8	1721	7.17	12	5.0	15	67.4
Malone, Pittsburgh	425	216	50.8	2444	5.75	15	3.5	18	62.5
Moon, Houston	488	256	52.5	3489	7.15	13	2.7	26	62.3
Trudeau, Indianapolis	417	204	48.9	2225	5.34	8	1.9	18	53.5

Rushing

	Att	Yds	Avg	TD
Warner, Seattle	319	1481	4.6	13
Brooks, Cincinatti	205	1087	5.3	5
Jackson, Pittsburgh	216	910	4.2	5
Abercrombie, Pittsburgh	214	877	4.1	6
McNeil, N.Y. Jets	214	856	4.0	5
Hampton, Miami	186	830	4.5	9
Winder, Denver	240	789	3.3	9
Allen, L.A. Raiders	208	759	3.6	5
Mack, Cleveland	174	665	3.8	10
Rozier, Houston	199	662	3.3	4

Pass Receiving

	No	Yds	Avg	TD
Christensen, L.A. Raiders	95	1153	12.1	8
Toon, N.Y. Jets	85	1176	13.8	8
Morgan, New England	84	1491	17.8	10
Anderson, San Diego	80	871	10.9	8
Collins, New England	77	684	8.9	5
Bouza, Indianapolis	71	830	11.7	5
Largent, Seattle	70	1070	15.3	9
Shuler, N.Y. Jets	69	675	9.8	4
Duper, Miami	67	1313	19.6	11
Brooks, Indianapolis	65	1131	17.4	8
D. Hill, Houston	65	1112	17.1	5

Scoring-Touchdowns

	TD	Rush	Pass	Pts
Winder, Denver	14	9	5	84
Warner, Seattle	13	13	0	78
Hampton, Miami	12	9	3	72
Walker, N.Y. Jets	12	0	12	72
Duper, Miami	11	0	11	66
Paige, Kansas City	11	0	11	66
Clayton, Miami	10	0	10	60
Collinsworth, Cincinnati	10	0	10	60
Mack, Cleveland	10	10	0	60
Morgan, New England	10	0	10	60

(a) 2 miscellaneous touchdowns.

Scoring-Kicking

	XP	XPA	FG	FGA	Pts
Franklin, New England	44	45	32	41	140
N.Johnson, Seattle	42	42	22	35	108
Karlis, Denver	44	45	20	28	104
Breech, Cincinnati	50	51	17	32	101
Lowery, Kansas City	43	43	19	26	100
Bahr, L.A. Raiders	36	36	21	28	99
Anderson, Pittsburgh	32	32	21	32	95
Reveiz, Miami	52	55	14	22	94
Zendejas, Houston	28	29	22	27	94
Leahy, N.Y. Jets	44	44	16	19	92

Punt Returns

	No	Yds	Avg	TD
Edmonds, Seattle	34	419	12.3	1
Willhite, Denver	42	468	11.1	1
Fryar, New England	35	366	10.5	1
Anderson, San Diego	25	227	9.1	0
Walker, L.A. Raiders	49	440	9.0	1
Woods, Pittsburgh	33	294	8.9	0
McNeil, Cleveland	40	348	8.7	1
J. Smith, Kansas City	29	245	8.4	0
Sohn, N.Y. Jets	35	289	8.3	0

Punters

	No	Yds	Avg
Stark, Indianapolis	76	3432	37.2
Roby, Miami	56	2476	37.4
Camarillo, New England	89	3746	33.1
Mojsiejenko, San Diego	72	3026	32.9
Gossett, Cleveland	83	3423	35.6
L. Johnson, Houston	88	3623	35.7
Colbert, Kansas City	99	4033	33.7
Kidd, Buffalo	75	3031	34.5
Guy, L.A. Raiders	90	3620	33.8

Interceptions

	No	Yds	TD
Cherry, Kansas City	9	150	0
Lippett, New England	8	76	0
McElroy, L.A. Raiders	7	105	0
Breeden, Cincinnati	7	72	1
Harden, Denver	6	179	2
Holmes, N.Y. Jets	6	29	0
Burruss, Kansas City	5	193	3
Brown, Seattle	5	58	1
Byrd, San Diego	5	45	0
Lyles, N.Y. Jets	5	36	0
Lynn, N.Y. Jets	5	36	0
Dixon, Cleveland	5	35	0

Kickoff Returns

	No	Yds	Avg	TD
Sanchez, Pittsburgh	25	591	23.6	0
McGee, Cincinnati	43	1007	23.4	0
Humphery, N.Y. Jets	28	655	23.4	1
Bell, Denver	23	531	23.1	0
Lang, Denver	21	480	22.9	0
Edmonds, Seattle	34	764	22.5	0
Starring, New England	36	802	22.3	0
Ellis, Miami	25	541	21.6	0
Bentley, Indianapolis	32	687	21.5	0
Adams, L.A. Raiders	27	573	21.2	0

Sacks

	No.		No.		No.
Jones, L.A. Raiders	15.5	Jones, Denver	13.5	Willis, Pittsburgh	12.0
Lee Williams, San Diego	15.0	O'Neal, San Diego	12.5	Pickel, L.A. Raiders	11.5
B.Smith, Buffalo	15.0	Green, Seattle	12.0	Townsend, L.A. Raiders	11.5

National Football Conference Leaders

Passing

Player, team	Atts	Com	YG	TD	Year
John Brodie, San Francisco	378	223	2,941	24	1970
Roger Staubach, Dallas	211	126	1,882	15	1971
Norm Snead, N.Y. Giants	325	196	2,307	17	1972
Roger Staubach, Dallas	286	179	2,428	23	1973
Sonny Jurgensen, Washington	167	107	1,185	11	1974
Fran Tarkenton, Minnesota	425	273	2,294	25	1975
James Harris, Los Angeles	158	91	1,460	8	1976
Roger Staubach, Dallas	361	210	2,620	18	1977
Roger Staubach, Dallas	413	231	3,190	25	1978
Roger Staubach, Dallas	461	267	3,586	27	1979
Ron Jaworski, Philadelphia	451	257	3,529	27	1980
Joe Montana, San Francisco	488	311	3,565	19	1981
Joe Thiesmann, Washington	252	161	2,033	13	1982
Steve Bartkowski, Atlanta	423	274	3,167	22	1983
Joe Montana, San Francisco	432	279	3,630	28	1984
Joe Montana, San Francisco	494	303	3,653	27	1985
Tommy Kramer, Minnesota	372	208	3,000	24	1986

Pass-Receiving

Year	Player, team	Ct	YG	TD
1970	Dick Gordon, Chicago	71	1,026	13
1971	Bob Tucker, Giants	59	791	4
1972	Harold Jackson, Philadelphia	62	1,048	4
1973	Harold Carmichael, Philadelphia	67	1,116	9
1974	Charles Young, Philadelphia	63	696	3
1975	Chuck Foreman, Minnesota	73	691	9
1976	Drew Pearson, Dallas	58	806	6
1977	Ahmad Rashad, Minnesota	51	681	2
1978	Rickey Young, Minnesota	88	704	5
1979	Ahmad Rashad, Minnesota	80	1,156	9
1980	Earl Cooper, San Francisco	83	567	4
1981	Dwight Clark, San Francisco	85	1,105	4
1982	Dwight Clark, San Francisco	60	913	5
1983	Roy Green, St. Louis	78	1,227	14
	Charlie Brown, Washington	78	1,225	8
	Earnest Gray, N.Y. Giants	78	1,139	5
1984	Art Monk, Washington	106	1,372	7
1985	Roger Craig, San Francisco	92	1,016	6
1986	Jerry Rice, San Francisco	86	1,570	15

Scoring

Player, team	TD	PAT	FG	Pts	Year
Fred Cox, Minnesota	0	35	30	125	1970
Curt Knight, Washington	0	27	29	114	1971
Chester Marcol, Green Bay	0	29	33	128	1972
David Ray, Los Angeles	0	40	30	130	1973
Chester Marcol, Green Bay	0	19	25	94	1974
Chuck Foreman, Minnesota	22	0	0	132	1975
Mark Moseley, Washington	0	31	22	97	1976
Walter Payton, Chicago	16	0	0	96	1977
Frank Corrall, Los Angeles	0	31	29	118	1978
Mark Moseley, Washington	0	39	25	114	1979
Ed Murray, Detroit	0	35	27	116	1980
Ed Murray, Detroit	0	46	25	121	1981
Wendell Tyler, L.A. Rams	13	0	0	78	1982
Mark Moseley, Washington	0	62	33	161	1983
Ray Wersching, San Francisco	0	56	25	131	1984
Kevin Butler, Chicago	0	51	31	144	1985
Kevin Butler, Chicago	0	36	28	120	1986

Rushing

Year	Player, team	Yds	Atts	TD
1970	Larry Brown, Washington	1,125	237	5
1971	John Brockington, Green Bay	1,105	216	4
1972	Larry Brown, Washington	1,216	285	8
1973	John Brockington, Green Bay	1,144	265	3
1974	Larry McCutcheon, Los Angeles	1,109	236	3
1975	Jim Otis, St. Louis	1,076	269	5
1976	Walter Payton, Chicago	1,390	311	13
1977	Walter Payton, Chicago	1,852	339	14
1978	Walter Payton, Chicago	1,395	333	11
1979	Walter Payton, Chicago	1,610	369	14
1980	Walter Payton, Chicago	1,460	317	15
1981	George Rogers, New Orleans	1,674	378	13
1982	Tony Dorsett, Dallas	745	177	5
1983	Eric Dickerson, L.A. Rams	1,808	390	18
1984	Eric Dickerson, L.A. Rams	2,105	379	14
1985	Gerald Riggs, Atlanta	1,719	397	10
1986	Eric Dickerson, L.A. Rams	1,821	404	11

American Football Conference Leaders

Passing

Player, team	Atts	Com	YG	TD	Year
Daryle Lamonica, Oakland	356	179	2,516	22	1970
Bob Griese, Miami	263	145	2,089	19	1971
Earl Morrall, Miami	150	83	1,360	11	1972
Ken Stabler, Oakland	260	163	1,997	14	1973
Ken Anderson, Cincinnati	328	213	2,667	18	1974
Ken Anderson, Cincinnati	377	228	3,169	21	1975
Ken Stabler, Oakland	291	194	2,737	27	1976
Bob Griese, Miami	307	180	2,252	22	1977
Terry Bradshaw, Pittsburgh	368	207	2,915	28	1978
Dan Fouts, San Diego	530	332	4,082	24	1979
Brian Sipe, Cleveland	554	337	4,132	30	1980
Ken Anderson, Cincinnati	479	300	3,754	29	1981
Ken Anderson, Cincinnati	309	218	2,495	12	1982
Dan Marino, Miami	296	173	2,210	20	1983
Dan Marino, Miami	564	362	5,084	48	1984
Ken O'Brien, N.Y. Jets	488	297	3,888	25	1985
Dan Marino, Miami	623	378	4,746	44	1986

Pass-Receiving

Year	Player, team	Ct	YG	TD
1970	Marlin Briscoe, Buffalo	57	1,036	8
1971	Fred Biletnikoff, Oakland	61	929	9
1972	Fred Biletnikoff, Oakland	58	802	7
1973	Fred Willis, Houston	57	371	1
1974	Lydell Mitchell, Baltimore	72	544	2
1975	Reggie Rucker, Cleveland	60	770	3
	Lydell Mitchell, Baltimore	60	554	4
1976	MacArthur Lane, Kansas City	66	686	1
1977	Lydell Mitchell, Baltimore	71	620	4
1978	Steve Largent, Seattle	71	1,168	8
1979	Joe Washington, Baltimore	82	750	3
1980	Kellen Winslow, San Diego	89	1,290	9
1981	Kellen Winslow, San Diego	88	1,075	10
1982	Kellen Winslow, San Diego	54	721	6
1983	Todd Christensen, L.A. Raiders	92	1,247	12
1984	Ozzie Newsome, Cleveland	89	1,001	5
1985	Lionel James, San Diego	86	1,027	6
1986	Todd Christensen, L.A. Raiders	95	1,153	8

Scoring

Player, team	TD	PAT	FG	Pts	Year
Jan Stenerud, Kansas City	0	26	30	116	1970
Garo Yepremian, Miami	0	33	28	117	1971
Bobby Howfield, N.Y. Jets	0	40	27	121	1972
Roy Gerela, Pittsburgh	0	36	29	123	1973
Roy Gerela, Pittsburgh	0	33	20	93	1974
O.J. Simpson, Buffalo	23	0	0	138	1975
Toni Linhart, Baltimore	0	49	20	109	1976
Errol Mann, Oakland	0	39	20	99	1977
Pat Leahy, N.Y. Jets	0	41	22	107	1978
John Smith, New England	0	46	23	115	1979
John Smith, New England	0	51	26	129	1980
Jim Breech, Cincinnati	0	49	22	115	1981
Marcus Allen, L.A. Raiders	14	0	0	84	1982
Gary Anderson, Pittsburgh	0	38	27	119	1983
Gary Anderson, Pittsburgh	0	45	24	117	1984
Gary Anderson, Pittsburgh	0	40	33	139	1985
Tony Franklin, New England	0	44	32	140	1986

Rushing

Year	Player, team	Yds	Atts	TD
1970	Floyd Little, Denver	901	209	3
1971	Floyd Little, Denver	1,133	284	6
1972	O.J. Simpson, Buffalo	1,251	292	6
1973	O.J. Simpson, Buffalo	2,003	332	12
1974	Otis Armstrong, Denver	1,407	263	9
1975	O.J. Simpson, Buffalo	1,817	329	16
1976	O.J. Simpson, Buffalo	1,503	290	8
1977	Mark van Eeghen, Oakland	1,273	324	7
1978	Earl Campbell, Houston	1,450	302	13
1979	Earl Campbell, Houston	1,697	368	19
1980	Earl Campbell, Houston	1,934	373	13
1981	Earl Campbell, Houston	1,376	361	10
1982	Freeman McNeil, N.Y. Jets	786	151	6
1983	Curt Warner, Seattle	1,446	335	13
1984	Earnest Jackson, San Diego	1,179	296	8
1985	Marcus Allen, L.A. Raiders	1,759	380	11
1986	Curt Warner, Seattle	1,481	319	13

Bert Bell Memorial Trophy Winners

The Bert Bell Memorial Trophy, named after the former NFL commissioner, is awarded annually to the outstanding rookies in a poll conducted by Murray Olderman of Newspaper Enterprise Assn.

1964	Charlie Taylor, Washington, WR
1965	Gale Sayers, Chicago, RB
1966	Tommy Nobis, Atlanta, LB
1967	Mel Farr, Detroit, RB
1968	Earl McCullouch, Detroit, WR
1969	Calvin Hill, Dallas, RB
1970	Raymond Chester, Oakland, TE
1971	AFC: Jim Plunkett, New England, QB
	NFC: John Brockington, Green Bay, RB
1972	AFC: Franco Harris, Pittsburgh, RB
	NFC: Willie Buchanon, Green Bay, DB
1973	AFC: Boobie Clark, Cincinnati, RB
	NFC: Chuck Foreman, Minnesota, RB
1974	Don Woods, San Diego, RB
1975	AFC: Robert Brazile, Houston, LB
	NFC: Steve Bartkowski, Atlanta, QB
1976	AFC: Mike Haynes, New England, CB
	NFC: Sammy White, Minnesota, WR
1977	Tony Dorsett, Dallas, RB
1978	Earl Campbell, Houston, RB
1979	Ottis Anderson, St. Louis, RB
1980	Billy Sims, Detroit, RB
1981	Lawrence Taylor, N.Y. Giants, LB
1982	Marcus Allen, L.A. Raiders, RB
1983	Eric Dickerson, L.A. Rams, RB
1984	Louis Lipps, Pittsburgh, WR
1985	Eddie Brown, Cincinnati, WR
1986	Rueben Mayes, New Orleans, RB

George Halas Trophy Winners

The Halas Trophy, named after football coach George Halas, is awarded annually to the outstanding defensive player in football in a poll conducted by Murray Olderman of Newspaper Enterprise Assn.

1966	Larry Wilson, St. Louis
1967	Deacon Jones, Los Angeles
1968	Deacon Jones, Los Angeles
1969	Dick Butkus, Chicago
1970	Dick Butkus, Chicago
1971	Carl Eller, Minnesota
1972	Joe Greene, Pittsburgh
1973	Alan Page, Minnesota
1974	Joe Greene, Pittsburgh
1975	Curley Culp, Houston
1976	Jerry Sherk, Cleveland
1977	Harvey Martin, Dallas
1978	Randy Gradishar, Denver
1979	Lee Roy Selmon, Tampa Bay
1980	Lester Hayes, Oakland
1981	Joe Klecko, N.Y. Jets
1982	Mark Gastineau, N.Y. Jets
1983	Jack Lambert, Pittsburgh
1984	Mike Haynes, L.A. Raiders
1985	Howie Long, L.A. Raiders
	Andre Tippett, New England
1986	Lawrence Taylor, N.Y. Giants

NEA/World Almanac All-Pro Team in 1986

Chosen by sports experts of the World Almanac and its 140 co-sponsoring newspapers; and its publisher, Newspaper Enterprise Assn., which distributed the results to over 600 newspapers.

First team	Offense	Second team
Jerry Rice, San Francisco	Wide receiver	Steve Largent, Seattle
Al Toon, N.Y. Jets	Wide receiver	Stanley Morgan, New England
Todd Christensen, L.A. Raiders	Tight end	Mark Bavaro, N.Y. Giants
Anthony Munoz, Cincinnati	Tackle	Gary Zimmerman, Minnesota
Brian Holloway, New England	Tackle	Jackie Slater, L.A. Rams
Bill Fralic, Atlanta	Guard	Randy Cross, San Francisco
Russ Grimm, Washington	Guard	Dan Fike, Cleveland
Dwight Stephenson, Miami	Center	Jay Hilgenberg, Chicago
Phil Simms, N.Y. Giants	Quarterback	Dan Marino, Miami
Joe Morris, N.Y. Giants	Running back	Curt Warner, Seattle
Eric Dickerson, L.A. Rams	Running back	Walter Payton, Chicago
Morton Anderson, New Orleans	Placekicker	Pat Leahy, N.Y. Jets

First team	Defense	Second team
Dexter Manley, Washington	End	Howie Long, L.A. Raiders
Dan Hampton, Chicago	End	Rulon Jones, Denver
Michael Carter, San Francisco	Nose guard	Bob Golic, Cleveland
Reggie White, Philadelphia	Tackle	Keith Millard, Minnesota
Karl Mecklenburg, Denver	Inside linebacker	Harry Carson, N.Y. Giants
Mike Singletary, Chicago	Inside linebacker	Kyle Clifton, N.Y. Jets
Rickey Jackson, New Orleans	Outside Linebacker	Andre Tippett, New England
Lawrence Taylor, N.Y. Giants	Outside linebacker	Wilbur Marshall, Chicago
Darrell Green, Washington	Cornerback	Albert Lewis, Kansas City
Hanford Dixon, Cleveland	Cornerback	Leroy Irvin, L.A. Rams
Dennis Smith, Denver	Strong safety	Leonard Smith, St. Louis
Ronnie Lott, San Francisco	Free safety	Deron Cherry, Kansas City
Rohn Stark, Indianapolis	Punter	Sean Landeta, N.Y. Giants

NFL Team Rankings in 1986

	Offense			Defense		
	Total	Rush	Pass	Total	Rush	Pass
Atlanta	17	3	25	7	16	7
Buffalo	19	21	15	24	9	27
Cincinnati	1	2	3	20	22	10
Chicago	7	1	20	1	2	2
Cleveland	9	22	8	19	18	15
Dallas	6	11	12	10	23	3
Denver	15	20	10	9	5	16
Detroit	24	15	19	15	26	4
Green Bay	18	23	14	12	21	5
Houston	16	19	13	13	20	8
Indianapolis	22	26	16	25	17	26
Kansas City	28	27	21	8	11	12
L.A. Raiders	14	13	11	3	10	9
L.A. Rams	23	4	28	5	8	11
Miami	2	25	1	26*	27	22
Minnesota	4	16	5	11	13	13
New England	13	28	4	16	24	6
New Orleans	21	8	23	14	4	21
N.Y. Giants	10	6	17	2	1	19
N.Y. Jets	11	18	9	26*	6	28
Philadelphia	25	9	26	17	19	14
Pittsburgh	20	7	24	18	15	18
St. Louis	26	14	22	4	25	1
San Diego	12	24	7	23	7	25
San Francisco	3	10	2	6	3	17
Seattle	8	5	18	22	12	23
Tampa Bay	27	12	27	28	28	24
Washington	5	17	6	21	14	20

*Tie.

All-Time Football Records

NFL, AFL, and All-American Football Conference

(at start of 1987 season)

Leading Lifetime Rushers

Player	League	Yrs	Att	Yards	Avg	Player	League	Yrs	Att	Yards	Avg
Walter Payton	NFL	12	3,692	16,193	4.4	O.J. Anderson	NFL	8	1,882	8,080	4.3
Jim Brown	NFL	9	2,359	12,312	5.2	Mike Pruitt	NFL	11	1,844	7,378	4.0
Franco Harris	NFL	13	2,949	12,120	4.1	Leroy Kelly	NFL	10	1,727	7,274	4.2
Tony Dorsett	NFL	10	2,625	11,580	4.4	Eric Dickerson	NFL	4	1,495	6,968	4.7
John Riggins	NFL	14	2,916	11,352	3.9	John Henry Johnson	NFL-AFL	13	1,571	6,803	4.3
O.J. Simpson	AFL-NFL	11	2,404	11,236	4.7	Wilbert Montgomery	NFL	9	1,540	6,789	4.4
Joe Perry	AAFC-NFL	16	1,929	9,723	5.0	Chuck Muncie	NFL	9	1,561	6,702	4.3
Earl Campbell	NFL	8	2,187	9,407	4.3	Mark van Eeghen	NFL	10	1,652	6,651	4.0
Jim Taylor	NFL	10	1,941	8,597	4.4	Lawrence McCutcheon	NFL	10	1,521	6,578	4.3
Larry Csonka	AFL-NFL	11	1,891	8,081	4.3	George Rogers	NFL	6	1,529	6,563	4.3

Most Yards Gained, Season — 2,105, Eric Dickerson, Los Angeles Rams, 1984.
Most Yards Gained, Game — 275, Walter Payton, Chicago Bears vs. Minnesota Vikings, Nov. 20, 1977.
Most Games, 100 Yards or more, Season — 12, Eric Dickerson, Los Angeles Rams, 1984.
Most Games, 100 Yards or more, Career — 77, Walter Payton, Chicago Bears, 1975-86.
Most Touchdowns Rushing, Career — 106, Jim Brown, Cleveland Browns, 1957-1965; Walter Payton, Chicago Bears, 1975-1986.
Most Touchdowns Rushing, Season — 24, John Riggins, Washington Redskins, 1983.
Most Touchdowns Rushing, Game — 6, Ernie Nevers, Chicago Cardinals vs. Chicago Bears, Nov. 8, 1929.
Most Rushing Attempts, Season — 407, James Wilder, Tampa Bay Buccaneers, 1984.
Most Rushing Attempts, Game — 43, Butch Woolfolk, N.Y. Giants vs. Philadelphia, Nov. 20, 1983; James Wilder, Tampa Bay Buccaneers vs. Pittsburgh, Sept. 30, 1984.
Longest run from Scrimmage — 99 yds., Tony Dorsett, Dallas vs. Minnesota, Jan. 3, 1983 (scored touchdown).

Leading Lifetime Passers

(Minimum 1,500 attempts)

Player	League	Yrs	Att	Comp	Yds	Pts*	Player	League	Yrs	Att	Comp	Yds	Pts*
Dan Marino	NFL	4	2,050	1,249	16,177	95.2	Neil Lomax	NFL	6	2,247	1,287	15,989	80.7
Joe Montana	NFL	8	2,878	1,818	21,498	91.2	Bart Starr	NFL	16	3,149	1,808	24,718	80.5
Otto Graham	AAFC-NFL	10	2,626	1,464	23,584	86.6	Fran Tarkenton	NFL	18	6,467	3,686	47,003	80.4
Dave Krieg	NFL	7	1,822	1,046	13,677	84.1	Johnny Unitas	NFL	18	5,186	2,830	40,239	78.2
Roger Staubach	NFL	11	2,958	1,685	22,700	83.4	Bert Jones	NFL	10	2,551	1,430	18,190	78.2
Danny White	NFL	11	2,546	1,517	19,068	83.2	Frank Ryan	NFL	13	2,133	1,090	16,042	77.6
Sonny Jurgensen	NFL	18	4,262	2,433	32,224	82.6	Bill Kenney	NFL	8	2,043	1,118	14,261	77.5
Len Dawson	NFL-AFL	19	3,741	2,136	28,711	82.6	Joe Theismann	NFL	12	3,602	2,044	25,206	77.4
Ken Anderson	NFL	15	4,452	2,643	32,667	82.0	Bob Griese	AFL-NFL	14	3,429	1,926	25,092	77.1
Dan Fouts	NFL	13	4,810	2,839	37,492	81.8	Gary Danielson	NFL	11	1,847	1,049	13,159	75.6

*Rating points based on performances in the following categories: Percentage of completions, percentage of touchdown passes, percentage of interceptions, and average gain per pass attempt.

Most Yards Gained, Season — 5,084, Dan Marino, Miami Dolphins, 1984.
Most Yards Gained, Game — 554, Norm Van Brocklin, Los Angeles Rams vs. New York Yankees, Sept. 18, 1951 (27 completions in 41 attempts).
Most Touchdowns Passing, Career — 342, Fran Tarkenton, Minnesota Vikings, 1961-66; N.Y. Giants, 1967-71; Vikings, 1972-78.
Most Touchdown Passing, Season — 48, Dan Marino, Miami Dolphins, 1984.
Most Touchdown Passing, Game — 7, Sid Luckman, Chicago Bears vs. New York Giants, Nov. 14, 1943; Adrian Burk, Philadelphia Eagles vs. Washington Redskins, Oct. 17, 1954; George Blanda, Houston Oilers vs. New York Titans, Nov. 19, 1961; Y.A. Tittle, New York Giants vs. Washington Redskins, Oct. 28, 1962; Joe Kapp, Minnesota Vikings vs. Baltimore Colts, Sept. 28, 1969.
Most Passing Attempts, Season — 623, Dan Marino, Miami Dolphins, 1986.
Most Passing Attempts, Game — 68, George Blanda, Houston Oilers vs. Buffalo Bills, Nov. 1, 1964 (37 completions).
Most Passes Completed, Season — 378, Dan Marino, Miami Dolphins, 1986.
Most Passes Completed, Game — 42, Richard Todd, N.Y. Jets vs. San Francisco 49ers, Sept. 21, 1980.
Most Consecutive Passes Completed — 20, Ken Anderson, Cincinnati vs. Houston, Jan. 2, 1983.
Most Consecutive Games, Touchdown Passes — 47, John Unitas, Baltimore Colts, 1956-1960.

Leading Lifetime Receivers

Player	League	Yrs	No	Yds	Avg	Player	League	Yrs	No	Yds	Avg
Charlie Joiner	NFL	18	750	12,146	16.2	Ozzie Newsom	NFL	9	541	6,698	12.4
Steve Largent	NFL	11	694	11,129	16.0	James Lofton	NFL	9	530	9,656	18.2
Charley Taylor	NFL	13	649	9,110	14.0	Bobby Mitchell	NFL	11	521	7,954	15.3
Don Maynard	AFL-NFL	15	633	11,834	18.7	Wes Chandler	NFL	9	516	8,316	16.1
Raymond Berry	NFL	13	631	9,275	14.7	Nat Moore	NFL	13	510	7,546	14.8
Harold Carmichael	NFL	14	590	8,985	15.2	Billy Howton	NFL	12	503	8,459	16.8
Fred Biletnikoff	AFL-NFL	14	589	8,974	15.2	Cliff Branch	NFL	12	501	8,685	17.3
Harold Jackson	NFL	16	579	10,372	17.9	John Stallworth	NFL	13	496	8,202	16.5
Lionel Taylor	AFL	10	567	7,195	12.7	Tommy McDonald	NFL	12	495	8,410	17.0
Lance Alworth	AFL-NFL	11	542	10,266	18.9	Ahmad Rashad	NFL	10	495	6,831	13.8

Most Yards Gained, Season — 1,746, Charley Hennigan, Houston Oilers, 1961.
Most Yards Gained, Game — 309, Stephone Paige, Kansas City Chiefs vs. San Diego Chargers, Dec. 22, 1985.
Most Pass Receptions, Season — 106, Art Monk, Washington Redskins, 1984.
Most Pass Receptions, Game — 18, Tom Fears, Los Angeles Rams vs. Green Bay Packers, Dec. 3, 1950 (189 yards).
Most Consecutive Games, Pass Receptions — 139, Steve Largent, Seattle Seahawks, 1976-1986.
Most Touchdown Passes, Career — 99, Don Hutson, Green Bay Packers, 1935-1945.
Most Touchdown Passes, Season — 18, Mark Clayton, Miami Dolphins, 1984.
Most Touchdown Passes, Game — 5, Bob Shaw, Chicago Cardinals vs. Baltimore Colts, Oct. 2, 1950; Kellen Winslow, San Diego vs. Oakland, Nov. 22, 1981.

Leading Lifetime Scorers

Player	League	Yrs	TD	PAT	FG	Total
George Blanda	NFL-AFL	26	9	943	335	2,002
Jan Stenerud	AFL-NFL	19	0	580	373	1,699
Lou Groza	AAFC-NFL	21	1	810	264	1,608
Jim Turner	AFL-NFL	16	1	521	304	1,439
Mark Moseley	NFL	16	0	482	300	1,382
Jim Bakken	NFL	17	0	534	282	1,380
Fred Cox	NFL	15	0	519	282	1,365
Gino Cappelletti	AFL	11	42	350	176	1,130
Don Cockroft	NFL	13	0	432	216	1,080
Garo Yepremian	AFL-NFL	14	0	444	210	1,074
Ray Wersching	NFL	14	0	412	209	1,039
Bruce Gossett	NFL	11	0	374	219	1,031
Pat Leahy	NFL	13	0	393	200	993
Sam Baker	NFL	15	2	428	179	977
Rafael Septien	NFL	10	0	420	180	960
Chris Bahr	NFL	11	0	397	187	958
Lou Michaels	NFL	13	1	386	187	955*
Roy Gerela	AFL-NFL	11	0	351	184	903
Bobby Walston	NFL	12	46	365	80	881
Pete Gogolak	AFL-NFL	10	0	344	173	863

*Includes safety.

Most Points, Season — 176, Paul Hornung, Green Bay Packers, 1960 (15 TD's, 41 PAT's, 15 FG's).
Most Points, Game — 40, Ernie Nevers, Chicago Cardinals vs. Chicago Bears, Nov. 28, 1929 (6 TD's, 4 PAT's).
Most Touchdowns, Season — 24, John Riggins, Washington Redskins, 1984 (24 rushing).
Most Touchdowns, Game — 6, Ernie Nevers, Chicago Cardinals vs. Chicago Bears, Nov. 28, 1929 (6 rushing); Dub Jones, Cleveland Browns vs. Chicago Bears, Nov. 25, 1951 (4 rushing, 2 pass receptions); Gale Sayers, Chicago Bears vs. San Francisco 49ers, Dec. 12, 1965 (4 rushing, 1 pass reception, 1 punt return).
Most Points After Touchdown, Season — 66, Uwe von Schamann, Miami Dolphins, 1984.
Most Consecutive Points After Touchdown — 234, Tommy Davis, San Francisco 49ers, 1959-1969.
Most Field Goals, Game — 7, Jim Bakken, St. Louis Cardinals vs. Pittsburgh Steelers, Sept. 24, 1967.
Most Field Goals, Season — 35, Ali Haji-Sheikh, N.Y. Giants, 1983.
Most Field Goals Attempted, Season — 49, Bruce Gossett, Los Angeles Rams, 1966; Curt Knight, Washington Redskins, 1971.
Most Field Goals Attempted, Game — 9, Jim Bakken, St. Louis Cardinals vs. Pittsburgh Steelers, Sept. 24, 1967 (7 successful).
Most Consecutive Field Goals — 23, Mark Moseley, Washington Redskins, 1981-1982.
Most Consecutive Games, Field Goal — 31, Fred Cox, Minnesota Vikings, 1968-1970.
Longest Field Goal — 63 yds., Tom Dempsey, New Orleans Saints vs. Detroit Lions, Nov. 8, 1970.
Highest Field Goal Completion Percentage, Season (20 attempts) — 95.24 Mark Moseley, Washington Redskins, 1982 (20 FG's in 21 attempts).

Pass Interceptions

Most Passes Had Intercepted, Game — 8, Jim Hardy, Chicago Cardinals vs. Philadelphia Eagles, Sept. 24, 1950 (39 attempts)
Most Passes Had Intercepted, Season — 42, George Blanda, Houston Oilers, 1962 (418 attempts).
Most Passes Had Intercepted, Career — 277, George Blanda, Chicago Bears, 1949-1958; Houston Oilers, 1960-1966; Oakland Raiders, 1967-1975 (4,000 attempts).
Most Consecutive Passes Attempted Without Interception — 294, Bart Starr, Green Bay Packers, 1964-1965.
Most Interceptions By, Season — 14, Dick Lane, Los Angeles Rams, 1952.
Most Interceptions By, Career — 81, Paul Krause, Washington Redskins, 1964-67; Minnesota Vikings, 1968-79.
Most Consecutive Games, Passes Intercepted By — 8, Tom Morrow, Oakland Raiders, 1962 (4), 1963 (4).

Punting

Most Punts, Career — 1,090, Dave Jennings, N.Y. Giants, 1974-1984; N.Y. Jets, 1985-1986.
Most Punts, Season — 114, Bob Parsons, Chicago Bears, 1981.
Highest Punting Average, Season (20 punts) — 51.40, Sam Baugh, Washington Redskins, 1940 (35 punts).
Longest Punt — 98 yds., Steve O'Neal, New York Jets vs. Denver Broncos, Sept. 21, 1969.

Kickoff Returns

Most Yardage Returning Kickoffs, Career — 6,922, Ron Smith, Chicago Bears, 1965; Atlanta Falcons, 1966-67; Los Angeles Rams, 1968-69; Chicago Bears, 1970-72; San Diego Chargers, 1973; Oakland Raiders, 1974.
Most Yardage Returning Kickoffs, Season — 1,345, Buster Rhymes, Minnesota Vikings, 1985.
Most Yardage Returning Kickoffs, Game — 294, Wally Triplett, Detroit Lions vs. Los Angeles Rams, Oct. 29, 1950 (4 returns)
Most Touchdowns Scored via Kickoff Returns, Career — 6, Ollie Matson, Chicago Cardinals, 1952 (2), 1954, 1956, 1958 (2); Gale Sayers, Chicago Bears, 1965, 1966 (2), 1967 (3); Travis Williams, Green Bay Packers, 1967 (4), 1969; Los Angeles Rams, 1971.
Most Touchdowns Scored via Kickoff Returns, Season — 4, Travis Williams, Green Bay Packers, 1967; Cecil Turner, Chicago Bears, 1970.
Most Touchdowns Scored via Kickoff Returns, Game — 2, Tim Brown, Philadelphia Eagles vs. Dallas Cowboys, Nov. 6, 1966; Travis Williams, Green Bay Packers vs. Cleveland Browns, Nov. 12, 1967; Ron Brown, Los Angeles Rams vs. Green Bay Packers, Nov. 24, 1985.
Most Kickoff Returns, Career — 275, Ron Smith, Chicago Bears, 1965; Atlanta Falcons, 1966-67; Los Angeles Rams, 1968-69; Chicago Bears, 1970-72; San Diego Chargers, 1973; Oakland Raiders, 1974.
Most Kickoff Returns, Season — 60, Drew Hill, Los Angeles Rams, 1981.
Longest Kickoff Return — 106 yds., Al Carmichael, Green Bay Packers vs. Chicago Bears, October 7, 1956; Noland Smith, Kansas City vs. Denver, Dec. 17, 1967; Roy Green, St. Louis Cardinals vs. Dallas Cowboys, Oct. 21, 1979 (all scored TD).

Punt Returns

Most Yardage Returning Punts, Career — 3,123, Billy Johnson, Houston, 1974-80, Atlanta, 1982-86.
Most Yardage Returning Punts, Season — 692, Fulton Walker, Miami-L.A. Raiders, 1985.
Most Yardage Returning Punts, Game — 207, Leroy Irvin, Los Angeles Rams vs. Atlanta Falcons, Oct. 11, 1981.
Most Touchdowns Scored via Punt Returns, Career — 8, Jack Christiansen, Detroit Lions, 1951-1958; Rick Upchurch, Denver Broncos, 1975-83.
Most Punt Returns, Career — 258, Emlen Tunnell, New York Giants, 1948-1958; Green Bay Packers, 1959-1961; Billy Johnson, Houston Oilers, 1974-1980; Atlanta Falcons, 1982-1986.
Most Punt Returns, Season — 70, Danny Reece, Tampa Bay Buccaneers, 1979.

Miscellaneous Records

Most Fumbles, Season — 17, Dan Pastorini, Houston Oilers, 1973; Warren Moon, Houston Oilers, 1984.
Most Fumbles, Game — 7, Len Dawson, Kansas City Chiefs vs. San Diego Chargers, Nov. 15, 1964.
Most Sacks, Season — 22, Mark Gastineau, New York Jets, 1984.
Winning Streak (Regular Season) — 17 games, Chicago Bears, 1933-34.
Most Seasons, Active Player — 26, George Blanda, Chicago Bears, 1949-1958; Houston Oilers, 1960-1966 and Oakland, 67-75.
Most Consecutive Games Played, Career — 282, Jim Marshall, Cleveland Browns, 1960; Minnesota Vikings, 1961-1979.

Jim Thorpe Trophy Winners

The Jim Thorpe Trophy goes to the most valuable player as chosen in a poll of NFL players.

Year	Winner
1955	Harlon Hill, Chicago Bears
1956	Frank Gifford, N.Y. Giants
1957	John Unitas, Baltimore Colts
1958	Jim Brown, Cleveland Browns
1959	Charley Conerly, N.Y. Giants
1960	Norm Van Brocklin, Philadelphia Eagles
1961	Y.A. Tittle, N.Y. Giants
1962	Jim Taylor, Green Bay Packers
1963	Jim Brown, Cleveland Browns; Y.A. Tittle, N.Y. Giants
1964	Lenny Moore, Baltimore Colts
1965	Jim Brown, Cleveland Browns
1966	Bart Starr, Green Bay Packers
1967	John Unitas, Baltimore Colts
1968	Earl Morrall, Baltimore Colts
1969	Roman Gabriel, Los Angeles Rams
1970	John Brodie, San Francisco 49ers
1971	Bob Griese, Miami Dolphins
1972	Larry Brown, Washington Redskins
1973	O.J. Simpson, Buffalo Bills
1974	Ken Stabler, Oakland Raiders
1975	Fran Tarkenton, Minnesota Vikings
1976	Bert Jones, Baltimore Colts
1977	Walter Payton, Chicago Bears
1978	Earl Campbell, Houston Oilers
1979	Earl Campbell, Houston Oilers
1980	Earl Campbell, Houston Oilers
1981	Ken Anderson, Cincinnati Bengals
1982	Dan Fouts, San Diego Chargers
1983	Joe Theismann, Washington Redskins
1984	Dan Marino, Miami Dolphins
1985	Walter Payton, Chicago Bears
1986	Phil Simms, N.Y. Giants

1987 NFL Player Draft

The following are the first round picks of the National Football League.

Team	Player	Pos.	College
1—Tampa Bay	Vinny Testaverde	QB	Miami
2—Indianapolis	Cornelius Bennett	LB	Alabama
3—Houston	Alonzo Highsmith	RB	Miami
4—Green Bay	Brent Fullwood	RB	Auburn
5—Cleveland	Mike Junkin	LB	Duke
6—St. Louis	Kelly Stouffer	QB	Colorado State
7—Detroit	Reggie Rogers	DE	Washington
8—Buffalo	Shane Conlan	LB	Penn State
9—Philadelphia	Jerome Brown	DT	Miami
10—Pittsburgh	Rod Woodson	DB	Purdue
11—New Orleans	Shawn Knight	DL	BYU
12—Dallas	Danny Noonan	DL	Nebraska
13—Atlanta	Chris Miller	QB	Oregon
14—Minnesota	D. J. Dozier	RB	Penn State
15—L.A. Raiders	John Clay	OT	Missouri
16—Miami	John Bosa	DE	Boston College
17—Cincinnati	Jason Buck	DE	BYU
18—Seattle	Tony Woods	LB	Pittsburgh
19—Kansas City	Paul Palmer	RB	Temple
20—Houston	Haywood Jeffires	WR	N.C. State
21—N.Y. Jets	Roger Vick	RB	Texas A&M
22—San Francisco	Harris Barton	OT	North Carolina
23—New England	Bruce Armstrong	OT	Louisville
24—San Diego	Rod Bernstine	TE	Texas A&M
25—San Francisco	Terrence Flagler	RB	Clemson
26—Chicago	Jim Harbaugh	QB	Michigan
27—Denver	Ricky Nattiel	WR	Florida
28—N.Y. Giants	Mark Ingram	WR	Michigan State

Pro Football Hall of Fame, Canton, Ohio

Herb Adderley
Lance Alworth
Doug Atkins
Morris (Red) Badgro
Cliff Battles
Sammy Baugh
Chuck Bednarik
Bert Bell
Bobby Bell
Raymond Berry
Charles Bidwell
George Blanda
Jim Brown
Paul Brown
Roosevelt Brown
Willie Brown
Dick Butkus
Tony Canadeo
Joe Carr
Guy Chamberlin
Jack Christiansen
Dutch Clark
George Connor
Jim Conzelman
Larry Csonka
Willie Davis
Len Dawson
Art Donovan
Paddy Driscoll
Bill Dudley
Turk Edwards
Weeb Ewbank
Tom Fears
Ray Flaherty
Len Ford
Dr. Daniel Fortmann
Frank Gatski
Bill George
Frank Gifford
Sid Gillman
Otto Graham
Red Grange
Joe Greene
Forrest Gregg
Lou Groza
Joe Guyon
George Halas
Ed Healey
Mel Hein
Pete Henry
Arnold Herber
Bill Hewitt
Clarke Hinkle
Elroy (Crazy Legs) Hirsch
Paul Hornung
Ken Houston
Cal Hubbard
Sam Huff
Lamar Hunt
Don Hutson
John Henry Johnson
Deacon Jones
Sonny Jurgensen
Walt Kiesling
Frank (Bruiser) Kinard
Curly Lambeau
Dick (Night Train) Lane
Jim Langer
Willie Lanier
Yale Lary
Dante Lavelli
Bobby Layne
Tuffy Leemans
Bob Lilly
Vince Lombardi
Sid Luckman
Link Lyman
Tim Mara
Gino Marchetti
George Marshall
Ollie Matson
Don Maynard
George McAfee
Mike McCormack
Hugh McElhenny
John (Blood) McNally
Mike Michalske
Wayne Millner
Bobby Mitchell
Ron Mix
Lenny Moore
Marion Motley
George Musso
Bronko Nagurski
Joe Namath
Greasy Neale
Ernie Nevers
Ray Nitschke
Leo Nomellini
Merlin Olsen
Jim Otto
Steve Owen
Clarence (Ace) Parker
Jim Parker
Joe Perry
Pete Pihos
Hugh (Shorty) Ray
Dan Reeves
Jim Ringo
Andy Robustelli
Art Rooney
Pete Rozelle
Gale Sayers
Joe Schmidt
O.J. Simpson
Bart Starr
Roger Staubach
Ernie Stautner
Ken Strong
Joe Stydahar
Fran Tarkenton
Charlie Taylor
Jim Taylor
Jim Thorpe
Y.A. Tittle
George Trafton
Charlie Trippi
Emlen Tunnell
Clyde (Bulldog) Turner
Johnny Unitas
Gene Upshaw
Norm Van Brocklin
Steve Van Buren
Doak Walker
Paul Warfield
Bob Waterfield
Arnie Weinmeister
Bill Willis
Larry Wilson
Alex Wojciechowicz

American Football League

Year	Eastern Division	Western Division	Playoff
1960	Houston Oilers (10-4-0)	L. A. Chargers (10-4-0)	Houston 24, Los Angeles 16
1961	Houston Oilers (10-3-1)	San Diego Chargers (12-2-0)	Houston 10, San Diego 3
1962	Houston Oilers (11-3-0)	Dallas Texans (11-3-0)	Dallas 20, Houston 17(b)
1963	Boston Patriots (8-6-1)(a)	San Diego Chargers (11-3-0)	San Diego 51, Boston 10
1964	Buffalo Bills (12-2-0)	San Diego Chargers (8-5-1)	Buffalo 20, San Diego 7
1965	Buffalo Bills (10-3-1)	San Diego Chargers (9-2-3)	Buffalo 23, San Diego 0
1966	Buffalo Bills (9-4-1)	Kansas City Chiefs (11-2-1)	Kansas City 31, Buffalo 7
1967	Houston Oilers (9-4-1)	Oakland Raiders (13-1-0)	Oakland 40, Houston 7
1968	New York Jets (11-3-0)	Oakland Raiders (12-2-0)(a)	New York 27, Oakland 23
1969	New York Jets (10-4-0)	Oakland Raiders (12-1-1)	Kansas City 17, Oakland 7(c)

(a) won divisional playoff (b) won at 2:45 of second overtime. (c) Kansas City defeated Jets to make playoffs.

Canadian Football League Championships

Winners of Eastern and Western divisions meet in championship game for Grey Cup (donated by Governor-General Earl Grey in 1909). Canadian football features 3 downs, 110-yard field, and each team can have 12 players on field at one time.

1956	Edmonton Eskimos 50, Montreal Alouettes 27
1957	Hamilton Tiger-Cats 32, Winnipeg Blue Bombers 7
1958	Winnipeg Blue Bombers 35, Hamilton Tiger-Cats 28
1959	Winnipeg Blue Bombers 21, Hamilton Tiger-Cats 7
1960	Ottawa Rough Riders 16, Edmonton Eskimos 6
1961	Winnipeg Blue Bombers 21, Hamilton Tiger-Cats 14
1962	Winnipeg Blue Bombers 28, Hamilton Tiger-Cats 27
1963	Hamilton Tiger-Cats 21, British Columbia Lions 10
1964	British Columbia Lions 34, Hamilton Tiger-Cats 24
1965	Hamilton Tiger-Cats 22, Winnipeg Blue Bombers 16
1966	Saskatchewan Roughriders 29, Ottawa Rough Riders 14
1967	Hamilton Tiger-Cats 24, Saskatchewan Roughriders 1
1968	Ottawa Rough Riders 24, Calgary Stampeders 21
1969	Ottawa Rough Riders 29, Saskatchewan Roughriders 11
1970	Montreal Alouettes 23, Calgary Stampeders 10
1971	Calgary Stampeders 14, Toronto Argonauts 11
1972	Hamilton Tiger-Cats 13, Saskatchewan Roughriders 10
1973	Ottawa Rough Riders 22, Edmonton Eskimos 18
1974	Montreal Alouettes 20, Edmonton Eskimos 7
1975	Edmonton Eskimos 9, Montreal Alouettes 8
1976	Ottawa Rough Riders 23, Saskatchewan Roughriders 20
1977	Montreal Alouettes 41, Edmonton Eskimos 6
1978	Edmonton Eskimos 20, Montreal Alouettes 13
1979	Edmonton Eskimos 17, Montreal Alouettes 9
1980	Edmonton Eskimos 48, Hamilton Tiger-Cats 10
1981	Edmonton Eskimos 26, Ottawa Rough Riders 23
1982	Edmonton Eskimos 32, Toronto Argonauts 16
1983	Toronto Argonauts 18, B.C. Lions 17
1984	Winnipeg Blue Bombers 47, Hamilton Tiger-Cats 17
1985	B.C. Lions 37, Hamilton Tiger-Cats 24
1986	Hamilton Tiger-Cats 39, Edmonton Eskimos 15

Football Stadiums

See index for major league baseball stadium seating capacity, and college football stadiums.

Name, location	Capacity
Alamo Stadium, San Antonio, Tex.	32,000
Anaheim Stadium, Anaheim, Cal.	69,007
Arrowhead Stadium, Kansas City, Mo.	78,198
Astrodome, Houston, Tex.	47,695
Atlanta-Fulton County Stadium	59,709
Baltimore Memorial Stadium	60,714
Buffalo War Memorial Stadium	46,206
Busch Stadium, St. Louis	51,392
Candlestick Park, San Francisco, Cal.	61,413
Cleveland Stadium	80,098
Cotton Bowl, Dallas, Tex.	72,000
Franklin Field, Philadelphia, Pa.	60,546
Gator Bowl, Jacksonville, Fla.	70,000
Giants Stadium, E. Rutherford, N.J.	76,891
Hoosier Dome, Indianapolis, Ind.	60,127
Hubert H. Humphrey Metrodome, Minneapolis	62,212
John F. Kennedy Stadium, Philadelphia, Pa.	105,000
Robert F. Kennedy Stadium, Wash., D.C.	55,750
Kezar Stadium, San Francisco, Cal.	59,636
Kingdome, Seattle, Wash.	64,752
Ladd Memorial Stadium, Mobile, Ala.	40,605
Lambeau Field, Green Bay, Wis.	56,189
Legion Field, Birmingham, Ala.	75,412
Liberty Bowl, Memphis, Tenn.	50,180
Los Angeles Memorial Coliseum	92,516
Louisiana Superdome, New Orleans	69,105
Mile High Stadium, Denver, Col.	75,123
Milwaukee County Stadium	55,958
Mississippi Memorial Stadium, Jackson	61,000
Oakland-Alameda County Coliseum	54,615
Orange Bowl, Miami, Fla.	75,500
Orlando Stadium, Orlando, Fla.	50,000
Pontiac Silverdome, Mich.	80,638
Portland Civic Stadium, Portland, Ore.	32,500
Rich Stadium, Buffalo, N.Y.	80,290
Riverfront Stadium, Cincinnati, Oh.	59,754
Joe Robbie Stadium, Miami, Fla.	75,000
Rose Bowl, Pasadena, Cal.	106,721
San Diego Jack Murphy Stadium, San Diego	60,100
Soldier Field, Chicago, Ill.	65,793
Sullivan Stadium, Foxboro, Mass.	61,890
Tampa Stadium, Tampa, Fla.	74,317
Texas Stadium, Irving, Tex.	63,855
Three Rivers Stadium, Pittsburgh, Pa.	59,000
Veterans Stadium, Philadelphia, Pa.	69,417

Professional Sports Arenas

The seating capacity of sports arenas can vary depending on the event being presented. The figures below are the normal seating capacity for basketball. (*) indicates hockey seating capacity. Domed stadiums can dramatically increase seating capacity for special occasions.

Name, location	Capacity
Arco Arena, Sacramento	10,333
Arena, The, St. Louis, Mo.	20,000-*17,666
Arizona Veteran's Memorial Coliseum, Phoenix	14,519
Baltimore Civic Center	13,043-*10,200
Boston Garden	14,890-*14,451
Buffalo Memorial Auditorium	17,900-*16,433(a)
Capital Centre, Landover, Md.	19,105-*18,130
Chicago Stadium	17,458-*17,317
Cincinnati Gardens	11,650-*10,606
Cobo Hall, Detroit	11,147
The Coliseum, Richfield Township, Oh.	20,900
Cow Palace, San Francisco	14,500-*12,195
Freedom Hall, Louisville, Ky.	16,613
Greensboro Coliseum	15,500-*13,280
Halifax Metro Centre	*9,552
Hartford Civic Center	*15,100
HemisFair Arena, San Antonio	15,800
Jefferson County Coliseum, Birmingham, Ala.	*16,753
Joe Louis Sports Arena, Detroit	*19,275
Kemper Arena, Kansas City	16,778
Kingdome, Seattle	40,192
Los Angeles Forum	17,505-*16,005
Los Angeles Memorial Sports Arena	15,371
Louisiana Superdome	47,284
Madison Square Garden, New York	19,591-*17,500
Maple Leaf Gardens, Toronto	*16,382(a)
Market Square Arena, Indianapolis	16,912-*15,822
McNichols Arena, Denver,	17,022-*16,399
Meadowlands Arena, E. Rutherford, N.J.	20,149-*19,040
Met. Sports Center, Bloomington, Minn.	*15,471
Milwaukee Arena	11,052-*8,946
Montreal Forum	*16,074
Nassau Veterans Memorial Coliseum, Uniondale, N.Y.	*16,002
Northlands Coliseum, Edmonton	*17,300(a)
Oakland Coliseum Arena	15,011
Olympia Stadium, Detroit	*16,673
Olympic Saddledome, Calgary, Alta	*16,673
The Omni, Atlanta	16,074
Pacific Coliseum, Vancouver, B.C.	*16,553
Pittsburgh Civic Arena	*16,033
Portland Memorial Coliseum	12,666
Quebec Coliseum	*15,434
Reunion Arena, Dallas	17,007
Riverfront Coliseum, Cincinnati	*15,794
Salt Palace, Salt Lake City	12,212-*10,594
San Diego Sports Arena	13,753-*13,039
Seattle Center Coliseum	14,200
Silverdome, Pontiac, Mich.	22,366
Spectrum, Philadelphia	17,941-*17,191
The Summit, Houston	16,016
Thomas and Mack Center, Las Vegas	18,500
Winnipeg Arena	*15,250

(a) includes standees

COLLEGE FOOTBALL

Annual Results of Major Bowl Games

(Note: Dates indicate the year that the game was played).

Rose Bowl, Pasadena

1902 Michigan 49, Stanford 0
1916 Wash. State 14, Brown 0
1917 Oregon 14, Pennsylvania 0
1918-19 Service teams
1920 Harvard 7, Oregon 6
1921 California 28, Ohio State 0
1922 Wash. & Jeff. 0, California 0
1923 So. California 14, Penn State 3
1924 Navy 14, Washington 14
1925 Notre Dame 27, Stanford 10
1926 Alabama 20, Washington 19
1927 Alabama 7, Stanford 7
1928 Stanford 7, Pittsburgh 6
1929 Georgia Tech 8, California 7
1930 So. California 47, Pittsburgh 14
1931 Alabama 24, Wash. State 0
1932 So. California 21, Tulane 12
1933 So. California 35, Pittsburgh 0
1934 Columbia 7, Stanford 0
1935 Alabama 29, Stanford 13
1936 Stanford 7, So. Methodist 0
1937 Pittsburgh 21, Washington 0
1938 California 13, Alabama 0
1939 So. California 7, Duke 3
1940 So. California 14, Tennessee 0
1941 Stanford 21, Nebraska 13
1942 Oregon St. 20, Duke 16 (at Durham)
1943 Georgia 9, UCLA 0
1944 So. California 29, Washington 0
1945 So. California 25, Tennessee 0
1946 Alabama 34, So. California 14
1947 Illinois 45, UCLA 14
1948 Michigan 49, So. California 0
1949 Northwestern 20, California 14
1950 Ohio State 17, California 14
1951 Michigan 14, California 6
1952 Illinois 40, Stanford 7
1953 So. California 7, Wisconsin 0
1954 Mich. State 28, UCLA 20
1955 Ohio State 20, So. California 7
1956 Mich. State 17, UCLA 14
1957 Iowa 35, Oregon St. 19
1958 Ohio State 10, Oregon 7
1959 Iowa 38, California 12
1960 Washington 44, Wisconsin 8
1961 Washington 17, Minnesota 7
1962 Minnesota 21, UCLA 3
1963 So. California 42, Wisconsin 37
1964 Illinois 17, Washington 7
1965 Michigan 34, Oregon St. 7
1966 UCLA 14, Mich. State 12
1967 Purdue 14, So. California 13
1968 Southern Cal. 14, Indiana 3
1969 Ohio State 27, Southern Cal 16
1970 Southern Cal 10, Michigan 3
1971 Stanford 27, Ohio State 17
1972 Stanford 13, Michigan 12
1973 So. California 42, Ohio State 17
1974 Ohio State 42, So. California 21
1975 So. California 18, Ohio State 17
1976 UCLA 23, Ohio State 10
1977 So. California 14, Michigan 6
1978 Washington 27, Michigan 20
1979 So. California 17, Michigan 10
1980 So. California 17, Ohio State 16
1981 Michigan 23, Washington 6
1982 Washington 28, Iowa 0
1983 UCLA 24, Michigan 14
1984 UCLA 45, Illinois 9
1985 So. California 20, Ohio State 17
1986 UCLA 45, Iowa 28
1987 Arizona St. 22, Michigan 15

Orange Bowl, Miami

1935 Bucknell 26, Miami (Fla.) 0
1936 Catholic U. 20, Mississippi 19
1937 Duquesne 13, Miss. State 12
1938 Auburn 6, Mich. State 0
1939 Tennessee 17, Oklahoma 0
1940 Georgia Tech 21, Missouri 7
1941 Miss. State 14, Georgetown 7
1942 Georgia 40, TCU 26
1943 Alabama 37, Boston Col. 21
1944 LSU 19, Texas A&M 14
1945 Tulsa 26, Georgia Tech 12
1946 Miami (Fla.) 13, Holy Cross 6
1947 Rice 8, Tennessee 0
1948 Georgia Tech 20, Kansas 14
1949 Texas 41, Georgia 28
1950 Santa Clara 21, Kentucky 13
1951 Clemson 15, Miami (Fla.) 14
1952 Georgia Tech 17, Baylor 14
1953 Alabama 61, Syracuse 6
1954 Oklahoma 7, Maryland 0
1955 Duke 34, Nebraska 7
1956 Oklahoma 20, Maryland 6
1957 Colorado 27, Clemson 21
1958 Oklahoma 48, Duke 21
1959 Oklahoma 21, Syracuse 6
1960 Georgia 14, Missouri 0
1961 Missouri 21, Navy 14
1962 LSU 25, Colorado 7
1963 Alabama 17, Oklahoma 0
1964 Nebraska 13, Auburn 7
1965 Texas 21, Alabama 17
1966 Alabama 39, Nebraska 28
1967 Florida 27, Georgia Tech 12
1968 Oklahoma 26, Tennessee 24
1969 Penn State 15, Kansas 14
1970 Penn State 10, Missouri 3
1971 Nebraska 17, Louisiana St. 12
1972 Nebraska 38, Alabama 6
1973 Nebraska 40, Notre Dame 6
1974 Penn State 16, Louisiana St. 9
1975 Notre Dame 13, Alabama 11
1976 Oklahoma 14, Michigan 6
1977 Ohio State 27, Colorado 10
1978 Arkansas 31, Oklahoma 6
1979 Oklahoma 31, Nebraska 24
1980 Oklahoma 24, Florida St. 7
1981 Oklahoma 18, Florida St. 17
1982 Clemson 22, Nebraska 15
1983 Nebraska 21, Louisiana St. 20
1984 Miami (Fla.) 31, Nebraska 30
1985 Washington 28, Oklahoma 17
1986 Oklahoma 25, Penn State 10
1987 Oklahoma 42, Arkansas 8

Sugar Bowl, New Orleans

1935 Tulane 20, Temple 14
1936 TCU 3, LSU 2
1937 Santa Clara 21, LSU 14
1938 Santa Clara 6, LSU 0
1939 TCU 15, Carnegie Tech 7
1940 Texas A&M 14, Tulane 13
1941 Boston Col. 19, Tennessee 13
1942 Fordham 2, Missouri 0
1943 Tennessee 14, Tulsa 7
1944 Georgia Tech 20, Tulsa 18
1945 Duke 29, Alabama 26
1946 Oklahoma A&M 33, St. Mary's 13
1947 Georgia 20, No. Carolina 10
1948 Texas 27, Alabama 7
1949 Oklahoma 14, No. Carolina 6
1950 Oklahoma 35, LSU 0
1951 Kentucky 13, Oklahoma 7
1952 Maryland 28, Tennessee 13
1953 Georgia Tech. 24, Mississippi 7
1954 Georgia Tech 42, West Virginia 19
1955 Navy 21, Mississippi 0
1956 Georgia Tech 7, Pittsburgh 0
1957 Baylor 13, Tennessee 7
1958 Mississippi 39, Texas 7
1959 LSU 7, Clemson 0
1960 Mississippi 21, LSU 0
1961 Mississippi 14, Rice 6
1962 Alabama 10, Arkansas 3
1963 Mississippi 17, Arkansas 13
1964 Alabama 12, Mississippi 7
1965 LSU 13, Syracuse 10
1966 Missouri 20, Florida 18
1967 Alabama 34, Nebraska 7
1968 LSU 20, Wyoming 13
1969 Arkansas 16, Georgia 2
1970 Mississippi 27, Arkansas 22
1971 Tennessee 34, Air Force 13
1972 Oklahoma 40, Auburn 22
*1972 (Dec.) Oklahoma 14, Penn State 0
1973 Notre Dame 24, Alabama 23
1974 Nebraska 13, Florida 10
1975 Alabama 13, Penn State 6
1977 (Jan.) Pittsburgh 27, Georgia 3
1978 Alabama 35, Ohio State 6
1979 Alabama 14, Penn State 7
1980 Alabama 24, Arkansas 9
1981 Georgia 17, Notre Dame 10
1982 Pittsburgh 24, Georgia 20
1983 Penn State 27, Georgia 23
1984 Auburn 9, Michigan 7
1985 Nebraska 28, Louisiana St. 10
1986 Tennessee 35, Miami (Fla.) 7
1987 Nebraska 30, Louisiana St. 15

*Penn St. awarded game by forfeit

Fiesta Bowl, Tempe

1971 Arizona St. 45, Florida St. 38
1972 Arizona St. 49, Missouri 35
1973 Arizona St. 28, Pittsburgh 7
1974 Okla. St. 16, Brigham Young 6
1975 Arizona St. 17, Nebraska 14
1976 Oklahoma 41, Wyoming 7
1977 Penn St. 42, Arizona St. 30
1978 UCLA 10, Arkansas 10
1979 Pittsburgh 16, Arizona 10
1980 Penn St. 31, Ohio St. 19
1981 Penn St. 26, USC 10
1983 (Jan.) Arizona St. 32, Oklahoma 21
1984 Ohio State 28, Pittsburgh 23
1985 UCLA 39, Miami 37
1986 Michigan 27, Nebraska 23
1987 Penn St. 14, Miami (Fla.) 10

Cotton Bowl, Dallas

1937 TCU 16, Marquette 6
1938 Rice 28, Colorado 14
1939 St. Mary's 20, Texas Tech 13
1940 Clemson 6, Boston Col. 3
1941 Texas A&M 13, Fordham 12
1942 Alabama 29, Texas A&M 21
1943 Texas 14, Georgia Tech 7
1944 Randolph Field 7, Texas 7
1945 Oklahoma A&M 34, TCU 0
1946 Texas 40, Missouri 27
1947 Arkansas 0, LSU 0
1948 So. Methodist 13, Penn State 13
1949 So. Methodist 21, Oregon 13
1950 Rice 27, No. Carolina 13
1951 Tennessee 20, Texas 14
1952 Kentucky 20, TCU 7
1953 Texas 16, Tennessee 0
1954 Rice 28, Alabama 6
1955 Georgia Tech 14, Arkansas 6
1956 Mississippi 14, TCU 13
1957 TCU 28, Syracuse 27
1958 Navy 20, Rice 7
1959 TCU 0, Air Force 0
1960 Syracuse 23, Texas 14
1961 Duke 7, Arkansas 6
1962 Texas 12, Mississippi 7
1963 LSU 13, Texas 0
1964 Texas 28, Navy 6
1965 Arkansas 10, Nebraska 7
1966 LSU 14, Arkansas 7
1967 Georgia 24, So. Methodist 9
1968 Texas A&M 20, Alabama 16
1969 Texas 36, Tennessee 13
1970 Texas 21, Notre Dame 17
1971 Notre Dame 24, Texas 11
1972 Penn State 30, Texas 6
1973 Texas 17, Alabama 13
1974 Nebraska 19, Texas 3
1975 Penn State 41, Baylor 20
1976 Arkansas 31, Georgia 10
1977 Houston 30, Maryland 21
1978 Notre Dame 38, Texas 10
1979 Notre Dame 35, Houston 34
1980 Houston 17, Nebraska 14
1981 Alabama 30, Baylor 2
1982 Texas 14, Alabama 12
1983 SMU 7, Pittsburgh 3
1984 Georgia 10, Texas 9
1985 Boston Coll. 45, Houston 28
1986 Texas A&M 36, Auburn 16
1987 Ohio St. 28, Texas A&M 12

Sun Bowl, El Paso

1936 Hardin Simmons 14, New Mex. St. 14
1937 Hardin-Simmons 34, Texas Mines 6
1938 West Virginia 7, Texas Tech 6
1939 Utah 26, New Mexico 0
1940 Catholic U. 0, Arizona St. 0
1941 Western Reserve 26, Arizona St. 13
1942 Tulsa 6, Texas Tech 0
1943 2d Air Force 13, Hardin-Simmons 7
1944 Southwestern (Tex.) 7, New Mexico 0
1945 Southwestern (Tex.) 35, U. of Mex. 0
1946 New Mexico 34, Denver 24
1947 Cincinnati 38, Virginia Tech 6
1948 Miami (O.) 13, Texas Tech 12
1949 West Virginia 21, Texas Mines 12
1950 Texas Western 33, Georgetown 20
1951 West Texas St. 14, Cincinnati 13
1952 Texas Tech 25, Col. Pacific 14
1953 Col. Pacific 26, Miss. Southern 7
1954 Texas Western 37, Miss. Southern 14
1955 Texas Western 47, Florida St. 20
1956 Wyoming 21, Texas Tech 14
1957 Geo. Washington 13, Tex. Western 0
1958 Louisville 34, Drake 20
1959 Wyoming 14, Hardin-Simmons 6
1960 New Mexico St. 28, No. Texas St. 8
1961 New Mexico St. 20, Utah State 13
1962 Villanova 17, Wichita 9
1963 West Texas St. 15, Ohio U. 14
1964 Oregon 21, So. Methodist 14
1965 Georgia 7, Texas Tech 0
1966 Texas Western 13, TCU 12
1967 Wyoming 28, Florida St. 20
1968 UTex El Paso 14, Mississippi 7
1969 Auburn 34, Arizona 10
1969 (Dec.) Nebraska 45, Georgia 6
1970 Georgia Tech. 17, Texas Tech. 9
1971 LSU 33, Iowa State 15
1972 North Carolina 32, Texas Tech 28
1973 Missouri 34, Auburn 17
1974 Mississippi St. 26, No. Carolina 24
1975 Pittsburgh 33, Kansas 19
1977 (Jan.) Texas A&M 37, Florida 14
1977 (Dec.) Stanford 24, Louisiana St. 14
1978 Texas 42, Maryland 0
1979 Washington 14, Texas 7
1980 Nebraska 31, Mississippi St. 17
1981 Oklahoma 40, Houston 14
1982 North Carolina 26, Texas 10
1983 Alabama 28, SMU 7
1984 Maryland 28, Tennessee 27
1985 Georgia 13, Arizona 13
1986 Alabama 28, Washington 6

Gator Bowl, Jacksonville

1946 Wake Forest 26, So. Carolina 14
1947 Oklahoma 34, N.C. State 13
1948 Maryland 20, Georgia 20
1949 Clemson 24, Missouri 23
1950 Maryland 20, Missouri 7
1951 Wyoming 20, Wash. & Lee 7
1952 Miami (Fla.) 14, Clemson 0
1953 Florida 14, Tulsa 13
1954 Texas Tech 35, Auburn 13
1955 Auburn 33, Baylor 13
1956 Vanderbilt 25, Auburn 13
1957 Georgia Tech 21, Pittsburgh 14
1958 Tennessee 3, Texas A&M 0
1959 Mississippi 7, Florida 3
1960 Arkansas 14, Georgia Tech 7
1961 Florida 13, Baylor 12
1962 Penn State 30, Georgia Tech 15
1963 Florida 17, Penn State 7
1964 No. Carolina 35, Air Force 0
1965 Florida St. 36, Oklahoma 19
1966 Georgia Tech 31, Texas Tech 21
1967 Tennessee 18, Syracuse 12
1968 Penn State 17, Florida St. 17
1968 Missouri 35, Alabama 10
1969 (Dec.) Florida 14, Tenn. 13
1971 (Jan.) Auburn 35, Mississippi 28
1972 Georgia 7, N. Carolina 3
1973 Auburn 24, Colorado 3
1973 (Dec.) Tex. Tech. 28, Tenn. 19
1974 Auburn 27, Texas 3
1975 Maryland 13, Florida 0
1976 Notre Dame 20, Penn State 9
1977 Pittsburgh 34, Clemson 3
1978 Clemson 17, Ohio State 15
1979 No. Carolina 17, Michigan 15
1980 Pittsburgh 37, So. Carolina 9
1981 No. Carolina 31, Arkansas 27
1982 Florida St. 31, West Va. 12
1983 Florida 14, Iowa 6
1984 Oklahoma St. 21, So. Carolina 14
1985 Florida St. 34, Oklahoma St. 23
1986 Clemson 27, Stanford 21

Bluebonnet Bowl, Houston

1959 Clemson 23, TCU 7
1960 Texas 3, Alabama 3
1961 Kansas 33, Rice 7
1962 Missouri 14, Georgia Tech 10
1963 Baylor 14, LSU 7
1964 Tulsa 14, Mississippi 7
1965 Tennessee 27, Tulsa 6
1966 Texas 19, Mississippi 0
1967 Colorado 31, Miami (Fla.) 21
1968 SMU 28, Oklahoma 27
1969 Houston 36, Auburn 7
1970 Oklahoma 24, Alabama 24
1971 Colorado 29, Houston 17
1972 Tennessee 24, Louisiana St. 17
1973 Houston 47, Tulane 7
1974 N. Carolina St. 31, Houston 31
1975 Texas 38, Colorado 21
1976 Nebraska 27, Texas Tech 24
1977 USC 47, Texas A&M 28
1978 Stanford 25, Georgia 22
1979 Purdue 27, Tennessee 22
1980 No. Carolina 16, Texas 7
1981 Michigan 33, UCLA 14
1982 Arkansas 28, Florida 24
1983 Oklahoma St. 24, Baylor 14
1984 W. Virginia 31, Tex. Christian 14
1985 Air Force 21, Texas 16
1986 Baylor 21, Colorado 9

Liberty Bowl, Memphis

1959 Penn State 7, Alabama 0
1960 Penn State 41, Oregon 12
1961 Syracuse 15, Miami 14
1962 Oregon State 6, Villanova 0
1963 Miss. State 16, N.C. State 12
1964 Utah 32, West Virginia 6
1965 Mississippi 13, Auburn 7
1966 Miami (Fla.) 14, Va. Tech 7
1967 N.C. State 14, Georgia 7
1968 Mississippi 34, Va. Tech 17
1969 Colorado 47, Alabama 33
1970 Tulane 17, Colorado 3
1971 Tennessee 14, Arkansas 13
1972 Georgia Tech 31, Iowa State 30
1973 No. Carolina St. 31, Kansas 18
1974 Tennessee 7, Maryland 3
1975 USC 20, Texas A&M 0
1976 Alabama 36, UCLA 6
1977 Nebraska 27, N. Carolina 17
1978 Missouri 20, Louisiana St. 15
1979 Penn St. 9, Tulane 6
1980 Purdue 28, Missouri 25
1981 Ohio State 31, Navy 28
1982 Alabama 21, Illinois 15
1983 Notre Dame 19, Boston Coll. 18
1984 Auburn 21, Arkansas 15
1985 Baylor 21, Louisiana St. 7
1986 Tennessee 21, Minnesota 14

Freedom Bowl, Anaheim

1984 Iowa 55, Texas 17
1985 Washington 20, Colorado 17
1986 UCLA 31, Brigham Young 10

Florida Citrus Bowl, Orlando

1947 Catawba 31, Maryville 6
1948 Catawba 7, Marshall 0
1949 Murray State 21, Sul Ross St. 21
1950 St. Vincent 7, Emory & Henry 6
1951 Morris Harvey 35, Emory & Henry 14
1952 Stetson 35, Arkansas St. 20
1953 East Texas St. 33, Tenn. Tech 0
1954 East Texas St. 7, Arkansas St. 7
1955 Neb.-Omaha 7, Eastern Kentucky 6
1956 Juniata 6, Missouri Valley 6
1957 West Texas St. 20, So. Miss. 13
1958 East Texas St. 10, So. Miss. 9
1958 (Dec.) East Texas St. 26, Missouri Valley 7
1960 (Jan.) Middle Tenn. 21, Presbyterian 12
1960 (Dec.) Citadel 27, Tenn. Tech 0
1961 Lamar 21, Middle Tennessee 14
1962 Houston 49, Miami (O.) 21
1963 Western Ky. 27, Coast Guard 0
1964 E. Carolina 14, Massachusetts 13
1965 East Carolina 31, Maine 0
1966 Morgan State 14, West Chester 6
1967 Tenn.-Martin 25, West Chester 8
1968 Richmond 49, Ohio U. 42
1969 Toledo 56, Davidson 33
1970 Toledo 40, William & Mary 12
1971 Toledo 28, Richmond 3
1972 Tampa 21, Kent State 18
1973 Miami (O.) 16, Florida 7
1974 Miami (O.) 21, Georgia 10
1975 Miami (O.) 20, South Carolina 7
1976 Okla. St. 49, Brigham Young 21
1977 Florida St. 40, Texas Tech 17
1978 N.C. State 30, Pittsburgh 17
1979 LSU 34, Wake Forest 10
1980 Florida 35, Maryland 20
1981 Missouri 19, Southern Miss. 17
1982 Auburn 33, Boston College 26
1983 Tennessee 30, Maryland 23
1984 Georgia 17, Florida St. 17
1985 Ohio St. 10, Brigham Young 7
1986 Auburn 16, USC 7

Peach Bowl, Atlanta

1968 LSU 31, Florida St. 27
1969 West Virginia 14, S. Carolina 3
1970 Arizona St. 48, N. Carolina 26
1971 Mississippi 41, Georgia Tech. 18
1972 N. Carolina St. 49, W. Va. 13
1973 Georgia 17, Maryland 16
1974 Vanderbilt 6, Texas Tech. 6
1975 W. Virginia 13, No. Carolina St. 10
1976 Kentucky 21, North Carolina 0
1977 N. Carolina St. 24, Iowa St. 14
1978 Purdue 41, Georgia Tech. 21
1979 Baylor 24, Clemson 18
1981 (Jan.) Miami 20, Virginia Tech. 10
1981 (Dec.) West Virginia 26, Florida 6
1982 Iowa 28, Tennessee 22
1983 Florida St. 28, North Carolina 3
1984 Virginia 27, Purdue 22
1985 Army 31, Illinois 29
1986 Va. Tech 25, N.C. State 24

Independence Bowl, Shreveport

1976 McNeese St. 20, Tulsa 16
1977 Louisiana Tech 24, Louisville 14
1978 E. Carolina 35, La. Tech 13
1979 Syracuse 31, McNeese St. 7
1980 So. Miss. 16, McNeese St. 14
1981 Texas A&M 33, Oklahoma St. 16
1982 Wisconsin 14, Kansas St. 3
1983 Air Force 9, Mississippi 3
1984 Air Force 23, Virginia Tech 7
1985 Minnesota 20, Clemson 13
1986 Mississippi 20, Texas Tech 17

All-American Bowl, Birmingham

1977 Maryland 17, Minnesota 7
1978 Texas A&M 28, Iowa St. 12
1979 Missouri 24, So. Carolina 14
1980 Arkansas 34, Tulane 15
1981 Mississippi St. 10, Kansas 0
1982 Air Force 36, Vanderbilt 28
1983 W. Virginia 20, Kentucky 16
1984 Kentucky 20, Wisconsin 19
1985 Georgia Tech 17, Michigan St. 14
1986 Florida St. 27, Indiana 13

Holiday Bowl, San Diego

1978 Navy 23, Brigham Young 16
1979 Indiana 38, Brigham Young 37
1980 Brigham Young 46, SMU 45
1981 Brigham Young 38, Wash. St. 36
1982 Ohio State 47, Brigham Young 17
1983 Brigham Young 21, Missouri 17
1984 Brigham Young 24, Michigan 17
1985 Arkansas 18, Arizona St. 17
1986 Iowa 39, San Diego St. 38

Aloha Bowl, Honolulu

1982 Washington 21, Maryland 20
1983 Penn State 13, Washington 10
1984 SMU 27, Notre Dame 20
1985 Alabama 24, USC 3
1986 Arizona 30, North Carolina 21

California Bowl, Fresno

1981 Toledo 27, San Jose St. 25
1982 Fresno St. 29, Bowling Green 28
1983 N. Illinois 20, Cal. State Fullerton 13
1984 Nevada-Las Vegas 30, Toledo 13
1985 Fresno St. 51, Bowling Green 7
1986 San Jose St. 37, Miami (Oh.) 7

College Football Teams

Division I Teams

Team	Nickname	Team colors	Conference	Coach	1986 record (W-L-T)
Air Force	Falcons	Blue & silver	Western Athletic	Fisher De Berry	6-5-0
Akron	Zips	Blue & Gold	Independent	Gerry Faust	7-4-0
Alabama	Crimson Tide	Crimson & white	Southeastern	Bill Curry	9-3-0
Alabama State	Hornets	Black & gold	Southwestern	Houston Markham	4-7-0
Alcorn State	Braves	Purple & gold	Southwestern	Theo Danzy	5-5-0
Appalachian State	Mountaineers	Black & gold	Southern	Sparky Woods	9-1-1
Arizona	Wildcats	Red & blue	Pacific Ten	Dick Tomey	8-3-0
Arizona State	Sun Devils	Maroon & gold	Pacific Ten	John Cooper	9-1-1
Arkansas	Razorbacks	Cardinal & white	Southwest	Ken Hatfield	9-2-0
Arkansas State	Indians	Scarlet & black	Independent	Lawrence Lacewell	9-1-1
Army	Cadets	Black, gold, gray	Independent	Jim Young	6-5-0
Auburn	Tigers	Orange & blue	Southeastern	Pat Dye	9-2-0
Austin Peay State	Governors	Red & white	Ohio Valley	Emory Hale	5-6-0
Ball State	Cardinals	Cardinal & white	Mid-American	Paul Schudel	6-5-0
Baylor	Bears	Green & gold	Southwest	Grant Teaff	8-3-0
Bethune-Cookman	Wildcats	Maroon & gold	Mid-Eastern	Larry Little	3-8-0
Boise State	Broncos	Orange & Blue	Big Sky	Skip Hall	5-6-0
Boston College	Eagles	Maroon & gold	Independent	Jack Bicknell	8-3-0
Boston Univ.	Terriers	Scarlet & white	Yankee	Steve Stetson	4-7-0
Bowling Green St.	Falcons	Orange & brown	Mid-American	Moe Ankney	5-6-0
Brigham Young	Cougars	Royal blue & white	Western Athletic	LaVell Edwards	8-4-0
Brown	Bruins, Bears	Brown, cardinal, white	Ivy	John Rosenberg	5-4-1

Team	Nickname	Team colors	Conference	Coach	1986 record (W-L-T)
Bucknell	Bisons	Orange & blue	Colonial	George Landis	3-7-0
California	Golden Bears	Blue & gold	Pacific Ten	Bruce Snyder	2-9-0
Central Michigan	Chippewas	Maroon & gold	Mid-American	Herb Deromedi	5-5-0
Cincinnati	Bearcats	Red & black	Independent	Dave Currey	5-6-0
Citadel	Bulldogs	Blue & white	Southern	Charles Taaffe	3-8-0
Clemson	Tigers	Purple & orange	Atlantic Coast	Danny Ford	7-2-2
Colgate	Red Raiders	Maroon	Colonial	Fred Dunlap	4-7-0
Colorado State	Rams	Green & gold	Western Athletic	Leon Fuller	6-5-0
Colorado	Buffaloes	Silver, gold & blue	Big Eight	Bill McCartney	6-5-0
Columbia	Lions	Blue & white	Ivy	Larry McElreavy	0-10-0
Connecticut	Huskies	Blue & white	Yankee	Tom Jackson	8-3-0
Cornell	Big Red	Carnelian & white	Ivy	Maxie Baughan	8-2-0
Dartmouth	Big Green	Dartmouth green & white	Ivy	Buddy Teevens	3-6-1
Davidson	Wildcats	Red & black	Colonial	Vic Gatto	0-9-0
Delaware	Fightin' Blue Hens	Blue & gold	Yankee	Tubby Raymond	8-3-0
Delaware State	Hornets	Red & blue	Mid-Eastern	William Collick	7-4-0
Duke	Blue Devils	Royal blue & white	Atlantic Coast	Steve Spurrier	4-7-0
East Carolina	Pirates	Purple & gold	Independent	Art Baker	2-9-0
East Tennessee St.	Buccaneers	Blue & gold	Southern	Mike Ayers	6-5-0
Eastern Illinois	Panthers	Blue & Gray	Gateway	Bob Spoo	10-1-0
Eastern Kentucky	Colonels	Maroon & white	Ohio Valley	Roy Kidd	8-2-1
Eastern Michigan	Hurons	Green & white	Mid-American	Jim Harkema	6-5-0
Eastern Washington	Eagles	Red & white	Big Sky	Dick Zornes	6-5-0
Florida	Gators	Orange & blue	Southeastern	Galen Hall	6-5-0
Florida A&M	Rattlers	Orange & green	Mid-Eastern	Ken Riley	5-6-0
Florida State	Seminoles	Garnet & gold	Independent	Bobby Bowden	7-4-1
Fresno State	Bulldogs	Cardinal & blue	Pacific Coast	Jim Sweeney	9-2-0
Fullerton State	Titans	Blue, orange, white	Pacific Coast	Gene Murphy	3-9-0
Furman	Paladans	Purple & white	Southern	Jimmy Satterfield	7-2-2
Georgia	Bulldogs	Red & black	Southeastern	Vince Dooley	8-3-0
Georgia Southern	Eagles	Blue & white	Independent	Erskine Russell	9-2-0
Georgia Tech	Yellow Jackets	Old gold & white	Atlantic Coast	Bobby Ross	5-5-1
Grambling State	Tigers	Black & gold	Southwestern	Eddie Robinson	7-4-0
Harvard	Crimson	Crimson	Ivy	Joe Restic	3-7-0
Hawaii	Rainbow Warriors	Green & white	Western Athletic	Bob Wagner	7-5-0
Holy Cross	Crusaders	Royal purple	Colonial	Mike Duffner	10-1-0
Houston	Cougars	Scarlet & white	Southwest	Jack Pardee	1-10-0
Howard	Bison	Blue & white	Mid-Eastern	Willie Jeffries	8-3-0
Idaho	Vandals	Silver & gold	Big Sky	Keith Gilbertson	8-3-0
Idaho State	Bengals	Orange & black	Big Sky	Jim Koetter	2-9-0
Illinois	Fighting Illini	Orange & blue	Big Ten	Mike White	4-7-0
Illinois State	Redbirds	Red & white	Gateway	Bob Otolski	5-5-0
Indiana	Fightin' Hoosiers	Cream & crimson	Big Ten	Bill Mallory	6-5-0
Indiana State	Sycamores	Blue & white	Gateway	Dennis Raetz	3-8-0
Iowa	Hawkeyes	Old gold & black	Big Ten	Hayden Fry	8-3-0
Iowa State	Cyclones	Cardinal & gold	Big Eight	Jim Walden	6-5-0
Jackson State	Tigers	Blue & white	Southwestern	W.C. Gorden	9-2-0
James Madison	Dukes	Purple & gold	Independent	Joe Purzycki	5-5-1
Kansas	Jayhawks	Crimson & blue	Big Eight	Bob Valesente	3-8-0
Kansas State	Wildcats	Purple & white	Big Eight	Stan Parrish	2-9-0
Kent State	Golden Flashes	Blue & gold	Mid-American	Glen Mason	5-6-0
Kentucky	Wildcats	Blue & white	Southeastern	Jerry Clairborne	5-5-1
Lafayette	Leopards	Maroon & white	Colonial	Bill Russo	6-5-0
Lamar	Cardinals	Red & white	Independent	Ray Alborn	2-9-0
Lehigh	Engineers	Brown & white	Colonial	Hank Small	5-6-0
Long Beach State	Forty-Niners	Brown & gold	Pacific Coast	Larry Reisbig	6-5-0
Louisiana State	Fighting Tigers	Purple & gold	Southeastern	Mike Archer	9-2-0
Louisiana Tech	Bulldogs	Red & blue	Independent	Carl Torbush	6-4-1
Louisville	Cardinals	Red, black, white	Independent	Howard Schnellenberger	3-8-0
Maine	Black Bears	Blue & white	Yankee	Tim Murphy	7-4-0
Marshall	Thundering Herd	Green & white	Southern	George Chaump	6-4-1
Maryland	Terps	Red, white, black & gold	Atlantic Coast	Joe Krivak	5-5-1
Massachusetts	Minutemen	Maroon & white	Yankee	Jim Reid	8-3-0
McNeese State	Cowboys	Blue & gold	Southland	Sonny Jackson	2-9-0
Memphis State	Tigers	Blue & gray	Independent	Charlie Bailey	1-10-0
Miami (Fla.)	Hurricanes	Orange, green, white	Independent	Jimmy Johnson	11-1-0
Miami (Ohio)	Redskins	Red & white	Mid-American	Tim Rose	8-3-0
Michigan	Wolverines	Maize & blue	Big Ten	Bo Schembechler	11-1-0
Michigan State	Spartans	Green & white	Big Ten	George Perles	6-5-0
Middle Tennessee St.	Blue Raiders	Blue & white	Ohio Valley	Boots Donnelly	6-5-0
Minnesota	Golden Gophers	Maroon & gold	Big Ten	John Gutekunst	6-5-0
Mississippi	Rebels	Red & blue	Southeastern	Billy Brewer	7-3-1
Mississippi State	Bulldogs	Maroon & white	Southeastern	Rocky Felker	6-5-0
Miss. Valley State	Delta Devils	Green & white	Southwestern	Ken Pettiford	4-4-1
Missouri	Tigers	Old gold & black	Big Eight	Woody Widenhofer	3-8-0
Montana	Grizzlies	Copper, silver, gold	Big Sky	Don Read	6-4-0
Montana State	Bobcats	Blue & gold	Big Sky	Earle Solomonson	3-8-0
Morehead State	Eagles	Blue & gold	Ohio Valley	Bill Baldridge	7-4-0
Morgan State	Bears	Blue & orange	Mid-Eastern	Jesse Thomas	1-9-0
Murray State	Racers	Blue & gold	Ohio Valley	Mike Mahoney	7-3-1
Navy	Midshipmen	Navy blue & gold	Independent	Elliot Uzelac	3-8-0
Nebraska	Cornhuskers	Scarlet & cream	Big Eight	Tom Osborne	9-2-0
Nevada-Las Vegas	Rebels	Scarlet & gray	Pacific Coast	Wayne Nunnely	6-5-0

Team	Nickname	Team colors	Conference	Coach	1986 record (W-L-T)
Nevada-Reno	Wolf Pack	Silver & blue	Big Sky	Chris Ault	11-0-0
New Hampshire	Wildcats	Blue & white	Yankee	Bill Bowes	7-4-0
New Mexico	Lobos	Cherry & silver	Western Athletic	Mike Sheppard	4-8-0
New Mexico State	Aggies	Crimson & white	Pacific Coast	Mike Knoll	1-10-0
Nicholls St.	Colonels	Red & grey	Independent	Phil Greco	9-2-0
North Carolina	Tar Heels	Blue & white	Atlantic Coast	Dick Crum	7-3-1
North Carolina A & T	Aggies	Blue & gold	Mid-Eastern	Maurice Forte	9-2-0
North Carolina State	Wolfpack	Red & white	Atlantic Coast	Dick Sheridan	8-2-1
North Texas State	Mean Green, Eagles	Green & white	Southland	Corky Nelson	6-4-0
Northeast Louisiana	Indians	Maroon & gold	Southland	Pat Collins	5-6-0
Northeastern	Huskies	Red & black	Independent	Paul Pawlak	4-6-0
Northern Arizona	Lumberjacks	Blue & gold	Big Sky	Larry Kentera	7-4-0
Northern Illinois	Huskies	Cardinal & black	Independent	Jerry Pettibone	2-9-0
Northern Iowa	Panthers	Purple & Old Gold	Gateway	Darrell Mudra	7-3-1
Northwestern	Wildcats	Purple & white	Big Ten	Francis Peay	4-7-0
Northwestern State	Demons	Burnt orange, purple, white	Southland	Sam Goodwin	5-5-1
Notre Dame	Fighting Irish	Gold & blue	Independent	Lou Holtz	5-6-0
Ohio State	Buckeyes	Scarlet & gray	Big Ten	Earle Bruce	9-3-0
Ohio Univ	Bobcats	Green & white	Mid-American	Cleve Bryant	1-10-0
Oklahoma	Sooners	Crimsom & cream	Big Eight	Barry Switzer	10-1-0
Oklahoma State	Cowboys	Orange & black	Big Eight	Pat Jones	6-5-0
Oregon	Ducks	Green & yellow	Pacific Ten	Rich Brooks	5-6-0
Oregon State	Beavers	Orange & black	Pacific Ten	Dave Kragthrope	3-8-0
Pacific	Tigers	Orange & black	Pacific Coast	Bob Cope	4-7-0
Penn State	Nittany Lions	Blue & white	Independent	Joe Paterno	12-0-0
Pennsylvania	Red & Blue, Quakers	Red & blue	Ivy	Ed Zubrow	10-0-0
Pittsburgh	Panthers	Gold & blue	Independent	Mike Gottfried	5-5-1
Prairie View A & M	Panthers	Purple & gold	Southwestern	Conway Hayman	3-8-0
Princeton	Tigers	Orange & black	Ivy	Ron Rogerson	2-8-0
Purdue	Boilermakers	Old gold & black	Big Ten	Fred Akers	3-8-0
Rhode Island	Rams	Blue & white	Yankee	Bob Griffin	1-10-0
Rice	Owls	Blue & gray	Southwest	Jerry Berndt	4-7-0
Richmond	Spiders	Red & blue	Yankee	Dal Shealy	4-7-0
Rutgers	Scarlet Knights	Scarlet	Independent	Dick Anderson	5-5-1
Sam Houston State	Bear Kats	Orange & white	Southland	Ron Rondleman	9-2-0
San Diego State	Aztecs	Scarlet & black	Western Athletic	Denny Stolz	8-3-0
San Jose State	Spartans	Gold & white	Pacific Coast	Claude Gilbert	9-2-0
South Carolina	Fighting Gamecocks	Garnet & black	Independent	Joe Morrison	3-6-2
South Carolina State	Bulldogs	Garnet & blue	Mid-Eastern	Dennis Thomas	5-6-0
Southern	Jaguars	Blue & gold	Southwestern	Marino Casem	5-5-1
Southern California	Trojans	Cardinal & gold	Pacific Ten	Larry Smith	7-4-0
Southern Illinois	Salukis	Maroon & white	Gateway	Ray Dorr	7-4-0
Southern Mississippi	Golden Eagles	Black & gold	Independent	Jim Carmody	6-5-0
SW Missouri St	Bears	Maroon & white	Gateway	Jesse Branch	3-7-0
SW Texas	Bobcats	Maroon & gold	Southland	John O'Hara	4-7-0
Southwestern La.	Ragin' Cajuns	Vermillion & white	Independent	Nelson Stokley	6-5-0
Stanford	Cardinal	Cardinal & white	Pacific Ten	Jack Elway	8-3-0
Stephen F. Austin St.	Lumberjacks	Purple & white	Southland	Jim Hess	5-6-0
Syracuse	Orangemen	Orange	Independent	Dick MacPherson	5-6-0
Temple	Owls	Cherry & white	Independent	Bruce Arians	6-5-0
Tennessee	Volunteers	Orange & white	Southeastern	John Majors	6-5-0
Tenn.-Chattanooga	Moccasins	Navy blue & gold	Southern	Buddy Nix	4-7-0
Tennessee State	Tigers	Blue & white	Independent	William Thomas	9-1-1
Tennessee Tech	Golden Eagles	Purple & gold	Ohio Valley	Jim Ragland	0-10-0
Texas	Longhorns	Orange & white	Southwest	David McWilliams	5-6-0
Texas-El Paso	Miners	Orange, white, blue	Western Athletic	Bob Stull	4-8-0
Texas A & M	Aggies	Maroon & white	Southwest	Jackie Sherrill	9-2-0
Texas Christian	Horned Frogs	Purple & white	Southwest	Jim Wacker	3-8-0
Texas Southern	Tigers	Maroon & gray	Southwestern	Lionel Taylor	2-8-1
Texas Tech	Red Raiders	Scarlet & black	Southwest	Spike Dykes	7-4-0
Toledo	Rockets	Blue & gold	Mid-American	Dan Simrell	7-4-0
Tulane	Green Wave	Olive green & sky blue	Independent	Mack Brown	4-7-0
Tulsa	Golden Hurricane	Blue & gold	Independent	George Henshaw	7-4-0
UCLA	Bruins	Navy blue & gold	Pacific Ten	Terry Donahue	7-3-1
Utah State	Aggies	Navy blue & white	Pacific Coast	Chuck Shelton	3-8-0
Utah	Utes	Crimson & white	Western Athletic	Jim Fassel	2-9-0
Vanderbilt	Commodores	Black & gold	Southeastern	Watson Brown	1-10-0
Villanova	Wildcats	Blue & white	Yankee	Andy Talley	8-1-0
Virginia	Cavaliers	Orange & blue	Atlantic Coast	George Welsh	3-8-0
VMI	Keydets	Red, white & yellow	Southern	Eddie Williamson	1-10-0
Virginia Tech	Gobblers, Hokies	Orange & marroon	Independent	Frank Beamer	8-2-1
Wake Forest	Demon Deacons	Old gold & black	Atlantic Coast	Bill Dooley	5-6-0
Washington	Huskies	Purple & gold	Pacific Ten	Don James	8-2-1
Washington State	Cougars	Crimson & gray	Pacific Ten	Dennis Erickson	3-7-1
Weber State	Wildcats	Purple & white	Big Sky	Mike Price	3-8-0
West Virginia	Mountaineers	Old gold & blue	Independent	Don Nehlen	4-7-0
Western Carolina	Catamounts	Purple & gold	Southern	Bob Waters	6-5-0
Western Illinois	Leathernecks	Purple & Gold	Gateway	Bruce Craddock	6-5-0
Western Kentucky	Hilltoppers	Red & white	Independent	Dave Roberts	4-6-1
Western Michigan	Broncos	Brown & gold	Mid-American	Al Molde	3-8-0
William & Mary	Indians	Green, gold, silver	Independent	Jimmye Laycock	9-2-0
Wisconsin	Badgers	Cardinal & white	Big Ten	Don Morton	3-9-0
Wyoming	Cowboys	Brown & yellow	Western Athletic	Paul Roach	6-6-0
Yale	Bulldogs, Elis	Yale blue & white	Ivy	Carmen Cozza	3-7-0
Youngstown St.	Penguins	Scarlet & white	Ohio Valley	Jim Tressel	2-9-0

College Football Conference Champions

	Atlantic Coast		Ivy League		Big Eight		Big Ten
1971	North Carolina	1971	Dartmouth, Cornell	1971	Nebraska	1971	Michigan
1972	North Carolina	1972	Dartmouth	1972	Nebraska	1972	Ohio State, Michigan
1973	No. Carolina St.	1973	Dartmouth	1973	Oklahoma	1973	Ohio State, Michigan
1974	Maryland	1974	Yale, Harvard	1974	Oklahoma	1974	Ohio State, Michigan
1975	Maryland	1975	Harvard	1975	Oklahoma, Nebraska	1975	Ohio State
1976	Maryland	1976	Yale, Brown	1976	Oklahoma, Colorado, Oklahoma State	1976	Michigan, Ohio State
1977	North Carolina	1977	Yale	1977	Oklahoma	1977	Michigan, Ohio State
1978	Clemson	1978	Dartmouth	1978	Nebraska, Oklahoma	1978	Michigan St., Michigan
1979	No. Carolina St.	1979	Yale	1979	Oklahoma	1979	Ohio State
1980	North Carolina	1980	Yale	1980	Oklahoma	1980	Michigan
1981	Clemson	1981	Yale, Dartmouth	1981	Nebraska	1981	Iowa, Ohio State
1982	Clemson	1982	Harvard, Dartmouth, Penn	1982	Nebraska	1982	Michigan
1983	Maryland	1983	Harvard, Penn	1983	Nebraska	1983	Illinois
1984	Maryland	1984	Penn	1984	Nebraska, Oklahoma	1984	Ohio State
1985	Maryland	1985	Penn	1985	Oklahoma	1985	Iowa
1986	Clemson	1986	Penn	1986	Oklahoma	1986	Michigan, Ohio State

	Mid-America		Southern		Southeastern		Southwest
1971	Toledo	1971	Richmond	1971	Alabama	1971	Texas
1972	Kent State	1972	East Carolina	1972	Alabama	1972	Texas
1973	Miami	1973	East Carolina	1973	Alabama	1973	Texas
1974	Miami	1974	VMI	1974	Alabama	1974	Baylor
1975	Miami	1975	Richmond	1975	Alabama	1975	Texas A&M, Texas, Arkansas
1976	Ball State	1976	East Carolina	1976	Georgia	1976	Houston
1977	Miami	1977	Tenn.-Chattanooga	1977	Alabama	1977	Texas
1978	Ball State	1978	Tenn.-Chattanooga, Furman	1978	Alabama	1978	Houston
1979	Central Michigan	1979	Tenn.-Chattanooga	1979	Alabama	1979	Houston, Arkansas
1980	Central Michigan	1980	Furman	1980	Georgia	1980	Baylor
1981	Toledo	1981	Furman	1981	Georgia, Alabama	1981	SMU
1982	Bowling Green	1982	Furman	1982	Georgia	1982	SMUL,8
1983	Northern Illinois	1983	Furman	1983	Auburn	1983	Texas
1984	Toledo	1984	Tenn.-Chattanooga	1984	Florida (title vacated)	1984	SMU, Texas
1985	Bowling Green	1985	Furman	1985	Tennessee	1985	Texas A&M
1986	Miami	1986	Appalachian St.	1986	LSU	1986	Texas A&M

	Pacific Ten		Western Athletic		Pacific Coast
1971	Stanford	1971	Arizona State	1971	Long Beach State
1972	USC	1972	Arizona State	1972	San Diego State
1973	USC	1973	Arizona State, Arizona	1973	San Diego State
1974	USC	1974	Brigham Young	1974	San Diego State
1975	UCLA, Cal.	1975	Arizona State	1975	San Jose St.
1976	USC	1976	Wyoming, Brigham Young	1976	San Diego State
1977	Washington	1977	Brigham Young, Arizona St.	1977	Fresno State
1978	USC	1978	Brigham Young	1978	Utah St., San Jose St.
1979	USC	1979	Brigham Young	1979	San Jose St.
1980	Washington	1980	Brigham Young	1980	Long Beach State
1981	Washington	1981	Brigham Young	1981	San Jose State
1982	UCLA	1982	Brigham Young	1982	Fresno State
1983	UCLA	1983	Brigham Young	1983	Cal State-Fullerton
1984	USC	1984	Brigham Young	1984	Nevada-Las Vegas
1985	UCLA	1985	Brigham Young, Air Force	1985	Fresno State
1986	Arizona State	1986	San Diego State	1986	San Jose State

Longest Division 1-A Winning Streaks

Wins	Team	Years	Ended by	Score
47	Oklahoma	1953-57	Notre Dame	7-0
39	Washington	1908-14	Oregon State	0-0
37	Yale	1890-93	Princeton	6-0
37	Yale	1887-89	Princeton	10-0
35	Toledo	1969-71	Tampa	21-0
34	Pennsylvania	1894-96	Lafayette	6-4
31	Oklahoma	1948-50	Kentucky	13-7
31	Pittsburgh	1914-18	Cleveland Naval Reserve	10-9
31	Pennsylvania	1896-98	Harvard	10-0
30	Texas	1968-70	Notre Dame	24-11
29	Michigan	1901-03	Minnesota	6-6
28	Alabama	1978-80	Mississippi State	6-3
28	Oklahoma	1973-75	Kansas	23-3
28	Michigan State	1950-53	Purdue	6-0
27	Nebraska	1901-04	Colorado	6-0
26	Cornell	1921-24	Williams	14-7
26	Michigan	1903-05	Chicago	2-0
25	Michigan	1946-49	Army	21-7
25	Army	1944-46	Notre Dame	0-0
25	Southern Cal	1931-33	Oregon State	0-0
25	Brigham Young	1983-85	UCLA	27-24

National College Football Champions

The NCAA recognizes as unofficial national champion the team selected each year by the AP (poll of writers) and the UPI (poll of coaches). When the polls disagree both teams are listed. The AP poll originated in 1936 and the UPI poll in 1950.

1936	Minnesota	1949	Notre Dame	1962	Southern Cal.	1975	Oklahoma
1937	Pittsburgh	1950	Oklahoma	1963	Texas	1976	Pittsburgh
1938	Texas Christian	1951	Tennessee	1964	Alabama	1977	Notre Dame
1939	Texas A&M	1952	Michigan State	1965	Alabama, Mich. State	1978	Alabama, So. Cal.
1940	Minnesota	1953	Maryland	1966	Notre Dame	1979	Alabama
1941	Minnesota	1954	Ohio State, UCLA	1967	Southern Cal.	1980	Georgia
1942	Ohio State	1955	Oklahoma	1968	Ohio State	1981	Clemson
1943	Notre Dame	1956	Oklahoma	1969	Texas	1982	Penn State
1944	Army	1957	Auburn, Ohio State	1970	Nebraska, Texas	1983	Miami (Fla.)
1945	Army	1958	Louisiana State	1971	Nebraska,	1984	Brigham Young
1946	Notre Dame	1959	Syracuse	1972	Southern Cal.	1985	Oklahoma
1947	Notre Dame	1960	Minnesota	1973	Notre Dame, Alabama	1986	Penn State
1948	Michigan	1961	Alabama	1974	Oklahoma, So. Cal.		

College Football Coach of the Year

(Selected by the American Football Coaches Assn. & the Football Writers Assn. of America)

	AFCA
1935	Lynn Waldorf, Northwestern
1936	Dick Harlow, Harvard
1937	Edward Mylin, Lafayette
1938	Bill Kern, Carnegie Tech
1939	Eddie Anderson, Iowa
1940	Clark Shaughnessy, Stanford
1941	Frank Leahy, Notre Dame
1942	Bill Alexander, Georgia Tech
1943	Amos Alonzo Stagg, Pacific
1944	Carroll Widdoes, Ohio St.
1945	Bo McMillin, Indiana
1946	Earl "Red" Blaik, Army
1947	Fritz Crisler, Michigan
1948	Bennie Oosterbaan, Michigan
1949	Bud Wilkinson, Oklahoma
1950	Charlie Caldwell, Princeton
1951	Chuck Taylor, Stanford
1952	Biggie Munn, Michigan St.
1953	Jim Tatum, Maryland
1954	Henry "Red" Sanders, UCLA
1955	Duffy Daugherty, Michigan St.
1956	Bowden Wyatt, Tennessee

	FWAA	AFCA
1957	Woody Hayes, Ohio St.	Woody Hayes, Ohio St.
1958	Paul Dietzel, LSU	Paul Dietzel, LSU
1959	Ben Schwartzwalder, Syracuse	Ben Schwartzwalder, Syracuse
1960	Murray Warmath, Minnesota	Murray Warmath, Minnesota
1961	Darrell Royal, Texas	Paul "Bear" Bryant, Alabama
1962	John McKay, USC	John McKay, USC
1963	Darrell Royal, Texas	Darrell Royal, Texas
1964	Ara Parseghian, Notre Dame	Frank Broyles, Arkansas; Ara Paraseghian, Notre Dame
1965	Duffy Daugherty, Michigan St.	Tommy Prothro, UCLA
1966	Tom Cahill, Army	Tom Cahill, Army
1967	John Pont, Indiana	John Pont, Indiana
1968	Woody Hayes, Ohio St.	Joe Paterno, Penn St.
1969	Bo Schembechler, Michigan	Bo Schembechler, Michigan
1970	Alex Agase, Northwestern	Charles McClendon, LSU; Darrell Royal, Texas
1971	Bob Devaney, Nebraska	Paul "Bear" Bryant, Alabama
1972	John McKay, USC	John McKay, USC
1973	Johnny Majors, Pittsburgh	Paul "Bear" Bryant, Alabama
1974	Grant Teaff, Baylor	Grant Teaff, Baylor
1975	Woody Hayes, Ohio St.	Frank Kush, Arizona St.
1976	Johnny Majors, Pittsburgh	Johnny Majors, Pittsburgh
1977	Lou Holtz, Arkansas	Don James, Washington
1978	Joe Paterno, Penn St.	Joe Paterno, Penn St.
1979	Earle Bruce, Ohio St.	Earle Bruce, Ohio St.
1980	Vince Dooley, Georgia	Vince Dooley, Georgia
1981	Danny Ford, Clemson	Danny Ford, Clemson
1982	Joe Paterno, Penn St.	Joe Paterno, Penn St.
1983	Howard Schnellenberger, Miami (Fla.)	Ken Hatfield, Air Force
1984	LaVell Edwards, Brigham Young	LaVell Edwards, Brigham Young
1985	Fisher De Berry, Air Force	Fisher De Berry, Air Force
1986	Joe Paterno, Penn St.	Joe Paterno, Penn St.

Heisman Trophy Winners

Awarded annually to the nation's outstanding college football player.

1935	Jay Berwanger, Chicago, HB	1953	John Lattner, Notre Dame, HB	1971	Pat Sullivan, Auburn, QB
1936	Larry Kelley, Yale, E	1954	Alan Ameche, Wisconsin, FB	1972	Johnny Rodgers, Nebraska, RB-R
1937	Clinton Frank, Yale, HB	1955	Howard Cassady, Ohio St., HB	1973	John Cappelletti, Penn State, RB
1938	David O'Brien, Tex. Christian, QB	1956	Paul Hornung, Notre Dame, QB	1974	Archie Griffin, Ohio State, RB
1939	Nile Kinnick, Iowa, HB	1957	John Crow, Texas A & M, HB	1975	Archie Griffin, Ohio State, RB
1940	Tom Harmon, Michigan, HB	1958	Pete Dawkins, Army, HB	1976	Tony Dorsett, Pittsburgh, RB
1941	Bruce Smith, Minnesota, HB	1959	Billy Cannon, La. State, HB	1977	Earl Campbell, Texas, RB
1942	Frank Sinkwich, Georgia, HB	1960	Joe Bellino, Navy, HB	1978	Billy Sims, Oklahoma, RB
1943	Angelo Bertelli, Notre Dame, QB	1961	Ernest Davis, Syracuse, HB	1979	Charles White, USC, RB
1944	Leslie Horvath, Ohio State, QB	1962	Terry Baker, Oregon State, QB	1980	George Rogers, So. Carolina, RB
1945	Felix Blanchard, Army, FB	1963	Roger Staubach, Navy, QB	1981	Marcus Allen, USC, RB
1946	Glenn Davis, Army, HB	1964	John Huarte, Notre Dame, QB	1982	Herschel Walker, Georgia, RB
1947	John Lujack, Notre Dame, QB	1965	Mike Garrett, USC, HB	1983	Mike Rozier, Nebraska, RB
1948	Doak Walker, SMU, HB	1966	Steve Spurrier, Florida, QB	1984	Doug Flutie, Boston College, QB
1949	Leon Hart, Notre Dame, E	1967	Gary Beban, UCLA, QB	1985	Bo Jackson, Auburn, RB
1950	Vic Janowicz, Ohio State, HB	1968	O. J. Simpson, USC, RB	1986	Vinny Testaverde, Miami, QB
1951	Richard Kazmaier, Princeton, HB	1969	Steve Owens, Oklahoma, RB		
1952	Billy Vessels, Oklahoma, HB	1970	Jim Plunkett, Stanford, QB		

Vince Lombardi Award

Honoring the outstanding lineman, sponsored by the Rotary Club of Houston

1970	Jim Stillwagon, Ohio State, MG	1976	Wilson Whitley, Houston, DT	1982	Dave Rimington, Nebraska, C
1971	Walt Patulski, Notre Dame, DE	1977	Ross Browner, Notre Dame, DE	1983	Dean Steinkuhler, Nebraska, G
1972	Rich Glover, Nebraska, MG	1978	Bruce Clark, Penn State, DT	1984	Tony Degrate, Texas, DT
1973	John Hicks, Ohio State, OT	1979	Brad Budde, USC, G	1985	Tony Casillas, Oklahoma, NG
1974	Randy White, Maryland, DT	1980	Hugh Green, Pittsburgh, DE	1986	Cornelius Bennett, Alabama, DE
1975	Lee Roy Selmon, Oklahoma, DT	1981	Kenneth Sims, Texas, DT		

All-Time Division 1-A Coaching Victories

Paul "Bear" Bryant	323	Joe Paterno	199	Vince Dooley	183
Amos Alonzo Stagg	314	Dana Bible	198	Carl Snavely	180
Glenn "Pop" Warner	313	Dan McGugin	197	Gil Dobie	180
Woody Hayes	238	Fielding Yost	196	Ben Schwartzwalder	178
Bo Schembechler	207	Howard Jones	194	Ralph Jordan	176
Jess Neely	207	John Vaught	190	Frank Kush	176
Warren Woodson	207	John Heisman	185	Bob Neyland	173
Eddie Anderson	201	Darrell Royal	184		

Eddie Robinson of Grambling State Univ. holds the record for most college football victories with 336 at the start of the 1987 season.

Outland Award

Honoring the outstanding interior lineman selected by the Football Writers' Association of America.

1946	George Connor, Notre Dame, T	1960	Tom Brown, Minnesota, G	1974	Randy White, Maryland, DE
1947	Joe Steffy, Army, G	1961	Merlin Olsen, Utah State, T	1975	Leroy Selmon, Oklahoma, DT
1948	Bill Fischer, Notre Dame, G	1962	Bobby Bell, Minnesota, T	1976	Ross Browner, Notre Dame, DE
1949	Ed Bagdon, Michigan St., G	1963	Scott Appleton, Texas, T	1977	Brad Shearer, Texas, DT
1950	Bob Gain, Kentucky, T	1964	Steve Delong, Tennessee, T	1978	Greg Roberts, Oklahoma, G
1951	Jim Weatherall, Oklahoma, T	1965	Tommy Nobis, Texas, G	1979	Jim Ritcher, No. Carolina St., C
1952	Dick Modzelewski, Maryland, T	1966	Loyd Phillips, Arkansas, T	1980	Mark May, Pittsburgh, OT
1953	J. D. Roberts, Oklahoma, G	1967	Ron Yary, Southern Cal, T	1981	Dave Rimington, Nebraska, C
1954	Bill Brooks, Arkansas, G	1968	Bill Stanfill, Georgia, T	1982	Dave Rimington, Nebraska, C
1955	Calvin Jones, Iowa, G	1969	Mike Reid, Penn State, DT	1983	Dean Steinkuhler, Nebraska, G
1956	Jim Parker, Ohio State, G	1970	Jim Stillwagon, Ohio State, LB	1984	Bruce Smith, Virginia Tech, DT
1957	Alex Karras, Iowa, T	1971	Larry Jacobson, Nebraska, DT	1985	Mike Ruth, Boston College, DT
1958	Zeke Smith, Auburn, G	1972	Rich Glover, Nebraska, MG	1986	Jason Buck, Brigham Young, DT
1959	Mike McGee, Duke, T	1973	John Hicks, Ohio State, G		

College Football Stadiums

School	Capacity
Alabama, Univ. of (Bryant-Denny Stad.), University	60,000
Arizona State Univ. (Sun Devil), Tempe	70,021
Arizona, Univ. of (Arizona Stad.), Tucson	51,952
Arkansas, Univ. of (Razorback Stad.) Fayetteville	52,055
Auburn Univ. (Jordan Hare Stad.), Auburn, Ala.	72,169
Baylor Univ. Stad., Waco, Tex.	48,500
Boston Coll. (Alumni Stad.), Boston, Mass.	32,000
Bowling Green State Univ. (Doyt Perry Field), Oh.	30,000
Brigham Young Univ. Stad., Provo, Ut.	65,000
Cal., Univ. of (Memorial Stad.), Berkeley	75,662
Clemson Univ. (Memorial Stad.), S.C.	79,725
Colorado, Univ. of (Folsom Field), Boulder	51,941
Duke Univ., (Wade Stad.), Durham, N.C.	33,941
E. Carolina Univ. (Ficklen Stad.), Greenville, N.C.	35,000
Florida State, (Campbell Stad.), Tallahassee	60,519
Florida, Univ. of (Florida Field), Gainesville	72,000
Georgia Tech. (Grant Field), Atlanta	46,000
Georgia, Univ. of (Sanford Stad.), Athens	82,122
Harvard Stad., Boston, Mass.	37,289
Hawaii, Univ. of (Aloha Stad.), Honolulu	50,000
Illinois, Univ. of (Memorial Stad.), Champaign	70,563
Indiana Univ. (Memorial Stad.), Bloomington	52,354
Iowa State (Cyclone-Jack Trice Stad.), Ames	50,000
Iowa, Univ. of (Kinnick Stad.), Iowa City	66,000
Kansas State Univ. Stad., Manhattan	42,000
Kansas, Univ. of (Memorial Stad.), Lawrence	51,500
Kent State Univ. (Dix Stad.), Kent, Oh.	30,400
Kentucky, Univ. of (Commonwealth), Lexington	58,000
La. State Univ. (Tiger Stad.), Baton Rouge	77,542
Louisville, Univ. of (Cardinal Stad.); Ky	35,500
Maryland, Univ. of (Byrd), College Park	45,000
Memphis State (Liberty Bowl), Tenn.	50,180
Michigan State Univ. (Spartan Stad.), E. Lansing	76,000
Michigan, Univ. of (Mich. Stad.), Ann Arbor	101,701
Mississippi St. Univ. (Scott Field)	41,000
Mississippi, Univ. of (Vaught-Hemingway Stad.), Univ.	41,000
Missouri, Univ. of (Faurot Field), Columbia	62,000
Nebraska, Univ. of (Memorial Stad.), Lincoln	73,650
Nevada-Las Vegas, Univ. of (Sam Boyd Silver Bowl)	32,000
New Mexico State Univ. (Memorial Stad.), Las Cruces	30,343
New Mexico, Univ. Stad., Albuquerque	30,646
North Carolina St. U. (Carter-Finley Stad.), Raleigh	53,500
North Carolina, Univ. of (Kenan Stad.), Chapel Hill	50,000
Northern Illinois Univ. (Huskie Stad.), DeKalb	30,998
Northwestern Univ. (Dyche Stad.), Evanston, Ill.	40,256
Notre Dame Stad., South Bend, Ind.	59,075
Ohio State Univ. (Ohio Stad.), Columbus	85,339
Oklahoma State (Lewis Stad.), Stillwater	50,440
Oklahoma, Univ. of (Owen Field), Norman	75,004
Oregon St. Univ. (Parker Stad.), Corvallis	40,593
Oregon, Univ. of (Autzen Stad.), Eugene	41,009
Penn. State Univ. (Beaver Stad.), University Park	83,370
Penn., Univ. of (Franklin Field), Phila.	60,546
Pittsburgh, Univ. of (Pitt. Stad.), Pa.	56,500
Princeton, (Palmer Stad.), Princeton, N.J.	45,725
Purdue, (Ross-Ade Stad.), Lafayette, Ind.	67,861
Rice Stad., Houston, Texas	70,000
So. Carolina, Univ. of (Williams-Brice), Columbia	72,400
So. Miss., Univ. of (Roberts Stad.), Hattiesburg	33,000
Stanford Stad., Stanford, Cal.	86,055
Syracuse Univ., (Carrier Dome), N.Y.	50,000
Tenn., Univ. of (Neyland Stad.), Knoxville	91,246
Texas A. & M. Univ. (Kyle Field), College Station	72,317
Texas Christian Univ. (Amon Carter Stad.) Ft. Worth	46,000
Texas-El Paso (Sun Bowl)	52,000
Texas Tech. Univ. (Jones Stad.), Lubbock	47,000
Texas, Univ. of (Memorial Stad.), Austin	80,000
Tulsa, Univ. of (Skelly Stad.), Okla.	40,235
U.S. Air Force Acad. (Falcon Stad.), Col.	52,153
U.S. Military Academy (Michie Stad.), West Point, N.Y.	39,867
U.S. Naval Academy (Navy-Marine Corps Mem. Stad.) Annapolis, Md.	30,000
Utah State Univ. (Romney Stad.), Logan	30,257
Utah, Univ. of (Robert Rice Stad.), Salt Lake City	36,000
Vanderbilt Stad., Nashville	41,000
Virginia Tech. (Lane Stad.), Blacksburg	51,000
Virginia, Univ. of (Scott Stad.), Charlottesville	42,000
Wake Forest (Groves Stad.), Winston-Salem, N.C.	31,500
Wash. State Univ. (Clarence D. Martin), Pullman	40,000
Washington, Univ. of (Husky Stad.), Seattle	59,800
West Va. Univ. (Mountaineer Field), Morgantown	63,500
Wisconsin, Univ. of (Camp Randall), Madison	77,280
Wyoming, Univ. of (Memorial), Laramie	33,500
Yale Bowl, New Haven, Conn.	70,896

North American Soccer League Champions

Year	Champion	Year	Champion	Year	Champion	Year	Champion
1967	Oakland Clippers (NPSL)	1971	Dallas Tornado	1976	Toronto Metros	1981	Chicago Sting
1967	Los Angeles Wolves (USA)	1972	New York Cosmos	1977	New York Cosmos	1982	New York Cosmos
1968	Atlanta Chiefs	1973	Philadelphia Atoms	1978	New York Cosmos	1983	Tulsa Roughnecks
1969	Kansas City Spurs	1974	Los Angeles Aztecs	1979	Vancouver Whitecaps	1984	Chicago Sting
1970	Rochester Lancers	1975	Tampa Bay Rowdies	1980	New York Cosmos	1985	league suspended

Boxing Champions by Classes

As of Sept. 15, 1987 the only generally accepted title holder was in the heavyweight division. There are numerous governing bodies in boxing including the World Boxing Council, the World Boxing Assn., the International Boxing Federation, the United States Boxing Assn., the North American Boxing Federation, and the European Boxing Union. Other organizations are recognized by TV networks and the print media. All the governing bodies have their own champions and assorted boxing divisions. The following are the recognized champions in the principal divisions of the World Boxing Association and the World Boxing Council.

	WBA	WBC
Heavyweight	Mike Tyson, U.S.	Mike Tyson, U.S.
Cruiserweight (not over 195 lbs.)	Evander Holyfield, U.S.	Carlos DeLeon, Puerto Rico
Light Heavyweight (not over 175 lbs.)	Virgil Hill, U.S.	Thomas Hearns, U.S.
Middleweight (not over 160 lbs.)	vacant	vacant
Jr. Middleweight (not over 154 lbs.)	Mike McCallum, U.S.	Lupe Aquino, U.S.
Welterweight (not over 147 lbs.)	Marlon Starling, U.S.	Lloyd Honeyghan, England
Jr. Welterweight (not over 140 lbs.)	Juan Coggi, Argentina	Tsuyoshi Hamada, Japan
Lightweight (not over 135 lbs.)	Edwin Rosario, Puerto Rico	Jose Luis Ramirez, Mexico
Jr. Lightweight (not over 130 lbs.)	Brian Mitchell, So. Africa	Julio Cesar Chavez, Mexico
Featherweight (not over 126 lbs.)	Antonio Esparragoza, Venezuela	Azumah Nelson, Ghana
Jr. Featherweight (not over 122 lbs.)	Louie Espinoza, U.S.	Jeff French, Australia
Bantamweight (not over 118 lbs.)	Chan Yong Park, So. Korea	Miguel Lora, Colombia
Flyweight (not over 112 lbs.)	Fidel Bassa, Colombia	Sot Chitalada, Thailand

Ring Champions by Years

*Abandoned title

Heavyweights

1882-1892	John L. Sullivan (a)
1892-1897	James J. Corbett (b)
1897-1899	Robert Fitzsimmons
1899-1905	James J. Jeffries (c)
1905-1906	Marvin Hart
1906-1908	Tommy Burns
1908-1915	Jack Johnson
1915-1919	Jess Willard
1919-1926	Jack Dempsey
1926-1928	Gene Tunney*
1928-1930	vacant
1930-1932	Max Schmeling
1932-1933	Jack Sharkey
1933-1934	Primo Carnera
1934-1935	Max Baer
1935-1937	James J. Braddock
1937-1949	Joe Louis*
1949-1951	Ezzard Charles
1951-1952	Joe Walcott
1952-1956	Rocky Marciano*
1956-1959	Floyd Patterson
1959-1960	Ingemar Johansson
1960-1962	Floyd Patterson
1962-1964	Sonny Liston
1964-1967	Cassius Clay* (Muhammad Ali) (d)
1970-1973	Joe Frazier
1973-1974	George Foreman
1974-1978	Muhammad Ali
1978-1979	Leon Spinks (e), Muhammad Ali*
1978	Ken Norton (WBC), Larry Holmes (WBC) (f)
1979	John Tate (WBA)
1980	Mike Weaver (WBA)
1982	Michael Dokes (WBA)
1983	Gerrie Coetzee (WBA)
1984	Tim Witherspoon (WBC); Pinklon Thomas (WBC); Greg Page (WBA)
1985	Tony Tubbs (WBA); Michael Spinks (IBF)
1986	Tim Witherspoon (WBA); Trevor Berbick (WBC); Mike Tyson (WBC); James (Bonecrusher) Smith (WBA).
1987	Mike Tyson (WBA).

(a) London Prize Ring (bare knuckle champion).
(b) First Marquis of Queensberry champion.
(c) Jeffries abandoned the title (1905) and designated Marvin Hart and Jack Root as logical contenders and agreed to referee a fight between them, the winner to be declared champion. Hart defeated Root in 12 rounds (1905) and in turn was defeated by Tommy Burns (1906) who immediately laid claim to the title. Jack Johnson defeated Burns (1908) and was recognized as champion. He clinched the title by defeating Jeffries in an attempted comeback (1910).
(d) Title declared vacant by the World Boxing Assn. and other groups in 1967 after Clay's refusal to fulfill his military obligation. Joe Frazier was recognized as champion by New York, 5 other states, Mexico, and So. America. Jimmy Ellis was declared champion by the World Boxing Assn. Frazier KOd Ellis, Feb. 16, 1970.
(e) After Spinks defeated Ali, the WBC recognized Ken Norton as champion. Norton subsequently lost his title to Larry Holmes.
(f) Holmes was stripped of his WBC title in 1984. He was the International Boxing Federation champion when he lost to Michael Spinks.

Light Heavyweights

1903	Jack Root, George Gardner
1903-1905	Bob Fitzsimmons
1905-1912	Philadelphia Jack O'Brien*
1912-1916	Jack Dillon
1916-1920	Battling Levinsky
1920-1922	George Carpentier
1922-1923	Battling Siki
1923-1925	Mike McTigue
1925-1926	Paul Berlenbach
1926-1927	Jack Delaney*
1927-1929	Tommy Loughran*
1930-1934	Maxey Rosenbloom
1934-1935	Bob Olin
1935-1939	John Henry Lewis*
1939	Melio Bettina
1939-1941	Billy Conn*
1941	Anton Christoforidis (won NBA title)
1941-1948	Gus Lesnevich, Freddie Mills
1948-1950	Freddie Mills
1950-1952	Joey Maxim
1952-1960	Archie Moore
1961-1962	vacant
1962-1963	Harold Johnson
1963-1965	Willie Pastrano
1965-1966	Jose Torres
1966-1968	Dick Tiger
1968-1974	Bob Foster*, John Conteh (WBA)
1975-1977	John Conteh (WBC), Miguel Cuello (WBC), Victor Galindez (WBA)
1978	Mike Rossman (WBA), Mate Parlov (WBC), Marvin Johnson (WBC)
1979	Victor Galindez (WBA), Matthew Saad Muhammad (WBC)
1980	Eddie Mustava Muhammad (WBA)
1981	Michael Spinks (WBA), Dwight Braxton (WBC)
1983	Michael Spinks
1986	Marvin Johnson (WBA); Dennis Andries (WBC)
1987	Thomas Hearns (WBC); Leslie Stewart (WBA); Virgil Hill (WBA).

Middleweights

1884-1891	Jack "Nonpareil" Dempsey
1891-1897	Bob Fitzsimmons*
1897-1907	Tommy Ryan*
1907-1908	Stanley Ketchel, Billy Papke
1908-1910	Stanley Ketchel
1911-1913	vacant
1913	Frank Klaus, George Chip
1914-1917	Al McCoy
1917-1920	Mike O'Dowd
1920-1923	Johnny Wilson
1923-1926	Harry Greb

1926-1931	Tiger Flowers, Mickey Walker
1931-1932	Gorilla Jones (NBA)
1932-1937	Marcel Thil
1938	Al Hostak (NBA), Solly Krieger (NBA)
1939-1940	Al Hostak (NBA)
1941-1947	Tony Zale
1947-1948	Rocky Graziano
1948	Tony Zale, Marcel Cerdan
1949-1951	Jake LaMotta
1951	Ray Robinson, Randy Turpin, Ray Robinson*
1953-1955	Carl (Bobo) Olson
1955-1957	Ray Robinson
1957	Gene Fullmer, Ray Robinson, Carmen Basilio
1958	Ray Robinson
1959	Gene Fullmer (NBA); Ray Robinson (N.Y.)
1960	Gene Fullmer (NBA); Paul Pender (New York and Mass.)
1961	Gene Fullmer (NBA); Terry Downes (New York, Mass., Europe)
1962	Gene Fullmer, Dick Tiger (NBA), Paul Pender (New York and Mass.)*
1963	Dick Tiger (universal).
1963-1965	Joey Giardello
1965-1966	Dick Tiger
1966-1967	Emile Griffith
1967	Nino Benvenuti
1967-1968	Emile Griffith
1968-1970	Nino Benvenuti
1970-1977	Carlos Monzon*
1977-1978	Rodrigo Valdez
1978-1979	Hugo Corro
1979-1980	Vito Antuofermo
1980	Alan Minter, Marvin Hagler
1987	Ray Leonard* (WBC)

Welterweights

1892-1894	Mysterious Billy Smith
1894-1896	Tommy Ryan
1896	Kid McCoy*
1900	Rube Ferns, Matty Matthews
1901	Rube Ferns
1901-1904	Joe Walcott
1904-1906	Dixie Kid, Joe Walcott, Honey Mellody
1907-1911	Mike Sullivan
1911-1915	vacant
1915-1919	Ted Lewis
1919-1922	Jack Britton
1922-1926	Mickey Walker
1926	Pete Latzo
1927-1929	Joe Dundee
1929	Jackie Fields
1930	Jack Thompson, Tommy Freeman
1931	Freeman, Thompson, Lou Brouillard
1932	Jackie Fields
1933	Young Corbett, Jimmy McLarnin
1934	Barney Ross, Jimmy McLarnin
1935-1938	Barney Ross
1938-1940	Henry Armstrong
1940-1941	Fritzie Zivic
1941-1946	Fred Cochrane
1946-1946	Marty Servo*; Ray Robinson (a)
1946-1950	Ray Robinson*
1951	Johnny Bratton (NBA)
1951-1954	Kid Gavilan
1954-1955	Johnny Saxton
1955	Tony De Marco, Carmen Basilio
1956	Carmen Basilio, Johnny Saxton, Basilio
1957	Carmen Basilio*
1958-1960	Virgil Akins, Don Jordan
1960	Benny Paret
1961	Emile Griffith, Benny Paret
1962	Emile Griffith
1963	Luis Rodriguez, Emile Griffith
1964-1966	Emile Griffith*
1966-1969	Curtis Cokes
1969-1970	Jose Napoles, Billy Backus
1971-1975	Jose Napoles
1975-1976	John Stracey (WBC), Angel Espada (WBA)
1976-1979	Carlos Palomino (WBC), Jose Cuevas (WBA)
1979	Wilfredo Benitez (WBC), Sugar Ray Leonard (WBC)
1980	Roberto Duran (WBC), Thomas Hearns (WBA), Sugar Ray Leonard (WBC)
1981-1982	Sugar Ray Leonard*
1983	Donald Curry (WBA); Milton McCrory (WBC)
1985	Donald Curry
1986	Lloyd Honeyghan (WBC)
1987	Mark Breland (WBA); Marlon Starling (WBA).

(a) Robinson gained the title by defeating Tommy Bell in an elimination agreed to by the NY Commission and the NBA. Both claimed Robinson waived his title when he won the middleweight crown from LaMotta in 1951.

Lightweights

1896-1899	Kid Lavigne
1899-1902	Frank Erne
1902-1908	Joe Gans
1908-1910	Battling Nelson
1910-1912	Ad Wolgast
1912-1914	Willie Ritchie
1914-1917	Freddie Welsh
1917-1925	Benny Leonard*
1925	Jimmy Goodrich, Rocky Kansas
1926-1930	Sammy Mandell
1930	Al Singer, Tony Canzoneri
1930-1933	Tony Canzoneri
1933-1935	Barney Ross*
1935-1936	Tony Canzoneri
1936-1938	Lou Ambers
1938	Henry Armstrong
1939	Lou Ambers
1940	Lew Jenkins
1941-1943	Sammy Angott
1944	S. Angott (NBA), J. Zurita (NBA)
1945-1951	Ike Williams (NBA; later universal)
1951-1952	James Carter
1952	Lauro Salas, James Carter
1953-1954	James Carter
1954	Paddy De Marco; James Carter
1955	James Carter; Bud Smith
1956	Bud Smith, Joe Brown
1956-1962	Joe Brown
1962-1965	Carlos Ortiz
1965	Ismael Laguna
1965-1968	Carlos Ortiz
1968-1969	Teo Cruz
1969-1970	Mando Ramos
1970	Ismael Laguna, Ken Buchanan (WBA)
1971	Mando Ramos (WBC), Pedro Carrasco (WBC)
1972-1979	Roberto Duran* (WBA)
1972	Pedro Carrasco, Mando Ramos, Chango Carmona, Rodolfo Gonzalez (all WBC)
1974-1976	Guts Ishimatsu (WBC)
1976-1977	Esteban De Jesus (WBC)
1979	Jim Watt (WBC), Ernesto Espana (WBA)
1980	Hilmer Kenty (WBA)
1981	Alexis Arguello (WBC), Sean O'Grady (WBA), Arturo Frias (WBA)
1982-1984	Ray Mancini (WBA)
1983	Edwin Rosario (WBC)
1984	Livingstone Bramble (WBA); Jose Luis Ramirez (WBC)
1985	Hector (Macho) Camacho (WBC)
1986	Edwin Rosario (WBA); Jose Luis Ramirez (WBC).

Featherweights

1892-1900	George Dixon (disputed)
1900-1901	Terry McGovern, Young Corbett*
1901-1912	Abe Attell
1912-1923	Johnny Kilbane
1923	Eugene Criqui, Johnny Dundee
1923-1925	Johnny Dundee*
1925-1927	Kid Kaplan*
1927-1928	Benny Bass, Tony Canzoneri
1928-1929	Andre Routis
1929-1932	Battling Battalino*
1932-1934	Tommy Paul (NBA)
1933-1936	Freddie Miller
1936-1937	Petey Sarron
1937-1938	Henry Armstrong*
1938-1940	Joey Archibald (b)
1940-41	Harry Jeffra
1942-1948	Willie Pep
1948-1949	Sandy Saddler
1949-1950	Willie Pep
1950-1957	Sandy Saddler*
1957-1959	Hogan (Kid) Bassey
1959-1963	Davey Moore
1963-1964	Sugar Ramos
1964-1967	Vicente Saldivar*
1968-1971	Paul Rojas (WBA), Sho Saijo (WBA)
1971	Antonio Gomez (WBA), Kuniaki Shibada (WBC)
1972	Ernesto Marcel* (WBA), Clemente Sanchez* (WBC), Jose Legra (WBC)

(*continued*)

1973	Eder Jofre (WBC)
1974	Ruben Olivares (WBA), Alexis Arguello (WBA), Bobby Chacon (WBC)
1975	Ruben Olivares (WBC), David Kotey (WBC)
1976	Danny Lopez (WBC)
1977	Rafael Ortega (WBA)
1978	Cecilio Lastra (WBA), Eusebio Pedrosa (WBA)
1980	Salvador Sanchez (WBC)
1982	Juan LaPorte (WBC)
1984	Wilfredo Gomez (WBC); Azumah Nelson (WBC)
1985	Barry McGuigan (WBA)
1986	Steve Cruz (WBA)
1987	Antonio Esparragoza (WBA)

(b) After Petey Scalzo knocked out Archibald in an overweight match and was refused a title bout, the NBA named Scalzo champion. The NBA title succession: Scalzo, 1938-1941; Richard Lemos, 1941; Jackie Wilson, 1941-1943; Jackie Callura, 1943; Phil Terranova, 1943-1944; Sal Bartolo, 1944-1946.

History of Heavyweight Championship Bouts

*Title Changed Hands

1889—July 8—John L. Sullivan def. Jake Kilrain, 75, Richburg, Miss. Last championship bare knuckles bout.

***1892**—Sept. 7—James J. Corbett def. John L. Sullivan, 21, New Orleans. Big gloves used for first time.

1894—Jan. 25—James J. Corbett KOd Charley Mitchell, 3, Jacksonville, Fla.

***1897**—Bob Fitzsimmons def. James J. Corbett, 14, Carson City, Nev.

***1899**—June 9—James J. Jeffries def. Bob Fitzsimmons, 11, Coney Island, N.Y.

1899—Nov. 3—James J. Jeffries def. Tom Sharkey, 25, Coney Island, N.Y.

1900—May 11—James J. Jeffries KOd James J. Corbett, 23, Coney Island, N.Y.

1901—Nov. 15—James J. Jeffries KOd Gus Ruhlin, 5, San Francisco.

1902—July 25—James J. Jeffries KOd Bob Fitzsimmons, 8, San Francisco.

1903—Aug. 14—James J. Jeffries KOd James J. Corbett, 10, San Francisco.

1904—Aug. 26—James J. Jeffries KOd Jack Monroe, 2, San Francisco.

***1905**—James J. Jeffries retired, July 3—Marvin Hart KOd Jack Root, 12, Reno. Jeffries refereed and presented the title to the victor. Jack O'Brien also claimed the title.

***1906**—Feb. 23—Tommy Burns def. Marvin Hart, 20, Los Angeles.

1906—Nov. 28—Philadelphia Jack O'Brien and Tommy Burns, 20, draw, Los Angeles.

1907—May 8—Tommy Burns def. Jack O'Brien, 20, Los Angeles.

1907—July 4—Tommy Burns KOd Bill Squires, 1, Colma, Cal.

1907—Dec. 2—Tommy Burns KOd Gunner Moir, 10, London.

1908—Feb. 10—Tommy Burns KOd Jack Palmer, 4, London.

1908—March 17—Tommy Burns KOd Jem Roche, 1, Dublin.

1908—April 18—Tommy Burns KOd Jewey Smith, 5, Paris.

1908—June 13—Tommy Burns KOd Bill Squires, 8, Paris.

1908—Aug. 24—Tommy Burns KOd Bill Squires, 13, Sydney, New South Wales.

1908—Sept. 2—Tommy Burns KOd Bill Lang, 2, Melbourne, Australia.

***1908**—Dec. 26—Jack Johnson KOd Tommy Burns, 14, Sydney, Australia. Police halted contest.

1909—May 19—Jack Johnson and Jack O'Brien, 6, draw, Philadelphia.

1909—June 30—Jack Johnson and Tony Ross, 6, draw, Pittsburgh.

1909—Sept. 9—Jack Johnson and Al Kaufman, 10, draw, San Francisco.

1909—Oct. 16—Jack Johnson KOd Stanley Ketchel, 12, Colma, Cal.

1910—July 4—Jack Johnson KOd Jim Jeffries, 15, Reno, Nev. Jeffries came back from retirement.

1912—July 4—Jack Johnson def. Jim Flynn, 9, Las Vegas, N.M. Contest stopped by police.

1913—Nov. 28—Jack Johnson KOd Andre Spaul, 2, Paris.

1913—Dec. 9—Jack Johnson and Jim Johnson, 10, draw, Paris. Bout called a draw when Jack Johnson declared he had broken his arm.

1914—June 27—Jack Johnson def. Frank Moran, 20, Paris.

***1915**—April 5—Jess Willard KOd Jack Johnson, 26, Havana, Cuba.

1916—March 25—Jess Willard and Frank Moran, 10, draw, New York.

***1919**—July 4—Jack Dempsey KOd Jess Willard, Toledo, Oh. Willard failed to answer bell for 4th round.

1920—Sept. 6—Jack Dempsey KOd Billy Miske, 3, Benton Harbor, Mich.

1920—Dec. 14—Jack Dempsey KOd Bill Brennan, 12, New York.

1921—July 2—Jack Dempsey KOd George Carpentier, 4, Boyle's Thirty Acres, Jersey City, N.J. Carpentier had held the so-called white heavyweight title since July 16, 1914, in a series established in 1913, after Jack Johnson's exile in Europe late in 1912.

1923—July 4—Jack Dempsey def. Tom Gibbons, 15, Shelby, Mont.

1923—Sept. 14—Jack Dempsey KOd Luis Firpo, 2, New York.

***1926**—Sept. 23—Gene Tunney def. Jack Dempsey, 10, Philadelphia.

1927—Sept. 22—Gene Tunney def. Jack Dempsey, 10, Chicago.

1928—July 26—Gene Tunney KOd Tom Heeney, 11, New York; soon afterward he announced his retirement.

***1930**—June 12—Max Schmeling def. Jack Sharkey, 4, New York. Sharkey fouled Schmeling in a bout which was generally considered to have resulted in the election of a successor to Gene Tunney, New York.

1931—July 3—Max Schmeling KOd Young Stribling, 15, Cleveland.

***1932**—June 21—Jack Sharkey def. Max Schmeling, 15, New York.

***1933**—June 29—Primo Carnera KOd Jack Sharkey, 6, New York.

1933—Oct. 22—Primo Carnera def. Paulino Uzcudun, 15, Rome.

1934—March 1—Primo Carnera def. Tommy Loughran, 15, Miami.

***1934**—June 14—Max Baer KOd Primo Carnera, 11, New York.

***1935**—June 13—James J. Braddock def. Max Baer, 15, New York.

***1937**—June 22—Joe Louis KOd James J. Braddock, 8, Chicago.

1937—Aug. 30—Joe Louis def. Tommy Farr, 15, New York.

1938—Feb. 23—Joe Louis KOd Nathan Mann, 3, New York.

1938—April 1—Joe Louis KOd Harry Thomas, 5, New York.

1938—June 22—Joe Louis KOd Max Schmeling, 1, New York.

1939—Jan. 25—Joe Louis KOd John H. Lewis, 1, New York.

1939—April 17—Joe Louis KOd Jack Roper, 1, Los Angeles.

1939—June 28—Joe Louis KOd Tony Galento, 4, New York.

1939—Sept. 20—Joe Louis KOd Bob Pastor, 11, Detroit.

1940—February 9—Joe Louis def. Arturo Godoy, 15, New York.

1940—March 29—Joe Louis KOd Johnny Paycheck, 2, New York.

1940—June 20—Joe Louis KOd Arturo Godoy, 8, New York.

1940—Dec. 16—Joe Louis KOd Al McCoy, 6, Boston.

1941—Jan. 31—Joe Louis KOd Red Burman, 5, New York.

1941—Feb. 17—Joe Louis KOd Gus Dorzaio, 2, Philadelphia.

1941—March 21—Joe Louis KOd Abe Simon, 13, Detroit.

1941—April 8—Joe Louis KOd Tony Musto, 9, St. Louis.

1941—May 23—Joe Louis def. Buddy Baer, 7, Washington, D.C., on a disqualification.

1941—June 18—Joe Louis KOd Billy Conn, 13, New York.

1941—Sept. 29—Joe Louis KOd Lou Nova, 6, New York.

1942—Jan. 9—Joe Louis KOd Buddy Baer, 1, New York.

1942—March 27—Joe Louis KOd Abe Simon, 6, New York.

1946—June 19—Joe Louis KOd Billy Conn, 8, New York.

1946—Sept. 18—Joe Louis KOd Tami Mauriello, 1, New York.

1947—Dec. 5—Joe Louis def. Joe Walcott, 15, New York.

1948—June 25—Joe Louis KOd Joe Walcott, 11, New York.

***1949**—June 22—Following Joe Louis' retirement Ezzard Charles def. Joe Walcott, 15, Chicago, NBA recognition only.

1949—Aug. 10—Ezzard Charles KOd Gus Lesnevich, 7, New York.

1949—Oct. 14—Ezzard Charles KOd Pat Valentino, 8, San Francisco; clinched American title.

1950—Aug. 15—Ezzard Charles KOd Freddy Beshore, 14, Buffalo.

1950—Sept. 27—Ezzard Charles def. Joe Louis in latter's attempted comeback, 15, New York; universal recognition.

1950—Dec. 5—Ezzard Charles KOd Nick Barone, 11, Cincinnati.

1951—Jan. 12—Ezzard Charles KOd Lee Oma, 10, New York.

1951—March 7—Ezzard Charles def. Joe Walcott, 15, Detroit.

1951—May 30—Ezzard Charles def. Joey Maxim, light heavyweight champion, 15, Chicago.

***1951**—July 18—Joe Walcott KOd Ezzard Charles, 7, Pittsburgh.

1952—June 5—Joe Walcott def. Ezzard Charles, 15, Philadelphia.

***1952**—Sept. 23—Rocky Marciano KOd Joe Walcott, 13, Philadelphia.

1953—May 15—Rocky Marciano KOd Joe Walcott, 1, Chicago.

1953—Sept. 24—Rocky Marciano KOd Roland LaStarza, 11, New York.

1954—June 17—Rocky Marciano def. Ezzard Charles, 15, New York.

1954—Sept. 17—Rocky Marciano KOd Ezzard Charles, 8, New York.

1955—May 16—Rocky Marciano KOd Don Cockell, 9, San Francisco.

1955—Sept. 21—Rocky Marciano KOd Archie Moore, 9, New York. Marciano retired undefeated, Apr. 27, 1956.

***1956**—Nov. 30—Floyd Patterson KOd Archie Moore, 5, Chicago.

1957—July 29—Floyd Patterson KOd Hurricane Jackson, 10, New York.

1957—Aug. 22—Floyd Patterson KOd Pete Rademacher, 6, Seattle.

1958—Aug. 18—Floyd Patterson KOd Roy Harris, 12, Los Angeles.

1959—May 1—Floyd Patterson KOd Brian London, 11, Indianapolis.

***1959**—June 26—Ingemar Johansson KOd Floyd Patterson, 3, New York.

***1960**—June 20—Floyd Patterson KOd Ingemar Johansson, 5, New York. First heavyweight in boxing history to regain title.

1961—Mar. 13—Floyd Patterson KOd Ingemar Johansson, 6, Miami Beach.

1961—Dec. 4—Floyd Patterson KOd Tom McNeeley, 4, Toronto.

***1962**—Sept. 25—Sonny Liston KOd Floyd Patterson, 1, Chicago.

1963—July 22—Sonny Liston KOd Floyd Patterson, 1, Las Vegas.

***1964**—Feb. 25—Cassius Clay KOd Sonny Liston, 7, Miami Beach.

1965—May 25—Cassius Clay KOd Sonny Liston, 1, Lewiston, Maine.

1965—Nov. 11—Cassius Clay KOd Floyd Patterson, 12, Las Vegas.

1966—Mar. 29—Cassius Clay def. George Chuvalo, 15, Toronto.

1966—May 21—Casslus Clay KOd Henry Cooper, 6, London.

1966—Aug. 6—Cassius Clay KOd Brian London, 3, London.

1966—Sept. 10—Cassius Clay KOd Karl Mildenberger, 12, Frankfurt, Germany.

1966—Nov. 14—Cassius Clay KOd Cleveland Williams, 3, Houston.

1967—Feb. 6—Cassius Clay def. Ernie Terrell, 15, Houston.

1967—Mar. 22—Cassius Clay KOd Zora Folley, 7, New York. Clay was stripped of his title by the WBA and others for refusing military service.

***1970**—Feb. 16—Joe Frazier KOd Jimmy Ellis, 5, New York.

1970—Nov. 18—Joe Frazier KOd Bob Foster, 2, Detroit.

1971—Mar. 8—Joe Frazier def. Cassius Clay (Muhammad Ali), 15, New York.

1972—Jan. 15—Joe Frazier KOd Terry Daniels, 4, New Orleans.

1972—May 25—Joe Frazier KOd Ron Stander, 5, Omaha.

***1973**—Jan. 22—George Foreman KOd Joe Frazier, 2, Kingston, Jamaica.

1973—Sept. 1—George Foreman KOd Joe Roman, 1, Tokyo.

1974—Mar. 3—George Foreman KOd Ken Norton, 2, Caracas.

***1974**—Oct. 30—Muhammad Ali KOd George Foreman, 8, Zaire.

1975—Mar. 24—Muhammad Ali KOd Chuck Wepner, 15, Cleveland.

1975—May 16—Muhammad Ali KOd Ron Lyle, 11, Las Vegas.

1975—June 30—Muhammad Ali def. Joe Bugner, 15, Malaysia.

1975—Oct. 1—Muhammad Ali KOd Joe Frazier, 14, Manila.

1976—Feb. 20—Muhammad Ali KOd Jean-Pierre Coopman, 5, San Juan.

1976—Apr. 30—Muhammad Ali def. Jimmy Young, 15, Landover, Md.

1976—May 25—Muhammad Ali KOd Richard Dunn, 5, Munich.

1976—Sept. 28—Muhammad Ali def. Ken Norton, 15, New York.

1977—May 16—Muhammad Ali def. Alfredo Evangelista, 15, Landover, Md.

1977—Sept. 29—Muhammad Ali def. Earnie Shavers, 15, New York.

***1978**—Feb. 15—Leon Spinks def. Muhammad Ali, 15, Las Vegas.

***1978**—Sept. 15—Muhammad Ali def. Leon Spinks, 15, New Orleans. Ali retired in 1979.

(Bouts when title changed hands only)

***1978**—June 9—(WBC) Larry Holmes def. Ken Norton, 15, Las Vegas.

***1980**—Mar. 31—(WBA) Mike Weaver KOd John Tate, 15, Knoxville.

***1982**—Dec. 10—(WBA) Michael Dokes KOd Mike Weaver, 1, Las Vegas.

***1983**—Sept. 23—(WBA) Gerrie Coetzee KOd Michael Dokes, 10, Richfield, Oh.

***1984**—Mar. 10—(WBC) Tim Witherspoon def. Greg Page, 12, Las Vegas, Nev.

***1984**—Aug. 31—(WBC) Pinklon Thomas def. Tim Witherspoon, 12, Las Vegas, Nev.

***1984**—Dec. 2—(WBA) Greg Page KOd Gerrie Coetzee, 8, Sun City, Bophuthatswana

***1985**—Apr. 29—(WBA) Tony Tubbs def. Greg Page, 15, Buffalo, N.Y.

***1985**—Sept. 21—(IBF) Michael Spinks def. Larry Holmes, 15, Las Vegas, Nev.

***1986**—Jan. 17—(WBA) Tim Witherspoon def. Tony Tubbs, 15, Atlanta, Ga.

***1986**—Mar. 23—(WBC) Trevor Berbick def. Pinklon Thomas, 12, Miami, Fla.

1986—Nov. 22—(WBC) Mike Tyson KOd Trevor Berbick, 2, Las Vegas.

1986—Dec. 12—(WBA) James (Bonecrusher) Smith KOd Tim Witherspoon, 1, New York.

1987—Mar. 7—(WBA) Mike Tyson def. James (Bonecrusher) Smith, 12, Las Vegas.

Table Tennis in 1986-87

U.S. National Closed Championship

Pittsburgh, Pa., Dec. 10-14, 1986

Men's Singles — Chartchai Teekaveerakit, Vienna, Va.
Women's Singles — In Sook Bhushan, Aurora, Col.
Men's Doubles — Sean O'Neill & Chartchai Teekaveerakit, Vienna, Va.
Women's Doubles — In Sook Bhushan & Diana Gee, Santa Clara, Cal.
Mixed Doubles — Sean O'Neill & Diana Gee.

World Championships

New Delhi, India, Feb. 18-Mar. 1, 1987

Men's Singles — Jiang Jialiang, China.
Women's Singles — He Zhili, China.
Men's Doubles — Chen Longcan & Wei Qingguang, China.
Women's Doubles — Hyun Jung & Yang Young Ja, South Korea.
Mixed Doubles — Hui Jun & Geng Lijuan, China.
Men's Team — China.
Women's Team — China.

Tennis

U.S. Open Champions

Men's Singles

Year	Champion	Final opponent	Year	Champion	Final opponent
1920	Bill Tilden	William Johnston	1954	E. Victor Seixas Jr.	Rex Hartwig
1921	Bill Tilden	Wallace Johnson	1955	Tony Trabert	Ken Rosewall
1922	Bill Tilden	William Johnston	1956	Ken Rosewall	Lewis Hoad
1923	Bill Tilden	William Johnston	1957	Malcolm Anderson	Ashley Cooper
1924	Bill Tilden	William Johnston	1958	Ashley Cooper	Malcolm Anderson
1925	Bill Tilden	William Johnston	1959	Neale A. Fraser	Alejandro Olmedo
1926	Rene Lacoste	Jean Borotra	1960	Neale A. Fraser	Rod Laver
1927	Rene Lacoste	Bill Tilden	1961	Roy Emerson	Rod Laver
1928	Henri Cochet	Francis Hunter	1962	Rod Laver	Roy Emerson
1929	Bill Tilden	Francis Hunter	1963	Rafael Osuna	F. A. Froehling 3d
1930	John Doeg	Francis Shields	1964	Roy Emerson	Fred Stolle
1931	H. Ellsworth Vines	George Lott	1965	Manuel Santana	Cliff Drysdale
1932	H. Ellsworth Vines	Henri Cochet	1966	Fred Stolle	John Newcombe
1933	Fred Perry	John Crawford	1967	John Newcombe	Clark Graebner
1934	Fred Perry	Wilmer Allison	1968	Arthur Ashe	Tom Okker
1935	Wilmer Allison	Sidney Wood	1969	Rod Laver	Tony Roche
1936	Fred Perry	Don Budge	1970	Ken Rosewall	Tony Roche
1937	Don Budge	Baron G. von Cramm	1971	Stan Smith	Jan Kodes
1938	Don Budge	C. Gene Mako	1972	Ilie Nastase	Arthur Ashe
1939	Robert Riggs	S. Welby Van Horn	1973	John Newcombe	Jan Kodes
1940	Don McNeill	Robert Riggs	1974	Jimmy Connors	Ken Rosewall
1941	Robert Riggs	F. L. Kovacs	1975	Manuel Orantes	Jimmy Connors
1942	F. R. Schroeder Jr.	Frank Parker	1976	Jimmy Connors	Bjorn Borg
1943	Joseph Hunt	Jack Kramer	1977	Guillermo Vilas	Jimmy Connors
1944	Frank Parker	William Talbert	1978	Jimmy Connors	Bjorn Borg
1945	Frank Parker	William Talbert	1979	John McEnroe	Vitas Gerulaitis
1946	Jack Kramer	Thomas Brown Jr.	1980	John McEnroe	Bjorn Borg
1947	Jack Kramer	Frank Parker	1981	John McEnroe	Bjorn Borg
1948	Pancho Gonzales	Eric Sturgess	1982	Jimmy Connors	Ivan Lendl
1949	Pancho Gonzales	F. R. Schroeder Jr.	1983	Jimmy Connors	Ivan Lendl
1950	Arthur Larsen	Herbert Flam	1984	John McEnroe	Ivan Lendl
1951	Frank Sedgman	E. Victor Seixas Jr.	1985	Ivan Lendl	John McEnroe
1952	Frank Sedgman	Gardnar Mulloy	1986	Ivan Lendl	Miloslav Mecir
1953	Tony Trabert	E. Victor Seixas Jr.	1987	Ivan Lendl	Mats Wilander

Men's Doubles

Year	Champions	Year	Champions
1940	Jack Kramer—Frederick Schroeder Jr.	1964	Dennis Ralston—Chuck McKinley
1941	Jack Kramer—Frederick Schroeder Jr.	1965	Roy Emerson—Fred Stolle
1942	Gardnar Mulloy—William Talbert	1966	Roy Emerson—Fred Stolle
1943	Jack Kramer—Frank Parker	1967	John Newcombe—Tony Roche
1944	Don McNeill—Robert Falkenburg	1968	Robert Lutz—Stan Smith
1945	Gardnar Mulloy—William Talbert	1969	Fred Stolle—Ken Rosewall
1946	Gardnar Mulloy—William Talbert	1970	Pierre Barthes—Nicki Pilic
1947	Jack Kramer—Frederick Schroeder Jr.	1971	John Newcombe—Roger Taylor
1948	Gardnar Mulloy—William Talbert	1972	Cliff Drysdale—Roger Taylor
1949	John Bromwich—William Sidwell	1973	John Newcombe—Owen Davidson
1950	John Bromwich—Frank Sedgman	1974	Bob Lutz—Stan Smith
1951	Frank Sedgman—Kenneth McGregor	1975	Jimmy Connors—Ilie Nastase
1952	Mervyn Rose—E. Victor Seixas Jr.	1976	Marty Riessen—Tom Okker
1953	Rex Hartwig—Mervyn Rose	1977	Bob Hewitt—Frew McMillan
1954	E. Victor Seixas Jr.—Tony Trabert	1978	Stan Smith—Bob Lutz
1955	Kosei Kamo—Atsushi Miyagi	1979	John McEnroe—Peter Fleming
1956	Lewis Hoad—Ken Rosewall	1980	Bob Lutz—Stan Smith
1957	Ashley Cooper—Neale Fraser	1981	John McEnroe—Peter Fleming
1958	Hamilton Richardson—Alejandro Olmedo	1982	Kevin Curren—Steve Denton
1959	Neale A. Fraser—Roy Emerson	1983	John McEnroe—Peter Fleming
1960	Neale A. Fraser—Roy Emerson	1984	Tomas Smid—John Fitzgerald
1961	Dennis Ralston—Chuck McKinley	1985	Ken Flach—Robert Seguso
1962	Rafael Osuna—Antonio Palafox	1986	Andres Gomez—Slobodan Zivojinovic
1963	Dennis Ralston—Chuck McKinley	1987	Stefan Edberg—Anders Jarryd

Mixed Doubles

Year	Champions	Year	Champions
1962	Margaret Smith—Fred Stolle	1975	Rosemary Casals—Dick Stockton
1963	Margaret Smith—Kenneth Fletcher	1976	Billie Jean King—Phil Dent
1964	Margaret Smith—John Newcombe	1977	Betty Stove—Frew McMillan
1965	Margaret Smith—Fred Stolle	1978	Betty Stove—Frew McMillan
1966	Donna Floyd Fales—Owen Davidson	1979	Greer Stevens—Bob Hewitt
1967	Billie Jean King—Owen Davidson	1980	Wendy Turnbull—Marty Riessen
1968	Mary Ann Eisel—Peter Curtis	1981	Anne Smith—Kevin Curren
1969	Margaret S. Court—Marty Riessen	1982	Anne Smith—Kevin Curren
1970	Margaret S. Court—Marty Riessen	1983	Elizabeth Sayers—John Fitzgerald
1971	Billie Jean King—Owen Davidson	1984	Manuela Maleeva—Tom Gullikson
1972	Margaret S. Court—Marty Riessen	1985	Martina Navratilova—Heinz Gunthardt
1973	Billie Jean King—Owen Davidson	1986	Raffaella Reggi—Sergio Casal
1974	Pam Teeguarden—Geoff Masters	1987	Martina Navratilova—Emilio Sanchez

Women's Singles

Year	Champion	Final opponent	Year	Champion	Final opponent
1936	Alice Marble	Helen Jacobs	1962	Margaret Smith	Darlene Hard
1937	Anita Lizana	Jadwiga Jedrzejowska	1963	Maria Bueno	Margaret Smith
1938	Alice Marble	Nancye Wynne	1964	Maria Bueno	Carole Graebner
1939	Alice Marble	Helen Jacobs	1965	Margaret Smith	Billie Jean Moffitt
1940	Alice Marble	Helen Jacobs	1966	Maria Bueno	Nancy Richey
1941	Sarah Palfrey Cooke	Pauline Betz	1967	Billie Jean King	Ann Haydon Jones
1942	Pauline Betz	Louise Brough	1968	Virginia Wade	Billie Jean King
1943	Pauline Betz	Louise Brough	1969	Margaret Court	Nancy Richey
1944	Pauline Betz	Margaret Osborne	1970	Margaret Court	Rosemary Casals
1945	Sarah P. Cooke	Pauline Betz	1971	Billie Jean King	Rosemary Casals
1946	Pauline Betz	Doris Hart	1972	Billie Jean King	Kerry Melville
1947	Louise Brough	Margaret Osborne	1973	Margaret Court	Evonne Goolagong
1948	Margaret Osborne duPont	Louise Brough	1974	Billie Jean King	Evonne Goolagong
1949	Margaret Osborne duPont	Doris Hart	1975	Chris Evert	Evonne Goolagong
1950	Margaret Osborne duPont	Doris Hart	1976	Chris Evert	Evonne Goolagong
1951	Maureen Connolly	Shirley Fry	1977	Chris Evert	Wendy Turnbull
1952	Maureen Connolly	Doris Hart	1978	Chris Evert	Pam Shriver
1953	Maureen Connolly	Doris Hart	1979	Tracy Austin	Chris Evert Lloyd
1954	Doris Hart	Louise Brough	1980	Chris Evert Lloyd	Hana Mandlikova
1955	Doris Hart	Patricia Ward	1981	Tracy Austin	Martina Navratilova
1956	Shirley Fry	Althea Gibson	1982	Chris Evert Lloyd	Hana Mandlikova
1957	Althea Gibson	Louise Brough	1983	Martina Navratilova	Chris Evert Lloyd
1958	Althea Gibson	Darlene Hard	1984	Martina Navratilova	Chris Evert Lloyd
1959	Maria Bueno	Christine Truman	1985	Hana Mandlikova	Martina Navratilova
1960	Darlene Hard	Maria Bueno	1986	Martina Navratilova	Helena Sukova
1961	Darlene Hard	Ann Haydon	1987	Martina Navratilova	Steffi Graf

Women's Doubles

Year	Champions	Year	Champions
1940	Alice Marble—Mrs. Sarah P. Fabyan	1964	Billie Jean Moffitt—Karen Susman
1941	Mrs. S. P. Cooke—Margaret Osborne	1965	Carole C. Graebner—Nancy Richey
1942	A. Louise Brough—Margaret Osborne	1966	Maria Bueno—Nancy Richey
1943	A. Louise Brough—Margaret Osborne	1967	Rosemary Casals—Billie Jean King
1944	A. Louise Brough—Margaret Osborne	1968	Maria Bueno—Margaret S. Court
1945	A. Louise Brough—Margaret Osborne	1969	Francoise Durr—Darlene Hard
1946	A. Louise Brough—Margaret Osborne	1970	M. S. Court—Judy Tegart Dalton
1947	A. Louise Brough—Margaret Osborne	1971	Rosemary Casals—Judy Tegart Dalton
1948	A. Louise Brough—Mrs. M. O. du Pont	1972	Francoise Durr—Betty Stove
1949	A. Louise Brough—Mrs. M. O. du Pont	1973	Margaret S. Court—Virginia Wade
1950	A. Louise Brough—Mrs. M. O. du Pont	1974	Billie Jean King—Rosemary Casals
1951	Doris Hart—Shirley Fry	1975	Margaret Court—Virginia Wade
1952	Doris Hart—Shirley Fry	1976	Linky Boshoff—Ilana Kloss
1953	Doris Hart—Shirley Fry	1977	Betty Stove—Martina Navratilova
1954	Doris Hart—Shirley Fry	1978	Martina Navratilova—Billie Jean King
1955	A. Louise Brough—Mrs. M. O. du Pont	1979	Betty Stove—Wendy Turnbull
1956	A. Louise Brough—Mrs. M. O. du Pont	1980	Billie Jean King—Martina Navratilova
1957	A. Louise Brough—Mrs. M. O. du Pont	1981	Anne Smith—Kathy Jordan
1958	Darlene Hard—Jeanne Arth	1982	Rosemary Casals—Wendy Turnbull
1959	Darlene Hard—Jeanne Arth	1983	Martina Navratilova—Pam Shriver
1960	Darlene Hard—Maria Bueno	1984	Martina Navratilova—Pam Shriver
1961	Darlene Hard—Lesley Turner	1985	Claudia Kohde-Kilsch—Helena Sukova
1962	Maria Bueno—Darlene Hard	1986	Martina Navratilova—Pam Shriver
1963	Margaret Smith—Robyn Ebbern	1987	Martina Navratilova—Pam Shriver

Davis Cup Challenge Round

Year	Result	Year	Result	Year	Result
1900	United States 5, British Isles 0	1930	France 4, United States 1	1961	Australia 5, Italy 0
1901	(not played)	1931	France 3, Great Britain 2	1962	Australia 5, Mexico 0
1902	United States 3, British Isles 2	1932	France 3, United States 2	1963	United States 3, Australia 2
1903	British Isles 4, United States 1	1933	Great Britain 3, France 2	1964	Australia 3, United States 2
1904	British Isles 5, Belgium 0	1934	Great Britain 4, United States 1	1965	Australia 4, Spain 1
1905	British Isles 5, United States 0	1935	Great Britain 5, United States 0	1966	Australia 4, India 1
1906	British Isles 5, United States 0	1936	Great Britain 3, Australia 2	1967	Australia 4, Spain 1
1907	Australia 3, British Isles 2	1937	United States 4, Great Britain 1	1968	United States 4, Australia 1
1908	Australasia 3, United States 2	1938	United States 3, Australia 2	1969	United States 5, Romania 0
1909	Australasia 5, United States 0	1939	Australia 3, United States 2	1970	United States 5, W. Germany 0
1910	(not played)	1940-45	(not played)	1971	United States 3, Romania 2
1911	Australasia 5, United States 0	1946	United States 5, Australia 0	1972	United States 3, Romania 2
1912	British Isles 3, Australasia 2	1947	United States 4, Australia 1	1973	Australia 5, United States 0
1913	United States 3, British Isles 2	1948	United States 5, Australia 0	1974	South Africa (default by India)
1914	Australasia 3, United States 2	1949	United States 4, Australia 1	1975	Sweden 3, Czech. 2
1915-18	(not played)	1950	Australia 4, United States 1	1976	Italy 4, Chile 1
1919	Australasia 4, British Isles 1	1951	Australia 3, United States 2	1977	Australia 3, Italy 1
1920	United States 5, Australasia 0	1952	Australia 4, United States 1	1978	United States 4, Great Britain 1
1921	United States 5, Japan 0	1953	Australia 3, United States 2	1979	United States 5, Italy 0
1922	United States 4, Australasia 1	1954	United States 3, Australia 2	1980	Czechoslovakia 4, Italy 1
1923	United States 4, Australasia 1	1955	Australia 5, United States 0	1981	United States 3, Argentina 1
1924	United States 5, Australasia 0	1956	Australia 5, United States 0	1982	United States 3, France, 0
1925	United States 5, France 0	1957	Australia 3, United States 2	1983	Australia 3, Sweden 1
1926	United States 4, France 1	1958	United States 3, Australia 2	1984	Sweden 3, United States 0
1927	France 3, United States 2	1959	Australia 3, United States 2	1985	Sweden 3, W. Germany 2
1928	France 4, United States 1	1960	Australia 4, Italy 1	1986	Australia 3, Sweden 2
1929	France 3, United States 2				

All-England Champions, Wimbledon

Men's Singles

Year	Champion	Final opponent	Year	Champion	Final opponent
1933	Jack Crawford	Ellsworth Vines	1963	Chuck McKinley	Fred Stolle
1934	Fred Perry	Jack Crawford	1964	Roy Emerson	Fred Stolle
1935	Fred Perry	Gottfried von Cramm	1965	Roy Emerson	Fred Stolle
1936	Fred Perry	Gottfried von Cramm	1966	Manuel Santana	Dennis Ralston
1937	Donald Budge	Gottfried von Cramm	1967	John Newcombe	Wilhelm Bungert
1938	Donald Budge	Wilfred Austin	1968	Rod Laver	Tony Roche
1939	Bobby Riggs	Elwood Cooke	1969	Rod Laver	John Newcombe
1940-45	not held		1970	John Newcombe	Ken Rosewall
1946	Yvon Petra	Geoff E. Brown	1971	John Newcombe	Stan Smith
1947	Jack Kramer	Tom P. Brown	1972	Stan Smith	Ilie Nastase
1948	Bob Falkenburg	John Bromwich	1973	Jan Kodes	Alex Metreveli
1949	Ted Schroeder	Jaroslav Drobny	1974	Jimmy Connors	Ken Rosewall
1950	Budge Patty	Frank Sedgman	1975	Arthur Ashe	Jimmy Connors
1951	Dick Savitt	Ken McGregor	1976	Bjorn Borg	Ilie Nastase
1952	Frank Sedgman	Jaroslav Drobny	1977	Bjorn Borg	Jimmy Connors
1953	Vic Seixas	Kurt Nielsen	1978	Bjorn Borg	Jimmy Connors
1954	Jaroslav Drobny	Ken Rosewall	1979	Bjorn Borg	Roscoe Tanner
1955	Tony Trabert	Kurt Nielsen	1980	Bjorn Borg	John McEnroe
1956	Lew Hoad	Ken Rosewall	1981	John McEnroe	Bjorn Borg
1957	Lew Hoad	Ashley Cooper	1982	Jimmy Connors	John McEnroe
1958	Ashley Cooper	Neale Fraser	1983	John McEnroe	Chris Lewis
1959	Alex Olmedo	Rod Laver	1984	John McEnroe	Jimmy Connors
1960	Neale Fraser	Rod Laver	1985	Boris Becker	Kevin Curren
1961	Rod Laver	Chuck McKinley	1986	Boris Becker	Ivan Lendl
1962	Rod Laver	Martin Mulligan	1987	Pat Cash	Ivan Lendl

Women's Singles

Year	Champion	Year	Champion	Year	Champion	Year	Champion
1946	Pauline Betz	1957	Althea Gibson	1968	Billie Jean King	1979	Martina Navratilova
1947	Margaret Osborne	1958	Althea Gibson	1969	Ann Haydon-Jones	1980	Evonne Goolagong
1948	Louise Brough	1959	Maria Bueno	1970	Margaret Court	1981	Chris Evert Lloyd
1949	Louise Brough	1960	Maria Bueno	1971	Evonne Goolagong	1982	Martina Navratilova
1950	Louise Brough	1961	Angela Mortimer	1972	Billie Jean King	1983	Martina Navratilova
1951	Doris Hart	1962	Karen Hantze-Susman	1973	Billie Jean King	1984	Martina Navratilova
1952	Maureen Connolly	1963	Margaret Smith	1974	Chris Evert	1985	Martina Navratilova
1953	Maureen Connolly	1964	Maria Bueno	1975	Billie Jean King	1986	Martina Navratilova
1954	Maureen Connolly	1965	Margaret Smith	1976	Chris Evert	1987	Martina Navratilova
1955	Louise Brough	1966	Billie Jean King	1977	Virginia Wade		
1956	Shirley Fry	1967	Billie Jean King	1978	Martina Navratilova		

French Open Champions

Year	Men	Women	Year	Men	Women
1968	Ken Rosewall	Nancy Richey	1978	Bjorn Borg	Virginia Ruzici
1969	Rod Laver	Margaret Smith Court	1979	Bjorn Borg	Chris Evert Lloyd
1970	Jan Kodes	Margaret Smith Court	1980	Bjorn Borg	Chris Evert Lloyd
1971	Jan Kodes	Evonne Goolagong	1981	Bjorn Borg	Hana Mandlikova
1972	Andres Gimeno	Billie Jean King	1982	Mats Wilander	Martina Navratilova
1973	Ilie Nastase	Margaret Court	1983	Yannick Noah	Chris Evert Lloyd
1974	Bjorn Borg	Chris Evert	1984	Ivan Lendl	Martina Navratilova
1975	Bjorn Borg	Chris Evert	1985	Mats Wilander	Chris Evert Lloyd
1976	Adriano Panatta	Sue Barker	1986	Ivan Lendl	Chris Evert Lloyd
1977	Guillermo Vilas	Mima Jausovec	1987	Ivan Lendl	Steffi Graf

Harness Racing

Source: U.S. Trotting Assn.; records to Sept. 15, 1987

Trotting Records

Asterisk (*) denotes record taken in time trial. Times—seconds in fifths.

One mile records (mile track)

All-age — 1:52.1 — Mack Lobell, Springfield, Ill., Aug. 21, 1987.
Two-year-old — 1:55.3 — Mack Lobell, Lexington, Ky., Oct. 3, 1986.
Three-year-old — 1:53.2 — Prakas, Du Quoin, Ill., Aug. 31, 1985.

(Half-mile track)

All-age — 1:56.4 — Nevele Pride, Saratoga Springs, N.Y., Sept. 6, 1969.
Two-year-old — 1:58.3 — Petri Kosmos, Delaware, Oh., Sept. 15, 1987.
Three-year-old — 1:57 — Armbro Devona, Delaware Oh., Sept. 19, 1985

Pacing Records

One mile records (mile track)

All-age — *1:49.1 — Niatross, Lexington, Ky., Oct. 1, 1980.
Two-year-old — 1:52.3 — Rumpus Hanover, Lexington, Ky. Sept. 25, 1986.
Three-year-old — *1:49.1 — Niatross, Lexington, Ky., Oct. 1, 1980.

(Half-mile track)

All age — 1:51 — Falcon Seelster, Delaware, Oh., Sept. 19, 1985.
Two-year-old — 1:55.2 — Barberry Spur, Delaware, Oh., Sept. 19, 1985 & Jate Lobell, Louisville, Ky., Sept. 6, 1986.
Three-year-old — 1:51 — Falcon Seelster, Delaware, Oh., Sept. 19, 1985.

The Hambletonian (3-year-old trotters)

Year	Winner	Driver	Purse	Year	Winner	Driver	Purse
1949	Miss Tilly	Fred Egan	$69,791	1969	Lindy's Pride	Howard Beissinger	$124,910
1950	Lusty Song	Del Miller	75,209	1970	Timothy T	John Simpson Sr.	143,630
1951	Mainliner	Guy Crippen	95,263	1971	Speedy Crown	Howard Beissinger	128,770
1952	Sharp Note	Bion Shively	87,637	1972	Super Bowl	Stanley Dancer	119,090
1953	Helicopter	Harry Harvey	117,118	1973	Flirth	Ralph Baldwin	144,710
1954	Newport Dream	Del Cameron	106,830	1974	Christopher T	Bill Haughton	160,150
1955	Scott Frost	Joe O'Brien	86,863	1975	Bonefish	Stanley Dancer	232,192
1956	The Intruder	Ned Bower	98,591	1976	Steve Lobell	Bill Haughton	263,524
1957	Hickory Smoke	John Simpson Sr.	111,126	1977	Green Speed	Bill Haughton	284,131
1958	Emily's Pride	Flave Nipe	106,719	1978	Speedy Somolli	Howard Beissinger	241,280
1959	Diller Hanover	Frank Ervin	125,284	1979	Legend Hanover	George Sholty	300,000
1960	Blaze Hanover	Joe O'Brien	144,590	1980	Burgomeister	Bill Haughton	293,570
1961	Harlan Dean	James Arthur	131,573	1981	Shiaway St. Pat	Ray Remmen	838,000
1962	A.C. Os Viking	Sanders Russell	116,312	1982	Speed Bowl	Tommy Haughton	875,750
1963	Speedy Scot	Ralph Baldwin	115,549	1983	Duenna	Stanley Dancer	1,080,000
1964	Ayres	John Simpson Sr.	115,281	1984	Historic Freight	Ben Webster	1,219,000
1965	Egyptian Candor	Del Cameron	122,245	1985	Prakas	Bill O'Donnell	1,272,000
1966	Kerry Way	Frank Ervin	122,540	1986	Nuclear Kosmos	Ulf Thoresen	1,172,082
1967	Speedy Streak	Del Cameron	122,650	1987	Mack Lobell	John Campbell	1,046,300
1968	Nevele Pride	Stanley Dancer	116,190				

Little Brown Jug (3-year-old pacers)

Year	Winner	Driver	Purse	Year	Winner	Driver	Purse
1963	Overtrick	John Patterson Sr.	$68,294	1976	Keystone Ore	Stanley Dancer	$153,799
1964	Vicar Hanover	Billy Haughton	66,590	1977	Gov. Skipper	John Chapman	150,000
1965	Bret Hanover	Frank Ervin	71,447	1978	Happy Escort	Bill Popfinger	186,760
1966	Romeo Hanover	George Sholty	74,616	1979	Hot Hitter	Herve Filion	226,455
1967	Best of All	James Hackett	84,778	1980	Niatross	Clint Galbraith	207,000
1968	Rum Customer	Billy Haughton	104,226	1981	Fan Hanover(A)	Glen Garnsey	243,779
1969	Laverne Hanover	Billy Haughton	109,731	1982	Merger	John Campbell	328,900
1970	Most Happy Fella	Stanley Dancer	100,110	1983	Ralph Hanover	Ron Waples	358,800
1971	Nansemond	Herve Filion	102,944	1984	Colt Forty Six	Chris Boring	366,717
1972	Strike Out	Keith Waples	104,916	1985	Nihilator	Bill O'Donnell	350,730
1973	Melvin's Woe	Joe O'Brien	120,000	1986	Barberry Spur	Bill O'Donnell	407,680
1974	Ambro Omaha	Billy Haughton	132,630	1987	Jaguar Spur	Dick Stillings	412,330
1975	Seatrain	Ben Webster	147,813				

(A) First filly to win the Little Brown Jug.

Annual Leading Money-Winning Horses

Trotters

Year	Horse	Dollars	Year	Horse	Dollars	Year	Horse	Dollars
1962	Duke Rodney	206,113	1971	Fresh Yankee	293,960	1980	Classical Way	350,410
1963	Speedy Scot	144,403	1972	Super Bowl	437,108	1981	Shiaway St. Pat	480,095
1964	Speedy Scot	235,710	1973	Spartan Hanover	262,023	1982	Speed Bowl	672,084
1965	Dartmouth	252,348	1974	Delmonica Hanover	252,165	1983	Jole De Vie	1,007,705
1966	Noble Victory	210,696	1975	Savoir	351,385	1984	Baltic Speed	1,062,611
1967	Carlisle	231,243	1976	Steve Lobell	338,770	1985	Prakis	1,610,608
1968	Nevele Pride	427,440	1977	Green Speed	584,405	1986	Royal Prestige	1,052,114
1969	Lindy's Pride	323,997	1978	Speedy Somolli	362,404			
1970	Fresh Yankee	359,002	1979	Chiola Hanover	553,058			

Pacers

Year	Horse	Dollars	Year	Horse	Dollars	Year	Horse	Dollars
1962	Henry T. Adios	220,302	1971	Albatross	558,009	1980	Niatross	1,414,313
1963	Overtrick	208,833	1972	Albatross	459,921	1981	McKinzie Almahurst	936,418
1964	Race Time	199,292	1973	Sir Dalrae	307,354	1982	Fortune Teller	1,313,175
1965	Bret Hanover	341,784	1974	Armbro Omaha	345,146	1983	Ralph Hanover	1,711,990
1966	Bret Hanover	407,534	1975	Silk Stockings	336,312	1984	On The Road Again	1,751,695
1967	Romulus Hanover	277,636	1976	Keystone Ore	539,762	1985	Nihilator	1,864,286
1968	Rum Customer	355,618	1977	Governor Skipper	522,148	1986	Redskin	1,407,263
1969	Overcall	373,150	1978	Abercrombie	703,260			
1970	Most Happy Fella	387,239	1979	Hot Hitter	826,542			

Harness Horse of the Year

(Chosen by the U.S. Trotting Assn. and the U.S. Harness Writers Assn.)

1948	Rodney	1958	Emily's Pride	1968	Nevele Pride	1978	Abercrombie
1949	Good Time	1959	Bye Bye Byrd	1969	Nevele Pride	1979	Niatross
1950	Proximity	1960	Adios Butler	1970	Fresh Yankee	1980	Niatross
1951	Pronto Don	1961	Adios Butler	1971	Albatross	1981	Fan Hanover
1952	Good Time	1962	Su Mac Lad	1972	Albatross	1982	Cam Fella
1953	Hi Lo's Forbes	1963	Speedy Scot	1973	Sir Dalrae	1983	Cam Fella
1954	Stenographer	1964	Bret Hanover	1974	Delmonica Hanover	1984	Fancy Crown
1955	Scott Frost	1965	Bret Hanover	1975	Savior	1985	Nihilator
1956	Scott Frost	1966	Bret Hanover	1976	Keystone Ore	1986	Forrest Skipper
1957	Torpid	1967	Nevele Pride	1977	Green Speed		

(continued)

Leading Drivers

Races Won

Year	Driver		Year	Driver		Year	Driver		Year	Driver	
1963	Donald Busse	201	1970	Herve Filion	486	1976	Herve Filion	445	1982	Herve Filion	495
1964	Bob Farrington	312	1971	Herve Filion	543	1977	Herve Filion	441	1983	Eddie Davis	470
1965	Bob Farrington	310	1972	Herve Filion	605	1978	Herve Filion	423	1984	Michel Lachance	466
1966	Bob Farrington	283	1973	Herve Filion	445	1979	Ron Waples	443	1985	Michel Lachance	592
1967	Bob Farrington	277	1974	Herve Filion	637	1980	Herve Filion	474	1986	Michel Lachance	770
1968	Herve Filion	407	1975	Daryl Buse	360	1981	Eddie Davis	404			
1969	Herve Filion	394					Herve Filion	404			

Money Won

Year	Driver	Dollars	Year	Driver	Dollars	Year	Driver	Dollars
1962	Stanley Dancer	760,343	1971	Herve Filion	1,915,945	1980	John Campbell	3,732,306
1963	Bill Haughton	790,086	1972	Herve Filion	2,473,265	1981	Bill O'Donnell	4,065,608
1964	Stanley Dancer	1,051,538	1973	Herve Filion	2,233,302	1982	Bill O'Donnell	5,755,067
1965	Bill Haughton	889,943	1974	Herve Filion	3,474,315	1983	John Campbell	6,104,082
1966	Stanley Dancer	1,218,403	1975	Carmine Abbatiello	2,275,093	1984	Bill O'Donnell	9,059,184
1967	Bill Haughton	1,305,773	1976	Herve Filion	2,241,045	1985	Bill O'Donnell	10,207,372
1968	Bill Haughton	1,654,172	1977	Herve Filion	2,551,058	1986	John Campbell	9,515,055
1969	Del Insko	1,635,463	1978	Carmine Abbatiello	3,344,457			
1970	Herve Filion	1,647,837	1979	John Campbell	3,308,984			

Sports Halls of Fame

The following is a list of the location of the halls of fame for various sports:

Baseball, professional: Cooperstown, N.Y.
Baseball, Little League: Williamsport, Pa.
Basketball: Springfield, Mass.
Bowling: St. Louis, Mo.
Boxing: Canastota, N.Y.
Football, college: King's Island, Oh.
Football, professional: Canton, Oh.
Football, Canadian: Hamilton, Ont.
Golf, PGA: Palm Beach Gardens, Fla.
Greyhound racing: Abilene, Kan.
Hockey, NHL: Toronto, Ont.
Hockey, U.S.: Eveleth, Minn.
Lacrosse: Baltimore, Md.
Rodeo Cowboy: Oklahoma City, Okla.
Skating, figure: Colorado Springs, Col.
Skating, speed: Newburgh, N.Y.
Skiing: Ishpeming, Mich.
Soccer: Oneonta, N.Y.
Softball: Oklahoma City, Okla.
Swimming: Ft. Lauderdale, Fla.
Tennis: Newport, R.I.
Track & Field, national: Charleston, W. Va.
Track & Field, U.S.: Angola, Ind.
Trotting: Goshen, N.Y.
Volleyball: Holyoke, Mass.
Wrestling: Stillwater, Okla.

Sports on Television

Source: Sports 1986, Nielsen Media Research

	Household rating %	% Viewing Audience			
		Men	Women	Teens	Children
Football					
NFL Super Bowl	45.8	48	37	8	7
ABC-NFL (Monday eves.)	18.5	60	31	6	9
CBS-NFL	15.2	56	33	6	5
NBC-NFL	12.3	54	32	7	7
College bowl games	12.2	54	35	5	6
College football reg. season	8.2	55	34	5	6
Baseball					
World Series	28.6	52	40	5	3
All-star game	20.3	49	36	12	3
Regular season	6.3	49	35	6	10
Horse racing					
Average all	6.7	47	47	3	3
Basketball					
NBA average	6.8	58	26	8	8
NCAA average	6.0	58	28	7	7
Bowling					
Pro tour	5.1	45	43	6	6
Golf	4.1	52	40	4	4
Tennis					
Wimbledon	3.9	39	45	7	9
Tournament average	3.2	41	44	5	10
Multi-sports					
ABC Wide World of Sports	7.4	48	37	6	9
CBS Sports-Sunday	5.1	50	37	5	8
Sportsworld-Sunday	4.4	48	36	7	9

NCAA Wrestling Champions

Year	Champion	Year	Champion	Year	Champion	Year	Champion	Year	Champion
1963	Oklahoma	1968	Oklahoma State	1973	Iowa State	1978	Iowa	1983	Iowa
1964	Oklahoma State	1969	Iowa State	1974	Oklahoma	1979	Iowa	1984	Iowa
1965	Iowa State	1970	Iowa State	1975	Iowa	1980	Iowa	1985	Iowa
1966	Oklahoma State	1971	Oklahoma State	1976	Iowa	1981	Iowa	1986	Iowa
1967	Michigan State	1972	Iowa State	1977	Iowa State	1982	Iowa	1987	Iowa State

SKIING

U.S. National Alpine Championships in 1987

Men's Downhill—Doug Lewis.
Men's Super G—Tiger Shaw.
Men's Slalom—Bob Ormsby.
Men's Giant Slalom—Felix McGrath.
Men's Combined—Tiger Shaw.

Women's Downhill—Pam Fletcher.
Women's Super G—Pam Fletcher.
Women's Slalom—Tamara McKinney.
Women's Giant Slalom—Debbie Armstrong.
Women's Combined—Pam Fletcher.

World Cup Alpine Champions

Men

1967	Jean Claude Killy, France	1974	Piero Gros, Italy	1981	Phil Mahre, U.S.
1968	Jean Claude Killy, France	1975	Gustavo Thoeni, Italy	1982	Phil Mahre, U.S.
1969	Karl Schranz, Austria	1976	Ingemar Stenmark, Sweden	1983	Phil Mahre, U.S.
1970	Karl Schranz, Austria	1977	Ingemar Stenmark, Sweden	1985	Marc Girardelli, Luxembourg
1971	Gustavo Thoeni, Italy	1978	Ingemar Stenmark, Sweden	1986	Marc Girardelli, Luxembourg
1972	Gustavo Thoeni, Italy	1979	Peter Luescher, Switzerland	1987	Pirmin Zurbriggen, Switzerland
1973	Gustavo Thoeni, Italy	1980	Andreas Wenzel, Liechtenstein		

Women

1967	Nancy Greene, Canada	1974	Annemarie Proell, Austria	1981	Marie-Theres Nadig, Switzerland
1968	Nancy Greene, Canada	1975	Annemarie Proell, Austria	1982	Erika Hess, Switzerland
1969	Gertrud Gabl, Austria	1976	Rose Mittermaier, W. Germany	1983	Tamara McKinney, U.S.
1970	Michele Jacot, France	1977	Lise-Marie Morerod, Switzerland	1984	Erika Hess, Switzerland
1971	Annemarie Proell, Austria	1978	Hanni Wenzel, Liechtenstein	1985	Michela Figini, Switzerland
1972	Annemarie Proell, Austria	1979	Annemarie Proell Moser, Austria	1986	Maria Walliser, Switzerland
1973	Annemarie Proell, Austria	1980	Hanni Wenzel, Liechtenstein	1987	Maria Walliser, Switzerland

Chess

Chess dates back to antiquity. Its exact origin is unknown. The strongest players of their time, and therefore regarded by later generations as world champions, were Francois Philidor, France; Alexandre Deschappelles, France; Louis de la Bourdonnais, France; Howard Staunton, England; Adolph Anderssen, Germany and Paul Morphy, United States. In 1866 Wilhelm Steinitz of Austria defeated Adolph Anderssen and claimed the title of world champion. The official world champions since the title was first used follow:

1866-1894 Wilhelm Steinitz, Austria
1894-1921 Dr. Emanuel Lasker, Germany
1921-1927 Jose R. Capablanca, Cuba
1927-1935 Dr. Alexander A. Alekhine, France
1935-1937 Dr. Max Euwe, Netherlands
1937-1946 Dr. Alexander A. Alekhine, France
1948-1957 Mikhail Botvinnik, USSR
1957-1958 Vassily Smyslov, USSR
1958-1959 Mikhail Botvinnik, USSR
1960-1961 Mikhail Tal, USSR
1961-1963 Mikhail Botvinnik, USSR
1963-1969 Tigran Petrosian, USSR
1969-1972 Boris Spassky, USSR
1972-1975 Bobby Fischer, U.S. (a)
1975-1985 Anatoly Karpov, USSR
1985 Gary Kasparov, USSR

(a) Defaulted championship after refusal to accept International Chess Federation rules for a championship match, April 1975.

United States Champions

Unofficial champions	
1857-1871	Paul Morphy
1871-1876	George Mackenzie
1876-1880	James Mason
1880-1889	George Mackenzie
1889-1890	S. Lipschutz
1890	Jackson Showalter
1890-1891	Max Judd
Official champions	
1891-1892	Jackson Showalter
1892-1894	S. Lipschutz
1894	Jackson Showalter
1894-1895	Albert Hodges
1895-1897	Jackson Showalter
1897-1906	Harry Pillsbury
1906-1909	vacant
1909-1936	Frank Marshall
1936-1944	Samuel Reshevsky
1944-1946	Arnold Denker
1946-1948	Samuel Reshevsky
1948-1951	Herman Steiner
1951-1954	Larry Evans
1954-1957	Arthur Bisguier
1957-1961	Bobby Fischer
1961-1962	Larry Evans
1962-1968	Bobby Fischer
1968-1969	Larry Evans
1969-1972	Samuel Reshevsky
1972-1973	Robert Byrne
1973-1974	Lubomir Kavalek, John Grefe
1974-1977	Walter Browne
1978-1980	Lubomir Kavalek
1980-1981	(tie) Larry Evans, Larry Christiansen, Walter Browne
1981-1983	(tie) Walter Browne, Yasser Seirawan
1983	(tie) Walter Browne Larry Christiansen Roman Dzindzichashvili
1984-1985	Lev Alburt
1986	Yasser Seirawan

The World Cup

The World Cup, emblematic of International soccer supremacy, was won by Argentina on June 29, 1986, with a 3-2 victory over W. Germany. It was the 2d time Argentina has won the event. Winners and sites of previous World Cup play follow:

Year	Winner	Final opponent	Site
1930	Uruguay	Argentina	Uruguay
1934	Italy	Czechoslovakia	Italy
1938	Italy	Hungary	France
1950	Uruguay	Brazil	Brazil
1954	W. Germany	Hungary	Switzerland
1958	Brazil	Sweden	Sweden
1962	Brazil	Czechoslovakia	Chile
1966	England	W. Germany	England
1970	Brazil	Italy	Mexico City
1974	W. Germany	Netherlands	W. Germany
1978	Argentina	Netherlands	Argentina
1982	Italy	W. Germany	Spain
1986	Argentina	W. Germany	Mexico City

1986 Final Round

Quarterfinals
France 5, Brazil 4
W. Germany 4, Mexico 1
Argentina 2, England 1
Belgium 6, Spain 5

Semifinals
W. Germany 2, France 0
Argentina 2, Belgium 0

Championship
Argentina 3, W. Germany 2

TRACK AND FIELD

World Track and Field Records

As of Sept. 1987

*Indicates pending record; a number of new records await confirmation. The International Amateur Atheletic Federation, the world body of track and field, recognizes only records in metric distances except for the mile.

Men's Records

Running

Event	Record	Holder	Country	Date	Where made
100 meters	*9.83 s.	Ben Johnson	Canada	Aug. 30, 1987	Rome
200 meters	19.72 s.	Pietro Mennea	Italy	Sept. 17, 1979	Mexico City
400 meters	43.86 s.	Lee Evans	U.S.	Oct. 18, 1968	Mexico City
800 meters	1 m., 41.73 s.	Sebastian Coe	Gr. Britain	June 10, 1981	Florence, Italy
1,000 meters	2 m., 12.18 s.	Sebastian Coe	Gr. Britain	July 11, 1981	Oslo
1,500 meters	3 m., 29.46 s.	Said Aouita	Morocco	Aug. 23, 1985	W. Berlin
1 mile	3 m., 46.32 s.	Steve Cram	Gr. Britain	July 27, 1985	Oslo
2,000 meters	*4 m., 50.81 s.	Said Aouita	Morocco	July 1987	Paris
3,000 meters	7 m., 32.1 s.	Henry Rono	Kenya	June 27, 1978	Oslo
5,000 meters	*12 m., 58.39 s.	Said Aouita	Morocco	July 23, 1987	Rome
10,000 meters	27 m., 13.81 s.	Fernando Mamede	Portugal	July 2, 1984	Stockholm
20,000 meters	57 m., 24.2 s.	Jos Hermens	Netherlands	May 1, 1976	Netherlands
25,000 meters	1 hr., 13 m., 55.8 s.	Toshihiko Seko	Japan	Mar. 22, 1981	New Zealand
30,000 meters	1 hr., 29 m., 18.8 s.	Toshihiko Seko	Japan	Mar. 22, 1981	New Zealand
3,000 meter stpl	8 m., 05.4 s.	Henry Rono	Kenya	May 13, 1978	Seattle
Marathon	2 hr., 7 m., 12 s.	Carlos Lopes	Portugal	Apr. 20, 1985	Rotterdam

Hurdles

Event	Record	Holder	Country	Date	Where made
110 meters	12.93 s.	Renaldo Nehemiah	U.S.	Aug. 19, 1981	Zurich
400 meters	47.02 s.	Edwin Moses	U.S.	Aug. 31, 1983	Koblenz, W. Ger.

Relay Races

Event	Record	Holder	Country	Date	Where made
400 mtrs.	37.83 s.	(Graddy, Brown, Smith, Lewis)	U.S.	Aug. 11, 1984	Los Angeles
800 mtrs. (4×200)	1 m., 20.26 s.	USC	U.S.	May 27, 1978	Tempe, Ariz.
1,600 mtrs. (4×400)	2 m., 56.1 s.	(Matthews, Freeman, James, Evans)	U.S.	Oct. 20, 1968	Mexico City
3,200 mtrs. (4×800)	7 m., 03.89 s.	National team	Gr. Britain	Aug. 30, 1982	London

Field Events

Event	Record	Holder	Country	Date	Where made
High jump	*7 ft., 11½ in.	Patrik Sjoberg	Sweden	June 30, 1987	Stockholm
Long jump	29 ft., 2½ in.	Bob Beamon	U.S.	Oct. 18, 1968	Mexico City
Triple jump	58 ft., 11½ in.	Willie Banks	U.S.	June 16, 1985	Indianapolis
Pole vault	*19 ft., 9¼ in.	Sergei Bubka	USSR	July, 1987	Prague
16 lb. shot put	*75 ft., 2 in.	Alessandro Andrei	Italy	Aug. 12, 1987	Viareggio, Italy
Discus throw	243 ft.	Juergen Schult	E. Germany	June 6, 1986	E. Germany
Javelin throw	343 ft., 10 in.	Uwe Hohn	E. Germany	July 20, 1984	E. Berlin
16 lb. hammer throw	284 ft., 7 in.	Yuri Sedykh	USSR	Aug. 30, 1986	Stuttgart
Decathlon	8,646 pts.	Daley Thompson	Gr. Britain	Aug. 8-9, 1984	Los Angeles

Walking

Event	Record	Holder	Country	Date	Where made
30 km.	2 h., 7 min., 59.8 s.	Jose Martin	Spain	Aug. 4, 1979	Barcelona
50 km.	3 hr., 41 m., 39 s.	Raul Gonzales	Mexico	May 25, 1978	Norway

Women's Records

Running

Event	Record	Holder	Country	Date	Where made
100 meters	10.76 s.	Evelyn Ashford	U.S.	Aug. 22, 1984	Zurich
			E. Germany	June 10, 1979	E. Berlin
200 meters	21.71 s.	Marita Koch	E. Germany	July 21, 1984	Potsdam
		Heike Drechsler	E. Germany	Aug. 29, 1986	Stuttgart
400 meters	47.60 s.	Marita Koch	E. Germany	Oct. 6, 1985	Canberra
800 meters	1 m., 53.28 s.	Jarmila Kratochvilova	Czech.	July 26, 1983	Munich
1,500 meters	3 m., 52.47 s.	Tatyana Kazankina	USSR	Aug. 13, 1980	Zurich
1 mile	4 m., 16.71 s.	Mary Decker Slaney	U.S.	Aug. 21, 1985	Zurich
2,000 meters	5 m., 28.69 s.	Maricica Puica	Romania	July 11, 1986	London
3,000 meters	8 m., 22.62 s.	Tatyana Kazankina	USSR	Aug. 26, 1984	Leningrad
5,000 meters	14 m., 37.33 s.	Ingrid Kristiansen	Norway	Aug. 5, 1986	Stockholm
10,000 meters	30 m., 13.74 s.	Ingrid Kristiansen	Norway	July 11, 1986	Oslo
Marathon	2 h., 21 m., 06 s.	Ingrid Kristiansen	Norway	Apr. 21, 1985	London

Hurdles

Event	Record	Holder	Country	Date	Where made
100 meters	*12.25 s.	Ginka Zagorcheva	Bulgaria	Aug., 1987	Greece
400 meters	*52.94 s.	Marina Stepanova	USSR	Sept. 17, 1986	USSR

Field Events

Event	Record	Holder	Country	Date	Where made
High jump	*6 ft., 10¼ in.	Stefka Kostadinova	Bulgaria	Aug., 1987	Rome
Shot put	*74 ft., 3 in.	Natalya Lisouskaya	USSR	June, 1987	Moscow
Long jump	24 ft., 5½ in.	Heike Drechsler	E. Germany	June 21, 1986	USSR

Event	Record	Holder	Country	Date	Where made
Discus throw	**244 ft., 7 in.**	Zdena Silvaha	Czechoslovakia	Aug. 26, 1984	Prague
Javelin	***258 ft., 10 in.**	Petra Felke	E. Germany	July 23, 1987	Leipzig
Heptathlon	**7,161 pts.**	Jackie Joyner-Kersee	U.S.	Aug. 1-2, 1986	Houston

Relay Races

Event	Record	Holder	Country	Date	Where made
400 mtrs. (4×100)	**41.37 s.**	National team	E. Germany	Oct. 6, 1985	Canberra
800 mtrs. (4×200)	**1 m., 28.15 s.**	National team	E. Germany	Aug. 9, 1980	E. Germany
1,600 mtrs. (4×400)	**3 m., 15.92 s.**	National team	E. Germany	June 3, 1984	E. Germany
3,200 mtrs. (4×800)	**7 m., 50.17 s.**	National team	USSR	Aug. 5, 1984	Moscow

World Track and Field Indoor Records

As of Sept., 1987

The International Amateur Athletic Federation began recognizing world indoor track & field records as official on January 1, 1987. Prior to that, there were only unofficial world indoor bests. World indoor bests set prior to January 1, 1987 are subject to approval as world records providing they meet the prescribed IAAF world records criteria, including drug testing. To be accepted as a world indoor record, a performance must meet the same criteria as a world record outdoors except that a track performance can't be set on an indoor track larger than 200 meters. *record pending.

Men

Event	Record	Holder	Country	Date	Where made
50 meters	***5.55**	Ben Johnson	Canada	Jan. 31, 1987	Ottawa
60 meters	***6.41**	Ben Johnson	Canada	Mar. 7, 1987	Indianapolis
200 meters	***20.36**	Bruno Marie-Rose	France	Feb. 22, 1987	Lievin
400 meters	**45.41**	Thomas Schoenlebe	E. Germany	Feb. 9, 1986	Vienna
800 meters	**1:44.91**	Sebastian Coe	Gr. Britain	Mar. 12, 1983	Cosford
1,000 meters	***2:18.00**	Igor Lotarev	USSR	Feb. 14, 1987	Moscow
1,500 meters	**3:35.6**	Eamonn Coghlan	Ireland	Feb. 20, 1981	San Diego
1 Mile	**3:49.78**	Eamonn Coghlan	Ireland	Feb. 27, 1983	E. Rutherford
3,000 meters	**7:39.2**	Emiel Puttemans	Belguim	Feb. 18, 1973	New York
5,000 meters	**13:20.4**	Suleiman Nyambui	Tanzania	Feb. 6, 1981	New York
50-meter hurdles	**6.25**	Mark McKoy	Canada	Mar. 5, 1986	Kobe
60-meter hurdles	***7.46**	Greg Foster	U.S.	Mar. 6, 1987	Indianapolis
High Jump	***7 ft. 10¾ in.**	Patrik Sjoberg	Sweden	Feb. 1 1987	Piraeus
Pole Vault	***19 ft. 7 in.**	Sergey Bubka	USSR	Mar. 17, 1987	Turin
Long Jump	**28 ft. 10¼ in.**	Carl Lewis	U.S.	Feb. 27, 1984	New York
Triple Jump	***58 ft. 3¼ in.**	Mike Conley	U.S.	Feb. 27, 1987	New York
Shot Put	***73 ft. ½ in.**	Werner Gunthor	Switzerland	Feb. 8, 1987	Magglingen

Women

Event	Record	Holder	Country	Date	Where made
50 meters	***6.06**	Angella Issajenko	Canada	Jan. 31, 1987	Ottawa
60 meters	**7.00**	Nellie Cooman-Fiere	Holland	Feb. 23, 1986	Madrid
200 meters	***22.27**	Heike Drechsler	E. Germany	Mar. 7, 1987	Indianapolis
400 meters	**49.59**	Jarmila Kratochvilova	Czechoslovakia	Mar. 7, 1982	Milan
800 meters	***1:58.42**	Sigrun Wodars	E. Germany	Jan. 10. 1987	Vienna
1,000 meters	**2:34.8**	Brigitte Kraus	W. Germany	Feb. 19, 1978	Dortmund
1,500 meters	**4:00.8**	Mary Decker-Slaney	U.S.	Feb. 8, 1980	New York
1 Mile	**4:20.5**	Mary Decker-Slaney	U.S.	Feb. 19, 1982	San Diego
3,000 meters	**8:39.79**	Zola Budd	Gr. Britain	Feb. 8, 1986	Cosford
5,000 meters	**15:34.5**	Margaret Groos-Thomas	U.S.	Feb. 20, 1981	Blacksburg
50-meter hurdles	***6.71**	Cornelia Oschkenat	E. Germany	Feb. 24, 1987	Berlin
60-meter hurdles	***7.74**	Yordanka Dankova	Bulgaria	Feb. 15, 1987	Sofia
High Jump	***6 ft. 8¾ in.**	Stefka Kostadinova	Bulgaria	Mar. 8, 1987	Indianapolis
Long Jump	***24 ft. ¼ in.**	Heike Dreschler	E. Germany	Feb. 27, 1987	New York
Shot Put	**73 ft. 10 in.**	Helena Fibingerova	Czechoslovakia	Feb. 19, 1977	Jablonec

Evolution of the World Record for the One-Mile Run

The table below shows how the world record for the one-mile has been lowered in the past 120 years.

Year	Individual, country	Time
1868	William Chinnery, Britain	**4:29**
1868	W. C. Gibbs, Britain	**4:28.8**
1874	Walter Slade, Britain	**4:26**
1875	Walter Slade, Britain	**4:24.5**
1880	Walter George, Britain	**4:23.2**
1882	Walter George, Britain	**4:21.4**
1882	Walter George, Britain	**4:19.4**
1884	Walter George, Britain	**4:18.4**
1894	Fred Bacon, Scotland	**4:18.2**
1895	Fred Bacon, Scotland	**4:17**
1895	Thomas Conneff, U.S.	**4:15.6**
1911	John Paul Jones, U.S.	**4:15.4**
1913	John Paul Jones, U.S.	**4:14.6**
1915	Norman Taber, U.S.	**4:12.6**
1923	Paavo Nurmi, Finland	**4:10.4**
1931	Jules Ladoumegue, France	**4:09.2**
1933	Jack Lovelock, New Zealand	**4:07.6**
1934	Glenn Cunningham, U.S.	**4:06.8**
1937	Sydney Wooderson, Britain	**4:06.4**
1942	Gunder Haegg, Sweden	**4:06.2**
1942	Arne Andersson, Sweden	**4:06.2**
1942	Gunder Haegg, Sweden	**4:04.6**
1943	Arne Andersson, Sweden	**4:02.6**
1944	Arne Andersson, Sweden	**4:01.6**
1945	Gunder Haegg, Sweden	**4:01.4**
1954	Roger Bannister, Britain	**3:59.4**
1954	John Landy, Australia	**3:58**
1957	Derek Ibbotson, Britain	**3:57.2**
1958	Herb Elliott, Australia	**3:54.5**
1962	Peter Snell, New Zealand	**3:54.4**
1964	Peter Snell, New Zealand	**3:54.1**
1965	Michel Jazy, France	**3:53.6**
1966	Jim Ryun, U.S.	**3:51.3**
1967	Jim Ryun, U.S.	**3:51.1**
1975	Filbert Bayi, Tanzania	**3:51**
1975	John Walker, New Zealand	**3:49.4**
1979	Sebastian Coe, Britain	**3:49**
1980	Steve Ovett, Britain	**3:48.8**
1981	Sebastian Coe, Britain	**3:48.53**
1981	Steve Ovett, Britain	**3:48.40**
1981	Sebastian Coe, Britain	**3:47.33**
1985	Steve Cram, Britain	**3:46.32**

Track and Field Events in 1987

80th Annual Millrose Games

New York, N.Y., Feb. 13, 1987

Men

60 Yds.—Lee McRae, Univ. of Pittsburgh. **Time—0:06.12.**
60-Yd. High Hurdles—Greg Foster, World Class Athletics. **Time—0:06.98.**
400 Meters—Antonio McKay, unattached. **Time—0:47.39.**
500 Yds.—Michael Franks, Athletics West. **Time—1:01.85.**
600 Yds.—Ian Morris, Puma TC. **Time—1:08.47.**
800 Meters—Stanley Redwine, Athletics West. **Time—1:51.08.**
1,000 Meters—Sammy Koskei, Kenya. **Time—2:20.08.**
One Mile—Eamonn Coghlan, Ireland. **Time—3:55.91.**
3,000 Meters—Jose Luis Gonzalez, Spain. **Time—7:54.23.**
Pole Vault—Earl Bell, Pacific Coast Club. **18 ft. 4¾ in.**
High Jump—Doug Nordquist, Asics TC. **7 ft. 4¼ in.**

Women

60 Yds.—Gwen Torrance, Univ. of Georgia. **Time—0:06.63.**
60-Yd. High Hurdles—Lavonna Martin, Univ. of Tennessee. **Time—0:07.50.**
400 Meters—Ilrey Oliver, Univ. of Tennessee. **Time—0:54.10.**
800 Meters—Joetta Clark, Athletics West. **Time—2:04.39.**
One Mile—Lynn Williams, Canada. **Time—4:36.71.**
High Jump—Katrena Johnson, Univ. of Arizona. **6 ft. 2¼ in.**

USA/Mobil Indoor Championships

New York, N.Y., Feb. 27, 1987

Men

55 Meters—Lee McRae, Univ. of Pittsburgh. **Time—0:06.14.**
55-Meter Hurdles—Greg Foster, World Class AC. **Time—0:06.99.**
400 Meters—Antonio McKay, unattached. **Time—0:47.00.**
500 Meters—Ian Morris, Karamu Flyers. **Time—1:01.55.**
800 Meters—Stanley Redwine, Athletics West. **Time—1:48.13.**
One Mile—Eamonn Coghlan, New York AC. **Time—3:59.25.**
3,000 Meters—Doug Padilla, Athletics West. **Time—7:51.03.**
High Jump—Igor Paklin, USSR. **7 ft. 7¾ in.**
Long Jump—Brian Cooper, McNeese St. **26 ft. 11¾ in.**
Pole Vault—Earl Bell, Pacific Coast Club. **18 ft. 9¼ in.**
Shot Put—Ulf Timmermann, E. Germany. **70 ft. 11¾ in.**
Triple Jump—Mike Conley, Tyson International. **58 ft. 3¼ in.**

Women

55 Meters—Anelia Nuneva, Bulgaria. **Time—0:06.64.**
55-Meter Hurdles—Cornelia Oschkenat, E. Germany. **Time—0-07.37.**
200 Meters—Grace Jackson, Atoms TC. **Time—0:23.51.**
400 Meters—Diane Dixon, Atoms TC. **Time—0:52.20.**
800 Meters—Christine Wachtel, E. Germany. **Time—2:03.51.**
One Mile—Doine Melinte, Romania. **Time—4:30.29.**
3,000 Meters—Maricica Pulca, Romania. **Time—8:43.49.**
High Jump—Tamara Bykova, USSR. **6 ft. 3½ in.**
Long Jump—Heike Drechsler, E. Germany. **24 ft.¼ in.**
Shot Put—Ilona Briesenick, E. Germany. **66 ft. 4½ in.**

NCAA Indoor Championships

Oklahoma City, Okla., Mar. 14, 1987

Men

55 Meters—Lee McRae, Univ. of Pittsburgh. **Time—0:06.13.**
500 Meters—Roddie Haley, Univ. of Arkansas. **Time—0:59.90.**
1,000 Meters—Robin Van Helden, LSU. **Time—2:21.64.**
One Mile—Michael Stahr, Georgetown. **Time—4:02.33.**
3,000 Meters—Joe Falcon, Univ. of Arkansas. **Time—7:56.79.**
55-Meter Hurdles—Keith Talley, Univ. of Arkansas. **Time—0:07.13.**
High Jump—James Lott, Univ. of Texas. **7 ft. 6 in.**
Triple Jump—Frank Rutherford, Univ. of Houston. **56 ft. 1 in.**
Shot Put—Lars Nilsen, SMU. **66 ft. 5 in.**
Team champion—Univ. of Arkansas.

Women

55 Meters—Gwen Torrence, Univ. of Georgia. **Time—0:06.56.**
500 Meters—Linetta Wilson, Univ. of Nebraska. **Time—1:08.89.**
1,000 Meters—Trena Hull, UNLV. **Time—2:41.08.**
One Mile—Suzy Favor, Univ. of Wisconsin. **Time—4:41.68.**
3,000 Meters—Vicki Huber, Villanova. **Time—9:11.16.**
55-Meter High Hurdles—LaVonna Martin, Univ. of Tennesee. **Time—0:07.57.**
Triple Jump—Yvette Bates, USC. **45 ft. 3 in.**
Team champion—LSU.

USA/Mobil Outdoor Championships

San Jose, Cal., June 24-27, 1987

Men

100 Meters—Mark Witherspoon, Santa Monica TC. **Time—0:10.04.**
200 Meters—Carl Lewis, Santa Monica TC. **Time—0:20.12.**
400 Meters—Harry Reynolds, Ohio St. **Time—0:44.46.**
800 Meters—Johnny Gray, Santa Monica TC. **Time—1:45.14.**
1,500 Meters—Jim Spivey, Athletics West. **Time—3:43.66.**
5,000 Meters—Sidney Maree, Puma TC. **Time—13:51.45.**
3,000-Meter Steeplechase—Henry Marsh, Athletics West. **Time—8:20.26.**
110-Meter Hurdles—Greg Foster, World Class AC. **Time—0:13.29.**
400-Meter Hurdles—Edwin Moses, Team Adidas. **Time—0:47.99.**
20-Km. Walk—Tim Lewis, **Time—1:24.12**
High Jump—Jerome Carter. **7 ft. 7 in.**
Pole Vault—Joe Dial, Athletics West. **19 ft. ¼ in.**
Long Jump—Carl Lewis. **28 ft. 4½ in.**
Triple Jump—Mike Conley. **58 ft. 7½ in.**
Discus—John Powell, Mazda. **217 ft. 3 in.**
Hammer —Judd Logan. **259 ft. 4 in.**
Javelin—Duncan Atwood. **271 ft. 5 in.**
Shot Put—John Brenner, Mazda. **69 ft. 9 in.**

Women

100 Meters—Diane Williams, Puma TC. **Time—0:10.90.**
200 Meters—Pam Marshall, Mazda. **Time—0:21.06.**
400 Meters—Lillie Leatherwood-King, Reebok. **Time—0:49.95.**
800 Meters—Essie Washington, Santa Monica TC. **Time—1:59.07.**
1,500 Meters—Regina Jacobs, L.A. TC. **Time—4:03.70.**
3,000 Meters—Mary Knisely, New Balance TC. **Time—8:57.60.**
10,000-Meter Walk—Maryanne Torrellas, Reebok. **Time—47:23.08**
100-Meter Hurdles—LaVonna Martin, Coast Athletics. **Time—0:12.80.**
400-Meter Hurdles—Judy Brown-King, Athletics West. **Time—0:54.45.**
Long Jump—Jackie Joyner-Kersee, World Class AC. **23 ft. 4½ in.**
Shot Put—Ramona Pagel, Mazda TC. **62 ft. 3 in.**
Javelin—Karin Smith, Coast Athletics. **203 ft. 8 in.**
Discus—Connie Price, Coast Athletics. **212 ft. 5 in.**

NCAA Outdoor Championships

Baton Rouge, La., June 3-6, 1987

Men

100 Meters—Raymond Stewart, Texas Christian. **Time—0:10.14.**
200 Meters—Floyd Heard, Texas A&M. **Time—0:20.03**
400 Meters—Harry Reynolds, Ohio. **Time—0:44.12.**
1,500 Meters—Abdi Bile, George Mason. **Time—3:35.79.**
5,000 Meters—Dean Crowe, Boston Univ. **Time—13:43.40.**
110-Meter Hurdles—Eric Reid, LSU. **Time—0:13.51.**
Javelin—Dag Wennlund, Texas-Austin. **252 ft. 10 in.**
Shot Put—Garry Frank, Mississippi St. **65 ft. 3 in.**
Triple Jump—Frank Rutherford, Houston. **56 ft. 1 in.**
Discus—Clifford Felkins, Abiline Christian. **200 ft. 1 in.**
High Jump—Tom Smith, Illinois St. **7 ft. 5 in.**
Men's Champion—UCLA

Women

100 Meters—Gwen Torence, Georgia. **Time—0:11.25.**
200 Meters—Gwen Torence. **Time—0:22.37.**
400 Meters—Lillian Leatherwood, Alabama. **Time—0:50.90.**
800 Meters—Julie Jenkins, BYU. **Time—2:02.52.**
1,500 Meters—Suzanne Favor, Wisconsin. **Time—4:09.85.**
3,000 Meters—Vicki Huber, Villanova. **Time—8:54.41.**
5,000 Meters—Annie Schweitzer, Texas. **Time—15:46.00.**
100-Meter Hurdles—Lavona Martin, Tennessee. **Time—0:13.05.**
High Jump—Hazel Thomas, Abilene Christian. **6 ft. 2 in.**
Triple Jump—Sheila Hudson, California. **45 ft. 2½ in.**
Discus—Laura Lavine, Washington St. **184 ft. 2 in.**
Shot Put—Regina Cavanaugh, Rice. **56 ft. 10¾ in.**
Long Jump—Sheila Echols, LSU. **22 ft. 9¼ in.**
Women's Champion—LSU.

World Championships

Rome, Italy, Aug. 24-Sept. 6, 1987

Men

100 Meters—Ben Johnson, Canada. **Time—0:09.83.**
400 Meters—Thomas Schoenlebe, E. Germany. **Time—0:44.33.**
800 Meters—Billy Konchellan, Kenya. **Time—1:43.06.**
1,500 Meters—Abdi Bile, Somalia. **Time—3:36.80.**
5,000 Meters—Said Aouita, Morocco. **Time—13:26.44.**
3,000-Meter Steeplechase—Francesco Panetta, Italy. **Time—8:08.57.**
10,000 Meters—Paul Kipkoech, Kenya. **Time—27:38.63.**
Marathon—Douglas Wakihura, Kenya. **Time—2.11:48.**
110-Meter Hurdles—Greg Foster, U.S. **Time—0:13.21.**
400-Meter Hurdles—Edwin Moses, U.S. **Time—0:47.46.**
20-Km. Walk Maurizio Damilano, Italy. **Time—1:20.45.**
High Jump—Patrik Sjoberg, Sweden. **7ft. 9¾ in.**
Pole Vault—Sergei Bubka, USSR. **19 ft. 2¼ in.**
Long Jump—Carl Lewis, U.S. **28 ft. 5½ in.**
Triple Jump—Christo Markov, Bulgaria. **58 ft. 8½ in.**
Discus—Jurgen Schult, E. Germany. **225 ft. 6 in.**
Hammer—Sergei Litvinov, USSR. **276 ft. 6 in.**
Javelin—Sebbo Raty, Finland. **244 ft. 1 in.**
Decathlon—Torsten Voss, E. Germany. **8,680 pts.**

Women

100 Meters—Silke Gladisch, E. Germany. **Time—0:10.90.**
200 Meters—Silke Gladisch. **Time—0:21.74.**
400 Meters—Olga Bryzgina, USSR. **Time—0:49.38.**
800 Meters—Sigrun Wodars, E. Germany. **Time—1:55.26.**
1,500 Meters—Tatiana Samolenko, USSR. **Time—3:58.56.**
3,000 Meters—Tatiana Samolenko. **Time—8:38.73.**
10,000 Meters—Ingrid Kristiansen, Norway. **Time—31:05.85.**
100-Meter Hurdles—Gilka Zagorcheva, Bulgaria. **Time—0:12.34.**
400-Meter Hurdles—Sabine Busch, E. Germany. **Time—0:53.62.**
Marathon—Rosa Mota, Portugal. **Time—2.25:17.**
Long Jump—Jackie Joyner-Kersee, U.S. **24 ft. 1¼ in.**
Shot Put—Natalia Lisovskaia, USSR. **69 ft. 8¼ in.**
Javelin—Fatima Whitbread, Gr. Britain. **251 ft. 5 in.**
Discus—Martina Hellmann, E. Germany. **235 ft.**
High Jump—Stefka Kostadinova, Bulgaria. **6 ft. 10¾ in.**
Heptathlon—Jackie Joyner-Kersee. **7,128 pts.**

National Track & Field Hall of Fame

Indianapolis, Ind.

Jesse Abramson
Dave Albritton
Horace Ashenfelter
Andy Bakjian
Weems Baskin
James Bausch
Bob Beamon
Percy Beard
Dee Boeckman
Tom Botts
Ralph Boston
Bill Bowerman
Avery Brundage
Jim Bush
Lee Calhoun
Alice Coachman (Davis)
Harold Connolly
Tom Courtney
Dean Cromwell
Glenn Cunningham
William Curtis
Willie Davenport
Glenn Davis
Harold Davis
Mildred (Babe) Didrikson
Harrison Dillard
Ken Doherty
Bill Easton
James (Jumbo) Elliott
Lee Evans
Barney Ewell
Ray Ewry
Mae Faggs (Starr)
Dan Ferris
John Flanagan
Dick Fosbury
Bob Giegengack
Fortune Gordien
John Griffith
Archie Hahn
Brutus Hamilton
Glenn Hardin
Ted Haydon
Billy Hayes
Bob Hayes
Ward Haylett
Bud Held
Ralph Higgins
Harry Hillman
Jim Hines
Bud Houser
DeHart Hubbard
Edward Hurt
Wilbur Hutsell
Bruce Jenner
Rafer Johnson
Hayes Jones
Thomas Jones
Payton Jordan
John Kelley
Abel Kiviat
Alvin Kraenzlein
Ron Laird
Clyde Littlefield
Bob Mathias
Randy Matson
Mildred McDaniel
Edith McGuire (DuVall)
Ted Meredith
Ralph Metcalfe
Billy Mills
Madeline Manning-Mims
Bobby Morrow
Michael Murphy
Lon Myers
Parry O'Brien
Al Oerter
Harold Osborn
Jesse Owens
Charlie Paddock
Mel Patton
Eulace Peacock
Steve Prefontaine
Joie Ray
Greg Rice
Bob Richards
Betty Robinson (Schwartz)
Ralph Rose
Wilma Rudolph
Jim Ryun
Jackson Scholz
Bob Seagren
Mel Sheppard
Dave Sime
Robert Simpson
Tommie Smith
Larry Snyder
Andy Stanfield
Les Steers
Helen Stephens
James Sullivan
Dink Templeton
John Thomas
Earl Thomson
Jim Thorpe
Eddie Tolan
Bill Toomey
Forrest Towns
Wyomia Tyus
LeRoy Walker
Stella Walsh
Cornelius Warmerdam
Martha Watson
Willye White
Mal Whitfield
Fred Wilt
Lloyd "Bud" Winter
John Woodruff
Dave Wottle
Frank Wykoff
Joe Yancey
George Young

GOLF

United States Open

Year	Winner
1901	Willie Anderson
1902	L. Auchterlonie
1903	Willie Anderson
1904	Willie Anderson
1905	Willie Anderson
1906	Alex Smith
1907	Alex Ross
1908	Fred McLeod
1909	George Sargent
1910	Alex Smith
1911	John McDermott
1912	John McDermott
1913	Francis Ouimet*
1914	Walter Hagen
1915	Jerome Travers*
1916	Chick Evans*
1917-18	(Not played)
1919	Walter Hagen
1920	Edward Ray
1921	Jim Barnes
1922	Gene Sarazen
1923	Bobby Jones*
1924	Cyril Walker
1925	Willie MacFarlane
1926	Bobby Jones*
1927	Tommy Armour
1928	John Farrell
1929	Bobby Jones*
1930	Bobby Jones*
1931	Wm. Burke
1932	Gene Sarazen
1933	John Goodman*
1934	Olin Dutra
1935	Sam Parks Jr.
1936	Tony Manero
1937	Ralph Guldahl
1938	Ralph Guldahl
1939	Byron Nelson
1940	Lawson Little
1941	Craig Wood
1942-45	(Not played)
1946	Lloyd Mangrum
1947	L. Worsham
1948	Ben Hogan
1949	Cary Middlecoff
1950	Ben Hogan
1951	Ben Hogan
1952	Julius Boros
1953	Ben Hogan
1954	Ed Furgol
1955	Jack Fleck
1956	Cary Middlecoff
1957	Dick Mayer
1958	Tommy Bolt
1959	Billy Casper
1960	Arnold Palmer
1961	Gene Littler
1962	Jack Nicklaus
1963	Julius Boros
1964	Ken Venturi
1965	Gary Player
1966	Billy Casper
1967	Jack Nicklaus
1968	Lee Trevino
1969	Orville Moody
1970	Tony Jacklin
1971	Lee Trevino
1972	Jack Nicklaus
1973	Johnny Miller
1974	Hale Irwin
1975	Lou Graham
1976	Jerry Pate
1977	Hubert Green
1978	Andy North
1979	Hale Irwin
1980	Jack Nicklaus
1981	David Graham
1982	Tom Watson
1983	Larry Nelson
1984	Fuzzy Zoeller
1985	Andy North
1986	Ray Floyd
1987	Scott Simpson

*Amateur

Professional Golfer's Association Championships

Year	Winner
1921	Walter Hagan
1922	Gene Sarazen
1923	Gene Sarazen
1924	Walter Hagen
1925	Walter Hagen
1926	Walter Hagen
1927	Walter Hagen
1928	Leo Diegel
1929	Leo Diegel
1930	Tommy Armour
1931	Tom Creavy
1932	Olin Dutra
1933	Gene Sarazen
1934	Paul Runyan
1935	Johnny Revolta
1936	Denny Shute
1937	Denny Shute
1938	Paul Runyan
1939	Henry Picard
1940	Byron Nelson
1941	Victor Ghezzi
1942	Sam Snead
1944	Bob Hamilton
1945	Byron Nelson
1946	Ben Hogan
1947	Jim Ferrier
1948	Ben Hogan
1949	Sam Snead
1950	Chandler Harper
1951	Sam Snead
1952	James Turnesa
1953	Walter Burkemo
1954	Melvin Harbert
1955	Doug Ford
1956	Jack Burke
1957	Lionel Hebert
1958	Dow Finsterwald
1959	Bob Rosburg
1960	Jay Hebert
1961	Jerry Barber
1962	Gary Player
1963	Jack Nicklaus
1964	Bob Nichols
1965	Dave Marr
1966	Al Geiberger
1967	Don January
1968	Julius Boros
1969	Ray Floyd
1970	Dave Stockton
1971	Jack Nicklaus
1972	Gary Player
1973	Jack Nicklaus
1974	Lee Trevino
1975	Jack Nicklaus
1976	Dave Stockton
1977	Lanny Wadkins
1978	John Mahaffey
1979	David Graham
1980	Jack Nicklaus
1981	Larry Nelson
1982	Ray Floyd
1983	Hal Sutton
1984	Lee Trevino
1985	Hubert Green
1986	Bob Tway
1987	Larry Nelson

Masters Golf Tournament Champions

Year	Winner
1934	Horton Smith
1935	Gene Sarazen
1936	Horton Smith
1937	Byron Nelson
1938	Henry Picard
1939	Ralph Guldahl
1940	Jimmy Demaret
1941	Craig Wood
1942	Byron Nelson
1943-1945	(Not played)
1946	Herman Keiser
1947	Jimmy Demaret
1948	Claude Harmon
1949	Sam Snead
1950	Jimmy Demaret
1951	Ben Hogan
1952	Sam Snead
1953	Ben Hogan
1954	Sam Snead
1955	Cary Middlecoff
1956	Jack Burke
1957	Doug Ford
1958	Arnold Palmer
1959	Art Wall Jr.
1960	Arnold Palmer
1961	Gary Player
1962	Arnold Palmer
1963	Jack Nicklaus
1964	Arnold Palmer
1965	Jack Nicklaus
1966	Jack Nicklaus
1967	Gay Brewer Jr.
1968	Bob Goalby
1969	George Archer
1970	Billy Casper
1971	Charles Coody
1972	Jack Nicklaus
1973	Tommy Aaron
1974	Gary Player
1975	Jack Nicklaus
1976	Ray Floyd
1977	Tom Watson
1978	Gary Player
1979	Fuzzy Zoeller
1980	Severiano Ballesteros
1981	Tom Watson
1982	Craig Stadler
1983	Severiano Ballesteros
1984	Ben Crenshaw
1985	Bernhard Langer
1986	Jack Nicklaus
1987	Larry Mize

British Open Golf Champions

Year	Winner
1930	Bobby Jones
1931	Tommy Armour
1932	Gene Sarazen
1933	Denny Shute
1934	Henry Cotton
1935	Alf Perry
1936	Alf Padgham
1937	T.H. Cotton
1938	R.A. Whitcombe
1939	Richard Burton
1940-45	(Not played)
1946	Sam Snead
1947	Fred Daly
1948	Henry Cotton
1949	Bobby Locke
1950	Bobby Locke
1951	Max Faulkner
1952	Bobby Locke
1953	Ben Hogan
1954	Peter Thomson
1955	Peter Thomson
1956	Peter Thomson
1957	Bobby Locke
1958	Peter Thomson
1959	Gary Player
1960	Kel Nagle
1961	Arnold Palmer
1962	Arnold Palmer
1963	Bob Charles
1964	Tony Lema
1965	Peter Thomson
1966	Jack Nicklaus
1967	Roberto de Vicenzo
1968	Gary Player
1969	Tony Jacklin
1970	Jack Nicklaus
1971	Lee Trevino
1972	Lee Trevino
1973	Tom Weiskopf
1974	Gary Player
1975	Tom Watson
1976	Johnny Miller
1977	Tom Watson
1978	Jack Nicklaus
1979	Seve Ballesteros
1980	Tom Watson
1981	Bill Rogers
1982	Tom Watson
1983	Tom Watson
1984	Seve Ballesteros
1985	Sandy Lyle
1986	Greg Norman
1987	Nick Faldo

Professional Golf Tournaments in 1987

Date	Event	Winner	Score	Prize
Jan. 11	MONY Tournament of Champions, Carlsbad, Cal.	Mac O'Grady	278	$90,000
Jan. 18	Bob Hope Chrysler Classic, Palm Springs	Corey Pavin	341	162,000
Jan. 25	Phoenix Open, Ariz.	Paul Azinger	268	108,000
Feb. 1	A.T.&T. National Pro-Am, Pebble Beach, Cal.	Johnny Miller	278	108,000
Feb. 8	Hawaiian Open, Honolulu	Corey Pavin	*270	108,000
Feb. 15	Andy Williams Open, La Jolla, Cal.	George Burns	266	90,000
Feb. 22	Los Angeles Open	T.C. Chen	*275	108,000
Mar. 1	Doral Ryder, Miami, Fla.	Lanny Wadkins	277	180,000
Mar. 8	Honda Classic, Coral Springs, Fla.	Mark Calcavecchia	279	108,000
Mar. 15	Bay Hill Classic, Orlando, Fla.	Payne Stewart	264	108,000
Mar. 22	U.S.F.&G. Classic, New Orleans, La.	Ben Crenshaw	268	90,000
Mar. 29	Tournament Players Championship, Ponte Vedra, Fla.	Sandy Lyle	*274	180,000
Apr. 5	Greater Greensboro Open, N.C.	Scott Simpson	282	108,000
Apr. 12	Masters Tournament, Augusta, Ga.	Larry Mize	*285	162,000
Apr. 19	Heritage Classic, Hilton Head, S.C.	Davis Love 3d	271	117,000
Apr. 26	Houston Open, The Woodlands, Tex.	Jay Haas	*276	108,000
May 3	Las Vegas Invitational	Paul Azinger	271	225,000
May 10	Byron Nelson Classic, Irving, Tex.	Fred Couples	*266	108,000
May 17	Colonial National Tournament, Ft. Worth, Tex.	Keith Clearwater	266	108,000
May 24	Atlanta Classic, Atlanta, Ga.	Dave Barr	265	108,000
May 31	Memorial Tournament, Dublin, Oh.	Don Pooley	272	140,000
June 7	Kemper Open, Potomac, Md.	Tom Kite	270	126,000
June 14	Westchester Classic, Harrison, N.Y.	J.C. Snead	*276	108,000
June 21	U.S. Open, Southampton, N.Y.	Scott Simpson	277	150,000
June 28	Greater Hartford Open, Conn.	Paul Azinger	269	126,000
July 5	Canadian Open, Oakville, Ont.	Curtis Strange	276	108,000
July 12	Anheuser-Busch Classic, Williamsburg, Va.	Mark McCumber	267	110,000
July 26	Buick Open, Grand Blanc, Mich.	Robert Wren	262	108,000
Aug. 2	St. Jude Memphis Open, Tenn.	Curtis Strange	275	130,000
Aug. 9	PGA Championship, Palm Beach Gardens, Fla.	Larry Nelson	*287	150,000
Aug. 16	The International, Castle Rock, Col.	John Cook	+11 pts.	180,000
Aug. 23	Western Open, Oak Brook, Ill.	D.A. Weibring	207	144,000
Aug. 30	World Series of Golf, Akron, Oh.	Curtis Strange	275	144,000
Sept. 6	B.C. Open, Endicott, N.Y.	Joey Sindelar	266	72,000
Sept. 13	Bank of Boston Classic, Sutton, Mass.	Sam Randolph	199	90,000
Sept. 21	Greater Milwaukee Open	Gary Hallberg	269	108,000
Sept. 27	Southwest Classic, Abilene, Tex.	Steve Pate	272	72,000

Women

Date	Event	Winner	Score	Prize
Feb. 8	Sarasota Classic, Sarasota, Fla.	Nancy Lopez	281	$30,000
Mar. 1	Kemper Open, Princeville, Ha.	Jane Geddes	276	45,000
Mar. 22	Tucson Open, Tucson, Ariz.	Betsy King	281	30,000
Apr. 5	Dinah Shore Invitational, Rancho Mirage, Cal.	Betsy King	*283	80,000
Apr. 12	Kyocera Classic, San Diego, Cal.	Ayako Okamoto	275	30,000
Apr. 19	Santa Barbara Open, Cal.	Jan Stephenson	215	45,000
May 3	S & H Classic, St. Petersburg, Fla.	Cindy Hill	271	33,000
May 10	United Virginia Bank Classic, Suffolk, Va.	Jody Rosenthal	209	37,500
May 17	Chrysler-Plymouth Classic, Middletown, N.J.	Ayako Okamoto	215	33,000
May 24	Mazda Championship, Kings Island, Oh.	Jane Geddes	275	52,000
May 31	Corning Classic, Corning, N.Y.	Cindy Rarick	275	41,250
June 7	McDonald's Classic, Wilmington, Del.	Betsy King	278	75,000
June 14	Mayflower Classic, Indianapolis, Ind.	Colleen Walker	278	52,500
June 21	Lady Keystone Open, Hershey, Pa.	Ayako Okamoto	208	45,000
June 28	Rochester Invitational, N.Y.	Deb Richard	280	45,000
July 5	Jamie Farr Toledo Classic, Oh.	Jane Geddes	200	34,000
July 12	Du Maurier Classic, Laval, Que.	Jody Rosenthal	272	60,000
July 19	Boston Five Classic, Danvers, Mass.	Jane Geddes	277	45,000
July 28	U.S. Women's Open, Edison, N.J.	Laura Davies	*285	55,000
Aug. 9	Henredon Classic, High Point, N.C.	Mary Beth Zimmerman	206	45,000
Aug. 23	Atlantic City Classic, Absecon, N.J.	Betsy King	207	33,750
Aug. 30	World Championship of Women's Golf, Buford, Ga.	Ayako Okamoto	282	81,500
Sept. 6	Rail Charity Classic, Springfield, Ill.	Rosie Jones	208	30,000
Sept. 13	Cellular One-Ping Championship, Portland, Ore.	Nancy Lopez	210	33,750
Sept. 20	Safeco Classic, Kent, Wash.	Jan Stephenson	277	33,750
Sept. 27	San Jose Classic, Cal.	Jan Stephenson	205	45,000

*Won playoff.

U.S. Women's Open Golf Champions

Year	Winner	Year	Winner	Year	Winner	Year	Winner
1948	"Babe" Zaharias	1958	Mickey Wright	1968	Susie Maxwell Berning	1978	Hollis Stacy
1949	Louise Suggs	1959	Mickey Wright	1969	Donna Caponi	1979	Jerilyn Britz
1950	"Babe" Zaharias	1960	Betsy Rawls	1970	Donna Caponi	1980	Amy Alcott
1951	Betsy Rawls	1961	Mickey Wright	1971	JoAnne Carner	1981	Pat Bradley
1952	Louise Suggs	1962	Marie Lindstrom	1972	Susie Maxwell Berning	1982	Janet Alex
1953	Betsy Rawls	1963	Mary Mills	1973	Susie Maxwell Berning	1983	Jan Stephenson
1954	"Babe" Zaharias	1964	Mickey Wright	1974	Sandra Haynie	1984	Hollis Stacy
1955	Fay Crocker	1965	Carol Mann	1975	Sandra Palmer	1985	Kathy Baker
1956	Mrs. K. Cornelius	1966	Sandra Spuzich	1976	JoAnne Carner	1986	Jane Geddes
1957	Betsy Rawls	1967	Catherine Lacoste*	1977	Hollis Stacy	1987	Laura Davies

*Amateur

PGA Leading Money Winners

Year	Player	Dollars	Year	Player	Dollars	Year	Player	Dollars
1946	Ben Hogan	42,556	1960	Arnold Palmer	75,262	1974	Johnny Miller	353,201
1947	Jimmy Demaret	27,936	1961	Gary Player	64,540	1975	Jack Nicklaus	323,149
1948	Ben Hogan	36,812	1962	Arnold Palmer	81,448	1976	Jack Nicklaus	266,438
1949	Sam Snead	31,593	1963	Arnold Palmer	128,230	1977	Tom Watson	310,653
1950	Sam Snead	35,758	1964	Jack Nicklaus	113,284	1978	Tom Watson	362,429
1951	Lloyd Mangrum	26,088	1965	Jack Nicklaus	140,752	1979	Tom Watson	462,636
1952	Julius Boros	37,032	1966	Billy Casper	121,944	1980	Tom Watson	530,808
1953	Lew Worsham	34,002	1967	Jack Nicklaus	188,988	1981	Tom Kite	375,699
1954	Bob Toski	65,819	1968	Billy Casper	205,168	1982	Craig Stadler	446,462
1955	Julius Boros	65,121	1969	Frank Beard	175,223	1983	Hal Sutton	426,668
1956	Ted Kroll	72,835	1970	Lee Trevino	157,037	1984	Tom Watson	476,260
1957	Dick Mayer	65,835	1971	Jack Nicklaus	244,490	1985	Curtis Strange	542,321
1958	Arnold Palmer	42,407	1972	Jack Nicklaus	320,542	1986	Greg Norman	653,296
1959	Art Wall Jr.	53,167	1973	Jack Nicklaus	308,362			

LPGA Leading Money Winners

Year	Winner	Dollars	Year	Winner	Dollars	Year	Winner	Dollars
1954	Patty Berg	16,011	1965	Kathy Whitworth	28,658	1976	Judy Rankin	150,734
1955	Patty Berg	16,492	1966	Kathy Whitworth	33,517	1977	Judy Rankin	122,890
1956	Marlene Hagge	20,235	1967	Kathy Whitworth	32,937	1978	Nancy Lopez	189,813
1957	Patty Berg	16,272	1968	Kathy Whitworth	48,379	1979	Nancy Lopez	215,987
1958	Beverly Hanson	12,629	1969	Carol Mann	49,152	1980	Beth Daniel	231,000
1959	Betsy Rawls	26,774	1970	Kathy Whitworth	30,235	1981	Beth Daniel	206,977
1960	Louise Suggs	16,892	1971	Kathy Whitworth	41,181	1982	JoAnne Carner	310,399
1961	Mickey Wright	22,236	1972	Kathy Whitworth	65,063	1983	JoAnne Carner	291,404
1962	Mickey Wright	21,641	1973	Kathy Whitworth	82,854	1984	Betsy King	266,771
1963	Mickey Wright	31,269	1974	JoAnne Carner	87,094	1985	Nancy Lopez	416,472
1964	Mickey Wright	29,800	1975	Sandra Palmer	94,805	1986	Pat Bradley	492,021

1987 Rifle and Pistol Individual Championships

Source: National Rifle Association

National Outdoor Rifle and Pistol Championships

Pistol — Erich Buljung, Ft. Benning, Ga., 2627-104X.
Civilian Pistol — Allen B. Fulford, Vienna, Ga. 2608-115X.
Woman Pistol — Ruby E. Fox, Parker, Ariz., 2570-79X.
Senior Pistol — Joseph C. White, Rockville, Md., 2587-109X.
Collegiate Pistol — Philip J. Bradley, Savannah, Ga., 2512-67X.
Smallbore Rifle Prone — Lones W. Wigger Jr., Colorado Springs, Col., 6394-528X.
Civilian Smallbore Rifle Prone — Lones W. Wigger Jr., 6394-528X.
Woman Smallbore Rifle Prone — Gwendolyn H. Fox, Downers Grove, Ill., 6390-510X.
Senior Smallbore Rifle Prone — Richard F. Hanson, Punta Gorda, Fla., 6388-492X.
Collegiate Smallbore Rifle Prone — Webster M. Wright III, Annapolis, Md., 6393-521X.
Smallbore Rifle 3-Position — Karen E. Monez, Weatherford, Tex., 2303-36.
Civilian Smallbore Rifle 3-Position — Lones W. Wigger Jr., 2297-19.
Woman Smallbore Rifle 3-Position — Karen E. Monez, 2303-36.
Senior Smallbore Rifle 3-Position — Robert A. Makielski, Mishawaka, Ind., 2103-30.
Collegiate Smallbore Rifle 3-Position — Michael E. Anti, Jacksonville, N.C., 2270-31.
Highpower Rifle — Greg A. Strom, Ft. Benning, Ga., 2356-79X.
Civilian Highpower Rifle — Eric Luhmann, Clovis, Cal., 2328-64X.
Woman Highpower Rifle — Kathy M. Livingstone, Fallston, Md., 2299-57X.
Senior Highpower Rifle — George A. Pratt, Pownal, Vt., 2258-41X.
Collegiate Highpower Rifle — Byron R. Bjordahl, Minot, N.D., 2284-45X.

U. S. NRA International Shooting Championships

English Match — W.F. Beard, Indianapolis, Ind., 1790.
Smallbore Free Rifle — D.J. Durben, Colorado Springs, Col., 3499.
Air Rifle — D.J. Durben, 1863.
Woman Air Rifle — L.K. Meili, Colorado Springs, Col., 1668.
Woman Standard Rifle Prone — M.L. Godlove, Macon, Ga., 1774.
Woman Standard Rifle 3-Position — D.L. Wigger, Colorado Springs, Col., 1743.
Free Pistol — E.M. Buljung, Ft. Benning, Ga., 1202.
Rapid Fire Pistol — J.T. McNally, Columbus, Ga., 1280.
Center Fire Pistol — R. Arredondo, Columbus, Ga., 1178.
Standard Pistol — J.R. Dorsey, Spokane, Wash., 1159.
Air Pistol — E.M. Buljung, 1246.
Woman Air Pistol — J.D. Gladwell, Big Pine Key, Fla., 843.
Woman Sport Pistol — B. Blocksome, Hartselle, Ala., 1259.

National Indoor Rifle and Pistol Championships

Smallbore Rifle 4-Position — Lones W. Wigger, Jr., Colorado Springs, Col., 800.
Smallbore Rifle International — Kurt H. Fitz-Randolph, Palm Bay, Fla., 1184.
Smallbore Rifle 3-Position — Lones W. Wigger Jr., 1192.
Woman Smallbore Rifle 4-Position — Denise L. Loring, Ft. Benning, Ga., 797.
Woman Smallbore Rifle International — Wanda R. Jewell, Columbus, Ga., 1176.
Woman Smallbore Rifle 3-Position — Wanda R. Jewell, 1180.
Conventional Pistol — Charles E. Baxter, Argyle, Tex., 890.
Woman Conventional Pistol — Judith L. Kemp, Bloomington, Cal., 866.
International Free Pistol — Eugene G. Ross, Saugus, Cal., 561.
Woman International Free Pistol — Dorothea A. Martin, Detroit, Mich., 511.
International Standard Pistol — E.M. Buljung, Ft. Benning, Ga., 583.
Woman International Standard Pistol — Judith L. Kemp, 545.
Air Pistol — Darius R. Young, Winterburn, Alberta, Can., 579.
Woman Air Pistol — Patricia A. Zidek, Hopwell Jct., N.Y., 550.
Air Rifle — Carl R. Bernosky, Gordon, Pa., 589.
Woman Air Rifle — Pat Spurgin, Billings, Mont., 588.

Notable Sports Personalities

Henry Aaron, b. 1934: Milwaukee-Atlanta outfielder hit record 755 home runs; led NL 4 times.
Kareem Abdul-Jabbar, b. 1947: Milwaukee, L.A. Lakers center; MVP 6 times; leading scorer twice; playoff MVP, 1971, 1985; all-time leading NBA scorer.
Grover Cleveland Alexander, (1887-1950): pitcher won 374 NL games; pitched 16 shutouts, 1916.
Muhammad Ali, b. 1942: 3-time heavyweight champion.
Ken Anderson, b. 1949: Cinn. Bengals quarterback led AFC in passing 4 times.
Mario Andretti, b. 1940; won Indy 500, 1969; Grand Prix champ, 1978.
Eddie Arcaro, b. 1916: jockey rode 4,779 winners including the Kentucky Derby 5 times; the Preakness and Belmont Stakes 6 times each.
Henry Armstrong, b. 1912: boxer held feather-, welter-, lightweight titles simultaneously, 1937-38.
Arthur Ashe, b. 1943: U.S. singles champ, 1968, Wimbledon champ, 1975.
Red Auerbach, b. 1917: coached Boston Celtics to 9 NBA championships.
Ernie Banks, b. 1931: Chicago Cubs slugger hit 512 NL homers: twice MVP.
Roger Bannister, b. 1929: Briton ran first sub 4-minute mile, May 6, 1954.
Rick Barry, b. 1944: NBA scoring leader, 1967; ABA, 1969.
Sammy Baugh, b. 1914: Washington Redskins quarterback held numerous records upon retirement after 16 pro seasons.
Elgin Baylor, b. 1934: L.A. Lakers forward; 1st team all-star 10 times.
Bob Beamon, b. 1946: long jumper won 1968 Olympic gold medal with record 29 ft. 2½ in.
Jean Beliveau, b. 1931: Montreal Canadiens center scored 507 goals; twice MVP.
Johnny Bench, b. 1947: Cincinnati Reds catcher; MVP twice; led league in home runs twice, RBIs 3 times.
Patty Berg, b. 1918: won over 80 golf tournaments: AP Woman Athlete-of-the-Year 3 times.
Yogi Berra, b. 1925: N.Y. Yankees catcher; MVP 3 times; played in 14 World Series.
Raymond Berry, b. 1933: Baltimore Colts receiver caught 631 passes.
Larry Bird, b. 1956: Boston Celtics forward; chosen MVP 1984-86, playoff MVP, 1984, 1986.
George Blanda, b. 1927: quarterback, kicker; 26 years as active player, scoring record 2,002 points.
Wade Boggs, b. 1958; AL Batting champ, 1983, 1985-87.
Bjorn Borg, b. 1956: led Sweden to first Davis Cup, 1975; Wimbledon champion, 5 times.
Mike Bossy, b.1957; N.Y. Islanders right wing scored over 50 goals 8 times.
Jack Brabham, b. 1926: Grand Prix champ 3 times.
Terry Bradshaw, b. 1948; Pittsburgh Steelers quarterback led team to 4 Super Bowl titles.
George Brett, b. 1953: Kansas City Royals 3d baseman led AL in batting, 1976, 1980; MVP, 1980.
Lou Brock, b. 1939: St. Louis Cardinals outfielder stole record 118 bases, 1974; record 938 career; led NL 8 times.
Jimmy Brown, b. 1936: Cleveland Browns fullback ran for 12,312 career yards; MVP 3 times.
Paul "Bear" Bryant, (1913-1983), college football coach with 323 victories.
Maria Bueno, b. 1939: U.S. singles champ 4 times; Wimbledon champ 3 times.
Dick Butkus, b. 1942: Chicago Bears linebacker twice chosen best NFL defensive player.
Dick Button, b. 1929: figure skater won 1948, 1952 Olympic gold medals; world titlist, 1948-52.
Walter Camp, (1859-1925): Yale football player, coach, athletic director; established many rules; promoted All-America designations.
Roy Campanella, b. 1921: Brooklyn Dodgers catcher; MVP 3 times.
Earl Campbell, b. 1955: NFL running back; NFL MVP 1978-1980.
Rod Carew, b. 1945: AL infielder won 7 batting titles; MVP, 1977.
Steve Carlton, b. 1944: NL pitcher won 20 games 5 times, Cy Young award 4 times.
Billy Casper, b. 1931: PGA Player-of-the-Year 3 times; U.S. Open champ twice.
Wilt Chamberlain, b. 1936: center was NBA leading scorer 7 times; MVP 4 times.
Bobby Clarke, b. 1949: Philadelphia Flyers center led team to 2 Stanley Cup championships: MVP 3 times.
Roberto Clemente, (1934-1972): Pittsburgh Pirates outfielder won 4 batting titles; MVP, 1966.
Ty Cobb, (1886-1961): Detroit Tigers outfielder had record .367 lifetime batting average, 12 batting titles.
Sebastian Coe, b. 1956: Briton won Olympic 1,500-meter run, 1980, 1984.
Nadia Comaneci, b. 1961: Romanian gymnast won 3 gold medals, achieved 7 perfect scores, 1976 Olympics.
Maureen Connolly, (1934-1969): won tennis "grand slam," 1953; AP Woman-Athlete-of-the-Year 3 times.
Jimmy Connors, b. 1952: U.S. singles champ 5 times; Wimbledon champ twice.
James J. Corbett, (1866-1933): heavyweight champion, 1892-97; credited with being the first "scientific" boxer.
Angel Cordero, b. 1942: jockey won over 6,000 races; leading money winner, 1976, 1982-83.
Margaret Smith Court, b. 1942: Australian won U.S. singles championship 5 times; Wimbledon champ 3 times.
Bob Cousy, b. 1928: Boston Celtics guard led team to 6 NBA championships: MVP, 1957.
Dizzy Dean, (1911-1974): colorful pitcher for St. Louis Cardinals "Gashouse Gang" in the 30s; MVP, 1934.
Jack Dempsey, (1895-1983); heavyweight champion, 1919-26.
Eric Dickerson, b. 1960: L.A. Rams running back ran for NFL record 2,105 yds., 1984.
Joe DiMaggio, b. 1914: N.Y. Yankees outfielder hit safely in record 56 consecutive games, 1941; MVP 3 times.
Leo Durocher, b. 1906: manager won 3 NL pennants.
Gertrude Ederle, b. 1906: first woman to swim English Channel, broke existing men's record, 1926.
Julius Erving, b. 1950: MVP and leading scorer in ABA 3 times; NBA MVP, 1981.
Phil Esposito, b. 1942: NHL scoring leader 5 times.
Chris Evert, b. 1954: U.S. singles champ 6 times, Wimbledon champ 3 times.
Patrick Ewing, b. 1962: center led Georgetown Univ. to 1984 NCAA championship.
Ray Ewry, (1873-1937): track and field star won 8 gold medals, 1900, 1904, and 1908 Olympics.
Juan Fangio, b. 1911: Argentine World Grand Prix champion 5 times.
Bob Feller, b. 1918: Cleveland Indians pitcher won 266 games; pitched 3 no-hitters, 12 one-hitters.
Peggy Fleming, b. 1948: world figure skating champion, 1966-68; gold medalist 1968 Olympics.
Whitey Ford, b. 1928: N.Y. Yankees pitcher won record 10 World Series games.
Dick Fosbury, b. 1947: high jumper won 1968 Olympic gold medal; developed the "Fosbury Flop."
Jimmy Foxx, (1907-1967): Red Sox, Athletics slugger; MVP 3 times; triple crown, 1933.
A.J. Foyt, b. 1935: won Indy 500 4 times; U.S. Auto Club champ 7 times.
Joe Frazier, b. 1944: heavyweight champion, 1970-73.
Lou Gehrig, (1903-1941): N.Y. Yankees 1st baseman played record 2,130 consecutive games; MVP, 1936.
George Gervin, b. 1952: leading NBA scorer, 1978-80, 1982.
Althea Gibson, b. 1927: twice U.S. and Wimbledon singles champ.
Bob Gibson, b. 1935: St. Louis Cardinals pitcher won Cy Young award twice; struck out 3,117 batters.
Frank Gifford, b. 1930: N.Y. Giants back; MVP, 1956.
Dwight Gooden, b. 1964: N.Y. Mets pitcher was NL Rookie of Year, 1984; Cy Young award, 1985.
Otto Graham, b. 1921: Cleveland Browns quarterback; all-pro 4 times.
Red Grange, b 1903: All-America at Univ. of Illinois; played for Chicago Bears, 1925-35.
Joe Greene, b. 1946: Pittsburgh Steelers lineman; twice NFL outstanding defensive player.
Wayne Gretzky, b. 1961: Edmonton Oilers center scored record 92 goals, 212 pts., 1982; MVP, 1980-87.
Lefty Grove, (1900-1975): pitcher won 300 AL games; 20-game winner 8 times.
Tony Gwynn, b. 1960: NL batting champ, 1984, 1987.
Walter Hagen, (1892-1969): won PGA championship 5 times. British Open 4 times.
George Halas, (1895-1983); founder-coach of Chicago Bears; won 5 NFL championships.
Bill Hartack, b. 1932: jockey rode 5 Kentucky Derby winners.
Doug Harvey, b. 1930: Montreal Canadiens defenseman; Norris Trophy 7 times.
Bill Haughton, b. 1923: harness racing driver won Little Brown Jug 4 times, Hambletonian 4 times.
John Havlicek, b. 1940: Boston Celtics forward scored over 26,000 NBA points.
Eric Heiden, b. 1958: speed skater won 5 1980 Olympic gold medals.

Carol Heiss, b. 1940: world champion figure skater 5 consecutive years, 1956-60; won 1960 Olympic gold medal.
Rickey Henderson, b. 1958; AL outfielder stole record 130 bases, 1982.
Sonja Henie, (1912-1969): world champion figure skater, 1927-36; Olympic gold medalist, 1928, 1932, 1936.
Ben Hogan, b. 1912: won 4 U.S. Open championships, 2 PGA, 2 Masters.
Larry Holmes, b. 1949: WBC heavyweight champ 1978-84.
Rogers Hornsby, (1896-1963): NL 2d baseman batted record .424 in 1924; twice won triple crown; batting leader, 1920-25.
Paul Hornung, b. 1935: Green Bay Packers runner-placekicker scored record 176 points, 1960.
Gordie Howe, b. 1928: hockey forward holds NHL career records in goals, assists, and points; NHL MVP 6 times.
Carl Hubbell, b. 1903: N.Y. Giants pitcher; 20-game winner 5 consecutive years, 1933-37.
Bobby Hull, b. 1939: NHL all-star 10 times.
Catfish Hunter, b 1946: pitched perfect game, 1968; 20-game winner 5 times.
Don Hutson, b. 1913: Green Bay Packers receiver caught NFL record 99 touchdown passes.
Reggie Jackson, b. 1946: slugger led AL in home runs 4 times; MVP, 1973; hit 5 World Series home runs, 1977.
Bruce Jenner, b. 1949: decathlon gold medalist, 1976.
Jack Johnson, (1878-1946): heavyweight champion, 1910-15.
Magic Johnson, b. 1959: NBA MVP 1987; playoff MVP 1980, 1982.
Rafer Johnson, b. 1935: decathlon gold medalist, 1960.
Walter Johnson, (1887-1946): Washington Senators pitcher won 413 games.
Bobby Jones, (1902-1971); won "grand slam of golf" 1930; U.S. Amateur champ 5 times, U.S. Open champ 4 times.
Deacon Jones, b. 1938: L.A. Rams lineman; twice NFL outstanding defensive player.
Michael Jordan, b. 1963: NBA leading scorer, 1987.
Sonny Jurgensen, b. 1934: quarterback named all-pro 5 times.
Duke Kahanamoku, (1890-1968): swimmer won 1912, 1920 Olympic gold medals in 100-meter freestyle.
Harmon Killebrew, b. 1936: Minnesota Twins slugger led AL in home runs 6 times.
Jean Claude Killy, b. 1943: French skier won 3 1968 Olympic gold medals.
Ralph Kiner, b. 1922: Pittsburgh Pirates slugger led NL in home runs 7 consecutive years, 1946-52.
Billie Jean King, b. 1943: U.S. singles champ 4 times; Wimbledon champ 6 times.
Bob Knight, b. 1940: Indiana U. basketball coach lead team to NCAA championships, 1976, 1981, 1987.
Olga Korbut, b. 1955: Soviet gymnast won 3 1972 Olympic gold medals.
Sandy Koufax, b. 1935: Dodgers pitcher won Cy Young award 3 times; lowest ERA in NL, 1962-66; pitched 4 no-hitters, one a perfect game.
Guy Lafleur, b. 1951: Montreal Canadiens forward led NHL in scoring 3 times; MVP, 1977, 1978.
Tom Landry, b. 1924: Dallas Cowboys head coach since 1960.
Rod Laver, b. 1938: Australian won tennis "grand slam," 1962, 1969; Wimbledon champ 4 times.
Ivan Lendl, b. 1960: U.S. singles champ, 1985-87.
Sugar Ray Leonard, b. 1956: former world welterweight champ.
Carl Lewis, b. 1961: track and field star won 4 1984 Olympic gold medals.
Vince Lombardi, (1913-1970): Green Bay Packers coach led, team to 5 NFL championships and 2 Super Bowl victories.
Joe Louis, (1914-1981): 1914: heavyweight champion, 1937-49.
Sid Luckman, b. 1916: Chicago Bears quarterback led team to 4 NFL championships; MVP, 1943.
Connie Mack, (1862-1956): Philadelphia Athletics manager, 1901-50; won 9 pennants, 5 championships.
Bill Madlock, b. 1951: NL batting leader 4 times.
Moses Malone, b. 1955: NBA center was MVP 1979, 1982, 1983.
Mickey Mantle, b. 1931: N.Y. Yankees outfielder; triple crown, 1956; 18 World Series home runs.
Pete Maravich, b. 1948: guard scored NCAA record 44.2 ppg during collegiate career; led NBA in scoring, 1977.
Alice Marble, b. 1913: U.S. singles champ 4 times.
Rocky Marciano, (1923-1969): heavyweight champion, 1952-56; retired undefeated.
Dan Marino, b. 1961: Miami Dolphins quarterback passed for NFL record 5,084 yds, 1984.
Roger Maris, (1934-1985): N.Y. Yankees outfielder hit record 61 home runs, 1961; MVP, 1960 and 1961.
Billy Martin, b. 1928: baseball manager led N.Y. Yankees to World Series title, 1977.
Eddie Mathews, b. 1931: Milwaukee-Atlanta 3d baseman hit 512 career home runs.
Christy Mathewson, (1880-1925): N.Y. Giants pitcher won 373 games.
Bob Mathias, b. 1930: decathlon gold medalist, 1948, 1952.
Don Mattingly, b. 1961: N.Y. Yankees 1st baseman won 1984 AL batting title; MVP, 1985.
Willie Mays, b. 1931: N.Y.-S.F. Giants center fielder hit 660 home runs; twice MVP.
Willie McCovey, b. 1938: S.F. Giants slugger hit 521 home runs; led NL 3 times.
John McEnroe, b. 1959: U.S. singles champ, 1979-81, 1984; Wimbledon champ, 1981, 1983-84.
John McGraw, (1873-1934): N.Y. Giants manager led team to 10 pennants, 3 championships.
Debbie Meyer, b. 1952: swimmer won 200-, 400-, and 800- meter freestyle events, 1968 Olympics.
George Mikan, b. 1924: Minneapolis Lakers center selected in a 1950 AP poll as the greatest basketball player of the first half of the 20th century.
Stan Mikita, b. 1940: Chicago Black Hawks center led NHL in scoring 4 times; MVP twice.
Joe Montana, b. 1956: QB led 49ers to Super Bowl championships, 1982, 1985.
Archie Moore, b. 1913: world light-heavyweight champion, 1952-62.
Howie Morenz, (1902-1937): Montreal Canadiens forward chosen in a 1950 Canadian press poll as the outstanding hockey player of the first half of the 20th century.
Joe Morgan, b. 1943: National League MVP, 1975, 1976.
Thurman Munson, (1947-1979): N.Y. Yankees catcher; MVP, 1976.
Dale Murphy, b. 1956: Atlanta Braves outfielder chosen NL MVP 1982, 1983.
Stan Musial, b. 1920: St. Louis Cardinals star won 7 NL batting titles; MVP 3 times; NL record 3,630 hits.
Bronko Nagurski, b. 1908: Chicago Bears fullback and tackle; gained over 4,000 yds. rushing.
Joe Namath, b. 1943: quarterback led N.Y. Jets to 1969 Super Bowl title.
Martina Navratilova, b. 1956: Wimbledon champ 8 times, U.S. champ 1983-1984; 1986-87.
Byron Nelson, b. 1912: won 11 consecutive golf tournaments in 1945; twice Masters and PGA titlist.
Ernie Nevers, (1903-1976): Stanford star selected the best college fullback to play between 1919-1969.
John Newcombe, b. 1943: Australian twice U.S. singles champ; Wimbledon titlist 3 times.
Jack Nicklaus, b. 1940: PGA Player-of-the-Year, 1967, 1972; leading money winner 8 times; won Masters 6 times.
Chuck Noll, b. 1931: Pittsburgh Steelers coach led team to 4 Super Bowl titles.
Paavo Nurmi, (1897-1973): Finnish distance runner won 6 Olympic gold medals, 1920, 1924, 1928.
Al Oerter, b. 1936: discus thrower won gold medal at 4 consecutive Olympics, 1956-68.
Bobby Orr, b. 1948: Boston Bruins defenseman; Norris Trophy 8 times; led NHL in scoring twice, assists 5 times.
Mel Ott, (1909-1958): N.Y. Giants outfielder hit 511 home runs; led NL 6 times.
Jesse Owens, (1913-1980): track and field star won 4 1936 Olympic gold medals.
Satchel Paige, (1906-1982): pitcher starred in Negro leagues, 1924-48; entered major leagues at age 42.
Arnold Palmer, b. 1929: golf's first $1 million winner; won 4 Masters, 2 British Opens.
Jim Palmer, b. 1945: Baltimore Orioles pitcher; Cy Young award 3 times; 20-game winner 7 times.
Floyd Patterson, b. 1935: twice heavyweight champion.
Walter Payton, b. 1954: Chicago Bears running back has most rushing yards in NFL history; leading NFC rusher, 1976-80.
Pele, b. 1940: Brazilian soccer star scored 1,281 goals during 22-year career.
Bob Pettit, b. 1932: first NBA player to score 20,000 points; twice NBA scoring leader.
Richard Petty, b. 1937: NASCAR national champ 6 times; 7-times Daytona 500 winner.
Laffit Pincay Jr., b. 1946: leading money-winning jockey, 1970-74, 1979.
Jacques Plante, (1929-1986): goalie, 7 Vezina trophies; first goalie to wear a mask in a game.
Gary Player, b. 1935: South African won the Masters, U.S. Open, PGA, and twice the British Open.
Annemarie Proell Moser, b. 1953: Austrian skier won the World Cup championship 6 times.
Willis Reed, b. 1942: N.Y. Knicks center; MVP, 1970; playoff MVP, 1970, 1973.
Jim Rice, b. 1953: Boston Red Sox outfielder led AL in home runs, 1977-78, 1983; MVP 1978.
Maurice Richard, b. 1921: Montreal Canadiens forward scored 544 regular season goals, 82 playoff goals.

Branch Rickey, (1881-1965): executive instrumental in breaking baseball's color barrier, 1947; initiated farm system, 1919.
Oscar Robertson, b. 1938: guard averaged career 25.7 points per game; record 9,887 career assist; MVP, 1964.
Brooks Robinson, b. 1937: Baltimore Orioles 3d baseman played in 4 World Series; MVP, 1964.
Frank Robinson, b. 1935: slugger MVP in both NL and AL; triple crown winner, 1966; first black manager in majors.
Jackie Robinson, (1919-1972): broke baseball's color barrier with Brooklyn Dodgers, 1947; MVP, 1949.
Larry Robinson, b. 1951: Montreal Canadiens defenseman won Norris trophy, 1977, 1980.
Sugar Ray Robinson, b. 1920: middleweight champion 5 times, welterweight champion.
Knute Rockne, (1888-1931): Notre Dame football coach, 1918-31; revolutionized game by stressing forward pass.
Pete Rose, b. 1941: won 3 NL batting titles; hit safely in 44 consecutive games, 1978; has most major league hits.
Wilma Rudolph, b. 1940: sprinter won 3 1960 Olympic gold medals.
Bill Russell, b. 1934: Boston Celtics center led team to 11 NBA titles; MVP 5 times; first black coach of major pro sports team.
Babe Ruth, (1895-1948): N.Y. Yankees outfielder hit 60 home runs, 1927; 714 lifetime; led AL 11 times.
Johnny Rutherford, b. 1938: auto racer won Indy 500 3 times.
Nolan Ryan, b. 1947: pitcher struck out record 383 batters, 1973; pitched record 5 no-hitters.
Gene Sarazen, b. 1902: won PGA championship 3 times, U.S. Open twice; developer of sand wedge.
Gale Sayers, b. 1943: Chicago Bears back twice led NFC in rushing.
Mike Schmidt, b. 1949: Phillies 3d baseman led NL in home runs, 1974-76, 1980-81, 1983-84, 1986; NL MVP, 1980, 1981, 1986.
Tom Seaver, b. 1944: pitcher won NL Cy Young award 3 times, won 311th major league games.
Bill Shoemaker, b. 1931: jockey rode 3 Kentucky Derby and 5 Belmont Stakes winners; leading career money winner.
Eddie Shore, (1902-1985): Boston Bruins defenseman; MVP 4 times, first-team all-star 7 times.
Al Simmons, (1902-1956): AL outfielder had lifetime .334 batting average.
O.J. Simpson, b. 1947: running back rushed for 2,003 yds., 1973; AFC leading rusher 4 times.
George Sisler, (1893-1973): St. Louis Browns 1st baseman had record 257 hits, 1920; batted .340 lifetime.
Billy Smith, b. 1950: N.Y. Islanders goalie led team to 4 Stanley Cup championships.
Sam Snead, b. 1912: PGA and Masters champ 3 times each.
Warren Spahn, b. 1921: pitcher won 363 NL games; 20-game winner 13 times; Cy Young award, 1957.
Tris Speaker, (1885-1958): AL outfielder batted .344 over 22 seasons; hit record 793 career doubles.
Mark Spitz, b. 1950: swimmer won 7 1972 Olympic gold medals.
Amos Alonzo Stagg, (1862-1965): coached Univ. of Chicago football team for 41 years, including 5 undefeated seasons; introduced huddle, man-in-motion, and end-around play.
Willie Stargell, b. 1941: Pittsburgh Pirate slugger chosen NL, World Series MVP, 1979.
Bart Starr, b. 1934: Green Bay Packers quarterback led team to 5 NFL titles and 2 Super Bowl victories.
Roger Staubach, b. 1942: Dallas Cowboys quarterback; leading NFC passer 5 times.
Casey Stengel, (1890-1975): managed Yankees to 10 pennants, 7 championships, 1949-60.
Jackie Stewart, b. 1939: Scot auto racer retired with 27 Grand Prix victories.
John L. Sullivan, (1858-1918): last bareknuckle heavyweight champion, 1882-1892.
Fran Tarkenton, b. 1940: quarterback holds career passing records for touchdowns, completions, yardage.
Gustave Thoeni, b. 1951: Italian 4-time world alpine ski champ.
Jim Thorpe, (1888-1953): football All-America, 1911, 1912; won pentathlon and decathlon, 1912 Olympics.
Bill Tilden, (1893-1953): U.S. singles champ 7 times; played on 11 Davis Cup teams.
Y.A. Tittle, b. 1926: N.Y. Giants quarterback; MVP, 1961, 1963.
Lee Trevino, b. 1939: won the U.S. and British Open championships twice.
Bryan Trottier, b. 1956: N.Y. Islanders center led team to 4 consecutive Stanley Cup championships, 1980-83.
Wyomia Tyus, b. 1945: sprinter won 1964, 1968 Olympic 100-meter dash.
Johnny Unitas, b. 1933: Baltimore Colts quarterback passed for over 40,000 yds.; MVP, 1957, 1967.
Al Unser, b. 1939: Indy 500 winner, 4 times.
Bobby Unser, b. 1934: Indy 500 winner 3 times.
Fernando Valenzuela, b. 1960: L.A. Dodgers pitcher won Cy Young award, 1981.
Norm Van Brocklin, (1926-1983): quarterback passed for game record 554 yds., 1951; MVP, 1960.
Honus Wagner, (1874-1955): Pittsburgh Pirates shortstop won 8 NL batting titles.
Tom Watson, b. 1949; golfer won British Open 5 times.
Johnny Weissmuller, (1903-1984): swimmer won 52 national championships, 5 Olympic gold medals; set 67 world records.
Jerry West, b. 1938: L.A. Lakers guard had career average 27 points per game; first team all-star 10 times.
Kathy Whitworth, b. 1939: women's golf leading money winner 8 times: first woman to earn over $300,000.
Ted Williams, b. 1918: Boston Red Sox outfielder won 6 batting titles; last major leaguer to hit over .400: .406 in 1941: .344 lifetime batting average.
Helen Wills, b. 1906: winner of 7 U.S., 8 British, 4 French women's singles titles.
John Wooden, b. 1910: coached UCLA basketball team to 10 national championships.
Mickey Wright, b. 1935: won LPGA championship 4 times, Vare Trophy 5 times; twice AP Woman-Athlete-of-the-Year.
Carl Yastrzemski, b. 1939: Boston Red Sox slugger won 3 batting titles, triple crown, 1967.
Cy Young, (1867-1955): pitcher won record 511 major league games.
Babe Didrikson Zaharias, (1914-1956): track star won 2 1932 Olympic gold medals; won numerous golf tournaments.

Water Ski Champions in 1987

44th Annual National Water Ski Championships

West Palm Beach, Fla., Aug. 12-15, 1987

Men's Overall—Rick Anderson, Anderson, S.C., 2,998.7 pts.
Men's Slalom—Rafe Armstrong, Duck Hill, Miss., 54½ buoys.
Men's Tricks—Rick Anderson, 6,960 pts.
Men's Jump—Scott Hardt, North Brook, Ill., 161 feet.
Women's Overall—Jill Norman, Mt. Gilead, N.C. 2,489 pts.
Women's Slalom—Gina Goehner, Sacramento, Cal. 53 buoys.
Women's Tricks—Michelle Mason, Boynton Beach, Fla., 5,520 pts.
Women's Jump—Renee Aurich, Clemson, S.C., 111 feet.

28th Annual Masters Water Ski Tournament

Callaway Gardens, Ga., May 23–24, 1987

Men's Overall—Carl Roberge, Orlando, Fla., 2,510.5 pts.
Men's Slalom—Andy Mapple, Great Britain, 57½ buoys.
Men's Tricks—Cory Pickos, Eagle Lake, Fla., 10,220 buoys.
Men's Jump—Sammy Duvall, Windermere, Fla., 189 feet.
Women's Overall—Deena Brush, Windermere, Fla., 2,569.6 pts.
Women's Slalom—Camille Duvall, Windermere, Fla., 58 buoys.
Women's Tricks—Judy Messer, Canada, 6,580 pts.
Women's Jump—Deena Brush, 144 feet.

1987 U.S. Open

West Palm Beach, Fla., Aug. 16, 1987

Men's Overall—Carl Roberge, Orlando, Fla., 3,331.0 pts.
Men's Slalom—Andy Mapple, England, 64 buoys.
Men's Tricks—Cory Pickos, Eagle Lake, Fla., 10,250 buoys.
Men's Jump—Mike Hazelwood, Great Britain, 196 feet.
Women's Overall—Deena Brush, Windermere, Fla., 3,046.9 pts.
Women's Slalom—Jennifer Leachman, Orlando, Fla., 63 buoys.
Women's Tricks—Britt Larsen, Madison Wis., 5,280 pts.
Women's Jump—Deena Brush, 142 feet.

10th Pan American Games

Indianapolis, Ind., Aug. 15-29, 1987

As expected, the United States dominated the 1987 Pan American games by winning a total of 369 medals, including 169 gold medals. Cuba finished second with 175 medals, highlighted by a gold medal in baseball and 10 of 12 gold medals in boxing. The most stunning upset at the games was Brazil's 120-115 victory over the highly favored U.S. basketball team. A total of 6,032 athletes and officials from 38 countries took part in the games.

The games were marred by the disqualification of 6 athletes from 5 countries for testing positive for banned drugs. There were several clashes between members of the Cuban delegation and Cuban-American and anti-Castro demonstrators. The 11th Pan Am games will be held in Cuba in 1991.

Final Medals Standings

Country	Gold	Silver	Bronze	Total
United States	168	118	83	369
Cuba	75	52	48	175
Canada	30	57	75	162
Brazil	14	14	33	61
Argentina	12	14	22	48
Mexico	9	11	18	38
Puerto Rico	3	6	20	29
Venezuela	3	11	12	26
Colombia	3	8	13	24
Jamaica	2	3	8	13
Dominican Republic	0	3	9	12
Costa Rica	3	4	4	11
Uruguay	2	2	3	7
Chile	1	2	4	7
Peru	0	4	2	6
Ecuador	0	1	5	6
Bahamas	0	2	3	5
Panama	0	3	1	4
Suriname	1	0	1	2
Trinidad & Tobago	0	1	1	2
U.S. Virgin Islands	0	1	1	2
Guatemala	0	0	2	2
Antilles	0	0	1	1
Bermuda	0	0	1	1
El Salvador	0	0	1	1
Guyana	0	0	1	1
Paraguay	0	0	1	1

BASEBALL

Cy Young Award Winners

Year	Player, club
1956	Don Newcombe, Dodgers
1957	Warren Spahn, Braves
1958	Bob Turley, Yankees
1959	Early Wynn, White Sox
1960	Vernon Law, Pirates
1961	Whitey Ford, Yankees
1962	Don Drysdale, Dodgers
1963	Sandy Koufax, Dodgers
1964	Dean Chance, Angels
1965	Sandy Koufax, Dodgers
1966	Sandy Koufax, Dodgers
1967	(NL) Mike McCormick, Giants
	(AL) Jim Lonborg, Red Sox
1968	(NL) Bob Gibson, Cardinals
	(AL) Dennis McLain, Tigers
1969	(NL) Tom Seaver, Mets
	(AL) (tie) Dennis McLain, Tigers
	Mike Cuellar, Orioles
1970	(NL) Bob Gibson, Cardinals
	(AL) Jim Perry, Twins
1971	(NL) Ferguson Jenkins, Cubs
	(AL) Vida Blue, A's
1972	(NL) Steve Carlton, Phillies
	(AL) Gaylord Perry, Indians
1973	(NL) Tom Seaver, Mets
	(AL) Jim Palmer, Orioles
1974	(NL) Mike Marshall, Dodgers
	(AL) Jim (Catfish) Hunter, A's
1975	(NL) Tom Seaver, Mets
	(AL) Jim Palmer, Orioles
1976	(NL) Randy Jones, Padres
	(AL) Jim Palmer, Orioles
1977	(NL) Steve Carlton, Phillies
	(AL) Sparky Lyle, Yankees
1978	(NL) Gaylord Perry, Padres
	(AL) Ron Guidry, Yankees
1979	(NL) Bruce Sutter, Cubs
	(AL) Mike Flanagan, Orioles
1980	(NL) Steve Carlton, Phillies
	(AL) Steve Stone, Orioles
1981	(NL) Fernando Valenzuela, Dodgers
	(AL) Rollie Fingers, Brewers
1982	(NL) Steve Carlton, Phillies
	(AL) Pete Vuckovich, Brewers
1983	(NL) John Denny, Phillies
	(AL) LaMarr Hoyt, White Sox
1984	(NL) Rick Sutcliffe, Cubs
	(AL) Willie Hernandez, Tigers
1985	(NL) Dwight Gooden, Mets
	(AL) Bret Saberhagen, Royals
1986	(NL) Mike Scott, Astros
	(AL) Roger Clemens, Red Sox

The Sporting News Gold Glove Awards in 1986

National League

Keith Hernandez, New York, first base.
Ryne Sandberg, Chicago, second base.
Mike Schmidt, Philadelphia, third base.
Ozzie Smith, St. Louis, shortstop.
Dale Murphy, Atlanta, outfield.
Tony Gwynn, San Diego, outfield.
Willie McGee, St. Louis, outfield.
Jody Davis, Chicago, catcher.
Fernando Valenzuela, Los Angeles, pitcher.

American League

Don Mattingly, New York, first base.
Frank White, Kansas City, second base.
Gary Gaetti, Minnesota, third base.
Tony Fernandez, Toronto, shortstop.
Jesse Barfield, Toronto, outfield.
Kirby Puckett, Minnesota, outfield.
Gary Pettis, California, outfield.
Bob Boone, California, catcher.
Ron Guidry, New York, pitcher.

The following are the players at each position who have won the most Gold Gloves since the award was instituted in 1957.

First base:	Keith Hernandez	9
	George Scott	8
Second base:	Bill Mazeroski	8
	Frank White	8
Third base:	Brooks Robinson	16
	Mike Schmidt	10
Shortstop:	Luis Aparicio	9
	Mark Belanger	8
Outfield:	Roberto Clemente	12
	Willie Mays	12
	Al Kaline	10
	Paul Blair	8
	Dwight Evans	8
	Garry Maddox	8
Catcher:	Johnny Bench	10
	Jim Sundberg	6
Pitcher:	Jim Kaat	16
	Bob Gibson	9

National Baseball Hall of Fame and Museum

Cooperstown, N.Y.

Aaron, Hank
Alexander, Grover Cleveland
Alston, Walt
Anson, Cap
Averill, Earl
Aparicio, Luis
Appling, Luke
Baker, Home Run
Bancroft, Dave
Banks, Ernie
Barrow, Edward G.
Beckley, Jake
Bell, Cool Papa
Bender, Chief
Berra, Yogi
Bottomley, Jim
Boudreau, Lou
Bresnahan, Roger
Brock, Lou
Brouthers, Dan
Brown (Three Finger), Mordecai
Bulkeley, Morgan C.
Burkett, Jesse C.
Campanella, Roy
Carey, Max
Cartwright, Alexander
Chadwick, Henry
Chance, Frank
Chandler, Happy
Charleston, Oscar
Chesbro, John
Clarke, Fred
Clarkson, John
Clemente, Roberto
Cobb, Ty
Cochrane, Mickey
Collins, Eddie
Collins, James
Combs, Earle
Comiskey, Charles A.
Conlan, Jocko
Connolly, Thomas H.
Connor, Roger
Coveleski, Stan
Crawford, Sam
Cronin, Joe
Cummings, Candy
Cuyler, Kiki
Dandridge, Ray
Dean, Dizzy
Delahanty, Ed
Dickey, Bill
DiHigo, Martin
DiMaggio, Joe
Doerr, Bobby
Drysdale, Don
Duffy, Hugh
Evans, Billy
Evers, John
Ewing, Buck
Faber, Urban
Feller, Bob
Ferrell, Rick
Flick, Elmer H.
Ford, Whitey
Foster, Andrew
Foxx, Jimmy
Frick, Ford
Frisch, Frank
Galvin, Pud
Gehrig, Lou
Gehringer, Charles
Gibson, Bob
Gibson, Josh
Giles, Warren
Gomez, Lefty
Goslin, Goose
Greenberg, Hank
Griffith, Clark
Grimes, Burleigh
Grove, Lefty
Hafey, Chick
Haines, Jesee
Hamilton, Bill
Harridge, Will
Harris, Bucky
Hartnett, Gabby
Heilmann, Harry
Herman, Billy
Hooper, Harry
Hornsby, Rogers
Hoyt, Waite
Hubbard, Cal
Hubbell, Carl
Huggins, Miller
Hunter, Catfish
Irvin, Monte
Jackson, Travis
Jennings, Hugh
Johnson, Byron
Johnson, William (Rudy)
Johnson, Walter
Joss, Addie
Kaline, Al
Keefe, Timothy
Keeler, William
Kell, George
Kelley, Joe
Kelly, George
Kelly, King
Killebrew, Harmon
Kiner, Ralph
Klein, Chuck
Klem, Bill
Koufax, Sandy
Lajoie, Napoleon
Landis, Kenesaw M.
Lemon, Bob
Leonard, Buck
Lindstrom, Fred
Lloyd, Pop
Lombardi, Ernie
Lopez, Al
Lyons, Ted
Mack, Connie
MacPhail, Larry
Mantle, Mickey
Manush, Henry
Maranville, Rabbit
Marichal, Juan
Marquard, Rube
Mathews, Eddie
Mathewson, Christy
Mays, Willie
McCarthy, Joe
McCarthy, Thomas
McCovey, Willie
McGinnity, Joe
McGraw, John
McKechnie, Bill
Medwick, Joe
Mize, Johnny
Musial, Stan
Nichols, Kid
O'Rourke, James
Ott, Mel
Paige, Satchel
Pennock, Herb
Plank, Ed
Radbourn, Charlie
Reese, Pee Wee
Rice, Sam
Rickey, Branch
Rixey, Eppa
Roberts, Robin
Robinson, Brooks
Robinson, Frank
Robinson, Jackie
Robinson, Wilbert
Roush, Edd
Ruffing, Red
Rusie, Amos
Ruth, Babe
Schalk, Ray
Sewell, Joe
Simmons, Al
Sisler, George
Slaughter, Enos
Snider, Duke
Spahn, Warren
Spalding, Albert
Speaker, Tris
Stengel, Casey
Terry, Bill
Thompson, Sam
Tinker, Joe
Traynor, Pie
Vance, Dazzy
Vaughan, Arky
Waddell, Rube
Wagner, Honus
Wallace, Roderick
Walsh, Ed.
Waner, Lloyd
Waner, Paul
Ward, John
Weiss, George
Welch, Mickey
Wheat, Zach
Wilhelm, Hoyt
Williams, Billy
Williams, Ted
Wilson, Hack
Wright, George
Wright, Harry
Wynn, Early
Yawkey, Tom
Young, Cy
Youngs, Ross

All-Star Baseball Games, 1933-1987

Year	Winner	Score	Location
1933	American	4-2	Chicago
1934	American	9-7	New York
1935	American	4-1	Cleveland
1936	National	4-3	Boston
1937	American	8-3	Washington
1938	National	4-1	Cincinnati
1939	American	3-1	New York
1940	National	4-0	St. Louis
1941	American	7-5	Detroit
1942	American	3-1	New York
1943*	American	5-3	Philadelphia
1944*	National	7-1	Pittsburgh
1945	(not played)		
1946	American	12-0	Boston
1947	American	2-1	Chicago
1948	American	5-2	St. Louis
1949	American	11-7	New York
1950	National (1)	4-3	Chicago
1951	National	8-3	Detroit
1952	National	3-2	Philadelphia
1953	National	5-1	Cincinnati
1954	American	11-9	Cleveland
1955	National (2)	6-5	Milwaukee
1956	National	7-3	Washington
1957	American	6-5	St. Louis
1958	American	4-3	Baltimore
1959	National	5-4	Pittsburgh
1959	American	5-3	Los Angeles
1960	National	5-3	Kansas City
1960	National	6-0	New York
1961	National (3)	5-4	San Francisco
1961	Called-rain	1-1	Boston
1962	National (3)	3-1	Washington
1962	American	9-4	Chicago
1963	National	5-3	Cleveland
1964	National	7-4	New York
1965	National	6-5	Minnesota
1966	National (3)	2-1	St. Louis
1967	National (4)	2-1	Anaheim
1968*	National	1-0	Houston
1969	National	9-3	Washington
1970*	National (2)	5-4	Cincinnati
1971*	American	6-4	Detroit
1972*	National	4-3	Atlanta
1973*	National	7-1	Kansas City
1974*	National	7-2	Pittsburgh
1975*	National	6-3	Milwaukee
1976*	National	7-1	Philadelphia
1977*	National	7-5	New York
1978*	National	7-3	San Diego
1979*	National	7-6	Seattle
1980*	National	4-2	Los Angeles
1981*	National	5-4	Cleveland
1982*	National	4-1	Montreal
1983*	American	13-3	Chicago
1984*	National	3-1	San Francisco
1985*	National	6-1	Minneapolis
1986*	American	3-2	Houston
1987*	National (5)	2-0	Oakland

(1) 14 innings, (2) 12 innings, (3) 10 innings, (4) 15 innings (5) 13 innings. *Night game.

Little League World Series in 1987

The team from Taiwan won the 1987 Little League World Series by defeating the team from Irvine (Cal.) 21-1 at Williamsport, Pa. on Aug. 29. It was the 12th Little League championship in 19 years for Taiwan.

Major League Pennant Winners, 1901–1987

National League

Year	Winner	Won	Lost	Pct	Manager
1901	Pittsburgh	90	49	.647	Clarke
1902	Pittsburgh	103	36	.741	Clarke
1903	Pittsburgh	91	49	.650	Clarke
1904	New York	106	47	.693	McGraw
1905	New York	105	48	.686	McGraw
1906	Chicago	116	36	.763	Chance
1907	Chicago	107	45	.704	Chance
1908	Chicago	99	55	.643	Chance
1909	Pittsburgh	110	42	.724	Clarke
1910	Chicago	104	50	.675	Chance
1911	New York	99	54	.647	McGraw
1912	New York	103	48	.682	McGraw
1913	New York	101	51	.664	McGraw
1914	Boston	94	59	.614	Stallings
1915	Philadelphia	90	62	.592	Moran
1916	Brooklyn	94	60	.610	Robinson
1917	New York	98	56	.636	McGraw
1918	Chicago	84	45	.651	Mitchell
1919	Cincinnati	96	44	.686	Moran
1920	Brooklyn	93	60	.604	Robinson
1921	New York	94	56	.614	McGraw
1922	New York	93	61	.604	McGraw
1923	New York	95	58	.621	McGraw
1924	New York	93	60	.608	McGraw
1925	Pittsburgh	95	58	.621	McKechnie
1926	St. Louis	89	65	.578	Hornsby
1927	Pittsburgh	94	60	.610	Bush
1928	St. Louis	95	59	.617	McKechnie
1929	Chicago	98	54	.645	McCarthy
1930	St. Louis	92	62	.597	Street
1931	St. Louis	101	53	.656	Street
1932	Chicago	90	64	.584	Grimm
1933	New York	91	61	.599	Terry
1934	St. Louis	95	58	.621	Frisch
1935	Chicago	100	54	.649	Grimm
1936	New York	91	62	.597	Terry
1937	New York	95	57	.625	Terry
1938	Chicago	89	63	.586	Hartnett
1939	Cincinnati	97	57	.630	McKechnie
1940	Cincinnati	100	53	.654	McKechnie
1941	Brooklyn	100	54	.649	Durocher
1942	St. Louis	106	48	.688	Southworth
1943	St. Louis	105	49	.682	Southworth
1944	St. Louis	105	49	.682	Southworth
1945	Chicago	98	56	.636	Grimm
1946	St. Louis	98	58	.628	Dyer
1947	Brooklyn	94	60	.610	Shotton
1948	Boston	91	62	.595	Southworth
1949	Brooklyn	97	57	.630	Shotton
1950	Philadelphia	91	63	.591	Sawyer
1951	New York	98	59	.624	Durocher
1952	Brooklyn	96	57	.627	Dressen
1953	Brooklyn	105	49	.682	Dressen
1954	New York	97	57	.630	Durocher
1955	Brooklyn	98	55	.641	Alston
1956	Brooklyn	93	61	.604	Alston
1957	Milwaukee	95	59	.617	Haney
1958	Milwaukee	92	62	.597	Haney
1959	Los Angeles	88	68	.564	Alston
1960	Pittsburgh	95	59	.617	Murtaugh
1961	Cincinnati	93	61	.604	Hutchinson
1962	San Francisco	103	62	.624	Dark
1963	Los Angeles	99	63	.611	Alston
1964	St. Louis	93	69	.574	Keane
1965	Los Angeles	97	65	.599	Alston
1966	Los Angeles	95	67	.586	Alston
1967	St. Louis	101	60	.627	Schoendienst
1968	St. Louis	97	65	.599	Schoendienst

American League

Year	Winner	Won	Lost	Pct	Manager
1901	Chicago	83	53	.610	Griffith
1902	Philadelphia	83	53	.610	Mack
1903	Boston	91	47	.659	Collins
1904	Boston	95	59	.617	Collins
1905	Philadelphia	92	56	.622	Mack
1906	Chicago	93	58	.616	Jones
1907	Detroit	92	58	.613	Jennings
1908	Detroit	90	63	.588	Jennings
1909	Detroit	98	54	.645	Jennings
1910	Philadelphia	102	48	.680	Mack
1911	Philadelphia	101	50	.669	Mack
1912	Boston	105	47	.691	Stahl
1913	Philadelphia	96	57	.627	Mack
1914	Philadelphia	99	53	.651	Mack
1915	Boston	101	50	.669	Carrigan
1916	Boston	91	63	.591	Carrigan
1917	Chicago	100	54	.649	Rowland
1918	Boston	75	51	.595	Barrow
1919	Chicago	88	52	.629	Gleason
1920	Cleveland	98	56	.636	Speaker
1921	New York	98	55	.641	Huggins
1922	New York	94	60	.610	Huggins
1923	New York	98	54	.645	Huggins
1924	Washington	92	62	.597	Harris
1925	Washington	96	55	.636	Harris
1926	New York	91	63	.591	Huggins
1927	New York	110	44	.714	Huggins
1928	New York	101	53	.656	Huggins
1929	Philadelphia	104	46	.693	Mack
1930	Philadelphia	102	52	.662	Mack
1931	Philadelphia	107	45	.704	Mack
1932	New York	107	47	.695	McCarthy
1933	Washington	99	53	.651	Cronin
1934	Detroit	101	53	.656	Cochrane
1935	Detroit	93	58	.616	Cochrane
1936	New York	102	51	.667	McCarthy
1937	New York	102	52	.662	McCarthy
1938	New York	99	53	.651	McCarthy
1939	New York	106	45	.702	McCarthy
1940	Detroit	90	64	.584	Baker
1941	New York	101	53	.656	McCarthy
1942	New York	103	51	.669	McCarthy
1943	New York	98	56	.636	McCarthy
1944	St. Louis	89	65	.578	Sewell
1945	Detroit	88	65	.575	O'Neill
1946	Boston	104	50	.675	Cronin
1947	New York	97	57	.630	Harris
1948	Cleveland	97	58	.626	Boudreau
1949	New York	97	57	.630	Stengel
1950	New York	98	56	.636	Stengel
1951	New York	98	56	.636	Stengel
1952	New York	95	59	.617	Stengel
1953	New York	99	52	.656	Stengel
1954	Cleveland	111	43	.721	Lopez
1955	New York	96	58	.623	Stengel
1956	New York	97	57	.630	Stengel
1957	New York	98	56	.636	Stengel
1958	New York	92	62	.597	Stengel
1959	Chicago	94	60	.610	Lopez
1960	New York	97	57	.630	Stengel
1961	New York	109	53	.673	Houk
1962	New York	96	66	.593	Houk
1963	New York	104	57	.646	Houk
1964	New York	99	63	.611	Berra
1965	Minnesota	102	60	.630	Mele
1966	Baltimore	97	63	.606	Bauer
1967	Boston	92	70	.568	Williams
1968	Detroit	103	59	.636	Smith

National League

Year	East Winner	W	L	Pct	Manager	West Winner	W	L	Pct	Manager	Playoff winner
1969	N.Y. Mets	100	62	.617	Hodges	Atlanta	93	69	.574	Harris	New York
1970	Pittsburgh	89	73	.549	Murtaugh	Cincinnati	102	60	.630	Anderson	Cincinnati
1971	Pittsburgh	97	65	.599	Murtaugh	San Francisco	90	72	.556	Fox	Pittsburgh
1972	Pittsburgh	96	59	.619	Virdon	Cincinnati	95	59	.617	Anderson	Cincinnati
1973	N.Y. Mets	82	79	.509	Berra	Cincinnati	99	63	.611	Anderson	New York
1974	Pittsburgh	88	74	.543	Murtaugh	Los Angeles	102	60	.630	Alston	Los Angeles
1975	Pittsburgh	92	69	.571	Murtaugh	Cincinnati	108	54	.667	Anderson	Cincinnati
1976	Philadelphia	101	61	.623	Ozark	Cincinnati	102	60	.630	Anderson	Cincinnati
1977	Philadelphia	101	61	.623	Ozark	Los Angeles	98	64	.605	Lasorda	Los Angeles
1978	Philadelphia	90	72	.556	Ozark	Los Angeles	95	67	.586	Lasorda	Los Angeles
1979	Pittsburgh	98	64	.605	Tanner	Cincinnati	90	71	.559	McNamara	Pittsburgh

	East					West					Playoff
Year	Winner	W	L	Pct	Manager	Winner	W	L	Pct	Manager	winner
1980	Philadelphia .	91	71	.562	Green	Houston	93	70	.571	Virdon	Philadelphia
1981(a)	Philadelphia .	34	21	.618	Green	Los Angeles . . .	36	21	.632	Lasorda	(c)
1981(b)	Montreal . . .	30	23	.566	Williams, Fanning	Houston	33	20	.623	Virdon	Los Angeles
1982	St. Louis . . .	92	70	.568	Herzog	Atlanta	89	73	.549	Torre	St. Louis
1983	Philadelphia .	90	72	.556	Corrales, Owens	Los Angeles . . .	91	71	.562	Lasorda	Philadelphia
1984	Chicago. . . .	96	65	.596	Frey	San Diego	92	70	.568	Williams	San Diego
1985	St. Louis . . .	101	61	.623	Herzog	Los Angeles . . .	95	67	.586	Lasorda	St. Louis
1986	N.Y. Mets. . .	108	54	.667	Johnson	Houston	96	66	.593	Lanier	New York
1987	St. Louis . . .	95	67	.586	Herzog	San Francisco . .	90	72	.556	Craig	St. Louis

American League

	East					West					Playoff
Year	Winner	W	L	Pct	Manager	Winner	W	L	Pct	Manager	winner
1969	Baltimore . . .	109	53	.673	Weaver	Minnesota	97	65	.599	Martin	Baltimore
1970	Baltimore . . .	108	54	.667	Weaver	Minnesota	98	64	.605	Rigney	Baltimore
1971	Baltimore . . .	101	57	.639	Weaver	Oakland	101	60	.627	Williams	Baltimore
1972	Detroit	86	70	.551	Martin	Oakland	93	62	.600	Williams	Oakland
1973	Baltimore . . .	97	65	.599	Weaver	Oakland	94	68	.580	Williams	Oakland
1974	Baltimore . . .	91	71	.562	Weaver	Oakland	90	72	.556	Dark	Oakland
1975	Boston.	95	65	.594	Johnson	Oakland	98	64	.605	Dark	Boston
1976	New York . . .	97	62	.610	Martin	Kansas City	90	72	.556	Herzog	New York
1977	New York . . .	100	62	.617	Martin	Kansas City	102	60	.630	Herzog	New York
1978	New York . . .	100	63	.613	Martin, Lemon	Kansas City	92	70	.568	Herzog	New York
1979	Baltimore . . .	102	57	.642	Weaver	California.	88	74	.543	Fregosi	Baltimore
1980	New York . . .	103	59	.636	Howser	Kansas City	97	65	.599	Frey	Kansas City
1981(a)	New York . . .	34	22	.607	Michael	Oakland	37	23	.617	Martin	(d)
1981(b)	Milwaukee . .	31	22	.585	Rodgers	Kansas City	30	23	.566	Frey, Howser	New York
1982	Milwaukee . .	95	67	.586	Rodgers, Kuenn	California.	93	69	.574	Mauch	Milwaukee
1983	Baltimore . . .	98	64	.605	Altobelli	Chicago	99	63	.611	LaRussa	Baltimore
1984	Detroit	104	58	.642	Anderson	Kansas City	84	78	.519	Howser	Detroit
1985	Toronto	99	62	.615	Cox	Kansas City	91	71	.562	Howser	Kansas City
1986	Boston.	95	66	.590	McNamara	California.	92	70	.568	Mauch	Boston
1987	Detroit	98	64	.605	Anderson	Minnesota	85	77	.525	Kelly	Minnesota

(a) First half; (b) Second half, (c) Montreal and L.A. won the divisional playoffs; (d) N.Y. and Oakland won the divisional playoffs.

Baseball Stadiums

National League

Team		Surface	Home run distances (ft.) LF	Center	RF	Seating capacity
Atlanta Braves.	Atlanta-Fulton County Stadium	Natural grass	330	402	330	52,003
Chicago Cubs	Wrigley Field.	Natural grass	355	400	353	38,143
Cincinnati Reds	Riverfront Stadium	Artificial	330	404	330	52,392
Houston Astros	Astrodome	Artificial	330	400	330	45,000
Los Angeles Dodgers. . . .	Dodger Stadium.	Natural grass	330	395	330	56,000
Montreal Expos	Olympic Stadium	Artificial	325	404	325	59,123
New York Mets	Shea Stadium	Natural grass	000	410	000	55,001
Philadelphia Phillies	Veterans Stadium.	Artificial	330	408	330	64,538
Pittsburgh Pirates	Three Rivers Stadium.	Artificial	335	400	335	54,438
St. Louis Cardinals	Busch Stadium	Artificial	330	414	330	53,138
San Diego Padres.	Jack Murphy Stadium	Natural grass	330	405	330	58,433
San Francisco Giants	Candlestick Park	Natural grass	335	400	335	58,000

American League

Team		Surface	LF	Center	RF	Seating capacity
Baltimore Orioles	Memorial Stadium.	Natural grass	309	405	309	54,002
Boston Red Sox.	Fenway Park.	Natural grass	315	420	302	33,583
California Angels	Anaheim Stadium	Natural grass	333	404	333	64,573
Chicago White Sox	Comiskey Park	Natural grass	347	409	347	44,087
Cleveland Indians	Cleveland Stadium	Natural grass	320	400	320	74,208
Detroit Tigers	Tiger Stadium	Natural grass	340	440	325	52,806
Kansas City Royals	Royals Stadium	Artificial	330	410	330	40,625
Milwaukee Brewers	Milwaukee County Stadium	Natural grass	315	402	315	53,192
Minnesota Twins.	Hubert H. Humphrey Metrodome	Artificial	343	408	327	55,244
New York Yankees	Yankee Stadium.	Natural grass	312	410	310	57,545
Oakland A's	Oakland Coliseum	Natural grass	330	400	330	49,219
Seattle Mariners.	Kingdome	Artificial	316	410	316	59,438
Texas Rangers	Arlington Stadium	Natural grass	330	400	330	43,508
Toronto Blue Jays.	Exhibition Stadium.	Artificial	330	400	330	43,737

Molitor Hits in 39 Consecutive Games

Paul Molitor of the Milwaukee Brewers hit safely in 39 consecutive games during the 1987 season. It was the fifth longest hitting streak in modern major league history. The following are the longest consecutive-game hitting streaks since 1900.

Player, Team, Year	Games
Joe DiMaggio, New York (A), 1941	56
Pete Rose, Cincinnati, 1978	44
George Sisler, St. Louis (A), 1922	41
Ty Cobb, Detroit, 1911	40
Paul Molitor, Milwaukee, 1987	39
Tommy Holmes, Boston (N), 1945	37
Ty Cobb, Detroit, 1917	35
Dom DiMaggio, Boston (A), 1949	34
Benito Santiago, 1987	34
George McQuinn, St. Louis (A), 1938	34
George Sisler, St. Louis (A), 1925	34
Heinie Manush, Washington, 1933	33
Rogers Hornsby, St. Louis (N), 1922	33
Ken Landreaux, Minnesota, 1980	31
Rico Carty, Atlanta, 1970	31
Willie Davis, Los Angeles, 1969	31
Sam Rice, Washington, 1924	31
George Brett, Kansas City, 1980	30
Ron LeFlore, Detroit, 1976	30
Stan Musial, St. Louis (N), 1950	30
Goose Goslin, Detroit, 1934	30
Tris Speaker, Boston (A), 1912	30

Home Run Leaders

National League

Year		HR
1925	Rogers Hornsby, St. Louis	39
1926	Hack Wilson, Chicago	21
1927	Hack Wilson, Chicago; Cy Williams, Philadelphia	30
1928	Hack Wilson, Chicago; Jim Bottomley, St. Louis	31
1929	Charles Klein, Philadelphia	43
1930	Hack Wilson, Chicago	56
1931	Charles Klein, Philadelphia	31
1932	Charles Klein, Philadelphia, Mel Ott, New York	38
1933	Charles Klein, Philadelphia	28
1934	Collins, St. Louis; Mel Ott, New York	35
1935	Walter Berger, Boston	34
1936	Mel Ott, New York	33
1937	Mel Ott, New York; Joe Medwick, St. Louis	31
1938	Mel Ott, New York	36
1939	John Mize, St. Louis	28
1940	John Mize, St. Louis	43
1941	Dolph Camilli, Brooklyn	34
1942	Mel Ott, New York	30
1943	Bill Nicholson, Chicago	29
1944	Bill Nicholson, Chicago	33
1945	Tommy Holmes, Boston	28
1946	Ralph Kiner, Pittsburgh	23
1947	Ralph Kiner, Pittsburgh; John Mize, New York	51
1948	Ralph Kiner, Pittsburgh; John Mize, New York	40
1949	Ralph Kiner, Pittsburgh	54
1950	Ralph Kiner, Pittsburgh	47
1951	Ralph Kiner, Pittsburgh	42
1952	Ralph Kiner, Pittsburgh; Hank Sauer, Chicago	37
1953	Ed Mathews, Milwaukee	47
1954	Ted Kluszewski, Cincinnati	49
1955	Willie Mays, New York	51
1956	Duke Snider, Brooklyn	43
1957	Hank Aaron, Milwaukee	44
1958	Ernie Banks, Chicago	47
1959	Ed Mathews, Milwaukee	46
1960	Ernie Banks, Chicago	41
1961	Orlando Cepeda, San Francisco	46
1962	Willie Mays, San Francisco	49
1963	Hank Aaron, Milwaukee, Willie McCovey, San Francisco	44
1964	Willie Mays, San Francisco	47
1965	Willie Mays, San Francisco	52
1966	Hank Aaron, Atlanta	44
1967	Hank Aaron, Atlanta	39
1968	Willie McCovey, San Francisco	36
1969	Willie McCovey, San Francisco	45
1970	Johnny Bench, Cincinnati	45
1971	Willie Stargell, Pittsburgh	48
1972	Johnny Bench, Cincinnati	40
1973	Willie Stargell, Pittsburgh	44
1974	Mike Schmidt, Philadelphia	36
1975	Mike Schmidt, Philadelphia	38
1976	Mike Schmidt, Philadelphia	38
1977	George Foster, Cincinnati	52
1978	George Foster, Cincinnati	40
1979	Dave Kingman, Chicago	48
1980	Mike Schmidt, Philadelphia	48
1981	Mike Schmidt, Philadelphia	31
1982	Dave Kingman, New York	37
1983	Mike Schmidt, Philadelphia	40
1984	Mike Schmidt, Phil.; Dale Murphy, Atlanta	36
1985	Dale Murphy, Atlanta	37
1986	Mike Schmidt, Philadelphia	37
1987	Andre Dawson, Chicago	49

American League

Year		HR
1925	Bob Meusel, New York	33
1926	Babe Ruth, New York	47
1927	Babe Ruth, New York	60
1928	Babe Ruth, New York	54
1929	Babe Ruth, New York	46
1930	Babe Ruth, New York	49
1931	Babe Ruth, Lou Gehrig, New York	46
1932	Jimmy Foxx, Philadelphia	58
1933	Jimmy Foxx, Philadelphia	48
1934	Lou Gehrig, New York	49
1935	Jimmy Foxx, Philadelphia, Hank Greenberg, Detroit	36
1936	Lou Gehrig, New York	49
1937	Joe DiMaggio, New York	46
1938	Hank Greenberg, Detroit	58
1939	Jimmy Foxx, Boston	35
1940	Hank Greenberg, Detroit	41
1941	Ted Williams, Boston	37
1942	Ted Williams, Boston	36
1943	Rudy York, Detroit	34
1944	Nick Etten, New York	22
1945	Vern Stephens, St. Louis	24
1946	Hank Greenberg, Detroit	44
1947	Ted Williams, Boston	32
1948	Joe DiMaggio, New York	39
1949	Ted Williams, Boston	43
1950	Al Rosen, Cleveland	37
1951	Gus Zernial, Chicago-Philadelphia	33
1952	Larry Doby, Cleveland	32
1953	Al Rosen, Cleveland	43
1954	Larry Doby, Cleveland	32
1955	Mickey Mantle, New York	37
1956	Mickey Mantle, New York	52
1957	Roy Sievers, Washington	42
1958	Mickey Mantle, New York	42
1959	Rocky Colavito, Cleveland, Harmon Killebrew, Washington	42
1960	Mickey Mantle, New York	40
1961	Roger Maris, New York	61
1962	Harmon Killebrew, Minnesota	48
1963	Harmon Killebrew, Minnesota	45
1964	Harmon Killebrew, Minnesota	49
1965	Tony Conigliaro, Boston	32
1966	Frank Robinson, Baltimore	49
1967	Carl Yastrzemski, Boston, Harmon Killebrew, Minn.	44
1968	Frank Howard, Washington	44
1969	Harmon Killebrew, Minnesota	49
1970	Frank Howard, Washington	44
1971	Bill Melton, Chicago	33
1972	Dick Allen, Chicago	37
1973	Reggie Jackson, Oakland	32
1974	Dick Allen, Chicago	32
1975	George Scott, Milwaukee; Reggie Jackson, Oakland	36
1976	Graig Nettles, New York	32
1977	Jim Rice, Boston	39
1978	Jim Rice, Boston	46
1979	Gorman Thomas, Milwaukee	45
1980	Reggie Jackson, New York; Ben Oglivie, Milwaukee	41
1981	Bobby Grich, California; Tony Armas, Oakland; Dwight Evans, Boston; Eddie Murray, Baltimore	22
1982	Gorman Thomas, Milwaukee; Reggie Jackson, California	39
1983	Jim Rice, Boston	39
1984	Tony Armas, Boston	43
1985	Darrell Evans, Detroit	40
1986	Jesse Barfield, Toronto	40
1987	Mark McGwire, Oakland	49

Runs Batted In Leaders

National League

Year		RBI
1952	Hank Sauer, Chicago	121
1953	Roy Campanella, Brooklyn	142
1954	Ted Kluszewski, Cincinnati	141
1955	Duke Snider, Brooklyn	136
1956	Stan Musial, St. Louis	109
1957	Hank Aaron, Milwaukee	132
1958	Ernie Banks, Chicago	129
1959	Ernie Banks, Chicago	143
1960	Hank Aaron, Milwaukee	126
1961	Orlando Cepeda, San Francisco	142
1962	Tommy Davis, Los Angeles	153
1963	Hank Aaron, Milwaukee	130
1964	Ken Boyer, St. Louis	119
1965	Deron Johnson, Cincinnati	130

American League

Year		RBI
1952	Al Rosen, Cleveland	105
1953	Al Rosen, Cleveland	145
1954	Larry Doby, Cleveland	126
1955	Ray Boone, Detroit, Jack Jensen, Boston	116
1956	Mickey Mantle, New York	130
1957	Roy Sievers, Washington	114
1958	Jack Jensen, Boston	122
1959	Jack Jensen, Boston	112
1960	Roger Maris, New York	112
1961	Roger Maris, New York	142
1962	Harmon Killebrew, Minnesota	126
1963	Dick Stuart, Boston	118
1964	Brooks Robinson, Baltimore	118
1965	Rocky Colavito, Cleveland	108

Year		RBI
1966	Hank Aaron, Atlanta	127
1967	Orlando Cepeda, St. Louis	111
1968	Willie McCovey, San Francisco	105
1969	Willie McCovey, San Francisco	126
1970	Johnny Bench, Cincinnati	148
1971	Joe Torre, St. Louis	137
1972	Johnny Bench, Cincinnati	125
1973	Willie Stargell, Pittsburgh	119
1974	Johnny Bench, Cincinnati	129
1975	Greg Luzinski, Philadelphia	120
1976	George Foster, Cincinnati	121
1977	George Foster, Cincinnati	149
1978	George Foster, Cincinnati	120
1979	Dave Winfield, San Diego	118
1980	Mike Schmidt, Philadelphia	121
1981	Mike Schmidt, Philadelphia	91
1982	Dale Murphy, Atlanta; Al Oliver, Montreal	109
1983	Dale Murphy, Atlanta	121
1984	Mike Schmidt, Phil.; Gary Carter, Montreal	106
1985	Dave Parker, Cincinnati	125
1986	Mike Schmidt, Philadelphia	119
1987	Andre Dawson, Chicago	137

Year		RBI
1966	Frank Robinson, Baltimore	122
1967	Carl Yastrzemski, Boston	121
1968	Ken Harrelson, Boston	109
1969	Harmon Killebrew, Minnesota	140
1970	Frank Howard, Washington	126
1971	Harmon Killebrew, Minnesota	119
1972	Dick Allen, Chicago	113
1973	Reggie Jackson, Oakland	117
1974	Jeff Burroughs, Texas	118
1975	George Scott, Milwaukee	109
1976	Lee May, Baltimore	109
1977	Larry Hisle, Minnesota	119
1978	Jim Rice, Boston	139
1979	Don Baylor, California	139
1980	Cecil Cooper, Milwaukee	122
1981	Eddie Murray, Baltimore	78
1982	Hal McRae, Kansas City	133
1983	Cecil Cooper, Milwaukee; Jim Rice, Boston	126
1984	Tony Armas, Boston	123
1985	Don Mattingly, New York	145
1986	Joe Carter, Cleveland	121
1987	George Bell, Toronto	134

Batting Champions

National League

Year	Player	Club	Pct.
1924	Rogers Hornsby	St. Louis	.424
1925	Rogers Hornsby	St. Louis	.403
1926	Eugene Hargrave	Cincinnati	.353
1927	Paul Waner	Pittsburgh	.380
1928	Rogers Hornsby	Boston	.387
1929	Lefty O'Doul	Philadelphia	.398
1930	Bill Terry	New York	.401
1931	Chick Hafey	St. Louis	.349
1932	Lefty O'Doul	Brooklyn	.368
1933	Charles Klein	Philadelphia	.368
1934	Paul Waner	Pittsburgh	.362
1935	Arky Vaughan	Pittsburgh	.385
1936	Paul Waner	Pittsburgh	.373
1937	Joe Medwick	St. Louis	.374
1938	Ernie Lombardi	Cincinnati	.342
1939	John Mize	St. Louis	.349
1940	Debs Garms	Pittsburgh	.355
1941	Pete Reiser	Brooklyn	.343
1942	Ernie Lombardi	Boston	.330
1943	Stan Musial	St. Louis	.357
1944	Dixie Walker	Brooklyn	.357
1945	Phil Cavarretta	Chicago	.355
1946	Stan Musial	St. Louis	.365
1947	Harry Walker	Philadelphia	.363
1948	Stan Musial	St. Louis	.376
1949	Jackie Robinson	Brooklyn	.342
1950	Stan Musial	St. Louis	.346
1951	Stan Musial	St. Louis	.355
1952	Stan Musial	St. Louis	.336
1953	Carl Furillo	Brooklyn	.344
1954	Willie Mays	New York	.345
1955	Richie Ashburn	Philadelphia	.338
1956	Hank Aaron	Milwaukee	.328
1957	Stan Musial	St. Louis	.351
1958	Richie Ashburn	Philadelphia	.350
1959	Hank Aaron	Milwaukee	.355
1960	Dick Groat	Pittsburgh	.325
1961	Roberto Clemente	Pittsburgh	.351
1962	Tommy Davis	Los Angeles	.346
1963	Tommy Davis	Los Angeles	.326
1964	Roberto Clemente	Pittsburgh	.339
1965	Roberto Clemente	Pittsburgh	.329
1966	Matty Alou	Pittsburgh	.342
1967	Roberto Clemente	Pittsburgh	.357
1968	Pete Rose	Cincinnati	.335
1969	Pete Rose	Cincinnati	.348
1970	Rico Carty	Atlanta	.366
1971	Joe Torre	St. Louis	.363
1972	Billy Williams	Chicago	.333
1973	Pete Rose	Cincinnati	.338
1974	Ralph Garr	Atlanta	.353
1975	Bill Madlock	Chicago	.354
1976	Bill Madlock	Chicago	.339
1977	Dave Parker	Pittsburgh	.338
1978	Dave Parker	Pittsburgh	.334
1979	Keith Hernandez	St. Louis	.344
1980	Bill Buckner	Chicago	.324
1981	Bill Madlock	Pittsburgh	.341
1982	Al Oliver	Montreal	.331
1983	Bill Madlock	Pittsburgh	.323
1984	Tony Gwynn	San Diego	.351
1985	Willie McGee	St. Louis	.353
1986	Tim Raines	Montreal	.334
1987	Tony Gwynn	San Diego	.369

American League

Year	Player	Club	Pct.
1924	Babe Ruth	New York	.378
1925	Harry Heilmann	Detroit	.393
1926	Henry Manush	Detroit	.378
1927	Harry Heilmann	Detroit	.398
1928	Goose Goslin	Washington	.379
1929	Lew Fonseca	Cleveland	.369
1930	Al Simmons	Philadelphia	.381
1931	Al Simmons	Philadelphia	.390
1932	Dale Alexander	Detroit-Boston	.367
1933	Jimmy Foxx	Philadelphia	.356
1934	Lou Gehrig	New York	.363
1935	Buddy Myer	Washington	.349
1936	Luke Appling	Chicago	.388
1937	Charlie Gehringer	Detroit	.371
1938	Jimmy Foxx	Boston	.349
1939	Joe DiMaggio	New York	.381
1940	Joe DiMaggio	New York	.352
1941	Ted Williams	Boston	.406
1942	Ted Williams	Boston	.356
1943	Luke Appling	Chicago	.328
1944	Lou Boudreau	Cleveland	.327
1945	George Stirnweiss	New York	.309
1946	Mickey Vernon	Washington	.353
1947	Ted Williams	Boston	.343
1948	Ted Williams	Boston	.369
1949	George Kell	Detroit	.343
1950	Billy Goodman	Boston	.354
1951	Ferris Fain	Philadelphia	.344
1952	Ferris Fain	Philadelphia	.327
1953	Mickey Vernon	Washington	.337
1954	Roberto Avila	Cleveland	.341
1955	Al Kaline	Detroit	.340
1956	Mickey Mantle	New York	.353
1957	Ted Williams	Boston	.388
1958	Ted Williams	Boston	.328
1959	Harvey Kuenn	Detroit	.353
1960	Pete Runnels	Boston	.320
1961	Norm Cash	Detroit	.361
1962	Pete Runnels	Boston	.326
1963	Carl Yastrzemski	Boston	.321
1964	Tony Oliva	Minnesota	.323
1965	Tony Oliva	Minnesota	.321
1966	Frank Robinson	Baltimore	.316
1967	Carl Yastrzemski	Boston	.326
1968	Carl Yastrzemski	Boston	.301
1969	Rod Carew	Minnesota	.332
1970	Alex Johnson	California	.328
1971	Tony Oliva	Minnesota	.337
1972	Rod Carew	Minnesota	.318
1973	Rod Carew	Minnesota	.350
1974	Rod Carew	Minnesota	.364
1975	Rod Carew	Minnesota	.359
1976	George Brett	Kansas City	.333
1977	Rod Carew	Minnesota	.388
1978	Rod Carew	Minnesota	.333
1979	Fred Lynn	Boston	.333
1980	George Brett	Kansas City	.390
1981	Carney Lansford	Boston	.336
1982	Willie Wilson	Kansas City	.332
1983	Wade Boggs	Boston	.361
1984	Don Mattingly	New York	.343
1985	Wade Boggs	Boston	.368
1986	Wade Boggs	Boston	.357
1987	Wade Boggs	Boston	.363

National League Records in 1987

Final standings

Eastern Division

Club	W	L	Pct	GB
St. Louis	95	67	.586	—
New York	92	70	.568	3
Montreal	91	71	.562	4
Philadelphia	80	82	.494	15
Pittsburgh	80	82	.494	15
Chicago	76	85	.472	18½

Western Division

Club	W	L	Pct	GB
San Francisco	90	72	.556	—
Cincinnati	84	78	.519	6
Houston	76	86	.469	14
Los Angeles	73	89	.451	17
Atlanta	69	92	.429	20½
San Diego	65	97	.401	25

National League Championship Series

St. Louis 5, San Francisco 3
San Francisco 5, St. Louis 0
St. Louis 6, San Francisco 5
San Francisco 4, St. Louis 2
San Francisco 6, St. Louis 3
St. Louis 1, San Francisco 0
St. Louis 6, San Francisco 0

Club Batting

Club	Pct	AB	R	H	HR	SB
New York	**.268**	5601	823	1499	192	159
Cincinnati	**.266**	5560	783	1478	192	169
Montreal	**.265**	5527	741	1467	120	166
Pittsburgh	**.264**	5536	723	1464	131	140
Chicago	**.264**	5583	720	1475	209	109
St. Louis	**.263**	5500	798	1449	94	248
San Diego	**.260**	5456	668	1419	113	198
San Francisco	**.260**	5608	783	1458	205	126
Atlanta	**.258**	5428	747	1401	152	135
Philadelphia	**.254**	5475	702	1390	169	111
Houston	**.253**	5485	648	1386	122	162
Los Angeles	**.252**	5517	635	1389	125	128

Club Pitching

Club	ERA	CG	IP	H	R	BB	SO
San Francisco	**3.68**	19	1471	1407	669	547	1038
Los Angeles	**3.72**	29	1455	1415	675	565	1097
Houston	**3.84**	13	1441	1363	678	525	1137
New York	**3.84**	16	1454	1407	698	510	1032
St. Louis	**3.91**	10	1466	1484	693	533	873
Montreal	**3.92**	16	1450	1428	720	446	1012
Philadelphia	**4.18**	13	1448	1453	749	587	877
Pittsburgh	**4.20**	25	1445	1377	744	562	914
Cincinnati	**4.24**	7	1452	1486	752	485	919
San Diego	**4.27**	14	1433	1402	763	602	897
Chicago	**4.55**	11	1434	1524	801	628	1024
Atlanta	**4.63**	16	1427	1529	829	587	837

Individual Batting

Leaders—Based on 502 plate appearances.

Player, club	Pct	AB	R	H	HR	RBI
Gwynn, San Diego	**.370**	589	119	218	7	54
Guerrero, Los Angeles	**.338**	545	89	184	27	89
Raines, Montreal	**.330**	530	123	175	18	68
Kruk, San Diego	**.313**	447	72	140	20	91
James, Atlanta	**.312**	494	80	154	10	61
Clark, San Francisco	**.308**	529	89	163	35	91
Galarraga, Montreal	**.305**	551	72	168	13	90
Smith, St. Louis	**.303**	600	104	182	0	75
Thompson, Philadelphia	**.302**	527	86	159	7	43
Bonilla, Pittsburgh	**.300**	466	58	140	15	77

Individual Pitching

Leaders—Based on 162 inning.

Pitcher, club	W	L	ERA	G	IP	H	BB	SO
Ryan, Houston	8	16	**2.76**	34	211	154	87	270
Dunne, Pittsburgh	13	6	**3.03**	23	163	143	68	72
Hershiser, Los Angeles	16	16	**3.06**	37	264	247	74	190
Reuschel, Pitts.-S.F.	13	9	**3.09**	34	227	207	42	107
Gooden, New York	15	7	**3.21**	25	179	162	53	148
Welch, Los Angeles	15	9	**3.22**	35	251	204	86	196
Scott, Houston	16	13	**3.23**	36	247	199	79	233
Dravecky, S.D.-S.F.	10	12	**3.43**	48	191	186	64	138
Magrane, St. Louis	9	7	**3.54**	27	170	157	60	101
Hammaker, San Francisco	10	10	**3.58**	31	168	159	57	107

Individual Batting (at least 115 at-bats); Individual Pitching (at least 50 innings)

Atlanta Braves

Batting	Avg	AB	R	H	HR	RBI
James	**.312**	494	80	154	10	61
Murphy	**.295**	566	115	167	44	105
Griffey	**.286**	399	65	114	14	64
Hall	**.284**	292	54	83	3	24
Oberkfell	**.280**	508	59	142	3	48
Simmons	**.277**	177	20	49	4	30
Perry	**.270**	533	77	144	12	74
Hubbard	**.264**	443	69	117	5	38
Ramirez	**.263**	179	22	47	1	21
Virgil	**.247**	429	57	106	27	72
Blauser	**.242**	165	11	40	2	15
Thomas	**.231**	324	29	75	5	39
Roenicke	**.219**	151	25	33	9	28
Nettles	**.209**	177	16	37	5	33

Pitching	W	L	ERA	IP	BB	SO	Sv
Dedmon	3	4	**3.91**	89	42	40	4
Z. Smith	15	10	**4.09**	242	91	130	
Alexander	5	10	**4.13**	117	27	64	
Acker	4	9	**4.16**	114	51	68	14
Puleo	6	8	**4.23**	123	40	99	
Garber	8	10	**4.41**	69	28	48	10
Palmer	8	11	**4.90**	152	64	111	
Mahler	8	13	**4.98**	197	85	95	
Assenmacher	1	1	**5.10**	54	24	39	2
Glavine	2	4	**5.54**	50	33	20	

Chicago Cubs

Batting	Avg	AB	R	H	HR	RBI
Mumphrey	**.333**	309	41	103	13	44
Dernier	**.317**	199	38	63	8	21
Sandberg	**.294**	523	81	154	16	59
Trillo	**.294**	214	27	63	8	26
Martinez	**.292**	459	70	134	8	36
Dawson	**.287**	621	90	178	49	137
Dayett	**.277**	177	20	49	5	25
Palmeiro	**.276**	221	32	61	14	30
Durham	**.273**	439	70	120	27	63
Moreland	**.266**	563	63	150	27	88
J. Davis	**.248**	428	57	106	19	51
Dunston	**.246**	346	40	85	5	22
Noce	**.228**	180	17	41	3	14
Sundberg	**.201**	139	9	28	4	15

Pitching	W	L	ERA	IP	BB	SO	Sv
Trout	6	3	**3.00**	75	27	32	
Smith	4	10	**3.12**	83	32	96	36
DiPino	3	3	**3.15**	80	34	61	4
Noles	4	2	**3.50**	64	27	33	2
Sutcliffe	18	10	**3.68**	237	106	174	
Sanderson	8	9	**4.29**	144	50	106	2
Lancaster	8	3	**4.90**	132	51	78	
Moyer	12	15	**5.10**	201	97	147	
Lynch	2	9	**5.38**	110	48	80	4
Maddux	6	14	**5.61**	155	74	101	

Cincinnati Reds

Batting	Avg	AB	R	H	HR	RBI
Daniels	.334	368	73	123	26	64
Concepcion	.319	279	32	89	1	33
Davis	.293	474	120	139	37	100
Jones	.290	359	53	104	10	44
Bell	.284	522	74	148	17	70
Esasky	.272	346	48	94	22	59
Diaz	.270	496	49	134	15	82
Stillwell	.258	395	54	102	4	33
O'Neill	.256	160	24	41	7	28
Oester	.253	237	28	60	2	23
Parker	.253	589	77	149	26	97
Larkin	.244	439	64	107	12	43
Francona	.227	207	16	47	3	12

Pitching	W	L	ERA	IP	BB	SO	Sv
Williams	4	0	2.30	105	39	60	2
Franco	8	5	2.52	82	227	61	32
Murphy	8	5	3.04	100	32	99	3
Perry	5	2	3.56	81	25	39	2
Robinson	7	5	3.68	154	43	99	4
Hoffman	9	10	4.37	158	49	87	
Power	10	13	4.50	204	71	133	
Landrum	3	2	4.71	65	34	42	2
Gullickson	10	11	4.85	165	39	89	
Browning	10	13	5.02	183	61	117	
Hume	2	4	5.36	84	43	33	

Houston Astros

Batting	Avg	AB	R	H	HR	RBI
Young	.321	274	44	88	1	15
Hatcher	.296	564	96	167	11	63
Ashby	.288	386	53	111	14	63
Bass	.284	592	83	168	19	85
Doran	.283	625	82	177	16	79
Walling	.283	325	45	92	5	33
C. Reynolds	.254	374	35	95	4	28
Davis	.251	578	70	145	27	93
Caminiti	.246	203	10	50	3	23
Cruz	.241	365	47	88	11	38
Puhl	.230	122	9	28	2	15

Pitching	W	L	ERA	IP	BB	SO	Sv
Smith	2	3	1.65	60	21	73	24
Ryan	8	16	2.76	211	87	270	
Scott	16	13	3.23	247	79	233	
Andersen	9	5	3.45	101	41	94	5
Darwin	9	10	3.59	195	69	134	
Deshales	11	6	4.62	152	57	104	
Knepper	8	17	5.27	177	54	76	

Los Angeles Dodgers

Batting	Avg	AB	R	H	HR	RBI
Guerrero	.338	545	89	184	27	89
Marshall	.294	402	45	118	16	72
Hatcher	.282	287	27	81	7	42
Sax	.280	610	84	171	6	46
Shelby	.277	476	61	132	21	69
Scioscia	.265	461	44	122	6	38
Anderson	.234	265	32	62	1	13
Stubbs	.233	386	48	90	16	52
Ramsey	.232	125	18	29	0	12
Woodson	.228	136	14	31	1	11
Landrum	.222	117	13	26	1	10
Trevino	.222	144	16	32	3	16
Hoffman	.220	132	10	29	0	10
Duncan	.215	261	31	56	6	18
Garner	.206	238	29	49	5	23
Landreaux	.203	182	17	37	6	23

Pitching	W	L	ERA	IP	BB	SO	Sv
Hershiser	16	16	3.06	264	74	190	1
Welch	15	9	3.22	251	86	196	
Pena	2	7	3.50	87	37	76	11
Hillegas	4	3	3.57	58	31	51	
Holton	3	2	3.89	83	32	58	2
Valenzuela	14	14	3.98	251	124	190	
Young	5	8	4.47	54	17	42	11
Honeycutt	2	12	4.59	115	45	92	
Leary	3	11	4.76	107	36	61	1
Howell	3	4	4.91	55	29	60	1

Montreal Expos

Batting	Avg	AB	R	H	HR	RBI
Raines	.330	530	123	175	18	68
Galarraga	.305	551	72	168	13	90
Wallach	.298	593	89	177	26	123
Foley	.293	280	35	82	5	28
Webster	.281	588	101	165	15	63
Law	.273	436	52	119	12	56
Candaele	.272	449	62	122	1	23
Nichols	.265	147	22	39	4	20
Brooks	.263	430	57	113	14	72
Fitzgerald	.240	287	32	69	3	36
Winningham	.239	347	34	83	4	41
Reed	.213	207	15	44	1	21

Pitching	W	L	ERA	IP	BB	SO	Sv
Burke	7	0	1.19	91	17	58	18
Perez	7	0	2.30	70	16	58	
McGaffigan	5	2	2.39	120	42	100	12
Martinez	11	4	3.30	144	40	84	
McClure	6	1	3.44	52	20	33	5
St. Claire	3	3	4.03	67	20	43	7
Parrett	7	6	4.21	62	30	56	6
Smith	10	9	4.37	150	31	94	
Sebra	6	15	4.42	177	67	156	
Heaton	13	10	4.52	193	37	105	
Youmans	9	8	4.64	116	47	94	
Tibbs	4	5	4.99	83	34	54	

New York Mets

Batting	Avg	AB	R	H	HR	RBI
Magaden	.318	192	21	61	3	24
Teufel	.308	299	55	92	14	61
Mazzilli	.306	124	26	38	3	24
Wilson	.299	385	58	115	9	34
Hernandez	.290	587	87	170	18	80
Dykstra	.285	431	86	123	10	43
Strawberry	.284	532	108	151	39	104
McReynolds	.276	590	86	163	29	95
Johnson	.265	554	93	147	36	99
Santana	.255	439	41	112	5	44
Lyons	.254	130	15	33	4	24
Backman	.250	300	43	75	1	23
Carter	.235	523	55	123	20	83

Pitching	W	L	ERA	IP	BB	SO	Sv
Gooden	15	7	3.21	179	53	148	
Leach	11	1	3.22	131	29	61	
Sisk	3	1	3.46	78	22	37	3
Aguilera	11	3	3.60	115	33	77	
Cone	5	6	3.71	99	44	68	1
Fernandez	12	8	3.81	156	67	134	
Myers	3	6	3.96	75	30	92	6
Mitchell	3	6	4.11	111	36	57	
McDowell	7	5	4.16	88	28	32	25
Darling	12	8	4.29	207	96	167	
Orosco	3	9	4.44	77	31	78	16

Philadelphia Phillies

Batting	Avg	AB	R	H	HR	RBI
Thompson	.302	527	86	159	7	43
James	.293	358	48	105	17	54
Schmidt	.293	522	88	153	35	113
G. Gross	.286	133	14	38	1	12
Hayes	.277	556	84	154	21	84
Samuel	.272	655	113	178	28	100
Wilson	.264	569	55	150	14	54
Stone	.256	125	19	32	1	16
Parrish	.245	466	42	114	17	67
Schu	.235	196	24	46	7	23
Jeltz	.232	293	37	68	0	12
Aguayo	.206	209	25	43	12	21
Daulton	.194	129	10	25	3	13

Pitching	W	L	ERA	IP	BB	SO	Sv
Bedrosian	5	3	2.83	89	28	74	40
Tekulve	6	4	3.09	105	29	60	3
Ritchie	3	2	3.75	62	29	45	3
M. Jackson	3	10	4.20	109	56	93	1
Carman	13	11	4.22	211	69	125	
K. Gross	9	16	4.35	200	87	110	
Ruffin	11	14	4.35	204	73	93	
Rawley	17	11	4.39	229	86	123	

(continued)

Pittsburgh Pirates

Batting	Avg	AB	R	H	HR	RBI
Lind	.322	143	21	46	0	11
Bonilla	.300	466	58	140	15	77
LaValliere	.300	340	33	102	1	36
Pedrique	.294	252	24	74	1	27
Van Slyke	.293	564	93	165	21	82
Bream	.275	516	64	142	13	65
Cangelosi	.275	182	44	50	4	18
Ray	.273	472	48	129	5	54
Ortiz	.271	192	16	52	1	22
Morrison	.264	348	41	92	9	46
Bonds	.261	551	99	144	25	59
Reynolds	.260	335	47	87	7	51
Diaz	.241	241	28	58	16	48
Coles	.227	119	20	27	6	24
Belliard	.207	203	26	42	1	15

Pitching	W	L	ERA	IP	BB	SO	Sv
J. Robinson	8	9	2.85	123	54	101	14
Dunne	13	6	3.03	163	68	72	
Walk	8	2	3.31	117	51	78	
Gott	1	2	3.41	87	40	90	13
Drabek	11	12	3.88	176	46	120	
Fisher	11	9	4.52	185	72	117	
Taylor	2	3	5.74	53	28	37	
Smiley	5	5	5.76	75	50	58	4
Kipper	5	9	5.94	110	52	83	

St. Louis Cardinals

Batting	Avg	AB	R	H	HR	RBI
Smith	.303	600	104	182	0	75
Coleman	.289	623	121	180	3	43
Pendleton	.286	583	82	167	12	96
Clark	.286	419	93	120	35	106
Oquendo	.286	248	43	71	1	24
McGee	.285	620	76	177	11	105
Ford	.285	228	32	65	3	26
Herr	.263	510	73	134	2	83
Morris	.261	157	22	41	3	23
Lake	.251	179	19	45	2	19
Pena	.214	384	40	82	5	44
Lindeman	.208	207	20	43	8	28

Pitching	W	L	ERA	IP	BB	SO	Sv
Dayley	9	5	2.66	61	33	63	4
Worrell	8	6	2.66	94	34	92	33
Magrane	9	7	3.54	170	60	101	
Mathews	11	11	3.73	197	71	108	
Horton	8	3	3.82	125	42	55	7
Tudor	10	2	3.84	96	32	54	
Cox	11	9	3.88	199	71	101	
Forsch	11	7	4.32	179	45	89	
Dawley	5	8	4.47	96	38	65	2
Tunnell	4	4	4.84	74	34	49	
O'Neal	4	2	5.32	66	26	37	

San Diego Padres

Batting	Avg	AB	R	H	HR	RBI
Gwynn	.369	590	119	218	7	54
Kruk	.313	447	72	140	20	91
Ready	.309	350	69	108	12	54
Santiago	.300	546	64	164	18	79
Martinez	.273	447	59	122	15	70
Salazar	.254	189	13	48	3	17
Wynne	.250	188	17	47	2	24
Mack	.239	238	28	57	4	25
Brown	.237	287	34	68	12	40
Cora	.237	241	23	57	0	13
Jefferson	.230	422	59	97	8	29
Flannery	.228	276	23	63	0	20
Templeton	.222	510	42	113	5	48

Pitching	W	L	ERA	IP	BB	SO	Sv
Gossage	5	4	3.12	52	19	44	11
Booker	1	1	3.16	68	30	17	1
Nolte	2	6	3.21	67	36	44	
McCullers	8	10	3.72	123	59	126	16
Show	8	16	3.84	206	85	117	
M. Davis	9	8	3.99	133	59	98	2
Jones	9	7	4.14	145	54	51	
Grant	7	9	4.24	163	73	90	1
Comstock	2	1	4.61	56	31	59	1
Whitson	10	13	4.73	205	64	135	
Hawkins	3	10	5.05	117	49	51	
S. Davis	2	7	6.18	62	36	37	

San Francisco Giants

Batting	Avg	AB	R	H	HR	RBI
Aldrete	.325	357	50	116	9	51
Clark	.308	529	89	163	35	91
Maldonado	.292	442	69	129	20	85
Uribe	.291	309	44	90	5	30
Leonard	.280	503	70	141	19	63
Mitchell	.280	464	68	130	22	70
Brenly	.267	375	55	100	18	51
Thompson	.262	420	62	110	10	44
Milner	.252	214	38	54	4	19
C. Davis	.250	500	80	125	24	76
Speier	.249	317	39	79	11	39
Melvin	.199	246	31	49	11	31
Williams	.188	245	28	46	8	21

Pitching	W	L	ERA	IP	BB	SO	Sv
Reuschel	13	9	3.09	227	42	107	
Garrelts	11	7	3.22	106	55	127	12
D. Robinson	11	7	3.42	108	40	79	19
Dravecky	10	12	3.43	191	64	138	
Hammaker	10	10	3.58	168	57	107	
Downs	12	9	3.63	186	67	137	1
LaCross	13	10	3.68	171	63	79	
Lefferts	5	5	3.83	98	33	57	6
Krukow	5	6	4.80	163	46	104	

Earned-Run Average Leaders

National League

Year	Player, club	G	IP	ERA
1969	Juan Marichal, San Francisco	37	300	2.10
1970	Tom Seaver, New York	37	291	2.81
1971	Tom Seaver, New York	36	286	1.76
1972	Steve Carlton, Philadelphia	41	346	1.98
1973	Tom Seaver, New York	36	290	2.07
1974	Buzz Capra, Atlanta	39	217	2.28
1975	Randy Jones, San Diego	37	285	2.24
1976	John Denny, St. Louis	30	207	2.52
1977	John Candelaria, Pittsburgh	33	231	2.34
1978	Craig Swan, New York	29	207	2.43
1979	J. R. Richard, Houston	38	292	2.71
1980	Don Sutton, Los Angeles	32	212	2.21
1981	Nolan Ryan, Houston	21	149	1.69
1982	Steve Rogers, Montreal	35	277	2.40
1983	Atlee Hammaker, San Fran.	23	172	2.25
1984	Alejandro Pena, Los Angeles	28	199	2.48
1985	Dwight Gooden, New York	35	276	1.53
1986	Mike Scott, Houston	37	275	2.22
1987	Nolan Ryan, Houston	34	211	2.76

American League

Year	Player, club	G	IP	ERA
1969	Dick Bosman, Washington	31	193	2.19
1970	Diego Segui, Oakland	47	162	2.56
1971	Vida Blue, Oakland	39	312	1.82
1972	Luis Tiant, Boston	43	179	1.91
1973	Jim Palmer, Baltimore	38	296	2.40
1974	Catfish Hunter, Oakland	41	318	2.49
1975	Jim Palmer, Baltimore	39	323	2.09
1976	Mark Fidrych, Detroit	31	250	2.34
1977	Frank Tanana, California	31	241	2.54
1978	Ron Guidry, New York	35	274	1.74
1979	Ron Guidry, New York	33	236	2.78
1980	Rudy May, New York	41	175	2.47
1981	Steve McCatty, Oakland	22	186	2.32
1982	Rick Sutcliffe, Cleveland	34	216	2.96
1983	Rick Honeycutt, Texas	25	174	2.42
1984	Mike Boddicker, Baltimore	34	261	2.79
1986	Dave Stieb, Toronto	36	265	2.48
1986	Roger Clemens, Boston	33	254	2.48
1987	Jimmy Key, Toronto	36	261	2.76

ERA is computed by multiplying earned runs allowed by 9, then dividing by innings pitched.

Most Valuable Player

Baseball Writers' Association

National League

Year	Player, team
1931	Frank Frisch, St. Louis
1932	Charles Klein, Philadelpha
1933	Carl Hubbell, New York
1934	Dizzy Dean, St. Louis
1935	Gabby Hartnett, Chicago
1936	Carl Hubbell, New York
1937	Joe Medwick, St. Louis
1938	Ernie Lombardi, Cincinnati
1939	Bucky Walters, Cincinnati
1940	Frank McCormick, Cincinnati
1941	Dolph Camilli, Brooklyn
1942	Mort Cooper, St. Louis
1943	Stan Musial, St. Louis
1944	Martin Marion, St. Louis
1945	Phil Cavarretta, Chicago
1946	Stan Musial, St. Louis
1947	Bob Elliott, Boston
1948	Stan Musial, St. Louis
1949	Jackie Robinson, Brooklyn
1950	Jim Konstanty, Philadelphia
1951	Roy Campanella, Brooklyn
1952	Hank Sauer, Chicago
1953	Roy Campanella, Brooklyn
1954	Willie Mays, New York
1955	Roy Campanella, Brooklyn
1956	Don Newcombe, Brooklyn
1957	Henry Aaron, Milwaukee
1958	Ernie Banks, Chicago
1959	Ernie Banks, Chicago
1960	Dick Groat, Pittsburgh
1961	Frank Robinson, Cincinnati
1962	Maury Wills, Los Angeles
1963	Sandy Koufax, Los Angeles
1964	Ken Boyer, St. Louis
1965	Willie Mays, San Francisco
1966	Roberto Clemente, Pittsburgh
1967	Orlando Cepeda, St. Louis
1968	Bob Gibson, St. Louis
1969	Willie McCovey, San Francisco
1970	Johnny Bench, Cincinnati
1971	Joe Torre, St. Louis
1972	Johnny Bench, Cincinnati
1973	Pete Rose, Cincinnati
1974	Steve Garvey, Los Angeles
1975	Joe Morgan, Cincinnati
1976	Joe Morgan, Cincinnati
1977	George Foster, Cincinnati
1978	Dave Parker, Pittsburgh
1979	(tie) Willie Stargell, Pittsburgh Keith Hernandez, St. Louis
1980	Mike Schmidt, Philadelphia
1981	Mike Schmidt, Philadelphia
1982	Dale Murphy, Atlanta
1983	Dale Murphy, Atlanta
1984	Ryne Sandberg, Chicago
1985	Willie McGee, St. Louis
1986	Mike Schmidt, Philadelphia

American League

Year	Player, team
1931	Lefty Grove, Philadelphia
1932	Jimmy Foxx, Philadelphia
1933	Jimmy Foxx, Philadelphia
1934	Mickey Cochrane, Detroit
1935	Henry Greenberg, Detroit
1936	Lou Gehrig, New York
1937	Charley Gehringer, Detroit
1938	Jimmy Foxx, Boston
1939	Joe DiMaggio, New York
1940	Hank Greenberg, Detroit
1941	Joe DiMaggio, New York
1942	Joe Gordon, New York
1943	Spurgeon Chandler, New York
1944	Hal Newhouser, Detroit
1945	Hal Newhouser, Detroit
1946	Ted Williams, Boston
1947	Joe DiMaggio, New York
1948	Lou Boudreau, Cleveland
1949	Ted Williams, Boston
1950	Phil Rizzuto, New York
1951	Yogi Berra, New York
1952	Bobby Shantz, Philadelphia
1953	Al Rosen, Cleveland
1954	Yogi Berra, New York
1955	Yogi Berra, New York
1956	Mickey Mantle, New York
1957	Mickey Mantle, New York
1958	Jackie Jensen, Boston
1959	Nellie Fox, Chicago
1960	Roger Maris, New York
1961	Roger Maris, New York
1962	Mickey Mantle, New York
1963	Elston Howard, New York
1964	Brooks Robinson, Baltimore
1965	Zoilo Versalles, Minnesota
1966	Frank Robinson, Baltimore
1967	Carl Yastrzemski, Boston
1968	Denny McLain, Detroit
1969	Harmon Killebrew, Minnesota
1970	John (Boog) Powell, Baltimore
1971	Vida Blue, Oakland
1972	Dick Allen, Chicago
1973	Reggie Jackson, Oakland
1974	Jeff Burroughs, Texas
1975	Fred Lynn, Boston
1976	Thurman Munson, New York
1977	Rod Carew, Minnesota
1978	Jim Rice, Boston
1979	Don Baylor, California
1980	George Brett, Kansas City
1981	Rollie Fingers, Milwaukee
1982	Robin Yount, Milwaukee
1983	Cal Ripken Jr., Baltimore
1984	Willie Hernandez, Detroit
1985	Don Mattingly, New York
1986	Roger Clemens, Boston

Rookie of the Year

Baseball Writers' Association

1947—Combined selection—Jackie Robinson, Brooklyn, 1b

1948—Combined selection—Alvin Dark, Boston, N.L. ss

National League

Year	Player, team
1949	Don Newcombe, Brooklyn, p
1950	Sam Jethroe, Boston, of
1951	Willie Mays, New York, of
1952	Joe Black, Brooklyn, p
1953	Jim Gilliam, Brooklyn, 2b
1954	Wally Moon, St. Louis, of
1955	Bill Virdon, St. Louis, of
1956	Frank Robinson, Cincinnati, of
1957	Jack Sanford, Philadelphia, p
1958	Orlando Cepeda, S.F., 1b
1959	Willie McCovey, S.F., 1b
1960	Frank Howard, Los Angeles, of
1961	Billy Williams, Chicago, of
1962	Ken Hubbs, Chicago, 2b
1963	Pete Rose, Cincinnati, 2b
1964	Richie Allen, Philadelphia, 3b
1965	Jim Lefebvre, Los Angeles, 2b
1966	Tommy Helms, Cincinnati, 2b
1967	Tom Seaver, New York, p
1968	Johnny Bench, Cincinnati c
1969	Ted Sizemore, Los Angeles, 2b
1970	Carl Morton, Montreal, p
1971	Earl Williams, Atlanta, c
1972	Jon Matlack, New York, p
1973	Gary Matthews, S.F., of
1974	Bake McBride, St. Louis, of
1975	John Montefusco, S.F., p
1976	(tie) Butch Metzger, San Diego, p Pat Zachry, Cincinnati, p
1977	Andre Dawson, Montreal, of
1978	Bob Horner, Atlanta, 3b
1979	Rick Sutcliffe, Los Angeles, p
1980	Steve Howe, Los Angeles, p
1981	Fernando Valenzuela, Los Angeles, p
1982	Steve Sax, Los Angeles, 2b
1983	Darryl Strawberry, New York, of
1984	Dwight Gooden, New York, p
1985	Vince Coleman, St. Louis, of
1986	Todd Worrell, St. Louis, p

American League

Year	Player, team
1949	Roy Sievers, St. Louis, of
1950	Walt Dropo, Boston, 1b
1951	Gil McDougald, New York, 3b
1952	Harry Byrd, Philadelphia, p
1953	Harvey Kuenn, Detroit, ss
1954	Bob Grim, New York, p
1955	Herb Score, Cleveland, p
1956	Luis Aparicio, Chicago, ss
1957	Tony Kubek, New York, if-of
1958	Albie Pearson, Washington, of
1959	Bob Allison, Washington, of
1960	Ron Hansen, Baltimore, ss
1961	Don Schwall, Boston, p
1962	Tom Tresh, New York, if-of
1963	Gary Peters, Chicago, p
1964	Tony Oliva, Minnesota, of
1965	Curt Blefary, Baltimore, of
1966	Tommie Agee, Chicago, of
1967	Rod Carew, Minnesota, 2b
1968	Stan Bahnsen, New York, p
1969	Lou Piniella, Kansas City, of
1970	Thurman Munson, New York, c
1971	Chris Chambliss, Cleveland, 1b
1972	Carlton Fisk, Boston, c
1973	Al Bumbry, Baltimore, of
1974	Mike Hargrove, Texas, 1b
1975	Fred Lynn, Boston, of
1976	Mark Fidrych, Detroit, p
1977	Eddie Murray, Baltimore, dh
1978	Lou Whitaker, Detroit, 2b
1979	(tie) John Castino, Minnesota, 3b Alfredo Griffin, Toronto, ss
1980	Joe Charboneau, Cleveland, of
1981	Dave Righetti, New York, p
1982	Cal Ripken Jr., Baltimore, ss, 3b
1983	Ron Kittle, Chicago, of
1984	Alvin Davis, Seattle, 1B
1985	Ozzie Guillen, Chicago, ss
1986	Jose Canseco, Oakland, of

American League Records in 1987

Final standings

Eastern Division

Club	W	L	Pct	GB
Detroit	98	64	.605	—
Toronto	96	66	.593	2
Milwaukee	91	71	.562	7
New York	89	73	.549	9
Boston	78	84	.481	20
Baltimore	67	95	.414	31
Cleveland	61	101	.377	37

Western Division

Club	W	L	Pct	GB
Minnesota	85	77	.525	—
Kansas City	83	79	.512	2
Oakland	81	81	.500	4
Seattle	78	84	.481	7
Chicago	77	85	.475	8
California	75	87	.463	10
Texas	75	87	.463	10

American League Championship Series

Minnesota 8, Detroit 5
Minnesota 6, Detroit 3
Detroit 7, Minnesota 6
Minnesota 5, Detroit 3
Minnesota 9, Detroit 5

Club Batting

Club	Pct	AB	R	H	HR	SB
Boston	**.278**	5586	842	1554	174	77
Milwaukee	**.276**	5625	862	1552	163	176
Seattle	**.272**	5508	760	1499	161	174
Detroit	**.272**	5649	896	1535	225	106
Toronto	**.269**	5635	845	1514	215	126
Texas	**.266**	5564	823	1478	194	120
Cleveland	**.263**	5606	742	1476	187	140
Kansas City	**.262**	5499	715	1443	168	125
New York	**.262**	5511	788	1445	196	105
Minnesota	**.261**	5441	786	1422	196	113
Oakland	**.260**	5511	806	1432	199	140
Baltimore	**.258**	5576	729	1437	211	69
Chicago	**.258**	5538	748	1427	173	138
California	**.252**	5570	770	1406	172	125

Club Pitching

Club	ERA	CG	IP	H	R	BB	SO
Toronto	**3.74**	18	1454	1323	655	567	1064
Kansas City	**3.86**	44	1424	1424	691	548	923
Detroit	**4.02**	33	1456	1430	735	563	976
Chicago	**4.30**	29	1447	1436	746	537	792
Oakland	**4.32**	18	1445	1442	789	531	1042
New York	**4.36**	19	1446	1475	758	542	900
California	**4.38**	20	1457	1481	803	504	941
Seattle	**4.49**	39	1430	1503	801	497	919
Milwaukee	**4.62**	28	1464	1548	817	529	1039
Minnesota	**4.63**	16	1427	1465	806	564	990
Texas	**4.63**	20	1444	1388	849	760	1103
Boston	**4.77**	47	1436	1584	825	517	1034
Baltimore	**5.01**	17	1439	1555	880	547	870
Cleveland	**5.28**	24	1422	1566	957	606	849

Individual Batting

Leaders—Based on 502 plate appearances.

Player, club	Pct	AB	R	H	HR	RBI
Boggs, Boston	**.363**	551	108	200	24	89
Molitor, Milwaukee	**.353**	465	114	164	16	75
Trammell, Detroit	**.343**	597	109	205	28	105
Puckett, Minnesota	**.332**	624	96	207	28	99
Mattingly, New York	**.327**	569	93	186	30	115
Seitzer, Kansas City	**.323**	641	105	207	15	83
Fernandez, Toronto	**.322**	578	90	186	5	67
Franco, Cleveland	**.319**	495	86	158	8	52
Sheets, Baltimore	**.316**	469	74	148	31	94
Yount, Milwaukee	**.312**	635	99	198	21	103

Individual Pitching

Leaders—Based on 162 inning.

Pitcher, club	W	L	ERA	G	IP	H	BB	SO
Key, Toronto	17	8	**2.76**	36	261	210	66	161
Viola, Minnesota	17	10	**2.90**	36	251	230	66	197
Clemens, Boston	20	9	**2.97**	36	281	248	83	256
Saberhagen, Kansas City	18	10	**3.36**	33	257	246	53	163
Morris, Detroit	18	11	**3.38**	34	266	227	93	208
Leibrandt, Kansas City	16	11	**3.41**	35	240	235	74	151
Clancy, Toronto	15	11	**3.54**	37	241	234	80	180
Bannister, Chicago	16	11	**3.58**	34	228	216	49	124
Stewart, Oakland	20	13	**3.68**	37	261	224	105	205

Individual Batting (at least 115 at-bats); Individual Pitching (at least 50 innings)

Baltimore Orioles

Batting	Avg	AB	R	H	HR	RBI
Sheets	**.316**	469	74	148	31	94
B. Ripkin	**.308**	234	27	72	2	20
Murray	**.277**	618	89	171	30	91
Dwyer	**.274**	241	54	66	15	33
Knight	**.256**	563	46	144	14	65
Lynn	**.253**	396	49	100	23	60
C. Ripkin	**.252**	624	97	157	27	98
Kennedy	**.250**	512	51	128	18	62
Lacy	**.244**	258	35	63	7	28
Gerhart	**.243**	284	41	69	14	34
Young	**.240**	363	46	87	16	39
Wiggins	**.232**	306	37	71	1	15
Burleson	**.209**	206	26	43	2	14

Pitching	W	L	ERA	IP	BB	SO	Sv
Schmidt	10	5	**3.77**	124	26	70	1
Williamson	8	9	**4.03**	125	41	73	3
Boddicker	10	12	**4.18**	226	78	152	
Griffin	3	5	**4.36**	74	33	42	1
Habyan	6	7	**4.80**	116	40	64	1
Neidenfuer	3	5	**4.99**	52	22	37	13
Bell	10	13	**5.45**	165	78	111	
Arnold	0	0	**5.77**	53	17	18	
Dixon	7	10	**6.43**	105	27	91	5
Ballard	2	8	**6.59**	69	35	27	
McGregor	2	7	**6.64**	85	35	39	

Boston Red Sox

Batting	Avg	AB	R	H	HR	RBI
Boggs	**.363**	551	108	200	24	89
Greenwell	**.328**	412	71	135	19	89
Evans	**.305**	541	109	165	34	123
Barrett	**.293**	559	72	164	3	43
Horn	**.278**	158	31	44	14	34
Benzinger	**.278**	223	36	62	8	43
Rice	**.277**	404	66	112	13	62
Burks	**.272**	558	94	152	20	59
Romero	**.272**	235	23	64	0	14
Owen	**.259**	437	50	113	2	48
Marzano	**.244**	168	20	41	5	24
Henderson	**.234**	184	30	43	8	25
Gedman	**.205**	151	11	31	1	13
Sullivan	**.169**	160	11	27	2	10

Pitching	W	L	ERA	IP	BB	SO	Sv
Clemens	20	9	**2.97**	281	83	256	
Bolton	1	0	**4.38**	61	27	49	
Schiraldi	8	5	**4.41**	83	40	93	6
Hurst	15	13	**4.41**	238	76	190	
Stanley	4	15	**5.01**	152	42	67	
Sellers	7	8	**5.28**	139	61	99	
Crawford	5	4	**5.33**	72	32	43	
Gardner	3	6	**5.42**	89	42	70	10
Nipper	11	12	**5.43**	174	62	89	

California Angels

Batting	Avg	AB	R	H	HR	RBI
Ray	.346	127	16	44	0	15
Buckner	.286	469	39	134	5	74
Joyner	.285	564	100	161	34	117
Downing	.272	567	110	154	29	77
White	.263	639	103	168	24	87
Polidor	.263	137	12	36	2	15
Schofield	.251	479	52	120	9	46
Howell	.245	449	64	110	23	64
Jones	.245	192	25	47	8	28
Boone	.242	389	42	94	3	33
Hendrick	.241	162	14	39	5	25
McLemore	.236	433	61	102	3	41
DeCinces	.234	453	65	106	16	63
Pettis	.208	394	49	82	1	17

Pitching	W	L	ERA	IP	BB	SO	Sv
Minton	5	4	3.08	76	29	35	10
Buice	6	7	3.39	114	40	109	17
Lucas	1	5	3.63	74	35	44	3
Fraser	10	10	3.92	176	63	106	1
Witt	16	14	4.01	247	84	192	
Lazorko	5	6	4.59	117	44	55	
Finley	2	7	4.67	90	43	63	
Sutton	11	11	4.70	191	41	99	
Candelaria	8	6	4.71	116	20	74	
Reuss	4	5	5.25	82	17	37	
McCaskill	4	6	5.67	74	34	56	

Chicago White Sox

Batting	Avg	AB	R	H	HR	RBI
Calderon	.293	542	93	159	28	83
Baines	.293	505	59	148	20	93
Williams	.281	391	48	110	11	50
Lyons	.280	193	26	54	1	19
Guillen	.279	560	64	156	2	51
Manrique	.258	298	30	77	4	29
Boston	.258	337	51	87	10	29
Walker	.256	566	85	145	27	94
Fisk	.256	454	68	116	23	71
Hill	.239	410	57	98	9	46
Redus	.236	475	78	112	12	48
Hairston	.230	126	14	29	5	20
Hulett	.217	240	20	52	7	28
Hassey	.214	145	15	31	3	12

Pitching	W	L	ERA	IP	BB	SO	Sv
Thigpen	7	5	2.73	89	24	52	16
LaPoint	6	3	2.94	82	31	43	
Bannister	10	11	3.58	228	49	124	
DeLeon	11	12	4.02	206	97	153	
Dotson	11	12	4.17	211	86	114	
Searage	2	3	4.20	55	24	33	2
Long	8	8	4.37	169	28	72	1
James	4	6	4.67	54	17	34	10
Winn	4	6	4.79	94	62	44	6
Davis	1	5	5.73	55	29	25	
Nielson	3	5	6.24	66	25	23	2

Cleveland Indians

Batting	Avg	AB	R	H	HR	RBI
Franco	.319	495	86	158	8	52
Tabler	.307	553	66	170	11	86
Jacoby	.300	540	73	162	32	69
Butler	.295	522	91	154	9	41
Hall	.280	485	57	136	18	76
Allanson	.266	154	17	41	3	16
Hinzo	.265	257	31	68	3	21
Carter	.264	588	83	155	32	106
Castillo	.250	220	27	55	11	31
Snyder	.236	577	74	136	33	82
Bando	.218	211	20	46	5	16
Bell	.216	125	14	27	2	13
Dempsey	.177	141	16	25	1	9

Pitching	W	L	ERA	IP	BB	SO	Sv
Jones	6	5	3.15	91	24	87	8
Farrell	5	1	3.39	69	22	28	
Gordon	0	3	4.09	50	15	23	1
Bailes	7	8	4.64	120	47	65	6
Candiotti	7	18	4.78	201	93	111	
Huismann	2	3	5.04	50	12	38	2
Swindell	3	8	5.10	102	37	97	
Vande Berg	1	0	5.10	72	21	40	
Yett	3	9	5.25	97	49	59	1
Schrom	6	13	6.50	153	57	61	
Akerfelds	2	6	6.75	74	38	42	

Detroit Tigers

Batting	Avg	AB	R	H	HR	RBI
Trammell	.343	597	109	205	28	105
Herndon	.324	225	32	73	9	47
Nokes	.289	461	69	133	32	87
Heath	.281	270	34	76	8	33
Madlock	.279	326	56	91	14	50
Gibson	.277	487	95	135	24	79
Lemon	.277	470	75	130	20	75
Bergman	.273	172	25	47	6	22
Whitaker	.265	604	110	160	16	59
Sheridan	.259	421	57	109	6	49
Evans	.257	499	90	128	34	99
Brookens	.241	444	59	107	13	59
Morrison	.205	117	15	24	4	19
Coles	.181	149	14	27	4	15

Pitching	W	L	ERA	IP	BB	SO	Sv
Alexander	9	0	1.53	88	26	44	
Henneman	11	3	2.98	96	30	75	7
Morris	18	11	3.38	266	93	208	
Tanana	15	10	3.91	218	56	146	
Terrell	17	10	4.05	244	94	143	
Thurmond	0	1	4.23	61	24	21	5
King	6	9	4.89	116	60	89	9
Robinson	9	6	5.37	127	54	98	
Petry	9	7	5.61	134	76	93	

Kansas City Royals

Batting	Avg	AB	R	H	HR	RBI
Seitzer	.323	641	105	207	15	83
Tartabull	.309	582	95	180	34	101
Brett	.290	427	71	124	22	78
Wilson	.279	610	97	170	4	30
Bosley	.279	140	13	39	1	16
Pecota	.276	156	22	43	3	14
Smith	.251	167	26	42	3	8
White	.245	563	67	138	17	78
Quirk	.236	296	24	70	5	33
B. Jackson	.235	396	46	93	22	53
Balboni	.207	386	44	80	24	60
Salazar	.205	317	24	65	2	21
Owen	.189	164	17	31	5	14

Pitching	W	L	ERA	IP	BB	SO	Sv
Saberhagen	18	10	3.36	257	53	163	
Leibrandt	16	11	3.41	240	74	151	
Black	8	6	3.60	122	35	61	1
Gubicza	13	18	3.98	241	120	166	
D. Jackson	9	18	4.02	224	109	152	
Farr	4	3	4.15	91	44	88	1
Gleaton	4	4	4.26	50	28	44	5

Milwaukee Brewers

Batting	Avg	AB	R	H	HR	RBI
Molitor	.353	465	114	164	16	75
Schroeder	.332	250	35	83	14	42
Yount	.312	635	99	198	21	103
Brock	.299	532	81	159	13	85
Surhoff	.299	395	50	118	7	68
Gantner	.272	265	37	72	4	30
Braggs	.269	505	67	136	13	77
Felder	.266	289	48	77	2	31
Riles	.261	276	38	72	4	38
Sveum	.252	535	86	135	25	95
Cooper	.248	250	25	62	6	36
Deer	.238	474	71	113	28	80
Manning	.228	114	21	26	0	13
Paciorek	.228	101	16	23	2	10
Castillo	.224	321	44	72	3	28

Pitching	W	L	ERA	IP	BB	SO	Sv
Plesac	5	6	2.61	79	23	89	23
Crim	6	8	3.67	130	39	56	12
Higuera	18	10	3.85	261	87	240	
Wegman	12	11	4.24	225	53	102	
Clear	8	5	4.48	78	55	81	6
Nieves	14	8	4.88	195	100	163	
Aldrich	3	1	4.94	58	13	22	
Bosio	11	8	5.24	170	50	150	2
Knudson	4	4	5.37	62	14	26	

(continued)

Minnesota Twins

Batting	Avg	AB	R	H	HR	RBI
Puckett	.332	624	96	207	28	99
Hrbek	.285	477	85	136	34	90
Smalley	.275	309	32	85	8	34
Davidson	.267	150	32	40	1	14
Larkin	.266	233	23	62	4	28
Gagne	.265	437	68	116	10	40
Brunansky	.259	532	83	138	32	85
Gaetti	.257	584	95	150	31	109
Bush	.253	293	46	74	11	46
Gladden	.249	438	69	109	8	38
Baylor	.245	388	67	95	16	63
Lombardozzi	.238	432	51	103	8	38
Newman	.221	307	44	68	0	29
Launder	.191	288	30	55	16	43

Pitching	W	L	ERA	IP	BB	SO	Sv
Viola	17	10	2.90	251	66	197	
Berenguer	8	1	3.94	112	47	110	4
Blyleven	15	12	4.01	267	101	196	
Straker	8	10	4.37	154	59	76	
Reardon	8	8	4.48	80	28	83	31
Atherton	7	5	4.54	79	30	51	2
Frazier	5	5	4.98	81	51	58	2
Niekro	7	13	5.33	147	64	84	
Carlton	6	14	5.74	152	86	91	1
Smithson	4	7	5.94	109	38	53	

New York Yankees

Batting	Avg	AB	R	H	HR	RBI
Mattingly	.327	569	93	186	30	115
Randolph	.305	449	96	137	7	67
Henderson	.291	358	78	104	17	37
Easler	.281	167	13	47	4	21
Washington	.279	312	42	87	9	44
Kittle	.277	159	21	44	12	28
Winfield	.275	575	83	158	27	97
Meacham	.271	203	28	55	5	21
Royster	.265	196	26	52	7	27
Salas	.250	160	21	40	6	21
Ward	.248	529	65	131	16	78
Cerone	.243	284	28	69	4	23
Cotto	.235	149	21	35	5	20
Pagliarulo	.234	522	76	122	32	87
Pasqua	.233	318	42	74	17	42
Tolleson	.221	349	48	77	1	22
Skinner	.137	139	9	19	3	14

Pitching	W	L	ERA	IP	BB	SO	Sv
Stoddard	4	3	3.50	92	30	78	8
Righetti	8	6	3.51	95	44	77	31
Hudson	11	7	3.61	154	57	100	
Guidry	5	8	3.67	117	38	96	
Rhoden	16	10	3.86	181	61	107	
John	13	6	4.03	187	47	63	
Rasmussen	9	7	4.75	146	55	89	
Clements	3	3	4.95	80	30	36	7
Allen	0	8	5.93	74	36	42	

Oakland A's

Batting	Avg	AB	R	H	HR	RBI
McGwire	.289	557	97	161	49	118
Lansford	.289	554	89	160	19	76
Polonia	.287	435	78	125	4	49
Steinbach	.284	391	66	111	16	56
M. Davis	.265	494	69	131	22	72
Griffin	.263	494	69	130	3	60
Canseco	.257	630	81	162	31	113
Bernazard	.250	507	73	127	14	49
Gallego	.250	124	18	31	2	14
Phillips	.240	379	48	91	10	46
Murphy	.233	219	39	51	8	35
Jackson	.220	336	42	74	15	43
Tettleton	.194	211	19	41	8	26
Javier	.185	151	22	28	2	9

Pitching	W	L	ERA	IP	BB	SO	Sv
Eckersley	6	8	3.03	115	17	113	16
Stewart	20	13	3.68	261	105	205	
Leiper	2	1	3.78	52	18	33	1
G. Nelson	6	5	3.93	123	35	94	3
Ontiveros	10	8	4.00	150	50	97	1
Young	13	7	4.08	203	44	124	
Plunk	4	6	4.74	95	62	90	2
Lamp	1	3	5.08	56	22	36	
Rijo	2	7	5.90	82	41	67	
Andujar	3	5	6.08	60	26	32	

Seattle Mariners

Batting	Avg	AB	R	H	HR	RBI
Brantley	.302	351	52	106	14	54
P. Bradley	.297	603	101	179	14	67
Davis	.295	580	86	171	29	100
Kingery	.280	354	38	99	9	52
S. Bradley	.278	342	34	95	5	43
Quinones	.276	478	55	132	12	56
Reynolds	.275	530	73	146	1	35
Phelps	.259	332	68	86	27	68
Valle	.256	324	40	83	12	53
Nixon	.250	132	17	33	3	12
Presley	.247	575	78	142	24	88
Moses	.246	390	58	96	3	38
Christensen	.242	132	19	32	2	12
Matthews	.235	119	10	28	3	15

Pitching	W	L	ERA	IP	BB	SO	Sv
Reed	1	2	3.42	81	24	51	7
Wilkinson	3	4	3.66	76	21	73	10
Guetterman	11	4	3.81	113	35	42	
Langston	19	13	3.84	272	114	262	
Morgan	12	17	4.65	207	53	85	
Moore	9	19	4.71	231	84	115	
Bankhead	9	8	5.42	149	37	95	
Trujillo	4	4	6.17	65	26	36	1

Texas Rangers

Batting	Avg	AB	R	H	HR	RBI
Petralli	.302	202	28	61	7	31
Fletcher	.287	588	82	169	5	63
O'Brien	.286	569	84	163	23	88
O'Malley	.274	117	10	32	1	12
Stanley	.273	216	34	59	6	37
Incaviglia	.271	509	85	138	27	80
Browne	.271	454	63	123	1	38
Wilkerson	.268	138	28	37	2	14
Parrish	.268	557	79	149	32	100
Sierra	.263	643	97	169	30	109
Brower	.261	303	63	79	14	46
McDowell	.241	407	65	98	14	52
Porter	.238	130	19	31	7	21
Buechele	.237	363	45	86	13	50
Slaught	.224	237	25	53	8	16

Pitching	W	L	ERA	IP	BB	SO	Sv
Mohorcic	7	6	2.99	99	19	48	16
Williams	8	6	3.23	108	94	129	6
Hough	18	13	3.79	285	124	223	
Kilgus	2	7	4.13	89	31	42	
Russell	5	4	4.44	97	52	56	3
Guzman	14	14	4.67	208	82	143	
Harris	5	10	4.86	140	56	106	
Witt	8	10	4.91	143	140	160	
Loynd	1	5	6.10	69	38	48	1

Toronto Blue Jays

Batting	Avg	AB	R	H	HR	RBI
Fernandez	.322	578	90	186	5	67
Mulliniks	.310	332	37	103	11	44
Bell	.308	610	111	188	47	134
Moseby	.282	592	106	167	26	96
Leach	.282	195	26	55	3	25
Whitt	.269	446	57	120	19	75
Fielder	.269	175	30	47	14	32
Barfield	.263	590	89	155	28	84
Lee	.256	121	14	31	1	11
Beniquez	.251	255	20	64	8	47
McGriff	.247	295	58	73	20	43
Upshaw	.244	512	68	125	15	58
Liriano	.241	158	29	38	2	10
Gruber	.235	341	50	80	12	36
Iorg	.210	310	35	65	4	30

Pitching	W	L	ERA	IP	BB	SO	Sv
Henke	0	6	2.49	94	25	128	34
Key	17	8	2.76	261	66	161	
Eichhorn	10	6	3.17	127	52	96	4
Clancy	15	11	3.54	241	80	180	
Flanagan	6	8	4.06	144	51	93	
Stieb	13	9	4.09	185	87	115	
Musselman	12	5	4.15	89	54	54	3
Cerutti	11	4	4.40	151	59	92	
Nunez	5	2	5.01	97	58	99	
Johnson	3	5	5.13	66	18	27	
Niekro	7	13	6.10	135	60	64	

1987 World Series

First Game

St. Louis	ab	r	h	bi	Minnesota	ab	r	h	bi
Coleman lf	4	0	0	0	Gladden lf	4	1	2	5
Smith ss	4	0	0	0	Gagne ss	5	0	0	0
Herr 2b	4	0	0	0	Puckett cf	5	0	1	0
Lindeman 1b	4	1	2	0	Gaetti 3b	5	1	2	0
McGee cf	3	0	2	0	Baylor dh	5	1	1	0
Pena c	3	0	0	1	Brunansky rf	3	1	1	0
Lake c	0	0	0	0	Davidson rf	0	0	0	0
Oquendo rf	3	0	0	0	Hrbek 1b	2	2	1	2
Pagnozzi dh	3	0	1	0	Larkin 1b	0	0	0	0
Lawless 3b	3	0	0	0	Lombardozzi 2b	3	3	2	2
Magrane p	0	0	0	0	Laudner c	3	1	1	1
Forsch p	0	0	0	0	Viola p	0	0	0	0
Horton p	0	0	0	0	Atherton p	0	0	0	0
Totals	**31**	**1**	**5**	**0**	**Totals**	**35**	**10**	**11**	**10**

St. Louis.	0	1	0	0	0	0	0	0	0—	1
Minnesota.	0	0	0	7	2	0	1	0	x—	10

DP - St. Louis 1, Minnesota 1. LOB - St. Louis 3, Minnesota 7. 2B - Lindeman, Gaetti, Gladden. HR - Gladden 1, Lombardozzi 1. SB - Gladden 1.

St. Louis	ip	h	r	er	bb	so
Magrane L, 0-1	3	4	5	5	4	1
Forsch	3	4	4	4	2	0
Horton	2	3	1	1	0	1
Minnesota						
Viola W, 1-0	8	5	1	1	0	5
Atherton	1	0	0	0	0	0

How runs were scored—One in Cardinals second: Lindeman doubled. Lindeman went to third on a fly ball and scored on Pena's groundout.

Seven in Twins fourth: Gaetti, Baylor, and Brunansky singled. Hrbek singled scoring Gaetti and Baylor. Lombardozzi walked. Laudner singled scoring Brunansky. Gladden hit a home run.

Two in Twins fifth: Hrbek walked. Lombardozzi hit a home run.

One in Twins seventh: Lombardozzi singled. Gladden doubled scoring Lombardozzi.

Second Game

St. Louis	ab	r	h	bi	Minnesota	ab	r	h	bi
Coleman lf	4	1	1	0	Gladden lf	5	0	1	1
Smith ss	4	0	1	0	Gagne ss	4	0	1	1
Herr 2b	4	0	0	0	Puckett cf	4	1	1	0
Driessen 1b	4	1	1	1	Hrbek 1b	3	1	1	0
McGee cf	4	0	1	1	Gaetti 3b	3	2	2	1
Pendleton dh	4	1	1	0	Bush dh	3	1	1	2
Ford rf	3	1	2	0	Larkin ph	1	0	0	0
Oquendo 3b	4	0	1	0	Brunansky rf	3	1	0	0
Pena c	4	0	1	2	Lombardozzi 2b	3	0	0	0
Cox p	0	0	0	0	Smalley ph	1	0	1	0
Tunnell p	0	0	0	0	Newman pr-2b	0	0	0	0
Dayley p	0	0	0	0	Laudner c	3	2	2	3
Worrell p	0	0	0	0	Blyleven	0	0	0	0
					Berenguer p	0	0	0	0
					Reardon p	0	0	0	0
Totals	**35**	**4**	**9**	**4**	**Totals**	**33**	**8**	**10**	**8**

St. Louis.	0	0	0	0	1	0	1	2	0—	4
Minnesota.	0	1	0	6	0	1	0	0	x—	8

LOB - St. Louis 5, Minnesota 5. 2B - Bush, Gagne, Driessen, Smalley. HR - Gaetti 1, Laudner 1. SB - Coleman 1.

St. Louis	ip	h	r	er	bb	so
Cox L, 0-1	3 2/3	6	7	7	2	3
Tunnell	2 1/3	3	1	1	1	1
Dayley	1 1/3	0	0	0	0	1
Worrell	2/3	1	0	0	1	0
Minnesota						
Blyleven W, 1-0	7	6	2	2	1	8
Berenguer	1	3	2	2	0	0
Reardon	1	0	0	0	0	0

How runs were scored—One in Twins second: Gaetti hit a home run.

Six in Twins fourth: Puckett and Hrbek singled. Gaetti walked. Bush doubled scoring Puckett and Hrbek. Brunansky walked. Laudner singled scoring Gaetti and Bush. Gladden singled scoring Brunansky. Gagne doubled scoring Laudner.

One in Cardinals fifth: Pendleton singled. Ford walked. Pendleton later scored on Pena's groundout.

One in Twins sixth: Laudner hit a home run.

One in Cardinals seventh: Ford and Oquendo singled. Pena singled scoring Ford.

Two in Cardinals eighth: Coleman singled. Driessen doubled scoring Coleman. McGee singled scoring Driessen.

Third Game

Minnesota	ab	r	h	bi	St. Louis	ab	r	h	bi
Gladden lf	4	0	1	0	Coleman lf	4	1	1	2
Gagne ss	3	1	0	0	Smith ss	4	0	2	1
Puckett cf	3	0	1	0	Herr 2b	4	0	1	0
Gaetti 3b	4	0	0	0	Driessen 1b	4	0	0	0
Brunansky rf	4	0	1	1	Worrell p	0	0	0	0
Hrbek 1b	4	0	0	0	McGee cf	4	0	2	0
Laudner c	3	0	2	0	Ford rf	4	0	1	0
Bush ph	1	0	0	0	Oquendo 3b	3	1	1	0
Lombardozzi 2b	3	0	0	0	Pena c	2	1	1	0
Straker p	2	0	0	0	Tudor p	2	0	0	0
Larkin ph	1	0	0	0	Pendleton ph	0	0	0	0
Berenguer p	0	0	0	0	Lindeman 1b	0	0	0	0
Schatzeder p	0	0	0	0					
Totals	**32**	**1**	**5**	**1**	**Totals**	**31**	**3**	**9**	**3**

Minnesota.	0	0	0	0	0	1	0	0	0—	1
St. Louis.	0	0	0	0	0	0	3	0	x—	3

DP - Minnesota 1. LOB - Minnesota 6, St. Louis 7. 2B - McGee, Laudner, Coleman. 3B - Puckett. SB - Coleman 2 (3).

Minnesota	ip	h	r	er	bb	so
Straker	6	4	0	0	2	4
Berenguer L, 0-1	1/3	4	3	3	0	0
Schatzeder	1 2/3	1	0	0	0	1
St. Louis						
Tudor W, 1-0	7	4	1	1	2	7
Worrell S, 1	2	1	0	0	0	1

How runs were scored—One in Twins sixth: Gagne and Puckett walked. Brunansky singled scoring Gagne.

Three in Cardinals seventh: Oquendo and Pena singled. Coleman doubled scoring Oquendo and Pena. Smith singled scoring Coleman.

Fourth Game

Minnesota	ab	r	h	bi	St. Louis	ab	r	h	bi
Gladden lf	5	0	1	0	Coleman lf	4	1	1	0
Newman 2b	3	0	1	0	Smith ss	4	1	0	0
Baylor ph	1	0	1	0	Herr 2b	3	1	2	0
Puckett cf	4	0	1	1	Lindeman 1b	4	1	2	2
Gaetti 3b	3	0	1	0	McGee cf	4	0	2	2
Brunansky rf	4	0	0	0	Pena c	3	1	1	0
Hrbek 1b	4	0	1	0	Oquendo rf	4	1	1	0
Laudner c	3	0	0	0	Lawless 3b	4	1	1	3
Butera c	0	0	0	0	Mathews p	1	0	0	0
Gagne ss	4	1	1	1	Forsch p	2	0	0	0
Viola p	1	0	0	0	Dayley p	1	0	0	0
Schatzeder p	0	0	0	0					
Larkin ph	0	1	0	0					
Niekro p	0	0	0	0					
Smalley ph	1	0	0	0					
Frazier p	0	0	0	0					
Davidson ph	1	0	0	0					
Totals	**34**	**2**	**7**	**2**	**Totals**	**34**	**7**	**10**	**7**

Minnesota.	0	0	1	0	1	0	0	0	0—	2
St. Louis.	0	0	1	6	0	0	0	0	x—	7

DP - St. Louis 1. LOB - Minnesota 10, St. Louis 9. 2B - McGee, Coleman. HR - Gagne 1, Lawless 1. SB - Gaetti 1, Brunansky 1, Coleman 4.

Minnesota	ip	h	r	er	bb	so
Viola L, 1-1	3 1/3	6	5	5	3	4
Schatzeder	2/3	2	2	2	1	1
Niekro	2	1	0	0	1	1
Frazier	2	1	0	0	0	2
St. Louis						
Mathews	3 2/3	2	1	1	2	3
Forsch W, 1-0	2 2/3	4	1	1	1	3
Dayley S, 1	2 2/3	1	0	0	0	2

How runs were scored—One in Twins third: Gagne hit a home run.

One in Cardinals third: Smith walked. Herr singled. Lindeman singled scoring Smith.

Six in Cardinals fourth: Pena walked. Oquendo singled. Lawless hit a home run scoring Pena and Oquendo. Coleman and Herr walked. Lindeman singled scoring Coleman. McGee doubled scoring Herr and Lindeman.

One in Twins fifth: Larkin walked. Gladden singled. Puckett singled scoring Larkin.

Fifth Game

Minnesota	ab	r	h	bi	St. Louis	ab	r	h	bi
Gladden lf	3	1	1	0	Coleman lf	3	2	1	0
Gagne ss	4	1	1	0	Smith ss	4	1	2	1
Baylor ph	1	0	0	0	Herr 2b	4	0	0	0
Puckett cf	4	0	0	0	Driessen 1b	3	1	1	0
Hrbek 1b	4	0	1	0	Dayley p	0	0	0	0
Gaetti 3b	4	0	1	2	Worrell p	0	0	0	0
Brunansky rf	4	0	1	0	McGee cf	4	0	0	0
Laudner c	2	0	0	0	Ford rf	4	0	1	2
Newman ph	1	0	0	0	Oquendo 3b	4	0	2	0
Lombardozzi 2b	2	0	1	0	Pena c	4	0	3	0
Smalley ph	0	0	0	0	Johnson pr	0	0	0	0
Blyleven p	1	0	0	0	Lake c	0	0	0	0
Larkin ph	1	0	0	0	Cox p	2	0	0	0
Atherton p	0	0	0	0	Lindeman 1b	1	0	0	0
Reardon p	0	0	0	0					
Bush ph	1	0	0	0					
Totals	32	2	6	2	**Totals**	33	4	10	3

Minnesota	0	0	0	0	0	0	0	2	0—2
St. Louis	0	0	0	0	0	3	1	0	x—4

LOB - Minnesota 9, St. Louis 8. 3B - Gaetti. SB - Gladden 2, Coleman 2 (6), Smith 2 (2), Johnson 1.

Minnesota	ip	h	r	er	bb	so
Blyleven L, 1-1	6	7	3	2	1	4
Atherton	⅓	0	1	1	1	0
Reardon	1⅔	3	0	0	0	3
St. Louis						
Cox W, 1-1	7⅓	5	2	2	3	6
Dayley	⅓	0	0	0	0	0
Worrell S, 2	1⅓	1	0	0	2	0

How runs were scored—Three in Cardinals sixth: Coleman and Smith singled. Driessen walked. Ford singled scoring Coleman and Smith. Driessen scored on an infield error.

One in Cardinals seventh: Coleman walked, went to second on a balk, and stole third. Smith singled scoring Coleman.

Two in Twins eighth: Gladden and Gagne singled. Gaetti tripled scoring Gladden and Gagne.

Sixth Game

St. Louis	ab	r	h	bi	Minnesota	ab	r	h	bi
Coleman lf	5	0	0	0	Gladden lf	5	1	2	0
Smith ss	4	1	1	0	Gagne ss	5	1	1	0
Herr 2b	5	1	3	1	Puckett cf	4	4	4	1
Driessen 1b	2	1	1	0	Gaetti 3b	5	1	1	1
Pagnozzi ph	1	0	0	0	Baylor dh	3	2	2	3
Morris rf	2	0	0	0	Bush ph	1	0	0	0
McGee cf	4	1	2	1	Brunansky rf	4	1	1	1
Pendleton dh	3	1	2	1	Hrbek 1b	4	1	1	4
Ford rf	1	0	0	0	Laudner c	5	0	0	0
Lindeman rf	3	0	0	0	Lombardozzi 2b	4	0	3	1
Oquendo 3b	3	0	1	2					
Pena c	3	0	1	0					
Totals	36	5	11	5	**Totals**	40	11	15	11

St. Louis	1	1	0	2	1	0	0	0	0—5
Minnesota	2	0	0	0	4	4	0	1	x—11

E - McGee, Lindeman. DP - Minnesota 1. LOB - St. Louis 8, Minnesota 9. 2B - Driessen, Lombardozzi, Gaetti. 3B - Gladden. HR - Herr 1, Baylor 1, Hrbek 1. SB - Puckett 1, Pendleton 2 (2). SF - Oquendo.

St. Louis	ip	h	r	er	bb	so
Tudor L, 1-1	4	11	6	6	1	1
Horton	1	2	1	1	0	0
Forsch	⅔	0	2	2	2	0
Dayley	⅓	1	1	1	0	0
Tunnell	2	1	1	0	1	0
Minnesota						
Straker	3	5	4	4	1	2
Schatzeder W, 1-0	2	1	1	1	2	1
Berenguer	3	3	0	0	0	1
Reardon	1	2	0	0	0	0

How runs were scored—One in Cardinals first: Herr hit a home run.

Two in Twins first: Gladden tripled. Puckett singled scoring Gladden. Baylor singled scoring Puckett from second.

One in Cardinals second: Pendleton walked. Oquendo singled scoring Pendleton from second.

Two in Cardinals fourth: Driessen doubled. McGee singled, Driessen to third (McGee to second on throw). Pendleton hit an infield single scoring Driessen; McGee to third. Oquendo hit a sacrifice fly scoring McGee.

One in Cardinals fifth: Smith walked. McGee singled scoring Smith from third.

Four in Twins fifth: Puckett singled. Gaetti doubled scoring Puckett. Baylor homered scoring Gaetti. Brunansky singled. Lombardozzi singled scoring Brunansky from second.

Four in Twins sixth: Gagne singled. Puckett walked. Baylor was intentionally walked after a passed ball moved runners to second and third. Hrbek homered (on Dayley's first pitch in relief of Forsch) scoring Gagne, Puckett, and Baylor.

One in Twins eighth: Puckett singled. Bush (pinch hitting for Baylor) was safe on an error; Puckett to third. Brunansky grounded out scoring Puckett.

Seventh Game

St. Louis	ab	r	h	bi	Minnesota	ab	r	h	bi
Coleman lf	4	0	0	0	Gladden lf	5	0	1	1
Smith ss	4	0	0	0	Gagne ss	5	1	2	1
Herr 2b	4	0	1	0	Puckett cf	4	0	2	1
Lindeman 1b	3	1	1	0	Gaetti 3b	3	0	0	0
Ford ph	1	0	0	0	Baylor dh	3	0	1	0
McGee cf	4	1	1	0	Brunansky rf	3	2	1	0
Pena dh	3	0	2	1	Hrbek 1b	3	0	0	0
Oquendo rf	3	0	0	0	Laudner c	3	1	2	0
Lawless 3b	3	0	0	0	Lombardozzi 2b	2	0	1	1
Lake c	3	0	1	1	Smalley ph	0	0	0	0
					Newman 2b	1	0	0	0
Totals	32	2	6	2	**Totals**	32	4	10	4

St. Louis	0	2	0	0	0	0	0	0	0—2
Minnesota	0	1	0	0	1	1	0	1	x—4

E - Lindeman. LOB - St. Louis 3, Minnesota 10. 2B - Puckett, Pena, Gladden. SB - Gaetti 2, Pena 1. HBP - Baylor by Magrane.

St. Louis	ip	h	r	er	bb	so
Magrane	4⅓	5	2	2	1	4
Cox L, 1-2	⅔	2	1	1	3	0
Worrell	3	3	1	1	1	2
Minnesota						
Viola W, 2-1	8	6	2	2	0	7
Reardon S, 1	1	0	0	0	0	0

How runs were scored—Two in Cardinals second: Lindeman singled. McGee singled. Pena singled scoring Lindeman from second. Lake singled scoring McGee from third.

One in Twins second: Baylor was hit by a pitch. Brunansky singled. Laudner singled. Lombardozzi singled scoring Brunansky from second (after Baylor had been thrown out at home on single by Laudner).

One in Twins fifth: Gagne singled. Puckett doubled (off Cox in relief of Magrane) scoring Gagne.

One in Twins sixth: Brunansky and Hrbek walked. Smalley, pinch hitting for Lombardozzi, walked. Gagne got an infield single scoring Brunansky.

One in Twins eighth: Laudner singled. Gladden doubled scoring Laudner.

World Series MVPs

1955 Johnny Podres, Brooklyn (NL)
1956 Don Larsen, New York (AL)
1957 Lew Burdette, Milwaukee (NL)
1958 Bob Turley, New York (AL)
1959 Larry Sherry, Los Angeles (NL)
1960 Bobby Richardson, New York (AL)
1961 Whitey Ford, New York (AL)
1962 Ralph Terry, New York (AL)
1963 Sandy Koufax, Los Angeles (NL)
1964 Bob Gibson, St. Louis (NL)
1965 Sandy Koufax, Los Angeles (NL)
1966 Frank Robinson, Baltimore (AL)
1967 Bob Gibson, St. Louis (NL)
1968 Mickey Lolich, Detroit (AL)
1969 Donn Clendenon, New York (NL)
1970 Brooks Robinson, Baltimore (AL)
1971 Roberto Clemente, Pittsburgh (NL)
1972 Gene Tenace, Oakland (AL)
1973 Reggie Jackson, Oakland (AL)
1974 Rollie Fingers, Oakland (AL)
1975 Pete Rose, Cincinnati (NL)
1976 Johnny Bench, Cincinnati (NL)
1977 Reggie Jackson, New York (AL)
1978 Bucky Dent, New York (AL)
1979 Willie Stargell, Pittsburgh (NL)
1980 Mike Schmidt, Philadelphia (NL)
1981 Ron Cey, Pedro Guerrero, Steve Yeager, Los Angeles (NL)
1982 Darrell Porter, St. Louis (NL)
1983 Rick Dempsey, Baltimore (AL)
1984 Alan Trammell, Detroit (AL)
1985 Bret Saberhagen, Kansas City (AL)
1986 Ray Knight, New York (NL)
1987 Frank Viola, Minnesota (AL)

St. Louis Cardinals

	g	ab	r	h	2b	3b	hr	rbi	so[1]	bb	avg	po	a	e	pct
Terry Pendleton dh-ph	3	7	2	3	0	0	0	1	1	1	.429	0	0	0	—
Willie McGee cf	7	27	2	10	2	0	0	4	8	0	.370	18	1	1	.950
Tony Pena c-dh	7	22	3	9	1	0	0	4	1	3	.409	32	1	1	.971
Curt Ford rf-ph	5	13	1	4	0	0	0	2	1	1	.308	5	0	0	1.000
Jim Lindeman 1b-rf	6	15	3	5	1	0	0	2	2	0	.323	23	1	3	.923
Jose Oquendo rf-3b	7	24	2	6	0	0	0	2	3	1	.250	6	10	0	1.000
Tom Herr 2b	7	28	2	7	0	0	1	1	1	2	.250	22	15	0	1.000
Ozzie Smith ss	7	28	3	6	0	0	0	2	3	2	.214	7	18	0	1.000
Tom Pagnozzi dh	2	4	0	1	0	0	0	0	0	0	.250	0	0	0	—
Dan Driessen 1b	4	13	3	3	2	0	0	1	1	1	.231	27	1	0	1.000
Vince Coleman lf	7	28	5	4	2	0	0	2	8	2	.143	8	0	0	1.000
Tom Lawless 3b	3	10	1	1	0	0	1	3	4	0	.100	1	5	1	.857
Danny Cox p	3	2	0	0	0	0	0	0	1	0	.000	1	1	0	1.000
Bob Forsch p	3	2	0	0	0	0	0	0	0	0	.000	1	0	0	1.000
John Morris rf	1	2	0	0	0	0	0	0	0	0	.000	2	0	0	1.000
John Tudor p	2	2	0	0	0	0	0	0	2	0	.000	0	4	0	1.000
Ken Dayley p	4	1	0	0	0	0	0	0	1	0	.000	0	0	0	—
Greg Mathews p	1	1	0	0	0	0	0	0	0	0	.000	0	1	0	1.000
Ricky Horton p	2	0	0	0	0	0	0	0	0	0	—	0	1	0	1.000
Vance Johnson pr	1	0	0	0	0	0	0	0	0	0	—	0	0	0	—
Steve Lake c	3	3	0	1	0	0	0	1	0	0	.333	0	0	0	—
Joe Magrane p	2	0	0	0	0	0	0	0	0	0	—	0	0	0	—
Lee Tunnell p	2	0	0	0	0	0	0	0	0	0	—	0	1	0	1.000
Todd Worrell p	4	0	0	0	0	0	0	0	0	0	—	0	0	0	—
Totals	**7**	**232**	**26**	**60**	**8**	**0**	**2**	**25**	**37**	**13**	**.259**	**153**	**60**	**6**	**.977**

Minnesota Twins

	g	ab	r	h	2b	3b	hr	rbi	so	bb	avg	po	a	e	pct
Roy Smalley ph	4	2	0	1	1	0	0	0	0	1	.500	0	0	0	—
Steve Lombardozzi 2b	6	17	3	7	1	0	1	4	2	2	.412	9	22	0	1.000
Don Baylor dh	5	13	3	5	0	0	1	3	0	1	.385	0	0	0	—
Kirby Puckett cf	7	28	5	10	1	1	0	3	0	2	.357	11	1	1	.923
Dan Gladden lf	7	31	3	9	2	1	1	7	3	3	.290	12	0	0	1.000
Gary Gaetti 3b	7	27	4	7	2	1	1	4	5	1	.259	5	10	0	1.000
Tim Laudner c	7	22	4	7	1	0	1	4	4	4	.318	39	2	0	1.000
Al Newman 2b-ph	4	5	0	1	0	0	0	0	1	1	.200	1	1	0	1.000
Kent Hrbek 1b	7	24	4	5	0	0	1	6	2	4	.208	58	1	0	1.000
Tom Brunansky rf	7	25	5	5	0	0	0	2	4	3	.200	12	0	0	1.000
Randy Bush dh-ph	4	6	1	1	1	0	0	2	1	0	.167	0	0	0	—
Greg Gagne ss	7	30	5	6	1	0	1	3	4	1	.200	4	19	2	.920
Gene Larkin 1b-ph	5	3	1	0	0	0	0	0	0	1	.000	1	0	0	1.000
Les Straker p	2	2	0	0	0	0	0	0	2	0	.000	1	0	0	1.000
Bert Blyleven p	2	1	0	0	0	0	0	0	1	0	.000	0	1	0	1.000
Mark Davidson rf	2	1	0	0	0	0	0	0	0	0	.000	0	0	0	—
Sal Butera c	1	0	—	—	—	—	—	—	—	—	—	—	—	—	—
Frank Viola p	3	1	0	0	0	0	0	0	1	0	.000	0	4	0	1.000
Keith Atherton p	2	0	0	0	0	0	0	0	0	0	—	0	0	0	—
Juan Berenguer p	3	0	0	0	0	0	0	0	0	0	—	0	0	0	—
George Frazier p	1	0	0	0	0	0	0	0	0	0	—	0	1	0	1.000
Joe Niekro p	1	0	0	0	0	0	0	0	0	0	—	0	1	0	1.000
Jeff Reardon p	4	0	0	0	0	0	0	0	0	0	—	0	0	0	—
Dan Schatzeder p	2	0	0	0	0	0	0	0	0	0	—	0	0	0	—
Totals	**7**	**238**	**38**	**64**	**10**	**3**	**7**	**38**	**30**	**24**	**.269**	**153**	**63**	**3**	**.986**

Pitching Summary

St. Louis Cardinals

	g	cg	ip	h	r	bb	so	hb	wp	w	l	pct	er	era
Todd Worrell	4	0	7	6	1	4	3	0	0	0	0	.000	1	1.28
Ken Dayley	3	0	4⅔	2	1	0	3	0	0	0	0	.000	1	1.93
Lee Tunnell	2	0	4⅓	4	2	2	1	0	0	0	0	.000	1	2.08
Greg Mathews	1	0	3⅔	2	1	2	3	1	1	0	0	.000	1	2.46
John Tudor	2	0	11	15	7	3	8	0	0	1	1	.500	7	5.73
Ricky Horton	2	0	3	5	2	0	1	0	0	0	0	.000	2	6.00
Danny Cox	3	0	11⅔	13	10	8	9	0	1	1	2	.333	10	7.72
Bob Forsch	3	0	6⅓	8	7	5	3	1	0	1	0	1.000	7	9.95
Joe Magrane	2	0	7⅓	9	7	5	5	1	0	0	1	.000	7	8.59
Totals	**7**	**0**	**59**	**64**	**38**	**29**	**36**	**3**	**2**	**3**	**4**	**.429**	**37**	**5.64**

Minnesota Twins

	g	cg	ip	h	r	bb	so	hb	wp	w	l	pct	er	era
Jeff Reardon	4	0	4⅔	5	0	0	3	0	0	0	0	.000	0	0.00
George Frazier	1	0	2	1	0	0	2	0	0	0	0	.000	0	0.00
Phil Niekro	1	0	2	1	0	1	1	1	0	0	0	.000	0	0.00
Bert Blyleven	2	0	13	13	5	2	12	0	0	1	1	.500	4	2.77
Les Straker	2	0	9	9	4	3	5	0	0	0	0	.000	4	4.00
Frank Viola	3	0	19⅔	17	8	3	16	0	0	2	1	.666	8	3.73
Dan Schatzeder	3	0	4⅓	4	3	3	4	0	0	1	0	1.000	3	6.23
Keith Atherton	2	0	1⅓	0	1	1	0	0	0	0	0	.000	1	6.75
Juan Berenguer	3	0	4⅓	10	5	0	1	0	0	0	1	.000	5	10.39
Totals	**7**	**0**	**60**	**60**	**26**	**13**	**44**	**1**	**0**	**4**	**3**	**.571**	**25**	**3.75**

Composite Score By Innings

St. Louis	1	4	1	8	5	0	5	2	0	—	26
Minnesota	2	2	1	13	8	7	1	4	0	—	38

(1) Note: so, bb, po, a, pct through six games.

World Series Results, 1903-1987

1903 Boston AL 5, Pittsburgh NL 3
1904 No series
1905 New York NL 4, Philadelphia AL 1
1906 Chicago AL 4, Chicago NL 2
1907 Chicago NL 4, Detroit AL 0, 1 tie
1908 Chicago NL 4, Detroit AL 1
1909 Pittsburgh NL 4, Detroit AL 3
1910 Philadelphia AL 4, Chicago NL 1
1911 Philadelphia AL 4, New York NL 2
1912 Boston AL 4, New York NL 3, 1 tie
1913 Philadelphia AL 4, New York NL 1
1914 Boston NL 4, Philadelphia AL 0
1915 Boston AL 4, Philadelphia NL 1
1916 Boston AL 4, Brooklyn NL 1
1917 Chicago AL 4, New York NL 2
1918 Boston AL 4, Chicago NL 2
1919 Cincinnati NL 5, Chicago AL 3
1920 Cleveland AL 5, Brooklyn NL 2
1921 New York NL 5, New York AL 3
1922 New York NL 4, New York AL 0, 1 tie
1923 New York AL 4, New York NL 2
1924 Washington AL 4, New York NL 3
1925 Pittsburgh NL 4, Washington AL 3
1926 St. Louis NL 4, New York AL 3
1927 New York AL 4, Pittsburgh NL 0
1928 New York AL 4, St. Louis NL 0
1929 Philadelphia AL 4, Chicago NL 1
1930 Philadelphia AL 4, St. Louis NL 2
1931 St. Louis NL 4, Philadelphia AL 3
1932 New York AL 4, Chicago NL 0
1933 New York NL 4, Washington AL 1
1934 St. Louis NL 4, Detroit AL 3
1935 Detroit AL 4, Chicago NL 2
1936 New York AL 4, New York NL 2
1937 New York AL 4, New York NL 1
1938 New York AL 4, Chicago NL 0
1939 New York AL 4, Cincinnati NL 0
1940 Cincinnati NL 4, Detroit AL 3
1941 New York AL 4, Brooklyn NL 1
1942 St. Louis NL 4, New York AL 1
1943 New York AL 4, St. Louis NL 1
1944 St. Louis NL 4, St. Louis AL 2
1945 Detroit AL 4, Chicago NL 3
1946 St. Louis NL 4, Boston AL 3
1947 New York AL 4, Brooklyn NL 3
1948 Cleveland AL 4, Boston NL 2
1949 New York AL 4, Brooklyn NL 1
1950 New York AL 4, Philadelphia NL 0
1951 New York AL 4, New York NL 2
1952 New York AL 4, Brooklyn NL 3
1953 New York AL 4, Brooklyn NL 2
1954 New York NL 4, Cleveland AL 0
1955 Brooklyn NL 4, New York AL 3
1956 New York AL 4, Brooklyn NL 3
1957 Milwaukee NL 4, New York AL 3
1958 New York AL 4, Milwaukee NL 3
1959 Los Angeles NL 4, Chicago AL 2
1960 Pittsburgh NL 4, New York AL 3
1961 New York AL 4, Cincinnati NL 1
1962 New York AL 4, San Francisco NL 3
1963 Los Angeles NL 4, New York AL 0
1964 St. Louis NL 4, New York AL 3
1965 Los Angeles NL 4, Minnesota AL 3
1966 Baltimore AL 4, Los Angeles NL 0
1967 St. Louis NL 4, Boston AL 3
1968 Detroit AL 4, St. Louis NL 3
1969 New York NL 4, Baltimore AL 1
1970 Baltimore AL 4, Cincinnati NL 1
1971 Pittsburgh NL 4, Baltimore AL 3
1972 Oakland AL 4, Cincinnati NL 3
1973 Oakland AL 4, New York NL 3
1974 Oakland AL 4, Los Angeles NL 1
1975 Cincinnati NL 4, Boston AL 3
1976 Cincinnati NL 4, New York AL 0
1977 New York AL 4, Los Angeles NL 2
1978 New York AL 4, Los Angeles NL 2
1979 Pittsburgh NL 4, Baltimore AL 3
1980 Philadelphia NL 4, Kansas City AL 2
1981 Los Angeles NL 4, New York AL 2
1982 St. Louis NL 4, Milwaukee AL 3
1983 Baltimore AL 4, Philadelphia NL 1
1984 Detroit AL 4, San Diego NL 1
1985 Kansas City AL 4, St. Louis NL 3
1986 New York NL 4, Boston AL 3
1987 Minnesota AL 4, St. Louis NL 3

Major League Leaders in 1987

National League

Home Runs

Dawson, Chicago, 49; Murphy, Atlanta, 44; Strawberry, New York, 39; Davis, Cincinnati, 37; Johnson, New York, 36; Clark, St. Louis, 35; Schmidt, Philadelphia, 35; Clark, San Francisco, 35.

Runs Batted In

Dawson, Chicago, 137; Wallach, Montreal, 123; Schmidt, Philadelphia, 113; Clark, St. Louis, 106; Murphy, Atlanta, 105; McGee, St. Louis, 105; Strawberry, New York, 104; Davis, Cincinnati, 100; Samuel, Philadelphia, 100.

Stolen Bases

Coleman, St. Louis, 109; Gwynn, San Diego, 56; Hatcher, Houston, 53; Davis, Cincinnati, 50; Raines, Montreal, 50.

Runs

Raines, Montreal, 123; Coleman, St. Louis, 121; Davis, Cincinnati, 120; Gwynn, San Diego, 119; Murphy, Atlanta, 115.

Hits

Gwynn, San Diego, 218; Guerrero, Los Angeles, 184; Smith, St. Louis, 182; Coleman, St. Louis, 180; Dawson, Chicago, 178; Samuel, Philadelphia, 178.

Doubles

Wallach, Montreal, 41; Galarraga, Montreal, 40; Smith, St. Louis, 40; Dykstra, New York, 38.

Triples

Samuel, Philadelphia, 15; Gwynn, San Diego, 13; McGee, St. Louis, 11; Van Slyke, Pittsburgh, 11; Coleman, St. Louis, 10.

Pitching (15 decisions)

Martinez, Montreal, 11-4, .733; Dunne, Pittsburgh, 13-6, .684; Gooden, New York, 15-7, .682; Deshales, Houston, 11-6, .647; Sutcliffe, Chicago, 18-10, .643.

Strikeouts

Ryan, Houston, 270; Scott, Houston, 233; Welch, Los Angeles, 195; Hershiser, Los Angeles, 190; Valenzuela, Los Angeles, 190.

Saves

Bedrosian, Philadelphia, 40; Smith, Chicago, 36; Worrell, St. Louis, 33; Franco, Cincinnati, 32; McDowell, New York, 25.

American League

Home Runs

McGwire, Oakland, 49; Bell, Toronto, 47; Evans, Detroit, 34; Evans, Boston, 34; Hrbek, Minnesota, 34; Joyner, California, 34; Tartabull, Kansas City, 34; Snyder, Cleveland, 33.

Runs Batted In

Bell, Toronto, 134; Evans, Boston, 123; McGwire, Oakland, 118; Joyner, California, 117; Mattingly, New York, 115; Canseco, Oakland, 113; Gaetti, Minnesota, 109; Sierra, Texas, 109.

Stolen Bases

Reynolds, Seattle, 60; Wilson, Kansas City, 59; Redus, Chicago, 52; Molitor, Milwaukee, 45; Henderson, New York, 41.

Runs

Molitor, Milwaukee, 114; Bell, Toronto, 111; Downing, California, 110; Whitaker, Detroit, 110; Evans, Boston, 109; Trammell, Detroit, 109.

Hits

Puckett, Minnesota, 207; Seitzer, Kansas City, 207; Trammell, Detroit, 205; Boggs, Boston, 200; Yount, Milwaukee, 198.

Doubles

Molitor, Milwaukee, 41; Boggs, Boston, 40; Calderon, Chicago, 38; Mattingly, New York, 38; Whitaker, Detroit, 38.

Triples

Wilson, Kansas City, 15; P. Bradley, Seattle, 10; Polonia, Oakland, 10; Yount, Milwaukee, 9.

Pitching (15 decisions)

Cerutti, Toronto, 11-4, .733; Guetterman, Seattle, 11-4, .733; Musselman, Toronto, 12-5, .706; Clemens, Boston, 20-9, .690; John, New York, 13-6, .684.

Strikeouts

Langston, Seattle, 262; Clemens, Boston, 256; Higuera, Milwaukee, 240; Hough, Texas, 223; Morris, Detroit, 208.

Saves

Henke, Toronto, 34; Reardon, Minnesota, 31; Righetti, New York, 31; Plesac, Milwaukee, 23; Buice, California, 17.

Pitchers with 300 Major League Wins

Pitcher	Wins	Pitcher	Wins	Pitcher	Wins	Pitcher	Wins
Cy Young	511	Warren Spahn	363	Eddie Plank	325	Tom Seaver	311
Walter Johnson	416	Kid Nichols	360	Don Sutton	321	Charles Radbourn	308
Grover C. Alexander	373	Tim Keefe	346	Phil Niekro	318	Lefty Grove	300
Christy Mathewson	373	Steve Carlton	329	Mickey Welch	316	Early Wynn	300
Pud Galvin	365	John Clarkson	328	Gaylord Perry	314		

All-Time Home Run Leaders

Player	HR	Player	HR	Player	HR	Player	HR
Hank Aaron	755	Ernie Banks	512	Frank Howard	382	Lee May	354
Babe Ruth	714	Mel Ott	511	Darrell Evans	381	Dick Allen	351
Willie Mays	660	Lou Gehrig	493	Orlando Cepeda	379	George Foster	348
Frank Robinson	586	Stan Musial	475	Tony Perez	379	Ron Santo	342
Harmon Killebrew	573	Willie Stargell	475	Norm Cash	377	John (Boog) Powell	339
Reggie Jackson	563	Carl Yastrzemski	452	Rocky Colavito	374	Joe Adcock	336
Mike Schmidt	530	Dave Kingman	442	Gil Hodges	370	Dave Winfield	332
Mickey Mantle	536	Billy Williams	426	Ralph Kiner	369	Bobby Bonds	332
Jimmy Foxx	534	Duke Snider	407	Jim Rice	364	Hank Greenberg	331
Ted Williams	521	Al Kaline	399	Joe DiMaggio	361	Don Baylor	331
Willie McCovey	521	Johnny Bench	389	John Mize	359	Willie Horton	325
Ed Mathews	512	Graig Nettles	389	Yogi Berra	358	Dwight Evans	325

World Almanac All-Major League Baseball Team

The team was chosen by a panel of sports experts on behalf of the World Almanac.

Position	Player, team	Position	Player, team
First base	Don Mattingly, N.Y. Yankees	Catcher	Benito Santiago, San Diego Padres
Second base	Juan Samuel, Philadelphia Phillies	Designated hitter	Paul Molitor, Milwaukee Brewers
Third base	Wade Boggs, Boston Red Sox	Right-hand pitcher	Roger Clemens, Boston Red Sox
Shortstop	Alan Trammell, Detroit Tigers	Left-hand pitcher	Frank Viola, Minnesota Twins
Left field	George Bell, Toronto Blue Jays	Relief pitcher	Todd Worrell, St. Louis Cardinals
Center field	Kirby Puckett, Minnesota Twins	Rookie of the Year	Mark McGwire, Oakland A's
Right field	Andre Dawson, Chicago Cubs	Player of the Year	Alan Trammell, Detroit Tigers

NCAA Baseball Champions

1947	California	1958	USC	1969	Arizona St.	1980	Arizona
1948	USC	1959	Oklahoma St.	1970	USC	1981	Arizona St.
1949	Texas	1960	Minnesota	1971	USC	1982	Miami, Fla.
1950	Texas	1961	USC	1972	USC	1983	Texas
1951	Oklahoma	1962	Michigan	1973	USC	1984	Cal. St.-Fullerton
1952	Holy Cross	1963	USC	1974	USC	1985	Miami, Fla.
1953	Michigan	1964	Minnesota	1975	Texas	1986	Arizona
1954	Missouri	1965	Arizona St.	1976	Arizona	1987	Stanford
1955	Wake Forest	1966	Ohio St.	1977	Arizona St.		
1956	Minnesota	1967	Arizona St.	1978	USC		
1957	California	1968	USC	1979	Cal. St.-Fullerton		

The 1987 Bud Light U.S. Triathlon Series

The World Almanac perpetual trophy was awarded to Mike Pigg of Acrata, Cal. and Kirsten Hanssen of Denver, Col. as the overall men's and women's 1987 Bud Light U.S. Triathlon Series National Champions.

U.S. Gymnastics Championships in 1987

Scott Johnson of Colorado Springs, Col. scored 114.70 points to win the men's overall title at the 1987 U.S. Gymnastics Championships in Kansas City, Mo. Kristie Phillips of Baton Rouge, La. took the women's crown.

Ten Most Dramatic Sports Events, Nov. 1986—Oct. 1987

Selected by The World Almanac Sports Staff

—Ben Johnson of Canada broke the world record in the 100-meter dash in a clocking of 9.83 seconds at the World Championship games in Rome. He broke the record set by Calvin Smith in 1983.

—Penn State became the national champions of college football when they forced 5 interceptions and defeated the number-one ranked Miami Hurricanes 14-10 in the Fiesta Bowl. It was the second national title for the Nittany Lions.

—Sugar Ray Leonard won a 12-round split decision over Marvelous Marvin Hagler to win the WBC middleweight title. Leonard had fought only one bout in 5 years because of an eye injury.

—Keith Smart hit a 17-foot jump shot with 5 seconds remaining in the game to give Indiana Univ. a 74-73 victory over Syracuse Univ. in the finals of the NCAA basketball tournament. It was the fifth national championship for the Hoosiers and the third under coach Bob Knight.

—The U.S. yacht *Stars & Stripes* defeated the Australian yacht *Kookaburra III,* 4-0, in the best-of-seven series of races off Fremantle, Australia to recapture the America's Cup. Skipper Dennis Connor avenged the 1983 loss of the Cup to the yacht *Australia.*

—Paul Molitor of the Milwaukee Brewers hit safely in 39 consecutive games. It was the fifth longest streak in modern major league history.

—John Elway of the Denver Broncos threw a touchdown pass to Mark Jackson with 39 seconds remaining in the game to tie the score and climax a 98-yard drive in the AFC championship game against the Cleveland Browns. The Broncos won the game on a field goal in overtime. (They were defeated by the N.Y. Giants in Super Bowl XXI.).

—Don Mattingly of the New York Yankees hit home runs in 8 consecutive games to tie the major league record. The record was set by Dale Long of the Pittsburgh Pirates in 1956.

—Larry Mize rolled in a 140-foot chip shot in a playoff against Greg Norman to win the Masters Golf Tournament.

—In the first World Series where all seven games were won by the home team, the Minnesota Twins, after winning only 85 games in the regular season, won the 1987 World Series.

Auto Racing

Indianapolis 500 Winners

Year	Winner	Chassis	Engine	MPH	Purse	Runner up
1952	Troy Ruttman	Kuzma	Offenhauser	128.922	$230,100	Jim Rathmann
1953	Bill Vukovich	Kurtis Kraft 500A	Offenhauser	128.740	246,300	Art Cross
1954	Bill Vukovich	Kurtis Kraft 500A	Offenhauser	130.840	269,375	Jim Bryan
1955	Bob Sweikert	Kurtis Kraft 500C	Offenhauser	128.209	270,400	Tony Bettenhausen
1956	Pat Flaherty	Watson	Offenhauser	128.490	282,052	Sam Hanks
1957	Sam Hanks	Epperly	Offenhauser	135.601	300,252	Jim Rathmann
1958	Jimmy Bryan	Epperly	Offenhauser	133.791	305,217	George Amick
1959	Rodger Ward	Watson	Offenhauser	135.857	338,100	Jim Rathmann
1960	Jim Rathmann	Watson	Offenhauser	138.767	369,150	Rodger Ward
1961	A.J. Foyt	Watson	Offenhauser	139.130	400,000	Eddie Sachs
1962	Rodger Ward	Watson	Offenhauser	140.293	426,152	Len Sutton
1963	Parnelli Jones	Watson	Offenhauser	143.137	494,031	Jim Clark
1964	A.J. Foyt	Watson	Offenhauser	147.350	506,625	Rodger Ward
1965	Jim Clark	Lotus	Ford	151.388	628,399	Parnelli Jones
1966	Graham Hill	Lola	Ford	144.317	691,809	Jim Clark
1967	A.J. Foyt	Coyote	Ford	151.207	737,109	Al Unser
1968	Bobby Unser	Eagle	Offenhauser	152.882	809,627	Dan Gurney
1969	Mario Andretti	Hawk	Ford	156.867	805,127	Dan Gurney
1970	Al Unser	P.J. Colt	Ford	155.749	1,000,002	Mark Donohue
1971	Al Unser	P.J. Colt	Ford	157.735	1,001,604	Peter Revson
1972	Mark Donohue	McLaren	Offenhauser	163.465	1,011,846	Al Unser
1973	Gordon Johncock	Eagle	Offenhauser	159.014(a)	1,011,846	Billy Vukovich
1974	Johnny Rutherford	McLaren	Offenhauser	158.589	1,015,686	Bobby Unser
1975	Bobby Unser	Eagle	Offenhauser	149.213(b)	1,101,322	Johnny Rutherford
1976	Johnny Rutherford	McLaren	Offenhauser	148.725(c)	1,037,775	A.J. Foyt
1977	A.J. Foyt	Coyote	Ford	161.331	1,116,807	Tom Sneva
1978	Al Unser	Lola	Cosworth	161.363	1,145,225	Tom Sneva
1979	Rick Mears	Penske	Cosworth	158.899	1,271,954	A.J. Foyt
1980	Johnny Rutherford	Chaparral	Cosworth	142.862	1,502,425	Tom Sneva
1981	Bobby Unser	Penske	Cosworth	139.085	1,609,375	Mario Andretti
1982	Gordon Johncock	Wildcat	Cosworth	162.026	2,067,475	Rick Mears
1983	Tom Sneva	March	Cosworth	162.117	2,411,450	Al Unser
1984	Rick Mears	March	Cosworth	163.621	2,795,399	Roberto Guerrero
1985	Danny Sullivan	March	Cosworth	152.982	3,261,025	Mario Andretti
1986	Bobby Rahal	March	Cosworth	170.722	4,001,450	Kevin Cogan
1987	Al Unser	March	Cosworth	162.175	4,490,375	Roberto Guerrero

(a) 332.5 miles. (b) 435 miles. (c) 255 miles. Race record—170.722 MPH, Bobby Rahal, 1986.

Notable One-Mile Speed Records

Date	Driver	Car	MPH
1/26/06	Marriott	Stanley (Steam)	127.659
3/16/10	Oldfield	Benz	131.724
4/23/11	Burman	Benz	141.732
2/12/19	DePalma	Packard	149.875
4/27/20	Milton	Dusenberg	155.046
4/28/26	Parry-Thomas	Thomas Spl.	170.624
3/29/27	Seagrave	Sunbeam	203.790
4/22/28	Keech	White Triplex	207.552
3/11/29	Seagrave	Irving-Napier	231.446
2/ 5/31	Campbell	Napier-Campbell	246.086
2/24/32	Campbell	Napier-Campbell	253.96
2/22/33	Campbell	Napier-Campbell	272.109
9/ 3/35	Campbell	Bluebird Special	301.13
11/19/37	Eyston	Thunderbolt 1	311.42
9/16/38	Eyston	Thunderbolt 1	357.5
8/23/39	Cobb	Railton	368.9
9/16/47	Cobb	Railton-Mobil	394.2
8/ 5/63	Breedlove	Spirit of America	407.45
10/27/64	Arfons	Green Monster	536.71
11/15/65	Breedlove	Spirit of America	600.601
10/23/70	Gabelich	Blue Flame	622.407
10/9/79	Barrett	Budweiser Rocket	638.637*
10/4/83	Noble	Thrust 2	633.6

*not recognized as official by sanctioning bodies.

World Grand Prix Champions

Year	Driver
1951	Jan Fangio, Argentina
1952	Alberto Ascari, Italy
1953	Alberto Ascari, Italy
1954	Juan Fangio, Argentina
1955	Juan Fangio, Argentina
1956	Juan Fangio, Argentina
1957	Juan Fangio, Argentina
1958	Mike Hawthorne, England
1959	Jack Brabham, Australia
1960	Jack Brabham, Australia
1961	Phil Hill, United States
1962	Graham Hill, England
1963	Jim Clark, Scotland
1964	John Surtees, England
1965	Jim Clark, Scotland
1966	Jack Brabham, Australia
1967	Denis Hulme, New Zealand
1968	Graham Hill, England
1969	Jackie Stewart, Scotland
1970	Jochen Rindt, Austria
1971	Jackie Stewart, Scotland
1972	Emerson Fittipaldi, Brazil
1973	Jackie Stewart, Scotland
1974	Emerson Fittipaldi, Brazil
1975	Nicki Lauda, Austria
1976	James Hunt, England
1977	Niki Lauda, Austria
1978	Mario Andretti, U.S.
1979	Jody Scheckter, So. Africa
1980	Alan Jones, Australia
1981	Nelson Piquet, Brazil
1982	Keke Rosberg, Finland
1983	Nelson Piquet, Brazil
1984	Niki Lauda, Austria
1985	Alain Prost, France
1986	Alain Prost, France

CART Champions

(U.S. Auto Club Champions prior to 1979)

Year	Driver
1959	Rodger Ward
1960	A. J. Foyt
1961	A. J. Foyt
1962	Rodger Ward
1963	A. J. Foyt
1964	A. J. Foyt
1965	Mario Andretti
1966	Mario Andretti
1967	A. J. Foyt
1968	Bobby Unser
1969	Mario Andretti
1970	Al Unser
1971	Joe Leonard
1972	Joe Leonard
1973	Roger McCluskey
1974	Bobby Unser
1975	A. J. Foyt
1976	Gordon Johncock
1977	Tom Sneva
1978	Tom Sneva
1979	Rick Mears
1980	Johnny Rutherford
1981	Rick Mears
1982	Rick Mears
1983	Al Unser
1984	Mario Andretti
1985	Al Unser
1986	Bobby Rahal

Grand Prix for Formula 1 Cars in 1987

Grand Prix	Winner, car
Austrian	Nigel Mansell, Williams-Honda
Belgian	Alain Prost, McLaren TAG
Brazilian	Alain Prost, McLaren TAG
British	Nigel Mansell, Williams-Honda
Detroit	Ayrton Senna, Lotus-Renault
French	Nigel Mansell, Williams-Honda
German	Nelson Piquet, Williams-Honda
Hungarian	Nelson Piquet, Williams-Honda
Italian	Nelson Piquet, Williams-Honda
Monaco	Ayrton Senna, Lotus-Honda
Portuguese	Alain Prost, McLaren-TAG
San Marino	Nigel Mansell, Williams-Honda
Spanish	Nigel Mansell, Williams-Honda

Le Mans 24-Hour Race in 1987

Derek Bell, Hans Stuck, and Al Holbert drove their Porsche 962C to victory in the 1987 Le Mans 24-hour race. They covered 2,978.108 miles at an average speed of 124.087 miles per hour.

NASCAR Racing in 1987

Winston Cup Grand National Races

Date	Race, site	Winner	Car	Average MPH
Feb. 15	Daytona 500, Daytona Beach, Fla.	Bill Elliott	Ford	176.263
Mar. 1	Goodwrench 500, Rockingham, N.C.	Dale Earnhardt	Chevrolet	117.556
Mar. 8	Miller High Life 400	Dale Earnhardt	Chevrolet	81.520
Mar. 15	Motorcraft 500, Atlanta, Ga.	Ricky Rudd	Ford	133.689
Mar. 29	Transouth 500, Darlington, S.C.	Dale Earnhardt	Chevrolet	122.540
Apr. 5	First Union 400, N. Wilkesboro, N.C.	Dale Earnhardt	Chevrolet	94.103
Apr. 12	Valleydale Meats 500, Bristol, Tenn.	Dale Earnhardt	Chevrolet	75.621
Apr. 26	Sovran Bank 500, Martinsville, Va.	Dale Earnhardt	Chevrolet	72.808
May 3	Winston 500, Talladega, Ala.	Davey Allison	Ford	154.228
May 31	Budweiser 500, Dover, Del.	Davey Allison	Ford	112.958
June 14	Miller High Life 500, Pocono, Pa.	Tim Richmond	Chevrolet	122.166
June 21	Budweiser 400, Riverside, Cal.	Tim Richmond	Chevrolet	102.183
June 28	Miller American 400, Brooklyn, Mich.	Dale Earnhardt	Chevrolet	148.454
July 4	Firecracker 400, Daytona Beach, Fla.	Bobby Allison	Buick	161.074
July 19	Summer 500, Long Pond, Pa.	Dale Earnhardt	Chevrolet	121.737
July 26	Talladega 500, Talladega, Ala.	Bill Elliott	Ford	171.293
Aug. 10	Watkins Glen International, N.Y.	Rusty Wallace	Pontiac	90.682
Aug. 16	Champion Spark Plug 400, Brooklyn, Mich.	Bill Elliott	Ford	138.648
Aug. 22	Busch 500, Bristol, Tenn.	Dale Earnhardt	Chevrolet	90.373
Sept. 6	Southern 500, Darlington, S.C.	Dale Earnhardt	Chevrolet	—
Sept. 13	Wrangler 400, Richmond, Va.	Dale Earnhardt	Chevrolet	67.074
Sept. 20	Delaware 500, Dover, Del.	Ricky Rudd	Ford	124.706
Sept. 27	Goody's 500, Martinsville, Va.	Darrell Waltrip	Chevrolet	76.410
Oct. 4	Holly Farms 400, N. Wilkesboro, N.C.	Terry Labonte	Chevrolet	96.002
Oct. 11	Oakwood Homes 500, Concord, N.C.	Bill Elliott	Ford	128.443

Daytona 500 Winners

Year	Driver, car	Avg. MPH
1962	Fireball Roberts, Pontiac	152.529
1963	Tiny Lund, Ford	151.566
1964	Richard Petty, Plymouth	154.334
1965	Fred Lorenzen, Ford (a)	141.539
1966	Richard Petty, Plymouth (b)	160.627
1967	Mario Andretti, Ford	146.926
1968	Cale Yarborough, Mercury	143.251
1969	Lee Roy Yarborough, Ford	160.875
1970	Pete Hamilton, Plymouth	149.601
1971	Richard Petty, Plymouth	144.456
1972	A. J. Foyt, Mercury	161.550
1973	Richard Petty, Dodge	157.205
1974	Richard Petty, Dodge (c)	140.894
1975	Benny Parsons, Chevrolet	153.649
1976	David Pearson, Mercury	152.181
1977	Cale Yarborough, Chevrolet	153.218
1978	Bobby Allison, Ford	159.730
1979	Richard Petty, Oldsmobile	143.977
1980	Buddy Baker, Oldsmobile	177.602
1981	Richard Petty, Buick	169.651
1982	Bobby Allison, Buick	153.991
1983	Cale Yarborough, Pontiac	155.979
1984	Cale Yarborough, Chevrolet	150.994
1985	Bill Elliott, Ford	172.265
1986	Geoff Bodine, Chevrolet	148.124
1987	Bill Elliott, Ford	176.263

(a) 322.5 miles. (b) 495 miles. (c) 450 miles.

Grand National Champions (NASCAR)

Year	Driver
1956	Buck Baker
1956	Buck Baker
1957	Buck Baker
1958	Lee Petty
1959	Lee Petty
1960	Rex White
1961	Ned Jarrett
1962	Joe Weatherly
1963	Joe Weatherly
1964	Richard Petty
1965	Ned Jarrett
1966	David Pearson
1967	Richard Petty
1968	David Pearson
1969	David Pearson
1970	Bobby Isaac
1971	Richard Petty
1972	Richard Petty
1973	Benny Parson
1974	Richard Petty
1975	Richard Petty
1976	Cale Yarborough
1977	Cale Yarborough
1978	Cale Yarborough
1979	Richard Petty
1980	Dale Earnhardt
1981	Darrell Waltrip
1982	Darrell Waltrip
1983	Bobby Allison
1984	Terry Labonte
1985	Darrell Waltrip

Notable Sports Records

During 1986-87, there were many record-breaking performances in sports. The following are the major accomplishments of the year.

Baseball

The past baseball season became known as the year of the home run. Home run records set during the year include:

—Most home runs in a season (4,458); most American League home runs (2,634); and most National League home runs (1,824).
—Cleveland, Detroit, Kansas City, Oakland, Texas, Toronto, the Chicago Cubs, and the New York Mets set team home run records.
—a record 28 players hit at least 30 home runs during the season.
—Baltimore pitchers allowed the most home runs by one team in a season (226).
—Don Mattingly of the N.Y. Yankees hit home runs in 8 consecutive games to tie the major league record.
—Don Mattingly hit 6 bases loaded home runs to set a major league record.
—Mark McGwire of Oakland set a major league record for most home runs by a rookie (49).
—Eddie Murray of Baltimore became the first major leaguer to hit home runs from both sides of the plate in consecutive games.
—The Toronto Blue Jays set a major league record by hitting 10 home runs in a game against the Baltimore Orioles.

Other baseball records include:

—Don Baylor established a major league record by being hit by a pitch for the 244th time.
—Don Mattingly tied a major league record with 22 putouts in a game.
—Cal Ripkin Jr. of Baltimore ended his consecutive innings streak at 8,243, which is believed to be the longest in major league history.
—Bob Boone of California set a major league record by catching his 1,919th major league game.
—Geno Petralli of Texas tied a major league record with 6 passed balls in a game.
—Darryl Strawberry and Howard Johnson of the N.Y. Mets became the first major league teammates to have at least 30 home runs and 30 stolen bases in the same year.
—Kirby Puckett of Minnesota had 10 hits in 2 consecutive 9-inning games to set an American League record and tie the major league record.
—The Milwaukee Brewers set a major league record by winning their first 13 games.
—Steve Bedrosian of Philadelphia set a major league record by recording a save in 13 straight appearances.
—Joe and Phil Niekro's 530th win passed the Perry brothers in career major league pitching victories.
—The Salt Lake Trappers of the rookie Pioneer League won 29 straight games, the most in professional baseball history.
—The outfield of the St. Louis Cardinals set a major league record by failing to record a putout in 13 innings against the Phillies.
—The N.Y. Mets and the L.A. Dodgers used 8 pitchers in an inning, a major league record.
—Benito Santiago of the San Diego Padres set major league records for a consecutive-game hitting streak for a rookie and a catcher (34).
—Rob Murphy of Cincinnati set a major league record for relief appearances by a left-handed pitcher (87).
—Jack Clark of St. Louis walked in 16 consecutive games to set a major league record.

Football

—Charlie Joiner set a new NFL record for pass reception yardage (12,146 yds.).
—Marcus Allen of the L.A. Raiders ran for 100 or more yards in 10 consecutive games for a new NFL record.
—Steve Largent of Seattle caught a pass in his 139th consecutive game to extend his NFL record in 1986.
—Quarterback Randall Cunningham of Philadelphia was sacked an NFL record 72 times during the 1986 season.
—Dave Jennings of the N.Y. Jets finished the 1986 season with an NFL record 1,090 career punts.
—Walter Payton of Chicago set an NFL record in 1987 when he scored his 107th rushing touchdown.
—Kevin Sweeney of Fresno St. set a major-college career passing record in 1986 (10,623 yds.).
—Columbia Univ. set a major college record by losing 35 consecutive football games.

Hockey

—Wayne Gretzky of Edmonton set a record for most Stanley Cup playoff points (183).
—The Edmonton Oilers scored a Stanley Cup record 13 goals in a game against the L.A. Kings.

Basketball

—Dick Baldwin won his 876th coaching victory at Broome Community College in Binghamton, N.Y. to set a record for most collegiate basketball coaching wins.
—Michael Jordan of Chicago became the first NBA guard to score over 3,000 points in a season.
—The Boston Celtics set an NBA record by winning 33 consecutive playoff games at home.
—The L.A. Lakers set an NBA record by scoring the first 29 points in a game against the Sacramento Kings. The Kings tied the league mark by scoring only 4 points in the quarter.

Track

—Ben Johnson set a world record in the 100-meter dash (9.83 seconds).
—Edwin Moses lost a 400-meter hurdles race ending a 122-race winning streak, the longest in the history of track.
—Said Aouita of Morocco set world records in the 2,000 meter run (4:50.81), and the 5,000 meter run (12:58.39).

Tennis

—Steffi Graf, age 17, became the youngest woman to win the French Open singles tennis title.

American Power Boat Assn. Gold Cup Champions

Year	Boat	Driver	Year	Boat	Driver
1972	Atlas Van Lines	Bill Munsey	1980	Miss Budweiser	Dean Chenoweth
1973	Miss Budweiser	Dean Chenoweth	1981	Miss Budweiser	Dean Chenoweth
1974	Pay'N Pak	George Henley	1982	Atlas Van Lines	Chip Hanauer
1975	Pay 'N Pak	George Henley	1983	Atlas Van Lines	Chip Hanauer
1976	Miss U.S.	Tom D'Eath	1984	Atlas Van Lines	Chip Hanauer
1977	Atlas Van Lines	Bill Muncey	1985	Miller American	Chip Hanauer
1978	Atlas Van Lines	Bill Muncey	1986	Miller American	Chip Hanauer
1979	Atlas Van Lines	Bill Muncey	1987	Miller American	Chip Hanauer

Tour de France in 1987

Stephen Roche of Ireland won the Tour de France, the world's most prestigious bicycle endurance race. He became the first Irishman to win the event since it was first held in 1903. His time for the 3-week, 2,547-mile race was 115 hours 27 minutes 42 seconds. Pedor Delgado of Spain finished second.

Deaths, Nov. 1, 1986—Oct. 21, 1987

A

Abel, I.W., 79; labor leader who helped found United Steelworkers of America; pres., 1965-77; Malvern, Oh., Aug. 10.
Abel, Walter, 88; actor whose career in the theater and in films spanned 50 years; Essex, Conn., Mar. 26.
Andrews, V.C., 50; author of books dealing with adolescent and family problems against a background of suspense; Virginia Beach, Va., Dec. 19.
Angel, Heather, 77; character actress who appeared in over 60 films; Santa Barbara, Cal., Dec. 13.
Anouilh, Jean, 77; French playwright, *The Waltz of the Toreadors; Becket;* Lausanne, Switzerland, Oct. 3.
Arnaz, Desi, 69; musician, actor, and producer who created and starred in the *I Love Lucy* TV sitcom in the 1950s; Del Mar, Cal., Dec. 2.
Astaire, Fred, 88; dancer and singer who was a major star of 30 film musicals 1933-1968; Los Angeles, June 22.
Astor, Mary, 81; actress who appeared in over 100 films, *The Maltese Falcon;* Woodland Hills, Cal., Sept. 24.

B

Baird, Bil, 82; puppeteer popular on TV in the 1950s; New York, Mar. 18.
Baker, Carlos, 77; literary critic, author, biographer of Hemingway; Princeton, N.J., Apr. 18.
Baldrige, Malcolm, 64; U.S. Secretary of Commerce since 1981; Walnut Creek, Cal., July 25.
Bennett, Michael, 44; choreographer and director who created the musical, *A Chorus Line;* Tucson, Ariz., June 2.
Bergman, Jules, 57; science editor for ABC News for 25 years; New York, Feb. 12.
Bethea, Larry, 30; defensive lineman for the Dallas Cowboys, 1978-83; Newport, Va., Apr. 23.
Bishop, Jim, 79; newspaper columnist and author, *The Day Lincoln Was Shot;* Delray Beach, Fla., July 26.
Bolger, Ray, 83; dancer and actor best known as the Scarecrow in *The Wizard of Oz;* Los Angeles, Jan. 15.
Brannum, Hugh, 77; actor who played Mr. Green Jeans on TV's *Captain Kangaroo;* E. Stroudsburg, Pa., Apr. 19.
Brattain, Walter, 85; inventor who shared the 1956 Nobel Prize in Physics for the invention of the transistor; Seattle, Oct. 12.
de Broglie, Louis, 94; French physicist who won the 1929 Nobel Prize for his wave theory; Paris, Mar. 19.
Bremner, John B., 66; journalism teacher; Ponce Inlet, Fla., July 30.
Brown, Clarence, 97; film director who was nominated 6 times for an Oscar; Santa Monica, Cal., Aug. 17.
Bryant, Boudleaux, 67; composer of country music, including Everly Brothers hits; Knoxville, Tenn., June 25.
Burke, Michael, 70; executive who headed the N.Y. Yankees baseball team and Madison Square Garden; Ireland, Feb. 5.
Burnham, James, 82; founding editor of *The National Review* magazine; Kent, Conn., July 28.
Burns, Arthur, F., 83; economist and diplomat who headed Federal Reserve Board, 1970-78; Baltimore, June 26.
Burton, Sala, 61; U.S. representative from California since 1983; Washington, D.C., Feb. 1.
Butterfield, Paul, 44; harmonica player who led a blues band popular in the 1960s; Los Angeles, May 4.

C

Caldwell, Erskine, 83; author of over 50 novels including *Tobacco Road* and *God's Little Acre;* Paradise Valley, Ariz., Apr. 11.
Campbell, Archie, 72; comedian featured on TV's *Grand Ole Opry* and *Hee Haw;* Knoxville, Tenn., Aug. 29.
Carlson, Frank, 94; U.S. senator from Kansas, 1951-69; Concordia, Kan., May 30.
Carter, Tim Lee, 76; U.S. representative from Kentucky, 1965-81; Glascow, Ky., Mar. 27.
Casey, William, 74; director of the U.S. Central Intelligence Agency, 1981-87; Glen Cove, N.Y., May 6.
Caspary, Vera, 87; novelist and screenwriter, New York, June 13.
Clancy, King, 83; hockey hall of famer who was a NHL player, coach, referee, and executive; Toronto, Nov. 10.
Cochet, Henri, 85; French tennis star of the 1920s and 1930s; Paris, Apr. 1.
Coco, James, 56; character actor who appeared in films, TV and the theater; New York, Feb. 25.
Coe, Peter, 59; British stage director; England, May 25.
Colonna, Jerry, 82; comic actor who appeared with Bob Hope for 25 years; Woodland Hills, Cal., Nov. 21.
Crothers, Scatman, 76; actor and singer whose show business career spanned 60 years; Los Angeles, Nov. 22.
Curtis, Charlotte, 58; columnist for the *N.Y. Times;* Columbus, Oh., Apr. 16.

D

D'Alesandro Jr., Thomas, 84; mayor of Baltimore, 1947-59; Baltimore, Aug. 23.
Damon, Cathryn, 56; actress who won an Emmy for her role in *Soap;* Los Angeles, May 4.
Daniels, Dominick, V., 78; U.S. representative from New Jersey, 1959-76; Jersey City, July 17.
Daugherty, Duffy, 72; head football coach at Michigan State Univ., 1954-72; Santa Barbara, Cal., Sept. 25.
Davis, Eddie "Lockjaw", 65; jazz tenor saxophonist; Culver City, Cal., Nov. 3.
Delaney, James J., 86; New York Democrat who spent 32 years in the U.S. House of Representatives; Tenafly, N.J., May 24.
Dionne, Elzire, 77; Canadian woman who gained worldwide fame by giving birth to 5 identical girls, May 28, 1934; North Bay, Ont., Canada, Nov. 22.
Dolan, John "Terry", 36; a leading political spokesman for the new right of the 1980s; Washington, D.C., Dec. 28.

E

Eaker, Ira C., 91; commander of U.S. air forces in Europe in World War II; Camp Springs, Md., Aug. 6.
Egan, Richard, 65; actor in 1950's films; Santa Monica, Cal., July 20.

F

Flavin, Joseph B., 58; Singer Corp. head since 1975; Norwalk, Conn., Oct. 7.
Fong, Benson, 70; actor whose career in films and TV spanned more than 40 years; Los Angeles, Aug. 1.
Ford 2d, Henry, 70; head of the auto making company that was founded by his grandfather, Detroit, Sept. 29.
Fosse, Bob, 60; choreographer and director in theater and films, *Cabaret;* Washington, D.C., Sept. 23.
Fredericks, Carlton, 76; host of radio nutrition show for some 30 years; Yonkers, N.Y., July 28.

G

Gaines, Lee, 73; singer and founder of the Delta Rhythm Boys vocal group; Helsinki, Finland, July 15.
Gerhardsen, Einar, prime minister of Norway, 1945-51, 1955-65; Lilleborg, Norway, Sept. 19.
Gleason, Jackie, 71; comedian and actor who was a major TV star in the 1950s; Ft. Lauderdale, Fla., June 24.
Gingold, Hermoine, 89; English-born actress of films and the theater; New York, May 24.
Goodell, Charles E., 60; U.S. Senator from New York, 1968-71; a leading opponent of the Vietnam War; Washington, D.C., Jan. 21.
Grant, Cary, 82; actor who starred in films for over 30 years beginning in the 1930s; Davenport, Ia., Nov. 29.
Green, Edith, 77; U.S. representative from Oregon, 1955-75; Tualatin, Ore., Apr. 21.
Greene, Lorne, , 72; star of the *Bonanza,* TV series; 1959-73; Santa Monica, Cal., Sept. 11.
Greenwood, Joan, 65; British stage and film actress; London, Feb. 27.
Gross, H.R., 88; U.S. representative from Iowa, 1949-75; Washington, D.C., Sept. 22.
Guldahl, Ralph, 75; a leading 1930's golfer; Sherman Oaks, Cal., June 11.

H

Haley, Sir William, 86; British journalist who headed the *Manchester Guardian,* the *Times of London,* and the BBC; Jersey, U.K., Sept. 6.
Harlow, Bryce, 70; presidential advisor in the Eisenhower and Nixon adminstrations; Arlington, Va., Feb. 17.
Hartman, Elizabeth, 45; actress who starred in films in the 1960s; Pittsburgh, June 10.
Hayes, Woody, 74; football coach who led the Ohio State team for 28 years, 1951-78; Upper Arlington, Oh., Mar. 12.
Haynes, Lloyd, 52; actor who starred in the *Room 222,* TV series in the 1970s; Coronado, Cal., Dec. 31.
Hayworth, Rita, 68; actress and dancer; a Hollywood leading lady in the 1940s and 1950s; New York, May 14.
Hazeltine, Matt, 53; football linebacker for the San Francisco 49ers, 1955-58; Los Altos, Cal., Jan. 14.
Heidt, Horace, 85; band leader who starred with his "Musical Knights" on radio and TV; Los Angeles, Dec. 1.
Heller, Walter, 71; economist who was an advisor to Presidents Kennedy and Johnson; Silverdale, Wash., June 15.
Hess, Rudolf, 93; Nazi leader during their rise to power in the 1930s; W. Berlin, Aug. 17.
High, Johnny, 30; basketball player who played for the Phoenix Suns; Phoenix, June 13.
Holman, Bill, 84; cartoonist who created and drew "Smokey Stover"; New York, Feb. 27.
Howser, Dick, 51; baseball manager who led the Kansas City Royals to a world series championship in 1985; Kansas City, June 17.
Huie, William Bradford, 76; author who wrote about the South of the civil rights era; Guntersville, Ala., Nov. 22.
Huston, John, 81; film maker, *The Maltese Falcon; The Treasure of Sierra Madre;* Middletown, R.I., Aug. 28.

J

Jackson, Travis, 83; baseball hall of famer with the N.Y. Giants in the 1920s and 1930s; Waldo, Ark., July 27.

Johnson, Gus, 48; basketball player in the NBA, 1963-72, mostly for the Baltimore Bullets; Akron, Oh., Apr. 28.

K

Kaye, Danny, 74; comedian and entertainer on stage and in films; Los Angeles, Mar. 3.
Kaye, Nora, 67; a leading American ballerina of the 1940s and 1950s; Los Angeles, Feb. 28.
Kaye, Sammy, 77; bandleader who led one of the most popular "swing era" bands; Ridgewood, N.J., June 2.
Kennedy, Madge, 96; stage and silent film star; Woodland Hills, Cal., June 9.
Keyserling, Leon, 79; chairman of the Council of Economic Advisors under Truman; Washington, D.C., Aug. 9.

L

Lake, Arthur, 81; actor who played Dagwood in the "Blondie" film series of the 1940s; Indian Wells, Cal., Jan. 9.
Lanchester, Elsa, 84; character actress in films and the theater for over 50 years; Woodland Hills, Cal., Dec. 26.
Landon, Alf, 100; governor of Kansas who was the Republican presidential candidate in 1936; Topeka, Oct. 12.
Lash, Joseph P., 77; journalist and biographer who won a 1971 Pulitzer Prize for *Eleanor and Franklin;* Boston, Aug. 22.
Layne, Bobby, 59; hall of fame quarterback who starred for the Detroit Lions and Pittsburgh Steelers in the 1950s; Lubbock, Tex., Dec. 1.
Lennon, Anton A., 80; U.S. representative from North Carolina, 1957-73; Wilmington, N.C., Dec. 28.
LeRoy, Mervyn, 86; director of more than 75 movies; *Little Caesar; Mister Roberts;* Beverly Hills, Cal., Sept. 13.
Lescoulie, Jack, 75; TV personality who co-hosted NBC's *Today* show in the 1950's; Memphis, July 22.
Levi, Primo, 67; writer who drew upon his experiences as a victim of the Holocaust; Turin, Italy, Apr. 11.
Levine, Joseph E., 81; film producer and distributor; Greenwich, Conn., July 31.
Levinson, Richard, 52; writer who helped create the *Colombo* and *Murder, She Wrote* TV series; Los Angeles, Mar. 12.
Liberace, 67; flamboyant pianist and entertainer; Palm Springs, Cal., Feb. 4.
Lifar, Serge, 81; dancer and choreographer who was a major influence in modern French ballet; Lausanne, Switzerland, Dec. 15.
Locke, Bobby, 69; South African golfer who won the British Open 4 times; Johannesburg, Mar. 9.
Luboff, Norman, 70; composer and choir director; Bynum, N.C., Sept. 22.
Luce, Clare Boothe, 84; playwright, U.S. representative from Conn., and diplomat; widow of Henry R. Luce; Washington, D.C., Oct. 9.

M

MacBeth, Donald, 37; jockey whose mounts earned over $40 million; Ocala, Fla., Mar. 1.
MacDonald, John D., 70; novelist whose 70+ books included the "Travis McGee" series; Milwaukee, Dec. 28.
MacLean, Alistair, 64; author of adventure novels, *The Guns of Navarrone;* Munich, Feb. 2.
MacMillan, Harold, 92; prime minister of Great Britain, 1957-63; Sussex, England, Dec. 29.
Madden, Ray, 95; U.S. representative from Indiana, 1943-77; Washington, D.C., Sept. 28.
Marquand, Richard, 49; British film director, *The Return of the Jedi;* near London, Sept. 4.
Martin, Dean Paul, 35; actor and musician; son of Dean Martin; San Bernadino, Cal., Mar. 25.
Martin, Quinn, 65; TV producer, *The Fugitive; Barnaby Jones;* Rancho Santa Fe, Cal., Sept. 5.
Marvin, Lee, 63; actor who usually played tough guys in films; Tucson, Ariz., Aug. 29.
McConnell, Gen. John Paul, 78; U.S. Air Force chief of staff in the 1960s; Bethesda, Md., Nov. 21.
McKenna, Siobhan, 64; Irish-born stage actress; Dublin, Nov. 16.
McKinney, Stewart B., U.S. representative from Connecticut; Washington, D.C., May 7.
McMahon, Don, 57; relief pitcher and coach with several major league baseball teams; Los Angeles, July 22.
Mitchell, Dale, 65; baseball player who spent 11 seasons in the major leagues mostly with the Cleveland Indians; Tulsa, Okla., Jan. 5.
Molotov, Vyacheslav M., 96; a member of the Soviet leadership, 1921-57; Moscow, Nov. 8.
Moorhead, William S., 64; U.S. representative from Pennsylvania, 1959-81; Baltimore, Aug. 3.
Moss, Howard, 64; poet and poetry editor of the *New Yorker* magazine; New York, Sept. 16.
Murchinson, Clint W., 63; businessman who created the Dallas Cowboys football team; Dallas, Mar. 30.
Murphy, Turk, 71; jazz trombonist; San Francisco, May 30.
Myrdal, Gunnar, 88; Swedish economist and sociologist; Stockholm, May 17.

N

Negri, Pola, 88; silent screen "vamp"; San Antonio, Aug. 1.
Nolen, William, 58; physician whose book, *The Making of a Surgeon* was a 1970 best seller; Minneapolis, Dec. 20.
Northrop, John H., 95; U.S. scientist who shared the 1947 Nobel Prize in chemistry; Wickenburg, Ariz., May 27.

O

O'Boyle, Patrick Cardinal, 91; archbishop of Washington, D.C., 1948-73; Washington, D.C., Aug. 10.
O'Konski, Alvin, 83; U.S. representative from Wisconsin, 1943-73; co-author of the G.I. Bill of Rights; Kewaunee, Wis., July 8.
Owens, Harry, 84; bandleader and composer, "Sweet Leilani"; Eugene, Ore., Dec. 12.

P

Page, Geraldine, 62; stage and film actress who won an Oscar for *A Trip to Bountiful;* New York, June 13.
Peller, Clara, 86; actress who gained fame with her "Where's the Beef" TV commercial; Chicago, Aug. 10.
Poage, W.R., 87; U.S. representative from Texas, 1937-79; Temple, Tex., Jan. 3.
Preston, Robert, 68; actor; best known as the star of *The Music Man;* Santa Barbara, Cal., Mar. 21.

R

Rey, Alejandro, 57; character actor who appeared in some 50 films; Los Angeles, May 21.
Rich, Buddy, 69; jazz drummer; Los Angeles, Apr. 2.
Richards, Sir Gordon, 82; jockey who was the British champion 26 times; Kintbury, England, Nov. 10.
Robison, Howard, 71; U.S. representative from New York, 1958-75; Rehoboth Beach, Del., Sept. 26.
Rogers, Carl R., 85; psychotherapist and author who was instrumental in the encounter group movement of the 1960s; La Jolla, Cal., Feb. 4.
Rogerson, Ron, 44; head football coach at Princeton Univ.; New Hampshire, Aug. 8.
Rosenberg, Edgar, 62; TV producer; husband of Joan Rivers, Philadelphia, Aug. 14.
Rowan, Dan, 65; co-host of TV's *Rowan and Martin's Laugh-In;* Englewood, Fla., Sept. 22.
Rustin, Bayard, 75; civil rights leader who helped organize the 1963 march on Washington; New York, Aug. 24.

S

Scott, Randolph, 89; actor who was a leading man in western films in the 1940s and 1950s; Los Angeles, Mar. 2.
Segovia, Andres, 94; Spanish classic guitarist who was one of the major concert performers of the century; Madrid, June 2.
Shawn, Dick, 63; comic actor in films and the theater; La Jolla, Cal., Apr. 17.
Singh, Charan, 85; prime minster of India in 1979; India, May 29.
Smalls, Charlie, 43; composer and lyricist, *The Wiz;* Bruges, Belgium, Aug. 27.
Stewart, Michael, 63; author of Broadway musicals, *Bye Bye Birdie; Hello, Dolly;* New York, Sept. 20.
Stoessel, Walter J. Jr., 66; diplomat; ambassador to Poland, USSR, W. Germany; Washington, D.C., Dec. 9.
Sullivan, Maxine, 75; jazz singer; New York, Apr. 7.
Susskind, David, 66; TV talk-show host; movie and TV producer; New York, Feb. 22.

T

Taylor, Kent, 80; actor who appeared in films for more than 50 years; Los Angeles, Apr. 11.
Taylor, Gen. Maxwell D., 85; military leader and envoy; Washington, D.C., Apr. 19.
Tosh, Peter, 42; Jamaican reggae singer, Kingston, Sept. 11.
von Trapp, Maria, 82; leader of the Trapp Family Choir which inspired the musical *The Sound of Music;* Morrisville, Vt., Mar. 28.
Tudor, Antony, 79; choreographer who transformed classical ballet; New York, Apr. 19.

U

Unruh, Jesse, 64; California political leader; Marina del Rey, Cal., Aug. 4.

V

Vanos, Nick, 24; basketball player for the Phoenix Suns; nr. Detroit, Nov. 15
Villency, Maurice, 85; furniture designer; Brookville, N.Y., Jan. 11.

W

Walston, Bobby, 58; end, placekicker for the NFL's Philadelphia Eagles; Elk Grove Village, Ill., Oct. 7.
Warhol, Andy, 58; artist who was a founder of the Pop Art movement; New York, Feb. 21.
Wellstood, Dick, 59; jazz pianist; Palo Alto, Cal., July 24.
Wheeler, Hugh, 75; British-born playwright, screenwriter, and mystery novelist; Pittsfield, Mass., July 26.
Wilson, Earl, 79; Broadway gossip columnist for more than 40 years; Yonkers, N.Y., Jan. 16.
Wydler, John W., 63; U.S. representative from New York, 1963-81; Washington, D.C., Aug. 4.

XYZ

Young, Dick, 69; sports columnist and reporter for New York City newspapers for 50 years; New York, Aug. 31.
Zorinsky, Edward, 58; U.S. senator from Nebraska since 1977; Omaha, Mar. 6.

Off-Beat News Stories of 1987

Which way to the Planet of the Apes? — A Soviet satellite on a flight to conduct research on the effects of weightlessness to help pave the way for manned interplanetary travel, was taken over by a monkey who was running amok. Yerosha, whose name means troublemaker, a second monkey, and an assortment of rats, fish, and insects blasted off from earth after completing a training course in simulated space flight. During the flight, Yerosha freed its left arm from a restraining cuff and began tinkering with everything within reach, pushing buttons on the control panel, playing with a cap fitted with electrodes attached to its head, jeopardizing research and causing havoc. The Soviet news agency Tass reported that Yerosha, and the other better behaved monkey, Dryoma, whose name means sluggishness, had proved to be "excellent operatives, and had demonstrated a brilliant mastery of the program of experiments."

Monkey business — John Schneider, an A.S.P.C.A. animal-care technician, got a call while on duty at Kennedy International Airport that there were monkeys loose on one of the planes. He went to a plane which included among its cargo 20 crates of monkeys—100 in all. He determined that only one monkeey was loose, a 20-inch female macaque. The beast was finally captured after an hour-and-a-half chase throughout the airplane with the other monkeys cheering on their fellow primate. "She was feisty, angry, and jetlagged," explained Schneider after his victory.

Jailbird — Richard Garner was sentenced to jail for 3 years for holding a macaw for ransom. Garner denied taking the 2-foot-tall bird named Bow, but pleaded guilty to demanding $1,500 for its safe return.

L.A. Law — The first Canine Court in the U.S. opened in Los Angeles and was expected to save the city $3,500 a day, the sum spent prosecuting some 1,500 misdemeanor cases involving dogs each year. Canine Court will handle such villains as barkers, escapers, jogger-chasers, and garbage snoopers. Biters will continue to have their cases heard in human court.

A dog may be your best friend, but ... — The canine world suffered a setback when a Rochester, N.Y. federal judge ruled that "a dog is not a person" and "does not have the legal status to sue anybody." A $50,000 suit was filed on behalf of Ari, a 15-year-old, blind, arthritic, and nearly deaf dog, claiming that the canine suffered "physical and emotional damage" when USAir baggage handlers left the animal on an airport conveyor belt.

Why? ... Because we like you! — Voters in Georgia are no longer able to vote for Mickey Mouse. The cartoon character was a popular write-in choice. The State Senate passed a bill which directs election officials to ignore any write-in votes cast for a person who has not filed a notice of a write-in candidacy.

Don't believe everything you read — When the 7th edition of the Baseball Encyclopedia is published, Lou Proctor, listed in previous editions as a member of the 1912 St. Louis Browns, will be missing. It was discovered that Proctor was actually a press-box telegraph operator who decided to enter his name in the box score. He remained a "player" with a one-game career until researchers weeded him out.

"Here she comes, Miss Siberia!" — A beauty contest sponsored by the Young Communist League and labor unions, the first of its kind in Siberia, was won by Lyudmilla Semdyakina, a student at an Institute for railroad engineers. Some 10,000 women from Irkutsk, a city of 600,000 near the Mongolian border, were judged on their ability in dancing, rhythmic exercise, social skills, and bearing. A newspaper report said that Semdyakina was judged "the most charming and attractive." It said she loves sports and ballet, likes to read, mixes well with others and "unlike some of her peers, she does not smoke." The chairman of the contest's jury remarked "It's clear that the formation of a discotheque 'standard' of behavior and appearance, which some of the girls tried to follow, was beneath all criticism from the esthetic point of view."

"Is this what Shirley MacLaine drinks?" — When Pepsi-Cola began to sell their product in Thailand they began their advertising campaign with their American slogan "Come alive, you're in the Pepsi generation." They later realized that the Thai translation they were using said, "Pepsi brings your ancestors back from the dead."

Hot potato — Dave Bresnahan, a catcher for Williamsport in baseball's Eastern League, threw a potato to third base in order to pick off a baserunner. The baserunner, thinking that the potato was a ball, broke for home. He was met at the plate and tagged out by Bresnahan, who had the real ball. Bresnahan was charged with an error, fined $50, and released from the team the following day.

Two, for Dollar Bill — Senator Bill Bradley was asked the best way for the Democratic Party to choose their next presidential candidate. Bradley, who played for 10 years in the National Basketball Association, said that he preferred jump shots from the top of the key.

What would Snow White say? — The Little People's Association in Australia called it "disgusting and appalling" when The Australian People magazine announced that their charity event between teams from Australia and England would include a "dwarf-throwing and bowling contest." David Naylor, editor of the magazine, explained, "We're going to strap a skateboard to their stomachs and roller skates to their arms, and roll them down an expansive floor toward the skittles." Naylor defended the event. He said, "The two dwarfs we are using are not representing other dwarfs. They are professional stunt men who like being thrown. They are professional projectiles."

Original Skin — The leaves will be removed and Adam and Eve will be completely nude in the Brancacci Chapel in Florence, Italy. During the restoration of the Renaissance master Masaccio's fresco "Expulsion from the Garden of Eden," it was discovered that leaves covering Adam and Eve had beeen added in the 16th century. Ornella Casazza, artistic director of the restoration said, "It was part of a movement to cover the part of the body considered sinful."

The line-up was X-rated — In London, Andrew Greene used a toy pistol and wore a stocking mask when robbing gasoline stations in the nude. He explained that he didn't want to be identified by his clothes. Holdup victims identified Greene by his physique, vaccination marks, and skin blemishes.

Hold the pickles — A Stockton, Cal. man ordered 3 cheeseburgers from a drive-in stand but left without them, telling an employee he had forgotten his note. Minutes later, he returned with a gun and his note which contained a demand for money. He collected $45 and fled—without his cheeseburgers.

Keep these on ice — John E. Powell, a work-release inmate, was caught smuggling 8 cans of beer into prison and sentenced to an additional 15 years. Powell's attorney noted that the law for smuggling beer into prison is the same as for smuggling a weapon, and explained "If he had run away he would have gotten a lower sentence."

Pass the napkins — The Environmental Protection Agency received a letter from a man asking if he could get dioxin-caused cancer from eating toilet paper. Dioxin can appear in trace amounts in bleached white paper, probably arising from chlorine bleach. The letter writer explained that he suffered from pica, a craving for non-food substances, and had been eating unscented bleached white toilet paper for close to 20 years.

You *can* take it with you — As part of the community's 100th anniversary celebration, the town of Wilkinsburg, Pa. planned to open a time capsule that had been buried in 1962. At that time, the City Council, to prevent vandals from digging up the capsule, had held a special closed meeting to decide where the stainless steel box would be buried. Time passed and all those at the meeting died without telling anyone where the capsule had been buried. The ceremony of the opening of the time capsule was cancelled, since no one knew where it was.

You *can* go home again — . . .And we will always remember when the nation held its breath and noses as Islip, N.Y. cast its garbage upon the waters and began a 155-day, 6,000 mile odyssey that saw the barge *Mobro* and its cargo of 3,186 tons of garbage turned away from 6 states as well as Mexico, Belize, and the Bahamas. Finally, the trash was burned and 400 tons of ashes were returned and buried in Islip.

QUICK REFERENCE INDEX